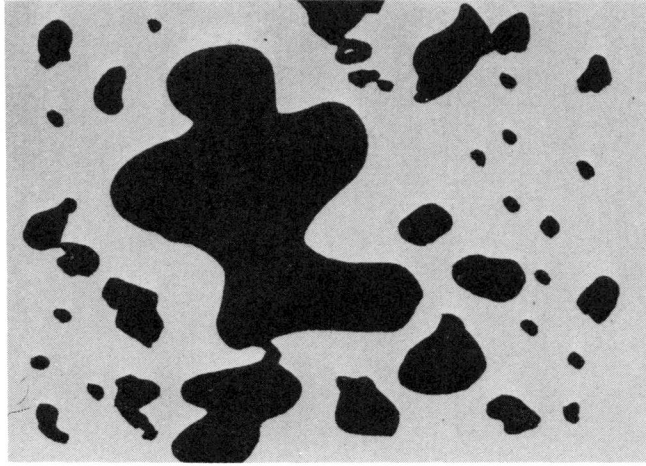

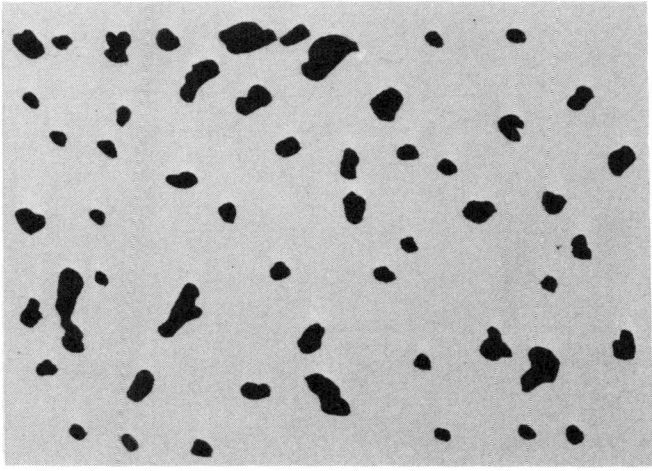

JANE'S
MERCHANT SHIPS
1982

Alphabetical list of advertisers

Classified list of advertisers

JANE'S MERCHANT SHIPS

Compiled and edited by
R A Streater and D G Greenman

1982

JANE'S
"Jane's" is a registered trade mark

Published by Jane's Publishing Company Limited,
238 City Road, London EC1V 2FU, England

ISBN 0 7106-0168-9

Made and produced by Simon Books Limited,
Cumbrae Lodge, Ditton Hill, Surbiton, Surrey KT6 5EN

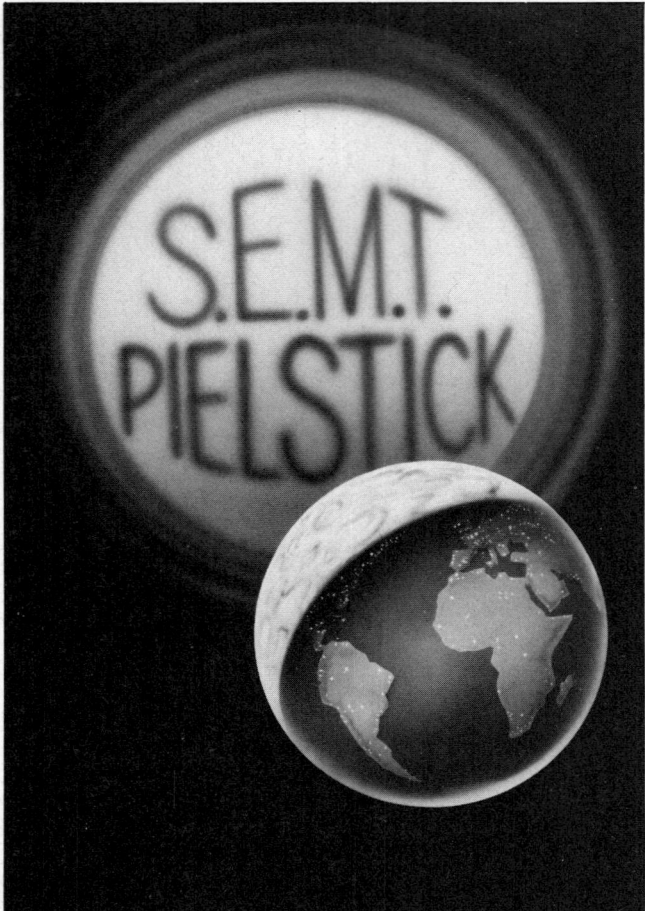

Contents

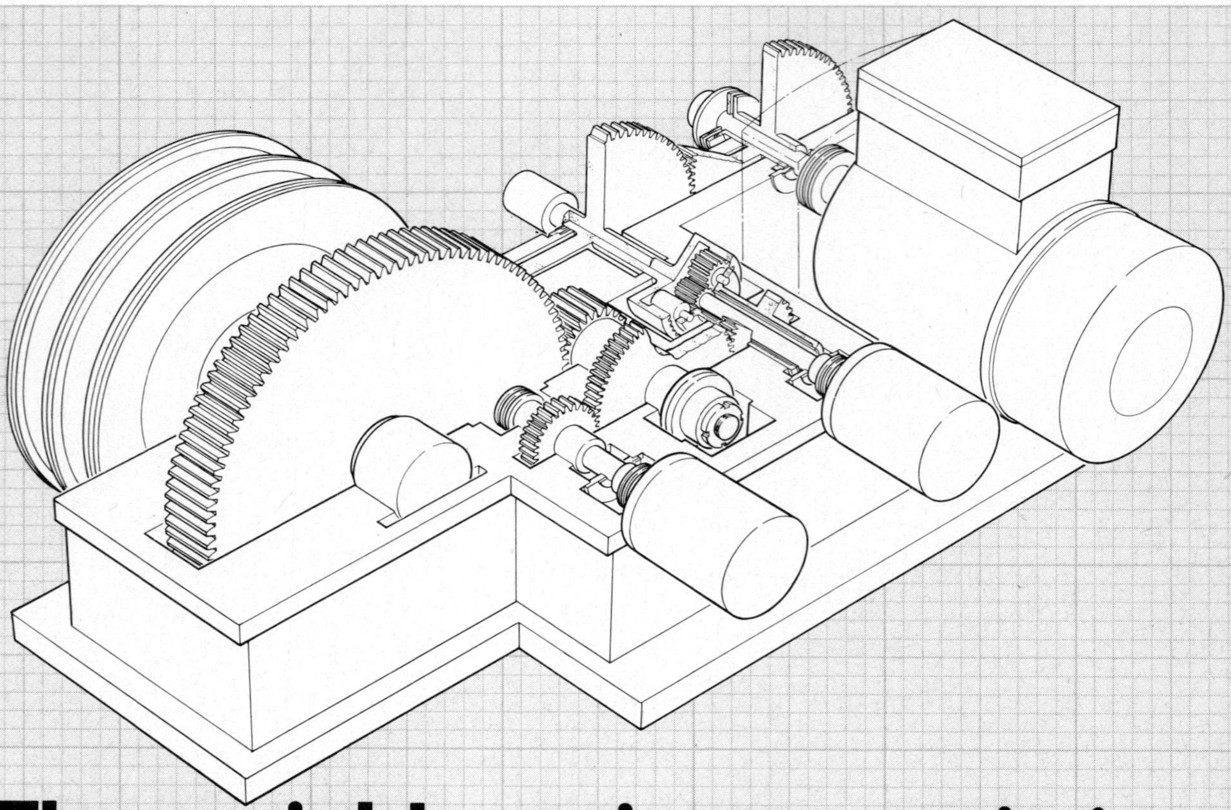

Foreword to Jane's Merchant Ships
by
Captain John Moore, RN
Editor, Jane's Fighting Ships

The primary purposes of maritime reference publications is to ensure the accurate recognition of ships and to provide the requisite information on their capabilities. It was for these two reasons that, during the Second World War, every well-found British submarine carried a copy of *Talbot-Booth's Merchant Ships* and a copy of *Jane's Fighting Ships* in the control room. Both had the great advantage of being "Unclassified" and could, therefore, be readily available. The moment of a sudden sighting in low visibility is no time to start rooting through the contents of a safe in search of the right Confidential Book.

In recent years the subject of Ship Recognition has received too little attention in navies—even the modern radar screen is no substitute for the human eye. With modern merchant fleets still carrying over 96% of the world's freight and many of those from the Warsaw Pact having a dual role as naval auxiliaries, swift and accurate recognition is essential in both peace and war. It was, therefore, a great pleasure to me when Jane's Publishing Company agreed to produce this work on Talbot-Booth's invaluable contribution. Since well before the last war he has worked selflessly on his subject, frequently having to battle against official prejudice and apathy. That at last the two books should be published under the same imprint is, I believe, an acknowledgement of the interdependence of two major branches of the great sweep of seapower.

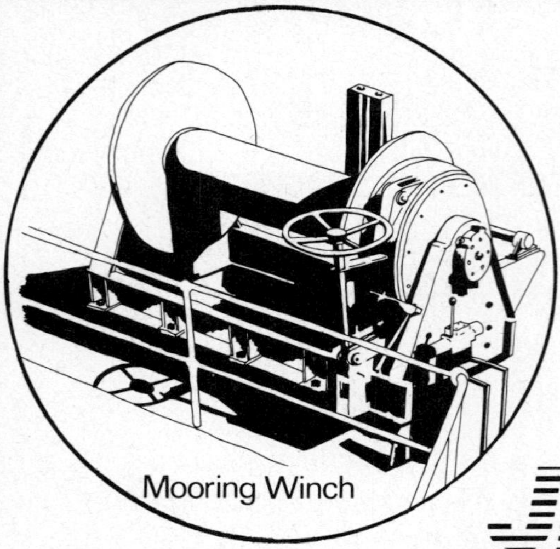
Mooring Winch

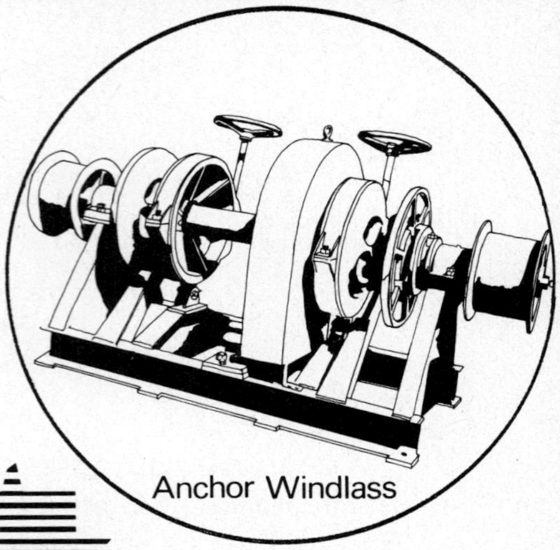
Anchor Windlass

INTRODUCTION

The first *Jane's Merchant Ships* is a major event in the long history of Lt Cdr E C Talbot-Booth RD, RNR, and his, often one man, fight to keep extensive files of ship information available to the free world at all times. Captain John Moore has accurately summed up the situation in his foreword and there is very little to add except the heartfelt thanks of myself, and my colleague David Greenman, for all the training, help and assistance received from our mentor over many years, and the sincere hope that one day we may come a little closer to his vast skill and knowledge of the subject.

One of the problems that has dogged this work for years is the fact that, in peacetime, those in high positions regard the task as an extra expense that can be spared. It seems that very little thought is generally put to "what would we have to use in the event of conflict". The following precis from a speech which appeared in the *Nautical Magazine* echoes many of these sentiments and is worthy of a further reprint.

MERCHANT FLEETS ARE VITAL TO WESTERN SECURITY

'Co-operation between Western industrialised nations in the operation of their merchant fleets should be as close as had been accomplished in the military sphere within NATO', urged Hans D. Druegg, President, Hapag-Lloyd (America) Inc., when speaking at the second ILA Employers' Educational Foundation Conference at Dublin. He said that an analysis titled, 'Western Security: What has changed? What should be done?' recently published by four international affairs institutes in the U.S.A., France, Britain and Germany, did not contain a single word on the role of merchant fleets in this context, let alone their shortcomings. After pointing out how vital merchant shipping had been to Britain during the last war, referring to the post-war growth of Soviet naval and merchant shipping and giving examples of vital commodities to Western countries which had to be carried by sea, he continued: 'In spite of the rapid increase of ocean-borne trade during the last 30 years and Western nations' growing dependence on their sea-lanes, the percentage of the merchant fleets of the West European countries and the United States under their national flags has dropped from 85 per cent of total world tonnage in 1939 to 40 per cent, or less than half, of the 400 million tons of world tonnage in 1980.' This was due to more and more shipowners putting at least part of their tonnage under so-called open registries (flags of convenience), under the flags of Liberia and Panama. He added: 'Our economies with their high standards of living have become too expensive for operators of bulk carriers and tankers to remain competitive in world markets, where freight rates are still determined solely by supply and demand.' Other major beneficiaries in the expansion of trade had been Greece, Japan and the Soviet Union. Mr. Druegg continued: 'Our governments will have to act fairly promptly in finding ways and means—be it tax reliefs, less stringent safety or social standards or otherwise—to render operation under national flags attractive again, if this trend is to be reversed. To abolish these open registries altogether—as the Russians for obvious reasons so fervently demand—would, however, not solve the problem. On the contrary, it would raise the overall transport bill for bulk shipments and drive even more western operators out of business. We should, therefore, draw a clear distinction between 'substandard ships'—which in fact should be stopped by international safety standards and strict port controls—as against flags of convenience.' In liner shipping, free enterprise and private companies were being more and more curtailed in their operations by escalating governmental interference and bureaucracy from different quarters all over the world. They also had to wrestle with inflationary cost increases. Mr Druegg said that threats to free enterprise shipping originated from four different directions. Certain developing countries were seeking to aid their young national merchant fleets by flag-protective legislation directing trade to their own ships, but part of these discriminatory measures could be mitigated by Western lines being accorded associated status within those conferences. In US trades contrary to all other Western countries liner conferences had been regulated since 1916 under the Shipping Act, practically prohibiting their members from rationalising their services to any reasonable extent, as is common practice in most other trades. 'The deplorable financial state of some of the surviving American carriers is a direct consequence of trying to export a domestic antitrust philosophy into international business.' The third threat was to the Soviet merchant fleet. Although Soviet foreign overseas trade of liner cargo was next to nothing, they had built up the largest general cargo fleet in the world and had succeeded in establishing regular cross trade services on the major Western trade routes as well as in trades between the industrialised nations and developing countries. They used liner conference tariffs as an umbrella for their quotations, which they set much lower as necessary to attract whatever cargo they wished to carry. 'Should this turn out as a notional operational loss, so what. Did you ever hear of a Soviet company going bankrupt?' The fourth threat to Western shipping was caused by the lack of protection received from their own Western governments. Private companies could not fight against political rates set by foreign governments or against other political market distortions. If the cake thus became too small, they simply had to go out of business once and for all and the state traders would take their place. The Soviets had a great number of medium-size general cargo ships and Ro-Ro ships suitable for rapid military support operations, but Western merchant fleets could not compete to any extent in this sector. Their oversize bulker units and container ships have been built under purely commercial criteria, and if profitability of liner services was not improved soon by appropriate steps, then the size of this fleet capacity would shrink rapidly for lack of capital. Mr Druegg said: 'What is urgently required is a similar close co-operation in the operation of our merchant fleets among western industrialised nations as has been successfully accomplished in the military sphere within NATO. This means that we have to give the private sector sufficient operational freedom to organise themselves at an optimum level, and at the same time government protection against outside, non-commercial distortions of the market.'

(Nautical magazine).

THE WORLD'S FLEETS

The world recession has continued to have a drastic effect on the size of the fleets under individual flags around the globe. Surplus conventional tonnage is still being replaced by larger and more specialised ships with the exception of the tanker market which is going through its own separate crisis.

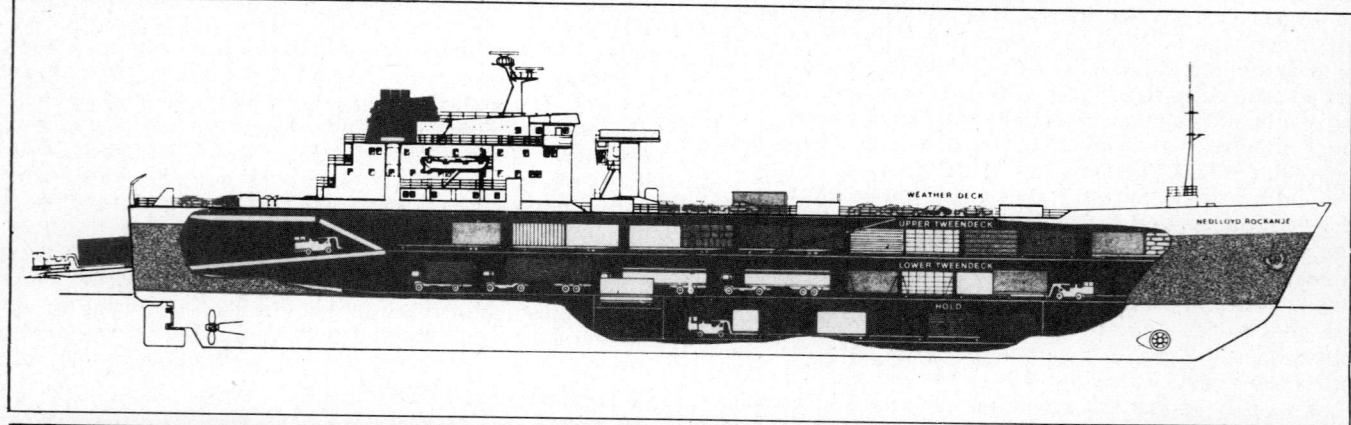

THE UNITED KINGDOM

Perhaps one of the most significant features of British shipping over the past decade has been the rapid drop in the number of vessels and men operating under the Red Ensign. In August 1981 the total fleet was at its lowest level for more than 10 years and the decline is accelerating. The statistics to June 1981 showed a combined fleet of only 1087 ships of 33.2 million tonnes deadweight, compared with a 1975 figure of 1624 vessels of more than 50 million tonnes. Correspondingly the number of men employed at sea has dropped from 80,000 in 1975 to 59,000 in 1981. In late 1981 the tonnage was being forecast at less than 30 million in 1982.

Jim Slater of the National Union of Seamen stated that in the past five years 300 ships had been sold to flags of convenience. The General Council of British Shipping stated in September 1981 that in the previous three months a further 15 vessels had left the British registry and only a single new one, a ferry, had been added. By November the same council had announced the tenth successive monthly drop, now totalling 100 ships since the beginning of the year.

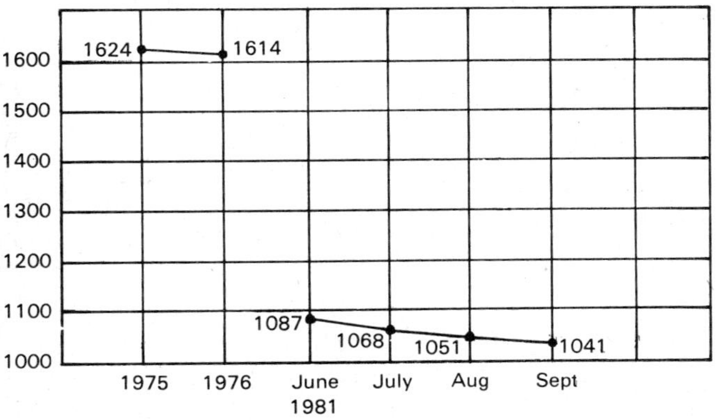

Table 1. Total number of ships on British Register

EEC

The situation within the whole of the EEC is very similar to that in the UK and the following tables will illustrate the state of the total fleets within the community.

Composition of EEC and World fleet at 1st July 1980

	Total	"10"	World		EEC as % of World
	No	mn dwt	No	mn dwt	(by dwt)
General Cargo	5670	30.7	23236	120.9	25.4
Cellular container	191	4.3	4325	142.6	29.3
Ore/bulk carrier	1254	41.8	4325	142.6	29.3
Combination carrier	121	13.5	452	48.7	27.6
Passenger & ferry	417	0.9	1214	2.3	36.9
Total dry cargo	7635	91.2	29889	325.7	28.0
Tanker	1557	84.7	7232	340,2	24.9
Chemical tanker	117	0.7	649	3.8	18.4
Liquefied gas carrier	140	1.7	631	7.7	22.4
Total tanker	1814	87.1	8512	351.6	24.8
Total all ships	9467	178.2	38401	677.3	26.3

Table 2. Composition of EEC and world fleet at July 1, 1980

EEC and world fleet 1975-80

	*EEC		World		EEC as % of World
July 1	No	mn dwt	No	mn dwt	(by dwt)
1970*	8333	77.4	31813	332.8	23.3
1975	7197	117.4	34934	544.2	21.6
1976	7012	123.8	35666	598.4	20.7
1977	6494	119.2	36208	637.2	18.7
1978	6431	120.6	36880	658.7	18.3
1979	6124	114.0	37668	669.0	17.0
1980	5979	111.2	38401	677.3	16.4

*Excludes Greece which joined the EEC on Jan 1, 1981, and has 3,488 trading vessels with a combined deadweight of 66,992,000 tons

Table3. EEC.and world fleet 1970, 1975-80

GREECE

Greece announced in August 1981 that its merchant fleet, now the second largest in the world, totalled over 50 million tons gross, which contributed over $139bn. to the country's invisible earnings, a rise of 22% over the previous year. Upon entry into an enlarged EEC of 10 countries the addition of the Greek tonnage gave the community control of over one third of the world's cargo carrying tonnage.

HONG KONG

During 1980 the small Crown Colony of Hong Kong moved into third place in the world's shipping table, behind Japan and Greece and now ahead of the United Kingdom, mainly due to very heavy buying in the year.

JAPAN

Depending on the way the tables are calculated, the size of relative fleets varies by the addition of tonnage belonging to a country but operating under a flag of convenience or by just calculating the flag ships. Calculating in gross or deadweight also makes variations. Japan is now firmly placed as the premier fleet with over 33mn tons gross under the Japanese flag and a further 29mn tons under other flags. The Japanese Government is, like numerous other countries, worried about the trend to flags of convenience, seeing a threefold increase in the past decade, and is now making movements to ensure that its own industry is protected for the future carrying of essentials.

INDIA

The emergence of the Indian merchant fleet over the past years is a very good example of a new country doing well in the commercial fields and managing to make a significant contribution to its own financial position with the sensible use of a well planned merchant fleet. In the decade to 1980 the Indian fleet increased by 167% to stand at a total of 383 ships.

USA

The traditional use of flags of convenience by the major US ship operators has caused many worries over the years but the latest figures show that many of the percentages of cargo carried to and from the US have dropped alarmingly Overall, US-flag ships only carry 1.1% of the nation's bulk exports and 1.4% of imports. American operators of Panamanian and Liberian flag fleets have already announced that they plan to increase their fleets in line with the anticipated increase in the coal trade.

USSR

The further expansion and trends within the merchant fleet of the USSR is very difficult to anticipate because of conflicting reports, but the conclusion seems to be that the expansion will continue. In July 1981 it was reported that the fleet consisted of 1750 vessels and that a further 250 would be delivered by 1985 to increase the total to 2000. In a report in October however it was stated that many of the new ships would be replacements for old tonnage. Despite this confusion the present fleet tops the 30mn. tonnes deadweight mark compared with only 5.4mn tonnes as recently as 1960. Not only is this a more than spectacular rise, it also represents one of the major threats to the West in the tactics of the USSR in obtaining freight, often leaving the free world outside, as the subsidised rates they offer cannot ever be matched except by way of even heavier governmental subsidies. This is a never ending downward spiral that, so far, has not been answered—but must be before the Soviet fleet dominates the world's trade routes.

PEOPLE'S REPUBLIC OF CHINA

China has continued its expansion in 1981 by maintaining its very high ratio of second-hand purchases in relation to most other countries. The relative ages of the ships is now far less than they used to be, and the fleet is rapidly emerging as one of the finest in the world. With over 9mn tonnes under its own flag and a further 2mn under Chinese controlled Hong Kong companies, flying the Panamanian flag, the fleet is now comparable in size to those of West Germany and Spain. Much of the 'new' tonnage is bulk carriers, purchased in the main from the United Kingdom and Greece.

SOUTH AMERICA

Cuba has now risen to the exalted position of fourth in the table of South-American ship owners with a 12-fold increase since 1950. Brazil still leads the way with an addition of over 651000 grt to its fleet in the past year and now representing

44% of the total fleets of the 17 countries. Argentina and Venezuela are the only countries to show any significant drop in size.

SHIPBUILDING

By the latter half of 1981 the World order book for new ships seemed to have developed a slow upward trend with the order books healthier than at any time since 1977. However, with the advent of much larger ships it is easy to be lulled into a false sense of optimism. As with all other aspects of shipping the order books can be judged by means of ships on order or total tonnage. The two following tables show firstly the drop since 1969 of the number of ships on order at any one time, and the second shows the total order book at the end of June 1981 by way of tonnage.

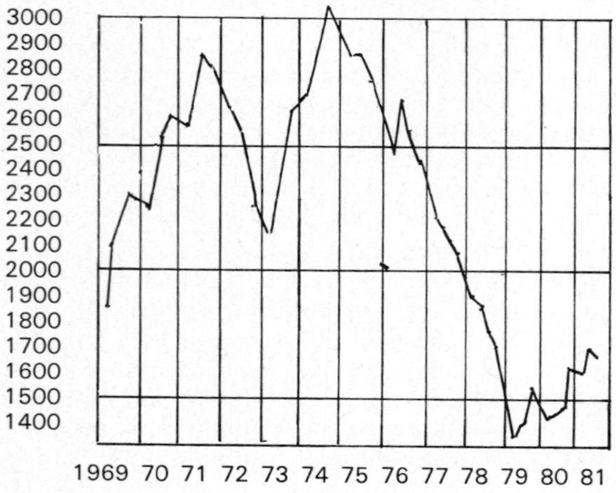

Table 4. Total ships on order

Leading countries	Under construction *gross tons*	Orders not commenced *gross tons*	Total order book *gross tons*
Japan	5 645 349 (+ 776 961)	9 034 440 (+ 601 581)	14 679 789 (+ 1 378 542)
Korea	698 791 (+ 18 512)	2 013 830 (+ 193 395)	2 712 621 (+ 211 907)
Spain	925 234 (+ 34 537	1 599 739 (+ 420 154)	2 524 973 (+ 385 617)
Brazil	880 941 (- 20 425)	733 991 (- 148 880)	1 614 932 (- 169 305)
**China,	34 549 (*)	272 443 (*)	1 601 243 (+ 386 192)
Taiwan,	367 351 (+ 124 645)	926 900 (- 45 445)	
Poland	747 (+ 59 723)	793 888 (- 71 360)	1 541 084 (- 11 637)
U.S.A.	586 521 (- 94 546)	835 924 (- 183 119)	1 422 445 (- 277 665)
Germany,	461 924 (- 120 468)	586 785 (+ 186 521)	1 048 709 (+ 66 053)
France	696 538 (- 18 770)	294 635 (+ 13 655)	991 173 (- 5 115)
Yugoslavia	462 336 (+ 111 094)	501 323 (- 63 360)	963 659 (+ 47 734)
Denmark	145 795 (- 79 624)	759 430 (+ 118 415)	905 225 (+ 38 791)
United Kingdom	652 187 (- 59 272)	237 508 (+ 101 429)	889 695 (+ 42 157)
Sweden	406 059 (- 34 950)	365 298 (+ 4 199)	771 357 (- 30 751)
Italy	442 624 (+ 15 578)	153 820 (- 35 750)	596 444 (- 20 172)
Belgium	384 924 (- 28 175)	210 960 (+ 22 400)	595 884 (- 5 775)
Norway	368 339 (- 2 872)	226 772 (+ 17 568)	595 111 (+ 14 696)
India	202 981 (+ 105)	359 155 (+ 88 000)	562 136 (+ 88 105)

***Information incomplete* **Information not available*

Table 5.

From a report, in August, that the shipbuilding market was continuing its recovery, with an air of optimism, by the end of September *Lloyds List* was reporting a slump on new orders of more than one million tons, largely caused by the Japanese being unable to compete.

Although it has already been reported that the capacity of the present bulk fleet exceeds the demand, by a considerable percentage, it is anticipated that bulk carriers will replace tankers as the new mainstay of shipbuilding. New and more economical designs have become the order of the day, and the anticipated increased demand for coal will help to justify the yard's optimism in this direction. The world is beginning to realise the need for conservation of oil and use of coal both on land and at sea, as a viable alternative. Many new designs of coal burning ships are being developed without the fear of the old methods of stoking the boilers. These new ships, using a pulverised dust feed method, similar to that employed in some modern power stations, will be as clean as present oil burning ships. Current Japanese experiments could well lead to more sail-assisted ships. To see a tanker being driven by wind is surely the ultimate in reversals of trend that has happened for decades. Perhaps we will yet see a tanker driven by coal and assisted by wind.

Hand in hand with the development of new ships and the rise of the multi-purpose bulker the development in tankers is back to smaller designs, of up to 150,000 tonnes deadweight, able to pass through the Suez Canal.

The two-masted 1,600 dwt products tanker "Shin Aitoku Maru" of Aitoku Co., Ltd. undergoing successful trial runs.

"Mini-Lace" in motor-sailing mode.

In February 1981 the USSR announced plans for a new type of ship that encompassed this trend towards specialised ships in two directions: Firstly, the vessel would be a combination LASH/Container ship but would, in addition, have heavy lift capacity. Also, and most important, it would be nuclear powered. Since neither the "Savannah", "Mutsu" or the "Otto Hahn" seem to have been commercial successes in this field it is an interesting development, but one which was backed up later in the year by a paper at the annual symposium of the Chartered Institute of Transport in Brisbane, in which Mr. J. Jenkins of Overseas Containers Australia stated that he thought that nuclear power was eventually going to be the viable alternative, as oil became more expensive and coal became uneconomic for smaller ships and the liner trades.

Nuclear fuels were not the only controversial announcement from the Soviet Union during the year. In September they announced a scientific project investigating the possibilities of using ions as a form of propulsion. While there are still many and varied problems to be overcome, the basis of the system seems to be nests of plates beneath the hull of the ship which can act as electrodes. when direct current is passed through them. Water passing through the plates is then charged to the same polarity as an adjacent magnet. The reactive force thereby caused is, it is hoped, directed into propulsive power to move the vessel.

From Norway in September came another scientific project—using wave action to assist propulsion. Already tested with models, the concept involves the use of a foil propeller installed under the ship's keel, which moves up and down with the motion of the vessel through the water, working on the theory that 72% of a wave's power is in its top 10%.

Already delivered in 1981 is an Australian vessel that runs on oil and bottled gas, loaded from shore tanks. In November 1981 firm orders were placed for other dual-propulsion ships; Bulk coal carriers for Bulkships, ordered from Italy's Italcantieri yards, are to be oil/coal powered.

WORLD SHIPBUILDING

JAPAN

For many years the Japanese yards have dominated shipbuilding but 1981 showed a move away from this, although by the end of the year they were still very much the world leaders. During the first part of the year they made great strides towards reducing their capacity and had managed to get down to 51% of the peak 1974 figure. But the pressure still continued from the rest of the world for the Japanese share to be reduced even more. In June, the Organisation of Economic Development and Co-operation reported that Japan had secured 2.6 million of the 3.8 million tons ordered in the first quarter of the year. By comparison, yards belonging to the Association of West European Shipbuilders had secured orders for only 1.1 million tons. By late in the year the Japanese yards were announcing that they had recovered from the shipbuilding slump that had caused them a lot of cut-back and recession and they were again capturing over half the new orders from around the world. At the end of June, they were, in fact, building 34% of all the world's ships on order at that time.

UNITED KINGDOM

Apart from the warship division, British Shipbuilders overall picture in 1981 was again one of gloom, although the general picture seemed to be brightening. The head of London-based Liberty Marine even went so far as to say publicly that the British yards were too modest and played down their product, whereas the Far Eastern and Communist builders tended to oversell. In an article in the Sunday Telegraph of 15th Dec 1981 the head of British Shipbuilding, Mr Robert Atkinson, stated "From the start I said I would run British Shipbuilders as a business—and that is what I am doing. I don't care a fig about politicians or unions. My task is simply to get the corporation back into profitability, and when I achieve that, everybody will be better off." Since taking office this seems to be the case, and on the record so far, perhaps the chairman will be right, with his planned break even by 1984. Perhaps he might also take notice of the statement from Liberty Marine and let the corporation be seen to sell. The complete absence of any representation of the British shipbuilding industry at the Europoort Exhibition in Amsterdam this past November makes one wonder why we are not doing so well, and if perhaps we should be seen to do better. A position of eleventh in the world is very low.

SHIP DISPOSALS

The face of the secondhand market and the scrapping of ships has overall remained unchanged over the last year—dismal. In spite of minor surges and spates of false optimism the general market has been towards the breaking up of many ships that, in earlier years, would still have had many useful years ahead. The slump in the world demand for oil and the corresponding surplus of tonnage has meant the breaker's yard for many tankers now uneconomic to their owners. In the first six months of 1981 the world's tanker fleet was cut by a staggering 2 million tonnes deadweight, including 23 VLCCs. In September, shipbrokers John Jacobs reported that slow steaming—now as low as 10 knots—for most VLCCs had produced some 43 million tonnes of under-utilized ships, while storage, excess port time and the carriage of part cargoes had reduced the capacity even further. Eventually it is anticipated that up to half the world's tankers face early scrapping with the continuing decline of the "answer to all problems" VLCC and ULCC carriers, some already scrapped after less than ten years in commercial service.

A similar picture of gloom was painted by London shipping consultant H P Drewry in July for many of the world's bulk ships, especially vessels of over 50,000 tonnes, where there is serious overtonnage.

The only question that never seems to get asked is "If the often forecast world revival in trade does come then how will it be transported?" From the analysis of the facts and figures so far collated it seems to be "In ships of Comecon, China and other expanding countries". Perhaps the answer is the reason why the question isn't asked.

SHIP LOSSES AND DISASTERS

The subject of the safety of ships falls into two distinct categories: Firstly, there is design factor, which is becoming more prevalent in this era of "standard ship types" and, secondly, the faults caused by owners trying to economise on maintenance and general safety habits.

Early in 1981, 27 ships were checked as to design safety, in Japan, as the result of the loss of the "Onomichi Maru" in 1980 after breaking in two. The safety of bulk carriers has become a topic of concern since the loss of the "Berge Vanga" and the "Derbyshire." Further losses of a significant nature like the German lighter-carrier "Munchen" and tanker break-ups, like the "Energy Concentration," "Tanio" and "Kurdistan," have now become a major problem, but unfortunately the experts estimate it will take years to come to any firm conclusions, and by then the face of shipping will have changed again. Overall, however, the picture is better, with total losses in 1981 down £22million on the previous year. What is not so satisfactory is the loss of nine ships and 241 lives without logical explanation. A report in September on tanker accidents by three leading organisations proved that in most cases human failings were the biggest factor. One wonders how far this spreads to other incidents and whether modern ship design and complexity, with all its electronics etc., is getting beyond the present seamen. That is not to say that the men are not up to the mark, but rather that the ships are advancing more rapidly than the training and too much importance is being put on electronic warnings etc., rather than the seaman's eyes, skills and knowledge.

"Reform the laws against the sub-standard operator" has long been the call of the traditional shipping companies and, although the figures often speak out against them, the "flag of convenience operators" are forever claiming innocence. Both the Intergovernmental Maritime Consultative Organisation (IMCO) and the International Shipping Federation made impassioned pleas during the year for more to be done, but it remains a thorny problem as to how to take action against these operators in International waters. While in port any action would be the responsibility of the country being visited, as many of these vessels never call in ports of their home registry.

Flag of Convenience vessels accounted for more than half the total number of vessels lost in May, and for almost half the vessels involved in other incidents. Out of the 19 ships lost in September, 10 were under Greek, Panamanian or Liberian registry.

Tankers continued to feature very badly in casualty returns with almost 700 major incidents reported between 1973 and 1978. The Liberian registry accounted for 42% of this total.

RoRo vessels have also become the centre of controversy within the past year. Losses, some in unusual circumstances, have led to a train of thought towards possible unsafe design and operation. The losses of the "Mauritius II" and the 1979- completed "Zenobia" added a fair amount of fuel to this theory. The latter vessel had to make for port in Greece in February after developing a 45% list. Upon discharge, 25% of its cargo of cars was discovered to have been damaged. Four months later, in June, the ship again developed a serious list and had to be towed into port. After having water pumped into her ballast tanks by tugs to right her, she again developed a list and eventually sank.

Another casualty was the German RoRo vessel "Ems:" After a collision she sank in less than five minutes.

The Norwegian Bureau—Det Norske Veritas, reported to the "RoRo 81" conference, in Hamburg, that 12 of 28 losses since 1965 were due to either operational neglect or shifting cargo. This tended to endorse the builders' and operators' claims that it was, in fact, not the design of the ships that was the problem. This statement was also backed by the influential Swedish Club, and by The Salvage Association.

Apart from the tragedy to ships and men in the cases of ship loss there are also the problems of explosion and pollution to take into account. The annual report of the Advisory Committee on Oil Pollution of the Sea said, in June, that the national and international action against pollution still remained ineffective, despite promises of the government. This, of course, also included the problem of pollution from spilled bunkers and tank-washings. Calls have also been made for "havens" to be made available for crippled and distressed vessels. At present these 'lepers' of the marine world are turned away at almost every port, when the safety of a protected berth is needed most. The Port of Rotterdam is now taking steps to provide this service, on the theory that one has to take a few bad apples with all the good ones, in return for financial guarantees.

Similar problems arise in the discharge of gas in a crisis, and in this matter the UK was reported to lag far behind the USA and Norway in developing a safety system and provide the necessary men fully-trained to operate it. World maritime authorities are drawing up a convention to deal with the carriage of hazardous and noxious substances by sea. Plans are now well advanced for a diplomatic conference in London in 1982, when the scheme may well be taken an important stage further under the auspices of IMCO. The aim is to provide compensation for damage caused to casualties by high risk products such as chemicals and liquified gas.

Mr James Paffett, who, until his retirement, was general manager of the National Maritime Institute, warned a meeting in Newcastle, in October 1981, that while the causes of explosions in oil tankers were quite well known, "with gas tankers we enter the realm of some uncertainty". The total energy released if a large modern gas carrying ship were to explode would equal that of a nuclear weapon detonating. Other hazards included accidental escape of the gas at very low temperatures (minus 180°C) which could make the hull as brittle as glass, or if lost into the sea would be warmed up sufficiently by the water and boil. Under some circumstances this boiling could cause ebullition in the form of a thudding bump—virtually an explosion.

PORTS AND HARBOURS

The rise and fall of the fortunes of the world's ports and harbours does not seem to follow the usual pattern of decline in the Western World and the rise of the third world, but more the attitudes and determination of the individual ports and unions, and the environment.

Despite the world trade recession, the port of Hamburg had a 22.9% increase in its container handling in 1980. Apparently this is no coincidence as Hamburg had been consistently expanding over the past few years with this in mind.

The Jacksonville Port Authority in Florida announced an amazing 517% increase in general cargo over a three month period, ending December 1980.

At the same time, the US port, Houston, was reporting a decline, particularly in oil, which had dropped by 33%, although overall volume was up by 21%.

In the United Kingdom, the plight of London and Southampton continue and the Mersey Docks and Harbour Board reported a decline of 20% at Liverpool, to underline the ports demise.

Taiwan, on the other hand, is set to grow as a nation of the sea, if government plans to develop the island as a transhipment centre succeed.

Over the past decade the decline of the traditional port and the rise of the specialised container and oil port seem to be continuing, with a particular emphasis on major developments in suitable areas for transhipment. This in itself will almost certainly continue to affect the reduction in conventional vessels and also the traditional dockworkers' jobs of stevedoring the ship handling.

THE JOLLY ROGER

Captain Morgan and his contempories would not believe their luck, if they were to come alive, in this modern age of piracy. Over the past year the pirates and their rewards have featured regularly in the pages of the shipping press and, from time to time, the world's newspapers.

In the closing months of 1980 the American cargo ship "Poet" disappeared, along with her entire crew, while crossing the Atlantic. Lloyds of London and UK-based Insurance companies settled a £1 million claim for the vessel in February 1981, dismissing a claim from US news agencies that the vessel had been hijacked by the Mafia, for use in a heroin-running operation from Iran. The loss was officially attributed to a "freak storm" but the piracy claim was not altogether surprising in view of the formation in London of "The International Maritime Bureau", an organisation with maritime fraud as its main brief.

By June 1981 Thailand had asked the United Nations for £18million worth of equipment to help fight pirates in the South China Seas. Claims had been made that half the vessels arriving in Thailand, Malaysia and Singapore with Vietnamese refugees had been attacked, and there were probably in excess of 20,000 pirates operating in the area.

In September 1980 it was reported in *Lloyds List* that 2 Japanese vessels had been piracy targets in the notorious Phillips Channel. The 27,000 dwt container vessel "Hakata Maru" and the 80,000 ton "Diana" were both attacked and boarded and, shortly after that, the Shell-chartered tanker "Mammoth Monarch" suffered a similar skirmish whilst travelling through the channel at 12 knots.

Nigeria, and the coast of West Africa in general, also feature very frequently in these acts, along with the coastal areas of Columbia. Nearer to home, in Spain, the problem is not so much at sea as in port, with 45% of all cargo losses in 1980 being of Spanish origin.

These are only a few of the numerous reports over the year but they serve to highlight a problem that is fast becoming a worldwide epidemic. The pirates' targets, in the main, seem to be cash and valuables when attacking the larger merchantmen, but it seems only a matter of time before we are faced with further atrocities similar to the China Seas murders. Taking armed guards on board in areas of high risk is one of the methods now being used by some companies, but, increasingly, calls are being made for a multi-national sea-borne defence force.

It was inevitable that a new form of piracy would be involved, using modern technology—and it has: Fraud on paper. A special report in the *Journal of Commerce* in August 1981 illustrated the new method of using documentary credits to make the "haul". The report, from the International Maritime Bureau, stated, "Fraud, not theft, is the most likely problem to be encountered in Hong Kong". It warns that the new methods being used have forced fraud prevention into a subordinate position, with the onus for detecting possible tricks falling squarely on the consignee.

ACKNOWLEDGEMENTS

The invaluable help given by Lt. Cdr. E. C. Talbot-Booth, Director of the Ship Recognition Corps, has already been mentioned, but in addition we would also like to express our thanks to the Corps President and Committee for their faith and backing during this project and also to the publishers for their faith and perseverance to enable the book to be finished.

We would also like to express our thanks to the shipbuilders, manufacturers and companies who have kept us regularly supplied with information on their activities and to the many people in the shipping press that have provided material for use in the book. There are many individuals who have regularly supplied valuable information to whom we are indebted. Lack of space prevents us from naming them all but we would like to especially thank Peter Cundall and Stuart Dobson of New Zealand, Tony Smith of Walsall, Norman Thompson of London and Captain Eric Askew of Stockport.

Finally a word of thanks to Phillip Neumann, of FotoFlite, of Ashford, for his valuable assistance in the supplying of photographs in the new-building section and to the pilot of the plane and his photographer for so many good shots.

R. A. STREATER
Bromley, Kent.
December 1981.

MERCHANT SHIPS NEW BUILDINGS 1981

This section is devoted to a selection of the major merchant ship newbuildings in 1981. The fact that it takes many months for all the information to filter through means that not only are there some specific details missing but also some vessels omitted, especially those delivered late in the year. Details are from the worlds major yards, and where information conflicts, as it often does in new deliveries, the yards pre-delivery data has been used, where available. Much of this detail is, of course, subject to amendment and correction after delivery.

THE TEXT

The text for each entry has been gathered to give a clear and concise precis of each vessel. Where two or more known identical ships have been delivered they are cross referenced. The text has been collated as follows:

NAME
FLAG: abbreviated as in the ship recognition section. Full list of abbreviations can be found in the appropriate section.
TYPE
GRT: Gross Registered Tonnage
DWT: Dead Weight Tonnage.
DIMENSIONS: Length × breadth × draught—in metres
Note: Length (unless otherwise stated) is overall
(BB) length overall including bulbous bow (where known)
(BP) length between perpendiculars.

MACHINERY: bhp—brake horse-power.
shp—shaft horse-power
ENGINES: either builder (designer)
or designer/builder (where different).
SPEED:
OWNERS:
MANAGERS: if appropriate
BUILDERS:
YARD NUMBER:

Vessels that have already changed name or were launched under a previous name are listed under both and cross referenced.

A

ACCOLADE II (Au)
Type Limestone Carrier; 7500 DWT; Dimensions 108.63 × 23 × 6; Machinery Natural Gas/Motor 1650 bhp each; Engine builders Fuji/Caterpillar; 11 knots; Owners Adelaide Brighton Cement Ltd; Builders Carrington Slipways NSW; Yard No. 146.

ACE CONCORD (Br)
Type Container; 31071 GRT; 30220 DWT: Dimensions 207(BP) × 32.2 × 10.7; Machinery Motor 40220 bhp; Engine Builders Sulzer/IHI; 25.6 Knots; Owners Diamond Concord Shipping Co. Ltd., (C.Y. Tung Group); Builders Ishikawajima Do Brazil; Yard No. 116.

Ace Concord *(FotoFlite)*

ADDARRAQ (Mo)
Type Chemical Tanker; 14500 GRT; 24000 DWT; Dimensions 163 (BP) × 24.8 × 9.75; Machinery Motor 12000 bhp; Engine builders Sulzer/CCM; 15.4 Knots; Owners Marphocean; Builders Chantiers de France, Dunkerque; Yard No. 313.

ADRIA (It)
Type RoRo Cargo; 7010 GRT; 1000 DWT; Dimensions 148.32 × 22.71 × 6.32; Machinery Motor 15000 bhp; Engine builders GMT; Owners 'Adriatica' S.p.A. di Navigazione; Builders Cantieri Navali Riuniti S.p.A., Ancona; Yard No. 873.

AFRICAN EVERGREEN (Li)
Type Cargo; 5400 GRT; 7381 DWT; Dimensions 128 (BP) × 19 × 5.64; Machinery Motor 5200 bhp; Engine builders Mitsubishi-/Akasaka; 15 Knots; Owners African Evergreen Sg; Builders Shimoda DY Co. Ltd., Shimoda; Yard No. 315.

AFRICAN FERN - **sister of AFRICAN EVERGREEN (q.v.)**
Yard No. 316.

AFRICAN GARDENIA - **sister of AFRICAN EVERGREEN (q.v.)**
Yard No. 317.

AITOKU MARU (Ja)
Type Tanker; 699 GRT; 1600 DWT; Dimensions 66 × 10.6 × 4.75; Machinery (Sail - 160 sq metres) Motor 1600 bhp; Engine builders Daihatsu; 11.04 Knots; Owners Aitoku KK; Builders Imamura Zosen KK; Yard No. 271.

AKADEMIK ALEXSANDR NESMEYANOV (Ru)
Type Research (B86 Type); 4950 GRT; 1810 DWT; Dimensions 110.9 × 16.6 × 5.7; Machinery Motor 6400 bhp; Engine builders Sulzer/Zgoda; 16 Knots; Owners USSR; Builders Stocznia Szczecinska im A. Warskiego, Szczecin; Yard No. B86/02.

AKADEMIK ARTOBOLEVSKIY (Ru)
Type Cargo; 6300 GRT; 5600 DWT; Dimensions 133.08 × 18.04 × 7.68; Machinery Motor 13200 bhp; Engine builders Sulzer/H. Cegielski; 20.75 Knots; Owners USSR; Builders Stocznia Gdanska Im. Lenina, Gdansk; Yard No. B437/442.

Akademik Mstislav Keldysh *(FotoFlite)*

AKADEMIK MSTISLAV KELDYSH (Ru)
Type Research; 5500 GRT; Dimensions 122.2 × 17.8 × 5.9; Machinery Motor 5820 bhp; Engine builders Wartsila Vasa; 16 Knots; Owners USSR; Builders Hollming Oy, Rauma; Yard No. 0224.

Albula *(Centromar)*

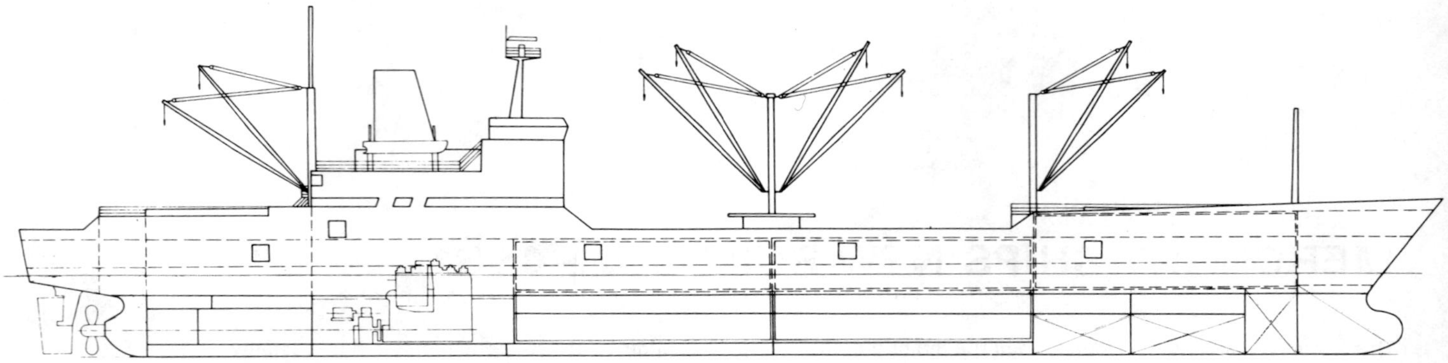

ALBULA (Sd)
Type Cargo; 8950 GRT; 11000 DWT; Dimensions 152.41 × 22.6 × 9.451; Machinery Motor 14780 bhp; Engine builders Sulzer/H. Cegielski; 21.9 Knots; Owners St. Gotthard, Schiffahrts A.G; Managers Suisse - Outremar Reederei A.G; Builders Stocznia Gdanska im. Lenina, Gdansk; Yard No. B360/01.

ALCA (Sp)
Type Cargo; 6900/9721 GRT; 12000/15000 DWT; Dimensions 148.06 × 19.26 × -/8.98; Machinery Motor 7500 bhp; Engine builders MAN/Bazan; Owners Maritima Astur S.A; Builders Empresa Nacional 'Bazan' de C.N.M.S.A., El Ferrol; Yard No. C1.

ALEXANDER (Li)
Type Ore/Bulk/Oil; 37914 GRT; 75714 DWT; Dimensions 240.72 × 32.67 × 14.34; Machinery Motor 16533 bhp; Engine builders MAN/Bremer Vulkan; 15.8 Knots; Owners Setenata Ltd; Managers Suisse - Outremer Reederei A.G; Builders Bremer Vulkan, Vegesack; Yard No. 1015.

ALGOWOOD (Ca)
Type Bulk (Gt Lakes); 22500 GRT; 32000 DWT; Dimensions 222.4 × 23.29 × 8.61; Machinery Motor 7500 bhp; Engine builders Mak; Owners Algoma Central Railway; Builders Collingwood Shipyards, Collingwood; Yard No. 219.

ALMUDENA (Sp)
Type Container; 11950 GRT; 17300 DWT; Dimensions 170 (BP) × 27 × 9.5; Machinery Motor 23900 bhp; Engine builders B & W/AESA; 21.7 Knots; Owners Trasatlantica; Builders Astilleros Espanoles S.A., Puerto Real; Yard No. 26.

ALTONIC - see GOLD AFRICA

AMAL TWO (Pa)
Type LGC; 3040 GRT; 3996 DWT; Dimensions 102.01 × — × 5.61; Machinery Motor 3200 bhp; Engine builders Akasaka; Owners Sun Iris Marine S.A; Builders Kishigami Zosen K.K., Akitsu; Yard No. 1403.

AMANDA (Fi)
Type Chemical Tanker; 1600 GRT; 3000 DWT; Dimensions 80(BP) × 14 × 6.2; Machinery Motor 3000 bhp; 13.8 Knots; Owners Polttoaine Osuuskunta; Builders Oy Navire AB., Naantali; Yard No. NH-72.

AMAPA (Bz)
Type RoRo/Cargo/Ferry; 500 GRT; 560 DWT; Dimensions 56.11 × — × 3.18; Machinery Motor 1000 bhp; Engine builders Daihatsu/Ishikawajima do Brasil; Owners E.N.A.S.A; Builders INCONAV, Rio de Janeiro; Yard No. 146.

AMARANTA (FRG)
Type Cargo; 8000 GRT; Dimensions 122.96(BP) × 20.2 × —; Machinery Motor 8160 bhp; 16.5 Knots; Owners Peter Dohle Schiffahrts K.G; Builders J.J. Sietas, Hamburg; Yard No. 827.

AMBIA FAIR (Li)
Type Ore/Bulk/Oil; 40000 GRT; 76000 DWT; Dimensions 235.1 × 32.2 × 14.2; Machinery Motor 15400 bhp; Engine builders B & W; 14.83 Knots; Owners L. Hoegh; Builders Hyundai Heavy Industries Co., Ltd., Ulsan; Yard No. 148.

AMBIA FINJO- sister of AMBIA FAIR (q.v.)
Yard No. 149.

AMERICAN REPUBLIC (US)
Type Bulk; 12158 GRT; 23110 DWT; Dimensions 192.37(BP) × 20.72 × —; Machinery Twin Screw Motor 7200 bhp; Engine builders General Motors; 15 Knots; Owners American Steamship Company; Builders Bay Shipbuilding Corporation, Sturgeon Bay, Wis.; Yard No. 724.

AMSTELVLIET (Ne)
Type Bulk; 22973 GRT; 38000 DWT; Dimensions 201.61 × 28 × 11.91; Machinery Motor 15000 bhp; Engine builders B & W/Bryansk; Owners Nedlloyd Bulk BV; Builders G. Dimitrov Shipyard, Varna; Yard No. 066.

AMSTELVOORN - sister of AMSTELVLIET (q.v.)
Yard No. 067.

ANA MARIA DE PANDO (Sp)
Type Chemical Tanker; 19566 GRT; 39340 DWT; Dimensions 168 (BP) × 32 × 10; Machinery Motor 11200 bhp; Engine builders B & W/AESA; 15.2 Knots; Owners M. Antares; Builders Ast. Espanoles S.A., Sestao, Bilbao; Yard No. 247

ANASTASIA (Gr)
Type Bulk ("Pri 26/15"); 15570 GRT; 26148 DWT; Dimensions 173.18 × 26.67 × 9.75; Machinery Motor 13300 bhp; Engine builders MAN/Mecanica Pesada; Owners International Freighting Corp; Builders C.C.N., Niteroi; Yard No. 112.

ANATOLIY VASILYEV (Ru)
Type RoRo Cargo/Cont; 15638 GRT; 22447 DWT; Dimensions 205.42 × 31.15 × 9.7; Machinery Motor 27000 bhp; Engine builders MAN; 21.75 Knots; Owners USSR; Builders Valmet Oy, Helsingin Telakka, Vuosaari, Helsinki; Yard No. 304.

ANDHIKA PALACE (Pa)
Type Cargo; 4351 GRT; 6940 DWT; Dimensions 100 (BP) × 17.6 × 6.87; Machinery Motor 4500 bhp; Engine builders Mitsubishi/Kobe; 12.5 Knots; Owners Sanzo Enterprise; Builders Higaki Zosen KK, Imabari; Yard No. 257.

ANDHIKA PARAMITA - sister of ANDHIKA PALACE (q.v.)
Yard No. 258.

ANJERITA (No)
Type Vehicle Carrier; 11700 GRT; 12000 DWT; Dimensions 167 (BP) × 29.2 × 8.5; Machinery Motor 10200 bhp; Engine builders B & W; 18.9 Knots; Owners Ugland Management Co. A/S; Builders Tsuneishi Zosen KK., Numakuma; Yard No. 473.

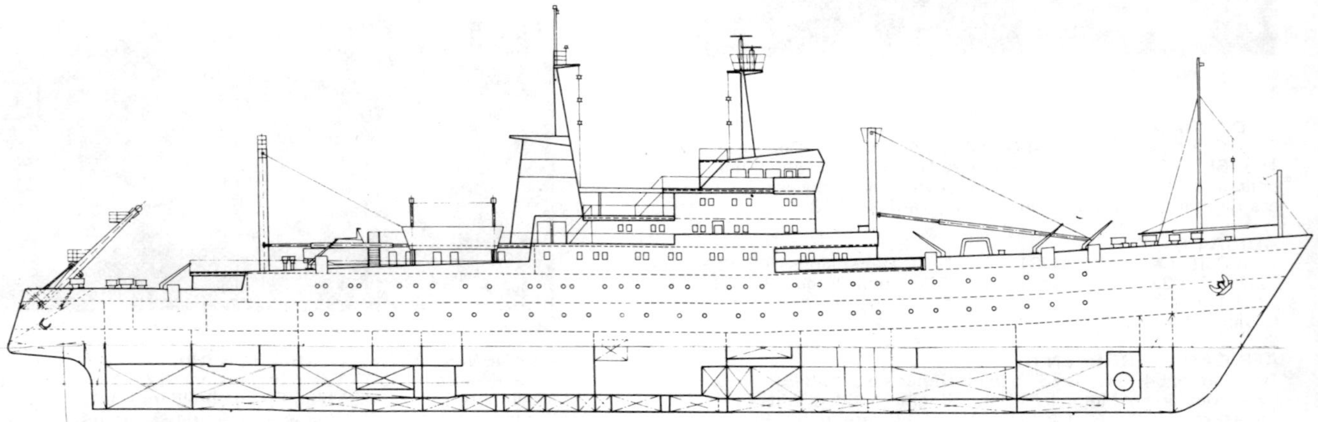

Akademik Aleksandr Nesmeyanov *(Centromar)*

ANSGARITOR (FRG)
Type Bulk; 35000 GRT; 63578 DWT; Dimensions 215.4 × 32.2 × 12.9; Machinery Motor 13680 bhp; Engine builders Sulzer/IHI; 14.9 Knots; Owners Part. M.S. 'Ansgaritor'; Builders IHI, Aioi; Yard No. 1746.

ANTIGUA (FRG)
Type Chemical Tanker; 2500 GRT; 4428 DWT; Dimensions 92 (BP) × 15.5 × 5.95; Machinery Motor 4000 bhp; Engine builders Mitsubishi/Kobe; 14 Knots; Owners Kompass Schiffahrtskontor; Builders Ernst. Menzer Schiffswerft, Hamburg; Yard No. 510.

ANTONIO MACEO (Cu)
Type Bulk; 15988 GRT; 25000 DWT; Dimensions 185.2 × — × 10.23; Machinery Motor 12000 bhp; Engine builders Sulzer/H. Cegielski; Owners Empresa Navegacion Mambisa; Builders G. Dimitrov Shipyard, Varna; Yard No. 141.

ANTONIO MACHADO (Sp)
Type Cargo; 9630 GRT; 15240 DWT; Dimensions 144.13 × 21.47 × 8.9; Machinery Motor 6150 bhp; Engine builders B & W/Ast. Espanoles; Owners Maritima de Cementos y Graneles; Builders Astilleros Espanoles S.A., Factoria de Olaveaga, Bilbao; Yard No. 324.

AOBASAN MARU (Ja)
Type Bulk; 71500 GRT; 132400 DWT; Dimensions 260 (BP) × 43 × 16.3; Machinery Motor 20400 bhp; Engine builders Sulzer/IHI; 15 Knots; Owners Mitsui OSK; Builders I.H.I. Kure; Yard No. 2755.

APULIA – sister of **ADRIA (q.v.)**
Builders Italcantieri S.p.A., Genova; Yard No. 4375.

ARATZ (Sp)
Type Fishing (Tuna); 1150 GRT; 1090 DWT; Dimensions 65.11 × — × 5.5; Machinery Motor 4640 bhp; Engine builders Alpha/C-ons. Echevarria; Onwners Atuneros del Atlantico S.S; Builders Ast. Luzuriaga S.A., Pasajes; Yard No. 220.

ARCHERY (Pa)
Type Cargo; 4752 GRT; 7970 DWT; Dimensions 116.13 × — × 7.2; Machinery Motor 6160 bhp; Engine builders B & W/Mitsui; Owners Majestic Shipping Ltd., S.A; Builders Iwagi Zosen KK, Iwagi; Yard No. 22.

ARCTIC – see **MAERSK PINTO**

ASAHI MARU No. 2 (Ja)
Type Tanker; 24021 GRT; 37182 DWT; Dimensions 166 (BP) × 30.0 × 11.02; Machinery Motor 12600 bhp; Engine builders Mitsubishi/Ube Kosan; 14.5 Knots; Owners Asahi Tanker K.K: Builders Kasado Dock Co. Ltd., Kudamatsu; Yard No. 320.

ASCONA (Gr)
Type Bulk; 30500 GRT; 59970 DWT; Dimensions 215 (BP) × 32.2 × 12.4; Machinery Motor; Engine builders B & W/Hitachi; 15.1 Knots; Owners Ascona Shipping Corp. (Liberia); Builders Hitachi Zosen, Maizuru; Yard No. 4662.

ASIA UNITY (Pa)
Type Bulk; 30000 GRT; 58420 DWT; Dimensions 213 (BP) × 32.2 × 11.48; Machinery Motor 14400 bhp; Engine builders Sulzer/TMMC: 14.9 Knots; Owners Dawn Maritime Corp; Builders China Shipbuilding Corp., Keelung; Yard No. 189.

ASIAN FRIENDSHIP (Pa)
Type Cargo; 3786 GRT; 6200 DWT; Dimensions 105.31 × 6.5; Machinery Motor 2600 bhp; Engine builders Akasaka Diesels; Owners Faygo S.S. Co. S.A; Builders Kochi Jukogyo K.K., Kochi; Yard No. 2178.

ASIAN PROGRESS (Br)
Ex PACIFIC PEACE 1981. Type Bulk; 36031 GRT; 60000 DWT; Dimensions 224 (BP) × 32 × 14.2; Machinery Motor 15200 bhp; Engine builders B & W/Hyundai; 14.5 Knots; Owners Panocean No. 2; Builders Hyundai Heavy Industries, Ulsan; Yard No. 155.

ASIAN STAR (Ja)
Type Cargo; 3600 GRT; 6200 DWT; Dimensions 110 (BP) × 19 × 6.9; Machinery Motor 6700 bhp; Engine builders Ito; 14 Knots; Owners Eastern Car Liner; Builders Kegoya Dock K.K., Kure; Yard No. 827.

ASTRAFEDERICO (Ar)
(Launched as CIUDAD DE SAN FERNANDO). Type Bulk; 18000 GRT; 25750 DWT; Dimensions 178.01 × 22.92 × 9.84; Machinery Motor 11500 bhp; Engine builders Gray/A.F.N.E: Owners Astramar Compania Argentina de Nav; Builders Ast. Argentinos Rio de la Plata, Tigre; Yard No. 142.

ATHENIAN VICTORY (Cy)
Type Tanker; 18495 GRT; 29940 DWT; Dimensions 178.87 × 25.33 × 11.1; Machinery Motor 10600 bhp; Engine builders B & W/Bryansk; Owners Blue Saronic Shipping Co. Ltd; Managers Athenian Tankers Management S.A; Builders Kherson Shipyard, Kherson; Yard No. 1911.

ATHENIAN XENOPHON – **sister of ATHENIAN VICTORY (q.v.)**
Yard No. 1912.

ATHINA K. (Gr)
Type Cargo; 11980 GRT; Owners Anstar; Builders Kherson Shipyard, USSR; Yard No. 2021.

ATLANTIC (Li)
Type Passenger; 30000 GRT; Dimensions 172 (BP) × 27.35 × 7.35; Machinery Motor; Engine builders GMT; 23.5 Knots; Builders Const. Nav. et Ind. de la Mediterranee (C.N.I.M.) La Seyne; Yard No. 1432.

ATLAS CHALLENGER (Li)
Type Tanker; 34000 GRT; 39600 DWT; Dimensions 169 (BP) × 32 × 12.8; Machinery Motor 11400 bhp; Engine builders Sulzer/'3 Maj'; 15.1 Knots; Owners Commodore Maritime Co; Builders Brodogradiliste '3 Maj', Rijeka; Yard No. 606.

AUGUST THYSSEN (Li)
Type Bulk/Oil; 37914 GRT; 75300 DWT; Dimensions 235 (BP) × 32.24 × 14.76; Machinery Motor 16520 bhp; Engine builders MAN/BV; 15.75 Knots; Owners City Corp; Managers Suisse - Outremar Reederei; Builders Bremer Vulkan, Vegesack; Yard No. 1016.

AUSTRALIAN GRAIN (Li)
Type Bulk (Fortune); 13200 GRT; 22000 DWT; Dimensions 155.45 × 22.86 × 9.99; Machinery Motor 8000 bhp; Engine builders Pielstick/IHI; Owners Co-op International Co; Builders I.H.I., Tokyo; Yard No. 2756.

AUTHOR – **see BENARMIN**

AUTOESTRADA (Bz)
Type RoRo Cargo; 4804 GRT; 6895 DWT; Dimensions 133.51 × — × 7.08; Machinery Twin Screw Motor 7800 bhp; Engine builders Sulzer/Zgoda; Owners Companhia de Navegacao Lloyd Brasileiro; Builders Stocznia Gdanska Im. Lenina, Gdansk; Yard No. B485/01.

AUTOVIA – **sister of AUTOESTRADA (q.v.)**
Yard No. B485/02.

AUTOMOBILE VENTURE – **see EUROPEAN VENTURE**

AVILA (Ja)
Type Tanker; 41000 GRT; 65500 DWT; Dimensions 227 (BP) × 32.2 × 12.5; Machinery Motor 13200 bhp; Engine builders Sulzer/IHI; 14.4 Knots; Owners Japan Line; Builders I.H.I., Aioi; Yard No. 2757.

AWOBASAN MARU (Ja)
Type Bulk/Ore; 71500 GRT; 132400 DWT; Dimensions 260 × 4.3 × 16.3; Machinery Motor 20400 bhp; Engine builders Sulzer-/IHI; 14.5 Knots; Owners Mitsui OSK Line & Sawayama SS. Co; Builders I.H.I., Kure; Yard No. 2755.

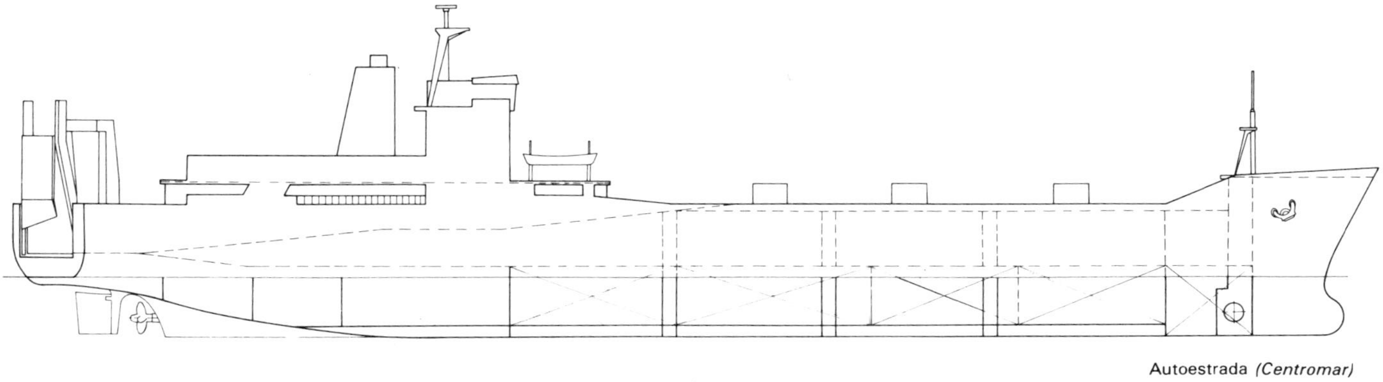

Autoestrada *(Centromar)*

AYDIN GULER (Tu)
Type Ferry; 456 GRT; 180 DWT; Dimensions 58.2 × 10.62 × 2.4; Machinery Twin Screw Motor 750 bhp; Engine builders Stork-Werkspoor; Owners D.B. Sehir Hatlari Isletmesi; Builders Denizcilik Bankasi T.A.O., Istinye, Istanbul; Yard No. 40.

AYUBIA - sister of MURREE (q.v.)
Yard No. 1409.

B

BAKENGRACHT - sister of BARENTZGRACHT (q.v.)
Yard No. 1183.

BALDER CABOT (Br)
Type Diving Support; 1599 GRT; 1604 DWT; Dimensions 72.07 × 16.41 × 4.7; Machinery Twin Screw Motor 5424 bhp; Engine builders Alco/MLW; 14 Knots; Owners Deasea Ltd; Managers Parley Augustsson (Management) A/S; Builders Marystown Shipyard Ltd., Newfoundland; Yard No. 29.

BALDER HOPE (Pa)
Type Bulk; 9900 GRT; 18400 DWT; Dimensions 137 (BP) × 22.86 × 9.27; Machinery Motor 8000 bhp; Engine builders Mitsubishi-/Kobe; 17 Knots; Owners Fairway Transportation; Builders Sasebo Heavy Industries Co. Ltd., Sasebo; Yard No. 298.

BALIKESIR I (Tu)
Type Ore; 12200 GRT; 18000 DWT; Dimensions 154.01 × 22.43 × 9.14; Machinery Motor 9000 bhp; Engine builders Sulzer-/Brodogradiliste '3 Maj'; Owners D.B. Deniz Nakliyati T.A.S; Builders Golcuk Naval Yard, Golcuk, Turkey; Yard No. 56.

BALTICO (Sp)
Bulk; 2203 GRT; 4000 DWT; Dimensions 79.66 × 13.8 × 5.68; Machinery Motor 1400 bhp; Engine builders B & W; 10.5 Knots; Owners Cia. Nav. Surena; Builders Ast. Del Cantabrico de Riera, Gijon; Yard No. 140.

BARBAROSSA - see IBN AL-AKFANI

BARENTZGRACHT (Ne)
Type Cargo; 1599/3467 GRT; 3444/6151 DWT; Dimensions 80.22 × 16.11 × 5.99/8.48; Machinery Motor 3000 bhp; Engine builders Hanshin Nainenki Kogyo; Owners C.V. Scheepvaart Onderneming 'Barentzgracht'; Builders Miho Zosensho KK, Shimizu; Yard No. 1165.

BARON KINNAIRD (Br)
Type Bulk (Prinasa 26/15); 17300 GRT; 26500 DWT; Dimensions 173.16 × 26.6; Machinery Motor 11305 bhp; Engine builders MAN/Mecapesa; 15.4 Knots; Owners Lyle & Hogarth; Builders Cia Comercia & Navegacao, Rio de Janeiro; Yard No. 142.

BAUMARE - sister of DANELOCK (q.v.)
Owners T. Klaveness; Yard No. 883.

BENARMIN (Br)
Ex AUTHOR 1981. Type Container; 28000 GRT; 23000 DWT; Dimensions 203.99 × — × 10; Machinery Motor 29000 bhp; Engine builders Sulzer/Cegielski; 22 Knots; Owners T & J Harrison; Chartered to Ben Line; Builders Stocznia Gdanska im Lenina, Gdansk; Yard No. B463/103.

BENNY QUEEN (Ja)
Type LPG; 46000 GRT; 44900 DWT; Dimensions 214 × 32.2 × 10.96; Machinery Motor 15200 bhp; Engine builders B & W/Mitsui; 15.3 Knots; Owners Showa Line; Builders Nippon Kokan K.K., Tsu; Yard No. 72.

BERGE CHARLOTTE - sister of LAGOVEN SINAMAICA (q.v.)
Owners Star Breeze Shipping; Managers A. P. Moller; Yard No. 1226.

BERGE ENTERPRISE (No)
Type Tanker; 203000 GRT; 320000 DWT; Dimensions 325 (BP) × 65 × 21.9; Machinery Motor 40900 bhp; Engine builders B & W/Mitsui; 16.05 Knots; Owners Sig Bergesen DY Co; Builders Mitsui Eng. & SB., Chiba; Yard No. 112.

BERGE HELENE - see LAGOVEN SINAMAICA

BERGE SUND (No)
Type LPG/Ammonia; 45200 GRT; 55200 DWT; Dimensions 223 × 34.2 × 13; Machinery Motor 23450 bhp; Engine builders Sulzer/Wartsila; 16.7 Knots; Owners Sig. Bergesen DY; Builders Oy Wartsila, Turku; Yard No. 1234.

BERNARDO DE ZAMACOLA - see MARIA INES

BERNINA - sister of ALBULA (q.v.)
Yard No. B360/02.

BERRIA (Sp)
Type Cement Carrier; 3353 GRT; 8103 DWT; Dimensions 106.84 × 15.83 × 6.78; Machinery Motor 4400 bhp; Engine builders Deutz/Hijos de J. Barreras; Owners Naviera de Cantabria S.A; Builders Ast. Construcciones S.A., Rios; Yard No. 253.

BEURSGRACHT - sister of BARENTGRACHT (q.v.)
Yard No. 1179.

BHARATENDU (In)
Type Cargo; 11311 GRT; 15700 DWT; Dimensions 152.51 (BB) × 22.66 × 9.59; Machinery Motor 9350 bhp; Engine builders B & W/Tvornica Dizel Motora 'Uljanik'; Owners The Shipping Corporation of India; Builders Brodogradiliste i Tvornica Dizel Motora 'Uljanik', Pula; Launched 1978. Lengthened and completed 1981; Yard No. 320.

BHASA - see VELEBIT (sister of BHARATENDU)

BHAVA BHUTI - sister of BHARATENDU (q.v.)
Launched as BHUSHAN; Yard No. 321.

BHAVU BHUTI - see TRIGLAV
Yard No. 319.

BHUSHAN - see BHAVA BHUTI

BICKERSGRACHT - sister of BARENTZGRACHT (q.v.)
Yard No. 1166.

BILLY JEANNE A (Li)
Type Tanker; 43000 GRT; 79999 DWT; Dimensions 243.82 (BB) × 41.6 × 12.2; Machinery Motor 15800 bhp; Engine builders B & W/Mitsui; 14.6 Knots; Owners New Resolution Carriers Corp; Builders Sanoyasu Dockyard Co. Ltd., Mizushima; Yard No. 1037.

BITLIS (Tu)
Type Ore; 12000 GRT; 18000 DWT; Dimensions 154.01 × 22.43 × 9.12; Machinery Motor 9000 bhp; Engine builders Sulzer-/Brodogradiliste '3 Maj'; Owners D. B. Deniz Nakliyati T.A.S; Builders Denizcilik Bankasi, T.A.O., Camialti; Yard No. 203.

BLAS DE LEZO - see MARIA FRANCISCA

BLUE EXCELSIOR (Li)
Type Tanker; 22150 GRT; 38000 DWT; Dimensions 172 (BP) × 31.4 × 10.95; Machinery Motor 12000 bhp; Engine builders B & W/Mitsui; 14.5 Knots; Owners Blue Excelsior Maritime; Builders Onomichi Dockyard Co. Ltd; Yard No. 297.

BLUE RIDGE - sister of SIERRA MADRE (q.v.)
Yard No. 415.

BONTEGRACHT - sister of BARENTZGRACHT (q.v.)
Yard No. 1180.

Bore Queen *(Builders)*

BORE QUEEN (Fi)
Type RoRo Cargo; 6849 GRT; 7984 DWT; Dimensions 142.1 × 23.0 × 7.62; Machinery Motor 6000 bhp; Engine builders Mak; 17.5 Knots; Owners Oy Bore Line; Builders Rauma Repola Oy, Rauma; Yard No. 261.

BOTANY TRANSCENDENT (Ja)
Type Chemical Tanker; 4600 GRT; 7800 DWT; Dimensions 107.02 × — × 8.02; Machinery Motor 4500 bhp; Engine builders Akasaka/Mitsubishi; Owners Mitshuama, Kisen, K.K; Builders K. K. Taihei Kogyo, Akitsu; Yard No. 1438.

BOTANY TRIBUTE (Pa)
Type Tanker; 4688 GRT; 7700 DWT; Dimensions 107.02 × 17.23 × 8.02; Machinery Motor 4500 bhp; Engine builders Sulzer/Mitsubishi; Owners Argus Overseas Shipping Co; Builders Kochi Jukogyo K.K., Kochi; Yard No. 2162.

BRAZIL VENTURE (Li)
Type Bulk; 18610 GRT; 32680 DWT; Dimensions 183 × 27.69 × 10.88; Machinery Motor 12600 bhp; Engine builders Sulzer/IHI; Owners Boston Shipping Ltd; Managers Venture Shipping (Managers) Ltd; Builders Kanda Zosensho KK, Kure; Yard No. 256.

BRIGITTE (Be)
Type Cargo 2000 GRT; 3609 DWT; Dimensions 110.1 × 11.41 × 3.83; Machinery Twin Screw Motor 1700 bhp; Engine builders Caterpillar; Owners Rudiger Clemens Janssens; Builders N. V. Scheepswerf van Rupelmonde, Rupelmonde; Yard No. 448.

Castillo de Monterrey *(Motor Ship)*

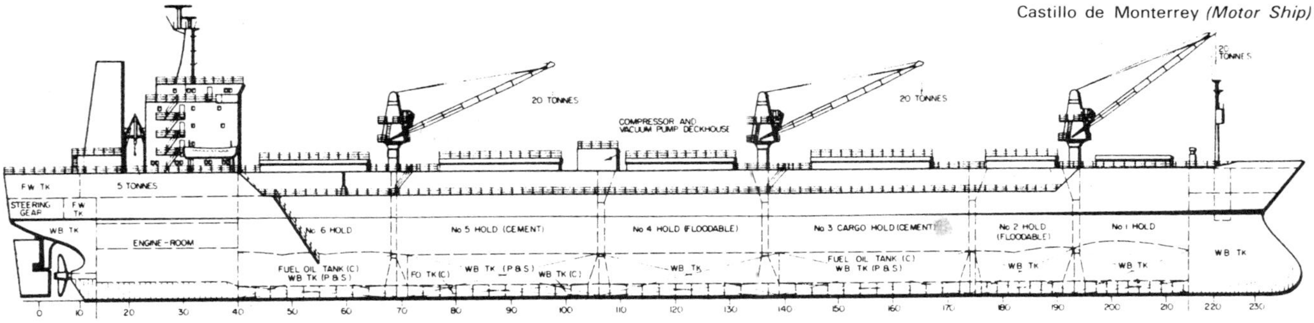

BRILLIANT VENTURE (Li)
Type Bulk; 29710 GRT; 58412 DWT; Dimensions 22.99 × 32.26 × 5.47; Machinery Motor 13100 bhp; Engine builders B & W/Mitsui; Owners Brilliance Carriers Inc; Builders Koyo Dockyard Co. Ltd., Mihara; Yard No. 1002.

Broere Aquamarine *(FotoFlite)*

BROERE AQUAMARINE (Ne)
Type Tanker; 3338 GRT; 4428 DWT; Dimensions 87 (BP) × 16 × 6.2; Machinery Motor 4400 bhp; Engine builders Deutz; 13.5 Knots; Owners Gebr. Broere; Builders Batservice Verft A/S, Mandal; Yard No. 660.

BUCREST - sister of BURSEA (q.v.)
Yard No. 559.

BUENA VENTURA (Gr)
Type Tanker; 29909 GRT; 55880 DWT; Dimensions 218 (BP) × 32.2 × 11.85; Machinery Motor 13100 bhp; Engine builders B & W/Mitsui; 14.3 Knots; Owners Sea Tankers Overseas Ltd; Builders Koyo Dockyard Co. Ltd., Mihara; Yard No. 1010.

BUNGA KANTAN (My)
Type Bulk; 18400 GRT; 31300 DWT; Dimensions 170 (BP) × 27.6 × 10.8; Machinery Motor 12600 bhp; Engine builders Sulzer/IHI; 16.6 Knots; Owners Malaysian International Shipping Corp; Builders Kanda Zosensho KK, Kawajiri or Kure; Yard No. 261.

BUNGA KESIDANG (My)
Type Bulk; 35000. GRT; 64400 DWT; Dimensions 217 (BP) × 32.2 × 12.37; Machinery Motor 14400 bhp; Engine builders Sulzer/Mitsubishi; 14.7 Knots; Owners Malaysian International Shipping Corp; Builders Namura Zosensho K.K., Imari Yard No. 849.

BURSEA (Pp)
Type Landing Craft; 499 GRT; 364 DWT; Dimensions 39.68 × 9.2 × 3.03; Machinery Motor Twin Screw 299 bhp; Engine builders Deutz; Owners Burns Philp (New Guinea) Ltd.; Builders Sing Koon Seng (Pte) Ltd, Singapore; Yard No. 556.

BURWAVE - sister of BURSEA (q.v.)
Yard No. 557.

C

CADDIE (Li)
Type Tanker; 49100 GRT; 81880 DWT; Dimensions 233(BP) × 39.36 × 18.19; Machinery Motor 17400 bhp; Engine builders B&W; 15.3. Knots; Owners Superline; Builders Ast. y. Talleres del Noroeste S.A., El Ferrol; Yard No. 259.

CAMBOURNE (Br)
Type Dredger/Sand Carrier; 3122 GRT; 5270 DWT; Dimensions 97.31 × 17.02 × 6.31; Machinery Twin Screw Motor 3114 bhp; Engine builders Mirrlees Blackstone Ltd; 12 Knots; Owners Civil & Marine Aggregate Co.; Builders Ailsa S.B. Co. Ltd., Troon; Yard No. 556.

CANOPUS (Li)
Type Tanker; 18402 GRT; 31000 DWT; Dimensions 164(BP) × 26 × 11.2; Machinery Motor 10800 bhp; Engine builders Sulzer/Mitsubishi; 15. Knots; Owners Canopus Tankers; Builders Hyundai Heavy Industries, Ulsan; Yard No. 141.

CAP CAROLINA (Sp)
Type Supply; 1041 GRT; 1200 DWT; Dimensions 60.23 × — × 4.81; Machinery Motor Twin Screw 8640 bhp; Engine builders Sulzer/Ast. Espanoles S.A.; Owners Compania Auxilaire Petrolifera S.A.; Builders Ast. Construcciones S.A., Meira; Yard No. 159.

CAP ISABEL - sister of CAP CAROLINA (q.v.)
Yard No. 160.

CAPE ARNHEM - sister of BARON KINNAIRD (q.v.)
Yard No. 124.

CAPE FINISTERRE - sister of BARON KINNAIRD (q.v.)
Yard No. 136.

CAPE THISTLE (Li)
Type Tanker; 17500 GRT; 29900 DWT; Dimensions 165 (BP) × 25 × 10.7; Machinery Motor 11200 bhp; Engine builders B & W/Mitsui; 15.5 knots; owners Elwyn Shipping; Builders Hayashikane Shipbuilding & Eng., Shimonoseki; Yard No. 1242.

CAPE TRAFALGAR - sister of BARON KINNAIRD (q.v.)
Yard No. 137.

CAPTAIN X. KYRIAKOU - sister of ATHENIAN VICTORY (q.v.)
Yard No. 1910.

CARIBE (Sp)
Type Cargo; 1415 GRT; 2253 DWT; Dimensions 78.85 × 11.87 × 5.0; Machinery Motor 1800 bhp; Engine builders MaK; Owners Navicar S.A.; Builders Ast. y. Talleres Celaya S.A., Bilbao; Yard No. 175

CARLA A. HILLS (Ja)
Type Tanker; 21400 GRT; 34950 DWT; Dimensions 168 (BP) × 30.4 × 10.95; Machinery Motor 11400 bhp; Engine builders Sulzer/Mitsubishi; 15.9 knots; owners Chevron Transport Corporation; Builders Mitsubishi Heavy Industries, Kobe; Yard No. 1114.

CARLINKA (Ja)
Type Tanker; 17265 GRT; 29900 DWT; Dimensions 162.01 (BP) × — × —; Machinery Motor 10800 bhp; Engine builders Mitsubishi/Kobe Hatsudoki; Owners K.K. Abo Shoten; Builders Minami - Nippon Zosen K.K., Usuki; Yard No. 534.

CAROL MARU (Ja)
Type LGC; 2999 GRT; 3402 DWT; Dimensions 99.8 × — × 5.41; Machinery Motor 3800 bhp; Engine builders Akaska; Owners Seifukumaru; Managers Kumazawa Kaiun KK; Builders Usuki Tekkosho, Usuki; Yard No. 1517.

CARRIANNA ORCHID (Li)
Type Bulk; 18420 GRT; 3200 DWT; Dimensions 172 (BP) × 26.6 × 10.7; Machinery Motor 11400 bhp; Engine Builders Sulzer/-Sumitomo; 14.5 knots; Owners Skyline Shipping; Builders Minami - Nippon K.K., Shitanoe; Yard No. 538.

CARRIANNA ROSE - sister of CARRIANNA ORCHID (q.v.)
Owners Swan Shipping; Yard No. 537.

CARWOOD (Pa)
Type Cargo; 4183 GRT; Dimensions 74.6 (BP) × 16 × 5.97; Machinery Motor 3000 bhp; Engine builders Hanshin; 12.7 knots; Owners Shipping Carrier Co.; Builders Miho Shipyard Co. Ltd.; Yard No. 1162.

CASTILLO DE JAVIER (Sp)
Type Cement Carrier; 28000 GRT; 44800 DWT; Dimensions 189.25 × 31 3 × 11.85; Machinery Motor 12300 bhp; Engine Builders B & W/AESA; 15.4 knots; Owners Elcano; Builders Ast. Espanoles, Sestao, Bilbao; Yard No. 226.

CASTILLO DE MONTERREY - sister of CASTILLO DE JAVIER (q.v.)
Yard No. 227.

Contender Argent *(Motor Ship)*

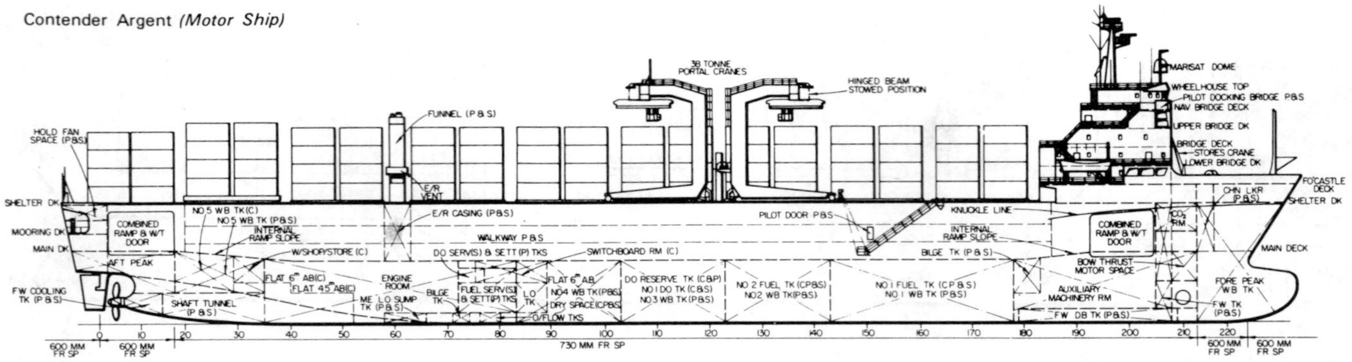

CATERINA (Sp)
Type Tanker, Oil/Chemical; 11626 GRT; 15456 DWT; Dimensions 149.03 × — × 8.85; Machinery Motor 6150 bhp; Engine builders B & W/Ast Espanoles S.A.; Owners MARPETROL; Builders Astilleros Espanoles S.A., Factoria de Sevilla, Sevilla; Yard No. 236.

Caterina *(FotoFlite)*

CATHERINE VENTURE (Li)
Type Bulk; 60500 GRT; 120000 DWT; Dimensions 253 (BP) × 42 × 15.85; Machinery Motor 18400 bhp; Engine builders B & W/Mitsui; Owners Dearene Shipping Ltd.; Builders Mitsui Eng. & SB. Co. Ltd., Tamano; Yard No. 1229.

CELTIC YANA (Li)
Type Bulk; 35000 GRT; 61140 DWT; Dimensions 217 (BP) × 32 × 12.51; Machinery Motor 14400 bhp; Engine Builders Sulzer/Mitsubishi; 14.5 knots; Adoria Shipping; Builders Namura Shipbuilding Co. Ltd., Imari; Yard No. 846.

CHAMPION - sister of E.L.M.A. CINCO (q.v.)
Owners Reederei Projex; Yard No. 404.

CHANG YUN (Tw)
Type Tanker; 127000 GRT; 210000 DWT; Dimensions 300 (BP) × 54.5 × 18.2; Machinery Motor 30600 bhp; Engine builders Sulzer/TMMC; 15.2 knots; Owners Chinese Petroleum Corp; Builders China Shipbuilding Corp., Kaohsiung; Yard No. 151.

CHEMICAL VENTURE (Li)
Type Chemical Tanker; 18600 GRT; 29900 DWT; Dimensions 162 (BP) × 25.4 × 10.6; Machinery Motor 11200 bhp; Engine builders B & W/Mitsui; 15.1 knots; Owners Pearl Carriers Inc.; Builders Minami - Nippon Zosen, KK, Usuki; Yard No. 536.

CHIE MARU No 5 (Ja)
Type Tanker; 699 GRT; 1750 DWT; Dimensions 68.56 × 11.03 × 4.5; Machinery Motor 1800 bhp; Engine Builders Hanshin Nainenki Kogyo; Owners Yawatahama Shosen KK; Builders Kurinoura Dock K.K., Japan; Yard No. 156.

CHIMO (No)
Type Bulk (Fortune Type); 13881 GRT; 21170 DWT; Dimensions 164.34 (BB) × 22.92 × 9.85; Machinery Motor 8000 bhp; Engine builders Pielstick/IHI; 15 knots; Owners K/S A/S Chimo & Co.; Managers Paal Wilson & Co. A/S; Builders I.H.I., Tokyo; Yard No. 2744.

CHIOS (Gr)
Type Tanker; 23000 GRT; 39830 DWT; Dimensions 168 (BP) × 30 × 11.9; Machinery Motor 10800 bhp; Engine Builders Sulzer/Mitsubishi; Owners Earl Maritime; Builders Mitsubishi Heavy Industries Ltd., Nagaskaki; Yard No. 1873.

CHIZUKAWA MARU (Ja)
Type Tanker; 39000 GRT; 60200 DWT; Dimensions 219 (BP) × 32.2 × 12.19; Machinery Motor 14000 bhp; Engine builders MAN/Mitsubishi; 14.8 knots; Owners Kasumigaseki KK; Builders Mitsubishi Heavy Industries Ltd., Kobe; Yard No. 1127.

CHUL JIN (Ko)
Type Cargo; 956 GRT; 1500 DWT; Dimkensions 66.81 × 12.22 × 4.10; Machinery Motor 1400 bhp; Engine builders Hanshin Nainenki Kogyo; Owners Han Jin Transportation Co. Ltd.; Builders Busan SB. & Eng. Co. Ltd., Busan; Yard No. 332.

CHUN HI (Ko)
Type Cargo; 1592 GRT; 2616 DWT; Dimensions 82.66 × 12.2 × —; Machinery Motor 1800 bhp; Engine builders Hanshin/Ssang Yong; Owners Chun Jyung Shipping; Builders Dae Sun SB & Eng. Co. Ltd., Busan; Yard No. 251.

CHUN JI - sister of CHUN HI (q.v.)
Yard No. 256.

CITY OF OXFORD (Br)
Type Container; 1599 GRT; 4184 DWT; Dimensions 96 (BP) × 16.5 × 5.5; Machinery Motor 5000 bhp; Engine Builders Doxford; 14.5 knots; Owners Ellerman City Liners; Builders Appledore Shipbuilders, Appledore; Yard No. 125.

CIUDAD DE SALAMANCA (Sp)
Type RoRo Cargo/Ferry; 7500 GRT; — DWT; Dimensions 125 (BP) × 20.5 × —; Machinery Motor; Engine builders MAN/Bazan; 21 knots; Owners Trasmediterranea; Builders Union Nav. de. Levante. S.A., Valencia; Yard No. 142.

CIUDAD DE SAN FERNANDO see ASTRAFEDERICO.

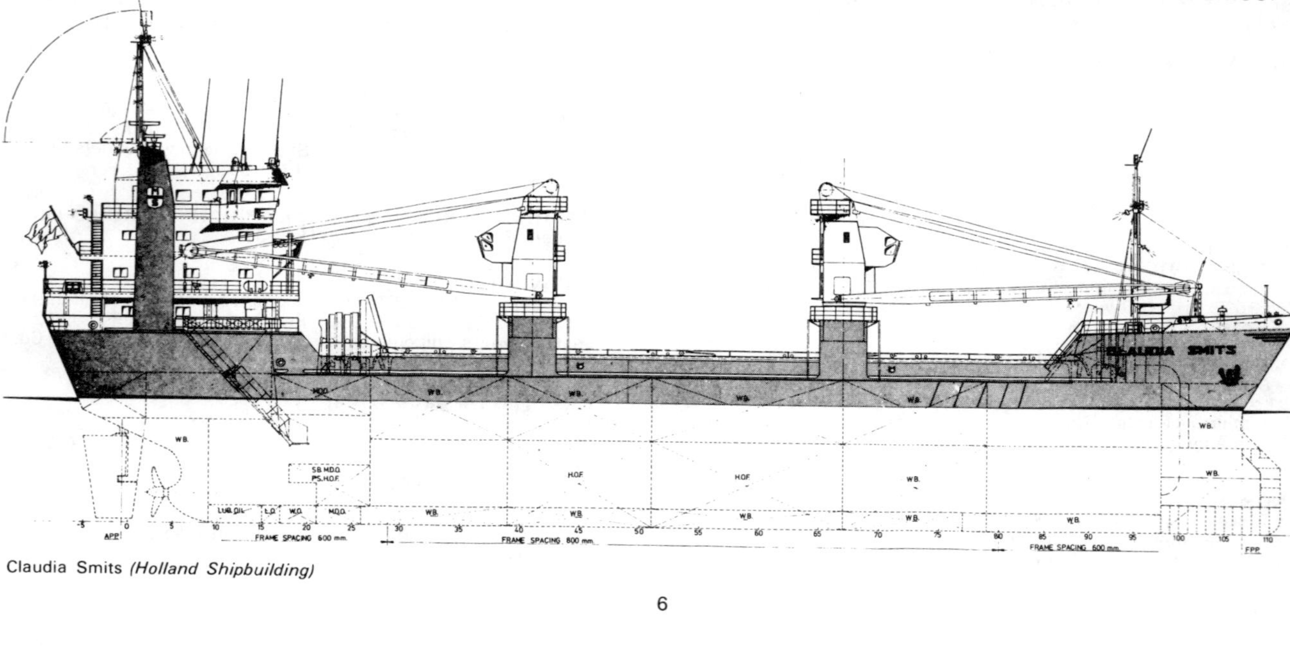

Claudia Smits *(Holland Shipbuilding)*

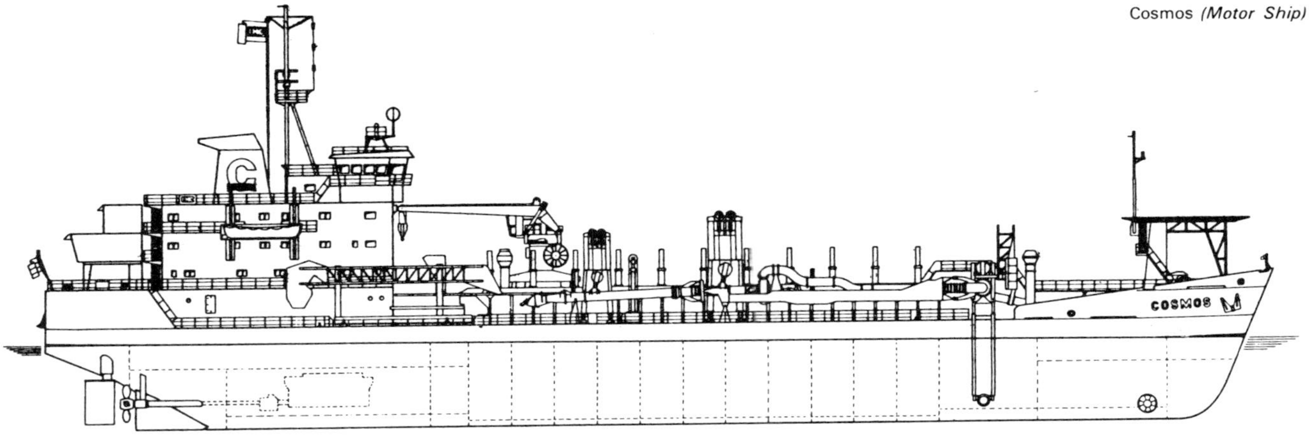

Cosmos *(Motor Ship)*

CLAUDIA SMITS (Ne)
Type Cargo; 3460 GRT; 3123/6020 DWT; Dimensions 84.18 × 17 × 5.74/8.38; Machinery Motor 2500 bhp; Engine builders Stork Werkspoor; 12 knots; Owners M. Smits; Builders De Groot & Van Vliet Scheepsw. en Mach, Slikkerveer; Yard No. 404.

COAST RANGE (US)
Type Tanker; 24500 GRT; 37500 DWT; Dimensions 190.81 (BP) × 30.48 × 10.06; Machinery Steam Turbine; Engine builders General Electric; 16.6 knots; Owners West Coast Shipping; Builders National Steel & SB., San Diego; Yard No. 416.

COLUMBIA NEPTUNE (Li)
Type Tanker; 33000 GRT; 58950 DWT; Dimensions 216 (BP) × 32.2 × 12.19; Machinery Motor 12900 bhp; Engine Builders B & W/Mitsui; 15 knots; Owners Intercom Petroleum; Managers C.Y. Tung; Builders Tsuneishi Zosen K.K., Numakuma; Yard No. 472.

COLUMBIA STAR (US)
Type Bulk; 40000 GRT; 61500 DWT; Dimensions 304.8 × 32 × 8.38; Machinery Motor 14000 bhp; Engine builders General Motors; Owners Oglebay Norton Co.; Builders Bay Shipbuilding & D.D. Co., Sturgeon Bay; Yard No. 726.

COMANDANTE REVELLO (It)
Type RoRo Cargo; 19000 GRT; 28500 DWT; Dimensions 194.37 × 32.29 × 10.8; Machinery Motor 22500 bhp; Engine Builders Grandi Motori Trieste; 19 knots; Owners Andrea Merzario S.p.A.; Builders Italcantieri S.p.A., Monfalcone; Yard No. 4371.

CONCORD - see EASTMED QUEEN.

CONTENDER ARGENT (Br)
Type Container/RoRo Cargo; 12000 GRT; 18500 DWT; Dimensions 173 × 30.4 × 8.2; Machinery Motor 10530 bhp; Engine builders Pielstick/Lindholmen; 19 knots; Owners Sea Containers; Builders Cant. Nav. Breda, S.p.A., Venice; Yard No. 292.

CONTENDER BEZANT - sister of CONTENDER ARGENT (q.v.)
Yard No. 293.

CONUS (Au)
Type Tanker; 26324 GRT; 38850 DWT; Dimensions 177.71 (BB) × — × 10.68; Machinery Motor 10260 bhp; Engine builders Sulzer/Mitsubishi; 14.5 knots; Owners Shell Co. of Australia Ltd.; Builders Mitsubishi Heavy Industries Ltd., Kobe; Yard No. 1110.

Coral Essberger *(FotoFlite)*

CORAL ESSBERGER (FRG)
Type Chemical Tanker; 1600 GRT; 2860 DWT; Dimensions 74.5 (BP) × 13.38 × 5.34; Machinery Motor 2000 bhp; Engine Builders MaK; 12.5 knots; Owners John T. Essberger; Builders Busumer Werft G.m.b.H., Busum; Yard No. 1438.

CORAL TEMSE (Be)
Type LPG; 6762 GRT; 8365 DWT; Dimensions 110 (BP) × 18.5 × 8.6; Machinery Motor 6330 bhp; Engine builders MAN/ACEC; 16 knots; Owners Exmar S.A. & Marine Service Belgium S.A.; Builders Boelwerf S.A., Temse, Belgium; Yard No. 1505.

CORTINA (Sw)
Type Chemical Tanker; 6350 GRT; 10700 DWT; Dimensions 121.5 (BP) × 18.5 × 7.2; Machinery Motor 6300 bhp; Engine builders MaK; 14.8 knots; Owners Reederei Joel Backman & Soner; Builders Schichau Unterweser AG, Bremerhaven; Yard No. 2276.

COSMOS (Ne)
Type Dredger/Anti-pollution; 5000 GRT; 9500 DWT; Dimensions 113.6 × 20 × 7.28; Machinery Motor 10400 bhp; Engine builders Stork Werkspoor; 13.7 knots; Owners Nederland State Waterways; Builders I.H.C. Smits BV., Kinderdyk; Yard No. Co1137.

COSTA ARABICA (It)
Type Container/RoRo; 22126 GRT; 27300 DWT; Dimensions 156.8 (BP) × 27.3 × 11.45; Machinery Motor 22400 bhp; Engine Builders GMT; 17 knots; Owners Renesso S.p.A; Builders Italcantieri, S.p.A, Monfalcone, Trieste; Yard No. 4373.

COSTA LIGURE - sister of COSTA ARABICA (q.v.)
Yard No. 4374.

Costa Arabica *(FotoFlite)*

COSTA RICA (FRG)
Type Cargo; 9200 GRT; 11500 DWT; Dimensions 145.85 × — × 7.65; Machinery Motor ; 16.8 knots; Owners H. Schuldt; Builders Stocznia Szczecinska A. Warskiego, Szczecin; Yard No. B430/12.

COSTAS KONIALIDIS - see KOSTAS KONIALIDIS

COTE D'AZUR (Fr)
Type RoRo Ferry; 8000 GRT; Dimensions 122.3 (BP) × 22.5 × 5; Machinery Motor 23400 bhp; Engine builders Pielstick/Atlantique; Owners S.N.C.F; Builders Atelier & Chantier du Havre; Yard No. 256.

Cote D'Azur *(FotoFlite)*

C. V. RAMAN (In)
Type Tanker; 27000 GRT; 40870 DWT; Dimensions 170 × 31 × 9.14; Machinery Motor 8415 bhp; Engine builders Sulzer/Mitsubishi; 13.8 knots; Owners Shipping Corporation of India; Builders Mitsubishi Heavy Industries, Kobe; Yard No. 1116.

Danelock *(Shipping World & Shipbuilder)*

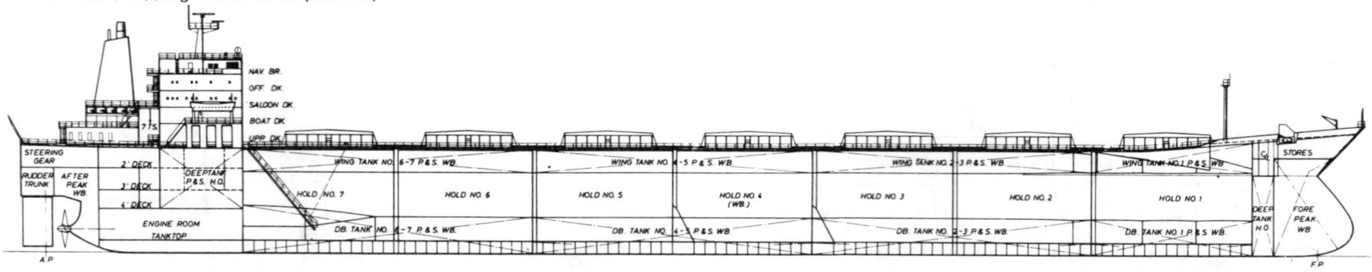

D

DA QING 218 (RC)
Type Tanker; 3890 GRT; 6038 DWT; Dimensions 99.98 (BP) × 14.94 × 7; Machinery Motor 4400 bhp; Engine Builders B & W/Hitachi; 13 knots; Owners Peoples Republic of China; Builders Malta Drydocks; Yard No. 139.

DAIJU MARU No 2 (Ja)
Type Tanker; 699 GRT; 1702 DWT; Dimensions 73 × — × 4.652; Machinery Motor 1600 bhp; Engine builders Akasaka; Owners Daiju Kaiun K.K; Builders Shirahama Zosen K.K., Honai; Yard No. 101.

DANA (De)
Type Research/Fishing; 2483 GRT; 890 DWT; Dimensions 78.44 × 14.81 × 5.7; Machinery Motor 4650 bhp; Engine builders B & W; Owners Govt. of the Kingdom of Denmark; Builders Dannebrog Vaerft A/S, Aarhus; Yard No. 175.

DANELOCK (Li)
Type Bulk; 33539 GRT;64000 DWT; Dimensions 225.0 (BB) × 32.24 × 13.1; Machinery Motor 15400 bhp; Engine builders B & W/Mitsui; 15 knots; Owners Turnville Shipping Ltd.; Managers Wheelock Marden; Builders B & W Skibsvaerft, Kobenhaven; Yard No. 881.

DANIELA (Bz)
Type Bulk; 26512 GRT; 38049 DWT; Dimensions 191.8 (BP) × 27.2 × 10.35; Machinery Motor 13100 bhp; Engine builders B & W/Villares; 15.2 knots; Owners Empresa de Nav. Alianca, S.A.; Builders Industrias Reunidas Caneco, Rio de Janeiro; Yard No. 224.

DARYA KAMAL (Br)
Type Bulk; 17716 GRT; 31000 DWT; Dimensions 181 (BP) × 23.1 × 10.65; Machinery Motor 12000 bhp; Engine builders Sulzer/-Clark Hawthorn; 15 knots; Owners Quadrant Shipping (Kishinchand Chelleram Group); Builders Sunderland Shipbuilders, Deptford; Yard No. 860.

DELEGAT (Ru)
Type Tanker; 4821 GRT; 5873 DWT; Dimensions 105 (BP) × 17 × 7.02; Machinery Motor 3500 bhp; Engine builders B & W/Bryansk; 14 knots; Owners U.S.S.R.; Builders Rauma-Repola, Rauma; Yard No. 269.

DEMA PHOSPHATE (Pa)
Type Bulk; 13913 GRT; 25446 DWT; Dimensions 169 × 23 × 9.99; Machinery Motor 9380 bhp; Engine Builders B & W/Hitachi; 15.6 knots; Owners Sevenseas Maritime Carriers; Builders Osaka Shipbuilding. Osaka; Yard No. 401.

DHAN (Kh)
Type Cement Carrier; 8500 GRT; 12550 DWT; Dimensions 130 (BP) × 21 × 8.1; Machinery Motor 4000 bhp; Engine builders MaK/Ube; 10.5 knots; Owners Gulf Cement; Builders Shikoku Dock Co. Ltd., Takamatsu; Yard No. 814.

Diplomat *(FotoFlite)*

DIPLOMAT (US)
Type RoRo Cargo; 13400 GRT; 9094 DWT; Dimensions 168.8 × 21.6 × 6.45; Machinery Motor 10000 bhp; Engine builders Stork - Werkspoor; 17.2 knots; Owners Co-ordinated Caribbean Transport Inc.; Builders Jos. L. Meyer, Papenburg (Ems); Yard No. S597.

DMITRIY POKROVICH (Ru)
Type Fish Factory; 3000 GRT; Dimensions 93.91 (PB) × 15.93 × 5.76; Machinery Motor 5200 bhp; Engine builders Sulzer/Zgoda; Owners U.S.S.R.; Builders Stocznia Gdanska im Lenina, Gdansk; Yard No. B408/19.

Docebeta *(FotoFlite)*

DOCEBETA (Bz)
Type Bulk; 40000 GRT; 70000 DWT; Dimensions 241.87 × 32.26 × 12.96; Machinery Motor 17400 bhp; Engine builders Sulzer-/Ishikawajima do Brasil; Owners Docenave; Builders Verolme Est. Reunidos do Brasil S.A., Jacuacanga; Yard No. B55.

DOCEBRISA - sister of DOCEBETA (q.v.)
Yard No. B56.

DOCEBRUMA - sister of DOCEBETA (q.v.)
Yard No. B57.

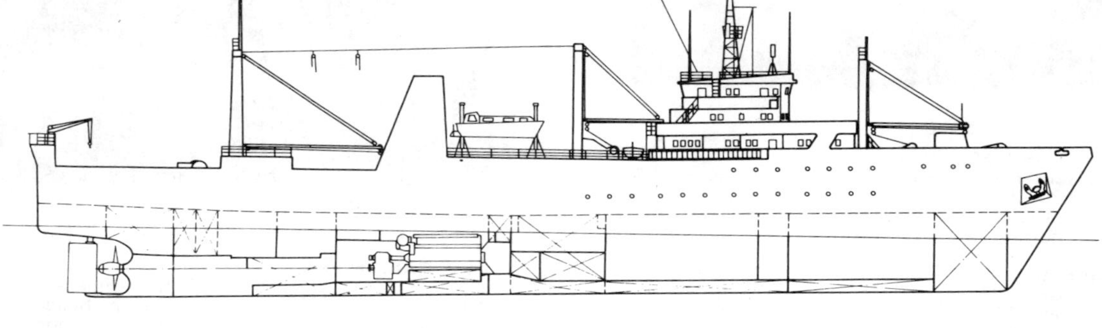

Dmitriy Pokrovich *(Centromar)*

Donald Redford *(Port of Manchester)*

DONALD REDFORD (Br)
Type Hopper/Dredger; 595 GRT; 750 DWT; Dimensions 43.01 × 10.7 × 3.6; Machinery Motor 640 bhp; Engine builders A.P.E. Allen; Owners W & G Industrial Leasing Ltd.; Managers Manchester Ship Canal Co.; Builders Ferguson Bros (Port Glasgow) Ltd.; Yard No. 484.

DOROTHEA SCHULTE (FRG)
Type LPG; 4950 GRT; 6095 DWT; Dimensions 110.9 × 15.5 × 7.52; Machinery Motor 5910 bhp; Engine builders B & W; 14.2 knots; Owners Bernhard Schulte; Builders Jos. L. Meyer, Papenburg (Ems); Yard No. S595.

DORSCH (FRG)
Type Tanker; 6355 GRT; 10854 DWT; Dimensions 122 (BP) × 18.5 × 8.3; Machinery Motor 6000 bhp; Engine builders MaK; 14.5 knots; Owners Carl Buttner; Builders Berner Schiffswerft, Bardenfleth; Yard No. 1375.

DUKE OF HOLLAND II (Ne)
Type RoRo Ferry; 1600 GRT; Dimensions 80 × 17.3 × 4.4; Machinery Motor 4000 bhp; 14 knots; Owners Norfolk Line. B.V.; Builders Amels B.V., Makkum; Yard No. 375.

DURRINGTON (Br)
Type Bulk; 7673 GRT; 11990 DWT; Dimensions 137.6 (BB) × 18.67 × 7.92; Machinery Motor 6500 bhp; Engine builders Stork-Werkspoor; 14 knots; Owners Stephenson Clarke Shipping Ltd.; Builders Verolme Scheepswerf Heusden B.V., Heusden; Yard No. 982.

Dyvi Swan *(FotoFlite)*

DYVI SWAN (No)
Type Tanker/Semi Submersible-Heavylift; 18000 GRT; 33200 DWT; Dimensions 170.8 (BP) × 32.26 × 9.99; Machinery Motor 13100 bhp; Engine builders B & W/Fredriksstad; 14.75 knots; Owners J-E. Dyvi A/S; Builders Kaldnes Mek Verksted A/S, Tonsberg; Yard No. 217.

Elma Cinco *(Builders)*

E

E.L.M.A. CINCO (FRG)
Ex ESTETURM 1981. Type Container; 4999 GRT; 7950 DWT; Dimensions 117.2 (BP) × 20 × 6.06; Machinery Motor 6000 bhp; Engine builders MAN/ Kawaski; 15.02 Knots; Owners M/S 'Esteturm' Hauschildt KG; Managers Bauer & Hauschildt KG. Charter to E.L.M.A; Builders Rickmers Werft, Bremerhaven; Yard No. 398.

EAGLE 1 (US)
Type Hopper/Dredger; 4200 GRT; 4940 DWT; Dimensions 96.63 × — × —; Machinery Twin Screw Motor 7460 bhp; Engine builders Alco Engine Div. of White Industrial; Owners Eagle Dredging Corp; Builders Avondale Shipyards Inc., Avondale; Yard No. 2320.

EASTERN RANGER (Li)
Type Tanker; 34000 GRT; 55000 DWT; Dimensions 216 (BP) × 32.2 × 11.7; Machinery Motor 1400 bhp; Engine builders Sulzer/Sumitomo; 15.3 Knots; Owners Yeaman Shipping; Builders Oshima Zosen, Nagasaki; Yard No. 10052.

EASTMED QUEEN (FRG)
Ex CONCORD 1981. Type Cargo; 1588 GRT; 4059 DWT; Dimensions 92.3 × 15.45 × 5.79; Machinery Motor 2000 bhp; Engine builders Deutz; 15 knots; Owners Jakob Winter; Builders J. J. Sietas, Hamburg; Yard No. 884.

EASTWIND (Gr)
Type Bulk; 16700 GRT; 26200 DWT; Dimensions 163 (BP) × 26.3 × 9.58; Machinery Motor 11550 bhp; Engine builders Sulzer/Sumitomo; Owners Westwind Africa Line; Builders Oshima Zosen, Nagasaki; Yard No. 10055.

EASY RIDER (Gr)
Type RoRo Cargo; 4618 GRT; 5500 DWT; Dimensions 148.44 × 20.22 × 9.34; Machinery Twin Screw Motor 12000 bhp; Engine builders MWM; Owners Castello Shipping & Naviglad Shipping; Builders Nuovo Cantieri Apuania S.p.A., Marina di Carrara; Yard No. 2119.

EGGARLOCK (Li)
Type Bulk; 15140 GRT; 27000 DWT; Dimensions 182.8 (BP) × 22.86 × 9.45; Machinery Motor 10500 bhp; Engine builders B & W/Mitsui; 14.6 Knots; Owners Essex Carriers; Builders Nipponkai Heavy Industries, Toyama; Yard No. 217.

EIHO MARU (Ja)
Type Tanker; 999 GRT; 2350 DWT; Dimensions 72.01 (BP) × — × 5.01; Machinery Motor 1100 bhp; Engine builders Hanshin Nainenki Kogyo; Owners Yokohama Yusosen KK & Sanpo Unyu KK; Builders K. K. Matsuura Zosen, Kinoe; Yard No. 282.

EIYO MARU (Ja)
Type Bulk/Wood Chip; 36500 GRT; 43000 DWT; Dimensions 189.00 × 32.2 × 11.0; Machinery Motor 12000 bhp; Engine builders Sulzer/IHI; 14.8 Knots; Owners Mitsui O.S.K. Lines Ltd., & Inui Kisen K.K; Builders I.H.I., Aioi; Yard No. 2745.

EL CHALLENGER (Pa)
Type Bulk; 15900 GRT; 26300 DWT; Dimensions 170.77 (BP) × 22.7 × 10.39; Machinery Motor 10800 bhp; Engine builder Sulzer; 15 Knots; Owners Litonjua Shipping; Builders Austin & Pickersgill, Sunderland; Yard No. 1402.

EL CRUSADER (Pa)
Type Bulk; 24600 DWT; Dimensions 172 (BP) × 22.8 × 10.21; Machinery Motor 12000 bhp; Engine builders Sulzer/Cegielski; 15.3 Knots; Owners Inter-Royal Sg., Co., S.A; Builders G. Dimitrov; Yard No. 142.

EL QUINTO (Sp)
Type RoRo Cargo; 1040 GRT; 1960 DWT; Dimensions 74.71 × 14.38 × 4.57; Machinery Motor 2200 bhp; Engine builders B & W/Cons. Echevarria; Owners Compania Madrilena de Navegacion, S.A; Builders Ast. Construcciones, S.A., Meira; Yard No. 161.

El Sexto *(FotoFlite)*

EL SEXTO – sister of EL QUINTO (q.v.)
Yard No. 162.

EL TOR (Eg)
Type Passenger/RoRo/Cargo/Ferry; 4609 GRT; 800 DWT; Dimensions 105.97 (BB) × 17.3 × 4.13; Machinery Twin Screw Motor 9900 bhp; Engine builders Nordberg/A/S Bergens; 19 Knots; Owners MISR Edco Shipping Co., Ltd; Builders A/S Bergens M/V, Bergen; Yard No. 794.

ELGIN (Li)
Launched as LAKE DROVILLE. Type Ore/Bulk; 86208 GRT; 17600 DWT; Dimensions 285 (BP) × 50 × 17; Machinery Motor 23900 bhp; Engine builders B & W/Mitsui; 14 Knots; Owners Bulkers Ltd; Managers Anglo Nordic Bulkships (Management) Ltd; Builders Nippon Kokan K.K., Tsu. Yard No. 71.

ELIZA HEEREN (FRG)
Type Cargo; 999 GRT; 2347 DWT; Dimensions 79.71 (BB) × 14.03 × 5.07; Machinery Motor 1770 bhp; Engine builders Mak; 12 Knots; Owners Johann Heeren; Builders Schiffswerft Heinrich Brand K.G., Oldenburg; Yard No. 206.

ELSEBETH VESTA (De)
Type Cargo; 499 GRT; 1300 DWT; Owners P/R Elsebeth Vesta; Managers Jorgen Jensen Partrederiet; Builders Nordsovaerftet A/S, Ringkobing; Yard No. 149.

EMILE D. (Be)
Type Cargo; 2500 GRT; 3500 DWT; Owners Antwerp Maritime BV; Builders Fulton NV, Ruisbruek; Yard No. 140.

ERIMA CHIEF (Pp)
Type RoRo/Cargo/Landing Craft; 263 GRT; 301 DWT; Dimensions 33.53 × 9.28 × 2.6; Machinery Twin Screw Motor 558 bhp; Owners Steamships Trading Co., Ltd; Builders Land & Sea Construction Services, Singapore; Yard No. 021.

ESQUIMAL - see FRIGO TENERIFE

ESSO AVON (Br)
Type Tanker; 1599 GRT; 3200 DWT; Dimensions 84 (BP) × 13.5 × 5.5; Machinery Motor bhp; Engine builders Deutz; Owners Esso Petroleum Co., Ltd; Builders N.V. Nieuwe Noord Nederlandsche Scheepswerven, Groningen; Yard No. 401.

Esso Finlandia *(Builders)*

ESSO FINLANDIA (Fi)
Type Tanker; 4000 GRT; 7000 DWT; Dimensions 100 (BP) × 17.5 × 7.3; Machinery Motor 5020 bhp; Engine builders Warsila/Vasa; 14 Knots; Owners Esso Petroleum; Builders Oy Navire, Naantali; Yard No. NY-70.

ESSO HIDAKA MARU (Ja)
Type Tanker; 995 GRT; 2359 DWT; Dimensions 81.79 × — × 5.1; Machinery Motor 2300 bhp; Engine builders Akasaka; Owners Esso Senpaku, K.K; Builders Kurinoura Dock K.K., Japan; Yard No. 158.

ESSO JURONG (Pa)
Type Tanker; 3265 GRT; 5200 DWT; Dimensions 107.07 × — × 6.15; Machinery Motor 3200 bhp; Engine builders Akasaka; Owners Esso Far East Ships Inc; Builders Shimoda Dockyard Co., Ltd., Shimoda; Yard No. 313.

Esterel *(Builders)*

ESTEREL (Fr)
Type Passenger/Vehicle Ferry; 1300 GRT; 2200 DWT; Dimensions 145 × 23.8 × 6.3; Machinery Motor 37000 bhp; Engine builders Pielstick/Atlantique; 23.5 Knots; Owners Soc. Nat. Mar. Corse Mediterranee; Builders Dubigeon-Normandie, S.A., Nantes; Yard No. 162.

ESTETURM - see E.L.M.A. CINCO

Estrella *(FotoFlite)*

ESTRELLA (No)
Type Paper Carrier; 1599 GRT; 3543 DWT; Dimensions 96 (BP) × 17.5 × 5.2; Machinery Motor 3780 bhp; Engine builders MWM; 14 Knots; Owners Det Bergenske Dampskibsselskab; Builders Kleven/Loland Verft, Leirvik i Sogn; Yard No. 35/45.

ETERNAL FUJI (Pa)
Type Cargo; 15800 GRT; 22500 DWT; Dimensions 157 (BP) × 26.5 × 10.3; Machinery Motor 10500 bhp; Engine builders B & W/Mitsui; 15.7 Knots; Owners Escaba Naviera; Builders Hashihama Zosen, Tadotsu; Yard No. 810.

ETERNITY VENTURE (Li)
Type Bulk; 30000 GRT; 58420 DWT; Dimensions 213 (BP) × 32.2 × 12.4; Machinery 14000 bhp; Engine builders Sulzer/IHI; 14.9 Knots; Owners Triumph Carriers Inc; Managers Venture Shipping (Management) Ltd; Builders China S.B., Kaohsiung; Yard No. 180.

Europa *(Builders)*

EUROPA (FRG)
Type Passenger; 35000 GRT; 6500 DWT; Dimensions 196 × 27.5 × 8.35; Machinery Twin Screw Motor 14460 bhp; Engine builders MAN/Bremer Vulkan; 22 Knots; Owners Hapag-Lloyd AG; Builders Bremer Vulkan, Bremen-Vegesack; Yard No. 1001.

EUROPEAN VENTURE (Li)
(launched as AUTOMOBILE VENTURE) Type Vehicles Carrier; 15576 GRT; 17637 DWT; Dimensions 190.0 (BB) × 32.24 × 8.92; Machinery Motor 16800 bhp; Engine builders Sulzer/Sumitomo; Owners Transworld Carriers Inc; Builders Sumitomo Heavy Industries Ltd., Oppama Shipyard, Yokosuka; Yard No. 1083.

EVA (Li)
Type Tanker; 86105 DWT; Dimensions 233 (BP) × 39.35 × 12.95; Machinery Motor 1680 bhp; Engine builders Sulzer/AESA; 15.2 Knots; Owners Eva Armadora; Builders Ast. y. Talleres del Noroeste; Yard No. 257.

EVA VENTURE - see KOSTAS KONIALIDIS

Everdina *(FotoFlite)*

EVERDINA (Ja)
Type LPG; 2450 GRT; 3043 DWT; Dimensions 87.03 (BP) × — × 5.27; Machinery Motor 3200 bhp; Engine builders Akasaka; Owners Jinyu Kaiun, KK; Builders Tokushima Zosen Sangyo KK, Komatsushima; Yard No. 1450.

EXTREMAR (Sp)
Type Cargo; 1590 GRT; 2100 DWT; Dimensions 84.03 × — × 5.0; Machinery Motor 2100 bhp; Engine builders Deutz/Hijos de J. Barreras; Owners Naviera Extremena S.A; Builders Ast. del Cadagua, Bilbao; Yard No. 114.

F

FAIRFIELD VENTURE - sister of BUENA VENTURA (q.v.)
Owners Tavli Tankers; Yard No. 1011.

FAIRWIND VENTURE (Li)
Type Bulk; 31077 GRT; 58420 DWT; Dimensions 222.99 × — × 12.4; Machinery Motor 14400 bhp; Engine builders Sulzer/Taiwan Mach. Corp; Owners Dah Wah Shipping; Builders China SB Corp., Keelung Division, Keelung; Yard No. 179.

FAMILY ANTHONY - sister of ATHINA K (q.v.)
Owners Helamco Shg. Co; Yard No. 2020.

FAMILY FOTINI - sister of ATHINA K (q.v.)
Owners Family Shg. Co; Yard No. 2022.

FEDERAL ELBE (Li)
Type Bulk; 14806 GRT; 23323 DWT; Dimensions 176.5 × — × 10.46; Machinery Motor 11200 bhp; Engine builders MAN/Rostock; Owners Sanaliotis Shipping Corp; Builders VEB Mathias-Thesen Werft, Wismar; Yard No. 125.

Federal Maas *(FotoFlite)*

FEDERAL MAAS (Be)
Type Bulk; 22283 GRT; 35630 DWT, Dimensions 22.49 (BB) × 23.22 × 9.72; Machinery Motor 11600 bhp; Engine builders B & W/Cockerill; Owners N.V. UBEM S.A; Builders N.V. Cockerill Yards, Hoboken; Yard No. 894.

FEDERAL THAMES - sister of FEDERAL MAAS (q.v.)
Yard No. 895.

FELICIA (Pa)
Type Bulk; 16912 GRT; 32191 DWT; Dimensions 179.0 × 25.45 × 11.16; Machinery Motor 10500 bhp; Engine builders B & W/Mitsui; 16.2 Knots; Owners Eridanus Carriers Corp., S.A; Builders Tsuneishi Zosen, Namakuma; Yard No. 476.

FENLOCK (Li)
Type Bulk; 31000 GRT; 69000 DWT; Dimensions 225 (BP) × 32.2 × 12.65; Machinery Motor 15200 bhp; Engine Builders B & W; 12.65 Knots; Owners Escudo Shipping; Builders Kasado Dock Co., Ltd., Kudamatsu; Yard No. 321.

FIGARO - sister of MADAME BUTTERFLY (q.v.)
Yard No. 582.

FINLANDIA (Fi)
Type Passenger/RoRo Cargo/Ferry; 25678 GRT; 3898 DWT; Dimensions 166.02 × 31.26 × 6.72; Machinery Twin Screw Motor 31200 bhp; Engine builders Pielstick/Wartsila; 22 Knots; Owners Finland Steamship Co., Ltd; Builders Oy Wartsila Ab, Turku/Abo; Yard No. 1251.

FINNEAGLE (Sw)
Type RoRo Cargo; 15952 GRT; 20300 DWT; Dimensions 194.01 × 28.0 × 9.00; Machinery Twin Screw Motor 21600 bhp; Engine builders Sulzer/H. Cegielski; 19.5 Knots; Owners O. T. Rederierna; Builders Kockums Varv AB., Malmo; Yard No. 577.

Finneagle *(Builders)*

FLAMINIA (It)
Type RoRo/Cargo/Ferry; 10500 GRT; 3250 DWT; Dimensions 136.0 (BB) × 30.0 × 5.9; Machinery Twin Screw Motor 19200 bhp; Engine builders Grandi Motori Trieste; 22.25 Knots; Owners Tirrenia S.p.A.di Navigazione; Builders Italcantieri S.p.A., Castellammare di Stabia; Yard No. 4352.

FLEET ENDEAVOUR (Br)
Type Tanker; 381 GRT; 935 DWT; Dimensions 60.81 × 6.05 × 2.9; Machinery Motor 320 bhp; Engine builders Kelvin; 9.5 Knots; Owners John H. Whitaker (Tankers) Ltd; Builders Yorkshire DD Co., Ltd., Hull; Yard No. 271.

FLINDERS TIDE (Au)
Type Supply; 925 GRT; 1500 DWT; Dimensions 51.11 × 12.55 × 4.65; Machinery Twin Screw Motor 3000 bhp; Engine builders General Motors; 12 Knots; Owners Tidewater Port Jackson Marine Pty Ltd; Managers Tidwater Inc; Builders Carrington Slipways Pty Ltd., Newcastle NSW; Yard No. 145.

FORMOSA ONE (Li)
Type Chemical Tanker; 13800 GRT; 30200 DWT; Dimensions 167 (BP) × 27.8 × 10.5; Machinery Motor 12000 bhp; Engine builders B & W/Mitsui; 17 Knots; Owners Formosa Plastics Marine Corp; Builders Nippon Kokan K.K., Shimizu; Yard No. 387.

FORMOSA TWO - sister of FORMOSA ONE (q.v.)
Yard No. 388.

FORT TORONTO (Br)
Type Chemical Tanker; 19982 GRT; 31745 DWT; Dimensions 169.55 (BB) × 27.33 × 11.21; Machinery Motor 11200 bhp; Engine builders B & W/Mitsui; 15 Knots; Owners Canadian Pacific (Bermuda) Ltd; Managers Canadian Pacific Steamships Ltd; Builders Sanoyasu Dockyard Co., Ltd., Mizushima; Yard No. 1036.

FRANCES BAY (Au)
Type RoRo/Landing Craft; 1599 GRT; Dimensions 80 × 15 × 4; Machinery Motor 3000 bhp; Engine builders Deutz; 11 Knots; Owners V. B. Perkins; Builders Selco Shipyard (Pte) Ltd., Singapore; Yard No. 294.

Frankfurt Express *(FotoFlite)*

FRANKFURT EXPRESS (FRG)
Type Container; 58385 GRT; 37000 DWT; Dimensions 287.7 × 32.2 × 13; Machinery Twin Screw Motor 54400 bhp; Engine builders MAN; 23.5 Knots; Owners Hapag-Lloyd; Builders Howaldtswerke-Deutsche-Werft, Kiel; Yard No. 168.

Finlandia *(Motor Ship)*

FRELLSEN ANNETTE (De)
Type Cargo; 1599 GRT; 4380 DWT; Dimensions 101.33 × 17.12 × 5.2; Machinery Twin Screw Motor 3668 bhp; Engine builders Mak; Owners I. M. Frellsen Shipping; Builders I/S Orskovs Stallskibsvaerft, Frederikshavn; Yard No. 116.

FRELLSEN BIRGITTE - sister of FRELLSEN ANNETTE (q.v.)
Yard No. 117.

FRIDTJOF NANSEN (No)
Type LPG; 1990 GRT; 4000 DWT; Dimensions 83.15 (BP) × 14 × 6.28; Machinery Motor; Engine builders Wichmann; 13 Knots; Owners Langfeldts Rederi; Builders Kristiansands Mek Verksted; Yard No. 236.

FRIGO LAS PALMAS (Sp)
Ex POLA SUR 1981. Type Cargo; 2172 GRT; 3475 DWT; Dimensions 94.5 (BP) × 16 × 6.3; Machinery Motor 4400 bhp; Engine builders Deutz/Barreras; 15.3 Knots; Owners Canomar S.A; Builders S.A. Juliana Constructora Gijonesa, Gijon; Yard No. 269.

FRIGO TENERIFE - sister of FRIGO LAS PALMAS (q.v.)
ex ESQUIMAL 1981. Yard No. 268.

FROSTA (No)
Type Tanker; 24000 GRT; 36200 DWT; Dimensions 174 × 30 × 10.67; Machinery Motor 11200 bhp; Engine builders B & W/Mitsui; 14.8 Knots; Owners Mowinckels; Builders Sanoyasu Dockyard Co. Ltd., Mizushima; Yard No. 1039.

FUGAKU MARU (Ja)
Type Vehicles Carrier; 9725 GRT; 6002 DWT; Dimensions 149.92 × 22.84 × 7.02; Machinery Motor 16000 bhp; Engine builders MAN/Mitsubishi; Owners Fujiki Kaiun KK; Builders Mitsubishi Heavy Industries Ltd., Nagasaki; Yard No. 1869.

FUJI GAS - see VIGAS

FULL CRY (Pa)
Type Chemical Tanker; 3500 GRT; 6500 DWT; Dimensions 90 (BP) × 16 × 7.8; Machinery Motor 3600 bhp; Engine builders Mak; 13.5 Knots; Owners Achise Maritime Inc; Builders De Groot & Van Vliet Scheepswerf & Maschinefabriek BV., Slikkerveer; Yard No. 403.

FYRBJORN (Sw)
Type Buoy Tender; 476 GRT; 250 DWT; Dimensions 40.06 × 10.55 × 3.3; Machinery Motor 1360 bhp; Engine builders Hedemora; Owners Govt. of the Kingdom of Sweden; Builders A/B Asi-Verken, Amal; Yard No. 130.

G

GA YANG (Ko)
Type Cement Carrier; 4800 GRT; 7500 DWT; Dimensions 106.03 (BP) × — × 7.01; Machinery Motor 4000 bhp; Engine builders Hanshin; Owners Ssang Yong Shipping Co. Ltd; Builders Kyokuyo Zosen Tekko KK, Chofu; Yard No. 310.

GAL COSTA (Bz)
Type RoRo Cargo/Ferry; 944 GRT; 1135 DWT; Dimensions 71.02 × 14.08 × 2.87; Machinery Twin Screw Motor 1860 bhp; Engine builders B & W/Industrias Villares; Owners Companhia de Navegacao Bahiana S.A; Builders Est. EBIN/So S.A., Porto Alegre; Yard No. 107.

GALLANT LION (Br)
Type Bulk; 76000 GRT; 128500 DWT; Dimensions 268 (BP) × 42 × 16; Machinery Motor 17600 bhp; Engine builders B & W/Hitachi; 14.5 Knots; Owners Gallant Shipping; Builders Kawasaki Heavy Industries Ltd., Sakaide; Yard No. 1332.

GALLEON AGATE (Pi)
Type Cargo; 13886 GRT; 19409 DWT; Dimensions 163.07 (BB) × 23.09 × 9.92; Machinery Motor 11200 bhp; Engine builders B & W/Hitachi; Owners Galleon Shipping Corp; Builders Naikai Zosen, Setoda; Yard No. 458.

Galleon Agate *(Builders)*

Galleon Emerald *(Builders)*

GALLEON EMERALD - sister of GALLEON AGATE (q.v.)
Builders Hitachi Zosen, Hiroshima Works, Innoshima; Yard No. 4655.

GARCIA LORCA (Sp)
Type Bulk; 25000 GRT; 44000 DWT; Dimensions 189 (BP) × 29 × 11.6; Machinery Motor 11200 bhp; Engine builders B & W/AESA; 14.8 Knots; Owners Maritima de Cementos y Graneles S.A; Builders Ast. Espanoles S.A., Factoria de Sestao, Bilbao; Yard No. 242.

GAZ FAR EAST (Ja)
Type LGC; 2991 GRT; 3826 DWT; Dimensions 102.01 × — × 5.67; Machinery Motor 3600 bhp; Engine builders Hanshin; Owners Shokuyu Tanker KK; Builders K.K. Ichikawa Zosensho, Ise; Yard No. 1347.

GAZ PACIFIC - sister of DOROTHEA SCHULTE (q.v.) Owners Friedrich A. Detien; Yard No. S598.

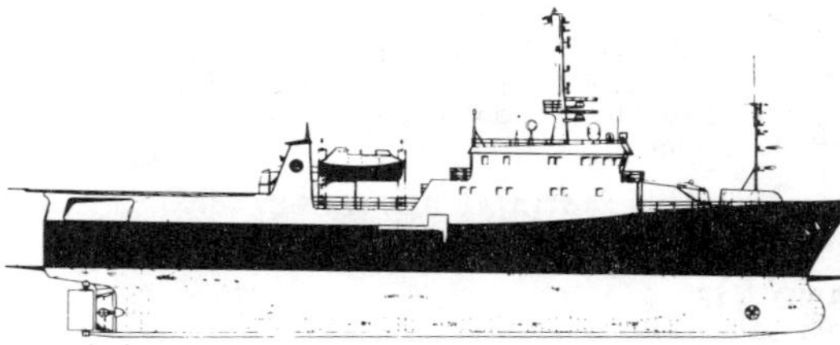

Geco Echo *(Ship and Boat International)*

GECO ECHO (No)
Type Survey; 1400 GRT; 1000 DWT; Dimensions 70.3 × 12.5 × 5.25; Machinery Motor 3600 bhp; Engine builders Normo; 16 Knots; Owners G.E.C.O. A/S; Builders A. M. Liaaen A/S

GECO GAMMA (No)
Type Research; 1599 GRT; 2300 DWT; Dimensions 66 (BP) × 15.6 × 6.4; Machinery Motor 4524 bhp; Engine builders Normo; 14.7 Knots; Owners G.E.C.O. A/S; Builders Trosvik Verksted A/S, Brevik; Yard No. 132.

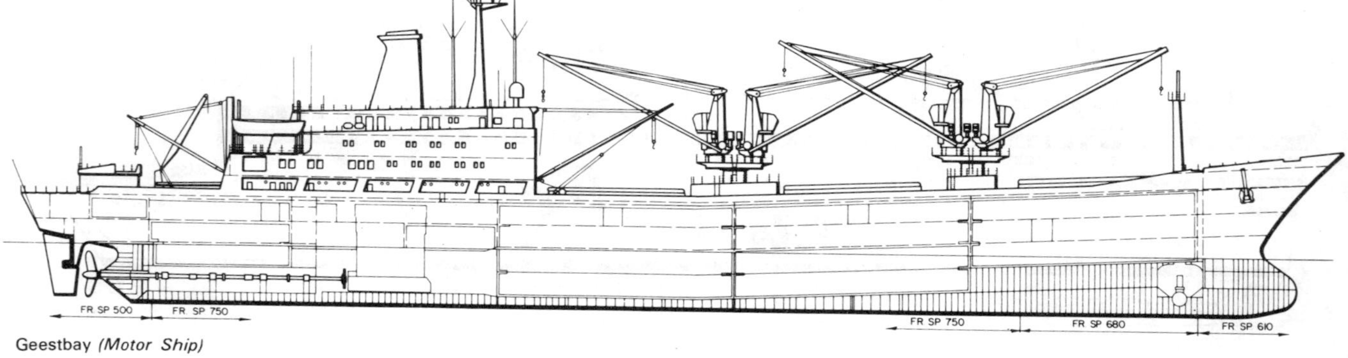

Geestbay *(Motor Ship)*

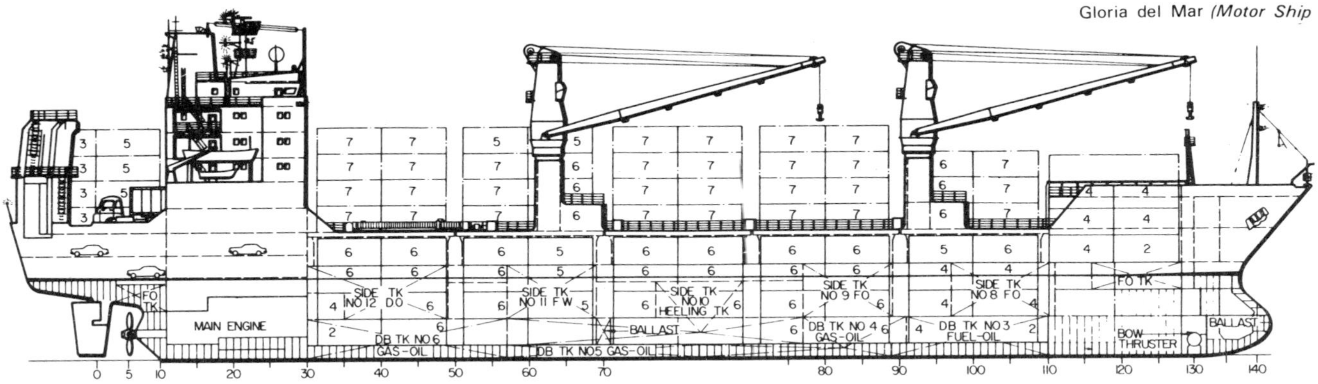

Gloria del Mar *(Motor Ship*

GEESTBAY (Br)
Type Reefer/Container; 9750 DWT; Dimensions 159.07 × 21.3 × 8.82; Machinery Motor 13100 bhp; Engine builders B & W/Kincaid; 21 Knots; Owners Geest Line; Builders Smiths Dock, South Bank, Tees; Yard No. 1346.

Geestbay *(FotoFlite)*

GEESTPORT - sister of GEESTBAY (q.v.)
Yard No. 1347.

GEHAN AL SADAT II (Eg)
(launched as NICOLAOS CONDARAS) Type Cargo; 3472/5844 GRT; 5887/8207 DWT; Dimensions 127.36 (BB) × 18.27 × 8.06; Machinery Motor 4800 bhp; Engine builders 'Zgoda' Zaklady Urzadzen; Owners The Pharaonic Shipping Co; Builders Est EBIN/SO S.A., Porto Alegre; Launched 1977; Lenthened & completed 1980; Yard No. 105.

GELTRUDE A (It)
Type Bulk; 28000 GRT; 49000 DWT; Dimensions 184 (BP) × 32.2 × 12.4; Machinery Motor 13100 bhp; Engine builders B & W; Owners Ferruzzi S.p.A; Builderrs Italcantierr S.p.A., Castellamare; Yard No. 4377.

GEMA PHOSPHATE (Pa)
Type Bulk; 13913 GRT; 25854 DWT; Dimensions 178.31 (BB) × 23.0 × 10.02; Machinery Motor 9380 bhp; Engine builders B & W/Hitachi; 14.8 Knots; Owners Seven Seas Maritime Carriers Co. S.A; Managers Hong Kong Borneo Shipping Co. Ltd; Builders Osaka Zosensho, Osaka; Yard No. 401.

GENERAL MANUEL BELGRANO (Ar)
Type Cargo (Modified SD-14); 9236 GRT; 14910 DWT; Dimensions 134.15 (BP) × 20.42 × 8.84; Machinery Motor 8000 bhp; Engine builders Doxford; 15 Knots; Owners E.L.M.A; Builders Ast. y. Fabricas Navales Del Estado, Ensenada; Yard No. 52..

GEORGE H. WEYERHAEUSER - sister of CARLA A HILLS (q.v.)
Yard No. 1121.

GERANIUM (Pa)
Type Bulk; 10121 GRT; 17280 DWT; Dimensions 148.11 × — × 9.35; Machinery Motor 8000 bhp; Engine builders Mitsubishi-/Kobe Hatsudoki; Owners Kraft Line, S.A. & Maritime Bootes S.A; Builders Shikoku Dockyard Co. Ltd., Takamatsu; Yard No. 812.

GERHARD (FRG)
Type Tanker; 1599 GRT; 4155 DWT; Dimensions 84 (BP) × 15 × 5.66; Machinery Motor 2475 bhp; Engine builders MWM; 12.2 Knots; Owners Leth & Co; Builders Krogerwerft G.M.b.H., Rendsburg; Yard No. 1503.

Ghannouch *(Builders)*

GHANNOUCH (Tn)
Type Chemical Tanker; 4765 GRT; 6000 DWT; Dimensions 116.59 × — × 7.3; Machinery Motor 5200 bhp; Engine builders Pielstick/Alsthom-Atlantique; 15 Knots; Owners Gabeschimie Transport; Builders Soc. Nouvelle des At. & Ch. de La Rochelle-Pallice; Yard No. 1232.

GLACIAR PERITO MORENA (Ar)
Type Reefer; 8480 GRT; 6000 DWT; Dimensions 135.3 (BP) × 21 × 8; Machinery Motor 13300 bhp; Engine builders Sulzer/AFNE; 20 Knots; Owners ELMA; Builders Ast. Alianza S.A., Buenos Aires; Yard No. 35.

GLOBE OCEANIC (Pa)
Type Chemical Tanker; 14000 GRT; 21800 DWT; Dimensions 146 (BP) × 25 × 9.7; Machinery Motor 7920 bhp; Engine builders B & W/Mitsui; 15 Knots; Owners Tokyo Spechride Tankers Co; Managers Iino Kaiun KK; Builders Kurushima Dockyard, Uwajima; Yard No. 2163.

GLOBE ORIENT (Ja) - sister of GLOBE OCEANIC (q.v.)
Yard No.2153.

GLOBE OVERSEAS (Ja) - sister of GLOBE OCEANIC (q.v.)
Yard No. 2147.

GLORIA DEL MAR (Sp)
Type RoRo/Reefer; 3975 GRT; 9000 DWT; Dimensions 122.77 × 19.4 × 9.02; Machinery Motor 6600 bhp; Engine builders Deutz-/Barreras; 14.5 Knots; Owners Telde S.A; Managers Navimol; Builders Enrique Lorenzo y Cia, Vigo (Vulcano Group); Yard No. 398; Sold December 1981 to overseas buyers.

GLORIA ELENA (Pa)
Type Cement Carrier; 7000 GRT; 13700 DWT; Dimensions 136 × 21.7 × 8.12; Machinery Motor; Engine builders B&W; 15 knots; Owners Mar. del Golfo S.A; Builders J. J. Sietas, Hamburg; Yard No. 801.

Glorious Ace *(Builders)*

GLORIOUS ACE (Ja)
Type Vehicles Carrier; 16880 GRT; 17440 DWT; Dimensions 190.0 × 32.0 × 7.9; Machinery Motor 16800 bhp; Engine builders B & W/Hitachi; 19 Knots; Owners Mitsui O.S.K. Lines Ltd., & Baba Daiko Shosen KK; Builders Hitachi Zosen, Ariake Works, Nagasu; Yard No. 4673.

Golar Spirit

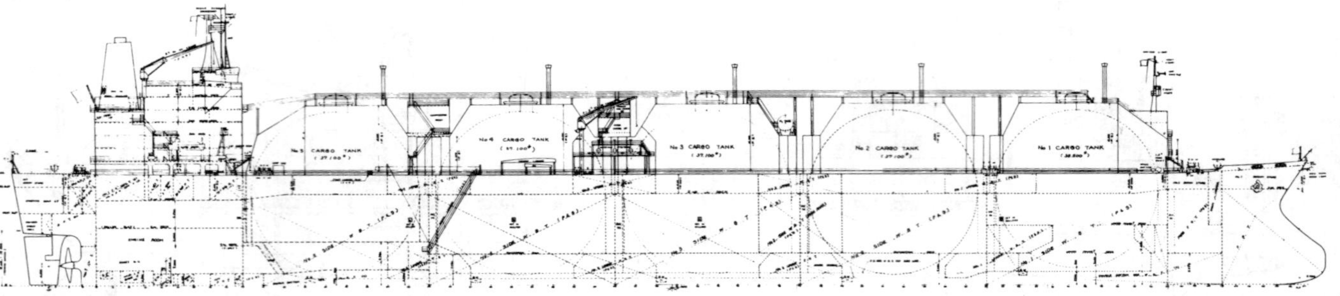

GOLAR SPIRIT (Li)
Tyoe LNG; 88000 GRT; 76700 DWT; Dimensions 289 × 44.6 × 11.4; Machinery Steam Turbine; Engine builders Kawasaki; 19.8 Knots; Owners Cryogenic (Gotaas-Larsen Shipping Corp); Builders Kawasaki Heavy Industries, Sakaide; Yard No. 1220.

GOLD AFRICA (Pa)
ex ALTONIC 1981. Type Container; 8000 GRT; 8500 DWT; Dimensions 106.5 (BP) × 18.2 × 8; Machinery Motor 7385 bhp; Engine builders MAN/Kawasaki; 15 Knots; Owners Valdosta Sg. Corp; Builders China SB. Corp., Keelung; Yard No. 105.

GOLDEN CRUX No5 (Ja)
Type LGC; 2370 GRT; 2700 DWT; Dimensions 83 (BP) × 13.8 × 5.4; Machinery Motor 3200 bhp; Engine bukiders Akasaka; Owners Kumazawa Kaiun; Builders Uchida Zosen KK, Ise; Yard No. 815.

GOLDEN KYOSEI MARU (Ja)
Type Chemical Tanker; 3700 GRT; 6000 DWT; Dimensions 99.8 (BP) × 16 × 6.7; Machinery Motor 5200 bhp; Engine builders Makita; Owners Kyoei Kisen KK; Builders Honda Zosen, Saeki; Yard No. 691.

GRACIA DEL MAR - sister of GLORIA DEL MAR (q.v.)
Yard No. 399.

GRAND EAGLE (Li)
Type Tanker; 44000 GRT; 79999 DWT; Machinery Motor; Engine builders Pielstick/NKK; Owners Bracknell Shipping Ltd; Builders Sumitomo Heavy Industries, Oppama.

GRAZIELA FERRAZ (Bz)
Type Bulk (Pri 26/15); 17893 GRT; 26500 DWT; Dimensions 162 (BP) × 26.6 × 9.72; Machinery Motor 13300 bhp; Engine builders MAN/Mecapesa; 15.4 Knots; Owners C.B.d.T; Builders Companhia Comercio e Navegacao, Rio de Janeiro; Yard No. 128.

GREEN MARU No3 (Ja)
Type Asphalt Tanker; 699 GRT; 1300 DWT; Dimensions 64.93 × — × 4.3; Machinery Motor 1600 bhp; Engine builders Akasaka; Owners Nippon Tokushusen KK; Builders Kurinoura Dock K.K., Japan; Yard No. 161.

GUAPORO - sister of GUARUJA (q.v.)
Yard No. 1217.

Guara *(Builders)*

GUARA - sister of GUARUJA (q.v.)
Yard No. 1216.

GUARUJA (Bz)
Type LGC; 6662 GRT; 4514 DWT; Dimensions 109.91 (BB) × 20.00 × 5.8; Machinery Motor 5280 bhp; Engine builders B & W/Mitsui; 15.75 Knots; Owners Petrobras; Builders Mitsui Eng. & SB. Co. Ltd., Ichihara; Yard No. 1215.

GUIARD (Sp)
Type Reefer; 3650 GRT; Dimensions 94.5 (BP) × 16 × 6.3; Machinery Motor 4940 bhp; Engine builders B & W/AESA; 15.3 Knots; Owners Navifrisa; Builders S. A. Julian Constructora Gijonesa, Gijon; Yard No. 277.

GUNNAR SEIDENFADEN - sister of GUNNAR THORSON (q.v.)
Yard No. 119.

GUNNAR THORSON (De)
Type Pollution Patrol; 869 GRT; 684 DWT; Dimensions 55.61 × — × 3.87; Machinery Motor 2320 bhp; Engine builders B & W; Owners Govt. of the Kingdom of Denmark; Builders I/S Orskovs Staalskibsvaerft, Frederikshavn; Yard No. 118.

H

HAKUYO MARU (Ja)
Type Cargo (Reefer); 2800 GRT; 3000 DWT; Dimensions 90 (BP) × 15.5 × 6.27; Machinery Motor; Engine builders Mitsubishi-/Kobe Hatsuodoki; Owners Nomura Kaiun; Builders Kishigami Zosen K.K., Akitsu; Yard No. 1428.

Hanne Lupe *(Builders)*

HANNE LUPE (De)
Type Asphalt Tanker; 1600 GRT; 2870 DWT; Dimensions 86 × 12.4 × 5.04; Machinery Motor 1475 bhp; Engine builders Deutz; 11.7 Knots; Owners Rederiet Hans Petersen; Builders Werft Nobiskrug G.m.b.H., Rendsburg.

HARBEL TAPPER (Li)
Type Cargo; 8500 GRT; 11700 DWT; Dimensions 130 (BP) × 22 × 6.9; Machinery Motor 6160 bhp; Engine builders B & W/Mitsui; 15.1 Knots; Owners PMC IV Corp; Builders Koyo Dock K.K., Mihara; Yard No. 876.

HARTING (Br)
Type Cargo; 1589 GRT; 4300 DWT; Dimensions 91.27 × 14.58 × 5.81; Machinery Motor 3300 bhp; Engine builders Mirrlees Blackstone; 14 Knots; Owners Stephenson Clarke Shipping Ltd; Builders Clelands SB Co. Ltd., Wallsend; Yard No. 354.

HARUKAWA MARU (Ja)
Type Bulk; 10000 GRT; 17600 DWT; Dimensions 136 (BP) × 22.86 × 9; Machinery Motor 7000 bhp; Engine builders Mitsubishi/Akasaka; 13.7 Knots; Owners Shinsei Kaiun; Builders Watanabe Zosen K.K., Kakata; Yard No. 212.

HAYAZURU MARU (Ja)
Type RoRo Cargo/Ferry; 1330 GRT; 620 DWT; Dimensions 71.58 × 13.62 × 3.5; Machinery Motor 1600 bhp; Engine builders Daihatsu; Owners Eiyu Shoji, Y.K; Builders Fukuoka Zosen, Fukuoka; Yard No. 1085.

HEBE (No)
Type LGC; 1999 GRT; 2950 DWT; Dimensions 76.74 × 14.03 × 6.77; Machinery Motor 2640 bhp; Engine builders Polar/Nohab; Owners A/S Helengas; Managers Helge R. Myhre; Builders Moss Rosenberg Verft A/S, Moss; Yard No. 195.

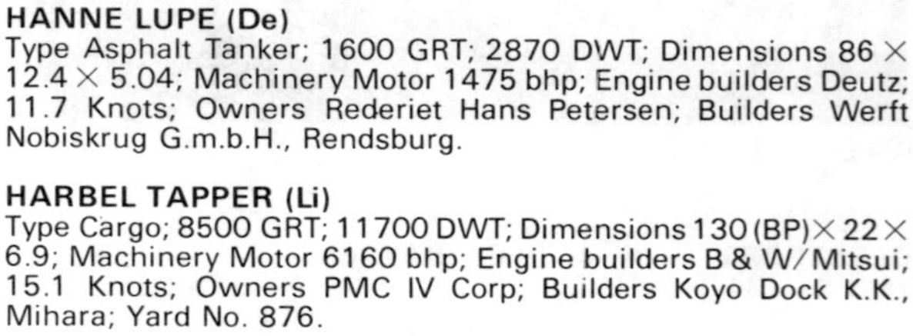

Hebe *(Builders)*

HERACLITO DANTAS (Bz)
Type Bulk; 11188 GRT; 15780DWT; Dimensions 146.01 × 21.24 × 8.88; Machinery Motor 7050 bhp; Engine builders B & W/Villares; Owners H. Dantas Comercio Nav & Indust. Ltda; Builders Industrias Reunidas Caneco, Rio de Janeiro; Yard No. 217.

HERCEGNOVI (Ys)
Type Cargo; 9698 GRT; 13900 DWT; Dimensions 156.85 (BP) × 21.85 × 9.02; Machinery Motor 9300 bhp; Engine builders MAN/Rostock; Owners Jugoslavenska Oceanska Plovidba; Builders VEB Warnowwerft, Warnemunde; Yard No. 422.

HILCO SKIER (No)
Type Cargo; 6764/9064 GRT; -/12475 DWT; Dimensions 156.17 (BB) × 23.04 × -/9.8; Machinery Motor 20100 bhp; Engine builders Sulzer/A/S Horten Verft; 22 Knots; Owners K/S Hilco Skier A/S & Co; Managers Irgens Larsen A/S; Builders A/S Framnaes M/V, Sandefjord; Yard No. 194.

HILDE DEL MAR (Sp)
Type Cargo; 1990/2882 GRT; 3400/5950 DWT; Dimensions 127.18 × 15.78 × 16.44; Machinery Motor 7500 bhp; Engine builders MAN/Bazan; Owners SBC Container Lines S.A; Builders Ast. de Huelva S.A., Huelva; Yard No. 107.

HIRADO (Ja)
Type Bulk; 20500 GRT; 34000 DWT; Dimensions 165 (BP) × 28.2 × 11.33; Machinery Motor 10650 bhp; Engine builders Mitsubishi/Kobe; 14.05 Knots; Owners Sankyu/Manno; Builders Tohuku SB. Co. Ltd., Shiogama; Yard No. 194.

HISATOKU MARU (Ja)
Type Chemical Tanker; 1995 GRT; 3606 DWT; Dimensions 76.51 (BP) × — × 6.01; Machinery Motor 3200 bhp; Engine builders Ito Tekkosho; Owners Shintoku Kaiun K.K; Builders Hayashikane SB. & Eng. Co. Ltd., Nagasaki; Yard No. 901.

HO MING No2 (Pa)
Type Cargo; 6600 GRT; 11000 DWT; Dimensions 112 (BP) × 20 × 8.2; Machinery Motor 6000 bhp; Engine builders Akasaka; Owners Balsa Navigacion; Builders Taihei Kogyo K.K., Akitsu; Yard No. 145.

HO MING No3 - sister of HO MING No 2 (q.v.)
Yard No. 1452.

HOEGH BISCAY (No)
(Sold France Nov. 1981) Type RoRo Cargo; 16744 GRT; 22300 DWT; Dimensions 186.6 × 32.29 × 9.01; Machinery Motor 17400 bhp; Engine builders Sulzer/H. Cegielski; 18 Knots; Owners A/S Arcadia; Managers Leif Hoegh & Co. A/S; Builders Stocznia Gdynska im Komuny Paryskiej, Gdynia; Yard No. B484/03.

Hoegh Falcon *(FotoFlite)*

HOEGH FALCON (No)
Type Bulk/Oil; 47000 GRT; 81000 DWT; Dimensions 251 (BP) × 32.24 × 14.8; Machinery Motor 15147 bhp; Engine builders B & W; 15.1 Knots; Owners L. Hoegh & Co., A/S; Builders Howaldtswerke-Deutsche Werft; Yard No. 169.

HOEGH FAVOUR - sister of HOEGH FALCON (q.v.)
Yard No. 170.

Hoegh Trader *(Builders)*

HOEGH TRADER (No)
Type Vehicles Carrier; 22000 GRT; 26300 DWT; Dimensions 213 × 32.26 × 10.5; Machinery Motor; Engine builders Sulzer/Cegielski; 17 Knots; Owners L. Hoegh & Co., A/S; Builders Stocznia im Komuny Paryskiej, Gdynia; Yard No. B487/01.

HOEGH TRANSPORTER - sister of HOEGH TRADER (q.v.)
Yard No. B487/02.

HOJU MARU (Ja)
Type Vehicles Carrier; 4500 GRT; 3000 DWT; Dimensions 107.02 (BP) × — × 6.1; Machinery Motor 15280 bhp; Engine builders Hitachi; Owners Fukuju Kigyo K.K. & Toyofuji Kaiun KK; Builders Towa Zosen K.K., Shimonoseki; Yard No. 530.

HOLSATIC (Sg)
Type Cargo; 6165 GRT; 8514 DWT; Dimensions 118.01 (BB) × — × 8.01; Machinery Motor 7385 bhp; Engine builders MAN/Kawasaki; 15.75 Knots; Owners Hanseatische Handels und Schiffahrtsges Neptun (HK) Ltd; Managers Reederei Hans Beilken C.H.G; Builders China SB., Corp., Keelung; Yard No. 103.

Holstenracer *(FotoFlite)*

HOLSTENRACER (FRG)
Type Cargo ("Key 12" type); 8700 GRT; 12590 DWT; Dimensions 146.01 × 23 × 8.16; Machinery Motor 11200 bhp; Engine builders Mak; 18 Knots; Owners Reederei Claus-Peter Offen; Builders A.G. "Weser" Seebeckwerft, Bremerhaven; Yard No. 1022.

HOUSTON ACCORD (Li)
Type Tanker; 36000 GRT; 63550 DWT; Dimensions 235 × 32.2 × 12.3; Machinery Motor 15800 bhp; Engine builders B & W/Mitsui; 15.4 Knots; Owners Houston Accord Tankers Inc; Builders Tsuneishi Zosen KK., Numakuma; Yard No. 464.

HOWARD SMITH (Au)
Type OBO; 26519 GRT; 43300 DWT; Dimensions 177.02 × 33.08 × 11.83; Machinery Motor 14400 bhp; Engine builders Mitsubishi/Kobe; Owners Howard Smith Industries Pty. Ltd; Builders Kasado Dock Co., Kudamatsu; Yard No. 323.

HUAL TRACER (Li)
Type Vehicles Carrier; 12783 GRT; 12500 DWT; Dimensions 180.0 × 29.2 × 7.5; Machinery Motor 11200 bhp; Engine builders B & W/Mitsui; 17.5 Knots; Owners Barra Car Carrier Inc; Builders Kanasashi Zosensho, Toyohashi; Yard No. 1301.

HUAL TRAPPER - sister of HUAL TRACER (q.v.)
Yard No. 1302.

HUANGPU CAREER (Pa)
Type Bulk; 13371 GRT; 23987 DWT; Dimensions 160.38 × 24.64 × 9.95; Machinery Motor 10500 bhp; Engine builders Hitachi; Owners Huangpu Maritime Carriers Inc; Builders Imabari Zosen, Imabari; Yard No. 397.

HUNAN (Br)
Type Bulk; 24200 GRT; 39900 DWT; Dimensions 174 (BP) × 29 × 11.35; Machinery Motor 13100 bhp; Engine builders B & W/Mitsui; 15.83 Knots; Owners China Navigation; Builders Mitsui Eng. & SB. Co Ltd., Tamano; Yard No. 1232.

HUNJIANG (RC)
Type Cargo (SD 14 type); 9296 GRT; 15200 DWT; Dimensions 144.02 × 20.45 × 8.87; Machinery Motor 7600 bhp; Engine builders Sulzer/Clark Hawthorn; 15 Knots; Owners China Ocean Shipping Co; Managers China Merchants Steam Navigation Co. Ltd; Builders Austin & Pickersgill Ltd., Sunderland; Yard No. 1403.

HYDROLOCK - sister of DANELOCK (q.v.)
Yard No. 884.

HYUNDAI ATLANTIC (Ko)
Type Bulk; 31000 GRT; 60000 DWT; Dimensions 215 (BP) × 32.2 × 12.45; Machinery Motor 15200 bhp; Engine builders B & W/Hyundai; 17 Knots; Owners Asia Merchant Marine; Builders Hyundai Heavy Industries Co. Ltd., Ulsan; Yard No. 161.

HYUNDAI PACIFIC (Ko)
Type Bulk; 71000 GRT; 113184 DWT; Dimensions 164.52 × 40.85 × 16.73; Machinery Motor 18500 bhp; Engine builders Sulzer/Sumitomo; Owners Asia Merchant Marine; Builders Hyundai Heavy Industries Co. Ltd., Ulsan; Yard No. 146.

I

IBN AL-AKFANI (FRG)
Launched as BARBAROSSA; Type Container; 17519 GRT; 18800 DWT; Dimensions 163.81 × 28.55 × 10.33; Machinery Motor 14460 bhp; Engine builders MAN; 18.25 Knots; Owners Barbarossa Schiffahrts G.m.b.H., & Co. K.G; Managers Horst-Werner Janssen; Builders Thyssen Nordseewerke G.m.b.H., Emden; Yard No. 467.

IBUKI MARU (Ja)
Type Fishing; 2577 GRT; 3635 DWT; Dimensions 91.39 × — × 5.5; Machinery Motor 4400 bhp; Engine builders B & W/Hitachi; Owners Nippon Suisan K.K; Builders Naikai Zosen, Taguma Shipyard, Innoshima; Yard No. 464.

Igloo Finn *(Motor Ship)*

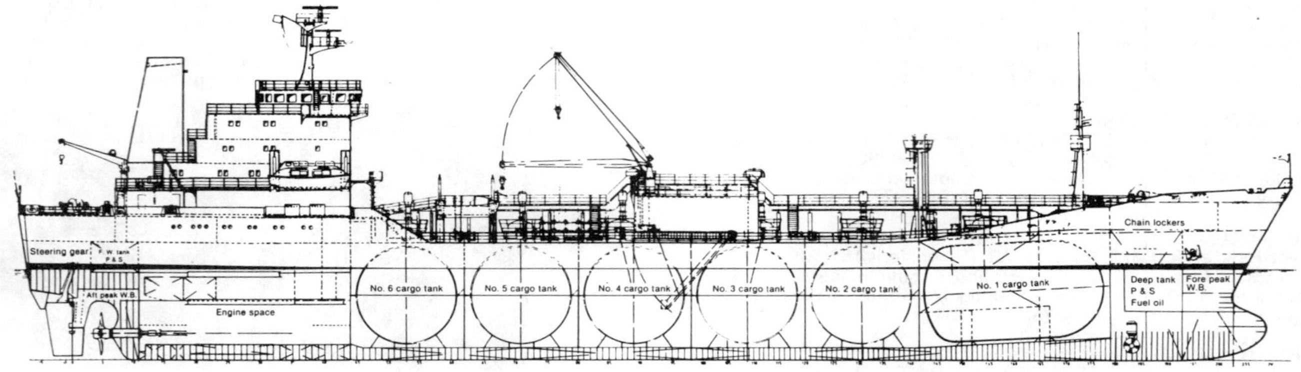

IGLOO FINN (No)
Type Chemical Tanker/LPG; 8000 GRT; 11200 DWT; Dimensions 128 × 21.3 × 9.45; Machinery Motor 7590 bhp; Engine builders Sulzer; 16 Knots; Owners A/S Havtor Management; Builders Moss Rosenberg Verft; Yard No. 197.

IKAN KERAPU (Sg)
Type Bulk; 31624 GRT; 64954 DWT; Dimensions 224.01 (BB) × 31.86 × 13.33; Machinery Motor 14400 bhp; Engine builders Sulzer/Mitsubishi; 16.65 Knots; Owners Kerapu Shipping Pte. Ltd; Managers Pacific Carriers Pte. Ltd; Builders Mitsubishi Heavy Industries Ltd., Kobe; Yard No. 1112.

IKAN TONGKOL (Sg)
Type Bulk; 77500 GRT; 130330 DWT; Dimensions 258 (BP) × 43 × 16.3; Machinery Motor 20400 bhp; Engine builders Sulzer-/Mitsubishi; 15.6 Knots; Owners Tongkol Shipping; Builders Mitsubishi Heavy Industries Ltd., Nagasaki; Yard No. 1865.

INA LEHMANN (FRG)
Type Cargo; 999 GRT; 2574 DWT; Dimensions 81.64 × — × 5.06; Machinery Motor 1287 bhp; Engine builders MWM; 13 Knots; Owners Reederei Hans Lehmann OHG; Builders J. J. Sietas Schiffsw., Hamburg; Yard No. 870.

ING. KRAUSSE (Ar)
Type Tanker; 4620 GRT; 6000 DWT; Dimensions 104.2 (BP) × — × 6.7; Machinery Motor 5800 bhp; Engine builders Sulzer/AFNE; Owners Govt. of the Argentine Republic (YPF); Builders ASTAR-SA, Tigre; Yard No. 144.

INTERMAR ALLIANCE (Li)
Type Tanker; 49100 GRT; 80000 DWT; Dimensions 244 × 39.4 × 12.19; Machinery Motor 17400 bhp; Engine builders B & W/Mitsui; Owners Intermarine Carriers Co; Builders Ast. y Talleres del Noroeste, El Ferrol; Yard No. 154.

INVERLOCK - sister of FENLOCK (q.v.)
Yard No. 322.

INZHENER YERMOSHKIN (Ru)
Type RoRo Cargo/container; 14345 GRT; 20075 DWT; Dimensions 227.3 × 30 × 9.87; Machinery Gas Turbine 2x25000 shp; 25 Knots; Owners U.S.S.R; Builders "Chernomorskiy" Shipyard, Nikolayev.

IOLAIR (Br)
Type Emergency Support; 17000 GRT; 19600 Dspl; Dimensions 102 (over pontoons) × 51.5 (over pontoons) × 6.54/15.25; Machinery 6 × Diesel Electric 6 × 4423; Engine builders MAN; 12 Knots; Owners BP/National Oil; Builders Scott Lithgow; Yard No. 1200.

IRIAN JAYA (Ia)
Type Dredger; 5100 GRT; Dimensions 105 (BP) × 18 × 6.25; Machinery Motor 7600 bhp; Engine builders MWM; 12 Knots; Owners Ministry of Transport; Builders Orenstein & Koppel AG, Lubeck; Yard No. 761.

Iolair *(David Brown Gear Industries Ltd.)*

IRISHGATE (Br)
Type Tanker; 1599 GRT; 3300 DWT; Dimensions 93.15 × 13.44 × 5.19; Machinery Motor 2250 bhp; Engine builders Mak/Ube; Owners Portland Overseas Shipping Ltd; Managers Hull Gates Shipping Co; Builders Kanrei Zosen, Naruto; Yard No. 291.

IRON PRINCE (Au)
Type Bulk/Ore Carrier; 15200 GRT; 21500 DWT; Dimensions 155.45 (BP) × 22.86 × 9.95; Machinery Motor 9000 bhp; Engine builders Sulzer/IHI; 14.7 Knots; Owners Broken Hill Proprietary Co; Builders I.H.I., Kure; Yard No. 2780.

IRON SPENCER - sister of IRON WHYALLA (q.v.)
Yard No. 2732.

IRON WHYALLA (Au)
Type Bulk; 77400 GRT; 141435 DWT; Dimensions 285.5 (BB) × 47.1 × 15.27; Machinery Motor 20400 bhp; Engine builders Sulzer/IHI; 14.25 Knots; Owners Broken Hill Pty. Co. Ltd; Builders I.H.I., Kure; Yard No. 2731.

IRVING OCEAN (Ca)
Type Tanker; 24000 GRT; 38601 DWT; Dimensions 191.8 × 27.49 × 11.09; Machinery Motor 12000 bhp; Engine builders Sulzer; Owners Irving Oil Ltd; Managers Kent Line Ltd; Builders Saint John SB. & DD. Co. Ltd., St. John N.B; Yard No. 1123.

IVER LIBRA (Li)
Type Chemical Tanker; 13310 GRT; 20000 DWT; Dimensions 145 (BP) × 22.7 × 9.6; Machinery Motor 8040 bhp; Engine builders B & W/Mitsui; 14.4 Knots; Owners Norsino Shipping; Builders Hayashikane Shipbuilding & Eng., Shimonoseki; Yard No. 1246.

IVER TAURUS - sister of IVER LIBRA (q.v.)
Yard No. 1245.

IWAKUNI MARU (Ja)
Type LGC; 7300 GRT; 4900 DWT; Dimensions 104 (BP) × 20 × 5.9; Machinery Motor 4500 bhp; Engine builders Mitsubishi-/Kobe; 13.5 Knots; Owners Shimazu Kaiun; Builders Hitachi Shipbuilding & Eng. Co., Hiroshima; Yard No. 4666.

J

JACINTH (No)
Type Tanker; 39148 GRT; 60000 DWT; Dimensions 224.09 × 32.24 × 13.43; Machinery Motor 14400 bhp; Engine builders Sulzer/Sumitomo Heavy Industries; 15.1 Knots; Owners A/S Kosmos; Managers Anders Jahre; Builders Nippon Kokan K.K., Tsurumi Shipyard, Yokohama; Yard No. 984.

JALAGOURI (In)
Type Cargo; 13505 GRT; 20854 DWT; Dimensions 162.13 (BB) × 22.94 × 10.34; Machinery Motor 9100 bhp; Engine builders MAN; Builders Hindustan Shipyard Ltd., Visakapatnam; Yard No. 171013.

JAPAN STORK (Ja)
Type Tanker; 55000 GRT; 80750 DWT; Dimensions 232.52 × 44.0 × 12.19; Machinery Motor 17000 bhp; Engine builders Sulzer/Mitsubishi; 16.8 Knots; Owners Japan Line Ltd; Builders Mitsubishi Heavy Industries Ltd., Nagasaki; Yard No. 1871.

Jaraconda *(Builders)*

JARACONDA (No)
Type Bulk; 35921 GRT; 59570 DWT; Dimensions 224.52 × 32.26 × 12.4; Machinery Motor 14400 bhp; Engine builders Sulzer/Hitachi Zosen; 17 knots; Owners A/S Kosmos; Managers Anders Jahre; Builders Hitachi Zosen, Hiroshima Works, Innoshima; Yard No. 4668.

JARAMA (No)
Type Ore/Bulk/Oil; 42105 GRT; 77673 DWT; Dimensions 243.82 × 32.29 × 14.34; Machinery Motor 15800 bhp; Engine builders B & W/A/S Fredriksstad M/; 15.3 knots; Owners A/S Kosmos; Managers Anders Jahre; Builders A/S Fredriksstad M/V, Fredriksstad; Yard No. 4389

JARMINA - sister of JARAMA (q.v.)
Yard No. 439.

Jasaka *(Builders)*

JASAKA - sister JARACONDA (q.v.)
Yard No. 4669.

JASPER (Pa)
Type Builk Carrier; 13600 GRT; 22000 DWT; Dimensions 155.4 (BP) × 22.9 × 9.8; Machinery Motor 8000 bhp; Engine builders Pielstick/IHI; 15 knots; Owners Chrysolte Marine; Builders IHI, Tokyo; Yard No. 2760.

JAVAZEE - see MELTON VOYAGER

JAYAKARTA (Ia)
Type Container; 14990 GRT; 20500 DWT; Dimensions 157 (BP) × 28.4 × 9.65; Machinery Motor 14460 bhp; Engine builders Man; 19 knots; Owners Djakarta Lloyd; Builders Flensburger Schiffsbau Gesellschaft, Flensburg; Yard No. 658.

JINMU MARU (Ja)
Type Vehicles Carrier; 17361 GRT; 17427 DWT; Dimensions 186.01 (BP) × 30.01 × 9.32; Machinery Motor 16800 bhp; Engine builders Mitsubishi Heavy Industries; Owners Nippon Yusen Kaisha & Okada Shosen K.K.; Builders Imabari Zosen, Marugame; Yard No. 1077.

JINTO MARU - sister of JINMU MARU (q.v.)
Yard No. 1086.

JO CLIPPER (No)
Launched as POLUX. Type Chemical Tanker; 18706 GRT; 33695 DWT; Dimensions 182.71 × 29.51 × 10.00; Machinery Motor 13100 bhp; Engine builders B & W/Nylands Verksted; Owners A/S Rederiet Odfjell; Builders A/S Ankerlokken Verft, Floro; Yard No. 114.

JO LONN (No)
Type Tanker; 23000 GRT; 38400 DWT; Dimensions 168.2 (BP) × 32 × 10.67; Machinery Motor 15200 bhp; Engine builders B & W; 15.3 knots; Owners J.O. Odfjell A/S; Builders Bergens Mek. Verksteder (Aker Group); Yard No. 823.

JOHN B WATERMAN (US)
Type Ro/Ro cargo/container; 18500 GRT; 23500 DWT; Dimensions 195.7 (BP) × 32.2 × 10.1; Machinery Steam Turbine 32000 shp; 20.9 knots; Owners Waterman Steamship Corp.; Builders Sun Shipbuilding & D.D. Co., Chester; Yard No. 679.

JOLLY SPRITE (Li)
Type Tanker; 49071 GRT; 97069 DWT; Dimensions 253.02 × 44.46 × 12.8; Machinery Motor 20400 bhp; Engine builders Sulzer/IHI; Owners Penmarine Ltd.; Builders Sasebo Heavy Industries Co. Ltd., Sasebo; Yard No. 285.

JUKO MARU (Ja)
Type Ore/Bulk/Oil; 42651 GRT; 70681 DWT; Dimensions 236 × 32.2 × 13.5; Machinery Motor 12100 bhp; Engine builders MAN/Kawasaki; 14.4 knots; Owners Dolphin Shipping Ltd.; Builders Kawasaki Heavy Industries, Sakaide; Yard No. 1293.

JULIA - sister of ADRIA (q.v.)
Builders Cant dell'alto Adriatico, Trieste; Yard No. 211.

JUSTICIA (ES)
Type Tuna Fishing Seiner; 1146 GRT; 1610 DWT; Dimensions 69.02 × — × —; Machinery Motor 4200 bhp; Engine builders Soc. Alsacienne de Const. Mec de Mulhouse; 16.75 knots; Owners Govt. of the Republic of El Salvador; Builders At. & Ch. de la Manche, Dieppe; Yard No. 1285.

K

KAGHAN - sister of MURREE (q.v.)
Yard No. 1408.

Kaghan *(FotoFlite)*

KAIJYO MARU No 20 (Ja)
Type Cargo; 499 GRT; 1446 DWT; Dimensions 66.6 × — × —; Machinery Motor 1500 bhp; Engine builders Hanshin Nainenki Kogyo; Owners G.K. Marui Kaiun Shokai; Builders Miura Zosen, Saeki; Yard No. 618.

KAPETAN YANNIS (Gr)
Type Bulk Carrier; 30852 GRT; 60000 DWT; Dimensions 224.5 × 32.2 × 12.3; Machinery Motor 14400 bhp; Engine builders Sulzer/Sumitomo; 15.6 knots; Owners Pikal Shipping Corp.; Builders Nippon Kokan KK., Tsurumi; Yard No. 982.

KAPITAN KHLEBNIKOV (Ru)
Type Icebreaker; 10471 GRT; 14900 Displacement; Dimensions 132.4 × 26.5 × 8.5; Machinery Triple screw diesel-electric 6 × 3050 bhp; Engine builders Sulzer/Wartsila; 19 knots; U.S.S.R; Builders Oy Wartsila (Helsinki); Yard No. 430.

KAPITAN SERGIYEVSKIY (Ru)
Type Container; 4827 GRT; 5720 DWT; Dimensions 130 × 17.3 × 6.9; Machinery Motor 6100 bhp; Engine builders B & W/Bryansk; 16 knots; Owners U.S.S.R.; Builders Vyborg Shipyard, Vyborg.

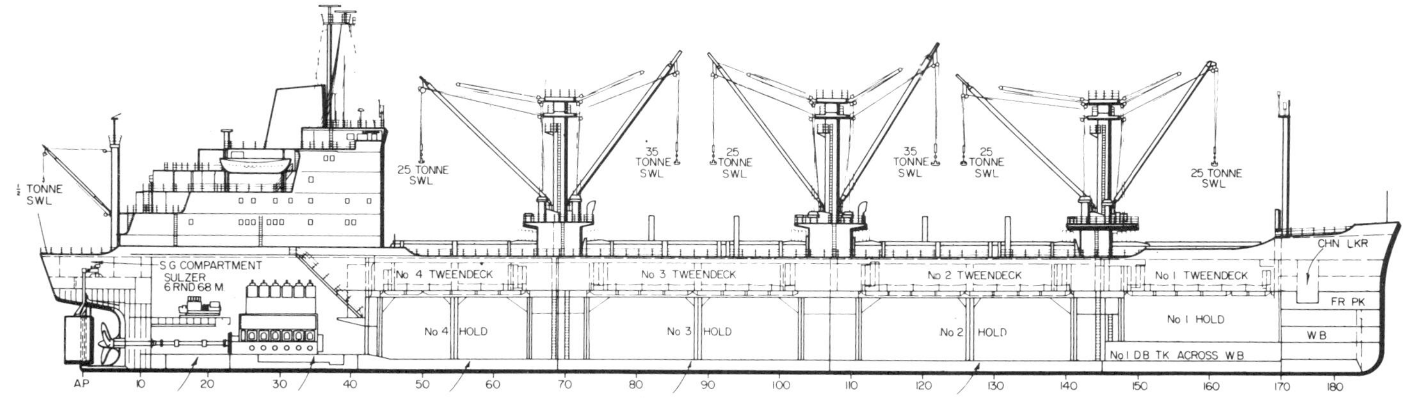

Kaghan *(Motor Ship)*

KAPITAN VOOLENS (Ru)
Type Cargo; 1400 GRT; 2500 DWT; Dimensions 82.5 (BP) × 12.6 × 5.05; Machinery Motor 2500 bhp; Engine builders Vasa/Wartsila; 12.2 knots; Owners U.S.S.R.; Builders Rauma-Repola, Uusikaupunki; Yard No. 305.

KAPTAN ISMAIL CILLIOGLU (Tu)
Type Cargo; 1600 GRT; 2800 DWT; Dimensions 81.21 × 13.03 × 5.35; Machinery Motor 1230 bhp; Engine builders Skoda/CKD Praha; Owners Yusuf Cillioglu; Builders Denizcilik Anonim Sirketi Beykoz Tersanesi, Beykoz; Yard No. 32.

KASHIRSKOYE (Ru)
Type Fish Carrier; 6300 DWT; Dimensions 123.93 × 17.05 × ; Machinery Motor 6100 bhp; Engine builders Sulzer/Cegielski; 15.75 knots; Owners U.S.S.R.; Builders Stocznia Szczecinska im Warskiego; Yard No. B432/443.

KASTANIA (Pa)
Type Cargo; 3811 GRT; 6486 DWT; Dimensions 99.68 × 16.31 × 6.82; Machinery Motor 3800 bhp; Engine builders Hanshin Nainenki Kogyo; Owners Rokko Shipping Co. S.A.; Builders Higaki Zosen K.K., Imabari; Yard No. 250.

KATHY O - sister of NORDIC TRADER (q.v.)
Yard No. 807.

KAUPANGER (No)
Type Chemical tanker; 33000 DWT; Dimensions 174.6 (BP) × 29.5 × 10; Machinery Motor 11900 bhp; Engine builders B & W; 15.6 knots; Owners Westfal Larsen; Builders Ankerlokken Verft Floro; Yard No. 115.

KAYU LAPIS EMPAT (Pa)
Type Cargo; 4304 GRT; Dimensions 100.01 × 17.61 × 8.67; Machinery Motor; Engine builders Mitsubishi/Kobe Hatsudoki; 12 knots; Owners Hilford Maritime; Builders Imai Zosen, Kochi; Yard No. 506.

KAZIMIERZ PULASKI - sister of TADEUSZ KOSCIUSKO (q.v.)
Builders Ch. de l'Atlantique, St. Nazaire; Yard No. M27.

KEMIRA (Fi)
Type Chemical Tanker; 5547 GRT; 8250 DWT; Dimensions 112.71 × — × 8.15; Machinery Motor 5600 bhp; Engine builders Sulzer/Oy Wartsila; Owners Kemira O/Y; Managers O/Y Finnlines Ltd.; Builders M. Kleven M/V., Ulsteinvik; Yard No. 34.

KENWOOD (Ja)
Type Cargo; 2496 GRT; 6269 DWT; Dimensions 89.52 (BP) × 17.42 × 6.73; Machinery Motor 3600 bhp; Engine builders Akasaka; Owners Kurushima Marine KK; Builders Kishigami Zosen, Akitsu; Yard No. 1430.

KENYO MARU (Ja)
Type Tanker; 54786 GRT; 81283 DWT; Dimensions 220 (BP) × 44 × 12.19; Machinery Motor 17000 bhp; Engine builders Sulzer/Mitsubishi; Owners Taiyo Shosen Kaisha & Nippon Yusen Kaisha; Builders Mitsubishi Heavy Industries, Nagasaki; Yard No. 1872.

KEPWAVE (Sg)
Type Bulk Carrier; 59200 GRT; 120000 DWT; Dimensions 253 (BP) × 42 × 15.85; Machinery motor 18400 bhp; Engine builders B&W/Mitsui; 14.1 knots; Owners Kepsula Shipping (Pte.) Ltd.; Managers Kopal Management; Builders Mitsui Eng. & S.B., Tamano; Yard No. 1227.

KERTAU (Pa)
Type Cargo; 2499 GRT; 6000 DWT; Dimensions 89.5 (BP) × 17.42 × 6.65; Machinery Motor 3600 bhp; Engine builders Hanshin Nainenki Kogyo; Owners Caceres (Panama) Ltd. S.A.; Builders Kochi Jukogyo K.K., Kochi; Yard No. 2177.

KHAIRPUR (Pk)
Type Cargo; 11500 GRT; 15000 DWT; Dimensions 145 (BP) × 22.8 × 9.2; Machinery Motor 11400 bhp; Engine builders Sulzer/Cegielski; 17 knots; Owners Pakistan National Sg. Corp.; Builders Stocznia Gdanska im Lenina, Gdansk; Yard No. B346/02.

KINABALU ENAMBELAS (Li)
Type Cargo; 4654 GRT; 7750 DWT; Dimensions 114.28 × 17.6 × 7.2; Machinery Motor 4400 bhp; Engine builders B & W/Mitsui; Owners Kinabalu Enambelas Shipping Corp.; Builders Kochi Jukogyo, Kochi; Yard No. 2185.

KINOKAWA MARU (Ja)
Type Tanker; 25000 GRT; 35000 DWT; Dimensions 165 (BP) × 30 × 10.3; Machinery Motor 12950 bhp; Engine builders Sulzer/Mitsubishi; 15 knots; Owners Kawasaki Kisen; Builders Imabari S.B., Imabari; Yard No. 1078.

KINTERBURY (Br)
Type Cargo; 1393 GRT; 685 DWT; Dimensions 70.39 × 12.25 × 4.48; Machinery Motor 3042 bhp; Engine builders Mirrlees Blackstone; Owners Govt of the United Kingdom (MOD-Navy); Builders Appledore Shipbuilders Ltd., Appledore; Yard No. 130.

KOH JIN (Li)
Type Vehicles Carrier; 16713 GRT; 19422 DWT; Dimensions 190 (BP) × — × 9.64; Machinery Motor 16880 bhp; Engine builders MAN/Kawasaki; Owners Lorraine Maritime; Builders Kurushima Dock Co. Ltd., Onishi; Yard No. 2132.

KONKAR DORIS (Gr)
Type Cargo; 16000 GRT; 24500 DWT; Dimensions 193 (BP) × 22.9 × 10.2; Machinery Motor 11200 bhp; Engine builders B & W/Uljanik; 16.8 knots; Owners Konkar Doris Corp.; Builders Brodogradiliste "Uljanik", Pula; Yard No. 335.

KONKAR THETIS - sister of KONKAR DORIS (q.v.)
Yard No. 336.

KONKAR TRITON - sister of KONKAR DORIS (q.v.)
Yard No. 343.

KONSTANTIN FOMTSHENKO - sister of DMITRIY POKROVICH (q.v.)
Yard No. B408/16.

KONSTANTIN SIMONOV (Ru)
Type Ro/Ro Passenger Ferry; 9800 GRT; 1350 DWT; Dimensions 124.82 × — × 5.46; Machinery Twin Screw Motor 17400 bhp; Engine builders Sulzer/Zgoda; Owners U.S.S.R.; Builders Stocznia Szczecinska im A Warskiego; Yard No. B493/03.

KOREAN WONIS SEVEN (Ko)
Type Container; 25000 GRT; 25000 DWT; Dimensions 193.6 (BP) × — × —; Machinery Motor 30150 bhp; Engine builders Sulzer/Hyundai; Owners Korea Shipping Corp. Ltd.; Builders Hyundai Heavy Industries Co. Ltd., Ulsan; Yard No. 151.

KOSTAS KONIALIDIS (Gr)
(May be COSTAS KONIALIDIS) ex EVA VENTURE 1981
Type Bulk; 29800 GRT; 57000 DWT; Dimensions 222.99 × 32.26 × 9.1; Machinery Motor 13100 bhp; Engine builders B & W/Mitsui; Owners Kelso Panama S.A.; Managers Olympic Maritime S.A.; Builders Koyo Dockyard Co. Ltd, Japan; Yard No. 1007.

KRISLOCK - sister of WORLD ACCLAIM (q.v.)
Yard No. 1013.

KRONPRINS FREDERIK (De)
Type RoRo Ferry/Train Ferry; 11000 GRT; 4490 DWT; Dimensions 143.2 (BP) × 23.1 × 5.64; Machinery Twin Screw Motor 6 × 3840 bhp; Engine builders Alpha/B & W; 18.9 knots; Owners Danske Statsbaner; Builders Nakskov Skibsvaerft.

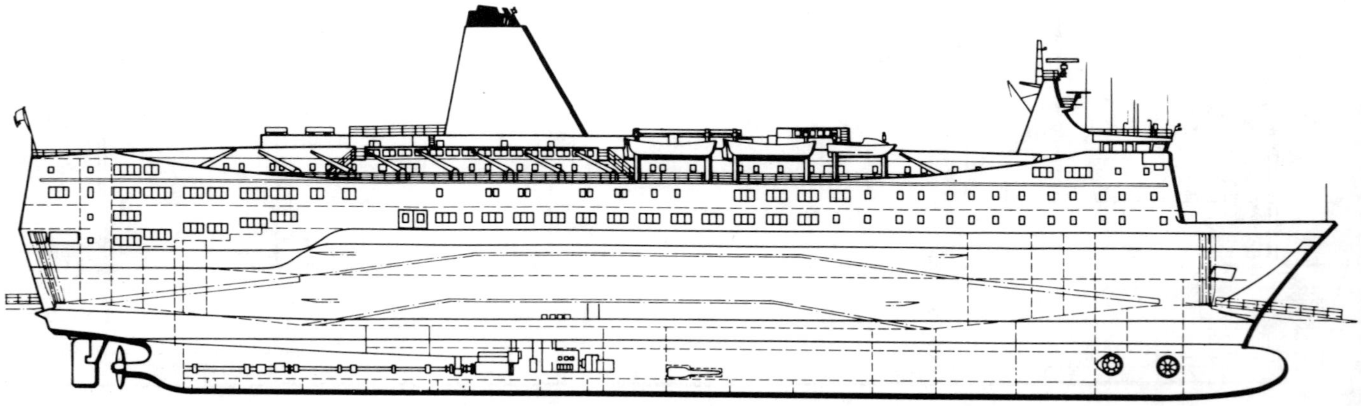

Kronprinsessan Victoria *(Motor Ship)*

Kronprinsessan Victoria *(Builders)*

KRONPRINSESSAN VICTORIA (Sw)
Type Ro/Ro Pass. Ferry; 15000 GRT; 3100 DWT; Dimensions 150 × 26 × 6; Machinery Twin Screw Motor 4 × 5220 bhp; Engine builders Vasa/Wartsila; 21 knots; Owners Sessan Line; Builders Gotaverken Arendal; Yard No. 908.

KROPOTKIN (Ru)
Type Tanker/Replenishment; 4816 GRT; 5873 DWT; Dimensions 115.5 × 17.02 × 7.0; Machinery Motor 3500 bhp; Engine Builders B & W/Bryansk; 14.25 knots; Owners U.S.S.R.; Builders Rauma-Repola Oy, Rauma/Raumo; Yard No. 263.

KUKULKAN (Me)
Type Tuna Fishing; 990 GRT; Dimensions 67.52 × — × 5.79; Machinery Motor 3600 bhp; Engine builders General Motors; Owners Atunera del Carmen; Builders Campbell Industries, San Diego, California; Yard No. 128.

KULIKOVO - sister of KASHIRSKOYE (q.v.)
Yard No. B432/442.

KUNIANG (Li)
Type Bulk; 31007 GRT; 65535 DWT; Dimensions 224.01 (BB) × 32.26 × 13.09; Machinery Motor 15200 bhp; Engine builders B & W/Hyundai; Owners Malaren Corp.; Builders Hyundai Heavy Industries Co. Ltd., Ulsan; Yard No. 144.

KUWAIT EXPRESS - sister of FINNEAGLE (q.v.)
Yard No. 578.

KYOEI MARU No 21 (Ja)
Type Cargo; 499 GRT; 1600 DWT; Dimensions 58.8 (BP) × — × 4.3; Machinery Motor 1800 bhp; Owners Kyoae Kaiun; Builders Mategata Zosen K.K., Namikata; Yard No. 202.

KYOKUWA MARU (Ja)
Type Tanker; 71700 GRT; 11990 DWT; Dimensions 230 (BP) × 46 × 16.08; Machinery Motor 23800 bhp; Engine builders Sulzer/Mitsubishi; 14.6 knots; Owners Taiyo Kaiun Kaisha; Builders Mitsubishi Heavy Industries, Shimonoseki; Yard No. 1875.

KYRIAKI (Gr)
Type Bulk Carrier; 38000 GRT; 60000 DWT; Dimensions 214 (BP) × 32.2 × 12.3; Machinery Motor 14400 bhp; Engine builders Sulzer/Sumitomo; 15.1 knots; Owners Etal Shipping; Managers Glaski Group; Builders Nippon Kokan KK, Tsurumi; Yard No. 983.

Kyushu Maru *(FotoFlite)*

KYUSHU MARU (Ja)
Type Car Carrier; 16867 GRT; 17650 DWT; Dimensions 190 × 32.2 × 8.92; Machinery Motor; Engine builders B & W/Hitachi; Owners Nissan Motor Car Carrier Co.; Builders Hitachi Zosen (Hiroshima); Yard No. 4683.

L

LA ESTANCIA (Br)
Type Bulk; 26191 GRT; 39900 DWT; Dimensions 175.3 (BP) × — × 11.7; Machinery Motor 12000 bhp; Engine builders Sulzer/Cegielski; 14 knots; Owners Buries Markes Ltd.; Builders Stocznia Gdynska im Komuny Paryskiej, Gdynia; Yard No. B518/03.

LA PAMPA (Br)
Type Bulk; 42500 GRT; 75900 DWT; Dimensions 219.5 (BP) × 32.23 × 14.82; Machinery Motor 15400 bhp; Engine builders B & W/Kincaid; 13.5 knots; Owners Buries Markes; Builders Sunderland Shipbuilders, Deptford; Yard No. 861.

LA SIERRA - sister of LA ESTANCIA (q.v.)
Yard No. B518/04.

LADY DIANA (Au)
Launched as LONGBOW. Type Supply; 990 GRT; 1500 DWT; Dimensions 58.48 × 13.87 × 4.9; Machinery Twin Screw Motor 5750 bhp; Engine builders General Motors; 14 knots; Owners International Offshore Maintenance Services (Australasia) Pty, Ltd.; Builders N.S.W. Govt. Eng. & SB. Undertaking (State Dockyard) Newcastle, N.S.W.; Yard No. 102.

LAGOVEN SINAMAICA (Ve)
Ex BERGE HELENE (Ve). Type Tanker; 31849 GRT; 53500 DWT; Dimensions 205 (BP) × 32 × 11.6; Machinery Motor 18400 bhp; Engine builders B & W/Mitsui; Owners Lagoven; Builders Mitsui Eng. & SB. Co. Ltd., Chiba; Yard No. 1225.

LAKE OROVILLE - see ELGIN.

LEANDROS (Gr)
Type Bulk; 30644 GRT; 54540 DWT; Dimensions 219.92 × 32.2 × 12.32; Machinery Motor 17400 bhp; Engine builders Sulzer/Cegielski; Owners Merit Holdings Corp.; Managers Leandros Shipping Co.; Builders Santierul Naval Mangalia, Mangalia; Yard No. 900/20.

LEINSTER (Ih)
Type Passenger/RoRo Cargo/Ferry; 6812 GRT; Dimensions 112 (BP) × 18.5 × 4.82; Machinery Twin Screw Motor 18000 bhp; Engine builders Mak; 20 knots; Owners British and Irish Steam Packet Co.; Builders Verolme, Cork Dockyards, Cork; Yard No. 979.

LEIRO (No)
Type Cargo; 499 GRT; Dimensions 75.95 × 13.7 × —; Machinery Motor 2035 bhp; Engine builders Wichmann; 10 knots; Owners Paal Wilson & Co A/S (Norway-Rhine Line); Builders Mjellem & Karlsen, Bergen; Yard No. 124.

LEONID IVANOV - sister of DMITRIY POKROVICH (q.v.)
Yard No. B408/18.

LEONID NOVOSPASSKIY - sister of DMITRIY POKROVICH (q.v.)
Yard No. B408/15.

LEV TOLSTOY (Ru)
Type Passenger/Ferry; 6680 GRT; Dimensions 134.5 × 21 × 5.3; Machinery Motor 17400 bhp; Engine builders Sulzer/Zgoda; 19 knots; Owners U.S.S.R; Builders Stocznia Szczecinska im A. Warskiego, Szczecin; Yard No. B492/02.

LEXA MAERSK (De)
Type Container; 30694 GRT; 31600 DWT; Dimensions 212.48 (BB) × 32.26 × 12.22; Machinery Motor 40920 bhp; Engine builders B & W; Owners A/S D/S Svendborg & D/S af 1912 A/S; Managers A.P. Moller; Builders Odense Staalskibsvaerft A/S, Lindo; Yard No. 85.

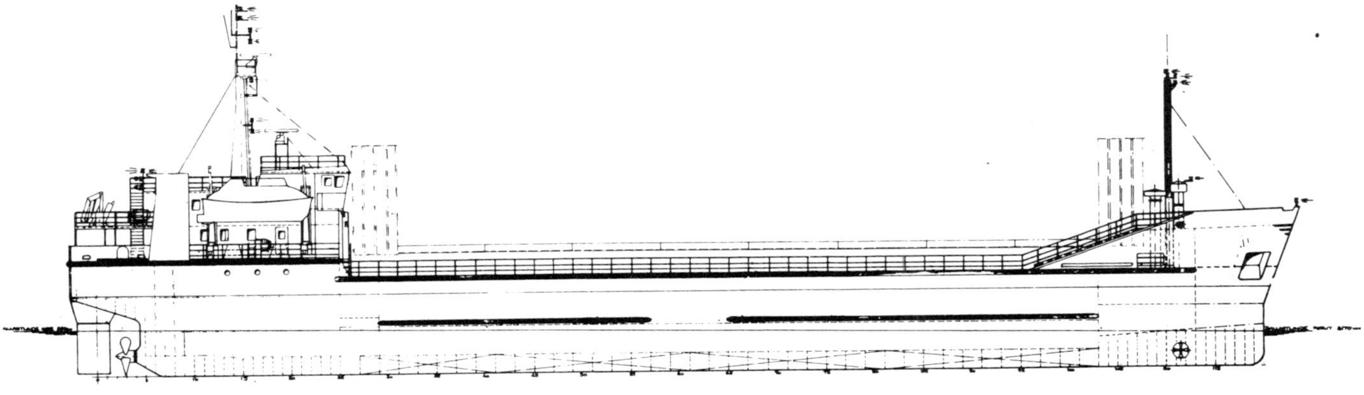

Leiro *(Zosen)*

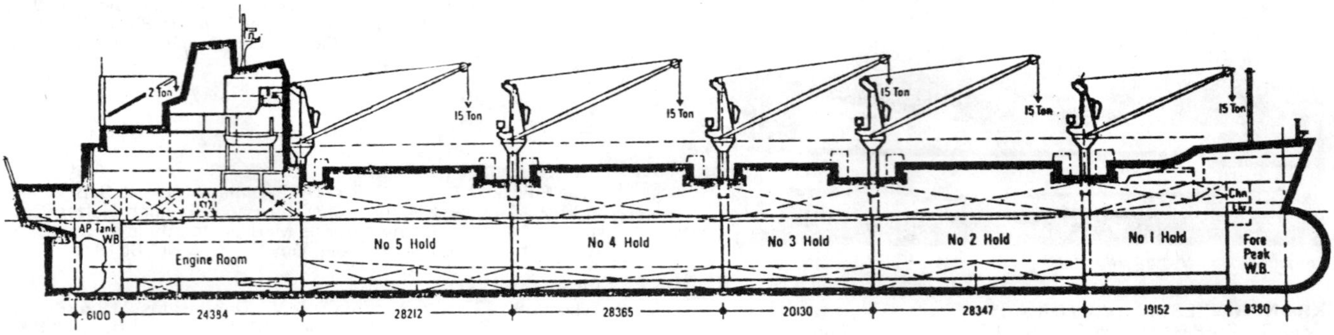

Lord Curzon

LIBERTY BELL VENTURE (Li)
Type Tanker; 34000 GRT; 54930 DWT; Dimensions 216 (BP) × 32.2 × 11.7; Machinery Motor 14400 bhp; Engine builders Sulzer/Sumitomo; 15.5 knots; Owners Garland Carriers; Builders Oshima Zosen, Nagasaki; Yard No. 10051.

LICA MAERSK - sister of LEXA MAERSK (q.v.)
Yard No. 86.

LIESEL ESSBERGER - sister of CORAL ESSBERGER (q.v.)
Yard No. 1425.

LINGEGAS (Ne)
Type LGC; 1600 GRT; 3297 DWT; Dimensions 82.5 (BP) × 14 × 6.5; Machinery Motor 2500 bhp; Engine builders Deutz; 13.4 knots; Owners B.V. Lusitania Lijn; Managers Sloman-Neptun Schiffahrts; Builders BV. Scheepswerf 'Waterhuizen', J. Pattje; Yard No. 345.

LIPNO (Cz)
Type Cargo; 6890/10416 GRT; 11000/15173 DWT; Dimensions 145.7 × 21.65 × 9.1; Machinery Motor 7200 bhp; Engine builders Sulzer/Brodogradiliste '3 Maj'; Owners Czechoslovak Ocean Shipping International Joint Stock Co.; Builders Brodogradiliste '3 Maj', Rijeka; Yard No. 603.

LLOYD ARGENTINA (Bz)
Type Cargo ("SD14" type); 9100 GRT; 14800 DWT; Dimensions 140.98 × 20.55 × 8.82; Machinery Motor 8400 bhp; Engine builders MAN/Halberstadt; 15 knots; Owners Companhia de Nav. Lloyd Brasileiro; Builders Cia. Comercio e Nav. CCN Maua Shpyd., Niteroi; Yard No. 145.

LOJA (Ec)
Type Tanker; 11096 GRT; 26000 DWT; Dimensions 153.5 (BP) × 22.9 × 9.45; Machinery Motor 12000 bhp; Engine builders Sulzer/Mitsubishi; Owners Flopec; Builders Korea Shipbuilding & Eng. Corp., Busan; Yard No. 2005.

LONGBOW - see LADY DIANA.

LORD BYRON (Br)
Type Bulk ("Cardiff" type); 16421 GRT; 26354 DWT; Dimensions 175.14 (BB) × 25.53 × 9.96; Machinery Motor 11600 bhp; Engine builders B & W/Kincaid; 15.5 knots; Owners Bishopsgate Marine Hire Purchase Ltd.; Managers H. Scullard & Sons Ltd.; Builders Govan Shipbuilders Ltd., Govan, Glasgow; Yard No. 251.

LORD CURZON - sister of LORD BYRON (q.v.)
Launched as Lord Jellicoe. Yard No. 252.

LORD JELLICOE - see LORD CURZON.

LOS MOLINUCOS (Sp)
Type Cement Carrier; 3498 GRT; 6205 DWT; Dimensions 106.18 × — × 6.78; Machinery Motor 4400 bhp; Engine builders Deutz/Hijos de J. Barreras S.A.; Owners Naviera de Cantabria S.A.; Builders Astilleros del Atlantico S.A., Santander; Yard No. 210.

Lotus Maru *(FotoFlite)*

LOTUS MARU (Ja)
Type Tanker; 17265 GRT; 29525 DWT; Dimensions 162 (BP) × 25.4 × 10.65; Machinery Motor 11200 bhp; Engine builders Kawasaki; Owners Sumitomo Shintaku Ginko; Builders Kurushima Dockyard Co. Ltd., Onishi; Yard No. 2148.

LUCKY RIDER (Gr)
Type RoRo/cargo; 7000 GRT; 5500 DWT; Dimensions 128 (BP) × 20.2 × 6; Machinery Motor 6000 bhp; Engine builders MWM; 19 knots; Owners Castello; Builders Nuovi Cant. Apuania S.p.A., Spezia; Yard No. 2120.

LUKOMORYE - sister of KROPOTKIN (q.v.)
Yard No. 267.

LURO (Sw)
Type Chemical Tanker; 2337 GRT; 3889 DWT; Dimensions 86.01 × — × 5.99; Machinery Motor 2950 bhp; Engine builders Polar/-Nohab Diesel A/B; Owners Thunrederierna; Builders A/B Falkenbergs Varv., Falkenberg; Yard No. 177.

M

M. JACINTO VERDAGUER (Sp)
Type Cargo; 9633 GRT; 15400 DWT; Dimensions 144.13 × — × 8.96; Machinery Motor 6150 bhp; Engine builders B & W/Ast. Espanoles S.A.; Owners Maritima de Cementos y Graneles S.A.; Builders Ast. Espanoles S.A., Factoria de Olaveaga, Bilbao; Yard No. 323.

M. LUISA DE PANDO (Sp)
Type Chemical Tanker; 19566 GRT; 39340 DWT; Dimensions 168 (BP) × 32 × 10; Machinery Motor 11200 bhp; Engine builders B & W/AESA; 15.2 knots; Owners Antares; Builders A.E.S.A., Sestao; Yard No. 246.

MACAYE (Sp)
Type Bulk; 20487 GRT; 35000 DWT; Dimensions 197.7 × — × 11.0; Machinery Motor 11550 bhp; Engine builders Sulzer/Ast. Espanoles S.A.; Owners Naviera Sokorri S.A.; Builders Ast. Espanoles S.A., Factoria de Sevilla, Sevilla; Yard No. 230.

Madame Butterfly *(FotoFlite)*

MADAME BUTTERFLY (Sw)
Type Vehicles Carrier; 18728 GRT; 27500 DWT; Dimensions 198.12 × 32.25 × 9.5; Machinery Motor 18400 bhp; Engine builders B & W/Gotaverken; 20.3 knots; Owners Wallenius Line; Builders Kockums A/B, Malmo; Yard No. 581.

MAERSK DETECTOR (De)
Type Tug/Supply; 1157/1598 GRT; 1600/2160 DWT; Dimensions 65.82 × — × —/5.99; Machinery Twin Screw Motor — bhp; Engine Builders Mak; Owners A/S D/S Svendborg & D/S af 1912 A/S; Builders Frederikshavn Vaerft A/S, Frederikshavn; Yard No. 394.

MAERSK DISPATCHER - sister of MAERSK DETECTOR (q.v.)
Yard No. 395.

MAERSK PINTO - sister of HOLSATIC (q.v.)
Launched as ARCTIC Yard No. 104.

MAERSK SEBAROK - sister of MAERSK SENTOSA (q.v.)
Yard No. 4682.

MAERSK SELETAR - sister of MAERSK SENTOSA (q.v.)
Yard No. 4679.

Maersk Sentosa *(Builders)*

MAERSK SENTOSA (Sg)
Type Bulk; 30741 GRT; 64797 DWT; Dimensions 224.5 × 32.2 × 12.96; Machinery Motor; Engine builders B & W/Hitachi; 17.29 knots; Owners Maersk Company (Singapore) Pte. Ltd.; Builders Hitachi Zosen, Ariake; Yard No. 4678.

MAERSK WIND (Li)
Type Vehicles Carrier; 9354 GRT; 7300 DWT; Dimensions 153.12 (BB) × 26.04 × 7.82; Machinery Motor 13100 bhp; Engine builders B & W/Mitsui; Owners Astral Carriers Ltd.; Managers A.P. Moller; Builders Oshima Zosen, Nagasaki; Yard No. 10047.

MAHMUD-UL HASAN (Pk)
Type Hopper/Dredger; 2257 GRT; 3980 DWT; Dimensions 82.81 × 15.24 × 6.58; Machinery Twin Screw Motor 3150 bhp; Engine builders MAN; Owners Karachi Port Trust; Builders Dubigeon-Normandie S.A., Grand Quevilly; Yard No. 2554.

MAN WO (Br)
Type Ferry; 519 GRT; 100 DWT; Dimensions 43.21 × — × —; Machinery Motor 1025 bhp; Engine builders M.T.U. Friedrichshafen; 13 knots; Owners The Hongkong & Yaumati Ferry Co. Ltd.; Builders Hong Kong Shipyard Ltd., Kowloon, Hong Kong.

MANA
Type Container; 7100 DWT; Dimensions 110.9 (BP) × 20.8 × 6.23; Machinery Motor 7000 bhp; Engine builders Mitsubishi-/Kobe; 16 knots; Owners Panwind Shipping; Builders Mie Shipyard; Yard No. 198.

MANABI (Ec)
Type Tanker; 26999 GRT; Dimensions 205.5 (BP) × 31 × 11.9; Machinery Motor 16800 bhp; Engine Builders Sulzer/Mitsubishi; 16 knots; Owners Flopec; Builders Korea Shipbuilding & Eng. Corp. Busan; Yard No. 5001.

MARACA - sister of MARAU (q.v.)
Yard No. B53.

MARACAIBO MARU (Ja)
Type Tanker; 37860 GRT; 63005 DWT; Dimensions 219 (BP) × 32.2 × 12.5; Machinery Motor 14000 bhp; Engine builders MAN/Mitsubishi; 14.5 knots; Owners Yamashita-Shinnihon S.S. Co.; Builders Mitsubishi Heavy Industries, Kobe; Yard No. 1118.

MARAU (Bz)
Type Ore/Bulk/Oil; 77929 GRT; 133752 DWT; Dimensions 274.02 × 43.57 × 16.12; Machinery Motor 29000 bhp; Engine builders Sulzer/Ishikawajima do Brasil; 16 knots; Owners Petrobras; Builders Verolme Est. Reunidos do Brasil S.A., Jacuacanga; Yard No. B52.

MARCO ALBELAY (Sp)
Type Bulk Carrier; 19800 GRT; 35000 DWT; Dimensions 185 (BP) × 24.2 × 11.11; Machinery Motor 10900 bhp; Engine builders B & W/AESA; 15.3 Knots; Owners Marcosa; Builders Astilleros Espanoles, Seville; Yard No. 237.

MARIA (Li)
Type Container; 6700 GRT; 7100 DWT; Dimensions 110.9 (BP) × 20.8 × 6.23; Machinery Motor 7000 bhp; Engine builders Mitsubishi/Kobe; 16.5 Knots; Owners Panwind Shipping; Builders Mie Zosen, Yokkaichi; Yard No. 198.

MARIA FRANCISCA (Sp)
ex Blas de Lezo 1981 Type Cargo; 3679 GRT; 6637 DWT; Dimensions 130.34 × - × 6.64; Machinery Motor 7500 bhp; Engine builders MAN/Bazan; Owners Naviera Gorbea S.A; Builders Soc. Met. Duro Felguera, Gijon; Yard No. 154.

MARIA INES - sister of MARIA FRANCISCA (q.v.)
ex Bernardo de Zamacola 1981; Type Cargo; 3645/6152 GRT; 6700/9407 DWT; Dimensions 130.36 × 19.28 × 6.64/8.01; Machinery Motor 7500 bhp; Engine builders MAN/Bazan; Owners Naviera Gorbea S.A; Builders S. A. Juliana Const. Gijonesa, Gijon; Yard No. 267.

MARIANA (Fr)
Type LNG; Dimensions 83 × 14.3 × 4.4; Machinery Motor 2400 bhp; Engine builders Crepelle; 12 Knots; Owners Services et Transports Armement; Builders At et Ch. du Sud-Ouest, Bordeaux; Yard No. 1187.

MARIGOLA (It)
Type Chemical Tanker; 6950 GRT; 12000 DWT; Dimensions 142.24 × 18.6 × 8.09; Machinery Motor 8250 bhp; Engine builders GMT; 16 Knots; Owners Carbocoke S.p.A. di Navigazione; Builders M & B Benetti, Viareggio; Yard No. 120.

MARITIME REGION - see SIRI BHUM

MARITIME VICTOR (Pa)
Type Bulk Carrier; 22300 GRT; 36000 DWT; Dimensions 180 (BP) × 28.4 × 11; Machinery Motor 13300 bhp; Engine builders Sulzer/Mitsubishi; 15.5 Knots; Owners Bultrade Nav. Corp; Builders Osaka Shipbuilding, Osaka; Yard No. 402.

MARMARA (Sp)
Type Tanker; 6128 GRT; 10000 DWT; Dimensions 123 (BP) × 19 × 7.85; Machinery Motor 2×2400 bhp; Engine builders Deutz-/Barreras; 14.5 Knots; Builders Astilleros del Cantabrico y Riera, Gijon; Yard No. 134.

Mataram *(FotoFlite)*

MATARAM (Ia)
Type Container; 12000 GRT; 17000 DWT; Dimensions 146 (BP) × 25.5 × 9.5; Machinery Motor 12390 bhp; Engine builders MAN; 17 Knots; Owners Djakarta Lloyd; Builders Schlichting Werft, Lubeck; Yard No. 1428.

MATSUKAZE (Ja)
Type Tanker; 10550 GRT; 16000 DWT; Dimensions 149.61 × - × 8.65; Machinery Motor 6000 bhp; Engine builders B & W/Akasaka; Owners Central Marine K.K; Builders Mie Zisen K.K., Yokkaichi; Yard No. 207.

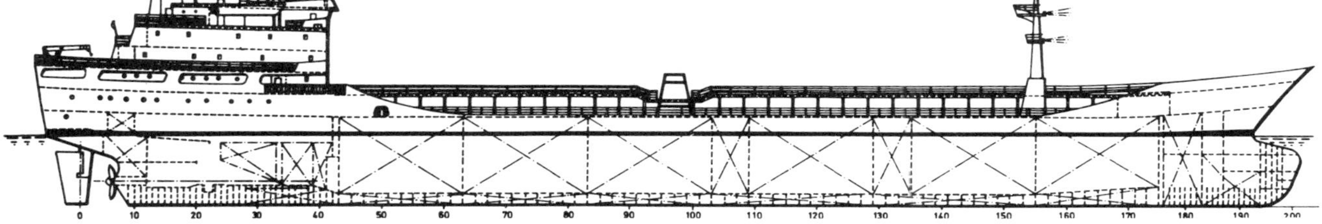

Marigola *(Motor Ship)*

MAURANGER (No)
Type Chemical Tanker; 18716 GRT; 33000 DWT; Dimensions 174.6 (BP) × 29.5 × 10; Machinery Motor 11900 bhp; Engine builders B & W; 15.6 Knots; Owners Westfal-Larsen & Co; Builders Ankerlokken, Floro; Yard No. 115.

MAZOWIA (Pd)
Type Ferry/RoRo Cargo; 7400 GRT; Dimensions 120 (BP) × 19.7 × 5.3; Machinery Motor 16800 bhp; Engine builders Sulzer/Zgoda; 20 Knots; Owners Polska Zegluga Baltycka; Builders Stocznia Szczecinska; Yard No. B490.

MEANDROS (Gr)
Type Tanker; 23000 GRT; 39830 DWT; Dimensions 168 (BP) × 30 × 11.9; Machinery Motor 10800 bhp; Engine builders Sulzer-/Mitsubishi; Owners Countess Shipping; Builders Mitsubishi Heavy Industries, Nagasaki; Yard No. 1874.

MEDI SEA (FRG)
Type Cargo/Container; 14500 GRT; 19400 DWT; Dimensions 163.04 (BP) × 25.03 × 8.06; Machinery Motor 15200 bhp; Engine builders Sulzer/Cegielski; 19 Knots; Owners B. Schuldt; Builders Stocznia Szczecinska, Szczecin.

MEDI STAR - sister of MEDI SEA (q.v.)

MEDITERRANEAN SHEARWATER (Br)
Type Nuclear Fuel Carrier; 2300 GRT; 1150 DWT; Dimensions 70.5 (BP) × 12.5 × 4.5; Machinery Motor 1866 bhp; Engine builders Ruston; 11 Knots; Owners Pacific Nuclear Transport; Builders Swan Hunter, Hebburn; Yard No. 115.

MEIYO MARU (Ja)
Type Vehicles Carrier; 15000 GRT; 16800 DWT; Dimensions - × - × 9.01; Machinery Motor 17400 bhp; Engine builders Mitsui; Owners Y. K. Meiji Kaiun; Builders Imabari Zosen, Marugame; Yard No. 1079.

MEKHANIK KRULL - sister of KAPITAN VOOLENS (q.v.)
Yard No. 306.

MELTON EXPLORER (Ne)
ex POOLZEE 1981; Type Cargo; 1599/2721 GRT; 3550/4800 DWT; Dimensions 81.6 × 15 × 6.05/7.23; Machinery Motor 3000 bhp; Engine builders Deutz; 12 Knots; Owners Noondlijn B.V; Builders Amels B.V., Makkum; Yard No. 373.

MELTON VOYAGER - sister of MELTON EXPLORER (q.v.)
Ex JAVAZEE.

MERCANDIAN MERCHANT II (De)
Type RoRo Cargo; 1599 GRT; 3400 DWT; Dimensions 105.5 × 18.8 × 5; Machinery Motor 5000 bhp; Engine builders Mak; 15.5 Knots; Owners Mercandia Rederierne (Per Henriksen); Builders Frederikshavn Vaerft, Fredrikshavn; Yard No. 391.

MERCANDIAN SUPPLIER II - sister of MERCANDIAN MERCHANT II (q.v.)

MERCURIA (Ja)
Type Cargo; 2499 GRT; 5200 DWT; Dimensions 89.5 (BP) × 16 × 6.15; Machinery Motor 3200 bhp; Engine builders Akasaka; Owners Kotoku Kaiun; Builders Hakata Zosen, Fukuoka; Yard No. 252.

MERWEGAS (Ne)
Type LGC; 1600 GRT; 3350 DWT; Dimensions 74.5 (BP) × 14 × 6.5; Machinery Motor 3000 bhp; Engine builders Deutz; 13.5 Knots; Owners BV Lusitania Linj; Managers Sloman-Neptun Schiffahrt; Builders B.V. Sch. Gebr. Van. Diepen, Waterhuizen; Yard No. 1018.

METHONI (Gr)
Type Tanker; 34200 GRT; 54918 DWT; Dimensions 219 (BP) × 32.2 × 11.7; Machinery Motor 14400 bhp; Engine builders Sulzer/Sumitomo; 15.5 Knots; Owners Metromar Corp; Builders Oshima Zosen, Nagasaki; Yard No. 10050.

MIYAJIMA MARU (Ja)
Type Cargo; 499 GRT; 1515 DWT; Dimensions 71.05 × 12.02 × 4.16; Machinery Motor 1800 bhp; Engine builders Fuji Seisakusho; Owners Nakanishi Kisen K.K; Builders Matsuura Tekko Zosen, Higashino; Yard No. 284.

MOBIL ENDEAVOUR (Li)
Type Tanker; 20000 GRT; Dimensions 162 (BP) × 30 × 10.77; Machinery Motor 11000 bhp; Engine builders Sulzer/Sumitomo; 15.3 Knots; Owners Mobil Shipping & Transportation; Builders Sumitomo Heavy Industries, Yokosuka; Yard No. 1091.

MOBILITY (Pa)
Type Cargo; 4318 GRT; 7071 DWT; Dimensions 100.01 (BP) × - × 6.88; Machinery Motor 3800 bhp; Engine builders Mitsubishi-/Kobe Hatsudoki; Owners Fumania Shipping S.A; Builders Imai Zosen, Kochi; Yard No. 505.

MONTE ROSA (FRG)
Type Container; 21900 GRT; 24000 DWT; Dimensions 174.2 (BP) × 28 × 10.02; Machinery Motor 14400 bhp; Engine builders Sulzer; 19 Knots; Owners Hamburg Sud; Builders A. G. 'Weser', Seebeckwerft, Bremerhaven; Yard No. 1029.

MONTLHERY (Fr)
Type RoRo Cargo; 1600 GRT; 2200 DWT; Dimensions 115 (BP) × 18 × 5.25; Machinery Motor 6000 bhp; Engine builders Pielstick-/Atlantique; 15.5 Knots; Owners A.T.A. Walon S.A. & SFTM; Builders Soc. Nouvelle des Ateliers et Ch. de la Rochelle-Pallice; Yard No. 1233.

MOSMAN STAR (Li)
Type Bulk; 18664 GRT; 33496 DWT; Dimensions 170 (BP) × 27.6 × 10.88; Machinery Motor 12600 bhp; Engine builders Sulzer/I-HI; 15 Knots; Owners Rowley Shipping; Managers Venture Shipping (Managers) Ltd; Builders Kanda Zosensho, Kure; Yard No. 258.

MOSOR CARRIER (Sw)
Type Tanker; 25000 GRT; 36900 DWT; Dimensions 169 (BP) × 32 × 10; Machinery Motor 10900 bhp; Engine builders B & W/Uljanik; 15 Knots; Owners Lennart Kihlberg; Builders Brodogradiliste 'J.L.Mosor', Trogir; Yard No. 181.

MOUNT KING - sister of MOUNT SANTA (q.v.)
Yard No. 255.

MOUNT SANTA (Pa)
Type Cargo; 4400 GRT; 6974 DWT; Dimensions 100 (BP) × 17.6 × 6.87; Machinery Motor 4500 bhp; Engine builders Mitsubishi-/Kobe; 12.5 Knots; Owners Marciana Naviera S.A; Builders Higaki Zosen K.K., Imabari; Yard No. 256.

MULTITANK ADRIA - sister of MULTITANK ASCANIA (q.v.)
Yard No. 806.

MULTITANK ARCADIA - sister of MULTITANK ASCANIA (q.v.)

MULTITANK ARMENIA - sister of MULTITANK ASCANIA (q.v.)
Yard No. 793.

MULTITANK ASCANIA (FRG)
Type Chemical Tanker; 1599 GRT; 3560 DWT; Dimensions 93.05(BB) × 14 × 5.45; Machinery Motor 2340 bhp; Engine builders B & W; 13.5 Knots; Owners Tankreederei Ahrenkiel; Builders J. J. Sietas Schiffsw, Hamburg; Yard No. 768.

MURREE (Pk)
Type Cargo ('SD 18' type); 7924/11941 GRT; -/17815 DWT; Dimensions 152.03 × 22.86 × 9.49; Machinery Motor 10400 bhp; Engine buildersSulzer/Clark Hawthorn; Owners Pakistan National Shipping Corp; Builders Austin & Pickersgill Ltd., Southwick, Sunderland; Yard No. 1407.

MYS-KHRUSTALNY - sister of KROPOTKIN (q.v.)
Yard No. 264.

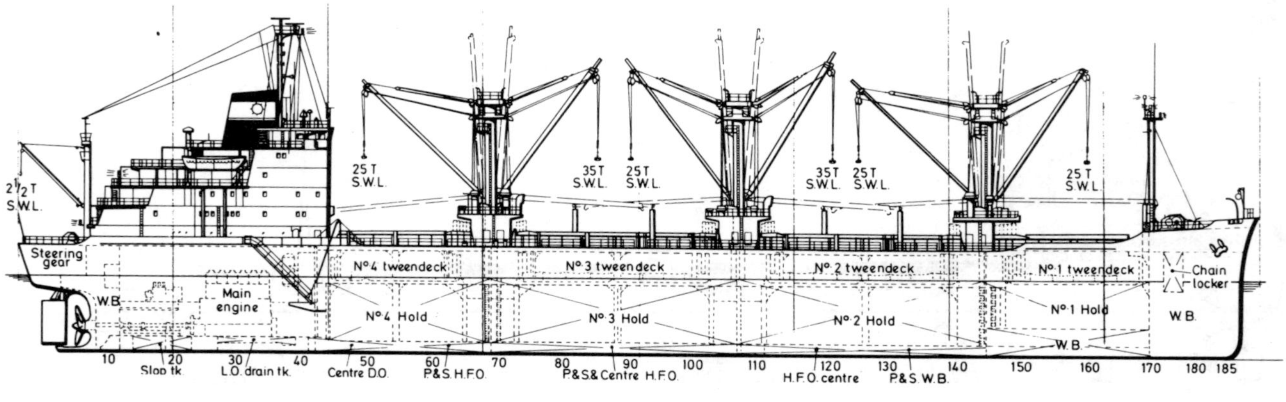

Murree (Shipbuilding & Marine Eng. Int.)

N

NADA II (Li)
Type Vehicle Carrier; 9000 GRT; 10600 DWT; Dimensions 147 (BP) × 26.8 × 7.5; Machinery Motor 10500 bhp; Engine builders B & W/Hitachi; Owners Nada II Shipping Co; Managers Chung Gai Ship Management Co; Builders Watanabe Zosen K.K., Hakata; Yard No. 211.

NAIKAI MARU No15 (Ja)
Type Cargo; 499 GRT; 1385 DWT; Dimensions 70.01 × – × 4.3; Machinery Motor 1600 bhp; Engine builders Niigata Eng. Co. Ltd; Owners Naikai Shosen K.K; Builders Murakami Hide Zosen K.K., Hakata; Yard No. 187.

NAMDALINGEN (No)
Type Bulk; 1199 GRT; 2000 DWT; Dimensions 69.24 (BP) × 14.7 × 5.92; Machinery Motor 1695 bhp; Engine builders Normo; 13.65 Knots; Owners Viktor Meland; Builders Tronderverftet; Yard No. 46.

NAN HUA (Tw)
Type Container; 8000 GRT; 8365 DWT; Dimensions 106.5 (BP) × 18.2 × 8; Machinery Motor 7385 bhp; Engine builders MAN-/Kawasaki; 15 Knots; Owners Nan Tai Line; Builders China Shipbuilding Corp., Keelung; Yard No. 152.

NAPO (Ec)
Type Tanker; 19500 GRT; 30000 DWT; Dimensions 168 (BP) × 28 × 10.5; Machinery Motor 14400 bhp; Engine builders Sulzer-/Mitsubishi; 16 Knots; Owners Flopec; Builders Korea Shipbuilding, Busan; Yard No. 3012.

NARA (Bz)
Type Tanker; 10000 GRT; 17900 DWT; Dimensions 153 (BP) × 23.4 × 7.92; Machinery Motor 6325 bhp; Engine builders Sulzer-/Ishibras; 13.7 Knots; Owners Petrobras; Builders Ishikawajima do Brasil, Rio de Janeiro; Yard No. 96.

Nauticas Mexico *(Schaart Fotografile)*

NAUTICAS MEXICO (Me)
Type Cargo/Training; 9860 GRT; 12000 DWT; Dimensions 140 (BP) × 21 × 9.2; Machinery Motor 11400 bhp; Engine builders Sulzer; 18 Knots; Owners Mexican Govt; Builders BV Scheepswerf en Masch. 'De Merwede' Hardinxveld; Yard No. 628.

NAVIGATOR (FRG)
Type Cargo; 999 GRT; 2400 DWT; Dimensions 73.7 (BP) × 12.8 × 4.6; Machinery Motor 1500 bhp; Engine builders MaK; 10 Knots; Owners M.S. 'Navigator' Scheep; Builders C. Luhring, Brake; Yard No. 8101.

NAWABSHAN - sister of KHAIRPUR (q.v.)
Yard No. B346/01.

NEAPOLIS (Gr)
Type Tanker; 29700 GRT; 60150 DWT; Dimensions 219 (BP) × 32.2 × 12.9; Machinery Motor 13680 bhp; Engine builders Sulzer/IHI; 14.9 Knots; Owners Maritime Petroleum Carriers; Builders I.H.I., Aioi; Yard No. 2741.

NEPRYADVA (Ru)
Type Cable Ship; 1900 GRT; Dimensions 75.9 × 12.6 × 3; Machinery Diesel/Electric 1620 bhp; Engine builders Wartsila-/Vasa; 11 Knots; Owners U.S.S.R; Builders Oy Wartsila, Helsinki; Yard No. 434.

NEPTUNE PAVO - sister of NEPTUNE PEGASUS (q.v.)
Yard No. 1748.

NEPTUNE PEGASUS (Sg)
Type Tanker; 39000 GRT; 80700 DWT; Dimensions 232 × 41.6 × 12.75; Machinery Motor 15960 bhp; Engine builders Pielstick/I.H.I; 14.75 Knots; Owners Neptune Eta Lines Pte. Ltd; Builders I.H.I., Kure; Yard No. 1747.

NEW IDEAL (Li)
Type Tanker; 45200 GRT; 85334 DWT; Dimensions 234 (BP) × 41.6 × 12.2; Machinery Motor 15800 bhp; Engine builders B & W/Mitsui; 14.6 Knots; Owners New Ideal Shipping; Builders Sanoyasu Dockyard Co., Mizushima; Yard No. 1038.

New Katsura *(Builders)*

NEW KATSURA (Ja)
Type RoRo Passenger-Ferry; 6773 GRT; 3249 DWT; Dimensions 141.31 × 22.7 × 5.4; Machinery Twin Screw Motor; Engine builders Pielstick/IHI; 19.7 Knots; Owners Maritime Credit Corp. and Osaka Kochi Tokkyu Ferry Co; Builders Naikai Zosen (Hitachi Zosen), Setoda; Yard No. 465.

NEW MAIL (Pa)
Type Bulk Carrier; 12370 GRT; 20500 DWT; Dimensions 142 (BP) × 24 × 9.6; Machinery Motor 8040 bhp; Engine builders Sulzer-/Mitsubishi; 15.4 Knots; Owners New Mail Line; Builders Shin-Yamamoto Shipbuilding Co., Kochi; Yard No. 255.

NICHIAS MARU No12 (Ja)
Type Asphalt Tanker; 699 GRT; 1250 DWT; Dimensions 63 × – × 4.33; Machinery Motor; Owners Daiei Kisen K.K; Builders Kinoura Zosen, Imabari; Yard No. 63.

NICHIYO MARU (Ja)
Type LGC; 699 GRT; 786 DWT; Dimensions 55.02 (BP) × – × 4.05; Machinery Motor 1600 bhp; Engine builders Akasaka; Owners Meiyo Shosen K.K; Builders Daiko Dockyard Co. Ltd., Osaka; Yard No. 121.

NICOLAOS CONDARAS - see GEHAN AL SADAT II

NIELS ONSTAD (No)
Type Bulk Carrier; 73500 GRT; 12400 DWT; Dimensions 258 (BP) × 42 × 16; Machinery Motor 22000 bhp; Engine builders MAN-/Kawasaki; 16.7 Knots; Owners Onstad Shipping; Builders Kawasaki Heavy Industries, Kobe; Yard No. 1328.

NIHO MARU (Ja)
Type Tanker; 499 GRT; 1150 DWT; Dimensions 59.11 × – × 4.2; Machinery Motor 1200 bhp; Engine builders Hanshin Nainenki Kogyo; Owners Nippo Senpaku K.K; Builders Hakata Zosen K.K., Hakata; Yard No. 237.

NIKITA MITCHENKO (Ru)
Type Cargo; 11736 GRT; 13449 DWT; Dimensions 162.39 × 22.2 × 9.17; Machinery Motor 10600 bhp; Engine builders B & W/Bryansk; 18 Knots; Owners U.S.S.R; Builders Kherson Shipyard, Kherson.

NILZA - sister of NARA (q.v.)
Yard No. 93.

NISSHO MARU (Ja)
Type Tanker; 142500 GRT; 257882 DWT; Dimensions 340.62 × 54.5 × 19.70; Machinery Motor 30600 bhp; Engine builders Sulzer/IHI; 14.5 Knots; Owners Idemitsu Tanker K.K; Builders I.H.I., Kure; Yard No. 2708.

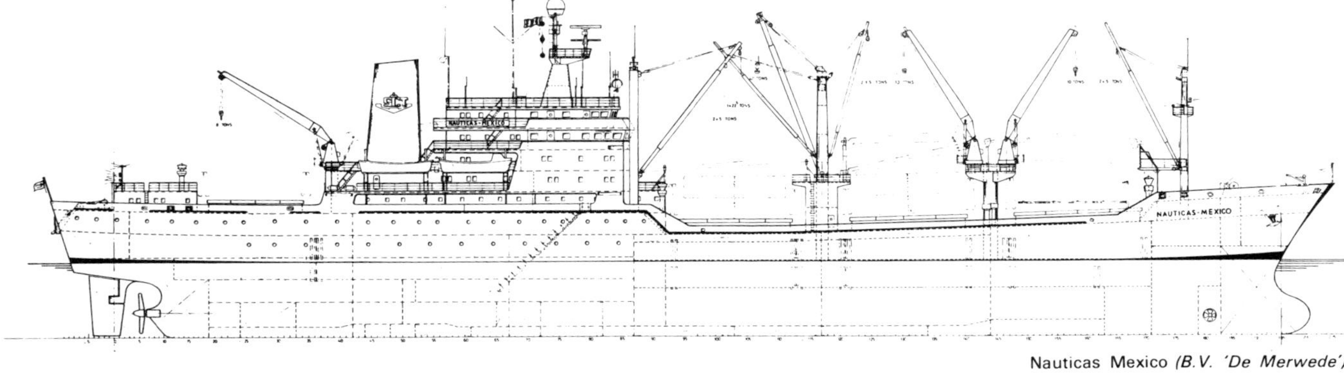

Nauticas Mexico *(B.V. 'De Merwede')*

NISSHO MARU (Ja)
Type Bulk Carrier; 14232 GRT; 23900 DWT; Dimensions 150 (BP) × 24.6 × 9.8; Machinery Motor 9380 bhp; Engine builder Mitsubishi/Kobe; 13.7 Knots; Owners Dainichi Kaiun; Builders Imabari Shipbuilding Co., Imabari; Yard No. 400.

Nordic Link *(FotoFlite)*

NORDIC LINK (Sw)
Type RoRo Cargo; 5200 GRT; 6500 DWT; Dimensions 110.8 (BP) × 21 × 6.1; Machinery Motor 6420 bhp; Engine builders Pelstick/Lindholmen; 14.5 Knots; Owners Rederi AB Sea-Link; Builders Finnboda Varv, Stockholm; Yard No. 414.

NORDIC MONARCH (Pa)
Type Bulk; 30892 GRT; 58420 DWT; Dimensions 223.02 × 32.29 × 11.58; Machinery Motor 14000 bhp; Engine builders Sulzer/Taiwan Mach. Corp; Owners Teh Tung Enterprise Corp; Builders China SB. Corp., Kaohsiung; Yard No. 188.

NORDIC SANKO - sister of NORDIC MONARCH (q.v.)
Yard No. 187.

NORDIC SUN (Li)
Type Tanker; 11781 GRT; 20000 DWT; Dimensions 145 (BP) × 22.7 × 9.6; Machinery Motor 8040 bhp; Engine builders B & W/Mitsui; 14 Knots; Owners Welland Shipping Co; Builders Hayashikane Shipbuilding & Eng. Shimonoseki; Yard No. 1244.

NORDIC TRADER (Li)
Type Tanker; 20085 GRT; 36724 DWT; Dimensions 161 (BP) × 30 × 11.2; Machinery Motor 11700 bhp; Engine builders IHI; Owners Nordic Tanker, Inc; Managers Swire Pacific Offshore Services; Builders Hashihama Shipbuilding Co., Imabari; Yard No. 808.

NORDSTAR (Sg)
Type Cargo; 1598/4691 GRT; 4555/7350 DWT; Dimensions 120.53 × 17.84 × 6.5; Machinery Motor 4000 bhp; Engine builders Mitsubishi /Akasaka; 14.5 Knots; Owners Senang Shipping Pte. Ltd; Builders Singapore SB & Eng. Ltd., Singapore; Yard No. 137.

NORSE FALCON (Bs)
Type Tanker; 54420 GRT; 87324 DWT; Dimensions 220 (BP) × 42.3 × 13.5; Machinery Motor 15800 bhp; Engine builders B & W/Uddevalla; 15.3 Knots; Owners Cardigan Shipping Co; Builders Uddevallavarvet, Uddevalla; Yard No. 307.

NORTHERN LIGHT (Li)
Type Bulk; 31007 GRT; 65592 DWT; Dimensions 224.01 × 32.26 × 12.45; Machinery Motor 15200 bhp; Engine builders B & W/Hyundai; Owners Timor Navigation Ltd; Builders Hyundai Heavy Industries Co. Ltd., Ulsan; Yard No. 145.

NORTHERN SUN (US)
Type Tanker; 1533 GRT; 2295 DWT; Dimensions 74.68 × 13.72 × 4.4; Machinery Twin Screw Motor 1900 bhp; Engine builders General Motors; Owners Sun Transport Inc; Builders Mangone SB. Corp., Houston, Texas; Yard No. 129.

NOSIRA LIN - sister of DARYA KAMAL (q.v.)
Owners Nosira Shipping Ltd; Yard No. 17.

NOSIRA SHARON - sister of DARYA KAMAL (q.v.)
Owners Nosira Shipping Ltd; Yard No. 18.

NS CARRIER (Ja)
Type Oil/Molasses Tanker; 3494 GRT; 6230 DWT; Dimensions 99.24 × – × 6.71; Machinery Motor 3800 bhp; Engine builders Hanshin Nainenki Kogyo; Owners Daiichi Kaiun K.K; Builders Nishi Zosen K.K., Imabari; Yard No. 310.

O

OAK RIVER - sister of BUENA VENTURA (q.v.)
(launched as Salena); Owners Triumphant; Yard No. 1001.

OAK STAR (Pa)
Type Bulk Carrier; 15140 GRT; 27000 DWT; Dimensions 182.8 (BP) × 22.86 × 13.5; Machinery Motor 10700 bhp; Engine builders B & W; 14.7 Knots; Owners Mansfield Shipping Ltd; Builders Nipponkai Heavy Industries, Toyama; Yard No. 219.

OCEAN EVER (Ko)
Type Bulk; 29116 GRT; 46855 DWT; Dimensions 216.97 × 32.09 × –; Machinery Motor 11850 bhp; Engine builders Sulzer/Mitsubishi; 16 Knots; Owners Pan Ocean Bulk Carriers Ltd; Builders Korea SB & Eng. Corp., Busan; Yard No. 4001.

OCEAN FAME (Ja)
Type Bulk Carrier; 13900 GRT; 23900 DWT; Dimensions 150(BP) × – × –; Machinery Motor 9380 bhp; Engine builders Sulzer/Mitsubishi; 13.7 Knots; Owners Ohama Kisen; Builders Imabari Shipbuilding Co., Imabari; Yard No. 404.

OCEAN PASSAT (Li)
Type Vehicle Carrier; 15670 GRT; 10905 DWT; Dimensions 155 (BP) × 27.6 × 7.8; Machinery Motor 12006 bhp; Engine builders MAN/Kawasaki; 18 Knots; Owners Lorraine Car Carrier Corp; Builders Kurushima Dock Co., Inoshi; Yard No. 2150.

OCEAN TRADER (Pa)
Type Bulk; 23400 GRT; 23900 DWT; Dimensions 150 (BP) × 24.6 × 9.8; Machinery Motor 9900 bhp; Engine builders Mitsubishi; Owners Ladarien Nav; Builders Imabari Zosen, Imabari; Yard No. 399.

OCEAN VICTORIA (Ja)
Type Tanker; 6123 GRT; 10987 DWT; Dimensions 113.7(BP) × – × 8.5; Machinery Motor 6000 bhp; Engine builders Mitsubishi/Kobe Hatsukoki; Owners Monsuhra; Builders Asakawa Zosen, Imabari; Yard No. 300.

OGDEN NILE (Li)
Type Tanker; 38500 GRT; 57650 DWT; Dimensions 220 (BP) × 32.24 × 11.58; Machinery Motor 13600 bhp; Engine builders Sulzer/Sumitomo; 14.5 Knots; Owners Ogden Nile Transport; Builders Sumitomo Heavy Industries, Oppama, Yokosuka; Yard No. 1082.

OGDEN VOLGA - sister of OGDEN NILE (q.v.)
Owners Ogden Volga Transport; Yard No. 1081.

OKTANIA (Sw)
Type Tanker; 20000 GRT; 35000 DWT; Dimensions 168 (BP) × 32.2 × 10; Machinery Motor 12200 bhp; Engine builders B & W/Uddevalla; 15.5 Knots; Owners Oljekonsumenternas Forbund; Builders Uddevallavarvet, Uddevalla; Yard No. 312.

Olau Hollandia *(FotoFlite)*

OLAU HOLLANDIA (FRG)
Type Passenger /RoRo Cargo/Ferry; 15200 GRT; 2700 DWT; Dimensions 153.4 × 24.7 × 5.8; Machinery Twin Screw Motor 20800 bhp; Engine builders Pielstick/Blohm & Voss AG; 22.25 Knots; Owners Partenreederei M.S. 'Olau Hollandia'; Managers Olau Linie (UK) Ltd; Builders A. G. 'Weser' Seebeckwerft, Bremerhaven; Yard No. 1028.

ORANUS (No)
Type Tanker; 23300 GRT; 38500 DWT; Dimensions 168 (BP) × 32 × 10.67; Machinery Motor 11900 bhp; Engine builders B & W; 14.8 Knots; Owners Combiflex; Builders Ahkerlokken Verft, Floro; Yard No. 15.

ORIENTAL CRANE (Ja)
Type Chemical Tanker; 3946 GRT; 7000 DWT; Dimensions 104(BP) × 16.03 × 7.0; Machinery Motor 4500 bhp; Engine builders Akasaka; Owners Yamato Kisen K.K; Builders Kurinoura Dock K.K., Japan; Yard No. 7001.

ORION MARU (Ja)
Type Bulk; 38000 GRT; 60000 DWT; Dimensions 218 (BP) × 32.2 × 12.74; Machinery Motor 13100 bhp; Engine builders B & W/Mitsui; 14.2 Knots; Owners Daiichi Chuo K.K; Builders Hashihama Zosen KK, Imabari; Yard No. 812.

OSAKA MARU (Ja)
Type Container; 31900 GRT; Dimensions 195 (BP) × 32.2 × 10.6; Machinery Motor 20400 bhp; Engine builders Sulzer/Mitsubishi; 19 Knots; Owners Mitsui OSK Lines; Builders Mitsubishi Heavy Industries, Kobe; Yard No. 1125.

OSCO STREAM (No)
Type Tanker; 20000 GRT; 34000 DWT; Dimensions 177.1 (BP) × 27.8 × 10.6; Machinery Motor 10200 bhp; Engine builders B & W/Mitsui; 15 Knots; Owners Ole Schroeder; Builders Samsung SB. Co., Seoul; Yard No. 1012.

OSCO SURF - sister of **OSCO STREAM** (q.v.)
Yard No. 1013.

OT Acid *(FotoFlite)*

OT ACID (Sw)
Type Chemical Tanker; 5721 GRT; 8800 DWT; Dimensions 122.6 (BP) × 19 × 6.92; Machinery Motor 5800 bhp; Engine builders Sulzer/Zgoda; 14.5 Knots; Owners OT-Rederierna; Builders A/B Oskarshamns Varv; Yard No. 433.

OT PHOSPHOROUS - sister of **OT ACID** (q.v.)

OT SULPHUR - sister of **OT ACID** (q.v.)
Yard No. 432.

OYASHIMA MARU (Ja)
Type Ore Carrier; 78000 GRT; 126500 DWT; Dimensions 248.4 × 43 × 16.3; Machinery Motor 20450 bhp; Engine builders Sulzer-/Mitsubishi; 15.7 Knots; Owners Nippon Yusen Kaisha; Builders Mitsubishi Heavy Industries, Nagasaki; Yard No. 1879.

OXY TRADER (US)
Type Tug-Pusher; 1200 GRT; Dimensions 40.85 × – × 11.0; Machinery Twin Screw Motor; Engine builders Pielstick/Colt Industries; Owners Suwannee River Finance Inc; Builders Avondale Shipyards Inc., Westwego; Yard No. 2324.

OYAMBRE (Sp)
Type Cement Carrier; 3498 GRT; 6205 DWT; Dimensions 106.18 (BB) × 15.83 × 6.78; Machinery Motor 4400 bhp; Engine builders Deutz/Hijos de J. Barreras; Owners Naviera de Cantabria S.A; Builders Ast. del Atlantico S.A., Santander; Yard No. 209.

P

PACIFIC CHARGER (Li)
Type Bulk/Log; 9900 GRT; 18109 DWT; Dimensions 137 (BB) × 22.86 × 9.27; Machinery Motor 8000 bhp; Engine builders Mitsubishi; 15 Knots; Owners Ocean Chargers Co; Builders Sasebo Heavy Industries Co. Ltd., Sasebo; Yard No. 294.

PACIFIC MARU (Ja)
Type Cargo; 17500 GRT; 22100 DWT; Dimensions 160 (BP) × 27 × 10; Machinery Motor 12950 bhp; Engine builders Sulzer/Mitsubishi; 18.5 Knots; Owners Mitsui OSK Lines; Builders Mitsubishi Heavy Industries, Shimonoseki; Yard No. 834.

PACIFIC PEACE - see **ASIAN PROGRESS**

Pacific Prestige *(Builders)*

PACIFIC PRESTIGE (Br)
Type Bulk; 35840 GRT; 63000 DWT; Dimensions 224.52 × 32.2 × 12.9; Machinery Motor 15200 bhp; Engine builders B & W/Hitachi; 14.9 Knots; Owners Malleus Shipping (C. Y. Tung); Builders Hitachi Zosen, Maizuru Works, Maizuru; Yard No. 4663.

PACIFIC PRIDE (Br)
Type Bulk; 37562 GRT; 64919 DWT; Dimensions 222.93 × 32.26 × 12.78; Machinery Motor 15200 bhp; Engine builders B & W/Mitsui; 16.25 Knots; Owners Greenburg Shipping Ltd., (C. Y. Tung); Managers Golden Peak Maritime Agencies; Builders Tsuneishi Shipbuilding, Fukuyama; Yard No. 463.

PACIFIC PROGRESS (Br)
Type Bulk; 32000 GRT; 60000 DWT; Dimensions 215 (BP) × 32.2 × 14.2; Machinery Motor 15200 bhp; Engine builders B & W/Hyundai; 16.8 Knots; Owners Molloy Shipping Ltd; Builders Hyundai Heavy Industries, Ulsan; Yard No. 154.

PACIFIC SUNSHINE (Ko)
Type Container; 21136 GRT; 22500 DWT; Engine builders Sulzer; Owners Korea Marine Transport; Builders Korea Shipbuilding, Busan; Yard No. 2006.

PALAPUR - sister of **PALOMA** (q.v.)
Yard No. 123.

PALOMA (FRG)
Type Bulk/Container (MBC type); 16230 GRT; 23000 DWT; Dimensions 178.01 × – × 10.09; Machinery Motor 11200 bhp; Engine builders MAN; 15.5 Knots; Owners Laeisz; Builders VEB Mathias-Thesen-Werft, Wismar, DDR; Yard No. 122.

PANAM CLIPPER (Pa)
Type Chemical Tanker; 4056 GRT; 7000 DWT; Dimensions 107.02 (BP); × 16.45 × 7.45; Machinery Motor 5000 bhp; Engine builders Mitsubishi/Daihatsu; 13.5 Knots; Owners Futuro Brilliante Navegacion; Builders Fukuoka Zosen, Fukuoka; Yard No. 1086.

PANAMA MARU (Ja)
Type Container; 17500 GRT; 22100 DWT; Dimensions 160 (BP) × 27 × 10; Machinery Motor 10120 bhp; Engine builders Sulzer-/Mitsubishi; 16.7 Knots; Owners Mitsui OSK; Builders Mitsubishi Heavy Industries, Shimonoseki; Yard No. 835.

PAQUISHA (Ec)
ex RIO PALORA 1981; Type Reefer; 6975 GRT; 9315 DWT; Dimensions 144.46 × 18.32 × 9.2; Machinery Motor 11400 bhp; Engine builders Sulzer/A/S Horten Verft; 21 Knots; Owners Flota Bananera Ecuatoriana S.A; Builders Drammen Slip & Verk., Drammen; Yard No. 93.

PARAMOUNT ACE (Pa)
Type Vehicles Carrier; 13730 GRT; 13834 DWT; Dimensions 186.01 × 32 × 9.0; Machinery Motor 16800 bhp; Engine builders B & W/Mitsui; 19.6 Knots; Owners Pacific Overseas No I Bulk Carriers Inc; Managers Golden Peak Maritime Agencies; Builders Tsuneishi Zosen, Numakuma; Yard No. 471.

PARANDOWSKI (Pd)
Type Cargo; 14000 GRT; 16300 DWT; Machinery Motor 10800 bhp; Engine builders Sulzer/Cegielski; 16.5 Knots; Owners Chinese-Polish Joint Stock Co; Builders Stocznia Gdanska im Lenina, Gdansk; Yard No. B348/01.

PARITA (Fi)
Type Tanker; 24500 GRT; 45200 DWT; Dimensions 185 (BP) × 32.2 × 11.58; Machinery Motor 13600 bhp; Engine builders Sulzer/Wartsila; 15.3 Knots; Owners Oy Gustav Paulig; Builders Oy Wartsila, Turku; Yard No. 1254.

PASTAZA - sister of **NAPO** (q.v.)
Yard No. 3011.

PATHFINDER (Pa)
Type Bulk; 34160 GRT; 47000 DWT; Dimensions 200 (BP) × 32.2 × 11; Machinery Motor 12400 bhp; Engine builders B & W/Hitachi; 14.95 Knots; Owners Pan-Ore Transportation; Builders Hitachi Zosen, Hiroshima; Yard No. 4685.

PATRICIA (Br)
Type Buoy/Lighthouse Tender; 2500 GRT; Dimensions 77.8 (BP) × 13.8 × 6.9; Machinery Twin Screw Diesel Electric 4020 bhp; Engine builders Ruston; 14 Knots; Owners Trinity House; Builders Robb Caledon Shipbuilding, Leith; Yard No. 530.

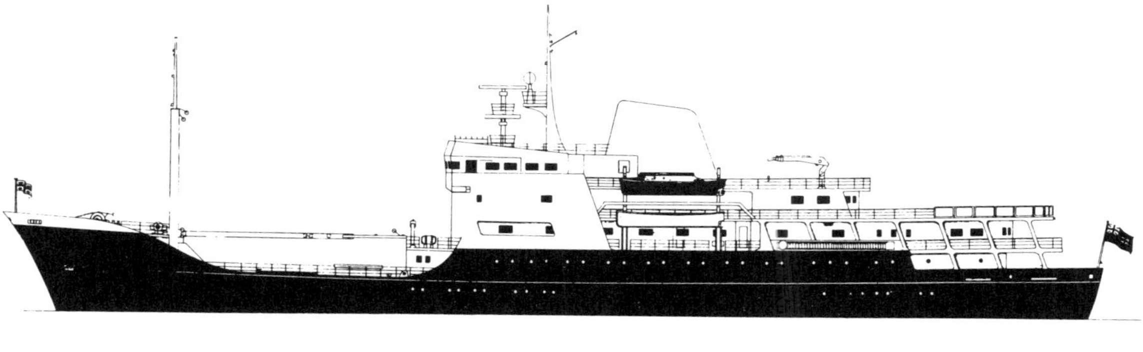
Patricia

Pertamina 1023 *(Builders)*

PERTAMINA 1023 (Pa)
Launched as PRANEDYA TRITYA: Type Tanker; 10882 GRT; 18065 DWT; Dimensions 157.99 (BB) × 25.84 × 7.02; Machinery Motor 6160 bhp; Engine builders B & W/Hitachi Zosen; 14 Knots; Owners PERTAMINA; Builders Hitachi Zosen, Maizuru Works, Maizuru; Yard No. 4675.

PETER MAERSK (De)
Type Tanker; 28300 GRT; 38000 DWT; Dimensions 175 (BP) × 32.2 × 11; Machinery Motor 13100 bhp; Engine builders B & W/Mitsui; 15.25 Knots; Owners A. P. Moller; Builders IHI, Kure; Yard No. 2709.

PETR MASHEROV (Ru)
Type RoRo Cargo/Container; 12800 GRT; 18000 DWT; Dimensions 187.87 (BB) × 28.22 × 9.64; Machinery Motor 20800 bhp; Engine builders Sulzer/Zgoda; 20.5 Knots; Owners U.S.S.R; Builders Stocznia Gdanska im Lenina, Gdansk; Yard No. B481/07.

PILAR - sister of ALMUDENA (q.v.)
Yard No. 25.

PILOS (Gr)
Type Bulk ('Fortune' type); 13800 GRT; 22000 DWT; Dimensions 155.45 (BP) × 22.85 × 9.85; Machinery Motor 7800 bhp; Engine builders Pielstick/IHI; 15 Knots; Owners Pilos Shipping; Builders IHI, Tokyo; Yard No. 2764.

PINGWO VENTURE (Li)
Type Bulk; 15544 GRT; 27300 DWT; Dimensions 165 (BP) × 25 × 10.2; Machinery Motor 11400 bhp; Engine builders Sulzer/IHI; 14.75 Knots; Owners Campion Shipping Co; Builders Hayashikane SB & Eng. Co. Ltd., Shimonoseki; Yard No. 1239.

PIONEER SPIRIT (Pa)
Type Bulk; 28000 GRT; 57400 DWT; Dimensions 213 (BP) × 32.2 × 12.45; Machinery Motor 13100 bhp; Engine builders B & W/Mitsui; 14.7 Knots; Owners Eastern Bulkships Inc; Builders Koyo Dockyard Co., Mihara; Yard No. 1020.

PISHCHEVAYA PROMYSHIENNOST (Ru)
Type Fish Factory; 15750 GRT; Dimensions 177 (BP) × 24.6 × 7.2; Machinery Motor 8900 bhp; Engine builders B & W: 14.5 Knots; Owners U.S.S.R; Builders Stocznia Gdanska im Lenina, Gdansk; Yard No. B670/06.

PLANTIN (Be)
Type Container; 27500 GRT; 23000 DWT; Dimensions 175 (BP) × 27.5 × 10.8; Machinery Motor 21100 bhp; Engine builders B & W: & Knots; Owners CMB; Builders NV Boelwerf, Tamise; Yard No. 1502.

PLUTO - sister of CANOPUS (q.v.)
Yard No. 140.

POHJOLA (Fi)
Type Cargo; 1376 GRT; 2700 DWT; Dimensions 82.38 (BB) × 12.78 × 5.05; Machinery Motor 2500 bhp; Engine builders Vaasa/Oy Wartsila; 12 Knots; Owners Rauma-Repola O/Y; Builders Rauma-Repola OY, Uusikaupunki/Nystad; Yard No. 302.

POLA SUR - see FRIGO LAS PALMAS

POLAR QUEEN (No)
Type Research/Sealer Survey; 955 GRT; 1100 DWT; Dimensions 65.11 × 13.06 × 5.25; Machinery Motor 4500 bhp; Engine builders Atlas-MaK; Owners G. C. Rieber & Co. A/S; Builders G. Eides Sonner A/S, Hoylandsbygd; Yard No. 111.

POLLY BRISTOL (Br)
Type Drill Ship; 7764 DWT; Dimensions 136.8 (BP) × 27 × 7.5; Machinery Twin Screw Diesel Electric 17000 bhp; Engine builders S.A.C.M; 12 Knots; Owners KCA Offshore Drilling; Builders IHC-Gusto/Boele's Sch. Bolnes.

POLUX - see JO CLIPPER

POLYSTAR (No)
Type Tanker; 39609 GRT; 61438 DWT; Dimensions 205 × 32.2 × 12.82; Machinery Motor 16200 bhp; Engine builders B & W/Mitsui; 15.68 Knots; Owners K/S Rasmussen Tankers A/S; Builders Mitsui Eng. & SB Co. Ltd; Yard No. 1211.

POLYSUNRISE - sister of POLYSTAR (q.v.)
Yard No. 1212.

PONTOKRATIS (Gr)
Type Bulk; 15852 GRT; 28738 DWT; Dimensions 179.89 × 23.14 × 10.65; Machinery Motor 11400 bhp; Engine builders Sulzer/IHI; Owners Amphitrite Maritime SA; Builders Hakodate Dock Co., Muroran; Yard No. 703.

POOLZEE - see MELTON EXPLORER

POROS ISLAND (Gr) sister of SIFNOS ISLAND
Type Cargo; 11000 GRT; 15470 DWT; Dimensions 137 (BP) × 21 × 9.04; Machinery Motor 6000 bhp; Engine builders Pielstick/I.H.I.; 14.5 Knots; Owners Sifnos Maritime; Builders I.H.I., Tokyo; Yard No. 2763.

PRANEDYA TRITYA - see PERTAMINA 1023

PRECIOUS (Li)
Type Bulk; 31000 GRT; 60000 DWT; Dimensions 224.42 × 32.26 × 12.45; Machinery Motor 14000 bhp; Engine builders Sulzer-/Mitsubishi; Owners Precious Navigation Inc; Managers Teh-Hu Cargocean Management Co. Ltd; Builders Hyundai Heavy Industries Co. Ltd., Ulsan; Yard No. 147.

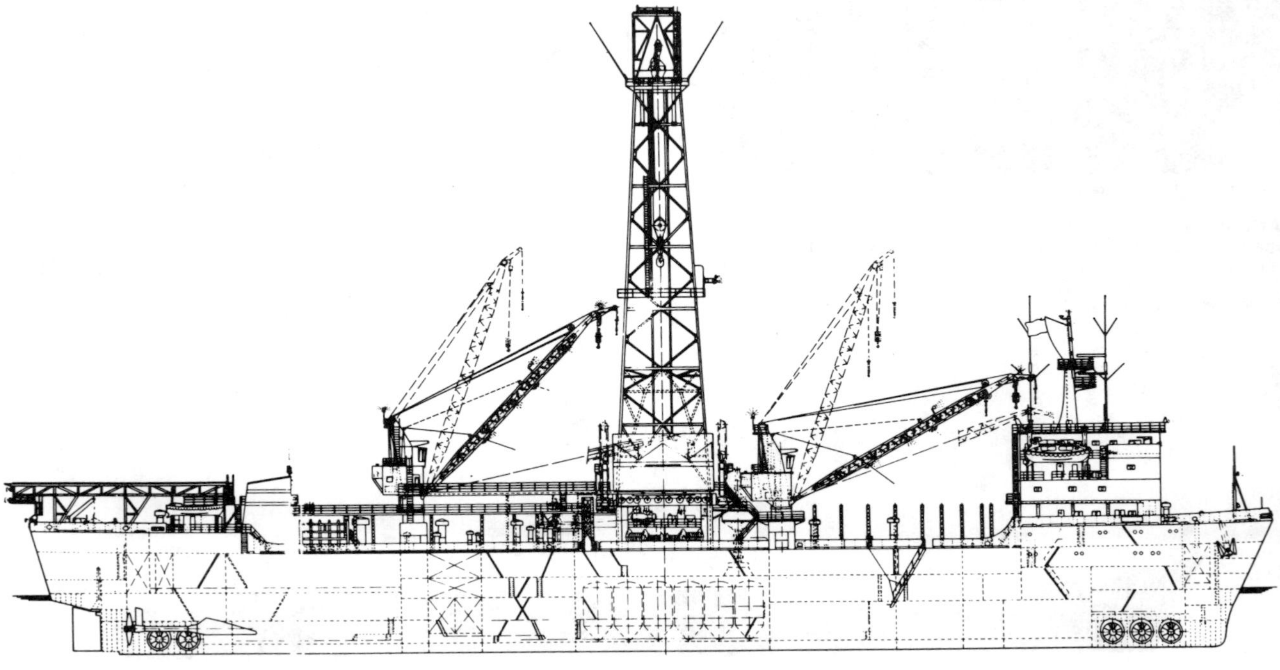

Polly Bristol *(The Naval Architect)*

Poolzee *(Holland Shipbuilding)*

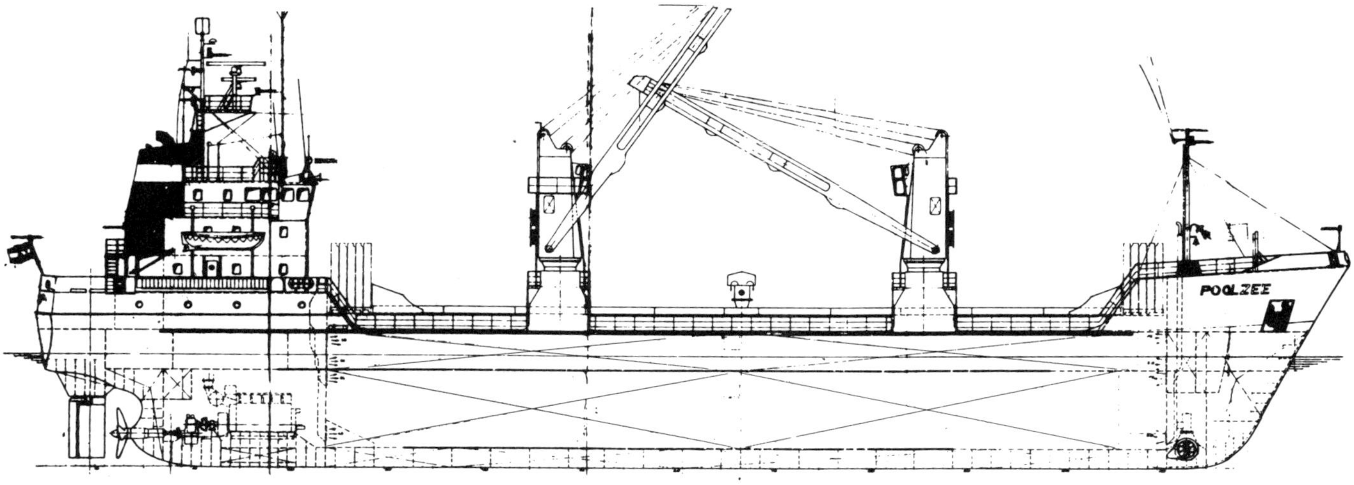

PRIDE OF TEXAS (US)
Type Bulk (Future 32); 23500 GRT; 35839 DWT; Dimensions 178 (BP) × 28.4 × 10.72; Machinery Motor 15600 bhp; Engine builders Enterprise (Delaval); 15 Knots; Owners Falcon Carriers Inc; Builders Levingston Shipbuilding, Orange, Texas; Yard No. 751.

PRIMA MAERSK - sister of PETER MAERSK (q.v.)
Yard No. 2710.

PRIMORYE (Ru)
Type Dredger; 1000 GRT; 2000 DWT; Dimensions 80.02 × 15.14 × 4.1; Machinery Twin Screw Motor 1470 bhp; Engine builders Sulzer/Jugoturbina; Owners U.S.S.R; Builders Brodogradiliste 'Split', Split; Yard No. 305.

Princesse Clementine *(FotoFlite)*

PRINCESSE CLEMENTINE
Type Hydrofoil Ferry ('JETFOIL' type); 329 GRT; Dimensions 27.44 × 9.5 × 2.51/5.3; Machinery Gas Turbine 7600 shp; Engine builders Allison/General Motors; 43 Knots; Owners Regie voor Maritiem Transport; Builders Boeing Marine Systems, Seattle; Yard No. 0019.

PRINS FREDERIK HENDRIK - sister of PRINS MAURITS (q.v.)
Yard No. 198.

PRINS MAURITS (Ne)
Type LGC; 2584 GRT; 3588 DWT; Dimensions 81.87 × 14.00 × 6.5; Machinery Motor 3000 bhp; Engine builders Deutz; 13.5 Knots; Owners A. Veder Gas Carriers; Builders Ysselwerf B.V., Rotterdam; Yard No. 197.

PRINSES STEPHANIE - sister of PRINCESSE CLEMENTINE (q.v.) Yard No 0020

PRINSESSE RAGNHILD (No)
Type Passenger/RoRo Cargo/Ferry; 16000 GRT; 3000 DWT; Dimensions 170.01 × 24.36 × 5.8; Machinery Twin Screw Motor 23673 bhp; Engine builders Stork-Werkspoor; Owners Anders Jahre; Builders Howaldtswerke-Deutsche Werft, Kiel; Yard No. 164.

PRODUCT SPLENDOR (Br)
Type Tanker; 17804 GRT; 29820 DWT; Dimensions 174.02 × 25.43 × 10.68; Machinery Motor 10880 bhp; Engine builders B & W/Mitsui; Owners Tradax Export SA; Builders Minami-Nippon Zosen, Usuki; Yard No. 535.

PROJECT ORIENT (NA)
Type Container/Heavy Lift/RoRo; 9768 GRT; 11810 DWT; Dimensions 138.5 × 21.5 × 8.5; Machinery Motor 5880 bhp; Engine builders Mak; 16 Knots; Owners Bulk Cargo Nav. Corp; Builders Schiffswerft Martin Jansen, Leer; Yard No. 170.

PROLIV NADEZHDY (Ru)
Type Fish Carrier; 13021 GRT; 11560 DWT; Dimensions 172.09 × 23.04 × 8.1; Machinery Motor 10600 bhp; Engine builders B & W/Bryansk; 18.75 Knots; Owners U.S.S.R; Builders "61 Kommunar" Shipyard, Nikolayev.

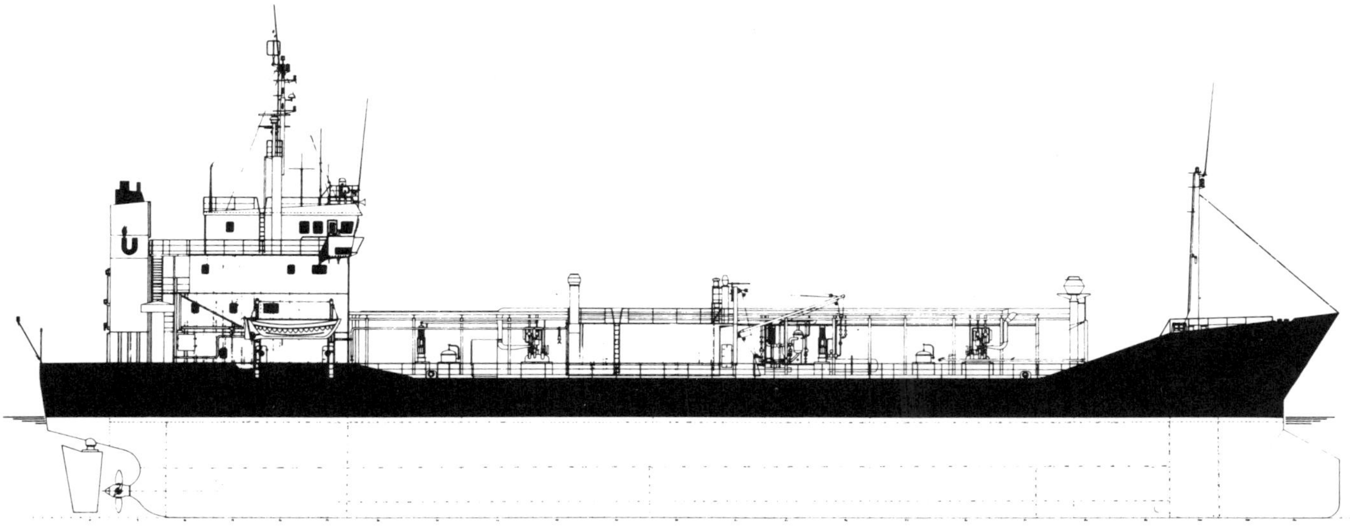

Prins Frederick Hendrik *(Holland Shipbuilding)*

Quatsino Sound

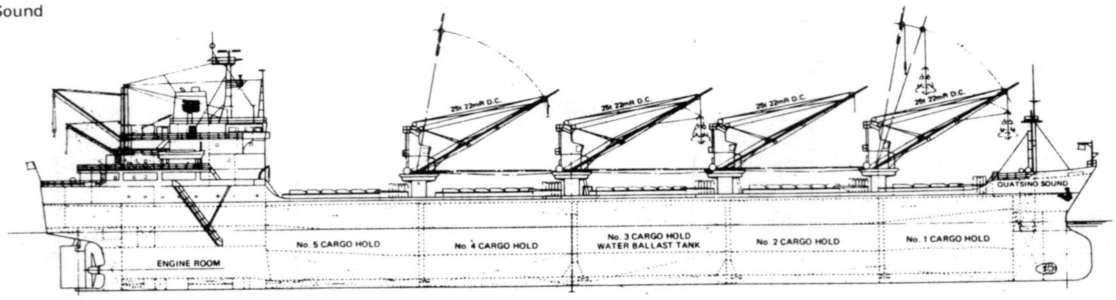

Q

QUATSINO SOUND (Li)
Type Bulk; 15568 GRT; 29348 DWT; Dimensions 160 × 27.2 × 9.75; Machinery Motor 12000 bhp; Engine builders Sulzer/Mitsubishi; 17 Knots; Owners Utah Transport Inc; Builders Mitsubishi Heavy Industries, Shimonoseki; Yard No. 832.

QUEEN OF OAK BAY - sister of QUEEN OF SURREY (q.v.)
Builders Burrard-Yarrows Corp., Victoria, B.C; Yard No. 550.

QUEEN OF SURREY (Ca)
Type Passenger/RoRo Cargo/Ferry; 6700 GRT; 700 DWT; Dimensions 139.35 × 27.59 × 5.51; Machinery Motor 11860 bhp; Engine builders Mak; Owners British Columbia Ferry Corp; Builders Burrard Yarrows Corp., Vancouver; Yard No. 100.

R

RACISCE (Ys)
Type Cargo; 7000 GRT; 9251 DWT; Dimensions 151 × 21.6 × 8.7; Machinery Motor 16520 bhp; Engine builders MAN/Split; 21 Knots; Owners Mediteranska-Plovidba; Builders Split Shipyard; Yard No. 303.

RAKNES (No)
Type Cargo; 3600 GRT; 4500 DWT; Owners Kristian Jebsens Rederi; Builders Storviks Mek. Verksted, Kristiansand N; Yard No. 92.

RAMDANE ABANE (Ag)
Type LNG Carrier; 74200 GRT; 75000 DWT; Dimensions 262 (BP) × 42 × 13.3; Machinery turbine 32000 shp; Engine builders Stal-Laval/Atlantique; Owners Cie. Nationale Algerienne de Nav; Builders Ch. de l'Atlantique, St. Nazaire; Yard No. L26.

RANI PADMINI (In)
Type Bulk Carrier; 42141 GRT; 75000 DWT; Dimensions 236.38 × 32 × 13.88; Machinery Motor 20500 bhp; Engine builders B & W/Harland & Wolff; 15.85 Knots; Owners The Shipping Corporation of India; Builders Cochin Shipyard, Cochin; Yard No. 001.

RAS AL ZOUR (Ku)
Type Tanker; 16000 GRT; 28000 DWT; Dimensions 160 (BP) × 24.8 × 10.97; Machinery Motor 13500 bhp; Engine builders B & W; 15.5 Knots; Owners Kuwait Oil Tanker Co; Builders China Shipbuilding Corp., Keelung; Yard No. 196.

RAVEN ARROW (Br)
Type Bulk; 24399 GRT; 38000 DWT; Dimensions 174 (BP) × 29 × 11.59; Machinery Motor 13100 bhp; Engine builders B & W/Mitsui; Owners Kriship Shipping; Builders Mitsui Eng. & Shipbuilding, Chiba; Yard No. 1228.

RAYMOND A. WHEELER (US)
Type Dredger; 9930 GRT; Dimensions 124.7 (BP) × 23.8 × –; Machinery Motor 2×5250 bhp; Engine builders Cooper-Bessemer; Managers US Corps of Engineers; Builders Avondale Shipyards Inc; Yard No. 2322.

Rayna *(Builders)*

RAYNA (Li)
Type Bulk Carrier; 32293 GRT; 60010 DWT; Dimensions 224.5 × 32.2 × 12.4; Machinery Motor 14400 bhp; Engine builders Sulzer/Hitachi; 16 Knots; Owners Epos Marine Corp; Builders Hitachi Zosen, Hiroshima; Yard No. 4672.

REGENT OAK (Pa)
Type Bulk/log Carrier; 16427 GRT; 30228 DWT; Dimensions 166.81 (BP) × 26.02 × 10.65; Machinery Motor 11850 bhp; Engine builders Sulzer/IHI; 15.2 Knots; Owners Regent Oak Shipping Co; Builders Tsuneishi Shipbuilding Co; Yard No. 467.

REGENT PALM (Pa)
Type Bulk; 16074 GRT; 27125 DWT; Dimensions 191.29 × 22.94 × 9.49; Machinery Motor 10700 bhp; Engine builders B & W/Mitsui; Owners Regent Palm Shipping Co., S.A; Managers Regent Shipping Ltd; Builders Aft section- Nipponkai Heavy Ind. Co. Ltd., Toyama; Yard No. 216; Fwd. section: Rinkai Kogyo KK, Setoda; Yard No. 48.

REGENT TAMPOPO (Pa)
Type Bulk Carrier; 16800 GRT; 27000 DWT; Dimensions 183 (BP) × 23 × 10; Machinery Motor 10600 bhp; Engine builders B & W; 16.3 Knots; Owners Regent Shipping Co; Builders Dalian Shipyard, People's Republic of China; Yard No. B2701.

REINA DEL CANTABRICO (Sp)
Type RoRo Cargo; 2650 GRT; 4600 DWT; Dimensions 103 (BP) × 18.35 × 6.2; Machinery Motor 6000 bhp; Engine builders Deutz-/Barreras; 18.5 Knots; Owners Cia. Nav. Astur-Andaluza; Builders Hijos de J. Barreras, Vigo; Yard No. 1461.

RENOVATION (Ga)
Type RoRo Cargo/Landing Craft; 940 GRT; 400 DWT; Dimensions 66.32 × – × 13.2; Machinery Triple Screw Motor 1080 bhp; Engine builders General Motors; Owners Damen Marine Services; Builders Scheepswerf Ravenstein, Deest; Yard No. 998.

RICH ARROW (Ja)
Type Tanker; 9990 GRT; 16550 DWT; Dimensions 138 (BP) × 22.4 × 9.1; Machinery Motor 8300 bhp; Engine builders B & W/Hitachi; 14.2 Knots; Owners Fuyo Kaiun; Builders Usuki Tekkosho, Saeki; Yard No. 1302.

RICH STAR (Ja)
Type Tanker; 8000 GRT; Dimensions 125 (BP) × 19.4 × 9.25; Machinery Motor 6000 bhp; Engine builders Mitsubishi/Akasaka; 13 Knots; Owners Fuyoh Kaiun; Builders Kyokiyo SB & Iron Works, Chofu; Yard No. 311.

RIJEKA (Ys)
Type Cargo; 10000 GRT; 17000 DWT; Dimensions 160 (BP) × 23.5 × 9.5; Machinery Motor 11200 bhp; Engine builders B & W/Uljanik; 16.6 Knots; Owners Jugoslavenska Oceanska Plovidba; Builders Uljanik Shipbuilding Industries, Pula; Yard No. 332.

RIO BRANCO (Bz)
Type Bulk Carrier; 21733 GRT; 38097 DWT; Dimensions 183 (BP) × 27.6 × 10.23; Machinery Motor 12000 bhp; Engine builders Sulzer/Ishikawajima do Brasil; 15 Knots; Owners Lloyd Brasileiro; Builders EMAQ-Engenharia e Maquinas, Rio de Janeiro; Yard No. 306.

RIO GRANDE - sister of RIO BRANCO (q.v.)
Yard No. 307.

RIO LUJAN
Type Tanker; 8000 DWT; Dimensions 114.5 (BP) × 20 × 5.79; Machinery Motor 4246 bhp; Engine builders B & W/Hitachi; 12 knots; Owners Rio Lujan Navigation; Principe Menghi y Penco; Yard No. 150.

RIO PALORA - see PAQUISHA.

RIO TINTO (Sp)
Type Tanker; 124499 GRT; 271465 DWT; Dimensions 326.73 × 55.05 × 20.0; Machinery Steam 36000 shp; Engine builders General Electric/Ast. Espanoles; Builders Ast. Espanoles S.A., Factoria de Puerto Real; Yard No. 7.

RIVER DART - sister of RIVER TAMAR (q.v.)
Builders Nordsovaerftet, Ringkobing; Yard No. 148.

RIVER TAMAR (Br)
Type low air draught coaster; 499 GRT; 800 DWT; Dimensions 49.99 × 9.2 × 5.25; Machinery Motor 467 bhp; Engine builders Callesen; Owners General Freight Co.; Builders James W. Cook & Co., Wivenhoe; Yard No. 1465.

River Tamar *(Builders)*

RODENBEK (FRG)
Type Chemical tanker; 1600 GRT; 3900 DWT; Dimensions 91.7 (BP) × 13.6 × 8.64; Machinery Motor 2450 bhp; Engine builders Mak; 12.5 knots; Owners Chemical Cargo Transport; Builders Busumer Werft G.m.b.H., Busum; Yard No. 1439.

ROLL GALICIA (Sp)
Type Ro/Ro Cargo; 3000 GRT; 5500 DWT; Dimensions 112.8 (BP) × 18.35 × 6.2; Machinery Motor 10000 bhp; Engine builders MAN/Bazan; 17 knots; Owners Interoll; Builders Enrique Lorenzo y Cia., Vigo; Yard No. 401.

ROLL VIGO - sister of ROLL GALICIA (q.v.)
Yard No. 400.

ROMEO (Pi)
Type Cargo; 800 GRT; 1000 DWT; Dimensions 65.11 × — × 3.65; Machinery Motor; Engine builders Hanshin Nainenki Kogyo; Owners Candano Shipping Lines Inc.; Builders Mayon Docks Inc, Tabaco; Yard No. 001.

ROSE (Ja)
Type Bulk Carrier; 15000 GRT; 25400 DWT; Dimensions 141.8 (BP) × 26 × 10.4; Machinery Motor 10800 bhp; Engine builders Sulzer/Mitsubishi; 14 knots; Owners Orient Leasing; Builders Imabari Zosen K.K., Imabari; Yard No. 406.

RYBAK VLADIVOSTOCKA - sister of PISHCHEVAYA PROMYSHIENNOST (q.v.)
Yard No. B670/05.

RYOHYOSHI MARU (Ja)
Type Tanker; 1500 GRT; 2650 DWT; Dimensions 78.42 (BP) × - × 5.51; Machinery Motor; Engine builders Akasaka; Owners Nippon Kaiun KK; Builders Kishimoto Zosen, Japan; Yard No. 506.

RYOHYU MARU No. 3 (Ja)
Type Oil/Chemical Tanker; 699 GRT; 980 DWT; Dimensions 52.02 (BP) × — × 4.25; Machinery Motor 1200 bhp; Engine builders Hanshin Nainenki Kogyo; Owners Yamane Kaiun K.K.; Builders Imamura Zosen, Kure; Yard No. 268.

S

SAGALAND (Sw)
Type RoRo Cargo/Ferry; 3500 GRT; Dimensions 145 × 24 × 6; Machinery Motor 4 × 4500 bhp; Engine builders Pielstick/Lindholmen; 18.5 knots; Owners Svelast, Rederi AB Svea & Gotlands Bolaget; Builders Kalmar Varv, Kalmar; Yard No. 453.

St. Christopher *(FotoFlite)*

ST. CHRISTOPHER (Br)
Type Passenger/RoRo Cargo/Ferry; 6996 GRT; 2092 DWT; Dimensions 129.62 (BP) × 21.62 × 4.72; Machinery Twin Screw Motor 20800 bhp; Engine builders Pielstick/A.P.E. Crossley; 19.5 knots; Owners Barclays Mercantile Industrial Finance Ltd.; Managers Sealink UK Ltd.; Builders Harland & Wolff Ltd., Belfast; Yard No. 1716.

ST. DAVID (Br)
Type Ro/Ro pass. ferry; 8200 GRT; 1755 DWT; Dimensions 129.4 × 21 × 4.72; Machinery Twin Screw Motor 2 × 10400 bhp; Engine builders Pielstick/Crossley; 19.5 knots; Owners Sealink (UK) Ltd.; Builders Harland & Wolff (Belfast; Yard No. 1717.

ST. MICHAELIS (FRG)
Type Tanker; 26000 GRT; 45300 DWT; Dimensions 174 (BP) × 32.2 × 10.6; Machinery Motor 12520 bhp; Engine builders MAN; 14.5 knots; Owners Hamburg Sudamerikanische; Builders A.G. "Weser", Bremen; Yard No. 1413.

Saint Oran *(Builders)*

SAINT ORAN (Br)
Type RoRo/Cargo/Tanker; 573 GRT; 719 DWT; Dimensions 53.29 × 9.17 × 3.36; Machinery Motor 644 bhp; Engine builders Mirrlees Blackstone; 10 knots; Owners J & A Gardner & Co. Ltd.; Builders J.W. Cook & Co. Ltd., Wivenhoe; Yard No. 1464.

ST. PETRI - sister of ST. MICHAELIS (q.v.)
Yard No. 1412.

SAINT VINCENT (Pi)
Type Bulk; 10670 GRT; 18600 DWT; Dimensions 143 (BP) × — × 9.10; Machinery Motor 8400 bhp; Engine builders B & W/Mitsui; Owners A.P. Madrigal Steamship Co.; Builders Minami-Nippon Zosen K.K., Usuki; Yard No. 539.

Sainte Alexandrine *(FotoFlite)*

SAINTE ALEXANDRINE (Pa)
Type Cargo; 8832 GRT; 18770 DWT; Dimensions 150.2 × — × 9.05; Machinery Motor 9000 bhp; Engine Builders MAN/Schwermaschbau Halberstadt; Owners Blakenham Shipping; Builders VEB Schiffswerft 'Neptun', Rostock; Yard No. 436.

SALENA - see OAK RIVER

SALLY MAERSK (De)
Type LPG; 14000 GRT; 17500 DWT; Dimensions 142 (BP) × 25 × 9.9; Machinery Motor 13050 bhp; Engine builders B & W; 17 knots; Owners A.P. Moller; Builders Odense Staalskibs. A/S, Lindo; Yard No. 89.

SALLY STOVE (No)
Type Bulk Carrier; 38000 GRT; 60000 DWT; Dimensions 214 (BP) × 32.2 × 12.3; Machinery Motor 14400 bhp; Engine builders Sulzer/Sumitomo; 15.6 knots; Owners Lorentzen's Skibs. A/S; Builders Nippon Kokan K.K., Tsurumi; Yard No. 985.

SALMONPOOL (Br)
Type Bulk Carrier; 23785 GRT; 43800 DWT; Dimensions 195 (BP) × 27.2 × 11.76; Machinery Motor 14200 bhp; Engine builders Sulzer/Sumitomo; 15.8 knots; Owners Ropner Shipping Co.; Builders Eleusis Shipyards S.A., Athens; Yard No. 10011.

SANDHAYAK (In)
Type Research; 2050 GRT; Dimensions 78.31 (BP) × — × 3.75; Machinery Twin Screw Motor; Engine builders MAN/Garden Reach Workshops; Owners Govt. of the Republic of India (Navy Dept); Builders Garden Reach SB & E Ltd., Calcutta; Yard No. 1026.

SANEI MARU (Ja)
Type Cargo; 1351 GRT; 3586 DWT; Dimensions 80.02 (BP) × — × —; Machinery Motor 2200 bhp; Engine builders Akasaka; Owners Asami Kisen K.K.; Builders Kochi Jukogyo (Eiho Zosen) KK, Kochi; Yard No. 1443.

SANKO CHERRY (Li)
Type OBO; 37322 GRT; 69600 DWT; Dimensions 227 (BP) × 32.2 × 13.5; Machinery Motor 11930 bhp; Engine builders MAN/Kawasaki; 14.4 knots; Owners Peacock Tankship Ltd.; Builders Kawasaki Heavy Industries, Sakaide; Yard No. 1296.

SANSAN VENTURE (Li)
Type Bulk Carrier; 30000 GRT; 57000 DWT; Dimensions 213 (BP) × 32.2 × 9.14; Machinery Motor 13100 bhp; Engine builders B & W/Mitsui; Owners Zenith Carriers; Managers Venture Shipping (Managers) Ltd.; Builders Koyo Dockyard Co., Mihara; Yard No. 1000.

SANTA BARBARA (Pa)
Type Bulk Carrier; 12370 GRT; 20500 DWT; Dimensions 142 (BP) × 24 × 9.6; Machinery Motor 7200 bhp; Engine builders MaK-/Mitsubishi; Owners Golden Mariner Shipping S.A.; Builders Watanabe Shipbuilding Co., Hakata; Yard No. 213.

SANTA VITORIA MARU (Ja)
Type Bulk; 35000 GRT; 61000 DWT; Dimensions 218.00 (BP) × 32.00 × 12.3; Machinery Motor 16880 bhp; Engine builders MAN/Mitsubishi; 16.2 knots; Owners Mitsubishi Ore Transport Co.; Builders Tsuneishi Zosen, Numakuma; Yard No. 460.

Santong *(FotoFlite)*

SANTONG (Pa)
Type LGC; 2990 GRT; 3500 DWT; Dimensions 94.01 (BP) × — × 5.4; Machinery Motor 3200 bhp; Engine builders Akasaka; Owners Eastern Heaven Shipping S.A.; Builders Kochi Jukogyo K.K., Kochi; Yard No. 2161.

SANYO MARU (Ja)
Type Cargo; 499 GRT; 1100 DWT; Dimensions 60.03 (BP) × 9.63 × 4.05; Machinery Motor 1200 bhp; Engine builders Hanshin Nainenki Kogyo; Owners Ohyama Kisen K.K.; Builders Miura Zosen, Saeki; Yard No. 621.

SAO SEBASTIAO (Bz)
Type Bulk Carrier; 11188 GRT; 15780 DWT; Dimensions 136 (BP) × 21.2 × 8.7; Machinery Motor 7050 bhp; Engine builders B & W/Villares; 14.45 knots; Owners Mansur Nav.; Builders Industrias Reunidas Caneco, Rio de Janeiro; Yard No. 231.

SARGASSO (Pa)
Type LPG Carrier; 6200 GRT; 6000 DWT; Dimensions 112 (BP) × 19. 4 × 6.5; Machinery Motor; Engine builders Akasaka; Owners DK Line; Builders Taihei Kogyo KK., Akitsu; Yard No. 1421.

SCANDIC ESSAR (Sg)
Type Tanker; 4309 GRT; 6700 DWT; Dimensions 100 (BP) × 17 × 7; Machinery Motor 4500 bhp; Engine builders Mitsubishi/Kobe; 14.5 knots; Owners Scandia Shipping; Builders Dong Hae Shipyard, Ulsan; Yard No. 8028.

SCANDIC VENTURE (Sg)
Type Tanker; 11135 GRT; 19500 DWT; Dimensions 138.5 (BP) × 23 × 9.4; Machinery Motor 6160 bhp; Engine builders B & W; 13.25 knots; Owners Guls Tankers Inc.; Builders Samsung Shipbuilding Co., Seoul; Yard No. 1007.

SEA ARCHITECT (Pa)
Type Cargo; 7507/12984 GRT; 12000/17500 DWT; Dimensions 164.32 × 22.92 × —/9.74; Machinery Motor 11200 bhp; Engine builders B & W/Mitsui; Owners Sea Architect Shipping Inc.; Builders Shanghai Shipyard Chung Hua, Shanghai; Yard No. 7211.

SEABEX ONE (FRG)
Type Offshore/diving support; 2990 DWT; Dimensions 106.8 × 21 × 5.5; Machinery Twin Screw Motor 4400 bhp; Engine builders MaK/AEG; 11.9 knots; Owners Seabex G.m.b.H.; Builders Werft Nobiskrug G.m.b.H.; Yard No. 705.

SEIKYU MARU (Ja)
Type Bulk Carrier; 12370 GRT; 20800 DWT; Dimensions 142 (BP) × 24 × 9.6; Machinery Motor 7800 bhp; Engine builders Sulzer-/Mitsubishi; 15.4 knots; Owners Kyosai Maru; Builders Shin-Yamamoto Zosen., Kochi; Yard No. 256.

SEKI OAK (Ja)
Type Tanker; 23123 GRT; 37350 DWT; Dimensions 170.52 × — × 11.0; Machinery Motor 11700 bhp; Engine builders Pielstick/I-HI; Owners Sekihyo Seibaku K.K.; Builders Hashihama Zosen, Tadotsu; Yard No. 806.

SELENA (FRG)
Type Cargo; 499/999 GRT; 1515/2290 DWT; Dimensions 80.02 × 11.41 × 4.25; Machinery Motor 599 bhp; Engine builders Deutz; Owners Amasis Bereederungs G.m.b.H.; Builders Detlef Hegemann Rolandwerft G.m.b.H., Bremen; Yard No. 110.

SEMYON LAPSHENKOV (Ru)
Type Fish Factory (B408 type); 3000 GRT; 1800 DWT; Dimensions 93.91 (BP) × — × —/5.76; Machinery Motor 5200 bhp; Engine builders Sulzer/'Zgoda' Zaklady Urzadzen Technicznych; Owners U.S.S.R.; Builders Stocznia Gdanska im. Lenina, Gdansk; Yard No. B408/14.

SERAFINO FERRUZZI (It)
Type Bulk Carrier; 30000 GRT; 49000 DWT; Dimensions 184 (BP) × 32.2 × 12.4; Machinery Motor 13100 bhp; Engine builders B & W; 16.4 knots; Owners Lloyd Triestino S.p.A.; Builders Italcantieri S.p.A., Genoa; Yard No. 4376.

SETUN - sister of NEPRYADVA (a.v.)
Yard No. 435.

SHAAM - sister of DHAN (q.v.)
Yard No. 813.

SHELL MARKETER (Br)
Type Tanker; 1599 GRT; 2575 DWT; Dimensions 74.5 (BP) × 13.1 × 5.03; Machinery Motor 3000 bhp; Engine builders Mirrlees-Blackstone; 13 knots; Owners Shell Oil UK.; Builders Clelands Shipbuilding Co., Wallsend; Yard No. 355.

SHELL SEAFARER - sister of SHELL MARKETER (q.v.)
Builders Goole Shipbuilding, Goole; Yard No. 599.

Shin-Kakogawa Maru *(Builders)*

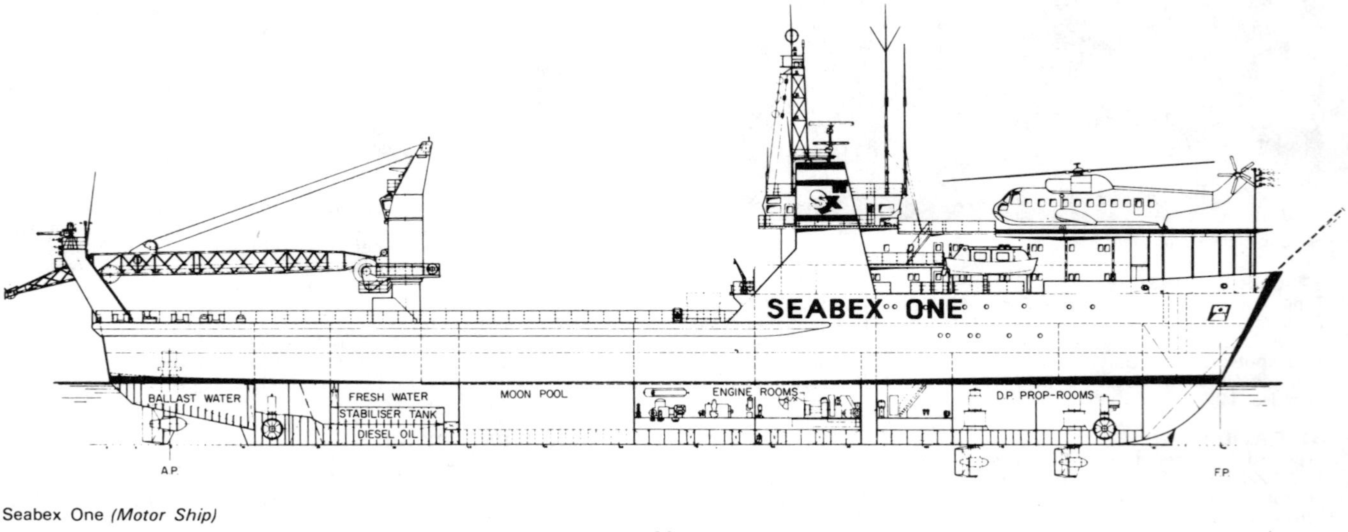

Seabex One *(Motor Ship)*

SHIN-KAKOGAWA MARU (Ja)
Type Bulk Carrier; 71792 GRT; 124292 DWT; Dimensions 259.51 × 43 × 16.1; Machinery Motor; Engine builders B & W/Hitachi; 17 knots; Owners Yamashita-Shinnihon S.S. Co.; Builders Hitachi Zosen, Ariake; Yard No. 4665.

SHIN-KASHU MARU see SHINKASU MARU

SHIN OGISHIMA MARU (Ja)
Type Bulk; 98511 GRT; 194109 DWT; Dimensions 300.00 × 50 × 18.27; Machinery Motor 23900 bhp; Engine builders B & W/Mitsui; 14 knots; Owners Nippon Yusen Kaisha (NYK); Builders Nippon Kokan K.K., Tsu; Yard No. 70.

SHINANO MARU (Ja)
Type Bulk; 77500 GRT; 132960 DWT; Dimensions 270.01 × 43.00 × 16.3; Machinery Motor 30400 bhp; Engine builders Sulzer/Mitsubishi; Owners Nippon Yusen Kaisha (NYK); Builders Mitsubishi Heavy Industries Ltd., Nagasaki; Yard No. 1868.

SHINEI MARU (Ja)
Type Bulk; 76958 GRT; 134176 DWT; Dimensions 270.01 × 43.00 × 16.25; Machinery Motor 20400 bhp; Engine builders Sulzer/Mitsubishi; 14.25 knots; Owners Shinwa Kaiun K.K.; Builders Mitsubishi Heavy Industries Ltd., Nagasaki; Yard No. 1863.

SHINKASHU MARU (Ja)
Type Container; 31000 GRT; 25700 DWT; Dimensions 207 (BP) × 31 × 10.6; Machinery Motor 31300 bhp; Engine builders Sulzer-/IHI; Owners Yamashita-Shinnihon SS. Co.; Builders Hitachi Zosen, Hiroshima; Yard No. 4691.

SHINKO MARU (Ja)
Type Cargo; 499 GRT; 1117 DWT; Dimensions 57.03 (BP) × — × 4.05; Machinery Motor 1300 bhp; Engine builders Yanmar Diesel; Owners Shinko Kaiun K.K.; Builders Kochi Jukogyo (Kaisei Zosen) KK, Kochi; Yard No. 1448.

SHINZAN MARU No 12 (Ja)
Type Cargo; 499 GRT; 1105 DWT; Dimensions 65 × 11.21 × 3.82; Machinery Motor 1200 bhp; Engine builders Hanshin Nainenki Kogyo; Owners Syoshin Kaiun G.K.; Builders Miura Zosen, Saeki; Yard No. 617.

SHIROTAE MARU (Ja)
Type Bulk; 76747 GRT; 140152 DWT; Dimensions 264.02 (BP) × — × 16.3; Machinery Motor 18990 bhp; Engine builders MAN-/Mitsubishi; 14 knots; Owners Nippon Yusen Kaisha (NYK); Builders Namura SB. Co. Ltd., Imari; Yard No. 843.

SHOEI MARU No 2. (Ja)
Type LGC; 697 GRT; 750 DWT; Dimensions 55.02 (BP) × — × 4.01; Machinery Motor 1600 bhp; Engine builders Niigata Eng. Co. Ltd.; Owners Seiwa Unyu KK; Builders Shirahama Zosen K.K., Honai; Yard No. 100.

SHOEI MARU No 33 (Ja)
Type Cargo; 499 GRT; 1600 DWT; Dimensions 65.03 (BP) × — × 4.6; Machinery Motor 1750 bhp; Engine builders Hanshin Nainenki Kogye; Owners Daiei Kaiun K.K.; Builders K.K. Yoshida Zosen Kogyo, Arida; Yard No. 355.

SHOHO MARU (Ja)
Type Bulk Carrier; 44000 GRT; 68500 DWT; Dimensions 217 (BP) × 36 × 13.6; Machinery Motor 14000 bhp; Engine builders MAN/Mitsubishi; 15.85 knots; Owners Shinwa Kaiun; Builders Mitsubishi Heavy Industries, Nagasaki; Yard No. 1881.

SHOWA MARU (Ja)
Type Tanker; 57500 GRT; 90000 DWT; Dimensions 236 (BP) × 39.6 × 13.7; Machinery Motor 18600 bhp; Engine builders B & W/Mitsui; 15 knots; Owners Showa Kaiun; Builders Hashihama Shipbuilding Co., Imabari; Yard No. 809.

SIBI - sister of KHAIRPUR (q.v.)
Yard No. B346/03.

SIBIRSKIY 2116 (Ru)
Type Sea/river cargo; 3550 DWT; Dimensions 123 (BP) × 15.8 × 3.2; Machinery Motor 1800 bhp; Engine builders Russki; 10 knots; Owners U.S.S.R.; Builders Hollming Oy, Rauma; Yard No. 233.

SIBIRSKIY 2117 - sister of SIBIRSKIY 2116 (q.v.)
Yard No. 234.

SIBIRSKIY 2118 - sister of SIBIRSKIY 2116 (q.v.)
Yard No. 235.

SIBIRSKIY 2119 - sister of SIBIRSKIY 2116 (q.v.)
Yard No. 236.

SIBIRSKIY 2123 - sister of SIBIRSKIY 2116 (q.v.)
Builders Valmet Oy, Turku; Yard No. 386.

SIBIRSKIY 2124 - sister of SIBIRSKIY 2116 (q.v.)
Builders Valmet Oy, Turku; Yard No. 387.

SIERRA MADRE (US)
Type Tanker; 24500 GRT; 37500 DWT; Dimensions 190.81 (BP) × 30.48 × 10.06; Machinery Steam Turbine; Engine builders General Electric; 16.6 knots; Owners West Coast Shipping; Builders National Steel & Shipbuilding, San Diego; Yard No. 417.

SIFNOS ISLAND (Pa)
Type Cargo ("Freedom Mk II" type); 10900 GRT; 15470 DWT; Dimensions 137 (BP) × 21 × 9.04; Machinery Motor 6000 bhp; Engine builders Pielstick SEMT/IHI; 14.5 knots; Owners Sifnos Maritime SA; Builders IHI, Tokyo; Yard No. 2763.

SILVER PINE (Ja)
Type Bulk; 13000 GRT; 21500 DWT; Dimensions 155.23 × 22.89 × 9.96; Machinery Motor 8040 bhp; Engine builders B & W/Mitsui; Owners Manno Kisen K.K.; Builders Tohoku Zosen, Shiogama; Yard No. 193.

Silvia Regina *(Builders)*

SILVIA REGINA - sister of FINLANDIA (q.v.)
Owners Stockholms Rederi "Svea"; Yard No. 1252.

SIMON BOLIVAR (Ru)
Type Container; 8000 GRT; Owners U.S.S.R.; Builders Georgi Dimitrov Shipyard, Varna; Yard No. 201.

SINDBAD (FRG)
Type Cargo; 499 GRT; 1769 DWT; Dimensions 82.48 × — × 3.54; Machinery Motor 600 bhp; Engine builders Deutz; Owners Matthiesen Schiffahrts K.G.; Builders Schiffsw. Hugo Peters, Wewelsfleth; Yard No. 580.

SIOUX (FRG)
Type Tanker; 1599 GRT; 3660 DWT; Dimensions 98.3 × 13.7 × 5.81; Machinery Motor 2250 bhp; Engine builders MaK; 13 knots; Owners Atlantic-Rhederei F & W Joch; Builders Paul Lindenau G.m.b.H, Kiel; Yard No. S191.

SIRI BHUM (Pa)
Launched as Maritime Region. Type Container; 4374 GRT; 6994 DWT; Dimensions 109.71 (BB) × 20.07 × 6.97; Machinery Motor 6000 bhp; Engine builders Pielstick/IHI; Owners Fulfed Shipping Co. Inc.; Managers International Maritime Carriers Ltd.; Builders Usuki Tekkosho, Usuki; Yard No. 1511.

Sirt *(FotoFlite)*

SIRT (Ly)
Type Cargo; 7200 GRT; 10000 DWT; Dimensions 125.82 (BP) × 19 × —; Machinery Motor 7000 bhp; Engine builders MAN; 15.9 knots; Owners General National Maritime Transport Co.; Builders VEB Schiffswerft Neptun, Rostock, DDR.

SLAPY (Cz)
Type Cargo; 6890/10416 GRT; 11000/15326 DWT; Dimensions 145.7 × 21.65 × 9.12; Machinery Motor 7200 bhp; Engine builders Sulzer/Brodogradiliste '3 Maj'; Owners Czechoslovak Ocean Shipping International Joint Stock Co.; Builders Brodogradiliste '3 Maj', Rijeka; Yard No. 601.

SLETFJORD (No)
Type Chemical Tanker; 1546 GRT; 2952 DWT; Dimensions 71.6 (BP) × 12.6 × 5.76; Machinery Motor 2700 bhp; Engine builders MWM; 12.75 knots; Owners Skibs. A/S Karlander; Builders Aukra Bruk A/S, Aukra; Yard No. 73.

Smolensk *(FotoFlite)*

SMOLENSK - sister of ANATOLIY VASILYEV (q.v.)

SOUTH SEAS (US)
Type Tuna Fishing; 1165 GRT; Dimensions 68.13 × — × —; Machinery Motor 3600 bhp; Engine builders General Motors; Owners Caribbean Marine Service Inc.; Builders J.M. Martinac SB Corp., Tacoma, Wa.; Yard No. 224.

SOYO (Ja)
Type Cargo; 1999 GRT; 4500 DWT; Dimensions 78.01 (BP) × — × 6.7; Machinery Motor 2800 bhp; Engine Builders Makita Diesel; Owners Kinkai Sekiyu K.K.; Builders Kochi Jukogyo K.K., Kochi; Yard No. 2173.

SPICA (Li)
Type Vehicle carrier; 15000 GRT; 13600 DWT; Dimensions 180.08 (BP) × 32.2 × 8.8; Machinery Motor 15300 bhp; Engine builders Pielstick/IHI; 19.1 knots; Owners Sakura Marine; Builders Kanasashi Shipbuilding Co., Toyohashi; Yard No. 1305.

Sriwijawa *(Builders)*

SRIWIJAYA (Ia)
Type Container; 11000 GRT; 16731 DWT; Dimensions 146 (BP) × 25.5 × 9.5; Machinery Motor 12390 bhp; Engine builders MAN; 17 knots; Owners Djakarta Lloyd; Builders Schlichting Werft (Harmstorf Group); Yard No. 1426.

STAD FLEX (No)
Type Offshore/Supply; 2500 DWT; Dimensions 76.2 (BP) × 18 × 4.3; Machinery Motor 5200 bhp; Engine builders Nohab Polar; 14 knots; Owners Sv. Farstad/Ivaran; Builders Ulstein Group; Yard No. 170.

STAD SENIOR (No)
Type Tug/Supply; 492/1400 GRT; 1100/1900 DWT; Dimensions 68.03 × 14.71 × 4.711/—; Machinery Twin Screw Motor bhp; Engine builders A/S Bergens M/V; 16 knots; Owners K/S Stad Senior A/S & Co.; Managers Sverre Farstad & Co.; Builders Ulstein Hatlo A/S, Ulsteinvik; Yard No. 169.

STAR EAGLE (No)
Type Bulk Carrier; 24200 GRT; 38000 DWT; Dimensions 170 (BP) × 29.4 × 11.97; Machinery Motor 13100 bhp; Engine builders B & W/Mitsui; Owners Star Shipping A/S; A/S Billabong; Builders Mitsui Engineering & Shipbuilding, Tamano; Yard No. 1234.

STAR OF TEXAS - sister of PRIDE OF TEXAS (q.v.)
Yard No. 752.

STATE OF GUJARAT (In)
Type Cargo ("Pioneer" type); 11400 GRT; 16800 DWT; Dimensions 131.2 (BP) × 22.8 × 10.36; Machinery Motor 9100 bhp; Engine builders MAN/GRW; 15.7 knots; Owners The Shipping Corporation of India; Builders Hindustan Shipyard, Visakhapatnam; Yard No. 171015.

STATE OF HARYANA - sister of STATE OF GUJARAT (q.v.)
Yard No. 171014.

STEFAN STARZYNSKI - sister of TADEUSZ KOSCIUSKO (q.v.)
Builders Ch. de l'Atlantique, St. Nazaire; Yard No. N27.

STELLA POLLUX (Ne)
Type Tanker; 1499 GRT; 2272 DWT; Dimensions 67.01 × — × 5.51; Machinery Motor 1500 bhp; Engine builders Wartsila; Owners Red. Theodora BV; Builders Nieuwe Noord Nederlandse Scheeps., Groningen; Yard No. 400.

STEN (Ja)
Type Tanker; 1100 GRT; 1763 DWT; Dimensions 69.53 × — × 4.31; Machinery Motor 1400 bhp; Engine builders Yanmar Diesel Eng.; Owners Nippo Unyu Shokai K.K.; Builders Kitanihon Zosen K.K., Hachinohe; Yard No. 166.

STENA DANICA (Sw)
Type Ro/Ro Cargo/Passenger Ferry; 16300 GRT; 3300 DWT; Dimensions 135 (BP) × 28 × 6.05; Machinery Motor 4 × 8700 bhp; Engine builders Sulzer; 22 knots; Owners Stena Line; Managers Sten A. Olsson; Builders Chantiers de France, Dunkerque; Yard No. 309.

STENA JUTLANDICA - sister of STENA DANICA (q.v.)
Yard No. 310.

STEPHANOS D. PATERAS (Gr)
Type Bulk; 30650 GRT; 54400 DWT; Machinery Motor 17400 bhp; Engine builders Sulzer/Cegielski; Owners New World Shipping Corp.; Managers Diamantis Pateras & Sons; Builders Santierul Naval Mangalia, Mangalia; Yard No. 900/94.

SULISKER (Br)
Type Fishery Protection; 1177 GRT; 337 DWT; Dimensions 71.33 × 11.64 × 4.66; Machinery Twin Screw Motor 5640 bhp; Engine builders Ruston Diesels Ltd.; 18 knots; Owners Govt. of the United Kingdom (Min. of Agriculture, Fisheries & Food); Builders Ferguson Bros (Port Glasgow) Ltd., Port Glasgow; Yard No. 483.

SUN ACE (Ja)
Type Vehicles Carrier; 9132 GRT; 11058 DWT; Dimensions 147.02 (BP) × — × 8.22; Machinery Motor 12600 bhp; Engine builders Mitsubishi/Kobe Hatsudoki; Owners Nissen Kaiun K.K.; Builders Watanabe Zosen K.K., Hakata; Yard No. 210.

SUN GLORIOUS (Pa)
Type Bulk; 13403 GRT; 23900 DWT; Dimensions 150 (BP) × 24.6 × 9.8; Machinery Motor 9380 bhp; Engine builders Sulzer/Mitsubishi; 13.7 knots; Owners Mount Enterprise Corp.; Builders Imabari Zosen, Imabari; Yard No. 398.

SUN MERLION (Pa)
Type LGC; 2418 GRT; 2850 DWT; Dimensions 93.6 × — × 5.1; Machinery Motor 3200 bhp; Engine builders Akasaka; Owners Mount Enterprise Corp. S.A.; Builders Honda Zosen, Saiki; Yard No. 688.

SUNCOR CHIPPEWA (Li)
Type Chemical Tanker; 10200 GRT; 20000 DWT; Dimensions 145 (BP) × 22.7 × 9.6; Machinery Motor 8040 bhp; Engine builders B & W/Mitsui; 14 knots; Owners Sunchem Shipping Co.; Managers Sun Transport Inc.; Builders Hayashikane Shipbuilding & Eng., Shimonoseki; Yard No. 1243.

SUNNY CRANE (Ja)
Type Tanker; 3491 GRT; 6158 DWT; Dimensions 98.4 (BP) × — × 6.71; Machinery Motor 3900 bhp; Engine builders Akasaka; Owners Sun Marine KK; Builders Murakami Hide Zosen, Hakata; Yard No. 198.

SUNNY HOPE (Li)
Type Tanker; 33000 GRT; 58950 DWT; Dimensions 216 (BP) × 32.2 × 12.19; Machinery Motor 15200 bhp; Engine builders B & W/Mitsui; 15 knots; Owners Sunny Rock Shipping Inc.; Builders Tsuneishi Shipbuilding Co., Numakuma; Yard No. 466.

SUNSHINE OKINAWA (Ja)
Type Passenger/Cargo; 4500 GRT; 2650 DWT; Dimensions 120.53 (BP) × — × 5.85; Machinery Twin Screw Motor 14400 bhp; Engine builders Mitsubishi; Owners Ryukyu Kaiun KK; Builders Yamanishi Zosen, Ishonomaki; Yard No. 873.

SUSAN B - sister of DANELOCK (q.v.)
Yard No. 882.

SVENDBORG MAERSK - sister of SALLY MAERSK (q.v.)
Yard No. 90.

SYDSTRAUM (No)
Type Chemical Tanker; 1199 GRT; 2500 DWT; Dimensions 74.9 (BP) × 13 × 5.1; Machinery Motor 2250 bhp; Engine builders Normo; 13 knots; Owners Anders Utkilens Rederi; Builders Bolsones Verft, Molde; Yard No. 270.

T

TADEUSZ KOSCIUSZKO (Pd)
Type RoRo Cargo/Container; 25700 GRT; 21652 DWT; Dimensions 203 × 31.7 × 9.5; Machinery Motor 29000 bhp; Engine builders Sulzer/Cegielski; 20.7 knots; Owners Polskie Linie Oceaniczne; Builders Chantiers Navals de la Ciotat, La Ciotat; Yard No. 324

Tadeusz Kosciuszko *(FotoFlite)*

TAISEI MARU (Ja)
Type Training Ship; 5800 GRT; 3273 DWT; Dimensions 128.86 × 17.00 × 5.82; Machinery Steam 7000 shp; Engine builders Kawasaki Heavy Ind.; 17.5 knots; Owners Govt. of Japan (Ministry of Transportation); Builders Nippon Kokan K.K., Tsurumi Shipyard, Yokohama; Yard No. 981.

TAISHO MARU (Ja)
Type Cargo; 3990 GRT; 6845 DWT; Dimensions 98 (BP) × 16.8 × 7; Machinery Motor 3900 bp; Engine builders Akasaka; 12.4 knots; Owners Toda Kisen KK; Builders Murakami Hide Zosen, Hakata; Yard No. 192.

TAIYO MARU No 3 (Ja)
Type Cargo; 460 GRT; 949 DWT; Dimensions 58.63 × — × 3.92; Machinery Motor 1100 bhp; Engine builders Yanmar Diesel; Owners Taiyo Kaiun K.K.; Builders Maeno Zosen KK, Onoda; Yard No. 65.

TAK YANG (Ko)
Type Cement; 4692 GRT; 7500 DWT; Dimensions 106 (BP) × — × 7; Machinery Motor 4000 bhp; Engine builders Hanshin; Owners Ssang Yong Shipping Co.; Builders Shinhama Dock KK, Anan; Yard No. 726.

TARNVIND (Sw)
Type Chemical Tanker; 3750 GRT; 6200 DWT; Dimensions 105.52 × 15.73 × 7.8; Machinery Motor 4000 bhp; Engine builders Mak; Owners Tarntank Rederi A/B; Managers Sven Olaf Kristensson; Builders Kalmar Varv A/B, Kalmar and Marstrandsverken FEAB, Marstrand; Yard No. 451/—.

TARRACO AUGUSTA (Sp)
Type Tanker; 141640 GRT; 300070 DWT; Dimensions 341.61 × — × 22.18; Machinery Steam 36000 shp; Engine builders Kawasaki/Bazan; Owners ENPETROL; Builders 'ASTANO' Ast. y. Talleres del Noroeste S.A., El. Ferrol.; Yard No. 245.

TATSU MARU No 28 (Ja)
Type Cargo; 699 GRT; 1500 DWT; Dimensions 70.01 (BP) × — × —; Machinery Motor 2000 bhp; Engine builders Hanshin; Owners Mitsughio Bussan; Builders K.K. Yoshida Zosen Kogyo, Arida; Yard No. 356.

TATSUTA MARU (Ja)
Type LPG; 46000 GRT; 44900 DWT; Dimensions 214 (BP) × 32.2 × 10.5; Machinery Motor 15200 bhp; Engine builders B & W/Mitsui; 16.6 knots; Owners Nippon Yusen Kaisha; Builders Nippon Kokan K.K., Tsu; Yard No. 75.

TECUMSEH (FRG)
Type Tanker; 999 GRT; 2600 DWT; Dimensions 78.9 (BP) × 13 × 4.85; Machinery Motor 1800 bhp; Engine builders Deutz; 11.5 Knots; Owners Atlantic Reederei F & W Joch; Builders Meltem Beykoz Tersanesi, Istabul; Yard No. 38.

TENAGA EMPAT (Ma)
Type LGC; 66800 GRT; 68750 DWT; Dimensions 282.72 × — × 11.35; Machinery Steam 45000 shp; Engine builders Stal-Laval/Alsthom-Atlantique; Owners Malaysian International Shipping Corp., Berhad; Builders C.N.I.M., La Seyne; Yard No. 1428.

TENEI MARU (Ja)
Type Tanker; 39000 GRT; 60900 DWT; Dimensions 217.71 × 36.00 × 11.8; Machinery Motor 11700 bhp; Engine builders Pielstick/IHI; 14.1 Knots; Owners The Kyoei Tanker Co. Ltd; Builders I.H.I., Aioi; Yard No. 2751.

TENRYU MARU (Ja)
Type LPG; 47000 GRT; 53000 DWT; Dimensions 217 (BP) × 36.6 × 11.5; Machinery Motor 21600 bhp; Engine builders Sulzer/Mitsubishi; 17.5 Knots; Owners Nippon Yusen Kaisha; Builders Mitsubishi Heavy Industries, Nagasaki; Yard No. 1876.

TENSHA MARU No 7 (Ja)
Type Cargo; 699 GRT; 2100 DWT; Dimensions 62.21 (BP) × — × 5.1; Motor 2000 bhp; Engine builders Makita Diesel; Owners Wakamatsu Kaiun K.K; Builders Omishima Zosen, Ehime; Yard No. 1100.

TERRA (Ne)
Type Cargo; 2000 GRT; 3500 DWT; Dimensions 110.01 × 11.41 × 3.83; Machinery Motor 1860 bhp; Engine builders General Motors/Allison; Owners O. Slokkers & others; Builders Scheeps van Langerbrugge, Gent/Gand; Yard No. 6500.

TETSUUN MARU No. 15 (Ja)
Type Cargo; 499 GRT; 1400 DWT; Dimensions 70.01 × — × 4.15; Machinery Motor 1600 bhp; Engine builders Niigata Eng. Co. Ltd; Owners Tetsuun Kisen K.K; Builders Murakami Hide Zosen K.K., Hakata; Yard No. 188.

TEXACO WESTMINSTER (Br)
Type Tanker; 54076 GRT; 79622 DWT; Dimensions 236.8 (BP) × 39.9 × 12.18; Machinery Motor 15000 bhp; Engine builders Pielstick/IHI; 14.7 Knots; Owners Texaco Overseas Tankship Ltd; Managers Globtik Management Ltd; Builders IHI, Aioi; Yard No. 2718.

TFL Adams *(FotoFlite)*

TFL ADAMS (FRG)
Type Container; 15000 GRT; 21200 DWT; Dimensions 170.2 × 28.4 × 9.65; Machinery Motor 14460 bhp; Engine builders M.A.N; 19 Knots; Owners Artimon Schiffahrts; Managers H. W. Janssen G.m.b.H; Builders Flensburger Schiffs. Gesellschaft, Flensburg; Yard No. 657.

Thekla Wessels *(FotoFlite)*

THEKLA WESSELS (FRG)
Type Cargo; 999 GRT; 3030 DWT; Dimensions 99.83 × 11.41 × 4.32; Machinery Motor 1320 bhp; Engine builders Karl Liebknecht; Owners Wessels; Builders M.A.N. Unternehmensbereich GHH Sterkrade, Walsum; Yard No. 1143.

THORSDRAKE (No)
Type Bulk; 35000 GRT; 61200 DWT; Dimensions 213 (BP) × 32.2 × 12.2; Machinery Motor 15200 bhp; Engine builders B & W/Mitsui; Owners Thor Dahl; Builders Mitsui Eng. & Shipbuilding, Chiba; Yard No. 1233.

THUTMOSE (Eg)
Type Cargo ("Kaliningrad" type); 5741 GRT; 8230 DWT; Dimensions 129.93 × 17.84 × 7.84; Machinery Motor 4900 bhp; Engine builders B & W/Bryansk; 16 Knots; Owners The Egyptian Nav. Co; Builders Alexandria Shipyard, Alexandria; Yard No. 10018.

TIBERIUS (No)
Type Bulk Carrier; 77226 GRT; 128272 DWT; Dimensions 258 (BP) × 43 × 16.3; Machinery Motor 20400 bhp; Engine builders Sulzer/Mitsubishi; 15 Knots; Owners Wilh. Wilhelmsen; Builders Mitsubishi Heavy Industries, Nagasaki; Yard No. 1864.

Tomoe 85 *(Motor Ship)*

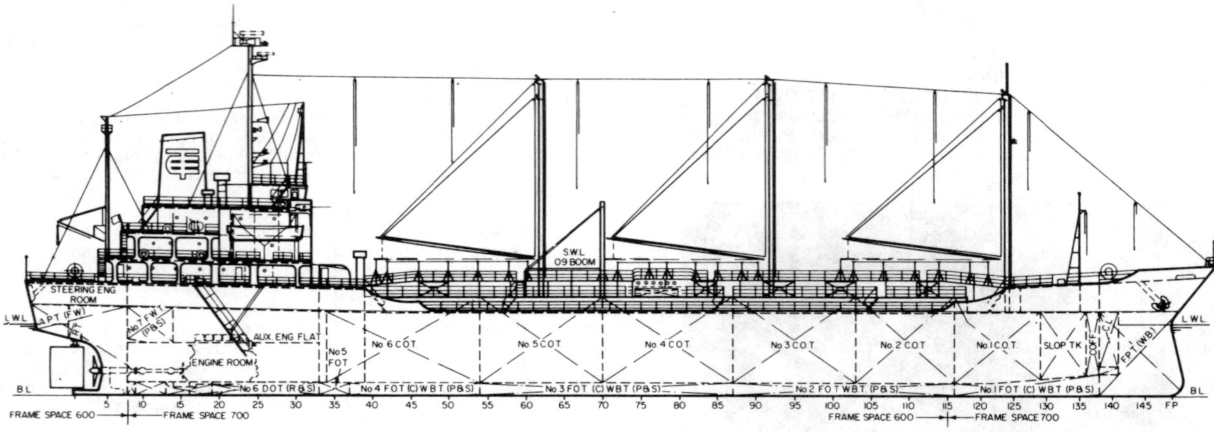

TIMBER ROYAL (Pa)
Type Cargo; 4400 GRT; 7000 DWT; Dimensions 100 (BP) × 17.6 × 6.87; Machinery Motor 3800 bhp; Engine builders Mitsubishi-/Akasaka; 12.3 Knots; Owners Ormus Shipping; Builders Imai Zosen KK, Kochi; Yard No. 509.

TIMBER STAR - sister of TIMBER ROYAL (q.v.)
Yard No. 510.

TIMOR (Ia)
Type Dredger; 4145 GRT; 4066 DWT; Dimensions 95.03 (BP) × — × 5.0; Machinery Twin Screw Motor 4200 bhp; Engine builders Niigata Eng. Co. Ltd; Owners Govt. of the Republic of Indonesia; Builders Ishikawajima Ship & Chemical Plant Co., Tokyo; Yard No. 516.

TOHO MARU (Ja)
Type Cargo; 698 GRT; 2223 DWT; Dimensions 68 (BP) × — × 4.85; Machinery Motor 1800 bhp; Engine builders Makita; Owners Toho Kaiun Y.K; Builders Kinoura Zosen, Hakata Yard No. 66.

TOKO MARU (Ja)
Type Tanker; 36014 GRT; 54000 DWT; Dimensions 215 (BP) × — × 11.5; Machinery Motor 13100 bhp; Engine builders B & W/Mitsui; Owners Toko Kaiun K.K; Builders Kurushima Dock Co. Ltd., Onishi; Yard No. 2151.

TOMOE 37 (Ja)
Type Tanker; 3500 GRT; 6200 DWT; Dimensions 100.2 (BP) × 15.5 × 6.75; Machinery Motor 3900 bhp; Engine builders Mitsubishi/Akasaka; 12.7 Knots; Owners Niwase Kaiun; Builders Asakawa Shipbuilding Co., Imabari; Yard No. 302.

TOMOE 85 (Ja)
Type Tanker; 3557 GRT; 6217 DWT; Dimensions 108.71 × 15.5 × 6.78; Machinery Motor 3900 bhp; Engine builders Mitsubishi-/Akasaka; 12.7 Knots; Owners Niwase Kaiun; Builders Asakawa Shipbuilding Co., Imabari; Yard No. 301.

TOMOE 103 (Ja)
Type Tanker; 5300 GRT; 10000 DWT; Dimensions 115.6 (BP) × 18.2 × 8.15; Machinery Motor 6000 bhp; Engine builders Mitsubishi/Akasaka; 13.5 Knots; Owners Niwase Kaiun; Builders Asakawa Shipbuilding Co., Imabari; Yard No. 305.

TORASUND (No)
Type Cargo; 2500 DWT; Dimensions 81 × 13 × —; Machinery Motor; 14 Knots; Owners A. Teigens A/S; Builders Skaalurens, Rosendal.

TORM VENTURE (Li)
Type Tanker; 18000 GRT; 29900 DWT; Dimensions 162 (BP) × 26 × 10.75; Machinery Motor 11200 bhp; Engine builders B & W/Hitachi; 15.7 Knots; Owners Prominence Carriers Inc; Builders Kanda Shipbuilding Co., Kure; Yard No. 259.

TOYOFUJI No. 6 (Ja)
Type Car Carrier; 4200 GRT; 3616 DWT; Dimensions 110 (BP) × 19.1 × 6.05; Machinery Motor 6000 bhp; Engine builders Mitsubishi; 15 Knots; Owners Toyofuji Kaiun KK; Builders Mitsubishi Heavy Industries, Shimonoseki; Yard No. 833.

TOYOFUJI No. 7 (Ja)
Type Car Carrier; 14200 GRT; 8860 DWT; Dimensions 178 (BP) × 29 × 8; Machinery Motor 15700 bhp; Engine builders B & W/Hitachi; 18 Knots; Owners Toyofuji Kaiun KK; Builders Naikai Shipbuilding & Eng. (Hitachi Zosen), Setoda; Yard No. 869.

TOYOKUNI MARU No. 2 (Ja)
Type Cargo; 699 GRT; 1500 DWT; Dimensions 68 (BP) × — × —; Machinery Motor 2000 bhp; Engine builders Hanshin Nainenki Kogyo; Owners Toyomasu Kaiso K.K; Builders Kochi Jukogyo (Eiho Zosen) K.K., Kochi; Yard No. 1402.

TOYOSAKI (Ja)
Type Chemical Tanker; 3242 GRT; 5628 DWT; Dimensions 94 × — × (BP) × 6.86; Machinery Motor 3800 bhp; Engine builders Akasaka; Owners Manno Marine Service K.K; Builders Honda Zosen, Saiki; Yard No. 687.

TOYOSHIO MARU (Ja)
Type Tanker; 999 GRT; 2300 DWT; Dimensions 74.02 (BP) × — × 5.0; Machinery Motor 20000 bhp; Engine builders Hanshin; Owners Nagashiki Kisen K.K; Builders Imamura Zosen, Kure; Yard No. 266.

TOYU MARU (Ja)
Type Tanker; 54000 GRT; 81280 DWT; Dimensions 230 (BP) × 42 × 12.2; Machinery Motor 13100 bhp; Engine builders B & W; Owners Toko Kaiun; Builders Kurushima Dock Co., Onishi; Yard No. 2142.

TRADEWIND - sister of EASTWIND (q.v.)
Yard No. 10056.

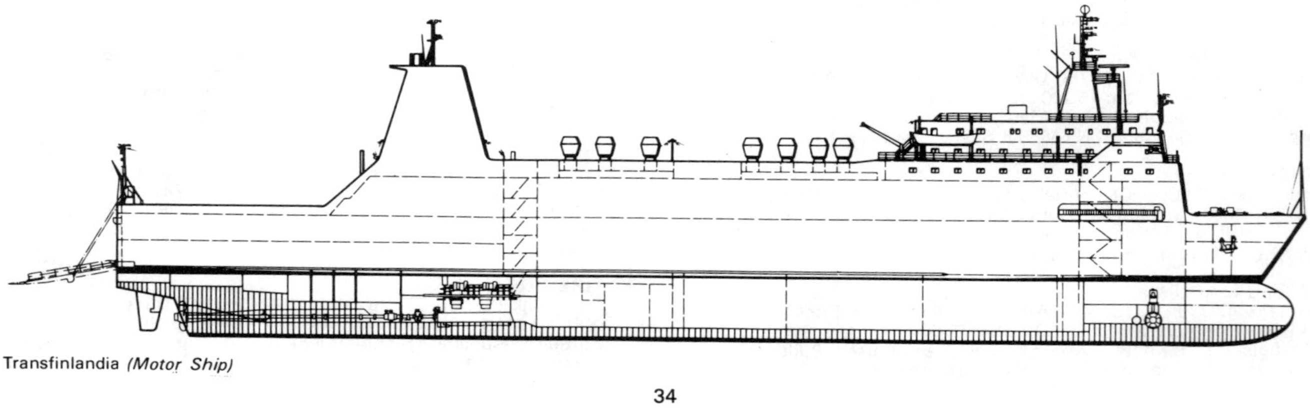

Transfinlandia *(Motor Ship)*

Travemunde *(Holland Shipbuilding)*

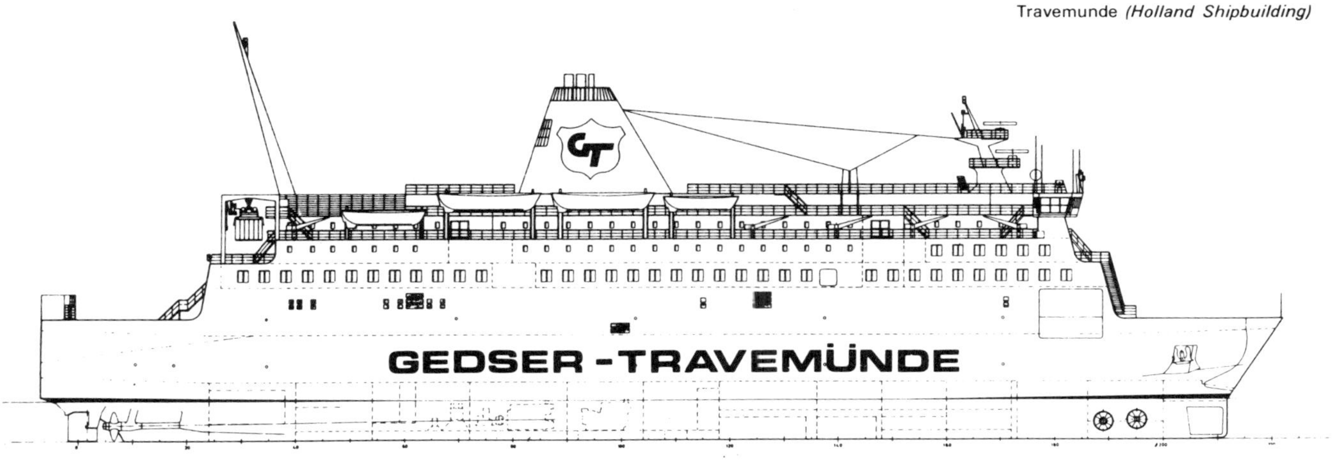

Transfinlandia *(Builders)*

TRANSFINLANDIA (FRG)
Type RoRo Cargo; 9500 GRT; 11000 DWT; Dimensions 175.8 × 24.6 × 7.27; Machinery Motor 16500 bhp; Engine builders B & W; 19.6 Knots; Owners Poseidon Schiffahrt OHG; Builders Flender Werft AG, Lubeck; Yard No. 623.

TRAQUAIR (Br)
Type LPG; 5500 GRT; 7130 DWT; Dimensions 106.5 (BP) × 18.3 × 8.1; Machinery Motor 6325 bhp; Engine builders Sulzer/Clark-Hawthorn; 16 Knots; Owners Anchor Line Ltd; Managers Geo. Gibson; Builders Ailsa Shipbuilding Co., Troon; Yard No. 557.

TRAVEMUNDE (De)
Type RoRo Passenger Ferry; 9000 GRT; Dimensions 137.4 × 22.6 × 4.95; Machinery Twin Screw Motor 4 × 4718 bhp; Engine builders Vasa/Wartsila; 19.4 Knots; Owners Gedser Travemunde Ruten; Builders Oy Wartsila, Helsinki; Yard No. 432.

TRELLEBORG (Sw)
Type Passenger/Vehicle/Train Ferry; 10000 GRT; 3800 DWT; Dimensions 170 × 22.45 × —; Machinery Motor 24000 bhp; Engine builders MAN; 18 Knots; Owners Swedish State Railways; Builders Oresundsvarvet AB (Gotaverken group), Landskrona; Yard No. 271.

Tresmares *(FotoFlite)*

TRESMARES (Sp)
Type Container; 1600 GRT; 3100 DWT; Dimensions 73.7 (BP) × 13.5 × 5.6; Machinery Motor 2000 bhp; Engine builders Sulzer/AESA; 11.5 Knots; Owners Maritima del Besaya; Builders Astilleros del Atlantico, Santander; Yard No. 211.

TRIBULUS (Br)
Type Bulk; 69230 GRT; 111500 DWT; Dimensions 264.52 × 40.87 × 16.73; Machinery Motor 18400 bhp; Engine builders B & W/Mitsui; Owners Shell Tankers (UK) Ltd; Builders Hyundai Heavy Industries Co. Ltd., Ulsan; Yard No. 142.

Tribulus *(FotoFlite)*

Tricula *(FotoFlite)*

TRICULA - sister of TRIBULUS (q.v.)
Yard No. 143.

TRIGLAV - sister of BHARATENDU (q.v.)
Launched as BHAVU BHUTI; Yard No. 319.

TROMA - sister of FROSTA (q.v.)
Yard No. 1040.

Tropicale *(Builders model.)*

TROPICALE (Li)
Type Cruise Liner; 30000 GRT; 5000 DWT; Dimensions 200 × 26.3 × 6.8; Machinery Motor 26000 bhp; Engine builders Sulzer; 21 Knots; Owners Festivale Maritime Inc; Builders Aalborg Vaerft A/S, Aalborg; Yard No. 234.

Trydakna *(Centromar)*

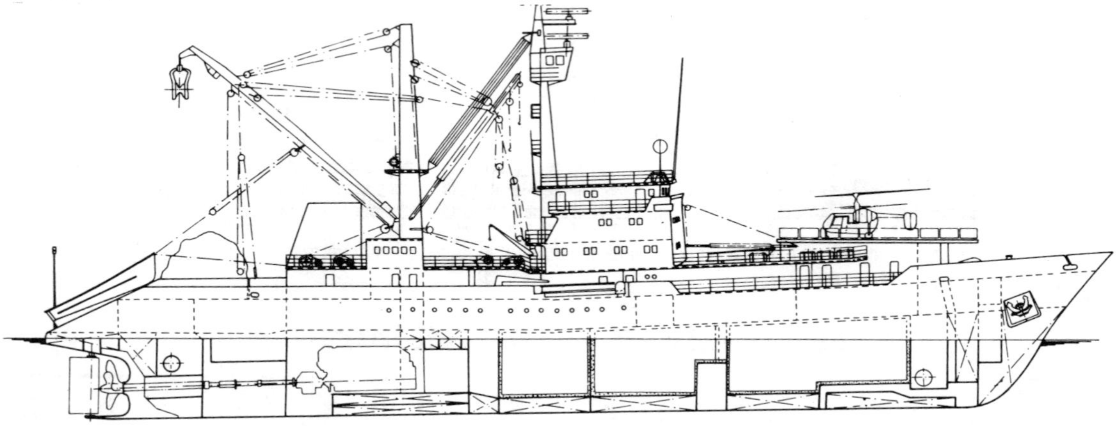

TRYDAKNA (Ru)
Type Fishing; 2900 GRT; 1850 DWT; Dimensions 84.99 × — × 6.0; Machinery Motor 5200 bhp; Engine builders Sulzer/"Zgoda"; 16 Knots; Owners U.S.S.R; Builders Stocznia Polnocna im Bohaterow Westerplatte, Gdansk; Yard No. B406/10.

TSURUFUJI MARU No. 18 (Ja)
Type Tanker; 1987 GRT; 3740 DWT; Dimensions 78.01 (BP) × — × 6.35; Machinery Motor 3200 bhp; Engine builders Akasaka; Owners Hinode Kaiun K.K; Builders Kochi Jukogyo K.K., Kochi; Yard No. 2167.

TUMA (Cu)
Type Cement Carrier; 3907 GRT; 5400 DWT; Dimensions 109.45 × 15.83 × 6.41; Machinery Motor 400 bhp; Engine builders B & W/AESA; Owners Marpesca; Builders Astilleros de Santander, Santander; Yard No. 154.

XXVI SYEZD KPSS (Ru)
Type Fish Factory/Trawler; 3385 GRT; 1815 DWT; Dimensions 103.1 × 16.03 × 5.9; Machinery Motor 6000 bhp; Engine builders Praha; 14 Knots; Owners U.S.S.R; Builders U.S.S.R.

U

UMM AL AISH (Ku)
Type Tanker; 55000 GRT; 80000 DWT; Dimensions 220 (BP) × 44 × 12.19; Machinery Motor 17000 bhp; Engine builders Sulzer/Mitsubishi; 16 Knots; Owners Kuwait Oil Tanker Co; Builders Mitsubishi Heavy Industries, Nagasaki; Yard No. 1866.

Umm al Aish *(FotoFlite)*

UMM AL MARADEM - sister of UMM AL AISH (q.v.)
Yard No. 1867.

UMM AL MATRABH - sister of UMM CASBAH (q.v.)
Yard No. 286.

UMM CASBAH (Ku)
Type Tanker; 55800 GRT; 80000 DWT; Dimensions 225 (BP) × 43 × 12.16; Machinery Motor 17000 bhp; Engine builders Sulzer/Mitsubishi; 16 Knots; Owners Kuwait Oil Tanker Co; Builders Sasebo Heavy Industries, Sasebo; Yard No. 287.

UNION DIAMOND (Ih)
Type Cargo; 980 GRT; 1400 DWT; Dimensions 70.01 × 11.26 × 3.57; Machinery Motor 999 bhp; Engine builders Mak; Owners Sagitta Shipping Ltd; Builders J. G. Hitzler Schiffwerft u. Maschinenfabrik, Lauenburg; Yard No. 766.

UNION MARS (Ih)
Type Cargo; 936 GRT; 1448 DWT; Dimensions 70.01 × 11.28 × 3.4; Machinery Motor 999 bhp; Engine builders Alpha Diesel A/S; 10.5 Knots; Owners Union Transport (London) Ltd; Builders A/S Nordsovaerftet, Ringkobing; Yard No. 146.

UNION PLUTO - sister of UNION MARS (q.v.)

UNION VENUS - sister of UNION MARS (q.v.)
Yard No. 147.

UNIVERSAL APOLLO (Pa)
Type Chemical Tanker; 3865 GRT; 6291 DWT; Dimensions 108.11 × 16.24 × 6.93; Machinery Motor 4500 bhp; Engine builders MaK/Ube Kosan; Owners Universal Apollo Enterprise S.A; Builders Ube Dock, Ube; Yard No. 162.

UNIVERSAL BENEFIT (Li)
Type Bulk; 16325 GRT; 30868 DWT; Dimensions 175.01 (BB) × 26.04 × 10.45; Machinery Motor 10400 bhp; Engine builders Pielstick/Nippon Kokan; 14.3 Knots; Owners Universal Emerald Maritime; Builders Nippon Kokan KK, Shimizu; Yard No. 385.

UNIVERSAL FRONTIER - sister of UNIVERSAL APOLLO (q.v.)
Yard No. 163.

UNIVERSAL MONARCH (Pa)
Type Tanker; 40839 GRT; 81282 DWT; Dimensions 229.55 (BB) × 44.05 × 11.93; Machinery Motor 15800 bhp; Engine builders B & W/Mitsui; 15 Knots; Owners Cygnus Maritime S.A; Builders Mitsui Eng. & SB. Co. Ltd., Ichihara; Yard No. 1214.

UNKAS - sister of SIOUX (q.v.)
Yard No. S192.

URGENCE (Br)
Type Cargo; 699 GRT; 1842 DWT; Dimensions 84.82 × 11.49 × 3.44; Machinery Motor 1240 bhp; Engine builders Alpha Diesel; 11 Knots; Owners Babyssa Ltd; Managers Crescent Shipping; Builders Cochrane Shipbuilders Ltd., Selby; Yard No. 112.

URIMARE (Ve)
Type Tanker; 33100 GRT; 61571 DWT; Dimensions 235.8 × 32.24 × 12.22; Machinery Motor 14000 bhp; Engine builders B & W/Mitsui; Owners Maraven S.A; Builders Onomichi Zosen, Onomichi; Yard No. 296.

UST-ILIMSK - sister of KROPOTKIN (q.v.)
Yard No. 265.

UST-IZHMA - sister of KROPOTKIN (q.v.)
Yard No. 268.

UST-KAN - sister of KROPOTKIN (q.v.)
Yard No. 226.

V

VALBRUNA (It)
Type Tanker; 12000 GRT; 19900 DWT; Machinery Motor 6300 bhp; Engine builders GMT; Owners G & A Montanari; Builders Cant. Nav. Breda, Venice; Yard No. 296.

VALDIVIA (Br)
Type Bulk; 35522 GRT; 65785 DWT; Dimensions 225.03 × 32.26 × 12.89; Machinery Motor 14000 bhp; Engine builders Sulzer/Mitsubishi; 14.5 Knots; Owners Aiden Shipping Co. Ltd; Managers Harrisons (Clyde) Ltd; Builders Namura SB. Co. Ltd., Imari; Yard No. 844.

Valentin Shaskin

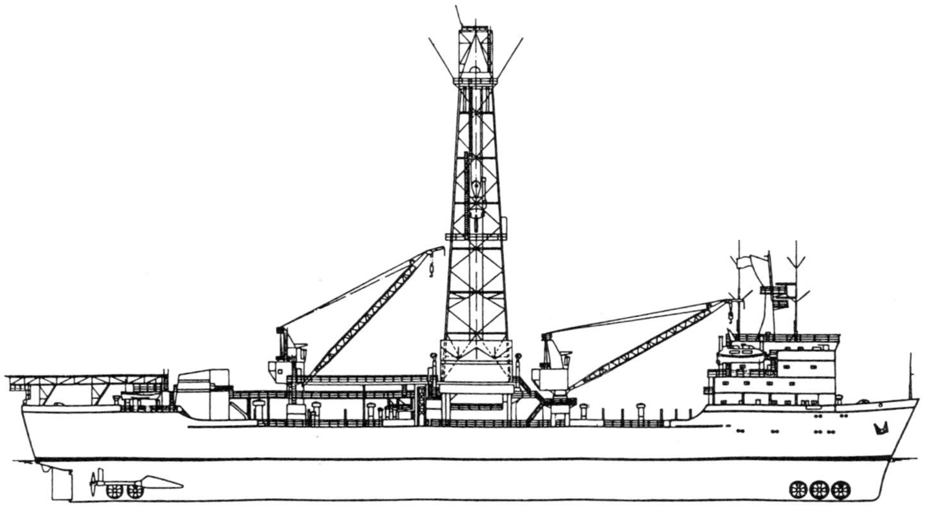

VALENTIN SHASKIN (Ru)
Type Drill Ship (Pelican type); 12000 GRT; 7000 DWT; Dimensions 149.4 × 24 × 7.3; Machinery Twin Screw Diesel-electric 2 × 3750 shp; Owners U.S.S.R; Builders Rauma-Repola Oy, Mantyluoto.

VALLE DE IBAIZABAL (Sp)
Type Cargo; 6300 GRT; 12790 DWT; Dimensions 138.56 (BB) × 21.04 × 9.26; Machinery Motor 7148 bhp; Engine builders B & W/Ast. Espanoles; Owners Compania Vasco Madrilena de Navegacion S.A; Builders T. Ruiz de Velasco S.A., Bilbao; Yard No. 147.

VASILIY SOLOVYEV SEDOY - sister of KONSTANTIN SIMONOV (q.v.)
Yard No. B492/04.

VELA (FRG)
Type Container; 999 GRT; 2800 DWT; Dimensions 95 × 13.5 × 4.25; Machinery Motor; Engine builders Mak; 12.5 Knots; Owners VEHA-Reederei G.m.b.H; Builders Martin Jansen, Leer; Yard No. 167.

VELAZQUEZ (Sp)
Type RoRo Cargo; 4400 GRT; 6600 DWT; Dimensions 121 (BP) × 21.5 × 6.7; Machinery Motor 2 × 5625 bhp; Engine builders MAN/Bazan; 17.5 Knots; Owners Lineas Maritimas Espanoles; Builders Empresa Nacional Bazan, San Fernando; Yard No. 212.

VELEBIT (Ys) - sister of BHARATENDU (q.v.)
(Launched as Bhasa); Yard No. 322.

VENTURE STAR (Li)
Type Bulk; 18648 GRT; 32587 DWT; Dimensions 183.01 (BB) × 27.69 × 10.88; Machinery Motor 12600 bhp; Engine builders Sulzer/IHI; Owners Concord Carriers Inc; Managers Venture Shipping (Managers) Ltd; Builders Kanda Zosensho K.K., Japan; Yard No. 255.

VENUS (Li)
Type Tanker; 46000 GRT; 80000 DWT; Dimensions 243.01 × — × 12.19; Machinery Motor 16800 bhp; Engine builders Sulzer/Hitachi Zosen; Owners Venus Tankers Inc; Builders Hyundai Heavy Industries Co. Ltd., Ulsan; Yard No. 128.

VERA KHORUZHAYA (Ru)
Type RoRo Cargo/Container; 3954 GRT; 4600 DWT; Dimensions 139.63 × 19.23 × 6.26; Machinery Motor 6100 bhp; Engine builders B & W Bryansk; 16.75 Knots; Owners U.S.S.R; Builders "A Zhdanov" Shipbuilding Yd., Leningrad.

VERDANT (Pa)
Type Bulk; 12650 GRT; 21500 DWT; Dimensions 145.7 × 22.86 × 9.9; Machinery Motor 8040 bhp; Engine builders B & W/Hitachi; 14 Knots; Owners Verdant Nav. S.A; Builders Tohoku Shipbuilding Co., Shiogama; Yard No. 201.

VERMILION HIGHWAY (Ja)
Type Vehicles Carrier; 17565 GRT; 16800 DWT; Dimensions 199.42 × — × 9.0; Machinery Motor 16800 bhp; Engine builders Sulzer/Mitsubishi; Owners Koyo Kaiun K.K; Builders Imabari Zosen, Marugame; Yard No. 1093.

VIATOR (No) - sister of ALEXANDER (q.v.)
Owners C. H. Sorenson & Sonner; Yard No. 1028.

VIBRENCE - sister of URGENCE (q.v.)
Owners Crescent Shipping; Yard No. 113.

VICHREN (Bu)
Type Bulk Carrier; 14850 GRT; 24605 DWT; Dimensions 172 (BP) × 22.8 × 10.21; Machinery Motor 12000 bhp; Engine builders Sulzer/Cegielski; 15.3 Knots; Owners Navigation Maritime Bulgare; Builders Georgi Dimitrov Shipyard, Varna; Yard No. 143.

VIGAS (Ja)
Launched as Fuji Gas; Type LGC; 2490 GRT; 3070 DWT; Dimensions 87 (BP) × — × 5.27; Machinery Motor 3200 bhp; Engine builders Akasaka; Owners Fuji Gas Line K.K; Builders Tokushima Zosen Sangyo, Komatsushima; Yard No. 1431.

VIKING HARRIER - sister of VIKING OSPREY (q.v.)
Yard No. 316.

VIKING LADY (No)
Type Tanker; 30745 GRT; 55000 DWT; Dimensions 198 (BP) × 32.25 × 12.6; Machinery Motor 12000 bhp; Engine builders Sulzer/Horten; 15.2 Knots; Owners K/S Olsen Daughter Tankers; Builders A/S Horten Verft, Horten; Yard No. 201.

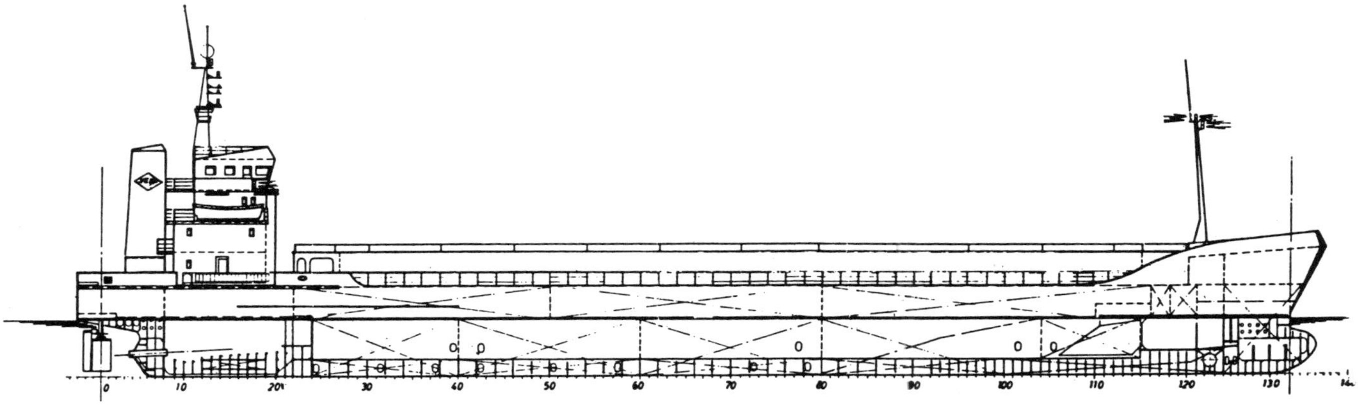

Vela

Viking Osprey *(Motor Ship)*

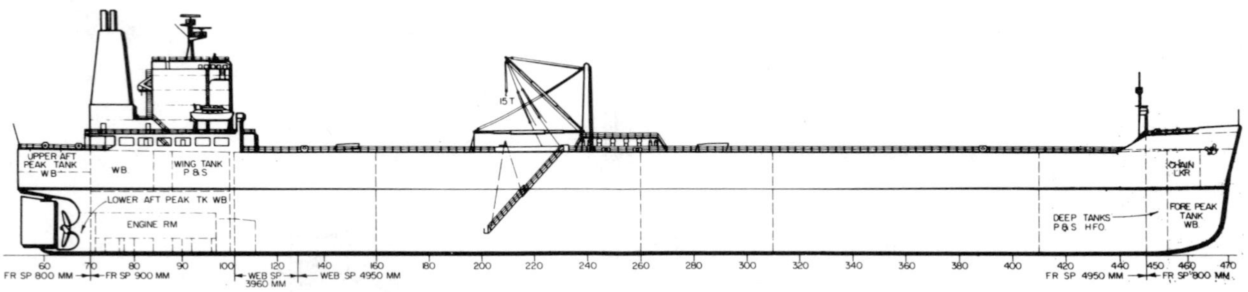

VIKING OSPREY (Sg)
Type Tanker; 42235 GRT; 88750 DWT; Dimensions 228.61 × 42.7 × 13.5; Machinery Motor 18500 bhp; Engine builders B & W/Uddevallavarvet; Owners Uller Shipping Co (Pte) Ltd; Managers Norse Management Co (Pte) Ltd; Builders Uddevallavarvet AB., Uddevalla; Yard No. 315.

VIKING VENTURE (Li)
Type Tanker; 17500 GRT; 29900 DWT; Dimensions 165 (BP) × 25 × 10.7; Machinery Motor 11200 bhp; Engine builders B & W/Mitsui; 15.5 Knots; Owners Kettering Shipping; Builders Hayashikane Shipbuilding & Eng. Shimonoseki; Yard No. 1241.

VIKTOR MURAVLENKO - sister of VALENTIN SHASKIN (q.v.)
Yard No. RR-16.

VIKTOR STRELTSOV - sister of DMITRIY POKROVICH (q.v.)
Yard No. B408/-.

VIOLETTA (Gr)
Type Bulk; 16500 GRT; 28600 DWT; Dimensions 170 (BP) × 23.1 × 10.65; Machinery Motor 11400 bhp; Engine builders Sulzer/IHI; 15 Knots; Owners Blue Tower Trading Corp; Builders Hakodate Dock Co., Muroran; Yard No. 706.

VISHVA PRAFULLA (In)
Type Cargo; 8940/12810 GRT; 13389/16146 DWT; Dimensions 152.03 × 22.97 × -/9.53; Machinery Motor 9900 bhp; Engine builders Sulzer/Clark Hawthorn; 15.75 Knots; Owners The Shipping Corporation of India Ltd; Builders Sunderland Shipbuilders Ltd., Pallion, Sunderland; Yard No. 16.

VOJVODINA (Ys)
Type Cargo; 9700 GRT; 14435 DWT; Dimensions 156.85 × 21.85 × 9.25; Machinery Motor 11200 bhp; Engine builders MAN/DMR; 18.25 Knots; Owners JUGOLINIJA; Builders VEB Warnowwerft, Warnemuende; Yard No. 421.

VOREDA - sister of VALDIVIA (q.v.)
Yard No. 845.

W

WAKAYAMA MARU (Ja)
Type Bulk; 65000 GRT; 135000 DWT; Machinery Motor 20400 bhp; Engine builders Sulzer/Sumitomo; Owners Daiichi Chuo Kisen; Builders Kurushima Dock Co., Onishi; Yard No. 2165.

WEST VIRGINIA (Pa)
Type Tanker; 42175 GRT; 79870 DWT; Dimensions 236.33 × 44.02 × 12.19; Machinery Motor 20400 bhp; Engine builders Sulzer/Mitsubishi; 16 Knots; Owners United States Trust Co. of New York; Builders Mitsubishi Heavy Industries Ltd., Nagasaki; Yard No. 1862.

West Virginia *(FotoFlite)*

WESTAFCARRIER (Pa)
Type Cargo; 3467 GRT; 6151 DWT; Dimensions 74.6 (BP) × 16 × 5.97; Machinery Motor; 3000 bhp; Engine builders Hanshin; 12.5 Knots; Owners West African Shipping Co; Builders Miho Shipyard Co., Shimizu; Yard No. 1161.

WHITE EXCELSIOR (Li)
Type Tanker; 22150 GRT; 38000 DWT; Dimensions 172 (BP) × 31.4 × 10.95; Machinery Motor 12000 bhp; Engine builders B & W/Mitsui; 14.5 Knots; Owners White Excelsior Maritime; Builders Onomichi Shipbuilding Co., Kobe; Yard No. 298.

WHITE SANPO II (Ja)
Type RoRo Passenger Ferry; 10181 GRT; 3725 DWT; Dimensions 141 (BP) × 23.6 × 5.6; Machinery Motor 23400 bhp; Engine builders Pielstick/NKK; 21.1 Knots; Owners Sanpo Kaiun Kaisha; Builders Hayashikane Shipbuilding & Eng., Shimonoseki; Yard No. 1240.

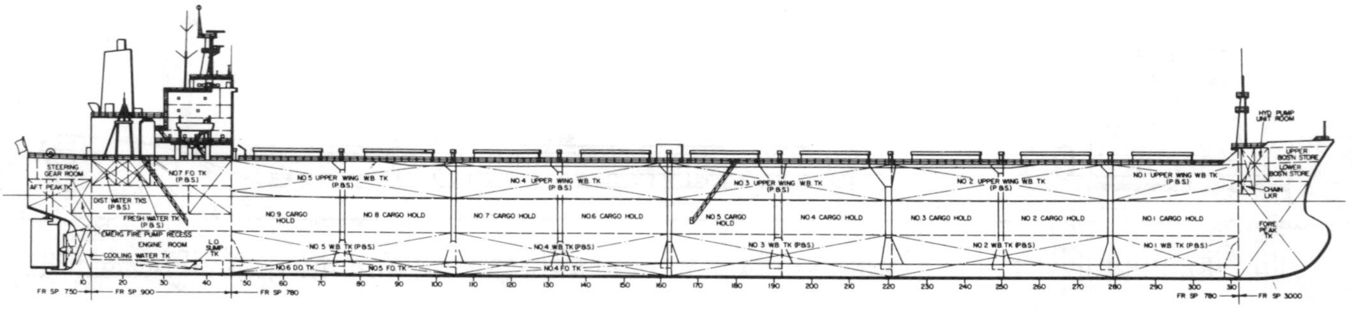

World Dulce *(Motor Ship)*

WIGGS (Br)
Type Cargo; 497 GRT; 1140 DWT; Dimensions 45.55 × 9.5 × 4.03; Machinery Twin Screw Motor 460 bhp; Engine builders Caterpillar; 7.5 Knots; Owners Eggar Forrester (Holdings) Ltd; Managers R. Lapthorn & Co. Ltd; Builders A/S Nordsovaerftet, Ringkobing; Yard No. 145.

WLADYSLAW SIKORSKI - sister of TADEUSZ KOSCIUSKO (q.v.)
Yard No. 325.

WORLD ACCLAIM (Li)
Type Bulk Carrier; 35980 GRT; 56271 DWT; Dimensions 213 (BP) × 32.2 × 12.35; Machinery Motor 13100 bhp; Engine builders B & W/Mitsui; Owners Liberian Biscayne Transportation; Managers World-Wide Shipping; Builders Koyo Dockyard Co., Mihara; Yard No. 1012.

WORLD BRIDGE (Pa)
Type Tanker; 24000 GRT; 38000 DWT; Dimensions 168 (BP) × 32.2 × 10.5; Machinery Motor 10600 bhp; Engine builders B & W/Mitsui; 14.2 Knots; Owners Spirit Co. Ltd; Builders Kanasashi Shipbuilding Co., Toyohashi; Yard No. 1303.

WORLD CLIFF (Pa)
Type Tanker; 42500 GRT; 80000 DWT; Dimensions 235 (BP) × 42 × 12.19; Machinery Motor 20500 bhp; Engine builders B & W/Hitachi; 15.6 Knots; Owners Maeda Co; Builders Imabari Shipbuilding Co., Marugame; Yard No. 1085.

WORLD DAWN - sister of WORLD ZEAL (q.v.)
Yard No. 1984.

WORLD DULCE (Pa)
Type Bulk; 63076 GRT; 1333361 DWT; Dimensions 170.9 (BB) × 43.06 × 16.35; Machinery Motor 18400 bhp; Engine builders B & W/Hitachi Zosen; 14.55 Knots; Owners Kingdom Co., S.A; Managers World Wide Shipping Agency Ltd; Builders Hitachi Zosen, Ariake Works, Nagasu; Yard No. 4642.

World Dulce *(Builders)*

WORLD EDEN (Br)
Type Bulk Carrier; 72940 GRT; 135921 DWT; Dimensions 268 (BP) × 42 × 16; Machinery Motor 18360 bhp; Engine builders B & W; Owners World Fairfax Shipping; Managers World-Wide Shipping; Builders Kawasaki Heavy Industries, Sakaide; Yard No. 1331.

WORLD GLEN (Pa)
Type Bulk; 14440 GRT; 26710 DWT; Dimensions 162 (BP) × 24.6 × 10.03; Machinery Motor 10550 bhp; Engine builders B & W/Hitachi; 14.75 Knots; Owners Prosperity Shipping Co; Builders Osaka Shipbuilding Co., Osaka; Yard No. 403.

WORLD KUDOS (Li)
Type Tanker; 40357 GRT; 79600 DWT; Dimensions 236.8 (BP) × 39.9 × 12.19; Machinery Motor 15960 bhp; Engine builders Sulzer/IHI; 14.7 Knots; Owners Gibbon Shipping Co; Builders IHI, Aioi; Yard No. 2682.

WORLD LIGHT - sister of WORLD EDEN (q.v.)
Yard No. 1330.

WORLD PRODUCT (Gr)
Type Tanker; 18300 GRT; 29900 DWT; Dimensions 162 (BP) × 26 × 10.8; Machinery Motor 12000 bhp; Engine builders B & W; 15 Knots; Owners Barking Shipping; Managers Niarchos Group; Builders Hellenic Shipyards, Skaramanga; Yard No. 1122.

WORLD ZEAL (Pa)
Type Tanker; 41911 GRT; 79900 DWT; Dimensions 243.85 (BB) × 12.19; Machinery Motor 20500 bhp; Engine builders B & W/Hitachi Zosen; Owners Renown Co., S.A; Managers World Wide Shipping Agency Ltd; Builders Imabari Zosen, Marugame; Yard No. 1083.

X

XENIA (Li)
Type Bulk; 15894 GRT; 29372 DWT; Dimensions 179.81 × 23.17 × 10.67; Machinery Motor 11400 bhp; Engine builders B & W/Hitachi; 15 Knots; Owners Manor Shipping Ltd; Builders The Hakodate Dock Co., Muroran; Yard No. 705.

Y

YAMAOKI MARU (Ja)
Type Bulk; 30000 GRT; 45200 DWT; Dimensions 182 (BP) × 32.2 × 12.10; Machinery Motor 14400 bhp; Engine builders Mitsubishi/Ube; 13.9 Knots; Owners Yamashita-Shinnihon Kisen KK; Builders Kasado Dock Co., Kudamatsu; Yard No. 326.

YAMASUGI MARU (Ja)
Type Cargo; 3702 GRT; 6436 DWT; Dimensions 97.97 (BP) × — × 6.84; Machinery Motor 3800 bhp; Engine builders Hanshin Nainenki Kogyo; Owners Yamada Kaiun K.K; Builders Higaki Zosen K.K., Imabari; Yard No. 252.

YANNIS C (Gr)
Type Bulk; 16500 GRT; 28640 DWT; Dimensions 170 (BP) 23.1 × 14.5; Machinery Motor 11400 bhp; Engine builders Sulzer/IHI; 15 Knots; Owners Archipelagos Sea Carriers Ltd; Builders The Hakodate Dock Co., Muroran; Yard No. 709.

YASHIROKAWA MARU (Ja)
Type Bulk; 76500 GRT; 144590 DWT; Dimensions 268 (BP) × 43 × 16; Machinery Motor 14070 bhp; Engine builders MAN/Kawasaki; 13.1 Knots; Owners Kawasaki Kisen Kaisha; Builders Kawasaki Heavy Industries, Sakaide; Yard No. 1335.

YERAL (Pa)
14850 GRT; 24600 DWT; Dimensions 172 (BP) × 22.8 × 10.21; Machinery Motor 12000 bhp; Engine builders Sulzer/Cegielski; 15.3 Knots; Owners DAL Deutsche Afrika Linien; Builders Georgi Dimitrov Shipyard, Varna; Yard No. 144.

YIN KIM (Pa)
Type Bulk; 13913 GRT; 25845 DWT; Dimensions 178.31 (BB) × 23.09 × 9.58; Machinery Motor 9380 bhp; Engine builders B & W/Hitachi Zosen; Owners New Southseas Maritime Carriers Co. Ltd; Managers Hong Kong Borneo Shipping Co; Builders Osaka Zosensho, Osaka; Yard No. 400.

YOKOHAMA MARU (Ja)
Type Vehicle Carrier; 17400 GRT; 14500 DWT; Dimensions 180 (BP) × 32.2 × 8.2; Machinery Motor 16800 bhp; Engine builders Sulzer/Sumitomo; 19.09 Knots; Owners Nissan Motor Car Carrier Co; Builders Sumitomo Heavy Industries, Oppama; Yard No. 1088.

YOU YI 11 (RC)
Type Cargo; 3566 GRT; 4500 DWT; Dimensions 95 (BP) × 15.2 × 6; Machinery Motor 3000 bhp; Engine builders Pielstick/NKK; 13 Knots; Owners COSCO; Builders Karachi Shipyard & Eng. Works, Karachi; Yard No. 173.

YOU YI 12 - sister of YOU YI 11 (q.v.)
Yard No. 174.

YUANJIANG - sister of HUNJIANG (q.v.)
Yard No. 1414.

YUKIKAZE (Ja)
Type Tanker; 499 GRT; 1200 DWT; Dimensions 55.02 (BP) × — × 4.25; Machinery Motor 1300 bhp; Engine builders Makita Diesel; Owners Eiko Kaiun K.K; Builders Hakata Zosen K.K., Hakata; Yard No. 251.

YURA (Ja)
Type Landing Craft; 1000 GRT; 500 DWT; Machinery Twin Screw Motor 1600 bhp; Engine builders Fuji Seisakusho; Owners Govt. of Japan (Defence Agency); Builders Sasebo Heavy Industries Co. Ltd., Sasebo; Yard No. 502.

YURIY KLEMENTYEV - sister of KAPITAN VOOLENS (q.v.)
Yard No. 304.

YUSHO MARU No. 35 (Ja)
Type Cargo; 699 GRT; 2200 DWT; Dimensions 68(BP) × — × —; Machinery Motor; 2000 bhp; Engine builders Makita Diesel; Owners Daito Kaiun Sangyo K.K; Builders Miura Zosen, Saeki; Yard No. 620.

YUZURU MARU (Ja)
Type Bulk; 76773 GRT; 140086 DWT; Dimensions 260.03 (BP) × — × 16.78; Machinery Motor 18990 bhp; Engine builders MAN-/Mitsubishi; Owners Yamashita-Shinnihon Kisen, KK; Builders Namura Shipbuilding, Imari; Yard No. 851.

Z

ZAGREB (Ys)
Type Multi-purpose Cargo; 10000 GRT; 17000 DWT; Dimensions 160 (BP) × 23.5 × 9.5; Machinery Motor 11200 bhp; Engine builders B & W/Uljanik; 16.6 Knots; Owners Jugolinija; Builders Brodogradiliste "Uljanik", Pula; Yard No. 332.

ZANNIS (Gr)
Type Bulk; 22857 GRT; 39900 DWT; Dimensions 182.10 × 29.00 × 11.37; Machinery Motor 13100 bhp; Engine builders B & W/Mitsui; 16.2 Knots; Owners Belsford Shipping Corp; Builders Mitsui Eng. & S.B. Co., Ltd., Ichihara; Yard No. 1222.

ZHOB - sister of KHAIRPUR (q.v.)
Yard No. B346/04.

ZIM KEELUNG (Is)
Type Container; 29373 GRT; 29547 DWT; Dimensions 210.22 × 36.28 × 11.5; Machinery Motor 35200 bhp; Engine builders Sulzer/"De Schelde"; 22.5 Knots; Owners Zim Israel Nav. Co; Builders Van der Giessen-de Noord BV, Krimpen; Yard No. 922.

Zim Keelung *(FotoFlite)*

ZIM SAVANNAH - sister of ZIM KEELUNG (q.v.)
Yard No. 923.

THE RECOGNITION SYSTEM

The system used in this book is designed to identify either individual ships or a group of very similar or identical ships.

The basis of the system is the noting of three features:

1) The PROFILE—definition: The funnel position (amidships or aft) and the arrangement of the superstructure.

2) The SEQUENCE—definition: The noting of certain prescribed features on the ship in the order in which they occur.

3) The HULL FORM—definition: The arrangement of castles, or islands, on the hull.

These features are reported in a simple abbreviated form which is described in the following pages, along with a fuller description of the coding features.

An important fact to remember is that, although many standard nautical terms are used in the system, they are often defined in a very different way. The term HULL FORM is a good example of this: Technically, it refers to the actual shape of the hull, but, in the recognition system, it is the arrangement of islands. All the features used in the system are classified purely by *appearance* and *never by function.* This is one reason why many everyday nautical terms, such as mast or kingpost, have been re-defined for the purposes of the recognition system.

To gain a thorough knowledge of the system it is essential to go through the pages of this manual slowly and in strict order. Learn the definitions and the methods as they are set out and, more importantly, apply them when coding a vessel. Although this may seem unnecessarily pedantic, the appearance of different ships can vary so much that it is left, finally, to the judgement of the observer to decide how a particular vessel should be coded.

The number of elements in the system has deliberately been kept to a minimum, in order to make it easily memorable. In the sequence, for example, there are only six classifications; kingpost, mast, crane, funnel, gantry and ramp. With the abundance of ships and the increasing diversity in design it is often very difficult to classify these features. By following the prescribed method it should be possible to decide on a classification but, if it is impossible to decide, the solution is to give an *alternative sequence.* Alternative codings can also, of course, be applied to the profile and the full form. Many of the vessels appearing in this book appear under two, or sometimes more, codings.

THE PROFILE

Definition: The Profile consists of two separate elements: The funnel position (amidships or aft) and the arrangement of the superstructure.

It is very important that the two elements (funnel and superstructure) are considered independently. In other words, after the funnel position has been decided it must be ignored when deciding the superstructure arrangement.

FUNNEL POSITION

There are two positions; amidships and aft.
Note that the ¾-aft position is regarded as funnel amidships if *any part* of the funnel touches it. Remember that the terms 'amidships' and 'aft' may be defined differently when used in another context.

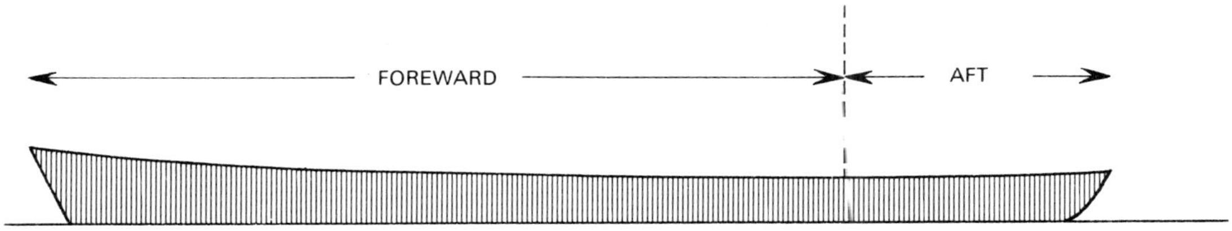

FUNNEL POSITION

SUPERSTRUCTURE

For the purposes of classifying a ship's profile, the superstructure is only the main bulk of accomodation, bridge, engine-room casing etc. Smaller structures, such as mast houses, docking bridges and islands, are not considered as superstructure. Although there can be confusion between islands and superstructure (this is also mentioned in the section on HULL FORM), islands apear as integral parts of the hull although they are raised above the upper deck.

DETERMINING THE PROFILE

There are *five* Profiles in the system.
They are reported as P1, P2, P3, P4 and P5.
The first two Profiles, P1 and P2, have the funnel amidships and the other profiles, P3, P4 and P5, have the funnel aft. Having decided whether the funnel is amidships or aft, the observer then looks at the superstructure to determine the actual Profile. The different arrangements are best shown by drawings.

P1

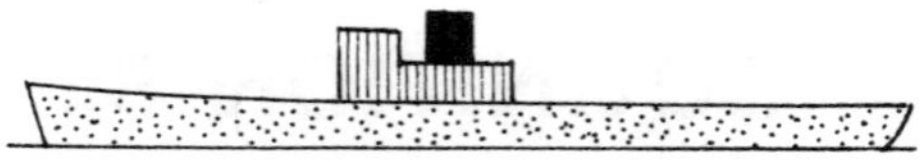

P2

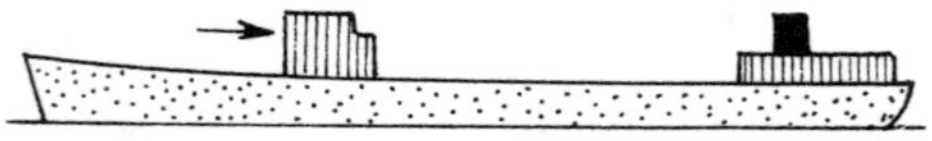

P3

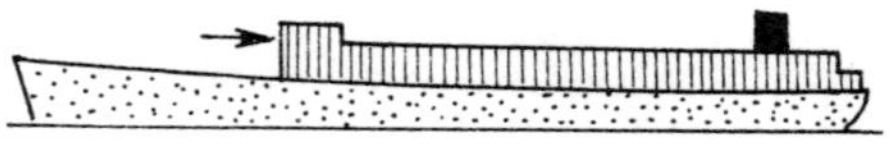

P3

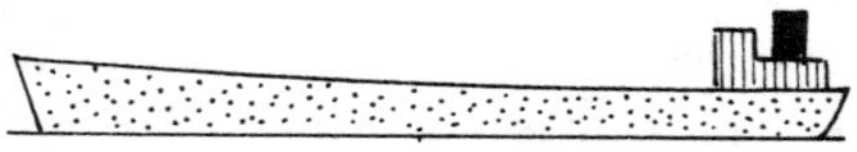

P4

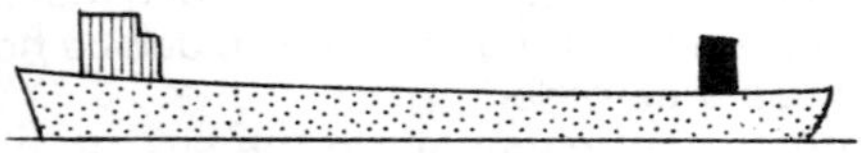

P5

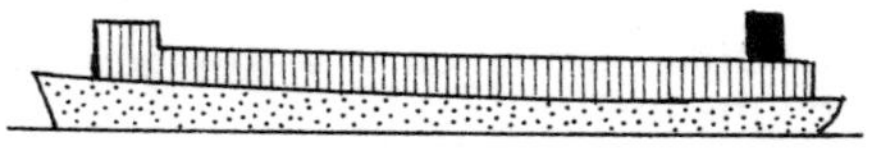

P5

IMPORTANT NOTE. The superstructure is analysed in a different way in the two groups of Profiles. In the funnel-amidships group it is the number of blocks of superstructure that determines the profile, regardless of where that superstructure is situated. In the funnel-aft Profiles, however, the distinguishing feature is the position of the bridge-front (foreward, amidships or aft) that determines the profile. The number of blocks of superstructure is irrelevant.

PROBLEMS IN POSITIONING THE FUNNEL OR SUPERSTRUCTURE ACCURATELY

As the observer normally has to judge by eye where the ¾-aft line falls on a ship, it is obvious that it may be very difficult to decide exactly where the funnel or bridge-front falls. If the observer is undecided the answer is, as stated previously, *give alternative Profiles.*

WORKED EXAMPLES

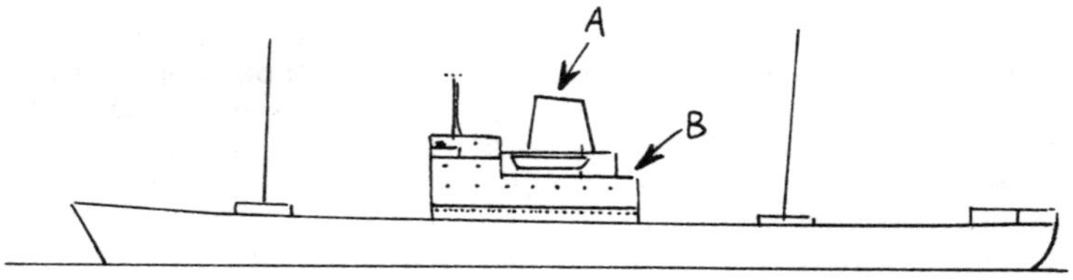

EXAMPLE ONE
1) Where is the funnel positioned?
The funnel (A) is positioned amidships.
Therefore, the profile is either P1 or P2.
2) How is the superstructure arranged?
The superstructure (b) is in one block.
Conclusion: The funnel is amidships; the superstructure is in one block, therefore the Profile is P2.

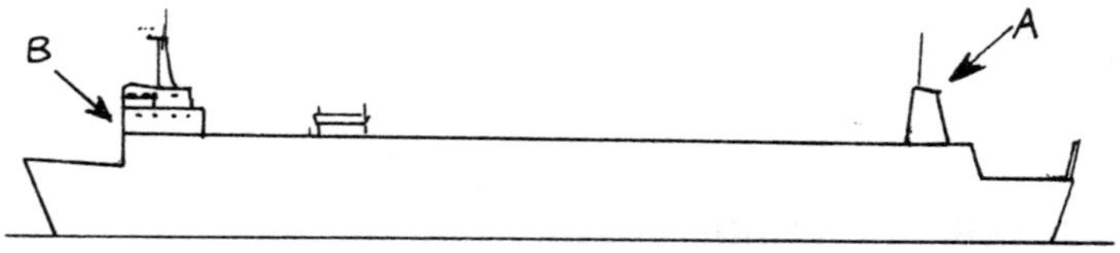

EXAMPLE TWO
1) Where is the funnel positioned?
The funnel (A) is positioned aft.
Therefore, the profile is P3, P4 or P5.
2) Where does the bridge-front fall?
The bridge-front falls foreward.
Conclusion: The funnel is aft; the bridge-front falls foreward, therefore the Profile is P5.

THE SEQUENCE

Definition: The noting of certain prescribed features on the ship in the order in which they occur (working foreward to aft).

There are six features which are coded as follows:

feature	*reported as*	*feature*	*reported as*
Kingpost	K	Funnel	F
Mast	M	Gantry	N
Crane	C	Ramp	R

Apart from the mast and the kingpost, which will be dealt with separately, all these features can be easily identified. It is important to remember that with all cargo gear it is the upright part and not the lifting device, derrick, jib etc., which is considered the principal feature.

The following drawings give the basic shapes of the sequence features:

The funnel is normally a prominent and obvious feature, and it has not been illustrated.

Cranes

Although they can be very similar to kingposts, cranes differ principally by the fact that they have a *width* as well as height, whereas the kingpost is merely an upright pole. This is well illustrated in a later section where an upright which is technically a crane has the appearance of a kingpost. Very small cranes, such as those installed to handle small lifeboats or liferafts, are usually too small to code.

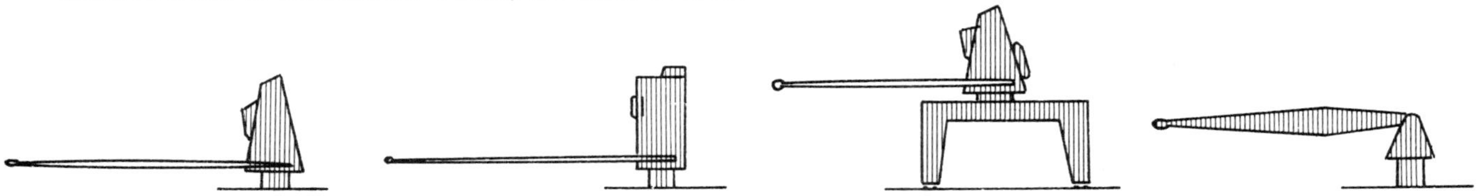

Gantries

As the drawings show, there are a wide variety of designs although the commonest is the one which gives the appearance of a "goalpost" from the side. A crane mounted on a gantry is always coded C, as illustrated in the crane drawings.

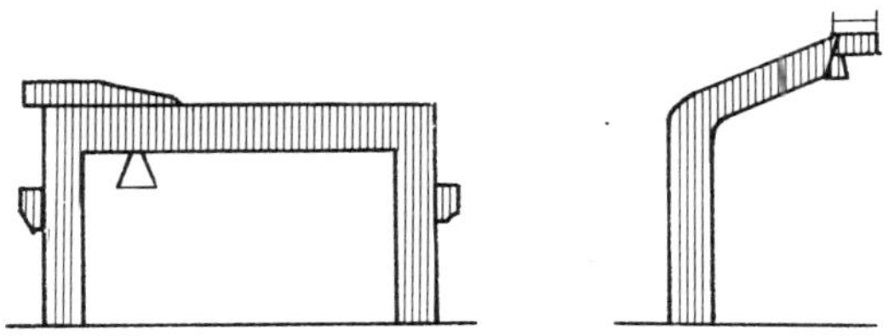

Ramps

Only the increasingly popular quarter and stern slewing ramps. The conventional type of stern ramp will simply appear as an upright if it rises above the upper deck or superstructure and may be coded as K or M, according to its height. Codeable ramps can be seen occasionally in the foreward parts of some vessels.

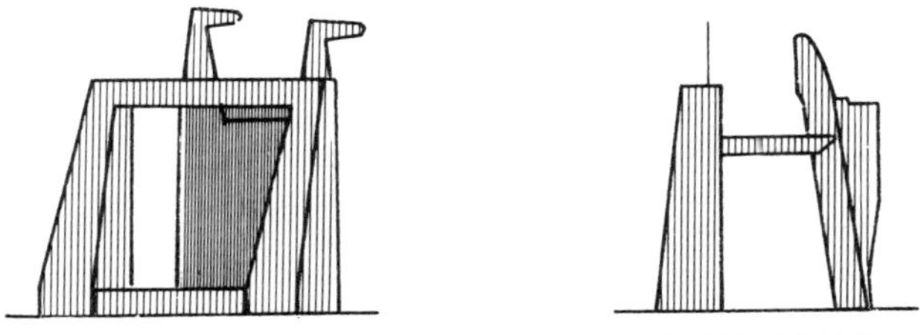

QUARTER RAMP SLEWING RAMP

Superimposed Features

If one coding feature is mounted on another the topmost feature is always coded first; e.g. a mast from a funnel is coded MF and a mast from a ramp is coded MR.

MASTS AND KINGPOSTS

Masts and kingposts must be considered together as they are both basically uprights poles. They are distinguished by their relative heights. Do not take into account any additions to the upright, such as derricks or a gaff, for example, when deciding upon a classification. The radar mast from the bridge and a mast from the funnel are *always* coded M. As with all the features in the sequence, it is important to forget their technical function and only remember how they are defined within the coding system. In some older vessels, kingposts are often arranged in pairs. These are coded as a *single* K as a ship is always coded from a perfect broadside view, which must be judged if the vessel is not actually seen broadside. This applies to every aspect of the coding system.

A larger selection of more detailed drawings of masts, kingposts, cranes etc. are given in a later section.

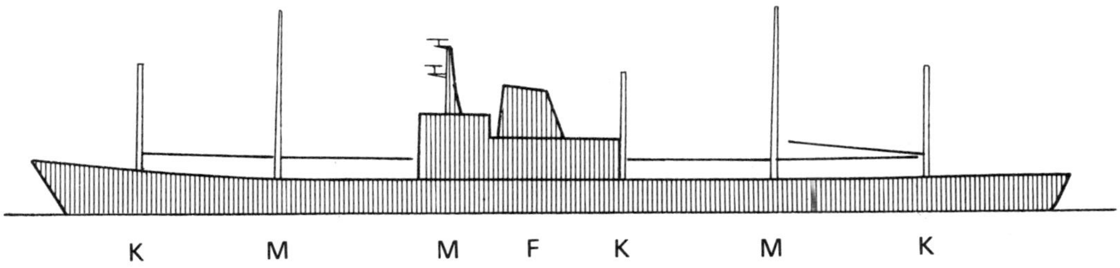

HULL FORM

Definition: The arrangement of castles or islands, on the hull. The reporting method is simple: The castles are numbered: I—Forecastle, 2—Midcastle, 3—Poop and the letter H is placed before the numerals; e.g. H13, H2 etc. A flush-decked vessel is simply reported as H.

There are a number of possible combinations, the following illustrations show the main ones:

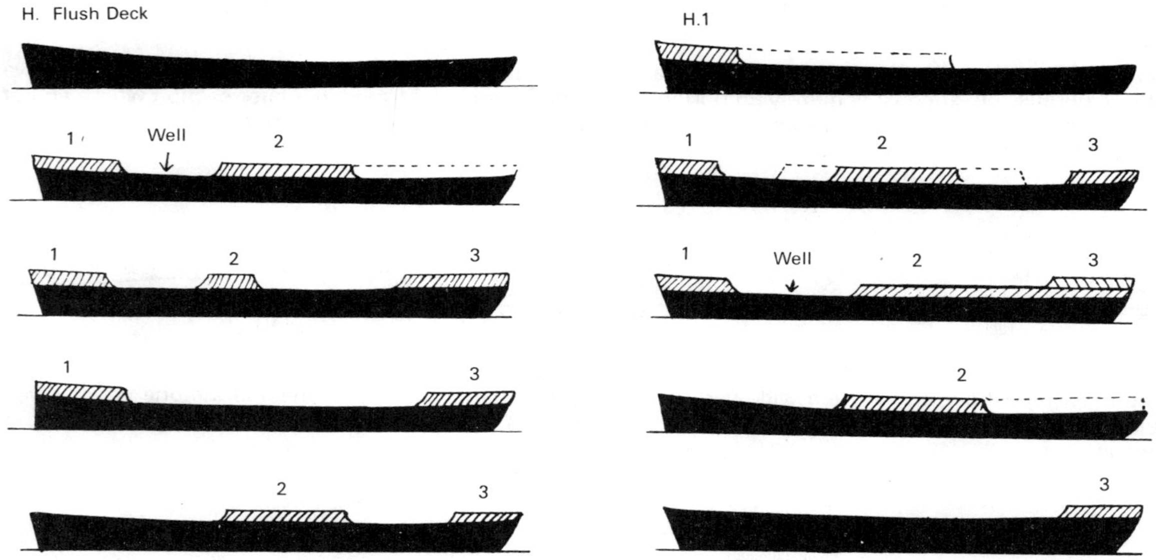

It is sometimes difficult to distinguish islands from superstructure. Islands can be simply defined as structures which stand proud from the upperdeck although incorporated into the shape of the hull. They are always solid although they may have portholes. Problems can arise when superstructure is built out practically to the hull sides and can, perhaps, only be identified by openings such as large windows. Passenger ships can be particularly difficult in this respect. The height of an island is normally about the same as one deck of superstructure, i.e. about 8′. However, there are exceptions: The modern ro/ro ship, for example, often has several decks above the upper-deck which are solidly plated and meet the sides of the hull. They give the appearance of very high islands and should be coded as such.

Other confusions in Hull Forms

As can be seen from the drawings of hull forms shown previously, the length of island can vary considerably. A forecastle may extend almost to the stern of a vessel but it is still reported as H1 although it may seem to be combined with a midcastle. The same would apply to a midcastle which runs into a poop, it is coded H2. This is only the case, however, if the island begins on, or forward of, the amidships line. If it begins aft of amidships it is regarded as a poop, H3. If an island begins near the stem but *not at it*, it cannot be regarded as a forecastle but must be a midcastle, H2. Although the islands are called forecastle and midcastle, this does not necessarily indicate their position on the hull. The only definite rules that can be made are that the forecastle must *begin at the stem* and the poop must end at, or very near, the stern.

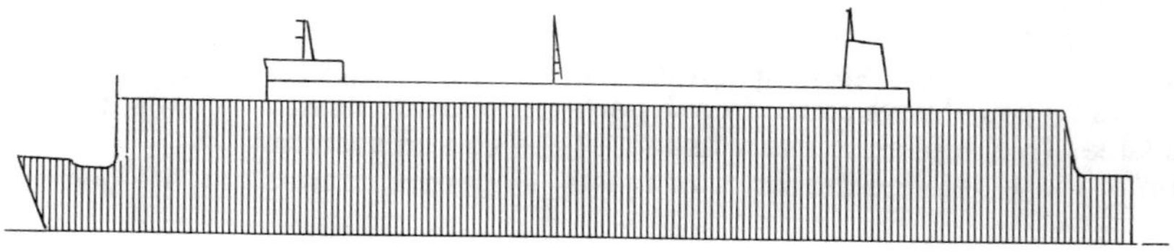

H2

H2

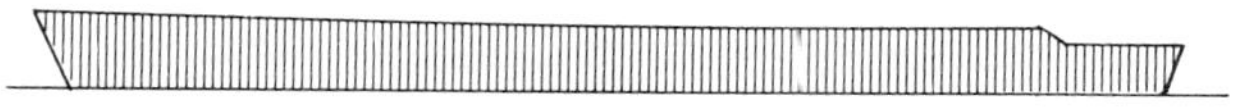

H1

Do not confuse islands with *bulwark plating.* Plating is only about half the height of an average island and should be easily distinguished.

Long hances, see "Glossary" for definition, often disguise an island and may give the impression of slighly exaggerated sheer. A hull of this type must be regarded as flush-decked, H.

FORECASTLE

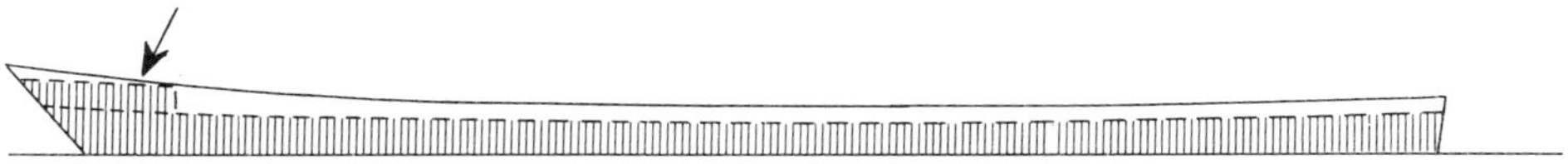

H

Another problem is the *trunk-deck,* a common feature on smaller tankers. If a vessel with a trunk-deck is seen silhouetted it may appear to be flush-decked. If the trunk-deck can be seen the islands should be coded, even though the trunk may be the same height as the islands.

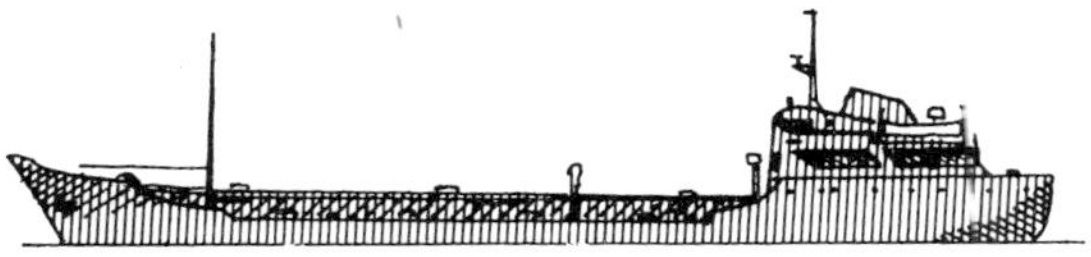

TRUNK DECK TANKER

ADDITIONAL RECOGNITION FEATURES

The next few pages contain features which, although not used in the body of this book, can provide useful recognition information beyond the basic features of Profile, Sequence and Hull Form.

Bows (B)

Actually *Stems* but coded *Bows* (B) to avoid confusion with *Sterns* (S)

For recognition purposes Bows or Sterns are grouped into three classes for coding although there are variations or modifications of most of them.

B.1 Straight, Plumb or Vertical. The oldest type which offers resistance to the seas.

B.2 Raking or Sloping and Curved and Raking. Angle varies greatly and Clipper or Cable bows come within this group.

B.3 Spoon, an outward curve, all rounded and not 'sitting' on the water, and **Icebreaking,** also with an outward curve but angular and straighter. Not always noticeable if ship is laden or in heavy seas.

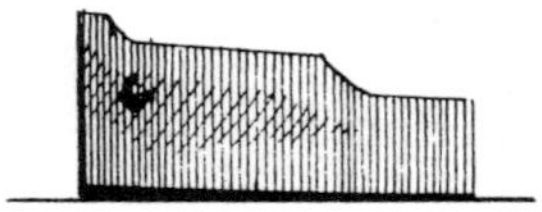

B1

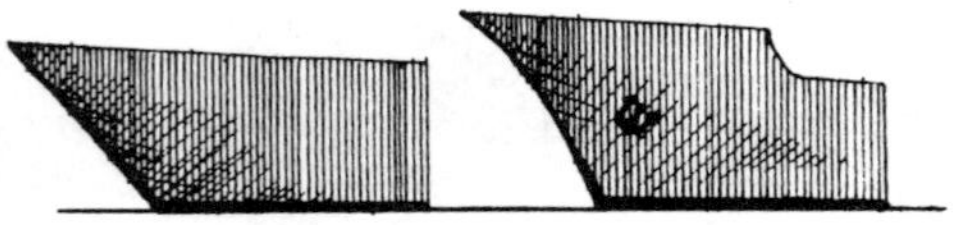

B2

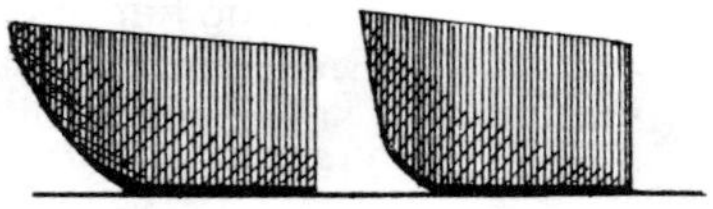

B3

Sterns (S)

Classified and reported in three groups although there are a few variations from the basic types.

S.1 Counter or Cut Away. The older type. Second drawing represents a tug or trawler type with deep overhanging counter.

S.2 Cruiser. Angle varies. There is a flat Transom stern but silhouetted it appears little different.

S.3 Cruiser Spoon. Particularly a feature of German or Russian built ships. The second drawing shows the stern of a typical Roll-on/Roll-off vessel.

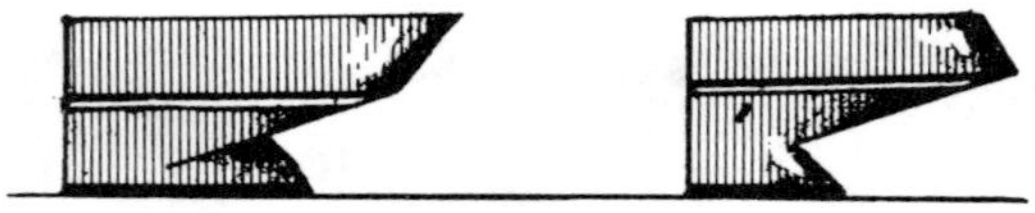

S1

S2

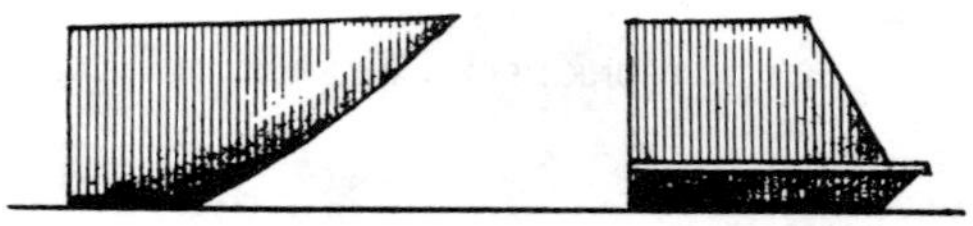

S3

1

2

3

4

ILLUSIONS
A ship in heavy weather may need some watching.
The drawings show the same ship pitching heavily when bows and sterns might be wrongly reported—S1 instead of S2 in Number 2 and B3 instead of B1 as in Number 4.

POSITIONING

The above view shows that ships with varying appearance can have the same basic reporting sequence. This can be overcome by dividing the ship into twelve equal parts and estimating each feature against the scale.

This is a most important step in identification for there are many ships with the same sequence and hull form but the positions and lengths vary considerably. The length of the vessel is divided into twelve equal parts, numbered 0 at the stem and 12 at the stern. Features which fall between dividing lines can be suffixed with a fraction, e.g. the kingpost on the vessel drawn below falls at $6\frac{3}{4}$. Any fraction can be used, according to the judgement of the observer.

The ship shown below is coded:

P4; KKMFK; H13;
F'clse length 1 - $1\frac{1}{2}$; Aftercastle length $8\frac{3}{4}$ - 12;
Mast at $9\frac{1}{2}$ Kingposts at 2, $6\frac{3}{4}$ and $10\frac{3}{4}$;
Superstructure lengths (four decks)
$9\frac{1}{3}$ - 11, $9\frac{1}{3}$ - 10,
$9\frac{1}{3}$ - 10, $9\frac{1}{3}$ - $9\frac{3}{4}$;
Funnel at $10\frac{1}{4}$.

Note: The superstructure decks are noted from the lower to the top and the funnel position is for the front of the funnel, at the base.

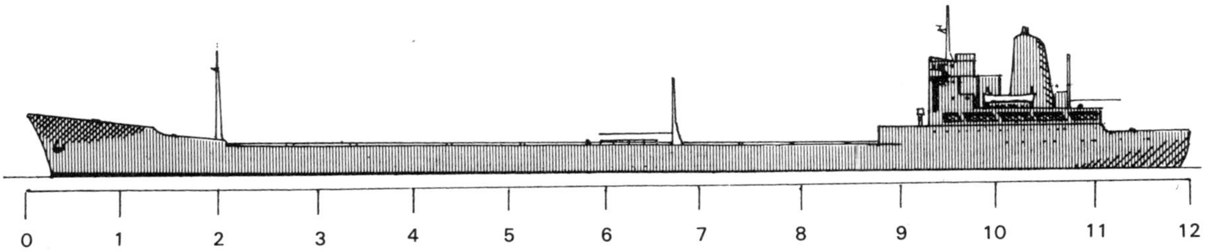

Masts (M)

Parts of a Mast

Very tall masts or masts with table tops very high up are common features of may German or Dutch built ships.

Masts are named from foreward: **Foremast, Mainmast, Mizzen** (or **Aftermast**).

Technically a mast is any pole set along the *centre-line* but for recognition purposes it is the *tallest* pole in a ship, either by itself or by reason of its being set on superstructure which *raises it above all other uprights,* such as a signal mast on the bridge.

A *Lower Mast* with topmast lowered is coded as a King-post.

Radar Masts are only coded if they are sufficiently tall or thick to show in the Distant View.

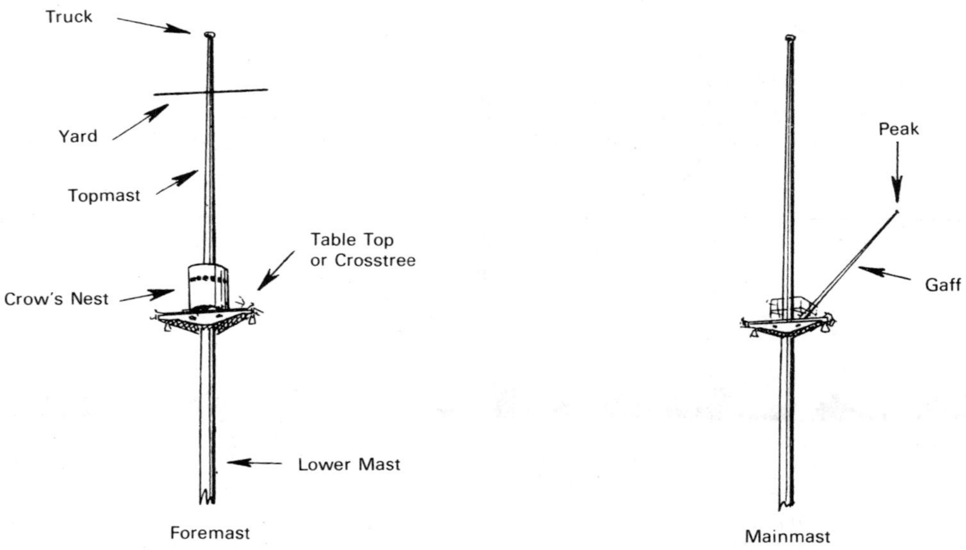

Types of Mast

There are many types of mast today and whenever possible in the Medium View, M should be amplified by more detail, such as M(GP) for a Goal-Post mast.

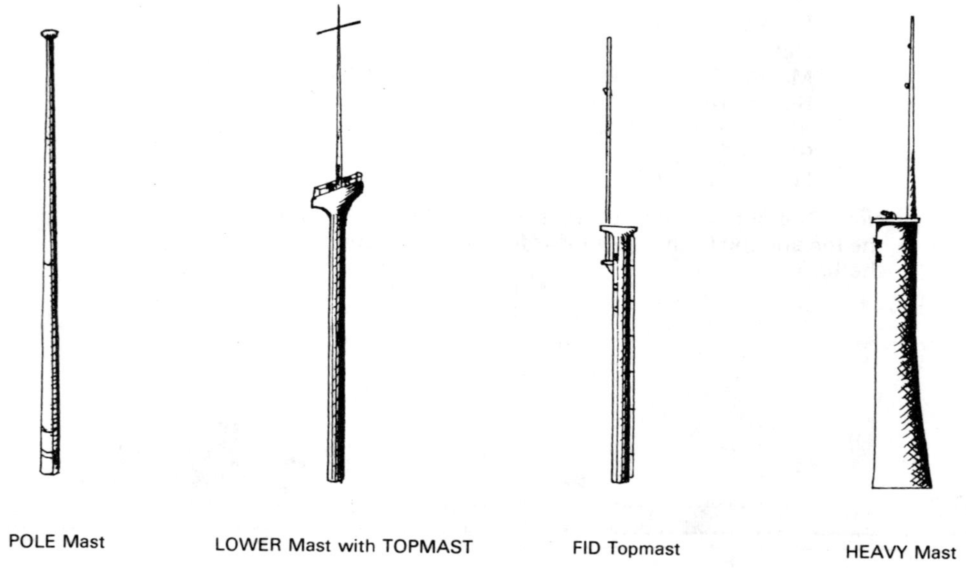

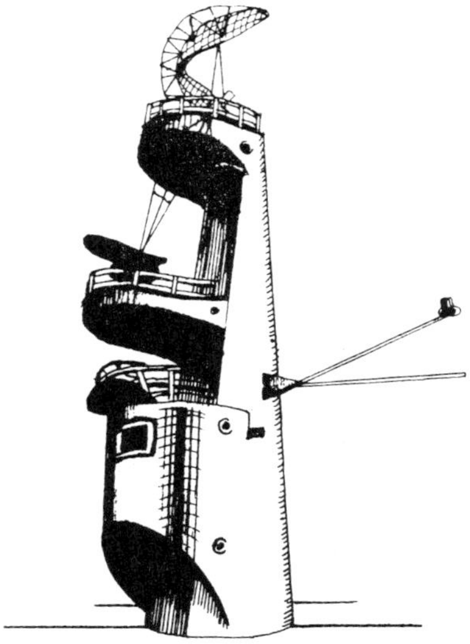

HEAVY 'Military' Mast fitted with variations in many ships. Scanners and look-out platforms incorporated in one structure.

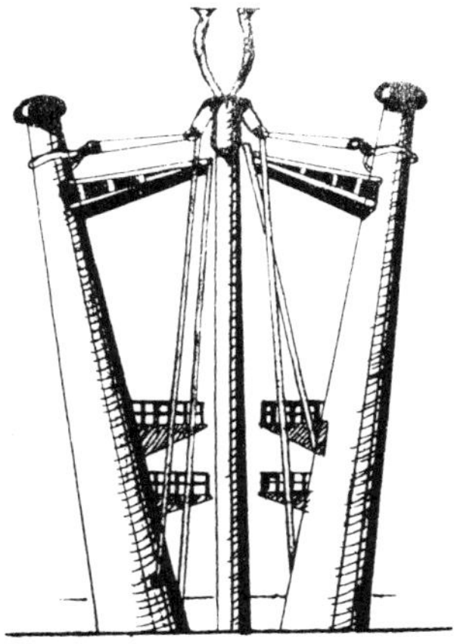

FRONT VIEW of STULCKEN Mast for very heavy lifts up to 300 tons or more. When seen broadside looks like a thick lower mast with topmast. Derrick may be stowed vertically or at an angle

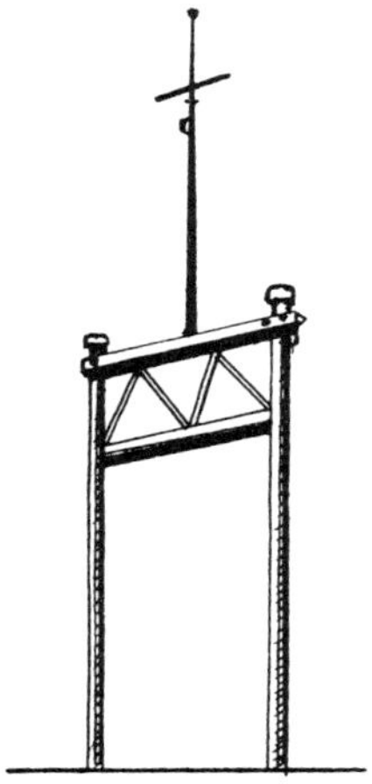

GOAL-POST Mast. M(GP)

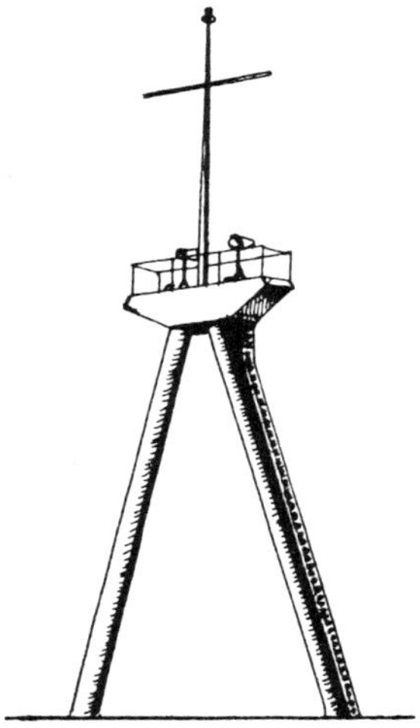

BI-POD Mast. M(B)

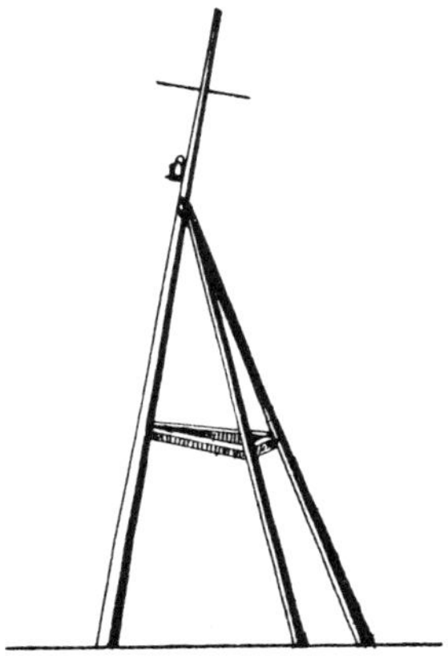

TRI-POD Mast. M(T)

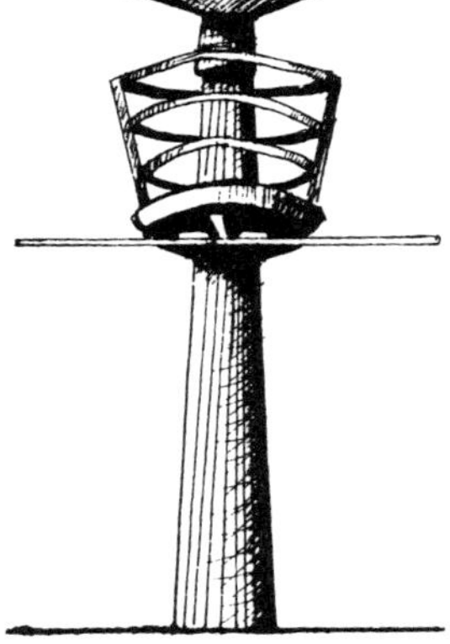

RADAR Mast or Pole. M(RP)

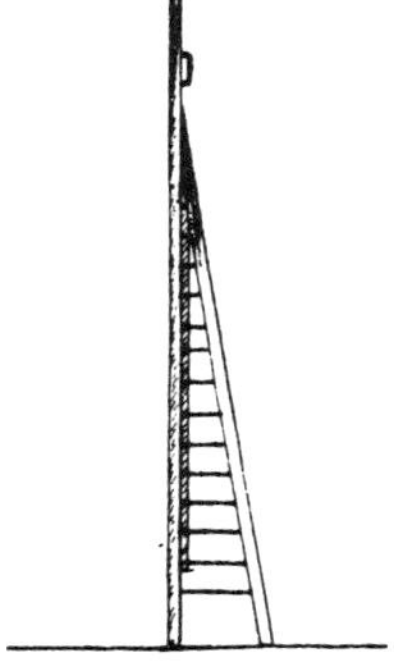

TOWER or LATTICE Mast

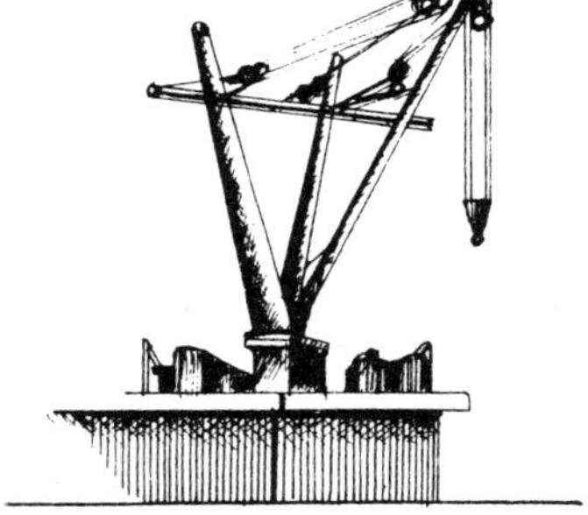

'Y' Mast

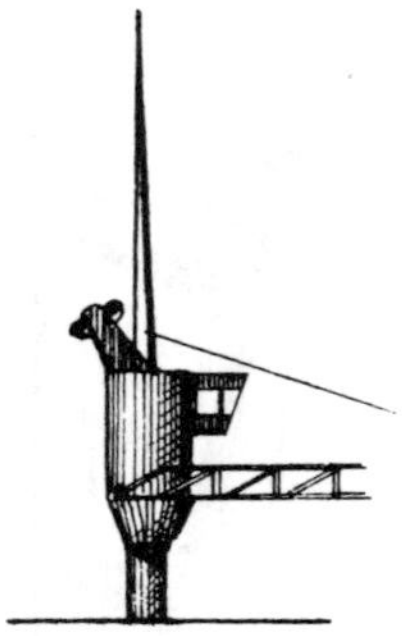

MAST from CRANE. M(C)

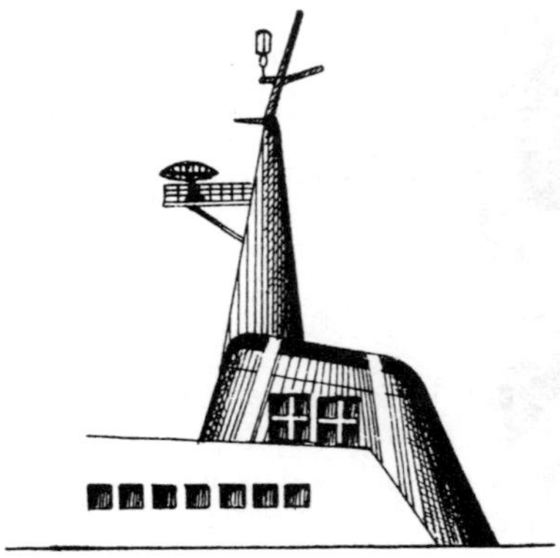

MAST from FUNNEL

Kingposts (K)
Although coded K, Kingposts are also known as Derrick Posts or Samson Posts.

They are generally similar to the lower portions of masts and indeed may well *be* lower masts with topmasts lowered.

They may be on the Centre Line (when this should be reported C.L.) or in pairs, three abreast or even four abreast. If a pair is joined it is coded as Goal-Post Kingpost - K(GP). They are erected near hatchways.

A **Kingpost Abreast** a mast or Funnel is not coded but is reported in the Close View

Hatch Gear for working the hatches may look like a Kingpost and if so, is reported as K.

Crutches for securing Derricks in coasters may, in a small ship, be proportionately large and should be reported as K.

Cranes may sometimes look like Kingposts, especially with Jibs down and may be coded K, if uncertain.

Kingposts rising from superstrucutre such as those near funnels on many tankers or bulk carriers are coded K, because although placed high, they are in themselves short and lower than the Mast.

Many of the Mast types are seen also in Kingposts - for example Bi-pods, Heavy, etc. are coded in the same manner: K(B), *K's against Bridge front* are not easy to distinguish.

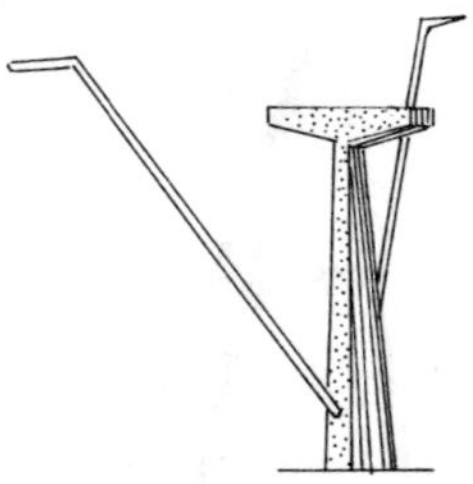

Centre-line LOWER MAST type

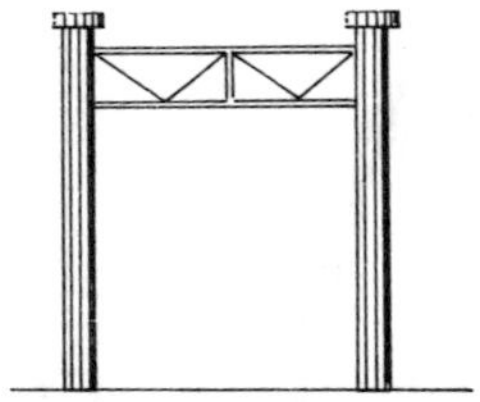

GOAL-POST Type

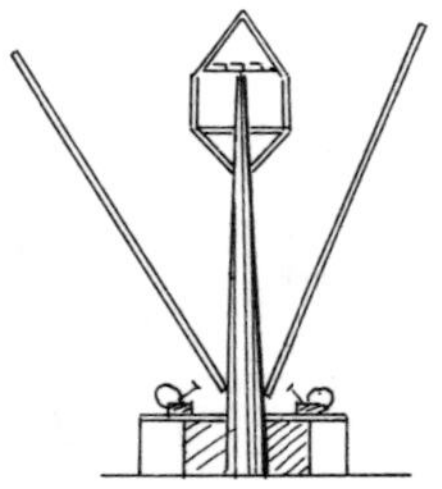

HALLEN Type (Variations) modern feature

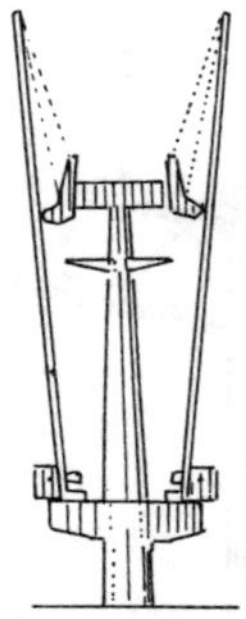

LIEBHERR CRANE - coded as K

Cranes (C)
Cranes, while always a feature in a few classes of ships are now rapidly supplanting Masts, Kingposts and Derricks.

Some are very large indeed but when the jib is stowed it is not always easy to distinguish them from Kingposts.

A further difficulty is that many run along the deck on rails and so make the classifying of ships according to the **Position** of leading features difficult.

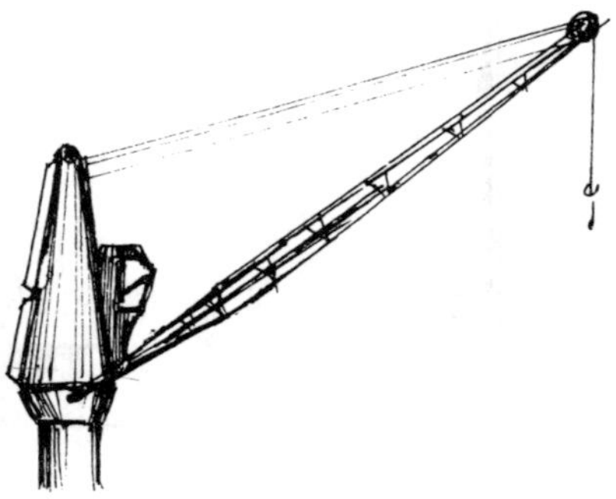

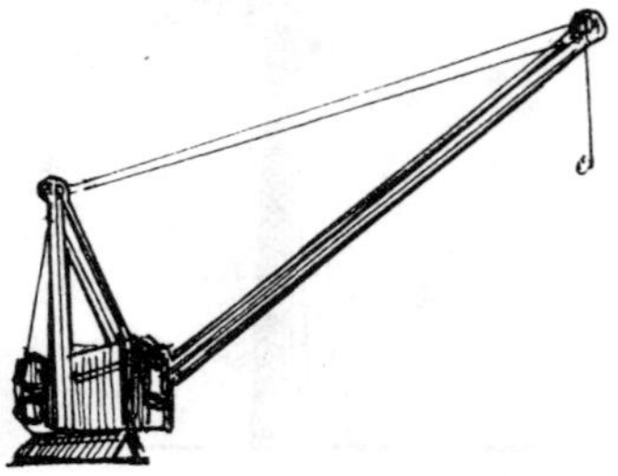

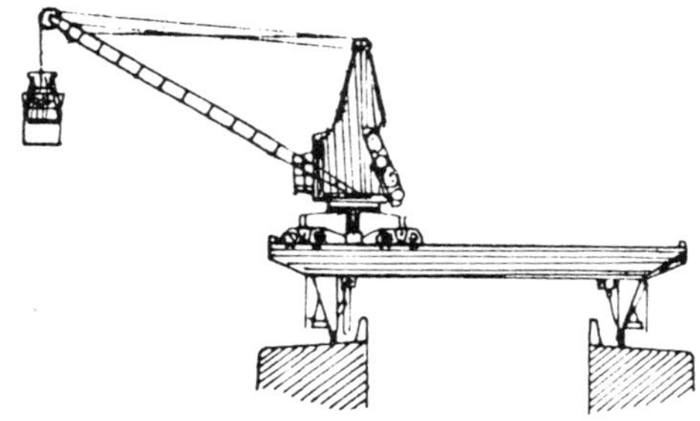

GRAB CRANE on Gantry. Coded as C not N.

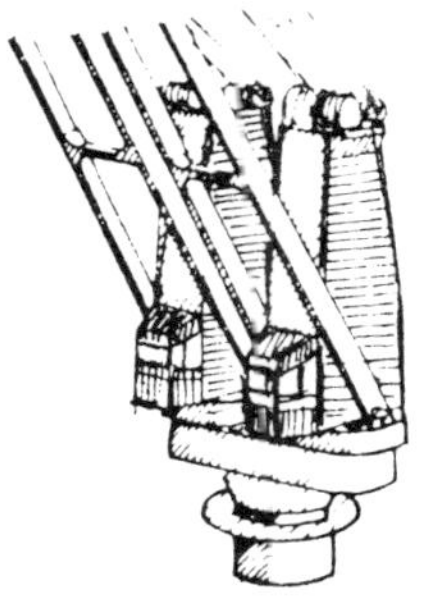

TANDEM CRANE. Each can swing on its individual axis or they can operate as a pair and swing on large base. Usually stowed amidships but may be seen fore and aft. Coded C or CC according to position.

Gantries (N)
Coded N so as not to confuse with Goal-Post Kingpost.

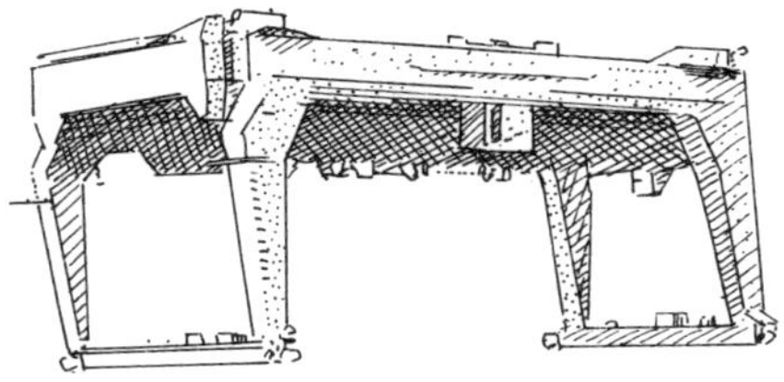

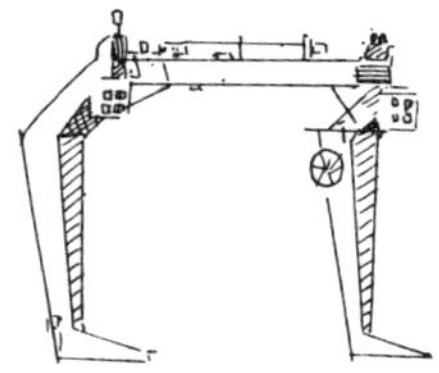

FUNNELS (F)

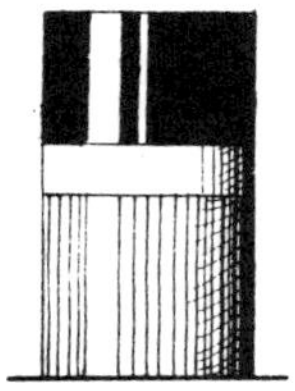

VERTICAL

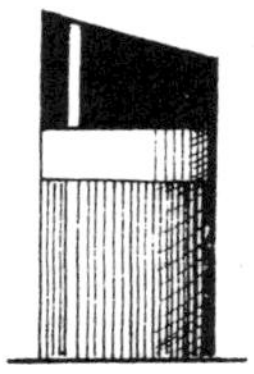

RAKING TOP

RAKING

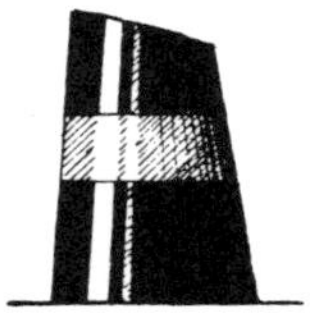

CONICAL

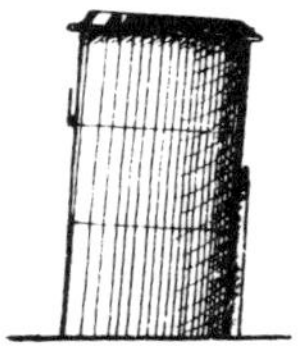

COWL TOP

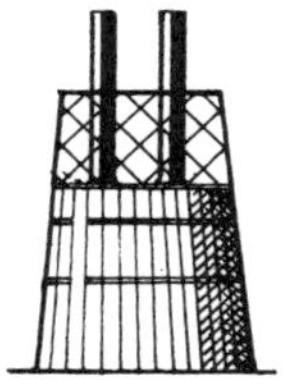

LATTICE WORK

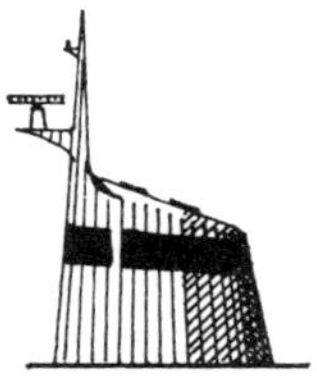

MAST AND FUNNEL COMBINED

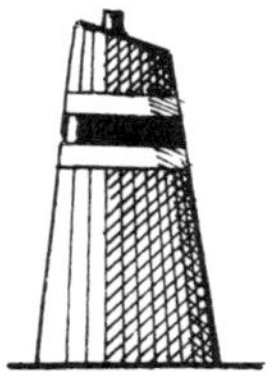

NARROW CONICAL

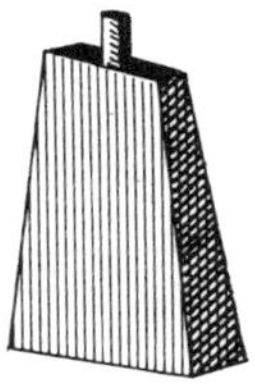

ANGULAR

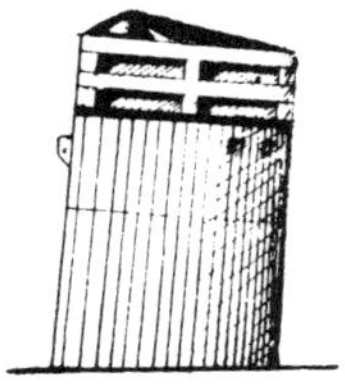

THORNYCROFT

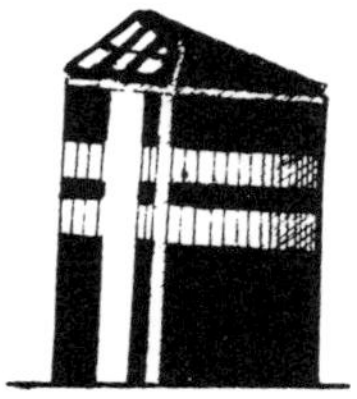

CLINKER SCREEN

CLINKER SCREEN (Small)

WING (US. Type)

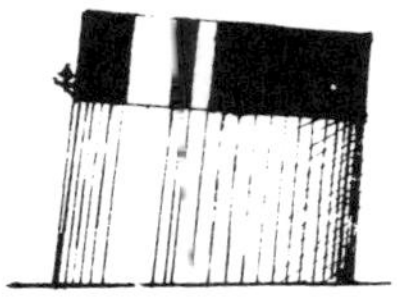

'MOTOR SHIP' Type

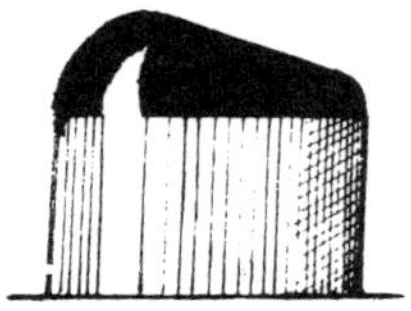

DOME TOP

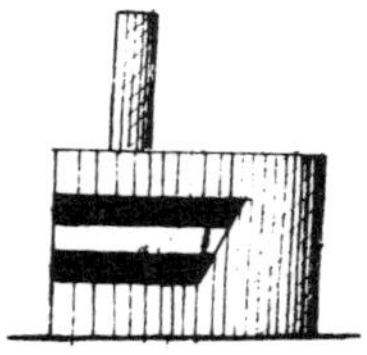

PROJECTING PIPE (Vary)

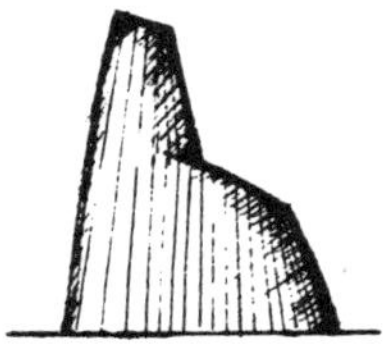

BOTTLE Type

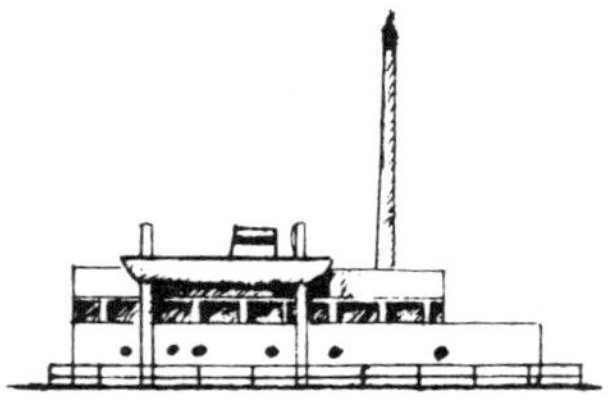

'KINGPOST' Type (Coded K or F/K))

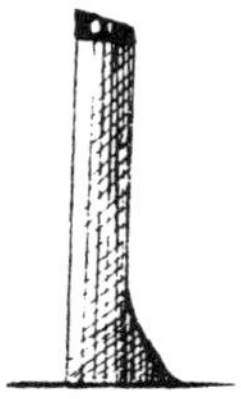

MATCH-STICK Type (Common in Tankers and usually abreast)

FERRY Type. One on either side of superstructure.

FUNNEL and BRIDGE merged.
A very common type in coasters.

Ventilators (V)
There are many different types and the cowls vary greatly in appearance. Some are characteristic of a particular nationality of build but this is no guide to recognition.

Very conspicuous ventilators and their positions are recorded.

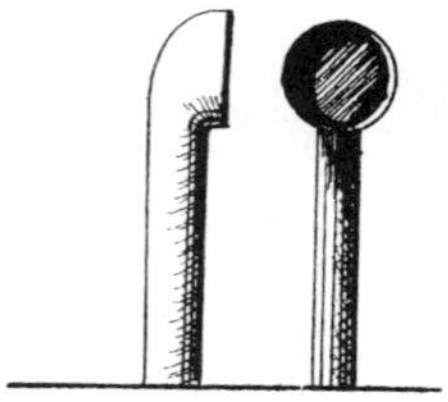

COWL

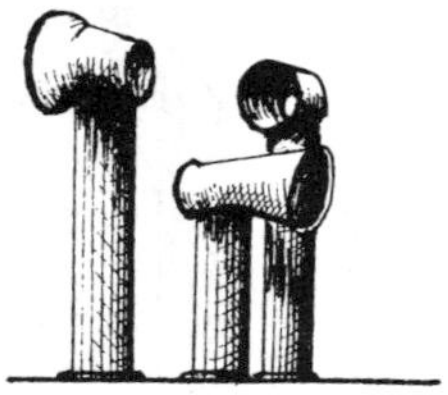

BONNET (German)

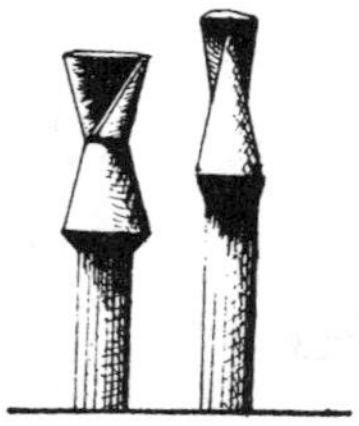

HOUR GLASS or
THISTLE (Finnish)

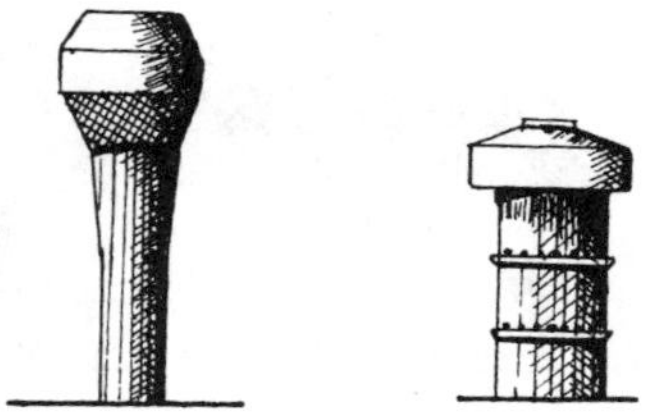

MUSHROOM (British)

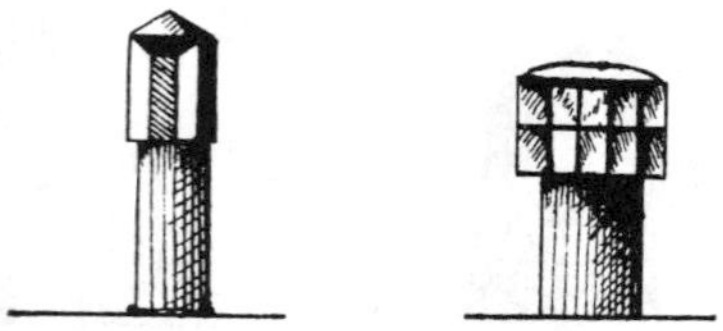

RATTLE (German)

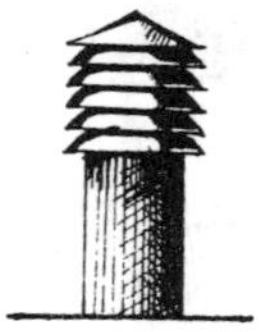

Scandinavian

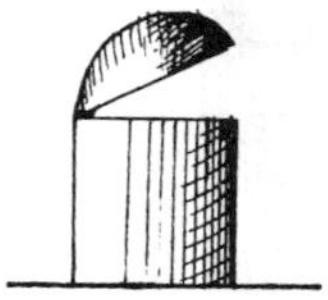

BOX (French)

SQUARE (British)

CANVAS WINDSAIL. In hot weather additional ventilation may be obtained by fixing canvas windsail, secured to the rigging.

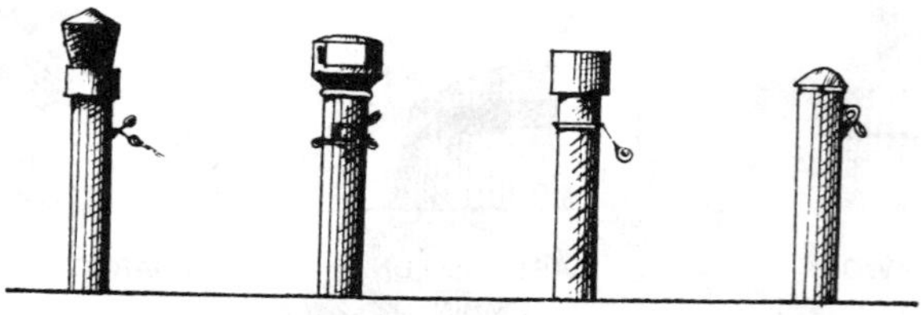

Ventilator tops to Kingposts

Deck Houses, Mast Houses or Winch Houses (DH)
These may be quite small, in which case they will be merely recorded as being in a position corresponding to one of the numbers in the 0 to 12 scale. They may, however, be sufficiently large to occupy a full sub-division or even more.

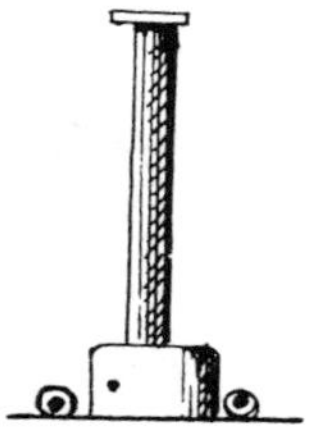

SMALL (Common)

LARGE (Common)

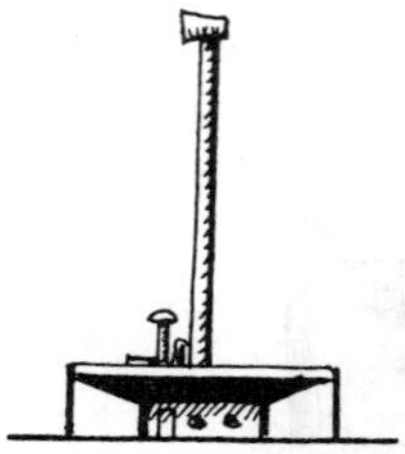

GERMAN TYPE

Heavy or Jumbo Derrick (HD)
Lashed vertically to mast or kingpost and should be reported. Sometimes mistaken for topmasts but as they stand away from mast quite considerably, the mistake should not be made.
Blocks and tackle protected by canvas when not in use.
See also Stulcken Derrick.

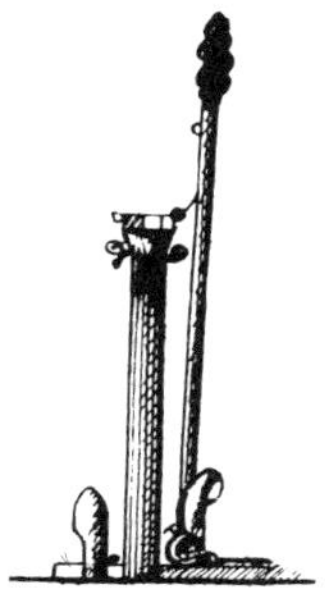

Lifeboats and Davits
Lifeboats are normally stowed on the boat deck or highest deck. Numbers give an indication of size of ship.

They are stowed under a variety of davit types but the two main ones are (1), those that sit direct on to the deck and (2), those with headroom beneath.

A small **'Accident boat'** is usually kept swung outboard in the vicinity of the bridge.

Gravity Davits

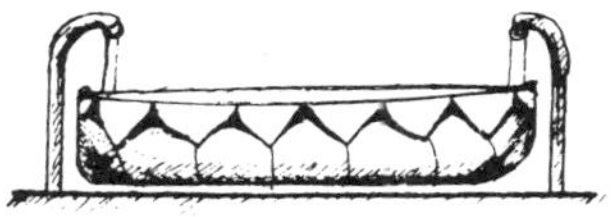

Goose or Swan Neck
(Boat on deck)

Nested Boats
(On deck)

Gravity Davits
(Above deck)

TONNAGE AND SIZE

Perhaps the most difficult thing in merchant ship identification is to form an estimation of size, whether it be of tonnage or of length. There is absolutely nothing in external appearance to guarantee either. Ships of almost identical outline may have huge variations and particularly is this so with engines-aft types.

Only experience can help to give a 'feeling' as to whether a ship is large or small and a graph of tonnage to length will only possibly give an approximately 70% accurate result to within 500 or more tons either way.

Merchant ships are shown in registers by **Gross Tonnage** and **Nett Tonnage** and these are measurements of **Volume** and *not* of **Weight.** 100 cubic feet of permanently enclosed space equalling 1 Gross ton.

Displacement and **Deadweight Tonnages** *are* a measurement in Tons **Weight** and the accompanying diagrams will show the differences.

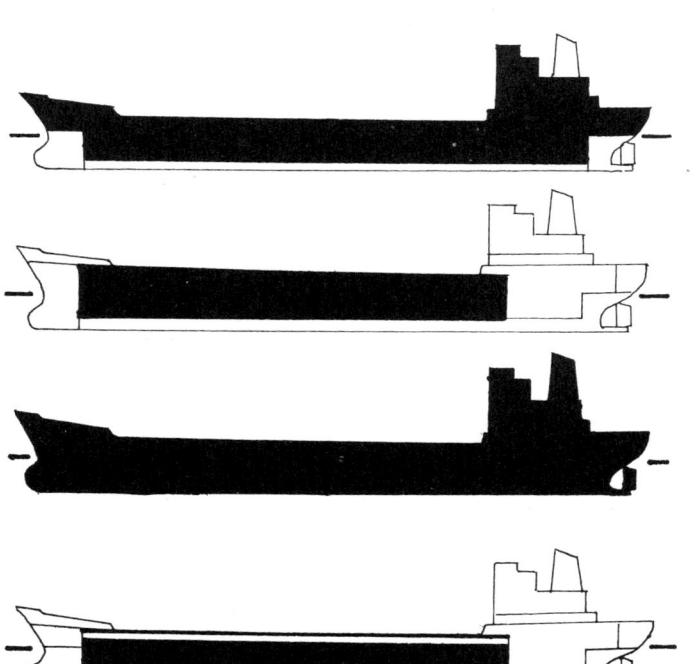

Gross Tonnage
Total *volume* of enclosed space. 100 Cubic feet = 1 Ton.

Nett Tonnage
The earning capacity. Same as Gross less crew quarters, boiler and engine rooms, fuel spaces, etc. Dock, canal and harbour dues are paid on this tonnage.

Displacement Tonnage
Total *weight* of ship and her contents which varies in light and loaded state but as registered usually means an average.

Deadweight Tonnage
Weight of cargo, fuel, etc. required to bring vessel from light to loaded or full displacement. Deadweight tonnage is often expressed in Tonnes. This is a metric unit equal to 1000 Kilograms, making it practically identical to the imperial ton. (1 tonne = 0.984 imperial tons)

A GUIDE TO AGE AND APPEARANCE

A Guide to Age

External appearance cannot be accepted as a reliable indication of age. Constructional features still regarded as 'modern' may be seen in ships built twenty or thirty years ago, while those of much more recent date may embody a few which have remained unchanged over the same period.

There has been an acceleration in recent years, largely on account of economic pressure and an urge towards fashion resulting in a somewhat dull uniformity, especially in passenger ships and tankers or bulk carriers.

Again, there are certain types of specialist ships which have been introduced only recently. Others have been rebuilt so that one may see a vessel with a heavily raking stem and modernized superstructure with an older counter stern, and engine aft types have had the bridge removed right aft.

The following generalizations may be of interest and of some little *help* provided that they are not accepted as *proof.*

General

	Modern	*Old*
Bows	Very raking or curved	Straight or slightly raking
Bridges	Heavy and enclosed	Open and flat-fronted
Cranes	Large and numerous	Small and scarce
Funnels	Short, fat or 'fancy'	Tall and thin
Hances	Very long and curved	Short and angular
Hull Form	Few islands	Three-island
Masts	Few, single or 'fancy'	More numerous and plain
Profile	Composite	Split
Sterns	Cruiser or spoon	Counter
Superstructures	Streamlined	Open and angular
Ventilators	Few and small	Large and numerous

Speed (Bow Waves and Wakes)

The water displaced by the bow is called the Bow Wave and is produced more by the hull shape than by the speed.

Older vessels with blunt bows piled up water in front but were generally slow. Often the faster the ship the smaller the wave and as the ship increases speed, the bow wave is formed further back and at high speed may merge with the wake to form one line of white water.

The track left by the ship is called the Wake. It is the product of the disturbed water caused by the hull passing through the water, and the water churned up by the screw.

It is more pronounced in modern high-powered vessels with smaller, fast-moving propellers.

Seen from the air the wake caused by a single screw and twin-screwed ships differs.

A deeply laden ship leaves a greater wake as the propeller causes a deeper disturbance of water. A vessel 'light' churns up a great amount of water but only for a short distance.

In addition to the age of vessels, weather conditions very naturally affect the appearance.

Bow wave as affected by stem forms

Impression of speed is accentuated by slim, raking ship and smoke depressed by wind.

A large liner with wash due almost entirely to very high speed.

A light ship with half immersed screw creating illusion of speed.

Colours

In peace time, colouring adds interest to and helps quite a lot in identification. Most companies have distinctive liveries and this forms a separate study. In addition to main hull colouring, such features as bands on hulls, boot-topping, islands, superstructure, funnels, masts, kingposts, derricks and even large ventilators, all help to build up a complete picture.

Names

Russian merchant ships have their name in Cyrillic characters on the bow and on the quarter or round the counter and in Roman characters on the bridge board. This latter may be a little confusing as the transliteration may not always conform to that with which one is familiar.

Bulgarian vessels follow a similar procedure.

Greek ships usually have the name in Roman characters on the bow and in Greek characters on the quarter and counter and not always having a bridge board.

Ships of Moslem countries usually have names on the bow in Arabic but possibly also in Roman characters alongside or below.

Among other countries which also generally follow this custom are: Japan, India, Israel, South Korea and both Chinas.

FLAGS

Merchant Ships usually wear certain flags at positions as indicated in *Figure 13* above and these may help identification.

(A) Jack—a small Ensign, National Flag or House Flag; worn in port.
(B) Courtesy or Destination Flag—Ensign of country being visited.
(C) 'Blue Peter'—'P' of International Code indicating that vessel is shortly sailing. Blue with white centre.
(D) Pilot Flag—Vertical, white-red: 'Pilot on Board' -Vertical, blue and yellow stripes: 'Require a Pilot'.
(E) Ship's Name—a 4-flag hoist from Code Book.
(F) House or Company Flag—usually only worn in port.
(G) Ensign worn here usually at sea.
(H) Ensign worn here usually in port.

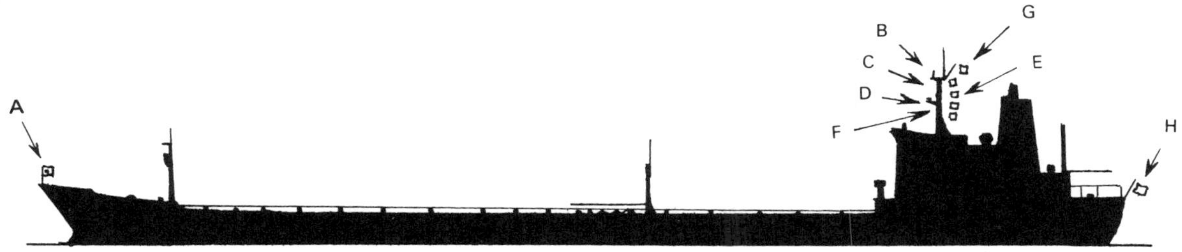

Contemporary practice of having one mast only means that flags may readily be 'masked' when worn from several halliards from the same yardarm and when combined with radar scanners, etc.

GLOSSARY

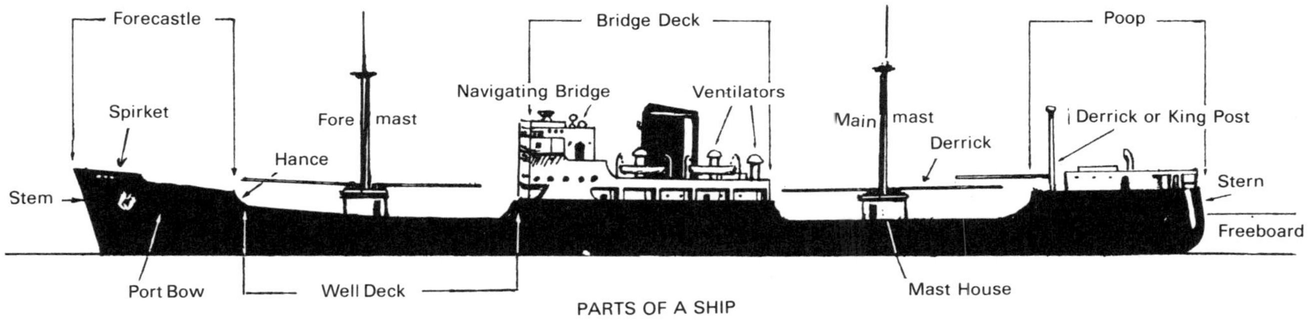

PARTS OF A SHIP

Parts of a Ship

Abaft	Behind an object
Aft	Towards the stern.
Aftercastle	Raised portion or 'Island' at after end of a vessel. Also termed the Poop.
Ahead	Directly in advance.
Amidships	Midway between stem and stern
Astern	Directly to the rear or behind a vessel.
Athwartships	Across a vessel: at right angles to centre line.
Ballast	Water, sand, etc. to give stability when ship is 'light' or empty of cargo.
Beam	Greatest width of vessel.
Boom	Same as Derrick.
Boot-Topping	Colour of paint along the waterline, between topsides and underwater surface.
Bow Wave	Wave formed under or near the bows when under way.
Bows	Adjacent to the stem: either side near front.
Bridge	Navigating platform running athwartships high up on front part of superstructure.
Bridge Deck	Mid-castle or 'Island' approximately amidships.
Broadside	Complete view of a ship from stem to stern—not foreshortened.
Bulk Cargo	Heavy dry cargo such as ore or coal or bulky like grain or timber.
Bulkhead	Watertight walls which subdivide the hull. Usually transverse.
Bulwark	Plating on deck at side to give shelter or protection in place of railings.
Bunkers	Fuel capacity or space in which fuel is carried.
Cab	Covered portion at outboard ends of bridge wings.
Castle	Raised portion or 'Island' above upper deck.
Catwalk	Raised gangway connecting castles, above the upper deck, especially in tankers.

Centre Line	Imaginary line drawn on deck from stem to stern.
Counter	Extreme stern of a ship. Sloping portion of a cutaway stern.
Crosstrees	Platform on top of lower mast or kingpost to which lifting gear is rigged. Also known as Table Tops.
Crow's Nest	Look out platform high up on foremast.
Davits	Curved fittings for supporting and handling boats.
Derrick	Long spar attached to foot of mast or kingpost for cargo handling.
Derrick Post	Vertical post to which derricks are fixed but shorter than a mast. Also known as Kingpost or Samson Post.
Docking Bridge	Athwartships platform aft used when ship is being navigated astern.
Draught	Depth from waterline to keel. Marked in feet or metres at stem and stern.
Ensign	Flag denoting nationality but not always the same as National Flag.
Ensign Staff	Flagstaff right aft from which ensign may be worn.
Flare	Slope outwards of ship's hull from waterline to upper deck, particularly at bows and stern.
Flush Deck	Uninterrupted top line without castles.
Flying Bridge	Another name for a Catwalk.
Fore and Aft	Along the length of a vessel.
Forecastle	Raised portion or island at foreward end.
Foreward	Towards the fore part—towards the stem.
Freeboard	Depth of hull from waterline to upper deck.
Freeing Ports	Openings in ship's side or bulwarks to allow water to run off. Also known as Scuppers.
Gaff	Light fore and aft spar sometimes fitted to aft mast from which ensigns are worn at sea.
Gallows	Inverted 'U' shaped fitting at sides or stern of a trawler for handling nets.
Hance	Curved or sloping portion of side plating at breaks of castles or islands.
Hatch	Opening in deck to give access to cargo holds.
Hatch Covers	Wood or steel coverings to hatch.
Hatch Gear	Short vertical posts between hatches for working covers. If very prominent should be coded as Kingposts.
Heavy Derrick	Particularly heavy derrick lashed against mast when at sea.
Hold	Compartment for cargo stowage below deck.
Island	Same as Castle. A raised portion of hull above upper deck.
Jack Staff	Small flagstaff in stem at which 'Jack' is worn.
Jumbo Derrick	Very heavy derrick—same as Heavy Derrick.
Kingpost	Same as Derrick Post.
Laden	A vessel with full cargo. Down to her load marks.
Light	A vessel riding light without cargo. 'In Ballast'.
Load Line	Horizontal lines painted on hull amidships to indicate depth to which vessel may be loaded under varying conditions.
Lower Mast	Heavily constructed lower portion of a mast if latter is in more than one section.
Mast	Vertical or raked pole to support derricks or for signalling purposes. Tallest verticals.
Mast House	Large deck house at base of mast or kingpost.
Midcastle	Raised portion or island amidships. Same as Bridge Deck.
Navigating Bridge	A term covering wheel house, chart room and athwartships platform high up on foreward part of superstructure.
Peak	Extreme outward end of Gaff.
Plimsoll Line	Same as Load Line.
Poop	Raised castle at stern; same as Aftercastle.
Port Side	That side of a vessel which is on the left when facing foreward. Indicated by RED.
Quarter	Adjacent to stern at either side.
Rake	Slope or inclination of mast or funnel.
Rubbing Strake	Heavy permanent wood, metal or rubber guard along the Hull to protect plating when going alongside. Prominent feature in coasters or small ships.
Samson Post	Same as Derrick Post or Kingpost.
Scuppers	Same as Freeing Ports.
Sheer	Slope upwards of hull at forward and after ends.
Signal Letters	A group of 4 letters of International Code allocated to a vessel for identification. The same as her radio call sign.
Spirketing Plate	Raised plating or screen above the upper deck at the stem: varies in length.
Starboard Side	That side of a vessel which is on the right hand when facing foreward. Indicated by GREEN.
Stem	Extreme foreward part of ship's hull. The cut-water.
Stern	Extreme after part of a ship.
Superstructure	Upperworks. Deckhouses, etc. on upper deck.
Tonnage	Size of a ship. As there are various forms of measurement a separate chapter is devoted to it.
Trunk Deck	Enclosed structure about two-thirds of the width of a ship joining the islands. Particularly in coastal tankers.
Wake	Disturbed water left astern.
Washports	Same as Freeing Ports or Scuppers.
Waterline	Line formed on hull by surface of water.
Weather Deck	A technical term for a light deck enclosed by plating. Frequently same as upper deck.
Well Deck	Portion of hull between castles or islands and approximately 7 to 8 feet lower.
Winch House	Same as Mast or Deckhouse.
Yard	A light spar rigged athwart a mast for signal purposes.

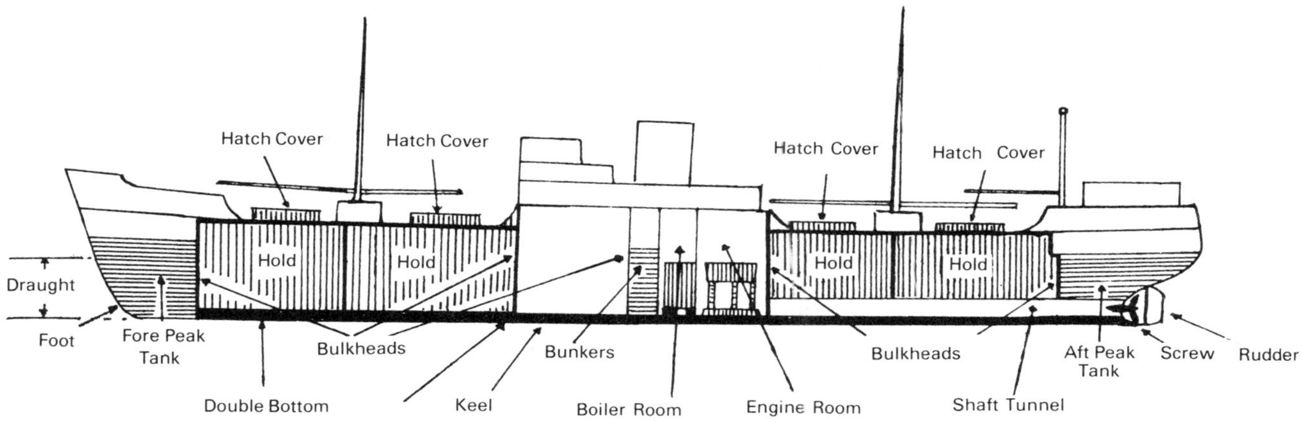
Hatch Cover
Hatch Cover
Hatch Cover
Hatch Cover
Hold
Hold
Hold
Hold
Draught
Foot
Fore Peak
Tank
Bulkheads
Bunkers
Bulkheads
Aft Peak
Tank
Screw
Rudder
Double Bottom
Keel
Boiler Room
Engine Room
Shaft Tunnel

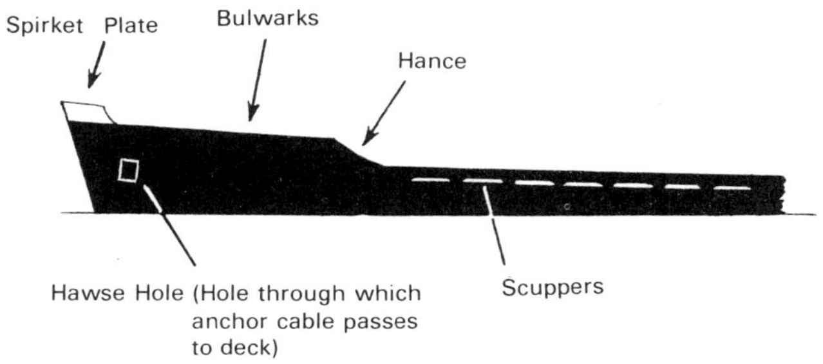
Spirket Plate
Bulwarks
Hance
Hawse Hole (Hole through which
anchor cable passes
to deck)
Scuppers

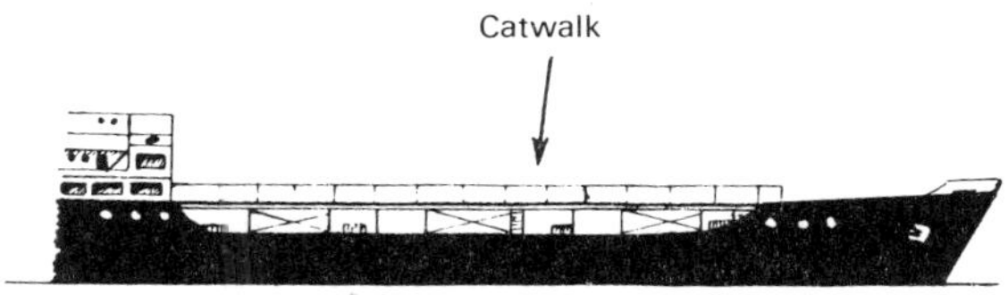
Catwalk

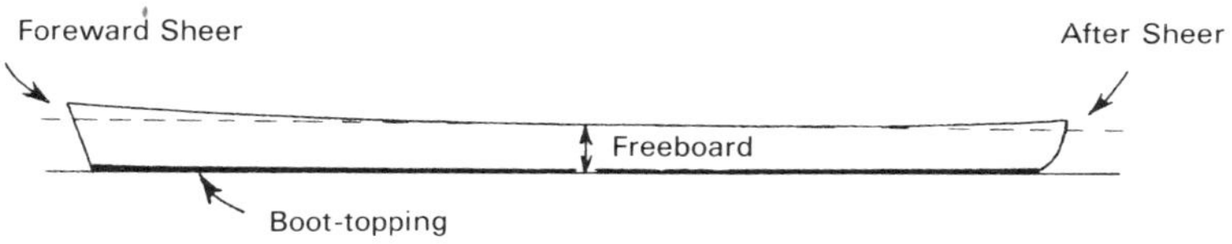
Foreward Sheer
After Sheer
Freeboard
Boot-topping

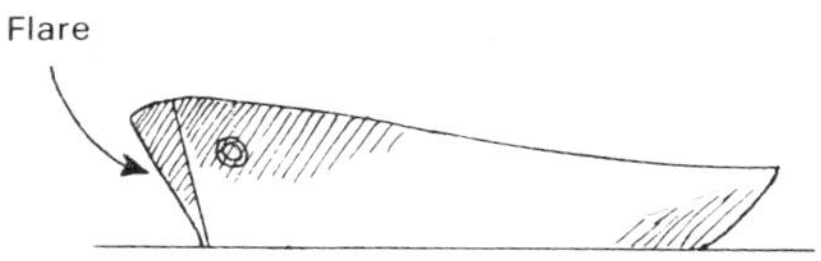
Flare

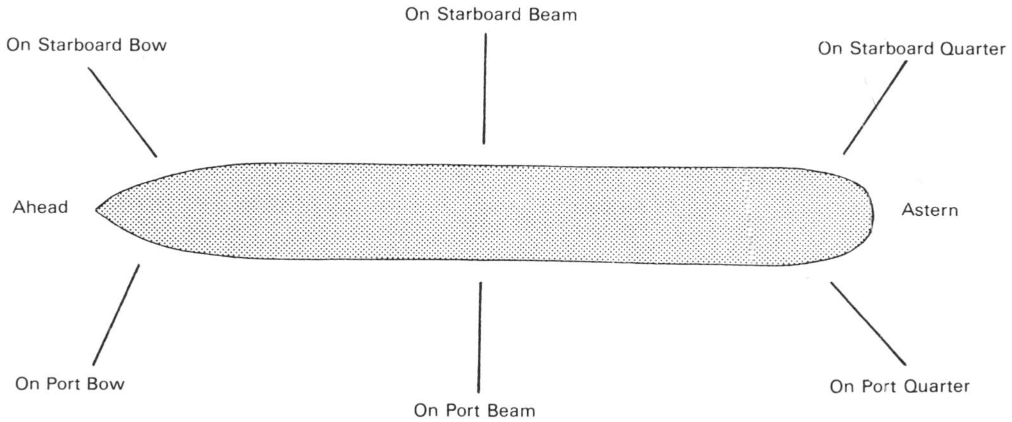
On Starboard Beam
On Starboard Bow
On Starboard Quarter
Ahead
Astern
On Port Bow
On Port Beam
On Port Quarter

ARRANGEMENT OF DRAWINGS

All drawings are to the scale of 1 inch = 200 feet (1:2400).

The drawings are arranged in *five sections*, corresponding to the five Profiles, P1-P5.

Within these main sections the drawings are arranged in *alphabetical order of sequence.* This simply means that the sequence is regarded in the same way as words in a dictionary, e.g. the following sequences are in alphabetical order: CCF. CCFK, CCMF etc. Vessels with twin funnels, i.e. funnels side-by-side, are coded as *single funnelled* ships, as only one funnel can be seen in the broadside view.

Within a particular sequence the drawings are further divided into Hull Forms. These are arranged in Numerical order thus—H, H1, H12, H123, H13, H2, H23, H3.

After having divided and sub-divided the drawings, one may still have several vessels with the same sequence and hull form. These groups are not very large as a rule, so we have made their arrangement conform to general guidelines rather than to strict rules. In most cases we have taken the coded features (Masts, Kingposts, Funnel, etc.) and their positioning as the initial distinguishing feature. Explained simply, this means that a vessel with its first coded feature at No. 2 on the grid would precede another with its first feature at No. 6, and and so on. If this system has, however, tended to split up two practically identical vessels which only vary by the positioning of one or two features, we have remained flexible. The type of vessel and size has also been taken into account.

As an aid to identification we have marked certain coded features on the drawings. Masts can be assumed to be on the Centre Line and kingposts in pairs if they are not marked. If they do not conform to this pattern they are marked, (CL for Centre Line or small silhouettes for goalpost, bi-pod, etc.) Most tripods are not indicated as they are obvious from the drawing.

On a vessel which has a line, for example, centre-line kingposts, the first post only is marked and the remainder simply arrowed (See drawing A below). If there is a combination of features, any that are marked with an arrow only are the same as the last feature foreward that was fully identified (See drawing B below).

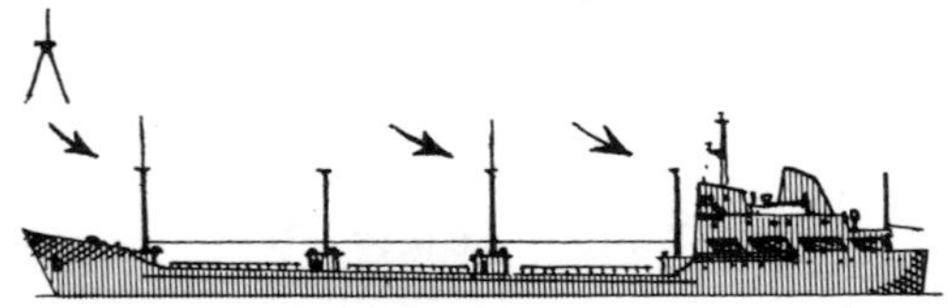

Drawing A

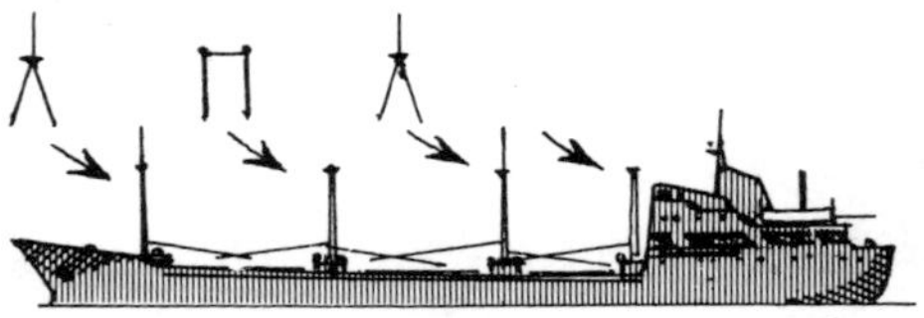

Drawing B

TEXT BENEATH DRAWINGS

This list follows the same order as the text.

Sequence — Following alphabetical order. Explained in previous sections detailing the Ship Recognition Corps reporting code. NOTE: if a feature recurs consecutively when coding a vessel it is indicated by an inferior number e.g. *KKKMFKK* is shown as K_3MFK_2.

Hull Form — Following a numerical order. Explained in previous sections.

Consecutive Number — The number is indexed. The numbers are not consecutive to allow for insertions.

Name — The spellings are taken from current registers.

Flag/County of Build — Abbreviated form (see following section). Where a vessel has been rebuilt or modified the country/countries where this was carried out are hyphenated after the original builder. A complete entry in this section could therefore appear like this: Li/Ja-Ja (wears the Liberian flag, built in Japan, modified in Japan). Communist flag vessels are indicated by an asterisk—*

Year of Build/Major Alteration or Completion — Example: 1956/65/72 (completed 1956, rebuilt 1965, further rebuilding 1972).

Type of Vessel — Abbreviated form (see following section)

Tonnage — GRT to nearest 100-tons. Smaller tonnages are shown exact. Other tonnages shown if the GRT is unavailable are dwt (deadweight) and dspl (full displacement). For open-/closed shelterdeck vessels both tonnages are shown.

Dimensions — Length overall x maximum draught. Stated in metres and taken to the nearest centimetre. Imperial measurements (to the nearest hundredth of a foot) follow in brackets. Open/closed shelterdeck vessels have both draughts. Length between perpendiculars (bp) is given if overall length is not available.

Machinery — Abbreviated form (see following section).

Speed — Service speed in knots.

Ex Names — From the most recent, working back.

Remarks — Special features, details of rebuilding, etc.

Sister Ships — Vessels built to same design as named vessel. May have very small differences.

Similar Ships — Vessels similar enough to the vessel drawn not to warrant a separate drawing. Differences may include—types of mast, kingpost, etc., superstructure, stanchions, funnel, etc.

Flags of sisters/similar ships — The flag of every vessel is shown. However, where there are large groups under the same flag, that flag is shown at the beginning of the group. If a group of similar ships follows a group of sisters and both groups have the same flag, the flag is not repeated for the similar group.

Appendix — Any entry which is updated by information in the Appendix is indicated by a small disc. A similar disc between entries indicates that a new drawing which appears in the Appendix belongs in that position. Its number is also given.

Abbreviations

Flag and Country of Build Abbreviations

These indicate the ensign worn at the time of compilation of the book, and country of build. It is not necessarily the same as nationality of owners.

Vessels may change their flag from time to time without changing ownership. This particularly applies to American or Greek owned tonnage which is frequently registered under so called Flags of Convenience such as Liberia, Lebanon, Panama.

Ab	Abu Dhabi
Ag	Algeria
Al	Albania
An	Angola
Ar	Argentina
As	Austria
Au	Australia
Be	Belgium
Bh	Bangladesh
Bi	Benin
Bm	Burma
Bn	Bahrain
Bo	Bolivia
Br	British and British Dependencies
Bs	Bahamas
Bu	Bulgaria
Bz	Brazil
Ca	Canada
Ch	Chile
Cn	Cameroun
Co	Colombia
CR	Costa Rica
Cu	Cuba
CV	Cape Verde
Cy	Cyprus
Cz	Czecholovakia
Db	Dubai
De	Denmark
DDR	Deutsch Democratic Republic (East)
Do	Dominica
Ec	Ecuador
Eg	Egypt
ES	El Salvador
Et	Ethiopia
Fa	Faroes
Fi	Finland
Fr	France
FRG	Federal Republic of Germany (West)
Ga	Gabon
Ge	Germany—Pre 1945
Gh	Ghana
Gm	Gambia
Gn	Guinea
Gr	Greece
Gu	Guatemala
Gy	Guyana
Ha	Haiti
HK	Hong Kong
Ho	Honduras
Hu	Hungary
Ia	Indonesia
Ic	Iceland
Ih	Ireland
In	India
Iq	Iraq
Ir	Iran
Is	Israel
It	Italy
Iv	Ivory Coast
Ja	Japan
Jm	Jamaica
Jo	Jordan
Ke	Kenya
Kh	Ras al Khaimah
Ko	South Korea
Ku	Kuwait
Le	Lebanon
Li	Liberia
Ly	Libya
Ma	Malta
Mb	Mocambique
Me	Mexico
Mg	Madagascar
Mn	Monaco
Mo	Morocco
Ms	Mauritius
Mt	Mauritania
Mv	Maldives
My	Malaysia
Na	Nauru
NA	Netherlands Antilles
Ne	Netherlands
Ng	Nigeria
Ni	Nicaragua
No	Norway
NZ	New Zealand
O	Oman
Pa	Panama
Pd	Poland
Pe	Peru
Pi	Philippines
Pk	Pakistan
Po	Portugal
Pp	Papua/New Guinea
Py	Paraquay
Qt	Qatar
RC	Peoples' Republic of China
RK	Peoples' Republic of North Korea
Rm	Rumania
Ru	U.S.S.R.
SA	South Africa
Sc	Seychelles
Sd	Switzerland
Se	Senegal
Sg	Singapore
Sh	Sharjah
Si	Saudi Arabia
SL	Sierra Leone
Sn	Surinam
So	Somalia
Sp	Spain
Sr	Sri Lanka (Ceylon)
Su	Sudan
Sw	Sweden
Sy	Syria
Ta	Tanzania
Tg	Togo
Th	Thailand
To	Tonga
Tr	Trinidad & Tobago
Tu	Turkey
Tw	Taiwan
UAE	United Arab Emirates
Ug	Uganda
Ur	Uruguay
US	United States of America
Va	Vanuatu
Ve	Venezuela
Vn	Vietnam
Ye	Yemen
Ys	Yugoslavia
Za	Zambia
Zr	Zaire

Abbreviations of Ship Types

Vessels of more than one function will have a combination of abbreviations from this list separated by an oblique stroke (e.g. C/HL).

A	Auxiliary
AT	Asphalt Tanker
B	Bulk Carrier
BC	Bulk/Car Carrier
BC/O	Bulk/Car/Ore
Bg	Barge Carrier
BO	Bulk/Oil Carrier
BT	Buoy Tender
BWC	Bulk Carrier—Wood Chip
C	General Dry Cargo Ship
Cble	Cable Ship
Cem	Cement Carrier
CG	Coast Guard Ship
Ch	Chemical Tanker
Con	Container Ship
ConR	Container Ship with Refrigerated Capacity
CP	Cargo Passenger Ship (Up to 12 passengers)
CS	Crane Ship
CTS	Cargo/Training Ship
D	Dredger
Dep	Depot Ship
Dk	Dock Ship
DS	Drilling Ship
F	Ferry (Probably carrying unberthed passengers)
FA	Fleet Auxiliary
FC	Fish Carrier
FF	Fish Factory
FFMS	Fishery Mother Ship
Fru	Fruit Ship
FT	Stern Trawling Factory Ship
FV	Fishing Vessel
HL	Heavy Lift Vessel
IB	Ice Breaker
LC	Landing Craft
LGC	Liquified Gas Carrier
Ls	Livestock Carrier
LT	Light Tender
M	Mining Ship
MT	Molasses Tanker
MTV	Missile Tracking Vessel
O	Ore Carrier
OBO	Ore/Bulk/Oil
OO	Ore/Oil
OSS	Offshore Support Ship
P	Passenger Ship
Pal	Pallets Carrier
PC	Passenger Cargo Ship (Over 12 passengers)
PCTF	Passenger, Cargo and Train Ferry
PLC	Pipe Laying
Plt	Pilot Vessel
Pp	Pipe Carrier
PR	Passenger Refrigerated Vessel
PRiv	Passenger (River)
PtCon	Part Container Ship
PTF	Passenger/Train Ferry
R	Cargo Vessel with large Refrigerated capacity
Rad	Radio Station
Riv	River Craft
Rmt	Replenishment Ship (Naval)
RoC	Ro/Ro Cargo Ship
RoRo	Roll-on/Roll-off (specific function unknown)
RoCF	Ro/Ro Cargo Ferry
RoPF	Ro/Ro Passenger Ferry
RoPCF	Ro/Ro Passenger Vehicle Ferry
RoVC	Ro/Ro Vehicle Carrier
RS	Research Ship (Including hydrographic, oceanographic, etc.)
Rst	Replenishment Ship (Naval)
RT	Replenishment Tanker (Naval)
Sal	Salvage Vessel
SCon	Semi Container Ship
SDT	Slop Disposal Tanker
Slu	Sludge Carrier
Sply	Supply Ship
Spt	Support Ship (Naval)
SS	Stern Trawler
STS	Stern Trawler/Sealer
TB	Bitumen Tanker
TC	Timber Carrier
TF	Train Ferry
Tg	Tug
Tk	Tanker
TPu	Tanker Pulp
Trlr	Trawler
TS	Training Ship
V	Vehicle Carrier (other than Ro/Ro)
Wa	Water Carrier
WF	Whale Factory Ship
Whlr	Whaler
WS	Weather Ship
WT	Wine Tanker
Y	Yacht

Engine Abbreviations

D-E	Diesel Electric
GT	Gas Turbine
M	Motor Vessel
N	Nuclear Power
Pdl	Paddle
R	Reciprocating
R & LPT	Reciprocating and Low Pressure Turbine
T	Turbine
T-E	Turbo Electric

All vessels are single screw unless otherwise stated:

TS	Twin Crew
TrS	Triple Screw
QS	Quadruple Screw

Profile 1

CKMKMKFKMK H1
00001 TAI YANG No 11. Ko/No 1947; FF; 7100; 155 × 5 (509 × 16); TM; 17; ex SHIN HUNG 1970; ex BATAAN 1967; Converted from cargo ship 1967.

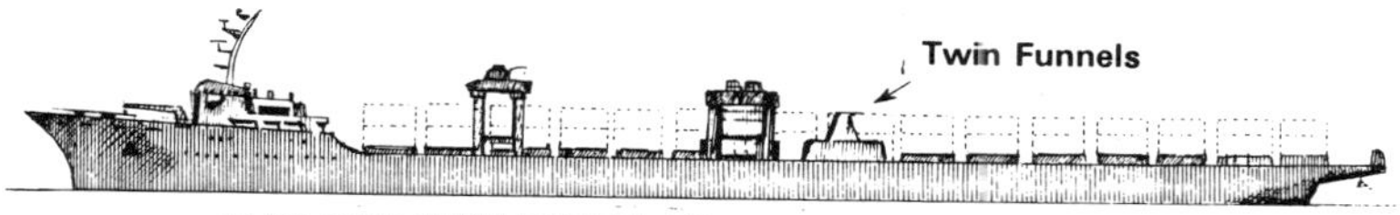

$CMN_2F/CMNFN/CMFN_2$ H1
● **00010 LASH ATLANTICO.** US/US 1972; Bg/Con; 26400; 250 × 10.7 (820 × 35.5); —; 21; Both Gantries (N) can move right aft thus altering sequence. Could also be P5. **"LASH"** type: Sisters (US flag) (overall lengths vary) **00011 LASH ITALIA 00012 LASH PACIFICO 00013 AUSTRAL LIGHTNING** ex LASH ESPANA 1976; ex AUSTRALIA BEAR 1975; ex PHILIPPINE BEAR 1975 **00015 DELTA MAR 00016 DELTA SUD 00017 DELTA NORTE 00018 DELTA CARIBE** ex LASH TURKIYE

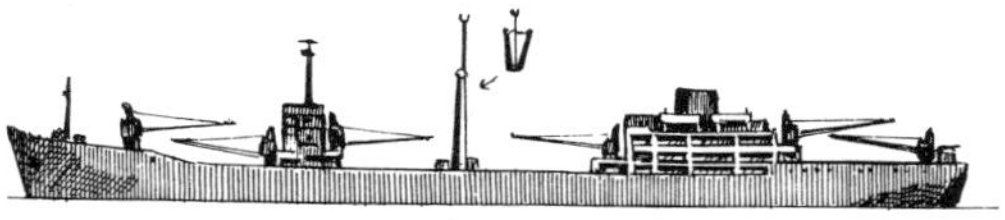

$KC_2MCMCFC_2H13$
● **00020 INVENTOR.** Br/Br 1964; C/HL; 6100/8800; 150.37 × 7.67/9.04 (493.34 × 25.17/29.69); M; —.

KCMKFCK H12
00030 SIRIUS. US/Br 1966; FA; 12300; 159.7 × 25.4 (524 × 25.5); M; 20; ex LYNESS 1981; Helicopter platform aft. Hull could be H. Sisters **00031 STROMNESS** (Br) **00032 TARBATNESS** (Br)

KFM H12
● **00040 RAJAH MAS.** My/Br 1955; P; 600; 51.2 × 2.6 (168 × 8.5); M; 10; ex REJANG 1969.

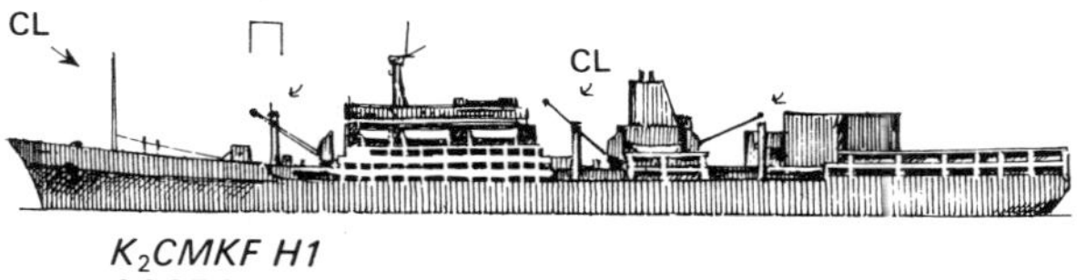

K_2CMKF H1
00050 FORT GRANGE. Br/Br 1978; Rst/FA; 16000; 183.78 × 9 (602.95 × 29.53); M; 20; Operated by the RFA; Helicopter platform. Sister **00051 FORT AUSTIN** (Br)

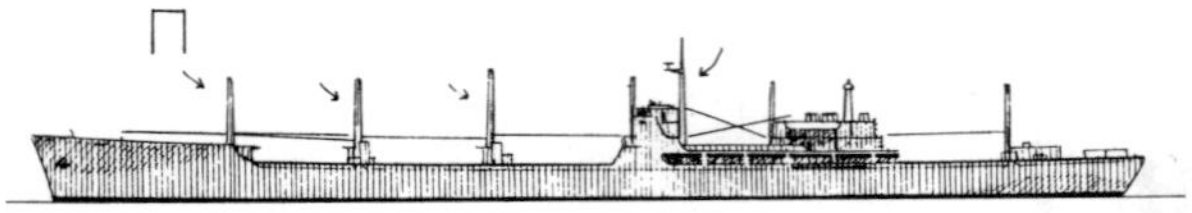

K_4MKFK H1
00060 ASHLEY LYKES. US/US 1962; P. Con; 11800; 179 × 10.3 (588 × 24.5); T; 18; Lengthened **'Pacer'** or **'Gulf Pride'** class. Sisters (US flag). **00061 BRINTON LYKES 00062 JAMES LYKES 00063 JEAN LYKES 00064 JOHN LYKES 00065 JOSEPH LYKES 00066 NANCY LYKES 00067 SOLON TURMAN 00068 MARJORIE LYKES 00069 THOMPSON LYKES 00070 ZOELLA LYKES**

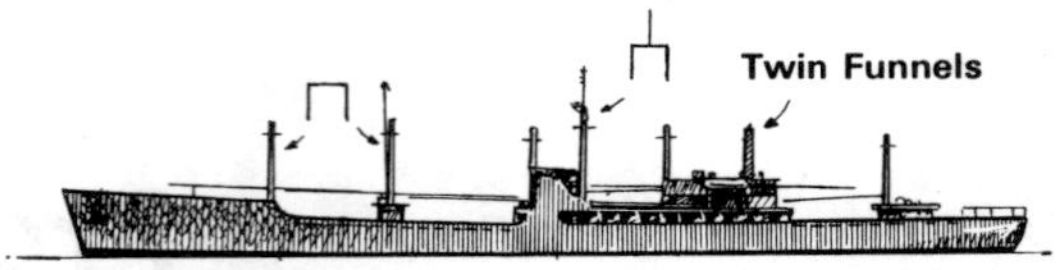

K_3MK_3/K_3MKFK H1
00080 ADABELLE LYKES. US/US 1963; S. Con; 9900; 150.8 × 10.3 (495 × 35.5); T; 18; Some ships have sequence $KMKM_2FK$. Sisters (US flag). **00081 AIMEE LYKES 00082 ALLISON LYKES 00083 CHARLOTTE LYKES 00084 CHRISTOPHER LYKES 00085 SHELDON LYKES**

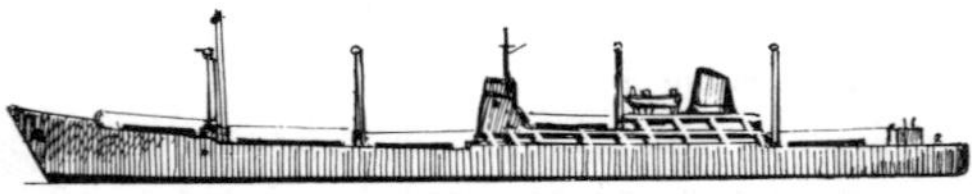

K_2MKFK H1
00090 GELA. Gr/Br 1962; C; 9600; 152 × 9.2 (499 × 30.5); M; 15; ex SOUTHGATE 1970; ex ARLINGTON COURT 1963.

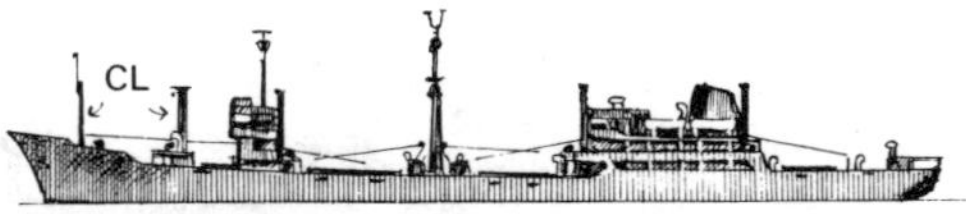

$K_2MKMKFK$ H1
00100 SEA PEARL. Cy/Br 1961; C/HL; 6000/8700; 149 × 9 (488 × 30); M; 16; ex CUSTODIAN 1979.

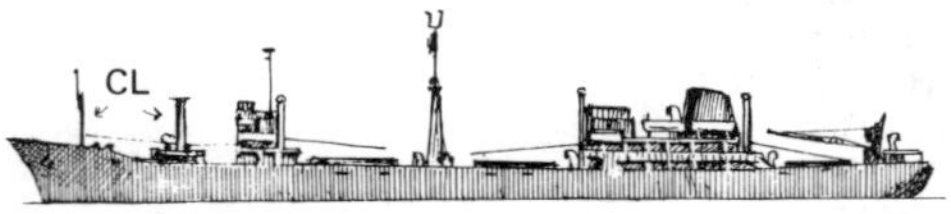

$K_2MKMKFKC$ H1
00110 KERO. Pe/Br 1961; C/HL; 6000/8700; 149 × 9 (488 × 30); M; 16; ex SEA LUCK 1979; ex TACTICIAN 1979.

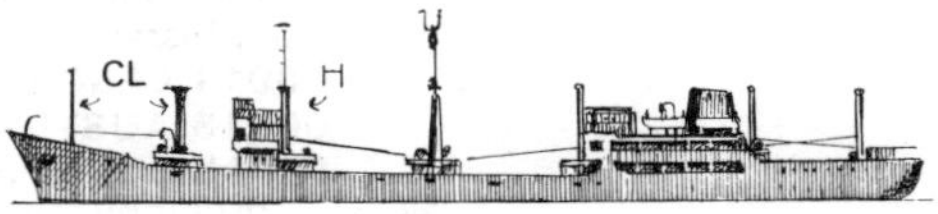

$K_2M_2KFK_2$ H1
00120 ELEFTHERIA. Gr/Br 1960; C/HL; 6400/8400; 150 × 9 (490 × 30); M; 15; ex ADVENTURER 1979.

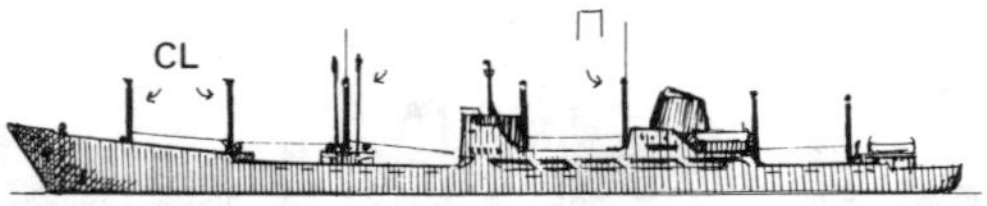

$K_2M_2KMFK_2$ H1
00130 ELBREEZE. Cy/Fr 1958; CP/R; 6600; 150 × 9 (490 × 30); M; 17.5; ex MAGELLAN 1979; Has a pole foremast. Sister **00131 SENANG ISLAND** (Sg); ex MARYLAND 1976

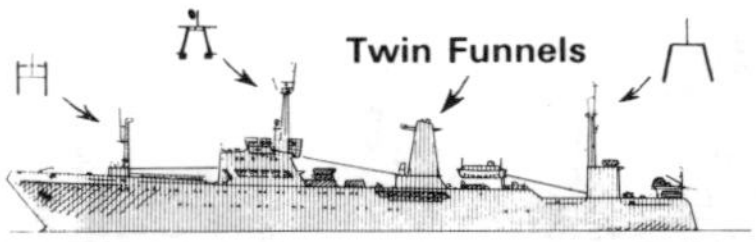

KMFK/KMFM H1
⋆00140 ADMIRAL GOLOVKO. Ru/Ru 1975; FT; 4500; 112.81 × 6.52 (370.11 × 21.39); M; 17; Sisters (Ru flag). **⋆00141 ADMIRAL KOLYSHKIN ⋆00142 ALEKSANDR TORTSYEV ⋆00143 IVAN SIVKO ⋆00144 KAPITAN TELOV ⋆00145 MARSHAL YAKUBOVSKIY ⋆00146 PYOTR SGIBNEV (or PETR SGIBNEV)**

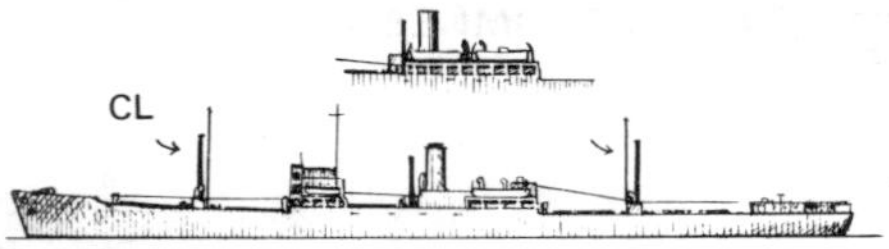

KMFK H
⋆00150 HOPING CHI SHI CHIU. RC/Ca 1943; C; 7000; 134 × 8.2 (422 × 27); R; 10; ex AEGEAN SEA; ex TAYGETOS; ex LAURENTIAN SEA; ex FORT BRANDON; Sisters (RC flag). **⋆00151 HOPING CHI SHI LIU;** ex ATHENS; ex AKKO; ex VANCOUVER CITY; ex FORT WALLACE; **⋆00152 HOPING CHI SHI WU;** ex KASERT; ex TERNATE; ex GOVERT FIINCK; ex OCEAN ATHLETE; **⋆00153 HOPING ER SHI CHI;** ex NORD SKY; ex TEMPLE BAR; ex FORT ST. JAMES; **⋆00154 HOPING SAN SHI;** ex GUNN; ex YAMASKA; ex YAMASKA PARK; **⋆00155 HOPING SHI SAN;** ex NUEVA GLORIA; ex LAKE OKANAGAN; ex RUPERT PARK; **⋆00156 HOPING WU SHI;** ex LONGFORD; ex MARIKA; ex TARSIAN; ex FORT ST. PAUL; **⋆00157 HOPING WU SHI I;** ex HEREFORD; ex NOVOR ISOBEL; ex FORT TICONDEROGA All these ships were built as WWII standard types.

KMKFK H1
⋆00160 NAN HAI 145. RC/Br 1943; C; 6000; 126.4 × 8 (415 × 26); R; 10; ex NORWIND 1967; ex GRAIGLWYD 1959; ex KINGSBOROUGH 1951; ex CHERTSEY 1947

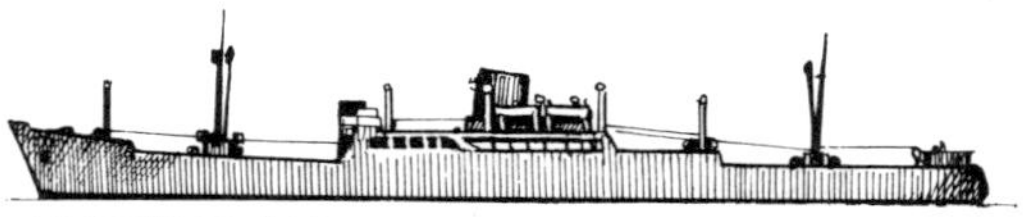

$KMKFK_2M$ H12

00170 CAPETAN NICOLAS. Cy/Br 1957; C/R; 11100; 156×9.3 (512×31); TSM; 18.5; ex CANOPIC 1975; KP also abreast funnel. Similar: **00171 UNITED VIGOUR** (Sg); ex DRINA 1977; ex CRETIC 1973

KMKFKM H1

00180 VASSILAKIS. Gr/Br 1958; C; 5400/9100; 140×7.8 (460×26); M; 14; ex ELENA M 1978; ex CAXTON 1968

KMKFM H1

00190 MELPO. Gr/Br 1960; C; 8500; 145×8.5 (476×28); M; 11.5; ex LOUKIA 1976; ex MAREANTES 1975; ex KAPTAYANNI 1973; ex BRIGHTON 1970;Laid up 1980. Sister **00191 SAMI** (Gr); ex KALLIMACHOS 1979; ex MICHAAL ANGELOS 1976; ex CAPTAIN LEMOS 1973; ex CLEARTON 1968

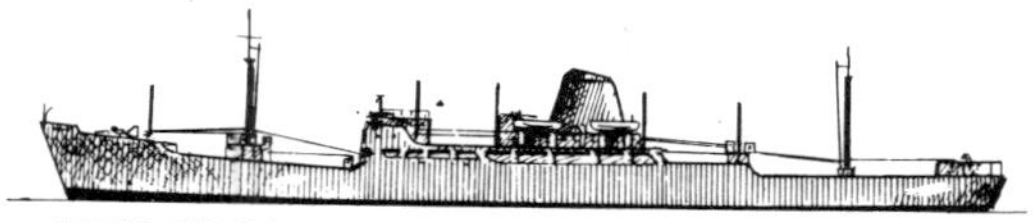

KMK_2FK_2M H12

● **00200 DESEADO.** Br/Br 1961; C/R; 11200; 156.3×9.6 (511×32); M; 17; ex IBERIC 1976 Sister **00201 IONIC** (Br)

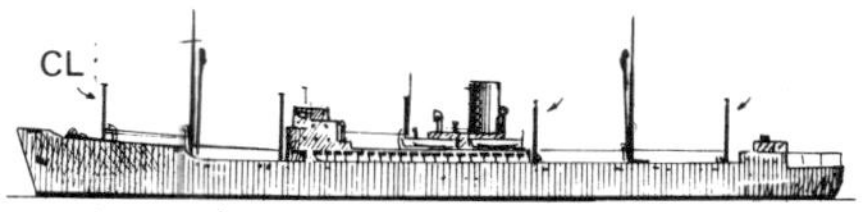

KMK_2FKMK H1

00210 TOPEKA. Pa/Ge 1938; C; 5100; 133.8×7.3 (438×24); M; 15; ex LACASIELLE 1976; ex TOGO 1968; ex STELLA MARINA 1956; ex TILTHORN 1954; ex SVALBARD 1954; ex TOGO 1947; Converted from passenger ship.

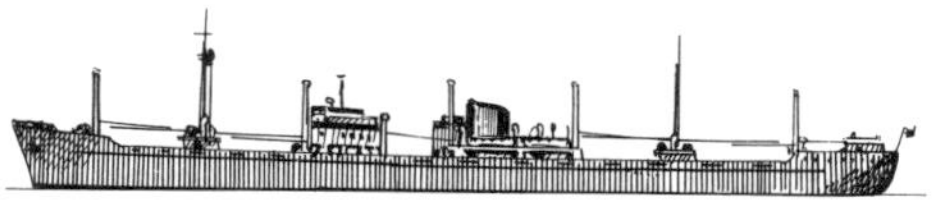

KMK_2FKMK H13

● **00220 EASTERN JADE.** Br/Ne 1949; CP; 5800; 144×7.9 (463×26); M; 16; ex UNIVERSAL ATLANTA 1977; ex SAGAJO 1974; ex MARGARET C ERTEL 1970; ex GLENVILLE 1966 Sister **00221 YAT HING**(Pa) ex RYTTERTIND 1978; ex BRONXVILLE 1971

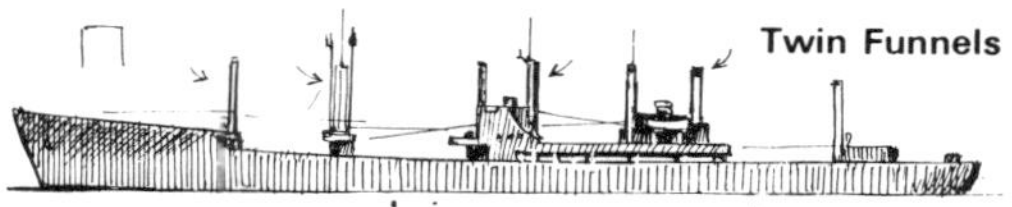

$KMKM_2FK/KMKM_2K_2$ H1

00230 ADABELLE LYKES. US/US 1963; S. Con; 9900; 150×10.3 (495×34.5); T; 18; Sisters (US flag). **00231 AIMEE LYKES 00232 ALLISON LYKES 00233 CHARLOTTE LYKES 00234 CHRISTOPHER LYKES 00235 SHELDON LYKES** Some ships K_3MK_3

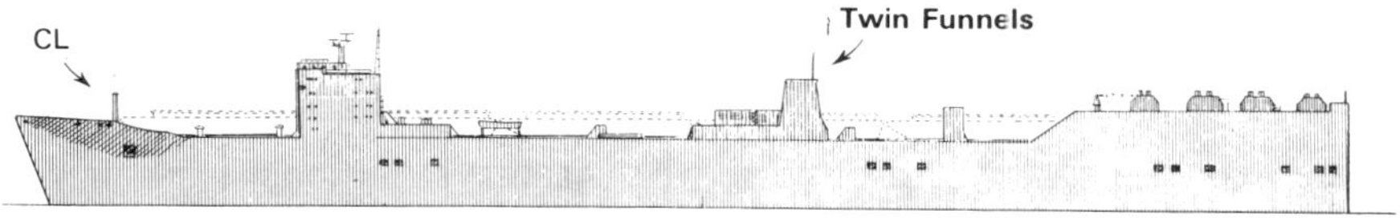

KM_2F H13

⋆**00240 YULIUS FUCHIK.** Ru/Fi 1978; Bg/Con; 22800/35900; 266.45×—/11 (874.18×—/36.09); TSM; 20; May be spelt **JULIUS FUCIK.** Sister ⋆**00241 TIBOR SZAMUELY** (Ru)

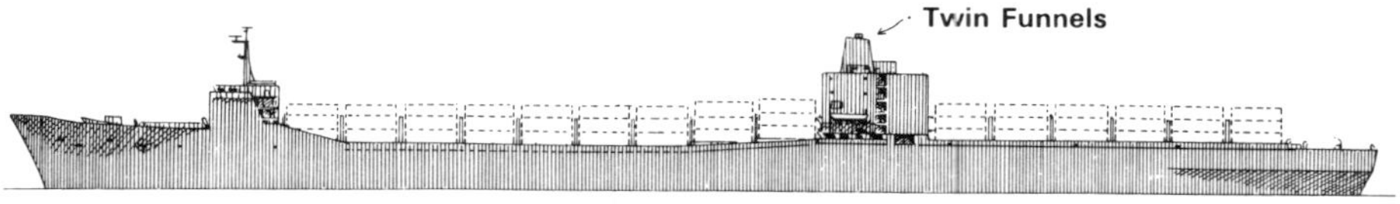

MF H1

● **00250 SEA-LAND COMMERCE.** US/FRG 1973; Con; 41100; 288×10.4 (946×34.5); TST; 33; Sisters (US flag). **00251 SEA-LAND ECONOMY 00252 SEA-LAND EXCHANGE 00253 SEA-LAND FINANCE 00254 SEA-LAND GALLOWAY 00255 SEA-LAND McLEAN 00256 SEA-LAND MARKET 00257 SEA-LAND RESOURCE 00258 SEA-LAND TRADE**

MFM H
00260 AFFAN ALBAHAR. Ia/Br 1931; C; 5400; 131 × 8 (430 × 27); M; 12.5; ex ADRI X 1963; ex HONGKONG FIR 1962; ex ANTRIM 1957; ex KAIMATA 1954; ex ARDENVOHR 1937

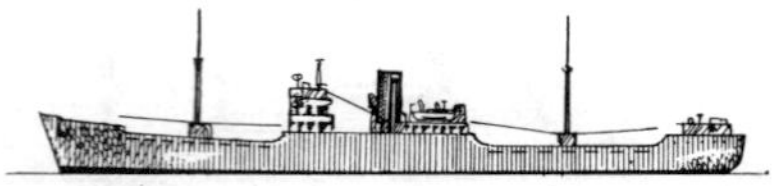

MFM H123
***00270 RIO JIBACOA.** Cu/Br 1946; C; 3700; 112 × 6.6 (368 × 22); R; 10; ex DUNDRENNAN 1957; ex COULBRECK 1954; KP abreast the funnel.

MFM H13
00280 ANNAJM. Si/Br 1960; C; 5400/7600; 137.9 × 8.24/8.79 (452.4 × 27/28.8); M; 13.5; ex ALFARAJ 1980; ex INDUSTRIA 1974; ex SILVERISLE 1965; Tall vent before bridge might look like a KP. KP also abreast funnel. Could be coded MKFM.

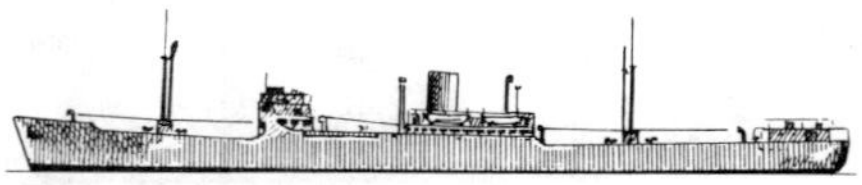

MKFKM H
***00290 YUNGLUTATION.** RC/Br 1949; C; 5400; 135 × 7.9 (443 × 26); M; 12.5; ex TRELYON 1963

MKFM H
● **00300 AGHIA MARINA.** Cy/Br 1954; C; 8800; 147.5 × 8.1 (484 × 27); M; 13.5 Sister **00301 ANTAGORAS** (Pa); ex CHIEF S.B. BAKARE 1978; ex AKTIS 1976; ex RODON 1973; ex AGHIOS NICOLAOS 1970

MKFM H
00310 DIMITRA K. Gr/Br 1952; C; 8300; 142.2 × 8.5 (466.5 × 27.89); M; 12; ex KANARIS 1980; ex KING MALCOLM 1972 Sister **00311 BANGKOK 2** (Pa); ex ELLI 2 1980; ex KING ALEXANDER 1972 Similar: **00312 TAICHUNG 2** (Pa) ex ELENI 2 1980; ex KING GEORGE 1957

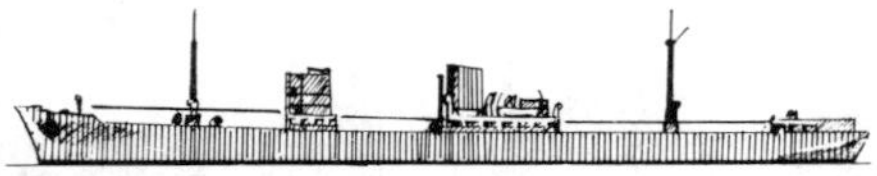

MKFM H
00320 RIO SEGUNDO. Ar/Br 1947; C; 5000; 134.4 × 7.8 (441 × 26); M; 11.

MKFM H
***00330 ALEKSANDROVSK.** Ru/Fi 1960; C; 5400; 139 × 7.9 (457 × 28); M; 14.5; Sisters (Ru flag). ***00331 ATKARSK *00332 BERDJANSK *00333 KISLOVODSK *00334 SRETENSK *00335 DOLINSK** (on naval service as a survey ship)

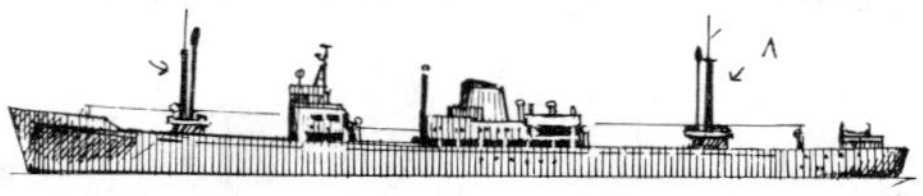

MKFM H
***00340 LJGOV** Ru/Fi 1961; C; 5400; 139 × 7.9 (457 × 26); M; 16 Sisters (Ru flag). ***00341 ALAPAYEVSK *00342 ALMETYEVSK *00343 CHERNYAKHOVSK**

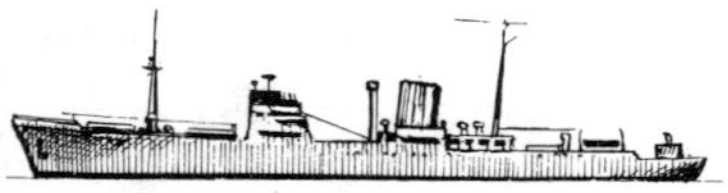

MKFM H
***00350 TAUYSK.** Ru/FRG 1956; R; 3800; 110.6 × 7 (363 × 23); M; 15; ex AMALIENBURG 1964; ex BONITA 1963

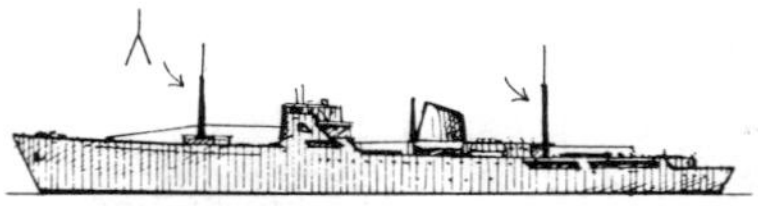

MKFM H
● **00351 OPALINE BAY.** Pa/Fr 1962; R; 4700; 115.27 × 6.1 (378.18 × 20.01); M; 17; ex LETHE 1979; ex ESPADON 1977

MKFM H1
00360 ARION. Cy/Br 1956; C; 7900; 140.5 × 8.6 (461 × 28.5); M; 12; ex NEFOS 1976; ex RODSLEY 1963

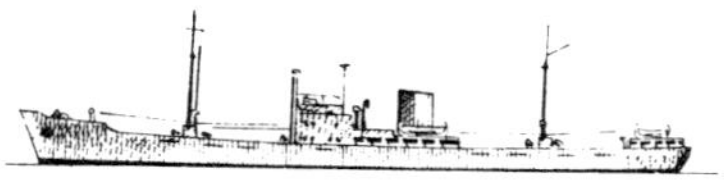

MKFM H1
00370 SAINT NECTARIOS. Gr/De 1947; C; 2700; 109.7 × 6.3 (360 × 21); M; 11; ex LEFTERIS M 1976; ex BRETAGNE 1969

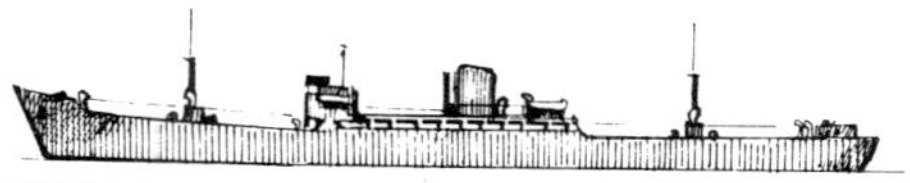

MKFM H1
00380 GLOBAL TRADER. Gr/Br 1960; C; 5700/8100; 140.8 × 8.9 (463 × 29.5); M; 13.5; ex BARON BELHAVEN 1967 Sisters (some ships may have a taller funnel). **00381 ERINI PATERA** (Gr); ex BORDAGAIN 1976; ex BARON GARIOCH 1968 **00382 PALMIS** (Gr); ex ARTIBA 1976; ex BARON KINNAIRD 1968 **00383 AGHIOS NICOLAOS** (Gr); ex BARON PENTLAND 1968; **00384 BORDABARRI** (Li); ex BARON WEMYSS 1968 **00385 FILIO AVGERIS** (Gr); ex DIRPHYS II 1980; ex BARON MINTO 1967

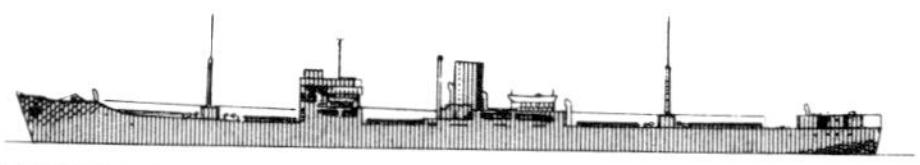

MKFM H1
● **00390 BLESSING FIVE**. Pa/Br 1957; C; 5500/7400; 139.38 × —/8.71 (457.28 × —/28.58); M; 12.5; ex LEONIDAS MICHALOS 1979; ex LUCY 1973

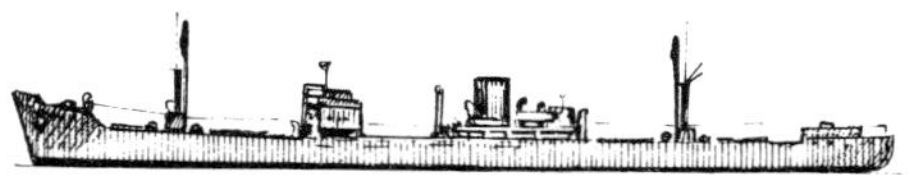

MKFM H1
★**00400 XING HUO**. RC/Br 1955;C; 8000; 140.5 × 8.4 (461 × 28); R & LPT; 12.5; ex HOPING WU SHI SSU; ex KYVERNITIS 1959; ex DIAMANTIS PATERAS 1957

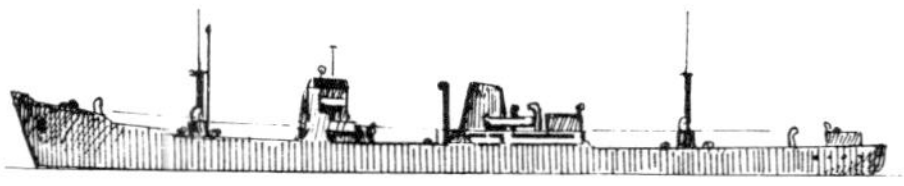

MKFM H1
00410 ELIKON. Cy/Br 1958; C; 5800/8400;140.8 × 8 (462 × 26.7); M; 13.5.

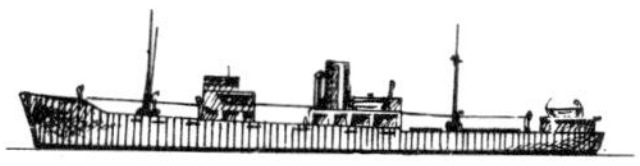

MKFM H1
00420 KASTELLORIZON. Cy/Sw 1946; C; 1600; 91.4 × 5.8 (300 × 19.3);M; 13; ex ELENI T 1973; ex ZATON 1968; ex ALGERIA 1964 Sister **00421 GAMBELA** (My); ex HONGKONG LINE 1975; ex PARAGON 1974; ex SLINDE 1965; ex INDUSTRIA 1962

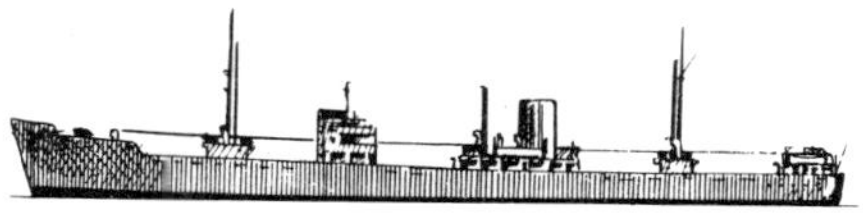

MKFM H1
● **00450 ADRIASTAR**. Cy/Da 1949; C; 4800; 132 × 7.8 (433 × 25.8); M; 14; ex GINA JULIANO 1976; ex NORTHWILD 1970; ex NORDHVAL 1969 Similar: **00451 GLORIASTAR** (Pa); ex ALBAMAR 1974; ex NORDVEST 1970 **00452 MARYSTAR** (Pa); ex ARETIS 1975; ex NORDKYN 1963

MKFM H1
★**00460 HOPING ER SHI CHIU**. RC/De 1935; C; 4600; 121.6 × 7.4 (399 × 24.6); TM; 12; ex ESBJORN 1958

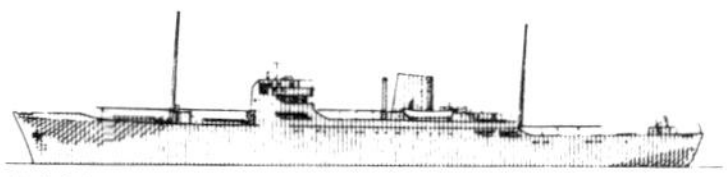

MKFM H1
00470 TAIBAH. Cy/Sw 1953; R; 3600; 110.47 × 7.01 (362.43 × 23); M; 16; ex FRESCA 1978; ex SOYOKAZE 1977; ex PENJA 1972

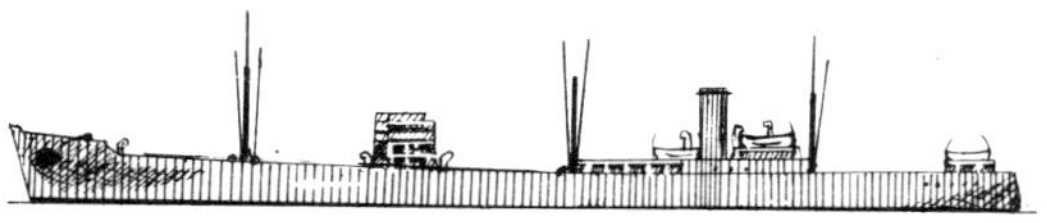

MKFM H1
00480 UNION ATLANTIC. Pa/Au 1953;O; 9600; 159 × 8 (523 × 27); T; 13; ex IRON WYNDHAM

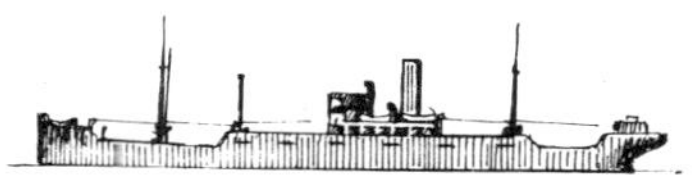

MKFM H123
00490 MAR GRANDE. Ar/De 1928; C; 3200; 103.6 × — (340 × —); M; 10; ex RIO GRANDE 1971; ex RIO IGUAZU 1967; ex BRETAGNE 1942

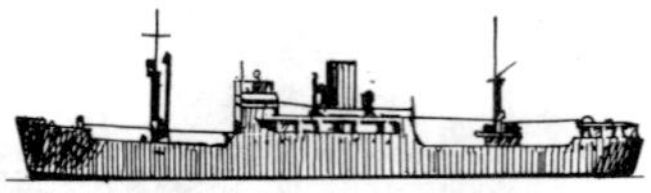

MKFM H123
⋆**00500 ROCHFORD**.RC/Br 1946; CP; 3400; 100 × 6.3 (328 × 20.7); R; 12;ex TAKSANG 1962

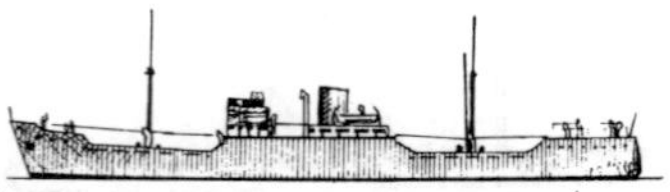

MKFM H123
00510 INCONFIDENTE. Bz/Ne 1937; C; 2900; 102.4 × 6.3 (336 × 20.5); TM; 10.

MKFM H123
00520 PRESIDENTE CASTILLO. Ar/Fr 1948; C; 6500/8700; 153 × 7.7 (502 × 25.7); M; 14; ex TARA 1961; ex CHARLES L.D. 1959

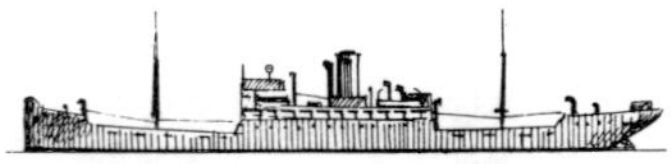

MKFM H123
⋆**00530 EFORIE.** Rm/Br 1918; C; 3500; 105 × 6.7 (345 × 22); R; 9; ex BEREZINA 1962; ex BRACONDALE 1934; ex SEATONIA; ex WAR HIGHWAY

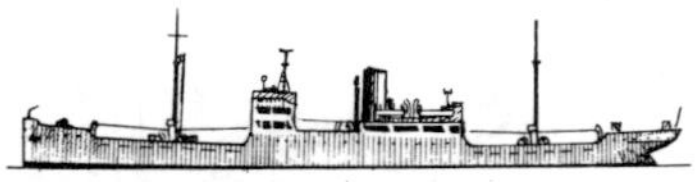

MKFM H123
⋆**00540 OTTO SCHMIDT.** Ru/Ne 1915; C; 4000; 112.5 × 6.5(360 × 22); R; 12; ex PSKOV 1935; ex BELLATRIX 1934

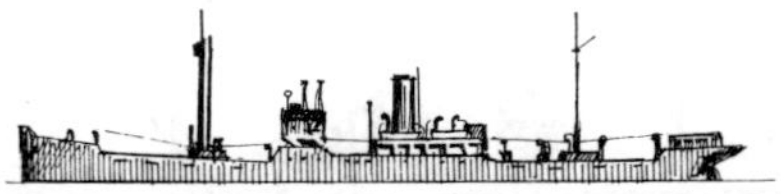

MKFM H123
⋆**00550 NOVGOROD.** Ru/US 1920; C; 5200; 120 × 7.3 (396 × 24); R; 11; ex PANAMA CITY 1945; ex EXBROOK 1935; ex OSSA

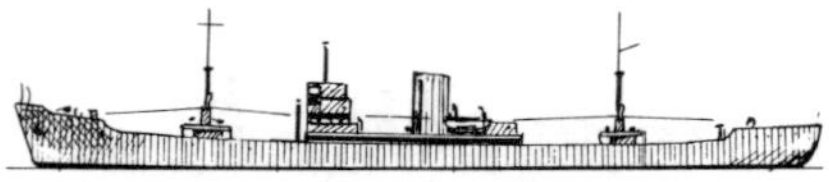

MKFM H13
● **00560 PANETOLIKON.** Sr/Br 1960; C; 7900; 137.8 × 8.8 (452 × 26.11); M; 13.5; ex INGLETON 1970; ex THISTLEROY 1966; KP abreast the funnel.

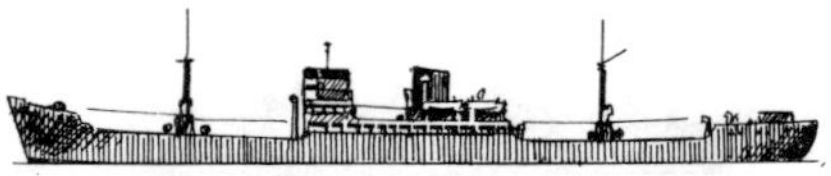

MKFM H13
00570 ANNAJM. Si/Br 1960; C; 5400/7600; 137 × 8.24/8.79 (452.4 × 27/28.8); M; 13.5; ex ALFARAJ 1980; ex INDUSTRIA 1974; ex SILVERISLE 1965; KP abreast funnel.

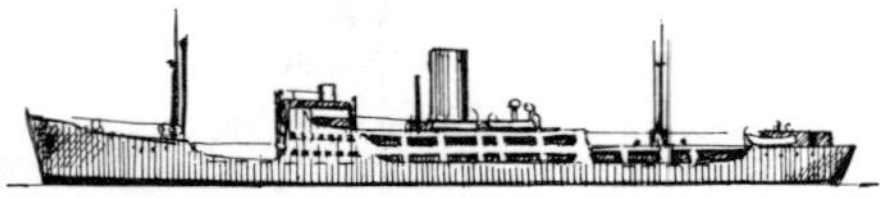

MKFM H13
● **00580 KOTA PANJANG.** Sg/Br 1949; P; 7400; 134 × 7.2 (440 × 23.7); M; 15.5; ex CHANGSHA 1969

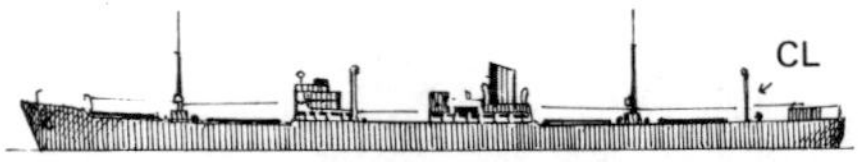

MKFMK H
00590 FRANCISCO MATARAZZO. Bz/Br 1947; C; 4900; 131 × 7.6 (430 × 25); R; 11.

MKFMK H1
00600 ANEL D'AZUR. Gr/Br 1957; C; 8300; 140.2 × 8.3 (460 × 27.4); M; 13; ex HERBERT MACAULAY; ex SUSSEX TRADER 1964 Sister **00601 SAFINA-E-ISMAIL** (Pk); ex ESSEX TRADER 1963

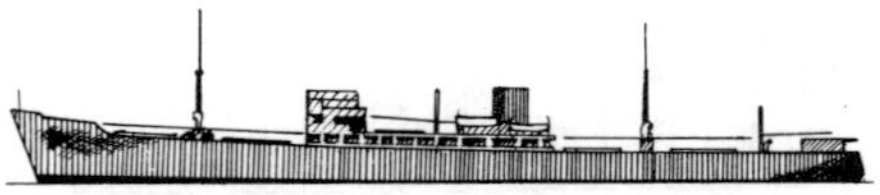

MKFMK H1
● **00610 SAUDI FORTUNE.** Sg/Br 1956; C; 5600/7900; 136.8 × 8.5 (449 × 28); M; 12.5; ex GLENMOOR 1976 Similar: **00611 EUCADIA** (Br); ex LINKMOOR 1968 **00612 GOURI SHANKAR** (In); ex RATNA MANJUSHREE 1974; ex INNESMOOR 1963 **00613 JHELUM** (Pk); ex KIRRIEMOOR 9164 **00614 RAVI** (Pk); ex JEDMOOR 1964

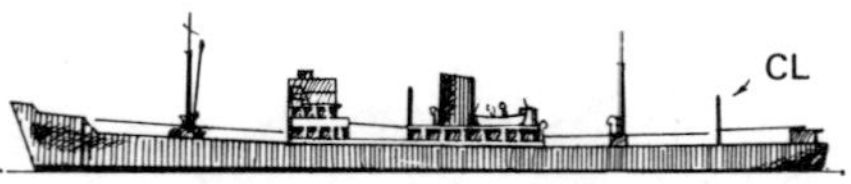

MKFMK H1
● **00620 ISTIKBAL.** Tu/Br 1949; C; 4800; 131.3 × 7.6 (432 × 25); R; 10.5; ex DENIZ 1962; ex STRATIDORE 1962

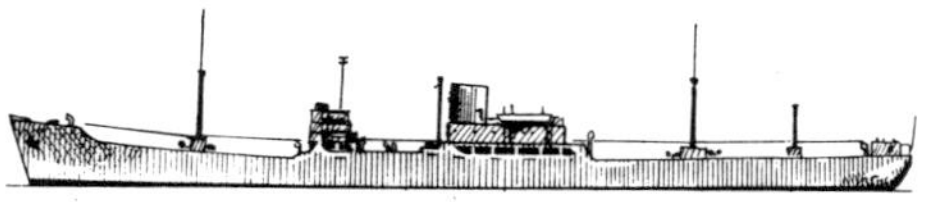

MKFMK H1
00630 FELICIE. Cy/Br 1960; C; 9000; 148 × 9.25 (485.5 × 30.35); M; 13.5; ex TARPON CLIPPER 1973; ex PEARL CLIPPER 1969

MKFMK H123
00640 ASTILLERO. Sp/Sp 1920; C; 3500; 104 × 6.6 (341 × 21.1); R; —; ex GAYARRE 1967; ex ARICHACHU 1939

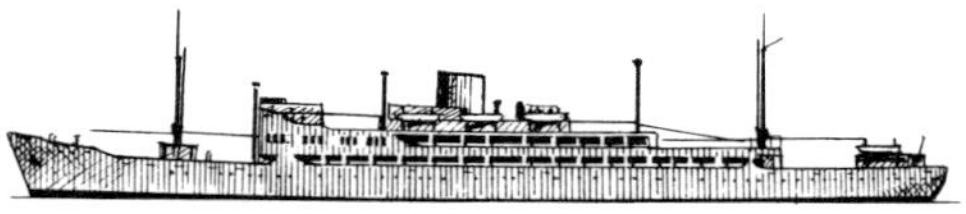

MK_2FKM H1
⋆**00650 GEORG BUCHNER.** DDR/Be 1951; PC; 11100; 153.6 × 8.4 (504 × 27.6); M; 16; ex CHARLESVILLE 1967; May be slightly altered in appearance.

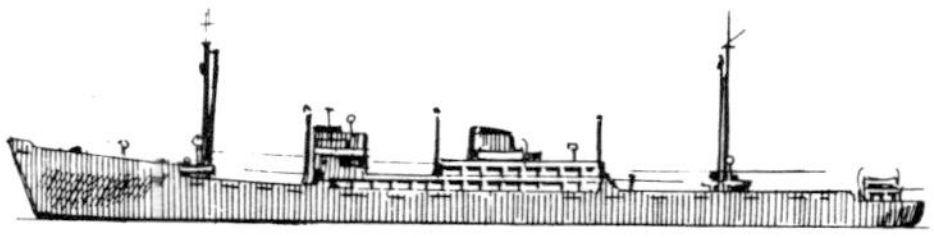

MK_2FKM H1
⋆**00660 SRBIJA.** Ys/Ne 1949; C; 6200/8400; 144.7 × 8 (475 × 25.4); M; 14; ex DRVAR 1949

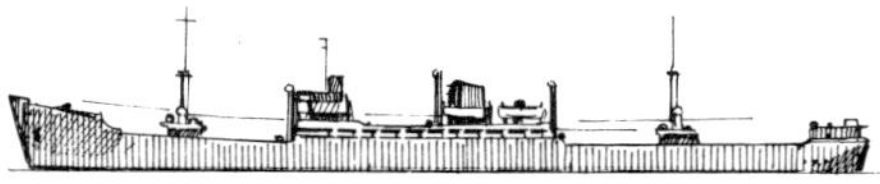

MK_2FKM H1
00670 WAN FU. Pa/Br 1950; CP; 9200; 149 × 9.8 (488 × 31.3); M; 15; ex SPALMATORI SEAMAN 1975; ex LOOSDRECHT 1968; ex LANGLEECLYDE 1961

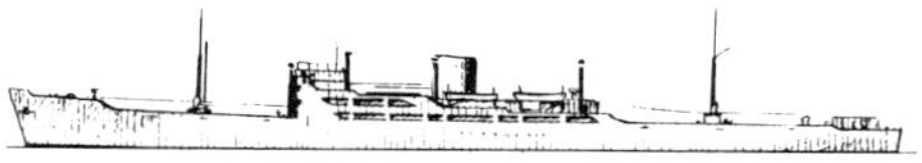

MK_2FKM H1
⋆**00680 STARLIGHT.** RC/Br 1944; C; 7400; 136.7 × 8.4 (449 × 27.1); M; 12.5; ex PARNON 1979; ex LA CUMBRE 1959; ex EMPIRE MACDERMOTT 1948

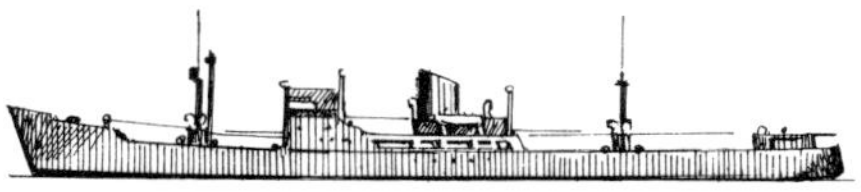

MK_2FKM H1
● **00690 LIDO.** Sg/Br 1957; C; 5371; 135.5 × 8.8 (415 × 29); M; 15; ex TAIWAN 1975; ex ALBANY 1971 Sisters **00691 LIBRA** (Sg); ex EUROPE 1976; ex PICARDY 1971 **00692 LIHO** (Sg); ex JAPAN 1976; ex THESSALY 1971

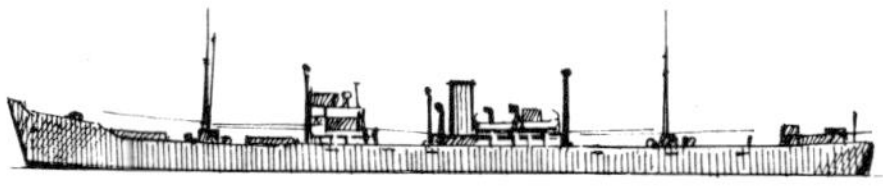

MK_2FKM H1
⋆**00700 HOPING WU SHI WU.** RC/Br 1943; C; 7000; 136.2 × 7.9 (447 × 26); R; 10; ex WISHFORD 1959; ex DEMETRIUS D.S. 1958; ex SCOTTISH MONARCH 1957; May be called **ZHAN DOU 55.**

MK_2FKM H1
00710 SUDELMAR II. Ur/No 1951; C; 5100; 134.7 × 7.7 (442 × 25.4); M; 15; ex SOLSYN 1975; ex THORSGAARD 1972 Sister **00711 KOTA SABAS** (Sg); ex THORSCAPE 1976

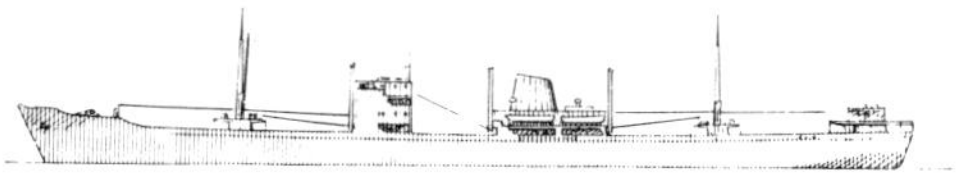

MK_2FKM H1
● ⋆**00720 YU QUAN SHAN.** RC/No 1959; C; 5800; 146.06 × 8.09 (479.2 × 26.54); M; 17; ex THORSRIVER 1977 Sisters ⋆**00721 LIU PAN SHAN** (RC); ex THORSHOPE 1978 ⋆**00722 LU LIANG SHAN** (RC); ex THORSTREAM 1978

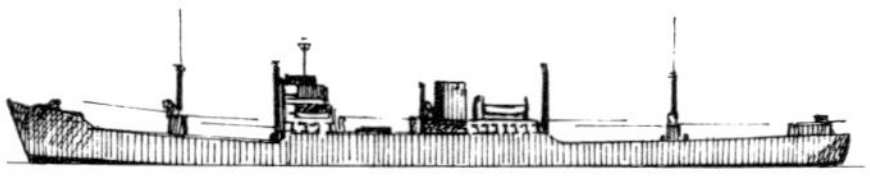

MK_2FKM H1
00730 PERMATARIS. Cy/Br 1941; C; 6500; 135 × 8.4 (455 × 27.3); M; 10; ex RHEINFELS 1968; ex ALCHIBA 1956; ex FRANS HALS 1946; ex EMPIRE RENNIE 1942

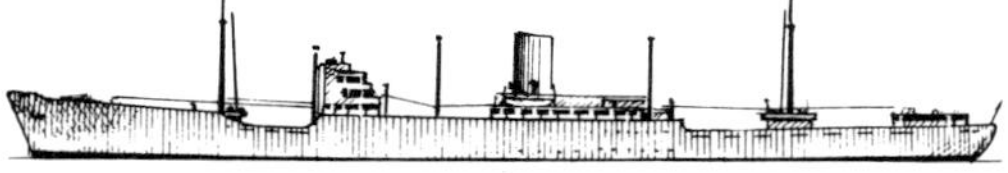

MK_2FKM H12
00740 BLITAR. Ia/Ne 1949; PC; 9400; 157 × 9.6 (515 × 21.3); TM; 16 Sister **00741 LANGKOES** (Ia)

MK_2FKM H123
00750 FOOCHOW. So/Br 1955; C; 7500; 145 × 7.7 (478 × 25.8); M; 13; ex KHUZISTAN 1973

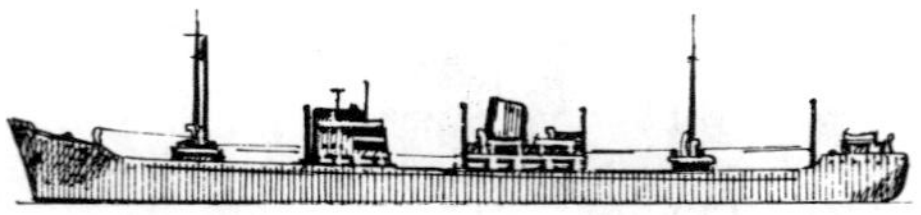

MK$_2$FKMK$_i$H13
00760 MARIYA. Sg/No 1951; CP; 5900; 143 × 7.8 (469 × 25.7); M; 15; ex TIMUR STAR 1975; ex KONGSFJORD 1972

MK$_2$FKMK H13
⋆**00770 CRNA GORA.** Ys/Ne 1951; C; 5800; 140.8 × 7.93 (462 × 26); M; 16.

MK$_2$FM H
⋆**00780 HOPING CHI SHI WU**. RC/US 1942; C; 7100; 134.7 × 8.2 (442 × 27); R; 11; ex KASERT 1960; ex TERNATE 1959; ex GOVERT FIINCK 1947; ex OCEAN ATHLETE 1943; May be called **ZHAN DOU 75.**

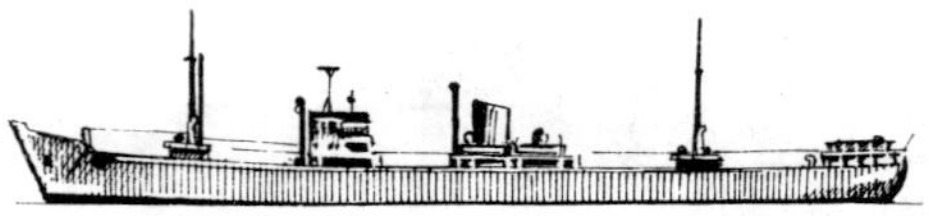

MK$_2$FM H1
00790 NISSOS ITHAKI. Gr/No 1953; C; 5200; 135.2 × 7.9 (443 × 26.1); M; 15; ex ROBIN HOOD 1973; ex NOREFJORD 1972

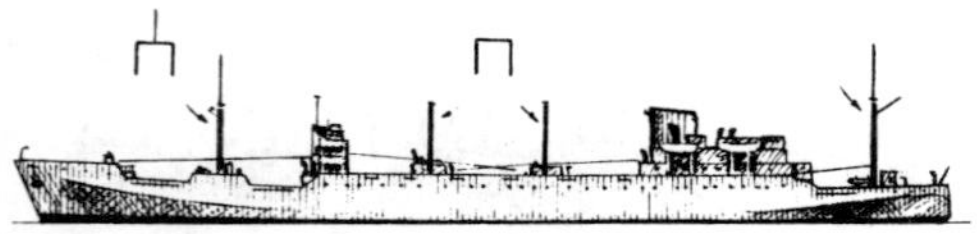

MK$_2$FM H12
00800 KAROTUA. Pk/Br 1958; C; 5800/8300; 148.6 × 8.6 (488 × 27.9); M; 15.5; ex WEYBRIDGE 1967; ex ROSSETTI 1964; ex WEYBRIDGE 1964 Sister **00801 SWAT** (Pk): ex WIMBLEDON 1967; ex PORT WIMBLEDON 1965; ex WIMBLEDON 1960

MK$_2$FM H13
00810 MOHAMMED ABBAS. Db/De 1929; C; 4300; 116 × 7.4 (381 × 24.9); TSM; 10.5; ex DUKEGAT 1969; ex URSULA SCHULTE 1966; ex SACHSENWALD 1953; ex SOMERVILLE 1950

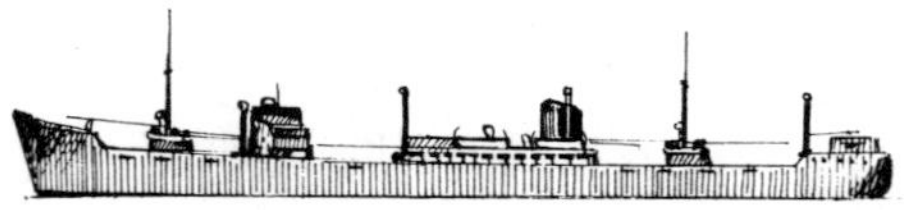

MK$_2$FMK H13
00820 KRONOS 1. Cy/Br 1950; C; 6200; 141.4 × 7.9 (464 × 29); M; 14; ex FOS 1978; ex DAN FODIO 1974; ex LA SIERRA 1959; Tall KP abreast funnel.

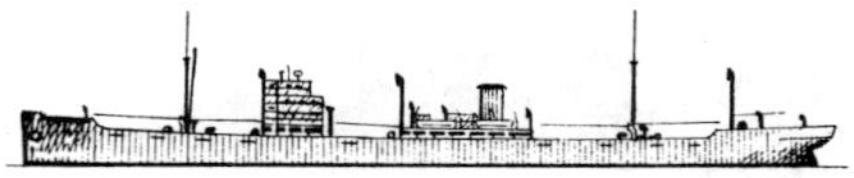

MK$_2$FMK H13
⋆**00830 HOPING SSU SHI PA**. RC/Fr 1926; C; 5400; 132 × 7.9 (433 × 26); M; 12; ex SUNNY PRINCE 1958; ex TIJUCA 1952; May be called **ZHAN DOU 48.**

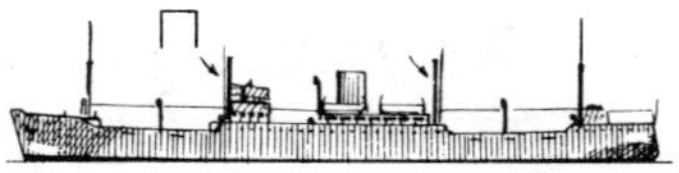

MK$_3$FK$_2$M H123
00840 CHRYSSOPIGI II. Gr/Fr 1951; C; 3700; 103 × 6.3 (338 × 21.6); M; 13; ex OUED - SOUS 1970

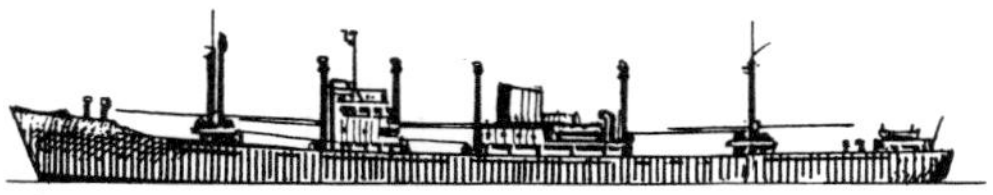

MK_3FKM H/H1
★**00850 ARCHANGELSK.** Ru/Fi 1952; C; 5700; 139.3 × 7.8 (457 × 25.9); M; 16; Sisters (Ru flag). ★**00851 BALTIYSK** ★**00852 BRATSK** ★**00853 IZHEVSK** ★**00854 KIROVSK** ★**00855 MICHURINSK** (RC flag) ★**00856 XUCHANG;** ex LIDICE 1967 Similar (bipod masts). **00857 ABULWAFA** (Eg); ex ACONCAGUA 1976 **00858 ABULFEDA** (Eg); ex ARAGUAYA 1976 **00859 HONOR SEA** (Pa); ex UNIVERSAL QUEEN 1977; ex ACTINIA 9174

MK_3FKMK H13
00890 LAGOS EXPRESS. Gr/No 1953; C; 6400; 152 × 8.4 (499 × 27.6); M; 17; ex TOWADA 1978; ex TAGUS 1975 Similar: **00891 LUK CHAU** (Pa); ex SOL PEMKO 1975; ex THALATTA 1970 **00892 KOTA MOLEK** (Sg); ex TIBER 1976; **00893 KOTA ALAM** (Sg); ex TUGELA 1976

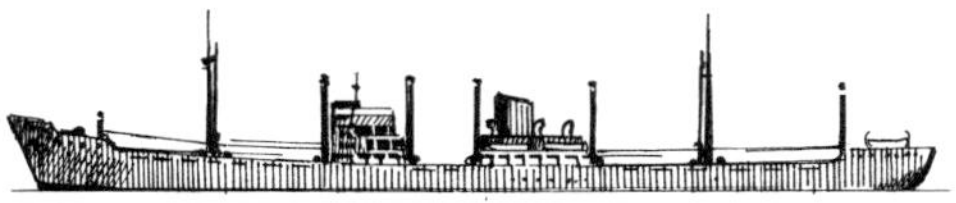

MK_3FKMK H13
00920 ROSSELLAEMME. It/Ne 1949; C; 6000; 146 × 8.2 (479 × 27); M; 15.2; ex HOOGKERK 1969 Sister **00921 ALBERTOEMME** (It); ex HEEMSKERK 1969

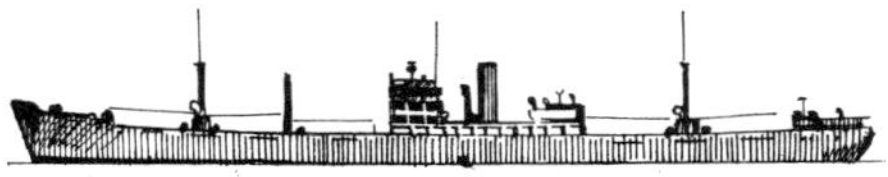

MKMFM H1
★**00940 ZHAN DOU 53** RC/Br 1945; C; 7100; 134.4 × 8.2 (441 × 27); R; 11; ex HOPING 53

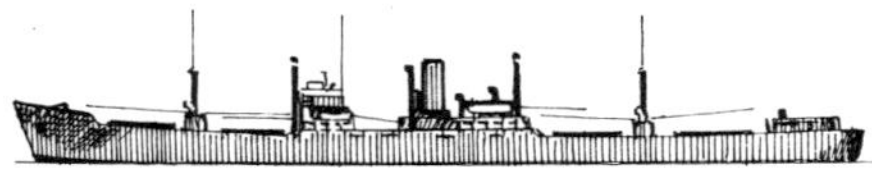

MKMKFKM H
★**00960 ZHAN DOU 51.** RC/Ca 1943; C; 7100; 134.4 × 8.2 (411 × 27); R; 11; ex HOPING 51 Similar (RC flag). ★**00961 ZHAN DOU 13;** ex HOPING 13 ★**00962 ZHAN DOU 76;** ex HOPING 76 ★**00963 ZHAN DOU 79;** ex HOPING 79

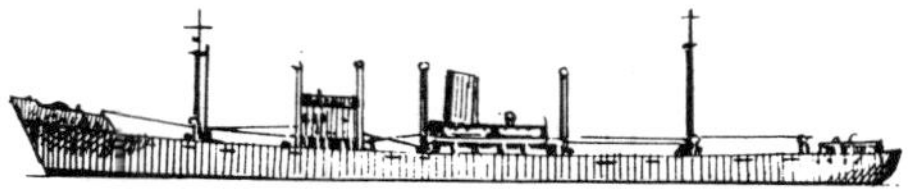

MK_3FKM H1
00870 MINOUTSI. Cy/Ne 1948; CP; 8400; 145 × 7.7 (476 × 25.5); M; 12.5; ex PROCYON 1966; ex ALBIREO 1963

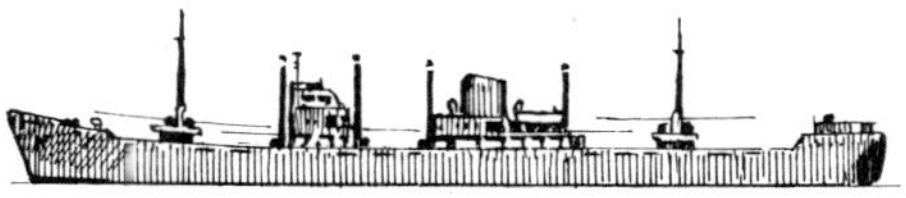

MK_3FKM H13
00880 BARU HOPE. Gr/Fi 1957; C; 5500; 139.91 × 7.83 (459.02 × 25.69); M; 16; ex ARTEMON 1980; ex ANGRA 1973 Similar: **00881 EFSTANTHIA** (Gr); ex ATHINAI II 1980; ex SPORADES 1978; ex ASYNJA 1972

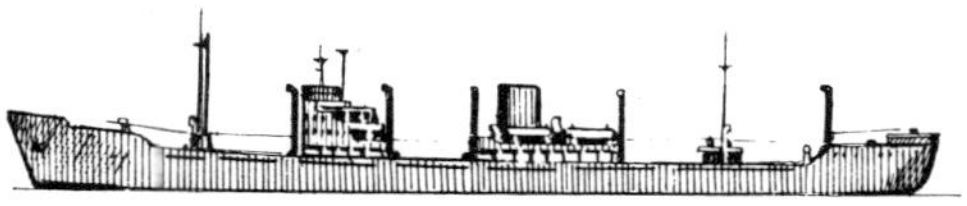

MK_3FKMK H13
00900 KOTA MAS. Sg/Sw 1953; C; 7000; 155.5 × 8.4 (510 × 27.6); M; 17.5; ex THEBEN 1978 Similar: **00901 TOYA** (Sg); ex THEMIS 1975

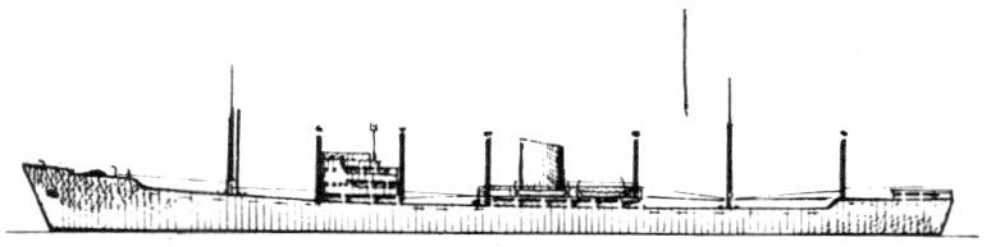

MK_3FKMK H13
00910 MINERVA. Gr/Sw 1949; C; 6100; 146 × 8.2 (479 × 29); M; 16; ex TALLEYRAND 1972

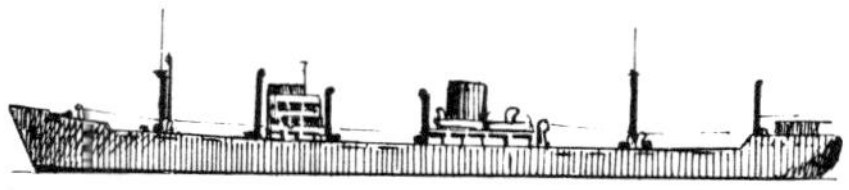

MK_3FMK H13
00930 MAXIMUS. Pa/Sw 1949; C; 4700; 130.7 × 8 (429 × 25.7); M; 15; ex KASSIOPI 1970; ex TENNESSEE 1968 Similar (Raking-topped funnel). **00931 AGILITY** (Gr); ex ION 1970; ex TEXAS 1968

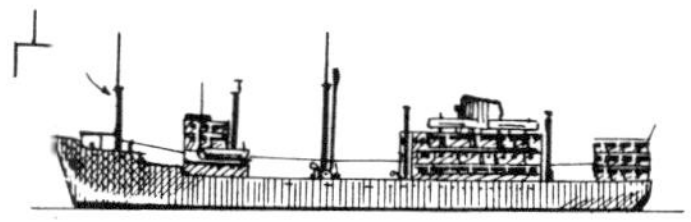

MKMKFK H1
00950 KIMANIS. Sg/Br 1951; PC; 3200; 96 × 5.6 (314 × 18.9); TSM; 12.5.

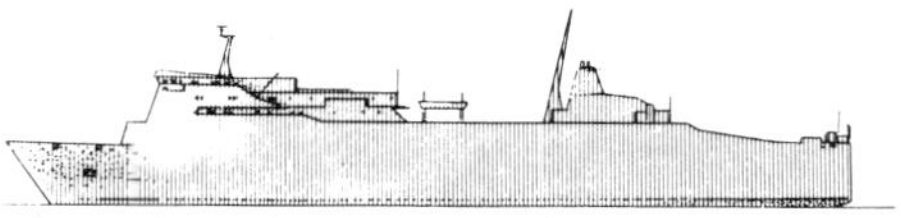

M_2F H2
00970 TRANSGERMANIA. FRG/FRG 1976; ROC; 5600; 135.45 × 6.05 (444.39 × 19.85); TSM; 19 Stern ramp.

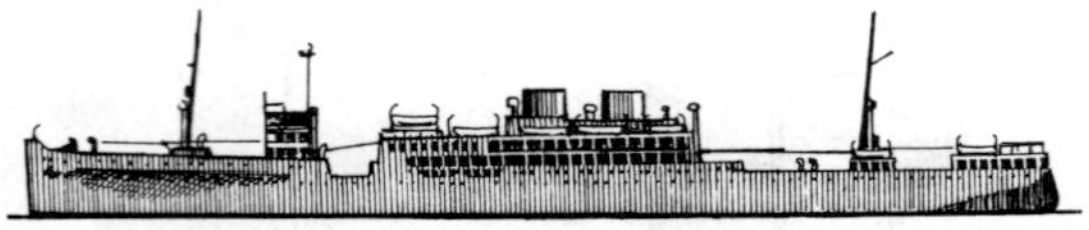

M_2F_2KM H12
⋆**00980 GUANGHUA.** RC/Br 1930; RC; 14200; 166 × 8.7 (545 × 29); TSM; 15; ex SLAPY 1960; ex MARIANNA 1960; ex HIGHLAND PRINCESS 1959

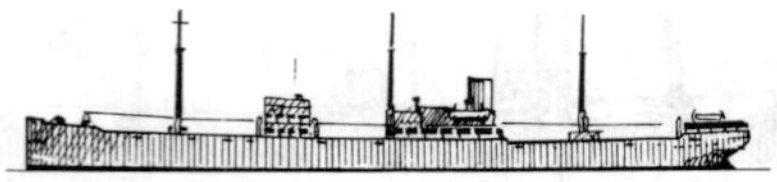

M_2FM H
00990 RODANTHI A. Gr/Ge 1924; C; 3800; 122 × 8 (400 × 26); TSM; 12.5; ex SLOWACKI 1974; ex RENA 1956; ex FORDEFJORD 1937; ex EMMA MAERSK

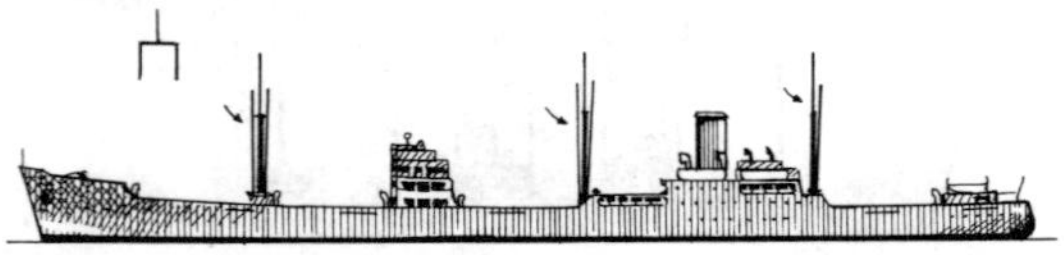

M_2FM H1
01000 UNION ATLANTIC. Pa/Au 1953; O; 9600; 159 × 8 (523 × 29); T; 14.5; ex IRON WYNDHAM 1976

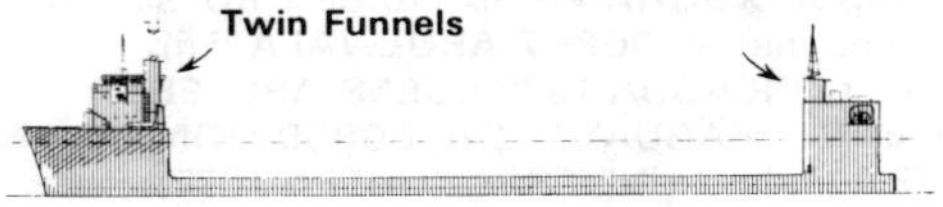

M_2FMF $H1_3$
01010 SUPER SERVANT 1. Ne/Ja 1979; ROC/HL; 10200; 139 × 6.18 (456 × 20.28); TSM; 13; Submersible—broken line shows extent of maximum immersion.

M_2KFM H
⋆**01020 LJGOV.** Ru/Fi 1961; C; 5400; 139.2 × 7.9 (457 × 25.8); M; 14.5 Sisters (Ru flag). ⋆**01021 ALAPAEVSK** ⋆**01022 ALMATEVSK** ⋆**01023 CHERNYAKHOVSK**

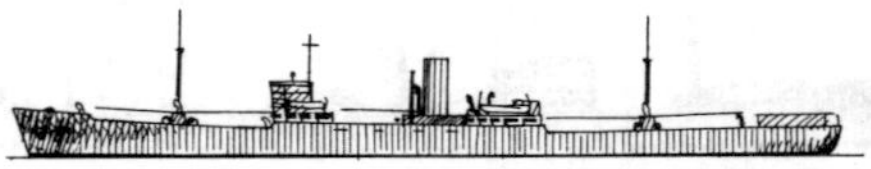

M_2KFM H
⋆**01030 ZHAN DOU 27.** RC/Ca 1944; C; 7000; 134.1 × 8.5 (440 × 27.75); R; 10; ex HOPING 27 Similar (RC flag). ⋆**01031 ZHAN DOU 30;** ex HOPING 30 ⋆**01032 ZHAN DOU 50;** ex HOPING 50 ⋆**01033 ZHAN DOU 52;** ex HOPING 52

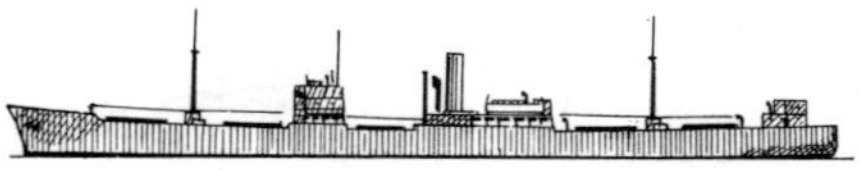

M_2KFM H
⋆**01040 HOPING SSU SHI CHI.** RC/Br 1941; C; 7200; 132.9 × 7.9 (436 × 26); R; 11; ex MASTRO STELIOS 1960; ex NORTON 1956; May be called **ZHAN DOU 47.** May no longer be in service.

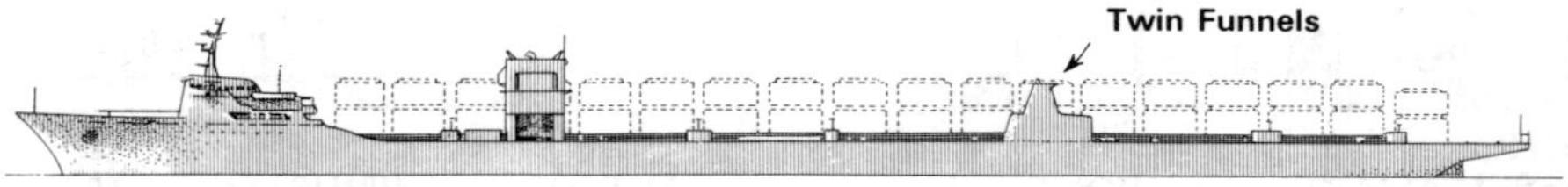

MNF H1
01050 STONEWALL JACKSON. US/US 1974; Bg; 32270; 272.55 × 11.62 (894.19 × 38.12); T; 22; **"LASH"** type Sisters **01051 ROBERT E. LEE 01052 SAM HOUSTON 01052 BUTTON GWINNETT;** ex GREEN VALLEY 1980 **01054 GEORGE WYTHE;** ex GREEN ISLAND 1980 **01055 WILLIAM HOOPER;** ex GREEN HARBOUR 1980 Probable sisters: **01056 BENJAMIN HARRISON 01057 EDWARD RUTLEDGE**

Profile 2

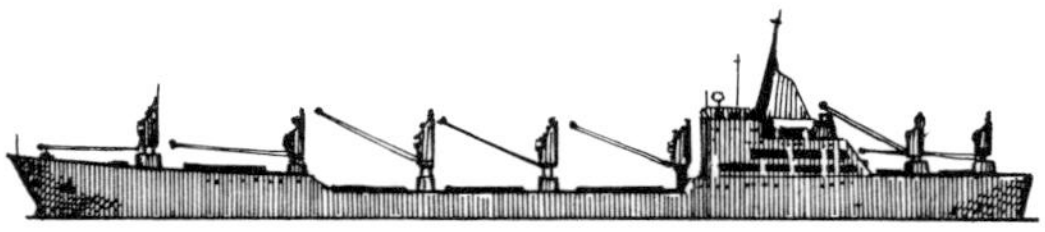

C_5MFC_2 H13
01060 ZAMBEZE. Fr/Fr 1971; C; 13200; 167 × 10.8 (548 × 35.75); M; 23 Sisters (Fr flag). **01061 ZEEBRUGGE 01062 ZELANDE**

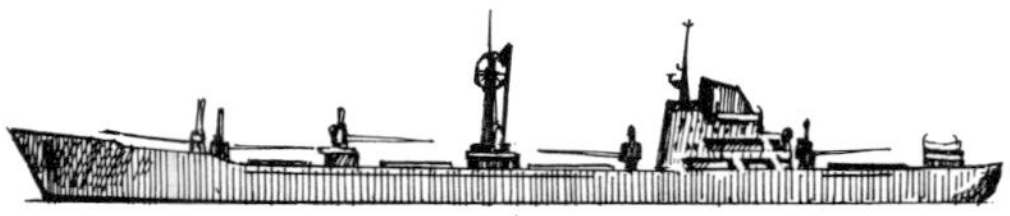

C_3MCMFC H1
⋆01070 BELORETSK. Ru/De 1962; C; 10500; 160.3 × 9.6 (526 × 31.7); M; 18.5 Sisters (Ru flag). **⋆01071 BELITSK ⋆01072 BELOVODSK ⋆01073 KOSMONAUT** Similar (Ru flag) **⋆01074 BEREZNIKI ⋆01075 BIYSK**

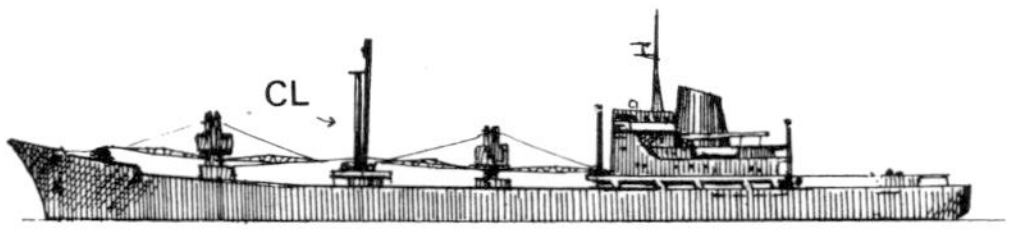

C_2KC_2KMFK H1
01080 EKA DAYA SAMUDERA. Ia/Br 1966; C; 7100/10300; 155 × 9.3 (509 × 30.6); M; —; ex ORCOMA 1979

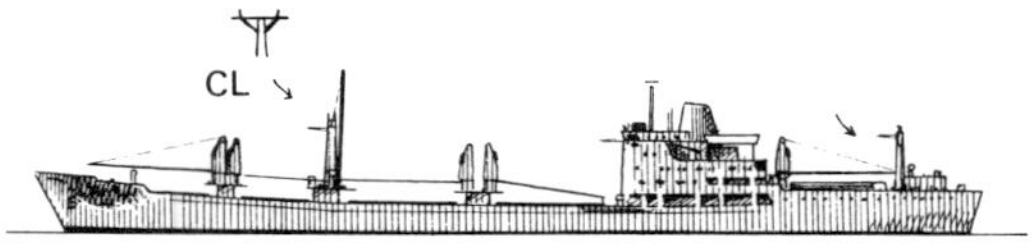

C_2KC_2MFCK H13
01090 GARNET. Pa/Sw 1968; C; 5900/9400; 153.9 × 8.6 (505 × 28.25); M; 18.5; ex MAIHAR 1978 Sister **01091 TURQUOISE** (Pa); ex MAHSUD 1978

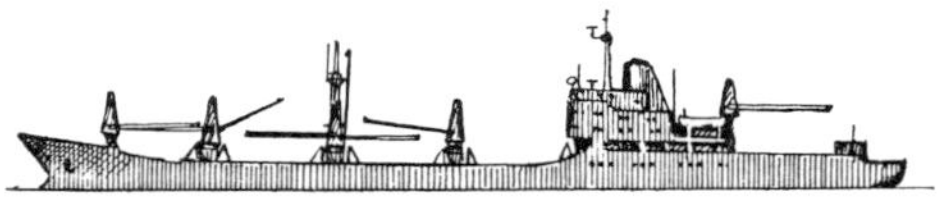

C_2KCMFC H13
⋆01100 PYATIDYESYATILETIYE KOMSOMOLA. Ru/Ru 1968; C; 3900/5600; 129.9 × 7.8 (426 × 25.7); M; 16.5; **"Kaliningrad" type.** Also known as **50 LETIYE KOMSOMOLA.**

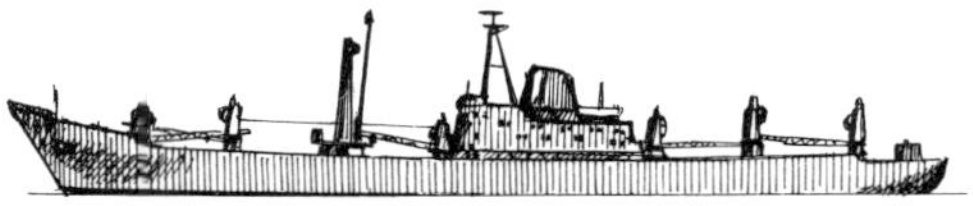

C_2KCMFC_3 H1
01110 MARIETTA. Gr/Br 1965; R; 6100/8300; 149 × 9.3 (489 × 30.65); M; 19; ex PORT ALBANY 1972 Sister **01111 JULIETTA** (Gr); ex PORT HUON1972 Similar (Conical funnel). **01112 ANGELIKI** (Gr); ex PORT BURNIE 1972

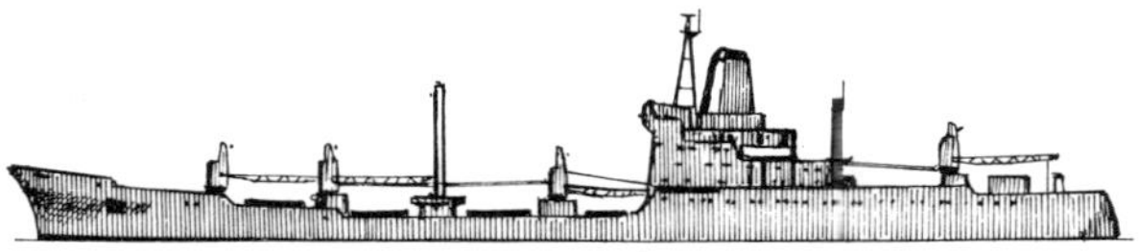

$C_2KCMFKC$ H13
01120 PORT CAROLINE. Br/Br 1968; R; 12400/16300; 186.5 × 10.8 (612 × 35.5); TSM; 21.5 Sister **01121 PORT CHALMERS** (Br)

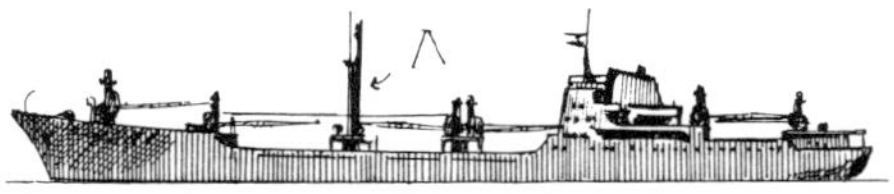

$C_2MC_2MFC_2$ H13
01140 PEMBA. Mb/Ja 1960; CP; 5100; 138 × 7.7 (454 × 25.2); M; 17; ex PORTO AMELIA 1976; ex TENOS 1970 Sister **01141 PABLOEVERETT** (Li); ex SAMOS 1978

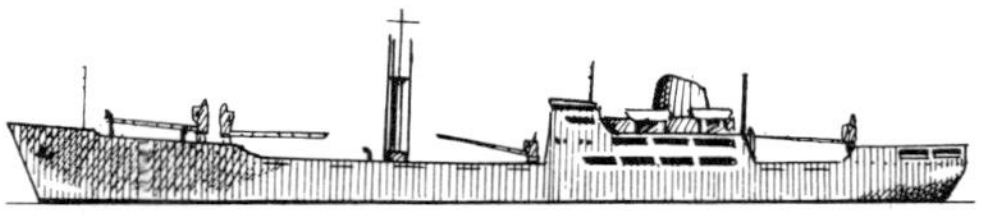

C_2MCFKC H1
01150 STRATHANNA. Br/Br 1966; C; 6300/8800; 153.3 × 8.4 (503 × 27.56); M; 17; ex REGISTAN 1975 Sister **01151 STRATHANGUS** (Br); ex SERBISTAN 1975

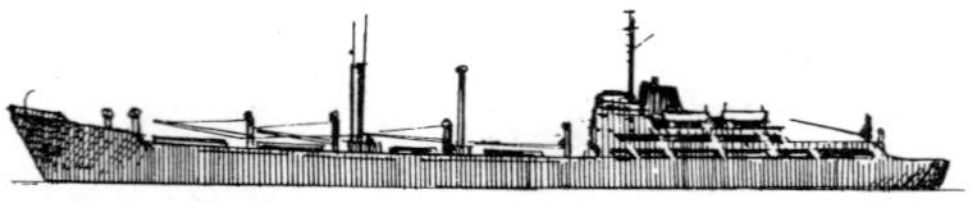

C_2MCKCMFC H1
⋆01160 KAIHUA. RC/Sw 1958; C; 6400/10100; 149.3 × 9.8 (490 × 32.1); M; 15.5; ex GAOYAN 1976; ex ARISTANAX 1973; ex W.R. LUNDGREN 1976

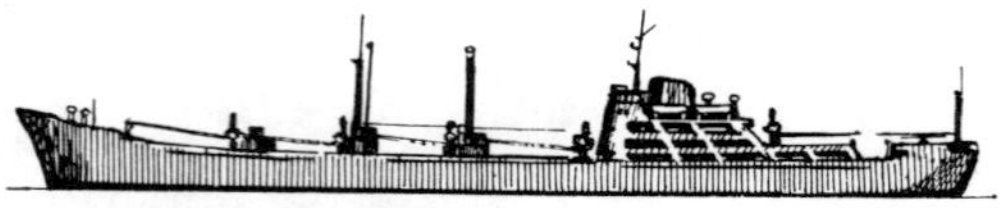

C_2MCKCMFCK H1
⋆01170 CHANGSHU. RC/Sw 1958; C/TS; 6900/10500; 149.3 × 9 (490 × 29.55); M; 15; ex CHIANG KIANG 1970; ex G.D. KENNEDY 1967

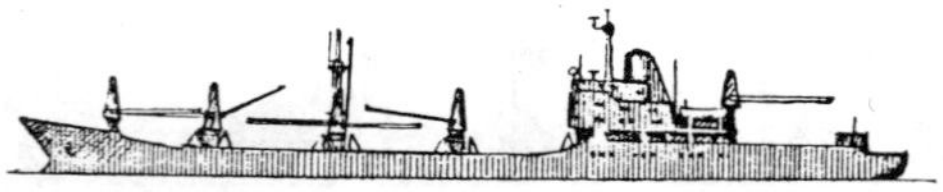

C_2MCMFC H13
⋆01180 PYATIDYESYATILETIYE KOMSOMOLA. Ru/Ru 1968; C; 3900/5600; 129.9 × 7.8 (426 × 25.7); M; 16.5; **"Kaliningrad" type.** Also known as **50 LETIYE KOMSOMOLA**

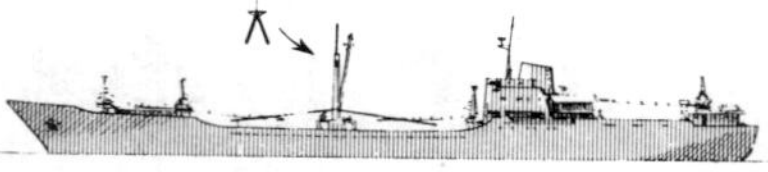

C_2MCMFC H13
01190 OAKWOOD. Pa/De 1964; C; 2600/4600; 121.01 × —/7.01 (397 × —/22.9); M; 16; ex NEPTUNE BERYL 1980; ex OLAU JARL 1970; ex CAP EGMONT 1970; ex CAP FLINDERS 1967; ex OLAU JARL 1966; ex SARDINIA 1966; ex OLAU JARL 1964 Sister **01191 TEAKWOOD** (Pa); ex NEPTUNE JASPER 1980; ex CAP NELSON 1970; ex OLAU KNUD 1966

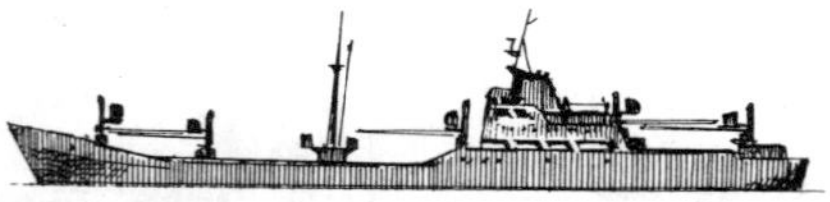

C_2MCMFC$_2$ H13
● **⋆01200 ZHEN ZHU QUAN.** RC/Br 1961; C; 6700; 129.88 × 7.79 M; 16; ex SUPACHAI BULAKUL 1980, ex SHENDI 1980; ex BOMBALA 1971 Sisters **01201 CHERRY SINGA** (Sg); ex MAHABHARAT 1980; ex BANKURA 1971 **01202 SEASPRITE** (Li); ex BUNGA KENANGA 1978; ex BULIMBA 1978 **01203 SPIJKENISSE** (Pa); ex MARIDI 1980; ex BARPETA 1971

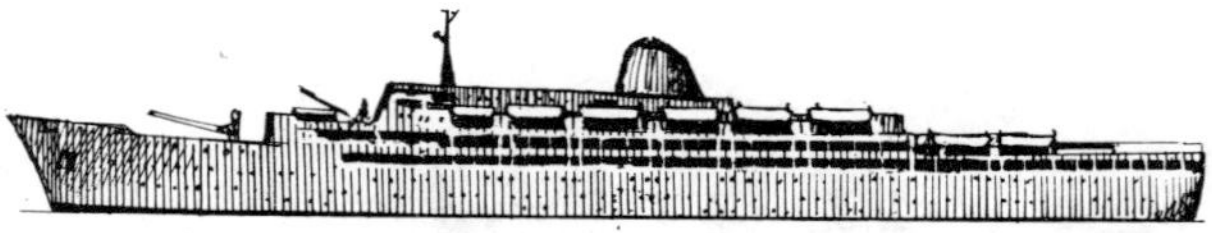

C_2MF H
01210 FAIR STAR. Li/Br 1957; P; 21500; 185.6 × 8.4 (609 × 27.7); TST; 20; ex OXFORDSHIRE 1964

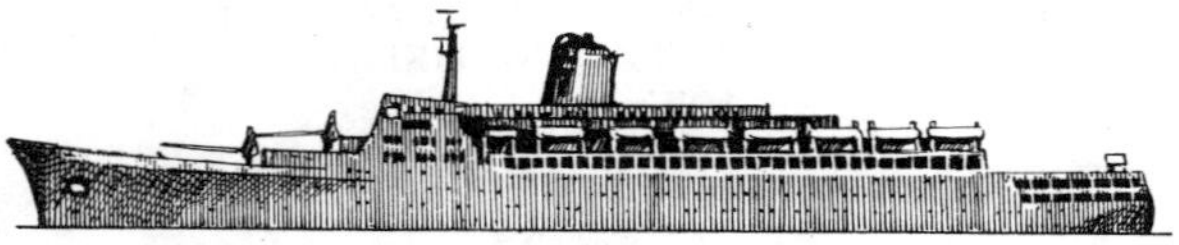

C_2MF
01220 FAIRWIND. Li/Br 1957; P; 16700; 185.3 × 8.9 (608 × 29.4); TST; 20; ex SYLVANIA 1968 Sister **01221 FAIRSEA** (Li); ex FAIRLAND 1971; ex CARINTHIA 1968

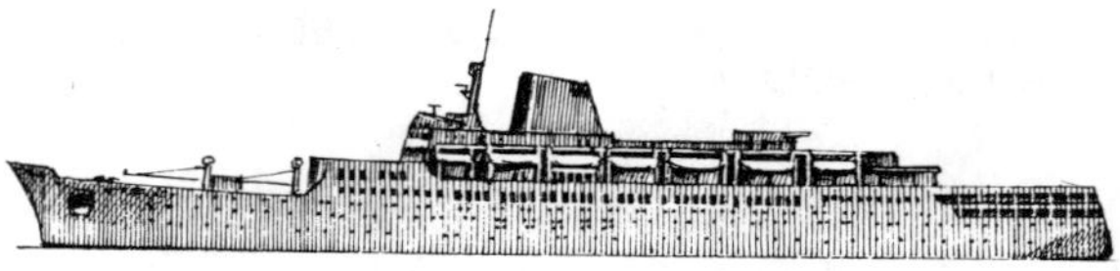

C_2MF H
01230 CARLA C. It/Fr 1952; P; 20000; 182.9 × 8.6 (600 × 28.2); TST; 23; ex FLANDRE 1968

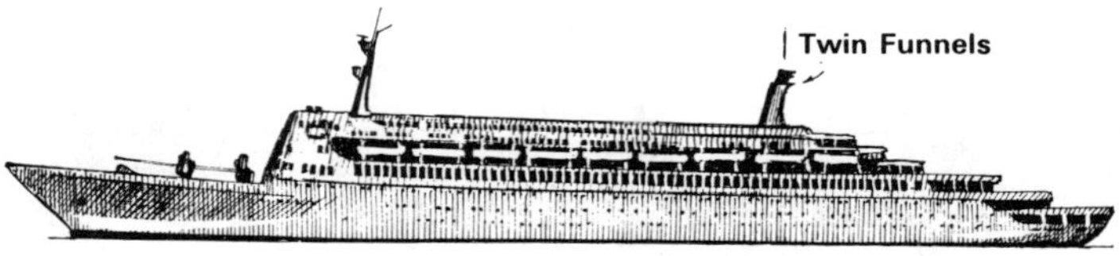

C_2MF H
01240 EUGENIO C. It/It 1966; P; 30600; 217 × 8.6 (773 × 28.4); TST; 27.

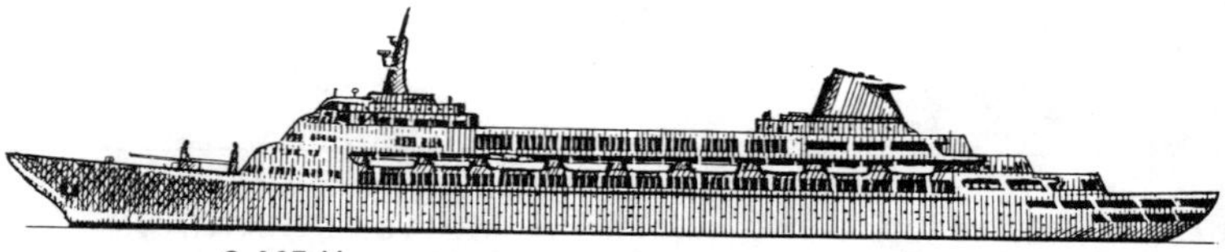

C_2MF H
01250 OCEANIC. Pa/It 1965; P; 27600; 238 × 8.6 (782 × 28.4); TST; 26.5.

$C_2MF_2C_2$ H
01260 ORIANA. Br/Br 1960; P; 41900; 245 × 9.75 (804 × 32); TST; 27.5.

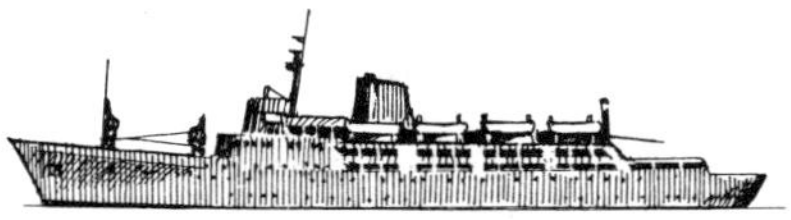

C_2MFK H
01270 CITTA DI NAPOLI. It/It 1962; P; 5700; 120.4 × 5.4 (395 × 17.9); TSM; 19.5 Sister **01271 CITTA DI NUORO** (It).

C_2MFK H1
● **01280 CAMPANIA FELIX.** It/It 1952; P; 5200; 116.7 × 5.5 (383 × 18); TSM; 17; May now be CMF. Similar: **01281 GOLDEN SUN** (Cy); ex ARBOREA 1976

C_2MFM H
01290 JUAN MARCH. Sp/Sp 1966; RoPCF; 6900; 130.8 × 5.4 (429 × 17.9); TSM; 21 Sisters (Sp flag). **01291 CIUDAD DE COMPOSTELA 01292 LAS PALMAS DE GRAN CANARIA 01293 SANTA CRUZ DE TENERIFFE**

C_2MFM H1
01300 NORDLYS. No/De 1951; P; 2200; 80.2 × 4.5 (263 × 14.9); M; 15.5 Sisters (No flag). **01301 NORDSTJERNEN 01302 POLARLYS**

C_2MFMC H
01310 AL KHAIRAT. Ku/Br 1960; P; 2900; 90.2 × 4.6 (296 × 15.2); M; 16; ex ST. CLAIR II 1977; ex SAINT CLAIR 1977

C_2MFMC H12
01320 SEIS MARINER. No/No 1955; CP; 1100; 76.1 × 5 (250 × 16.8); M; 15; ex ARA 1973. Sisters **01321 AGIOS NICOLAOS** (Mv); ex MABELLA 1977; ex URANUS 1972 **01322 VOLISSOS** (Cy); ex URSA

C_2M_2F
01330 VITTORE CARPACCIO. It/It 1963; P; 1200; 72.24 × 3.68 (237 × 12.07); M; 12.25; May be rebuilt—see ANTONELLO DA MESSINA.

C_2M_2F H
01340 ANTONELLO DA MESSINA. It/It 1963; Roc/F; 1200; 72.27 × 3.66 (237.10 × 12); M; —; Bow & stern doors/ramp. Converted from passenger; original sister VITTORE CARPACCIO may be similarly converted—which see:

C_2M_2F H
01350 HARALD JARL. No/No 1960; P; 2600; 87.4 × 4.6 (287 × 15.2); M; 16.

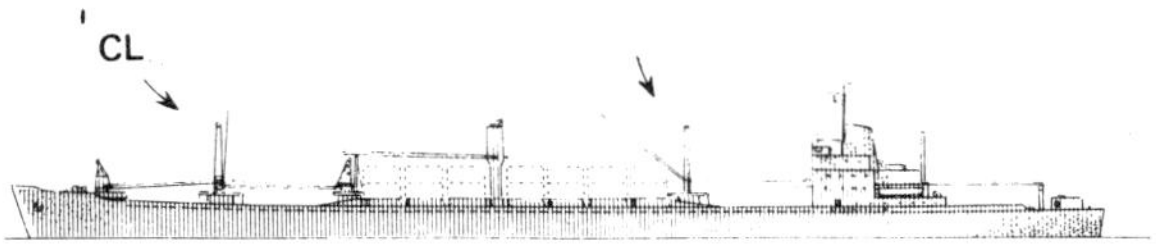

CKC_2KMFK H1
01360 ST. FRANCOIS. Fr/Br—Po 1970/78; C/Con; 12400; 174.53 × 8.49; M; 16; Modified **"SD 14"** type. Lengthened and converted 1978. Sister **01361 ST. PAUL** (Fr)

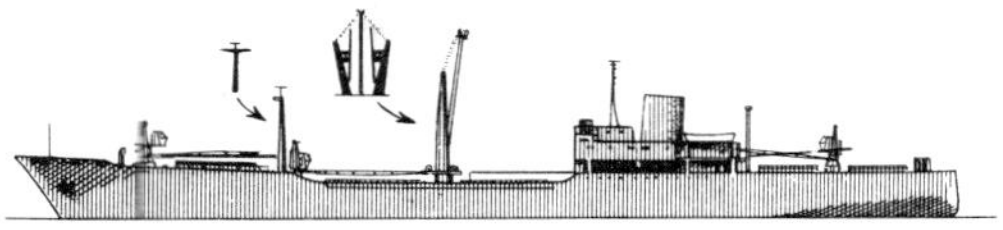

CKCKMFKC H13
01370 TIMARU STAR. Br/Br 1967; R; 6000/8400; 151.5 × 9 (497 × 29.6); M; —;

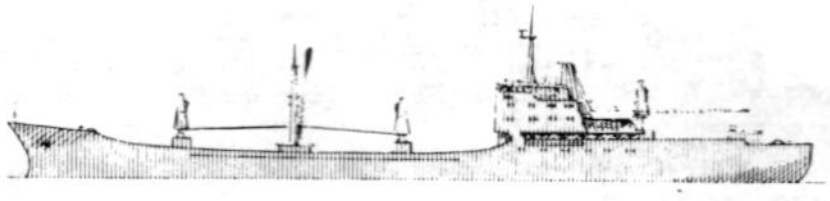

CKCMFC H13

● *01380 **'KALININGRAD'** type; —/Ru 1969; C; 3900/5600; 129 × 6.55/7.83 (426 × 21.9/25.69); M; 16; There are 2 types—the earlier ones having cranes by the foremast. Sisters (Ru flag). ***01381 DONETSKIY KOMSOMOLETS *01382 DONETSKIY KHIMIK *01383 DONETSKIY METALLURG *01384 DONETSKIY SHAKHTER *01385 KOMSOMOLETS *01386 BRYANSKIY MASHINOSTROITEL *01387 LENINSKIYE ISKRY *01388 KRASNOYARSKI KOMSOMOLETS *01389 KOMSOMOLETS ARMENII *01390 KOMSOMOLETS AZERBAYDZHANA *01391 KOMSOMOLETS GRUZII *01392 KOMSOMOLETS MOLDAVII *01393 KOMSOMOLETS NAKHODKI *01394 KOMSOMOLETS SPASSKA *01395 KOMSOMOLETS USSURIYSKA *01396 KOMSOMOLETS VLADIVOSTOKA *01397 KOMSOMOLETS ROSSII *01398 KOMSOMOLETS KAZAKHSTANA *01399 KOMSOMOLETS ADZHARII *01400 KOMSOMOLETS BYELORUSSII *01401 KOMSOMOLETS TURKMENII *01402 KOMSOMOLETS PRAVDA *01403 MOSKOVSKIY KOMSOMOLETS *01404 ZHDANOVSKIY KOMSOMOLETS *01405 30—LETYE POBEDY (or TRIDTSATILETIYE POBEDY) *01406 RABOCHAYA SMENA *01407 SMENA *01408 STARYY BOLSHEVIK:** (Rm flag); ***01409 SALAJ *01410 NASAUD:** (Eg flag). **01411 RAMSES II 01412 NEFERTITI 01413 ISIS 01414 AMOUN 01415 THUTMOSE 01416 AHMOS 01417 IKHNATON 01418 MEMPHIS**

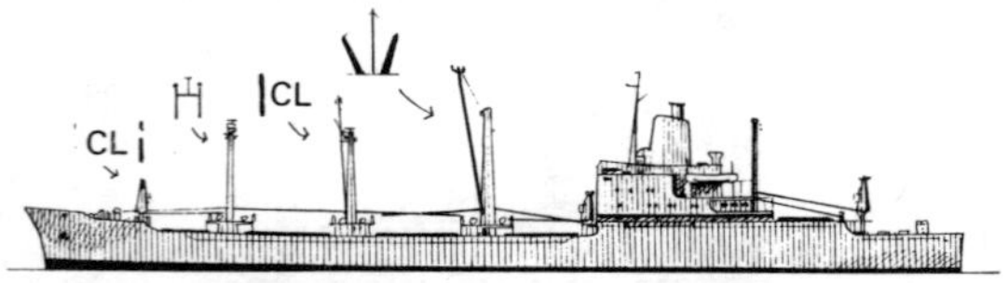

CK_3CMFKC H13

01420 FRIESENSTEIN. FRG/FRG 1967; CP; 7500/10500; 162.1 × 10 (532 × 32.1); M; 21; This vessel, with HOLSTENSTEIN and SCHWABENSTEIN, is to be rebuilt as a semi-container ship and may alter in appearance. Sisters **01421 HOLSTENSTEIN** (FRG) **01422 SCHWABENSTEIN** (FRG) **01423 RENAICO** (Ch); ex SACHSENSTEIN 1979 **01424 RAPEL** (Ch); ex BADENSTEIN 1979 **01425 SOUTH STAR** (Sg); ex BAYERNSTEIN 1980

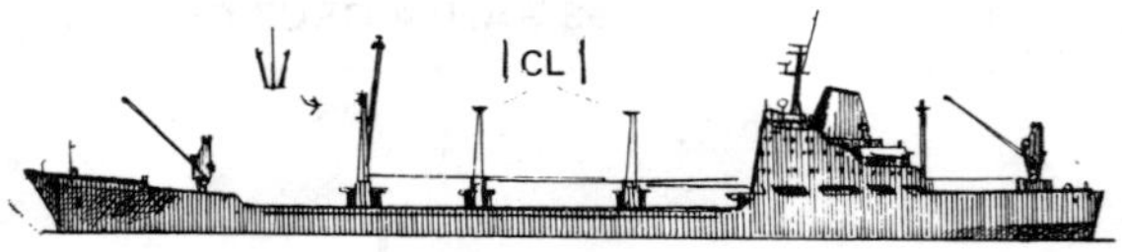

CK_3MFKC H13

01430 MONTERREY. Me/Ys 1971; Pt. Con; 12600; 173.1 × 10.1 (568 × 32.11); M; — Sister **01431 TOLUCA** (Me)

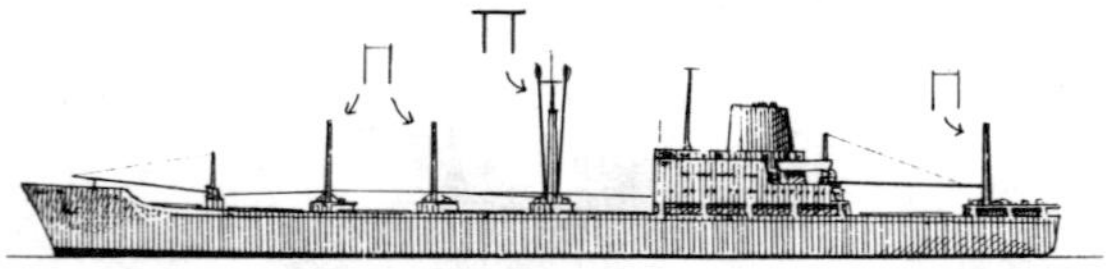

CK_2M_2FCK H1

● **01440 CECILIE MAERSK.** De/Sw 1967; CP; 11000; 170.6 × 10.4 (560 × 34.1); M; 22.5; Side Doors. Sisters (De flag). **01441 CORNELIA MAERSK 01442 CHASTINE MAERSK 01443 CHRISTIAN MAERSK 01444 CLARA MAERSK 01445 CLIFFORD MAERSK**

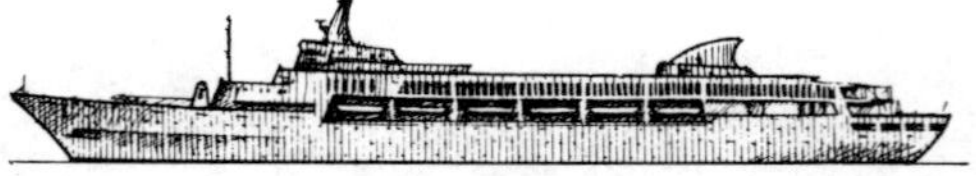

CKMF H

01450 ITALIA. It/It 1967; P; 12200; 149 × 6.4 (489 × 21.1); TSM; 19.

CKMF H1

01460 MUTIARA. My/My 1977; SS; 725 SWT; 71 × 4 (232.94 × 13.12); M; 16; Operated by Malaysian Navy. Helicopter deck aft.

$CKMFC_2$ H1

01470 CARMEN. Ch/Be 1957; C; 1500; 88 × 5.3 (289 × 17.5); M; 13; ex GERTRUD BRATT 1967 Sisters **01471 GLORIA L** (Ch); ex BELGIA 1967 ***01472 ZLARIN** (Ys); ex REINE ASTRID 1965

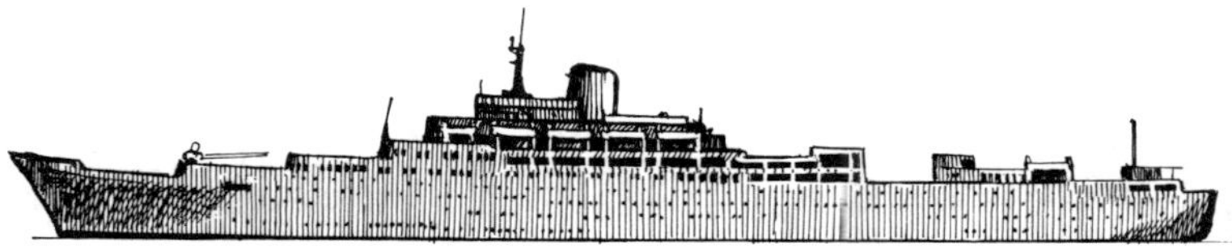

CKMFK H
01480 MARGARITA L. Pa/Br 1960; F; 34200; 238.6 × 9.8 '783 × 32.1); TST; 23.5; ex WINDSOR CASTLE 1978

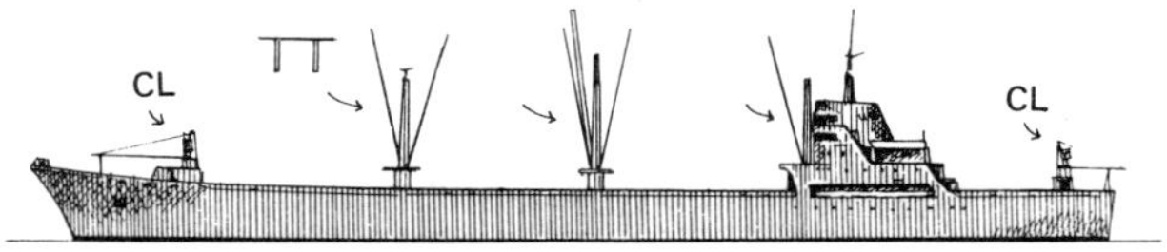

CKMKMFC H
01490 DEFIANCE. US/US 1969; RoVC/Con; 11800; 183.2 × 10.4 (603 × 34.1); T; 23.5; ex MORMACSEA 1970 Sisters (US flag). **01491 GREAT REPUBLIC;** ex MORMACSKY 1970 **01492 RED JACKET;** ex MORMACSTAR 1970 **01493 YOUNG AMERICA;** ex MORMACSUN 1970

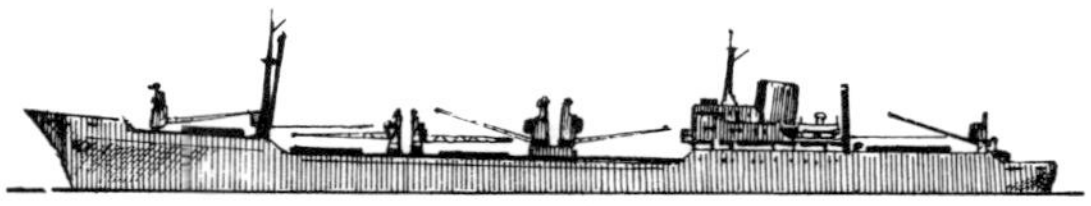

CMC_4MFKC H13
01500 HALIFAX STAR. Br/Br 1964; R; 6900/9200; 141 × 8.8 (463 × 29); M; 19 Sister **01501 LIGURIA** (Pa); ex NEW YORK STAR 1980

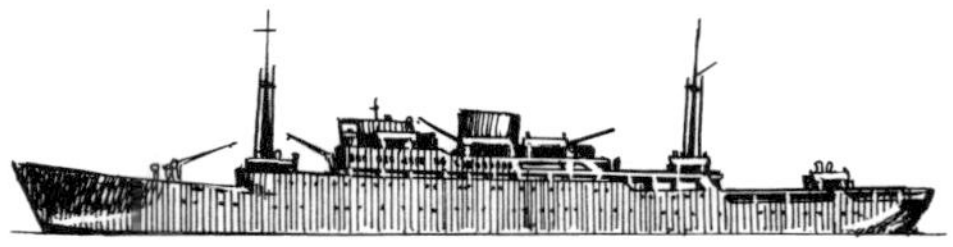

CMC_2FCM H2
01510 KOTA BALI. Sg/Ne 1950; CP; 9000; 146 × 7.2 (479 × 23.7); TSM; 16.5 ex TJIWANI 1974

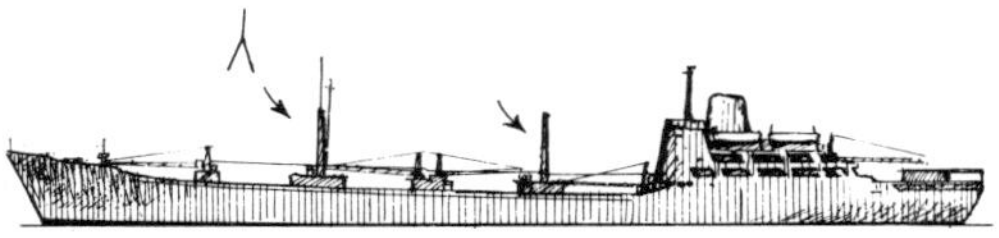

CMC_2KCMFC H13
● **01520 MIRRABOOKA.** Sw/Sw 1961; R; 8100/11300; 156 × 8.73/9.4 (513 × 28.64/30.8); M; 17 Sisters **01521 VENUS DEL MAR** (Ur); ex TEMNAREN 1979 **01522 POPI** (Gr); ex KLIPPAREN 1979

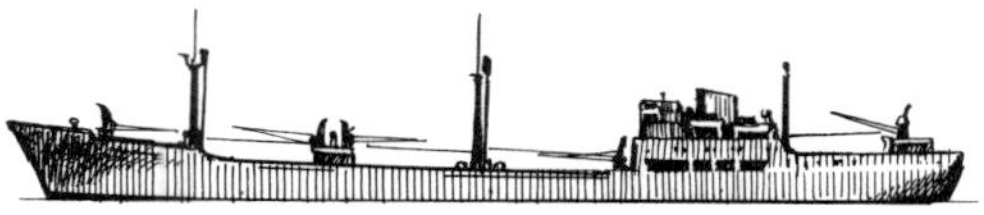

CMC_2MCFKC H13
01530 FEDON. Gr/Ne 1960; CP; 6700; 151 × 8 (496 × 26.2); M; 16; ex IFESTOS 1980; ex ALGORAB 1978 Sisters (RC flag). **⋆01531 LI SHUI;** ex TEXAS 1973; ex ALUDRA 1969 **⋆01532 GUANGSHUI;** ex TORTUGAS 1973; ex ALCHIBA 1969 **⋆01533 JIANSHUI;** ex TENNESEE 1973; ex ALNITAK 1969 **⋆01534 WENSHUI;** ex TAMPA 1973; ex ALAMAK 1969

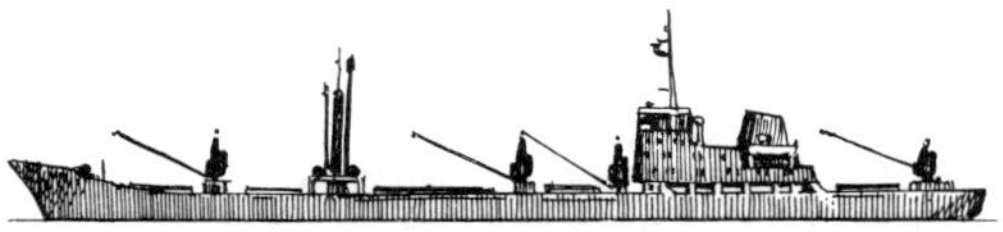

CMC_2MFC H1
⋆01540 OTRADNOE. Ru/Ja 1964; C; 11100; 157 × 9.4 (518 × 30.9); M; 18; Cranes abreast foremast. Sisters (Ru flag). **⋆01541 OLA ⋆01542 OREKHOV ⋆01543 ORSHA ⋆01544 OSTROGOZHSK**

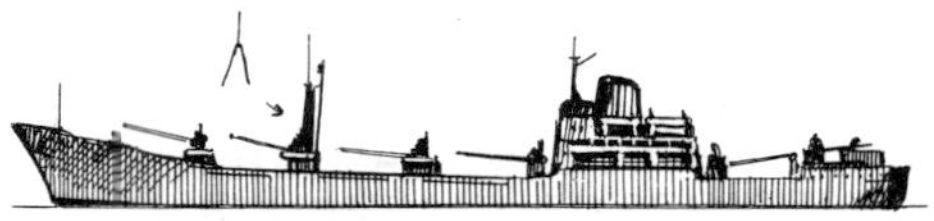

CMC_2MFC_2 H123
01550 HALLAREN. Gr/Sw 1960; R; 6700; 142.6 × 7.2 (468 × 23.9); M; 17 Sister **01551 VINGAREN** (Gr).

CMC_2MFC_2MC H13
● **⋆01560 METALLURG ANASOV.** Ru/Ru 1962; C; 8300/11200; 170 × 8.25/9.75 (558 × 27.07/32); T; 18; Ships vary slightly. Some have lighter masts or masts from funnel. Sisters (Ru flag). **⋆01561 AKADEMIK SHIMANSKIY ⋆01562 BRATSTVO ⋆01563 FREDERIK ZHOLIO-KYURI ⋆01564 KHIRURG VISHNEVSKIY ⋆01565 KRASNAYA PRESNYA ⋆01566 KRASNOE ZNAMYA ⋆01567 KRASNYY-OKTYABAR ⋆01568 KREML ⋆01569 LENINSKIY PIONER ⋆01570 METALLURG BARDIN ⋆01571 METALLURG KURAKO ⋆01572 PARIZHSKAYA KOMMUNA ⋆01573 RAVENSTVO ⋆01574 SVOBODA ⋆01575 TRANSBALT ⋆01576 VALENTINA TERESHKOVA ⋆01577 YUNYY LENINETS ⋆01578 YURIY GAGARIN**

CMCFCMC H
01580 AKDENIZ. Tu/FRG 1955; P; 8800; 144.7×6.1 (474×20.3); TSM; 18.5 Sister **01581 KARADENIZ** (Tu)

CMCFCMC H
01590 EGE. Tu/FRG 1955; P; 6000; 122×5.8 (402×19); M; 14 Sister **01591 IZMIR** (Tu)

CMCFCMC H
01600 GLORY II. Cy/Sw 1944; C; 1300; 89.9×4.9 (295×16.2); M; 13; ex EMMA D.P. 1976; ex MISENO 1973; ex GOTHIA 1963; ex BOHUS 1960

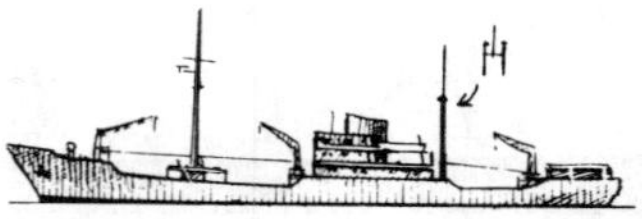

CMCFMC H123
01610 HINTHA. Pa/Ne 1955; C; 2800; 97×5.8 (318×19); M; 12.5; ex ANNITA 1976; ex AMRITHA 1972; ex VAN NECK 1969 Sister **01611 HANDARA** (Sg); ex VAN NOORT 1969

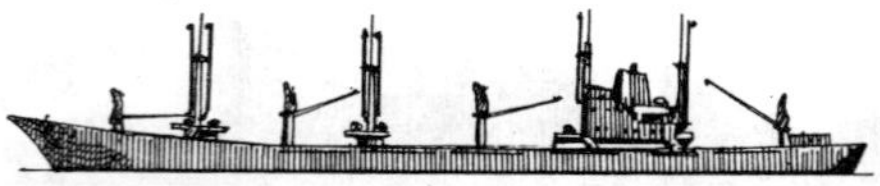

CMCMCMFMC H
● **01620 MARFRIO.** Ar/De 1970; R; 6100/8200; 136×6.92/9.32 (449×22.7/30.58); M; 19; ex LINDFIELD 1980; ex LIMPSFIELD 1977; ex OLAU ROLF 1973; ex CAP MELVILLE 1973 Sister **01621 SEA FROST** (Li); ex MAYFIELD 1980; ex OLAU PIL 1973; ex CAP COLVILLE 1972

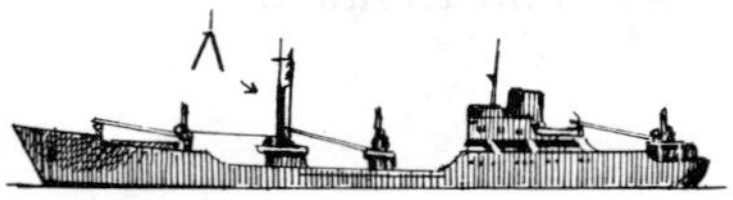

CMCMFC H13
● **01630 WILHELMINA.** Gr/Sw 1959; CP; 2500; 110×7.2 (362×23.7); M; 15; ex URSA 1973 Similar: ***01631 WEIDA** (DDR); ex OLAU DROT 1968; ex ADVISER 1967; ex OLAU DROT 1962; ex OLAV DROT 1961; Launched as HIBATA.

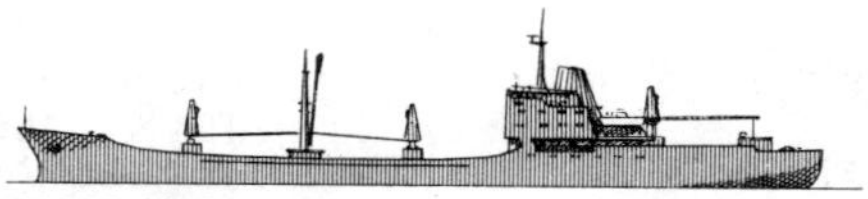

CMCMFC H13

● ***01640 'KALININGRAD'** type; —/Ru 1969; C; 3900/5600; 129×6.55/7.85 (426×21.49/25.69); M; 16; There are 2 types—the earlier ones having cranes by the foremast. Sisters (Ru flag). ***01641 DONETSKIY KOMSOMOLETS *01642 DONETSKIY KHIMIK *01643 DONETSKIY METALLURG *01644 DONETSKIY SHAKHTER *01645 KOMSOMOLETS *01646 BRYANSKIY MASHINOSTROITEL *01647 LENINSKIYE ISKRY *01648 KRASNOYARSKI KOMSOMOLETS *01649 KOMSOMOLETS ARMENII *01650 KOMSOMOLETS AZERBAYDZHANA *01651 KOMSOMOLETS GRUZII *01652 KOMSOMOLETS MOLDAVII *01653 KOMSOMOLETS NAKHODKI *01654 KOMSOMOLETS SPASSKA *01655 KOMSOMOLETS USSURIYSKA *01656 KOMSOMOLETS VLADIVOSTOKA *10657 KOMSOMOLETS ROSSII*01658 KOMSOMOLETS KAZAKHSTANA *01659 KOMSOMOLETS ADZHARII *01660 KOMSOMOLETS BYELORUSSII *01661 KOMSOMOLETS TURKMENII 01662 KOMSOMOLETS PRAVDA *01663 MOSKOVSKIY KOMSOMOLETS *01664 ZHDANOVSKIY KOMSOMOLETS *01665 30-LETIYE POBEDY (or TRIDTSATILETIYE POBEDY) *01666 RABOCHAYA SMENA *01667 SMENA *01668 STARYY BOLSHEVIK:** (Rm flag). ***01669 SALAJ *01670 NASAUD:** (Eg flag). **01671 RAMSES II 01672 NEFERTITI 01673 ISIS 01674 AMOUN 01675 THUTMOSE 01676 AHMOS 01677 IKHNATON 01678 MEMPHIS**

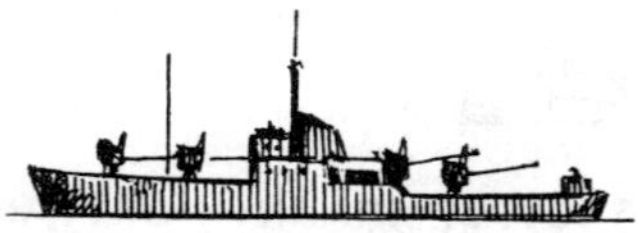

CMCMFC$_2$ H1
***01680 BRIONI.** Ys/Br 1962; C; 1600; 90×5.2 (295×17.1); M; 13; ex TUSKAR 1968

CMCMFC$_2$MC H13
01690 ARAB ALHIJAZ. Si/FRG 1957; CP; 5400/8100; 143-2×7.15/7.94 (470×23.46/26.05); M; 17; ex ELGAREN 1975

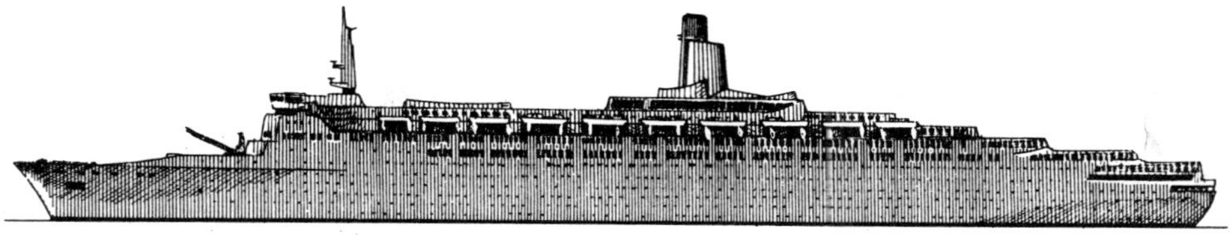

CMF H
01700 QUEEN ELIZABETH 2. Br/Br 1969; P; 67000; 293 × 10 (963 × 32.8); TST; 28.5.

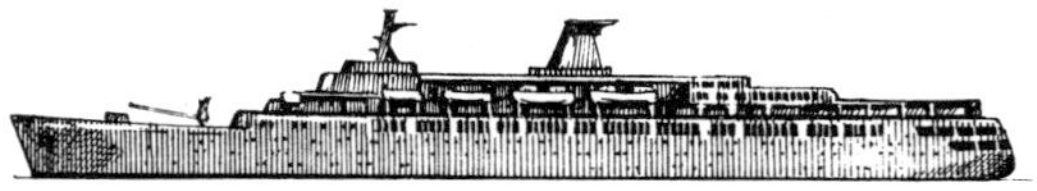

CMF H
01710 DAPHNE. Gr/Br-Gr 1959/75; P; 11700; 162 × 10 (533 × 32.1); TSM; 17; ex AKROTIRI EXPRESS 1974; ex PORT SYDNEY 1972; Rebuilt from a cargo ship 1975. Sister **01711 DANAE** (Gr) ex THERISSOS EXPRESS 1974; ex PORT MELBOURNE 1972

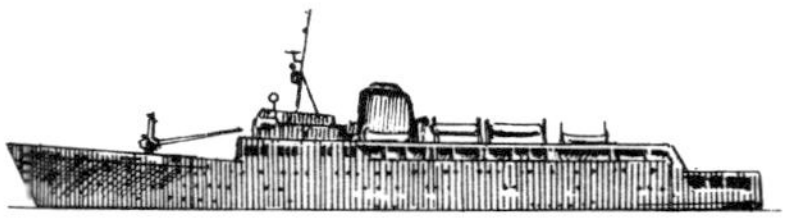

CMF H
01720 CALABRIA. It/It 1952; RoPf; 4800; 116.7 × 5.8 (383 × 19); TSM; 16.5. Sisters **01721 SANT ANDREA** (Gr) ex LAZIO 1980 **01722 SICILIA** (It) Possible sister: **01723 SARDEGNA** (It)

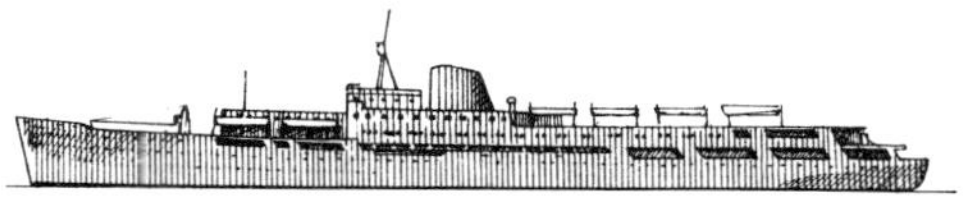

CMF H
01730 ROMANZA. Pa/Ge 1939; P; 7500; 148 × 6.7 (488 × 22); D-E; 16; ex AURELIA 1970; ex BEAVERBRAE 1954; ex HUASCARAN 1947

CMF H13
01740 PILOTO PARDO. Ch/Ne 1959; SS; 200 Dspl; 82-3 × 4.6 (269 × 15); D-E; 14; Antarctic patrol ship: Helicopter platform.

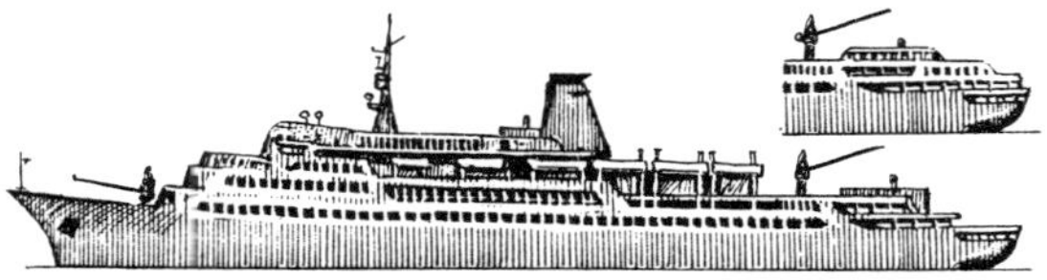

CMFC H
⋆01750 ALEKSANDR PUSHKIN. Ru/DDR 1965; P; 19900; 176 × 8 (577 × 26.1); TM; 20.5. Similar (Ru flag). **⋆01751 IVAN FRANKO ⋆01752 SHOTA RUSTAVELI ⋆01753 TARAS SHEVCHENKO ⋆01754 MIKHAIL LERMONTOV**

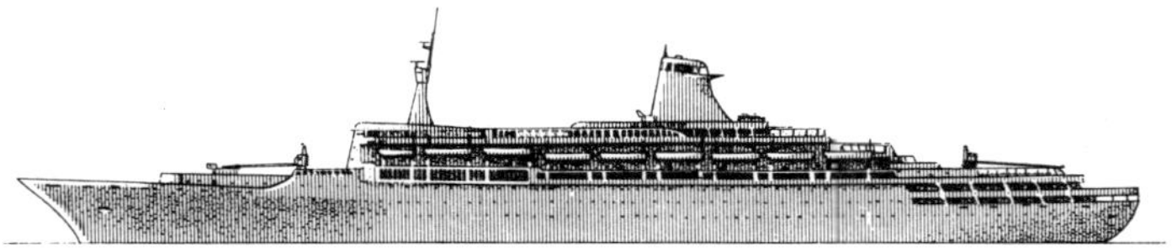

CMFC H
01760 GALILEO GALILEI. It/It 1963; P; 27900; 213.65 × 8.65 (700.95 × 28.38); TSM; 25.5 Sister **01761 GUGLIELMO MARCONI**

CMFCM H
⋆01770 BAO FENG. RC/De 1952; P; 2800; 93 × 4.4 (305 × 14.5); M; 15; ex KONGEDYBET 1979

CMF_2/CMF_2C H1
01780 POLAR STAR. US/US 1976; IB; 12100 displ; 121.6 × 9.5 (399 × 31); Trs GT × D-E; 18; Helicopter platform and hangar. Sister **01781 POLAR SEA.**

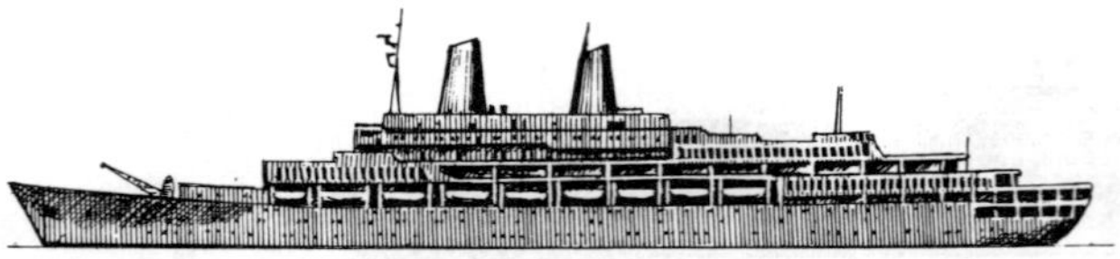

CMF_2K H
01790 ACHILLE LAURO. It/Ne 1947/65; P; 23600; 191 × 8.5 (627 × 28); TSM; 22; ex WILLEM RUYS 1965

CMF_2M H
01800 BOREA. Fi/Sw 1960; PF; 3900; 100 × 4.9; (330 × 16); R & T; 15; ex BORE 1978

CMF_2M H1
01810 PANDELIS. Gr/US 1944; P; 1160; 67 × 2.8 (220 × 9); TSM; 18; exB-A-M-29; ex JASPER

CMFK H
⋆01820 MINGHUA. RC/Fr 1962; P; 14200; 168 × 6.6 (551 × 21.9); TM; 22.5; ex ANCERVILLE 1973

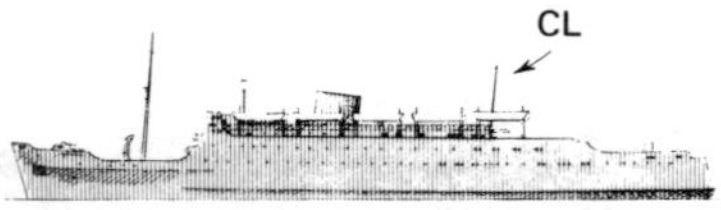

CMFK H12
● **01830 APHRODITE.** Gy/Br 1948; P; 4800; 111.82 × 4.6 (366.86 × 15.09); TSM; 17.5; ex LEINSTER 1 1969; ex LEINSTER 1968; Converted from ferry.

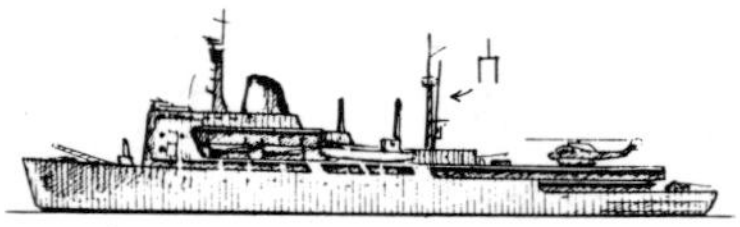

CMFKKM H1
01840 LOUIS S. ST. LAURENT. Ca/Ca 1967; 1B; 13000 Dspl; 111 × 9.4 (367 × 31); Trs D-E; —; Helicopter hangar and deck.

CMFKMC H
01850 HAKUREI MARU. Ja/Ja 1975; RS/SS; 1800; 87 × 5 (286 × 16.5); M; 15.

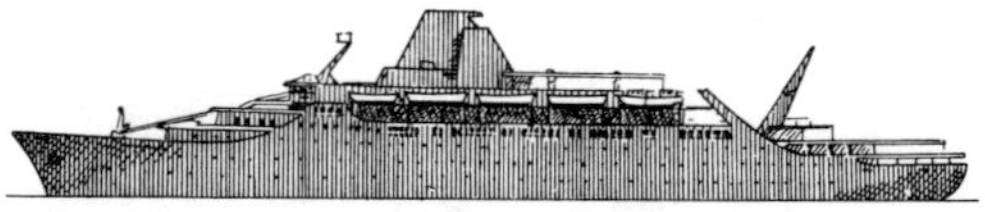

CMFM H
01860 ATLAS. Gr/Ne 1951/72; P; 9100; 153.3 × 8.6 (503 × 28.9); T; 17; ex RYNDAM 1972; ex WATERMAN 1968; ex RYNDAM 1968; Rebuilt 1972.

CMFM H
01870 STARWARD. No/FRG 1968; P; 12900; 160 × 6.3 (525 × 20.5); TSM; 21; Side Doors. Similar: **01871 SKYWARD** (No)

CMFM H
⋆01880 ABKHAZIA. Ru/Ge 1939/55; P; 6800; 131.7 × 5.4 (432 × 16); TS T-E; 17; ex LENSOVET; ex MARIENBERG; Completed in DDR in 1955.

CMFM H
01890 SAPPHO. Gr/Br 1966; RoPF; 6500; 140 × 54 (460 × 17.6); TSM; 18; ex SPERO 1973.

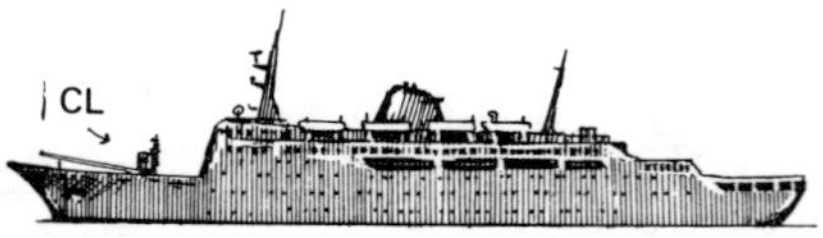

CMFM H
01900 DANA SIRENA. De/It 1970; RoPF; 6700; 125 × 5.2 (410 × 17.1); TSM; 21; ex DANA CORONA 1980; ex TREKRONER 1971 Similar: **01901 DANA CORONA** (De)—to be rebuilt; ex DANA SIRENA: EX AALBORGHUS

CMFM H
01910 KONG OLAV V. De/It 1968; RoPF; 8000; 125 × 5.2 (411 × 17); TSM; 21; Sister **01911 PRINCESSE MARGARETHE** (De);

CMFM H
01920 ENGLAND. De/De 1964; RoPF; 8100; 140 × 5.5 (459 × 18.1); TSM; 21.

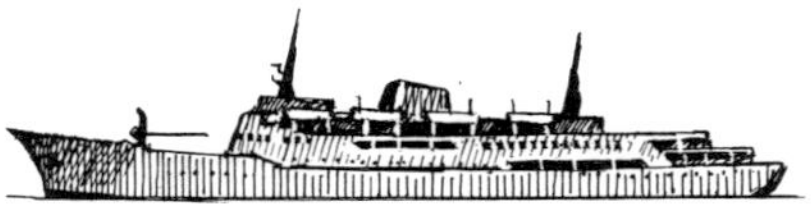

CMFM H
● **01930 PRINSEN**. Fi/De 1957; P; 4300; 121 × 5.2 (397 × 17.2); TSM; 20.5; ex PRINSESSAN 1978; ex PRINSESSEN 1971; ex PRINCESSE MARGRETHE 1968 Sister **01931 MIN FUNG** (Pa); ex BARONESSAN 1980; ex TAIWAN 1972; ex OLAV 1969; ex KONG OLAV V 1968

CMFM H
01940 KONG OLAV. No/No 1964; P; 2600; 87.5 × 4.6 (287 × 15.2); M; 16.5.

CMFM H
01950 NORDNORGE. No/No 1964; P; 2600; 87.5 × 4.6 (287 × 15.2); M; 16.5.

CMFM H
⋆**01960 ABRAU-DYURSO**. Ru/Bu 1964; P; 1000; 64 × 3 (211 × 10); M; 13 Sisters (Ru flag) ⋆**01961 ADZHIGOL** ⋆**01962 ALUPKA** ⋆**01963 ALUSHTA** ⋆**01964 AY-PETRI** ⋆**01965 AYTODOR** ⋆**01966 GURIEV** ⋆**01967 ADMIRAL LUNIN**; ex KARA-DAG 1974 ⋆**01968 PITSUNDA** ⋆**01969 SARYTCH** ⋆**01970 SOLOVKI**; ex VANEMUYNE 1968; ex ARTEK 1966 ⋆**01971 VASIL KOLAROV**

CMFM H
⋆**01980 GEORGI DIMITROV**. Bu/Bu 1957; P; 900; 62.7 × 3 (206 × 10); M; 12; Sister ⋆**01981 VASIL KOLAROV**

CMFM H
01990 OLDENBURG. FRG/FRG 1958; F; 300; 43.6 × 1.5 (143 × 5); TSM; 11.5

CMFM H
⋆**02000 MIN ZHUI**. RC/De 1961; P; 5000; 98 × 4.8 (322 × 14.11); M; 16; ex BORNHOLM 1980

CMFM H
⋆**02010 MAZOWSZE**. Pd/Hu 1955; P; 1000; 60.3 × 3 (198 × 10); TSM; 12; Crane may be removed.

CMFM H
02020 WAPPEN VON HAMBURG. FRG/FRG 1965; P; 4400; 109.7 × 4.2 (360 × 13.7); TSM; 21.5; ex LUCAYA 1966; ex WAPPEN VON HAMBURG 1965

CMFM H
02030 ALTE LIEBE. FRG/FRG 1962; P; 3800; 104 × 4 (341 × 13.2); TSM; 21; ex WAPPEN 1966; ex WAPPEN VON HAMBURG 1964

CMFM H
02040 TSUGARU MARU. Ja/Ja 1969; Cbl; 1700; 84.5 × 4.6 (278 × 15.1); M; 13.5

CMFM H1
02050 SWEET FAITH. Pi/De 1950; P; 3300; 104 × 4.9 (341 × 16); TSM; 20; ex H.P. PRIOR 1970; Crane may be removed.

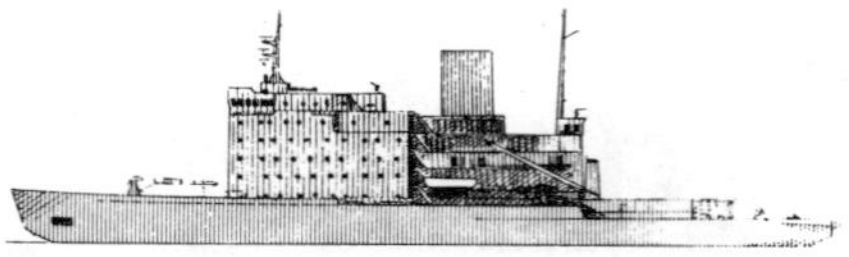

CMFM H1
⋆02060 KAPITAN SOROKIN. Ru/Fi 1977; IB; 10600; 131.88 × 8.5 (432.68 × 27.89); Trs D-E; 19; Helicopter deck. Sister **⋆02061 KAPITAN NIKOLAYEV** (Ru) Similar (sloping funnel; bridge front stepped): **⋆02062 KAPITAN DRANITSYN** (Ru); may be spelt **KAPITAN GRANITSYN ⋆02063 KAPITAN KLEBNIKOV** (Ru)

CMFM H12
02090 CAPE DON. Au/Au 1963; LT; 2100; 74 × 4.3 (243 × 14.4); M; —; Sisters **02091 CAPE MORETON** (Au) **02092 CAPE PILAR** (Au)

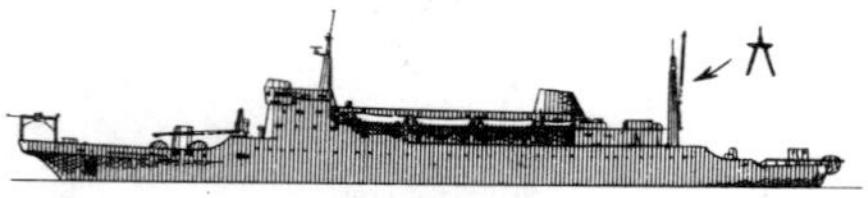

CMFM H2
⋆02110 INGUL. Ru/Fi 1962; Cbl; 5600; 130.41 × 5.21 (427.85 × 17.09); TS D-E; 14; **"KLASMA"** Class. Sister **⋆02111 JANA** (may be spelt **YANA**) (Ru).

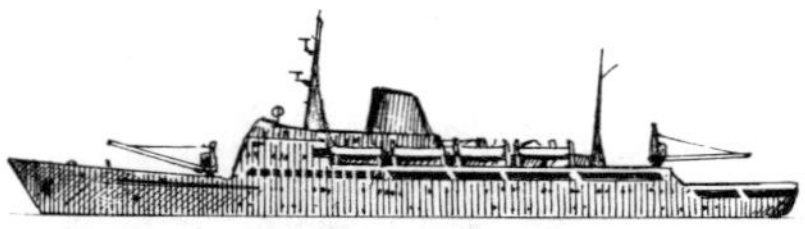

CMFMC H
⋆02140 BASHKIRIYA. Ru/DDR 1964; P; 5300; 122.15 × 5.27 (400.75 × 17.29); TSM; 17; May be modified like ESTONIA—Which see. Sister **⋆02141 KUBAN** (Ru); ex NADEZHDA KRUPSKAYA; (Naval troopship).

CMFMC H
⋆02160 ESTONIA. Ru/DDR 1960; P; 4900; 122 × 5.2 (401 × 17); TSM; 17. Sisters (Ru Flag) **⋆02161 LATVIYA ⋆02162 MIKHAIL KALININ** Similar (heavier mainmast) **⋆02163 ARMENIYA** Others of this type may be rebuilt like this.

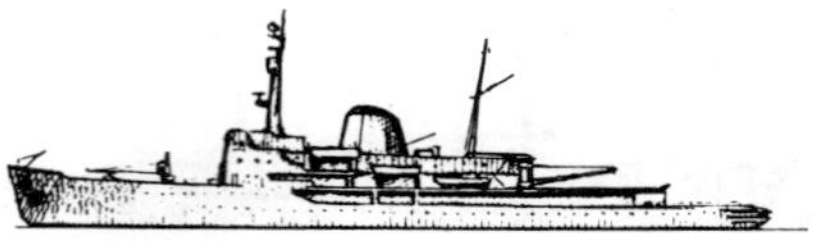

CMFM H1
⋆02070 MOSKVA. Ru/Fi 1960; IB; 9400; 122 × 10.7 (401 × 35.6); Trs D-E; 18; Helicopter Deck and 2 Helicopters Sisters (Ru flag). **⋆02071 KIEV ⋆02072 LENINGRAD ⋆02073 MURMANSK ⋆02074 VLADIVOSTOK**

CMFM H1
⋆02080 KAPITAN M. IZMAYLOV. Ru/Fi 1976; IB/Sal; 1400; 56.3 × .42 184 × 14); TSD-E; 14 Sisters **⋆02081 KAPITAN A. RADZHABOV** (Ru) **⋆02082 KAPITAN KOSOLAPOV** (Ru)

CMFM H12
02100 HOPEDALE. Ca/Ca 1960; PC; 1100; 57.3 × 3.8 (188 × 12.6); TSM; 13 Sister **02101 TAVERNER**

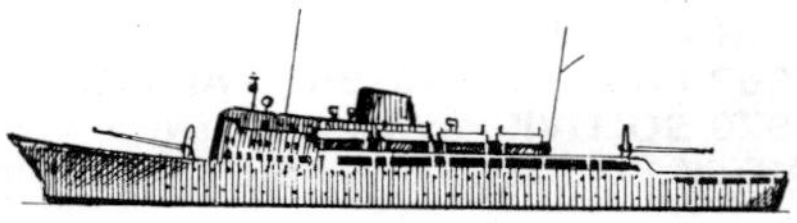

CMFMC H
⋆02120 BAYKAL. Ru/DDR 1964; P; 5200; 122.1 × 5.2 (401 × 17); TSM; 17. Similar—vary in details (Ru flag). **⋆02121 FELIKS DZERZHINSKY ⋆02122 GRIGORIY ORDZHONIKIDZE ⋆02123 KHABAROVSK ⋆02124 LITVA ⋆02125 MARIYA ULYANOVA ⋆02126 M. URITSKIY ⋆02127 NIKOLAYEVSK ⋆02128 PETROPAVLOVSK ⋆02129 PRIAMURYE ⋆02130 TURKMENIYA** Some of these may be rebuilt like ESTONIA (Which see)

CMFMC H
⋆02150 ADZHARIYA. Ru/DDR 1964; P; 5300; 122 × 5.2 (401 × 17); TSM; 17; May be modified like ESTONIA—which see.

CMFMC H
02170 ESPRESSO CORINTO. It/Fr 1967; RoPF; 6900; 130 × 5.3 (427 × 17.5); TSM; 21.5; ex AVENIR 1976.

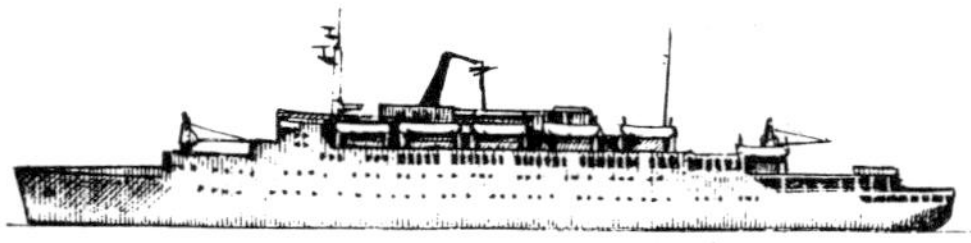

CMFMC H
⋆02180 STEFAN BATORY. Pd/Ne 1952; P; 15000; 153.3 × 8.7 (503 × 18.9); T; 16.5; ex MAASDAM 1965.

CMFMC H
02190 HUDSON. Ca/Ca 1963; IB/SS; 3700; 90.5 × 6.3 (197 × 20.7); TSD-E;-; Helicopter.

CMFMC H
02200 JOHN CABOT. Ca/Ca 1965; IB/Cbl; 5100; 95.4 × 6.7 (313 × 22); TS D-E;-; Helicopter.

CMFMC H
02210 SAUDI ARABIAN. Si/No 1966; RoPF; 8500; 140 × 5.3 (458 × 17.4); TSM; 20; ex GRAND FLOTEL 1980; ex ILE DE BEAUTE 1976; ex SUNWARD 1973.

CMFMC H
02220 HAKUREI MARU. Ja/Ja 1974; RS/SS; 1800; 87 × 5 (286 × 16.5); M; 15.

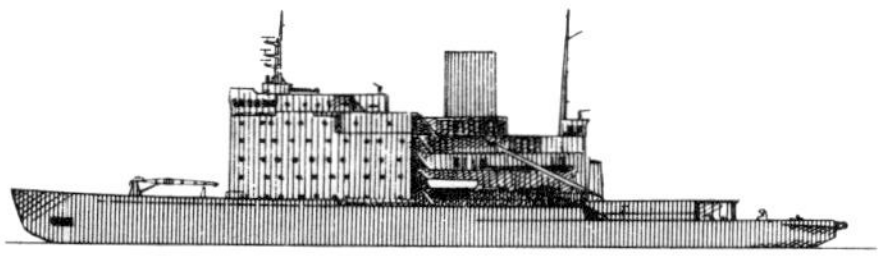

CMFMC H1
⋆02230 KAPITAN SOROKIN. Ru/Fi 1977; IB; 10600; 131.88 × 8.5 (432.68 × 27.89); TrS D-E; 19; Helicopter Deck. Sister (Ru flag). **⋆02231 KAPITAN NIKOLAYEV** Similar (sloping funnel top, bridge front stepped); **⋆02232 KAPITAN DRANITSYN** could be spelt **KAPITAN GRANITSYN ⋆02233 KAPITAN KLEBNIKOV.**

CMFMC H1
02240 VOIMA. Fi/Fi-Fi 1954/79; IB; —; 83.52 × — (274 × —); TSD-E; —; Rebuilt 1978-79.

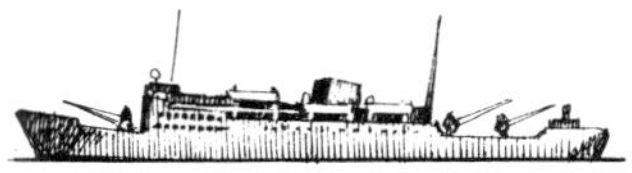

CMFMC$_2$ *H*
02250 BUCCANEER. Ec/Br 1950; PC; 2000; 87.2 × 4.5 (286 × 14.9); TSM; 14; ex ST. NINIAN 1976.

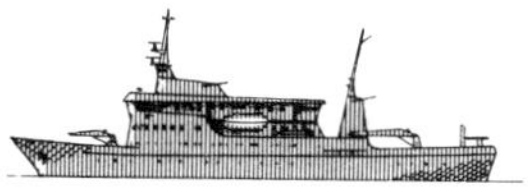

CMFMFC H
02260 DANA. De/De 1980; RS; —; 78.43 × 5.7 (257.32 × 18.7); M; 15.5.

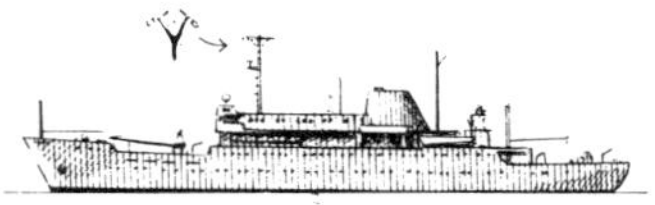

CMFMK H12
⋆02270 MUSSON. Ru/Pd 1967; RS; 3300; 97 × 5.2 (319 × 17.1); TSM; —; '**B88**' type; Sisters (Ru flag); **⋆02271 ERNST KRENKEL ⋆02272 GEORGIY USHAKOV ⋆02273 OKEAN ⋆02274 PASSAT ⋆02275 PRIBOY ⋆02276 PRILIV ⋆02277 VICTOR BUGAEV;** ex PORYV **⋆02278 VOLNA.**

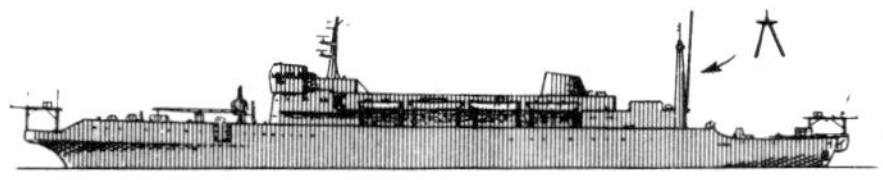

CMFMN H2
⋆02280 KATYN. Ru/Fi 1973; Cbl; 6000; 130.41 × 5.75 (427.8 × 18.86); TS D-E; 14; **"KLASMA"** class: also known as **KATUNJ;** Sisters (Ru flag). **⋆02281 DONETS ⋆02282 ZNA** (or **TSNA)** Possible sisters (may be KCMFMN—see INGURI) **⋆02283 ZEYA ⋆02284 TAVDA ⋆02285 KALAR**

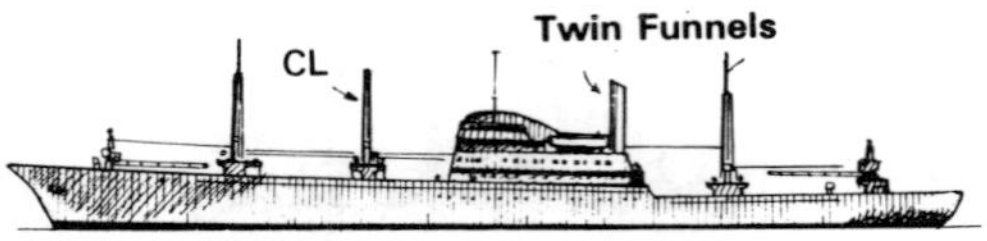

CMKFMC H1
● **02290 CAP SAN NICOLAS.** FRG/FRG 1961; R; 7600/9600; 153 × 7.54 8.46 (502 × 24.74/27.76); M; 19; Sisters (FRG flag): **02291 CAP SAN AUGUSTIN 02292 CAP SAN DIEGO 02293 CAP SAN LORENZO 02294 CAP SAN MARCO**

CMK_2FMK_3 H1
02300 JEFF DAVIS. US/US 1962; C; 8500/12800; 172 × —/9.63 (565 × —/31.59); T; —; ex CANADA BEAR 1975; ex CHINA BEAR 1974.

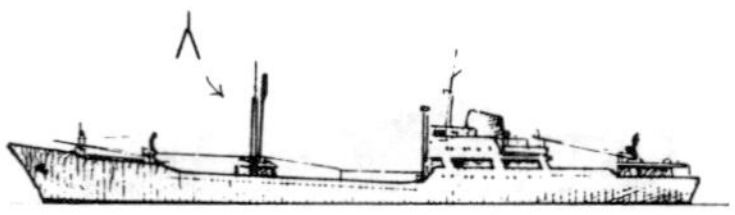

CMKMFC H13
⋆**02310 SCHWARZA.** DDR/De 1962; C; 2300/3500; 110 × 6/7.16 (362 × 19.69/23.49); M; 15; ex OLAU EGE 1968; ex BENEFACTOR 1967; Launched as OLAU EGE.

CMKMFKM H1
⋆**02320 FENG BAO.** RC/RC 1975; C; 10300; 161.5 × 9 (530 × 30); M; —; Cranes abreast mainmast; Sisters (RC flag). ⋆**02321 FENG LANG** ⋆**02322 FENG GUANG**

CM_2 H1
02330 COLONEL PLEVIN II. Fr/Fr 1962; ST; 1800; 78 × 5.6 (256 × 18.5); M; 14.5.

CM_2F H
● ⋆**02340 MARIA YERMOLOVA.** Ru/Ys 1974; P; 3900; 100 × 4.5 (328 × 14.1); TSM; 17; Sisters (Ru flag). ⋆**02341 ALLA TARASOVA** ⋆**02342 ANTONIA NEDZHDANOVA** ⋆**02343 LYUBOV ORLOVA** ⋆**02344 MARIYA SAVINA** ⋆**02345 OLGA ANDROVSKAYA** ⋆**02346 OLGA SADOVSKAYA**

CM_2F H
● ⋆**02350 KOLKHIDA.** Ru/Ru 1961; P; 3200; 101.5 × 4 (333 × 13); TSM; 14.5; Some ships have taller funnel; Some ships may not have crane. Sisters (Ru flag): ⋆**02351 BUKOVINA** ⋆**02352 KIRGHIZSTAN** ⋆**02353 MOLDAVIA** ⋆**02354 OSETIYA** ⋆**02355 TADZHAKISTAN** ⋆**02356 TALLINN** ex SVANETIYA ⋆**02357 TATARIYA** ⋆**02358 UZBEKISTAN** Possible sister (Ru flag): ⋆**02359 AFGHANISTAN**

CM_2F H
02370 LOFOTEN. No/No 1964; P; 2600; 87.4 × 4.6 (287 × 15.2); M; 16.5.

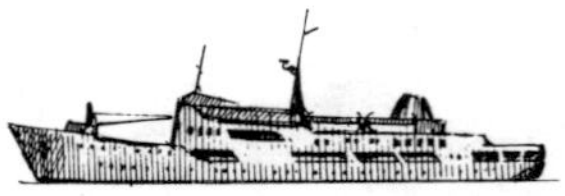

CM_2F H
02380 FINNMARKEN. No/FRG 1956; P; 2200; 81.3 × 4.5 (167 × 14.9); M; 16. Sister: **02381 RAGNVALD JARL** (No)

CM_2F H
02390 GENTILE DA FABRIANO. It/It 1962; P; 2200; 95 × 3.7 (312 × 12.4); TSM; 19.5. Sister **02391 ANDREA MANTEGNA** (It)

CM_2F H
02400 LONG LINES. US/FRG 1963; Cbl; 11300; 156 × 8.2 (512 × 26.9); TST-E; 15.

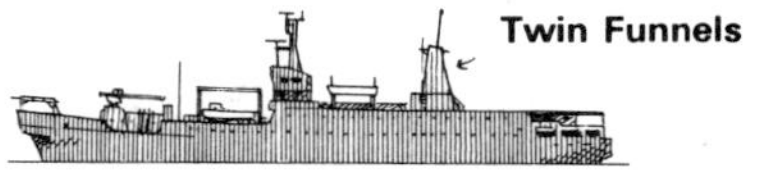

CM_2F H
02410 C. S. MONARCH. Br/Br 1975; Cbl; 3500; 95.4 × 4.8 (313 × 15.9); M; 15. Sister: **02411 C.S. IRIS** (Br)

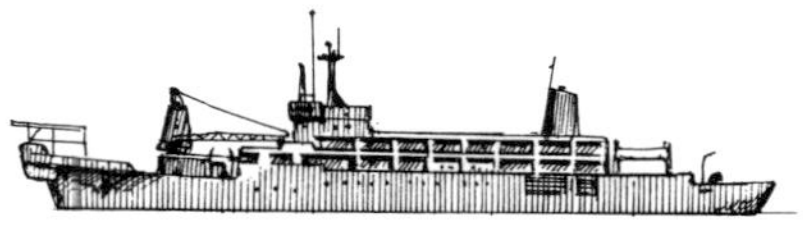

CM_2F H2
02420 KUROSHIO MARU. Ja/Ja 1975; Cbl; 3300; 119.3 × 5.6 (392 × 18.5); M; 16.5.

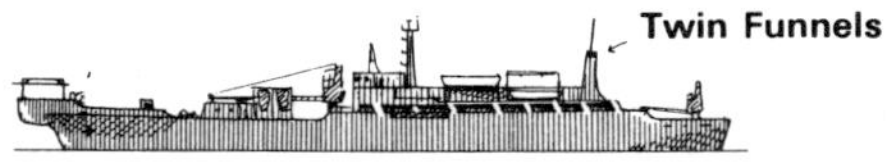

CM_2FC H
02430 KDD MARU. Ja/Ja 1967; Cbl; 4300; 114 × 6 (374 × 19.6); TSM; 16.

CM_2FC H
02440 BALTIC STAR. FRG/FRG 1963; P; 2800; 91.4 × 3.8 (300 × 12.1); TSM; 19.5; ex STENA FINLANDICA 1975; ex HELGOLAND 1972.

CM_2FC H
⋆**02450 DALMACIJA.** Ys/Ys 1964; P; 5400; 116.7 × 5 (383 × 16.9); TSM; 18. Sister: ⋆**02451 ISTRA** (Ys)

CM_2FK H
⋆**02460 AKADEMIK KRYLOV.** Ru/DDR; —; RS; 9100 Dsp; 147 × — (483 × —); M; 15

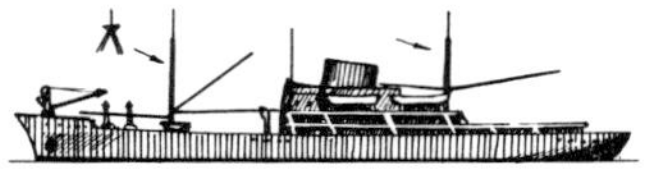

CM_2FM H1
02470 SAGARDEEP. In/Ys 1964; LT; 2800; 100 × — (327 × —); TSM; 19.75.

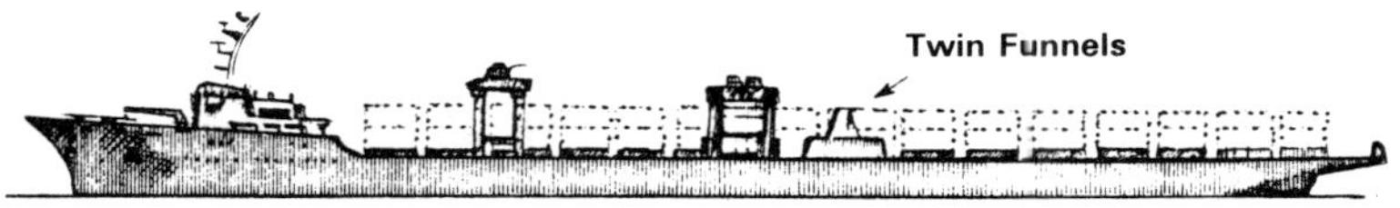

CMN_2F H1
● **02480 LASH ATLANTICO.** US/US 1972; Bg/Con; 26400; 250 × 10.7 (820 × 35.5); T; 21; Both gantries (N) can be moved right aft, thus altering sequence. Also coded P5; **"LASH"** type. Sisters (overall lengths vary) (US flag): **02481 LASH ITALIA 02482 LASH PACIFICO 02483 AUSTAL LIGHTNING;** ex LASH ESPANA 1976 **02484 AUSTRAL MOON;** ex AUSTRALIA BEAR 1975; ex PHILIPPINE BEAR 1975 **02485 DELTA MAR 02486 DELTA SUD 02487 DELTA NORTE 02488 DELTA CARIBE;** ex LASH TURKIYE

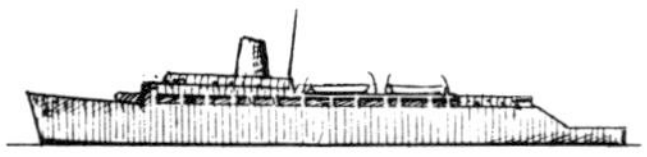

FM H1
02500 CAPE HENLOPEN. US/US 1944; PF; 1500; 96.3 × 3.1 (316 × 10.2); M; —; ex VIRGINIA BEACH 1964.

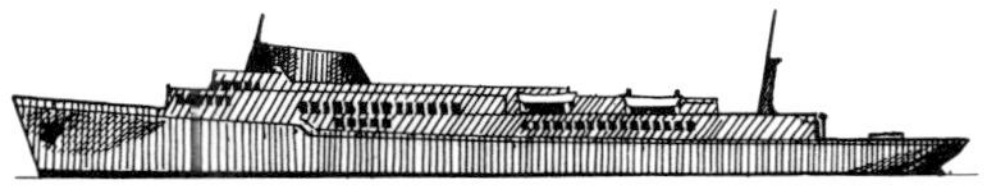

FM H1
02505 AQUARAMA. US/US 1945; RoPF; 12800; 150.9 × 5.2 (495 × 17.3); T; 19; ex MARINE STAR 1955.

FMC H1
02510 JEAN CHARCOT. Fr/Fr 1965; RS; 2100; 74.5 × 5 (244 × 16.5); TS D-E; 15.

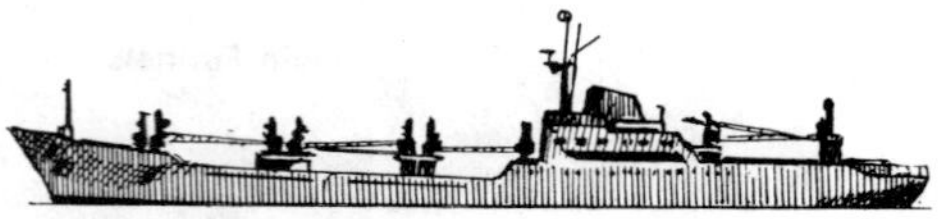

KC$_7$MFC$_2$ H13
02515 LUCERO DEL MAR. Ur/De 1963; C/R; 5900; 143 × 7.6 (469 × 25); M; 17; ex TIJUCA 1980; ex NORMA 1980.

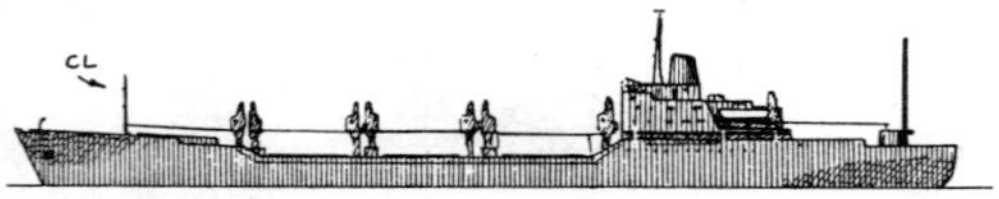

KC$_7$MFCK H13
***02520 IRKUTSK.** Ru/DDR 1968; C; 4800/8500; 151 × 8.8 (497 × 29.9); M; 17. Sisters (Ru flag): ***02521 IZHORA *02522 IZMAIL *02523 KARAGANDA *02524 TULA *02525 SANTIAGO DE CUBA**; ex ILOVAYSK 1976 ***02526 AKADEMIK FILATOV *02527 AKADEMIK IOSIF ORBELI *02528 AKADEMIK RYKACHEV *02529 AKADEMIK SHUKHOV *02530 AKADEMIK YURYEV**

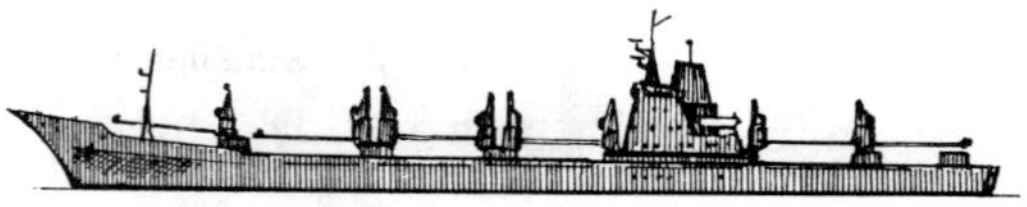

KC$_6$MFC$_2$ H1
● **02540 ACONCAGUA VALLEY.** Sw/F; 1968 R; 9600; 154 × 8.5 (506 × 28); M; 21. Sister: **02541 SAN JOAQUIN VALLEY** (Sw)

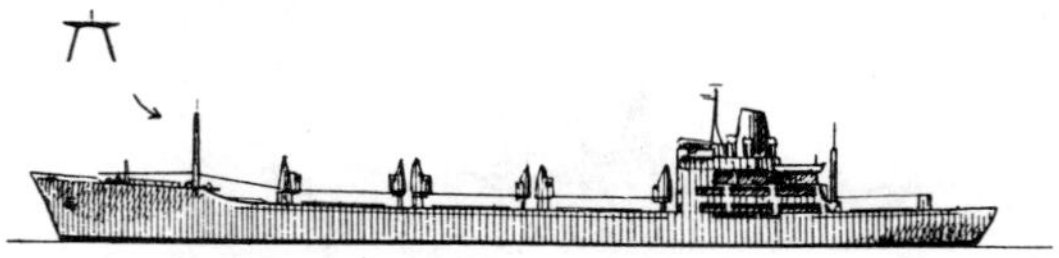

KC$_6$MFK H1
● **02550 SACRAMENTO MARU.** Ja/Ja 1967; C; 6700; 156 × 8.6 (511 × 28.4); M; 18.5. Sisters; **02551 SAN FRANCISCO MARU** (Ja) **02552 SAVANNAH MARU** (Ja) **02553 HELEN** (Ma); ex ST. LOUIS MARU 1981

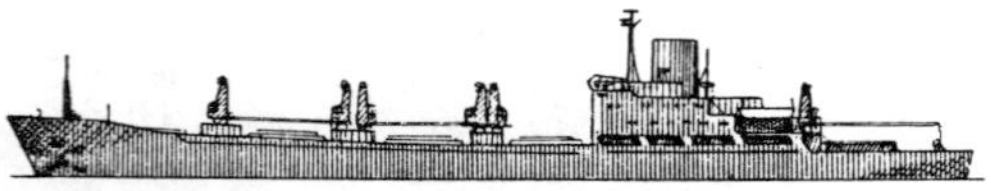

KC$_5$MFC H1
02560 AFRIC STAR. Br/Br 1975; R; 7600/8900; 155.8 × 9.2 (511 × 30.05); M; 24. Sisters **02561 ALMEDA STAR** (Br) **02562 ANDALUCIA STAR** (Br) **02563 AVELONA STAR** (Br) **02564 ALMERIA STAR** (Br) **02565 HIDLEFJORD** (No); ex AVILA STAR 1980

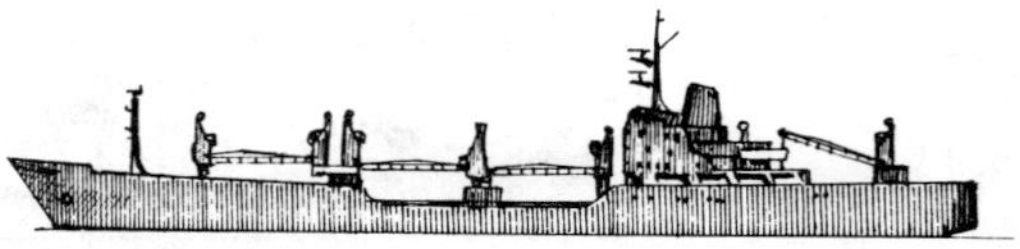

KC$_5$MFC H13
***02570 HAI QUAN.** RC/Fr 1969; R; 6700; 140 × 8.2 (459 × 26.9); M; 20.5; ex POINTE ALLEGRE 1979. Sisters: **02571 CALLAO** (Pe); ex POINTE DES COLIBRIS 1979 ***02572 YANG QUAN** (RC); ex POINTE MARLIN 1979

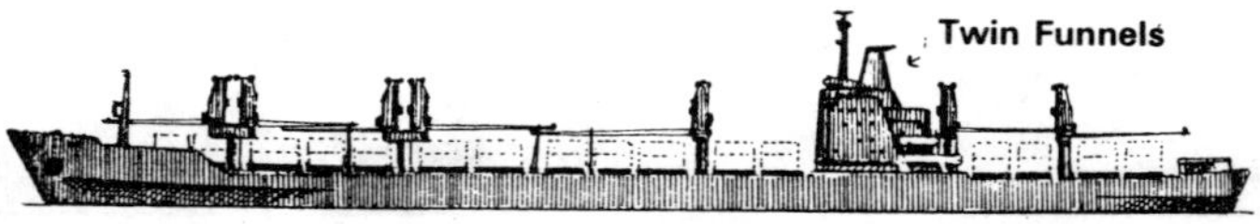

KC$_5$MFC$_2$ H1
● **02580 TAMARA.** Sw/Fi 1974; Con; 22300; 209 × 9.5 (686 × 31); TSM; 23. Sisters **02581 MALMROS MONSOON** (Br) **02582 NAGARA** (Sw)

KC$_5$MFC$_2$ H13
● **02590 ARGO.** Fi/Fi 1963; C; 3000/5000; 130.7 × 7.3 (430 × 24.1); M; 16. Lengthened 1970 Sister **02591 VIRGO** (Fi)

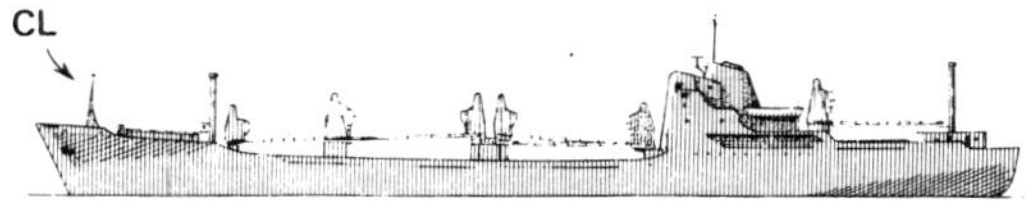

KC$_5$MFCK H13
02610 GAIETY. Br/Br 1964; C; 6700; 130.7 × 7.8 (429 × 25.6); M; 16.5; ex CUFIC 1977; ex NEWFOUNDLAND 1976; ex CUFIC 1974; ex NEWFOUNDLAND 1973. Sister: **02611 ARAB DABBOR** (Si); ex BOOKER VALIANT 1979; ex TROPIC 1978; ex NOVA SCOTIA 1976; ex TROPIC 1974; ex NOVA SCOTIA 1973

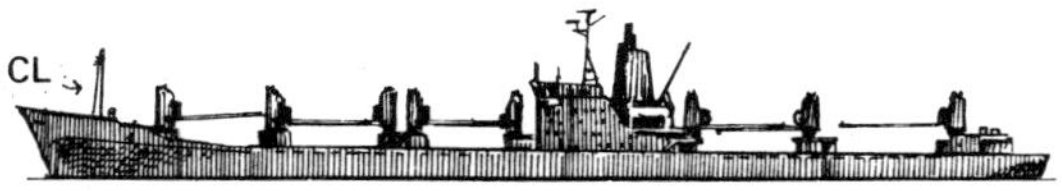

KC$_5$MFKC$_3$ H1
● **02630 SNOW FLAKE.** Sw/Fr 1972; R; 11400; 173 × 9.3 (569 × 30.5); M; 22.5; Side doors. Sisters (Sw flag): **02631 SNOW BALL 02632 SNOW CRYSTAL 02633 SNOW DRIFT 02634 SNOW FLOWER 02635 SNOW LAND 02636 SNOW STORM**

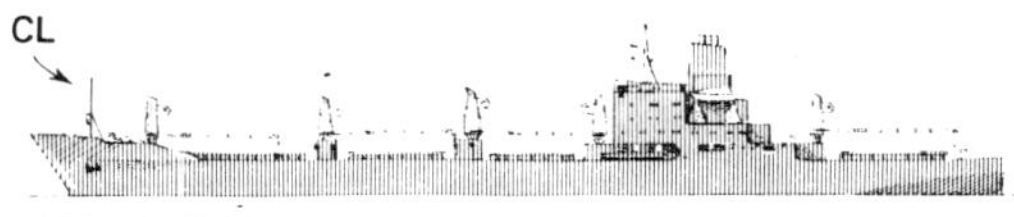

KC$_4$MFC H1
● **02650 HILCO SPRINTER.** No/No 1979; R; 6800/9100; 155.7 × 7.5/9.8 (510.9 × 24.6/32.1); M; 22 (trials). Sisters (No flag): **02651 HILCO SCAMPER 02652 HILCO SPEEDSTER**

KC$_5$MFC$_3$ H1
● **02600 SNOW FLAKE.** Sw/Fr 1972; R; 11400; 173 × 9 3 (569 × 30.5); M; 22.5; Side Doors. Sisters (Sw flag): **02601 SNOW BALL 02602 SNOW CRYSTAL 02603 SNOW DRIFT 02604 SNOW FLOWER 02605 SNOW LAND 02606 SNOW STORM**

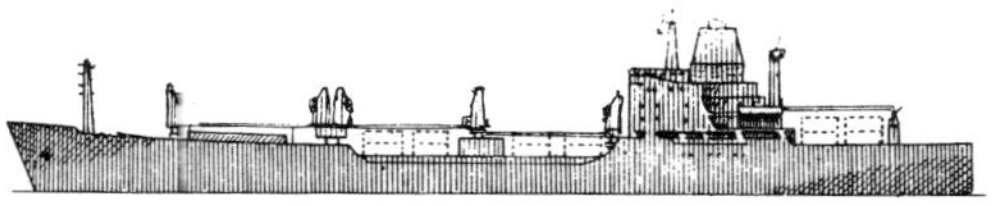

KC$_5$MFK H13
02620 POINTE SANS SOUCI. Fr/Fr 1973; Roc/Cor; 6500; 155.4 × 8.2 (510 × 26.9); M; 20; Stern ramp/door—side door. Sisters (Fr flag): **02621 POINTE LA ROSE 02622 POINTE MADAME**

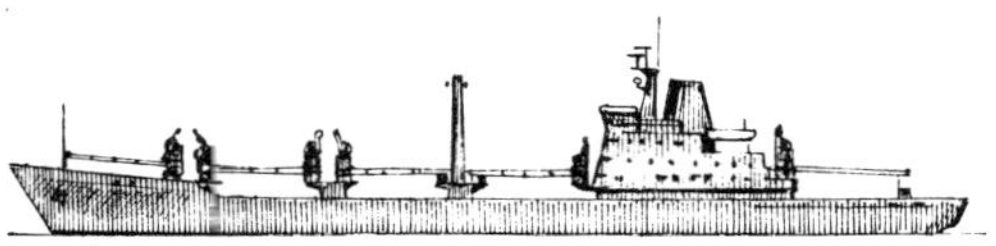

KC$_4$KCMFC H1
02640 ST. JOHN. Gr/Br 1971; C; 7100/9800; 153 × 9.1 (502 × 30.9); M; 18; ex CITY OF HULL 1980. Sisters (Gr flag): **02641 SEA LORD;** CITY OF LONDON 1980 **02642 MARIANTHE;** ex CITY OF LIVERPOOL 1980

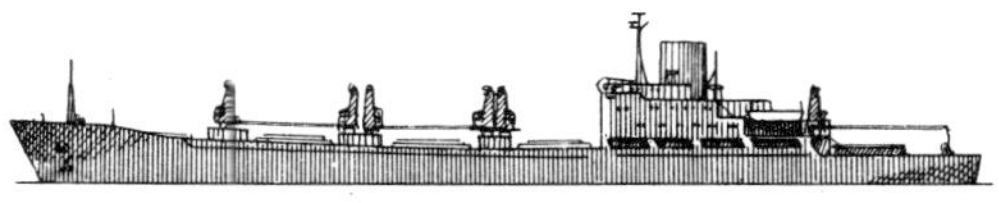

KC$_4$MFC H1
02660 AFRIC STAR. Br/Br 1975; R; 7600/9800; 155.8 × 9.2 (511 × 30.1); M; 24. Sisters: **02661 ALMEDA STAR** (Br) **02662 ANDALUCIA STAR** (Br) **02663 AVELONA STAR** (Br) **02664 ALMERIA STAR** (Br) **02665 HIDLEFJORD** (No); ex AVILA STAR 1980

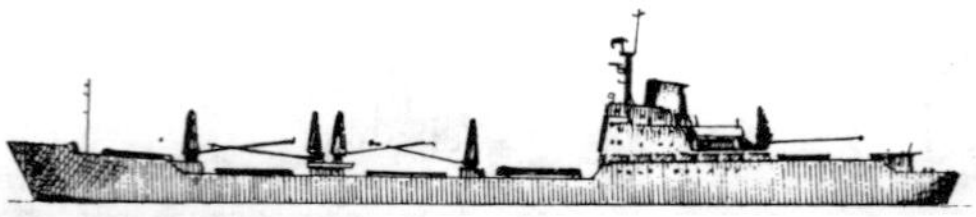

KC_4MFC H13

● ⋆**02670 SVETLOGORSK.** Ru/Ru 1970; C; 6300/8900; 152.7 × 9.3 (501 × 30.85); M; 17. Sisters (Ru flag): ⋆**02671 AKADEMIK EVGENIY PATON** ⋆**02672 ILYA KULIK** ⋆**02673 SEREBRYANSK** ⋆**02674 SEVAN** ⋆**02675 SYZRAN** Similar (Ru flag): ⋆**02676 SARNY** ⋆**02677 SEROV** ⋆**02678 SEVERODONETSK** ⋆**02679 SLAVYANSK** ⋆**02680 SVANETIYA** ⋆**02681 KOMSOMOLSKAYA SLAVA** ⋆**02682 SOCHI**

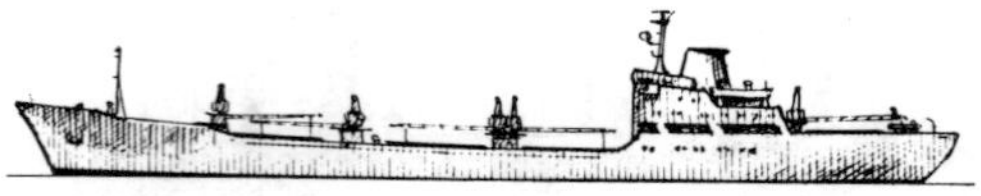

KC_4MFC H13

⋆**02690 NOVGOROD.** Ru/Fi 1967; C; 5800/8800; 150.9 × 9 (495 × 29.6); M; 18. Sisters (Ru flag):Sisters (Ru flag): ⋆**02691 NOVOSIBIRSK** ⋆**02692 NOVOKUZNETSK** ⋆**02693 NOVOKUIBYSHEVSK** ⋆**02694 NOVOMOSKOVSK** ⋆**02695 NOVOTROITSK** ⋆**02696 NOVOVYATSK** ⋆**02697 NOVOALTAISK** ⋆**02698 NOVOMIRGOROD** ⋆**02699 NOVOPOLOTSK** ⋆**02700 NOVODRUZHESK** ⋆**02701 NOVOLVOVSK** ⋆**02702 NOVZYBKOV** ⋆**02703 NOVOGRUDOK** ⋆**02704 NOVOVOLYNSK** Some later ships vary in superstructure. Some can be fitted with a heavy-lift derrick. See drawing under KC_2KC_2MFC.

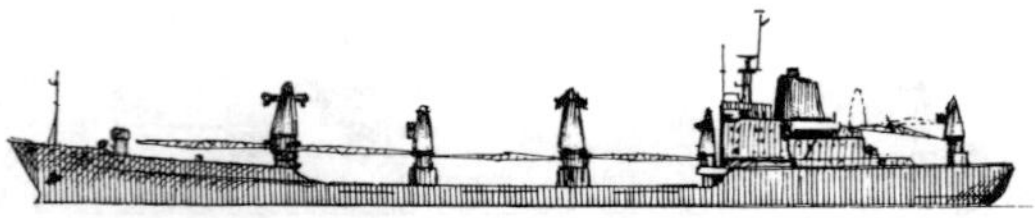

KC_4MFC H13

02710 NEDLLOYD NAGASAKI. Ne/Ne 1972; C; 12100; 165 × 9.7 (543 × 32); M; 21; ex STRAAT NAGASAKI 1978. Sisters (Ne flag): **02711 NEDLLOYD NAGOYA;** ex STRAAT NAGOYA 1978 **02712 NEDLLOYD NAPIER;** ex STRAAT NAPIER 1978 **02713 NEDLLOYD NASSAU;** ex STRAAT NASSAU 1978

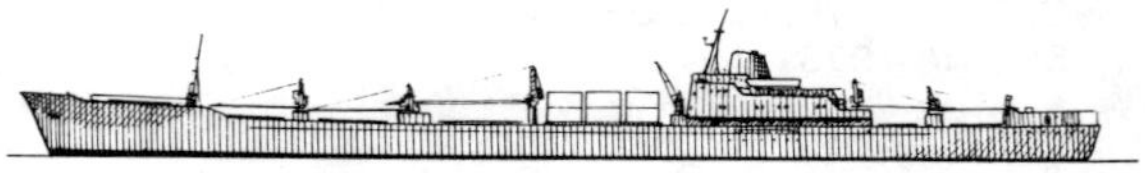

KC_4MFC_2 H1

● **02720 BRASILIA.** Sw/Sw 1968; Con; 10300; 173.3 × 8.7 (568 × 28.4); TSM; 18.5; Converted from cargo ship. Sisters (Sw flag): **02721 ROSARIO 02722 SANTOS** Similar (shorter funnel): **02723 MONTEVIDEO 02724 BUENOS AIRES**

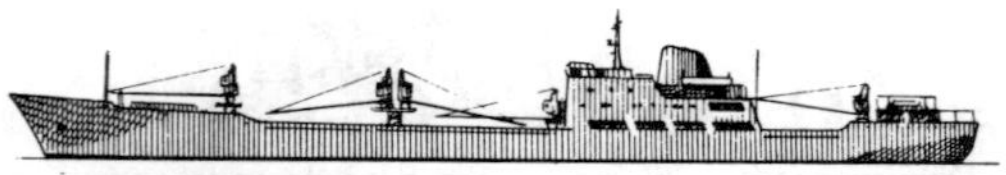

KC_4MFKC H13

02730 GARIFALIA C. Gr/Br 1970; C; 6400/9800; 155.7 × 9.2 (511 × 30.25); M; 17; ex STRATHAIRD 1979; ex NIGARISTAN 1975.

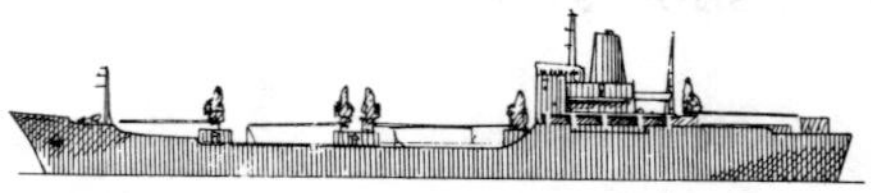

KC_4MFKC H13

02740 PENTA. Li/Ja 1969; R; 4700; 135 × 7.1 (443 × 23.2); M; 17; ex AOTEAROA 1972.

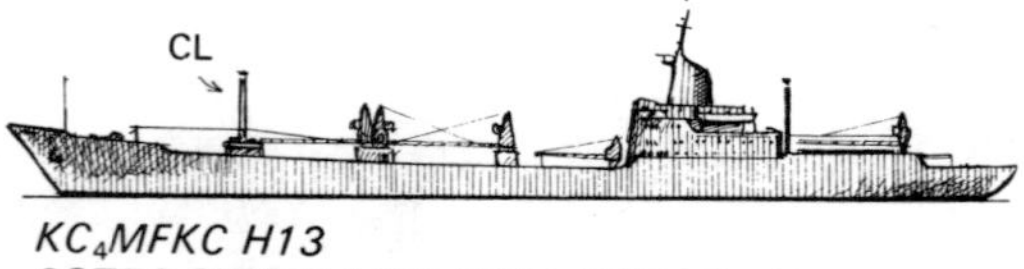

KC_4MFKC H13

02750 NEDLLOYD HOLLAND. Ne/Ja 1967; C; 7300/10200; 161.8 × 10 (531 × 33.1); M; 20; ex STRAAT HOLLAND 1978. Sisters (Ne flag): **02751 NEDLLOYD HOBART;** ex STRAAT HOBART 1978 **02752 NEDLLOYD HONSHU;** ex STRAAT HONSHU 1978 **02753 NEDLLOYD HONG KONG;** ex STRAAT HONG KONG 1978

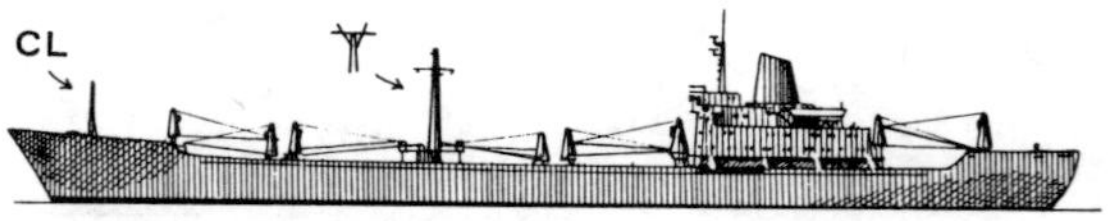

$KC_3KC_3MFC_2$ H13

02760 ANCHAN. Th/Ja 1967; C; 9900; 171 × 9.1 (563 × 30.1); M; 21; ex STRATHARDLE 1979. Sisters: **02761 BENJAMAS** (Th); ex STRATHBRORA 1979 **02762 TZELEPI** (Gr); ex CHUANCHOM 1980; ex STRATHCONON 1979.

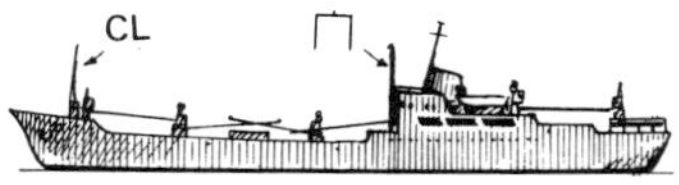

KC_3KMFC_2 H13
02770 BEI SHAN. Pa/Sw 1958; C; 3700; 106 × 7 (349 × 22.35); M; 15; ex BONNARD 1975. Sisters: **02771 NAN SHANG** (Pa); ex BRAQUE 1975 **02772 CARMEN A.** (Li); ex BOTTICELLI 1975.

KC_3KMFK H13
02780 MERCHANT PRINCE. Li/No 1959; C; 6300; 131 × 7.8 (430 × 25.8); M; 15; ex SEA HARE 1976; ex NOOR-E-RAZA 1975; ex ANTHONY 1974; ex BELANTHONY 1969; ex JALANTHONY 1964.

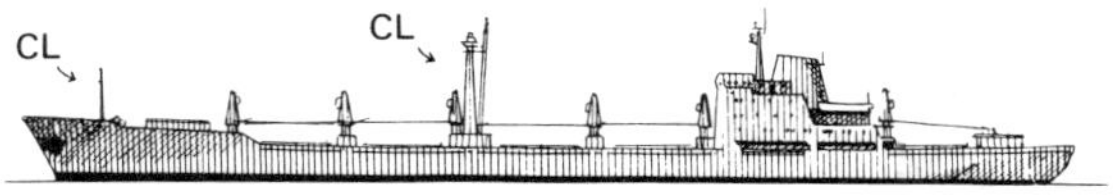

KC_3MC_2MFC H1
02790 ROCADAS. Po/Ru 1971; C; 12100; 169.86 × 10.06 (557.28 × 33.01); M; 18; ex TROPICO 1971; **"FEODOSIYA"** type. Similar: **02791 SERPA PINTO** (Po) ex TROPICALIA 1971 **02792 MONARCH** (Be) **02793 MONSOON** (Be) **02794 DIMITRIS** (Gr); ex IKAROS 1980. The following are Ru flag: **★02795 KAPITAN ALEKSEYEV ★02796 KAPITAN CHIRKOV ★02797 KAPITAN DZHURASHEVICH ★02798 KAPITAN KADETSKIY ★02799 KAPITAN KAMINSKIY ★02800 KAPITAN KUSHNARENKO ★02801 KAPITAN ANISTRATYENKO ★02802 KAPITAN GEORGIY BAGLAY ★02803 KAPITAN LEONTIY BORISENKO ★02804 KAPITAN LEV SOLOVYEV ★02805 KAPITAN MODEST IVANOV ★02806 KAPITAN SLIPKO.**

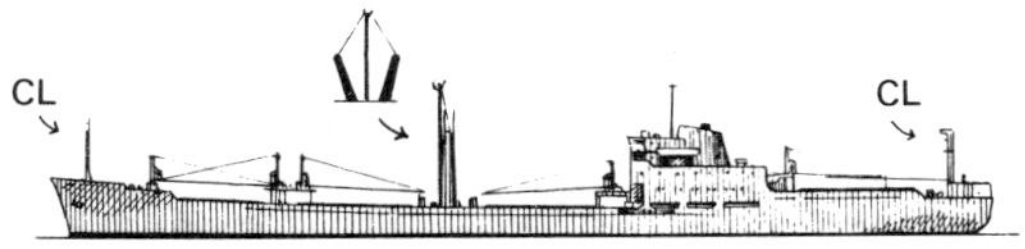

$KC_3MCMFCK$ H13
● **02810 HISTORIAN.** Br/Br 1968; C; 5600/8500; 150.6 × 8.9 (494 × 29.3); M; 18. Sister: **02811 MAGICIAN** (Br).

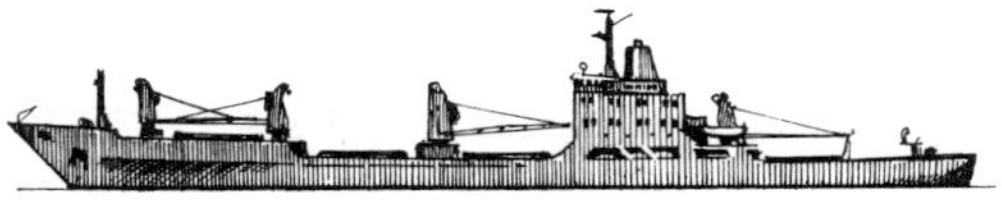

KC_3MFC H1
02830 PUNTA STELLA. It/It 1976; R; 7200/9400; 152.8 × 9.2 (503 × 30); M; 23. Sisters (It flag): **02831 PUNTA VERDE 02832 PUNTA SOLE 02833 PUNTA BIANCA** (see KC[2] MFC) may also have this sequence.

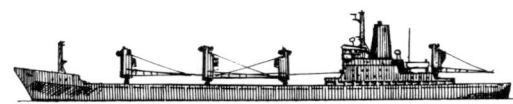

KC_3MFC H1
● **02860 LOCH MAREE.** Br/Br 1975; R; 8000/10400; 157.3 × 9.3 (516 × 30); M; 20.5. Sister: **02861 LOCH LOMOND** (Br).

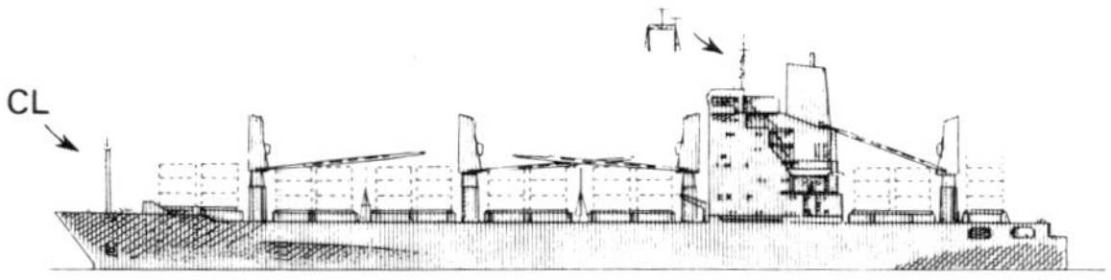

KC_3MFC H
02820 NEW ZEALAND CARIBBEAN. Br/FRG 1980; Ccn; 19600; 169.4 × 10.02 (555.77 × 32.87); M; 19.

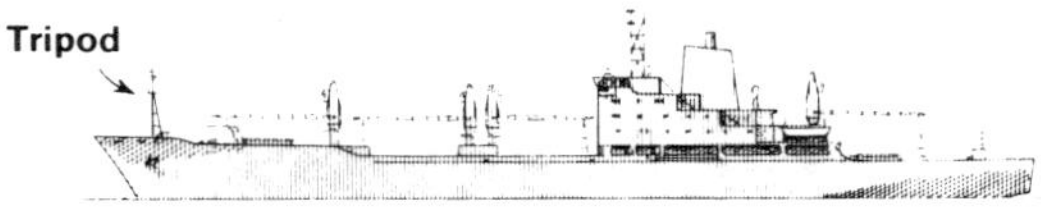

KC_3MFC H1
02840 POCANTICO. Be/Be 1979; R; 7000; 151.26 × 8.7 (496.26 × 28.54); M; 21. Sisters (Be flag): **02841 POCAHONTAS 02842 POTOMAC.**

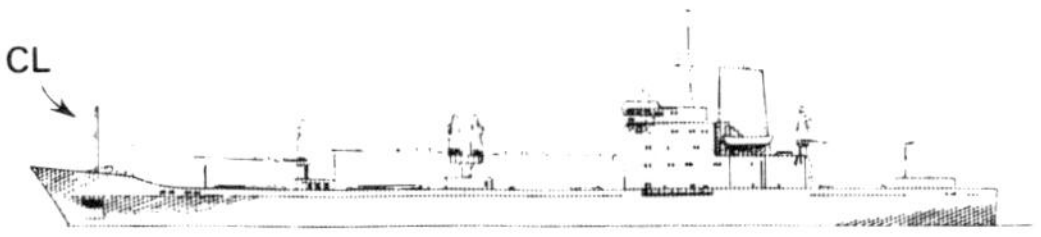

KC_3MFC H1
02850 HONOLULU. Ne/Ne 1979; R; 14500; 155 × 8.8 (508.53 × 28.87); M; 21.6. Sisters (Ne flag): **02851 CHRISTINA 02852 LANAI 02853 RIO FRIO.**

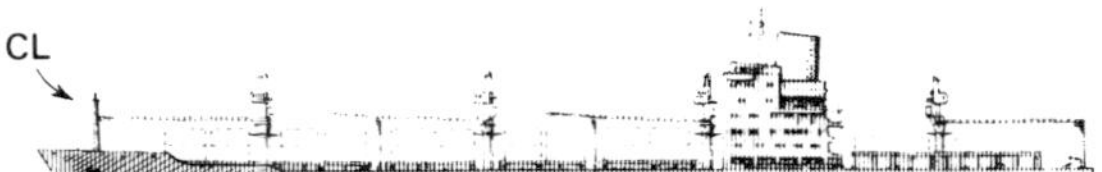

KC_3MFC H1
02870 AUSTRALIA STAR. Br/Br 1978; Con; 17100; 168.87 × 9.37 (554.04 × 30.74); M; 18. Sister: **02871 NEW ZEALAND STAR** (Br).

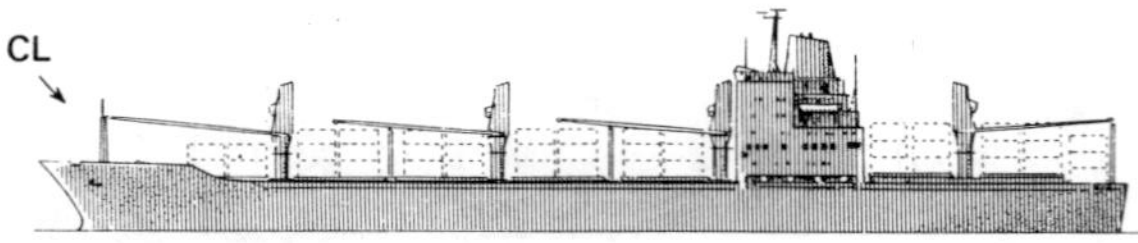

KC_3MFC H1
02880 WILLOWBANK. Br/Br 1980; Con; 18200; 171.13 × 9.35 (561.45 × 30.68); M; 19.

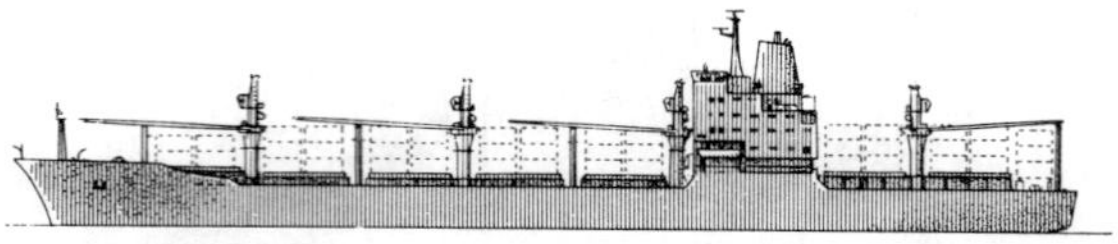

KC_3MFC H12
02890 DUNEDIN. Br/Br 1980; Con; 18140; 171.1 × 9.37 (561.35 × 30.74); M; 19.

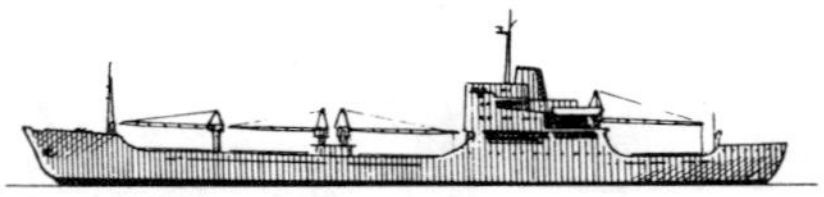

KC_3MFC H123
⋆02900 PERM. Ru/Ru 1969; C; 4800; 122 × 7.2 (400 × 23.5); M; 14.5. Sisters (Ru flag): **⋆02901 PALANGA ⋆02902 PAMIR ⋆02903 PARAMUSHIR ⋆02904 PAROMAY ⋆02905 PARGOLOVO ⋆02906 PAVLOVO ⋆02907 PECHENGA ⋆02908 PERTOMINSK ⋆02909 PETROKREPOST ⋆02910 PETROVSKIY ⋆02911 PETROZAVODSK ⋆02912 PLESETSK ⋆02913 POMORYE ⋆02914 PONOY ⋆02915 PROKOPYEVSK ⋆02916 PREZHEVALSK ⋆02917 PULKOVO ⋆02918 PUSHLAKHTA ⋆02919 PUSTOZERSK**

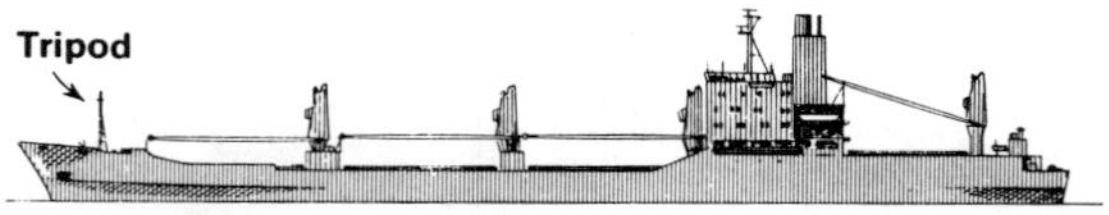

KC_3MFC H13
02930 WINTER WATER. Sw/Sw 1979; R; 11800; 169 × 10.1 (554.46 × 33.14); M; 21.9. Sisters (Sw flag): **02931 WINTER MOON 02932 WINTER SEA 02933 WINTER STAR 02934 WINTER SUN 02935 WINTER WAVE.**

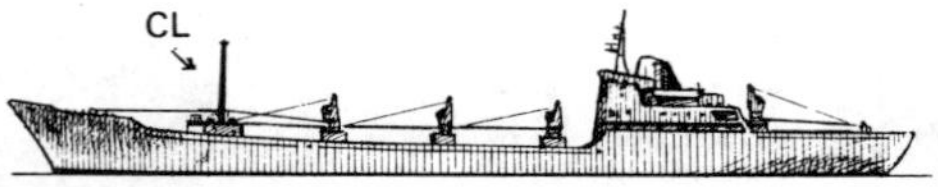

KC_3MFC H13
02940 COFFEE TRADER. Gr/Ne 1968; CP; 5200; 155 × 8.5 (477 × 28); M; 18; ex MERCURIUS 1980. Sister: **02941 AGIOS GIANNIS** (Gr); ex ELENA ALTOMARE 1980; ex NEPTUNUS 1979.

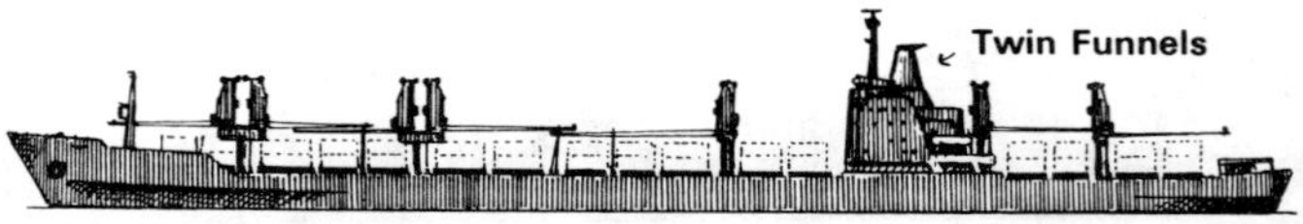

KC_3MFC_2 H1
● **02950 TAMARA.** Sw/Fi 1974; Con; 22300; 209 × 9.5 (686 × 31); M; 23. Sisters **02951 MALMROS MONSOON** (Br) **02952 NAGARA** (Sw)

KC_3MFC_2 H1
02960 LANKA KANTHI. Sr/Sw 1962; CP; 5700; 129 × 7.1 (424 × 23.4); M; 14.5; ex HUANGYAN 1973; ex DAWNING 1970; ex CONVALLARIA 1970.

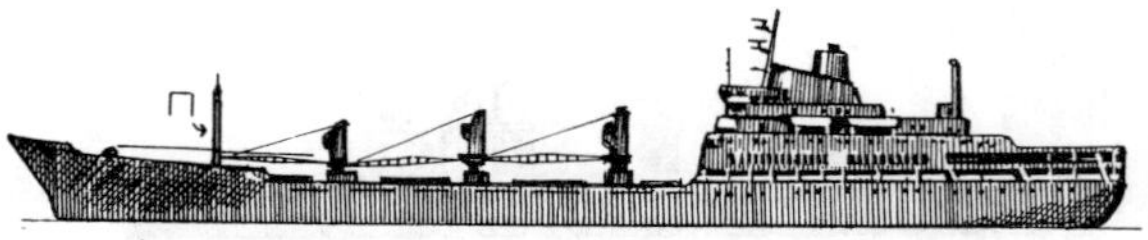

KC_3MFK H1
02970 SHIN SAKURA MARU. Ja/Ja 1972; PC; 13100; 175.6 × 9 (577 × 29.7); M; 20.5. Now converted to passenger ship & altered in appearance.

KC_3MFKC H
● **02980 TOEI MARU.** Ja/Ja 1973; R; 7400; 141.1 × 8.1 (463 × 26); M; 21. Sister: **02981 TOYU MARU** (Ja).

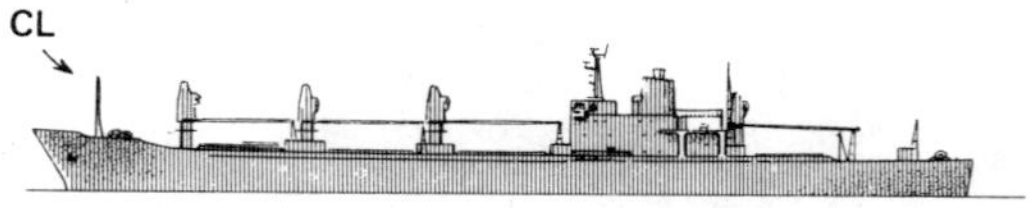

KC_3MFKC H1
02990 HAWAII. Ja/Ja 1979; R; 6500; 151.11 × 8.62 (495.77 × 28.28); M; —.

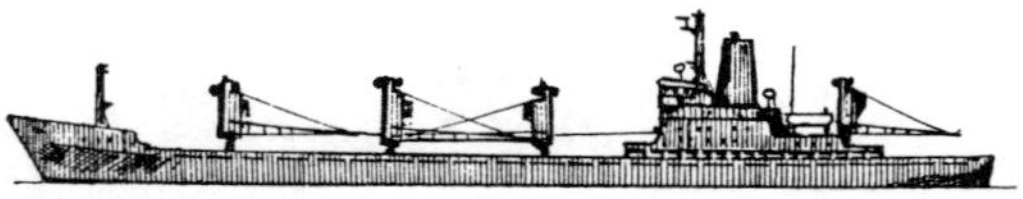

KC_3MFKC H1
● **03000 LOCH MAREE.** Br/Br 1975; R; 8000/10400; 157.3 × 9.3 (516 × 30); M; 20.5. Sister: **03001 LOCH LOMOND** (Br).

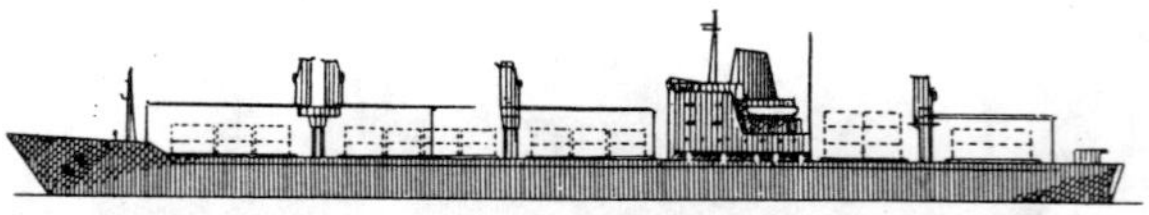

KC_3MFKC H1
03010 NEPTUNE EMERALD. Sg/Fi 1973; Con; 12700; 179 × 9.5 (590 × 31.2); M; 24. Sister: **03011 NEPTUNE SAPPHIRE** (Sg).

KC_3MFKC_3 H13
03020 NEPTUNE AGATE. Sg/No 1962; C; 6400; 134.4×7.1 (442×23.4); M; 15.5; ex CYGNUS 1970.

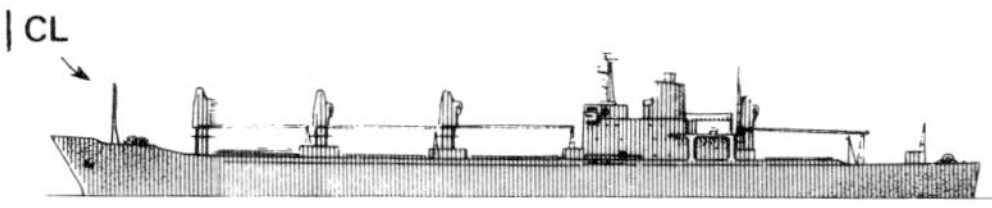

KC_3MFKCK H1
03030 HAWAII. Ja/Ja 1979; R; 6500; 151.11×8.62 (495.77×28.28); M; —.

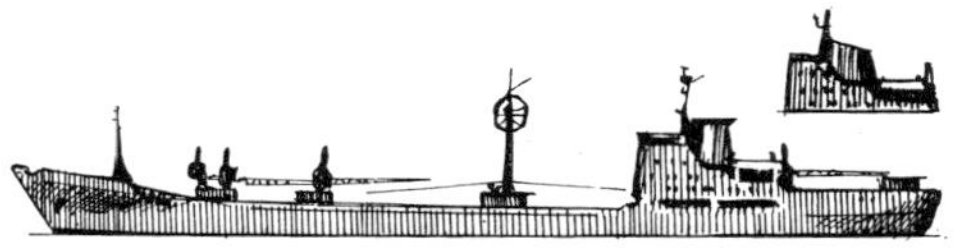

KC_3M_2FC H13
⋆03040 KASIMOV. Ru/Fi 1962; C; 9300; 147×9.1 (482×30); M; 15.25. Sisters (Ru flag): **⋆03041 KALININABAD ⋆03042 KANEV ⋆03043 KARACHAJEVO - CHERKESSIJA ⋆03045 KASPIJSK ⋆03046 KIMOVSK ⋆03047 KOVROV ⋆03048 KRASNOUFIMSK** Similar: **⋆03049 KRASNOGRAD.**

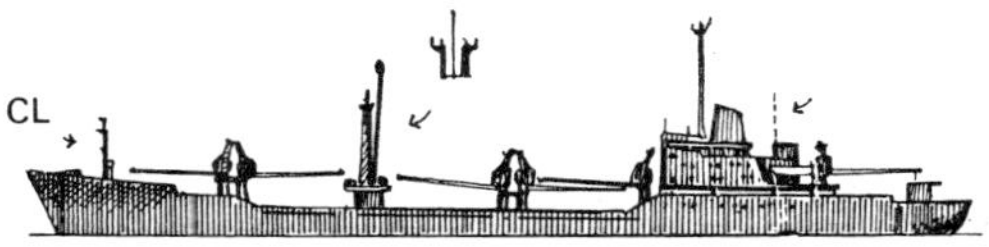

KC_2KC_3MFC/KC_2KC_3MFKC H13
⋆03060 HARRY POLLITT. Ru/DDR 1971; C; 9300; 151.5×9 (497×29.5); M; 17; Some sisters vary in details. Some have small kingpost abaft funnel as indicated in drawing. Sisters (Ru flag): **⋆03061 VALERIAN KUIBYSHEV ⋆03062 WILLIAM FOSTER ⋆03063 ANATOLIY LUNACHARSKIY ⋆03064 ANNA ULYANOVA ⋆03065 ALEKSANDR ULYANOV ⋆03066 DMITRIY ULYANOV ⋆03067 ILYA ULYANOV ⋆03068 NIKOLAY KRYLENKO ⋆03069 NIKOLAY POGODIN ⋆03070 OLGA ULYANOVA ⋆03071 VLADIMIR ILYCH ⋆03072 BORIS ZHEMCHUZIN.**

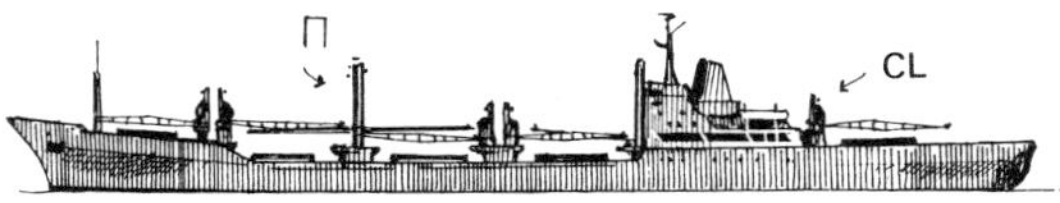

KC_2KC_2KMFC H13
● **03080 ITAIMBE.** Bz/Bz 1970; C; 10800; 161×9.7 (528×31.9); M; 20.5. Sisters (Bz flag): **03801 ITAITE 03082 ITANAGE 03083 ITAPUI 03084 ITAQUICE 03085 ITAGIBA 03086 ITAPAGE 03087 ITAPE 03087 ITAPUCA 03088 ITAQUATIA 03089 ITAPURA 03090 ITASSUCE 03091 COPACABANA 03092 FLAMENGO 03093 FROTARIO 03094 FROTASANTOS 03095 MARINGA 03096 OLINDA** (Po flag): **03097 CARVALHO ARAUJO.**

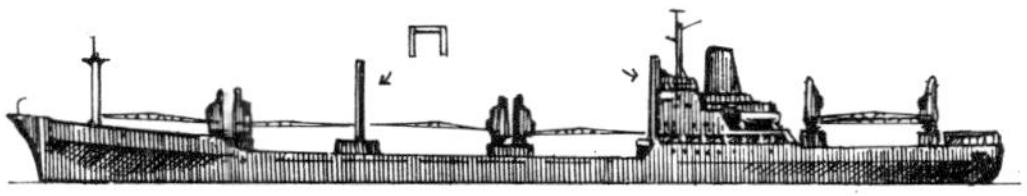

$KC_2KC_2KMFC_2$ H13
03100 PEREIRA d'ECA. Po/Bz 1972; C; 7800/11200; 161×9.6 (528×31.5); M; 20.5. probable sisters (Bz flag): **03101 MINERVA 03102 ZEUS 03103 NETUNO.**

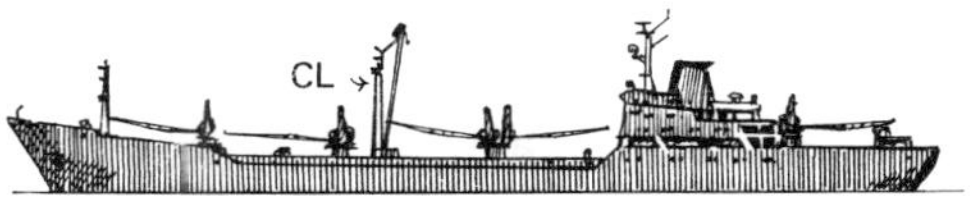

KC_2KC_2MFC H13
⋆03110 NOVGOROD. Ru/Fi 1967; Ci; 5800/8800; 150.9×9 (495×29.5); M; 18; Heavy lift derrick is not normally fitted. See alternative entry under KC^4MFC. Sisters (Ru flag): **⋆03111 NOVOSIBIRSK ⋆03112 NOVOKUZNETSK ⋆03113 NOVOKUIBYSHEVSK ⋆03114 NOVOMOSKOVSK ⋆03115 NOVOTROITSK ⋆03116 NOVOVYATSK ⋆03117 NOVOALTAISK ⋆03118 NOVOMIRGOROD ⋆03119 NOVOPOLOTSK ⋆03120 NOVODRUZHESK ⋆03121 NOVOLVOVSK ⋆03122 NOVOZYBKOV ⋆03123 NOVOGRUDOK ⋆03124 NOVOVOLYNSK.**

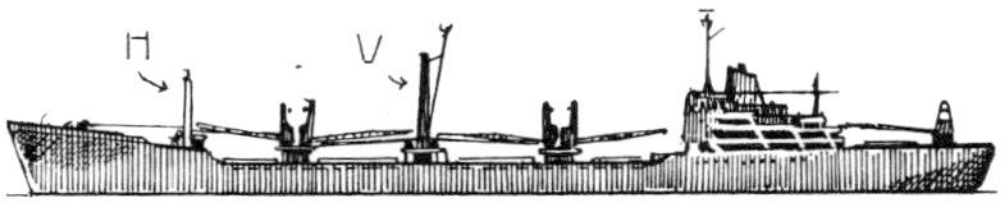

KC_2KC_2MFKC H13
⋆03130 HONG SHOU SHAN. RC/Fr 1966; C; 10400; 158×9.5 (516×32); M; 19; ex ANGO 1978. Sisters: **⋆03031 LIAN YUN SHAN** (RC) ex DUPLEIX 1978 **⋆03132 WU TAI SHAN** (RC) ex FORBIN 1978 **03133 BOUGAINVILLE** (Fr) **03134 SURCOUF** (Fr) **03135 TOURVILLE** (Fr).

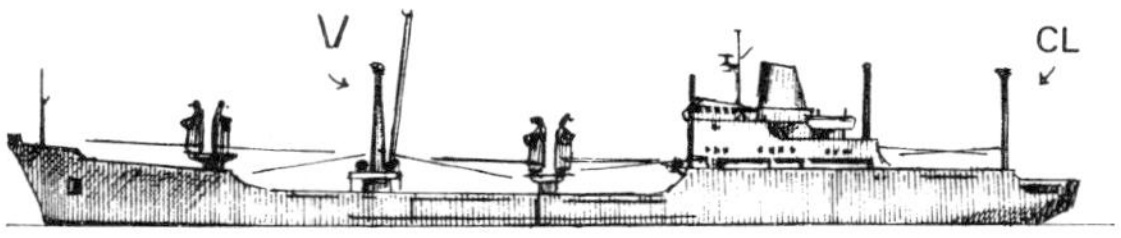

$KC_2KC_2KMFK_2$ H13
03140 AMSTERDAM. NA./Ne 1970; CP; 7200; 169×8.3 (555×27.1); M; 21; ex TRIDENT AMSTERDAM 1980; Side doors. Sisters **03141 ROTTERDAM** (NA); ex TRIDENT ROTTERDAM 1980 **03142 CARACAS** (Ve) **03143 VENEZUELA** (Ve).

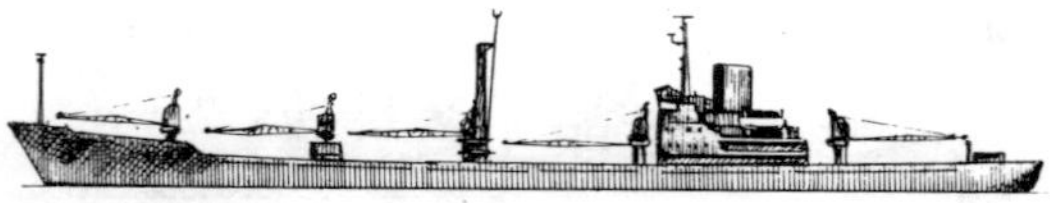

KC_2KCMFC H1
⋆**03150 KARL MARX.** DDR/DDR 1971; C; 11000; 166.4 × 9.5 (546 × 31.35); M; 21.5. Sister ⋆**03151 FRIEDRICH ENGELS** (DDR).

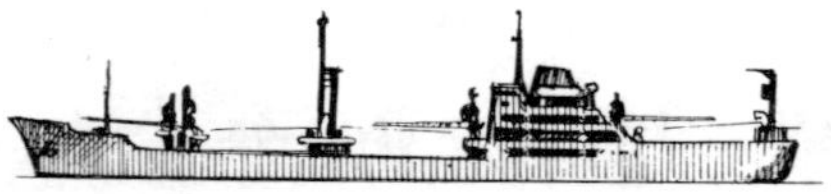

$KC_2KCMFCK$ H13
⋆**03170 JIANCHANG.** RC/Sw 1964; C 3600/5600; 124 × 8.2 (407 × 26.9); M; 17; ex STATESMAN 1977. Sisters (RC flag): ⋆**03171 JINCHANG** ex DISCOVERER 1977 ⋆**03172 YICHANG** ex NATURALIST 1977 ⋆**03173 WU CHANG** ex NOVELIST 1977 ⋆**03174 YONGCHANG** ex PHILOSOPHER 1977.

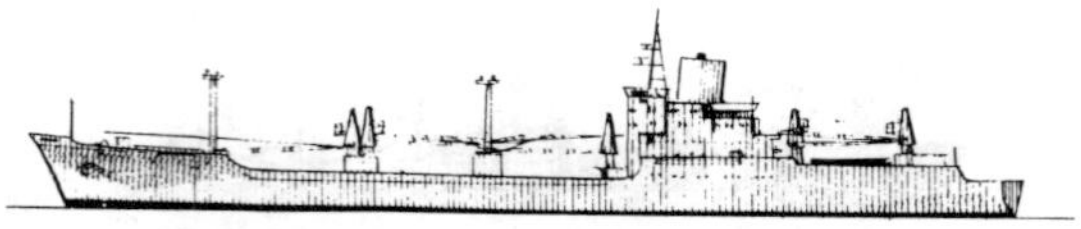

KC_2KCMFC_2 H13
03160 NEDLLOYD AMSTERDAM. Ne/Ne 1968; C; 7300/10500; 161 × 10.3 (528 × 33.7); M; 20; ex STRAAT AMSTERDAM 1978; ex SAFOCEAN AMSTERDAM 1976; ex STRAAT AMSTERDAM 1970. Sisters **03161 NEDLLOYD ADELAIDE** (Ne); ex SAFOCEAN ADELAIDE 1978; ex STRAAT ADELAIDE 1970 **03162 NEDLLOYD AUCKLAND** (Ne); ex SAFOCEAN AUCKLAND 1980; ex STRAAT AUCKLAND 1970 Possible sisters: **03163 VICTORIA 1** (Pa); ex NEDLLOYD AGULHAS 1980; ex STRAAT AGULHAS 1978 **03164 ACONCAGUA** (Ar); ex NEDLLOYD ALGOA 1980; ex STRAAT ALGOA 1978 **03165 NEDLLOYD ALBANY** (Ne); ex SAFOCEAN ALBANY 1980; ex STRAAT ACCRA 1970.

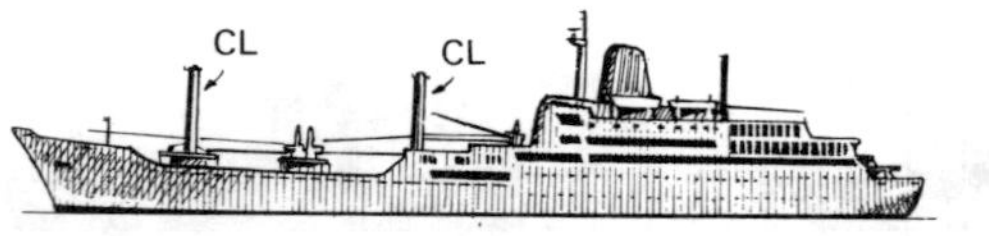

KC_2KCMFK H12
03180 CENTAUR. Sg/Br 1963; P/LS; 8000; 146 × 8 (481 × 26.4); TSM; 20.

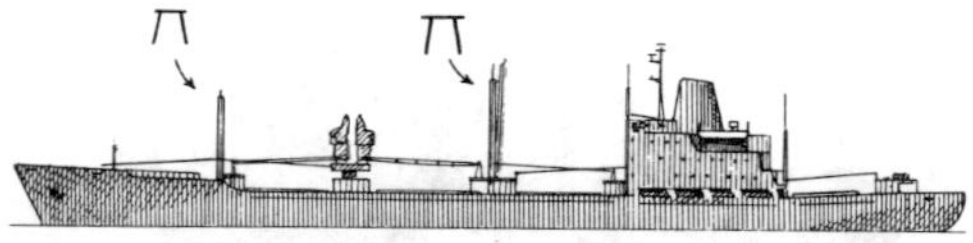

KC_2K_2MFK H1
03200 BUNGA ORKID. My/Ja 1971; C; 10700; 153 × 9.7 (502 × 31.9); M; 23. Sister **03201 BUNGA TANJONG** (My). possible sisters: **03202 BUNGA MELATI** (My). **03203 BUNGA SEROJA** (My).

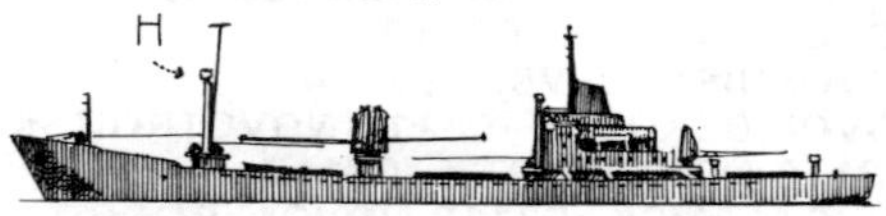

KC_2KMFC H1
03220 RONCESVALLES. Sp/Sp 1972; C; 5500; 140 × 7.5 —(460 × 24.6); —M: 18. Sisters (Sp flag): **03221 BELEN 03222 GALEONA 03223 VALVANUZ**

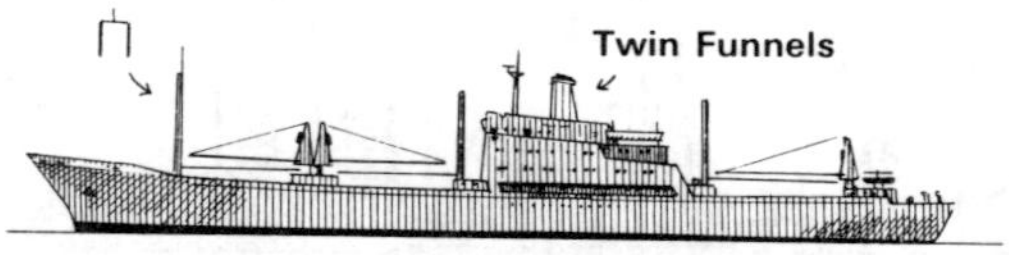

KC_2KMFKC H
● **03260 GEEST-TIDE.** Br/Br 1971; R; 5900; 149.3 × 8.5 (490 × 27.9); M; 21. Sisters (Br flag): **03261 GEESTCREST 03262 GEESTLAND 03263 GEESTSTAR**

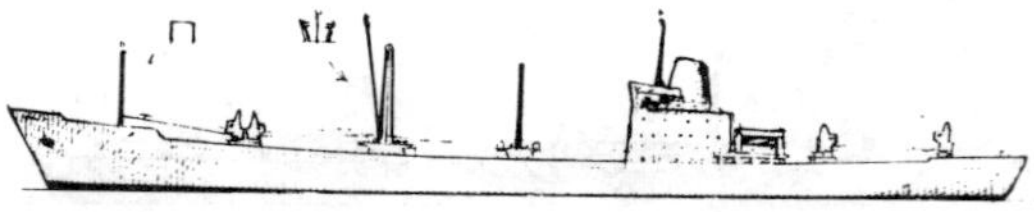

$KC_2K_2MFC_2$ H1
03190 MYKONOS. Gr/Br 1967; R; 9000/12300; 166 × 9.8 (546 × 32.4); M; 19; ex NZ AORANGI 1979; ex MAJESTIC 1974. Similar: **03191 SERIFOS** (Gr); ex N.Z. WAITANGI 1980; ex BRITANNIC 1974.

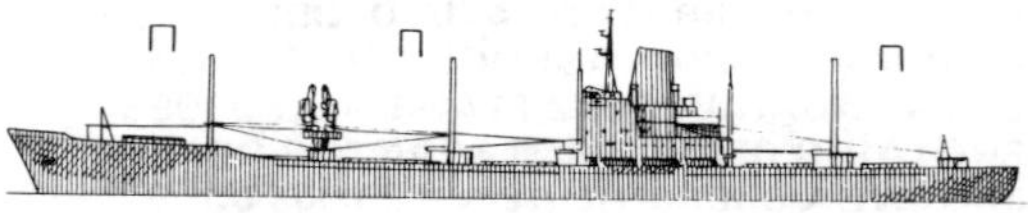

$KC_2K_2MFK_2$ H1
03210 BUNGA RAYA. My/Ja 1970; C; 11100; 162 × 9.1 (532 × 30.1); M; 19. Sister: **03211 BUNGA MELOR** (My).

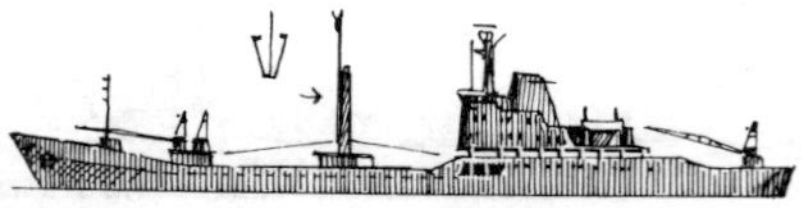

KC_2KMFC H13
● ⋆**03230 RADZIONKOW.** Pd/Pd 1973; C; 3500/5500; 124 × 7.3 (407 × 24.1); M; 15.5; 'B432' type Sisters (Pd flag): ⋆**03231 BOCHNIA** ⋆**03233 CHELM** ⋆**03233 GARWOLIN** ⋆**03234 HENRYK LEMBERG** ⋆**03235 OSTROLEKA** ⋆**03236 WIELICZKA** ⋆**03237 SKOCZOW** ⋆**03238 SIEMIATYCZE** (Ru flag): ⋆**03239 TARKHANSK** ⋆**03240 SARATOVSK** ⋆**03241 TEREKHOVSK** ⋆**03242 TERNOVSK** ⋆**03243 TITOVSK** ⋆**03244 TOKARYEVSK** ⋆**03245 TULSK** ⋆**03246 TRUNOVSK** ⋆**03247 TALNIKI** ⋆**03248 TARASOVSK** (Sy flag): **03249 AL YARMOUK 03250 BARADA** (Eg flag): **03251 AL ESRAA 03252 AL HAMRAA 03253 ASMAA**

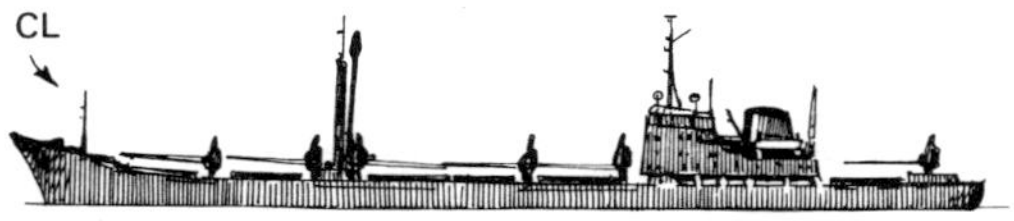

KC_2MC_3MFC H1
★**03270 OMSK** Ru/Ja 1961; C; 7500/10900; 155 × 9.6 (509 × 31.5); M; 17. Sisters (Ru flag): ★**03271 OKHOTSK** ★**03272 ORENBURG**

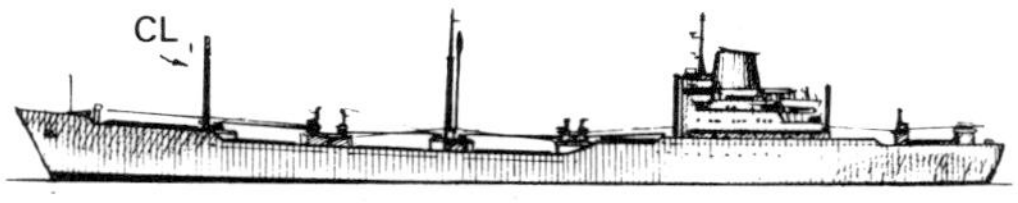

KC_2MC_2KMFKC H13
03290 HELLENIC PATRIOT. Gr/Ne 1962; C; 6800/9700; 159 × 8.6 (521 × 28.5); M; 17.5; ex MARIT 1975; ex NIPPON 1974.

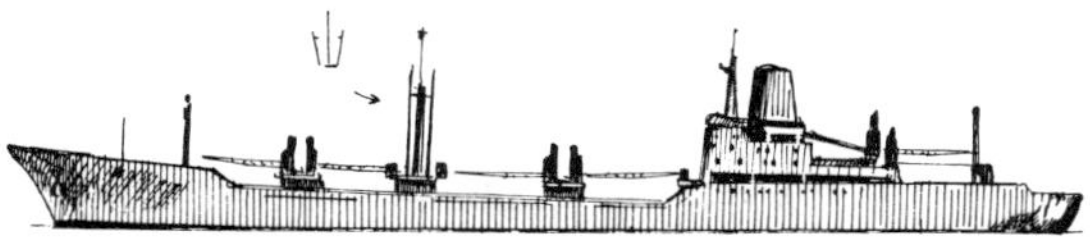

$KC_2MC_2MFC_2K$ H13
03320 PATROCLUS. Br/Ja 1966; C; 9600/12300; 172 × 10.2 (564 × 33.5); M; 21; ex GLENALMOND 1973. Sisters **03321 PHEMIUS (Br);** ex GLENFINLAS 1972 **03322 PHRONTIS** (Br); ex PEMBROKESHIRE 1972 **03323 PERSEUS** (Br); ex RADNORSHIRE 1972 **03324 PROTESILAUS** (Br) **03325 PEISANDER** (Br) **03326 ORIENTAL CHAMPION** (Li); ex PRIAM 1979 **03327 ORIENTAL MERCHANT** (Br); ex PROMETHEUS Some ships have slightly different sequences.

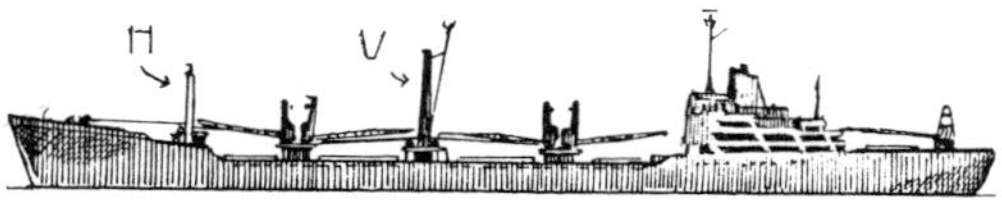

KC_2MC_2MFKC H13
★**03340 HONG SHOU SHAN.** RC/Fr 1966; C; 10400; 158 × 9.5 (516 × 32); M; 19; ex ANGO 1978. Sisters ★**03341 LIAN YUN SHAN** (RC); ex DUPLEIX 1978 ★**03342 WU TAI SHAN** (RC); ex FORBIN 1978 **03343 BOUGAINVILLE** (Fr) **03344 TOURVILLE** (Fr) **03345 SURCOUF** (Fr)

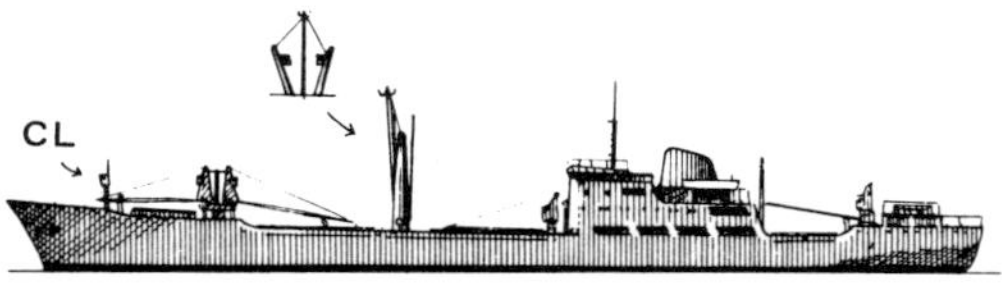

$KC_2MCMFKC$ H13
03370 AEOLIAN STAR. Gr/Br 1969; C; 6400/9600; 155.7 × 9.1 (511 × 30.2); M; 17.5; ex STRATHARLICK 1980; ex TABARISTAN 1975:

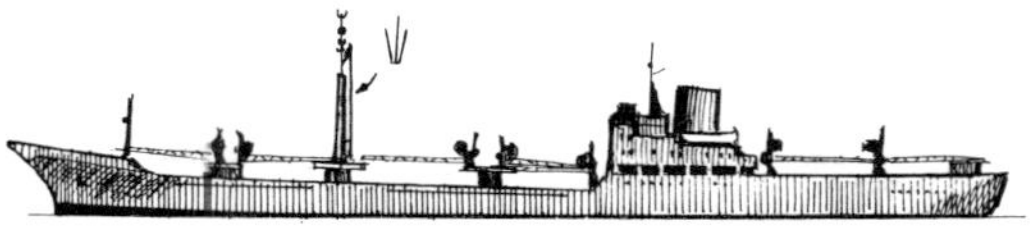

$KC_2MC_3MFC_2$ H13
03280 CORTINA. It/Br 1965; C; 8500; 160.3 × 0.3 (526 × 31.6); M; 19; ex CONCORDIA GULF 1974; ex AUSTRALIA STAR 1972.

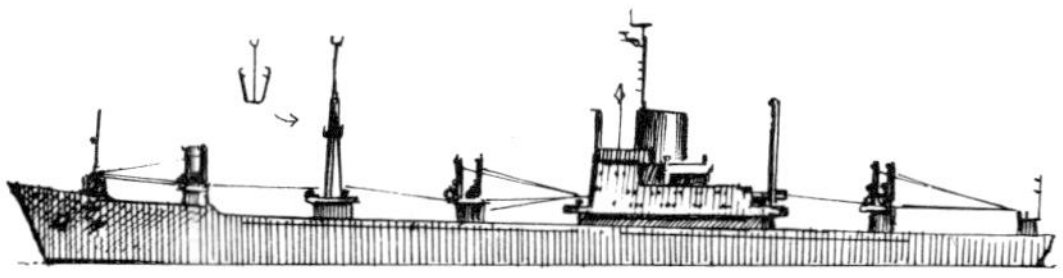

$KC_2MC_2KMFKC_2$ H1
03300 NEDLLOYD LEUVE. Ne/Ja 1966; C; 12900; 1.62 × 9.4 (532 × 29.9); M; 20; ex LEUVE LLOYD 1978. Sisters (Ne flag): **03301 NEDLLOYD LOIRE** ex LOIRE LLOYD 1978 **03302 NEDLLOYD LINGE** ex NEDER LINGE 1978

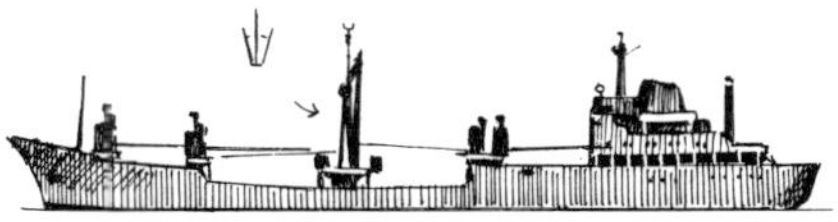

KC_2MC_2MFK H13
03330 TRADER. Br/Sw 1966; C/HL; 3500/5800; 127.4 × 8.2 (418 × 26.9); M; 16. Sister **03331 LINGUIST** (Br)

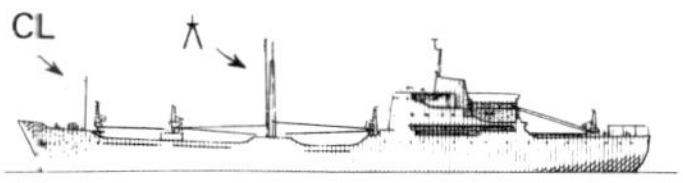

KC_2MCMFC H13
● **03350 ASSALAMAH.** Li/Au 1965; C; 2800/3900; 101.22 × 5.89/7.41 (332.01 × 19.32/24.31); M; —; ex NEPTUNE JADE 1976; ex MORESBY 1970

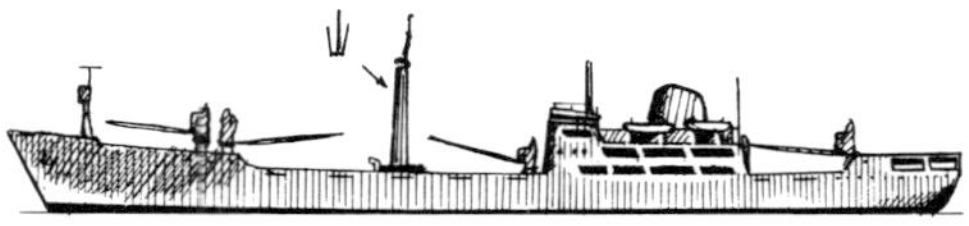

$KC_2MCMFKC$ H13
03360 STRATHAPPIN. Br/Br 1965; C; 7000/9300; 153.3 × 8.6 (503 × 28.2); M; M; ex SHAHRISTAN 1975. Sister **03361 STRATHALVIE** (Br); ex FLORISTAN 1975

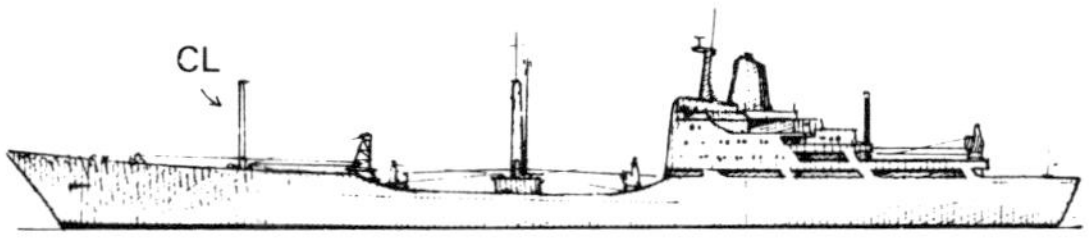

$KC_2MCMFKC$ H13
03380 REA B. Pa/Br 1967; C; 9400/11500; 171.6 × 10.1 (562 × 33.4); M; 21; ex DA VERRAZANO 1980; ex BENALBANACH 1962:

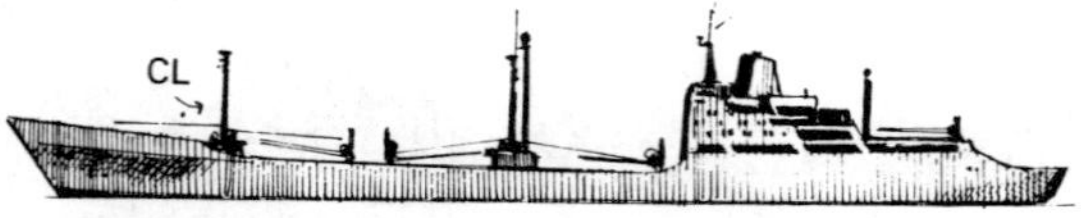

KC$_2$MCMFKC H13
03390 TINA B. Pa/Br 1965; C; 8800/11800; 171.6 × 10.2 (563 × 33.8); M; 21.5; ex DA NOLI 1980; ex BENLEDI 1972.

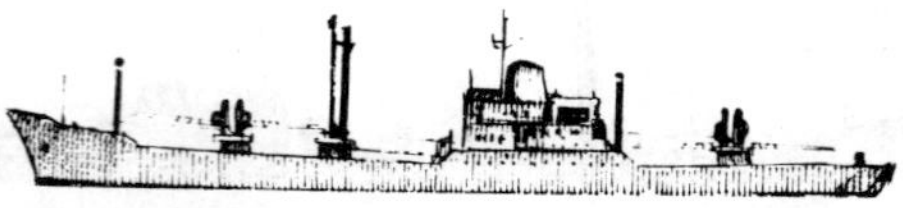

KC$_2$MCMFKC$_2$ H12
03400 CHAR HUI. Pa/Ja 1966; C; 6800/9100; 157 × 9.4 (514 × 31); M; 20; ex NEDLLOYD FIJI 1980; ex STRAAT FIJI 1978. Sisters (Pa flag): **03401 CHAR KUO;** ex NEDLLOYD FLORIDA 1980; ex STRAAT FLORIDA 1978 **03402 CHAR MOU;** ex NEDLLOYD FUTAMI 1980; ex STRAAT FUTAMI 1978 **03403 CHAR TAH;** ex NEDLLOYD FUSHIMI 1980; ex STRAAT FUSHIMI 1978

KC$_2$MFC H
● **03410 PLAYA DE LAS NIEVES.** Sp/Sp 1967; R; 2600; 110 × 6.5 (361 × 21.2); M; 19. Sisters **03411 PLAYA BLANCA** (Sp) **03412 USHAIA** (Ar); ex PLAYA DE NAOS 1979; ex PLAYA NAOS 1969.

KC$_2$MFC H1
03420 PUNTA BIANCA. It/It 1975; R; 9400; 152.8 × 9.1 (501 × 30); M; 23; May be KC^{3}MFC—See 'PUNTA STELLA'.

KC$_2$MFC H1
● **03430 IOS.** Pa/Ar 1970; C; 4000; 106.3 × 6.8 (348 × 22.4); M; 18; ex CIPOLLETI 1980.

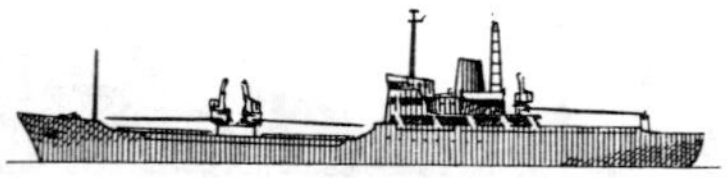

KC$_2$MFC H12
03440 HAYASHIKANE MARU NO.1. Ja/Ja 1967; C; 3700; 111 × 6.8 (364 × 22.6); M; 16. Sister **03441 HAYASHIKANE MARU NO.2** (Ja)

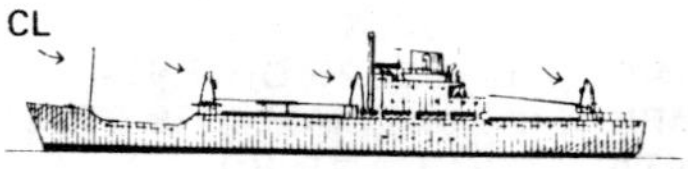

KC$_2$MFC H12
03450 POOLTA. Br/Br 1959; C- 2900; 100 × 4.9 (329 × 16.4); M; 11.

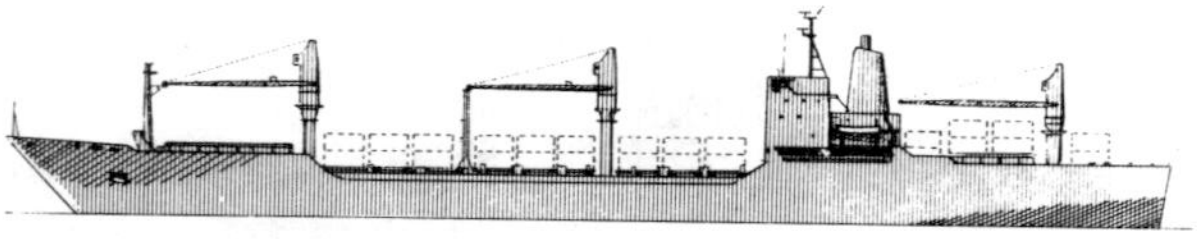

KCCMFC H13
03460 D'ALBERTIS. It/It 1978; C/Con; 17800; 186.44 × 10.02 (611.68 × 32.87); M; 23. Sisters (It flag): **03461 DA MOSTO 03462 PANCALDO**

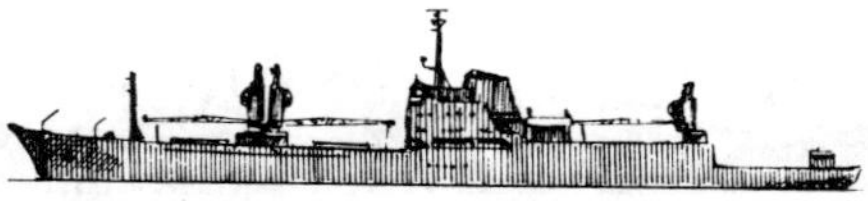

KC$_2$MFC H2
03470 LLOYD BAGE. Bz/Bz 1973; R; 6700; 140 × 8.3 (459 × 27.3); M; 21. Sister **03471 LLOYD SANTOS** (Bz)

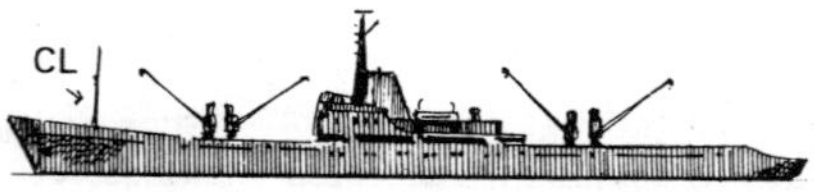

KC$_2$MFC$_2$ H
● **03480 ROYAL SEA.** Gr/Bz 1968; R; 4200; 126.2 × 7 (414 × 23); M; 18.5; ex INGA POLARIS 1980; ex ALBERTO COCOZZA 1978. Sisters **03481 ROYAL SKY;** (Gr) ex ANNA POLARIS 1979; ex FRIGO TEJO 1978 **03482 FRIGO TIETE;** (Bz) ex RAFAEL LOTITO.

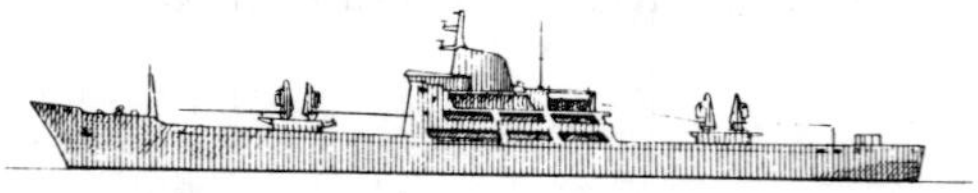

KC$_2$MFC$_2$ H1
● **03490 AQUILON.** Fr/Fr 1968; R; 4400/8600; 144.1 × 7.5 (473 × 24.8); M; 21.5. Sisters **03491 FORT SAINTE MARIE** (Fr) **03492 MARYBETH** (Li); ex FRIBOURG 1979 **03493 ORQUE** (Fr); ex IVONDRO 1974 **03494 NARVAL** (Fr) **03495 FAVORITA** (Sd) **03496 CAYENNE** (Li); ex BELOUGA 1980 **03497 JUNIPER** (Li); ex MARSOUIN 1980

KC_2MFC_2 H1
03500 VEGESACK. Gr/FRG 1959; R; 3100; 134.7×6.1 (442×20); M; 18. Sister **03501 WESERMUNDE** (Gr)

KC_2MFC_2 H1
● **03510 SAN BLAS.** Pi/Sw 1967; R; 6400; 149×8 7 (489×28.9); M; 20.25. Sisters **03511 SAN BRUNO** (Pi) **03512 SAN BENITO** (Fi) **03513 CORIANDER** (Li); ex OREGANO 1980; ex REGAN 1979; ex TASMANIC 1979

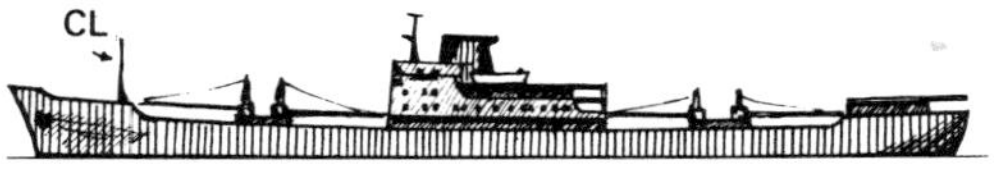

KC_2MFC_2 H13
03520 AUSTRALIC. Sw/Sw 1965; R; 6500/8000; 150×8.4; 490×27-6; M; 19. Sisters **03521 ANTILOPE** (Sw) **03522 ALTCAR** (Br); ex ARAWAK 1979 **03523 ARGONAUT II** (Li); ex ARGONAUT 1978 **03524 ARIEL I** (Sg); ex ARIEL 1978 **03525 AEGEAN REEFER** (Gr); ex ALBANY 1978

KC_2MFC_2 H13
03530 KAREPO. NZ/Hong Kong 1964; C; 3200; 99.3×5.7 (326×18.7); M; 13. Sister **03531 PACIFIC OCEAN** (Sg); ex KARETU 1980.

KC_2MFC_2 H2
03540 LLOYD BAGE. Bz/Bz 1973; R; 6700; 140×8.3 (459×27.3); M; 21. Sister **03541 LLOYD SANTOS** (Bz)

●
03545

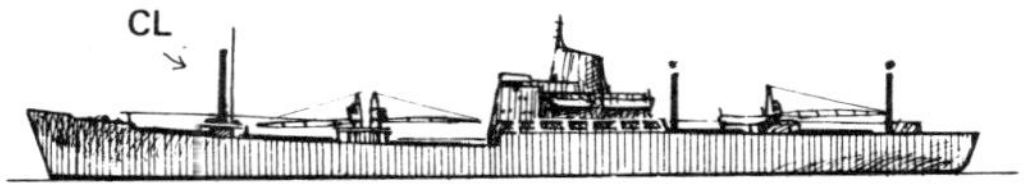

KC_2MFKCK H12
03550 OCEAN ENDURANCE. Pk/Br 1966; PC; 7500/10300; 153×9.2 (502×30.4); M; 17-5.

KC_2MFM H12
03560 ASAKAZE MARU. Ja/Ja 1967; R; 2800; 104×6.3 (342×20); M; 15.75. Sister **03561 HARUKAZE MARU** (Ja)

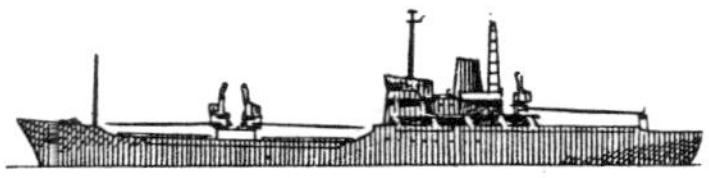

KC_2MFMC H12
03570 HAYASHIKANE MARU NO.1. Ja/Ja 1967; C; 3700; M; 16. Sister **03571 HAYASHIKANE MARU NO.2** (Ja):

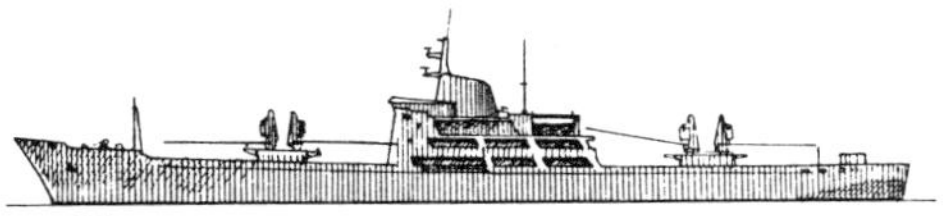

KC_2MFMC_2 H1
● **03580 AQUILON.** Fr/Fr 1968; R; 4400/8600; 144.1×7.5 (473×24.8); M; 21.5. Sisters **03581 FORT SAINTE MARIE** (Fr) **03582 MARYBETH** (Li); ex FRIBOURG 1979 **03583 ORQUE** (Fr); ex IVONDRO 1974 **03584 NARVAL** (Fr) **03585 FAVORITA** (Sd) **03586 CAYENNE** (Li); ex BELOUGA 1980 **03587 JUNIPER** (Li); ex MARSOUIN 1980

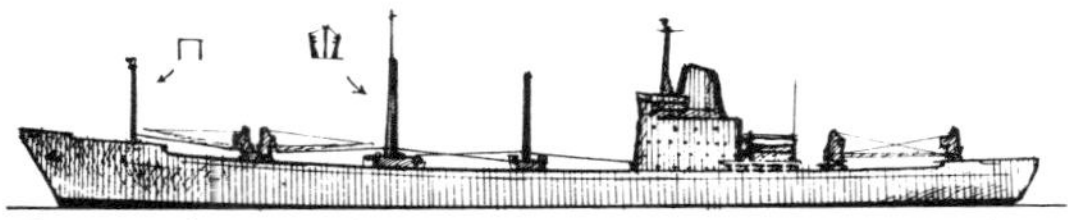

KC_2MKMFC_2 H1
03590 MYKONOS. Gr/Br 1967; R; 9000/12300; 166×9.8 (546×32.4); M; 19; ex NZ AORANGI 1979; ex MAJESTIC 1974. Similar **03591 SERIFOS** (Gr); ex NZ WAITANGI 1980; ex BRITANNIC 1974

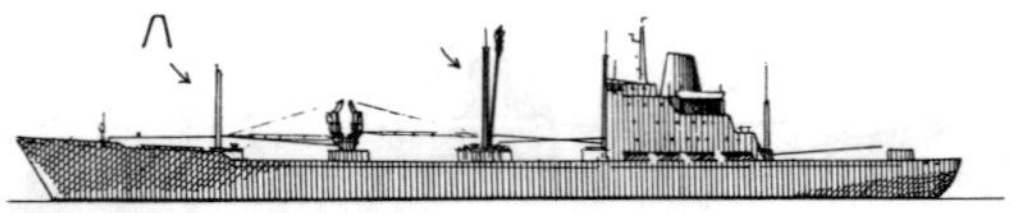

KC_2MKMFK H1
03600 BUNGA ORKID. My/Ja 1971; C; 10700; 153 × 9.7 (502 × 31.9); M; 23. Sister **03601 BUNGA TANJONG** (My) Possible sisters **03602 BUNGA MELATI** (My) **03603 BUNGA SEROJA** (My)

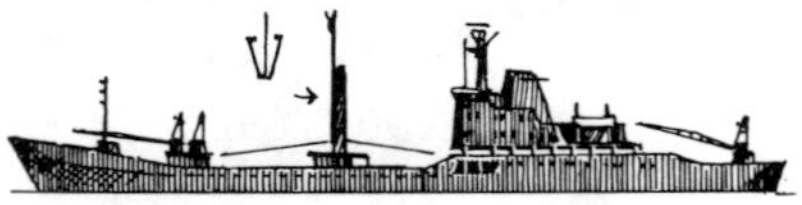

KC_2M_2FC H13
● ★**03620 RADZIONKOW:** Pd/Pd 1973; C; 3500/5500; 124 × 7.3 (407 × 24.1); M; 15.5; **'B432'** type. Sisters (Pd flag): ★**03621 BOCHNIA** ★**03622 CHELM** ★**03623 GARWOLIN** ★**03624 HENRYK LEMBERG** ★**03625 OSTROLEKA** ★**03627 SKOCZOW** ★**03628 SIEMIATYCZE** ★**03629 WIELICZKA** (Eg flag): **03630 AL ESRAA 03631 AL HAMRAA 03632 ASMAA** (Sy flag): **03633 AL YARMOUK 03634 BARADA** (Ru flag): ★**03635 TARKHANSK** ★**03636 SARATOVSK** ★**03637 TEREKHOVSK** ★**03638 TERNOVSK** ★**03639 TITOVSK** ★**03640 TOKARYEVSK** ★**03641 TULSK** ★**03642 TIMOFEYEVSK** ★**03643 TRUNOVSK** ★**03644 TALNIKI** ★**03645 TARASOVSK**

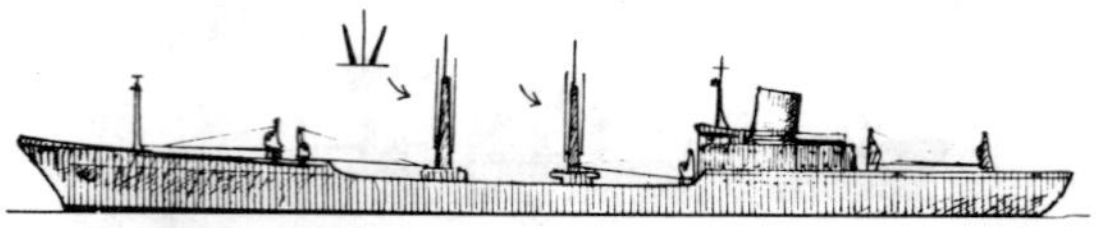

$KC_2M_2CMFC_2$ H13
03610 SOUTHLAND STAR: Br/FRG 1967; R; 7800/11300; 168.2 × 4.8 (552 × 32); M; 21.5; Both converted to container ships in 1977. May be altered in appearence. Sister **03611 WELLINGTON STAR** (Br); ex NEW ZEALAND STAR 1978

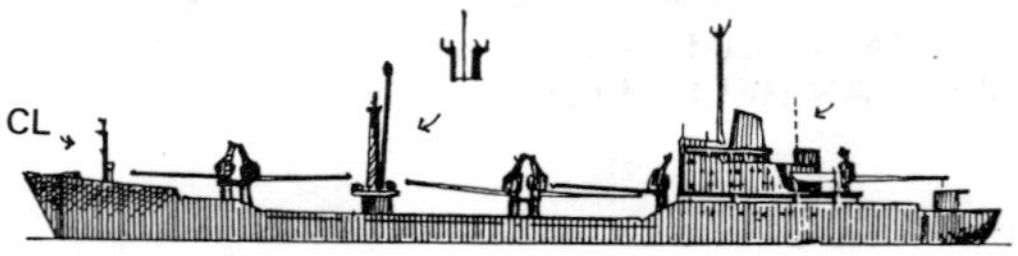

$KCKC_3MFC$ H13
★**03650 HARRY POLLITT.** Ru/DDR 1971; C; 9300; 151.5 × 9 (497 × 29.5); M; 17. Sisters(Ru flag)—ships may vary. ★**03651 VALERIAN KUIBYSHEV** ★**03652 BORIS ZHEMCHUZIN** ★**03653 WILLIAM FOSTER** ★**03654 ANATOLIY LUNACHARSKIY** ★**03656 ANNA ULYANOVA** ★**03657 ALEXSANDR ULYNOV** ★**03658 DIMITRIY ULYANOV** ★**03659 ILYA ULYANOV** ★**03660 NIKOLAY KRYLENKO** ★**03661 NIKOLAY POGODIN** ★**03662 OLGA ULYANOVA** ★**03663 VLADIMIR ILYCH**

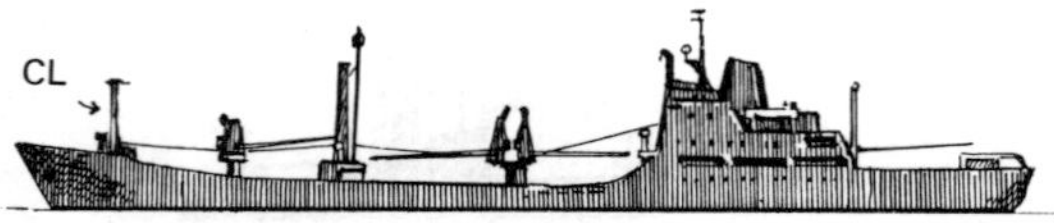

$KCKC_2KMFK$ H13
03670 CORABANK. Br/Br 1972; C; 7900/11400; 148.5 × 9.6 (520 × 31.7); M; 18.75. Sisters (Br flag). **03671 CLYDEBANK 03672 FORTHBANK 03673 IVYBANK 03674 MEADOWBANK 03675 MORAYBANK**

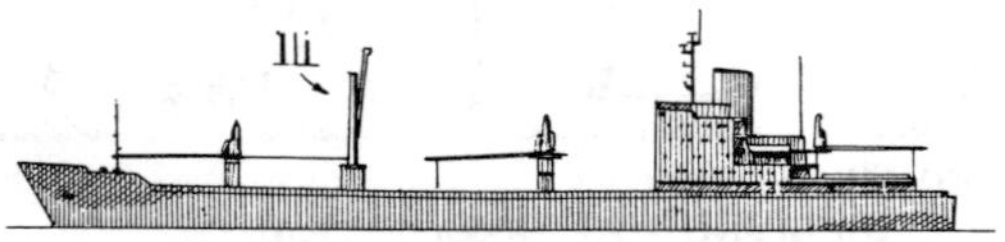

$KCKC_2MFC$ H1
★**03690 WARNEMUNDE.** Ru/DDR 1972; C; 11000; 150.2 × 8.9 (493 × 29); M; 19.25; **"MERCATOR"** type. Ships may vary slightly. Sisters (Ru flag). ★**03691 PALEKH** ★**03692 PAVLODAR** ★**03693 PAVLOGRAD** ★**03694 PESTOVO** ★**03695 PETRODVORETS** ★**03696 POLESSK** ★**03697 PRAVDINSK** ★**03698 PRIMORSK** ★**03699 PSKOV** ★**03700 PUTIVL** ★**03701 PERVOMAYSK** ★**03702 SALVADOR ALLENDE** ★**03703 WALTER ULBRICHT** ★**03704 DEKABRIST** ★**03705 NADEZHDA KRUPSKAYA** Possible similar (DDR flag): ★**03706 MUHLHAUSEN** ★**03707 NORDHAUSEN** ★**03708 SANGERHAUSEN** ★**03709 SONDERHAUSEN.**

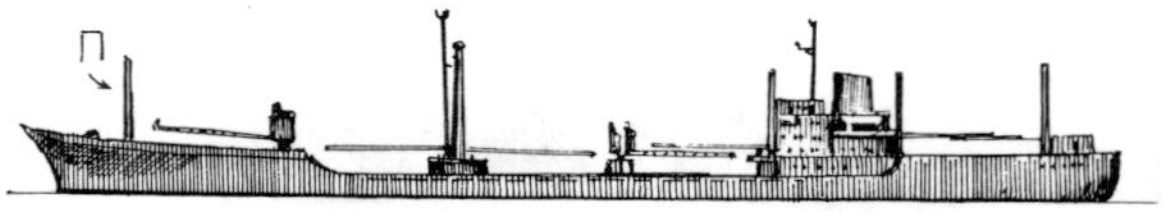

$KCKC_2KMFK_2$ H13
03680 ENGLAND MARU. Ja/Ja 1970; C; 9600; 175 × 9.1 (574 × 29.10); M; 20.5. Sisters. **03681 NEW GOLDEN PHOENIX** (Pa); ex GOLDEN PHOENIX 1979; ex SCOTLAND MARU 1979 **03682 SILVER PHOENIX** (Li); ex WALES MARU 1979

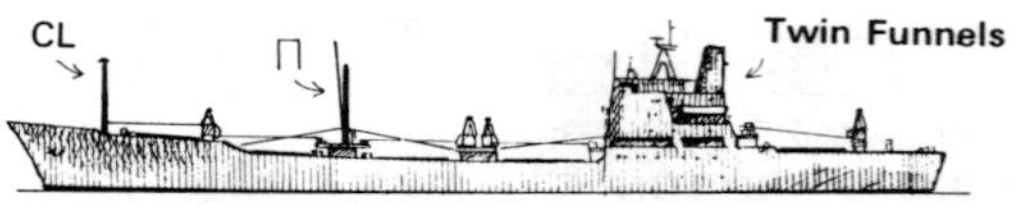

$KCKC_2MFC$ H13
03720 DIONE. Fr/Fr 1967; CP; 6000/9800; 149.3 × 7.4 (490 × 24.7); M; 17; ex SUFFREN 1978.

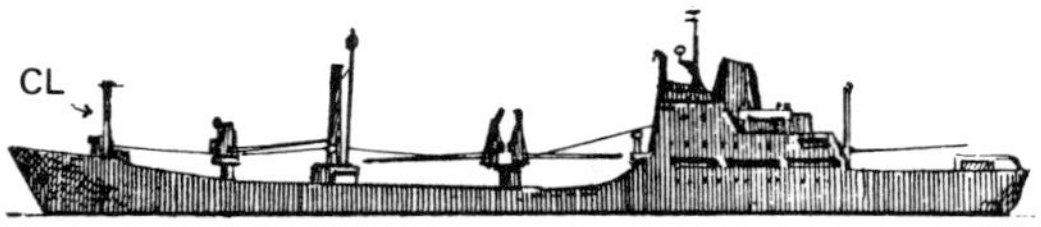

$KCKC_2MFK$ H13
03730 CORABANK. Br/Br 1972; C; 7900/11400; 148.5 × 9.6 (520 × 31.7); M; 18.75. Sisters (Br flag): **03731 CLYDEBANK 03732 FORTHBANK 03733 IVYBANK 03734 MEADOWBANK 03735 MORAYBANK.**

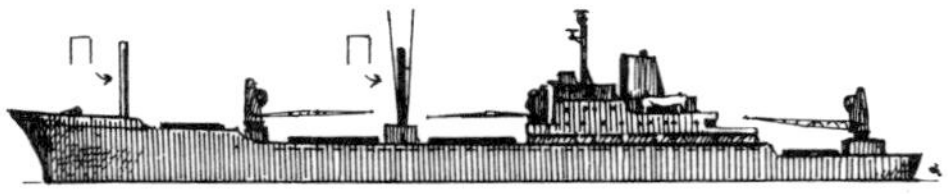

KCKCMFC H1
03760 MANISTEE. Br/Ja 1972; R; 6500; 144.5 × 7.4 (474 × 24.5); M; 20.5. Sisters (Br flag): **03761 MAGDALENA 03762 MANZANARES 03763 MAZATEC.**

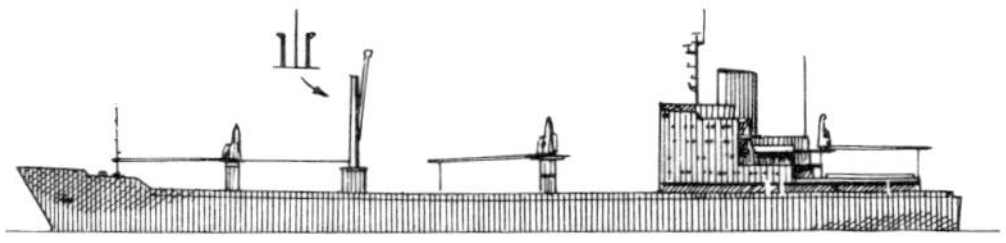

KCKCMFKC H1
***03810 WARNEMUNDE.** Ru/DDR 1972; C; 11000; 150.2 × 8.9 (493 × 29); M; 19.25; **'MERCATOR'** type. Ships may vary slightly. Sisters (Ru flag): ***03811 PALEKH *03812 PAVLODAR *03813 PAVOLGRAD *03814 PESTOVO *03815 PETRODVORETS *03816 POLESSK *03817 PRAVDINSK *03818 PRIMORSK *03819 PSKOV *03820 PUTIVL *03821 SALVADOR ALLENDE *03822 WALTER ULBRICHT *03823 DEKABRIST *03824 NADEZHDA KRUPSKAYA *03825 PERVOMAYSK** Possibly Similar (DDR flag): ***03826 MUHLHAUSEN *03827 NORDHAUSEN *03828 SANGERHAUSEN *03829 SONDERHAUSEN**

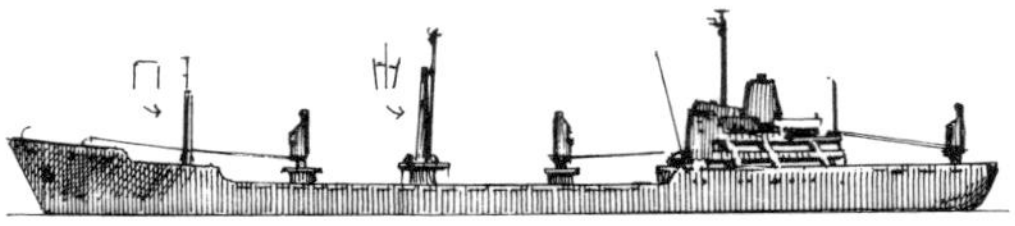

KCKCMFKC H13
● **03840 MAYON.** Pi/Fr 1970; C; 7500/10700; 157 × 9.7 (515 × 32); M; 18; ex VILLE DE HAMBOURG 1979. Sister: **03841 VILLE DE ROTTERDAM** (Fr).

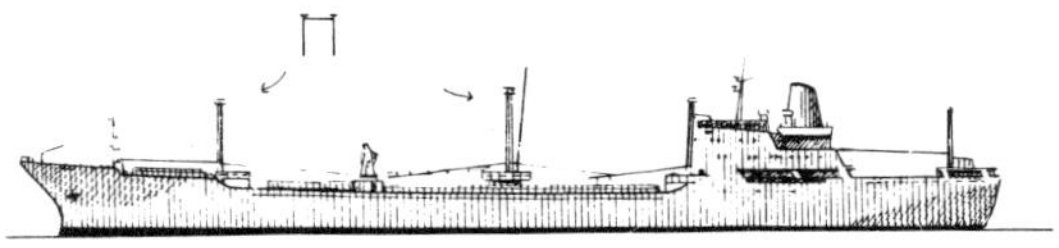

KCK_2MFK H13
03860 SKODSBORG. De/Ja 1967; C; 6200; 157 × 7.5 (515 × 24.4); M; 17.25; ex BANANA 1979. Sister: **03861 STJERNEBORG** (De); ex KINSHASA 1979.

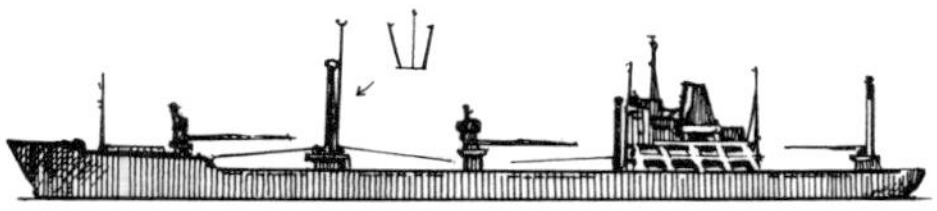

$KCKCKMFK_2$ H1
03740 JAPAN CAOBO; Li/Ja 1970; C; 8500; 148.7 × 8.7 (488 × 28.8); M; 15.75. Sister **03741 JAPAN CANELA** (Li)—number of cranes may vary.

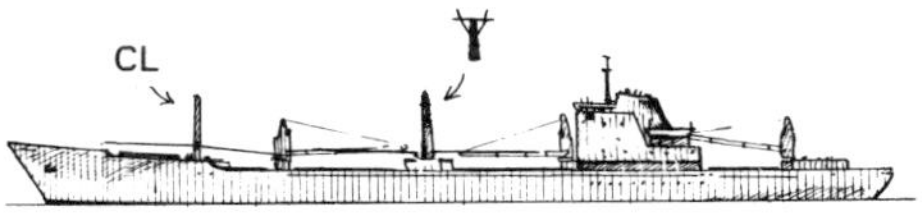

KCKCMFC H1
● **03750 JAVRON.** Fr/Fr 1966; C; 5500/7500; 141.7 × 9.7 (465 × 28.1); M; —; ex ILKON DALIO 1976; ex COVENTRY CITY 1974. Sister **03751 FREE SPIRIT** (Li); ex ILKON POLLY 1980; ex TORONTO CITY 1974.

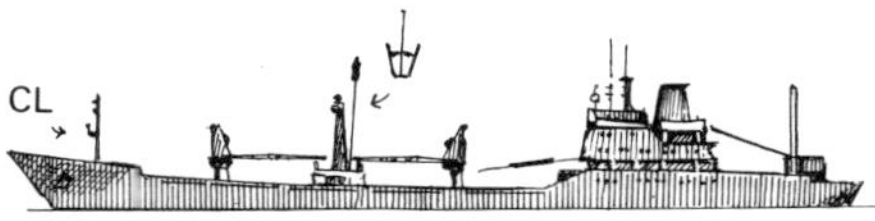

KCKCMFK H13
***03770 LENINSKAYA GVARDIYA.** Ru/Pd 1972; C; 6600; 135 × 7.5 (443 × 24.5); M; 15.5; **'B 46'** type: Sisters (Ru flag): ***03771 ALEKSANDR VINOKUROV *03772 ALEKSANDRA ARTYUKHINA *03773 ANDREY ANDREYEV *03774 FEDOR PETROV *03775 GLEB KRZHIZHANOVSKIY *03776 IOSIF DUBROVINSKIY *03777 IVAN BYELOSTOTSKIY *03778 IVAN POKROVSKIY *03779 IOHANNES LAURISTIN *03780 LEON POPOV *03781 LYUDMILA STAL *03782 MATVEY MURANOV *03783 MAXIM LITVINOV *03784 MIKHAIL VLADIMIRSKY *03785 MIKHAIL OLMINSKIY *03786 NIKOLAY SEMASHKA *03787 NIKOLAY SHVERNIK *03788 OLGA VARENTSOVA *03789 OSIP PYATNITSKIY *03790 PANTELEYMON LEPESHINSKIY *03791 PETR KRASIKOV *03792 SERGEY GUSEV *03793 SUREN SPANDARYAN *03794 VERA LEBEDYEVA *03795 VIKTOR KURNATOVSKIY *03796 VASILY SHELGUNOV *03797 YAAN ANVELT *03799 PAVEL DAUGE *03800 SVORTSOV—STEPANOV *03801 YEMELYAN YAROSLAVSKIY.**

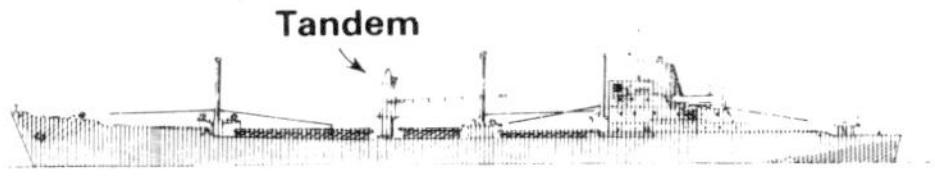

KCK_2MFK H1
03850 SANTA TERESA. Sg/Bz 1976; C; 9200; 140.98 × 8.82 (462.53 × 28.94); M; 15; **"MODIFIED SD 14" type.**

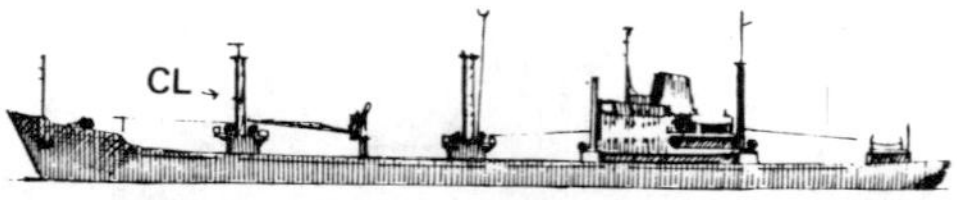

KCK_2MFM H1
⋆**03870 ALTENBURG.** DDR/DDR 1967; C; 5400/8500; 150.2 × 8.2 (493 × 26.11); M; 17; **"XD" Type.** Sisters (DDR flag): ⋆**03871 BERNBURG** ⋆**03872 BLANKENBURG** ⋆**03873 BOIZENBURG** ⋆**03874 EILENBURG** ⋆**03875 FREYBURG** ⋆**03876 MAGDEBURG** ⋆**03877 MEYENBURG** ⋆**03878 NAUMBURG** ⋆**03879 NIENBURG** ⋆**03880 ORANIENBURG** ⋆**03881 QUEDLINBURG** ⋆**03882 ROSTOCK** ⋆**03883 NEUBRANDENBURG** ⋆**03884 RONNEBURG** ⋆**03885 SCHWARZBURG.**

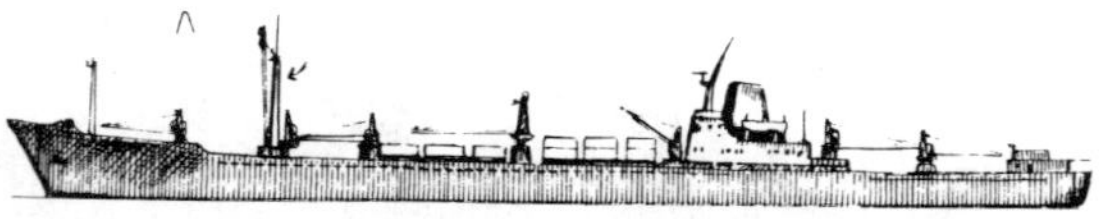

$KCMC_4MFC_2$ H1
03910 BAHIA BLANCA. Sw/Sw 1965/68; PtCon; 10400; 173 × 8.7 (569 × 28.7); M; 19; converted from general cargo & lengthened 1968.

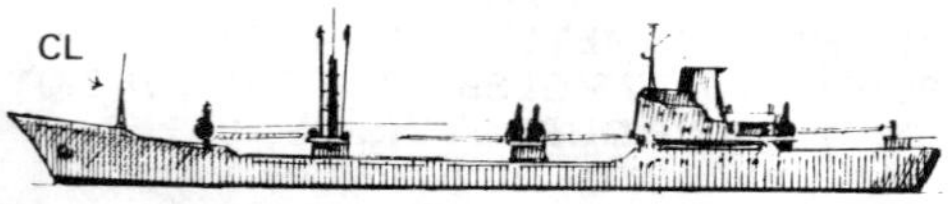

$KCMC_2MFC$ H13
03930 KLIN. Ru/Fi 1964; C; 6600/9400; 147 × 9.1 (482 × 30); M; 17.5. Sisters (Ru flag): ⋆**03931 KOMSOMOLETS ESTONII** ⋆**03932 KOMSOMOLETS KIRGIZII** ⋆**03933 KOMSOMOLETS LATVII** ⋆**03934 KOMSOMOLETS LITVY** ⋆**03935 KOMSOMOLETS TADZHIKISTANA** ⋆**03936 KOMSOMOLETS UZBEKISTANA** ⋆**03937 KOMMUNARSK** ⋆**03938 KRASNOGVARDEYSK** ⋆**03939 KRASNOKAMSK** ⋆**03940 KRASNODON** ⋆**03941 KRASNOUFIMSK** ⋆**03942 KRASNOURALSK** ⋆**03943 KRASNOZAVODSK** ⋆**03944 KRASNOE SELO.**

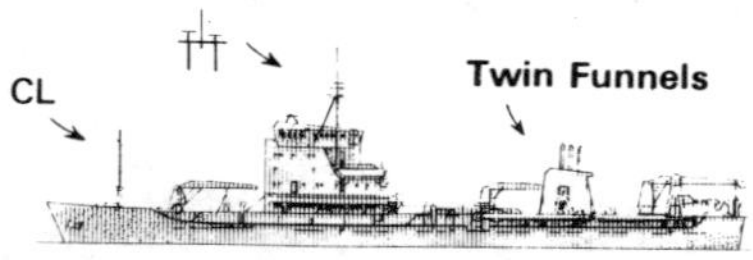

KCMCFC H13
03980 ALPHA BAY. Br/Ne 1980; D- 5700; 112 × 6.35 (367.45 × 20.83); M; 13.7.

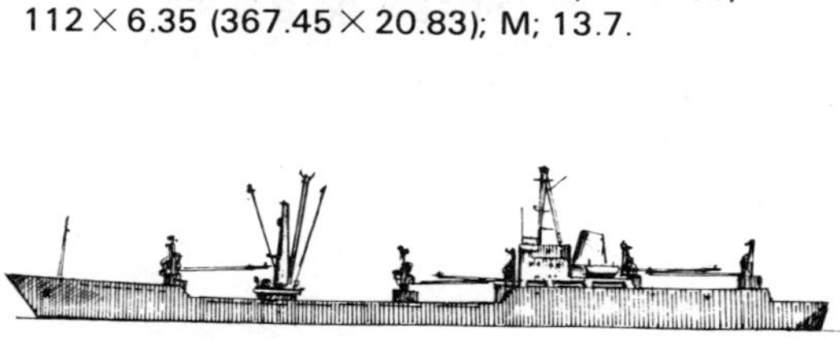

$KCMC_2MFC_2$ H13
03990 GAZELLA. It/It 1969; PtCon; 12400; 152.8 × 9.6 (534 × 31.10); M; 20. Sisters (It flag): **03991 CAPRIOLO 03992 CERVO 03993 TIGRE.**

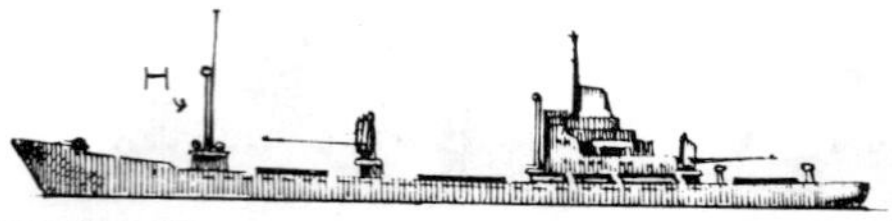

KCKMFC H1
03890 RONCESVALLES. Sp/Sp 1972; C; 5500; 140 × 7.5 (460 × 24.6); M; 18. Sisters (Sp flag): **03891 BELEN 03892 GALEONA 03893 VALVANUZ.**

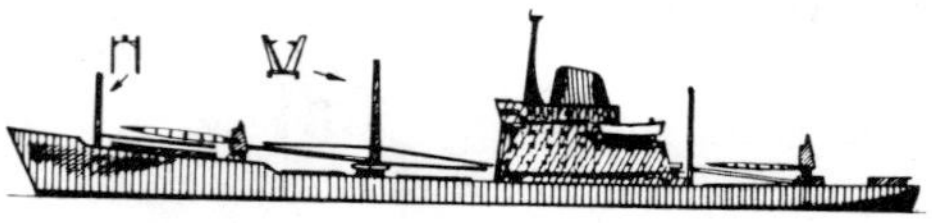

KCKMFKC H1
● **03900 SPARTAN REEFER.** Gr/Br 1964; R- 6400/7800; 147 × 8.8 (481 × 29.2); M; 18; ex LAURENTIC 1980. Sister **03901 PORT LAUNAY** (Gr); ex ZEALANDIC 1980.

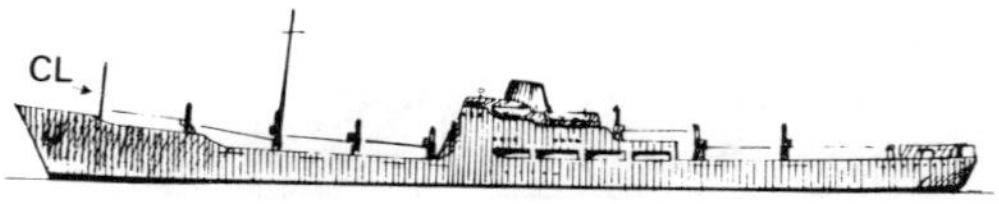

$KCMC_2FC_3$ H1
03920 UNITED VISION. Sg/Sw 1953; C; 6600/9000; 152.51 × 8.13/8.54 (500.36 × 26.67/28.02); TSM; 19; ex CANADA 1978; Cranes abreast foremast. Probably similar: **03921 UNITED VULCAN** (Sg); ex SILVER GATE 1977.

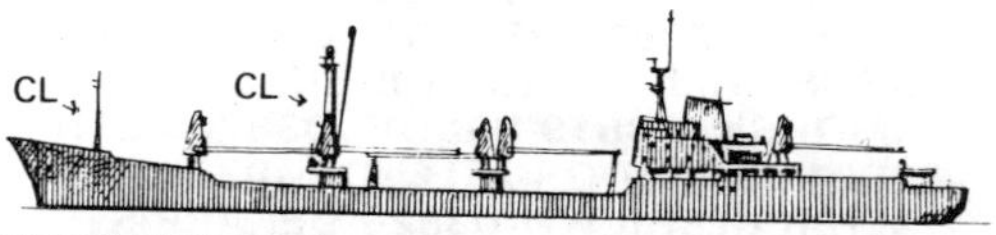

$KCMC_2MFC$ H13
⋆**03950 SOSNOGORSK.** Ru/Ru 1969; C; 6800/8900; 153 × 9.1 (501 × 29.8); M; 17; Cranes abreast mast. Sisters (Ru flag): ⋆**03951 SIDOR KOVPAK** ⋆**03952 SOKOL** ⋆**03953 SUZDAL** ⋆**03955 KAPITAN PLAUSHEVSKIY** ⋆**03956 STOLETIYE PARIZHSKOY KOMMUNY** ⋆**03957 IVAN KOROBTSOV** ⋆**03958 GENERAL VLADIMIR ZAIMOV** Some of the following may be KC^4MFC—Like SVETLOGORSK: ⋆**03959 VALERIY MEZHLAUK** ⋆**03960 VALENTIN KHUTORSKOY** ⋆**03961 KAPITAN LUKHMANOV** ⋆**03962 ALEKSANDR TSYURUPA** ⋆**03963 ANDREY LAVROV** ⋆**03964 KAPITAN SHANTSBERG** ⋆**03965 KLIM VOROSHILOV** ⋆**03966 KOMANDARM MATVEYEV** ⋆**03967 PROFESSOR BUZNIK** ⋆**03968 AKADEMIK YANGEL** Sisters (Cranes ahead of bridge may be abreast) (Eg flag): **03969 ISMAILIYA 03970 PORT SAID 03971 SUEZ 03972 ALEXANDRIA.**

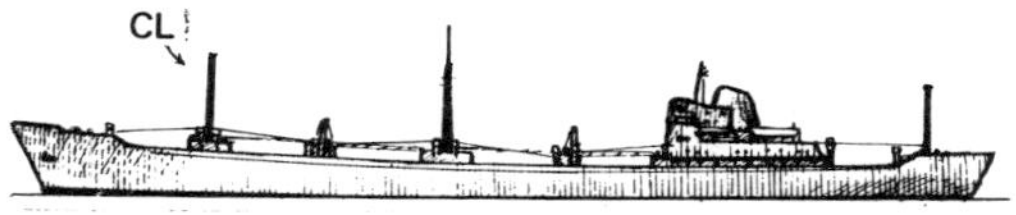

KCMCMFK H13
04000 PARACLETE. Pa/FRG 1958; C; 7900/11000; 157.2 × 9.5 (516 × 31); M; 16; ex EASTERN LOTUS 1979; ex SPRING FLOWER 1975; ex AMPAL 1972; May now be KMMFK like sister ship PARAGON—which see.

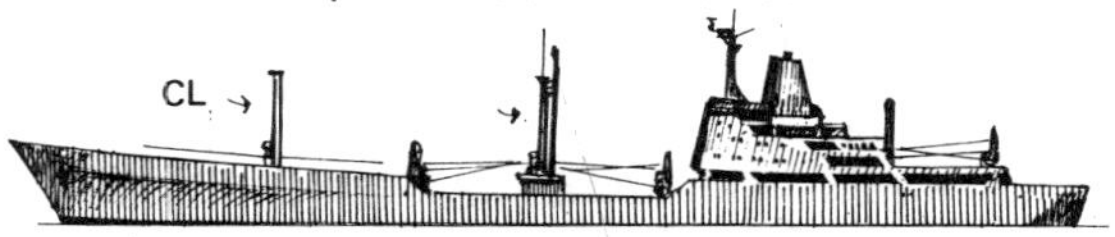

KCMCMFKC H13
● ⋆**04050 DA VERRAZANO.** It/Br 1967; C; 9400/11500; 171.6 × 10.1; (562 × 33.4); M; 21; ex BENALBANACH 1972:

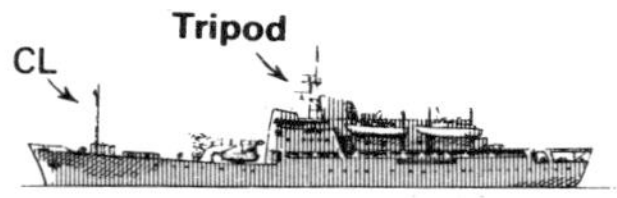

KCMF H
04060 MONOWAI. NZ/Br-Br 1960/77; SS; —; 90.33 × 5.21; (296.36 × 17.09); TSM; —; Operated by New Zealand Navy. Converted from cargo/passenger 1976/77. Helicopter deck:

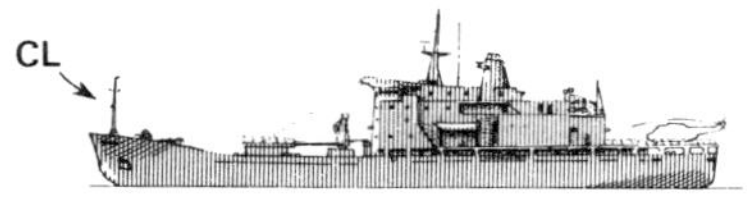

KCMF H1
04070 S. A. AGULHAS: SA/Ja 1978; RS/SS; 5400; 109.45 × 6.06 (359.09 × 19.88); M; 14.5; helicopter deck. Travelling crane in Foreward well:

KCMFC H
04090 VEGESACK: Gr/FRG 1959; R; 3100; 134.7 × 6.1 (442 × 20); M; 18. Sister: **04091 WESERMUNDE** (Gr).

KCMCMFK H13
⋆**04010 LENINSKAYA GVARDIYA.** Ru/Pd 1972; C; 6600; 135 × 7.5 (443 × 24.5); M; 15.5; **"B 46" type.** Sisters (Ru flag): ⋆**04011 ALEKSANDR VINOKUROV** ⋆**04012 ALEKSANDRA ARTYUKHINA** ⋆**04013 ANDREY ANDREYEV** ⋆**04014 FEDOR PETROV** ⋆**04015 GLEB KRZHIZHANOVSKIY** ⋆**04016 IOSIF DUBROVINSKIY** ⋆**04017 IVAN BYELOSTOTSKIY 04018 IVAN POKROVSKIY** ⋆**04019 IOHANNES LAURISTIN** ⋆**04020 LEON POPOV** ⋆**04021 LYUDMILA STAL** ⋆**04022 MATVEY MURANOV** ⋆**04023 MAXIM LITVINOV** ⋆**04024 MIKHAIL VLADIMIRSKY** ⋆**04025 MIKHAIL OLMINSKIY** ⋆**04026 NIKOLAY SEMASHKO** ⋆**04027 NIKOLAY SHVERNIK** ⋆**04028 OLGA VARENTSOVA** ⋆**04029 OSIP PYATNITSKIY** ⋆**04030 PANTELEYMON LEPESHINSKIY** ⋆**04031 PETR KRASIKOV** ⋆**04032 SERGEY GUSEV** ⋆**04033 SUREN SPANDARYAN** ⋆**04034 VERA LEBEDYEVA** ⋆**04035 VIKTOR KURNATOVSKIY** ⋆**04036 VASILY SHELGUNOV** ⋆**04037 YAAN ANVELT**
⋆**04038 YELENE STASOVA** ⋆**04039 PAVEL DAUGE** ⋆**04040 SVORTSOV—STEPANOV** ⋆**04041 YEMELYAN YAROSLAVSKIY**

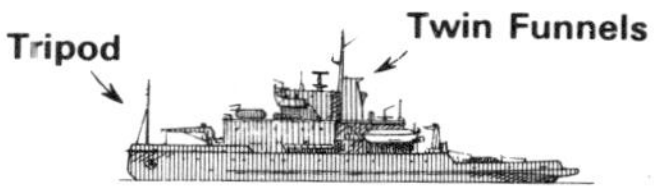

KCMF H1
⋆**04080 STROPTIVYY.** Ru/Fi 1979; Sal/Tg; 4200 dspl; 69.8 × 6.5 (229 × 21.33); M; 15. Sisters (Ru flag): ⋆**04081 SPRAVEDLIVYY** ⋆**04082 STAKHANOVETS** ⋆**04083 SIBIRKIJ** ⋆**04084 SUVOROVETS**

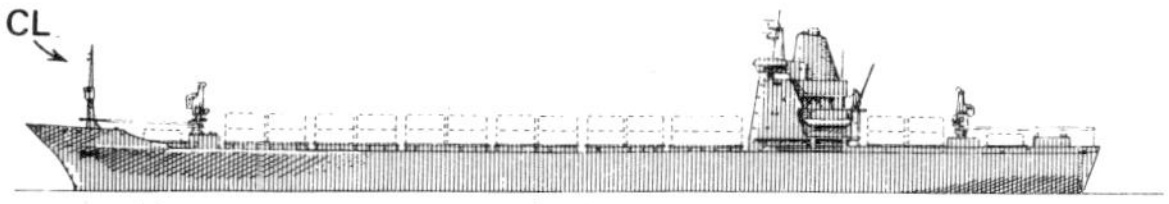

KCMFC H1
04100 SAN FRANCISCO: Sw/Fi 1970; Con; 16100; 174.25 × 10.08 (571.69 × 33.07); TSM; 23. Sister **04101 ANTONIA JOHNSON** (Sw). Others in this class may also have gantries removed—see AXEL JOHNSON etc.

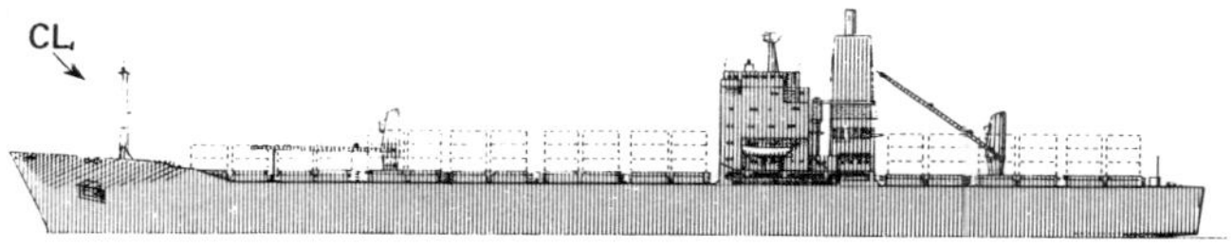

KCMFC H1
04110 INCOTRANS SPIRIT: Ne/Ne 1979; Con; 29400; 202 × 10.5 (662.73 × 34.45); M; 21. Sister **04111 INCOTRANS SPEED.**

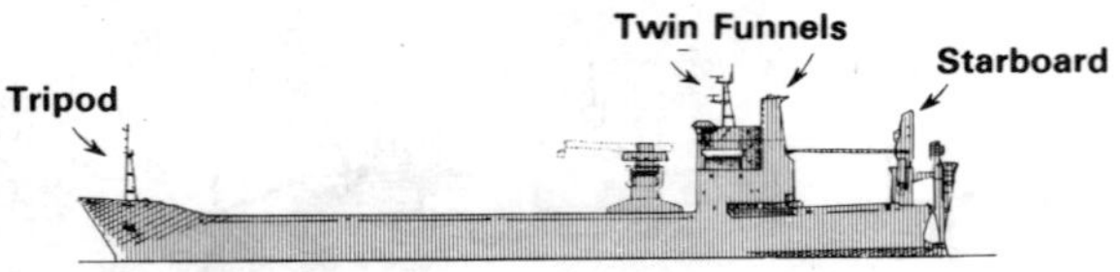

KCMFCR H1
⋆04120 LEDENICE. Ys/Ys; 1979; RoC/Con/C; 5600; 144.4 × 6.5 (473.75 × 21.33); M; 17.9; stern slewing ramp. travelling crane in foreward well. Sister **⋆04121 BRIBIR** (Ys).

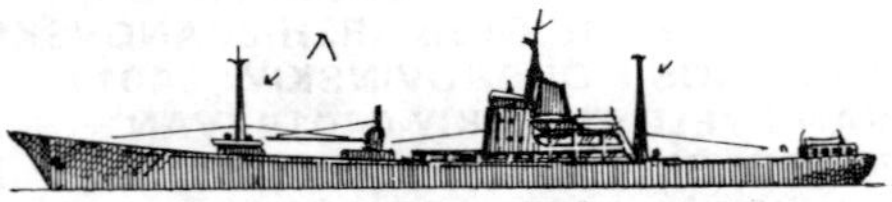

KCMFK H
04140 ISLAS GALAPAGOS. Ec/It 1968; R; 6600; 139 × 7.6 (457 × 25) M; —: Sisters **04141 RIO AMAZONAS** (Ec); **⋆04142 OCEANO PACIFICO** (Cu) **⋆04143 OCEANO INDIO** (Cu).

KCMFM H
04160 SCILLONIAN III. Br/Br 1977; P; 1200; 68 × 2.9 (224 × 9.5); M; 15.5.

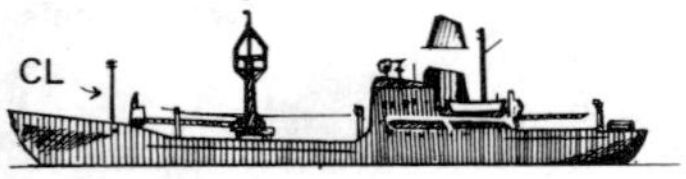

KCMFM H13
● **⋆04180 KIROVSKLES.** Ru/Fi 1962; TC/C; 2900; 102 × 5.7 (335 × 18.9); M; 12.25. Sisters (Ru flag): **⋆04181 BAYKALLES ⋆04182 KAMALES ⋆04183 KAMCHATSKLES ⋆04184 KARELYALES ⋆04185 KOLYMALES ⋆04186 KOTLASLES ⋆04187 KRASNOGORSKLES ⋆04188 KUNGURLES ⋆04189 KOVDALES ⋆04190 VOLOGDALES.**

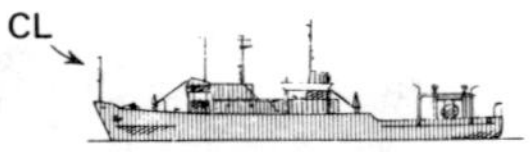

KCM$_2$FC H1
⋆04220 NAN HAI 502. RC/Ja 1979; SS/RS; 900; 65.7 × . (215.55 × —); M; 13.

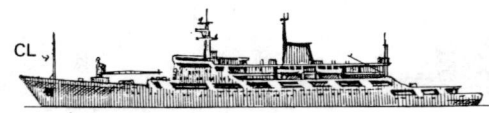

KCM$_2$FK H
⋆04240 ADMIRAL VLADIMIRSKIY. Ru/— 1975; RS; —; 147 × — (483 × —); —; 20. Sister **⋆04241 IVAN KRUZHENSTERN** Ru).

KCMFK H
04130 PROTEA. It/It 1952; P; 11400; 158.5 × 7.6 (522 × 25); TSM; 21.5; ex AFRICA 1976. Sister **04131 ANASTASIS** (Cy); ex VICTORIA 1979.

KCMFKCK H1
● **04150 JAMAICA PRODUCER.** Jm/Br 1962; R; 5800; 121 × 7.3 (397 × 24.3); M; 15.

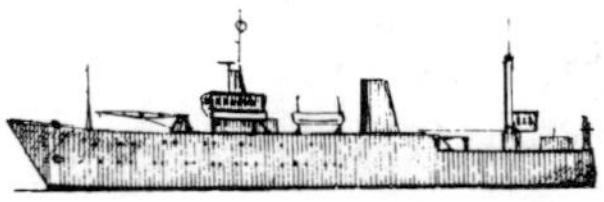

KCMFM H1
● **04170 SALMO.** Sw/Pd 1975; FT; 2500; 90.6 × 5.2 (297 × 17); M; 16.5; **"B 413" type.**

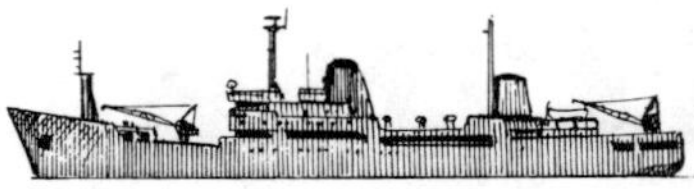

KCMFMFC H1
⋆04200 "TOMBA" CLASS. Ru/Ru 1975; Repair/FA; 5200 displ; 107 × 6 (351 × 20); M; —; Class of at least 3 ships operated by the Soviet Navy.

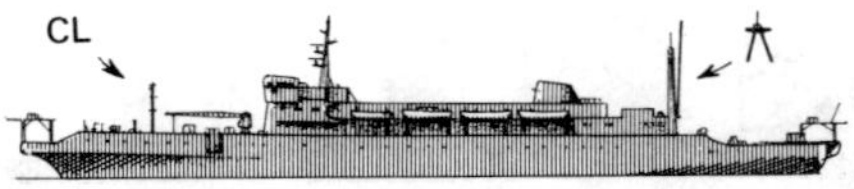

KCMFMN H2
⋆04210 INGURI. Ru/Fi 1978; Cbl; 6000; 130.41 × 5.75 (427.8 × 18.8); TS D-E; 14; Modified "KLASMA" type. Others in this class may also have this sequence—see DONETS.

KCM$_2$FC$_2$ H1
⋆04230 WILHELM FLORIN. DDR/DDR 1964; C; 5000/7700; 142.3 × 7.2 (467 × 23.7); M; 14.5. Sisters (DDR flag): **⋆04231 EDGAR ANDRE ⋆04232 ERNST SCHNELLER ⋆04233 WERNER SEELENBINDER.**

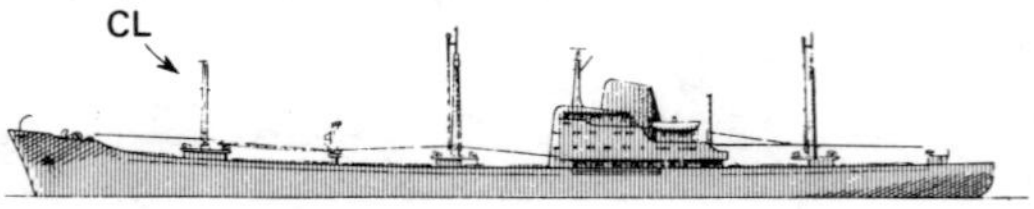

KCM$_2$FKM H1
04250 JALAJAYA. In/FRG 1966; C; 8300/10900; 158.43 × 8.53/9.66 (519.78 × 27.99/31.69); M; 16; Three original sisters (JALAJYOTI etc) may also have this sequence now.—which see.

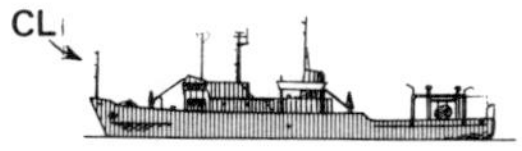

KCM_3FC H1
⋆04260 NAN HAI 502. RC/Ja 1979; SS/RS; 900; 65.7 × — (215.55 × —); M; 13.

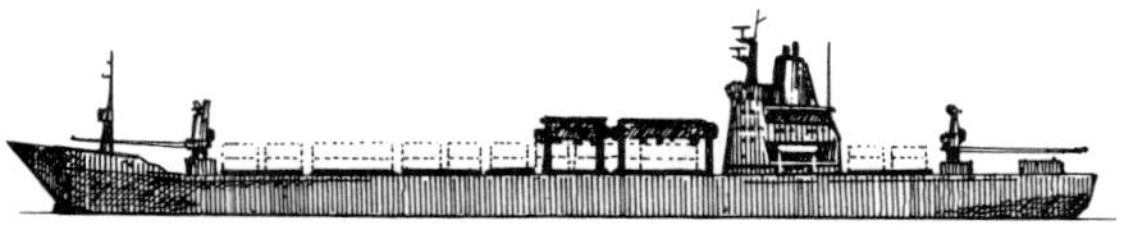

KCN_2MFC H1
04270 ANNIE JOHNSON. Sw/Fi 1969; Con; 16300; 174.3 × 10 (572 × 32.81); TSM; 23. Sister **04271 AXEL JOHNSON** (Sw) Similar (superstructure varies) **04272 MARGARET JOHNSON** (Sw) These vessels may now have gantries removed like SAN FRANCISCO—which see:

KFC H12
04280 DELTA BAY. Br/Br 1971; D; 8000; 132 × 10.3 (434 × 34); M; 13.5. Similar **04281 HUMBER RIVER** (Br).

KFM H
04290 ARKADIA. Gr/Be 1933; PC; 1000; 58 × 4.9 (190 × 16); M; 12.5; ex AMETHYSTE 1959; converted from general cargo.

KFM H
04300 MARSA. Ma/Br 1947; CP; 1800; 90.5 × 5.2 (297 × 17.3); R & LPT; 13.5; ex OLEOS 1974; ex MALCOLM PACE 1970; ex LEO 1967.

KFM H1
04310 TUI CAKAU II. Fiji/Fr 1961/71; RoC; 1800; 107 × 5.1 (360 × 17); M; 15.75; ex CAPITAINE SCOTT 1979; ex BLIDA 1978; Converted from cargo ship 1971, and lengthened. Bow and side doors.

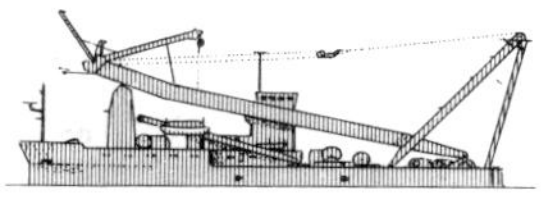

KFMC H1
04320 UGLEN. No/No 1978; Crane ship; 1600; 78.57 × 3.25 (257.76 × 10.66); TS D-E; 10; Drawing shows sheerlegs in stowed position. Twin funnels.

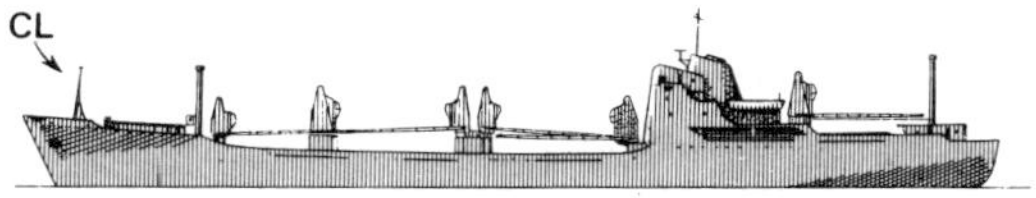

K_2C_5MFCK H13
04330 GAIETY. Br/Br 1964; C; 6700; 130.7 × 78 (429 × 25.6); M; 16.5; ex CUFIC 1977; ex NEWFOUNDLAND 1976; ex CUFIC 1974; ex NEWFOUNDLAND 1973. Sister **04331 ARAB DABBOR** (Si); ex BOOKER VALIANT 1979; ex TROPIC 1978; ex NOVA SCOTIA 1976; ex TROPIC 1974; ex NOVA SCOTIA 1973.

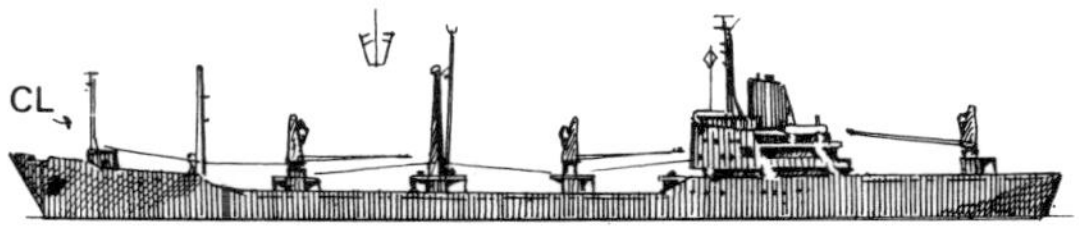

$K_2C_2KC_2MFC$ H13
⋆04340 HEL. Pd/De 1970; C; 7700/11000; 166.7 × 9.7 (547 × 31.9); M; 20.75. Sisters (Pd flag): **⋆04341 JASTARNIA-BOR ⋆04342 JURATA; ⋆04343 WLADYSLAWOWO. ⋆04344 KUZNICA**

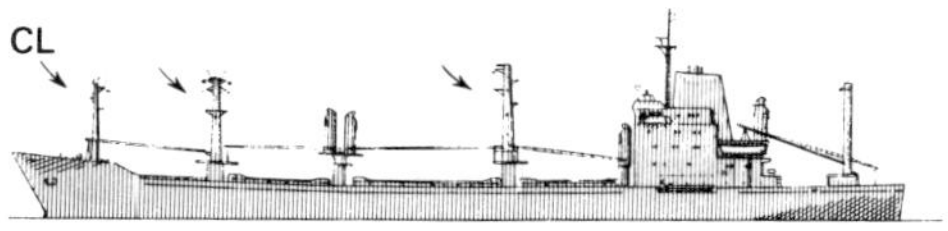

$K_2C_2KCMFCK$ H1
04350 ALDABI. Ne/Ne 1977; Pt.Con; 9800; 142 × 9.5 (466 × 31); M; approx. 16.25. Sisters (Ne flag): **04351 ALHENA 04352 ALNATI 04353 ALPHACCA.**

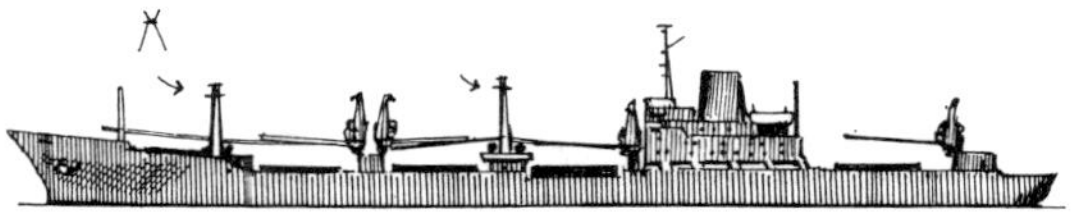

$K_2C_2KCMFKC$ H1
● **04360 WILD MARLIN.** Br/Ja 1968; R; 9500; 164 × 9.2 (540 × 30.2); M; 21; ex MANAPOURI 1977. Sister **04361 WILD MALLARD** (Br); ex MATAURA 1977.

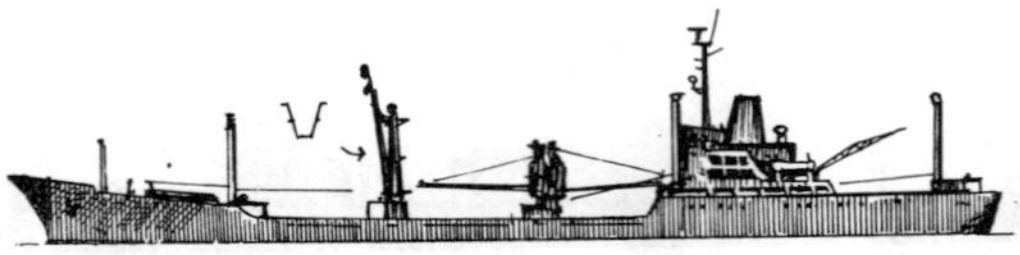

K_2C_2KMFK H13
04370 TACHIRA. Ve/Fi 1976; C; 10300; 159 × 9.8 (522 × 32); M; 18.25. Sisters (Ve flag): **04371 TRUJILLO 04372 ARAGUA 04373 FALCON.**

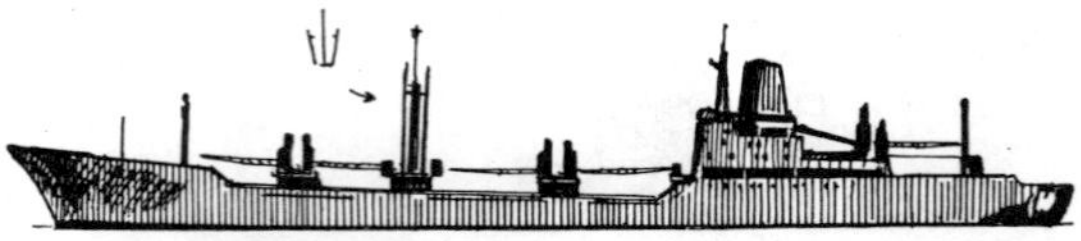

$K_2C_2MC_2MFC_2K$ H13
04380 PHRONTIS. Br/Ja 1966; C; 9600/12300; 172 × 10.2 (564 × 33.5); M; 21; ex PEMBROKESHIRE 1972. Sisters **04381 PATROCLUS** (Br); ex GLENALMOND 1973 **04382 PHEMIUS** (Br); ex GLENFINLAS 1972 **04383 PERSEUS** (Br); ex RADNORSHIRE 1972 **04384 PROTESILAUS** (Br) **04385 PEISANDER** (Br) **04386 ORIENTAL CHAMPION** (Li); ex PRIAM 1979 **04387 ORIENTAL MERCHANT** (Br); ex PROMETHEUS.

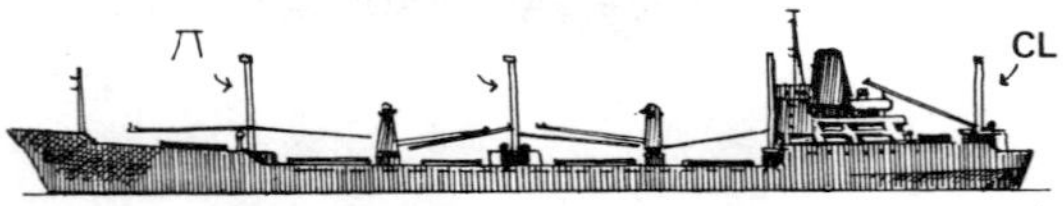

$K_2CKCKMFK$ H13
04390 NEDLLOYD KEMBLA. Ne/Ja 1971; C; 7900/12400; 162 × 10.4 (533 × 34); M; 17. Sisters (Ne flag); (Superstructure may vary slightly). **04391 NEDLLOYD KIMBERLEY 04392 NEDLLOYD KINGSTON 04393 NEDLLOYD KYOTO 04394 NEDLLOYD KATWIJK.**

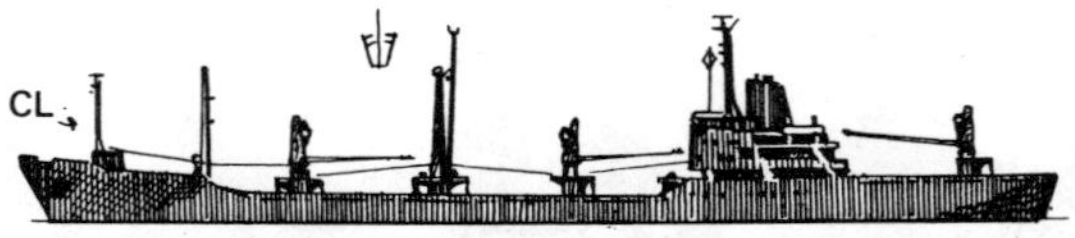

$K_2CKCMFC$ H13
⋆**04400 HEL.** Pd/De 1970; C; 7700/11000; 166.7 × 9.7 (547 × 31.9); M; 20.75. Sisters (Pd flag): ⋆**04401 JASTARNIA-BOR** ⋆**04402 JURATA** ⋆**04403 KUZNICA** ⋆**04404 WLADYSLAWOWO.**

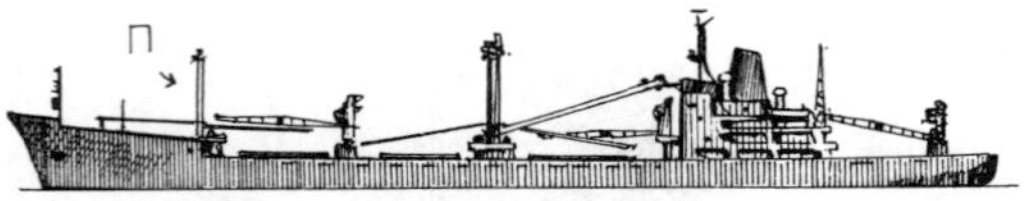

$K_2CKCMFKC$ H1
04410 CORINTO MARU. Ja/Ja 1970; C; 7300; 155.7 × 9.1 (511 × 20.6); M; 18.5. Sister **04411 CURACAO MARU** (Ja).

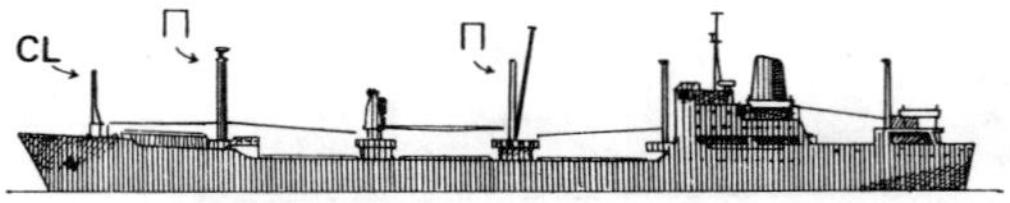

K_2CK_2MFK H13
04420 CHARLOTTENBORG. De/De 1972; C; 6700/9700; 153.6 × 9.4 (504 × 30.9); M; 18; ex AFRIKA 1979. Sister **04421 CHRISTIANSBORG** (De); ex BRETAGNE 1979.

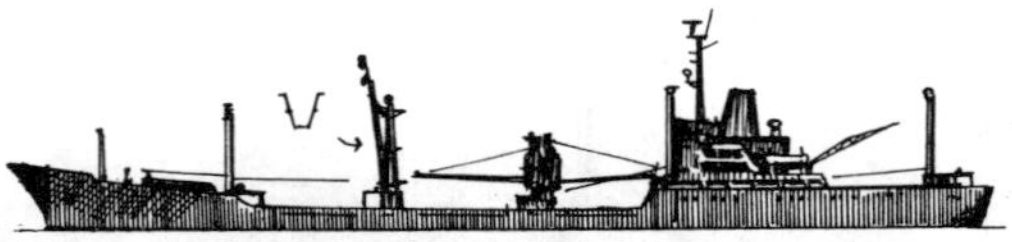

K_2CKMFK H13
04430 TACHIRA. Ve/Fi 1976; C; 10300; 159 × 9.8 (522 × 32); M; 18.25. Sisters (Ve flag). **04431 TRUJILLO 04432 ARAGUA 004433 FALCON**

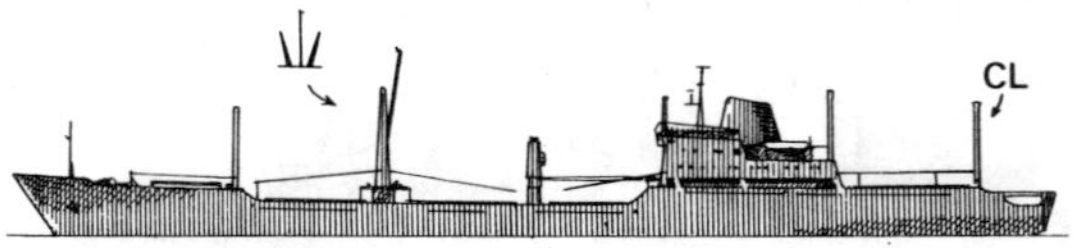

K_2CKMFK_2 H13
04440 CIUDAD DE MANIZALES. Co/Sp 1971; Pt.Con; 7300; 166 × 9.4 (545 × 30.9); M; 21. Sister **04441 CIUDAD DE MEDELLIN** (Co)

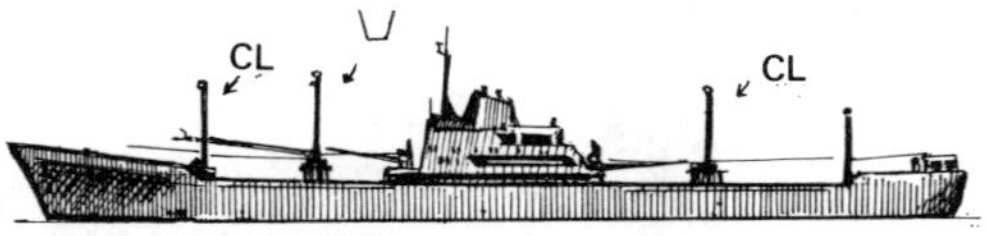

K_2CMFCK_2 H13
⋆**04450 DONGSHAN.** RC/FRG 1961; CP; 9900; 154 × 8.8 (505 × 29.1); M; 17; ex HAVLOM 1972.

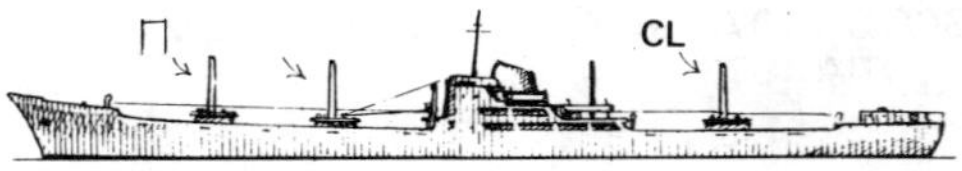

K_2CMFK_2 H1
● **04460 AUSTRIAN EXPLORER.** As/Fr 1952; C; 6000; 149.3 × 7.8 (490 × 25.5); M; 14.5; ex SAUZON 1976; ex LEOPOLD L.D. 1964. Sisters (Gr flag). **04461 ALDEA** ex ARZON 1977; ex ROBERT L.D. 1964 **04462 PERLA** ex MOMBASA 1974; ex CONCORDIA MOMBASA 1972; ex MOMBASA 1972; ex VALPARAISO 1971; ex LA HACIENDA 1965; ex FRANCOIS L.D. 1961

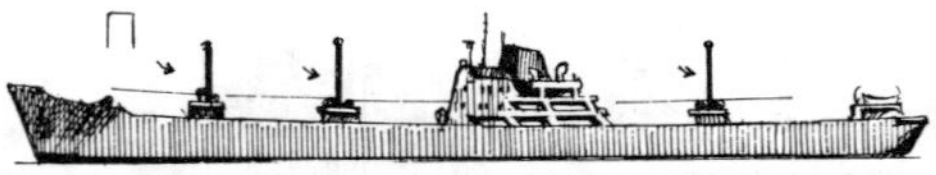

K_2FK H1
⋆**04470 BOKA.** Ys/Ys 1952; C; 6000; 149.3 × 7.8 (490 × 25.5); M; 13 Sisters ⋆**04471 LIKA PETKA** (Ys) ⋆**04472 SLAVONIJA** (Ys) ⋆**04473 TRECI MAJ** (Ys) ⋆**04474 ULJANIK** (Ys) **04475 ASSOCIATED GRAIN** (Tw); ex AMARILIS 1974; ex MARIEL 1967; ex RADNIK 1967

K_2FK_2 H1
04480 SAN FELICE. It/It 1959; C; 8900; 148.7×9.1 (488×29.8); M; 15.5.

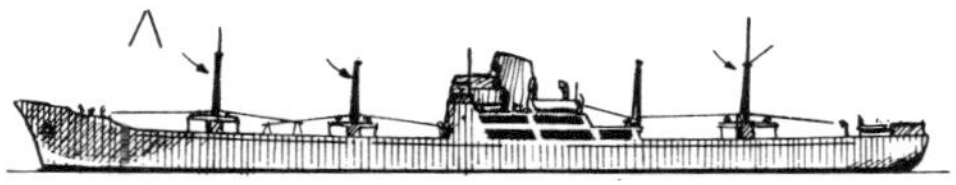

K_2FKM H1
04490 JALADUHITA. In/It 1958; C; 6000/8700; 146.3×8.8 (480×29.2); M; —; ex LUCLE 1959.

K_2FKM H13
★**04500 LIAZI.** Mb/Po 1957; CP; 1300; 78.6×4.3 (258×14); TSM; 11.25.

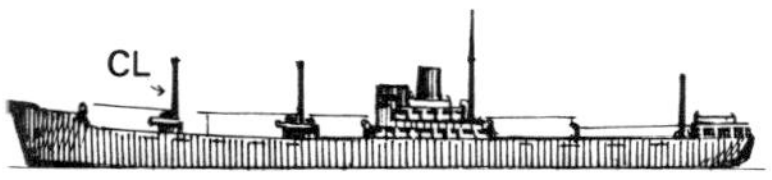

K_2FMK H1
04510 ELIPIDA. Gr/Sw 1946; C; 3500; 117×6.8 (383×22.7); M; 13; ex KARESUANDO 1969. Sisters (Pa flag). **04511 PIAMAR** ex DENEB 1978; ex TRES FLORES 1976; ex GINGER 1969; ex KVIKKJOKK 1967 **04512 TUREL** ex BERRY 1975; ex KARMAS 1967

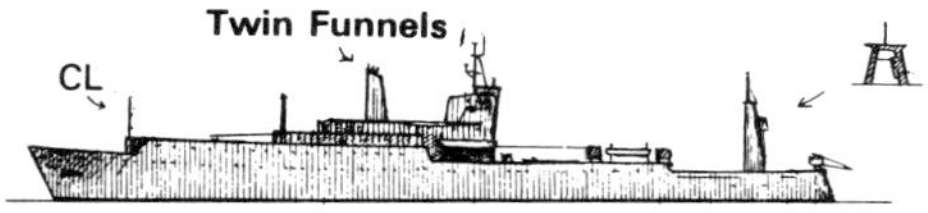

K_2FM_2 H2
★**04520 NATALIA KOVCHOVA.** Ru/Fr 1965; FT; 6300; 129×7 (423×23.1); D-E; 13.5. Sisters (Ru flag). ★**04521 ANATOLIY KHALIN** ★**04522 MARIA POLIVANOVA**

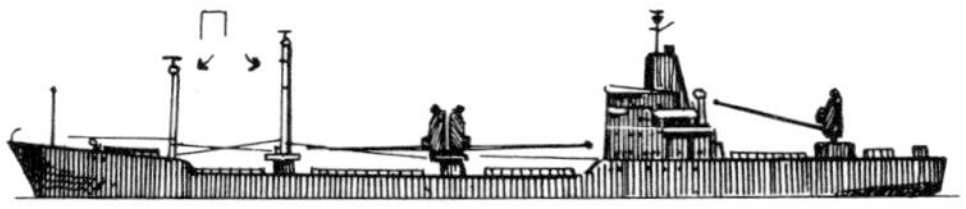

K_3C_2MFC H13
04530 SANTA CRUZ. Sg/FRG 1972; C; 6900/9800; 149×9.4 (488×30.7); M; 19; ex LLOYD MELBOURNE 1980; ex SANTA CRUZ 1979. Sister **04531 SANTA FE** (Sg)

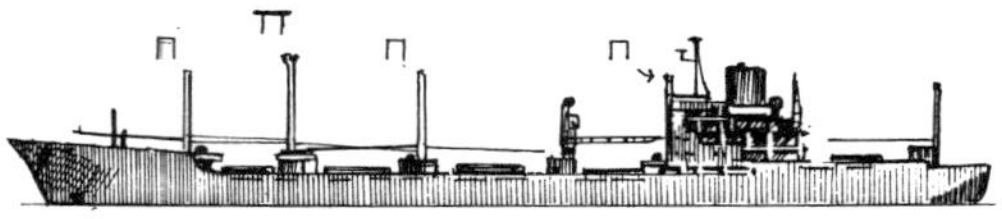

K_3CKMFK_2 H13
04540 FUTAMI MARU. Ja/Ja 1971; Pt. Con; 11000; 159×9.4 (522×30.8); M; 18.25.

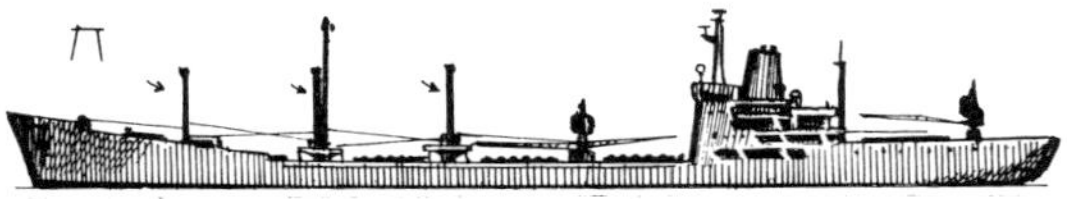

K_3CMFKC H13
04550 BREMEN MARU. Ja/Ja 1966; C; 10400; 166×9.1 (545×29.6); M; 22.75. Sisters (Ja flag). **04551 BARCELONA MARU** **04552 BERGEN MARU**

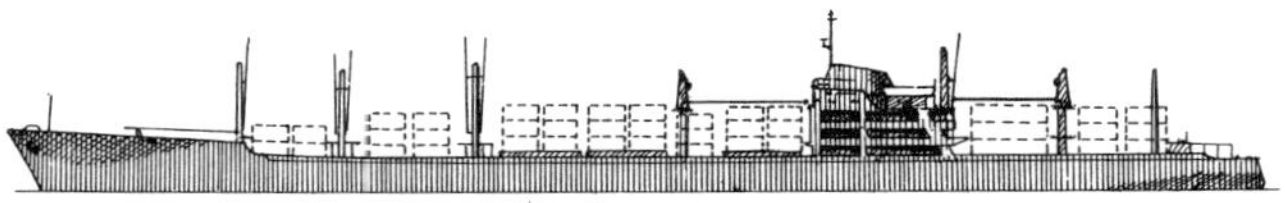

$K_3CMFKCK$ H1
04560 MORMACALTAIR. US/US 1965/76; Pt. Con; 14000; 203×9.5 (666×31.5); T; 21; Converted from cargo ship and lengthened 1976. Sister **04561 MORMACDRACO** (US)

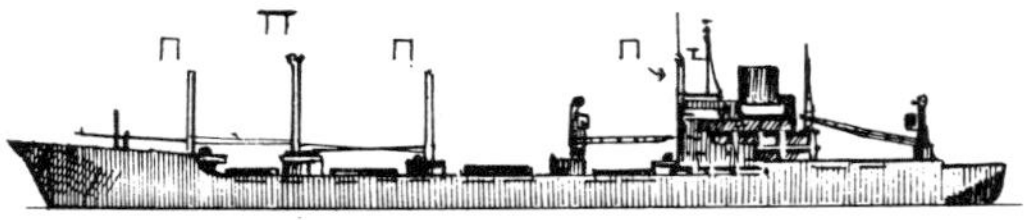

K_3CM_2FKC H13
04570 FUSHIMI MARU. Ja/Ja 1970; C; 10900; 158×9.4 (519×30.8); M; 18.25. Sister **04571 FUSO MARU** (Ja)

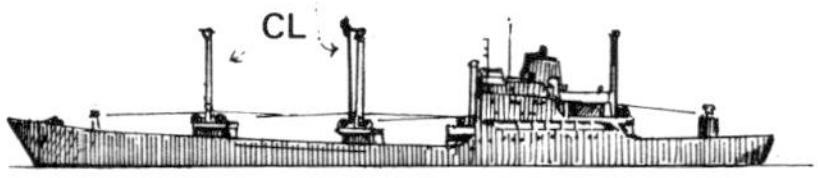

K_3FK H13
04580 LION OF ETHIOPIA. Et/Ne 1966; C; 5200; 121×8 (397×26); M; ex LION OF JUDAH 1975. Sister **04581 QUEEN OF SHEEBA** (Et)

K_3FKMK H13
● **04590 HOEGH ELAN.** No/Fr 1963; CP; 7200/10700; 157×9.4 (515×30.7); M; 15.5. Sister **04591 GURAMI** (Pa); ex HOEGH ELITE 1979

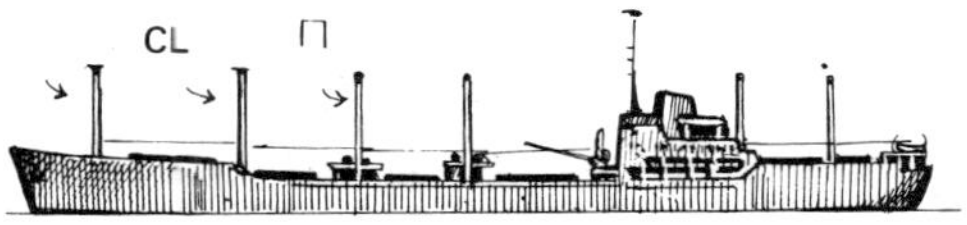

K_4CMFK_2 H13
★**04600 QUINGSHAN.** RC/FRG 1960; CP; 9300; 154×8.9 (505×29); M; 17.25; ex HAVSKAR 1972; Side doors.

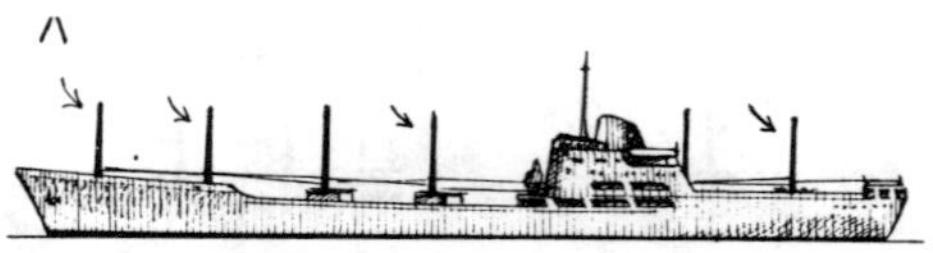

K_4CMFK_2 H13
★**04610 DE DU.** RC/Sw 1962; CP; 9600; 143 × 9.7 (469 × 31.9); M; 17; ex GAOYU 1973; ex HAVTJELD 1972; Side doors.

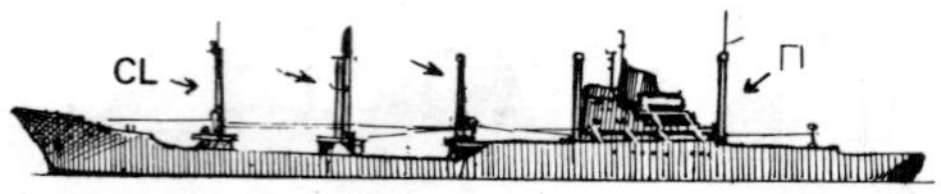

K_4FM H13
04620 MAR CANTABRICO. Sp/Sp 1967; C; 8300; 143 × 9.3 (468 × 30.6); M; 15.

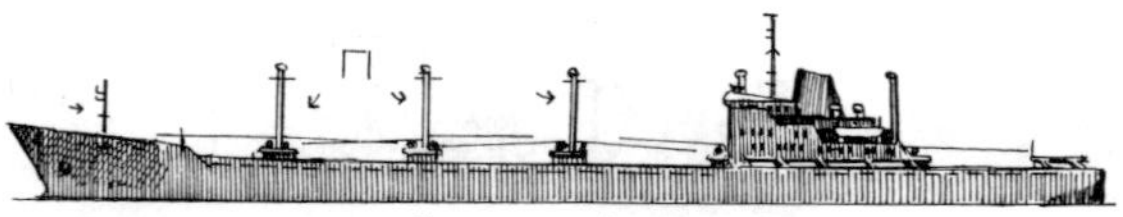

K_5MFK H1
04630 SAXONIA. Br/Da 1972; R; 8500/12000; 175 × 9.1 (575 × 30.1); M; 23.5; ex GLADIOLA 1976. Sisters (Br flag). **04631 SAMARIA;** ex CHRYSANTEMA 1976 **04632 SCYTHIA** ex IRIS QUEEN 1976 **04633 SERVIA** ex ORCHIDEA 1976

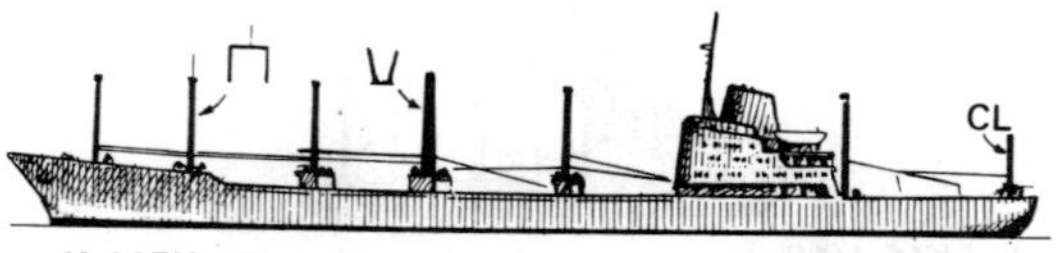

K_5MFK_2 /1
04640 BOLIVIA. Bo/FRG 1965; CP; 8100/10900; 165 × 9.7 (540 × 32); M; 21; ex ALEMANNIA 1979. Sisters (FRG flag)**04641 BAVARIA 04642 BORUSSIA 04643 HAMMONIA 04644 HOLSATIA 04655 THURINGA 04656 WESTFALIA**

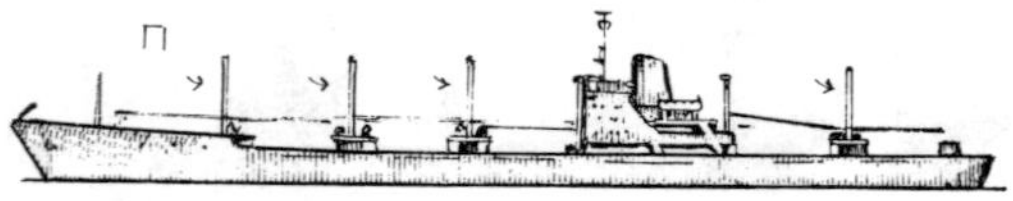

K_5MFK_2 H1
04650 ON SHUN. Pa/Ja 1968; C; 9800; 156 × 9.4 (555 × 31.1) M; 21.5; ex KOREAN FRONTIER 1978. Sisters (Pa flag). **04651 ON TAT** ex KOREAN EXPORTER 1978 **04652 ON WO** ex KOREAN PIONEER 1978 **04653 ON PING** ex KOREAN TRADER 1978

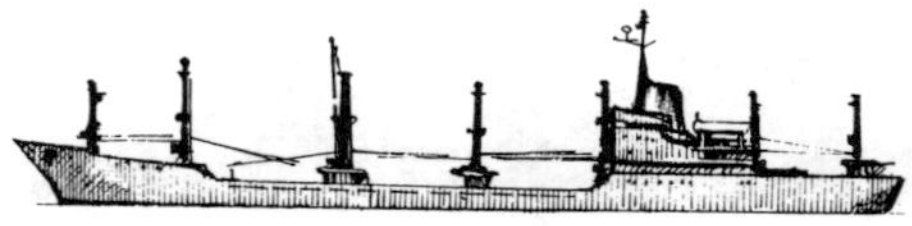

K_5MFK_2 H13
● **04660 TRIER.** FRG/FRG 1967; C; 5600/7300; 136 × 7.4/8.6 (446 × 24/28); M; 18.75. Sisters **04661 HAGEN** (FRG) **04662 HAMBURG** (FRG) **04663 HANNOVER** (FRG) **04664 HEIDELBERG** (FRG) **04665 HATTINGEN** (FRG) **04666 SPEYER** (FRG) **04667 CORAIN 1** (Pa); ex HANAU 1979 **04668 CORAIN 2** (Pa); ex HEILBRONN 1979

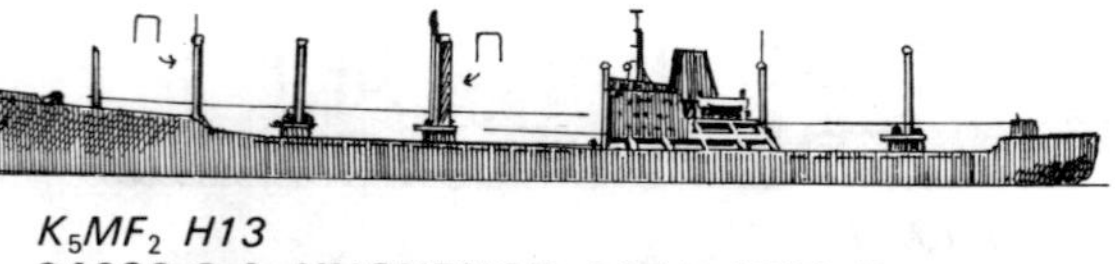

K_5MFK_2 H13
04670 DACEBANK. Br/Br 1979; C/Con; 12200; 161.82 × 9.95 (530.9 × 32.64); M; 16.6. Sisters (Br flag). **04671 PIKEBANK 04672 ROACHBANK 04673 RUDDBANK 04674 TENCHBANK 04675 TROUTBANK**

K_5MFK_2 H13
04680 S.A. CONSTANTIA. SA/Ja 1968; Pt. Con; 8900/12200; 182 × 9.3/9.6 (598 × 30.5/32); M; 21; Lengthened 1975. Sisters (SA flag). **04681 S.A. MORGENSTER 04682 S.A. VERGELEGEN**

K_5MF_2 H13
04690 S.A. HUGUENOT. SA/Ja 1966; Pt. Con; 8900/12300; 181.8 × 8.4/9.6 (596 × 27.3/32); M; 21; Lengthened 1974. Sister **04691 S.A. ALPHEN** (SA)

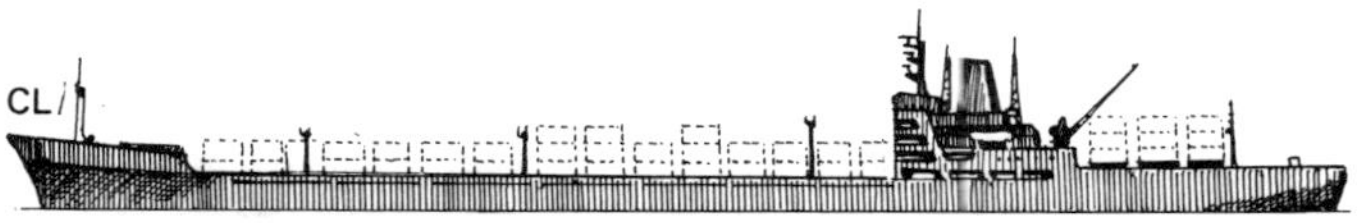

K_4MFCK H13
04700 AUSTRALIA MARU. Ja/Ja 1969; Con; 24000; 213 × 10.4 (699 × 34.5); M; 22.5. Similar: **04701 ASIA MARU** (Ja) **04702 BEISHU MARU** (Ja)

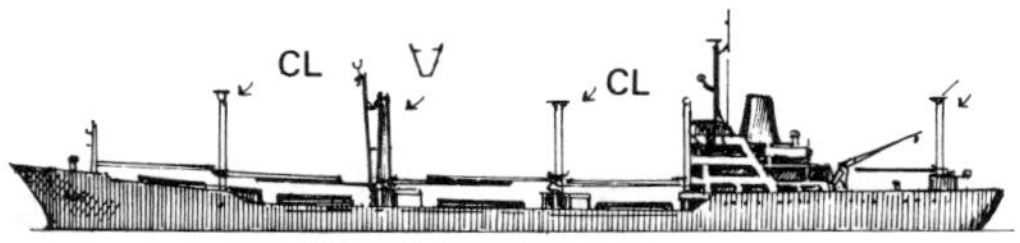

K_4MFCK H13
● **04710 HELLENIC PRIDE.** Gr/Fi 1971; CP; 6800/10300; 159 × 8.2/9.8 (523 × 27/32); M; 18. Sisters (Gr flag). **04711 HELLENIC FAITH 04712 HELLENIC SEA 04713 HELLENIC STAR 04714 HELLENIC SUN 04715 HELLENIC WAVE**

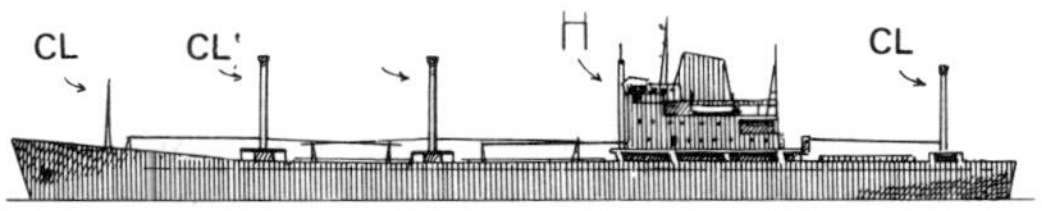

K_4MFK H/H1
04720 ANDES. Br/Br 1973; Pt. Con; 8400/12300; 162 × 8.6/9.8 (530 × 28/32.4); M; 18; ex ORDUNA 1980. Sisters **04721 ORTEGA** (Br) **04722 RUBENS** (Li); ex MORNING SUN 1980; ex ORBETA 1980.

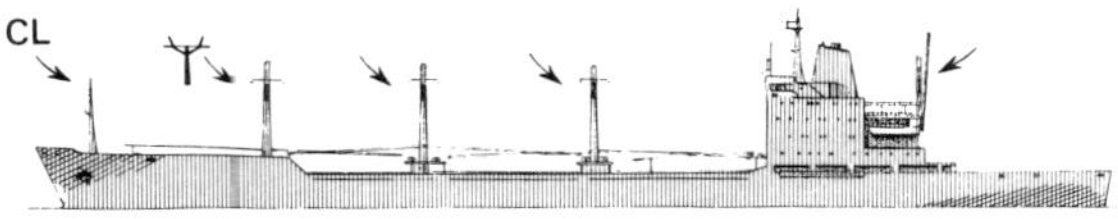

K_4MFK H1
04730 RIVER ADADA. Ng/Ys 1979; C/Con; 13200; 173 × 9.15 (567.59 × 30.02); M; 19. Sisters (Ng flag). **04731 RIVER OJI 04732 RIVER MAIDUH 04733 RIVER OLI 04734 RIVER GURARA 04735 RIVER OSHUN 04736 RIVER OGBESE 04737 RIVER MAJE**

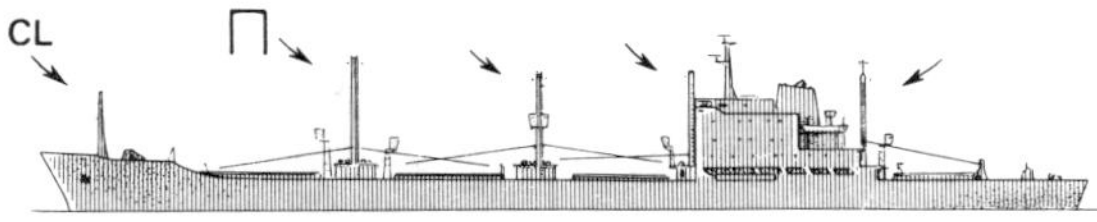

K_4MFK H1
04740 TASMAN REX. Ja/Ja 1979; R; 10200; 168.05 × 8.65 (551.35 × 28.38); M; 21.

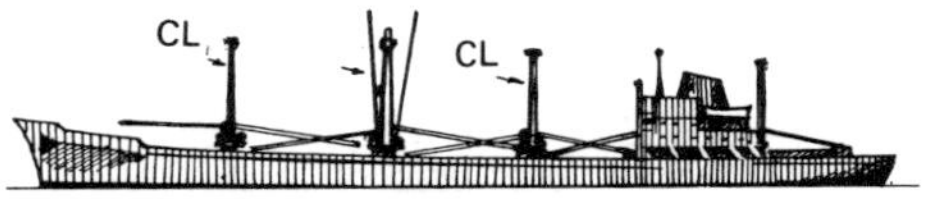

K_4MFK H1
04750 MANOLOEVERETT. Li/Ja 1965; C; 5900; 140 × 7.6 (458 × 24.11); M; 17. Sisters (Li flag). **04751 JOHNEVERETT 04752 HUGHEVERETT 04753 MURRAYEVERETT 04754 THOMASEVERETT**

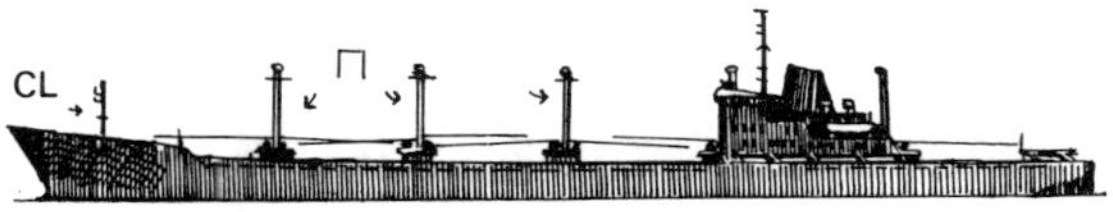

K_4MFK H1
04760 SAXONIA. Br/De 1972; R; 8500/12000; 175 × 9.1/— (575 × 30.1/—); M; 23.5; ex GLADIOLA 1976. Sisters (Br flag). **04761 SAMARIA** ex CHRYSANTEMA 1976 **04762 SCYTHIA** ex IRIS QUEEN 1976 **04763 SERVIA** ex ORCHIDEA 1976

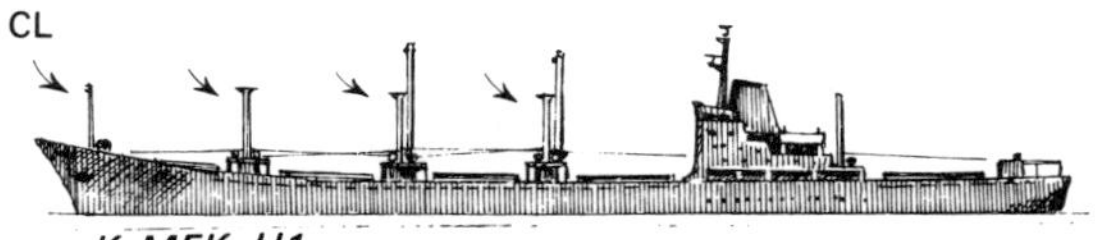

K_4MFK H1
04770 CRESTBANK. Br/Br 1978; C; 12200; 161.5 × 9.7 (529.86 × 31.82); M; 16. Sister **04771 FENBANK** (Br)

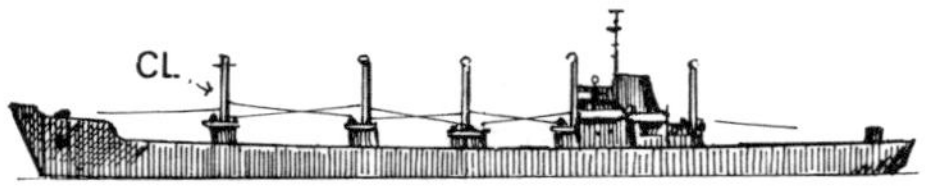

K_4MFK H1
04780 HELLENIC CHAMPION. Gr/Gr 1971; CP; 5900/9000; 143 × 7.8/8.8 (470 × 26/29); M; 16.5; **'SD 14' Liner type.** Sisters (Gr flag). **04781 HELLENIC CARRIER 04782 HELLENIC CHALLENGER 04783 HELLENIC IDEAL 04784 HELLENIC NAVIGATOR 04785 GRIGORIOS C IV** Similar ('SD 14' type) **04786 BELLE ISLE** (Br) **04787 BELLE ROSE** (Br) **04788 WESTLAND** (Ne)

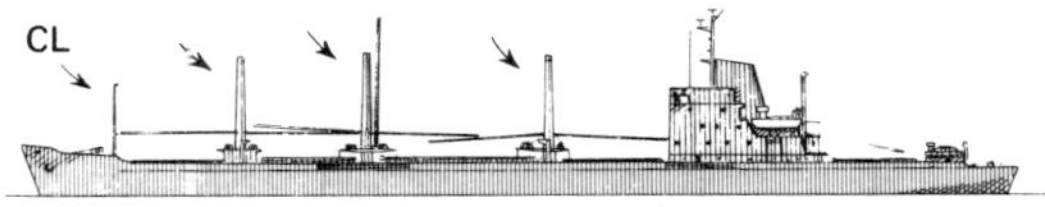

K_4MFK H1
● **04800 LLOYD MANDU.** Bz/Bz 1979; C; 11400; 160.02 × 9.21 (525 × 30.22); M; 17; **"PRINASA 121"** type. Sisters (Bz flag). **04801 AMALIA 04802 CAICARA 04803 JOANA** possible sister **04804 CELINA TORREALBA** probable sisters **04805 NICIA 04806 LLOYD TUPIARA 04807 LLOYD ALEGRETE**

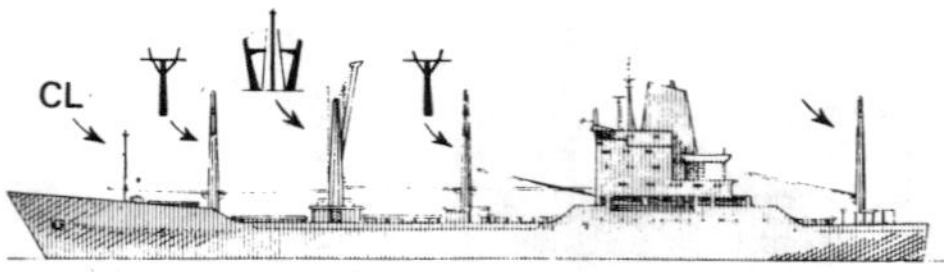

K_4MFK H12
04820 RIVER JIMINI. Ng/Ko 1979; C/Con; 7200/11000; 147.26 × 8.56/— (483.14 × 28.08/—); M; 16.1. Sisters (Ng flag). **04821 RIVER ABOINE 04822 RIVER ASAB 04823 RIVER OSSE 04824 RIVER RIMA 04825 RIVER MADA 04826 RIVER ANDONI 04827 RIVER GUMA 04828 RIVER KERAWA 04829 RIVER NGADA 04830 RIVER IKPAN** Similar (Gh flag) without Stulcken derrick. **04831 TANO RIVER 04832 VOLTA RIVER 04833 SISSILI RIVER 04834 KETA LAGOON**

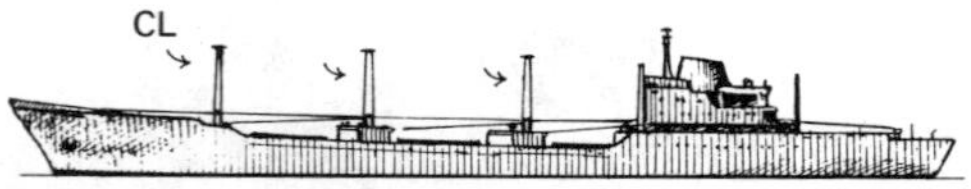

K_4MFK H13
⋆**04860 BAOTING.** RC/Fi 1965; C; 7300/9800; 151 × 8.6/9.7 (496 × 28/32); M; 18; ex DATUHO 1972; ex WIHURI 1971. Sisters (Pd flag).⋆**04861 MIKOLAJ REJ** ex WIRTA 1973 ⋆**04862 FRYCZ MODRZEWSKI** ex WILMA 1972

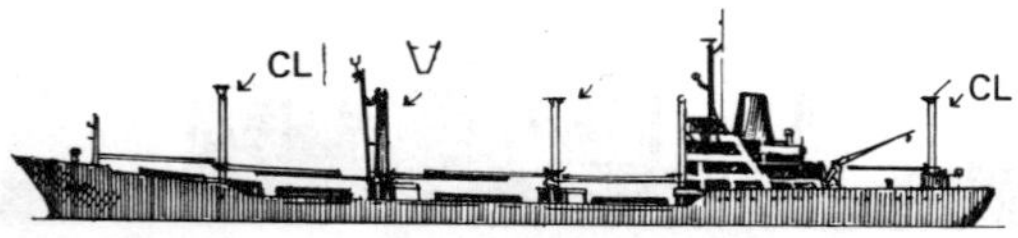

K_4MFK H13
● **04880 HELLENIC PRIDE.** Gr/Fi 1971; CP; 6800/10300; 159 × 8.2/9.8 (528 × 27/32); M; 18. Sisters (Gr flag). **04881 HELLENIC FAITH 04882 HELLENIC SEA 04883 HELLENIC STAR**
04884 HELLENIC SUN 04885 HELLENIC WAVE

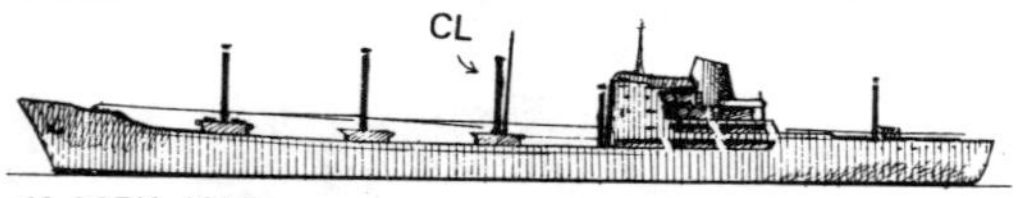

K_4MFK H13
04900 BORDATXOA. Li/Br 1964; C; 7800/10800; 157 × 8.5/9.6 (516 × 28/31.5); M; 16; ex SCOTSTOUN 1972

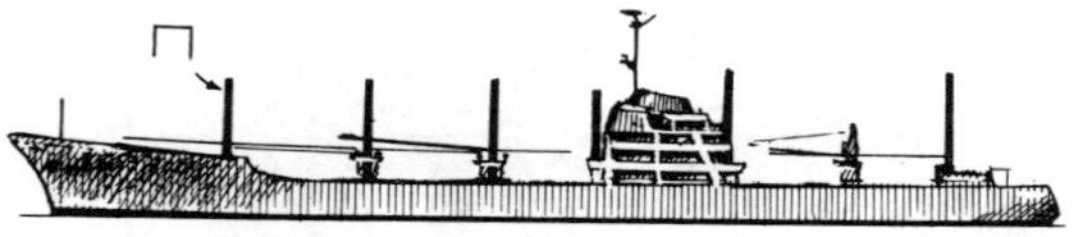

K_7MFKCK H1
04930 MORMACARGO. US/US 1964; Pt Con; 7200/10500; 168 × —/9.6 (551 × —/31.5); T; 21. Sisters (US flag). **04931 MORMACLYNX 04932 MORMACRIGEL 04933 MORMACVEGA**

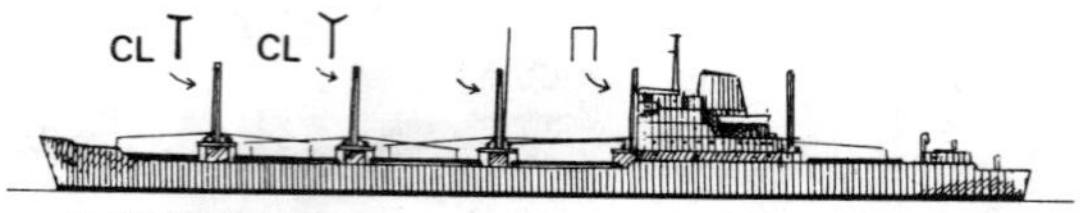

K_4MFK H1
● **04840 ARMADALE.** Br/Br 1970; C; 7200/10300; 160 × 8.2/9.2 (525 × 27/30.3); M; 16.5; **'SD 15'** type.

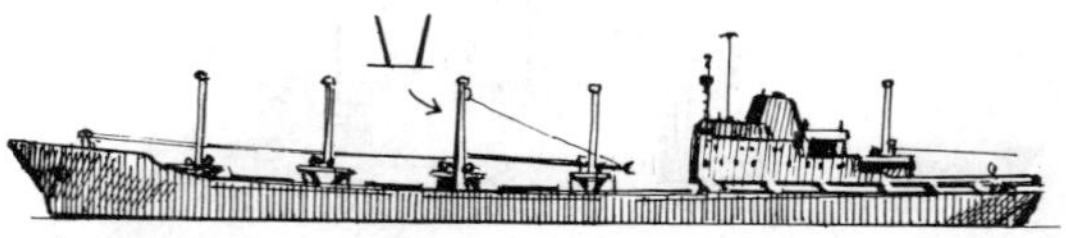

K_4MFK H1
04850 CIUDAD DE BOGOTA. Co/FRG 1964; CP; 11700; 166 × 9.1 (545 × 30.1); M; 19. Sisters (Co flag). **04851 CIUDAD DE BUCARAMANGA 04852 CIUDAD DE BUENAVENTURA 04853 CIUDAD DE CUCUTA 04854 REPUBLICA DE COLOMBIA 04855 RIO MAGDALENA 04856 REPUBLICA DEL ECUADOR**

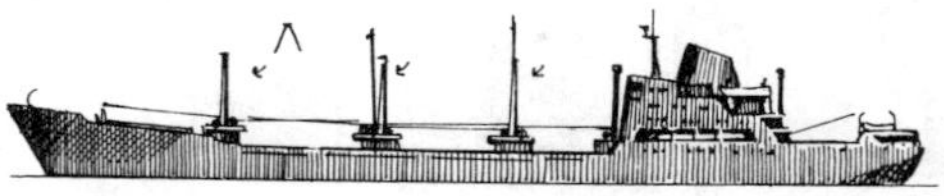

K_4MFK H13
⋆**04870 LJUTOMER.** Ys/Ys 1965; CP; 6200/8100; 146.4 × 8.2 (480 × 27); M; 17.5. Sister ⋆**04871 LJUBLJANA** (Ys)

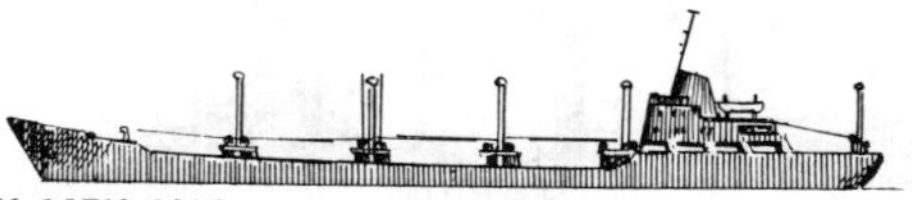

K_4MFK H13
04890 JULIO REGIS. Bz/Bz 1964; C; 6200/8300; 142 × 8.2/— (466 × 27/—); M; 18.5. Sister **04891 CELESTINO** (Bz)

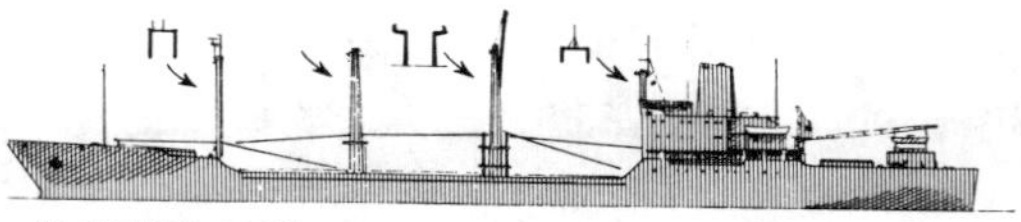

K_4MFKC H13
● ⋆**04910 XING CHENG.** RC/DDR 1973; C; 6300/9300; 144.99 × 7.3/— (492 × 23.95/—; M; 18; ex UNION AOTEAROA 1978; **"MERIDIAN" type.** Sisters (In flag). **04911 JALAMUDRA 04912 JALAMURUGAN 04913 VISHVA MOHINI 04914 VISHVA NANDINI 04915 VISHVA PRAYAS 04916 VISHVA KAUMUNDI** (DDR flag). ⋆**04917 DRESDEN;** ex HAWK 1979 ⋆**04918 HALLE;** ex MERLIN 1 1979 ⋆**04919 SUHL;** ex PHENIX 1 1979 ⋆**04920 KARL MARX STADT;** ex CROP 1980; ex CONDOR 1980 (Ys flag). ⋆**04921 DRVAR** ⋆**04922 KRASICA** ⋆**04923 KRK** ⋆**04924 MOSCENICE** ⋆**04925 MOTOVUN** ⋆**04926 TOPUSKO** (Li flag). **04927 CYNTHIA G;** ex FALCON 1979 **04928 MARCIA;** ex EAGLE 1979

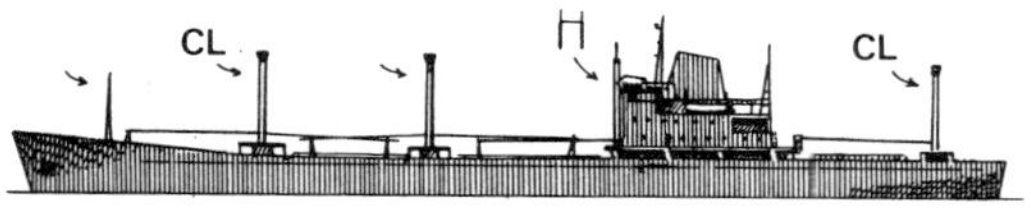

K_4MFK H/H1
04940 ANDES. Br/Br 1973; Pt. Con; 8400/12300; 162×8.6/9.8 (530×28/32.4); M; 18; ex ORDUNA 1980. Sisters **04941 ORTEGA** (Br) **04942 RUBENS** (Li); ex MORNING SUN 1980; ex ORBITA 1980.

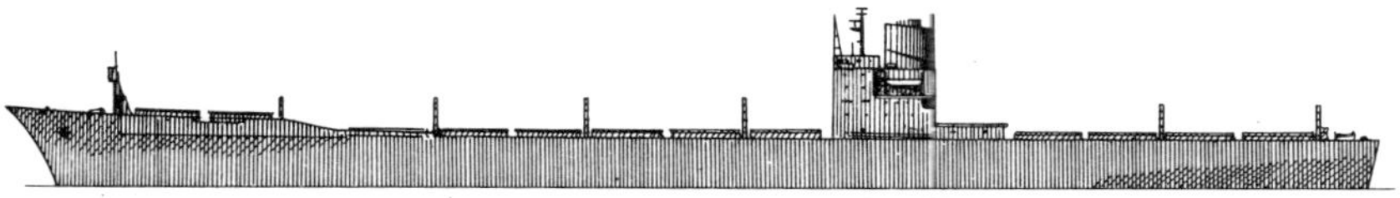

K_4MFK_2 H1
04950 VERRAZANO BRIDGE. Ja/Ja 1973; Con; 39500; 265×11.9 (868×39); TSM; 26.5. Similar: **04951 SEVEN SEAS BRIDGE** (Ja) **04952 HONG KONG CONTAINER** (Li)

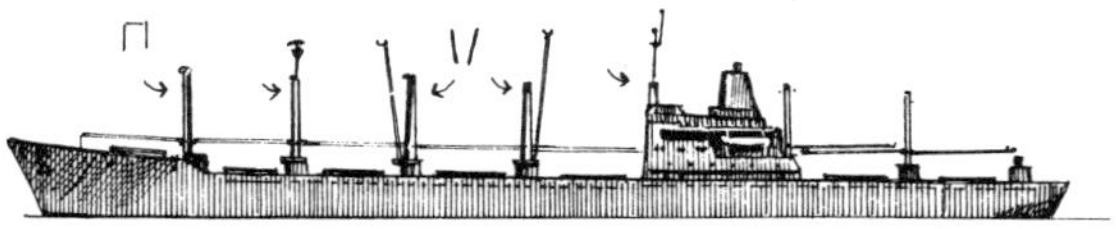

K_4MFK_2 H1
04960 SANTA BARBARA. US/US 1967; Pt. Con; 9300; 171×9.2 (560×30.4); T; 20; ex DELTA BOLIVIA 1980; ex SANTA BARBARA 1979. Sisters (US flag). **04961 SANTA CLARA** ex DELTA COLUMBIA 1980; ex SANTA CLARA 1972 **04962 SANTA CRUZ** ex DELTA ECUADOR 1980; ex SANTA CRUZ 1979 **04963 SANTA ELENA** ex; DELTA PANAMA 1980; ex SANTA ELENA 1979 **04964 SANTA ISABEL** ex DELTA PERU; ex SANTA ISABEL 1979 **04965 SANTA LUCIA** ex DELTA VENEZUELA 1980; ex SANTA LUCIA 1979

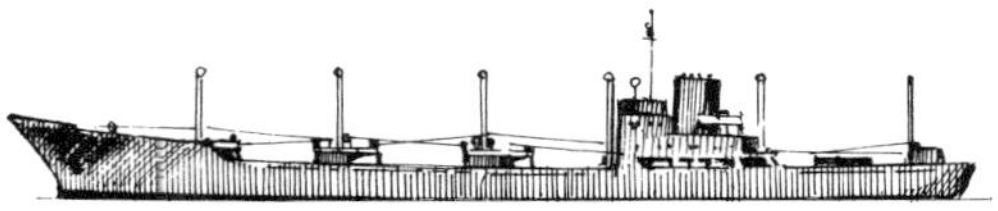

K_4MFK_2 H1
04970 OLIVINE. Pa/Ja 1965; C; 880; 151×8.8 (496×29.2); M; 17.5; ex DENMARK MARU 1979. Sister **04971 HOLLAND MARU** (Ja)

● 04975

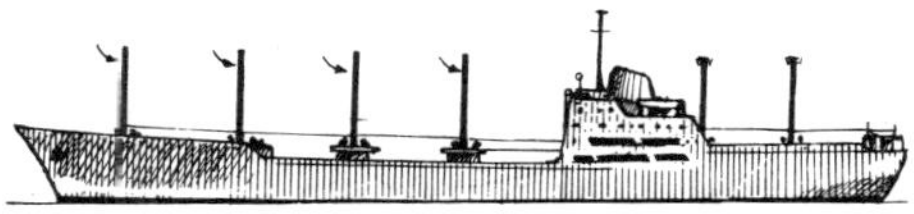

K_4MFK_2 H13
04980 GAOPENG. Pa/Sw 1956; CP; 5400; 143×8.1 (469×26.4); M; 17; ex HAVJO 1972.

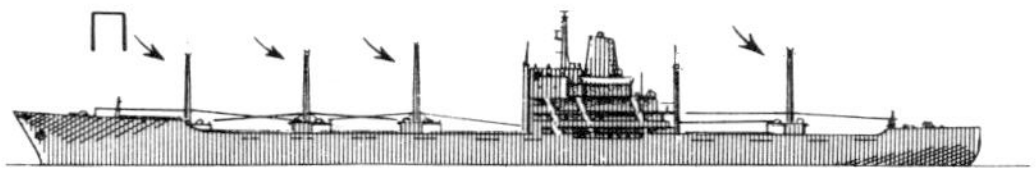

K_4MFK_2 H13
04990 TAI NING. Tw/Ja 1968; C; 10000; 155.4×9.45 (509.84×31); M; 18.25. Sister **04991 TAI SUN** (Tw)

K_4MFK_2 H13
● **05000 BENDEARG.** Br/Br 1964; C; 8200/11900; 162×8.6/— (533×28.3); M; 19.

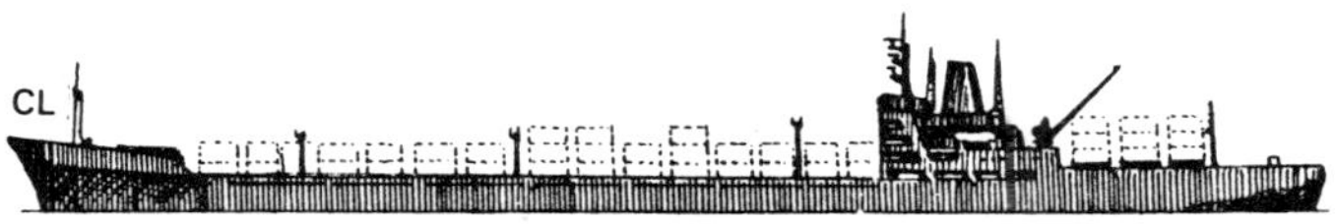

K_4MFK_2 H13
05010 AUSTRALIA MARU. Ja/Ja 1969; Con; 2400; 213×10.4 (699×34.5); M; 22.5. Similar: **05011 ASIA MARU** (Ja) **05012 BEISHU MARU** (Ja)

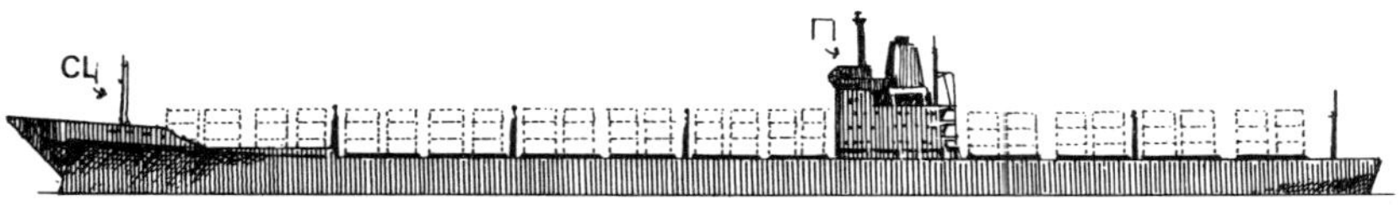

K_4MFK_3 H1
05020 DRAGOR MAERSK. De/Ja 1974; Con; 38500; 260×11.8 (851×38.6); TSM; 26.5; ex SVENDBORG MAERSK 1981; ex TFL CHARLESTON 1980; ex SEATRAIN CHARLESTON 1980; ex SVENDBORG MAERSK 1979.

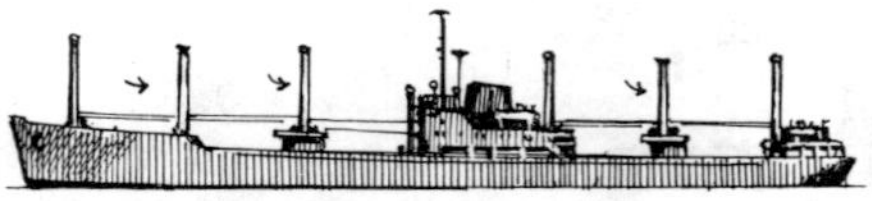

K_4MFK_3 H1
05030 FORTUNE WIND. Pa/Sw 1956; CP; 5000; 133 × 7.9 (435 × 25.6); M; 17; ex HAVTROLL 1971.

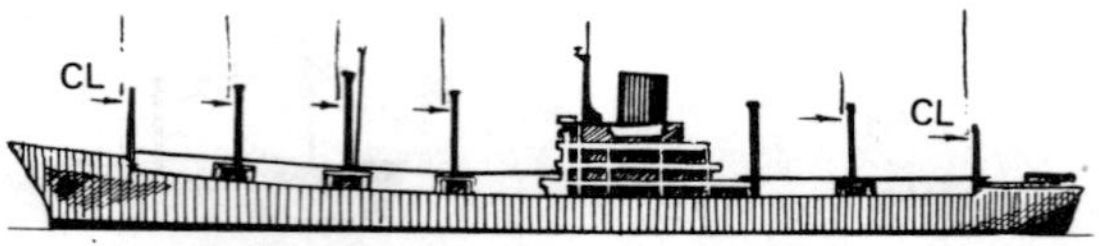

K_4MFK_3 H13
● **05040 HARVEST.** Br/Br 1962; R; 9600/11500; 166 × 9.1/9.5 (544 × 30.1/31.5); M; 20; ex GLENOGLE 1978. Sister ⋆**05041 QING HE CHENG** (RC); ex GLENFALLOCH 1978

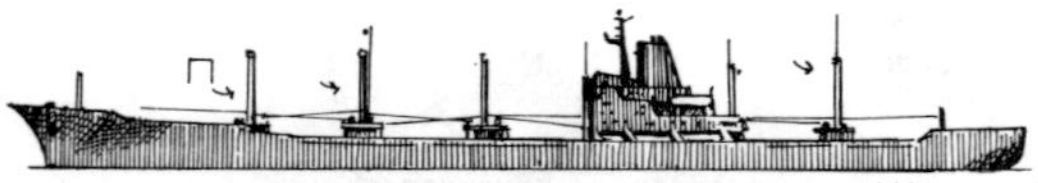

K_4MFKM H13
05050 PRESIDENT J KASAVUBU. Zr/Ja 1971; C; 7300; 157 × 9.4 (515 × 30.8); M; 18.75.

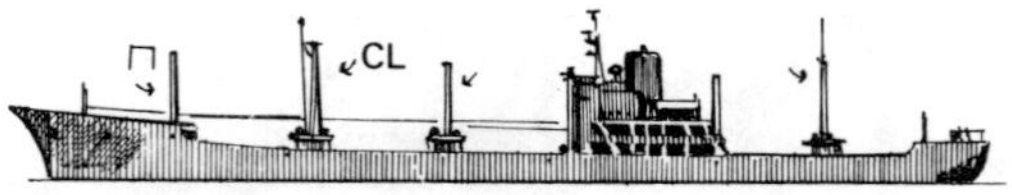

K_4MFKM H13
05060 UNION SUNRISE. Tw/Ja 1969; C; 10500; 159 × 9.7 (523 × 32.2); M; 19.

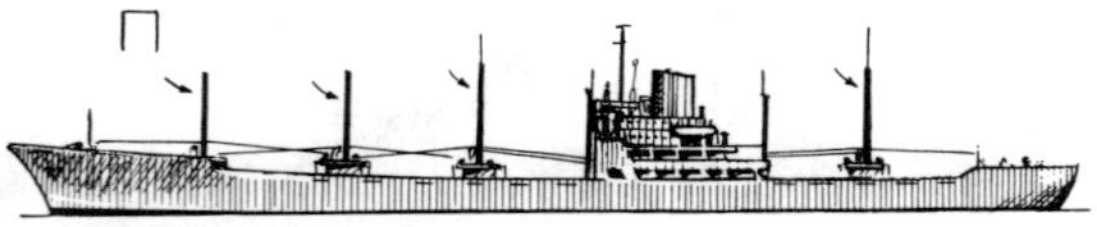

K_4MFKM H13
● **05070 IZUMO MARU.** Ja/Ja 1966; CP; 10100; 157 × 9.4 (517 × 31); M; 18.5. Sisters **05071 CHAR HO** (Pa); ex IBARAKI MARU 1978 **05072 IZUMI MARU** (Ja) **05073 IWASHIRO MARU** (Ja) Similar (Funnel and superstructure variations) **05074 AFRICAN EXPRESS** (Pa) ex YAMAGATA MARU 1979 **05075 ISE MARU** (Ja) **05076 IYO MARU** (Ja) **05077 ROYAL RUBY** (Pa) ex IWAKI MARU 1975 **05078 BRAZILIAN EXPRESS** (Pa) ex YAMAGUCHI MARU 1980

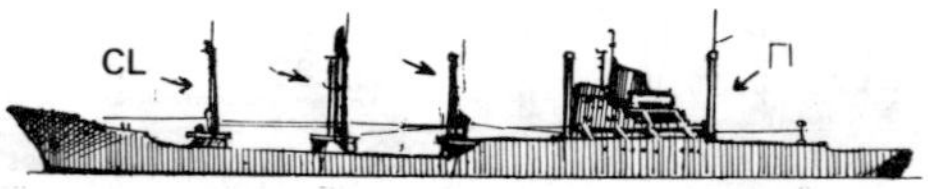

K_4MFM H13
05080 MAR CANTABRICO. Sp/Sp 1967; C; 8300; 143 × 9.3 (468 × 30.6); M; 15.

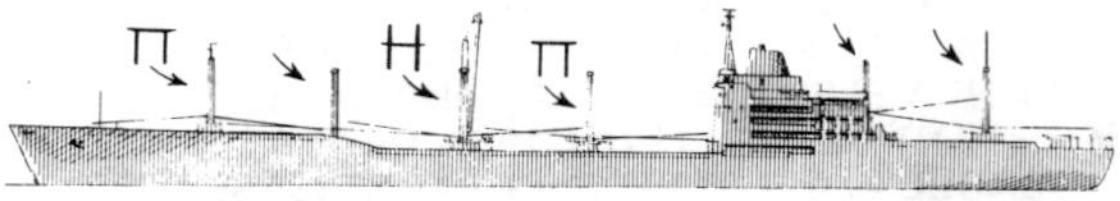

K_4MFKM H13
● **05090 IDAHO.** US/US 1969; C/Con; 9500; 176.49 × 9.4 (579.04 × 30.84); T; 23. Sisters (US flag) **05091 COLORADO 05092 MICHIGAN 05093 MONTANA 05094 WYOMING**

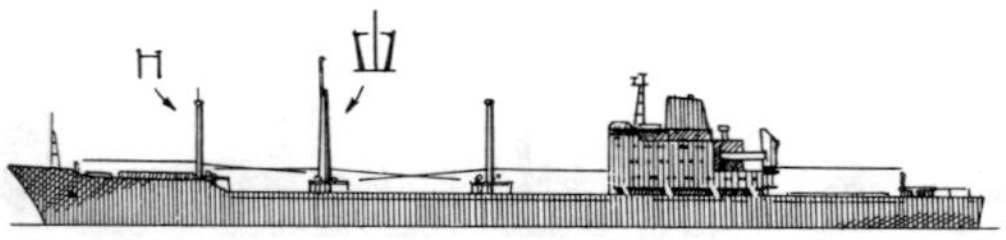

K_3MFC H1
⋆**05100 JIANG CHUAN.** RC/Ys 1973; C; 7500/10700; 157 × —/9.2 (519 × —/30.5); M; 18. Sisters (RC flag) ⋆**05101 HAN CHUAN 05102 YIN CHUAN** ⋆**05103 TONG CHUAN**

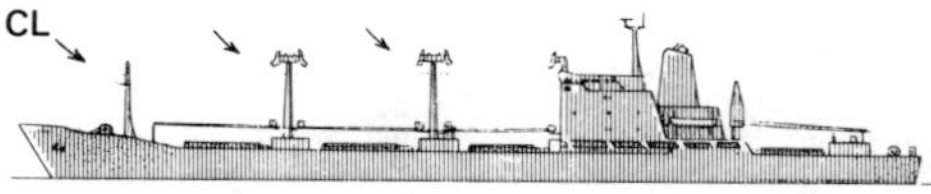

K_3MFC H1
05110 CANADIAN REEFER. De/De 1979; R; 8800; 144.35 × 10.14 (473.59 × 33.27); M; 22. Sister **05111 ECUADORIAN REEFER** (De) Sisters (Japanese Built) **05112 ASIAN REEFER** (De) **05113 BALKAN REEFER** (De)

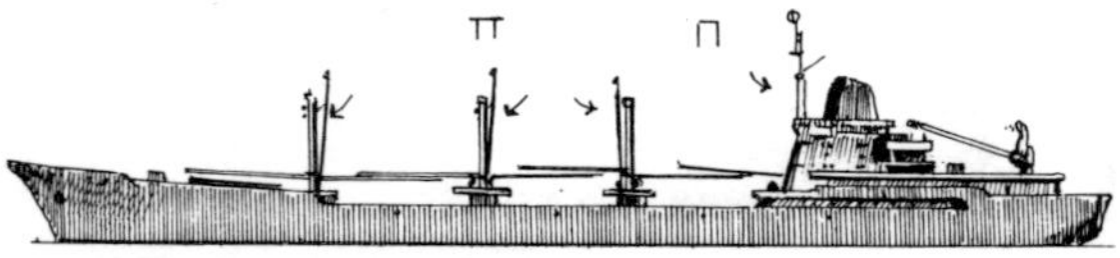

K_3MFC H13
● **05120 LEONCE VIELJEUX.** Fr/Fr 1970; C; 7900/12500; 171 × 7.7/9.7 (561 × 25.6/32); M; 19. Sisters (Fr flag). **05121 CHRISTIAN VIELJEUX 05122 THONON** ex ERIC VIELJEUX 1979 **05123 GEORGES VIELJEUX 05124 PIERRE VIELJEUX** Possibly similar **05125 PATRICK VIELJEUX 05126 TAJ** ex STEPHANE VIELJEUX 1979

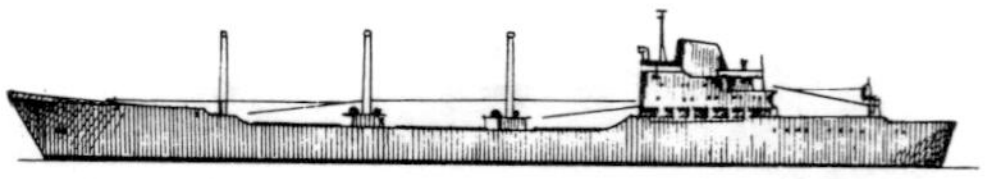

K_3MFC H13
⋆**05130 LETING.** RC/Fi 1966; C; 7400/9900; 151 × 8.6/9.7 (496 × 28/31.7); M; 18; ex WISA 1971.

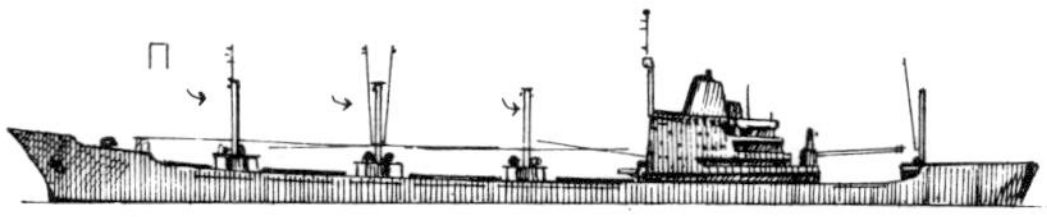

K_3MFCK H13
05140 IRAN HEJRAT. Ir/Fr 1967; C; 10200; 161 × 9.1 (529 × 29.8); M; 17.5; ex ARYA SARA 1980; ex LUCIE DELMAS 1973. Sisters (Ir flag).
05141 IRAN NEHZAT ex ARYA OMID 1980; ex HELENE DELMAS 1973
05142 IRAN SHAD ex ARYA SHAD 1980; ex IRMA DELMAS 1973
05143 IRAN BESAT ex IRAN PAKE 1980; ex ARYA PAKE 1980; ex MARIE DELMAS 1973

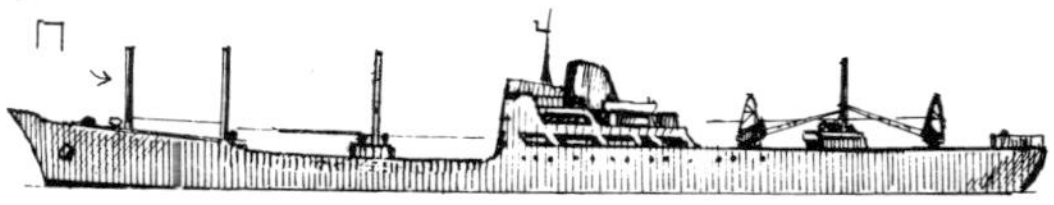

K_3MFCKC H12
05150 ODYSEFS. Gr/Br 1963; R; 11100; 165 × 9.8 (538 × 32.3); TSM; 18; ex MEDIC 1979.

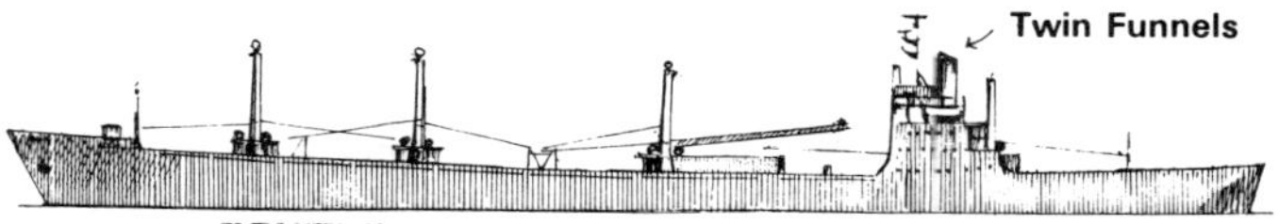

K_3MFK H
05160 ADM. WM. M. CALLAGHAN. US/US 1967; C/RoC; 24500; 211 × 8-9 (604 × 29); TSGT; 26; stern door.

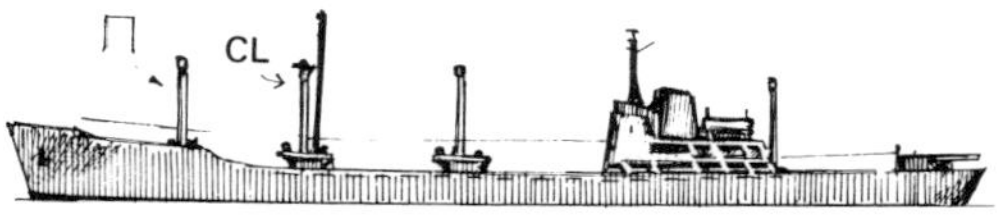

K_3MFK H1
05170 JALARAJAN. In/Br 1966; C; 11300; 160 × 9.4 (535 × 31); M; 16. Sisters (In flag) with stulcken derrick on second kingpost.
05171 JALARATNA 05172 JALARASHMI

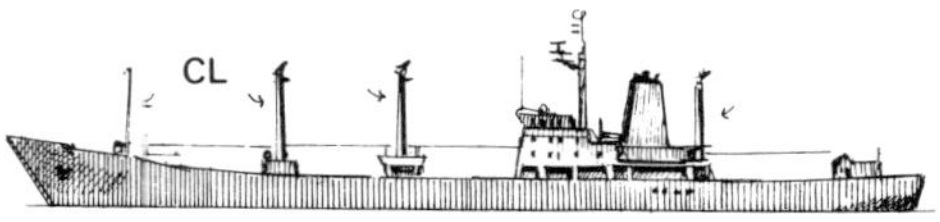

K_3MFK H1
05180 SAMOAN REEFER. De/De 1973; R; 5900; 145 × 8.8 (477 × 28.10); M; 22.5; side doors. Sister **05181 TUNISIAN REEFER** (De)

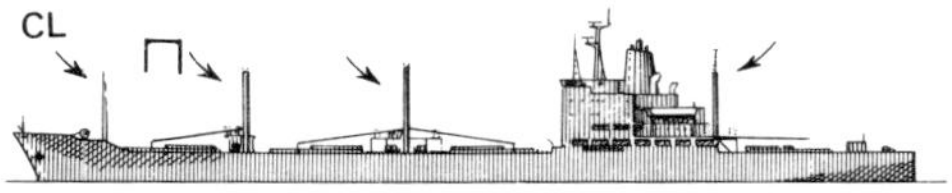

K_3MFK H1
05190 FUJI REEFER. Ja/Ja 1979; R; 7200; 144.95 × 8.07 (475.56 × 26.48); M; 20. Sisters (Ja flag). **05191 SAKURA REEFER 05192 ARIAKE REEFER 05193 AKEBONO REEFER 05194 TOKYO REEFER**

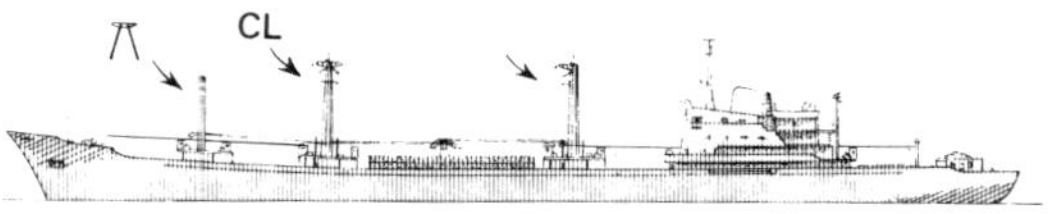

K_3MFK H1
● **050200 HUPEH.** Br/Ne 1961/76; C/Con; 9400; 162.54 × — (533.27 × —); M; 17; ex SIDONIA 1967; Lengthened and converted from cargo 1976.

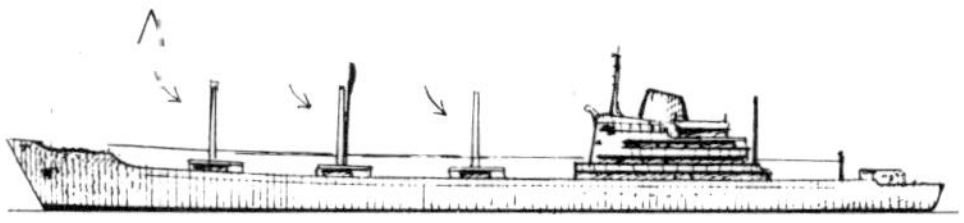

K_3MFK H1
● **05210 STRATHAVOCH.** Br/Br 1965; C; 6300/8500; 148 × 8.1/8.6 (485 × 26/28); M; 16.25; ex ARMANISTAN 1975; ex ELYSIA 1968. Sister **05211 GOLD STAR** (Li) ex ANAT 1974; ex SICILIA 1968

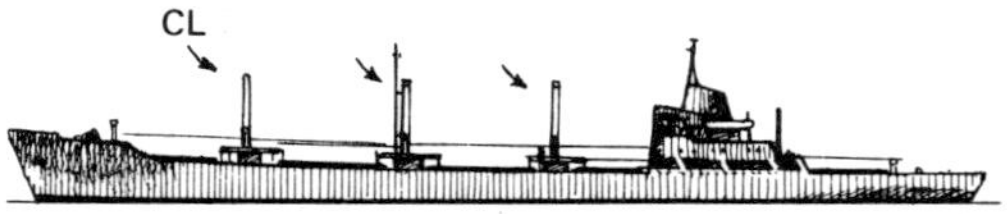

K_3MFK H1
05220 JOHN. Pa/Br 1967; C; 7900/10500; 156 × 8.8/9.6 (512 × 29/31.5); M; 16; ex LUTETIAN 1979

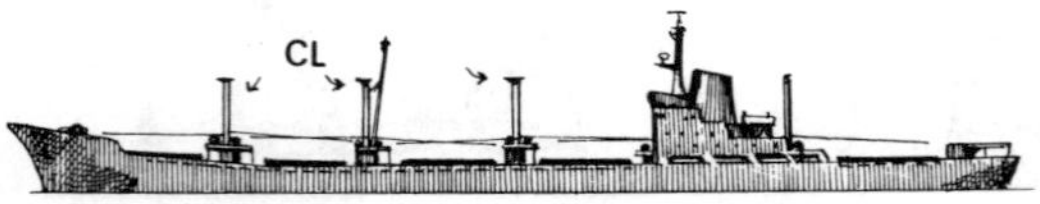

K_3MFK H1

● **05230 FLEETBANK.** Br/Br 1972; C; 7600/11500; 161 × —/9.7 (530 × —/32); M; 17. Sisters **05231 BEAVERBANK** (Br) **05232 BIRCHBANK** (Br) **05233 CEDARBANK** (Br) **05234 RIVERBANK** (Br) **05235 STREAMBANK** (Br) **05236 CLOVERBANK** (Br) ex SIENA 1979; ex CLOVERBANK **05237 FIRBANK** (Br) ex SIBONGA 1979; ex FIRBANK **55238 ALKAIOS** (Gr) ex NESSBANK 1981 **05239 AMPHION** (Gr) ex LAGANBANK 1981

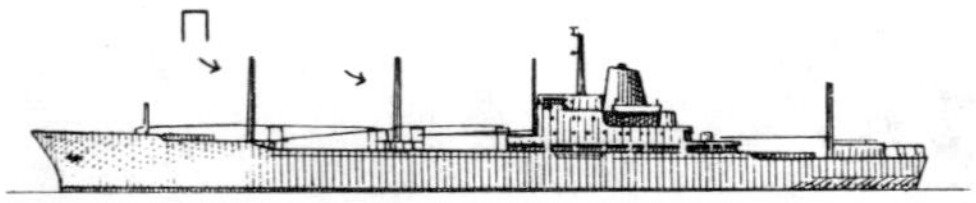

K_3MFK H1

05260 MATINA. Br/Ja 1969; R; 6400; 145 × 7.4 (474 × 24.4); M; 20.5. Sisters (Br flag) **05261 MORANT 05262 MOTAGUA 05263 MUSA**

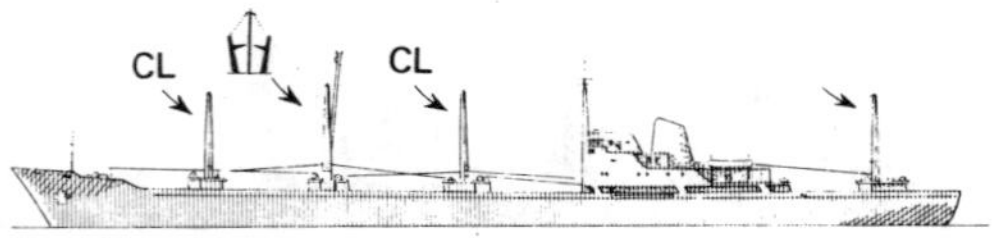

K_3MFK H1

05280 RIO ESQUEL. Ar/Ar 1976; C; 9100; 147.63 × 8.26 (484.35 × 27.1); M; 18. Sisters (Ar flag). **05281 RIO CINCEL 05282 RIO DESEADO 05283 RIO LIMAY 05284 RIO OLIVIA 05285 TIO TEUCO**

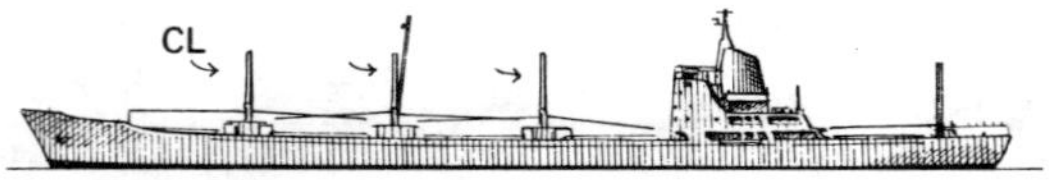

K_3MFK H1

05300 CAPETAN LUKIS. Gr/Br 1969; C; 10800; 159 × 9.7 (523 × 31.8); M; 17; ex MARIGO R 1979

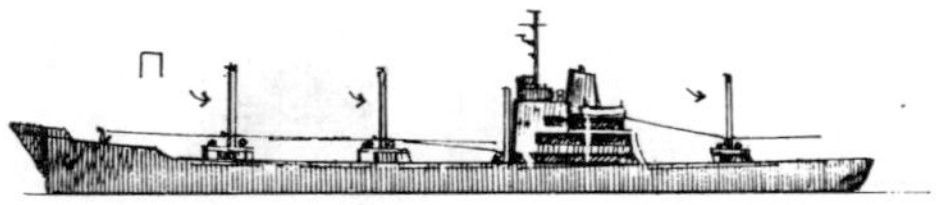

K_3MFK H1

05340 ADELFOTIS. Gr/Ja 1967; C; 7000; 138 × 8.7 (458 × 28.8); M; 16.25; ex JAPAN KAURI 1977. Sisters (Gr flag) **05341 KRONOS** ex JAPAN TOTARA 1977 **05342 NAFTILOS** ex JAPAN RIMU 1977

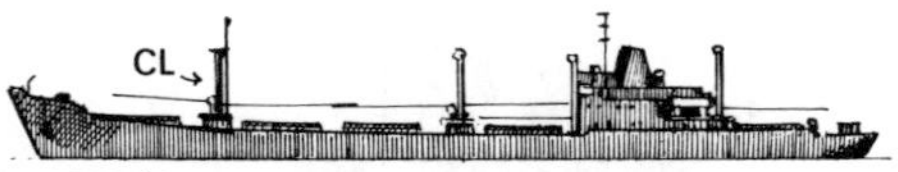

K_3MFK H1

05350 WATERLAND. Ne/Br 1974; C; 9000; 141 × 8.9 (463 × 29); M; 15; **'SD 14'** type.

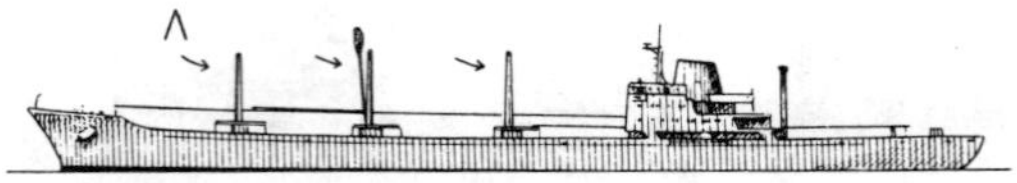

K_3MFK H1

05240 TAXILA. Pk/Ys 1968; C; 5900/8900; 155 × —/9.3 (507 × —/30.8); M; 18.15.

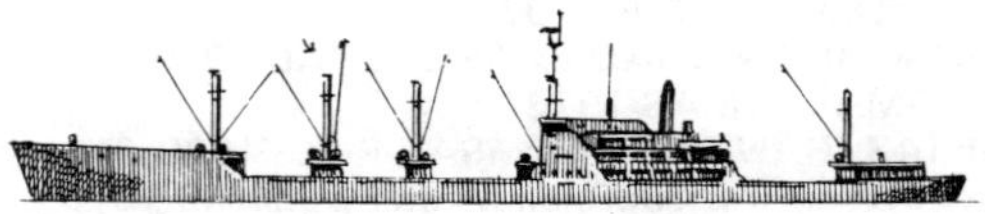

K_3MFK H1

05250 GULF BANKER. US/US 1964; CP; 9500; 151 × 9.8 (495 × 32); T; 18; **"Gulf Andes"** class. Sisters (US flag) **05251 GULF FARMER 05252 GULF MERCHANT 05253 GULF SHIPPER 05254 GULF TRADER**

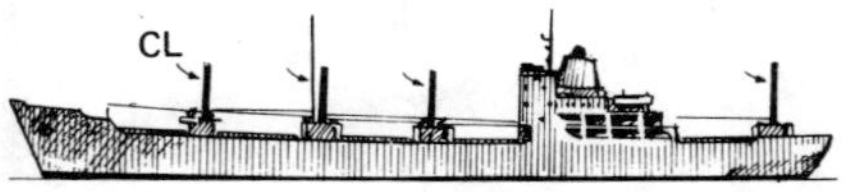

K_3MFK H1

05270 AL BARAT. Li/Br 1965; C; 8100; 141 × 8.8 (452 × 28.11); M; —; ex TENBURY 1974.

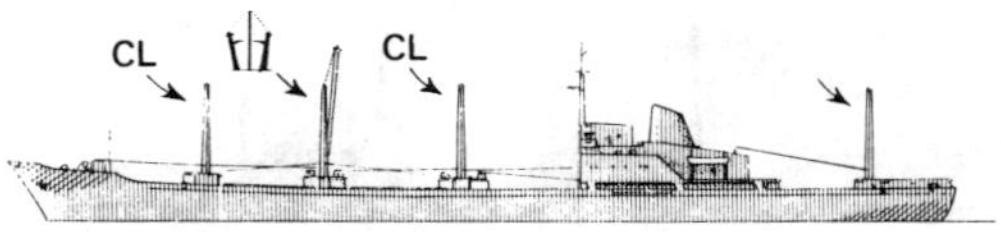

K_3MFK H1

● **05290 RIO CALCHAQUI.** Ar/Ar 1970; C; 10400; 152.71 × 8.68 (501.02 × 28.48); M; 17.5. Sisters (Ar flag) **05291 RIO DE LA PLATA 05292 RIO IGUAZU 05293 RIO PARANA 05294 RIO GUALEGUAY**

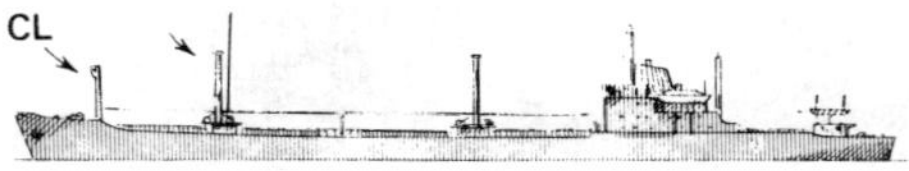

K_3MFK H1

● **05310 MORVIKEN.** No/Br 1978; C; 9100; 141 × 8.86 (462 × 29.07); M; 14.75; **"SD-14" Type.** Earlier vessels are KKMFK—which see. Sisters ⋆**05311 MAXIMO GOMEZ** (Cu); ex AUSTRALIND 1980 ⋆**05312 KIFANGONGO** (An); ex SEA HAWK 1979 ⋆**05313 LONDOGE** (An); ex AEGIRA 1979 ⋆**05314 THAI-BINH** (Vn) ⋆**05315 LUCNAM** (Vn) ⋆**05316 TO-LICH** (Vn) Probably similar (some may be KKMFK). ⋆**05317 SONG DUONG** (Vn); ex DALWORTH 1979 **05318 GLOBE TRADER** (Li) **05319 GOOD FAITH** (Li) Similar (Series IV) **05320 FUNING** (Br) **05321 DERWENT** (Br) **05322 BELLOC** (Br) **05323 BOSWELL**(Br) **05324 BRONTE** (Br) **05325 BROWNING** (Br) **05326 AFRICAN EXPRESS** (Ne) **05327 EUROPEAN EXPRESS** (Ne) **05328 EMPROS** (Gr)

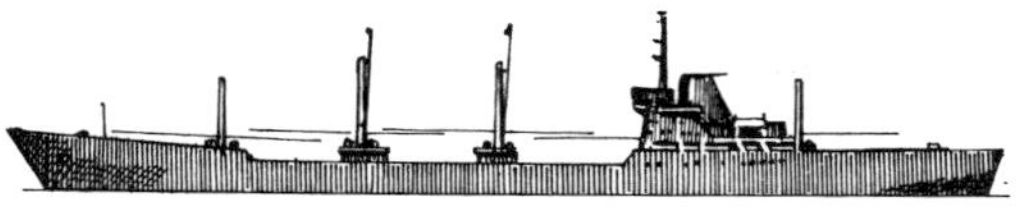

K_3MFK H13
05360 AMARALINA. Bz/Pd 1970; C; 6900/10200; 161 × 19.7 (528 × —/31.1); M; 20.5; **'B 444'** type. Similar (Bz flag) **05361 ITABERA 05362 ITATINGA 05363 BOTAFOGO 05364 BERNARDINO CORREA 05365 ARPOADOR** (Lengthened) **05366 FROTABEIRA 05367 MARIA DA PENHA** ex FROTATOKYO 1978.

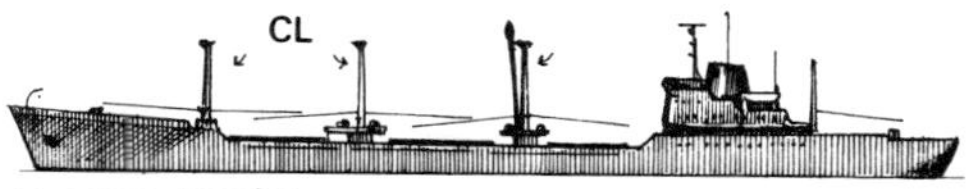

K_3MFK H13
***05370 ANTING.** RC/Fi 1970; C; 7000/9800; 151.8 × 8.7/9.8 (498 × 28.5/32); M; 18; ex KUNLUNGSHAN 1971. Sisters (RC flag) ***05371 CHANGTING** ex WUTAISHAN 1972 ***05372 HUATING**; ex LIUPANSHAN 1973 ***05373 JIANGTING**; ex DAHSUESHAN 1972 ***05374 WANGTING**; ex TAIHANSHAN 1971 Possibly ***05375 YANGTING *05376 YUTING**

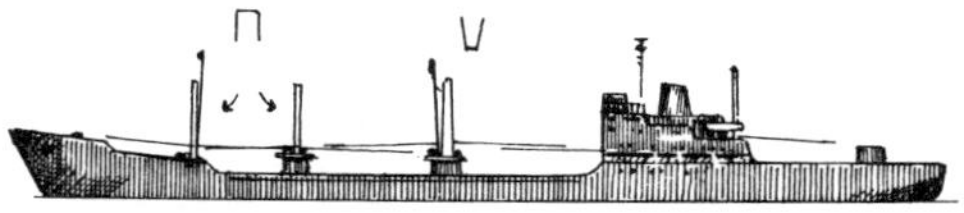

K_3MFK H13
● **05380 TAMATAVE.** Mg/DDR 1972; C; 9200; 151.8 × — 498 × —); M; 19.5; **"Ozean"** type Similar **05381 AUNIS** (Fr) **05382 HOLSTENTAL** (Li) ex ARMATAN 1975 **05383 STATE OF MEGHALAYA** (In) ex ORPHEE 1972 ***05384 FOCSANI** (Rm) ***05385 DRAGASANI** (Rm)

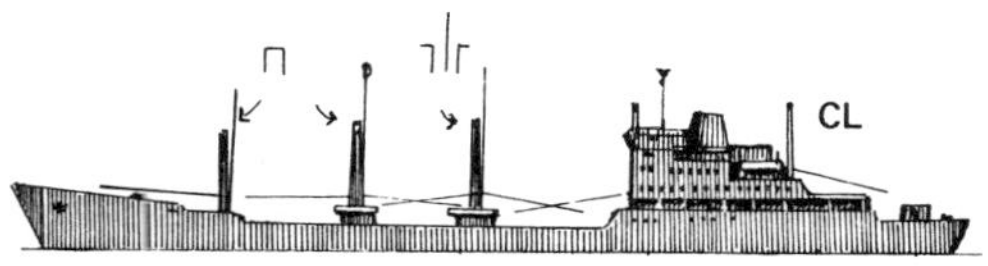

K_3MFK H13
***05390 QIMEN.** RC/DDR 1973; C; 9700; 151.8 × 9.3 (498 × 30.6); M; 17; **'Ozean'** type Similar ***05391 HAIFENG** (RC) ***05392 LONGMEN** (RC) ***05393 LUFENG** (RC) ***05394 YONGMEN** (RC) ***05395 XINFENG** (RC) ***05396 MIR** (Cz) ex SHIMEN.

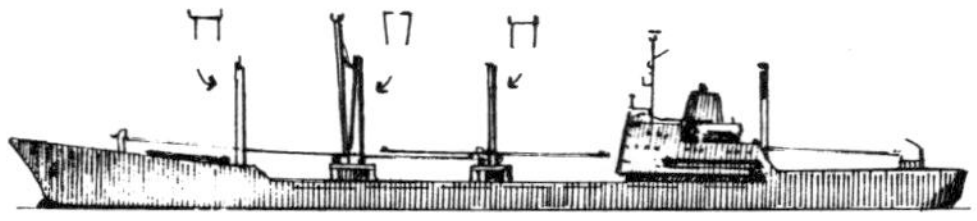

K_3MFK H13
05400 AFRICAN BERYL. Pa/DDR 1969; C; 9000; 151 × 9 (495 × 29.8); M; 17.5; ex SAINT MICHEL 1980; **'OZEAN'** type.

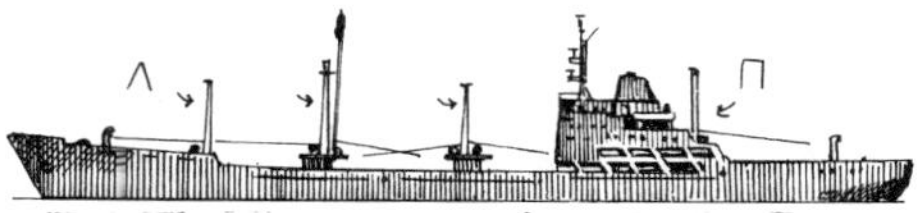

K_3MFK H13
***05410 VOLCHANSK.** Ru/DDR 1968; C; 9500; 150.8 × 8.9 (494 × 29.3); M; 16.5.

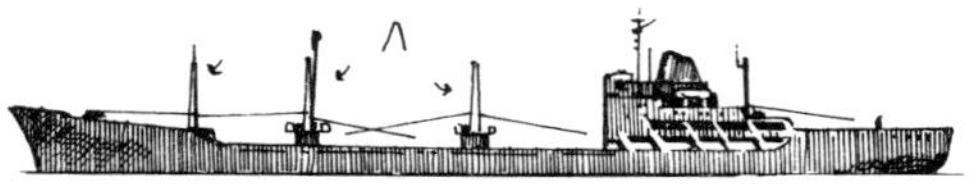

K_3MFK H13
05420 ANYI. Pa/DDR 1969; C; 5600; 151.2 × 9 (496 × 29.8); M; 20; ex NEPTUNE AMETHYST 1974; **'Ozean'** type Sister **05421 IRENES LOGIC** (Gr); ex CLISSON 1980; ex VELOCITY 1977; ex ANDU 1974; ex NEPTUNE AQUAMARINE 1974.

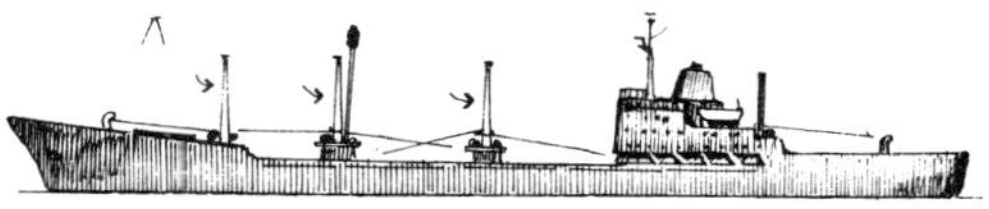

K_3MFK H13
05430 PALAWAN. Li/DDR 1969; C; 8800; 150.5 × 9 (495 × 29.8); M; 18.5; ex VILLE DE REIMS 1976. Sister **05431 CORREGIDOR** (Li); ex VILLE DE SETE 1978.

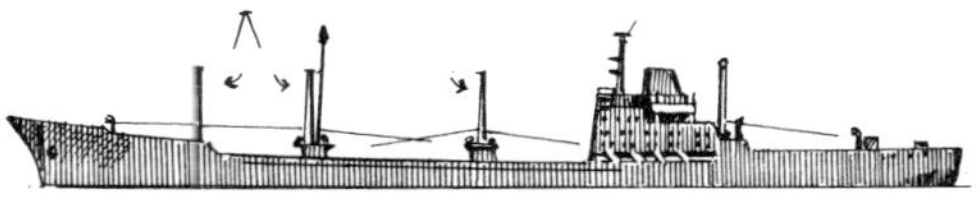

K_3MFK H13
***05440 HAIMEN.** RC/DDR 1968; C; 9500; 151 × 8.8 (494 × 29.3); M; —.

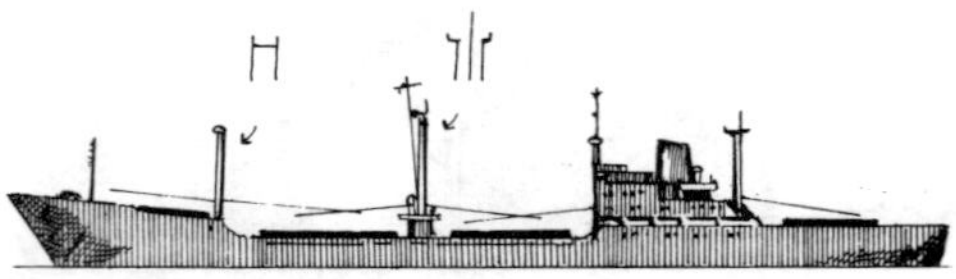

K_3MFK H13
05450 AFRICA PALM. Br/DDR 1971; C; 6300/9800; 152 × 7.6/9.4 (501 × 25/31); M; 18.5; ex JORUNA 1974; **'OZEAN'** type Sisters **05452 AUBRAC** (Fr); ex ANNE REED 1975 **05453 POLNORD** (No); ex KAREN REED 1980; ex NORTRANS KAREN 1980; ex KAREN REED 1975.

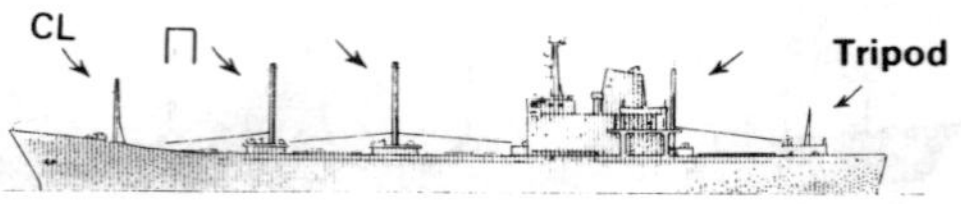

K_3MFK_2 H1
● **05460 FREEZER KING.** Ja/Ja 1978; R; 7700; 140.67 × 8.32 (461.52 × 27.3); M; 20. Sisters **05461 FREEZER PRINCE** (Ja) **05462 FREEZER QUEEN** (Ja) **05463 KHALIJ REEFER** (Ja) Possible Sisters **05465 KHALIJ FREEZER** (Ja) **05466 KHALIJ FROST** (Ja) **05467 KHALIJ COOLER** (Ja) **05468 FREEZER ACE** (Pa)

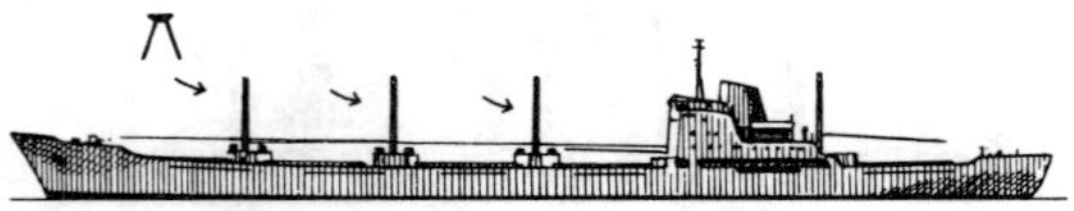

K_3MFK H13
● **05470 BENEFACTOR.** Br/Br 1971; C; 7800/11300; 163 × —/9.7 (540 × —/31.9); M; 18; ex ION. Sisters **05471 FAETHON** (Gr) **05472 FINIX** (Gr) **05473 IASON** (Gr) **05474 IKTINOS** (Gr) **05475 ION** (Gr) **05476 ATALANTI** (Li) Similar: **05477 FEAX** (Gr)

K_3MFK H13
● **05480 ISLA PINTA.** Li/FRG 1972; C; 3700/7200; 131 × 7/8.2 (431 × 23/27); M; 18; ex BARON 1979; ex WILHELM BORNHOFEN 1973. Sisters **05481 BATE BRIDGE** (Sg); ex ADVISER 1975; ex HANS BORNHOFEN 1973 **05482 ISLA GENOVESA** (Pa); ex MAX BORNHOFEN 1980; ex RAPID BRIDGE 1976; ex SPECIALIST 1974; ex MAX BORNHOFEN 1973 **05483 OPULENCE** (Pa); ex XIONG YUE CHENG 1981; ex ELISABETH BORNHOFEN 1978; ex CITOS 1975; ex ELISABETH BORNHOFEN 1973

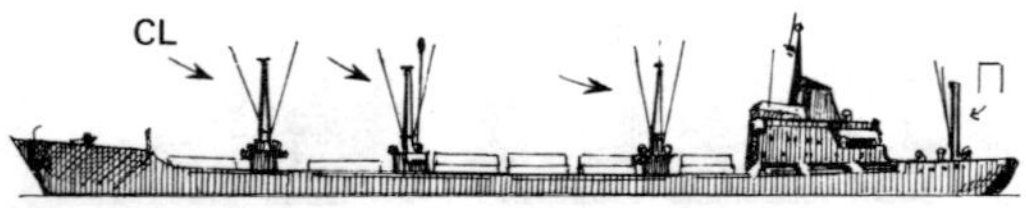

K_3MFK H13
● **05490 ESHKOL.** Is/Fr 1964; C; 4900/7700; 159 × 6.7/7.9 (522 × 22/30.1); M; 17.5; lengthened 1971. Sisters: **05491 ETROG** (Is) **05492 GOLD PILOT** (Li); ex HADAR 1977 **05493 ROGET** (Pa) ex YAFO 1980; ex DOLLY 1979; ex YAFO 1979.

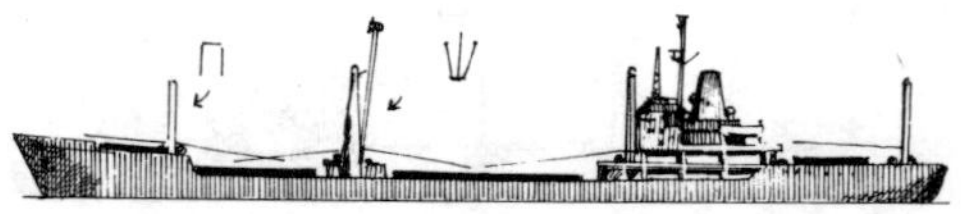

K_3MFK H13
05500 MACASSAR MARU. Ja/Ja 1964; : 9400; 150 × 9 (492 × 29.11); M; 16.

K_3MFK H13
05510 QUINCY. Gr/Br 1960; C; 7500/9400; 152.56 × 8.34/9.35 (500.52 × 27.36/30.68); M; 14.5; ex STRATHASLAK 1978; ex KOHISTAN 1976. Sisters: **05511 SOPHOCLES** (Pa) ex STRATHADDIE 1978 ex FARSISTAN 1975 **05512 NILE U** (Eg) ex STRATHATLOW 197878 ex GORJISTAN 1975.

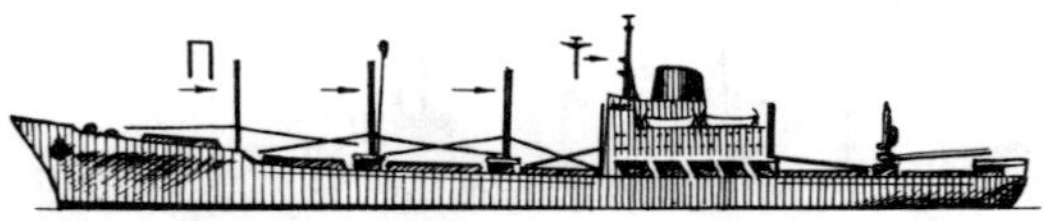

K_3MFKC H1
05520 ORIENTAL QUEEN. Tw/72 1966; C; 11100; 160 × 9.3 (523 × 30.1); M; 19.5.

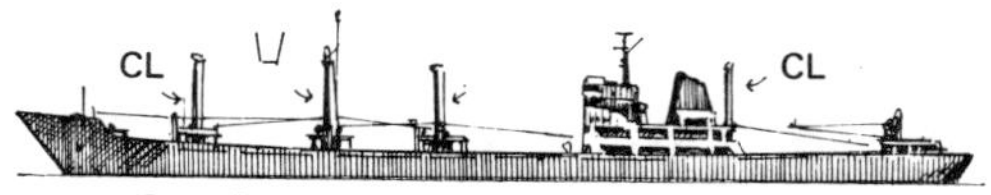

K_3MFKC H1
05530 RIO ABAUCAN. Ar/Sp 1973; C; 8600/10200; 150.9×7.6/8.2 (495×25/27.1); M; 18. Sisters (Ar flag): **05531 RIO LOS SAUCES 05532 RIO PILCOMAYO** Possible sisters: **05533 RIO CALINGASTA 05534 RIO MARAPA 05535 RIO NEUQUEN.**

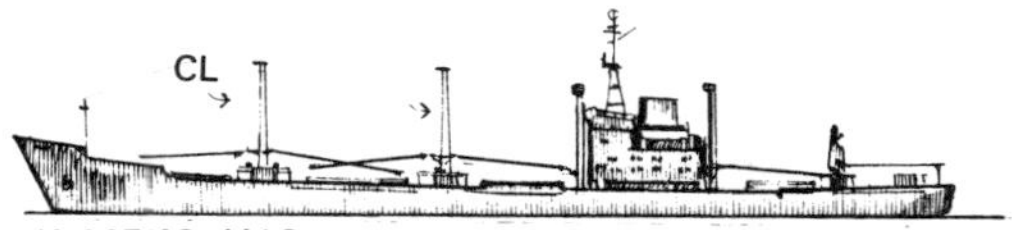

K_3MFKC H13
05540 GOOILAND. Ne/Ne 1969; C; 4800; 148×7 (484×23.4); M; 15.5.

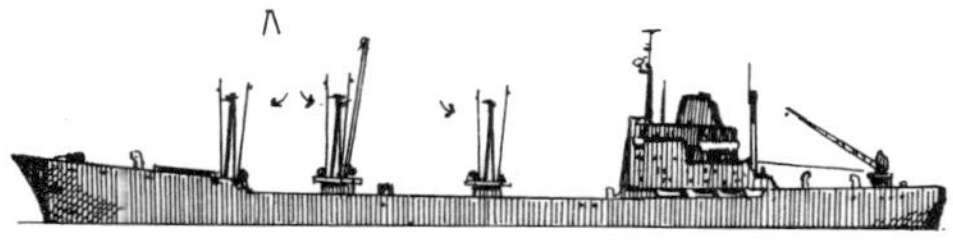

K_3MFKC H13
05550 IRENES MAGIC: Gr/DDR 1968; C; 8700; 151×8.8 (495×29); M; 16.5; ex ANJOU 1979. Possible Sister: **05551 PANAGHIA P** (Gr); ex AUVERGNE 1979.

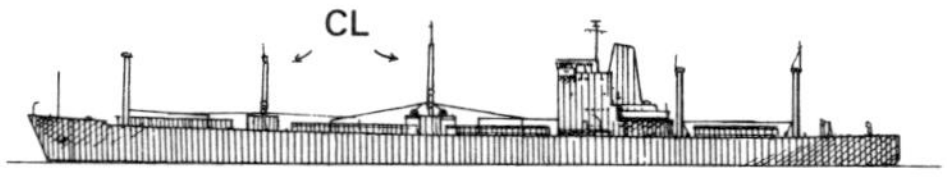

K_3MFK_2 H
⋆05560 MATIJA IVANIC; Ys/Be 1969; C; 6100/9300; 141×19.3 (461×131); M; 14; **'Unity'** type. Sisters (Ys flag): **⋆05561 MATIJA GUBEC ⋆05562 MARKO ORESKOVIC ⋆05563 MOSA PIJADE ⋆05564 PROMINA ⋆05565 SIBENIK.**

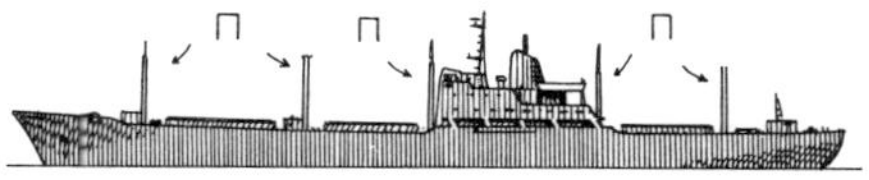

K_3MFK_2 H
05570 OVERSEA FRUIT Sg/Ja 1971; C; 6500; 134×7.5 (440×24.8); M; 18.5. Sister: **05571 PHILIPPINES FRUIT** (Sg); ex COMFORT 1977.

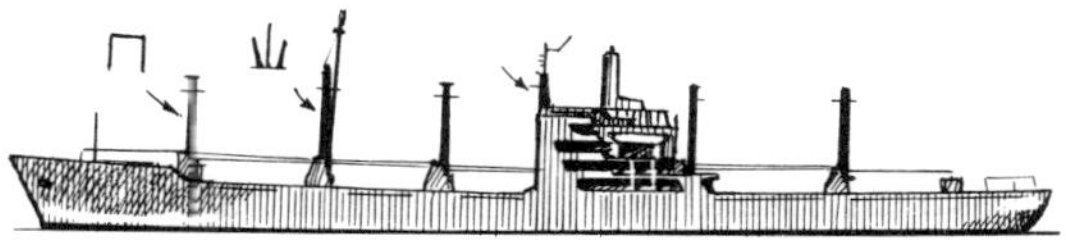

K_3MFK_2 H1
05580 ELIZABETH LYKES; US/US 1964; CP; 7400/11000; 165×8.5/9.9 (540×28/31.8); T; 20. Sisters (US flag): **05581 FREDERICK LYKES 05582 GENEVIEVE LYKES 05583 HOWELL LYKES 05584 LETITIA LYKES 05585 LOUISE LYKES 05586 MALLORY LYKES 05587 MASON LYKES 05588 RUTH LYKES 05589 STELLA LYKES 05590 VELMA LYKES.**

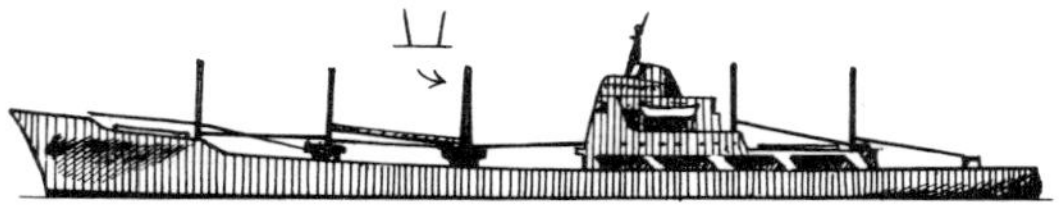

K_3MFK_2 H1
05600 SANTA JUANA; US/US 1966; C; 7200/11000; 165×—/9.5 (554×-/31.8); T; 21; ex DELTA AMERICA 1980; ex PRUDENTIAL SEAJET 1979. Sister **05601 SANTA ADELA** (US); ex DELTA AFRICA 1980; ex PRUDENTIAL OCEANJET 1979.

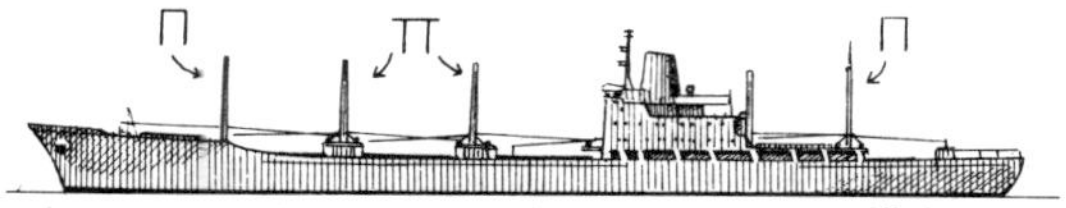

K_3MFK_2 H1
05610 LING YUNG; Tw/Ja 1968; C; 11200; 159×9 2 (522×30.5); M; 19.5. Sisters **05611 YEH YUNG** (Tw) **05612 EIDANGER** (Sg) ex SINGAPORE PRIDE 1976 **05613 VILLANGER** (Li) ex SINGAPORE TRIUMPH 1976.

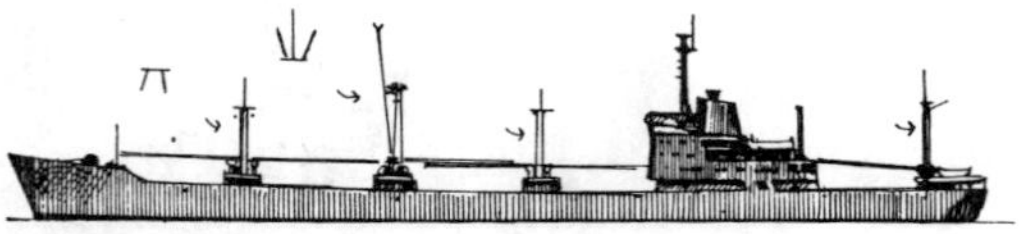

K_3MFK_2 H1
★05620 IGNATIY SERGEYEV Ru/Pd 1968; C; 10200; 154.5 × 9.5 (507 × 29.6); M; 16.5; **"B40/B401"** type **"KOMMUNIST"** class. Sisters (Ru flag): **★05621 GEORGIY CHICHERIN ★05622 GEORGIY DIMITROV ★05623 ERNST THALMANN ★05624 GIUSEPPE DI VITTORIO ★05625 50 LET SOVIET SOVIETSKOY ★05626 UKRAINY ★05627 HO CHIN MIN ★05628 INESSA ARMAND ★05629 IONA YAKIR ★05630 JEANNE LABOURBE ★05631 KARL LIEBKNECHT ★05632 KOMMUNIST ★05633 KOMMUNISTICHESKOYE ZNAMYA ★05634 BELA KHUN ★05635 DMITRY POLUYAN ★05636 NIKOLAY KREMLYANSKIY ★05637 FRIEDRICH ENGELS ★05638 ROSA LUXEMBURG ★05639 FRANTS BOGUSH ★05640 TOYVO ANTIKAYNEN** (Tu flag) **B442** type: **05641 GENERAL A. F. CEBESOY 05642 GENERAL K. ORBAY 05643 GENERAL R. GUMUSBALA 05644 GENERAL Z. DOGAN** (Pd flag): **★05645 KONIN.**

K_3MFK_2 H1
05690 EASTERN MARINER I Pa/Br 1959; C; 8000; 142.6 × 9.1 (468 × 30); M; 13; ex ANASTASIA 1980; ex BROOMPARK 1969.

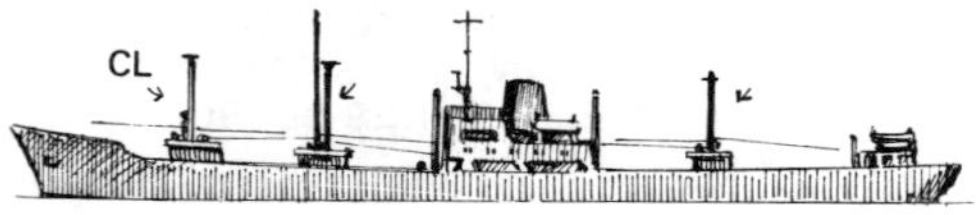

K_3MFK_2 H1
05700 FAMILY DELTA Gr/Br 1962; C; 7100/9900; 154.9 × 8.3/9.4 (508 × 27/.31); M; 16; ex DELTA 1980; ex SINGAPORE PROGRESS 1979; ex STRATHNAVER 1978; ex JUMNA 1975.

K_3MFK_2 H1
05720 NORTH SEA. Pa/Br 1959; C; 6400/8900; 146.3 × 8.21 (480 × 26.8/—); M; 15.5; ex SEA SWALLOW;.

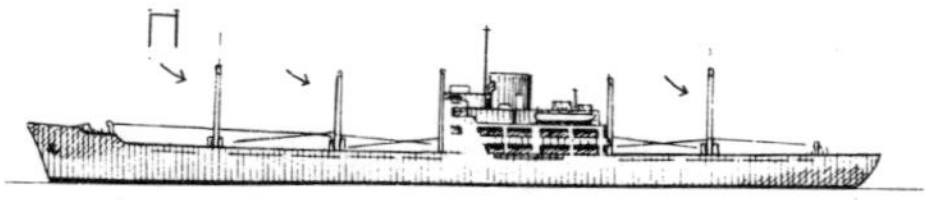

K_3MFK_2 H1
05730 HAN CHEONG. Ko/Ja 1957; C; 7300; 137.1 × 8.5 (450 × 28.1); M; 13.75; ex PACIFIC SHINHO 1978; ex TENKAI MARU 1972.

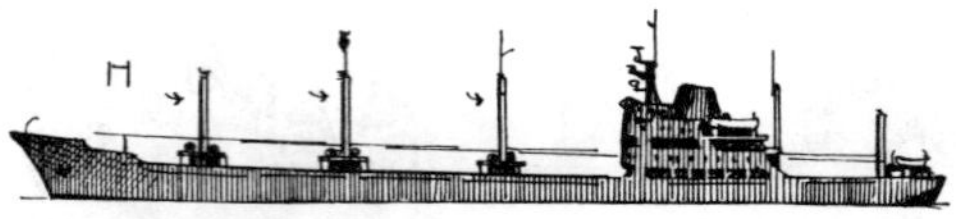

K_3MFK_2 H1
★05650 BAJAR; Ys/It 1969; C; 6200; 152.3 × — (500 × —); M; 18. Sisters (Ys flag): **05651 KRALJEVICA ★05652 PAZIN ★05653 KASTAV** Very similar: **★05654 KRANJCEVIC ★05655 GORAN KOVACIC.**

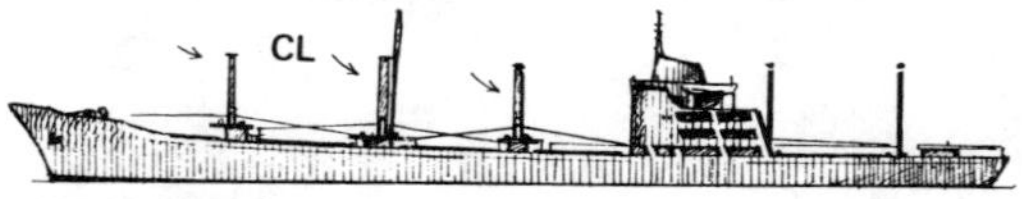

K_3MFK_2 H1
★05660 DUNHUANG RC/Br 1967; C; 8300/11400; 159 × 8.5/9.4 (523 × 27.3/31); M; - . Sister **★05661 JINSHA** (RC).

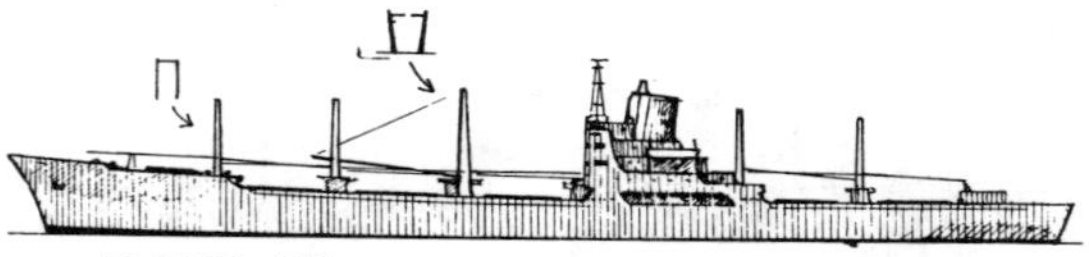

K_3MFK_2 H1
05670 AMERICAN CHALLENGER; US/US 1962; C; 8200/11100; 171 × -/9.6 (561 × -/31.7); T; 21. Sisters (US flag): **05671 AMERICAN CHAMPION 05672 AMERICAN CHARGER 05673 AMERICAN CHIEFTAIN 05674 AMERICAN CORSAIR 05675 AMERICAN COURIER 05676 PIONEER COMMANDER** ex AMERICAN COMMANDER 1967 **05677 PIONEER CONTENDER** ex AMERICAN CONTENDER 1966 **05678 PIONEER CONTRACTOR** ex AMERICAN CONTRACTOR 1966 **05679 PIONEER CRUSADER** ex AMERICAN CRUSADER 1966 **05680 PIONEER MOON** ex AMERICAN MOON 1962.

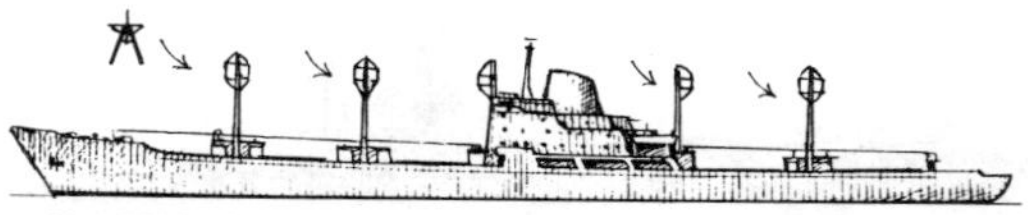

K_3MFK_2 H1
● **05710 FARES REEFER** Le/Br 1966; R; 8200; 161 × 8.6 (528 x 29.5); M; 19.5; ex WESTMORLAND 1980. Sisters **05711 REEFER PRINCESS** (Gr) ex TONGARIRO 1979 **05712 MAHSURI** (Sg) ex TEKOA 1980 **05713 MANDAMA** (Sg) ex TAUPO 1980.

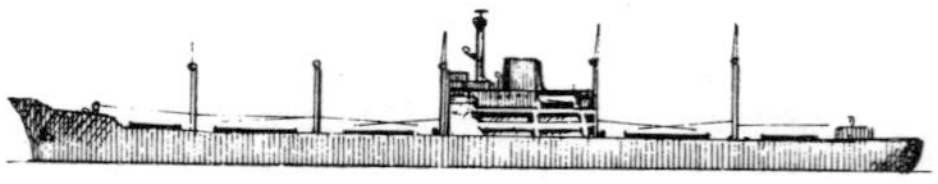

K_3MFK_2 H1
05740 SPARTA. Gr/Ja 1958; C; 8400; 4 × 8.6 (474 × 28.6); M; 13.5; ex PLATA STAR 1979; ex NORTHGATE 1977; ex HORAI MARU 1973.

K_3MFK_2 *H1*
05750 CHIEH JEN. Pa/Ja 1955; C; 7700; 140 × 8.4 (459 × 27.5); M; 14.5; ex SEIUN MARU 1973.

K_3MFK_2 *H1*
● **05760 CHRISTOS S.T. ARAPAKIS.** Cy/Ja 1961; C; 9000; 156 × 8.7 (513 × 28.6); M; 16.5; ex MAN HING 1979; ex ANDINO 1979; ex FLORIDA MARU 1973; Sisters **05761 PACIFIC ACE** (Pa) ex MISSISSIPPI MARU 1975 **05762 LAMBROS TSAGLIOTIS** (Gr) ex LOUISIANA MARU 1975 **05763 TENNESSEE MARU** (Ja) **05764 UNION KINGSTON** (Pa) ex SANSHIN VICTORY 1980; ex TEXAS MARU 1973.

K_3MFK_2 *H1*
05770 ATLANTIC NEPTUNE. Pa/Ja 1961; C; 9200; 156.01 × 9.2 (511.8 × 30.18); M; 18.25; ex MIKISHIMA MARU 1972.

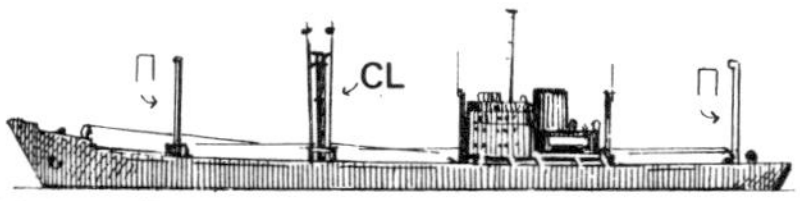

K_3MFK_2 *H1*
05780 SEALUCK II. Cy/Ja 1963; C; 5200; 124 × 7.2 (407 × 23); M; 14.25; ex ELENIA 1980; ex GANGES MARU 1974.

K_3MFK_2 *H12*
05790 OCEAN GREEN. Pa/Ja 1965; C; 4000; 113 × 7.1 (371 × 23); M; 14; ex TAI CHIAO 1972; S ster **05791 TUNG CHING** (Tu).

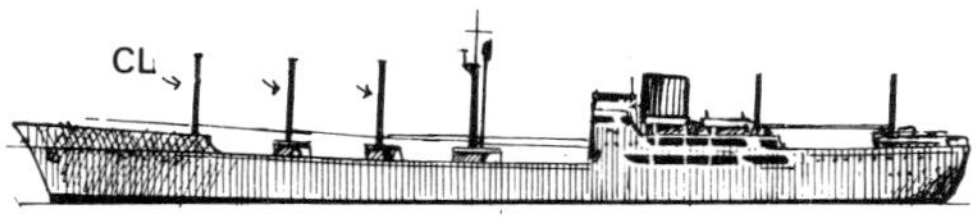

K_3MFK_2 *H13*
05800 KOTA CANTIK. Sg/Br 1962; CP; 7300/9700; 154× 8.4/9 (5 27.5/29); M; 18; ex CITY OF TORONTO 1978; ex CITY OF EASTBOURNE 1971; Sister **05801 KOTA CAHAYA** (Sg) ex CITY OF OTTAWA 1978; ex CITY OF GLASGOW 1971.

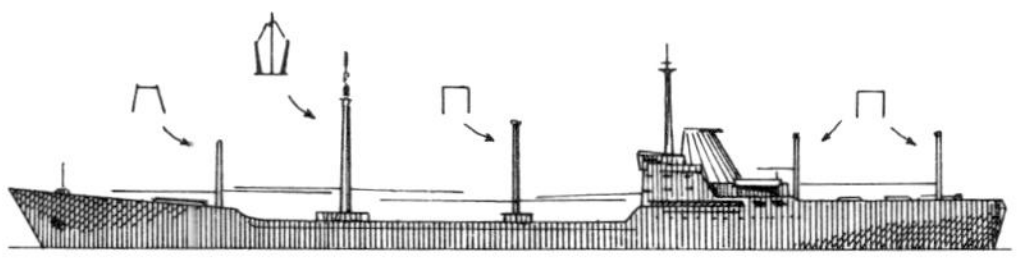

K_3MFK_2 *H13*
05810 SAO TOME. Po/Pa 1972; Pt.Con; 7000/11700; 161 x —/9.7 (518 × —/31.11); M; 21; **'B 434'** type
05811 SOFALA (Po).

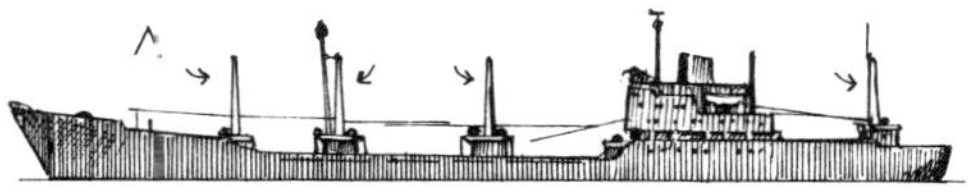

K_3MFK_2 *H13*
05820 JALAMOKAMBI. In/DDR 1972; C; 9600; 153 × 9.3 (500 × 30.9); M; 18.25; **'OZEAN'** type Sisters (In Flag): **05821 JALAMORARI 05822 JALAMANI 05823 JALAMOHAN 05824 JALAMAYUR 05825 JALAMANGALA 05826 JALAMATSYA 05827 JALAMOTI.**

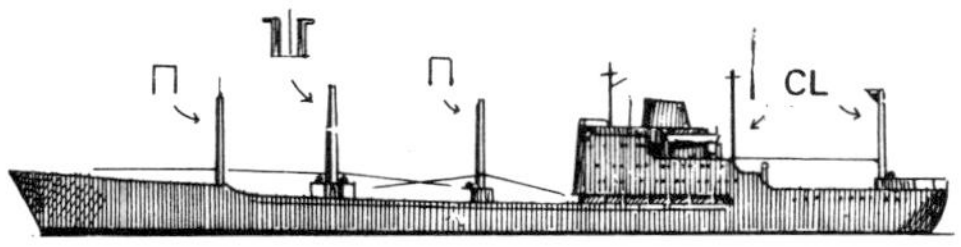

K_3MFK_2 *H13*
⋆**05830 HAIFENG.** RC/DDR 1969; C; 8900; 150.5 × 8.8 (494 × 29.3); M; 17; **'OZEAN'** type Sisters ⋆**05831 LUFENG** (RC) ⋆**05832 XINFENG** (RC).

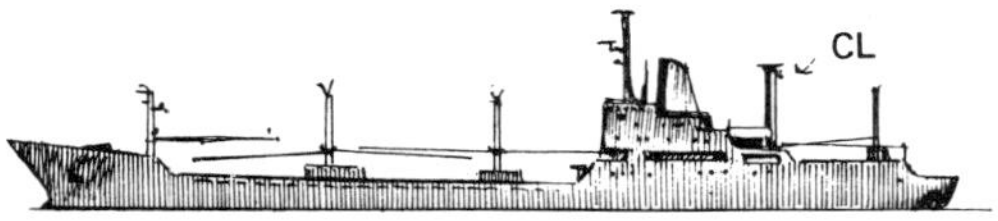

K_3MFK_2 *H13*
05840 FLAMAR PRIDE. Li/Fr 1969; R; 9600; 148.4 × 8.5 (487 × 28); M; 20.5; ex FORT LA REINE 1980; Sister **05841 FLAMAR PROGRESS** (Li) ex FORT PONTCHARTRAIN 1980.

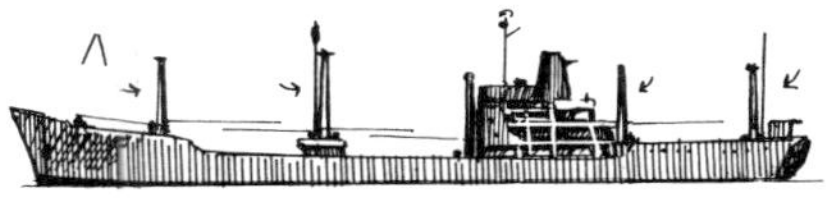

K_3MFK_2 *H13*
05850 DJAKARTA. Pa/Ja 1961; CP; 6000; 130 × 8.2 (426 × 27); M; 14.75; ex DJAKARTA MARU 1976.

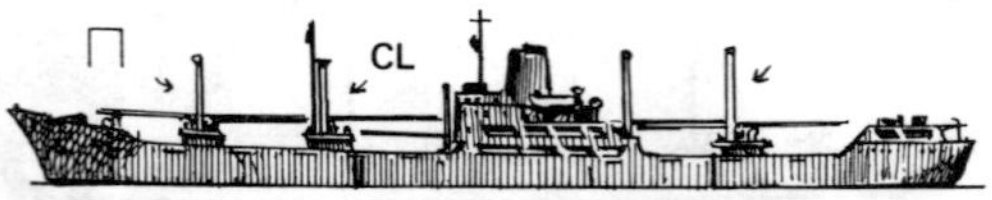

K_3MFK_2 H13
05860 FLORA C. Gr/Br 1960; C; 7500/9700; 154 × 8.4/9.4 (505 × 27.5/31); M; 14; ex JOIL 1976; ex ALDERMINSTER 1975; ex KINGS REACH 1970; ex PORT CAMPBELL 1966; ex CLARKSPEY 1961.

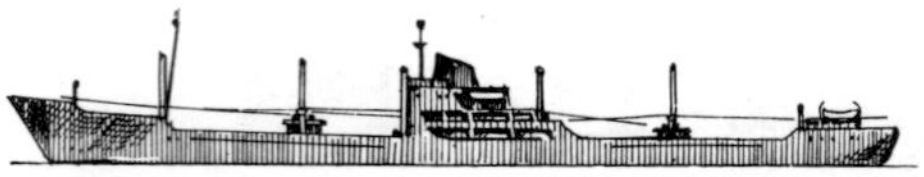

K_3MFK_2 H13
05870 LAKY. Gr/Sw 1956; C; 6100/8700; 142.4 × 8/9 (466 × 26/30; M; 14; ex KIMBERLEY 1979; ex CRETAN HARMONY 1976; ex HARMONY 1974; ex TRUTH 1971.

K_3MFK_2 H13
★**05880 PEPITO TEY.** Cu/Sw 1961; C; 6000/8800; 148.4 × 8.2/9.1 (487 × 27/30); M; 15; ex MARBLE ISLANDS 1975; ex HANSA 1972.

K_3MFK_2 H13
● **05890 MARMARAS.** Gr/Br 1961; C; 6400/8800; 141.7 × 8.1/8.6 (465 × 27/31.5); M; 14; ex DALLA 1980; Sisters **05891 DONGA** (Br) **05892 DUMBAIA** (Br) **05893 JOELLE** (Cy) ex REGU 1981; ex PEGU 1980.

K_3MFK_2 H13
05900 DEUTSCHLAND EXPRESS. Pa/FRG 1960; C; 8300; 144 × 7.9 (473 × 25.11); M; 15; ex GRIFFIN 1980; ex DEGANYA 1973; Sister **05901 ALIAKMON PROSPERITY** (Gr) ex SILVER 1974; ex SILVER LAND 1974; ex GEDERA 1973.

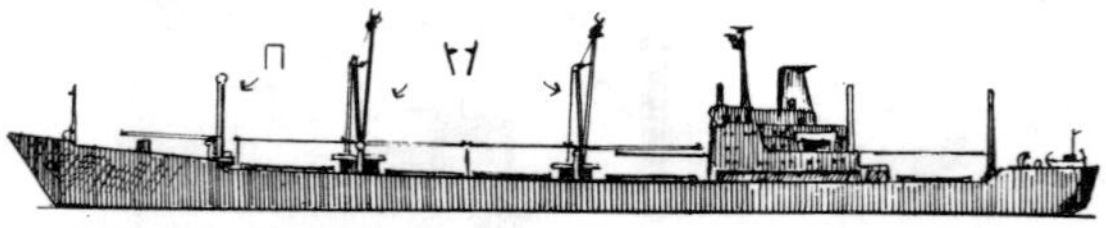

K_3MFK_2 H13
● **05910 FINN-AMER.** Fi/FRG 1971; RoC/Pt.Con; 7800/17000; 174 × 7.9/9.1 (572 × 26/30); M; 20;ex CONCORDIA AMER 1978; ex FINN-AMER 1977; stern and side doors Sisters **05911 FINNBUILDER** (Fi) ex CONCORDIA BUILDER 1978; ex FINNBUILDER 1977 **05912 FINNSAILOR** (Fi) ex CONCORDIA SAILOR 1978; ex FINNSAILOR 1976.

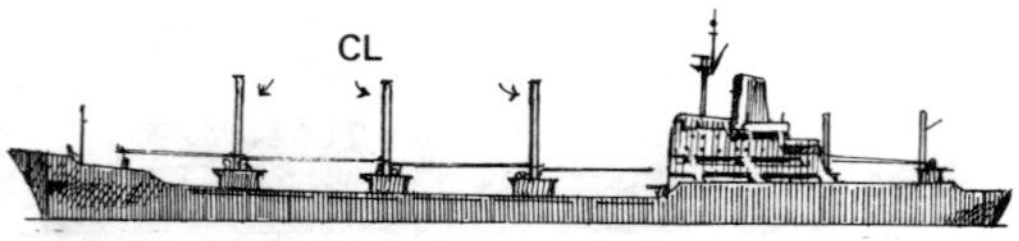

K_3MFK_2 H13
05920 BENSTAC. Br/Br 1968; C; 8300/12000; 162 × 8.6/10 (532 × 28/33); M; 22.

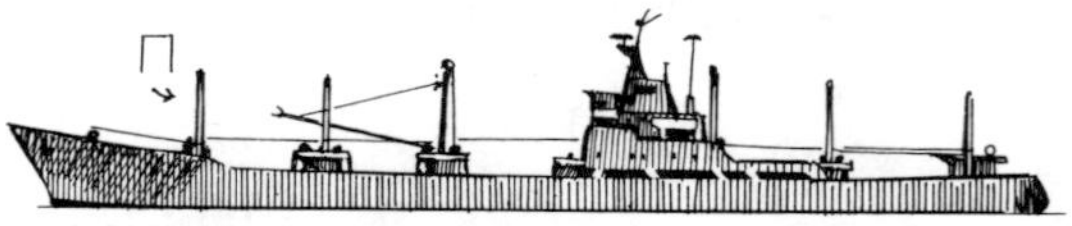

K_3MFK_3 H1
05930 AMERICAN RACER. US/US 1964; Pt.Con; 7500/11200; 166 × –/9.74 (542 × —/31.96); T; 21; Sisters (US flag): **05931 AMERICAN RANGER** **05932 AMERICAN RELIANCE** **05933 MORMACDAWN** ex AUSTRAL PATRIOT 1980; ex AMERICAN RESOLUTE 1969 **05934 MORMACMOON** ex AUSTRAL PILOT 1980; ex AMERICAN ROVER 1969.

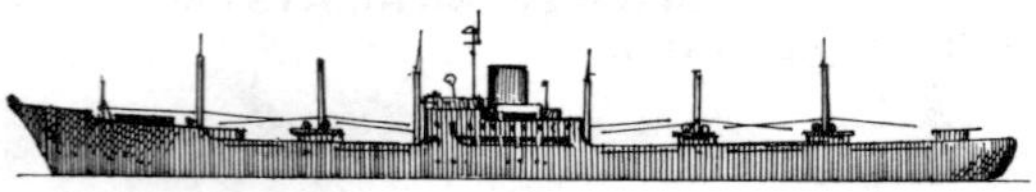

K_3MFK_3 H1
● **05940 ROYAL FORTUNE.** Pa/Ja 1959; C; 9100; 162.2 × 9.2 (532 × 30.1); M; 17.5; ex SEATTLE MARU 1975.

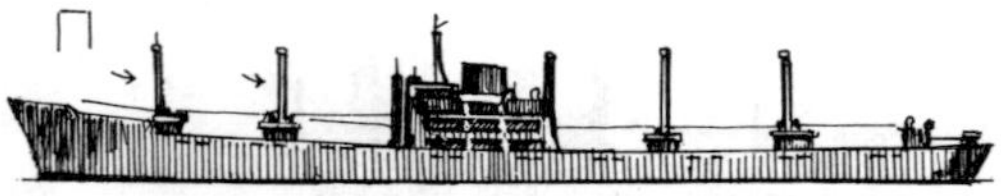

K_3MFK_3 H1
05950 KARA CAREER. Pa/Ja 1960; C; 9500; 160 × 9.3 (524 × 30.5); M; 18.5; ex BROOKLYN MARU 1975. Sister **05951 PRESIDENT GARCIA** (Pi) ex RIO TUXPAN 1979; ex MANHATTAN MARU 1975. Similar: **05952 HOWA MARU (Ja).**

K_3MFK_3 H1
● **05960 COMET.** US/US 1962; C; 11300; 174.3 × 9.4 (572 × 30.1); T; 20; ex AFRICAN COMET 1980. Sisters (US flag): **05961 DAWN** ex AFRICAN DAWN 1980 **05962 MERCURY** ex AFRICAN MERCURY 1980 **05963 METEOR** ex AFRICAN METEOR 1980 **05964 NEPTUNE** ex AFRICAN NEPTUNE 1980 **05965 SUN** ex AFRICAN SUN 1980.

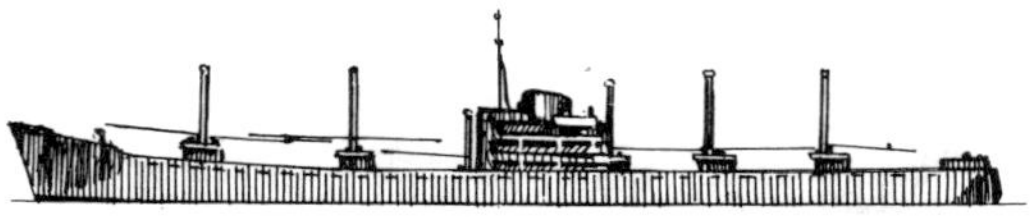

K_3MFK_3 H1
05970 ONWARD ELITE. Pa/Ja 1958; C; 9400; 157×8.8 (514×28.11); M; 18.25; ex MEGUROSAN MARU 1975. Similar: **05971 HAN GARAM** (Ko) ex SEA BRAVE 1979 ex MOMIJISAN MARU 1973 **05972 SEA DISCOVERER** (Pa) ex MATSUDOSAN MARU 1974.

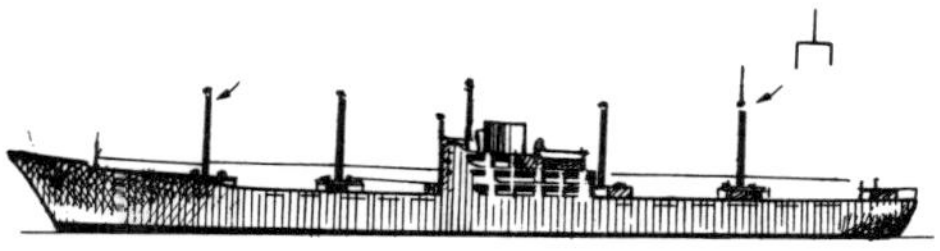

K_3MFKM H1
05980 LEAGE. Gr/Ja 1961; C; 8800; 154×9.2 (505×30.4); M; 18.5; ex TOSAHARU MARU 1975. Similar: **05981 SMINARCHOS FRANGISTAS** (Gr) ex YAMATOSHIMA MARU 1977 **05982 AEGEAN CAREER** (Pa) ex OCEAN FAITH 1977; ex SADOHARU MARU 1976.

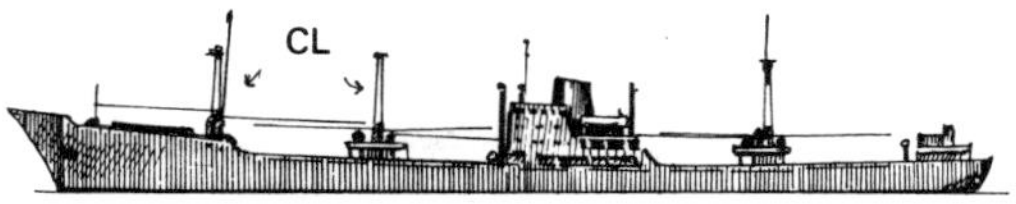

K_3MFKM H1
05990 AEOLIAN SEA. Gr/FRG 1958; CP; 9300; 153×9 (502×29.9); M; 15; ex CORTHIAN 1974; ex FERNPOINT 1969.

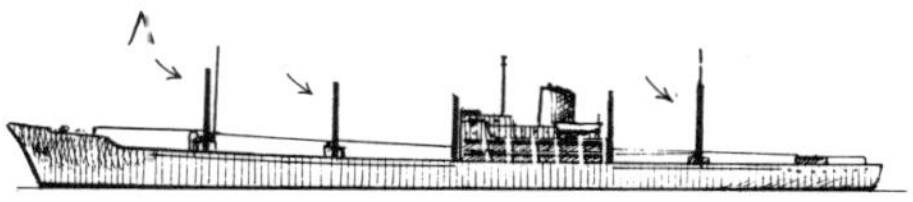

K_3MFKM H1
06000 GOLCONDA. Li/Ja 1962; C; 8200; 140.4×8.3 (461×27.3); M; 15.5; ex HOZUI MARU 1975.

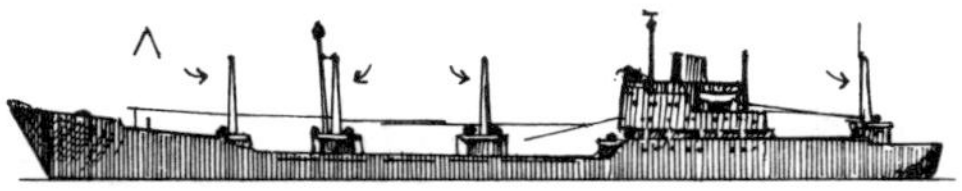

K_3MFKM H13
06010 JALAMOKAMBI. In/DDR 1972; C; 9600; 153×9.3 (500×30.9); M; 18.25; **'OZEAN'** type Sisters (In flag): **06011 JALAMORARI 06012 JALAMANGALA 06013 JALAMANI 06014 JALAMATSYA 06015 JALAMOHAN 06016 JALAMOTI 06017 JALAMAYOR.**

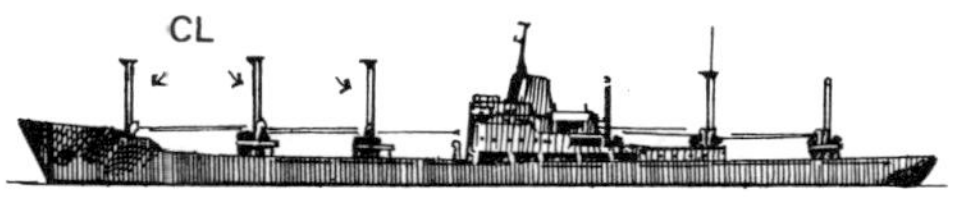

K_3MFKMK H1
06020 NACALA. Po/Hong Kong 1966; C; 9100; 149×9.1 (489×29.10); M; 18; ex HUNAN 1968.

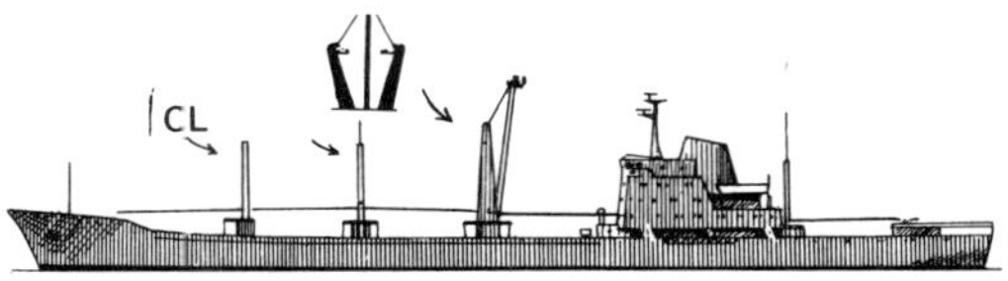

K_3MFM H1
⋆06030 HULIN; RC/Ys 1974; C; 6300/9700; 160×—/9.4 (525×—/30.10); M; 19.25. Sisters (RC Flag): **⋆06031 CHUNLIN ⋆06032 SONGLIN ⋆06033 TIANLIN ⋆06034 YANGLIN ⋆06035 YULIN ⋆06036 TAOLIN** Possible sister: **⋆06037 LONGLIN.**

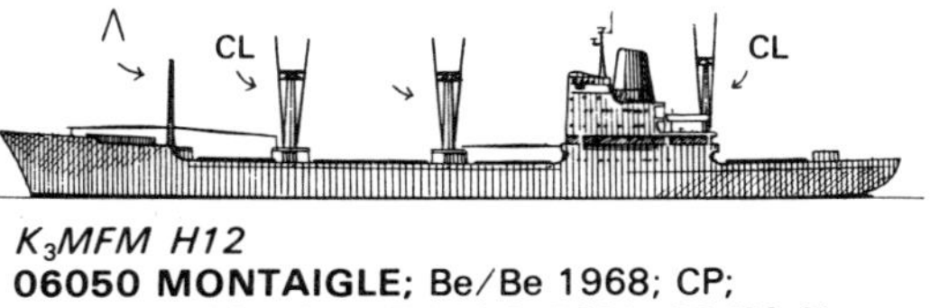

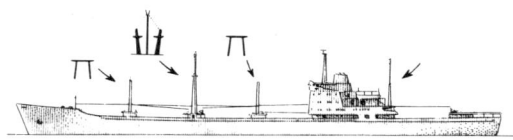

K_3MFM H1
⋆06040 URSUS; Pd/Pd 1972; C; 6400/10100; 154.7×—/8.97 (507.55×—/29.43); M; 17.75; **"B442"** type.

K_3MFM H12
06050 MONTAIGLE; Be/Be 1968; CP; 7100/11500; 161×7.9/9.9 (528×26/32.6); M; 19. Sisters (Be flag): **06051 MONTENAKEN 06052 MONTFORT 06053 MONTSALVA.**

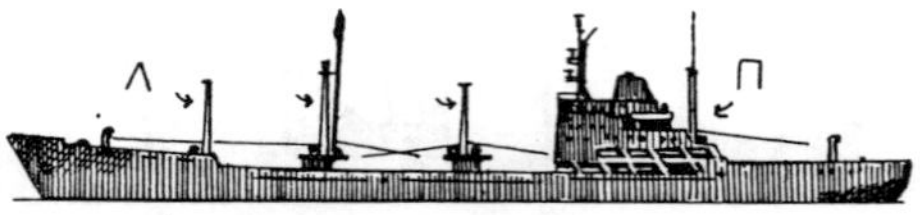

K_3MFM *H13*
● ⋆**06060 VELIKIYE LUKI;** Ru/DDR 1964; C; 9400; 150.6×8.8 (494×29.3); M; 16.5. Sisters ⋆**06061 VEREYA** (Ru) ⋆**06062 VELIZH** (Ru) ⋆**06063 CHAMWINO** (Ta); ex CHANGCHENG 1972; ex AL MUBARAKIAH 1972; ex JOLANDA 1966 Similar: ⋆**06064 JIANGMIN** (RC) ⋆**06065 YUMEN** (RC) **06066 PULAO BATAM** (Ia); ex HOEGH BREEZE 1979; ex JANECKE REED; **06067 AFRICAN AMBER** (Pa); ex CARIBA 1979 **06068 AFRICAN CORRAL** (Pa); ex CASSARATE 1980.

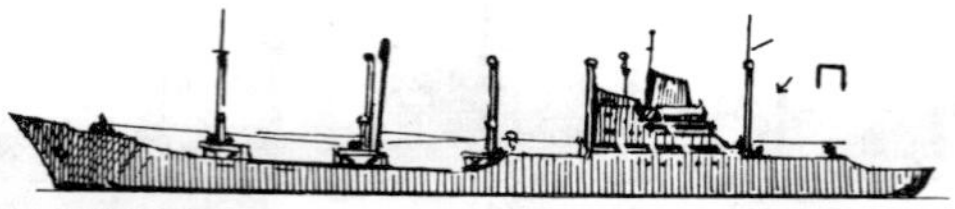

K_3MFM *H13*
06080 MIGHTY: Gr/Sp 1963; C; 6200/9400; 156.8×8/9.3 (515×26/30.3); M; 16; ex SINCERITY 1977; ex MOHELI 1977; ex CHATWOOD 1969.

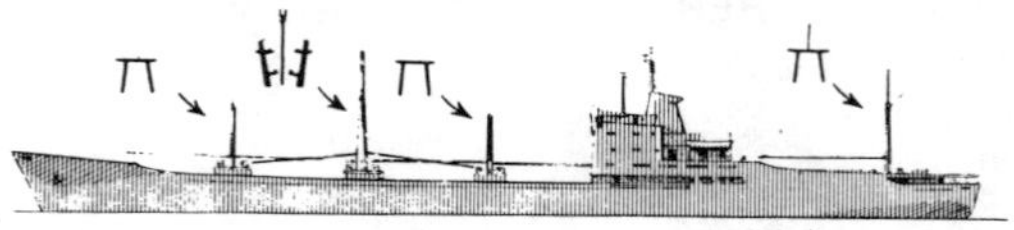

K_3MFM *H13*
⋆**06090 WLADYSLAW ORKAN;** Pd/Pd 1971; C; 6400/10100; 153.74×—/8.97 (504.4× /29.43); M; 18; Modified **"B442"** type. Sister ⋆**06091 LUCJAN SZENWALD.**

K_3MFMK *H1*
06100 RU YUNG; Tw/Ja 1962; C; 10400; 158×9.1 (518×29.8); M; 18.

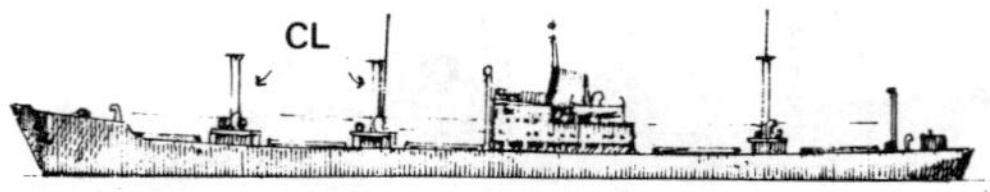

K_3MFMK *H1*
● **06110 AGIOS PANDELEIMON;** Gr/Br 1962; C; 9200; 151.9×8.8 (498×29); M; 14.5; ex CAPTAIN MICHAEL 1975; ex LLANWERN 1968.

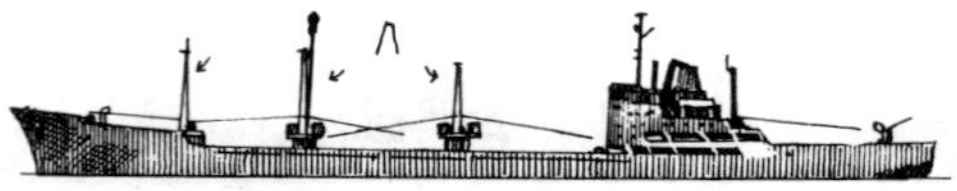

K_3MKFK *H13*
06120 ANUI; Pa/DDR 1969; C; 8700; 151.7×9.9 (496×29.7); M; 20; ex NEPTUNE AMETHYST 1974; **"OZEAN"** type. Sister **06121 IRENES LOGIC** (Gr); ex CLISSON 1980; ex VELOCITY 1977; ex ANDU 1974; ex NEPTUNE AQUAMARINE 1974.

K_3MKFKM *H13*
● **06130 BRAZILIAN EXPRESS;** Pa/Ja 1965; C; 10000; 161×9.3 (528×30.6); M; 19.5; ex YAMAGUCHI MARU 1980. Sister **06131 KYRA** (Gr); ex YAMASHIRO MARU 1974.

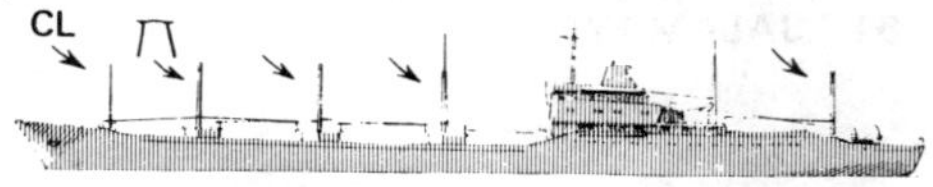

$K_3M_2FK_2$ *H13*
⋆**06140 CSOKONAI;** Hu/Pd 1976; C; 5300/8100; 145.37×—/9.08 (476.94× - /29.79); M; 18.5; **"B474"** type. Sister ⋆**06141 RADNOTI** (Hu) the following are identical but **"B478"** type: ⋆**06142 ALBA IULIA** (Rm) ⋆**06143 CURTEA DE ARGES** (Rm).

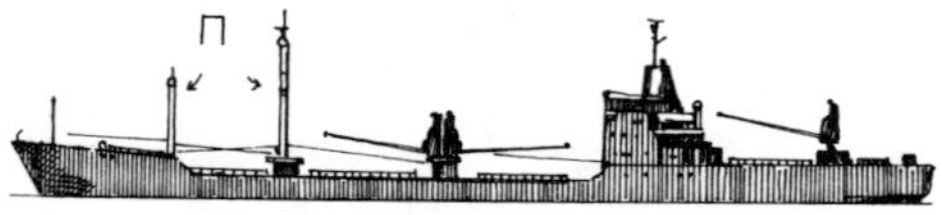

K_2MC_2MFKC *H13*
06150 SANTA FE; FRG/FRG 1972; C; 6900/9800; 148.6×7.9/9.4 (488×26/30.7); M; 19. Sister **06151 SANTA CRUZ** (FRG); ex LLOYD MELBOURNE 1980; ex SANTA CRUZ 1979.

K_2MF *H*
06160 DEVONIA; Br/Br 1956; P; 900; 64×3 (210×9.7); TSM; 15.5; ex SCILLONIAN 1977.

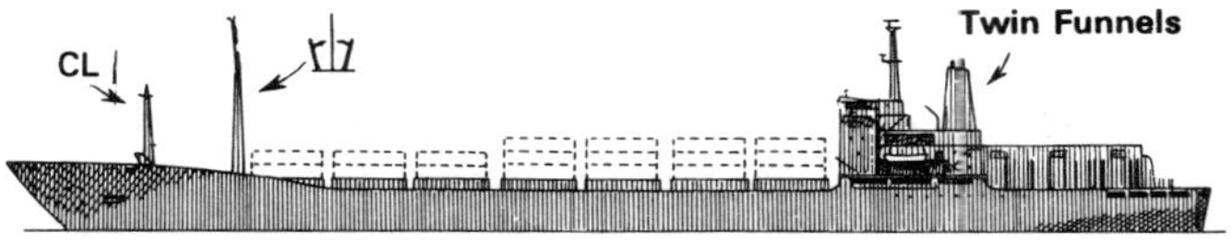

K_2MF H1
06170 AMERICANA; It/It 1974; Con/V. 22200; 208 × 10.3 (683 × 34.1); T; 23.5; Side door on port side. Sister **06171 ITALICA** (It).

K_2MF H1
06180 MARION DUFRESNE; Fr/Fr 1973; RS/C/P; 6600; 112.1 × 6.3 (368 × 20.8); M; 15.

K_2MF H13
● **06190 KHALIJ EXPRESS;** Sg/Br 1955/75; LS; 8100; 134 × 7.7 (440 × 25.3); T; 15; ex UNITED CHALLENGER 1976; ex MALAYSIA 1976; ex HUBERT 1964; Converted from cargo ship 1975.

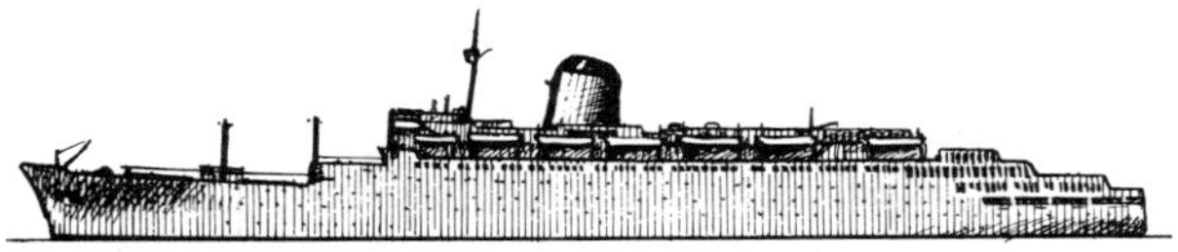

K_2MF H2
⋆**06200 LEONID SOBINOV;** Ru/Br 1954; P; 21400; 185 × 8.7 (608 × 28.7); TST; 20; ex CARMANIA 1973; ex SAXONIA 1962. Sister ⋆**06201 FEDOR SHALYAPIN** (Ru); ex FRANCONIA 1973; ex IVERNIA 1962.

K_2MFC H
06210 SWEET HOME; Pi/It 1956; PC; 5500; 120 × 5.8 (394 × 19); TSM; 18; ex CARALIS 1973.

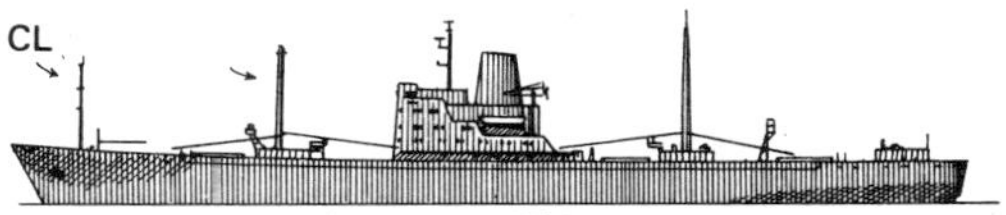

K_2MFK H
● **06220 WILD CORMORANT;** Br/FRG 1973; R; 7600; 155 × 8.8 (507 × 28.7); M; 22.5. Sisters (Br flag): **06221 WILD CURLEW 06222 CARIBBEAN UNIVERSAL** ex POLAR COSTA RICA 1980 **06223 EDINBURGH UNIVERSAL** ex POLAR HONDURAS 1980.

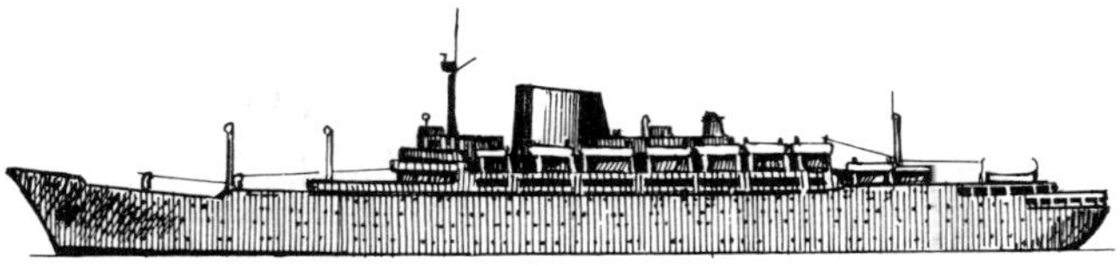

K_2MFK H
06230 OCEAN KING; Pa/It 1952; P; 27100; 207 × 8.5 (680 × 28); TSM; 21; ex GREAT SEA 1980; ex AUGUSTUS 1976.

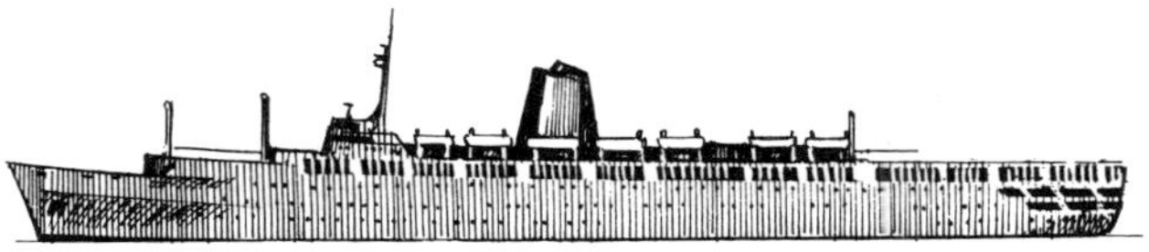

K_2MFK H
06240 CARNIVALE; Pa/Br 1956; P; 21700; 195 × 8.8 (640 × 29); TST; 21; ex QUEEN ANNA MARIA 1975; ex EMPRESS OF BRITAIN 1964.

K_2MFK H
06250 UNIVERSE; Li/US 1953; P; 14000; 172 × 8.6 (564 × 28.7); T; 20; ex UNIVERSE CAMPUS 1976; ex ATLANTIC 1971; ex BADGER MARINER 1957.

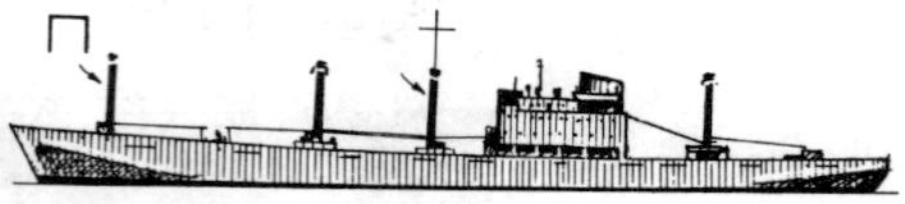

K_2MFK H
★**06260 GEORGI SAVA RAKOVSKY;** Bu/Br 1961; C; 8600; 141.8 × 8.9 (465 × 29.3); M; 14; ex WILLESDEN 1962.

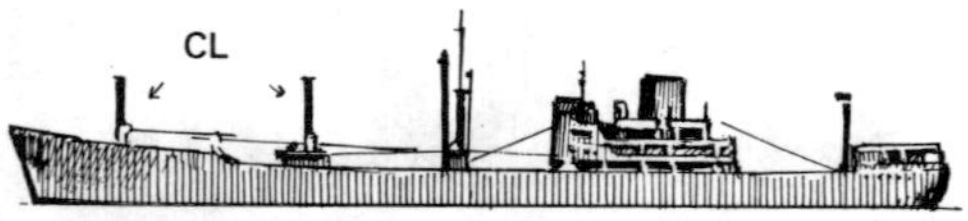

K_2MFK H1
★**06270 LUC NGAN;** Vn/Br 1963; C; 6800/9300; 153 × 7.8/8.8 (503 + 26/29); M; 17; ex AMBER STAR 1980; ex STRATHASSYNT 1978; ex TURKISTAN 1975.

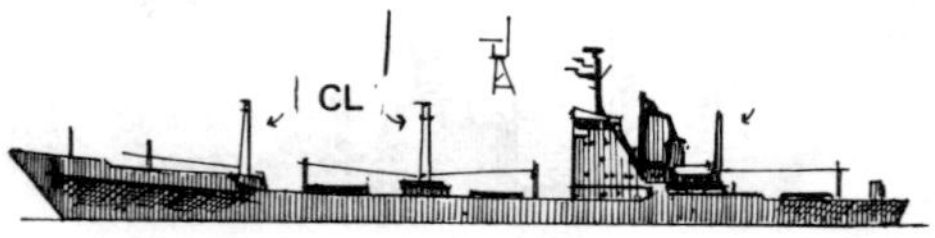

K_2MFK H1
● **06280 BREMERHAVEN;** FRG/No 1975; R; 6300/8400; 143.4 × 9.4 (470 × 31); M; 23.5. Sister (with tripod mast): **06281 BLUMENTHAL** (FRG).

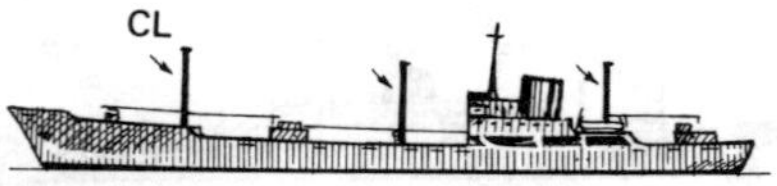

K_2MFK H1
● **06290 FRIO AEGEAN;** Pa/Br 1960; R; 3600; 120 × 6.1 (393 × 20.1); M; 18; ex CALAVITTORIA 1979; ex MENDOZA STAR 1967; ex CHATHAM 1962; Lengthened 1964. Sister **06291 CALAGARIBALDI** (Pa) ex SANTOS STAR 1966; ex CONSTABLE 1962.

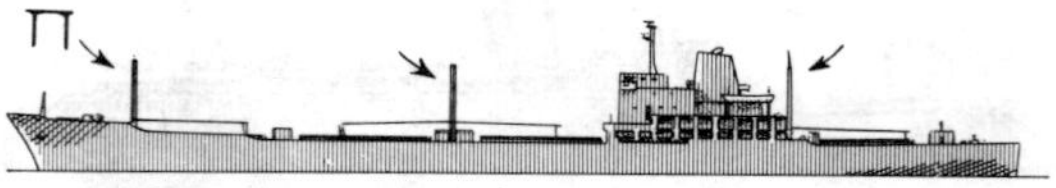

K_2MFK H1
06300 EXCELSIOR REEFER; Pa/Ja 1973; R; 10300; 163.02 × 8.99 (534.84 × 29.49); M; 20; ex RYUTU REEFER 1981. Sisters **06301 PACIFIC REEFER** (Pa) **06302 UNITY REEFER** (Pa); ex SONODA REEFER 1976 (Cu flag): ★**06303 GOLFO DE BATABANO** ★**06304 GOLFO DE GUACANAYBO** ★**06305 GOLFO DE GUANAHACABIBES** ★**06306 OCEANO ATLANTICO;** Launched as OCEAN REEFER ★**06307 OCEANO ARTICO**

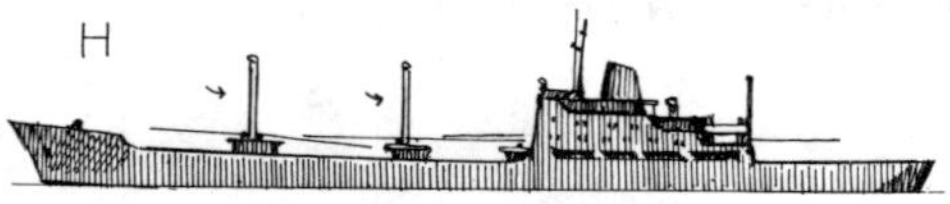

K_2MFK H1
● **06310 ORICA;** Ho/No 1965; T; 6000/8200; 148 × 8.5/9.1 (485 × 28/30); M; 20; ex AVOCADOCORE 1976. Sisters **06311 CHAITEN** (Ch) ex BANANACORE 1976 **06312 OMOA** (Ch) ex LEMONCORE 1976 **06313 OLANCHO** (Ch); ex MANGOCORE 1976 **06314 CONDORA** (Li) ex PERSIMMONCORE 1977 **06315 CONDATA** (Li) ex TANGARINECORE 1974 **06316 ROSEMARY** (Pa) ex GUAVA 1980; ex GUAVACORE 1974 **06317 ANONA** (FRG) ex ANONACORE 1974 **06317 CLEMENTINE** (FRG) **06318 PECAN** (FRG) **06319 NECTARINE** (FRG) ex NECTARINECORE 1975 **06320 PASADENA** (Pa) ex NAVELINA 1976; ex NAVELINACORE 1975 **06321 CHILLAN** (Ch) ex CEIBA 1980; ex MANDARINCORE 1976 **06322 ARIANE I** (Pa) ex SULTANA 1976 **06323 SATSUMA** (FRG) ex SATSUMACORE 1975 **06324 CHOLGUAN** (Ch) ex CORINTO 1980; ex SABRACORE 1976.

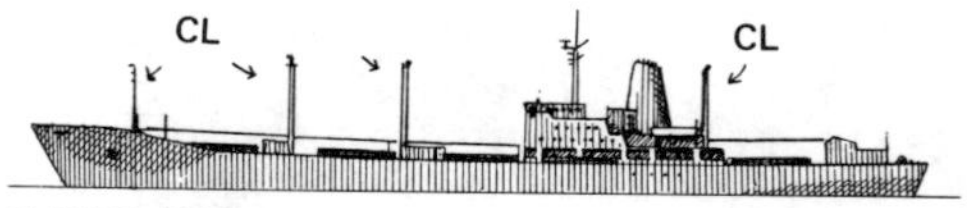

K_2MFK H1
06330 ARCTIC OCEAN; Li/De 1968; R; 6000; 145.3 × 8.8 (477 × 28.11); M; 22.5; ex ITALIAN REEFER 1978. Sisters **06331 INDIAN OCEAN** (Li) ex NIPPON REEFER 1978 **06332 PERSIAN REEFER** (De); **06333 ROMAN REEFER** (De) Similar: **06334 SAMOAN REEFER** (De) **06335 TUNISIAN REEFER** (De).

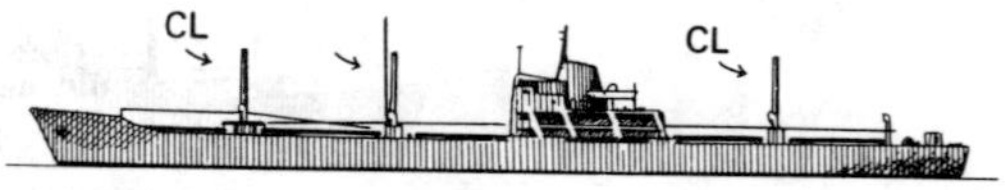

K_2MFK H1
● **06340 SKYMNOS;** Cy/Br 1962; C; 7000/9600; 151 × —/9.4 (496 × —130.5); M; 13; ex PHILIPPA 1974; ex SALAMAT 1974; ex WARKWORTH 1970.

K_2MFK H1

● **06350 LADY MADONNA.** Gr/Br 1965; R; 8000; 161.2 × 8.5 (529 × 28.3); M; 17.5; ex WINCHESTER UNIVERSAL 1980; ex WINCHESTER CASTLE 1980; ex CLAN RAMSAY 1977. Sisters **06351 BALMORAL UNIVERSAL;** (Br); ex BALMORAL CASTLE 1980; ex CLAN ROBERTSON 1976 **06352 KINPURNIE UNIVERSAL;** (Br); ex KINPURNIE CASTLE 1980; ex CLAN ROSS 1976 **06353 DOVER UNIVERSAL;** (Br); ex DOVER CASTLE 1979; ex CLAN RANALD 1977.

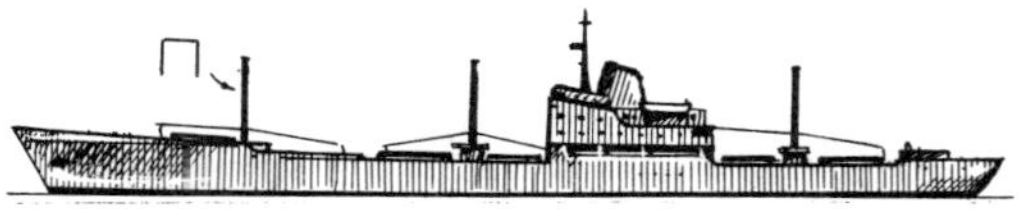

K_2MFK H1

● **06360 PASSAT UNIVERSAL.** Br/Br 1963; R; 6800; 158.4 × 7.6 (520 × 25); M; 17; ex LETABA 1979; ex S A LETABA 1977; ex LETABA 1966. Sisters (Br flag) **06361 PAMPERO UNIVERSAL** ex DRAKENSTEIN 1980; ex S.A. DRAKENSTEIN 1977; ex DRAKENSTEIN 1966 **06362 MISTRAL UNIVERSAL** ex HEXRIVIER 1979; ex S.A. HEXRIVIER 1978 **06363 PAPAGAYO UNIVERSAL** ex TZANEEN 1979; ex S.A. TZANEEN 1977; ex TZANEEN 1966 **06364 MONSONE UNIVERSAL** ex LANGKLOOF 1979; ex S.A. LANGKLOOF 1977; ex LANGKLOOF 1966 **06365 MELTEM UNIVERSAL** ex ZEBEDIELA 1980; ex S.A. ZEBEDIELIA 1977.

K_2MFK H1

06370 AL RIYADH. Si/No 1950; CP; 2800; 117 × 6.3 (380 × 20.4); M; 17; ex BENCOMO 1977.

K_2MFK H1

⋆**06380 ANTON SAEFKOW.** DDR/DDR 1965; C; 5000/7700; 142 × 7.2/8.5 (466 × 23.6/28); M. Similar (DDR flag): ⋆**06381 HEINZ KAPELLE** ⋆**06382 LIESELOTTE HERRMANN** ⋆**06383 RUDOLF BREITSCHIED** ⋆**06384 ALBIN KOBIS** ⋆**06385 BERNHARD BASTLEIN** ⋆**06386 MAX REICHPIETSCH** Possible Sisters: ⋆**06387 JOHN SCHEHR** ⋆**06388 GEORG SCHUMANN** ⋆**06389 MATHIAS THESEN**

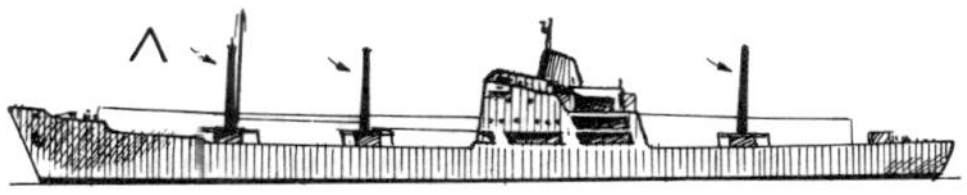

K_2MFK H1

06400 PUSSUR. Pk/Br 1965; C; 6200/8800; 152 × —/8.7 (498 × —/28.6); M; ex TEESTA.

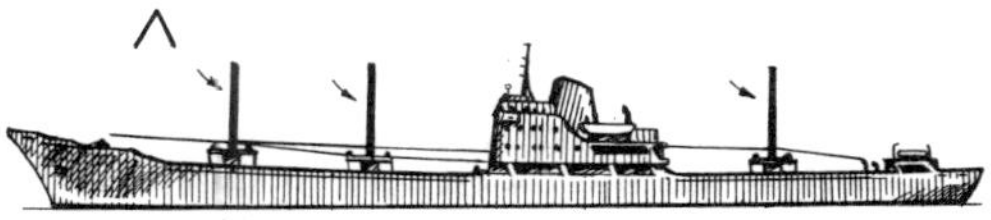

K_2MFK H1

● ⋆**06410 MARKO MARULIC.** Ys/Ys 1959; C; 6200/8900; 154 × —/9 (504 × —/29.7); M; 16. Sisters ⋆**06411 NATKO NODILO** (Ys) ⋆**06412 LUKA BOTIC** (Ys) ⋆**06413 SUBICEVAC** (Ys) ex GUNDULIC 1966 **06414 AGIOS KONSTANTINOS** (Gr) ex MURTER 1980; ex RUDER BOSKOVIC 1972.

K_2MFK H1

06420 DOLLY. Gr/Ys 1959; C; 5800/8800; 154 × —/9.1 (504 × —/29.7); M; 15.5; ex CELERINA 1976. Sisters **06421 ELEFTHERIOS T** (Gr); ex MOLESON 1974; ex GENERAL GUISAN 1970 ⋆**06422 MAOLIN** (RC); ex MINDANAO SEA 1977; ex CASTASEGNA 1973; ex CRUZEIRO DO SUL 1965.

K_2MFK H1

06430 COLUMBUS VERONICA. Pa/No 1958; CP; 7700; 139 × 8.8 (457 × 28.8); M; 14; ex EASTERN DOLPHIN 1980; ex DANISH MARINER 1977; ex ARISTONIKOS 1974; ex SUNCLIFF 1970; ex CONCORDIA SUNCLIFF 1965; ex SUNCLIFF 1964.

K_2MFK H1

06440 GOLDEN LION. Tw/Br 1956; C; 7900; 137×8.5 (449×27.7); M; 16; ex POLAMARY 1973; ex IRISH POPLAR 1972.

K_2MFK H1

06450 KYOMEI MARU. Ja/Ja 1956; C; 7600; 140×8.4 (459×27.6); M; 14.

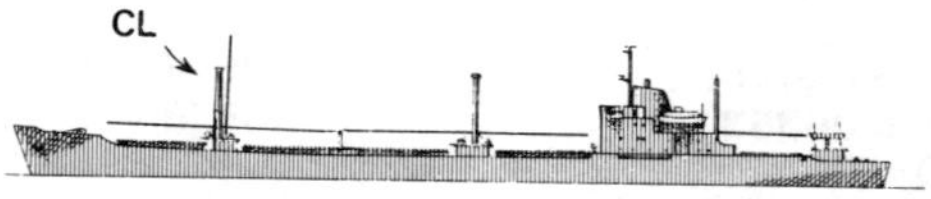

K_2MFK H1

● **06460 'SD 14' TYPE.** —/Br 1968 onwards; C; approx 9,000; 141×8.' (463×29); M; 14; Standard British 'Liberty' replacement" design. Built in UK & under licence in Ar; Bz and Gr. ships vary slightly in appearance (mast houses; taller superstructure; heavy derricks etc). (Br flag): **06461 ARDENHALL** ex DUNELMIA A76 **06462 LINDENHALL 06463 SEA MOON 06464 STRATHDEVON 06465 STRATHDIRK 06466 STRATHDOON 06467 STRATHDUNS 06468 VERGSTAR** ex MIGUEL DE LARRINAGA 1975 **06469 VERGRAY** ex RUPERT DE LARRINAGA 1975 **06470 WELSH TROUBADOUR** (Gr flag): **06480 AEGIS FAME 06481 AEGIS BANNER 06482 AEGIS TRADE 06483 LOYALTY 06484 ANNA DRACOPOULOS 06485 ATHENA** ex AKRI 1979; ex SYRIE **06486 ARIADNE 06487 ATHANASSIA 06488 MARI 06490 GIANNIS XILAS** ex COLIN **06491 DESPINA 06492 DORA PAPALIOS 06493 FROSSO K 06494 ITHAKI 06495 JADE BAY** ex RAMON DE LARRINAGA 1972 **06496 JOHN MICHALOS 06497 JUANITA HALKIAS** ex IOANNIS S 1974; ex PRODROMOS 1971 **06498 KONSTANTIS YEMELOS** ex HELLENIC RENAISSANCE **06499 MARIA K 06500 MARIA 06501 EPIMENIDIS** ex CAPE PRIDE 1980; ex TOGO 1976 **06502 ANAVISSOS** ex ARGOLIS 1980; ex JANEY 1980 **06503 IO** ex ALIOUSSA 1980; ex CARINA 1980 **06504 GOOD DOLPHIN** ex AEGIS VENTURE 1980; ex VENTURER 1977 **06505 GOOD SUN** ex MIMIS N PAPALIOS 1980 **06506 GOOD LORD** ex GEORGE N PAPALIOS 1980 **06507 GOOD PATRIOT** ex AEGIS ISLAND 1980; ex DEGEDO **06508 ALEXION HOPE** ex KONSTANTIS YEMELOS 1981 **06509 GIANNIS M** ex NEFOS II **06510 JOCASTA** ex NATAL 1977 **06511 AEGIS FREEDOM** ex NEA HELLAS 1976 **06512 NEOTIS 06513 NIKI 06514 PANAGHIS VERGOTTIS 06515 REA 06516 RINOULA 06517 ROSARIO 06518 SAN GEORGE 06519 SAMOS PROGRESS** ex SANTA AMALIA 1976 **06520 SCAPBREEZE 06521 SCAPWIND 06522 SEA TRADER 06523 SILVER CLOUD 06524 SKLERION 06525 STEPHANOS VERGOTTIS 06526 JUVENTUS** ex TANGANYIKA 1977 **06527 TAXIARCHIS 06528 TOXOTIS 06529 CAPETAN MARKOS 06530 TIGER BAY** ex HOLSTENBEK 1979; ex SANTA CLIO 1976 **06531 PHOEVOS** ex CITY OF EXETER 1979; ex STRATHDARE 1974 **06532 MAKRA** ex PATRICIA M 1980; ex PATRICIA 1979 **06533 GIORGIS** ex PORTO ALEGRE 1980; ex VERMELHA; ex BABITONGA 1974 **06534 AKARNANIA** ex LONDON BOMBARDIER **06535 KAPTAMICHALIS** ex NICOLAOS D.D. 1979 **06536 CAPE RION** ex ERAWAN **06537 AGIA SKEPI** ex CAPETAN GIANNIS. Possible Sisters: **06540 KATERINA DRACOPOULOS 06541 SEA LION** (Bz flag): **06550 L.L. PERU 06551 L.L. CHILE 06552 L.L. EQUADOR 06553 L.L. COLOMBIA 06554 LLOYD ANTUERPIA 06555 LLOYD HAMBURGO 06556 LLOYD LIVERPOOL 06557 LLOYD ROTTERDAM 06558 LLOYD BRAS 06559 LLOYD GENOVA 06560 LLOYD MARSELHA 06561 REGINA CELI 06562 SEMIRAMIS 06563 SERRA AZUL 06564 SERRA BRANCA 06565 SERRA DOURADA 06566 SERRA VERDE 06567 MONTE ALTO 06568 MONTE CRISTO 06569 MONTE PASCOAL** (Sg flag): **06580 ARACAJU 06581 CATHARINA OLDENDORFF 06582 DORTHE OLDENDORFF 06583 EIBE OLDENDORFF 06584 HILLE OLDENDORFF 06585 HINRICH OLDENDORFF 06586 IMME OLDENDORFF 06587 SANTA INES 06588 SANTA ISABELLA 06589 SANTA URSULA 06590 NEW WHALE** ex LONDON FUSILIER (Li flag): **06600 CERESIO 06601 MARSHA 06602 SACHA 06603 VIRTUS 06604 FUTURE HOPE 06605 DURBAN CARRIER** ex COSMOKRAT 1980 (Cu flag): ***06610 1 CONGRESO DEL PARTIDO** ex MAISI ***06611 MONCADA** ex BELIC ***06612 CARLOS MANUEL DE CESPEDES *06613 IGNACIO AGRAMONTE *06614 CALIXTO CARCIA** ex AJANNA 1980 (Pa flag): **06620 LADY ISABEL** ex COSMONAUT 1980 **06621 COLOSSUS** ex MERLION 1980; ex TRANSVAAL 1977; ex CLUDEN **06622 CLAUDIA KOGEL** ex SANTA MAJA 1976; ex SANTA MAYA 1971; ex SANTA MAJA **06623 JOSEF ROTH** ex SANTA VASSILIKI 1976 **06624 STAR I** ex STAR; ex COSMOSTAR 1974 **06625 THOMAS ROTH** ex SANTA KATERINA 1975 **06626 AGATE** ex WELSH TRIDENT 1978 **06627 QUARTZ** ex WELSH ENDEAVOUR 1978 **06628 SILAGA** ex ASIAN LINER 1980; ex LONDON CAVALIER 1979 **06629 NEW PANDA** ex DUNELMIA 1980 (Various flags): **06640 VARUNA KACHHAPI** (In); ex CAPETAN MANOLIS 1979 **06641 JALAPUTRA** (In); ex MOLDOVA 1976 **06642 BANGLAR BAANI** (Bh); ex INDUSTRIA 1979 ***06643 HOJI YA HENDA** (An); ex ANAX 1978 ***06644 EBO** (An); ex RIO CONQUISTA 1979 **06645 NIGER BASIN** (Ng); ex JUVENTUS 1978 **06646 NIGER VALLEY** (Ng); ex CARREL 1976 **06647 PARANA STAR** (Cy); ex HEINRICH ARNOLD SCHULTE 1977 **06648 FIRST JAY** (Cy); ex COSMOPOLITAN: ex LONDON GRENADIER **06649 GLASGOW** (Cy); ex AVALAKI 1980; ex NICOLA 1979 **06650 OCEAN ENVOY** (Pk) ***06651 RUMIJA** (Ys); ex ARRINO 1978 ***06652 MEI JIANG** (RC); ex ORMOS 1978 **06653 ANGOL** (Ch) **06654 ANAKENA** (Ch). See also under K^3MFK—MORVIKEN etc. Some of these vessels may have this sequence.

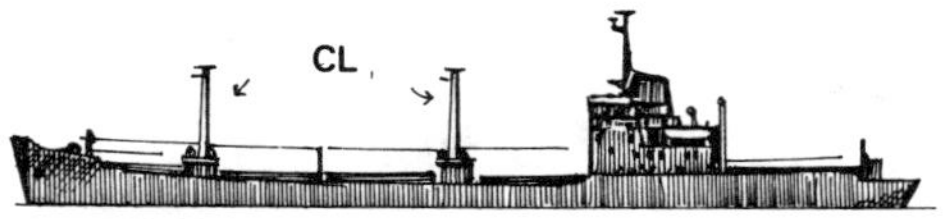

K_2MFK H1
● **06670 SALTA.** Ar/Br 1976; C; 9100; 141 × 8.9 (463 × 29); M; 15.5; Modified **'SD 14'** type. Sisters (Ar flag): **06671 JUJUY II 06672 TUCUMAN** Probable sisters (Ar. built): **06673 LIBERTADOR GENERAL JOSE DE SAN MARTIN 06674 PRIVATE RAMON CASTILLO 06675 NEUQUEN II 06676 ALMIRANTE STORNI 06677 DR. ATILIO MALVAGNI 06678 GENERAL BELGRANO.**

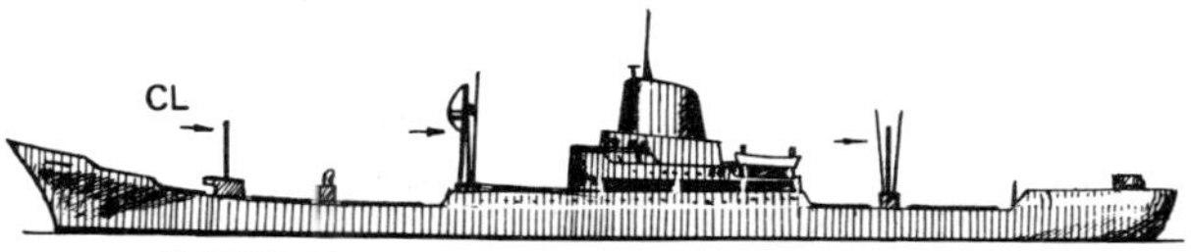

K_2MFK H123
06690 PAOLA C. It/Br 1965; R; 10500; 181 × 9.5 (593 × 3.1); TSM; 22.5; ex GOOD HOPE CASTLE 1978.
Sister:
06691 FRANCA C (It); ex SOUTHAMPTON CASTLE 1978.

K_2MFK H123
06700 CURITIBA. Bz/Br 1943; C; 1900; 80.1 × 5.4 (263 × 18); R; 10; ex SHETLAND 1959; ex ZEALAND 1954.

K_2MFK H123
06710 MALDIVE COURAGE. Mv/Br 1955; C; 5800; 137.20 × 7 (450 × 23); M; 12.5; ex OWERRI 1972.

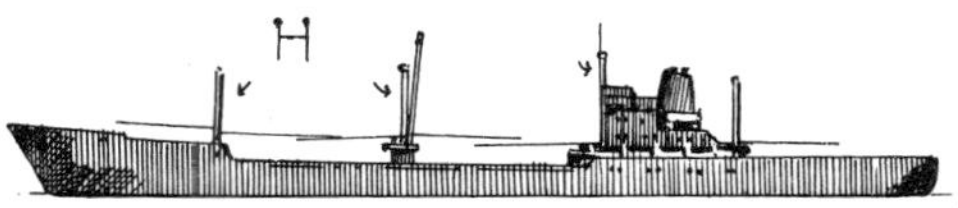

K_2MFK H13
06720 FLEVOLAND. Ne/DDR 1973; C; 6200/9800; 153 × 7.6/9.4 (501 × 25/31); M; 18.5; ex JOMARA; **'Ozean'** type.

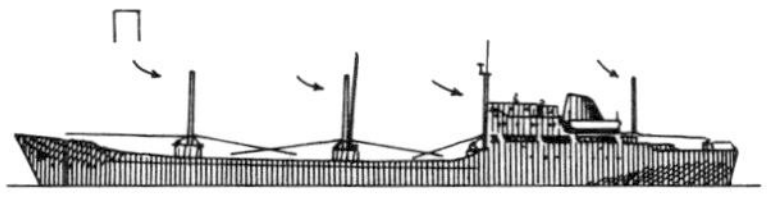

K_2MFK H13
06730 ELAZIG. Tu/No 1960; C; 3000/4800; 116.3 × 6.5/7.9 (382 × 21.5/26); M; 8; ex MAROSA 1960. Sister **06731 ARIANE** (Sg); ex HOEGH AILETTE 1972.

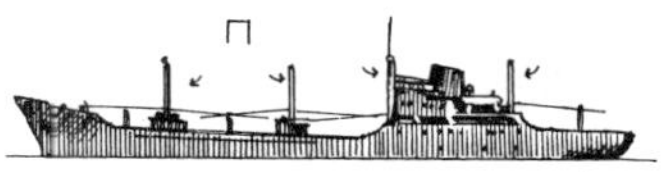

K_2MFK H13
06740 ISORA. Sp/Sp 1967; C; 1600; 96.7 × 5.7 (317 × 18.5); M; —; ex LAGO SAN MAURICIO 1975. Sister **06741 ARONA** (Sp); ex CARMEN M. PINILLOS 1975.

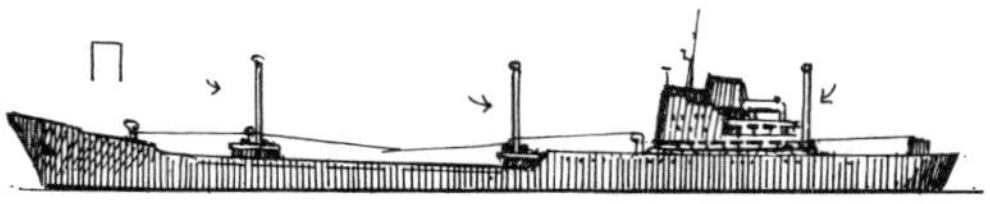

K_2MFK H13
06750 GARCIA MUNTE. Sp/Sp 1968; C; 9400; 154.5 × 8.9 (507 × 29); M; 18. Sister **06751 FRATERNITY** (Gr); ex TENACITY 1977; ex JOAQUIN PONTE NAYA 1975.

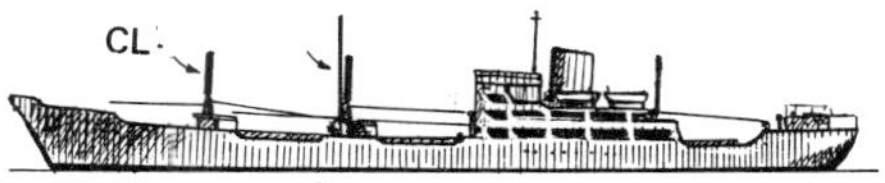

K_2MFK H13
06760 IOANNIS. Gr/Ne 1961; C; 4900/7000; 134 × 7.3/8.6 (440 × 24/28.5); M; 15.5; ex ADRIANOS 1979; ex DALESMAN 1978. Sister **06761 LINK TRUST**; ex EXPLORER 1978.

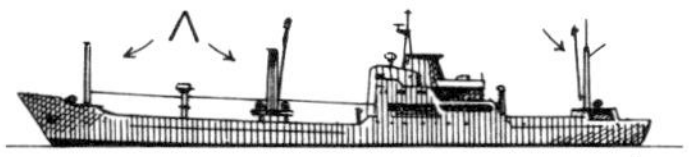

K_2MFK H13
⋆**06770 BEREZNIK.** Ru/Fi 1968; C/TC; 2700; 102 × 6.2 (335 × 20.2); M; 13.5; Ships vary in appearance. Sisters ⋆**06771 GUS-KHRUSTALNYY** ⋆**06772 KAPSUKAS** ⋆**06773 KASHINO** ⋆**06774 KARA** ⋆**06775 KALININGRAD** ⋆**06776 KAPITAN GASTELLO** ⋆**06777 KEDAYNYAY** ⋆**06778 KINGISEPP** ⋆**06779 KOPORYE** ⋆**06780 KRASNOBORSK** ⋆**06781 KOSTINO** ⋆**06782 KUZMINKI** ⋆**06783 KUPISHKIS** ⋆**06784 KUNTSEVO** ⋆**06785 LYUBAN** ⋆**06786 JOSE DIAS** ⋆**06787 TURKU** ⋆**06788 VORONEZH** ⋆**06789 SOFIA PEROVSKAYA** ⋆**06790 TSIGLOMEN** ⋆**06791 VELIKIYE USTYUG** ⋆**06792 KIKCHIK** ⋆**06793 KAMCHADAL.**

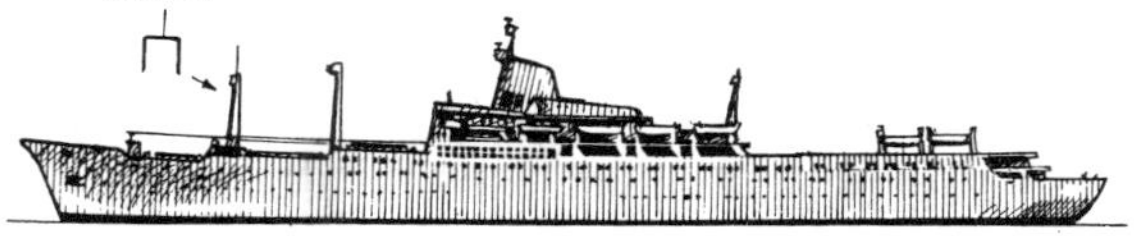

K_2MFK H2
06800 CHIDAMBARAM. In/Fr 1966; PC; 17200; 174 × 8 (571 × 26.3); TSM; 10; ex PASTEUR 1973.

K_2MFK H3

● **06810 ISLA PINTA.** Li/FRG 1972; C; 4000/6300; 131.2 × 7/8.2 (431 × 23/27); M; 18; ex BARON 1979; ex WILHELM BORNHOFFEN 1973. Sisters ⋆**06811 XIONG YUE CHENG** (RC); ex ELISABETH BORNHOFEN 1978; ex CITOS 1975; ex ELISABETH BORNHOFEN 1972 **06812 BATE BRIDGE** (Sg); ex ADVISER 1975; ex HANS BORNHOFEN 1973
06813 ISLA GENOVESA (FRG); ex MAX BORNHOFEN 1980; ex RAPIDBRIDGE 1976; ex SPECIALIST 1974; ex MAX BORNHOFEN 1973.

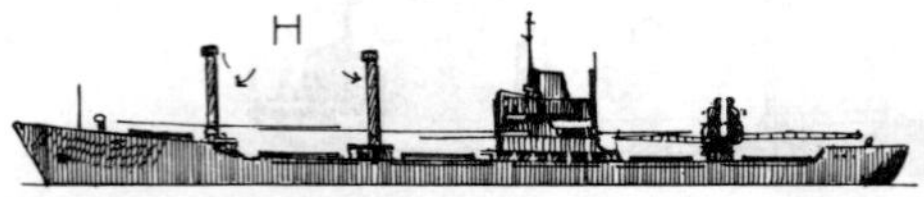

K_2MFKC_2 H13

06820 THAMESHAVEN. Ne/Br 1971; C; 9000; 143 × 8.5 (469 × 28); M; —.

K_2MFK_2 H

06830 MARDI GRAS. Pa/Br 1961; P; 18300; 198 × 8.8 (650 × 29); TST; 20; ex EMPRESS OF CANADA.

K_2MFK_2 H

06840 MONTEREY. US/US 1952/56; P; 14800; 172 × 9 (564 × 29.6); T; 20; ex FREE STATE MARINER 1956; converted from cargo ship 1956. Sister **06841 MARIPOSA** (US); ex PINE TREE MARINER 1956.

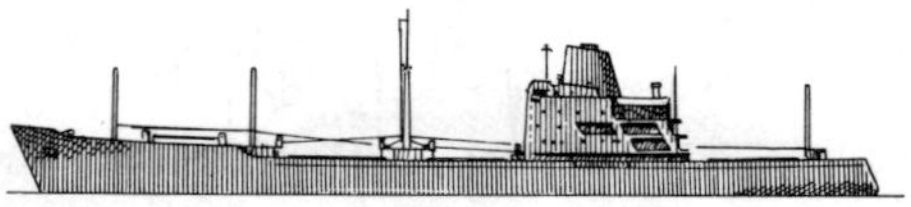

K_2MFK_2 H1

06850 KYMA. Gr/FRG 1960; R; 7800; 139.5 × 8.8 (458 × 28.9); M; 17; ex AMALRIC 1977.

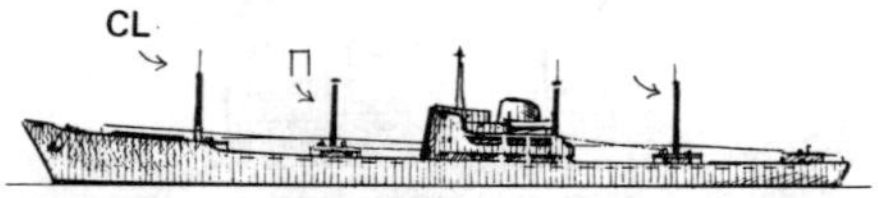

K_2MFK_2 H1

06860 MARITIME EXPLORER. Pa/Ja 1960; C; 6400; 132.4 × 7.6 (434 × 24.11); M; 15; ex NAGOASAN MARU 1971.

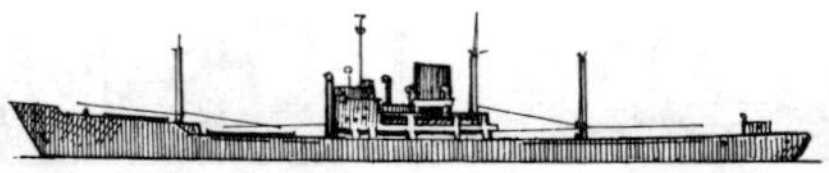

K_2MFK_2 H1

06870 RIO BRANCO. Gr/Ja 1961; C; 4100/5700; 128 × —/8 (420 × —/26.6); M; 15.25; ex KAPPA CHAMPION 1979; ex NEW GUINEA TRADER; ex WELLINGTON MARU 1971; ex SHOAN MARU 1967.

K_2MFK_2 H1

06880 PORT ALFRED. Br/Br 1961; R; 8300/10500; 152.3 × 8.7/9.5 (500 × 28.3/31.3); M; 17. Sisters **06881 MATANGI** (Br); ex PORT ST. LAWRENCE 1975.

K_2MFK_2 H1

⋆**06890 KOCHANOWSKI.** Pd/Ys 1962; CP; 5700/8200; 148.4 × 7.6/8.6 (487 × 25.1/28); M; 15.25. Sister ⋆**06891 WYSPIANSKI** (Pd).

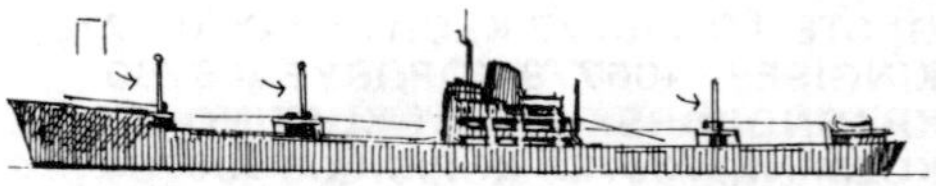

K_2MFK_2 H1

06900 THAI DEVELOPMENT. Pa/Tw 1956; CP; 6200/8700; 142 × 8.3/9.1 (467 × 27/30); M; 14; ex RANDA 1979; ex HOLTHEIM 1967.

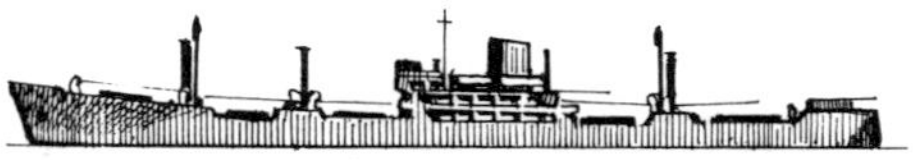

K_2MFK_2 H1
06910 GEORGY. Cy/Br 1954; C; 6000/8100; 141 × 7.8/8.5 (464 × 25.6/28); M; 13; ex GEORGE 1976; ex BARRISTER 1974. Sister **06911 AGHIA THALASSINI** (Gr); ex JOURNALIST 1973.

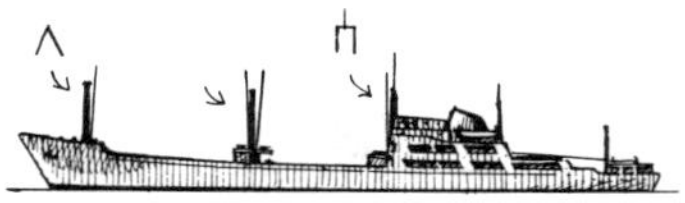

K_2MFK_2 H1
● **06930 AKRA DREPANON.** Gr/Fr 1958; C; 3500; 118 × 7.1 (386 × 23.3); M; 15.25; ex NISSOS SIFNOS 1979; ex SAINT RAPHAEL 1977.

K_2MFK_2 H1
06950 FAMILY ANGEL. Gr/Br 1963; C; 7000/9900; 154 × 8.3/9.4 (505 × 27.3/31); M; 15; ex SIAM BAY 1980; ex STRATHTRUIM 1977; ex TRENEGLOS 1974.

K_2MFK_2 H1
06970 YI. Ur/Fr 1956; CP; 8700; 145 × 9.1 (475 × 29.11); M; 15; ex PUNTA LOBOS 1980; ex GANJA 1973.

K_2MFK_2 H1
06990 CAPTAIN LYGNOS. Gr/Br 1966; C; 7400/9900; 155 × 8.3/9.4 (507 × 27.3/31); M; 16; ex DERBYSHIRE 1976. Sisters **06991 BORDAGAIN** (Li); ex WORCESTERSHIRE 1976 **06992 FURAMA** (Pa); ex WARWICKSHIRE.

K_2MFK_2 H1
● **07000 GEORGIOS.** Gr/Br 1958; C; 8100; 140 × 8.5 (460 × 28); M; 13; ex TARA SEA 1976; ex PREMIER PACIFIC 1975; ex LOMBARDY 1971; ex MANCHESTER FREIGHTER 1969; ex CAIRNFORTH 1965.

K_2MFK_2 H1
06920 ANNOOR. Pa/Br 1956; C; 8200; 145 × 8.9 (476 × 29.2); M; 15; ex ALIAKMON PIONEER 1979; ex IRISH MAPLE 1968.

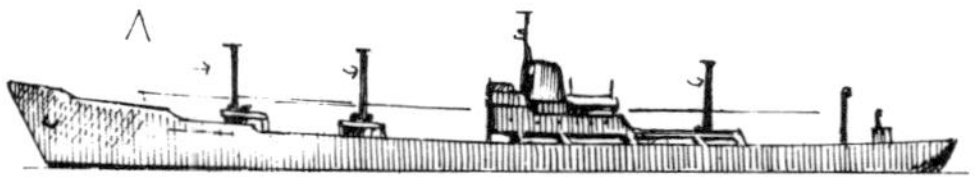

K_2MFK_2 H1
06940 EGTON. Br/Br 1962; C; 7200/10000; 155 × 8.3/9.3 (508 × 27.3/30); M; —.

K_2MFK_2 H1
● **06960 ADMINISTRATOR.** Br/Br 1958; C; 6900/8600; 149 × 8.1/9.3 (489 × 26/30.2); M; 15. Sisters **06961 HUMBER** (Br); ex AUTHOR 1978 **06962 EVLALIA** (Pa); ex PLAINSMAN 1979.

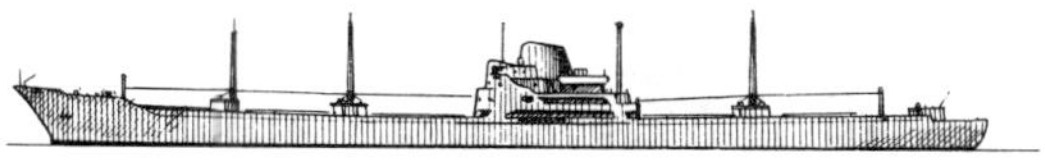

K_2MFK_2 H1
06980 VASILIS. Gr/Ne 1962; C; 10400; 158 × 9.7 (517 × 31.6); M; 14.25; ex WAARDRECHT 1976. Sisters **06981 PANAGIA ELEOUSSA** (Gr); ex MARIANA 1 1979; ex WIELDRECHT 1977 **06982 KHOOBCHAND** (Pa); ex ANDRIANA II 1979; ex WOENSDRECHT 1976.

K_2MFK_2 H1
● **07010 FAMILY UNITY.** Gr/Br 1965; C; 7600/10100; 155 × 8.4/9.5 (507 × 27.4/31); M; 15; ex ERNEBANK 1980. Sisters **07011 SHIRRABANK** (Br) **07012 SHINIAS** (Gr); ex BEECHBANK 1979 Similar: **07013 NIKITAS F.** (Gr); ex HOLLYBANK 1979 **07014 BRISTOL** (Cy); ex SPRUCEBANK 1979 **07015 GOOD LION** (Gr); ex TWEEDBANK 1979 **07016 GOOD BREEZE** (Gr); ex TAYBANK 1979.

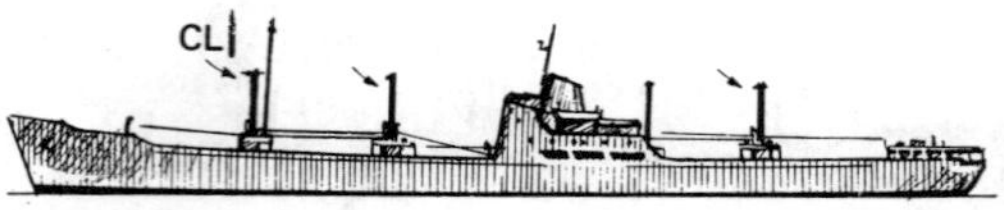

K_2MFK_2 *H1*
07020 ARGONAUT. Gr/Br 1964; C; 7600/10400; 156 × 8.5/9 (512 × 28/31); M; 14.5; ex HAZELBANK 1979. Sisters **07021 KAVO GROSSOS** (Gr); ex GOWANBANK 1979 **07022 KAVO YOSSONAS** (Gr); ex MAPLEBANK 1979 **07023 NAIRNBANK** (Br) **07024 LENDOUDIS KIKI** (Gr); ex ROWANBANK 1979 ***07025 KANG DONG** (RK); ex OCEANAUT 1980; ex IRISBANK 1979.

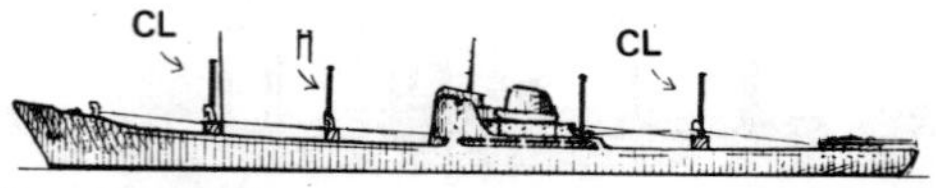

K_2MFK_2 *H1*
07030 IRINI G.F. Gr/Br 1962; C; 6200/8400; 148 × 8/8.8 (487 × 26/29); M; 14; ex INVERBANK 1978. Sisters (Gr flag): **07031 VALI PERO;** ex LAURELBANK 1979 **07032 GOOD SPIRIT;** ex OAKBANK 1978.

K_2MFK_2 *H1*
● **07040 UNION LISBON.** Pa/Ja 1960; C; 8300; 146 × 8.8 (480 × 29); M; 14.25; ex SOFIA 1980; ex CHOKAI MARU 1973. Sister **07041 PLUMA RICO** (Pa); ex SHUNKAI MARU 1977.

K_2MFK_2 *H1*
07050 GENIE. Gr/Br 1959; C; 7300/9600; 155 × —/9.2 (509 × —/30.4); M; 15; ex MISS CHANDRIS 1969.

K_2MFK_2 *H1*
07060 CONCORDIA LAGO. No/Br 1961; CP; 5000; 134.1 × 7.4 (440 × 24.5); M; 17; ex MONTROSE 1963.

K_2MFK_2 *H1*
07070 MALDIVE IMAGE. Mv/Br 1958; C; 6100/8500; 145 × —/9.4 (476 × —/31); M; 14; ex CARON P.E. 1979; ex RUPSA 1978; ex LA FALDA 1964; ex MONTCALM.

K_2MFK_2 *H1*
***07080 HUANGSHI.** RC/Br 1955; C; 6300; 145 × 8.2 (476 × 26.11); M; 13.5; ex SALINA 1966; ex LA ORILLA 1961.

K_2MFK_2 *H1*
07090 FORTUNE. Pa/Ja 1959; C; 6200/8700; 147 × —/8.8 (483 × —/29); M; 14; ex IOANNIS A 1980; ex TOWA MARU 1971.

K_2MFK_2 *H1*
***07100 HYOK SIN.** RK/Ja 1958; C; 8400; 149.59 × 8.79 (490.78 × 28.84); M; 13.5; ex KYOKUYO MARU 1974.

K_2MFK_2 *H1*
07110 KAADERSHAIKH. Cy/Br 1960; C; 6900/9800; 153 × 8.6/9.3 (501 × 28/30.3); M; 14.5; ex KONGSFJORD 1978; ex VISTAFJORD 1972.

K_2MFK_2 *H1*
07120 HWA GEK. Sg/Br 1961; CP; 7000/9200; 152 × —/19 (499 × —/29.7); M; 15; ex LONDONER 1971.

K_2MFK_2 *H12*
● **07130 TAMARA.** Gr/Br 1960; CP; 4700; 113.4 × 7.3 (501 × 28/30.3); M; 14.5; ex LANCASTRIAN PRINCE 1971.

K_2MFK_2 *H12*
07140 SEAMASTER II. PA/FRG 1958; C; 6700/9500; 155.9 × 8.3/9 (511 × 27.2/29.6); M; 13.5; ex MONSOON CURRENT 1975; ex OSSIAN 1971. Similar: **07141 KONISTRA** (Pa); ex METHAN 1969.

K_2MFK_2 H123
07150 CHI LEE. Pa/Ja 1953; C; 7000; 142.9×8.2 (469×27); M; 15; ex KEE LEE 1977; ex NIKKEI MARU 1971.

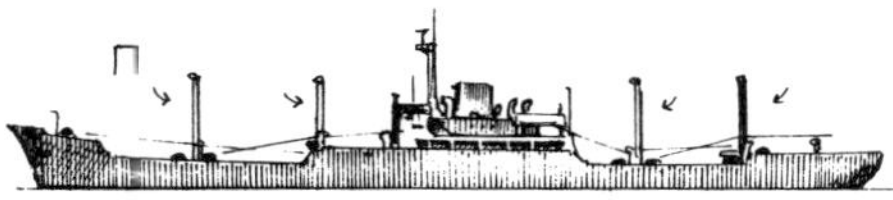

K_2MFK_2 H123
07160 SEA ROSE. Pa/Ja 1956; C; 6300; 137.6×8.2 (451×26.10); M; 14; ex MADRAS MARU 1975.

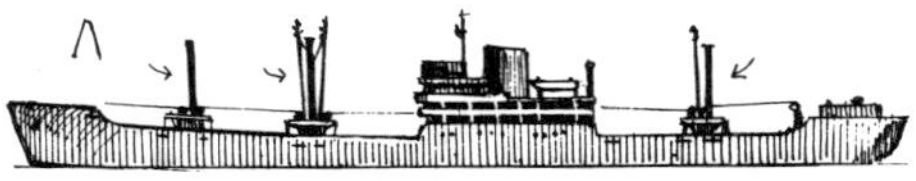

K_2MFK_2 H123
● **07170 PANSEPTOS.** Gr/Br 1964; C; 7500; 141.7×7.8 (465×15.5); M; 16; ex FREETOWN1978. Sisters **07171 MAHAPRIYA** (In); ex FIAN 1975 **07172 CAM AYOUS** (Cn); ex FORCADAS 1976 **07173 CAM AZOBE** (Cn); ex FOULANI 1976.

K_2MFK_2 H123
07180 ALEXANDERS TRUST. Gr/Br 1962; C; 7700 141.7×7.8 (465×15.5); M; 16; ex LEONOR MARIA 1980; ex FALABA 1978. Sister **07181 ALEXANDERS FAITH** (Gr); ex MAGDA JOSEFINA 1980; ex FOURAH BAY 1978.

K_2MFK_2 H123
● **07190 GOLDBEACH.** Cy/Br 1956; C; 5500; 137.2×7 (450×23); M; 12.5; ex MIMI METHENTIS 1976; ex OTI 1972.

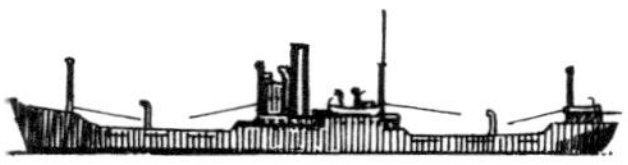

K_2MFK_2 H123
07200 EFSTATHIOS. Le/Br 1943; C; 2900; 100×6.3 (328×20.6); R; 9; ex WINGROVE 1961; ex MOYLE 1960; ex ICELAND 1956.

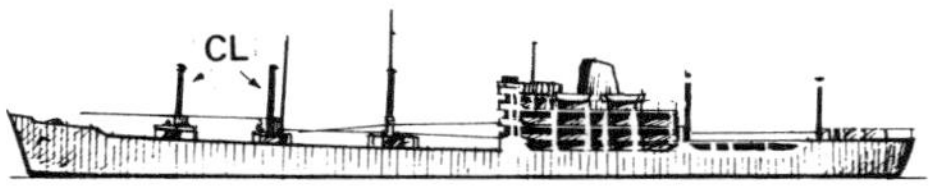

K_2MFK_2 H13
07210 EVANGELIA S. Gr/Br 1963; C; 6200/9200; 146.6×7.6/8.6 (481×25/28); M; 16; ex AGLAOS 1980; ex MAHOUT 1978. Sister **07211 MARKHOR** (Br).

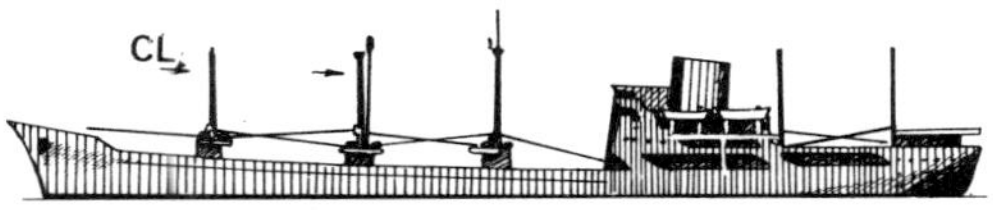

K_2MFK_2 H13
07220 RUBENS. Be/Br 1961; C; 7700/10300; 155.7×8.5/9.1 (511×28/30); M; 18; ex CITY OF CANTERBURY 1975; ex CAP CLEVELAND 1973; ex CITY OF ADELAIDE 1972.

K_2MFK_2 H13
● **07230 ARGIRO.** Gr/Br 1959; C; 7100/8800; 149.6×8.3/9.2 (491×27.3/30.3); M; 15.5, ex SHROPSHIRE 1972. Sisters **07231 KOTA MEWAH** (Sg); ex MOZAMBIQUE 1976; ex CHESHIRE 1968 **07232 BORDABEKOA** (Li); ex YORKSHIRE 1971; ex EASTERN PRINCESS 1964; ex YORKSHIRE 1963.

K_2MFK_2 H13
07240 EMMANUEL MARCOU. Gr/Sw 1960; C; 6100/8500; 148.3×—/9.1 (487×—/30); M; 13.75; ex WILLOWPOOL 1967.

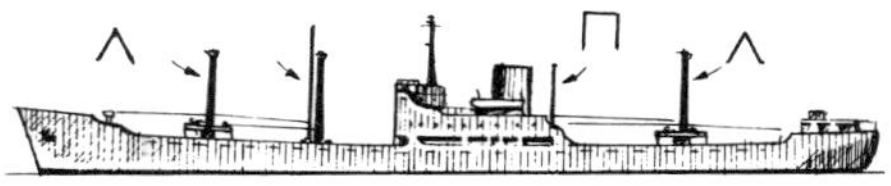

K_2MFK_2 H13
● **07250 ROGERS TRADER.** Br/HONG KONG 1962; CP; 5800; 128.7×7.5 (422×24.6); M; 11.5; ex KWEILIN 1974. Possibly Similar (Br flag):
07251 STRAITS STAR 07252 KWANTUNG; (could be MKFKM as "FORTUNE VICTORY").

K_2MFK_2 *H13*

● **07260 VEEJUMBO.** Ho/Br 1959; C; 5600/8200; 140.2×8.1/8.3 (460×26.6/27.3); M; 14; ex DEGEMA 1979. Sisters **07261 AGHIOS GEORGIOS III** (Gr); ex SAN GEORGIO III 1980; ex DEIDO 1979 **07262 GULF EAGLE** (Br); ex DIXCOVE 1978 **07263 FUMURRA** (Br); ex DUMURRA 1980 **07264 CLARE** (Gr); ex DUNKWA 1980 Similar (mast from funnel): **07265 LONE EAGLE** (Li); ex DARU 1978.

K_2MFK_2 *H13*

07270 EVOICOS GULF. Gr/Br 1963; C; 6300/8500; 147.3×8/8.9 (483×26/29); M; 15; ex LOSSIEBANK 1979; KP abreast funnel.

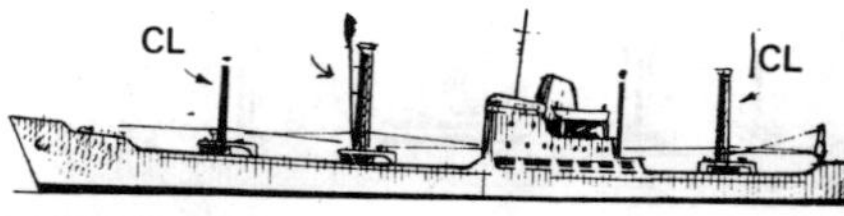

K_2MFK_2C *H13*

● **07280 GOLD BRIDGE.** Li/Fr 1964; C; 4800/7100; 138.6×7.4/8.6 (455×24.4/28); M; 17.5; ex MAZAL 1974. Sisters (Li flag): **07281 GOLD LEAF;** ex QESHET 1973 **07282 GOLD BEETLE;** ex NOGAH 1974.

K_2MFK_3 *H1*

07290 PARAMOUNT. Pa/Pd 1961; C; 6400; 153.7×8.4 (504×27.6); M; 16.5; ex LUCHON 1980; ex RHIN 1966; **'B 54'** type. Sister **07291 MARITIME OPTIMUM** (Pa) ex ABLON 1979; ex RHONE 1967; ex FRANCOIS L.D. 1961; ex CHARLES L.D Similar: ⋆**07292 LELEWEL** (Pd).

K_2MFK_3 *H1*

07300 GAYTA. Gh/FRG 1952; C; 1900/3000; 91×—/5.7 (299×—/19); M; 13; ex STELIOS MATSAS 1976; ex ANASTASSIA 1973; ex FREDRIK RAGNE 1968; ex FREDBORG 1961.

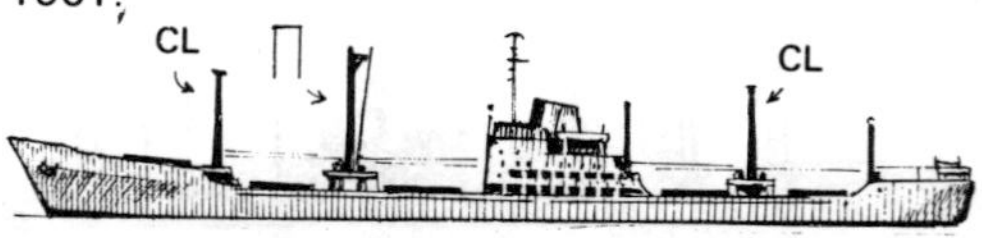

K_2MFK_3 *H13*

⋆**07310 MEISHAN.** Rc/FRG 1959; CP; 9800; 154×8.8 (505×29.1); M; 17; ex HAVSUL 1972.

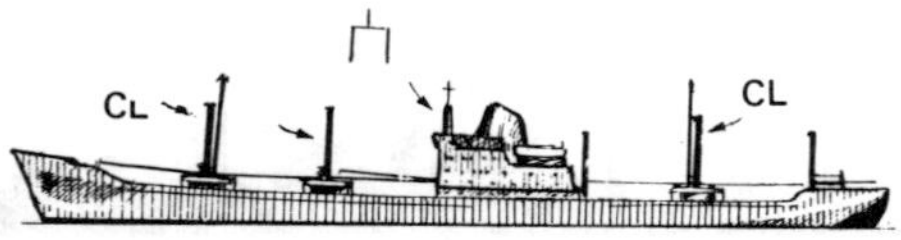

K_2MFK_3 *H13*

07320 DIMITRIOS A. Gr/Br 1963; C; 5400/7800; 141×—/8.7 (462×—/26.11); M; 16; ex MAURICE DELMAS 1978. Sister **07321 ALHAMBRA** (Gr) ex HENRI DELMAS 1977.

K_2MFK_3 *H13*

07330 SAFINA-E-HAIDER. Pk/Br 1963; CP; 6700/8900; 142×8.4/9.4 (465×27/30.5); M; —; ex LANCASHIRE 1970.

K_2MFK_3 *H13*

07340 CASTOR. Cy/Br 1963; C; 6400/8700; 147×8/8.9 (483×26/29); M; 15; ex ROYBANK 1979. Sister **07341 GOLDEN NIGERIA** (Pa) ex WEYBANK 1979.

K_2MFK_3 *H13*

07350 QUESTNORTH. Br/Br 1962 C; 6200/8600; 149×8/9 (489×26/29); M; 15; ex VEESKY 1980; ex FORRESBANK 1978.

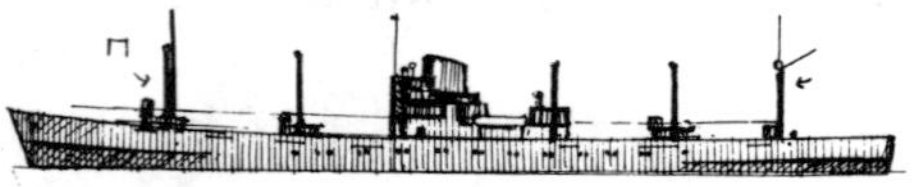

K_2MFK_2M *H*

07360 KOTA SUBUR. Sg/Br 1950; C; 5400/9000; 145×7.8/8.3 (475×25/27.3); M; 15; ex WENCHOW 1975; ex WENDOVER 1965.

K_2MFKM *H*

● **07370 CARTAGENA DE INDIAS.** Co/FRG 1958; CP; 5300; 145×7.2 (475×23.7); M; 17. Sisters (Co flag): **07371 CIUDAD DE BARRANQUILLA 07372 CIUDAD DE TUNYA 07373 MANUEL MEJIA.**

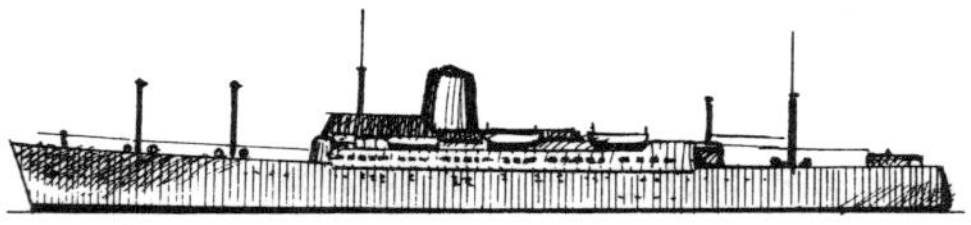

K_2MFKM H
07380 CRISTOBAL. US/US 1939; PC; 10200; 150.4 × 8 (493 × 26); TST; 17.5.

K_2MFKM H1
● **07390 REUNION.** Sg/Au 1953; C; 3700; 123.6 × 6.9 (406 × 22.8); M; 12; ex COLIN FOUR 1976; ex BOONAROO 1970. Sister **07391 TAIPING** (Sg) ex HANGCHOW 1977; ex BARALGA 1972.

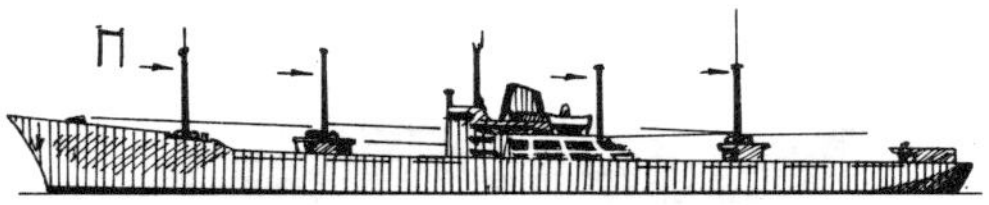

K_2MFKM H1
07400 AEGEAN CARRER. Pa/Ja 1962; C; 8600; 154 × 9.2 (505 × 30.4); M; 17; ex SADOHARU MARU 1976. Similar: **07401 SMINARCHOS FRANGISTAS** (Gr) ex YAMATOSHI MARU.

K_2MFKM H123
07410 CHEER SONG. Pa/Ja 1952; C; 7200; 142 × 8.3 (466 × 27.4); M; 15; ex CHIEH PENG; ex PORT ELIZABETH MARU 1972; ex KAMOGAWA MARU 1969.

K_2MFKM H13
07420 PINYA. Bm/Ja 1963; C; 5200/7400; 137.9 × 7.3/8.4 (452 × 23.6/27.5); M; 15. Sister **07421 MERGUI** (Bm).

K_2MFKM H13
● **07430 ARGIRO.** Gr/Br 1959; C; 7100/8800; 149.6 × 8.3/9.2 (491 × 27.3/30.3); M; 15.5; ex SHROPSHIRE 1972. Sisters **07431 KOTA MEWAH** (Sg) ex MOZAMBIQUE 1976; ex CHESHIRE 1968 **07432 BORDABEKOA** (Li) ex YORKSHIRE 1971; ex EASTERN PRINCESS 1964; ex YORKSHIRE 1963.

K_2MFKMK H1
07440 IRAN SEEYAM. Ir/Po 1974; C; 9200; 153 × 9.1 (501 × 30); M; 18; ex ARYA SUN 1980. Sisters ⋆**07441 MAJOR SUCHARSKI** (Pd) ⋆**07442 MARIAN BUCZEK** (Pd) **07443 IRAN SALAM** (Ir) ex IRAN ZAR 1980; ex ARYA ZAR 1980 **07444 IRAN KALAM** (Ir) ex IRAN SEEM 1980; ex ARYA SEEM 1980.

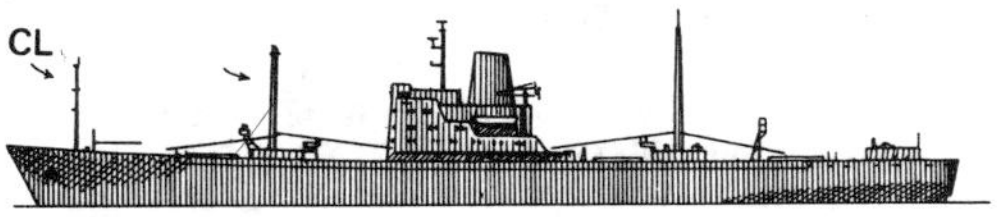

K_2MFM H
● **07450 WILD CORMORANT.** Br/FRG 1973; R; 7600; 154.5 × 8.7 (507 × 28,7); M; 22.5. Sisters (Br flag): **07451 WILD CURLEW 07452 EDINBURGH UNIVERSAL** ex POLAR HONDURAS 1980 **07453 CARIBBEAN UNIVERSAL** ex POLAR COSTA RICA 1980.

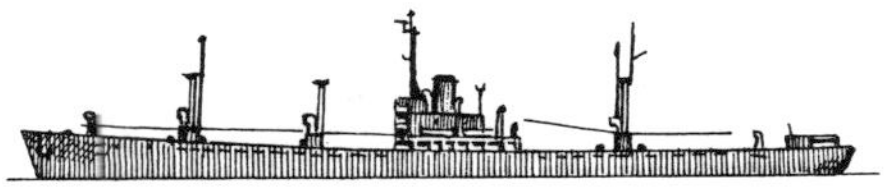

K_2MFM H
⋆**07460 ASKOLD.** Ru/US 1943; C; 7200; 134.6 × 8.4 (443 × 27.8); R; 10.5; ex HENRY L. PITTOCK; **'LIBERTY'** type.

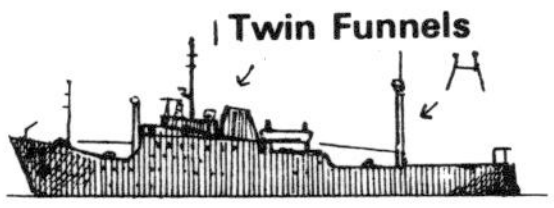

K_2MFM H
⋆**07470 'ATLANTIK'** type. Ru/DDR —; FT; 2200 approx; 82 × 5.3; 269 × 17.6; M; 14.25; Many **'ATLANTIK'** type ships may have this appearance. (see others under KMFM). Sisters ⋆**07471 BAROGRAF** ⋆**07472 DIPLOT** ⋆**07473 GEROI ADZHIMUSHKAYA** ⋆**07474 KURSOGRAF** ⋆**07475 MAKELIS BUKA** ⋆**07476 RODONIT** ⋆**07477 SERDOLIK.**

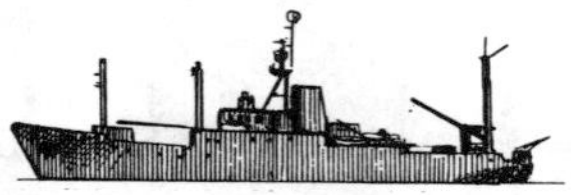

K_2MFM H
07480 SCOMBRUS. FRG/FRG 1975; FT; 2000; 81 × 5.8 (266 × 19); M; 16.

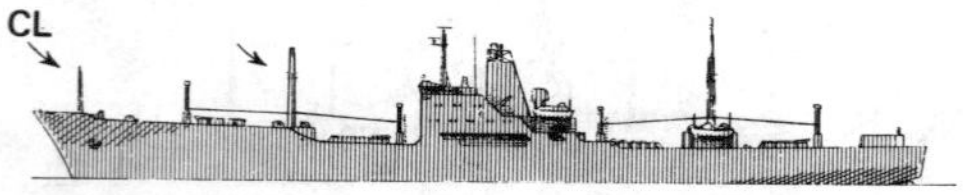

K_2MFM H1
● **07500 RAGNI BERG.** No/No 1978; R; 7000; 144.45 × 9.01 (473.92 × 29.56); M; 21.9; **"DRAMMEN"** type Sister **07501 ELISABETH BERG** (No) Similar: **07502 RIO CHONE** (Ec) **07503 RIO ESMERALDAS** (Ec) **07504 RIO BABAHOYA** (Ec).

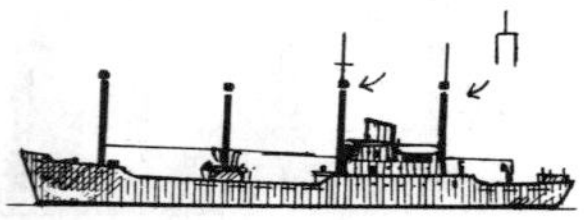

K_2MFM H12
● **07530 SEA GLORY.** Pa/Ne 1950; C; 1900; 90.8 × 4.4 (298 × 14.5); M; 10.5; ex EASTERN UNION 1980; ex SEA LUCK 1972; ex EASTERN LUCK 1970; ex SABANG 1968. Sisters **07531 EASTERN FORTUNE** (Pa) ex SEA UNITY 1972; ex EASTERN UNITY 1970; ex SAMBAS 1968 **07532 KOTA BINTANG** (Sg) ex SANANA 1968.

K_2MFM H13
⋆**07600 LENALES.** Ru/Fi 1964; C/TC; 2900; 102 × 6.2 (334 × 20.4); M; 13.75; May be other vessels of the **'BEREZNIK'** class with this appearance—see previous entry.

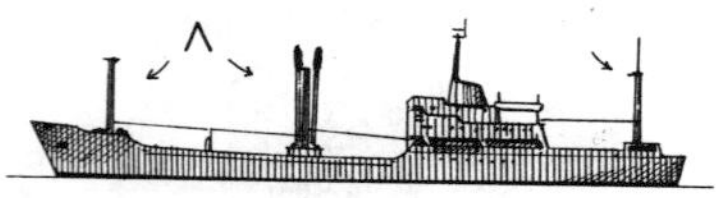

K_2MFM H13
⋆**07610 LYONYA GOLIKOV** Ru/DDR 1968; C; 3600; 105.7 × 6.8 (347 × 22.4); M; 13.75; May be other ships of this class with this sequence. See 'SHURA KOBER' class under *KM_2FM*.

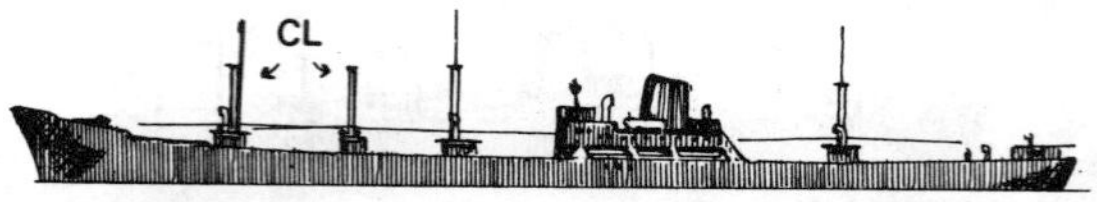

K_2MFM H1
● **07490 CHAR CHUN.** Pa/Br 1959; C; 7200/10300; 170.2 × —/9 (559 × —/29.4); M; 16.5; ex NICETO DE LARRINAGA 1972; Lengthened 1964.

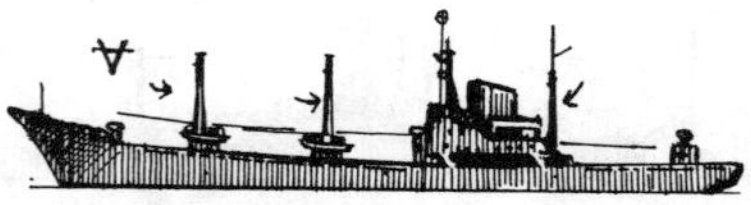

K_2MFM H1
● **07510 CHRISTL HERMANN.** Pa/Br 1967; C; 2600/4400; 114 × 6.5/7.4 (374 × 21.4/24.3); M; 15.25; ex DUBURG 1974. Sisters (Li flag): **07511 TOPAZ** ex TROYBURG 1973 **07512 TOURMALIN** ex GLUCKSBURG 1973.

K_2MFM H1
07520 MARION DUFRESNE. Fr/Fr 1973; RS/C/P; 6600; 112.1 × 6.3 (368 × 20.8); M; 15.

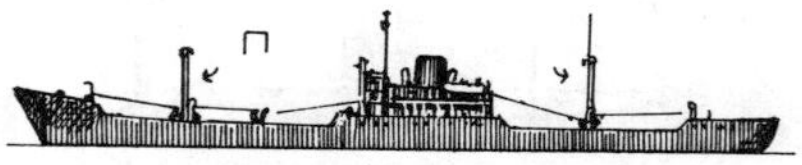

K_2MFM H123
● **07540 PHAEDON II.** Gr/Ja 1958; C; 4900; 119.4 × 7.5 (392 × 24.8); M; 12; ex NAGAURA MARU 1975. Sister **07541 PEMA** (Gr) ex DRAGON I 1975; ex ANAKAN MARU 1973.

K_2MFM H13
⋆**07550 'BEREZNIK'** class. Ru/Fi 1968; C/TC; 2700; 102 × 6.2 (334 × 20.4); M; 13.5; Ships vary. Radar mast often from bridge top. Similar (Ru flag): ⋆**07551 CHAZHMA** ⋆**07552 BLAGOVESHCHENSK** ⋆**07553 ILYINSK** ⋆**07554 ILICHOVO** ⋆**07555 KAMCHADAL** ⋆**07556 TOBOL** ⋆**07557 YANTARNYY** ⋆**07558 KRETINGA** ⋆**07559 KOZYREVSK** ⋆**07560 LOMONOSOVO** ⋆**07561 PRAVDA** ⋆**07562 MIRNYY** ⋆**07563 PALANA** ⋆**07564 VAGA** ⋆**07565 KHARLOV** ⋆**07566 KRASNOYARSK** ⋆**07567 LIGOVO** ⋆**07568 KAMCHATSKIY** ⋆**07569 KOMSOMOLETS** ⋆**07570 TURKU** ⋆**07571 LYUBAN** ⋆**07572 KINGISEPP** ⋆**07573 KRANSNOBORSK** ⋆**07574 VELIKIY USTYUG** ⋆**07575 TSIGLOMEN** ⋆**07576 KUPISHKIS** ⋆**07577 KALININGRAD** ⋆**07578 KUZMINKI** ⋆**07579 KOSTINO** ⋆**07580 KARA** ⋆**07581 GUS-KHRUSTALNYY** ⋆**07582 KOPORYE** ⋆**07583 KASHINO** ⋆**07584 KIKHCHIK** ⋆**07585 KAPITAN GASTELLO**⋆**07586 SOFIA PEROVSKAYA** ⋆**07587 JOSE DIAS** ⋆**07588 VORONEZH** ⋆**07589 KUNTSEVO** ⋆**07590 KIMRY** ⋆**07591 KEDAYNYAY** ⋆**07592 KAPSUKAS** ⋆**07592 TAMPERE** ⋆**07593 SHUSENSKOYE.**

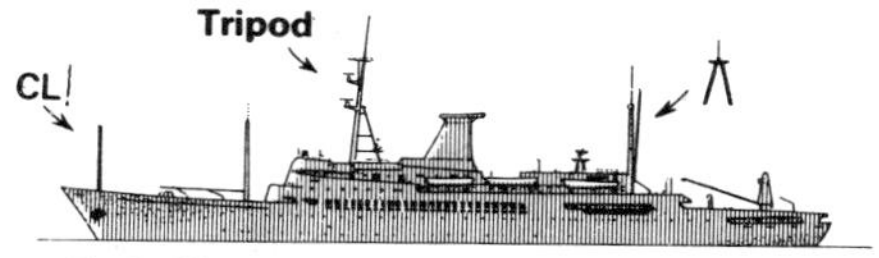

K_2*MFMC H*
⋆07620 AKADEMIK KURCHATOV. Ru/DDR 1966; RS; 5500; 123.88 × 6.06 (406.43 × 19.88); TSM; 18.25. Sister **⋆07621 AKADEMIK VERNADSKIY** (Ru) Similar (funnel top differs): **⋆07622 DMITRIY MENDELEYEV** (Ru) (may be spelt **DMITRIY MENDELEEV**).

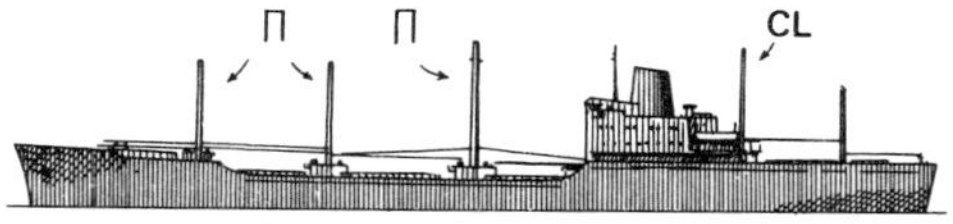

K_2*MFMK H13*
07650 BALINTAWAK. Pa/FRG 1969; C; 6200/10200; 148.6 × 8/9.4 (488 × 26.3/31); M; 19; ex ODER 1978. Sister **07651 ANTIPOLO** (Li) ex SAAR 1978.

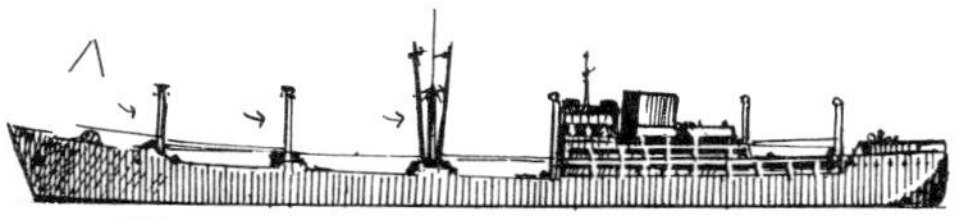

K_2*MKFK*$_2$ *H13*
07670 GULF HERON. Br/Br 1959; C; 7000/9000; 150.58 × —/8.86; M; 15; ex CLAN MACINDOE 1979. Sister **07671 GOLDEN CITY** (Sg) ex CLAN MACILWRAITH 1978.

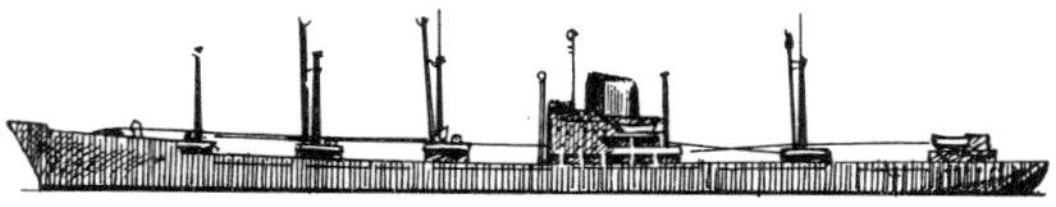

K_2*MKFKM H1*
07680 NEDLLOYD SEINE. Ne/Ne 1961; C; 8200; 166 × 8.8 (545 × 29); M; 18; ex SEINE LLOYD 1978. Sisters (Ne flag): **07681 NEDLLOYD SCHELDE** ex SCHELDE LLOYD 1978 **07682 NEDLLOYD SCHIE** ex SCHIE LLOYD 1978 **07683 NEDLLOYD MAIN** ex MAIN LLOYD 1978 **07684 NEDLLOYD MADISON** ex MADISON LLOYD 1978.

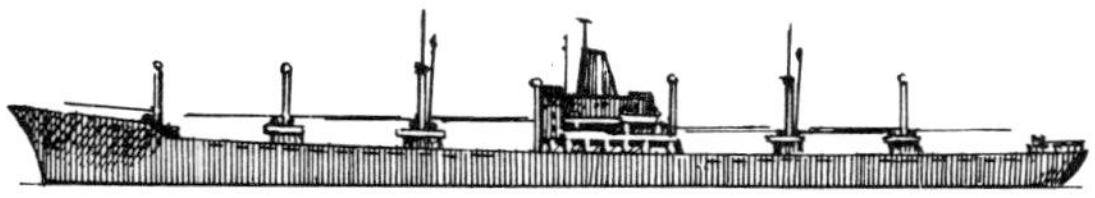

K_2*MKFKMK H1*
07710 'MARINER' class. US/US 1953; C; 9100/12500; 172 × —/9.6 (564 × —/31.7); T; 20. Similar (US flag): **07711 JOHN PENN** ex AMERICA BEAR 1973; ex JAPAN BEAR 1972; ex GRAND CANYON MARINER **07712 JOHN B WATERMAN** ex WASHINGTON BEAR 1972; ex TAR HEAL MARINER 1960 **07713 IBERVILLE** ex HONGKONG BEAR 1972; ex KEYSTONE MARINER 1960.

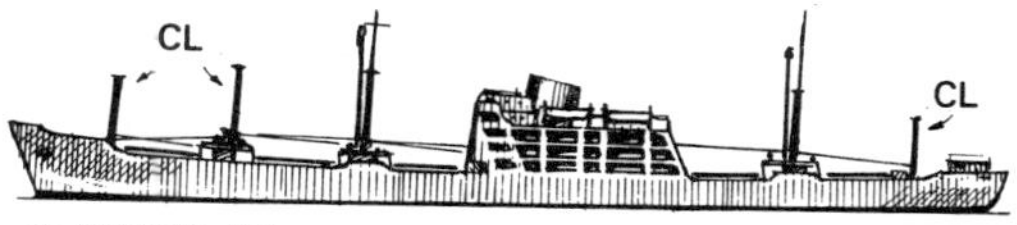

K_2*MFMK H1*
07630 SILVER RAYS. Pa/Br 1959; C; 7500/9400; 158.4 × 8/8.7 (620 × 26.3/28.9); M; 17; ex SEA FORTUNE 1980; ex ROTHERWICK CASTLE 1975.

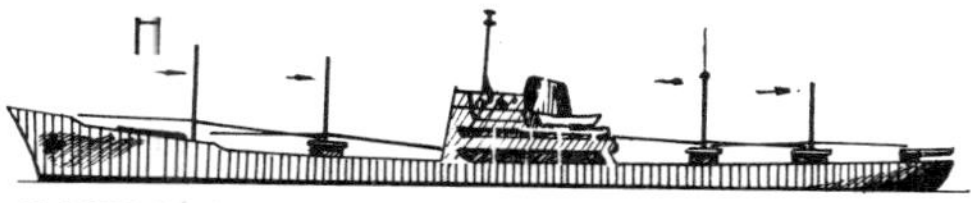

K_2*MFMK H1*
07640 EVER HARMONY. Pa/Ja 1962; C; 8200; 150 × 8.6 (492 × 28.3); M; 18; ex KASUGASAN MARU 1975.

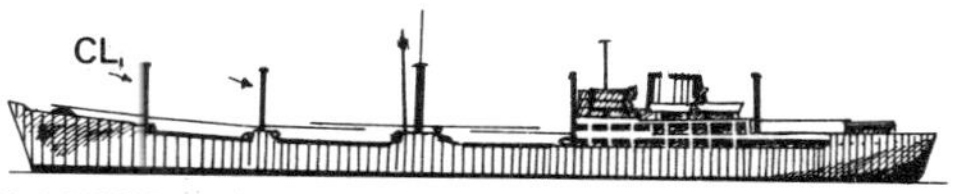

K_2*MKFK H13*
● **07660 CLAN GRAHAM.** Br/Br 1962; C; 6100/9000; 151.4 × 8.6 (497 × 28.2); M; 16. Sisters **07661 IRAN HEMMET** (Ir) ex ARYA MAN 1980; ex CLAN FORBES 1968 **07662 IRAN OKHUVAT** (Ir) ex ARYA SEP 1980; ex CLAN FARQUHARSON 1968 **07663 JALAPANKHI** (In) ex CLAN FERGUSSON 1965 **⋆07664 LU CHUN** (RC) ex ATLANTIC OCEAN 1975; ex ARYA FAR 1971; ex CLAN FINLAY 1968 **07665 NEW EAGLE** (Pa) ex CLAN MACNAB 1980 **07666 LICHIANG** (Sg) ex CLAN MACNAIR 1980 **07667 ENRIQUETA** (Pa) ex CLAN GRANT 1980.

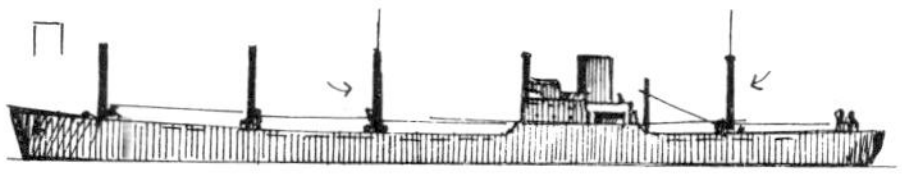

K_2*MKFKM H2*
07690 TONG JIT. Pa/US 1939; C; 6300; 139.9 × 8.2 (459 × 27); M; 15.5; ex TJIPANAS 1967; ex MORMACDOVE; ex ALCHIBA; ex MORMACDOVE; **"C 2"** type.

K_2*MKFKMK H1*
● **07700 EURYLOCHUS.** Pa/FRG 1960; C; 9500; 162.6 × 8 (534 × 26.3); T; 17.

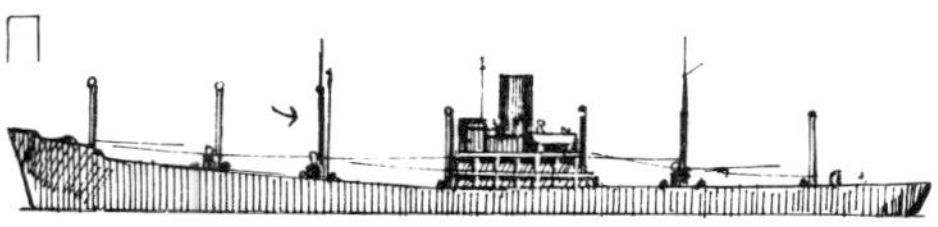

K_2*MKFKMK H1*
07720 'C 3' type. —/US 1943; CP; 7900; 150 × 9.1 (492 × 29.5); T; 16.5; May still be vessels of this type in service or in reserve.

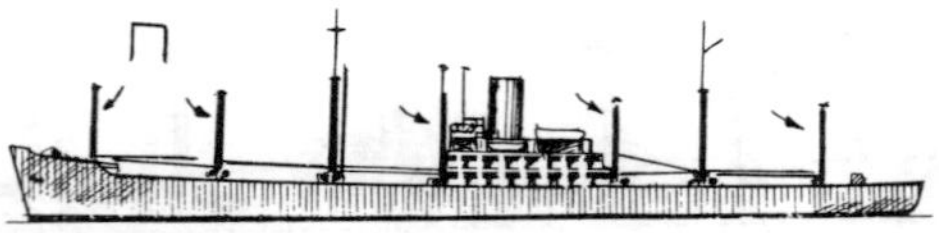

$K_2MKFKMK$ H1
07730 'C 3' type. —/US 1943; CP; 7900; 150×9.1 (492×29.5); T; 16.5; May still be some vessels of this type in service or in reserve.

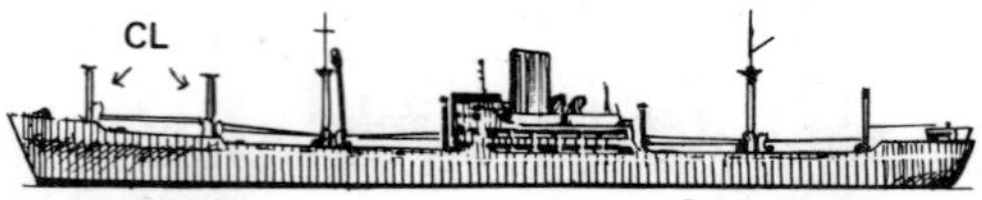

$K_2MKFKMK$
07740 TUDIS. Gr/Br 1952; CP; 6900/9700; 153.5×—/10 (504×—/33); T; 17; ex BENREOCH 1976.

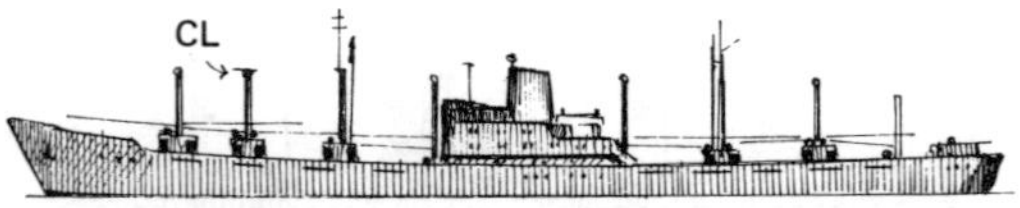

$K_2MKFKMK_2$ H1
● **07750 ETHA RICKMERS.** FRG/FRG 1958; C; 9200/12700; 166.6×8.6/9.7 (547×28.2/32); M; 18; ex ETHA 1975; ex MUNCHEN 1970. Sister. **07751 SOPHIE RICKMERS** (FRG); ex DRESDEN 1970.

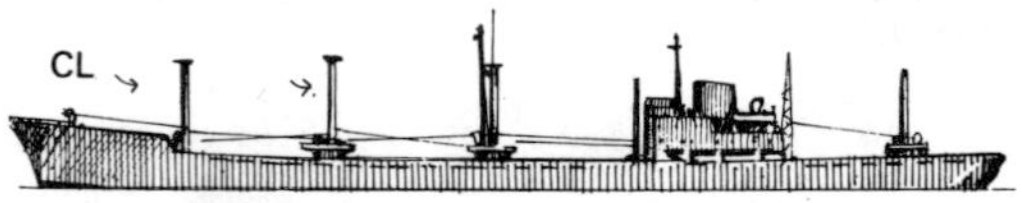

K_2MKMFK H1
● **07760 ZEA STAR.** Gr/Ja 1966; CP; 8900; 141×8.6 (463×28.2); M; 15.75; ex BISMARK CAREER 1980; GUATEMALA MARU 1978. Similar: (some may have cranes). **07761 HONDURAS MARU** (Ja) **07762 IONIAN CAREER** (Pa); ex EL SALVADOR MARU 1979 **07763 BAHAMA MARU** (Ja); ex VENEZUELA MARU (Ja) **07764 COLOMBIA MARU** (Ja); **07765 TREASURE ISLAND** (Pa); ex DOMINICA MARU 1980. **07766 HAITI MARU** (Ja);

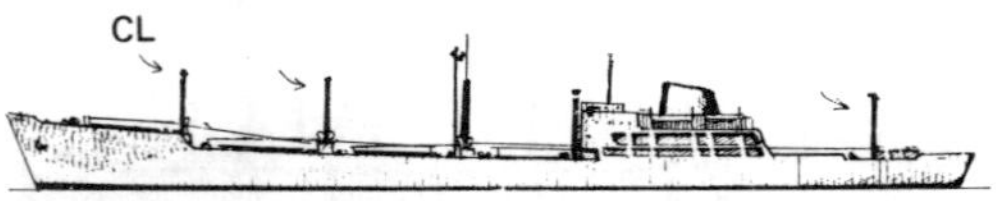

K_2MKMFK H1
● **07770 CLAN MACGILLIVRAY.** Br/Br 1962; C; 5900/8800; 154.8×7.4/8.7 (508×24.3/28.6); M; 16.5.Sisters: **07171 CLAN MACGREGOR** (Br) **07772 INDIAN TRIBUNE** (In); ex CLAN MACGOWAN 1970 Similar: (1 boat aside and larger mast houses). **07773 AFRICAN DIAMOND** (Li); ex CLAN ALPINE 1981.

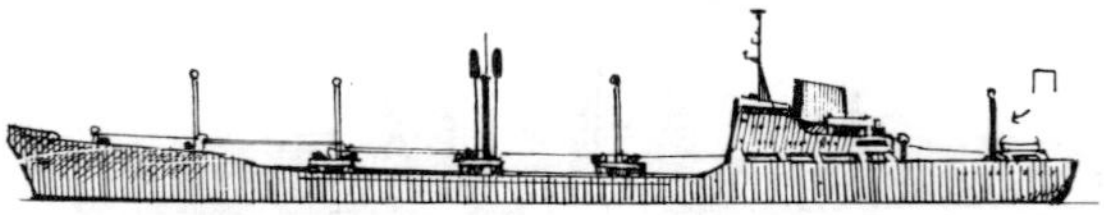

K_2MKMFK H13
● **07780 TOBIAS MAERSK.** De/De 1963; C; 12300; 170.7×8.9 (560×29.3); M; —. Sisters (De flag): **07781 THOMAS MAERSK 07782 TREIN MAERSK.**

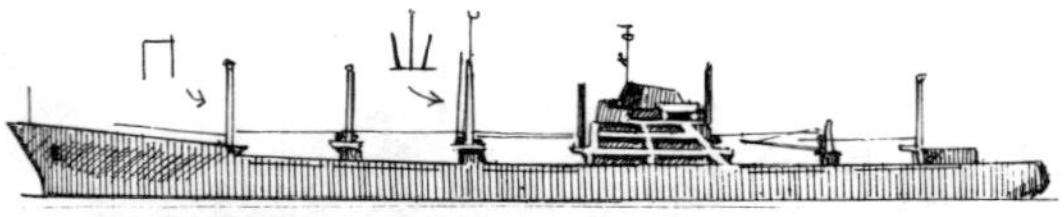

$K_2MKMFKCK$ H1
● **07790 MORMACARGO.** US/US 1964; Pt.Con; 7200/10500; 167.9×—(9.6 (551×—(31.6); T; 21. Sisters (US flag): **07791 MORMACLYNX 07792 MORMACALTAIR 07793 MORMACRIGEL 07794 MORMACVEGA 07795 MARMACDRACO.**

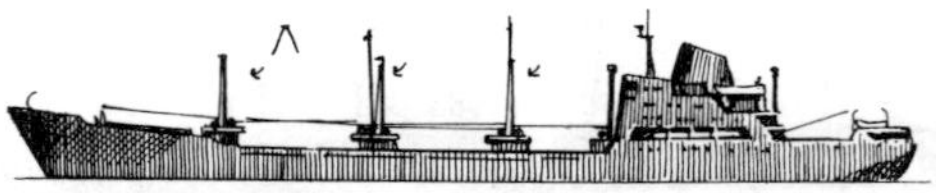

K_2MKMFK H13
⋆**07800 LJUTOMER.** Ys/Ys 1964; CP; 6200/8100; 146.4×—/8.2 (481×—/27), M; 17.5. Sister: ⋆**07801 LJUBLJANA** (Ys).

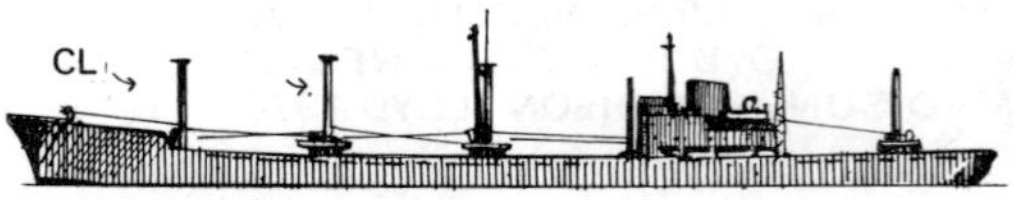

K_2MKMFK_2 H1
● **07810 BAHAMA MARU.** Ja/Ja 1970; CP; 8900; 141×8.6 (463×28.2); M; 15.75. Possibly Similar: **07811 HONDURAS MARU** (Ja) **07812 IONIAN CAREER** (Pa); ex EL SALVADOR MARU 1979 **07813 VENEZUELA MARU** (Ja) **07814 HAITI MARU** (Ja) **07815 TREASURE ISLAND** (Pa); ex DOMINICA MARU 1980 **07816 ZEA STAR** (Gr); ex BISMARK CAREER 1980; ex GUATEMALA MARU 1978. **07817 COLOMBIA MARU** (Ja);

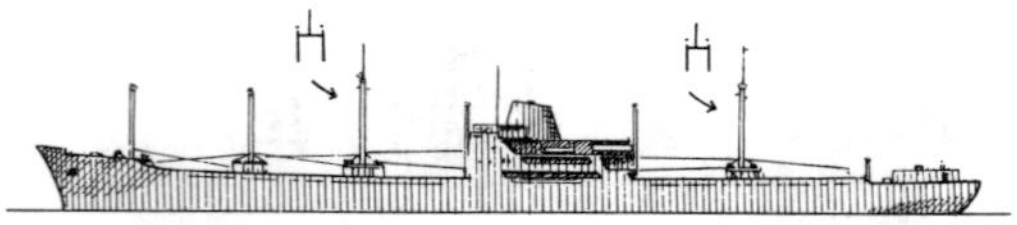

$K_2MKMFKM$ H1
● **07820 STATE OF TAMIL NADU.** In/It 1959; C; 7100; 152.6×7.9 (501×26); M; 12; ex GIMMI FASSIO 1970. Sisters: **07821 PENNY S.** (Pa); ex SEBASTIANO VENIER 1976; ex NANDO FA FASSIO 1971 **07822 FILOMENA LEMBO** (It); ex CARLIN FASSIO 1971 **07823 BAO SHAN** (Br); ex ZINAL 1980; ex GIUANIN FASSIO 1971.

$K_2MKMFKM$ *H1*
07830 NEDLLOYD SEINE. Ne/Ne 1961; C; 8200; 166×8.8 (545×29); M; 18; ex SEINE LLOYD 1978. Sisters (Ne flag): **07831 NEDLLOYD SCHELDE** (Ne); ex SCHELDE LLOYD 1978 **07832 NEDLLOYD SCHIE** (Ne); ex SCHIE LLOYD 1978 **07833 NEDLLOYD MAIN** (Ne); ex MAIN LLOYD 1978 **07834 NEDLLOYD MADISON** (Ne); ex MADISON LLOYD 1978.

$K_2MKMFKM$ *H1*
● **07840 BRAZILIAN EXPRESS.** Pi/Ja 1965; CP; 10000; 161×9.3 (528×30.6); M; 19.5; ex YAMAGUCHI MARU 1980. Sisters: **07841 KYRA** (Gr); ex YAMASHIRO MARU 1974 **07842 ROYAL RUBY** (Pa); ex IWAKI MARU 1975.

$K_2MKMFKMK$ *H1*
07850 EXPORT DEFENDER. US/US 1954; C; 9100; 171.8×9.4 (564×31); T; 20; ex PRESIDENT COOLIDGE 1974; ex CRACKER STATE MARINER 1956; Modified **"MARINER"** type. Sisters (US flag): **07851 EXPORT DIPLOMAT** ex PRESIDENT HAYES 1974; ex OLD DOMINION MARINER 1956 **07852 LONE STAR MARINER** ex EXPORT DEMOCRACY 1978; ex PRESIDENT ARTHUR 1974; ex LONE STAR MARINER 1979 **07853 HOOSIER MARINER** ex CARTER BRAXTON 1980; ex PRESIDENT BUCHANAN 1974; ex HOOSIER MARINER 1959.

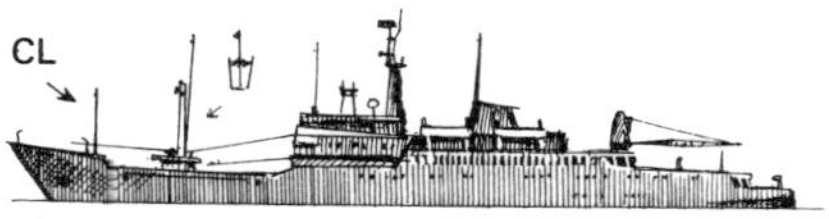

K_2M_2FC *H12*
⋆**07860 ANTONI GARNUSZEWSKI.** Pd/Pd 1974; C/TS; 6000; 122.2×7.4 (401×24.3); M; 15.75; **'B. 80'** type. Sisters: ⋆**07861 KAPITAN LEDOCHOWSKI** (Pd) ⋆**07862 NEPTUN** (Rm) ⋆**07863 NICOLA VAPTZAROV** (Bu).

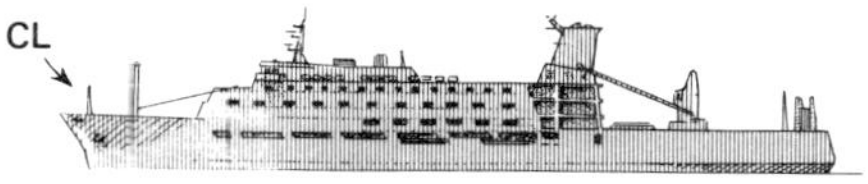

K_2M_2FCR *H*
07870 WAKASHIO MARU. Ja/Ja 1973; RoC; 5500; 124.92×5.51 (409.84×18.08); M; 24; stern ramp.

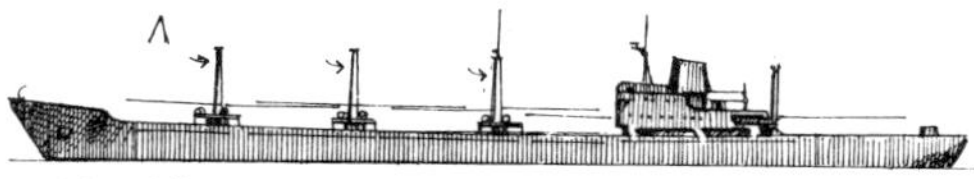

K_2M_2FK *H1*
07880 KEBAN. Tu/Ys 1971; C; 9000; 154.3×9.3 (506×30.6); M; —. Sisters (Tu flag); (sequence may vary). **07881 ARAS 07882 DICLE 07883 FIRAT 07884 GEDIZ 07885 MERIC.**

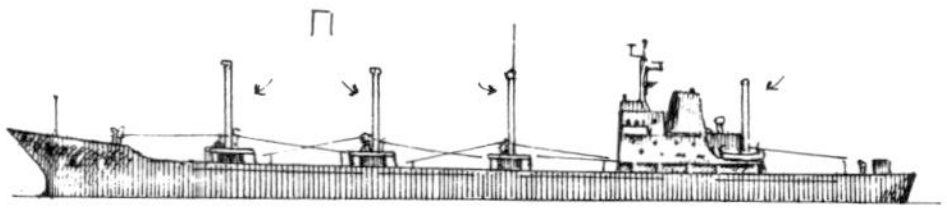

K_2M_2FK *H1*
07890 BETELGEUSE. Pa/Ys 1969; C; 6100/9400; 145×—/9.1 (476×29.10); M; 15.5; **'Zagreb'** type Sisters (Pa flag) **07891 ARCTURUS 07892 BELLATRIX 07893 DENEBOLA.**

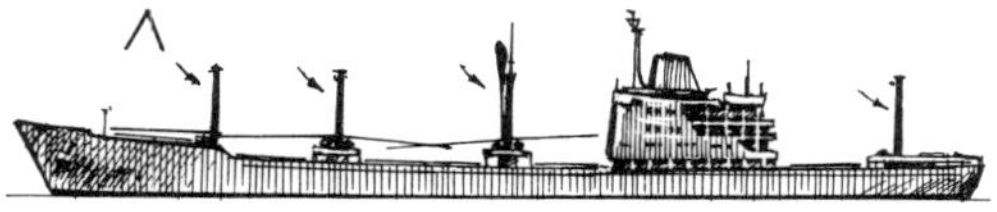

K_2M_2FK *H1*
⋆**07900 MINSK.** Ru/Pd 1964; C; 7400/9700; 155×7.4/9 (508×24.3/29.10); M; 17.25; **'B 44'** type. Sisters (Ru flag). ⋆**07901 MATSESTA** ⋆**07902 MARGELAN** ⋆**07903 MARIINSK** ⋆**07904 MARNEULI** ⋆**07905 MTSENSK** ⋆**07906 MEDYN** ⋆**07907 MEZHDURECHENSK** ⋆**07908 MEZHGORYE** ⋆**07909 MICHURIN** ⋆**07910 MILLEROVO** ⋆**07911 MOZHAISK** ⋆**07912 MOLOCHANSK** ⋆**07913 MORSHANSK** ⋆**07914 MUKACHEVO** ⋆**07915 MOLODOGVARDEYSK** ⋆**07916 MOZYR** ⋆**07917 MUROM** ⋆**07918 MYTISHCHI** ⋆**07919 ALEKSEY TOLSTOY** ⋆**07920 BORIS GORBATOV** ⋆**07921 DMITRIY FURMANOV** ⋆**07922 IVAN GONCHAROV** ⋆**07923 NIKOLAY NEKRASOV** ⋆**07924 SAMUIL MARSHAK** ⋆**07925 ANTON MAKARENKO** ⋆**07926 BORIS LAVRENEV** ⋆**07927 FEDOR GADKOV** ⋆**07928 ROMAN ROLLAN.**

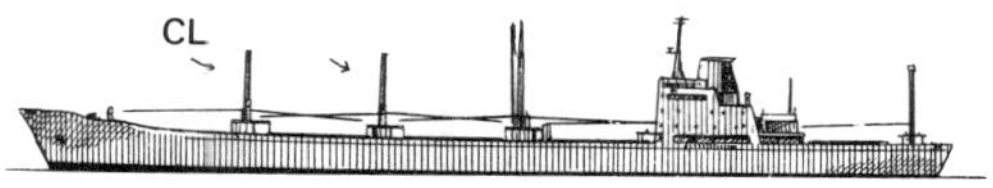

K_2M_2FK *H1*
07940 GARCILASO. Pe/Fi 1969; C; 5800/9500; 150.5×—/9.4 (494×—/30.8); M; —. Sisters (Pe flag). **07941 CHOCANO 07942 PALMA 07943 SABOGAL 07944 TELLO 07945 VALLEJO.**

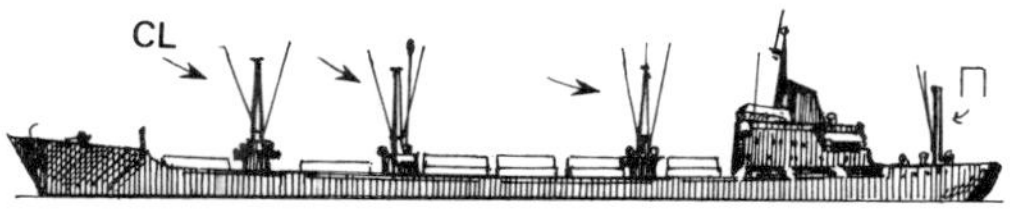

K_2M_2FK *H13*
● **07950 ESHKOL.** Is/Fr 1964; C; 4900/7700; 159.2×6 7/7.9 (522×22/26); M; 17.5; Lengthened 1971. Sisters. **07951 ETROG** (Is) **07952 GOLD PILOT** (Li); ex HADAR 1977 **07953 ROGET** (Pa); ex YAFO 1980; ex DOLLY 1979; ex YAFO 1979.

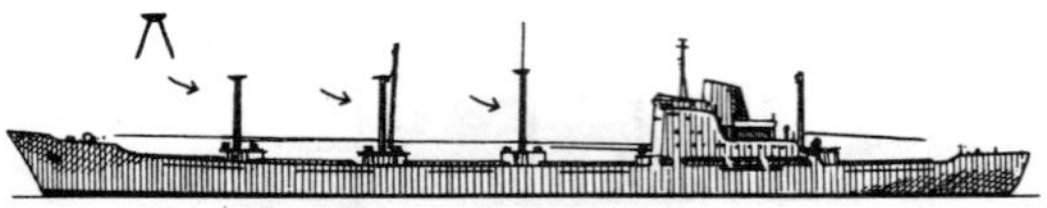

K_2M_2FK H13
● **07960 FEAX.** Gr/Br 1970; C; 11500; 164.5 × 9.7 (544 × 32); M; 17.

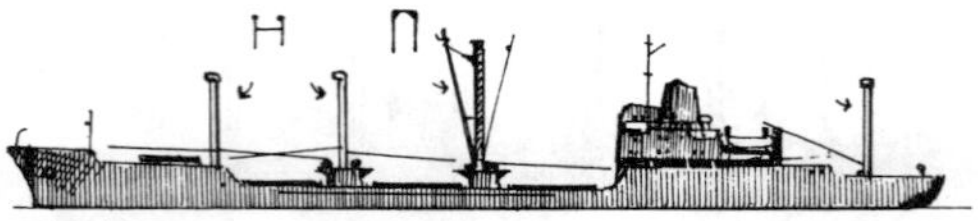

K_2M_2FK H13
07970 ALCOUTIM. Po/FRG 1968; C; 10500; 148.1 × 9.7 (487 × 31); M; 19; ex CASTORP 1972. Sister. **07971 AMARANTE** (Po); ex LUBECK 1972.

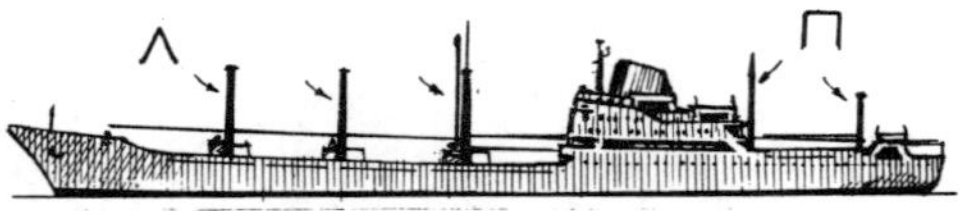

$K_2M_2FK_2$ H13
● ***07980 TUHOBIC.** Ys/Ys 1965; CP; 6800; 149 × 7.2 (489 × 23.8); M; 18. Sisters (Ys flag). ***07981 KLEK *07982 VISEVICA *07983 ZVIR.**

K_2M_2FKM H13
07990 BIA RIVER. Gh/Ja 1965; C; 4900/7500; 138.7 × —/8.5 (455 × —/28); M; —. Sister (Gh flag): **07991 OTI RIVER** Similar: **07992 SUBIN RIVER 07993 KLORTE LAGOON;** (Funnel heights vary).

K_2M_2FKMK H1
● **08000 MORMACSAGA.** US/US 1961; PtCon; 9300/12700; 172 × —/9.7 (565 × —/31.7); T; 20; ex M.M. DANT. Sisters (US flag): **08001 SANTA ANA** EX C.E. DANT **08002 MORMACSEA 08003 MORMACTIDE 08004 MARMACWAVE 08005 CALIFORNIA;** ex SANTA RITA 1980.

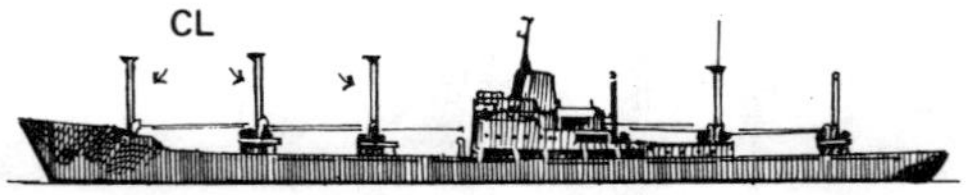

K_2M_2FKMK H1
08010 NACALA. Po/Hong Kong 1966; CP; 9100; 149 × 9.1 (489 × 29.10); M; 18; ex HUNAN 1968.

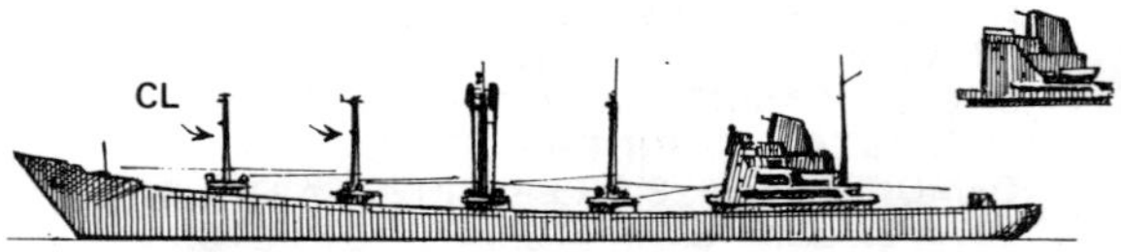

K_2M_2FM H1
08020 GOOD HERALD. Gr/Ne 1960; C; 7200; 163 × 8.2 (534 × 26.11); M; 17; ex GAASTERDYK 1978. Sister **08021 HELLENIC SKY** (Gr) ex GREBBEDYK 1974 Similar (See inset). **08022 HELLENIC GRACE** (Gr) ex GORREDYK 1974 **08023 H. CAPELO** (Po) ex MOERDYK 1973.

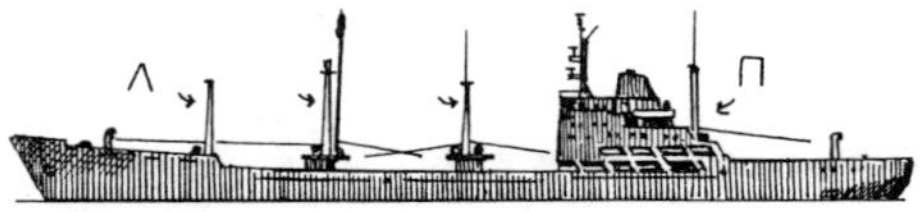

K_2M_2FM H13
***08030 VYBORG.** Ru/DDR 1964; C; 5500/8500; 151 × 7.2/8.9 (494 × 23.6/29); M; 16.5. Sisters (Ru flag): ***08032 VATUTINO *08032 VYAZMA *08033 VOLZHSK** Similar: ***08034 JIANG MEN** (RC).

K_2M_2FMK H1
● **08040 BLUE SKY.** Gr/Ja 1958; C; 8500; 144 × 8.9 (472 × 29.2); M; 13.5; ex ELKA 1974; ex NICHIWA MARU 1972.

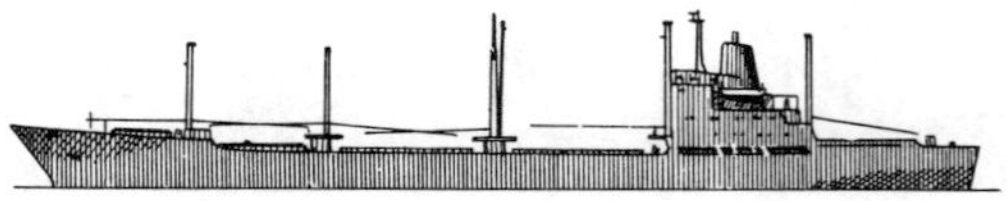

K_2M_3FK H13
● **08050 AFRICAN PIONEER.** Li/FRG 1971; CP; 6300/9200; 155 × 7.9/9.2 (509 × 26/30); M; 20; ex GUADALUPE 1980; ex NAXOS 1978; ex ROBERT BORNHOFEN 1972. Sister: **08051 COVADONGA** (Sp) ex RHODOS 1978; ex PETER BORNHOFEN 1973.

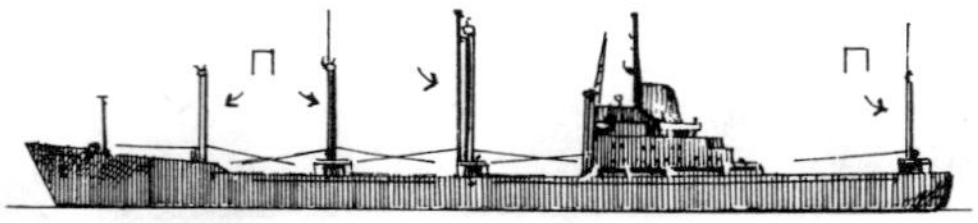

K_2M_4FM H1
08060 PANAGIOTIS A.L. Gr/Ja 1970; C; 4900/7700; 147 × 8.9 (482 × 29); M; 15; ex SAINT MATTHIEU 1981; ex HOEGH BONNY 1975; ex CENTRAL MARINER.

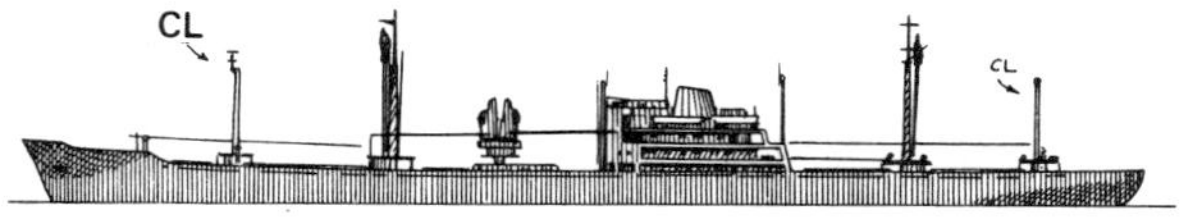

KMC$_2$KFKMK H1
08070 NEDLLOYD SPAARNEKERK. Ne/Ne 1962; C/Con; 8300; 180 × 8.1 (591 × 26.6); M; 17.5; ex SPAARNEKERK 1978. Sisters (Ne flag): **08071 NEDLLOYD SINOUTSKERK** ex SINOUTSKERK 1977 **08072 NEDLLOYD STEENKERK** ex STEENKERK 1978 **08073 NEDLLOYD STREEFKERK** ex STREEFKERK 1977 **08074 NEDLLOYD FRESCO** ex STRAAT FRESCO 1978 **08075 NEDLLOYD FORCADOS** ex STRAAT FORCADOS 1978 **08076 NEDLLOYD FUKUOKA** ex STRAAT FUKUOKA 1978.

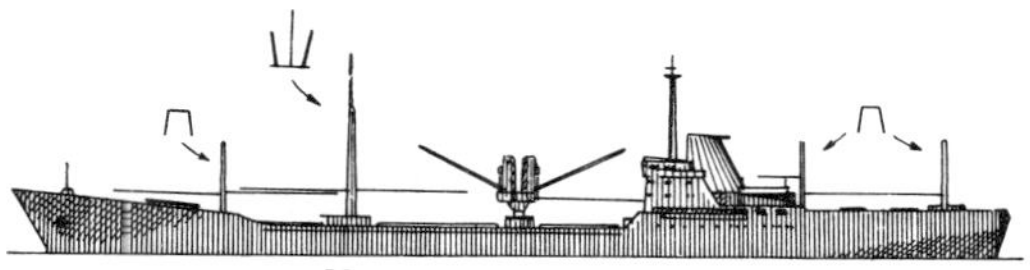

KMC$_2$MFK$_2$ H13
08080 CIUDAD DE MANTA. Ec/Pd 1972; C/Con; 7300/9700; 161 × 8.9/9.7 (528 × 29/3); M; 20.5; **"B434"** type. Sisters (Co flag): **08081 CIUDAD DE CALI 08082 CIUDAD DE IBAGUE.**

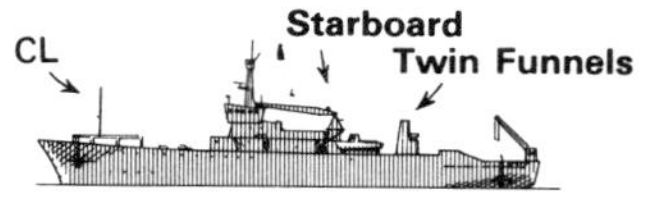

KMCF H1
08090 SUBSEA MARAUDER. Br/No 1967; Submersible Support Ship; 1500; 80.2 × 5.6 (263 × 18.6); M; 14; ex STAR PISCES 1980; ex GADUS 1976; converted from trawler 1976; Also reported as **SUBSEA BUCCANEER.**

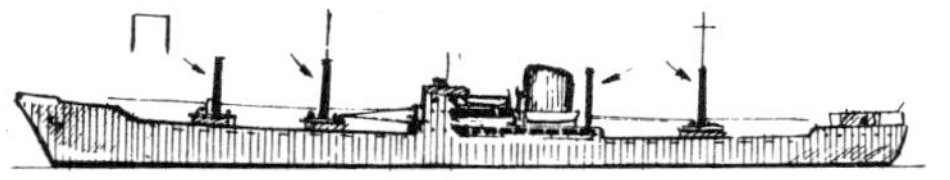

KMCFKM H13
08100 CLIMAX RUBY. Pa/Ja 1951; CP; 6000; 144 × 7.9 (471 × 26); M; 15; ex VAR 1974; ex CAPO NOLI 1973; ex LA ENSENADA 1960; ex PHILIPPE L.D. 1954.

KMCKFKMK H13
08110 NEW BEAR. Sg/De 1953; C; 6200/9000; 149 × 8.4/8.9 (488 × 27.6/29); M; 17.25; ex JESPER MAERSK 1977; ex CHASTINE MAERSK 1968.

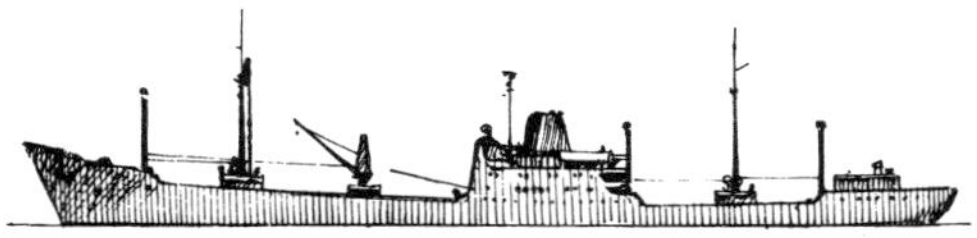

KMCMFKMK H123
08120 CHAI TRADER. Gr/Ne 1958; CP; 4800/6900; 146 × 6.5/7.4 (480 × 21.3/24); M; 14.5; ex STRAAT LAGOS 1978; ex VAN DER HAGEN 1967: Sisters (Sg flag): **08121 KOTA RATU** ex STRAAT LUANDA 1978; ex VAN LINSCHOTEN 1967 **08122 KOTA RAJA** ex STRAAT LUZON 1978; ex VAN SPILBERGEN.

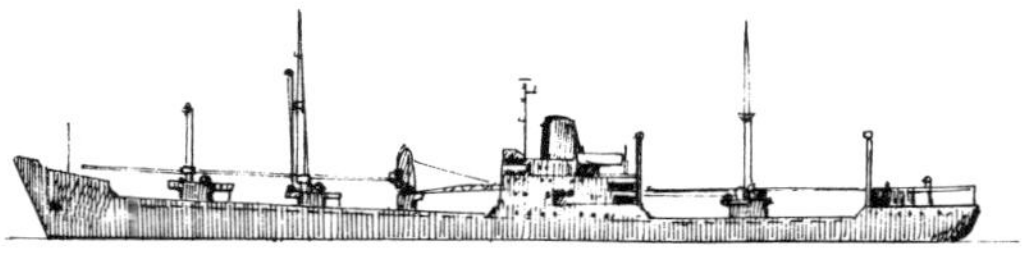

KMCMFKMK H123
08130 SAUDI ENTERPRISE. Si/Ne 1960; CP; 6200/8900; 158 × 7.3/8.3 (519 × 24/27.2); M; 16; ex NEDLLOYD CUMBERLAND 1978; ex STRAAT CUMBERLAND 1977: Sisters: **08131 KOTA CEMPAKA** (Sg) ex NEDLLOYD CLARENCE 1979; ex STRAAT CLARENCE 1978 **08132 CAPITAINE COOK** (Fr) ex NEDLLOYD CLEMENT 1979; ex STRAAT CLEMENT 1978; ex ASIA EXPRESS 1974; ex STRAAT CLEMENT 1973 **08133 MERCURY LAKE** (Pa) ex NEDLLOYD COLOMBO 1980; ex STRAAT COLOMBO 1977; ex ASIAN EXPLORER 1974; ex STRAAT COLOMBO 1973 **08134 CAPITAINE LA PEROUSE** (Fr) ex NEDLLOYD CHATHAM 1979; ex STRAAT CHATHAM 1978.

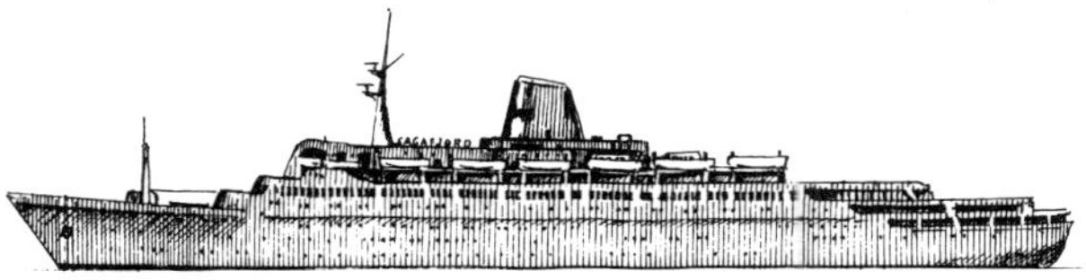

KMF H
08140 SAGAFJORD. No/Fr 1965; P; 24000; 189 × 8.2 (620 × 27.1); TSM; 20.

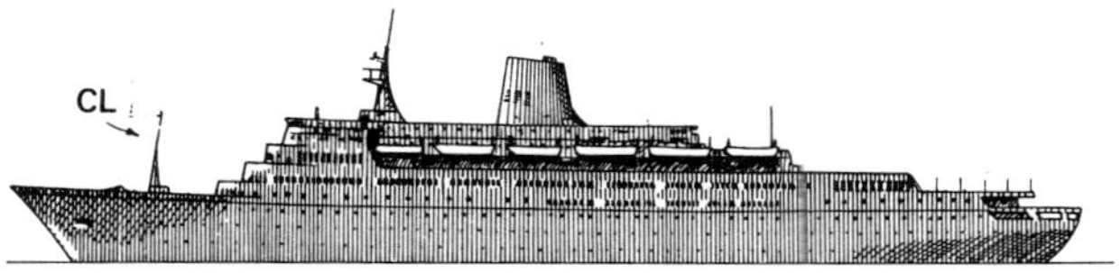

KMF H
08150 VISTAFJORD. No/Br 1973; P; 24900; 191 × 8.2 (627 × 27); TSM; 20.

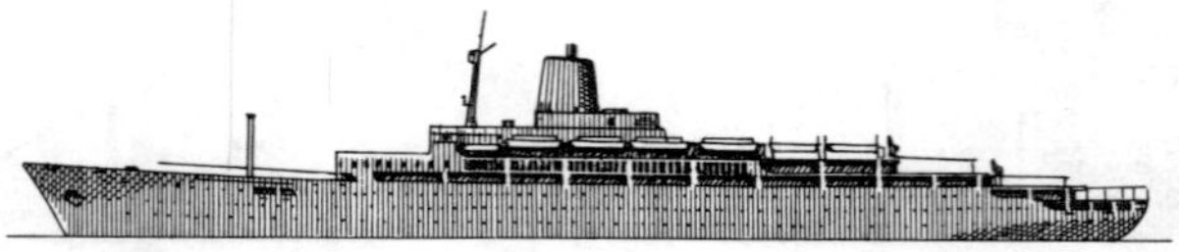

KMF H
08160 FEDERICO C. It/It 1958; P; 20400; 185 × 8.6 (606 × 28.5); TST; 21.

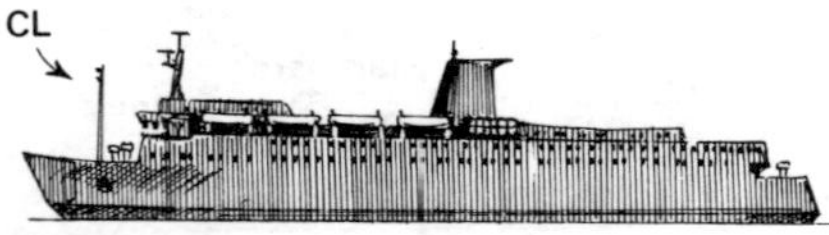

KMF H
⋆08170 POMERANIA. Pd/Pd 1978; RoPCF; 7400; 127.25 × 5.42 (417.49 × 17.78); M; 20.4; **"B490"** type. Sisters (Pd flag): **⋆08171 SILESIA ⋆08172 MAZOWIA.**

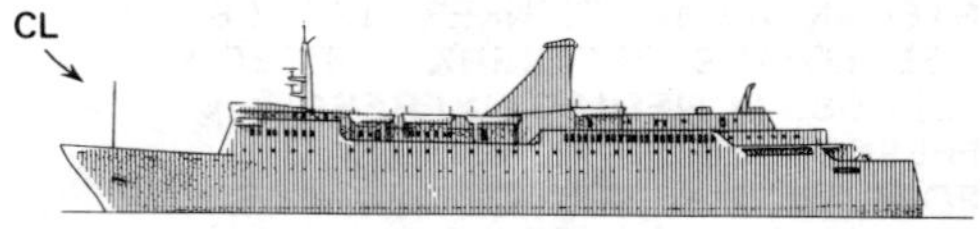

KMF H
08180 CIUDAD DE SEVILLA. Sp/Sp 1980; RoPCF; 7400; 138.5 × 5.5 (454.4 × 18.04); TSM; 21; stern door.

KMF H
08190 RODOS. Gr/US 1946; P; 2500; 95 × 4.2 (310 × 14); TSM; 18.

KMF H
08200 KRITI. Gr/Br 1929; P; 2100; 89 × 4.7 (293 × 15.5); R; 13; ex MELROSE ABBEY II 1959; ex MELROSE ABBEY 1958.

KMF H
08210 EL GRECO. Gr/Br 1936; P; 1200; 75 × 2.7 (245 × 9); TSM; 15; ex GALAXIAS 1966; ex NEA HELLAS 1964; ex ELLAS 1963; ex MARCHIONESS OF GRAHAM 1959.

KMF H
08220 NEPTUNO. Gr/Ys 1954; P; 600; 58 × 2.7 (189 × 8.10); TSM; 14.5; ex MELTEMI 1 1978; ex MARIBOR 1966. Sister: **08221 MELTEMI II** (Gr) ex MOSTAR 1966.

KMF H
08230 PONTA DELGADA. Po/Po 1962; P; 1100; 67 × 3.6 (220 × 11.6); M; 15.

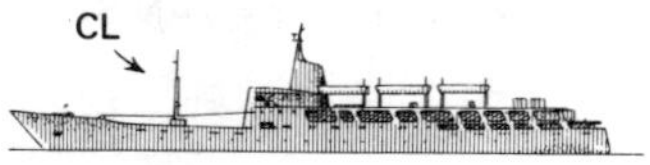

KMF H
08240 DON JULIO. Pi/Ja 1967; PC; 2100; 95.66 × 5.16 (313.85 × 16.93); M; 17.5.

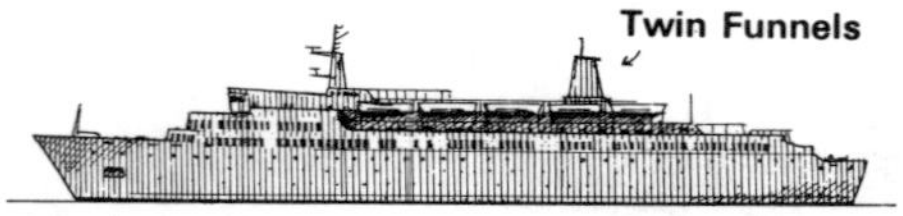

KMF H
08250 BOHEME. FRG/Fi 1968; P; 10300; 134 × 5.5 (441 × 18.1); TSM; 20.

KMF H
08260 MERMOZ. Fr/Fr 1957; P; 13800; 162 × 6.4 (532 × 21); TSM; 17; ex JEAN MERMOZ 1970.

KMF H
08270 AMERIKANIS. Gr/Br 1952; P; 16500; 176 × 7.8 (577 × 25.7); TST; 19.5; ex KENYA CASTLE; Rebuilt 1962.

KMF H
08280 LA PALMA Cy/Fr 1952; P; 10900; 150 × 7.4 (493 × 24.5); TSM; 17; ex LA PERLA 1980; ex DELPHI 1977; ex FERDINAND DE LESSEPS 1969: Possibly Similar: **08281 EROS** (Gr) ex CHRYSOVALANDOU II 1980; ex PATRA 1978; ex OLYMPIA 1972; ex PIERRE LOTI 1970 **08282 OCEANOS** (Gr) ex EASTERN PRINCESS 1976; ex ANCONA 1974; ex MYKINAI 1971; ex JEAN LABORDE 1970.

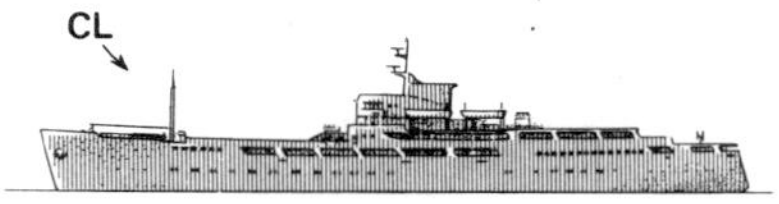

KMF H
08290 ROLAND VON BREMEN. FRG/De-FRG 1939/66; F; 4400; 114×5.91 (374×19.39); TSM; 19; ex INDIAN REEFER 1966; ex RIO GALLEGOS 1946; ex INDIAN REEFER 1942; converted from reefer 1966.

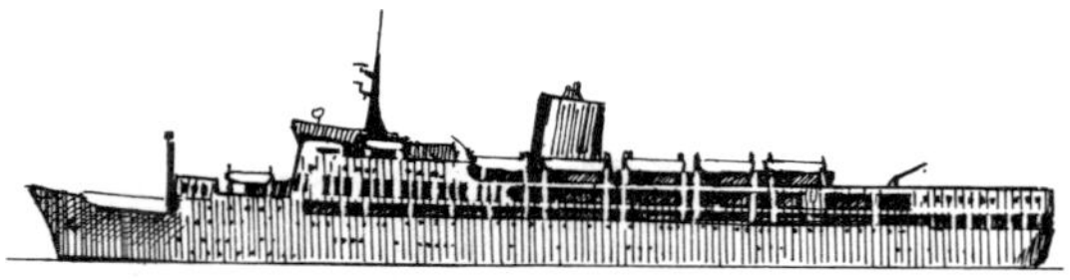

KMF H
08300 UGANDA. Br/Br 1952; P; 16900; 165×7.7 (540×25.3); TST; 16.

KMF H
08310 VICTORIA. Sp/Sp 1952; RoPF; 3300; 104×5 (340×16.9); TSM; 17; ex 5 DE AGOSTO 1952; stern door. Sister: **08311 VIRGEN DE AFRICA** (Sp).

KMF H
***08320 PERAST.** Ys/Ys 1962; PF; 335; 445×3 (146×9.10); TSM; 13. Sisters: (Ys flag) ***08321 POROZINA *08322 POSTIRA *08323 PUNAT.**

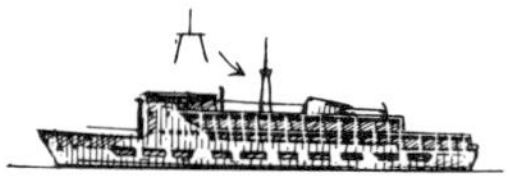

KMF H
08330 LEOPOLDO PERES. Bz/Ne 1954; P.Riv; 1400; 71×2.3; (234×7.10); TSM; 11. Sisters (Bz flag): **08331 AUGUSTO MONTENEGRO 08332 LAURO SODRE 08333 LOBO D'ALMADA.**

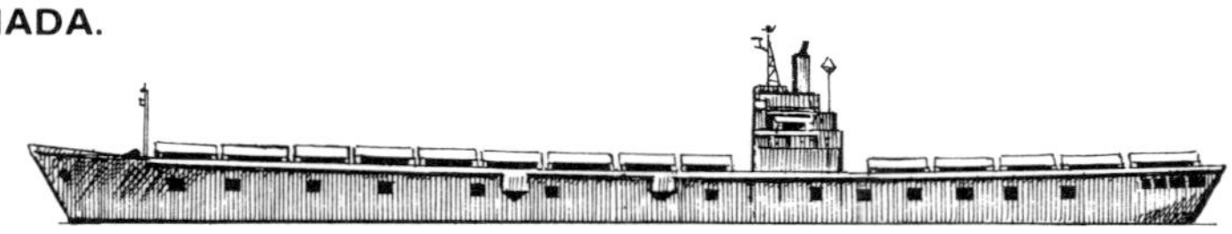

KMF H
08340 PONCE. US/US 1968; RoC; 15100; 213×8.6 (700×28.2); T; 25.5; ex PONCE DE LEON 1977; side doors. Sisters (US flag): **08341 BAYAMON** ex ERIC K. HOLZER 1977; ex BAYAMON; ex ERIC K. HOLZER 1975 **08342 FORTALEZA 08343 GULF BEAR** (lengthened 1976 now 241m); ex EL TAINO **08344 PUERTO RICO** Similar: (extra deck level forward of bridge.) **08345 WESTWARD VENTURE.**

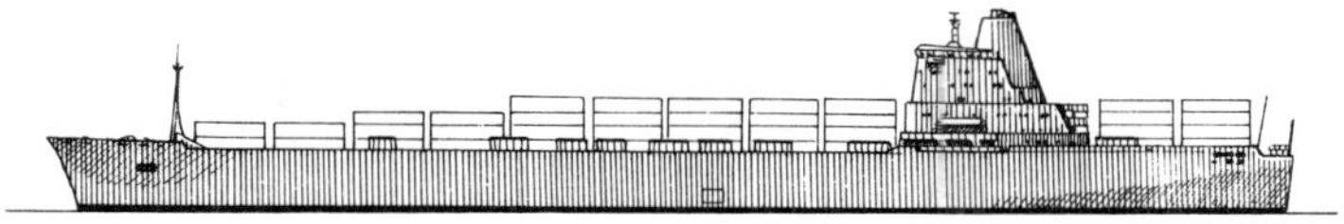

KMF H
08350 ATLANTIC CAUSEWAY. Br/Br 1969; RoC/Con; 14900; 212×9.3 (696×30.6); TST; 23; stern doors. Sisters: **08351 ATLANTIC CONVEYOR** (Br) **08352 ATLANTIC CINDERELLA** (Sw) **08353 ATLANTIC COGNAC** (Fr) **08354 ATLANTIC CHAMPAGNE** (Fr) **08355 ATLANTIC CROWN** (Ne).

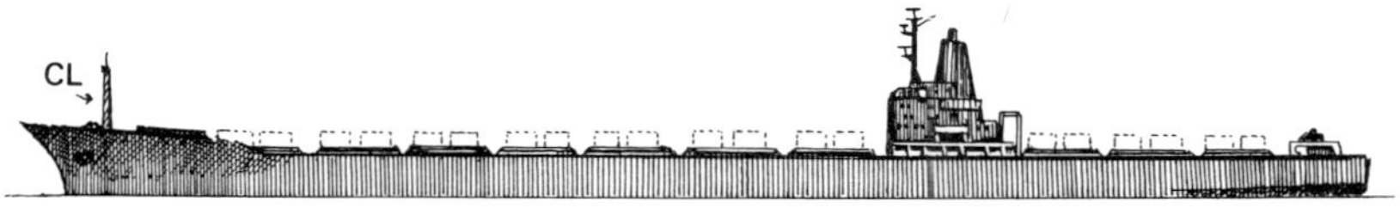

KMF H
08360 REMUERA BAY. Br/Br 1973; Con; 42000; 252×11 (827×32.6); TST; —; ex REMUERA 1977.

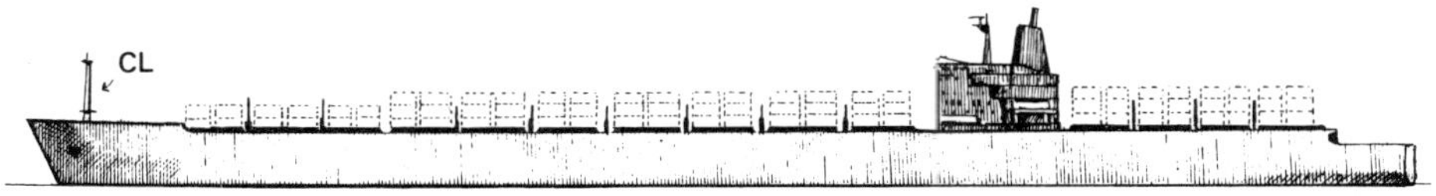

KMF H
08370 BREMEN EXPRESS. FRG/FRG 1972; Con; 57500; 187×12 (942×39.6); TST; 26. Sisters: **08371 HAMBURG EXPRESS** (FRG) **08372 HONGKONG EXPRESS** (FRG) **08373 TOKIO EXPRESS** (FRG) **08374 NEDLLOYD DEJIMA** (Ne) **08375 NEDLLOYD DELFT** (Ne).

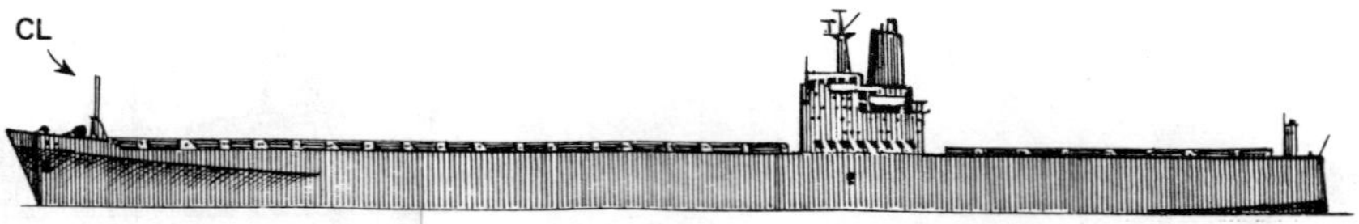

KMF H
08380 S.A. SEDERBERG. SA/Fr 1978; Con; 53000; 258.53 × 13 (841.48 × 42.65); TSM; 21. Sisters (SA flag): **08381 S.A. HELDERBERG 08382 S.A. WATERBERG 08383 S.A. WINTERBERG.**

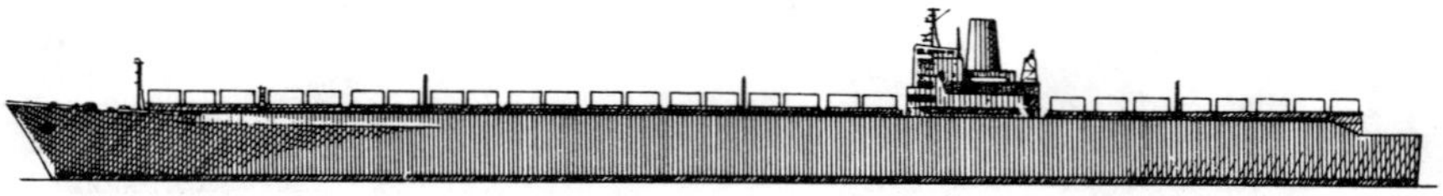

KMF H
08390 ELBE MARU. Ja/Ja 1972; Con; 51600; 269 × 11.9 (883 × 39.4); TrST; 27.5.

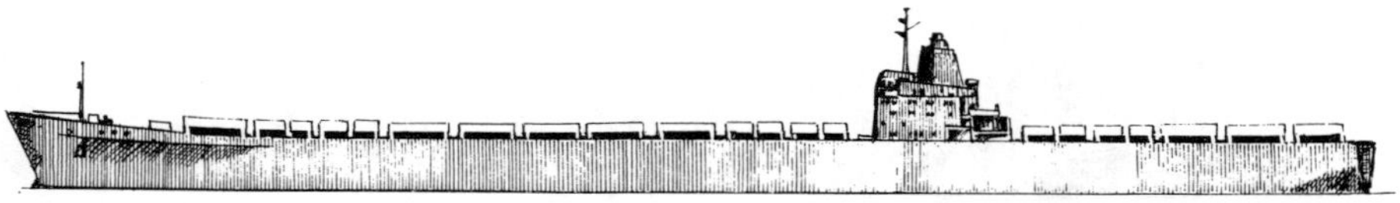

KMF H
● **08400 LIVERPOOL BAY.** Br/FRG 1972; Con; 58900; 290 × 13 (950 × 42.9); TST; 26. Sisters (Br flag): **08401 CARDIGAN BAY 08402 KOWLOON BAY 08403 OSAKA BAY 08404 TOKYO BAY.**

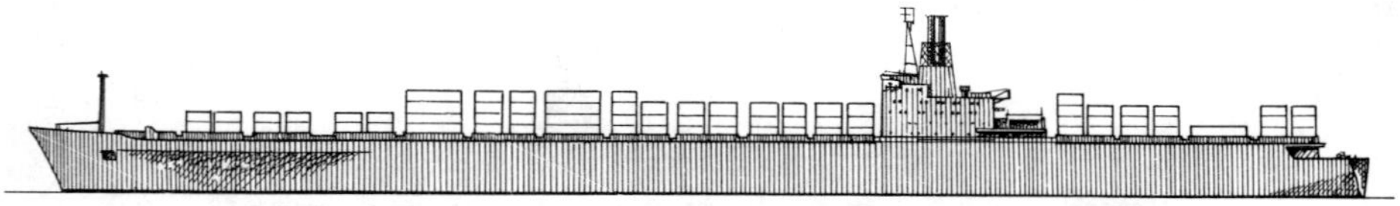

KMF H
08410 BENALDER. Br/FRG 1972; Con; 58400; 290 × 13 (950 × 42.7); TST; 26.5. Sisters (Br flag): **08411 BENAVON 08412 CITY OF EDINBURGH.**

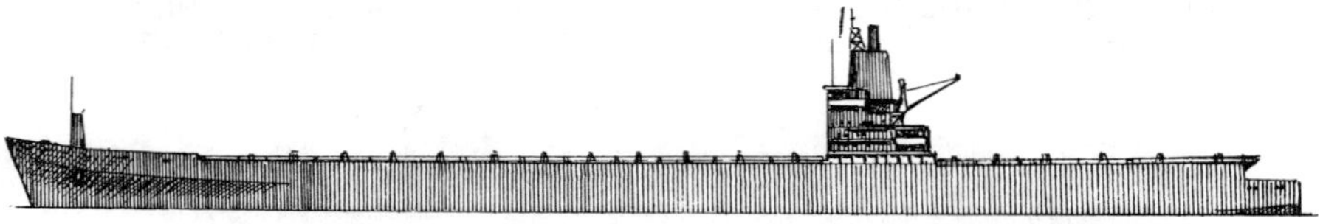

KMF H
08420 BARCELONA. Br/FRG 1977; Con; 53800; 258.55 × 13.02 (848.26 × 42.72); TSM; 21.5; ex TABLE BAY 1979. Sister: **08421 CITY OF DURBAN** (Br).

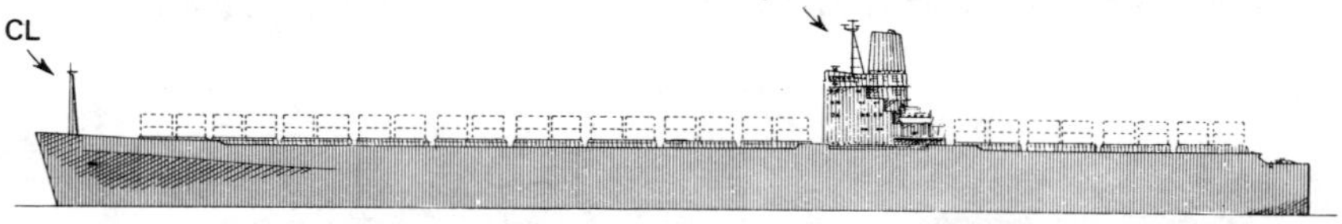

KMF H
08430 LARGS BAY. Ne/Ne 1977; Con; 52600; 258.5 × 13.03 (848.1 × 42.75); TSM; 21.5; ex NEDLLOYD HOUTMAN 1981. Sister: **08431 NEDLLOYD HOORN** (Ne).

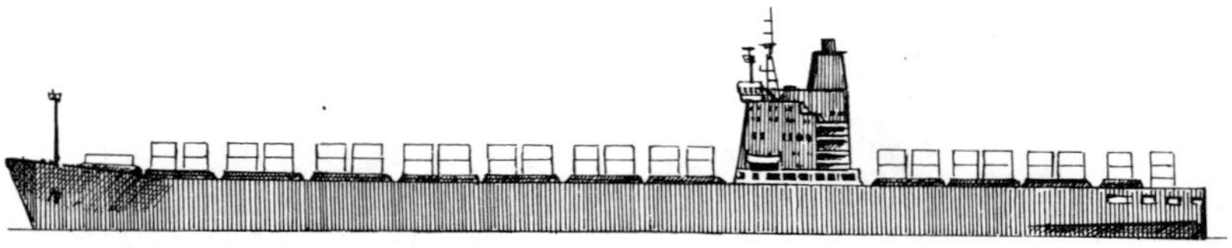

KMF H
08440 AUSTRALIAN VENTURE. Au/FRG 1977; Con; 44000; 249 × 11 (820 × 37); M; 24. Sisters: **08441 ACT 7** (Br) **08442 RESOLUTION BAY** (Br) **08443 MAIRANGI BAY** (Br) **08444 NEW ZEALAND PACIFIC** (NZ).

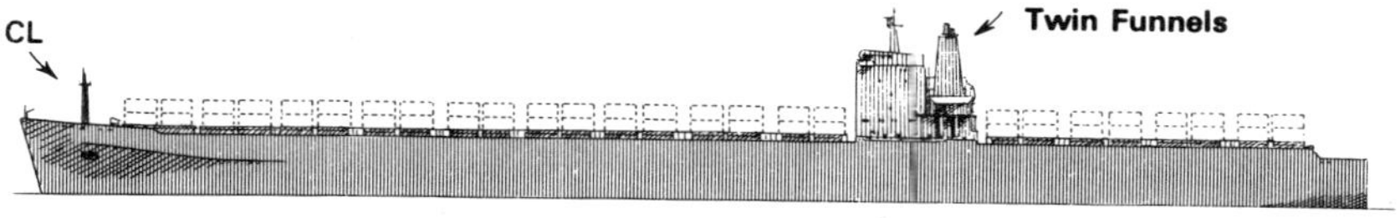

KMF H
08450 TRANSVAAL. FRG/FRG 1978; Con; 52600; 258.53 × 13.02 (848.2 × 42.72); TSM; 23.

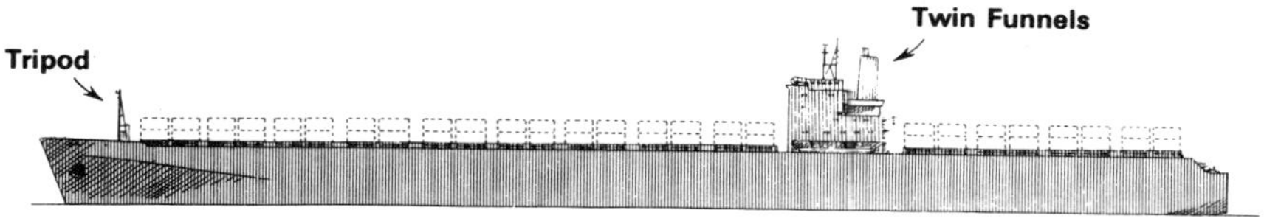

KMF H
08460 ORTELIUS. Be/Be 1978; Con; 52400; 258.53 × 13 (848.2 × 42.65); TSM; 22.75.

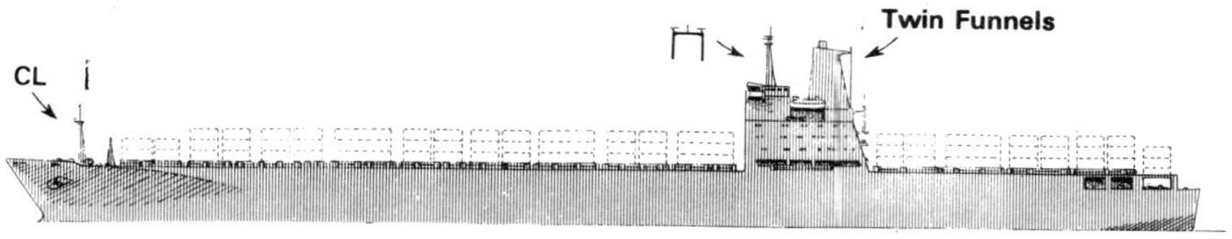

KMF H
08470 BUNGA PERMAI. My/Ja 1979; Con; 43500; 267 × 13 (875.98 × 42.65); M; 26. Sister: **08471 BUNGA SURIA** (My).

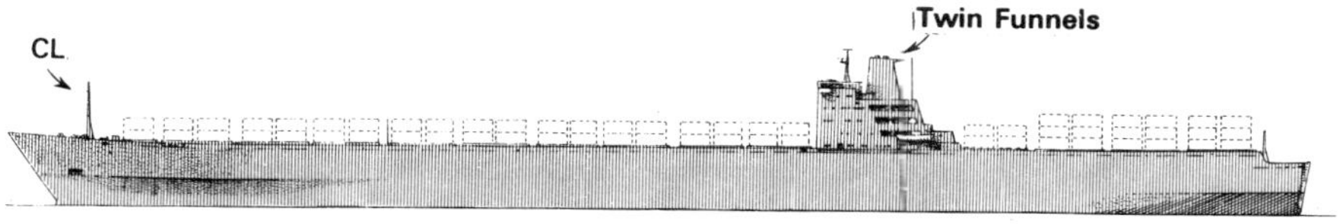

KMF H
08480 NIHON. Sw/Sw 1972; Con; 50800; 275.22 × 11.58 (902.95 × 37.99); TrSM; 26.

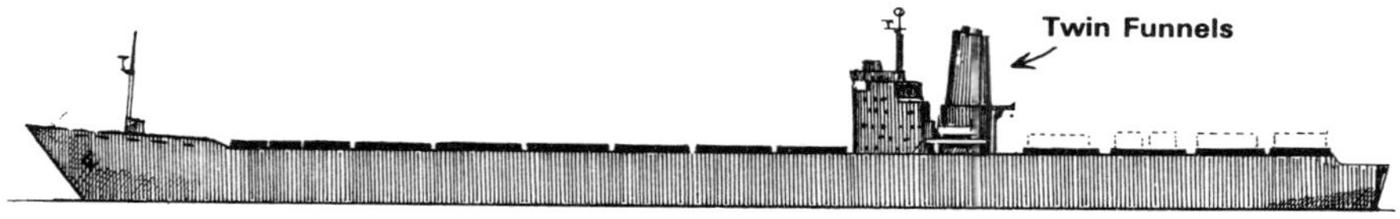

KMF H
08490 SELANDIA. De/De 1972; Con; 50000; 274.3 × 12 (900 × 38); TrSM; 26. Sister: **08491 JUTLANDIA** (De).

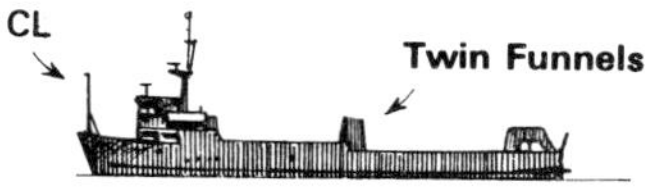

KMF H
08500 QORMI. Ma/Fr 1973; RoC; 1000; 74.99 × 3.2 (262.43 × 10.5); TSM; 13; ex POOLE ANTELOPE 1976. Sister: **08501 DAUPHIN DE CHERBOURG** (Fr).

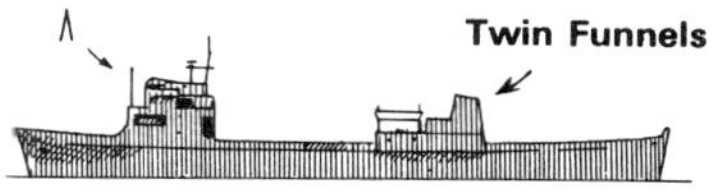

KMF H
08510 TANGO EXPRESS. Pa/It 1969; RoC; 1600; 105.5 × 5 (346 × 16.9); TSM; —; ex CORRIERE DELL'EST 1978; ex ESPRESSO CAMPANIA 1971. Sister: **08511 CORRIERE DEL SUD** (Pa) ex ESPRESSO CALABRIA 1971.

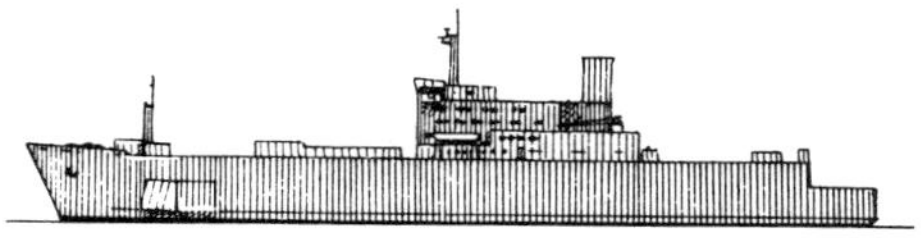

KMF H1
08520 POLARIS. Fi/Fi 1969; RoC; 6200; 137.4 × 5.7 (451 × 18.9); TSM; 18; ex FINNCARRIER 1975; Stern doors. Sisters (Fi flag): **08521 FINNFELLOW 08522 HANS GUTZEIT.**

KMF H1
⋆**08530 OSIJEK.** Ys/Ys 1954; PC; 600; TSM; 15.5; Sister: **08531 PATRIZIA** (It) ex NOVI SAD 1972.

KMF H1
08540 JHUFEL. Pi/Ja 1956; F; 780; 62.36 × 3 (204.59 × 9.84); M; 15; ex YUMEJI MARU 1979.

KMF H1
08550 MARILENA. Gr/Gr 1911; C; 1200; 71 × 5.5 (233 × 18.3); TSM; 16; ex COSTAKIS TOYALS 1960; ex MARIE 1946; ex PATRIS; ex CONQUEROR: ex EMERALD; ex MARYNTHEA; converted yacht.

KMF H1
08560 MUTIARA. My/My 1977; SS; 725 DWT; 71 × 4 (232.94 × 13.12); M; 16; Operated by Malaysian Navy. Helicopter deck aft.

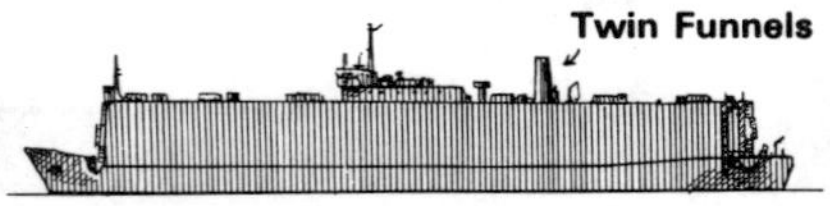

KMF H1
08570 AOI MARU. Ja/Ja 1968; RoVC; 2600; 124 × 5 (407 × 18.5); TSM; 20.

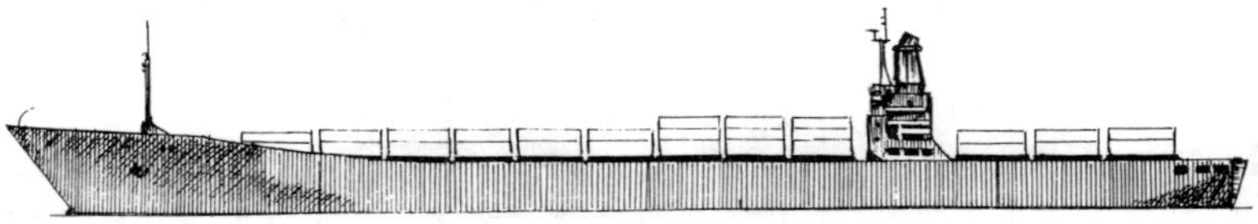

KMF H1
● **08580 EUROLINER.** FRG/FRG 1971; Con; 30900; 243 × 10.7 (799 × 35.2) M; 20. Sisters (FRG flag): **08581 EUROFREIGHTER 08582 ASIALINER 08583 ASIAFREIGHTER.**

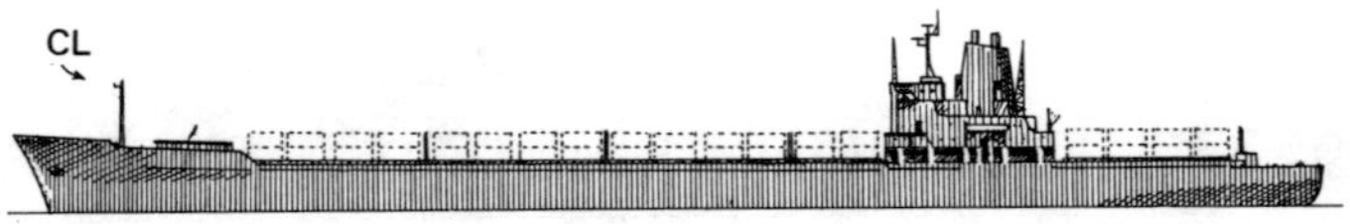

KMF H1
08590 TOHGO MARU. Ja/Ja 1970; Con; 23300; 212 × 9.5 (696 × 31.4); M; 23. Similar: **08591 YAMASHIN MARU** (Ja).

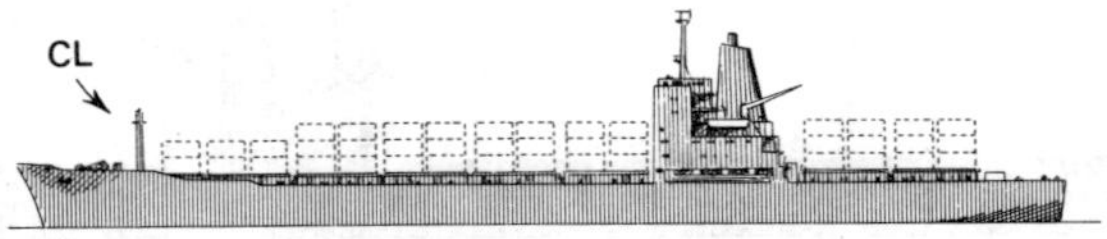

KMF H1
● **08600 ORIENTAL VENTURE.** Br/Br 1980; Con; 17400; 168.89 × 9.15 (554.1 × 30.02); M; 20; ex MANCHESTER VENTURE 1980; ex MARSEILLE 1980; ex MANCHESTER VENTURE 1979; ex SEATRAIN BENNINGTON 1979; ex MANCHESTER VENTURE 1977. Sister: **08601 ORIENTAL VANGUARD** (Br) ex MANCHESTER VANGUARD 1980; ex KEELUNG 1980; ex MANCHESTER VANGUARD 1979; ex SEATRAIN TRENTON 1978; ex MANCHESTER VANGUARD 1977.

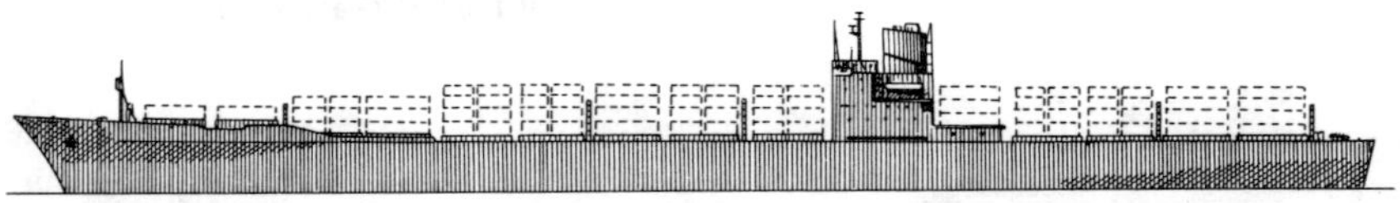

KMF H1
08610 VERAZZANO BRIDGE. Ja/Ja 1973; Con; 39500; 165 × 12 (868 × 39.4); TSM; 26.5. Sister: **08611 HONGKONG CONTAINER** (Li) Similar: **08612 SEVEN SEAS BRIDGE** (Ja).

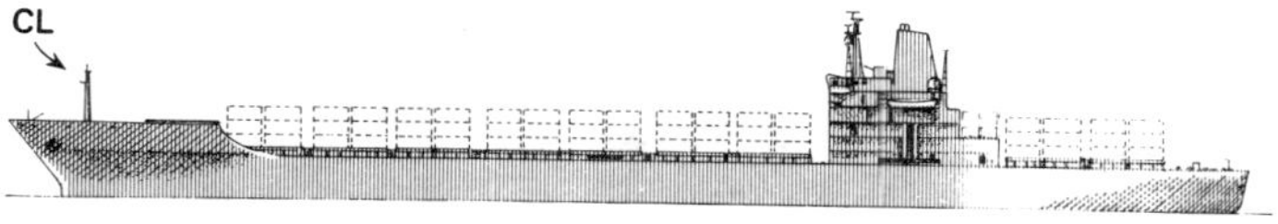

KMF H1

08620 CANBERRA MARU. Ja/Ja 1979; Con; 32200; 216.3 × 11.52 (709.64 × 37.8); M; 22.3.

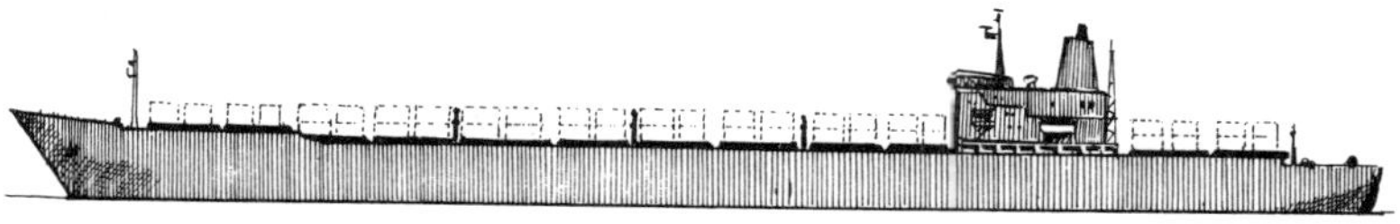

KMF H1

08630 TOHBEI MARU. Ja/Ja 1972; Con; 35500; 246 × 10.5 (807 × 34.7); T; 24.5. Sister: **08631 YASHIMA MARU** (Ja).

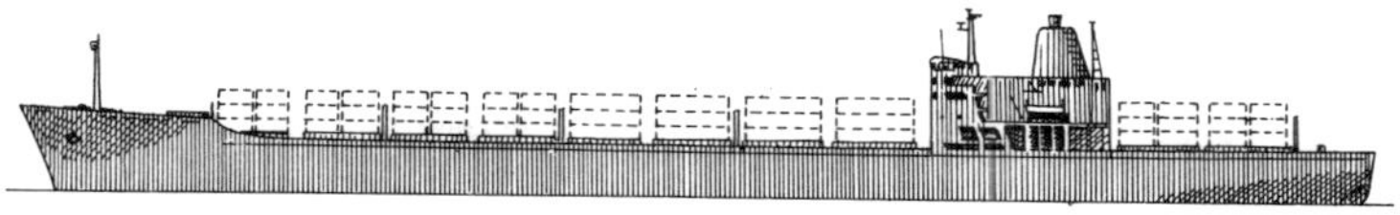

KMF H1

08640 JAPAN AMBROSE. Ja/Ja 1972; Con; 33300; 228 × 11; (748 × 30.6); T; 25.

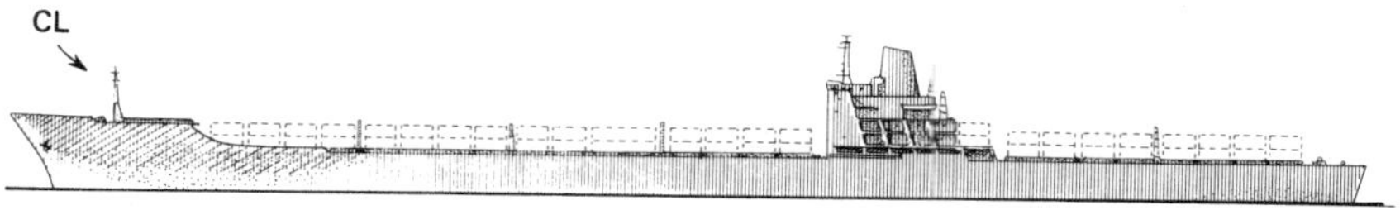

KMF H1

08650 NEW JERSEY MARU. Ja/Ja 1973; Con; 37800; 263.28 × 11.5 (863.78 × 37.73); TSM; 26.

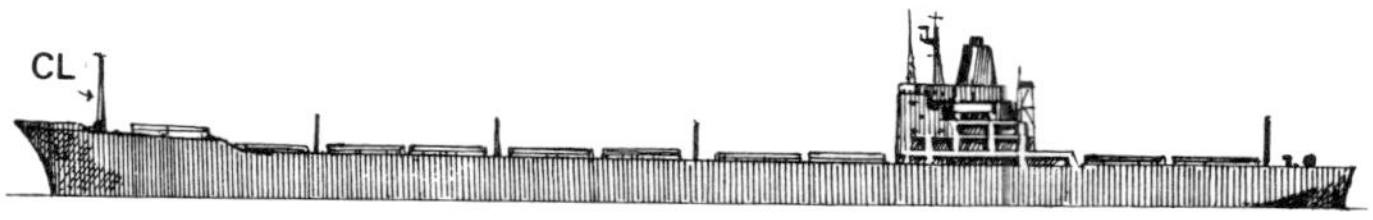

KMF H1

08660 PACIFIC ARROW. Ja/Ja 1973; Con; 30000; 219 × 11 (719 × 36.10); M; 22.

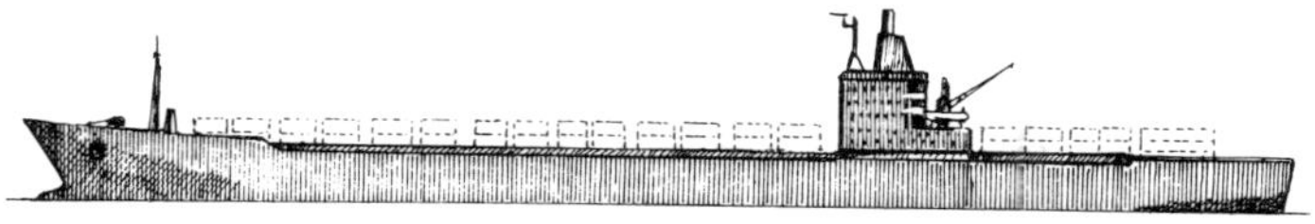

KMF H1

08670 ANDERS MAERSK. De/FRG 1976; Con; 26900; 211 × 11.2 (693 × 37); T; 26; This vessel and all its sisters have been lengthened and a revised drawing will eventually be published. The sequence is probably unaltered. Sisters (De flag): **08671 ADRIAN MAERSK 08672 ALBERT MAERSK 08673 ANNA MAERSK 08674 ARTHUR MAERSK 08675 AXEL MAERSK 08676 ARILD MAERSK 08677 ALVA MAERSK** Similar: (Longer forecastle). **08678 ARNOLD MAERSK.**

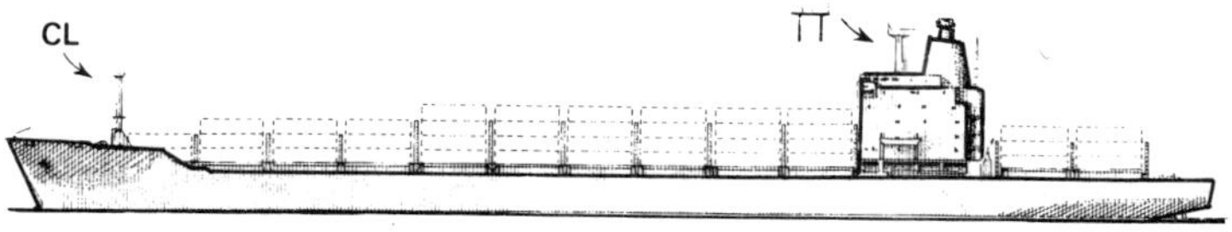

KMF H1

08680 SEA-LAND PATRIOT. US/Ja 1980; Con; 24900; 226.96 × 10 (744.42 × 32.8); M; 22; **"D-9"** class. Sisters (US flag): **08681 SEA-LAND DEFENDER 08682 SEA-LAND EXPLORER 08683 SEA-LAND DEVELOPER 08684 SEA-LAND EXPRESS 08685 SEA-LAND FREEDOM 08686 SEA-LAND INDEPENDENCE 08687 SEA-LAND MARINER 08688 SEA-LAND VOYAGER** The following sisters were built in Ko: **08689 SEA-LAND ENDURANCE 08690 SEA-LAND INNOVATOR.**

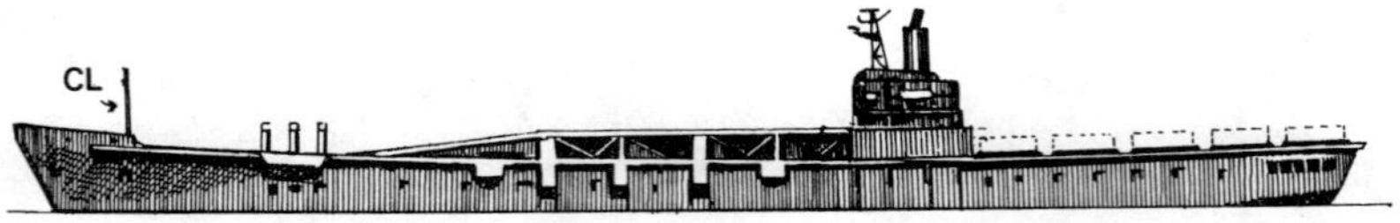

KMF H1
08710 GREAT LAND. US/US 1975; RoC: 17600; 241 × — (791 × —); T; 25.

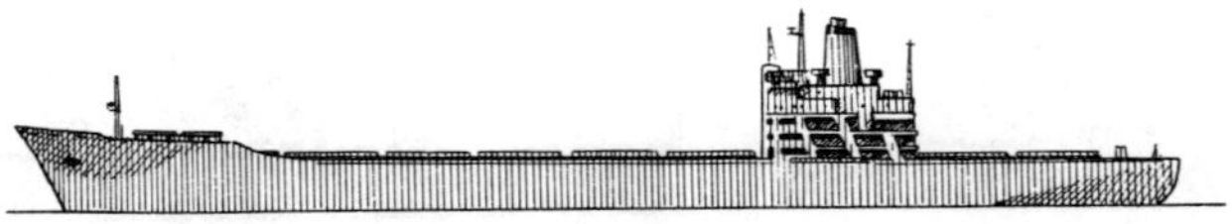

KMF H1
08720 JAPAN ACE. Ja/Ja 1968; Con; 16600; 188 × 9 (617 × 31.10); M; 22.75. Similar: **08721 KAZUKAWA MARU** (Ja) ex GOLDEN ARROW 1980.

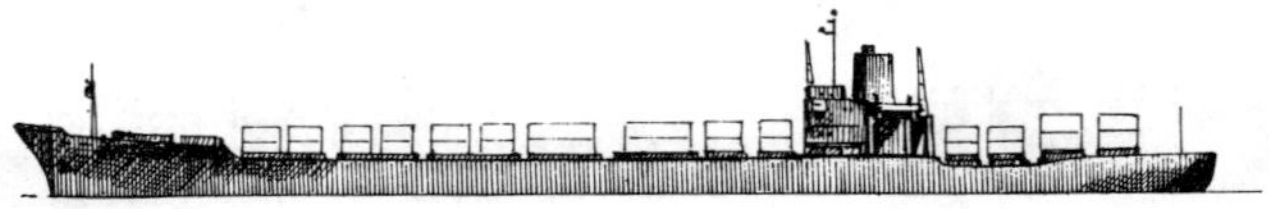

KMF H1
08730 GOLDEN GATE BRIDGE. Ja/Ja 1968; Con; 16900; 189 × 9.9 (620 × 33.6); M; 22.25.

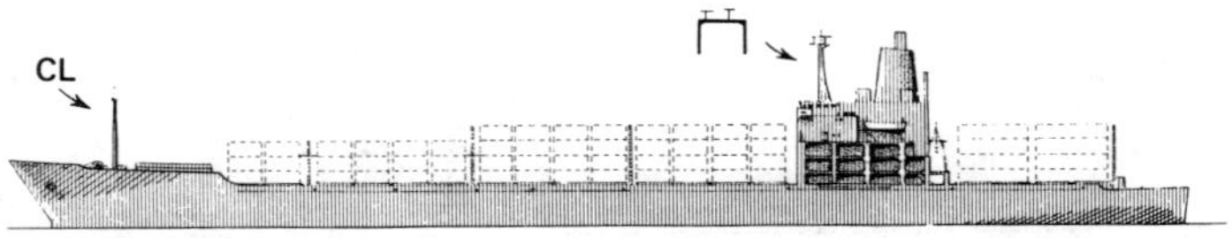

KMF H1
08740 HIRA MARU. Ja/Ja 1978; Con; 24800; 214.61 × 10.5 (704 × 34.45); M; 23.

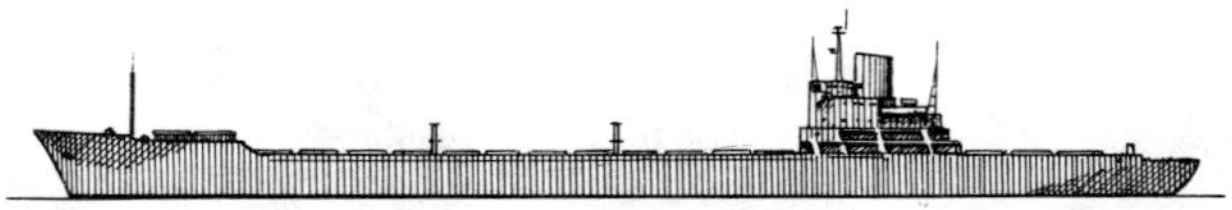

KMF H1
08750 KASHU MARU. Ja/Ja 1968; Con; 16600; 188 × 9.4 (617 × 30.11); M; 22.5.

KMF H1
08760 DRAGOR MAERSK. De/Ja 1974; Con; 38500; 261 × 11.7 (853 × 38.6); TSM; 26.5; ex SVENDBORG MAERSK 1980; ex TFL CHARLESTON 1980; ex SEATRAIN CHARLESTON 1980; ex SVENDBORG MAERSK 1979.

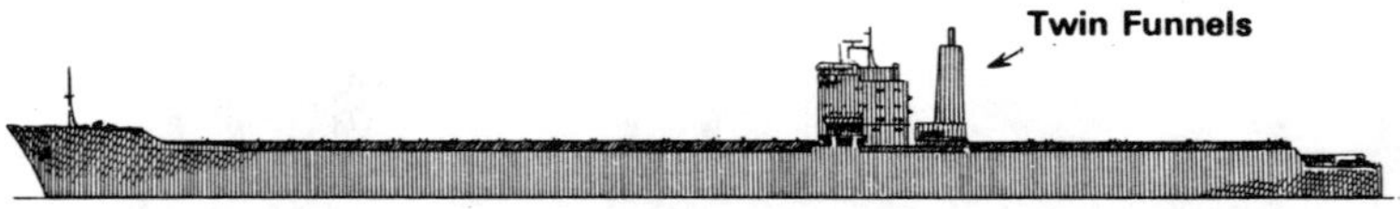

KMF H1
08770 ARIAKE. Br/FRG 1976; Con; 37500; 238 × 11.6 (781 × 38); TSM; 26.

●
08775

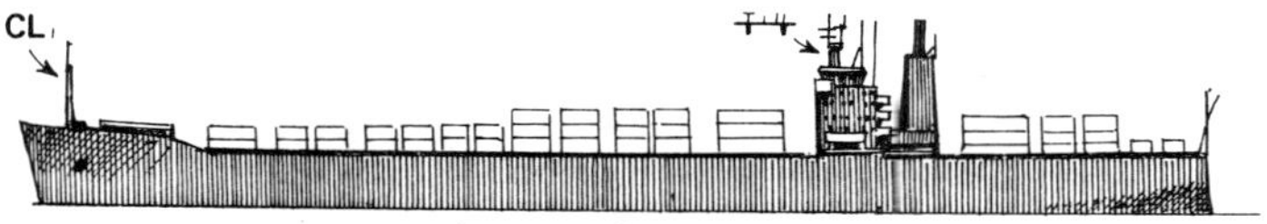

KMF H1
08780 DUSSELDORF EXPRESS. FRG/FRG 1977; Con; 32900; 209.94 × 11.02 (688.78 × 36.15); M; 22. Sisters (FRG flag): **08781 KOLN EXPRESS 08782 NURNBERG EXPRESS 08783 STUTTGART EXPRESS.**

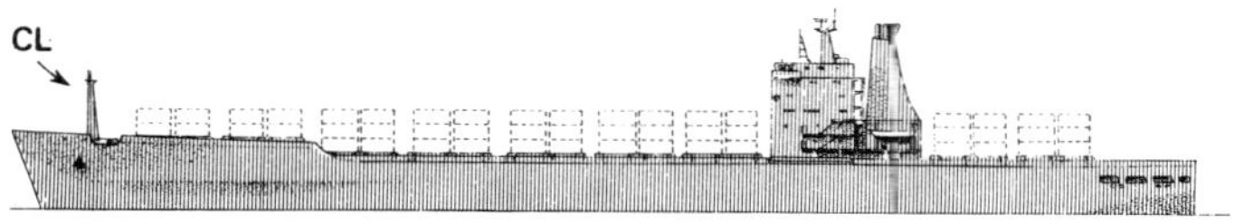

KMF H1
08790 FORT ROYAL. FR/Fr 1979; Con; 32200; 210 × 11.02 (688.98 × 36.15); TSM; 22. Sister: **08791 FORT FLEUR d'EPEE** (Fr).

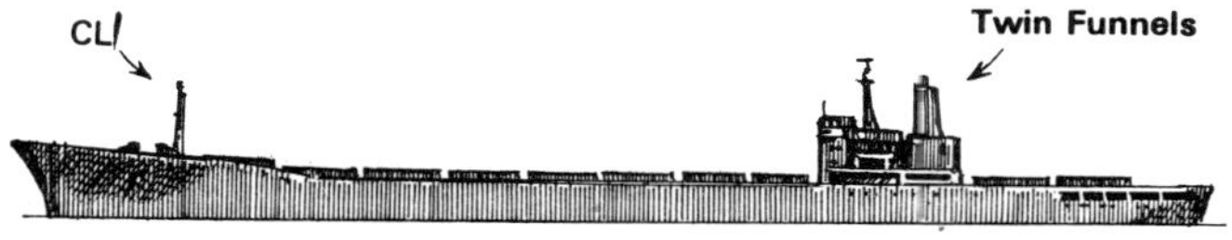

KMF H1
● **08800 KOREAN COMMANDER.** Ko/It 1971; Con; 25800; 208 × 10.4 (683 × 34.1); T; 23.5; ex TAEPING 1977. Sisters: **08801 ZIM CALIFORNIA** (Li) ex TAEHO 1976 **08802 ZIM GENOVA** (Is) **08803 ZIM HAIFA** (Is) **08804 ZIM NEW YORK** (FRG) **08805 ZIM TOKYO** (FRG) Similar: **08806 MEDITERRANEA** (It) **08807 NIPPONICA** (It) Similar (with garage abaft superstructure): **08808 AFRICA** (It) **08809 EUROPA** (It) **08810 S.A. LANGEBERG** (SA).

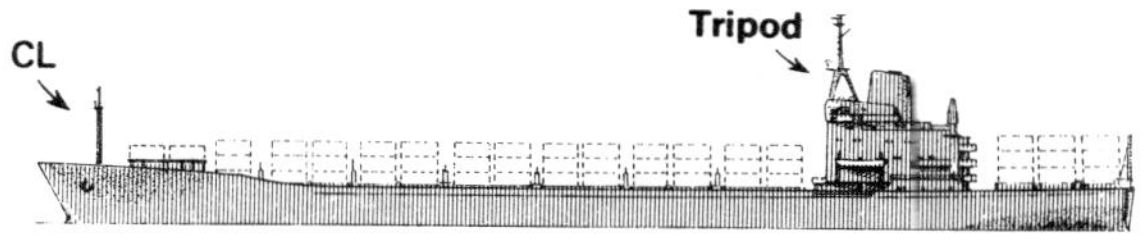

KMF H1
● **08830 LEVERKUSEN EXPRESS.** FRG/FRG-FRG 1970/78; Con; 16700; 176.49 × 10.59 (579 × 34.74); M; —; ex LEVERKUSEN 1978; converted from general cargo, lengthened & widened 1978. Sisters (FRG flag): **08831 ERLANGEN EXPRESS** ex ERLANGEN 1979 **08832 HOECHST EXPRESS** ex HOECHST 1979 **08833 LUDWIGSHAFEN EXPRESS** ex LUDWIGSHAFEN 1979.

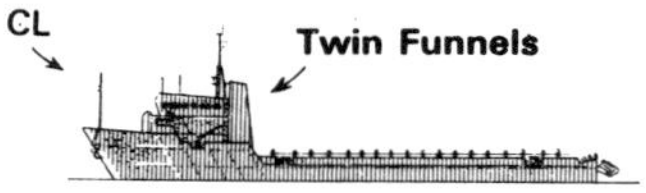

KMF H1
08840 STAR HERCULES. Br/Br 1980; Sply/Spt; 1600; 82.56 × 4.47 (270.87 × 14.67); TSM; 13.

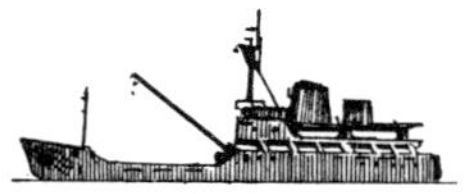

KMF H12
08850 MONTCALM. Ca/Ca 1957; IB/LT; 2000; 67 × 4.9 (220 × 16.4); TSM; 13. Similar (Ca flag): **08851 WOLFE 08852 SIR HUMPHREY GILBERT.**

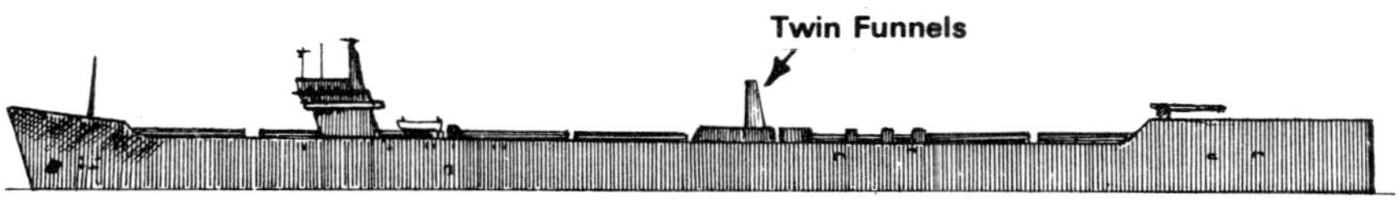

KMF H13
08860 ALMERIA LYKES. US/US 1972; Bg; 21700; 167 × 11.9 (876 × 38.2); T; 19.5; **'Seabee'** type; stern elevator. Sisters (US flag): **08861 DOCTOR LYKES 08862 TILLIE LYKES.**

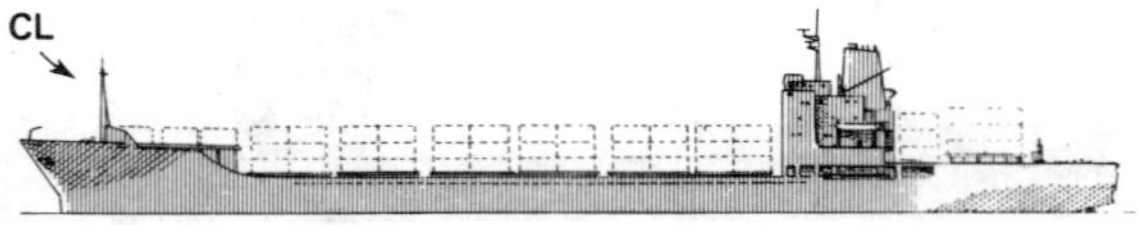

KMF H13

● **08870 SEATRAIN ORISKANY.** Li/Ja 1979; Con; 13800; 177.03 × 10.13 (383.96 × 33.23); M; 19. Sisters: **08871 SEATRAIN BENNINGTON** (FRG) **08872 SEATRAIN CHESAPEAKE** (Li **08873 SEATRAIN YORKTOWN** (Li) **08874 SEATRAIN INDEPENDENCE** (Li) **08875 TFL JEFFERSON** (Br) ex SEATRAIN SARATOGA 1980.

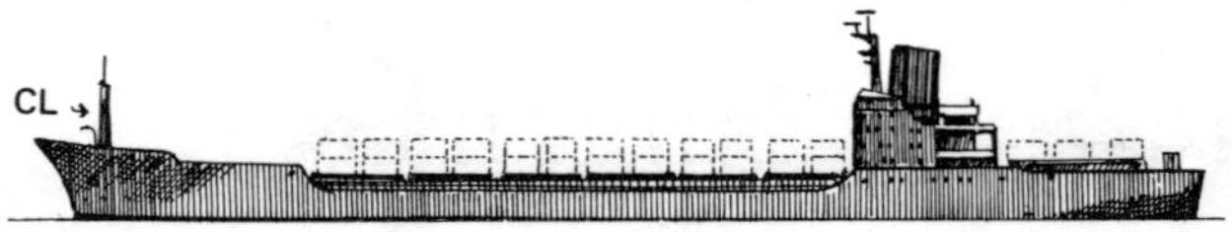

KMF H13

08880 CALIFORNIA STAR. Br/FRG 1971; Con; 19100; 189 × 10 (616 × 33); M; 21.5. Sister: **08881 COLUMBIA STAR** (Br).

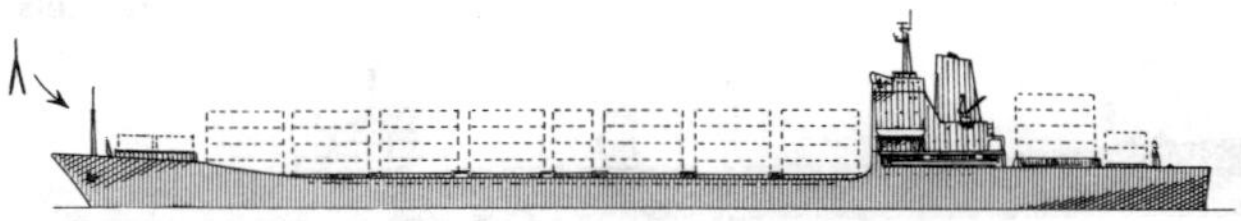

KMF H13

08890 EVER VALIANT. Pa/Ja 1977; Con; 14400; 186.75 × 10.02 (612.7 × 32.87); M; 22. Similar: **08891 EVER VICTORY** (Li) **08892 EVER VOYAGER** (Li) **08893 EVER VIGOR** (Tw) **08894 EVER VITAL** (Tw) probably similar: **08895 EVER VALOR** (Pa) **08896 EVER VALUE** (Pa).

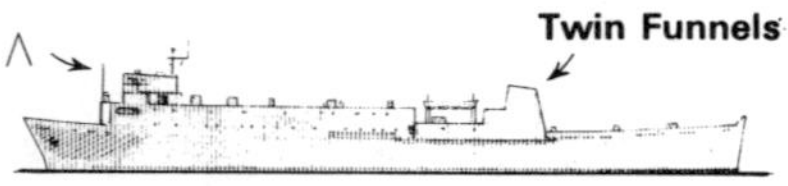

KMF H2

08900 FRECCIA DELL'OUEST. It/It 1975; RoCF; 2600; 117.51 × 5.066 (385.5 × 16.62); TSM; 20; CORRIERE DELL'OUEST 1979. Sister: **08901 FRECCIA DEL NORD** (It) ex CORRIERE DEL NORD 1979.

KMF H2

08920 CABLE RESTORER. SA/Br 1944; Cbl; 1500; 77 × 5 (255 × 17); TSR: 10; ex RETRIEVER III 1961; ex RETRIEVER 1960.

KMF H2

08940 HARSHA VARDHANA. In/In 1974; PC; 8900; 132.6 × 7 (435 × 23); M; 17.

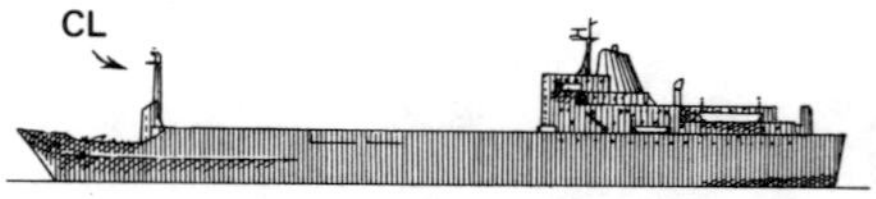

KMF H2

08910 FRECCIA BLU. It/It 1970; RoC; 4400; 133 × 6 (437 × 19.7); TSM; 21. Sister: **08911 FRECCIA ROSSA** (It).

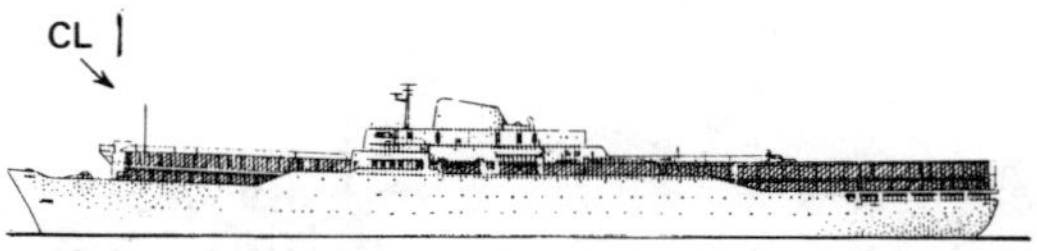

KMF H2

08930 PERSIA. Le/It 1953/77; LS; 8800; 159.09 × 8.35 (521.85 × 27.4); TSM; 19; ex ASIA 1975; converted from passenger 1977.

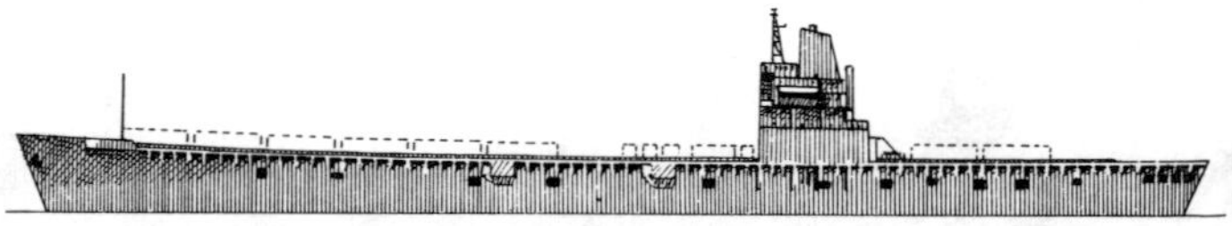

KMF H2

08950 LURLINE. US/US 1973; RoC/Con; 15300; 213 × 8.5 (700 × 28.1); T; 25; side doors. Sister: **08951 MATSONIA** (US).

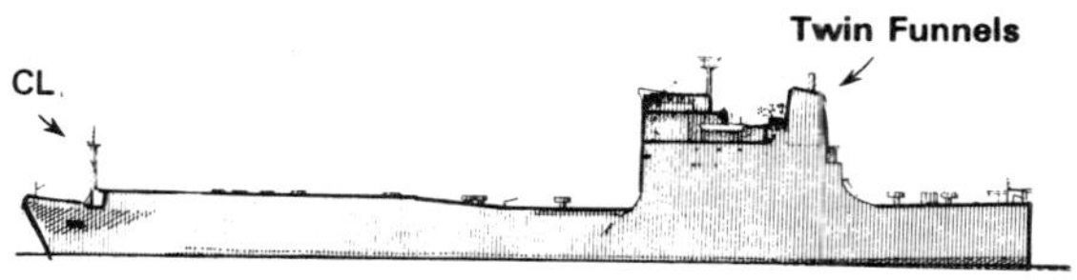

KMF H3

08960 FOSS DUNKERQUE. Fr/Fr 1978; RoC; 8700; 169.25 × 7.74 (555.2 × 25.3); M; 18.5; ex VILLE DE DUNKERQUE 1979; stern door/ramp. Side doors. Sister (Fr flag): **08961 FOSS HAVRE** ex VILLE DU HAVRE 1979 **08962 RO-RO MANHATTAN 08963 RO-RO GENOVA** ex QATAR EXPRESS 1981; ex RO-RO GENOVA 1980.

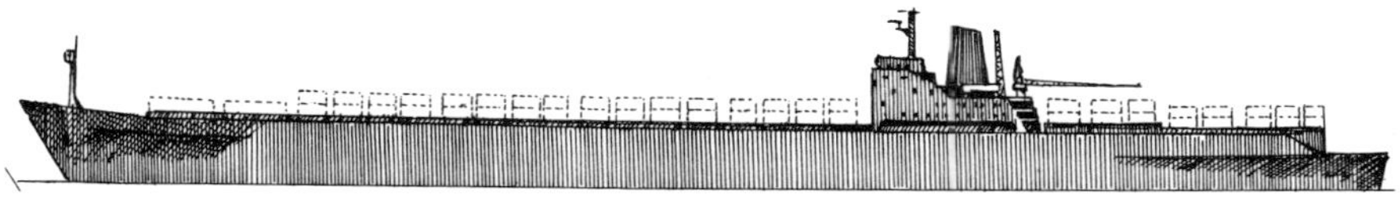

KMFC H

08970 TOYAMA. No/Ja 1972; Con; 52200; 275 × 11 (903 × 36.4); TSM; 26.25.

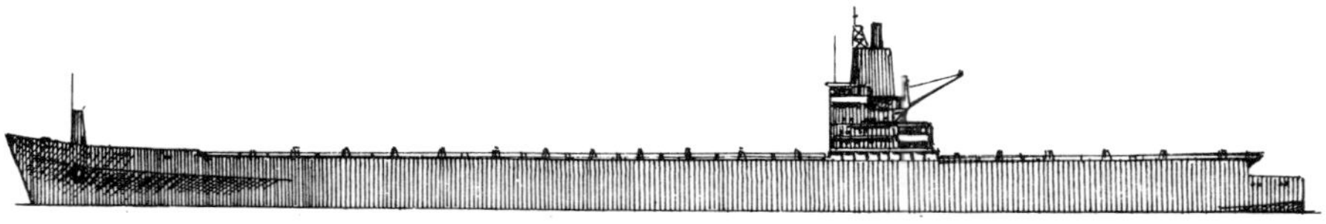

KMFC H

08980 BARCELONA. Br/FRG 1977; Con; 53800; 258.55 × 13.02 (848.26 × 42.72); TSM; 21.5; ex TABLE BAY 1979. Sister: **08981 CITY OF DURBAN** (Br).

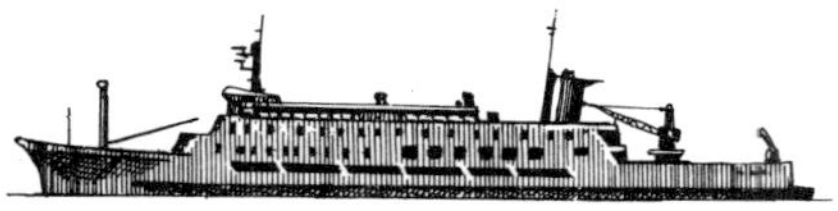

KMFC H

08990 KUROSHIO MARU. Ja/Ja 1971; F; 4900; 124 × 5.5 (407 × 17.10); TSM; 23.

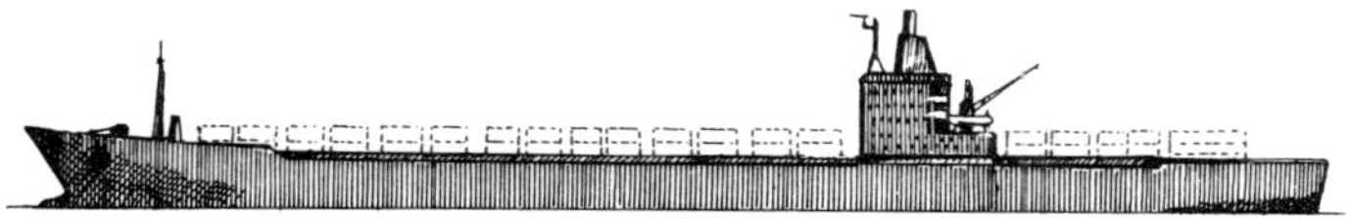

KMFC H1

09000 ANDERS MAERSK. De/FRG 1976; Con; 26900; 211 × 11.2 (693 × 37); T; 26; This vessel and all its sisters have been lengthened and a revised drawing will eventually be published. The sequence is probably unaltered. Sisters (De flag): **09001 ADRIAN MAERSK 09002 ALBERT MAERSK 09003 ANNA MAERSK 09004 ARTHUR MAERSK 09005 AXEL MAERSK 09006 ARILD MAERSK 09007 ALVA MAERSK** Similar (longer forecastle): **09008 ARNOLD MAERSK.**

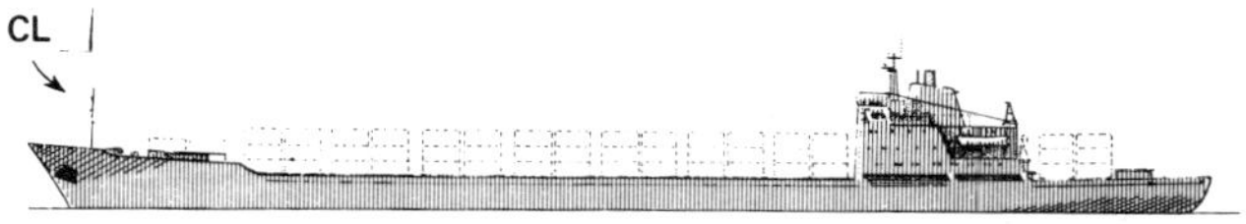

KMFC H1

09010 AL AHMADIAH. Ku/Ru-Sp 1969/80; Con; 14400; 194.33 × 9.5 (637.57 × 31.17); M; 18.5; converted from cargo of **"Feodosiya"** type 1980. Sisters (Ku flag): **09011 AL RUMAITHIAH 09012 AL SHAMIAH.**

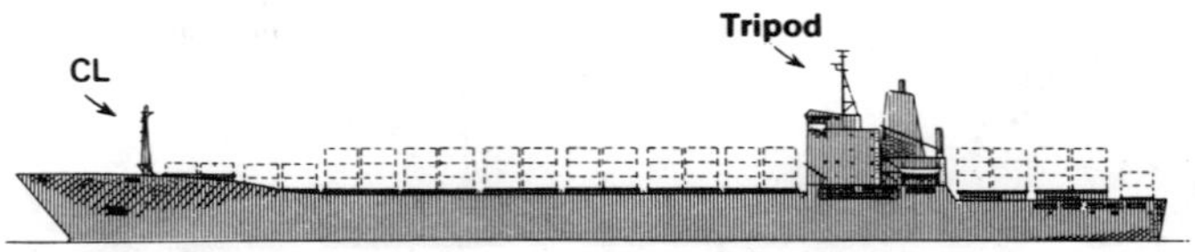

KMFC H1
09020 ERCOLE LAURO. It/It 1980; Con; 26800; 208.12 × 10.66 (682.81 × 34.97); M; 22.

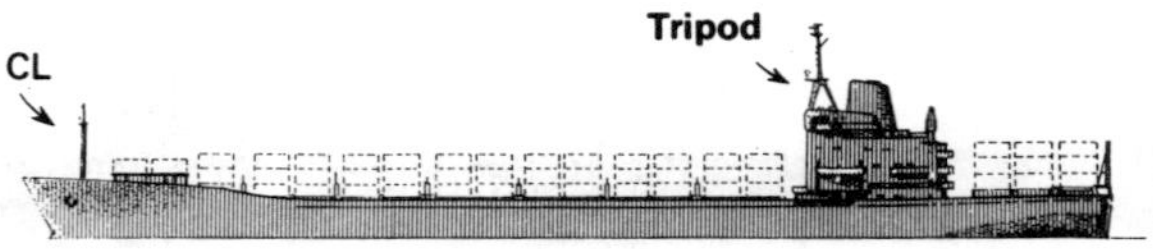

KMFC H1
● **09030 LEVERKUSEN EXPRESS.** FRG/FRG-FRG 1970/78; Con; 16700; 176.49 × 10.59 (579 × 34.74); M; 21; ex LEVERKUSEN 1978; Converted from general cargo, lengthened & widened 1978. Sisters (FRG flag): **09031 ERLANGEN EXPRESS** ex ERLANGEN 1979 **09032 HOECHST EXPRESS** ex HOECHST 1979 **09033 LUDWIGSHAFEN EXPRESS** ex LUDWIGSHAFEN 1979.

KMFC H1
09040 OIL ENDEAVOUR. Br/Fr-Br 1967/77; Diving Support; 1900; 84.82 × 5.64 (278.28 × 18.5); D-E; 14.5; ex MARIE DE GRACE 1976; converted from stern trawler.

KMFC H1
09050 SEAFORTH CLANSMAN. Br/Br 1977; OSS; 2000; 78.62 × 5 (257.9 × 16.4); TSM; 13; Diving support ship—stern ramp.

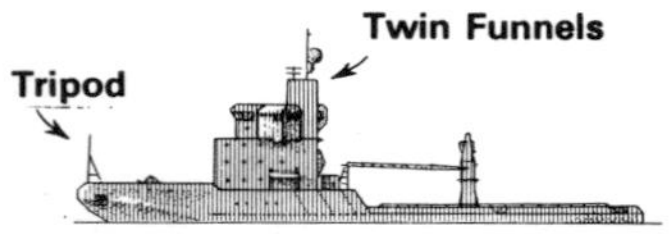

KMFC H1
09060 CANMAR KIGORIAK. Ca/Ca 1980; IB/Tg/Sply; 3600; 91.06 × 8.54 (298.75 × 28.02); M; 18.6 (max).

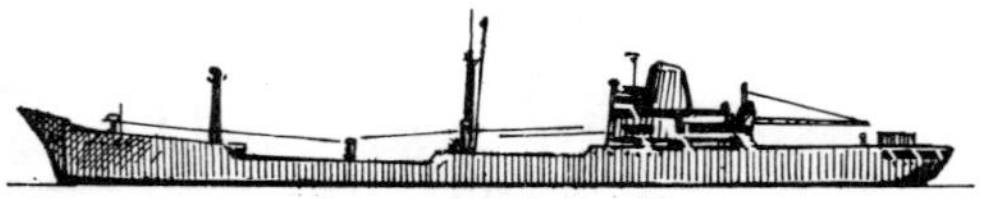

KMFC H12
09070 KEFALONIA SPIRIT. Cy/Sp 1965; C: 6000/8300; 146 × —/— (480 × —/—); M; 16; ex MONTE SAJA 1974. Sister: **09071 BANGLAR UPOHAR** (Bh) ex MONTE SOLLUBE 1973 Similar: **09072 BANGLAR ASHA** (Bh) ex MOSOR 1973; ex GARCIANI 1970.

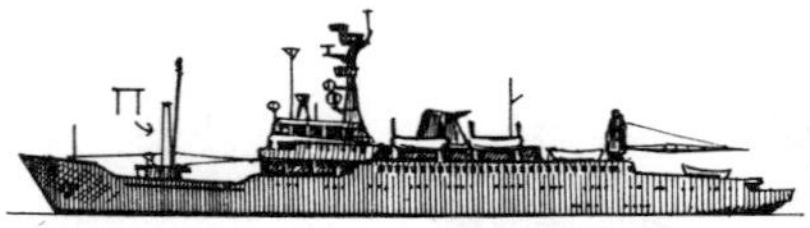

KMFC H12
⋆09080 PROFESSOR SHCHYOGOLEV. Ru/Pd 1970; C/TS; 6000; 122 × 7.3 (401 × 24.2); M; 15.5; **'B 80'** type. Sisters (Ru flag): **⋆09081 PROFESSOR KUDREVICH ⋆09082 PROFESSOR ANICHKOV ⋆09083 PROFESSOR PAVLENKO ⋆09084 PROFESSOR RYBALTOVSKIY ⋆09085 PROFESSOR KLYUSTIN ⋆09086 PROFESSOR YUSHENKO** Similar (light mast from funnel): **⋆09087 PROFESSOR UKHOV ⋆09088 PROFESSOR MINYAYEV.**

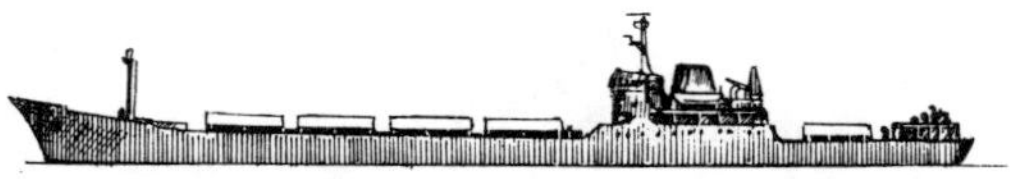

KMFC H12
09090 SUNHERMINE. Ca/Br 1965; Con; 9100; 151 × 8.1 (495 × 28.1); M; 17; ex INISHOWEN HEAD 1979; ex CAST BEAVER 1977; ex INISHOWEN HEAD 1973; Converted from cargo ship.

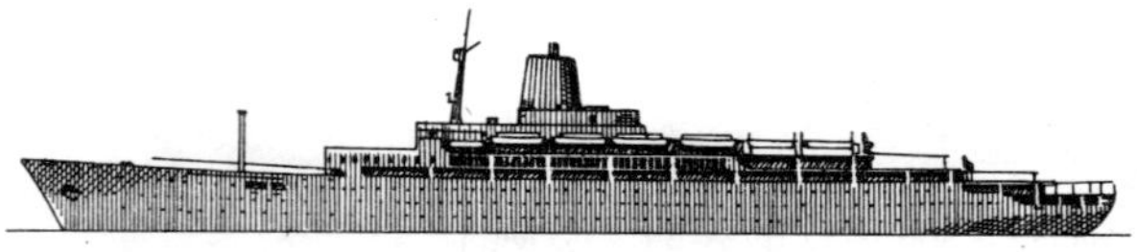

$KMFC_2$ H
09100 FEDERICO C. It/It 1958; P; 20400; 185 × 8.6 (606 × 28.5); TST; 21.

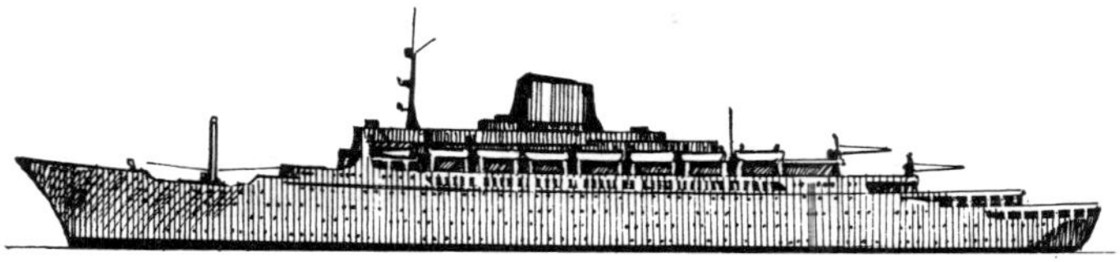

$KMFC_2$ H

● **09110 CRISTOFORD COLOMBO.** It/It 1954; P; 29400; 214 × 9.1 (701 × 30.4); TST; 23; Sold 1977 to the Venezuelan Government. To be used as a floating hotel.

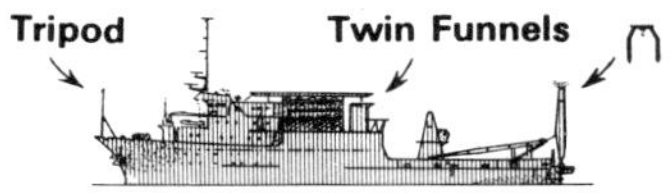

KMFCK H1

09120 SWAN OCEAN. Br/Fi 1979; Spt; 730 dwt; 77. × 5.35 (252.62 × 17.55); TSM; 14; Helicopter deck. Radar mast and "A" frame are hinged.

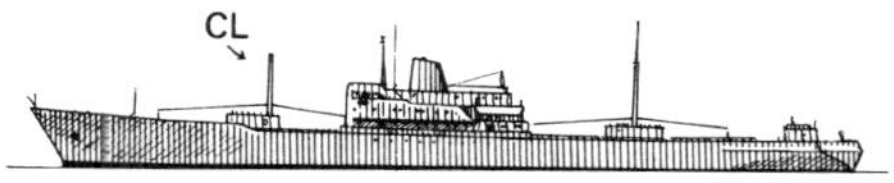

KMFCM H

09140 AFRICA. Gr/Be 1965; R; 5100; 135 × 6.5 (440 × 21.9); M; 20; ex FRUBEL AMERICA 1980. Sister: **09141 FRUBEL EUROPA** (Be).

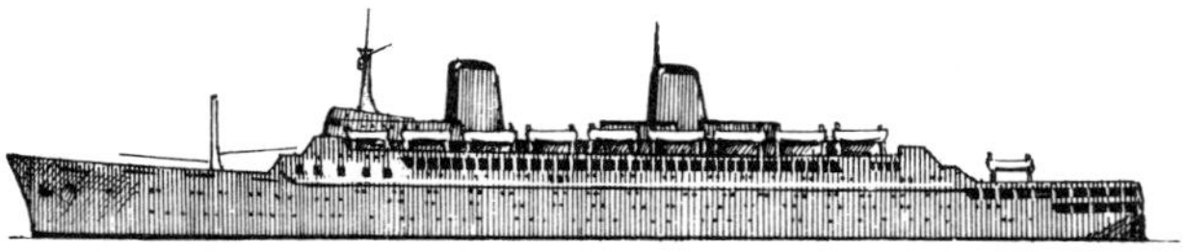

KMF_2 H

09150 BRITANIS. Gr/US 1932; P; 18300; 192 × 8.6 (630 × 28); TST; 21.5; ex LURLINE 1970; ex MATSONIA 1963; ex MONTEREY 1956.

KMF_2 H

09160 CONSTELLATION. Gr/Ys 1962; P; 12400; 150 × 5.5 (492 × 18.5); TSM; 18.5; ex DANAOS 1978; ex ANNA NERY 1978. Sister **09161 NIPPON MARU** (Ja) ex P.S. SEVEN SEAS 1978; ex ROSA DA FONSECA 1975.

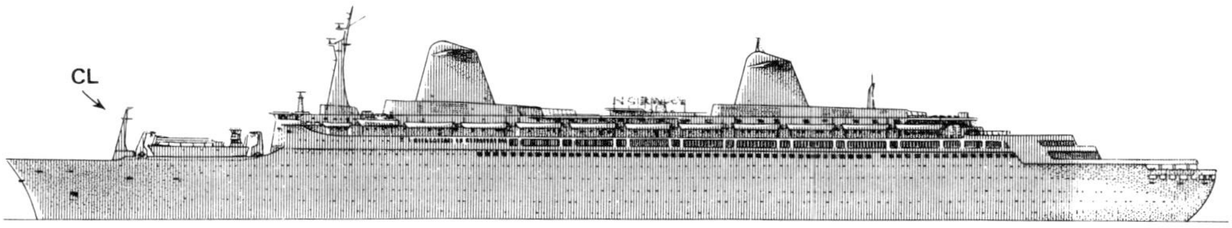

KMF_2K H

09165 NORWAY. No/Fr-FRG 1961/80; P; 70200; 315 × 10.3 (1034 × 34); TST; 17; ex France; Modernised and rebuilt 1979/80.

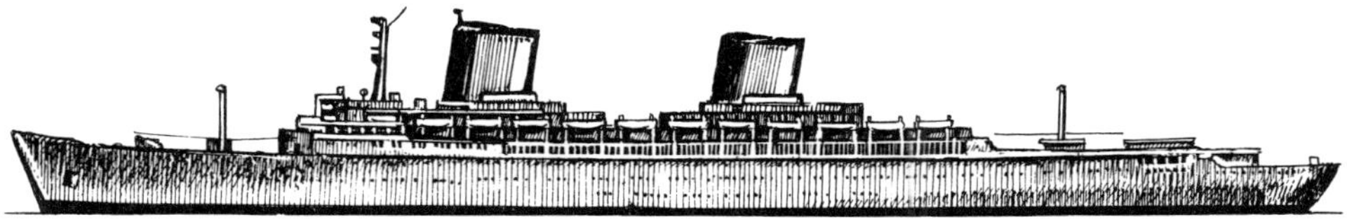

KMF_2K H

09170 UNITED STATES. US/US 1952; P; 38200; 301 × 10 (988 × 33); QST; 30.

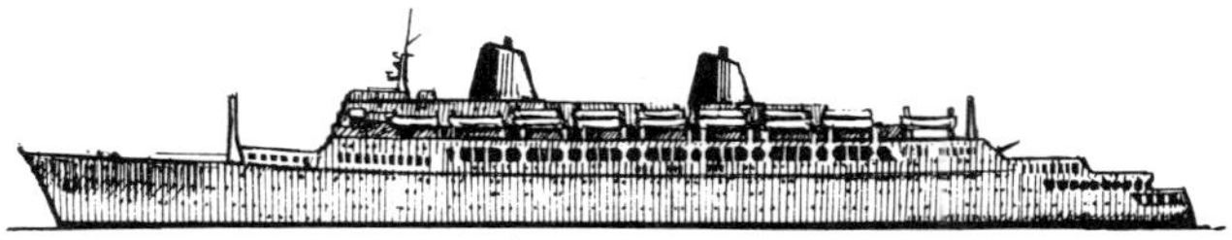

KMF_2K H

09180 ELLINIS. Gr/US 1932; P; 18600; 193 × 8.6 (634 × 28); TST; 21; ex LURLINE 1963.

KMF_2K *H*

09190 OCEANIC CONSTITUTION. US/US 1951; P; 20300; 208 × 9 (683 × 30); TST; 22.5; ex CONSTITUTION 1974. Sister: **09191 OCEANIC INDEPENDENCE** (US) ex INDEPENDENCE 1974.

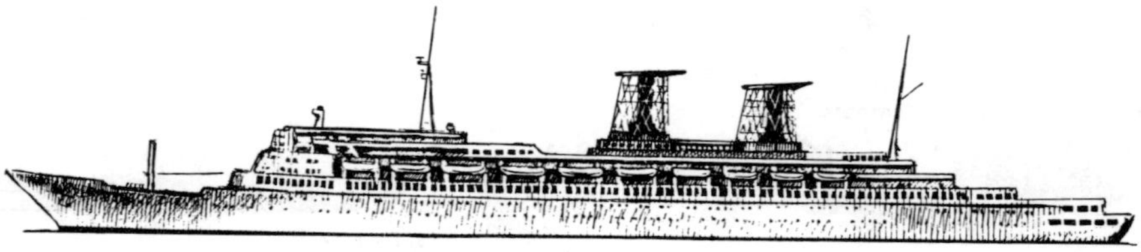

KMF_2M *H*

09200 MICHELANGELO. Ir/It 1965; P; 49500; 276 × 9.3 (906 × 30); TST; 26.5; Used as accomdation ships by the Iranian Navy. May be renamed. Sister: **09201 RAFFAELLO** (Ir).

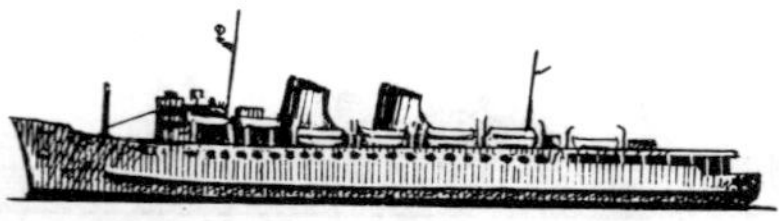

KMF_2M *H*

⋆09210 PRIAMURYE. Ru/Ru 1957; P; 5800; 119 × 6.7 (391 × 19); DE; 16. Sister: **⋆09211 ZABAYKALYE.**

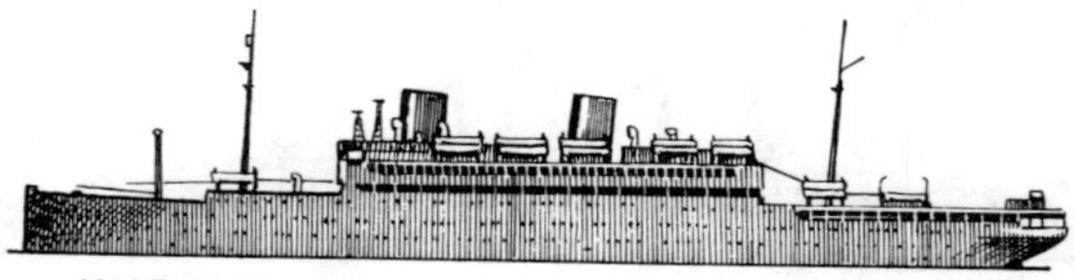

KMF_2M *H*

⋆09220 ADMIRAL NAKHIMOV. Ru/Ge 1925; P; 17100; 173 × 9 (568 × 30); TSR; 16; ex BERLIN 1947.

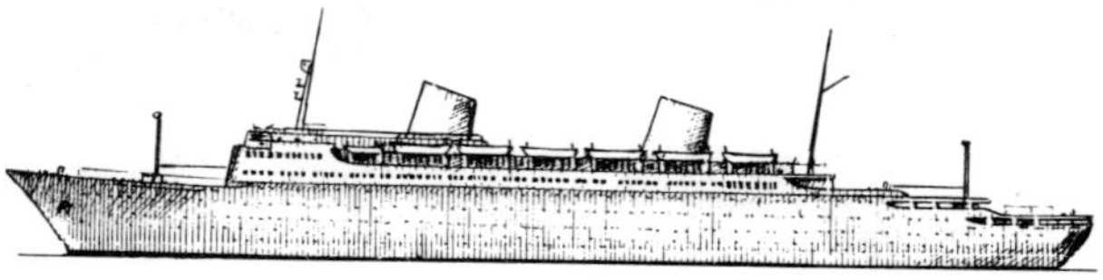

KMF_2MK *H*

09230 NAVARINO. Gr/It 1957; P; 23200; 193 × 8.2 (634 × 27); TSM; 19; ex GRIPSHOLM 1975.

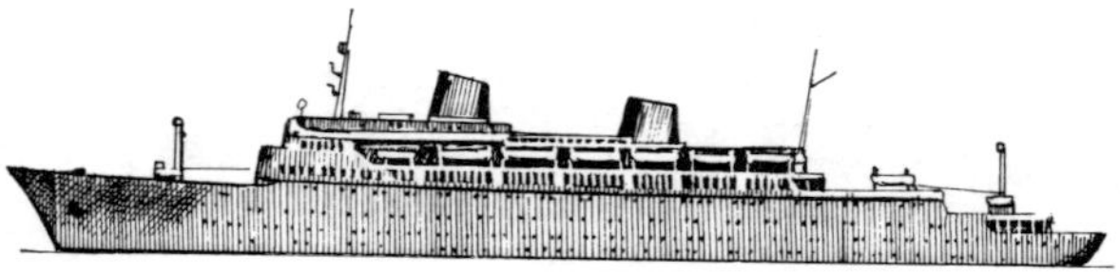

KMF_2MK *H*

● **09240 EUROPA.** FRG/Ne 1953; P; 21500; 182 × 8.2 (598 × 27); TSM; 19; ex KUNGSHOLM 1965; Satellite Navigation dome has now been fitted to foreward funnel.

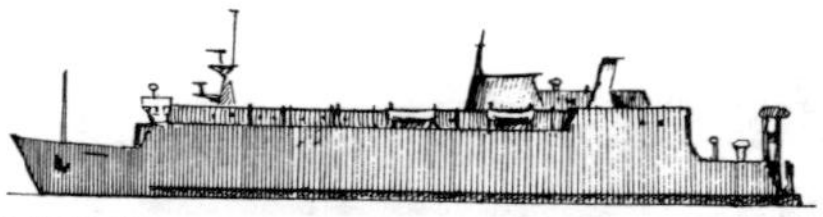

KMF_2MK *H*

⋆09250 MIKOLAJ KOPERNIK. Pd/No 1973; TF; 2600; 126 × 4.6 (412 × 150); TSM; 16. Sister: **⋆09251 JAN HEWELIUSZ** (Pd).

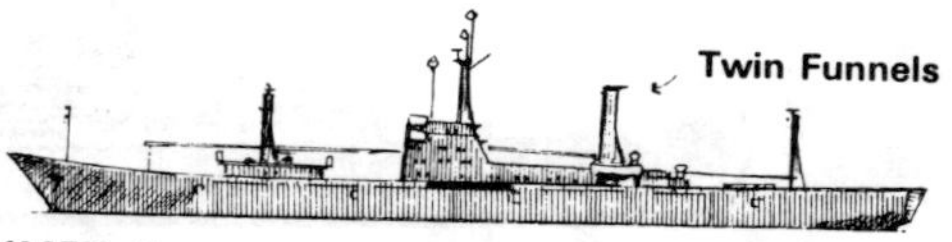

KMFK H

09260 POLAR ARGENTINA. Li/FRG 1968; R; 3800/5600; 148 × 6.6/8.2 (485 × 18.6/27); M; 23. Sisters (Li flag): **09261 POLAR BRASIL 09262 POLAR COLOMBIA 09263 POLAR ECUADOR 09264 POLAR PARAGUAY 09265 POLAR URUGUAY.**

KMFK H

09270 LIPARI. It/It 1956; PC; 1600; 86 × 3.8 (282 × 12.6); TSM; —.

KMFK H

09280 ST. MARGARETS. Br/Br 1944; Cbl; 1500; 76 × 4.8 (252 × 16.3); TSR; 12; Owned by Ministry of Defence.

KMFK H
09290 ANG PANGULO. Pi/Ja 1959; Y; 2200; 83 × 4.9 (275 × 17); TSM; 16.5; ex THE PRESIDENT; ex ROXAS; ex LAPU-LAPU; Presidential Yacht.

KMFK H
09300 ORION. Gr/It 1953; P; 6100; 127 × 5.4 (416 × 17.5); TST; 17; ex ACHILLEUS 1968.

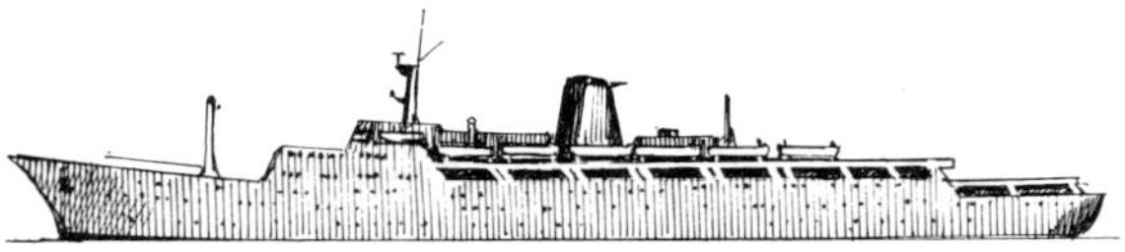

KMFK H
09310 FLAVIA. It/Br 1947; P; 15500; 169 × 8 (556 × 27); TST; 18; ex MEDIA 1961; Converted from passenger/cargo.

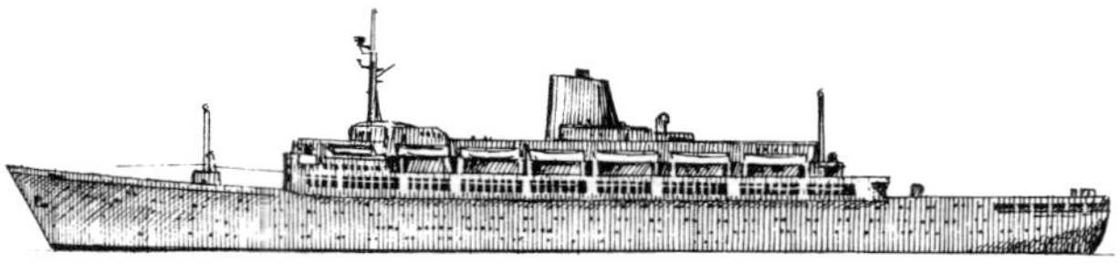

KMFK H
09320 STATENDAM. NA/Ne 1957; P; 24400; 196 × 8 (643 × 26.1); TST; 19.

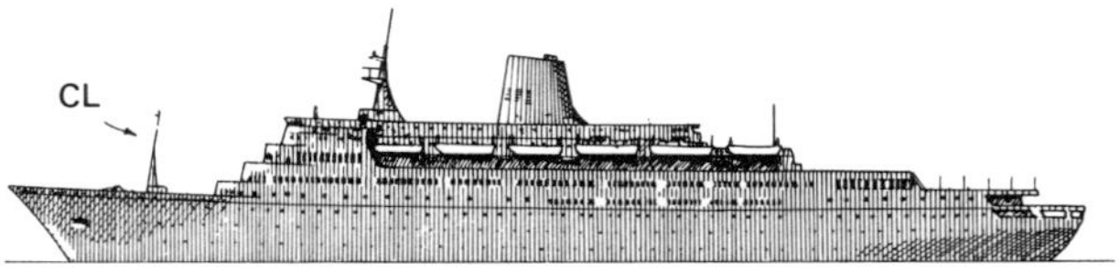

KMFK H
09330 VISTAFJORD. No/Br 1973; P; 24900; 191 × 8.2 (627 × 27); TSM; 20.

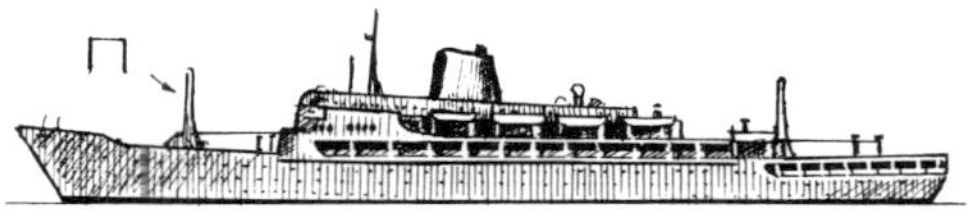

KMFK H
09340 VERACRUZ 1. Pa/FRG 1957; P; 9900; 149 × 6.6 (488 × 21.5); TST; 20; ex FREEPORT 1976; ex CARNIVALE 1974; ex THEODOR HERZL 1969.

KMFK H
09350 TERAAKA. Br/Ys 1959; C; 1000; 64.3 × 3.9 (211 × 12.11); M; 15; ex NINIKORIA 1975; ex OPATIJA 1968. Sister: **09351 FRANCISCO DE MIRANDA** (Ve) ex OREBIC 1967.

KMFK H
★**09360 GRUMANT.** Ru/De 1964; FT; 4700; 103 × 5.5 (337 × 18.3); M; 14. (differ from SKRYPLEV by having both KP.s on houses). Sisters (Ru flag): ★**09361 GEIZER** ★**09362 GLETCHER** ★**09363 KAPITAN SKORNYAKOV** ex GOLFSTRIM ★**09364 KURS** ★**09365 NAVIGATOR** ★**09366 SKAZOCHNIK ANDERSEN** Similar: ★**09368 PAVLOVO** ★**09369 PELENGATOR** ★**09370 PEREMYSHLJ** ★**09371 PRILUKI** ★**09372 PROKOPYEVSK** ★**09373 ZELENOBORSK** ★**09374 MAGNIT** ★**09375 BUSSOL** ★**09376 EKHOLOT** ★**09377 LOKATOR**

KMFK H
★**09380 SKRYPLEV.** Ru/De 1962; FT; 4700; 103 × 5.5 (337 × 18.3); M; 14. Sisters (Ru flag): ★**09381 DAVYDOV** ★**09382 SOVIETSK** ★**09383 VITUS BERING** Possible sisters: ★**09384 APETIT** ★**09385 KOMPAS** ★**09386 KONDOR** ★**09387 ZAPOLYARNYY.**

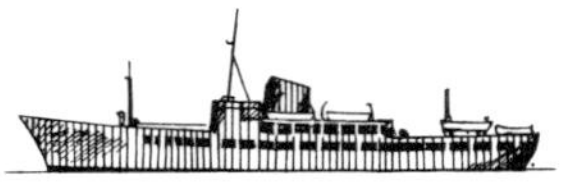

KMFK H
09390 ACHILLEUS. Gr/It 1952; Pc; 1700; 82 × 4.6 (269 × 13.1); TSM; 14; ex KOLOKOTRONIS 1971. Sisters (Gr flag): **09391 ALEXANDROS** ex KARAISKAKIS **09392 KANARIS 09393 MIAOULIS.**

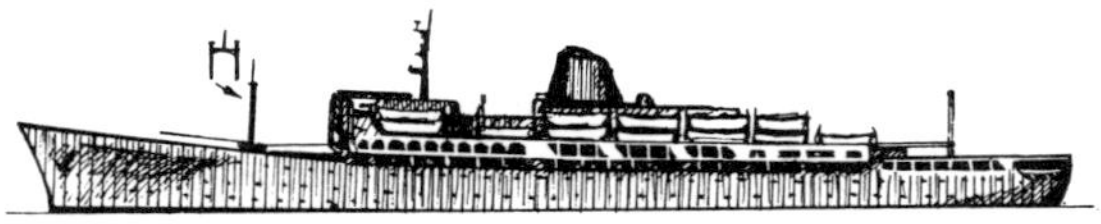

KMFK H
09400 IRPINIA. It/Br 1929; P; 13200; 164 × 7.2 (537 × 23.7); TSM; 18.5; ex CAMPANA 1955; ex RIO JACHEL 1946; ex CAMPANA 1943.

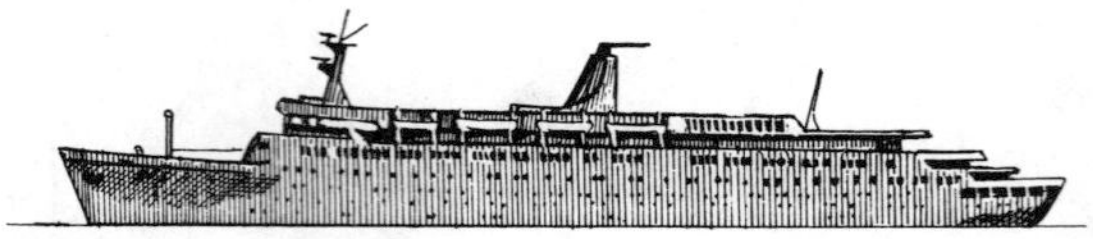

KMFK H
09410 STELLA SOLARIS. Gr/Fr 1953; P; 10600; 166 × 7.9 (545 × 26); TST; 21; ex STELLA V. 1970; ex CAMBODGE 1970.

KMFK H
09420 MARIANNA VI. Pa/Br 1951; P; 14100; 164 × 7.7 (537 × 25.1); TSM; 16; ex AUREOL 1974.

KMFK H
09430 NIPPON MARU. Ja/Ys 1962; P; 9700; 150 × 5 (493 × 17); TSM; —; ex P/S SEVEN SEAS 1977; ex ROSA DA FONSECA 1975.
Sister: **09431 CONSTELLATION** (Gr) ex DANAOS 1978; ex ANNA NERY 1978.

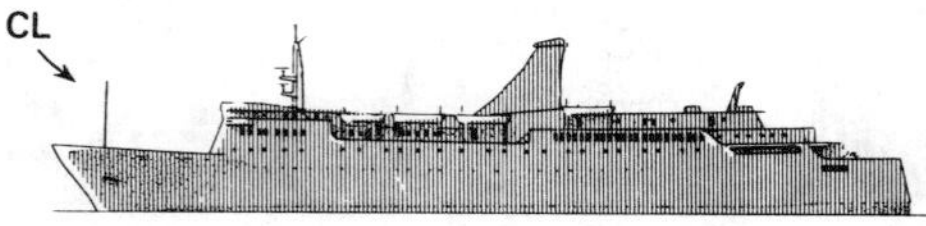

KMFK H
09440 CIUDAD DE SEVILLA. Sp/Sp 1980; RoPCF; 7400; 138.5 × 5.5 (454.4 × 18.04); TSM; 21; Stern door.

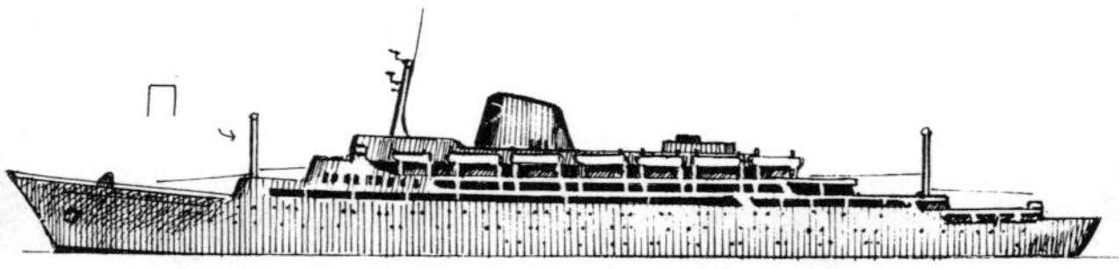

KMFK H
09450 INFANTE DOM HENRIQUE. Po/Be 1961; T; 23300; 196 × 8.2 (642 × 27); TST; 20.

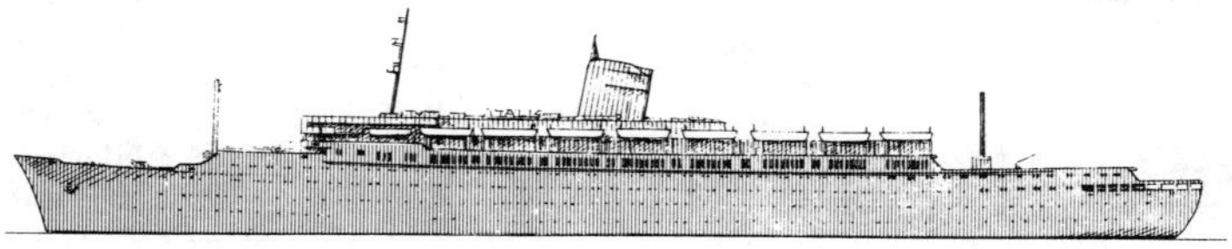

KMFK H
09460 NOGA. Pa/US 1940/79; P; 26400; 220.38 × 9.98 (723 × 32.74); TST; 22.5; ex ITALIS 1980; ex AMERICA 1979; ex AUSTRALIS 1978; ex AMERICA 1964; ex WEST POINT 1946; ex AMERICA 1942; Modernised 1979. Converted to floating hotel 1980; Probably altered in appearance.

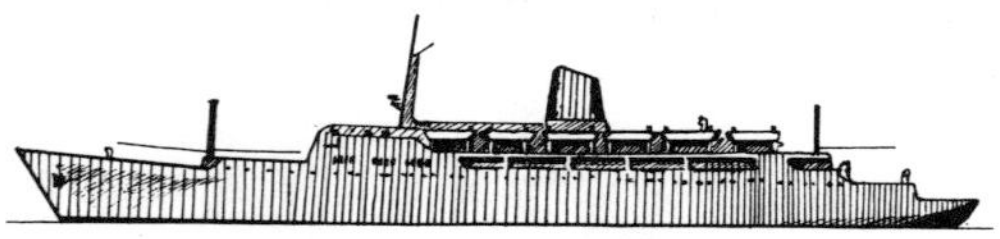

KMFK H
09470 FUNCHAL. Po/De 1961; P; 9800; 153 × 6.2 (501 × 20.3); TST; 20.

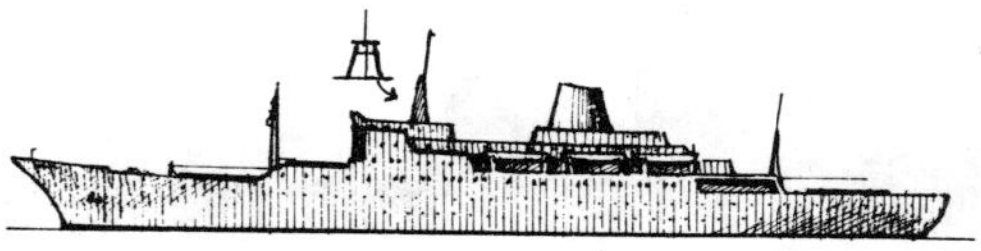

KMFK H
⋆09480 YAOHUA. Rc/Fr 1967; P; 10200; 149 × 6.6 (489 × 21.8); TSM; 21.

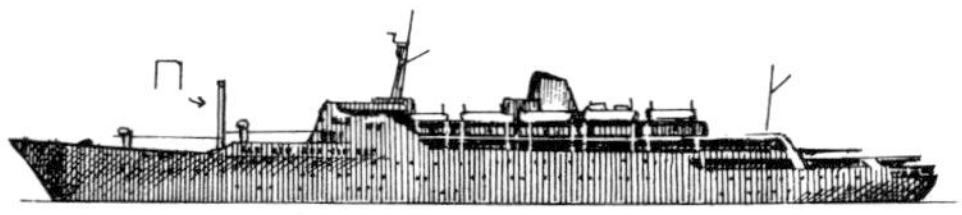

KMFK H
09490 CORAL PRINCESS. Br/Sp 1962; P; 9600; 146 × 5.5 (478 × 18); TSM; 17; ex PRINCESA LEOPOLDINA 1970. Sister: **09491 AQUAMARINE** (Gr) ex MARCO POLO 1978; ex PRINCESA ISABEL 1969.

KMFK H
09500 GUERVEUR. Fr/Fr 1966; RoPF; 500; 45.1 × 2.3 (148 × 7.8); TSM; 12.5.

KMFK H
09510 SOGNEFJORD. No/US 1943; PC; 9600; 146 × 5.5 (478 × 18); TSM; 15. Sister: **09511 SUNNFJORD II** (No) ex SUNNFJORD 1978.

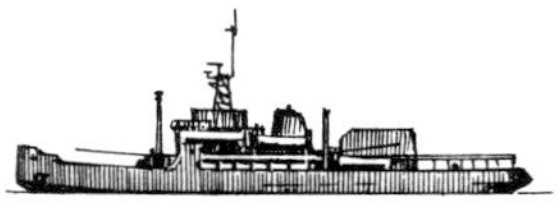

KMFK H
09520 LABRADOR. Ca/Ca 1953; IB; 3800; 82 × 9.1 (269 × 30.1); TSD-E; 16; Helicopter deck and hangar; operated by Canadian Coast Guard.

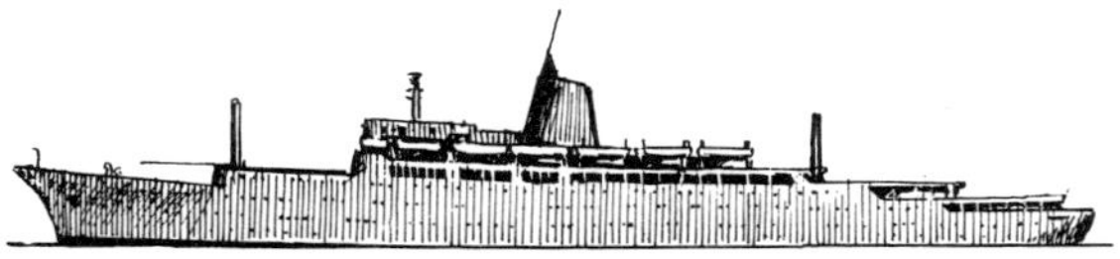

KMFK H
09530 THE VICTORIA. Gr/Br 1936; P; 11900; 173.4 × 8 (573 × 26.2); TSM; 16; ex VICTORIA 1977; ex DUNNOTTAR CASTLE 1958.

KMFK H
09540 TOBAGO. Br/Ne 1970; RoPF; 1100; 76 × 3.3 (250 × 11); TSM; 18; ex SANTA MARGARITA 1976; Bow and stern doors.

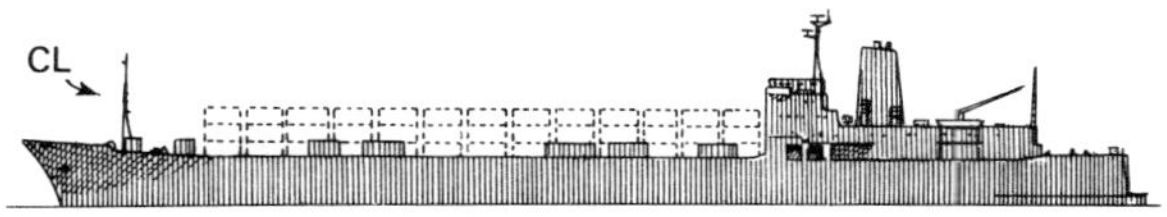

KMFK H
● **09550 HYOGO MARU.** Ja/Ja 1973; RoC/Con; 9100; 181 × 8.9 (594 × 29); M; 21. Similar (Au flag): **09551 AUSTRALIAN ENTERPRISE 09552 AUSTRALIAN EXPORTER** ex MATTHEW FLINDERS 1975 **09552 AUSTRALIAN SEAROADER.**

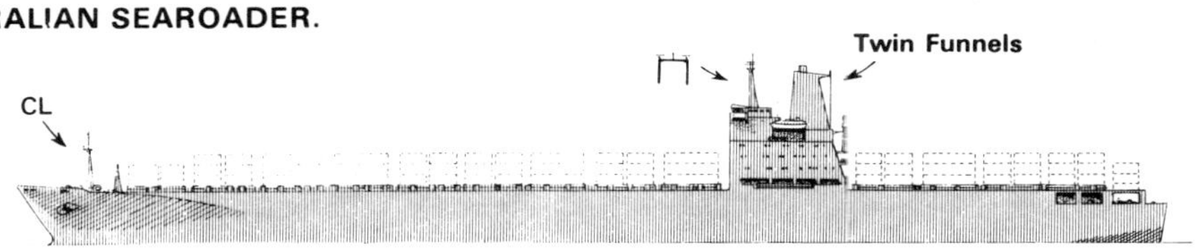

KMFK H
09560 BUNGA PERMAI. My/Ja 1979; Con; 43500; 267 × 13 (875.98 × 42.65); M; 26. Sister: **09561 BUNGA SURIA** (My).

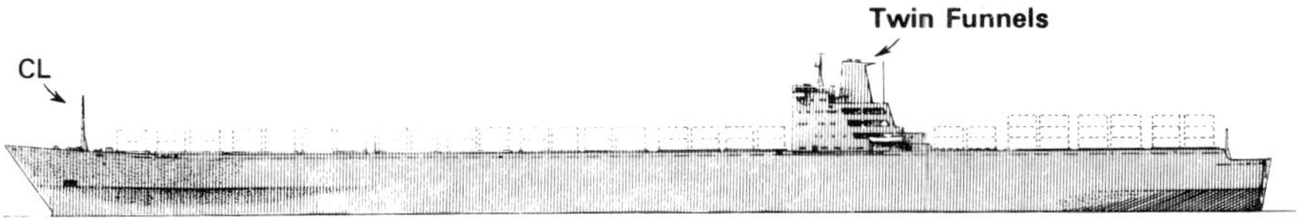

KMFK H
09570 NIHON. Sw/Sw 1972; Con; 50800; 275.22 × 11.58 (902.95 × 37.99); TrS M; 26.

KMFK H1
09580 HAWAIIAN CITIZEN. US/US 1944/60; Con; 12600; 150 × 9 (492 × 29.5); T; 16.5; ex SEA WREN 1947; Converted from a 'C 3' type; cargo ship in 1960.

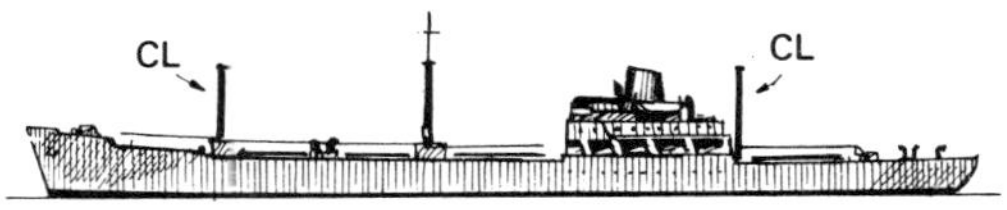

KMFK H1
09590 PEGASUS. Gr/Br 1963; C; 6900/9700; 153 × —/9.6 (501 × —/30.7); M; 16; ex NATALE 1981; ex HOPEPEAK 1969. Sisters: **09591 BLUE BAY** (Gr) ex LORD HASTINGS 1980; ex ELENI E.F. 1974; ex HOPECRAG 1971.

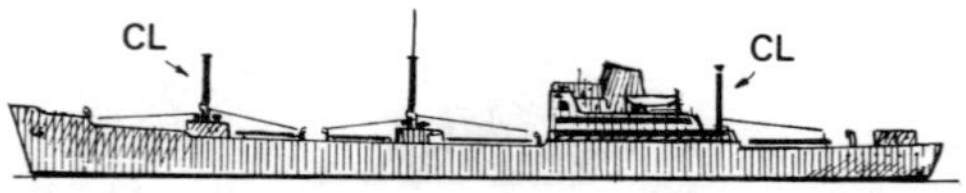

KMFK H1
● **09600 CHRYSOVALANDOU TRIA.** Cy/Br 1963; C; 9800; 148 × 9.1 (484 × 30); M; —; ex MARIKA VENIZELOS 1973; ex RADLEY 1968.

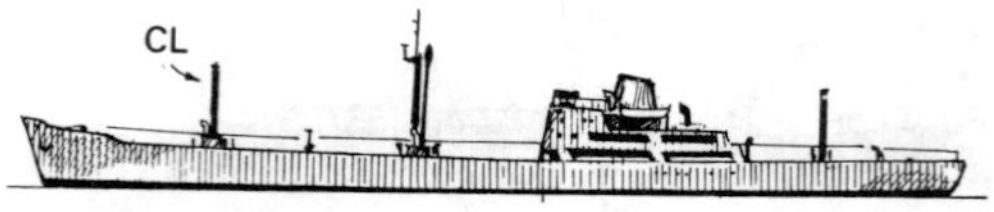

KMFK H1
● **09610 FANEROMENI.** Gr/Br 1961; C; 7200/9800; 153 × 8.5/9.6 (501 × 28/30.7); M; 15; ex SELENE 1975; ex HOPECREST 1969.

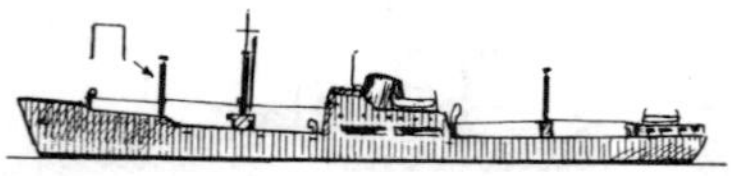

KMFK H1
● ⋆**09620 PENELOPE A.** Gr/De 1952; C; 2400; 110 × 6.1 (362 × 19.9); M; 15; ex ELSTER 1979; ex ERIK BANCK 1964.

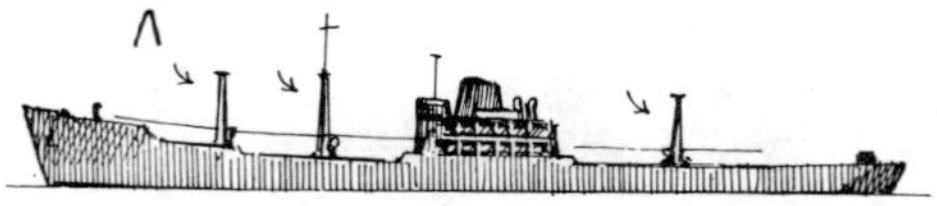

KMFK H1
09630 OSIA IRINI CHRYSOVALANDOU III. Gr/Br 1956; C; 6100/8400; 145 × 8.2 (476 × 26.11); M; 15; ex MARGARET H. 1977; ex RUNSWICK 1972.

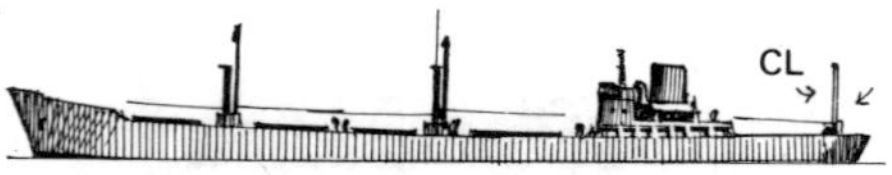

KMFK H1
● **09640 EGIDIA.** Br/Br 1962; C; 7800; 141 × 8.7 (461 × 28.7); M; 14.5; ex ALEXANDROS B. 1977; ex AVISFAITH 1971.

KMFK H1
09650 KYRIA. Cy/It 1951; C; 2100; 102 × 6 (362 × 20); M; 13.5; ex VALDARNO 1974. Sister: **09651 KONTEA** (Cy) ex VALLISARCO 1976.

KMFK H1
09660 JALANIDHI. Ia/Ja 1963; RS; 750; 54 × 3.4; 177 × 11.2; M; 12.

KMFK H1
09670 TORRES. It/It 1957; PC; 4200; 116 × 5 (381 × 17); M; 19.75.

KMFK H1
09680 ILLIRIA. Gr/It 1962; P; 3900; 101 × 5; (333 × 17); M; 18.

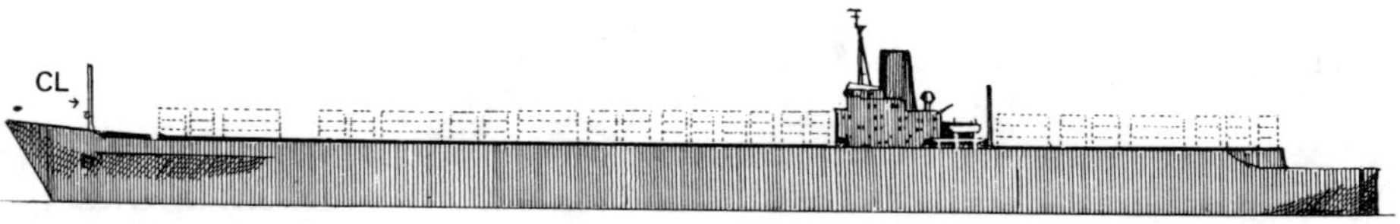

KMFK H1
09690 KORRIGAN. Fr/FRG 1973; Con; 57200; 289 × 13 (947 × 42.7); TST; 26.5.

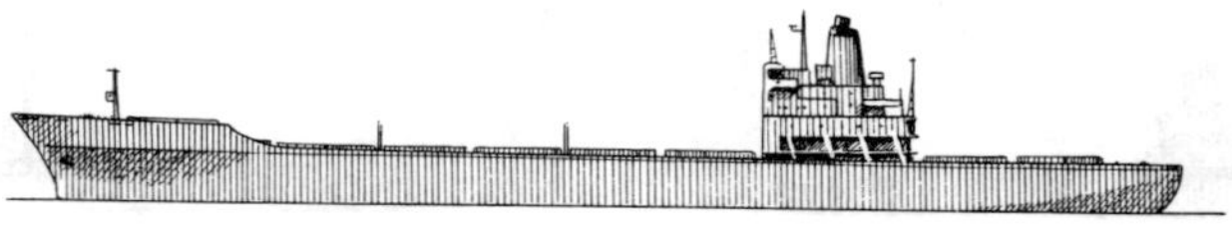

KMFK H1
09700 GOLDEN ARROW. Ja/Ja 1970; Con; 16600; 188 × 10.7 (617 × 35); M; 21.5.

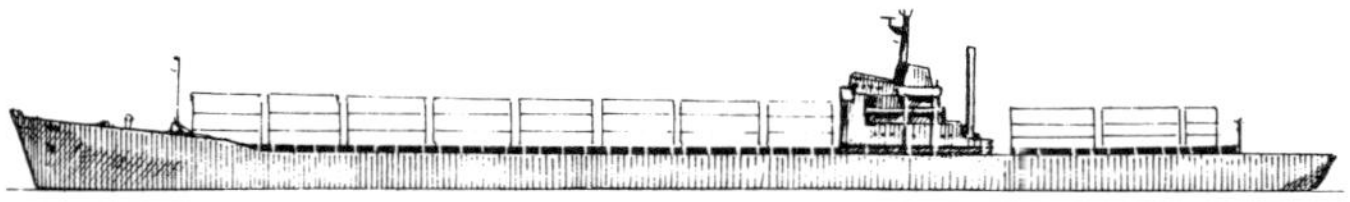

KMFK H1
09710 AMERICAN LANCER. US/US 1969; Con; 18900; 214 × 9.8 (701 × 32.2); T; 22. Sisters (US flag): **09711 AMERICAN LEGION 09712 AMERICAN LIBERTY 09713 AMERICAN LARK 09714 AMERICAN LYNX 09715 AMERICAN ASTRONAUT 09716 AMERICAN APOLLO 09717 AMERICAN AQUARIUS.**

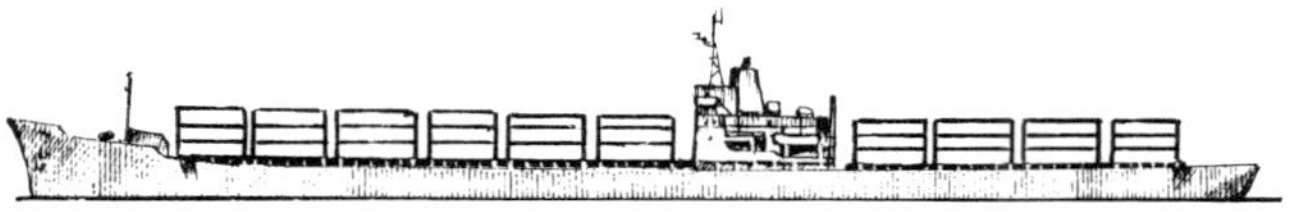

KMFK H1
09720 AMERICAN ACE. US/US 1953/70; Con; 15800; 202 × 9.1 661 × 29.6; T; 20; ex PIONEER MOON 1970; ex MOUNTAIN MARINER 1956; Lengthened and converted from cargo ship 1970. Sisters (US flag): **09721 AMERICAN ALLIANCE** ex PIONEER MILL 1970; ex SHOW ME MARINER 1956 **09722 AMERICAN ARGOSY** ex PIONEER MAIN 1970; ex COTTON MARINER 1956 **09723 AMERICAN ARCHER** ex PIONEER MIST 1970; ex PENINSULAR MARINER 1956 **09724 AMERICAN ACCORD** ex PIONEER MART 1971; ex SUNFLOWER MARINER 1956 **09725 AMERICAN LEADER** ex PIONEER MINX 1970; ex GOPHER MARINER 1956 **09726 AMERICAN LEGACY** ex PIONEER MING 1971; ex SILVER MARINER 1956 **09727 AMERICAN LEGEND** ex PIONEER MYTH 1971; ex PELICAN MARINER 1956.

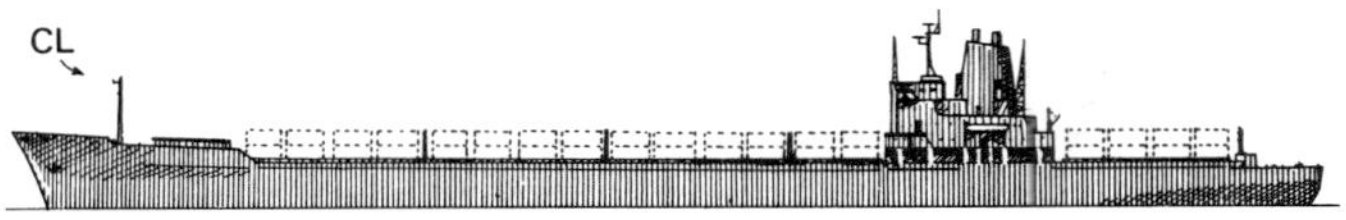

KMFK H1
09730 TOHGO MARU. Ja/Ja 1970; Con; 23300; 212 × 9.4 (696 × 31.2); M; 23. Similar: **09731 YAMASHIN MARU** (Ja).

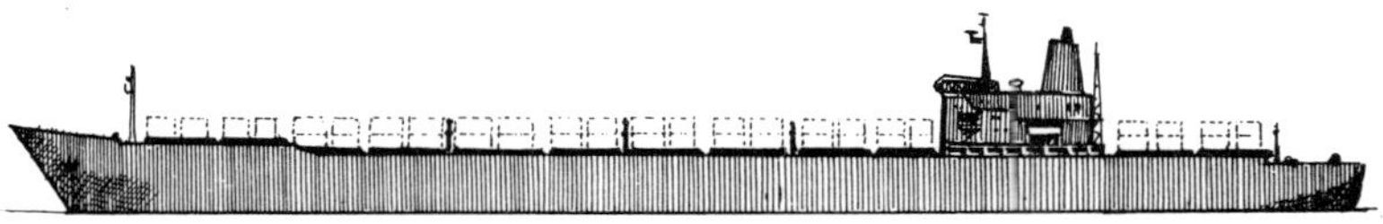

KMFK H1
09740 TOHBEI MARU. Ja/Ja 1972; Con; 35500; 246 × 10.6 (808 × 35); T; 24.75. Sister: **09741 YASHIMA MARU** (Ja).

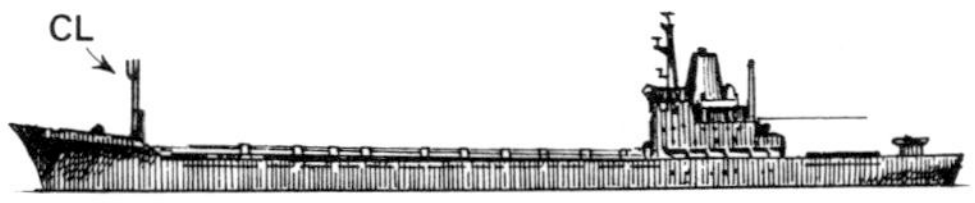

KMFK H1
09750 BUNGA ANGSANA. My/Ja 1972/77; Con; 11500; 155.96 × 8.68 (511.35 × 28.48); M; 17; Converted from general cargo 1977. Sister: **09751 BUNGA TERATAI** (My).

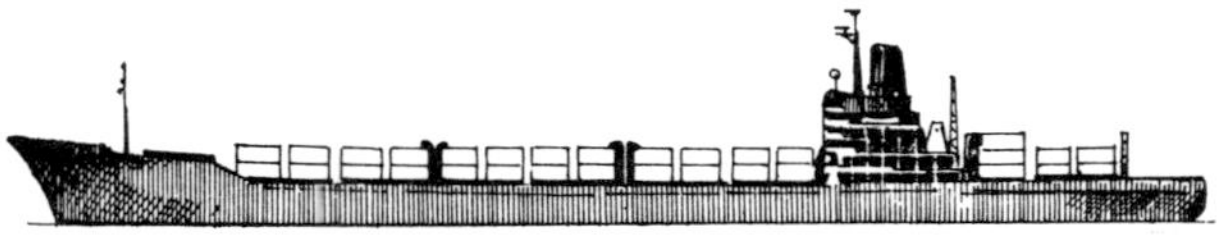

KMFK H1
09760 AMERICA MARU. Ja/Ja 1968; Con; 16400; 187 × 9.5 (614 × 31); M; 22.5.

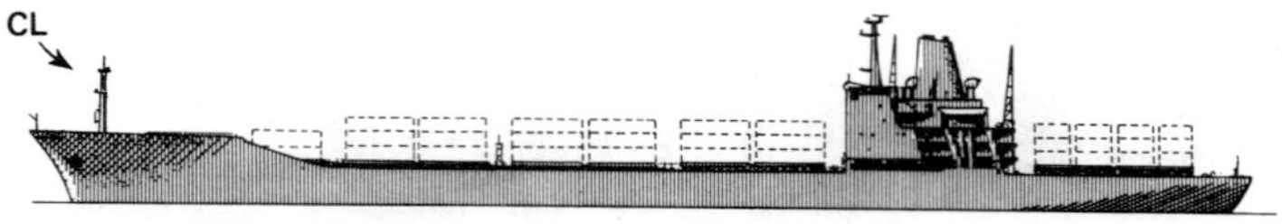

KMFK H1
09770 MONT BLANC MARU. Ja/Ja 1974; Con; 30000; 217 × 11.71 (711.94 × 38.42); M; 23.

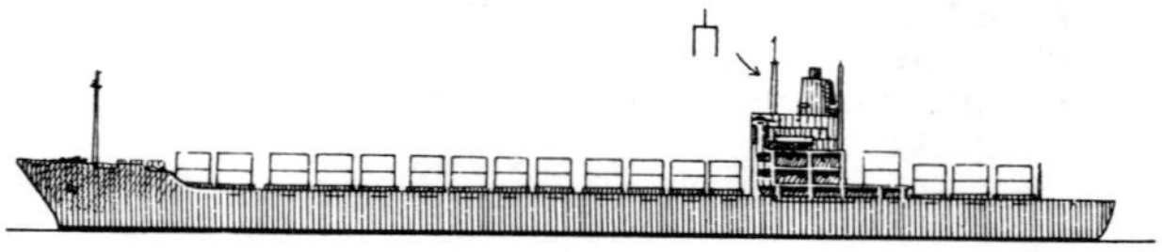

KMFK H1
09780 PACIFIC EXPRESS. Ko/Ja 1968; Con; 16200; 187 × 10.5 (614 × 34.3); M; 22.5; ex HAKONE MARU 1978. Sister: **09781 HARUNA MARU** (Ja).

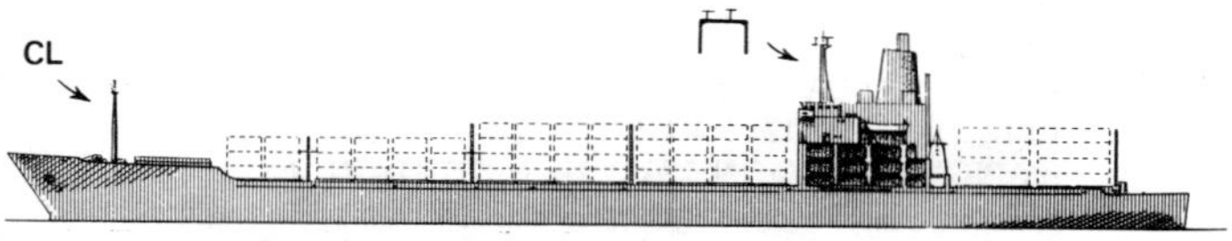

KMFK H1
09790 HIRA MARU. Ja/Ja 1978; Con; 24800; 214.61 × 10.5 (704 × 34.45); M; 23.

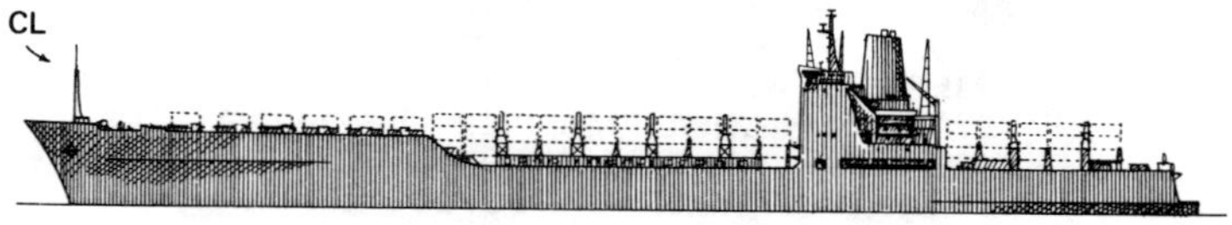

KMFK H1
09800 AUSTRALIAN EMBLEM. Au/Ja 1975; Roc/Con; 23200; 222.3 × 10.5 (731 × 35); M; 22.75; Stern door. Sister: **09801 AUSTRALIAN ESCORT** (Au) ex JAMES COOK 1976.

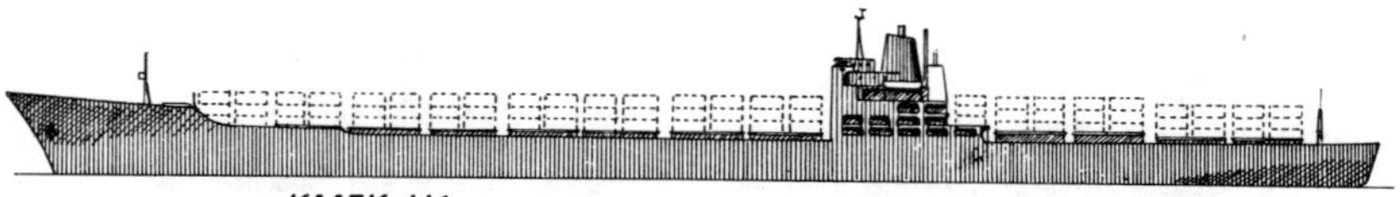

KMFK H1
09810 KISO MARU. Ja/Ja 1973; Con; 38500; 261 × 11.8 (857 × 38.6); TSM; 25.25.

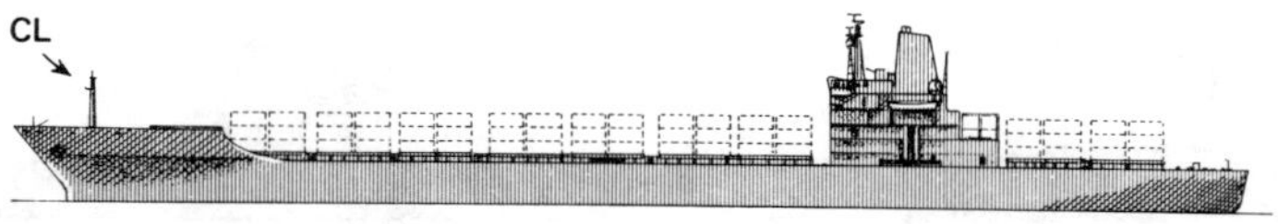

KMFK H1
09820 CANBERRA MARU. Ja/Ja 1979; Con; 32200; 216.3 × 11.53 (709.65 × 37.83); M; 22.3.

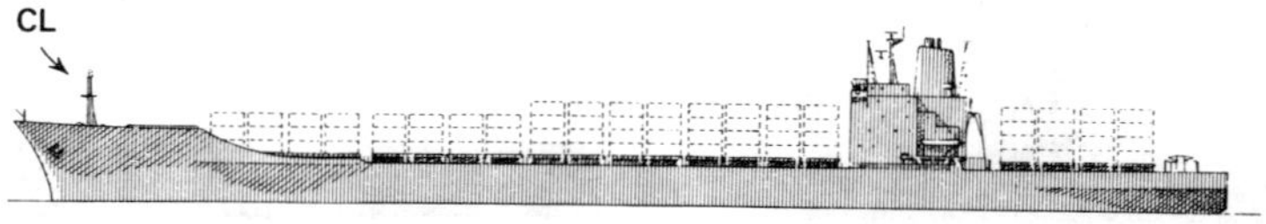

KMFK H1
09830 CHINA CONTAINER. Tw/Tw 1979; Con; 32500; 221.7 × 11.5 (727.36 × 37.73); M; 23. Similar—shorter (Tw flag): **09831 MING GALAXY 09832 MING GLORY 09833 MING MOON 09834 MING OCEAN 09835 MING STAR 09836 MING SUN 09837 MING UNIVERSE**

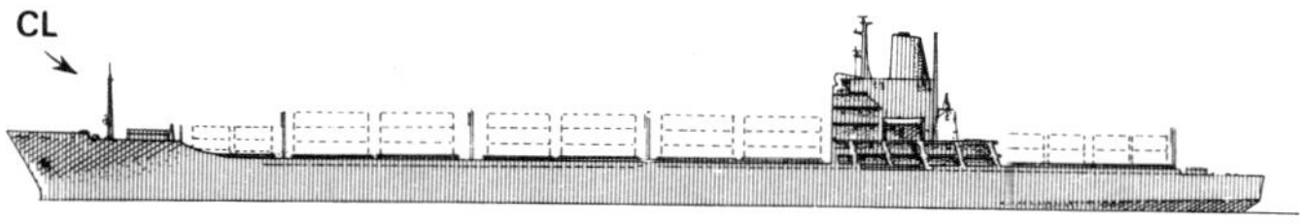

KMFK H1
09850 ALASKA MARU. Ja/Ja 1973; Con; 23600; 209 × 10.6 (686 × 35); M; 22.5.
Possible Sister: **09851 HAKUSAN MARU** (Ja).

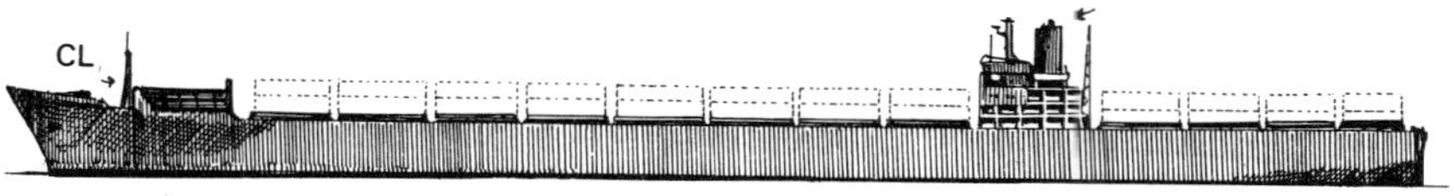

KMFK H1
09860 NEW YORK MARU. Ja/Ja 1972; Con; 38800; 263 × 11.5 (863 × 37.9); TSM; 24.75.

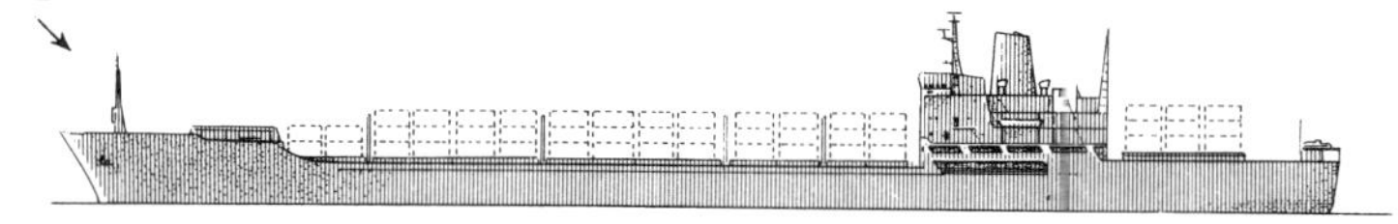

KMFK H1
09870 AOTEA. Br/Ja 1970; Con; 24400; 213 × 10.5 (700 × 34.5); M; 23; ex ARIAKE 1977.

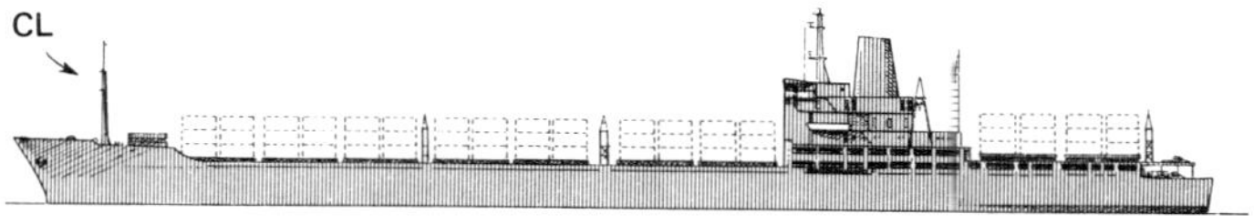

KMFK H1
09880 ARAFURA. Br/Ja 1972; Con; 25200; 211.49 × 10.53 (693.86 × 34.55); M; 23.

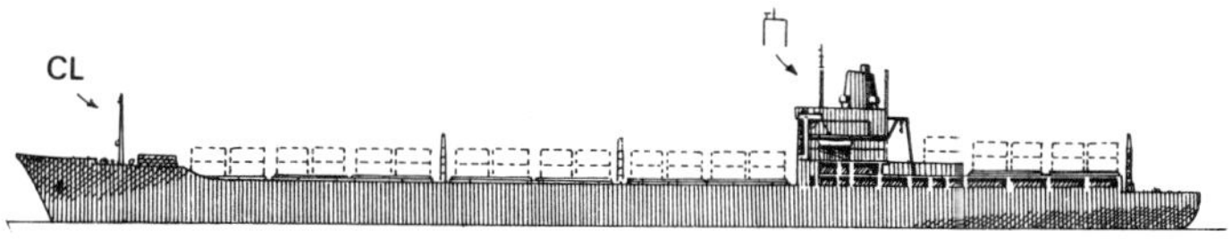

KMFK H1
● **09890 HAKOZAKI MARU** Ja/Ja 1969; Con; 23700; 212 × 9.4 (697 × 31.3); M; 23.

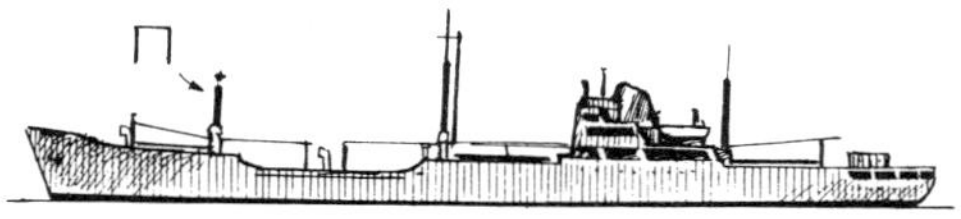

KMFK H12
09900 LUCHANA Sp/Sp 1964; C; 5900/8300; 145 × 7.9/9.7 (475 × 26/32); M;

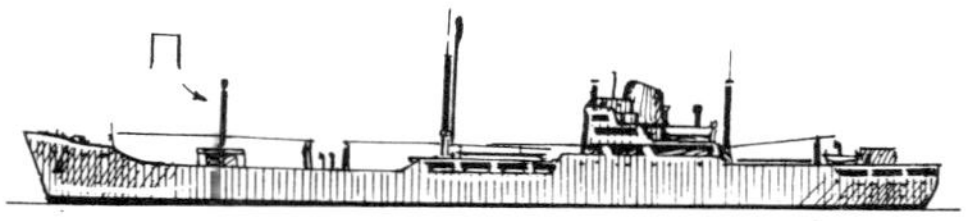

KMFK H12
⋆**09910 ULCINJ** Ys/Sp 1961; C; 5700/8200; 145 × —/9.1 (475 × —/29.9); M; 12.5; ex MARTIN ZUBIZARRETA 1969. Sisters: **09911 SALONAE** (Pa) ex MONTE PENELARA 1971 **09912 DEMARG** (Gr) ex BERMEO 1975.

KMFK H12
09920 CAMSELL. Ca/Ca 1959; IB/LT; 2000; 68.2 × 6.4 (224 × 21); TSD-E; 13; operated by Canadian Coast Guard.

KMFK H12
09930 MARIAM. Le/No 1919; C; 840; 63 × 4.2 (206 × 13.11); R; 9.5; ex SIRIUS 1963.

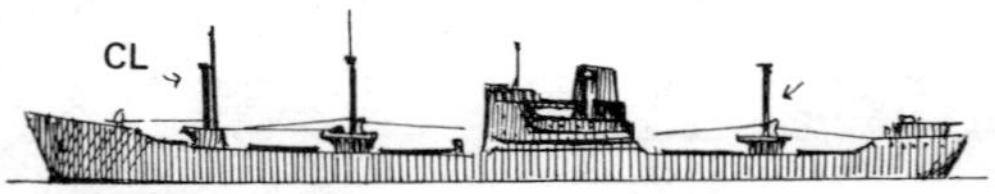

KMFK H13
09940 ALPAC ASIA. Br/Br 1962; C; 7500/10100; 153 × 9.4 (500 × 31); M; 15.5; ex SARA LUPE 1980; ex CARDIFF CITY 1972; KP. abreast funnel. Sister: **09941 ALPAC AFRICA** (Br) ex MARIA ELISA 1980; ex HOUSTON CITY 1972.

KMFK H13
09950 PENTA-Y. Sg/Br 1960; C; 10300; 155 × 9.2 (510 × 30.7); M; 15; ex TONG BENG 1978; ex EXECUTIVE VENTURE 1974; ex DEVON CITY; KP. abreast funnel. Sister: **09951 MALDIVE PROMOTER** (Mv) ex TONG JIT 1980; ex ALEXANDER A.S. 1973; ex ORIENT CITY 1972.

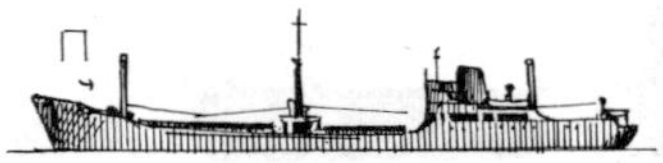

KMFK H13
09960 PICOBLANCO. Sp/Sp 1958; C; 2700; 96 × 6.1 (314 × 19.11); M; 13. Sisters: **09961 PICOVERDE** (Sp) **09962 INTER II** (Pa)—may be **INTERDOS;** ex PICOAZUL 1980.

KMFK H13
⋆**09970 ALEKSANDR DOVZHENKO.** Ru/Rm 1965; C/TC; 2700; 100 × 5.8 (330 × 18.11); M; 13.75. Sisters (Ru flag): ⋆**09971 GEORGIY VASILIEV** ⋆**09972 SERGEY EYZENSHTEYN** ⋆**09973 SERGEY VASILYEV** ⋆**09974 VSEVOLOD PUDOVKIN.**

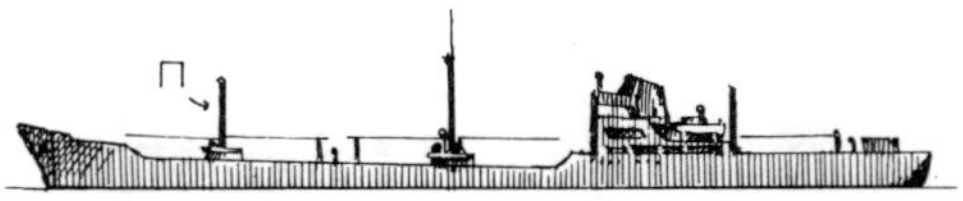

KMFK H13
09980 LAS ARENAS. Sp/Sp 1960; C; 6400/8700; 145 × 7.9/8.9 (475 × 26/29); M; 13. Sister: **09981 VALENTINA FRIAS** (Sp).

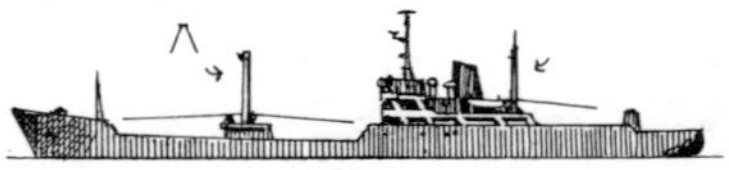

KMFK H13
09990 REIYO MARU. Ja/Ja 1967; C; 3400; 111 × 6.9 (365 × 23); M; 16. Possibly Similar: **09991 JUYO MARU** (Ja).

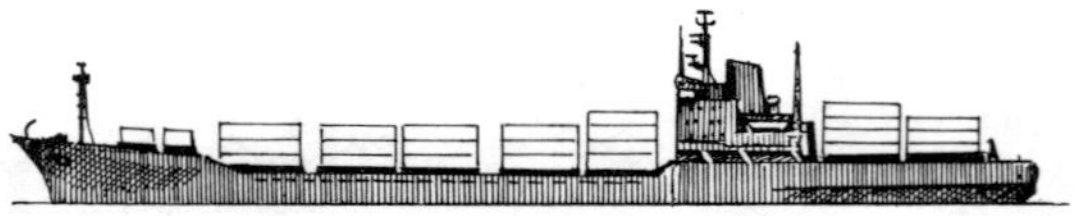

KMFK H13
10000 EVER SHINE. Pa/Ja 1976; Con; 10200; 160.8 × 9.4 (528 × 31); M; 20 Sisters (Pa flag): **10001 EVER SPRING 10002 EVER SUMMIT 10003 EVER SUPERB.**

●
10005

KMFK H2
10010 SALERNUM. It/It 1956; Cbl; 2800; 104 × 5.7 (342 × 19); TSM; 15.

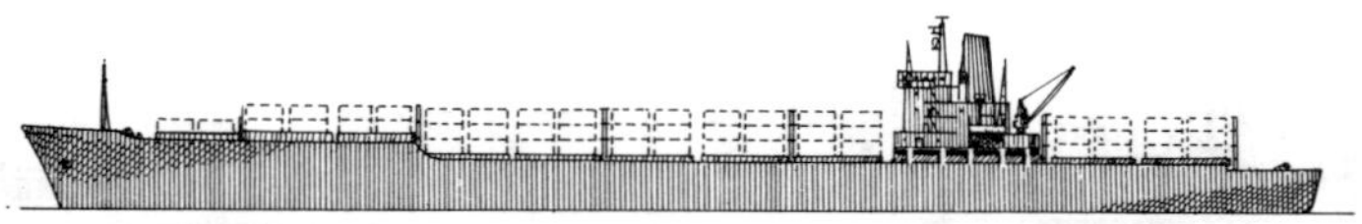

KMFKC H1
10020 ASIA MARU. Ja/Ja 1971; Con; 24300; 212 × 10.6 (699 × 35); M; 22.5.

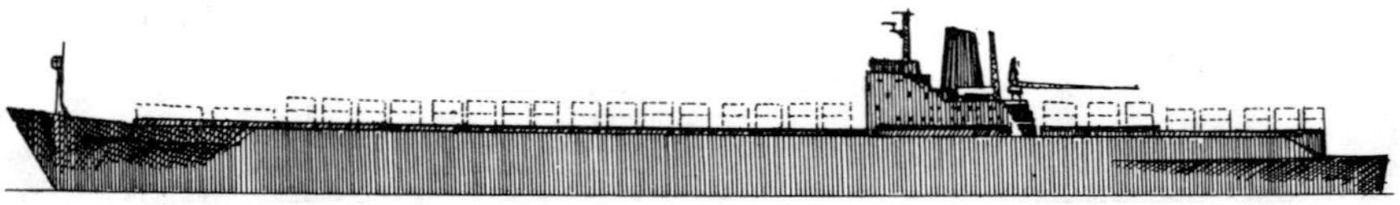

KMFKC H1
10030 TOYAMA. No/Ja 1972; Con; 52200; 275 × 11.1 (903 × 36.5); TrSM; 26.25.

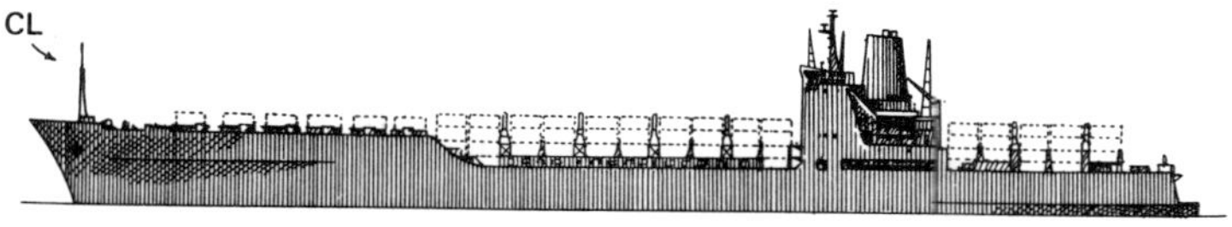

KMFKC H1
10040 AUSTRALIAN EMBLEM. Au/Ja 1975; RoRo Con; 23200; 222.3 × 10.5 (731 × 35); M; 22.75; Stern doors. Sister: **10041 AUSTRALIAN ESCORT** (Au) ex JAMES COOK 1976.

$KMFKC_2$ H
10050 AUSONIA. It/It 1957; PC; 11900; 159.3 × 6.5 (523 × 21.4); TST; 20.75.

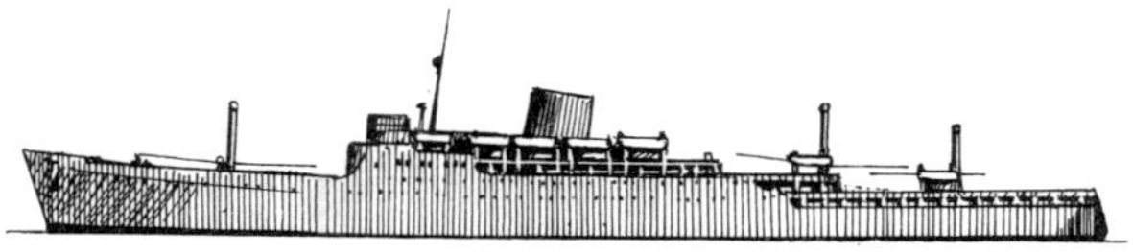

$KMFK_2$ H
10060 MEDITERRANEAN ISLAND. Gr/Br 1950; P; 16300; 181.2 × 8.9 (595 × 29.2); TSM; 18.5; ex PATRIS 1980; ex BLOEMFONTEIN CASTLE 1959.

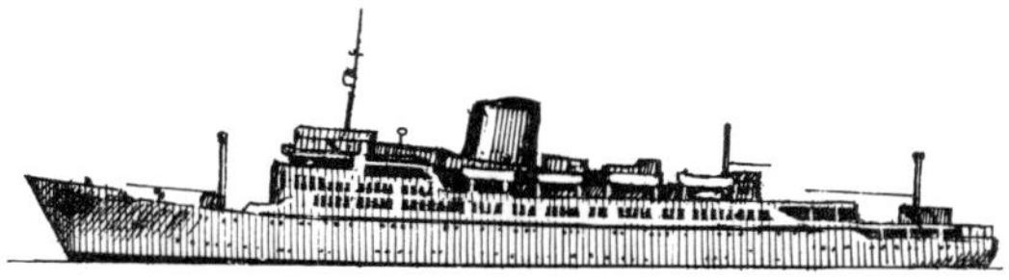

$KMFK_2$ H
⋆**10070 VARNA.** Bu/Br 1951; P; 13600; 157.3 × 7.3 (517 × 24); TST; 18; ex OCEAN MONARCH 1967.

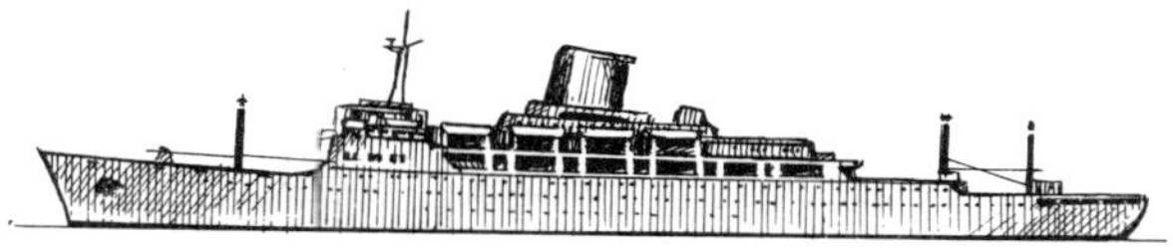

$KMFK_2$ H
10080 SANTA ROSA. US/US 1958; PC; 11400; 177.9 × 8.3 (584 × 27.3); TST; 20.

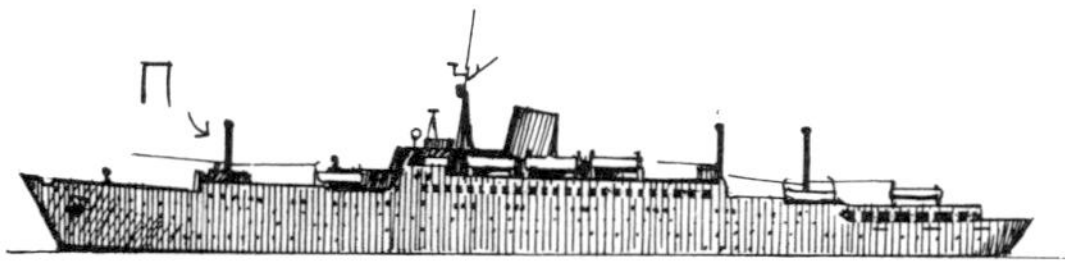

$KMFK_2$ H
⋆**10090 VOLKERFREUNDSCHAFT.** DDR/Sw 1948; PC; 12100; 160.1 × 7.5 (525 × 24.8); TSM; 19; ex STOCKHOLM 1960.

$KMFK_2$ H
⋆**10100 AFRICA CUBA.** Cu/Sp 1957; PC; 14200; 169.6 × 8.3 (556 × 27.3); TSM; 20; ex GOLDEN MOON 1978; ex CABO SAN ROQUE. Sister: **10101 NOOR JEHAN** (In) ex CABO SAN VICENTE 1975.

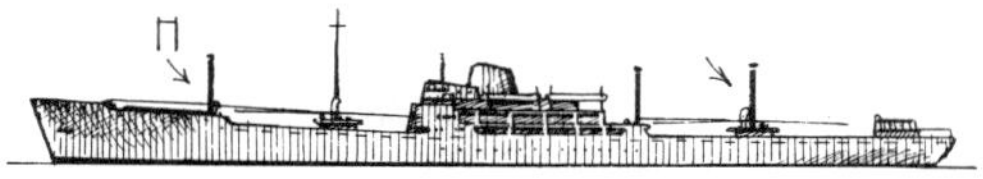

$KMFK_2$ H1
● **10110 CIUDAD DE TOLEDO.** Sp/Sp 1956; PC; 9800; 148.5 × 7.5 (487 × 24.8); M; 15.

$KMFK_2$ H1
⋆**10120 FELICITY.** RC/Br 1956; CP; 5600; 137 × 7.6/8.9 (450 × 25/29.3); T; 13.5; ex AVIS ORNIS 1970; ex NEW YORK CITY 1968.

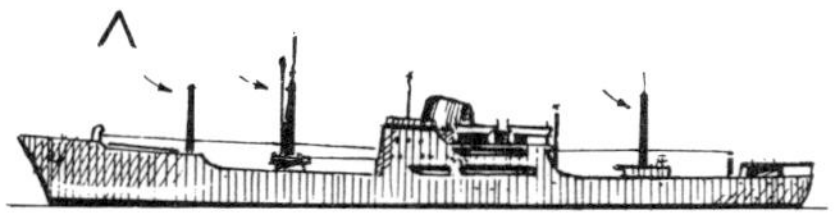

$KMFK_2$ H1
● **10130 NEW STAR.** Sg/Sw 1952; CP; 4100; 127 × 7.2 (417 × 23.4); M; 16; ex LEONOR 1973; ex DELOS 1971. Sister: **10131 NEW YELLOW SEA** (Pa) ex YELLOW SEA 1976; ex HALLBORG 1975; ex MILOS 1966.

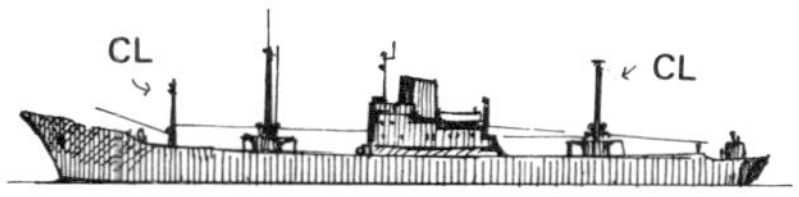

$KMFK_2$ H1
● **10140 MINSHAN.** Pa/FRG 1959; C; 3000/4900; 126.1 × 6.5/7.6 (414 × 21.6/25); M; 14.5; ex ILLSTEIN 1972. Sister: **10141 MINTSUNG** (Pa) ex WIEDSTEIN 1972.

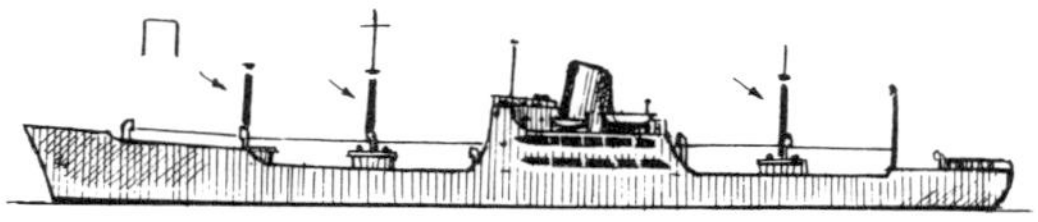

KMFKK H1
10150 AGILITY. Li/Br 1959; C; 7700/10400; 158 × —/9.8 (518 × —/31.4); M; 13.5; ex ION 1970; ex TEXAS 1968. Sisters: **10151 FAY C** (Gr) ex PROSPERITY 1977; ex ATLANTIC FURY 1975; ex DUKE OF MISTRA 1965 **10152 CHI GRAND** (Pa) ex MEGALUCK 1980; ex ATLANTIC FREEDOM 1973; ex DUKE OF ATHENS 1967.

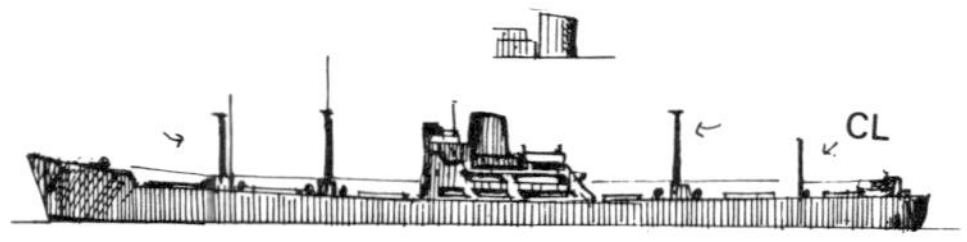

$KMFK_2$ H1
10160 IRENE'S BANNER. Gr/Br 1958; C; 8100; 139 × 8.5 (456 × 28); M; —; ex THOMASA 1975; ex ALIARTOS 1970; ex LORADORE 1966. Sister (Inset): **10161 EASTERN CONQUEST** (Pa) ex BACHDANG 1978; ex AL-KARIM 1978; ex SHAH-E-RAZA 1975; ex RIVERDORE 1974.

$KMFK_2$ H1
10170 CAPO SAN MARCO. It/Br 1960; C; 5000; 134 × 8.4 (440 × 27.3); M; —; ex MONTCALM 1971.

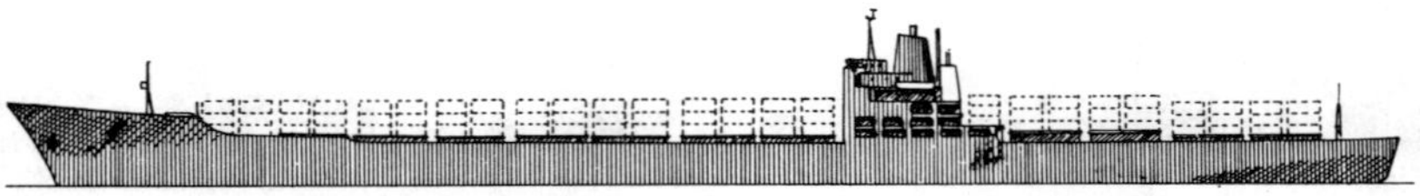

$KMFK_2$ H1
10180 KISO MARU. Ja/Ja 1973; Con; 38500; 261 × 11.8 (857 × 38.6); TSM; 25.24.

$KMFK_2$ H12
10190 POSIDON. Gr/Sp 1953; C; 4100; 112 × 6.9 (369 × 22); R; 10.5; ex MOHICAN 1968; ex PANOCEAN 1965; ex SEA STAR 1963; ex ANCUD 1961; ex TORREMOLINOS 1946; Launched 1946.

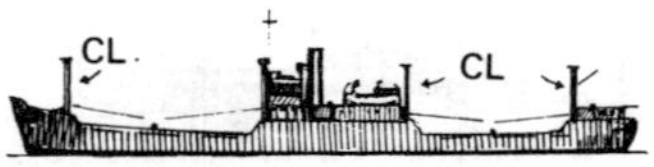

$KMFK_2$ H123
10210 RIO ATRATO. Co/US 1943; C; 2800; 100 × 6.4 (329 × 21); R; 9; ex RAMSDALI 1966; ex SAN JOHN P. 1965; ex ESTER 1963; ex KALO 1957; ex TATUK 1948; ex VICTORIA PARK 1946.

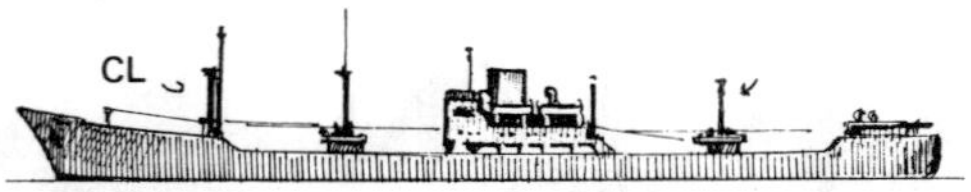

$KMFK_2$ H13
10230 IOANNIS. Gr/Br 1959; C; 6000/8400; 147 × 7.9/9 (482 × 26/29); M; 14; ex STRATHNEVIS 1978; ex NURJEHAN 1975; ex ADVOCATE 1973; ex NURJEHAN 1971.

$KMFK_2$ H2
★10250 WALTER DEHMEL. DDR/DDR 1963; FT; 2900; 85.3 × 5.3 (280 × 17.6); M; 13.5. Sisters (DDR flag): **★10251 BERNHARD KELLERMANN ★10252 PETER KAST ★10253 PETER NELL ★10254 RUDOLF LEONHARD.**

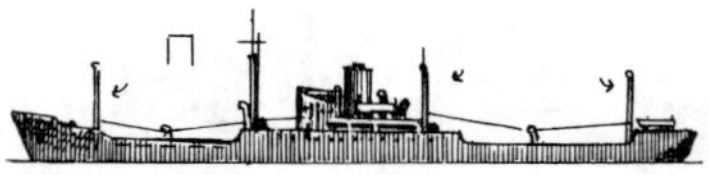

$KMFK_2$ H123
10200 ALMIRANTE LOBO. Sp/Sp 1954; Transport; 6700 DSPL; 111 × 9 (363 × 25.7); R; 12; Spanish Navy.

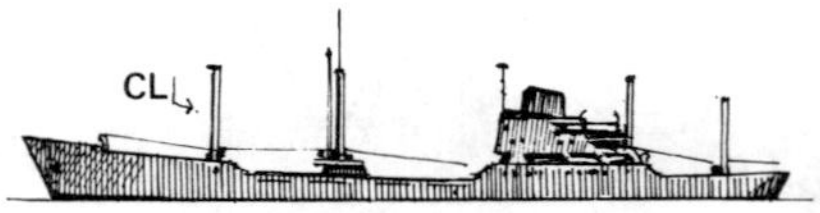

$KMFK_2$ H13
★10220 MILA GOJSALIC. Ys/FRG 1960; CP; 4500/6600; 139 × 7.2/8.8 (455 × 23/28.9); M; 16.5; ex BARBERBROOK 1975; ex FERNBROOK 1973. Sister: **10221 RAS DEDGEN** (Et) ex BARBERGATE 1975; ex FERNGATE 1973.

$KMFK_2$ H13
10240 RONSON. Gr/Br 1963; C; 6100; 142 × 8 (465 × 26.1); M; 15.5; ex AHMADU BELLO 1981. Sister: **10241 RONHILL** (Gr) ex NNAMDI AZIKIWE 1981.

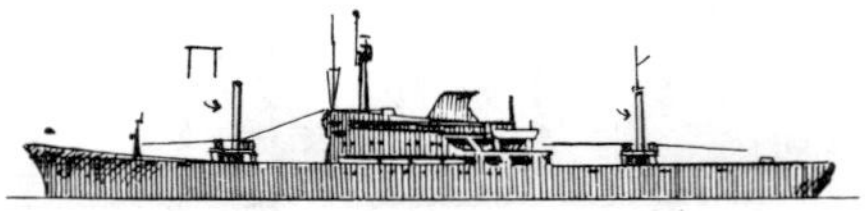

KMFKM H
★10260 BURAN. Pd/Pd 1972; FC; 2900/5100; 120 × —/7.3 (92 × —/24); M; 18; **'B 433'** type. Sisters (Pd flag): **★10261 HALNIAK ★10262 LEWANTER.**

KMFKM H1
● **★10270 HANOI.** Pd/Pd 1960; CP; 6900; 154 × 8.3 (505 × 27.4); M; 15.5; **'B 54'** type. Sisters: **★10271 PEKIN** (Pd) **★10272 PHENIAN** (Pd) Similar: **★10273 YI XING** (RC) ex KONOPNICKA 1979 **★10274 INTERNACIONAL** (Al) **★10275 GONZALEZ LINES** (Cu) **★10276 COMMANDANTE CAMILO CIENFUEGOS** (Cu).

KMFKM H1
⋆**10280 ROMER.** Pd/Pd 1964; CP; 5600; 146 × 7.6 (479 × 25.1); M; 16.25; **'B 516'** type. Similar (goalpost abaft superstructure). ⋆**10281 HENRYK JENDZHA** (Pd).

KMFKM H1
10290 VISHVA VIBHUTI. In/Pd 1966; C; 6100/9000; 153 × 7.7/8.9 (500 × 25.4/29); M; —; **'B 42'** type.
Sisters (In flag): **10291 VISHVA MAHIMA 10292 VISHVA KALYAN 10293 VISHVA RAKSHA.**

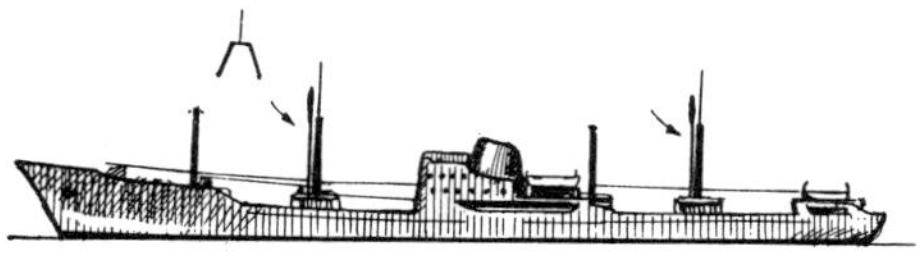

KMFKM H1
10300 NOTIS. Gr/De 1955; CP; 5100; 139 × 7.7 (457 × 25.3); M; —; ex TARRENS 1976; ex EQUADOR 1970; ex ECUADOR 1968. Sister: **10301 PROGRESS 1** (Pa) ex RAFAEL M 1980; ex RAPHAEL M 1980; ex TANA HAIQ 1973; ex BRASILIEN 1968.

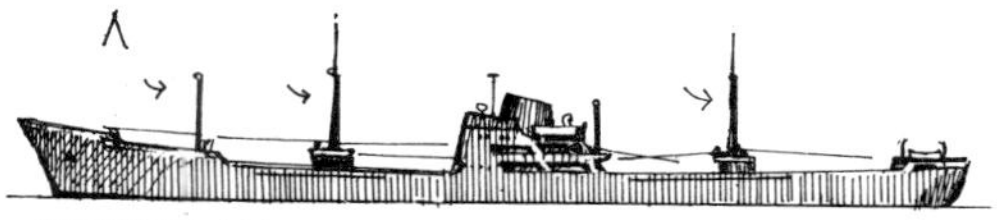

KMFKM H1
● ⋆**10310 KOROTAN.** Ys/Ys 1960; CP; 5800/8600; 149 × —/9.2 (488 × —/29.1); M; 14.5; ex TRBOVLJE 1960. Sisters: ⋆**10311 GORANKA** (Ys) ⋆**10312 TRBOVLJE** (Ys) ex KOROTAN 1960 **10313 RATNA USHA** (In) ex JALA RATNA USHA 1964; ex RATNA USHA 1963; ex ZRENNANIN 1961 **10314 VISHVA PRABHA** (In).

KMFKM H1
● **10320 NEW STAR.** Sg/De 1952; CP; 4100; 127 × 7.1 (417 × 23); M; 16; ex LEONOR 1973; ex DELOS 1971. Sister: **10321 NEW YELLOW SEA** (Pa) ex YELLOW SEA 1976; ex HALLBORG 1975; ex MILOS 1966.

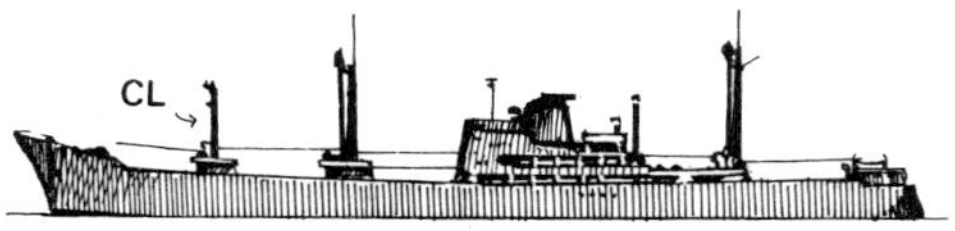

KMFKM H1
10330 LANTAO ISLAND. Li/FRG 1957; C; 6400; 145 × 8.3 (475 × 27.1); M; 17.5; ex OROPESA 1972; ex PACIFIC EXPORTER 1970; ex OROPESA 1970; ex ARAMAIC 1968. Sisters (Li flag): **10331 LAMMA ISLAND** ex OROYA 1972; ex PACIFIC RANGER 1971; ex OROYA 1970; ex ARABIC 1968 **10332 HONGKONG ISLAND** ex ORITA 1972; ex AFRIC 1968.

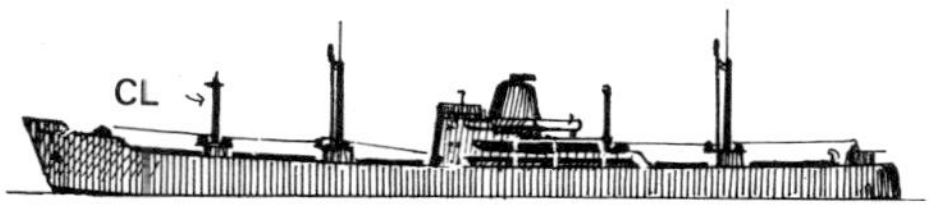

KMFKM H1
10340 AL KULSUM. Pk/Ne 1960; C; 7000/9900; 158 × 9.8 (517 × 32.2); M; 16.5; ex DORTHE OLDENDORFF 1970.

KMFKM H1
⋆**10350 STEFAN CZARNIECKI.** Pd/De 1967; CP; 6900/10200; 154 × 7.9/8.5 (504 × 26/28); M; 16. Sisters (Pd flag): **10351 GRUNWALD 10352 WESTERPLATTE.**

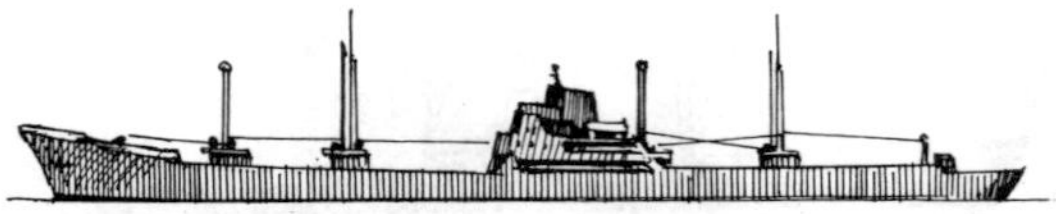

KMFKM H1

● **10360 ARTEMIDI IV.** Gr/Ne 1957; C; 10400; 157×9.6 (516×31.5); M; 16; ex LIMNOS 1976; ex ARGO OLLANDIA 1975; ex SANTA ALEXANDRA 1973; ex ARGO OLLANDIA 1968. Sisters: **10361 LANKA RATNA** (Sr) ex ARGO CHIOS 1975; ex SANTA FOTINI 1973; ex ARGO CHIOS 1969 **10362 AZOV SEA** (Pa) ex ISLAND MARINER 1973 **10363 KOTA ABADI** (Sg) ex ARGO ELLAS 1975; ex SANTA ANNA 1973; ex ARGO ELLAS 1969 **10364 ANTONIOS C.** (Gr) ex ALBIA 1975 Similar: **10365 KATIE** (Gr) ex KATWIJK 1979 ***10366 CHANGMING** (RC) ex ISLAND SKIPPER 1976 **10367 ATLAS** (Mo) ex ARGO AFAIA.

KMFKM H1

10370 LANKA RANI. (Sr/Ne 1961; C; 7100/10400; 157×8.4/9.6 (517×27.6/31.3); M; 16; ex FINNAMORE VALLEY 1971.

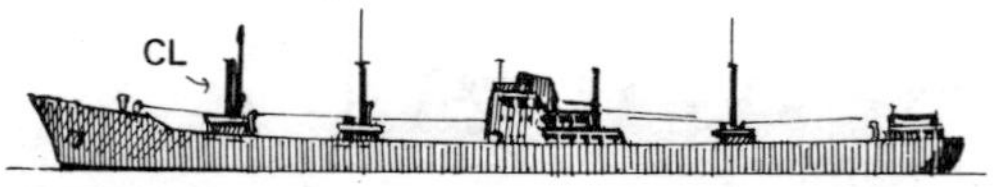

KMFKM H

● **10380 STATE OF KUTCH.** In/In 1956; C; 5300; 149×6.7 (499×22.2); M; 14. Sister: **10381 STATE OF ORISSA** (In).

KMFKM H1

10390 COLUMBUS VENTURE. Pi/Ja 1960; CP; 8300; 132×8.8 (434×28.11); M; 14.5; ex EASTERN GALAXY 1980.

KMFKM H1

● **10400 CAMINITO.** Ar/Br 1959; C; 8500; 139×8.9 (457×28.10); M; 13; ex TEWKESBURY 1972. Sisters: **10401 DIAMANDO** (Gr) ex WESTBURY 1978 **10402 EASTERN CONCORD** (Pa) ex BACHLONG 1979; ex CONFIDENCE EXPRESS 1979; ex PREMIER ATLANTIC 1973; ex SWAN RIVER 1971.

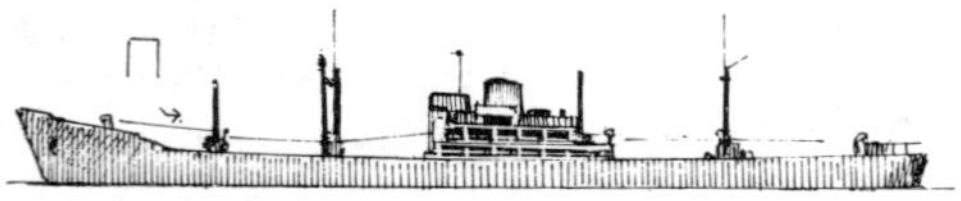

KMFKM H1

10410 JOHANNA U. Li/Br 1961; C; 6300/8500; 145×8.3/9.1 (477×27.6/30); M; 14.5; ex AUSTRALIND 1975.

KMFKM H123

***10420 KLARA ZETKIN.** Ru/Ru 1934; C; 4200; 111×6.7 (364×22); M; 9.75.

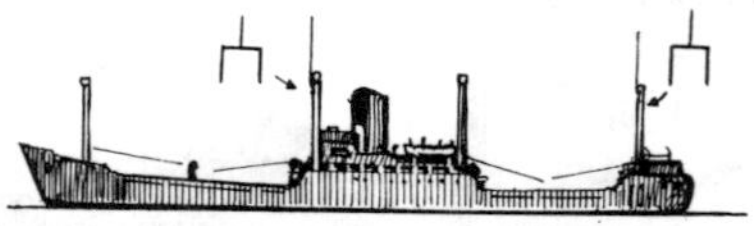

KMFKM H123

● ***10430 ANADYR.** Ru/Pd 1952; TC/C; 3600; 108×6.7 (355×22); R & LPT; 11.5; **'B 31'** type. Sisters (Ru flag): ***10431 ADAM MITSKEVICH *10432 ALEKSEY CHIRIKOV *10433 BELORUSSIYA *10434 CHEREMKHOVO *10435 JAN ANVELT *10436 YULIYA ZHEMAYTE *10435 KEMEROVO *10438 KHUDOZHNIK V. KRAYNEV *10439 KUZBASS *10440 MEKHANIK BONDIK** ex MOLOTOVSK 1957 ***10441 MIKHAIL LAZAREV *10442 NIKOLAY PRZHEVALSKIY *10443 NOVAYA ZEMLYA *10444 PETROPAVLOVSK—KAMCHATSKIY *10445 PRIMORSK *10446 PRIOZERSK *10447 PRIVOLZHSK *10448 SALOMEYA NERIS *10449 SARATOV *10450 SEVERNAYA ZEMLYA *10451 SEVEROMORSK *10452 SHAKHTY *10453 STEPAN KRASHENINNIKOV *10454 ULYANOVSK *10455 VASILIY GOLOVNIN *10456 VITUS BERING *10457 VORKUTA *10458 VYACHESLAV SHISHKOV *10459 KADIEVKA** (RC flag): ***10460 HOPING ER SHI SAN** ex RADOM 1956 ***10461 HOPING ER SHI SSU** ex LODZ 1956 ***10462 HOPING SAN SHI CHI** ex OSTRODA 1957 ***10463 HOPING SAN SHI CHIU** ex ROZEWIE 1957 ***10464 HOPING SAN SHI ER** ex KALISZ 1956 ***10465 HOPING SAN SHI PA** ex KARWIA 1957.

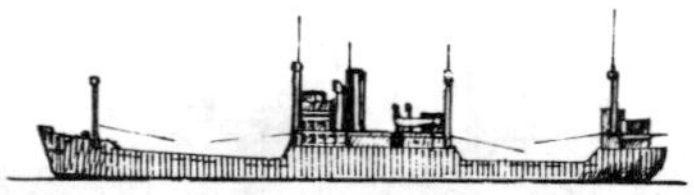

KMFKM H123

***10470 NAN HAI 157** RC/US 1945; C; 3300; 100×6.4 (329×21); R; 10; ex DUN YU 1951; ex MULGRAVE PARK 1946.

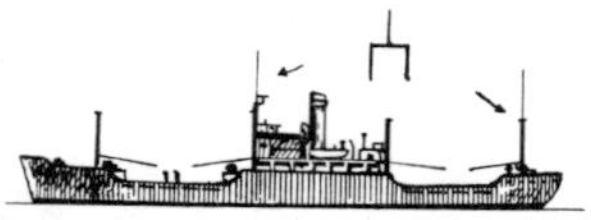

KMFKM H123

***10480 VOLODARSKIY.** Ru/Ru 1929; C; 2500; 97×5.8 (319×19); R; 8.75.

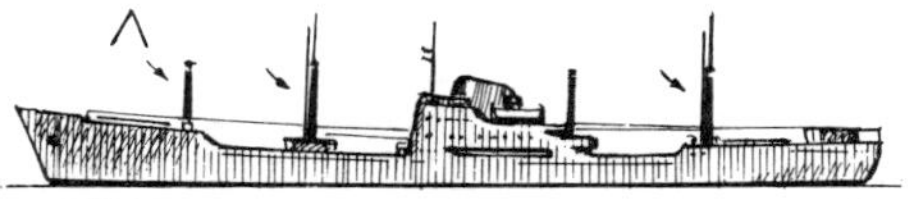

KMFKM H13
10490 DESANMAR. Gr/FRG; 1960; CP; 5100/7200; 138×7.2/8.6 (453×23.6/28.1); M; 16.5; ex EBEL 1980; ex BIRGITTE SKOU 1980. Sister: ⋆**10491 SHU YU QUAN** (RC) ex CHERRY CRYSTAL 1980; ex MAREN SKOU 1980.

KMFKM H13
10510 INDIAN INDUSTRY. In/In 1959; C; 5400; 118×7.5 (387×24.7); M; 13.

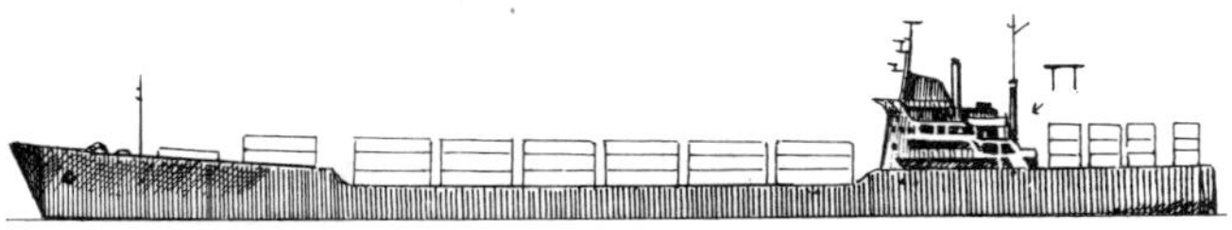

KMFKM H13
10530 PRESIDENT TAFT. US/US 1967; Con; 17300; 202.4×9.4 (664×30.10); T; 23. Sisters (US flag): **10531 PRESIDENT VAN BUREN 10532 PRESIDENT FILLMORE 10533 PRESIDENT McKINLEY.**

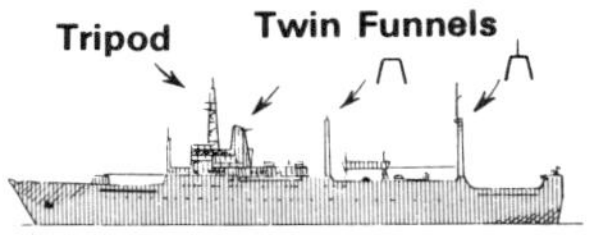

KMFKM H2
⋆**10540 REGULUS.** Pd/Pd 1976; FT; 2600; 89.06×5.6 (292.19×18.37); M; 17.75; **"B414"** type. Sisters (Pd flag): ⋆**10541 ANTARES** ⋆**10542 SAGITTA** Probable sisters (some may be like WLOCZNIK—which see): ⋆**10543 ANTARES** ⋆**10544 ARCTURUS** ⋆**10545 INDUS** ⋆**10546 POLLUX.**

KMFKMK H1
⋆**10590 BAO SHAN.** RC/FRG 1959; CP; 6500/8300; 155×8/9 (510×26/30); M; 17.5; ex MINGLANG 1975; ex WORMS 1972. Sisters: ⋆**10591 XIUSHAN** (RC) ex MINGLAO 1975; ex WIESBADEN 1972 ⋆**10592 YUSHAN** (RC) ex MINGWEI 1975; ex WEIN 1972; One of these ships may have been renamed **BA SHAN.**

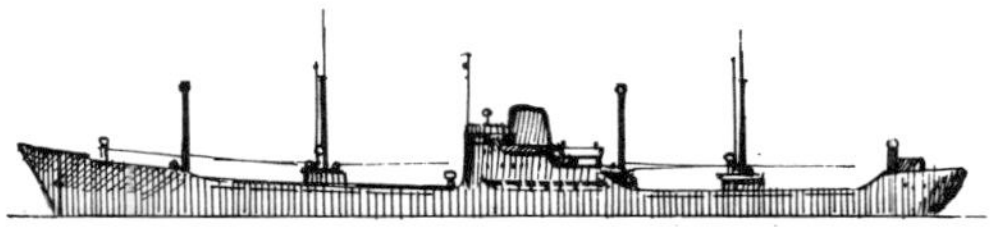

KMFKM H13
10500 MARIAELENA T. Cy/FRG 1957; C; 9500; 152×9.3 (496×31); M; 15; ex COSTAS METHENITIS 1978; ex SAN MIGUEL 1973; ex FLORES 1971; ex MERCIA 1969; ex SILKEN 1964.

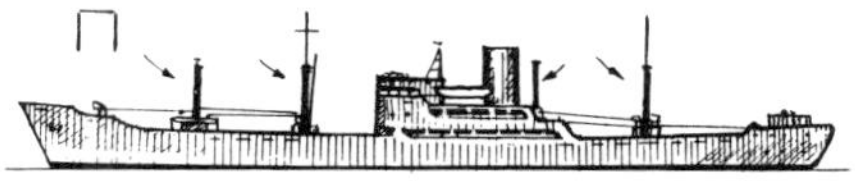

KMFKM H13
10520 KOTA BUANA. Sg/Hong Kong 1957; C; 9500; 152×9.3 (496×31); M; 15; ex CORAL CHIEF 1978; ex CORAL CHIEF 1977; ex CHEKIANG 1969. Sisters: **10521 STRAITS HOPE** (Sg) ex ISLAND CHIEF 1978; ex CHEFOO 1970 ⋆**10522 SONG GIANH** (Vn) ex KIM SENG 1977; ex FORTUNE GLORY 1971; ex CHUNGKING 1968.

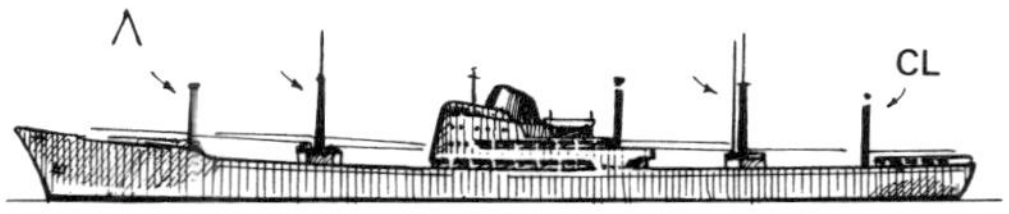

KMFKMK H1
⋆**10560 QIANJIN.** RC/Pd 1965; C; 6900; 154×8.3 (505×27.4); M; 15; ex HENRYK JENDZA; **'B 454'** type.

KMFKMK H1
● ⋆**10570 FRANCESCO NULLO.** Pd/Pd 1964; C; 5700/8600; 152.6×7.7/8.8 (501×25.4/29); M; 15.5; **"B41"** type. Sister (Pd flag): ⋆**10571 LENINO** Similar (larger funnel): ⋆**10572 ALEKSANDER ZAWADSKI** ⋆**10573 GWARDIA LUDOWA** ⋆**10574 LENINGRAD** ⋆**10575 JOZEF WYBICKI** ex SEBASTIAN KLONOWICZ ⋆**10576 PIOTR DUNIN** ⋆**10577 SMOLNY** ⋆**10578 STANISLAW DUBIOS** (RC flag) (some may have small funnels): ⋆**10579 CHANGNING** ⋆**10580 HAINING** ⋆**10581 JINING** ⋆**10582 XINGNING** ⋆**10583 YONGNING.**

KMFKMK H1
10600 ILIOS. Gr/Br 1962; C; 10700; 160×9.9 (526×32.3); M; 16.5; ex VASILIOS R 1977.

KMFKMK H1
⋆**10610 SIMFEROPOL.** Ru/Pd 1962; C; 6600/9200; 155 × 7.8/8.9 (508 × 26/29.3); M; 15; **'B 43'** type. Sisters (Ru flag): ⋆**10611 SALAVAT** ⋆**10612 SEMIPALATINSK** ⋆**10613 SLAVSK** ⋆**10614 SLUTSK** ⋆**10615 SOVIETSK.**

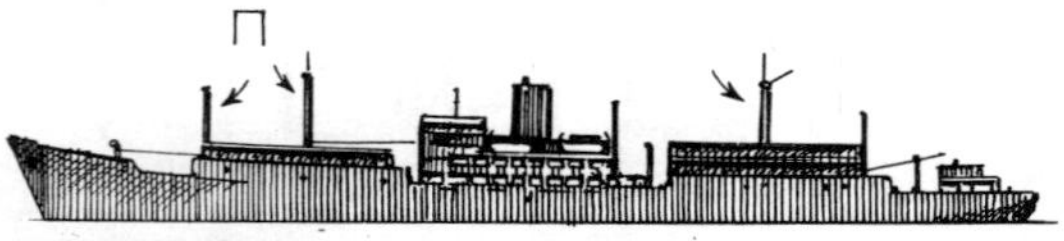

KMFKMK H1
● **10630 AL MESSILAH.** Ku/De 1947/70; LS; 8000; 165.03 × 9.23 (541.44 × 30.28); TSM; —; ex LINDA CLAUSEN 1974; ex KAMBODIA 1969; ex BRANDENBURG 1946; converted from general cargo. Side doors.

KMFKMK H123
10640 HOMER. Gr/Pd 1958; C/Tim; 2600; 95 × 5.5 (311 × 18.1); R; 12; ex KALLIOPI 1979; ex OPOLE 1977; **'B 32'** type. Others of this type may also have this sequence see BIELSKO under KMFMK.

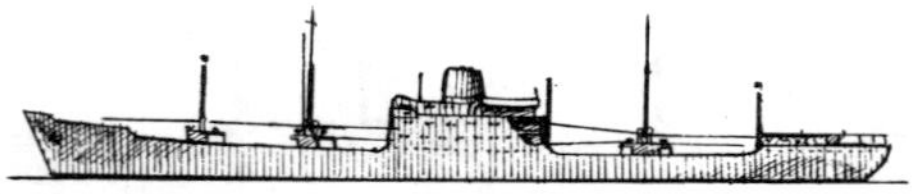

KMFKMK H123
10660 MIMOSA TRADER. Gr/Ne 1957; CP; 5300; 138 × 7.4 (455 × 24.6); M; 16; ex STRAAT JOHORE 1978.

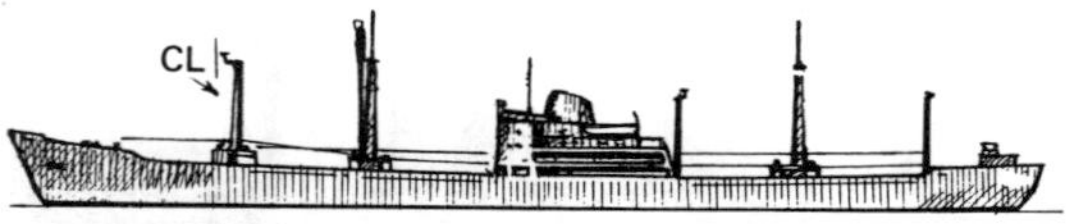

KMFKMK H13
10680 NEDLLOYD KOREA. Ne/Ne 1964; C; 7300/9900; 165 × 8/9 (541 × 26/29.8); M; 19; ex STRAAT KOREA 1977; ex KLOOSTERKERK 1971. Sister: **10681 NEDLLOYD KOBE** (Ne) ex STRAAT KOBE 1977; ex KOUDEKERK 1971.

KMFM H
⋆**10690 VOIKOV.** Ru/US 1943; C; 7200; 135 × 8.5 (442 × 27.9); R; 10; ex SAMUEL P LANGLEY **'Liberty'** type.

KMFM H
10710 AFRICA. Gr/Be 1965; Fru; 5100; 134 × 6.6 (441 × 21.6); M; 20; ex FRUBEL AMERICA 1980. Sister **10711 FRUBEL EUROPA** (Gr).

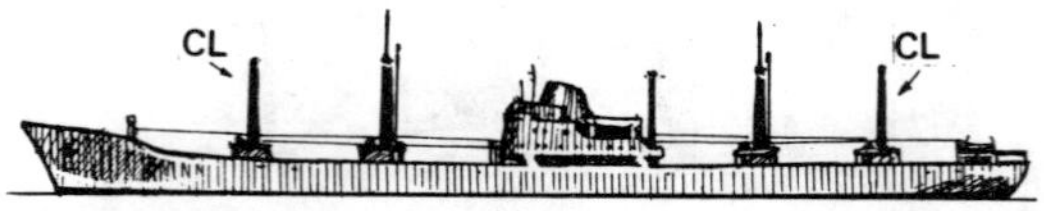

KMFKMK H1
● **10620 PINDAROS.** Gr/Sw 1963; C; 7900/10700; 162 × 8.7/9.5 (531 × 28.3/31); M; 16.5; ex LONDON CRAFTSMAN 1976. Sisters: **10621 PLOTINOS** (Gr) ex LONDON CITIZEN 1977 **10622 AGIA MARINA** (Gr) ex LONDON STATESMAN 1979 Similar: **10623 RIVA** (Gr) ex LONDON BANKER 1973 **10624 SINGAPORE FORTUNE** (Sg) ex LONDON ADVOCATE 1973 ⋆**10625 LIMING** (RC) ex LONDON TRADESMAN 1964.

KMFKMK H123
10650 SYNEBORIA. Gr/Ne 1956; CP; 5000/6600; 134 × 7.6/— (439 × 24.7/—); M; 16; ex JUPITER SUN 1976; ex STRAAT COOK 1974. Sisters (Sg flag): **10651 KOTA MELATI** ex STRAAT LOMBOK 1975 **10652 KOTA MAWAR** (Sg) ex STRAAT TORRES 1975.

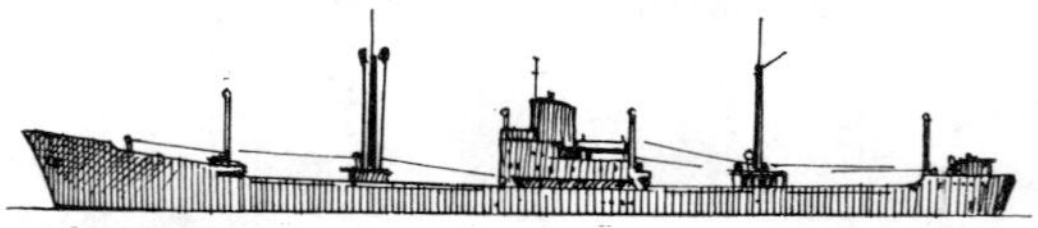

KMFKMK H13
10670 MANICA. Po/FRG 1961; CP; 9200; 157 × 9.2 (516 × 30.7); M; 18; ex KULMERLAND 1971. Sisters (Some may have a tall mast from bridge) **10671 MUNSTERLANDES** (Gr) ex MUNSTERLAND 1979 **10672 CONGO** (Po) ex NURNBERG 1971 **10673 MUXIMA** (Po) ex WOLFSBURG 1971 ⋆**10674 N'GOLA** (An) ex BLUMENTHAL 1971.

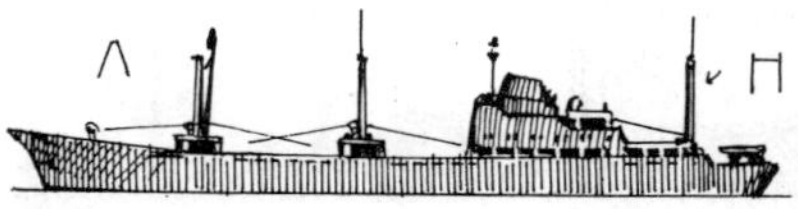

KMFM H
10700 MECIS FLAG. Le/Ys 1966; CP; 3300/5200; 120 × 7.2/— (395 × 23/—); M; 15.5; ex KORDOFAN 1980 Sisters **10701 MECIS PIONEER** (Le); ex EL GEZIRA 1980 **10702 MECIS LEADER** (Le); ex SENNAR 1980.

KMFM H
★**10720 YANIS RAYNIS.** Ru/Pd 1971; R; 5200; 119. 4×7.3 (393×23.11); M; 19; **'B.443'** Type. Sisters (Ru flag): ★**10721 ALEKSANDRA KOLLONTAY** ★**10722 HENRI BARBUSSE** ★**10723 LARISA REYSNER** ★**10724 KARLIS ZIEDINS** ★**10725 KLARA ZETKIN** ★**10726 MARINA RASKOVA** ★**10727 OTOMAR OSHKALIN** ★**10728 POLINA OSIPENKO** ★**10729 YANIS LENTSMANIS** ★**10730 JAKOV ALKSNIS** ★**10731 ZENTA OZOLA**

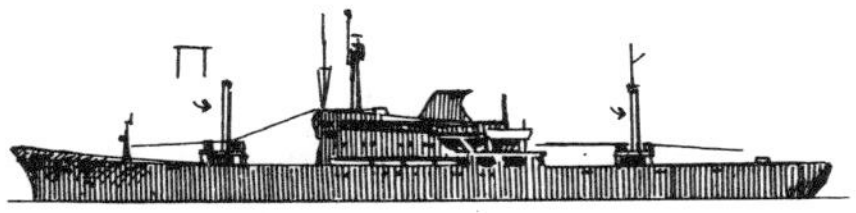

KMFM H
★**10760 BURAN;** Pd/Pd 1972; FC; 2900/5100; 120× -/7.3; (392× -/24); M; 18; **'B.433'** type. Sisters (Pd flag): ★**10761 HALNIAK** ★**10762 LEWANTER.**

KMFM H
★**10780 OKAH;** Ru/- 1959; P; 800; 61× - (200× -); M; 12.

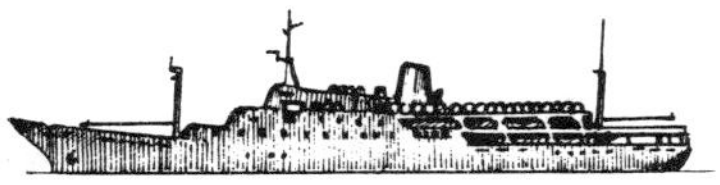

KMFM H
10800 NIHON MARU; Ja/Ja 1970; P; 3000; 106×4.6 (349×15.3); TSM; 20.5.

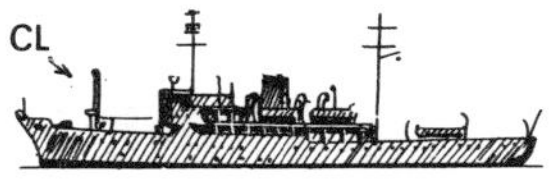

KMFM H
10820 HOKUTO MARU; Ja/Ja 1952; TS; 1600; 75.6×3.4 (248×11.4); T; 12.25.

KMFM H
● **10840 SACKR AL JAZIRAH;** Si/Fr 1967; RoVC/WT; 1300; 85×4.5 (279×15); TSM; 16; ex GIGNAC 1980.

KMFM H
● ★**10740 NIKOLAY KOPERNIK;** Ru/Pd 1974; R; 6400; 140×7.7 (460×25.6); M; 21.75; **'B.437'** type. Sisters (Ru flag): ★**10741 ARISTARKH BELOPOLSKIY** ★**10742 FEDOR BREDIKHIN** ★**10743 MIKHAIL LOMONOSOV** ★**10744 PAVEL PARENAGO** ★**10745 PAVEL SHTERNBERG** ★**10746 VASILIY FESENKOV** ★**10747 VASILIY STRUVE** ★**10748 IVAN POLZUNOV** ★**10749 IVAN KULIBIN** ★**10750 PROFESSOR POPOV** ★**10751 ILYA METCHNIKOV** ★**10753 AKADEMIK KHOKHLOV** (Ho flag): **10754 RIO SIXAOLA** ex RIO ULUA 1980 **10755 RIO CUYAMEL 10756 RIO SULACO** (Pd flag): ★**10757 GDYNSKI KOSYNIER** ★**10758 DZIECI POLSKIE** ★**10759 ZYRARDOW.**

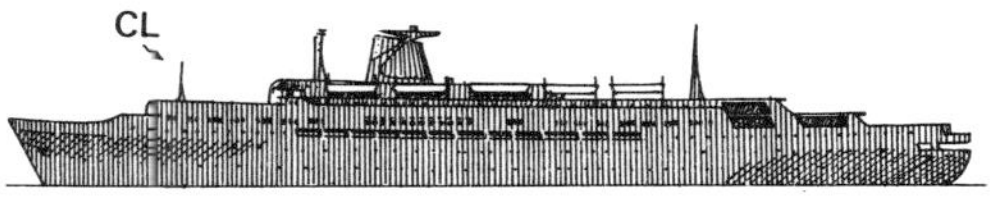

KMFM H
10770 ITHACA; Gr/FRG 1956; P; 9000; 153×8 (501×26.7); T; 19; ex AMELIA DE MELLO 1972; ex ZION 1966.

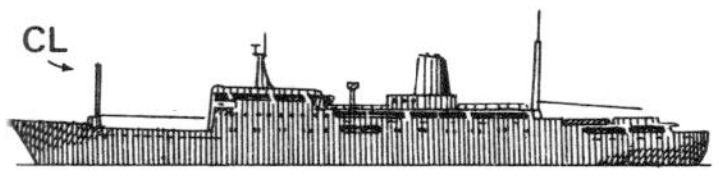

KMFM H
10790 TOKYO MARU; Ja/Ja 1969; PC; 3600; 111.2×5.5 (365×18); M; 18.5.

KMFM H
★**10810 SEJWAL;** Pd/Pd 1968; FT; 2500; 87×5 3 (286×17.7); M; 13.5; **'B.18'** type. Sisters (Pd flag): ★**10811 FOKA** ★**10812 KASZALOT** ★**10813 NARWAL** ★**10814 HOMAR** ★**10815 ORKA** ★**10816 FINWAL** ★**10817 LANGUSTA** ★**10818 PLETWAL.**

KMFM H
10830 TSUBAKI MARU; Ja/Ja 1948; F; 1000; 65×3.6 (214×12); M; 13; ex TERUKINI MARU No. 1 1959.

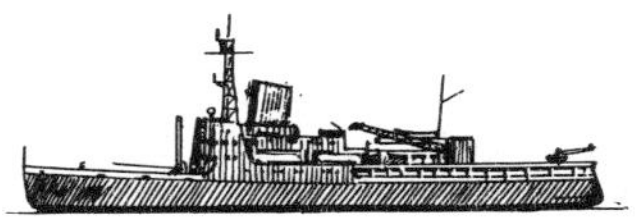

KMFM H
10850 d'IBERVILLE; Ca/Ca 1953; IB; 5700; 94.8×9.2 (311×30.5); TSR; 16.

KMFM H
10860 JOHN A MACDONALD; Ca/Ca 1960; IB/P; 6200; 96 × 8.5 (315 × 28.2); TrSD-E; 15.5; Helicopter deck. Canadian Coast Guard.

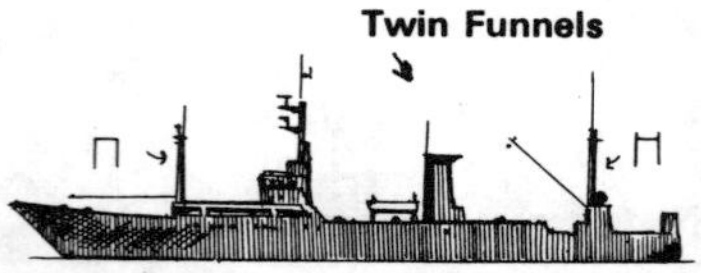

KMFM H1
⋆**10870 PULKOVSKIY MERIDIAN;** Ru/Ru 1974; FT; 3300; 104 × 5.9 (342 × 19.6); M; 15.5.

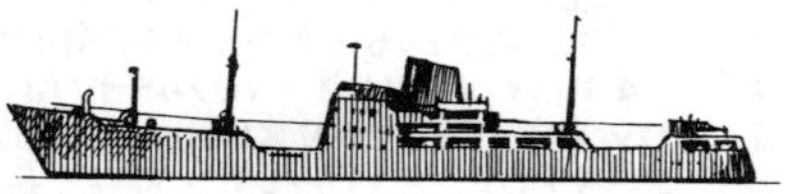

KMFM H1
⋆**10880 MALAKHOV KURGAN;** Ru/De 1953; FC; 3700/5500; 124 × 5.9/7.4 (407 × 19.6/24.5); M; 17.5; ex DOLORES 1964; ex BRAZILIAN REEFER 1963. Sisters (Ru flag): ⋆**10881 MATROS KOSHKA** ex DOMINGO 1964; ex MEXICAN REEFER 1964 ⋆**10882 SLAVA SEVASTOPOLYA** ex DARIEN 1964; ex PERUVIAN REEFER 1963.

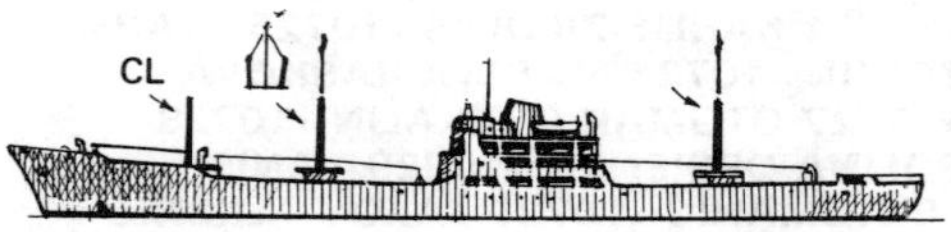

KMFM H1
● **10890 MILETO;** Li/Fr 1958; C; 8400; 144.5 × 9.2 (474 × 27.9); M; 15; ex FELICE d'AMICO 1974; ex TIDECREST 1966.

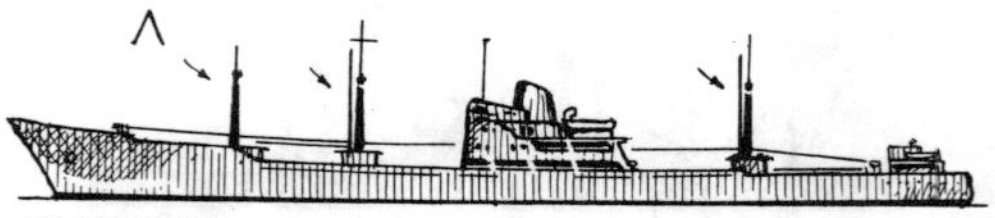

KMFM H1
10900 KERASOUS; Gr/Ys 1959; C; 6000/8800; 152 × 8.2/9.3 (500 × 27/30.6); M; - ; ex LAVAUX 1974. Similar: **10901 MACHITIS** (Gr) **10902 KAPITAN KAMARI** (Gr); ex HOPEWELL 1980; ex MASTER DASKALOS.

KMFM H1
10910 MINOTAURUS; Gr/Sp 1957; C; 4800; 132 × 7.5 (437 × 24.8); TSM; 16.5; ex CEFALLONIAN WAVE 1980; ex CABO SANTA MARTA 1979; ex PEDRO DE VALDIVIA.

KMFM H1
● **10920 M. ALEXAND;** Pa/Ne 1951; CP; 2100/3400; 107.5 × 6/- (353 × 19.7/-); M; 13; ex LADY SALLA 1977; ex NAUSIKA 1974; ex KASTOR 1970; ex RIMON 1965. Sister: **10921 ATHENA** (Gr); ex KRONIOS 1970; ex TAMAR 1965 Similar: **10922 CEFALLONIAN SEA** (Gr); ex DEGERO 1977 **10923 CEFALLONIAN SKY** (Gr); ex ECKERO 1977 Similar (larger): ⋆**10924 PULA** (Ys) ⋆**10925 ZADAR** (Ys).

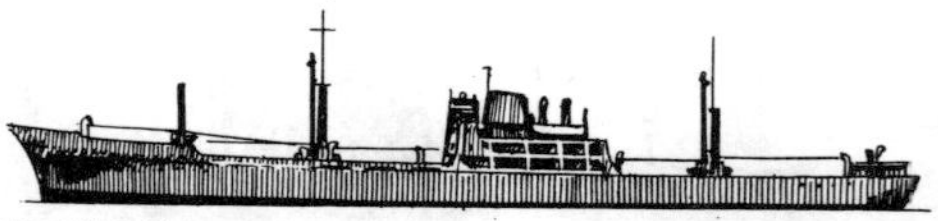

KMFM H1
10930 MONTE CARLO; Pa/FRG 1953; CP; 8900; 150 × 8.9 (493 × 29); M; 15; ex STAR FORTUNE 1980; ex MASTER STELIOS 1977. Similar: **10931 LINK LOVE** (Gr); ex MARGO **10932 LINK HARMONY** (Gr); ex MARIETTA E.

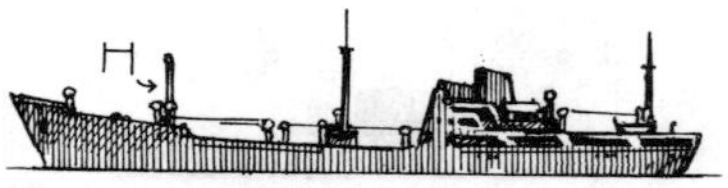

KMFM H1
● **10940 DUERO;** Sp/Sp 1961; C; 3300; 105.8 × 5.9 (347 × 19.6); M; 15. Sisters: **10941 TER** (Sp) **10942 ABU MISHARI AL KULAIB** (Ku) ex ARGA 1980.

KMFM H1
10950 VISHVA PRATAP; In/It 1956; C; 7100; 150 × 8; 386 × 27; M; 14.5; ex ELETTRA FASSIO1964.

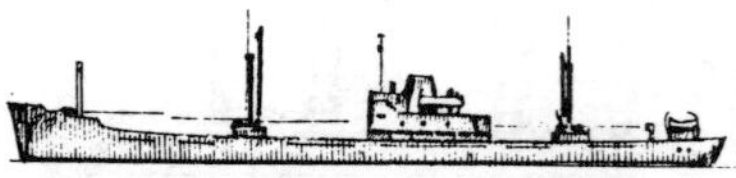

KMFM H1
10960 SARBO; Gr/FRG 1957; C; 3700; 111.1 × 6.2 (365 × 20.4); M; 14; ex ROSITA 1969.

KMFM H1
10970 MOSCHANTHY; Cy/FRG 1951; CP; 2400/4000; 98.4 × -/7.3 (323 × -/24); M; 13; ex TRANSQUEBEC 1967; ex IRMINGARD 1957.

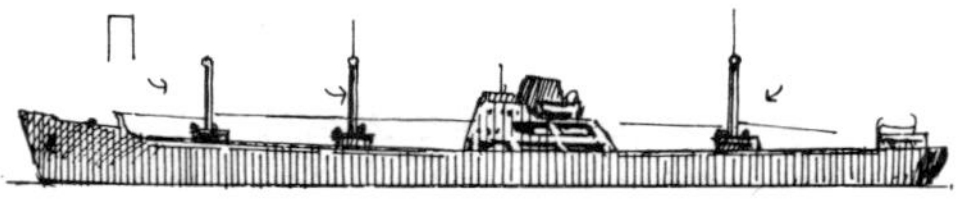

KMFM H1
● ⋆**10990 BOKA;** Ys/Ys 1958; C; 6300/9000; 146 × 7.9/8.5 (478 × 26/29.3); M; 13 Similar (Ys flag): ⋆**10991 LIKA** ⋆**10992 PETKA** ⋆**10993 SLAVONIJA** ⋆**10994 TRECI MAJ** ⋆**10995 ULJANIK** ⋆**10996 TREPCA** ⋆**10997 ZETA** **10998 AZIM** (Pa) ex ENDI; ex SPLENDID SUN; ex ENDI 1977; ex SPLENDID SUN 1976; ex MARJAN 1967 **10999 COMELUCK GLORY** (Tw) ex ASSOCIATED GRAIN 1977; ex AMARILIS 1974; ex MARIEL 1969; ex RADNIK 1967; ex JADRAN.

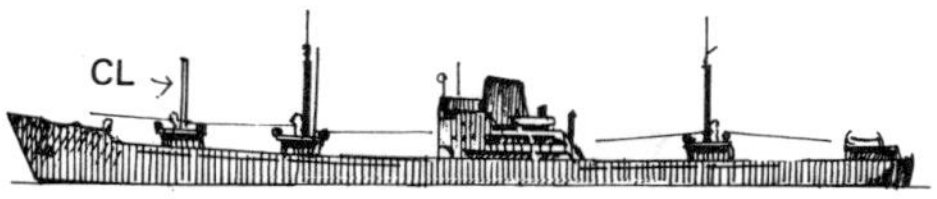

KMFM H1
● **11120 LENA;** It/FRG 1957; CP; 6400/8300; 144.3 × 7.9/8.5 (474 × 26/28); M; 13; ex ROSARIO LOFARO 1980; ex IRMGARD REITH 1973; ex CAROLA REITH 1972.

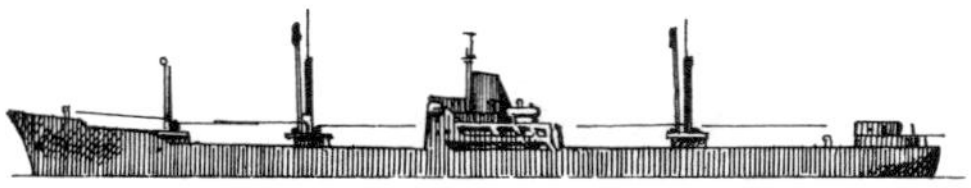

KMFM H1
11130 LANKA SHANTHI; Sr/Be 1964; C; 6500/9500; 146.9 × 8/9.2 (482 × 25.1/30.2); M; 14.5; ex HEERING ELSIE 1973; ex LOUCAS N 1970. Sister: **11131 IRENE D** (Gr) ex MASTER NICOS 1980.

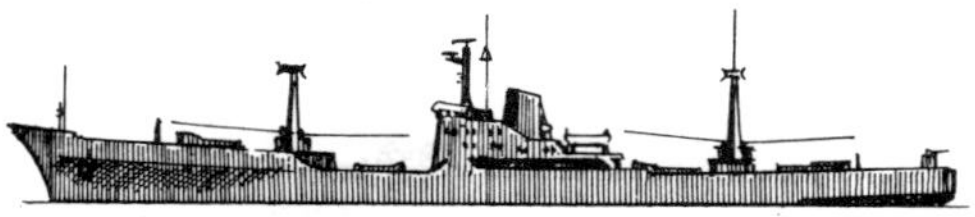

KMFM H1
11150 WILD GANNET; Br/No 1977; R; 5000/6900; 144.5 × 9 (474 × 29.8); M; 22.75; **'DRAMMEN'** type. Sister: **11151 WILD GREBE** (Br).

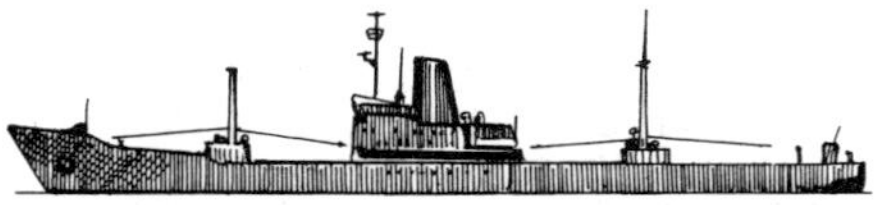

KMFM H1
11170 COYOLES; Li/Be 1967; R; 5200; 135.1 × 6.8 (443 × 22.4); M; 21; ex FRUBEL ASIA 1977. Sisters (Li flag): **11171 ESTRELLA** ex FRUBEL AFRICA **11172 GUAYAQUIL** ex FRUBEL OCEANIA **11173 SANTA MARTA** ex FRUBEL PRINSES PAOLA.

KMFM H1
10980 VITACALM; Gr/Br 1957; C; 9700; 152.9 × 8.8 (502 × 29); M; 15.5; ex DIONE 1975; ex MERCHANT ROYAL 1963.

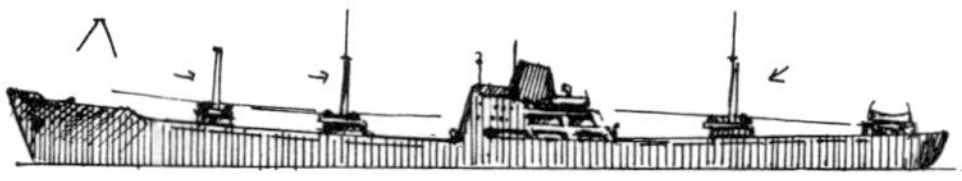

KMFM H1
⋆**11100 NIKOLA TESLA;** Ys/Ys 1957; C; 5900/8600; 146 × 7.8/9 (479 × 25.8/29.5); M; 14.

KMFM H1
● **11110 PATAGONIA ARGENTINA;** Ar/Ne 1962; C; 7200/9600; 152.6 × 8.4/9.2 (508 × 27.6/30.3); M; 13; ex HOLLANDS DREEF 1972. Sisters: **11111 PAMPA ARGENTINA** (Ar); ex HOLLANDS DIEP 1970 **11112 GREENVILLE** (Li); ex AMSTELHOEK 1973 **11113 HARLANDSVILLE** (Li); ex HOLLANDS DUIN 1973 **11114 BAYVILLE** (Li); ex AMSTELSTAD 1977.

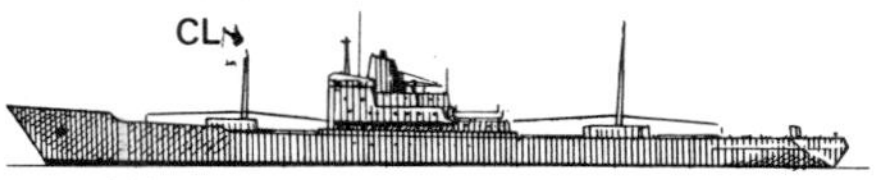

KMFM H1
⋆**11140 THEODOR STORM;** DDR/Be 1966; R; 5000; 135 × 6.8 (443 × 22.3); M; 21. Sister: ⋆**11141 THEODOR FONTANE** (DDR).

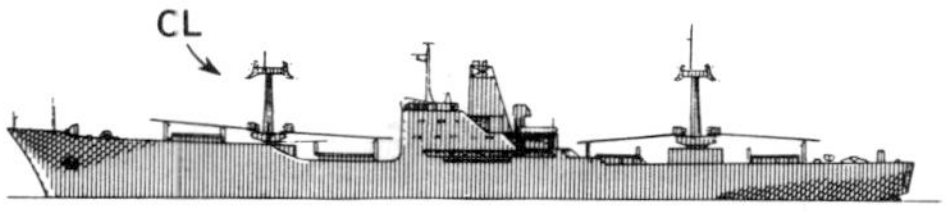

KMFM H1
11160 EMANUEL; No/No 1976; R; 5100/7000; 144.2 × 8.99 (473.1 × 29.49); M; 22.75; **"DRAMMEN"** type.

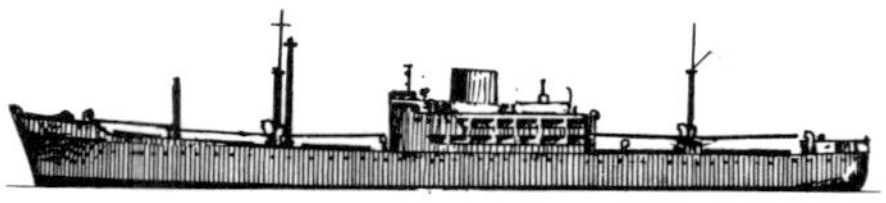

KMFM H1
11180 GANDA; Po/Br 1948; C; 5900; 135 × 7.9 (443 × 26); M; 13.

KMFM H1
● **11190 DYNAMIKOS;** Gr/FRG 1953; C; 5600/8500; 143.1 × 8/9 (470 × 26.5/30); M; 13.75; ex FREIENFELS 1972. Sisters: **11191 POLYMICHANOS** (Gr); ex FRAUENFELS 1973 **11192 THARALEOS** (Gr); ex DRACHENFELS 1972.

KMFM H1
⋆**11200 MURMANSK;** Ru/Hong Kong 1941; C; 7200; 136.8 × 7.9 (450 × 26); R; 9.5; ex EMPIRE STARLIGHT 1946; Rebuilt WW2 Standard ship.

KMFM H1
11210 MISAMIS OCCIDENTAL; Pi/Ja 1970; PC; 1900; 88.9 × 4.9 (292 × 16.1); M; 18.

KMFM H1
● **11220 HOKUTO MARU;** Ja/Ja 1976; TS; 5900; 125 × 5.8 (411 × 19); T; 18.

KMFM H1
11230 SHINTOKU MARU; Ja/Ja 1962; TS; 3500; 100.8 × 5.1 (331 × 16.1); M; 13.

KMFM H1
11240 CITY OF HYDRA; Gr/Br 1955; F; 1000; 58.6 × 2.8 (192 × 9.2); TSM; 12.5 ex CLAYMORE 1976.

KMFM H1
● **11250 SANTA MARIA DE LA CANDELARIA;** Sp/Sp 1964; F; 1200; 67.1 × 3.2 (220 × 10.5); TSM; 15. Possible Sisters (Sp flag): **11251 SANTA MARIA DE LA CARIDAD 11252 SANTA MARIA DE LAS NIEVES 11253 SANTA MARIA DE LA PAZ 11254 SANTA MARIA DEL PINO.**

KMFM H1
11260 EDRA; It/It 1962; F; 500; 64 × 2.7 (210 × 9); TSM; — .

KMFM H1
11270 AMARYLLIS; Ja/Ja 1967; Sal/Tg; 1800; 73 × 6 (240 × 19.8); TSM; 13.

KMFM H1
11290 TOULA; Sp/Sp 1963; FT; 1600; 73.9 × — (246 × —); M; 12.

KMFM H1
⋆**11300 KOPET-DAG;** Ru/Ru 1970; FT; 3300; 107.5 × 6.2 (353 × 20.4); D-E; 13. Sisters (Ru flag): ⋆**11301 ALTAY** ⋆**11302 AMBARCHIK** ⋆**11303 ASKANIYA** ⋆**11304 BELOMORY** ⋆**11305 ELBRUS** ⋆**11306 GOLFSTRIM** ⋆**11307 KHOLMOGORY** ⋆**11308 KIVACH** ⋆**11309 PAMIR** ⋆**11310 PEVEK** ⋆**11311 PODMOSKOVYE** ⋆**11312 POLESYE** ⋆**11313 KARPATY** ⋆**11314 BEREZNIKI** ⋆**11315 NOKUYEV** ⋆**11316 KARAKUMY** ⋆**11317 VOLGOBALT** ⋆**11318 ANDREY ANDREYEV** ⋆**11319 RZHEV** ⋆**11320 KHIBINY** ⋆**11321 DIKSON** ⋆**11322 PRIKARPATYE** ⋆**11323 ZAKAVKAZYE** ⋆**11324 KOTELNICH** ⋆**11325 POVOLZHYE** ⋆**11326 KARPOGORY** ⋆**11327 PRIONEZHYE** ⋆**11328 VERKHOYANY** ⋆**11329 ZAVOLZHYE** ⋆**11330 VALDAY.**

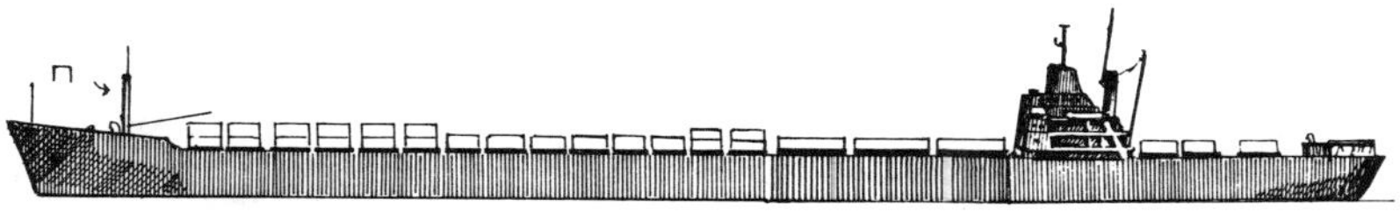

KMFM H1
11340 AUSTRAL ENVOY; US/US 1972/77; Con; 31000; 247,81 × 10.08 (813.02 × 33.07); T; 23; Lengthened 1977. Sisters (US flag): **11341 AUSTRAL ENTENTE 11342 AUSTRAL PIONEER 11343 AUSTRAL PURITAN.**

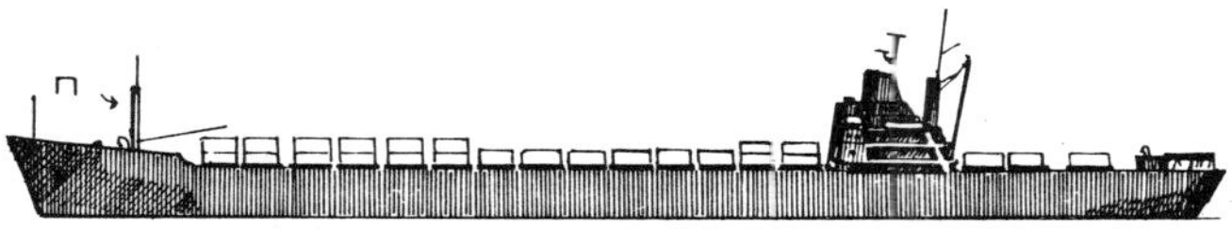

KMFM H1
● **11350 AUSTRAL ENSIGN.** US/US 1973, Con; 21200; 203.7 × 9.6 (669 × 31.5); T; 23; Sister (US flag); **11351 AUSTRAL ENDURANCE** Similar: **11352 PRESIDENT JEFFERSON 11353 PRESIDENT MADISON 11354 PRESIDENT PIERCE 11355 PRESIDENT JOHNSON**

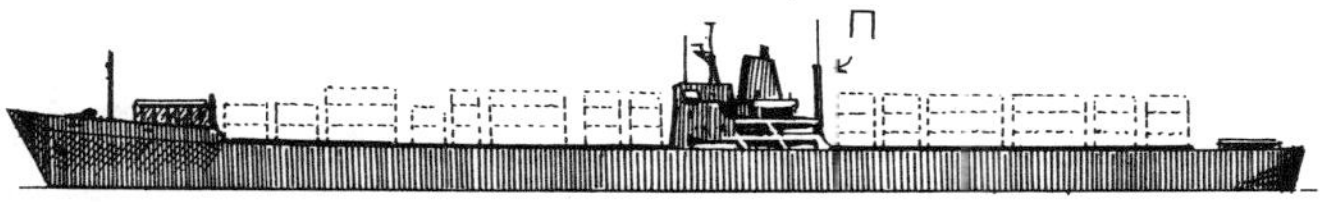

KMFM H1
11360 PRESIDENT EISENHOWER. US/US 1962; Con; 16500; 203.6 × 10.2 668 × 33.4; T; 20; ex PHILIPPINE MAIL 1975; lengthened and converted from a 'C.6' type cargo vessel 1972. Sisters (US flag): **11361 PRESIDENT KENNEDY** ex OREGON MAIL 1975 **11362 PRESIDENT ROOSEVELT** ex WASHINGTON MAIL 1975 **11363 PRESIDENT TRUMAN** ex JAPAN MAIL 1975.

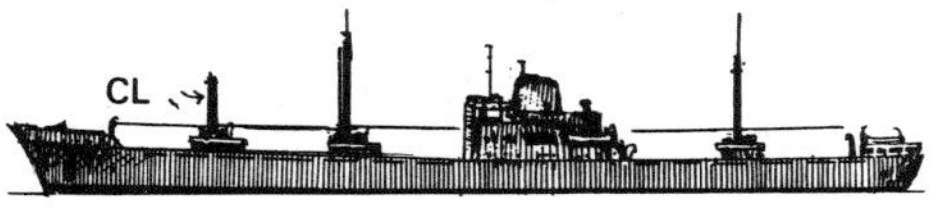

KMFM H1
● **11370 ALEXA.** Pa/FRG 1952; C; 8800; 143.5 × 8.5 (471 × 27.1); M; 13; ex DEMOCRITOS 1973; ex JULIA 1967.

KMFM H12
⋆**11380 BOROVICHI.** Ru/Ru 1965; RS; 5300; 122 × 4.7 (400 × 15.3); M; 15; Missile tracking vessel. Converted from cargo ship 1967. Sisters: (Ru flag): ⋆**11381 KEGOSTROV** ⋆**11382 MORZHOVETS** ⋆**11383 NEVEL.**

KMFM H12
11390 ASTRID. Pa/Sw 1944; C; 2700; 97.9 × 5.8 (321 × 19); R; 12; ex CATHRIN 1975; ex ARATON 1974.

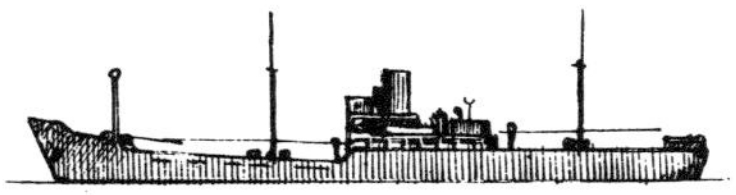

KMFM H12
11400 SOZER BIRADESLER. Tu/Sw 1946; CP; 3700; 104.5 × 6.3 (343 × 20.8); R & LPT; 10; ex ODEMIS 1976; ex HEIMDAL 1946.

KMFM H12
11410 DHARINI. In/Ca 1944; FA; 2900; 100 × 5.8 (324 × 19); R; 9; ex KETOWNA PARK 1953; Converted 1960 from cargo ship. Indian Navy.

KMFM H123
● ⋆**11430 KOSMONAUT PAVEL BELYAYEV.** Ru/Ru 1963; C; 4500; 122 × 7 (400 × 23); M; 14.5; ex VYTEGRALES 1974. Sisters (Ru flag): ⋆**11431 CHULMLES** ⋆**11432 ISAKOGORKA** ⋆**11433 IVAN CHERNYKH** ⋆**11434 KILDIN** ⋆**11435 KOSMONAUT VLADISLAV VOLKOV** ex YENISEYLES 1974 ⋆**11436 KRASNAYA GORKA** ⋆**11437 NAZAR GUBIN** ⋆**11438 NISHNIJ TAGIL** ⋆**11439 NOVAYA LADOGA** ⋆**11440 NOVAYA ZEMLYA** ⋆**11441 OKA** ⋆**11442 PORKHOV** ⋆**11443 SANGARLES** ⋆**11444 SEMYON KOSINOV** ⋆**11445 TAYMYR** ⋆**11446 VASYA ALEKSEEV** ⋆**11447 VOSKHOD** ⋆**11448 VOSTOK 2** ⋆**11449 VOSTOK 5** ⋆**11450 VOSTOK 6** ⋆**11451 VYTEGRA** ⋆**11452 YAMAL** ⋆**11453 ZOLOTITZA.**

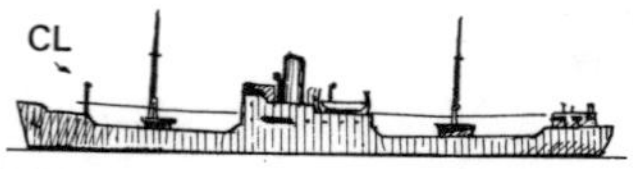

KMFM H123
● **11480 AFAMIA STAR.** Pa/Sw 1954; C; 2000; 90.5 × 5.3 (297 × 17.5); R; 11; ex ELENITSA S 1978; ex VAIGU 1973; ex MALLA 1966; ex SINIKKA 1959; ex GUNDEL 1958; ex NORDANVIK 1958.

KMFM H13
⋆**11510 ALEKSANDR DOVZHENKO.** Ru/Rm 1965; C/TC; 2700; 100 × 5.7 (330 × 18.11); M; 13.75. Sisters (Ru flag): ⋆**11511 GEORGIY VASILIEV** ⋆**11512 SERGEY EYZENSHTEYN** ⋆**11513 SERGEY VASILIEV** ⋆**11514 VSEVOLOD PUDOVKIN.**

KMFM H12
11420 TAISEI MARU. Ja/Ja 1948; TS; 2500; 95.2 × 4.5 (309 × 14.1); T; 10.5; ex OTARU MARU 1953.

KMFM H123
⋆**11460 BASKUNCHAK** Ru/Ru 1964; RS; 4900; 122.1 × 4.3 (400.3 × 14); M; 15; ex VOSTOK 4; Modified cargo vessels. Helicopter deck. Sisters (Ru flag); ⋆**11461 APSHERON** ex TOSNOLES ⋆**11462 DAURIYA** ex SUZDAL ⋆**11463 DIKSON** ex VAGALES ⋆**11464 DONBASS** ex KIRISHI ⋆**11465 SEVAN** ex VYBORGLES ⋆**11466 TAMAN** ex VOSTOK 3.

KMFM H123
11470 POSEIDONIA. Cy/Br 1948; P; 3800; 103.6 × 4.4 (340 × 14.8); TSM; 17; ex INNISFALLEN I 1969; ex INNISFALLEN 1969. Modified after superstructure and docking bridge removed c.1980.

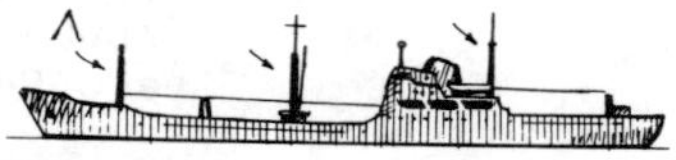

KMFM H13
● ⋆**11490 INDIGA.** Ru/Fi 1965; C/TC; 2900; 102 × 6 (334 × 19.6); M; 13.75. Sisters (Ru flag): ⋆**11491 JANALES** ⋆**11492 KHATANGALES** ⋆**11493 KOSTROMALES** ⋆**11494 KODINO** ⋆**11495 NEVALES** ⋆**11496 OLYUTORKA** ⋆**11497 DIKSON** ⋆**11498 KOLGUYEV** ⋆**11499 PERVOURALSK** ⋆**11500 SALDUS** ⋆**11501 SHEKSNALES** ⋆**11502 ZEYALES.**

KMFM H13
11520 PANKY. Pa/FRG 1958; C; 2300; 86.8 × 5.5 (285 × 18.4); M; 11.25; ex NOREN 1971.

KMFM H13
11530 CEFALLONIAN SPIRIT. Gr/FRG 1958; C; 2400/4000; 113 × 6.1/7.3 (370 × 20/24; M; 12.5; ex RUGEN; ex marivia 1963. Sisters: **10531 TRANSWORLD SAILOR** (Gr); ex VARILD 1977 **11532 SING TAO** (Sg); ex LOBIVIA 1972; ex GEORGIA 1961.

KMFM H13
11540 CLIMAX PEARL. Mv/Br 1956; C; 3100; 107 × 6.2 (351 × 20.3); M; 13.5; ex CITY OF IZMIR 1975; ex FLAMINIAN 1974. Sister: **11541 MALDIVE LOYALTY** (Mv); ex FLORIAN 1971.

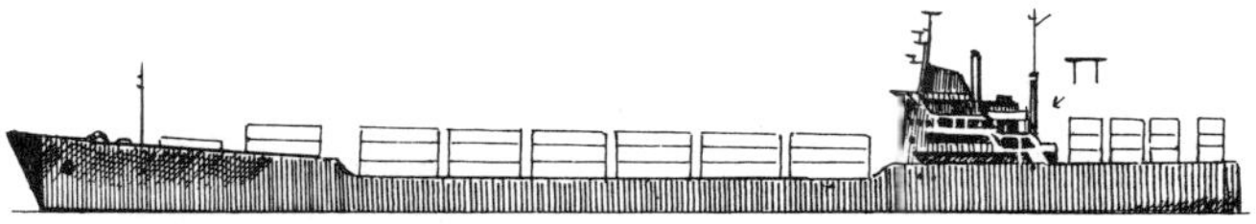

KMFM H13
11550 PRESIDENT TAFT. US/US 1967; Con; 17300; 202 × 9.3 (664 × 30.8); T; 23; converted from cargo ship and lengthened 1972. Sisters: **11551 PRESIDENT VAN BUREN** (US) **11552 PRESIDENT FILLMORE** (US) **11553 PRESIDENT MCKINLEY** (US).

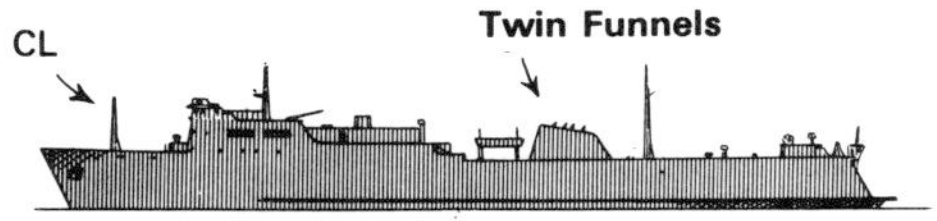

KMFM H2
11560 SIR ROBERT BOND. Ca/Ca 1975; RoC/TF; 10400; 135.34 × 5.11 (444.03 × 16.77); TSM; 17; stern door.

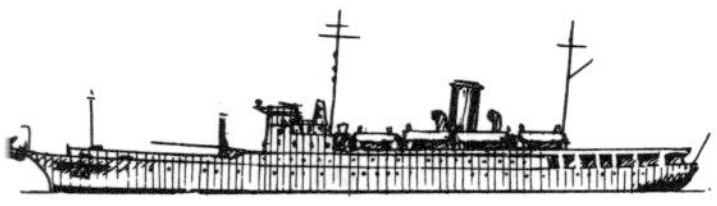

KMFM H2
11570 RECORDER. Br/Br 1954; Cbl; 3300; 103.6 × 5.5 (340 × 18.6); TrS; 11.

KMFM H2
⋆11580 KOMETA. Ru/Pd 1962; FT; 2900; 83. × 5.5 (273 × 18); M; 13; **'B.26'** type (early version) Sisters (Ru flag): **⋆11581 GRIGORIY POLUYANOV ⋆11582 ILYA KATUNIN ⋆11583 KILDIN ⋆11584 KOSMOS ⋆11585 KOLSKIY ⋆11586 MIKHAIL IVCHENKO ⋆11587 OLENEGORSK ⋆11588 PLANETA ⋆11589 PLUTONIY ⋆11590 PERLAMUTR ⋆11591 POLYARNYY ⋆11592 REVOLYUTSIYA ⋆11593 RYBACHIY ⋆11594 TRALFLOT ⋆11595 VOSKHOD ⋆11596 VSPOLOKH ⋆11597 ZARNITSA ⋆11598 BISON ⋆11599 LUNJ ⋆11600 MUROMSK ⋆11601 PARALLAKS ⋆11602 KIROVSK** ex TUR **⋆11603 OLENTUY ⋆11604 ONEKOTAN ⋆11605 SIYANIE** The following are converted to Fishery Research Trawlers: **⋆11606 PROGRESS ⋆11607 NIKOLAY KONONOV ⋆11608 POLYARNOYE SIYANIE.**

KMFM H2
⋆11610 SMOLNYY. Ru/Pd 1969; FT; 2900; 83.2 × 5.5 (273 × 18); M; 11.75; **'B.26'** type (later version). Sisters (Ru flag): **⋆11611 POLOTSK ⋆11612 SELIGER ⋆11613 KAPITAN DEMIDOV ⋆11614 KRASNOPUTILOVETS ⋆11615 LAZURNYY ⋆11616 NOVOKUIBYSHEVSK ⋆11617 PINAGORIY ⋆11618 VASILIY KOSENKHOV ⋆11619 VAYGACH ⋆11620 SLAVGOROD ⋆11621 VYBORGSKAYA STORONA ⋆11622 VYMPEL ⋆11623 BOLSHEVIK ⋆11624 SEVERYANIN ⋆11625 ANATOLIY BREDOV ⋆11626 NIKYEL ⋆11627 TIMOFEY KHRYUKIN** ex KAPITAN DEMIDOV **⋆11628 SULOY ⋆11629 ANTON LOPATIN ⋆11630 TOROS ⋆11631 SALYUT ⋆11632 NARVSKAYA ZASTAVA ⋆11633 ZODCHIY ⋆11634 LENINGRAD ⋆11635 ZELENETS** Similar (pole foremast): **⋆11636 YURIY KOSTIKOV** (Others may also have this feature).

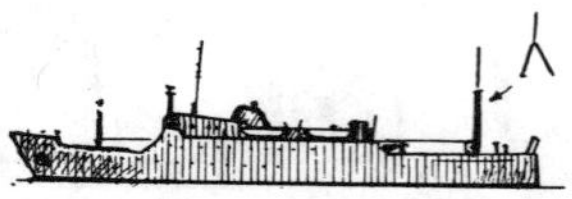

KMFM H2
⋆**11640 ANDROMEDA.** Pd/Pd 1964; FT; 2800; 85×5.5 (279×18); M; 12.5; **'B.15'** type. Sisters (Pd flag): ⋆**11641 DALMOR** ⋆**11642 FENIKS** ⋆**11643 AURIGA** ⋆**11644 MERKURY** ⋆**11645 VIRGO** ⋆**11646 JOWISZ** ⋆**11647 ANTLIA** ⋆**11648 ARIES** ⋆**11649 GENERAL RACHIMOW**

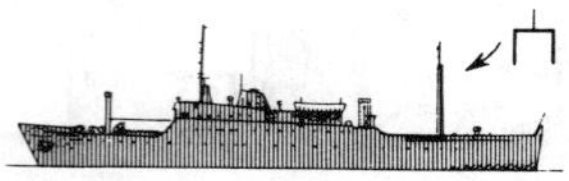

KMFM H2
⋆**11660 COLUMBA.** Pd/Pd 1967; FT; 2300; 83×5.5 (270×18.1); M; 12.5; **'B.15'** type. Sisters: (Pd flag); ⋆**11661 CRATER** ⋆**11662 CYGNUS** ⋆**11663 CENTAURUS** Probable sister: ⋆**11664 CETUS**

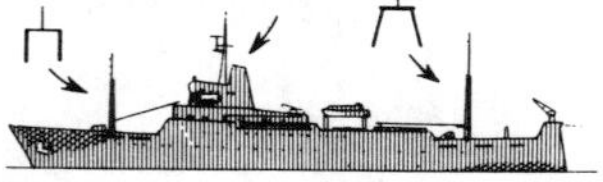

KMFM H2
⋆**11670 VEGA.** Pd/Pd 1973; FT; 2700; 88×5.6 (289×18.8); M; 15; **'B.419'** type. Sisters (Pd flag): ⋆**11672 DENEBOLA** ⋆**11673 PERSEUS** ⋆**11674 GEMINI** ⋆**11675 SIRIUS** (Rm flag): ⋆**11676 HARGHITA** ⋆**11677 IEZER** ⋆**11678 SEMENIC** ⋆**11679 CLABUCET** ⋆**11680 HARGHITA** ⋆**11681 INAU** ⋆**11682 MINDRA.**

KMFM H2
⋆**11690 PROFESOR SIEDLECKI** Pd/Pd 1971; ST/RS; 2800; 89.3×5.5 (293×18); D-E; 14; **'B.424'** type.

KMFM H2
⋆**11700 RETEZATUL.** Rm/Pd 1972; FT; 2700; 88×5.6 (289×18.4); M; 13.75; **'B.22'** type. Sisters: (Rm flag) ⋆**11701 MAREA NEAGRA** ⋆**11702 MOLDOVEANU** ⋆**11703 NEGOIU** ⋆**11704 SINOE** ex LEO ⋆**11705 DELTA DUNARII** ⋆**11706 CARAIMAN** ⋆**11707 CEAHLAU** launched as SATURN ⋆**11708 RAZELM** launched as LEPUS (Pd flag): ⋆**11709 TUCANA** ⋆**11710 LEPUS** ⋆**11711 LACERTA** ⋆**11712 SATURN** ⋆**11713 LYRA** ⋆**11714 TAURUS** ⋆**11715 CARINA** ⋆**11716 LIBRA.**

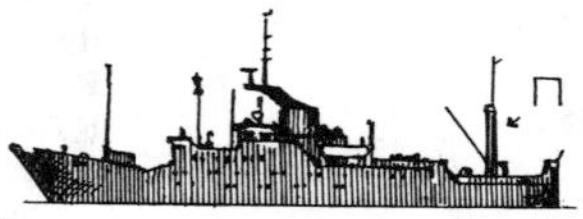

KMFM H2
⋆**11720 TARUSA.** Ru/Ru 1974; FT; 2300; 83.27×— (273×—); M; —. Sisters (Ru flag): ⋆**11721 BYKOVO 11722 BYELOMORSK** ⋆**11723 LOVOZYERO** ⋆**11724 MYS GROTOVYY** ⋆**11725 MYS KURILSKIY** ⋆**11726 MYS LOPATKA** ⋆**11727 MYS PROKOFYEVA** ⋆**11728 MYS RATMANOVA** ⋆**11729 MYS TAYMYR** ⋆**11730 MYS VAYGACH** ⋆**11731 MYS VORONINA** ⋆**11732 NAROCH** ⋆**11733 NEVYANSK** ⋆**11734 BORISPOL** ⋆**11735 DOMODYEDOVO** ⋆**11736 KRONSHTADT** ⋆**11737 MYS ARKTICHESKIY** ⋆**11738 TORZHOK** ⋆**11739 SOLOVIETSKIY** ⋆**11740 SHEREMTYEVO** ⋆**11741 GEROI ZAPOLYARYA** ⋆**11742 BIRYUSINSK** ⋆**11743 VNUKOVO** ⋆**11744 NOVYY MIR** ⋆**11745 ZELEZNOGORSK** ⋆**11746 ZNAMYA POBEDY** ⋆**11747 30-LETIYE POBEDY** ⋆**11748 MYS BUDYONNOGO** ⋆**11749 MYS CHELYUSKIN** ⋆**11750 MYS FRUNZE** ⋆**11751 MYS KRONOTSKIY** ⋆**11752 MYS OTRADNYY** ⋆**11753 MYS VODOPADNYY** ⋆**11754 URGAL** ⋆**11755 LINAKHAMARI** ⋆**11756 ZASHCHITNIK ZAPOLYARYA** ⋆**11757 KHAROVSK** ⋆**11758 TIKHOOKEANSKIY** ⋆**11759 TYNDA** ⋆**11760 MYS ILMOVYY** ⋆**11761 MYS KUZNETSOVA** ⋆**11762 MYS SILINA** ⋆**11763 MYS CHASOVOY** ⋆**11764 MYS CHAYKOVSKOGO** ⋆**11765 MYS GROZNYY** ⋆**11766 MYS SKALISTYY** ⋆**11767 MURMANSELD** ⋆**11768 DESYATAYA PYATILETKA** ⋆**11769 VERKHOVINA** ⋆**11770 MYS SVOBODNYY** ⋆**11771 SEVERSK** ⋆**11772 SOVGANSKIY KOMSOMOLETS** ⋆**11773 GANGUT** ⋆**11774 TSIMLYANSK** ⋆**11775 VYSOVSK** ⋆**11776 VYSHOGOROD** ⋆**11777 MYS TIKHIY** ⋆**11778 MYS DALNIY** ⋆**11779 NIKOLAYEVSKIY KORABEL** ⋆**11780 ANDREY MARKIN** ⋆**11781 ILYA VOLYNKIN** ⋆**11782 IYUN KORAN** ⋆**11783 TANTAL** ⋆**11784 XVI SZEZD PROFSOYUZOV** ⋆**11785 XVII SEYEZD VLKSM** ⋆**11786 MYS BABUSHKIN** ⋆**11787 MYS OSTROVSKOGO** ⋆**11788 MYS YUNONY.**

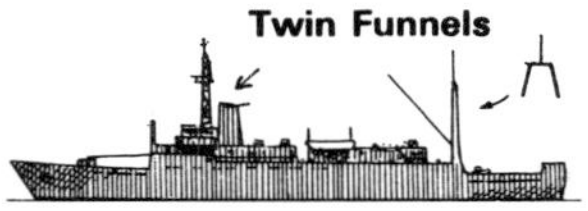

KMFM H2
★**11790 WLOCZNIK.** Pd/pd 1975; FT; 2600; 88.5 × 5.6 (291 × 18.4); M; 17.75; **'B.414'** type.

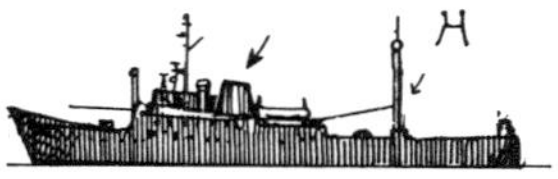

KMFM H2
★**11800 'ATLANTIK'** class; Ru/DDR 1966; FT; 2200; 82.1 × 5.1 (270 × 17); M; 13.5; Built 1966-1977. Similar (Ru flag): ★**11801 AIU-DAG** ★**11802 AKHILLES** ★**11803 AKHTUBA** ★**11804 AKHUN** ★**11805 AKMOLINSK** ★**11806 AKUSTIK** ★**11807 ALKA** ★**11808 ALEKSANDROVSK** ★**11809 ALEKSEY BORDUNOV** ★**11810 ALMA** ★**11811 ALSU** ★**11812 AMBERMA** ★**11813 AMGA** ★**11814 ASPHERON** ★**11815 ARDATOV** ★**11816 ARGUN** ★**11817 ARMENIYA** ★**11818 ARTEK** ★**11819 ARZAMAS** ★**11820 ASTRONOM** ★**11821 ATOLL** ★**11822 AVIATOR** ★**11823 AY-PETRI** ★**11824 AZURIT** ★**11825 BALTA** ★**11826 BATUMI**; ex ASKANIYA ★**11827 BAZALT** ★**11828 BEREZEN** ★**11829 BUREVESTNIK** ★**11830 BYELOVO**; ex MONGUGAY ★**11831 DARYAL** ★**11832 DNEPRODZERZHINSK** ★**11833 DRUZHBA SSSR-GDR**; ex KRUSTALNYY ★**11834 EISK** ★**11835 FEDOR GLADKOV** ★**11836 GELIOGRAF** ★**11837 GEROI ADZHIMUSHKAYA** ★**11838 ILMEN** ★**11839 ILYICHYOVSK** ★**11840 IMERITI** ★**11841 IZMAIL** ★**11842 KAKHETI** ★**11843 KANZATIP** ★**11844 KIROVOGRAD** ★**11845 KOBULETI** ex ZAPOROZHYE ★**11846 KORUND** ★**11847 KVADRANT** ★**11848 LENINOGORSK** ★**11849 LIMAN** ★**11850 LVOV** ★**11851 M. BORISOV** ex MARKSIST ★**11852 MEGANOM** ★**11853 MELITOPOL** ★**11854 METEORIT** ★**11855 MIKHAIL VIDOV** ex INITSIATOR ★**11856 MITRIDAT** ★**11857 NADEZHDA** ★**11858 NIKOLAY BROVTSYEV** ★**11859 NIKOLAYEV** ★**11860 OKTANT** ★**11861 OKTYABRSKOYE** ★**11862 OREL** ★**11863 ORLETS** ★**11864 ORLINOYE** ★**11865 PEREDOVIK** ★**11866 PETR LIZYUKOV** ★**11867 PISATEL** ★**11868 PITSUNDA** ★**11869 PLANERIST** ★**11870 PLUTON** ★**11871 POLEVOD** ★**11872 POLTAVA** ex KONDOR 1979 ★**11873 PRAVOVYED** ★**11874 PRILIV** ★**11875 PROLIV** ★**11876 PROMYSLOVIK** ★**11877 PROPAGANDIST** ★**11878 PROSVETITEL** ★**11879 PUBLIKIST** ★**11880 PYATIGORSK** ★**11881 POET** ★**11882 SADKO** ★**11883 SAKARTVELO** ★**11884 SALKHINO** ★**11885 SAPUN GORA** ★**11886 SERGEY KANDACHIK** ex ALATAU ★**11887 SHVENTOY** ★**11888 SIVASH** ★**11889 SKALISTYY** ★**11890 SOKOLINOYE** ★**11891 SOLNTSEDAR** ★**11892 SOPKA GEROYEV** ★**11893 SOYUZ 3** ★**11894 MIKHAIL KORNITSKIY** ex SOZIDATEL ★**11895 SUMY** ★**11896 TAGANROG** ★**11897 TAVRIDA** ★**11898 TIKHORETSK** ★**11899 TIMOFEY GORNOV** ★**11900 TSKHALTUBO** ★**11901 TULEN KABILOV** ★**11902 UGOLNYY** ★**11903 VASILY GOLOVKIN** ★**11904 VENERA IV** ★**11905 VOLKHOVSTROY** ★**11906 VOLNOMER** ★**11907 VZMORYE** ★**11908 YUKHAN SMUUL** ★**11909 YULIMISTE** ★**11910 YURIY MALAKHOV** ★**11911 YURNIEKS** ★**11912 YUZHNOMORSK** ex TAFUIN ★**11913 ZHELEZNOVODSK** ★**11914 ZHEMAYTIYA** ★**11915 ZOLOTOY KOLOS** The following are from a different yard: ★**11916 AGATOVYY** ★**11917 ARAGONIT** ★**11918 BARIT** ★**11919 BOKSIT** ★**11920 DIONIS** ★**11921 DOLOMIT** ★**11922 IZUMRUDNYY** ★**11923 KALINOVO** ★**11924 KALTAN** ★**11925 KARAGACH** ★**11926 KAVRAY** ★**11927 KHRUSTALNYY** ★**11928 KREMEN** ★**11929 KLIMOVO** ★**11930 MAKELIS BUKA** ★**11931 MRAMORNY** ★**11932 PIRIT** ★**11933 RODONIT** ★**11934 RUBINOVYY** ★**11935 SEDA** ★**11936 TESEY** ★**11937 ZYEMCHUSNYY** ★**11938 SERDOLIK** The following are Fishery Research Ships (some have alterations - extended boat deck etc): ★**11939 ALBA** ★**11940 ASTEROID** ★**11941 ARTEMIDA** ★**11942 BAKHCHISARAY** ★**11943 CHATYR-DAG** ★**11944 EVRIKA** ★**11945 FIOLENT** ★**11946 GERAKL** ★**11947 KAMENSKOYE** ★**11948 KARA-DAG** ★**11949 KHRONOMETR** ★**11950 MILOGRADOVO** ★**11951 PROFESSOR** ★**11952 PROFESSOR MESYATSYEV** ★**11953 SHANTAR** ★**11954 ZUND** ★**11955 ZVEZDA KRIMA** (Bu flag): ★**11956 ALKA** ★**11957 BEKAS** ★**11958 FLAMINGO** ★**11959 GLARUS** ★**11960 KONDOR** ★**11961 LIMOZA** ★**11962 LORNA** ★**11963 MELANITA** ★**11964 OLUSHA** ★**11965 PINGVIN** ★**11966 RALIDA** ★**11967 ZIKONIYA** (Cu flag) ★**11968 PLAYA COLORADO** ★**11969 PLAYA DUABA** ★**11970 PLAYA GIRON** ★**11971 PLAYITAS** ex PLAYA LARGA 1980 ★**11972 PLAYA VARADERO** ex PLAYA DE VARADERO 1980 (Rm flag): ★**11973 IALOMITA** ★**11974 JIUL** ★**11975 MILCOV** ★**11976 MURES** ★**11977 NEAJLOV** ★**11978 SIRET** ★**11979 SOMES** ★**11980 TROTUS.**

KMFM H2
11990 BRITISH VOYAGER; Br/Br 1959; Submersible support ship; 3000; 83.8 × 7.3 (275 × 23.5); D-E; —; ex VICKERS VOYAGER 1980; ex FAIRTRY II 1972; Converted from trawler 1973.

KMFMC H
⋆**12000 AKADEMIK KOROLYOV;** Ru/DDR 1967; RS; 5500; 124.3 × 6 (408 × 19.11); TSM; 18.25. Sisters (Ru flag); ⋆**12001 AKADEMIK SHIRSHOV** ⋆**12002 PROFESSOR VISE** ⋆**12003 PROFESSOR ZUBOV** (These may vary slightly).

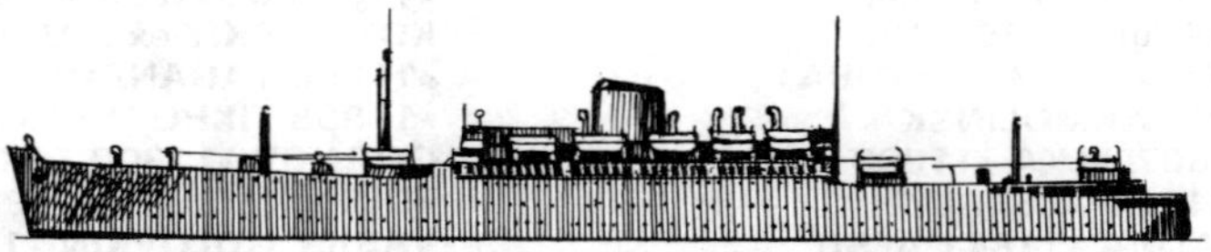

KMFMK H
⋆**12010 SOVIETSKIY SOYUZ;** Ru/Ge 1923; P; 23000; 205 × 9.6 (673 × 31.6); TST; 19.25; ex HANSA 1950; ex ALBERT BALLIN 1935; Lengthened 1934.

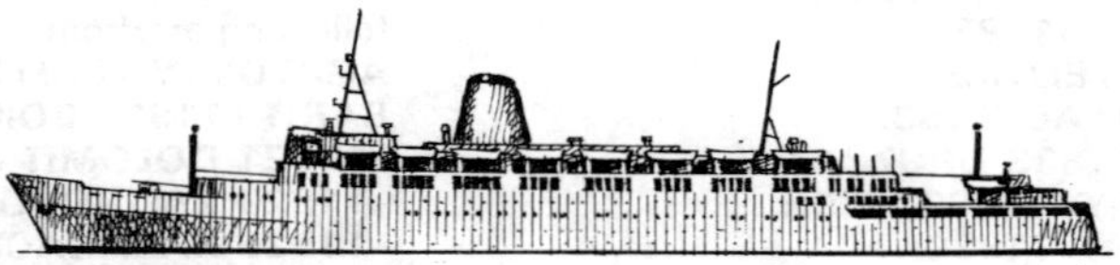

KMFMK H
12020 OLYMPIA; Gr/Br 1953; P; 17400; 186 × 8.5 (611 × 28.1); TST; 21.

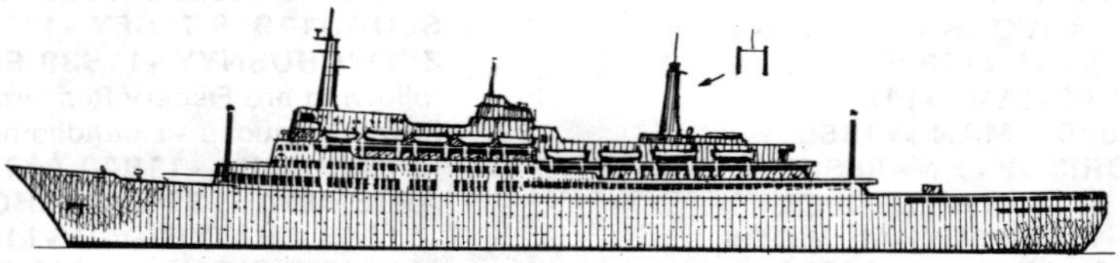

KMFMK H
12030 ROTTERDAM; NA/Ne 1959; P; 37800; 228 × 9 (749 × 29.8); TST; 21.5.

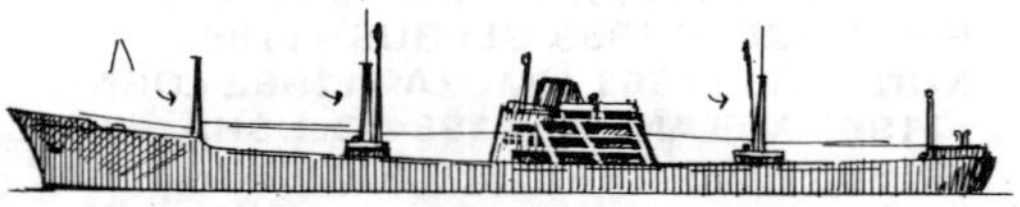

KMFMK H1
⋆**12040 PRIMORJE;** Ys/Ys 1961; C; 7000/9400; 155 × 8.2 (509 × 26.11); M; 18.5.

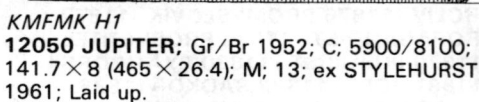

KMFMK H1
12050 JUPITER; Gr/Br 1952; C; 5900/8100; 141.7 × 8 (465 × 26.4); M; 13; ex STYLEHURST 1961; Laid up.

KMFMK H1
12060 SOULA K; Gr/FRG 1958; CP; 10600; 159 × 9.8 (522 × 32); M; 14; ex BIRGITTE CORD 1970; ex GRANE 1964.

KMFMK H1
12070 VISHVA VIVEK; In/FRG 1959; C; 10800; 159 × 9.2 (522 × 30.4); M; 14.5; ex FIGARO 1968.

KMFMK H1
12080 VENICE; Pa/Br 1958; C; 6800/8500; 145.7 × —/9.1 (478 × —/30); M; 14.5; ex CLEVELAND 1964.

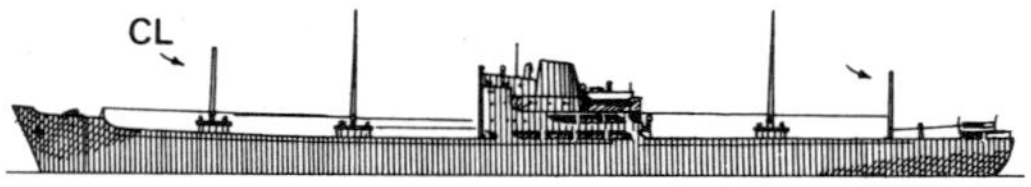

KMFMK H1
12100 PINGUIN; Pa/FRG 1959; CP; 10500; 159 × 9.5 (518 × 31.4); M; 14; ex LAZULI 1980; ex ARISTON 1975; ex GORDIAN 1971. Sisters: **12101 LUCIDITY** (Li); ex ARISTOFANIS 1974; ex TRAJAN 1970 **12102 SILVER CITY** (Gr) ex ARISTOKLIS 1976; ex NUMERIAN 1970 **12103 ARISTOFILOS** (Gr) ex JUSTINIAN 1970 Similar: **12104 PANAGHIA LOURION** (Gr) ex HADJITSAKOS 1972 **12105 LAERTIS** (Gr) ex CHIOS 1972.

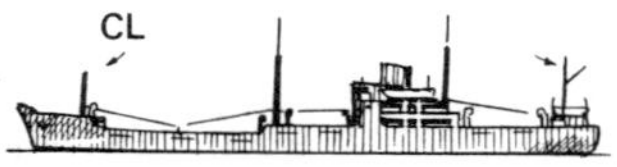

KMFMK H12
● **12130 AGIOS NICOLAOS;** Gr/Br 1946; CP; 2400; 90.2 × 5.5 (296 × 8.2); M; 10.5; ex GARTWOOD 1966.

KMFMK H123
12170 LINO MANCINO. It/No 1913; C; 1300; 75 × 4.5 (246 × 15); R; 10.5; ex DINO 1967; ex TERRA 1965; ex JAN 1963; ex MEDEMSAND 1957; ex DANIX 1951; ex VESLA 1946.

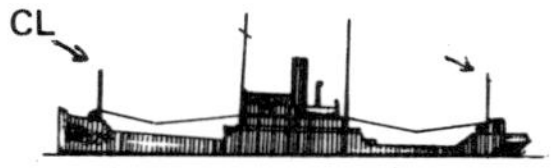

KMFMK H123
12180 GUDRUN. Le/No 1919; C; 1200; 73 × 4.6 (239 × 15); R; 9; ex RAGNHILD 1935.

KMFMK H123
12190 KEN SHENG. Pa/Ja 1951; C; 6800; 138 × 8.2 (453 × 27); R; 13.5; ex NISSEI MARU 1970.

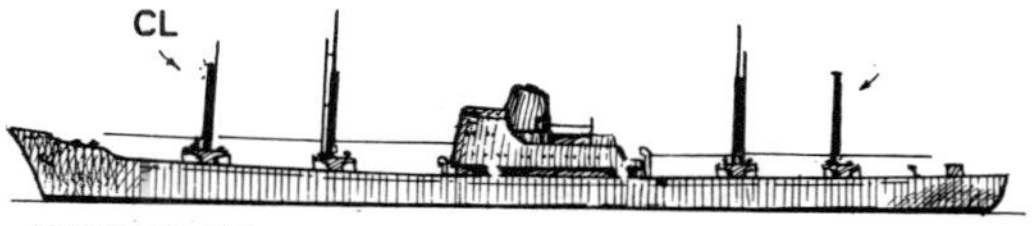

KMFMK H1
12090 KOTA AGUNG; Sg/FRG 1957; C; 11000; 158.1 × 9.6 (519 × 31.4); M; 15; ex ANTHONY II 1973.

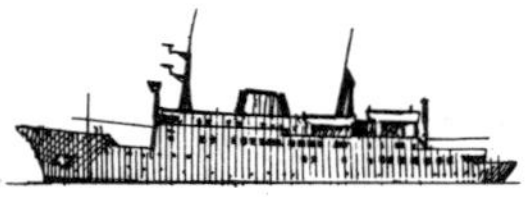

KMFMK H1
12110 KUNUNGUAK; De/De 1964; PC; 2300; 74.5 × 4 (244 × 13.1); M; 13.

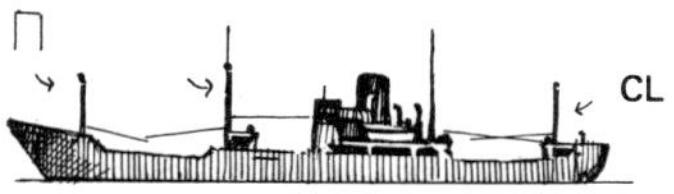

KMFMK H12
12120 RADIANT; In/Br 1957; C; 2200; 90.2 × 5.2 (296 × 17); R; —; ex WINGA 1967.

KMFMK H123
⋆**12140 LIPETSK.** Ru/Pd 1954; C; 2500; 94.7 × 5.5 (308 × 18); R; 11.5; **'B 32'** type. Similar (Ru flag): ⋆**12141 CHAPAYEVSK** ⋆**12142 CHERNOGORSK** ⋆**12143 CHERVONOGRAD** ⋆**12144 CHUGUYEV** ⋆**12145 CHIGIRIN** ⋆**12146 INGUL** ⋆**12147 KONSTANTINOVKA** ex CHRISTIAKOVO 1965 ⋆**12148 PROLETARSK** ⋆**12149 SHAKHTERSK** ex TEREK ⋆**12150 TOM** ⋆**12151 UKRAINE** (Al flag): ⋆**12152 LIRIJA** ⋆**12153 PARTIZANI** (RC flag): ⋆**12154 HOPING SAN SHI WU** ex WICKO 1956 ⋆**12155 HOPING SSU SHI 1** ex MAMRY 1957 ⋆**12156 HOPING SSU SHI** ex SNIARDWY 1957 ⋆**12157 HOPING SSU SHI ER** ex GARDNO 1956 ⋆**12158 NAN HAI 158** ex JAMNO 1956 ⋆**12159 HONG QI 159** ex NAN HAI 159; ex LEBSKO 1957 (Pd flag): ⋆**12160 BIELSKO** ⋆**12161 OPOLE** (Eg flag): **12162 BENHA 12163 TANTA** (Gr flag): **12164 EL HAG ABDALLA** ex ELLI; ex KALISZ 1976; ex SEWA **12165 EFI** ex TCZEW 1976; ex SENA (Cy flag): **12166 SUMMER BREEZE** ex MALBORK 1976 (Br flag): **12167 TULUM** ex GNIEZNO.

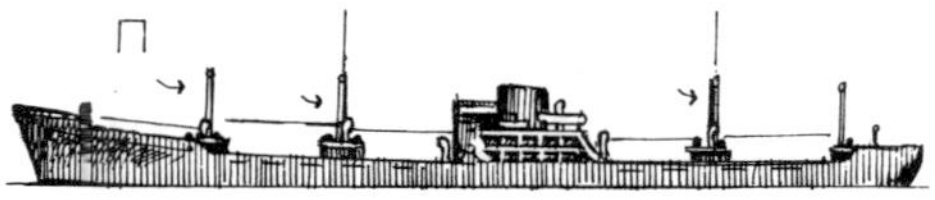

KMFMK H13
12200 EASTERN SEA. Pa/Br 1957; C; 10200; 157.92 × 9.58 (518 × 31.43); M; 14; ex YAT LUNG 1979; ex KAVO MATAPAS 1977; ex PEGASUS 1972. Sister: **12201 CHI YUEN** (Pa) ex CAPE AVANTI 1980; ex PROCYON 1972.

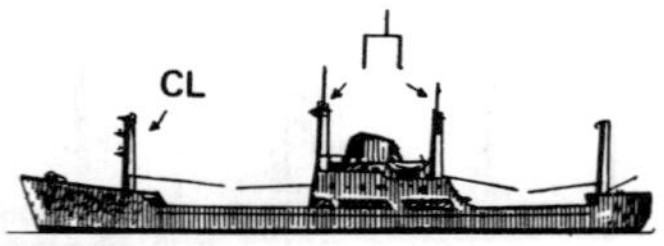

KMFMK H13
12210 DEMETRIS. Gr/Fr 1961; C; 3100; 99.2 × 5.7 (325 × 19); M; 19; ex REEFER PRINCESS 1979; ex FONTSY 1979; ex BOREE 1976. Sister: **12211 AMALTHEA** (Pa) ex AMALTHEE.

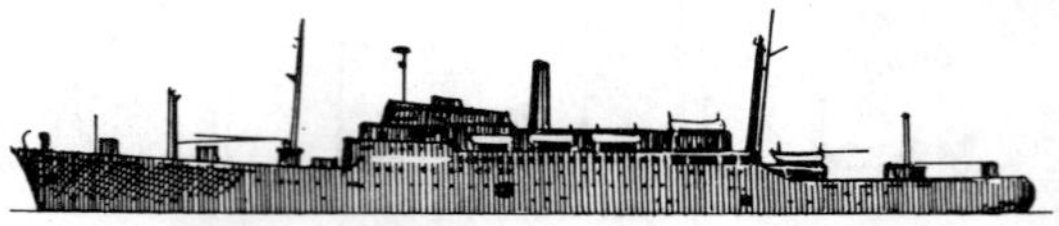

KMFMK H2
● **12220 STATE OF MAINE.** US/US 1952; PC/TS; 13300; 162.7 × 8.4 (534 × 27.6); T; 19.5; ex UPSHUR 1973; ex PRESIDENT HAYES 1952; Converted troopship.

KMFMK H2
● ⋆**12230 KERCH.** Ru/DDR 1961; FT; 1900; 79.8 × 5.2 (262 × 17); M; 12.5; **'TROPIK'** class—1961-1966. Similar (Ru flag): ⋆**12231 ABRANTSEVO** ⋆**12232 ALDERAMIN** ⋆**12233 ALIOT** ⋆**12234 ALMAK** ⋆**12235 ALUPKA** ⋆**12236 ALUSHTA** ⋆**12237 ANDROMEDA** ⋆**12238 ANTARES** ⋆**12239 ARGO** ⋆**12240 BALAKLAVA** ⋆**12241 BOLSHEVO** ⋆**12242 DENEB** ⋆**12243 DOBROVOLSK** ⋆**12244 ERIDAN** ⋆**12245 FEODOSIYA** ⋆**12246 GORECHJE** ⋆**12247 GURIYA** ⋆**12248 GURJEVSK** ⋆**12249 GURZUF** ⋆**12250 HERKULES** ⋆**12251 IVAN GOLUBETS** ⋆**12252 KAIRA** ⋆**12253 KALJMAR** ⋆**12254 KANOPUS** ⋆**12255 KARTLI** ⋆**12256 KASSIOPEYA** ⋆**12257 KLYAZMA** ⋆**12258 KOLKHIDA** ⋆**12259 KRASNODAR** ex MORSKAYA ZVEZDA ⋆**12260 KOREIZ** ⋆**12261 LANGUST** ⋆**12262 LEONID SEVRYUKOV** ex SARICH ⋆**12263 LIVADIYA** ⋆**12264 MTSKHETSA** ⋆**12265 MISKHOR** ⋆**12266 MIZAR** ⋆**12267 NADIR** ⋆**12268 N. FILCHENKOV** —may be **NIKOLAY FILCHENKOV** ⋆**12269 NIKOLSK** ⋆**12270 OREANDRA** ⋆**12271 ORION** ⋆**12272 OZERSK** ⋆**12273 PALLADA** ⋆**12274 PERSEY** ⋆**12275 PORECHIE** ⋆**12276 POTI** ex LEBEDJ ⋆**12277 REPINO** ⋆**12278 ROSLAVL** ⋆**12279 RUSLAN** ⋆**12280 RUSTAVI** ⋆**12281 RUZA** ⋆**12282 SALGIR** ⋆**12283 SATURN** ⋆**12284 SEMYON EMELYANOV** ⋆**12285 SHOTA RUSTAVELI** ⋆**12286 SIMEIZ** ⋆**12287 SIRIUS** ⋆**12288 SLAVSK** ⋆**12289 STRELETS** ⋆**12290 TBILISI** ⋆**12291 TSEFEY** ⋆**12292 TSENTAUR** ⋆**12293 VEGA** ⋆**12294 VOLOPAS** ⋆**12295 YALTA** ⋆**12296 YEVPATORIYE** ⋆**12297 YUZHNYY KREST** ⋆**12298 ZARAYSK** The following have been converted to Research Ships: ⋆**12299 BELOGORSK** ⋆**12300 FLAMINGO** ⋆**12301 KALLISTO** ⋆**12302 KERCHENSKIY** ⋆**12303 KOMSOMOLETS** ex YUZNYY KREST ⋆**12304 KOZEROG** ⋆**12305 LESNOY** ⋆**12306 LIRA** ⋆**12307 NAUKA** ⋆**12308 PEGAS** ⋆**12309 RADUGA** ⋆**12310 SHEDAR** (Bu flag): ⋆**12311 ALBATROS** ⋆**12312 BUREVESTNIK** ⋆**12313 FENIX** ⋆**12314 PELIKAN** ⋆**12315 TCHAIKA** (Gh flag): **12316 TROPIK** The following are used as Fish Carriers but may be similar: (DDR flag): ⋆**12317 GRANITZ** ⋆**12318 STUBNITZ.**

KMFMK H2
● ⋆**12320 'PUSHKIN'** class. Ru/DDR 1955/57; FT; 2500-3000; 84.5 × 5.5 (278 × 18); M; 12.5. Similar (Ru flag): ⋆**12321 DOSTOYEVSKIY** ⋆**12322 KAZAN** ⋆**12323 NEKRASOV** ⋆**12324 NOVIKOV-PRIBOY** ⋆**12325 SALTIKOV SHCHEDRIN** ⋆**12326 SERAFIMOVICH** ⋆**12327 YAROSLAVL.**

KMFMK H2
● ⋆**12330 'PUSHKIN'** class. Ru/DDR 1955; FT; 2500-300; 84.5 × 5.5 (278 × 18); M; 12.5. Sisters (Ru flag): ⋆**12331 GOGOL** ⋆**12332 PUSHKIN.**

KMFMK H2
⋆**12340** Modified **'PUSHKIN'** class. Ru/DDR 1955/57; FT; 2500/3000; 84.5 × 5.5 (278 × 18); M; 12.5. Similar (Ru flag): ⋆**12341 ASHKHABAD** ⋆**12342 CHEKHOV** ⋆**12343 DUSHANBE** ex STALINBAD ⋆**12344 IZHEVSK** ⋆**12345 KHABAROVSK** ⋆**12346 MURMANSK** ex VOROSHILOVGRAD ⋆**12347 NIKOLAY OSTROVSKIY** ⋆**12348 SEVERNOYE SIYANIE** ⋆**12349 SVERDLOVSK** ⋆**12350 ULYANOVSK** ⋆**12351 ZAVOLZHSK** ⋆**12352 ZLATOUST** ⋆**12353 ZHIGULEVSK.**

KMFMK H2
● ⋆**12360 'MAYAKOVSKIY'** class. Ru/Ru 1958/59; FT; 3200; 84.7 × 5.6 (278 × 18.4); M; 13.75; Distinguished from 'Modified Mayakovskiy class' by having a pole foremast. Similar (Ru flag): ⋆**12361 BELINSKIY** ⋆**12362 CHERNYSHEVSKIY** ⋆**12363 GLEB USPENSKIY** ⋆**12364 GRIBOYEDOV** ⋆**12365 KOLTSOV** ⋆**12366 KOROLENKO** ⋆**12367 KRISHYANS VOLDEMARS** ⋆**12368 LERMONTOV** ⋆**12369 LEV TOLSTOY** ⋆**12370 MAYAKOVSKIY** ⋆**12371 RADISHEV** ⋆**12372 ZHUKOVSKIY** (Gr flag): **12373 ANASTASIOS** ex REA 1979; ex KRYLOV 1965.

KMFMK H2

★**12380** Modified **"MAYAKOVSKIY"** class. Ru/Ru 1959/68; FT; 3200; 78×5.5 (256×18); M; 12. Similar (Ru flag): ★**12381 ADIMI** ★**12382 AFANASAY NIKITIN** ★**12383 AGAT** ★**12384 ALFONSAS CHEPONIS** ★**12385 ALEKSANDR MAKSUTOV** ★**12386 ALEKSEY GMYREV** ★**12387 ALEKSEY MAKHALIN** ★**12388 ALMAZ** ★**12389 AMETIST** ★**12390 AMURSK** ★**12391 ANISIMOVKA** ex KANGAUZ ★**12392 ANTCHAR** ★**12393 ANTON TAMMSAARE** ★**12394 ANTS LAYKMAA** ★**12395 ARALSK** ex ARSENYEV ★**12396 ARKOVO** ★**12397 ARSENEYEV** ★**12398 ASKOLD** ★**12399 ASTRA** ★**12400 AUGUST ALLE** ★**12401 BAKAYEVO** ex SIDIMI ★**12402 BAYKAL** ★**12403 BARABASH** ★**12404 BARABINSK** ★**12405 BASARGIN** ★**12406 BERILL** ★**12407 BIKIN** ★**12408 BORIS GORINSKIY** ★**12409 BIRSHTONAS** ★**12410 BIRYUZA** ★**12411 BRASLAV** ★**12412 BRILLIANT** ★**12413 BOSFOR** ★**12414 BYELKINO** ex SUYFUN ★**12415 DANKO** ★**12416 DIOMID** ★**12417 DMITRY FURMANOV** ★**12418 DRUSKININKAY** ★**12419 DZINTARYURA** ★**12420 EDUARD SYRMUS** ★**12421 EDUARD VEYDENBAUM** ★**12422 ELEKRENAY** ★**12423 ESTAFETA OKTYABRYA** ex UZBEKISTAN ★**12424 EVALD TAMMLAAN** ★**12425 FEDOR KRAYNOV** ★**12426 50 LET VLKSM** ★**12427 15 SYEZD VLKSM** ★**12428 GALIFAN BATARSHIN** ★**12429 GRANAT** ★**12430 GRIGORIY SHELIKOV** ★**12431 GUBERTAS BORISA** ★**12432 HANS LIEBERECHT** ★**12433 IMANT SUDMALIS** ★**12434 IOKHAN KYOLER** ★**12435 IONAS BILYUNAS** ★**12436 IOZAS VITAS** ★**12437 ITELMAN** ★**12438 IVAN DVORSKIY** ★**12439 IVAN CHERNOPYATKO** ★**12440 IVAN PANOV** ★**12441 IZUMRUD** ★**12442 JAAN KOORT** ★**12443 JAKHONT** ★**12444 JAKOV SMUSHKEVICH** ★**12445 JAN BERZIN** ★**12446 JAN FABRITSIUS** ★**12447 JAN RUDZUTAK** ★**12448 JOHANNES RUVEN** ★**12449 JUHAN SIUTISTE** ★**12450 JUOZAS VAREYKIS** ★**12451 JUOZAS GREYFENBERGIS** ★**12452 KAAREL LIYMAND** ★**12453 KAPITAN ANDREI TARAN** ★**12454 KAROLIS POZHELA** ★**12455 KASKAD** ★**12456 KAZAKHSTAN** ★**12457 KHERMAN ARBON** ★**12458 KINGAN** ★**12459 KHRUSTAL** ★**12460 KOMMUNIST** ★**12461 KOMMUNIST UKRAINY** ★**12462 KOMSOMOL UKRAINI** ★**12463 KORALL** ★**12464 KRAYEV** ★**12465 KRISTALL** ★**12466 KRISTIONAS DONELAYTIS** ★**12467 KRISTYAN RAUD** ★**12468 KUBA** ★**12469 LAGUNA** ★**12470 LAZURIT** ★**12471 LEON PAEGLE** ★**12472 LESOGORSK** ★**12473 LINARD LAYTSEN** ★**12474 LYUDAS GIRA** ★**12475 MALAKHIT** ★**12476 MAMIN-SIBIRYAK** ★**12477 MARK RESHETNIKOV** ★**12478 MART SAAR** ★**12479 MATIS PLUDON** ★**12480 MESKUPAS ADOMAS** ★**12481 MGACHI** ★**12482 MIKALOYUS CHYURLYONIS** ★**12483 MONGOLIYA** ★**12484 MRAMOR** ★**12485 NADEZHDINSK** ★**12486 NAKHODKA** ★**12487 NIKOLAY OSTROVSKIY** ★**12488 NOVAYA ERA** ★**12489 OPALA** ★**12490 OSKAR LUTS** ★**12491 OTROG** ★**12492 OZYORNYE KLYUCHI** ★**12493 PAKHACHA** ★**12494 PASIONARIYA** ★**12495 PECHENGA** ★**12496 PEREKAT** ★**12497 PETR. STUCHKA** ★**12498 PETRODVORETS** ★**12499 PIONER UKRAINY** ★**12500 PIONER ZAPOLYARYA** ★**12501 POSYET** ★**12502 PRIAMURYE** ex GLAFKI 1969 ★**12503 PRIOZERSK** ex MELITI 1969 ★**12504 PRANAS EYDUKYAVICHUS** ★**12505 PULKOVO** ★**12506 PUTIVL** ex THETIS 1969 ★**12507 PYOTR OVCHINNIKOV** ★**12508 RAPOLAS CHARNAS** ★**12509 ROBERT EYDEMAN** ★**12510 RUBIN** ★**12511 RUDOLF BLAUMANIS** ★**12512 SAKHALIN** ★**12513 SAMARGA** ★**12514 SAPFIR** ★**12515 SEMYON DEZHNEV** ★**12516 SERGEY YESENIN** ★**12517 SEROGLAZKA** ★**12518 SEVERNAYA PALMIRA** ★**12519 SEVEROMORSKIY KOMSOMOLETS** ★**12520 SHEVCHENKO** ★**12521 SHTURMAN YELAGIN** ★**12522 SHYAULYAY** ★**12523 SIBIRYAK** ★**12524 SNABZHENETS PERVYY** ★**12525 SOVGAVAN** ★**12526 SOVIETSKIE PROFSOYUZY** ★**12527 STANYUKOVICH** ★**12528 STAR** ★**12529 TADZHIKISTAN** ★**12530 TAYSHET** ★**12531 TAMAN** ★**12532 TEODOR NETTE** ★**12533 TERNEY** ★**12534 TIKHVIN** ★**12535 TOPAZ** ★**12536 TRETYAKOVO** ★**12537 TRUDOVYE RESERVY** ★**12538 TURGENEV** ★**12539 TURMALIN** ★**12540 VALENTIN KOTELNIKOV** ★**12541 VALERIY BYKOVSKIY** ★**12542 VASILY VINEVITIN** ★**12543 VITALIY BONIVUR** ★**12544 VITAUTAS MONTVILA** ★**12545 VITAUTAS PUTNA** ★**12546 VLADAS REKASHYUS** ★**12547 VLADIMIR ATLASOV** ★**12548 VOSKHOD** ★**12549 YANTAR** ★**12550 YARONIMAS UBORYAVICHUS** ex PERSEY 1966 ★**12551 YASHMA** ★**12551 YUBILEY OKTYABRYA** ★**12552 YUNOST** ★**12553 YUOZAS GARYALIS** ★**12554 YUOZAS VAREYKIS** ★**12555 ZIGMAS ANGARETIS** (Bu flag): ★**12556 BAKLAN** ★**12557 FREGATA** ★**12558 LEBED** (Gh flag): **12559 MANKOADZE**.

KMFMK H2

★**12570 AKADEMIK KNIPOVICH.** Ru/Ru 1964; RS; 2300; 84.7×5.8 (278×19); M; 13; **'Mayakovskiy'** class; both masts tripod. Similar (Ru flag): ★**12571 PERSEY III** ★**12572 PROFESSOR DERYUGIN** ★**12573 AKADEMIK BERG** ★**12574 ATLANT** ★**12575 ANDRUS YOKHANI** ★**12576 ARGUS** ★**12577 EKVATOR** ★**12578 GIZHIGA** ★**12579 NEPTUN** ★**12580 POSEYDON.**

KMFMK H2

★**12590 'LESKOV'** class. Ru/Pd 1960/63; FT; 2800; 84.6×5.3 (277×17.6); M; 12.5; **'B. 15'** type. Similar (Ru flag): ★**12591 DRUZHBA** ★**12592 GONCHAROV** ★**12593 KUPRIN** ★**12594 LESKOV** ex CHERNYSHEVSKI ★**12595 LUNNIK** ★**12596 MIR** ★**12597 MAMIN SIBIRYAK** ★**12598 ORBITA** ★**12599 SPUTNIK.**

KMFMK H2
★12610 JUPITER. Pd/Pd 1963; FT; 2300; 83 × 5.5 (272 × 18); M; 12.5; **'B. 15'** type. Sisters (Ru flag): **★12611 KASTOR ★12612 NEPTUN ★12613 PEGAZ ★12614 URAN**

KMFMK H2
★12620 BERTOLT BRECHT. DDR/DDR 1959; FT; 3000; 86 × 5.3 (281 × 17.4); M; 12.5. Similar (DDR flag): **★12621 ERIK WEINERT ★12622 F.C. WEISKOPF ★12623 JOHANNES R. BECKER.**

KMFMK H2
★12630 WALTER DEHMEL. DDR/DDR 1963; FT; 3000; 85.6 × 5.3 (281 × 17.5); M; 13.5. Sisters (DDR flag): **★12631 BERNHARD KELLERMANN ★12632 FRIEDRICH WOLF ★12633 PETER KAST ★12634 PETER NELL ★12635 RUDOLF LEONHARD.**

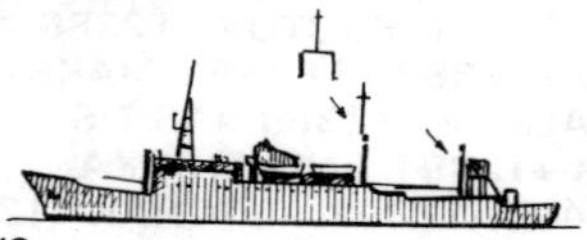

KMFMK H2
12640 JOY 18. Pa/Br 1954; FT; 2600; 85.6 × 7 (281 × 22.9); M; 12; ex FAIRTRY 1 1969; ex FAIRTRY 1959.

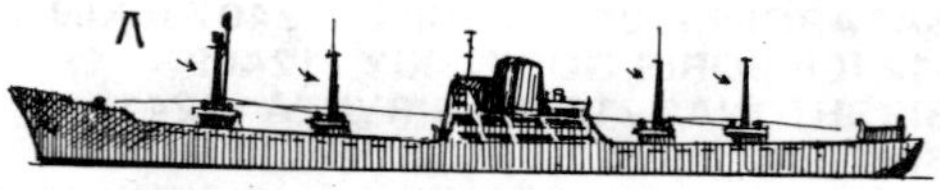

KMFMK H1
12650 SAN FELICE. It/It 1959; C; 8900; 148.7 × 9.1 (488 × 29.8); M; 15.5.

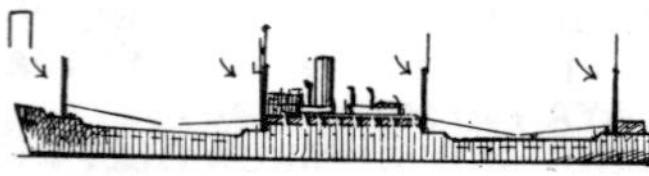

$KMFM_2$ H123
★12660 ARKTIKA. Ru/Br 1936; C/TC; 2900; 102.7 × 6 (338 × 20); R; 11. Sister: **★12661 IGARKA** (Ru).

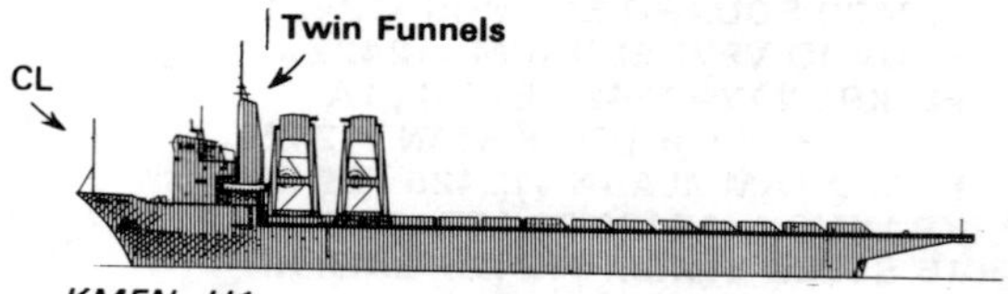

$KMFN_2$ H1
12670 DOCK EXPRESS 10. Ne/Ne 1979; Dk/RoC/HL; 5500; 153.76 × 8.9 (504.46 × 29.2); M; 16; Stern door. Sisters (Ne flag): **12671 DOCK EXPRESS 11 12672 DOCK EXPRESS 12.**

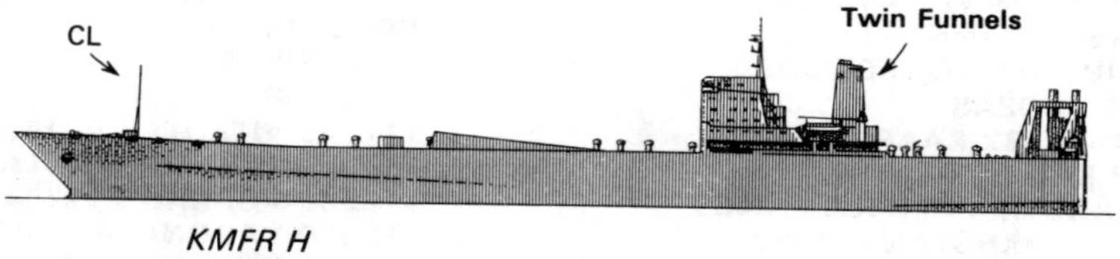

KMFR H
● **★12680 KAPITAN SMIRNOV.** Ru/Ru 1979; RoC/Con; 14300; 227.3 × 9.87 (745.74 × 32.38); TS GT/M; 25; Quarter ramp. Sister: **★12681 KAPITAN MEZENTSEV** (Ru) different type of ramp. One further sister on order.

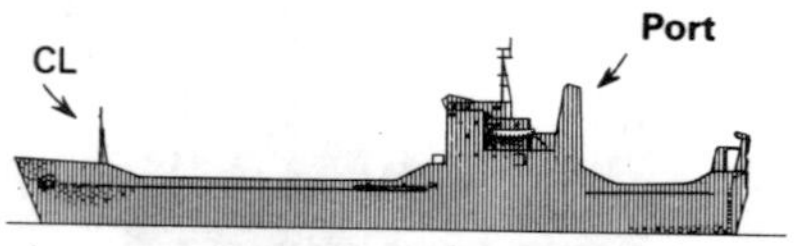

KMFR H123
12690 BELVAUX. Be/Be 1979; RoC; 3500; 116.7 × 6.2 (382.87 × 20.34); M; 15; Stern slewing ramp. Sister: **12691 CLERVAUX** (Be).

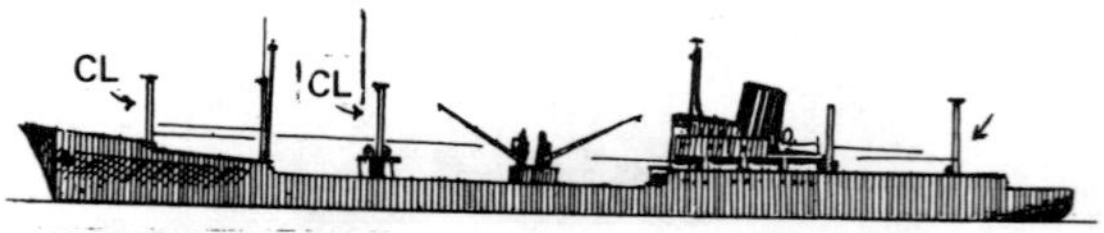

$KMKC_2MFK_2$ H13
12700 AMERICA STAR. Br/Br 1964; R; 7000/9300; 165 × 8.2/8.8 (541 × 27/29); M; —; Lengthened 1973.

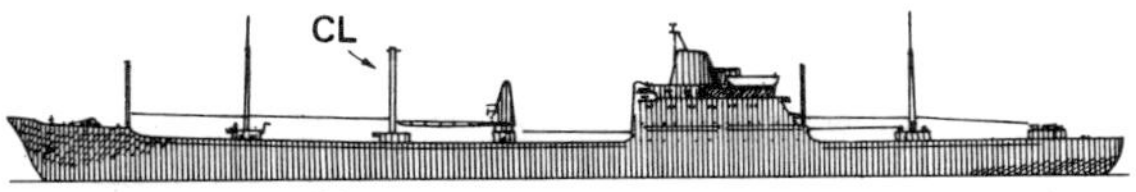

KMKCFKM H12
12710 NEDLLOYD FREMANTLE. Ne/Ne 1964; CP; 8200/10900; 177 × 8.1/9.4 (581 × 27/30.11); M; 20; ex STRAAT FREMANTLE 1977; ex ASIAN ENTERPRISE 1975; ex STRAAT FREMANTLE 1973. Sisters (Ne flag): **12711 NEDLLOYD FRANKLIN** ex STRAAT FRANKLIN **12712 NEDLLOYD FREETOWN** ex STRAAT FREETOWN; ex ASIAN ENSIGN 1975; ex STRAAT FREETOWN 1973 **12713 NEDLLOYD FRAZER** ex STRAAT FRAZER 1977; ex ASIAN ENDEAVOUR 1975; ex STRAAT FRAZER 1973.

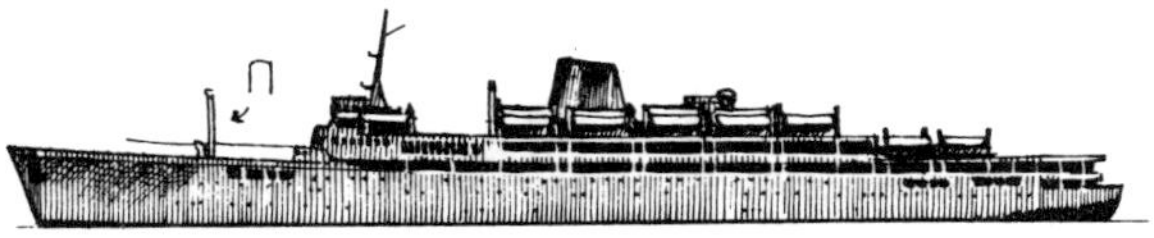

KMKF H
12740 ENRICO C. It/Br 1951; P; 13600; 176.7 × 7.5 (579 × 24.8); TST; 18.5; ex PROVENCE 1965.

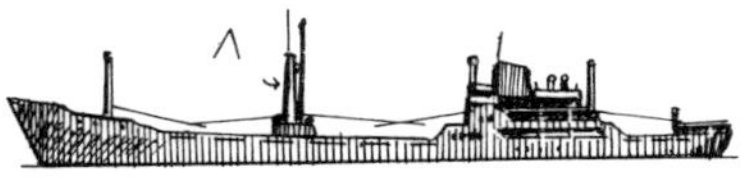

KMKFK H1
● **12760 CHINTA.** Gr/Sp 1959; C; 3200; 113 × 6.5 (371 × 21.6); M; 15; ex STEFANOEMME 1980; ex COMILLAS; ex BENIZAR 1967. Sister: **12761 IKAM** (Gr) ex FEDERICAEMME 1980; ex RUISENADA; ex BENIEL 1967.

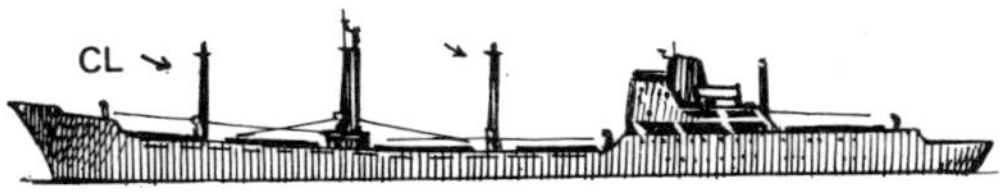

KMKFK H13
⋆**12790 BAIRE.** Cu/Sp 1966; C; 7000/9400; 157 × 8/9 (515 × 27/29.9); M; —. Sisters (Cu flag): ⋆**12791 CERRO PELADO** ⋆**12792 EL JIGUE** ⋆**12793 MAFFO** ⋆**12794 13 DE MARZO.**

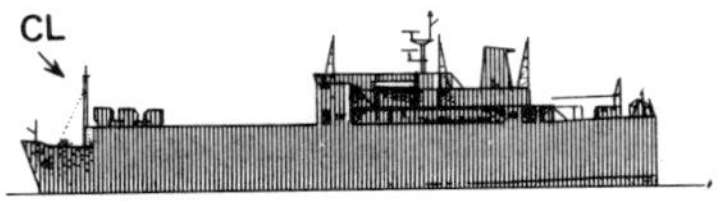

KMKFKC H2
12810 AUTOROUTE. Br/Ja 1979; RoVC; 2500; 100.01 × 4.21 (328.12 × 13.81); M; 15.25; Stern door/ramp.

KMKCMFK$_3$ H13
⋆**12720 YONG CHUN.** RC/Br 1963; CP; 8100/10900; 168 × 9/10.2 (550 × 30/33.6); M; 20; ex BENARMIN 1972. Sister: ⋆**12721 YICHUN** (RC) ex BENVALLA 1972.

KMKCMFKMK H1
● **12730 KRISTIN BAKKE.** No/Sw 1955; C; 9600; 154.5 × 8.8 (507 × 28.7); M; 17.

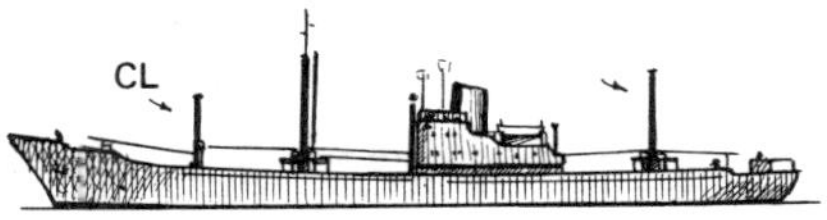

KMKFK H1
⋆**12750 XIANG SHAN.** RC/DDR 1957; CP; 4900; 126 × 7.5 (414 × 26.8); M; 14.5; ex MINAI 1976; ex SIEGSTEIN 1972. Sister: ⋆**12751 LEI SHAN** (RC) ex MINHAO 1977; ex SPREESTEIN 1972.

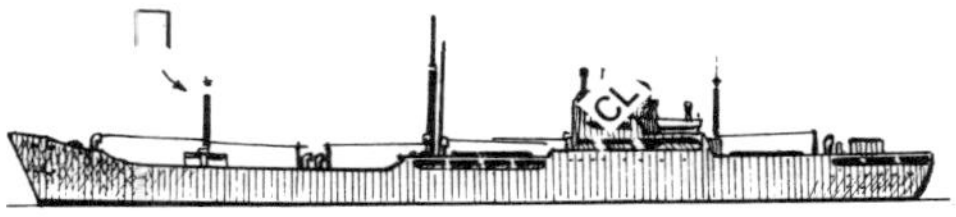

KMKFK H12
12770 SALONAE. Pa/Sp 1960; C; 8300; 145 × 8.9 (474 × 29); M; 14; ex MONTE PENALARA 1971. Sister: ⋆**12771 ULCINJ** (Ys) ex MARTIN ZUBIZARRETA 1969.

KMKFK H12
12780 SEAWAY FALCON. No/No 1975; Offshore Support Vessel; 1600; 80.1 × 4.4 (263 × 14.6); M; 14.

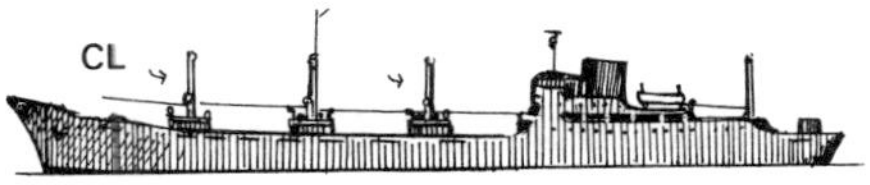

KMKFK H13
12800 BIBI. Li/Br 1961; CP; 4500; 127 × 7.2 (416 × 23.7); M; 15; ex LETITIA 1967.

KMKFK$_2$ H1
12820 EPAPHUS. Gr/Sw 1958; CP; 4700/7200; 134 × 7.6/9 (438 × 25/30); M; 16; ex IO 1980; ex KUNGSHAMN 1977; ex MARGARETA BRODIN 1971; ex RHODOS 1966; ex OTTO BANCK 1963.

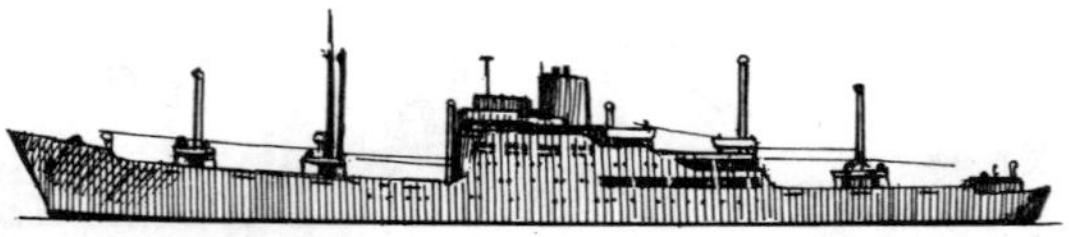

$KMKFK_2$ H1
12830 ORIENTAL HERO. Li/FRG 1954; CP; 8200; 164 × 8 (538 × 26.2); M; 17; ex FRANKFURT 1967. Sisters (Li flag): **12831 ORIENTAL LADY** ex BAYERNSTEIN 1967 **12832 ORIENTAL RULER** ex SCHWABENSTEIN 1967.

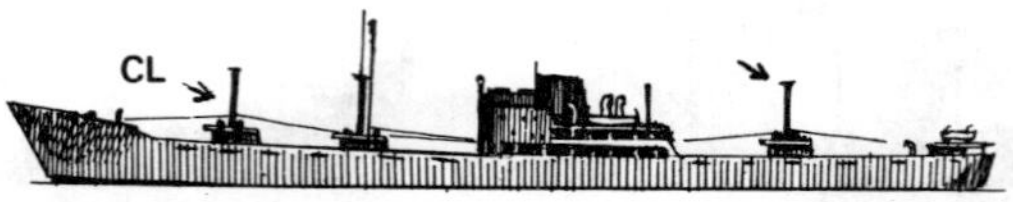

$KMKFK_2$ H1
12840 KIKI. Cy/Br 1957; C; 9700; 152 × 9.1 (499 × 30.1); M; 16; ex GARDENIA 1973; ex APOLLON 1969. Sisters: **12841 MOJAIL 5** (Ho) ex KAPETAN XILAS 1980; ex ATLAS 1973 **12842 HONG HOI** (Pa) ex ALEXANDROS 1974.

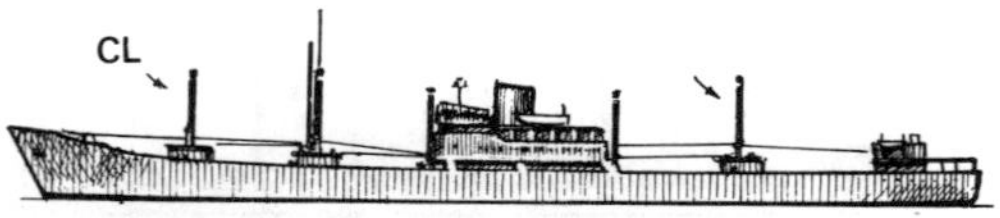

$KMKFK_2$ H1
12850 SILVER GATE. Sg/Br 1963; C; 7100/9900; 155 × 8.3/9.4 (508 × 27.4/30.1); M; —; ex STRATHNAIRN; ex KOHINUR 1975.

$KMKFK_2$ H1
12860 OLYMPIAS. Gr/FRG 1958; C; 5400; 131.4 × 6.6 (431 × 21.8); M; 14.75; ex BIRK 1973; ex LUTJENBURG 1968; ex FLAVIA 1964. Sisters (Gr flag): **12861 AMALINDA** ex HOLSTENDEICH; ex LECHSTEIN 1972 **12862 SYROS** ex HOLSTENFLEET; ex NABSTEIN 1972.

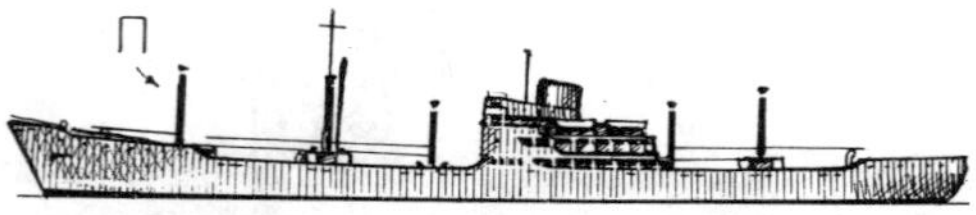

$KMKFK_2$ H13
12870 ISLAND TRADER. Pa/Br 1958; CP; 6000/8500; 152.4 × 7.3/8.4 (500 × 24/28); M; 14.5; ex PURNA SHANTI 1980; ex KANO PALM 1979. Sister: **12871 KATSINA PALM** (Br).

$KMKFK_2$ H13
● **12880 MASTRO MANOLIS.** Gr/FRG 1958; CP; 5600; 144 × 7.4 (473 × 23.7); M; 14; ex ANDONI PALM 1976.

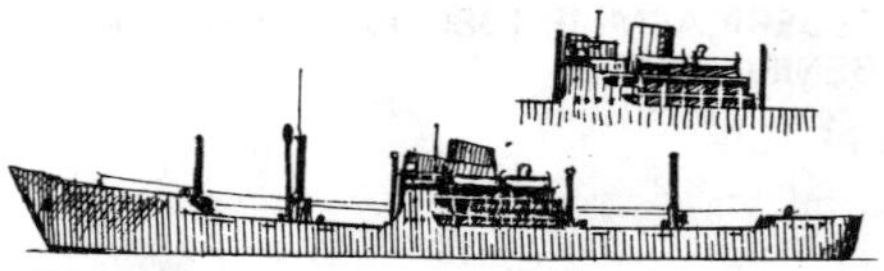

$KMKFK_2$ H13
● **12890 EUROPEAN LIBERTY.** Cy/Br 1957; CP; 5500; 139 × 7.2 (455 × 23.5); M; 14; ex CYPRUS SKY 1979; ex ELMINA PALM 1978. Sister: **12891 SEEPAYAL** (Br) ex ATHARI 1980; ex ENUGU PALM 1978 Similar (Inset): **12892 IRENES GRACE** (Cy) ex BADAGRY PALM 1972 **12893 ELSA K** (Gr) ex LENIO; ex BAMENDA PALM 1972.

$KMKFK_2$ H13
● **12900 EUROPEAN EXPRESS.** Pa/FRG 1961; C; 5600/8000; 144 × 7.2/8.5 (473 × 23.6/28); M; 14; ex EBONY 1980; ex JASPER—; ex OPAL—; ex BEER SHEVA 1976. Sister: **12901 LIA PERO** (Gr) ex PETROMARE STAR 1980; ex TEVERYA 1979; ex GOLD MOON 1977; ex TEVERYA 1976.

$KMKFK_2$ H13
● **12910 LAGOS PALM.** Br/Br 1961; CP; 6000; 144.5 × 7.6 (474 × 25.1); M; 16. Sisters; **12911 PERUVIAN TRADER** (Br) ex MINOA 1980; ex LOBITO PAL 1980; ex LOBITO PALM 1979 **12912 ARUNAKAMAL** (Br) ex HIND 1979; ex IBADAN PALM 1979 **12913 IKEJA PALM** (Br) **12914 DAPHNEMAR** (Pa) ex ILESHA PALM 1979 **12915 DIAMANT CAPTAIN** (Gr) ex ILORIN PALM 1979.

KMKFK$_3$ H1
12920 ROCKHAMPTON STAR. Br/Br 1958; C; 7500/9800; 154.59 × 8.63/9.32 (507.2 × 28.31/30.58); M; —.

KMKFK$_3$ H1
12930 GLADSTONE STAR. Br/FRG 1957; R; 8400/10600; 157 × —/9.3 (516 × —/30.5); M; 17.

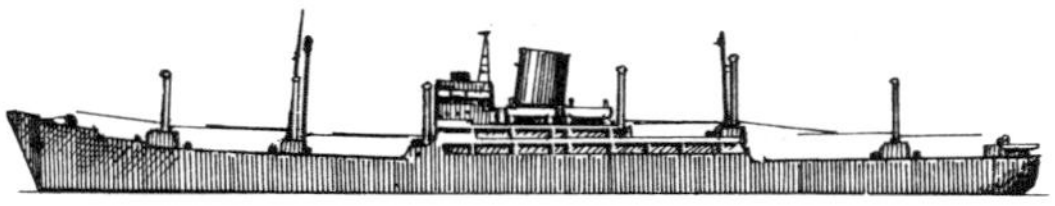

KMKFK$_3$ H1
12940 MAHMOUD. Cy/Br 1953; R; 10900; 160.3 × 9.3 (526 × 30.8); M; 16; ex OTAKI 1976.

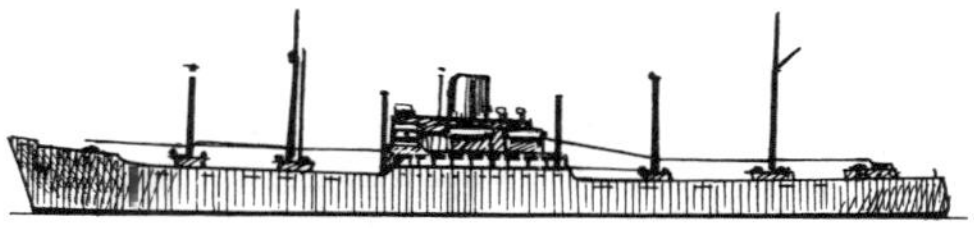

KMKFK$_2$M H12
12950 LORENZO d'AMICO. It/Br 1948; CP; 9600; 150 × 9.6 (493 × 31.5); M; 17; ex KAVO PEIRATIS 1970; ex SOESTDYK 1967.

KMKFK$_2$MK H123 |
● **12960 ANASSA.** Cy/Br 1953; C; 5400/7600; 148.5 × 7.35/8.65 (487.2 × 24.11/28.38); M; —; Ex ADRASTUS 1978. Sisters: **⋆12961 HONG QI 119** (RC) Ex HUNGMIEN 1977; ex DOLIUS 1972; ex GLENFRUIN 1972; ex DOLIUS 1970 **12962 HONG QI 137** (RC) ex HUNGSIA; ex DEMODOCUS 1973; ex GLENROY 1972; ex DEMODOCUS 1970 **12963 KAIGO** (Pa) ex DARANUS 1972; ex ACHILLES 1972 **12964 KAILOCK** (Pa) ex DEUCALION 1973; ex AJAX 1972 **12965 KAISING** (Pa) ex DIOMED 1973; ex GLENBEG 1972; ex DIOMED 1970 **12966 NIKOS** (Gr) ex AGAPENOR 1975.

KMKFKM H
12970 ARIS. Cy/Br 1954; C; 9600; 151 × 9.5 (495 × 31); M; 16; ex ARIS II 1972; ex TANTALLON CASTLE 1971.

KMKFKM H1
12980 KORINTHOS. Gr/FRG 1956; C; 6400/9000; 153.02 × 7.72/9.71 (502 × 25.33/31.86); M; 17; ex CAP ORTEGAL 1971. Sister: **12981 PENELOPE II** (Gr) ex CAP FINISTERRE 1972.

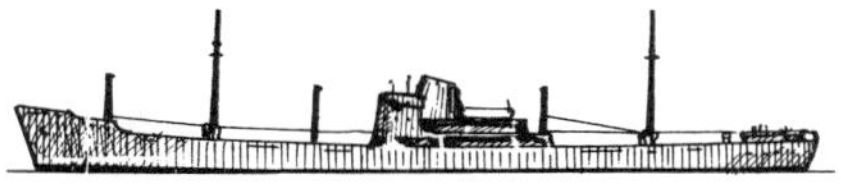

KMKFKM H1
12990 COVADONGA. Co/Br 1951; CP; 4200; 129 × 7 (424 × 22.9); M; 14; ex CIUDAD DE MEDELLIN 1969. Sisters: **12991 LIBERTADOR SIMON BOLIVAR** (Bo-Navy) ex LIBERTADOR BOLIVAR 1978; ex CIUDAD DE BARQUISIMENTO Similar: **12992 CIUDAD DE MARCAIBO** (Ve) **12993 PICHINCHA** (Ec) ex RIO GUAYAS 1979; ex CIUDAD DE QUITO 1977 **12994 DARIEN** (Co) ex MAITAMA 1974; ex CIUDAD DE MANIZALES 1970.

KMKFKM H1
13000 ROCK FERRY. Sc/Br 1958; C; 6500/9600; 160 × 8/8.6 (525 × 26/28.1); M; 14; ex TAI SHAN 1977; ex ARALUEN 1973.

KMKFKM H1
⋆13010 LENINOGORSK. Ru/Pd 1958; C; 9900; 154 × 8.7 (505 × 28.8); M; 16; **'B. 54'** type. Sisters (Ru flag): **⋆13011 BOLSHEVIK SUKHANOV ⋆13012 DEPUTAT LUTSKIY ⋆13013 LABINSK ⋆13014 LESOZAVODSK ⋆13015 PARTIZAN BONNIVUR ⋆13016 SOLNECHNOGORSK.**

KMKFKM H1
13020 PATRICIA U. Li/Br 1960; C; 7700; 139 × 8.8 (455 × 28.1); M; 17; ex TURAKINA 1977; May have mainmast removed.

KMKFKM H1
13030 ALSALMA. Bh/In 1958; C; 5100/7200; 144.96 × 6.48/7.33 (475.6 × 21.26/24.05); M; 12; ex JALAVEERA 1980.

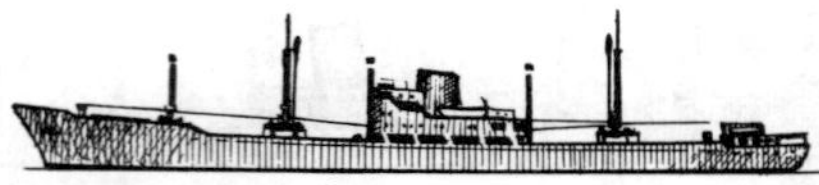

KMKFKM H1
● **13040 OURANIA.** Gr/FRG 1953; CP; 4200; 127 × 7.3 (415 × 23.1); M; 15; ex SCHAUENBURG 1970. Sisters: **13041 ARPA SUN** (Gr) ex STERN HASSELBURG 1974; ex HASSELBURG 1974; ex VOLTA VENTURE 1973; ex HASSELBURG 1972 **13042 ATHENS WAY** (Cy) ex MEXICAN TRADER 1976; ex VOLTA VIGILANCE 1973; ex SONDERBURG 1972.

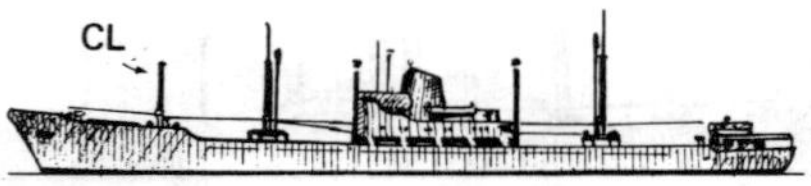

KMKFKM H1
13050 MEDI-SUN. Li/FRG 1959; CP; 3700/5700; 126 × 7.2/8.3 (414 × 23.6/27.3); M; 15.75; ex QUICHE 1980; ex MEDI-SUN 1979; ex VOLTA VIRTUE 1973; ex MEDI-SUN 1972; ex BREITENBURG 1971; ex SYLLUM 1970.

KMKFKM H1
13060 'VICTORY' type. Various flags/US 1945; C; 7600; 139 × 9.1 (455 × 29.6); T; 15; About 500 were built of which there are still a few in service under Taiwan and other flags. The United States Department of Commerce have over 100 'Victory' types laid up.

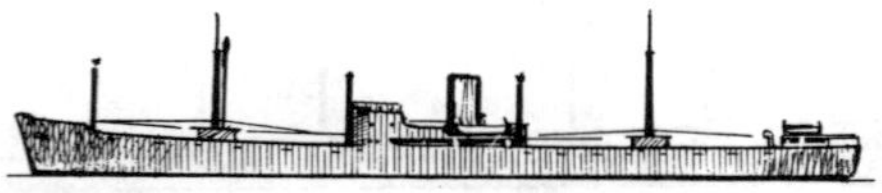

KMKFKM H1
13070 MAGNA SPES. Cy/De 1947; CP; 4800/7000; 134 × 8.08/— (440 × 26.6/^{8}); M; 14; ex SPALMATORI ISLANDS 1972; ex EVA CHRISTENSEN 1967; ex COLOMBIA 1966.

KMKFKM H1
13080 BACCHIS. Cy/FRG 1950; C; 2500; 89.3 × 6.4 (293 × 21.3); M; 14; ex LION OF MYKONOS 1975; ex LION OF MARATHON 1969; ex EVANGELOS 1966; ex CONSUL 1965; ex CONSUL ARLT 1962.

KMKFKM H1
● **13090 TOM.** Gr/Ne 1959; C; 6600/8000; 146.08 × 8/8.81 (479.27 × 26.25/28.9); M; 15; ex SEA GLORY 1979; ex LEIDERKERK 1978. Sister: **13091 MINA F** (Gr) ex SEA CHALLENGER 1980; ex NEDLLOYD LELYKERK 1978; ex LELYKERK 1977 Similar: **13092 KOTA JAYA** (Sg) ex NEDLLOYD BOVENKERK; ex BOVENKERK 1977.

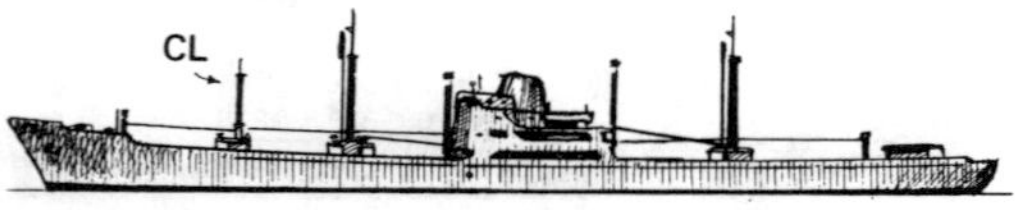

KMKFKM H1
⋆**13100 DONGMING.** RC/Ne 1964; C; 10400; 157 × 9.6 (516 × 31.6); M; 15; ex SEA AMBER 1973. Sister: ⋆**13101 KUNMING** (RC) ex SEA CORAL 1973.

KMKFKM H1
⋆**13110 TAIXING.** RC/Ne 1960; C; 7300/10400; 158 × 8.4/— (517 × 27.3/—); M; 16; ex BENIOWSKI 1971; ex ARGO ALTIS.

KMKFKM H1
⋆**13120 HUAI YIN.** RC/FRG 1959; CP; 6700/10000; 158 × 8.2/9.3 (518 × 27/30.6); M; 16; ex YELLOW SEA 1970; ex JAG JIWAN 1964; ex JALA JAG JIWAN 1963; ex JAG JIWAN 1959.

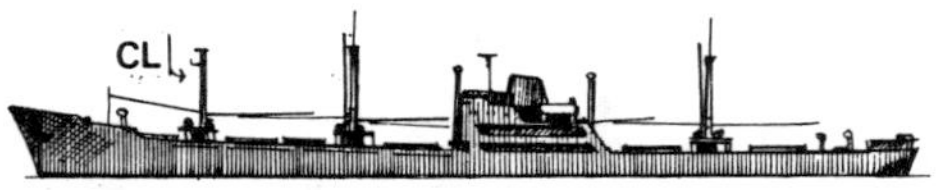

KMKFKM H1
⋆**13130 NANHUEI.** RC/Fi 1961; C; 6400/9100; 146 × 8.5/9.1 (479 × 28/30); M; 15.5; ex BRILLIANCE 1970; ex WIIRI 1970.

KMKFKM H1
13140 SEA EXPLORER. Li/Fi 1959; C; 9200; 146 × 9.3 (479 × 30); M; 14.5; ex LAMBROS M. FATSIS 1968; ex WESTERN TRADER 1967.

KMKFKM H1
13150 AURELIA DI MAIO. It/Fi 1961; C; 9000; 146 × 9.1 (479 × 29.1); M; 15.25; ex ANDREA GRITTI 1979; ex WILKE 1969.

KMKFKM H1
13160 LANKA DEVI. Sr/Br 1962; C; 7000/9900; 155.8 × 8.3/9.2 (511 × 27.3/30.2); M; 14.75; ex ARAMIS 1972.

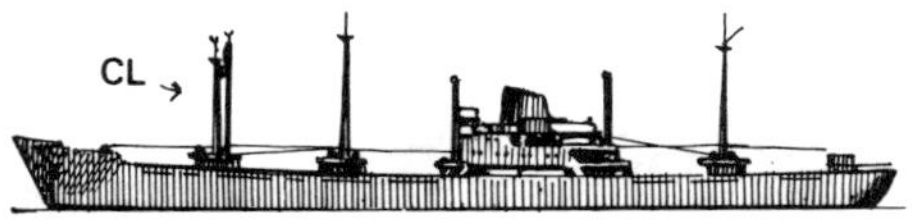

KMKFKM H1
13170 ADOM. Gh/FRG 1959; C; 5400; 140.2 × 7.7 (460 × 25.2); M; 16; ex VOLTA PEACE; ex KAMPERDYK 1972. Sisters: **13171 FERIAL** (Gh) ex ODUPON 1980; ex VOLTA WISDOM 1977; ex KORENDYK 1972 **13172 MARIKA J. LEMOS** (Cy) ex TJONGER; ex KATSEDYK 1973 ⋆**13173 BOROVNICA** (Ys) ex KINDERDYK 1970 ⋆**13174 BRANIK** (Ys) ex KERKEDYK 1970 ⋆**13175 BREZICE** (Ys) ex KLOOSTERDYK 1970.

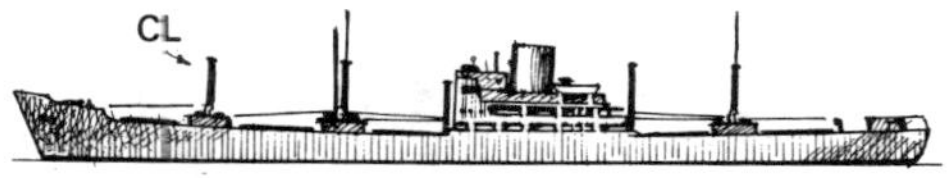

KMKFKM H1
13180 DINOS V. Cy/Br 1952; CP; 6200/9100; 144.8 x— (475 x—); M; 12.5; ex DINOS METHENITIS; ex OSWESTRY GRANGE 1971.

KMKFKM H1
● **13190 IQBALBAKSH.** Pk/Br 1963; CP; 7000/9900; 155.8 × —/9.4 (511 × —/31); M; 15; ex ARNA 1971.

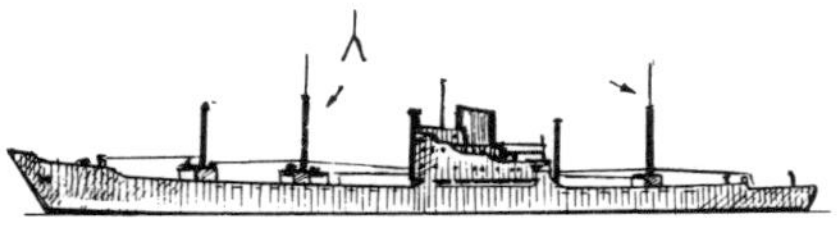

KMKFKM H1
● **13200 ATHENS DAY.** Cy/FRG 1954; C; 5100; 128.2 × 7.4 (421 × 24.3); M; 13.5; ex SILVIA 1972. Similar (No bi-pods): **13201 DIMITRIS** (Gr) ex CLIVIA 1972 **13202 NAXOS** (Gr) ex HOLSTENDAMM 1978; ex GOSLAR 1973; ex FRANZ 1959; ex FRANZ OHLROGGE 1958 **13203 EVDOKIA TSIRIS** (Cy) ex ALPHARD 1975.

KMKFKM H1
13210 LIEN CHANG. Pa/Br 1953; C; 5600/8400; 139.3 × 8.1/9.1 (457 × 26.8/29.1); M; 12.5; ex FONG LEE 1976; ex SANDRA 1973; ex QUEENSBURY 1971.

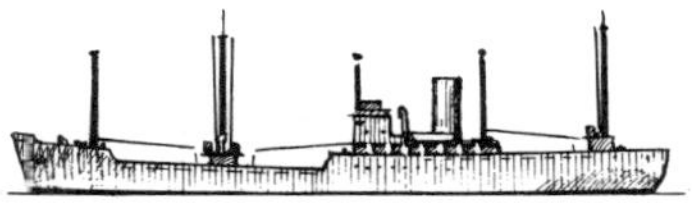

KMKFKM H12
13220 ATHINOULA. Gr/Br 1952; C; 3400; 105.21 × 6.82 (345.18 × 22.38); M; 11.75; ex KLEONIKO 1977; ex HUALIEN 1976; ex NEW BANGKOK 1975; ex KOWHAI 1973. Similar: **13221 MILOS IV** (Gr) ex ARNHEM 1977; ex WAIMEA 1975.

KMKFKM H13
13230 JANI. Ng/FRG 1954; CP; 8800; 146 × 8 (479 × 26.2); M; 13; ex AHMADU TIJANI 1980; ex SANTA RITA 1972. Sister: **13231 SAMOS SKY** (Gr) ex SANTA ROSA 1976.

KMKFKM H13
13240 AIHUA. Pa/FRG 1955; CP; 6800; 154.4 × 7.7 (507 × 25.4); M; 16; ex CAP NORTE 1973. Sister: **13241 AIMIN** (Pa) ex CAP VILANO 1974.

KMKFKM H13
13260 HERA. Li/FRG 1961; CP; 3300/5300; 127 × 6.8/7.7 (418 × 22.4/25.6); M; 14.5; ex MITRA 1977; ex LEORA 1976; ex LEADA 1971.

KMKFKM H13
13270 AVA. Bm/FRG 1963; C; 4900/7400; 135 × 7.2/— (455 × 23.6/—); M; 15.5. Sister: **13271 BASSEIN** (Bm).

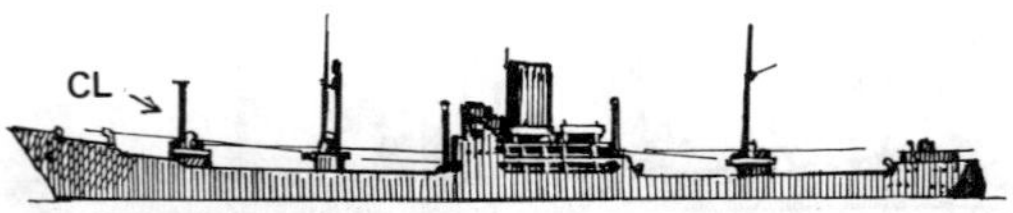

KMKFKM H13
13290 GULF FALCON. Br/Br 1958; C; 8200; 154.6 × 8.54 (507.4 × 28.02); M; 16; ex CITY OF AUCKLAND 1978. Sisters: **13291 BENVANNOCH** (Br) ex CITY OF RIPON **13292 EASTERN ENTERPRISE** (Sg) ex CITY OF WELLINGTON **13293 EASTERN ENVOY** (Sg) ex CITY OF NEWCASTLE.

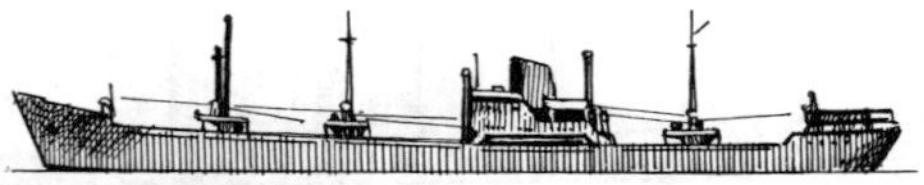

KMKFKM H13
● **13310 PRA RIVER.** Gh/Ne 1961; CP; 4900/7400; 140.5 × —/8.4 (461 × —/27.7); M; 15. Sisters (Gh flag): **13311 AFRAM RIVER 13312 BIRIM RIVER 13313 KULPAWN RIVER 13314 LAKE BOSOMTWE 13315 NASIA RIVER 13316 OFFIN RIVER 13317 OTCHI RIVER.**

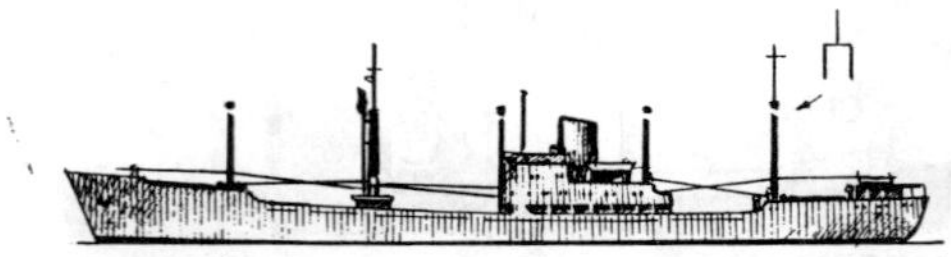

KMKFKM H13
13250 PUNTA ATALAYA. Pa/FRG 1956; CP; 4700/7000; 137.5 × 7.2/8.5 (451 × 23.6/28); M; 16; ex NOPAL PROGRESS 1974. Sister: **13251 LARA** (Cy) ex CREST LION 1979; ex AGHIOS LEFTERIS; ex KROHN TRADER; ex NOPAL TRADER 1974.

KMKFKM H13
13280 MARINA P. Gr/Be 1961; CP; 5200/7800; 141.2 × 7.8/8.8 (464 × 25.6/29); M; 16; ex MANAURE III 1980; ex GOOD LUCK 1977; ex ANVERS 1973. Sister: **13281 HELENA C** (Gr) ex GOOD HOPE 1975; ex GAND 1973.

KMKFKM H13
13300 GOLD STREAM. Li/Ja 1963; C; 4700/7100; 137.5 × 7.5/8.7 (451 × 24.6/28.6); M; 16.25; ex SAHAR 1974. Sister: **13301 GOLD MOUNTAIN** (Li) ex TSEDEK 1974.

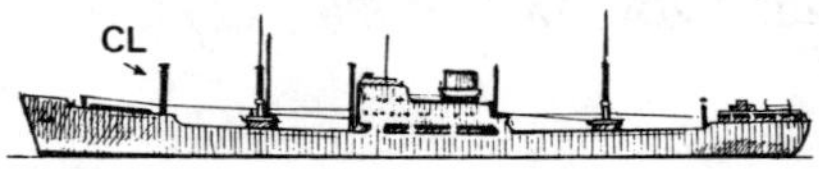

KMKFKM H13
13320 CONCORDIA SKY. Gr/No 1955; CP; 500; 130 × 7.5 (427 × 24.8); M; 17.

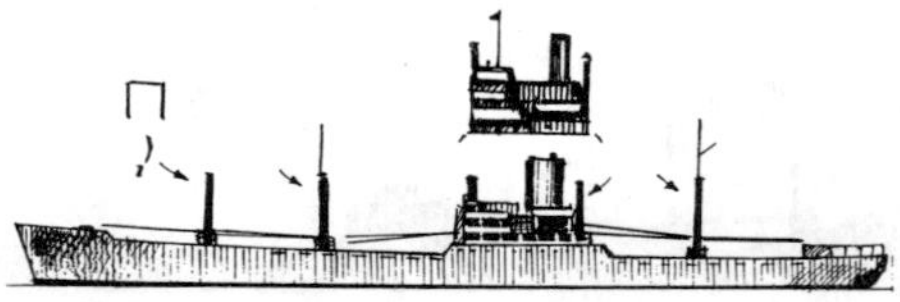

KMKFKM H2
13330 ERICSON. US/US 1946; C; 6100; 140.1 × 8.4 (460 × 27.8); T; 15; **'C. 2'** type. May be others of this type still in service.

KMKFKMK H1
13340 GEMURUH. Ia/It 1948; CP; 9400; 149 × 9.5 (489 × 31.2); M; 16.5; ex GIOVANNI D'AMICO 1974; ex FERNDALE 1967; Deepened 1971. Sister: **13341 GEMPITA** (Ia) ex MARIA CARLA D'AMICO 1974; ex FERNSIDE 1968.

KMKFKMK H1
13350 AL SHEHABIA. Sr/Sw 1963; CP; 4900/7300; 137.7 × 8/8.8 (452 × 26.3/28.1); M; 16.5; ex ELEN 1980; ex NEVA 1979; ex NOPAL NEVA; ex NOPAL ALKIMOS 1975; ex NOPAL REX 1973; ex EARLVILLE 1964. Sisters: **13351 JUNIOR K** (Le) ex ROSEVILLE 1974 **13352 MAKEVERETT** (Li) ex OAKVILLE 1968 **13353 TAMURAEVERETT** (Li) ex GRANVILLE 1967.

KMKFKMK H1
● **13360 STELLA C.** Gr/FRG 1954; CP; 7500; 154.8 × 8.3 (508 × 27.5); M; 16; ex WONORATO 1976. Sisters: **13361 LUCILLE** (Sg) ex WONOSARI 1977 **13362 SAUDI PRINCE** (Si) ex WONOSOBO **13363 KOTA MEGAH** (Sg) ex WONOGIRI 1976.

KMKFKMK H1
● ⋆**13370 FLORIAN CEYNOWA.** Pd/Pd 1957; CP; 6800; 153.9 × 8.4 (505 × 27.4); M; 14.75; **'B. 54'** type. Sisters: ⋆**13371 LINTONG** (RC) ex ORLIK 1967; ex HOPING WU SHI 1960; ex FRYDERYK SCHOPIN 1959 **13372 FAY III** (Gr) ex BOLESLAW BIERUT 1975.

KMKFKMK H1
● **13380 LAWANTI.** Pa/FRG 1956; CP; 6300; 155.5 × 8 (510 × 26.2); M; 17; ex ERLANGEN 1969. Sisters: **13381 TWADIKA** (Pa) ex GOTTINGEN 1969 **13382 AL SHUWAIKH** (Ku) ex CEENA 1971; ex TUBINGEN 1970 ⋆**13383 YING SHAN** (RC) ex MIN CHIANG; ex WEIMAR 1972 Similar (funnel and superstructure variations, twin KP foreward, etc.) **13384 KOTA BENAR** (Sg) ex BARTENSTEIN **13385 KOTA BAKTI** (Sg) ex BLANKENSTEIN **13386 DANIELA** (Pa) ex HAVELLAND **13387 JUTHA KARNCHANA** (Th) ex RHEINLAND **13388 JUTHA RAJATA** (Th) ex VOGTLAND 1977 **13389 FRANCA** (Pa) ex SAARLAND **13390 ZEA BEACH** (Pa) ex ZIRCON 1980; ex KALAHARI ⋆**13391 BAO SHAN** (RC) ex MINGLANG 1975; ex WORMS 1972 ⋆**13392 XIUSHAN** (RC) ex MINGYAO 1975; ex WIESBADEN 1972 ⋆**13393 BA SHAN** (RC) ex YUSHAN 1980; ex MINGWEI; ex WIEN.

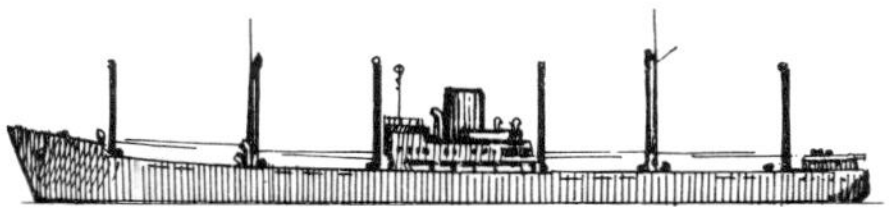

KMKFKMK H1
13400 BRAVO MARIA. Gr/Ne 1953; CP; 4500; 131.6 × 6.8 (432 × 22.5); M; 14; ex EEMLAND 1975.

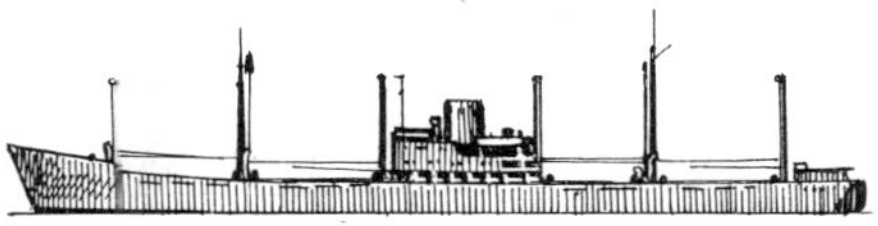

KMKFKMK H1
● **13410 KENNEMERLAND.** Ne/Ne 1957; CP; 5000; 131.7 × 7.2 (432 × 23.8); M; 14.5.

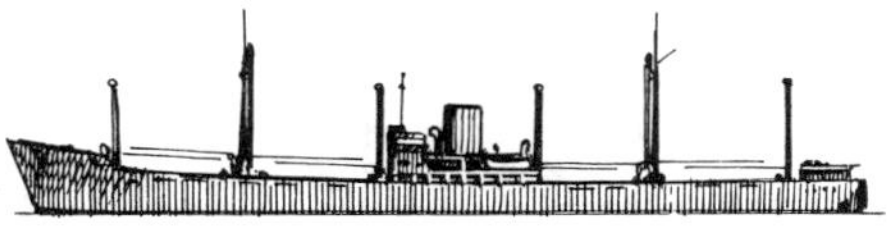

KMKFKMK H1
● **13420 BRAVO DENIS.** Gr/Ne 1951; C; 4000/6300; 131.07 × —/6.83 (432 × —/22.5); M; 14; ex GRAVELAND 1975.

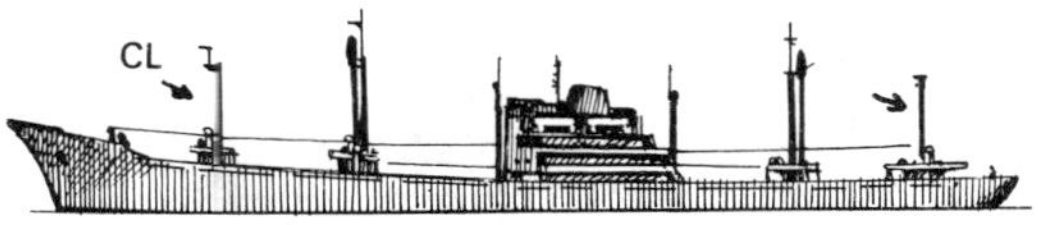

KMKFKMK H1
● **13430 NEDLLOYD SEROOSKERK.** Ne/Ne 1960; CP; 7300/9700; 161 × —/9 (528 × —/29.6); M; 17.5; ex SEROOSKERK 1977. Sister: **13431 NEDLLOYD SIMONSKERK** (Ne) ex SIMONSKERK 1977.

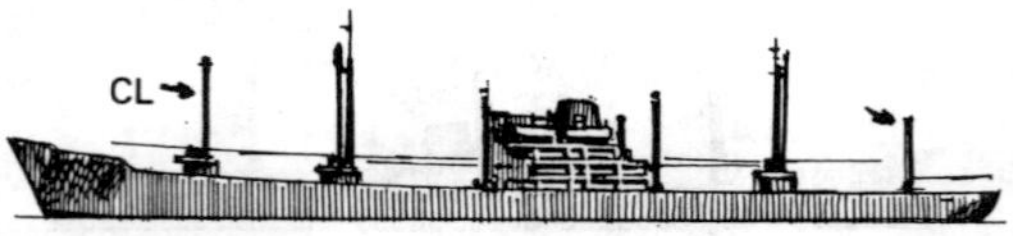

KMKFKMK H1
13440 GOOD SKIPPER. Gr/Ne 1957; C; 7000/9100; 154.64 × 8.02/8.9 (507.35 × 26.31/29.2); M; 17; ex ZONNEKERK 1977. Sister: **13441 TRANSWORLD GOLIATH** (Gr) ex ZUIDERKERK.

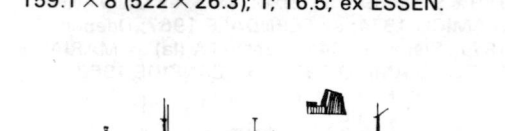

KMKFKMK H1
13450 ALAMOS. Sg/FRG 1953; CP; 6800; 159.1 × 8 (522 × 26.3); T; 16.5; ex ESSEN.

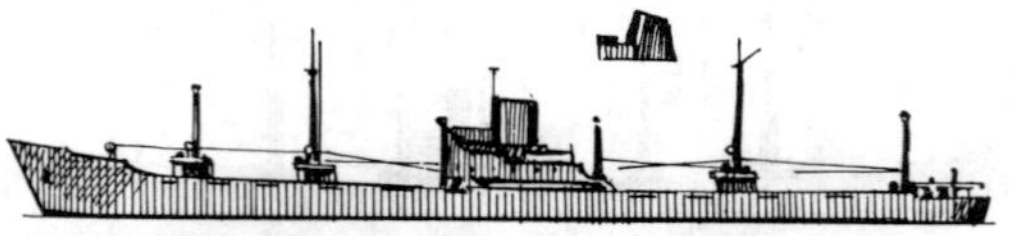

KMKFKMK H1
● **13460 FERNANDAEMME.** It/FRG 1952; CP; 5700; 152 × 7.6 (498 × 24.11); M; 16.5; ex BRANDENSTEIN 1972. Similar (conical funnel—see inset): **13461 BECENA** (Pa) ex KOLN 1973.

KMKFKMK H1
13470 MEIRU. Pa/FRR 1955; CP; 5600; 152 × 7.6 (498 × 26.1); M; 14.5; ex TANNSTEIN 1972. Sister: **13471 MEIKI** (Pa) ex TORSTEIN 1973.

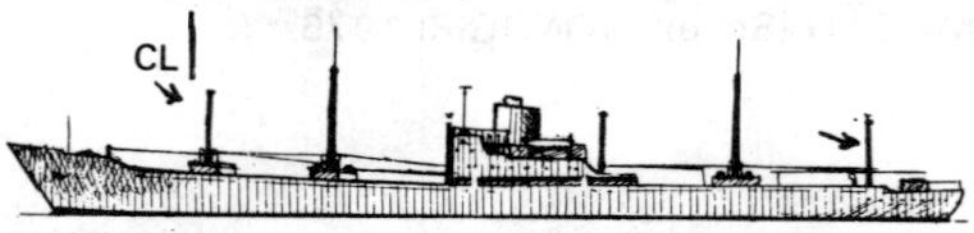

KMKFKMK H1
13480 PANTERA. Pa/FRG 1956; CP; 5900; 152 × 7.6 (498 × 24.1); M; 17.5; ex BISCHOFSTEIN 1977. Sisters: **13481 DIEGO** (Pa) ex BREITENSTEIN 1976 **13482 KOTA BERANI** (Sg) ex BIRKENSTEIN.

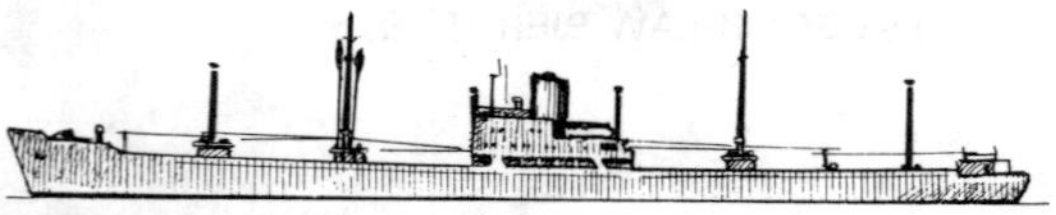

KMKFKMK H1
13490 NANHUA. Pa/FRG 1954; CP; 7000; 167 × 8 (542 × 26.2); M; 17.5; ex TRAVESTEIN 1973. Sisters (Pa flag): **13491 NANTAO** (Pa) ex WESERSTEIN 1973 Similar (taller KPs abaft funnel): **13492 NANKUO** (Pa) ex HAVELSTEIN 1973 **13493 NANCHENG** (Pa) ex WERRASTEIN 1973.

KMKFKMK H1
13500 GRIGORIOS D. Cy/FRG 1957; CP; 6500/9500; 163 × 8.9/9.1 (535 × 29.5/30); M; 17; ex NELA 1978; ex S.A. KUNENELAND; ex KUNENELAND 1974; ex CUXHAVEN 1971.

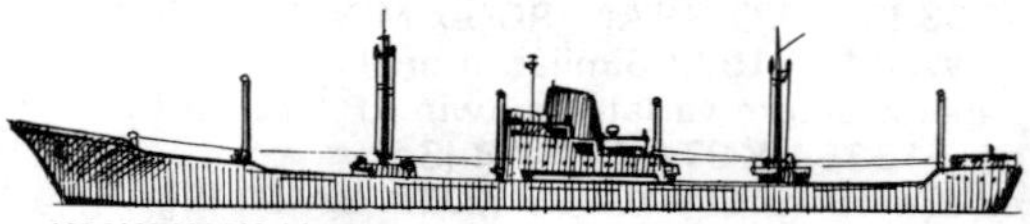

KMKFKMK H13
⋆**13510 N'GOLA.** An/FRG 1961; C; 6800/9400; 159 × 8/9.2 (520 × 26/30.4); M; 18.5; ex BLUMENTHAL 1971. Sisters: **13511 CONGO** (Po) ex NURNBERG 1971 **13512 MANICA** (Po) ex KULMERLAND 1971 **13513 MUXIMA** (Po) ex WOLFSBURG 1971 **13514 MUNSTERLANDES** (Gr) ex MUNSTERLAND.

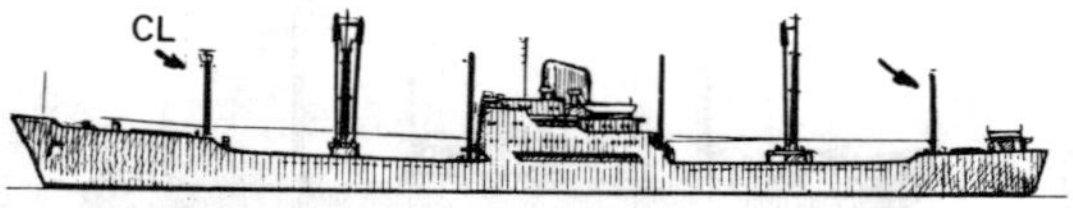

KMKFKMK H13
● **13520 NEDLLOYD RHONE.** Ne/FRG 1962; C; 7200/10000; 164 × 8.3/9.1 (537 × 27.6/29.11); M; 20; ex NEDER RHONE. Sister: **13521 NEDLLOYD RIJN** (Ne) ex NEDER RIJN.

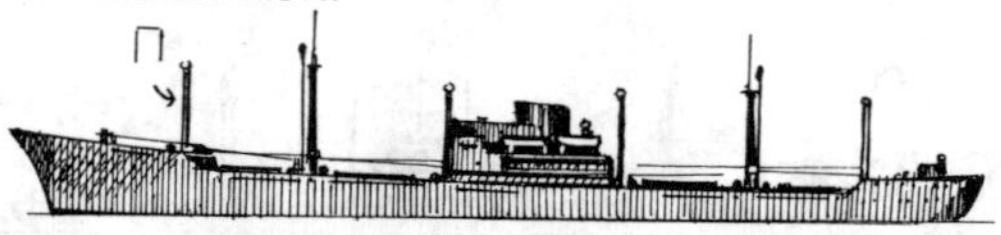

KMKFKMK H13
13530 KESNAR. Pa/Ne 1958; C; 6700; 151.19 × 7.99 (496 × 26.21); M; 16; ex ALKES 1978. Similar: **13531 KOTA SEJATI** (Sg) ex NIJKERK 1977.

KMKFKMK H13
13540 CONCORDIA TADJ. Gr/FRG 1958; CP; 6500; 150 × 8.8 (492 × 28.1); M; 17. Sisters: **13541 CONCORDIA TALEB** (No) **13542 CONCORDIA TAREK** (Gr).

KMKFKMK H13
⋆**13550 XING KONG.** RC/Br 1958; C; 7300; 153.24 × 8.3 (502.76 × 27.23); M; 16.25; ex TRINITY SPLENDOUR 1980; ex CLAN MENZIES 1979.

KMKFKMK H13
13570 BEIRA. Po/Po 1962; CP; 8600; 162 × 9.4 (531 × 31); M; 17.5; Lengthened and completed in 1963 in Ne.

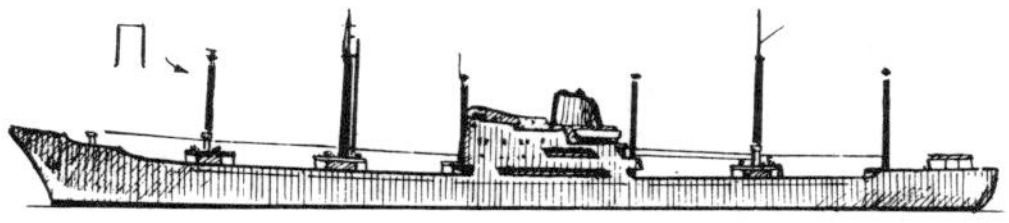

KMKFKMK H13
13580 PULAU BALI. Pa/FRG 1962; CP; 6800/9800; 157 × 8/9 (515 × 26/29); M; 16.5; ex HOEGH DYKE 1979. Similar: **13581 NOPAL VEGA** (Pa) ex CONCORDIA VEGA 1969; ex HOEGH DRAKE 1969.

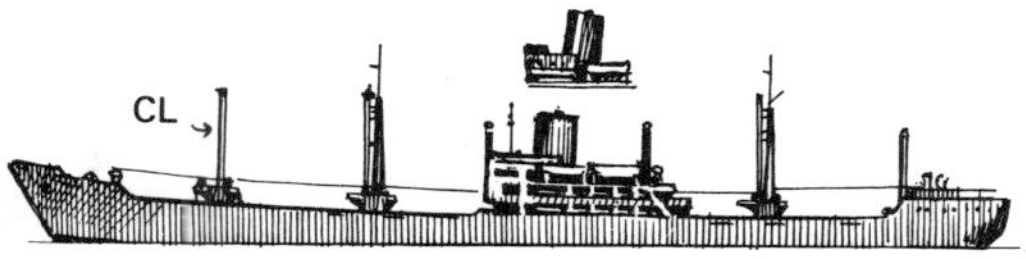

KMKFKMK H13
● **13560 FAULAD SARDAR.** In/FRG 1958; C; 7200/9400; 154.87 × 8.03/8.96 (508.1 × 26.35/29.4); M; 17.5; ex INDIAN STRENGTH 1979. Sisters (In flag): **13561 INDIAN TRIUMPH 13562 INDIAN TRUST** Similar (see inset): **13563 INDIAN SECURITY.**

KMKFKMK H13
● **13590 KOTA SEJARAH.** Sg/Ne 1956; CP; 6500/8300; 151 × 8/9 (495 × 26/29); M; 17; ex MERCURY RIVER; ex GIESSENKERK 1975. Sisters (It flag): **13591 ANNA C** ex OLDEKERK 1974 **13592 GIOVANNA C** ex OMMENKERK 1974.

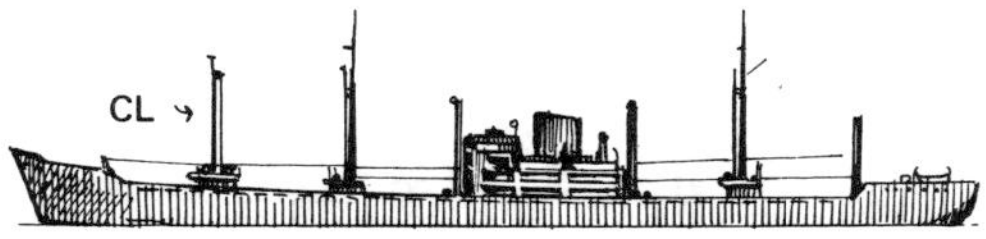

KMKFKMK H13
● **13600 GEMILANG.** Ia/Ne 1954; C; 7000; 150.35 × 8.55 (493.27 × 28.05); M; 16.5; ex OUWERKERK 1973.

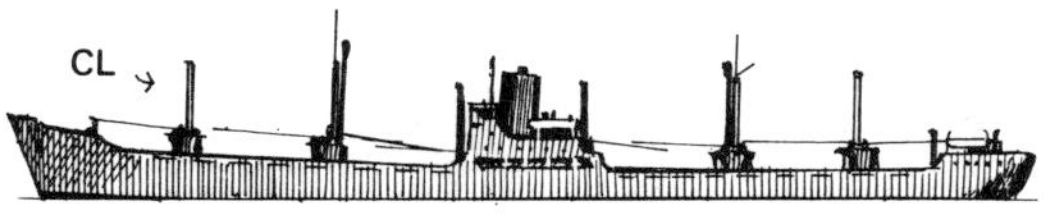

KMKFKMK H13
13620 INDIAN RELIANCE. In/FRG 1955; C; 7400; 162 × 8 (531 × 26.5); T; 17.5. Sister: **13621 INDIAN RENOWN** (In).

KMKFM H
13640 AFRICAN LION. Gr/Br 1958; C; 5800/8300; 142.3 × 7.9/8.8 (467 × 26/29); M; 12.5; ex KING HENRY 1972.

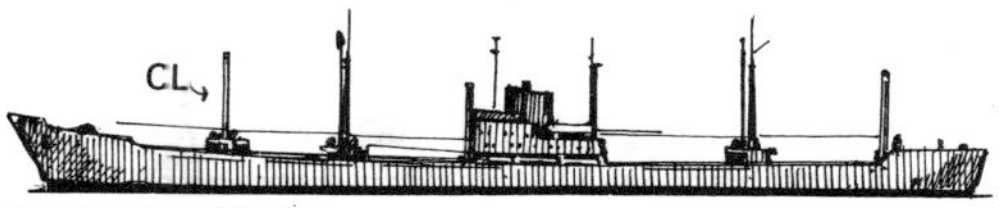

KMKFKMK H13
13610 LELLO DI MAIO. It/FRG 1961; CP; 6900/9200; 152 × 8.2/9.2 (497 × 27/30.4); M; 16.25; ex TANGA; ex NOVIA 1963.

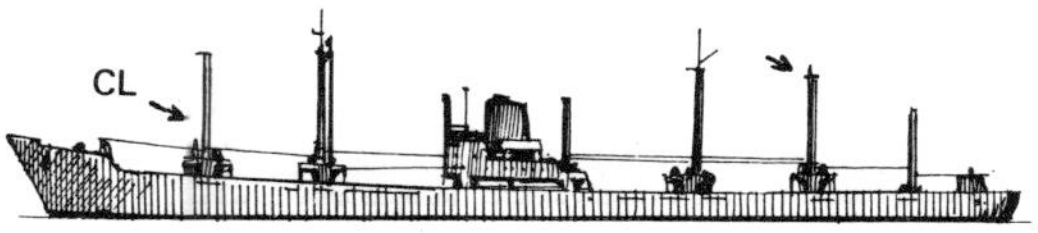

KMKFKMK$_2$ H1
13630 MOSELSTEIN. Pa/FRG 1954; C; 6900; 167.29 × 8 (548.85 × 26.25); M; 17.5; Lengthened and converted to motor ship 1964. Similar: **13631 NANWU** (Pa) ex NECKARSTEIN 1973.

KMKFM H1

● ⋆**13650 SUPER ATLANTIK** type. Ru/DDR 1972 onwards; FT; 4000; 102 × 5.2 (335 × 17); M; 15. Sisters (Ru flag): ⋆**13651 ADAYKHOKH** ⋆**13652 AKHILLEON** ⋆**13653 AUKSHAYTIKA** ⋆**13654 APOGEY** ⋆**13655 ARABAT** ⋆**13656 AZOV** ⋆**13657 BATILMAN** ⋆**13658 BERKUT** ⋆**13659 BAGRATIONOVSK** ⋆**13660 BIOSFERA** ⋆**13661 BORIS TSINDELIS** ⋆**13662 DONISAR** ⋆**13663 EDUARD CLAUDIUS** ⋆**13664 FOROS** ⋆**13665 GEYA** ⋆**13666 GALDOR** ⋆**13667 GRIGORIY TEREMTYEV** ⋆**13668 GRANIT** ⋆**13669 GEFEST** ⋆**13670 GARPUNNER PROKOPYENKO** ⋆**13671 GENERAL OSTRYAKOV** ⋆**13672 GRIGORIY OVODOVSKIY** ⋆**13673 IOSIF LAPUSHKIN** ⋆**13674 JAN RAINBERG** ⋆**13675 JOAKIM VACIETIS** ⋆**13676 KURSHAYA DUGA** ⋆**13677 KALPER** ⋆**13678 KOMMUNAR** ⋆**13679 LYUDMILA PAVLICHENKO** ⋆**13680 LEMBIT PERN** ⋆**13681 MAMAYEV KURGAN** ⋆**13682 MUSTYARV** ⋆**13683 MALAYA ZEMLYA** ⋆**13684 MYS CHAKO** ⋆**13685 PERIGEY** ⋆**13686 MEZOSFERA** ⋆**13687 MIKHAIL ORLOV** ⋆**13688 NIKOLAY BERAZIN** ⋆**13689 NIKOFOR PAVLOV** ⋆**13690 NIKOLAY TSYGANOV** ⋆**13691 NIKOLAY GRIBANOV** ⋆**13692 NARODNYY OPOLCHENETS** ⋆**13693 NOVOSOKOLNIKI** ⋆**13694 PATROKL** ⋆**13695 PRESIDENT PIK** ⋆**13696 PERIGEY** ⋆**13697 PEYPSI** ⋆**13698 PROMOTEY** ⋆**13699 PETROGRADSKAYA STORONA** ⋆**13700 RETAVAS** ⋆**13701 SALANTI** ⋆**13702 SERGEY LYULIN** ⋆**13703 SCHILUTE** ⋆**13704 SUVALKIYA** ⋆**13705 SAADYARV** ⋆**13706 STRATOSFERA** ⋆**13707 SUGAN** ⋆**13708 STRALSUNDSKIY KORABEL** ⋆**13709 SELENA** ⋆**13710 TRIPOSFERA** ⋆**13711 TRITON** ⋆**13712 TRUSEVIK MORYA** ⋆**13713 TEMRYUCHANIN** ⋆**13714 TAURAGE** ⋆**13715 TURAYDA** ⋆**13716 TSEMESSKAYA BUKHTA** ⋆**13717 TAMULA** ⋆**13718 URANIYA** ⋆**13719 VIYTNA** ⋆**13720 VAGULA** ⋆**13721 VASILIY FOMIN** ⋆**13722 VOROSHILOVGRAD** ⋆**13723 VASILIY REVYAKIN** ⋆**13724 YURMALA** ⋆**13725 YURBARKAS** ⋆**13726 YONAVA** ⋆**13727 ZVEZDA** ⋆**13728 ZNAMYA KERCHIL** ⋆**13729 ZEFIR** Probable Sister (Fisheries Training—may have differences): ⋆**13730 PRIZVANIE** (Rm flag): ⋆**13731 BAHLUI** ⋆**13732 BISTRITA** ⋆**13734 CERNA** ⋆**13735 CINDREWL** ⋆**13736 DORNA** ⋆**13737 JIJIA** ⋆**13738 PUTNA** ⋆**13739 TIRNAVA** (DDR flag): ⋆**13740 LUDWIG TUREK**

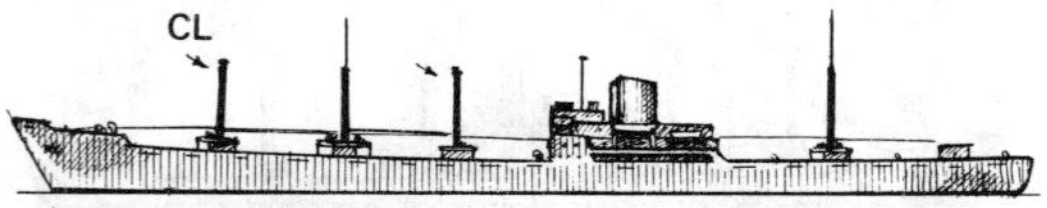

KMKFM H1
13750 CONSTANTINOS T. Gr/Br 1959; C; 11300; 161.2 × 9.5 (530 × 31); M; 15; ex N. ZOGRAFIA 1975; ex LORD GLADSTONE 1969.

KMKFM H1
13760 CLEOPATRA. Eg/US 1944; PC; 8200; 138.8 × 8.7 (445 × 28.7); T; 16.5; ex KHEDIVE ISMAIL 1956; ex UNITED VICTORY 1947; Modified **'VICTORY'** type.

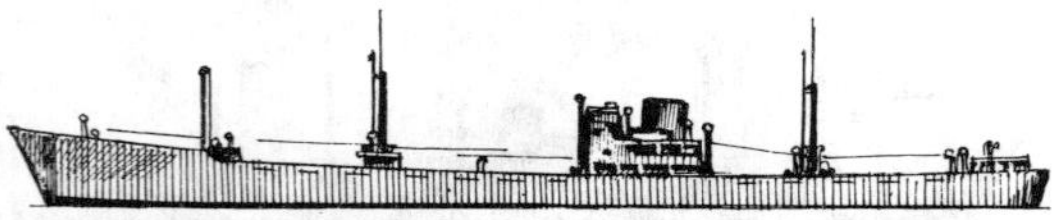

KMKFM H1
13770 PANTAZIS CAIAS. Cy/Ne 1954; C; 9600; 158.1 × 8.2 (519 × 27.1); M; 12.25; ex CROWBOROUGH BEACON 1970; Lengthened 1961.

KMKFM H1
13780 STARSTONE. Li/FRG 1956; C; 6100/9000; 153 × 8/9 (503 × 26/30); M; —; ex PEARLSTONE 1965.

KMKFM H1
13790 ILSE. Pa/FRG 1952; CP; 3900; 122 × 7.3 (401 × 23.9); M; 13; ex PAZIFIK 1972. Sister: **13791 KATAL** (Le) ex ATLANTIK I 1972; ex ATLANTIK 1972.

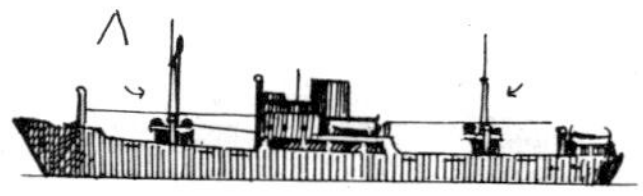

KMKFM H1

● **13800 RODONAS.** Gr/De 1952; CP; 1600; 92.3 × 6.1 (303 × 19.5); M; 13; ex ELVIRA M; ex BANGSBO 1968. Similar: **13801 RAS AL HADD** (Oman) ex KASTEL KONGO 1977; ex BASTHOLM 1967 **13802 ABUSABAA 1** (Cy) ex GUARDIAN 1979; ex CYPRIAN PRODUCER 1976; ex BORREBY 1967 **13803 COURAGE** (Cy) ex CYPRIAN TRADER 1976; ex BYGHOLM 1967.

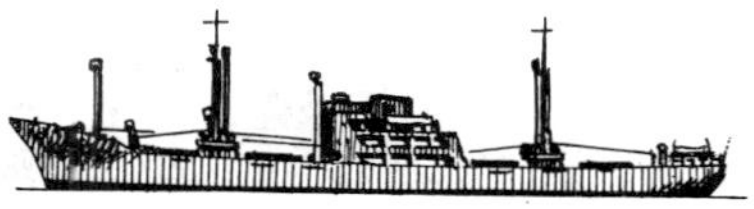

KMKFM H1

13810 GUIRIA. Ve/Ne 1955; CP; 3500; 116 × 6.3 (381 4 20.6); M; 14.75; ex ANZOATEGUI. Sisters (Ve flag): **13811 RENATA B** ex MERIDA 1979 **13812 LAS MOROCHAS** ex SUCRE 1979 **13813 YARACUY.**

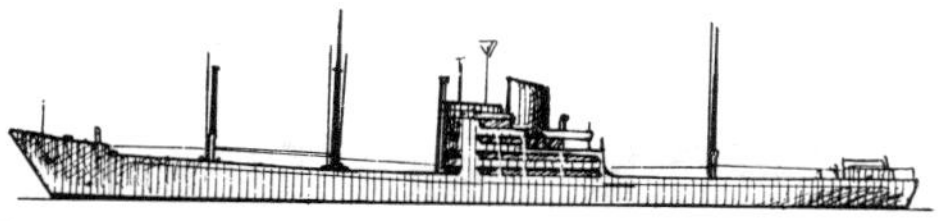

KMKFM H1

● **13820 STERNAL TRADER.** Pa/FRG 1958; CP; 5700/8600; 143 × 8/9 (470 × 26/29); M; —; ex AXENFELS; ex NARENDRA LAXMI 1972; ex AXENFELS 1972; ex SCHELDE 1969.

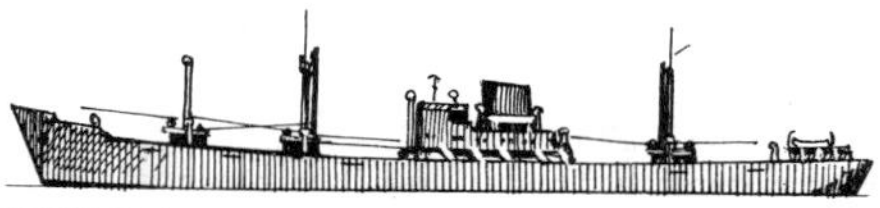

KMKFM H1

13830 ATHEN SKY. Gr/FRG 1956; C; 5000/7400; 142.55 × 7.69/8.56 (467.68 × 25.23/28.08); M; —; ex S.A. WALVIS BAY 1975; ex WALVIS BAY 1974; ex USAMBARA 1959.

KMKFM H12

⋆**13840 LAODONG.** RC/US 1940; C; 6000; 140 × 8.4 (459 × 27.8); M; 14; ex WARSZAWA 1963; ex BASTASEN 1951; ex AXEL SALEN 1951; ex SEA WITCH 1947; **'C.2'** type.

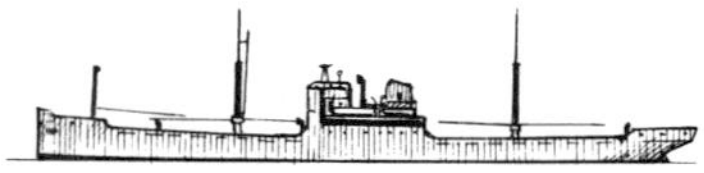

KMKFM H123

⋆**13850 MAMAIA.** Rm/Ru 1930; C; 4000; 112 × 7.3 (366 × 24); M; 11; ex FRIEDRICH ENGELS 1962.

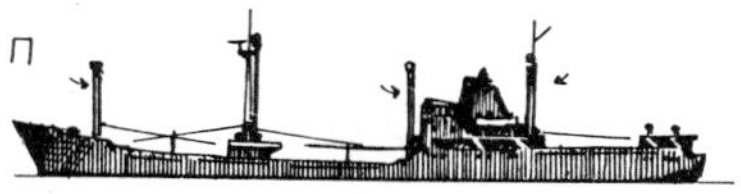

KMKFM H13

13860 TARA. Gr/FRG 1961; CP; 4000; 108 × 7.5 (354 × 24.4); M; 15; ex VARYKINO ADVENTURER 1970; ex PRINS MAURITS 1969.

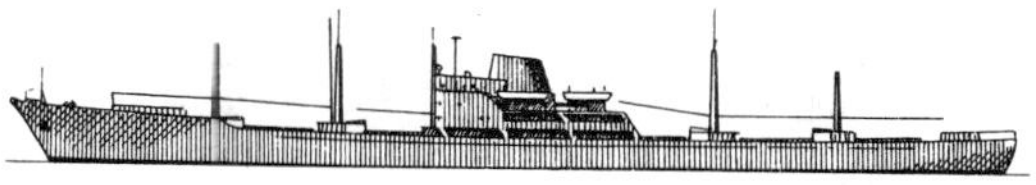

KMKFMK H1

13870 MING GIANT. Tw/Tw 1963; PC; 9800; 160 × 9.5 (525 × 31.3); M; 18; ex JING MING 1979; ex HAI CHIEN 1973; ex TAI SUN. Sister: **13871 MING CHALLENGER** (Tw) ex CHAO MING 1979; ex HAI HSIN 1973.

KMKFMK H1

13880 UNITED CONQUEST. Pa/Ja 1951; C; 6500; 153.4 × 8.2 (503 × 27); M; 16; ex TASMAN CAREER 1980; ex ACAPULCO MARU 1974; ex KYOEI MARU 1967.

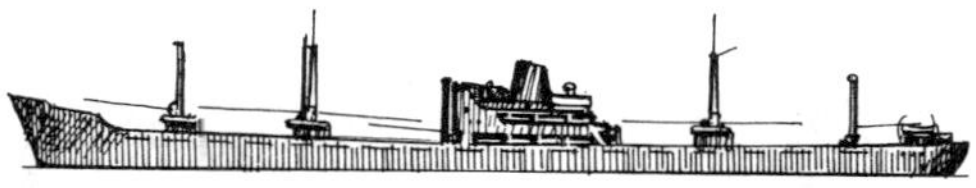

KMKFMK H1

13890 LUCIDITY. Li/FRG 1957; CP; 10600; 159 × 9.6 (522 × 31.6); M; 14; ex ARISTOFANIS 1974; ex TRAJAN 1970. Sisters: **13891 SILVER CITY** (Gr) ex ARISTOKLIS 1976; ex NUMERIAN 1970 **13892 ARISTOFILOS** (Gr) ex JUSTINIAN 1970 **13893 LAZULI** (Li) ex ARISTON 1975; ex GORDIAN 1971 **13894 LAERTIS** (Gr) ex CHIOS 1972 **13895 PANAGHIA LOURION** (Li) ex HADJITSAKOS 1972.

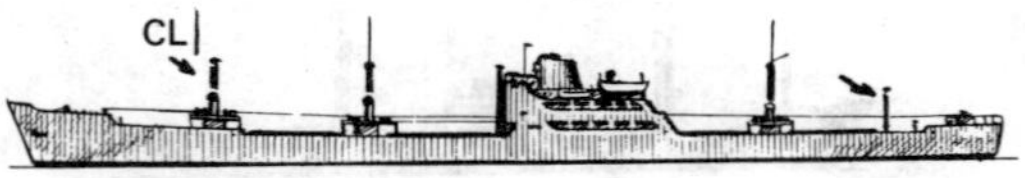

KMKFMK H1

13900 HYDRA GLAMOUR. Gr/Ja 1957; C; 7700/10100; 157.89 × —/9.63 (518 × —/31.59); T; 14.5; ex ARTA 1975; ex ATLANTIC SUN 1973. Sisters: **13901 HYDRA GLORY** (Gr) ex FLORINA 1975; ex LIBRA 1973; ex HAI TSUNG 1970; ex KALYMNOS 1961; ex ANDROS GLORY 1960 **13902 DON QUIXOTE** (Pa) ex PACIFIC HORIZON 1976; ex PYGMALION STAR 1976; ex SOVEREIGN DIAMOND 1975; ex ATTICOS 1974; ex SOUTHERN SUNRISE 1972; ex ATLANTIC SUNRISE 1972 **13903 ARAGON** (Cy) ex VALLE DE PICADURA 1977; ex IONICON 1974; ex IOANNIS 1972; ex NORTHERN SUNLIGHT 1964; ex ATLANTIC SUNLIGHT 1963.

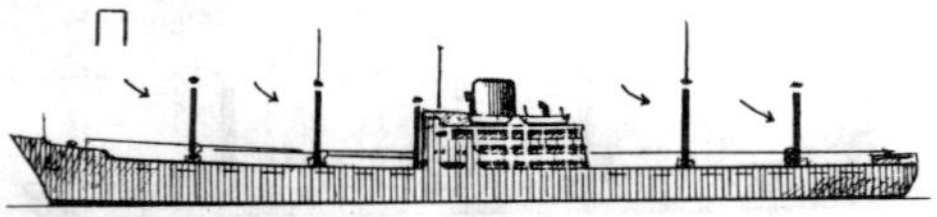

KMKFMK H1

● **13920 SWAN RIVER.** Ja/Ja 1951; C; 8200; 144.1 × 8.8 (473 × 28.7); M; 15.5; ex CHIEH TENG 1976; ex TARPONA 1974; ex ANDES MARU 1972; Converted to Livestock Carrier. Probably altered in appearance. Sister: **13921 CHIEH TEH** (Pa) ex STRONA 1974; ex ATLAS MARU 1972.

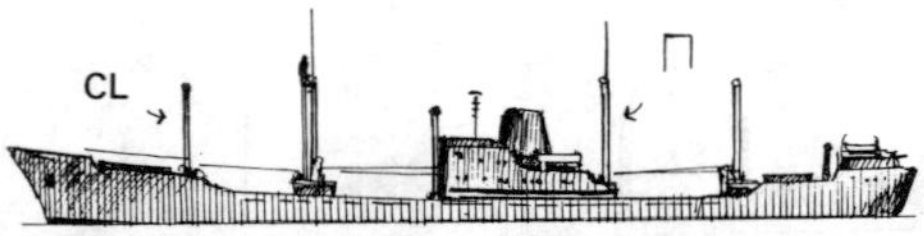

KMKFMK H13

⋆**13950 USKOK.** Ys/FRG 1961; C; 7400; 139.3 × 8.8 (457 × 29.6); M; 14.5; ex SILETTA 1968.

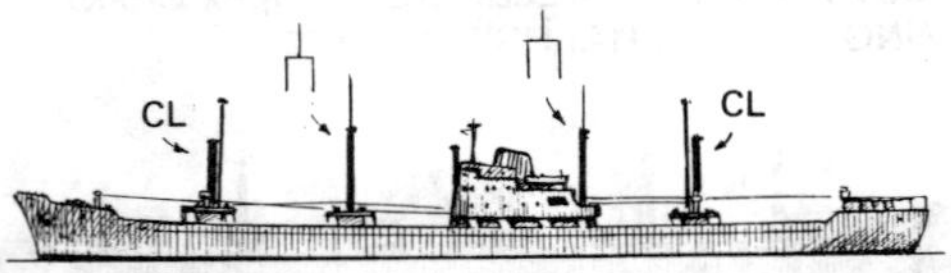

KMKFMK H13

⋆**13960 BAR.** Ys/Fr 1956; CP; 6300/8700; 145 × —/9.3 (475 × —/30.6); M; 14; ex ROALD AMUNDSEN 1968.

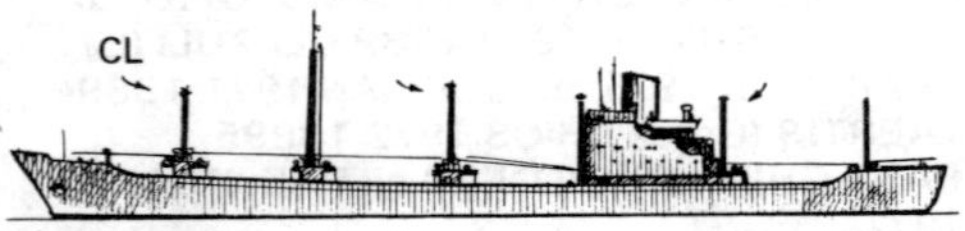

KMK$_2$FK$_2$ H13

● **13980 BUCHENSTEIN.** FRG/FRG 1958; CP; 6200/8500; 147 × 7.8/9 (482 × 25.6/29.4); M; 17.5. Sisters: **13981 BURGENSTEIN** (FRG) **13982 SANDRA S** (Pa) ex BUNTENSTEIN 1980.

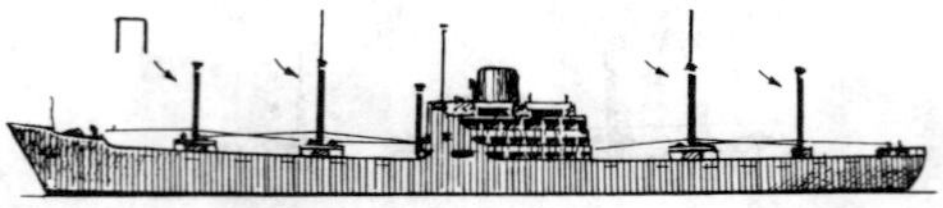

KMKFMK H1

● **13910 ORIENT LONDON.** Pa/Ja 1953; C; 8000; 144.3 × 8.8 (477 × 28.9); M; 15.5; ex OCEANIC LONDON; ex LONDON MARU 1972. Similar (Pole masts. After KP on House): **13911 GOLDEN SKY** (Pa) ex PHILIPPINE MARU 1977; **13912 VICTORY QUEEN** (Pa) ex EURYCHILI 1977; ex CHIEH HUI 1975; ex OCEANIC SUEZ 1973; ex SUEZ MARU 1972 **13913 UNION NEW YORK** (Pa) ex MONTEVIDEO MARU.

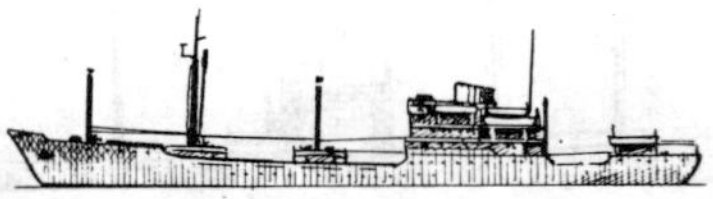

KMKFMK H123

13930 MALDIVE UNITY Mv/Ne 1954; PC; 4100; 110 × 6.7 (360 × 22.1); M; 14.5; ex HOUTMAN 1972.

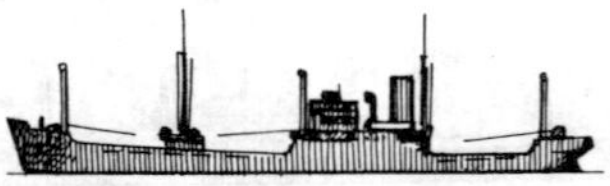

KMKFMK H123

13940 GUATARI. Ho/Br 1936; C; 2300; 102 × 6.8 (335 × 22.5); M; 9.5; ex GAMBALI 1979; ex GOLDEN DRAGON 1969; ex PRIMAL PROSPERITY 1968; ex MIRANDA 1968; ex CAROLINA 1967; ex KAURI 1963.

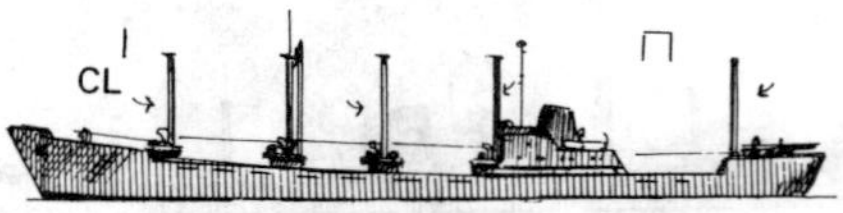

KMK$_2$FK H13

13970 SAO PAULO. Gr/No 1959; CP; 3700/5900; 127 × 6.9/7.2 (416 × 22.6/23.6); M; 15.5; ex FERNWAVE 1970.

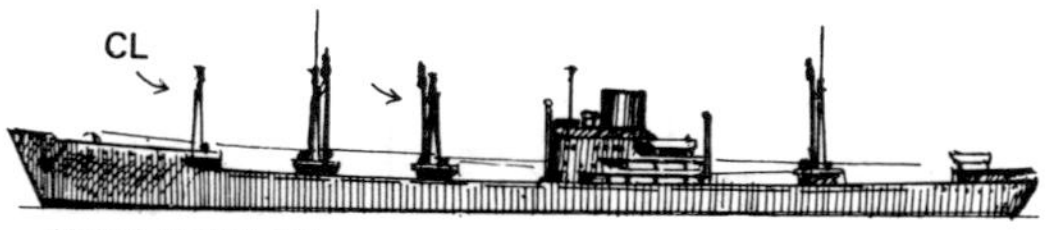

KMK_2FKM H1
● **13990 KOTA JASA.** Sg/Ne 1957; CP; 6800/9600; 161 × 8/8.9 (529 × 26/29.3); M; 18; ex NEDLLOYD MARNE 1980; ex MARNE LLOYD 1977. Sisters: **13991 GADING** (Pa) ex NEDLLOYD MERWE 1979; ex MERWE LLOYD 1977 **13992 KOTA SENTOSA** (Sg) ex NEDLLOYD MUSI; ex MUSI LLOYD 1978 **13993 NGOMEI CHAU** (Pa) ex NEDLLOYD MAAS 1979;ex MAAS LLOYD 1977 **13994 CHEUNG CHAU** (Pa) ex NEDLLOYD MERSEY 1979; ex MERSEY LLOYD 1977 **13995 GULUNGAN** (Pa) ex NEDLLOYD MISSISSIPPI 1979; ex MISSISSIPPI LLOYD 1977.

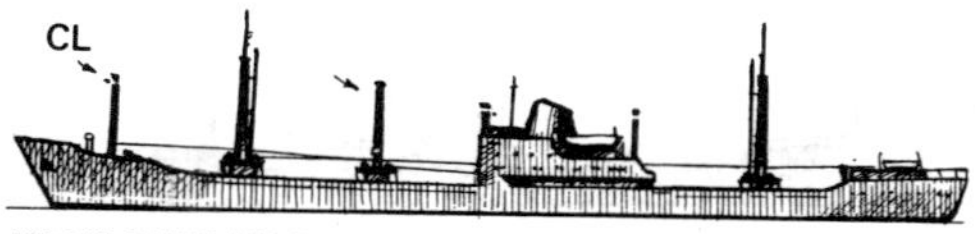

KMK_2FKM H13
● **14000 CONCORDIA VIKING.** Br/Sw 1960; CP; 6900; 150.8 × 8.8 (495 × 28.11); M; 17.

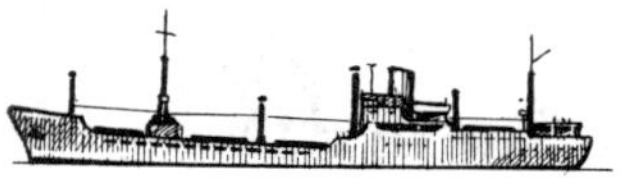

KMK_2FKM H13
● **14010 VOUNITSO.** Gr/It 1948; C; 2400; 93.2 × 5.6 (306 × 18.5); M; 12; ex KARTERADO 1976; ex NORDHEIDE 1973; ex GARNES 1966.

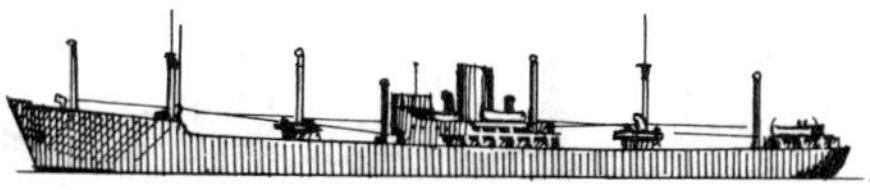

KMK_2FKMK H1
14020 FELICITY. Gr/De 1950; CP; 5300; 136 × 7.9 (446 × 25.10); M; 15; ex IOANNA 1971; ex LEOVILLE 1967.

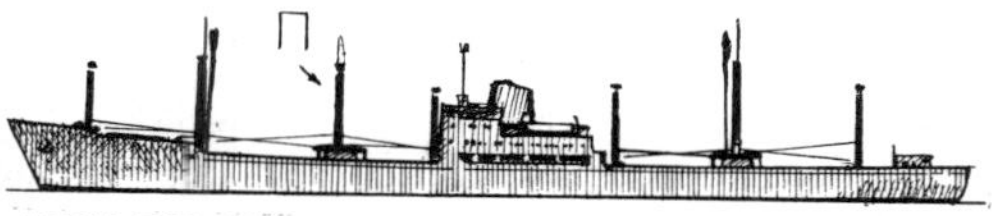

KMK_2FKMK H1
14030 HELLENIC HERO. Gr/Ja 1957; CP; 7100/10300; 152 × 8.3/9.5 (499 × 27/31.6); M; 16. Sister: **14031 HELLENIC SPIRIT** (Gr).

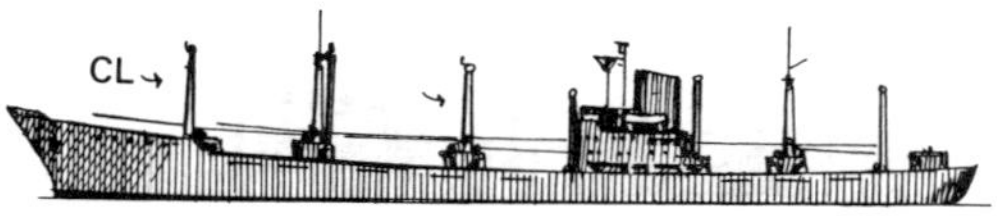

KMK_2FKMK H12
14040 REGENSTEIN. Sg/FRG 1960; CP; 9700; 161 × 9.3 (527 × 30.6); M; 17.5. Sister: **14041 RIEDERSTEIN** (Sg).

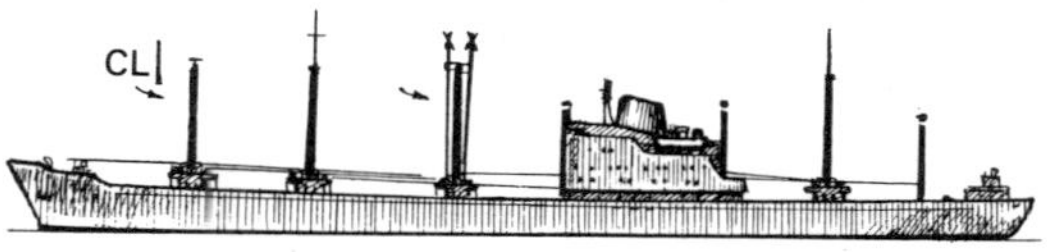

KMK_2FKMK H1
★**14050 HONG YIN.** RC/FRG 1960; CP; 7000/9900; 162 × 8/9 (533 × 26/30); M; 18.5; ex OSTFRIESLAND 1979; ex NEUHARLINGERSIEL 1970. Sister: ★**14051 DE YIN** (RC) ex ELBELAND 1979.

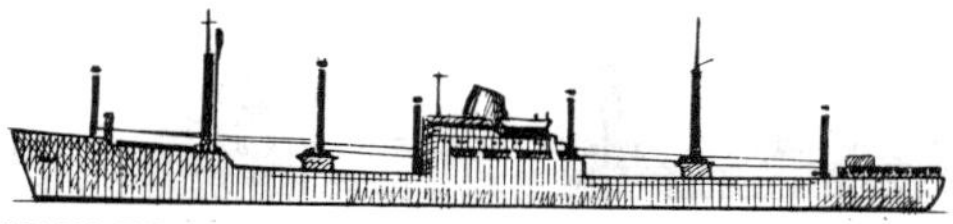

KMK_2FKMK H12
14060 JODY. Pa/Sw 1960; CP; 6000; 148 × 8.2 (484 × 26.8); M; 17.5; ex BLACK OSPREY 1976. Sister: **14061 NISSOS MYKONOS** (Gr) ex BLACK SWAN 1976.

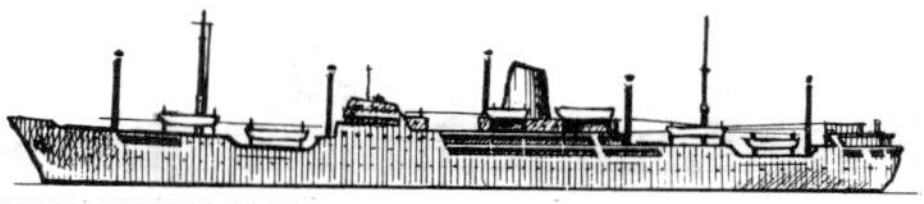

KMK_2FKMK H12
14070 SAFINA—E—ARAB. Pk/Sp 1962; CP; 8500; 141 × 7 (461 × 23.1); M; 15.

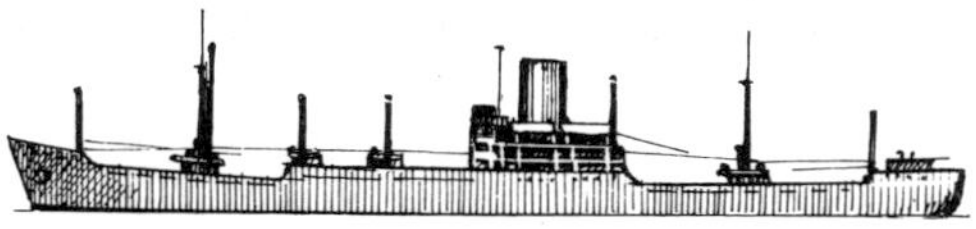

KMK_2FKMK H123
14080 EUROPE II. Gr/Br 1960; C; 6000/8200; 150.8 × 7.1/8.8 (495 × 23.3/28.10); M; 16.5; ex OPOBO 1979; ex RHEXENOR 1977; ex MARON 1975. Sisters (Gr flag): **14081 EUROPE** ex OWERRI 1979; ex STENTOR 1977; ex MEMNON 1975 **14082 ANNOULA II** ex MELAMPUS 1975.

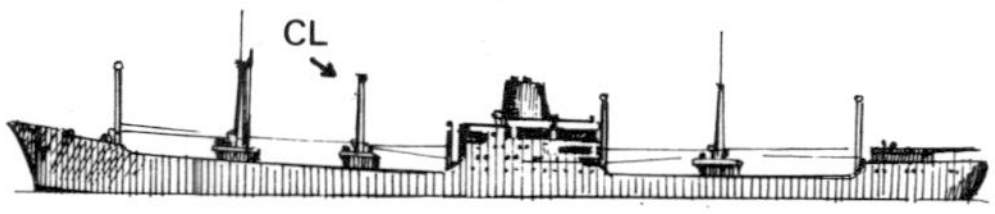

KMK_2FKMK H123
14090 OCEAN DIAMOND. Pa/Ne 1958; CP; 6900/9300; 154.2 × 8.1/9.4 (506 × 26.9/31); M; —; ex STRAAT MAGELHAEN 1979. Sisters: **14091 NEW SWAN** (Sg) ex NEDLLOYD RIO 1979; ex STRAAT RIO 1977 **14092 NEW DOVE** (Pa) ex WIN DOVE 1979; ex NEDLLOYD VAN DIEMEN 1979; ex STRAAT VAN DIEMEN 1974.

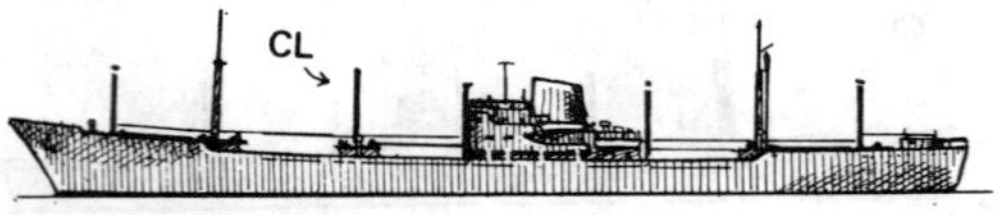

KMK_2FKMK H13
14100 RITA MAERSK. Li/De 1955; C; 6400; 152×8.5 (499×28); M; 18.5. Sister: **14101 SUSAN MAERSK** (Li).

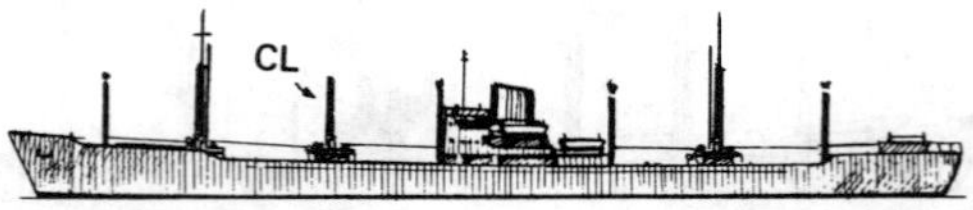

KMK_2FKMK H13
● **14110 LEDA MAERSK.** Li/De 1957; C; 6400; 151.54×8.36 (497.18×27.43); M; 17.5; Sold 1981.

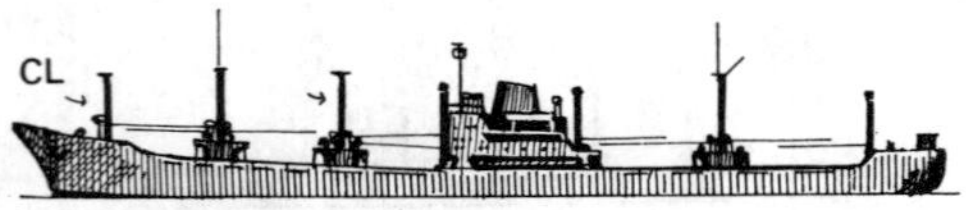

KMK_2FKMK H13
14120 ATTIKOS. Gr/FRG 1957; CP; 6500; 149.4×9 (490×29.3); M; 16; ex LOVERSUN 1977; ex LOPPERSUM 1974.

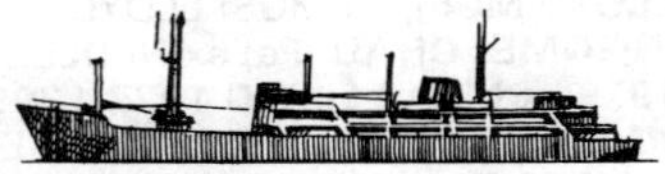

KMK_2FM H1
14130 YARA. Si/Au 1962; PC; 4100; 98.7×5.5 (334×18.2); M; 13; ex HONG KONG FIR 1974; ex KANGAROO 1973.

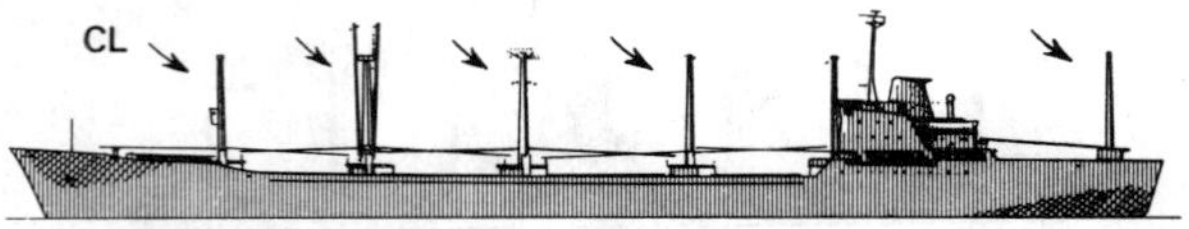

KMK_3MKF H13
14140 HOEGH OPAL. No/Fi 1967/75; C; 8200/12100; 182.61×8.05/9.4 (599.11×26.41/30.84); M; 17; lengthened 1975. Sisters (No flag): **14141 HOEGH ORCHID 14142 HOEGH ORRIS** Similar (taller funnel, etc.): **14143 HOEGH PILOT 14144 HOEGH PRIDE.**

KMK_2MFK H1
14150 CABO SANTA ANA. Sp/Ne 1961; C; 6200/8500; 144.2×8.1/8.8 (473×26.9/29); M; 16; ex KATENDRECHT 1974.

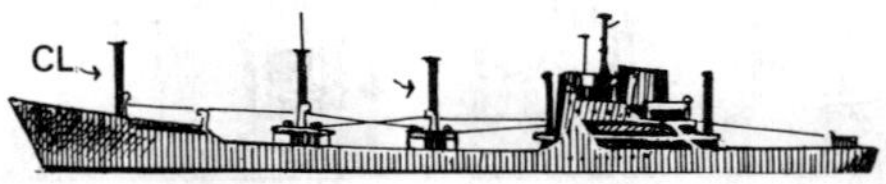

KMK_2MFK H1
14160 NAKORNTHON. Th/Br 1964; CP; 4400/6500; 134.1×7.2 /8 (440×23.8/26.7); M; 16; ex THONBURI 1973; ex HALIFAX CITY 1972.

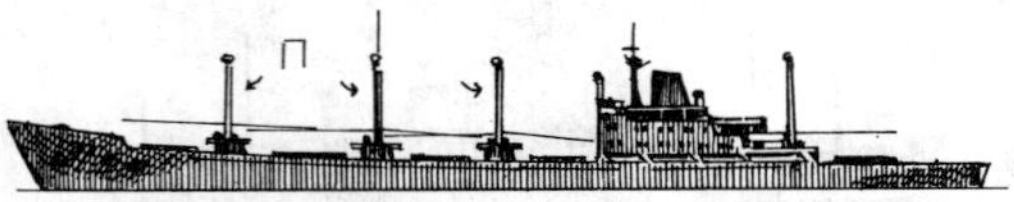

KMK_2MFK H1
14170 MORILLO. FRG/No 1971; R; 6900/9700; 155.8×8.6/9.2 (511×28.2/33); M; 22. Sisters: **14171 ATLANTIC OCEAN** (Li) ex TANGELO 1976 **14172 BRUNSLAND** (FRG) ex MARANGA 1976 **14173 CARINTHIA** (Br) ex CANTALOUP 1976 **14174 CARMANIA** (Br) ex ORANGE 1976 **14175 CHERRY** (FRG).

KMK_2MFK H1
14180 SAFOCEAN WELTEVREDEN. SA/Ne 1966; Pt.Con; 9000/12400; 192.2×—/9.1 (631×—/30); M; 21; ex S.A. WELTEVREDEN 1977; Lengthened 1975. Drawing shows ships before lengthening. Sister: **14181 SAFOCEAN NEDERBURG** (SA) ex S.A. NEDERBURG 1980.

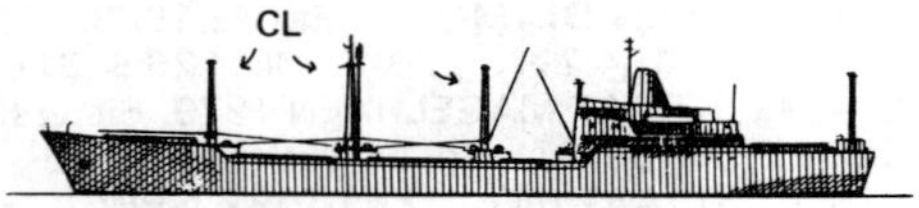

KMK_2MFK H13
● **14190 PEGASUS.** Gr/FRG 1969; C; 4500; 133.4×7.4 (438×24.4); M; 17.5; ex LOUISIANE 1980; ex HORNMEER 1975. Sisters (FRG flag): **14191 HORNGOLF 14192 HORNWIND.**

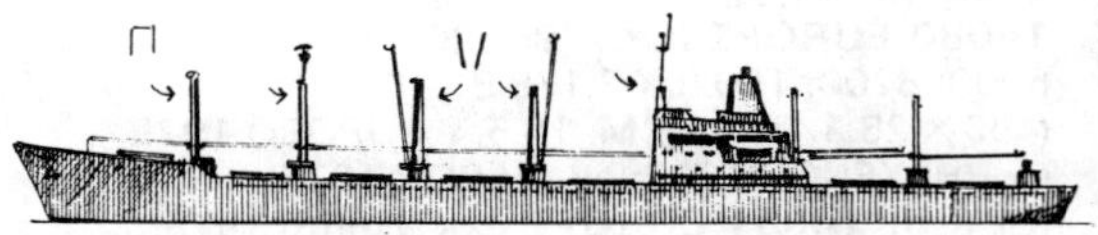

KMK_2MFK_2 H1
14200 SANTA BARBARA. US/US 1967; PtCon; 9300; 170.7×9.3 (560×36); T; 20; ex DELTA BOLIVIA 1980; ex SANTA BARBARA 1979. Sisters (US flag): **14201 SANTA ELENA** ex DELTA PANAMA 1980; ex SANTA ELENA 1979 **14202 SANTA CLARA** ex DELTA COLUMBIA 1980; ex SANTA CLARA 1979 **14203 SANTA CRUZ** ex DELTA ECUADOR 1980; ex SANTA CRUZ 1979 **14204 SANTA LUCIA** ex DELTA VENEZUELA 1980; ex SANTA LUCIA 1979 **14205 SANTA ISABEL** ex DELTA PERU 1980; ex SANTA ISABEL 1979.

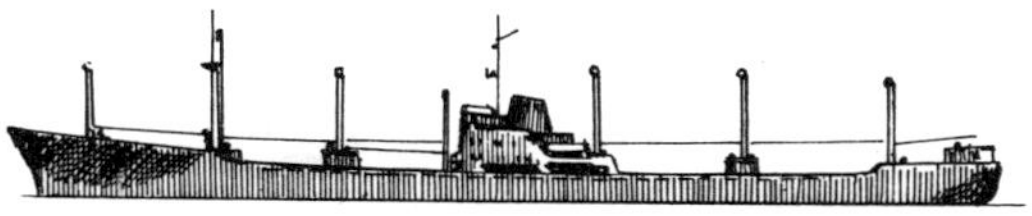

KMK$_2$MFK$_3$ H13
14210 CERAM SEA. Pa/Br 1958; CP; 5600/9900; 155.8 × 8.3/9.2 (511 × 27.3/30.3); M; 17; ex FERNSTATE 1976.

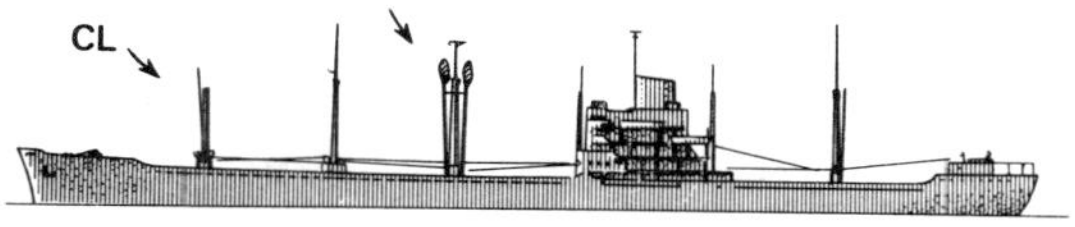

KMK$_2$MFKM H13
14220 SINKAI. Pa/Ne 1953; C; 8000/10500; 161.8 × 8.39/9.14 (530.84 × 27.53/29.99); M; 16.5; ex KARIMUN 1972.

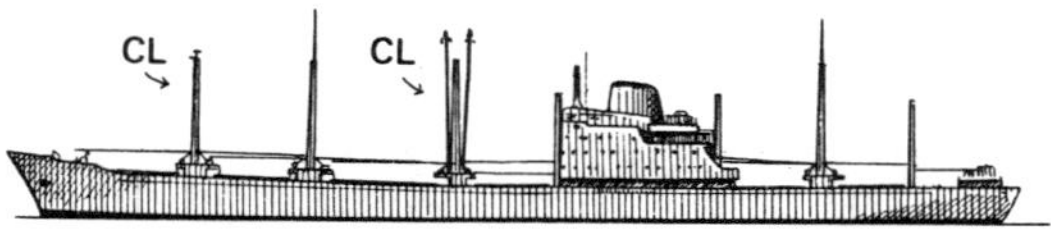

KMK$_2$MFKMK H1
⋆**14230 HONG YIN.** RC/FRG 1960; CP; 7000/9900; 162 × 8/9 (533 × 26/30); M; 18.5; ex OSTRIESLAND 1979. Sister: ⋆**14231 DE YIN** (RC) ex ELBELAND 1979.

KMK$_2$MFKMK H13
14240 JADE. Cy/De 1956; C; 6500; 149.69 × 8.4 (491.12 × 27.56); M; 17.25; ex STAR ANTARES 1980; ex SOLHOLT 1963; ex IVARAN 1962.

KMKM H
● **14250 NAKWA.** Gh/Ja 1964; ST; 2000; 79.5 × — (261 × —); M; 14.5.

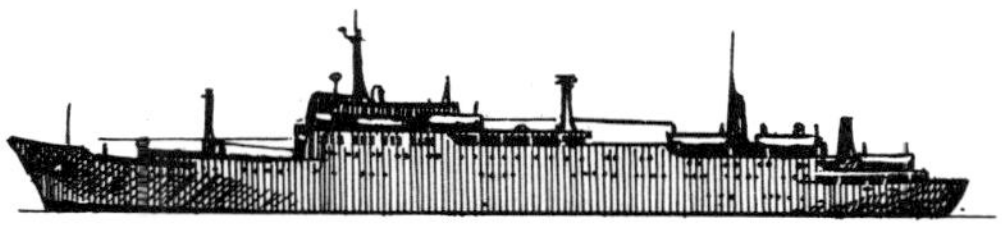

KMKMF H
14260 SAKURA. Ja/Ja 1962; PC; 12500; 157 × 8.6 (516 × 28.3); M; 17; ex SAKURA MARU 1972.

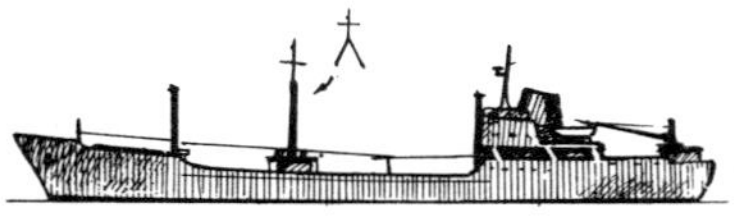

KMKMFC H13
14270 KWANGCHOW. Pa/De 1963; CP; 2300; 110 × 4.7 (362 × 15.6); M; 15; ex FRONTIER 1980; ex CRUSADER 1969.

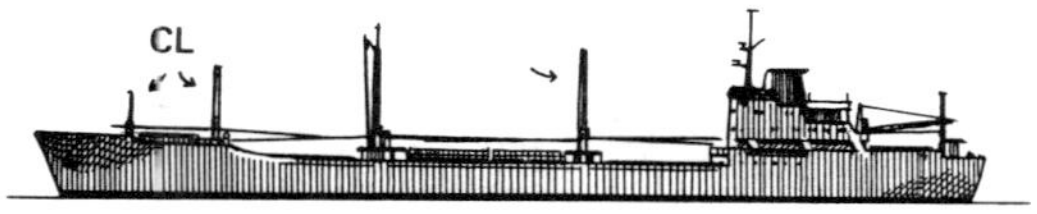

KMKMFCK H13
● **14280 POYANG.** Br/Fi 1964; CP; 8700; 152 × 8.6 (500 × 28.7); M; 16; ex ASIAN EXPORTER 1975; ex FINNBOSTON 1973; ex FINNENSO 1974. Similar: **14281 CORDILLERA** (Pa) ex FINNARROW 1980; ex VISAHOLM 1976; ex FINNARROW 1971 **14282 CORRAL** (Pa) ex MAH 1980; ex FINNENSO 1980 **14283 FERNANDOEVERETT** (Li) ex FINNHAWK 1980; ex MALTESHOLM 1976; ex FINNHAWK 1971 **14284 CONDOR** (Ch) ex PALLADIA 1980; ex FINNMAID 1979.

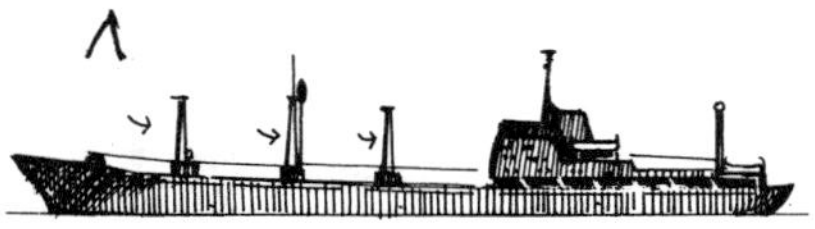

KMKMFK H
● **14290 KRYSTINA F.** Br/Pd 1958; CP; 3400; 124 × 6.5 (407 × 21.4); M; 14.5; ex KRYNICA 1979; **'B55'** type. Sisters (Pd flag): ⋆**14291 OLESNICA** ⋆**14292 POLANICA.**

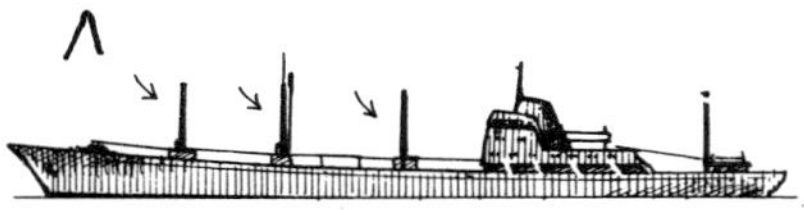

KMKMFK H
● ⋆**14300 BRODNICA.** Pd/Pd 1961; CP; 3400; 124 × 6.5 (407 × 21.4); M; 15.5; **'B55'** type. Sisters (Pd flag): ⋆**14301 BYDGOSZCZ** ⋆**14302 JAN ZIZKA** ⋆**14303 KRUSZWICA** ⋆**14304 SWIDNICA** ⋆**14305 SZCZAWNICA** ⋆**14306 WISLICA** (Gr flag): **14307 GIORGOS** ex LEGNICA 1980.

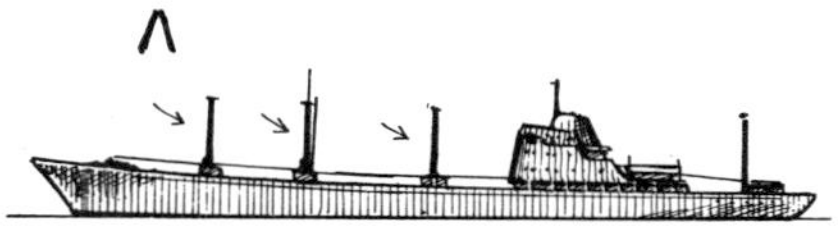

KMKMFK H
14310 CABO DE SAO ROQUE. Bz/Pd 1959; C; 3200/4600; 124 × 6.5/— (407 × 21.4/—); M; 15; **'B 55'** type. Sisters (Bz flag): **14311 CABO DE SANTA MARTA 14312 CABO FRIO.**

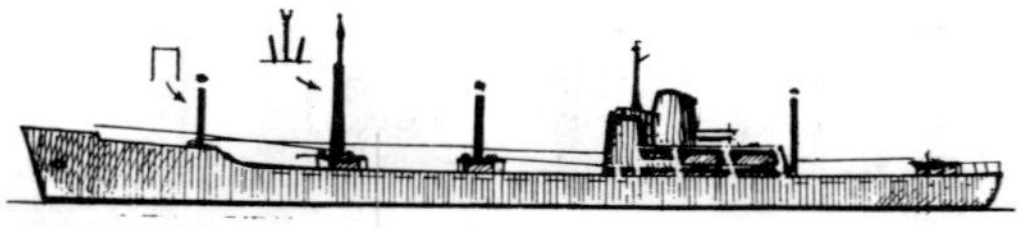

KMKMFK H1
14320 JALARASHMI. In/Br 1966; C; 11300; 160 × 9.4 (525 × 31); M; 16. Similar (stulcken masts): **14321 JALARAJAN** (In) **14322 JALARATNA** (In).

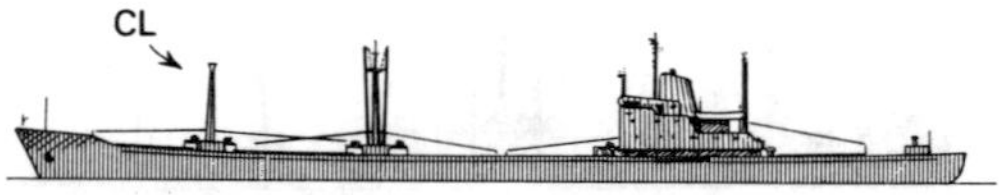

KMKMFK H1
● **14340 TILLY RUSS.** FRG/FRG 1967/74; C; 5200; 151.47 × 7.27/8.03 (496.95 × 23.85/26.35); M; 17.75; lengthened 1974. Sister: **14341 PAMPANA** (Pa) ex PAUL LORENZ RUSS 1979.

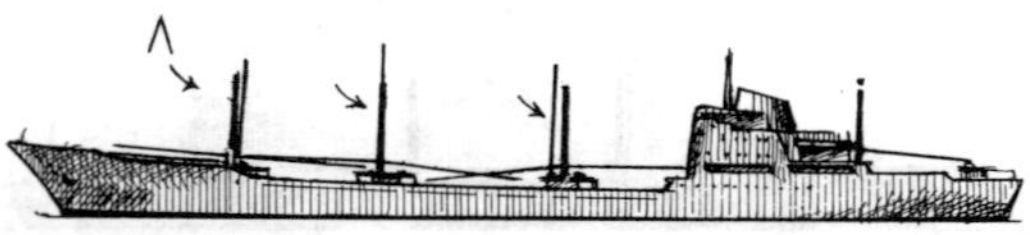

KMKMFK H13
● ⋆**14370 PULA.** Ru/Ys 1964; C; 8000/10100; 160 × /9.7 (525 × 26/32); M; 18. Sisters (Ru flag): ⋆**14371 ALEKSANDR BLOK** ⋆**14372 ALEKSANDR GERTSEN** ⋆**14373 ALEKSANDR GRIN** ⋆**14374 ALEKSANDR SERAFIMOVIC** ⋆**14375 ALEKSANDR VERMISHEV** ⋆**14376 ALISHER NAVOI** ⋆**14377 ANTON CHEKOV** ⋆**14378 ARKADY GAYDAR** ⋆**14379 DEMYAN BEDNYY** ⋆**14380 DMITRIY GULIA** ⋆**14381 DUBROVNIK** ⋆**14382 GAVRIIL DERZHAVIN** ⋆**14383 MAKHTUM-KULI** ⋆**14384 MUSA DZHALIL** ⋆**14384 NAZIM KHIKMET** ⋆**14386 NIKOLAY DUBROLYUBOV** ⋆**14387 NIKOLAY GOGOL** ⋆**14388 NIKOLAY KARAMZIM** ⋆**14389 NIKOLAY OGARYEV** ⋆**14390 OVANES TUMANYAN** ⋆**14391 SERGEY YESENIN** ⋆**14392 SULEYMAN STALSKIY** ⋆**14393 VISSARION BELINSKIY** ⋆**14394 VLADIMIR KOROLENKO** ⋆**14395 VLADIMIR MAYAKOVSKIY.**

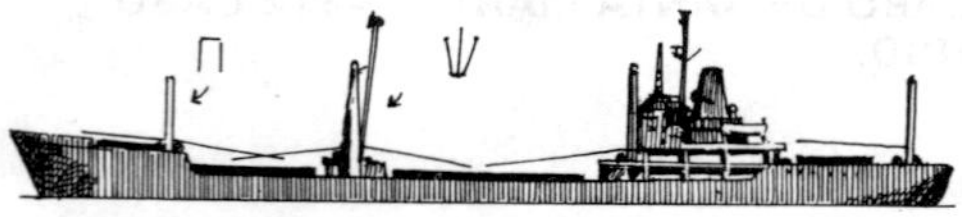

KMKMFK H13
14410 MACASSAR MARU. Ja/Ja 1970; C; 9400; 150 × 9 (492 × 29.11); M; 16.

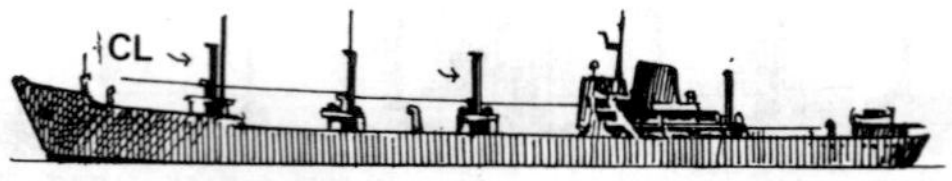

KMKMFK H1
● **14330 MARVALIENTE.** Ar/Br 1962; C; 6100/8300; 143 × 8.1/9 (470 × 26/29); M; —; ex BAXTERGATE 1972; ex MEDIATOR 1972; ex BAXTERGATE 1971.

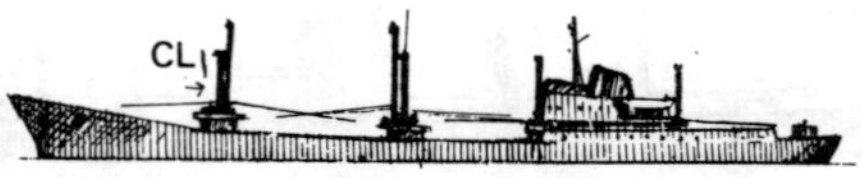

KMKMFK H1
14350 ATLANTICO. Sp/Br 1967; C; 4400/6400; 131.7.3/8.5 (430 × 23.6/28); M; 17.5; ex LUISE 1975; ex LUISE BORNHOFEN 1973.

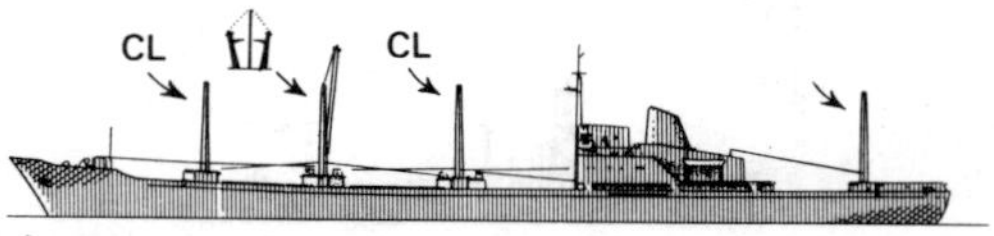

KMKMFK H1
● **14360 RIO CALCHAQUI.** Ar/Ar 1970; C; 10400; 152.71 × 8.68 (501.02 × 28.48); M; 17.5. Sisters (Ar flag): **14361 RIO DE LA PLATA 14362 RIO IGUAZU 14363 RIO PARANA 14364 RIO GUALEGUAY.**

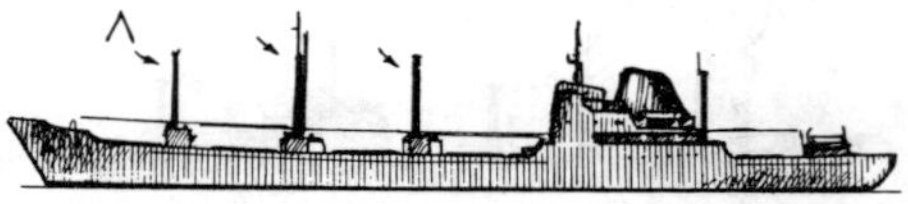

KMKMFK H13
● **14400 MAZZINI.** It/No 1966; C; 4500; 141 × 7.4 (463 × 24.5); M; 19; ex ALBERTA 1972. Sisters: **14401 ZANET** (Gr) ex MICHIGAN 1980 **14402 LABRADOR** (De) **14403 MARHABA** (In) ex ONTARIO 1979 **14404 CRISPI** (It) ex WISCONSIN 1972 **14405 D'AZEGLIO** (It) ex NEBRASKA 1972.

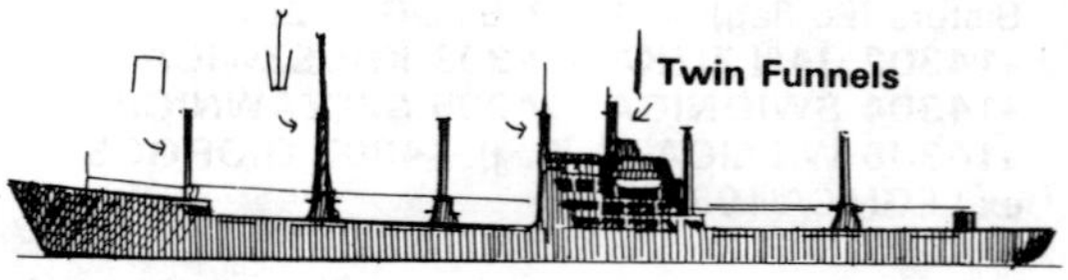

KMKMFK$_2$ H1
14420 ELIZABETH LYKES. US/US 1966; CP; 7400/11000; 165 × 8.5/10 (542 × 28/33); T; 20. Sisters (US flag): **14421 DOLLY TURMAN 14422 FREDERICK LYKES 14423 GENEVIEVE LYKES 14424 HOWELL LYKES 14425 LETITIA LYKES 14426 LOUISE LYKES 14427 MALLORY LYKES 14428 MASON LYKES 14429 RUTH LYKES 14430 STELLA LYKES 14431 VELMA LYKES.**

$KMKMFK_2$ H1
14440 EPAPHUS. Gr/Sw 1958; CP; 4700/7200; 134 × 7.6/9 (438 × 25/30); M; 16; ex IO 1980; ex KUNGSHAMN 1977; ex MARGARETA BRODIN 1971; ex RHODOS 1966; ex OTTO BANCK 1963.

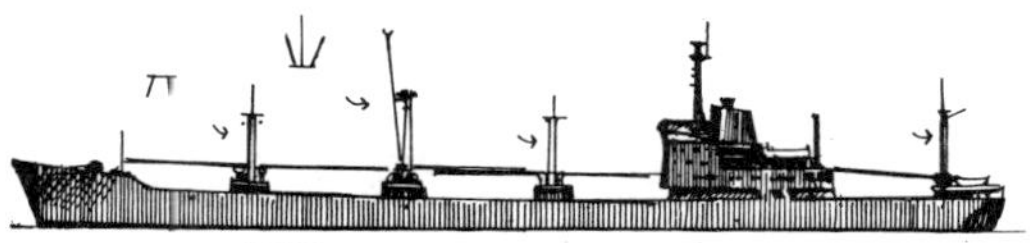

$KMKMFK_2$ H1
★**14450 IGNATIY SERGEYEV.** Ru/Pd 1968; C; 10200; 154.5 × 9.5 (507 × 29.6); M; 16.5; **'B40/B401'** type **'KOMMUNIST'** class. Similar (Ru flag): ★**14451 GEORGIY CHICHERIN** ★**14452 GEORGIY DMITROV** ★**14453 ERNST THALMANN** ★**14454 GIUSEPPE DI VITTORIO** ★**14455 50 LET SOVIETSKOY UKRAINY** ★**14456 HO CHI MIN** ★**14457 INESSA ARMAND** ★**14458 IONA YAKIR** ★**14459 JEANNE LABOURBE** ★**14460 KARL LIEBKNECHT** ★**14461 KOMMUNIST** ★**14462 KOMMUNISTICHESKOYE-ZNAMYA** ★**14463 BELA KHUN** ★**14464 DMITRY POLUYAN** ★**14465 NIKOLAY KREMLYANSKIY** ★**14466 FRIEDRICH ENGELS** ★**14467 ROSA LUXEMBURG** ★**14468 FRANTS BOGUSH** ★**14469 TOYVO ANTIKAYNEN** (Tu flag); (B442 type): **14470 GENERAL A. F. CEBESOY 14471 GENERAL K. ORBAY 14472 GENERAL R. GUMUSBALA 14473 GENERAL Z. DOGAN** (Pd flag): ★**14474 KONIN.**

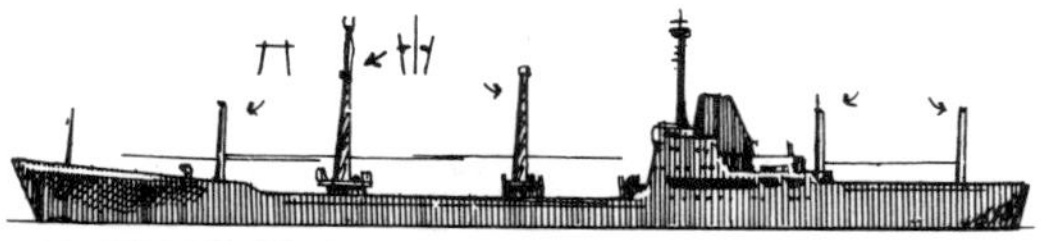

$KMKMFK_2$ H13
● ★**14480 FRANCISZEK ZUBRZYCKI.** Pd/Pd 1973; Con; 7200/10100; 161 × —/9.7 (529 × —/32); M; 21; **'B438'** type. Sisters (Pd flag): ★**14481 ALEKSANDR RYLKE** ★**14482 BRONISLAW LACHOWICZ** ★**14483 EUGENIUSZ KWIATKOWSKI** ★**14484 MIECZYSLAW KAUNOWSKI** ★**14485 ROMAN PAZINSKI** ★**14486 TADEUSZ OCIOSZYNSKI** Possible Sister: ★**14487 GENERAL STANISLAW POPLAWSKI** (Ec flag): **14488 ISLA SANTAY 14489 ISLA BALTRA** (Bz flag): **14491 CANTUARIA 14492 CALANDRINI.**

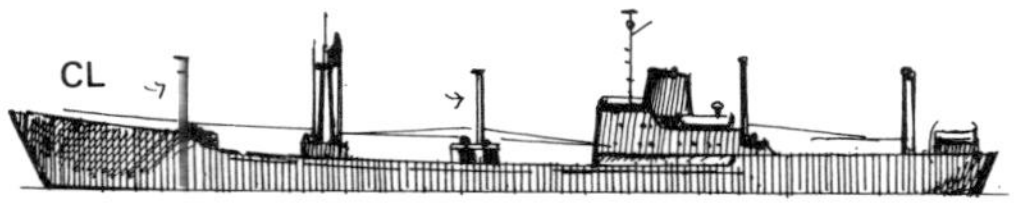

$KMKMFK_2$ H13
★**14500 LU CHENG.** RC/FRG 1966; CP; 10500; 156 × 9.2 (509 × 30.6); M; 19; ex S.A. TUGELALAND 1980; ex TUGELALAND 1974; ex CONCORDIA LAND 1973; ex TUGELND 1972.

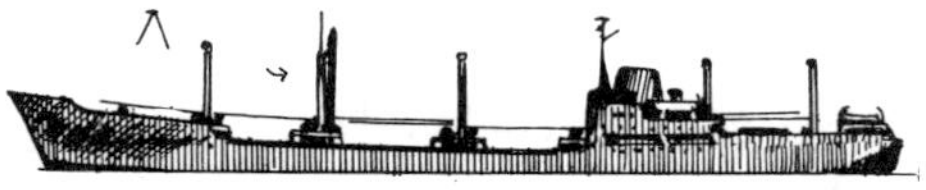

$KMKMFK_2$ H13
14510 SAUDI CROWN. Si/Sw 1962; C; 5300/7900; 141 × 7.8/8.8 (462 × 25.9/29); M; 16.5; ex SAUDI KING 1979; ex LENA CHRISTINA BRODIN 1965. Sister: **14511 ATROMITOS** (Gr) ex KARONGA 1979; ex LISA BRODIN 1965.

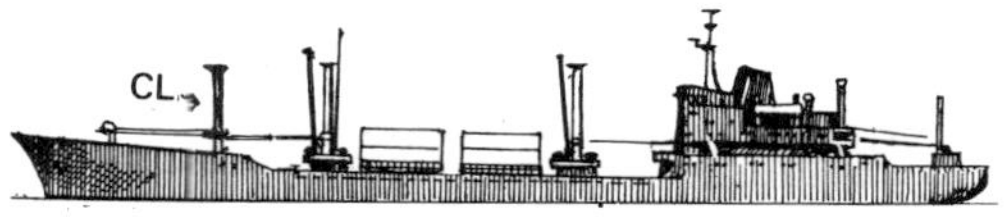

$KMKMFK_2$ H13
● **14520 FINNCLIPPER.** Fi/FRG 1962; Con; 6500 88800; 150 × 7/8.5 (493 × 23/28); M; 16; Converted from cargo ships and lengthened 1968. Sisters (Fi flag): **14521 FINNFOREST 14522 FINNEAGLE** ex TROLLEHOLM 1976; ex FINNEAGLE 1971.

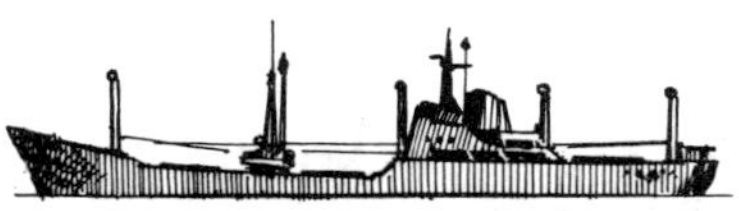

$KMKMFK_2$ H13
14530 DEXTER. Cy/FRG 1962; C; 2700; 108 × 7.5 (355 × 24.6); M; 15; ex LAMA 1979; ex LARA VIKING 1973; ex CONCORDIA LARA 1971; ex LARA VIKING 1970; ex SVANEFJELL 1969. Sisters (Po flag); **14531 CABO BOJADOR** ex FRIGOARTICO 1971; ex ALDENBURG 1968 **14532 CABO VERDE** ex SIREFJELL 1971.

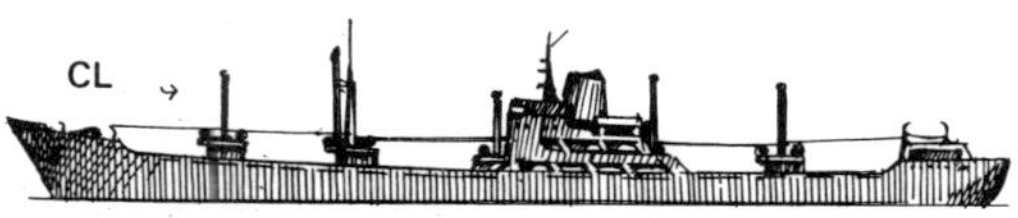

$KMKMFK_2$ H13
● ★**14540 DONG PING.** RC/Br 1962; C; 7500/9700; 159 × 8.4/9.4 (502 × 27.6/31); M; —; ex NORWEGIAN SEA 1976; ex SALIMIAH 1973; ex CLARKFORTH 1965. Sister: **14541 FLORA C** (Gr) ex JOLI 1976; ex ALDERMINSTER 1975; ex KINGS REACH 1970; ex PORT CAMPBELL 1966; ex CLARKSPEY 1961.

$KMKMFK_3$ H1
● **14550 MORMACGLEN.** US/US 1961; CP; 6600/9300; 147 × —/9.6 (483 × —/31.4); T; 19. Sisters (US flag): **14551 MORMACCAPE 14552 MORMACTRADE 14553 BAY** ex MORMACBAY 1977 **14554 COVE** ex MORMACCOVE 1977 **14555 LAKE** ex MORMACLAKE 1977 **14556 PRIDE** ex MORMACPRIDE 1977 **14557 SCAN** ex MORMACSCAN 1977.

$KMKMFK_2MK$ H123
● **14560 ANASSA.** Cy/Br 1953; C; 5400/7600; 148.5 × 7.35/8.65 (487.2 × 24.11/28.38); M; —; ex ADRASTUS 1978. Sisters: ⋆**14561 HONG QI 119** (RC) ex HUNGMIEN 1977; ex DOLIUS 1972; ex GLENFRUIN 1972; ex DOLIUS 1978 ⋆**14562 HONG QI 137** (RC) ex HUNGSIA; ex DEMODOCUS 1973; ex GLENROY 1972; ex DEMODOCUS 1970 **14563 KAIGO** (Pa) ex DARANUS 1972; ex ACHILLES 1972 **14564 KAILOCK** (Pa) ex DEUCALION 1973; ex AJAX 1972 **14565 KAISING** (Pa) ex DIOMED 1973; ex GLENBEG 1972; ex DIOMED 1970 **14566 NIKOS** (Gr) ex AGAPENOR 1975.

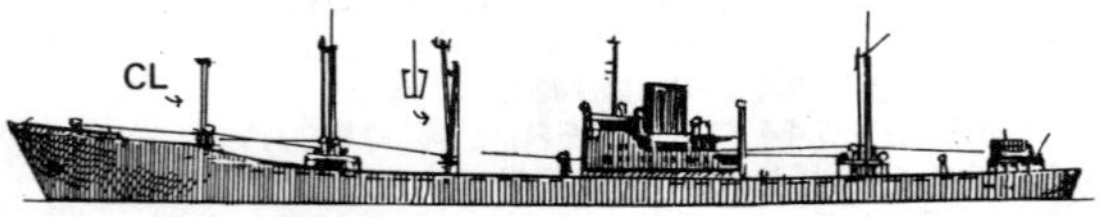

KMKMFKM H1
● **14570 HAMBURG EXPRESS.** Gr/FRG 1960; CP; 7000/9800; 167 × —/9.1 (548 × —/30); M; 17.5; ex KAAPLAND; ex S.A.KAAPLAND; ex KAAPLAND 1973. Lengthened 1970. Sister: **14571 RINI** (Gr) ex S.A.KRUGERLAND; ex KRUGERLAND 1974

KMKMFKM H1
⋆**14580 EMILIA PLATER.** Pd/Pd 1959; CP; 6700; 154 × 8.3 (506 × 27.6); M; 15.5; **'B54'** type. Sisters (Pd flag): ⋆**14581 ADOLF WARSKI** ⋆**14582 JAN MATEJKO** ⋆**14583 JANEK KRASICKI** ⋆**14584 LUDWIK SOLSKI.**

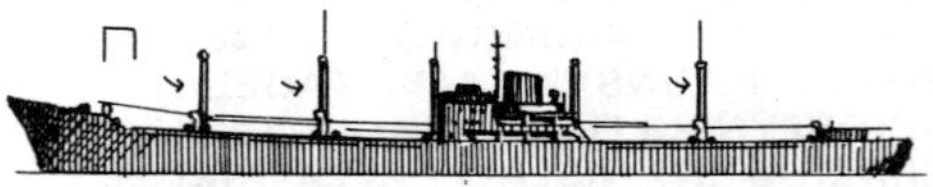

KMKMFKM H1
14590 SEA SUCCESS. Sg/Ja 1953; C; 8300; 142 × 8 (466 × 26); M; 14; ex AKIKAWA MARU 1973.

KMKMFKM H1
14600 CHEVALIER DARBY. Pa/Ja 1957; C; 7100; 136.63 × 8.37 (448.26 × 27.46); M; 13.25; ex MEDITERRANEAN DARBY 1975; ex HIKONE MARU 1973.

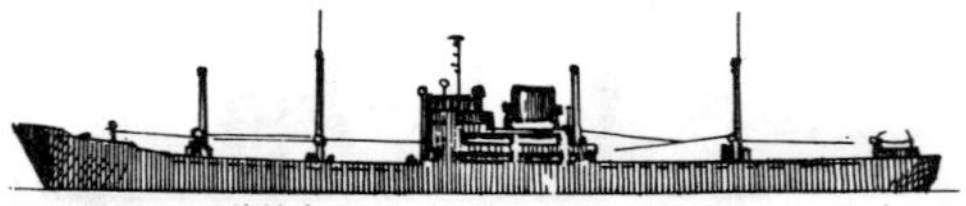

KMKMFKM H1
14610 EASTERN JUPITER. Pa/Ja 1957; C; 8700; 147 × 8.8 (483 × 29); M; 13.5; ex KENSHO MARU 1974.

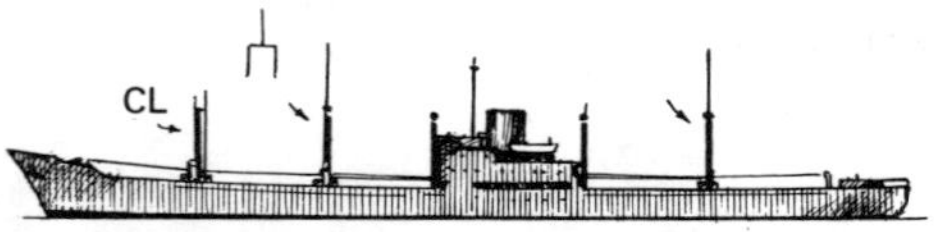

KMKMFKM H1
14620 CHAR YIH. Pa/Ja 1955; C; 8100; 143 × 8.1 (470 × 26.6); M; 14.25; ex TATEKAWA MARU 1976. Similar: **14621 CHITOS ARK** (Smaller funnel) (Pa) ex TERUKAWA MARU 1976 **14622 GOLDEN HERO** (Pa) ex HIKAWA MARU 1976 **14623 OCEAN ROYAL** (Sc) ex ASIA SEAGULL; ex TAGA MARU 1973.

KMKMFKM H1
⋆**14630 FENG QING;** RC/RC 1974; C; 10300; 161.6 × 9.1 (530 × 30); M; —.

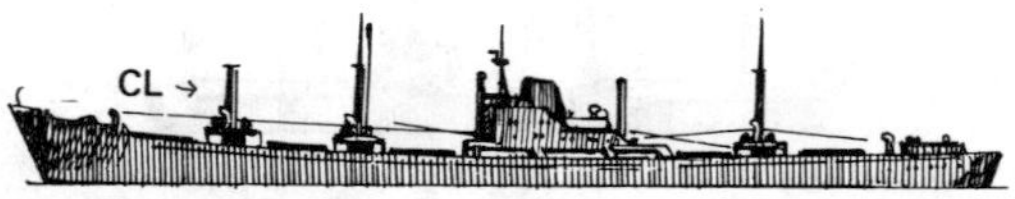

KMKMFKM H1
● **14640 IQBALBAKSH;** Pk/Br 1963; CP; 7000/9900; 155.8 × —/9.4 (511 × /31); M; 15; ex ARNA 1971.

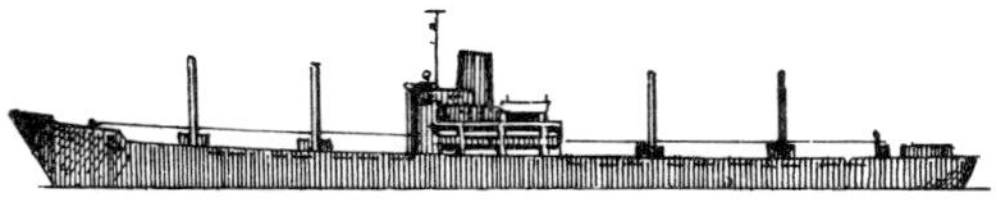

KMKMFKM H1
14650 UNION HONG KONG; Pa/Ja 1954; C; 7900; 148 × 8.8 (486 × 29); M; 14.75; ex SEIKAI MARU 1973.

KMKMFKM H1
14660 MARINA P; Gr/Be 1961; CP; 5200/7800; 141.2 × 7.8/8.8 (464 × 25.6/29); M; 16; ex MANAURE III 1980; ex GOOD LUCK 1977; ex ANVERS 1973. Sisters: **14661 HELENA C** (Gr) ex GOOD HOPE 1975; ex GAND 1973 **14662 SHABNAM** (Li) ex SCHERAZADE 1976; ex UNIOLYMPIA 1973; ex ESCAUT 1973.

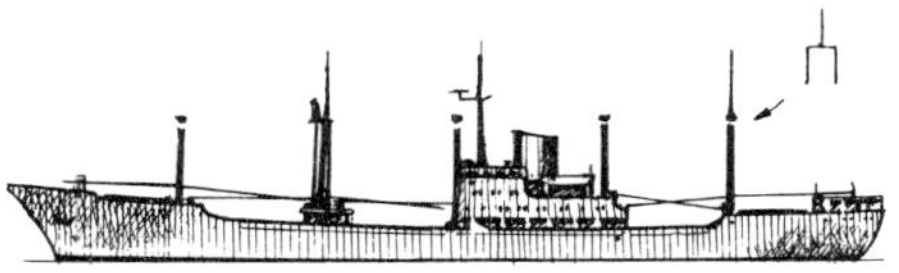

KMKMFKM H13
14670 PATEVERETT; Li/FRG 1960; CP; 7500; 143.2 × 8.5 (470 × 27.1); M; 17; ex NOPAL EXPRESS 1977. Similar (Lighter mast from bridge): **14671 LARA** (Cy) ex CREST LION 1979; ex AGHIOS LEFTERIS 1978; ex KROHN TRADER 1978; ex NOPAL TRADER 1974 **14672 PUNTA ATALAYA** (Li) ex NOPAL EXPRESS 1974.

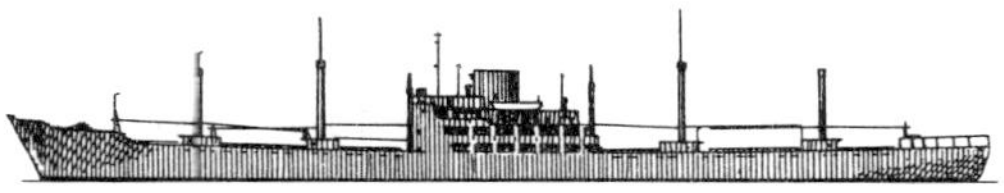

KMKMFKMK H1
14680 AZALEA BREEZE; Pa/Ja 1956; CP; 9100; 157 × 8.8 (516 × 29); M; 17.75; ex SATSUMA MARU 1974. Similar: **14681 TOKELAU** (Pa) ex SURUGA MARU 1976.

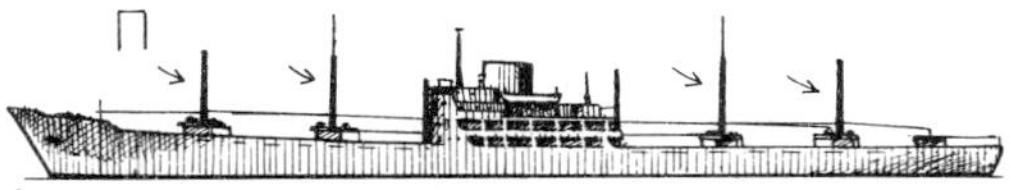

KMKMFKMK H1
14690 KOREAN RUNNER; Ko/Ja 1960; CP; 9300; 156.3 × 9 (513 × 30); M; 18; ex CRYSTAL LAUREL 1977; ex SETA MARU 1971.

KMKMFKMK H1
⋆**14700 DIVNOGORSK;** Ru/Pd 1961; C; 6400; 164 × 8.8 (505 × 29); M; 16; **'B 54'** type. Sister: ⋆**14701 MEDNOGORSK.**

KMKMFKMK H13
14710 TALAVERA; Br/FRG 1961; CP; 5100/7400; 143 × 7.7/8.5 (471 × 25.6/28); M; 17; ex NOPAL STAR 1977.

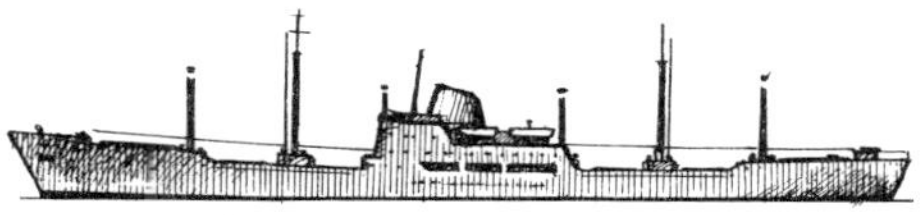

KMKMFKMK H13
14720 BRADEVERETT; Li/No 1953; CP; 5300; 143 × 7.9 (469 × 26); M; 16; ex BORGLAND 1970; ex CONCORDIA BORGLAND 1965; ex BORGLAND 1965.

KMKMFKMK H13
● **14730 BENARTY;** Br/Br 1963; C; 7300/10200; 155 × 8.5/9.2 (509 × 28/30.2); M; 16.

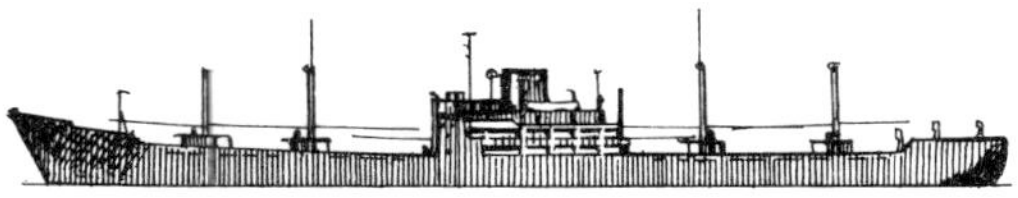

KMKMFKMK H13
14740 SAIKYO MARU; Ja/Ja 1961; CP; 9200; 156.4 × 9 (513 × 29.7); M; 18.25.

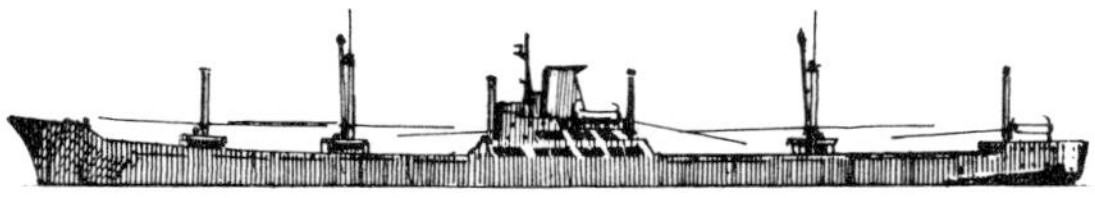

KMKMFKMK H13
14750 MALANGE; Po/Po 1971; C; 12200; 171.6 × 9.2 (563 × 30.2); M; 18. Sister: **14751 PORTO** (Po).

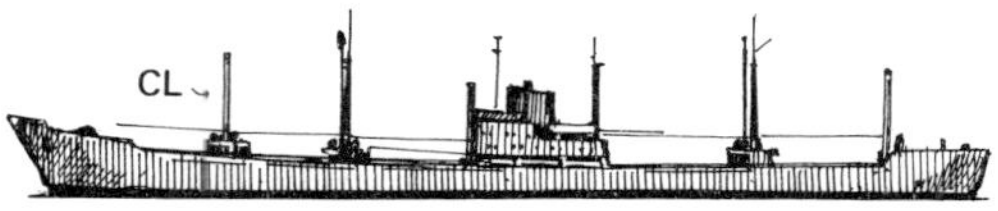

KMKMFKMK H13
14760 LELLO DI MAIO; It/FRG 1961; CP; 6400/8900; 151.6 × 8.2/9.2 (497 × 27/30); M; 16.25; ex TANGA; ex NOVIA 1963.

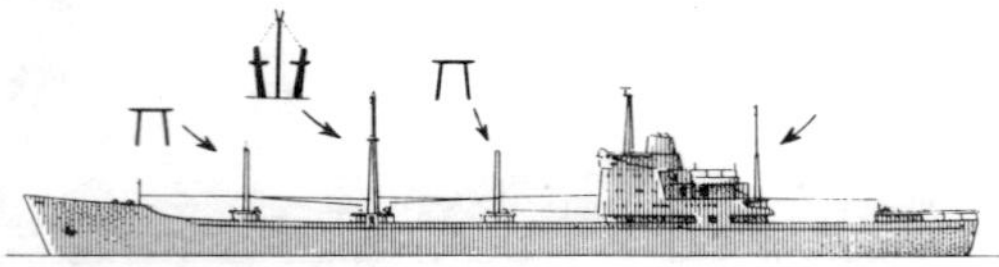

KMKMFM H1
★**14770 URSUS;** Pd/Pd 1972; C; 6400/10100; 154.7 × —/8.97 (507.55 × —/29.43); M; 17.75; **"B442"** type.

KMKMFM H1
14780 CONSTANTINOS T; Gr/Br 1959; C; 11300; 161.2 × 9.5 (530 × 31); M; 15; ex N. ZOGRAFIA 1975; ex LORD GLADSTONE 1969.

KMKMFM H1
14790 RUEY HSING; Tw/Ja 1957; C; 7900; 139.9 × 8.8 (459 × 28.1); M; 14; ex ORIENT WELFARE; ex KYOTAI MARU 1975. Sisters: **14791 CHAR HWA** (Pa) ex ORIENT STAR 1977; ex KYOSHIN MARU 1972 **14792 GOLDEN EAGLE** (Tw) ex VICRORY GENERAL 1980; ex CHIEH KANG; ex TOUN MARU 1973 **14793 NEW CASTLE** (Pa) ex YAMATO 1976; ex KYOZUI MARU 1972 **14794 AYESHA** (Cy) ex GEN-EI MARU 1973.

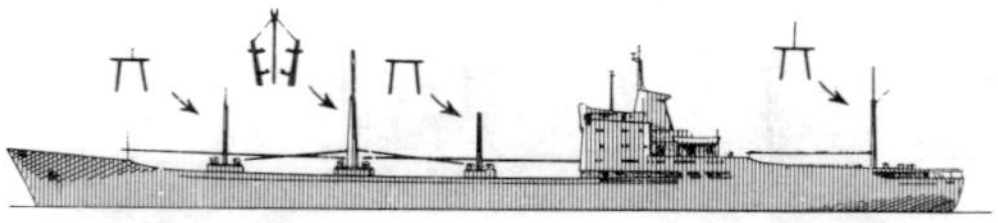

KMKMFM H13
★**14800 WLADYSLAW ORKAN;** Pd/Pd 1971; C; 6400/10100; 154.74 × —/8.97 (504.4 × —/29.43); M; 18; Modified **"B442"** type. Sister: ★**14801 LUCJAN SZENWALD** (Pd).

KMKMFMK H1
● **14810 PYRAMIDS U;** Eg/Ja 1960; C; 10000; 155.5 × 9 (510 × 29.10); M; 18.25; ex PHILIPPINE PRESIDENT MAGSAYSAY 1978. Sisters: **14811 GALLEON CORRAL** (Pi); ex PHILIPPINE PRESIDENT GARCIA **14812 GALLEON PEARL** (Pi) ex PHILIPPINE PRESIDENT QUIRINO **14813 GALLEON JADE** (Pi) ex PHILIPPINE PRESIDENT QUEZON **14814 SPHINX U** (Eg) ex PHILIPPINE PRESIDENT OSMENA **14815 PHILIPPINE PRESIDENT ROXAS** (Pi) Similar: **14816 PHILIPPINE ANTONIA LUNA** (Pi) ex PHILIPPINE LEYTE **14817 PHILIPPINE BATAAN** (Pi) **14818 PHILIPPINE RIZAL** (Pi).

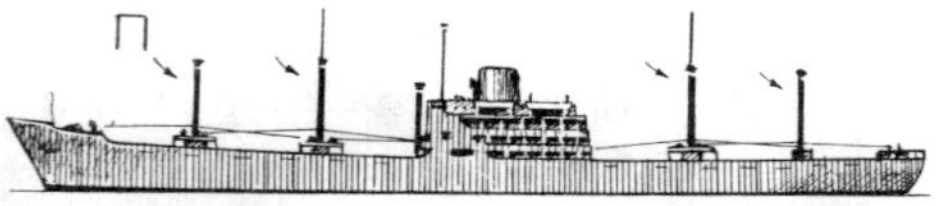

KMKMFMK H1
14820 ORIENT LONDON. Pa/Ja 1953; C; 8000; 144.3 × 8.8 (477 × 28.9); M; 15.5; ex OCEANIC LONDON: ex LONDON MARU 1972. Similar: (Pole masts. After KP on house) **14821 GOLDEN SKY** (Pa) ex Philippine Maru 1977 **14822 VICTORY QUEEN** (Pa) ex EURYCHILI 1977; ex CHIEH HUI 1975; ex OCEANIC SUEZ 1974; ex SUEZ MARU 1972.

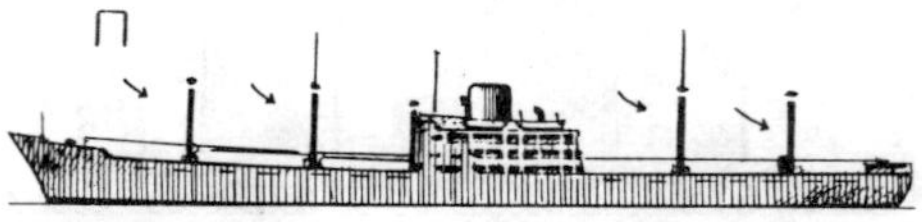

KMKMFMK H1
● **14830 SWAN RIVER.** Ja/Ja 1951; C; 8200; 144.1 × 8.8 (473 × 28.7); M; 15.5; ex CHIEH TENG 1976; ex TARPONA 1974; ex ANDES MARU 1972; converted to Livestock carrier. Probably altered in appearance. Similar: **14831 CHIEH TEH** (Pa) ex STRONA 1974; ex ATLAS MARU 1972.

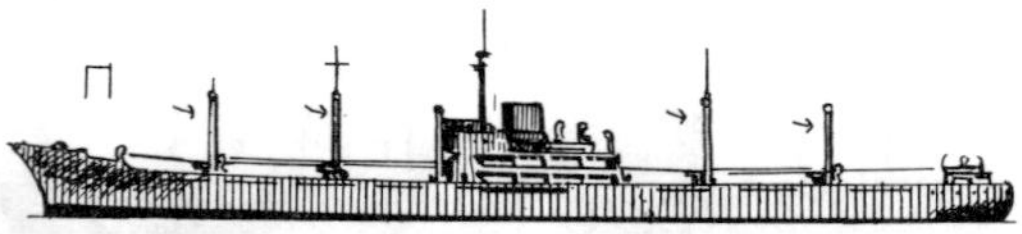

KMKMFMK H1
● **14840 NADER.** Pa/Ja 1951; C; 9600; 157 × 8.3 (515 × 27.3); M; 17.25; ex PACLOG PROVIDER; ex EASTERN PROVIDER 1974; ex KAMIKAWA MARU 1972.

KMKMFMK H1
14850 GREAT CONCORD. Pa/Ja 1957; CP; 8300; 143.3 × 8.5 (470 × 28); M; 14; ex NAGATO MARU 1975.

KMKMFMK H1
14860 DEVON EXPRESS. Li/Br 1954;LS; 1500; 90.1 × 5.2 (297 × 17); TSM; 14; ex LAIRDSGLEN 1974; converted from a cargo ship.

KMKMFMK H1
14870 APOSTOLOS K. Gr/Fr 1961; C/WT; 4500/6600; 130 × 7/8.1 (427 × 23/26.3); M; 15; ex JACQUES BINGEN 1972.

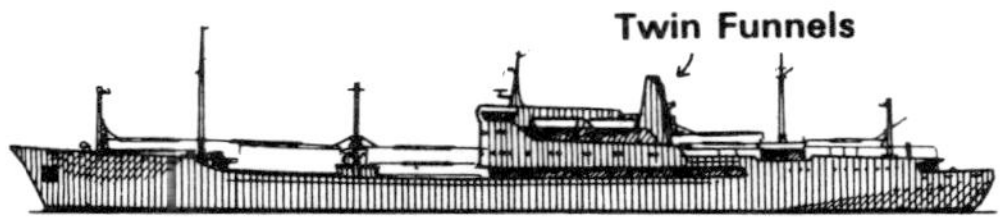

KMKMFMK H13
14880 OHRMAZD. Pk/Br 1968; PC; 8000/11000; 1577 × —/9 (515 × —/29.2); M; 19.

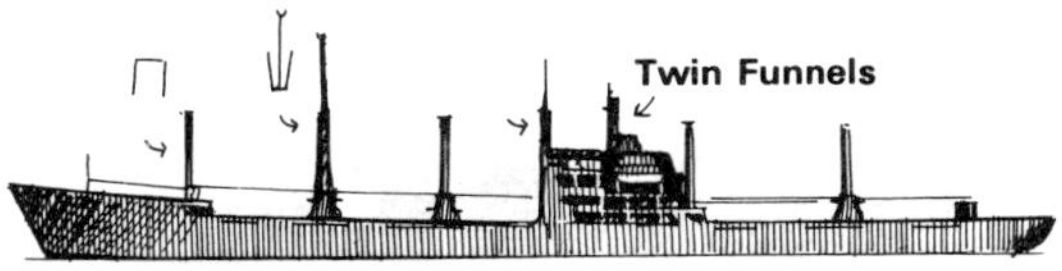

$KMKMK_3$ H13
14890 ELIZABETH LYKES. US/US 1966; CP; 7400/11000; 165 × 8.5/10 (542 × 28/33); T; 20. Sisters (US flag): **14891 DOLLY TURMAN 14892 FREDERICK LYKES 14893 GENEVIEVE LYKES 14894 HOWELL LYKES 14895 LETITIA LYKES 14896 LOUISE LYKES 14897 MALLORY LYKES 14898 MASON LYKES 14899 RUTH LYKES 14900 STELLA LYKES 14901 VELMA LYKES**

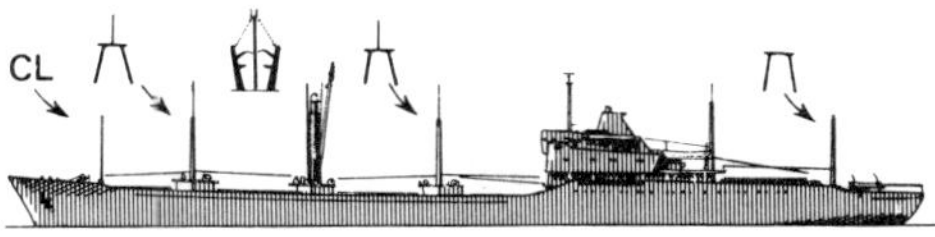

$KMKM_2FK_2$ H13
14910 VISHVA CHETANA. In/Pd 1969; C; 5400/8100; 145.37 × 7.36/9.09 (476.94 × 24.15/29.82); M; 17.5; ex VISHVA CHETNA 1969; launched as ZYGMUNT AUGUST; **'B445'** type. Sisters (In flag): **14911 VISHVA BINDU 14912 VISHVA SANDESH** launched as ZYGMUNT STARY **14913 VISHVA VIKAS** launched as WLADYSLAW JAGIELLO (Pd flag): **★14914 WLADYSLAW JAGIELLO ★14915 WLADYSLAW LOKIETEK ★14916 ZYGMUNT AUGUST ★14917 ZYGMUNT STARY ★14918 ZYGMUNT III WAZA ★14919 MIESZKO 1 ★14920 BOLESLAW CHOBRY ★14921 BOLESLAW SMIALY ★14922 BOLESLAW KRZYWOUSTY** (Ir flag): **14923 IRAN EKRAM** ex ARYA ROKH 1980 **14924 IRAN ELHAM** ex ARYA KISH 1980 **14925 IRAN GHEYAM** ex ARYA ROOZ 1980 (Fr flag) **14926 COURSON** ex ARYA DAD 1971; ex BOLESLAW KRZYWOUSTY (RC flag) **★14927 JIANG CHENG** ex WLADYSLAW IV.

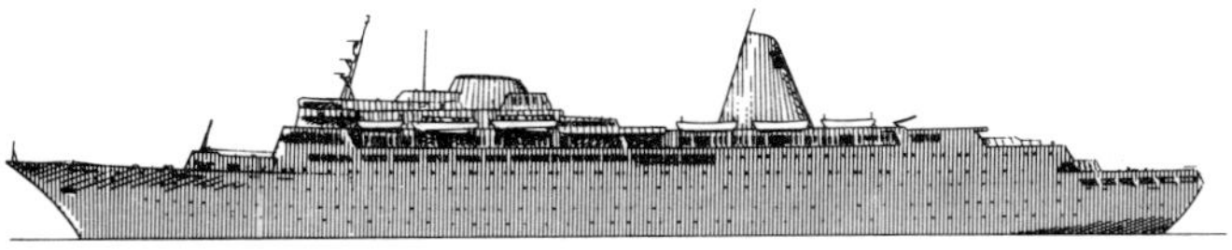

KM_2F H
14940 SEA PRINCESS. Br/Br-FRG 1966/79; P; 26700; 201.23 × 8.56 (approx) (660.2 × 28.08); TSM; 21; ex KUNGSHOLM 1978; rebuilt 1978/79.

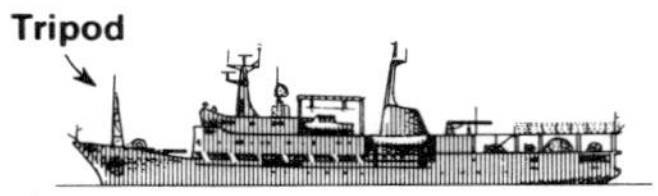

KM_2F H
14950 T.W. NELSON. US/Ja 1978; RS; 2600; 86.64 × 4.82 (284.25 × 15.81); M; 15.25; helicopter deck.

●
★14955

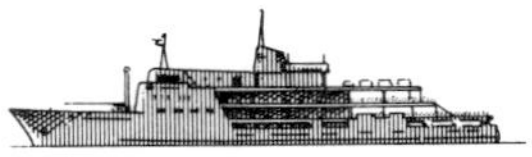

KM_2F H1
14970 DON VICENTE. Pi/Ja 1969; F; 1100; 77.35 × 3.77 (253.77 × 12.37); TSM; 17.

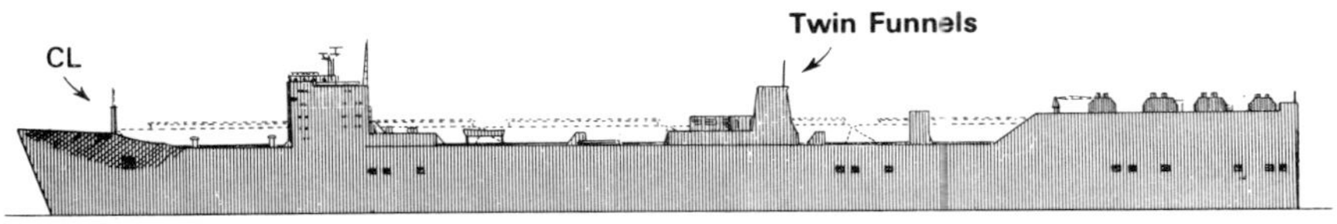

KM_2F H13
★14975 YULIUS FUCHIK. Ru/Fi 1978; Bg/Con; 22800/35900; 266.45 × —/11 (874.18 × —/36.09; TSM; 20; may be spelt **JULIUS FUCIK;** Deck stowage of barges indicated by dotted lines. Sister: **★14976 TIBOR SZAMUELY** (Ru).

●
14976

KM_2FC H
14980 DON CLAUDIO. Pi/Ja 1965; F; 2700; 93 × 5.4 (306 × 17.6); M; 18.5; ex OKINOSHIMA MARU.

KM_2FC H1
14990 MERCURY. Br/Br 1962; Cbl; 9000; 144.1 × 7.5 (473 × 24.7); TSD-E; 16.

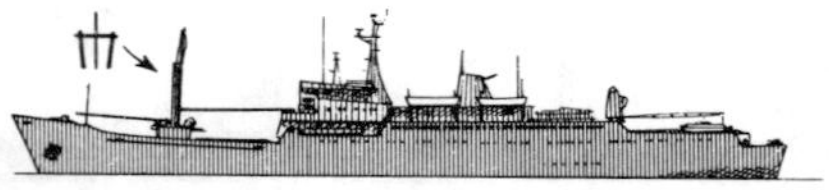

KM_2FC H12
⋆15000 'PROFESSOR' class. Ru/Pd 1970; CTS; 6000; 122 × 7.3 (401 × 24.2); M; **'B-80'** class. Several vessels of this class may have this sequence. Superstructure varies. Full list under KMFC H12 Professor Shchyogolev—which see.

KM_2FCM H13
⋆15020 DAI YUN SHAN. RC/De 1965; CP; 4800/7500; 137.5 × 7.1/8.7 (451 × 23/28.6); M; 17.5; ex JYTTE SKOU. Sisters: **⋆15021 BAI YUN SHAN** (RC) ex SUSANNE SKOU 1980 **⋆15022 HUANG PU JIANG** (RC) ex LOTTE SKOU 1980 **⋆15023 FU CHUNG JIANG** (RC) ex BENNY SKOU 1980.

KM_2FCR H
15030 KUROSHIO MARU. Ja/Ja 1971; F; 4900; 124 × 5.5 (407 × 17.1); TSM; 23.

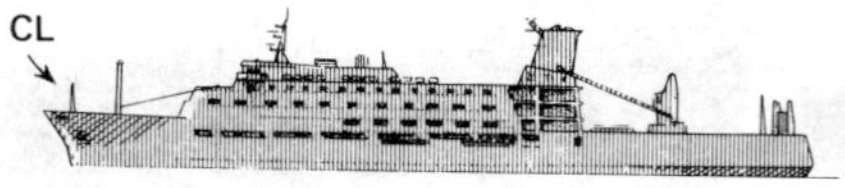

KM_2FCR H
15040 WAKASHIO MARU. Ja/Ja 1973; RoC; 5500; 124.92 × 5.51 (409.84 × 18.08; M; 24; stern ramp.

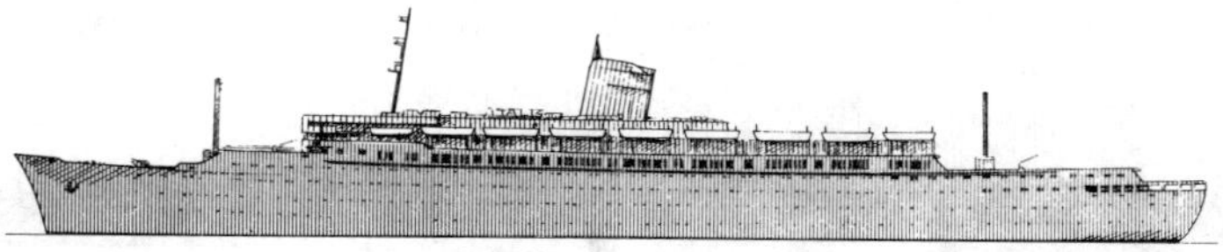

KM_2FK H
15050 NOGA. Pa/US 1940/79; P; 26400; 220.38 × 9.98 (723 × 32.74); TST; 22.5; ex ITALIS 1980; ex AMERICA 1979; ex AUSTRALIS 1978; ex AMERICA 1964; ex WEST POINT 1946; ex AMERICA 1942. Modernised c.1979; converted to a floating hotel in 1980; probably altered in appearance.

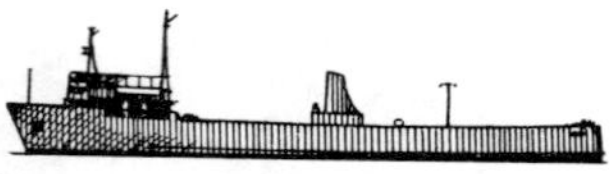

KM_2FK H
15060 GOLFO PARADISO. It/FRG 1968; RoC; 1500; 95 × — (312 × —); TSM; 16; stern door. Sister: **⋆15061 RAPOCA** (Ys) ex CARIBBEAN ENTERPRISE 1975.

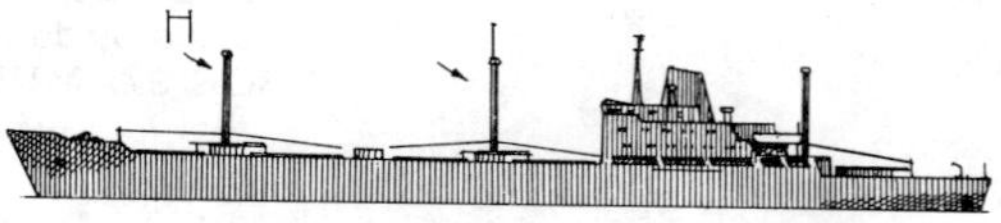

KM_2FK H1
15070 OLYMPIAN REEFER. Gr/No 1971; R; 7300/9700; 156 × 8.4/9.1 (511 × 27.6/30.1); M; 21; ex WILD AUK. Sister: **15071 DELPHIC REEFER** (Gr) ex WILD AVOCET 1980.

KM_2FK H1
★15080 KRAKOW. Pd/Pd 1965; CP; 3400/5500; 124 × 6.5/6.9 (407 × 21.6/23); M; 16; **'B455'** type. Sisters (Pd flag): **★15081 CZESTOCHOWA ★15082 GDYNIA II ★15083 LODS ★15084 LUBLIN ★15085 RADOM ★15086 RZESZOW ★15087 WARSZAWA**

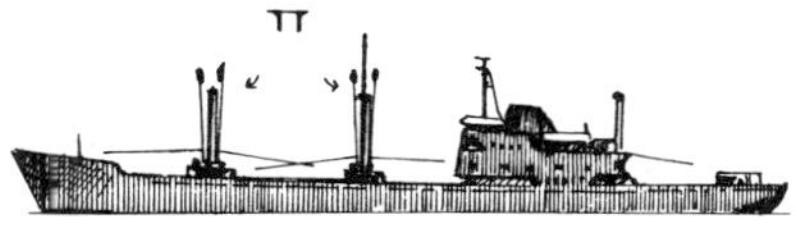

KM_2FK H1
★15090 KRIVAN. Cz/Pa 1970; CP; 3400/5500; 124 × 6.5/6.9 (407 × 21.6/23); M; 16; **'B 455'** type Sisters (Cz flag): **★15091 RADHOST ★15092 SITNO ★15093 BLANIK**

★15095

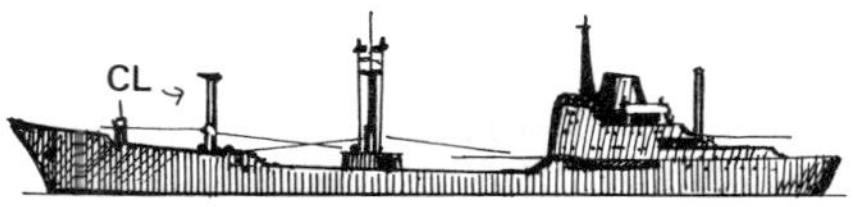

KM_2FK H13
★15100 FRANZ STENZER. DDR/Ja 1965; C; 6000/6400; 131 × 6.8/7.9 (430 22/26); M; 17; ex LLOYD HELSINKI; ex TRANSATLANTIC 1972. Sister: **15101 NYANDA** (Br) ex TRANSMICHIGAN 1973.

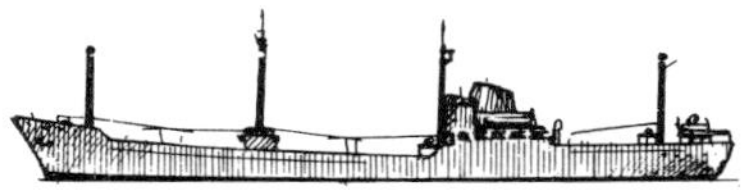

KM_2FK H13
15110 IRIS. Gr/FRG 1955; C; 5000; 116.7 × 7.8 (383 × 25.6); M; 12.5; ex UNITED VICTORY 1976; ex MARIEL 1973; ex NAGUILAN 1965; ex COMMERZ 1961. Sister: **15111 SEA HAWK** (Pa) ex ALLIPEN 1976; ex CONTINENT 1961.

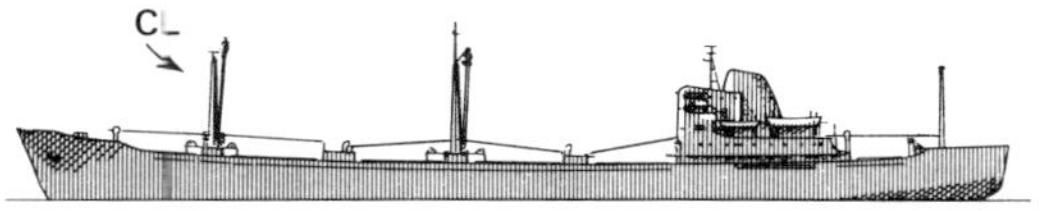

KM_2FK H13
15120 PARAGON. Pa/FRG 1958; C; 11100; 157.44 × 9.68 (516.54 × 31.76); M; 16; ex COUNT HUPITER 1978; ex LOTUS FLOWER 1976; ex NEGBA 1972. Sister: PARACLETE (see under KCMCMFK) may also have this sequence now.

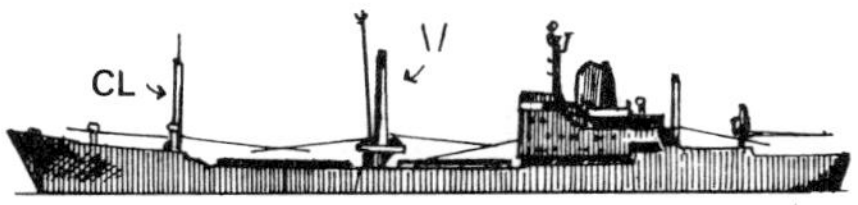

KM_2FKC H13
15130 BANGLAR SWAPNA. Bh/FRG 1971; C; 6900; 131 × 8.4 (429 × 27); M; 17.5; ex TRANSCANADA 1964. Sister: **15131 BANGLAR PROGOTI** (Bh) ex TRANSAMERICA 1974.

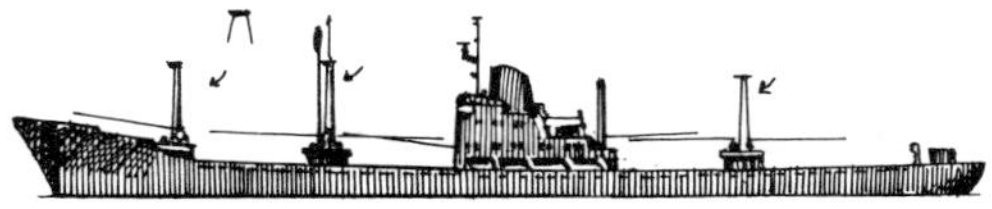

KM_2FK_2 H1
15140 LALAZAR. Pk/Pk 1973; C; 6000/9000; 154.7 × 9.2 (508 × 30.6); M; 17. Sister: **15141 SHALAMAR** (Pk) Possible sister: **15142 BAYNUNAH** (Sh).

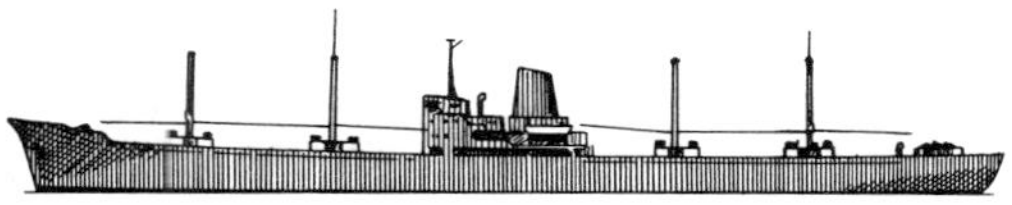

KM_2FK_2 H1
15150 PENELOPE. Gr/Ja 1962; C; 7000/10100; 158 × 8.3/9.5 (519 × 27.6/31.3); M; 15.

KM_2FK_3 H1
★15160 TIRANA. Al/Pd 1970; CP; 5800/8700; 153 × —/9 (502 × /29.9); M; 16.25; **'B41'** type.

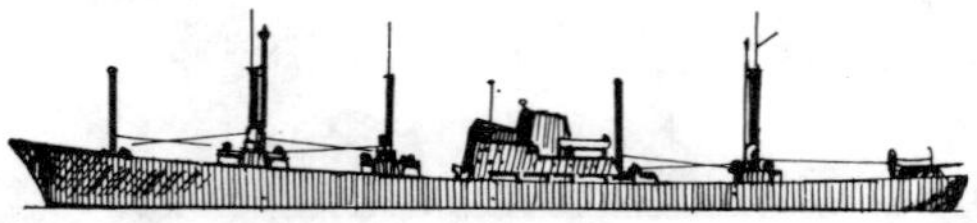

KM_2FKM H

● **15170 ATRA.** Pa/Sp 1960; CP; 5300; 145 7.3 (475 × 24); M; 17; ex RIO ATRATO 1980; ex CIUDAD DE ARMENIA 1977. Sisters (Co flag): **15171 CIUDAD DE PASTO 15172 CIUDAD DE PEREIRA** (Gr flag): **15173 HERCULUS** ex CEFALLONIAN AMBITION 1980; ex CIUDAD DE GUAYAQUIL 1980. Similar (Co flag): **15174 CIUDAD DE BARRANQUILLA 15175 CIUDAD DE TUNJA 15176 CARTAGENA DE INDIAS.**

KM_2FKM H1

⋆**15180 HANOI.** Pd/Pd 1960; CP; 6900; 154 × 8.3 (505 × 27.4); M; 15.5; **'B-54'** type. Sisters (Pd flag): ⋆**15181 PEKIN** ⋆**15182 PHENIAN** Similar: ⋆**15183 YI XING** (RC) ex KONOPNICKA ⋆**15184 INTERNACIONAL** (Al) ⋆**15185 GONZALEZ LINES** (Cu) ⋆**15186 COMMANDANTE CAMILO CIENFUEGOS** (Cu).

KM_2FKM H1

⋆**15190 DOMEYKO.** Pd/Pd 1962; CP; 5700; 146 × 7.7 (478 × 25.6); M; 16.5; **'B-516'** type Sisters (Pd flag): ⋆**15191 HEWELIUSZ** ⋆**15192 SNIADECKI** ⋆**15193 STASZIC.**

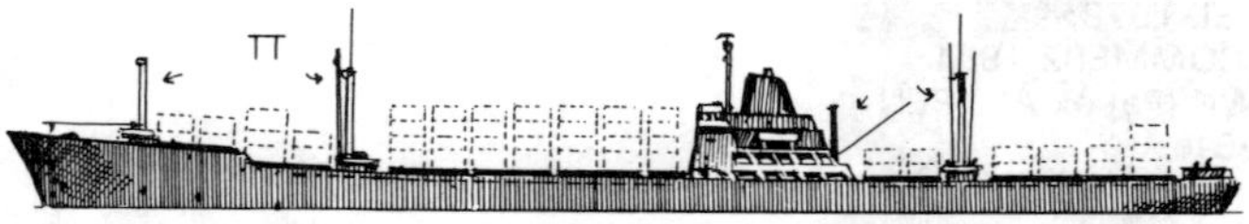

KM_2FKM H1

15200 PRESIDENT HARRISON. US/US 1966; Con; 16800; 204 × 10.2 (669 × 33.6); T; converted from a cargo ship and lengthened 1963. Sisters (US flag): **15201 PRESIDENT MONROE 15202 PRESIDENT POLK.**

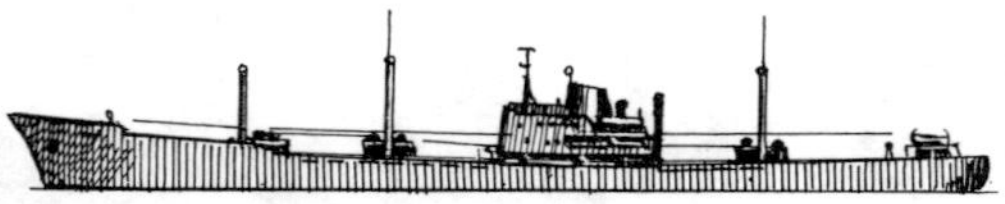

KM_2FKM H1

● ⋆**15210 SUMADIJA.** Ys/Ys 1961; C; 6300/9000; 152 × 8.1/9.3 (498 × 26.6/30.6; M; 15.75. Sister: ⋆**15211 MOSLAVINA** (Ys).

KM_2FKM H1

15220 RIVER NIGER. Ng/FRG 1968; C; 5400/7800; 137 × 7.6/8.7 (448 × 25/28.8); M; 16.5. Sisters (Ng flag): **15221 RIVER BENUE 15222 RIVER ETHIOPE 15223 RIVER OGUN.**

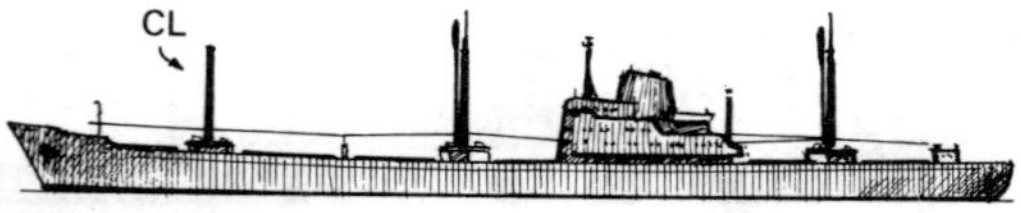

KM_2FKM H1

15230 JALAJYOTI. In/In 1966; C; 8300/10900; 158.43 × 8.5/9.66 (519.78 × 27.89/31.69; M; 16; ex APJ AMBAR 1966; may now be KCM²FKM—JALAJAYA. Possible Sisters: **15231 APJ AMBIKA** (In) **15232 APJ PRIYA** (In).

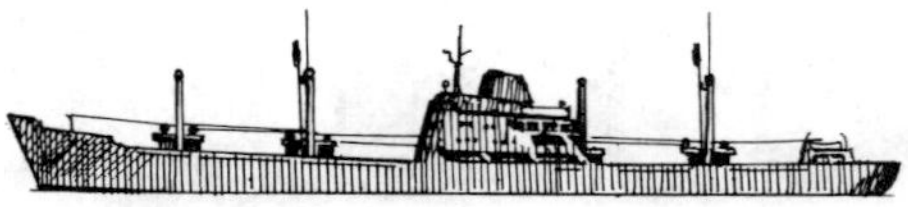

KM_2FKM H1

⋆**15240 BASKA.** Ys/Ys 1960; C; 4400/6700; 136 × 7.1/7.5 (447 × 23.6/24.9); M; 17.25. Sisters (Ys flag): ⋆**15241 DREZNICA** ⋆**15242 GROBNIK** ⋆**15243 NOVI VINODOLSKI.**

KM_2FKM H1

15250 BAGH-E-KARACHI. Pk/Ys 1964; C; 6100/9000; 155 × 8.2/9 (509 × 27/29.9); M; 17.5; Sisters (Pk flag): **15251 BAGH-E-DACCA 15252 CHENAB.**

KM_2FKM H13
15260 CHERRY CRYSTAL. Sg/FRG 1961; CP; 5200/7200; 138×7.2/8.6 (454 23.6/28.3); M; 16.5; ex MAREN SKOU 1980. **15261 DESANMAR** (Gr) ex EBEL 1980; ex BIRGITTE SKOU.

KM_2FKM H13
15270 BENYA RIVER. Gh/Br 1965; CP; 4900/7300; 139×—/8.5 (455×—/27.8); M; 17; Sisters (Gh flag): **15271 NAKWA RIVER 15272 KORLE LAGOON 15273 SAKUMO LAGOON** Similar; **15275 BIA RIVER 15276 OTI RIVER 15277 SUBIN RIVER 15278 KLORTE LAGOON.**

KM_2FKMK H1
***15280 HANKA SAWICKA.** Pd/Pd 1962; CP; 6900; 154.1×8.3 (506×27.4); M; 15.5; **'B-54'** type.

KM_2FKMK H1
***15290 JESENICE.**Ys/Ys 1960; C; 7000/9500; 155×8.2/9.5 (509×27/31.3); M; 18.5. Sisters: ***15291 KOSTRENA** (Ys) **15292 CHAMPEX** (Sd) ex KAPTASTAMATI 1972; ex TREBINJE 1968.

KM_2FKMK H1
***15300 ANDRZEJ STRUG.** Pd/Pd 1963; CP; 6900; 153×8.3 (502×27.2); M; 17; **B-54'** type ***15301 WLADYSLAW BRONIEWSKI.**

KM_2FKMK H1
● **15310 IRAN SEEYAM.** Ir/Po 1974; C; 9200; 153×9.1 (502×30); M; 18; ex ARYA SUN 1980. Sisters (Ir flag): **15311 IRAN KALAM** ex IRAN SEEM 1980; ex ARYA SEEM **15312 IRAN NAHAD** ex IRAN ZAR 1980; ex ARYA ZAR (Pd flag); ***15313 MAJOR SUCHARSKI** ***15314 MARIAN BUCZEK.**

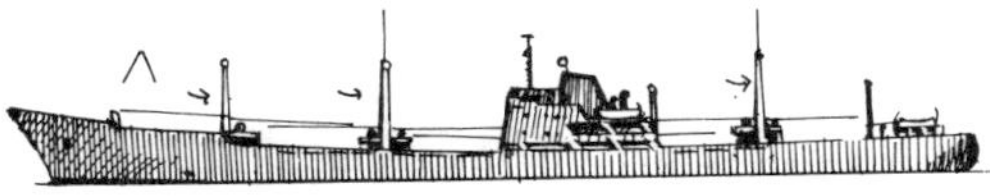

KM_2FKMK H1
● ***15320 BANAT.** Ys/Ys 1963; C; 6300/9000; 152×—/9 (498×—/29.5); M; 15. Sister; ***15321 METOHIJA** (Ys).

KM_2FKMK H1
● **15330 JORDAENS.** Be/Be 1963; CP; 7300/10300; 158×8.3/9.2 (517×27.3/30.4); M; 16.5. Sisters (Be flag): **15331 BREUGHEL 15332 MEMLING** ex RUBENS 1972 **15333 TENIERS.**

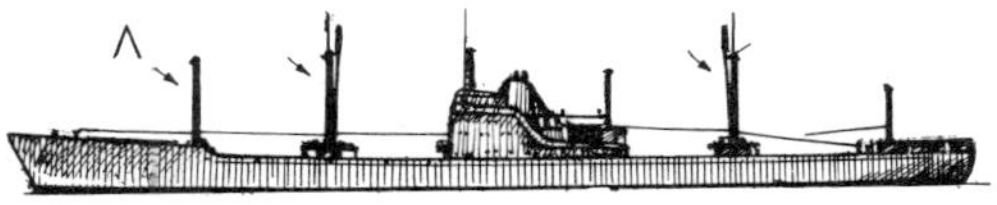

KM_2FKMK H1
● ***15340 FRANCESCO NULLO;** Pd/Pd 1964; C; 5700/8600; 152.6×7.7/8.8 (501×25.4/29); M; 15.5; **'B-41')** type. Sister: (Pd flag) ***15341 LENINO** Similar (larger funnels): ***15342 ALEKSANDER ZAWADSKI** ***15343 GWARDIA LUDOWA** ***15344 LENINGRAD** ***15345 JOZEF WYBICKI** ex SEBASTIAN KLONOWICZ ***15346 PIOTR DUNIN** ***15347 SNOLNY** ***15348 STANISLAW DUBOIS** Similar (some may have small funnel) (RC flag): ***15349 CHANGNING** ***15350 HAINING** ***15351 JINING** ***15352 XINGNING** ***15353 YONGNING.**

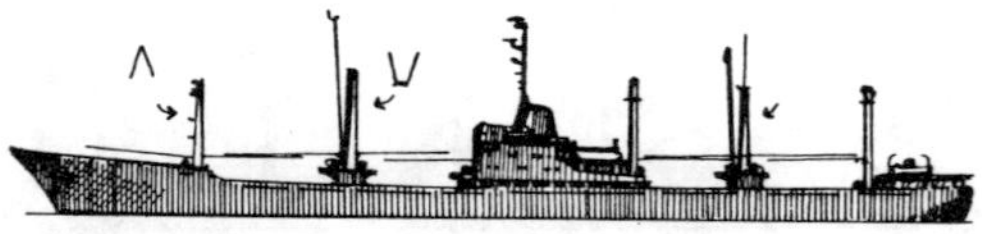

KM_2FKMK H1
● **15360 PONTEVEDRA.** Li/Pd 1971; CP; 5800/8700; 153×7.7/9.1 (502×25.3/30); M; 16.25; ex MORONI; ex LANGON 1971; **'B-41'** type. Probable sister ⋆**15361 PULKOWNIK DABEK** (Pd).

KM_2FKMK H1
15380 HADJI AGUS SALIM. Ia/Pd 1963; C; 6800; 154×8.2 (505×27.2); M; 15; **'B-454'** type. Sisters (Ia flag). **15381 JOHANNES LATUHARHARY 15382 SAM RATULANGIE.**

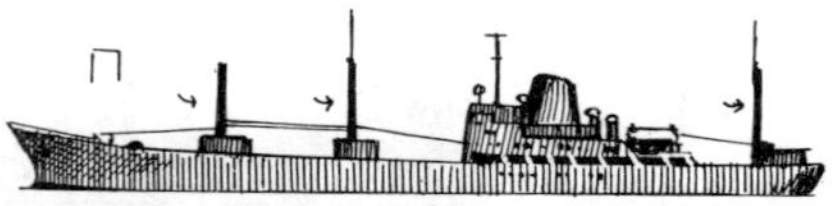

KM_2FM H
15390 LADY JOSEPHINE. Pa/Fr 1964; R; 4200; 125×7.6 (410×25); M; 20.75; ex FORT JOSEPHINE 1977. Sister. **15391 LORD TRINITE** (Pa) ex FORT TRINITE 1977.

KM_2FM H1
⋆**15410 ANTON SAEFKOW.** DDR/DDR 1965; C; 5000/7700; 142×7.2/8.5 (466×23.6/28); M; —. Similar (DDR flag) ⋆**15411 HEINZ KAPELLE** ⋆**15412 LIESELOTTE HERRMANN** ⋆**15413 RUDOLF BREITSCHEID** ⋆**15413 ALBIN KOBIS** ⋆**15414 BERNHARD BASTLEIN** ⋆**15415 MAX REICHPIETSCH** Possible sisters. ⋆**15416 JOHN SCHEHR** ⋆**15417 GEORG SCHUMANN** ⋆**15418 MATHIAS THESEN.**

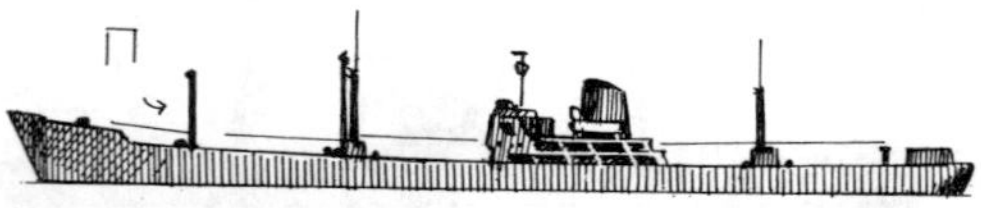

KM_2FM H1
15430 THEOTOKOS. Gr/Br 1957; C; 9200; 150.2×8.9 (493×29.3); M; 14; ex KING THESEUS.

KM_2FM H1
● ⋆**15450 OLKUSZ.** Pd/Pd 1960; CP; 3000; 114.3×6.3 (375×20.6); M; 15; **'B-59'** type. Sisters (Pd flag) ⋆**15451 OJCOW** ⋆**15452 OLIWA** ⋆**15453 ORLOWO** ⋆**15454 ORNETA** Similar (Ia flag) **15455 SAPUDI 15456 SANGIHE 15457 SALAJAR 15458 SAWU.**

KM_2FKMK H1
● **15370 PINDAROS.** Gr/Sw 1963; C; 7900/10700; 162×8.7/9.5 (531×28.3/31); M; 16.5; ex LONDON CRAFTSMAN 1976. Sisters **15371 PLOTINOS** (Gr) ex LONDON CITIZEN 1977 **15372 AGIA MARINA** (Gr) ex LONDON STATESMAN 1979 Similar **15373 RIVA** (Gr) ex LONDON BANKER 1973 **15374 SINGAPORE FORTUNE** (Sg) ex LONDON ADVOCATE 1973 ⋆**15375 LIMING** (RC) ex LONDON TRADESMAN 1964.

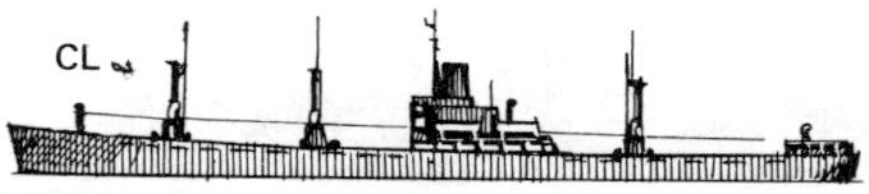

KM_2FM H
⋆**15400 ALEKSANDR SUVOROV.** Ru/US 1943; C; 7200; 135×8.5 (443×28); R; 10.75; ex ELIJAH P. LOVEJOY 1943; **'LIBERTY'** type. Sisters (Ru flag) ⋆**15401 DARYAL** ex ORATA 1963; ex WILFORD 1957 ex GEORGE WHITEFIELD 1947 ⋆**15402 VOLGOGRAD** ex STALINGRAD 1962; ex THOMAS F. FLAHERTY.

KM_2FM H1
⋆**15420 BUCURESTI.** Rm/Ys 1962; C; 6700/9200; 152×8.1/9 (500×26.4/29.8); M; 14. Similar (lower superstructure) ⋆**15421 DOBROGEA.**

KM_2FM H1
15440 VISHVA PRATAP. In/It 1957; C; 7100; 149.94 ×8.9 (491.93×29.2); M; 14.5; ex ELETTRA FASSIO 1964.

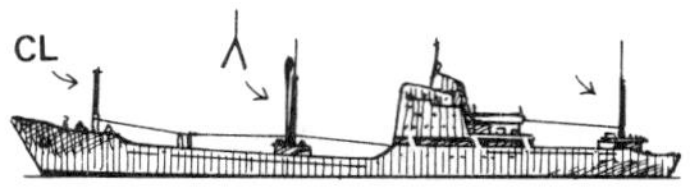

KM_2FM H13
★**15460 SINEGORSK**. Ru/DDR 1963; C; 3200; 106 × 6.6 (347 × 21.3); M; 12.5; ex GZHATSK 1974; **'POVONETS'** type. Sisters (Ru flag) ★**15461 BARGUZIN** ★**15462 BIRYUZA** ★**15463 BUKHTARMA** ★**15464 DALNEGORSK** ex TETYUKHE ★**15465 GORNO-ALTAYSK** ★**15466 GRISHA AKOPIAN** EX SULA ★**15467 GRUMANT** ★**15468 GULBENE** ★**15469 HELTERMAA** ★**15470 KAMCHATKA** ★**15471 KOKHTLA** ★**15472 KOVDOR** ★**15473 KYPU** ★**15474 MANYCH** ★**15475 MURMAN** ★**15476 NEVER** ★**15477 NIZHNEUDINSK** ★**15478 OLENEGORSK** ★**15499 PAYDE** ★**15480 PERESLAVL-ZALESSIK** ★**15481 SEGEZHA** ★**15482 SELEMDZHA** ★**15483 SEVORODVINSK** ★**15484 SHILKA** ★**15485 SPASSK-DALNIY** ★**15486 STEPAN KHALTURIN** ★**15487 SVIRSK** ★**15488 SYKTYVKAR** ★**15489 TUNGUSKA** ★**15490 USSURI** ★**15491 VILYANY** ★**15492 VYRU** ★**15493 ZAPOLYARNYY** Similar (Space Monitoring Ship) ★**15494 RISTNA**.

KM_2FM H13
★**15500 PYARNU**. Ru/DDR 1963; C; 3200; 106 × 6.7 (347 × 21.6); M; 13.75; **'POVONETS'** type. Sisters (Ru flag) ★**15501 NOVOVORONEZH** ★**15502 POVONETS**.

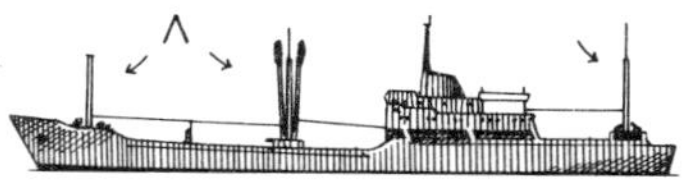

KM_2FM H13
★**15510 SHURA KOBER**. Ru/DDR 1971; C; 3600; 105.7 × 6.7 (347 × 21.6); M; 13.75; **'PIONER'** type. Sisters (Ru flag) ★**15511 ARKADIY KAMANIN** ★**15512 BORIYA TSARIKOV** ★**15513 GALYA KOMLEVA** ★**15514 KOLYA MYGATIN** ★**15515 LARA MIKHEYENKO** ★**15516 LYONYA GOLYKOV** ★**15517 MARAT KOZEY** ★**15518 NINA KUKOVEROVA** ★**15519 NINA SAGAYDAK** ★**15520 PAVLIK LARISHKIN** ★**15521 PIONER** ★**15522 PIONERSKAYA PRAVDA** ★**15523 PIONERSKAYA ZORKA** ★**15524 SASHA BORODULIN** ★**15525 SASHA KONDRATYEV** ★**15526 SASHA KOTOV** ★**15527 SASHA KOVALYOV** ★**15528 TOLYA KOMAR** ★**15529 TOLYA SHUMOV** ★**15530 TONYA BONDARCHUK** ★**15531 VALYA KOTIK** ★**15532 VALERIY VOLKOV** ★**15533 VASYA KOROBKO** ★**15534 VASYA SHISHKOVSKIY** ★**15535 VITYA CHALENKO** ★**15536 VITYA KHONENKO** ★**15537 VITYA SITNITSA** ★**15538 VOLODYA SCHERBATSEVICH** ★**15539 YUTA BONDAROVSKAYA** ★**15540 ZINA PORTNOVA**.

KM_2FMK H1
15550 MARITSA III. Pa/Br 1965; C; 7200/10600; 157.2 × 8.3/9.1 (516 × 27.6/30); M; 16; ex MARITSA 1974; ex EXNING 1973.

KM_2FMK H13
15560 EEMHAVEN. Ne/Ne 1963; CP; 5900/8300; 151.2 × 8.1/8.2 (496 × 26.3/26.8); M; —.

KM_2KFKMK H1
15570 OCEAN ACE. Pa/FRG 1956; CP; 6500; 157 × 8 (514 × 26.2); M; 17; ex MAERSK WIND; ex MONTFERLAND 1973. Sister **15571 OCEAN GLORY** (Pa) ex MAERSK WAVE; ex ZAANLAND 1973.

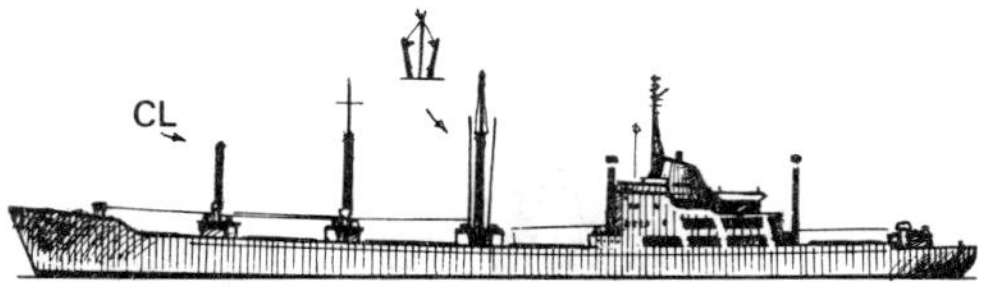

KM_2KMFK H1
★**15580 KRASZEWSKI**. Pd/De 1963; CP; 7200/10400; 153.3 × 8.3/9.1 (503 × 27.6/30); M; 16. Sister ★**15581 JIAXING** (RC) ex DLUGOSZ 1970.

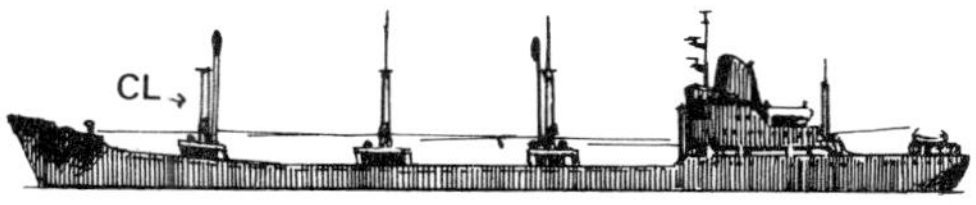

KM_2KMFK H13
15590 VISHVA KARUNA. In/In 1973; C; 7000/10000; 154 × 9.2 (506 × 30.6); M; 17.5. Sisters (In flag) **15591 VISHVA MADHURI 15592 VISHVA MAMTA 15593 VISHVA BANDHAN**.

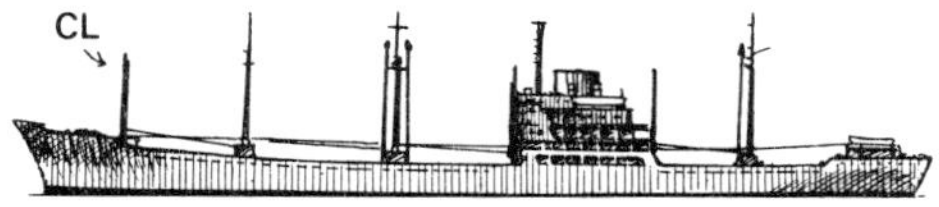

KM_2KMFKM H13
● **15600 JUTHA DHIPYA**. Th/Ne 1956; C; 8800; 145.3 × 8.8 (477 × 28.1); M; 17; ex BALONG 1976; ex BATANG 1956. Sisters **15601 GIANT PIONEER** (Pa) ex BANGGAI **15602 KOTA SELAMAT** (Sg) ex BATJAN **15603 MINDANAO CAREER** (Pa) ex SEA TREASURE; ex BATU.

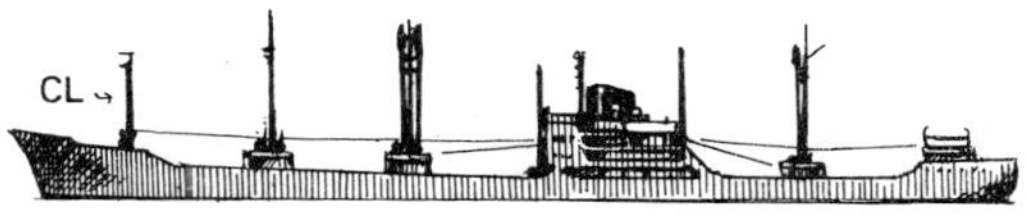

KM_2KMFKM H13
● **15610 NEDLLOYD EBRO**. Ne/Ne 1960; CP; 7300/10000; 159 × 8.3/9.3 (522 × 27.6/30.6); M; 17.5; ex NEDER EBRO 1977. Sisters **15611 NEDLLOYD EEMS** (Ne) ex NEDER EEMS 1977 **15612 KOTA MAJU** (Sg) ex NEDLLOYD ELBE; ex NEDER ELBE.

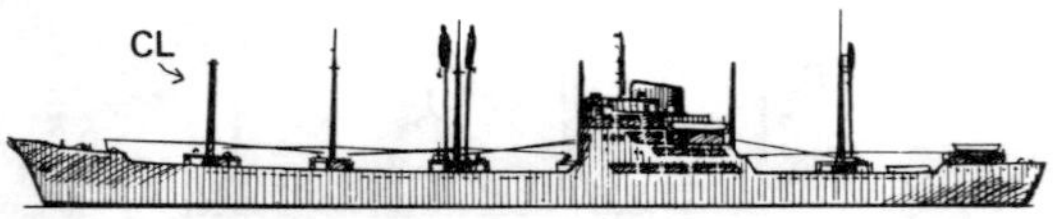

KM$_2$KMFKM H13
15620 NEDLLOYD KARAKORUM. Ne/Ne 1958; CP; 8000; 163.4 × 8.8 (536 × 29); M; 17; ex KARAKORUM 1977. Sisters **15621 NEDLLOYD WESER** (Ne) ex WESER 1977 **15622 KOTA JATI** (Sg) ex NEDLLOYD WAAL; ex NEDER WAAL.

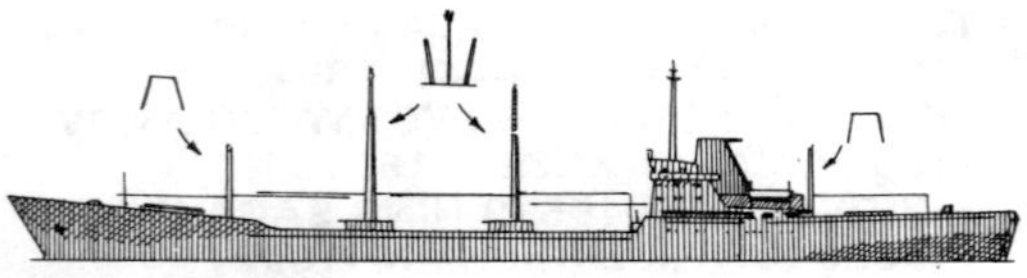

KM$_3$FK H13
15660 AMARALINA; Bz/Pd 1970; C; 6900/10200; 161 × —/9.7 (528 × —/31.11); M; 20.5; **'B-444'** type. Sisters **15661 ITABERA** (Bz) **15662 ITATINGA** (Bz) **15663 BOTAFOGA** (Bz) **15664 BERNARDINO CORREA** (Po) **15665 ARPOADOR** (Bz) Similar (lengthened): **15666 FROTABEIRA** (Bz) **15667 MARIA DA PENHA** (Bz) ex FROTATOKYO.

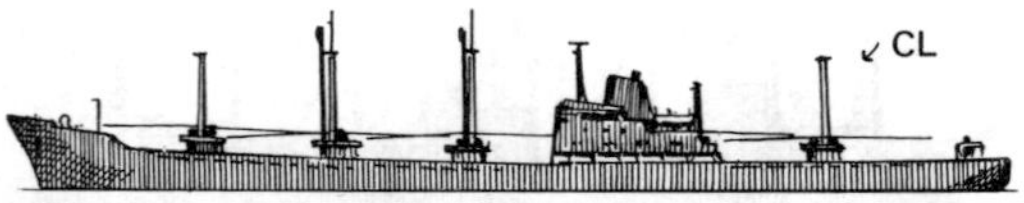

KM$_3$FK$_2$ H13
15680 JALAYAMUNA. In/FRG 1972; Pt.Con; 7800/10900; 158.4 × 8.5/9.6 (520 × 28/31.7); M; 16.25. Sister **15681 JALAYAMINI** (In).

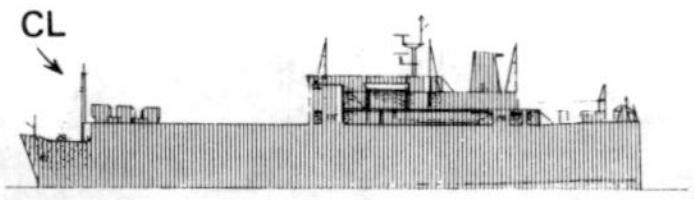

KM$_3$FMC H2
15690 AUTOROUTE. Br/Ja 1979; Ro VC; 2500; 100.01 × 4.21 (328.12 × 13.81); M; 15.25; Stern door/ramp.

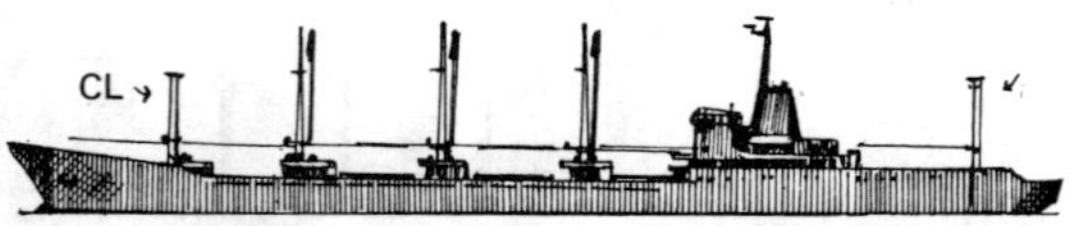

KM$_4$FK H13
● **15710 LA GUAIRA.** Ve/FRG 1970; C; 8400/11500; 165 × 9/9.8 (541 × 30/32.3); M; 22; ex CORALSTONE 1972. Sisters **15711 MARACAIBO** (Ve) ex RUBYSTONE 1972 **15712 ALKMAAR** (Ne) ex PEARLSTONE 1972 **15713 AMERSFOORT** (Ne) ex LOADSTONE 1972.

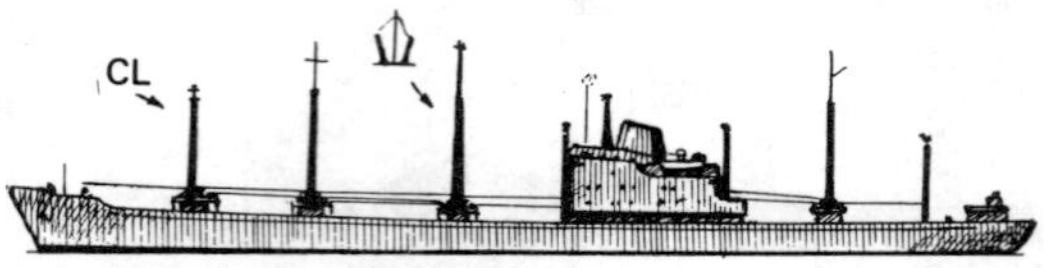

KM$_2$KMFKMK H13
15630 HANNOVERLAND. FRG/FRG 1966; CP; 7000/10200; 163 × 8/9 (534 × 26/30); M; 18. Sister **15631 LLOYD SYDNEY** (FRG) ex WESERLAND.

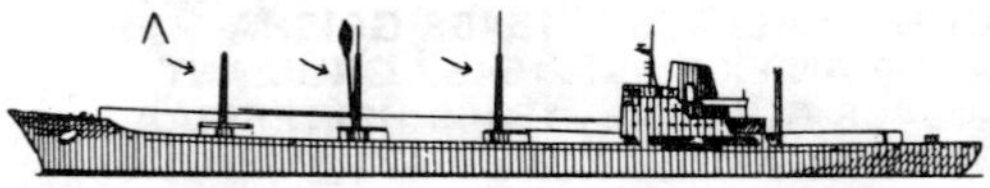

KM$_3$FK H1
15640 MOENJODARO. Pk/Ys 1968; C; 5900/8900; 154.5 × —/9.1 (507 × —/30); M; —. Sisters (Pk flag) **15641 RANGAMATI 15642 SUNDERBANS 15643 TAXILA** (Tu flag): **15644 ARAS 15645 DICLE 15646 FIRAT 15647 GEDIZ 15648 KEBAN 15649 MERIC.**

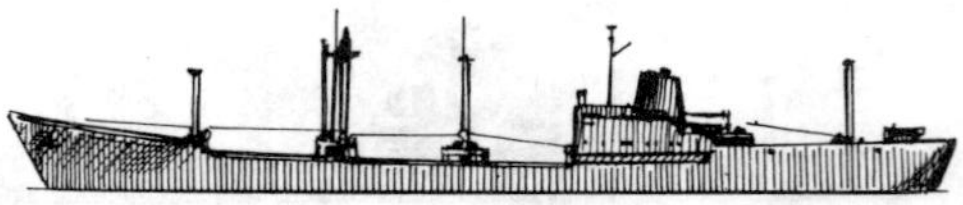

KM$_3$FK H13
● **15670 ARTICO.** Sp/FRG 1965; CP; 6400/9300; 156 × —/9 (511 × —/30); M; 18.25; ex TABORA 1974. Sisters **15671 NIKOS** (Gr) ex TAVETA 1975 **15672 STELLENBOSCH** (SA) **15673 TANGA** (As) ex LLOYD BRISBANE 1980; ex SWELLENDAM 1979 ⋆**15674 GEORG HANDKE** (DDR) ex TALANA 1977.

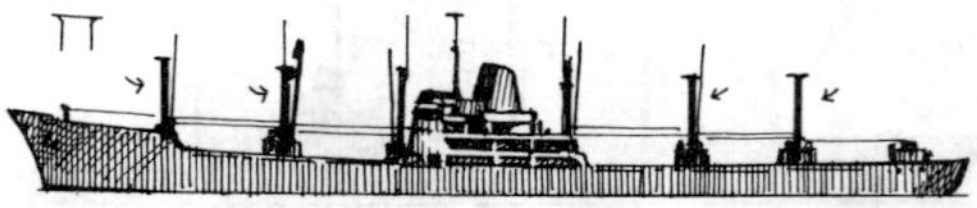

KM$_3$FMK$_2$
15700 AMBASSADOR. US/US 1960; C; 7800; 150.1 × 8.5 (493 × 28.1); T; 18.5; ex EXPORT AMBASSADOR 1980. Sisters (US flag) **15701 ADVENTURER** ex EXPORT ADVENTURER 1980 **15702 AIDE** ex EXPORT AIDE 1980 **15703 AGENT** ex EXPORT AGENT 1980 Vessels transferred to US Reserve Fleet.

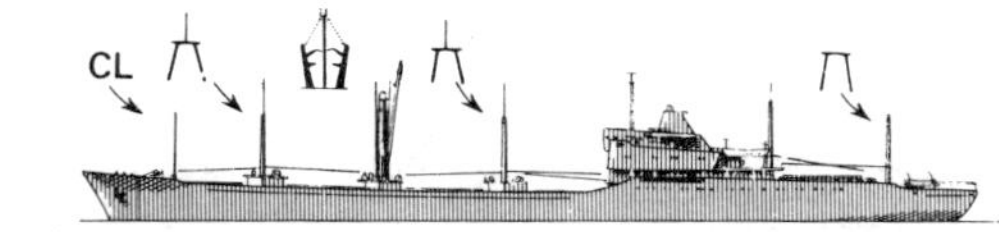

KMKM$_2$FK$_2$ H13
● **15720 VISHVA BINDU.** In/Pd 1969 C; 5400/8100; 145.3 × 7.5/9 (477 × 24.6/29.11); M; 17.5; **'B-445'** type. Sisters (In flag) **15721 VISHVA CHETANA** ex VISHVA CHETNA 1969; ex ZYGMUNT AUGUST **15722 VISHVA SANDESH** ex ZYGMUNT STARY **15723 VISHVA VIKAS** ex WLADYSLAW JAGIELLO (Pd flag) **⋆15724 WLADYSLAW JAGIELLO ⋆15725 WLADYSLAW LOKIETEK ⋆15726 ZYGMUNT AUGUST ⋆15727 ZYGMUNT STARY ⋆15728 ZYGMUNT III WAZA ⋆15729 MIESZKO I ⋆15730 BOLESLAW CHOBRY ⋆15731 BOLESLAW SMIALY ⋆15732 BOLESLAW KRZYWOUSTY** (Ir flag) **15733 IRAN ELHAM** EX ARYA KISH **15734 IRAN EKRAM** ex ARYA ROKH **15735 IRAN GHEYAM** ex ARYA ROOZ (RC flag) **⋆15736 JIANG CHENG** launched as WLADYSLAW IV (Fr flag) **15737 COURSON** ex ARYA DAD 1971; ex BOLESLAW KRZYWOUSTY.

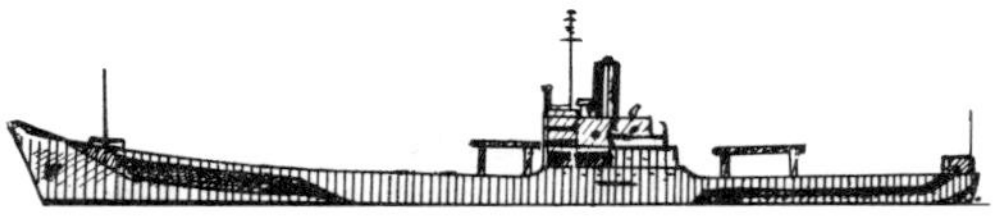

KNKMFNK H2
15770 PONCE. US/US 1944; Con; 10500; 154 × 7.7 (504 × 25.4); T; 15; ex LAND 1965; ex SANTA LEONOR 1964. Converted 'C2' cargo ship.

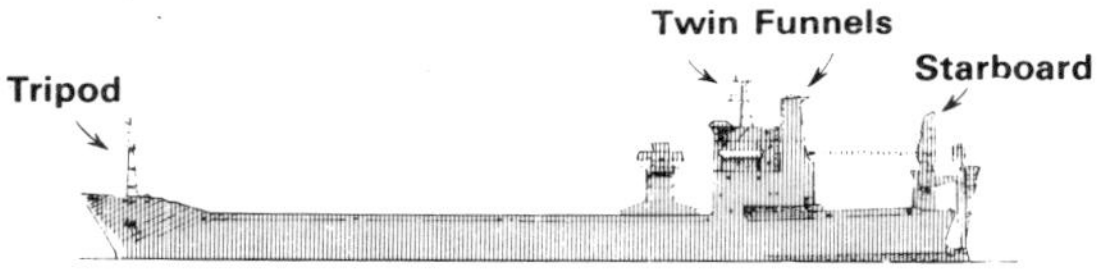

KNMFCR H1
⋆15790 LEDENICE. Ys/Ys 1979; Roc/Con/C 5600; 144.4 × 6.5 (473.75 × 21.33); M; 17.9; Travelling gantry with deck crane. Stern slewing ramp. Probable Sister: **⋆15791 BRIBIR** (Ys).

M H
15810 AYVALIK. Tu/Ne 1952; PC; 1900; 86 × 3.8 (285 × 12.6); TSM; 16. Sister: **15811 GEMLIK** (Tu).

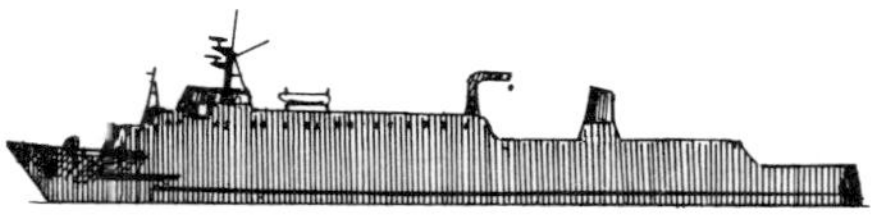

KMNF H2
15740 SURREY. De/De-Ne 1969/75; RoC; 4100; 132.7 × 5.8 (435 × 19); TSM 17.75. Stern door. Lengthened 1975.

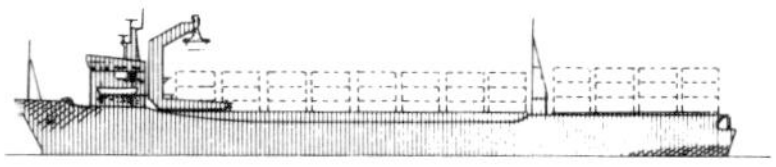

KMNMF H1
15750 TACKLER ARABIA. Br/Ja 1978; RoC/Con; 2800; 114.8 × 5.25 (376.6 × 17.22); M; 15.5; **"Tackler"** type. Sisters **15751 TACKLER DOSINIA** (Br) **15752 TAJIN** (Me).

KMNMFKMK H1
15760 LINCOLN. US/US 1962; Pt.Con; 13300; 172 × 9.6 (564 × 31.8); T; 20; ex PRESIDENT LINCOLN 1970. Sister **15761 TYLER** (US) ex PRESIDENT TYLER 1979; both vessels transferred to US Reserve Fleet.

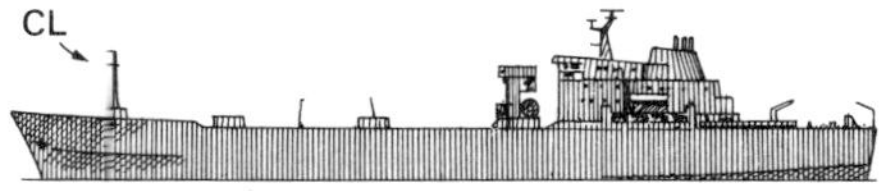

KNMF H12
15780 NEDLLOYD ROCKANJE. Ne/Fi 1972; RoC; 4300; 138 × 6.7 (451 × 21.1); TSM; 18; ex RHEINFELS 1976; ex ANTARES 1975; Stern door. Sisters: **15781 ORION** (Fi) **15782 SIRIUS** (Fi) **15783 BALTIC ENTERPRISE** (Br) **15784 BALTIC PROGRESS** (Br).

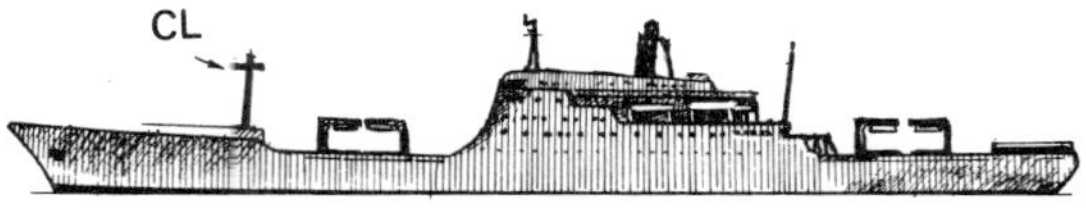

KNMFKN H12
15800 SANTA MAGDALENA. US/US 1963; PC/Con, 11200; 166 × 8.8 (545 × 29.1); T; 20. Sisters (US flag): **15801 SANTA MARIA 15802 SANTA MARIANA 15803 SANTA MERCEDES.**

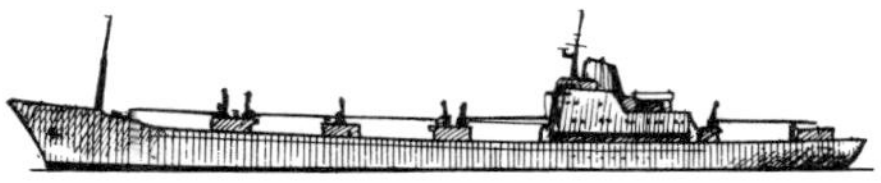

MC$_5$MFC H1
15820 BAMENDA. Fr/Sw 1964; R; 5800; 138.5 × 7.6 (454 × 25); M; 19.25; ex RIO NEGRO VALLEY 1970. Sister: **15821 MANOKA** (Fr) ex YAKIMA VALLEY 1970.

MC$_4$MFC H13
15830 NEDLLOYD WISSEKERK. Ne/Ne 1967; C; 7400/10700; 166.6 × 7.8/9.6 (546 × 25.6/31.6); M; 20. Sisters (Ne flag): **15831 NEDLLOYD WAALEKERK** ex WAALEKERK 1977 **15832 NEDLLOYD WILLEMSKERK** ex WILLEMSKERK 1977 **15833 NEDLLOYD WESTERKERK** ex WESTERKERK 1977.

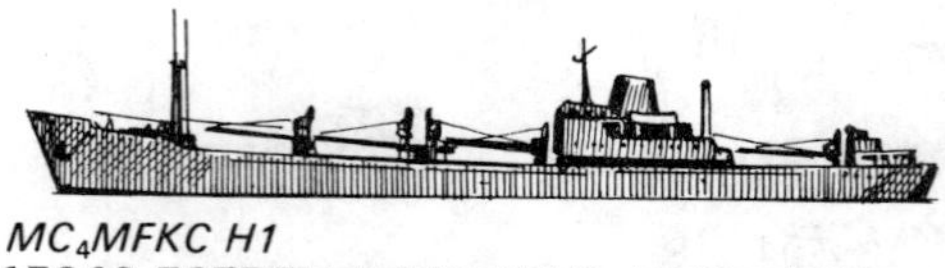

MC$_4$MFKC H1
15840 ESTRELLA DEL MAR. Ur/Sw 1961; CP; 5700/7500; 142.6 × 7.8/8.7 (46.8 × 25.6/28.6); M; 17; ex ESTRELLA.

MC$_3$KMFM
15850 TROJAN. Gr/De 1953; CP; 4600; 128 × 6.7 (420 × 22); M; 12.75; ex DOMINICA 1976; ex DOMINIC 1975; ex MAKATI 1967; ex JONNA DAN 1964; Lengthened 1967.

MC$_2$FM H1
15860 DORY. Gr/No 1954; C; 3000/4800; 121 × 6.6/7.3 (397 × 21.6/24); M; 15.75; ex MONTEVIDEO 1974.

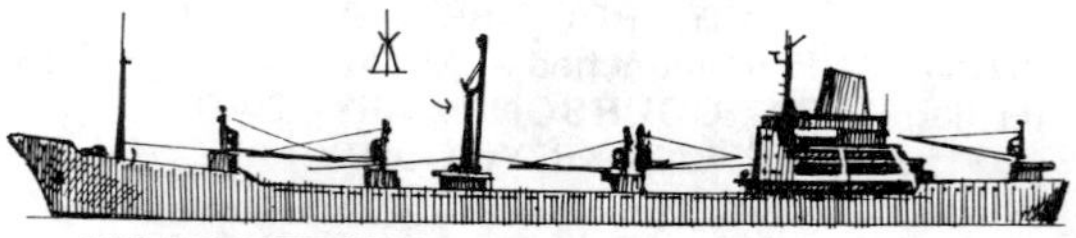

MC$_2$KC$_2$MFC H13
15870 RISHI ATRI. In/De 1966; CP; 7700; 164 × 8.6 (540 × 28.2); M; 20.75; ex ARANYA. Sisters: **15871 RISHI AGASTI** (In) ex AROSIA **15872 AZUMA** (Gr).

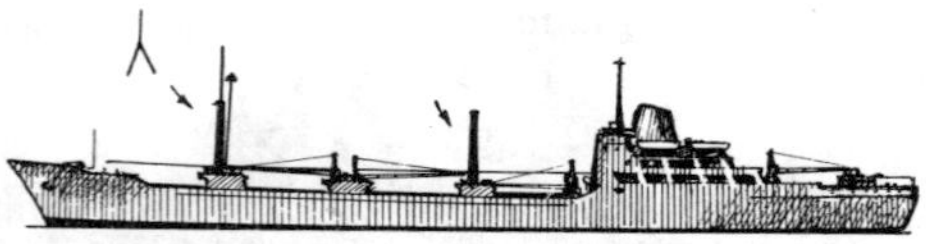

MC$_2$KCMFC H13
15880 IHABI. Eg/Sw 1962; CP; 6000/8500; 143.7 × 8/8.5 (471 × 26/28.3); M; 17.5; ex ALABAMA 1977. Sister: **15881 ELAMIR FAHD** (Eg) ex ARIZONA 1977.

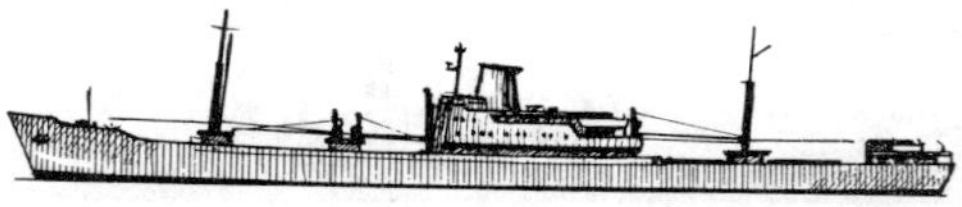

MC$_2$KFCM H1
15890 SAMOS SUN. Gr/Sw 1961; R; 6700; 149 × 8.5 (490 × 28); M; 18.5; ex LAKE EYRE 1975.

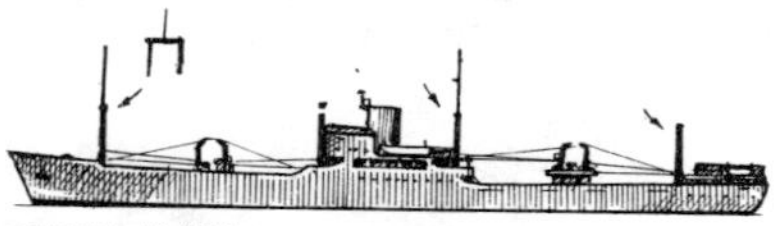

MC$_2$KFMC$_2$K H1
15900 TRIPOLI. Gr/Sw 1948; R; 4000; 120 × 7.1 (394 × 23.6); M; 16.5; ex KERKIRA 1965; ex ANTARCTIC OCEAN 1965.

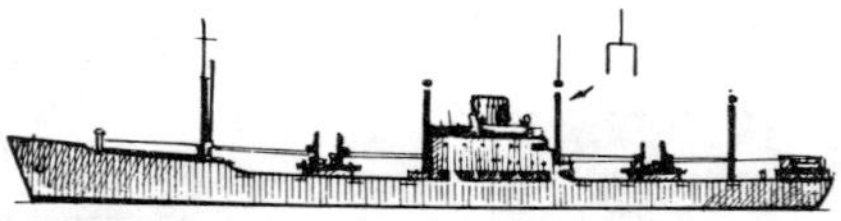

MC$_2$KFMC$_2$K H1
● **15910 AVRA.** Gr/Sw 1954; C; 4000; 130.89 × 7.19 (429.43 × 23.59); M; 16.5; ex VIDALAND 1978.

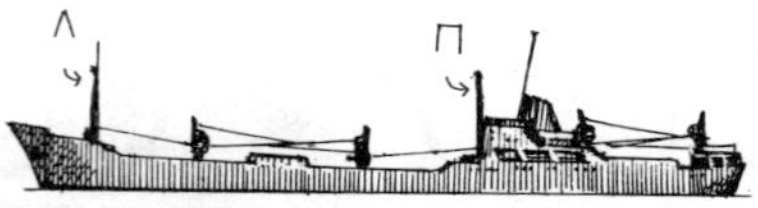

MC$_2$KMFC$_2$ H13
15920 JUN SHAN. Pa/No 1957; CP; 4500; 115.3 × 6.8 (378 × 22.6); M; 15.25; ex BRISEIS 1975.

MC$_2$KMFCK H13
● **15930 HADI.** Sh/Sw 1955; CP; 3800; 114 × 6.8 (375 × 22.6); M; 15.25; ex TELAURA 1980; ex BALKIS 1975. Similar (foremast bipod): **15931 TELANCA** (Cy) ex BAGHDAD 1975.

MC$_2$KMFKC$_2$K H1
15940 SANDYEVERETT. Li/Sw 1961; R; 6600; 150 × 8.5 (492 × 28); M; 19.5; ex LAKE ONTARIO 1976.

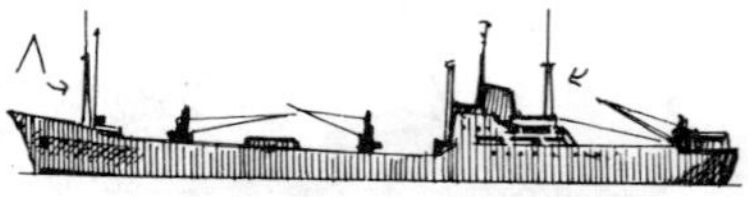

MC$_2$KMFMC H13
15950 GAO SHAN. Pa/No 1956; CP; 4500; 115.3 × 6.8 (378 × 22.6); M; 15.25; ex BOSPHORUS 1975.

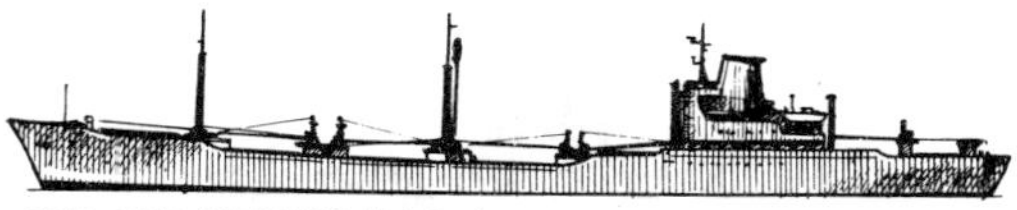

MC$_2$MC$_2$KMFKC H13
★**15960 QINGSHUI.** RC/Ne 1964; C; 6300/9400; 158.6 × 7.7/8.5 (521 × 25.4/28); M; 17.5; ex NARA. Sisters (RC flag): ★**15961 TIANSHUI** ex NICOBAR 1972 Similar: ★**15962 HENGSHUI** ex NAGASAKI 1972.

MC$_2$MFC H
15970 PLAYA DE LAS NIEVES. Sp/Sp 1967; CP; 2600; 110 × 6.4 (361 × 21); M; 19. Sisters: **15971 PLAYA BLANCA** (Sp) **15972 USHUAIA** (Ar) ex PLAYA DE NAOS.

MC$_2$MFC$_2$M H1
15980 KIRRIBILLI. Sw/Be 1956; CP; 7400/10700; 156 × 8.4/9 (511 × 27.6/30); M; 17.5.

MC$_2$MFK$_2$ H1
15990 BRUARFOSS. Pa/De 1960; C; 2300/3100; 102 × 6.3/6.8 (336 × 20.6/22.4); M; 15. Sister: **15991 SELFOSS** (Ic).

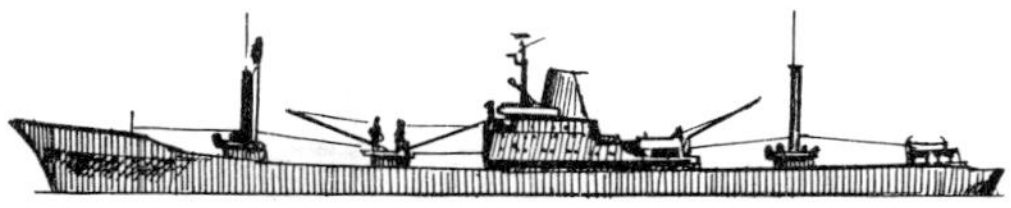

MC$_2$MFM H1
● **16000 PAROS.** Gr/Sw 1965; R; 6800/8900; 152.3 × 8/8.8 (500 × 26.3/28.1); M; 19.5; ex LOCH LONG 1976; ex PACIFIC OCEAN 1974.

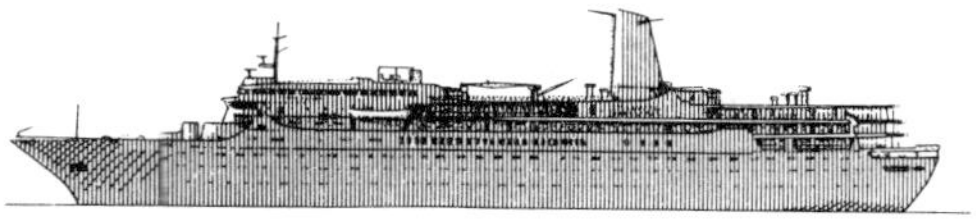

MCF H
16010 PROCYON. Pa/Ne-Sw 1972/75; LS; 5600; 148.11 × 6.83 (485.93 × 22.41); TSM; 14.75; ex LINDA CLAUSEN 1980; ex CUNARD AMBASSADOR 1975; Side doors. Converted from passenger 1975.

MCFCM H
● **16020 IRAN CREMONA.** Sg/Ne 1951; LS; 11600; 159.4 × 7.9 (523 × 25.11); TSM; 18; ex CREMONA 1976; ex PETREL 1974; ex YAPEYU 1969; Converted from a cargo ship 1968. Sister: **16021 CORMORAN** (Sg) ex ALBERTO DODERO 1969.

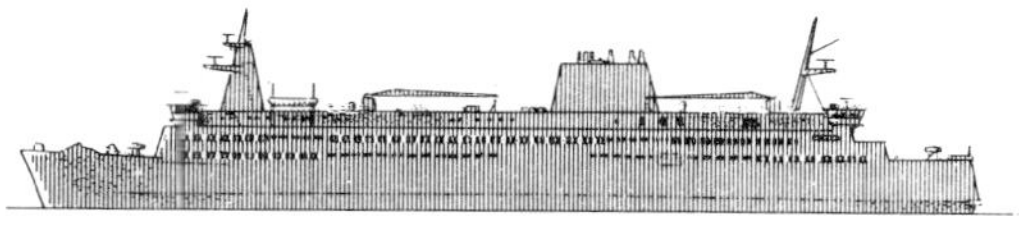

MCFCM H
16030 PRINS JOACHIM. De/De 1980; TF/RoPCF; 10600; 152 × 5.6 (498.69 × 18.37); TSM; 18. Bow and stern doors. Sisters: **16031 DRONNING INGRID 16032 KRONPRINS FREDERIK.**

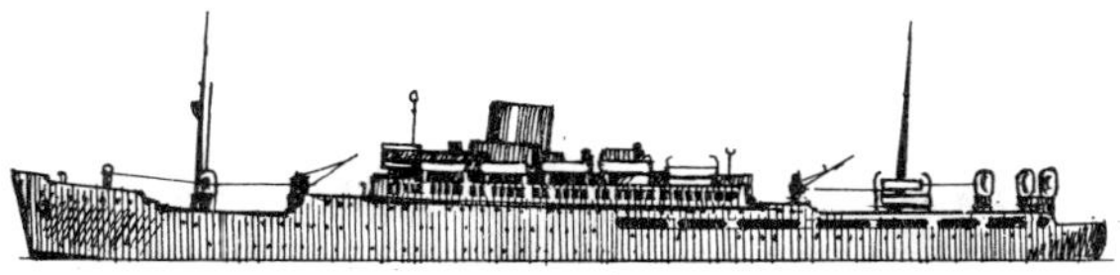

MCFCM H12
★**16040 ROSSIYA.** Ru/Ge 1938; PC; 17900; 182 × 7.1 (589 × 25); TSD-E; 15; ex EMPIRE WELLAND 1946; ex PATRIA 1945.

MCFM H
16050 NABIL. Le/Sw 1946; C; 1600; 80.42 × 5.07 (263.85 × 16.63); M; 12; ex ALEXIS 1973; ex FAY 1971; ex VELA 1968.

MCFM H1
16060 REA. Gr/Sw 1956; R; 3300/4300; 116.8 × 6.4/— (383 × 20.8/—); M; 17.5; ex LASTRIGONI 1974; ex COOLGARDIE 1969.

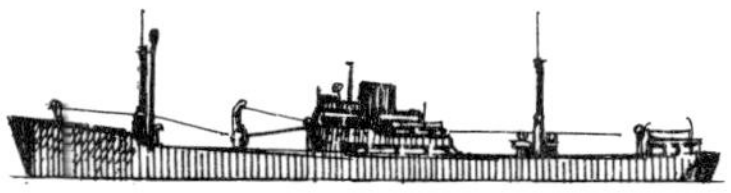

MCFM H1
16070 KRIOS. Gr/No 1955; C; 2700; 113.11 × 6.17 (371.1 × 20.24); M; —; ex THIRA 1980; ex FERNSPRING 1965. Sister: ★**16071 WEISSERITTZ** (DDR) ex FERNRIVER 1965.

MCFM H1
16080 LUCKY. Cy/It 1946; C; 3100; 117.5 × 6.4 (385 × 19.4); M; 14.5; ex CAGLIARI 1977.

MCFM H1
16090 TAREK. Gr/FRG 1953; CP; 4200; 114 × 7.6 (370 × 24.11); M; 15; ex NONI 1980; ex DARRAH 1974; ex RANTUM 1969.

MCFM H1
16100 HAKON JARL. No/De 1952; P; 2200; 80.8 × 4.5 (265 × 15.2); M; 15.

MCFM H12
⋆**16110 XX ANIVERSARIO.** Cu/Ne 1957; PC; 7500; 131.6 × 7 (432 × 23.8); M; 15.5; ex ORANJE NASSAU 1973. Sister: ⋆**16111 VIETNAM HEROICO** (Cu) ex PRINS DER NEDERLANDEN 1973.

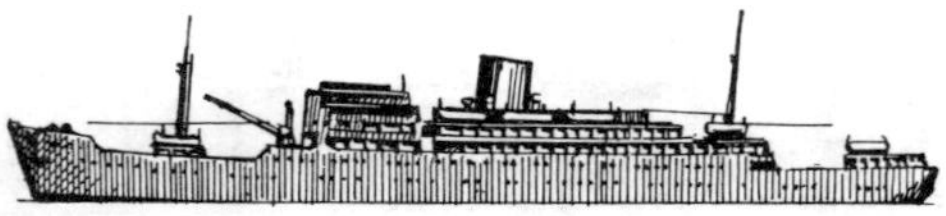

MCFM H12
⋆**16120 JIAN HUA.** RC/Fr 1951; PC; 9500; 150 × 6.9 (479 × 22.9); M; 16; ex FOCH 1967.

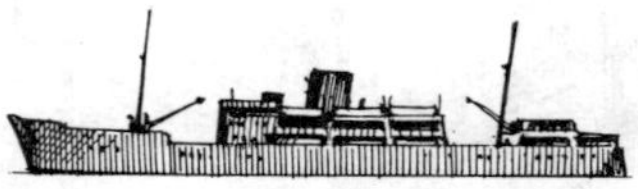

MCFMC H1
16130 ACHILLEUS. Cy/De 1939; PC; 2900; 99 × 4.8 (325 × 15.11); M; 17.5; ex HANS BROGE 1970; Lengthened 1955.

MCFMC$_2$ H
⋆**16140 UKRAINA.** Ru/De 1938; PC; 6400; 132 × 5.7 (432 × 15.9); TSM; 18; ex BASARABIA 1948.

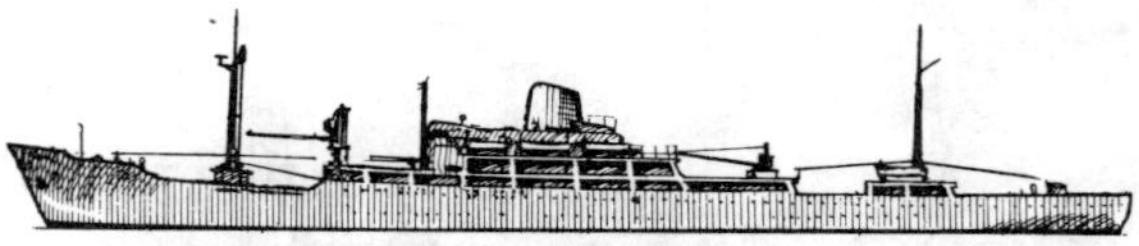

MCKFCM H12
⋆**16150 YU HUA.** RC/Ne 1958; PC; 11900/13600; 178 × 8.1/9 (584 × 26.8/29.5); TSM; 18.5; ex NIEUW HOLLAND 1974; ex RANDFONTEIN 1971.

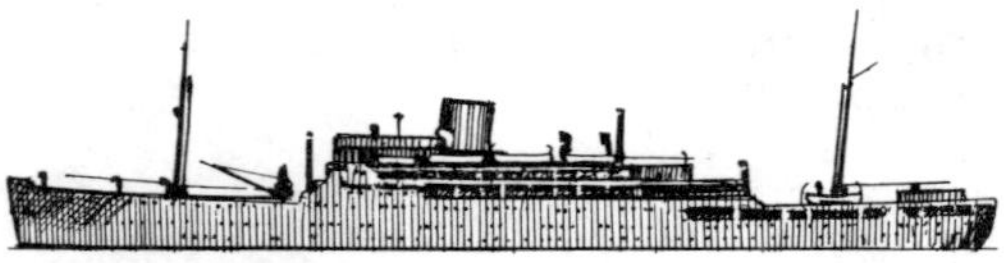

MCKFKM H1
⋆**16160 ILYCH.** Ru/Ge 1933; PC; 13100; 160 × 7.4 (524 × 24.8); TSM; 16; ex CARIBIA 1946; Rebuilt 1952.

MCKMFKCK H1
16170 RIO DE JANERIO. Gr/No 1957; CP; 3100/4900; 121 × 6.6/7.3 (397 × 21.8/24); M; 15.5.

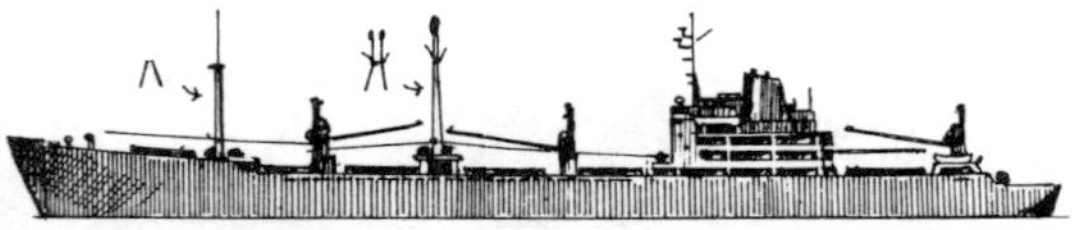

MCMCMFC H1
● **16180 TINOS.** Gr/De 1967; CP; 10900; 166 × 9.6 (545 × 31.7); M; 20.75; ex ALAMEDA.

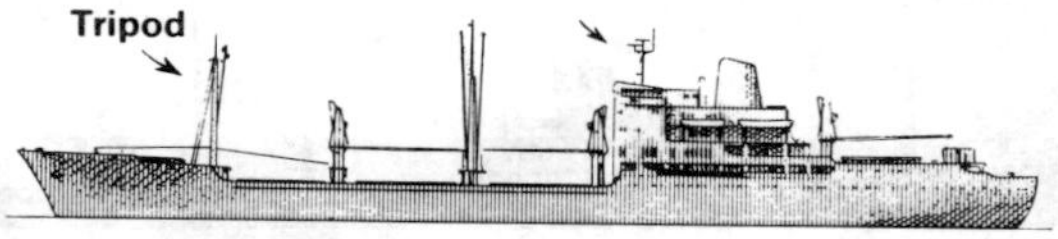

MCMCMFC H13
16190 FABIOLAVILLE. Be/Be 1972; PC; 9300/13500; 161.14 × 7.93/9.89 (528.67 × 26.05/32.48); M; 20. Sister: **16191 KANANGA** (Zr).

MCMF H1
16200 VOORSPELER. SA/Br 1965; C; 900; 68 × 4.2 (224 × 13.9); M; 12.

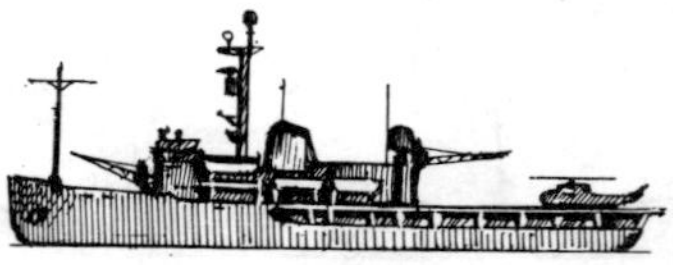

MCMFC H
16210 FUJI. Ja/Ja 1965; RS/IB; 5300 Disp; 100 × 8.8 (328 × 29); TSM; 17; Hangar and three helicopters.

MCMFCM H1
16220 ASTERI. Gr/FRG 1965; R; 6200; 137 × 7.9 (450 × 25.5); M; 20; ex HOOD RIVER VALLEY 1971. Sister: **16221 ATALANTI** (Gr) ex OKANAGAN VALLEY 1971.

MCMFK H
16230 DISCOVERY. Br/Br 1962; RS; 2700; 79.5 × 4.7 (261 × 15.6); D-E- —.

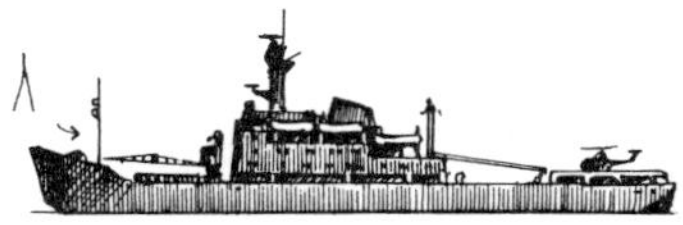

MCMFK H1
16240 BRANSFIELD. Br/Br 1970; RS; 4800; 99 × 6.7 (325 × 22); D-E; —.

MCMFK H1
16250 TOWUTI. Ia/Pd 1962; C; 3400; 96 × 4.5 (316 × 14.8); M; 12; **'B 450'** type. Sisters (Ia flag): **16251 TOBELO 16252 TOGARAN 16253 TOKALA 16254 TOLANDO 16255 TOMAKO 16256 TOMBATU.**

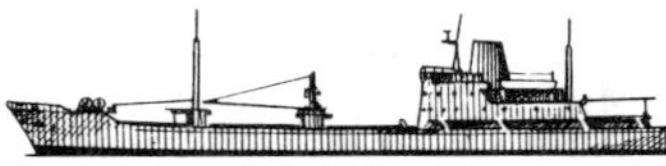

MCMFM H1
16260 EIGAMOIYA. Na/Br 1969; CP; 4400; 112 × 7.6 (367 × 25); M; 15.

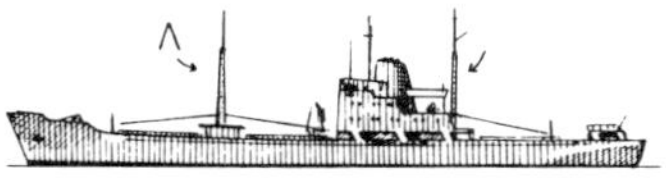

MCMFM H1
⋆**16270 JASLO.** Pd/De 1967; C; 2300; 101.5 × 6 (335 × 19.8); M; 15.

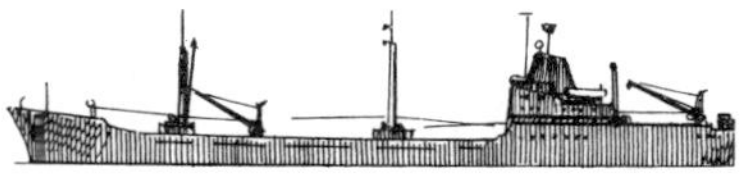

MCM_2FKC H13
16280 BHAIRAB. Pk/FRG 1961; CP; 3400/5400; 119 × 6.5 7.8 (390 × 21.4/25.6); M; 16; ex CAP COLORADO 1971; ex NORDERDIEK 1961.

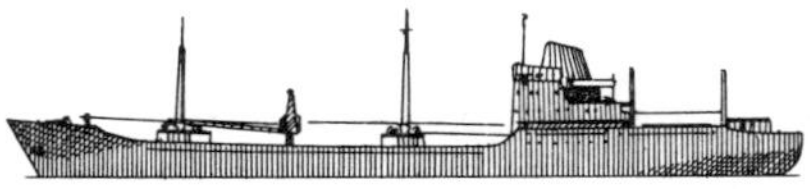

MCM_2FK_2 H13
16290 MIKELDEN. Cy/FRG 1964; CP; 3400/5300; 125.9 × 6.7/7.8 (413 × 22/25.6); M; 16.5; ex RIVER GONGOLA; ex POELDYK 1974.

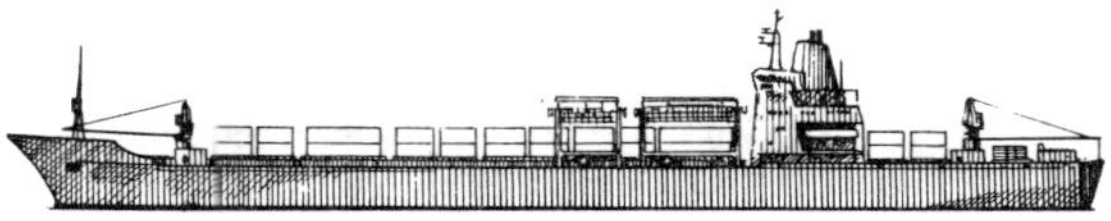

MCN_2MFC H1
16300 AXEL JOHNSON. Sw/Fi 1969; Con; 16300; 174.3 × 10 (572 × 23); TSM; 23. Sister: **16301 ANNIE JOHNSON** Similar: **16302 MARGARET JOHNSON** Gantries may have been removed.

MF H
16310 DOULOS. Ma/US 1914; PC; 6800; 130.3 × 5.6 (428 × 18.2); M; 15; ex FRANCA C; ex ROMA 1952; ex MEDINA 1949; Converted to a floating book exhibition ship. Re-engined 1952.

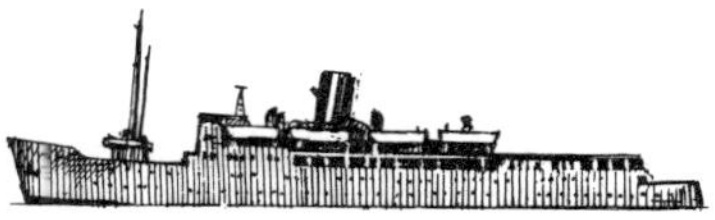

MF H
16320 HELLAS. Gr/Br 1935; CP; 4300; 108 × 4.6 (355 × 15.1); T; 16; ex TAROONA 1959.

MF H
⋆**16330 SHAO YAO.** RC/China 1947; P; 1600; 76.2 × 4.5 (250 × 15); R; 10; River service.

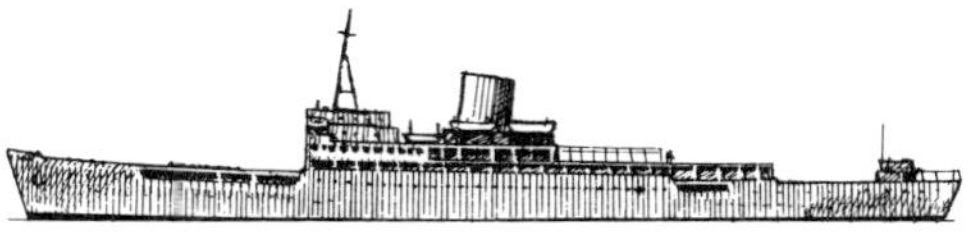

MF H
16340 SIRIUS. Gr/Br 1948; RoP; 8900; 151.8 × 8.4 (498 × 27.6); T; 15.5; ex CHANIA 1971; ex WARWICKSHIRE 1965.

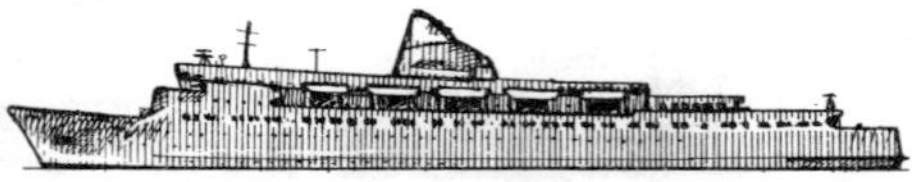

MF H
16350 BLACK WATCH/JUPITER. No/FRG 1966; RoP; 9500; 141.6 × 6.5 (466 × 22); TSM; 22; Serves as BLACK WATCH in winter and as JUPITER in summer. Sister: **16351 BLACK PRINCE/VENUS** (No).

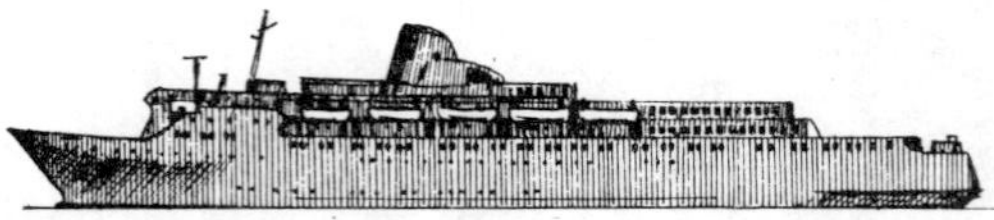

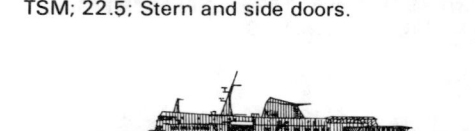

MF H
● **16360 BLENHEIM.** Br/Br 1970; RoPCF; 9200/10400; 149.3 × 6/6.7 (490 × 19.8/22); TSM; 22.5; Stern and side doors.

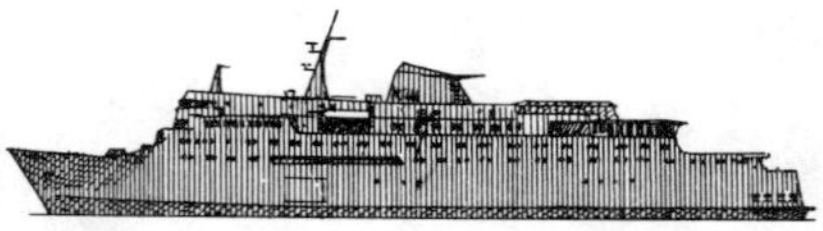

MF H
16370 COLUMBIA. US/US 1974; F; 3900; 127.4 × 5.3 (418 × 17.5); TSM; 21.

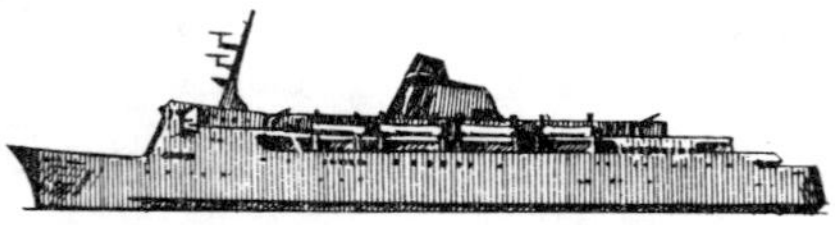

MF H
16380 ST. GEORGE. Br/Br 1968; RoP; 7400; 128 × 5 (420 × 16.5); TSM; 21; Bow and stern doors.

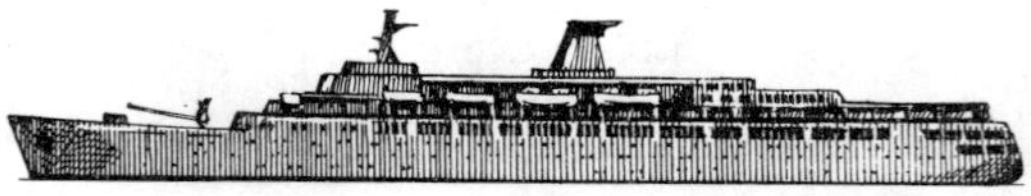

MF H
16390 DAPHNE. Gr/Br 1959; P; 11700; 162 × 10 (533 × 32.1); TSM; 17; ex AKROTIRI EXPRESS 1974; ex PORT SYDNEY 1972; Rebuilt from a cargo ship. Sister: **16391 DANAE** (Gr) ex THERISSOS EXPRESS 1974; ex PORT MELBOURNE 1972.

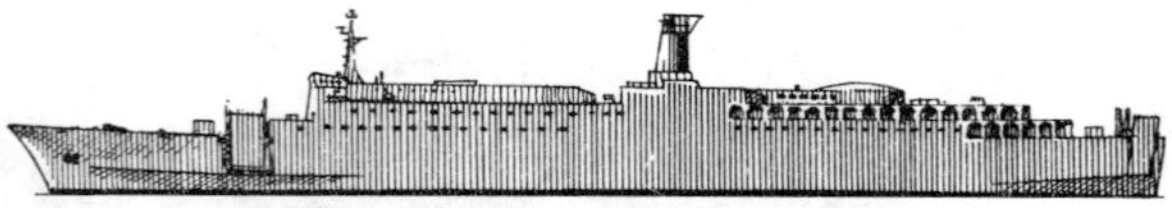

MF H
16400 SUN FLOWER. Ja/Ja 1972; RoPF; 11300; 185 × 6.4 (607 × 21); TSM; 24.75. Sisters (Ja flag): **16401 SUN FLOWER 2 16402 SUN FLOWER 5 16403 SUN FLOWER 8.**

MF H
16410 EMPRESS OF AUSTRALIA. Br/Au 1965; RoPF; 8200; 135.6 × 6.1 (445 × 20.1); TSM; 17.

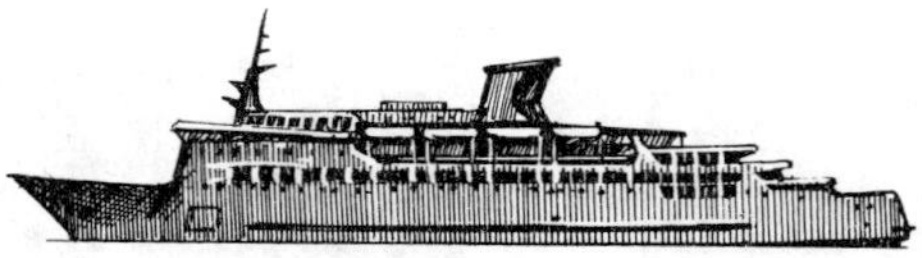

MF H
16420 MANUEL SOTO. Sp/Sp 1976; RoPF; 9100; 140.8 × 6.4 (462 × 21); TSM; 23.5. Sister: **16421 J.J. SISTER** (Sp).

MF H
⋆**16430 GULANG YU.** RC/Sp 1964; F; 6400; 130.3 × 4.2 (428 × 14); TSM; 18; ex MING YI 1979; ex CIUDAD DE BUENOS AIRES: Side doors. Sister: **16431 CITY OF RHODOS** (Gr) ex 33 ORIENTALES 1980.

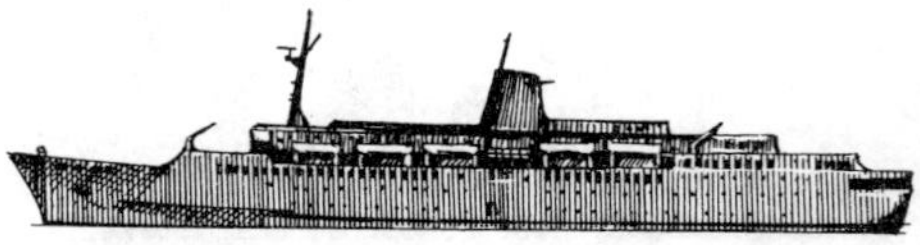

MF H
16440 PROVENCE. Fr/It 1974; RoP; 7800; TSM; 23; Bow and stern doors.

MF H
● **16450 PRINCE OF BRITTANY.** Sw/FRG 1970; RoP; 5500; 118.5 × 5 (389 × 16.5); TSM; —; ex PRINCE OF FUNDY; Bow, stern & side doors. Sister: **16451 SAINT PATRICK** (Ih) Similar: **16452 PETER WESSEL** (No).

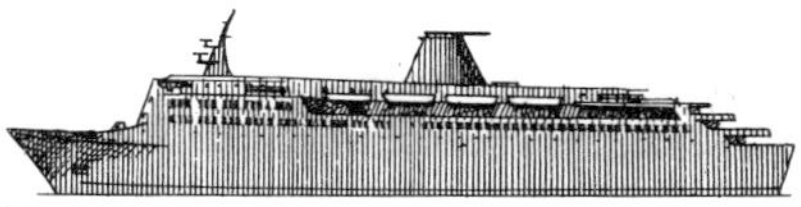

MF H
16460 STENA JUTLANDICA. Sw/Ys 1973; RoP; 6300; 124.9 × 5.3 (410 × 17.6); TSM; 22; Bow and stern doors. Sisters (Sw flag): **16461 STENA DANICA 16462 STENA NORDICA** Similar: **16463 STENA OLYMPICA 16464 SAINT KILLIAN** ex STENA SCANDINAVICA.

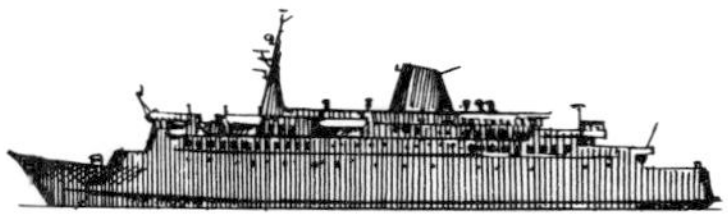

MF H
● **16470 KALLE III.** De/FRG 1974; RoPF; 4400; 118 × 5 (388 × 16.5); TSM; 21; ex KATTEGAT II. Sister: **16471 DJURSLAND II** (De).

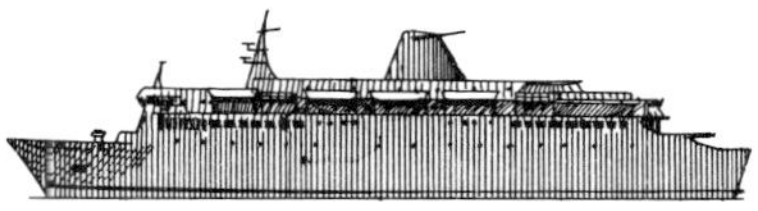

MF H
● **16480 TRAVEMUNDE.** De/FRG 1971; RoP; 4000; 118 × 5 (387 × 16.5); TSM; 21; Bow, stern & side doors.

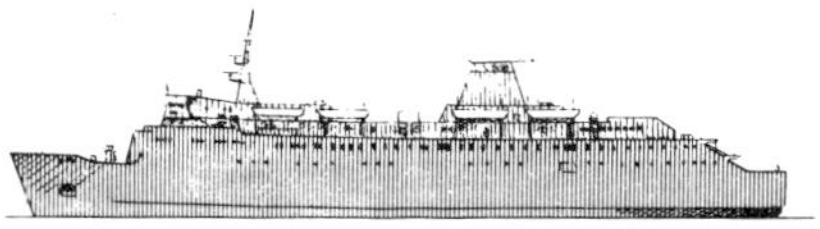

MF H
16490 CONNACHT. Ih/Ih 1978; RoPCF; 6000; 122.03 × 4.82 (400.36 × 15.81); TSM; 20; Bow & stern doors/ramps. Sister: **16491 LEINSTER** (Ih).

MF H
● **16500 QUEEN OF SURREY.** Ca/FRG 1969; RoP; 8800; 125 × 4.87 (410.1 × 15.98); TSM; 22.5; ex STENA DANICA 1974; Bow & stern doors.

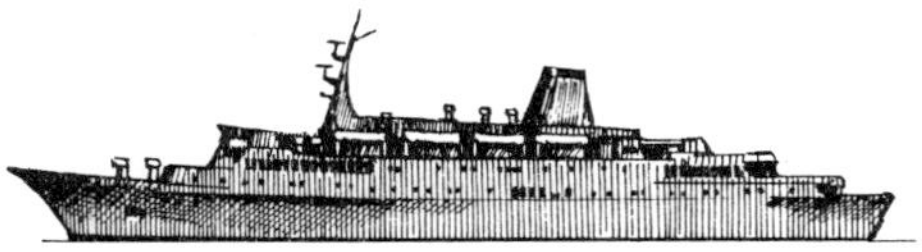

MF H
● **16510 PRINZ OBERON.** FRG/FRG 1970; RoP; 7900; 134 × 4.9 (440 × 16.3); TSM; 22; ex PRINS OBERON; Stern & side doors. Similar: **16511 PRINZ HAMLET** (FRG) **16512 GUSTAV VASA** (Sw) **16513 NILS DACKE** (Sw).

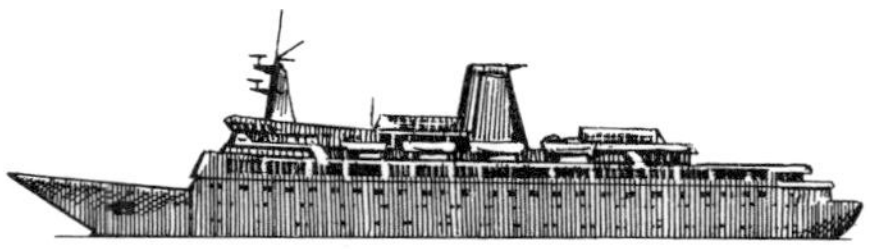

MF H
16520 GOLDEN ODYSSEY. Gr/De 1974; P; 6800; 130.2 × 5.2 (427 × 17.2); TSM; 21.

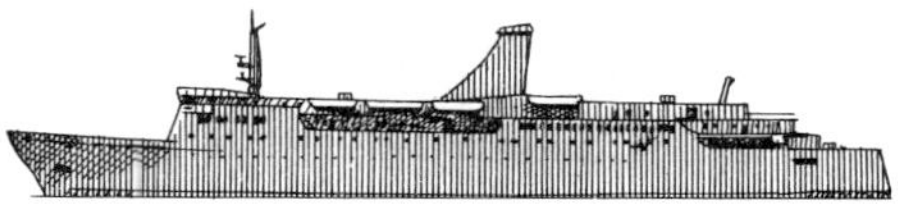

MF H
● **16530 CANGURO CABO SAN SEBASTIAN.** Sp/Sp 1972; RoP; 7500; 137.8 × 5.7 (452 × 18.1); TSM; 22.5; Stern door. Sisters (Sp flag): **16531 CANGURO CABO SAN JORGE 16532 CIUDAD DE BADAJOZ** Possible Sisters: **16533 CIUDAD DE SEVILLA 16534 CIUDAD DE CACERES.**

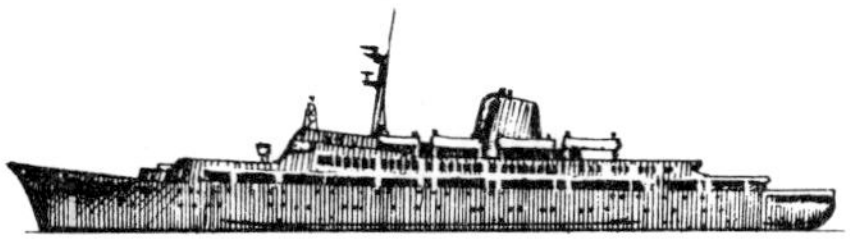

MF H
16540 JUPITER. Gr/Fr 1961; PC; 6300; 126.6 × 6.4 (415 × 21); M; 16; ex ALEXANDROS 1970; ex MOLEDET 1970; Also known as **ZEUS.**

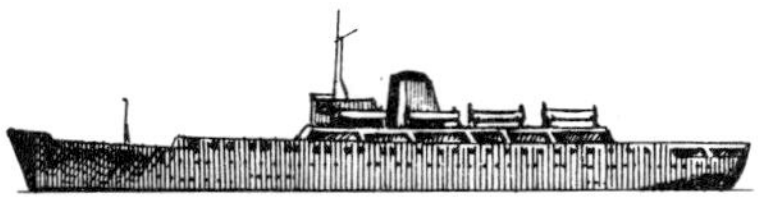

MF H
● **16550 MELINA.** Gr/Fr 1949; PC; 5100; 113.6 × 6.9 (373 × 22.8); T; 15; ex AZROU 1968. Similar: **16551 DELOS** (Gr) ex AZEMMOUR 1969.

MF H
● **16560 GOLDEN PRINCESS.** Gr/US 1944; PC; 3000; 94.7 × 4 (311 × 13); TSM; 18; ex ARTEMIS K 1980; ex ARTEMIS 1974; ex MYCONOS 1973; ex KYPROS 1964.

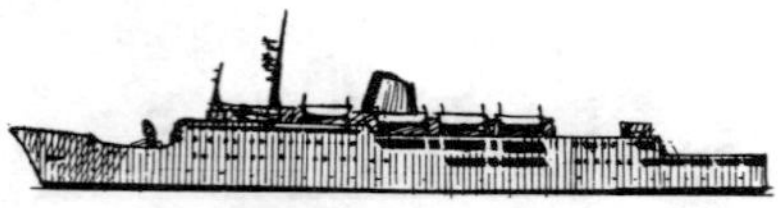

MF H
16570 GENNARGENTU. It/It 1965; RoP; 4900; 122 × 5.5 (411 × 16.3); TSM; 16.

MF H
16580 APOLLO III. Sw/Sw 1962; RoP; 4300; 101.4 × 4.8 (333 × 15.7); M; 16.5; Side doors.

MF H
● **16590 FIESTA.** Gr/Br 1946; P; 3200; 105 × 5.5 (341 × 16.2); TST; 20; ex CARINA 1964; ex BARROW QUEEN 1963; ex MONA'S QUEEN 1956.

MF H
16600 GALAXIAS. Gr/Br 1957; P; 4900; 104.32 × 4.81 (342.26 × 15.78); TSM; 17.5; ex SCOTTISH COAST 1969; Converted from ferry.

MF H
16610 ARGONAUT. Gr/Ge 1929; P; 4000; 93.2 × 5.6 (306 × 16); TSM; 13; ex ORION 1964; ex VIXON 1950; ex ORION 1947; Converted from a yacht 1947; Also known as **ARGONAFTIS.**

MF H
16620 KENTAVROS. Gr/US 1941; P; 2500; 94.9 × 4.6 (312 × 15); TSM; 15.5; ex BARNEGAT 1963; Former USN seaplane tender.

MF H
16630 ELENA P. Gr/Ge 1944; F; 1100; 68.3 × 2.7 (224 × 9); TSM; 14; ex LILLI SCARLETT 1964; ex HARALD IVERS 1954; ex M608 (German Minesweeper).

MF H
16640 POLIKOS. Gr/— 1943; C; —; 68.6 × 5 (225 × 16.5); TSM; 18; ex ATHINA 1961; ex ADRIS 1961; ex CYCLADES 1958; Built as HMS PERSIAN.

MF H
16650 EPOMEO PRIMO. It/Ys 1953; P; 630; 54.1 × 2.9 (178 × 9.8); TSM; 14.5; ex ALEKSA SANTIC 1971.

MF H
16660 DUC DE NORMANDIE. Fr/Sw 1958; F; 500; 45.6 × — (150 × —); M; 12; ex THOR VIKING 1973.

MF H
16670 SECHELT QUEEN. Ca/US 1947; RoPF; 5000; 96.9 × 4 (321 × 13.2); TSD-E; 16.5; ex CHINOOK II 1963; ex CHINOOK 1955.

MF H
16680 QUEEN OF SIDNEY. Ca/Ca 1960; RoPF; 3100; 102.4 × 3.8 (336 × 12.6); TSM; 8; ex SIDNEY 1963.

MF H
16690 ISLA DE MENORA. Sp/Ne 1961; RoPF; 1600; 78.9 × 2.9 (251 × 9.8); TSM; 15; ex LINDA SCARLETT 1971.

MF H
● **16700 HEBRIDES.** Br/Br 1964; RoPF; 1400; 71.6 × 2.7 (235 × 9); TSM; 14.5. Sister: **16701 COLUMBA** (Br).

MF H
16710 NAUSHON. US/US 1957; RoPF; 2700; 70 × 3.1 (230 × 10.3); TSR; 17; ex NANTUCKET 1975.

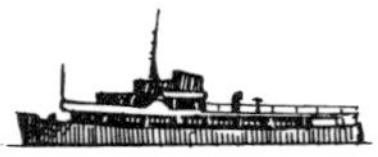

MF H
● ⋆**16720 VLADIMIR NAZOR.** Ys/Ys 1952; C; 430; 54.2 × 2.9 (178 × 9.8); TSM; 14. Sisters (Ys flag): ⋆**16721 VUK KARADZIC** ⋆**16723 NJEGOS** Similar (Passenger ships): **16724 CAMPANIA PRIMA** (It) ex IVAN CANKAR 1973 **16725 CAMPANIA SECONDA** (It) ex KOSTA RACIN 1973.

MF H
16730 BEYKOZ. Tu/Tu 1959; F; 500; 47.1 × 2.4 (153 × 8); TSM; —.

MF H
16740 AL RIYADH. Si/Ne 1978; Y; —; 64.64 × 3 (212 × 9.84); M; 21; Helicopter deck. Also known as **AL RIYAD.**

MF H
16750 GUSTAV AV KLINT. Sw/Sw 1941; RS; 500; 52 × 4.7 (170 × 15.7); M; 10; Rebuilt 1963.

MF H
⋆**16760 PALMA SORIANO.** Cu/Sp 1967; RoPF; 2000; 72.9 × 3.2 (239 × 10.7); TSM; —. Sister: ⋆**16761 JIBACOA.**

MF H
16770 LORD SELKIRK. Ca/Ca 1958; RoPF; 1800; 79 × 3.7 (259 × 12.1); TSM; —.

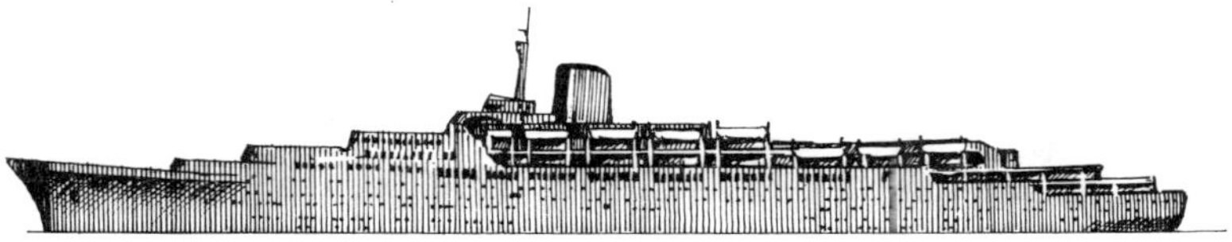

MF H
16780 FESTIVALE. Pa/Br-Ja 1961/78; P; 26600; 231.71 × 9.75 (760.2 × 31.99); TST; 23.5; ex S.A. VAAL 1977; ex TRANSVAAL CASTLE 1966; rebuilt 1978.

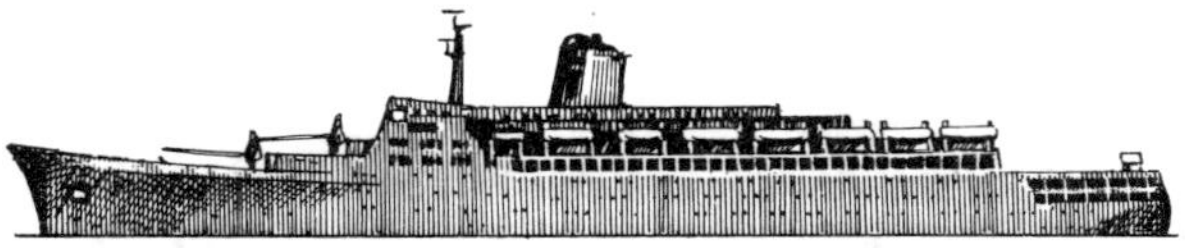

MF H
16790 FAIRWIND. Li/Br 1957; P; 16700; 185.3 × 8.9 (608 × 29.4); TST; 20; ex SYLVANIA 1968. Sister: **16791 FAIRSEA** (Li) ex FAIRLAND 1971; ex CARINTHIA 1968.

MF H
16800 MEDITERRANEAN SEA. Cy/Br 1953; RoPF; 16400; 164.9 × 6.4 (541 × 21); TSM;—; ex CITY OF EXETER 1972; converted from a Passenger Cargo Ship 1972. Sister: **16801 MEDITERRANEAN SKY** (Gr) ex CITY OF YORK 1971.

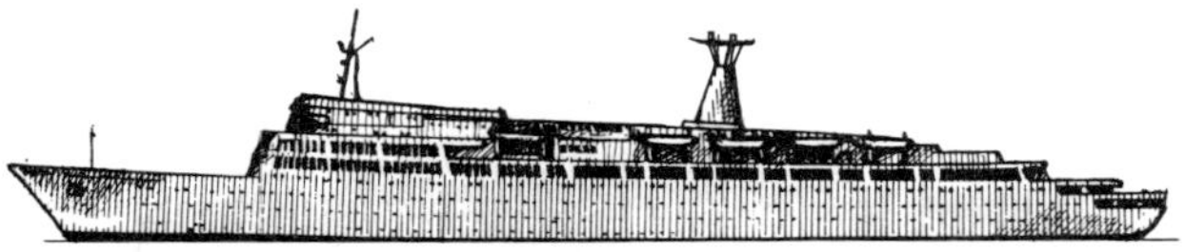

MF H
⋆**16810 MAKSIM GORKIY.** Ru/FRG 1969; P; 25000; 194.6 × 8.3 (627 × 27); TST; 23; ex HANSEATIC 1974; ex HAMBURG 1973.

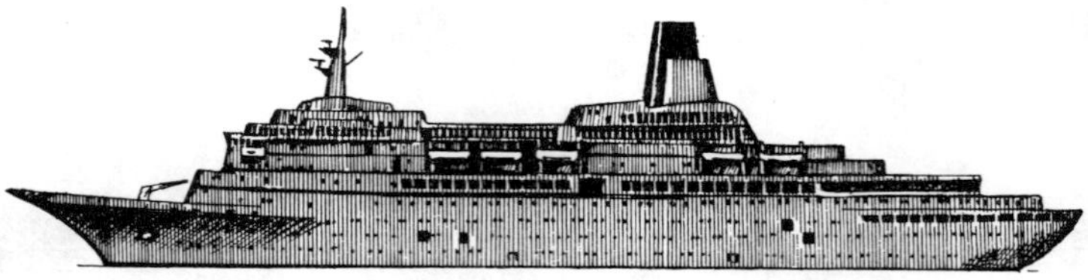

MF H
16820 ROYAL VIKING STAR. No/Fi 1972; P; 21800; 177.8 × 7.2 (583.6 × 23.9); TSM; 21.5. Sisters (No flag): **16821 ROYAL VIKING SEA 16822 ROYAL VIKING SKY.**

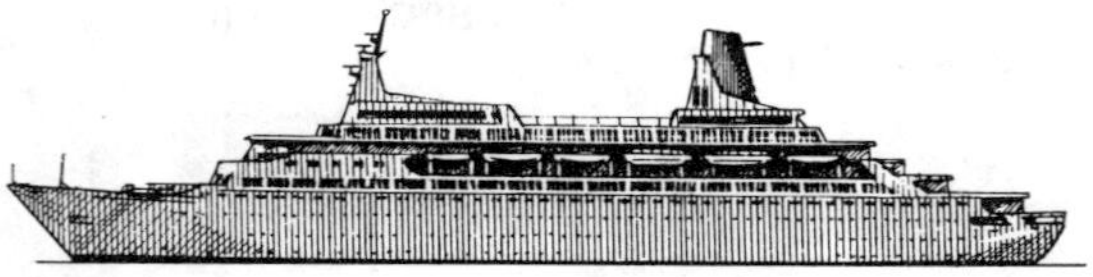

MF H
16830 PACIFIC PRINCESS. Br/FRG 1971; P; 19900; 168.7 × 7.7 (553.6 × 25.3); TSM; 21.5; ex SEA VENTURE 1975. Sister: **16831 ISLAND PRINCESS** (Br) ex ISLAND VENTURE 1972.

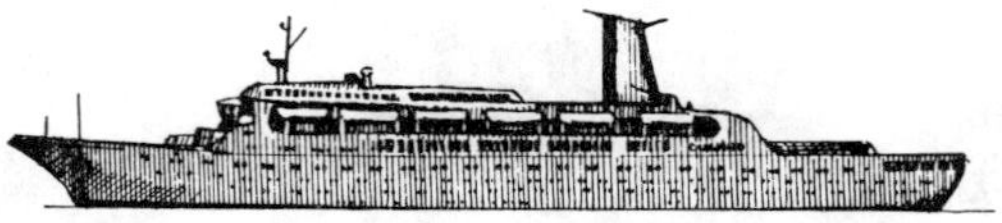

MF H
16840 SUNWARD II. No/Ne 1971; P; 14200; 148.1 × 5.9 (486 × 19.6); TSM; 21.5; ex CUNARD ADVENTURER 1977.

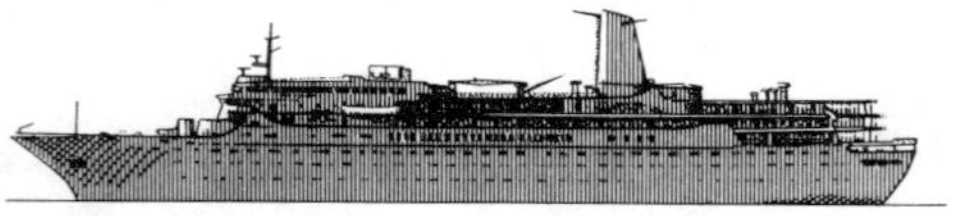

MF H
16850 PROCYON. Pa/Ne—Sw 1972/75; LS; 5600; 148.11 × 6.83 (485.93 × 22.41); TSM; 14.75; ex LINDA CLAUSEN 1980; ex CUNARD AMBASSADOR 1975; side doors; converted from Passenger 1975.

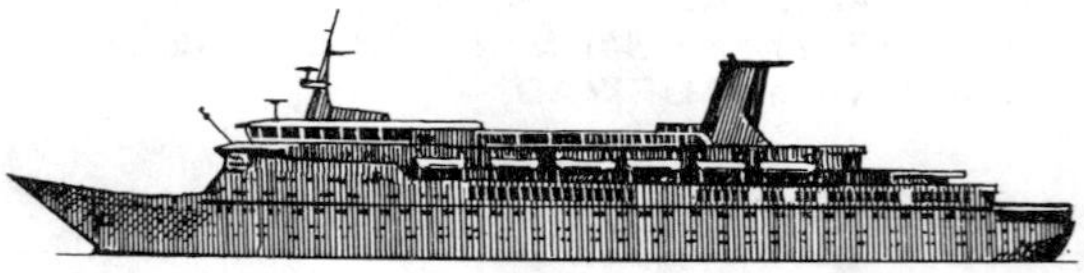

MF H
16860 CUNARD COUNTESS. Br/De 1976; P; 17500; 164 × 5.8 (538 × 19); TSM; 21.5. Sister; **16861 CUNARD PRINCESS** (Br) ex CUNARD CONQUEST 1977.

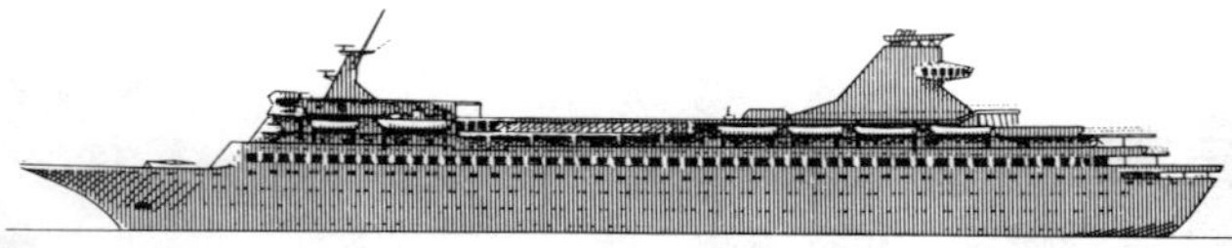

MF H
16870 SONG OF NORWAY. No/Fi 1969/78; P; 23000; 194.32 × — (637.47 × —); TSM; 20.5; lengthened 1978. Sister: **16871 NORDIC PRINCE** (No).

● 16875

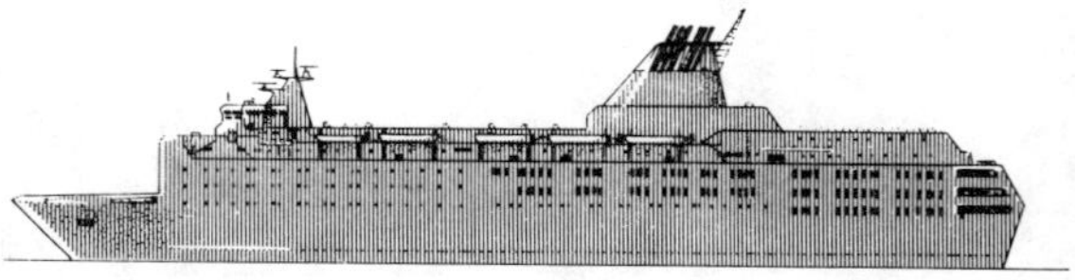

MF H
16880 VIKING SALLY. Fi/FRG 1980; RoPCF; 15600; 155.43 × 5.55 (509.94 × 18.21); TSM; 21.2; stern ramp.

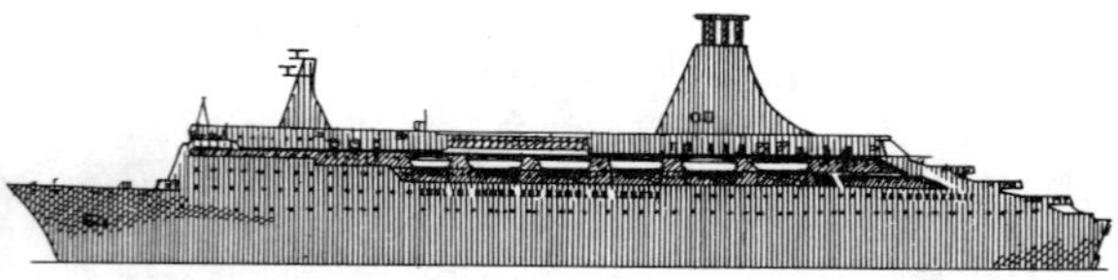

MF H
16890 TOR BRITANNIA. Sw/FRG 1975; RoPC; 15700; 182.4 × 6.3 (598.6 × 20.9); TSM; 26. Sister; **16891 TOR SCANDINAVIA** (Sw).

● 16895

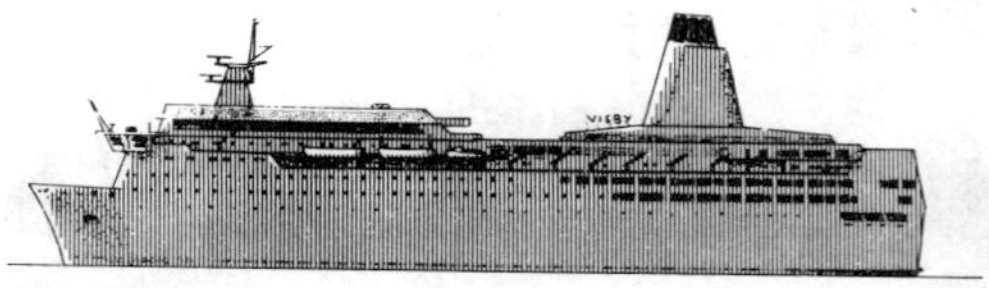

MF H
16900 VISBY. Sw/Sw 1980; RoPCF; 14900; 142.33 × 5.5 (466.96 × 18.04); TSM; 21; three stern door/ramps. Bow door/ramp; one sister ship on order.

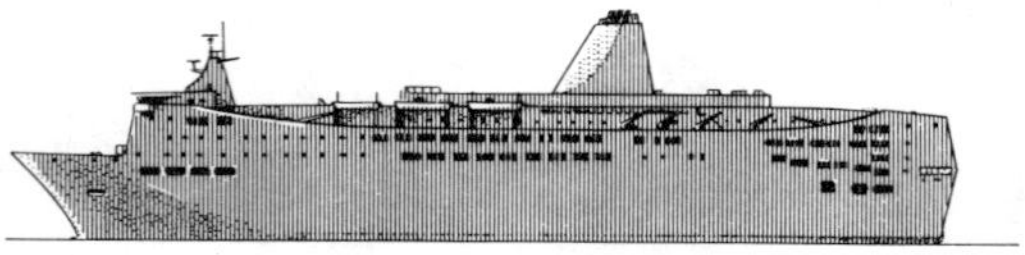

MF H
16910 KRONPRINSESSAN VICTORIA. Sw/Sw 1981; RoPCF; 15000; 150 × 6 (492.13 × 19.69); TSM —; three stern ramps. Bow door/ramp. Helicopter pad aft. One sister on order.

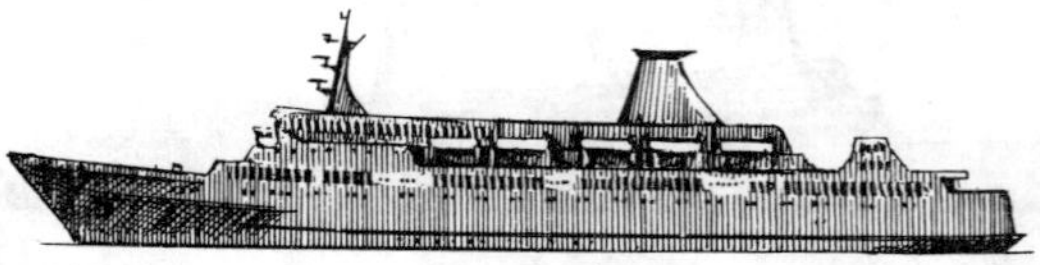

MF H
16920 KRONPRINS HARALD. No/FRG 1976; RoCF; 12800; 156.4 × 5.4 (513.6 × 5.18); TSM; 22.

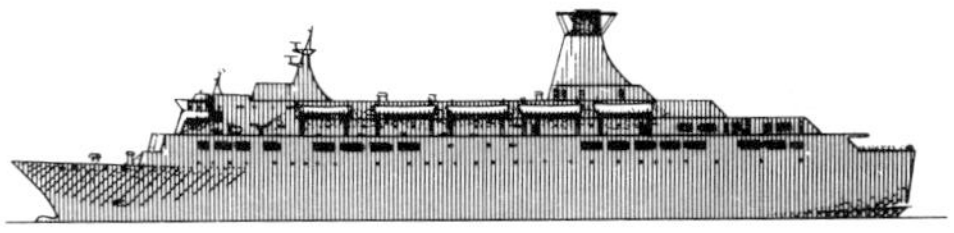

MF H
16930 HABIB. Tn/FRG 1978; P/RoC; 11200; 143.31 × 5.97 (470.18 × 19.59); TSM; 22; bow door/ramp, stern ramp.

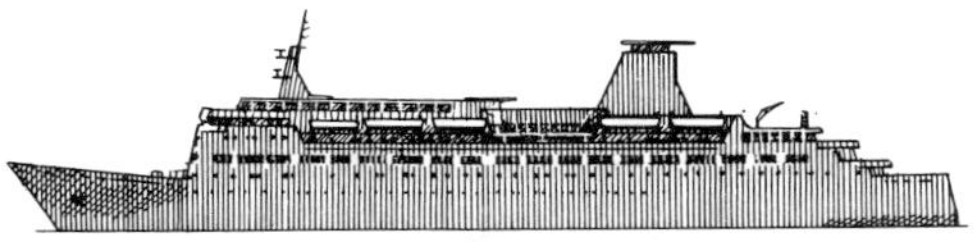

MF H
16950 TOLETELA. Ly/Sp 1974; RoCP; 10800; 151.5 × 6.5 (500.6 × 21.6); TSM; 22; ex MONTE TOLEDO 1977; stern & side doors. Sister: **16951 GARNATA** (Ly) ex MONTE GRANADA 1977.

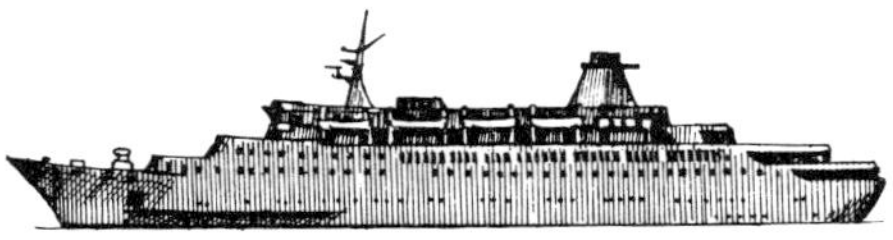

MF H
● **16970 CARIBE.** FRG/FRG 1968; RoPC; 10000; 134.5 × 5.5 (441.6 × 18); TSM; —; ex SVEA STAR 1976; ex FREEPORT 1974; ex FREEPORT 1 1974; ex FREEPORT.

MF H
● **16990 MARINE ATLANTICA.** Ca/FRG 1975; RoPF; 5400; 120 × 5.9 (394 × 19.3); TSM 20.25. Sisters: **16991 MARINE NAUTICA** (Ca) ex STENA NAUTICA 1974 **16992 STENA NORDICA** (Sw) ex HELLAS 1980; ex STENA NORDICA 1978 **16993 STENA NORMANDICA** (Sw) ex NORMANDICA; ex STENA NORMANDICA.

MF H
17020 SUN PRINCESS. Br/It 1972; P; 17400; 163.3 × 6.5 (536 × 21.6); TSM; 15.5 ex SPIRIT OF LONDON 1974.

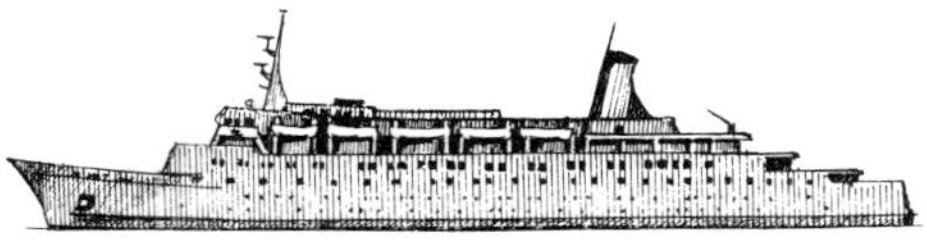

MF H
● **16940 AZUR.** Fr/Fr 1971; RoCP; 11600; 142.1 × 5.45 (466 × 18); TSM; 23; ex EAGLE 1975; stern door. Similar; **16941 SCANDINAVICA** (No) ex BOLERO **16942 MASSALIA** (Fr).

MF H
⋆**16960 ODESSA.** Ru/Br 1974; P; 13800; 136.3 × 5.8 (447.6 × 19); TSM; 19; ex COPENHAGEN 1975.

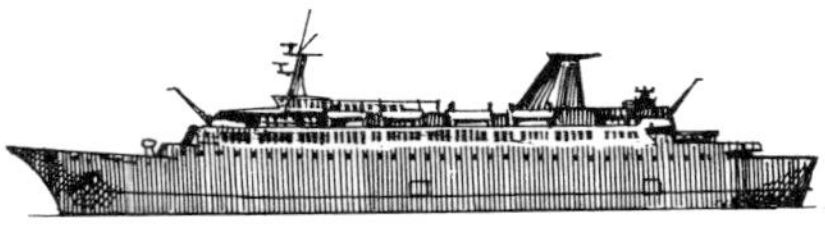

MF H
16980 DROTTEN. Sw/Ys 1972; RoCP; 6700; 123.9 × 5 (406.3 × 16.9); TSM; 20; ex VISBY 1980. Similar: **16981 GOTALAND** (Sw).

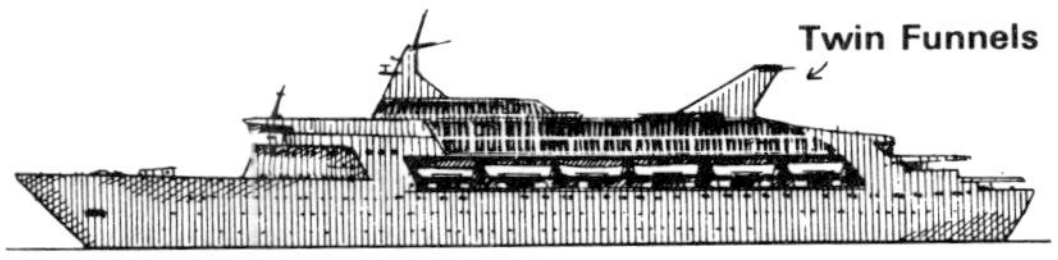

MF H
17000 SOUTHWARD. No/It 1971; P; 16600; 163.4 × 6.5 (536.6 × 21.6); TSM; 21.5.

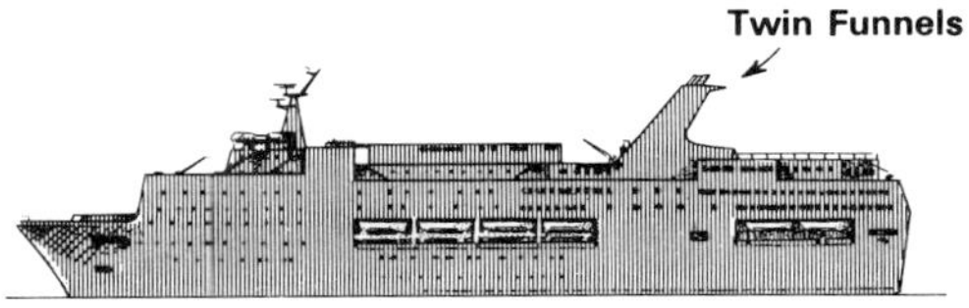

MF H
17010 VIKING SAGA. Fi/Fi 1980; RoPCF; 13900; 145.01 × 5.5 (475.75 × 18.04); TSM; 21; bow door/ramp. Stern ramp. Sister: **17011 VIKING SONG** (Fi).

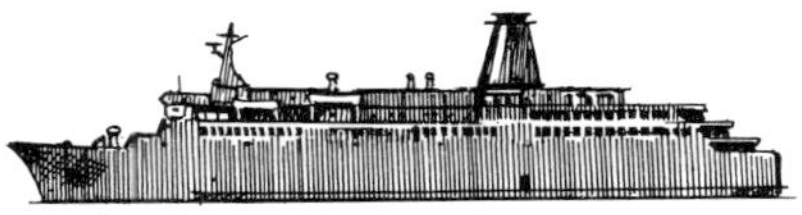

MF H
17030 EUROPAFARJAN III. Sw/FRG 1974; RoP; 4800; 118.7 × 5 (390 × 17); TSM; 20.75.

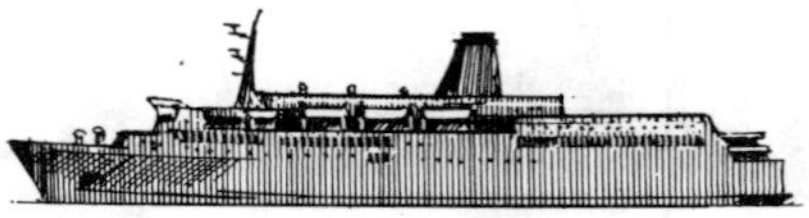

MF H
● **17040 NILS DACKE;** Sw/FRG 1975; RoP; 7900; 129 × 4.9 (424 × 16.5; TSM; 22; Stern doors.

MF H
17050 BOHEME; FRG/F 1968; P; 10300; 134.3 × 5.5 (440 × 18); TSM; —.

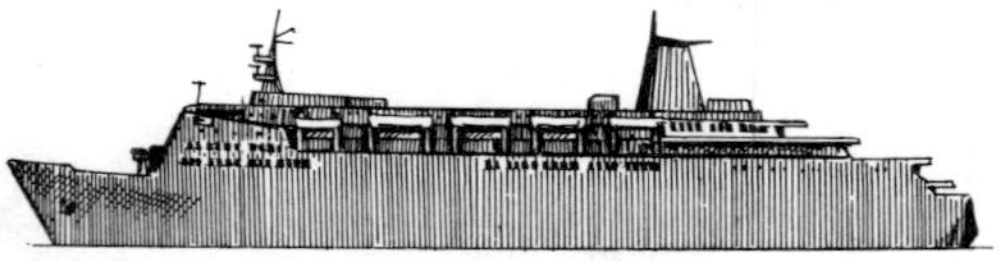

MF H
17060 NORLAND; Br/FRG 1974; RoPC; 13000; 153 × 6.2 (502 × 20.3); TSM; 19. Sister: **17061 NORSTAR** (Ne).

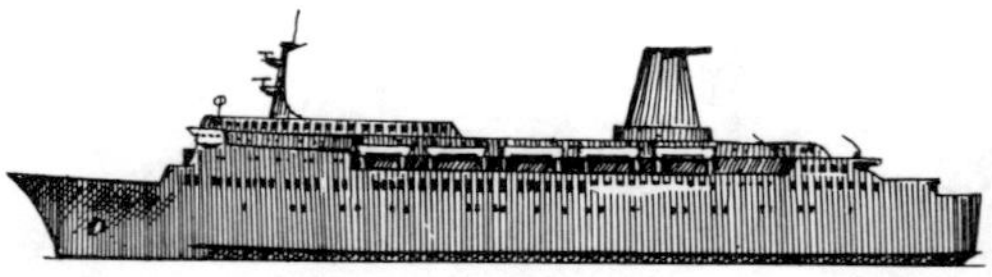

MF H
17070 PETER PAN; FRG/FRG 1974; RoPC; 12500; 148.9 × 5.5 (488 × 18); TSM; 22; Bow & stern doors. Sister: **17071 NILS HOLGERSSON** (FRG).

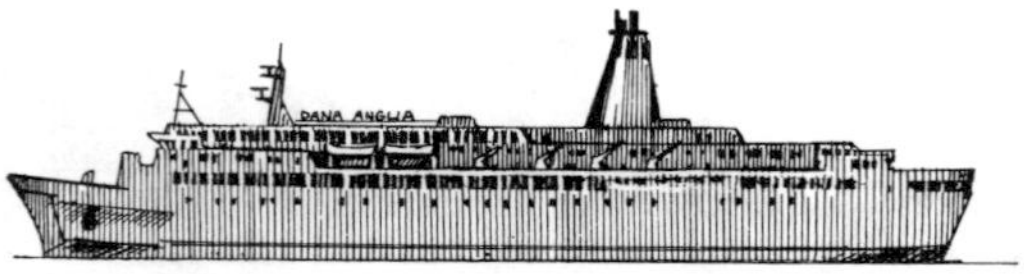

MF H
17080 DANA ANGLIA; De/De 1978; RoPCF; 14400; 152.91 × 5.71 (501.67 × 18.73); TSM; 21; Bow & stern doors.

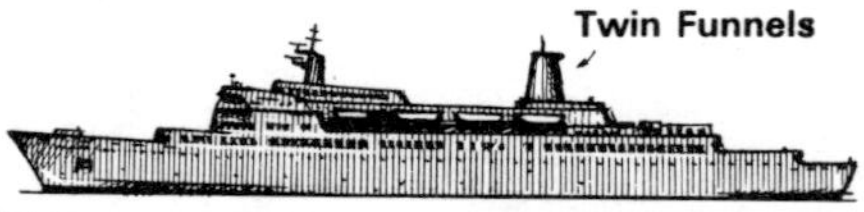

MF H
● **17090 PEER GYNT;** Sw/Fi 1966; RoCP; 7500; 134.5 × 5.7 (441 × 17.1); TSM; 21; ex SVEABORG; ex FINNPARTNER 1968. Sister: **17091 ROUSSILLON** (Fr) ex PRINZ HAMLET 1970; ex PRINS HAMLET 1969 Similar:**17092 PRINSESSAN** (Fi) ex FINNHANSA.

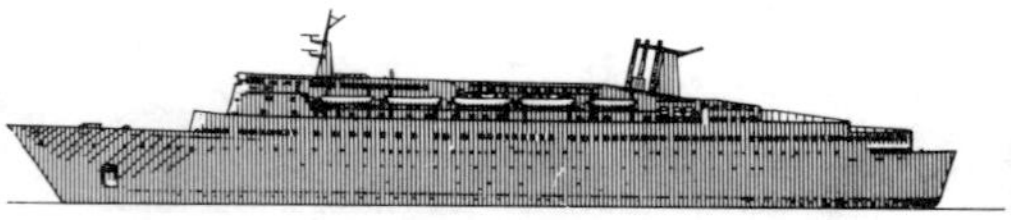

MF H
● **17100 FINNSTAR;** Fi/Fi 1967/78; P; 10300; 153,02 × 5.82 (502 × 19.09); TSM; approx 22; ex FINLANDIA 1978; Converted from RoPCF 1978.

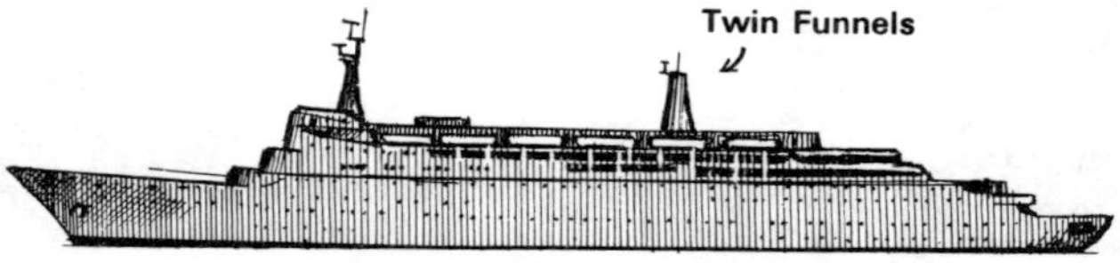

MF H
17110 DORIC; Pa/Fr 1964; P; 17900; 191.4 × 8.3 (628 × 27.4); TST; 20; ex HANSEATIC 1973; ex SHALOM 1067.

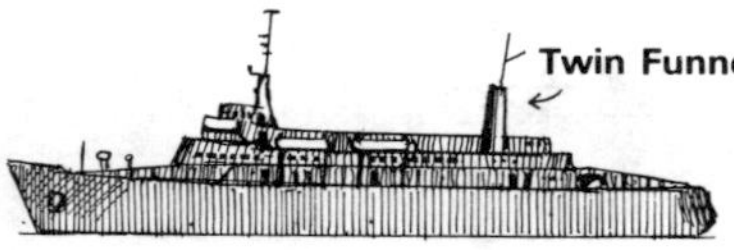

MF H
17120 NORWAVE; Br/FRG 1965; RoC; 3500; 108.8 × 5 (357 × 16.4); TSM; 15; Bow & stern doors. Sister: **17121 NORWIND** (Ne).

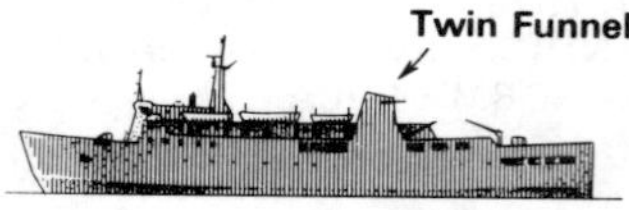

MF H
17130 PIETRO NOVELLI; It/It 1979; RoPCF; 1600; 91 × 4 (298.56 × 13.12); TSM; 18; Bow & stern doors. Sisters: **17131 PIERRA DELLA FRANCESCA** (It) (may be **PIERO DELLA FRANCESCA) 17132 MARMORICA** (It) Possible Sister: **17133 OGLASA** (It).

MF H
17140 GENERAL JOSE ARTIGAS; Ur/De 1960; RoPC; 2200; 86.5 × 4.4 (284 × 13.9); TSM; 17; ex BOTNIA EXPRESS 1975; ex PRINSESSAN CHRISTINA 1967.

MF H
17150 CAPTAIN CONSTANTINOS; Gr/Ne 1960; RoPCF; 6200; 120 × 4.9 (394 × 16); TSM; 21; ex KONINGIN WILHELMINA.

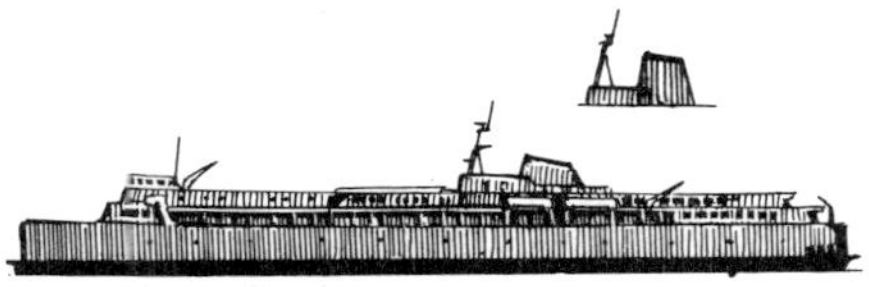

MF H
17160 QUEEN OF VICTORIA; Ca/Ca 1962; RoCF; 4900; 130 × 3.8 (427 × 12.6); TSM; 18; ex CITY OF VICTORIA 1963; Bow & stern doors; Lengthened 1970. Sisters (Ca flag): **17161 QUEEN OF VANCOUVER** ex CITY OF VANCOUVER 1963 **17162 QUEEN OF SAANICH 17163 QUEEN OF ESQUIMALT** Similar: **17164 QUEEN OF BURNABY 17165 QUEEN OF NANAIMO 17166 QUEEN OF NEW WESTMINISTER.**

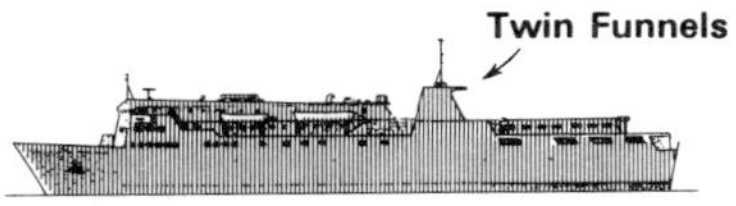

MF H
17170 CONCEPCION MARINO; Ve/No 1979; RoPCF; 6200; 105 × 3.8 (344.48 × 12.47); TSM; 17; Bow door/ramp & stern ramp. Sister: **17171 CACICA ISABEL** (Ve).

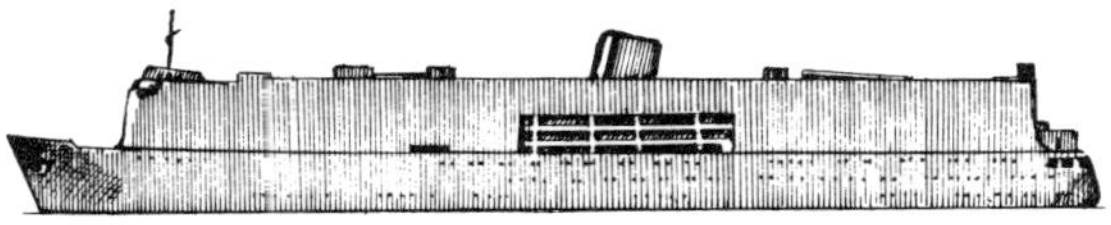

MF H
● **17180 HUAL TRAVELLER;** No/Br 1960/72; RoVC; 10900; 178 × 8.7 (584 × 28.6); TSM; 17.5; ex HOEGH TRAVELLER; ex ARANDA 1971; ex ARAGON 1969; Converted from a passenger cargo ship 1972. Sister: **17181 HUAL TROTTER** (No) ex HOEGH TROTTER; ex HOEGH TRANSIT 1972; ex ARAWA 1971; ex ARLANZA 1969.

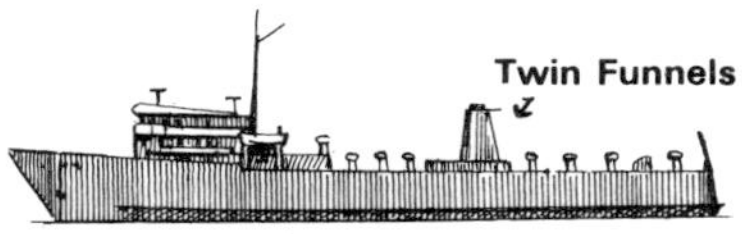

MF H
● **17190 LADY NINA;** FRG/No 1973; RoC; 1600; 108.6 × 5 (356 × 16.6); TSM; 17.5; ex LEILA; Bow & stern doors. Sisters (Br flag): **17191 LADY TONE** ex LAGAN BRIDGE 1981; ex ILKKA 1980 **17192 LADY CATHERINE** ex LUNE BRIDGE 1980; ex ANU 1980.

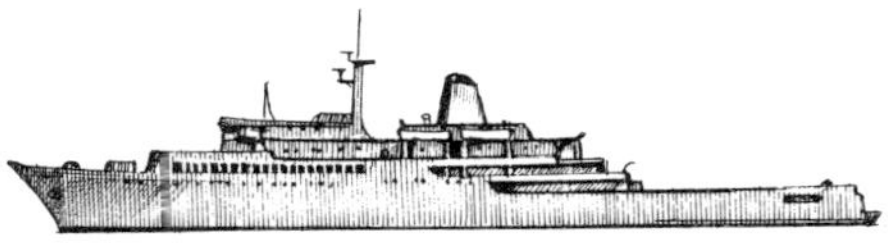

MF H1
17200 JERVIS BAY; Br/Au 1969; RoC; 6800; 135.7 × 6 1 (445 × 20); TSM; 17.5; ex AUSTRALIAN TRADER; Stern door.

MF H1
17210 CIUDAD DE TARIFA; Sp/Sp 1961; F; 3400; 103.2 × 5.1 (338 × 16.9); TSM; 17.

MF H1
17220 PRINCE NOVA; Ca/Ca 1964; RoF; 1800; 75.8 × 3.8 (249 × 12.4); TSM; —.

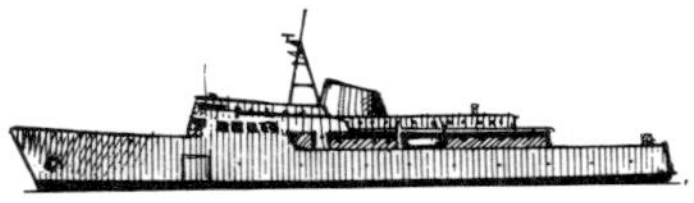

MF H1
17230 COHO; US/US 1959; F; 5300; 104.1 × 3.8 (342 × 12.6); TSM; —.

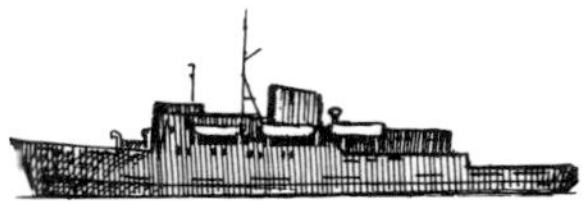

MF H1
17240 MONS CALPE; Br/Br 1954; RoF; 2000; 86.3 × 3.2 (283 × 10.6); TSM; —.

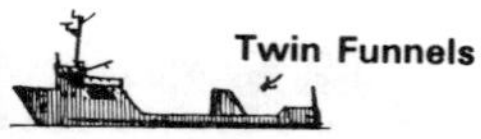

MF H1
17250 SOUND OF ISLAY; Br/Br 1969; RoF; 280; 43.4 × 1.6 (142 × 5.3); TSM; 10.75.

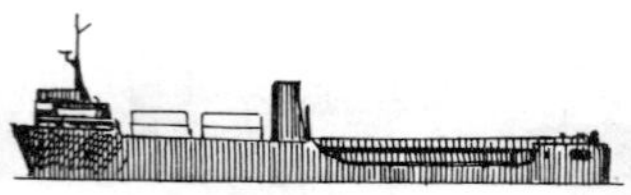

MF H13
17260 KIRK EXPRESS; Br/FRG 1968; RoC; 1600; 91.5 × 4.5 (300 × 14.1); TSM; 16; ex JAMAICAN PROVIDER.

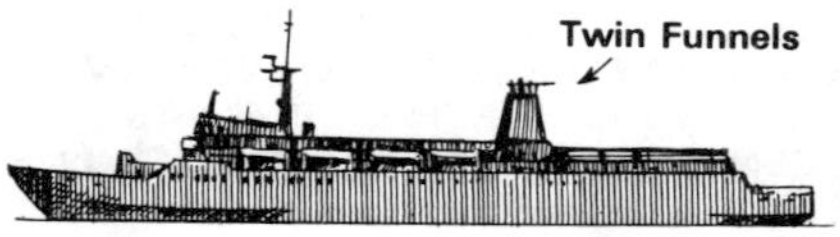

MF H2
17270 ESPRESSO CAGLIARI; It/It 1973; RoC; 4700; 125.5 × 5.5 (412 × 18.2); TSM; 21. Sisters (It flag): **17271 ESPRESSO LIVORNO 17272 ESPRESSO VENEZIA 17273 ESPRESSO RAVENNA.**

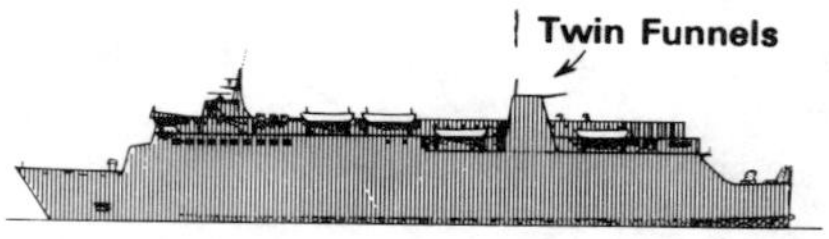

MF H2
17280 GEDSER; De/FRG 1976; RoPCF; 5300; 123.02 × 5.82 (403.61 × 19.09); TSM; 18.5; Bow & side doors. Stern door/ramp.

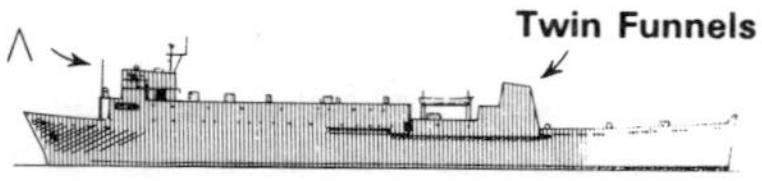

KMF H2
17290 FRECCIA DELL'OUEST; It/It 1975; RoCF; 2600; 117.5 × 4.9 (385 × 16.1); TSM; 20; ex CORRIERE DELL'OUEST. Sister: **17291 FRECCIA DEL NORD** (It) ex CORRIERE DEL NORD.

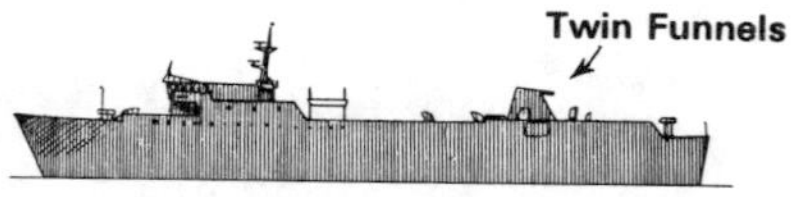

MF H2
17300 COUTANCES; Fr/Fr 1978; RoC; 2600; 110 × 4.5 (360.89 × 14.7); M; 17.5; Bow & stern door. Sister: **17301 PURBECK** (Fr).

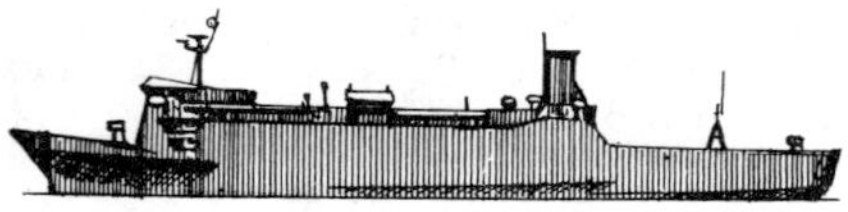

MF H2
● **17310 BRABANT;** FRG/FRG 1976; RoC; 3900; 127 × 5.4/6.6 (417 × 17.1/21.8); TSM; 19.5; ex ARGO 1977; Stern door.

MF H2
⋆**17320 ZARNITZA;** Ru/DDR 1957; F; 350; 39 × 2.9 (128 × 9.7); M; 10.5.

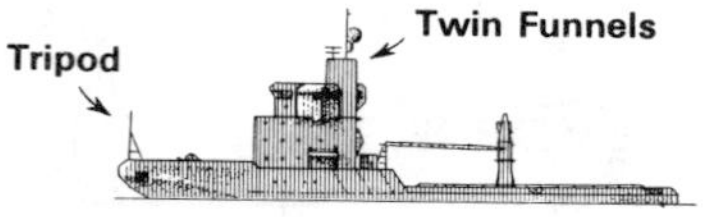

MFC H1
17330 CANMAR KIGORIAK; Ca/Ca 1980; IB/Tg/Sply; 3600; 91.06 × 8.54 (298.75 × 28.02); M; 18.6 (max).

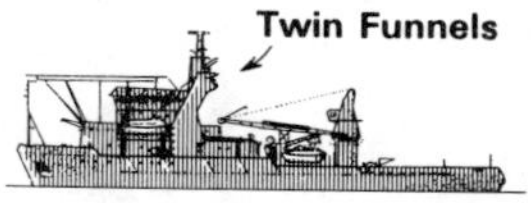

MFC H1
17340 WILDRAKE; No/No 1979; OSS; 1800; 77.8 × 4.6 (255.25 × 15.09); M; 14; Helicopter deck foreward.

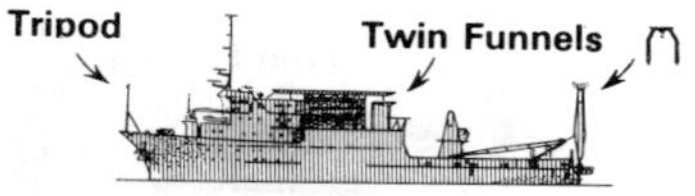

MFCKM H
17350 SWAN OCEAN; Br/Fi 1979; OSS; —; 77 × 5.35 (252.62 × 17.55); M; 14; Helicopter deck. Stern gantry.

MFCKM H1
17360 DR. FRIDTJOF NANSEN; No/No 1974; RS/ST; 500; 46.4 × 4.1 (152 × 13.5); M; 13.5.

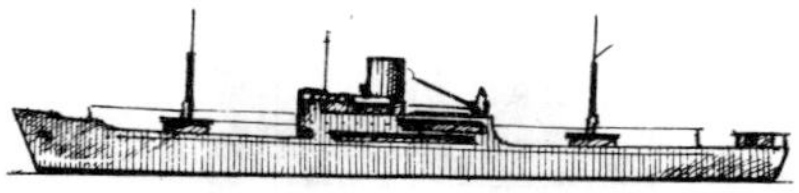

MFCM H1
17370 SINGWIND; Pa/Br 1962; C; 4400; 123.2 × 7.1 (404 × 23.5); M; —; ex GREEN ISLAND 1980; ex EASTERN RANGER 1974. Sister: **17371 CHEONGWIND** (Pa) ex LAMTONG CHAU 1980; ex SMARAGD RUTHIE 1979; ex TSING YI ISLAND.

MFCM H1
● **17380 SEAFORTH CAPE;** Br/FRG 1967; Submersible Support Ship; 1300; 79.7 × 4.7 (262 × 15.6); TSD-E; 10; ex TIKO I 1976; Converted Fish Factory/Stern Trawler. Stern ramp. Possibly Similar: **17381 SUBSEA I** (Br) ex NORTHSEA HUNTER 1976; ex ERICH OLLENHAUER 1975.

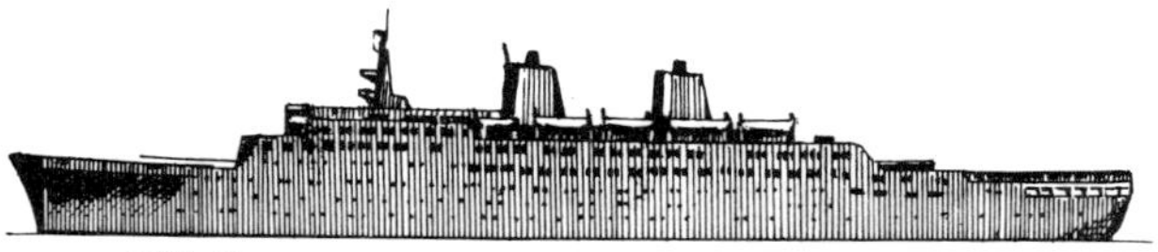

MF_2 H
17390 EMERALD SEAS; Pa/US 1944; P; 18900; 184 × 8 (604 × 27); TST; 19; ex ATLANTIS 1972; ex PRESIDENT ROOSEVELT 1970; ex LEILANI 1961; ex LAGUARDIA 1956; ex GENERAL W. P. RICHARDSON 1949.

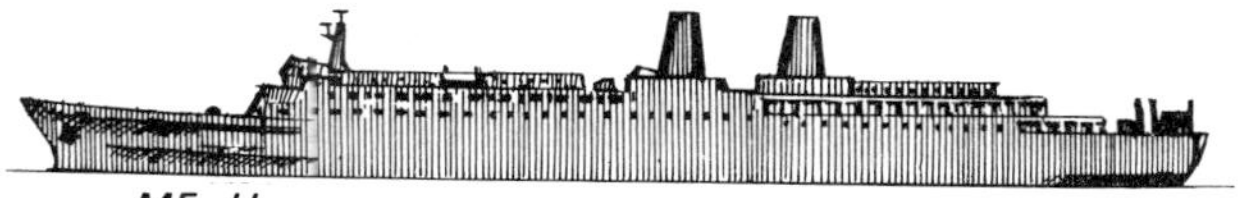

MF_2 H
17400 SUN FLOWER 11; Ja/Ja 1974; P/RoCF; 13600; 196 × 6.6 (643 × 21); TM; 25.

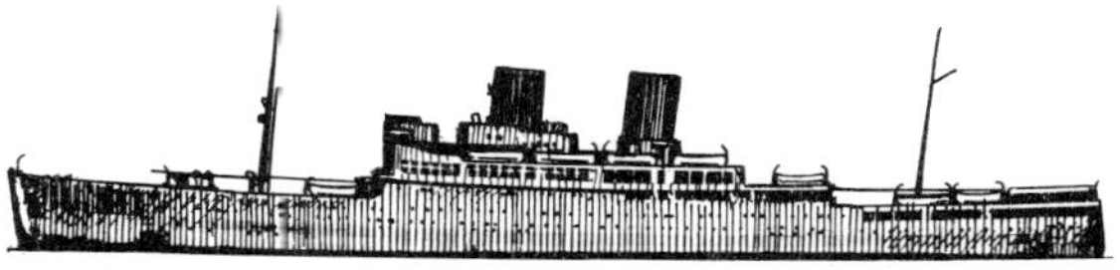

MF_2M H
17410 GUNUNG DJATI; Ia/Ge 1936; P; 17900; 176 × 8 (578 × 27); TSM; 17; ex EMPIRE CRWELL 1959; ex EMPIRE DOON 1949; ex PRETORIA 1945.

MF_2M H
17420 PRINCESS MARGUERITE; Ca/Br 1949; P; 5900; 114 × 4.6 (375 × 15); TSD-E; 23.5; Now used as a museum ship. Sister: **17421 PRINCESS PATRICIA** (Ca).

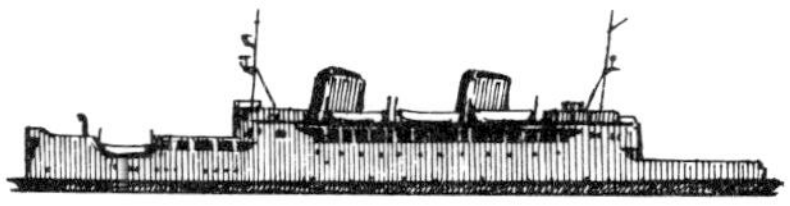

MF_2M H
17430 CARIDDI; It/It 1931/53; P/TF; 3100; 124 × 4 (407 × 13); TrS D-E; 13.5.

MF_2M H
17440 WAVERLEY; Br/Br 1947; P; 700; 73 × 1.9 (240 × 6); R; 14; Paddle steamer.

MF_2M H
● **17450 CIUDAD DE FORMOSA;** Ar/Sp 1963; PR; 4000; 105 × 2.4 (345 × 8); TrS M; 14. Sister: **17451 CIUDAD DE LA PLATA** (Ar).

MF_2M H
17460 DRONNING INGRID; De/De 1951; P/TF; 3000; 110 × 4 (363 × 13.5); TSM; —. Sister: **17461 FYN** (De).

MF_2M H
17470 OTOME MARU; Ja/Ja 1972; RoPF; 3500; 100.03 × 3.47 M; 19.5.

MF_2M H
⋆**17480 WARNEMUNDE;** DDR/DDR 1962; P/TF; 6100; 136 × 4.7 (449 × 16); TSM; 18.

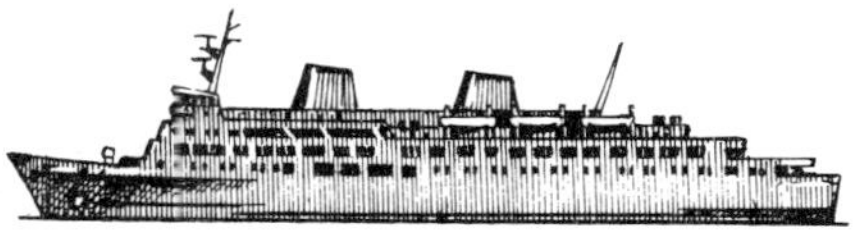

MF_2M H
17490 SKANDIA; Fi/Fi 1973; RoPF; 8500; 128 × 5.7 (420 × 19.5); TSM; 22; ex BORE I 1981.

MF_2M H
⋆17500 DOVATOR; Ru/DDR 1955; PR; 1400; 96 × 2.7 (316 × 9); M; 12. Sisters (Ru flag): **⋆17501 ALEKSANDR NEVSKII ⋆17502 ALIOSHA POPOVICH ⋆17503 ALTAI ⋆17504 BAGRATION ⋆17505 CHKALOV ⋆17506 DMITRI POZHARSKII ⋆17507 DMITRI DONSKOI ⋆17508 DOBRYNA NIKITCH ⋆17509 ERNST TELMAN ⋆17510 FRIDRICH ENGELS ⋆17511 G. V. PLEKHANOV ⋆17512 GENERAL CHERNIAKOVSKI ⋆17513 GOGOL ⋆17514 ILITCH ⋆17515 ILYA MUROMETS ⋆17516 KARL LIEBKNECHT ⋆17517 KARL MARX ⋆17518 KAVKAZ ⋆17519 KRUPSKAYA ⋆17520 KRYLOV ⋆17521 MATROSOV ⋆17522 MIKHAIL KUTUZOV ⋆17523 N. GASTELLO ⋆17524 RODINA ⋆17525 RYLYEV ⋆17526 TARAS SHEVCHENKO ⋆17527 TIMIRYAZEV ⋆17528 URAL ⋆17529 VYSHINSKII.**

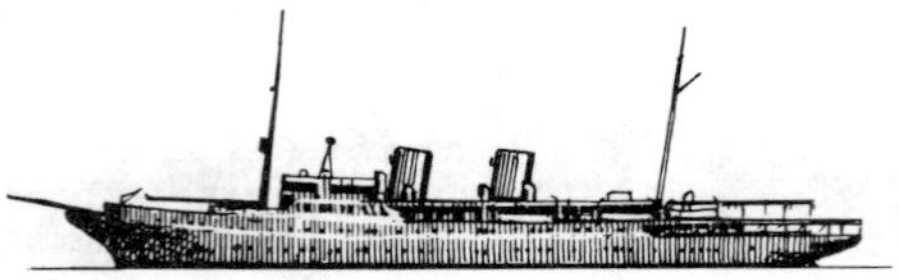

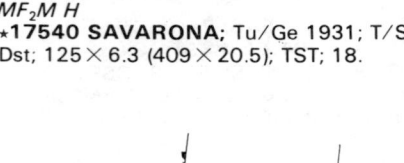

MF_2M H
⋆17540 SAVARONA; Tu/Ge 1931; T/S; 4700 Dst; 125 × 6.3 (409 × 20.5); TST; 18.

MF_2M H
17550 N. B. McLEAN; Ca/Ca 1930; IB; 3300; 79 × 6 (260 × 19.5); TSR; 13; KP's abreast both masts.

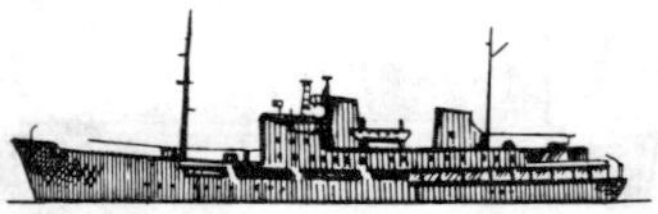

MF_2M H1
⋆17560 PETR LEBEDEV; Ru/Fi 1957; RS; 3600; 94 × 5.8 (309 × 19); M; 13.5; ex CHAPAYEV 1960. Sister: **⋆17561 SERGEI VAVILOV** (Ru) ex FURMANOV 1960.

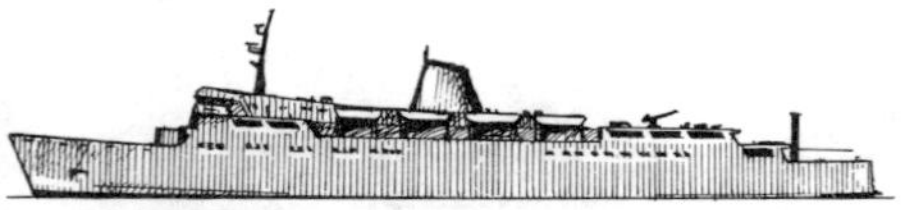

MFK H
17570 ARION; Gr/Br 1965; RoCP; 7800; 137,1 × 5.2 (450 × 16.7); TSM; 20; ex NILI; EX JAMAICA QUEEN 1969; ex NILI 1967.

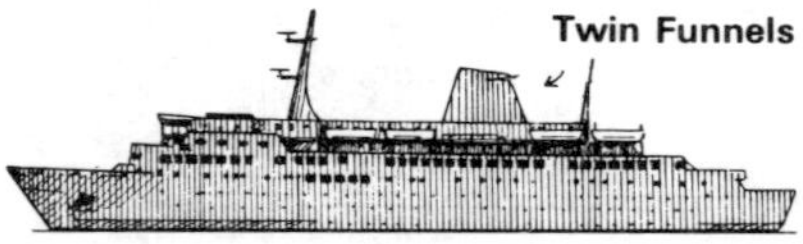

MFK H
● **17580 ROGALIN;** Fi/Fr 1972; RoCP: 7800; 126.9 × 5.2 (416 × 17.1); TSM; 21; ex AALLOTAR; Bow & stern doors. Sister: **17581 MEDITERRANEAN SUN** (Gr) ex REGINA; ex SVEA REGINA.

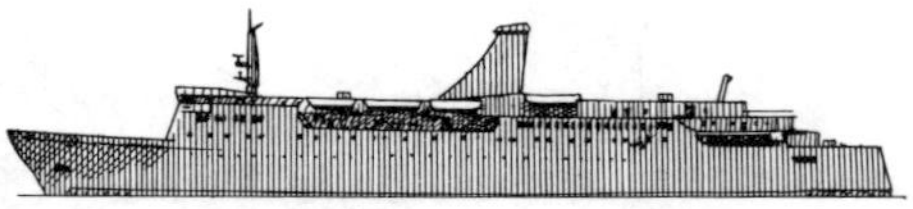

MFK H
● **17590 CANGURO CABO SAN SEBASTIAN;** Sp/Sp 1972; RoP; 7500; 137.8 × 5.7 (452 × 18.1); TSM; 22.5; Stern door. Sisters (Sp flag): **17591 CANGURO CABO SAN JORGE 17592 CIUDAD DE BADAJOZ** Possible sisters: **17593 CIUDAD DE SEVILLA 17594 CIUDAD DE CACERES.**

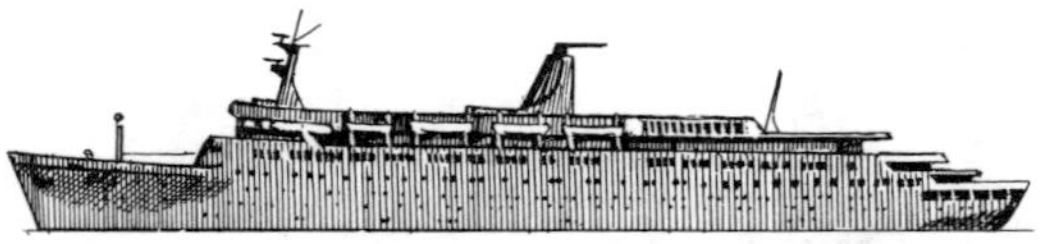

MFK H
17600 STELLA SOLARIS. Gr/Fr 1953; P; 10600; 166 × 7.9 (545 × 26); TST; ex STELLA I 1970; ex CAMBODGE 1970.

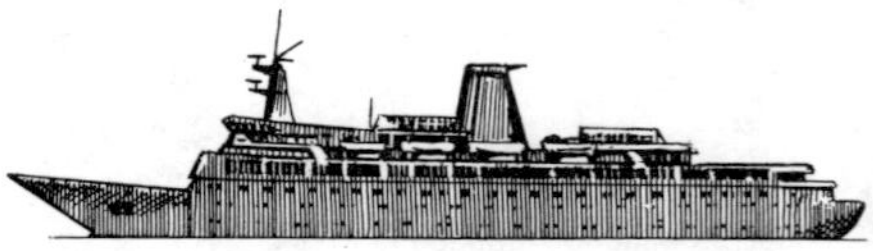

MFK H
17610 GOLDEN ODYSSEY. Gr/De 1974; P; 6800; 130.2 × 5.2 (427 × 17.2); TSM; 21.

MFK H
⋆**17620 SHUI HSIEN.** RC/Ca 1948; F; 3100; 86.6 × 3.7 (284 × 12); T; 14.

MFK H
17630 CIUDAD DE COLONIA. Ar/Ar 1939; F; 1300; 66.5 × 2.6 (218 × 8.6); TSD-E; 21.

MFK H2
17640 APOLLON II. Gr/Br 1952; P; 4800; 103.5 × 4.8 (340 × 15.1); TSM; 16; ex ACHILLEUS 1969; ex SEMIRAMIS II 1969; ex ORPHEUS 1969; ex IRISH COAST 1968.

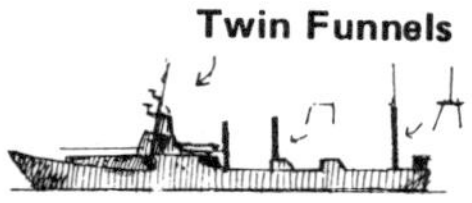

MFK_2M H
17650 MALENE OSTERVOLL. No/Br 1965; ST; 800; 63 × — (207 × —); D-E; —; ex ROSS INTREPID 1976; ex ROSS KENNEDY 1966; ex CAPE KENNEDY 1966.

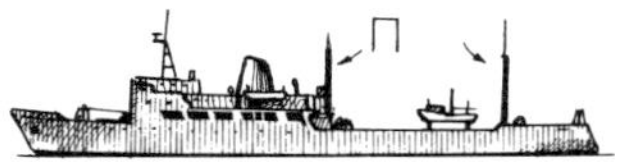

MFKM H
⋆**17660 GALATI.** Rm/Ja 1964; FT; 3600; 93.1 × 5 (305 × 16.3); M; 13. Sister: ⋆**17661 CONSTANTA** Rm).

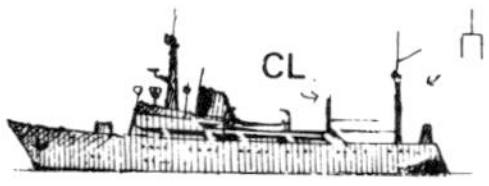

MFKM H
⋆**17670 ERNST HAECKEL.** DDR/DDR 1962; RS/ST; 1600; 67.7 × 4.9 (222 × 16.1); M; 11.5.

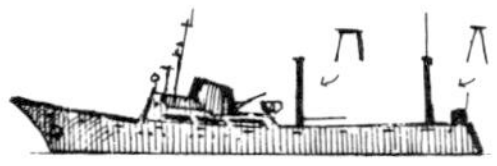

MFKM H
17680 SOUTHERN RANGER. SA/Br 1962; ST; 1400; 67.3 × — (240 × —); D-E; —; ex BLUEFIN; ex JUNELLA 1973.

MFKM H
17690 V.U. HAMMERSHAIMB. Fa/Br 1964; ST; 800; 63 × — (207 × —); D-E; —; ex ROSS VALIANT 1975.

MFKM H
17700 ARCTIC FREEBOOTER. Br/Br 1966; ST; 1200; 67.8 4 — (221 × —); M; —.

MFKM H
17710 DEFIANCE. Br/Br 1966; ST; 1100; 66.4 × 4.7 (218 × 15.6); M; 14.5.

MFKM H
17720 LADY PARKES. Br/Br 1966; ST; 1000; 67.8 × 4.6 (221 × 15.6); M; —. Sister; **17721 SIR FRED PARKES** (Br).

MFKM H
17730 ROSS VANGUARD. Br/Br 1966; ST; 1100; 65.7 × — (215 ×); M; —. Sister: **17731 ROSS ILLUSTRIOUS** (Br).

MFKM H
17740 ST. JASON. Br/Br 1967; ST; 1300; 66.2 × — (217 × —); M; 14. Sisters (Br flag): **17741 ST. JASPER 17742 ST. JEROME.**

MFKM H
17750 VICTORY. Br/Br 1965; ST; 1200; 74.6 × — (245 × —); D-E; —; May be a total loss.

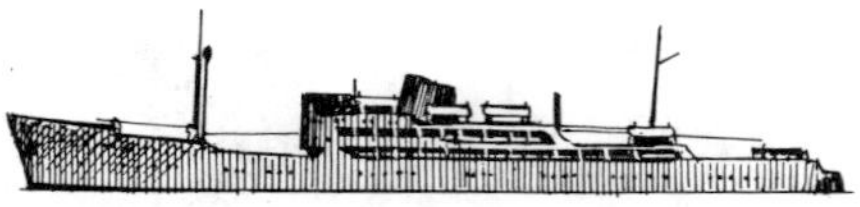

MFKM H
17760 KIM ANN. Sg/Br 1951; PC; 7700; 131.6 × 7.6 (432 × 25.8); TSM; 14.5; ex TIMOR 1974.

MFKM H
17770 ERLING JARL. No/It 1946; PC; 2100; 81.9 × 4.5 (269 × 14.1); M; 15. Sisters (No flag): **17771 MIDNATSOL 17772 VESTERALEN.**

MFKM H1
17780 ASPAKI. Cy/De 1956; C; 2700/3900; 108.4 × —/6.9 (356 × —/22.8); M; 14; ex VARRES 1976; ex BARMA 1974; ex EURODAWN 1972; ex OKLAHOMA 1970. Similar (Le flag): **17781 BAABDA** ex ATHOS 1973 **17782 BERYTE** ex SKYROS 1973.

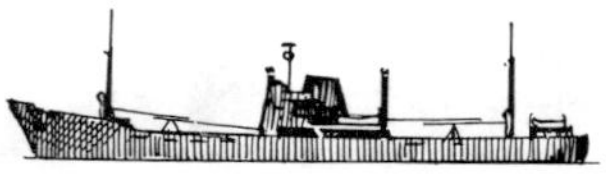

MFKM H1
● ⋆**17790 SALI.** Ys/FRG 1950; C; 2500; 88.7 × 6.3 (291 × 21); M; 12; ex HECTOR 1960. Sisters: **17791 ALEXANDROS K** (Cy) ex DARNLEY 1976; ex MYRIAM FIDELITY 1974; ex MANOLIOS L 1972; ex NIN 1972; ex HERCULES 1960. **17792 TAILIAT** (Pa) ex CHENG HSING; ex TA HUNG 1976; ex AGIA MARINA 1973; ex HESTIA 1970.

MFKM H1
17800 ANNOULA K. Pa/Ne 1953; C; 2200; 96 × 6 (315 × 19.7); R; 13; ex ANNA III; ex ANNITA 1973; ex PALLAS 1968.

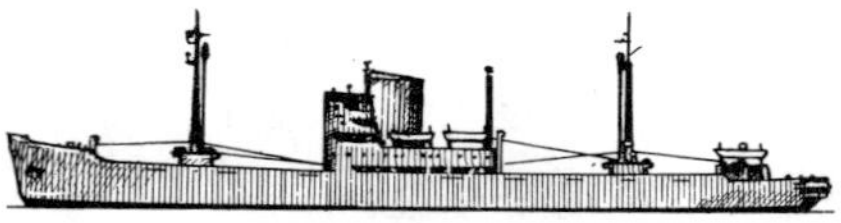

MFKM H1
⋆**17810 INDIGIRKA.** Ru/Ne 1957; C; 6000/7500; 130.2 × 7.9/8.2 (427 × 26/27); D-E; 15. Sisters (Ru flag): ⋆**17811 ANGARA** ⋆**17812 BAYKAL.**

MFKM H1
17820 KATIA. Gr/Br 1952; CP; 3700; 117.5 × 6.6 (368 × 21.5); M; 14.5; ex TABOR 1975.

MFKM H1
⋆**17830 FASTOV.** Ru/Fi 1958; C; 1700; 94.2 × 5.7 (309 × 18.7); M; 13.5. Sisters (Ru flag): ⋆**17831 FATEZH** ⋆**17832 FLORESHTY** ⋆**17833 FROLOVO** ⋆**17834 FRYAZINO.**

MFKM H1
17840 MONTE BRASIL. Po/Ne 1948; CP; 2400; 106.6 × 5.9 (350 × 19.4); M; 14. Sister: **17841 RIBEIRA GRANDE** (Po).

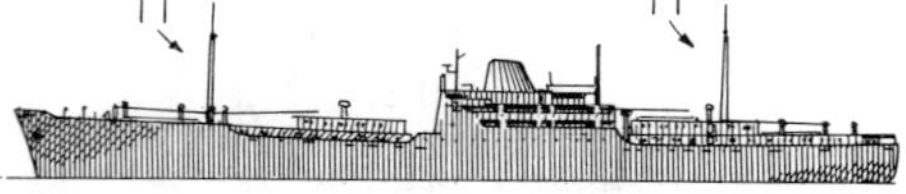

MFKM H12
● **17850 ORIENT CLIPPER.** Sc/Fr 1955; LS; 7000; 140.4 × 7.3 (461 × 24); TSM; 15; ex ELSEY FIR 1977; ex EUPHRATE 1973; converted from a cargo ship.

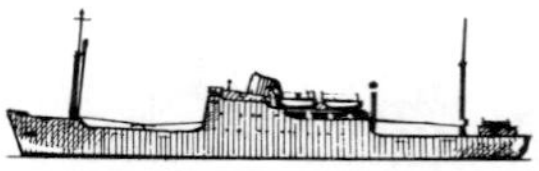

MFKM H12
17860 MALIGAYA. Pi/FRG 1950; C; 1300/1500; 82.8 × 4.8 (272 × 15.8); M; 12.5; ex ATHENA 1975; ex ADLER 1966.

MFKM H123
17870 KOTA RATNA. Sg/Ne 1959; CP; 2300/3300; 99.5 × 5.4/6.8 (326 × 17.11/22.4); M; 13.75; ex MERCURY GULF 1975; ex TJILIWONG 1972. Sisters (Sg flag): **17871 KOTA RIA** ex TJITARUM 1975 **17872 KOTA RUKUN** ex MERCURY COVE 1975; ex TJIMANUK 1972.

MFKM H123
17880 ZACHARIAS Z. Cy/Be 1949; C; 1600; 88.3 × 5.5 (310 × 18.1); M; 12; ex MARGUERITE 1966. Similar (Gr flag): **17881 PANTANASSA** ex FULMAR WISH 1975; ex NISSOS SERIFOS 1973; ex ALEPPO 1964; ex ALEGRITTA 1958; ex ESCAUT 1958.

MFKM H123
17890 ONBAK FADJAR. Ia/Ca 1945; C; 3100; 100 × 6.4 (329 × 21); R; 9.5; ex OCEAN FORTUNE 1968; ex CURRAN 1957; ex SUGAR PRODUCER 1956; ex MAKENA II 1950; ex OAKMOUNT 1948; ex OAKMOUNT PARK 1947. **'SCANDINAVIAN'** type.

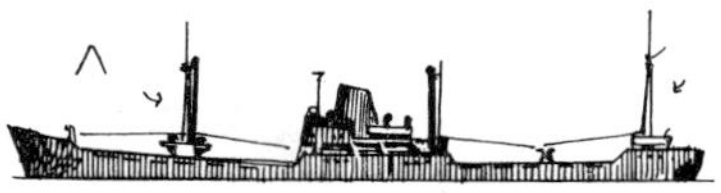

MFKM H123
⋆**17920 SHKIPER GIEK.** Ru/Pd 1959; C; 3700; 108.3 × 6.6 (355 × 21.8); R; 12.25; **'B-31'** type. Sisters (Ru flag): ⋆**17921 ADMIRAL SARYCHEV** ⋆**17922 ALEKSANDR BARANOV** ⋆**17923 ALEKSANDR POPOV** ⋆**17924 ALEKSANDR TEREKHIN** ⋆**17925 BOSHNYAKOVO** ⋆**17926 IVAN RYABOV** ⋆**17927 GORODETSKIY** ⋆**17928 KAPITAN GRITSUK** ex SHANTAR ⋆**17929 NIKOLAY BOSHNYAK** ⋆**17930 VELSK** ⋆**17931 ELETS** ⋆**17932 MOREKHOD** ⋆**17933 KUSKOV** Similar: **17934 DURRESI** (Al) Similar (converted to fish carrier): ⋆**17935 ARKHANGELSK** (Ru).

MFKM H2
⋆**17980 BODO UHSE;** DDR/DDR 1965; FT; 3200; 87.7 × 5.7 (288 × 18.9); M; 14. Sister: ⋆**17981 WILLI BREDEL** (DDR).

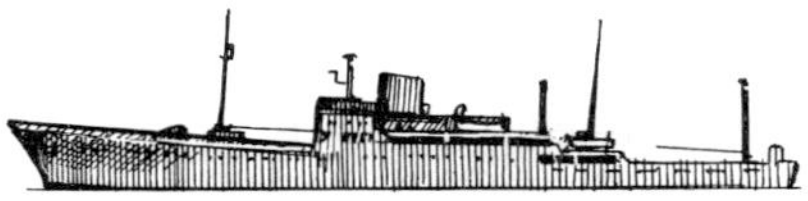

MFKMK H1
⋆**17990 MARTIN ANDERSEN NEXO;** DDR/FRG 1951; FF; 4800; 120.4 × 6 (395 × 19.7); M; 16.5; ex PEGASUS 1960; Converted from a cargo ship 1960.

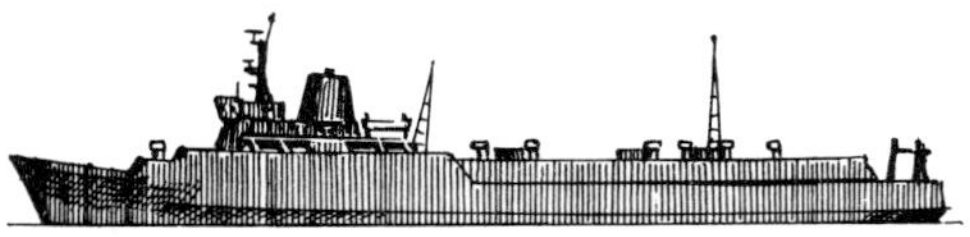

MFKMR H2
18000 SERENISSIMA EXPRESS; It/Ja 1976; RoC; 6800; 147.6 × 6.6 (484 × 21.8); M; 19.5; Stern and quarter doors. Sisters: **18001 ANGLIA EXPRESS** (It) **18002 ALLEMAGNA EXPRESS** (It).

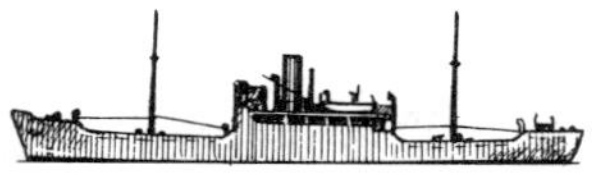

MFKM H123
17900 KAFAR. Pa/Ja 1948; CP; 2100; 90.3 × 5.8 (296 × 18.11); M; 10.5; ex YAMASHO MARU 1972; ex HOSHO MARU 1967.

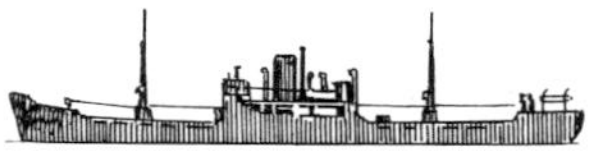

MFKM H123
17910 HEUNG AH No 7. Ko/Ja 1949; C; 2100; 90.4 × 6 (297 × 19.8); M; 9.5; ex FUKIHARU MARU 1967.

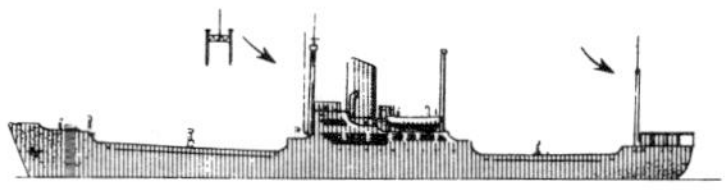

MFKM H123
● ⋆**17940 PETROVSK.** Ru/Pd 1957; C/B; 3800; 108.26 × 6.66 (355.8 × 21.85); R & LPT; 11.5; **'B31'** type. Others of this class may also be converted to gearless ships—see under KMFKM.

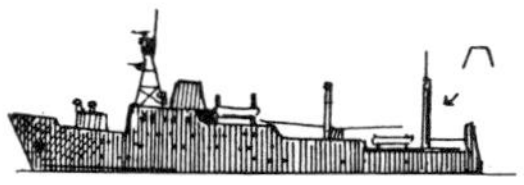

MFKM H2
⋆**17950 ZVYEROBOY;** Ru/Pd 1973; ST/S; 2000; 72.8 × 4.9 (239 × 16.2); D-E; 13; **'B-422'** type. Sisters: (Ru flag): ⋆**17951 LAPLANDIYA** ⋆**17952 SEREBRYANKA** ⋆**17953 BYELOKAMENKA** ⋆**17954 BYEREZINA** ⋆**17955 ZALESOVO** ⋆**17956 LIMENDA** ⋆**17957 ZAGORIANA** ⋆**17958 ZASLONOVO** ⋆**17959 ZYKOVO** ⋆**17960 ZVYAGIHO** ⋆**17961 TAYBOLA** ⋆**17962 GREMIKHA** ⋆**17963 ZAKHAROVO** ⋆**17964 ZVYERYEVO** ⋆**17965 ZUBOVO** ⋆**17966 VARSHUGA** ⋆**17967 TIERIBERKA** ⋆**17968 PROFESSOR SERGEY DOROFEYEV** ⋆**17969 PROFESSOR NESTOR SMYERNOV** ⋆**17970 TITOVKA** ⋆**17971 ZADORIE** ⋆**17972 ZAGORSKIY** ⋆**17973 ZUBARYEVO** ⋆**17974 MEZEN** ⋆**17975 KHARLOVKA.**

MFM H
⋆**18010 BALTIKA;** Ru/Ne 1940; PC; 7500; 135.7 × 6.3 (445 × 20.1); TST-E; 15; ex VYACHESLAV MOLOTOV 1957.

MFM H
⋆**18020 XIN HUA;** RC/No 1942; C; 2500; 88.2 × 4.6 (290 × 15.2); R; 13.5; ex SIGURD JARL 1960.

MFM H
18030 BALTIC STAR; Pa/Fi 1953; P; 2800; 92.7 × 4.9 (304 × 16); R; 15; ex MINISEA 1978; ex BORE NORD; ex BIRGER JARL 1973.

MFM H
18040 TAMPOMAS; Ia/Ne 1956; PC; 7200; 128.6 × 6.3 (422 × 20.8); M; 15.

MFM H
● **18050 CIUDAD DE CADIZ;** Sp/Sp 1951; PC; 6500; 121 × 7.3 (397 × 23.1); TSM; 18.

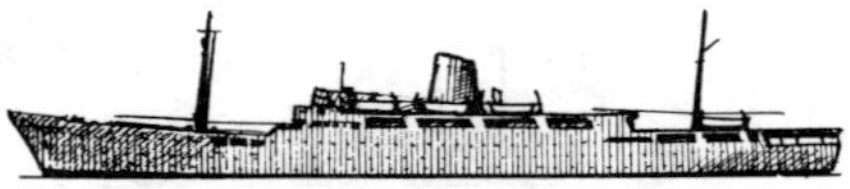

MFM H
18060 ISKENDERUN; Tu/It 1950; PC; 6600; 132 × 5.7 (433 × 18.9); TST; 16.5. Sister: **18061 SAMSUN**(Tu).

MFM H
18070 APOLLONIA; Gr/Br 1948; P; 5300; 122.6 × 6 (402 × 19.7); TST; 19.5; ex SIDI BEL ABBES 1963.

MFM H
18080 ROMANTICA; Gr/Br 1936; P; 3700; 99.5 × 7.6 (326 × 25); R; 13; ex MANSOUR 1960; ex AL-AMIR-SAUD 1956; ex FORT TOWNSHEND 1952.

MFM H
⋆**18090 MIKHAIL LOMONOSOV;** Ru/DDR 1957; RS; 3900; 102.4 × 6 (335 × 19.7); R; 13.

MFM H
18100 GANN; No/No 1950; F; 1500; 67.6 × 4.8 (222 × 15.9); M; 16; ex VIKINGFJORD; ex SANDNES 1974.

MFM H
⋆**18110 MIN CHU No 10;** RC/RC 1955; PC; 2700; 79.9 × 4.3 (262 × 14); R; 10.

MFM H
⋆**18120 MIN CHU No 14;** RC/RC 1958; PC; 2500; 90.5 × — (297 × —); R; 12. Sisters (RC flag): ⋆**18121 MIN CHU No 15** ⋆**18122 MIN CHU No 16.**

MFM H
⋆**18130 PETRODVORETS;** Ru/F 1938; PC; 2000; 77.5 × 5.2 (254 × 16); M; 13.25; ex BORE II 1950.

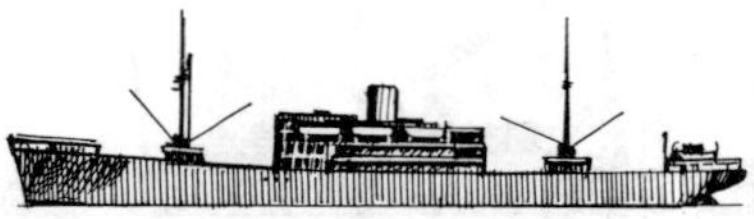

MFM H
18140 KENINGAU; Sg/Ne 1948; PC; 4900; 114.41 × 6.14 (375.36 × 20.14); M; 13.5; ex REYNIERSZ 1960.

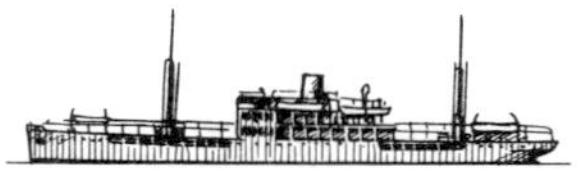

MFM H
18150 TIRTA MULIA; Pa/Ne 1935; C; 2100; 84.2 × 4.5 (276 × 14.9); M; 11; ex BAN HO HIN 1973; ex JANSSENS 1958. Similar (Ia flag): **18151 BIAN** ex CARINO 1962; ex KALIANDA 1960 **18152 KEBON AGUNG** ex KALOEKOE 1973 **18153 KAROSSA 18154 KAHAGIA IV** ex KEDAWUNG 1974; ex KASIMBAR 1973 **18155 KOMERING** ex GANA 1962; ex KAIMANA 1960 **18156 LEMATANG** ex VISO 1962; ex KALABAHI 1960 **18157 MUSI** ex MERITO 1962; ex KARATON 1960 **18158 OGAN** ex FAMA 1962; ex KALIANGET 1960.

MFM H
18160 CLANSMAN; Br/Br 1964; RoPC; 1700; 81 × 2.7 (266 × 9); TSM; 14.5; Bow & stern doors. Lengthened 1973.

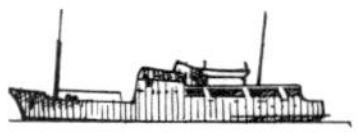

MFM H
18170 ORCADIA; Br/Br 1962; F/LS; 900; 50 × 2.9 (164 × 9.7); M; 12.

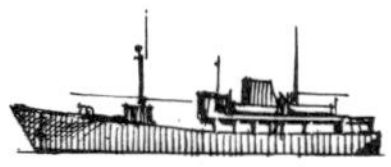

MFM H
18180 1 - 007; Bh/FRG 1964; F; 1000; 55.5 × 2.3 (182 × 7.6); TSM; 10.5; ex MONIRUL HAQUE 1975; ex E.P.S.C. ZAKIA 1967. Sisters (Bh flag): **18181 1 - 001** ex ALAUDDIN AHMED 1975 **18182 1 - 002** ex ABDUL MATIN 1975; ex E.P.S.C. ZUBEIDA 1967 **18183 C5 - 214** ex TAJUL ISLAM 1975.

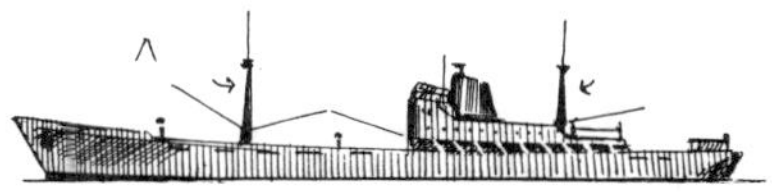

MFM H
18190 LEYTE GULF; Pi/Fr 1957; R; 3700; 113.4 × 7.1 (372 × 23.3); M; 17.5; ex FOULAYA 1969. Sisters (Gr flag): **18191 BIANCO** ex MATOUBA 1977 **18192 ANASTASIA** ex STORK 1980; ex SOUGUETA 1978.

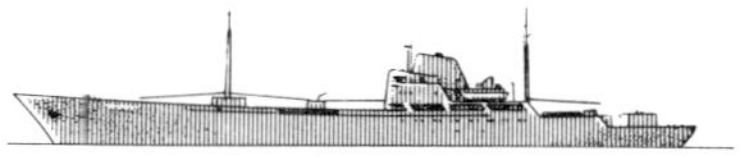

MFM H
● **18200 EL GAUCHO;** Pa/FRG 1960; C; 2100; 108.06 × 6.1 (354.53 × 20.01); M; 18; ex ELLAKI 1977; ex ALGOR 1972; ex BODETAL 1968. Sister (converted to LS - probably altered in appearance): **18201 EL PODRERO** (Pa) ex LINDAKI 1975; ex CALOR 1972; ex OKERTAL 1968.

MFM H
18210 WAJABULA; Ia/Fi 1959; C/F; 2500; 96.9 × 4.2 (318 × 13.11); M; 11; ex HALMAHERA 1963.

MFM H
18220 BYZANTINE ENTERPRISE; Gr/FRG 1961; R; 1600; 90 × —; (296 × —); M; 14; ex KETAMA.

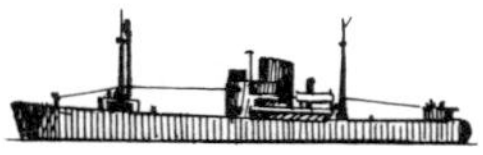

MFM H
● **18230 ILE DE SAINT PIERRE;** Fr/Br 1957; C; 1300; 70.9 × — (233 × —); M; 11.5; ex SANDPIPER 1967.

MFM H
18240 SARAH; Ca/Br 1956; C; 900; 70.8 × 3.9 (232 × 12.11); M; 11.5; ex GANNET 1968.

MFM H
18250 DESDEMONA; Ar/FRG 1952; C; 2100; 77.7 × 5.9 (255 × 19.6); M; 11. Sister: **18251 CLEOPATRA** (Ar).

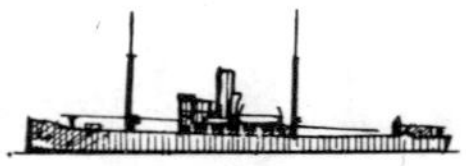

MFM H
18260 MANGANESE; Eg/Ge 1925; C; 960; 67.4 × 5.5 (221 × 18.2); R; —; ex LACONIA 1965; ex HERAKLEION 1948; ex EMPIRE CONTRACT 1945; ex WIEDAU 1945.

MFM H
⋆18280 KUBA; Ru/FRG 1955; FC; 3200; 130.5 × 6.1 (431 × 20); M; 16; ex QUARTETT 1963.

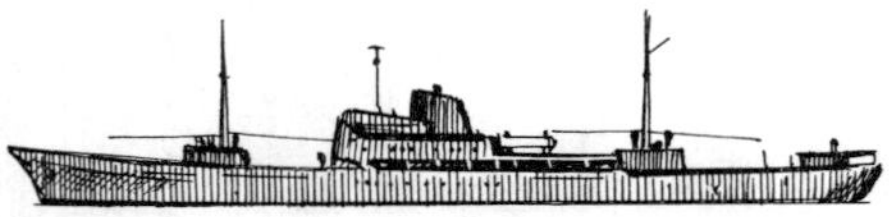

MFM H
18290 IANEVERETT; Li/FRG 1961; R; 5100; 136.1 × 7.8 (446 × 25.5); M; 19; ex HAR GILEAD 1971.

MFM H
⋆18310 ICHA; Ru/Be 1953; R; 6100; 132 × 7 (433 × 23.1); M; 18.5; ex CARIB 1964.

MFM H
18330 BALTIC FREEZER; Gr/Be 1960; R; 6200; 139.2 × 7.2 (457 × 23.7); M; —; ex ONDINE. Sister: **18331 MED FREEZER** (Gr) ex ORPHEUS.

MFM H
⋆18350 DE KASTRI; Ru/FRG 1952; R; 3000; 124.4 × 6.1 (408 × 19.9); M; 17; ex QUADRIVIUM 1964. Sister: **⋆18351 PALANA** (Ru) ex QUARTOLE 1964.

MFM H
18360 TSUNG HUEI; Pa/Fr 1953; C; 4900; 112.68 × 6.52 (369 × 69 × 21.39); M; 16; ex TA FONG 1978; ex FORT DESAIX 1969; May be spelt **TSING HUEI;** Possibly broken up.

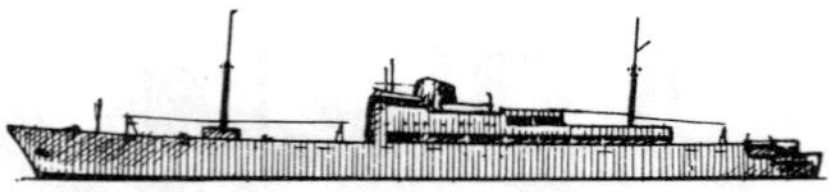

MFM H
⋆18270 HAVANA; Ru/FGR 1955; FC; 3100; 128.8 × 6.1 (423 × 20); M; 17; ex BRUNSHAUSEN 1963; Could be called **GAVANA.** Sisters (Ru flag): **⋆18271 BORA** ex BRUNSHOLM 1964 **⋆18272 MUSSON** ex BRUNSDEICH 1964 **⋆18273 PASSAT** ex BRUNSECK 1964 **⋆18274 PLAYA HIRON** ex BRUNSBUTTEL; May be called **PLAIYA KHIRON.**

MFM H
18300 SEVILLAN REEFER; Li/Sp 1967; C; 3200/4300; 134.3 × —/17.1 (441 × 23.3); M; 20; ex PORTUGALETE 1972. Sister: **18301 IKERIAN REEFER** (Li) ex IBERIAN REEFER; ex PLENCIA 1972.

MFM H
⋆18320 TSIKLON; Ru/FRG 1963; FC; 4700; 135.2 × 7.2 (444 × 23.7); M; 21; ex BRUNSHAUSEN 1966; Converted general cargo ship 1966. Sister: **18321 URAGAN** ex BRUNSBUTTEL 1967.

MFM H
18340 FRUCO; Pa/Fr 1956; R; 5000; 114.9 × 6.5 (377 × 21.5); M; 16.5; ex CUZCO 1973; ex FORT CAROLINE 1969. Similar (Pa flag): **18341 LORD CREVECOEUR** ex FORT CREVECOEUR 1976 **18342 LORD DE FRANCE** ex FORT DE FRANCE 1973 **18343 LORD FLEUR D'EPEE** ex FORT FLEUR D'EPEE 1975 **18344 LORD NIAGARA** ex FORT NIAGARA 1972 **18345 PEARL FRUIT** ex ATHLETE; ex HONEST SPRING; ex HARUKAZE 1977; ex TA SHUN 1973; ex ICA 1972; ex FORT ROYAL 1969.

MFM H
● **18370 DIMITRIOS K;** Gr/Fi 1958; R; 3400; 123.8 × 6.4 (406 × 21); M; 17; ex LANGSTONE 1974; ex SARACEN 1972. Similar: **18371 KASSOS** (Gr) ex FRUBEL JULIA 1966; ex AASE THORDEN 1958 **18372 KOS** (Gr) ex FRUBEL MARIA 1966; ex KARIN THORDEN 1958.

MFM H
18380 AUDACIA; Ur/No 1964; R; 4200; 128.1 × 7.8 (420 × 25.6); M; 19; ex PARA; ex VIKFROST 1977; ex THORSDROTT 1972. Sister: **18381 ISADORE HECHT** (Pa) ex CLYDEFIRTH 1980; ex VIKFRIO 1974; ex THORSOY 1972.

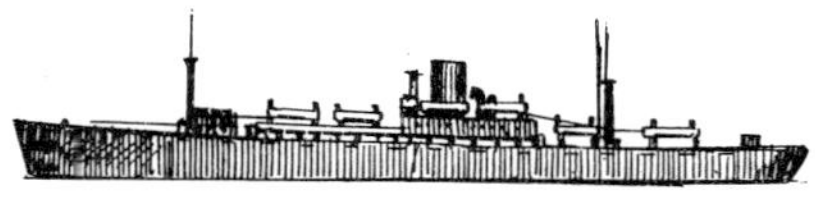

MFM H
18390 MISR; Eg/US 1943; C; 7400; 127.3 × 8.2 (418 × 26.9); T; 14; ex EMPIRE MACE 1947; ex CAPE ST ROQUE; Converted **C1'** type. Sister: **18391 AL SUDAN** (Eg) ex EMPIRE ARQUEBUS; ex CAPE ST VINCENT.

MFM H
● **18400 DEXENA;** Cy/FRG 1958; CP; 2300/3500; 106.2 × 7.4 (438 × 23.6); M; 14; ex ULSNIS 1976; ex VOLUMNIA 1969; ex LEALOTT 1966; ex VOLUMNIA 1963. Sisters: **18401 MARIA** (Gr) ex VIRGILIA 1974 **18402 TANIA** (Gr) ex ANEMOS 1972; ex POLARIS 1971; ex VALERIA 1963.

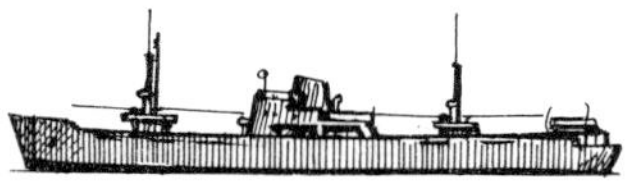

MFM H
18410 PANAY; Pi/No 1949; C; 2800; 95 × 5.6 (312 × 18.3); M; 14; ex MUI NAN 1951.

MFM H
18420 CARIBSTAR; Br/No 1948; C; 1100; 71 × 5.1 (246 × 16.1); M; 10; ex LA MOOR 1974; ex MAINA 1973; ex SINVELO 1972; ex VERA 1952.

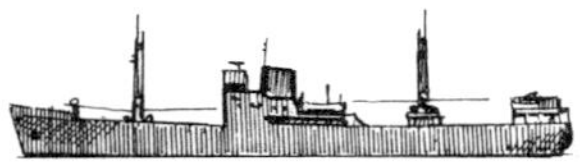

MFM H
● **18430 CASTLE GLORY;** Br/Sw 1952; C; 2200; 37 × 4.92 (285.43 × 16.14); M; 11.5; ex MARTA 1974; ex CAP VERT 1971; ex DJIRING 1969; Launched as BARRANQUILLA.

MFM H
18440 BALLENITA; Pa/No 1957; CP; 2200/2700; 95 × 5.4/6.4 (310 × 18/21); M; 15.

MFM H
18450 AVRA; Gr/Be 1954; C; 1800; 94 × 5.6 (309 × 16); M; 12; ex ALCA 1965.

MFM H
18460 ANNARITA SECONDA; It/Hong Kong 1967; RoC; 1100; 81.2 × 3.1 (267 × 10.6); M; 12.5; ex HOLMLEA 1975; ex SEAWAY PRINCESS 1970; Stern door.

MFM H
18470 DIMITRA M; Gr/De 1936; CP; 1700; 88 × 5.6 (288 × 18.3); M; 11.5; ex SANTA CRUZ 1970; ex MAROCCO 1966. Sister: **18471 MATHIOS** (Gr) ex MARIA T 1972; ex TUNIS 1966; ex BONANZA 1946; ex AQUILA 1945; ex TUNIS 1941.

MFM H
18480 ALKMINI A; Gr/Sw 1937; C; 2500; 100.97 × 5.69 (331.27 × 18.67); M; 12; ex MERCIA 1974; ex MYLLE 1969; ex FRIGG 1961; ex PAN 1957; ex ASTRI 1952; May be broken up.

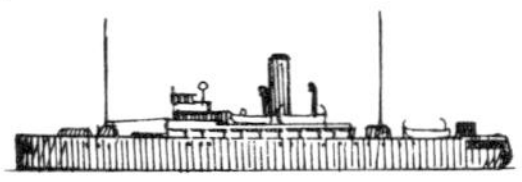

MFM H
★**18490 MIN CHU No 8;** RC/China 1924; C; 1900; 79.2 × 4.9 (260 × 16); R; 10.

MFM H
18500 DONA GLORIA; Pi/Sw 1947; C; 1800; 86 × 5.9 (282 × 19.6); M; 13; ex DON SULPICIO 1969; ex COLOMBIA 1964.

MFM H
● **18510 ORIENT;** Le/No 1950; C; 2100; 90 × 6.1 (295 × 20.2); R; 11; ex ODYSSEUS 1974; ex BLAAFJELD 1 1961.

MFM H
18520 GISMATALLAH; Si/Sw 1938; C; 1500; 87.6 × 5.4 (287 × 17.1); M; 13; ex CAROLA 1977; ex CAROLAEMME 1974; ex FREJA 1967. Sister: **18521 SPYROS** (Gr) ex GIANVITTORIOEMME 1973; ex FIDRA 1966.

MFM H
⋆**18530 GALIOLA;** Ys/Br 1954; C; 1100/1800; 79 × —/5.5 (260 × —/18); M; 13; ex ADJUTANT 1966. Sisters: (Ys flag) ⋆**18531 OTOK** ex HORIZONT 1973; ex RINGDOVE 1967; ⋆**18532 ORUDA** ex WHITEWING 1967.

MFM H
18540 SKULE; No/No 1949; TS; 700; 48 × 5.4 (167 × 17.6); M; 12; ex SOROY 1966.

MFM H
18550 SANDRA MARIA; Ia/It 1952; C; 800; 67.2 × 4.6 (221 × 15.2); M; 11.5; ex ALESSANDRA.

MFM H
⋆**18570 ORJULA.** Ys/Br 1948; C; 1000; 71.5 × 4.2 (235 × 13.11); M; 12; ex WOODCOCK 1964. Sister: ⋆**18571 RABAC (Ys)** ex LABIN 1967; ex PTARMIGAN 1963.

MFM H
18580 ARAFAT. Si/De 1924; C; 1200; 74.5 × 4.3 (245 × 14.1); M; 13.5; ex DANIA 1958; ex FREM 1953; Lengthened 1938.

MFM H
18590 TRONDELAG. No/No 1950; TS; 600; 49.2 × 3.5 (161 × 11.6); M; 12; ex AURE 1964.

MFM H
18600 ONGE. In/In 1969; F/LS; 1300; 68.3 × 2.9 (224 × 9.6); M; 12. Sister: **18601 YEREWA** (In).

MFM H
18610 GANN; No/FRG 1924; TS; 1600; 75 × 4.8 (146 × 15.9); TSM; 13; ex MARINA 1960; ex BRAND VI 1960; ex COURT ADELER 1956; ex KING 1950; ex TROUBADOUR 1948; ex WARRIOR; ex VANADIS; Converted yacht.

MFM H
18620 DANNEBROG. De/De 1931; Royal Yacht; 1100; 75 × 3.4 (246 × 11.2); TSM; 14.

MFM H
18630 ALSACE. Fr/Fr 1939; Cbl; 2100; 88.4 × 5.3 (289 × 17.6); TSR; 14.5.

MFM H
18640 AMPERE. Fr/Fr 1951; Cbl; 2200; 85.3 × 5.1 (289 × 16.1); TST; 15.

MFM H
18650 BODE THOMAS. Ng/Br 1960; BT; 1200; 62.8 × 3.5 (206 × 11.7); TSM; —.

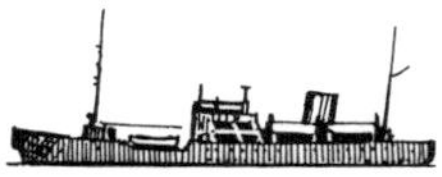

MFM H
18660 MERMAID. Br/Br 1959; LT; 1400; 67.4 × 4 (221 × 13); TSD-E; —. Sisters (Br flag): **18661 SIREN 18662 STELLA 18663 WINSTON CHURCHILL** (helicopter pad).

MFM H
18670 ARGUS. Br/Br 1948; LT; 1900; 81.4 × 4.1 (267 × 13.9); TSR 12. Sisters (Br flag): **18671 READY 18672 VESTAL.**

MFM H
18680 SAGAR. In/Br 1964; Plt; 2000; 83.6 × 4.7 (274 × 15.7); TSM; —. Sister: **18681 SAMUDRA** (In).

MFM H
18690 VIRGEN DEL CAMINO. Sp/Sp 1963; ST; 930; 61 × 5 (200 × 16.6); M; 14; ex MAR AUSTRAL 1967. Similar: ***18691 ISLA DE LA JUVENTUD** (Cu) ex ARMINZA 1967.

MFM H
18700 HESSEN. FRG/FRG. 1960; FT: 1000; 73 × 4.4 (239 × 14.3); D-E; —.

Twin Funnels

MFM H
18710 CORIOLANUS. Br/Br 1967; ST; 1100; 63.4 × 4.6 (208 × 15); M; 15.5. Sisters (Br flag): **18711 CASSIO 18712 OTHELLO 18713 ORSINO** (Research & Depot Ship).

Twin Funnels

MFM H
***18720 NORDSEE.** DDR/DDR 1966; FT; 640; 48.9 × 3.5 (160.3 × 11.4); M; 12. Sisters (DDR flag): ***18721 ATLANTIK *18722 BARENTSEE *18723 GROSSER BELT *18724 JAN MAYEN *18725 KATTEGAT *18726 LOFOTEN *18727 MALANGEN *18728 NORDMEER *18729 ORKNEY *18730 SILVER PIT *18731 SUND *18732 SVINOY *18733 SKAGERRAK.**

Twin Funnels

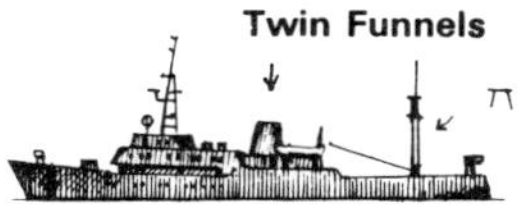

MFM H
***18740 LASKARA.** Pd/Pd 1968; FT; 1500; 75.6 × 5 (248 × 17); M; 14.5. **'B-29'** type. Sisters (Pd flag): ***18741 KABRYL *18742 KANARYJKA *18743 KANTAR *18744 KNIAZIK *18745 KOLEN *18746 KORWIN *18747 KULBAK *18748 KULBIN *18749 KUNATKA *18750 LATERNA *18751 LIKODYN *18752 LIKOMUR *18753 LIKOSAR *18754 LIKOWAL *18755 LODOWIK *18756 LUTJAN *18757 LUZYTANKA.**

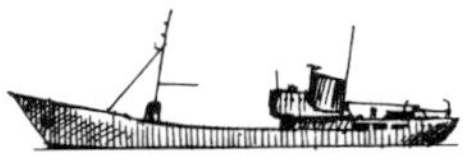

MFM H
18760 TYPICAL DEEP SEA TRAWLER. Approx 700-900; 64 to 70 × 5.1 to 5.5 (210 to 230 × 17 to 18); M; 15 approx.

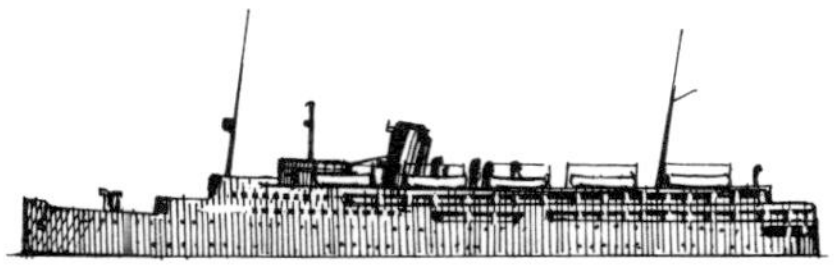

MFM H
18770 ANKARA. Tu/US 1927; P; 6200; 124.8 × 6.3 (409 × 20.8); TST; 19; ex SOLACE 1948; ex IROQUOIS 1948.

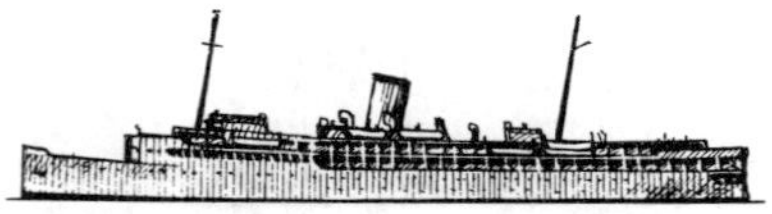

MFM H
18780 ELIZABETH A. Cy/US 1927; P; 5200; 115.6 × 6.1 (379 × 20.1); TST; 18; ex SAN ANDRES 1969; ex YARMOUTH 1966; ex YARMOUTH CASTLE 1957; ex QUEEN OF NASSAU 1957; ex YARMOUTH CASTLE 1954; ex YARMOUTH 1954.

MFM H
18790 WAH SHAN. Br/Ja 1934; F; 2100; 79 × 3.6 (259 × 12); TSM; 14; ex NISHIKI MARU 1971.

MFM H
18800 AKANE MARU. Ja/Ja 1948; F; 1000; 66 × 3.4 (200 × 10.6); TSM; 16. Sisters (Ja flag): **18801 AKASHI MARU 18802 AKEBONO MARU 18803 FUTABA MARU 18804 SAKURA MARU** (Pi flag): **18805 KATIPUNAN** ex HIKARI MARU 1974.

MFM H
18810 PRINCESS OF ACADIA. Ca/Ca 1971; RoF; 10100; 146.3 × 4.6 (480 × 15.3); TSM; 15.5; ex PRINCESS OF NOVA.

MFM H
18820 MANXMAN. Br/Br 1955; F; 2500; 105.1 × 3.7 (345 × 12.3); TST; 21.

MFM H
18830 QUEEN MARY. Br/Br 1933; F; 1000; 80.2 × 2.3 (263 × 7.5); TrST; 16; ex QUEEN MARY II 1976; ex QUEEN MARY 1935; May now be converted to a floating restaurant.

MFM H
18840 MARAKAZ. Tu/Ge 1938; PC; 1400; 80 × 3.4 (263 × 11.1); TST; 15.

MFM H
● **18850 LETO.** Gr/Br 1949; F; 1600; 82.9 × 2.4 (272 × 7.6); TSM; 18; ex OIA 1976; ex QUEEN OF THE CHANNEL 1968.

MFM H
18860 ROANA. Cy/De 1954; RoPF; 1300; 60.1 × 3.6 (197 × 11.8); M; 12.75; ex OSTERSOEN 1973.

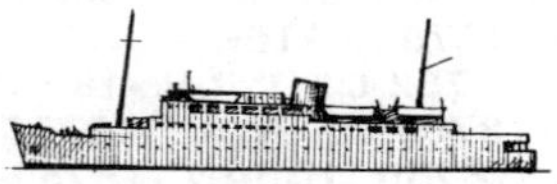

MFM H
18870 JOLLYEMME. It/De 1937; RoC; 1200; 82.3 × 4.2 (270 × 14.5); TSM; 14; ex LIDO 1974; ex JOLLYEMME 1973; ex PETER WESSEL II 1968; ex PETER WESSEL 1968; Bow & stern doors. Lengthened 1957.

MFM H
⋆**18880 MARINA.** Ys/De 1936; RoF; 1000; 71.8 × 3.4 (236 × 11.2); TSM; 14; ex CHRISTOFER POLHEM 1964; ex KRONPRINSESSAN INGRID 1935; Stern door. Lengthened 1950.

MFM H
18890 AGOSTINO LAURO. It/De 1935; F; 500; 60 × 3.6 (197 × 11.9); TSM; 14; ex ISEFJORD 1966.

MFM H
18900 BALMORAL. Br/Br 1949; F; 700; 62 × 2 (204 × 6.7); TSM; 14.5.

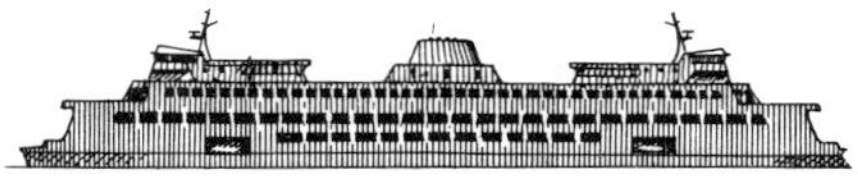

MFM H
18910 SPOKANE. US/US 1972; RoF; 3200; 134.1 × 5.2 (440 × 17.2); D-E; 20. Sister: **18911 WALLA-WALLA** (US).

MFM H
18920 QUEEN OF COQUITLAM. Ca/Ca 1976; RoF; 6600; 139.3 × 5.3 (457 × 17.8); M; 20. Sister: **18921 QUEEN OF COWICHAN** (Ca).

MFM H
18930 ARVEPRINS KNUD. De/De 1963; RoPC; 4800; 129.9 × 4.6 (426 × 15.1); TSM; 19; Bow and stern doors.

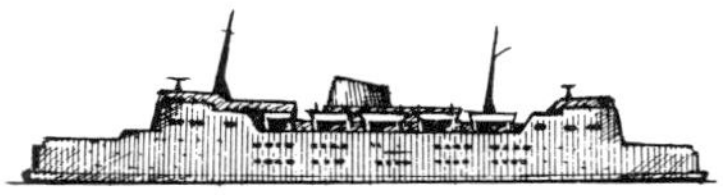

MFM H
18940 KNUDSHOVED. De/De 1961; RoC; 3900; 109.2 × 4.6 (358 × 15.1); TSM; 16. Sister (De flag): **18941 SPROGO** Similar: **18942 HALSSKOV.**

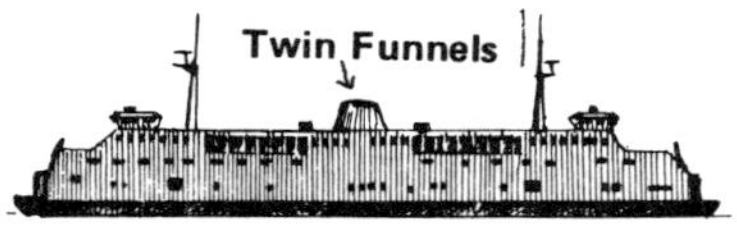

MFM H
18950 PRINSES CHRISTINA. Ne/Ne 1968; RoF; 3100; 113.6 × 4.6 (373 × 15.2); D-E; 18.5; Bow and Stern doors.

MFM H
18960 PRINSES MARGRIET. Ne/Ne 1963; RoF; 2300; 102 × 4.8 (345 × 15.1); D-E; 16. Sisters (Ne flag): **18961 PRINSES BEATRIX 18962 PRINSES IRENE.**

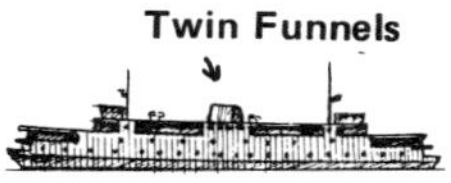

MFM H
18970 TEXELSTROOM. Ne/Ne 1966; RoF; 2700; 68 × —; (223 × —); D-E; —. Sister: **18971 MARSDIEP** (Ne).

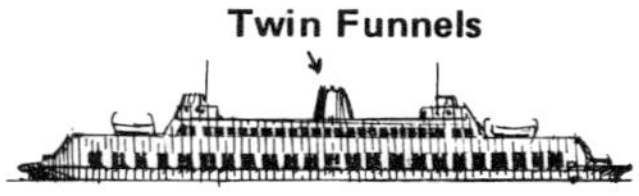

MFM H
18980 EVERGREEN STATE. US/US 1954; RoF; 1500; 94.5 × 4.6 (310 × 15); TSD-E; 15. Sisters (US flag): **18981 KLAHOWYA 18982 TILLIKUM.**

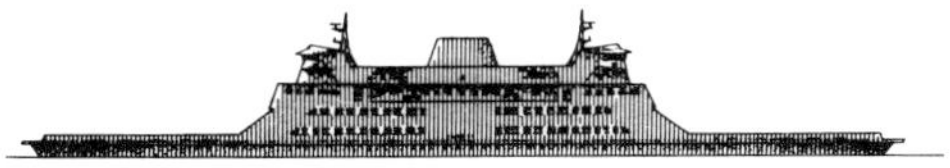

MFM H
18990 QUEEN OF ALBERNI. Ca/Ca 1976; RoPF/TF; 5300; 139.3 × 5.49 (457.02 × 18.01); TSM; 22.

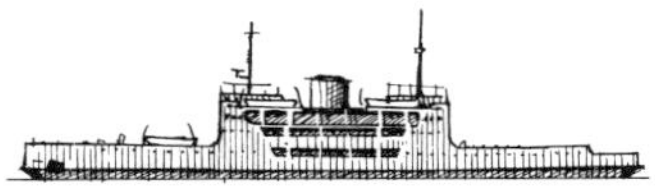

MFM H
19000 SECONDO ASPROMONTE. It/It 1948; RoC/TF; 1600; 97.7 × 3.8 (321 × 12.5); ex ASPROMONTE 1949. Sister: **19001 MONGIBELLO** (It).

MFM H
19010 HALSINBORG. De/De 1960; RoF/TF; 1050; 80.9 × 3.6 (265 × 11.1); D-E; 11. Similar (raised boats): **19011 HELSINGOR** (De).

MFM H
19020 CONFEDERATION. Ca/Ca 1962; RoF; 2400; 86.5 × 4.2 (284 × 13.9); TSD-E; —.

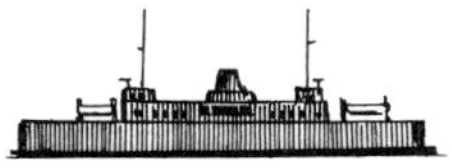

MFM H
19030 BASTO III. No/No 1968; RoF; 1200; 65.6 × 3.4 (215 × 11.2); M; —; Bow & stern doors.

MFM H
19040 KIZKULESI. Tu/Fr 1951; RoF; 1000; 60 × 3 (197 × 9.10); M; —. Sister: **19041 KASIMPASA** (Tu).

MFM H
19050 TRANS ST. LAURENT. Ca/Ca 1963; RoF; 2200; 79.8 × — (262 × —); TSM; —.

MFM H
19060 QUEEN OF THE ISLANDS. Ca/Ca 1963; RoF; 1700; 71.9 × — (236 × —); TSM; —; Bow & stern doors.

MFM H
19070 NOORD NEDERLAND. Ne/Sw 1960; RoF; 1100; 48 × 3.7 (158 × 11.6); TSM; —; ex PRIMULA 1976.

MFM H
19080 BETULA. Sw/FRG 1968; RoF; 2300; 71.3 × 4 (234 × 13.1); TSM; 14.5; Bow & stern doors. Similar (Sw flag): **19081 REGULA 19082 URSULA.**

MFM H
● **19090 SVEA SCARLETT.** Sw/FRG 1971; RoF; 3000; 86.3 × 4 (283 × 13.1); TSM; 17.

MFM H
● **19100 KORSOR.** De/De 1927; RoF/TF; 2400; 96.8 × 4.5 (318 × 14.9); TSM; 14.

MFM H
19110 PUERTO MONTT. Ch/FRG 1966; RoF; 3600; 93.9 × 4.3 (308 × 14.2); TSM; —; ex PRESIDENTE AGUIRRE CERDA 1974; ex KOBENHAVN 1973.

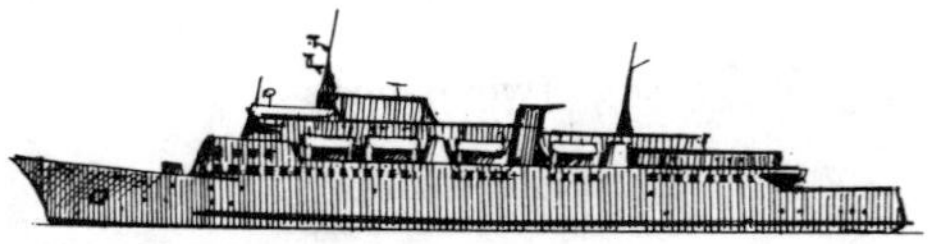

MFM H
19120 ESPRESSO OLBIA. It/FRG 1966; RoF; 7300; 138 × 5.5 (453 × 18); TSM; 23; ex TOR ANGLIA; Bow & stern doors.

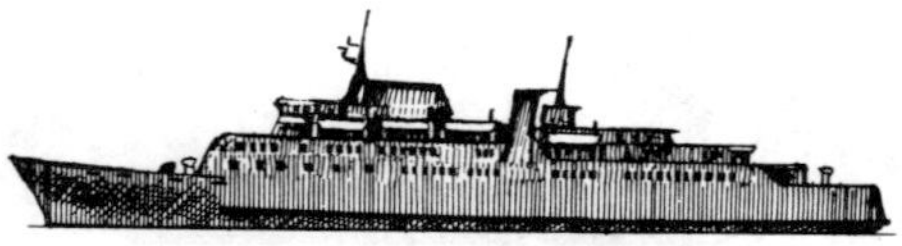

MFM H
19130 ARIADNE. Gr/FRG 1967; RoF; 10700; 138 × 5.5 (453 × 18); TSM; 23; ex TOR HOLLANDIA 1975; Bow & stern doors.

MFM H
● **19140 GELTING.** De/FRG 1963; RoF; 2500; 93.2 × 4 (306 × 13.2); TSM; 19; ex MILLE 1976; ex FALSTER 1968; ex GEDSTER 1968; Bow & stern doors. Sister: **19141 CORSICA NOVA** (Pa) ex CORSIKA NOVA 1979; ex EUROPAFARJAN II 1976; ex TRAVEMUNDE 1970 Similar: **19142 THJELVAR** (Sw) ex GOTLAND ★**19143 SKANDYNAWIA** (Pd) ex VISBY 1970.

MFM H
19150 CHRISTIAN IV. No/De 1968; RoC/TF; 2700; 87.3 × 4.1 (286 × 13.6); TSM; 19; Stern and side doors.

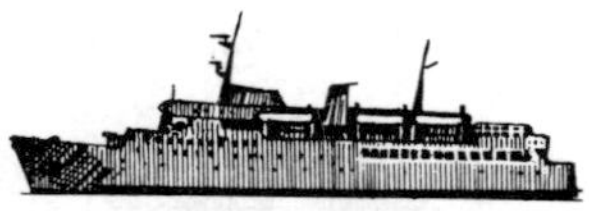

MFM H
19160 YESILADA. Tu/De 1968; RoF; 3100; 87.2 × 4.2 (186 × 13.9); TSM; 19.5; ex PETER WESSEL 1971.

MFM H
19170 SLAVIJA. De/Br 1963; RoF; 3000; 88.3 × 4.2 (290 × 13.9); TSM; —; ex SKIPPER CLEMENT 1976; ex JENS KOFOED 1965.

MFM H

● **19180 DANIA GLORIA.** De/De 1966; RoF; 2400; 92.7 × 4.2 (304 × 13.9); TSM; 19.5; ex METTE MO; ex METTE MOLS 1974. Sisters: **19181 CARAVAGGIO** (It) ex MAREN MO 1975; ex MAREN MOLS 1975 **19182 SMYRIL** (Fa) ex MORTEN MOLS 1975 **19183 TEISTEN** (Fa) ex MIKKEL MOLS 1980 Similar: **19184 ALMIRANTE LUIS BIRON** (Ve) ex LASSE 1973.

MFM H

19190 ALDONZA MANRIQUE. Ve/FRG 1964; RoF; 3100; 98.4 × 4.3 (323 × 14.2); TSM; 19; ex OLAU EAST 1975; ex JULLE 1975; ex HUNDESTED 1972; Bow & stern doors. Sister: **19191 CORSICA MARINA** (Pa) ex OLAU WEST; ex KALLE 1975; ex GRENAA 1971.

MFM H

19200 CHRYSANTHEMUM. Gr/FRG 1965; F; 1900; 77.6 × 3.4 (255 × 11.2); TSM; 18; ex MARIANNA 1975; ex HOLIDAY PRINCESS 1971; ex STELLA MARINA 1970; Side doors.

MFM H

19210 WILHEMSHAVEN. FRG/FRG 1963; F; 1600; 75 × 3.4 (246 × 11.2); TSM; 17.5.

MFM H

19220 POSEIDON. FRG/No 1964; F; 1100; 65.5 × 2.9 (215 × 9.1); TSM; —.

MFM H

19230 CAVO AZURO. Gr/FRG 1959; F; 900; 61.8 × 3.2 (203 × 10.6); TSM; 14.5; ex PORTOKALIS ILIOS 1980; ex ORANGE SUN 1967. Sister: **19231 HARLEKIN** (FRG) ex TOM KYLE 1977; ex ORANGE MOON 1961.

MFM H

19240 SKANE. Sw/Sw 1966; RoF/TF; 6500; 147.7 × 5.5 (484 × 17.5); TSM; —.

MFM H

19250 FENNIA. Fi/Sw 1966; RoF; 6400; 128.3 × 5 (421 × 16.5); TSM; 18.5; Bow & stern doors.

MFM H

19260 AGADIR. Mo/FRG 1969; RoF; 3800; 108.1 × 4.6 (355 × 15.1); TSM; 20; ex PRINZ HAMLET II 1974; ex VIKINGFJORD 1970; Bow, stern & side doors.

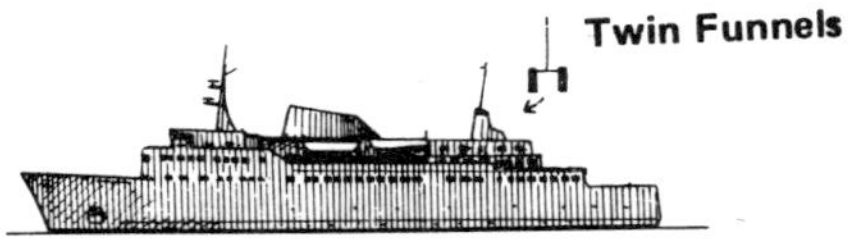

MFM H

19270 VILLA DE AGAETE. Sp/Fi 1970; RoF; 4100; 101.6 × 5 (334 × 16.6); TSM; 13; ex FLORIA 1975; Bow and stern doors.

MFM H

19280 CIUDAD DE LA LAGUNA. Sp/Fi 1967; RoF; 3500; 101.6 × 4.9 (334 × 16.2); TSM; 19; ex BOTNIA 1975.

MFM H

● **19290 OLAU KENT.** De/FRG 1970; RoPCF; 4200; 109 × 4.6 (357 × 15); TSM; 18.5; ex APOLLO 1976. Sisters: **19291 VIKING 1** (Fi) **19292 EARL GRANVILLE** (Br) ex VIKING 4 **19293 WASA EXPRESS** (Fi) ex VIKING 3 1976 **19294 BOTNIA EXPRESS** (Fi) ex DIANA 1979 **19295 COROMUEL** (Me) **19296 PUERTO VALLARTA** (Me).

MFM H

19300 FAIR LADY. FRG/FRG 1970; F; 900; 68.6 × 2.2 (225 × 7); TSM; 18.

MFM H

19310 SEEMOWE II. FRG/FRG 1969; F; 1000; 58.9 × 2.9 (193 × 9.8); TSM; 14; ex MALMO 1976.

MFM H

19320 ISLA DE CUBAGUA. Ve/Fi 1961; RoPF; 3700; 101.6 × 4.6 (334 × 15.2); TSM; 18; ex SKANDIA 1974; Bow and stern doors. Sister: **19321 ISLA DE COCHE** (Ve) ex NORDICA 1974.

MFM H

⋆**19330 WAWEL.** Pd/FRG 1965; RoPF; 3800; 110.2 × 4.4 (362 × 14.4); TSM; 20; ex GUSTAV VASA 1973; Bow and stern doors. Similar: **19331 IONIAN STAR** (Gr) ex LEIF ERIKSSON 1976; ex PRINS BERTIL 1966.

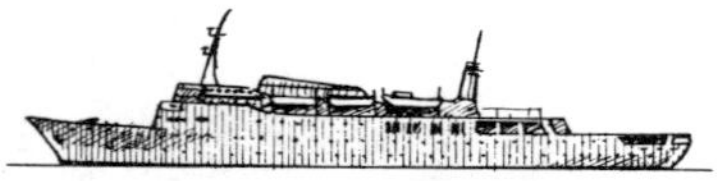

MFM H

⋆**19340 XING HU.** RC/Sp 1967; F; 4400; 104.9 × 4.3 (344 × 13.5); TSM; 19.5; ex DONA MONTSERRAT 1980; ex WEST STAR 1975; ex CABO IZARRA 1970.

MFM H

19350 LUCY MAUD MONTGOMERY. Ca/Fr 1965; RoCF; 4200; 86 × 3.9 (262 × 12.8); TSM; 17.5; ex STENA DANICA 1970; Bow and stern doors.

MFM H

19360 DANA SCARLETT. Sw/Sw 1964; RoCF; 1700; 65.3 × 3.2 (214 × 10.6); TSM; 14.75; Bow and stern doors. Similar (shorter top deck): **19361 CAROLA** (Sw).

MFM H

19370 GOTLANDIA. Sw/Sw 1965; RoPF; 1400; 71 × 3.8 (233 × 12.6); TSM; —; Bow and stern doors. Sister: **19371 BENITO JUAREZ** (Me) ex OLANNINGEN 1972.

MFM H

● **19380 ROTNA.** De/FRG 1962; RoPF; 2300; 88 × 4 (289 × 13.2); TSM; 16.5; ex KALLE 1971. Sister: **19381 CORSICA SERENA** (De).

MFM H

● **19390 POLHEM.** Sw/Sw 1964; RoPF; 2500; 78.5 × 3.9 (258 × 12.8); TSM; —; ex SCANIA EXPRESS 1976; ex SCANIA 1971.

MFM H

19400 HAMLET. Sw/FRG 1968; RoCF; 2100; 73.5 × 3.8 (241 × 12.6); TSM; 14.5; Bow and stern doors. Sister: **19401 OFELIA** (Sw).

MFM H
19410 AINOS. Gr/Sw 1964; F; 2400; 71.9 × — (236 × —); TSM; 17; ex MANIC; ex APOLLO 1968.

MFM H
19430 VIKING VICTORY. No/No 1964; RoPF; 3700; 99.5 × 4.4 (326 × 14.6); TSM; 20; ex VIKING I 1976; ex CARFERRY VIKING I; Bow & stern doors. Sisters: **19431 VIKING III** (No) **19432 EARL WILLIAM** (Br) ex CARFERRY VIKING II 1977; ex VIKING II 1964.

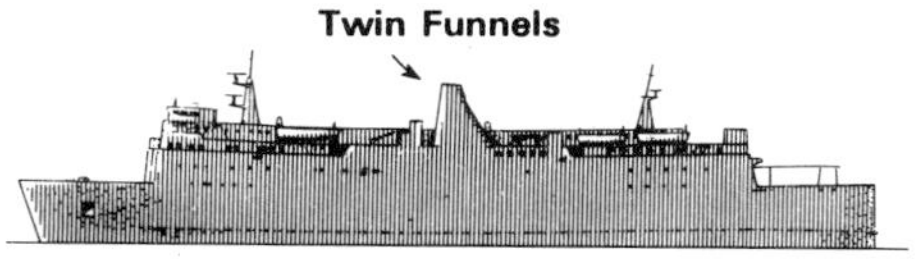

MFM H
19460 ST. ANSELM. Br/Br 1980; RoPF; 8200; 129.4 × 4.72 (424.54 × 15.49); TSM; 19.5; Bow and stern doors. Sister (Br flag): **19461 ST. CHRISTOPHER** Similar: **19462 ST. DAVID 19463 GALLOWAY PRINCESS** (bridge one deck lower).

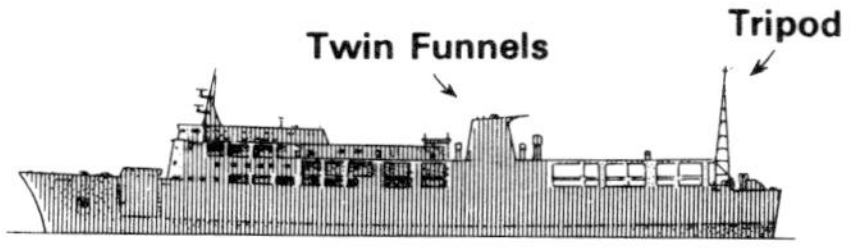

MFM H
19490 VELA. Ja/Ja 1979; RoPF; 3700; 120.58 × 5.3 (395.6 × 17.39); TSM; 20; Bow door/ramp. Stern door/ramp. Side doors/ramps.
Sister: **19491 VESTA** (Ja).

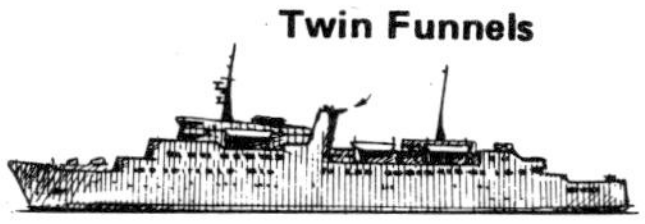

MFM H
19420 EARL GODWIN. Br/Sw 1966; RoPF; 4000; 99.2 × 4.4 (325 × 14.6); TSM; 20.25; ex SVEA DROTT 1975; Bow & stern doors.

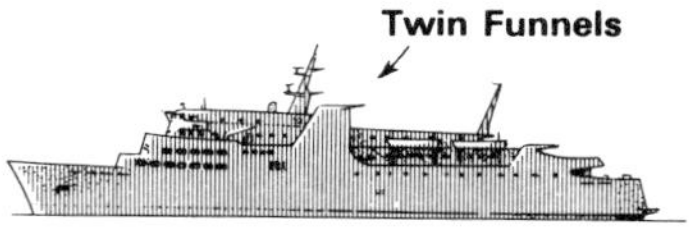

MFM H
19440 QUEEN OF PRINCE RUPERT. Ca/Ca 1966; RoPF; 5900; 101.12 × 4.64 (331.76 × 15.22); TSM; —; Bow & stern doors.

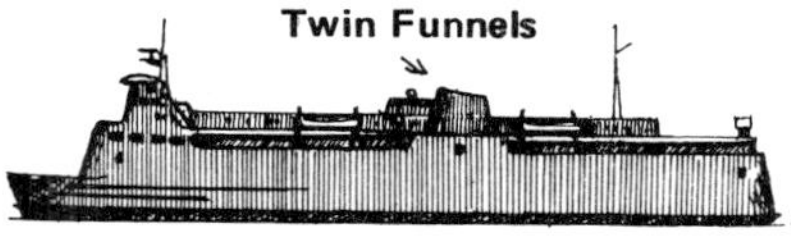

MFM H
19450 JOHN HAMILTON GRAY. Ca/Ca 1968; RoF/IB; 11300; 122.1 × 6.2 (401 × 20.3); TD-E; 18; Stern doors.

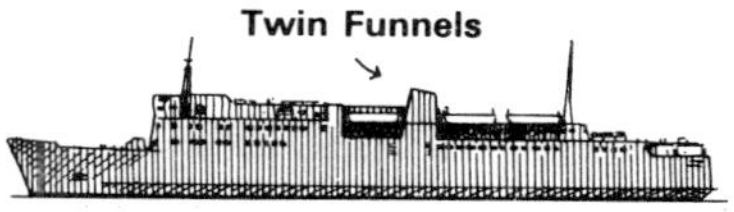

MFM H
19470 LION. Br/Br 1967; RoPF; 3900; 111 × 4.3 (365 × 14); TSM; 20.25; Bow and stern doors.

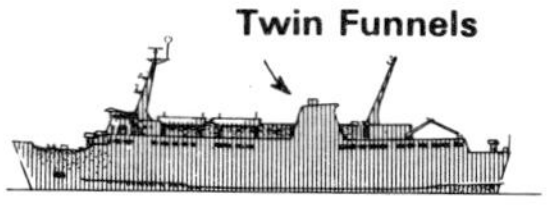

MFM H
19480 EMSLAND. FRG/Ja 1977; RoPF; 1600; 78.52 × 3.35 (257.61 × 10.99); TSM; 16; Bow door/ramp. Stern door/ramp.

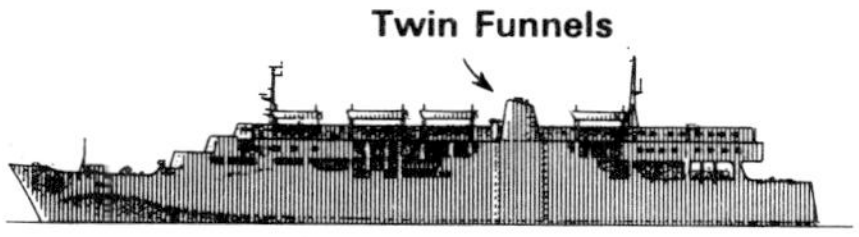

MFM H
19500 TASSILI. Ag/Ja 1971; RoPF; 10200; 130.38 × 5.62 (427.76 × 18.44); TSM; —; ex CENTRAL NO. 1 1973; Bow, stern and side doors.

MFM H
● **19510 KAMOME.** Ja/Ja 1975; RoPF; 2700; 90.5 × 4 (297 × 13.2); TSM; —.

MFM H
19520 HAYATOMO MARU. Ja/Ja 1971; RoCF; 3400; 105 × 4.4 (344 × 14.6); TSM; 18.25; ex TOSA 1977.

MFM H
19530 OSADO MARU. Ja/Ja 1969; RoPF; 1900; 82 × 3.45 (269.03 × 11.32); TSM; 16.5.

MFM H
19540 AMBROSE SHEA. Ca/Ca 1967; RoPF; 9500; 120.6 × 6.3 (396 × 20); TD-E; 16.5; Stern door.

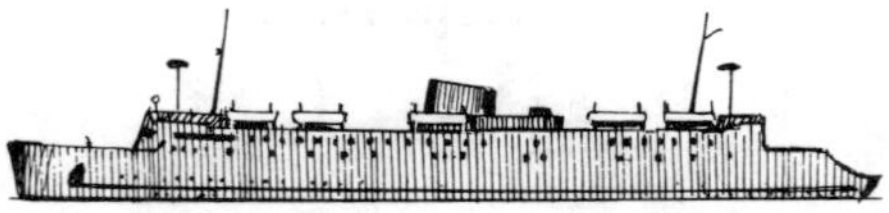

MFM H
19550 THEODOR HEUSS. FRG/FRG 1957; TF; 5600; 136 × 4.9 (446 × 16); TD-E; —.

MFM H
19560 CITY OF MIDLAND 41. US/US 1941 RoPF/TF; 4000; 124 × 5.7 (407 × 18.7); TSM; 18. Sisters (US flag): **19561 BADGER 19562 SPARTAN.**

MFM H
19570 PRINSESSE ANNE-MARIE. De/De 1960; RoCF; 3500; 103.4 × 4.6 (339 × 15); TSM; 18.

MFM H
19580 CORSICA STAR. Pa/No 1961; F; 2400; 87.4 × 4.4 (287 × 14.6); TSM; 17; ex NORDEK 1973; ex KATTEGAT 1969.

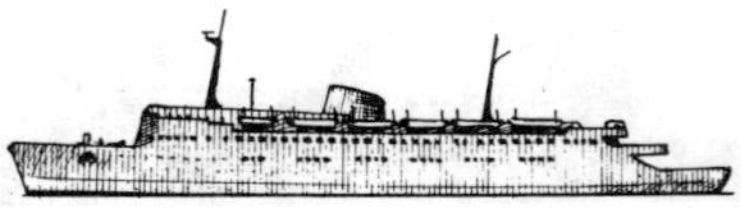

MFM H
19590 KONG FREDERIK IX. De/De 1954; RoPF; 4100; 114.3 × 4.5 (375 × 14.1); TSM; 18. Similar: **19591 PRINSESSE BENEDIKTE** (De).

MFM H
19600 MARINE CRUISER. Br/Au 1959; RoPF; 4100; 113.3 × 4.7 (372 × 15.7); TSM; 17.75; ex PRINCESS OF TASMANIA 1975; Stern door.

MFM H
19610 AGIOS GEORGIOS. Gr/De 1956; RoCF; 2000; 70.9 × 3.7 (232 × 12.1); TSM; 15; ex MASTROGIORGIS 1976; ex ABSALON 1975.

MFM H
19620 SCANIA. Sw/De 1972; RoCF; 2200; 74.2 × 3.8 (243 × 12.6); TSM; 14.5; Bow, stern and side doors.

MFM H
19630 AL ANOUD. Eg/Fi 1955; RoPF; 2200; 84.4 × 4.5 (277 × 15); TSM; 17; ex WASA EXPRESS 1975; ex THJELVAR 1964; ex PRINSESSAN MARGARETHA 1962; Side and stern doors.

MFM H
19640 SAUDI GOLDEN ARROW. Si/No 1960; RoCF; 2200; 87.5 × 4.4 (287 × 14.6); TSM; —; ex EUROPAFERGEN.

MFM H
19650 NORDSCHAU. FRG/De 1956; RoCF; 2000; 70.9 × 3.7 (233 × 12.6); TSM; 14.75; ex GRIPEN 1976.

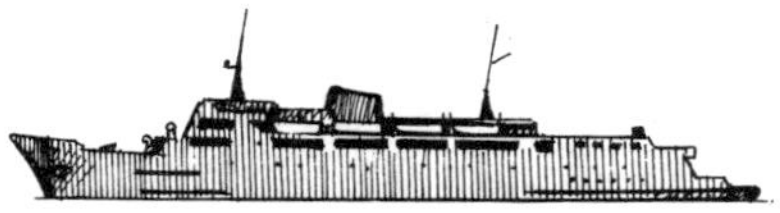

MFM H
19660 SAINT GERMAIN. Fr/De 1951; RoF/TF; 3100; 115.8×4.1 (380×13.6); TSM; 16.5.

MFM H
19680 YOTEI MARU. Ja/Ja 1965; RoCF/TF; 5400; 140×5.2 (433×17.1); TSM; 18; Stern door. Sisters (Ja flag): **19681 TAISETU MARU 19682 HAKKODA MARU 19683 MASHU MARU 19684 MATSUMAE MARU 19685 TSUGARU MARU 19686 TOWADA MARU.**

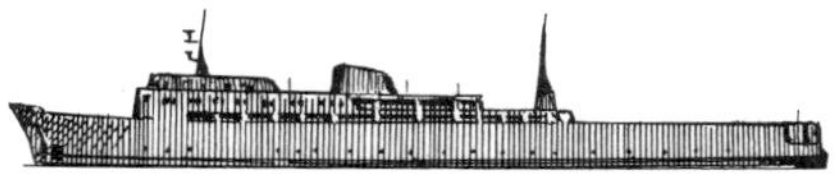

MFM H
19710 FERRY HANKYU. Ja/Ja 1968; RoF; 5000; 127×4.5 (416×15); TSM; 18. Sister: **19711 FERRY KANPU** (Ja) ex HANKYU MARU No 6.

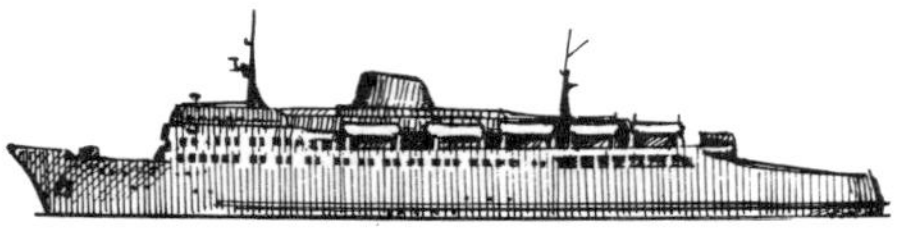

MFM H
19730 HOMERUS. Gr/De 1958; RoF/TF; 6500; 137.7×5.4 (452×17.9); TSM; 18; ex TRELLEBORG; Stern door.

MFM H
19750 REGGIO. It/It 1960; RoPF/TF; 3700; 126.8×4.3 (416×14); TSM; 15; Bow and stern doors.

MFM H
19760 SAN FRANCESCO DI PAOLA. It/It 1964; RoPF/TF; 4000; 128.5×4.3 (422×14.7); TSM; 15; Bow and side doors.

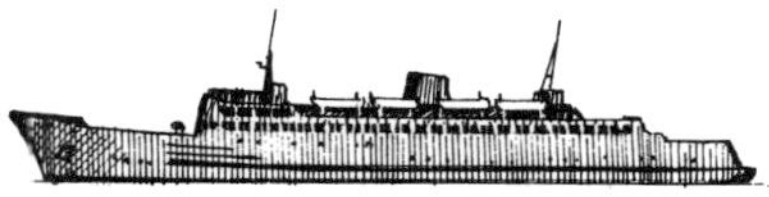

MFM H
19670 COMPIEGNE. Fr/Fr 1958; RoPF; 3500; 115×4 (377×13.1); TSM; 20; Stern door.

MFM H
19690 ISHIKARI MARU. Ja/Ja 1957; RoCF/TF; 3400; 120×4.7 (394×15.5); TSM; 15; ex TOWADA MARU 1969.

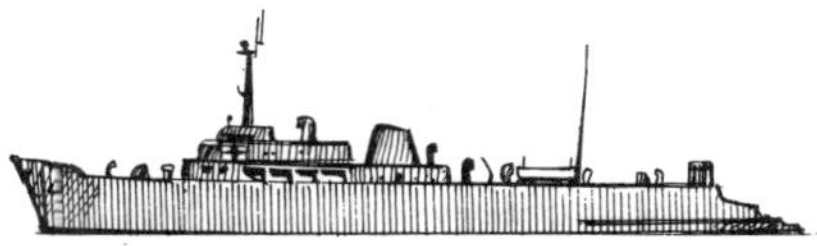

MFM H
19700 HIYAMA MARU. Ja/Ja 1955; TF; 3400; 119.2×4.7 (393×15.6); TSM; 15. Sister: **19701 SORACHI MARU** (Ja).

MFM H
19720 PRINCESS OF VANCOUVER. Ca/Br 1955; RoF/TF; 5600; 126.8×4.5 (416×15); TSM; 15.5.

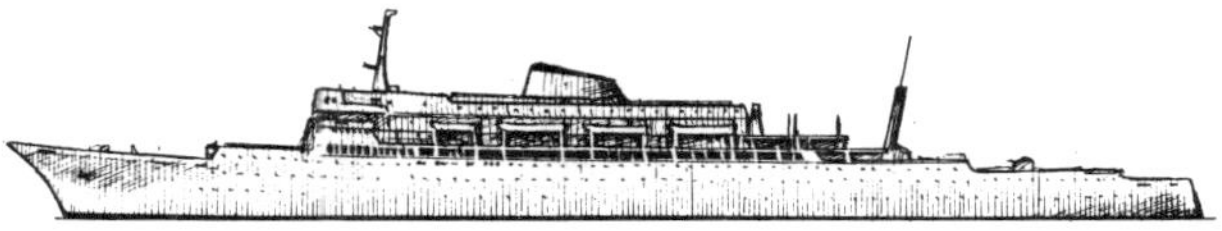

MFM H
19740 VOLENDAM. Pa/US 1958; P; 15300; 188.2×8.4 (617.6×28); TST; 23; ex MONARCH SUN; ex VOLENDAM 1975; ex BRASIL 1972. Sister: **19741 VEENDAM** (Pa); ex MONARCH STAR; ex VEENDAM 1976; ex BRASIL 1975; ex VEENDAM 1974; ex ARGENTINA 1972.

MFM H
19770 NICOLAS MIHANOVICH. Ar/Ar 1962; F; 1800; 89.6×2.6 (294×8.7); TrS D-E; 16.

MFM H
19780 QUEEN OF TSAWWASSEN. Ca/Ca 1960; RoF; 3100; 102.4 × 3.8 (336 × 12.6); TSM; —; ex TSAWWASSEN 1962.

MFM H
19790 ABEGWEIT. Ca/Ca 1947; RoF; 6700; 113.5 × 5.8 (373 × 19); TSD-E; 15.

MFM H
19800 GREENPORT. US/US 1936; F; 2400; 106.7 × 3.2 (350 × 10.6); TSR; 13; ex NEW JERSEY; ex PRINCESS ANNE 1964.

MFM H
19810 LE CONTE. US/US 1974; RoF; 1300; 71.9 × 3.9 (236 × 13); TSM; 15.5.

Twin Funnels

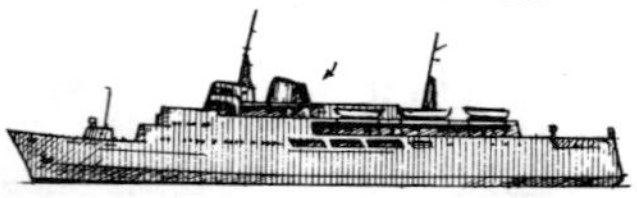

MFM H
19830 KIMOLOS. Pa/Ne 1962; RoF; 2600; 96.5 × 4.1 (317 × 12.11); TSM; 18; ex FREE ENTERPRISE 1 1980; ex FREE ENTERPRISE 1964; Stern door.

MFM H
19840 AL ZAHER. Si/Br 1952; RoF; 3300; 110.4 × 3.9 (362 × 12.11); TST; 19.5; ex LORD WARDEN 1980; Stern door and ramp.

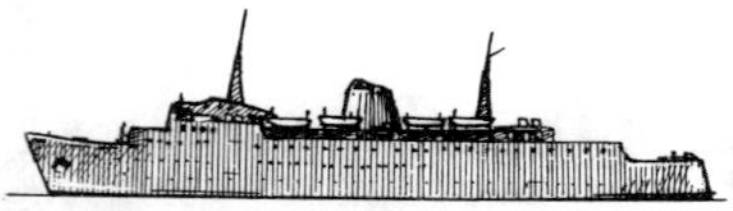

MFM H
19850 CALEDONIAN PRINCESS. Br/Br 1961; RoF; 4000; 107.6 × 3.7 (353 × 12); TST; 19; Stern door.

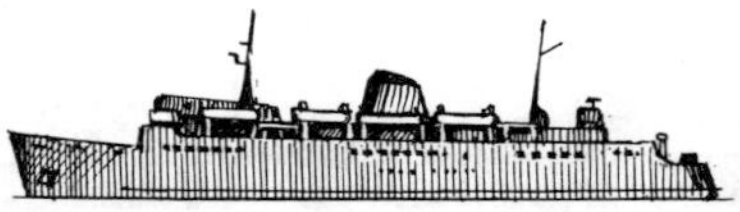

MFM H
● **19860 EARL SIWARD.** Br/Br 1965; RoF; 3600; 112.5 × 3.9 (369 × 12.9); TST; 19.5; ex DOVER 1977; Stern door.

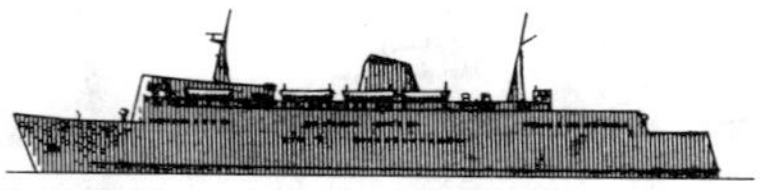

MFM H
● **19870 EARL LEOFRIC.** Br/Br 1965; RoPF; 3500; 112.48 × 3.88 (369.03 × 12.73); TST; 19.5; ex HOLYHEAD FERRY 1 1976; Bow door, stern door/ramp.

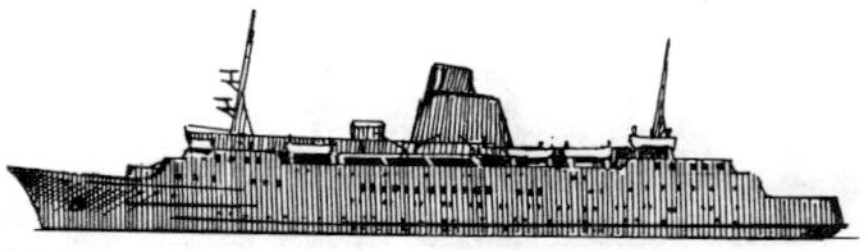

MFM H
19880 ST. EDMUND. Br/Br 1974; RoPF; 9000; 130.1 × 5.2 (427 × 17); TSM; 21; Bow and stern doors.

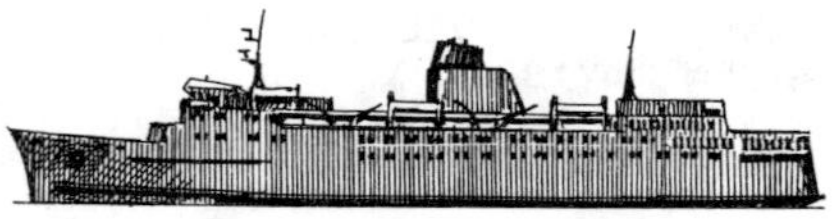

MFM H
19890 ST. COLUMBA. Br/De 1977; RoF; 7800; 128.6 × 4.7 (425 × 16); TSM; 19.5.

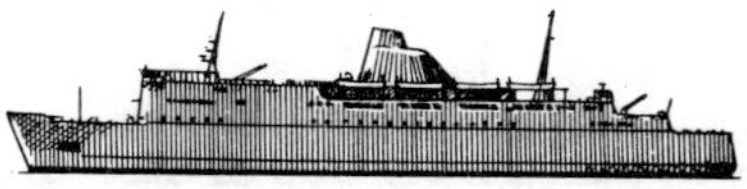

MFM H
19900 HENGIST. Br/Fr 1972; RoF; 5600; 118.1 × 4.1 (387 × 13.6); TSM; 19.5; Bow & stern doors. Sisters (Br flag): **19901 HORSA 19902 SENLAC**

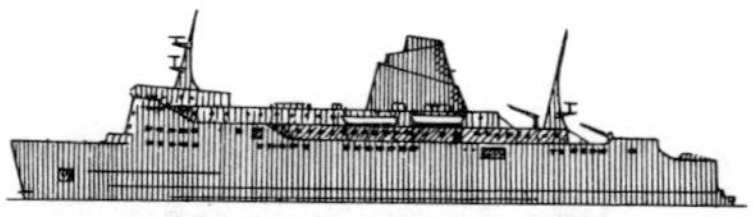

MFM H
19910 CHARTRES. Fr/Fr 1974; RoF/TF; 4600; 115.4 × 4.2 (379 × 13.8); TSM; 20.5; Bow and stern doors.

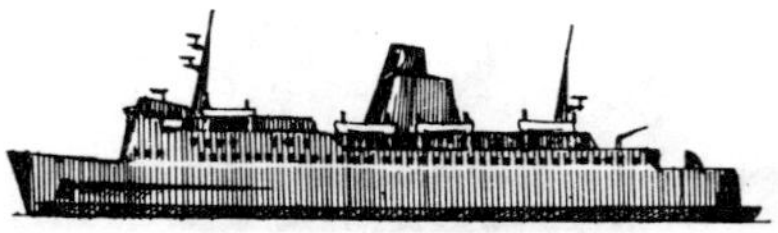

MFM H
19920 VORTIGERN. Br/Br 1969; RoF; 4400; 114.6 × 4.1 (376 × 13.4); TSM; 19.5; Bow and stern doors.

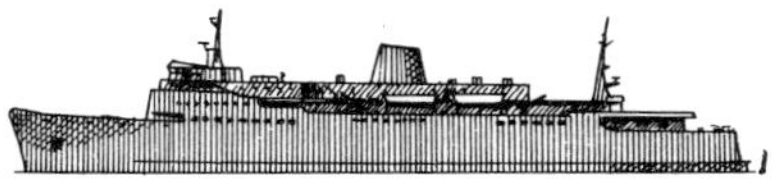

MFM H
19930 PRINS PHILIPPE. Be/Be 1973; RoF; 5100; 118 × 4.2 (387 × 13.8); TSM; 22; Bow and stern doors. Sister: **19931 PRINCE LAURENT.**

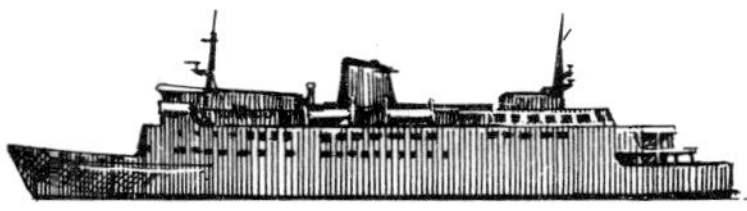

MFM H
19940 PRINCESSE MARIE CHRISTINE. Be/Be 1975; RoF; 5500; 118.4 × 4.5 (387 × 15); TSM; 22; Bow and stern doors. Sisters (Be flag): **19941 PRINSES MARIA ESMERALDA 19942 PRINS ALBERT**

MFM H
19950 ARATIKA. NZ/Fr 1974; RoF/TF; 3900; 127.7 × 4.9 (419 × 16.2); TSM; 17.5; Stern door. Converted 1977.

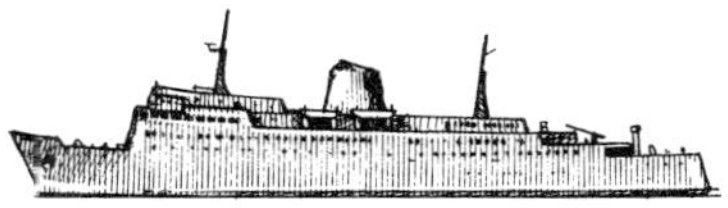

MFM H
19960 ARANUI. NZ/Br 1966; RoF/TF; 4500; 112.2 × 4.8 (368 × 15.8); TSD-E; 17.

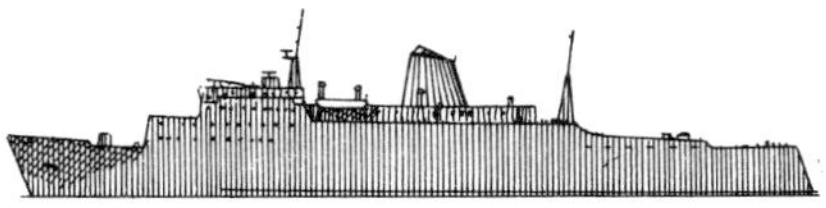

MFM H
19970 ARAHANGA. NZ/Br 1972; RoF/TF; 39''; 127.5 × 4.9 (418 × 16); TSM; 17; Stern door.

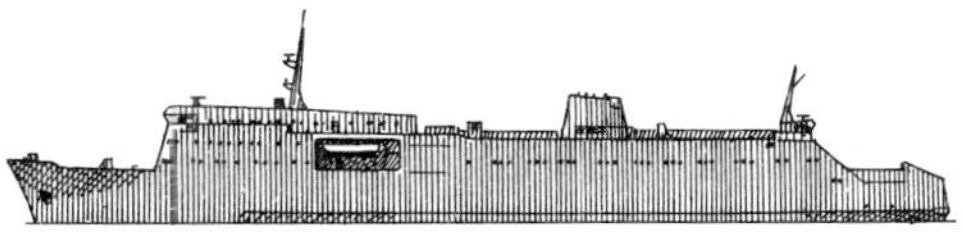

MFM H
19980 GOTALAND. Sw/De 1973; RoF/TF; 5200; 148. × 5.6 (486 × 18.6); TSM; 18.5; Stern and side doors. Sister; **19981 SVEALAND** (Sw).

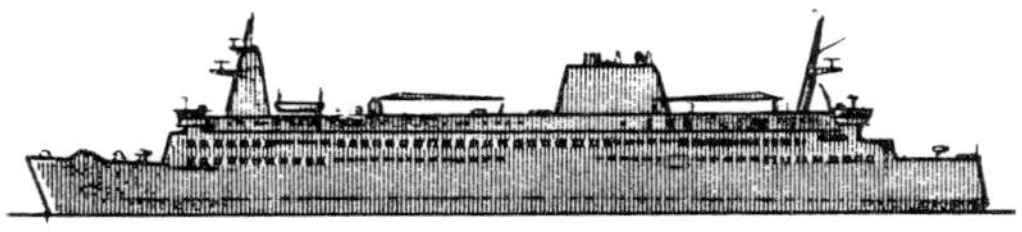

MFM H
19990 PRINS JOACHIM. De/De 1980; RoPF/TF; 10600; 152 × 5.6 (498.69 × 18.37); TSM; 18; bow and stern ramps. Sisters (De flag): **19991 DRONNING INGRID. 19992 KRONPRINS FREDERIK**

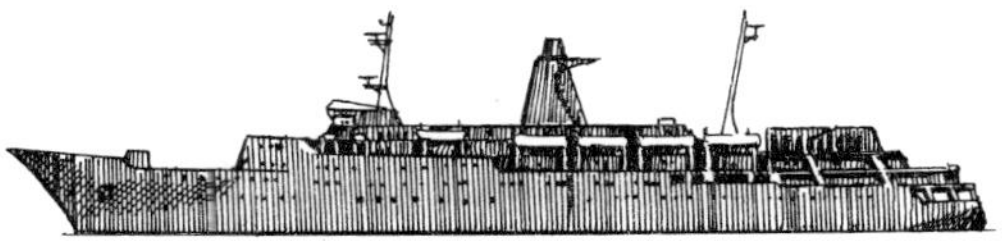

MFM H
20000 RANGATIRA NZ/Br 1972; RoF; 9400; 152.6 × 5.3 (500 × 17.6); TST-E; 21; Stern door. Being used as a floating hotel.

MFM H
20010 MAID OF KENT Br/Br 1959; RoF; 3900; 113.7 × 4 (373 × 13); TST; 19; Stern door.

MFM H
20020 CHANTILLY. Fr/Fr 1965; RoF; 3400; 109.9 × 4 (361 × 13); TSM; 20.

MFM H
20030 PRINCESSE ASTRID. Be/Be 1968; RoF; 3200; 118 × 3.8 (387.4 × 12.8); TSM; 22; stern door.

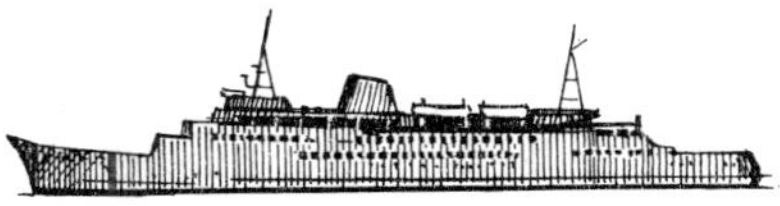

MFM H
20040 PRINSES PAOLA. Be/Be 1966; F; 3400/3800; 117.1 × —/3.8 (385 × —/12.8); TSM; 24.

MFM H
20050 ROI BAUDOUIN. Be/Be 1965; RoF; 3200; 117.8 × 3.8 (387 × 12.5); TSM; 21; Stern door.

MFM H
20060 KONINGIN FABIOLA. Be/Be 1962; RoF; 3100; 117.3 × 3.8 (385 × 12.6); TSM; 20; Stern door.

MFM H
20070 AEGEON. Gr/Be 1958; RoF; 2800; 116.9×3.9 (383×12.9); TSM; 21; ex ARTEVELDE 1976; Bow and stern doors.

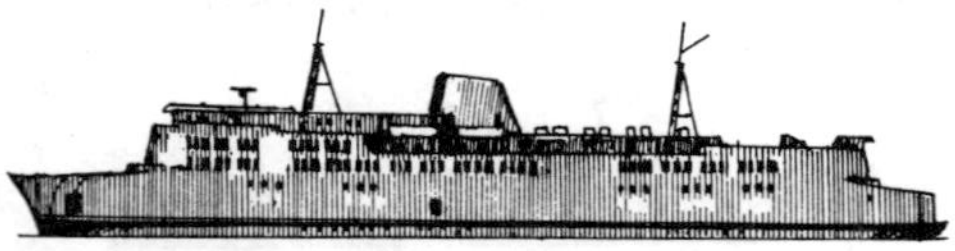

MFM H
20090 DANMARK. De/De 1968; RoF/TF; 6400; 144.5×5.5 (474×18); TSM; 17; Bow and stern doors.

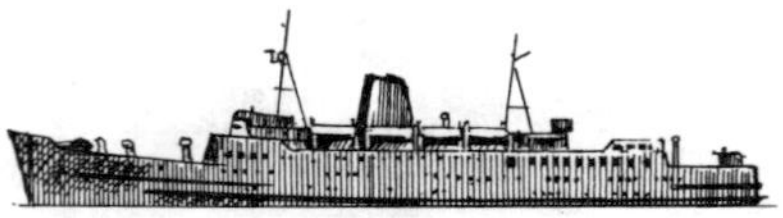

MFM H
20100 DUKE OF LANCASTER. Br/Br 1956; RoF; 4500; 114.6×4.5 (375.9×14.1); TST 19; Stern door.

MFM H
20120 LA PAZ. Me/Ja 1964; RoF; 2500; 109×4.3 (358×14.2); TSM; —; Bow door.

MFM H
20140 ALZAHRAA. Eg/Sw 1968; RoF/TF; 5600; 115.7×4.9 (379.8×16); TSM; —; ex DROTTNINGEN; Bow and stern doors.

MFM H
20160 OLAU FINN; Fi/Sw 1966; RoF; 8000; 141.2×5.5 (463×18); TSM; 18; ex FINNPARTNER 1976; ex STENA ATLANTICA 1973; ex SAGA 1971; Stern door.

MFM H
20170 HOLGER DANSKE; No/FRG 1961; RoF; 3700; 109.8×4.2 (360×13.1); TSM; —.

MFM H
20080 NAJD. Pa/Be 1956; F; 3400/3800; 144×—/4 (374×—/13); TSM; 22; ex ROI LEOPOLD III. Sisters: **20081 REINE ASTRID** (Be) **20082 NAJD II** (Si) ex ABHA 1980; ex KONINGIN ELISABETH 1978.

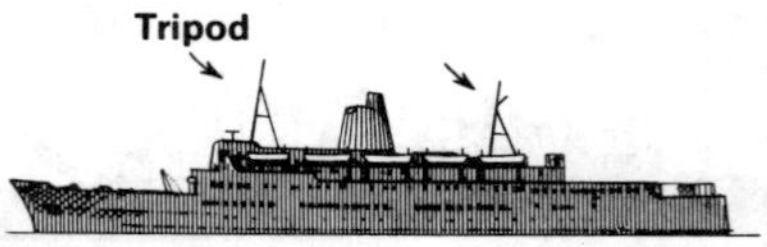

MFM H
20110 NEPTUNIA. Cy/Br 1956; P/RoC; 4400; 114.64×4.52 (376×12×14.83); TST; —; ex DUKE OF ARGYLL 1975; Rebuilt. Further modernised. Aft superstructure extended and docking bridge removed.

MFM H
20130 MALASPINA. US/US 1963; RoF; 2900; 124.2×4.9 (407.8×16); TSM; —; Lengthened 1972. Stern door.

MFM H
20150 STENA SAGA; Sw/Sw 1967; RoF; 8900; 141.2×5.5 (463×17.6); TSM; —; ex STENA OCEANICA; ex PATRICIA; Stern door. Similar (wings on funnel): **20151 KNOSSOS** (Gr) ex SAGA; ex HISPANIA 1972; ex SVEA 1969.

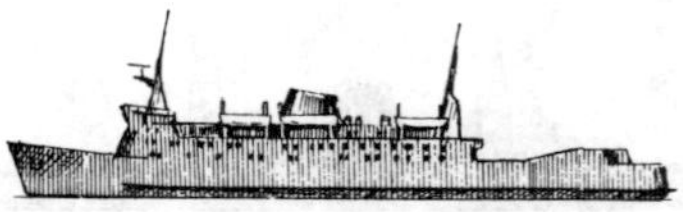

MFM H
● **20180 MONA'S QUEEN;** Br/Br 1972; RoF; 3000; 104.5×3.6 (343×12); TSM; 21. Possible Sister: **20181 LADY OF MANN** (Br).

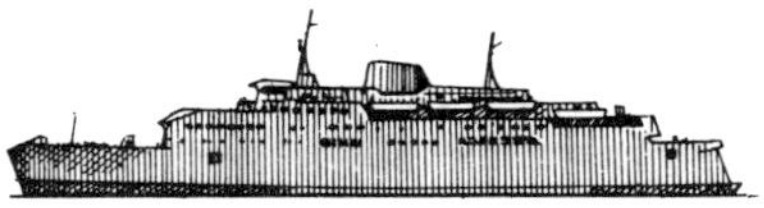

MFM H
20190 FREE ENTERPRISE IV; Br/Ne 1969; RoF; 5000; 117.5 × 4.3 (385.6 × 14.3); TrSM; 20.75; Bow and stern doors. Sisters: **20191 FREE ENTERPRISE V** (Br) **20192 FREE ENTERPRISE VI** (Br).

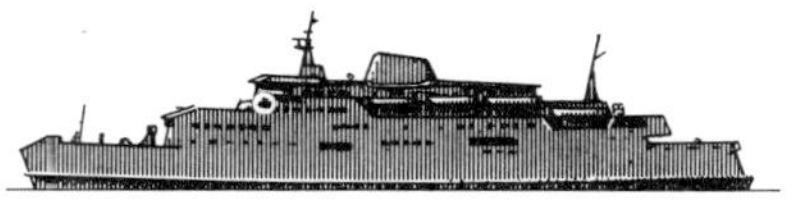

MFM H
20200 FREE ENTERPRISE VII; Br/Ne 1973; RoPF; 5000; 117.51 × 4.38 (385.53 × 14.37); TrSM; 21; Bow and stern doors. Mainmast further aft than on "Free Enterprise IV" - which see. Similar (longer): **20201 FREE ENTERPRISE VIII** (Br).

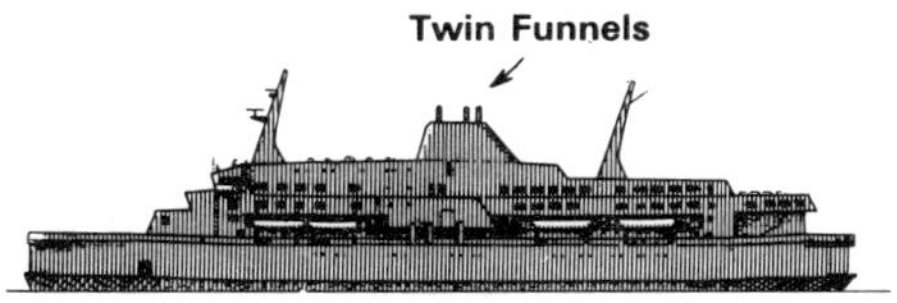

MFM H
20210 SPIRIT OF FREE ENTERPRISE; Br/FRG 1979; RoPF; 8000; 131.96 × 5.71 (432.94 × 18.73); TrSM; 22; Bow and stern doors. Sisters (Br flag): **20211 HERALD OF FREE ENTERPRISE 20212 PRIDE OF FREE ENTERPRISE.**

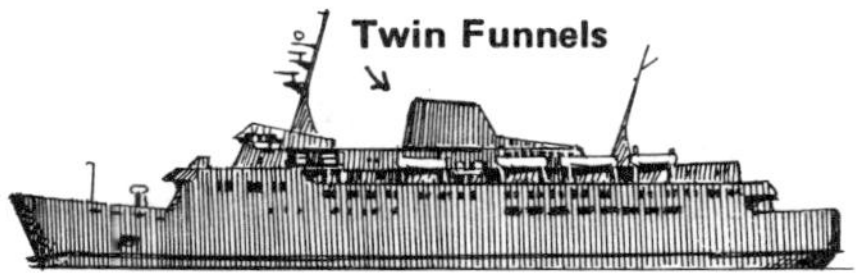

MFM H
20220 VIKING VENTURER; Br/De 1975; RoF; 6400; 128.8 × 4.5 (422.3 × 15); TrSM; 20.75; Bow and stern doors. Sisters (Br flag): **20221 VIKING VALIANT 20222 VIKING VISCOUNT 20223 VIKING VOYAGER.**

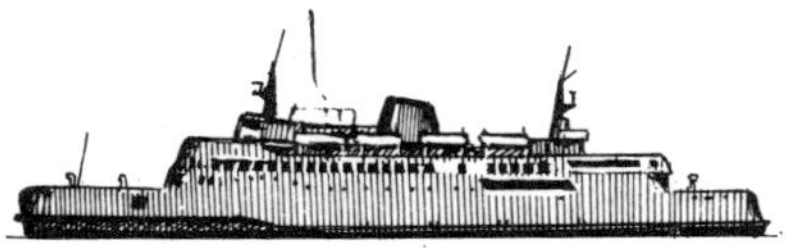

MFM H
20230 FREE ENTERPRISE III; Br/Ne 1966; RoF; 4700; 117.5 × 4 (385 × 13); TSM; 20; Bow and stern doors.

MFM H
20240 BLUENOSE; Ca/Ca 1955; RoF; 6400; 105.4 × 5 (346 × 16.7); TSM; 18.5.

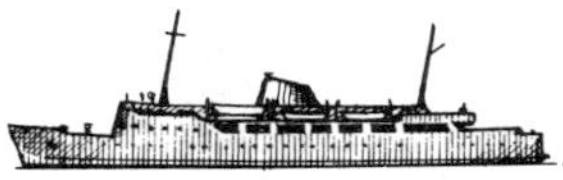

MFM H
⋆20250 SVETI STEFAN; Ys/De 1958; RoF; 1600; 85.5 × 4 (281 × 13); TSM; 15; ex DJURSLAND 1965; Bow and stern doors.

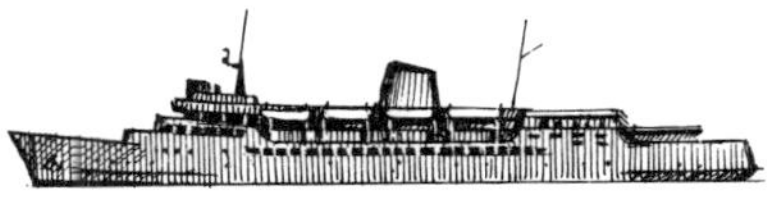

MFM H
20260 EGNATIA; Gr/Fr 1960; RoF; 6200; 115.40 × 4.1 (379 × 13.6); TSM; 18; Bow and stern doors.

MFM H
20270 ESPRESSO AZZURRO; It/It 1965; 5300; 126.3 × 5.3 (415 × 17.6); TSM; —; ex CANGURO AZZURRO: Bow and stern doors/ramp. Sisters (It flag): **20271 CANGURO BIANCO 20272 CANGURO BRUNO 20273 CANGURO VERDE 20274 ESPRESSO ROSSO** ex CANGURO ROSSO.

MFM H
20280 VILLANDRY; Fr/Fr 1964; RoF; 3400; 104.9 × 4 (344 × 13); TSM; 21; Bow and stern doors. Sister: **20281 VALENCAY** (Fr).

MFM H
20290 PRINSESSAN DESIREE; Sw/De 1971; RoF; 5800; 123.4 × 5.2 (405 × 17.6); TSM; 21.5; Bow and stern doors.

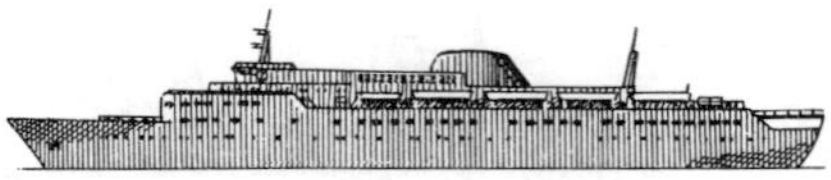

MFM H
20300 ILMATAR; Fi/Fi 1964; P; 7200; 128.3 × 4.4 (421 × 14.6); TrSM; 20; Side doors. Lengthened 1973. Extensively modified in 1978/79 and may have changes in appearance.

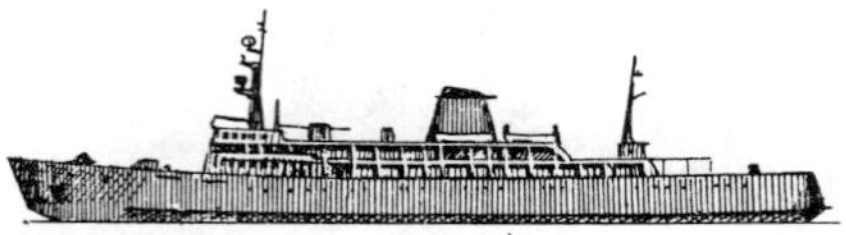

MFM H
● ⋆**20310 SAKHALIN - 1;** Ru/Ru 1963; RoF/TF; 5000; 127 × 6.2 (417 × 20.3); D-E; 18; Stern door. Sisters (Ru flag): ⋆**20311 SAKHALIN -2** ⋆**20312 SAKHALIN -3** ⋆**20313 SAKHALIN - 4** ⋆**20314 SAKHALIN - 5.**

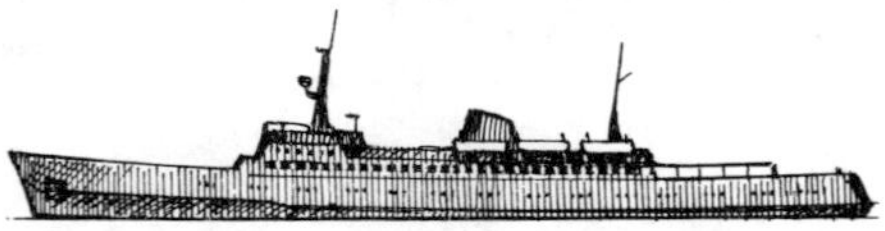

MFM H
⋆**20320 SOVIETSKIY AZERBAIDZHAN;** Ru/Ru 1963; RoF/TF; 8800; 133.6 × 4.5 (438 × 15.1); Tr SD-E; 14; Stern door. Sisters (Ru flag); ⋆**20321 SOVIETSKIY TURKMENISTAN** ⋆**20322 SOVIETSKIY KAZAKHSTAN** ⋆**20323 SOVIETSKIY UZBEKISTAN** ⋆**20324 GAMID SULTANOV.**

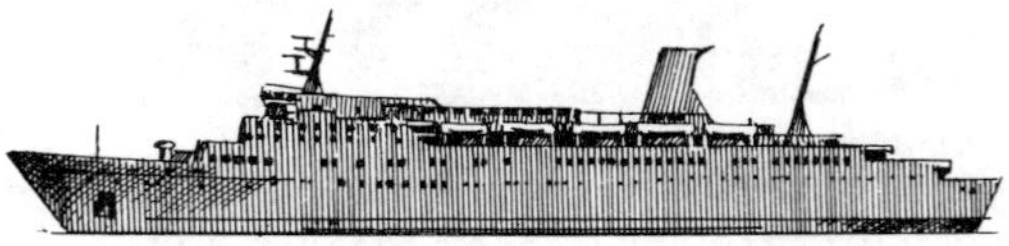

MFM H
20330 PRINSESSAN BIRGITTA; Sw/Fi 1974; RoF; 8800; 152.4 × 5.6 (500 × 20); TSM; 24; Bow and stern doors.

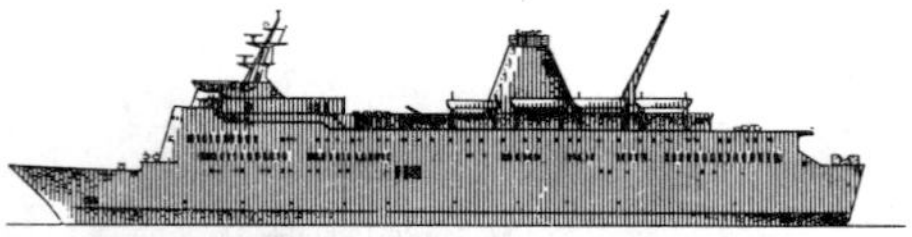

MFM H
20340 TURELLA; Fi/Fi 1979; RoPF; 10500; 136.11 × 5.5 (446.56 × 18.04); TSM; 21.3; Bow ramp and two stern ramps. Side door. Sister (extra superstructure fwd of funnel): **20341 ROSELLA** (Fi).

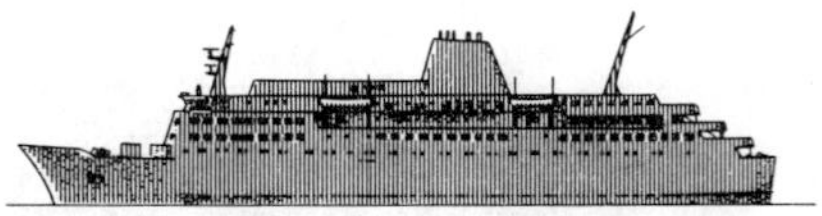

MFM H
20350 POVL ANKER; De/De 1978; RoPF; 8200; 121.19 × 5.15 (397.6 × 16.9); TSM; 20; Bow door/ramp. Two stern doors/ramps. Side doors. Sister: **20351 JENS KOFOED** (De).

●
⋆20353

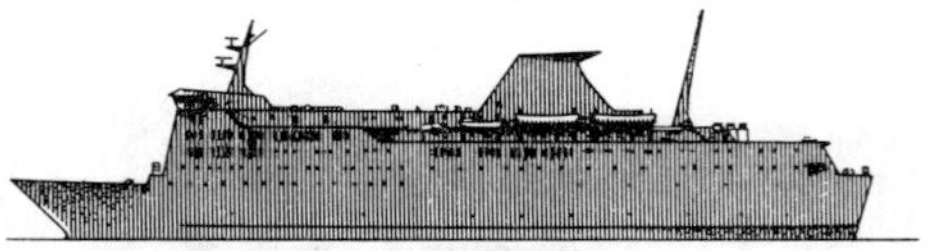

MFM H
20360 DIANA II; Sw/FRG 1979; RoPF; 11700; 137.2 × 5.65 (450.13 × 18.54); TSM; 21.5; Bow door/ramp. Two stern ramps.

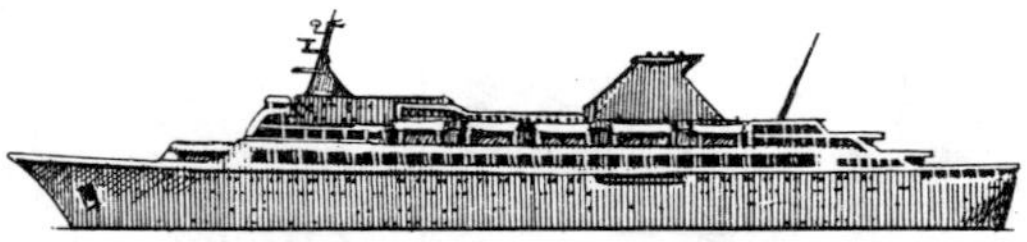

MFM H
⋆**20370 BYELORUSSIYA;** Ru/Fi 1975; RoP; 16600; 157 × 6.2 (516 × 20.4); TSM; 21.25; Bow, stern and side doors. Sisters (Ru flag): ⋆**20371 GRUZIYA** ⋆**20372 AZERBAYDZHAN** ⋆**20373 KARELIYA** ⋆**20374 KAZAKHSTAN.**

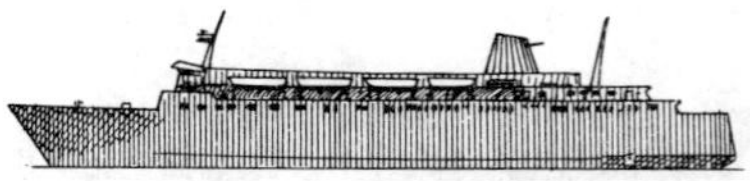

MFM H
20380 STELLA SCARLETT; Sw/FRG 1974; RoF; 4200; 115.2 × 4.5 (378 × 15); TSM; 19.25; Bow and stern doors.

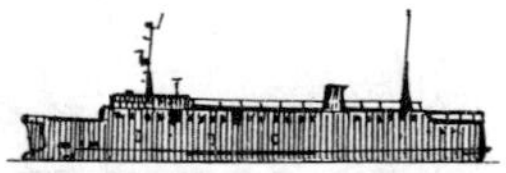

MFM H
20390 KII MARU; Ja/Ja 1964; F; 1600; 73.7 × 3.6 (242 × 12); TSM; 14.

MFM H
20400 FERRY FUKUE; Ja/Ja 1978; RoPF; 1900; 79.66 × 3.7 (261.35 × 12.14); TSM; 17.25; Bow and stern ramp/doors.

MFM H
20410 TRUVA; Tu/Fr 1967; RoF; 3400; 91.6×4.2 (300.6×14); TSM; 19.

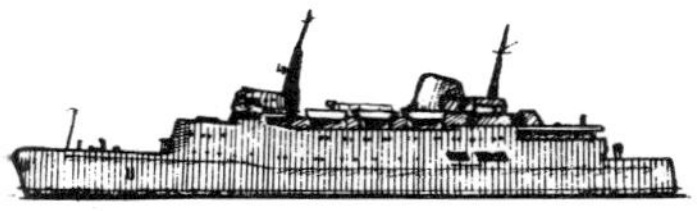

MFM H
20420 FREE ENTERPRISE II; Br/Ne 1965; RoF; 4000; 108.1×4 (355×13.3); TSM; 19; Bow and stern doors.

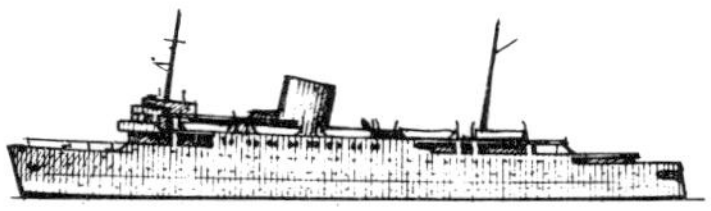

MFM H
20430 PRINCE GEORGE; Ca/Ca 1948; P; 5800; 106.7×5.4 (350×17.7); TSR; 15.5.

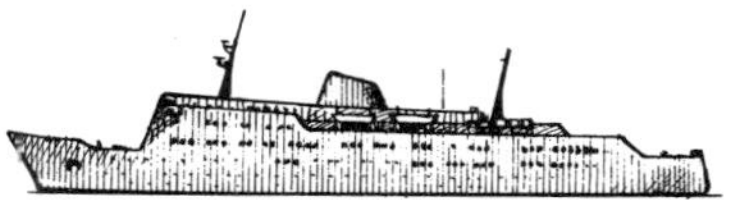

MFM H
20440 MAZATLAN; Me/De 1965; RoF; 5000; 108.9×4.6 (357×15.3); TSM; 17.5; ex AKERSHUS 1973; Bow door, ramp and side doors.

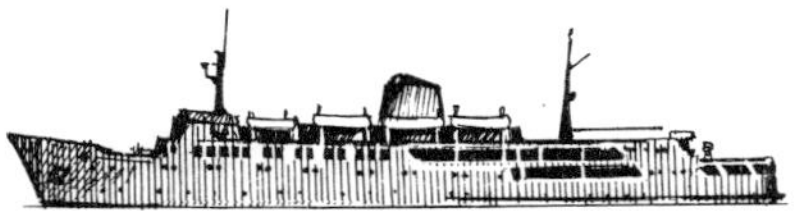

MFM H
20450 TYRSUS; It/It 1961; RoF/TF; 4300; 119.9×5.3 (393×15.1); TSM; 16. Sister: **20451 HERMAEA** (It).

MFM H
20460 ATLANTIS; Gr/It 1965; RoP; 4500; 97.2×4.2 (319×13.1); TSM; 17; ex ADONIS 1976; Stern and side doors. Sister: **20461 JASON** (Gr) ex EROS 1966.

MFM H
20470 KONINGIN JULIANA; Ne/Br 1968; RoF; 6700; 131×5 (430×16.9); TSM; 21; Bow and stern doors.

MFM H
20480 NORTHERN CRUISER; Ca/Br 1962; RoF; 1400; 57.7×2.8 (189.6×9.6); M; —; ex N. A. COMEAU 1977.

MFM H
20490 HOLYHEAD; Gr/Br 1947; P; 3700; 97.95×4.19 (321.36×13.75); TST; 15; ex ST DAVID 1970.

MFM H
20500 MANX MAID; Br/Br 1962; RoF; 2700; 104.8×3.8 (344×12.3); TST; 21; Side doors. Sister: **20501 BEN-MY-CHREE** (Br).

MFM H
● **20510 CAESAREA;** Br/Br 1960; F; 4000; 98.2×4.1 (322×13.7); TSM; 19.5. Sister: **20511 GOLDEN STAR** (Gr) ex SARNIA.

MFM H
20520 APOLLON; Gr/Fr 1952; C; 2900; 95.5×3.2 (313×10.6); TST; 22; ex LISIEUX 1966.

MFM H
20530 ATHENS EXPRESS; Gr/Be 1949; RoF; 2600; 114.3×3.8 (372×12.5); TSM; 20; ex LETO 1976; ex PRINSES JOSEPHINE CHARLOTTE 1976; ex CAR FERRY 1952; Stern door.

MFM H
● **20540 DRONNING MARGRETHE II;** De/De 1973; RoF/TF; 5600; 133.5×4.5 (438×15); TSM; 18.5; Bow door.

MFM H
⋆20550 HA LONG; Vn/FRG 1961; RoF; 7000; 138.3 × 5.5 (454 × 18); TSM; 19.5; ex KRONPRINS HARALD 1975; Side doors.

MFM H
● **20560 PRINSESSE RAGNHILD;** No/FRG 1966; RoF; 7700; 140.8 × 5.8 (463 × 18.1); TSM; 21.5; Side doors.

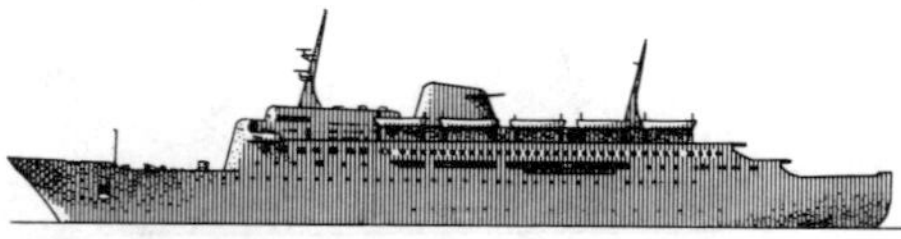

MFM H
20570 WINSTON CHURCHILL; De/It 1967; RoF; 8700; 140.7 × 5.5 (460 × 18.1); TSM; 23; Bow door and ramp. Stern door and ramp.

MFM H
20580 ORPHEUS; Gr/Br 1948/70; P; 5100; 111.82 × 4.88 (366.86 × 16.01); TSM; 15; ex THESEUS 1969; ex MUNSTER I 1968; ex MUNSTER 1968; Converted from ferry 1970.

MFM H
20590 STELLA OCEANIS; Gr/It 1965; P; 4000; 105.1 × 4.5 (365 × 13.11); TSM; 17; ex APHRODITE 1966.

MFM H
20600 APPIA; It/It 1961; F; 6100; 122.5 × 5.5 (402 × 16.3); TSM; 17.

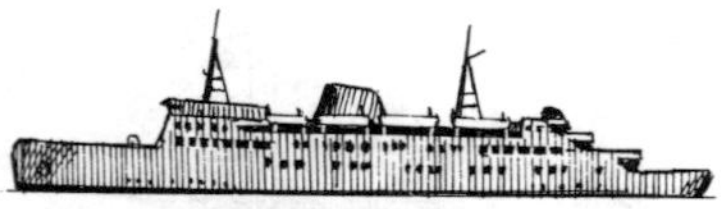

MFM H
20610 PRINSESSE ELISABETH; De/De 1964; RoF; 3600; 103.4 × 4.6 (339 × 15.1); TSM; 18.

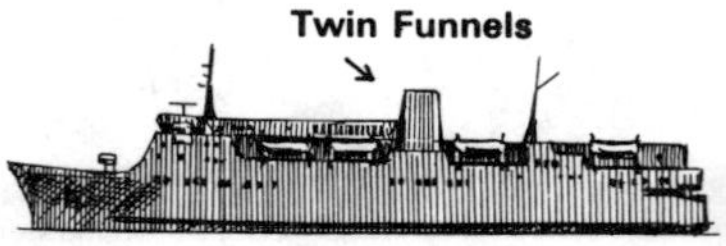

MFM H
● **20620 BORGEN;** No/De 1975; RoF/TF; 5300; 109 × 5 (358 × 16.6); TSM; 21; Bow door and ramp. Stern door and ramp.

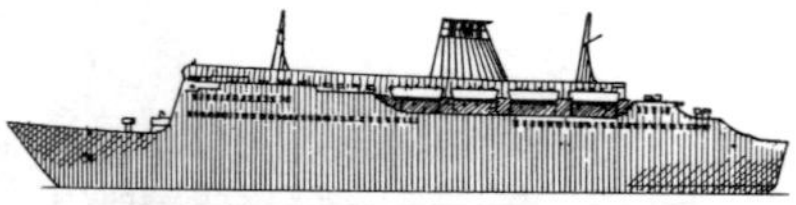

MFM H
20630 AURELLA; Fi/FRG 1973; RoF; 7200; 125.6 × 5.3 (412 × 17.5); TSM; 23; Bow and stern doors.

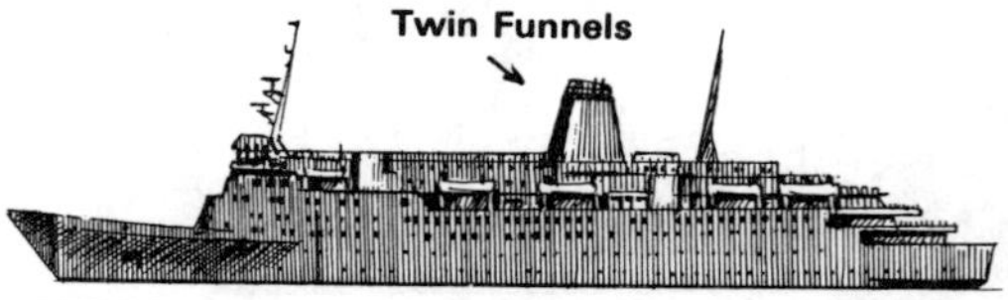

MFM H
● **20640 SILJA STAR;** Fi/Fr 1975; RoF; 12300; 153.1 × 5.1 (500.6 × 17); TSM; 22; ex BORE STAR 1971; Bow door and ramp. Stern door and ramp. Sisters: **20641 SVEA** (Fi) **20642 CORONA** (Sw) **20643 WELLAMO** (Fi).

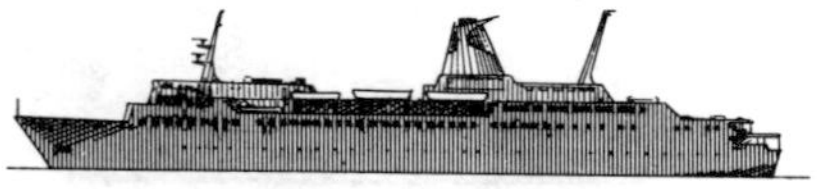

MFM H
⋆20650 AYVAZOVSKIY; Ru/Fr 1977; P; 7100; 121.49 × 4.4 (398.59 × 14.44); TSM; 18.25.

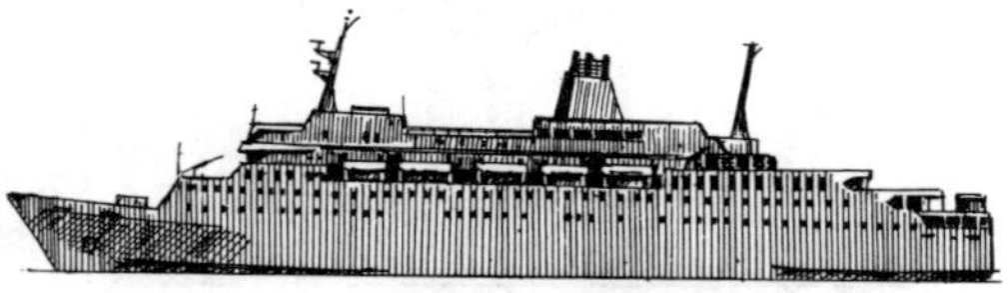

MFM H
20660 NAPOLEON; Fr/Fr 1976; RoF; 14900; 155 × 6.4 (509 × 21); TSM; 23.5.

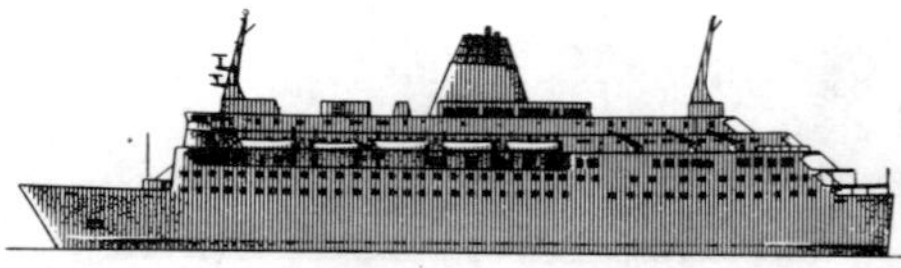

MFM H
● **20670 CYRNOS;** Fr/Fr 1979; RoPF; approx 12000; 138.65 × 6.16 (454.89 × 20.21); TSM; 22; Bow and stern ramp/doors. Similar: **20671 LIBERTE** (Fr).

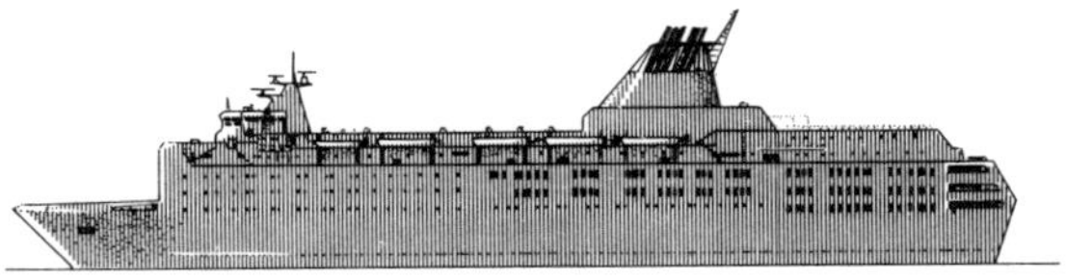

MFM H
20680 VIKING SALLY; Fi/FRG 1980; RoPF; 15600; 155.43 × 5.55 (509.94 × 18.21); TSM; 21.2; Bow door/ramp. Two stern ramps.

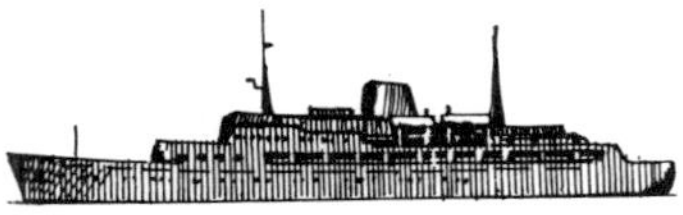

MFM H
★20690 MIN CHU No 18; RC/RC 1960; P; 2500; 107 × — (350 × —); TSM; 16.

MFM H
20700 NEPTUNE; Gr/De 1955; P; 2400; 90.2 × 5.4 (296 × 18); M; 18; ex METEOR 1971.

MFM H
20710 KURENAI MARU; Ja/Ja 1960; F; 3000; 86.7 × 3.9 (285 × 12.9); TSM; 18. Sister: **20711 MURASAKI MARU** (Ja).

MFM H
20720 NAIEFF; Qt/FRG 1957; Y; 2800; 90.2 × 3.7 (296 × 12.1); TSD-E; 19.5; ex STELLA SOLARIS 1971; Converted from a passenger ship.

MFM H
20730 RADIOSA; Gr/Br 1947/72; P; 1600; 76.66 × 3.72 (251.51 × 12.2); TSM; 12; ex EXETER 1972; ex WINCHESTER 1971; Converted from cargo ship.

MFM H
20740 XANADU; Pa/FRG 1955; P; 2600; 89.5 × 3.8 (293 × 12.6); TSD-E; 18; ex PACIFIC STAR 1972; ex POLAR STAR 1970; ex DELOS 1967; ex WAPPEN VON HAMBURG 1960.

MFM H
● **20750 ORNEN;** De/De 1962; RoF; 1900; 78.8 × 4 (259 × 13.2); TSM; 15; Side doors.

MFM H
20760 ORESUND; Sw/Sw 1960; RoF; 2000; 72.1 × 4.1 (236 × 13.4); TSM; 16.5.

MFM H
20770 AETHALIA; It/It 1956; RoF; 1300; 72.3 × 3.5 (237 × 11.7); TSM; 14.

MFM H
20780 NORDSEE I; FRG/FRG 1961; F; 981; 59.7 × 2.8 (196 × 9.3); TSM; 15.5; ex KOBENHAVN 1975; ex HEIN GODENWIND 1969.

MFM H
★20790 BELINSKIY; Ru/DDR 1955; P.Riv; 1100; 65.2 × 2.4 (214 × 8); M; 12. Sisters (Ru flag): **★20791 BALKHASH ★20792 BAYKAL ★20793 CHERNISHEVSKIY ★20794 ISYK KOL ★20795 KOROLENKO ★20796 KOTOVSKIY ★20797 LADOGA ★20798 LENINSKIY ★20799 MAMIN SIBIRYAK ★20800 MEKHANIK KALUSHNIKOV ★20801 MEKHANIK KULUBIN ★20802 ONEGA ★20803 RADISHEV ★20804 SERGEI TSENSKAY ★20805 SEVAN.**

MFM H
20810 HABICHT II; FRG/FRG 1959; F; 900; 54.3 × 3.1 (178 × 10.3); TSM; 15; ex BALTICA I; ex ORESTAD 1973; ex ALTE LIEBE 1962.

MFM H
20820 EVANGELISTRIA; Gr/US 1943; F; 1000; 54.9 × — (184 × —); TSM; —; ex DESPINA 1969; Converted warship.

MFM H
20830 KRISTINA BRAHE; Fi/US 1943; F; 1000; 56.5 × 2.6 (185 × 8.6); TSM; 15; ex SUNNHORDLAND 1974; Converted warship.

MFM H
● **20840 JUAN;** Pi/Ja 1963; F; 1500; 64.1 × 3.3 (211 × 12.4); TSM; 14.5; ex RAMON ABOITIZ; ex YOSHINO MARU 1974.

MFM H
20850 ARABI; Si/Br 1960; LS; 2700; 94.6 × 4 (310 × 13.1); TSM; 13.5; ex SLIEVE DONARD 1976.

MFM H
● **20860 ARRAN;** Br/Br 1953; RoF; 540; 56.7 × 2.3 (186 × 7.5); TSM; 15.5; Side doors. Sisters: **20861 MED SUN** (Gr) ex BUTE 1980 **20862 COWAL** (Br).

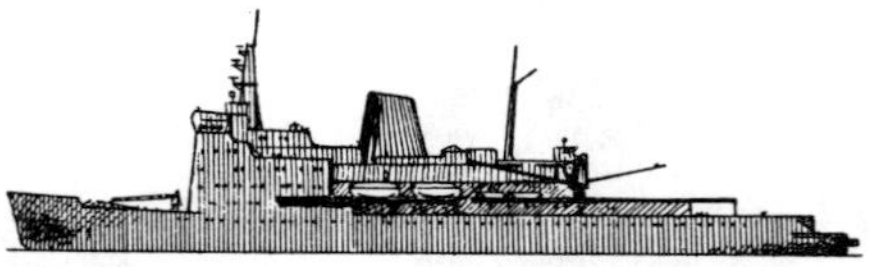

MFM H
⋆**20870 YERMAK;** Ru/Fi 1973; IB; 12200; 135 × 11 (445 × 37); Tr SD-E; 19. Sisters (Ru flag): ⋆**20871 ADMIRAL MAKAROV** ⋆**20872 KRASIN.**

MFM H
⋆**20880 PERKUN;** Pd/Br 1963; IB/Sal; 1200; 56.5 × 5 (185 × 16.3); TSD-E; 10.

MFM H
20890 WYUNA. Br/Br 1953; Plt; 1300; 63.6 × 4.8 (209 × 15); TSD-E; —.

MFM H
20900 FRANCE I. Fr/Fr 1959; RS; 1900; 76.4 × — (251 × —); TSD-E; 14.75. Sister: **20901 FRANCE II** (Fr).

MFM H
20910 ALIDADE. Fr/Fr 1964; TS; 640; 45.8 × 2.9 (150 × 9.3); M; 13.5.

MFM H
20920 WESTWARD HO. Br/Br 1938; F; 600; 60.9 × 1.8 (200 × 6); TSM; 15; ex VECTA 1966.

MFM H
● **20930 BRADING.** Br/Br 1948; F; 1000; 61 × 2.1 (200 × 7); TSM; 14. Sisters (Br flag): **20931 SOUTHSEA 20932 PRINCE IVANHOE** ex SHANKLIN 1980.

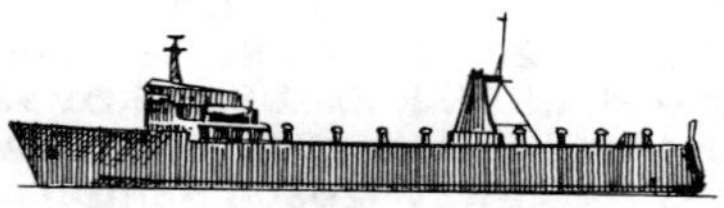

MFM H
20940 DOMINO. Br/No 1972; RoC; 1600; 108.5 × 5 (356 × 16.9); TSM; 17; Stern door.

MFM H
● **20950 PIONEER.** Br/Br 1974; RoF; 1100; 67.5 × 2.4 (221.6 × 8); TSM; 16; Stern door and ramp.

MFM H1
● **20960 HIZB-UL-BAHR.** Bh/Fr 1953; PC; 11700; 162 × 6.9 (532 × 20); TSM; 16; ex EASTERN QUEEN 1977; ex PRESIDENT 1972; ex GENERAL MANGIN 1969.

MFM H1
20970 ARIANE. Pa/Br 1951; P; 6700; 138.4 × 5.8 (454 × 19); T; 19; ex BON VIVANT 1979; ex FREEPORT II 1974; ex ARIADNE 1973; ex PATRICIA 1957.

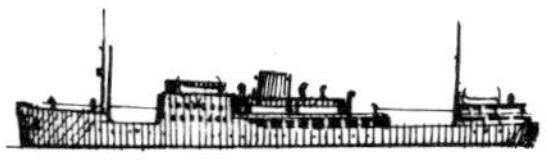

MFM H1
20980 CIUDAD DE IBIZA. Sp/De 1929; PC; 3100; 98.9 × 5.4 (324 × 17.8); TSM; 14.5; ex ESBJERG 1947; Rebuilt 1946.

MFM H1
⋆**20990 JAMHURI.** Ta/Br 1956; F; 1500; 66.6 × 4 (219 × 13.1); TSM; 13; ex SEYYD KHALIFA 1963.

MFM H1
21000 AQUA STAR. Br/Br 1951; RS; 650; 54.3 × 3.8 (178 × 12.6); M; 11; ex ST. OLA 1975.

MFM H1
21010 STAUPER. No/No 1929; Repair Ship; 850; 57.4 × 5 (188 × 16.6); M; 12; ex TUNGENES 1965; ex ROGALAND 1964; Converted Passenger Cargo Ship.

MFM H1
21020 SWEET GRACE. Pi/FRG 1968; PC/F; 1500; 88.02 × 4.82 (288.78 × 15.81); M; 15.75.

MFM H1
21030 CAGAYAN DE ORO. Pi/Ja 1955; P; 1500; 77.2 × 4.7 (253 × 15.6); TSM; —; ex CAGAYAN 1956.

MFM H1
21040 PATRICIA. Br/Br 1938; Tender; 1100; 70.7 × 3.9 (232 × 13); TSD-E; 10.

MFM H1
21050 STAR OF ASSUAN. Eg/Br 1948; PC; 5500; 119.9 × 7.2 (398 × 23.7); M; 13.5.

MFM H1
21060 EL HASSAN. Eg/It 1959; PC; 4400; 109.2 × 5.9; PC; 4400; 109.2 × 5.9 (358 × 19.3); TSM; 15.75; ex BRENNERO. Sisters: **21061 ABU EL KASSEM** (Eg) ex BERNINA **21062 STELVIO** (It).

MFM H1
21070 REINA DEL FRIO. Ar/De 1927; R; 1600; 84.8 × 5.5 (278 × 18); R; 11; ex FREEZER QUEEN 1960; ex BRUARFOSS 1957.

MFM H1
21080 FREIA IV. Pa/De 1936; RoF; 1500; 78 × 4 (257 × 13); M; 15; ex FREIA 1975; Side doors.

MFM H1
21090 SWEET ROSE. Pi/Pi 1960; F; 1800; 84.8 × 4.8 (278 × 15.6); M; 13.75; ex GENERAL ROXAS 1965. Similar: **21091 DONA ANITA** (Pi) ex DONA ANA 1976; ex GOVERNOR B. LOPEZ 1966.

MFM H1
● **21100 EL PODRERO.** Pa/FRG 1959; R; 2100; 108.1 × 6.1 (355 × 19.11); M; 18; ex LINDAKI 1975; ex CALOR 1972; ex OKERTAL 1968.

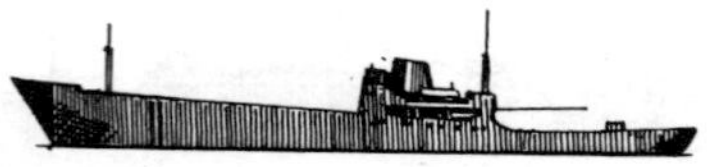

MFM H1
21110 TUI CAKAU II. Fiji/Fr 1961; RoF; 1800; 107 × 5.1 (360 × 17); M; 15.75; ex CAPITAINE SCOTT; ex BLIDA; Converted from Cargo 1971; Lengthened 1971; Bow and side doors.

MFM H1
21120 LOGOS. Sg/De 1949; PC; 2300; 82 × 5.6 (269 × 18.5); M; 13; ex UMANAK 1971; At present being used as a Missionary ship.

MFM H1
● **21130 BLUE OCEAN.** Si/FRG 1953; R; 3000; 115.4 × 6.3 (379 × 20.7); M; 16.5; ex DANAE 1974; ex FRANCHINA FASSIO 1970.

MFM H1
21140 AINIKOLAS. Ho/Fr 1959; C/WT; 1600/2400; 93 × 5.3/7 (306 × 17.6/23); M; 15; ex ELLY V 1980; ex RELIZANE 1975.

MFM H1
21150 BRIGHT FRUIT. Pa/FRG 1955; R; 3000; 126 × 5.8 (413 × 20); M; 17; ex BLUE FRUIT 1977; ex CHEN CHENG 1973; ex AHRENSBURG 1968.

MFM H1
21160 TAI YUAN. Tw/FRG 1955; R; 2800; 120.1 × 6.2 (424 × 20.1); M; 16.5; ex TAI YUN 1967; ex HORNCAP 1967.

MFM H1
21170 CABO BOJEADOR. Li/Fi 1958; R; 2800; 126.2 × 6.1 (414 × 20.1); M; 16.5; ex FRIGOARTICO 1971; ex ALDENBURG 1968. Sister: **21171 CABO SAN AGUSTIN** (Li) ex FRIGOANTARTICO 1972; ex ARTLENBURG 1968.

MFM H1
21180 NISSOS RHODOS. Pa/It 1957; R; 3200; 114.7 × 6.3 (376 × 20.8); M; 16; ex ANNETTE 1976; ex MARCIA 1975; ex MARZIA TOMELLINI FASSIO 1970.

MFM H1
★21190 INEY. Ru/De 1957; R; 3400; 123.8 × 6.4 (406 × 21); M; 18; ex TRUBADUR 1964; ex BRITA THORDEN 1963.

MFM H1
21200 KASSOS. Gr/Sw 1956; R; 3400; 123.8 × 6.4 (406 × 21); M; 18; ex FRUBEL JULIA 1966; ex AASE THORDEN 1958. Sister: **21201 KOS** (Gr) ex FRUBEL MARIA 1966; ex KARIN THORDEN 1958.

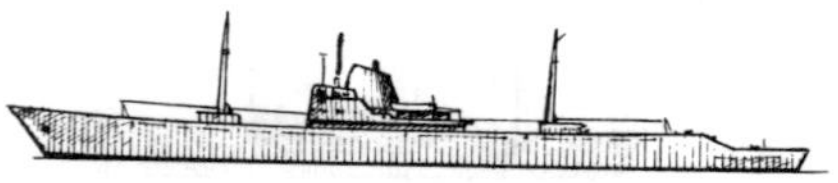

MFM H1
21210 MULTI FROST. Gr/FRG 1958; R; 4000; 126.1 × 7 (414 × 23); M; 17.5; ex NORTHERN FROST; ex CACIQUE NAMANCURA 1973; ex CAP CORRIENTES 1969. Sister: **★21211 MARKO POLO** (Ys) ex CRUX 1973; ex CAP DOMINGO 1970.

MFM H1
★21220 ARAGVI. Ru/FRG 1960; R; 3600; 120.6 × 7.1 (396 × 23.3); M; 18.5. Sisters (Ru flag): **★21221 INGUR ★21222 KURA.**

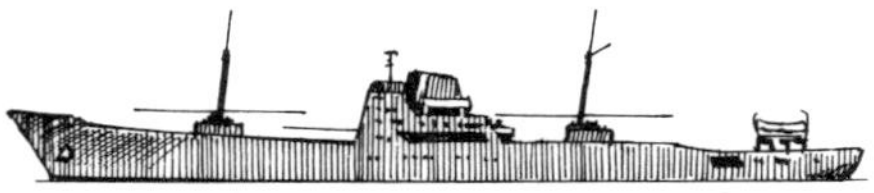

MFM H1
⋆**21230 LA LIMA**. Cu/De 1959; R; 3400/4800; 132.5 × 6.2/8 (435 × 20.4/26.3); M; 19; ex REALENGO 18 1966; ex ALGENEB 1966; ex YUGALA 1966.

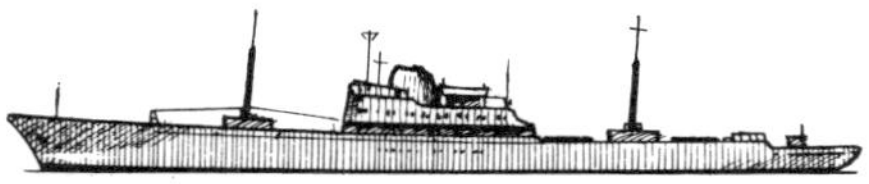

MFM H1
⋆**21260 SCHTORM**. Ru/FRG 1964; R/FC; 3400; 136 × 6.3 (446 × 20.3); M; 18. Sisters (Ru flag): ⋆**21261 BRIS** ⋆**21262 BURJA** ⋆**21263 TAYFUN** ⋆**21264 VETER.**

MFM H1
21270 SARANGANI. Li/FRG 1955; C; 2900; 134.55 × 6.07 (441.44 × 19.92); M; 18; ex NORDENHAM 1973.

MFM H1
⋆**21280 OCEANO ANTARTICO.** Cu/De 1949; R; 2700; 110.8 × 6.3 (364 × 20.8); M; 16; ex COOLADY 1969; ex COOLANGATTA 1969; ex FRUIT QUEEN.

MFM H1
21300 NAJD. So/Ne 1950; R; 2600; 110.9 × 6.4 (364 × 20.7); M; —; ex JOLE FASSIO; ex OCEAN QUEEN 1951.

MFM H1
● **21320 SANSTEFANO**. Pa/FRG 1955; R; 2600/3800; 119.89 × 5.96/6.14 (393.4 × 19.55/20.14); M; 16.5; ex CALASETTA 1974; ex BARCELONA STAR 1965; ex PIRAUS 1965.

MFM H1
21340 UNION REEFER. Pa/De 1959; R; 5000; 132.9 × 7.9 (436 × 26); TSM; 18; ex CHILEAN REEFER. Sister: **21341 FAIR REEFER** (Pa) ex ECUADORIAN REEFER.

MFM H1
● **21240 BENADIR**. So/FRG 1964; R; 4800; 136 × 6.6 (444 × 21.3); M; 21; ex BRUNSLAND 1971. Sisters: **21241 BRUNSHAUSEN** (FRG) **21242 BRUNSBUTTEL** (FRG) **21243 RONIREL** (Sg) ex LILY 1977; ex BRUNSHOLM 1972 **21244 PLAYAS** (Li) ex ASPASSIA 1977; ex BRUNSKAPPEL 1972 **21245 AVANTI** (Pa) ex TARO 1980; ex ROSARIA 1977; ex BRUNSKOOG 1972 **21246 SUSIE U** (Li) ex ELITA 1976; ex BRUNSECK 1971 **21247 ROYAL STAR** (Gr) ex VERA U 1980; ex KATINGAKI 1976; ex BRUNSGARD 1971. (Ru flag): ⋆**21248 TSIKLON** ex BRUNSHAUSEN 1966 ⋆**21249 URAGAN** ex BRUNSBUTTEL 1967 ⋆**21250 DNEPROVSKIY LIMAN** ex BRUNSTOR 1975 ⋆**21251 DNESTROVISKIY LIMAN** ex BRUNSHOEFT 1975.

MFM H1
21290 REA. Gr/De 1956; R; 4300; 116.8 × 6.4 (383 × 20.8); M; 17.5; ex LASTRIGONI 1974; ex COOLGARDIE 1969.

MFM H1
⋆**21310 PLOD**. Ys/FRG 1960; R; 3400/4700; 134.6 × 6.1/6.5 (442 × 20.1/21.5); M; 18.5; ex PENTELIKON 1974.

MFM H1
21330 SAN BERNARDINO. Li/FRG 1959; R; 3100; 129 × 6.1 (424 × 20.2); M; 18.5; ex HARSON 1972; ex ALSTERBLICK 1970.

MFM H1
● **21350 ATLANTIC FREEZER**. Gr/De 1958; R; 4700; 132.47 × 7.89 (434.61 × 25.89); TSM; 18; ex APOLLONIAN GRACE 1977; ex BELGIAN REEFER 1973.

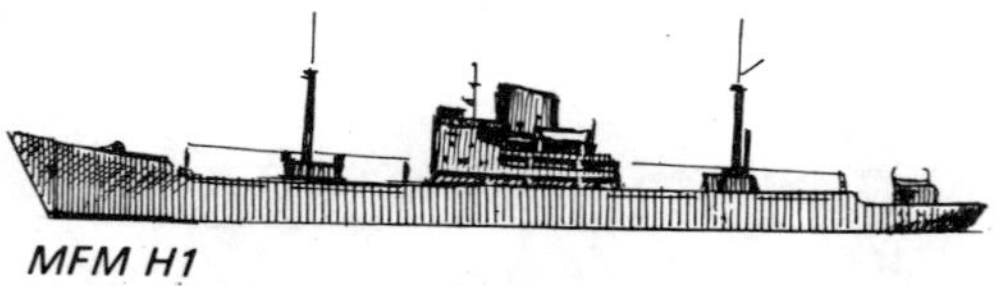

MFM H1
21360 CHOAPA. Ch/De 1964; R; 7900; 148.1 × 8.6 (486 × 26.4); M; 20.5; ex THURO MAERSK 1975. Sister: **21361 PACIFIC OCEAN** (Li) ex MAGLEBY MAERSK 1975.

MFM H1
21370 APOLLONIAN LIGHT. Gr/Fr 1962; R; 5300/6700; 152.3 × —/8.1 (450 × —/26.1); T; 18.75; ex BALLADE 1972.

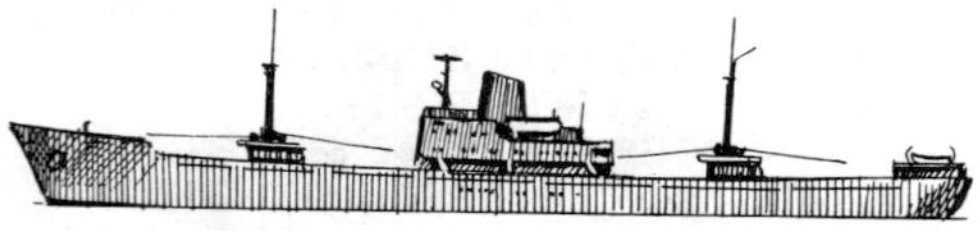

MFM H1
● **21380 ROSY.** It/Sw 1960; R; 6700/8100; 150.3 × —/8.4 (493 × —/27.6); T; 19; ex RIO 1980; ex ANTARTIDE 1978; ex ANTILLA 1977; ex ANTIGUA 1972.

MFM H1
21390 MALAYAN REEFER. Pi/Sw 1960; R;. 8100; 148 × 8.4 (488 × 27.6); M; 18.5; ex ATITLAN 1977. Sister: **21391 ATLANTIDE** (Sw).

MFM H1
● **21400 FREDEVERETT.** Li/Sw 1956; R; 4900; 135.4 × 7.6 (444 × 25.1); M; 18.5; ex HISPANIOLA 1972. Sisters: **21401 CABO BOLINAO** (Li) ex CAYMAN 1971 ⋆**21402 ICHA** (Ru) ex CARIB 1964 Similar: **21403 ANNAFLORA** (Pa) ex CALABELLA 1974; ex GENOVA STAR 1966.

MFM H1
21410 JERRYEVERETT. Li/Sw 1960; R; 4900; 133.4 × 7.6 (438 × 25.1); M; 18; ex CORAL SEA 1969. Sisters (Li flag): **21411 EWALDEVERETT** ex PEARL SEA 1972 **21412 WADEEVERETT** ex CRYSTAL SEA 1972.

MFM H1
21420 CARLEVERETT. Li/Sw 1962; R; 4900; 131.1 × 7.1 (430 × 23.2); M; 18; ex NORTHLAND. Sister: **21421 KELLYEVERETT** (Li) ex NORTH ISLE.

MFM H1
⋆**21430 VOCE.** Ys/De 1961; R; 4700; 132.6 × 7.8 (435 × 25.3); M; 19.5; ex DRAGOR MAERSK 1974.

MFM H1
21440 CHALMEVERETT. Li/Sw 1960; R; 5000; 134.1 × 7.6 (440 × 25.1); M; 17.75; ex BALTIC SEA 1969. Sister: **21441 FLORA II** (Li) ex NORTH SEA 1970.

MFM H1
⋆**21450 SHKVAL.** Ru/Sw 1963; R; 4200; 126.4 × 7.3 (415 × 24); M; 17; ex BAKKE REEFER 1975.

MFM H1
21460 SAMOS SEA. Gr/No 1965; R; 5700; 128.1 × 7.8 (420 × 25.6); M; 19; ex GOLAR FRUIT 1977. Sister: **21461 SAMOS STORM** (Gr) ex GOLAR TRYG 1977.

MFM H1
● **21470 CARIBBEAN ARROW.** Pa/FRG 1952; C; 3700; 106.4 × 6.8 (349 × 22.4); M; 13; ex MARTHA S 1975; ex RIA M 1974; ex ARMONIA 1973; ex FREATTYS 1972; ex DIANA 1970; ex CIUDAD DE BUCARAMANGA 1965; ex BRUNSHAUSEN 1953. Sister: **21471 NEDON** (Cy) ex CIUDAD DE SANTA MARTA Similar: **21472 ZAMIRA** (Co) ex CIUDAD DE POPAYAN **21473 FORTUNE CARRIER** (Br) ex TERE G 1976; ex MARGARITA M 1975; ex CIUDAD DE NEIVA 1974.

MFM H1
21500 EVITA TH. Pa/Ne 1951; C; 1800; 82 × 4 (269 × 13.11); M; 13; ex EVITA 1974; ex SAFI 1973. Sister: **21501 ESTEBAN S** (Me) ex LORETO 1975; ex MOGADOR 1964.

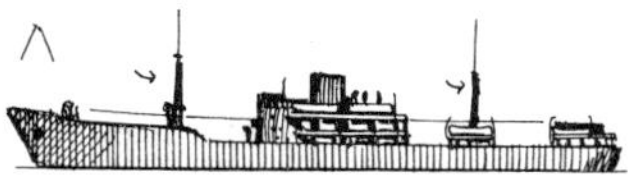

MFM H1
21520 LOO CHONG. Pa/Sw 1949; C; 1900; 95.26 × 5.56 (312.53 × 18.24); M; 13; ex LOON CHONG 1979; ex HERMOD 1971.

MFM H1
● **21540 BOUAR.** Le/De 1949; C; 1800; 100.97 × 6.5 (331.27 × 21.33); M; 13.5; ex MELOS 1968.

MFM H1
● **21550 ELLITSA.** Gr/Sw 1945; C; 1800; 99.3 × 5.6 (326 × 18.5); M; 13; ex BECKY 1975.

MFM H1
21570 BATANGHARI. Ia/Ne 1957; C; 2600; 87 × 3.9 (285 × 12.11); M; 11.5. Sisters (Ia flag): **21571 BENGAWAN 21572 BOGOWONTO 21573 BRANTAS.**

MFM H1
21480 HEBE. Fr/Fr 1960; C/WT; 5200; 118.2 × 7.1 (388 × 23.6); M; 19.

MFM H1
21490 GEMA. Pa/Ne 1959; R; 2700/3800; 115 × 6.1/6.8 (377 × 22/22.10); M; 17; ex SALTA 1977; ex BRUNSTAL 1970; ex BALEARES 1966.

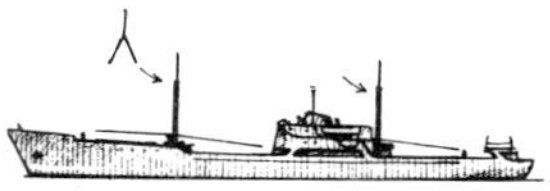

MFM H1
★**21510 VARAZDIN.** Ys/Ys 1958; C; 1000; 83.4 × 4.3 (274 × 14.3); M; 13.25; ex VODICE 1976; ex VARAZDIN 1969. Sisters (Ys flag): ★**21511 PIROT** ★**21512 ZEMUN** ex KAPRIJE 1976; ex ZEMUN 1969.

MFM H1
21530 RENEE. Pi/Sw 1954; CP; 1800; 100.2 × 5.6 (329 × 18.5); M; 13.5; ex RANI 1973; ex VALENCIA 1968. Sister: **21531 VICTORIA K** (Le) ex KOTRONAS VILLAGE 1980; ex DARLING; ex DIMITRAKIS 1973; ex RAGUNDA 1971; ex ALMERIA 1967 Similar (Bi-pod masts): **21532 SINNO M. E. II** (Le) ex BEIRUT TRUST 1980; ex IRENE I 1974; ex IRENE 1970.

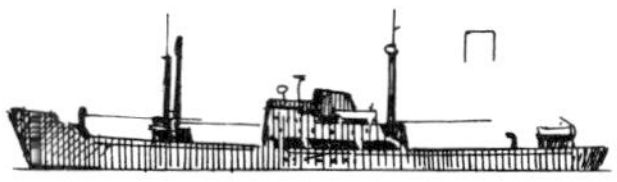

MFM H1
★**21560 FALESHTY.** Ru/Fi 1959; C; 1700; 94.5 × 5.7 (309 × 18.7); M; 13.5. Sisters (Ru flag): ★**21561 FARAB** ★**21562 FAYZABAD** ★**21563 FIRYUZA** ex FIROZA ★**21564 FRYANOVO** ★**21565 SEINE** ex FIROVO 1960.

MFM H1
★**21580 JANA.** Ru/FRG 1955; FC; 3800; 111.2 × 6.2 (365 × 21); M; 14. Sisters (Ru flag): ★**21581 INDIGIRKA** ★**21582 KONDA** ★**21583 KULOY** ★**21584 NEMAN** ★**21585 TULOMA** ★**21586 UMANJ.**

MFM H1
21590 VISAYAS. Pi/FRG 1963; C; 4300; 117×7.6 (384×25); M; —.

MFM H1
⋆21610 AMGUEMA. Ru/Ru 1962; C; 8100; 133×8.9 (436×30); D-E; 15; Polar service. Sister (Ru flag): **⋆21611 PENZHINA** Similar (some have helicopter deck): **⋆21612 GIZHIGA ⋆21613 KAPITAN BONDARENKO ⋆21614 KAPITAN GOTSKIY ⋆21615 KAPITAN KONDRATYEV ⋆21616 KAPITAN MARKOV ⋆21617 KAPITAN MYSHEVSKIY ⋆21618 NAVARIN ⋆21619 PAVEL PONOMARYEV ⋆21620 VANKAREM ⋆21621 VASILIY FEDOSEYEV ⋆21622 MIKHAIL SOMOV** (Research ship).

MFM H1
21640 VAVY K. Le/FRG 1956; CP; 2600/4100; 114.4×6.5/7.6 (375×21.5/24.11); M; 14; ex JOHNNY K 1972; ex NICOSIA 1971; ex BRAUNSFELD 1967; ex LUDWIGSBURG 1966.

MFM H1
21660 MICHAEL V. Gr/FRG 1953; C; 2800; 118.6×6.2 (385×20.6); M: 12; ex FRIENDSHIP I 1977; ex WARNOW 1977; ex LEON DENS 1962; ex SIARO 1958. Similar: **21661 LUCY** (Gr) ex KALLIARCHOS 1979; ex SEA PEARL 1976; ex MALOJA 1973.

MFM H1
⋆21680 VIET BAO. Vn/FRG 1956; C; 2700; 106×6.3 (345×20.9); R; 13.

MFM H1
⋆21600 ZELENOGORSK. Ru/Ne 1955; C/FC; 3600; 114.7×6.5 (377×18); M; 13. Sisters (Ru flag): **⋆21601 BALTIYSK ⋆21602 CHERNYAKHOVSK ⋆21603 GVARDEYSK ⋆21604 SVETLOGORSK.**

MFM H1
⋆21625 OLYUTORKA. Ru/Sw 1955; R; 5900; 132×7.6 (433×25); M; 18; ex SAN BLAS 1964.

MFM H1
21630 LAGADA STAR. Gr/FRG 1954; CP; 2700/4200; 114.8×6.5/7.6 (377×21.5/25); M; 14; ex NAHOST TRANSPORTER 1977; ex CHRISTEL VINNEN 1977; ex TROYBURG 1966.

MFM H1
21650 NEW HYDE. Pa/FRG 1958; CP; 2600/4100; 115×6.5/7.6 (377×21.5/24.11); M; 14.5; ex SUN KWONG 1979; ex EDWIN REITH 1973. Sister: **21651 NEW HERO** (Ps) ex SUN SANG 1980; ex MAGDALENA REITH 1972.

MFM H1
● **21670 SAC BARCELONA.** Sp/Sp 1963; C; 5000; 124.7×7.2 (409×23.9); T; 14.5.

MFM H1
● **21690 AMSTERDAM.** Gr/Fr 1952; C/WT; 3700; 118.7×6.2 (388×20.4); M; 14.5; ex JADEFAHRT 1970; ex PRESIDENT CHARLES LEFEBVRE 1969.

MFM H1
21700 EL NIL. Eg/It 1953; C; 2700; 111 × 6 (365 × 19.8); M; 14.5.

MFM H1
21710 HOE AIK. Sg/De 1949; C; 2900; 94.67 × 6.48 (310.6 × 21.26); M; 17; ex EAST CAPE 1980; ex LAGARFOSS.

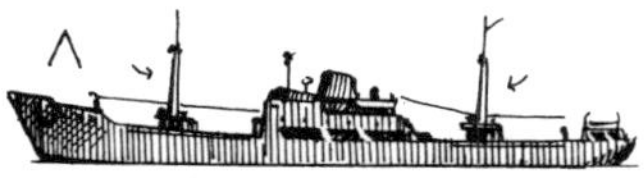

MFM H1
★21720 POBJEDA. Ys/Ys 1958; C; 1600; 94.5 × 5.5 (310 × 18.11); M; 14.75. Sisters: **★21721 BRATSTVO ★21722 SLOBODA.**

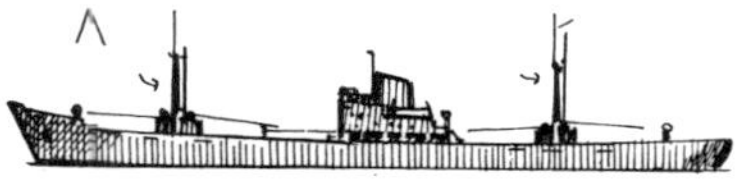

MFM H1
21730 ADOLF VINNEN. FRG/FRG 1955; C; 3000/4900; 124.3 × 6.6/7.5 (408 × 21.8/247); M; 13.5.

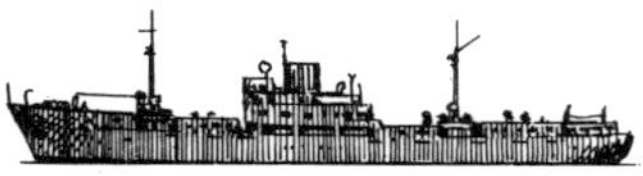

MFM H1
21740 NAHED. Si/It 1948; LS; 3200; 98.9 × 5.4 (324 × 17.1); M; 14.5; ex CIMBRIA 1975; ex DUCHY OF NORMANDY 1960; ex VERNA CLAUSEN 1955.

MFM H1
21750 FORTUNA REEFER. Br/Sw 1953; R; 2300; 104.2 × 6.1 (342 × 20); M; 16; ex BONZO 1975; ex BAJAMAR 1968; ex LEEWARD ISLANDS 1964. Sister: **21751 NATHALIE D** (Pa) ex HAMDAN 1976; ex NATHALIE D 1974; ex BAMBI 1974; ex MARDINA REEFER 1972; ex BAMBI 1971; ex BANADEROS 1968; ex WINDWARD ISLANDS 1964.

MFM H1
● **21760 OLGA.** Gr/Sw 1945; C; 1200/2100; 80.7 × 5.2/5.7 (265 × 17.2/18.8); M; 12; ex CHRYSSOULA 1972; ex LADY SOPHIA 1968; ex FERNEBO 1960.

MFM H1
21770 SEYHAN. Tu/No 1950; CP; 3100; 113.4 × 6.2 (372 × 20.3); R; 12; ex NORVIKEN 1955.

MFM H1
● **21780 SYMON.** Pa/It 1950; C; 2100; 97.4 × 6 (319 × 19.7); M; 12; ex TEA 1975; ex MARTERESA 1973; ex MARIA TERESA 1971; ex MARIA TERESA G. 1963. Sister: **21781 NIMOS** (Gr) ex MARIA FAUSTA; ex MARIA FAUSTA G 1963.

MFM H1
★21790 PANAGURISHTE. Bu/De 1951; C; 1600; 87.1 × 5.5 (286 × 18.2); R; 12.5; ex ARCTURUS 1970; ex ELSE NIELSEN 1963.

MFM H1
★21800 CHIPKA. Bu/Ge 1938; C; 2200; 97.9 × 5.8 (321 × 18); R; 11.5.

MFM H1
21810 DONA PAMELA. Pi/Sw 1950; C; 1400/2300; 88.8 × 5.2/— (291 × 17.2/—); M; 14; ex GOTHONG; ex CAP SPARTEL 1963; ex CAP GRIS NEZ 1956.

MFM H1
21820 PANAGIA CHRYSSOPIGI. Gr/Sw 1944; C; 2700; 103.8×7.3 (341×24); M; 13.5; ex SWIFT SKIPPER; ex FAST DOLPHIN 1974; ex SANTA ANTHOUSA 1970; ex BORDABERE 1968; ex FLENSBURG 1961; ex ATOMENA 1955.

MFM H1
● **21830 CASTLE GLORY.** Br/Sw 1952; C; 2200; 87×4.9 (285×16.2); M; 11.5; ex MARTA 1974; ex CAP VERT 1971; ex DJIRING 1969; ex BARRANQUILLA.

MFM H1
● **21840 MYSTRAS.** Gr/Sw 1950; C; 1500; 87×4.9 (285×16.2); M; 11.5; ex NAVARINO BAY 1972; ex IMMEN 1969. Similar (taller funnel): **21841 ORIENT** (Le) ex ODYSSEUS 1974; ex BLAAFJELD 1 1961.

MFM H1
21850 ALEXIA. Cy/Sw 1949; C; 1300; 88.8×5.2 (291×16.11); M; 12; ex ARNARFELL 1973.

MFM H1
21860 WINHO. Pa/FRG 1950; C; 1900/3100; 100.4×5.5/6.7 (329×18/22); M; 14.5; ex OCEAN PEACE 1972; ex MEROPI 1972; ex LAS PALMAS 1971.

MFM H1
21870 MELILLA. Gr/FRG 1952; C; 1700; 93.7×5.7 (307×18.9); M; 14.

MFM H1
● **21880 LAS PALMAS.** Gr/Sw 1948; C; 1600; 88.8×5.2 (291×16.11); M; 12; ex DELFI 1973; ex KATIA.

MFM H1
● **21890 LILLA.** Pa/FRG 1950; C; 2700; 96.5×6.2 (316×20.5); M; 10.5; ex JOACHIM SCHULTE 1972; ex HEINRICH SCHULTE 1963.

MFM H1
21900 BEAUTY ROSE. Pa/No 1951; C; 1400; 78.6×5.3 (258×17.3); R; 10.5; ex HWA CHANG 1973; ex CHICHOW FROG 1970; ex KRISTINA 1968; ex KOLLBRYN 1958.

MFM H1
★**21910 ILMEN.** Ru/No 1943; C; 200; 79.9×5.3 (260×18); R; 11; ex KOLLAA 1948.

MFM H1
21920 KRANTOR. Gr/Ne 1947; C; 1500; 78.6×5.5 (258×18); M; 12; ex CITTA DI ATENE; ex PRINS FREDERIK HENDRIK 1966. Sister: **21921 MICHELE GAROFANO** (It) ex PRINS FREDERIK WILLEM 1966.

MFM H1
21930 SAN GEORGE. Cy/FRG 1950; C; 1400; 76.69×5.5 (251.61×18.04); M; 13; ex RABAT 1969.

MFM H1
21940 KALYMNOS. Gr/De 1948; PC; 1500; 72.8×3.8 (239×12.6); TSM; —; ex ARCADIA 1969; ex KALYMNOS 1968; ex HEKLA 1966. Similar: **21941 NWAKUSO** (Ng) ex VENTURA BEACH; ex LUCAYA 1973; ex ESJA 1969.

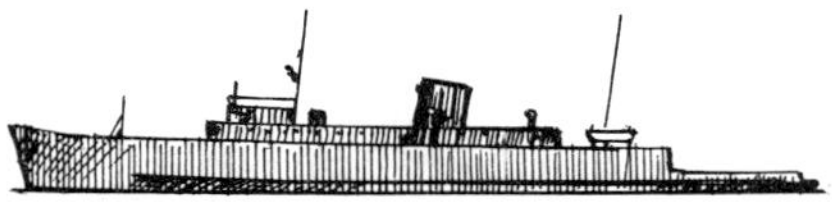

MFM H1
21950 ESSEX FERRY. Br/Br 1957; RoF/TF; 3100; 121.9 × 3.7 (400 × 12.1); TSM; 12.25. Sister: **21951 NORFOLK FERRY.**

MFM H1
21960 ASA-THOR. De/De 1965; RoF/TF; 3500; 131.7 × 4.5 (452 × 15); TSM; —.

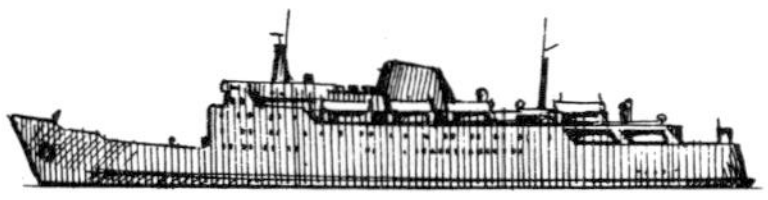

MFM H1
21970 ULSTER PRINCE. Br/Br 1967; RoPF; 4300; 115 × 4.1 (378 × 13.6); TSM; 17; Stern door. Sister: **21971 ULSTER QUEEN** (Br).

MFM H1
● **21980 SANTA MARIA DEL PINO.** Sp/Sp 1963; PC; 1200; 67 × 3.2 (220 × 10.5); TSM; 15. Sisters (Sp flag): **21981 SANTA MARIA DE LA CARIDAD 21982 SANTA MARIA DE LAS NIEVES 21983 SANTA MARIA DE LA PAZ** Some, or all, of these may be KMFM.

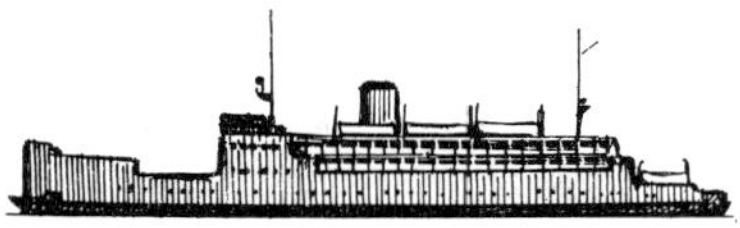

MFM H1
21990 SCILLA. It/It 1931; RoF/TF; 2800; 111.4 × 3.8 (366 × 12.6); TSD-E;15.5; Bow and side doors.

MFM H1
22000 NORGE. No/Br 1937; Royal Yacht; 1700 (T.Y.M.); 80.1 × 4.6 (263 × 15.2); TSM; 17; ex PHILANTE.

MFM H1
22010 BONAVISTA. Ca/Br 1956; PC; 1200; 65.5 × 5 2 (215 × 17.2); M; 12. Similar: **22011 NONA** (Ca).

MFM H1
22020 LAURO EXPRESS. It/US 1943; RoCF; 500; 57.8 × 2.7 (190 × 8); TSM; 15; ex HAUGESUND 1973; ex H.M.S. KILBURNIE.

MFM H1
22030 JYLLAND. Ma/US 1943; PC; 800; 57.3 × 2.6 (185 × 8.4); TSM; 15; ex H.M.S. KILBRIDE.

MFM H1
22040 PRINCESS OF NEGROS. Pi/Hong Kong 1962; F; 500; 61.7 × 3.2 (203 × 10.7); TSM; —.

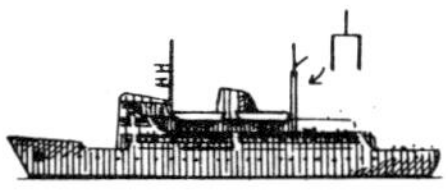

MFM H1
22050 PRINSES MARGRIET. Ne/Ne 1966; TS; 1600; 69 × 4.5 (226 × 15); M; —.

MFM H1
22060 CITY OF PIRAEUS. Gr/Br 1953; F; 500; 50.3 × 1.7 (165 × 5.8); TSM; 14; ex MAID OF ARGYLL 1975. Sister: **22061 ALA** (Pa) ex MAID OF SKELMORLIE 1972.

MFM H1
● **22070 IONA.** Br/Br 1970; RoCF; 1300; 74.3 × 3 (241 × 10); TSM; 16; Side doors and stern door/ramp.

MFM H1
22080 BIRD OF PARADISE. Br/Br 1960; F; 1300; 60.6 × 3 (199 × 10); TSM; 13. Sister: **22081 SCARLET IBIS** (Br).

MFM H1
22090 BAR HAVEN. Ca/Br 1948; P; 1100; 65.2 × 5.1 (214 × 16.1); R; 11.5. Sister: **22091 SPRINGDALE** (Ca).

MFM H1
22100 MARTERESA. It/Br 1941; C; 500; 47.3 × 4.5 (155 × 14.8); M; —; ex SERVANNAISE 1963; ex NADOR 1955; ex TILTHORN 1952; ex H.M.S. INCHMARNOCK; Converted trawler 1947.

MFM H1
22110 EVANGELISTRIA. Gr/Br 1943; Trlr; 500; 49.9 × 4.4 (164 × 14.6); M; 10; ex GRASSHOLM 1956.

MFM H1
22120 SEIUN MAUR. Ja/Ja 1968; TS; 5000; 114.6 × 5.8 (376 × 19); M; 16.5.

MFM H1
22130 BAFFIN. Ca/Ca 1957; IB/RS; 3500; 87 × 5.7 (286 × 18.1); TSM; 15.5.

MFM H1
22140 OCEANIC. FRG/FRG 1968; Tg/Sal; 2000; 87.2 × 6 (286 × 19); M; 22.

MFM H1
⋆**22150 MB 18.** Ru/Fi 1977; Tg; 1500; 63.51 × 5.2 (208.37 × 17.06); M; 13. Sisters (Ru flag): ⋆**22151 MB 15** ⋆**22152 MB 105** ⋆**22153 MB 119.**

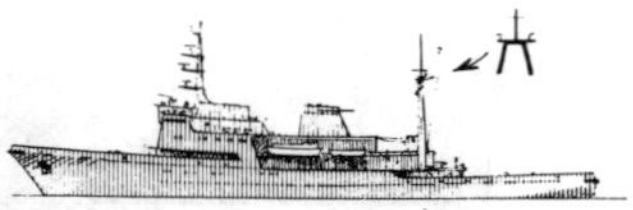

MFM H1
⋆**22160 YAGUAR.** Ru/Ru 1976; Tg/Sal; 2800; 92.79 × 5.8 (304.43 × 19.03); M; 18.5. Sister: (Ru flag) ⋆**22161 BARS** Similar (USSR Naval Service) **INGUL** class: ⋆**22162 MASHUK** ⋆**22163 PAMIR** (possibly renamed **INGUL**).

MFM H1
22170 JOHN ROSS. Br/SA 1976; Tg/Sal; 2800; 94.6 × 9 (311 × 30); M; 20; ex S.A. JOHN ROSS 1977. Sister: **22171 WOLRAAD WOLTEMADE** (Br) ex S.A. WOLRAAD WOLTEMADE.

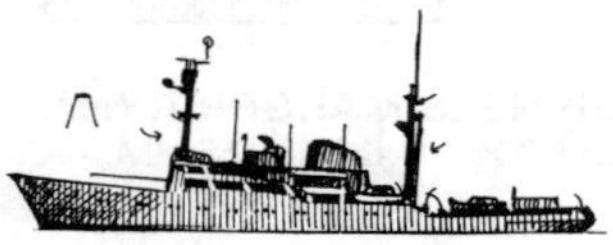

MFM H1
● ⋆**22180 NIKOLAI ZUBOV.** Ru/Pd 1964; RS/SS; 2700 Dspl; 90 × 4.6 (295 × 15); TSM; 16.5. Sisters (Ru flag): ⋆**22181 ALEKSEY CHIRIKOV** ⋆**22182 ANDREY VILKITSKIY** ⋆**22183 BORIS DAVIDOV** ⋆**22184 FEDOR LITKE** ⋆**22185 SEJMEN CHELYUSKIN** ⋆**22186 SEJMEN DEZHNEV** ⋆**22187 T. BELLINGSGAUSEN** ⋆**22188 VASILIY GOLOVNIN** The following are Intelligence Collectors: ⋆**22189 GAVRIL SARITCHEV** ⋆**22190 KHARITON LAPTEV.**

MFM H1
⋆**22200 KAPITAN CHECHKIN.** Ru/Fi 1977; IB; 1700; 77.6 × 3.25 (254.59 × 10.66); TrS D-E; 14; River Service. Sisters (Ru flag): ⋆**22201 KAPITAN CHADAYEV** ⋆**22202 KAPITAN PLAHIN** ⋆**22203 KAPITAN ZARUBIN** ⋆**22204 KAPITAN BUKAYEV** ⋆**22205 KAPITAN KRUTOV.**

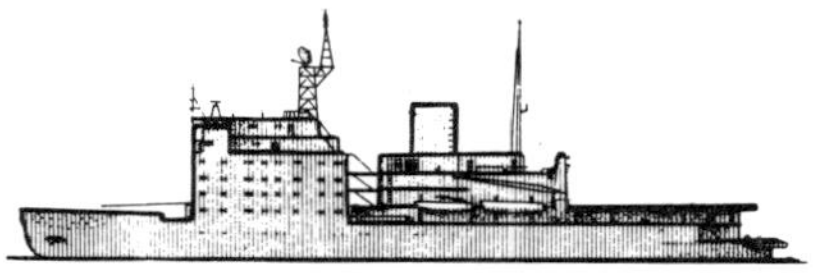

MFM H1
22210 ALMIRANTE IRIZAR. Ar/Fi 1978; IB/P; 10100; 119.31 × 9.5 (391.44 × 31.17); TSM; 16.5; Helicoper deck.

MFM H1
⋆**22250 KAPITAN M. IZMAYLOV.** Ru/Fi 1976; IB/Sal; 1400; 56.3 × 4.2 (184 × 14); TSD-E; 14. Sisters (Ru flag): ⋆**22251 KAPITAN A. RADZHABOV** ⋆**22252 KAPITAN KOSOLAPOV.**

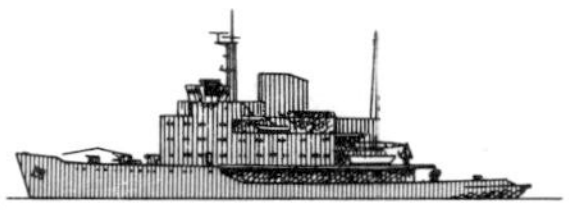

MFM H1
22260 VOIMA. Fi/Fi-Fi 1954/79; IB; —; 83.52 × — (274 × —); TS D-E; —; Rebuilt 1978-79.

MFM H1
22270 THULE. Sw/Sw 1953; IB; 1900; 62.2 × 4.9 (204 × 15.11); TrS D-E; 13.

MFM H1
22290 SOTIR. Gr/Br 1942; Sal; 1100; 66.1 × 4.8 (216 × 13); TSR; 12; ex SALVENTURE; On loan from British Government.

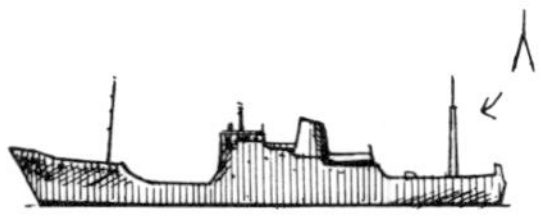

MFM H1
22310 TAURUS. FRG/FRG 1964; Tg; 1600; 78 × 5.3 (256 × 17.6); M; 15; ex HANS PICKENPACK 1974; Converted trawler 1974.

Twin Funnels

MFM H1
⋆**22330 BELONA.** Pd/Pd 1964; FT; 1000; 69.3 × 5 (228 × 16.7); M; 13.5; **'B-23'** type. Sisters (Pd flag): ⋆**22331 ALBAKORA** ⋆**22332 BARAKUDA** ⋆**22333 BARBATA** ⋆**22334 BARWENA** ⋆**22335 DORADA** ⋆**22336 GRANIK** ⋆**22337 KONGER** ⋆**22338 RAMADA** ⋆**22339 TARPOL** ⋆**22340 TASERGAL.**

MFM H1
⋆**22220 DOBRINYA NIKITICH.** Ru/Ru 1961; IB; Approx. 2300; 68 × 5.5 (223 × 18.9); TrS D-E; 13.75. Sisters (Ru flag)—Some are Naval manned: ⋆**22221 AFANASIY NIKITIN** ex LEDOKOL 2 ⋆**22222 BURAN** ⋆**22223 EROFFREY KHABAROV** ex LEDOKOL 5 ⋆**22224 FEDOR LITKE** ⋆**22225 GEORGIY SEDOV** ⋆**22226 ILYA MUROMETS** ⋆**22227 IVAN MOSKVITIN** ⋆**22228 IVAN KRUZENSHTERN** ex LEDOKOL 6 ⋆**22229 MENDELEYEV** ex PETR PAKHTUSOV; ex LEDOKOL 10 ⋆**22230 PERESVET** ⋆**22231 PLUG** ⋆**22232 SADKO** ⋆**22233 SEMYON DEZHNEV** ⋆**22234 SEMEN CHELYUSKIN** ex LEDOKOL 8 ⋆**22235 VASILIY POYARKHOV** exLEDOKOL 4 ⋆**22236 VASILIY PRONCHISHCHEV** ex LEDOKOL 1 ⋆**22237 VLADIMIR RUSANOV** ex LEDOKOL 7 ⋆**22238 YURIY LISYANSKIY** ex LEDOKOL 9 ⋆**22239 VYUGA.**

MFM H1
22280 CANOPUS. Bz/Ja 1958; SS; 1500 Dspl; 78 × 3.7 (256 × 12.2); TSM; 15. Sister: **22281 SIRIUS** (Bz).

Twin Funnels

MFM H1
22300 CIROLANA. Br/Br 1970; ST/RS; 1700; 72.5 × 5 (238 × 17); D-E; 14.

MFM H1
22320 THALASSA. Fr/Fr 1960; ST/RS; 1200; 66.1 × 4.6 (217 × 15.1); M; 12.

Twin Funnels

MFM H1
⋆**22350 RYBAK MORSKI.** Pd/Pd 1976; FT; 2600; 89 × 5.2 (292 × 17); M; 15.25; **'B-89'** type. Sister: ⋆**22351 ADMIRAL ARCISZEWSKI** (Pd).

MFM H1
22360 CLAYMORE. Br/Br 1978; RoPF; 450 dwt; 76.9 × 2.72 (252.3 × 8.92); TSM; 15.5; Stern ramp and side ramps.

MFM H1
22370 BRANDAL. Ca/Ca 1965; RS; 500; 41.6 × — (136 × —); M; —; Converted stern trawler.

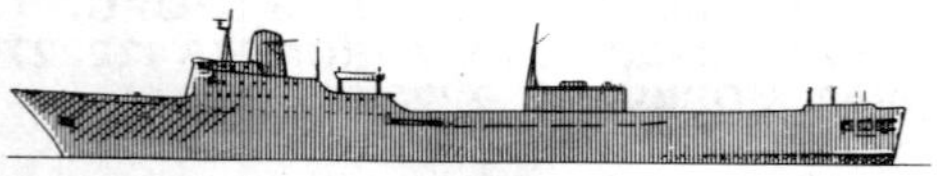

MFM H1
22380 STAFFETTA ADRIATICA. It/It 1969; RoC; 4700; 141.03 × 5.88 (462.7 × 19.29); TSD-E; 19; ex CANGURO GIALLO 1973; Stern door. Sisters (It flag): **22381 STAFFETTA JONICA** ex CANGURO GRIGIO 1973 **22382 STAFFETTA TIRRENICA** ex CANGURO BIONDO 1973 **22383 CANGURO FULVO.**

MFM H12
22390 AL TAIF. Si/Br 1949; F; 5300; 121 × 4.52 (397 × 14.); TSM; 15; ex CAMBRIA; May be known as **ALTAIF.**

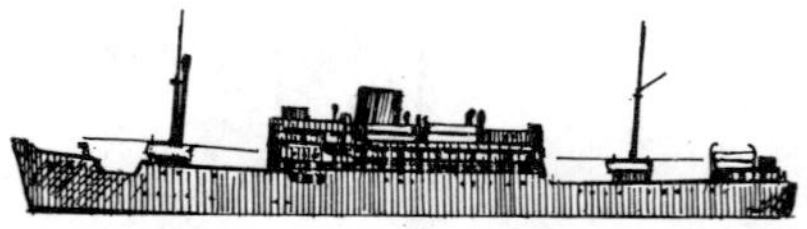

MFM H12
22400 DAMAN. In/Br 1946; PC; 4900; 121.5 × 6.7 (399 × 22); M; 14; ex DUMRA 1976. Sister: **22401 DWARKA** (Br).

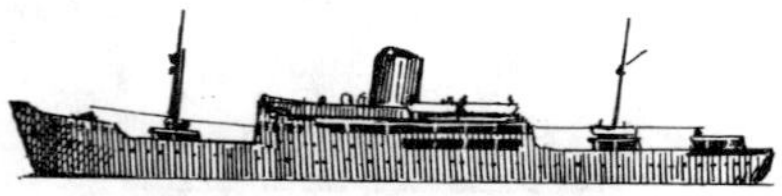

MFM H12
22410 ZAMZAM. Cy/It 1952; PC; 5200; 116.9 × 5.8 (383 × 19.1); TSM; 18; ex MESSAPIA 1975.

MFM H12
22420 AVARE. Bz/Br 1949; C; 2700; 99.4 × 5.8 (326 × 19); R; 12.5; ex SAO MIGUEL 1972; ex VALBORG NIELSEN 1960.

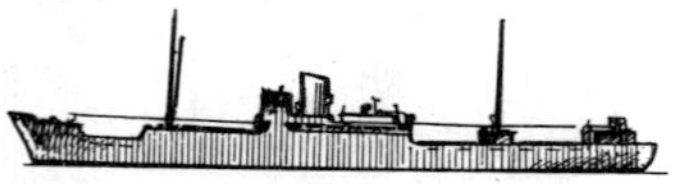

MFM H12
⋆22430 SUNNY BOY. RC/Br 1950; C; 2500; 101.8 × 5.8 (334 × 18.11); R; —; ex NEPOS 1960; ex FANA 1959.

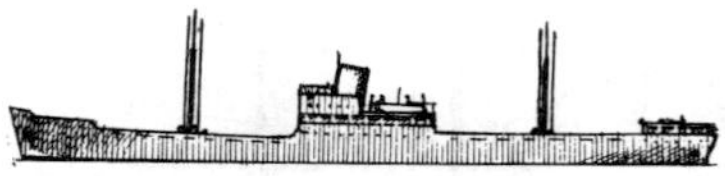

MFM H12
22440 ANTHI L. Gr/Fr 1954; C; 3700; 112.3 × 6.8 (368 × 21.4); R; 11.5; ex ARAYA 1973; ex ANTEE 1969.

MFM H12
⋆22450 SMOLNYY. Ru/Ru 1929; PC; 3700; 104 × 5.7 (341 × 16); M; 11.5. Similar: **⋆22451 KOOPERATSIYA** (Ru).

MFM H12
22460 GAMSOLO. Pa/Br 1947; C; 3200; 101.8 × 6.8 (334 × 19.5); M; 12; ex KEREDJA 1977; ex GAMSOLO 1974; ex FILIKOS 1973; ex MACO TRADER 1973; ex NIKOLAOS KATSOULIS 1968; ex ENGLAND 1967.

MFM H12
22470 SAVILCO. Gr/Ge 1938; C; 1800; 79.3 × 5.4 (260 × 17.7); M; 13; ex NISSOS THASSOS 1970; ex WICKENBURGH 1963; ex MARGECA 1947; ex EMPIRE CONINGSBY 1946; ex ADLER 1945.

MFM H12
22480 EFFIGYNY. In/Br 1954; C; 1600; 88.1 × 5.2 (289 × 17.2); R; 13; ex CLANGULA 1965.

MFM H12
22490 AMBERES. Ar/Br 1930; C;1500; 87.7×3.7 (288×11.2); TSM; 11; Converted to a barge. Similar (Ar flag): **22491 CARDIFF 22492 GENOVA.**

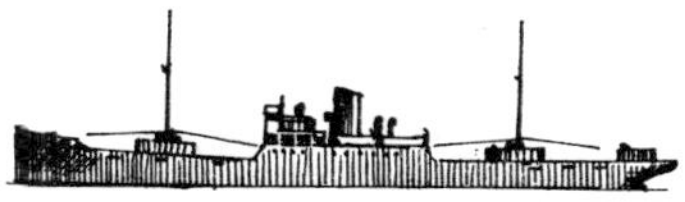

MFM H12
⋆**22500 RION.** Ru/Ru 1931; FC; 3100; 102.5×6.4 (338×21); M; 12. Similar: ⋆**22501 NEVA** (Ru).

MFM H12
22510 SELAMAT. Pa/Hong Kong 1937; C; 690; 52.8×4.1 (173×13.5); M; 19; ex SOON HUAT 1961; ex LA PALOMA 1958; ex PALOMA 1958; ex MULIAMA 1957.

MFM H12
● **22520 COMARA.** Pa/Br 1937; C; 750; 54×3.3 (177×11); M; 8.5; ex DAMADORA DEL MAR 1962; ex COMARA 1956; Converted to a barge.

MFM H12
22530 ANNA MARIA LAURO. It/— 1913; F; 900; 67.9×2.8 (214×9.6); TSM; —; ex ISOLA DEL SOLE 1965; ex KEHRWIEDER 1963; ex GLUCKAUF 1960; ex BUBENDEY.

MFM H12
22540 YEREWA. In/In 1965; PC; 1600; 68.3×2.9 (224×9.7); TSM; 12. Sister: **22541 ONGE** (In).

MFM H12
⋆**22550 ROBERT KOCH.** DDR/DDR 1955; Hospital Ship; 1100; 66.1×4.8 (217×15.7); M; 14.

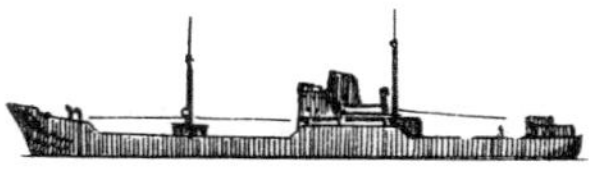

MFM H12
22560 UNIBAKSH. In/FRG 1956; C; 2700; 92×5.9 (302×19.5); M; 12; ex ROSANNA 1977; ex JALATAPI 1974.

MFM H12
22570 MARSO. Po/Po 1955; PC; 1000; 59.7×3.7 (196×12); M; 11; ex CEDROS 1973.

MFM H12
22580 VENUS II. Do/It 1947; C; 900; 67.2×4.1 (199×13.11); M; 10.5; ex ANDY; ex GRETA H. 1959; ex BAKKE BOY 1952; ex VAGAN 1951.

MFM H12
22590 MARIA SIGMA. Gr/Ge 1905; C; 800; 59.5×4.3 (195×14); M; 11; ex MARKELLA 1974; ex HOPE 1971; ex ELEFTHERIA 1971; ex SKANSEODDE 1968; ex ALEXANDRIA 1948.

MFM H12
22600 JURANDY. Bz/US 1920; C; 1400; 69.2×5.1 (227×16.9); R; —; ex RIO BRAVO 1955; ex LLOYD CUARTO 1952; ex TAKU 1946; ex ORMES 1939.

MFM H12
22610 SLUSKEN. Pa/No 1919; C; 650; 53.8×4.1 (176×13.6); R; —; ex MAGNHILD 1959; ex BRAS 1956; ex RAFTSUND 1946; ex BRAS.

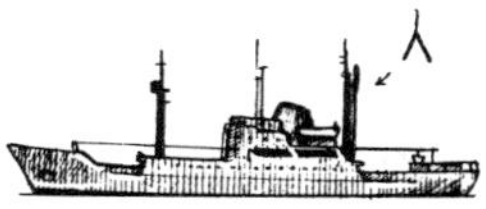

MFM H12
22620 NELLA DAN. De/De 1961; PC; 2200; 75.2×6.6 (245×21.7); M; 13.

MFM H12
22630 AMAMI MARU. Ja/Ja 1968; F; 1500; 83.1 × 4.1 (273 × 13.3); M; 17.

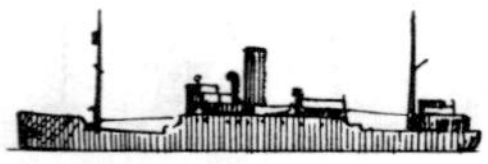

MFM H12
22640 CAPE YORK. Tw/Au 1925; LT; 1500; 71.8 × 4.5 (235 × 14.8); R; 10.

MFM H12
22650 ELCANO. Pi/Ja 1955; PC; 2000; 87.3 × 5 (288 × 16.7); M; —. Sister: **22651 LEGAZPI** (Pi) ex LEGASPI 1980.

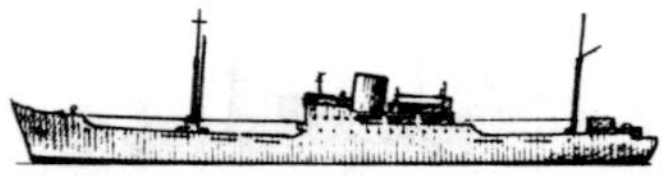

MFM H12
22660 OMAR. Ma/Br 1956; C; 2500; 102 × 5.9 (335 × 19.4); M; 12; ex RODANIA 1975; ex ELEFTHEROTRIA 1972; ex NORTHUMBRIAN PRINCE 1968.

MFM H12
22670 SPERUS. Br/Br 1939; CP; 900; 64.3 × 4 (211 × 13); TSM; 12; ex HESPERUS.

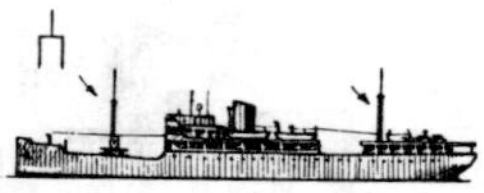

MFM H12
***22680 HUNG YU.** RC/—; CP; 2500; 73.2 × — (240 × —); —; —.

MFM H12
22690 GILBERT J. FOWLER. Br/Br 1971; Sludge Carrier; 2500; 91 × 5.4 (299 × 17.6); TSM; 12.75. Sister: **22691 CONSORTIUM I** (Br).

MFM H12
22700 KYRIAKI. Cy/Ge 1925; C; 950; 67.9 × 4.2 (223 × 13.9); M; 11.5; ex PSARA 1971; ex GREETSIEL 1962; ex SEEMOWE 1957; ex PATRICIA 1955; ex VESTJYDEN 1954; ex VIBEKE MAERSK 1946.

MFM H12
● **22710 CITTA DI META.** It/Br 1959; RoF; 670; 58.3 × 1.8 (191 × 6); TSM; 14; ex CARISBROOKE CASTLE 1974; Bow door and ramp. Sister: **22711 OSBORNE CASTLE** (Br).

MFM H12
***22720 SUCHAN.** Ru/Ru —; MTV; 3800; 144.8 × 6.1 (475 × 20); TSR; 15. Similar (Ru flag): ***22721 CHUKOTKA *22722 SAKHALIN *22723 SIBIR.**

MFM H12
22730 MEI PYA. Bm/Br 1954; LT; 900; 61 × 3.8 (200 × 12.6); R; 11.

MFM H12
22740 NEPTUNE. US/US 1946; Cbl; 4000; 112.8 × 5.8 (170 × 18); TSR 14; ex WILLIAM H.G. BULLARD; Helicopter deck. Sister: **22741 ALBERT J. MEYER** (US).

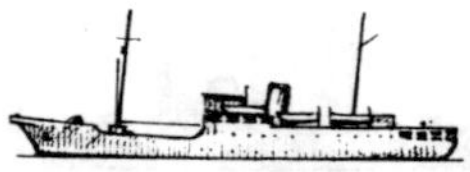

MFM H12
22750 ISOLDA. Ih/Ih 1953; Patrol Craft; 1200; 71 × 4 (233 × 12.11); TSR; 12.5; Irish Navy. Former lighthouse tender.

MFM H12
22760 LORD NELSON. Br/FRG 1961; FT; 900; 67.6 × 7.2 (222 × 23.8); M; —.

Twin Funnels

MFM H12
22770 TAIYO MARU No 62. Ja/Ja 1960; FT; 1500; 75 × 5.3 (245 × 17.4); M; 12.5. Sisters: **22771 CHALLWA No 2** (Pv) ex TAIYO MARU No 73 1976 **22772 SAM WON No 27** (Pa) ex TAIYO MARU No 61 1974 (Ja flag): **22773 TAIYO MARU No 63 22774 TAIYO MARU No 67 22775 TAIYO MARU No 68 22776 TAIYO MARU No 71 22777 TAIYO MARU No 72.**

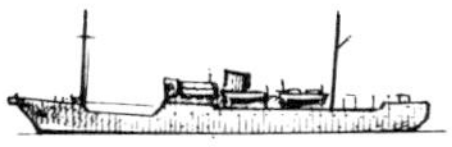

MFM H12
● **22800 ATLANTA.** Ih/Br 1959; LT; 1200; 70.7 × 4.8 (232 × 16); TSD-E; —.

MFM H123
● ⋆**22820 MONTE CASSINO.** Pd/Pd 1957; C; 3700; 108.2 × 6.6 (355 × 21.8); M; 12; **'B-511'** type.

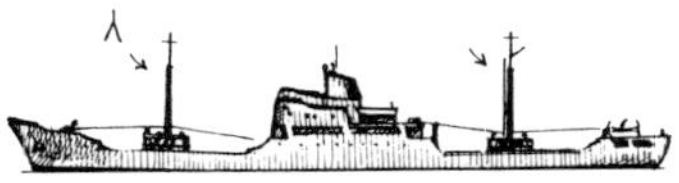

MFM H123
● ⋆**22840 ANDIZHAN.** Ru/DDR 1958; C; 3200; 104.2 × 6.6 (341 × 22); M; 12.5; **'LEVANT'** or **'KOVEL'** type. Sisters (Ru flag): ⋆**22841 BARABINSK** ⋆**22842 BIKIN** ⋆**22843 BOTSMAN ZOTOV** ex MONGUGAY ⋆**22844 CHELYABINSK** ⋆**22845 DALNERECHENSK** ex IMAN 1973 ⋆**22846 DALNIY** ⋆**22847 DAUGAVA** ⋆**22848 EMETSK** ⋆**22849 EYSK** ⋆**22850 HOROL** ⋆**22851 IZHMA** ⋆**22852 KHOLMOGORY** ⋆**22853 JASNOMORSK** ⋆**22854 KAPITAN VOOLENS** ex AMATA 1967 ⋆**22855 KOVEL** ⋆**22856 KYARDLA** ⋆**22857 LAZAREV** ⋆**22858 LOKSA** ⋆**22859 LUDZA** ⋆**22860 MAHTRA** ⋆**22861 MGA** ⋆**22862 MURMASH** ⋆**22863 NAGAEVO** ⋆**22864 NAMANGAN** ⋆**22865 POLYARNYY** ⋆**22866 POSYET** ⋆**22867 RAKVERE** ⋆**22868 RAZDOLNOYE** ⋆**22869 REVDA** ⋆**22870 RAZLIV** ⋆**22871 RENI** ⋆**22872 REPINO** ⋆**22873 SALSK** ⋆**22874 SARANSK** ⋆**22875 SHENKURSK** ⋆**22876 SOBOLEVO** ⋆**22877 SIGULDA** ⋆**22878 SYRVE** ⋆**22879 SINEGORSK** ⋆**22880 TURUKHANSK** ⋆**22881 VANINO** Ships vary slightly. Some have large radar mast from bridge. (Vn flag): ⋆**22882 HONG HA** ex ZAISAN ⋆**22883 SONGDA** ex SINEGORSK 1974 ⋆**22884 SONG KHAN** ex TURKESTAN 1975

MFM H12
22780 SEISELLA. Br/Br 1969; ST; 1100; 69.6 × 4.6 (229 × 15); M; —; ex SOUTHELLA 1980.

MFM H12
⋆**22790 Modified LEVANT or KOVEL type.** Ru/DDR c1958; —; 3400; M; 12.5; Modified from cargo vessel. May be Naval Auxilliary. Possible names (Ru flag): ⋆**22791 LAKHTA** ⋆**22792 VENUTA** ⋆**22793 VILYUY.**

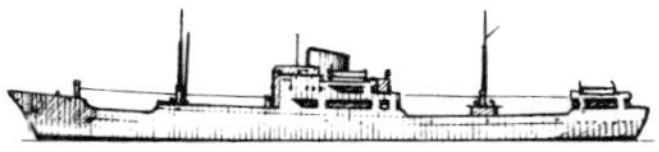

MFM H123
22810 BARBA. Pa/De 1954; C; 2800; 101.2 × 6 (332 × 19.7); M; 13; ex EURABIA WAVE 1979; ex SPERBER 1975; ex ABELONE VENDILA 1962.

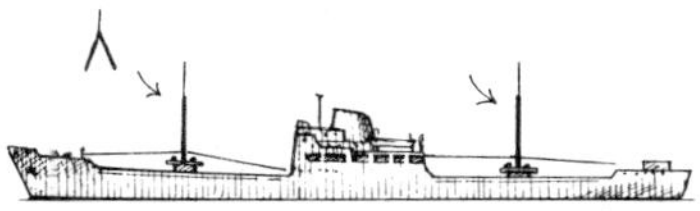

MFM H123
● **22830 DESANMAR.** Cy/Pd 1960; C; 3800; 108.2 × 6.6 (355 × 21.1); M; 14; ex TORRES **'B-31'** type. Sisters: **22831 MOSQUEIRO** (Bz) **22832 GUARUJA** (Bz) **22833 LEBLON** (Cy) **22834 VAL-DE-CAES** (Bz) ex DOM AMBROGIO 1967; ex TAMBAU 1961 (Cy flag): **22835 MERITA** ex LINA 1980; ex ITAPUA 1980 **22836 IOANNIS III** ex ANNA L; ex IRACEMA **22837 CIDADE DE ALCANTARA** (Bz) ex WALDEMAR PINHEIRO 1980; ex DOM ALEXANDRE 1967; ex BOA VIAGEM 1961

MFM H123
● **22890 MALDIVE CARRIER.** Pa/Br 1954; C; 2600; 95 × 5.8 (311 × 19); M; 11.5; ex RICKIE MILLER 1976; ex MINKARA 1970.

MFM H123
22900 NICOLO MARIA. It/it 1946; C; 1600; 84 × — (276 × —(; M; 11.5; ex ROSANGELA MARTINI 1974; ex ROSEANGELA MARTINI SECONDO 1964; ex VERGPORT 1962; ex MARIA VITTORIA 1957.

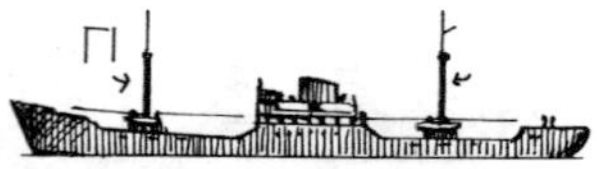

MFM H123
22910 ANNA MARTINI. It/It 1947; C; 1600; 84 × 5.3 (275 × 17.5); M; 12; ex SAN CARLO 1961; ex SABAUDIA.

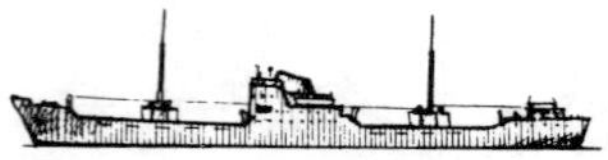

MFM H123
22920 KAROLOS. Cy/Br 1954; C; 2300; 93 × 5.7 (304 × 18.7); M; 10; ex STAVSUND 1968; ex HAMINA 1966.

MFM H123
22930 DEEPA RAYA. Ia/Ja 1948; PC; 2000; 89.6 × 5.6 (294 × 18.5); M; 11.5; ex BACHTERA KITA; ex TOKACHISAN MARU No 2 1962; ex TOKATISAN MARU 1960.

MFM H123
22940 LUIGI MARTINI. It/It 1942; C; 1600; 84.2 × 5.3 (276 × 17.6); M; 10.5; ex VERGMONT 1961; ex CARBONELLO 1956.

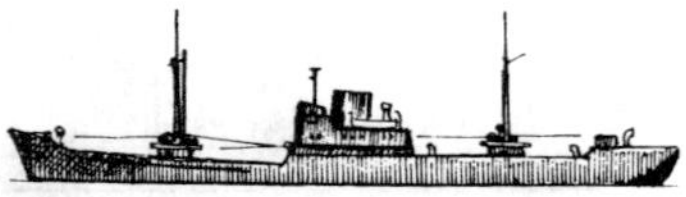

MFM H123
● **22950 TANIA.** Gr/FRG 1957; CP; 3600; 106.2 × 7.4 (348 × 24.6); M; 15; ex ANEMOS 1972; ex POLARIS 1971; ex VALERIA 1963. Sisters: **22951 MARIA** (Gr) ex VIRGILIA 1974 **22952 DEXENA** (Cy) ex ULSNIS 1976; ex VOLUMNIA 1969; ex LEALOTT 1966; ex VOLUMNIA 1963.

MFM H123
⋆**22960 SONG TRA LY.** Vn/Ja 1958; C; 3200; 106.2 × 6.4 (348 × 21.1); M; 12; ex PIONEER STAR, ex GOLDEN STAR; ex MINESHIMA MARU 1973. Similar: **22961 KWEI YING** (Pa) ex DYNAMIC ENTERPRISE 1974; ex KYOTO MARU 1970; ex TAISEI MARU 1967 **22962 KASAYSAYAN** (Pi) ex DIAMOND 1976; ex DIAMOND FLEUR 1973; ex TAIMEI MARU 1967 **22963 MING PING** (Pa); ex QUARRY BAY 1977; ex AN KANG 1976; ex UNITED ENDEAVOUR 1974; ex FOREMOST 1974; ex CONFIDENCE 1973; ex SANMEI MARU 1970; ex KOWA MARU 1969; ex SHOHO MARU 1967.

MFM H123
22970 SRI CHOL. Th/Ja 1958; C; 3400; 106.2 × 6.4 (348 × 21.1); M; 12; ex HIRA SHIMA MARU 1969.

MFM H123
22980 PETROS. Gr/De 1954; CP; 1600; 86 × 4.9 (283 × 16); M; 11; ex ANGELIKI 1976; ex ELPIS 1973; ex RIGMOR NIELSEN 1968.

MFM H123
22990 WESTGATE. Pa/Sw 1938; C; 1800; 97.5 × — (320 × —); TSM; 15; ex SAFCO I 1958; ex DUALA 1951.

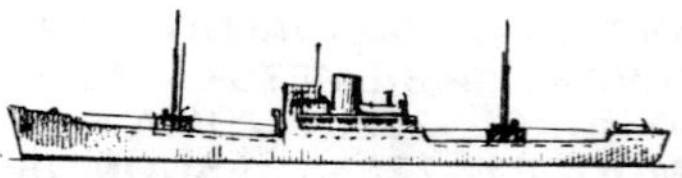

MFM H123
23000 MARY K. Gr/Ja 1957; C; 3200; 104.6 × 6.2 (343 × 20.5); M; 13; ex CARMENZITA 1975; ex VANESSA 1974; ex TOSEI MARU 1970.

MFM H123
23010 HAPPY. Pa/Br 1952; C; 2900; 103.7 × 6.2 (340 × 20.6); R; 10; ex HONEY 1975; ex LOZAN 1972; ex HAWKINGE 1965.

MFM H123
23020 SAMENA. Bz/Ca 1948; CP; 4300; 120 × 7.1 (393 × 23.6); R; 12; ex SIDERURGICA NOVE 1969; ex HEBE 1953.

MFM H123
23030 MING HO. Pa/Ja 1957; C; 3300; 105.7 × 6.4 (347 × 21); M; 12; ex MOUNT DAVIS; ex AN SHUN; ex YUNAN 1973; ex YUNAN MARU 1971; ex NISSHIN MARU 1967. Sister: **23031 NAGARAT** (Th) ex EASTER COMET, 1980; ex CHOZAN MARU 1957.

MFM H123
⋆**23060 INGUL.** Ru/Ru 1959; FC; 1600; 73.1 × 4.5 (262 × 17); M; 9.5.

MFM H123
23080 KRONOS. Pa/Br 1936; C; 800; 72 × 4 (237 × 13); TSM; 13.5; ex SAN MARCO 1974; ex LAIRDSCREST 1968.

MFM H123
● **23100 FALISEA.** My/Ca 1948; C; 1200; 74 × 4.3 (242 × 14); M; 12; ex CARTAXO 1972. Sister: **23101 PORT PYLOS** (Gr) ex PORTO FRIO 1980; ex TRANSFRIO 1978; ex COLARES 1966.

MFM H123
⋆**23120 MIN CHU No 13.** RC/Ja —; CP 2200; 98.1 × — (322 × —); R; 11.

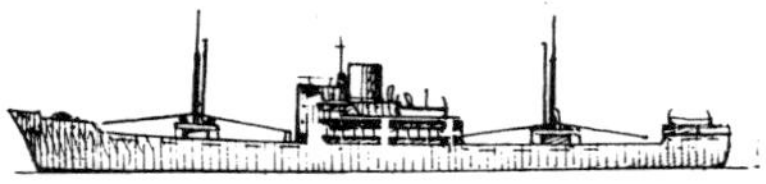

MFM H13
23130 KAPITAN ASLAN. Tu/Ja 1955; CP; 4200; 118 × 6.6 (387 × 21.6); T; 15.5; ex KAYSERI 1971.

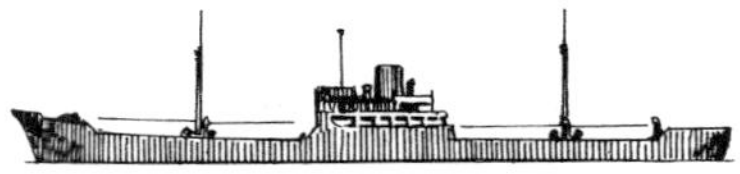

MFM H123
23040 KRUNG SIAM. Th/Ja 1957; CP; 4500; 113.9 × 7.5 (374 × 24.6); M; 12; ex ENOURA MARU 1970. Sister: **23041 SOVEREIGN RUBY** (Gr) ex YASUKUNI MARU 1971.

MFM H123
⋆**23050 MIN CHU No 9.** RC/RC 1954; C; 2200; 82.6 × 5.2 (271 × 17); R; 11.

MFM H123
23070 OROSEI. It/Fr 1952; Ch; 1800; 79.3 × 5.8 (260 × 19.1); R; —; ex CHLOE 1962; Converted from cargo ship. May be altered in appearance.

MFM H123
23090 DAMMAM. Si/Br 1927; C; 1300; 86 × 5.4 (282 × 17.7); M; 12; ex PALACIO 1958.

MFM H123
23110 TRANSAFRICAN I. Pa/Ne 1937; C; 200; 46 × 2.6 (152 × 8.5); M; 8.5; ex CASANA 1968; ex HADA 1948. Sister: **23111 OMAR** (Le) ex LASSI 1970; ex SAAD 1968; ex ZERO 1966; ex SANTONI 1958; ex GLADAN 1957; ex INLAND 1944; ex KARANAN 1939.

MFM H13
● **23140 EURYDICE.** Gr/Br 1957; C; 4900; 132.3 × 7.5 (434 × 24.7); M; 14.75; ex CITY OF GUILDFORD. Sisters: **23141 CITY OF DUNDEE** (Cy) ex DUNDEE 1980; ex CITY OF DUNDEE 1979 **23142 SUERTE** (Gr) ex CITY OF GLOUCESTER **23143 CITY OF LEEDS** (Cy) ex LEEDS 1980; ex CITY OF LICHFIELD **23144 ISLAND OF MARMARA** (Gr) ex CITY OF ST. ALBANS **23145 RIO DIAMANTO** (Gr) ex CITY OF WORCESTER.

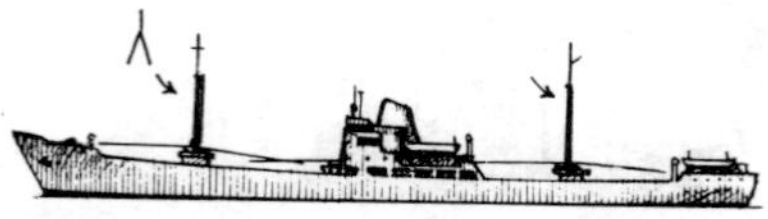

MFM H13
23150 LUCY. Gr/FRG 1952; C; 2900/4800; 118.6 × 6.2/7.7 (389 × 20.6/24.1); M; 13; ex KALLIARCHOS 1979; ex SEAPEARL 1976; ex MALOJA 1973.

MFM H13
23160 TAITUNG. Li/Fr 1957; C; 4700; 128.9 × 6.7 (423 × 21.1); M; 14.5; ex GALATEE 1976. Sisters: **23161 ARIANA** (Gr) ex PROTEE 1973 **23162 NEW STAR** (Pa); ex JAKARTA 1978; ex THESEE.

MFM H13
23170 ARAMIL. Sp/Sp 1963; C; 2500; 92.3 × 6.4 (303 × 21); M; 12.5.

MFM H13
● **23180 SEA BEAUTY.** Pa/Br 1949; CP; 2200/3200; 99.6 × 5.7/6.9 (327 × 18.6/20); M; 12; ex TYHI 1980; ex MILOS III 1979; ex CASTRENZA 1975; ex CRISTALLINA 1968.

MFM H13
23190 SAIBURI. Th/Hong Kong 1937; C; 600; 49.2 × 3.6 (161 × 11.8); M; 9; ex HUNG HAI 1948; ex MOAMOA 1946.

MFM H13
23200 AGIOS NECTARIOS. Cy/FRG 1955; CP; 1600; 84 × 4.5 (277 × 15); M; 12; ex ANTOFAGASTA 1977.

MFM H13
23210 VENUS II. Do/It 1947; C; 900; 67 × 4.2 (221 × 13.7); M; 10.5; ex ANDY; ex GRETA H 1959; ex BAKKE BOY 1952; ex VAGAN 1951; Lengthened 1960.

MFM H13
23220 DON CAMILO. Pi/FRG 1951; CP; 2400; 105 × 6.2 (345 × 20.3); M; 16; ex LICHTENSTEIN 1968. Sister: **23221 DONA JULIETA** (Pi) ex DON LORENZO; ex LIEBENSTEIN 1968.

MFM H13
23230 WAHENO. Pa/FRG 1959; C; 4200; 114.9 × 7.7 (377 × 25.4); M; 14.5; ex KAETHE JEBSEN 1977. Sister: **23232 WAH FAI** (Pa) ex CLARA JEBSEN.

MFM H13
23240 CAVO SIDERO. Gr/FRG 1954; CP; 2700; 93.6 × 7.1 (307 × 18.7); M; 14; ex PIRAEUSBURG 1973; ex CASABLANCA 1973.

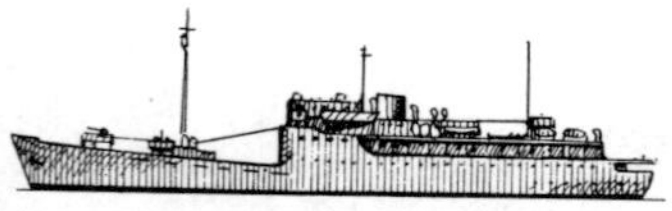

MFM H2
23250 BAHIA AGUIRRE. Ar/Ca 1950; Transport; 3800; 95 × 7.9 (335 × 13.8); TSM; 16; Argentine Navy. Sister: **23251 BAHIA BUEN SUCESO** (Ar).

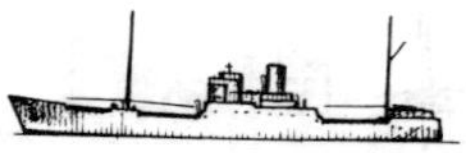

MFM H2
23260 AL MADANI. Ku/Br 1937; C; 800; 68 × 4.9 (223 × 16.1) M; 9; ex TOULA 1975; ex NISSOS SIFNOS 1969; ex CRANE 1964.

MFM H2
23270 OURANOUPOLIS. Gr/Br 1949; C; 1200/1600; 79 × 4.6/5.7 (259 × 15.2/17.5); TSM; 12; ex AUK 1965.

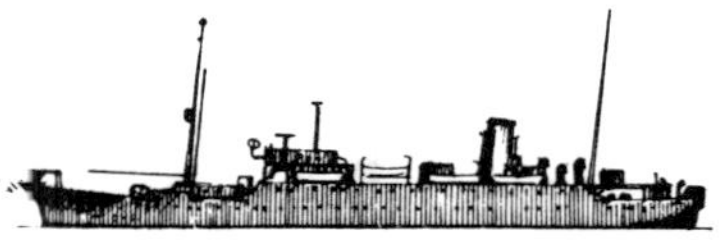

MFM H2
23280 JOHN W MACKAY. Br/Br 1922; Cbl; 4100; 110.2 × 7.7 (361.6 × 25.6); TSR; 11.5.

MFM H2
23290 MARIB. Ye/Ne 1938; C; 460; 47.9 × 2.8 (157 × 9.3); M; —; ex FRONTIER 1952.

MFM H2
23300 RIO SAMO. Sp/Ca 1941; C; 800; 62.6 × 5.3 (205 × 17.6); M; 14.5; ex LA CEIBA 1947; ex ARVIDA.

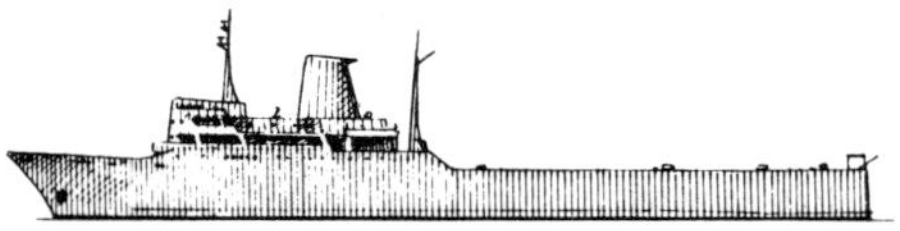

MFM H2
23310 EUROPIC FERRY. Br/Br 1968; RoCF; 4200; 137.6 × 4.6 (451 × 15.2); TSM; 19.25; Stern door.

MFM H2
23320 KAMASIN. Pa/Br 1958; RoCF; 1600; 103 × 4.4 (338 × 14.5); TSM; 14; ex IONIC FERRY 1976; Stern door/Ramp. Sister: **23321 NASIM II** (Pa) ex BARDIC FERRY 1976.

MFM H2
● **23330 CERDIC FERRY.** Br/Br 1961; RoCF; 2500; 110.2 × 3.9 (361 × 12.1); TSM; 14; Stern door/ramp. Sister (Br flag): **23331 DORIC FERRY** Similar (lengthened): **23332 GAELIC FERRY.**

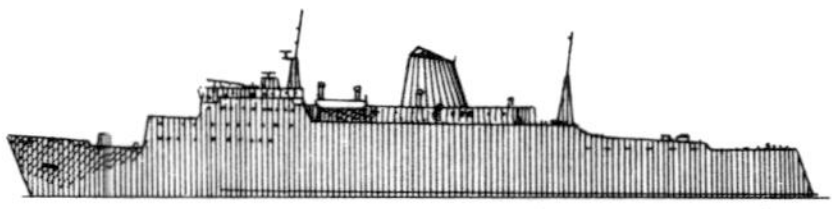

MFM H2
23340 ARAHANGA. NZ/Br 1972; RoC/TF; 3900; 127.5 × 4.9 (418 × 16.1); TSM; 17; stern door.

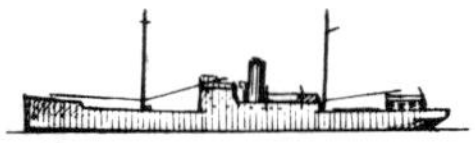

MFM H2
23350 JURANDY. Bz/US 1920; C; 1400; 69.2 × 5.1 (227 × 17.1); R; —; ex RIO BRAVO 1955; ex LLOYD CUARTO 1952; ex TAKU 1946; ex ORMES 1939.

MFM H2
23360 IJZER. Be/Be 1954; LS; 1200; 66.9 × 3.6 (220 × 11.1); M; 15.

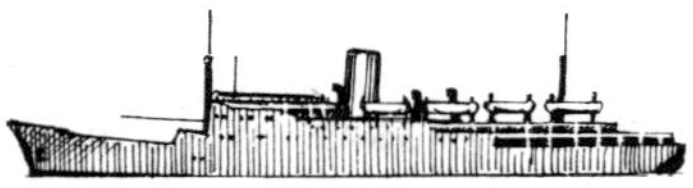

MFM H2
⋆23370 MIN CHU No 3. RC/Ja 1940; CP; 3200; 103.9 × 4.3 (431 × 14); R & LPT; 13.5.

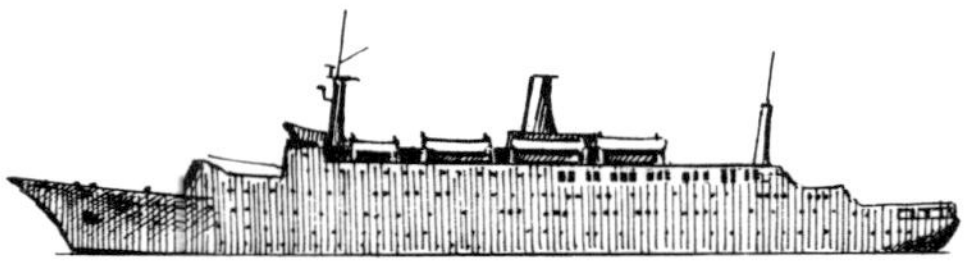

MFM H2
23380 WORLD RENAISSANCE. Gr/Fr 1966; P; 11700; 150 × 6.2 (492 × 20.5); TSM; 18.5; ex HOMERIC; ex RENAISSANCE.

MFM H2
⋆23390 ZVEZDA. Ru/DDR 1957; F; 350; 39.3 × 3.5 (129 × 11.4); M; 10. Sisters (Ru flag): **⋆23391 ZARNITSA ⋆23392 YUG.**

MFM H2
23400 CABLE ENTERPRISE. Br/Br 1964; Cbl; 4400; 113.2 × 5 (371 × 19.1); TSD-E; 15. Similar: **23401 RETRIEVER** (Br).

MFM H2
★**23410 RYBAK;** Ru/DDR 1968; ST; 1000; 63,1 × 4.8 (207 × 15.6); M; —; **'JUNGE WELT'** class. Sisters: ★**23411 RYBACHKA** (Ru) (DDR flag): ★**23412 ARTHUR BECKER** ★**23413 BRUNO TESCH** ★**23414 CARLO SCHONHAAR** ★**23415 ELVIRA EISENSCHNEIDER** ★**23416 ERICH STEINFURTH** ★**23417 EUGEN SCHONHAAR** ★**23418 GRETE WALTER** ★**23419 HANNO GUNTHER** ★**23420 HEINZ KAPELLE** ★**23421 HEINZ PRIESS** ★**23422 HERBERT BAUM** ★**23423 HERBERT TSCHAPE** ★**23424 HERTA LINDER** ★**23425 KARL WOLF** ★**23426 MAGNUS POSER** ★**23427 PETER GORING** ★**23428 PHILIPP MULLER** ★**23429 RUDI ARNT** ★**23430 RUDOLF SCHWARZ** ★**23431 WALTER BARTH** ★**23432 WERNER KUBE.**

MFM H2
★**23440 AFALA;** Bu/Pd 1974; FT; 2500; 89 × 5.2 (292 × 17.3); M; 15.5; **'B-418'** type. Sisters: (Bu flag): ★**23441 AKTINJA** ★**23442 ALFEUS** ★**23443 ARGONAUT** ★**23444 FIZALIA** ★**23445 KAPRELA** ★**23446 OFELIA** ★**23447 ROTALIA** ★**23448 SAGITA** (Pd flag): ★**23449 AMAREL** ★**23450 BONITO** ★**23451 DELFIN** ★**23452 GARNELA** ★**23453 GRINWAL** ★**23454 HAJDUK** ★**23455 HUMBAK** ★**23456 KALMAR** ★**23457 MORS** ★**23458 PARMA** ★**23459 REKIN** ★**23460 WALEN** The following are identical but **'B-417'** type: (Pd flag): ★**23461 KOLIAS** ★**23462 MANTA** ★**23463 MARLIN** ★**23464 ORCYN** ★**23465 ORLEN** ★**23466 OTOL** ★**23467 PROFESSOR BOGUCKI** ★**23468 TAZAR** ★**23469 TUNEK** (Iq flag): **23470 AL AHWAR 23471 AL KAHLA 23472 AL RAZAZA 23473 SAWA;** Launched as SAIRA.

MFM H2
★**23480 LUCHEGORSK class;** Ru/Ru 1969; FT; 3000; 83,9 × 5.7 (275 × 19); M; 12. Sisters (Ru flag): ★**23481 MATEMATIK** ★**23482 MYS SINYAVINA** ★**23483 MYS YEGOROVA** ★**23484 MYS YELAGINA** ★**23485 RUSNE** ★**23486 LUNOKHOD I** ★**23487 SIMYAVINO** ★**23488 VIKTOR KHUDYAKOV** ★**23489 MYS BELKINA** ★**23490 LUCHEGORSK** ★**23491 MYS BOBROVA** ★**23492 MYS GAMOVA** ★**23493 MYS KRYLOVA** ★**23494 MYS LAZARYEVA** ★**23495 MYS OBRUCHYEVA** ★**23496 MYS BARANOVA** ★**23497 MYS GRINA** ★**23498 MYS MALTSYEVA** ★**23499 MYS NADEZHDY** ★**23500 MYS OREKHOVA** ★**23501 MYS OSIPOVA** ★**23502 MYS YERMAK** ★**23503 MYS YUDINA** ★**23504 RUDOLF SIRGE** ★**23505 RUDOLF VAKMAN** ★**23506 SAMSHIT** ★**23507 SUDUVA** ★**23508 TRAKAY** ★**23509 TURKUL** ★**23510 TYMLAT** ★**23511 VOLDEMAR AZIN** ★**23512 BURAN** ★**23513 IVAN GREN** ★**23514 KVARTS** ★**23515 OTTO RYASTAS** ★**23516 TIRASPOL** ★**23517 VULKAN** ★**23518 ALEKSANDR BOGOLYUBOV** ★**23519 KUULUNDA** ★**23520 GDOV** ★**23521 KRECHET** ★**23522 XV SYEZD PROFSOYUZOV** ★**23523 DZUKIYA** ★**23524 DZINTERKRASTS** ★**23525 VALKA** ★**23526 TRUSKAVETS** ★**23527 PSKOV** ★**23528 ALEKSANDRIT** ★**23529 TIGIL** ★**23530 PETROZAVODSK** ★**23531 KARGOPAL** ★**23532 NIKOLAYEVSKIY KOMSOMOLETS** ★**23533 PAUDZHA** ★**23534 FEODOR OKK** ★**23535 IOKHANNES SEMPER** ★**23536 KARAGAT** ★**23537 MIKHAIL BARSUKOV** ★**23538 MYS SHELIKHOVA** ★**23539 KAZALINSK** ★**23540 PETROKREPOST** ★**23541 SAMARA** ★**23542 KAZATIN** ★**23543 KOMSOMOL** ★**23544 LATVII** ★**23545 TOLBACHIK** ★**23546 TUMAN-2** ★**23547 DAYNAVA** ★**23548 DZINTARZEME** ★**23549 AKVAMARIN** ★**23550 GRAD** ★**23551 KALAR** ★**23552 KALITVA** ★**23553 KANDALAKSHA** ★**23554 KHAYRYUZOVO** ★**23555 KIRIR** ★**23556 KLYUCHEYSKOY** ★**23557 KOTAYKA** ★**23558 KORENGA** ★**23559 KRASNOGVARDEYETS** ★**23560 KUSHKA** ★**23561 LABRADOR** ★**23562 MALKI** ★**23563 MEDIK** ★**23564 METEOROLOG** ★**23565 MARS - 2** ★**23566 NIDA** ★**23567 NIKOLAY PAPIVIN** ★**23568 PASSAT - 2** ★**23569 RIKHARD MIRRING** The following are Fishery Research Vessels: ★**23570 IKHTIANDR** ★**23571 PROGRESS** ★**23572 SALEKHARD** ★**23573 VOLZHANIN**

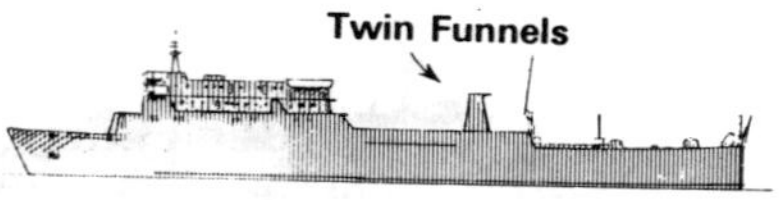

MFM H2
23580 WUPPERTAL; FRG/FRG 1977; RoC; 1600; 116.31 × 5.3 (381.59 × 17.39); TSM; 16; ex CANAIMA 1979; ex WUPPERTAL 1978; Stern ramp.

MFM H23
★**23590 PAMYATI KIROVA;** Ru/US 1943; FFMS; 8500; 134 × 8.1 (442 × 28); R; 10; ex HORACE BUSHNELL 1943; Converted **'LIBERTY'** type cargo ship.

MFM H3
23600 CHARRUA; Bz/Sw 1951; C; 1900; 95.4 × 5.8 (313 × 19); M; 15; ex CARLSHAM 1953. Sister: **23601 SAO JOSE** (Bz) ex MINUANO 1977.

MFMC H
23610 MIMIKA L; Gr/De 1949; P; 4200; 114.5 × 5.6 (375 × 18.3); TSM; 20; ex COPENHAGEN 1969; ex KRONPRINSESSE INGRID 1969.

MFMC H
23620 FEDERAL MAPLE; Br/Ca 1961; PCF; 3200; 90.8 × 4.7 (298 × 15.7); M; 15.

MFMC H
23630 REGINA MARIS; Sg/FRG 1966; P; 5800; 118 × 5 (387 × 16.5); TSM; 20; ex FRANKFURT I 1980; ex MERCATOR I 1979; ex REGINA MARIS 1976.

MFMC H
⋆**23640 VLADIMIR KAVRAYSKIY;** Ru/— 1962; RS; 2500 Dspl; 68 × 5.5 (223 × 18.1); TrSM; 13.75; Converted from 'Dobrynya Nikitch class' (IB); Helicopter platform aft.

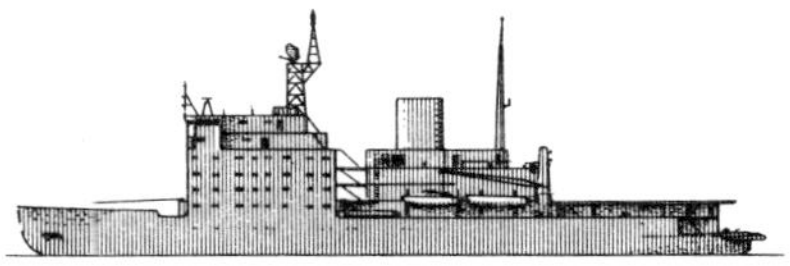

MFMC H1
23650 ALMIRANTE IRIZAR; Ar/Fi 1978; IB/P; 10100; 119.31 × 9.5 (391.44 × 31.17); TSM; 16.5; Helicopter deck.

MFMC H1
23660 TOR; Sw/Fi 1964; IB; 4200; 84.5 × 6.2 (277 × 20.4); TSD-E; 18. Similar: **23661 TARMO** (Fi) **23662 VARMA** (Fi) **23663 NJORD** (Sw).

MFMC H1
23670 ALE; Sw/Fi 1973; IB; 488 Dspl; 46 × 5 (151 × 16.3); TSM; 14.

MFMCK H13
23680 JOHN BISCOE; Br/Br 1956; RS; 1600; 67.06 × 5.01 (220 × 16.44); D-E; 11; Antarctic research.

MFMF H2
⋆**23690 SASSNITZ;** DDR/FRG 1959; P/RoVC; 6200; 137 × 5.8 (450 × 19); TSM; 18.

MFMF H
● **23700 OLAU KENT;** De/FRG 1970; RoPCF; 4200; 109 × 4.6 (357 × 15); TSM; 18.5; ex APOLLO 1976. Sisters: **23701 VIKING I** (Fi) **23702 WASA EXPRESS** (Fi) ex VIKING III 1976 **23703 COROMUEL** (Me) **23704 PUERTO VALLARTA** (Me) **23705 BOTNIA EXPRESS** (Fi) ex DIANA 1979 **23706 EARL GRANVILLE** (Br) ex VIKING 4 1980.

MFMF H
23710 IONIAN STAR; Gr/FRG 1964; PRoCF; 6100; 115 × 4.7 (378 × 15); TM; 20; ex LIEF ERIKSSON 1976; ex PRINS BERTIL 1966. Similar: ⋆**23711 WAWEL** (Pd) ex GUSTAV VASA 1973.

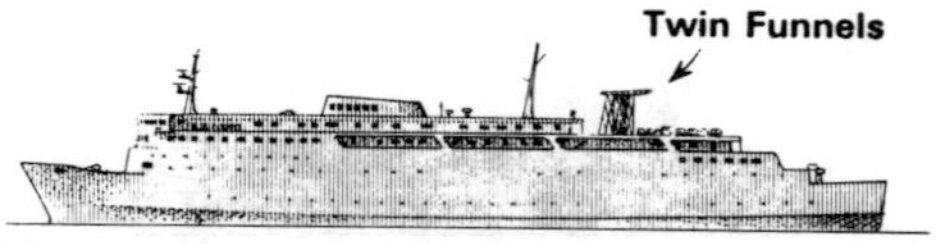

MFMF H
23720 IZU MARU No 3; Ja/Ja 1972; RoPF; 7500; 137.85 × 5.61 (452.26 × 18.41); TSM; 21.5; ex CASSIOPEIA: Bow and stern ramps. Sister: **23721 IZU MARU No 11;** ex ALBATROSS.

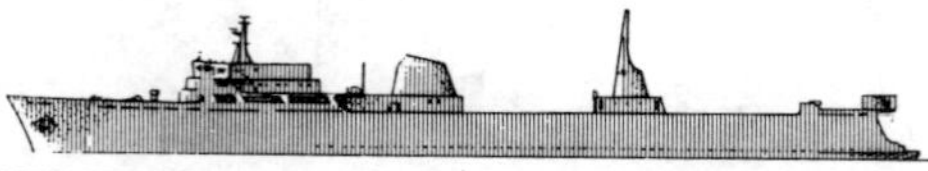

MFMF H
23730 HITAKA MARU; Ja/Ja 1969; PF; 4100; 144.5 × 5.2 (474 × 17); M; 18. Sisters (Ja flag): **23731 HIYAMA MARU 23732 ISHIKARI MARU 23733 OSHIMA MARU 23734 SORACH MARU 23735 TOKACHI MARU.**

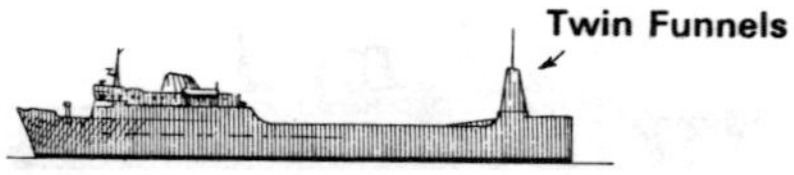

MFMF H2
23740 CALA MARSAL; Sp/Sp 1971; RoC; 900; 88.91 × 4.18 (291.69 × 13.71); m; 17. Sister: **23741 CALA LLONGA** (Sp).

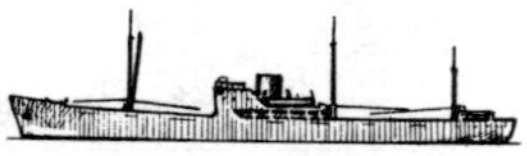

MFMK H
23750 MEROWAH; My/Br 1949; CP: 1200; 80.2 × 5.1 (236 × 16.8); M; 12; ex ORIBI 1971; ex KONG DAG 1958.

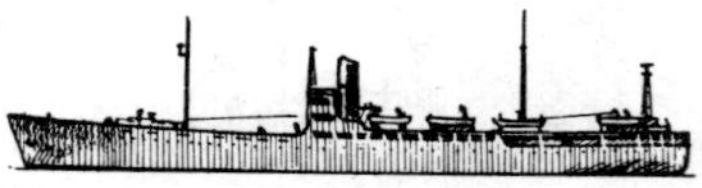

MFMK H
***23760 BATAYSK;** Ru/Pd 1955; TS; 4900; 108.3 × 6.1 (355 × 21); R; 11.5; Converted from **'B-31'** type cargo vessel.

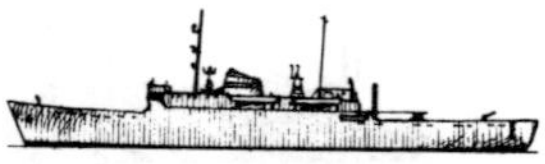

MFMK H
***23770 ALEKSANDR IVANOVICH VOEYKOV;** Ru/Ru 1959; RS; 3200; 84.7 × 5.5 (278 × 18); M; 13; Also known as **A.I. VOEYKOV;** Converted **'MAYAKOYSKIY'** class trawler. Sister: ***23771 YU M SHOKALSKIY** (Ru).

MFM H
23780 ORPHEUS; Gr/Br 1948/70; P; 5100; 111.82 × 4.88 (366.86 × 16.01); TSM; 15; ex THESEUS 1969; ex MUNSTER I 1968; ex MUNSTER 1968; Converted from ferry 1970.

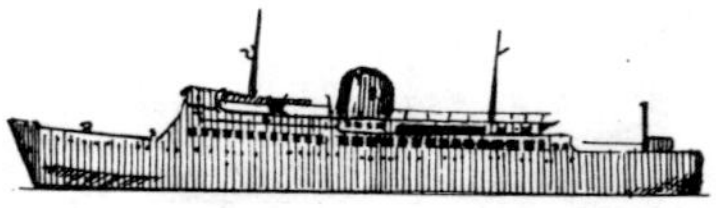

MFMK H
23790 AL PASHA; Si/Fr 1969; P; 5300; 108.7 × 4.8 (357 × 16.8); TSM; 18; ex NAPOLEON 1974; Side doors.

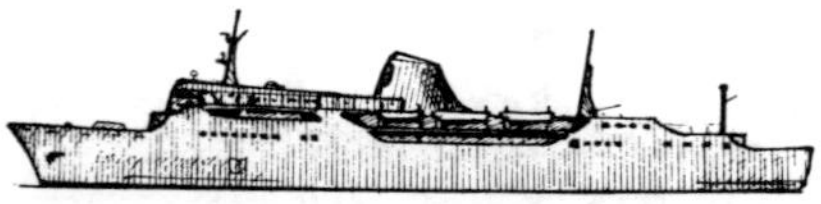

MFMK H
23800 VERGINA; Gr/Be 1964; RoF; 6400; 127.8 × 5.1 (419 × 16.1); TSM; 18; ex GOLDEN SKY 1980; ex SAUDI MOON; ex EL GRECO 1976; ex DAN 1976; ex BILU 1967.

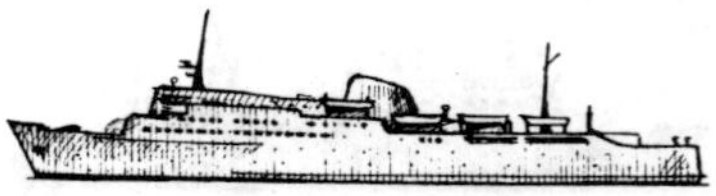

MFMK H
23810 SAMAINA; Gr/FRG 1962; RoF; 3800; 110 × 4.5 (361 × 14.8); TSM; 18; ex MARY POPPINS 1976; ex GOSTA BERLING 1975; ex ESCAPADE 1967; ex GOSTA BERLING 1967; ex NILS HOLGERSSON 1967.

MFMK H
23820 ST. CLAIR; Br/FRG 1965; RoF; 4500; 123.3 × 4.8 (404 × 15.7); TSM; —; ex TERJE VIGEN 1977; ex S F PANTHER 1975; ex PETER PAN 1973. Sister: **23821 EUROPAFARJAN IV** ex OLIVER TWIST 1978.

MFMK H
23830 ELBJORN; De/De 1954; IB; 900; 47 × 4.4 (157 × 14.5); D-E; 14.

MFMK H1
23840 EVANGELISTRIA IV; Pa/As 1959; ST; 1200; 75.9 × 4.4 (249 × 16); TSM; —.

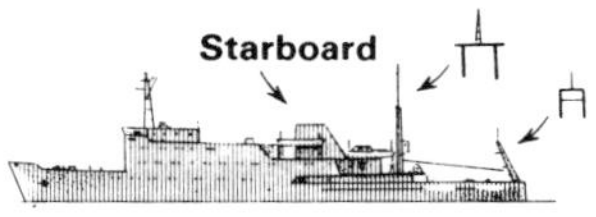

MFMK H1
⋆**23860 PLUTON;** Ru/Pd 1978; RS; approx 2000 dst; 82 × 4 (268.9 × 13.1); M; 18. Sisters (Ru flag): ⋆**23861 GIDROLOG** ⋆**23862 PEGAS** ⋆**23863 PERSEY** ⋆**23864 SENEZH** ⋆**23865 STRELETS** ⋆**23866 TAYGA** ⋆**23867 YUG** ⋆**23868 ZODIAC.**

MFMK H1
23890 NICOLAOS RIGAS; Gr/It 1958; C; 3600; 103.4 × 7.5 (339 × 24.8); M; 12.5; ex AUSTRALE 1976; ex UT PROSPERATIS 1969; ex SAN SEBASTIANO 1962.

MFMK H1
23910 NORTHERN ICE; Cy/FRG 1959; R; 4100; 126 × 7 (413 × 23); M; 17.75; ex CACIQUE YANQUETRUZ 1973; ex CAP VALIENTE 1970.

MFMK H1
● **23930 SIMALI 1.** Th/FRG 1951; CP; 2700/4300; 116.3 × —/7.3 (382 × —/24); M; 13; ex SIAM QUEEN 1976; ex NIKITAS II 1974; ex NORDHAFF 1971; ex NAGUILAN 1969; ex ATLAS 1959. Sister: **23931 DIANA** (Gr) ex NORDMARK 1974; ex DON PEDRO 1967; ex LEVANTE 1066.

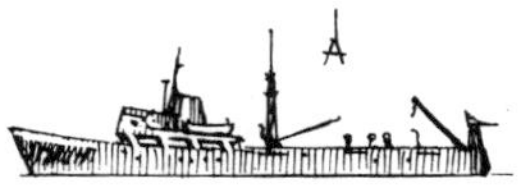

MFMK H1
23850 WESTERN ARCTIC; Pa/It 1965; FT; 1600; 74.4 × 4.9 (244 × 16); D-E; —; ex ASPA TERZO 1979.
Sister: **23851 ASPA QUARTO** (It).

MFMK H1
⋆**23870 MIN CHU No 17;** RC/RC 1959; PC; 2500; 90.5 × — (297 × —); M; 12.5.

MFMK H1
⋆**23880 NORILSK;** Ru/It 1951; PC; 3500; 101.9 × 5.5 (334 × 17.11); TSM; 13.

MFMK H1
23900 ZOE II; Gr/It 1956; C; 2700; 111 × 7.2 (365 × 23.8); M; 15; ex THESEUS 1980; ex TASSOS TSIRIS 1979; ex INDIANA 1975.

MFMK H1
23920 GIL EANES. Po/Po 1955; Hospital and Depot Ship; 3500; 98.6 × 5.5 (324 × 18); TSM;

MFMK H1
23940 DANBJORN. De/De 1965; IB; 3000; 75.4 × 6 (247 × 19.8); TSD-E; —. Sister: **23941 ISBJORN** (De).

MFMK H1
23950 ODEN. Sw/Fi 1957; IB; 3400; 83.5 × 7 (274 × 23); TSD-E; —.

MFMK H1
23960 HANSE. FRG/Fi; 1965; IB; 2800; 74.7 × 5.9 (245 × 19.2); TSD-E; —.

MFMK H1
★23970 KAPITAN BELOUSOV. Ru/Fi 1955; IB; 3700; 83.2 × 7 (273 × 23); TSD-E; 15. Sisters (Ru flag): **★23971 KAPITAN MELEKHOV ★23972 KAPITAN VORONIN.**

MFMK H1
23980 MURTAJA. Fi/Fi 1959; IB; 2700; 74.2 × 5.8 (243 × 19); TSD-E; —. Sister: **23981 KARHU** (Fi) Similar (Heavy foremast): **23982 SAMPO** (Fi).

MFMK H1
23990 ABERTHAW FISHER. Br/Br 1966; RoC; 2400; 86.6 × 4.6 (284 × 15.1); TSD-E; 11. Sister: **23991 KINGSNORTH FISHER** (Br).

MFMK H12
24000 DANIA. Pa/Br 1957; PC; 1800; 72.1 × 5 (238 × 16.5); R; 12.5; ex HATIM; ex CHRISTOS K; ex DARWIN 1973.

MFMK H12
24010 BRITISH VISCOUNT. Br/Ih 1960; Submersible Support Ship; 1600; 88 × 5.1 (280 × 16.1); —; —; ex VICKERS VISCOUNT 1980; ex MEATH; Converted Livestock Carrier.

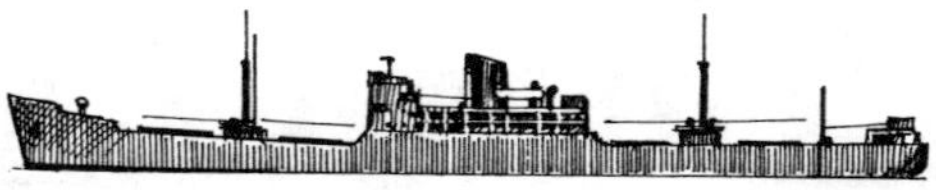

MFMK H12
★24020 MIHO PRACAT. Ys/Br 1959; C; 6200/8800; 145.7 × —/9.2 (478 × —/30.2); M; 12.5; ex DURHAM TRADER 1965.

MFMK H123
★24030 VOLGOLES. Ru/Pd 1960; C/TC; 4600; 123.9 × 6.9 (406 × 22.8); M; 14.75; **'B-514'** type. Similar (Ru flag): **★24031 ABAGURLES ★24032 ABAKANLES ★24033 ALAPAYEVSKLES ★24034 ALATYRLES ★24035 ALDANLES ★24036 ANADYRLES ★24037 ANDOMALES ★24038 ANGARSKLES ★24039 ARKHANGELSKLES ★24040 BRYANSKLES ★24041 DVINOLES ★24042 KAPITAN BELOSHAPKIN** ex ADIMILES **★24043 KOMILES ★24044 PRIMORLES ★24045 SEVERLES** The following are of the later **'B-45'** type (Ru flag): **★24047 BELOMORSKLES ★24048 ALTAYLES ★24049 ARGUN ★24050 AMURSKLES ★24051 ANGARLES ★24052 BALAKHNALES ★24053 BUREYALES ★24054 BRATSKLES ★24055 BUKHARA ★24056 BARNAUL ★24057 BELOZERSKLES ★24058 BEREZINALES ★24059 BAYKONUR ★24060 BOBRUYSKLES ★24061 BRASLAVLES ★24062 BODAYBO ★24063 DARASUN ★24064 DZHURMA ★24065 GRODEKOVO ★24066 ELEKTROSTAL ★24067 KRASKINO ★24068 KUNGUR ★24069 KANDALAKSHALES ★24070 KRANSK ★24071 KHATANGA ★24072 KHOLMSK ★24073 KOVDA ★24074 MIRONYCH ★24075 MEKHANIK RYBASHUK ★24076 NORDVIK ★24077 NARYAN—MAR ★24078 NIKOLAY MIRONOV ★24079 OREKHOVO—ZUYEVO ★24080 PORONIN ★24081 KAPITAN ABAKUMOV** ex TULOMALES **★24082 PRIDYATLES ★24083 PUTYATIN ★24084 POBYEDINO ★24085 RUZA ★24086 RUBTSOVSK ★24087 SAKHALINLES ★24088 SHADRINSK ★24089 SAYANLES ★24090 SEGEZHALES ★24091 SALEKHARD ★24092 SHATURA ★24093 RAYCHIKHINSK ★24094 SELENGALES ★24095 SUNGARI ★24096 TOBOLLES ★24097 TAYGONOS ★24098 TULOMA ★24099 TYUMEN ★24100 TAYGA ★24101 TAYSHEN ★24102 ULAN-UDE ★24103 URALLES ★24104 VETUGALES ★24105 VYCHEGDALES ★34106 VILYUYLES ★24107 VOSRESENSK ★24108 VALDAYLES ★24109 VOLGA** ex KONOSHALES **★24110 VORKUTA ★24111 ZABAYKALSK**

MFMK H13
24120 CHRISTINA. Pa/Br 1948; C; 3000; 109 × 6.4 (358 × 20.11); R; 10.5; ex BASIL 1968; ex DUNSTAN 1966; ex SALLUST 1958; ex DUNSTA 1951.

MFMK H13
24130 WATAMPONE. Ia/FRG 1959; C; 2200; 85 × 5.2 (279 × 17.1); M; 12. Sisters (Ia flag): **24131 WAKOLO 24132 WANDEBORI 24133 WARISANO 24134 WATUDAMBO.**

MFMK H13
24140 MAURITIUS. Br/FRG 1955; PC; 2100; 84.8 × 5.2 (278 × 17.1); M; 11.5.

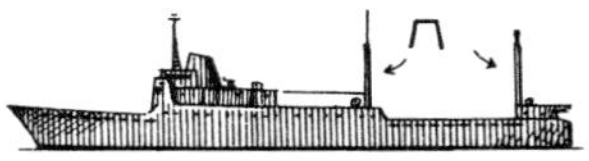

MFMK H2
● **24150 SEEFREEZE ATLANTIC.** US/US 1969; FT; 1600; 90 × 5.7 (314 × 18.6); D-E; —; Sister: **24151 ROYAL SEA** (US) ex SEEFREEZE PACIFIC 1973.

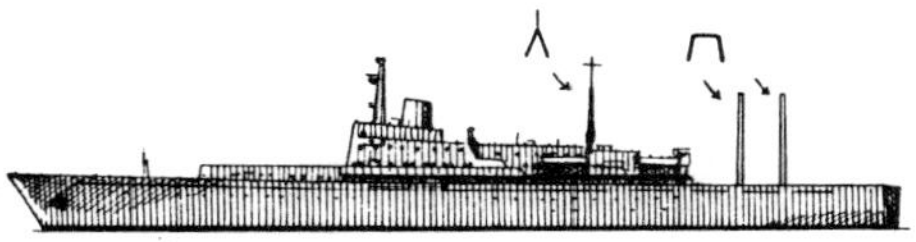

$MFMK_2$ H
★**24160 JUNGE GARDE.** DDR/DDR 1967; FT; 10200; 141.4 × 7.8 (464 × 25.9); D-E; 14. Sister: ★**24161 JUNGE WELT** (DDR).

MFMKM H1
24170 ANTON DOHRN. FRG/FRG 1963; RS/ST; 1900; 83.3 × 5.2 (230 × 17.1); D-E; —; ex WALTHER HERWIG 1972.

MFM_2 H
24180 MEROWAH. My/Br 1949; CP; 1200; 80.2 × 5.1 (263 × 16.8); M; 12; ex ORIBI 1971; ex KONG DAG 1958.

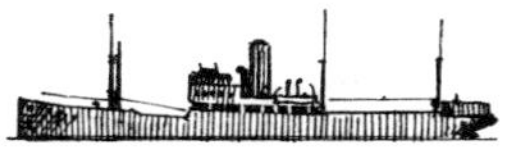

MFM_2 H
24190 ANITA. Pa/No 1928; C; 1200; 77 × 5 (253 × 16.5); R; 12.5; ex BONN 1961.

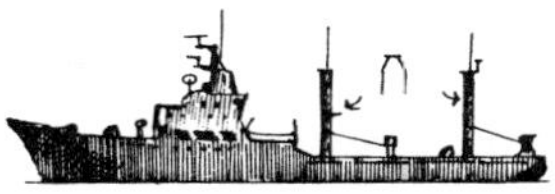

MFM_2 H1
24200 CIDADE DE AVEIRO. Po/Po 1966; ST; 2300; 83.4 × 5.6 (273 × 18.8); D-E; —.

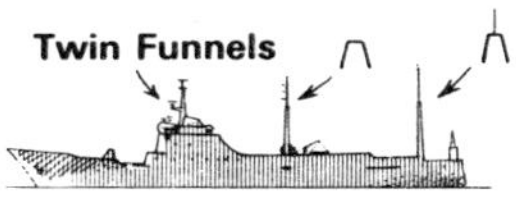

MFM_2 H12
● **24210 PRINCESS ANNE.** Br/Br 1974; ST; 1500; 72.79 × 5.18 (238.8 × 16.99); M; 14.25.

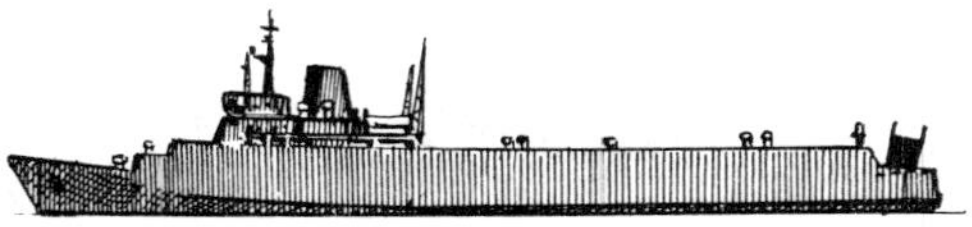

MFMR H
24220 TOKYO MARU Ja/Ja 1976; RoCF; 6700; 147.5 × 6.6 (484 × 21.7); M; 19.

MFN H
24230 TUSTUMENA. US/US 1964; F; 2200; 90 × 4.4 (295 × 14.6); TSM; —; Lengthened 1969.

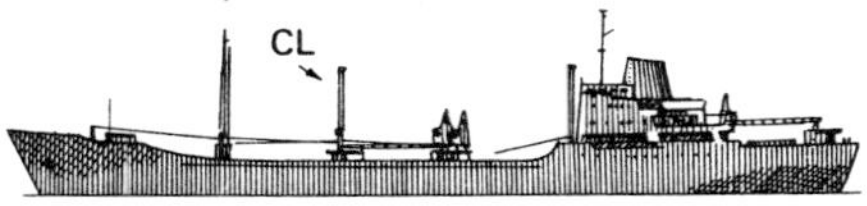

MKC_2KMFC H13
24240 SCHLOSS TARASP. Sd/Fi 1961; C; 4200; 135 × 8.6 (443 × 28); M; 16; ex TATRINA 1980; ex THEBELAND 1976; Lengthened 1963. Sisters: ★**24241 RUI CHANG** (RC) ex TYRUSLAND **24242 BRIGHTNESS** (Pa) ex TROJALAND.

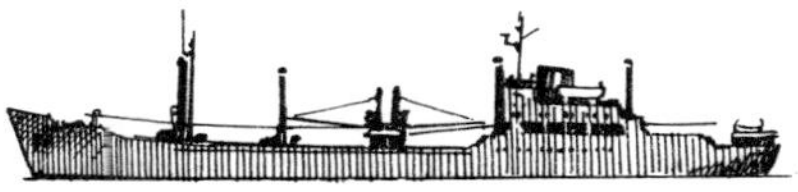

MKC_2KMFK H13
● ★**24250 AMAL EXPRESS.** Hu/FRG 1956; C; 3500; 119.79 × 6.5 (394 × 21.4); M; 15; ex TIMMERLAND 1975. Sisters: **24251 BRAVOALTONA** (Gr) ex ALTONA 1976; ex THULELAND 1975 **24252 TUNDRALAND** (Ca).

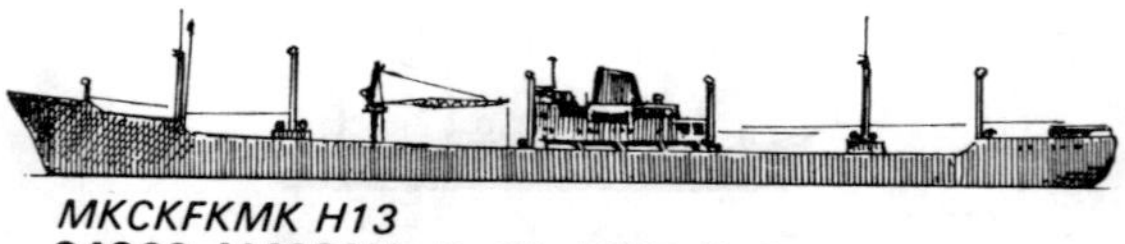

MKCKFKMK H13
24260 ALMONA. Pa/Br 1957; Pt.Con; 7700/10100; 171.7×8.1/9.1 (564×26.8/30); M; 18; ex WARRI EXPRESS 1980; ex TEMERAIRE 1978; Lengthened and converted from cargo vessel 1970.

MKCMFKM H1
● **24280 RIO CORRIENTES.** Ar/Ys 1962; C; 8500; 157.3×8.3 (516×27.3); M; —. Sisters (Ar flag): **24281 RIO CARCARANA 24282 RIO COLORADO 24283 LAGO NAHUEL HUAPI 24284 LAGO LACAR 24285 LAGO TRAFUL.**

MKCMFKMK H13
● **24300 MARTHA BAKKE.** No/Sw 1960; Pt.Con; 10000; 186.7×8.5 (613×28); M; 19.25; Lengthened & converted from cargo vessel 1970. Sister (No flag): **24301 RAGNA BAKKE** Similar: **24302 EMMA BAKKE.**

MKFCM H1
24320 UGOLINO VIVALDI. It/It 1947; C; 7100; 147.8×7.9 (485×25.11); M; 15.5; ex FERRUCCIO BUONAPACE 1947.

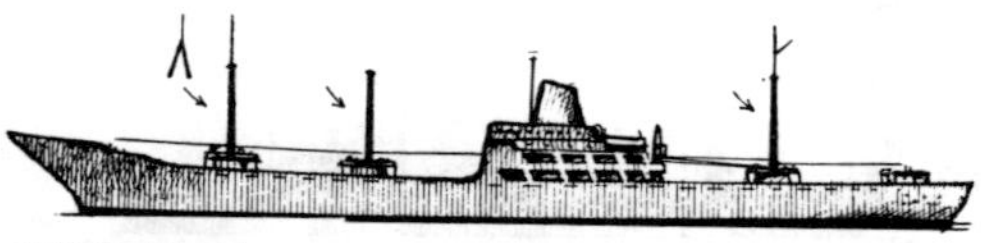

MKFCM H1
24340 PALATINO. It/It 1963; CP; 7000; 153.5×7.8 (504×25.9); M; —. Sisters (It flag): **24341 ESQUILINO 24342 QUIRINALE 24343 VIMINALE.**

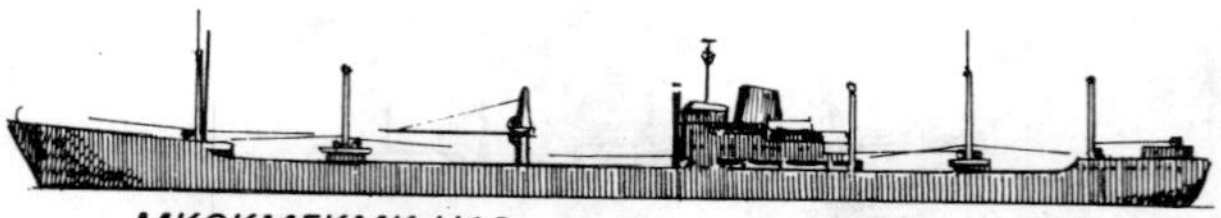

MKCKMFKMK H13
24270 APLI CHAU. Pa/FRG 1958; Pt.Con; 8600/11700; 188.7×7.9/8.6 (619×26/28.3); M; 18; ex TAGAYTAY; Lengthened & converted from a cargo ship 1970. Sisters (Pa flag): **24271 GINA** ex TAI PING 1980 **24272 SUNSHINE ISLAND** ex TEMA; ex TRAVIATA 1977 Similar (first KP is centre line): **24273 REGINA S** ex TARANTEL.

MKCMFKM H13
● **24290 VAUCLUSE.** Fr/Fr 1965; C; 7800; 175.3×8 (575×26.4); M; 18; Lengthened 1972. Sisters (Pa flag): **24291 CHAR YUENG** ex VAR 1980 **24292 CHAR KANG** ex VIENNE Probable Sisters: **24293 CHAR HANG** ex VELAY 1979; **24294 CHAR LY** ex VANOISE 1979.

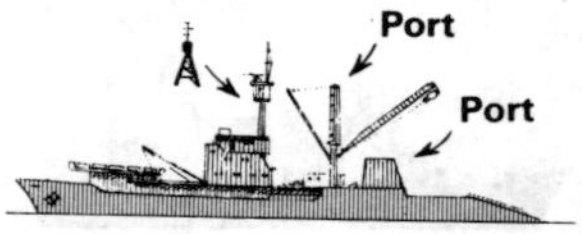

MKF H
● ⋆**24310 RODINA.** Ru/Pd 1978; FF; 1800dwt; 85×6 (moulded) (278.87×16.96); M; 16; Tuna Seiner. Helicopter deck forward. Further vessels on order for USSR.

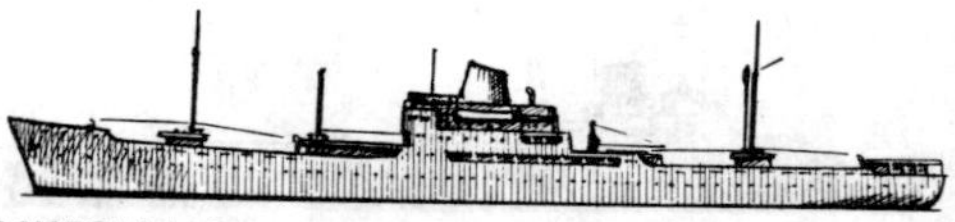

MKFCM H1
24330 MARCO POLO. It/It 1948; C; 7000; 147.8×7.9 (485×25.11); M; 15.5; ex NICOLO GIANI. Sister (It flag): **24331 ANTONIOTTO USODIMARE** ex VITTORIO MOCCAGATTA Possibly Similar: **24332 AMERIGO VESPUCCI** ex GUISEPPE MAJORANA.

MKFCM H1
24350 ROSANDRA. It/It 1956; C; 5000; 130.4 × 7.3 (428 × 24); M; 15. Similar (bi-pod KP's): **24351 ISONZO** (It).

MKFCM H13
24360 MUNDSBURG. Sg/FRG 1954; CP; 5100; 117.6 × 7.6 (386 × 25); M; 15; ex ROCIO 1977; ex ALPHA 1976; ex TAPPUZ 1969. Sister: **24361 CORK** (Pa) ex LEONIDAS A 1979; ex BETA 1973; ex READING I 1972; ex BETA 1972; ex DAGAN 1969.

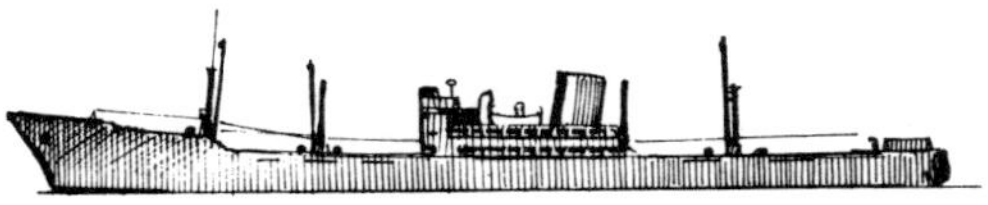

MKFK₂ H1
● **24370 OBESTAIN.** Pa/Br 1957; C; 6200/7700; 144.08 × 8.23/8.79 (473 × 27/30); M; 15; ex RONSARD 1980.

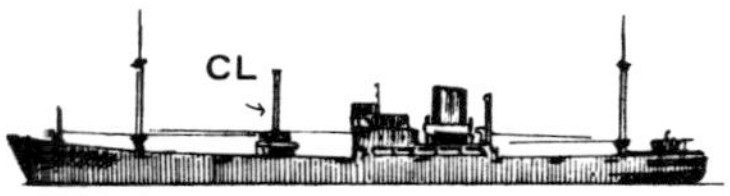

MKFKM H
● **24380 ANDINO.** ES/Ne 1956; CP; 1800; 109 × 5.3 (358 × 17.6); M; 14.5; ex ANA 1980; ex CRISPIN 1974. Sisters: **24381 AMALIA** (Gr) ex ANGIE 1980; ex CYRIL 1978; ex SHERIDAN 1967 **24382 BAROUK** (Le) ex CUTHBERT 1977; ex SPENSER 1967.

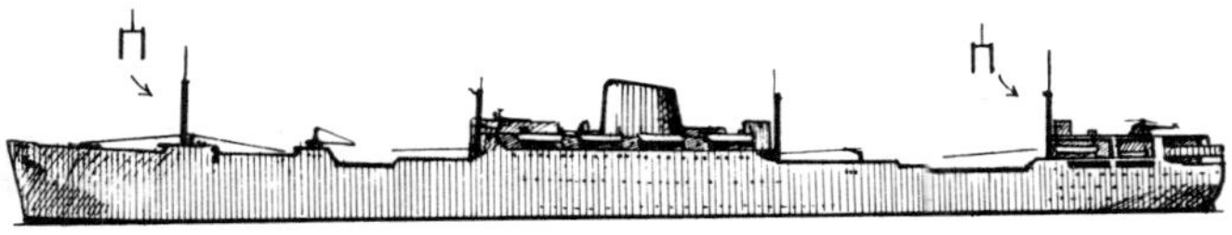

MKFKM H
⋆**24390 YURIY DOLGORUKIY.** Ru/Ge 1926; WF; 25400; 207.4 × 12 (680 × 39.6); TST; 16; ex HAMBURG 1951; Lengthened 1933; Converted from passenger cargo ship 1960.

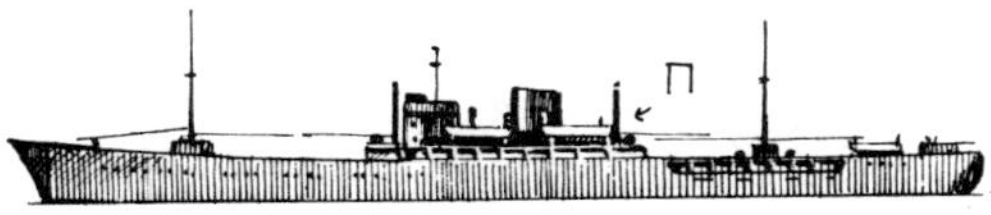

MKFKM H
24400 MIYAJIMA MARU. Ja/Ja 1953; C; 8300; 151.3 × 8.3 (496 × 27.4); M; 14.5; May be a Whale Factory Ship.

MKFKM H1
24410 NAI MONREALE. It/It 1964; C; 9500; 148.4 × 9.5 (487 × 29.1); M; 16.5; ex MONREALE 1975.

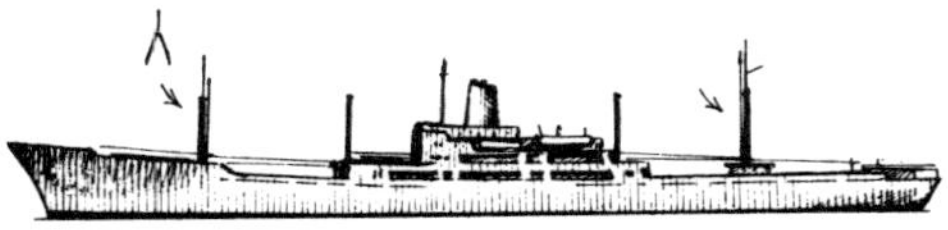

MKFKM H1
24420 TOLMIDIS. Gr/It 1959; C; 9500; 148 × — (486 × —); T; 16.5; ex MONFIORE 1973.

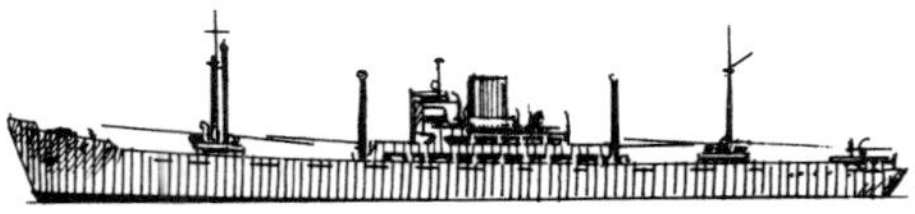

MKFKM H1
24430 RIO CUARTO. Ar/It 1950; C; 5200; 143.1 × 7.5 (470 × 24.6); M; 15. Sister: **24431 RIO QUINTO** (Ar).

MKFKM H1
● **24440 CIUDAD DE PAMPLONA.** Sp/Sp 1964; PC; 7700; 133.1 × 7.6 (437 × 25); M; 16. Sister: **24441 VILLA DE BILBAO** (Sp).

MKFKM H1
24450 LAGO ALUMINE. Ar/Ar 1965; C; 6100; 145 × 7.5 (476 × 24.6); M; 16. Sister: **24451 LAGO ARGENTINO** (Ar).

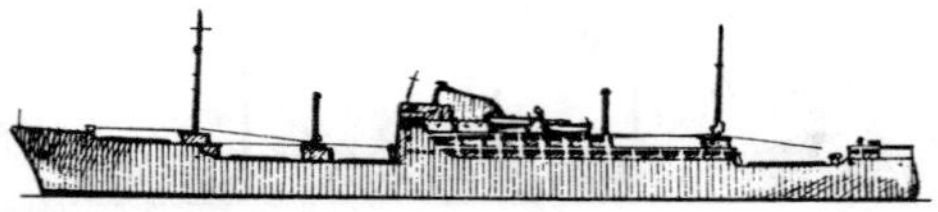

MKFKM H1
24460 VALMAS. Gr/Br 1954; CP; 6400/8300; 144 × 8.2/9.2 (472 × 27/30.3); M; 14; ex DESPINA R 1974; ex ST. MARIE 1967; ex ST. JOHN 1965. Sister: **24461 LUCKY TWO** (Pa) ex YUNNAN 1971; ex ST. ESSYLT 1965.

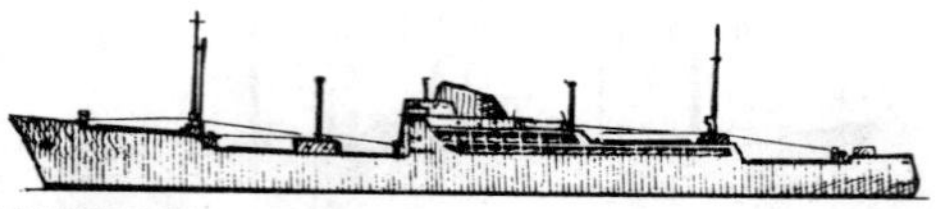

MKFKM H1
● **24470 MARIA SOFIA.** Gr/Br 1961; C; 9100; 144 × 8.6 (472 × 27.9); M; 15; ex HERMIONE 1979; ex HERMISTON 1970; ex ST. ROSARIO 1963.

MKFKM H1
24480 MEDCAPE. Gr/Br 1962; C; 6200/8800; 144 × 8.1/9.2 (473 × 26.3/30.2); M; 15; ex ALIKRATOR 1976; ex TEAKWOOD 1970.

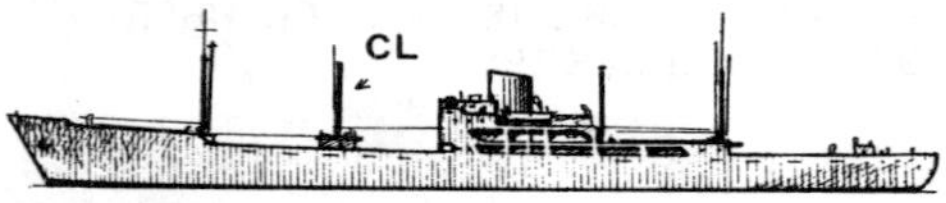

MKFKM H1
24490 HELLENIC GLORY. Gr/Br 1956; CP; 7500; 148.1 × 8.2 (486 × 26.9); M; 16. Sister: **24491 HELLENIC TORCH** (Gr).

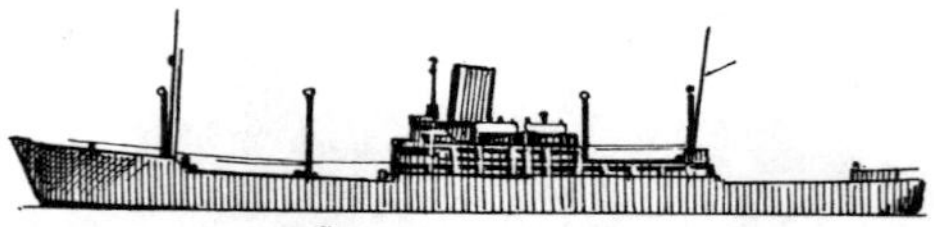

MKFKM H1
24500 TRUTHFUL. (Pa/Br 1954; CP; 8800; 143.8 × 9.3 (472 × 30.6); M; 16; ex WAN YU 1977; ex SUCCESSFUL ENTERPRISE 1972; ex WAITAKI 1970; ex WHAKATANE 1964.

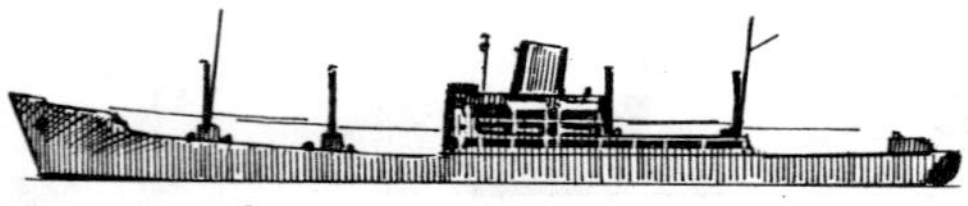

MKFKM H1
24510 REEFER QUEEN. Gr/Br 1962; C; 7600; 148.8 × 8.6 (488 × 28.2); M; 16.5; ex PIAKO. Sister: **24511 AEGEAN SKY** (Gr) ex SOMERSET.

MKFKM H1
24520 GOOD NAVIGATOR. Cy/Be 1956; CP; 8800; 147 × 9 (482 × 29.4); M; 16; ex LUKUGA 1972. Sister: **24521 GOOD MARINER** (Cy) ex LULUA 1972.

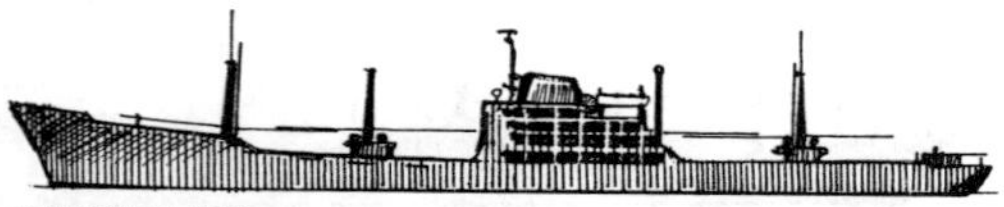

MKFKM H1
24530 BRUNELLA. Pa/Fr 1959; C; 6900; 156.6 × 8.1 (514 × 26.5); M; 18; ex MALAIS 1978. Sisters: **24531 MARINIQUAIS** (Fr) **24532 PATRICIA S** (Pa) ex MARQUISIEN Similar: **24533 VENTOUX** (Fr) **24534 VIVARAIS** (Fr) **24535 FORUM PROGRESS** (Gr) ex PAULINA 1980; ex VOSGES 1978.

MKFKM H1
24540 MASTER TONY K. Le/De 1959; C; 4100/6100; 126.9 × 7.31/8.41 (416 × 24/27.6); M; 16.5; ex GRETE SKOU 1974. Sisters: **24541 DELFINI V** (Pa) ex FLORA V 1980; ex VICTORIA U 1979; ex MARIA U 1978; ex HANNE SKOU 1974 **24542 MELANTHO C** (Gr) ex METTE SKOU 1979.

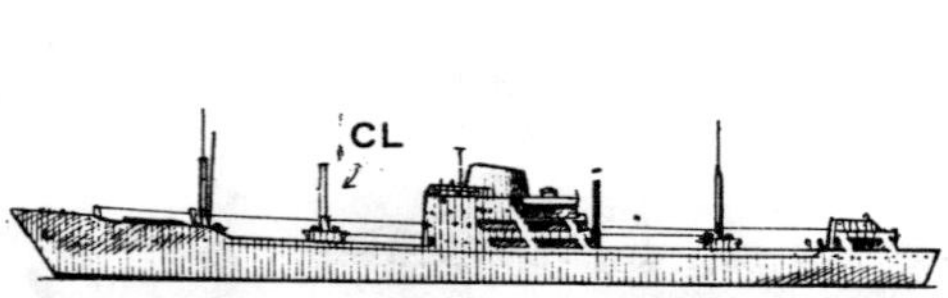

MKFKM H1
24550 HORIZONA. Pa/De 1958; PC; 6700/9300; 146.6 × 8.1/9.2 (481 × 26.8/30.1); M; 15.75; ex TORM GUNHILD; ex GUNHILD TORM 1974. Similar: **24551 DOROS** (Gr) ex MONT AIGOUAL 1974; ex HOLTHAV 1963.

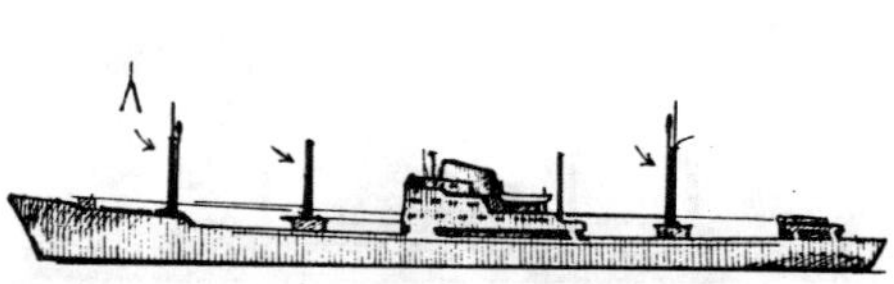

MKFKM H1
⋆**24560 SIENKIEWICZ.** Pd/De 1959; CP; 5300/7700; 138.7 × 7.8/8.7 (455 × 25.7/28.7); M; 16.25. Sister: ⋆**24561 ZEROMSKI** (Pd).

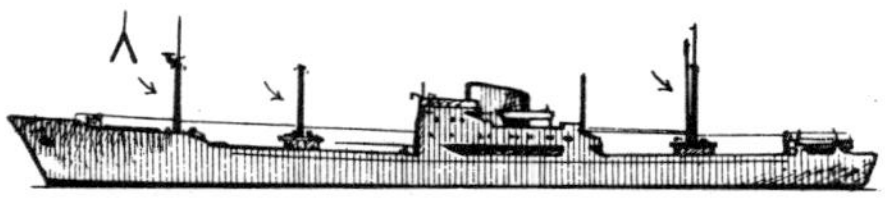

MKFKM H1
● **24570 GELORA 1.** Ia/De 1957; CP; 5300; 137.4 × 7.7 (451 × 25.4); M; 15; ex UNISTATE 1971; ex ALABAMA 1971. Sisters: **24571 ENAMEL** (Cy) ex MULUNGUSHI; ex MINNESOTA 1969 ★**24572 UJAMAA** (Ta) ex PENNSYLVANIA 1969 **24573 FILIA** (Gr) ex ENRICO DANDOLO 1977; ex ARIZONA 1967 **24574 KITMEER** (Ug) ex UGANDA 1980; ex COLORADO 1968.

MKFKM H1
24600 OCEAN TRADERS. Pa/Sw 1957; CP; 5200; 132.9 × 7.9 (436 × 25.11); M; 17; ex AMIR KHOSROW; ex IRAN ZAMIN 1977; ex EGDA 1973.

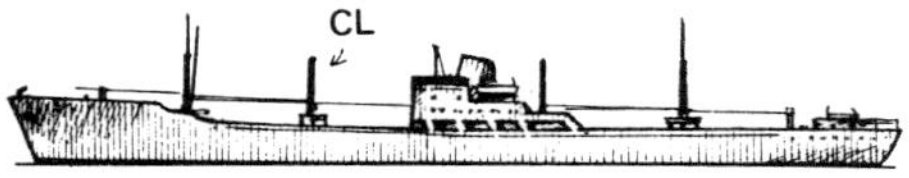

MKFKM H1
● **24620 POLYXENE G.** Gr/Sw 1957; C; 8500; 142.4 × 9.2 (467 × 29.8); M; 15; ex CONCORDIA GLEN; ex POLYXENE G. 1973.

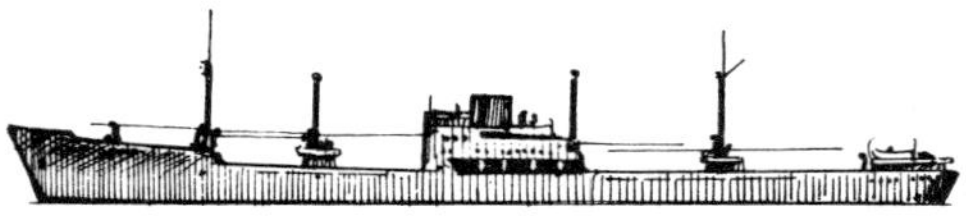

MKFKM H1
24640 YAT LEE. Pa/Sw 1950; CP; 8100; 147.7 × 8.7 (485 × 28.7); M; 17; ex SHANSI 1977; ex BERGANGER 1969. Sister: **24641 YAT SHING** (Pa) ex SOOCHOW 1977; ex MOLDANGER 1970.

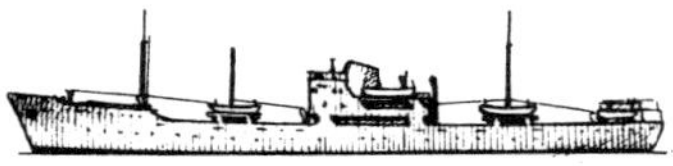

MKFKM H1
● **24660 AFFLUENT COUNTRY.** Pa/Sw 1949; PC; 2200; 104 × 5.8 (341 × 18.1); M; 14; ex HOI HOUW 1974. Sister: **24661 BUNGA BUTANG** (My) ex HOI WONG 1973.

MKFKM H1
24680 FAST BREEZE. Gr/De 1952; C; 4600; 115.1 × 7.4 (378 × 24.4); M; 15.25; ex AYIOS NIKOLAS 1976; ex ATHAINIKOLAS 1974; ex SANTA EVDOCIA 1973; ex OLAU GORM 1970; ex GRETA DAN 1963.

MKFKM H1
● **24580 EL QUETZAL.** Pa/De 1958; CP; 4900/7100; 137.6 × 7.5/8 (452 × 24.7/26.1); M; 16; ex TORM ALICE; ex ALICE TORM 1974.

MKFKM H1
24590 SEA GULL III. Pa/No 1954; CP; 7000; 134.7 × 8.4 (442 × 27.7); M; 15; ex PUNTA LARA 1980; ex ANTARTICO 1976; ex HARDANGER 1969.

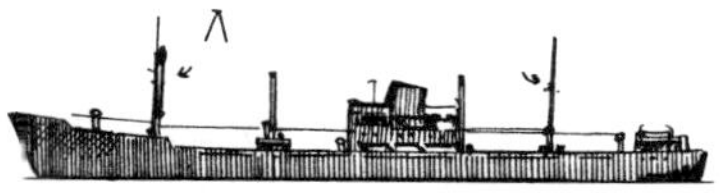

MKFKM H1
24610 POSEIDON C. Pa/Sw 1956; C; 3600; 108.8 × 5.9 (357 × 19.5); M; 15; ex RIODON 1979; ex DRUCILLA U 1975; ex FARIDA 1972.

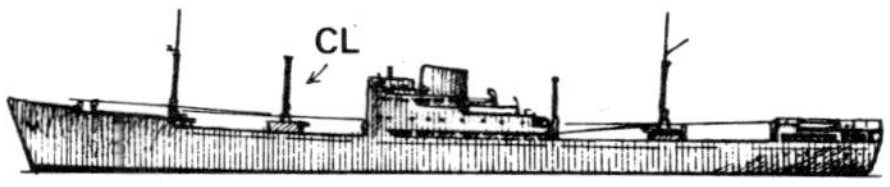

MKFKM H1
★**24630 PETER BERON.** Bu/Br 1949; C; 7400; 139.3 × 8.4 (457 × 27.7); M; 15; ex ALKAID 1971; ex BRANDANGER 1965.

MKFKM H1
24650 FOOCHOW. Pa/Sw 1955; PC; 2700/3900; 109 × 6/7.6 (357 × 19.8/25); M; 15; ex HOI YING.

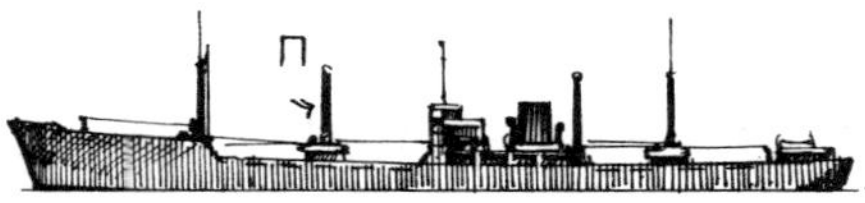

MKFKM H1
24670 KOSMAS K. Cy/Ja 1951; C; 7100; 137.95 × 8.47 (453 × 27.9); M; 12.5; ex MAGNOLIA 1976; ex MEITOKU MARU 1970.

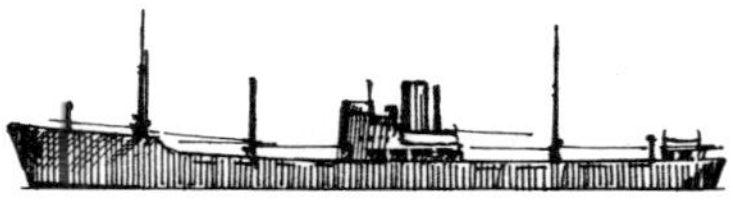

MKFKM H1
24690 THERAIOS. Gr/Sw 1935; C; 2700; 113 × 7 (370 × 21.6); M; 14; ex BROWIND 1966; ex BIRKALAND 1960.

MKFKM H1
● **24700 LILIANE.** Gr/Fr 1955; CP; 6500; 149 × 7.9 (489 × 26); M; 16; ex GODAVERY 1977. Similar: **24701 BADR** (Si) ex ESSAYONS 1975; ex SINDH 1970 **24702 TAKIS H** (Gr) ex SI-KIANG **24703 SIAM RAINBOW** (Pa) ex TIGRE 1977; **24704 GEORGIS K** (Gr) ex YALOU 1976.

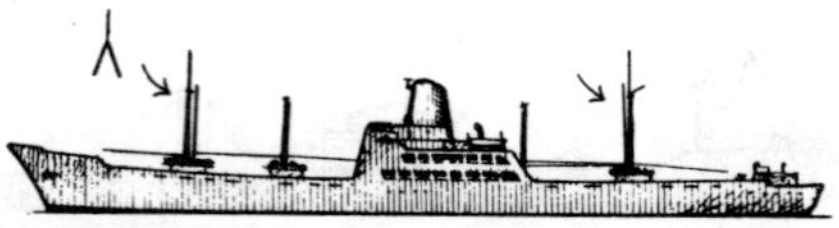

MKFKM H1
● **24710 AQUILEIA.** It/It 1955; C; 4900; 130.4 × 7.3 (428 × 24); M; 15. Sister: **24711 PIAVE** (It).

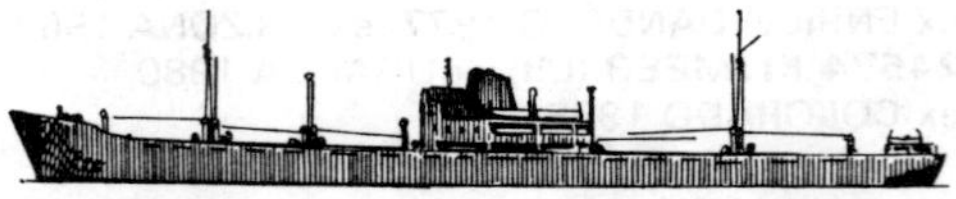

MKFKM H1
24720 LOBITO. Po/Po 1959; C; 6000; 145 × 8 (475 × 26.6); M; 14.

MKFKM H1
⋆**24730 HONG CHUN.** RC/Br 1957; C; 6900/9600; 153.6 × —/9.7 (504 × —/32); M; 15.5; ex CRETE SEA 1977; ex GRECIAN EMBLEM 1974.

MKFKM H1
⋆**24740 MARSHAL GOVOROV.** Ru/Sw 1939; C; 5100; 134.9 × 7.8 (443 × 25.4); M; 13; ex BORE X 1946.

MKFKM H1
24750 GRACE. Gr/Sw 1958; CP; 8600; 147.8 × 9.2 (485 × 30); M; 15; ex ATHENS GRACE 1977; ex ATHENS GLORY 1976; ex ARISTEFS 1974; ex SUNRANA 1970.

MKFKM H1
24760 STAR ALTAIR. Sw/Sw 1959; C; 6100/9000; 147.8 × 8.2/9.1 (485 × 26.1/29.11); M; —; ex VIMEIRA 1965; ex PORT DENISON 1965; ex VIMEIRA 1960; ex FAIR LADY. Probable Sister: **24761 PINELOPI** (Gr) ex STAR ALDEBARAN; ex KENSINGTON.

MKFKM H1
24770 FERE. Pa/FRG 1961; CP; 5200/7600; 139 × 7.6/8.6 (456 × 25/28.3); M; 15; ex TONKOUI; ex USAMBARA 1973.

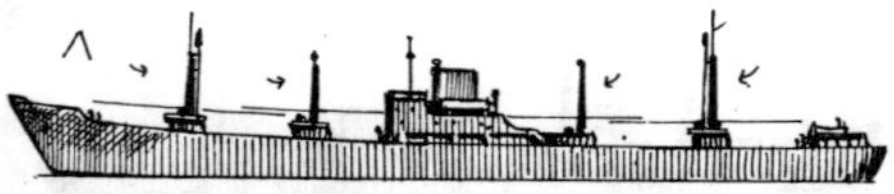

MKFKM H1
24780 PAUL RICKMERS. Sg/FRG 1955; C; 5400/7800; 147.3 × 7.6/8.7 (483 × 25/28.6); M; 14.5. Sister: **24781 MAIJIN** (Pa) ex R.C. RICKMERS 1973.

MKFKM H1
● **24790 TONG HONG.** Sg/Br 1955; C; 6000/8300; 147.8 × 8.1/9.1 (485 × 26.7/29.3); M; 14.5; ex AGIOS NIKOLAS 1976; ex ESPEN 1963.

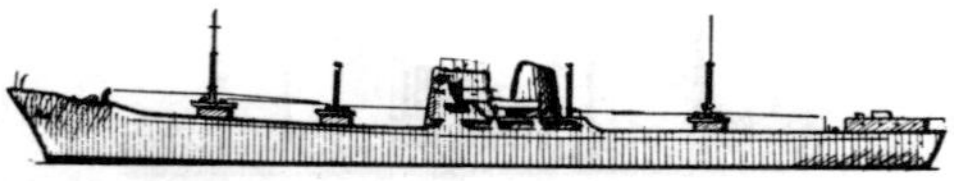

MKFKM H1
24800 STAMATIOS G. EMBIRICOS. Gr/Br 1956; C; 8900; 148.1 × 9.2 (486 × 29.7); M; —.

MKFKM H1
24810 GEMALA. Ia/Sw 1962; CP; 6300/9000; 145 × 8/8.9 (475 × 26.4/29.3); M; 14.5; ex RAVNAAS 1973.

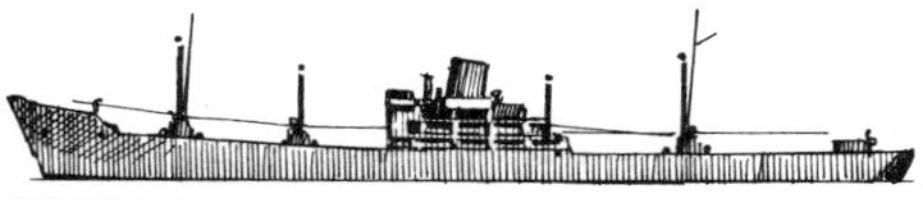

MKFKM H1
24820 GOLDEN HAVEN. Sg/Br 1952; C; 6200; 140.3 × 8.4 (460 × 27.2); M; 14; ex HOWRA 1972; ex LIMERICK 1969; ex ENTON 1955.

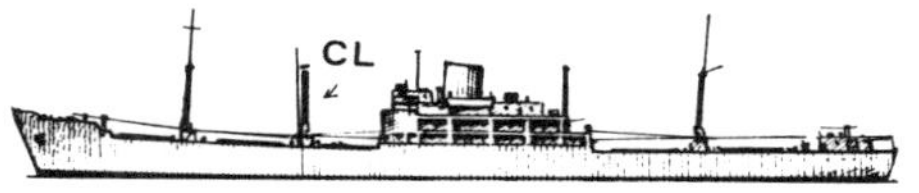

MKFKM H1
24830 SINGAPORE 2. Pa/Br 1962; C; 8100; 140.32 × 8.43 (460 × 27.2); M; 14; ex ISLAMI TAAJ 1980; ex STRATHINCH 1979; ex ANTRIM 1975.

MKFKM H1
24840 GLORY PHOENIX. Pa/Ja 1956; C; 7100; 136 × 8.3 (446 × 27.5); M; 13.75; ex GIANT TARZAN 1977; ex DURBAN MARU 1975; ex TENKO MARU 1964.

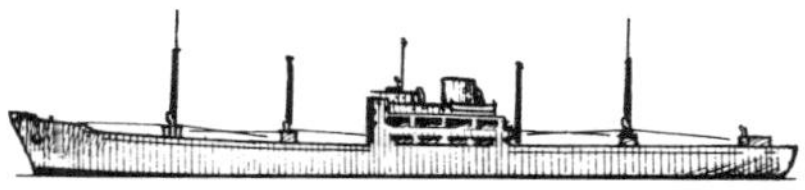

MKFKM H1
24850 GEORGIS. Gr/Ja 1956; C; 4100/5800; 125.9 × 7.2/— (412 × 23.8/—); M; 12.5; ex GIORGIS; ex MARIKA M; ex GLORIA 1977; ex CRETAN PALM 1977; ex MIHARU MARU 1975.

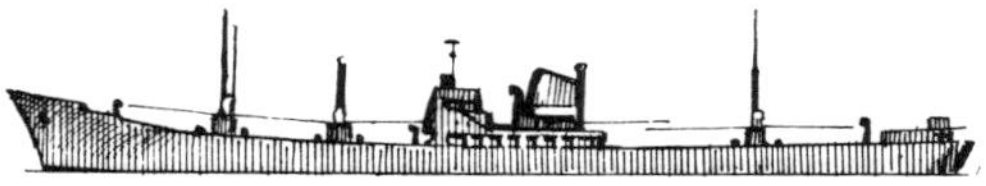

MKFKM H1
● **24860 MALDIVE SEAFARER.** Mv/Br 1957; C; 6100/8300; 148.4 × —/8.7 (487 × —/28.3); M; 14; ex AEGIS BEAUTY; ex FIRBANK 1973. Similar: **24861 NEWTON** (Li) ex TEAKBANK 1975 **24862 CAPETAN COSTAS** (Cy) ex YEWBANK 1974 **24863 BANGLAR POLYXENI** (Gr) ex FERNMOOR 1973; ex STREAMBANK 1971 **24864 GOLDEN SEASON** (Sg) ex RIVERBANK 1974 **24865 NEWTIDE** (Li) ex WAVEBANK 1976.

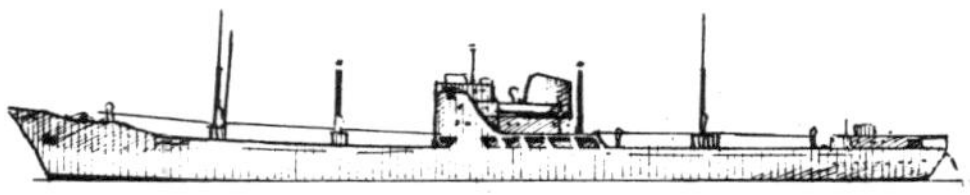

MKFKM H1
● **24870 NEW LARK.** Sg/Br 1961; C; 6200/8400; 148.8 × 7.9/8.8 (488 × 26/29); M; 14; ex LARCHBANK. Similar: **24871 VEESTAR** (Cy) ex WILLOWBANK **24872 WEIRBANK** (Br) **24873 GEORGIA F** (Gr) ex BESSIE 1979; ex TESTBANK 1978.

MKFKM H1
⋆**24880 VLORA.** Al/It 1960; C; 8600; 147.7 × 9 (485 × 29.6); M; —; ex ILICE 1961.

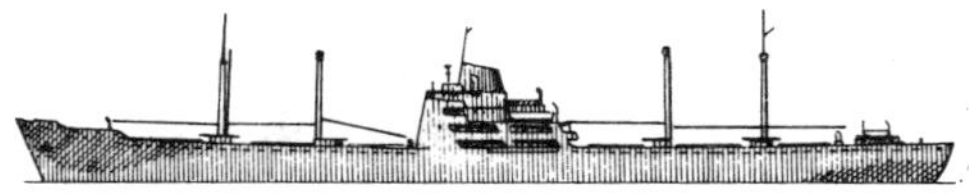

MKFKM H1
⋆**24910 VIETNAM THUONG TIN I.** Vn/It 1956; C; 6300; 148.6 × 8.1 (488 × 26.4); M; 14.25; ex SONIA 1969; ex VILLE DE DIEGO SUAREZ 1965; ex PIETRO CANALE 1962.

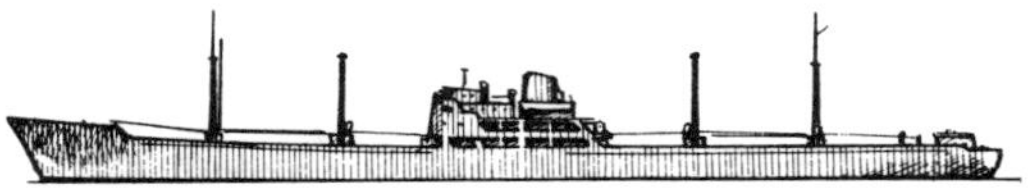

MKFKM H1
24920 MALDIVE PEACE. Mv/Ja 1956; C; 10000; 158 × 9.5 (519 × 30.4); M; 14.5; ex SCOPI 1980; ex CRETAN LIFE 1977; ex JURKO TOPIC 1973; ex ANTE TOPIC 1964. Sister: **24921 MALDIVE NEIGHBOUR** (Mv) ex ANGELIKI 1980; ex JURKO TOPIC 1978; ex OLGA TOPIC 1973.

MKFKM H1
● **24890 ATREO.** It/It 1957; C; 8700; 147.6 × 9.1 (484 × 29); M; 15. Sister: ⋆**24891 VAMPO** (Al) ex FINEO 1969 Similar: **24892 MOSCHA D** (Gr) ex ARGOLIS 1975; ex AZOTEA 1964 **24893 GOODWISH** (Cy) ex NINNY FIGARI 1971 **24894 THEANO** (Cy) ex SUNPALERMO 1972 ⋆**24895 HONG QI 118** (RC) ex JOLLITY 1977; ex SUNETNA 1964 ⋆**24896 JIANDE** (RC) ex MIRTO 1973 **24897 GREENLAND SEA** (Pa) ex GIOVE 1973 Similar (Conical Funnel): **24898 SAFINA-E-REHMAT** (Pk) ex FEDERICO PARODI 1965 **24899 ELVIUBA** (Pa) ex LATTUGA 1977; ex GIORGIO PARODI 1965.

MKFKM H1
24930 MALDIVE PROGRESS. Mv/Ja 1955; C; 10000; 158 × 9.5 (519 × 30.4); M; 16; ex MPARMPA CHRISTOS 1980.

MKFKM H1
⋆**24940 URSA.** Ys/FRG 1958; R; 1800/2900; 101.7 × —/6.8 (334 × —/22.4); M; 15.5; ex VERDAGUER 1971.

MKFKM H1
● ⋆**24960 SALI.** Ys/FRG 1950; C; 2500; 88.7 × 6.3 (291 × 21); M; 12; ex HECTOR 1960. Similar: **24961 ALEXANDROS K** (Cy) ex DARNLEY 1976; ex MYRIAM FIDELITY 1974; ex MANOLIS L 1972; ex NIN 1972; ex HERCULES 1960 **24962 TAILIAT** (Pa) ex CHENG HSING; ex TA HUNG 1976; ex AGIA MARINA 1973; ex HESTIA 1970.

MKFKM H1
24990 CAMPECHE. Me/Sw 1954; C; 2300; 107.6 × 5.9 (353 × 19.4); M; 14.75; ex GUNVOR BROVIG 1963. Sister: **24991 BREAKSEA** (Pa) ex JALAPA 1979; ex KIRSTEN BROVIG 1964.

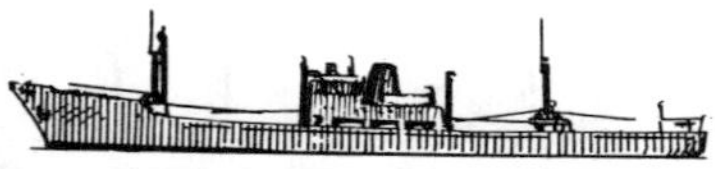

MKFKM H1
● **25010 ATHINAI.** Gr/Ja 1956; CP; 2900; 111.6 × 6.4 (366 × 21.2). Sisters (Gr flag): **25011 HOLLANDIA 25012 TURKIA.**

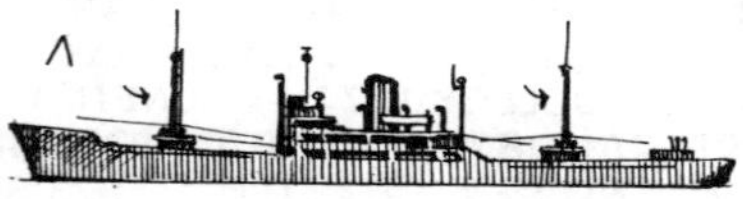

MKFKM H1
⋆**25030 HOPING.** RC/RC 1958; C; 5000; 115.5 × 6.7 (379 × 22); R; 12; may be called **HEPING.**

MKFKM H1
⋆**25050 ZHAN DOU No 72.** RC/RC 1960; C; 4700; 115.5 × 6.7 (379 × 22); R; 12; ex HOPING No 72.
Sister: ⋆**25051 LIAO YUAN** (RC).

MKFKM H1
24950 WHITE SHARK. Gr/FRG 1952; C; 1600; 93.6 × 5.4 (307 × 17.9); M; 12; ex ARCTURUS 1976.

MKFKM H1
⋆**24970 NADIR.** Ys/FRG 1957; C; 2900; 101.9 × 6.8 (334 × 18.1); M; —; ex ZENIT 1973; ex SAILOR PRINCE 1970; ex VELARDE 1969.

MKFKM H1
⋆**24980 CHONGMING.** RC/It 1941; CP; 8400; 144 × 8.2 (472 × 26.1); M; 14; ex MALGORZATA FORNALSKA 1965; ex GIUSEPPE CANEPA 1955; ex LUCIANO MANARA 1953.

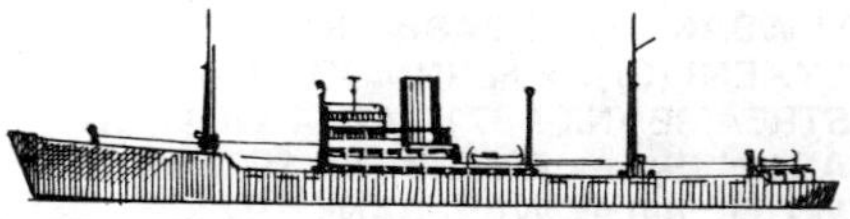

MKFKM H1
⋆**25000 MICKIEWICZ.** Pd/De 1943/47; CP; 4300; 132 × 7.8 (433 × 25.2); M- 14.5; ex GLADYS DAN 1950; ex HELGA DAN 1947; ex FRANKENLAND.

MKFKM H1
⋆**25020 ZHAN DOU No 28.** RC/RC 1958; C; 4700; 115.5 × 6.7 (379 × 22); R; 12; ex HOPING No 28; KP abreast funnel.

MKFKM H1
⋆**25040 ZHAN DOU No 71.** RC/RC 1961; C; 4700; 115.5 × 6.7 (379 × 22); R; 12; ex HOPING No 71.

MKFKM H1
⋆**25060 LENA.** Ru/Ne 1954; C; 5900/7300; 130.2 × —/8.2 (427 × —/26.11); D-E; 15. Sisters (Ru flag): ⋆**25061 YENISEY** ⋆**25062 OB** (Helicopter plaftform aft).

MKFKM H1

● **25070 MARIA.** Gr/Br 1959; R; 5400; 117.7 × 8 (386 × 25.1); M; 13.5; ex MIMI M 1974; ex ELEUTHERA 1971. Sisters (Gr flag): **25071 LELA** ex EMMA M 1974; ex CHANDELEUR 1971; ex CIENFUEGOS 1968 **25072 COMMENCEMENT** ex ELDINA 1975; ex SOMERS ISLE 1971.

MKFKM H1

● **25080 ANTONIA.** Gr/FRG 1959; CP; 4500; 115.6 × 7.4 (379 × 24.1); M; 13.5; ex ANNLEEA U 1977; ex DAHOMEYKUST 1972.

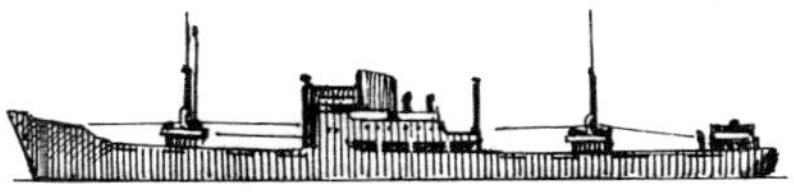

MKFKM H1

25090 ARISTOTELIS. Cy/Br 1948; CP; 3900; 118.1 × 7.2 (388 × 23.9); M; 14.5; ex PANODI; ex PANTIN 1977; ex EMMA METHENITIS 1974; ex TRANSAMERICA 1967; ex THORSHALL 1960. Similar: **25091 GEORGIOS K** (Gr) ex DMITRI METHENITIS 1975; ex HEIN HOYER 1969; ex THORSISLE 1966.

MKFKM H1

25100 DOLLY. Gr/FRG 1955; CP; 3100/4900; 119 × 6.8/8.1 (390 × 22.5/26.6); M; 15; ex CANDIA 1971 ex ESPERANZA 1968. Similar; **25101 CONFIDENCE** (Pa) ex FREIBURG 1972 (RC flag): ★**25102 HONG SHAN** ex SIEHCHIM 1976; ex PLYM 1973; ex KREFELD 1971 ★**25103 LAN SHAN** ex SIEHMIN 1976; ex OMEGA 1973; ex SOLINGEN 1972 ★**25104 CANG SHAN** ex SIEHTING: ex SILVER CLOUD 1973; ex REMSCHEID 1971.

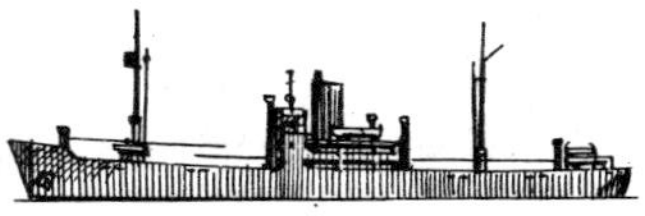

MKFKM H1

25110 GOLD STAR II. Th/De 1950; CP; 3600; 97.7 × 6.5 (321 × 21.4); R; 13; ex NEW TEH HU 1973; ex SLETHOLM 1962; ex OLAU BJARKE 1962; ex OLAV BJARKE 1961; ex TESSA DAN 1957.

MKFKM H1

25120 EL SALVADOR. Ni/Sw 1953; C; 2400; 109 × 5.9 (358 × 18.5); M; 14.5; ex FAROS 1953. Similar: **25121 LUCY** (Pa) ex EL CENTROAMERICANO 1973; ex GUDMUNDRA 1971 **25122 MANAGUA** (Ni).

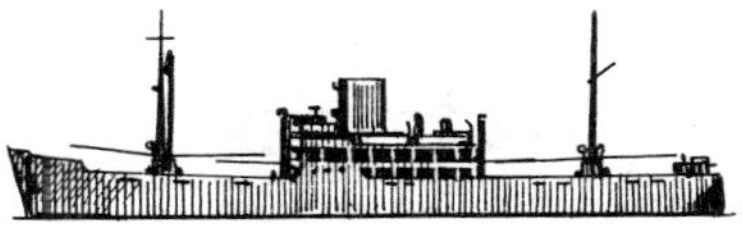

MKFKM H1

● **25130 KASTRIANI III.** Gr/Br 1949; C; 3400; 111.8 × 7.8 (367 × 25.7); M; 14; ex AMARNA 1975; ex ASSYRIA 1968; ex AMARNA 1967. Sister: **25131 CHRYSSOULA II** (Gr) ex ASSIOUT 1973.

MKFKM H1

25140 RAMIRO PEREZ. Sp/Sp 1957; CP; 2300; 105.7 × 6.1 (347 × 20.1); M; 16.2; ex TORRES DE CUARTE 1969. Sister: **25141 JUAN CLAUDIO** (Sp) ex TORRES DE SERRANOS 1969.

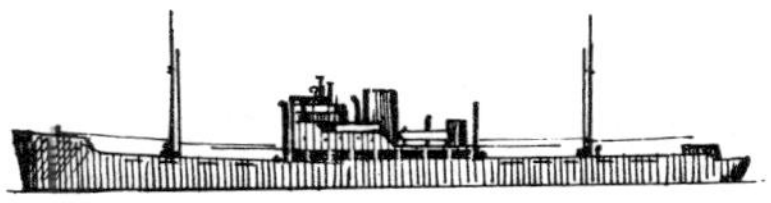

MKFKM H1

★**25150 ADMIRAL SENYAVIN.** Ru/Ge 1928; C; 5400; 119.2 × 6.8 (393 × 23); M; 13; ex PHOENICIA 1949.

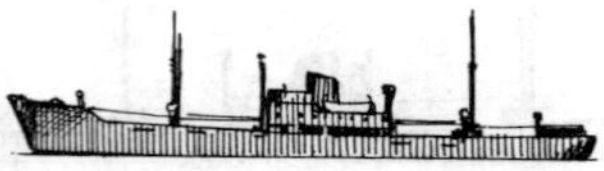

MKFKM H1
25160 SOUGERKA. Gr/Sw 1949; C; 1400; 91.2×6.4 (299×21); M; 13; ex LAD 1975; ex GOODWILL 1972; ex MODE 1968. Sister: **25161 YI SHANG** (Tw) ex WAN CHANG 1971; ex MIMER 1969.

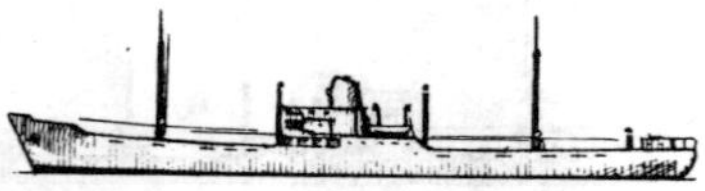

MKFKM H1
● **25180 LONDINON.** Gr/FRG 1950; C; 2700; 109.4×6.4 (359×20.1); R & LPT; 12; ex ANTARES 1966.

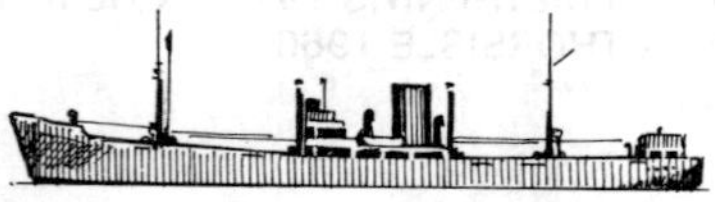

MKFKM H1
25190 LIH FONG. Pa/De 1948; C; 2200/4200; 109.48×6.33/6.93 (359.19×20.77/22.74); M; 13; ex OCEAN SPEWAY ex PING CHAU 1977; ex CLEMENTINE 1968; ex HERTA MAERSK 1967. Sister: **25191 RICKY** (Pa) ex GULF QUEEN; ex UNIPACIFIC 1977; ex KARANA II 1974; ex UNITY 1970; ex BRIGANTINE 1968; ex JESSIE MAERSK 1967; ex JESSIE GULWA 1961; ex JESSIE MAERSK 1958.

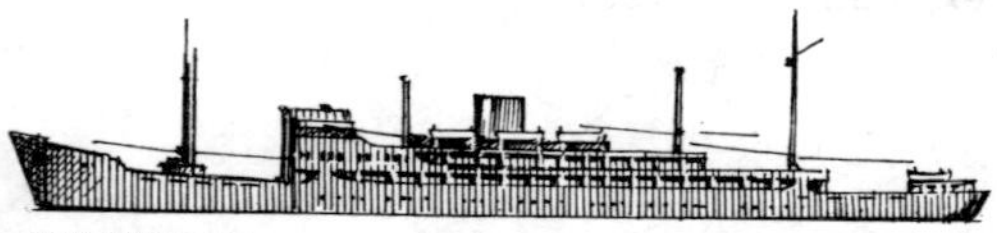

MKFKM H1
⋆**25220 GEORG BUCHNER.** DDR/Be 1951; PC; 11100; 153.7×8.4 (504×27.6); M; 16; ex CHARLESVILLE 1967.

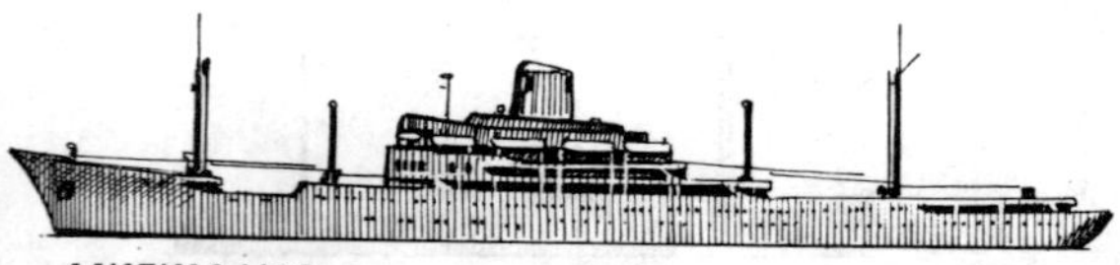

MKFKM H12
⋆**25230 SHANGHAI.** RC/Be 1957; PC; 12800/13500; 170×8.2/8.6 (558×27/28.2); T; 16.5; ex CATHAY; ex BAUDOUINVILLE 1961.

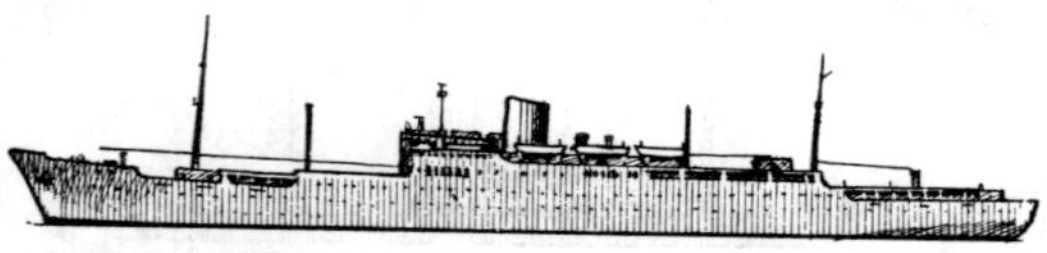

MKFKM H12
25250 LE HAVRE ABETO. Pa/Fr 1952; PC; 12000; 163.6×8.5 (537×27.1); TSM; 16; ex CHARLES TELLIER 1967.

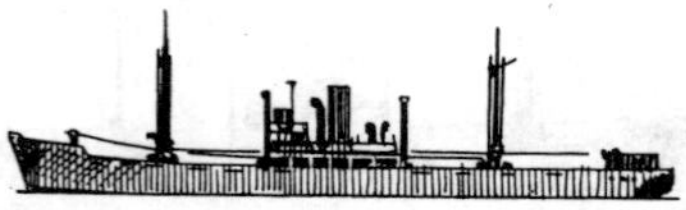

MKFKM H1
25170 'HANSA' type. c1947; C; 2700; 109.6×6.3 (360×20.8); R & LPT; 11; Standard WW2 design built in occupied countries. Sisters: **25171 PESQUERA** (Cy) ex MESSALA; ex LEADER TWO 1970; ex P. XILAS 1969; ex MIRA 1963; ex DANHOLM 1955; ex STENSNAES **25172 KR. AVINASH** (In) ex SAINT BERTRAND 1963; ex JACQUES DUROUX 1957; ex SPIEKEROOG 1947 **25173 KINGFORD** (So) ex HENRI STORY 1960 ⋆**25174 SERPUKOV** (Ru) ex MEKHANIK AFANASIEV.

MKFKM H1
⋆**25200 PUERTO DE VITA.** Cu/Ne 1951; C; 3400; 126.1×7.1 (410×23.5); M; 15; ex EQUUS; ex PYGMALION JUPITER 1976; ex SOVEREIGN SAPPHIRE 1975; ex TRITON AMBASSADOR 1973; ex FINNTRADER 1970.

MKFKM H1
25210 WELL VOY No 1. Pa/FRG 1953; C; 1600; 99.1×5.6 (325×18.2); M; 15.5; ex RITAPOINT; ex WAH PO; ex GLORY STAR; ex SHINTOKO MARU 1975; ex EXPERT MARU; ex SOUTHERN DRAGON 1973; ex SILVER SWAN 1970; ex BALTIC IMPORTER 1969. Sister: **25211 MONCALVO** (It) ex MEDOV ITALIA 1973; ex BALTIC TRADER 1971.

MKFKM H12
25240 MEI ABETO. Pa/Fr 1952; PC; 12700; 163.6×8.5 (537×27.1);TSM; 16; ex LOUIS LUMIERE 1967.

MKFKM H12
25260 ELPIS C. Gr/Fr 1957; C; 8800; 144.8×7.8 (475×25.8); M; —; ex PORT MAN 1977; ex TOBAGO 1976. Sisters: **25261 KIMKO STORK** (Pa) ex PORT CARTIER; ex TOCANSA 1975.

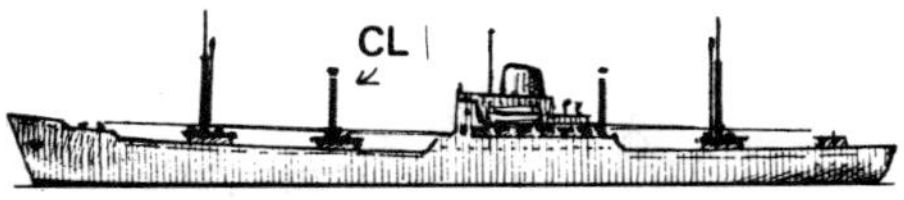

MKFKM H12

● **25270 ERECHTHION.** Gr/Fr 1958; C; 7400; 140.5 × 7.9 (461 × 26); M; 17.25; ex TABOA 1977. Sisters: **25271 DABEMA** (Iv) ex OWENDO; ex TALASSA 1974 **25272 TANAGREA** (Gr) ex TANAGRA 1975 **25273 EVALI** (Gr) ex TATIANA 1976 **25274 KOSSOU** (Iv) ex TAYGA 1968 **25275 PACTOLOS** (Gr) ex ARIADNI P.A. 1980; ex AKROU 1977; ex TIDRA 1973; ex TIMIA Similar: **25276 ASIA CARRIER** (Pa) ex ILOMBA 1979; ex NYANGA 1977; ex TAMBA **25277 ASIA CARRIER III** (Pa) ex LOTOFA 1979; ex MANDJI 1977; ex TESSA 1974.

MKFKM H12

25300 SEAWIND. Gr/FRG 1957; CP; 1800/2900; 101.9 × 5.5/7.1 (334 × 18/23.3); M; 15.75; ex MOSKA 1980; ex BALTIC EXPRESS.

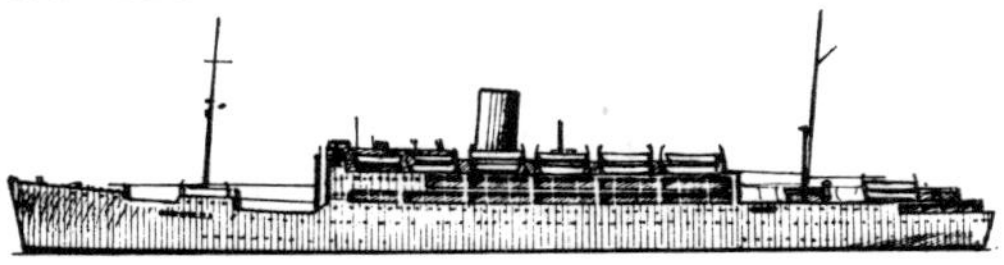

MKFKM H12

25310 NANCOWRY. In/Br 1948; PC; 10300; 157 × 8.3 (507 × 27.3); TST; 16; ex KARANJA 1976.

MKFKM H12

25330 BARBARA. It/Fi 1940; C; 1000; 68 × 4.6 (223 × 16); M; 11; ex PEYRA; ex ANDREA CAMALICH 1970; ex ALDA 1966; ex FROST 1961.

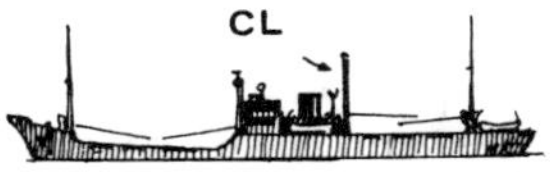

MKFKM H12

25350 LASS. Cy/FRG 1951; C; 1500; 82.5 × 4.8 (272 × 15.8); M; 11; ex HELUAN 1972.

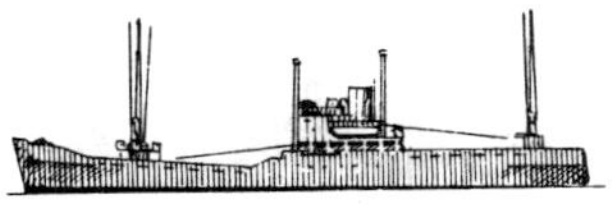

MKFKM H12

25370 HATI SENANG. My/Br 1950; C; 2500; 93.1 × 5.3 (306 × 17.5); TSM; 9.75; ex KAWATI 1980; ex KAWATIRI 1972. Sisters: **25371 BERJAYA** (My) ex TUNG LEE; ex BONATRADE 1974; ex KONUI 1969 **25372 TUNG PAO** (Pa) ex KARANA III 1974; ex PALADIN 1969; ex KAITANGATA 1968.

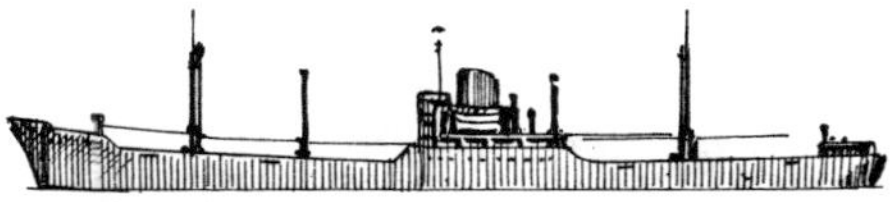

MKFKM H12

25280 ALRANA. Ku/Fr 1954; C; 6800; 140.1 × 7.98 (460 × 26.3) M; 14; ex ENIF 1980; ex STEFANIA ex LOUDIMA 1972.

MKFKM H12

25290 MARI. Cy/Br 1954; CP; 3500/4700; 113.4 × —/8 (373 × —/26.3); M; 13; ex MARIBER 1977; ex NAFTILOS 1973; ex MANDRAKI 1972; ex ENGISH PRINCE 1969; ex BEECHMORE 1965. Similar; **25291 TEMI** (cy) ex MELTIMI 1977; ex JATA 1976; ex ELIAS L 1973; ex MERCHANT PRINCE 1968; ex SYCAMORE 1965; ex WALSINGHAM 1957; ex SYCAMORE 1955.

MKFKM H12

25320 ARIS. Gr/FRG 1951; C; 2500; 92.7 × 6.1 (304 × 21); R; 12; ex KORMORANOS; ex CHALLENGER S; ex ILSABE OLDENDORF 1969; ex HERMAN SAUBER 1960.

MKFKM H12

25340 BAHAGIA VI. Ia/No 1950; C; 1100; 70 × 4.6 (230 × 15.2); R; 11.5; ex DAYA KURNIA 1975; ex SLIDRE BARAT 1973; ex BERBY 1965.

MKFKM H12

25360 FAROS. Gr/Br 1956; Cem; 2700; 94.5 × 5.8 (310 × 18.1); M; 11; ex BURWAH. Similar **25361 MACEDON** (Br).

MKFKM H12

25380 TSIN YUEN. Sg/Br 1953; C; 2000; 81 × 5; (266 × 16.6); M; 11; ex KING LUCK 1980; ex KARAMU 1972.

MKFKM H12
25390 MALDIVE REPUBLIC. Mv/Br 1958; C; 2100; 81.8 × 4.9 (268 × 16.2); M; 10; ex PATEENA 1975.

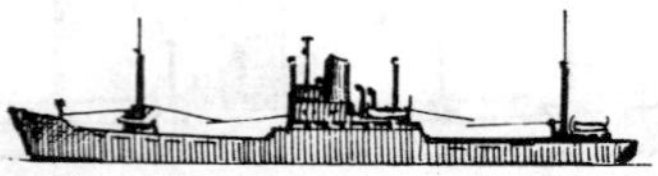

MKFKM H12
● **25400 DIANA.** Gr/FRG 1951; C; 2800; 116.3 × 6.4 (382 × 21); M; 14; ex NORDMARK 1974; ex DON PEDRO 1967; ex LEVANTE 1966.

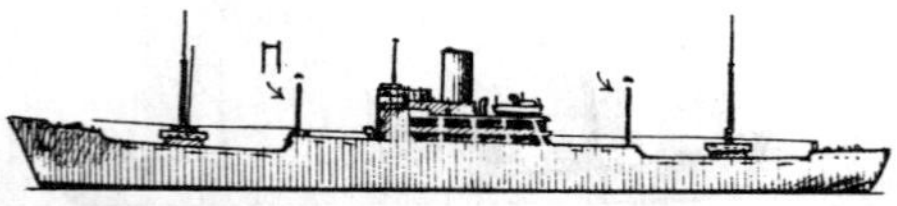

MKFKM H123
25410 GISELLA. Cy/Ja 1952; C; 6600; 139.3 × 8.3 (457 × 26.1); M; 13.5; ex BEGONIA 1975; ex SHOUN MARU 1970.

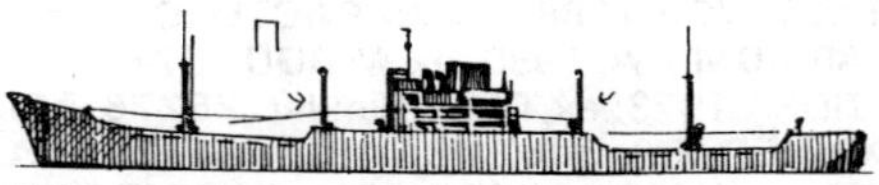

MKFKM H123
25420 JUPITER V. Pa/Ja 1953; C; 6600; 137.4 × 8.3 (451 × 27.3); M; 14; ex OCEAN FRIEND 1977; ex SUN PO 1975; ex TAIYU MARU 1969.

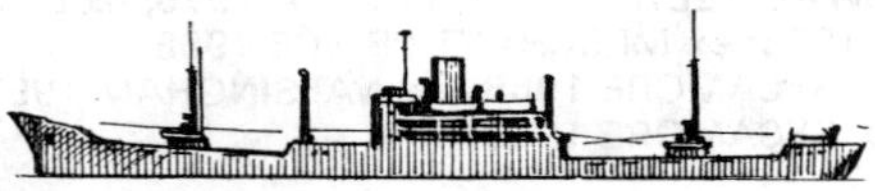

MKFKM H123
25430 TIMOR CAREER. Pa/Ja 1951; CP; 6800; 136.2 × 8.4 (447 × 27.7); M; 13; ex LUCKY KINGWAH 1977; ex GREEN BANK 1977; ex FIJI MARU 1974; ex GEKKO MARU No 2 1964; ex GEKKO MARU 1963.

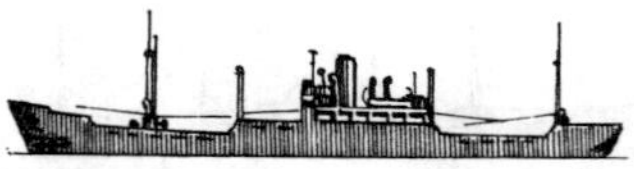

MKFKM H123
25440 J.R. ONE. Pi/Ja 1949; C; 3200; 98.6 × 6.4 (324 × 21); M; 11.5; ex DONA PAZ 1974; ex DONA HORTENICIA 1969; ex TOMOKAWA MARU 1966.

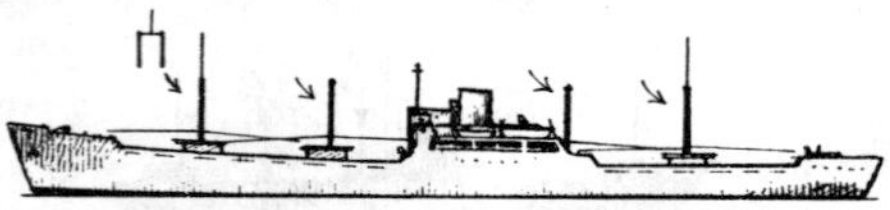

MKFKM H123
25450 DESPINA AII. Gr/Ja 1952; C; 6900; 141.5 × 7.9 (450 × 26); M; 14; ex GOODLUCK 1973; ex ACHAIKA HARMONY 1970; ex HOKKAI MARU 1970.

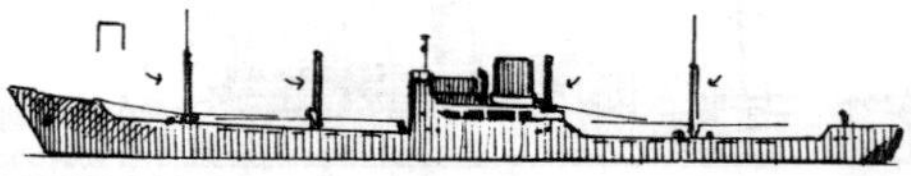

MKFKM H123
25460 FAIRSHIP. Pa/Ja 1952; C; 6900; 141.5 × 7.9 (464 × 25.9); M; 14.5; ex SEIZAN MARU 1975.

MKFKM H123
25470 SRI THAMARACH. Th/Ja 1958; C; 4100; 116 × 6.9 (381 × 22.8); M; 11.5; ex KASHIMA MARU 1970.

MKFKM H123
25480 GOLDEN GLOBE. Sg/Br 1957; C; 2700; 93.6 × 5.8 (307 × 19.4); M; 12.5; ex ABEL TASMAN 1975.

MKFKM H123
⋆**25490 SIVASH.** Ru/Fi 1950; C; 2500; 90 × 5.6(295 × 18); 9.75; Modified **'HANSA'** class.

MKFKM H123
25500 NIKOLAOS G. Gr/Ne 1953; C; 2600; 99.2 × 5.6 (326 × 18.5); M; 12.5; ex SOFIA; ex MARGARETA 1977.

MKFKM H123
25510 DIMITRIOS G. Gr/Ne 1958; C; 2700; 99.2 × 5.7 (326 × 19); M; 14; ex AGNETA 1977.

MKFKM H123
⋆**25520 HOPING CHI SHI CHI.** RC/US 1943; C; 1900; 78.9 × 5.5 (259 × 18); R; 10; ex HANSFORD 1960; ex INCHULVA 1959; ex ELKANAH CROMWELL 1951; **'JEEP'** type; may be called **ZHAN DOU 77.**

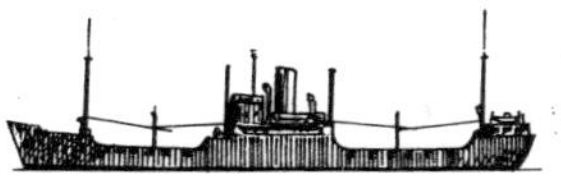

MKFKM H123
● **25530 NICOLAOS G.** Cy/No 1952; C; 1900; 84.7 × 5.4 (278 × 17.9); R; 11.5; ex WESTON 1976; ex VELOX 1970; ex LEKNES 1967; ex AUN 1963.

MKFKM H123
● ★**25550 'KHASAN'** class. Ru/Fi c1954; C; 2600; 90.5 × 5.6 (295 × 18); R; 10. Sisters (Ru flag): ★**25551 AMDERMA** ★**25552 ALCHEVSK** ★**25553 ARMAVIR** ★**25554 DNESTR** ★**25555 DONETS** ★**25556 DONETSK** ex STALINO ★**25557 IMANDRA** ★**25558 MIRGOROD** ★**25559 MOGILÉV** ★**25560 PINSK** ★**25561 PRIKUMSK** ★**25562 PYATIGORSK** ★**25563 RYAZHSK** ex BUDJONNOVSK ★**25564 SLAVYANKA** ex VOROSHILOVGRAD ★**25565 YENISEYSK** ★**25566 ZAPADNAYA DVINA** (RC flag): ★**25567 HOPING ER SHI ER** ex RUNA 1956 ★**25568 HOPING ER SHI I** ex RITA 1955 ★**25569 HOPING SAN SHI SAN** ex RAGNI 1956 ★**25570 HOPING SAN SHI I** ex ROSITA 1956 ★**25571 HOPING SHI PA** ex ROSA 1955 ★**25572 HOPING SHI CHIU** ex RENATA 1955 (Pa flag): **25573 VOLO** ex VOLOKOLAMSK

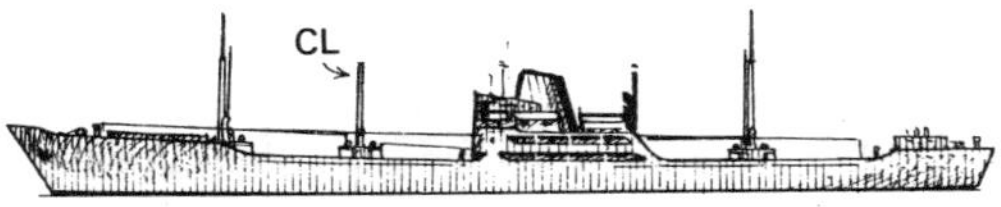

MKFKM H13
25610 JALADHRUV. In/In 1956; C; 6500; 155.28 × 7.86 (509 × 25.1); M; 17. Sisters (In flag): **25611 FAULAD SARKAR** ex JALADHARMA 1981 **25612 PRABHU SAKHI** ex JALADHIR 1981 **25613 PRABHU PARVATI** ex JALADHARATI 1980.

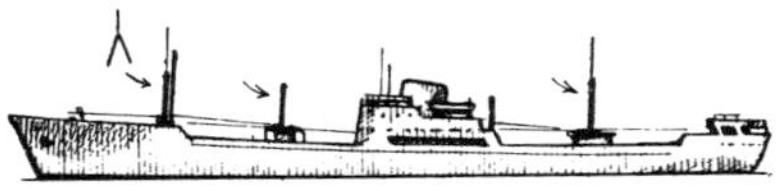

MKFKM H13
25640 SONORA. Me/De 1955; CP; 3300; 121.3 × 6.4 (398 × 21.1); M; 16; ex GINA MARIA 1977; ex CORNEVILLE 1971.

MKFKM H123
★**25540 ZHAN DOU No 49.** RC/RC 1959; C; 2400; 93.3 × 5.8 (306 × 19); R; 10; ex HOPING No 49. Similar (RC flag): ★**25541 ZHAN DOU No 65** ex HOPING No 65 ★**25542 ZHAN DOU No 66** ex HOPING No 66.

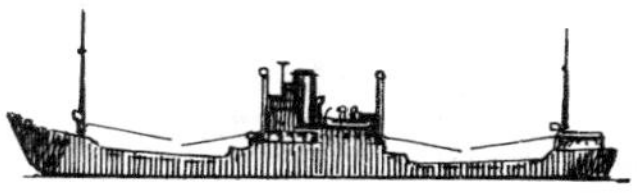

MKFKM H123
25580 ALEXANDROS A. Cy/Fi 1947; C; 2100; 90.4 × 5.6 (297 × 18.6); R; 10; ex KUNGSO 1971. Similar: **25581 GALATEA** (Pa) ex PATRIA 1967.

MKFKM H123
★**25590 LEONID KRASIN.** Ru/No 1913; C; 1800; 84.4 × 5.3 (277 × 18); R; 9; ex BRANN; ex STAVN ex BRAGER.

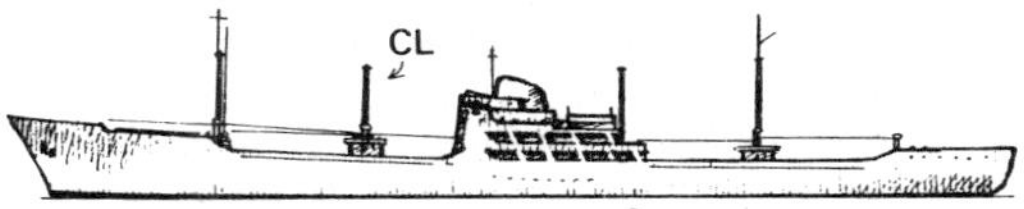

MKFKM H13
25600 EASTERN PIONEER. Pa/Fr 1958; CP; 11100; 159.7 × 9.6 (524 × 30.7); M; 15; ex NIGER STAR 1980; ex KING MINOS 1976.

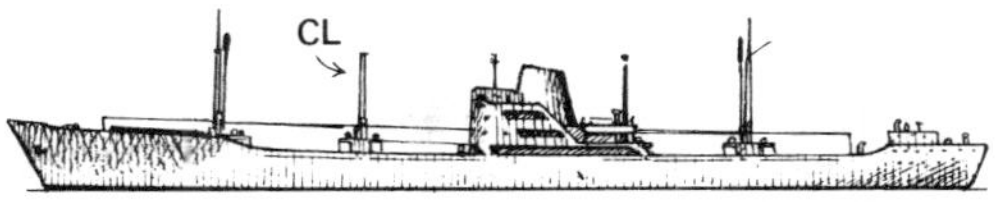

MKFKM H13
25620 VISHVA NIDHI. In/In 1961; CP; 6200; 155.2 × 7.8 (509 × 25.9); M; 17. Similar (In flag): **25621 STATE OF RAJAHSTAN 25622 STATE OF UTTAR PRADESH.**

MKFKM H13
25630 GOOGI Z. Pa/It 1953; C; 3600; 128.6 × 6.6 (422 × 21.8); M; 15; ex ATHINAI 1980.

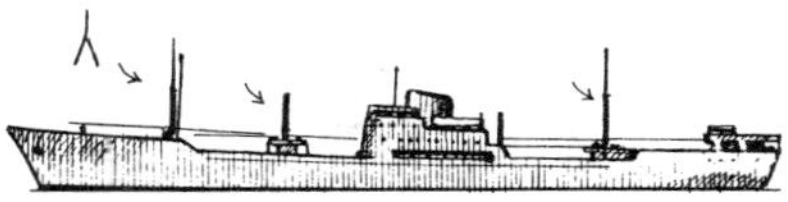

MKFKM H13
★**25650 PEIKIANG.** RC/De 1958; C; 3200/5200; 122.7 × 6.6/7.4 (403 × 21.1/24.4); M; 16; ex TITANIA 1971; ex CRESTVILLE 1961.

MKFKM H13
25660 NEW SEA PIONEER. Pa/FRG 1959; C; 6800/9400; 154.9 × 8/9 (508 × 26.3/29.9); M; 15.5; ex SEA PIONEER 1976; ex ARIEL 1972; ex ARIANA 1966.

MKFKM H13
25680 SISES. It/It 1948; PC; 8800; 144.7 × 8.6 (474 × 25.1); M; 17.5.

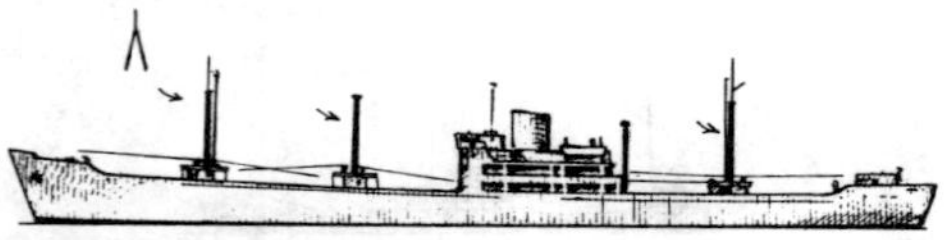

MKFKM H13
25700 ROSARIO DOS. Pa/Be 1958; C; 6200/8900; 147.12 × 8.28/9.27 (483 × 27/32); M; 13; ex MOBEKA. Sisters: **25701 RESURGENCE EXPRESS** (Li) ex MOERO 1973 **25702 GOOD STAR** (Gr) ex MOHASI **25703 LORETO** Pa) ex MOKOTO **25704 MOLIRO** (Be) ⋆**25705 HYANG SAN** (RK) ex GOOD FIGHTER 1980; ex MOKAMBO **25706 ASIA PALMO** (Ko) ex OKITO 1980; ex JOSEPH OKITO 1975; ex CONGO MOKO 1967 **25707 MPOLO** (Zr) ex MAURICE MPOLO 1976; ex CONGO ZOLO 1967.

MKFKM H13
25730 JALAGIRIJA. In/Br 1963; C; 10700; 155.6 × 9.2 (510 × 30); M; 15.5; ex ROSEWOOD 1968.

MKFKM H13
● **25750 FORTUNE VICTORY.** Pa/Hong Kong 1959; C; 4000/5700; 128.7 × 6.9/7.5 (422 × 22.8/24.8); M; —; ex ORIENT VICTORY 1976; ex KWEICHOW 1974; ex NORMAN 1968; ex KWEICHOW 1966.

MKFKM H13
25770 JALADURGA. In/FRG 1960; C; 6300/9200; 154 × 7.8/9.2 (505 × 25.7/30); M; 17. Sister: **25771 JALADUTA** (In).

MKFKM H13
25670 GEVO 1. Le/FRG 1952; C; 6200; 144.5 × 7.7 (474 × 25.7); M; 13.5; ex VASIL DRUMEV 1981; ex ALFERATZ 1970; ex ALLOBROGIA 1965. Sister: **25671 LUCKY PENNY** (Cy) ex BASILEA.

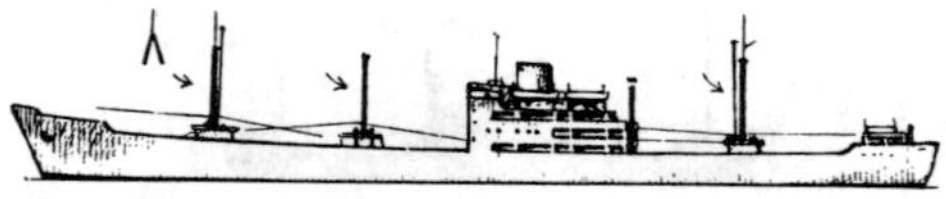

MKFKM H13
25690 PAZ. Sg/Be 1960; CP; 6400/9200; 147.1 × 6.4/9.3 (483 × 21/29.1); M; 14; ex MONTALTO. Sister: **25691 ALEXANDROS P** (Gr) ex FORTUNE GLORY 1980; ex MONTHOUET 1979.

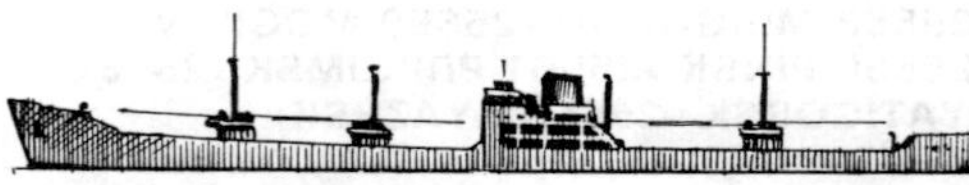

MKFKM H13
● **25710 ALIAKMON BREEZE.** Gr/FRG 1958; C; 9900; 157.2 × 9.1 (516 × 29.9); M; 15.75; ex BELINDA 1969.

MKFKM H13
● **25720 PLEIAS.** Gr/Br 1963; C; 7700/10700; 155.6 × 8/8.9 (510 × 26.1/29.4); M; —; ex SILVERLEAF 1968.

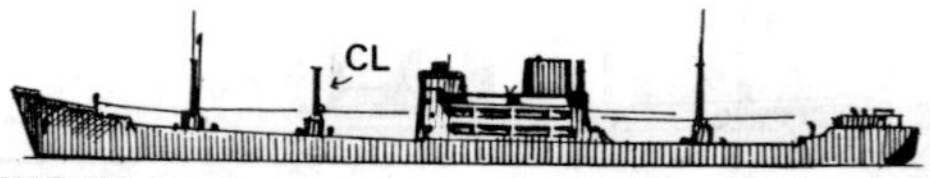

MKFKM H13
25740 OSIA IRINI CHRYSOVALANDOU. Gr/Br 1955; C; 8000; 141.5 × 8.4 (464 × 26.11); M; 15; ex GEORGETTA 1975; ex ELLISPONTOS 1970; ex LEEDS CITY 1967.

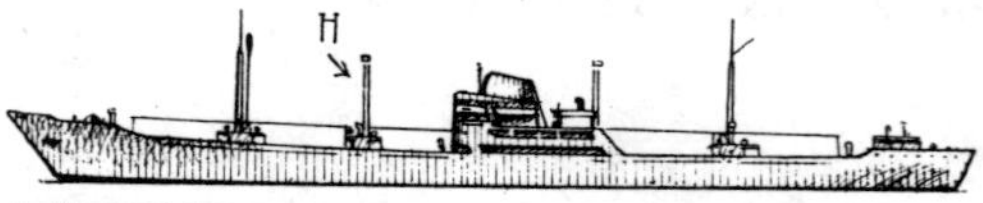

MKFKM H13
25760 JYOTI-VINOD. In/FRG 1955; CP; 6200; 152.1 × 7.7 (499 × 25.2); M; 14.75; ex JALAZAD 1980.

MKFKM H13
25780 VISHVA JYOTI. In/FRG 1959; C; 6200/9200; 154 × 7.8/9.2 (505 × 25.7/30); M; 17; ex JALA VISHVA JYOTI 1961; ex VISHVA JYOTI. Sisters (In flag): **25781 VISHVA KIRTI 25782 VISHVA MANGAL 25783 VISHVA MAYA 25784 STATE OF PUNJAB** (Bh flag): **25785 BANGLAR DOOT** ex VISHVA PREM 1972 (Rm flag): ⋆**25786 VRANCEA** ex VISHVA SHANTI 1972.

MKFKM H13
25810 ENARXIS. Cy/FRG 1956; CP; 9200; 149.4 × 9 (490 × 29.6); M; 15; ex VLIST 1972. Sister: **25811 VICTORIA U** (Li) ex PISHTAZ IRAN 1980; ex ROTTE.

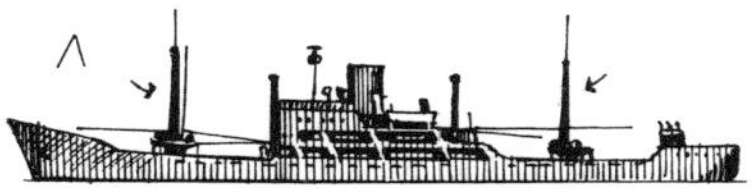

MKFKM H13
⋆**25830 YOU YI.** RC/RC 1959; C; 4900; 116.4 × 6.7 (382 × 22); R; 12.

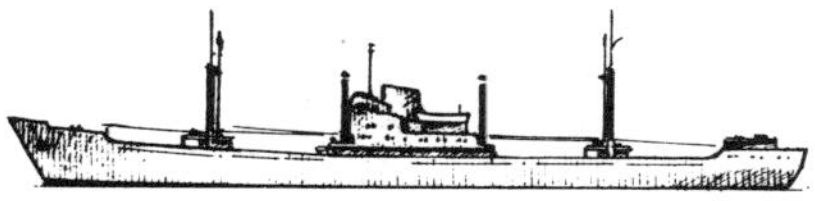

MKFKM H13
● **25860 OMEGA KASSOS;** Gr/FRG 1961; CP; 3400/5400; 126.3 × 6.8/7.8 (414 × 22.3/25.9); M; 16.5; ex VIKTORIA ROTH; ex MAILAND 1973. Sisters: **25861 MAH 2** (Th) ex POROS ISLAND 1980; ex TUNIS 1974 **25862 MAHARASHMI** (In) ex MADRID 1974; ex SLOMAN MADRID.

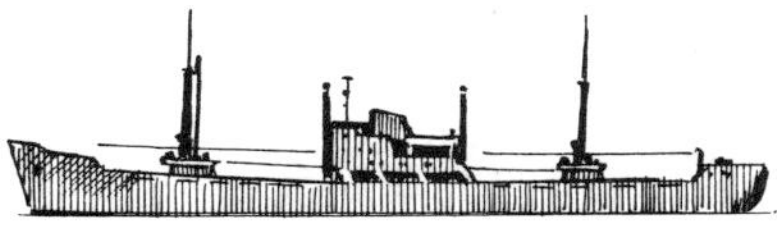

MKFKM H13
● **25880 AKRA SOUNION;** Gr/Ne 1960; CP; 4500; 113.9 × 7.1 (390 × 22.1); M; 14; ex LIBERIAKUST 1971. Sister: **25881 AKRA RION** (Gr) ex TOGOKUST 1971.

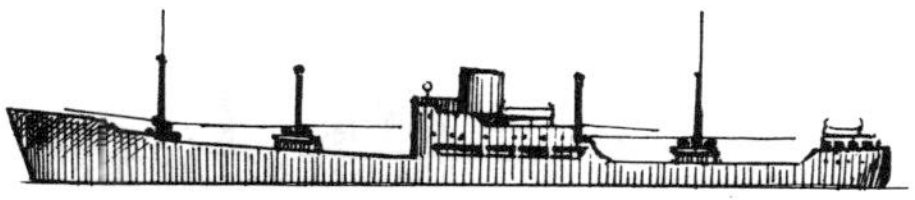

MKFKM H13
25790 SANTA LUCIA II. Pa/Sw 1955; CP; 5100; 140.5 × 7.8 (461 × 25.7); M; 15; ex LARS MELING; ex HOEGH MELING 1977; ex LARS MELING 1969.

MKFKM H13
25800 SUTLEJ. Pk/FRG 1957; C; 6000/8900; 151.3 × 8.1/9.1 (496 × 26.6/29.9); M; —; ex KALLIOPI PATERAS 1965. Sister: **25801 PANAGIOTIS XILAS** (Gr) ex ISAPOSTOLOI 1973; ex DIAMANTIS PATERAS 1972.

MKFKM H13
25820 DJATINEGARA. Ia/Ja 1958; C; 8800; 148.3 × 8.7 (487 × 28.8); M; 14; ex WEST BREEZE 1973.

MKFKM H13
⋆**25840 SEVERODVINSK;** Ru/Pd 1958; FF; 10000: 155 × 8.2 (510 × 26.11); TSR & LPT; 14.5; **'B-62'** type. Sisters (Ru flag): ⋆**25841 ARMAN** ⋆**25842 CHUKOTKO** ⋆**25843 IVAN FEDEROV** ⋆**25844 JOHANNES VARES** ⋆**25845 PECHENGA** ⋆**25846 RIGA** ⋆**25847 SOVIETSKAYA KAMCHATKA** ⋆**25848 SOVIETSKAYA SAKHALIN** ⋆**25849 SOVIETSKAYA LITVA** ⋆**25850 SVIATOGOR.**

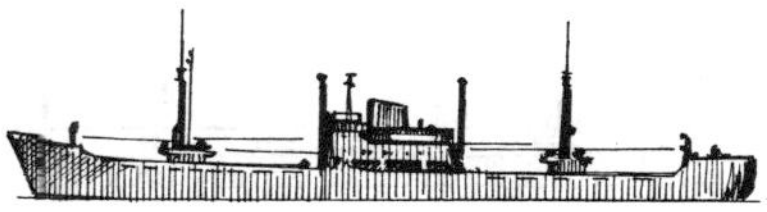

MKFKM H13
25870 PICHIT SAMUT; Th/Ne 1954; CP; 3400; 118.4 × 6.4 (388 × 21); M; 13.5; ex BENINKUST. Sister: **25871 YACU TAITO** (Pe) ex UNIVERSE 1974; ex CAMEROUNKUST 1969.

MKFKM H13
25890 LEO SOLING; Sg/FRG 1958; CP; 3300/5100); 120.9 × 6.6/7.9 (397 × 21.1/25.11); M; 14; ex ISERLOHN 1974. Sister: **25891 LEO STAR** (Sg) ex MARBURG 1974.

MKFKM H13

● **25900 NAJADE;** Cy/FRG 1961; C; 3100/4800; 121.2×6.8/7.8 (380×22.3/25.9); M; 16. Sister: **25901 ATHENS SEA** (Cy) ex NEREUS 1976.

MKFKMK H1

● **25920 HOUDA STAR;** Cy/Sw 1949; C; 5200; 135×7.9 (443×25.11); M; 14; ex PEGASOS III; ex PROSPERITAS 1976; ex VIBRAN NJORD 1968; ex CONCORDIA VIBRAN 1967; ex VIBRAN NJORD 1966; ex LANGFONN 1964.

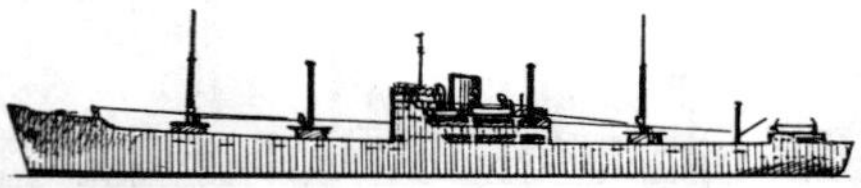

MKFKMK H1

25940 LAMTONG CHAU; Pa/De 1947; C; 5100; 134.4×7.9 (441×25.9); M; 15; ex EASTERN MOON 1971; ex HOEGH SILVERMOON 1960.

MKFKMK H1

● **25960 EURABIA WIND;** Le/Sw 1952; C; 1900; 98.1×5.9 (322×19.3); M; 14; ex KAP ARKONA 1975; ex INGRID GORTHON 1966.

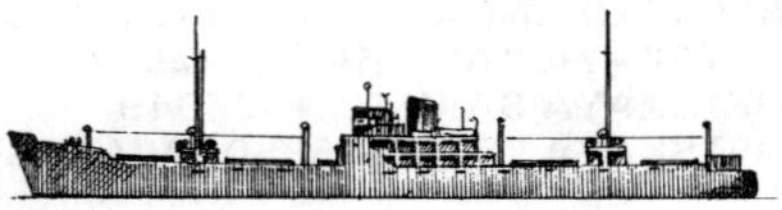

MKFKMK H1

● **25970 AMSTERDAM;** Gr/Fr 1952; C; 3700; 118.7×6.2 (389×20.4); M; 14.5; ex JADEFAHRT 1970; ex PRESIDENT CHARLES LEFEBVRE 1969.

MKFKMK H13

25990 HERMION; No/Ne 1959; CP; 9500; 155.9×8.8 (511×28.9); M; 17.5; ex HOYANGER 1974; Side doors.

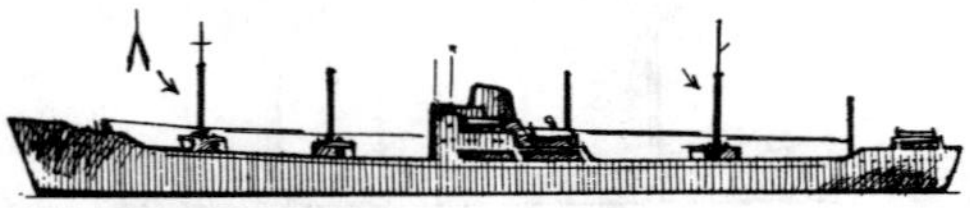

MKFKMK H13

26000 GENERAL PAEZ; Ve/Sw 1958; C; 9700; 151.6×9.3 (497×30.7); M; 15; ex HOSANGER 1976.

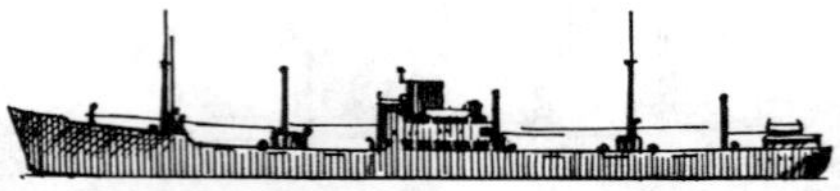

MKFKMK H1

25910 AL DAHRAN; Si/Sw 1946; CP; 4700; 138.7×7.3 (455×24); M; 16; ex BERNY 1976; ex RYDBOHOLM 1964. Similar: **25911 DANAOS** (Cy) ex CANADIA 1966; ex GREKLAND 1965; ex STEGEHOLM 1963.

MKFKMK H1

25930 GENEVE; Sd/Ys 1960; C; 6400/9300; 152.9×8.1/9 (502×26.7/29.8); M; —.

MKFKMK H1

⋆**25950 NING HUA;** RC/Sw 1958; C; 6300/9400; 149×9 (449×29.6); M; 15; ex NEW EAST SEA 1976; ex EAST SEA 1972; ex VINGROM 1967. Sister: **25951 SAI JONG** (Ko) ex LONGTA 1965; ex VINNI 1964 Similar: ⋆**25952 TANGSHAN** (RC) ex VARDA 1966.

MKFKMK H123

⋆**25980 HONG QI No 108;** RC/Br 1960; C; 7000/8700; 150×8.2/9 (490×26.7/29.6); T; 17.5; ex YUNGMING 1975; ex HUMI NASITA 1973; ex MALANCHA 1971; ex ALAUNIA 1969. Sister: ⋆**25981 HONG QI No 107** (RC); ex YUNGJIAN 1975; ex HUMI MAHIS 1973; ex MACHARDA 1971; ex ANDANIA 1969.

MKFKMK H13

26010 OLIVEBANK; Br/Br 1962; C; 6300/8500; 147.3×7.9/8.9 (483×26/29.3); M; 15. Sister: **26011 GLOBAL MED** (Li) ex TERRIE U 1980; ex GLOBAL MED 1980; ex SPRINGBANK 1978.

MKFKMK H13
26020 EURABIA OCEAN; Le/Br 1957; C; 6300/8600; 147.3×7.9/8.6 (483×26/28); M; 15; ex ARIS CARRIER 1977; ex CARRONBANK 1974. Similar: **26021 KOTA RAKYAT** (Sg) ex CLOVERBANK 1971 **26022 RENA K** (Gr) ex CRESTBANK 1973 **26023 LANKA KEERTI** (Sr) ex DARTBANK 1975 **26024 CHI HO** (Pa) ex CHIEH SHENG 1976; ex GARRYBANK 1974 **26025 NEWCREST** (Li) ex ASHBANK 1976 **26026 AVONBANK** (Br) **26027 NEWARK** (Li) ex PINEBANK 1976 **26028 NEWBEACH** (Li) ex NEWBREEZE 1977; ex ROSEBANK 1976 **26029 BLUE WAVE** (Gr) ex ELMBANK 1976 **26030 GOLDEN LAGOS** (Pa) ex OLIVEBANK 1978.

MKFM H
● ⋆**26060 YONG KANG.** RC/No 1960; C; 2500/3800; 102.1×6.06/7.46 (335×19.88/24.48); M; 14; ex HENGSHAN 1977; ex BEAVERELM 1971; ex ROGA 1962. Similar: **26061 CONNY** (Ho) ex MATHIOS NICOLAS 1979; ex STATHINA 1974; ex MARS 1979 ⋆**26062 YUHAI** (RC) ex MOUNTHWA; ex SNEFJELD 1967 **26063 MAHAJAK FOUNDER** (Pa) ex TAURUS 1980; ex PHUTNAKORN; ex GOLDEN CHRYSANTHEMUM 1976; ex SWIFT DRAGON 1972; ex NARDO 1968 ⋆**26064 MULDE** (DDR) ex SUNIMA 1965.

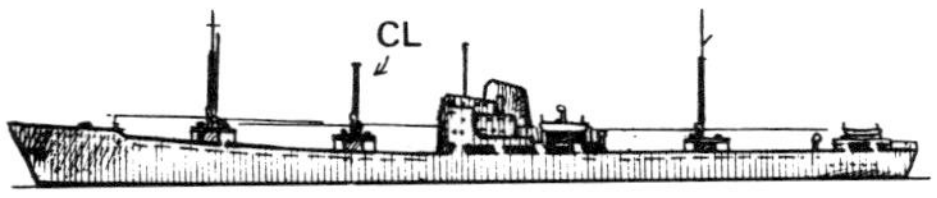

MKFM H
26080 DONG MYUNG. Ko/FRG 1955; CP; 8700; 143.5×8.6 (471×28.2); M; 13; ex NORDSTERN 1965. Similar: **26081 NORDWIND** (FRG) **26082 BREMEN** (Pa) ex NORDLAND 1970.

MKFM H
26100 AGIOS GERASSIMOS. Gr/FRG 1954; C; 8200; 144.3×8.8 (473×29); M; 13; ex RIVER ROSE 1976; ex PROGRESSUS 1974; ex PRESIDENT 1974; ex PROBITAS 1972; ex NEFELI 1970; ex WIDAR 1967. Similar: **26101 CAMELIA** (Cy) ex BELLO F. 1969; ex BALDUR 1965 **26102 NAMYANG DRAGON** (Ko) ex AEGIR 1965.

MKFM H
26040 GEMAR; Ia/FRG 1955; C; 5300; 143.7×7.6 (471×24.11); M; 13.25; ex GEERT HOWALDT 1972.

MKFM H
26050 ESKISEHIR. Tu/No 1953; CP; 2500; 102.8×6.3 (337×20.9); R; 12; ex BJORGSUND 1953. Sister: **26051 ZIYA KALKAVAN II** (Tu) ex S. MANIOGLU 1979; ex KIRSEHIR 1978 Similar (flat-topped funnel): **26052 NEVSEHIR** (Tu) ex DALHEIM 1955.

MKFM H
26070 FRIO DOLPHIN. Gr/De 1963; R; 2400; 106.9×5.8 (351×18.2); M; 15.5; ex KALIMANTAN FORTUNE; ex C. JOYCE 1976; ex PETUNIA 1974. Sister: **26071 AL GILANI** (In) ex C. RANEE 1976; ex MAGNOLIA 1974.

MKFM H
26090 ENNA G. Na/Ne 1961; PC; 9300; 139×8.6 (456×28.3); M; —; ex PRINSES MARGRIET 1970. Now rebuilt.

MKFM H
● **26110 NIKOLAOS A.** Gr/FRG 1952; C; 7300; 143.7×7.6 (471×24.1); M; 12.5; ex ANNROSE 1975; ex BREEZE 1973; ex WILDROSE 1973; ex FRANCISKA HENDRIK FISSER 1968. Sister: **26111 NEW WAN FU** (Pa) ex EASTERN METEOR 1977; ex HERTA ENGELINE FRITZEN 1964 Similar (with mast houses): **26112 AURORA** (Gr) ex MACHIAVELLI 1980; ex GENOVA 1978; ex CARL JULIUS 1977; ex ILSE SCHULTE 1957 **26113 AIS GIORGIS** (Gr) ex AGHIOS NECTARIOS 1980; ex SPLENDOR 1976; ex PRIMROSE 1973; ex KAREN REED 1968.

MKFM H

● **26120 DONA MARGARITA.** Li/Br 1956; C; 6300/8600; 147.4 × —/8.9 (483 × —/29.4); M; 13.5; ex MARIRITA 1966; ex DONA MARGARITA 1963. Sister: **26121 SHANI Z** (Pa) ex JUBILEE 77; ex DONA OURANIA 1977 Similar (taller bridge): **26122 ISOBEL** (Li) ex DONA EDIE 1961.

MKFM H

26130 AKROPOLIS. Cy/Br 1937; C; 5300; 133.9 × 7.7 (439 × 25.5); M; 10.5; ex OTHON; ex MARITSA Z 1969; ex THOMAS MUNTZER 1963; ex HAULERWIJK 1958; ex FOREST 1951.

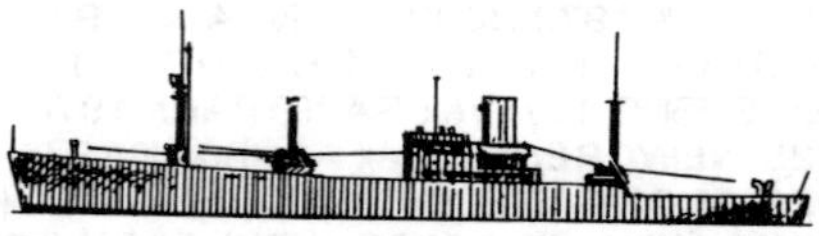

MKFM H

26140 NORTEMAR. Ur/US 1944; C; 5200; 125.7 × 7.6 (412 × 24.1); M; 14; ex SIRANGER 1959; ex NARVIK 1946; ex CAPE RIVER 1944; Standard WW2 **'C.1'** type. Sister: **⋆26141 RYTTERHOLM** (RC) ex STROM FOREST 1970; ex SUNROSE 1962; ex ALF LINDEBERG 1954; ex CAPE NORTH 1943; May be others of this type still in service.

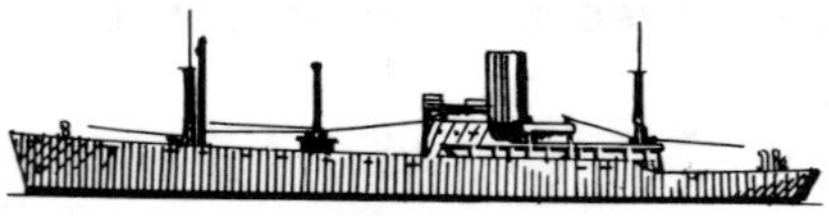

MKFM H

26150 'C-1' type. —/US c/1944; C; 5200; 125.7 × 7.6 (412 × 24.1); M; 14; May be some of this type still in service. Note extended superstructure.

MKFM H

⋆26160 KHOLMSK. Ru/Ge 1943; —; 3000; 90.5 × 7.3 (296 × 24); R; 10.5.

MKFM H

26170 DAVAO CITY. Pi/De 1956; PC; 1500; 89.3 × 5.7 (293 × 18.8); M; 12; ex TAGBILARAN CITY 1972; ex BELLONA 1972; Probably has more superstructure decks.

MKFM H

26180 ELLOBA. Pa/No 1951; CP; 3000; 98.7 × 6.9 (324 × 19.7); M; 13; ex BLUE SKY 1980; ex NIA 1977; ex RITA V 1970; ex MASUNA V 1966; ex GEFFEN 1965; ex MIM 1952.

MKFM H

26190 APOLLO. Gr/De 1937; CP; 2300; 104.1 × 6 (342 × 19.11); M; 13; ex CARMEN 1975; ex LIBERTY 1975; ex UNIFORCE 1975; ex OLYMPIC 1974; ex MAYA 1968; ex MATEO 1966; ex SUNDAAA 1962; ex GUDRUN MAERSK 1955.

MKFM H

26200 AL QASEEM. Si/Fr 1957; R; 2800; 115.5 × 5.8 (379 × 19.1); M; 16; ex BAMBARA 1973.

MKFM H

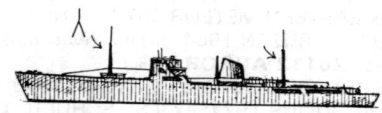

26210 KHALIJ SKY. Gr/Fr 1960; C; 4900; 114.94 × 6 (377.1 × 19.69); M; 18; ex TARPON 1978. Sister: **26211 OPALINE BAY** (Pa) ex LETHE 1980; ex ESPADON 1977.

MKFM H1

⋆26220 SOVIETSKAYA ARKTIKA. Ru/Br 1951; FC; 9000; 140.6 × 7 (461 × 26); M; 12; ex STANHOPE 1954.

MKFM H1
26230 PAOLO D'AMICO. It/It 1957; C; 8800; 151 × 8.9 (496 × 29); M; 15.5. Similar: **26231 CESARE D'AMICO** (It).

MKFM H1
● **26240 DINA.** Cy/Ne 1954; C; 5300; 138.6 × 7.6 (455 × 24.11); M; 14.5; ex WHITE ROSE 1973.

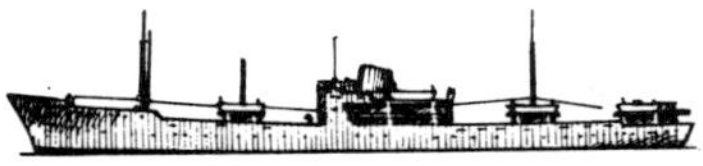

MKFM H1
26250 FOOCHOW. Pa/Sw 1955; PC; 2700/3900; 108.9 × 6/7 (357 × 19.8/22.11); M; 15; ex HOI YING 1981.

MKFM H1
26260 NOVEMBER SEVENTH. Pa/No 1948; CP; 2000; 99.8 × 5.6 (328 × 18.6); M; 14; ex TERESA 1977; ex MONICA 1972; ex PROMINENT 1966.

MKFM H1
● **26270 AFFLUENT COUNTRY.** Pa/SW 1949; PC; 2200; 104 × 5.7 (341 × 18.1); M; 14; ex HOI HOUW 1974. Sister: **26271 BUNGA BUTANG** (My) ex HOI WONG 1973.

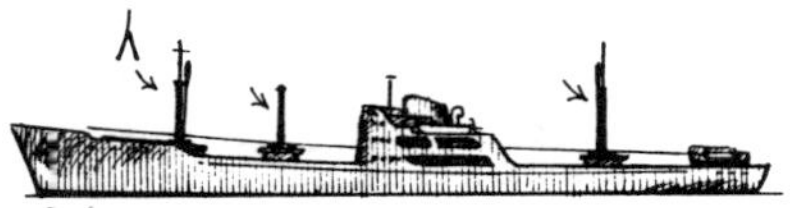

MKFM H1
26280 CEFALLONIAN GLORY. Gr/De 1955; CP; 4100; 120.1 × 7.4 (394 × 24.5); M; 14.25; ex UCKERMARK; ex LOTTE SKOU 1964.

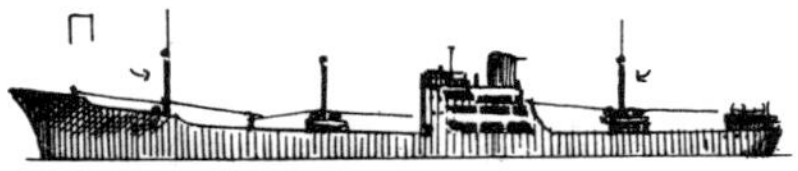

MKFM H1
26290 DELTA SIGMA PI. Pa/No 1954; CP; 4000; 118.3 × 6.8 (388 × 22.3); R; 11.5; ex AMARANTOS; ex ADVENT; ex PIONEER EAGLE; ex HWA LUNG; ex MAHAVIKRAM 1973; ex MAHA JAG TARA 1967; ex JAG TARA 1964; ex MAGNUS STOVE.

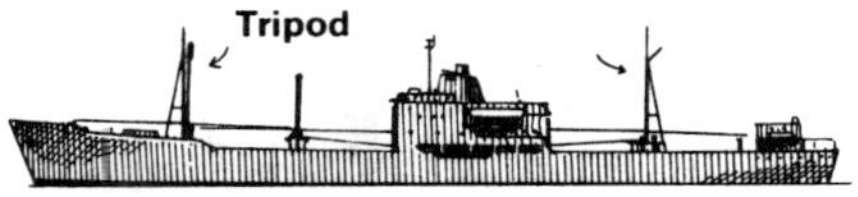

MKFM H1
26300 NAVIKAPOL. Pa/Sw 1954; CP; 4200; 132.2 × 7.7 (434 × 25.7); M; 18; ex LINDENSTEIN 1976; ex CLARY THORDEN 1965.

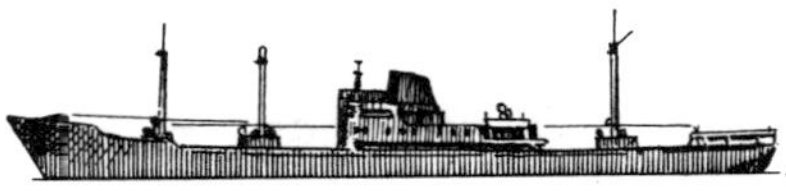

MKFM H1
26310 ATLANTIC FREEZER. Pa/Sp 1956; PC; 4000; 118.4 × 7.2 (388 × 23.8); M; 19; ex NISSOS KERKYRA 1980; ex MONTE ARUCAS 1976.

MKFM H1
● ⋆**26320 TRIGLAV.** Ys/Ys 1954; C; 3100; 119.4 × 6.7 (392 × 22); M; 16. Sisters (Ys flag): ⋆**26321 LOVCEN** ⋆**26322 VELEBIT.**

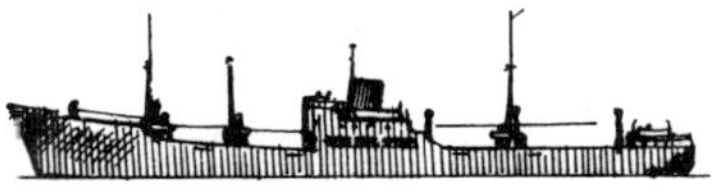

MKFM H1
26330 DYNAMIC 1. Gr/Sw 1947; C; 2200; 106.7 × 5.9 (350 × 19.3); M; 14.5; ex OLYMPIOS APOLLON 1979; ex AMBELOS; ex BENGAZI 1968.

MKFM H1
● **26340 EUGENIA V.** Gr/Sw 1952; CP; 3300/5300; 121.9 × 7.1/— (400 × 23.4/—); M; 15; ex PROMETHEUS; ex ADAJO 1975; ex USEDOM 1971; ex OTHEM 1962.

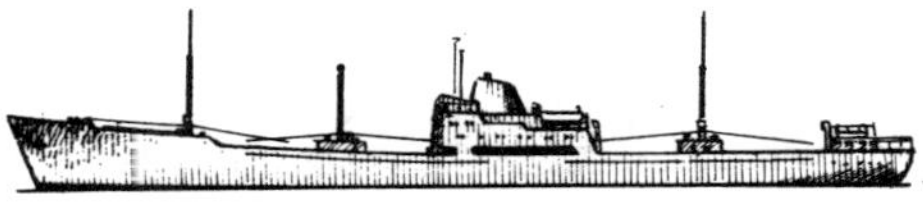

MKFM H1
26350 YUVALI. Li/FRG 1957; CP; 4000/6500; 143.2 × 6.6/— (470 × 21.7/—); TSM; 16.5; ex YUVAL 1975; ex VIVA; ex CAPE BRETON 1973; ex HORNLAND 1973. Sister: **26351 LI SHAN** (Pa) ex HORNSTERN 1975.

MKFM H1
26360 MAN CHEONG. Pa/Sw 1958; C; 4100/6400; 130.9 × 7.2/8.2 (430 × 23.9/26.1); M; 14.5; ex KAPTANIKOS 1979; ex NESSHORN 1972; ex FINNBOARD 1970.

MKFM H1
26370 POSEIDON C. Pa/Sw 1956; C; 3600; 108.82 × 5.92 (357 × 19.5); M; 15; ex RIODON 1979; ex DRUCILLA U 1975; ex FARIDA 1972. **26371 HOPE** (Ni) ex FOLIAS 1972; ex FORTUNA 1965.

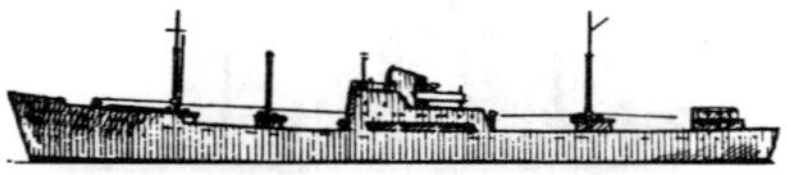

MKFM H1
26380 ARACTOS BRIDGE. Pa/Sw 1956; CP; 3400/5200; 121.9 × 7.7/8.2 (400 × 25.3/26.1); M; 16; ex ADAM S; ex PILHAMN 1972; ex INGRID BRODIN 1971.

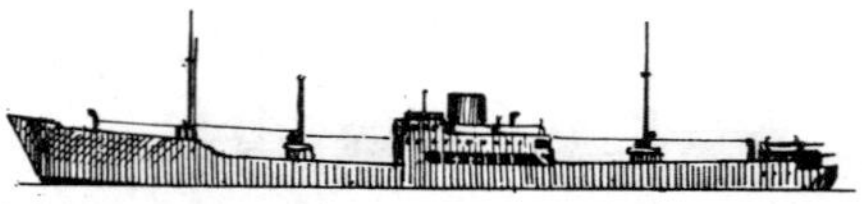

MKFM H1
26390 EASTERN VALOUR. Pa/Sw 1948; CP; 3800; 128.8 × 7.1 (421 × 23.4); M; 14.5; ex AMRONTO 1976; ex LYNGENFJORD 1970.

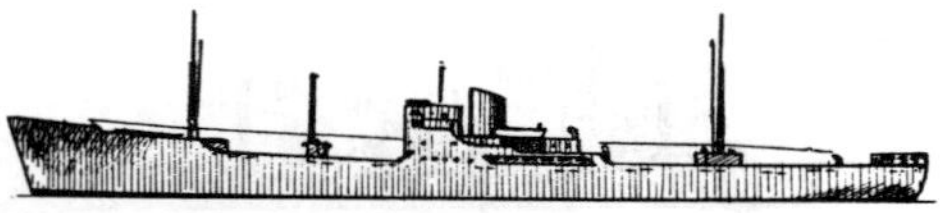

MKFM H1
● **26400 AGAPI.** Gr/Br 1955; C; 8900; 146.6 × 9.3 (481 × 30.7); M; 14.5; ex RENA 1975; ex CAPETAN CARRAS 1969. Sister: **26401 IOANIS XILAS** (Gr) ex STARLIGHT 1966; ex CAPETAN PSARROS 1958.

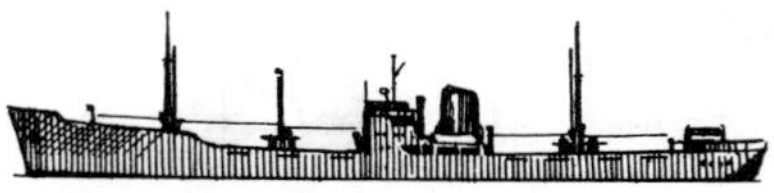

MKFM H1
26410 ELENI A. Gr/De 1943; CP; 3800; 117.7 × 7.4 (386 × 24); M; 13.5; ex HUGO KOLLATAJ 1975; ex BENNY SKOU.

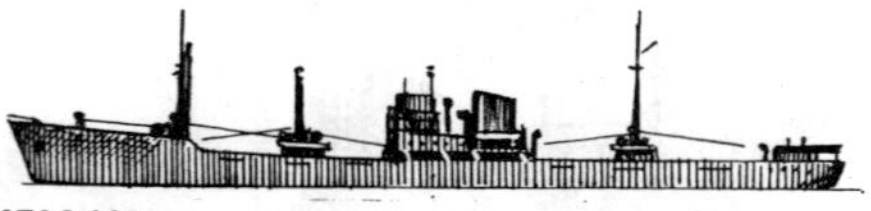

MKFM H1
26420 SANIX BELLE. Pa/FRG 1954; CP; 3700; 121.8 × 6.6 (430 × 21.6); M; 12.5; ex EL GAVILAN; ex HORNKLIFF 1972.

MKFM H1
26430 RIO SAN JUAN. Ar/De 1936; R; 2300; 108 × 5.8 (354 × 18.11); M; 12; ex AMERICAN REEFER 1942.

MKFM H1
● **26440 NORTH COUNTESS.** Gr/Br 1958; C; 10700; 159.1 × 9.5 (522 × 31.1); M; —. Similar (Inset): **26441 NORTH EMPRESS** (Gr).

MKFM H1
⋆**26450 JOSE ANTONIO ECHEVARRIA.** Cu/Fr 1949; CP; 9100; 142.4 × 8.9 (480 × 29.1); M; 17; ex VILLE 1970; ex VILLE DE TAMATAVE 1970.

MKFM H1
26460 KOTA FAJAR. Sg/Br 1957; C; 9800; 152.8 × 9.3 (501.8 × 30.6); M; 14; ex POLYXENE C 1973.

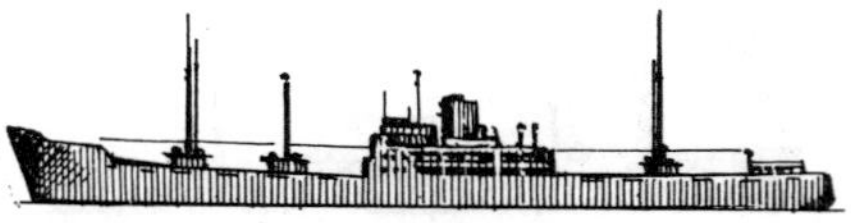

MKFM H1
⋆**26470 FOSHAN.** RC/Fr 1949; C; 5100; 129.5 × 7.3 (425 × 23.11); T; 13.5; ex JULIUS FUCIK 1965; ex VOLTA 1954.

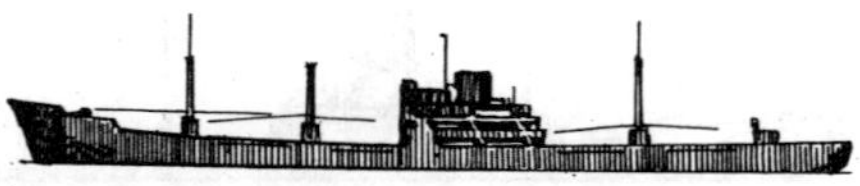

MKFM H1
26480 MING UNITY. Tw/Ja 1957; C; 7300; 132.2 × 8.6 (434 × 28.3); M; 14.5; ex YUNN MING 1977; ex HAI MIN 1963.

MKFM H1
26490 ZAK. Pa/Br 1962; C; 7300/10000; 154.9 × 8.3/9.3 (508 × 27.3/30.6); M; 15; ex STRATHTAY; ex TREBARTHA 1975. Sister: **26491 EVIA** (Gr) ex STRATHTEVIOT; ex TREFUSIS 1975.

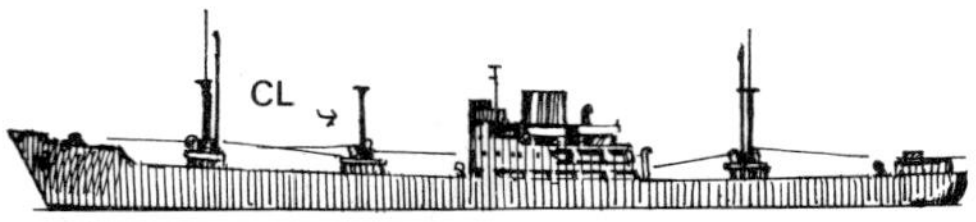

MKFM H1
26500 LENDOUDIS EVANGELOS. Gr/Br 1961; C; 6300/8600; 148.7 × 8.2/8.9 (488 × 26.5/29.4); M; —; ex TREVALGAN 1973.

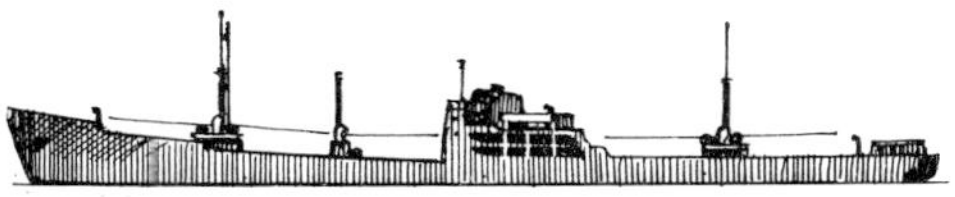

MKFM H1
26510 HIOS. Gr/Br 1958; C; 6800/9800; 145.5 × 8.5/9.2 (477 × 27.1/30.3); M; —; ex GEORGIOS C 1975; ex HUNTSFIELD 1969.

MKFM H1
⋆**26520 DANJIANG.** RC/Fr 1957; CP; 5800/8000; 145.4 × 7.9/8.7 (477 × 26/28.5); M; 16; ex VILLE DE DUNKERQUE 1976. Sister: ⋆**26521 LIU KIANG** (RC) ex VILLE DE ROUEN 1976 Similar: **26522 PROFITIS ELIAS** (Gr) ex GUYANE 1976; ex VILLE DE DJIBOUTI 1965.

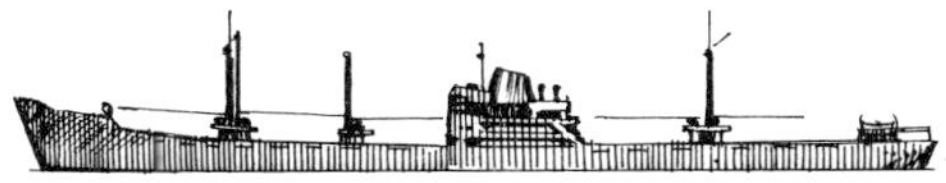

MKFM H1
26530 KAPETANIKOS. Gr/Ne 1958; C; 8600; 145.6 × 8.7 (478 × 28.7); M; —; ex NORTH DUCHESS 1976. Sister: **26531 EUROPEAN MARCHIONESS** (Li) ex NORTH MARCHIONESS 1980.

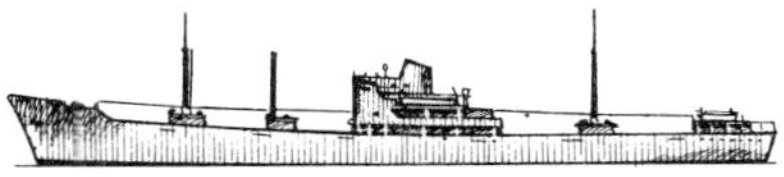

MKFM H1
26540 TREPSA. Cy/Sw 1947; C; 5300; 121.8 × 7.2 (400 × 23.3); M; 16; ex RIVER SES 1972; ex LIA 1968.

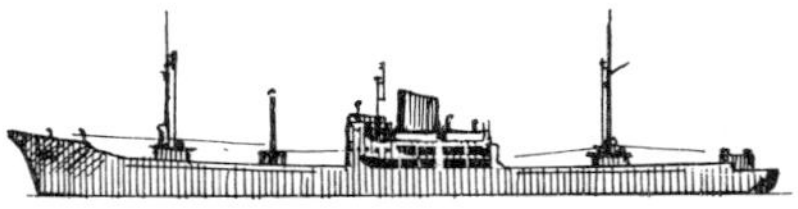

MKFM H1
26550 UNITED PIONEER. Pa/Ys 1952; C; 2800; 117.1 × 6.4 (384 × 20.11); M; —; ex STAR 1975; ex AVALA 1970. Sister: **26551 UNITED PROSPERITY** (Pa) ex ALGA 1975; ex DINARA 1971.

MKFM H1
26560 OPAL. Cy/It 1940; C; 3600; 116.9 × 6.7 (383 × 21.11); M; —; ex DAFFODIL 1976; ex KIM 1975; ex VOJVODINA 1969; ex SREM 1951; ex BALCIC.

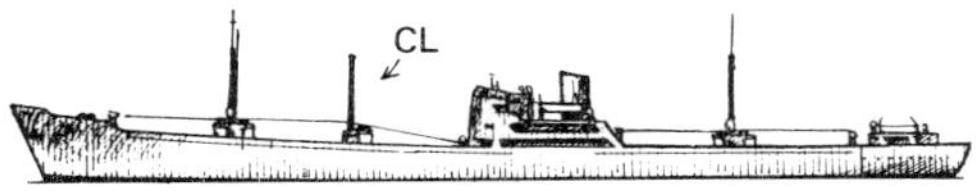

MKFM H1
● **26570 BONITA 1.** Pa/FRG 1958; C; 5700; 151.7 × 7.6 (498 × 25.1); M; 12.75; ex EMAR 1980; ex EFOR 1977; ex PROVIDENTIA 1974; ex KARPFANGER 1970. Sister: **26571 MIGHTY BREEZE** (Pa) ex PALMYRA 1980; ex KERSTEN MILES 1971 Similar: **26572 PEARL CITY** (Pa) ex CALYSO N 1980; ex SIMON VON UTRECHT 1971.

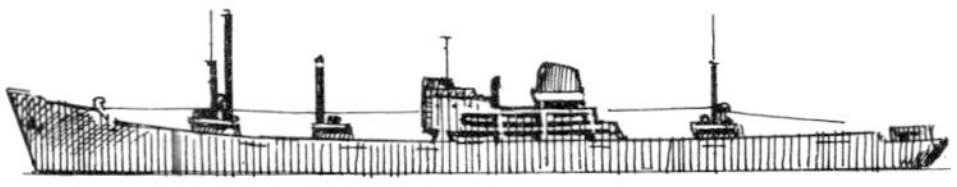

MKFM H1
26580 UNITY. Gr/Br 1954; C; 6200/8600; 147.8 × 8.1/8.9 (485 × 26.7/29.3); M; —; ex VASILAKIS 1974; ex PINDAR 1970.

MKFM H1
26590 PEARL DELTA. Pa/Br 1953; C; 5900; 141.8 × 8.7 (465 × 28.5); M; 14; ex COSTAFLORA 1980; ex LETO 1967; ex PEARLSTONE 1954.

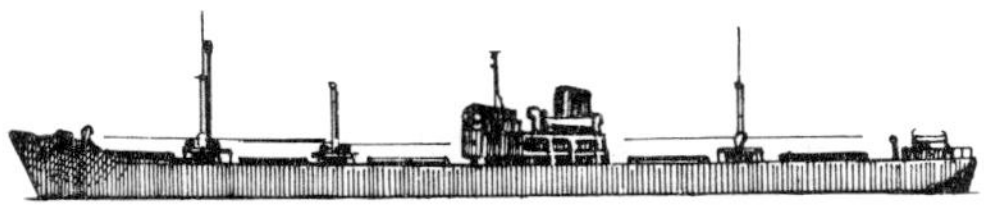

MKFM H1
26600 BYZANTINE MONARCH. Gr/Br 1959; C; 9400; 152.2 × 9.5 (500 × 31.2); M; 13.75; ex SCOTTISH MONARCH 1968.

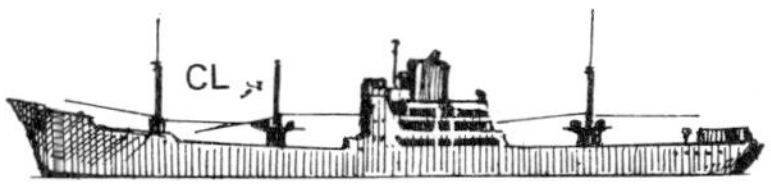

MKFM H1
26610 GULF UNITY. Sh/Br 1955; C; 5100; 114.9 × 7.3 (377 × 24); R & LPT; 13; ex KHALID 1975; ex FULKA 1973; ex AGIA SOPHIA 1971; ex ANATOLIAN 1968; ex ASCANIA 1968; ex ANATOLIAN 1968; ex ASCANIA 1966; ex CITY OF DURHAM 1964; ex ANATOLIAN 1963.

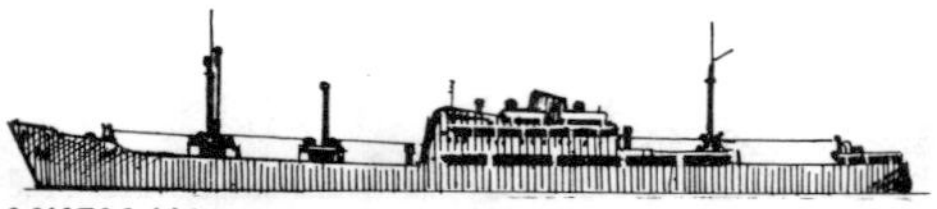

MKFM H1
26620 GURU ANGADH. Pa/De 1949; PC; 8700; 140×8.4 (459×27.9); M; 15.75; ex GULF MAJESTY 1980; ex ASTREE 1976; ex ILE DE LA REUNION 1972.

MKFM H1
26640 ZYGOS. Pa/FRG 1957; C; 6400; 144.3×7.9 (473×25.11); M; 13.25; ex TID 1980; ex LUXEMBOURG 1980; ex HELGA HOWALDT 1965.

MKFM H1
26660 JUVENA. Gr/FRG 1956; CP; 4900; 138.9×7.6 (456×25); M; 15.25; ex UBENA 1977. Sister: **26661 SAPLA** (Bh) ex BLUE TIGER 1980; ex DOCTOR LELLO 1976; ex USARAMO 1974.

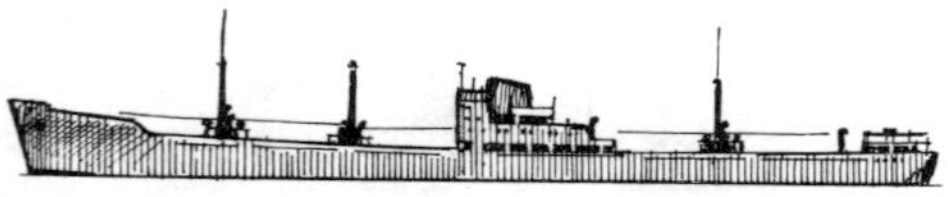

MKFM H1
26680 SAN NICOLAOS. Li/Sw 1957; CP; 9000; 145×9.3 (476×29.3); M; 15.25; ex CAPTO 1968.

MKFM H1
● **26690 SAINI.** Gr/Sw 1957; CP; 6300/9000; 145×8/9.2 (476×26.4/29.3); M; —; ex POLA NINA; ex LOA 1977; ex FOLGA 1970.

MKFM H1
★**26710 TAISHAN.** RC/Sw 1957; CP; 2700/4400; 112.5×6.4/7.5 (369×20.9/24.7); M; 13; ex NORDICA 1968.

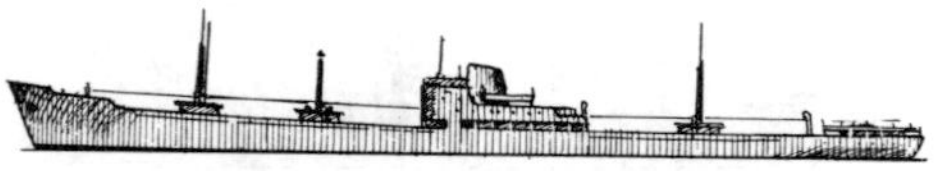

MKFM H1
★**26730 LONGHUA.** RC/Sw 1959; C; 8800; 145×9.4 (476×30.1); M; 14; ex BIBO 1975; ex ARISTOKRATIS 1974; ex KOLLBJORG 1969. Sister: **26731 VITASEA** (Gr) ex ARISTOVOULOS 1975; ex KOLLGRIM 1970.

MKFM H1
26630 ELLI. Gr/FRG 1958; CP; 6400; 144.3×7.9 (473×25.11); M; 12.5; ex MACHIAVELLI 1980; ex ALFRED THEODOR 1979.

MKFM H1
26650 GAY FIDELITY. Gr/FRG 1956; C; 5600/8200; 149.4×8.2/9 (490×26.1/29.6); M; 15; ex CATHARINA OLDENDORF 1974.

MKFM H1
● **26670 EASTAR.** Gr/Ja 1957; C; 6500/9400; 148.5×— (487×—); M; 14; ex SKARVA 1973; ex EDDA 1964. Sisters: **26671 WESTERN NAV** (PA) ex WESTAR 1980; ex SPILDRA 1973; ex SIGLAND 1964 **26672 KUSU ISLAND** (Sg) ex BOLMAREN; ex ARTEMEDI III 1976; ex SEFRA 1975; ex CAPE OF GOOD HOPE 1961 **26673 AMAR** (Gr) ex E.D. PAPALIOS **26674 PROMETHEUS** (Gr) ex OCEAN PROSPER 1968; ex SURNA 1965; ex CAPE AGULHAS 1961; ex SIRA **26675 THEANTO A.S.** (Gr) ex POLARIS 1970.

MKFM H1
26700 STELLA. Gr/Sw 1957; C; 6400/8900; 144.99×8.03/9.35 (475.69×26.35/30.68); M; 14.5; ex SUNPOLYNESIA 1971.

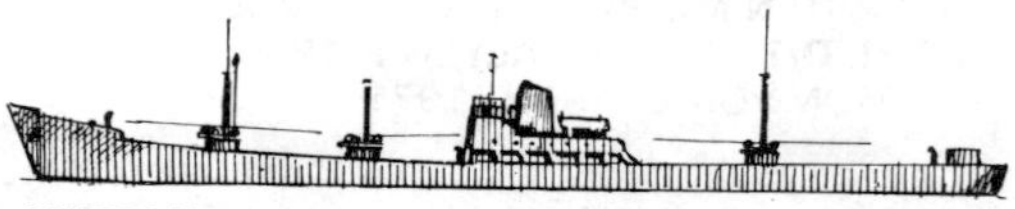

MKFM H1
26720 TACAMAR VI. Pa/Fr 1961; C; 11000; 158×9.6 (518×30.9); M; 15.5; ex TEPUY 1980; ex ANTONIOS COULOUTHROS.

MKFM H1
26740 YZONA. Cy/Sw 1952; C; 3300; 103.7×6.5 (340×21.4); M; 13; ex SEABREEZE 1973; ex NORMA 1968; ex NORINDA 1963.

MKFM H1

● **26750 AGIA EFIMIA.** Gr/FRG 1951; CP; 3800; 131.6 × 6.6 (432 × 21.7); M; 13.5; ex EUNA 1976; ex ANITA 1972. Similar: **26751 BENGUELA CURRENT** (Li) ex BALKAN **26752 AUSTRIAN MERCHANT** (As) ex THERESA 1976; ex WINDHUK 1972 **26753 LONGTIME** (Pa) ex LUCEDY 1976; ex NATAL D 1972; ex NATAL 1969.

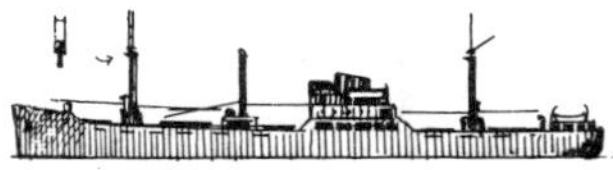

MKFM H1

26760 HONG ENG. Sg/Ne 1955/60; C; 2000; 92.97 × 5.44 (305 × 17.1); M; 12.5; ex ATLANTIC KLIF 1974; ex PRINS CASIMIR 1967; Lengthened 1960. Sister: **26761 ARAXOS** (Gr) ex MARINOS 1973; ex MINA 1971; ex GAELIC PRINCE 1970; ex MINA 1969; ex PRINS WILLEM V 1967.

MKFM H1

26770 BARAO DE JACEGUAY. Bz/Bz 1963; C; 3600/5000; 116.7 × —7.1 (383 × —/23.3); M; 12.5. Sisters (Bz flag): **26771 BARAO DO RIO BRANCO 26772 JACY RAMOS** ex BARAO DO AMAZONAS.

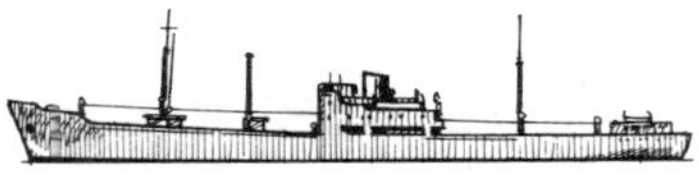

MKFM H1

26780 PELEUS. Gr/Sw 1950; C; 2300; 108.82 × 5.94 (357 × 19.6); M; 15; ex GRUNDSUNDA 1970.

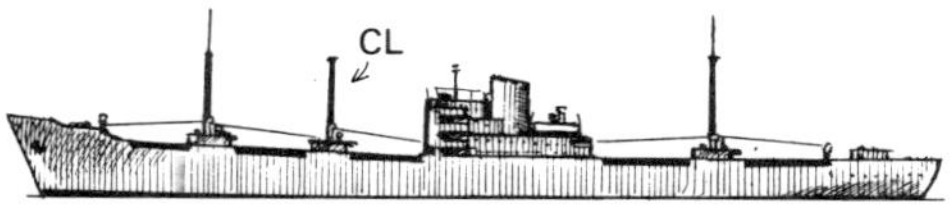

MKFM H1

● **26790 HUMANITY.** Gr/FRG 1957; C; 8500; 148.3 × 8.8 (486 × 28.11); M; 14; ex ANANGEL AMBITION 1973; ex STAD DELFT 1973. Sisters (Gr flag): **26791 CHARITY** EX ANANGEL FAITH 1973; ex STAD GOUDA 1972 **26792 DIGNITY** ex ANANGEL PROVIDENCE 1973; ex STAD UTRECHT 1972.

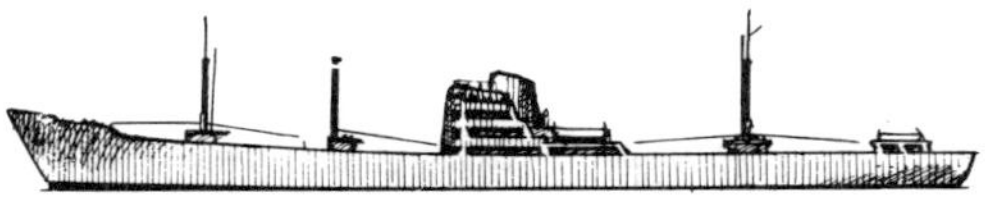

MKFM H1

● ⋆**26800 GUANG PING.** RC/FRG 1958; C; 9300; 153.7 × 9.3 (504 × 30.5); M; —; ex MIRTOAN SEA 1976; ex DIMITRA 1973; ex CONTINENTAL MERCHANT 1969; ex OTTERBURN 1966; ex CONTINENTAL CARRIER 1962. Sisters: **26801 SANTIAGO** (Gr) ex CONTINENTAL PIONEER 1968 **26802 UNISTAR** (Sg) ex SONIA M.G. 1980; ex PEGASO 1980; ex CONTINENTAL SHIPPER 1968; ex WOODBURN 1966; ex CONTINENTAL TRADER 1962 **26803 STATE OF MAHARASHTRA** (In) ex OREGON LEADER 1960; ex CONTINENTAL LEADER.

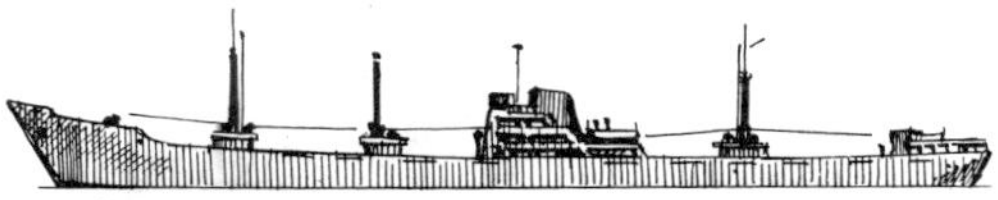

MKFM H1

⋆**26810 HONG QI 138.** RC/FRG 1957; C; 9500; 153.7 × 9 (504 × 29.7); M; 15; ex NEW SAPPHIRE 1980; ex SAPPHIRE 1976; ex SPARTO 1970; ex CAPTANTONIS 1963. Similar: **26811 ZEENA** (Pa) ex KYRAKATINGO 1973 **26812 VARUNA ADHAR** (In) ex LOK ADHAR 1979; ex HOOGHLY; ex DIMITRIS.

MKFM H1

26820 CYNTHLEMA. Li/FRG 1956; C; 9000; 149.7 × 7.9 (491 × 26); T; 14.5; ex EURYDAMAS.

MKFM H1
26830 AL HASAN. Pk/FRG 1958; C; 9200; 153.7 × 9.3 (504 × 30.2); M; 15; ex HELGA SCHRODER 1965.

MKFM H1
26850 GORGO Gr/De 1958; C; 5000/7100; 140 × 7.9/8.3 (459 × 26/27.4); M; 16.5; ex NORDHOLM 1974. Sister: **26851 MALDIVE NAVIGATOR** (Mv) ex AL QASIM 1976; ex AL RASHEED 1976; ex NORDGLIMT 1974.

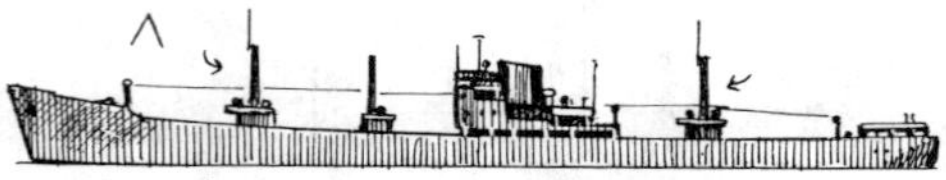

MKFM H1
26860 VIRA. Gr/Sw 1956; C; 5300/7800; 143.6 × 7.6/8.7 (471 × 25/28.7); M; 15; ex MAUTRIC 1973; ex ARAGONA 1968.

MKFM H1
26880 MAROUKO. Gr/Br 1957; C; 9000; 152.8 × 9.4 (501 × 30.1); M; 14; ex LORD BYRON 1975. Sister: **26881 AGIA VARVARA** (Gr) ex ARMA 1976; ex LORD CODRINGTON 1968.

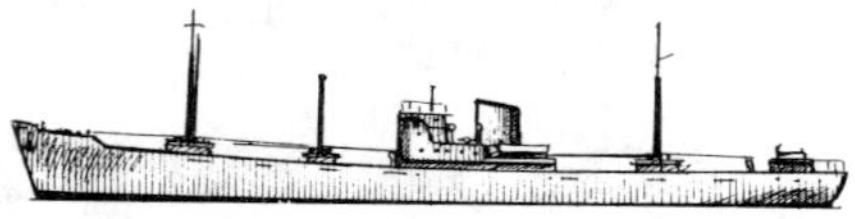

MKFM H1
26890 INTERHARMONY. Gr/FRG 1953; CP; 3600; 131.8 × 6.6 (432 × 21.6); M; 13; ex BLUE ALBACORE 1980; ex HORNBERG 1971.

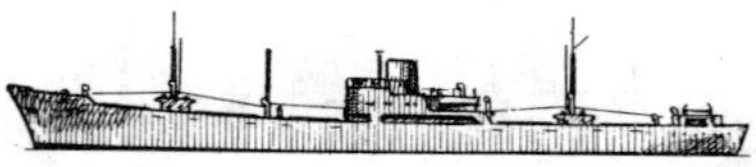

MKFM H1
26910 QUEEN SEA. Cy/FRG 1955; C; 2800/4600; 116.7 × —/7.1 (380 × —/23.3); M; 12.75; ex DANIEL 1979; ex DALBEK 1974.

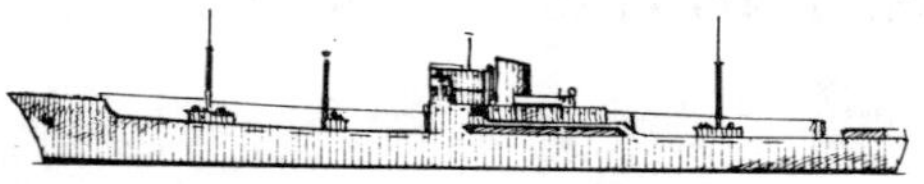

MKFM H1
⋆**26930 CHEUNG CHAU.** RC/Br 1956; C; 8600; 142.4 × 8.9 (467 × 29.3); M; —; ex ATALANTI M. LIVANOS 1964.

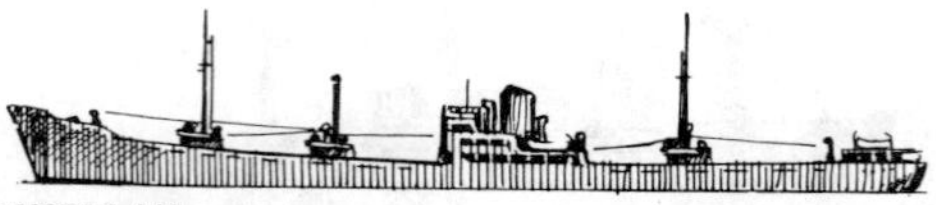

MKFM H1
26840 AURORA. No/FRG 1954; CP; 6200; 143.6 × 7.6 (471 × 25.1); M; 12.25; ex MACHIAVELLI 1980; ex GENOVA 1978; ex CARL JULIUS 1977; ex ILSE SCHULTE 1957. Sister: **26841 AIS GIORGIS** (Gr) ex AGHIOS NECTARIOS 1980; ex SPLENDOUR; ex PRIMROSE 1973; ex KAREN REED 1968.

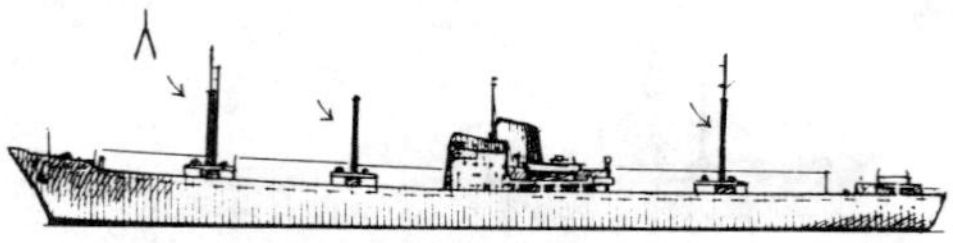

MKFM H1
● **26870 JUPITER D.** Pa/FRG 1955; CP; 6400; 147.9 × 8 (485 × 25.9); M; 13; ex M. ROSARIO D 1980; ex CINZIA D'AMATO 1973; ex KLAUS LEONHARDT 1969. Sisters: **26871 ALBIS** (Li) ex BERND LEONHARDT 1972 **26872 AURELIA** (Cy) ex EIBE OLDENDORFF 1974 **26873 ALIARTOS** (Cy) ex HINRICH OLDENDORFF 1974 **26874 PERAST** (Ma) ex MARBRAVA 1974; ex PROVENIERSSINGEL 1971 **26875 STATE OF ASSAM** (In) ex COOLSINGEL 1959 **26876 STATE OF BIHAR** (In) ex STATENSINGEL 1960 Similar: **26877 WHITE SEA** (Pa) ex FRANK LEONHARDT 1972.

MKFM H1
26900 MATHIOS. Gr/Sw 1953; C; 2000; 105 × 5.7 (346 × 18.7); M; 13.5; ex RECKNITZ; ex LAGNO 1965.

MKFM H1
⋆**26920 SONG JIANG.** RC/De 1945; C; 5000; 134.3 × 7.8 (441 × 25.7); M; 13; ex POKOJ 1966; ex DANSBORG 1951.

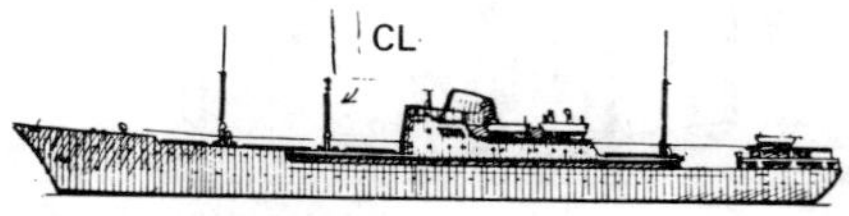

MKFM H1
26940 PRIMERO DE JUNIO. Me/Sp 1959; P/TS (Troopship); 6800; 130.8 × 6.9 (429 × 22.6); M; 17; ex MONTE ANAGA 1974; Mexican Navy.

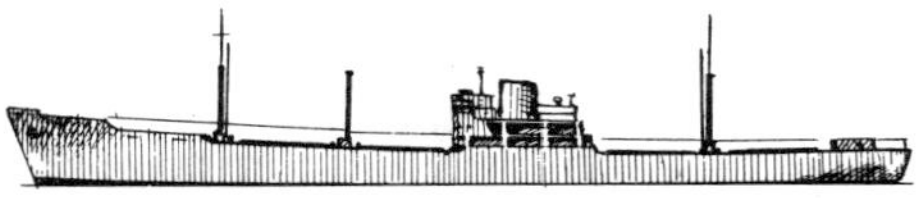

MKFM H1
26950 IRIS. Gr/Br 1954; C; 6000; 143.1 × 8.2 (470 × 27.1); M; 13; ex DORIS 1973. Similar: **26951 EASTERN SUCCESS** (Pa) ex DORIEFS 1980.

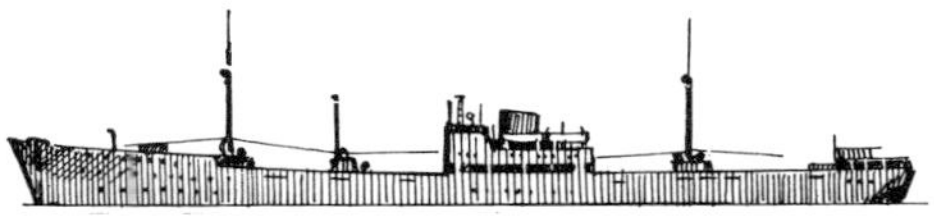

MKFM H1
★26960 ATLANTIKA. Ru/Sw 1954; C; 5500/8600; 143 × 6.5/7.6 (462 × 21.4/25); M; 13.5; ex ARAGONA 1954.

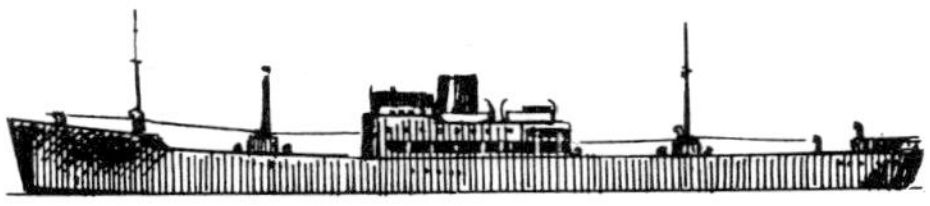

MKFM H1
26970 PRIAMOS. Cy/Sw 1945; C; 5800; 144.6 × 7.8 (474 × 25.8); M; 16.75; ex AMPHITRITE 1972; ex WANGARATTA 1967.

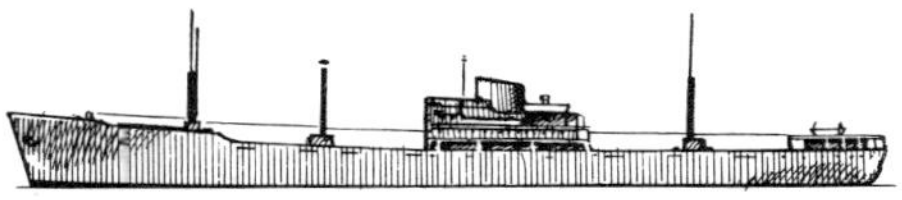

MKFM H1
26980 TELAMON. Gr/Br 1954; C; 7900; 139.6 × 8.2 (458 × 26.11); M; —; ex PANTELIS 1977; ex TEMPLE HALL 1969. Sisters: **26981 NORTH WAVE** (Gr) ex AEGEAN NAVIGATOR 1977; ex LAURICE FIDELITY 1974; ex HUMANITY 1973; ex DEUTERORNIS 1971; ex DUNSTER 1969; ex TEMPLE LANE 1968 **26982 AMINAH A** (Cy) ex IRINI; ex TEMPLE MAIN 1969.

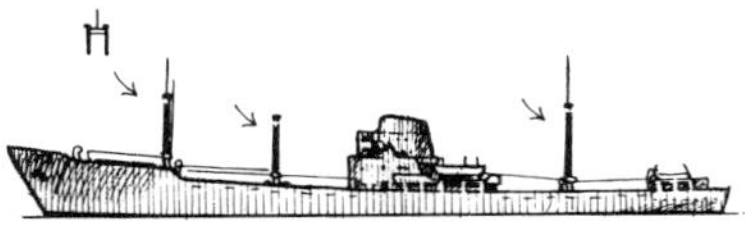

MKFM H1
● **★26990 STAVROPOL.** Ru/Pd 1953; C; 2800; 114.1 × 6.3 (374 × 20.9); M; 12.75; ex GDYNIA 1954; **'B-50'** type. Sisters: **★26991 TAGANROG** (Ru) ex SZCZECIN 1955 **26992 GULF KARIM** (Pa) ex DANSK 1980; ex GDANSK **26993 PACIFICO** (Ec) ex KOPERNIK 1977; ex LODZ 1953 **26994 VASSILIKI** (Gr) ex NOWA HUTA 1976; ex WARSZAWA.

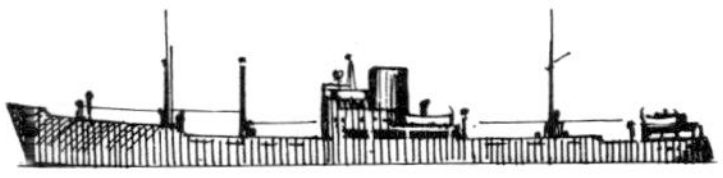

MKFM H1
27000 TAYABAS BAY. Pi/De 1945; F; 2600; 110 × 6 1 (361 × 19.11); M; 14.5; ex TEKLA 1965; ex TEKLA TORM 1964; ex TEKLA 1951; Possibly altered in appearance.

MKFM H1
27010 BLUE PEARL. Pa/Br 1952; C; 6000; 144.1 × 7.9 (473 × 25.9); M; 12; ex YANNIS 1974; ex ASHOKA JAYANTI 1970; ex BARRINGTON COURT 1963.

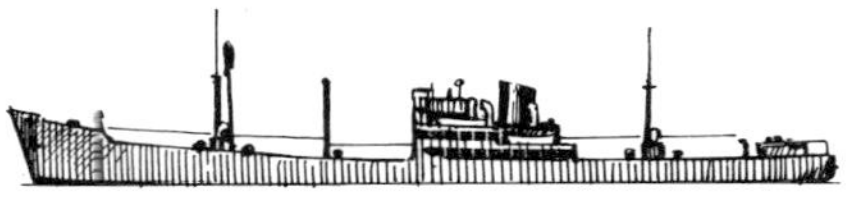

MKFM H1
27020 ESPEROS. Pa/Br 1949; CP; 4400; 129.6 × 7.2 (425 × 23.6); M; 13; ex BELAS.

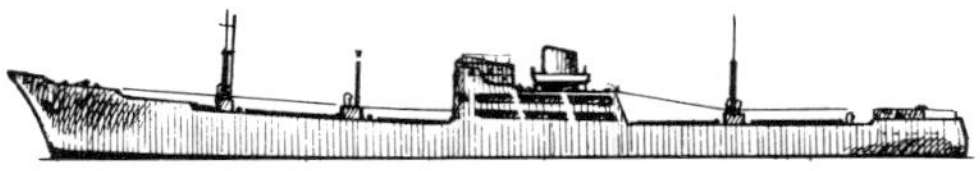

MKFM H1
27030 JALAGOMATI. In/Ys 1958; C; 6500/9100; 152 × 8.1/9 (499 × 26.8/29.6); M; 14.5; ex JALASILTONHALL 1963; ex SILTONHALL.

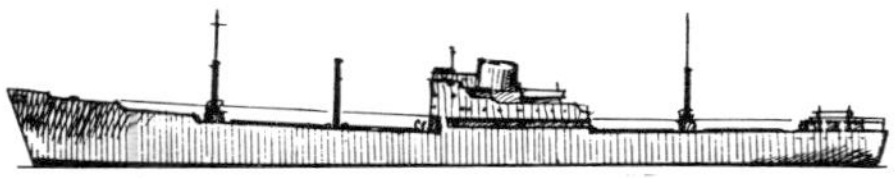

MKFM H1
27040 LADY ERA. Gr/Br 1956; C; 8100; 139.5 × 8.3 (458 × 27.3); M; 13; ex STANWEAR 1966.

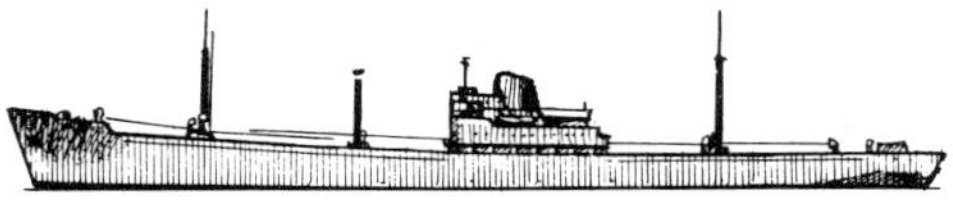

MKFM H1
27050 GALATIA. Li/Ja 1956; C; 6400/9500; 148.5 × —/9.5 (487 × —/30.6); M; 13.5. Sister: **27051 GALINI** (Li).

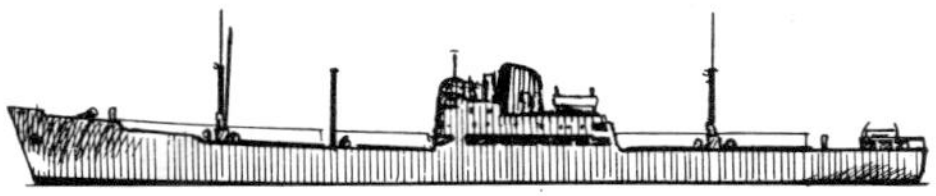

MKFM H1
● **27060 TAMIL PERIYAR E.V.R.** In/Br 1957; C; 8200; 139.4 × 8.5 (476 × 27); M; 12; ex INDIAN ENDEAVOUR 1975; ex RATNA CHANDRALEKHA 1972; ex ERRINGTON COURT 1963.

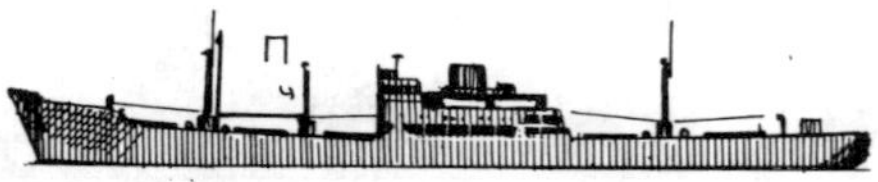

MKFM H1
★**27070 CONRADO BENITEZ.** Cu/Ca 1947; C; 6700; 133.1 × 8.6 (437 × 28.3); M; 15; ex CANADIAN CONSTRUCTOR 1962. Sister: ★**27071 MANUEL ASCUNCE** (Cu) ex CIUDAD DE DETROIT 1962; ex CANADIAN CRUISER 1960.

MKFM H1
● **27080 DONA KATERINA.** Li/Br 1957; C; 7000/9700; 155.2 × 8.3/9.3 (509 × 27.4/30.4); M; 13.25.

MKFM H1
● **27090 YOUTH GIANT.** Pa/Sw 1950; CP; 2200; 103.3 × 5.7 (339 × 18.9); M- 14.5; ex LOON SHENG; ex CHUNG LIEN II; ex VENEZIA 1967.

MKFM H1
27100 TAKIS ALEXAKOS. Cy/Br 1957; C; 9200; 146 × 9.5 (479 × 9.3 (479 × 30$1); M; 14.5; ex TAKIS 1974; ex BARBADINOS 1973; ex ETOLIS 1972; ex CYPRIAN 1968; ex ARGOBEAM 1966. ex CAPETAN CHIOTIS.

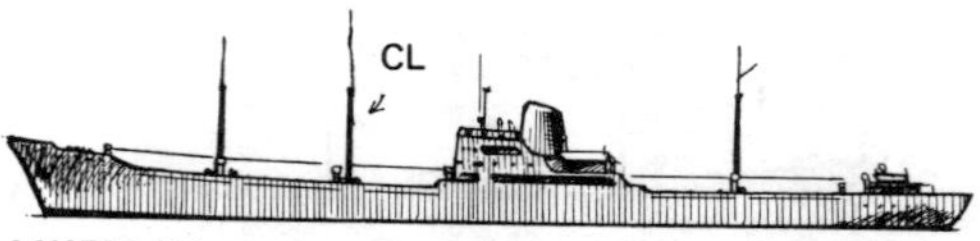

MKFM H1
27110 PADMA. Pk/FRG 1958; C; 6900/9300; 153.1 × 8/9.1 (502 × 26.4/29.1); M; 14.5; ex ALBERT VOGLER 1964.

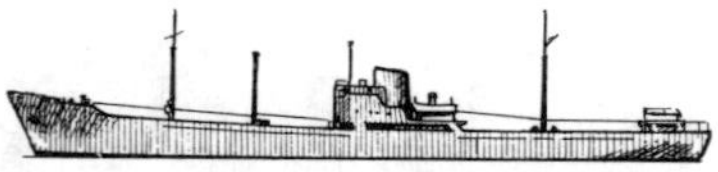

MKFM H1
27120 MAZDA. Pa/FRG 1958; C; 2500/4000; 111.4 × 6.1/6.9 (365 × 20.2/22.8); M; 13.5; ex MARS 1980; ex CENTRA 1980; ex SCHWARZENBEK 1972. Sisters: **27121 TOYOTA** (Pa) ex CENTRA STAR 1980; ex FISCHBEK 1974 **27122 GEORGIA** (Gr) ex EURABIA 1980; ex WANDSBEK 1971.

MKFM H1
27130 STARLIGHT SPLENDOUR. In/FRG 1958; C; 3900; 109.1 × 6.9 (358 × 22.1); R & LPT; 12.5; ex LASBEK 1971.

MKFM H1
27140 MED TRADER. Cy/FRG 1956; C; 2500/3900; 109.3 × —/6.29 (358 × —/22.1); M; 12.5; ex MARGO TRANSOCEANIC 1978; ex CHRISTIANA 1974; ex EILBEK 1971.

MKFM H1
27150 INTERAMICITY. Gr/FRG 1951; CP; 3600; 131.7 × 6.6 (432 × 21.6); M; 13; ex BLUE MARLIN 1979; ex HORNSUND 1969.

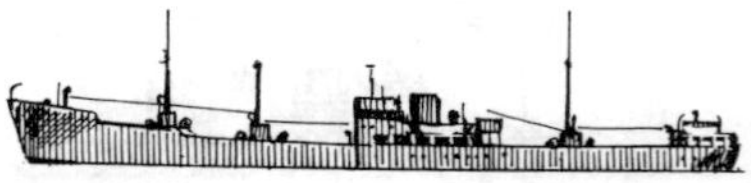

MKFM H1
27160 TONG HAI. Pa/Sw 1944; CP; 3200; 116.2 × 7.2 (381 × 23.9); TSM; 14.5; ex WORTHY DOWN 1964; ex TEMNAREN 1961.

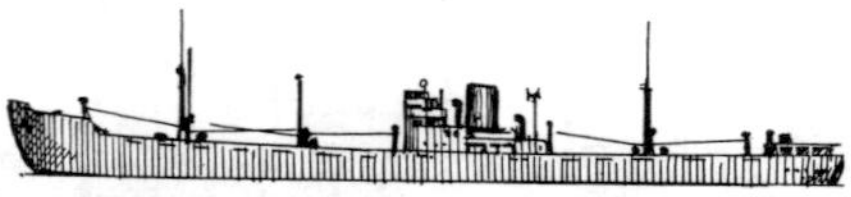

MKFM H1
27170 TOPAZ III. So/Ge 1935; C; 4700; 131.2 × 7.8 (431 × 25.6); M; 12.5; ex ARGOLIS 1973; ex SONNAVIND 1963.

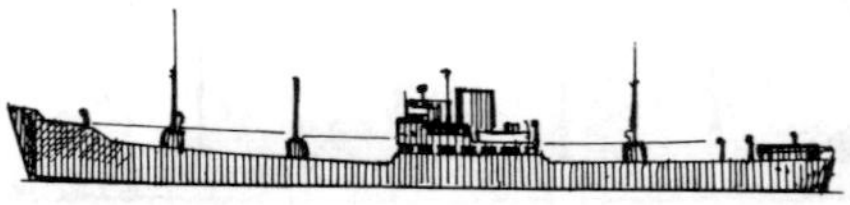

MKFM H1
★**27180 EDWARD DEMBOWSKI.** Pd/Sw 1941; C/TS; 6200; 131.7 × 7.8 (432 × 25.9); M; 12; ex SVEN SALEN 1954.

MKFM H1
27190 RAINFROST. Gr/Ne 1960; R; 4800; 120.4 × 7.2 (395 × 23.6); M; 18.25; ex VICTOR 1980; ex MUNGO 1977.

MKFM H1
27200 SAN JOSE. Pi/No 1948; CP; 1300; 84.7 × 4.8 (278 × 15.8); M; 12; ex FANAFJORD 1971; ex DELFINUS 1970; Lengthened 1962. Similar: **27201 CORAL** (Cy) ex CITTA DI MARSIGLIA; ex CANOPUS 1965.

MKFM H1
27210 ABOABO. Gh/No 1965; ST; 1500; 70.6 × 4.8 (232 × 15.9); M; —. Sisters (Gh flag): **27211 AGYIMFRA 27212 ADA 27213 ASUBONE 27214 CHECHEKU 27215 FANOMA 27216 SHAMA** (Is flag): **27217 AZGAD III**.

MKFM H1
27220 MITSA K. Gr/FRG 1957; CP; 3900; 106.7 × —/7.4 (350 × —/24.2); M; 14.6; ex HELGA DAN 1974.

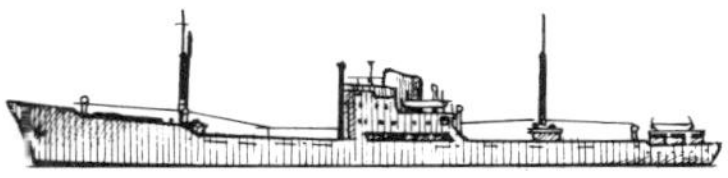

MKFM H1
27230 MALDIVE STAR. Mv/Ne 1955; C; 2900; 112.9 × 6.4 (371 × 21.1); M; 13.5; ex FINNSTAR 1973; ex RAIMO RAGNAR 1959. Sister: **27231 JOHN P** (Gr) ex PANOREA 1976; ex FINNBIRCH 1973; ex MARTTI RAGNAR 1959.

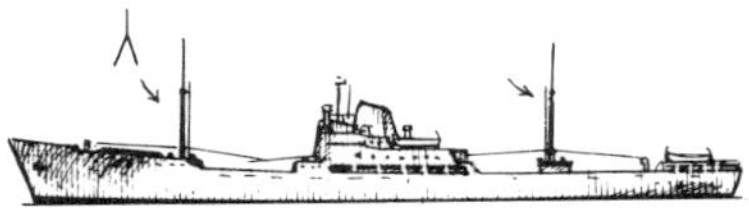

MKFM H1
27240 AUSTRIAN TRADER. As/FRG 1954; C; 2900/4300; 115.98 × 6.35/7.24 (380.51 × 20.83/23.75); M; 13; ex SISTER CLIO 1974; ex NESTOR 1974.

MKFM H1
● **27250 MICHAEL K**. Gr/FRG 1954; CP; 4400; 120 × 7.2 (393 × 23.8); M; 15; ex SYRTE 1976; ex NORDFELS 1975; ex NIEDERSACHSEN 1967.

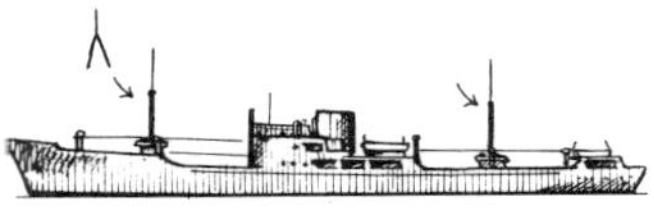

MKFM H1
27260 HOE HING. Sg/No 1955; CP; 1700; 101 × 5.6 (331 × 18.4); M; 14.5; ex MANUELLA PRIDE 1974; ex CALYPSO 1973; ex ULYSSES OGYGIA 1971; ex NAXOS 1970. Sister: **27261 BILKIS** (Pa) ex GEORGE BOWER 1971; ex ANDROS 1969.

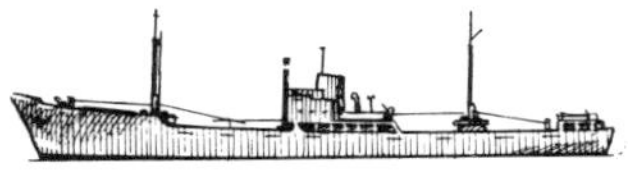

MKFM H1
27270 TERPANDROS. Gr/FRG 1953; C; 3000; 97 × 6.6 (310 × 21.8); M; 13; ex BELLA 1971; ex WALDECK 1969.

MKFM H1
27280 VEGA. Pa/FRG 1954; C; 2200; 108.2 × 6.1 (355 × 20.1); M; 13; ex ARIES 1967.

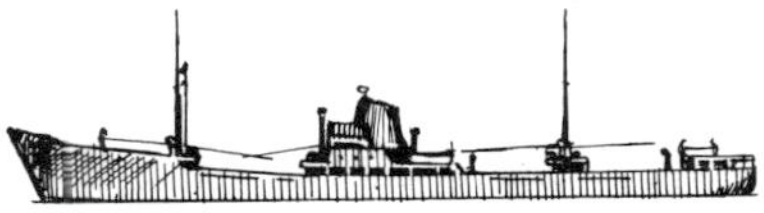

MKFM H1
27290 EAGLE. Cy/FRG 1953; CP; 2700; 115.6 × 6.4 (379 × 20.1); M; 14; ex ELENA 1976; ex EDE MARMSTORF 1972; ex ALDEBARAN 1969. Sister: **27291 KASSOS** (Cy) ex CARSS; ex ALGENIB 1962.

MKFM H1
27300 HONDURAS. Ni/FRG 1955; C; 2400; 107.91 × 6.19 (354.04 × 20.31); M; 15.5. Similar: **27301 CATHERINE** (Cy) ex HELENA STAR 1977; ex ISA BIANCA 1973; ex MONT JOLY 1971; ex CHRISTOBAL 1963; ex NICARAO 1961.

MKFM H1
27330 FARIDPUR. Bh/Ne 1959; C; 3200/4700; 117.5 × —/7.7 (385 × —/25.1); M; 14; ex MADHUMATI 1973; ex MARY NUBEL 1968.

MKFM H1
⋆**27350 VIRPAZAR.** Ys/FRG 1951; C; 5300; 146.92 × 7.68 (482 × 25.2); M; 12; ex CAPTAIN OTTAVIO 1974; ex KLAUS SCHOKE 1971. Similar: **27351 MERANTI** (Ia) ex BERNHARD HOWALDT 1972.

MKFM H1
27370 RIGOLETO. Br/FRG 1951; C; 2500/4000; 100 × —/7.1 (328 × —/23.4); M; 12.5; ex DENNIS B 1976; ex MIRYA 1974; ex MERAK 1973; ex BEATE BOLTEN 1967; ex BOCHUM 1960; ex ERNST BLUMENFELD 1959.

MKFM H1
27400 MINIMO. Pa/FRG 1961; CP; 2600/3700; 108.4 × 6.3/7.4 (356 × 209/24.1); M; 14; ex BYBLOS; ex RATZEBURG 1972. Similar (taller funnel): **27401 FRESENBURG** (FRG) Similar (boats on deck): **27402 YACU RUNA** (Pe) ex VESTA 1972; ex ARMIN RUSS 1967; ex STUBBENHUK 1964.

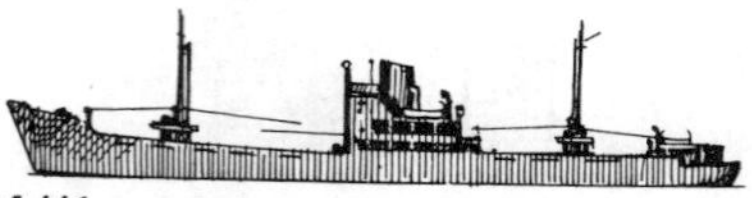

MKFM H1
27310 PATRAS. Gr/FRG 1952; CP; 2600; 115.6 × 6.3 (379 × 20.8); M; 13; ex GALATA 1974. Sisters: **27311 SANTA KATERINA** (Pa) ex CAIRO 1967 **27312 KALIA** (Cy) ex MEDSKY 1980.

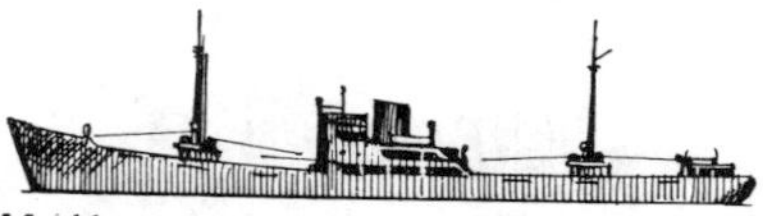

MKFM H1
● **27320 SWIFT SEAGULL.** Gr/FRG 1953; C; 3000; 116.7 × 6.5 (383 × 21.3); M; 14; ex FAST ROVER 1975; ex MONSUN 1972; ex EDMUND HUGO STINNES 1964; ex ANDREA 1957.

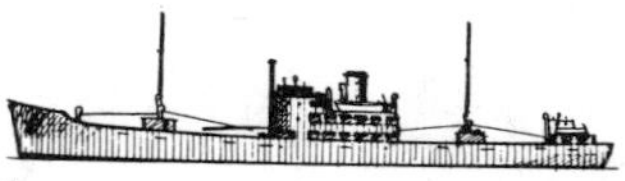

MKFM H1
27340 DIONE. It/No 1941; C; 2000; 96.1 × 5.7 (345 × 18.1); R; 12.5; ex DANVIG 1951; ex LALI 1948.

MKFM H1
● **27360 SIULI.** Bh/FRG 1953; CP; 2800; 110.4 × 6.5 (362 × 21.4); M; 14; ex CORDILLERA; ex NAUMBERG 1969. Sister: **27361 BULSOOK** (Pa) ex JANE PHOENIX 1973; ex WEISSENBURG 1971.

MKFM H1
27380 KOWLOON VOYAGER. Pa/No 1957; C; 2500/3900; 108.2 × 6.3/7.3 (355 × 20.8/23.11); M; 14; ex UNION KOWLOON 1980; ex MAH BULAKUL 1979; ex SUSANNE 1973.

MKFM H1
27390 HOLSTENWALL. Li/FRG 1956; CP; 3100/4700; 116.5 × 6.9/7.6 (382 × 22.8/24.11); M; 14; ex DON ROBERTO 1971; ex ROBERT BORNHOFEN 1971.

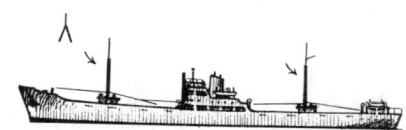

MKFM H1
● **27410 ASPASSIA M.** Gr/FRG 1953; C; 3400/4800; 121.5 × 6.4/7.4 (399 × 21.1/24.2); M; 12.5; ex ERNST MITTMANN 1972; ex BORNHEIM 1965.

MKFM H1
27420 THRIVING COUNTRY. Pa/FRG 1954; C; 2800; 110.4 × 6.4 (362 × 21.2); M; —; ex UNITED GLORY; ex GOLDEN SWAN 1972; ex ENAREN 1968.

MKFM H1
27430 ASTRONAFTIS. Gr/No 1960; C; 2500/3900; 108.2 × 6.3/7.5 (355 × 20.8/24.8); M; 14.5; ex SUNDOVE 1969; ex SPURT 1965; ex MABELLA 1963.

MKFM H1
27440 SCAPLAKE. Gr/Ne 1953; C; 3900; 126 × 7.1 (413 × 23.4); M; 15; ex GINA 1971; ex FINNPULP 1968. Sister: **27441 TUMI** (Pe) ex GRACIA 1972; ex FINNSAILOR 1968.

MKFM H1
27450 CHERRY MOLEK. Pa/FRG 1953; CP; 4400; 116.7 × 6.9 (383 × 22.8); M; 14; ex DUENDAS 1980; ex ZENO 1979; ex BARBARA 1971.

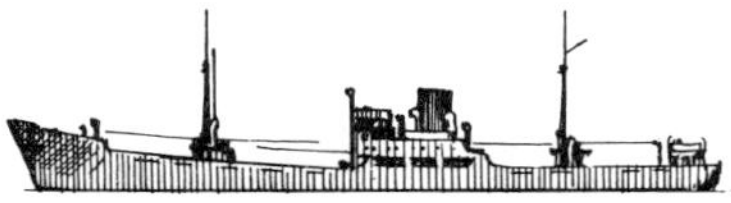

MKFM H1
⋆27460 RABA. Hu/FRG 1951; C; 2700; 110.39 × 6.42 (362 × 21.2); M; 14; ex DUISBURG 1971.

MKFM H1
27470 UNITED ENTERPRISE. Pa/Ja 1957; C; 4700; 117.5 × 7 (386 × 23); M; 13.25; ex ASAHI MARU 1974.

MKFM H1
27480 HAPPY WILLING. Pa/FRG 1958; CP; 5800; 129.1 × 8.1 (424 × 26.5); M; 14.5; ex KITSA S 1980; ex LEANNA 1972; ex DANHOLM 1965.

MKFM H1
27490 CRYSTAL. Sg/Sw 1958; CP; 3200; 104.8 × 6.8 (344 × 22.6); M; —; ex AASE NIELSEN 1972.

MKFM H1
● **27500 ANTIGONI TSIRIS.** Cy/FRG 1956; C; 4000; 109.8 × 6.6 (360 × 21.8); M; 12.5; ex PALMSEA 1977; ex JIM STEVE 1976; ex NEPTUN TRADER 1974; ex NEPTUN 1972.

MKFM H1
27510 VALIANT I. Pa/FRG 1953; C; 3800; 111 × 6.7 (364 × 22.1); M; 13; ex CARIBBEAN FLOWER; ex CRISTINA I 1975; ex PISCO 1974; ex LIZANDRO F; ex WILLI REITH 1968; ex BERLIN 1964.

MKFM H1
⋆27520 DUNA. Hu/FRG 1951; CP; 2400; 102.2 × 6.3 (312 × 20.8); M; 12.5; ex ELISABETH BORNHOFEN 1970. Sister: **27521 FLAMINGO** (Gr) ex NORDLANDER 1974; ex KARL GRAMMERSTORF 1968.

MKFM H1
27530 ROSELEN Gr/FRG 1954; C; 2700; 111.5 × 6.7 (365 × 21.11); M; 13; ex TAMPICO 1969; ex BEATE BOLTEN 1958.

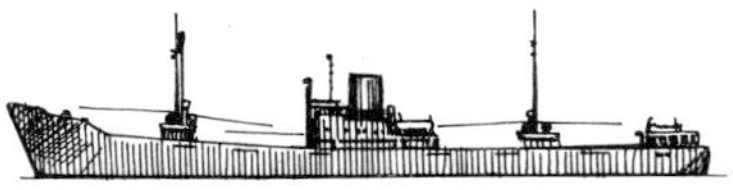

MKFM H1
27540 DONA LOLITA. Ho/FRG 1952; CP; 2700; 111 × 6.7 (365 × 22); M; 14; ex ARIZONA 1975; ex EL GAVILAN 1973; ex EL CAFETERO 1970.

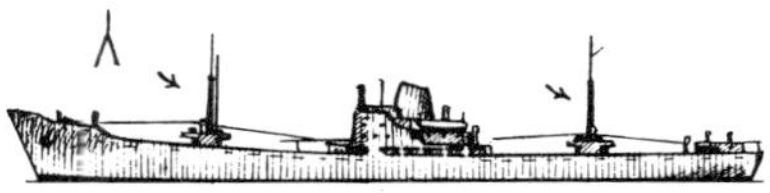

MKFM H1
27550 MICHAEL V. Gr/FRG 1953; C; 2800; 118.6 × 6.2 (385 × 20.6); M; 12; ex FRIENDSHIP 1; ex WARNOW; ex LEONS DENS 1962; ex SIARO 1958.

MKFM H1
27560 NEW HYDE. Pa/FRG 1958; CP; 2600/4100; 115 × 6.5/7.6 (377 × 21.5/24.11); M; 14.5; ex SUN KWONG 1979; ex EDWIN REITH 1973. Sister: **27561 NEW HERO** (Pa) ex SUN SANG 1980; ex MAGDALENA REITH 1972.

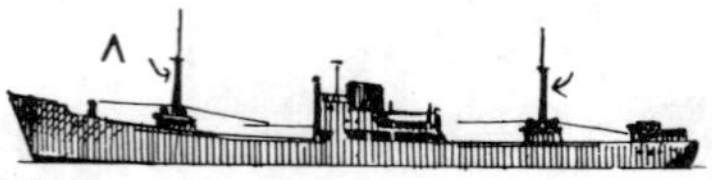

MKFM H1
● **27570 ELEISTRIA V.** Cy/Sw 1955; C; 2500/4000; 110.7 × 6.2/7.4 (363 × 20.3/24.3); M; 13; ex OLYMPIAS 1973; ex I.W.WINCK 1969. Sister: **27571 ELENIK** (Gr) ex EBBA 1976; ex ELSIE WINCK 1966.

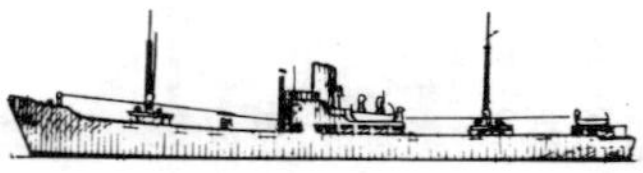

MKFM H1
27580 FERAX. Pa/FRG 1950; C; 1700; 100.2 × 5.4 (328 × 17.8); R & LPT; 10.5; ex SABA 1973; ex FERAX 1972; ex DUBURG 1963.

MKFM H1
27590 EL SALVADOR. Ni/Sw 1953; C; 2400; 109 × 5.9 (358 × 19.5); M; 14.5; ex FAROS 1953. Similar: **27591 LUCY** (Pa) ex EL CENTROAMERICANO 1973; ex GUDMUNDRA 1971 **27592 MANAGUA** (Ni).

MKFM H1
● **27600 DIONI.** Gr/Sw 1954; CP; 2900; 91.4 × 7 (300 × 23); M; 12.5; ex SISSY 1974; ex MILO 1970; ex ESBJORN GORTHON 1966.

MKFM H1
27610 MALDIVE CREST. Mv/No 1956; CP; 1900; 91 × 5.8 (299 × 19); M; 13; ex SUPREME TRADER 1980; ex SLEMBE 1973; ex CAROLINE SMITH 1968; Lengthened 1959.

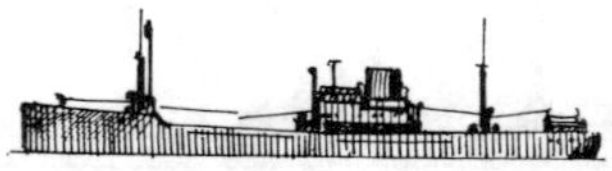

MKFM H1
● **27620 TANIA P.** (Pa/Br 1953; C; 1900; 90.6 × 5.6 (297 × 18.3); M; 12; ex NIKITAS M 1980; ex ALCYON 1975; ex RUTENFJELL 1965; Lengthened 1960. Similar: **27621 PACIFIC MULIA** (Pa) ex ARTA 1980; ex RAVNEFJELL 1967.

MKFM H1
27630 MARLEN. Gr/No 1951; CP; 1900; 90.6 × 5.5 (297 × 18.2); M; 12; ex ASTERI 1969; ex VESLEFJELL 1965; ex SEA CARRIER 1964; ex VESLEFJELL 1960; Lengthened 1960.

MKFM H1
27640 JANUSHA. In/Br 1953; CP; 8000; 142 × 8.3 (466 × 27.3); R; —; ex NORTH QUEEN 1959.

MKFM H1
27650 AGAPI II. Cy/Ne 1953; CP; 1800; 93 × 5.4 (305 × 17.8); M; 13; ex SOPHIE; ex JOLIETTE 1972; Lengthened 1959.

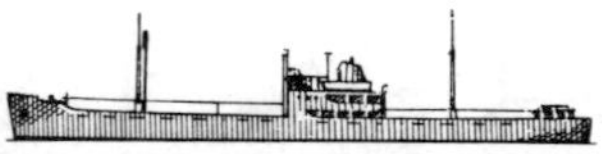

MKFM H1
27660 BONANZA. Cy/Be 1947; C; 1600; 93 × 5.4 (306 × 17.9); M; 12; ex SENEGAL 1977; ex LABRADOR 1966; ex FALCO 1956; ex ARDEA 1954; Lengthened 1959.

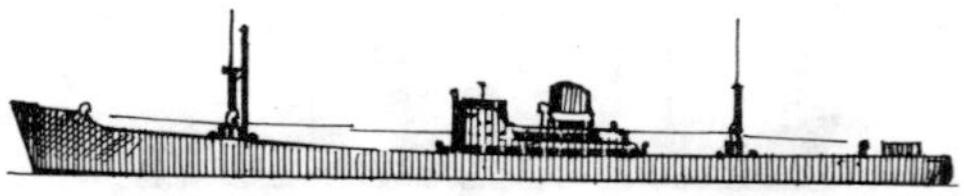

MKFM H1
27670 NIKOS A. Gr/Br 1956; C; 8400; 148.3 × 8.8 (486 × 28.11); M; —; ex KING AEGEUS.

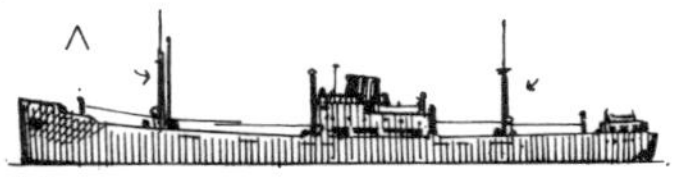

MKFM H1
27680 STELIOS II. Gr/Be 1954/64 C; 3300; 101.94 × 6.82; (334 × 22.4); M; 13; ex DIMITRIS GEORGOS 1976; ex FRANS GORTHON 1971; Lengthened 1964. Sisters (Gr flag): **27681 RODOS** ex ABOUKIR FORT 1980; ex VIRONA 1976; ex IVAN GORTHON 1971 **27682 MARGARET** ex AFRO 1972; ex LOUISA GORTHON 1970.

MKFM H1
● **27690 CHRISOULA K.** Gr/FRG 1954; C; 2300/3700; 106.5 × —/7.3 (349 × —/23.1); M; 13.5; ex ANNA B 1980; ex DORA OLDENDORFF 1970. Similar: **27691 AUSTRIAN IMPORTER** (As) ex MICHELE MAGLIONE 1977; ex CAPITANO VITO 1973; ex LUDOLF OLDENDORFF 1970 **27692 AETOPETRA** (Pa) ex CONSTANTINOS 1979; ex FLOTTBEK 1968 **27693 YUHENG** (Pa) ex RODENBEK 1972.

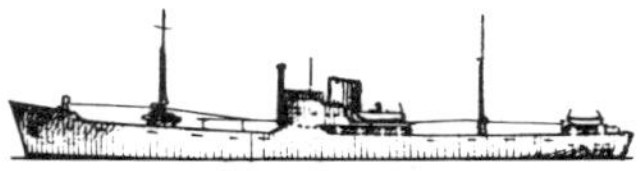

MKFM H1
27700 MARINA. Gr/Sw 1948; C; 1900; 98.9 × 6.7 (324 × 18.1); M; 13; ex ARLA 1972; ex HOEGH BELLE 1960; ex HOEGH BELL 1950; Lengthened 1953.

MKFM H1
27710 DELFIN DE SALAZAR. Sp/Sp 1958; CP; 2500; 105.6 × 6.1 (347 × 20.1); M; 16.5; ex EL SALAZAR 1972. Sisters (Sp flag): **27711 DELFIN ADRIATICO** ex EL PRIORATO 1972 **27712 DELFIN DEL CANTABRICO** ex EL BAZTAN 1972.

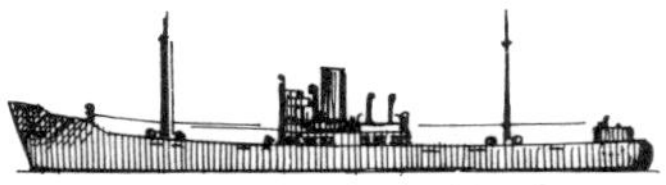

MKFM H1
27720 PATRAI. Gr/FRG 1947; CP; 2800; 109.6 × 6.3 (359.3 × 20.6); R & LPT; 10; ex EMPIRE PATRAI 1953; ex EMPIRE TOWY 1950. Similar: **27721 ULISSE I** (Gr).

MKFM H1
27730 PHOENIX. Gr/Br 1948; CP; 2100/3300; 99.5 × 5.8/6.4 (327 × 18.11/21); R; 11.5; ex ARISTIDIS S 1976; ex IRINI M; ex VOCO 1963; ex LOVLAND 1960.

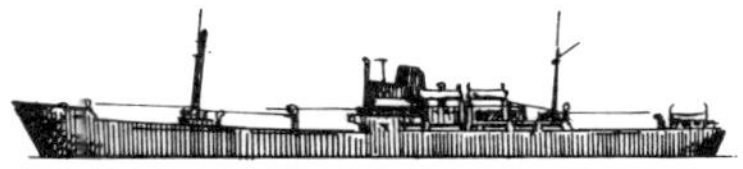

MKFM H1
27740 RITA MARIA. Po/Po 1953; C; 3700; 112.4 × 5.8 (369 × 19); M; 14.

MKFM H1
★**27750 TIHA.** Ys/FRG 1959; WT; 1800/3000; 101.7 × 5.5/6.7 (334 × 19/22); M; —; ex VARGAS 1971.

MKFM H1
27760 RAFIG II. Ly/No 1955; R; 1600; 90.2 × 5.4 (296 × 17); M; 15; ex BETTY MAE 1975; ex ARMASAL I 1974; ex MARDINA COOLER 1973; ex VIKFROST 1972; ex VERA 1966.

MKFM H1
27770 JAMILK. Le/Ne 1956; C; 1500/2300; 93.7 × 5.2/6.2 (307 × 17.6/20.3); M; 14; ex SPEEDMEDIT 1975; ex POLARIS 1973. Sister: **27771 ZENA** (Le) ex SPEEDAFRIC 1975; ex ASTREA 1973.

MKFM H1
● **27780 NEKTARIOS.** Cy/Br 1947; C; 1500; 83.2 × 5.2 (273 × 16.11); TSM; 12; ex TANIA MARIA 1973; ex KOSTANDIS FOTINOS 1971; ex DARINIAN 1970. Sister: **27781 AMORGOS** (Gr); ex LUCIAN 1964 **27782 MABUHAY** (Pi) ex CROSBIAN 1967.

MKFM H1
● **27790 KOTA PANJANG.** Sg/Br 1949; PC; 7100; 134.1 × 7.2 (440 × 23.7); M; 15.5; ex CHANGSHA 1969.

MKFM H12
27800 TJUT NJAK DHIEN. Ia/Ne 1959; PC; 8500; 138.9 × 8.6 (456 × 28.3); M; 16.5; ex PRINSES IRENE 1965.

MKFM H12
27810 HANAN. Sy/Br 1946; C; 2000; 93.9 × 5.9 (308 × 19.3); R; 12; ex GERMANIA 1977; ex KITTIWAKE 1955.

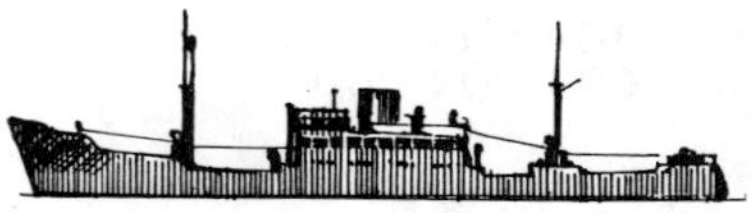

MKFM H12
27820 EUDOCIA. Gr/Br 1948; C; —; 111.6 × 8 (366 × 26.3); M; 13; ex KARNAK 1971. Sister: **27821 ELIAS** (Gr) ex MEMPHIS 1972.

MKFM H12
27830 STAR OF RIYADH. Si/FRG 1926; C; 1900; 89.7 × 5.6 (294 × 18.5); M; 11.5; ex FOTIS P 1966; ex ELSE SKOU 1963; ex BIRKENAU 1947; ex BARBARA 1933.

MKFM H12
27840 STAR OF LUXOR. Eg/It 1948; PC; 6400; 124.36 × 7.27 (408 × 23.1); M; 14. Sister: **27841 PORT SAID** (Eg).

MKFM H12
● **27850 SCALRAY.** Cy/FRG 1956; C; 2600; 108.4 × 6.3 (356 × 20.9); M; 13; ex LIBYAN TRADER 1975; ex GERDA SCHNELL 1974; ex SELMA NIMTZ 1963.

MKFM H12
● **27860 EVANGELOS B.** Cy/FRG 1952; C; 2200/3600; 104 × —/7.4 (341 × —/24.3); M; 12.5; ex TRIADA; ex EDUA 1974; ex MILFORD 1973; ex HILDE MITTMANN 1970; ex HILDEGARD 1964; ex HILDEGARD Z. NIMTZ 1962; ex HILDEGARD 1952.

MKFM H12
27870 COBARGO. Br/Br 1956; C; 1900; 76.9 × 4.3 (252 × 14); M; 10; ex KUMALLA 1973.

MKFM H12
27880 MALDIVE EXPRESS. Mv/Br 1949; C; 1800; 75.7 × 4.6 (248 × 14.11); M; 9.5; ex HARWOOD 1976; ex KAMONA 1965.

MKFM H12
27890 MAMANI. Sg/Br 1949; C; 930; 56.9 × 3.7 (187 × 12.3); TSM; 10; ex MAMATU 1973; ex MAMAKU 1973.

MKFM H12
27900 SINAR SURYA. My/De 1934; C; 1100; 68.6 × 3.9 (225 × 12.8); M; 10.5; ex SRI MAKHOTA; ex OCEAN LIFE 1973; ex UNION PACIFIC 1972; ex WYRALLAH 1969; ex COLORADO DEL MAR 1967; ex TAMATA 1966; ex COLORADO DEL MAR 1964; ex WYRALLAH 1961.

MKFM H12
27910 KING HORSE. Sg/Br 1955; C; 2000; 81.6 × 4.9 (268 × 15.11); M; 11; ex NAVAU 1971.

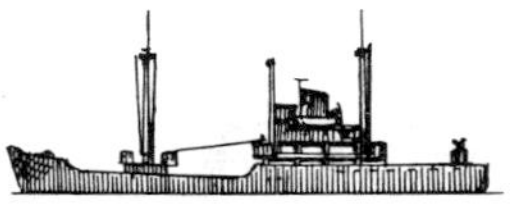

MKFM H12
27920 KING STAR. Sg/Br 1957; C; 1900; 76.9 × 4.5 (252 × 14.1); M; 11; ex KOONYA 1971.

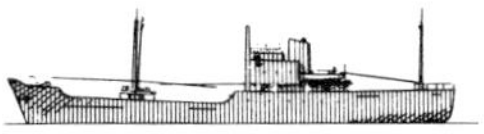

MKFM H12
27930 ARABIAN VICTORY. Pa/Br 1955; C; 1400; 71.07 × 4.47 (233.17 × 14.67); M; —; ex ASIAN QUEEN 1980; ex JOHN MONASH 1976; ex MARRA 1966.

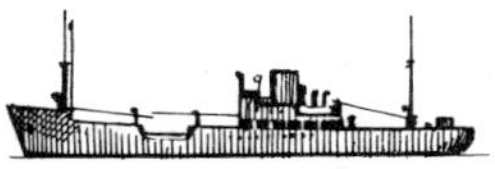

MKFM H12
27940 OSCAR. Cy/Br 1950; CP; 1000; 72.1 × 4.9 (237 × 16.2); M; 12; ex PANAGIA TOURLIANI 1972; ex EYSTEIN JARL 1968.

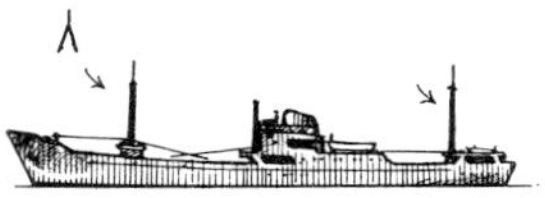

MKFM H12
● **27950 JANAKI.** In/Be 1958; CP; 1200; 80.6 × 4.8 (264 × 15.6); M; 12.5. Sister: **27951 VIJAYA VISANT** (In) ex JAHNAVI 1977.

MKFM H12
27960 BHOJA MARINER. Pa/FRG 1952; CP; 1200; 80.1 × 4.3 (263 × 14.2); M; 12; ex IRINI P 1980; ex SLOMAN ALGIER 1976; ex CASTOR 1969. Sisters: **27961 CHRISTOS M** (Cy) ex MINOS 1977; ex JASON 1976 **27962 ORIENTAL SURVEYOR** (Pa) ex POLLUX 1974.

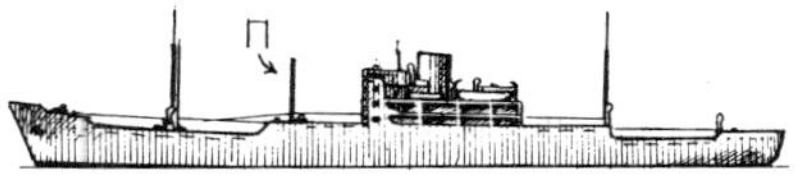

MKFM H123
27970 EASTERN NEPTUNE. Sg/Ja 1953; C; 4800; 122.7 × 7.5 (403 × 24.8); M; 13.75; ex GORDON SKIPPER 1976; ex OCEAN JUPITER 1972; ex KOWA MARU 1970; ex MANTETSU MARU No5 1957.

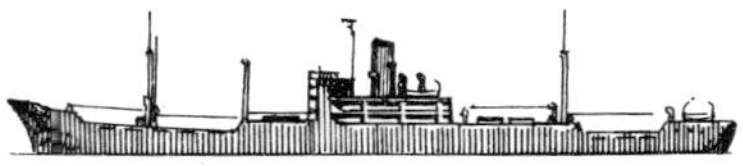

MKFM H123
27980 HENON. Pa/Ja 1949; C; 3600; 113 × 6.9 (371 × 22.8); M; 13; ex LUKITA 1977; ex TAIEI MARU 1970; ex KANSAI MARU 1967.

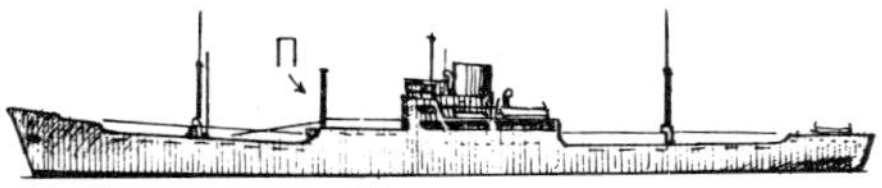

MKFM H123
27990 ANGY. Gr/Ja 1953; C; 6700; 136.9 × 8.3 (449 × 27.1); M; 14; ex CAMPANULA 1975; ex HIKOSHIMA MARU 1970.

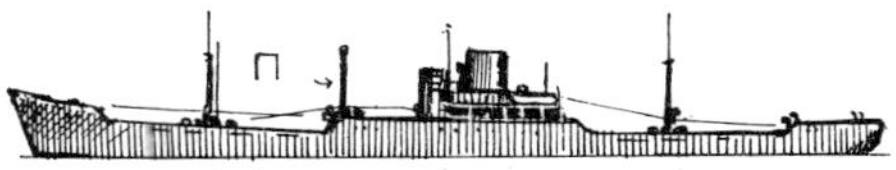

MKFM H123
28000 CHEER SPIRIT. Pa/Ja 1953; C; 6600; 136.9 × 8.3 (449 × 27.1); M; 14; ex TA PENG No1; ex ANHUI 1973; ex MADAGASCAR MARU 1972; ex TOZAI MARU No 1964. Similar: **28001 KENWA MARU** (Ja).

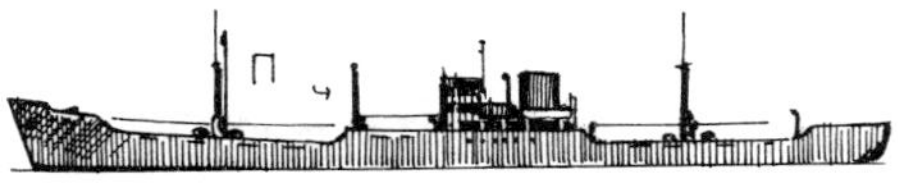

MKFM H123
28010 MILFORD. Pa/Ja 1951; C; 6200; 136.6 × 8 (447 × 26.1); M; 14; ex MICHAELSON PEARL 1974; ex GEMINI PIONEER 1973; ex SAMOA MARU 1972; ex USA MARU 1967.

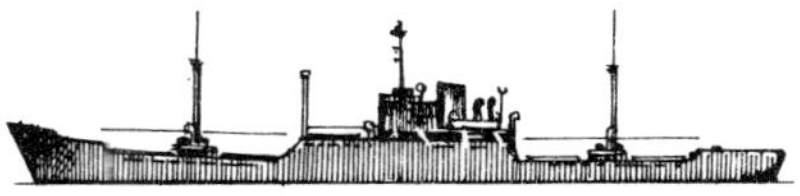

MKFM H123
28020 TAMIL ANNA. In/Ja 1958; C; 4900; 122.8 × 7.5 (403 × 24.8); M; 12.75; ex YAMAHANA MARU 1975.

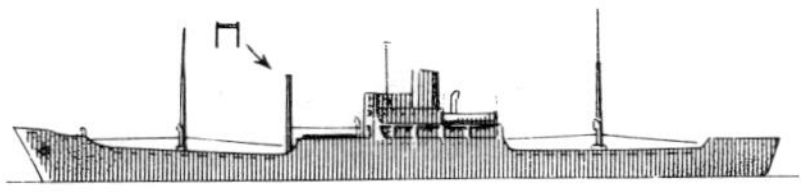

MKFM H123
● **28030 SEA KING.** Db/Ja 1951; C; 4600; 121.21 × 7.31 (399 × 24.2); M; 12; ex GOLDEN VENTURE 1980; ex NACHISAN 1976; ex NACHISAN MARU 1971.

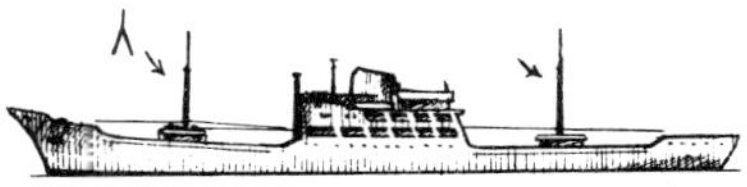

MKFM H123
28040 TAI YUNG. Tw/It 1963; CP; 4000; 114.9 × 7 (377 × 23); M; 13.5.

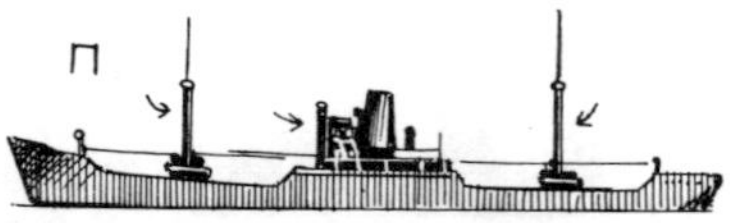

MKFM H123
28050 FORTUNE PIONEER. Pa/Ja 1952; CP; 3800; 113.5 × 7.2 (372 × 23.8); M; 12.5; ex BETSY 1976; ex DAIZO MARU 1968.

MKFM H123
● **28080 MANDOULA.** Pa/Ja 1952; C; 2400; 92.3 × 6.1 (303 × 20); M; 10.5; ex IBUKISAN MARU 1971; ex TOYOURA MARU 1969.

MKFM H123
28090 CHIEH SHENG. Pa/Ja 1951; C; 5000; 120.7 × 7.4 (396 × 24.2); T; 12.75; ex BURMA MARU 1971; ex GINKO MARU 1956. Similar: **28091 WELL KEEPER** (Pa) ex VENTURA SKY 1980; ex BELEM 1979; ex TANJONG 1976; ex BELLE MICHAELS 1974; ex DELTA 1970; ex TAIKO MARU 1970.

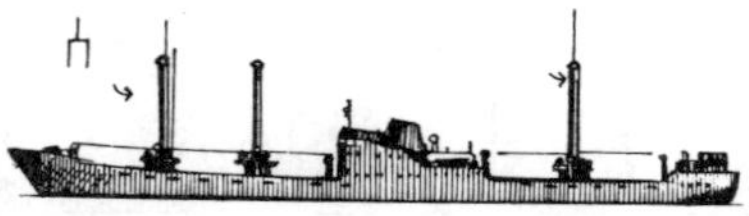

MKFM H123
● **28120 PROODOS.** Gr/It 1958; C; 4200; 113.6 × 7.7 (373 × 25.7); M; 14.75; ex DIAKAN PROGRESS 1976; ex GOLDEN CONDOR 1970; ex LUCKY DRAGON 1969; ex PIEK 1968. Sister: **28121 ZEA SKY** (Gr) ex DESIGNER 1975; ex SEAMERCHANT 1971; ex HAPPY BIRD 1969; ex GREEN DRAGON 1969; ex PAN 1968 Similar: **28122 ANVERSA** (Gr) ex PRONTO 1968.

MKFM H13
28150 AKIS S. Gr/Sw 1957; C; 4000/6200; 130.7 × 7.1/8.2 (429 × 23.4/27.1); M; 14.5; ex MIREILLE 1974; ex DALHEM 1970.

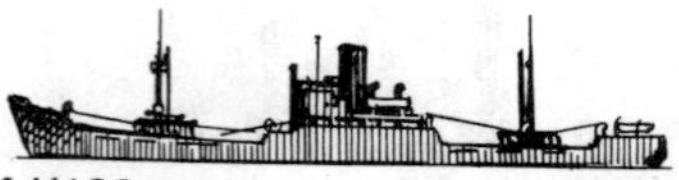

MKFM H123
⋆28060 'KOLOMNA' type. —/DDR 1956; C; 3300; 102.4 × 6.6 (335 × 21.8); R & LPT; 12.5. Sisters (Ru flag): **⋆28061 NEZHIN ⋆28062 SMELA ⋆28063 BALASHOV ⋆28064 KOTLAS** Some others are probably Naval Depot Ships. (RC flag): **⋆28065 ZHAN DOU 44** ex HOPING No44 **⋆28066 ZHAN DOU 45** ex HOPING No45 **⋆28067 NAN HAI No155 ⋆28068 NAN HAI No156** (Gr flag): **28069 LION OF CHAERONEA** ex SMARAGDI 1968; ex ROSTOCK 1965 Some have no mast houses. Similar: **⋆28070 ANGARSK** (Ru)—KP ahead of bridge much lower. Also drawn as MMFM—other Russian vessels may also be like this.

MKFM H123
28100 PETROS. Gr/De 1954; C; 1600; 86 × 4.9 (284 × 16.2); M; 11; ex ANGELIKI 1976; ex ELPIS 1973; ex RIGMOR NIELSEN 1968.

MKFM H123
28110 NAKHODA VANANCA. Ir/Ne 1939; C; 370; 53.5 × 3.1 (175 × 10.1); M; 8.5; ex ARVI 1968; ex COSTIS 1964; ex SIGYN 1961; ex AEGIR 1939.

MKFM H13
28130 RIO QUEQUEN. Ar/Br 1949; R; 3200; 116.1 × 6 (381 × 19.1); TSM; 14; ex ARTICO.

MKFM H13
28140 PRIMO ARABIA. Pa/Br 1955; C; 8300; 145.9 × 8.9 (479 × 29.2); M; 13.5; ex ALEXANDROS SKOUTARIS; ex ALEXANDROS S 1971; ex ST. JOANNA 1967; ex CAPE YORK 1965.

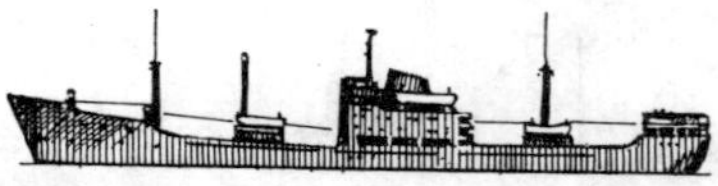

MKFM H13
⋆28160 LUO DING. RC/No 1964; PC; 3200/4500; 110.6 × 6.5/7.6 (363 × 21.4/24.11); M; 14; ex HOI KUNG.

MKFM H13
28170 LANKA KALYANI. Sr/De 1960; C; 5200; 122.7 × 7.4 (403 × 24.8); M; 16; ex HANKIANG 1973; ex TEMA 1971; ex BROOKVILLE 1963.

MKFM H13
28180 ARCADIA. Gr/Sw 1958; C; 6400; 130.7 × 8.2 (429 × 27.1); M; 15.5; ex SKELDERVIK 1972.

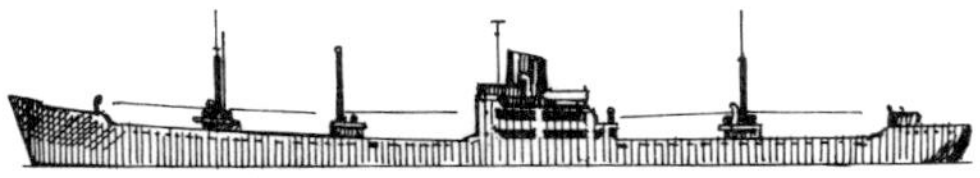

MKFM H13
★**28190 HONG QI 116.** RC/It 1957; C; 6400/8600; 151 × 8.9 (495 × 29.2); M; 14; ex FEITA 1977; ex NARA 1972; ex CALLIOPE 1961. Sister: ★**28191 HONG QI 115** (RC) ex FEIHANG 1977; ex NAUSICAA 1972; ex MARY SOPHIA 1961.

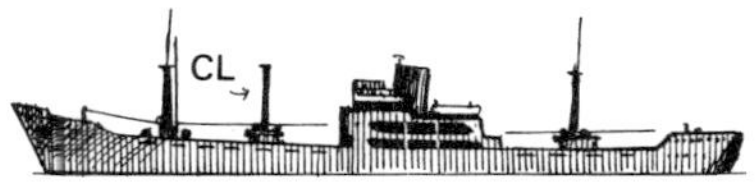

MKFM H13
28200 BATROUN. Le/Br 1960; C; 3400; 111.8 × 6.4 (367 × 21); M; —; ex CITY OF FAMAGUSTA 1977; ex ARCADIAN 1974. Sister: **28201 MALDIVE LOYALTY** (Mv) ex FLORIAN 1971.

MKFM H13
28210 GEORGIOS LENTOUDIS. Gr/FRG 1956; C; 8800; 149.4 × 9 (490 × 29.5); M; 13.5; ex AEGEAN DOLPHIN 1973.

MKFM H13
★**28220 HONG MING.** RC/Ne 1959; C; 6300/8600; 150.1 × 8.2/8.8 (492 × 26.11/29); M; 13; ex BANDA SEA 1976; ex AMSTELMOLEN 1972. Sisters (RC flag): ★**28221 YONG MING** ex JAVA SEA 1976; ex AMSTELSUIS 1972 ★**28222 SAN MING** ex BALI SEA 1976; ex AMSTELVELD 1972.

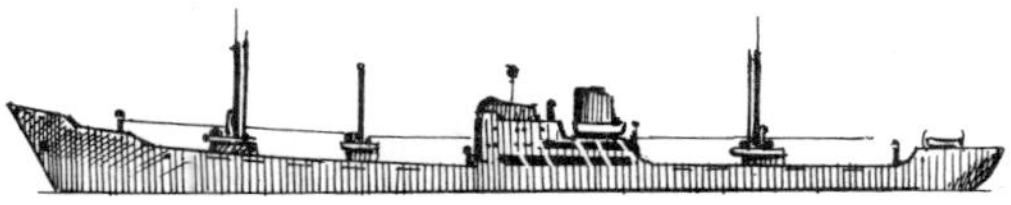

MKFM H13
28230 ORPHEUS. Gr/FRG 1956; C; 9900; 155.2 × 9.3 (509 × 30.6); M; 15.75. Similar: ★**28231 GUIYIN** (RC) ex SIUNGFEI 1976; ex PHOEVOS 1974.

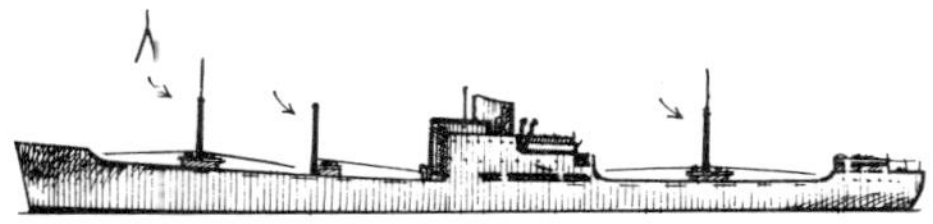

MKFM H13
28240 MAN WAH. Li/Br 1957; CP; 8800; 144 × 8.9 (473 × 29.2); T; 13.5; ex SUNVICTOR 1975; ex VICTOR 1974; ex SUNVICTOR 1969.

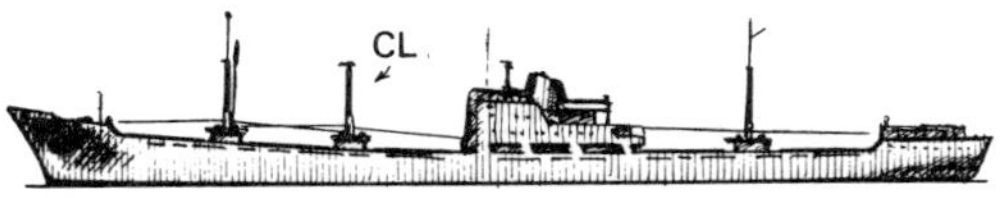

MKFM H13
★**28250 XING MING.** RC/Ne 1961; CP; 9100; 154.7 × 8.8 (508 × 29); M; —; ex FUCHUNKIANG 1976; ex ELIN HOPE 1970.

MKFM H13
● **28260 KALLIXENOS.** Gr/FRG 1960; C; 7300/10000; 157.8 × 9.3 (518 × 30.7); M; —; ex ERMIS; ex ALKMAN 1974.

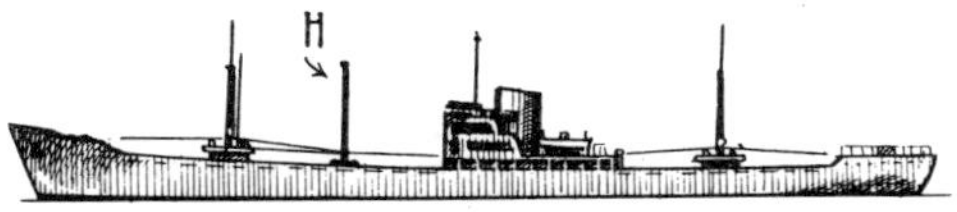

MKFM H13
28270 ELPIDA. Gr/Ne 1956; C; 8400; 145.98 × 8.76 (478.94 × 28.74); M; 12.5; ex AMSTELMEER 1969.

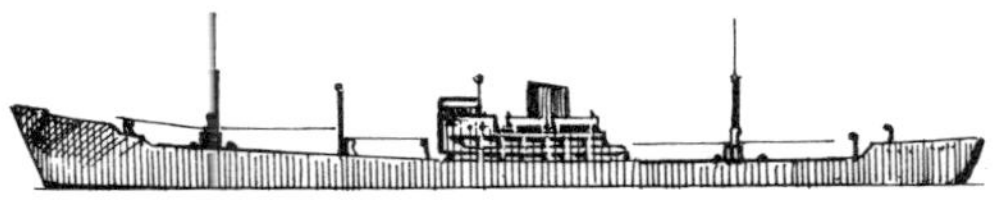

MKFM H13
28280 ASPYR. Gr/Br 1960; C; 9600; 152.2 × 9.3 (499 × 30.7); M; 12.5; ex DURMITOR; ex SILVERBECK 1965.

MKFM H13
● **28290 JALAGOURI.** In/Br 1957; C; 5900/8100; 137.95 × 7.9/8.79 (452.59 × 25.92/28.84); M; —; ex SILVERFORCE 1964. Similar: **28291 MYRTOS** (Pa) ex ILOK; ex ASTAREA 1976; ex HERCEGOVINA 1972; ex SILVERPOINT 1965.

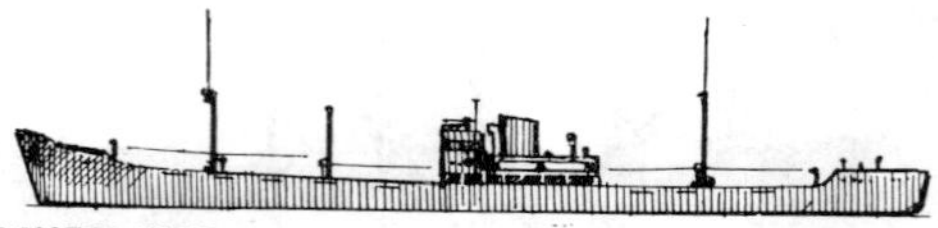

MKFM H13
★**28300 MAKEDONIJA.** Ys/FRG 1950; C; 600; 145.2 × 7.4 (476 × 24.1); M; 14; ex VIKTORIA.

MKFM H13
● **28310 DENIZHANLAR.** Tu/Br 1946; C; 7400; 136.9 × 8.2 (448 × 26.9); R; 11; ex MUSTAFA 1974; ex CLAN MURDOCH 1961; ex HESPERIA 1960; ex EMPIRE SOUTHWOLD.

MKFM H13
28320 THAI RAINBOW. Pa/FRG 1955; C; 3400; 99.1 × 7.1 (325 × 23.1); M; 13.5; ex MICHAEL JEBSEN.

MKFM H13
28330 ELDE. Gr/FRG 1958; C; 500; 118 × 7.9 (387 × 26); M; —; ex KASEM SAMUT; ex TUMLAREN 1970.

MKFM H13
● **28340 EURYDICE.** Gr/Br 1957; C; 4900; 132.3 × 7.5 (434 × 24.7); M; 14.75; ex CITY OF GUILDFORD. Sisters: **28341 CITY OF DUNDEE** (Cy) ex DUNDEE 1980; ex CITY OF DUNDEE 1979 **28342 SUERTE** (Gr) ex CITY OF GLOUCESTER **28343 CITY OF LEEDS** (Cy) ex LEEDS 1980; ex CITY OF LICHFIELD **28344 ISLAND OF MARMARA** (Gr) ex CITY OF ST. ALBANS **28345 RIO DIAMANTO** (Gr) ex CITY OF WORCESTER.

MKFM H13
28350 BEITEDDINE. Le/Br 1960; C; 3400; 111.5 × 6.4 (366 × 21); M; 13.5; ex CITY OF LIMASSOL 1977; ex RAPALLO 1975.

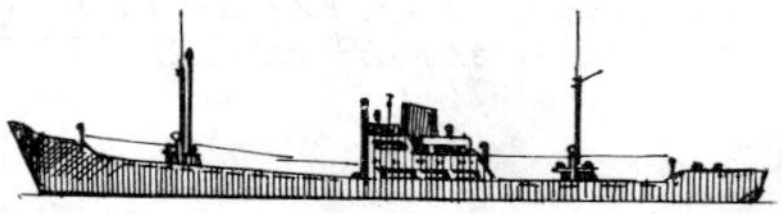

MKFM H13
● **28360 SAN SPYRIDON IV.** Cy/FRG 1953; CP; 2700; 117.4 × 6.5 (385 × 21.4); M; 13.5; ex AGHIOS SPYRIDON 1975; ex MASSIMOEMME 1973; ex PEPERKUST 1968.

MKFM H13
28370 ANTON ROTH. Cy/FRG 1959; CP; 3200/4900; 119 × 6.4/7.6 (390 × 21.11/24.1); M; 14.25; ex STEINHOFT 1971. Sister: **28371 EASTERN ABLE** (Pa) ex ORNA 1976; ex ALBION 1973; ex HERMANN RUSS 1973; ex STEINDAMM 1964.

MKFM H13
28380 MAPLE LEAF. Pa/FRG 1956; CP; 5000; 116.5 × 8 (382 × 26.1); M; 13; ex GLORIA SEA; ex UNIVERSAL KING; ex LISSY SCHULTE 1973; ex LUISE BORNHOFEN 1965.

MKFM H13
28390 SURAKARTA. Ia/Ja 1955; C; 3500; 117.2 × 6.6 (385 × 21.6); M; 11; ex EAST BREEZE 1974; ex EASTERN MUSE 1970; ex EAST BREEZE.

MKFM H13
28400 MEDMARE. Gr/FRG 1955; C; 3900; 128.3 × 6.92 (420.93 × 22.7); M; 14.25; ex PANFAN 1975; ex ULANGA 1974.

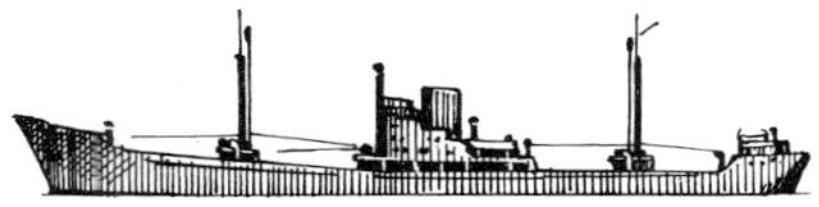

MKFM H13
28410 ALEXANDROUPOLIS. Li/FRG 1958; CP; 3300/5100; 122.1 × 6.8/7.8 (400 × 22.4/25.8); M; 14.5; ex NETA 1976; ex LAMDA 1973; ex LEARINA 1971.

MKFM H13
28420 GREAT GEORGE. Cy/FRG 1958; CP; 5100; 122 × 7.8 (400 × 25.8); M; 14.5; ex BINTANG KEJORA: ex ARGESTIS 1973; ex SPICA 1971; ex LEAPAUL 1967. Similar: **18421 DIMITRA A** (Gr) ex HIDDENSEE; ex LEALOTT 1963.

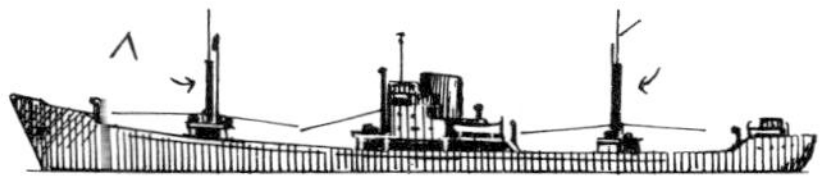

MKFM H13
28430 IRINI S.K. Gr/FRG 1956; C; 3200/5200; 128.73 × 6.52/— (421 × 20.11/—); M; 13; ex YANNIS ; ex FRANKRIG 1975.

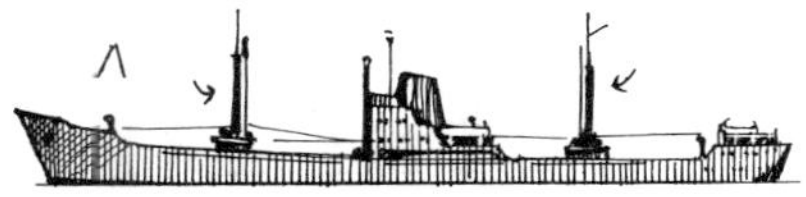

MKFM H13
28440 CLARITA. Cy/FRG 1959; C; 3300/5000; 120.8 × 6.7/7.9 (396 × 21.9/25.11); M; 15; ex CLARITA SCHRODER.

MKFM H13
28450 GREAT MAURICE. Cy/FRG 1959; CP; 5000; 119.8 × 7.9 (393 × 26); M; 14.5; ex BINTANG PAGI 1977; ex APELIOTIS 1973; ex ZOSMA 1971; ex WAHEHE 1965. Sister: **28451 CADMUS** (Gr) ex RIMA TSIRIS 1981; ex BINTANG LIMA 1977; ex APARKTIAS 1973; ex GEMMA 1971; ex WADAI 1965.

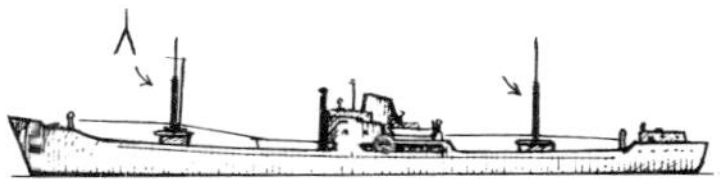

MKFM H13
28460 MARIE. Gr/Sw 1958; C; 4200; 111.1 × 7.2 (365 × 23.1); M; 12.5; ex BEGONIA 1969.

MKFM H13
28470 ANDROS. Gr/FRG 1958; CP; 3400/5100; 119.8 × 6.9/8 (393 × 22.9/26.1); M; 14; ex HOLSTENBURG 1978; ex CORONADO 1973; ex KARIN BORNHOFEN 1971.

MKFM H13
28480 MARLEN. Gr/FRG 1957; C; 3400/5100; 119.8 × 7/7.9 (393 × 22.1/26.1); M; 14; ex MAGDALENE VINNEN 1979.

MKFM H13
● ⋆**28490 STANISLAVSKIY.** Ru/Be 1956; C; 3100; 120.4 × 6.7 (395 × 22.1); M; 14. Sisters (Ru flag): **⋆28491 IVAN MOSKVIN ⋆28492 LEONID LEONIDOV ⋆28493 NEMIROVICH-DANCHENKO ⋆28494 VASILIY KACHALOV.**

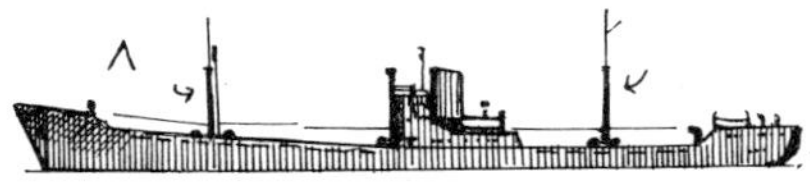

MKFM H13
28500 FERROL. Pa/FRG 1953; C; 2600/4700; 124.4 × 6.2/7.5 (408 × 20.3/24.6); M; 12; ex EDDA CORDS 1971.

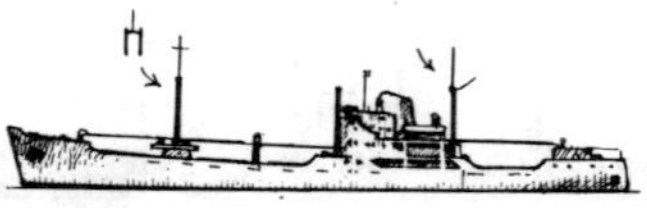

MKFM H13
28510 GEORGE F. Gr/Br 1959; CP; 3800; 99.1 × 7.3 (325 × 24.1); M; 12; ex QUEBEC 1976; ex ALICE BOWATER 1969. Similar (Gr flag): **28511 KRETAN SPIRIT** ex CONSTANCE BOWATER **28512 KRETAN GLORY** ex NINA BOWATER 1977 **28513 ALEXANDRA** ex AGINOR; ex GIGI 1976; ex GLADYS BOWATER 1972 **28514 TASSOS K** ex CHARLOTTE; ex PHYLLIS BOWATER 1973.

MKFM H2
★**28540 BELI.** Ys/Sw 1938; C; 900; 71.9 × 4.6 (236 × 15.2); M; 12; ex PLATAK 1967; ex WIRIL 1961. Similar: ★**28541 RASA** (Ys) ex PLAVNIK 1967; ex WARIA 1961.

MKFM H23
● **28560 PROODOS.** Gr/It 1958; C; 4200; 113.6 × 7.7 (373 × 25.7); M; 14.75; ex DIAKAN PROGRESS 1976; ex GOLDEN CONDOR 1970; ex LUCKY DRAGON 1969; ex PIEK 1968. Sister: **28561 ZEA SKY** (Gr) ex DESIGNER 1975; ex SEAMERCHANT 1971; ex HAPPY BIRD 1969; ex GREEN DRAGON 1969; ex PAN 1968 Similar: **28562 ANVERSA** (Gr) ex PRONTO 1968.

MKFMK H
28590 SAADEDDIN. Le/No 1947; C; 1300; 80.5 × 5.1 (264 × 16.9); M; 12; ex AMAL; ex ATLE JARL 1972; ex ARCTURUS 1958. Sister: **28591 CITTA DI GENOVA** (It) ex CENTAURUS 1963.

MKFM H2
28520 GYDA. Gr/Br 1920; C; 3200; 109.6 × 6.5 (350 × 21.2); M; 10; ex GYDA C 1976; ex GYDA 1969; ex J.C. ERTEL 1966; ex LISE 1956; ex CETUS 1953; ex MOTO 1936.

MKFM H2
28530 KORALLE. Ca/Sw 1937; CP; 800; 70.6 × 4.6 (232 × 15.2); M; 12; ex WIROS 1959.

MKFM H2
28550 TINOS. Cy/Ne 1938; C; 530; 58.8 × 4.6 (193 × 15.1); M; 10.5; ex DEMETRA 1 1980; ex CHRISTOS II 1977; ex DRAKE 1966.

MKFM H3
● **28570 DENIZHANLAR.** Tu/Br 1946; C; 7400; 136.9 × 8.2 (448 × 26.9); R; 11; ex MUSTAFA 1974; ex CLAN MURDOCH 1961; ex HESPERIA 1960; ex EMPIRE SOUTHWOLD.

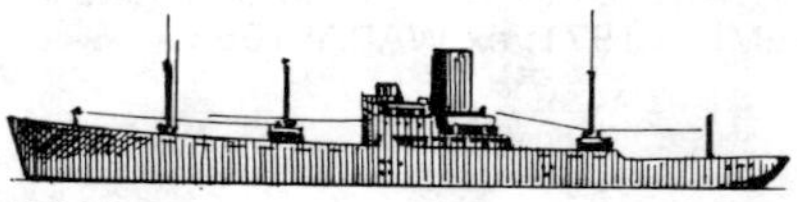

MKFMK H
28580 'C1' type. —/US 1944; C; 6900; 125.6 × 7.5 (412 × 24.1); T or M; 13; May be some of this type in service.

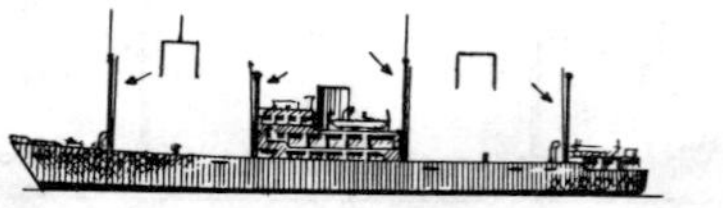

MKFMK H
28600 CLIMAX EMERALD. Mv/Fr 1951; C/WT; 2800; 95.8 × 6 (314 × 19.1); M; 13; ex PROSPER SCHIAFFINO 1973. Sister: **28601 CLIMAX SAPPHIRE** (Mv) ex CATHERINE SCHIAFFINO 1973.

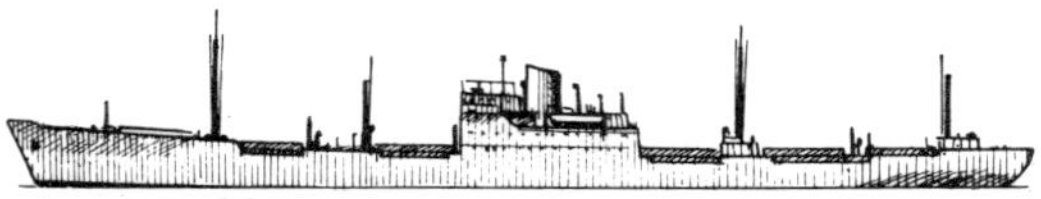

MKFMK H

28610 KAVO ALKYON. Gr/FRG 1961; C; 10900; 162.9 × 9.4 (534 × 30.9); M; 14; ex STAD KAMPEN 1968. Similar: **28611 KAVO DELFINI** (Gr) ex STAD MAASTRICHT 1968 **28612 ANGELIKI** (Gr) ex PORT ANTONIO 1973; ex STAD DEN HAAG 1972 **28613 OCEAN** (Sg) ex OCEAN INTREPID 1980; ex PORT ROYAL 1973; ex STAD ZWOLLE 1972 **28614 AVAX** (Gr) ex PORT MARIA 1973; ex STAD VLAARDINGEN 1972.

MKFMK H1

***28620 KVARNER.** Ys/Sw 1946; C; 3200; 121.4 × 6.9 (398 × 22.9); M; 15; ex ALIDA GORTHON 1961.

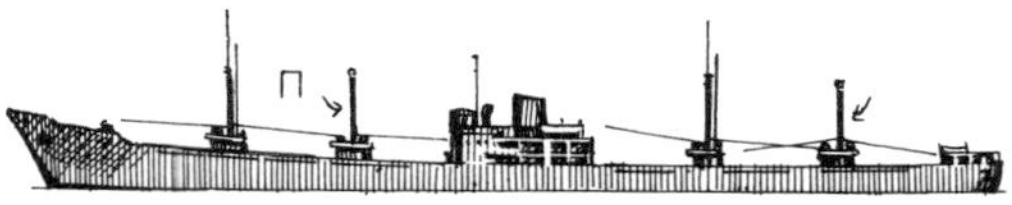

MKFMK H1

28630 MALDIVE PRIZE. Mv/Ja 1956; C; 9800; 158.1 × 9.5 (519 × 30.7); M; 14.5; ex YINKA FOLAWIYO 1980; ex OCEAN SEIGNEUR 1975; ex CAPETAN YEMELOS 1959. Sister: **28631 UNILION** (Sg) ex SITIA SUN 1980; ex JOHNNY B 1978; ex MARIA A.L. 1973; ex CARDAMILITIS 1970; ex PAPHIAN 1969; ex CAPETAN YIANNIS 1966.

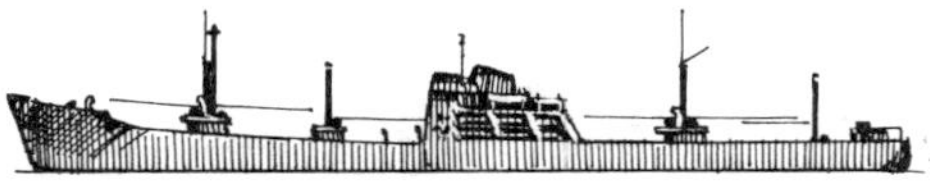

MKFMK H1

28640 ARIES. Gr/Br 1960; C; 5400/7800; 142.9 × 8/8.7 (469 × 26.3/28.6); M; —; ex ALEKOS K; ex INCHONA 1975; ex GLANELY 1969.

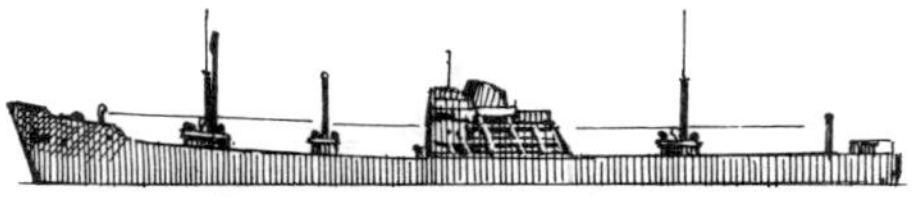

MKFMK H1

28650 SWEDE TONIA. Gr/Br 1961; C; 5500/7600; 140.4 × —/8.7 (461 × —/28.6); M; —; ex MARYTONIA 1976; ex LANDWADE 1972.

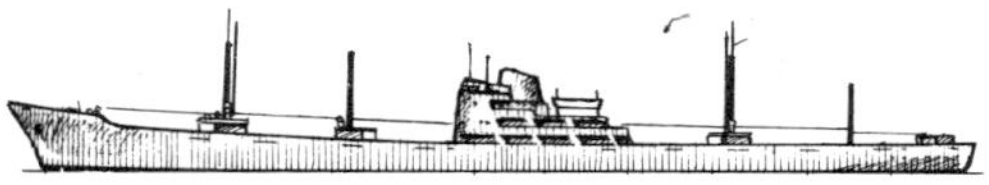

MKFMK H1

● **28660 MARIA.** Gr/FRG 1962; C; 9500; 153.7 × 9 (504 × 29.6); M; 15. Sister: **28661 PALASAUR** (Pa) ex NIKOS NASOS 1980; ex DESPINA.

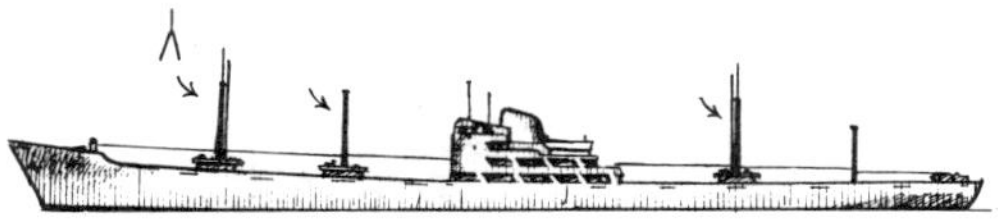

MKFMK H1

28670 MYRTIDIOTISSA. Gr/FRG 1957; C; 9300; 153.7 × 9 (504 × 29.6); M; 14; ex IOANNIS 1958. Sister: **28671 OTHON** (Gr).

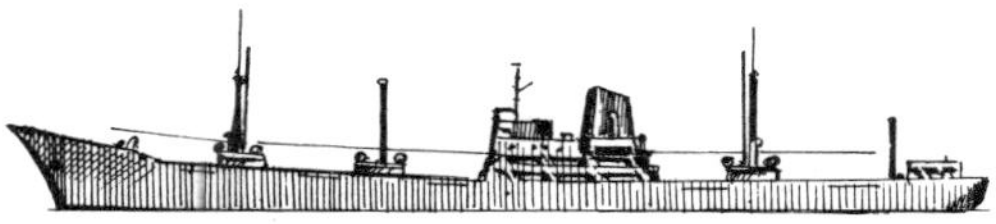

MKFMK H1

28680 AVRA. Gr/Ys 1959; C; 6000/8900; 152.3 × 8.3/9.2 (500 × 27.4/30.3); M; 15; ex AGIOS FANOURIOS 1976; ex PLATON 1974; ex KYVERNITIS 1972.

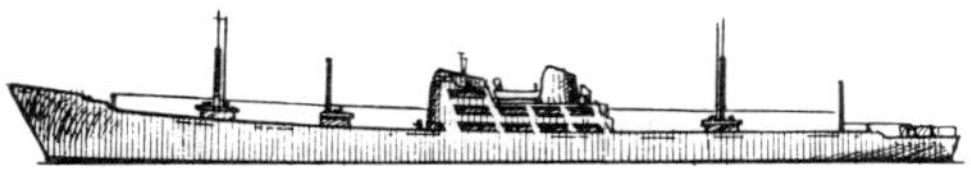

MKFMK H1

28690 DIMITRIS P. Pa/Br 1956; C; 8800; 149.6 × 8.7 (491 × 28.6); M; M; ex STAMOS.

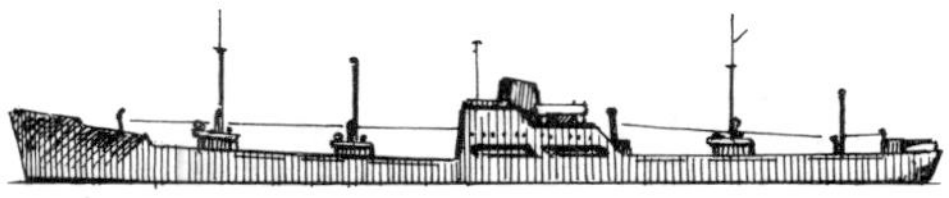

MKFMK H1

28700 MAN AN. Pa/Sw 1957; C; 6300/9500; 149 × 8/9 (489 × 26.1); M; 15; ex ANGELINA 1980; ex THORFRID 1969.

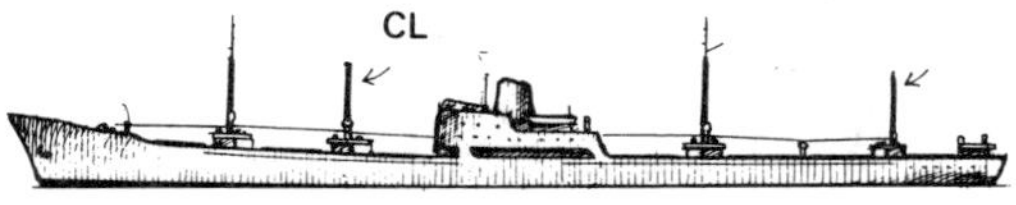

MKFMK H1

28710 ARACTOS GLORY. Li/FRG 1957; C; 9900; 157.9 × 9.4 (516 × 29.11); M; 14.5; ex MARIVANA MARIA; ex ESPERANTO 1974; ex DOMSHEIDE 1970. Similar: **28711 MAI RICKMERS** (Sg) ex ERIK BLUMENFELD 1965.

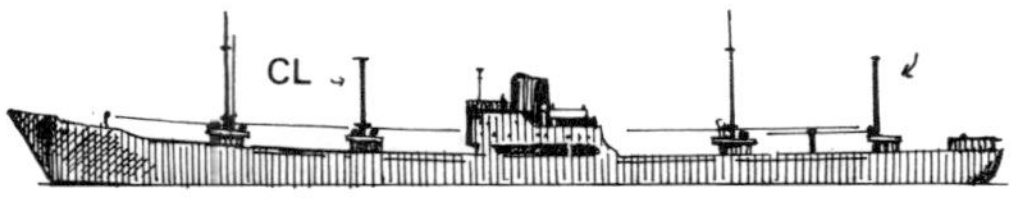

MKFMK H1

28720 DRASTIRIOS. Gr/FRG 1957; C; 10200; 157.9 × 9.1 (518 × 30); M; 14; ex MADISON FRIENDSHIP 1973.

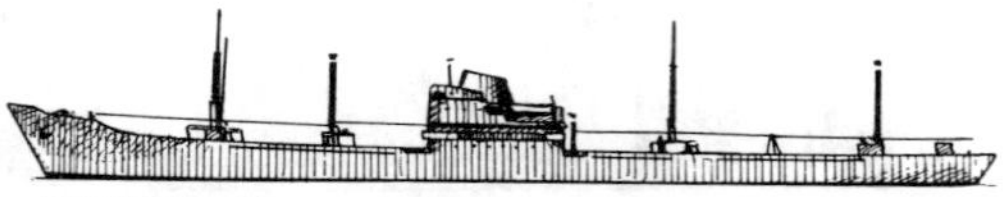

MKFMK H1
28730 AGIAPARASKEVI. Gr/FRG 1957; CP; 10300; 157 × 9.2 (515 × 30.3); M; 14.5; ex HAR CARMEL 1973. Sisters: **28731 VASSILIS KATSIKIS** (Gr) ex ADELFOTIS 1973; ex HAR CANAAN 1972 **28732 EASTERN EMERALD** (Sg) ex TITIKI; ex DESPINA PONTIKOS 1975; ex HAR TABOR 1972 ⋆**28733 RENATO GUITART** (Cu) ex JADE ISLANDS; ex JOHANNES RUSS 1972.

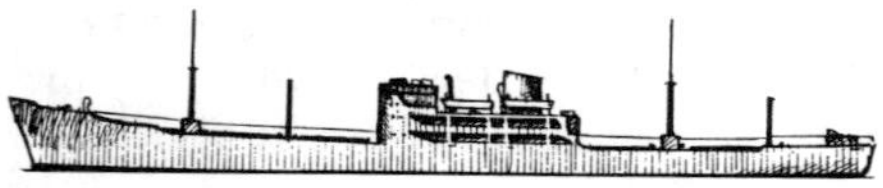

MKFMK H1
28760 LITA 1. Pa/Br 1953; C; 7800; 145.7 × 8.4 (478 × 27.5); M; 12.5; ex LITA 1977; ex KIM 1975; ex DIMITRAKIS 1973; ex JAG RAKSHAK 1965; ex LAKE PENNASK 1963; ex JERSEY SPRAY 1956. Sister: **28761 IRENES CHARITY** (Cy) ex IRENE XILAS; ex IRENES CHARITY 1977; ex IRENE XILAS; ex LAKE ATLIN 1965; ex JERSEY MIST 1956.

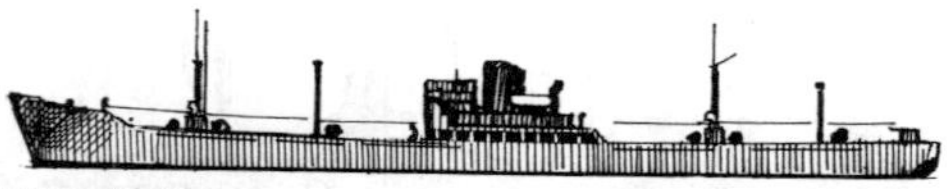

MKFMK H1
28790 LAVENDER. Cy/Br 1955; C; 8300; 145.2 × 8.7 (459 × 28.5); M; 13; ex AYIA MARKELLA 1968. Sister: **28791 CORDI** (Gr) ex COSTIS 1975.

MKFMK H1
28810 ELLEROS. Gr/FRG 1952; C; 2800; 115.7 × 6.4 (380 × 20.1); M; 13.5; ex AGAIS 1969.

MKFMK H1
● **28830 SIMALI 1.** Th/FRG 1951; CP; 2700; 116.3 × 7.3 (382 × 24); M; 13; ex SIAM QUEEN 1976; ex NIKITAS II 1974; ex NORDHAFF 1971; ex NAGUILAN 1969; ex ATLAS 1959. Sister: **28831 DIANA** (Gr) ex NORDMARK 1974; ex DON PEDRO 1967; ex LEVANTE 1966.

MKFMK H1
28740 UNIKING. Sg/Br 1958; C; 9600; 154.7 × 9.6 (508 × 30.6); M; 14.5; ex ANGELIC WINGS 1980; ex ERMIS 1968. Sister: **28741 ANGELIC POWER** (Gr) ex ERMOUPOLIS 1968.

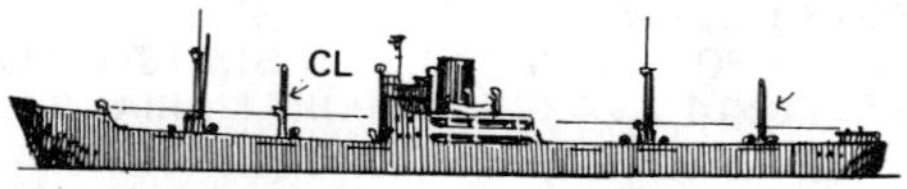

MKFMK H1
⋆**28750 BOGDAN KHMELNITSKY.** Ru/Br 1954; C; 7300; 136 × 8.2 (446 × 27); R & LPT; 11.75; ex STANPOOL.

MKFMK H1
28770 MANSOOR. Pk/FRG 1958; C; 8600/10600; 157.9 × 8.4/9.2 (518 × 27.7/30.3); M; 14; ex MUJAHID 1967; ex THOR 1966; ex FRITZ THYSSEN 1965.

MKFMK H1
28780 UJONG KULON. Ia/FRG 1957; C; 10400; 157.4 × 9.2 (516 × 30.3); M; 14; ex LADEN 1975; ex SPARTO 1974; ex ANITA THYSSEN 1971; ex VALE 1970.

MKFMK H1
28800 SEA HORSE. Le/Sw 1951; C; 2300; 107.55 × 5.87; M; 14; ex TOLLENSE 1978; ex ITAJAI 1965. Sister: **28801 LOULLIA** (Pa) ex ZSCHOPAU.

MKFMK H1
28820 CEFALLONIAN STAR. Gr/FRG 1952; PC; 2700; 110 × 6.4 (361 × 21); M; 11; ex SPREE; ex ELSE 1962.

MKFMK H1
● **28840 BARBARA B.** Br/FRG 1955; CP; 3900; 106.5 × 7.3 (387 × 21.3); M; 13.5; ex SUSAN 1980; ex DESIREE; ex AUGUST PETERS; ex CONGO 1960. Sister: **28841 KING EAST** (Pa) ex HWA YUNG 1980; ex NEW KAOHSIUNG 1978; ex EVA JR 1972; ex MIA MAURER 1971; ex ELBE 1963.

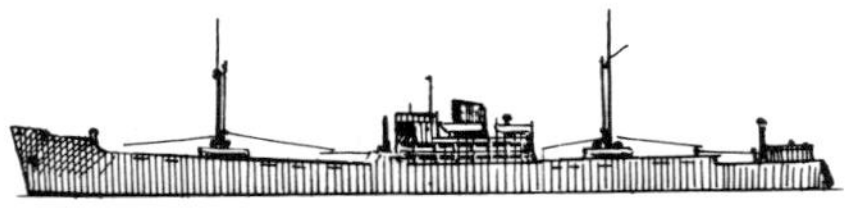

MKFMK H1
● **28850 AGIA MARINA.** Cy/Ca 1948; C; 4300; 128.1 × 6.8 (420 × 22.3); M; 15; ex NOTIOS HELLAS; ex BARBARA; ex LA COUBRE 1972. Similar: **28851 ASIR** (Si) ex GUADELOUPE 1972; ex CANTELEU 1953 **28852 HEJAZ** (Si) ex ALBERT LE BORGNE 1969 **28853 SANTA LUCIA** (Pa) ex TLEMCEN 1972 **28854 IBN SINA** (Ag) ex SAINT FERROL 1969 **28855 ALMAR II** (Vr) ex SAINT CLAIR 1967 **28856 CHRYS** (Cy) ex LILI 1975; ex NICOS H 1975; ex SAINTE MAXIME 1972 ⋆**28857 YI CHI** (RC).

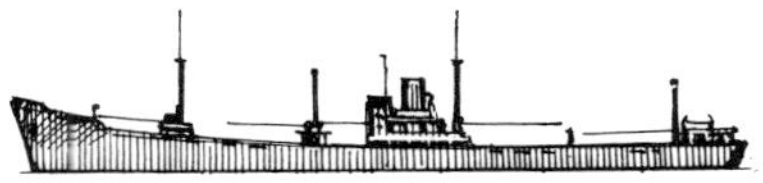

MKFMK H1
28860 DALIA A. Gr/Sw 1945; C; 3400; 116.7 × 6.9 (383 × 22.6); M; 12.5; ex GRODZIEC 1975; ex CETUS 1962; ex KAJTUM 1959. Sister: **28861 MILENA A** (Gr) ex FEJOWIEC 1975; ex CORA 1962; ex KENGIS 1959.

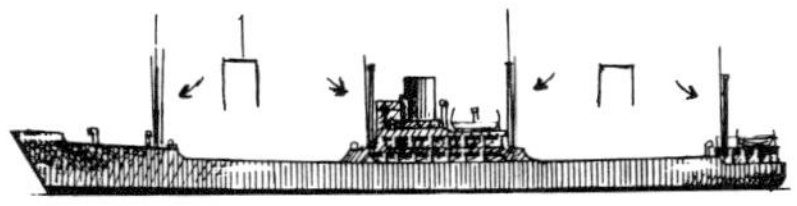

MKFMK H1
● **28870 ANGE SCHIAFFINO.** Fr/Fr 1951; C/WT; 5400; 126.3 × 7.2 (414 × 23.9); M; 14. Sister: **28871 CAPITAINE WALLIS** (Fr) ex MARIE-LOUISE SCHIAFFINO 1974.

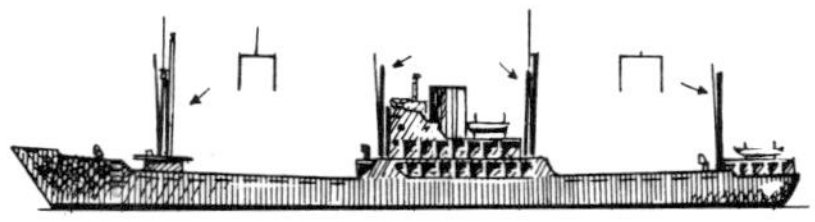

MKFMK H1
28880 TAMBA. Se/Fr 1956; C/WT; 5000; 119.4 × 7.3 (394 × 24); M; 14; ex LAURENT SCHIAFFINO. Sister: **28881 ILE DE LA MARTINIQUE** (Fr) ex ROSE SCHIAFFINO.

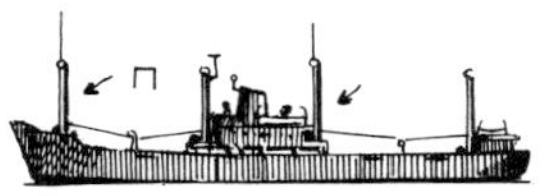

MKFMK H1
28890 NOGAR LOIRA. Sp/Sw 1944; C; 1200; 80.8 × 5.2 (265 × 17.2); M; 10.5; ex FITO; ex FORSVIK 1952.

MKFMK H1
28900 THISBE. Gr/Fr 1951; C; 2300/3400; 100.3 × 5/6.7 (329 × 19.9/21.1); R & LPT; 12.5; ex LADY CLIO 1970; ex THISBE 1964; ex NORMAND 1956; ex NABEUL 1955.

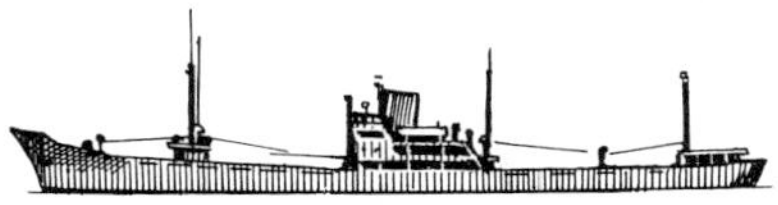

MKFMK H1
28910 RIHENG. Pa/FRG 1955; C; 2900; 119.5 × 6.5 (392 × 21.4); M; 14; ex LIHENG 1976; ex CADIZ 1972; ex FALKENTAL 1961.

MKFMK H1
28920 ANTONY. Pa/FRG 1954; C; 2400/3700; 108.2 × 6.1/7.2 (355 × 20.6/23.9); M; 13; ex ELISABETH BERGER 1971.

MKFMK H1
28930 ODIGITRIA B. Cy/Ne 1949; C; 2900; 91.8 × 5.6 (301 × 18.5); M; 12; ex NISSOS PAROS 1973; ex PACAYA 1964; ex IJSSEL 1961. Sister: **28931 AGIOS FANOURIOS VI** (Gr) ex PANAGOULA D 1977; ex AGIOS FANOURIOS 1977; ex PANAGOULA D; ex NISSOS SKYROS 1974; ex TAKANA 1964; ex MAAS 1961.

MKFMK H1
28940 SUDARSAN SHAKTI. In/Ge 1945; C; 1800; 92.2 × 5.6 (301 × 18.5); R; 10.5; ex UNIGOOLNAR 1979; ex ARSTERTURM 1969; ex BALTIC FIR 1956; ex BALTRADER 1952; ex EMPIRE GAFFER 1947; ex BETSDORF 1945; **'HANSA'** type.

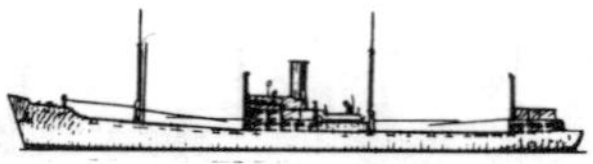

MKFMK H1
★**28950 CHRISTO SMIRNENSKI.** Bu/Be 1946; C; 1700; 91.8 × 5.6 (355 × 18.5); R; 11; ex SCALDIS 1949; **'HANSA'** type.

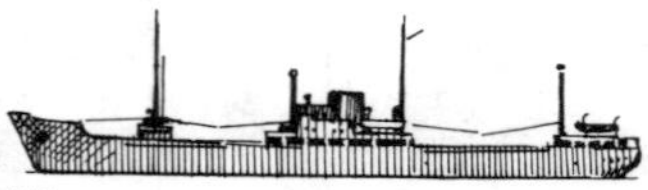

MKFMK H1
28960 PRECIOUS STAR. Pa/FRG 1953; CP; 2100/3300; 101 × 5.7/7 (331 × 18.1/23.1); M; 13.75; ex PHUTPHITHAK 1977; ex GOLDEN ROSE 1976; ex SUPER DRAGON 1972; ex LUGANO 1967.

MKFMK H1
★**28970 GLEB USPENSKY.** Ru/Be 1951; C; 1700; 92.1 × 5.7 (302 × 18); M; 13. Sisters (Ru flag): ★**28971 LEV TOLSTOY** ex STALINGRAD ★**28972 SALTYKOV-SHCHEDRIN** (Sg flag): **28973 SUMBER TUNAS 104** ex HENRIETTA 1975; ex TANDJUNG ALANG 1972; ex VISSARION BELINSKIY 1958 **28974 SUMBER TUNAS 102** ex EVELYNA 1975; ex TANDJUNG SENE 1972; ex NIKOLAI NEKRASOV 1958 **28975 SUMBER TUNAS 101** ex VICTORIA 1975; ex TANDJUNG RAYA 1972; ex ALEKSANDR RADISHEV 1958 **28976 SUMBER TUNAS 103** ex BEAU EAGLE 1975; ex TANDJUNG SOPI 1973; ex ALEKSANDR HERZEN 1958.

MKFMK H1
★**28980 IVAN BABUSHKIN.** Ru/Be 1956; C; 1800; 101.1 × 5.8 (333 × 18.1); M; 13. Sisters (Ru flag): ★**28981 NIKOLAY CHERNYSHEVSKIY** ★**28982 NIKOLAY OSTROVSKIY** ★**28983 VASILIY DOKUCHAEV** ★**28984 YAKOV SVERDLOV.**

MKFMK H1
● ★**28990 SKENDERBEG.** Al/Bu 1959; C; 1900; 92.5 × 4.7 (304 × 15.8); M; 13; ex G. KASTRIODI. Sisters: ★**28991 BURGAS** (Bu) ★**28992 PKHEN HOA** (RK) ★**28993 MIR** (RK).

MKFMK H1
2900 EAGLE. Pa/Be 1949; C; 1800; 92.1 × 5.6 (302 × 18.6); M; 12; ex BALTCHIK 1980; ex NIKOLA VAPTZAROV 1976; Modified **'HANSA'** type.

MKFMK H1
● ★**29010 JISKRA.** Cz/Bu 1962; C; 1700; 92.4 × 5.6 (303 × 18.6); M; 13. Sisters: ★**29011 SLIVEN** (Bu) ★**29012 GABROVO** (Bu).

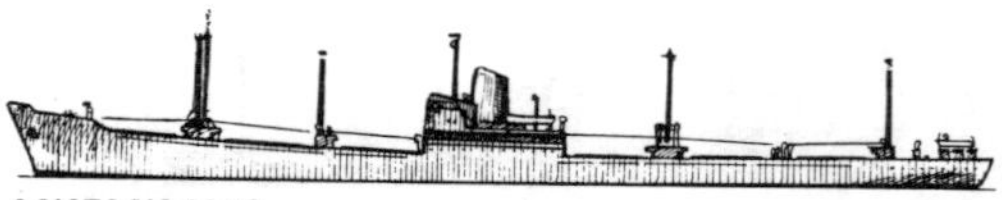

MKFMK H12
29020 SEAMASTER II. Pa/FRG 1958; C; 6700/9500; 155.9 × 8.3/9 (511 × 27.2/29.6); M; 13.5; ex MONSOON CURRENT 1975; ex OSSIAN 1971. Possibly Similar: **29021 KONISTRA** (Pa) ex METHAN 1969.

MKFMK H12
29030 MESAWA. Pa/Ge 1935; C; 1400; 73.9 × 4.1 (243 × 13.5); M; 9; ex MEDDUNO 1969; ex BASONGO 1967; ex ANBAN 1965; ex MOLOPO 1964; ex SELAT SINGKEP 1964; ex NYORA 1963; ex EMPIRE CONIFER 1947; ex ADRIAN 1945.

MKFMK H12
29040 SUMBER TUNAS III. Sg/FRG 1955; CP; 2200; 101.9 × 5.4 (334 × 17.9); M; 16; ex OCEAN CHEER 1969; ex VALDES 1968. Sister: **29041 SUMBER TUNAS II** (la) ex OCEAN TRUST 1969; ex VELAZQUEZ 1968.

MKFMK H123
29050 ADRIANA. Pa/Ja 1948; C; 2200; 90.5 × 5.6 (297 × 18.6); M; 10.5; ex WAN KHIM 1974; ex GLORY No 3 1972; ex TURTLE No 5 1969; ex POTI No 1 1967; ex TESHIOSAN MARU 1965.

MKFMK H123
★29060 LICUNGO. Mb/Br 1948; CP; 1000; 77.9 × 3.9 (256 × 12.11); TSM; 11.

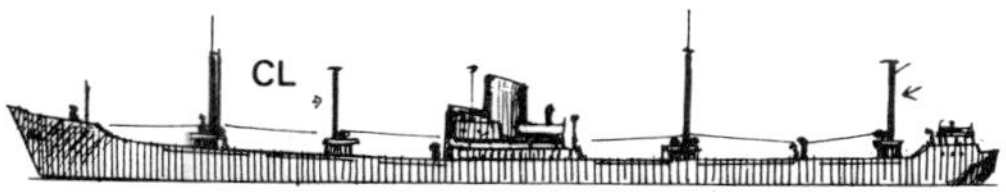

MKFMK H123
★29070 HONG QI 106. RC/FRG 1957; C; 7200/10100; 156.1 × 8.1/9 (512 × 26.8/29.7); M; 14; ex IRISH SEA 1975; ex HENRIETTE WILHELMINE SCHULTE 1973. Sisters: **29071 ARCADIAN STAR** (Gr) ex MADDALENA 1977; ex ILSE SCHULTE 1971 **29072 FRATZESCOS M** (Cy) ex NELSON 1980; ex GREEN PARK; ex ANNA PRESTHUS 1971; ex BOCHUM 1965; ex VIRGINIA BOLTEN 1960 Similar: **29073 MALDIVE NOVEL** (Mv) ex TONIA 1977; ex CAPE ANN 1977; ex CHRISTIAN RUSS 1972.

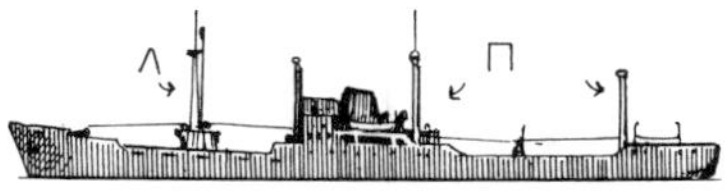

MKFMK H123
29080 CAVO DORO; Sg/Sp 1956; CP; 3900; 113.2 × 6.8 (371 × 22.4); M; 13.75; ex KWATANIREH; ex EMOTAN; ex ALMUDENA 1974; ex IBERICO 1961.

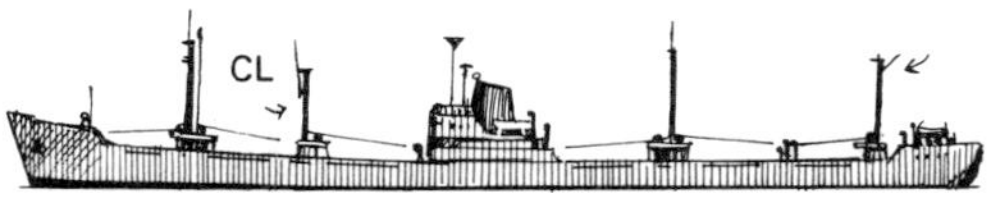

MKFMK H13
29090 ATHENAIS; Gr/FRG 1958; C; 6700/9400; 155.9 × 8.3/9.4 (512 × 26.8/29.6); M; 14; ex HELGA OLDENDORFF 1974. Sister: **29091 ASPIS** (Gr) ex JOHANNA OLDENDORFF.

MKFMK H13
29100 FOURKERO II; Gr/Ys 1963; C; 7300/10200; 162.49 × 8.2/9.4 (533 × 26.11/30); M; 15; ex FILADELPHOS 1981; ex ARYA SAM 1977; ex FILADELPHUS 1975; ex LEANDROS 1974. Sisters: **29101 DIMITRIOS** (Gr) **★29102 PODGORA** (Ys) ex MITERA KALLIOPI 1971.

MKFMK H13
29110 ENDEAVOUR; Gr/FRG 1957; C; 6200/8600; 148 × —/9.3 (486 × —/30.6); M; 14.75; ex GRECIAN ISLES. Sister: **29111 GRECIAN VALOUR** (Gr).

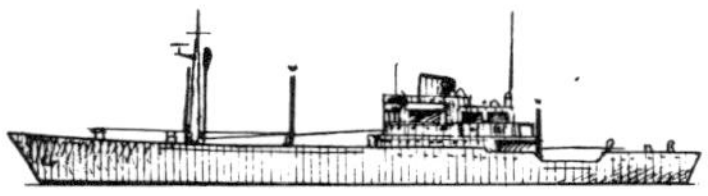

MKFMK H13
29120 ROUMANIA; Gr/Ne 1954; CP; 3700; 109.7 × 6.7 (360 × 22.1); M; 15; ex PRINSES MARIA 1969; ex VAN WAERWYCK 1966.

MKFMK H13
29130 MALDIVE ENVOY; Mv/Br 1955; CP; 2200; 96.9 × 5.3 (318 × 17.4); M; 12.5; ex SEALAND 1970.

MKFMK H2
29140 RIVER SIDE; Pa/Sw 1935; C; 1000; 78.3 × 4.6 (257 × 15.2); M; 10; ex ARISTIDES 1979; ex MARGIT 1965; ex WARUN 1957.

MKFMK H2
29150 OMID; Ir/Sw 1945; C; 600; 63.4 × 3.6 (208 × 11.1); M; 11; ex RABEHA 1975; ex HOODA 1972; ex BELLA 1970; ex TENTO 1964; ex RONNSKAR.

MKFMKC H
● **29160 IDEFJORD;** No/Sw 1960/76; Con; 3500/5500; 129.1 × 7.1/8.1 (424 × 24.4/26.6); M; 15.5; Converted from cargo ship 1976.

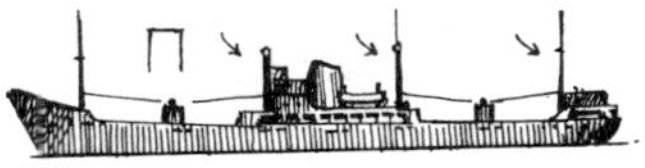

MKFM$_2$ H1
● **29170 ATTILIO IEVOLI;** It/Fr 1957; C/WT; 1600; 95.6 × 5.3 (314 × 17.4); M; 13.75; ex CAP TAINARON 1974; ex CAP SIM 1968.

MKFM$_2$ H12

● **29180 OLYMPIOS ZEUS;** Cy/FRG 1956; C; 1600; 84.2 × 4.8 (265 × 15.9); M; 11.75; ex MARTHA PETERS; ex TETUAN 1963.

MKFM$_2$ H12

29190 BHADRAVATI; In/FRG 1953; C; 2600; 100.8 × 6.1 (331 × 20); R & LPT; —; ex TRAVEMUNDE 1964.

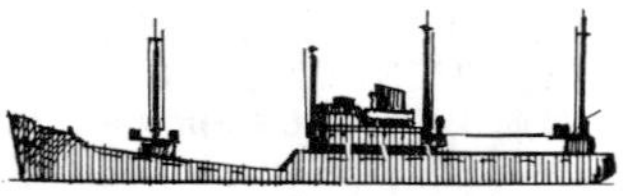

MKFM$_2$ H12

29200 HATI BAIK; My/Br 1956; C; 2600; 93.9 × 5.3 (308 × 17.5); TSM; 11; ex KATOA 1980; ex KAITOA 1972.

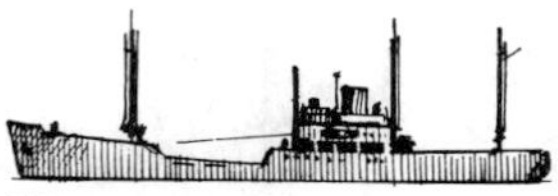

MKFM$_2$ H12

29210 ENDURANCE; Pa/Au 1954; C; 3400; 97.1 × 5.7 (288 × 18.7); TSM; 10; ex DONGARA 1972; ex WANGARA 1966; Lengthened 1967.

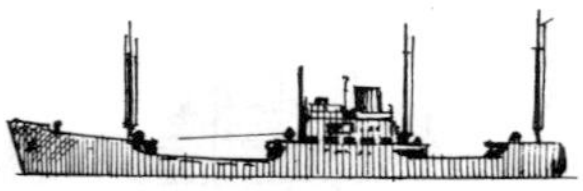

MKFMK H12

● **29220 WHITEHALL;** Pa/Au 1953; C; 2200; 87.9 × 5.7 (288 × 18.7); TSM; 10; ex COLLIN TWO 1976; ex WINDARRA 1970; ex WARRINGA 1953.

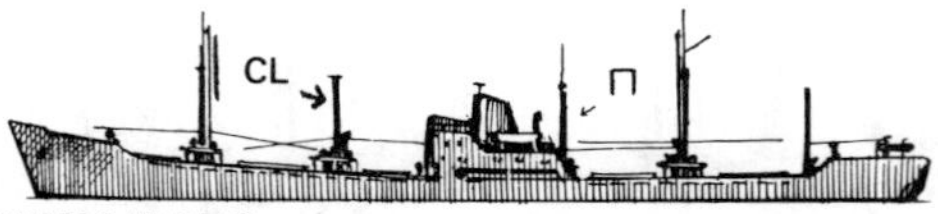

MKFM$_2$K H13

29230 ROSS SEA; Pa/FRG 1956; C; 5900/8700; 145.9 × 8.2/9.1 (497 × 26.1/30); M; 15; ex SENATOR POSSEHL 1971. Sister: **29231 PALIZZI** (It) ex LUBECK 1969.

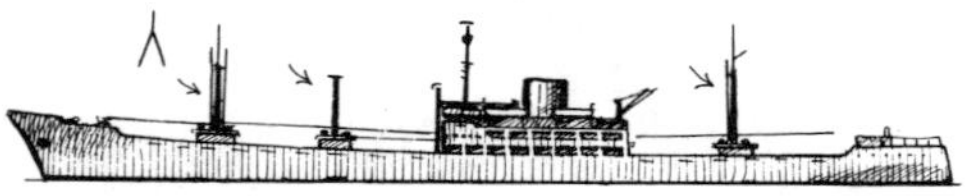

MK$_2$FCM H13

● **29240 YUEN CHAU;** Pa/De 1956; Pt. Con; 6400; 149.7 × 7.7 (491 × 25.2); M; 16.75; ex SINA LOA. Sisters: **29241 PING CHAU** (Pa) ex SARGODMA **29242 NEW GLOBE** (Sg) ex SAMOA 1976 **29243 PACLOG SEALINK** (Pa) ex SONGKHLA 1974 **29244 ZUIDER SEA** (Pa) ex SUMBAWA 1972 Similar (Pole masts): ⋆**29245 CELEBES SEA** (RC) ex PANAMA 1972 ⋆**29246 BERING SEA** (RC) ex PRETORIA 1972 ⋆**29247 KARA SEA** (RC) ex MAGDALA 1972 **29248 ILEOLUJI** (Ng) ex SIBONGA 1975.

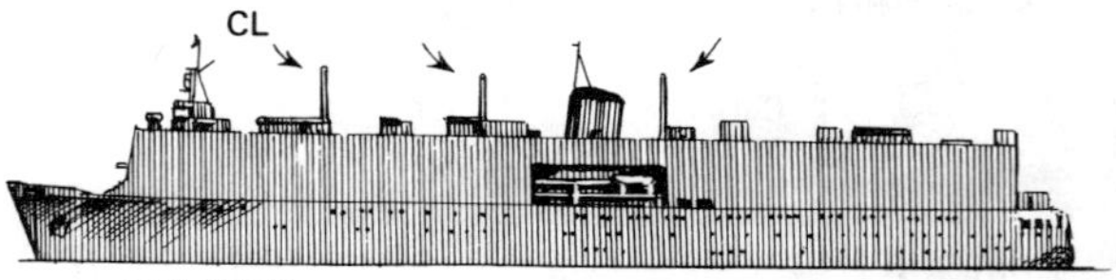

MK$_2$FK H

● **29260 HUAL AKARITA;** Li/Br 1959/72; RoVC; 10900; 178.01 × 8.66 (584.02 × 28.41); TSM; 17.5; ex AKARITA 1977; ex AKAROA 1971; ex AMAZON 1968; Converted from passenger/cargo. Side doors.

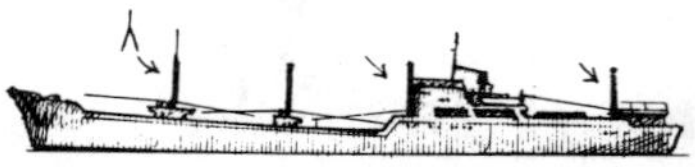

MK$_2$FK H13

29270 LEON PROM; Fr/Sw 1958; C; 3700; 106.6 × 6.9 (350 × 22.7); M; 15; ex CORDOVA 1967.

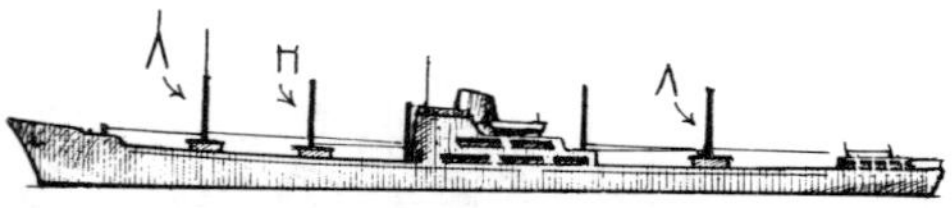

MK$_2$FK$_2$ H1

29280 CHANG HUA; So/Sw 1957; c; 8700; 147.8 × 9.1 (485 × 29.11); M; —; ex HEMISPHERE; ex DAGRUN 1963.

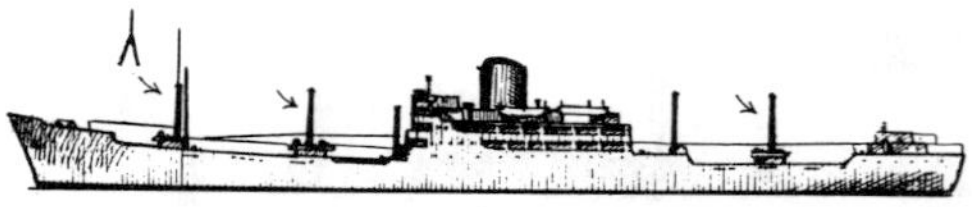

MK$_2$FK$_2$ H123

29290 ALWAHA; Ku/Br 1960; C; 6000/8300; 151.5 × —8.5 (497 × —/28.2); T; —; ex EURYTION 1977; ex MATHURA 1972.

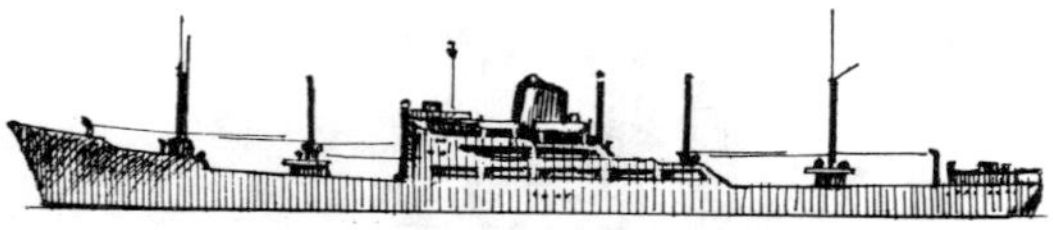

MK$_2$FK$_2$M H1

● **29300 KASTOR;** Gr/Sw 1950; CP; 7500; 160.4 × 8.2 (526 × 16.11); TSM; 19.5; ex POLYDOROS; ex CIRRUS 1976. Sister: **29301 CUMULUS** (Gr) ex ELENOS 1977; ex CUMULUS 1976.

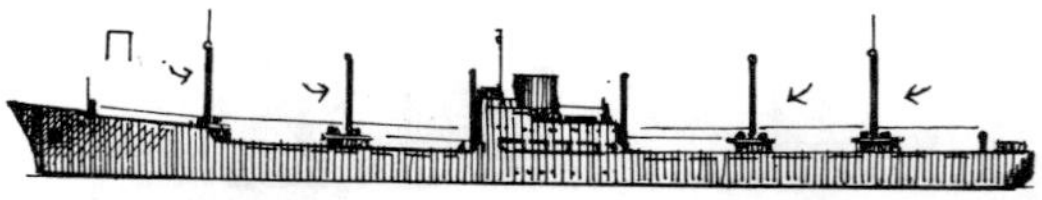

MK$_2$FK$_2$M H1

29310 UNION HODEIDAH; Pa/Ja 1958; C; 10100; 162.4 × 9.4 (533 × 30.2); M; 17.5; ex ORIENT HARMONY 1980; ex NEVADA MARU 1976.

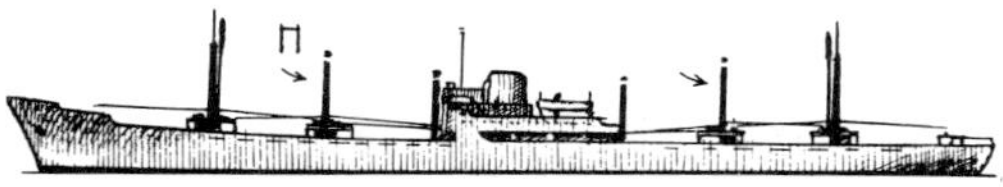

MK_2FK_2M H1
● **29320 HANBORI;** Ko/Ja 1960; C; 9100; 156.14 × 9.2 (512 × 30.2); M; 18; ex MARITIME GRACE 1979; ex HOUSTON MARU 1975. Sister: **29321 EASTERN LEADER** (Pa) ex NORFOLK MARU 1980 Similar: **29322 TACOMA MARU** (Ja).

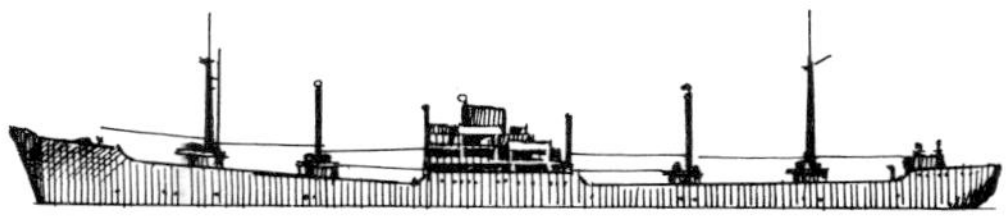

MK_2FK_2M H123
● **29330 MERCURY GULF;** Pa/Ne 1954; C; 7800/10200; 157.99 × 8.52/9.91 (518 × 28/31.9); M; 16.5; ex STRAAT MOZAMBIQUE 1977. Sister: **29331 SAUDI SUN** (Pa) ex MERCURY BAY 1980; ex STRAAT BALI 1977.

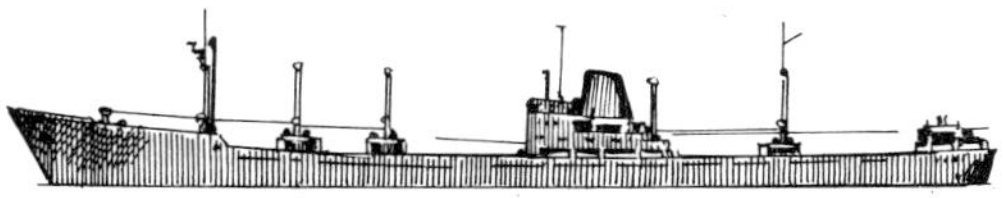

MK_2FKM H1
29340 MIN CHIANG; Pa/No 1960; CP; 5900/8300; 156.5 × 7.6/8.5 (513 × 25.6/27.1); M; 15.5; ex SIRANGER; Lengthened 1971.

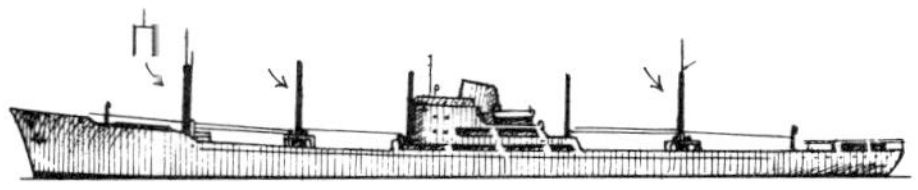

MK_2FKM H1
⋆**29350 TONG HUA;** RC/Sw 1958; C; 6300/8600; 142.5 × 8.3/9.1 (467 × 27.4/29.1); M; 15; ex ARAFURA SEA 1976; ex TYSLA 1972; ex BAY MASTER 1965; ex GOLDEN MASTER 1960.

MK_2FKM H1
● ⋆**29360 NANXIANG;** RC/Sw 1959; C; 6200/8700; 142.4 × 8.28/9.04 —; M; 15; ex ANTARTICA 1971; ex OLDER 1964. Sisters: ⋆**29361 DUNHUA** (RC) ex EAST FORTUNE 1970; ex SOLLEN 1963 **29362 TANIA** (Sg) ex HOEGH AUGVALD 1978; ex AUGVALD 1969 **29363 LINK FAITH** (Gr) ex LILIKA; ex TIGRIS 1971; ex TAMARA 1970; ex TIGRIS 1967; ex ANJAN 1963 **29364 MARACANA I** (Pa) ex MARACANA 1980; ex ARQUERO 1977; ex TRUDE 1974; ex GRUNO TRUDE 1973; ex HOEGH TRUDE 1973; ex GRUNO TRUDE 1971; ex PORTHOS 1970.

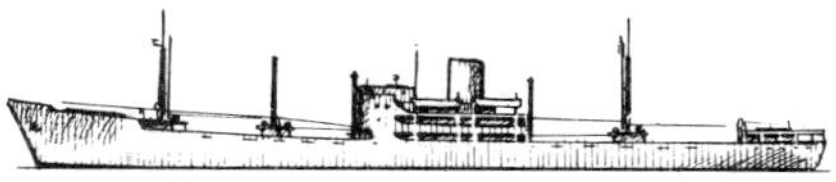

MK_2FKM H1
29370 AGIOS GERASSIMOS; Gr/Br 1956; CP; 4400/6200; 130.4 × 7.1/8.3 (428 × 23.2/27.1); M; 14.5; ex PACIFIC KLIF 1978; ex CRUX 1969; ex CONCORDIA CRUSADER 1968; ex CRUX 1968; ex SUNRISE 1967; ex CRUX 1964.

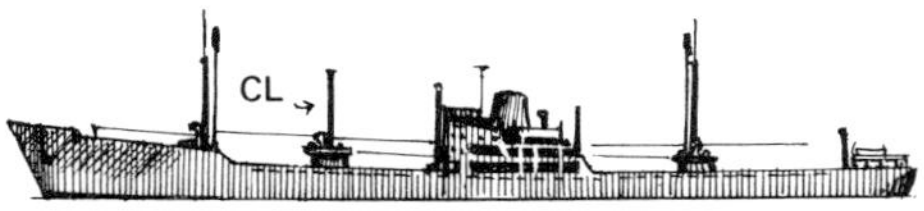

MK_2FKM H1
29380 HELLENIC DESTINY; Gr/FRG 1960; CP; 7300; 154.6 × 8 (507 × 26.2); M; 17. Sisters (Gr flag): **29381 HELLENIC LAUREL 29382 HELLENIC SPLENDOUR.**

MK_2FKM H1
29390 ANNA BAKKE; No/Sw 1950; C; 6100; 144.8 × 7.8 (475 × 25.8); M; 17. Sister: **29391 GJERTRUD BAKKE** (No).

MK_2FKM H1
● **29400 LIMA;** Pe/FRG 1958; CP; 7000/9100; 153 × 8/9 (502 × 26.3/29.8); M; 15.5; ex KENOSHA 1976; ex HALDOR VIRIK 1966; ex NEPTUN 1958. Similar: **29401 DJATILUHUR** (Ia) ex ANNE REED 1968.

MK_2FKM H1
29410 DIAMANTIS; Gr/Sw 1956; CP; 6100/8200; 142.5 × 8.1/9 (467 × 26.5/29.8); M; 14.75; ex CAPETAN LAZAROS; ex POLYDORA 1975; ex MONT BLANC 1972; ex SUNOAK 1961. Sister: **29411 EVANGELOS M 1.** (Gr) ex ACHAIOS 1979.

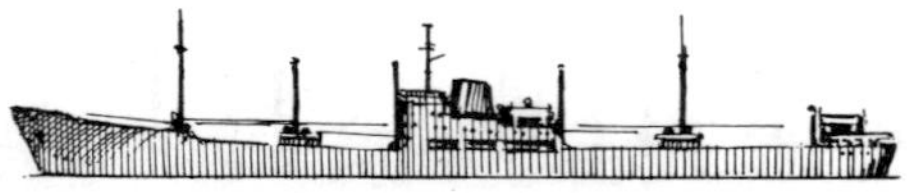

MK_2FKM H1
29420 TEGAL; Ia/No 1955; CP; 5700; 142.3 × 7.9 (467 × 26); M; 16; ex HORDA 1974.

MK_2FKM H1
29430 KOTA MELUR; Sg/Sw 1954; CP; 3800; 129 × 7.1 (423 × 23.5); M; 14.5; ex HALLVARD 1977.

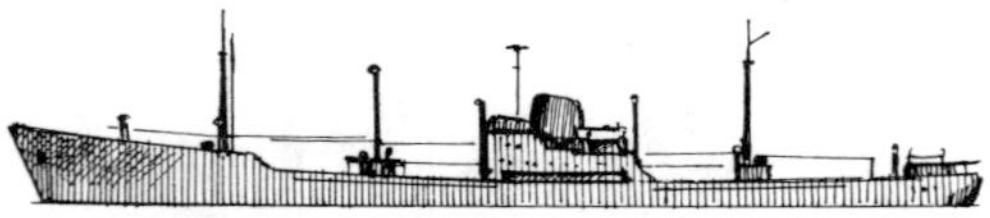

MK_2FKM H1
29440 MONTE CHRISTO; Li/FRG 1959; CP; 6400/9000; 150.9 × 7.7/8.9 (495 × 25.3/29.4); M; 16.5; ex HORNBELT 1977. Sister: **29441 TACNA** (Pe) ex HORNSEE 1972.

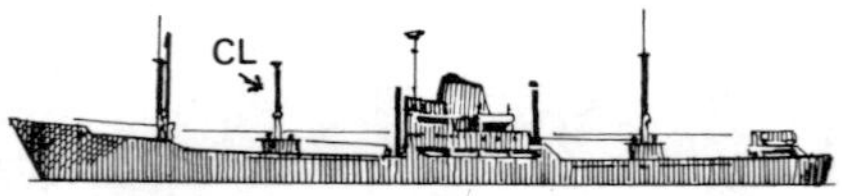

MK_2FKM H1
● **29450 CEFALLONIAN AMBITION.** Gr/De 1953; C; 4000/5700; 129.2 × 7.4/7.7 (424 × 24.5/25.6); M; 16; ex VOGTLAND; ex FREYA TORM 1965. Possible Sister: **29451 SYNARISTIA** (Gr) ex SPREEWALD 1974; ex BIRGITTE TORM 1965.

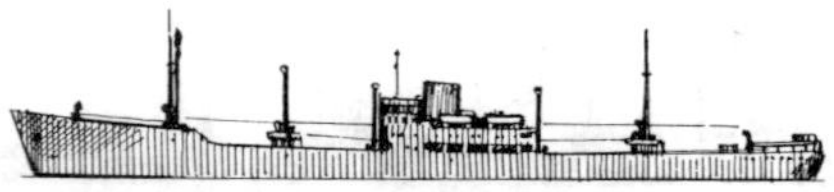

MK_2FKM H1
29460 PISTIS. Gr/Sw 1955; CP; 3800; 129.1 × 7.1 (423 × 23.4); M; 14; ex DRAMMENSFJORD 1974. Sister; **29461 ELPIS** (Gr) ex TANAFJORD 1974.

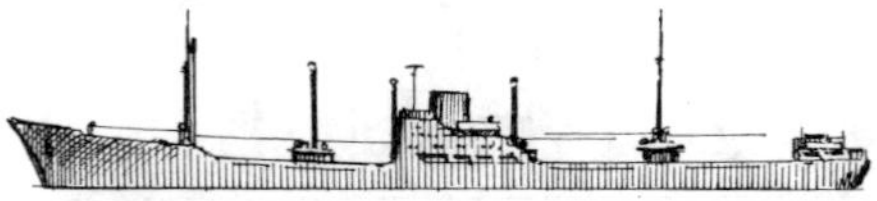

MK_2FKM H1
● **29470 SEAHORSE.** Gr/No 1953; CP; 6500; 132.6 × 8.5 (435 × 27.11); M; 14.75; ex HARPEFJELL 1970; ex ORIENTE 1959; ex HARPEFJELL 1954. Similar; **29471 SURABAYA** (Ia) ex CURLING 1975; ex BYKLEFJELL 1970; ex PUERTO SOMOZA 1958; ex BYKLEFJELL 1956.

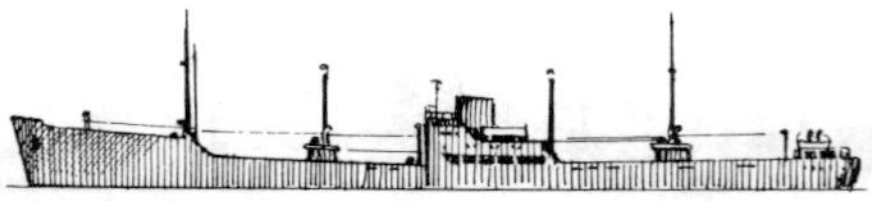

MK_2FKM H1
29480 CAPETAN GIORGIS. Gr/Sw 1950; CP; 5100; 132.6 × 7.9 (435 × 26); M; 15; ex PRINS PHILIPS WILLEM 1969; ex RUGDEFJELL 1966; ex HAVFALIK 1964.

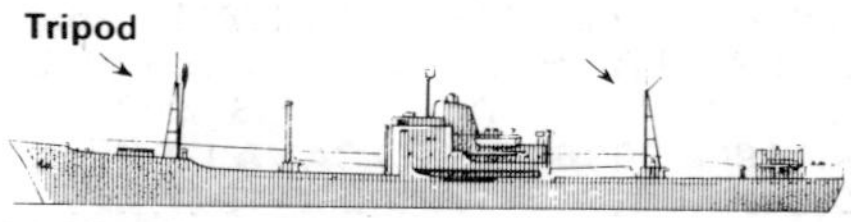

MK_2FKM H1
29490 NAVIKAPOL. Pa/Sw 1954; CP; 4200; 132.2 × 7.7 (434 × 25.1); M; 18; ex LINDENSTEIN 1976; ex CLARY THORDEN 1965.

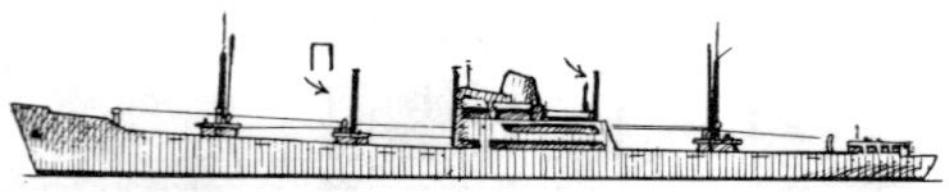

MK_2FKM H1
29500 STATE OF TRAVANCORE-COCHIN. In/FRG 1954; CP; 6200; 146.9 × 7.6 (482 × 25); M; 13.5.

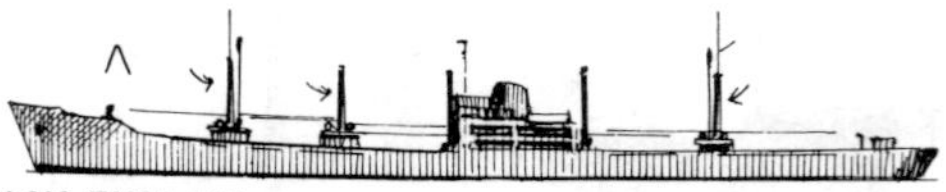

MK_2FKM H1
29510 CERVINIA II. Pa/It 1959; C; 8600; 145.5 × 8.8 (477 × 29); M; —; ex CERVINIA 1980; ex LORENZO MARCELLO 1964. Similar: **29511 PSARA** (Gr) ex SOVERIGN FAYLENNE 1976; ex EMMA 1974; ex LAZZARO MOCENIGO 1973; ex CORTINA 1966; ex LAZZARO MOCENICO 1963.

MK_2FKM H1
29520 DJATIANOM. Ia/Sw 1956; CP; 8800; 147.8 × 9.1 (485 × 29.11); M; —; ex MORVIKEN 1965. Similar: **29521 ST. DEMETRIUS** (Gr) ex HOEGH GUNVOR 1973; ex GUNVOR 1969; ex BOTNE 1966 **29522 CHANG HUA** (So) ex HEMISPHERE; ex DAGRUN 1963.

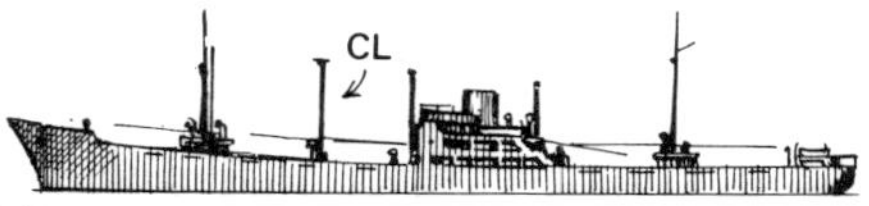

MK$_2$FKM H1
29530 PANTJARAN SINAR. Ia/FRG 1951; CP; 5100; 134.3 × 7.5 (441 × 24.6); M; 13; ex ODENWALD 1966.

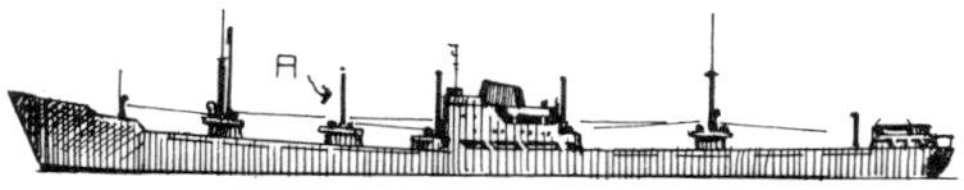

MK$_2$FKM H1
★**29550 ZUNHUA.** RC/Sw 1961; C; 5900/8900; 147.8 × 8.3/9.3 (485 × 26.9/29.11); M; —; ex WEDDELL SEA 1975; ex SALVADA 1971. Sisters: ★**29551 XING HUA** (RC) ex CHANGPAISHAN 1970; ex SALDURA 1967 ★**29552 YONG DING** (RC) ex PATRICE 1977; ex PATRICIA 1976; ex SALAMBRIA 1973 ★**29553 DE HUA** (RC) ex EASTGLORY 1975; ex SALDANHA 1967; ex SUNNY QUEEN **29554 DIAKLIS** (Gr) ex DESPINA R; ex DAWN GRANDEUR 1976; ex SALVINA 1972.

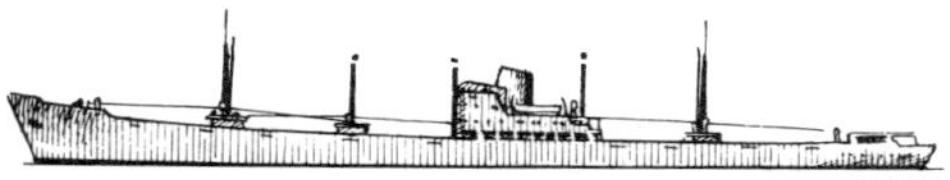

MK$_2$FKM H1
29570 ATLAS PREMIER. Ko/FRG 1952; C; 5800; 146.9 × 7.7 (482 × 25.8); M; 13.5; ex DITMAR KOEL 1971; ex BLUMENAU 1964; ex VOSSBROOK 1954.

MK$_2$FKM H1
29590 TACUARI. Ur/FRG 1956; CP; 6200/8800; 146.3 × 8.1/9.1 (480 × 26.8/30); M; 13.5; ex MOSLANE 1967; ex SUNMOSS 1964; ex SUN MOSTUN 1956.

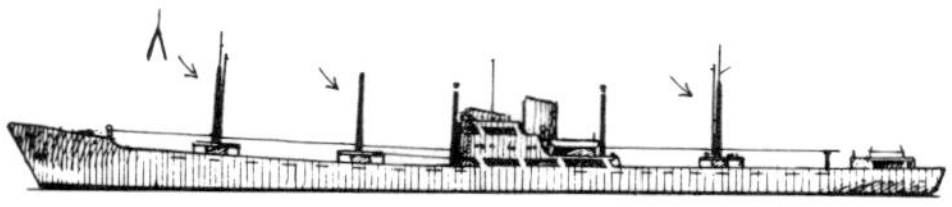

MK$_2$FKM H1
29610 BLACK SEA. Pa/FRG 1958; CP; 6000/10600; 147.9 × 7.8/8.5 (485 × 25.9/27.9); M; 14; ex INDUS 1972; ex ARYA INDUS 1970; ex INDUS 1968. Sister: ★**29611 LINYIN** (RC) ex BALTIC SEA 1977; ex MAAS 1973.

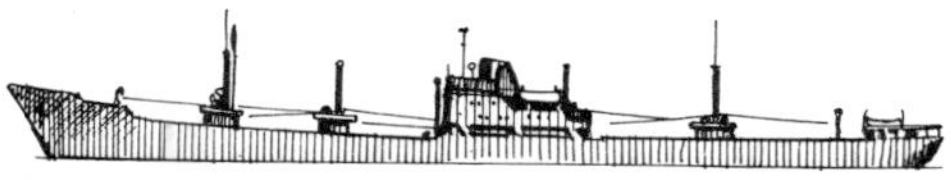

MK$_2$FKM H1
29540 STAR ALTAIR. Sw/Sw 1959; CP; 6100/9000; 147.8 × 8.2/9.1 (485 × 26.1/29.11); M; —; ex VIMEIRA 1965; ex PORT DENISON 1965; ex VIMEIRA 1960; ex FAIR LADY. Sister: **29541 DIAMANTENIA** (Gr) ex NEWPORT 1980; ex ARISTOGEITON 1974; ex GISNA 1969 Probable Sister: **29542 PINELOPI** (Gr) ex STAR ALDEBARAN; ex KENSINGTON.

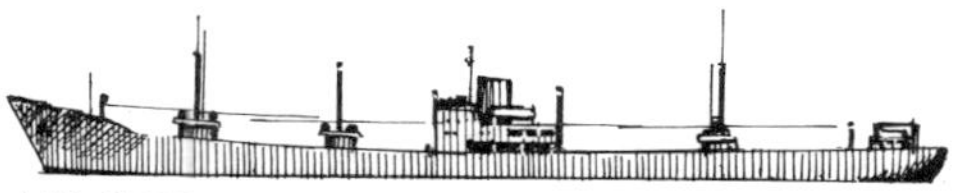

MK$_2$FKM H1
29560 QUELIMANE. Po/Sw 1963; CP; 6100/8700; 147.8 × 8.2/9.1 (485 × 26.2/29.9); M; 15; ex EVINA 1968.

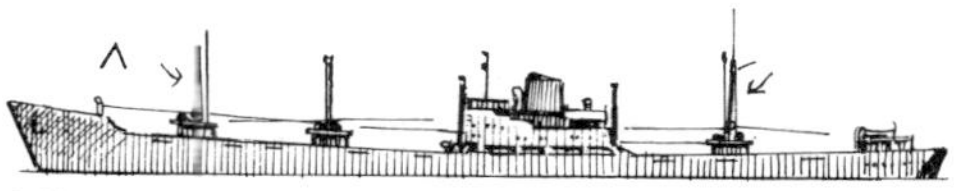

MK$_2$FKM H1
29580 PACIFIC CURRENT. NA/FRG 1953; CP; 6200/850 ; 150.1 × 7.8/8.6 (492 × 25.8/28.5); M; 14.75; ex ADRIAN 1974.

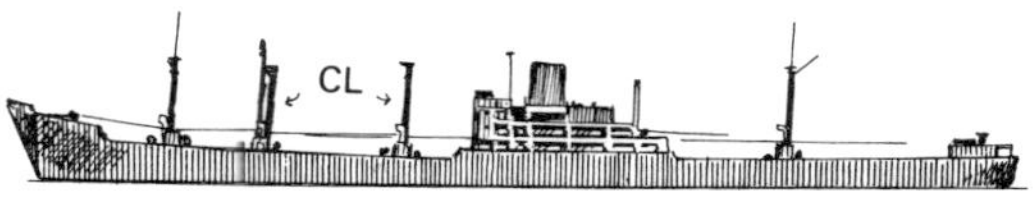

MK$_2$FKM H1
29600 GOLDEN FORTUNE. Sg/Br 1959; C; 7200/9500; 160.1 × 8.1/8.6 (525 × 26.3/28.2); M; —; ex STRATHINVER 1976; ex GALWAY 1975; Lengthened 1967.

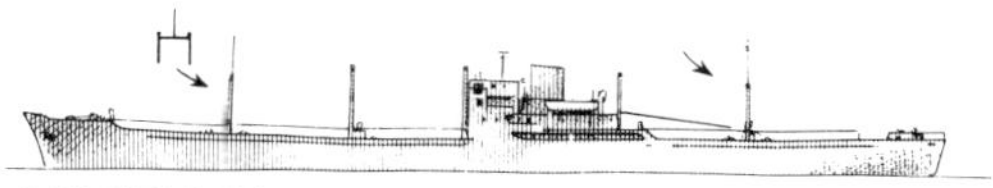

MK$_2$FKM H1
29620 TILEMACHOS. Gr/Br 1958; C; 6500; 146.01 × 8.51 (479.04 × 27.92); M; —; ex STAR BELLATRIX 1978; ex CAPETAN CARDAMILITIS 1959.

MK$_2$FKM H1
29630 'VICTORY' type. —/US 1944/47; C; 7600; 138.7 × 8.7 (455 × 28.7); T; —; May still be some of this type in service.

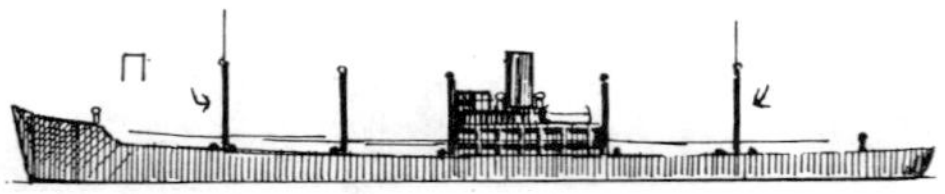

MK_2FKM H1
29640 MODIFIED 'C-3' type. —/US 1943; C; 7900; 150 × 8.9 (492 × 29.1); T; 16. May still be some of this type in service.

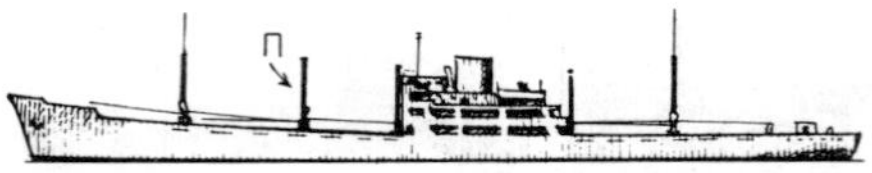

MK_2FKM H1
29650 ISABELITA. Cy/Ja 1955; C; 5400/7500; 135.4 × —/8.6 (444 × —/28.2); M; 13.5; ex ISABELA 1974; ex FILOTIS 1972; ex ASAKA MARU 1969.

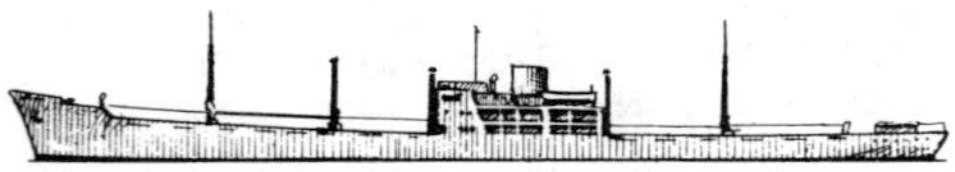

MK_2FKM H1
29660 ORIENT VICTORY. Pa/Ja 1960; C; 8700; 149.3 × 8.9 (480 × 29.1); M; 15; ex TAIKYU MARU 1974. Sister: **29661 GREEN BRIGHT** (Pa) ex EVER BRIGHT 1977; ex TAITEN MARU 1973.

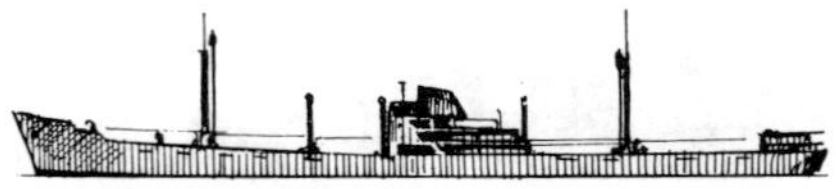

MK_2FKM H1
● **29670 RIO AMAZONAS.** Co/Ca 1953; C; 4300; 128.2 × 6.8 (421 × 22.3); M; 15; ex CIUDAD DE CALI 1972.

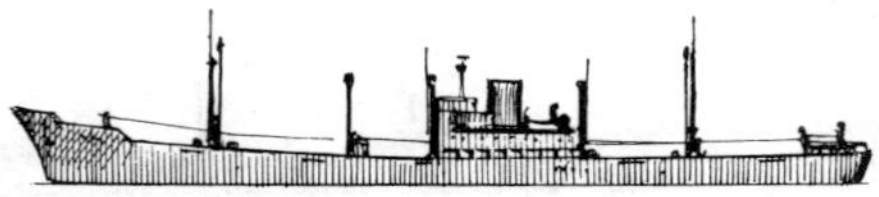

MK_2FKM H1
29680 NASOS. Gr/Fr 1951; C; 4700; 130.5 × 7.4 (439 × 24.6); M; 16; ex ATHAINASOS 1975; ex SUMA TRADER 1973; ex PICARDIE 1971.

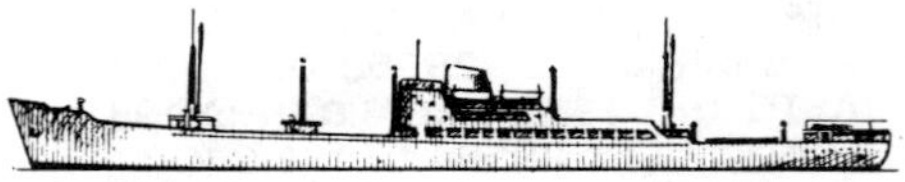

MK_2FKM H1
29690 KALLISTO. Gr/Sw 1956; CP; 5400; 139.9 × 7.7 (459 × 25.5); M; 17.5; ex KARPO 1976; ex INDIANA 1976.

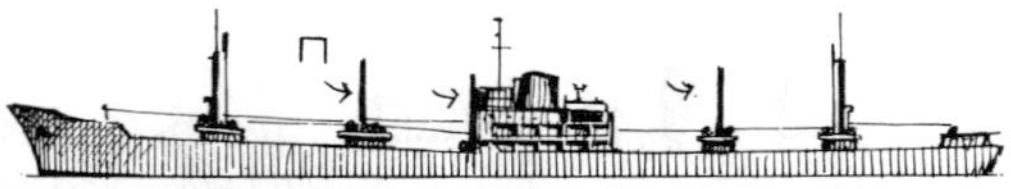

MK_2FKM H1
● **29700 WEIKO.** Pa/Ja 1958; C; 9300; 156.6 × 9.3 (514 × 30.6); ex YAMAWAKA MARU 1973. Sisters: **29701 WEILI** (Pa) ex YAMATAKA MARU 1973 **29702 MERSINIDI** (Pa) ex YAMAAKI MARU 1974.

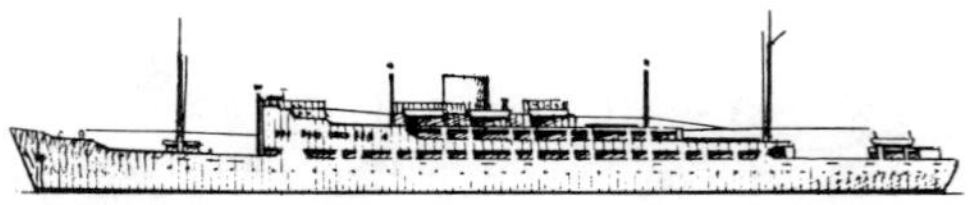

MK_2FKM H1
⋆**29710 GEORG BUCHNER.** DDR/Be 1951; PC; 11100; 153.7 × 8.4 (504 × 27.6); M; 16; ex CHARLESVILLE 1967.

MK_2FKM H12
29720 RIO BERMEJO. Ar/Br 1950; C; 7100; 149.7 × 7.9 (491 × 25.11); M; 15. Sisters (Ar flag): **29721 RIO BELEN 29722 RIO BELGRANO**

MK_2FKM H12
29730 CHRYANTHI. Cy/Br 1958; C; 8200; 140 × 9.4 (459 × 31); T; —; ex CARRIGAN HEAD 1972.

MK_2FKM H123
29740 BERNADETTE No 1. Pa/Ja 1954; C; 5600/7000; 145.2 × —/8.2 (476 × —/26.1); M; 14; ex YASUKUNI 1977; ex YASUKUNI MARU 1969.

MK_2FKM H123
29750 CHEER KING. Pa/Ja 1953; CP; 7600; 150.5 × 8.4 (494 × 27.7); M; 16; ex GUIN SAN; ex ASTORIA MARU 1974.

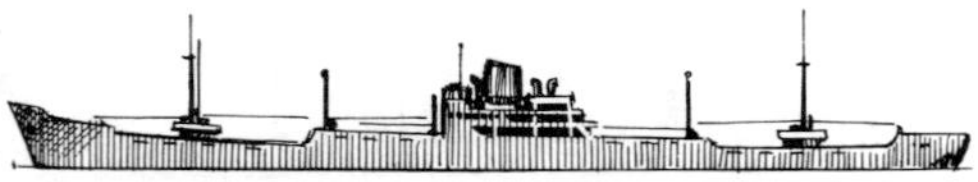

MK_2FKM H123
29760 CHIEH HSING. Pa/Ja 1952; C; 7600; 151 × 8.4 (495 × 27.7); TSM; 15.5; ex TOMISHIMA MARU 1972.

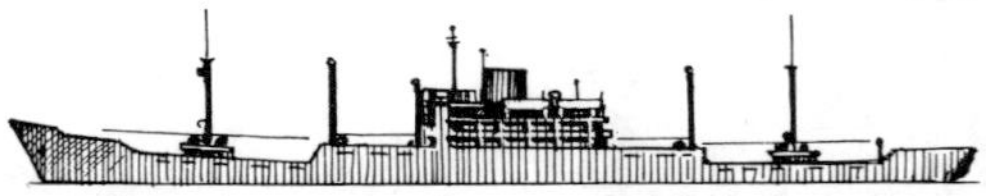

MK_2FKM H123
29770 CELEBES CAREER. Pa/Ja 1954; CP; 7600; 151 × 8.4 (496 × 27.7); TSM; 16; ex SAMOA MARU No2 1976; ex AKI MARU 1972. Sisters (Pa flag): **29771 UNION FRATERNITY** ex ATSUTA MARU 1977 **29772 GOLDEN DEFENDER** ex THUNDERBIRD; ex ARIMA MARU 1973 Similar: **29773 PAVLO** (Cy) ex KORAI MARU 1972.

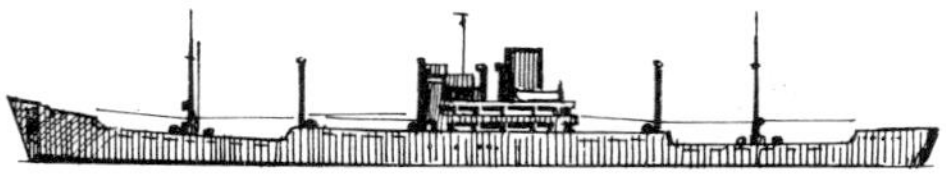

MK_2FKM H123
29780 CHIEH LAI. Pa/Ja 1952; C; 7000; 145.2 × 8.1 (476 × 26.1); M; 14.25; ex PORT LOUIS MARU 1972; ex WAKO MARU 1964.

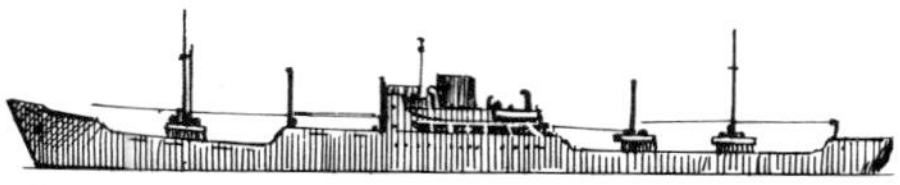

MK_2FKM H123
29790 BANDA CAREER. Pa/Ja 1952; CP; 7100; 141.4 × 8.1 (464 × 26.1); M; 13; ex CARNELIAN 1975; ex SARABAYA MARU 1975.

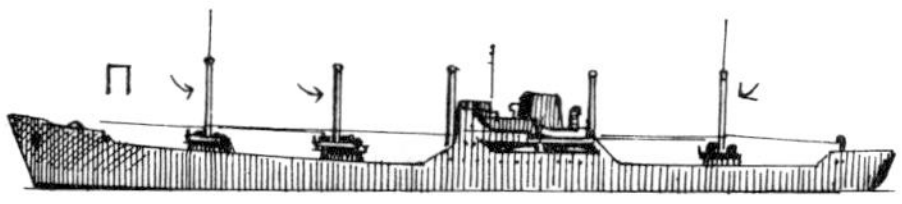

MK_2FKM H123
29800 SOUTHERN ENTERPRISE. Li/Ja 1953; C; 7500; 141.1 × 8.1 (452 × 26.1); M; 14; ex KENYO MARU 1973.

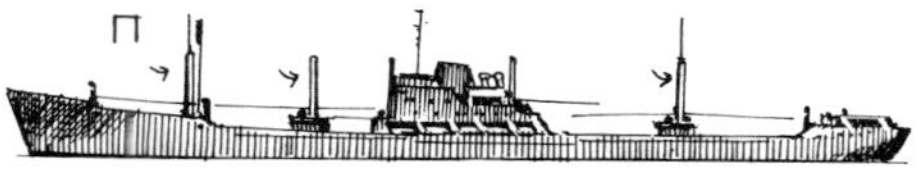

MK_2FKM H13
● **29810 ONYX ISLANDS.** Pa/Sw 1962; C; 6100/8500; 142.7 × 8/9.1 (467 × 26.5/29.8); M; 15; ex EGERO 1972.

MK_2FKM H13
29820 TSING CHAU. Li/De 1950; CP; 5000; 139.9 × 7.9 (459 × 25.1); M; 15; ex ALIOTH 1970; ex BLACK HAWK 1967.

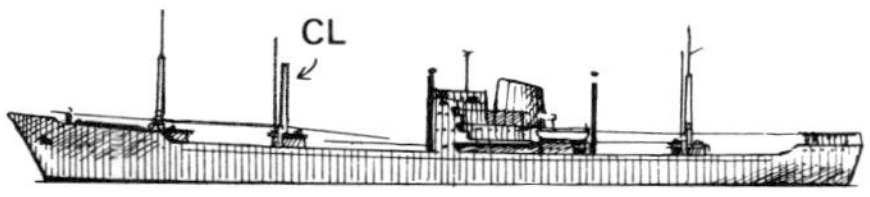

MK_2FKM H13
● **29830 BANGRAK.** Sg/De 1958/60 C; 5900; 136.43 × 6.73 (447.6 × 22.08); M; 14.75; ex KNUD MAERSK; Lengthened 1960. Sisters: **29831 CHERRY LAJU** (Sg) ex JENS MAERSK **29832 CHERRY SINDIA** (Sg) ex SVEND MAERSK.

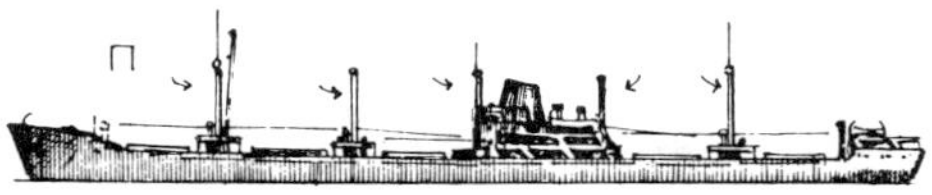

MK_2FKM H13
29840 ZULAIHA. Sg/Fr 1959; C; 8800; 144.9 × 9.1 (475 × 29.1); M; 15; ex EASTERN PROSPERITY 1980; ex TATRA 1977; ex SISTINA 1966.

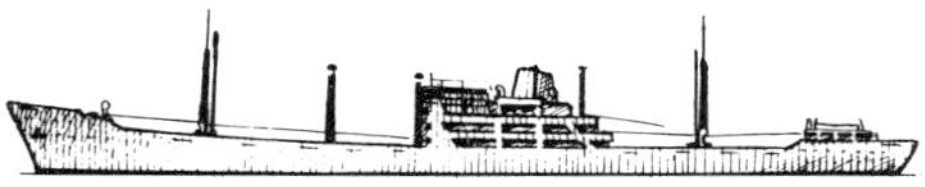

MK_2FKM H13
29850 UNITED EXPORTER. Pa/Ja 1950; C; 7900; 143.4 × 9 (470 × 29.6); M; 14; ex UNITED EXPLORER; ex ANTON STJEPOV 1976; ex TONI 1973; ex YAMA 1968.

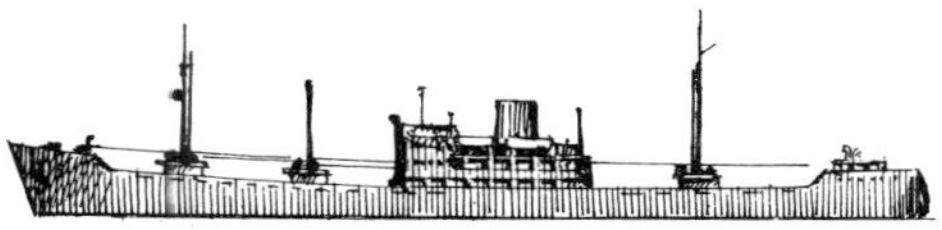

MK_2FKM H13
⋆**29860 CELEBES SEA.** RC/Ja 1950; C; 6600/8800; 146.7 × 8.1/— (481 × 27.8/—); M; 16; ex PANAMA 1972.

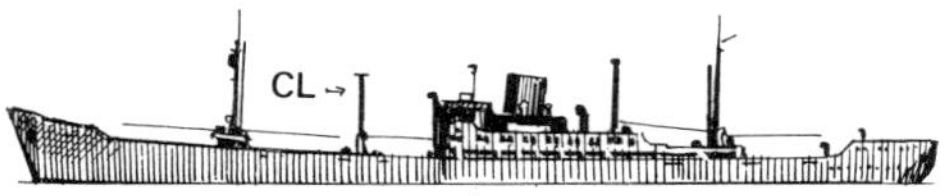

MK_2FKM H13
29870 EUROSAILOR. Gr/FRG 1952; CP; 6800; 146.1 × 7.5 (455 × 24.9); M; 13; ex BARING 1977; ex ALBUR II 1972; ex SANTA ISABEL 1968. Similar; **29871 ALEXI H** (Pa) ex PAPPIS P 1980; ex BRIGHT SKY 1977; ex ANGOL 1969; ex SANTA URSULA 1964.

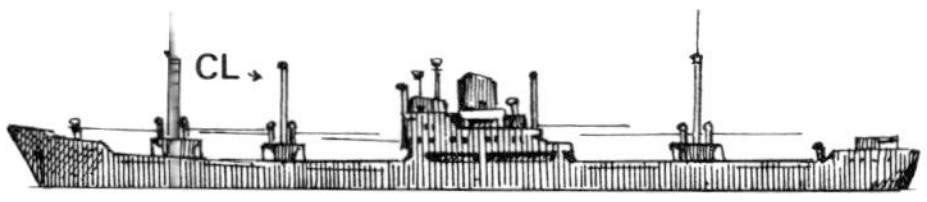

MK_2FKM H13
29880 DAVOS. Sd/FRG 1961; C; 8900; 149.4 × 9.1 (487 × 29.1); M; 15; ex YEMELOS 1973; ex STEINTOR 1971.

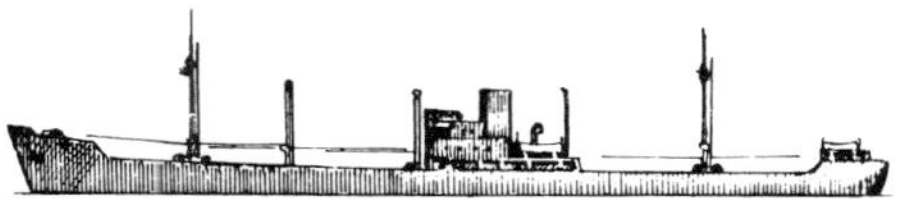

MK_2FKM H13
29890 GIORGIS P. Cy/Fr 1949; C; 6800; 139.9 × 7.2 (459 × 23.9); M; 13; ex CRIOS II 1976; ex FRANK DELMAS 1971; ex OLINDA.

MK_2FKM H13
29000 PANORMOS. Cy/Sw 1961; C; 6000/8800; 148.4 × —/9.3 (487 × —/30.5); M; 15; ex SALMELA 1972.

MK_2FKM H13
29910 VICMAR STAR. Gr/FRG 1956; C; 6100/10700; 146.4 × 8.3/9.3 (480 × 27/30.5); M; 15; ex BELLE RIVE 1973; ex HIMMERLAND 1966. Sister: **29911 KLIO** (Gr) ex LISIANNE; ex GIMLETUN 1969; ex MOSTUM 1965.

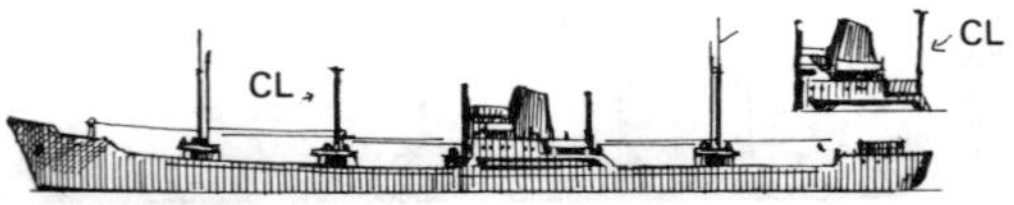

MK_2FKM H13
29920 KHADIJAAN. Pa/FRG 1956; C; 6100/8900; 146 × 8.2/9.1 (479 × 26.11/29.1); M; 15; ex ROMAN EMPEROR 1976; ex SVOLDER 1974; ex HOEGH SVOLDER 1972; ex SVOLDER 1970. Similar (inset): **29921 BANGLAR MAITRI** (Bh) ex BANGLA REGO 1974; ex REGO 1973 **29922 SOPHIA II** (Pa) ex SOPHIA MINERVA 1978; ex HOEGH FRAM 1977; ex MINERVA 1974 **29923 INNAREN** (Gr) ex EPTANISSOS 1977; ex BOGATYR 1973; ex LEIV ERIKSSON 1965.

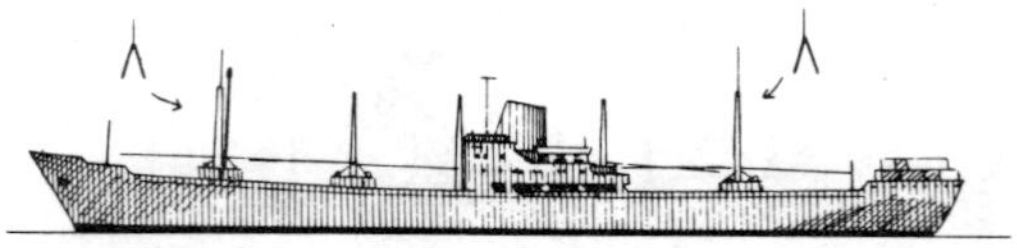

MK_2FKM H13
29930 AGATE ISLANDS. Pa/Sw 1959; CP; 5900/8700; 148.3 × 8.2/9.1 (487 × 26.11/29.1); M; 15.5; ex BROTT 1973.

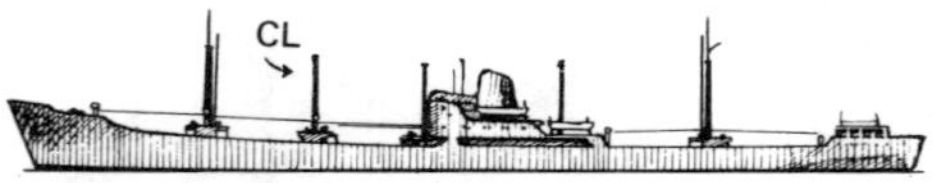

MK_2FKM H13
⋆**29940 USHIRIKA.** Ta/FRG 1956; CP; 8900; 145.9 × 9.2 479 × 30.1); M; 14; ex NANTONG 1967; ex THORSDRAKE 1967.

MK_2FKM H13
● ⋆**29950 XIANG YIN.** RC/FRG 1956; C; 8700; 145.3 × 9.1 (480 × 29.1); M; 15; ex ARCTIC OCEAN 1976; ex BLUE MASTER 1964. Sister: **29951 HELLAN** (Pa) ex AETOS 1975; ex MARIO G. GEORGILIS 1971; ex MILLROSS 1962 Similar: **29952 RAJAAN** (Pa) ex HOPEWELL 1976; ex ST. LAWRENCE 1973; ex KOSTANTIS M 1971; ex SOMERVILLE 1969.

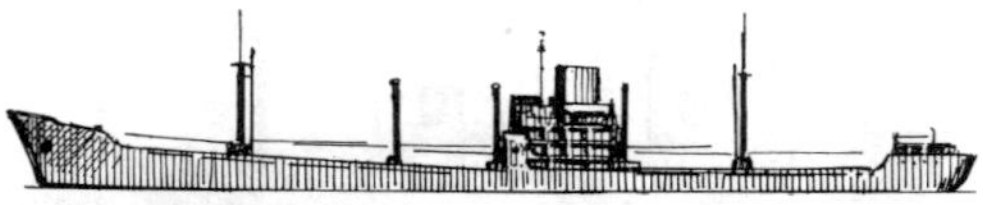

MK_2FKM H13
29960 GEMBIRA. Ia/Ne 1953; CP; 9500; 105.6 × 8.6 (494 × 28.3); M; 16; ex BAWEAN 1973.

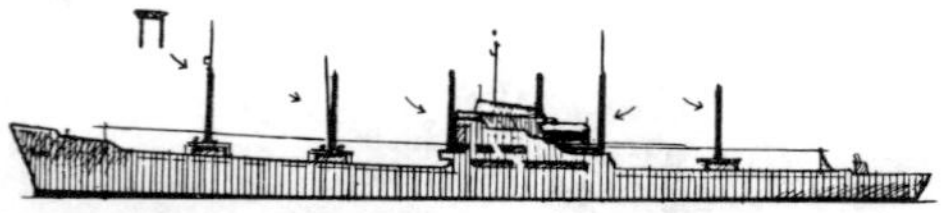

MK_2FKMK H1
29970 SCHUYLER OTIS BLAND. US/US 1951; C; 8900; 145.7 × 9.1 (478 × 30); T; 18.5; operated by Military Sealift Command.

MK_2FKMK H1
● **29980 PEARL VALLEY.** Pa/Sw 1953; CP; 3700/6000; 130.1 × 7/8.4 (427 × 23.4/27.7); M; 16; ex BIANCA 1980; ex GABON TRADER 1979; ex VISHAMN 1974; ex DISA 1971.

MK_2FKMK H1
⋆**30000 PING YIN.** RC/FRG 1962; CP; 6300/10000; 155.9 × 7.7/9.1 (511 × 25.6/30); M; 17.5; ex PACIFIC OCEAN 1974; ex TRANSVAAL 1972. Sister: ⋆**30001 SHAN YIN** (RC) ex INDIAN OCEAN 1974; ex TANGANYIKA 1971.

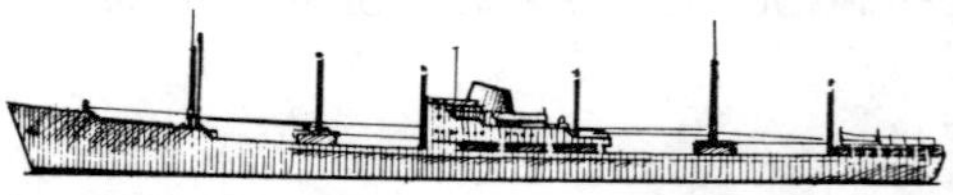

MK_2FKMK H1
30010 STAR FIVE. Cy/Sw 1955; CP; 5700; 147.6 × 8.4 (484 × 26.7); M; 17; ex BETTY 1979; ex GAY FAITH 1975; ex BLACK EAGLE 1973.

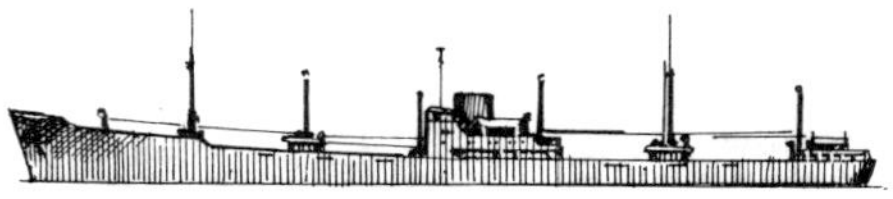

MK$_2$FKMK H1

● **30020 ZEA SILVER.** Gr/Sw 1953; CP; 5000; 132.5 × 7.9 (435 × 25.11); M; 15.5; ex HOE SENG 1975; ex AUD PRESTHUS 1973; ex HAVMOY 1967.

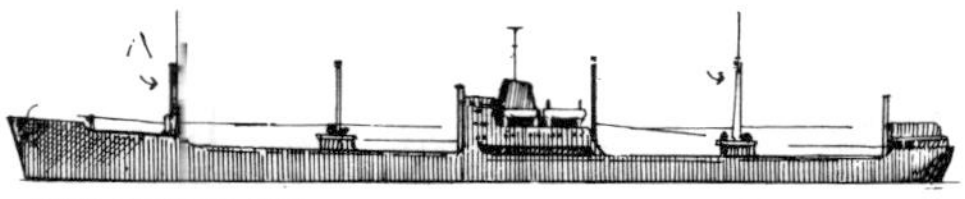

MK$_2$FKMK H1

⋆**30030 KANG DING.** RC/Sw 1956; CP; 10400; 151.6 × 9.3 (497 × 30.7); M; 14.75; ex OCEANTRAVEL 1970; ex NORTHERN CLIPPER 1963.

MK$_2$FKMK H1

⋆**30040 HONG QI 120.** RC/Ne 1956; CP; 6000; 147.5 × 8.1 (484 × 26.4); M; 15; ex MINFUNG 1976; ex WITMARSUM 1972.

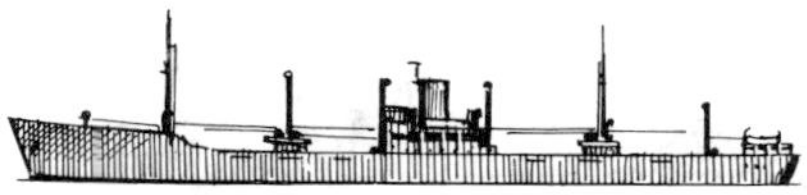

MK$_2$FKMK H1

30050 APOSTOLOS M. Pa/Sw 1939; C; 3400; 123.9 × 6.9 (407 × 22.6); TSM; 16; ex CYCLADES 1971; ex SAGOLAND 1963.

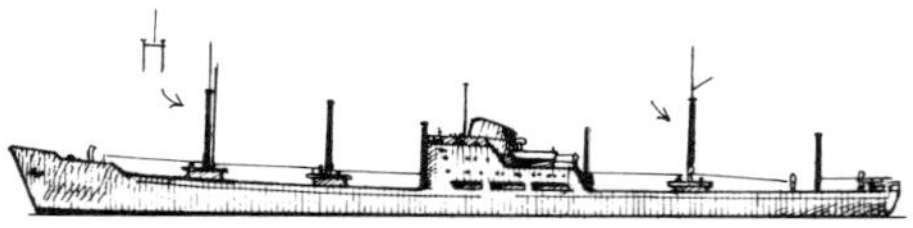

MK$_2$FKMK H1

⋆**30060 XUAN HUA.** RC/Sw 1956; C; 6000/9000; 141.08 × 8.19/9.21 (463 × 26.9/30.1); M; 14; ex STEED 1976; ex BROLAND 1970; ex O.A. BRODIN 1961.

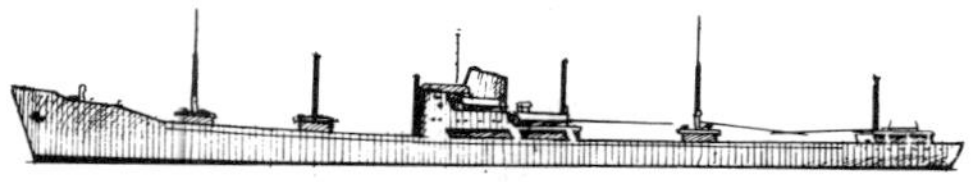

MK$_2$FKMK H1

30070 DIAMOND. Cy/Sw 1957; C; 6600/9800; 151.2 × —/9.5 (496 × —/31.1); M; 14; ex JOHNNY; ex ORIENT 1968. Similar: **30071 SAMUDRA VIJAY** (In) ex JALAGOPAL; ex SITANJA.

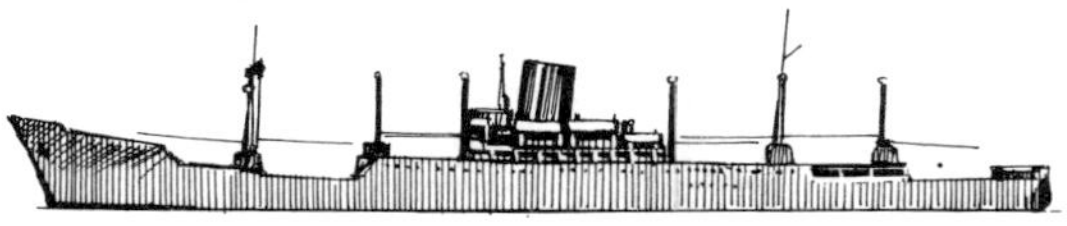

MK$_2$FKMK H12

● **30080 EASTERN ACADEMY.** Li/Br 1958; R; 10800/13000; 160.4 × 9/9.8 (526 × 31.6/32.2); TSM; —; ex OTAIO 1976.

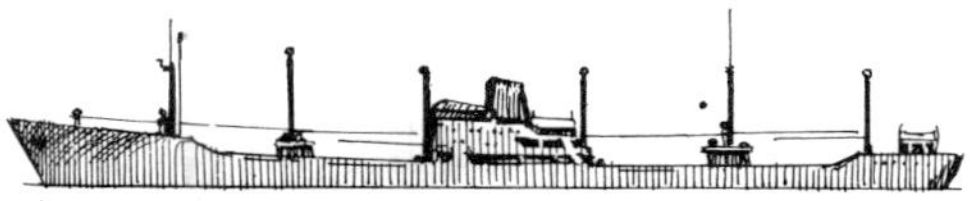

MK$_2$FKMK H13

30090 KOTA TANJONG. Sg/FRG 1956; CP; 9600; 151.2 × 8.1 (496 × 26.1); M; 17.5; ex EASTERN CAPE 1972; ex HOEGH CAPE 1967. Sister: ⋆**30091 HONG QI 134** (RC) ex BIHUA; ex EASTERN CLIFF 1972; ex HOEGH CLIFF 1967.

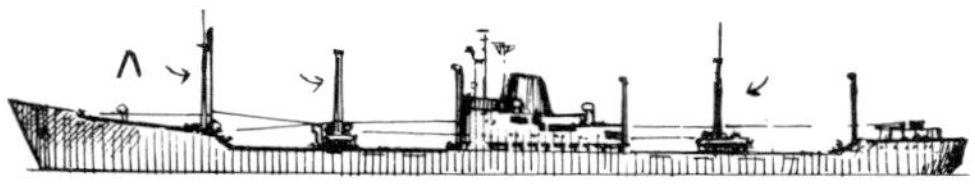

MK$_2$FKMK H13

30100 ASCARYA. Pa/No 1956; C; 5300/8200; 142 × 8.2/8.9 (466 × 26.1/29.5); M; 16.5; ex TORONTO 1973. Similar: **30101 BANGLAR PREETI** (Bh); ex TURANDOT 1976.

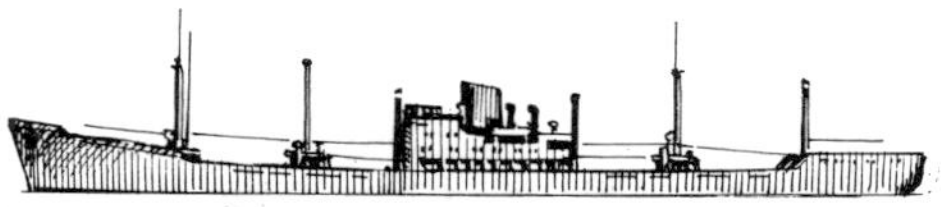

MK$_2$FKMK H13

30110 KOTA MUNI. Sg/Ne 1954; C; 8500; 143.7 × 8.8 (472 × 28.1); M; 17, ex TOREADOR 1973.

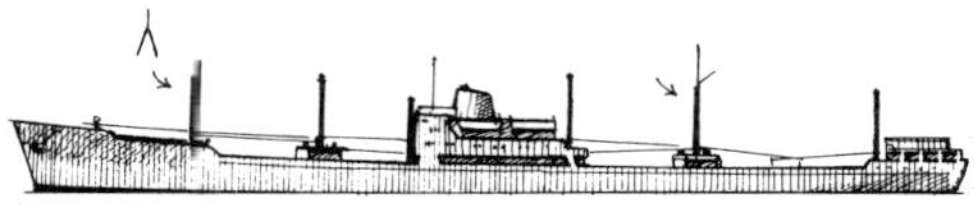

MK$_2$FKMK H13

⋆**30120 KANG DING.** RC/Sw 1956; CP; 10400; 151.6 × 9.3 (497 × 30.7); M; 14.75; ex OCEANTRAVEL 1970; ex NORTHERN CLIPPER 1963.

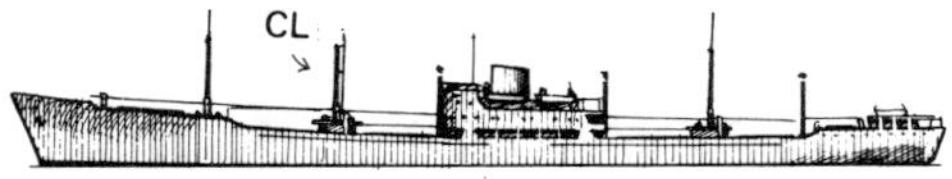

MK$_2$FKMK H13

30130 FAIZI. Ir/Sw 1955; C; 6100/8300; 147.05 × 7.86/8.23 (482 × 25.9/27); M; 17; ex IRAN SHAHR 1977; ex MINIKOI 1972. Sister (RC flag): ⋆**30131 WUDU** ex BAIYEN 1976; ex SABANG 1972 Similar: ⋆**30132 NINGDU** ex BINING 1976; ex KOTO 1973.

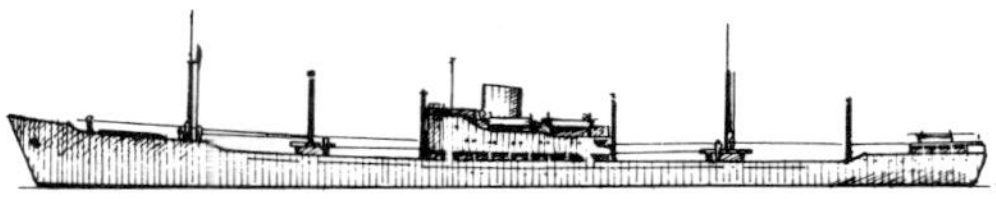

MK$_2$FKMK H13

30140 EDDY. Cy/Sw 1952; CP; 7000; 154.9 × 8.3 (508 × 27.3); TSM; 17.75; ex ANDROMACHI; ex BURMA 1976.

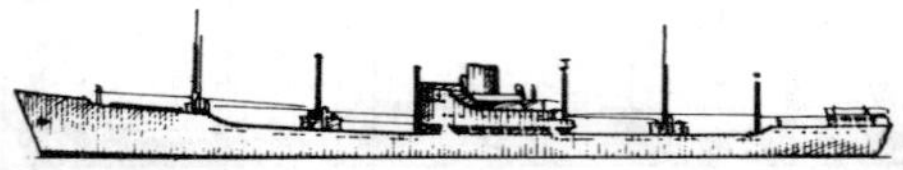

MK_2FKMK H13
30150 DELIMA. Pa/Sw 1950; C; 4900/7900; 138.5 × 7.7/8.6 (454 × 25.2/28.1); M; 14; ex BERYL 1972; ex PRODROMOS VITA 1970; ex BROTRADE 1968; ex KUNGALAND 1966.

MK_2FKMK H13
● **30160 KALMAR.** Gr/Sw 1951; CP; 4000; 131.3 × 8.4 (431 × 27.7); M; 16.5; ex MYSON 1976; ex CONCORDIA MYSON 1972; ex MYSON 1971; ex VIBYHOLM 1969. Sister: **30161 NEW HYSAN** (Pa) ex SEA CHALLENGER 1973; ex BRAHEHOLM 1967 Similar (longer): **30162 LITO** (Gr) ex BRORIVER 1975; ex MALTESHOLM 1969.

MK_2FKMK H13
30170 RAMONEVERETT. Li/Fi 1960; CP; 5800/8000; 147.1 × 7.9/9.1 (482 × 25.9/29.9); M; 17; ex MANDALAY. Sister (Goalpost Kingposts at either end of superstructure): **30171 OHIO** (Cy) ex DAFNOS 1980; ex SAMELAND 1978; ex SVANEHOLM 1973 Similar: **30172 DAFNOS** (Gr).

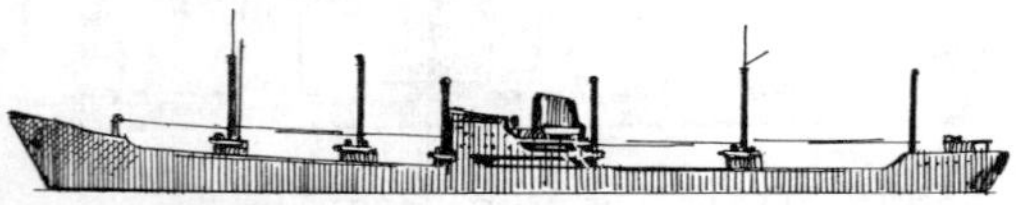

MK_2FKMK H13
30180 PULAU NIAS. Pa/FRG 1959; CP; 6700/9800; 157.1 × 8/9.3 (516 × 26.4/30.6); M; 16.5; ex HOEGH DENE 1979.

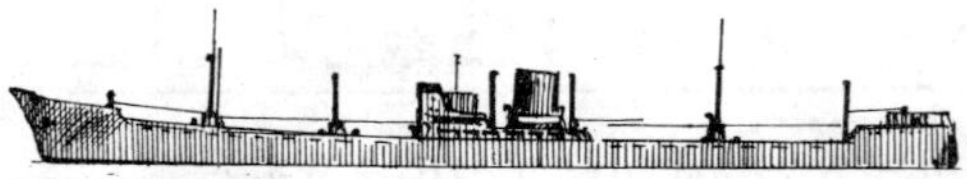

MK_2FKMK H13
30190 MAYSTAR. Pa/Br 1957; C; 6300/8600; 147.3 × 7.9/8.6 (483 × 26/28); M; 15; ex NEPTUN 1980; ex EURABIA OCEAN 1980; ex ARIS CARRIER 1977; ex CARRONBANK 1974. Similar: **30191 KOTA RAKYAT** (Sg) ex CLOVERBANK 1971 **30192 RENA K** (Gr) ex CRESTBANK 1973 **30193 LANKA KEERTI** (Sr) ex DARTBANK 1975 **30194 NEWCREST** (Li) ex ASHBANK 1976 **30195 FORTUNE STAR** (Pa) ex AVONBANK **30196 AEGIS GRACE** (Gr) ex MINCHBANK 1972 **30197 NEWBEACH** (Li) ex NEWBREEZE 1977; ex ROSEBANK 1976 **30198 BLUE WAVE** (Gr) ex ELMBANK 1976 **30199 GOLDEN LAGOS** (Pa) ex OLIVEBANK 1978.

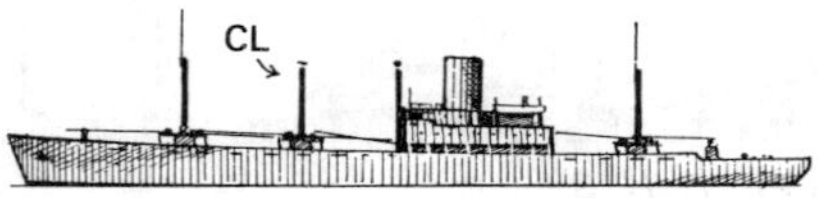

MK_2FM H1
30210 'C-1' type. —/US c.1943; C; 6700; 127.4 × 8.4 (419 × 27.7); T; 14; There may be some of this type in service.

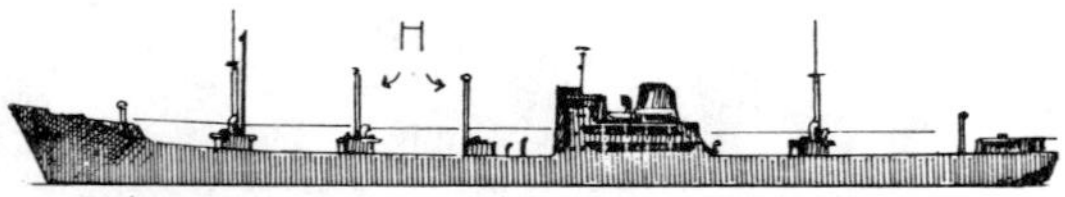

MK_2FM H1
30220 EFCHARIS. Gr/Br 1958; C; 7300/10000; 164.9 × 8.1/9.1 (541 × 26.7/29.11); M; 13.5; ex PATAGONIA 1974; ex HARPALYCE 1972. Sister: **30221 VICTORY FIVE** (Pa) ex IRINIKOS 1980; ex HARPAGUS 1973 Similar: **30222 SABRINA** (Pa) ex FILIKOS 1980; ex HARPALYCUS 1975.

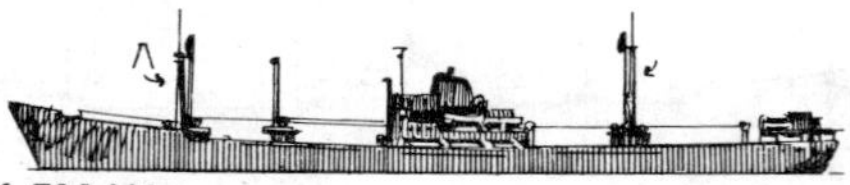

MK_2FM H1
30230 CHRISTOS K. Sg/Sw 1957; C; 4000/6200; 130.9 × 7.2/8.3(428 × 23.5/27.6); M; 14.25; ex NOPAL SUN; ex MARTIN THORE 1966.

MK_2FM H1
● **30240 LU CHIANG.** Pa/De 1955; CP; 4300; 131.3 × 7.5 (431 × 24.8); M; —; ex ANTONIA 1971; ex THOR ODLAND 1966.

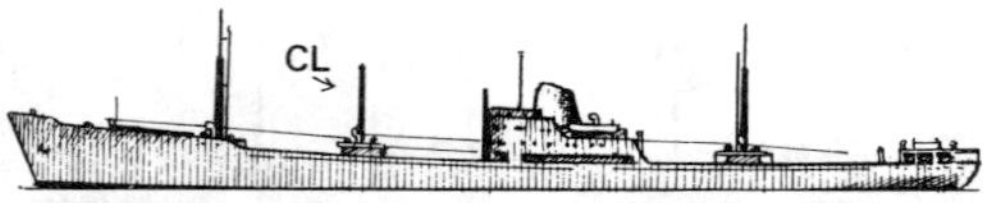

MK_2FM H1
⋆**30250 JIANGYIN.** RC/FRG 1958; C; 6800/9500; 153.1 × 8.1/9.1 (502 × 26.3/29.8); M; 15.5; ex HWANG HO 1970; ex HENRI G 1968. Sister: **30251 ULIANG** (Pa) ex MALAGA 1972; ex HEERING MILLE 1965; ex ROLV JARL 1965.

MK_2FM H1
● **30260 SYNARISTIA.** Gr/De 1952; CP; 4000/5700; 129.4 × 7.3/7.7 (425 × 24.1/25.2); M; 16; ex SPREEWALD 1974; ex BIRGITTE TORM 1965. Sister: **30261 SINALITHIA** (Gr) ex LAUSITZ 1977; ex ESTRID TORM 1966.

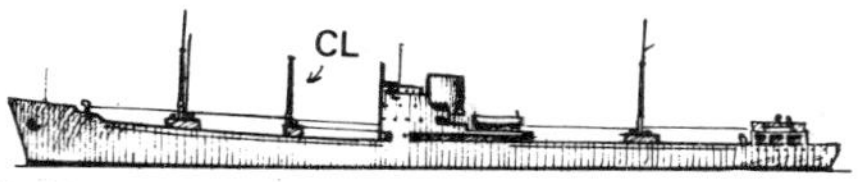

MK2FM H1
30270 BANGLAR TARANI. Bh/De 1962; C; 4700/6700; 133.5 × 7.8/8.6 (438 × 25.8/28.3); M; 14.5; ex GAUTATYR 1973.

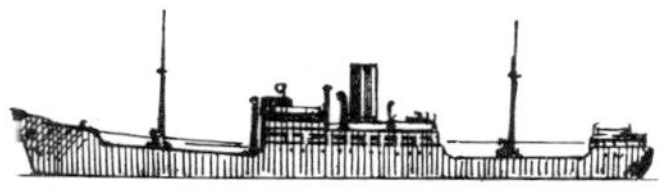

MK2FM H123
★**30280 STARFORD;** RC/Br 1950; CP; 3500; 101.1 × 6.3 (332 × 20.7); R; 11.5; ex FUNING 1964. Similar: ★**30281 WISHFORD** (RC).

MK2FM H13
30290 PETER RICH; Pa/FRG 1958; CP; 7000/9500; 153.2 × 8/9.1 (503 × 26.3/29.9); M; 14; ex CAPTAIN ANGELO 1980; ex ANGEL 1970; ex WOODVILLE 1970.

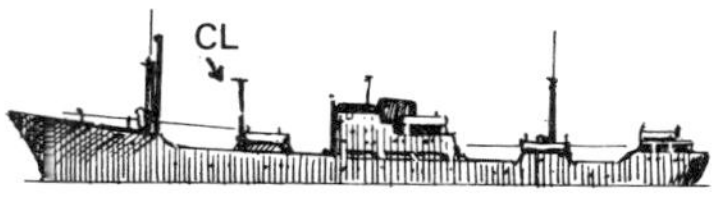

MK2FM H13
● **30300 TAIPOOSEK;** Br/No 1962; CP; 4600; 110.5 × 7.6 (363 × 25); M; 15.5.

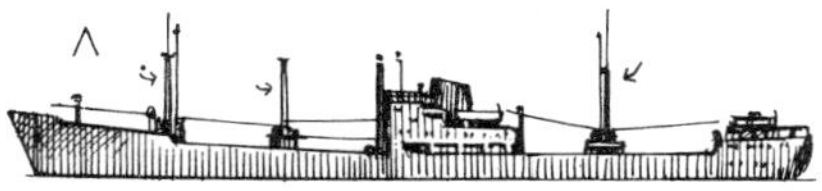

MK2FM H13
30310 ARPA; Gr/No 1955; C; 4000; 125.5 × 7.1 (412 × 23.4); M; 14.5; ex PALMA 1973.

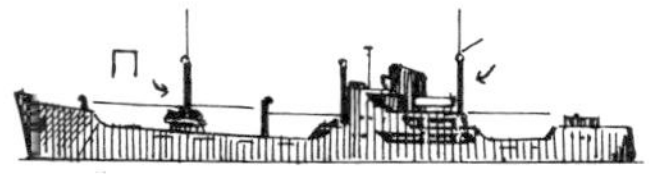

MK2FM H13
30320 GEORGE F; Gr/Br 1059; CP; 3800; 99.1 × 7.3 (325 × 24.1); M; 12; ex QUEBEC 1976; ex ALICE BOWATER 1969. Similar (Gr flag): **30321 KRETAN SPIRIT** ex CONSTANCE BOWATER **30322 AGINOR** ex GIGI 1976; ex GLADYS BOWATER 1972; **30323 KRETAN GLORY** ex NINA BOWATER 1977 **30324 TASSOS K** ex CHARLOTTE; ex PHYLLIS BOWATER 1973.

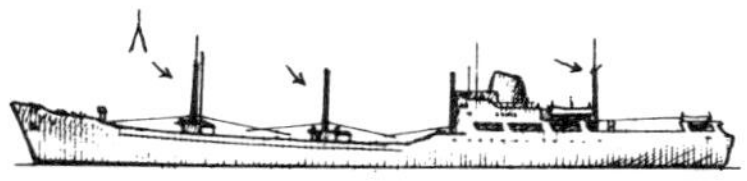

MK2FM H13
30330 GRAN CANARIA; Gr/Sw 1957; C; 2900; 114.5 × 6.2 (376 × 20.6); M; 15; ex FREDERICA 1965. Sister: **30331 ACORES** (Po) Similar: ★**30332 HONG QI 165** (RC) ex BAODI; ex SVENSKSUND 1973 ★**30333 YUQUAN** (RC) ex STOCK **30334 STOCKSUND** (Gr) ex CAP YORK 1970; ex STOCKSUND 1969 **30335 VERNA** (NA) ex MARION 1966; ex MARONIA 1963; ex MARION.

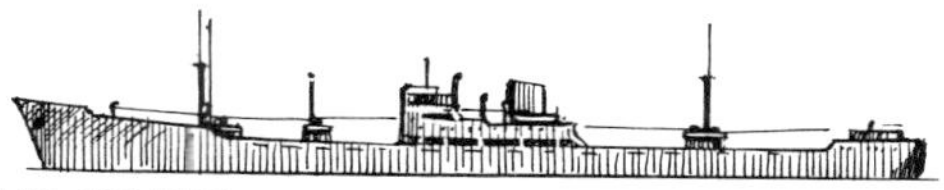

MK2FM H13
30340 PRIMO ARABIA; Pa/Br 1955; C; 8300; 145.9 × 8.9 (479 × 27.5); M; 13.5; ex ALEXANDROS SKOUTARIS; ex ALEXANDROS S 1971; ex ST JOANNA 1967; ex CAPE YORK 1965.

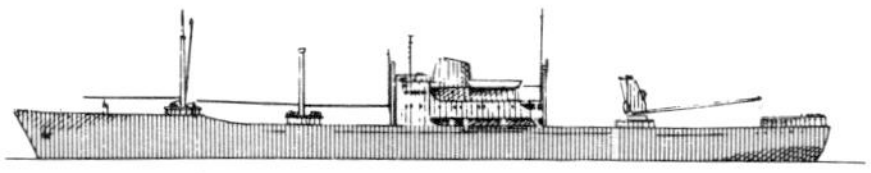

MK2FMC H1
● **30350 JEBEL ALI 2;** Gr/Sw 1958; C; 3600; 129.11 × 7.12 (423.59 × 23.36); M; 14.5; ex DIAMANT 1980; ex SKIENSFJORD 1977.

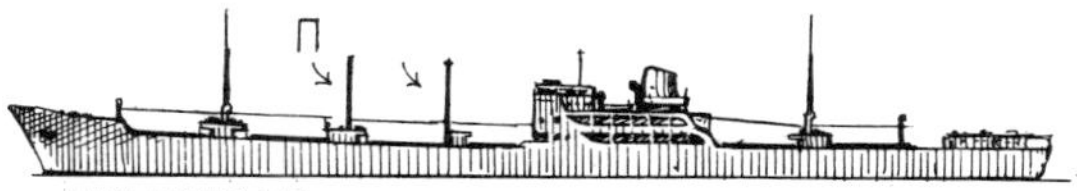

MK2FMK H1
30360 EFCHARIS; Gr/Br 1958; C; 7300/10000; 164.9 × 8.1/9.1 (541 × 26.7/29.11); M; 13.5; ex PATAGONIA 1974; ex HARPALYCE 1972. Sister: **30361 VICTORY FIVE** (Pa) ex IRINIKOS 1980; ex HARPAGUS 1973 Similar: **30362 SABRINA** (Pa) ex FILIKOS 1980; ex HARPALYUS 1975.

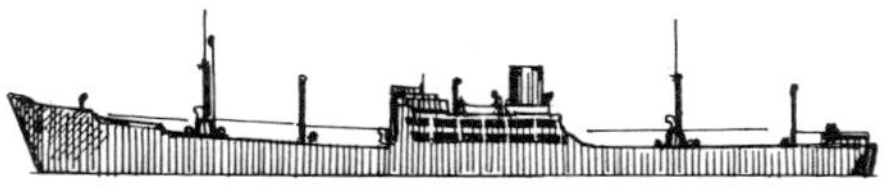

MK2FMK H1
30370 LITA I; Pa/Br 1953; C; 7800; 145.7 × 8.4 (448 × 25.6); M; 12.5; ex LITA; ex KIM 1975; ex DIMITRAKIS 1973; ex JAG RAKSHAK 1965; ex LAKE PENNASK 1963; ex JERSEY SPRAY 1956. Sister: **30371 IRENES CHARITY** (Pa) ex IRENE XILAS 1977; ex IRENES CHARITY 1977; ex IRENE XILAS; ex LAKE ATUN 1965; ex JERSEY MIST 1956.

MK_2FMK H13

● **30380 PATROCLOS;** Cy/Br 1955; C; 7700; 138.69 × — (455.02 × —); M; 14; ex FOYLEBANK 1973; KP abreast the funnel. Sisters: **30381 EASTERN SATURN** (Pa) ex GOLDEN SEA 1974; ex POLA ANNA 1973; ex LAGANBANK **30382 PARIS** (Cy) ex NESSBANK 1973.

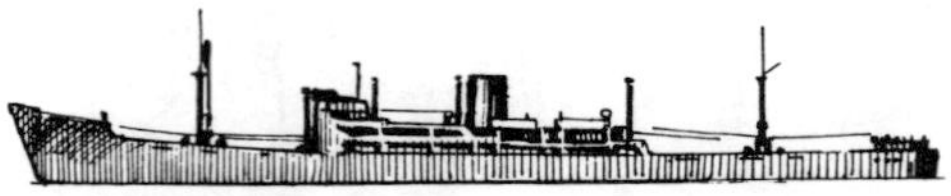

MK_3FKM H1

30390 WAN FU; Pa/Br 1950; CP; 9200; 148.7 × 9.5 (471 × 29.9); M; 15; ex SPALMATORI SEAMAN 1975; ex LOOSDRECHT 1968; ex LANGLEECYDE.

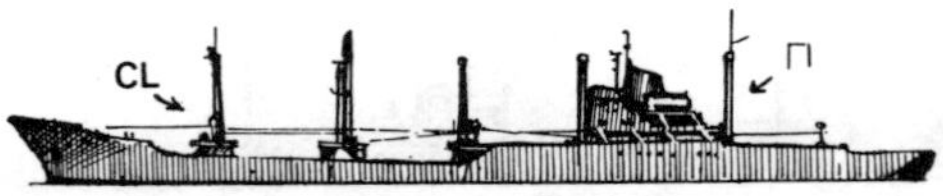

MK_3FM H12

30400 MAR CANTABRICO; Sp/Sp 1967; C; 8300; 142.5 × 9.4 (468 × 30.6); M; —.

MK_3FM H13

30410 LUIGI D'AMICO; It/It 1964; C; 9100; 156.9 × 9.1 (515 × 29.9); M; —; ex ORIENT MARINER 1969.

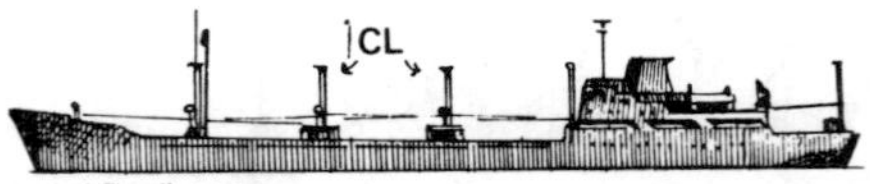

MK_3MFCK H13

⋆**30420 XINCHANG;** RC/Fi 1963; CP; 4200/6400; 134.7 × 7.3/8.2 (445 × 23.1/26.1); M; 16; ex SUNNANLAND 1977; ex SAGAHOLM 1972. Sisters (RC flag): ⋆**30421 YIDU** ex ODENSHOLM 1971 ⋆**30422 JIANGDU** ex VRETAHOLM 1971 ⋆**30423 CHANGDU** ex BLANKAHOLM 1971.

● 30425

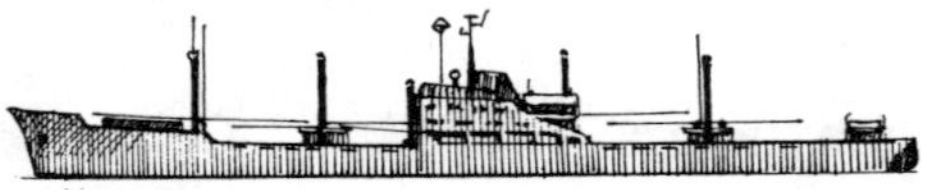

MK_2MFK_2 H1

⋆**30430 NORWID;** Pd/Fr 1962; C; 5500/7800; 141.1 × 7.6/8.7 (463 × 24.11/28.8); M; 16.5.

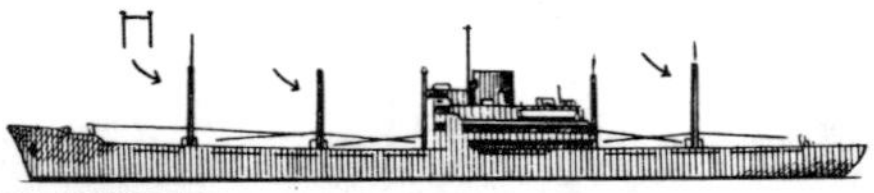

MK_2MFK_2 H1

30440 HAN GEONG; Ko/Ja 1957; C; 7300; 137.32 × 8.56 (451 × 28.4); M; 13.75; ex PACIFIC SHINHO 1975; ex TENKAI MARU 1972.

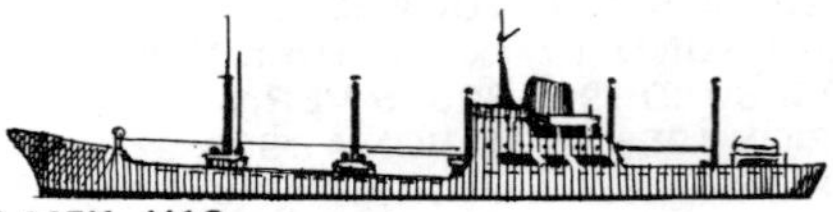

MK_2MFK_2 H13

● **30450 KARANA AMPAT;** Ia/No 1960; CP; 5600; 126 × 7.8 (413 × 25.6); M; 16; ex BRIMANGER 1973.

MK_2MFK_3 H1

30460 THOMAS NELSON; US/US 1962; C; 8700/12500; 172.2 × —/9.6 (565 × —/31.8); T; 20; ex NATHANAEL GREENE 1977; ex PHILIPPINE BEAR 1975.

MK_2MFK_3 H1

30470 HOWA MARU; Ja/Ja 1962; C; 9200; 156 × 9 (512 × 29.8); M; 16.25.

MK_2MFK_3 H13

30480 BAUPRE ISLAND; Pa/Sw 1953; CP; 6900; 155.8 × 8.2 (511 × 27); M; 17; ex SAUDI GLORY 1976; ex THORSISLE 1975; ex BONANZA 1970. Sister: **30481 ROSSEVERETT** (Pa) ex BUFFALO.

MK_2MFK_3 H13

30490 KOTA TIMUR; Sg/Br 1955; CP; 6400; 156 × 8.5 (512 × 27.1); M; 16.5; ex FERNMOOR 1975.

MK_2MFK_2M H1
30500 EASTERN RUBY; Pa/Ja 1959; C; 9100; 156.1 × 9.2 (512 × 30.6); M; 17.5; ex CHICAGO MARU 1980.

MK_2MFK_2M H1
30510 BOSTON MARU; Ja/Ja 1962; CP; 9000; 156.5 × 9.4 (513 × 30.11); M; 18.5. Sister: **30511 HAMPTON MARU** (Ja).

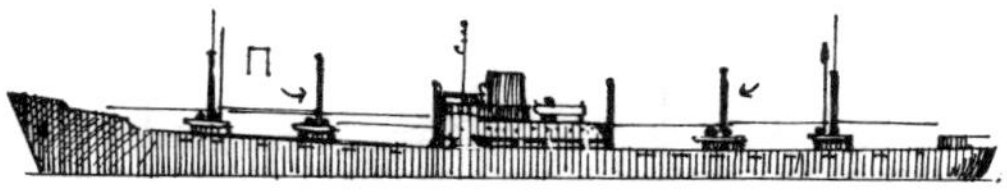

MK_2MFK_2M H1
● **30520 HAN BORI;** Pa/Ja 1960; C; 9100; 156.1 × 9.2 (512 × 30.2); M; 17.75; ex MARITIME GRACE 1980; ex HOUSTON MARU 1975. Sisters (Ja flag): **30521 TACOMA MARU 30522 EASTERN LEADER** (Pa) ex NORFOLK MARU 1980.

MK_2MFKM H
30530 RIO DULCE; Ar/Sp 1964; C; 5900; 149.6 × 7.2 (491 × 23.9); M; 19.5. Sister: **30531 RIO SALADO** (Ar).

MK_2MFKM H1
30540 AEOLIAN SEA; Gr/FRG 1958; CP; 9300; 153 × 9.1 (502 × 29.11); M; 15; ex CORTHIAN 1974; ex FERNPOINT 1969.

MK_2MFKM H1
● **30550 DJATILUHUR;** Ia/No 1961; CP; 7100/9300; 153.2 × —/9.1 (503 × —/29.11); M; 15; ex ANNE REED 1968. Sister: **30551 DJATIBARANG** (Ia) ex CARINA Similar: **30552 LIMA** (Pe) ex KENOSHA 1976; ex HALDOR VIRIK; ex NEPTUN 1958.

MK_2MFKM H1
⋆30570 TONG HUA; RC/Sw 1958; C; 6300/8600; 142.5 × 8.3/9.1 (467 × 27.2/29.11); M; 15; ex ARAFURA SEA; ex TYSLA 1972; ex BAY MASTER 1965; ex GOLDEN MASTER 1960.

MK_2MFKM H1
● **30580 TANIA;** Si/Sw 1958; C; 6200/8600; 142.42 × 8.05/9.21 (467.26 × 26.41/30.22); M; 15; ex HOEGH AUGVALD; ex AUGVALD. Similar: **30581 LINK FAITH** (Gr) ex SITIA HOPE; ex LILIKA 1978; ex TIGRIS 1971; ex TAMARA 1970; ex TIGRIS 1967; ex ANJAN 1963 **⋆30582 DUNHUA** (RC) ex EASTFORTUNE 1970; ex SOLLEN 1963.

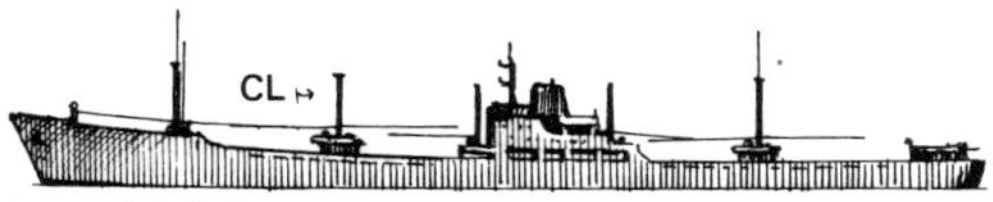

MK_2MFKM H1
30590 GOLDEN JEDDAH; Pa/FRG 1961; CP; 7000/9500; 153 × 8.1/9 (502 × 26.5/29.8); M; 15; ex LONGAVI; ex HIRAM 1968.

MK_2MFKM H1
● **30600 CEFALLONIAN AMBITION;** Gr/De 1953; C; 4000/5700; 129.2 × 7.4/7.7 (424 × 24.6/25.6); M; 16; ex VOGTLAND; ex FREYA TORM 1965.

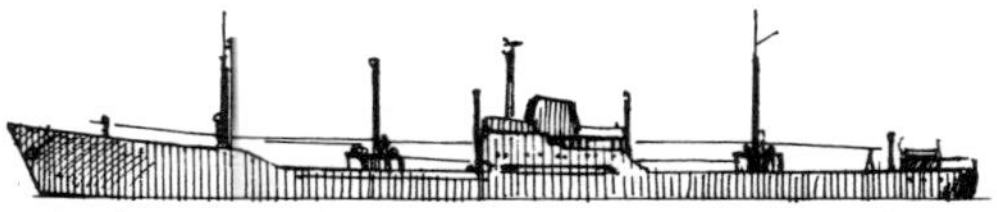

MK_2MFKM H1
30610 MONTE CRISTO; Li/FRG 1959; CP; 6400/9000; 150.9 × 7.7/8.9 (495 × 25.3/29.4); M; 16.5; ex HORNBELT 1977. Sister: **30611 TACNA** (Pe) ex HORNSEE 1972.

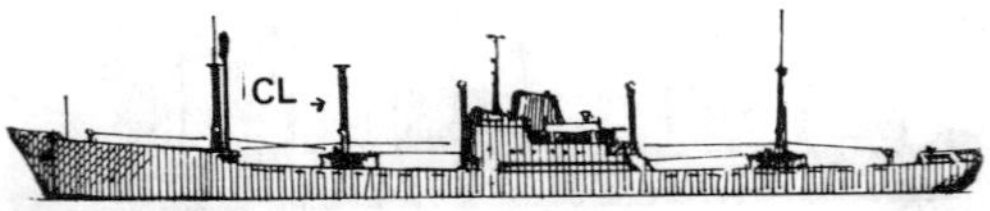

MK_2MFKM H1
30620 TOPAZ ISLANDS; Pa/Ne 1963; C; 6300/9000; 152.3 × 8.1/9 (526 × 26.5/29.7); M; —; ex PENDRECHT 1973; ex HURLEY BEACON 1967. Sisters: **30621 OPAL ISLANDS** (Pa) ex POOLDRECHT 1973; ex BRECON BEACON 1968 **30622 AMBER ISLANDS** (Pa) ex PAPENDRECHT 1973; ex HOLSWORTHY BEACON 1968.

MK_2MFKM H1
30650 TINDALO; Pi/Ja 1960; C; 6600; 147.8 × 8.9 (485 × 29.3); M; —. Sister: **30651 NATIONAL STEEL TWO** (Pi) ex PHILIPPINE ADMIRAL 1974; ex DAGOHOY 1964.

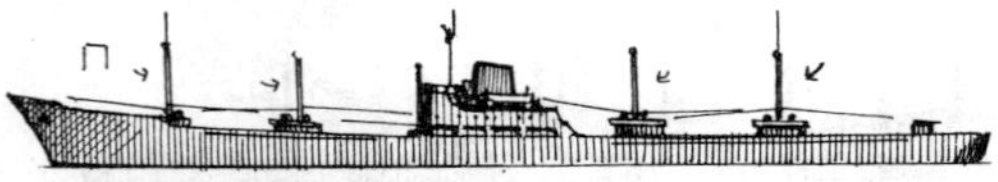

MK_2MFKM H1
● **30670 CHRISTOS S T ARAPAKIS;** Cy/Ja 1961; C; 9000; 156.3 × 8.7 (513 × 28.6); M; 16.5; ex MAN HING 1981; ex ANDINO 1979; ex FLORIDA MARU 1973. Sister: **30671 PACIFIC ACE** (Pa) ex MISSISSIPPI MARU 1975.

MK_2MFKM H1
30690 UNIVERSE STAR; Pa/Ja 1960; CP; 9000; 144 × 8.9 (475 × 29.3); M; 14.5; ex GENERAL LIM.

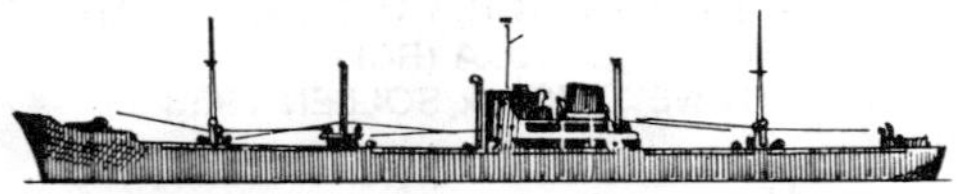

MK_2MFKM H1
30710 GOOD HOPE; Cy/Ja 1956; C; 8800; 147.3 × 8.6 (483.6 × 28.3); M; 15; ex HOPE 1980; ex UNIHOPE 1978; ex YOSHINOSAN MARU 1976.

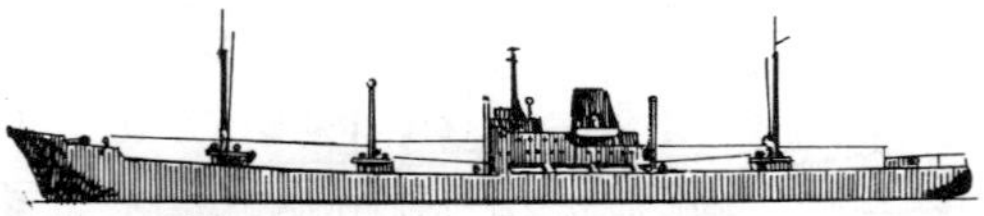

MK_2MFKM H1
30730 PACIFIC RIDE; Li/Ja 1960; CP; 9500; 149.2 × 9.1 (490 × 30); M; 18; ex PACIFIC PRIDE 1980; ex TRANSOCEAN MERCHANT 1977.

MK_2MFKM H1
30630 CAPETAN GEORGIS; Gr/Sw 1950; CP; 5100; 132.6 × 7.9 (435 × 25.11); M; 15; ex PRINS PHILIPS WILLEM 1969; ex RUGDEFJELL 1966; ex HAVFALK 1964.

MK_2MFKM H1
30640 TEGAL; Ia/No 1955; CP; 5700; 142.3 × 8 (467 × 26); M; 15; ex HORDA 1974.

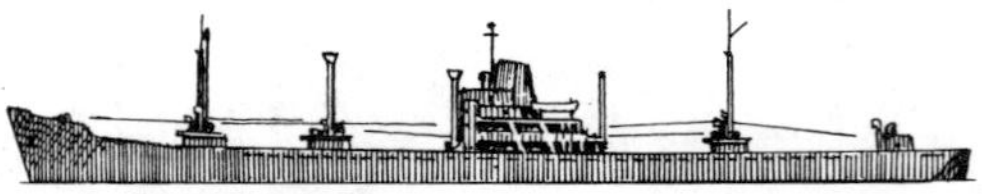

MK_2MFKM H1
30660 GENCLIK; Tu/It 1961; CP; 9000; 150.8 × 8.9 (495 × 29.3); M; 16.5.

MK_2MFKM H1
● **30680 APOSTOLOS A;** Pa/Ja 1959; C; 6000/8400; 149.3 × —/9.1 (490 × —/29.2); M; 14; ex KLADNO 1973.

MK_2MFKM H1
30700 CHIEH JEN; Pa/Ja 1955; C; 7700; 140 × 8.4 (459 × 27.5); M; 14.5; ex SEIUN MARU 1973.

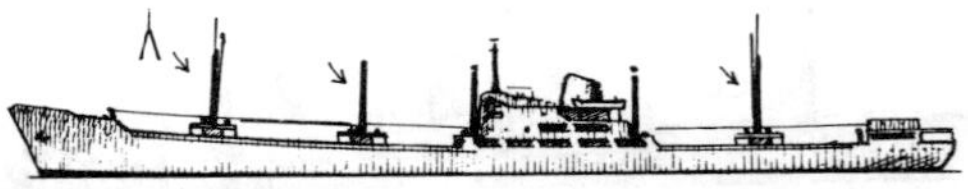

MK_2MFKM H1
30720 MAHAVIJAY; In/Ja 1962; C; 6500/9100; 149.3 × 8/9.1 (490 × 26.3/29.4); M; 14; ex MAHA JAG VIJAY 1976; ex JAG VIJAY 1975. Sister: **30721 MAHABIR** (In) ex JAG SHANTI 1973.

MK_2MFKM H1
⋆**30740 ASIA-AFRIKA;** RC/FRG 1960; CP; 6200/9000; 147.9 × 8.2/9.1 (485 × 26.9/29.11); M; 15; ex YAFEL 1967; ex GYDA 1967. Similar (taller radar mast): **70741 KADERBAKSH** (Pk) ex GYLFE 1965.

MK_2MFKM H1
30750 JALAKIRTI; In/Ja 1961; C; 6900/9200; 153 × 7.7/8.7 (502 × 25.4/28.7); M; 16.5. Sisters (In flag): **30751 JALAKALA 30752 JALAKENDRA 30753 JALAKRISHNA 30754 JALAKANTA 30755 VISHVA SEVA 30756 VISHVA TIRTH 30757 STATE OF MADHYA PRADESH 30758 STATE OF MYSORE 30759 STATE OF WEST BENGAL.**

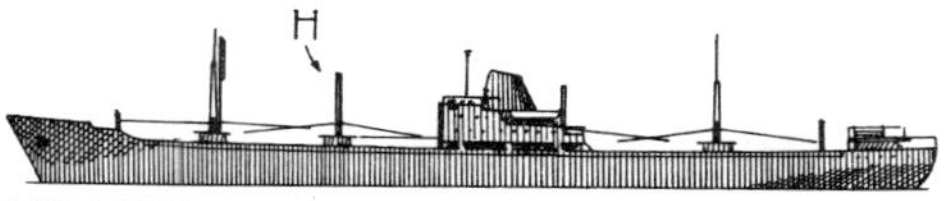

MK_2MFKM H1
30770 DIAMANTENIA; Gr/Sw 1960; C; 8600; 147.8 × 8.8 (485 × 29); M; 14; ex NEWPORT 1980; ex ARISTOGEITON 1974; ex GISNA 1969. Sister: **30771 STAR ALTAIR** (Sw) ex VIMEIRA 1965; ex PORT DENISON 1965; ex VIMEIRA 1960; ex FAIR LADY. Probable Sister: **30772 PINELOPI** (Gr) ex STAR ALDEBARAN; ex KENSINGTON.

MK_2MFKM H1
● **30780 AEOLIAN WIND;** Gr/Sw 1960; CP; 6100/8500; 142.4 × 8/9 (467 × 26.5/29.8); M; 15.25; ex IRAN ZAMIN 1973; ex CYCLADIAN 1973; ex HERMION 1972.

MK_2MFKM H1
30790 HUNG HSING; Tw/Bz 1963; C; 8500/11300; 155.5 × 8.3/9.4 (510.6 × 27.6/31); T; 18.25; ex OCEAN FELLOWS 1980; ex CORINNA 1977; ex PEREIRA CARNEIRO 1973. Sister: **30791 KATINA MATHEO** (Cy) ex BOLINA 1977; ex HENRIQUE LAGE 1973.

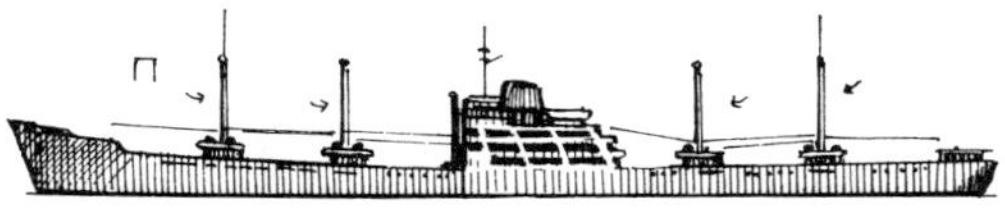

MK_2MFKM H1
30800 PHILIPPINE BATAAN; Pi/Ja 1960; CP; 9900; 156.1 × 9.2 (512 × 30.1); M; 18.25. Sister: **30801 PHILIPPINE ANTONIO LUNA** (Pi) ex PHILIPPINE LEYTE.

MK_2MFKM H1
30810 AMIRAL S OKAN; Tu/Tu 1970; C; 9800; 155.5 × 9 (509 × 29.1); M; 18. Sister: **30811 AMIRAL S ALTINCAN** (Tu).

MK_2MFKM H1
30820 MERSINIDI; Pa/Ja 1961; C; 9200; 156.6 × 9.3 (514 × 30.6); M; —; ex YAMAAKI MARU 1974. Sister: **30821 WEILI** (So) ex YAMATAKA MARU 1973.

MK_2MFKM H1
⋆**30830 JIN PING;** RC/Ja 1958; C; 9200; 156.6 × 9.3 (514 × 30.6); M; 18; ex WEIMIN 1976; ex YAMAKIMI MARU 1973. Sister: **30831 WEIKUO** (Pa) ex YAMAWAKA MARU 1973.

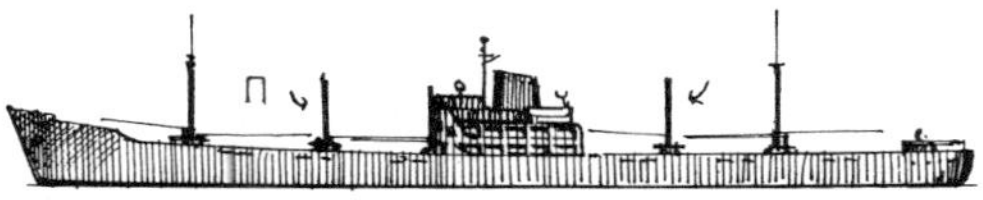

MK_2MFKM H1
30840 PRESIDENT MAGSAYSAY; Pi/Ja 1957; C; 9100; 151.3 × 9 (496 × 29.7); M; 16; ex KOSEI MARU 1972. Sisters: **30841 RIO BALSAS** (Me) ex KOHOH MARU 1972 **30842 PRESIDENT QUIRINO** (Pi) ex RIO BRAVO 1980; ex KOBU MARU 1974 **30843 PRESIDENT ROXAS** (Pi) ex RIO YAQUI 1980; ex KOTEI MARU Similar: **30844 BAIMA** (Pa) ex KOMAHARU MARU 1972 **30845 BAIPAO** (Pa) ex SHIGAHARU MARU 1973 ⋆**30846 DONGPING** (RC) ex BAISIUNG 1977; ex TAGAHARU MARU 1973 **30847 CAPTAIN JOHN** (Gr) ex CAPTAIN GEORGE; ex IGAHARU MARU 1974.

MK_2MFKM H1
30860 LEVANTES; Li/Ja 1960; CP; 8800; 148.9 × 9 (489 × 30); M; 13.5; ex MEIWA MARU 1970.

MK_2MFKM H12
30870 LOK VAIBHAV; In/Ja 1966; CP; 4600; 114×7.1 (375×23.6); M; 16.5; ex RICH TRADER 1975.

MK_2MFKM H12
30880 ANGEL; Pa/Ja 1965; C; 4400; 111.9×7.1 (365×23.6); M; 16; ex ASIA FRUIT 1975; ex CHEN FONG 1972; ex AN TAI 1968.

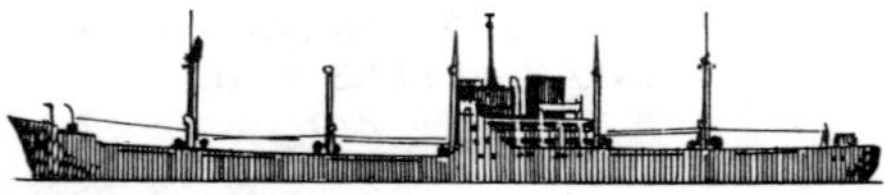

MK_2MFKM H12
30890 SEA QUEEN I; Pa/Ja 1958; C; 6400; 137.6×8.2 (451.3×27); M; 14; ex BOMBAY MARU 1975.

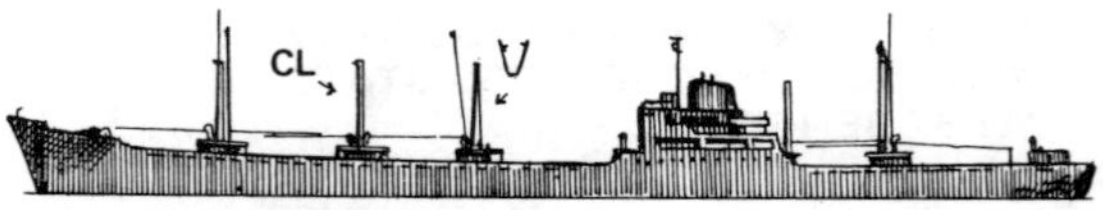

MK_2MFKM H12
30900 CONCORDIA ION; Gr/Fr 1963; C; 7800; 172.4×8.4 (566×27.3); M; 16.5; ex ION 1980; ex CIRCEA 1977 Lengthened 1971. Sisters: **30901 POLYDORA** (Gr) ex CYPRIA 1977; **30902 CONCORDIA DANAOS** (Gr) ex DANAOS 1980; ex CAPRAIA 1977.

MK_2MFKM H123
30910 CELEBES CAREER; Pa/Ja 1954; CP; 7600; 151×8.4 (495×27.7); TSM; 16; ex SAMOA MARU No 2 1975; ex AKI MARU 1972. Similar: **30911 PRINCESS EMERALD** (Pa) ex ARITA MARU.

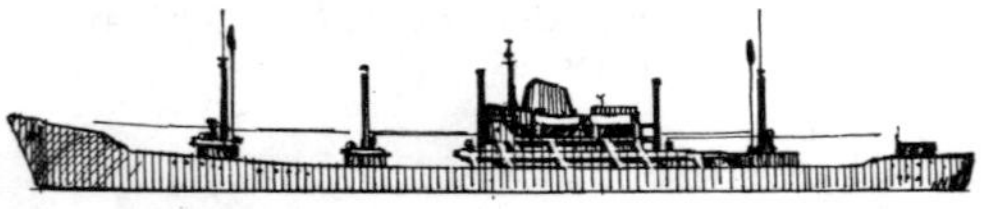

MK_2MFKM H13
30920 SETIABUDHI; Ia/Ja 1961; PC; 7300/9600; 152.5×8.3/— (500×27.3/—); M; 16. Sisters: **30921 M H THAMRON** (Ia) **30922 DJATISARI** (Ia) ex SINESIS 1965; ex H.O.S.TJOKROAMINOTO 1965.

MK_2MFKM H13
⋆**30930 CHANGDE;** RC/Sw 1964; CP; 9000; 148.4×9.1 (487×30); M; —; ex PEONY 1970; ex BONDE.

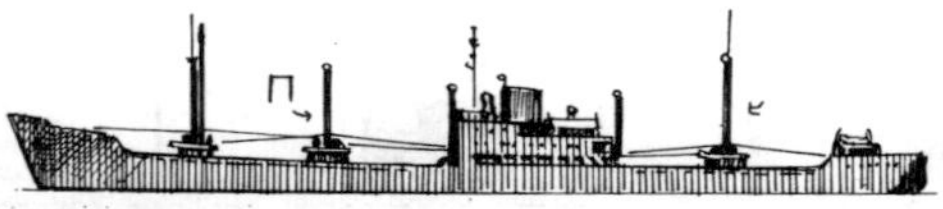

MK_2MFKM H13
● **30940 ZAMBOANGA;** Pi/Ja 1960; C; 9600; 144×28.9 (474×28.9); M; 16. Similar: **30941 MAN SING** (Pa) ex PACIFIC GLORY 1980; ex MARIA ROSELLO 1977.

MK_2MFKM H13
● **30950 MANILA.** Pi/Ja 1959; C; 8200; 146.4×8.9 (480×29.4); M; 17.

MK_2MFKM H13
30960 ENARXIS. Cy/FRG 1956; CP; 9200; 149.4×9 (480×30); M; 15; ex VLIST 1972. Sister: **30961 VICTORIA U** (Li) ex PISHTAZ IRAN 1980; ex ROTTE.

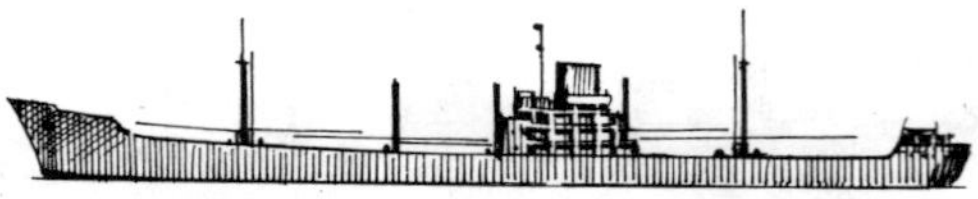

MK_2MFKM H13
30970 GEMBIRA. Ia/Ne 1953; CP; 9500; 150.6×8.6 (494×28.3); M; 16; ex BAWEAN 1972.

MK_2MFKMK H1
⋆**30980 SHAN YIN.** RC/FRG 1961; C; 6300/9600; 155.9×7.7/9.1 (511×25.5/29.11); M; 17.5; ex INDIAN OCEAN 1974; ex TANGANYIKA 1971. Sister: ⋆**30981 PING YIN** (RC) ex PACIFIC OCEAN 1974; ex TRANSVAAL 1972.

MK_2MFKMK H1
● **30990 BOLA No 1.** Pa/Sw 1956; C; 8600; 142.4×9.2 (467×29.8); M; 14; ex JOYFUL; ex WAN HO 1976; ex JAG RATNA 1973; ex SKAUBO 1963; May be a total loss. Similar: ⋆**30991 NANXING** (RC) ex ANTARCTICA 1971; ex OLDER 1964.

MK_2MFKMK H1
31000 HAN GARAM. Ko/Ja 1959; C; 9500; 156.57 × 8.8; M; 18; ex SEA BRAVE 1978; ex MOMIJISAN MARU 1974. Sisters: **31001 HAN NURI** (Ko) ex SEA DISCOVERER 1978; ex MATSUDOSAN MARU 1974. **31002 UNIQUE CHALLENGE** (Pa) ex ONWARD ELITE; ex MEGUROSAN MARU 1970.

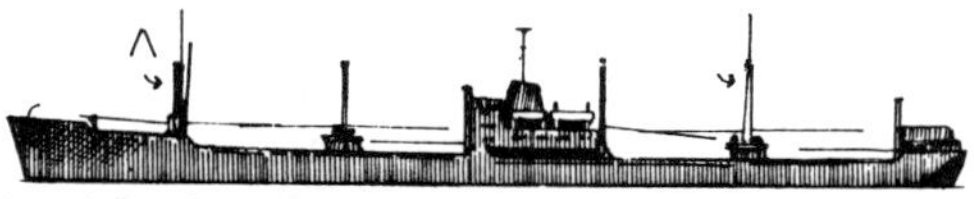

MK_2MFKMK H1
⋆31030 KANG DING. RC/Sw 1956; CP; 10400; 151.6 × 9.3 (498 × 30.6); M; 14.75; ex OCEANTRAVEL 1970; ex NORTHERN CLIPPER 1963.

MK_2MFKMK H13
⋆31050 LENINSKIY KOMSOMOL. Ru/Ru 1960; C; 12000; 170 × 9.7 (558 × 32); T; 19. Sisters (Ru flag): **⋆31051 FIZIK LEBEDYEV ⋆31052 FIZIK VAVILOV ⋆31053 METALLURG BAYKOV.**

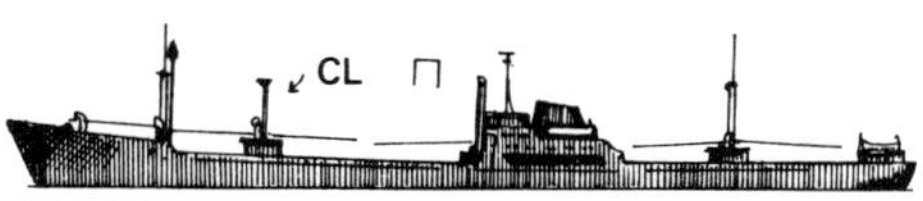

MK_2MFM H1
31070 HOLLAND. Gr/Ja 1961; CP; 4900; 145.7 × 7.2 (478 × 23.6); M; 16.5; Lengthened 1969; ex ARMADA CLIPPER 1980; ex HOLLAND 1979.

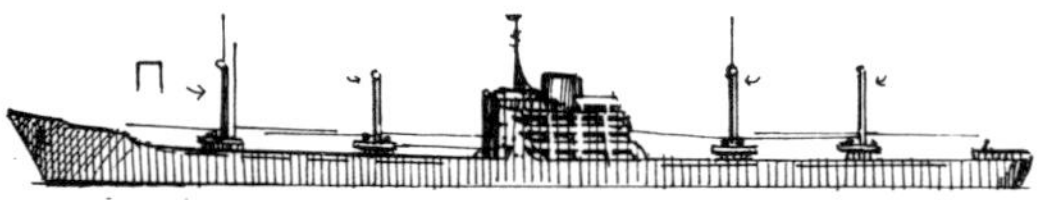

MK_2MFMK H1
31090 UNION CONCORD. Tw/Ja 1961; C; 10100; 158.1 × 9 (519 × 29.9); M; 18.

MK_2MFMK H1
31110 VICTORY KING. Pa/Ja 1951; C; 6400; 152.2 × 8.3 (500 × 27.6); M; 16.5; ex TA PENG No 2 1977; ex AKAGISAN MARU 1975. Similar (Pa flag): **31111 UNIQUE ENTERPRISES** ex AKIBASAN MARU 1974 **31112 AN HENG** ex EURYSHUNLI; ex AWAJISAN MARU. **31113 POHENG** ex EURYTEHLI 1977; ex AWOBASAN MARU.

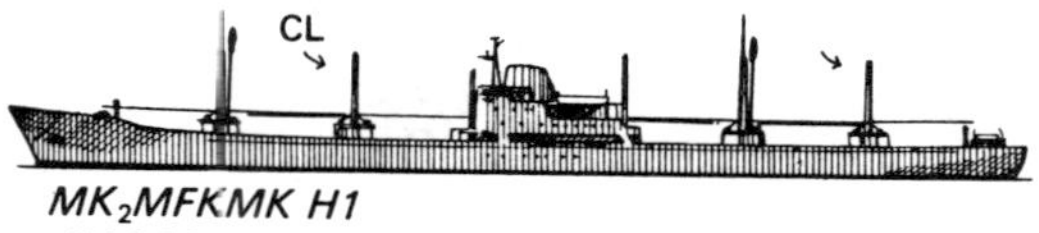

MK_2MFKMK H1
⋆31010 VICTORIA DE GIRON. Cu/Sw 1969; C; 11000; 161.9 × 9.8 (531 × 32.6); M; —. Sisters (Cu flag): **⋆31011 PLAYA LARGA ⋆31012 BAHIA DE COCHINOS.**

MK_2MFKMK H1
⋆31020 XUAN HUA. RC/Sw 1956; C; 6000/9000; 141.08 × 8.19/9.21; (462.86 × 26.87/30.22); M; 14; ex STEED 1976; ex BROLAND 1970; ex O.A. BRODIN 1961.

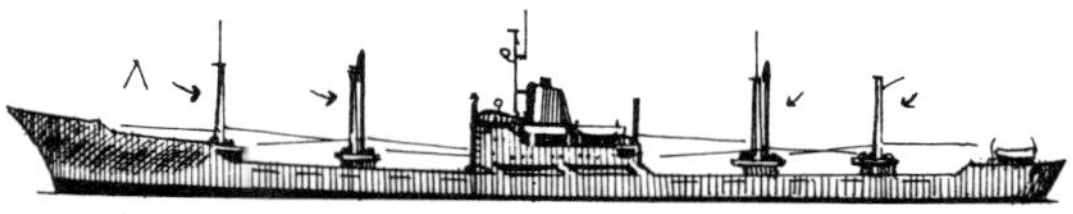

MK_2MFKMK H13
31040 HONG QI. RC/RC 1964; C; 11500; 171 × — (560 × —); T; —.

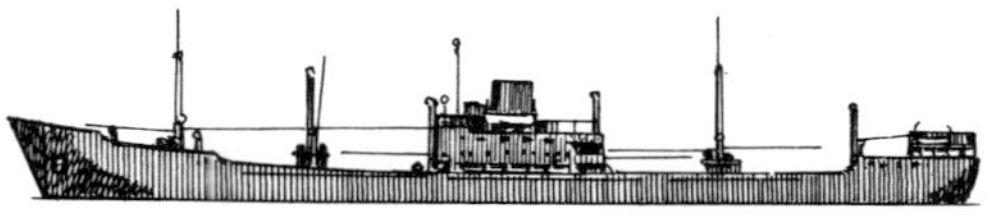

MK_2MFKMK H13
31060 KOTA SETIA. Sg/FRG 1957; CP; 6500/8700; 149.4 × 7.8/8.4 (490.6 × 25.9/27.6); M; 17; ex HERMES 1975; ex TRAVANCORE; ex STUREHOLM 1970.

MK_2MFM H1
⋆31080 JIANGYIN. RC/FRG 1958; C; 6800/9500; 153.1 × 8.1/9 (502 × 26.3/30); M; 15.5; ex HWANG HO 1970; ex HENRI G 1968. Sister: **31081 ULIANG** (Pa) ex MALAGA 1972; ex HEERING MILLE 1965; ex ROLV JARL 1965.

MK_2MFMK H1
31100 MOGAMISAN MARU. Ja/Ja 1956; C; 9600; 156.6 × 8.5 (514 × 27.11); M; 17.25). Similar (foremast and after KP not on houses): **31101 HADOKASAN MARU** (Ja).

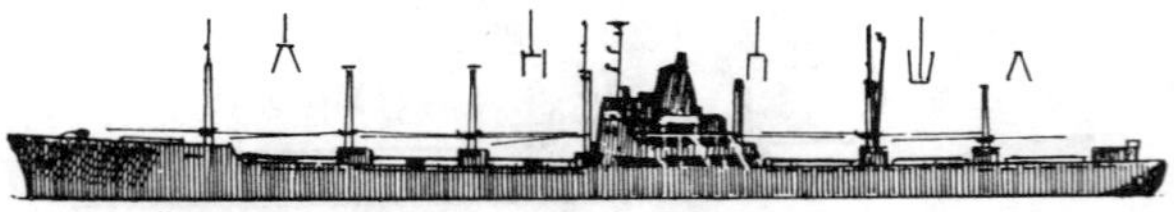

MK_2M_2FKMK H1
31120 PRESIDENT ADAMS. US/US 1968; Pt.Con; 11600/15900; 184.4 × 9.5/10.7 (605 × 31.3/35); T; 21; ex ALASKAN MAIL. Sisters (US flag): **31121 PRESIDENT CLEVELAND** ex AMERICAN MAIL 1978 **31122 PRESIDENT JACKSON** ex INDIAN MAIL 1978 **31123 PRESIDENT WILSON** ex HONG KONG MAIL 1978 **31124 PRESIDENT TAYLOR** ex KOREAN MAIL 1978.

MKM H2
31130 KIRKELLA. Br/Br 1965; ST; 1200; 69.4 × — (228 × —); D-E —. Similar: **31132 SWANELLA** (Br) **31133 NORTHERN HORIZON** (Br) ex MARBELLA 1980 **31134 SOUTHERN FIGHTER** (SA) ex YELLOWFIN 1977; ex NORTHELLA 1973.

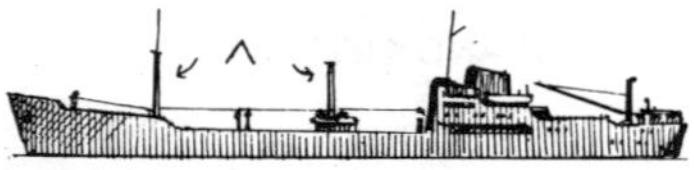

MKMFC H13
31140 EASTERN POWER. Pa/De 1956; CP; 2400/3300; 105.2 × 5.8/— (345 × 19.2/—); M; 14; ex EASTERN PROGRESS 1976; ex SALAMAUA 1974; ex IBERIA 1969. Sister: **31141 ALEXANDROS** (Gr) ex BASEL; ex VENERANDA M. 1973; ex MASSILIA 1970.

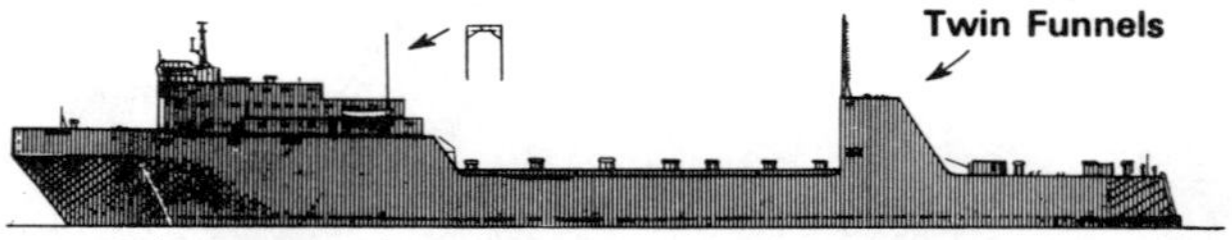

MKMF H1
***31150 GEROITE NA SEVASTOPOL.** Bu/No 1978; RoC/TF; 9600; 185.45 × 7.42 (608.43 × 24.34); TSM; 19; Stern door. Sister: ***31151 GEROITE NA ODESSA** (Bu) Similar (Ys built): ***31152 GEROI PLEVNY** (Ru) ***31153 GEROI SHIPKI** (Ru).

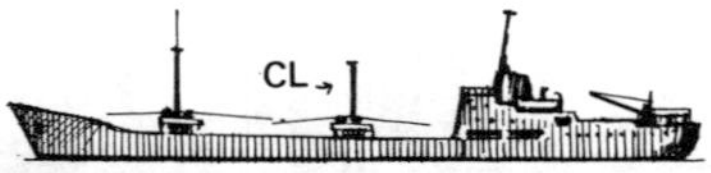

MKMFC H13
● **31160 CAPITAINE LA PEROUSE.** Fr/Sw 1951; CP; 2400; 105.5 × 5.7 (346 × 18.11); M; 15.5; ex TUI CAKAU; ex CAPITAINE LA PEROUSE 1975; ex NEGOSKY 1973; ex BAYARD 1972.

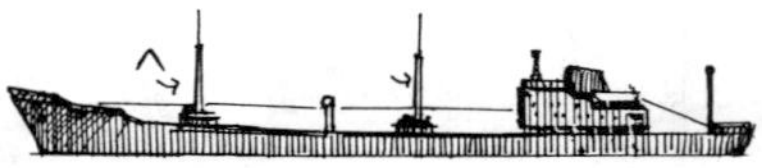

MKMFK H1
● **31170 TEVEGA.** Cy/Sw 1961; C; 4500; 115.1 × 7.5 (378 × 24.7); M; 15; ex NORDIA 1974; ex NORDIC.

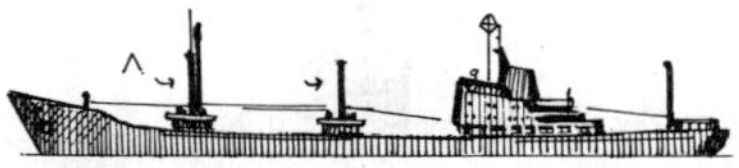

MKMFK H1
***31180 GRUDZIADZ.** Pd/Pd 1963; C; 2900; 113.5 × 6.4 (373 × 20.2); M; 15.5; **'B-49'** type. Sisters (Pd flag): ***31181 GLOGOW *31182 GORLICE.**

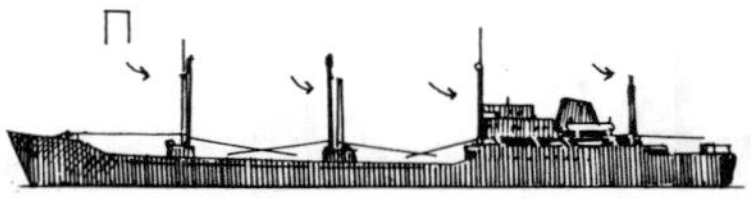

MKMFK H13
● **31190 ARIANE.** Sg/No 1958; C; 4800; 116.2 × 8 (381 × 26); M; 15.5; ex HOEGH AILETTE 1972. Sisters: **31191 ELAZIG** (Tu) ex MAROSA 1960 **31192 AURORE** (Sg) ex HOEGH AURORE 1972 **31193 HORIZON** (Pa) ex CONCORDIA LORD 1970; ex LORD VIKING 1969 **31194 NUEVA ESPARTA** (Ve) ex LISE 1960.

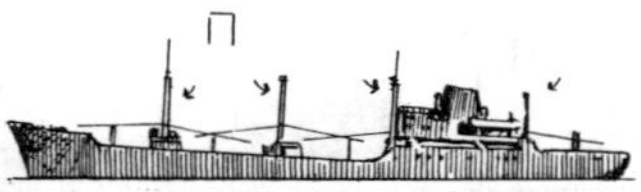

MKMFK H13
31200 ISORA. Sp/Sp 1967; C; 1600; 96.7 × 5.7 (317 × 18.6); M; —; ex LAGO SAN MAURICIO 1975. Sister: **31201 ARONA** (Sp) ex CARMEN M. PINILLOS 1975.

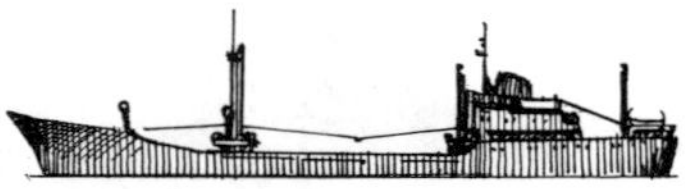

MKMFK H13
31210 NISSOS ANDROS. Gr/FRG 1961; C; 2000/2900; 102.4 × 5.7/6.9 (336 × 18.7/22.8); M; 13; ex TOMMY 1980; ex LORD NELSON 1978; ex SKOTLAND 1973; ex GRONLAND 1972.

$MKMFK_2$ H1
31220 MOUNT CARIBBEAN. Pa/Ja 1962; C; 6500; 133 × 8.2 (437 × 20.7); M; 14.75; ex MEIHOHSAN MARU. Sister: **31221 TAMY** (Sg) ex MEISHUSAN MARU 1974.

MKMFK$_2$ H1
31230 YANNIS. Gr/Br 1963; C; 11200; 164.4 × 9.5 (539 × 31.3); M; 16.

MKMFK$_2$ H13
31250 HAI LEE. No/FRG 1959; CP; 4900/7200; 138.1 × 7.2/8.6 (453 × 23.6/28); M; 16; ex MAKEFJELL 1972.

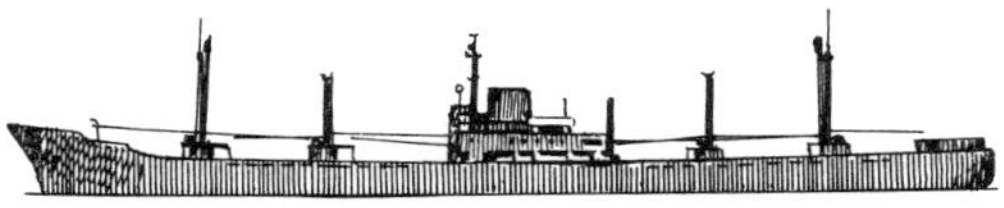

MKMFK$_2$M H1
● **31270 TACOMA MARU.** Ja/Ja 1962; C; 9200; 156.1 × 9.2 (512 × 30); M; 18.25.

MKMFKM H
⋆**31280 EASTERN LION.** RC/Br 1952; C; 5500/7500; 141.8 × 7.9/8.3 (465 × 26/27); M; 13.5; ex JAG KETU 1967; ex WINDSOR 1963.

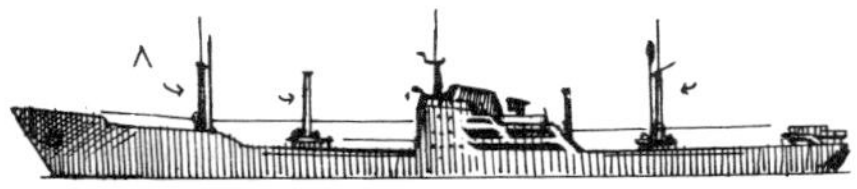

MKMFKM H1
● **31300 NAGLAN.** Le/De 1962; CP; 4200; 126.9 × 7.3 (416.4 × 24); M; 17; ex HELLE SKOU. Sisters: **31301 DAMIAN** (Gr) ex INGER SKOU **31302 KIRSTEN SKOU** (De) **31303 CARENERO** (Ve) ex MADS SKOU **31304 MARIE SKOU** (De) **31305 MELANTHO C** (Gr) ex METTE SKOU.

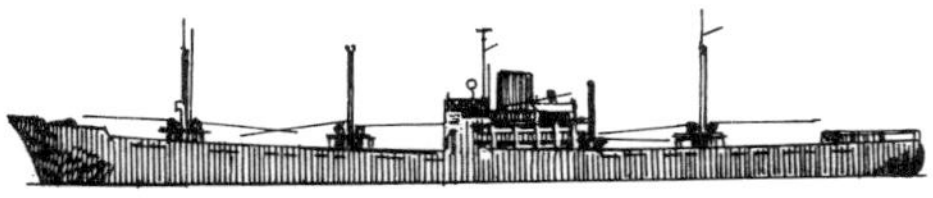

MKMFKM H1
⋆**31330 SONG NHUE.** Vn/Ja 1960; CP; 7200; 136.6 × 8.4 (448 × 26.9); M; 14.75; ex UNIQUE STAR 1980; ex CARIBBEAN STAR 1975; ex SOEI MARU 1970.

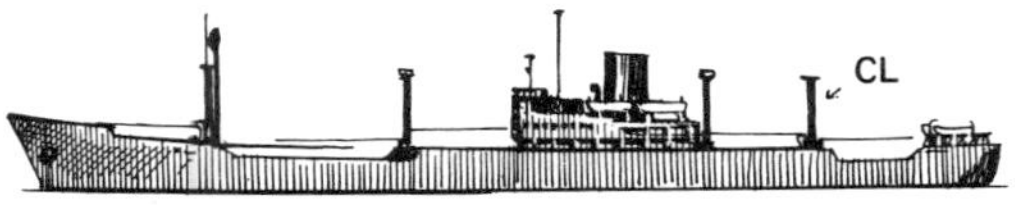

MKMFK$_2$ H123
31240 CHI KONG. Pa/Br 1959; C; 6000/8100; 155.8 × 6.5/8.6 (511 × 21.4/28.3); M; 15; ex STRATHAROS; ex BAHARISTAN 1975.

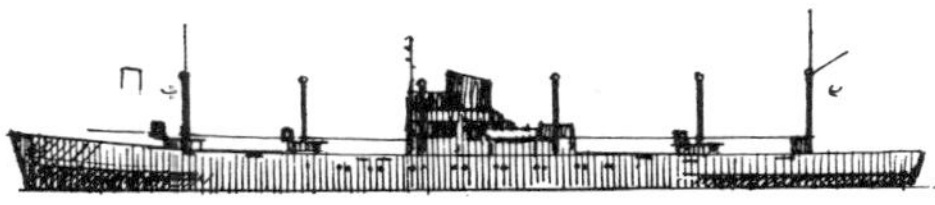

MKMFK$_2$M H
31260 KOTA SUBUR. Sg/Br 1950; C; 5400/9000; 145 × 7.8/8.3 (476 × 25.6/27); M; 15; ex WENCHOW 1975; ex WENDOVER 1965. Sister: **31261 MALDIVE EXPLORER** (Mv) ex WANLIU 1975; ex WANSTEAD 1964; ex RAEBURN 1964; ex WANSTEAD 1963; ex PORT WANSTEAD 1960; ex WANSTEAD 1957.

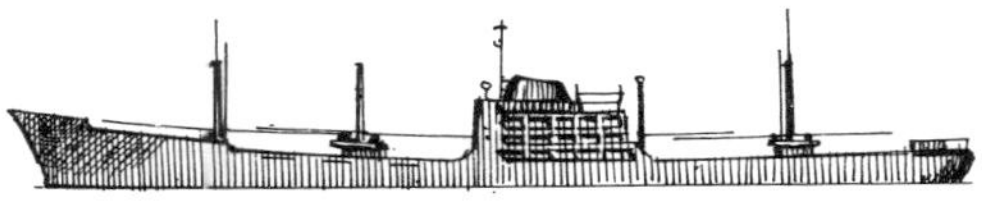

MKMFKM H1
31290 VIVARAIS. Fr/Be 1960; C; 6900; 156 × 8 (512 × 26.5); M; 18. Sisters: **31291 VENTOUX** (Fr) **31292 FORUM PROGRESS** (Gr) ex PAULINA 1980; ex VOSGES 1978 Similar: **31293 BRUNELLA** (Pa) ex MALAIS 1978 **31294 MARTINIQUAIS** (Fr) **31295 PATRICIA S** (Pa) ex MARQUISIEN.

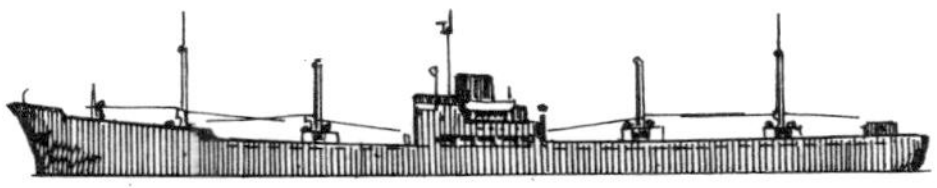

MKMFKM H1
31320 SILVER EAGLE. Tw/Ja 1959; C; 8300; 143 × 8.1 (469 × 26.5); M; 14.75; ex VICTORY GODDESS 1980; ex CHIEH HWANG 1979; ex GOH SHU MARU 1974.

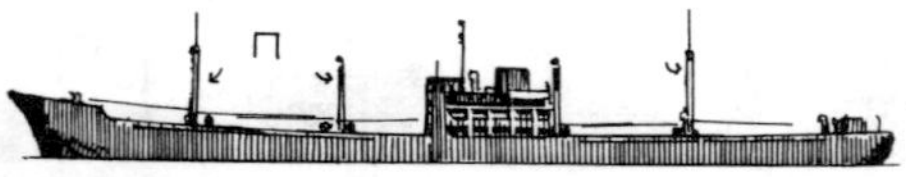

MKMFKM H1
31340 JIN YANG No 13. Ko/Ja 1957; C; 7600; 138×8.7 (453×28.6); M; 14.25; ex PAPEETE 1976; ex TOKELAU MARU 1972; ex EISHUN MARU 1971.

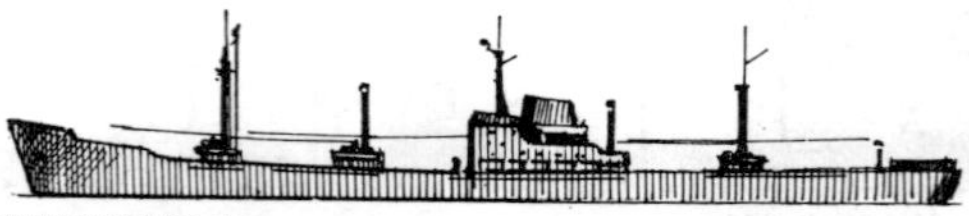

MKMFKM H1
31350 RAVNANGER. No/Sw 1963; C; 8900; 145×8.9 (476×29.3); M; 15.

MKMFM H1
31360 MEDROCK. Gr/Sw 1965; C; 9000; 145×8.9 (476×29.3); M; 15; ex FAUSKANGER 1980.

MKMFKM H1
31370 MOKARIA. Be/Be 1964; CP; 7200/10900; 159.3×8.1/9.5 (523×26.8/30.3); M; 15.

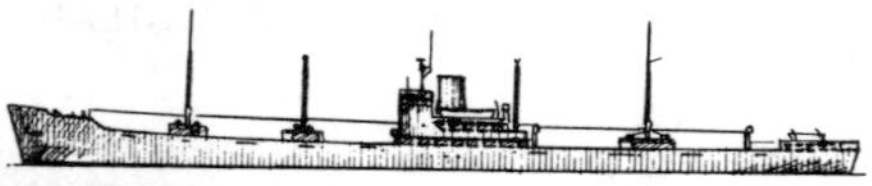

MKMFKM H1
● **⋆31380 MARSHAL GOVOROV.** Ru/Sw 1939; C; 5100; 134.9×7.8 (443×26); M; 13; ex BORE X 1946.

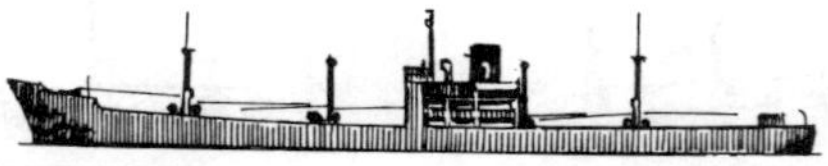

MKMFKM H1
31390 PEACE ROSE. Ko/Ja 1957; CP; 5800; 126×8 (414×26.3); M; 12.25; ex MIKUMO MARU 1975. Similar: **31391 MUNAKATA MARU** (Ja).

MKMFKM H1
● **31400 ANGELINA.** Gr/Br 1963; CP; 7300/10200; 162.1×8.4/9.4 (532×27.7/30.7); M; 17; ex WENDUYNE 1973; ex APSLEYHALL 1969.

MKMFKM H1
31410 ALASSIR. Li/It 1958; C; 6300/8600; 148.6×—/9.3 (488×—/30.2); M; —; ex SILVERSTONE; ex SUNSTONE. Sister: **31411 GOLDSTONE** (Li) ex MOONSTONE.

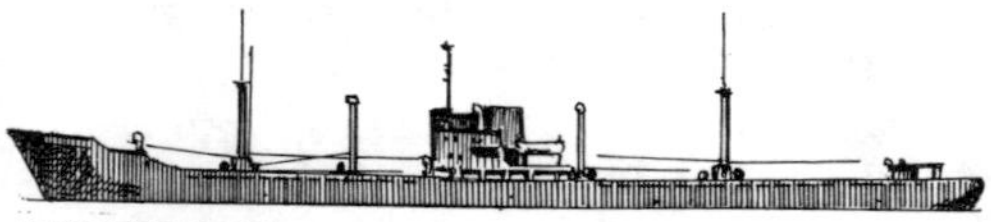

MKMFKM H1
31420 ISHER. Pa/Ja 1957; C; 6600/9800; 157.2×8.4/9.5 (516×27.6/31.2); M; 13.5; ex SWEDE MARIA 1980; ex JANE IOTA 1976; ex CLUNEPARK 1973.

MKMFKM H1
31430 ORIENT SUCCESS. Pa/Ja 1958; C; 7700; 139.6×8.6 (458×28.1); M; 13.5; ex SAKISHIMA MARU 1974.

MKMFKM H1
31440 ANTHIA. Cy/Br 1964; C; 7600/11000; 164.4×9.6 (539×31.6); M; —; ex NEPHELE 1975; ex KATHERINE 1973. Sisters: **31441 PEARL ISLAND** (Gr) **31442 GRACE FIVE** (Pa) ex PEARL MERCHANT.

MKMFKM H1
31450 MALIAKOS. Gr/Ja 1962; C; 6600/9700; 156.9×8.4/9.5 (515×27.6/31.5); M; —; ex ATHENIAN; ex VAN STAR 1969; ex DONA NANCY 1968.

MKMFKM H1
⋆31460 NANPING. RC/Ja 1964; CP; 9100; 156.5×9.3 (513×30.6); M; 18.25; ex FLORES SEA 1974; ex DON ANTONIO 1972.

MKMFKM H1
31470 LEIXOES. Po/Ja 1963; C; 9800; 158×9.3 (519×30.6); M; 15; ex EASTERN UME 1969.

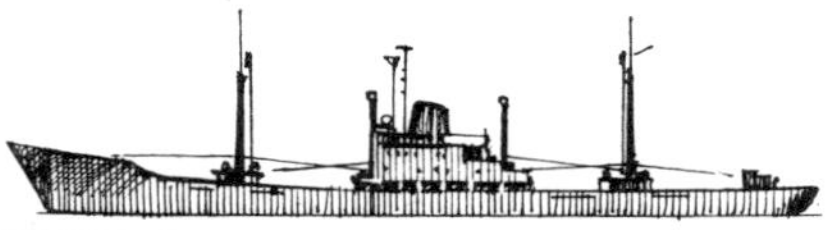

MKMFKM H1
31480 CAPTAIN GLYPTIS. Gr/FRG 1963; C; 3400/5300; 126.6 × 6.5/7.6 (415 × 21.5/25); M; —; ex CAROLA 1980; ex CALANDA 1979.

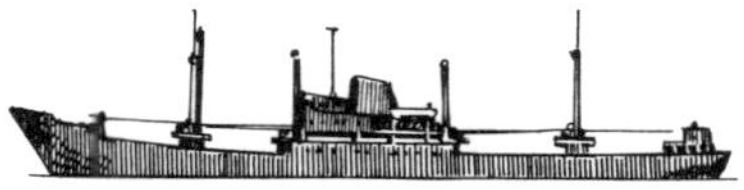

MKMFKM H12
31490 KRIOS. Gr/FRG 1960; C; 2700/4100; 111.6 × 6.3/7.5 (366 × 20.8/24.7); M; 14; ex ODETTE 1980; ex NETANYA 1978. Sister: **31491 KRATILAOS** (Gr) ex DIMO 1980; ex LIBERTY 1978; ex NAHARIYA 1976.

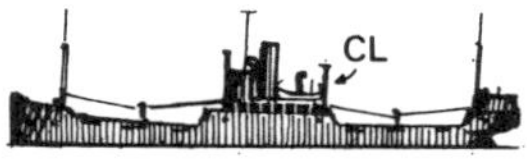

MKMFKM H123
31500 AGIOS FANOURIS III. Cy/Br 1947; C; 1300; 71.4 × 4.3 (234 × 14); M; 12; ex TREMCO UNITY 1972; ex MATA 1971; ex NISSOS MYCONOS 1969; ex LINGESTROOM 1965.

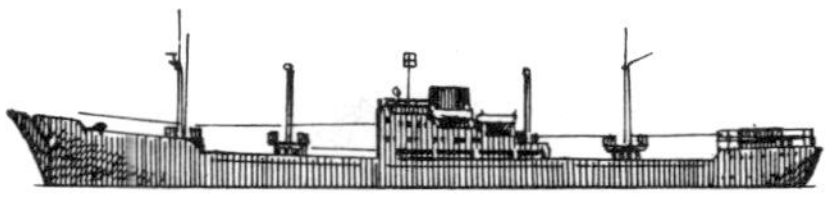

MKMFKM H13
31510 SENIOR K. Le/Ne 1958; CP; 5200/7200; 128.8 × —/8.5 (422 × —/28); M; 16; ex PORSANGER 1972.

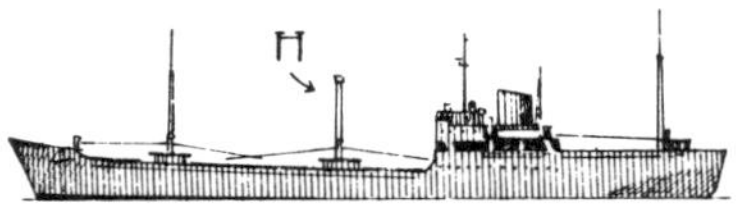

MKMFKM H13
31520 EL ZANJON. Pa/Ja 1959; C; 3800; 113.6 × 6.8 (373 × 22.4); M; 12; ex CARIBBEAN PEARL; ex ZIPOUNAS 1976; ex YUBARI MARU 1970.

MKMFKM H13
31530 GOOD MASTER. Gr/Ne 1962; CP; 6200/8900; 147.2 × 8.3/9 (483 × 27.3/29.8); M; 15; ex MOL.

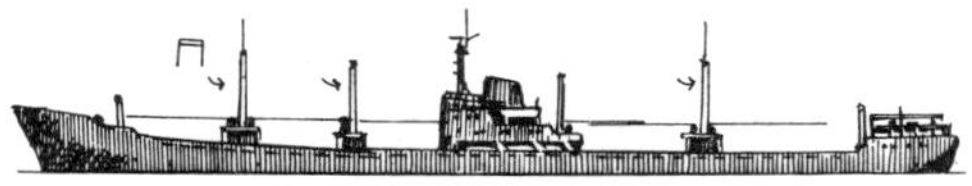

MKMFKM H13
31540 THEOSKEPASTI. Gr/Sw 1961; CP; 8900; 148.4 × 9.1 (487 × 30); M; 15; ex LAJA; ex HOLTHILL 1969.

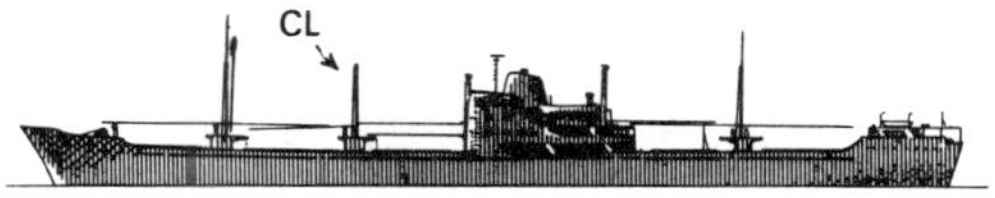

MKMFKM H13
31550 KOTA MANIS. Sg/FRG 1956; C; 6400/9200; 149.36 × 8.11/8.97 (490 × 26.61/29.43); M; 15; ex TULANE 1977; ex SKAUTROLL 1966.

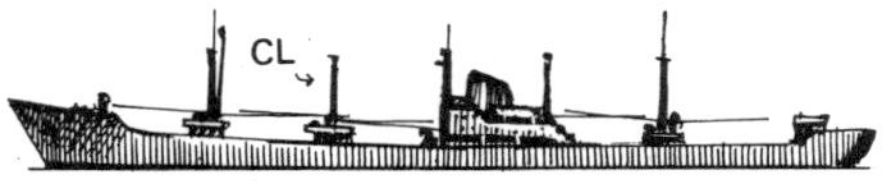

MKMFKM H13
● **31560 BISCAYA GOLF.** Sg/Ne 1959; C; 6700; 145 × 8.3 (443 × 27.1); M; 18; ex IVORY MOON: ex EMILIE DELMAS.

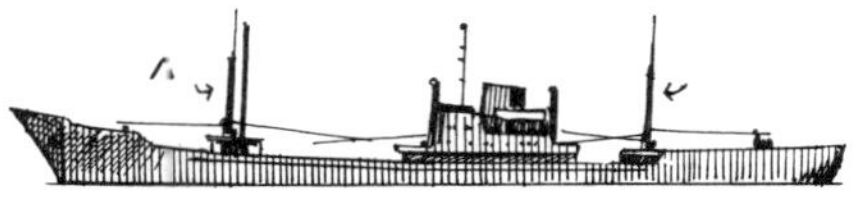

MKMFKM H13
31570 GEMINI. Gr/FRG 1966; CP; 5500; 127.4 × 7.6 (415 × 25.1); M; 15.5; ex CARL OFFERSEN.

MKMFKMK H1
31580 DAIWA MARU. Ja/Ja 1962; C; 9200; 156 × 9 (512 × 29.8); M; 17.25.

MKMFKMK H1
31590 SILVER DRAGON. Tw/Ja 1957; C; 8400; 143.11 × 8.1 (469.52 × 26.58); M; 14.5; ex VICTORY GLEAM 1981; ex CHILE MARU 1974. Sister: **31591 GOLDEN DRAGON** (Tw) ex VICTORY GLORY 1980; ex PERU MARU 1974.

MKMFKMK H1
● **31600 TRADER.** Gr/Br 1962; C; 7000/9900; 155.2 × —/9.3 (509 × —/30.6); M; 14.5; ex PEARL TRADER.

MKMFKMK H1
31610 ANTHIA. Cy/Br 1964; C; 7600/1100; 164.4 × 9.6 (539 × 31.6); M; —; ex NEPHELE 1975; ex KATHERINE 1973. Sisters: **31611 PEARL ISLAND** (Gr) **31612 GRACE FIVE** (Pa) ex PEARL MERCHANT.

MKMFKMK H13
⋆31620 TANG YIN. RC/FRG 1960; C; 7800/9200; 151.4 × 8.3/9.3 (497 × 27/30.4); M; 16; ex ARABIAN SEA 1974; ex HANSE 1971.

MKMFM H
31630 SHAMS. Pk/Ja 1960; PC; 8900; 143.3 × 6.7 (470 × 22.1); TSM; 17.

MKMFM H
● **31640 MARE ARABICO.** It/It 1964; R; 5100; 132.9 × 6.4 (436 × 21); M; 18.5. Sisters: **31641 MARE CARIBICO** (It) **31642 BANANA EXPRESS** (Pa) ex MARE SOMALO 1978 **31643 JUBA** (So) ex MARE ITALICO 1974.

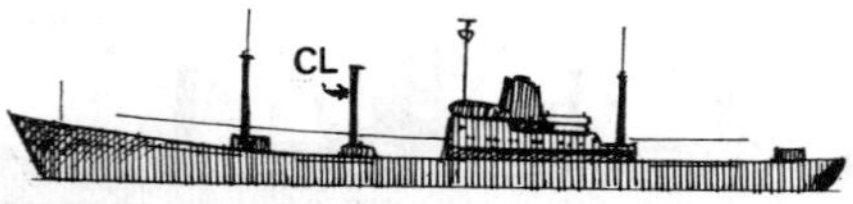

MKMFM H
● **31650 BIAFRA.** Fr/FRG 1965; R; 5700; 131.4 × — (431 × —); M; 20.5.

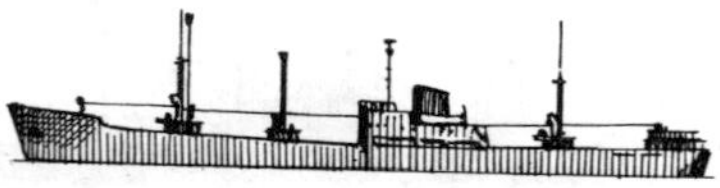

MKMFM H
31660 ALEXANDROS A. Gr/No 1958; CP; 2400/3800; 108.2 × 6.3/7.4 (355 × 20.1/24.3); M; 13.5; ex UNSTRUT; ex ARCTIC TERN 1965. Similar (more conical funnel) (Gr flag): **31661 CEFALLONIAN GRACE** ex MULDE; ex SUNIMA 1965 **31662 CEFALLONIAN DESTINY** ex BODE; ex ARCTIC GULL 1965.

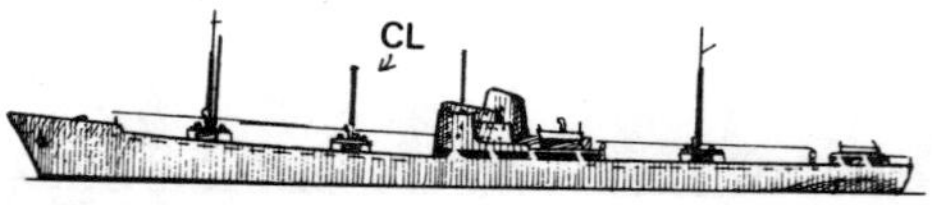

MKMFM H
31670 CENTAUROS. Gr/FRG 1955; CP; 8700; 143.5 × 8.6 (471 × 28.2); M; 13; ex RODANTHI-A 1979; ex NORWIND 1977. Similar: **31671 STELLINA** (Pa) ex MYCENE 1980; ex BREMEN 1979; ex NORDLAND 1970.

MKMFM H1
● **⋆31680 SOVIETSKAYA ARTIKA.** Ru/Br 1951; FC; 900; 140.6 × 7 (461 × 26); M; 12; ex STANHOPE 1954; Converted from general cargo.

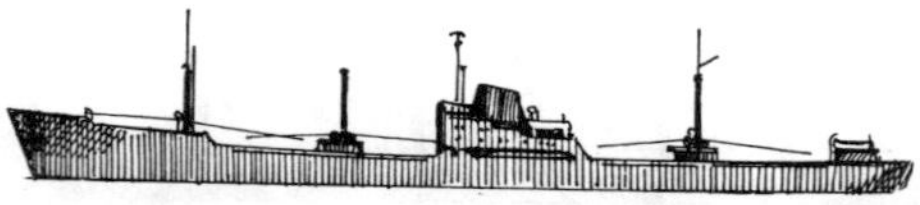

MKMFM H1
31690 MANILA BAY. Pa/FRG 1957; CP; 4000/6400; 143.2 × 6.6/— (470 × 21.7/—); TSM; 16.5; ex SUVA 1980; ex YUVALI 1978; ex YUVAL 1975; ex VIVA; ex CAPE BRETON 1973; ex HORNLAND 1973. Sister: **31691 LI SHAN** (Pa) ex HORNSTERN 1975.

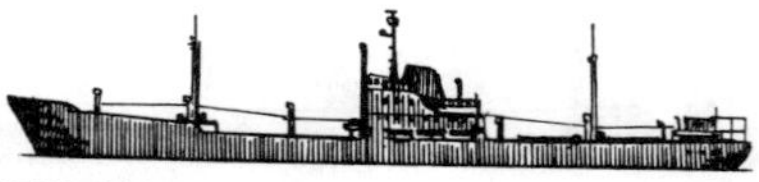

MKMFM H1
31700 KATINA. Cy/Ne 1959; C; 2900; 116.6 × 6.4 (383 × 21); M; 14; ex SOMMARO 1973.

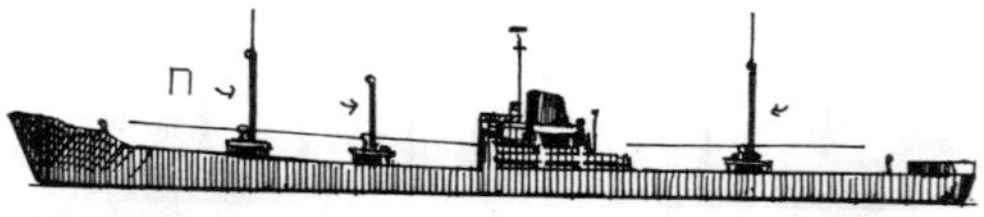

MKMFM H1
31710 MING HONESTY. Tw/Ja 1958; C; 9500; 149 × 9.5 (489 × 30.6); M; 14; ex HUNG MING; ex HAI SHAN 1973. Similar: **31711 PAPACOSTAS** (Gr) ex ARTEMIDI II 1974; ex PLEIADES 1970.

MKMFM H1
● **31720 AMINA.** Pa/Fr 1962; C; 11100; 158 × 9.6 (518 × 30.5); M; —; ex AEGEAN MARINER.

MKMFM H1
31730 EASTERN NAV. Pa/Ja 1957; C; 6500/9400; 148.52 × —/9.53 (487.27 × —/31.27); M; 14; ex EASTAR 1979; ex SKARVA 1973; ex EDDA 1964. Sisters: **31731 WESTERN NAV** (Pa) ex WESTAR 1979; ex SPILDRA 1973; ex SIGLAND 1964 **31732 KUSU ISLAND** (Sg) ex BOLMAREN 1978; ex ARTEMEDI III 1976; ex SEFRA 1975; ex CAPE OF GOOD HOPE 1961 **31733 PROMETHEUS** (Gr) ex OCEAN PROSPER 1968; ex SURNA 1965; ex CAPE AGULHAS 1961; ex SIRA **31734 THEANTO A. S.** (Gr) ex POLARIS 1970 **31735 AMAR** (Gr) ex E.D. PAPALIOS 1979; ex FENIX 1966.

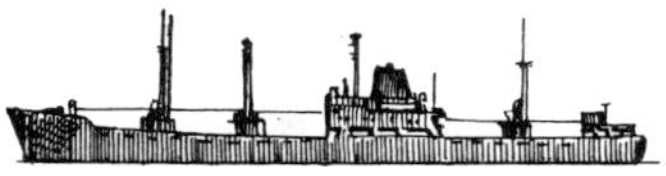

MKMFM H1
⋆**31740 YONG KANG.** RC/No 1960; C; 2500/3800; 102.1 × 6.06/7.46 (335 × 19.88/24.48); M; 14; ex HENGSHAN 1977; ex BEAVERELM 1971; ex ROGA 1962.

MKMFM H1
31750 DESPINA. Gr/Ne 1958; CP; 2300; 105.4 × 6.1 (346 × 19.10); M; 15; ex WERRA; ex FRAVIZO 1964.

MKMFM H1
⋆**31760 ROSENORT.** DDR/No 1962; C; 2400/3800; 108.2 × 6.3/7.4 (355 × 20.9/24.1); M; 15; ex NYCO 1963.

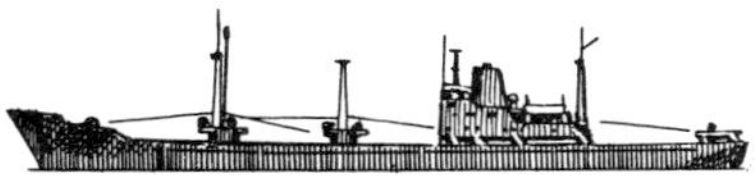

MKMFM H1
⋆**31770 LEWANT II.** Pd/De 1967; C; 3000; 114.5 × 6.3 (375 × 20.6); M; —.

MKMFM H1
31780 PETEN II. Gu/FRG 1951; CP; 1400/2200; 86.5 × 5.4/6.4 (274 × 17.1/20.11); M; 13.5; ex PALERMO 1973; ex SLOMAN PALERMO 1965; ex PALERMO 1962.

MKMFM H12
31790 KAO SAH. Pa/Ja 1959; C; 2600; 92 × 6.1 (302 × 20); M; 13; ex TAKASAGO MARU 1973.

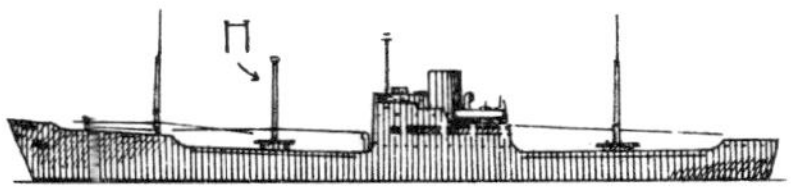

MKMFM H123
● **31800 SILK.** Gr/Ja 1956; C; 5000; 122.8 × 7.6 (403 × 25); M; 13; ex SILVER FIR; ex CEYLON MARU 1974. Sisters (Gr flag): **31801 APOSTOLOS M. 1.** ex SILVER SUN 1979; ex CANBERRA MARU 1972 **31802 ADAMANTIOS S** ex SILVER DOLPHIN 1974; ex COLOMBO MARU 1972.

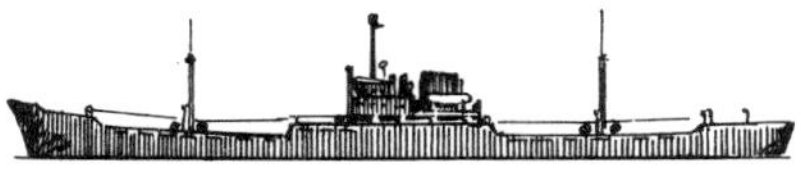

MKMFM H123
31810 KARANA ENAN. Ia/Ja 1960; C; 4800; 120.8 × 7.4 (396 × 24.6); M; 13; ex OCEANIC 1977; ex SHIGESHIMA MARU 1969.

MKMFM H123
31820 DEWI. Pa/Ja 1957; CP; 4900; 120.8 × 7.3 (396 × 24); M; 12.5; ex ASANO No 1 1977; ex NIKKO MARU 1973.

MKMFM H123
⋆**31830 ARZAMAS.** Ru/FRG 1955; C; 3300; 102.4 × 6.6 (329 × 21.6); R & LPT; 12.5.

MKMFM H13
***31840 VERKHOYANSKLES** class. Ru/Ru 1965; C; 3000; 104.5 × 6.1 (343 × 20.11); M; 13.25. Similar (Ru flag): ***31841 SIBIRLES *31842 SUKHONALES *31843 EGVEKINOT *31844 KORSAKOV *31845 SIBIRTSYEVO** ex MANZOVKA ***31846 TERNEY. *31847 VYATKALES *31848 YAKUTSKLES *31849 AJAN *31850 SELENGA *31851 OMOLON *31852 VZMORYE *31853 PROKOPIY GALUSHIN *31854 YANA *31855 ALDAN *31856 LAKHTA *31857 KEM *31858 KONDOPOGO *31859 UNZHA** (Rumanian built—Ru flag): ***31860 KILIYA *31861 KRYMSK *31862 KATANGLI *31863 KIRENSK *31864 KOREIZ *31865 KRASNOARMEYSK *31866 KRASNOPOLYE *31867 KRASNOTURINSK *31868 ANTON-BUYUKLY *31869 KAZATIN *31870 KUSTANAY *31871 KUZNETSK *31872 LEONID SMIRNYKH *31873 STEPAN SAVUSHKIN *31874 BORIS NIKOLAICHUK *31875 CHERNIGOV *31876 EVGENIY CHAPLANOV *31877 KARAGA *31878 KAVALEROVO *31879 KULUNDA *31880 TUSHINO *31881 TYMOVSK.**

MKMFM H13
● **31930 CHARALAMBOS M. PATERAS.** Gr/Yu 1960; C; 9300; 153.2 × 9.3 (503 × 29.9); M; 14; ex CAPETAN NICOLAS 1961.

MKMFM H13
31940 ELPIDA. Gr/Ne 1956; C; 8400; 145.98 × 8.76 (478.94 × 28.74); M; 12.5; ex AMSTELMEER 1969.

MKMFM H13
● **31960 KASEM SAMUT.** Th/FRG 1958; C; 5000; 118 × 8 (387 × 26); M; —; ex TUMLAREN 1970.

MKMFM H13
● **31980 LUZON.** Pi/Ja 1959; C; 4800; 115.1 × 7.8 (379 × 26); M; 14.

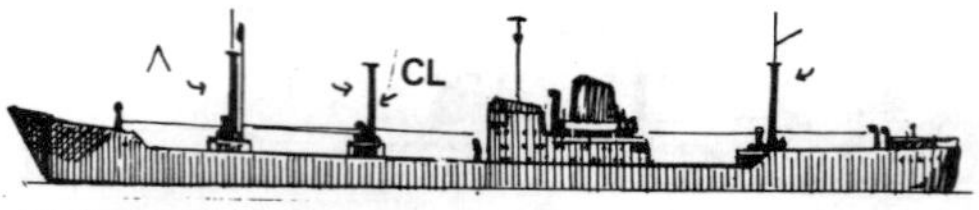

MKMFM H13
31900 CUZCO. Pe/DDR 1961; C; 6900/8900; 150.3 × 7.9/8.6 (493 × 25.9/28.4); M; 14.5; ex CASTAGNOLA 1975.

MKMFM H13
31910 AKIS S. Gr/Sw 1957; C; 3900/6200; 130.7 × 7.1/8.2 (428 × 23.4/27.1); M; 14.5; ex MIREILLE 1974; ex DALHEM 1970.

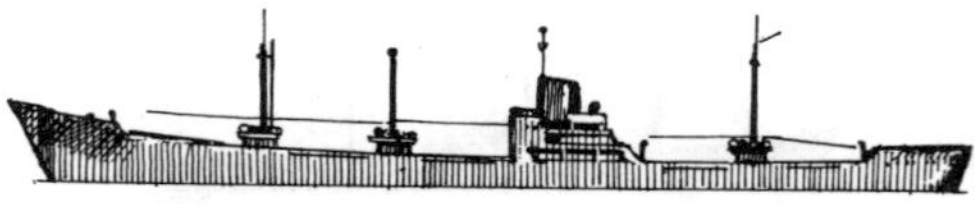

MKMFM H13
● ***31920 HONG MING.** RC/Ne 1959; C; 6300/8600; 150 × 8.2/8.8 (492 × 26.3/29); M; 13; ex BANDA SEA 1976; ex AMSTELMOLEN 1972. Sisters (RC flag): ***31921 SAN MING** ex BALI 1976; ex AMSTELVELD 1972 ***31922 YONG FING** ex JAVA SEA 1976; ex AMSTELSLUIS 1972.

MKMFM H13
31950 R.S.A. SA/Ja 1961; PC; 1600; 68.9 × — (227 × —); M; 11.5.

MKMFM H13
31970 EFFY. Gr/FRG 1955; C; 5000; 117.6 × 7.6 (373 × 25); M; 15; ex YEHUDA 1969.

MKMFM H13
● **31990 VOULLA.** Iv/FRG 1960; CP; 5100; 117 × 7.6 (384 × 25); M; 14; ex ARAUCO 1970.

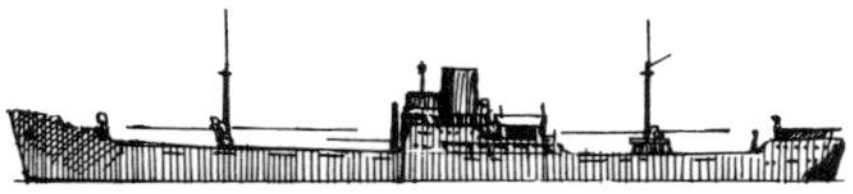

MKMFM H13
● **32000 ISLAND OF MARMARA.** Gr/Br 1960; C; 4800/7000; 132.1×7.6/8.1 (434×24.7/26.2); M; 14.75; ex CITY OF ST. ALBANS. Sisters: **32001 SUERTE** (Pa) ex CITY OF GLOUCESTER **32002 RIO DIAMANTO** (Gr) ex CITY OF WORCESTER **32003 CITY OF DUNDEE** (Cy) ex DUNDEE 1980; ex CITY OF DUNDEE 1979 **32004 CITY OF LEEDS** (Cy) ex LEEDS 1980; ex CITY OF LICHFIELD 1979.

MKMFMK H1
32010 ARCHANGELOS G. Gr/Ja 1960; C; 10100; 158×9.5 (519×31); M; —.

MKMFMK H1
● **32020 AVRA.** Gr/Ys 1959; C; 6000/8900; 152.3×8.3/9.2 (500×27.6/30.3); M; 15; ex AGIOS FANOURIOS 1976; ex PLATON 1974; ex KYVERNITIS 1972.

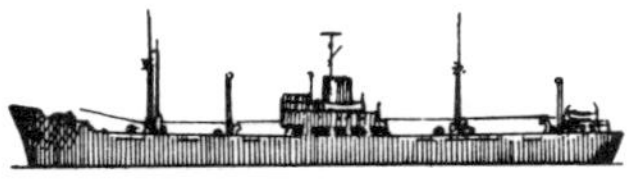

MKMFMK H1
32030 AL LOULOUAH. Ku/Sw 1946; CP; 1800; 98×5.9 (322×19.3); M; 14; ex TROPICAL RAINBOW 1977; ex GULF PEARL 1976; ex UNIVERSAL CHICAGO 1975; ex STOLTERJO 1974; ex DANAE IV 1972; ex STOLTERJO 1970; ex NILS GORTHON 1959.

MKMFMK H12
32040 SELENE G. Br/FRG 1959; C; 10400; 157×9.2 (516×30.3); M; 14.5; ex SIRA 1975. Sister: **32041 PARGA** (Gr) ex SIMOA 1976.

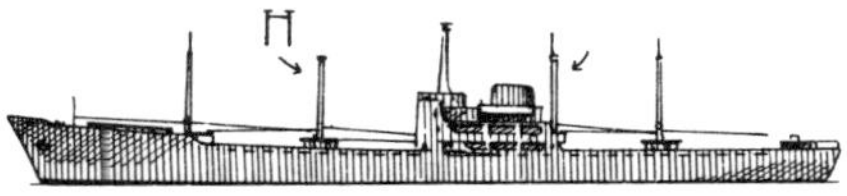

$MKMFM_2$ H1
32050 MARITIME EXPLORER. Pa/Ja 1960; C; 6400; 132.4×7.6 (434×25); M; 15; ex NAGAOSAN MARU 1971.

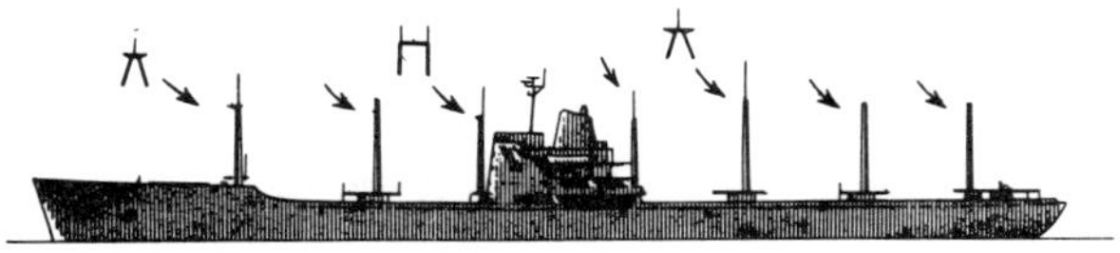

$MKM_2FM_2K_2$ H1
32060 H. H. HESS. US/US 1965; C; 9400/12400; 171.8×—/9.6 (564×—/31.6); T; 20; ex CANADA MAIL; U.S. Military Sealift Command.

● ⋆32065

M_2 H
32070 PAN ANTILLES. Li/US 1960; Con; 4700; 110.3×4.8 (361×15.11); TSM; 16; ex FLORIDIAN 1974. Sister: **32071 ALEUTIAN DEVELOPER** (Li) ex NEW YORKER 1976.

M_2 H
32080 KOUTOURIARIS S.V. Gr/FRG 1957; ST; 1300; 79.4×3.9 (227×13); D-E; —; ex HEINRICH MEINS 1970.

M_2F H
⋆**32090 AMBASADOR.** Ys/Ys 1958; PC; 2600; 90×4.7 (296×15.6); TSM; 17.5; ex JEDINSTVO 1979.

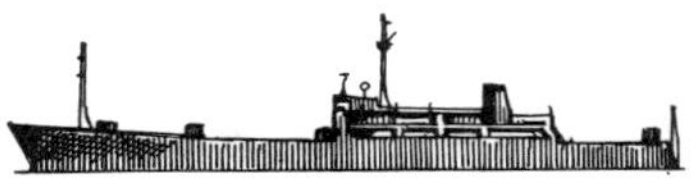

M_2F H
32100 RORO DANIA. FRG/No 1972; RoC; 500; 105.3×3.3 (346×11); TSM; 17; ex NANOMARK 1974. Sisters (FRG flag): **32101 RORO ANGLIA** ex SAILORMARK 1974 **32102 RORO CIMBRIA** ex LANDMARK 1974 Similar: **32103 L'ISERE** (Fr); ex JOLLY GIALLO 1976; ex TRAILER EXPRESS 1974.

M_2F H
32110 THE PHILIPPINE TOURIST. Pi/Br 1953; P; 4800; 114×5.4 (374×17.7); M; 16; ex BRAEMAR 1975.

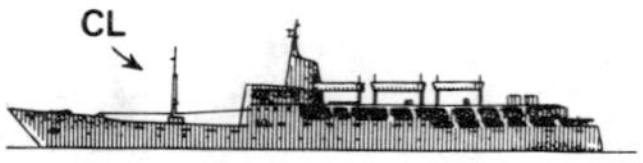

M_2F H
32120 DON JULIO. Pi/Ja 1967; PC; 2100; 95.66 × 5.16 (313.85 × 16.93); M; 17.5.

M_2F H
32140 SUADIYE. Tu/Tu 1964; F; 600; 67 × 2.6 (220 × 8.6); TSM; —.

M_2F H
32160 HARBIYE. Tu/Br 1961; F; 800; 69.7 × 2.7 (229 × 8.8); TSR; 15. Sisters (Tu flag): **32161 A. KAVAGI 32162 ATAKOY** ex GENCLIK 1961 **32163 IHSAN 32164 KALMAZ 32165 INKILAP 32166 KANLIKA 32167 PENDIK 32168 TURAN 32169 EMEKSIZ 32170 KUZGUNCUK.**

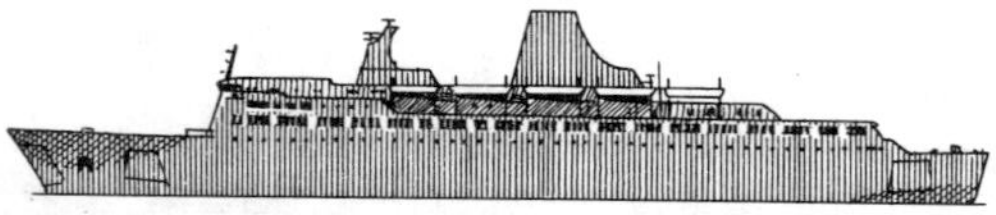

M_2F H
32200 DANA REGINA. De/De 1974; RoPCF; 12200; 153.7 × 6 (504 × 20); TSM; 21.5; Bow, stern & port side doors.

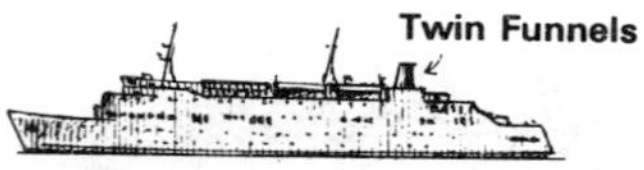

M_2F H
32220 HAMMERSHUS. De/FRG 1967; RoPCF; 2900; 86.4 × 3.8 (283 × 12.6); TSM; 18; Side door.

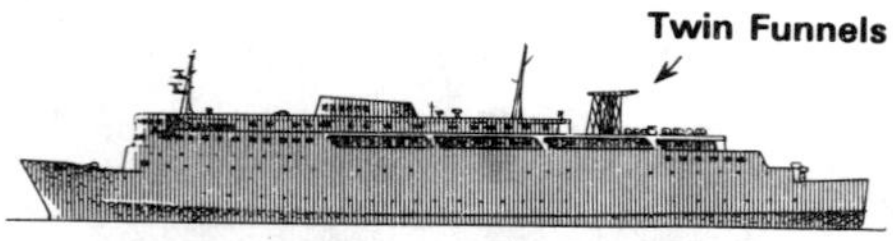

M_2F H
32240 IZU MARU No. 3. Ja/Ja 1972; RoPF; 7500; 137.85 × 5.61 (452.26 × 18.41); TSM; 21.5; ex CASSIOPEIA; Bow and stern ramps. Sister: **32241 IZU MARU No 11** (Ja) ex ALBATROSS.

M_2F H
32130 ISCHIA. It/Br 1948; RoPCF; 1500; 87.9 × 2.6 (288 × 8.6); TSM; 19; ex AUTOCARRIER 1973; ex ROYAL SOVEREIGN 1967; Converted from passenger ship.

M_2F H
32150 FENERBAHCE. Tu/Br 1952; F; 1000; 73.1 × 3.4 (240 × 11.2); TSM; —. Sisters (Tu flag): **32151 DOLMABAHCE 32152 PASABAHCE.**

M_2F H
32180 GALLURA. It/It 1968; F; 4900; 123 × 5.5 (404 × 18); TSM; —.

M_2F H
32190 MATANUSKA. US/US-US 1963/78; RoPF; 3000; 124.36 × 4.98 (408 × 16.34); TSM; 18; Lengthened 1978.

M_2F H
32210 ARMORIQUE. Fr/Fr 1972; RoPCF; 5700; 116.6 × 4.3 (382 × 14); TSM; 18; ex TERJE VIGEN 1975; Bow & stern doors.

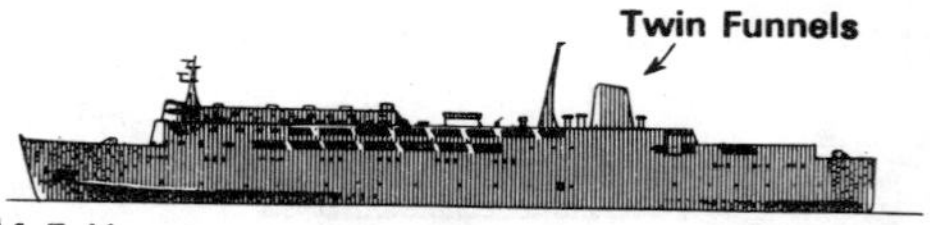

M_2F H
32230 HANKYU No. 16. Ja/Ja 1972; RoC/F; 5700; 135.49 × 5.23 (444.52 × 17.16); TSM; 21; ex TSUKUSMI. Sister: **32231 HANKYU No. 17** (Ja) ex HAKATA.

M_2F H
32250 PENN AR BED. Fr/Fr 1974; RoPCF; 2900; 109.5 × 5.5 (359 × 18); TSM; 19.

M_2F H
32260 PRESIDENTE DIAZ ORDAZ. Me/No 1961; RoPCF; 2900; 90.3×4.1 (296×13.6); TSM; 18; ex CORT ADELER 1970; Bow and stern doors.

M_2F H
32270 QUEEN OF VICTORIA. Ca/Ca 1962; RoPCF; 4900; 130×3.8 (427×12.6); TSM; 18; ex CITY OF VICTORIA 1963; Lengthened 1970; Bow & stern doors. Sister: **32271 QUEEN OF VANCOUVER** (Ca) ex CITY OF VICTORIA 1963.

M_2F H
32280 CALEDONIA. Br/No 1966; RoPCF; 1200; 61.8×3.2 (203×10.4); TSM; 15; ex STENA BALTICA 1970.

M_2F H
★**32290 ILIRIJA.** Ys/FRG 1963; RoPCF; 2000; 80.5×4.1 (264×14.6); TSM; 16.5; ex BORNHOLMERPILEN 1971.

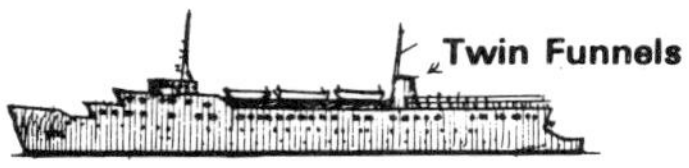

M_2F H
32300 POLAR EXPRESS. Fi/De 1963; RoPCF; 2900; 91.3×4.2 (299×13.9); TSM; 18; ex PRINSESSAN MARGARETHA 1970; Bow door.

M_2F H
● ★**32310 GRYF.** Pd/FRG 1962; RoPCF; 3000; 96×4.7 (315×14); TSM; 16; ex FINNDANA 1967; ex HANSA EXPRESS 1966; Bow and stern doors.

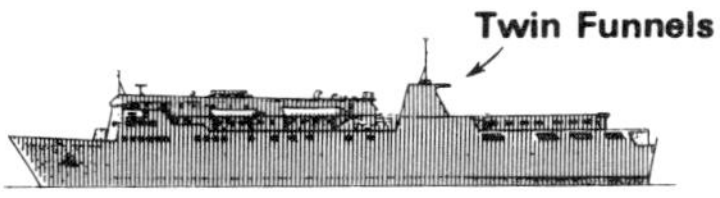

M_2F H
32320 CONCEPCION MARINO. Ve/No; 1978; RoPF; 6200; 105.01×3.9 (344.52×12.8); TSM; 17; Bow and stern doors. Sister: **32321 CACICA ISABEL** (Ve).

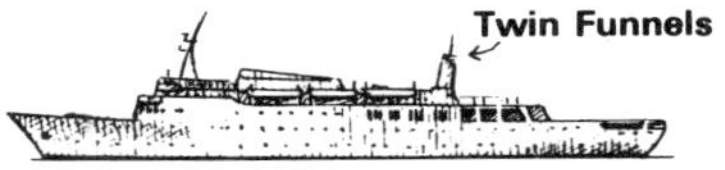

M_2F H
● **32330 DONA MONTSERRAT.** Pi/Sp 1967; CPF; 4400; 104.9×4.3 (344×13.5); TSM; 19.5; ex WEST STAR 1975; ex CABO IZARRA 1970.

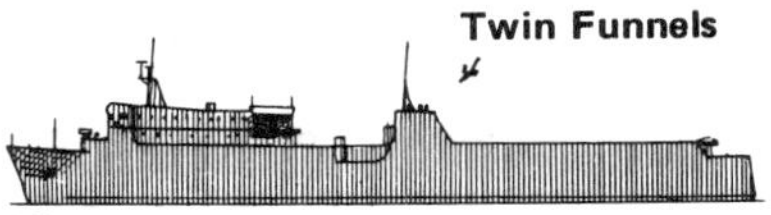

M_2F H
32340 STENA SAILOR. Sw/Ih 1975; RoCV; 2400; 119×4.6 (391×15); TSM; 18; ex DUNDALK 1980; Bow and stern ramps and doors.

M_2F H
32350 CAPO BIANCO. It/De 1960; RoPCF; 2300; 88.5×4.6 (290×15); TSM; 17.5; ex FLAMINIA NOVA 1974; ex HOLMIA 1971; ex CALMAR NYCKEL 1965; ex PRINS BERTIL 1964; Bow and stern doors.

M_2F H
32360 MERZARIO SYRIA. Sw/Sw 1968; RoCV; 1100; 89.3×4.1 (293×14); M; 18; ex SCANDIC 1977; Stern door.

M_2F H
32370 BUFFALO. Br/FRG 1974; RoC; 3500; 125×3.8 (410×13); TSM; 19.5.

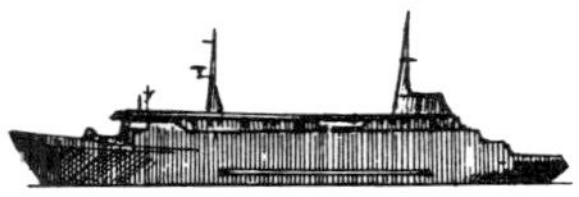

M_2F H
32380 AQUILA. It/No 1964; C; 500; 87.8×3.8 (288×12.6); M; 15; ex ANGLIA 1973; ex DYVI ANGLIA 1971.

M_2F H
32390 MAR CARIBE. Li/FRG 1967; RoC; 2600; 104 × 5.4 (342 × 18); Stern door. Similar: **32391 RHONE** (Fr) ex RHONETAL; ex NORCAPE; ex RHONETAL.

M_2F H
32400 VIKING IV. No/No 1967; RoC; 1200; 92 × 4.7 (301 × 15.6); TSM; 15; Stern and side doors.

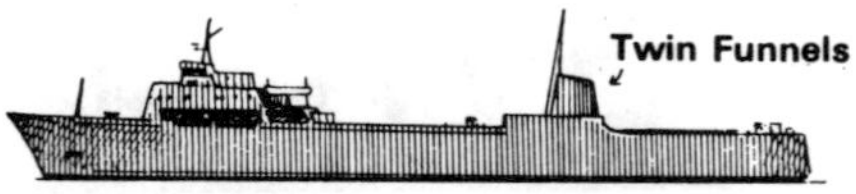

M_2F H
32410 JOLLY BIANCO. It/FRG 1969; RoC; 2900; 129.3 × 5 (424 × 17); TSM; 17; ex SERVUS; Stern door and ramp.

M_2F H
32420 STELLA MARIS II. Gr/FRG 1960; P; 2700; 88.2 × 4.4 (289 × 11.6); TSM; 18.5; ex BREMERHAVEN 1965.

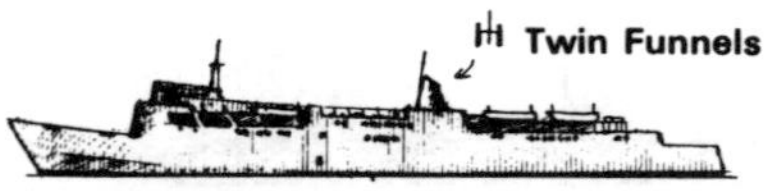

M_2F H
32430 CORSE. Fr/Fr 1966; RoPCF; 4600; 115 × 4.4 (378 × 14.6); TSM; 21; Bow and stern doors. Sister: **32431 COMTE DE NICE** (Fr) ex PROVENCE 1966.

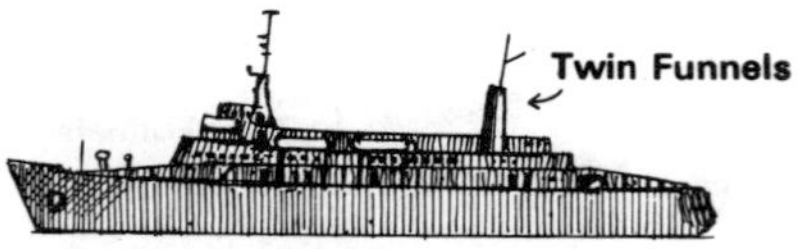

M_2F H
32440 NORWAVE. Br/FRG 1965; RoPCF; 3500; 108.8 × 4.9 (356 × 16); TSM; 15; Bow and stern doors. Sister: **32441 NORWIND** (Ne).

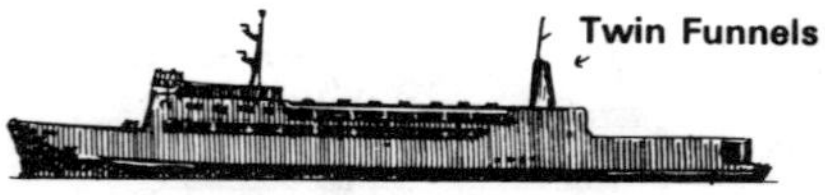

M_2F H
32450 FERRY GOLD. Ja/Ja 1970; PF; 4100; 117.5 × 4.4 (385 × 14.6); TSM; 18. Sisters (Ja flag): **32451 FERRY PEARL 32452 FERRY RUBY.**

M_2F H
● **32460 FUJI.** Ja/Ja 1965; PCF; 2900; 91.7 × 4.2 (301 × 13.6); M; 18.5.

M_2F H
32470 COBALT MARU. Ja/Ja 1967; PF; 3200; 89.3 × 3.9 (293 × 13); TSM; 13.5. Possible Sister: **32471 IVORY MARU** (Ja) Similar (Smaller): **32472 SUMIRE MARU** (Ja).

M_2F H
32480 IYO MARU. Ja/Ja 1974; RoPCF; 3100; 89.4 × 3.7 (276 × 12.2); TSM; 15.25. Sister: **32481 TOSA MARU** (Ja).

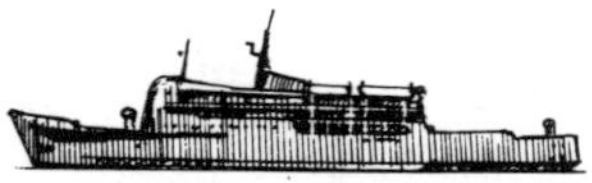

M_2F H
32490 TROUBRIDGE. Br/Au 1961; RoPCF; 2000; 91.4 × 3.7 (300 × 12.1); TSM; 14.5.

M_2F H
32500 DRAGON. Br/Fr 1967; RoPCF; 6100; 134.6 × 4.8 (440 × 15.9); TSM; 19. Sister: **32501 LEOPARD** (Fr).

M_2F H
32510 DEUTSCHLAND. FRG/FRG 1972; RoPCF; 6100; 144.1 × 5.9 (473 × 19.3); TD-E; 19.5; Bow and stern doors.

M_2F H
32520 PROVENCE. Fr/Fr 1974; RoPCF; 7800; 142.3 × 5.8 (467 × 19); TSM; 23; Bow, side & stern doors.

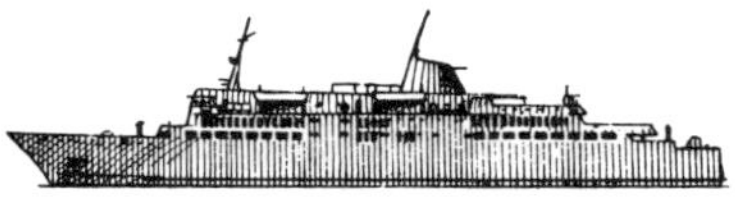

M_2F H
32530 MALTA EXPRESS. It/FRG 1968; RoPCF; 3900; 115 × 4.8 (377 × 15.6); TSM; —; ex GEDSER 1976.

M_2F H
● **32540 BOCCACCIO.** It/It 1970; RoPCF; 6900; 131 × 5 6 (430 × 18.3); TSM; 22. Sisters (It flag): **32541 CARDUCCI 32541 LEOPARDI 32543 MANZONI 32544 PASCOLI 32545 PETRARCA.**

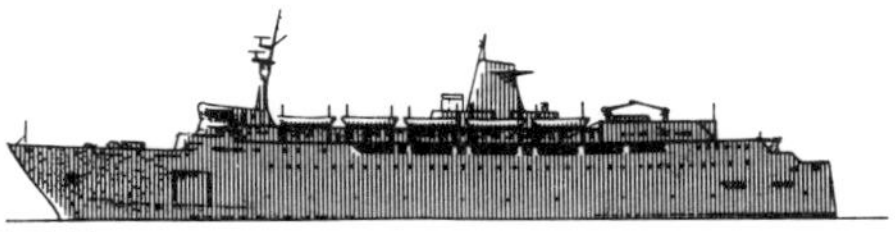

M_2F H
● **32550 DELEDDA.** It/It 1978; RoPCF; 6500; 131.02 × 5.62; (429.86 × 18.44); TSM; 20.5; Stern and side doors. Sister: **32551 VERGA** (It).

M_2F H
32560 SAINT ELOI. Fr/Fr 1972; RoPCF; 4600; 114.6 × 4.1 (376 × 13); TSM; 19.5.

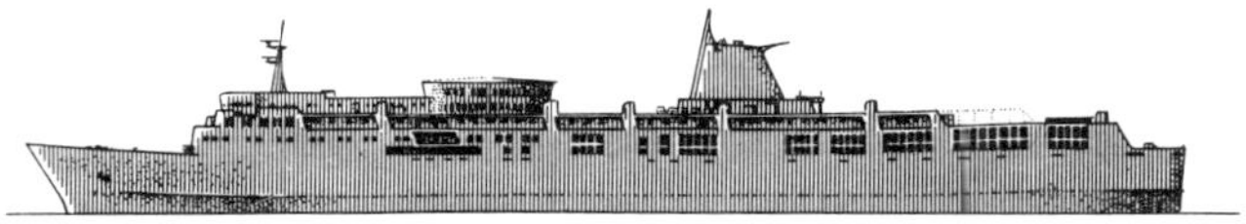

M_2F H
32570 ISHIKARI. Ja/Ja 1974; RoPCF; —; 188.4 × —(618.11 × —); TSM; 23.5; Lengthened 1980. Sister: **32571 DAISETSU** (Ja).

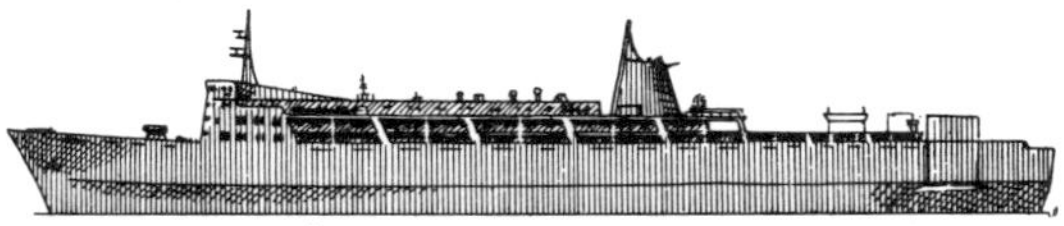

M_2F H
32580 ARKAS. Ja/Ja 1972; RoPCF; 9700; 167.2 × 6.3 (548 × 20.6); TSM; 21. Sister: **32581 ALBIREO** (Ja) Similar: **32582 MARIMO** (Ja).

M_2F H
32590 GARYOUNIS. Ly/Ja 1973; P/RoC; 9600; 166.53 × 6.47 (546.36 × 21.23); TSM; 20.5; ex MASHU 1977.

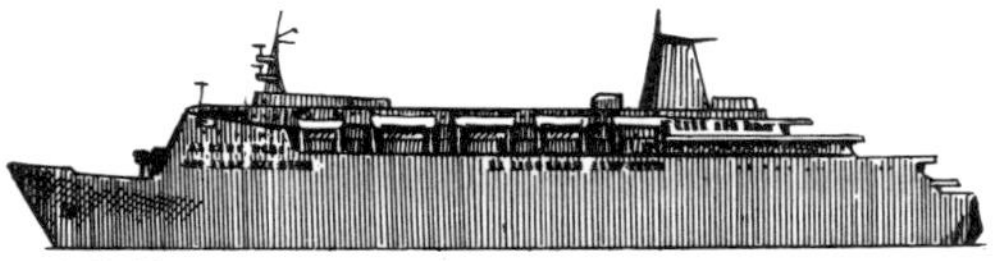

M_2F H
32600 NORLAND. Br/FRG 1974; RoPCF; 13000; 153 × 6.2 (502 × 20.3); TSM; 19; Stern door and ramp and side door. Sister: **32601 NORSTAR** (Ne).

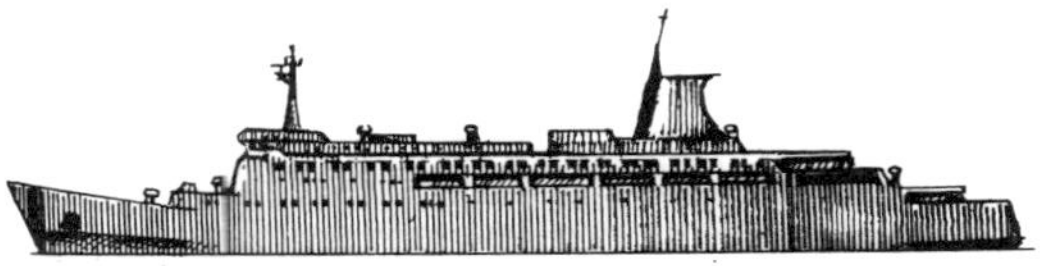

M_2F H
32610 MIMITSU MARU. Ja/Ja 1973; RoPCF; 9600; 160 × — (525 × —); TSM; 27. Similar: **32611 TAKACHIHO MARU** (Ja).

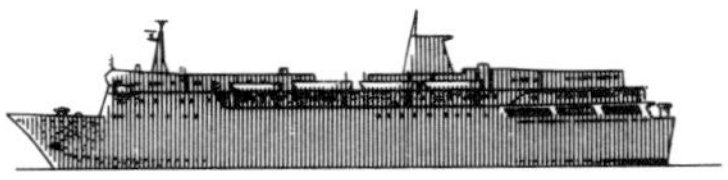

M_2F H
32620 EL ARISH. Eg/No 1980; RoPCF; 4600; 105 × 4.13 (344.5 × 13.55); TSM; 19; Stern door/ramp. Sister: **32621 EL TOR** (Eg).

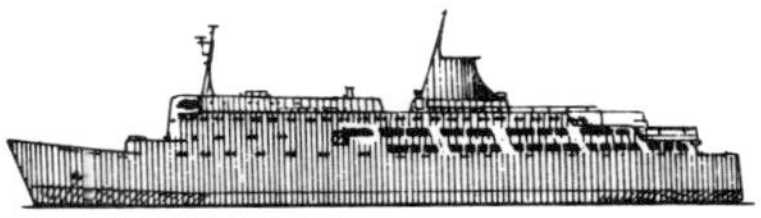

M_2F H
32630 SAINT PAULIA. Ja/Ja 1971; RoPCF; 6000; 118 × 5.7 (387 × 19); TSM; 16. Sister: **32631 ZERALDA** (Ag) ex BOUGAINVILLEA 1976 Similar: **32632 HOGGAR** (Ag) ex HIBISCUS 1976 **32633 TIPAZA** (Ag) ex PHENIX 1976 **32634 HAMAYU** (Ja) **32635 HUA LIEN** (Tw).

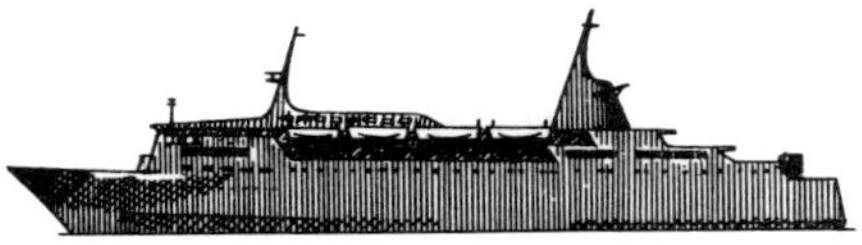

M_2F H
32640 CASTALIA. Gr/Ja 1974; RoPCF; 8500; 132 × 5.3 (433 × 17.6); TSM; 18.

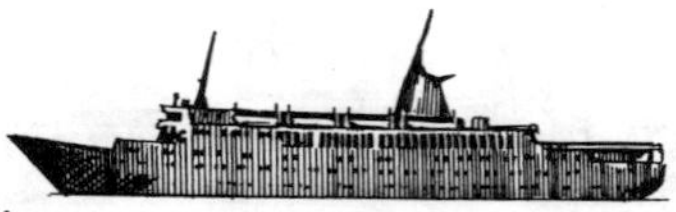

M_2F H

32650 AQUARIUS. Gr/Gr 1972; P; 4600; 103.7×4.7 (340×15.6); TSM; 19.5.

M_2F H

32660 TAI SHAN. Br/Ja 1972; F; 2100; 78.64×3.18 (258×10.43); TSM; 17.5. Sister (Br flag): **32661 LO SHAN 32662 NAM SHAN.**

M_2F H

32670 TIZIANO. It/It 1970; RoPCF; 3500; 101.2×4.3 (332×14); TSM; 18.

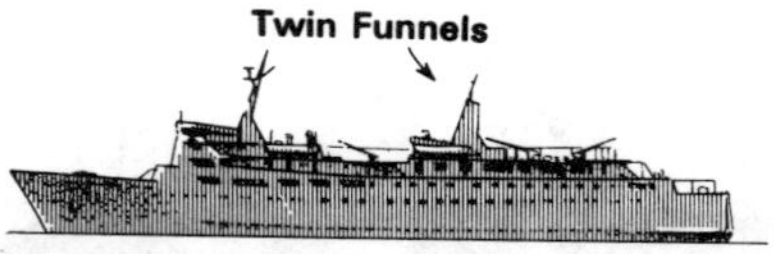

M_2F H

32680 NUITS ST. GEORGE. Fr/Fr 1966; RoPCF; 4800; 114.99×4.92 (377.26×16.14); TSM; 19.5; ex FRED SCAMARONI 1980; Bow and stern doors; Side doors.

M_2F H

32690 JACOPO TINTORETTO. It/It 1966; PF; 2700; 100×4.3 (328×14.3); TSM; 18.

M_2F H

32700 POSEIDON. FRG/No 1964; PF; 1100; 65.5×2.9 (215×9.6); TSM; —.

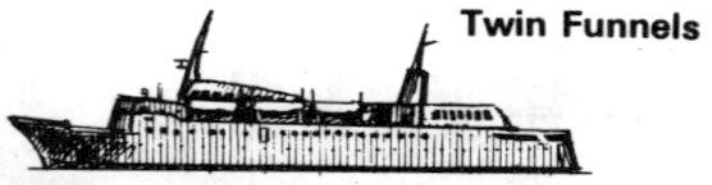

M_2F H

***32710 LIBURNIJA.** Ys/Ne 1965; RoPCF; 3000; 89.2×4.2 (292×14); TSM; 15; Bow and stern doors.

M_2F H

32720 INNISFALLEN. Ih/Ih 1969; RoPCF; 4800; 118.3×4.5 (388×13.6); TSM; 20; ex LEINSTER 1980; Bow and stern doors. Sister: **32721 CORSICA VIVA** (Pa) ex INNISFALLEN 1980.

M_2F H

32730 MUNSTER. Ih/FRG 1968; RoPCF; 4100; 110.2×4.5 (362×14.6); TSM; 21.5; Bow and stern doors.

M_2F H

32740 LA VALLETTA. It/It 1971; RoPCF; 2100; 89.5×4.3 (297×14); TSM; 16; Bow and stern doors.

M_2F H

32750 NISSOS CHIOS. Gr/Ys 1967; RoPCF; 3200; 97.5×4.8 (320×15.9); TSM; 18; ex KAPELLA: Bow and stern doors.

M_2F H

32760 PRINSES BEATRIX. Ne/Ne 1978; RoPCF; 9400; 131.02×5.17 (429.86×16.96); TSM; 21; Bow and stern doors/ramps.

M_2F H

● **32770 MARELLA.** Fi/Ys 1970; RoPCF; 3900; 99.2×4.8 (325×16); TSM; 18; Bow and stern doors.

M_2F H

32780 TIGER. Br/De 1972; RoPCF; 4000; 104.04×4.37 (341.34×14.38); TSM; 20.25; ex KATTEGAT 1978; Bow & stern doors; Also known as **'n.f. TIGER'**. Sister: **32781 PANTHER** (Br) ex LASSE II; ex DJURSLAND 1974; also known as **'n.f. PANTHER'**.

M_2F H
32790 ANTRIM PRINCESS. Br/Br 1967; RoPCF; 3600; 112.6 × 3.7 (369 × 12.3); TSM; 19.5. Similar: **32791 AILSA PRINCESS** (Br).

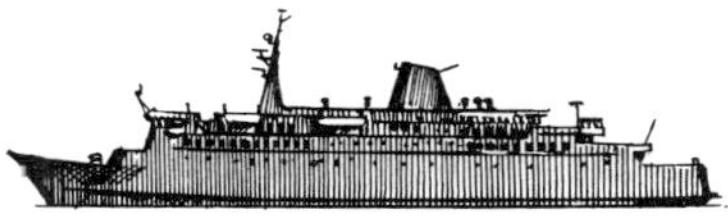

M_2F H
● **32800 KALLE III.** De/FRG 1974; RoPCF; 4400; 118 × 5 (388 × 16.9); TSM; 21; Bow and stern doors. Sister: **32801 DJURSLAND II** (De) Similar: **32802 TRAVEMUNDE** (De).

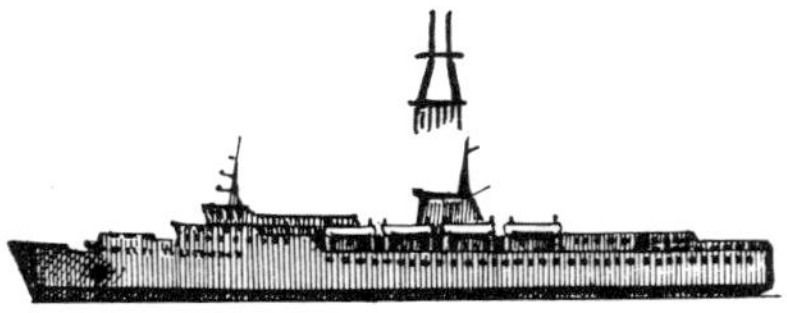

M_2F H
32810 PRINCESSAN CHRISTINA. Sw/De 1969; RoPCF; 5700; 123.5 × 5.2 (405 × 17); TSM; 20.5; ex PRINSESSAN CHRISTINA 1980; Bow and stern doors.

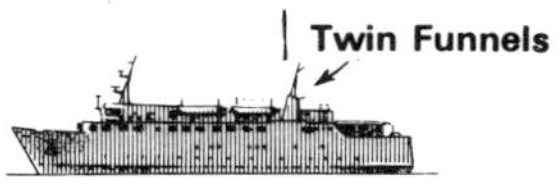

M_2F H
32820 SOLIDOR. Fr/FRG 1965; RoC/F; 900; 63.61 × 3.48 (208.7 × 11.42); TSM; 15; ex LANGELAND 1977; Bow door.

M_2F H
32830 DISKO. De/De 1968; PC; 2200; 70.5 × 4 (230 × 13); M; 14.

M_2F H
32840 LINDBLAD EXPLORER. Pa/Fi 1969; P; 2300; 72.9 × 4.2 (239 × 14); M; 15; Side door.

M_2F H
32850 WORLD DISCOVERER. Sg/FRG 1973; P; 3400; 71.4 × 4.2 (234 × 14); M; 16.5; ex BEWA DISCOVERER 1973.

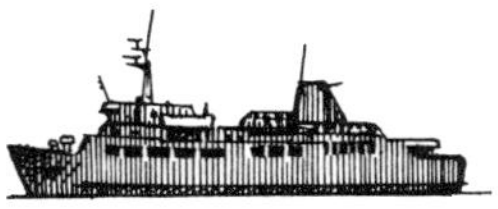

M_2F H
32860 LANGELAND II. De/Ne 1977; RoPCF; 1600; 70.01 × 3.81 (229.69 × 12.5); TSM; 15.5; Bow and stern doors; Also known as **LANGELAND TO.**

M_2F H
32870 ST. OLA. Br/Br 1974; RoPCF; 1300; 70.2 × 4 (230 × 13); TSM; 15; Bow and stern doors.

32880 A. REGINA. Pa/Sw 1967; RoPCF; 5200; 111 × 4.8 (361 × 16); TSM; 23.5; ex STENA GERMANICA; Bow and stern doors. Sister: **32881 VIKING VI** (Fi) ex WICKERSHAM 1974; ex STENA BRITANNICA 1968.

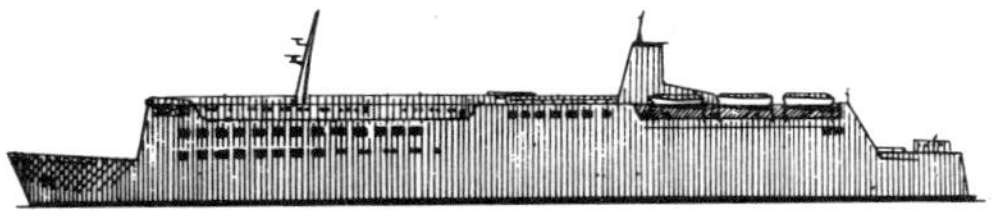

M_2F H
⋆**32890 RUGEN.** DDR/DDR 1972; RoPCF/F; 6500; 152 × 5.6 (500 × 18.3); TSM; 20.5; Stern and side doors.

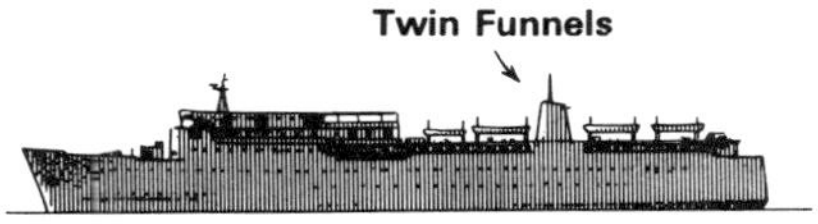

M_2F H
32900 SOL PHRYNE. Cy/Ja 1948; RoC/F; 5900; 118.67 × — (389.34 × —); TSM; 17; ex AEOLIS 1977; ex TAISETSU MARU 1967.

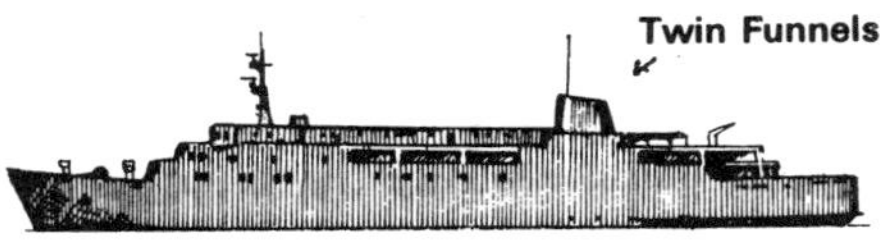

M_2F H
32910 CANDIA. Gr/Ja 1971; RoPCF; 5800; 130 × 5.5 (427 × 18); TSM; 19.5; ex CENTRAL No2 1972. Possible Sister: **32911 RETHIMNON** (Gr) ex CENTRAL No5 1972.

M_2F H
32920 VENUS. Ja/Ja 1975; RoCF; 3500; 120 × 4.9 (395 × 16); TSM; 20.

M_2F H
32930 FREDERICK CARTER. Ca/Ca 1968; RoC/TF; 12200; 148.1 × 6.4 (486 × 21); TSM; 18; Stern doors.

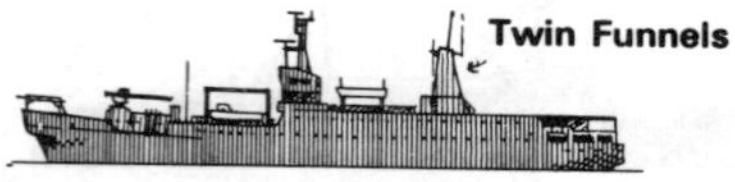

M_2F H
32940 C.S. MONARCH. Br/Br 1975; Cbl; 3900; 95.4 × 4.8 (313 × 15.6); M; 15. Sister: **32941 C.S. IRIS** (Br).

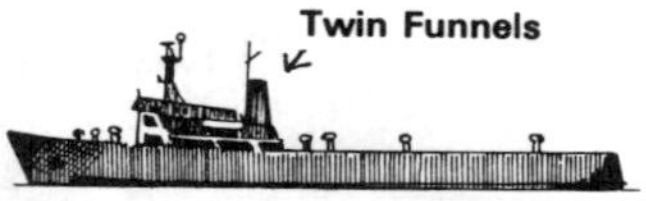

M_2F H
32950 SCHIAFFINO. Fr/FRG 1970; RoC; 1000; 97 × 4.1 (319 × 13.6); TSM; 16; ex NECKARTAL 1974; Stern door. Sisters: **32951 COTENTIN** (Fr) ex SAALETAL 1974; ex THULE 1971 **32952 ST. MAGNUS** (Br) ex DORSET; ex ULSTER SPORTSMAN 1976; ex DONAUTAL 1974 **32953 POINTER** (Br) ex PRESELI 1977; ex ANTWERPEN 1974.

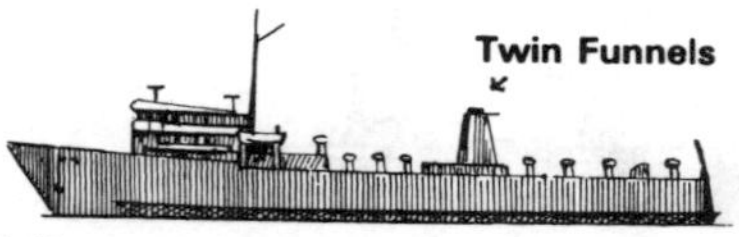

M_2F H
32960 LADY NINA. Br/No 1973; RoC; 1600; 108.6 × 4.9 (356 × 16); TSM; 17.5; ex LEILA; Bow and stern doors. Sisters: **32961 LADY TONE** (Br) ex LAGAN BRIDGE 1981; ex ILKKA 1980 **32962 LADY CATHERINE** (FRG) ex LUNE BRIDGE 1981; ex ANU 1980 **32963 LALLI** (Br).

M_2F H
● **32970 JOLLY BLU.** It/Ne 1969; RoC; 1600; 108.5 × 5 (356 × 17); TSM; —; ex TOR MERCIA 1975. Sisters: **32971 DESTRO** (Br) **32972 STARMARK** (Fi) Similar (Lengthened): **32973 JOLLY MARRONE** (It) ex TOR SCANDIA 1976.

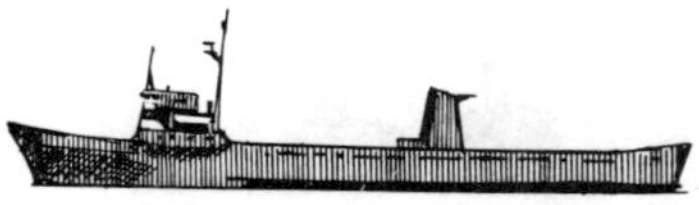

M_2F H
● **32980 ESPRESSO LIGURIA.** It/It 1967; RoC; 2000; 104.7 × 5.1 (343 × 16.1); TSM; 19; Stern doors. Sisters (It flag): **32981 ESPRESSO SARDEGNA 32982 ESPRESSO SICILIA 32983 ESPRESSO TOSCANA 32984 ESPRESSO LOMBARDIA.**

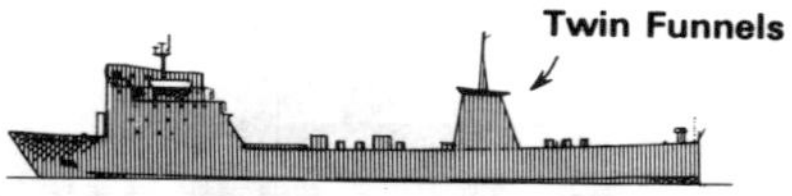

M_2F H
32990 KAPTAN SAIT OZEGE. Tu/FRG 1977; RoC; 2200; 110.52 × 4.98 (362.6 × 16.34); TSM; 17; Bow & stern door/ramp. Sister: **32991 KAPTAN NECDET OR** (Tu).

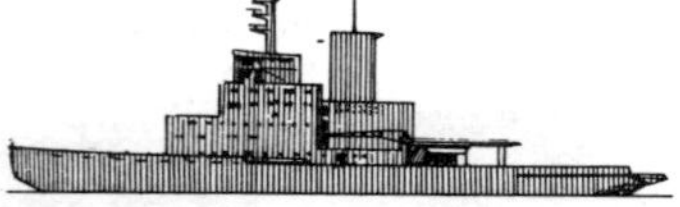

M_2F H
33000 ATLE. Sw/Fi 1974; IB; 6900; 104.6 × 8.3 (343 × 27.3); TSD-E; 18.5. Sisters: **33001 FREJ** (Sw) **33002 URHO** (Fi) **33003 SISU** (Fi).

M_2F H
33010 NORTREFF. No/No 1955; Trlr; 960; 65.9 × 4.9 (216 × 16.4); M; 14; Converted Whaler.

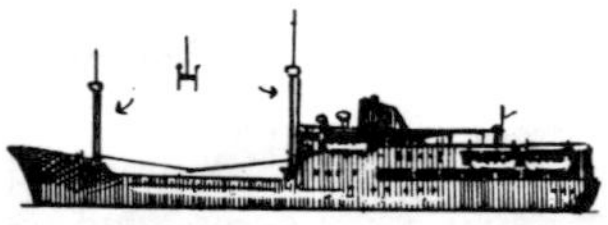

M_2F H1
33020 FERNANDO ESCANO. Pi/FRG 1968; CP; 1800; 89.4 × 4.1 (293 × 13.3); M; —; ex FERNANDO ESCANO II 1980.

M_2F H1
33030 MOIRA. Li/Br 1962; Con; 4700; 113.1 × 7.2 (371 × 23.1); M; 14; ex C.P. EXPLORER 1973; ex BEAVERPINE 1971; Converted cargo ship.

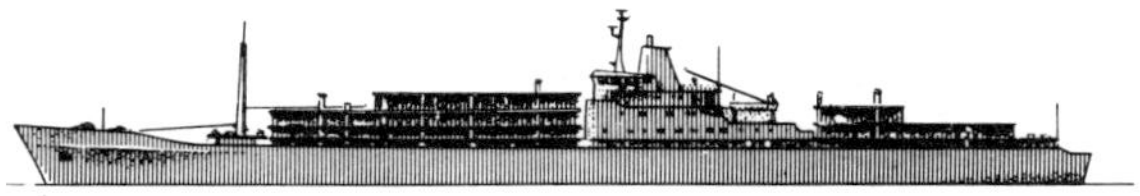

M_2F *H1*
33040 AL-KHALEEJ. Ku/Sw-Hong Kong 1965/75/78; LS; 7700/10100; 160 × — (524.9 × —); M; 19.5; ex WHITE OCEAN 1975; Converted from reefer 1975; Lengthened 1978.

M_2F *H1*
33050 CAP FALCONERA. It/De 1937; F; 2300; 100 × 4.9 (328 × 16.1); TSM; 19; ex EXPRESS FERRY ANGELINA LAURO; ex CORSICA EXPRESS 1975; ex KONPRINS OLAV 1967.

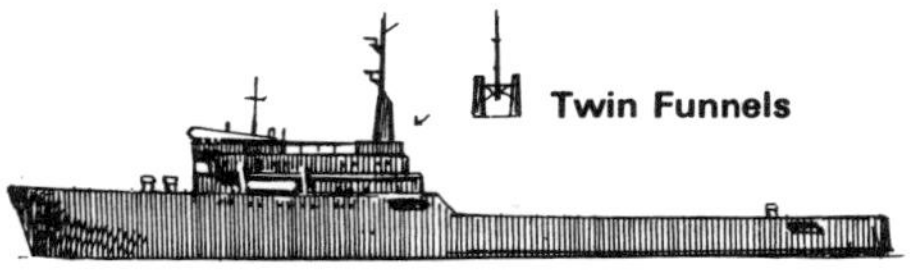

M_2F *H1*
33060 SYDNEY TRADER. Br/Au 1969; RoC; 6300; 136.7 × 6.4 (449 × 21.1); TSM; 17.5; Stern door. Sisters (Br flag): **33061 BRISBANE TRADER 33062 TOWNSVILLE TRADER.**

M_2F *H1*
33070 SALVISCOUNT. Sg/Br 1971; Tg; 2000; 80.7 × 7.4 (265 × 24.3); M; 18; ex LLOYDSMAN 1980.

M_2F *H1*
33080 HERMES. Gr/Ys 1956; P; 2600; 90.1 × 4.5 (296 × 15.3); TSM; 18; ex MESSAGER 1976; ex JUGOSLAVIJA 1971; This vessel has received modifications, including the filling in of the forward well & plating over part of the after superstructure.

M_2F *H1*
33090 CAMBRIDGE FERRY. Br/Br 1963; RoC/TF; 3300; 122.8 × 3.7 (440 × 12.2); TSM; 13.5.

●
33095

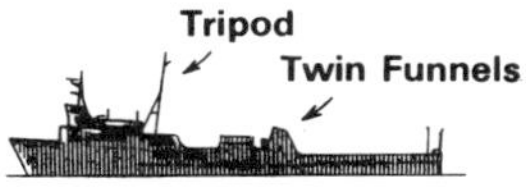

M_2F *H1*
33100 SATURN. Br/Br 1977; RoC/F; 900; 69.53 × 2.44 (228.12 × 8.01); TSM; 14; Stern ramp; Port and starboard side ramps.

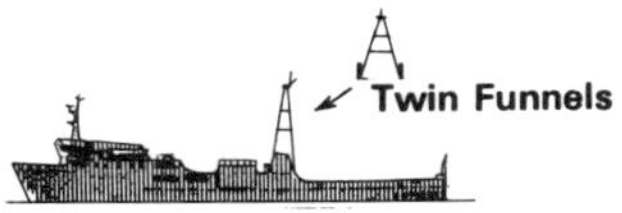

M_2F *H1*
33110 JUNO. Br/Br 1974; RoC/F; 900; 69.17 × 2.41 (226.94 × 7.91); TSM; 14; Stern door and side doors. Sister: **33111 JUPITER** (Br).

M_2F *H1*
33120 SAOS. Gr/De 1964; RoC/F; 700; 54.9 × 3 (180 × 9.1); TSM; 11; ex DROGDEN.

M_2F *H1*
33130 QUINTANA ROO. Me/No 1969; RoC/F; 550; 49.4 × 2.5 (162 × 8.3); TSM; 14; ex SOUND OF JURA 1976; Bow door and stern ramp.

M_2F *H1*
33140 ATLANTIS. Gr/Gr 1973; Y; 2600; 115.8 × 4.3 (380 × 14); TSM; 22.

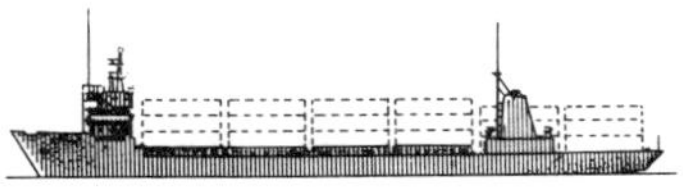

M_2F *H1*
33150 DESAFIO. Sp/Sp 1979; Con; 2000; 103.45 × 6.43 (339.4 × 21.1); M; 15.

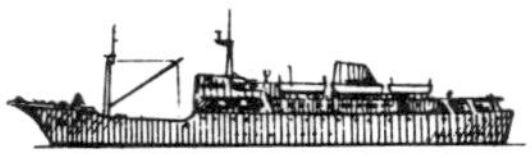

M_2F *H12*
33160 GRANUAILE. Ih/Br 1970; BT/LT 2000; 80.7 × 4 (265 × 13.1); TSM; 13.5.

M_2F H12
33170 OLOHAVA. To/Br 1965; F; 500; 47.8 × 2.9 (157 × 9.6); TSM; 13; ex QUEEN OF THE ISLES 1971.

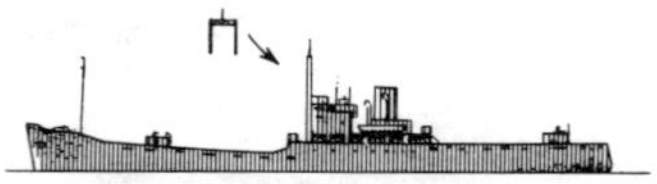

M_2F H12
33190 SOUTHERN GLORY. My/Au 1951; C/B; 2400; 93.07 × 5.34 (305.35 × 17.52); TSM; 10; ex SOUTHERN CROSS; ex LISA MILLER 1979; ex KAROON 1968.

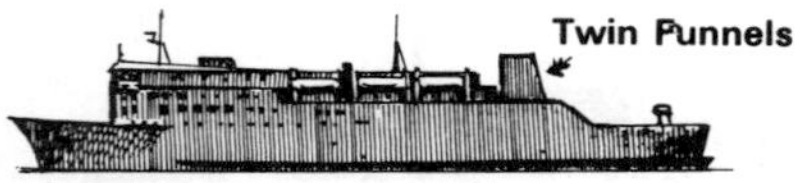

M_2F H2
33210 CORNUAILLES. Fr/No 1977; RoF; 3000; 109.7 × — (360 × —); TSM; 19; Bow and stern doors.

M_2F H2
33220 BREIZH-IZEL. Fr/Hong Kong 1970; RoC; 2700; 111.66 × 4.97 (366.34 × 16.31); TSM; 17.5; ex INICHIOS EXPRESS 1980; ex RATA HILLS 1978; ex WANAKA 1976; Stern door. INIKIOS EXPRESS No 2 (See under MMFC) may now be similar.

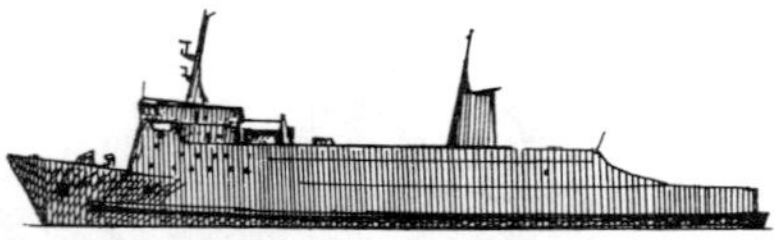

M_2F H2
33250 SVEALAND. Sw/De 1971; RoF; 4000; 118 × 5 (387 × 16.9); TSM; 18.5; Stern and side doors.

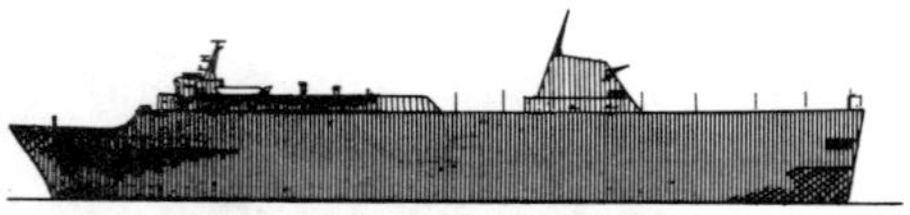

M_2F H2
33270 DORA BALTEA. It/It 1975; RoC; 3500; 135.52 × 6 (444.62 × 19.67); TSM; 18.5; Stern door/ramp. Side doors/ramps. Similar (Larger): **33271 DORA RIPARIA** (It).

M_2F H12
33180 ATALANTE. Gr/Fr 1953; P; 13100; 167.3 × 7.9 (549 × 25.9); TSM; 17; ex TAHITIEN 1972.

M_2F H2
33200 FULDATAL. FRG/FRG 1971; RoC; 1600; 114.9 × 5.7 (377 × 18.1); TSM; 17; ex NORCOVE 1975; ex FALCON 1972; ex FULDATAL. Sisters: **33201 TRAVETAL** (Sg) **33202 WESERTAL** (FRG) ex MEYER EXPRESS 1973; ex WESERTAL 1972 Similar: **33203 WUPPERTAL** (FRG) ex CANAIMA 1977.

M_2F H2
33230 HALLEY. Pa/Au 1961; RoC; 1700; 98.3 × 4.6 (323 × 15.1); TSM; 14.5; ex BASS TRADER 1975; Stern door.

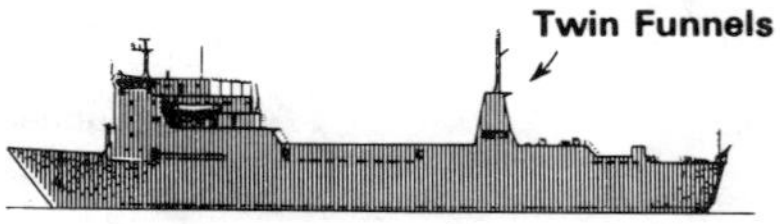

M_2F H2
33240 DR. ADNAN BIREN. Tu/No 1979; RoC; 2400; 113.4 × 5.51 (372 × 18.08); M; 15; Stern door/ramp. Sister: **33241 TRANSDENIZ** (Tu).

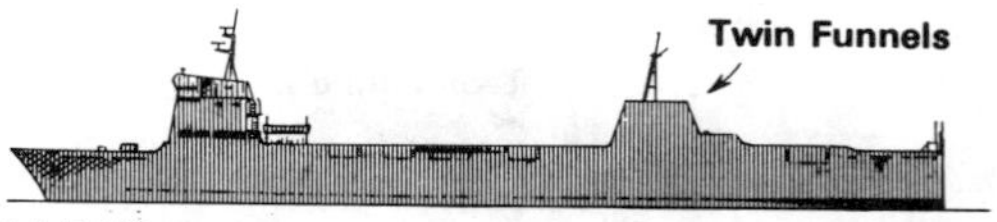

M_2F H2
33260 CICERO. Br/Br 1978; RoC; 5100; 147.12 × 6.88 (482.68 × 22.57); TSM; 18; Stern door/ramp. Sister: **33261 CAVALLO** (Ca).

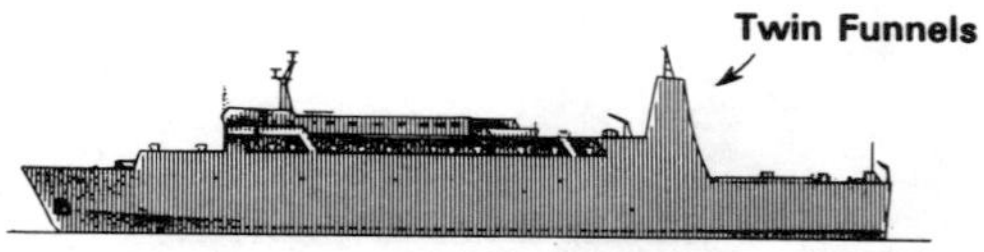

M_2F H2
33280 BALTIC EAGLE. Br/Fi 1979; RoC; 6400; 137.12 × 8.21 (449.87 × 26.94); TSM; 18. Two stern doors/ramps. Sister: ⋆**33281 INOWROCLAW** (Pd).

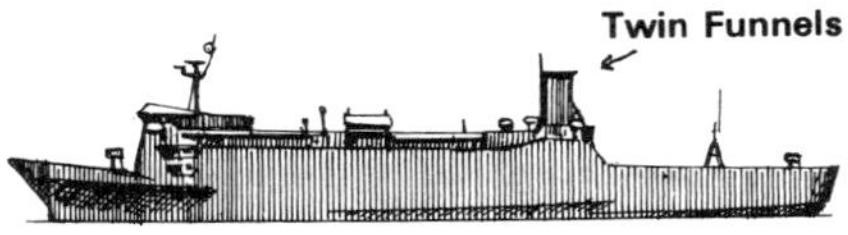

M_2F H2
● **33290 BRABANT.** FRG/FRG 1976; RoC; 3900; 127 × 5.4/6.6 (417 × 17.1/21.8); TSM; 19.5; ex ARGO 1977; Stern door.

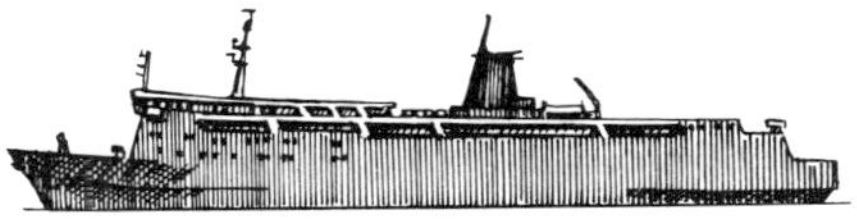

M_2F H2
33300 ARGO. Ja/Ja 1973; RoF; 7000; 132 × 5.5 (434 × 18.2); TSM; 19.5. Sister: **33301 ALNASL** (Ja).

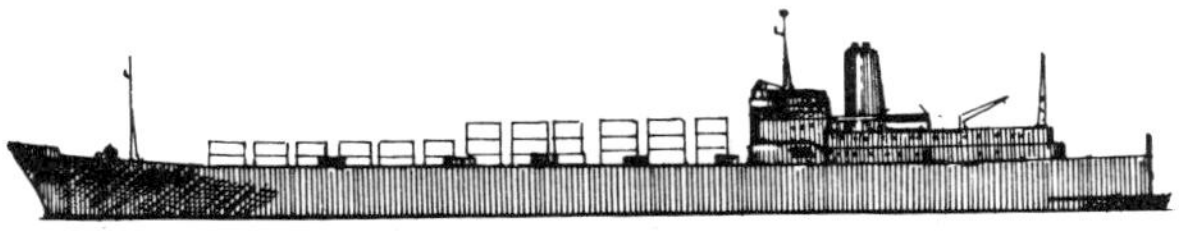

M_2FC H
33310 AUSTRALIAN ENTERPRISE. Au/Ja 1969; RoC; 9300; 181.8 × 9 (596 × 29.5); M; 21; Lengthened. Stern door. Sisters: **33311 AUSTRALIAN EXPLORER** (Au) ex MATTHEW FLINDERS 1975 Sister (Unlengthened): **33312 AUSTRALIAN SEAROADER** (Au) Similar: **33313 HYOGO MARU** (Ja).

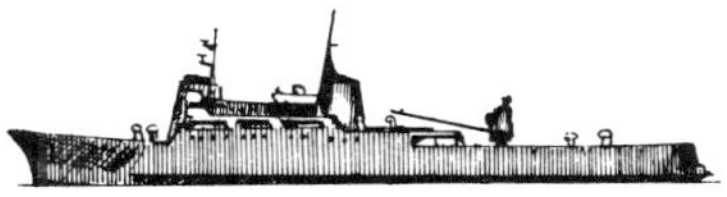

M_2FC H
33320 INIKIOS EXPRESS No 2. NZ/Hong Kong 1967; RoC; 2900; 111.7 × 5 (366 × 16.9); TSM; 16.5; ex COASTAL RANGER; Stern door. Crane may be removed. See BREIZH-IZEL under MMF.

M_2FC H
⋆**33330 FRITZ HECKERT.** DDR/DDR 1961; P; 7400; 141.3 × 5.5 (463 × 18.3); TSGT; 17.

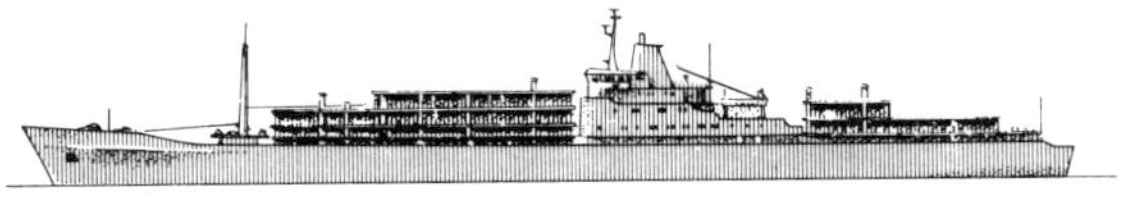

M_2FC H1
33340 AL-KHALEEJ. Ku/Sw-Hong Kong 1965/75/78; LS; 7700/10100; 160 × — (524.93 × —); M; 19.5; ex WHITE OCEAN 1975; Converted from reefer 1975. Lengthened 1978.

M_2FC H1
● **33350 GLEN SANNOX.** Br/Br 1957; RoF; 1100; 78.2 × 2.3 (257 × 9.1); TSM; 18; Stern door/ramp. Side doors.

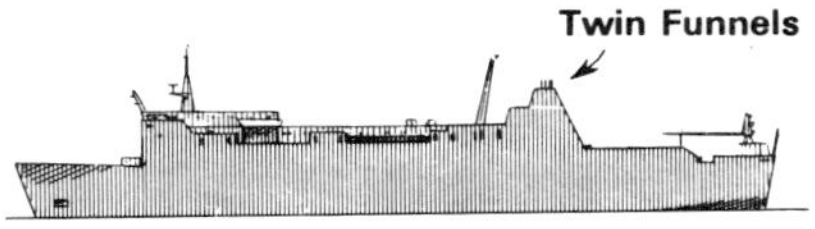

M_2FC H2
33360 LE MANS. Fr/Fr 1978; RoC; 4200; 120.33 × 5.9 (394.78 × 19.36); TSM; 16; Stern door/ramp. Side doors.

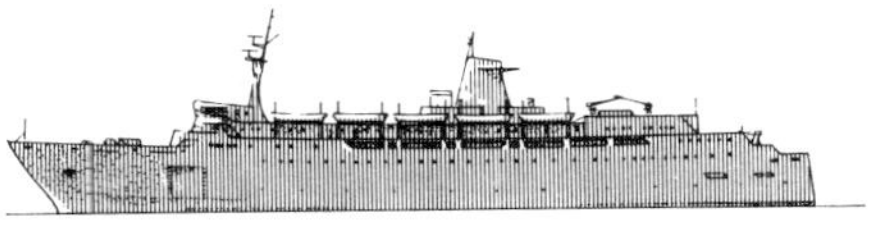

M_2FC_2 H
33370 DELEDDA. It/It 1978; RoPCF; 6500; 131.02 × 5.61 (429.86 × 18.41); TSM; 20.5; Stern and side doors. Sister: **33371 VERGA** (It).

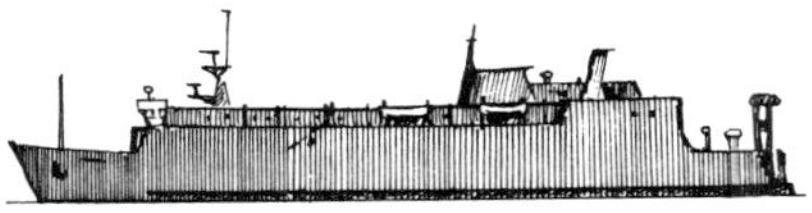

M_2F_2K H
⋆**33380 MIKOLAJ KOPERNIK.** Pd/No 1973; TF 2600; 126 × 4.6 (412 × 150; TSM; 16. Similar: ⋆**33381 JAN HEWELIUSZ** (Pd)

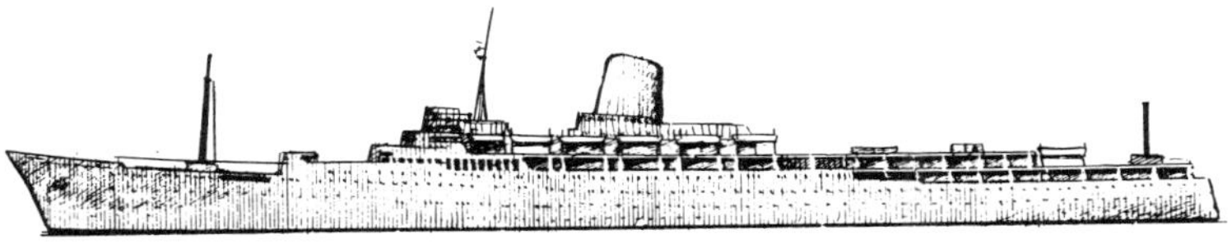

M_2FK H
33390 OCEAN QUEEN. Pa/Br 1958; P; 27100/28400; 232.7 × 9.7/9.8 (763 × 32.2/32.5); TST; 22.5; ex PENDENNIS CASTLE 1976.

M_2FK H

33400 CIUDAD DE BARCELONA. Sp/Sp 1955; PC; 5200; 106.4×5 (348×16.5); TSM; 17.5; ex PLAYA DE FORMENTOR 1956. Sister: **33401 CIUDAD DE BURGOS** (Sp) ex PLAYA DE PALMANOVA Similar: **33402 CIUDAD DE GRANADA** (Sp).

M_2FK H

● **33410 CIUDAD DE HUESCA.** Sp/Sp 1954; PC; 2000; 79.1×5.3 (259×17.5); M; —; ex HUESCA 1956.

M_2FK H

33420 TERAAKA. Br/Ys 1959; PC; 1000; 64.4×4 (211×13); M; 15; ex NINIKORIA; ex OPATIJA 1968. Sister: **33421 FRANCISCO DE MIRANDA** (Ve) ex OREBIC 1967.

M_2FK H

33430 KONG SVERRE. Ms/US 1943; F; 1300; 65.5×— (215×—); TSM; 15; ex STAVANGER 1973; ex KILCHATTAN.

M_2FK H

33440 KOKAN SEWAK. In/Ys 1964; C; 1900; 76.9×4.3 (252×14.2); TSM; 15. Sister: **33441 KONKAN SHAKTI** (In) ex SARITA 1977.

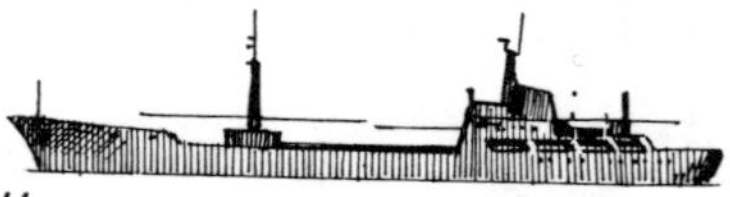

M_2FK H

● **33450 REMJAY.** Br/Fr 1966; R; 4300; 111.8×6.5 (367×21.4); M; 19.75; ex AEGEAN DESTINY 1980; ex MATUPI 1980; ex HARVEST GOLD; ex FRIGOMAR 1975; ex OYONNAX 1971.

M_2FK H

33460 CEBU CITY. Pi/Ja 1972; PC/F; 2500; 98.76×5.21; (324×17.09); M; 18.

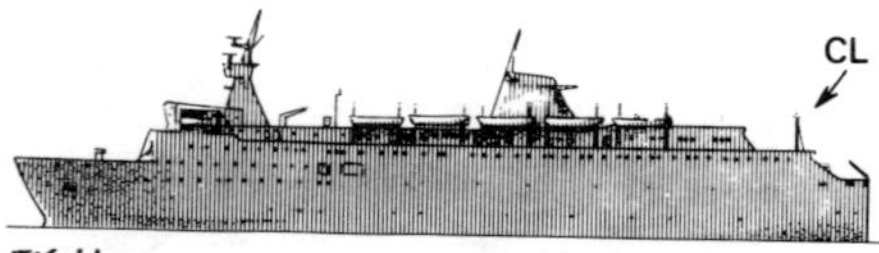

M_2FK H

33470 DOMIZIANA. It/It 1979; RoPCF; 10500; 136×5.9 (446.19×19.36); TSM; 20; Stern ramp. Side doors. Sisters (It flag): **33471 CLODIA 33472 NOMENTANA 33473 EMILIA 33474 AURELIA 33475 TIBURTINA** Possible sister: **33476 FLAMINIA.**

M_2FK H

33490 PIERRE VIDAL. Fr/Fr 1966; ST; 1200; 77×— (253×—); M; 14.5. Similar: **33491 JOSEPH DUHAMEL** (Fr) **33492 GRAND PECHE.**

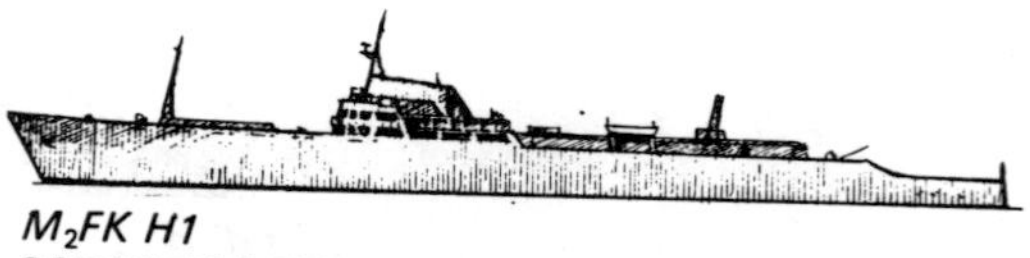

M_2FK H1

33500 ALASKA. Li/Ja 1959; RoC/TF; 5600; 157.9×5.6 (518×18.4); TST; 16.5; ex CITY OF NEW ORLEANS 1964; Bow door.

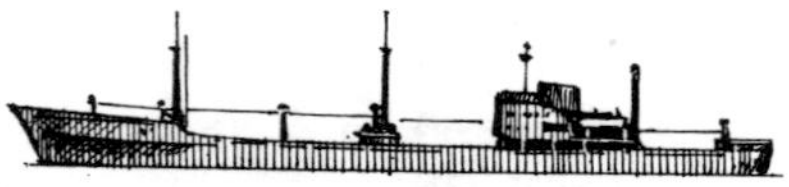

M_2FK H1

33510 REEFER CITY. Sg/FRG 1962; R; 3500; 118.9×6.6 (390×21.9); M; 15.5; ex BALTIC SUN 1973.

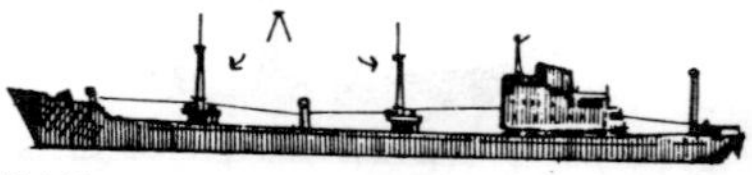

M_2FK H1

● **33520 TEVEGA.** Cy/Sw 1961; C; 4500; 115.1×7.5 (378×24.5); M; 15; ex NORDIA 1974; ex NORDIC.

M_2FK H12
33530 PONTA GARCIA. Po/Po 1960; CP; 1800; 97.4 × 5.2 (320 × 17.2); M; 12.

M_2FK H12
● **33540 KOSTER.** No/Ge 1929; F; 1000; 58.6 × — (192 × —); M; 13; ex KRONPRINSESSE MARTHA 1974; ex RYFYLKE 1945; ex KRONPRINSESSE MARTHA; re-engined and lengthened 1958.

M_2FK H12
33550 CARL KAMPF. FRG/FRG 1957; ST; 680; 58.8 × — (193 × —); M; 14.

M_2FK H12
33560 CARL WIEDERKEHR. FRG/FRG 1959; FT; 700; 67.3 × 4.3 (221 × 14); M; 14.

M_2FK H12
33570 BREMERHAVEN. FRG/FRG 1961; FT; 940; 73.8 × — (242 × —); M; 15.

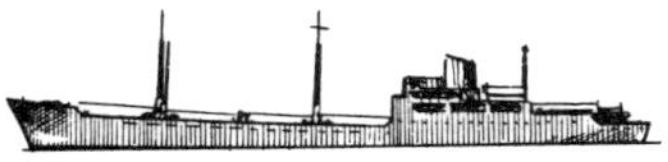

M_2FK H13
⋆**33580 SARAJEVO.** Ys/Ys 1949; C; 3100; 101.9 × 6.6 (334 × 21.8); M; 14.5. Sisters (Ys flag): ⋆**33581 SKOPJE** ⋆**33582 TITOGRAD** ⋆**33583 ZAGREB.**

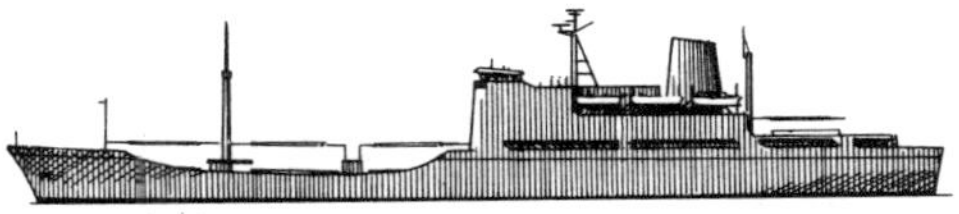

M_2FK H13
⋆**33590 JOSE MARTI.** Cu/De 1977; C/TS; 10000; 149.1 × 9 (489 × 30); M; 16.5. Sister: **33591 IBN KHALDOON** (Iq).

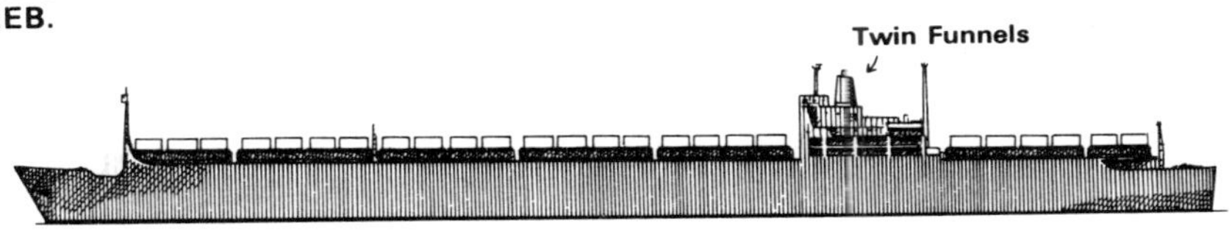

M_2FK H2
33600 KAMAKURA MARU. Ja/Ja 1971; Con; 51100; 261 × 12 (856 × 39.1); M; —; To be lengthened. Sisters (Ja flag): **33601 KITANO MARU 33602 KURAMA MARU 33603 RHINE MARU.**

M_2FK_2 H
33610 KOKAN SEWAK. In/Ys 1964; C; 1900; 76.9 × 4.3 (252 × 14.2); TSM; 15. Sister: **33611 KONKAN SHAKTI** (In) ex SARITA 1977.

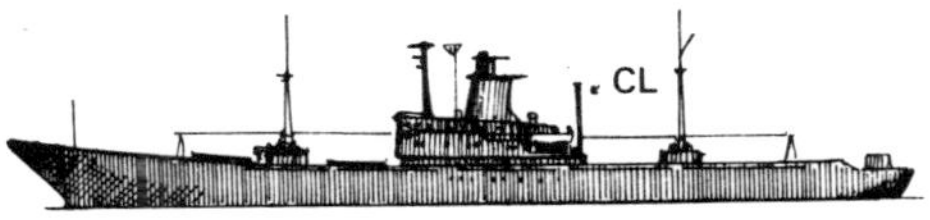

M_2FKM H
⋆**33620 EYSKIY LIMAN.** Ru/FRG 1968; R; 3400; 139 × 6.5/7.6 (456 × 21/25.2); M; 22.75; ex SLOMAN ALSTERPARK 1975. Sister: ⋆**33621 AKHTARSKIY LIMAN** (Ru) ex SLOMAN ALSTERTOR.

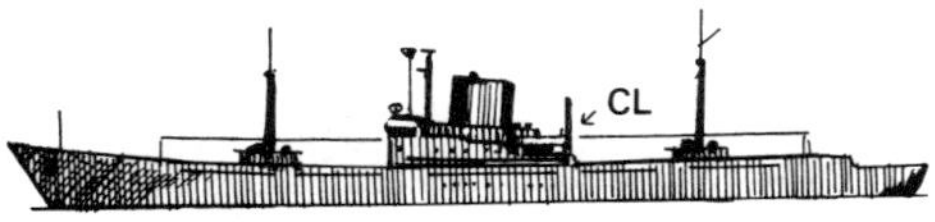

M_2FKM H
33630 UNITED REEFER. Pa/FRG 1966; R; 3400/4900; 139 × 6.4/7.6 (456 × 21.1/24.1); M; 22; ex PEKARI. Sisters (Pa flag): **33631 GRAND UNITED** ex PERSIMMON **33632 GRAND UNION** ex PICA **33633 GRAND FAIR** ex PIROL.

M_2FKM H
33640 ICE PILOT. Gr/FRG 1964; R; 3800/5300; 141.8 × 6.3/7.3 (465 × 20.6/23.1); M; 21; ex FROSTFJORD ex PISANG 1971. Sisters (Gr flag): **33641 ICE MERCHANT** ex SNEFJORD; ex PUNA 1972 **33642 SYROS** ex PONGAL 1974.

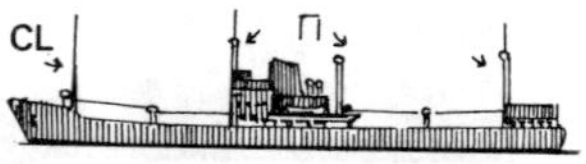

M_2FKM H1
33670 DAGUS. Pa/Ne 1953; C; 1500; 89.9 × 5.2 (295 × 17); M; 14; ex CHRISTOS 1980; ex IRENE STAR 1977; ex CAP KRIOS 1970; ex CAP BLANC 1969.

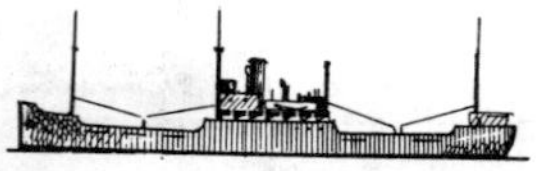

M_2FKM H123
⋆**33690 ZHAN DOU 16.** RC/US 1945; C; 1900; 78.9 × 5.5 (259 × 18); R; 11; ex HOPING 16.

M_2FKM H123
⋆**33710 NAN HAI 175.** RC/US 1944; C; 1900; 78.9 × 5.5 (259 × 18); R; 10.5; ex LIN SHEN 1958; ex HAI LIEN 1946; ex E.C. GARDNER 1946. Sister: ⋆**33711 BAHIA SANTIAGO DE CUBA** (Cu) ex PEBANE 1956; ex PHINAS WINSOR 1948.

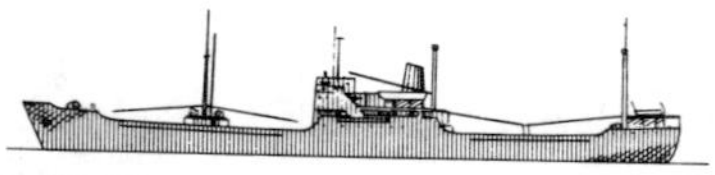

M_2FKM H123
33740 SANTO ANDRE. Bz/Pd 1958; C; 3600; 108.26 × 6.65 (355.18 × 21.82); M; —; **'B-31'** type. Sister: **33741 SANTO AMARO** (Bz).

M_2FKM H
33650 MED FREEZER. Gr/Be 1961; R; 6100; 139.2 × 7.2 (457 × 23.7); M; —; ex ORPHEUS. Sister: **33651 BALTIC FREEZER** (Gr) ex ONDINE.

M_2FKM H1
⋆**33660 WUXI.** RC/Ys 1958; C; 9300; 149.3 × 8.9 (490 × 29.2); M; 15; ex MIR 1967; ex POLET.

M_2FKM H123
⋆**33680 CHE HAI No 1.** RC/RC 1960; C; 2400; 93.3 × 5.8 (306 × 19); R; 10. Sister: ⋆**33681 CHE HAI No 2** (RC).

M_2FKM H123
⋆**33700 ZHAN DOU 14.** RC/US 1943; C; 1900; 78.9 × 5.5 (259 × 18); R; 11; ex HOPING 14.

M_2FKM H123
33720 HAI RYONG. Ko/Ja 1949; C; 2700; 96.6 × 6.3 (317 × 20.1); M; 10.5; ex TAI JIN MARU 1966.

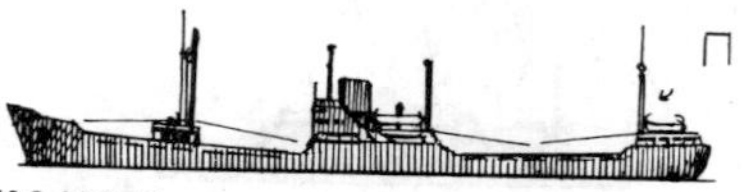

M_2FKM H123
33730 LATAKIA. Eg/Pd 1958; C; 3800; 108.3 × 6.7 (356 × 21.7); M; —; **'B-31'** type. Sister: **33731 YEMEN** (Eg).

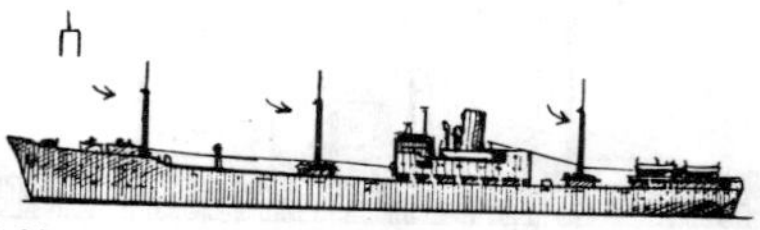

M_2FM H
⋆**33750 ANTARKTIKA.** Ru/No 1948; C; 6500; 117.4 × 6.7 (384 × 22.2); R; 11; ex MANNY 1954.

M_2FM H
33760 ALGAZAYER. Eg/FRG 1962; PC; 4400; 108 × 4.4 (354 × 14.7); M; 15.5. Sister: **33761 SYRIA** (Eg).

M_2FM H
33770 AKLAN. Pi/Ja 1955; P; 1100; 68.9 × 3.9 (226 × 13); M; 14; ex TAKACHIMO MARU.

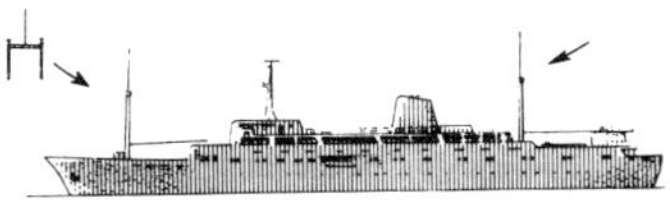

M_2FM H
● **33780 DONA ANA.** Pi/Ja 1966; PC; 3000; 97.6 × 4.5 (320 × 15); M; 19.5; ex OTOHIME MARU 1976.

M_2FM H
33790 DONA FLORENTINA. Pi/Ja 1965; PCF; 2100; 95.7 × 5.2 (313 × 16.11); M; 17.5.

M_2FM H
33800 TACLOBAN CITY. Pi/Ja 1962; C; 2000; 91 × 4.5 (299 × 14.6); M; 18.5; ex NAMINOUE MARU 1976.

M_2FM H
● **33810 DAVAO.** Br/FRG 1964; R; 3400/4900; 137.6 × 6.4/7.8 (451 × 20.11/25.9); M; 20; ex POLARLIGHT 1974. Similar: **33811 DARIEN** (Br) ex POLARSTEIN 1974.

M_2FM H
33820 ELSFLETH. Gr/Fr 1962; C; 4600; 139.1 × 7.2 (457 × 23.7); M; 18. Similar: **33821 MINDEN** (Gr) **33822 NIENBURG** (Gr).

M_2FM H
33830 ATLANTIS. Gr/No 1960; R; 5800; 133.3 × 7.2 (437 × 23.5); ex HIDLEFJORD. Sister: **33831 DEBRAEVERETT** (Li) ex BYFJORD 1976.

M_2FM H
33840 FRUCO. Pa/Fr 1956; R; 5000; 114.9 × 6.5 (377 × 21.5); M; 16.5; ex CUZCO 1973; ex FORT CAROLINE 1969. Sisters (Pa flag): **33841 LORD DE FRANCE** ex FORT DE FRANCE 1973 **33842 LORD CREVECOEUR** ex FORT CREVECOEUR 1973 **33843 LORD FLEUR D'EPEE** ex FORT FLEUR D'EPEE 1973 **33844 LORD D'ORLEANS** ex FORT D'ORLEANS 1973 **33845 LORD NIAGARA** ex FORT NIAGARA 1973 **33846 HONEST SPRING** ex HAROKAZE 1976; ex TA SHUN 1973; ex ICA 1972; ex FORT ROYAL 1969.

M_2FM H
33850 BRUNSKAMP. FRG/FRG 1965; R; 3400/4700; 136 × 6.2/6.6 (446 × 20.4/24.6); M; 21; ex BLEXEN 1975; ex AUGUSTENBURG 1972.

M_2FM H
33860 MARE ANTARTICO. It/It 1966; R; 7000; 142.4 × 7.5 (466 × 24.7); M; 20. Sisters (It flag): **33861 MARE ARTICO 33862 MARE AUSTRALE 33863 MARE BOREALE**

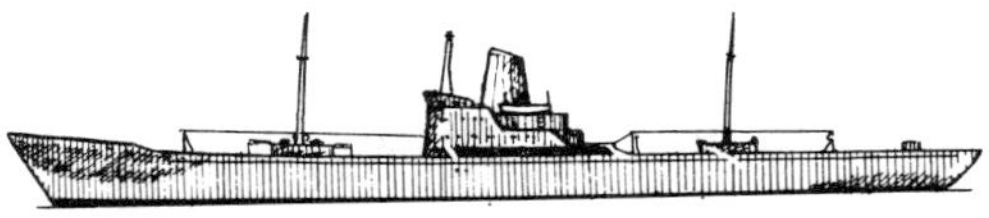

M_2FM H
⋆**33870 FERDINAND FREILIGRATH.** DDR/Br 1967; R; 5600; 152.7 × 7.6 (501 × 25); M; 22; ex PARMA II 1974; ex PARMA 1973. Sister: ⋆**33871 GEORG WEERTH** (DDR); ex PADUA 1974.

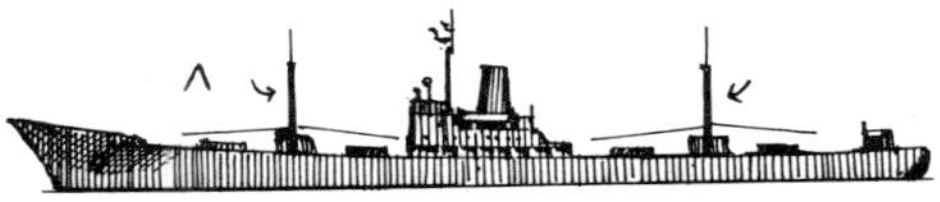

M_2FM H
33880 DAVAO. Li/Ja 1964; R; 5000; 142.1 × 7.3 (466 × 23.22); M; 20; ex ECUADOR MARU 1964. Sister: **33881 MINDANAO** (Li) ex CAPTAIN COOK; ex COSTA RICA MARU 1975.

M_2FM H
33890 APPLE BLOSSOM. Li/Ja 1969; R; 7000; 141 × 8.1 (463 × 27); M; —; ex BANAGRANDE 1977.

M_2FM H
⋆**33910 KOTOVSKIY.** Ru/It 1968; R; 4100; 121.7 × 7.5 (401 × 24); M; 18. Sisters (Ru flag): ⋆**33911 NIKOLAY SHCHORS** ⋆**33912 PARKHOMENKO** ⋆**33913 SERGEI LAZO** ⋆**33914 CHAPAEV.**

M_2FM H
● **33930 CORINTHIAN REEFER;** Gr/No 1968; R; 4200; 128 × 7.8 (420 × 26.6); M; 19; ex VIKFREEZER. Sister: **33931 AUDACIA** (Ur) ex PARA; ex VIKFROST 1977.

M_2FM H
33940 BRUNSRODE; FRG/FRG 1968; R; 3300; 135.9 × 6.5 (446 × 21.6); M; 22. Sister: **33941 BRUNSWICK** (FRG).

M_2FM H
33960 KARUKERA; Fr/Fr 1963; R; 5400; 120.7 × 7.2 (396 × 23.6); M; 18.25.

M_2FM H
33970 FLAMINGO; Gr/Sp 1963; R; 4700; 137.3 × — (450.6 × —); M; 18; ex ASSOUBA 1980; ex HAR BASHAN 1973; ex ATLANTIC ARROW 1967; ex NORTHPOLE 1966. Sisters: **33971 ELINA** (Gr) ex AZAGUIE 1980; ex HAR BOKER 1973; ex PACIFIC ARROW 1967; ex SOUTH POLE 1966 **33972 ARCTIC MARINER** (Gr) ex AL MANSOUR; ex ARTICO 1973.

M_2FM H
33900 LIMON. Li/No 1968; R; 6700; 139.4 × 7.9 (457 × 26); M; 22.5; ex GOLAR FREEZE 1976. Sister (Used as a fish carrier): ⋆**33901 BRESTSKAYA KREPOST** (Ru) ex GOLAR NEL 1975.

M_2FM H
33920 ORPHEUS. Li/FRG 1966; R; 5500; 148 × 8 (486 × 26); M; 23; ex AHRENSBURG. Sister: **33921 ANGELBURG** (FRG) Similar: **33922 ALDENBURG** (FRG) **33923 ARTLENBURG** (FRG) **33924 ODYSSEUS** (Li) ex ASSEBURG.

M_2FM H
● **33950 ISLA VERDE;** Li/Ne 1964; R; 4300; 148.8 × 8.8 (488 × 28.11); M; 21; ex NORTH STAR 1975; ex GEESTBAY 1973. Sisters: **33951 KIMOLOS** (Gr) ex GEESTPORT 1973 **33952 DOHA** (Qt) ex GEESTHAVEN 1975 **33953 NYOMBE** (Pi) ex GEESTCAPE 1975.

M_2FM H
⋆**33980 POLYUS;** Ru/DDR 1962; RS; 3900; 112 × 6 (368 × 20); D-E; 13.5.

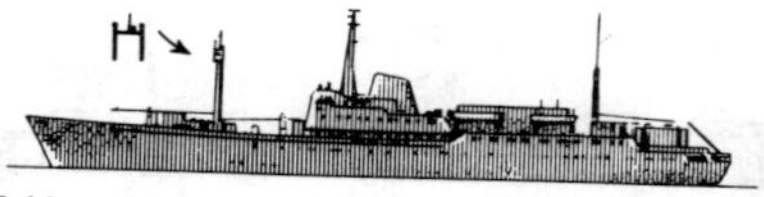

M_2FM H
⋆**33990 BAYKAL;** Ru/DDR 1964; RS; 3900; 111.56 × 6 (366 × 19.69); D-E; 13.5. Sister: ⋆**33991 BALKHASH** (Ru).

M_2FM H
34000 SOYA; Ja/Ja —; RS; 4400 Dspl; 79.3×5.6 (260×18.9); M; 12.

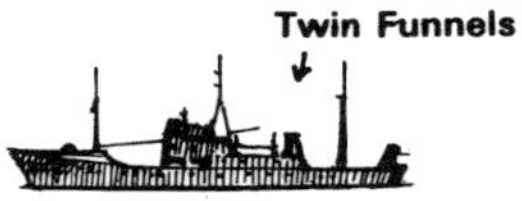

M_2FM H
34010 LONGVA; No/No 1962; RS; 800; 63×4.9 (206×16); M; 13.

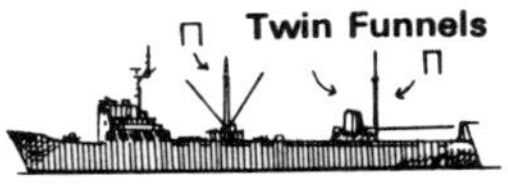

M_2FM H
34020 TAIYO MARU No 68; Ja/Ja 1961; ST; 1500; 75.5×5.5 (248×18); M; 14.25. Sisters (Ja flag): **34021 TAIYO MARU No 67 34022 TAIYO MARU No 71 34023 TAIYO MARU No 72 34024 TAIYO MARU NO 73.**

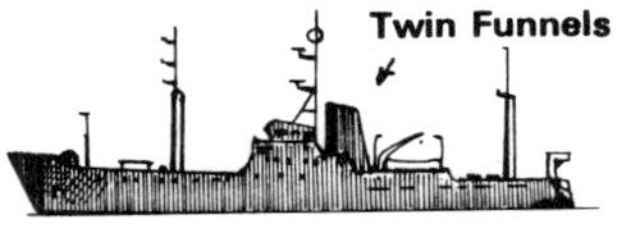

M_2FM H
34030 HARENGUS; FRG/FRG 1972; ST; 1700; 81×5.3 (263×17.6); M; 16.

M_2FM H
34040 MARIA PAOLINA G; It/It 1956; RS: 1900; 78.21×4.47 (257×14.9); M; 13; ex NOLI 1962; ex CAPO FARO 1961.

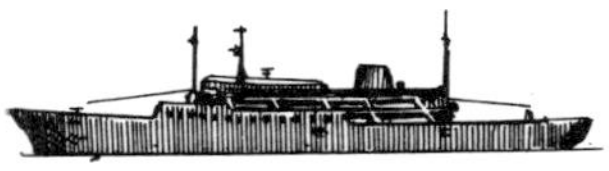

M_2FM H
34050 HIBISCUS; Ja/Ja 1971; RoPCF; 6000; 118×5.7 (388×19); TM; 19.

M_2FM H
34060 FRITHJOF; FRG/FRG 1968; RS; 1600; 76×5.2 (250×17); D-E; 16.

M_2FM H
34070 CUMULUS; Ne/Ne 1963; RS/WS; 2000; 71.1×4.6 (233×15.1); M; 12.75.

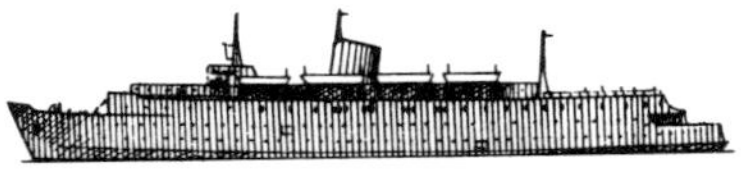

M_2FM H
● **34080 ARIANE II;** Pa/Br 1950; P; 3500; 114.9×4.6 (377×15); TST; 17.

M_2FM H
34090 EL DJAZAIR; Ag/Ja 1972; RoPCF; 12100; 130.38×5.62 (427.76×18.44); TSM; 19.5; ex CENTRAL No 3 1973; Bow door. Side door. Stern door.

M_2FM H1
⋆**34100 AMGUEMA;** Ru/Ru 1962; C; 8100; 133×8.9 (437×29); D-E; 15. Sisters (Ships vary slightly - Ru flag): ⋆**34101 GIZHIGA** ⋆**34102 KAPITAN BONDARENKO** ⋆**34103 KAPITAN MARKOV** ⋆**34104 KAPITAN GOTSKIY** ⋆**34105 KAPITAN KONDRATYEV** ⋆**34106 KAPITAN MYSHEVSKIY** ⋆**34107 NAVARIN** ⋆**34108 PENZHINA** ⋆**34109 VANKAREM** ⋆**34110 VASILIY FEDOSEYEV** ⋆**34111 PAVEL PONOMARYEV.**

M_2FM H1
34120 KERASOUS; Gr/Ys 1959; C; 6000/8000; 152.3×8.2/9.3 (500×26.9/29.1); M; 14; ex LAVAUX 1971. Sisters: **34121 MACHITIS** (Gr) **34122 KAPITAN KAMARI** (Pa) ex HOPEWELL 1980; ex MASTER DASKALOS 1979.

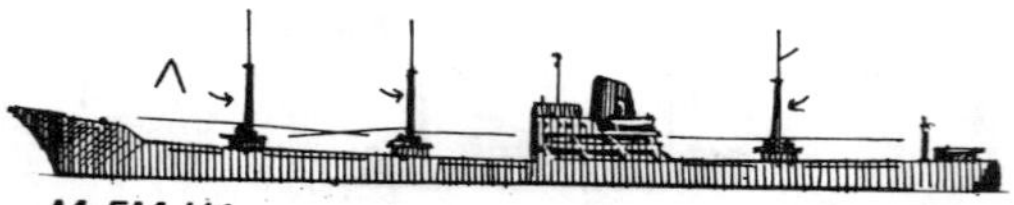

M_2FM *H1*
34130 ANAMARIA; Gr/Ys 1958; C; 9000; 152.5 × 9.2 (500 × 29.7); M; 14; ex ANGELIKI L 1972; ex CAPTAIN M LYRAS 1964. Sister: **34131 ARCAMARE** (Gr) ex EFPLOIA 1973.

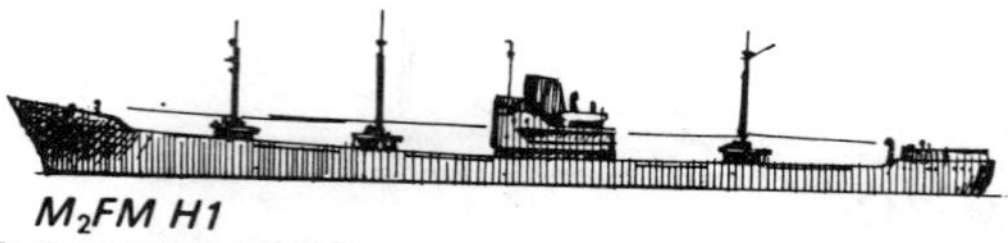

M_2FM *H1*
● **34140 GREENVILLE;** Li/Ne 1960; C; 6900/9500; 155.1 × 8.3/9.1 (509 × 27.6/30); M; 13; ex AMSTELHOEK 1973. Sisters: **34141 HARLANDSVILLE** (Li) ex HOLLANDS DUIN 1973 **34142 PAMPA ARGENTINA** (Ar) ex HOLLANDS DIEP 1970 **34143 PATAGONIA ARGENTINA** (Ar) ex HOLLANDS DREEF 1972.

M_2FM *H1*
⋆**34150 BOKA;** Ys/Ys 1958; C; 6300/8900; 146.11 × 7.9/8.5 (482 × 26/28); M; 13. Sisters (Ys flag): ⋆**34151 LIKA** ⋆**34152 PETKA** ⋆**34153 SLAVONIJA** ⋆**34154 TRECI MAJ** ⋆**34155 TREPCA ULJANIK** Similar: **34156 AZIM** (Pa) ex ENDI; ex SPLENDID SUN **34157 COMELUCK GLORY** (Tw); ex ASSOCIATED GLORY 1977; AMARILIS 1974.

M_2FM *H1*
34160 TONG HOE; Sg/Ne 1952; C; 6500; 146 × 8.3 (479 × 26.7); M; 14; ex TARA 1971.

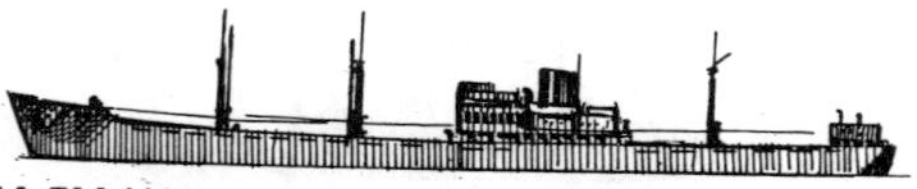

M_2FM *H1*
34170 EVANDROS; Gr/Ne 1947; C; 5300; 137.5 × 7.5 (451 × 24.6); M; 13; ex VASILIS 1974; ex TAMPO 1963.

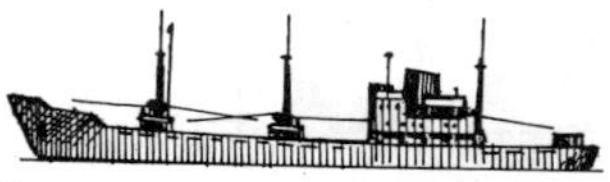

M_2FM *H1*
34180 MALDIVE TRUST; Mv/Br 1960; C; 2500; 100.1 × 5.9 (330 × 19.4); M; 13.5; ex AARO 1972.

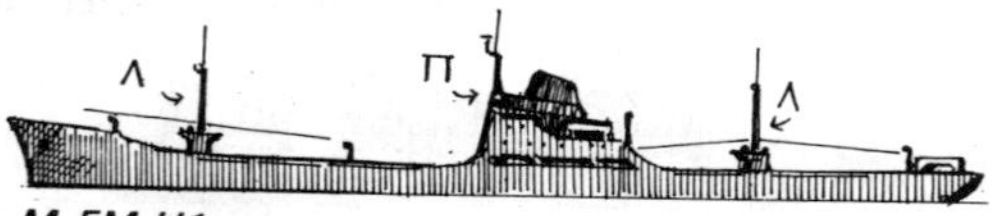

M_2FM *H1*
34190 PATRAI; Li/Fr 1961; C/O; 10400; 152 × 9.2 (499 × 30.2); M; 14; ex CALYMENE 1973. Sister: **34191 PATRIS** (Gr) ex ILE SAINT LOUIS 1972; ex HALONIA 1968.

M_2FM *H1*
● **34200 BONITA;** Ec/No 1970; R; 4900/6700; 140.7 × 8.3/9 (462 × 27/30); M; 22.5; ex BERING 1975; ex BERINGCORE 1975; **'DRAMMEN'** type. Sisters: **34201 ALASKA I** (FRG) ex ALASKA: ex ALASKACORE 1975; ex SLEVIK 1969 **34202 ANTARCTIC** (FRG) ex ANTARCTICORE 1975 **34203 SMARA** (Mo) ex CAYMAN 1976; ex GREENLAND 1975 **34204 FRIGOANTARTICO** (Po) **34205 FRIGOARTICO** (Po) **34206 NORDLAND V** (Pa) ex NORDLAND 1980 **34207 ICELAND** (FRG) **34208 CHIOS PRIDE** (Gr) ex TUSCAN STAR; ex LABRADOR CLIPPER 1975 **34209 ANDANIA** (Br) ex GLASGOW CLIPPER 1976 **34210 BOLIVAR** (Li) ex GOLAR FROST 1976 **34211 HILCO GIRL** (No) ex GOLAR GIRL **34212 SIERRA NEVADA** (Ve) ex RAGNI-BERG 1977; ex GOLAR RAGNI 1976; ex KONGSFJELL **34213 WILD FULMAR** (Br) **34214 KING EGBERT** (Br) ex LIVERPOOL CLIPPER 1976 ⋆**34215 ERNST MORITZ ARNDT** (DDR) ex KING EDMUND; ex BRISTOL CLIPPER 1976 **34216 ALAUNIA** (Br) ex CARDIFF CLIPPER 1977 **34217 IFNI** (Mo) **34218 IMILCHIL** (Mo) **34219 IMOUZZER** (Mo) ⋆**34220 THEODOR KORNER** (DDR) **34221 SALINAS** (Br) ex LONDON CLIPPER 1976 **34222 ALSATIA** (Br) ex EDINBURGH CLIPPER 1977 **34223 ANDRIA** (Br) ex TEESIDE CLIPPER 1977 **34224 SIJILMASSA** (Mo) ex KUNGSHAMN; ex LAPLAND 1976 **34225 CHIOS CLIPPER** (Gr) ex TROJAN STAR 1980; ex NEWCASTLE CLIPPER 1976.

M_2FM H1
⋆**34240 ILYA METCHNIKOV**; Ru/Fr 1956; C; 4100/5600; 129.7 × 6.8/7.5 (426 × 22.5/24.8); T; 14. Sisters (Ru flag): ⋆**34241 IVAN PAVLOV** ⋆**34242 IVAN SECHENOV** ⋆**34243 NIKOLAY BURDYENKO** ⋆**34244 NIKOLAY PIROGOV** ⋆**34245 SERGEY BOTKIN.**

M_2FM H1
34270 GOLDEN LIGHT. Gr/FRG 1959; R; 3000; 125.84 × 6.4 (412.86 × 21); M; 18; ex EL PUNTAL 1977; ex ASSEBURG 1968.

M_2FM H1
⋆**34290 SHKVAL**. Ru/Sw 1963; R; 4200; 126.4 × 7.3 (415 × 24); M; 17; ex BAKKE REEFER 1975.

M_2FM H1
34310 HEBE. Fr/Fr 1960; R/WT; 5200; 118.2 × 7.1 (388 × 23.6); M; 19.

M_2FM H1
⋆**34330 JOHN BRINCKMAN**. DDR/Sw 1964; R; 4600/6300; 138.8 × —/7.9 (455 × —/25.11); M; 19; ex BELNIPPON 1973. Sister: ⋆**34331 FRITZ REUTER** (DDR) ex PACIFIC EXPRESS 1973.

M_2FM H1
● **34350 INDIA ROSEWOOD**. Pa/Ja 1958; C; 3300; 113.9 × 6.7 (374 × 22.3); M; 12; ex THE SUNFLOWER 1975; ex OCEAN MERCURY 1972; ex TOKUWA MARU 1970.

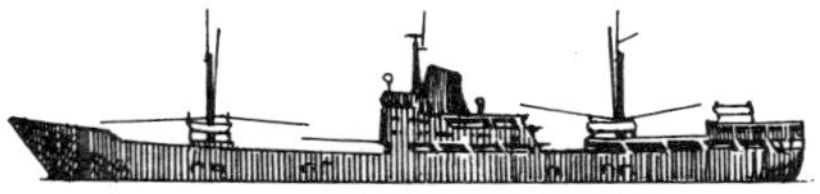

M_2FM H1
34250 FILIPINAS. Pi/FRG 1968; C; 5000; 121 × 7.7 (397 × 25.3); M; —.

M_2FM H1
● ⋆**34260 FRANO SUPILO**. Ys/Ys 1961; C; 2000/3100; 106.2 × —/5.9 (348 × —/19.6); M; 14. Sisters (Ys flag): ⋆**34261 MATKO LAGINJA** ⋆**34262 IVAN MAZURANIC** ⋆**34263 OMIS**.

M_2FM H1
● **34280 MINDANAO**. Pi/FRG 1959; R; 3400; 134.58 × 6.11 (442 × 20.1); M; 18; ex HORNKOOG 1970.

M_2FM H1
34300 PONTOS. Be/Be 1969; R; 3900/5800; 149.2 × 6.2/7.8 (489 × 20.7/25.8); M; 22. Sister: **34301 POMONA**.

M_2FM H1
34320 GEMA. Pa/Ne 1959; R; 2700/3800; 114.97 × 6.12/6.82 (377 × 20.2/22.38); M; 17; ex SALTA 1977; ex BRUNSTAL 1970; ex BALEARES 1966.

M_2FM H1
34340 AMANDAEVERETT. Li/Sw 1963; R; 4800; 131.1 × 7.4 (430 × 24.2); M; 18; ex BAKKE COOLER 1976.

M_2FM H1
⋆**34360 SOPOT**. Pd/De 1966; C; 2000/3000; 99.6 × 5.7/6.3 (327 × 19/22.3); M; 14.25. Sisters (Pd flag): ⋆**34361 SANDOMIERZ** ⋆**34362 SANOK** ⋆**34363 SLUPSK**.

M_2FM *H1*

● ***34370 DEBLIN.** Pd/Pd 1961; C; 1300; 86.4 × 4.6 (284 × 15.2); M; 14.5; **'B-513'** type. Sisters: ***34371 KOSZALIN *34372 WOLIN 34373 ODLI** (Pa) ex MODLIN 1980.

M_2FM *H1*

34380 HAYASHIO MARU. Ja/Ja 1960; Sal; 1200; 66.8 × 4.5 (219 × 14.9); M; 13.5.

M_2FM *H1*

34390 KOYO MARU. Ja/Ja 1967; Sal/Tg; 2100; 85.5 × 6 (280.6 × 19.9); M; 17.25.

M_2FM *H1*

***34400 SUI JIU 201.** RC/Ja 1975; Sal/Tg; 2200; — × 6.1 (— × 20); M; 18.75. Sister: ***34401 HUI JIU 101** (RC).

M_2FM *H12*

34410 JUYO MARU. Ja/Ja 1968; R; 3400; 111.1 × 6.9 (365 × 22.6); M; 16.

M_2FM *H12*

34420 COBARGO. Br/Br 1956; C; 1900; 76.9 × 4.3 (252 × 14); M; 10; ex KUMALLA 1973.

M_2FM *H12*

34430 MAMANI. Sg/Br 1949; C; 900; 56.9 × 3.7 (187 × 12.3); TSM; 10; ex MAMATU 1973; ex MAMAKU 1973.

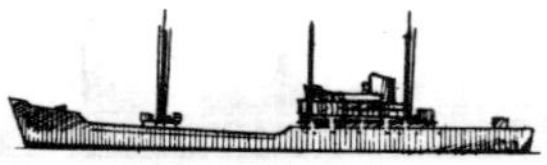

M_2FM *H12*

34440 KING HORSE. Sg/Br 1955; C; 1900; 81.6 × 4.9 (268 × 15.11); M; 11; ex NAVUA 1971.

M_2FM *H12*

34450 OKINAWA MARU. Ja/Ja 1956; C; 1600; 82.1 × 5 (269 × 16.5); M; 16.5.

Twin Funnels

M_2FM *H12*

34460 LONGVA. No/No 1962; RS; 800; 63 × 4.9 (206 × 16); M; 13.

M_2FM *H123*

● ***34470 ANDIZHAN.** Ru/DDR 1958; C; 3200; 104.2 × 6.6 (341 × 22); M; 12.5; **'LEVANT'** or **'KOVEL'** type. Some ships may vary slightly. Some have large radar mast from bridge. Similar (Ru flag): ***34471 BARABINSK *34472 BIKIN *34473 BOTSMAN ZOTOV** ex MONGUGAY ***34474 CHELYABINSK *34475 DALNERECHENSK** ex IMAN 1973 ***34476 DALNIY *34477 DAUGAVA *34478 EMETSK *34479 EYSK *34480 HOROL *34481 IZHMA *34482 KHOLMOGORY *34483 JASNOMORSK *34484 KAPITAN VOOLENS** ex AMATA 1967 ***34485 KOVEL *34486 KYARDLA *34487 LAZAREV *34488 LOKSA *34489 LUDZA *34490 MAHTRA *34491 MGA *34492 MURMASHI *34493 NAGAEVO *34494 NAMANGAN *34495 POLYARNYY *34496 POSYET *34497 RAKVERE *34498 RAZDOLNOYE *34499 REVDA *34500 RAZLIV *34501 RENI *34502 REPINO *34503 SALSK *34504 SARANSK *34505 SHENKURSK *34506 SOBOLEVO *34507 SIGULDA *34508 SYRVE *34509 SINEGORSK *34510 TURUKHANSK *34511 VANINO *34512 ZAISAN *34513 SONGDA** (Vn) ex SINEGORSK 1974 ***34514 SONG KHAN** (Vn) ex TURKESTAN 1975.

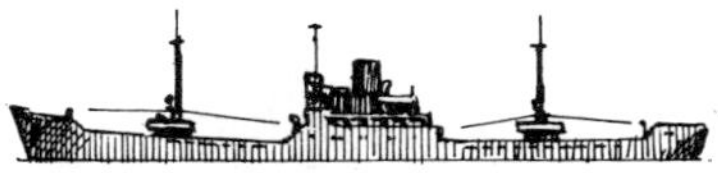

M_2FM H123
● **34530 TWIGHT.** Pa/Ja 1956; C; 4000; 113.5 × 6.8 (372 × 22.2); M; 11; ex GREEN LAKE; ex NASIPIT MARU 1972.

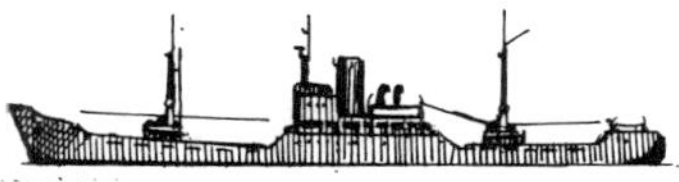

M_2FM H123
★34540 ANGARSK. Ru/DDR 1956; C; 3300; 102.42 × 6.65 (335 × 23.8); T; 12.5.

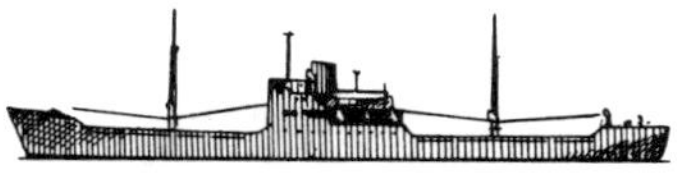

M_2FM H123
34550 SHIEH FU. Pa/Ja 1958; C; 3400; 106.2 × 6.4 (348.6 × 21.3); M; 12; ex CHEVALIER BERTHA; ex EIKO MARU 1974; ex KASASHIMA MARU 1969.

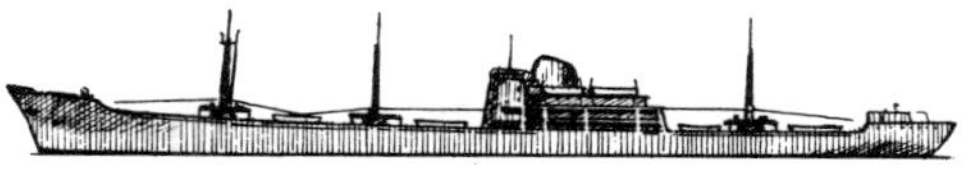

M_2FM H13
34560 KOTA MAHA. Sg/Ne 1957; CP; 6700; 149.4 × 8.6 (490 × 27.6); M; 17.25; ex STRAAT TOWA 1977; ex TOWA 1966.

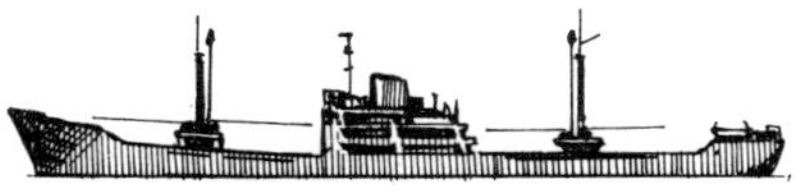

M_2FM H13
34570 MIMAR SINAN. Tu/Ja 1961; CP; 5400; 124.5 × 7.8 (409 × 25.8); M; 14.5.

M_2FM H13
34580 GAZI OSMAN PASA. Tu/Ja 1961; CP; 3700; 106.6 × 6.7 (350 × 21.11); M; 13. Sisters (Tu flag): **34581 MITHAT PASA 34582 27 MAYIS.**

M_2FM H13
34590 DENIZLI. Tu/Ja 1955; C; 3000; 102.4 × 6.2 (336 × 204); M; 14.

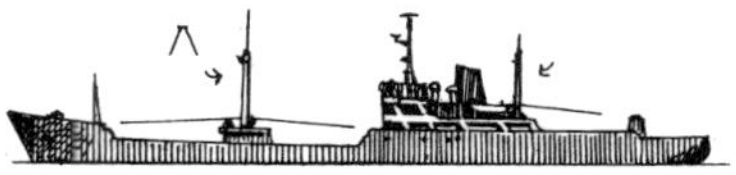

M_2FM H13
34600 RENO MARU. Ja/Ja 1967; R; 3400; 111.1 × 6.9 (364 × 22.6); M; 16.

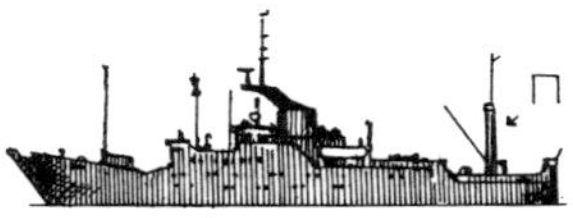

M_2FM H2
● **★34610 TARUSA.** Ru/Ru 1974; FT; 2300; 83.27 × — (273 × —); M; —. Sisters (Ru flag): **★34611 BYKOVO ★34612 BYELOMORSK ★34613 LOVOZYERO ★34614 MYS GROTOVYY ★34615 MYS KURILSKIY ★34616 MYS LOPATKA ★34617 MYS PROKOFYEVA ★34618 MYS RATMONOVA ★34619 MYS TAYMYR ★34620 MYS VAYGACH ★34621 MYS VORONINA ★34622 NAROCH ★34623 NEVYANSK ★34624 BORISPOL ★36425 DOMODYEDOVO ★34626 KRONSHTADT ★34627 MYS ARKTICHESKIY ★34628 TORZHOK ★34629 SOLOVIETSKIY ★34630 SHEREMTYEVO ★34631 GEROI ZAPOLYARYA ★34632 BIRYUSINSK ★34633 VNUKOVO ★34634 NOVYY MIR ★34635 ZELEZNOGORSK ★34636 ZNAMYA POBEDY ★34637 30-LET POBEDY ★34638 MYS BUDYONNOGO ★34639 MYS CHELYUSKIN ★34640 MYS FRUNZE ★34641 MYS KRONOTSKIY ★34642 MYS OTRADNYY ★34643 MYS VODOPADNYY ★34644 URGAL ★34645 LINAKHAMARI ★34646 ZASHCHITNIK ★34647 ZAPOLYARYA ★34648 KHAROVSK 34649 TIKHOOKEANSKIY ★34650 TYNDA ★34651 MYS ILMOVYY ★34652 MYS KUZNETSOVA ★34653 MYS SILINA ★34654 MYS CHASOVOY ★34655 MYS CHAYKOVSKOGO ★34656 MYS GROZNYY ★34657 MYS SKALISTYY ★34658 MURMANSELD ★34659 DESYATAYA PYATILETKA ★34660 VERKHOVINA ★34661 MYS SVOBODNYY ★34662 SEVERSK ★34663 SOVGANSKIY KOMSOMOLETS ★34664 GANGUT ★34665 TSIMLYANSK ★34666 VYOVSK ★34667 VYSHOGOROD ★34668 MYS TIKHIY ★34669 MYS DALNIY ★34670 NIKOLAYEVSKIY KORABEL ★34671 MYS BABUSKIN ★34672 MYS OSTROVSKOGO ★34673 MYS YUNONY.**

M_2FM H2

34690 PANAMIN II. Pi/Ja 1965; C; 1500; 73.4 × 4 (241 × 13); M; 15.25; ex TERUKUNI MARU 1975.

M_2FMC H

⋆**34710 ZENIT.** Ru/DDR 1961; TS; 4400; 104.9 × 6.2 (344 × 20); M; 13.75. Sisters (Ru flag): ⋆**34711 GORIZONT** ⋆**34712 MERIDIAN.**

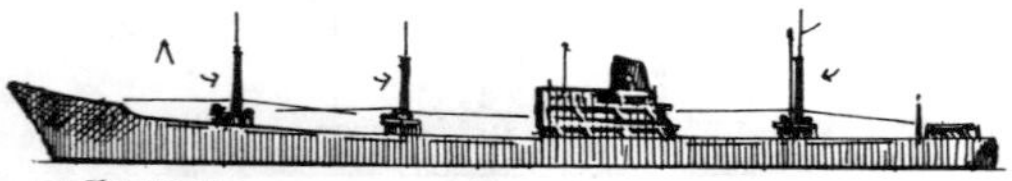

M_2FMK H1

34730 ARCAMARE. Gr/Ys 1959; C; 6200/9000; 152.3 × 8.1/9.2 (500 × 26.8/29.7); M; —; ex EFPLOIA 1973.

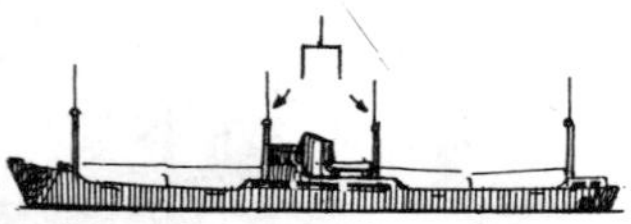

M_2FM_2 H1

34750 FLORY. Gr/Fr 1958; C/WT; 2900; 98.9 × 6.9 (325 × 22.7); M; 16; ex NELEE. Sister: **34751 ANNOULA TSIRIS** (Cy) ex CIRCE.

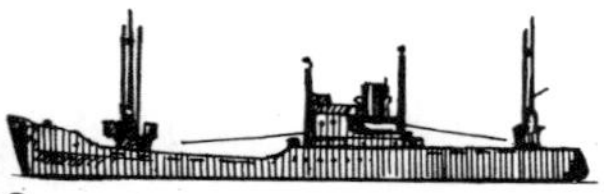

M_2FM_2 H12

34770 TUNG PAO. Pa/Br 1948; C; 2400; 93.1 × 5.3 (305 × 17.6); TSM; 9.75; ex KARANA III 1974; ex PALADIN 1969; ex KAITANGATA 1968. Sisters: **34771 HATI SENANG** (My) ex KAWATI 1980; ex KAWATRI 1972 **34772 BERJAYA** (My) ex TUNG LEE; ex BONATRADE 1974; ex KONUI 1969.

M_2FM H2

34700 BAHIA AGUIRRE. Ar/Ca 1950; Transport; 3800; 95 × 7.9 (335 × 13.8); TSM; 16; Argentine Navy. Sister: **34701 BAHIA BUEN SUCESO.**

M_2FMC H

34720 HAKUHO MARU. Ja/Ja 1966; RS; 3200; 94.9 × 5.5 (311 × 18); TSD-E; 12.5.

M_2FMK H1

34740 G. O. SARS. No/No 1970; RS/ST; 1400; 70 × 5 (230 × 16); M; 15.

M_2FM_2 H12

34760 MALDIVE REPUBLIC. Mv/Br 1958; C; 2100; 81.8 × 4.9 (268 × 16); M; 10; ex PATEENA 1975.

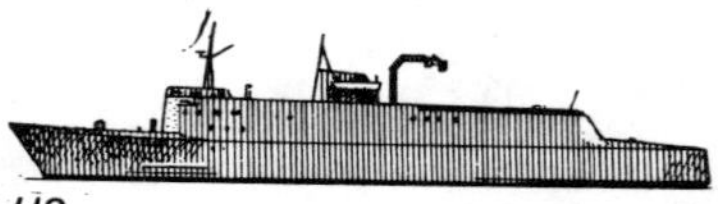

M_2FN H2

● **34780 STAFFORD.** De/De 1967; RoC; 2600; 124.2 × 5 (407 × 16.6); TSM; 19.5; Stern door. Lengthened 1973. Sister: **34781 SOMERSET** (De).

M_2K H/H1

34790 METEOR. FRG/FRG 1964; RS/ST; 2600; 82.1 × 5.1 (269 × 16.11); D-E; —.

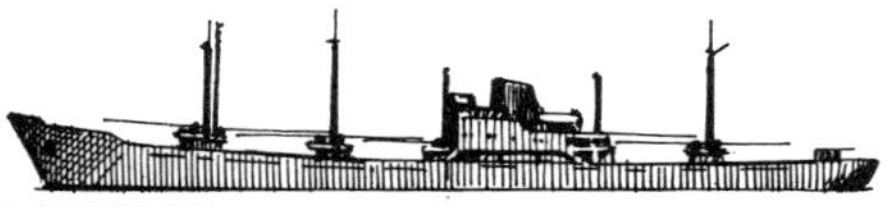

M_2KFKM H1
★34800 BOROVNICA. Ys/Ne 1956; CP; 5100/7200; 140.2 × 7.7/7.9 (460 × 25.1/25.11); M; 16; ex KINDERDYK 1970. Sisters: **★34801 BRANIK** (Ys) ex KERKEDYK 1970 **★34802 BREZICE** (Ys) ex KLOOSTERDYK 1970 **34803 REMCO** (Gh) ex ADOM 1980; ex VOLTA PEACE 1977; ex KAMPERDYK 1972 **34804 FERIAL** (Gh) ex ODUPON 1980; ex VOLTA WISDOM 1977; ex KORENDYK 1972 **34805 MARIKA J. LEMOS** (Cy) ex TJONGER; ex KATSEDYK 1973.

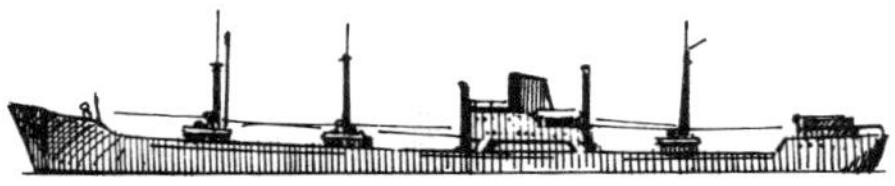

M_2KFKM H13
● **34830 AFRAM RIVER.** Gh/Ne 1962; CP; 4900/7400; 140.5 × — (461 × —/28); M; 15. Sisters (Gh flag): **34831 BIRIM RIVER 34832 KULPAWN RIVER 34833 NASIA RIVER 34834 OFFIN RIVER 34835 OTCHI RIVER 34836 PRA RIVER 34837 LAKE BOSOMTWE.**

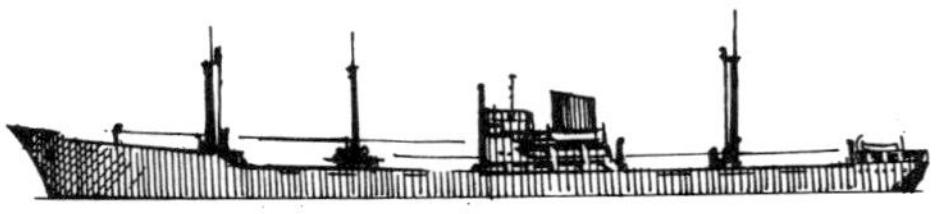

M_2KFM H1
34870 CHRISTINA B. Gr/Ne 1952; C; 5000/7600; 140 × 7.6/7.7 (459 × 24.9/25.6); M; —; ex CHRISTINA 1979; ex CAPTAIN JOHN TSAVARIS; ex LEKHAVEN 1969. Similar: **34871 GOLDEN HORSE** (Sg) ex PARKHAVEN 1973.

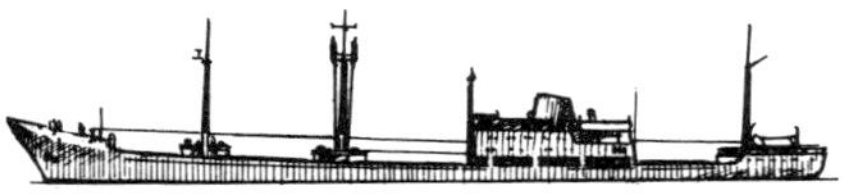

M_2KFM H13
34890 BRAVO ARES. Gr/Ne 1959; CP; 4200/6100; 129.2 × 6.5/7.3 (424 × 21.6/24); M; 16.25; ex ARES 1977; Lengthened 1966. Sisters: **34891 DENIS M** (Gr) ex ACHILLES **34892 MARIKA T** (Cy) ex ARCHIMEDES 1977 **34893 ARISTOTELES** (Ne) **34894 BRAVO CERES** (Gr) ex CERES 1977 **34895 ASTEROID** (Gr) ex DIOGENES 1978 **34896 COSMOS** (Ho) ex GANYMEDES **34897 YACU CASPI** (Pe) ex HERCULES **34898 ALKYON** (Gr) ex ULYSEES **34899 NIKI R** (Gr) ex HERMES **34900 BRAVO KATERINA** (Gr) ex PALAMEDES **34901 PERICLES** (Gr).

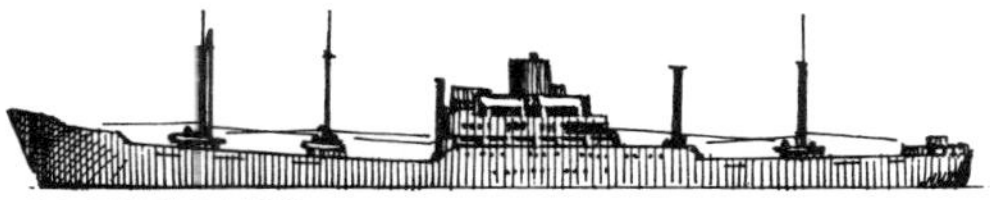

M_2KFKM H12
34810 HONG KONG SUCCESS. Li/Ne 1957; PC; 11200; 153.7 × 9.2 (504 × 30.1); T; 16; ex ORIENTAL FANTASIA 1972; ex DINTELDYK 1970.

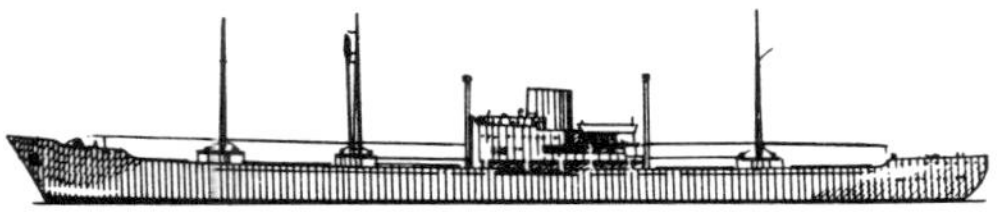

M_2KFKM H13
34820 AMSTELLAND. Ne/Ne 1962; CP; 6800; 157.8 × 8 (518 × 26.9); M; 17.5.

M_2KFKM_2K H1
34850 RAVENS. Cy/Be 1947; CP; 8000; 166.5 × 8.8 (546 × 28.1); TrSM; 17.25; ex RAVENSTEIN 1971; ex BASTOGNE 1955.

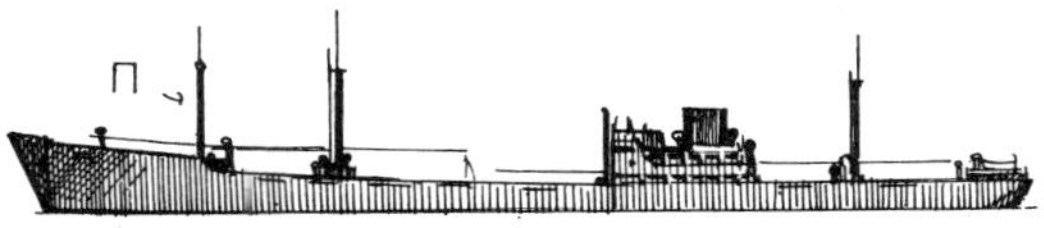

M_2KFM H1
34860 PANTAZIS CAIAS. Cy/Ne 1954; C; 9600; 158.3 × 8.5 (519 × 27.1); M; 12.25; ex CROWBOROUGH BEACON 1970; Lengthened 1961.

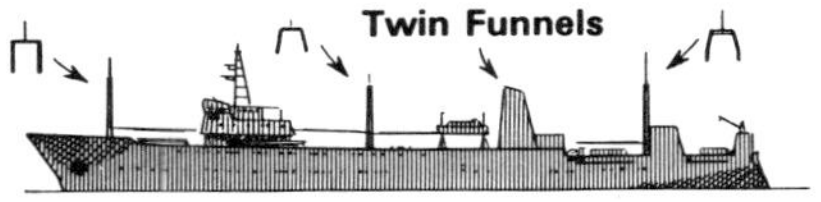

M_2KFM H1
★34880 SPRUT. Ru/Pd 1978; FT; 4800; 119 × 6.5 (390.42 × 21.33); M; 15; **'B-400'** type. Sisters (Ru flag): **★34881 ARKHIMED ★34882 PLUNGE ★34883 PRUZANIY ★34884 PASVALIS** At least 1 further vessel on order.

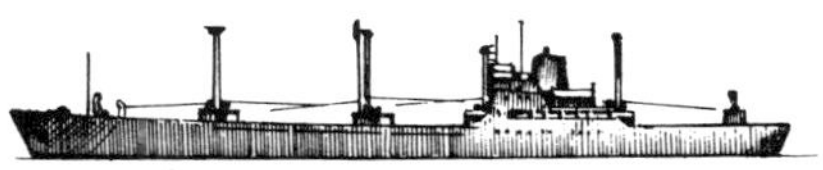

M_2KFM H13
34910 LION OF ETHIOPIA. Et/Ne 1966; C; 5200; 121 × 7.9 (397 × 26); M; —; ex LION OF JUDAH 1975. Sister: **34911 QUEEN OF SHEEBA** (Et).

M_2KFM_2 *H12*

34920 CLIMAX JADE. Mv/Br 1956; C; 3700; 105.3 × 6.8 (345 × 22.4); M; 12.5; ex KAITUNA 1975. Sisters: **34921 CLIMAX TOPAZ** (Mv) ex KAIMIRO 1975 **34922 SANTA URSULA** (Pa) ex KATEA 1976 **34923 IMPERIAL STAR** (Pa) ex CORAL SEA 1977; ex KAWERAU 1975 **34924 MALDIVE AMBASSADOR** (Mv) ex KORAKI 1975 **34925 SOUTH PACIFIC** (Mv) ex KORANUI 1975.

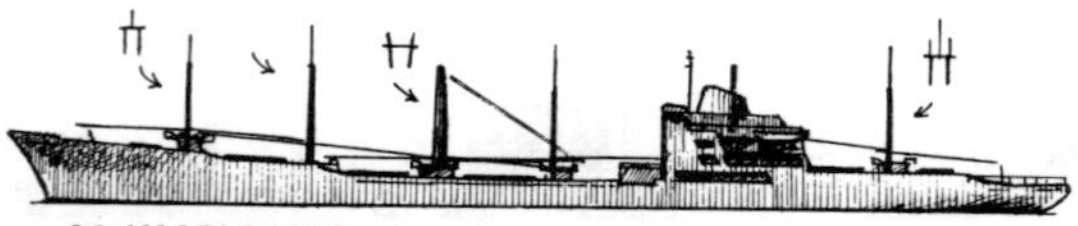

M_2KMFM *H13*

● **34950 ACONCAGUA II.** Ch/Ja 1965; CP; 10900; 168.4 × 9.3 (553 × 30.7); T; 20; ex ACONCAGUA 1980; ex ACONCAGUA II 1965. Sisters: **34951 COPIAPO II** (Ch) ex COPIAPO 1980; ex COPIAPO II **34952 ALLIANCE SUCCESS** (Gr) ex IMPERIAL II 1981; ex IMPERIAL 1980; ex IMPERIAL II.

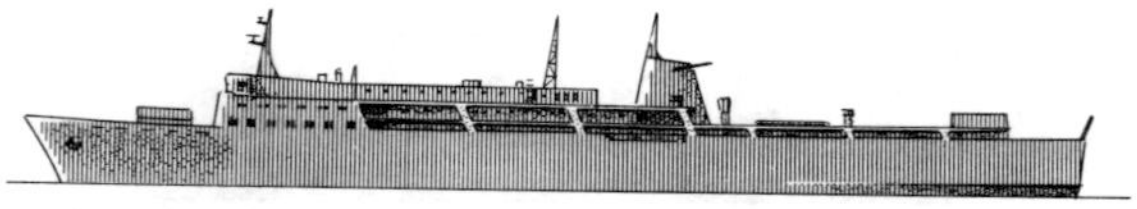

M_3F *H*

34980 MARIMO. Ja/Ja 1971; RoCPF; 9200; 166 × 6.3 (545 × 20.6); TSM; 20.75; Stern door and ramp. 2 side doors & ramps.

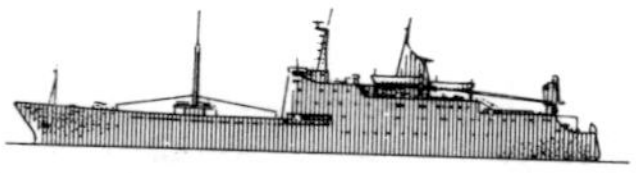

M_3FC *H*

⋆**35000 HAIO.** RC/Ja 1973; PC; 3300; 100.51 × 5.68 (329.76 × 18.64); M; 14; Name may be **HAI OU.**

M_3FKM *H1*

● **35020 SANSHIN PIONEER.** Pa/Ja 1960; C; 6000; 130.6 × 8.5 (428 × 28); M; 15; ex MALACCA MARU 1971.

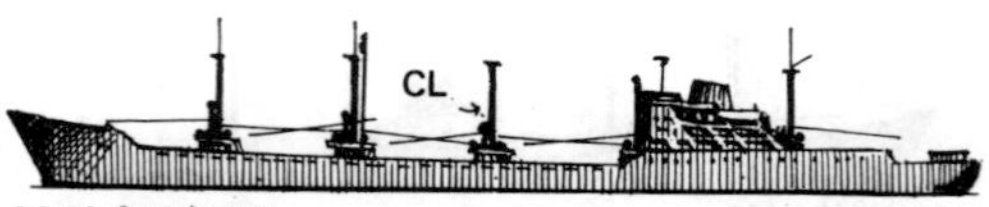

M_2K_2FM *H13*

34930 LUIGI D'AMICO. It/Sp 1964; C; 9100; 156.9 × 7.9 (519 × 29.9); M; —; ex ORIENT MARINER 1969.

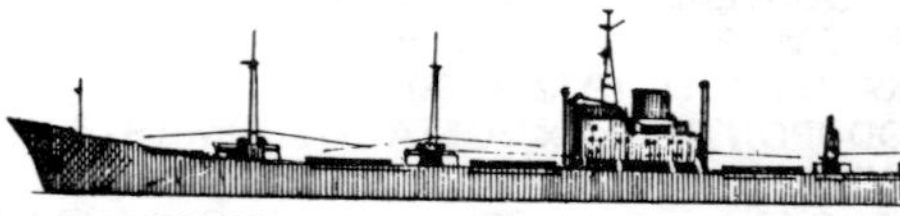

M_2KMFKC *H1*

34940 GOOILAND. Ne/Ne 1969; C; 4900; 147.5 × 7.1 (484 × 23); M; 15.5.

M_2KMFM *H1*

⋆**34960 WISMAR.** DDR/DDR 1968; CP; 3700/5700; 129.4 × 6.7/7.6 (424 × 22/25); M; 16; **'AFRIKA'** type. Sisters (DDR flag): ⋆**34961 FREDERIC JOLIOT CURIE** ⋆**34962 STOLLBERG** ⋆**34963 WITTENBERG.**

M_3 *H*

34970 BHANGURANSI. Th/De 1927; C; 700; 64 × 2.9 (210 × 9.9); TSM; 10.

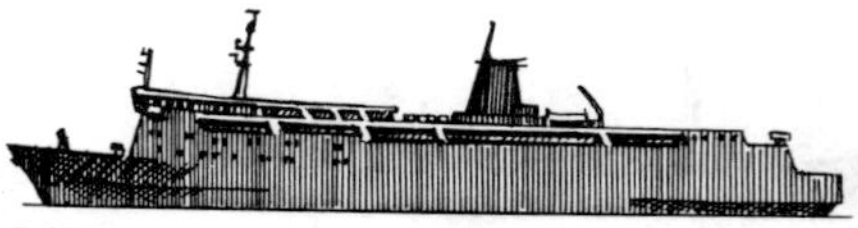

M_3F *H2*

34990 ARGO. Ja/Ja 1973; RoCF; 6900; 132 × 5.5 (433 × 18); TSM; 19.5. Sister: **34991 ALNASL** (Ja).

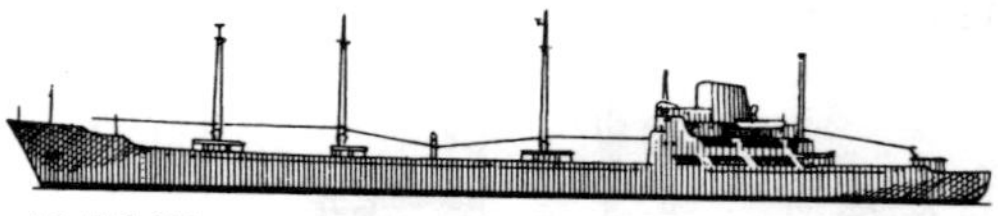

M_3FK *H1*

35010 AMBER. Cy/Ne 1962; C; 10600; 157.4 × 9.7 (516 × 32); M; 16.5; ex CENTAURUS 1973.

M_3FKM *H1*

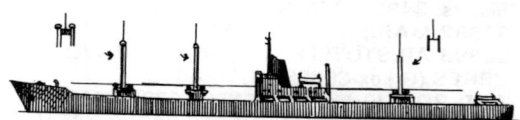

⋆**35030 ZHENJIANG.** RC/Fr 1966; C; 7800/10900; 158 × 8.5/9.4 (520 × 28/31); M; —. Sister: ⋆**35031 JIUJIANG** (RC).

M_3FKM H13
35040 SAKUMO LAGOON. Gh/Br 1964; CP; 4800/7300; 138.5 × 7.3/8.4 (454 × 23.11/27.8); M; 17. Sisters (Gh flag): **35041 BENYA RIVER 35042 NAKWA RIVER 35043 KORLE LAGOON.**

M_3FM H12
35050 HENG SHAN. Tw/Ja 1960; C; 4000; 110.8 × 6.4 (363 × 21); M; 13.5; ex TAISETSUSAN MARU 1972.

M_3FM H13
★35060 MALAYA VISHERA. Ru/Ru 1964; C; 2900; 104.5 × 5.8 (343 × 20.11); M; 12.5. Sister: **★35061 MALOYAROSLAVYETS** (Ru).

M_3FM_2 H12
35070 MARINA. Pa/As 1960; C; 4100; 103.6 × 7 (341 × 22.1); M; 12.5; ex MUNDOORA 1977.

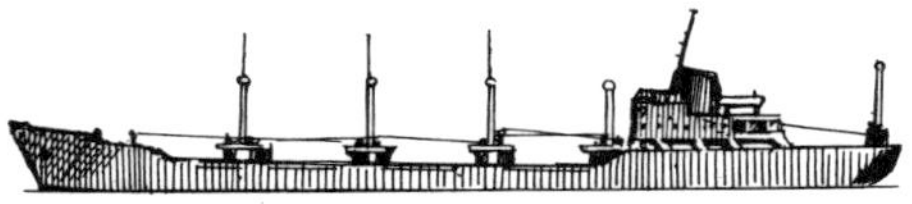

M_3KMFK H13
35080 CELESTINO. Bz/Bz 1968; C; 6200/8300; 142.3 × 8.2/9.2 (467 × 27/30); M;

M_4 H
35090 FUJI MARU. Ja/Ja 1968; ST/FF; 3900; 102.3 × 5.9 (336 × 19.6); M; 13.75. Similar (Ja flag): **35091 HARUNA MARU 35092 KONGO MARU 35093 NIITAKA MARU 35094 TSUDA MARU.**

MNF H1
35100 ACADIA FOREST. Li/Ja 1969; BC; 38900; 261.4 × 12.1 (857 × 40); M; 19; **'LASH'** type. Similar: **35101 ATLANTIC FOREST** (Li) **35102 BILDERDYK** (Ne).

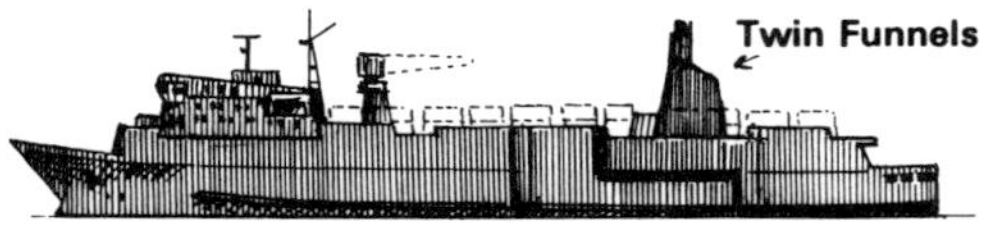

MNF H2
● **35110 DANA FUTURA.** De/De 1975; RoC; 6000; 144 × 7 (474 × 23); TSM; 22.5; ex DROSSELFELS; ex DAMMAN EXPRESS 1976; ex DANA FUTURA 1976. Sister: **35111 DANIA HAFNIA** (De) ex DRACHENFELS; ex DANA GLORIA 1976.

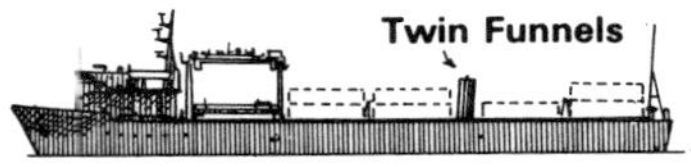

MNFM H
35120 BAYANO. Br/Sp 1972; Con; 4100; 104.3 × 5.8 (344 × 19); TSM; 17.5; Sister: **35121 BARRANCA** (Sp).

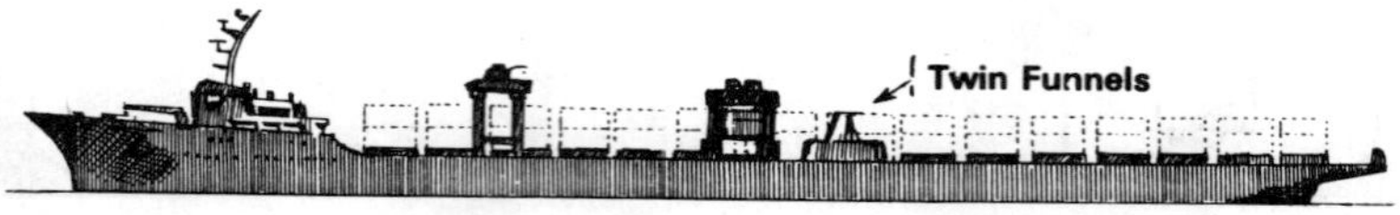

MN_2F H1

● **35130 LASH ATLANTICO.** US/US 1972; L/Con; 26400; 250 × 10.7 (820 × 35.5); T- 21; Both gantries (N) can move—thus altering sequence. Could also be P5. **'LASH'** type. Sisters (US flag) (overall lengths vary): **35131 LASH ITALIA 35132 LASH PACIFICO 35133 AUSTRAL LIGHTNING** ex LASH ESPANA 1976; ex AUSTRAL BEAR 1975; ex PHILIPPINE BEAR 1975 **35134 DELTA MAR 35135 DELTA SUD 35136 DELTA NORTE 35137 DELTA CARIBE** ex LASH TURKIYE.

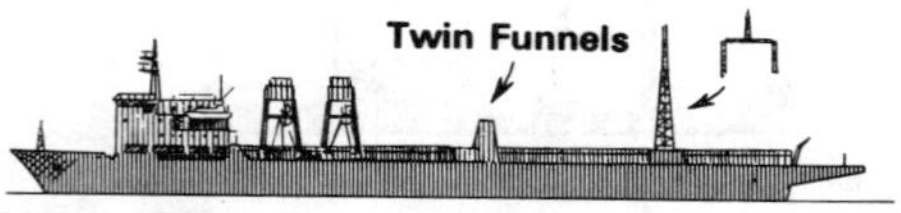

MN_2FM H

⋆35150 STAKHANOVETS KOTOV. Ru/Fi 1978; RoC/Dk; 4300; 135.53 × 6.2 (444.65 × 20.34); TSM; 14.25; Stern door. Sisters (Ru flag): **⋆35151 STAKHANOVETS PETRASH ⋆35152 STAKHANOVETS YERMOLENKO.**

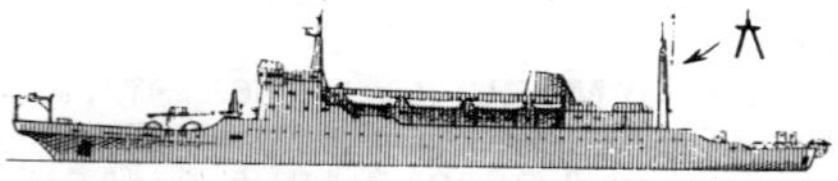

NCMFM H2

⋆35170 INGUL. Ru/Fi 1962; Cbl; 5600; 130.41 × 5.2 (427.85 × 17.06); TSD-E; 14; **"KLASMA"** class. Sister: **⋆35171 JANA** (Ru) (may be spelt **YANA**).

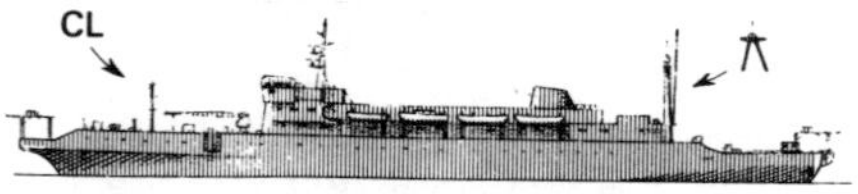

NKCMFMN H2

⋆35190 INGURI. Ru/Fi 1978; Cbl; 6000; 130.41 × 5.75 (427.85 × 18.86); TSD-E; 14; **"KLASMA"** class. Probably has sister ships under construction.

MN_2FK H1

35160 DOCKLIFT 1. Pa/Ne 1972; Dk; 2400; 105.7 × 5 (347 × 17); TSM; 12.75; Stern Ramp.

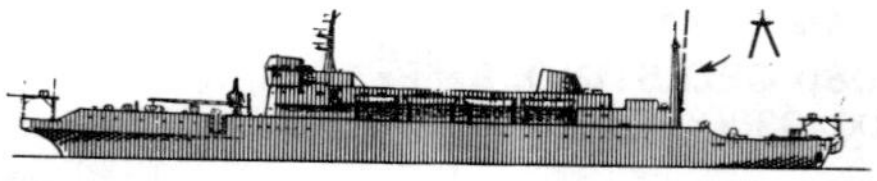

NCMFMN H2

⋆35180 KATUNJ. Ru/Fi 1973; Cbl; 6000; 130.41 × 5.75 (427.85 × 18.86); TSD-E; 14; May be spelt **KATUN. "KLASMA"** class. Sisters: **⋆35181 DONETS** (Ru) **⋆35182 TSNA** (Ru) (may be spelt **ZNA**).

NMFNM H/H1

35200 GATEWAY CITY. US/US 1943/57; Con; 9000; 137.2 × 7.6 (468 × 25); T; 16; ex IBERVILLE 1974; Converted from cargo ship 1957.

Profile 3

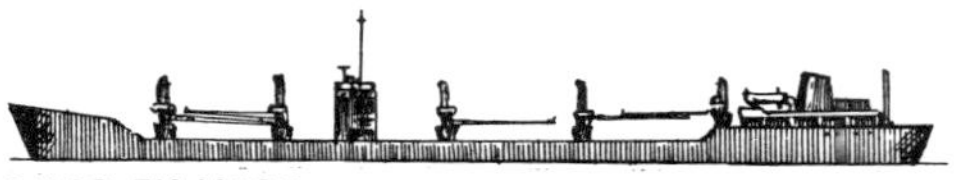

C_2MC_3FK H123
35210 ANGELIKE DYNAMIS. Gr/Ja 1962; B; 9500; 145.4 × 9.2 (477 × 30.2); M; 14; ex AGGELIKI 1976; ex DOROTHY ANN 1970.

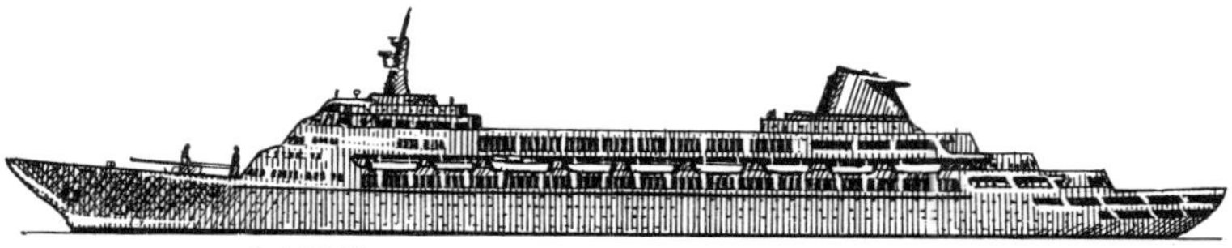

C_2MF H
35220 OCEANIC. Pa/It 1965; P; 27600; 238.44 × 8.63 (782.28 × 28.31); TST; 26.5.

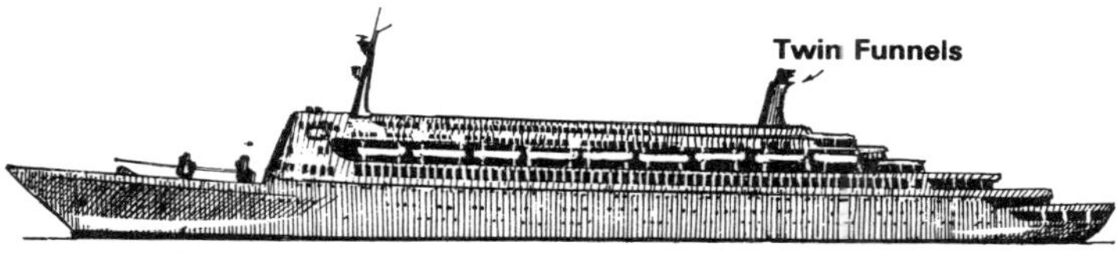

C_2MF H
35230 EUGENIO C. It/It 1966; PC; 30600; 217.5 × 8.6 (713.5 × 28.2); TST; 27.

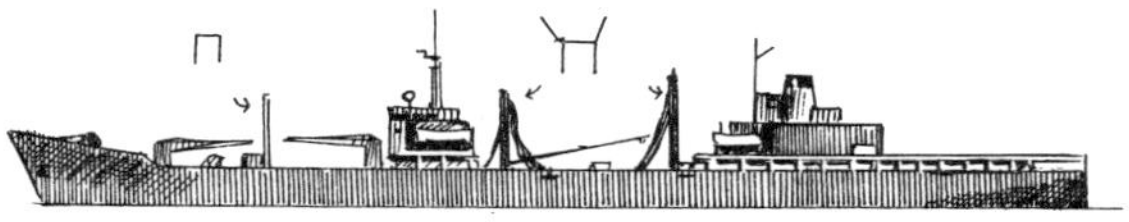

$CKCMK_2MF$ H1
35240 ZUIDERKRUIS. Ne/Ne 1975; Spt/FA; 16900 Dspl; 169.6 × 8.2 (566 × 27); T; 21; **'POOLSTER'** class. 5 helicopters.

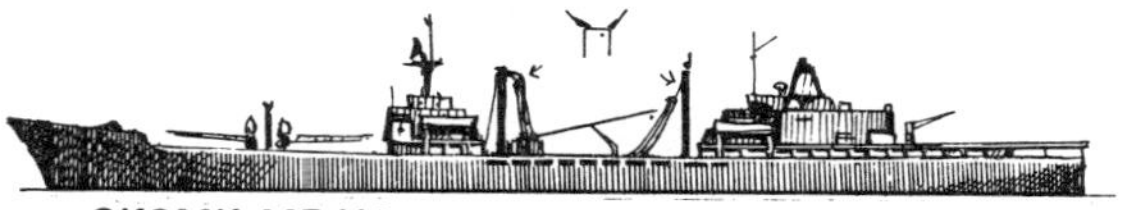

$CKCMK_2MF$ H1
35250 POOLSTER. Ne/Ne 1964; Spt/FA; 16800. Dspl; 169.6 × 8.2 (556 × 27); T; 21; 5 helicopters.

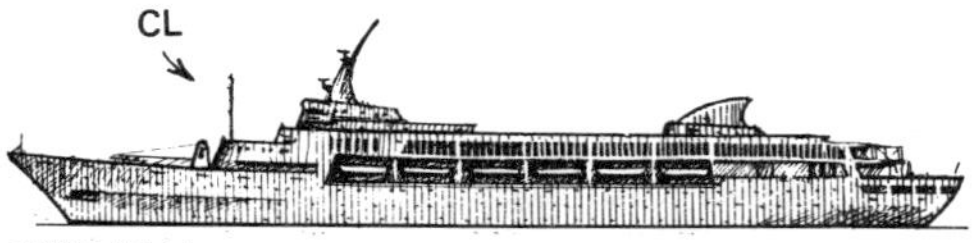

C(K)MF H
35260 ITALIA. It/It 1967; PC; 12200; 149 × 6.4 (489 × 21.01); M; 19.

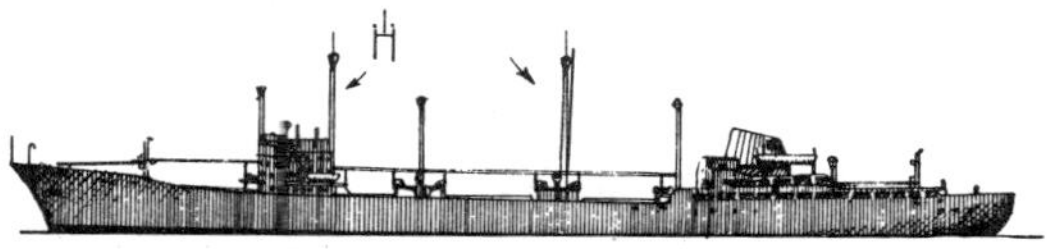

CKMKMKFC H
● **★35270 SCHWERIN.** DDR/DDR 1957; C; 6500/9400; 157.4 × 8.4/9.7 (516.4 × 27.6/31.71); TSM; 15. Sisters: **★35271 HANGZOU** (RC) ex DUKLA 1965; ex SOLIDARITAT **★35272 LANZHOU** (RC) ex ORAVA 1975; ex ZEROMSKI 1959; ex VOLKERFREUNDSCHAFT 1957 **★35273 SIERRA MAESTRA** (Cu) **35274 SAUDI INDEPENDENCE** (Pa) ex LEIPZIG 1980 **35275 SAUDI TRADER** (Pa) ex KARL-MARX-STADT 1980 **35276 SAUDI PRIDE** (Pa) ex GERA 1980 Some of these ships may have first crane removed like EURABIA FRIENDSHIP-which see.

CMC_2F H13
35280 TAINARON. Li/Sw 1955/75; DS; 9900; 177.65 × 9.12 (582 × 29.92); M; 15; ex BOLIVAR 1969; ex CERRO BOLIVAR 1968; Converted from Ore Carrier 1975.

CMCFM H
● **35290 LAKE LOTHING.** Br/Br 1955; D; 660; 50.42 × 4.11 (165.42 × 13.48); M; 9. Similar (Br flag): **35291 GRASSENDALE 35291 KENFIG.**

CMCMF H123
35300 PAUL HEROULT. Pa/Fr 1959; O; 6300; 128.15 × 7.95 (420.44 × 26.09); M; 14.5.

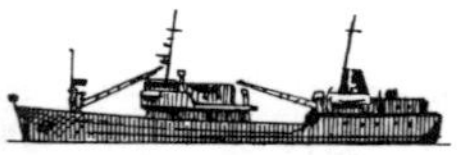

CMCMF H3–
***35310 KASPIY.** Ru/DDR 1968; FV; 1100; 65.51 × 3.61 (214.93 × 11.83); M; 10.75. Sisters (Ru flag): ***35311 NEVEZHIS *35312 NEVKA *35313 OKA *35314 LENA** Probable Sisters: ***35315 AKHTUBA *35316 AMU-DARYA *35317 FONTANKA *35318 GORKY *35319 INDIGIRKA** (fish carrier) ***35320 KAMA *35321 KAPITAN EVSEYEV** ex SYR-DARYA 1971 ***35322 KURA *35323 KOLYMA *35324 LENINGRADETS *35325 OB *35326 PSKOVITYANKA *35327 RAZLIV *35328 RADVILISKIS *35329 ROKISHKIS *35330 SUKHONA *35331 SVIR *35332 TAMAN *35333 VYCHEGDA *35334 50 LET VLKSM *35335 ANADYR** Similar: ***35336 RAND-1 *35337 RAND-2 *35338 RAND-3 *35339 RAND-4.**

CMF H
35350 FINNMARKEN. No/FRG 1956; PC; 2200; 81.31 × 4.51 (266.8 × 14.8); M; 16. Sister: **35351 RAGNVALD JARL** (No).

CM_2F H
35360 LOFOTEN. No/No 1964; PC; 2600; 87.43 × 4.62 (286.8 × 15.17); M; 16.75.

CM_2F H
***35370 KOLKHIDA.** Ru/Ru 1961; P; 3200; 101.5 × 4 (333 × 13); TSM; 14.5. Sisters—Some ships have taller funnel. Some may not have crane. (Ru flag): ***35371 BUKOVINA *35372 KIRGHIZSTAN *35373 MOLDAVIA *35374 TADZHAKISTAN *35375 TALLINN** ex SVANETIYA ***35376 TATARIYA *35377 UZBEKISTAN** Possible Sister: ***35378 AFGHANISTAN** Similar—Rebuilt with enclosed superstructure and taller funnel: ***35379 OSETIYA.**

CM_2F H
***35390 IZUMRUD.** Ru/Ru 1970; RS; 3900; 99.37 × 5.4 (326 × 17.75); D-E; 13.75.

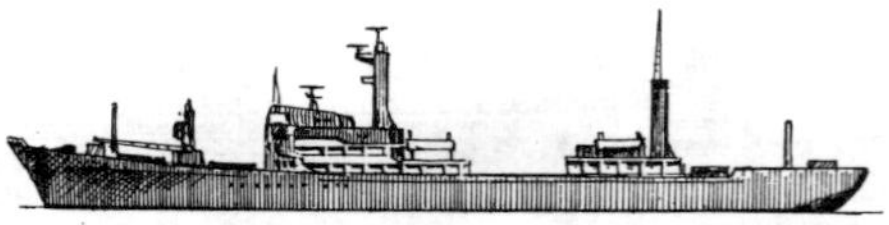

CM_2F H
35400 MUTSU. Ja/Ja 1969; RS/C; 8200; 130.46 × 6.9 (428 × 22.67); NT; 16.5.

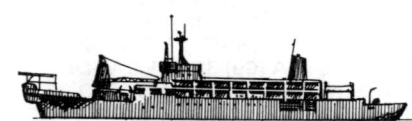

CM_2F H
35410 KUROSHIO MARU. Ja/Ja 1975; Cbl; 3300; 119.31 × 5.59 (391.44 × 18.34); M; 16.5.

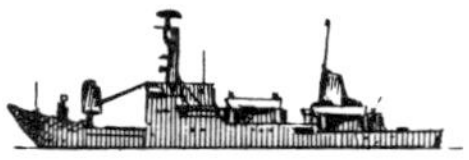

CM_2F H
⋆35420 DMITRY OVTSYN. Ru/Fi 1970; RS; 1100; 66.83 × 4.12 (219.26 × 13.52); M; 13.75. Possible Sisters (Ru flag): Some may be like SERGEY KRAVKOV—H1—next entry; **⋆35421 DMITRY LAPTEV ⋆35422 DMITRY STERLEGOV ⋆35423 EDUARD TOLL ⋆35424 NIKOLAY YEVGENOV ⋆35425 NIKOLAY KOLOMEYTSYEV ⋆35426 STEPAN MALYGIN ⋆35427 VALERIAN ALBANOV ⋆35428 VLADIMIR SUKHOTSKIY.**

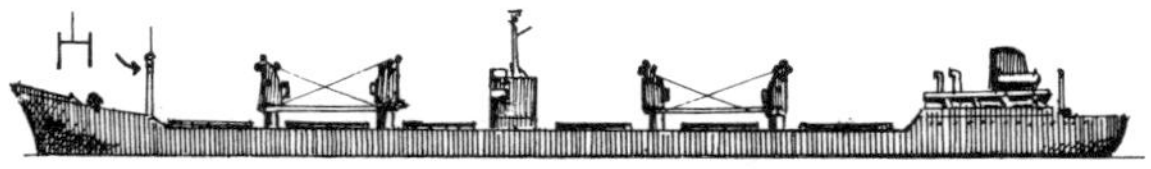

KC_2MC_2FK H123
35460 AQUARIUS. It/It 1960; B; 12800; 174.83 × 9.98 (573.6 × 32.74); M; 14. Possibly Similar (It flag): **35461 CORONA AUSTRALE 35462 AURIGA** May be other ships of this class with this appearance. See PIVIERE.

KC_2MF H3
⋆35480 BOJNICE. Cz/Hu 1966; C; 1400; 81.39 × 3.1 (267.03 × 10.16); TSM; 12. Sisters: **⋆35481 LEDNICE** (Cz) **⋆35482 CEGLED** (Hu) **⋆35483 SZEKESFEHERVAR** (Hu) **⋆35484 UJPEST** (Hu).

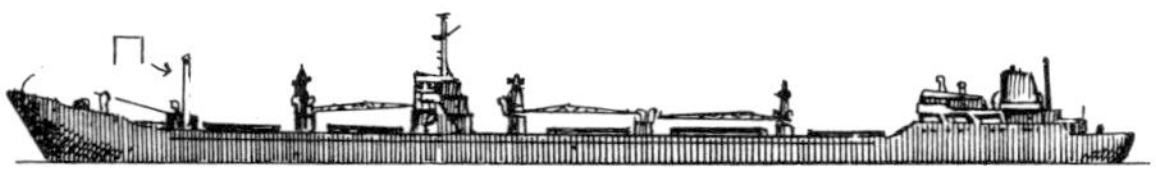

$KCMC_2FK$ H13
35500 PETER L. Gr/Ja 1961; B; 13400; 178.98 × 9.55 (587.2 × 31.33); M; 16.5. Probable Sister: **35501 CAPTAIN JOHN L** (Gr).

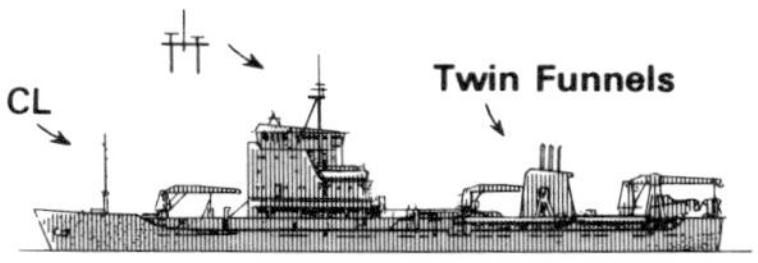

KCMCFC H13
35520 ALPHA BAY. Br/Ne 1980; D; 5700; 112 × 6.25 (367.45 × 20.5); TSM; 13.7; Split hopper suction dredger.

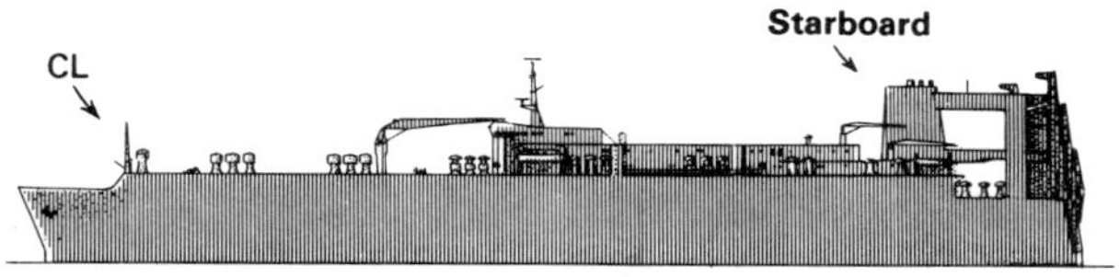

KCMCFR/KCMFR H2
35530 SKAUBORD. No/No 1979; RoC; 31100; 182.51 × 12.02 (598.79 × 39.44); M; 14.8; Stern quarter ramp/door.

CM_2F H1
⋆35440 SERGEY KRAVKOV. Ru/Fi 1974; RS; 1100; 68.23 × 4.15 (223.85 × 13.62); M; 13.5; Some units of DMITRY OVTSYN type—previous entry—may have this appearance.

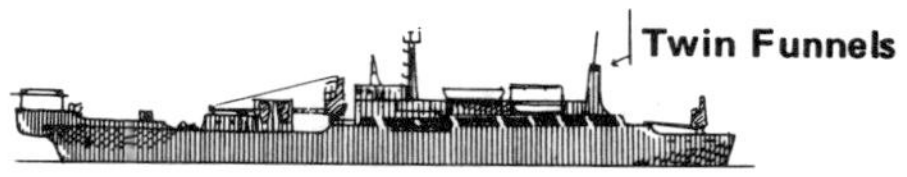

CM_2FC H
35450 KDD MARU. Ja/Ja 1967; Cbl; 4200; 114 × 6.32 (374 × 20.73); TSM; 16.

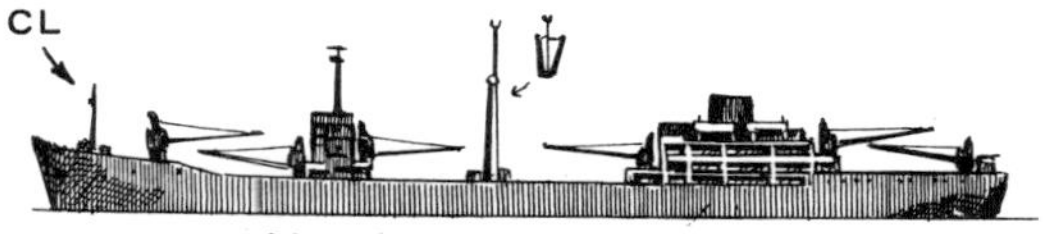

$KC_2MCMCFC_2$ H13
● **35470 INVENTOR.** Br/Br 1964; C/HL; 6100/8800; 150.37 × 7.67/9.04 (493.34 × 25.17/29.69); M; —.

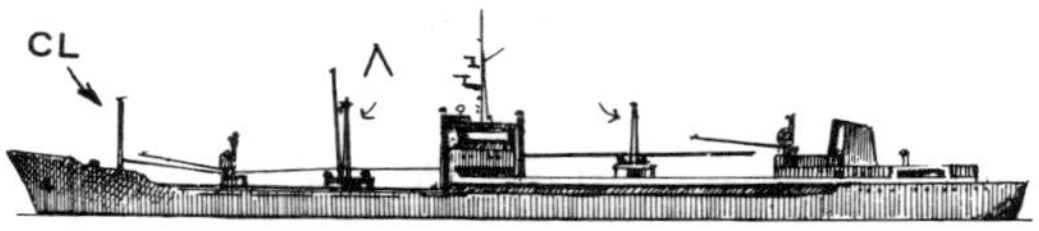

KCK_2MK_2CF H13
35490 PADANG. Ia/De 1964; C; 7600; 159.5 × 8.1 (523.3 × 26.6); M; 18.25; ex ANDORRA.

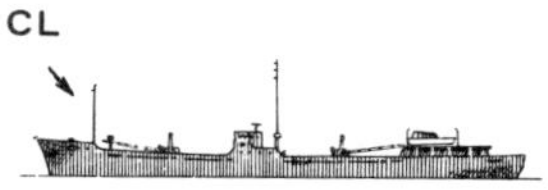

KCMCF H12
⋆35510 JERKO TOMASIC. Ys/Ys 1958; C; 1000; 77.15 × 3 (253.12 × 9.84); TSM; 12; ex PRIVALA 1978; ex TAMNAVA 1971. Similar (now converted to fishing craft—probably altered in appearance): **⋆35511 KRISTO MARINOVIC** (Ys) ex PRAPATNA 1975; ex KOLUBARA 1971 **⋆35512 MARKO MILAT** (Ys) ex PLITVINE 1975.

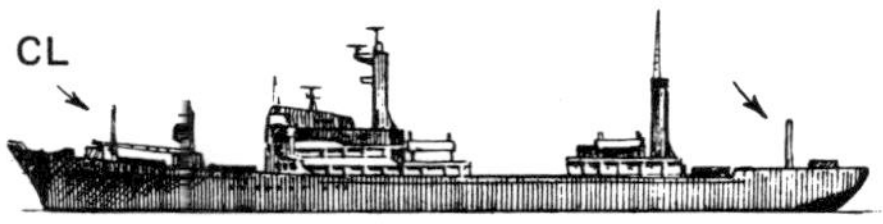

KCM_2FK H
35540 MUTSU. Ja/Ja 1969; RS/C; 8200; 130.46 × 6.9 (428 × 22.67); NT; 16.5.

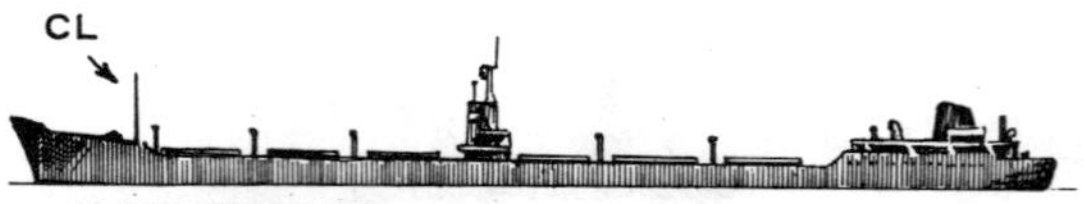

K_4MK_2FK H123
35550 LOCARNO. Li/It 1960; B; 11200; 166.53 × 9.32 (546.36 × 30.56); M; —; ex ALCIONE 1979; ex GIOVANNI QUERIOLO 1976.

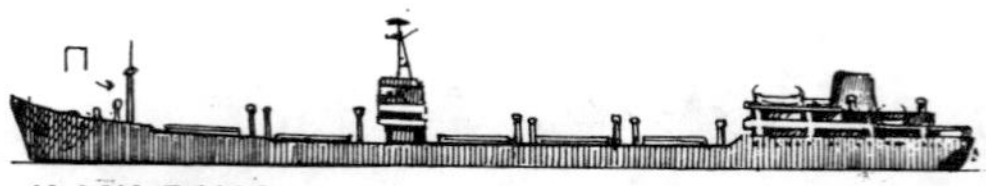

K_4MK_5F H13
35560 BIRKHALL. Li/FRG 1957; B; 8300; 149.99 × 8.57 (492.09 × 28.13); M; 14; ex SKRIM 1970.

K_3MF H13
35570 HAMID. Le/Br 1942; C; 500; 61.47 × 3.26 (201.68 × 10.7); M; 10.5; ex AL-AMIN 1972; ex ULSTER SPINNER 1968; ex GUERNSEY COAST 1955; ex ULSTER DUKE 1947.

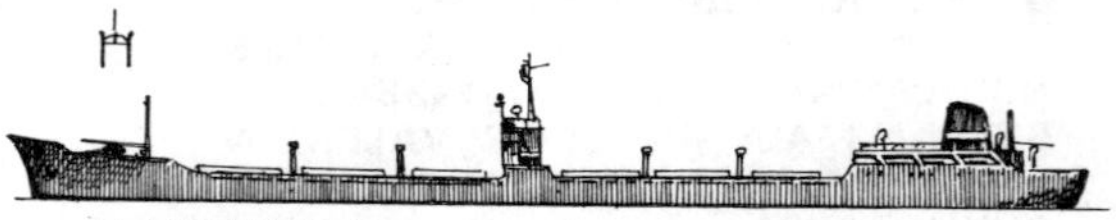

K_3MK_2FK H123
● **35580 PIVIERE.** It/It 1960; B; 11200; 165.49 × 9.25 (524.95 × 30.35); M; 15; ex SENATORE 1974; ex SENATORE G.B. BIBOLINI 1969. Sisters: **35581 LOCARNO** (Li) ex ALCIONE 1979; ex GIOVANNI QUEIROLO 1976 **35582 GIOVANNI ANSALDO** (It) **35583 CARLO CANEPA** (It) **35584 COCLERDUE** (It) ex PUNTA MESCO 1973; ex GUIDO DONEGANI 1969 Similar (Goalpost forward): **35585 ORSA MINORE** (It).

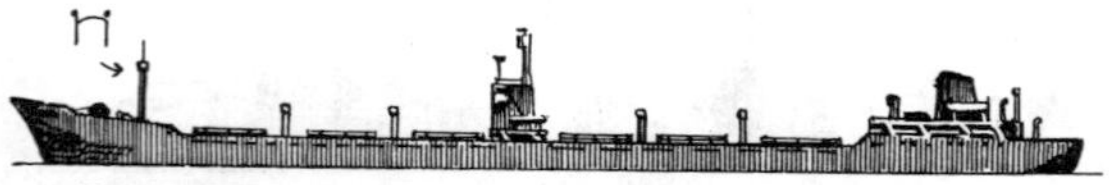

K_3MK_2FK H13
35590 ACCIAIERE. It/It 1957; B; 11300; 165.46 × 9.3 (542.85 × 30.51); M; 13. Sisters: **35591 CORONA BOREALE** (It) **35592 LAMINATORE** (It) Similar (Pole mast forward): **35593 COCLERTRE** (It) ex CORALLINA 1980 **35594 AUCTORITAS** (It) **35595 THOMAS A** (Gr) ex CONCORD 1 1976; ex LADY RITA 1976; ex PUGLIOLA 1973; ex ALBERTO LOLLI GHETTI 1965 **35596 WHITE RIVER** (Gr) ex WHITE ROVER 1980; ex WHITE RIVER 1976.

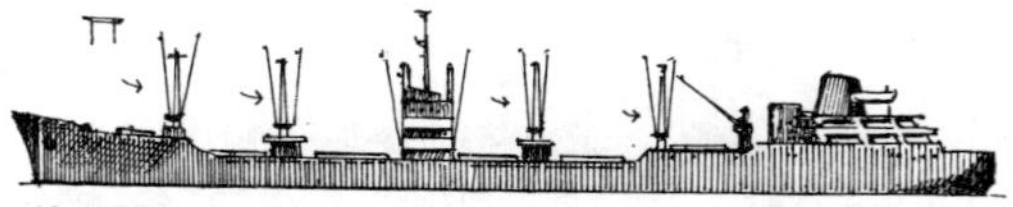

K_3MK_3CF H13
35600 BAY. US/US 1961; C; 7900/10700; 150.27 × —/9.32 (493 × 30.58); T; 18.5; ex EXPORT BAY 1980. Sisters (US flag): **35601 BUILDER** ex EXPORT BUILDER 1980 **35602 BUYER** ex EXPORT BUYER 1980 **35603 EXPORT BANNER.**

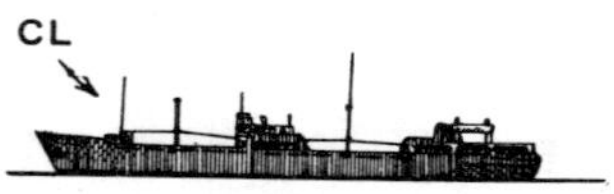

K_2MF H
35610 LEROS. Cy/Hu 1958; C; 1200; 80.4 × 3.1 (263.8 × 10.7); TSM; 12; ex LEROS II 1977; ex KRATEROS 1976; ex THEOFANIS L 1975; ex TINA 1973; ex HAZAM 1970.

K_2MF H13
35620 IRVINGWOOD. Br/Ca 1952/57; Tk; 2500; 79.23 × 5.81 (259.94 × 19.06); M; 10; Converted from general cargo 1957.

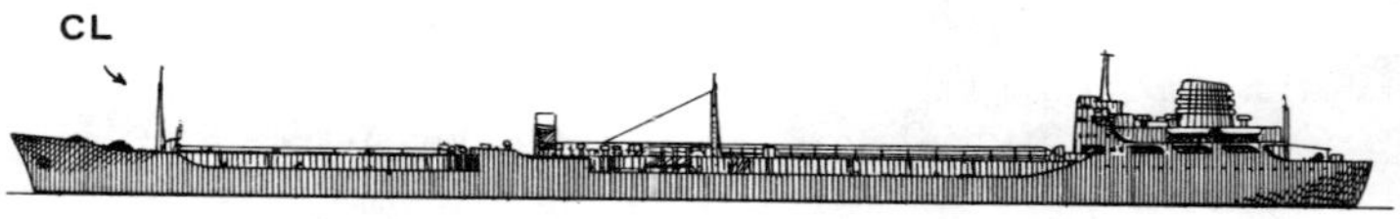

K_2MFK H123
35630 CONTOVELLO. Li/Ja 1961; LGC/Tk; 30100; 221.47 × 11.84 (726.61 × 38.85); M; 16; ex GREAT CRANE 1980; ex GOHSHU MARU 1973.

K_2MKF H

35640 MAGED. Ly/Hu 1960; C; 1200; 81.92 × 3.09 (268.77 × 10.14); TSM; 11; ex CHRISTINA 1975; ex BADACSONY 1970. Sisters: **35641 AREF** (Ly) ex VITTORIA 1975; ex CSEPEL 1970 **35642 SUNNY L** (Pa) ex ANNAMINA K 1980; ex CARPENTER 1977; ex NINGPO VIOLET 1975; ex DUNAUJVAROS 1974 **35643 BUILDER** (Sg) ex NINGPO LILAC 1975; ex BORSOD 1974 **35644 DECORATOR** (Sg) ex NINGPO ORCHID 1975; ex SZEGED 1974.

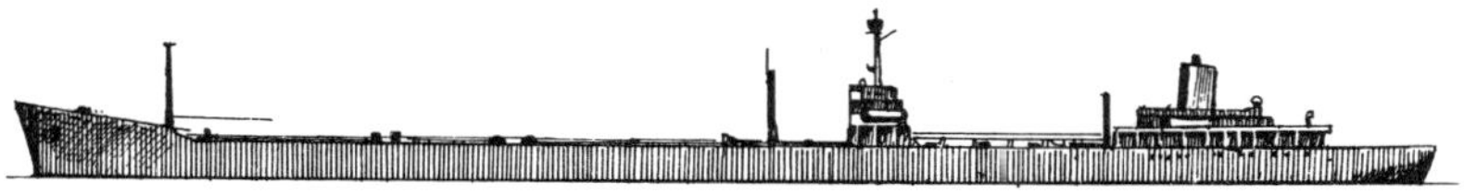

K_2MKF H1

35650 BALTIMORE TRADER. US/US 1955/71; Tk; 31100; 243.85 × 12.16 (800 × 39.9); ST; 17.5; ex P.W. THIRTLE 1971; Aft sections built 1955. Forward and cargo sections built 1971.

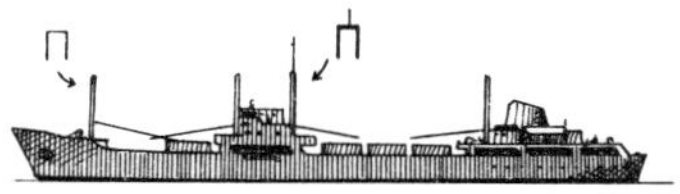

K_2MKF H1

● **35660 SPAN QUARTA.** It/Fi 1960/70; C; 1500/2500; 100.44 × 4.92/5.64 (329.53 × 16.15/18.5); M; 13.5; ex INHA; Lengthened 1970. Sisters: **35661 KATERINA** (Gr) ex INIO ⋆**35662 TAI WU SHAN** (RC) ex CHENGPA SHAN 1980; ex TELLUS 1970 ⋆**35663 TAI YANG SHAN** (RC) ex TABI SHAN 1980; ex TITANIA ⋆**35664 JORDAN** (Eg) ex TRITON 1976.

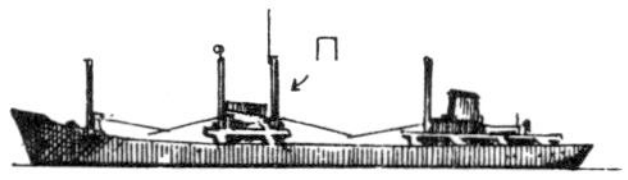

K_2MKF H1

● ⋆**35670 LUN.** Ys/Fi 1958; C; 1400; 89.03 × 4.88 (292.1 × 16.01); M; 13; ex INARI 1974. Sister: ⋆**35671 RAD** (Ys) ex IVALO 1974 Similar: **35672 SKOPELOS SEA** (Gr) ex HEROS 1974 **35673 NIKOLAKIS** (Cy) ex POSEIDON 1974 **35674 HEROIC SAILOR** (Cy) ex SALLA **35675 ETTORE** (Cy) ex MIRA 1974.

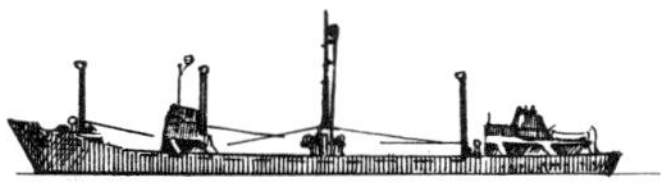

K_2MKF H1

35680 ALCYONE. Cy/FRG 1956; C; 1800; 95 × 5.64 (311.7 × 18.5); M; 12.5. Sisters: **35681 RIGEL** (Pa) ex ALCOR 1980 **35682 ATTIKON** (Cy) ex ALIOTH 1975.

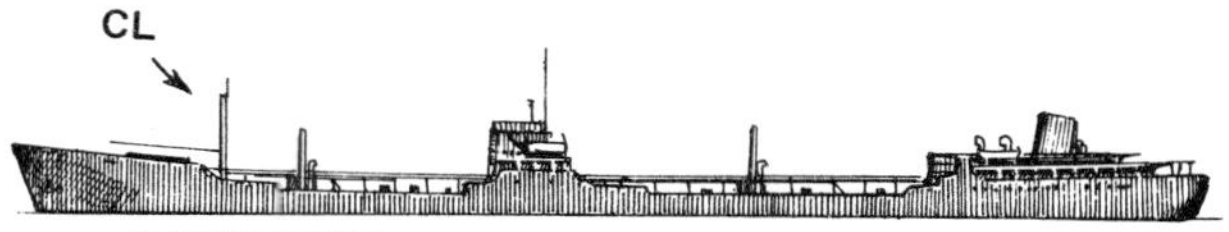

K_2MKF H123

35690 PETROLA 33. Gr/Br 1951; Tk; 16500; 190 × 10.29 (623.36 × 33.75); M; 14; ex PETROLA XXXIII 976; ex MARIANNA II 1975; ex BOLETTE 1964. Sister: **35691 PETROLA 34** (Gr) ex PETROLA XXXIV 1976; ex MARGARITA II 1975; ex DALFONN 1966.

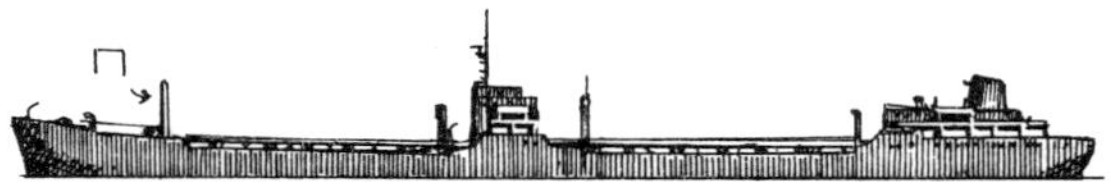

K_2MKF H123

35700 EGNAZIA. It/Sw 1958; Tk; 12500; 170.69 × 9.63 (560 × 31.6); M; —; ex POINT LACRE 1973.

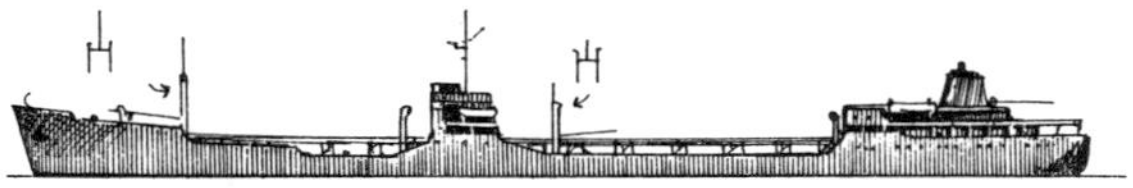

K_2MKF H123

35710 VOLUNTAS. It/Sw 1957; Tk; 12400; 170.72 × 9.63 (560.11 × 31.59); M; 14; ex PEPITA 1977. Similar: **35711 STOLT MARGARETA** (Gr) ex ANNIKEN 1974; ex MARGARETA 1961 **35712 EASTERN MARINER** (Tw) **35713 ALEXANDROS** (Cy) ex WILANA 1969

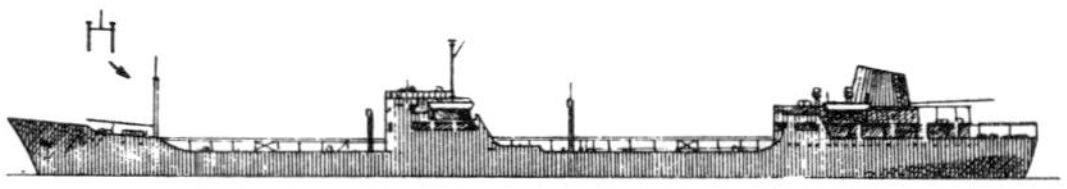

K_2MKF H123

⋆**35720 DA QING No 36.** RC/No 1957; Tk; 10200; 162.29 × 9.32 (532.45 × 30.56); M; 14.5; ex TA CHING No 36; ex VIVI 1970.

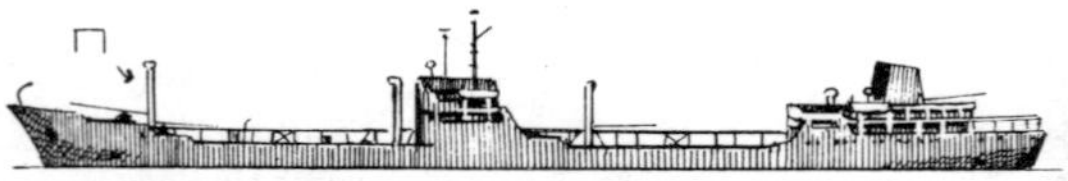

K_2MKF H123
35730 POLYVOS. Gr/No 1955; Tk; 10400; 162.29 × 9.31 (532.45 × 30.55); M; 14.5; ex VARVARA 1970. Similar: **35731 CAMELLIA B** (Gr) ex ROSE B; ex VENITA 1974.

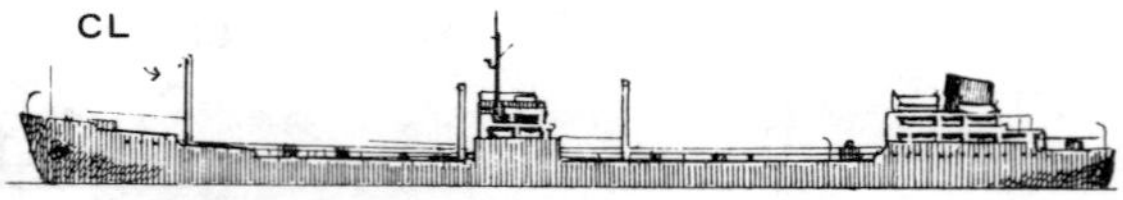

K_2MKF H123
35740 BANGLAR ALO. Bh/De 1960; Tk; 12300; 170.64 × 9.41 (559.84 × 30.88); M; 16; ex STOLT VIDAR 1976; ex STOLT SVEVE 1974; ex SVEVE 1971; ex NAKSKOV 1970. Sister: **35741 GARZAN** (Bh) ex ASIA 1960.

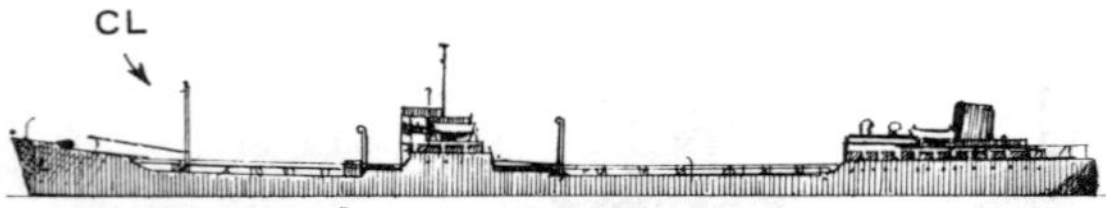

K_2MKF H123
● **35750 ALLISON STAR.** Li/Br 1960; Tk; 12500; 170.62 × 9.75 (559.78 × 32); M; 15; ex OCEAN TRADER 1972; ex ANCO QUEEN 1971; ex ATHELQUEEN 1966. Similar: **35751 ABELARDO L. RODRIGUEZ** (Me) ex PRESIDENTE ABELARDO L. RODRIGUEZ 1968; ex PEMEX 65-2 1966; ex NORDNES **35752 SPETSAI** (Gr) ex WHITE DOLPHIN 1976; ex STOLT DOLPHIN 1975; ex STOLT DESIREE 1975; ex STOLT SAGONA 1972; ex SAGONA 1967 **35753 MELITI** (Li).

K_2MKF H123
35760 ALRUBAYIA. Pa/Gr 1943; C; 900; 74.07 × 4.26 (243.01 × 14); M; 11; ex ELEISTRIA; ex SOUTHERN COAST 1967; ex FORTH 1962; ex COLEBROOKE 1959; ex SOUTHERN COAST 1955.

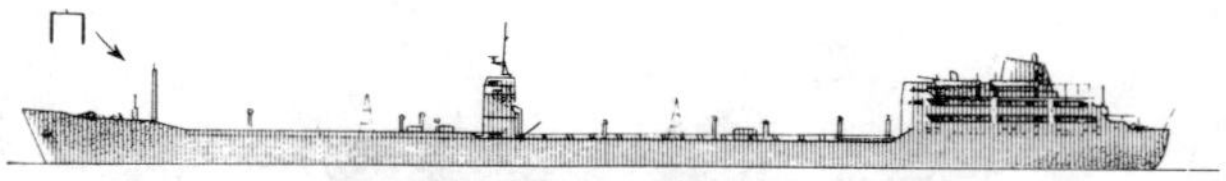

K_2MKF H13
35770 FFM-VIRIHAURE. Sw/Sw 1958/69; Tk/Ch; 15800; 181.82 × 10.36 (596.52 × 33.99); M; 14.5; ex VIRIHAURE 1970; Converted from ore/oil 1969.

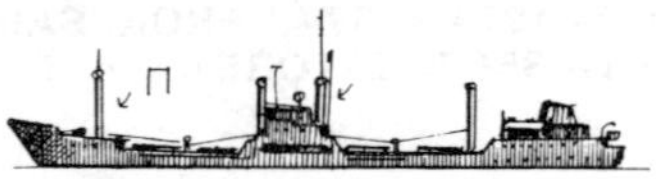

K_2MKF H13
35780 GIZAN. Si/Ys 1960; C; 1900/3100; 96.6 × —/6.97 (316.93 × —/22.87); M; 13.5; ex PORTLAND 1979; ex ALSTERDAMM 1973; ex MORAVA 1969; ex CIRCLE 1960.

K_2MKF H13
35790 ALRUBAYIA. Pa/Gr 1943; C; 900; 74.07 × 4.26 (243.01 × 14); M; 11; ex ELEISTRIA; ex SOUTHERN COAST 1967; ex FORTH 1962; ex COLEBROOKE 1959; ex SOUTHERN COAST 1955.

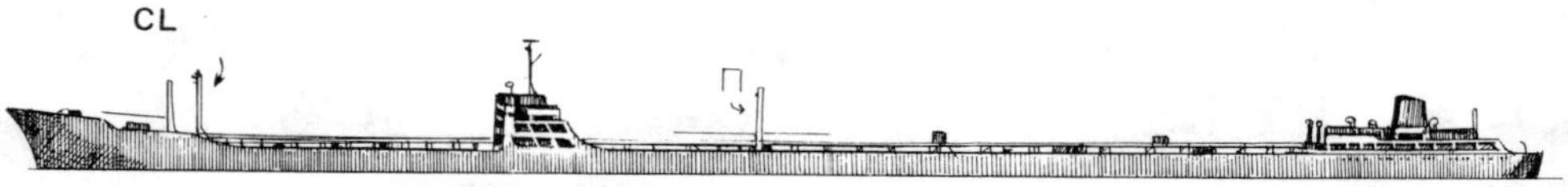

K_2MKFK H1
35800 LAKE PALOURDE. Li/US 1959; Tk; 61300; 297.01 × 15.69 (974.44 × 51.48); T; —; Lengthened 1965.

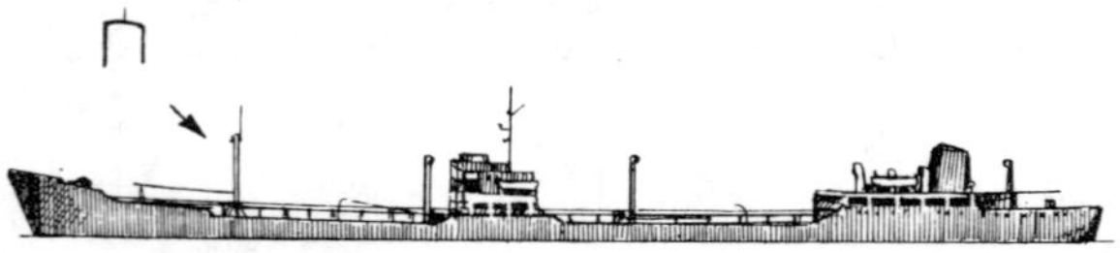

K_2MKFK H13
● **35810 ALDERAMINE.** It/It 1954; Tk; 12600; 172.24 × 9.6 (565.1 × 31.5); M; 15. Similar: **35811 ANDROMEDA** (It) **35812 BREZZA** (It) **35813 AURORA** (Cy) ex ATHENIAN AURORA 1980; ex ASTRAL 1975; ex AURORA 1974.

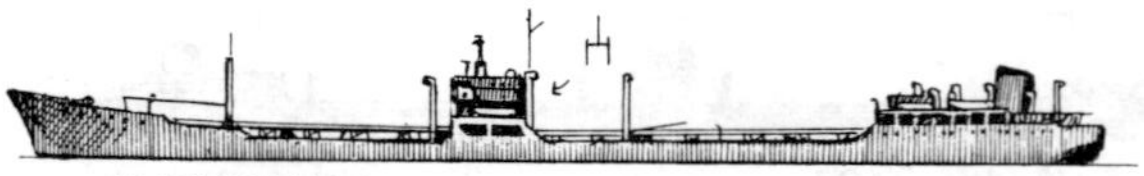

K_2MKFK H13
35820 CORTEMAGGIORE. It/It 1955; Tk; 12600; 172.24 × 9.6 (565.1 × 31.5); M; 15. Sister: **35821 PIBIDUE** (It) ex GIUSEPPINA NAPOLEONE 1973; ex CASSIOPEA 1968.

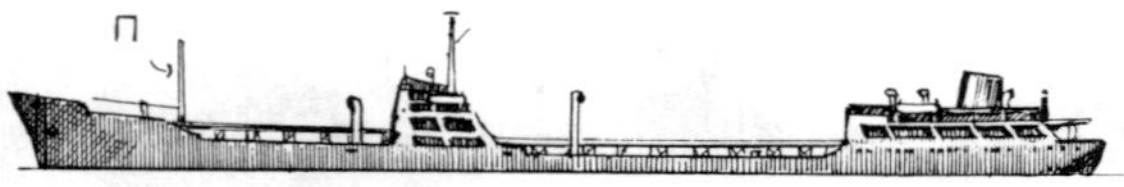

K_2MKFK H13
35830 SALAMBO. Li/Sw 1956; Tk; 12700; 169.81 × 9.25 (557.12 × 30.35); M; 15; ex PORT CROS 1976; ex TAIFUN 1974; ex MARIEBORG 1968.

K_2MK_2F H123
35840 SASSTOWN. Li/Ja-US 1943/64; Tk; 17500; 199.68 × 10.47 (655.12 × 34.33); T-E; 14; ex HESS FUEL 1963; ex CONASTOGA 1953; Aft section launched as HOBKIRKS HILL; Forward and cargo sections built Ja. 1963. Aft section built US 1943. Lengthened 1969. Sister: **35841 TIMBO** (Li) ex HESS VOYAGER 1963; ex RED CANYON 1956.

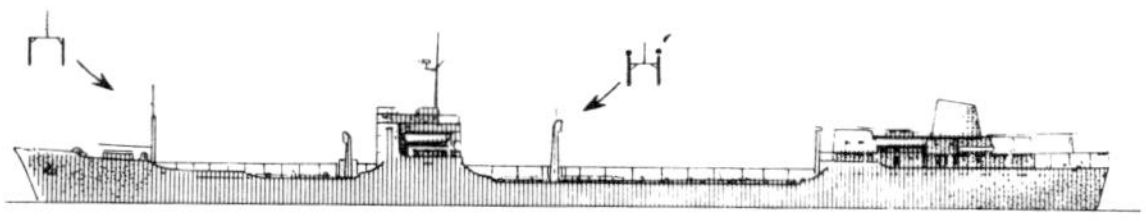

K_2MK_2F H123
35850 VASSILIS. Gr/Sw 1958; Tk; 12400; 170.72 × 9.63 (560.1 × 31.59); M; 15; ex LIFJORD 1972; ex ACINA 1961.

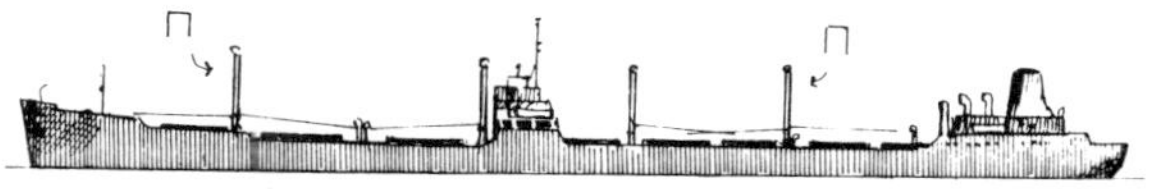

K_2MK_2F H123
35860 MERRIMAC. US/US-FRG 1944/62; B; 16000; 183.65 × 10.6 (602.53 × 33.6); T-E; 14.5; ex EASTHAMPTON 1965; ex LYRA 1962; ex AMANDA 1961; ex ALEXANDRA 1955; ex JAMES ISLAND 1948; Lengthened & converted from T-2 tanker 1962. Similar: **35861 LORANA** (Pa) ex PENN LEADER 1974; ex PEARY 1970; ex NORINA 1968; ex GRANAPOLIS : EX WESTHAMPTON 1963; ex MONTAUK POINT 1962; ex GULFPEAK 1960; ex GOLDEN HILL 1948.

K_2MK_2F H13
35870 MISS MARIETTA. Gr/FRG 1966; C; 22200; 204.96 × 11.37 (672.44 × 37.3); M; —. Sisters (Gr flag): **35871 MICHALAKIS 35872 MARY 35873 MASTER PETROS.**

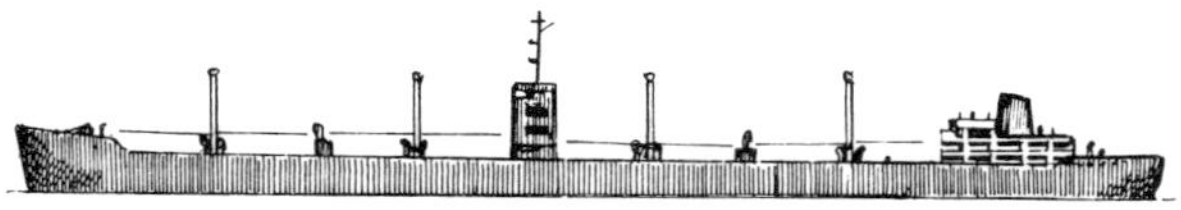

K_2MK_2F H13
35880 FAITH FIVE. Li/Ja 1959; B; 13100; 178.98 × 9.98 (587.21 × 32.74); M; 13.5; ex PUNTO BANCO 1981; ex CHI CHANG; ex NIKKO MARU 1972.

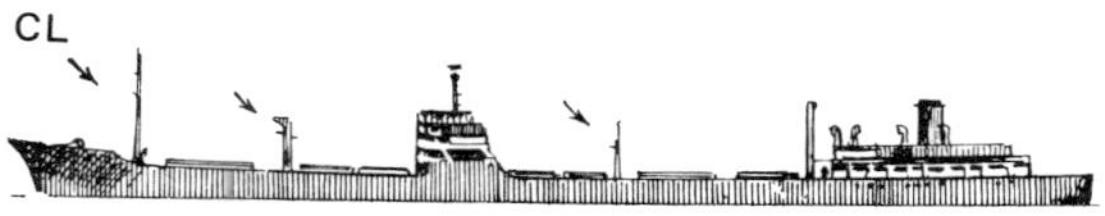

K_2MK_2F H2
35890 POLYTIMI ANDREADIS. Gr/US-Gr 1943/63; B; 14400; 172.37 × 10.1 (565.52 × 33.14); T-E; —; ex FORT NIAGARA 1948; Converted from a T-2 tanker and lengthened.

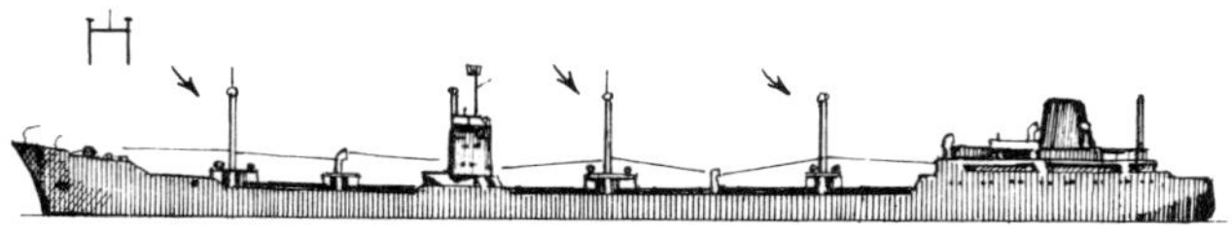

K_2MK_2FK H13
● **35900 ARCHANGELOS.** Gr/Ys 1963; B; 15900; 191.47 × 10.86 (628.18 × 35.63); M; 16; ex ARCHANGEL 1968; ex ARCHANGELOS 1963. Sisters: **35901 ALFITO** (Gr) ex MEANDROS 1980 **35902 THEOFANO LIVANOS** (Gr) Similar: ⋆**35903 HUA TAI** (RC) ex ATLANTIC CHAMPION 1978 **35904 ATLANTIC EAGLE** (Gr) **35905 ATLANTIC STAR** (Gr) **35906 INTERFELICITY** (Gr) ex IAMATIKOS 1980; ex SOUTHERN BREEZE 1973; ex ATLANTIC BREEZE 1972 **35907 EVROS** (Gr) **35908 MATHILDE** (Pa) ex THERMOPYLAI; ex KAPETANISSA 1976; ex KALLIOPI PATERAS 1972. **35909 NESTOS** (Li)

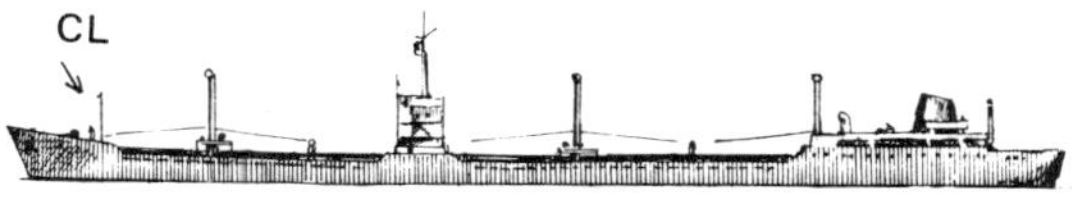

K_2MK_2FK H13
35910 SAINT MARCEL. Li/It 1961; B; 11200; 166.1 × 9.37 (544.95 × 30.74); M; 15.75; ex PORTOFINO 1968. Sister: **35911 SAINT RAPHAEL** (Li) ex PORTOVENERE 1968.

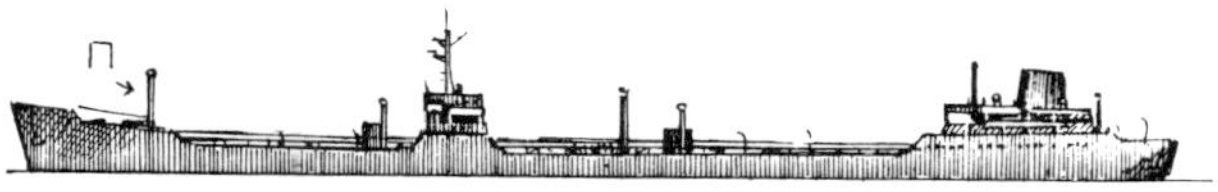

K_2MK_3FK H123
⋆**35920 CUU LONG I.** Vn/Sw 1964; Tk; 12900; 170.67 × 9.74 (559.94); M; 15; ex GRENANGER 1975. Sister: ⋆**35921 CUU LONG II** (Vn) ex AUSTANGER 1975.

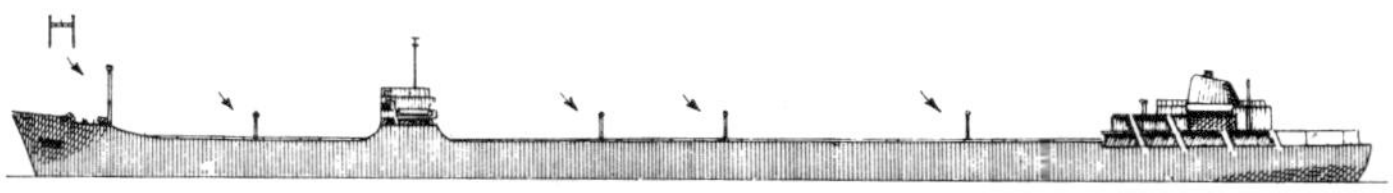

K_2MK_3FK H123
35930 DOMINIQUE. Li/Be 1959/66; B; 1900; 213.32 × 11.21 (699.87 × 36.78); T; —; ex RESOLUTE 1974; Lengthened and deepened 1966.

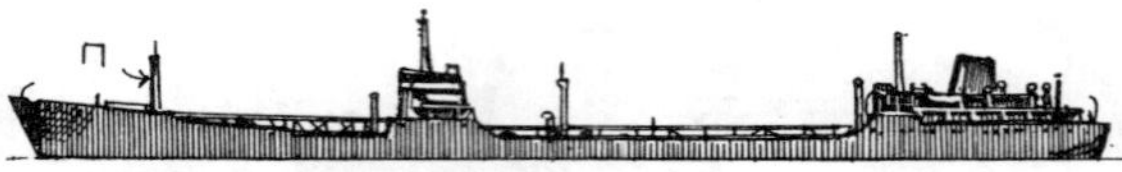

K_2MK_3FK H123
35940 BANGLAR KHEYA. Bh/Sw 1961; Tk; 12400; 170.72 × 9.63 (560.1 × 31.6); M; 15; ex ANJA 1976; ex WILCHIEF 1972.

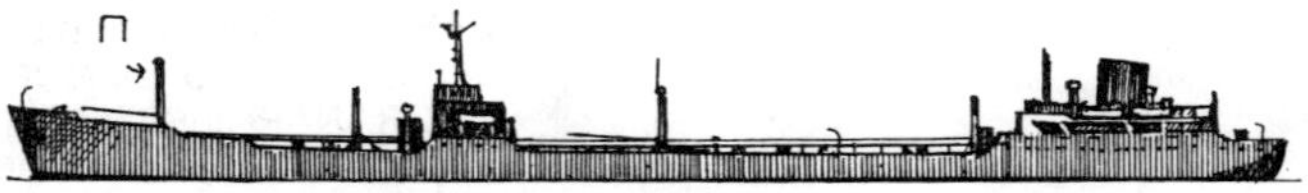

K_2MK_3FK H123
● **35950 RODOSTO.** Gr/No 1960; Tk; 20400; 200.95 × 10.9 (629.28 × 35.76); M; 15.75; ex HALLANGER 1973. Sister: **35951 ANSON** (Cy) ex STORANGER 1969.

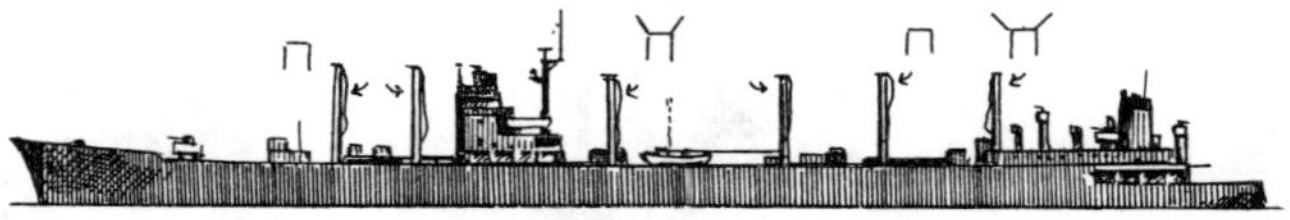

K_2MK_4F H1
35960 ASHTABULA. US/US 1943; RT/FA; 34000 Dspl; 196 × 10.7 (644 × 35); TST; 18; Jumboised 'T-3' type. Sisters: **35961 CALOOSAHATCHEE** (US) **35962 CANISTEO** (US).

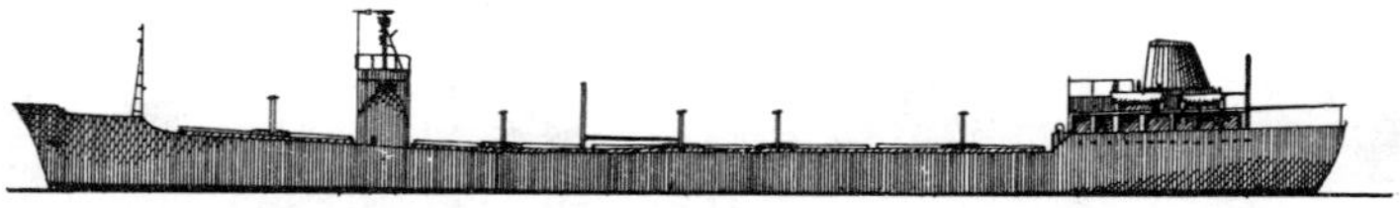

K_2MK_5FK H13
35970 MORVEN. Li/It 1961; OO; 17500; 212.15 × 10.78 (696 × 35.37); M; 14; Launched as OLIN MATHIESON.

K_2MK_2MF H
⋆**35980 HONG QI 112; & ALAMAR.** May now have this appearance. See next entry.

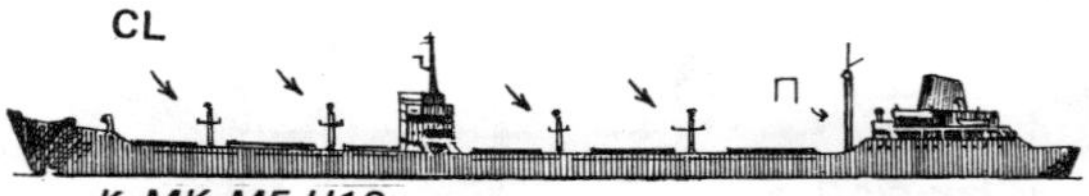

K_2MK_2MF H13
⋆**35990 HONG QI 112.** RC/FRG 1957; C; 11900; 166.5 × 9.05 (546.26 × 29.69); M; 14; ex NEW RED SEA 1976; ex RED SEA 1976; ex PRAUNHEIM 1972. Sister: **35991 ALAMAR** (Cy) ex BERKERSHEIM 1972 These two ships may now be like previous drawing.

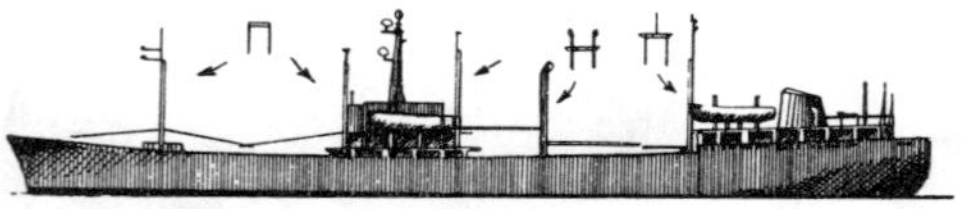

K_2MK_2MFK H
36000 SHIKISHIMA MARU. Ja/Ja 1961; FF; 9200; 145.9 × 7.85 (478.67 × 25.75); M; 14.75.

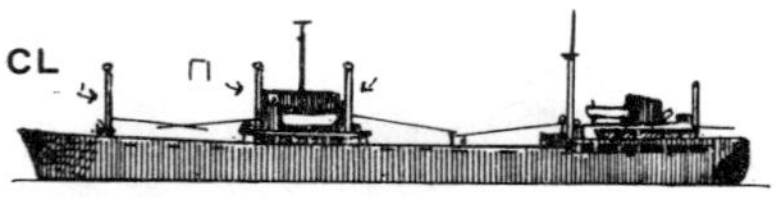

K_2MKMFK H
36010 POSSIDONIA. Gr/Ja 1955; C; 5100; 113.14 × 7.98 (371.19 × 26.18); M; 12.5; ex ITSUKISHIMA MARU 1977.

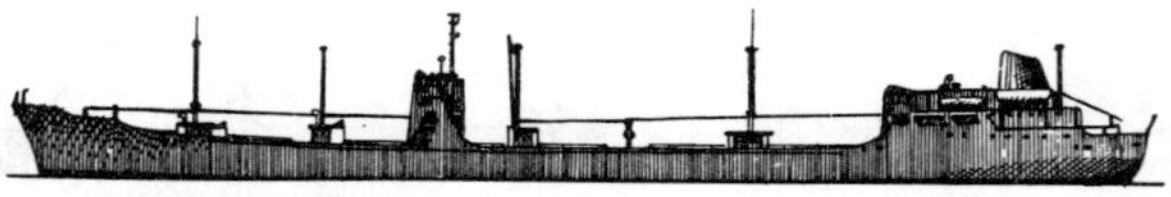

K_2MKMFK H13
36020 GREEK FRIENDSHIP. Gr/Ja 1963; B; 13500; 177.83 × 9.55 (583.43 × 31.33); M; 16.5; ex IONIAN SKIPPER 1980. Sister: **36021 IONIAN MARINER** (Li).

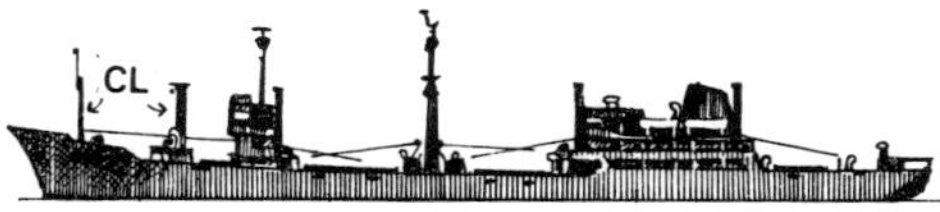

K_2MKMKFK H1
36030 SEA PEARL. Cy/Br 1961; C/HL; 6000/8700; 148.8 × 7.93/9.12 (488.19 × 26/29.92); M; —; ex CUSTODIAN.

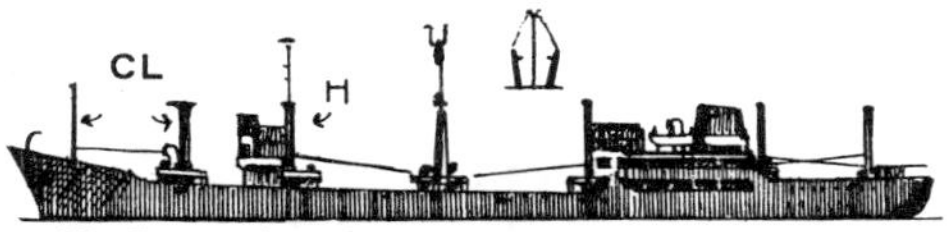

$K_2M_2KFK_2$ H13
36050 ADVENTURER. Br/Br 1960; C/HL; 6400/8400; 149.43 × —/9 (490.26 × —/29.53); M; 15.

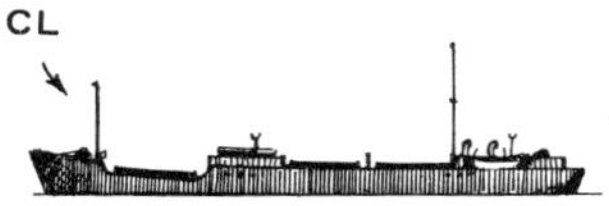

KM H12
● **36070 BLACKWELL POINT.** Pa/Br 1951; C; 1800; 82.45 × 5.2 (270.5 × 17.06); M; 11; ex BLACKWALL POINT. Sisters: **36071 GRAINVILLE** (Ih) ex BATTERSEA 1980 **36072 CHRISTOFOROS** (Gr) ex EPIC 1976; ex BIRLING 1975; ex THOMAS HARDIE 1968 **36073 GRANITT** (No) ex HORSHAM 1973; ex MURDOCH 1966 **36074 LINERA** (Br) ex LA MOLINERA 1972; ex SANDERSTEAD 1967; ex SAMUEL CLEGG 1967 **36075 FABIO SAVERIO** (It) (deepened 1970) ex CAPTAIN ALBERTO 1975; ex BRIGHTLING 1970; ex FALCONER BIRKS 1970 **36076 TITIKA** (Gr) ex KEYNES 1975; ex ACCUM 1967.

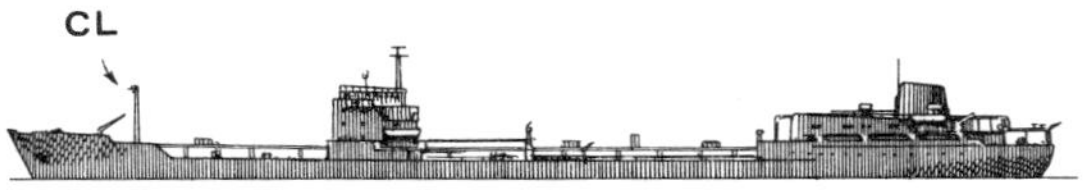

KMCF H123
36090 TERVI. Fi/Fi 1963; Tk; 11100; 164.83 × 9.2 (540.78 × 30.18); M; 14.5. Probable Sister: **36091 PALVA** (Fi).

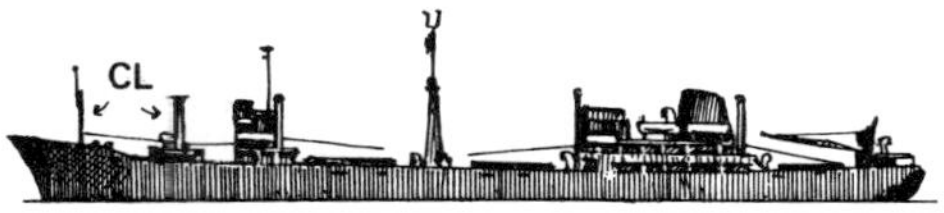

K_2MKMKFKC H1
36040 KERO. Pe/Br 1961; C/HL; 6000/8700; 148.8 × 7.93/9.11 (488.19 × 26/29.92); M; —; ex SEA LUCK 1980; ex TACTICIAN 1979.

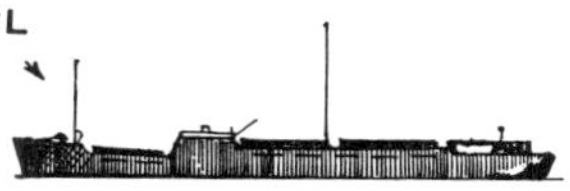

KM H12
● **36060 TARRING.** Br/Br 1958; C; 1900; 83.88 × 5.2 (275.2 × 17.09); M; —; ex LAMBETH 1970. Sisters: **36061 TSIMENTION** (Gr) ex KINGSTON 1971 **36062 VASSILIS IV** (Gr) ex MARO; ex CHRIS 1974; ex ACYRC 1972; ex CROYDON 1971 **36063 WORTHY** (Cy) ex WORTHING 1977; ex DULWICH 1970 **36064 ELEISTRIA II** (Gr) ex FULHAM IX 1970.

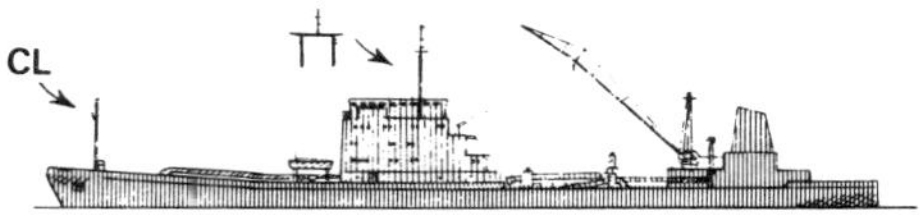

KMCF H
36080 NORDSEE. FRG/FRG 1978; D; 8700; 131.76 × 6.9 (432.28 × 22.64); TSM; 11.25.

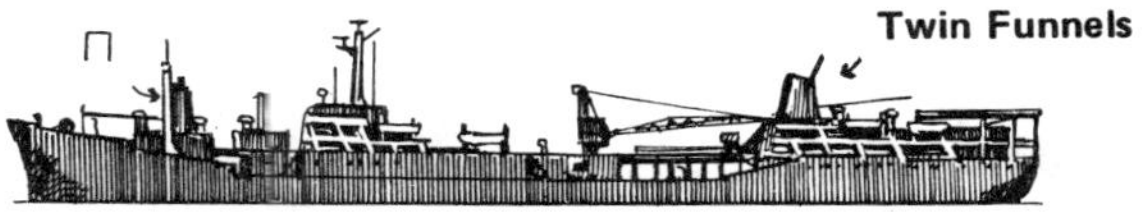

KMCF H123
36100 FORTIES KIWI. Br/Br 1960/76; OSS; 11000; 160.1 × 9.18 (525.26 × 30.12); M; 14.5; ex BRITISH KIWI 1976; Converted from a tanker.

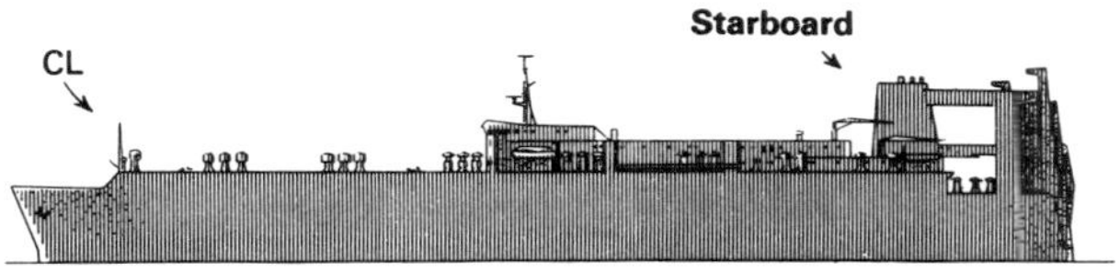

KMCFR H2
36110 SKAUGRAN. No/No 1979; RoC; 31100; 182.5 × 11.99 (598.75 × 39.34); M; 14.8; Stern quarter ramp/door.

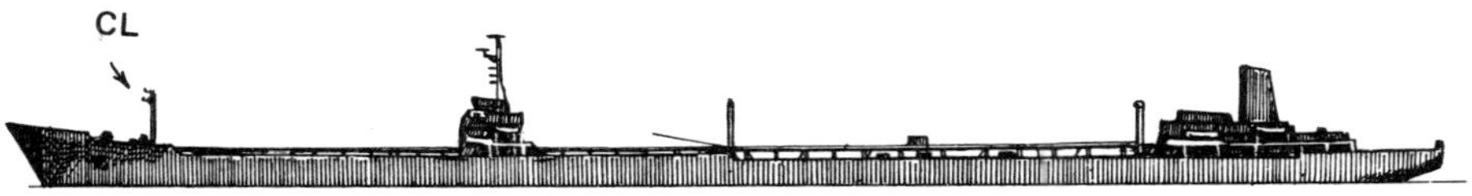

KMCKF H1
36120 ENSKERI. Fi/FRG 1970; Tk; 62400; 274.3 × 15.43 (899.93 × 50.62); M; 17. Sister: **36121 TIISKERI** (Fi).

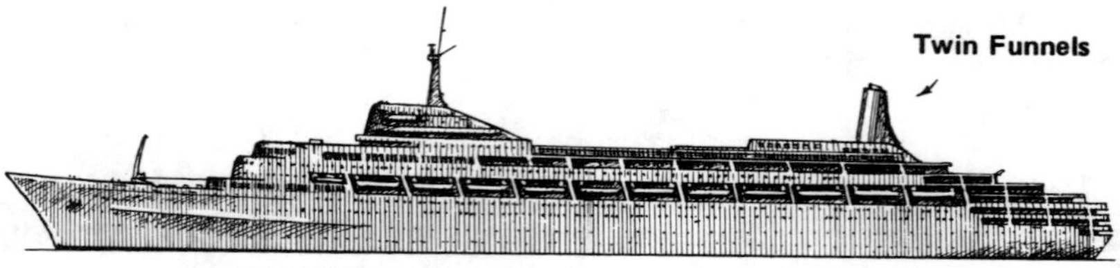

KMF H
36130 CANBERRA. Br/Br 1961; P; 44000/44800; 149.49×45/9.99 (818.54×28.01/32.78); TST-E; 27.5.

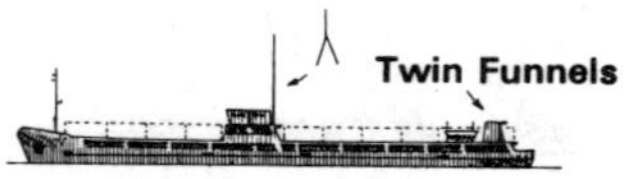

KMF H
★36140 SCHIFF DER DEUTSCH-SOWJETISCHEN FREUNDSCHAFT. Ru/DDR 1977; Riv/C/Con; —; 82×2.5 (269.2×8.57); TSM; 20.75.

KMF H
36150 AMINUL BAHR. Bh/Ne 1953; D; 900; 78.95×— (259.02×—); TSR; —.

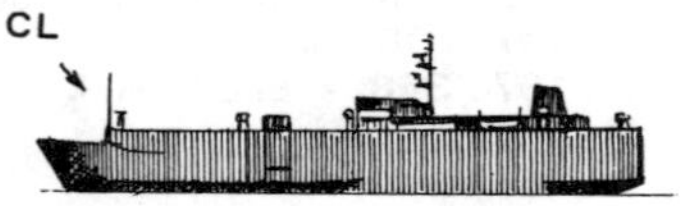

KMF H
36160 AUTOWEG. No/No 1973; RoVC; 500; 91.8×3.86 (301.18×12.66); M; 14.

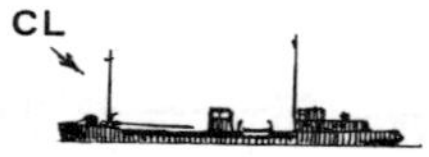

KMF H
36170 BLACKPOOL. Br/Br 1962; Tk; 530; 52.2×2.91 (171.26×9.55); M; —; ex UNO 1972. Sister: **36171 BRADFORD** (Br) ex TORO 1972.

KMF H12
36190 ANWAR. Le/Br 1941; C; 900; 64.32×4.1 (211.02×13.45); M; 10; ex AGHIOS SPYRIDON 1970; ex LOCHEE 1966; ex GOWRIE 1948; ex EMPIRE CAPE 1945.

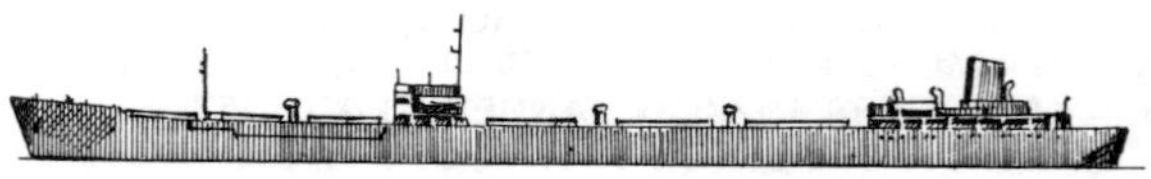

KMF H12
36200 SILVER FIR. Li/Br 1950/60 B; 12900; 174.15×9.9 (571.36×32.48); M; 13.5; ex SILVER STAR 1972; ex SAN MATEO 1960; ex VIKFOSS 1955; Converted from a tanker.

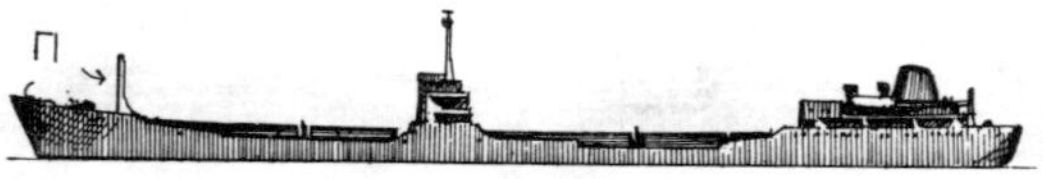

KMF H123
● **36210 MICHALIS.** Gr/Br 1961; O; 10600; 155.66×8.54 (510.7×28.02); M; 13; ex DUKESGARTH 1976. Sisters: **36211 DAPO SAILOR** (Gr) ex MONKSGARTH 1977 **36212 DAPO STAR** (Gr) ex QUEENSGARTH 1977 **36213 THEOSKEPASTI** (Pa) ex KNIGHTSGARTH 1975.

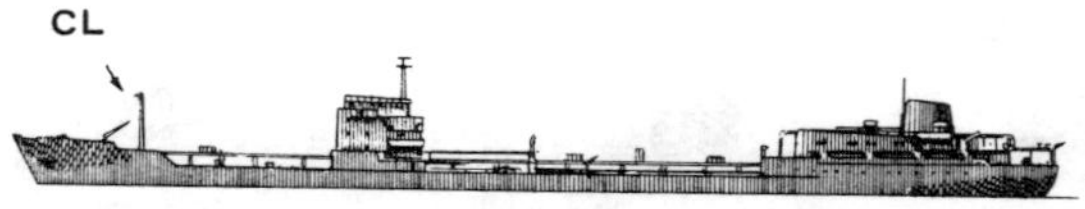

KMF H123
36220 TERVI. Fi/Fi 1963; Tk; 11100; 164.83×9.2 (540.78×30.18); M; 14.5. Probable Sister: **36221 PALVA** (Fi).

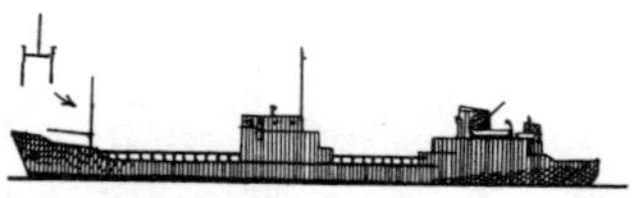

KMF H123
36230 PETROLA 13. Gr/Ne 1952; AT; 2300; 92.74×5.74 (304.27×18.83); M; 10.5; ex PETROLA XIII 1976; ex PETRO ASPHALT II; ex ESSO CALOR 1973; ex ESSO LE CAROUBIER 1968.

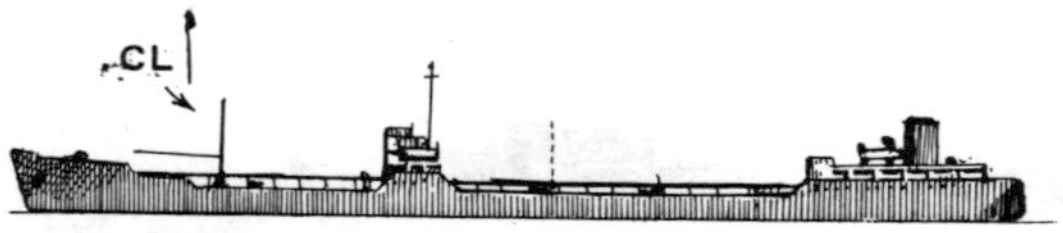

KMF H123
● **36240 WINDRATI.** So/Br 1952; Tk; 10500; 159.42×8.87 (523.03×29.1); M; 13; ex SEA JASPER 1966; ex WHEATFIELD 1964.

KMF H123
★36250 PEVEK. Ru/Fi 1958; Tk; 3100; 105.11×6.13 (344.85×20.1); M; 13.5. Sisters (Ru flag): **★36251 ARTYOM ★36252 BALTA ★36253 MOZYR ★36254 PIRYATIN ★36255 VENTSPILS ★36256 VILYUYSK ★36257 ZOLOTOY ROG ★36258 KOKAND.**

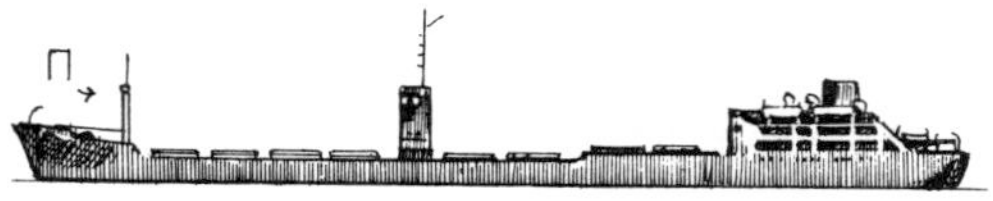

KMF H13
⋆36270 MAXHUTTE; DDR/Sw 1955; OO; 8500; 149 × 8.48 (488.85 × 27.83); M; 13.5; ex LEDARO 1975; ex VINDAFJORD 1974.

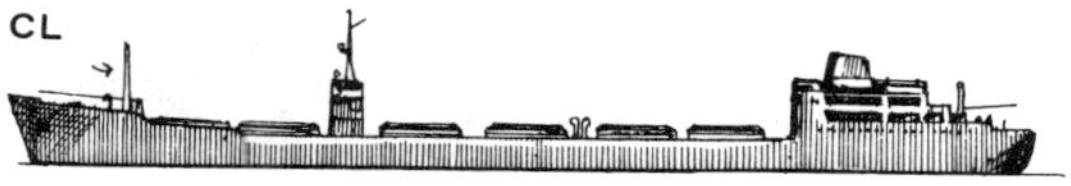

KMF H13
● **36280 FLAG SUPPLIER;** Pa/Sw 1956; O; 13400; 163.35 × 9.65 (536.91 × 31.66); M; 15; ex RIESA; ex CASSIOPEIA 1965. Sister: **36281 TELLHOLM** (Fi) ex DANWOOD SNOW 1975; ex SILVER CITY 1974; ex NORTRANS ENTERPRISE 1973; ex BULK ENTERPRISE 1970 Similar: **36282 TAKA** (Gr) ex WORLD SKILL 1971.

KMF H13
36290 ANINGA; It/FRG 1960; O; 9100; 166.43 × 9.42 (546.03 × 30.91); M; 15.5; ex TYNE ORE 1975. Sister: **36291 SEQUOIA** (It) ex QUIJOTE; ex TEES ORE 1975.

KMF H13
36300 FFM VIRIHAURE; Sw/Sw 1958; Tk/Ch; 15800; 181.82 × 10.36 (596.52 × 33.99); M; 14.5; ex VIRIHAURE 1970; Converted from ore/oil carrier 1969. Similar: **36301 KANARIS** (Gr) ex PAPANICOLIS 1974; ex VITTANGI 1970 **⋆36302 ZWICKAU** (DDR) ex VITAFORS 1969.

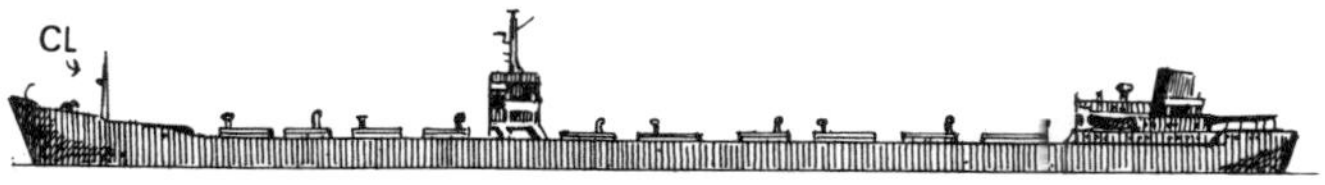

KMF H13
36310 REGAL STAR; Gr/Ja 1961; B; 23500; 204.12 × 11.75 (669.69 × 38.55); M; 16; ex JANECKE 1973; ex JANECKE MAERSK 1965. Sister: **36311 SOTIR** (Gr) ex MARCHEN 1973; ex JESPER MAERSK 1965.

KMF H13
36320 CAPO MANNU; It/Br 1944; Tk; 2400; 92 × 5.49 (301.84 × 18.01); R; 9; ex JANSON 1966; ex MOBILSUD 1964; ex CASSIAN 1954; ex REFAST 1953; ex EMPIRE PYM 1946.

KMF H13
36330 COVODORO; Mv/Br 1959; Tk; 948; 64.17 × 3.47 (210.53 × 11.38); M; 9; ex FIRLE 1976. Sister: **36331 ENAYATALLAH** (Si) ex MALDIVE ADVENTURE 1977; ex FRISTON 1975.

KMF H13
36340 BOLD KNIGHT; Br/FRG 1960; Tk; 464; 51.72 × 2.44 (169.69 × 8); M; 9.5. Probable Sister: **36341 PORTFIELD** (Br) ex BLACK KNIGHT 1980.

KMFC H1
⋆36350 QI LI HAI; RC/Be 1965; O; 33000; 229.67 × 12.4 (753.51 × 40.68); M; —; ex MINERAL SERAING.

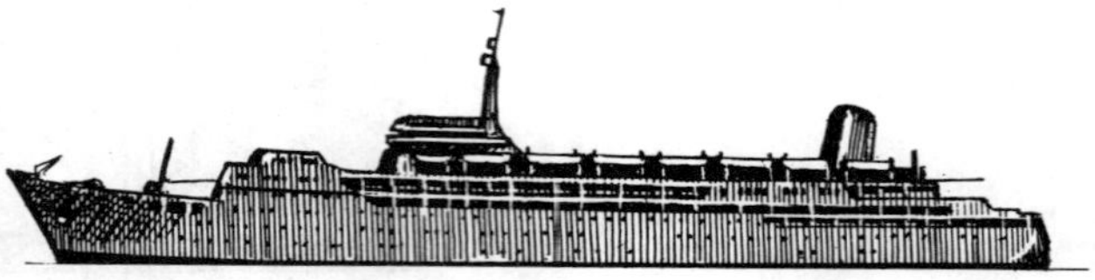

KMFK H
36360 AZURE SEAS; Pa/Br 1955; P; 16500; 184.06×7.98 (603.87×26.18); TST; 20; ex CALYPSO 1980; ex SOUTHERN CROSS 1973.

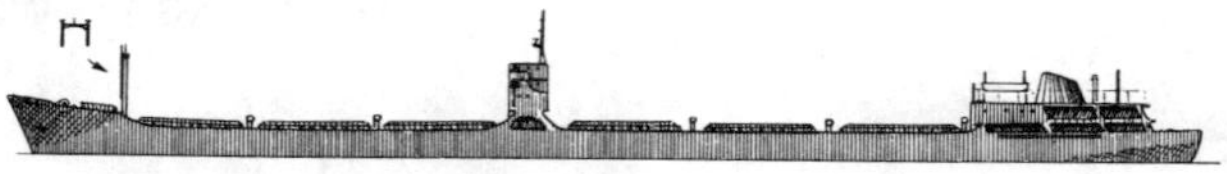

KMFK H1
36370 AMPHIOPEA; Gr/Fr 1962; O; 19400; 188.6×10.3 (618.77×33.79); M; —; ex AMPHIOPE 1980.

CL

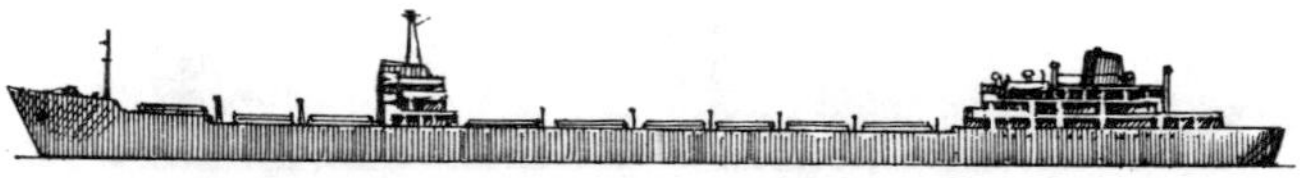

KMFK H1
36380 MARIVIC; Gr/Ja 1962; B; 23800; 204.2×11.78 (669.95×38.65); M; 15.5; ex IRON CAVALIER; ex NAESS CAVALIER 1966. Sister: **36381 KAVO XIFIAS** (Gr) ex NORDIC RAMBLER 1975; ex IRON CLIPPER 1975; ex NAESS CLIPPER 1964.

CL

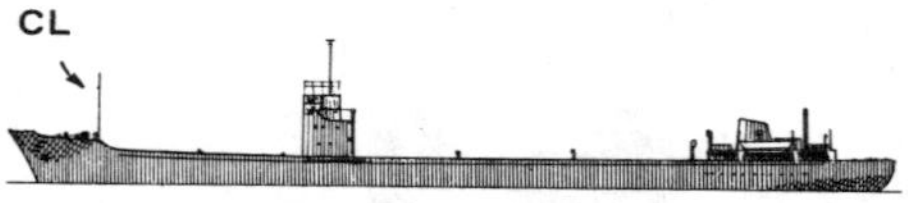

KMFK H1
● **36390 AFOVOS;** Gr/Ne 1958; B; 7300; 139.07×9.23 (456.27×30.29); M; 13.5; ex NICOLAS MARIS; ex KREEFT 1965. Sister: ⋆**36391 PERELIK** (Bu) ex ALIOTH 1970; ex RHONE 1968; ex ALIOTH 1967; ex TWEELINGEN 1965.

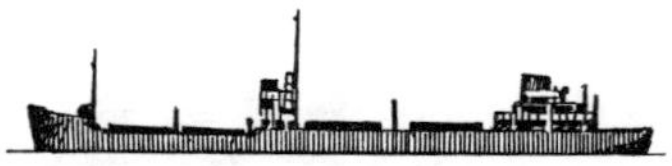

KMFK H12
● **36400 CAPITAN CARLO;** It/Br 1958; C; 3100; 97.54×6.27 (320×20.57); M; 11; ex MATHIOS 1976; ex SAINT ANDREAS 1975; ex SOUTHWARK 1968.

KMFK H123
● **36410 MICHALIS;** Gr/Br 1961; O; 10600; 155.66×8.54 (510.7×28.02); M; 13; ex DUKESGARTH 1976. Sisters: **36411 DAPO SAILOR** (Gr) ex MONKSGARTH 1977 **36412 DAPO STAR** (Gr) ex QUEENSGARTH 1977 **36413 THEOSKEPASTI** (Pa) ex KNIGHTSGARTH 1975.

CL

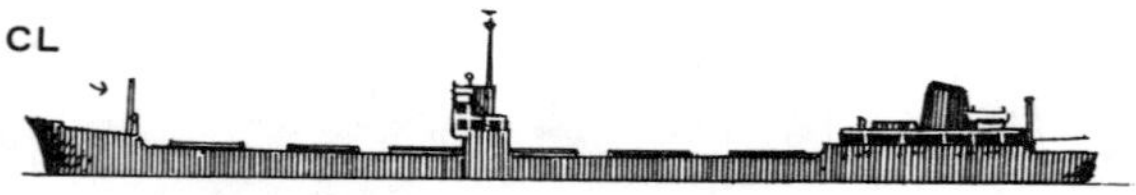

KMFK H123
36420 SPRINGTIME; Pa/It 1959; B; 11300; 166.02×9.4 (544.69×30.84); M; —; ex LIBIA CUOMO 1980; ex FEZZANO 1977; ex FALCON 1970.

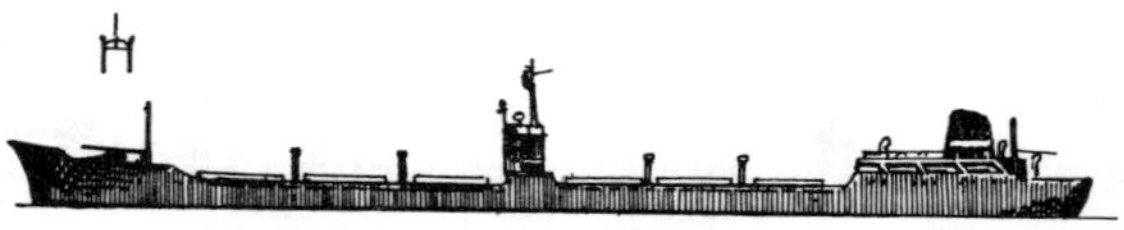

KMFK H123
36430 PIVIERE; It/It 1960; B; 11200; 165.49×9.25 (542.5×30.35); M; 15; ex SENATORE 1974; ex SENATORE G B BIBOLINI 1969. Sisters: **36431 LOCARNO** (Li) ex ALCIONE 1979; ex GIOVANNI QUEIROLO 1976

● **36432 GIOVANNI ANSALDO** (It) **36433 COCLERDUE** (It) ex PUNTA MESCO 1973; ex GUIDO DONEGANI 1969 **36434 CARLO CANEPA** (It) Similar (goal post forward): **36435 ORSA MINORE** (It).

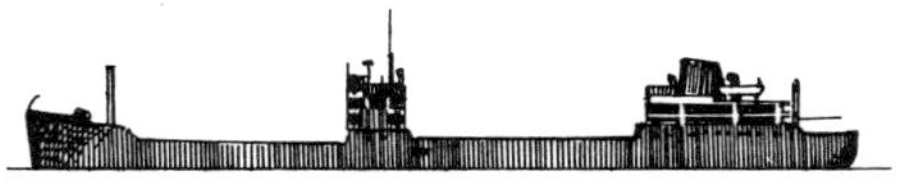

KMFK H123
36440 LSCO TAWI-TAWI; Pi/Br 1960; O; 5300; 130.23 × 7.79 (427.26 × 25.56); M; 11; ex KLAR 1976; ex CRINAN 1974.

KMFK H123
36450 ALASKAN TRADER; Gr/Sw 1954; Tk; 11600; 170.52 × 9.55 (559.5 × 31.34); M; 14.5; ex IRENES CHARISMA 1979; ex SWORD; ex HOEGH SWORD 1965.

KMFK H13
36460 FFM VIRIHAURE; Sw/Sw 1958; Tk/Ch; 15800; 181.82 × 10.36 (596.52 × 33.99); M; 14.5; ex VIRIHAURE 1970; Converted from ore/oil carrier 1969. Similar: **36461 KANARIS** (Gr) ex PAPANICOLIS 1974; ex VITTANGI 1970 ⋆**36462 ZWICKAU** (DDR) ex VITAFORS 1969.

CL

KMFK H13
36470 ATHANASIA COMNINOS; Cy/Sw 1956; O/Ch; 13600; 163.3 × 9.95 (535.76 × 32.64); M; 15; ex BISKOPSO 1974.

CL

KMFK H13
● **36480 FLAG SUPPLIER;** Pa/Sw 1956; O; 13400; 163.35 × 9.65 (536.91 × 31.66); M; 15; ex RIESA; ex CASSIOPEIA 1965. Sister: **36481 TELLHOLM** (Fi) ex DANWOOD SNOW 1975; ex SILVER CITY 1974; ex NORTRANS ENTERPRISE 1973; ex BULK ENTERPRISE 1970 Similar: **36482 TAKA** (Gr) ex WORLD SKILL 1971.

KMFK H13
36490 ACCIAIERE; It/It 1957; B; 11300; 165.46 × 9.3 (542.85 × 30.51); M; 13. Sisters: **36491 CORONA BOREALE** (It) **36492 LAMINATORE** (It) Similar (Pole mast forward): **36493 COCLERTRE** (It) ex CORALLINA 1980 **36494 AUCTORITAS** (It) **36495 THOMAS A** (Gr) ex CONCORD I 1976; ex LADY RITA 1976; ex PUGLIOLA 1973; ex ALBERTO LOLLI GHETTI 1965 **36496 WHITE RIVER** (Gr) ex WHITE ROVER 1980; ex WHITE RIVER 1976.

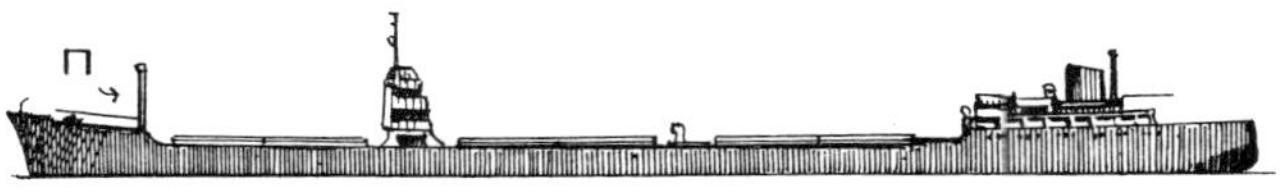

KMFK H13
36510 KRIOS; Gr/FRG 1959; B; 17000; 195.79 × 10.63 (642.36 × 34.88); M; 15; ex FIONA 1971.

CL

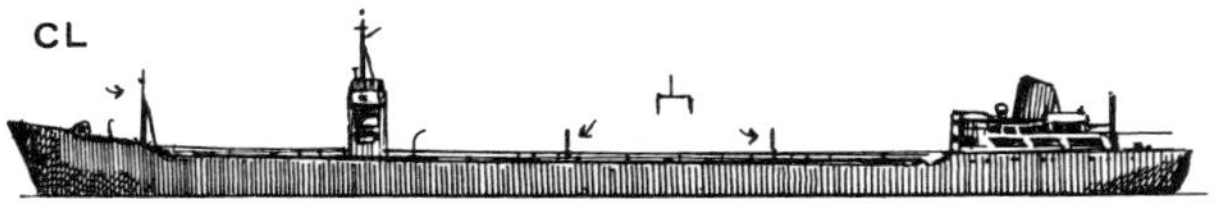

KMFK H13
36520 CONALCO; Li/FRG 1959; O; 8800; 184.31 × 9.41 (604.69 × 30.87); M; 14.5; ex OLIN 1974. Sisters (Li flag): **36521 REVERE 36522 BURNSIDE** ex MATHIESON 1974.

KMFK H13
36530 DEEPSEA MINER II; Li/FRG 1959; M; 8200; 166.43 × 9.41 (546.03 × 30.87); M; 15; ex WESER ORE 1976; Converted ore carrier.

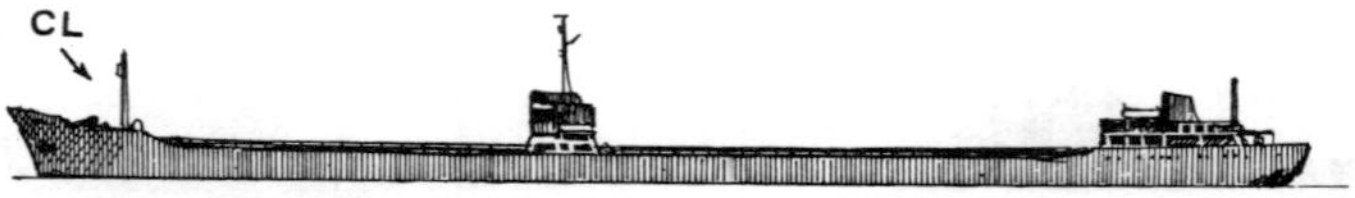

KMFK H13
36540 SENORITA MARIA; Gr/Ja 1962; B; 22300; 204.02 × 11.8 (669.36 × 38.71); M; 15.5; ex THEOFOROS 1980; ex EUGENIA 1971; ex DARIUS 1971; ex NAESS CLARION 1969.

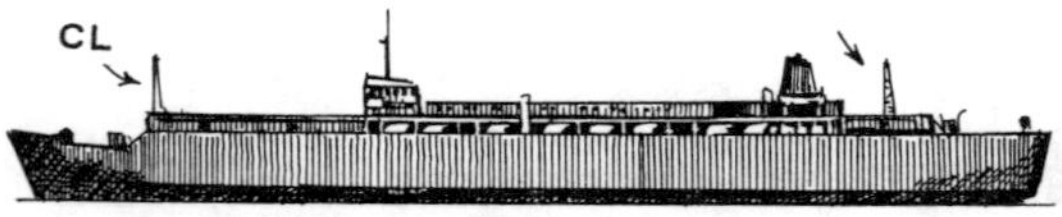

KMFK H2
36550 PERENNIAL ACE; Pa/Ja 1974; RoVC; 10900; 161.68 × 6.71 (530.45 × 22.01); M; 18.5.

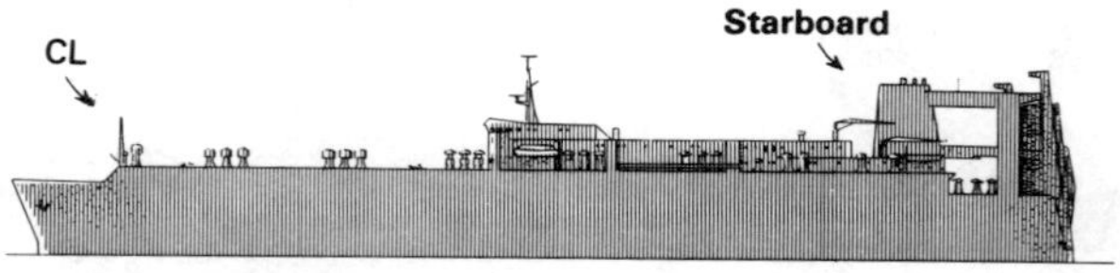

KMFR H2
36560 SKAUGRAN; No/No 1979; RoC; 31100; 182.5 × 11.99 (598.75 × 39.34); M; 14.8; Stern quarter ramp/door.

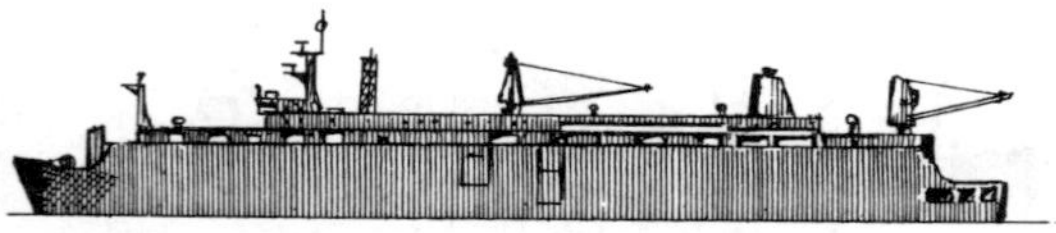

KMKCFC H2
36570 EASTERN HIGHWAY; Ja/Ja 1977; RoVC; 11400; 152.3 × 7.62 (499.67 × 25); M; 18.5.

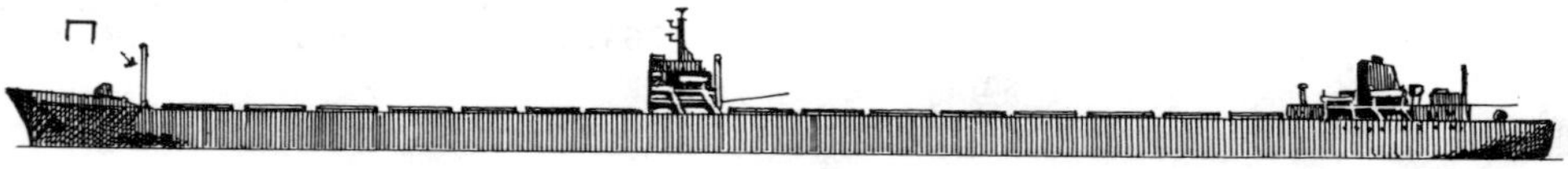

KMKF H
36580 WEILEE; Tw/Ja 1962/73; OO; 6460; 296.48 × 16.59 (972.7 × 54.43); T; 16.25; ex MARCONA PROSPECTOR 1977; ex PROSPECT 1977; ex MARCONA PROSPECTOR 1977; ex SAN JUAN PROSPECTOR 1974; Lengthened and deepened 1973.

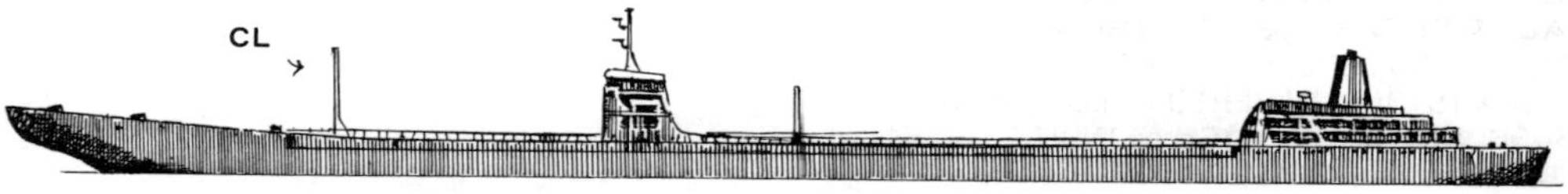

KMKF H
36590 MANHATTAN; US/US 1962/69; Tk/IB; 62400; 306.48 × 16.09 (1005.51 × 52.79); TST; 17.5; Converted from tanker, lengthened and widened.

KMKF H
36600 HORYU MARU; Ja/Ja 1964; Cem; 7700; 140.01 × 7.42 (459.35 × 24.34); M; 13.

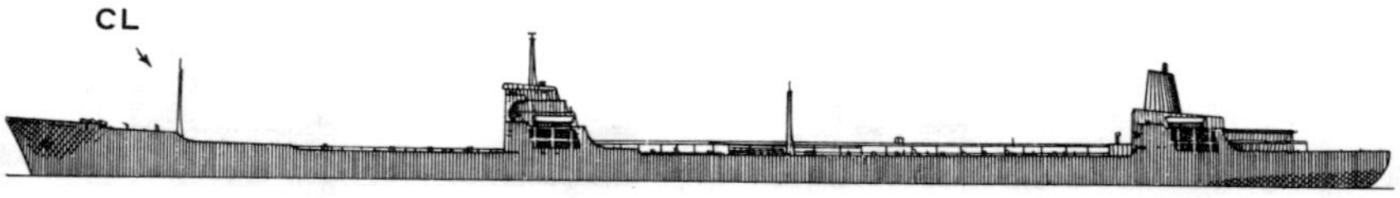

KMKF H1
36610 OVERSEAS NATALIE; US/US 1961; Tk; 41000; 262.14 × 14.05 (860.04 × 46.1); T; 17; ex WESTERN HUNTER; ex ORION HUNTER 1964.

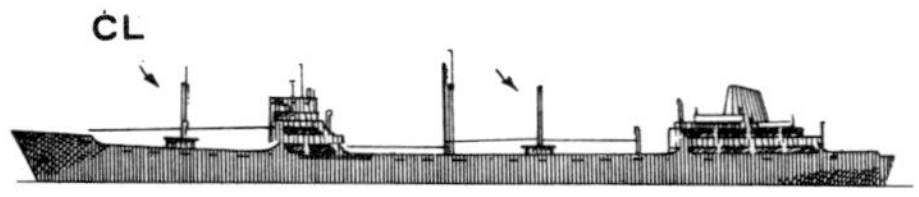

KMKF H1
● **36620 MIZAR**; Pa/It 1956; C; 5545/7441; 139.15 × 7.89/8.78 (456.53 × 25.88/28.8); M; 12.5; ex PIVA 1980; ex MARCO U MARTINOLI 1966. Sister: ⋆**36621 TARA** (Ys) ex MARCIA ANGELA MARTINOLI 1966.

KMKF H123
36630 PRIMERO; Fi/De 1959; Tk; 13600; 175.17 × 9.46 (574.71 × 31.04); M; 15.25.

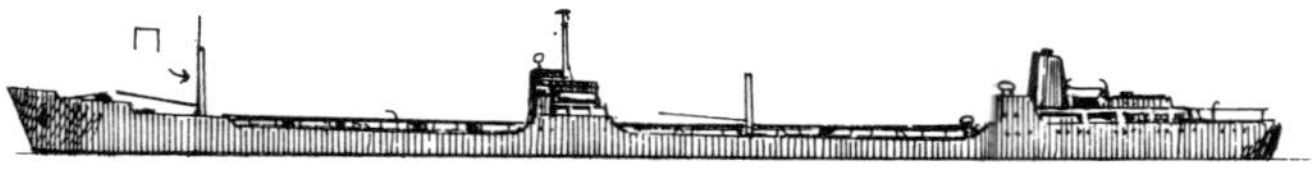

KMKF H123
36640 ALLEGIANCE; US/US 1956; Tk; 19400; 201.48 × 10.85 (661.02 × 35.6); T; 17; ex CITIES SERVICE BALTIMORE. Sister: **36641 BANNER** (US) ex CITIES SERVICE MIAMI 1976.

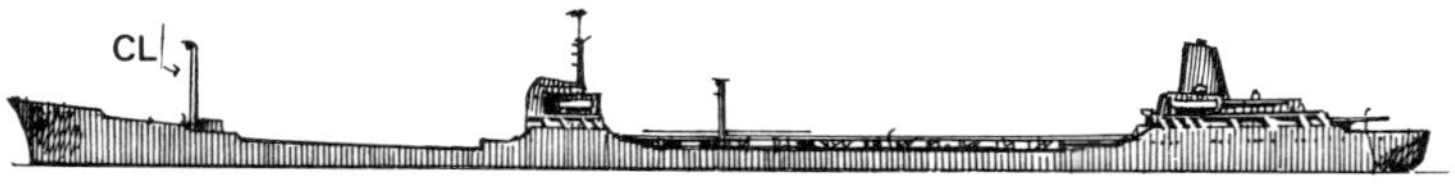

KMKF H123
36650 MONTICELLO VICTORY. US/US 1961; Tk; 28500; 222.44 × 12.14 (736.35 × 39.81); T; 16. Sister (US flag): **36651 MONTPELIER VICTORY** Similar (US flag): **36652 MOUNT WASHINGTON 36653 MOUNT VERNON VICTORY 36654 OVERSEAS JOYCE** ex MAYFLOWER 1966 **36655 COVE TRADE** ex TRANSEASTERN 1977.

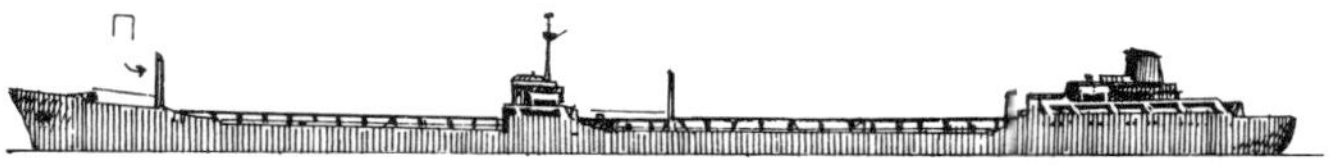

KMKF H123
36660 TEXACO ROCHESTER. Br/Be 1959; Tk; 22000; 203.16 × 10.98 (666.54 × 36.02); T; 17; ex CALTEX BRISTOL 1968.

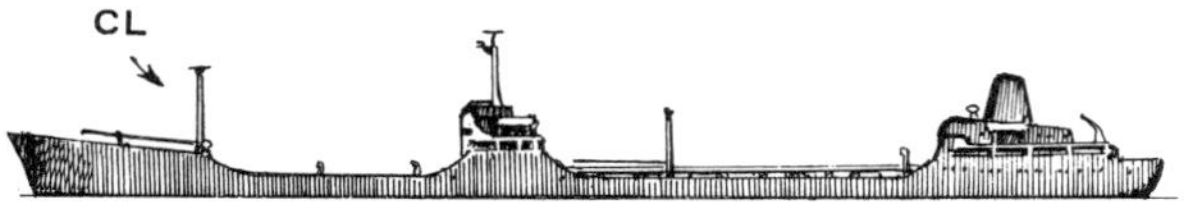

KMKF H123
36670 TEXACO GEORGIA. US/US 1964; Tk; 16500; 184.31 × 10.64 (604.69 × 34.9); T; 17.5. Sisters (US flag): **36671 TEXACO MARYLAND 36672 TEXACO MASSACHUSETTS 36673 TEXACO MONTANA 36674 TEXACO RHODE ISLAND**.

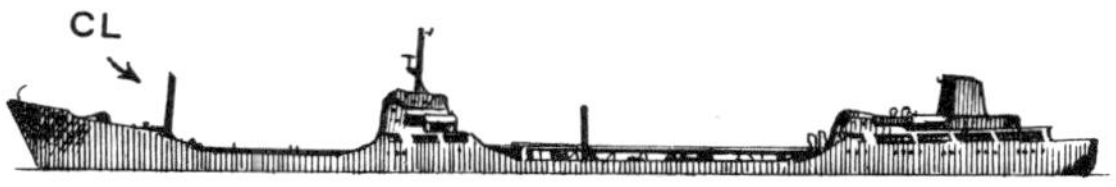

KMKF H123
● **36680 TEXACO SKANDINAVIA**. No/No 1962; Tk; 13200; 176.33 × 9.64 (578.51 × 31.63); M; 15. Sister: **36681 TEXACO NORGE** (No) Similar: **36682 TEXACO OSLO** (No) **36683 TEXACO GLOUCESTER** (Br) ex REGENT EAGLE 1969.

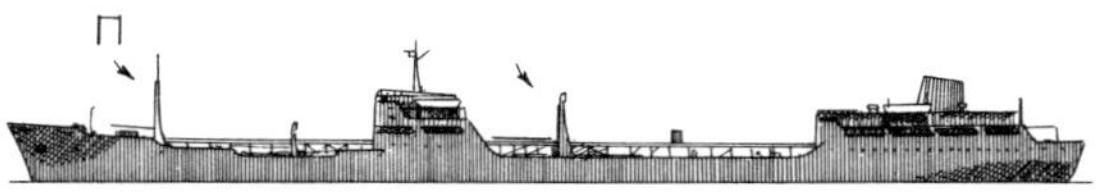

KMKF H123
36690 FOLIA. Li/No 1960 Tk; 12200; 169.73 × 9.67 (556.86 × 31.73); M; 14; ex STOLT FILIA 1980; ex STOLT ARGOBAY; ex STOLT HAWK 1973; ex OSTHAV 1968. Sister: **36691 SEA BREEZE** (Li) ex VERMONT 1977; ex JONWI 1962.

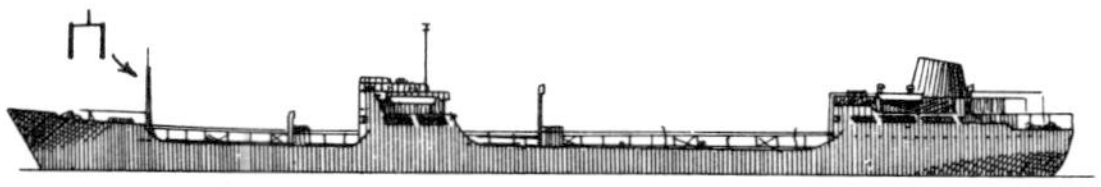

KMKF H123
⋆**36700 DA QING No 37**. RC/No 1958; Tk; 11100; 167.65 × 9.48 (550.03 × 31.1); M; 14.5; ex PET 1970; ex NORSK VIKING 1969; ex FARMAND 1963.

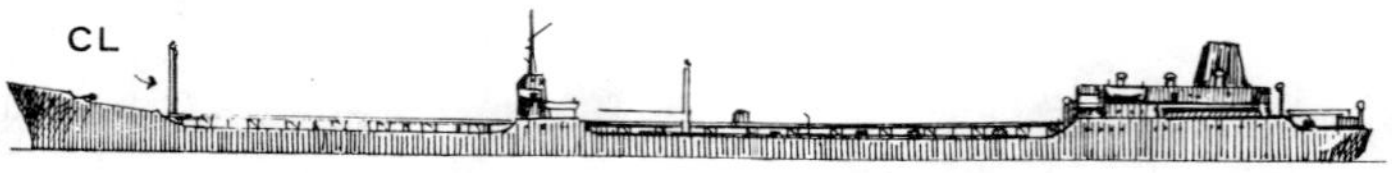

KMKF H123

● ⋆**36710 JIN HU**. RC/Sw 1963; Tk; 26400; 215.22 × 11.95 (706.1 × 39.2); M; 16; ex WANYI 1973; ex ANTILLA 1973; ex TIGRE 1969.

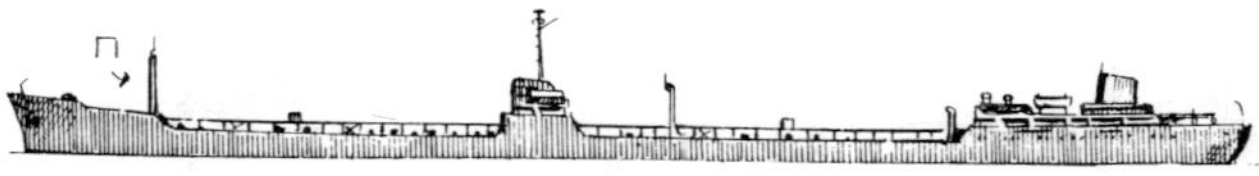

KMKF H123

⋆**36720 QI LIN HU**. RC/De 1960; Tk; 16200; 194.24 × 10.67 (637.27 × 35.01); M; —; ex CHINSHAKIANG 1977; ex GJERTRUD MAERSK 1971.

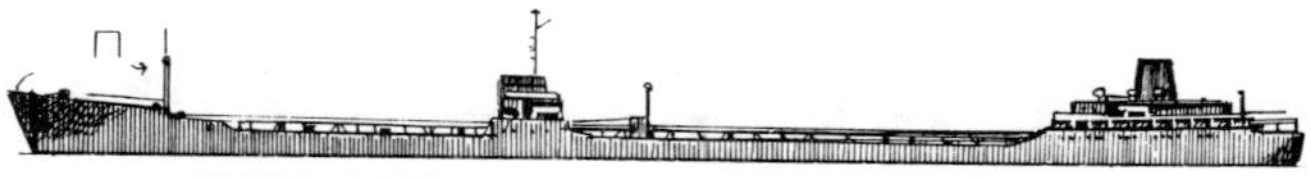

KMKF H123

36730 GOTA RIVER. Pa/Sw 1962; Tk; 22400; 208.03 × 11.56 (682.51 × 37.93); M; —.

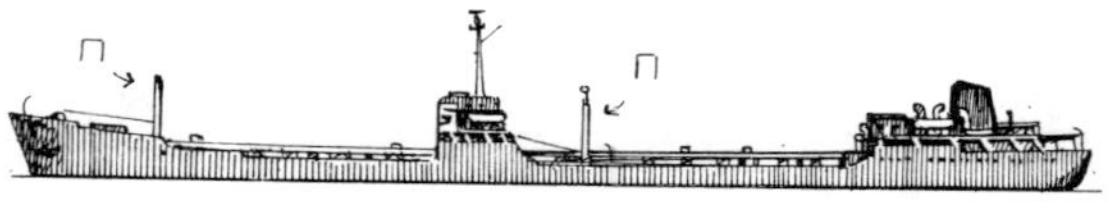

KMKF H123

36740 MONEMVASIA. Gr/Ja 1956; Tk; 12400; 170.69 × 9.34 (560 × 30.64); M; 15; ex SARONIS; ex ETHALI 1972; ex ELSBORG 1968. Sisters: **36741 PUNTA ANGELES** (Ch) ex SONAP II 1975; ex TUBORG 1975 ⋆**36742 CHUN HU** (RC) ex BINJIANG 1976; ex VIBORG 1975 Similar: **36743 MOLLENDO** (Pe-navy) ex AMALIENBORG 1967.

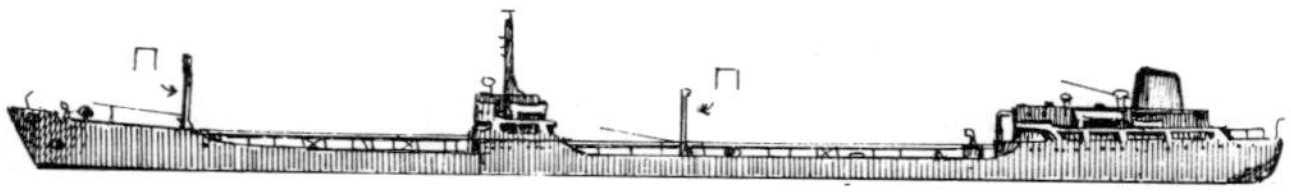

KMKF H123

36750 TURBIE. Pa/FRG 1957; Tk; 21200; 202.57 × 11.02 (664.6 × 36.25); M; 15.25; ex SAINT ANNA 1980; ex AGNH 1980; ex ST. GRIGOROUSA 1977; ex HOEGH FAIR 1969. Sister: ⋆**36751 SILBA** (Ys) ex HOEGH FAVOUR 1966.

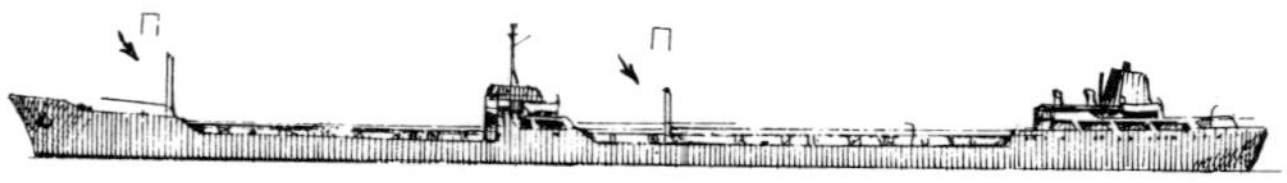

KMKF H123

36760 AGIOS VLASIOS V. Li/Ja 1956; Tk; 20100; 201.15 × 10.82 (659.94 × 35.5); T; 16.5.

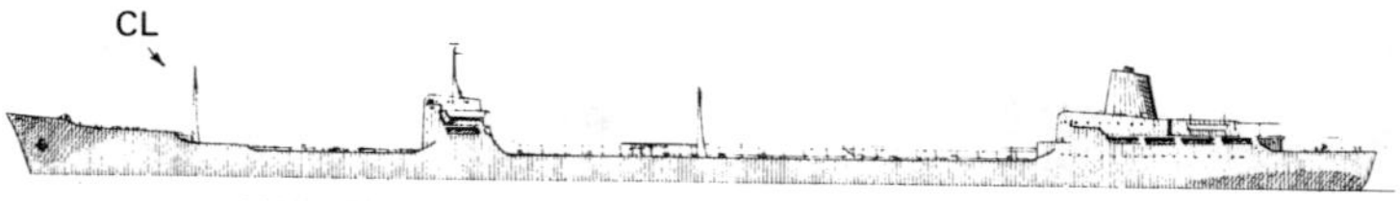

KMKF H123

36770 TEXACO ANACORTES. Pa/Ja 1961; Tk; 26300; 224.34 × 12 (736.02 × 39.37); T; 16. Similar (US built—Pa flag): **36771 TEXACO BRIGHTON** ex BRIGHTON 1971 **36772 TEXACO MAINE** ex MAINE 1960.

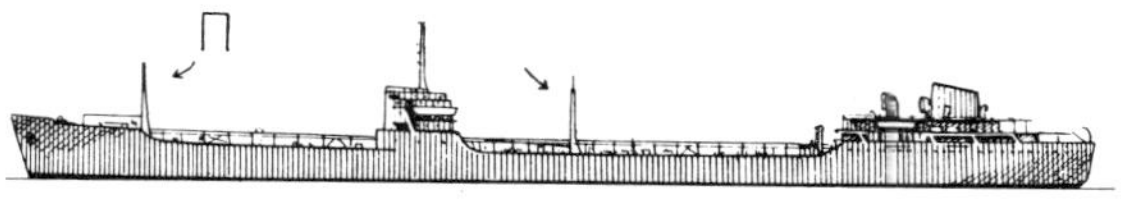

KMKF H123
36780 KAMPOS. Gr/Ja 1958; Tk; 13000; 170.69 × 9.82 (560.01 × 32.22); M; 14.75; ex ELPHINE 1975; ex ARTHUR MAERSK 1973. Similar: **36781 PYRROS V** (Gr) ex PALAEMON 1977; ex CHARLES P 1970; ex ANDERS MAERSK 1965 **36782 SILVER PACE** (Li) ex ALVA MAERSK 1968.

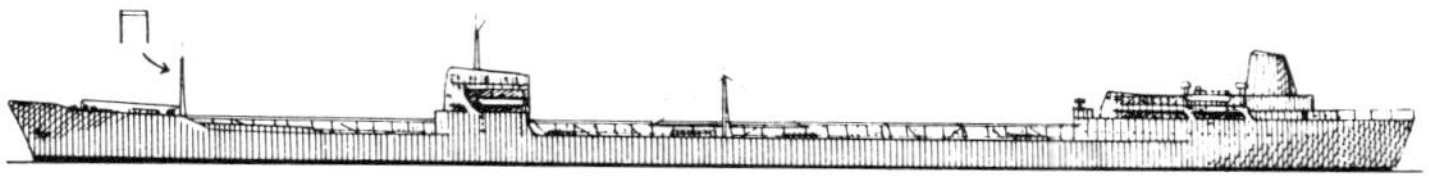

KMKF H123
36790 TZINA M. Gr/Sw 1963; Tk; 28000; 220.73 × 11.83 (724.18 × 38.81); M; 16; ex ERIC K FERNSTROM 1970; ex ERIC FERNSTROM.

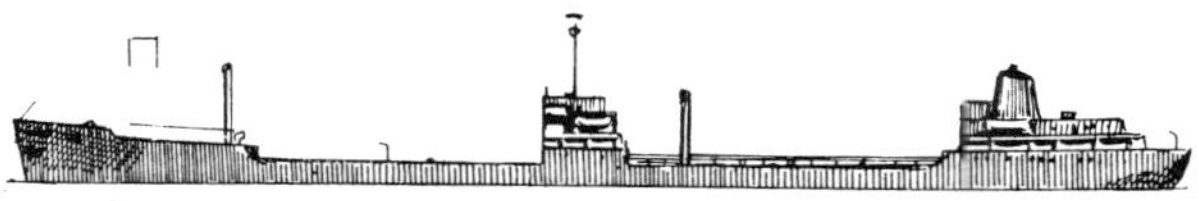

KMKF H123
36800 AMERICAN EXPLORER. US/US 1959; Tk; 22500 Dwt; 187.5 × 9.8 (615 × 32); T; 20; operated by Military Sealift Command.

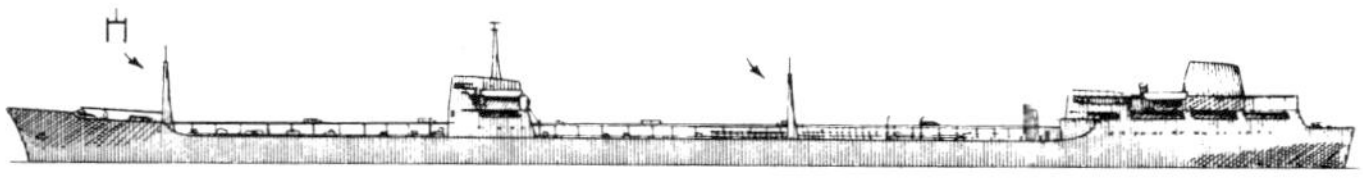

KMKF H123
⋆36820 TOUNDYA. Bu/No 1963; Tk; 26800; 213.62 × 11.76 (700.85 × 38.58); M; 15.5; ex BUGANDA 1969.

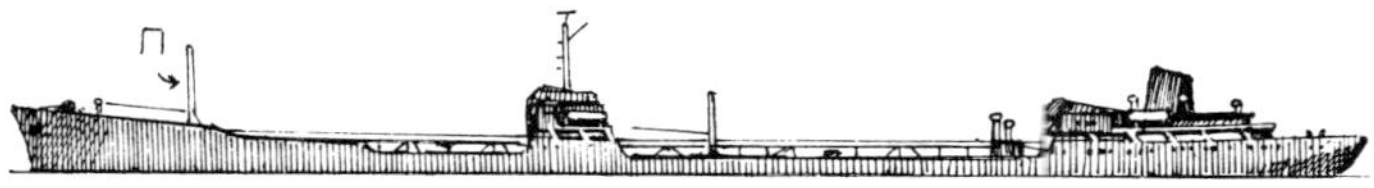

KMKF H123
36830 DAFFODIL B. Gr/Sw 1961; Tk; 22300; 212.86 × 11.24 (698.36 × 36.88); M; 16.25; ex LONDON INDEPENDENCE 1976. Sisters (Gr flag): **36831 TULIP B** ex OVERSEAS AMBASSADOR 1976 **36832 THIAKI** ex OVERSEAS DISCOVERER 1976.

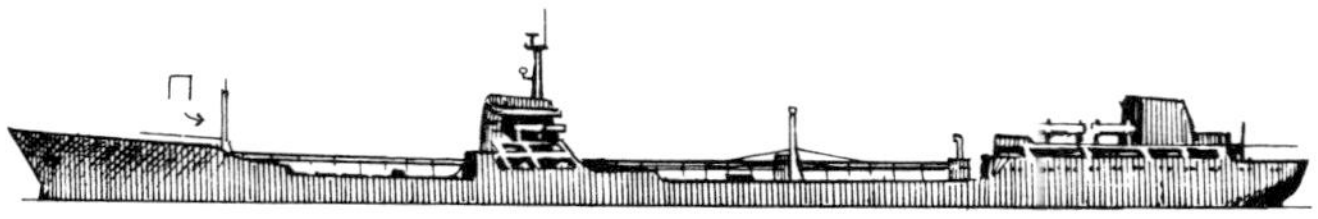

KMKF H123
⋆36840 PEKIN. Ru/Ru 1959; Tk; 20300; 202.8 × 11.98 (665.35 × 39.32); T; 17.5. Sisters (Ru flag): **⋆36841 BUCHAREST ⋆36842 BUDAPEST ⋆36843 PHENIAN ⋆36844 PRAGA ⋆36845 VARSHAVA ⋆36846 ULAN-BATOR.**

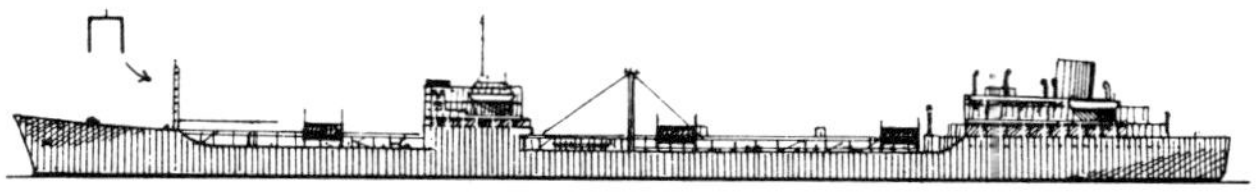

KMKF H123
● **36850 ESSO YORK.** Br/Br 1955; Tk; 17200; 191.93 × 10.26 (629.69 × 34.78); T; 16.75. Similar (US flag): **36851 NEW YORK GETTY** ex FLYING A—NEW YORK 1968 **36852 DELAWARE GETTY** ex FLYING A—DELAWARE 1968.

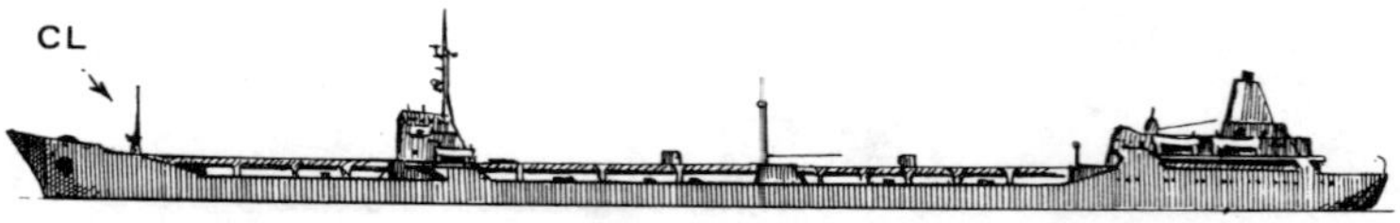

KMKF H123
★36860 SOFIYA. Ru/Ru 1963; Tk; 31800; 230.51 × 11.81 (756.27 × 38.89); T; 16.5. Sisters (Ru flag): **★36861 AKHTUBA** ex HANOI 1969 **★36862 BELGRAD ★36863 BRATISLAVA ★36864 GDYNIA ★36865 HAVANA ★36866 VARNA ★36867 DRESDEN ★36868 GDANSK ★36869 MAURICE THOREZ ★36870 OTTO GROTEVOHL ★36871 PALMIRO TOGLIATTI ★36872 GEORGE GEORGIU-DEZH ★36873 KOMSOMOLETS KUBANI ★36874 BURGAS ★36875 GEROI BRESTA ★36876 KHULIO ANTONIO MELYA ★36877 RICHARD SORGE ★36878 PYATIDYESYATILYETIYE OKTYABRYA** (also known as **50 LETIYE OKTYABRYA**) **★36879 KOMSOMOLETS LENINGRADA ★36880 MEKHANIK AFANASYEV ★36881 BORODINO** (Gr flag): **36882 VORRAS** ex HASSI MESSAOUD 1980.

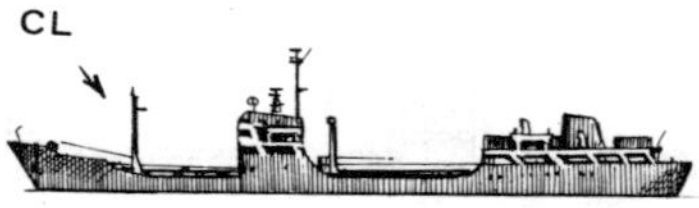

KMKF H123
★36890 ARGON. Ru/Fi 1963; Tk; 3400; 105.39 × 6.22 (345.77 × 20.42); M; 14.25. Sisters (Ru flag): **★36891 ALUKSNE ★36892 APE ★36893 AKTASH ★36894 AKSAY ★36895 ABRENE ★36896 AMURSK ★36897 APSHERONSK ★36898 ARAKS ★36899 ANAPKA ★36900 LYUBERTSY ★36901 SINEGORSK ★36902 ALEKSEYEVKA ★36903 ALEKSEYEVSK ★36904 ANIVA ★36905 ALAGIR ★36906 ALEYSK ★36907 ALEKSIN ★36908 ANAPA ★36909 EVENSK ★36910 ABAGUR ★36911 ARDATOV ★36912 DARNITZA ★36913 EREBUS ★36914 INKERMAN ★36915 VOLFRAM ★36916 IMAN ★36917 RADIY ★36918 ABAKAN ★36919 TYUMENNEFT ★36920 YUGLA** (Cu flag): **★36921 CUBA** ex ARTSYZ 1962.

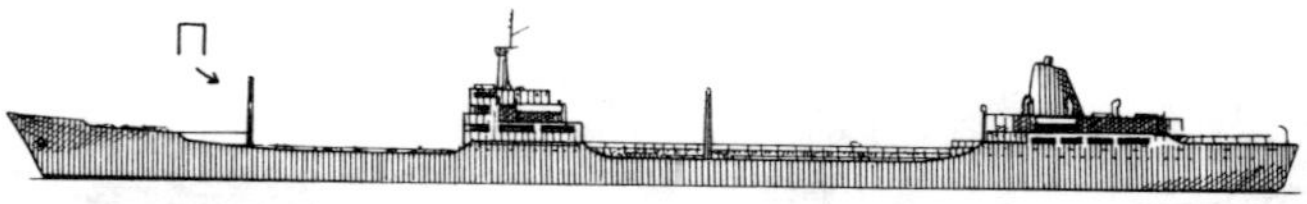

KMKF H123
36930 ECOL SPEZIA. It/It 1958/76; SDT; 21700; 200.01 × 10.88 (656.2 × 35.69); T; 16.25; ex BLUE RANGER 1976; ex MABRUK 1973; ex POLINICE 1972; Converted from tanker 1976.

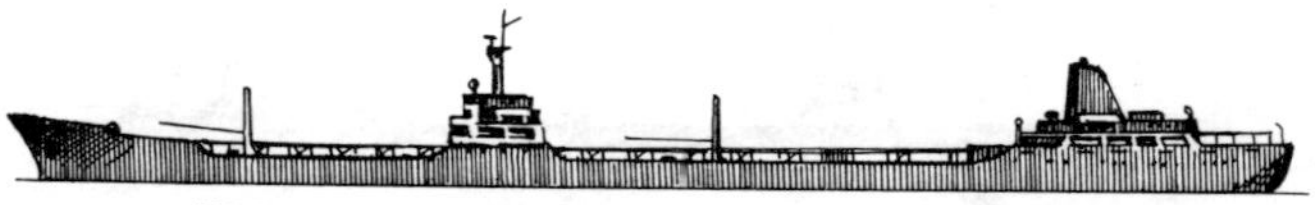

KMKF H123
★36940 GIUSEPPE GARIBALDI. Ru/It 1959/61; Tk; 20700; 203.08 × 10.43 (666.27 × 34.22); T; 15.5; launched as MARIA ADELAIDE; also known as **DZHUZEPPE GARIBALDI.**

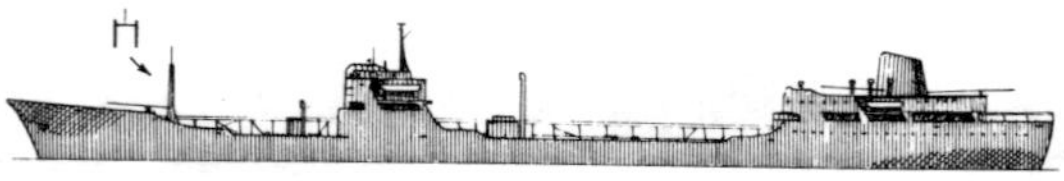

KMKF H123
★36950 DA QING No 34. RC/No 1958; Tk; 10200; 165.13 × 9.3 (541.77 × 30.51); M; 15; ex ANNE 1970; ex BELSTAR 1964.

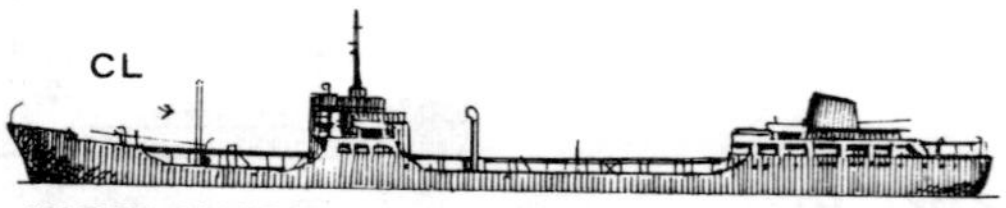

KMKF H123
36960 PIBIMARE PRIMA. It/De 1955; Tk; 8900; 154.84 × 8.66 (508 × 28.41); M; 13; ex STOLT FREDDY 1969; ex STOLT NIAGARA 1967; ex FREDDY 1964.

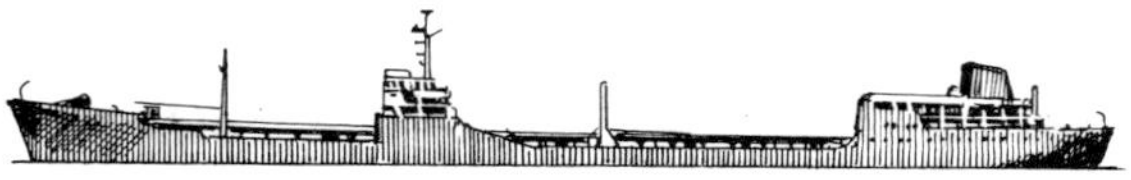

KMKF H123
36970 ALSAD ALAALY. Eg/FRG 1960; Tk; 13200; 170.69 × 9.4 (560 × 30.84); M; 15.

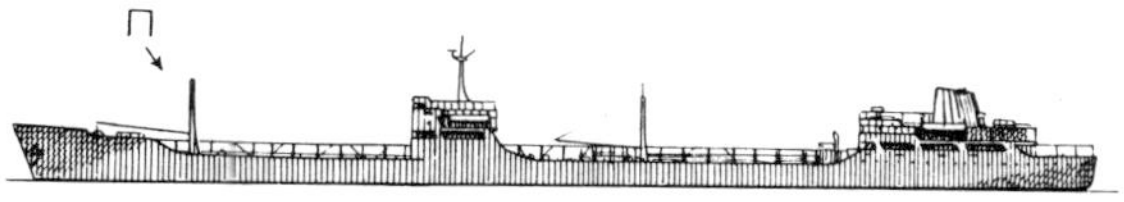

KMKF H123
● **36980 YANNIS K**. Pa/De 1961; Tk; 13100; 170.72 × 9.67 (560.1 × 31.73); M; 15; ex JULIUS HELM 1979; ex FU KANG; ex ANFOO 1976; ex LUGANO 1975; ex RONABAY 1973; ex STIGSTAD 1963.

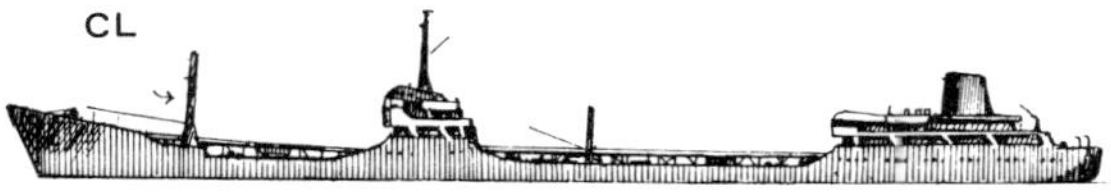

KMKF H123
36990 KALLIPOLIS. Gr/Br 1959; Tk; 13400; 169.6 × 9.58 (556.43 × 31.43); M; 15; ex TEXACO DURHAM 1975; ex REGENT FALCON 1972. Similar: **36991 TEXACO OSLO** (No).

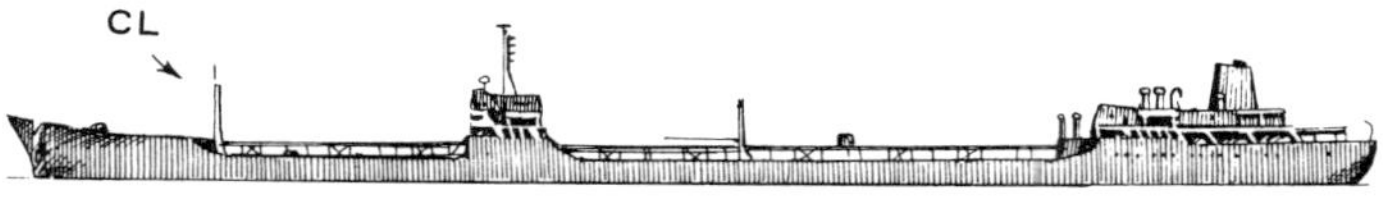

KMKF H123
⋆**37000 MIR**. Ru/Ja 1960; Tk; 25000; 214.03 × 11.38 (702.2 × 37.32); T; 16.25; launched as KATE N.L.

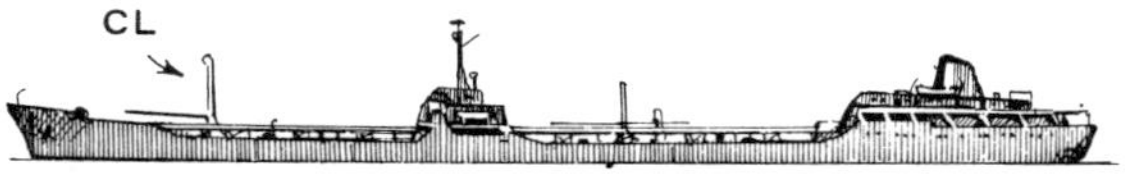

KMKF H123
37010 ABIDA. Ne/Ne 1958; Tk; 12200; 170.42 × 9.08 (559.12 × 29.79); M; 14.5. Sisters (Ne flag): **37011 ACILA 37012 ACMAEA 37013 ALINDA** ex SAN ERNESTO 1964 **37014 ACTEON**.

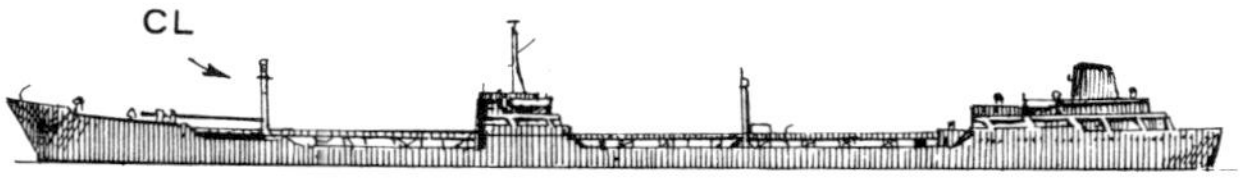

KMKF H123
37020 PERMINA SAMUDRA V. Li/FRG 1958; Tk; 16000; 189.14 × 10.91 (620.53 × 35.79); M; —; ex LINDOS 1971; ex BENSTREAM 1967; ex RING CHIEF 1964.

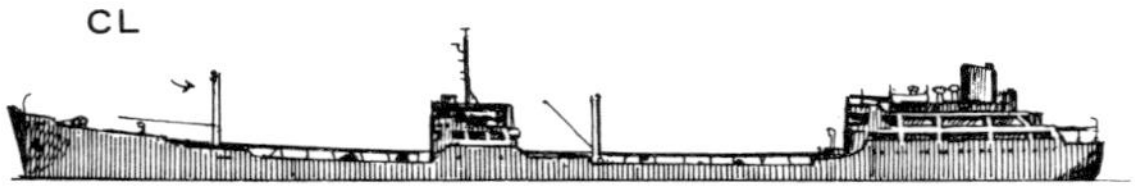

KMKF H123
37030 PERMINA 107. Li/Br 1955; Tk; 12000; 169.63 × 9.09 (556.53 × 29.81); T; 14; ex PSARA 1969; ex CAPETAN MIKES 1967; ex KALDFONN 1965.

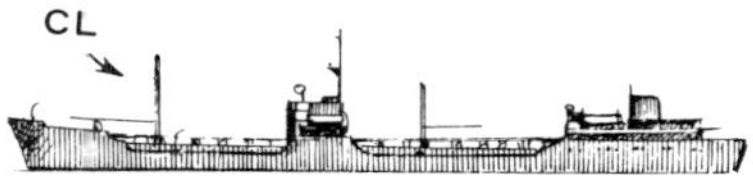

KMKF H123
37040 STORIONE. It/No 1953/62; Tk; 3400; 114.05 × 6.04 (374.18 × 19.82); M; 12.5; ex ALESSANDRO A 1975; ex NORDGARD 1970; Lengthened 1962.

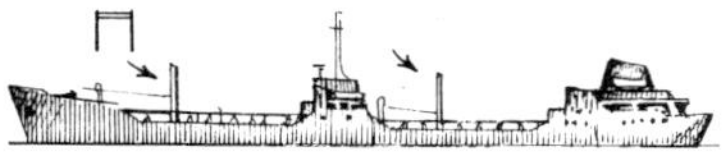

KMKF H123
37050 CAMPOALEGRE. Sp/Sp 1960; Tk; 3800; 109.4 × 5.88 (358.92 × 19.29); M; 13. Sisters (Sp flag): **37051 CAMPOLLANO 37052 CAMPOSECO**.

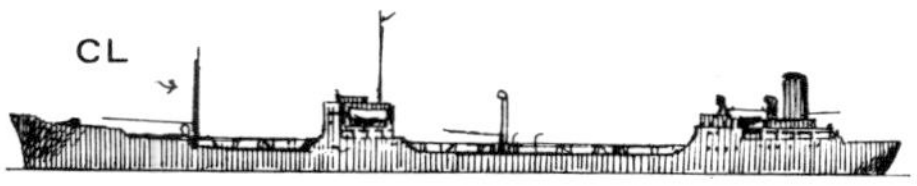

KMKF H123
● **37060 AL SALIMI V**. Si/Br 1957; Tk/MT; 7500; 139.88 × 7.79 (458.92 × 25.56); M; 12; ex MAORI 1979; ex ATHELCREST 1971.

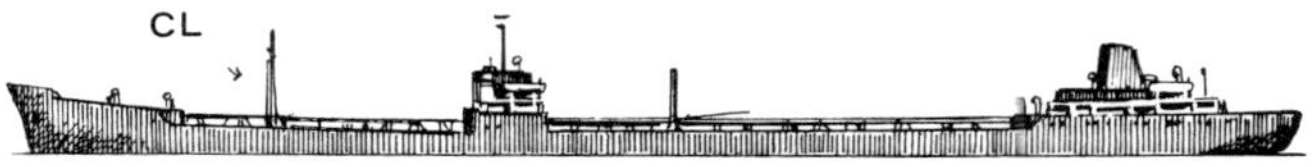

KMKF H123
37070 TSUBAME MARU. Ja/Ja 1956; Tk; 20800; 202.47 × 10.91 (664.27 × 35.79); T; 16. Similar: **37071 TSUBAME MARU No 2**.

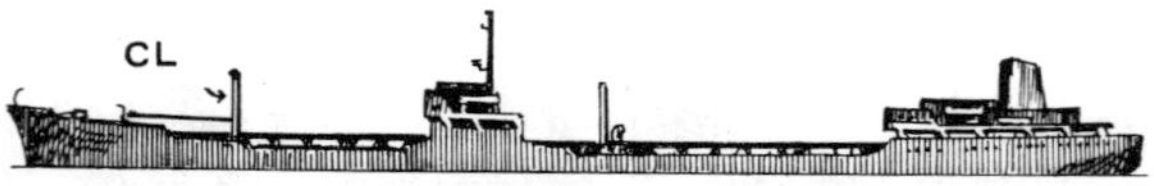

KMKF H123
37080 VARKIZA. Gr/Br 1960; Tk/Ch; 13400; 177.02 × 9.77 (580.77 × 32.05); M; 15; ex TINOS TRADER 1978; ex PANAGHIA A 1977; ex STOLT PIONEER; ex STOLT FALCON; ex ORLANDO 1966.

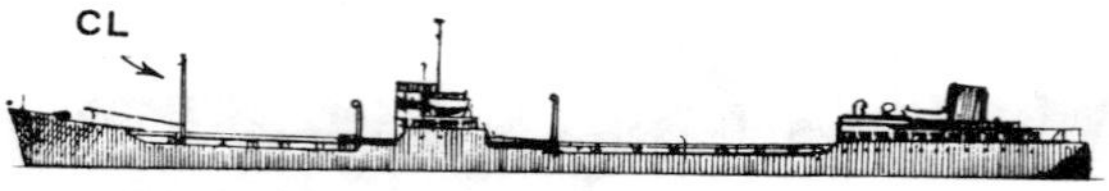

KMKF H123
● **37090 MELITI.** Li/Br 1957; Tk; 11700; 167.49 × 9.4 (549.51 × 30.92); M; 13;. Similar: **37091 SPETSAI** (Gr) ex WHITE DOLPHIN 1976; ex STOLT DOLPHIN 1975; ex STOLT DESIREE 1975; ex STOLT SAGONA 1972; ex SAGONA 1967. **37092 ABELADO L.RODRIGUEZ** (Me) ex PRESIDENT ABELADO L.RODRIGUEZ 1968; ex PEMEX 65-2 1966; ex NORDNES. **37093 ALLISON STAR** (Li) ex OCEAN TRADER 1972; ex ANCO QUEEN 1971; ex ATHELQUEEN.

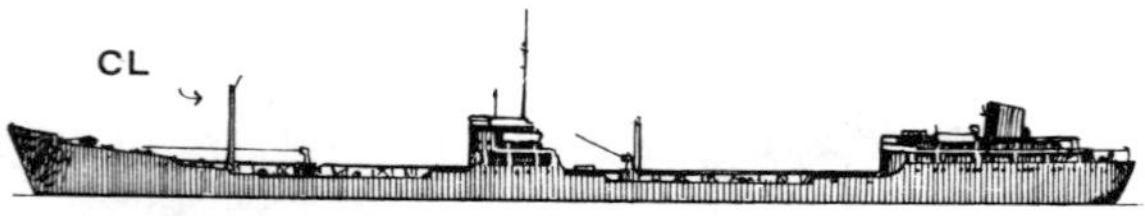

KMKF H123
37100 PETROLA 33. Gr/Br 1951; Tk; 16500; 190 × 10.28 (623.36 × 33.73); M; 14; ex PETROLA XXXIII; ex MARIANNA III. Similar: **37101 PETROLA 34** (Gr) ex PETROLA XXXIV 1976; ex MARGARITA II 1975; ex DALFONN 1966. ***37102 VIT** (Bu) ex HEMUSSITE 1970; ex BRITTA 1966.

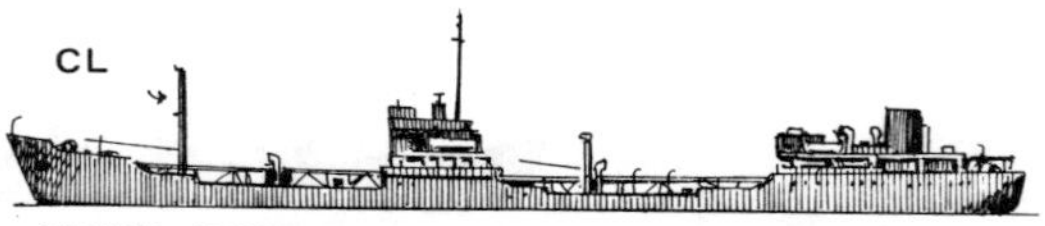

KMKF H123
37110 LSCO TRIDENT. Pi/Br 1954; Tk; 9500; 157.54 × 8.84 (516.86 × 2904); M; 12.5; ex LORENZO 1971; ex REGENT ROYAL 1968.

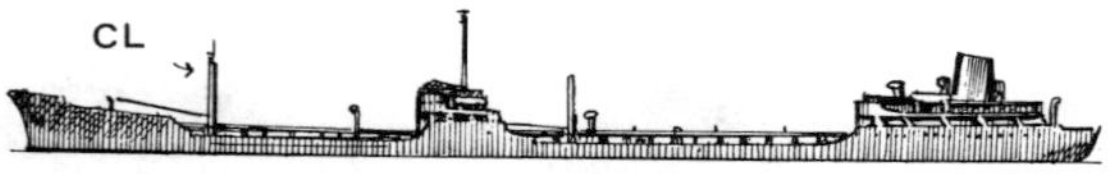

KMKF H123
37120 ELISABETH J. Pa/Sw 1959; Tk; 12700; 169.81 × 9.55 (557.12 × 31.33); M; 16; ex SERIFOS 1980; ex EVELYN 1979; ex ALFMAR 1972; ex SAGA SILVER 1969; ex BEDUIN 1967.

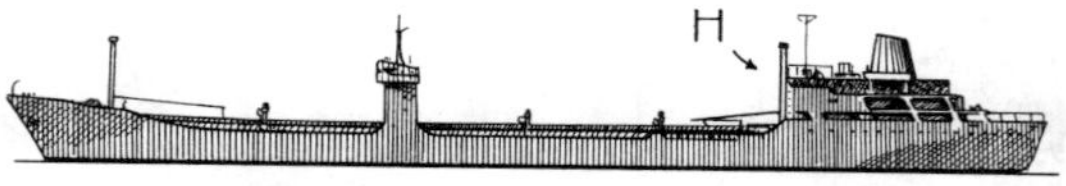

KMKF H123
37130 ELQUI. Ch/FRG 1960; B; 13400; 165.61 × 9.75 (543.67 × 31.99); T; 15.

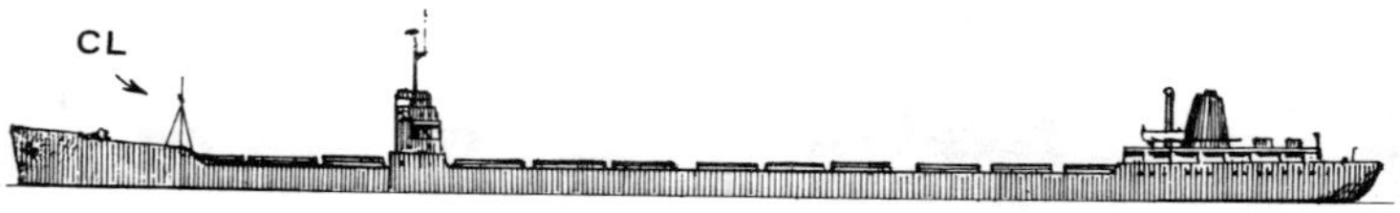

KMKF H123
37140 ORE PRINCE. Li/Ja 1956; O; 16200; 224.19 × 11.48 (735.53 × 37.69); T; 15.25.

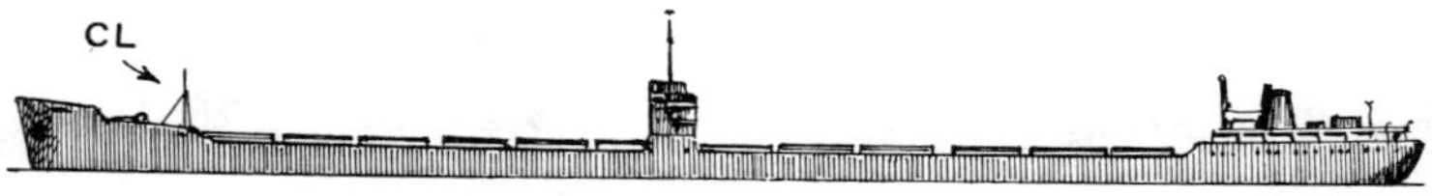

KMKF H123
● **37150 ORE JUPITER.** Li/Ja 1959; O; 18100; 228.91 × 11.69 (751.02 × 38.36); T; 15.5. Sisters (Li flag): **37151 ORE MERIDIAN 37152 ORE METEOR 37153 ORE NEPTUNE 37154 ORE SATURN 37155 ORE VENUS.**

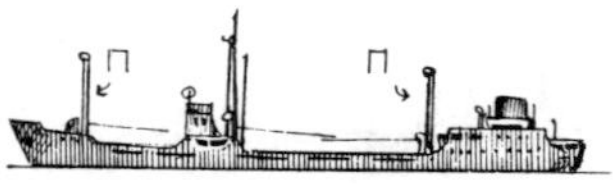

KMKF H123
37160 ANNA MADRE. It/Ne 1949/62; C; 1600; 85.58 × 4.82 (280.77 × 15.81); M; 13.5; ex VRIJBURGH 1967; lengthened 1962.

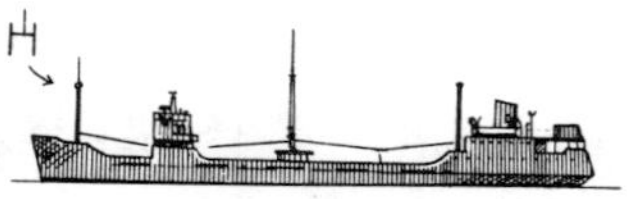

KMKF H123
37170 NIKITAS. Cy/Fi 1942/51 C; 2300; 88.5 × 5.18 (290.35 × 16.99); M; 10; ex SANTA PAOLA 1972; ex EMIL BERGER 1969; ex GENOA.

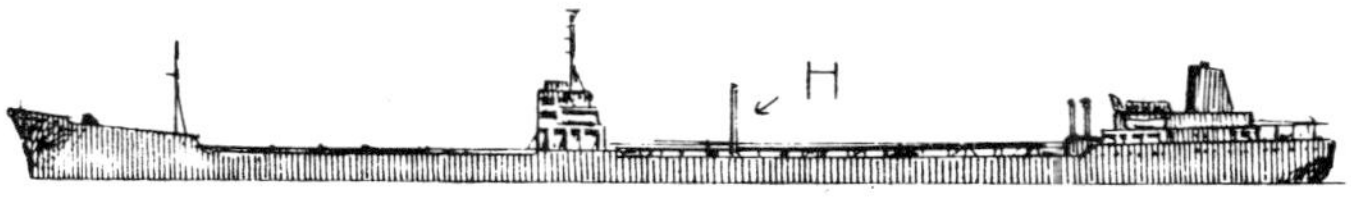

KMKF H13
37180 KYMO. Li/Ja 1956; Tk; 24200; 211.72 × 11.31 (694.62 × 37.2); T; 16.5. Sister: **37181 NEFELI** (Li).

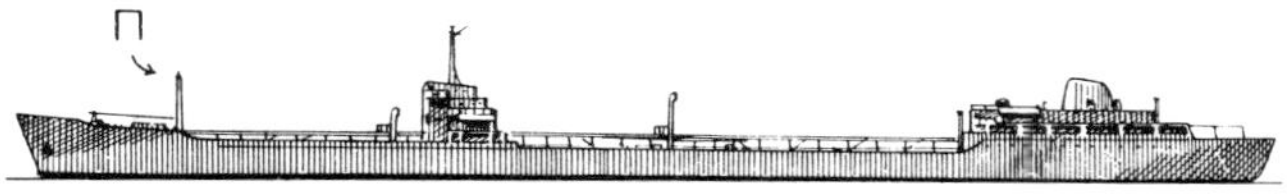

KMKF H13
37190 APHRODITE TRANSOCEANIC. Gr/Sw 1956; Tk; 18700; 198.13 × 10.86 (650.03 × 35.63); M; 14; ex BRANITA 1977.

KMKF H13
37200 COASTAL TEXAS. Li/Ja 1964; Tk; 44700; 248.04 × 13.15 (814 × 43.1); T; —; ex STAVROS G. LIVANOS 1977.

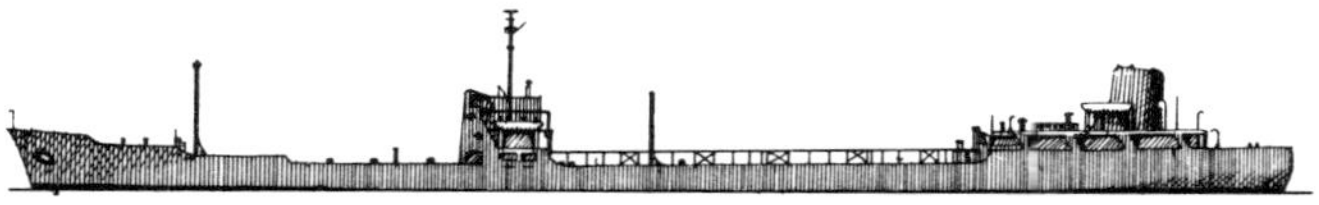

KMKF H13
37210 YOUSSEF B. Pa/Ja 1959; Tk; 21700; 203.56 × 10.61 (667.88 × 34.81); M; 15.5; ex KOWA MARU 1978.

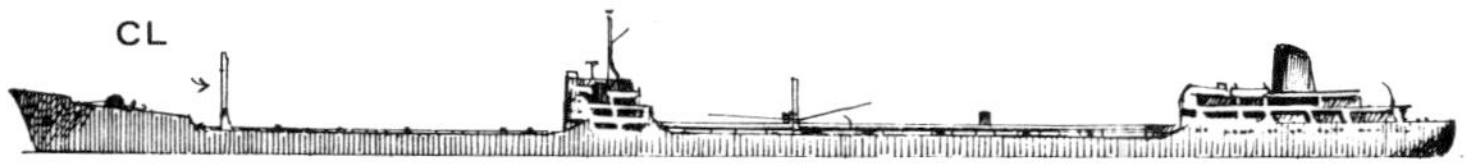

KMKF H13
● **37220 EDWARD STEVINSON.** Br/Br 1961; Tk; 31000; 229.67 × 12.38 (753.51 × 40.62); T; 16.5. Sister: **37221 KAYESON** (Br).

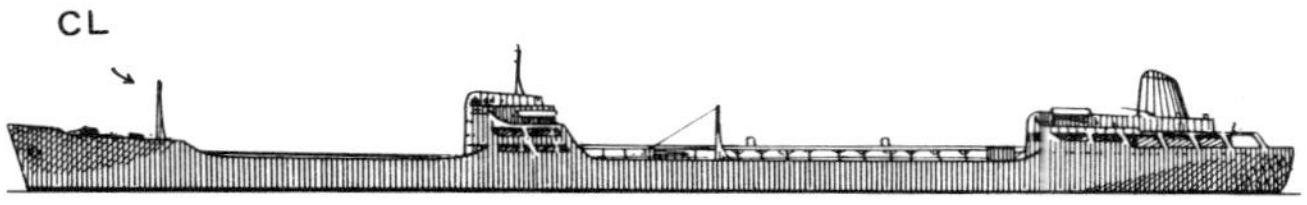

KMKF H13
● **37230 ESTRELLA ARGENTINA.** Ar/Ne 1960; Tk; 22100; 202.72 × 10.5 (665.09 × 34.45); T; 15; ex VIDENA 1969. Sister: **37231 VIANA** (Ne).

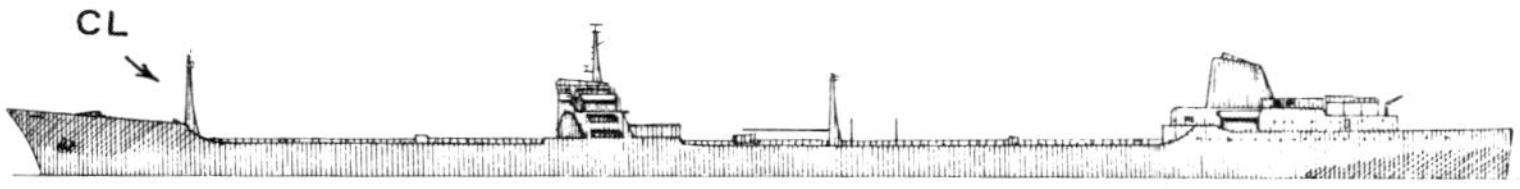

KMKF H13
● **37240 TEXACO VENEZUELA.** Pa/FRG 1964; Tk; 32800; 237.81 × 13.23 (777.59 × 43.91); T; 17.

KMKF H13
37250 FREEDOM. Li/Tw 1960; Tk; 23100; 213.37 × 11.69 (700.03 × 38.35); T; 17.5. Sister: **37251 FAITH** (Li).

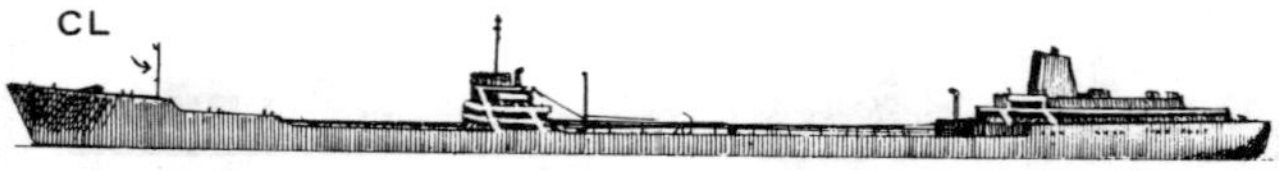

KMKF H13
● **37260 CHILBAR.** US/US 1959; Tk; 19300; 202.9 × 11.14 (665.68 × 36.55); T; 17.5; ex EAGLE TRAVELER. Sisters (US flag): **37261 METON** ex EAGLE VOYAGER 1977 **37262 BALDBUTTE** ex BARBARA JANE 1973 **37263 EXXON SEATTLE** ex ESSO SEATTLE 1973; ex SAROULA 1964.

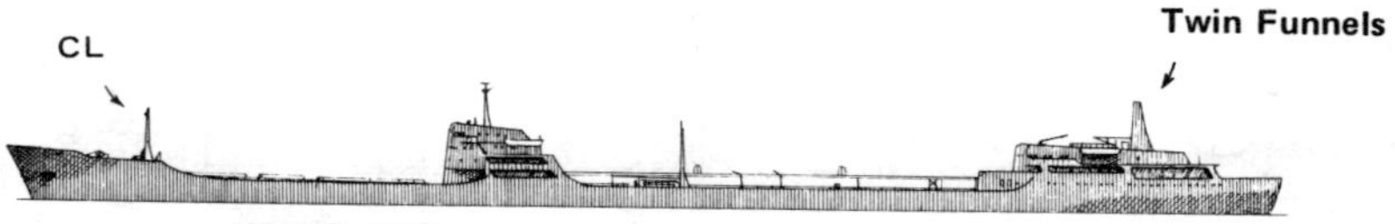

KMKF H13
37270 ONDINA. Ne/Ne 1961; Tk; 31000; 228.61 × 12.19 (250.03 × 39.99); T; 16.75.

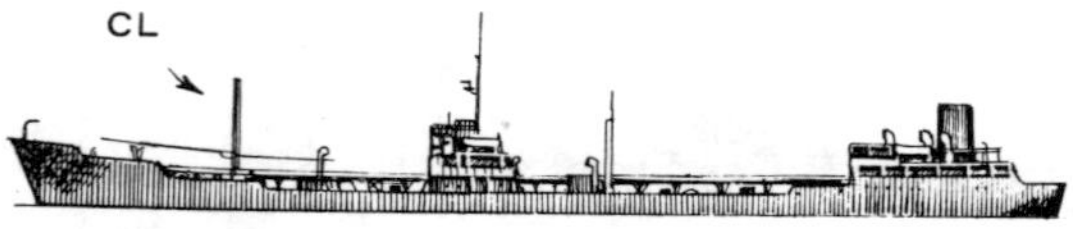

KMKF H13
37280 LAZARO CARDENAS. Me/Br 1955; Tk; 11100; 165.21 × 9.09 (542.03 × 29.82); M; 14.5; ex PRESIDENTE CARDENAS 1968; ex PEMEX 65 1965; ex HERMES 1965.

KMKF H13
37290 EIFEL. FRG/FRG 1963; RT/FA; 4700 Dspl; 102 × 7.1 (334 × 23.3); M; 13; ex FRIEDRICH JUNG 1963.

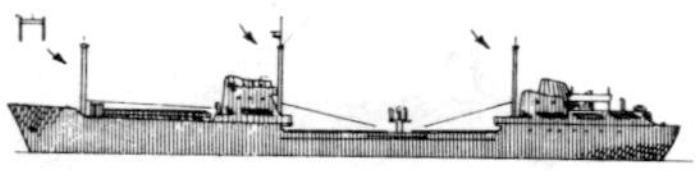

KMKF H13
⋆37300 PLOVDIV. Bu/Sw 1960; C; 4900; 106.76 × 7.51 (350.26 × 24.46); M; 14.5; ex FAUST 1966.

KMKF H13
⋆37310 PLISKA. Bu/Sw 1959; C; 4500; 106.41 × 7.53 (349.11 × 24.7); M; 13.5; ex FIDELIO 1966. Sister: **⋆37211 RUSSE** (Bu) ex FALSTAFF 1966.

KMKF H13
37320 BINTANG SAMUDRA III. In/FRG 1954; C; 690/1100; 68.89 × 371/4.37 (226.02 × 12.17/14.34); M; 12; ex CHERRY LAJU 1972; ex HABICHT 1969.

KMKF H13
37330 BERRY. Fr/FRG 1958; RS/FA; 2700 Dspl; 86.7 × 4.6 (285 × 15); M; 15; ex MEDOC 1964; Converted cargo ship.

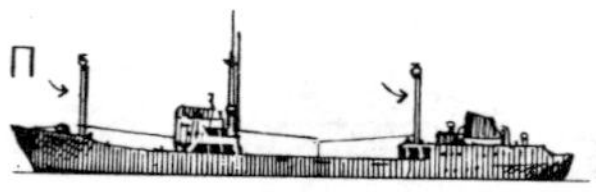

KMKF H13
● **37340 ARIS VI.** Gr/FRG 1955; C; 1200; 86.72 × 4.59 (284.51 × 15.06); M; 14; ex BARROW 1977; ex CORINTHIAN TRADER 1975; ex AGHIOS LAZAROS 1973; ex VILLEGAS 1970. Sisters: **37341 SEAMOON 1** (Bh) ex SYLHET 1977; ex PASNI 1973; ex BALTIC COMET 1966 **37342 NIVES** (It) ex VIVES 1970.

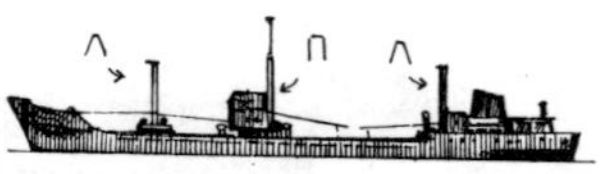

KMKF H13
● **37350 SHARON H.** Pa/FRG 1956; C; 1400/2100; 86.59 × 5.41 6.37 (284.09 × 17.75/20.9); D-E; 12.5; ex PHGH 1980; ex SOUTHERNER 1977; ex ST. HELEN 1972; ex ELISABETH SCHULTE 1971.

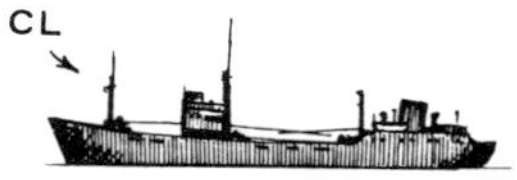

KMKF H3
37360 KIM GUAN. Pa/Br 1950; C; 1400 66.6 × 5.06 (218.5 × 16.6); M; 11; ex KINGFISH 1969; ex CHOPIN 1966; ex AKASSA 1966 ex CHOPIN 1965; ex RADJA MASS 1964; ex PLADDA 1963.

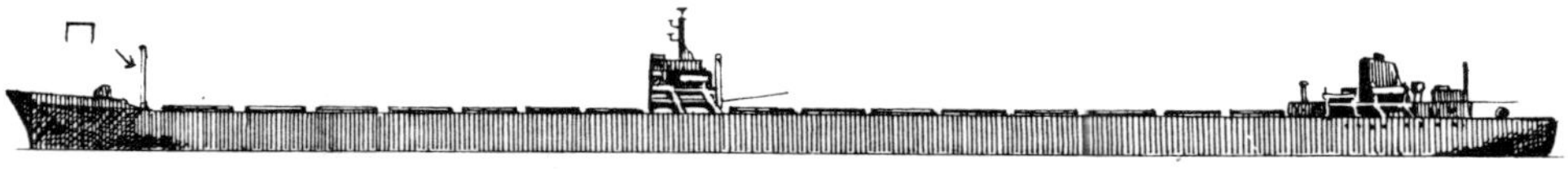

KMKFK H
37370 WEILEE. Tw/Ja 1962/73; OO; 64600; 296.48 × 16.59 (972.7 × 54.43); T; 16.25; ex MARCONA PROSPECTOR 1977; ex PROSPECT 1977; ex MARCONA PROSPECTOR 1974; ex SAN JUAN PROSPECTOR 1974. Lengthened and deepened 1973.

KMKFK H
37380 LUISA. Pa/Ne 1966; D; 3100; 95.64 × 5.94 (313.78 × 19.49); TSM; —. Sister: **37381 ORANJESTAD** (NA) ex YOLANDA 1970.

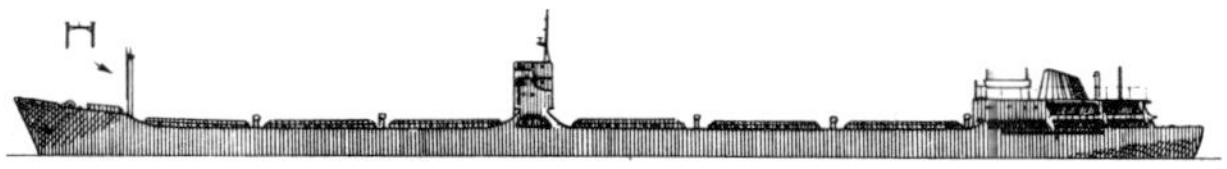

KMKFK H1
37390 AMPHIOPE. Fr/Fr 1962; O; 19400; 188.6 × 10.3 (618.77 × 33.79); M; —.

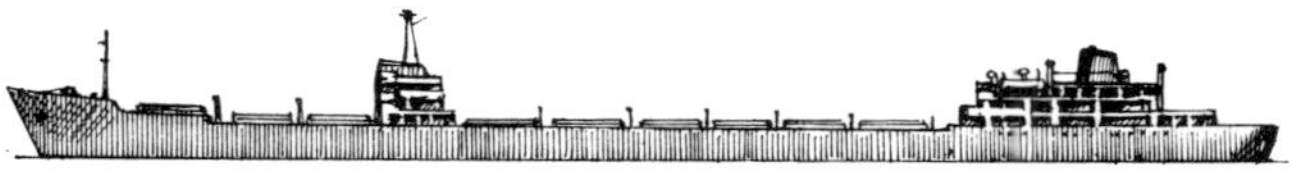

KMKFK H1
37400 MARIVIE. Gr/Ja 1962; B; 23800; 204.2 × 11.78 (669.95 × 38.65); M; 15.5; ex IRON CAVALIER; ex NAESS CAVALIER 1966. Sister: **37401 KAVO XIFIAS** (Gr) ex NORDIC RAMBLER 1975; ex IRON CLIPPER 1975; ex NAESS CLIPPER 1964.

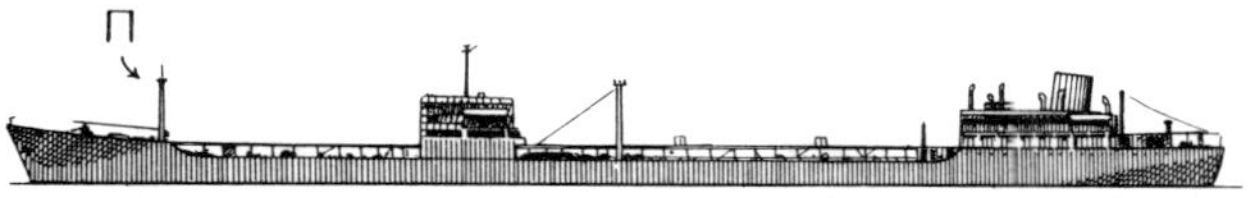

KMKFK H123
37410 GOODHOPE. Li/Br 1955; Tk; 17600; 191.93 × 10.26 (629.69 × 33.66); T- 16; ex ESSO EXETER. Similar: **37411 PETROLA 23** (Gr) ex PETROLA XXIII 1976; ex ESSO GOTHENBURG 1975; ex ESSO NEDERLAND 1962 Similar (FRG built): **37412 PETROMAR BAHIA BLANCA** (Ar) ex ESSO DUSSELDORF 1966.

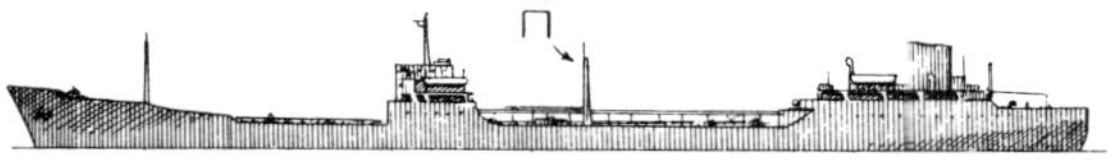

KMKFK H123
37420 FEOSO STAR. Pa/Ja 1958; Tk; 12800; 170.59 × 9.48 (559.68 × 31.1); M; 15.5; ex STELLA 1976; ex AIVA 1974; ex EIWA MARU 1968.

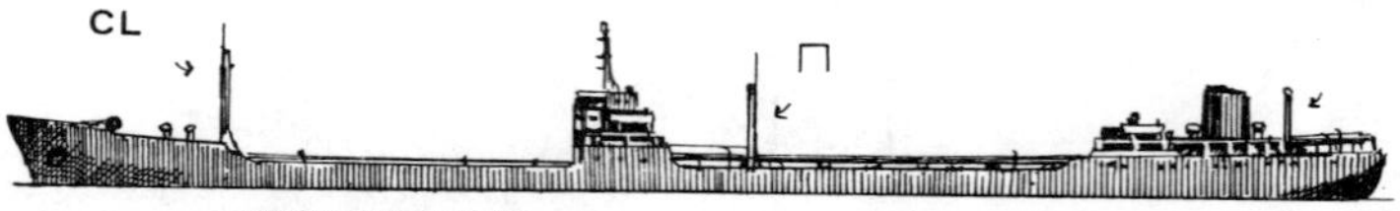

KMKFK H123
37430 CAROLYN. Li/Ja 1962; Tk; 30500; 218.02 × 11.81 (715.29 × 38.75); M; 16.25; ex YUYO MARU 1976.

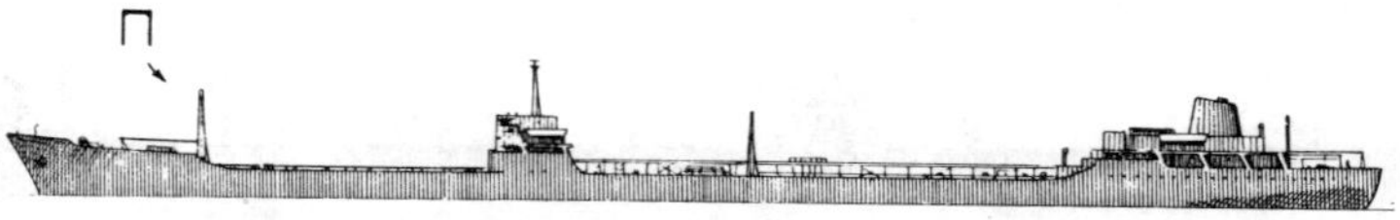

KMKFK H123
37440 OSWEGO CONCORD. Li/Ja 1963; Tk; 28600; 212.48 × 11.98 (697.11 × 39.3); T; 16.75; ex RICHARD C. SAUER 1966. Sister: **37441 OSWEGO PEACE** (Li) ex CHARLES E. SPAHR 1966.

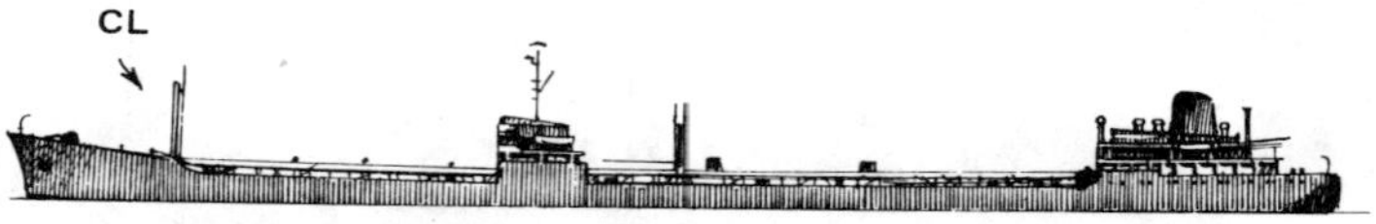

KMKFK H123
● **37450 PETROMAR CORDOBA.** Ar/FRG 1960; Tk; 24500; 211.23 × 11.32 (693 × 37); T; 17; ex ESSO HANNOVER 1968. Sister: **37451 PETROMAR ROSARIO** (Ar) ex ESSO NURNBERG.

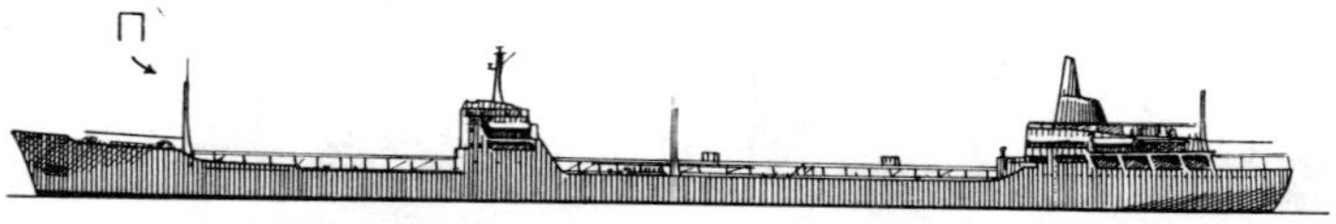

KMKFK H123
● **37460 ALEXANDRA CONWAY.** Pa/Ne 1959; Tk; 24600; 213.37 × 11.54 (700.03 × 37.86); T; —; ex BORGHOLM 1966.

KMKFK H123
37470 GEORGIOS K. Gr/It 1954; Tk; 20400; 200.01 × 10.9 (656.2 × 35.76); T; 16; ex GALISSA 1973; ex MIRELLA D'AMICO 1972.

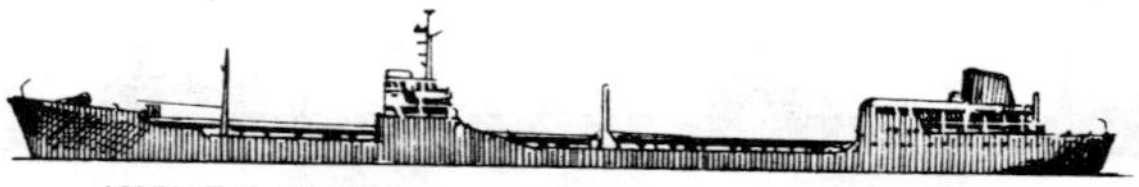

KMKFK H123
37480 ALSAD ALAALY. Eg/FRG 1960; Tk; 13200; 170.69 × 9.4 (560 × 30.84); M; 15.

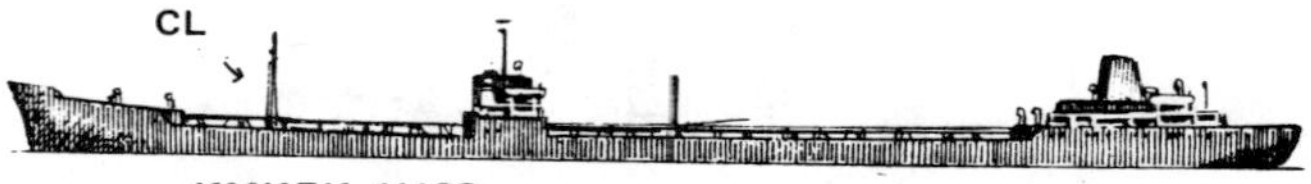

KMKFK H123
37490 TSUBAME MARU. Ja/Ja 1956; Tk; 20800; 202.47 × 10.91; (664.27 × 35.79); T; 16. Similar: **37491 TSUBAME MARU No2** (Ja).

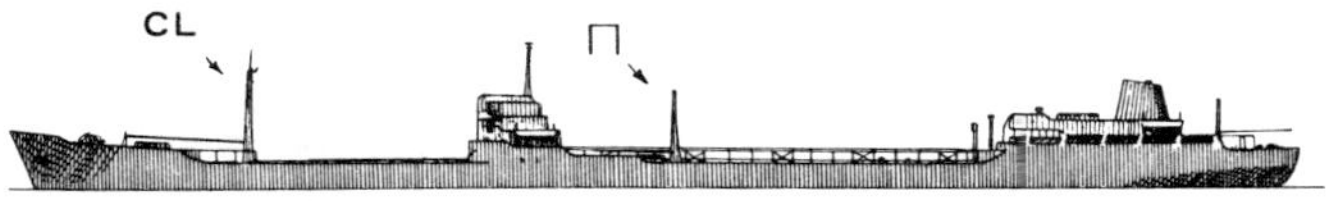

KMKFK H123
37500 WHITE BEACH. Pa/Ja 1956; Tk; 19800; 203.18 × 10.07 (666.6 × 33.04); T; 16; ex ATHENIAN RUNNER 1975; ex MARIETTA 1972.

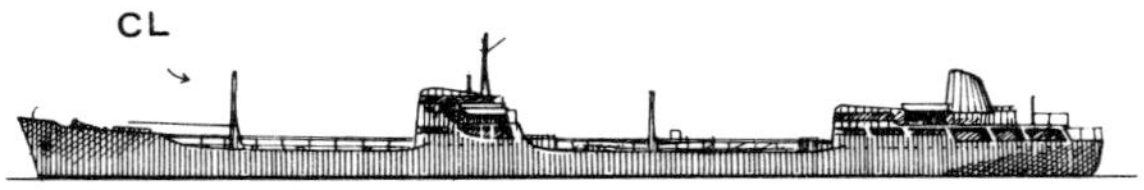

KMKFK H123
37510 ALINDA. Br/Br 1959; Tk; 12300; 170.39 × 9.36 (559.02 × 30.71); T; 15.5; ex SAN ERNESTO 1964. Sisters (Br flag): **37511 ACAVUS 37512 AMASTRA 37513 ASPRELLA 37514 AULICA 37515 ACHATINA 37516 STONEGATE** (Pa flag): **37517 UJE** ex AMORIA.

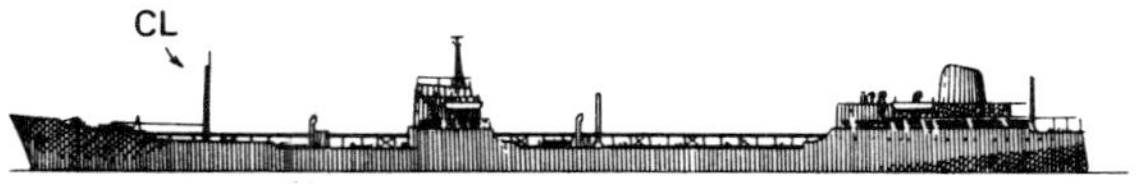

KMKFK H123
37530 HATTAN. Gr/Br 1958; Tk; 12400; 170.69 × 9.44 (560 × 30.97); M; 14.5; ex YANNIS P.V.; ex MARIONGA 1976; ex CORHAVEN 1965.

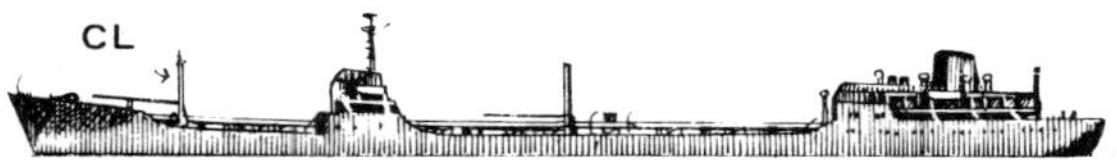

KMKFK H123
37540 HIPPO. Gr/FRG 1960; Tk; 13100; 170.69 × 9.69 (560 × 31.79); M; —; ex STOLT HIPPO 1980; ex DARIEN 1974; ex FABIO 1964.

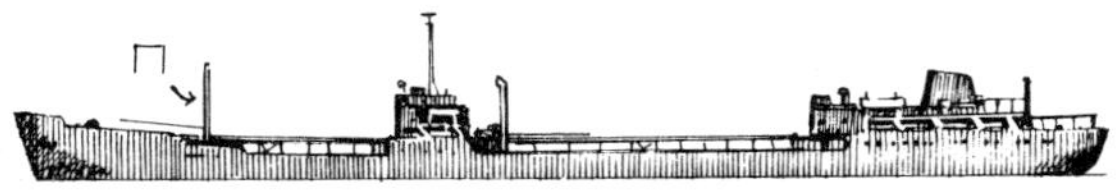

KMKFK H123
● **37550 DEA BROVIG.** No/No 1962; Tk; 12900; 170.69 × 9.6 (560 × 31.5); M; 14; ex GYLFE 1976; ex NINA BORTHEN 1968.

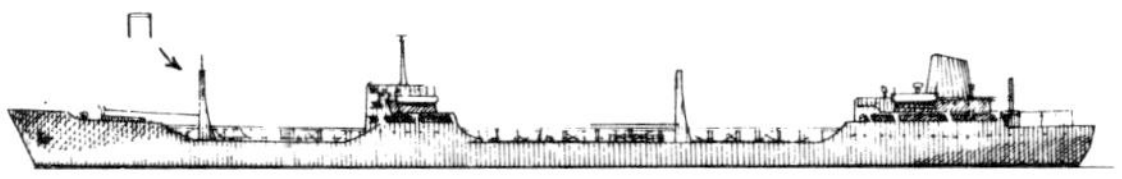

KMKFK H123
● **37560 EGEON.** Gr/Sp 1959; Tk; 12200; 172.17 × 9.44 (564.86 × 30.97); M; 15; ex RIBNICA 1976; ex MARIA DE LOS DOLORES Similar: **37561 GLOBE ASIMI** (Br) ex ASTORGA 1980 Possible Similar: **37562 GALE** (Li) ex VARUNA VAHINI; ex ARTOLA 1973.

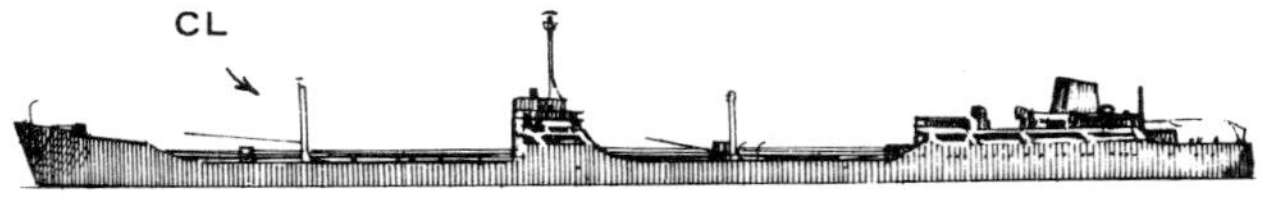

KMKFK H123
37570 GEORGIOS V. Gr/Br 1961; Tk; 18800; 196.07 × 10.86 (643.29 × 35.63); M; 15.75; ex GEORGE PEACOCK 1969. Similar: **37571 MIDAS TOUCH** (Li) ex GALAXIAS; ex NORSK DROTT 1968.

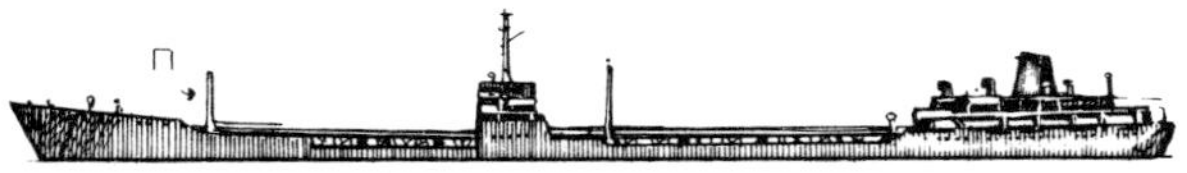

KMKFK H123
37580 MAGDA. Cy/Be 1959; Tk; 16800; 187.18 × 10.14 (616.08 × 33.27); M; 16.75; ex ACAMAR 1973; ex HECTOR HAWK 1968.

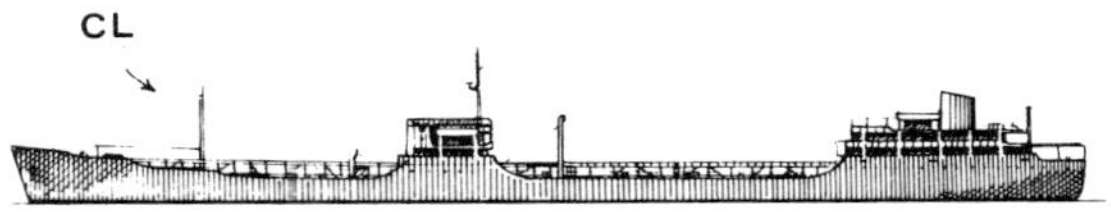

KMKFK H123
37590 POLLUCE. It Br 1958; Tk; 12600; 169.53 × 9.35 (556.2 × 31.27); M; —; ex FERNHAVEN 1967.

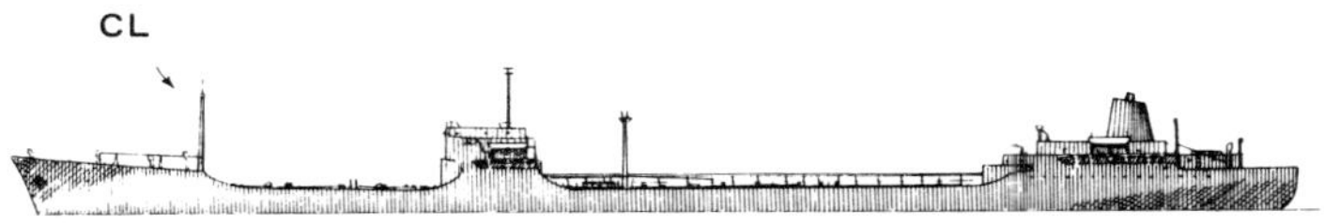

KMKFK H123
37600 WASHINGTON TRADER. US/US 1959; Tk; 24500; 217.08 × 11.53 (712.2 × 37.83); T; 17; ex THETIS 1975. Sister: **37601 ACHILLES** (US) Possibly Similar: **37602 SOUTHWEST CAPE** (Li) ex G.S. LIVANOS 1973.

KMKFK H123
37610 TRANSUD II. Li/FRG 1960; Tk; 16000; 187.2 × 10.18 (614.17 × 33.4); M; 15.25; ex SAN JUAN 1977; ex NEBO 1974; ex TOPAZ 1960.

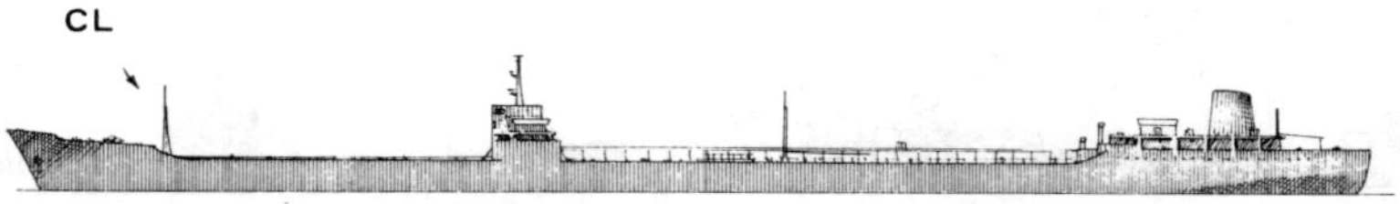

KMKFK H123
37620 KAPETAN MARKOS N. L. Gr/Ja 1962; Tk; 39200; 236.23 × 13.74 (775.03 × 45.08); M; 15.75; ex ISE MARU 1972.

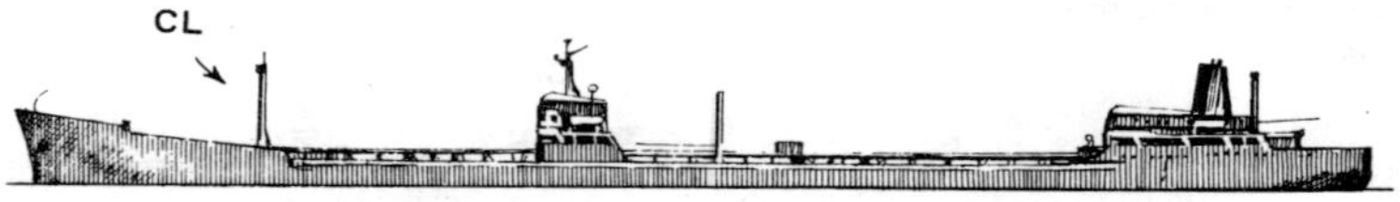

KMKFK H123
37630 MARIPRIMA. Li Sw 1961; Tk; 30200; 227.34 × 12.01 (745.87 × 39.4); T; 16.75; ex ESSO STOCKHOLM 1977.

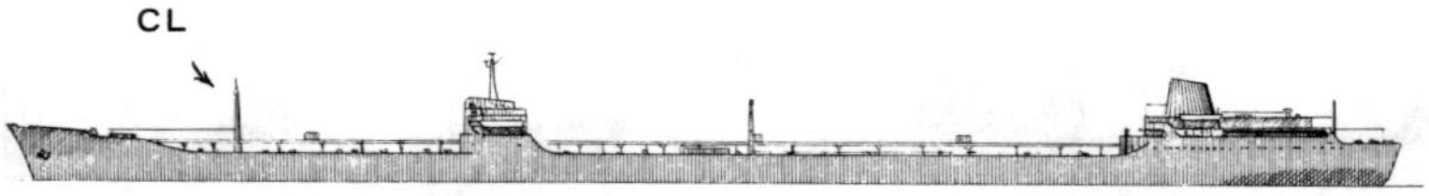

KMKFK H123
⋆**37640 YIN HU.** RC/Sw 1964; Tk; 35000; 235.87 × 12.21 (773.85 × 40.06); M; 15.5; ex HARWI 1974. May be spelt **YINHU.**

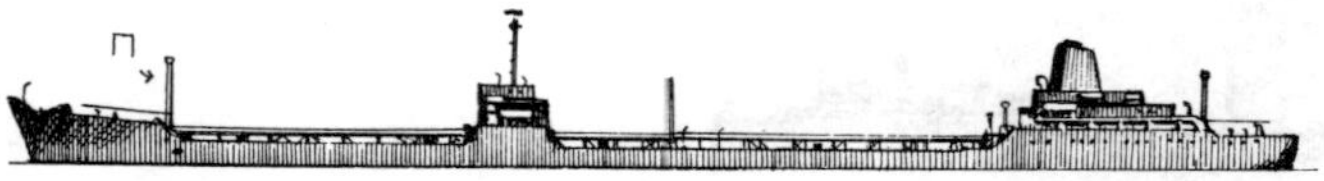

KMKFK H123
37650 SOUTHERN CONQUEST. Li/Be 1959; Tk; 18200; 201.51 × 10.64 (661.12 × 34.91); T; 16; ex CONQUEST 1977; ex NORTHERN CONQUEST 1975; ex ATLANTIC CONQUEST 1963. Sister: **37651 SOUTHERN CONQUEROR** (Li) ex NORTHERN CONQUEROR 1975; ex ATLANTIC CONQUEROR 1963.

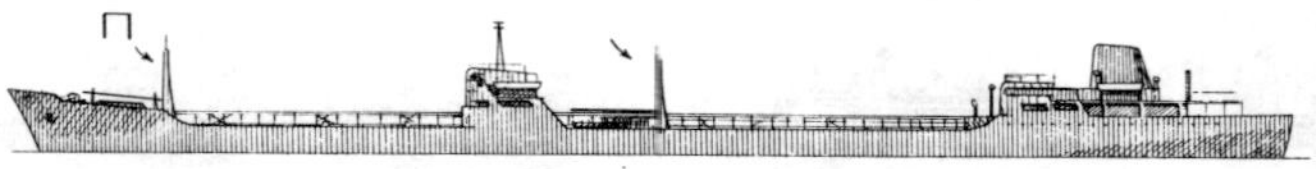

KMKFK H123
● **37660 TYCHOS.** Gr/Ja 1956; Tk; 20300; 203.18 × 10.82 (666.6 × 35.5); T; 16; ex TAURUS 1972.

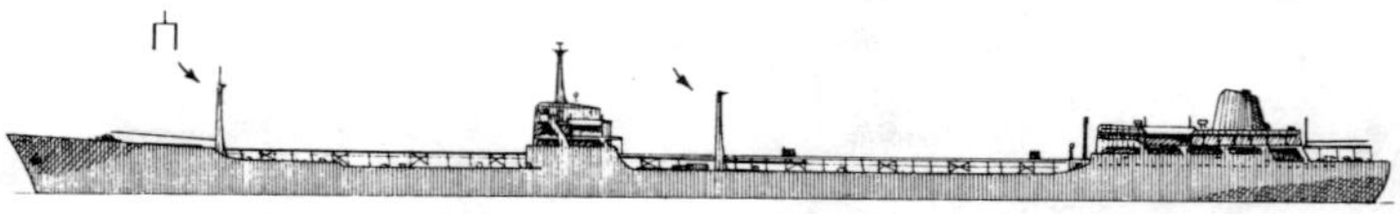

KMKFK H123
37670 PERMINA SAMUDRA XIV. Li/Ja 1961; Tk; 31400; 217.39 × 12.6 (713.22 × 41.34); T; —; ex WARUKIN CORP; ex MOSCLIFF 1969. Similar: **37671 DONA RITA** (Li) ex NAESS VOYAGER 1968.

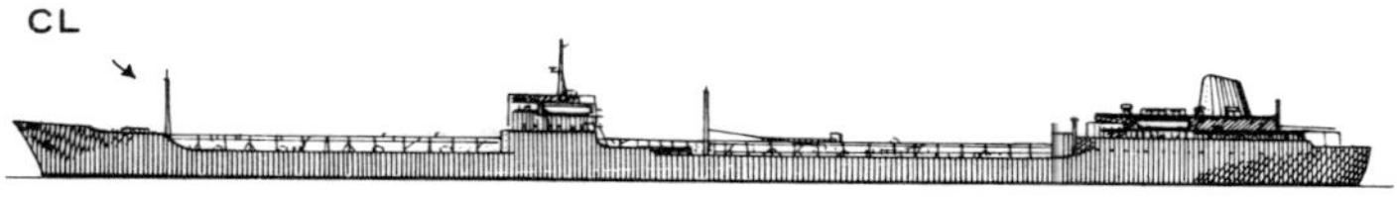

KMKFK H123
37680 POLYKARP. No/Sw 1964; Tk; 26600; 215.22 × 11.95 (706.1 × 39.21); M; 15.5. Similar: **37681 RION** (Gr) ex POLYCASTLE 1980.

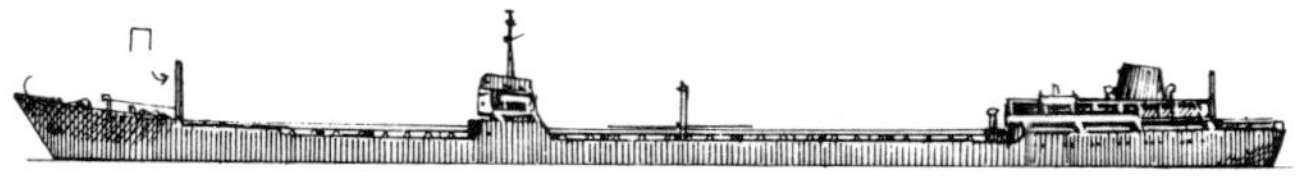

KMKFK H123
37690 TETA M. Gr/Sw 1960; Tk; 20100; 200.51 × 11.34 (657.84 × 37.2); M; —; ex EMMA FERNSTROM 1969.

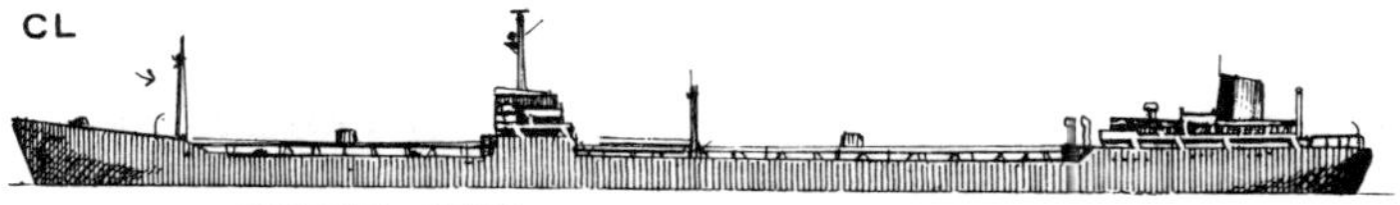

KMKFK H123
37700 ATHINA. Pa/De 1964; Tk; 21600; 209.15 × 11.27 (686.19 × 36.98); M; 15.5; ex OLUF MAERSK 1980; ex KAREN MAERSK 1978. Sister: **37701 HENNING MAERSK** (De).

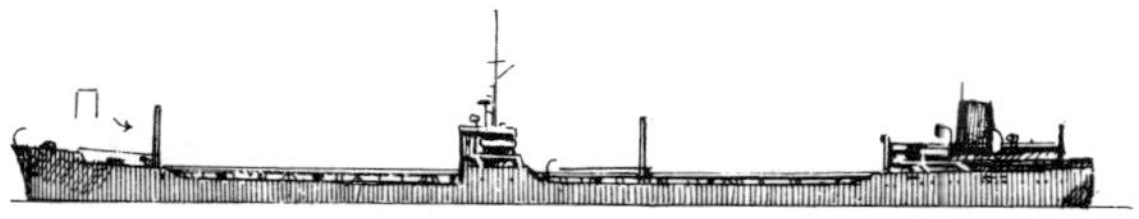

KMKFK H123
37710 KAVO YOSSONAS. Gr/De 1957; Tk; 12900; 170.64 × 9.77 (559.84 × 32.05); M; 15; ex AVANTI 1972.

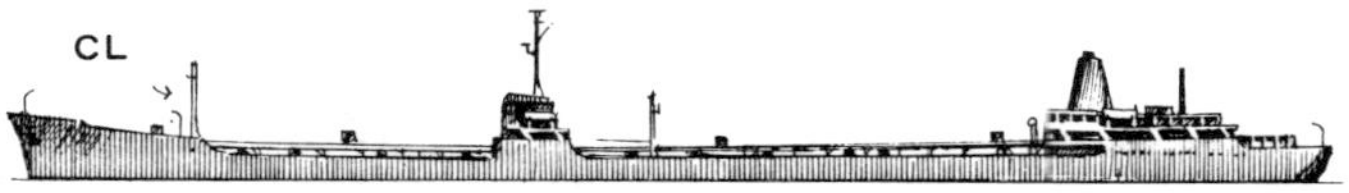

KMKFK H123
37720 E. M. TSANGARIS. Gr/De 1960; Tk; 25100; 212.1 × 11.69 (695.87 × 38.35); T; —; ex CAROLINE MAERSK 1971; ex CAROLINE. Sister: **37721 LUJAN DE CUYO** (Ar) ex KRISTINE MAERSK 1972.

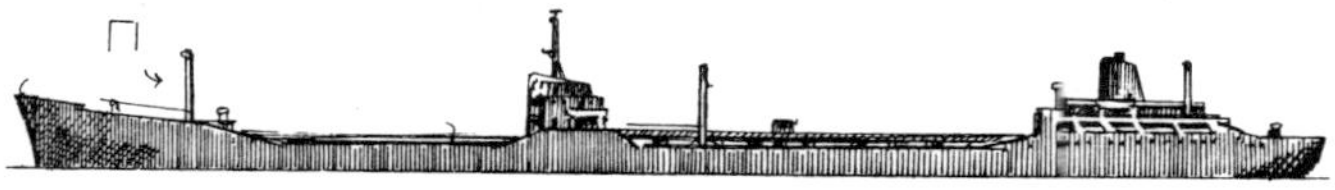

KMKFK H123
37730 GUERNICA. Sp/Sp 1962; Tk; 21600; 202.67 × 10.75 (664.93 × 35.27); T; 16.25. Sister: **37731 BILBAO** (Sp).

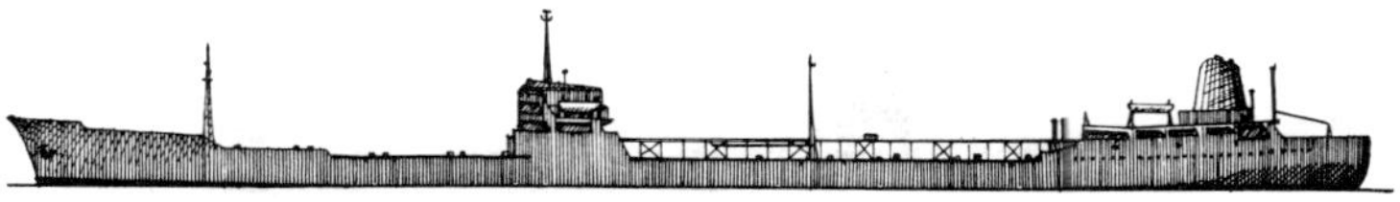

KMKFK H123
37740 AL HUSSEIN B. Pa/Ja 1962; Tk; 28200; 224.34 × 11.53 (736.02 × 37.83); M; 15.5; ex PACIFIC CENTURY.

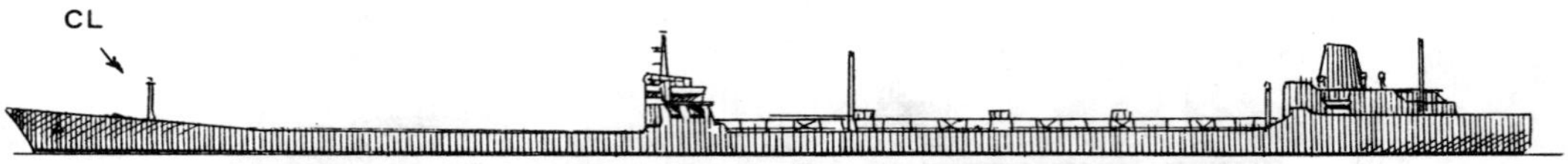

KMKFK H13
37750 ENERGY TRANSPORT. Li/Ja 1969; Tk; 99300; 326.02 × 19.34 (1069.62 × 63.45); T; 15.75.

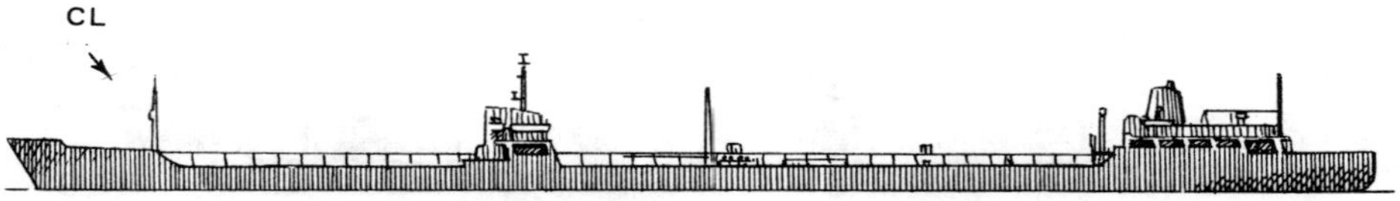

KMKFK H13
● **37760 ORIENTAL DRAGON.** Li/Ja 1965; Tk; 23200; 289.31 × 16.76 (949.18 × 54.99); T; —; Anchored in Jakarta. Being used as oil storage vessel.

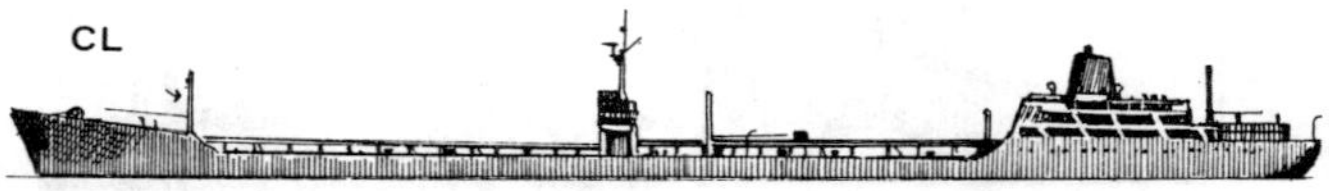

KMKFK H13
● **37770 COMMONWEALTH.** Li/It 1958; Tk; 23200; 212.02 × 11.2 (692.7 × 37); T; —; ex GRAND COMMONWEALTH 1974; ex CORCO EL TIGRE 1970; ex AGIP RAVENNA 1967.

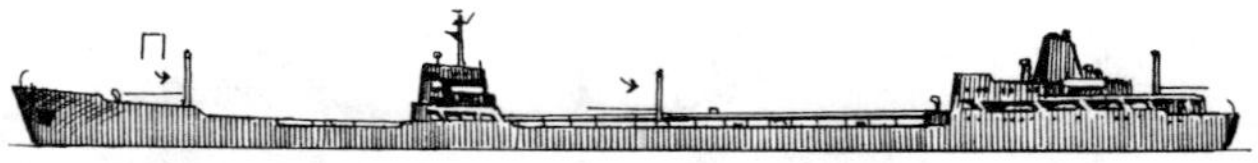

KMKFK H13
⋆**37780 TRUD.** Ru/Ys 1960; Tk; 17900; 192.36 × 10.24 (631.1 × 33.59); T; 16; ex FRATERNITY.

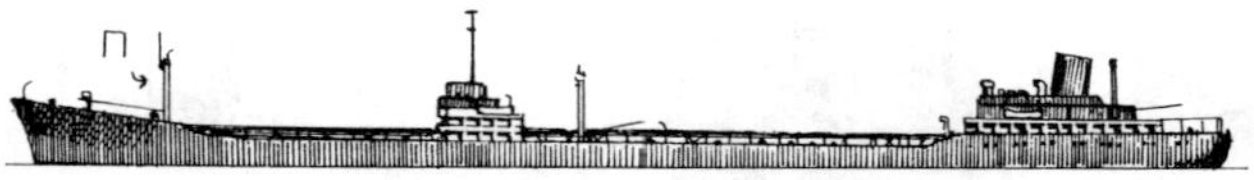

KMKFK H13
37790 EXXON FLORENCE. US/US 1954; Tk; 17400; 191.42 × 10.23 (628.02 × 33.56); T; 16; ex ESSO FLORENCE 1973. Possible Sisters (US flag): **37791 EXXON CHESTER** ex ESSO CHESTER 1973 **37792 EXXON HUNTINGTON** ex ESSO HUNTINGTON 1973 **37793 EXXON NEWARK** ex ESSO NEWARK 1973 **37794 EXXON BANGOR** ex ESSO BANGOR 1973 **37795 SABINE** ex ESSO LIMA 1972 **37796 SAN MARCOS** ex TRANSPANAMA 1976; ex OCEAN PIONEER 1968; ex ESSO JACKSONVILLE 1964; ex ESSO SUEZ 1962 Similar (Be built—Ar flag): **37797 PETROMAR CAMPANA** ex ESSO ANTWERP 1961.

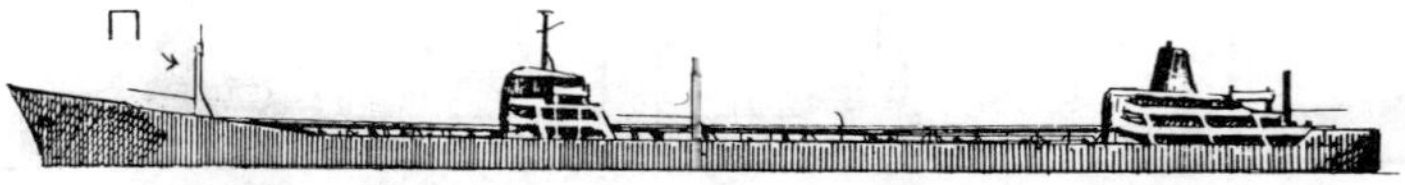

KMKFK H13
37810 PETROLA 36. Gr/Sw 1960; Tk; 26500; 213.21 × 11.59 (699.51 × 38.02); T; 17.25; ex PETROLA XXXVI 1976; ex SPIRO 1975; ex PETROLA XVII; ex ESSO BRUSSELS 1973.

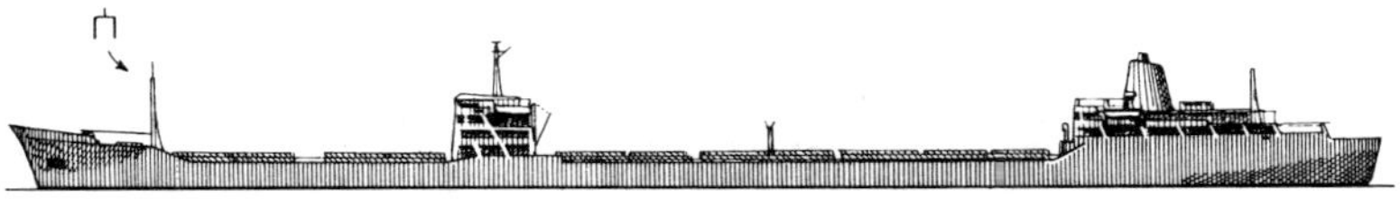

KMKFK H13
37820 PINDOS. Gr/Fr 1964; OO; 37800; 240.22 × 12.89 (788.12 × 42.29); T; 16.5; ex AZOV; ex SOYA BALTIC 1973.

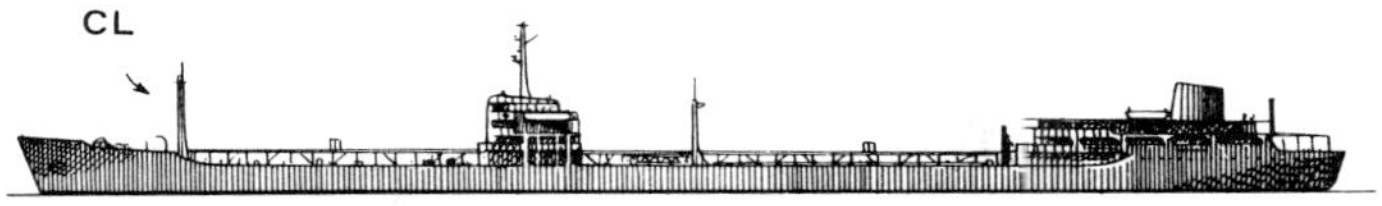

KMKFK H13
37830 MARIE MAERSK. De/De 1962; Tk; 21600; 209.15 × 10.75 (686.19 × 35.27) M; 15.

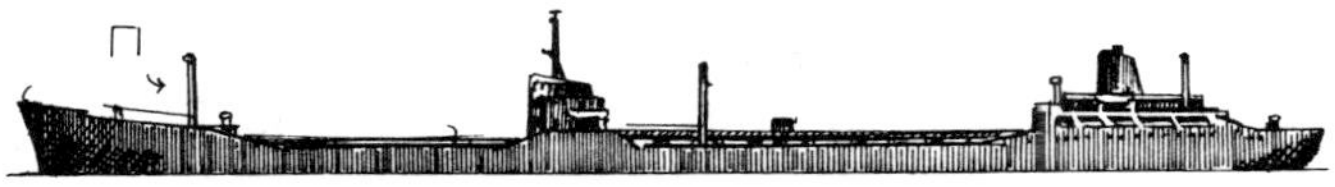

KMKFK H13
37840 GUERNICA. Sp/Sp 1962; Tk; 21600; 202.67 × 10.75 (664.93 × 35.27); T; 16.25. Sister: **37841 BILBAO** (Sp).

KMKFK H13
● **37850 PALLIUM;** Br/FRG 1959; Tk; 13000; 170.69 × 9.43 (560.03 × 30.94); T; 14.5. Sister: **37851 PARTULA** (Br).

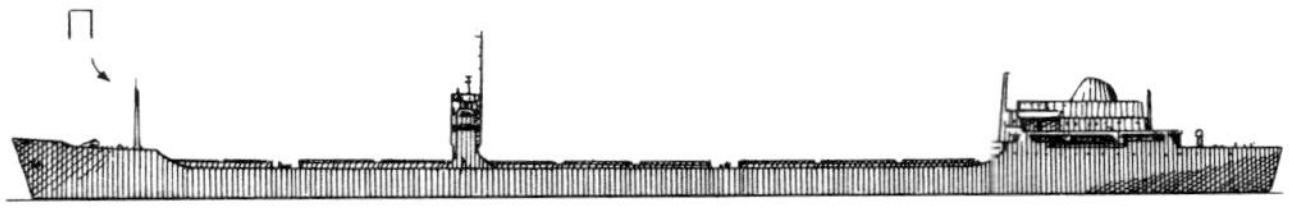

KMKFK H13
37860 SANTISIMA TRINIDAD; Ar/Fr 1963; O; 14700; 199.02 × 10.97 (652.95 × 33.99); M; 14; ex SKAMANDROS 1977; ex GERALD L D 1973. Sister: ★**37861 SUN CHON** (RK) ex COSMOS FAITH; ex PIERRE L D 1977.

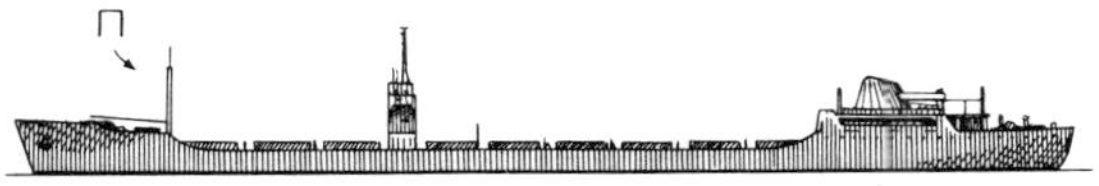

KMKFK H13
37870 ANINGA; It/FRG 1961; O; 9100; 166.43 × 9.42 (546.03 × 30.91); M; 15.5; ex TYNE ORE 1975. Sister: **37871 SEQUOIA** (It) ex TEES ORE 1975.

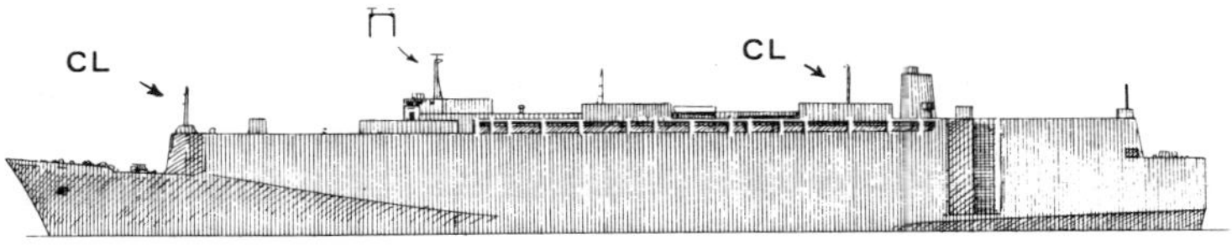

KMKFK H2
37880 JINYU MARU; Ja/Ja 1974; Ro/VC; 16100; 224.98 × 9.32 (738.12 × 30.58); M; 20.5; Side doors.

KMKFM H1
37890 ESTADO DA GUANABARA; Bz/Br 1973; D; 5000; 104.02 bp × 8.39 (341.27 × 27.53); TSM; 13; ex GUANABARA 1977.

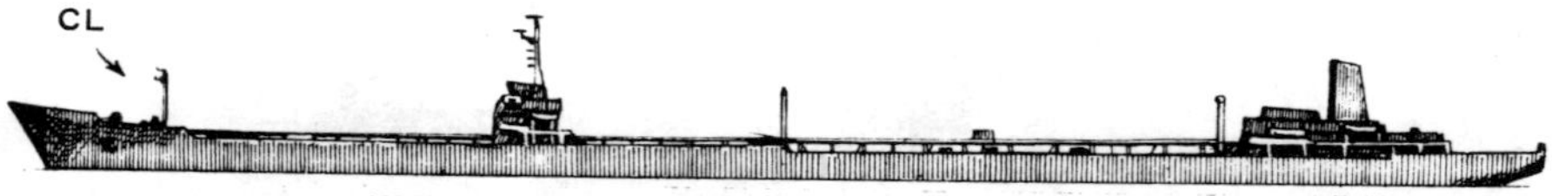

KMK$_2$F H1
37900 ENSKERI; Fi/FRG 1970; Tk; 62400; 274.3 × 15.43 (899.93 × 50.62); M; 17. Sister: **37901 TIISKERI** (Fi).

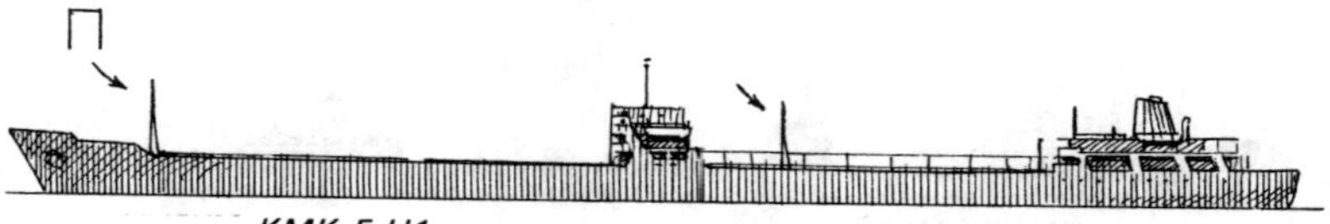

KMK$_2$F H1
37910 PRESIDENTE DEODORO; Bz/Ja 1960/67; Tk; 29900; 241.05 × 12.26 (790.85 × 40.22); T; —; Lengthened and deepened 1967. Sister: **37911 PRESIDENTE FLORIANO** (Bz).

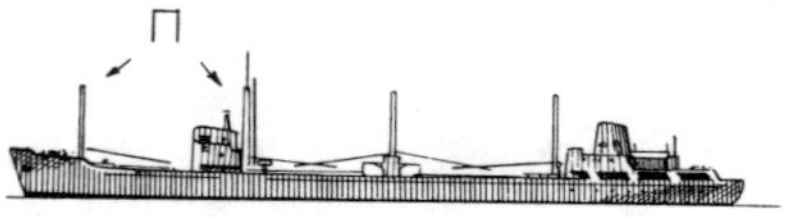

KMK$_2$F H1
37920 ILKON TAK; Li/Br 1959; C; 3000/4400; 115.27 × 6.55/7.47 (374.18 × 21.49/24.51); M; 15; ex MANCHESTER FAITH 1970; ex CAIRNESK 1966; ex MANCHESTER FAITH 1965. Sister: **37921 PANAGIS K** (Pa);ex EFI 1980; ex ILKON NIKI 1979; ex MANCHESTER FAME 1970; ex CAIRNGLEN 1966; ex MANCHESTER FAME 1965.

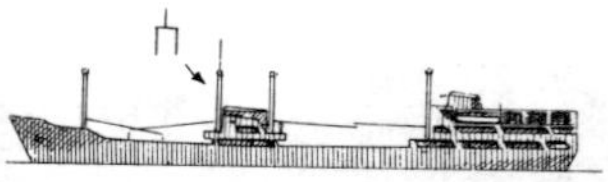

KMK$_2$F H1
37930 MARTINA; Pi/Sw 1957; CP; 1400; 89.08 × 4.88 (292.26 × 16,01); M; 13; ex VEGA 1973; Converted from cargo ship.

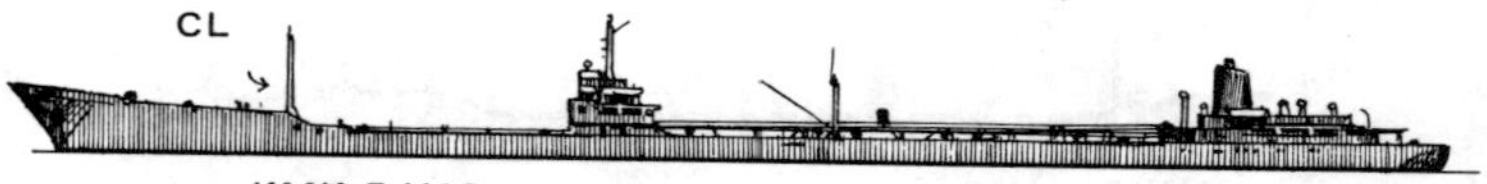

KMK$_2$F H12
● **37940 ANGEL PARK;** Ko/US-Ja 1953/65; Tk; 31300; 233.53 × 11.79 (766.17 × 38.68); T; 12; ex LAS PIEDRAS 1967.

KMK$_2$F H12
37950 MATCO AVON; Br/FRG-Ja 1964/68/76; Tk; 43700; 266.68 × 14.11 (874.93 × 46.29); T; 16.25; Lengthened and deepened 1968. Converted tanker 1976. Used for offshore loading.

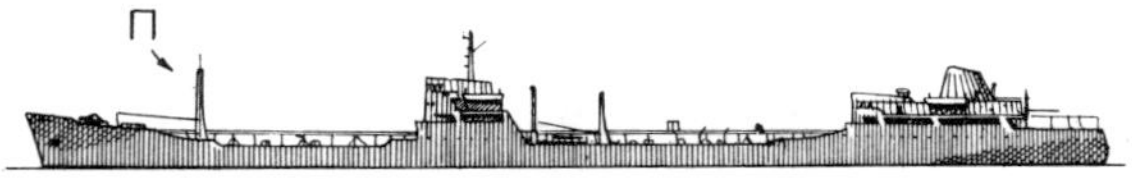

KMK_2F H123
● **37960 APOIKIA;** Gr/Ne 1959; Tk; 13000; 170.67 × 9.55 (559.94 × 31.34); M; 14; ex LONDON HARMONY 1976.

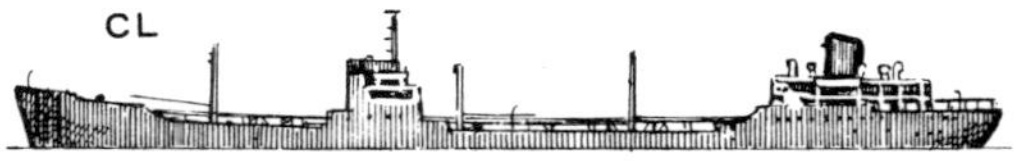

KMK_2F H123
37970 THERMOPYLAI; Gr/No 1955; Tk; 9000; 156.62 × 8.72 (513.85 × 28.61); M; 13.5; ex ANINA 1978; ex FOSSLAND 1963; ex SLEMDAL 1961.

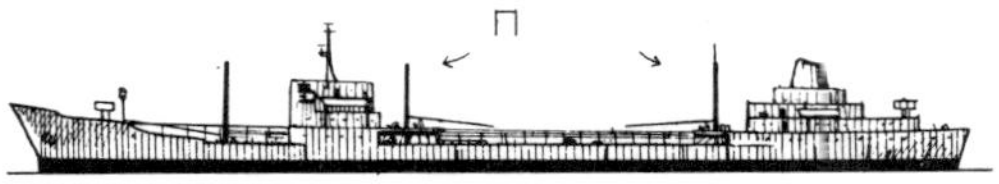

KMK_2F H123
37980 ARAUCANO; Ch/De 1967; RT/FA; 17300 Dspl; 151.8 × 8.8 (498 × 29); M; 15.5.

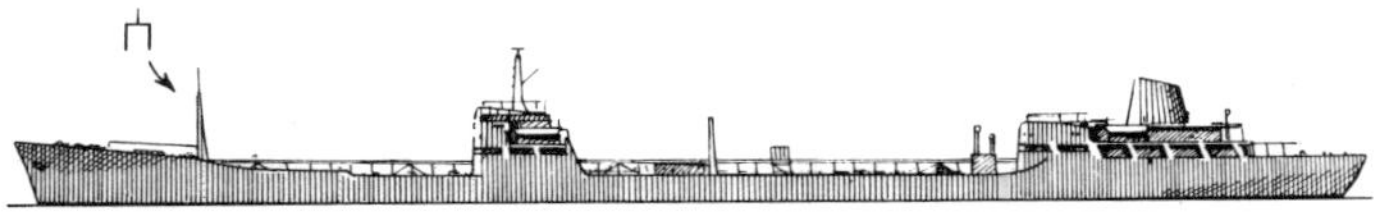

KMK_2F H123
37990 DAFFODIL B; Gr/Sw 1961; Tk; 22300; 212.86 × 11.24 (698.36 × 36.88); M; 16.25; ex LONDON INDEPENDENCE 1976. Sisters (Gr flag): **37991 TULIP B;** ex OVERSEAS AMBASSADOR 1976 **37992 THIAKI** ex OVERSEAS DISCOVERER 1976.

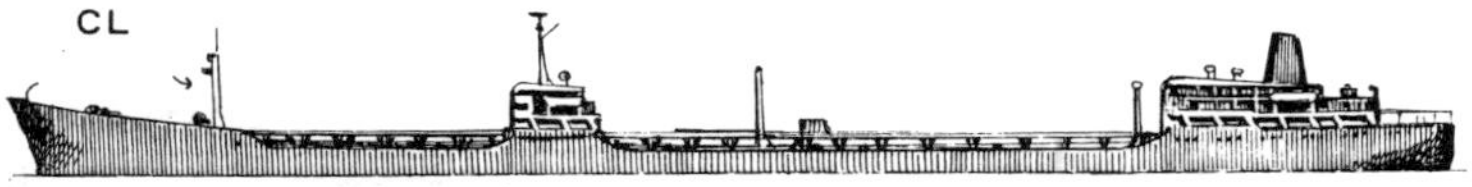

KMK_2F H123
● **38000 LONG PHOENIX;** No/FRG 1961; Tk; 29700; 225.74 × 12.03 (740.62 × 39.48); M; 16.5; ex ESSO NORWAY 1970; ex NORWAY 1970; ex ESSO NORWAY 1968.

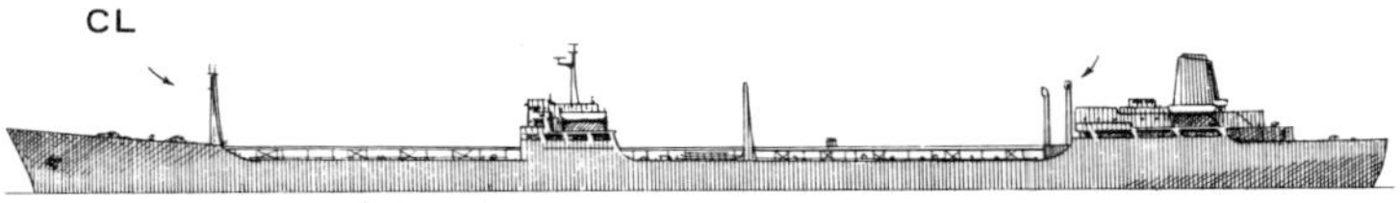

KMK_2F H123
38010 EXXON BOSTON; US/US 1960; Tk; 30700; 225.56 × 12.02 (740.03 × 39.42); T; 16.5; ex ESSO BOSTON 1973. Sister: **38011 EXXON BALTIMORE** (US) ex ESSO BALTIMORE 1973.

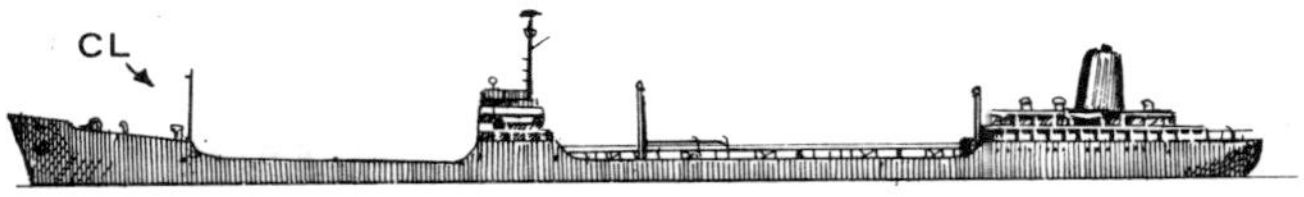

KMK_2F H123
38020 GULFCREST; US/US 1959; Tk; 18000; 196.55 × 10.56 (644.85 × 34.64); T; 17. Sisters: (US flag): **38021 GULFPRIDE 38022 GULFSOLAR 38023 GULFSUPREME 38024 GULFSPRAY.**

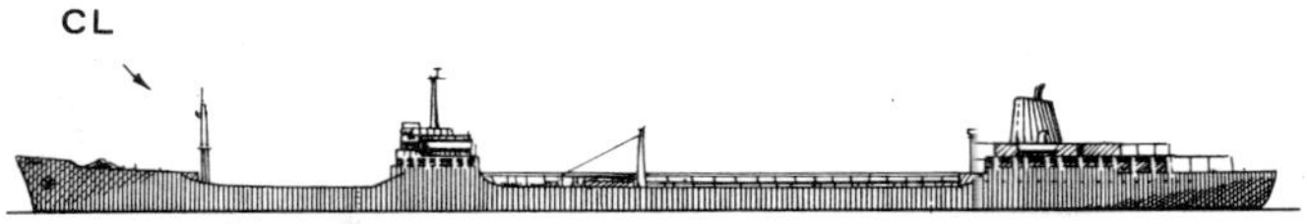

KMK_2F H123
38030 OGDEN CHALLENGER; US/US 1960; Tk; 20500; 201.48 × 10.86 (661.02 × 35.63); T; 16.5; ex PENN CHALLENGER 1974. Similar: **38031 COVE SAILOR** (US) ex ERNA ELIZABETH.

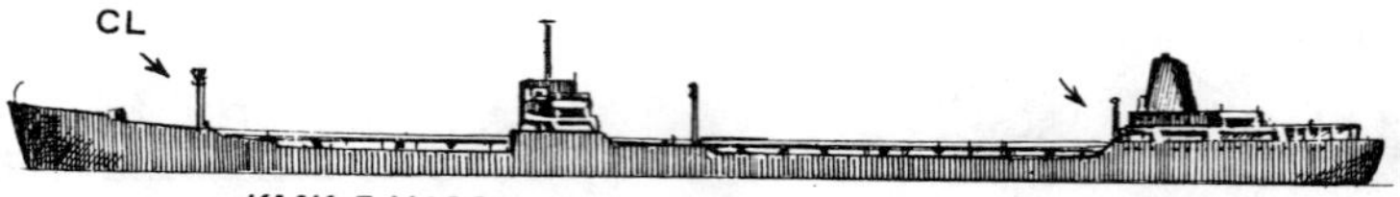

KMK_2F H123
38040 PENNSYLVANIA SUN; US/US 1959; Tk; 26300; 227.08 × 11.96 (745 × 39.25); T; 17. Sister: **38041 TEXAS SUN** (US).

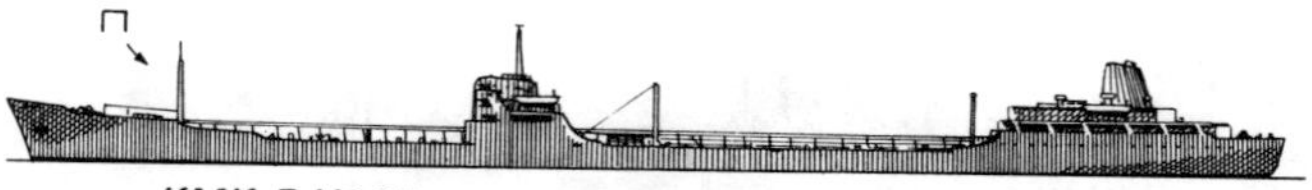

KMK_2F H123
38050 CHEVRON EINDHOVEN; Ne/Ja 1958; Tk; 21800; 201.17 × 10.81 (660 × 35.46); T; 16.5; ex CALTEX EINDHOVEN 1968.

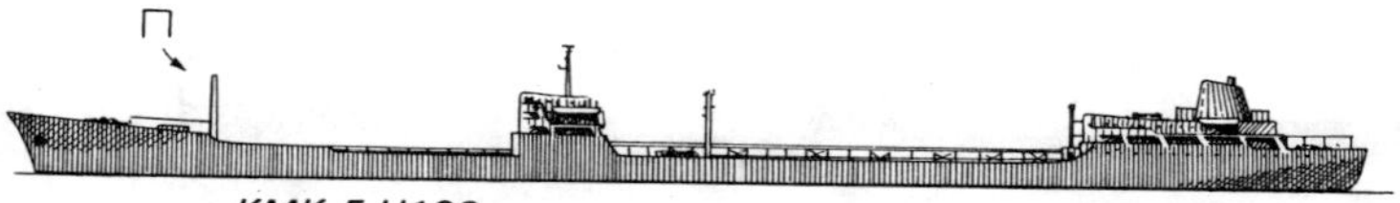

KMK_2F H123
● **38060 PHILLIPS TEXAS;** Li/Ja 1961; Tk; 28800; 224.52 × 11.94 (736.61 × 39.17); T; 16.25; ex DENMARK GETTY 1966.

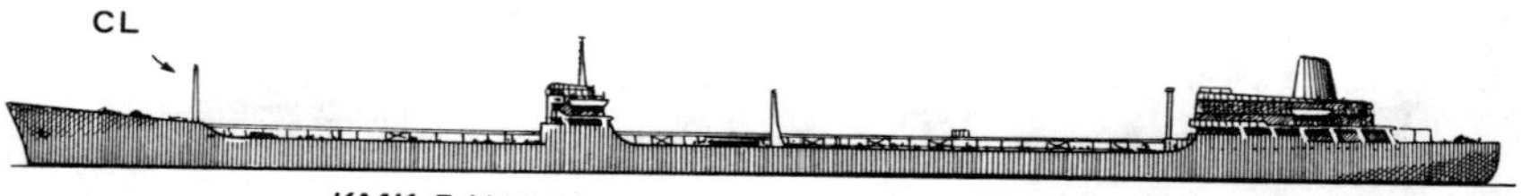

KMK_2F H123
● **38070 PETROLA 27;** Gr/FRG 1964; Tk; 53300; 262.54 × 15.01 (861.35 × 49.25); T; 17; ex PETROLA XXVII 1976; ex ESSO LONDON 1975. Similar: **38071 ESSO WARWICKSHIRE** (Br); Converted for loading crude oil at sea.

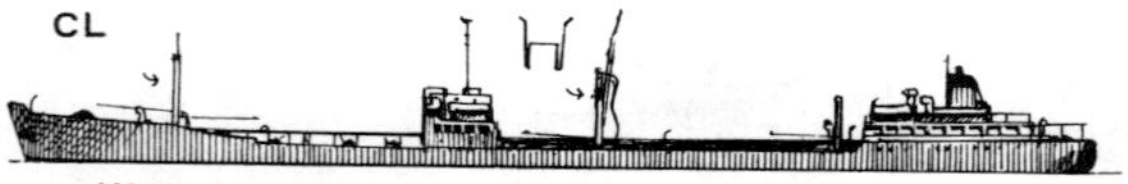

KMK_2F H123
38080 ISERE; Fr/Fr 1959; RT/FA; 26700 Dspl; 170.4 × 9.3 (559 × 30.3); T; 16; ex LA MAYENNE; ex CALTEX STRASBOURG.

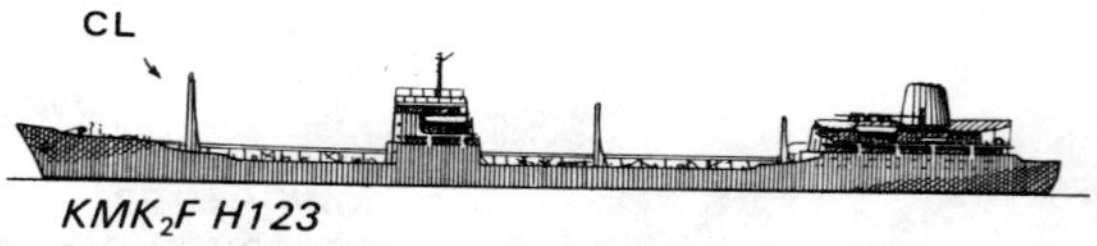

KMK_2F H123
38090 MERSIN; Tu/FRG 1955; Tk; 11300; 165.18 × 9.17 (541.93 × 30.09); M; 14.5; ex FAUST 1962.

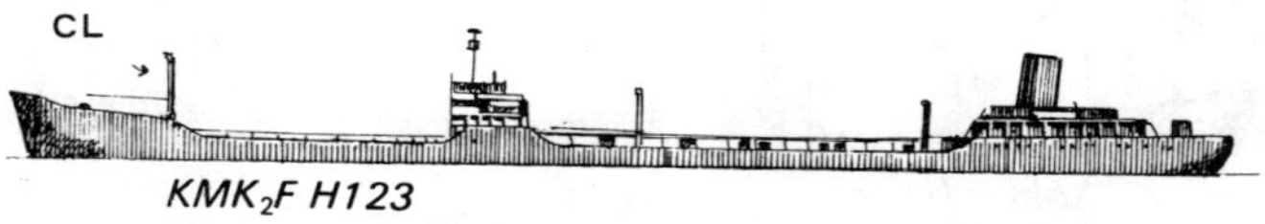

KMK_2F H123
38100 MOBIL FUEL; US/US 1957; Tk; 18700; 196.5 × 10.55 (644.68 × 34.61); T; 16.5. Sisters (US flag): **38101 MOBIL LUBE 38102 MOBIL POWER.**

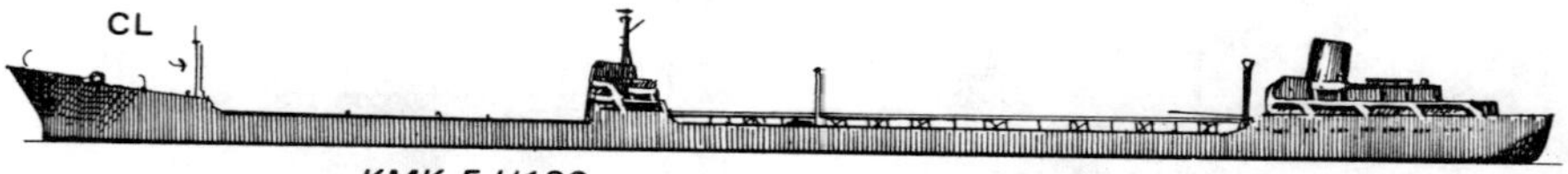

KMK_2F H123
● **38110 MOBIL COMET;** Li/Ja 1963; Tk; 58400; 270.62 × 15.42 (888 × 50.75); T; 17.25.

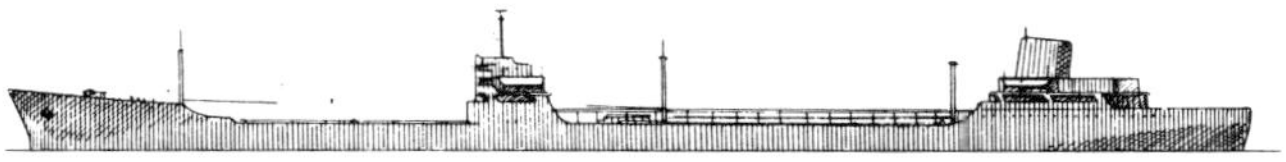

KMK_2F H123
38120 MOBIL OIL; US/US 1959; Tk; 18600; 195.38 × 10.84 (641.01 × 35.55); T; 17.25. Sister: **38121 MOBIL AERO** (US).

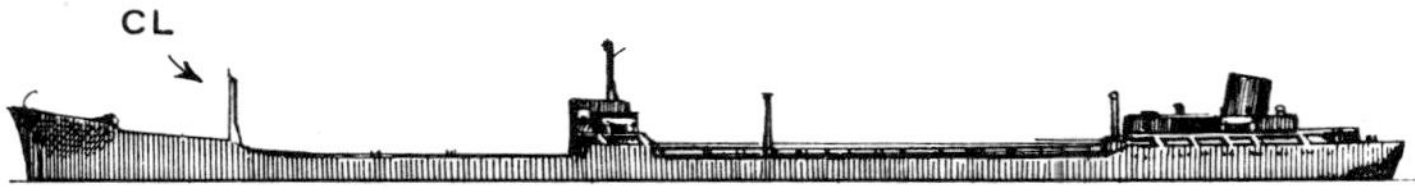

KMK_2F H123
● **38130 MOBIL VIGILANT;** Li/FRG 1964; Tk; 31300; 224.04 × 10.98 (735.04 × 36.02); T; 16.75. Similar: **38131 ATHENIAN** (Li) ex EGMONT 1972 **38132 TASSO** (FRG).

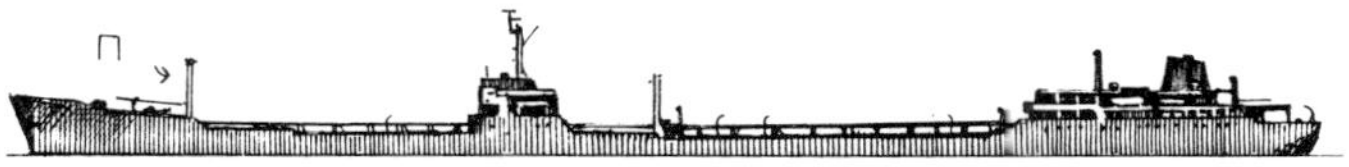

KMK_2F H123
38140 OMAR B; Pa/Sw 1960; Tk; 22400; 208.03 × 11.58 (682.51 × 37.98); M; —; ex FINALE 1980; ex BERGEMASTER 1968. Similar: **38141 AL MORGAN** (Eg) ex BERGESUND 1967.

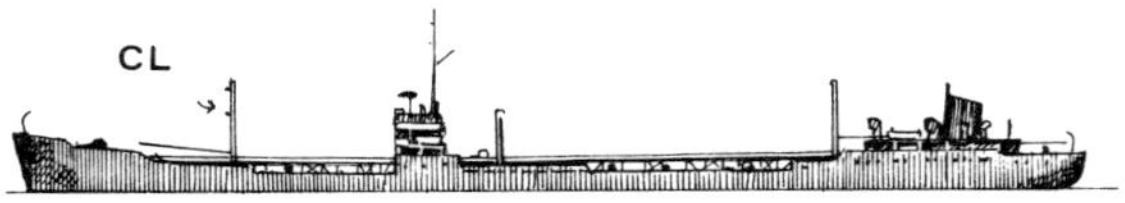

KMK_2F H123
38150 CHARLIE; Fi/De 1952; Tk; 12200; 169.78 × 9.58 (557.02 × 31.42); M; 14.5; ex MESSIDOR 1967.

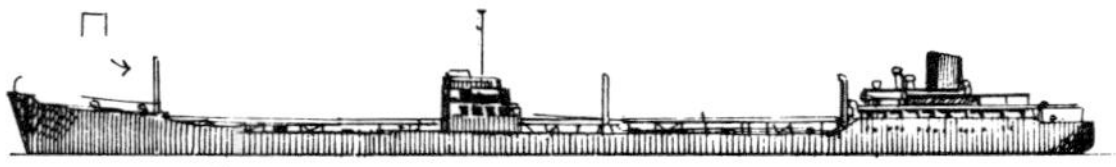

KMK_2F H123
38160 KOREA EDINBURGH; Ko/Br 1956; Tk; 11800; 170.39 × 9.62 (559.1 × 31.7); T; 15; ex TEXACO EDINBURGH 1971; ex CALTEX EDINBURGH 1968.

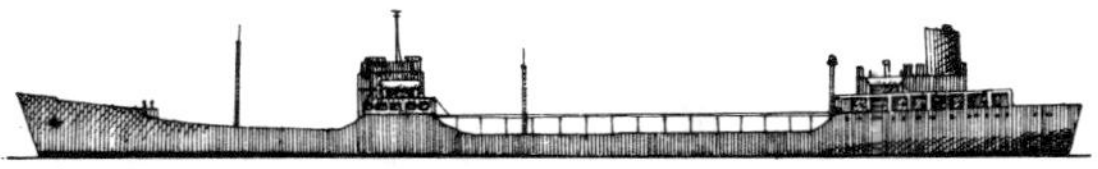

KMK_2F H123
38170 KEYSTONER; US/US 1953; Tk; 11400; 168 × 9.35 (551.18 × 30.67); T; 15.

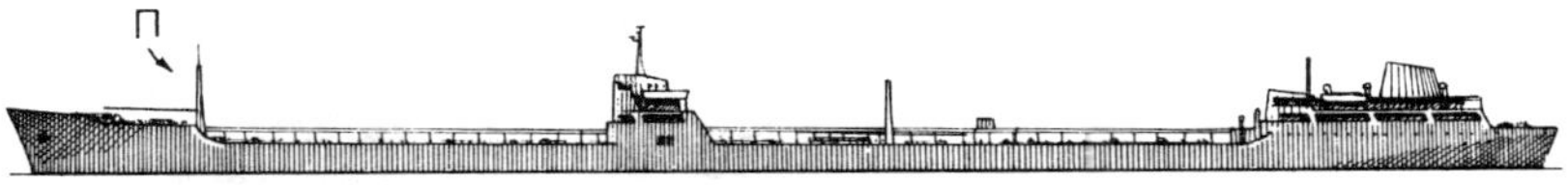

KMK_2F H123
38180 STATHEROS; Gr/No 1964; Tk; 41400; 253.02 × 13.65 (830.1 × 45); M; 17; ex CARDO 1975.

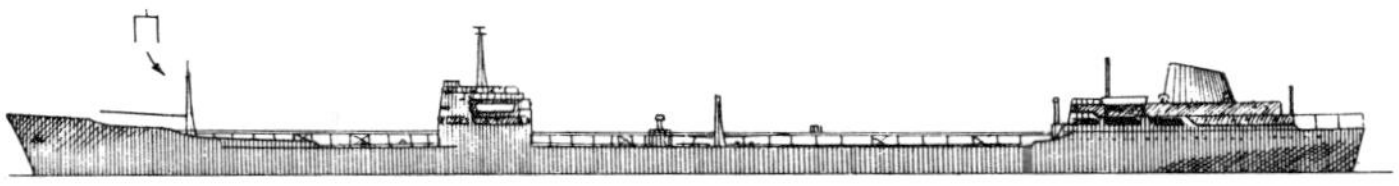

KMK_2F H123
38190 SANNY; Fi/Sw 1960; Tk; 26000; 213.42 × 11.39 (700.2 × 37.36); TSM; 16.5; ex HARRY TRAPP 1968. Sister: **38191 DAGNY** (Fi) ex O T TONNEVOLD 1967 Similar (KP's on aft superstructure nearer funnel): **38192 CABO CORRIENTES 1** (Ar) ex SVEN SALEN 1977.

KMK_2F H123
⋆**38200 ZEITZ;** DDR/De 1962; Tk; 25500; 208.59 × 11.61 (684.35 × 38.09); M; 16.5; ex DAGHILD 1969.

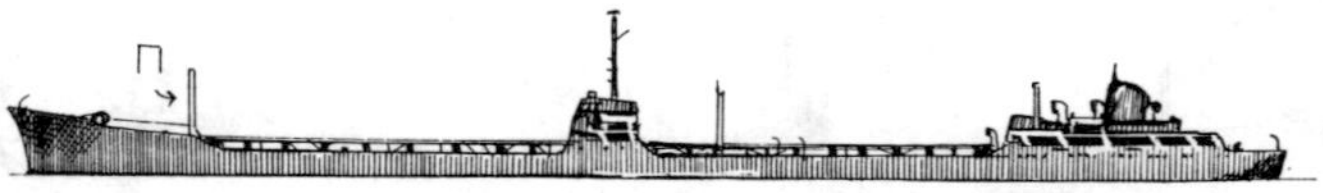

KMK_2F H123
38210 PAVLOS V; Gr/De 1958; Tk; 18300; 200.13 × 10.36 (656.59 × 33.99); M; 16.5; ex RAINBOW; ex GLOBAL LEADER: ex THOMAS G CHIMPLES 1977; ex MATHEOS 1972; ex FLOREAL 1968. Sister: **38211 TAMMANNA** (Sr) ex MONACO 1975; ex MAURITIUS 1974; ex MONSEAU 1971.

KMK_2F H123
38220 CEPHALONIA; Gr/Ja 1959; Tk; 24300; 213.65 × 11.44 (700.95 × 37.54); T; 17.25.

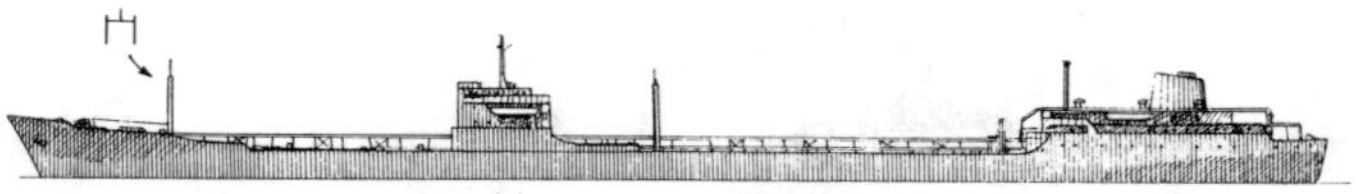

KMK_2F H123
38230 GEORGIOS; Gr/Sw 1960; Tk; 23500; 208.03 × 11.56 (682.51 × 37.93); M; 15; ex HOEGH FULMAR 1968.

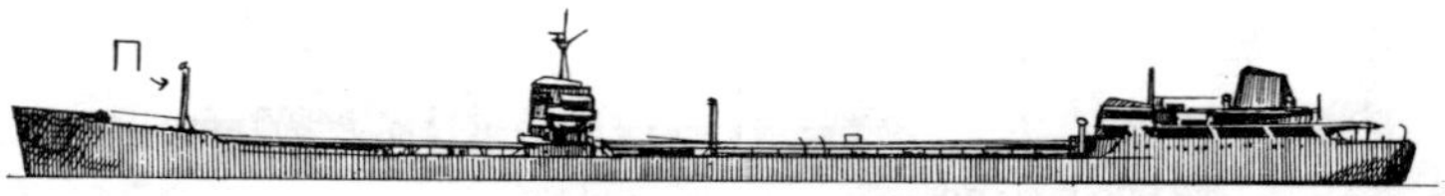

KMK_2F H123
38240 ST NICOLAS; Gr/No 1963; Tk; 31200; 223.73 × 12.55 (734.02 × 41.17); M; 16.5; ex CHALLENGER COLOCOTRONIS 1977; ex BERGE ODEL 1971. Sister: **38241 CHRISTINA** (Gr) ex FEARLESS COLOCOTRONIS 1976; ex BERGE JARL 1969.

KMK_2F H123
38250 CHERRY VESTA; Sg/Sw 1963; Tk; 25400; 213.44 × 11.45 (700.26 × 37.57); M; —; ex NEGO SHANG 1976; ex MIKE 1973; ex YANXILAS 1970; VILJA 1969.

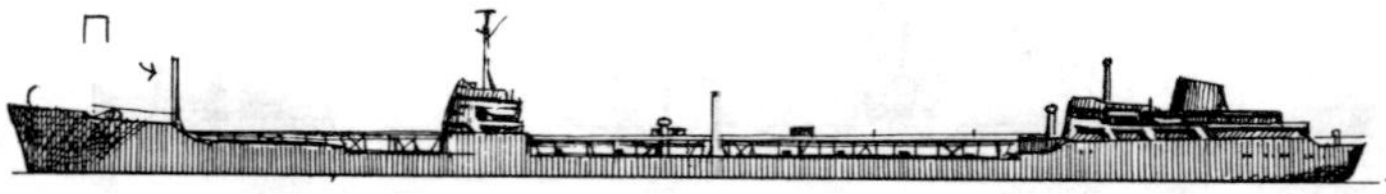

KMK_2F H123
38260 NEIL ARMSTRONG; Gr/Sw 1960; Tk; 25500; 213.42 × 11.41 (700.2 × 37.42); TSM; 15.25; ex GERINA 1969; ex VARENNA 1967.

KMK_2F H123
38270 FEOSO AMBASSADOR; Pa/Sw 1961; Tk; 24800; 213.42 × 11.81 (700.2 × 37.57); M; 17; ex SCHWEDT 1979; ex SEA SERPENT 1969.

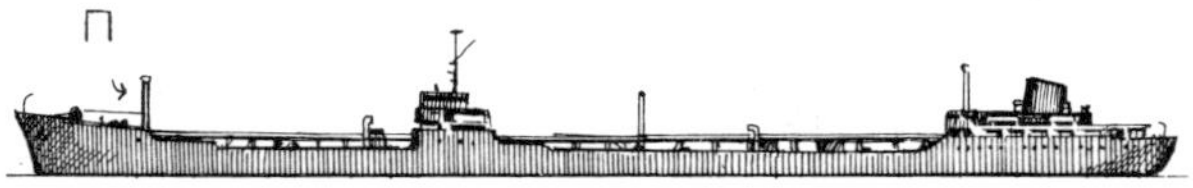

KMK_2F H123
● **38280 PHOENIX STAR;** Li/Sw 1957; Tk; 15400; 184.51 × 10.25 (605.6 × 33.7); M; 15.75; ex ARGO TRADER 1977; ex OCEAN STAR 1975; ex SEVEN STAR 1966.

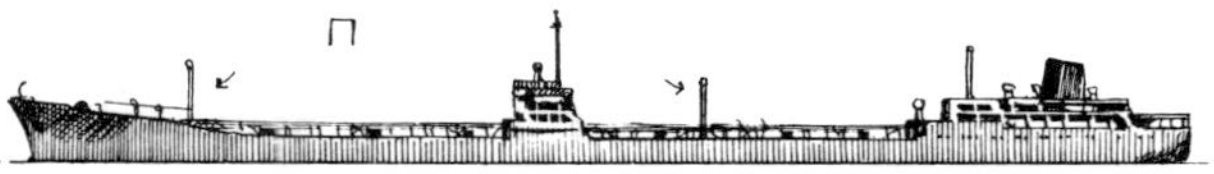

KMK_2F H123
38290 PERMINA SAMUDRA VII; Li/Br 1955; Tk; 16000; 180.8 × 1017 (593.18 × 33.38); T; —; ex SIRIUS 1971.

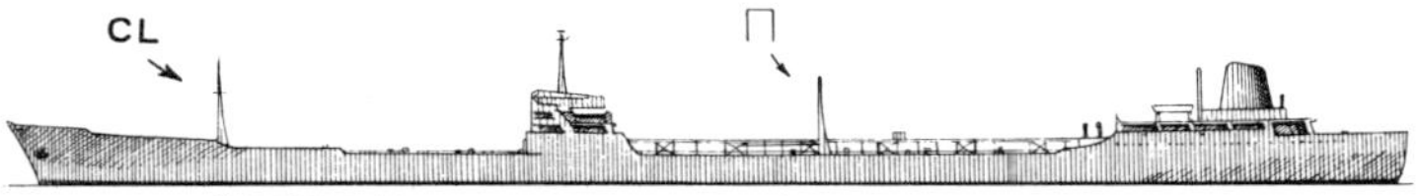

KMK_2F H123
38300 PEDOULAS; Gr/Ja 1962; Tk; 28200; 224.34 × 11.91 (736.02 × 39.08); M; 16; ex AMOCO CHALLENGER 1980; ex OCEAN CHALLENGER 1977; ex ASTRO PRINCE 1975; ex TANGO MARU 1973.

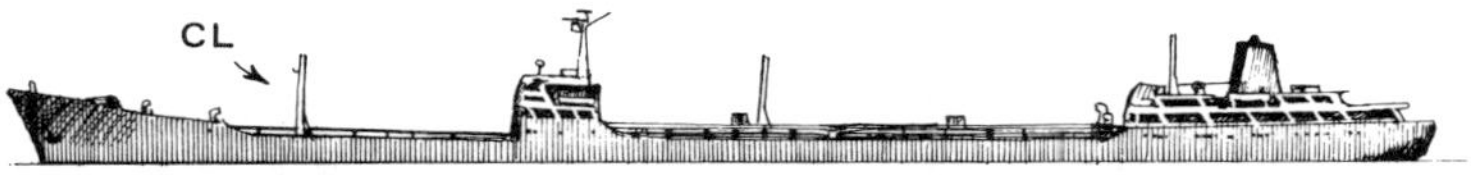

KMK_2F H123
38310 VENTURE LOUISIANA; Li/Fr 1964; Tk; 32000; 227.52 × 12.29 (746.46 × 40.33); T; 16.5; ex AZAY-LE-RIDEAU.

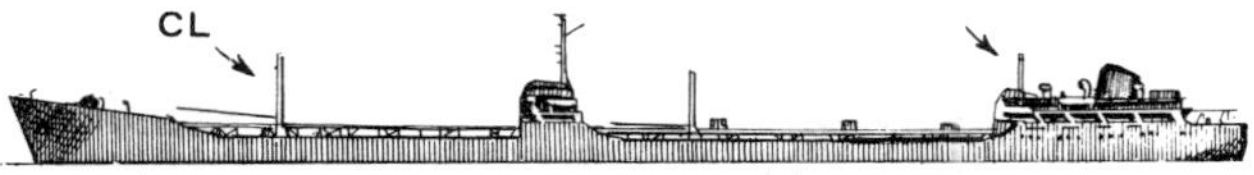

KMK_2F H123
38320 MIDAS TOUCH; Gr/Br 1961; Tk; 18600; 196.22 × 10.52 (643.77 × 34.51); M; 15; ex GALAXIAS; ex NORSK DROTT 1968.

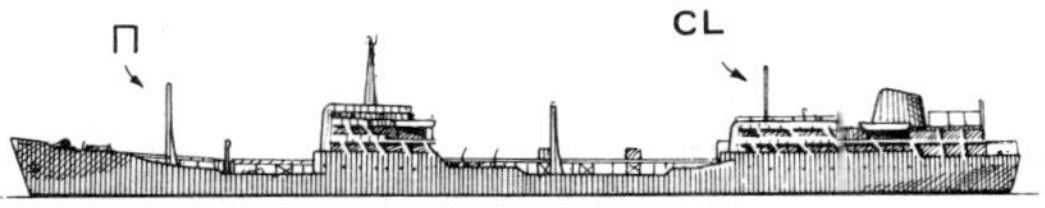

KMK_2F H123
● ⋆**38330 DA QING 235;** RC/Br 1959; Tk; 10700; 160.17 × 9.14 (525.5 × 30); M; 14.5; ex TINGJIANG; ex BRITISH TRUST 1976. Similar: ⋆**38331 DA QING 136** (RC) ex ZHUJIANG; ex BRITISH FULMAR 1976 **38332 ORIENTAL UNITY** (Li) ex BRITISH CYGNET 1977; ex B P EXPLORER 1969; ex B P ENDEAVOUR 1967; ex BRITISH CYGNET 1964 **38333 ORIENTAL BANKER** (Li) ex ORIENTAL ENDEAVOUR 1977; ex BRITISH CORMORANT 1977 **38334 ORIENTAL PEACE** (Li) ex BRITISH OSPREY 1977 **38335 HANJIANG** (Pa) ex BRITISH GANNET 1976 **38336 SUNJIANG** (Br) ex BRITISH KESTREL 1976 **38337 WENJIANG** (Br) ex BRITISH CURLEW 1976 **38338 NOAH VI** (Ir) ex BRITISH SWIFT 1977 **38339 LOT** (Fr) ex BRITISH ROBIN 1977 **38340 BRITISH GULL** (Br) **38341 PENHORS** (Fr) ex BRITISH MALLARD 1978.

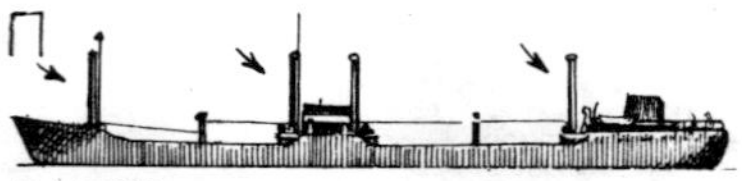

KMK_2F H123
● **38350 MALDIVE CORAL;** Mv/No 1953; C; 2400; 11.82 × 6.01 (366.86 × 19.73); M; 14; ex PAPUAN CHIEF 1975; ex MARSINA 1970; ex PAPUAN CHIEF 1969; ex BAHIA 1966; ex ITALIAN 1966; ex BAHIA 1964.

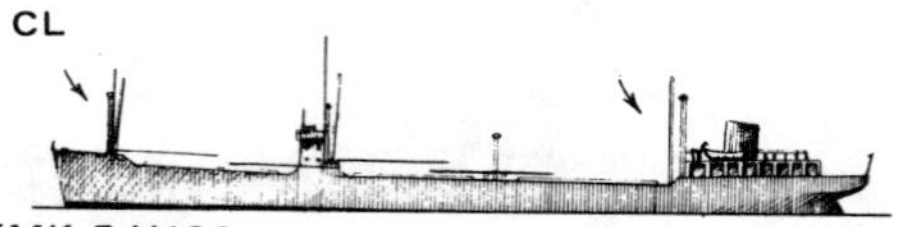

KMK_2F H123
⋆38360 BUGA; Ys/Br 1926; C/HL; 7200; 130.41 × 7.47 (427.85 × 24.51); TSM; 11.5; ex NEW ZEALAND VENTURE 1970; ex BELPAREIL 1965.

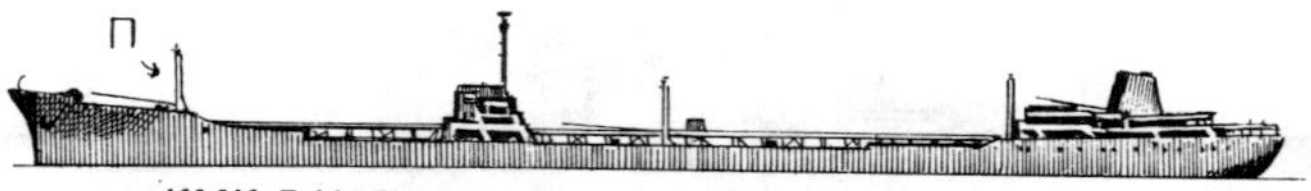

KMK_2F H13
● **38370 LONDON CONFIDENCE;** Br/Ne 1962; Tk; 21400; 202.62 × 10.86 (664.76 × 35.63); M; 14.5.

KMK_2F H13
38380 COASTAL TEXAS; Li/Ja 1964; Tk; 44700; 248.04 × 13.15 (814 × 43.1); T; —; ex STAVROS G LIVANOS 1977.

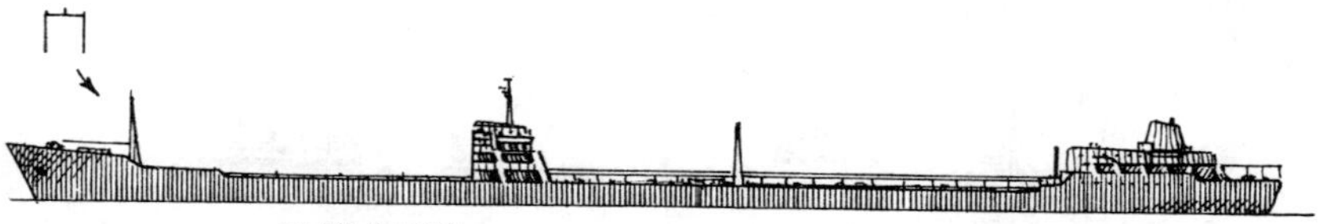

KMK_2F H13
38390 OKLAHOMA; Li/Ja 1963; Tk; 47400; 255.3 × 15.4 (837.6 × 50.41); T; 16.5; ex PHILLIPS OKLAHOMA; ex CALIFORNIA GETTY 1966. Sister: **38391 PHILLIPS OREGON** (Li) ex OREGON GETTY 1967.

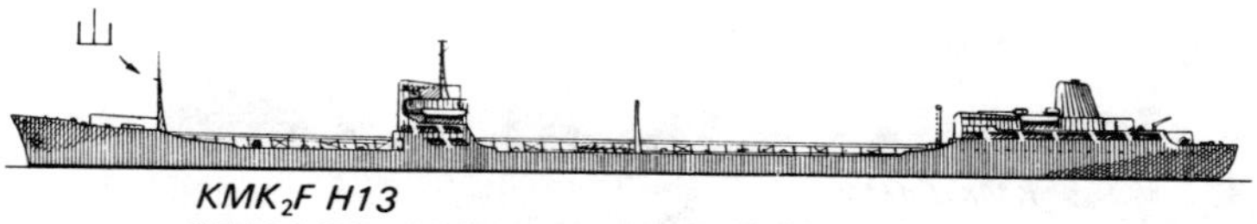

KMK_2F H13
38400 TEXACO PLYMOUTH; Br/Ja 1960; Tk; 31100; 223.5 × 11.79 (733.27 × 38.69); T; —; ex CALTEX PLYMOUTH 1968.

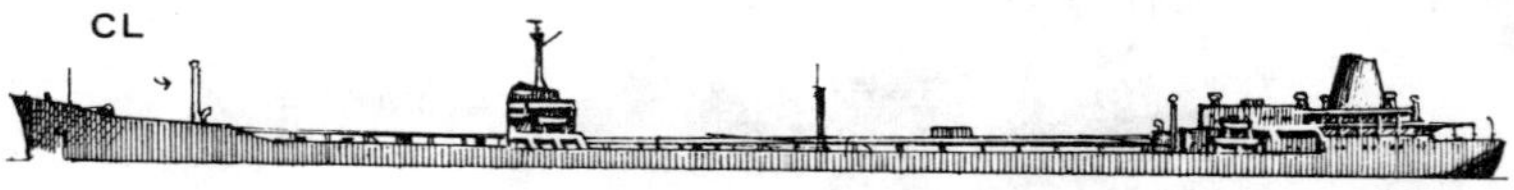

KMK_2F H13
38410 AMER B; Pa/Sw 1963; Tk; 34600; 236.18 × 11.74 (774.87 × 38.5); M; 16; ex HANTOS BREEZE; ex GLOBTIK VENUS; ex TUNDRA BREEZE 1974; ex GLOBTIK MERCURY 1972; ex BRALANTA 1969. Similar: **38411 ARCTIC STAR** (Li) ex PALMA 1976.

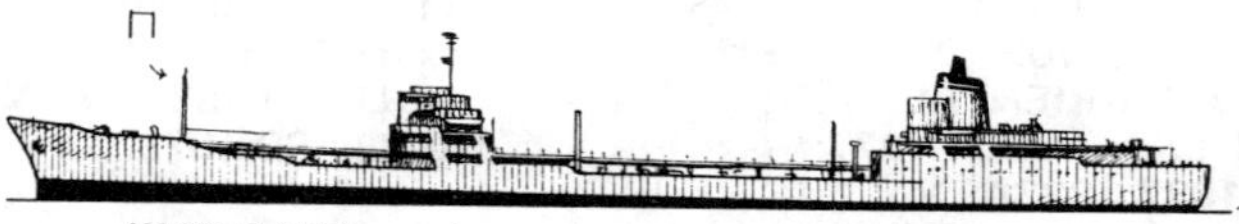

KMK_2F H13
38420 MAUMEE; US/US 1956; Tk; 25000 Dwt; 189 × 9.8 (620 × 32); T; 18; Operated by Military Sealift Command. Sisters (US flag): **38421 SHOSHONE 38422 YUKON.**

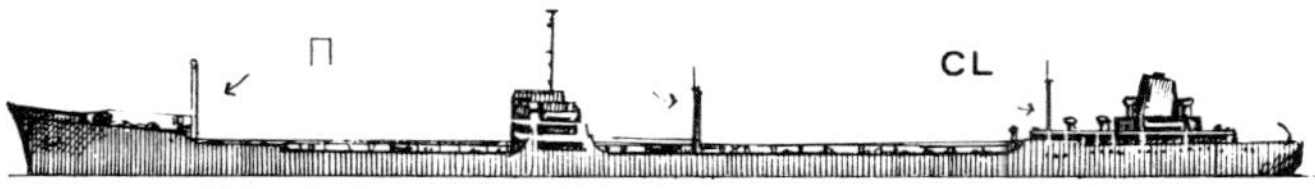

KMK$_2$F H13
38430 ROKOS V; Gr/Ja 1956; Tk; 21000; 203.56 × 11.04 (667.85 × 36.23); T; 17.25.

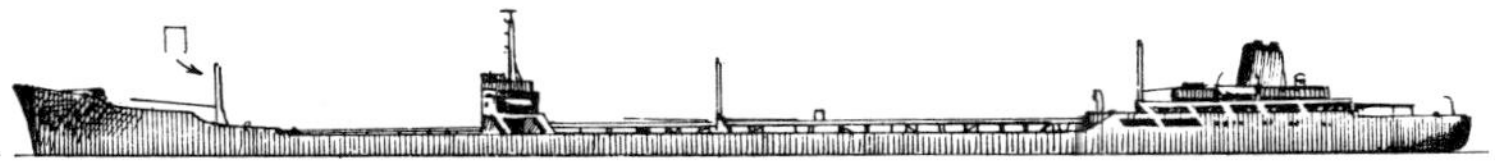

KMK$_2$F H13
38440 GEORGE VERGOTTIS; Li/Ja 1966; Tk; 30600; 236.23 × 12.38 (775.03 × 40.61); M; —. Sister: **38441 IONIAN COMMANDER** (Li).

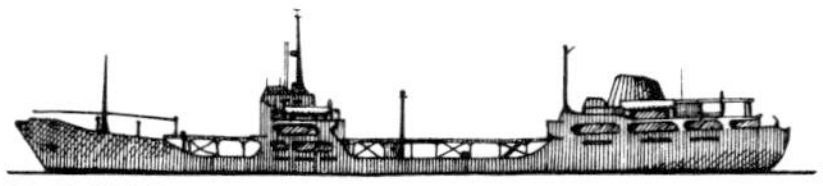

KMK$_2$F H13
38450 GABRIEL DA FONSECA; Bz/FRG 1959; Tk; 4700; 122.87 × 7.28 (403.12 × 23.88); M; 14.

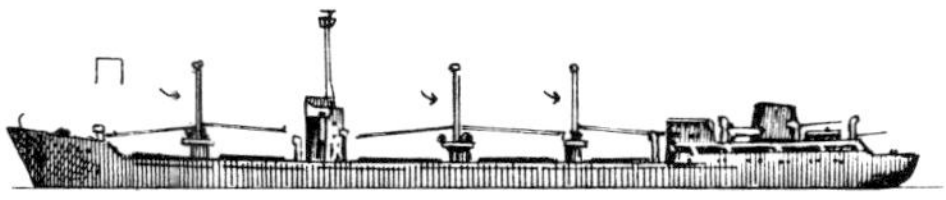

KMK$_2$F H13
38460 PRIMA KING; Sg/FRG 1955; C; 8700; 144.66 × 8.43 (474.61 × 27.67); M; 12.5; ex NIDAR 1968; ex ESTELLO 1962.

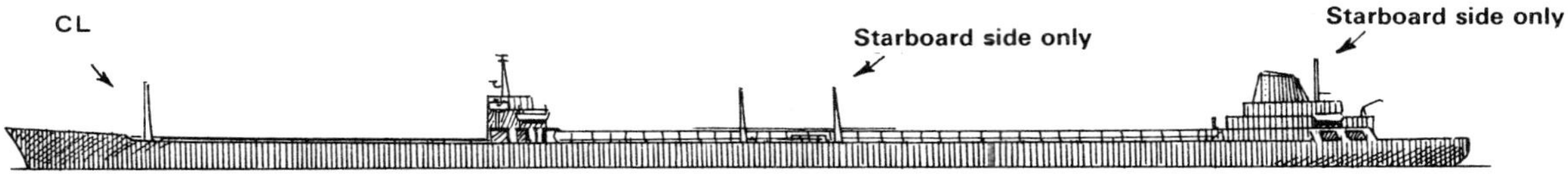

KMK$_2$FK H
38470 SHOJU MARU; Ja/Ja 1969; Tk; 109100; 315.37 × 18.85 (1034.68 × 61.83); T; 16.

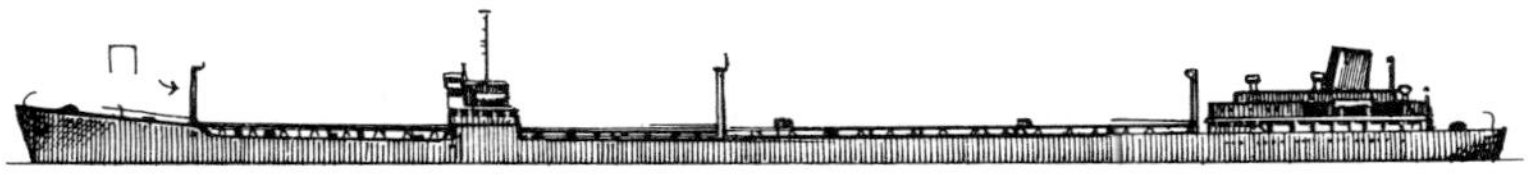

KMK$_2$FK H12
● **38480 ESSO CHILE**; Pa/It 1957/62; Tk; 29100; 235.67 × 13.06 (773.2 × 42.83); T; 15.5; Lengthened and deepened 1962.

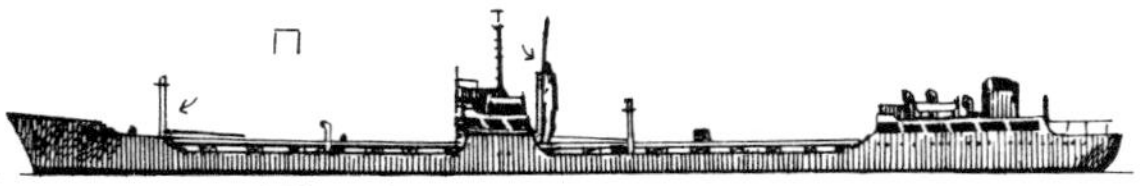

KMK$_2$FK H123
38490 PEARLEAF; Br/Br 1960; RT/FA; 12400; 173.2 × 9.2 (568 × 30); M; 16.

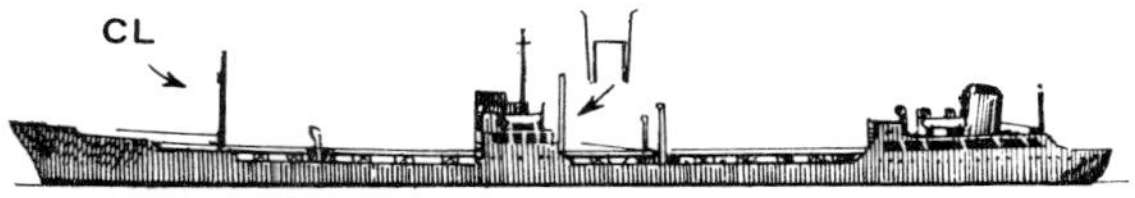

KMK$_2$FK H123
38500 PLUMLEAF; Br/Br 1960; RT/FA; 26500 Dspl; 163 × 9.2 (560 × 30); M; 15.5.

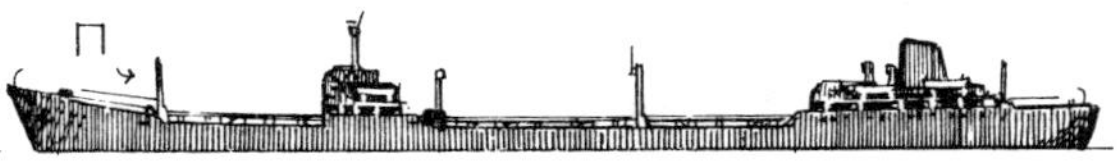

KMK$_2$FK H123
38510 MATA PRIMA; It/Sp 1956; Tk; 12600; 171.61 × 9.51 (563.02 × 31.21); M; 14; ex MATA 1973; ex PUENTES DE G RODRIGUEZ 1972. Sister: **38511 GRIFONE** (It) ex PUERTOLLANO 1972.

KMK$_2$FK H123
38520 CARAIBI; It/Sp 1957; Tk; 12700; 170.62 × 9.51 (559.78 × 31.2); M; 14; ex VALMASEDA 1975. Similar: **38521 CAMPANAR** (Sp) ex COMPOSTILLA 1974 **38522 CAMPAZAS** (Sp) ex RIBAGORZANA 1974.

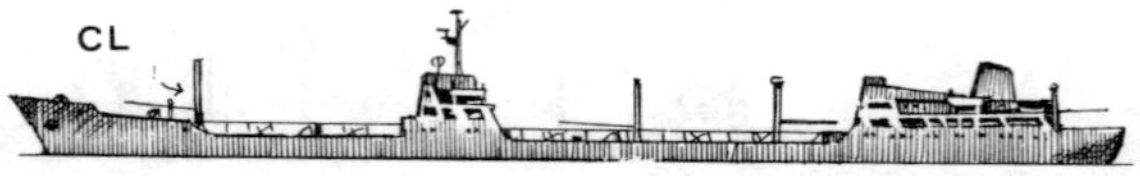

KMK_2FK H123
★**38530 PLYAVINYAS;** Ru/Pd 1967; Tk; 12600; 176.89 × 9.5 (580.35 × 31.17); M; 16.25; **'B-70'** type. Sisters (Ru flag): ★**38531 LIMBAZHI** ★**38532 PREYLI** ★**38533 RIGA** ★**38534 VALMIERA** ★**38535 TALSY** ★**38536 TSESIS.**

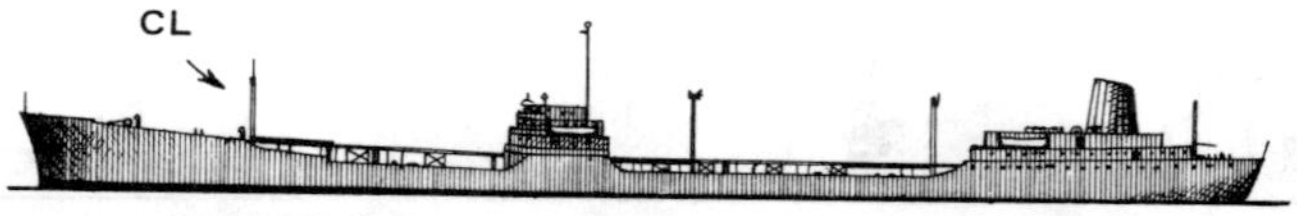

KMK_2FK H123
38540 DELAWARE SUN; US/US 1953; Tk; 18800; 195.38 × 1081 (641 × 35.46); T; 16.5. Sisters (US flag): **38541 EASTERN SUN 38542 WESTERN SUN 38543 NEW JERSEY SUN.**

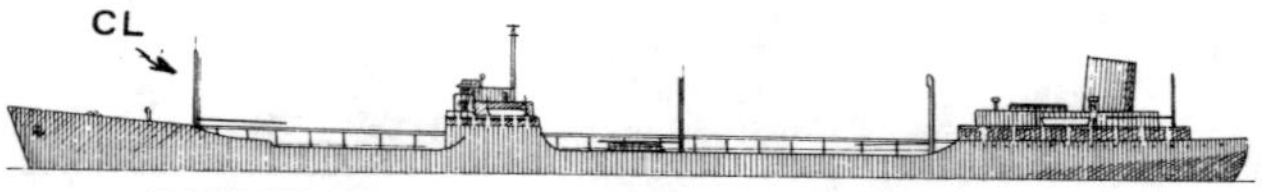

KMK_2FK H123
38550 COVE COMMUNICATOR; US/US 1954; Tk; 18800; 195.41 × 10.81 (641.11 × 35.46); T; 16.5; ex ATLANTIC COMMUNICATOR 1976.

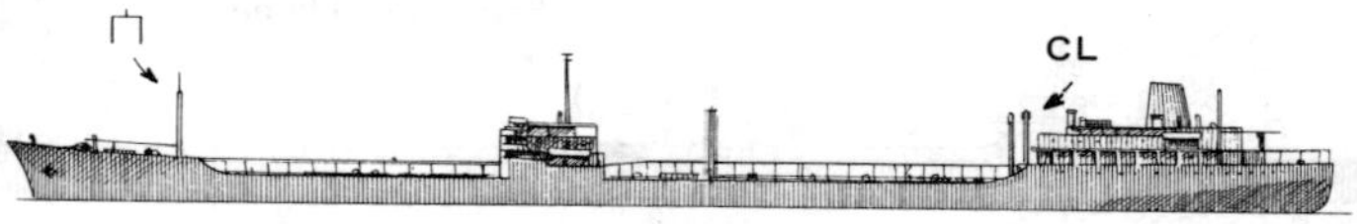

KMK_2FK H123
38560 LAGOVEN MARACAIBO; Ve/Ja 1959/64; Tk; 24100; 212.15 × 10.95; (696.03 × 35.92); T; 15; ex ESSO MARACAIBO 1976; Lengthened 1964. Sister: **38561 LAGOVEN CARACAS** (Ve) ex ESSO CARACAS 1976.

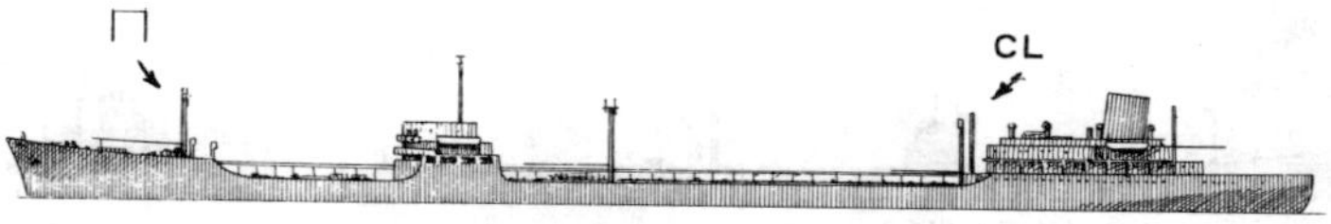

KMK_2FK H123
38570 EXXON GETTYSBURG; US/US 1957; Tk; 23700; 217.94 × 11.84 (715.03 × 38.85); T; 18.25; ex ESSO GETTYSBERG 1973. Sisters (US flag): **38571 EXXON JAMESTOWN** ex ESSO JAMESTOWN 1973 **38572 EXXON LEXINGTON** ex ESSO LEXINGTON 1973 **38573 EXXON WASHINGTON** ex WASHINGTON 1973.

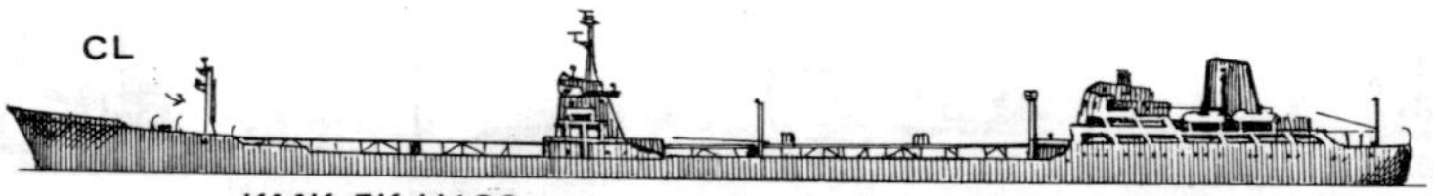

KMK_2FK H123
★**38580 GIORDANO BRUNO;** Ru/It 1964; Tk; 31300; 227.01 × 12.14 (744.78 × 39.83); M; 15.75. Sisters (Ru flag): ★**38581 FEDOR POLETAEV** ★**38582 LEONARDO DA VINCI.**

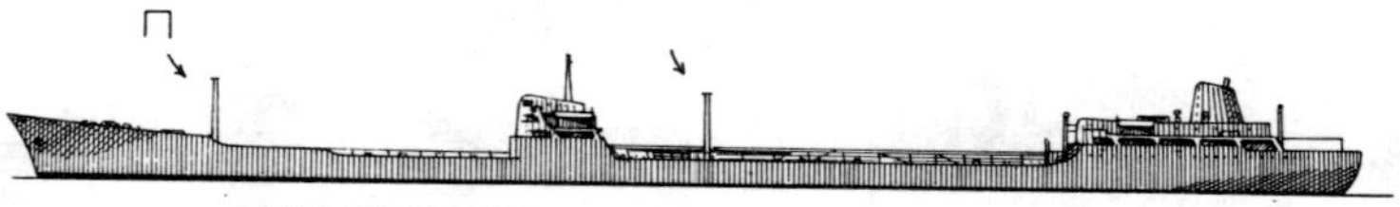

KMK_2FK H123
38590 DONA RITA; Li/Ja 1960; Tk; 28700; 224.52 × 11.94 (736.61 × 39.16); T; 16.5; ex NAESS VOYAGER 1968. Similar: **38591 PERMINA SAMUDRA XIV** (Li) ex WARUKIN CORP; ex MOSCLIFF 1969.

KMK_2FK H123
38600 GOTHIC LADY; Pa/Sw 1962; Tk; 21500; 208.92 × 10.88 (685.43 × 35.71); M; 15.25; ex HOLMA 1974.

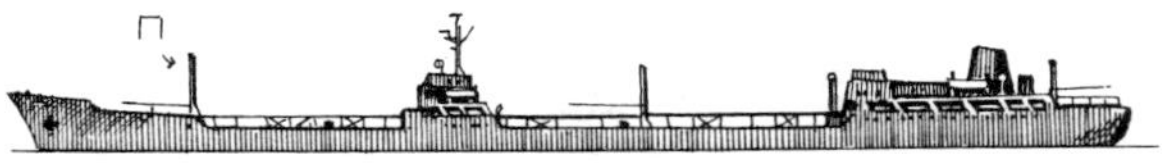

KMK_2FK H123
● ★**38610 BAUSKA;** Ru/Pd 1962; Tk; 12600; 176.94 × 9.55 (580.51 × 31.33); M; 15.25; ex PROFESOR HUBER: **'B-70'** type. Sisters: ★**38611 BALAKLAVA** (Ru) ★**38612 BALDONE** (Ru) ★**38613 BALVY** (Ru) ★**38614 DA QING No 17** (RC) ex PROF. M. T. HUBER 1964.

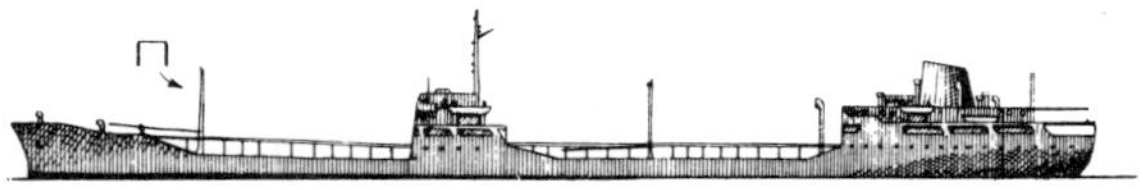

KMK_2FK H123
★**38620 HONG HU.** RC/Ys 1959; Tk; 13300; 170.69 × 9.5 (560 × 31.17); M; —; ex OSTRAVA 1965; ex ISTINA 1959.

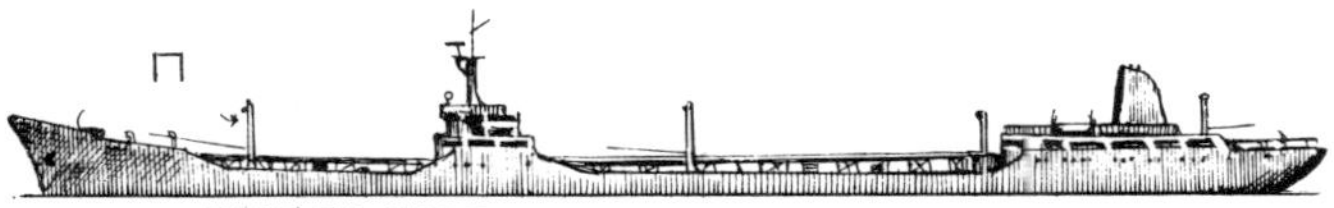

KMK_2FK H123
38630 SICILMOTOR. It/It 1958; Tk; 20600; 204.81 × 10.89 (671.95 × 35.73); M; 16.5.

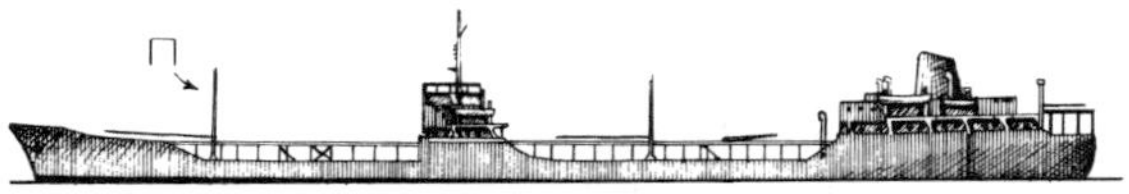

KMK_2FK H123
★**38640 IZ.** Ys/Ys 1960; Tk; 12800; 170.69 × 9.76 (560 × 32.02); M; 15.25.

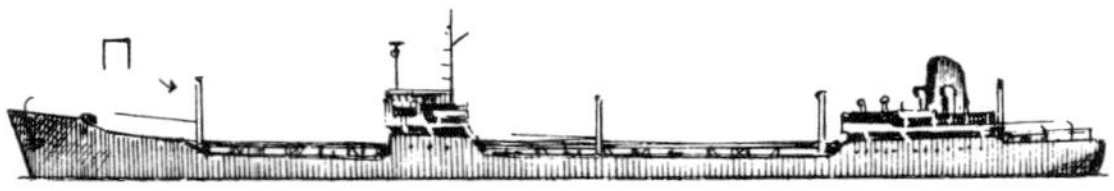

KMK_2FK H123
38650 CATHERINE. Gr/Yu 1960; Tk; 13000; 170.69 × 9.77 (560 × 32.04); M; 15; ex STOLT CATHERINE 1980; ex STOLT AEGEAN 1978; ex STOLT GEMINI 1973; ex DIOSKUROI 1969.

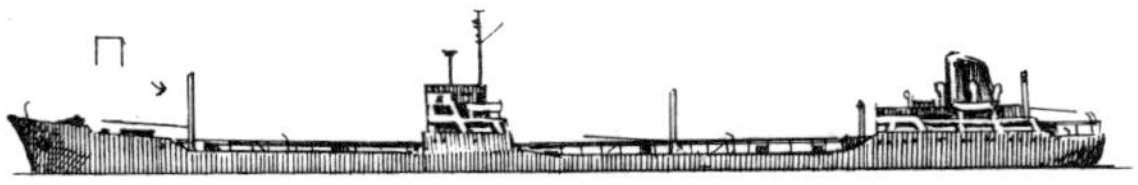

KMK_2FK H123
38660 HONESTAS. It/Pd 1961; Tk; 13700; 170.67 × 9.45 (559.94 × 31); M; 15; ex BESKIDY 1977; Ice strengthened. Sister: **38661 SANROCCO** (Pa) ex KARPATY 1978.

KMK_2FK H123
38670 CAMPORROJO. Sp/Sp 1963; Tk; 7000; 141.79 × 7.76 (465.2 × 25.46); M; 13.7. Sister (Sp flag): **38671 CAMPOGULES** Possible Sisters (Sp flag): **38672 CAMPOCERRADO 38673 CAMPOAZUR 38674 CAMPORRUBIO.**

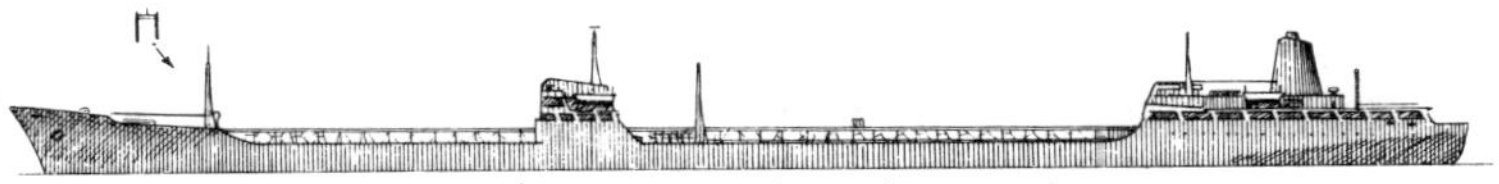

KMK_2FK H123
38680 ATA. Tu/Fr 1962; Tk; 31000; 230.33 × 11.94 (755.68 × 39.17); T; —; launched as TENAX.

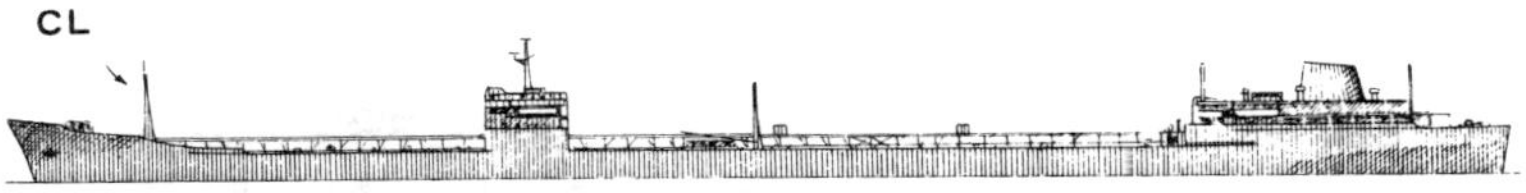

KMK_2FK H123
★**38690 DA QING No 253.** RC/De 1974; Tk; 33800; 236.23 × 12.42 (775.03 × 40.73); M; 16.5; ex JIAN HU 1977; ex VESTHAV 1974. Sister: **38691 THRACIAN SHIRLEY** (Gr) ex BALDER BORG; ex HERBORG 1977; ex SAMNANGER 1973.

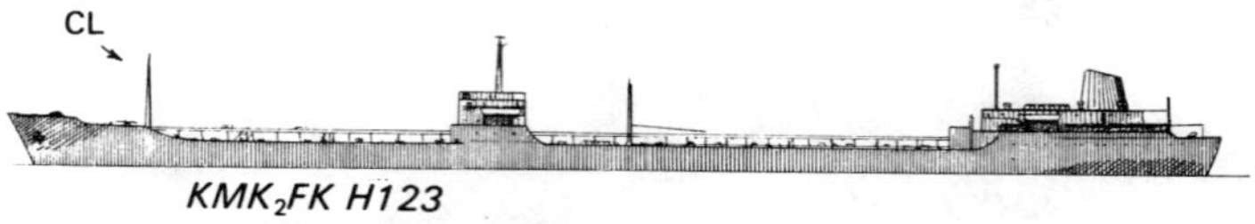

KMK₂FK H123

★**38700 DA QING No 251.** RC/Sw 1964; Tk; 26600; 215.22 × 11.94 (706.1 × 39.17); M; 15.25; ex PINGHU; ex GULDREGN 1974; ex REGINA 1973; ex NOVA 1967.

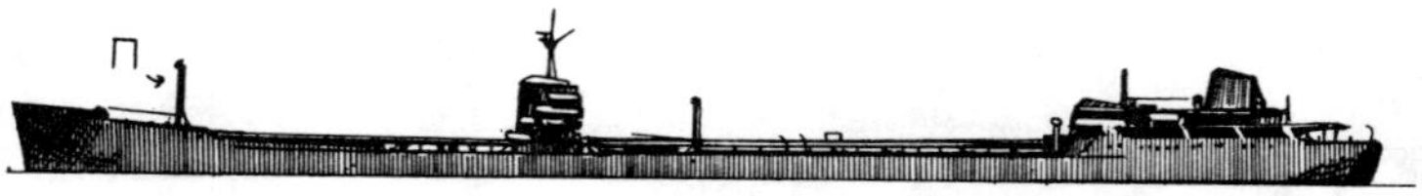

KMK₂FK H123

38710 ST. NICOLAS. Gr/No 1963; Tk; 31200; 223.73 × 12.55 (734.02 × 41.17); M; 16.5; ex CHALLENGER COLOCOTRONIS 1977; ex BERGE ODEL 1971. Sister: **38711 CHRISTINA** (Gr) ex FEARLESS COLOCOTRONIS 1976; ex BERGE JARL 1969.

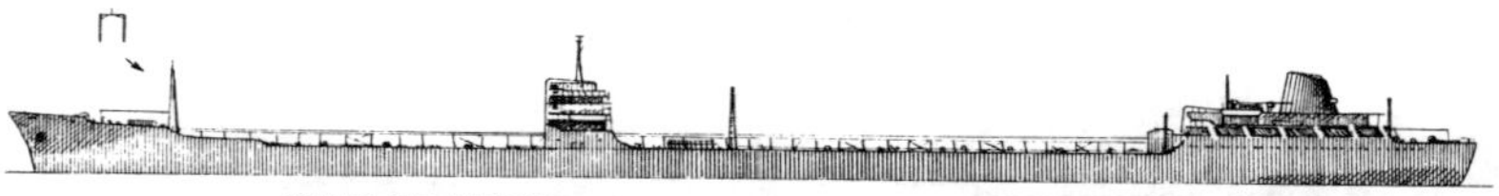

KMK₂FK H123

38720 CITTA DI SAVONA. It/Fr 1963; Tk; 36700; 242.91 × 12.85 (767.93 × 42.15); M; —; ex BERGE CHARLES 1968. Sister: **38721 GERMIK** (Tu) ex BERGE RACINE 1967.

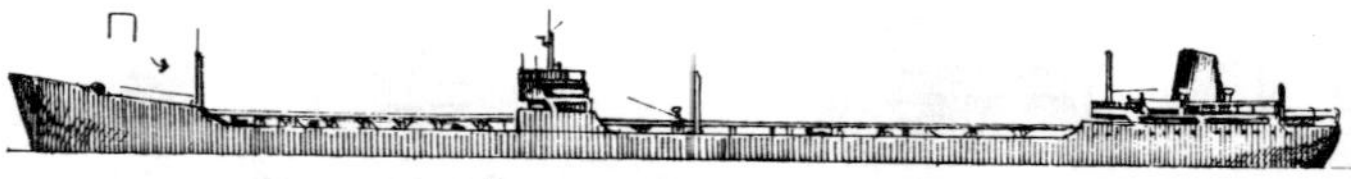

KMK₂FK H123

38730 SCAPMOUNT. Gr/Sw 1961; Tk; 22000; 208.03 × 11.56 (682.51 × 37.94); M; 16.5; ex MIRFAK 1973; ex TOSCANA 1972.

Similar: **38731 EUGENIA II** (Pa) ex DANA 1974; ex NOTO 1974; ex TORINO 1969. ★**38732 WOLFEN** (DDR) ex TARIM 1968.

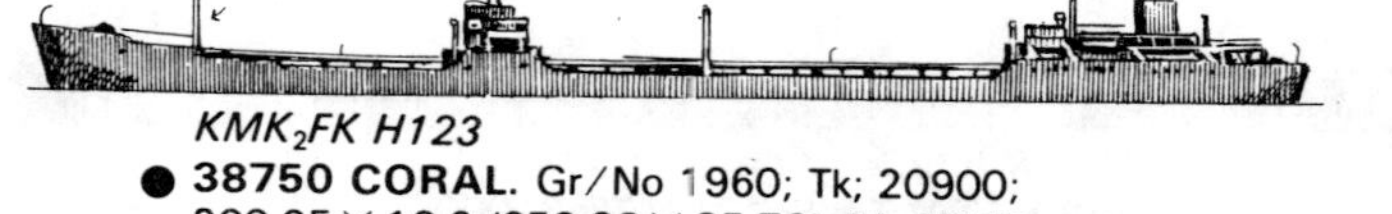

KMK₂FK H123

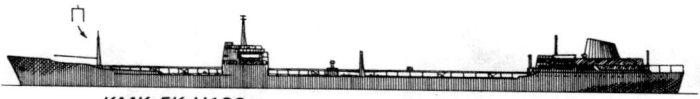

38740 SANNY. Fi/Sw 1960; Tk; 26000; 213 × 11.39 (700.2 × 37.36); TSM; 16.5; ex HARRY TRAPP 1968. Sister: **38741 DAGNY** (Fi) ex O.T. TONNEVOLD 1967.

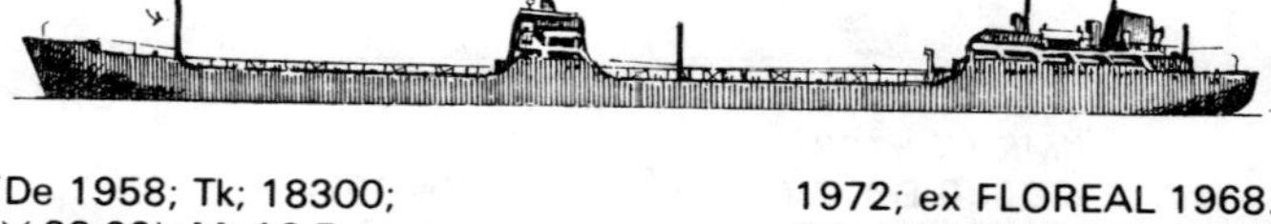

KMK₂FK H123

● **38750 CORAL.** Gr/No 1960; Tk; 20900; 200.95 × 10.9 (659.28 × 35.76); M; 15.75; ex ANSON 1989; ex STORANGER 1969. Sister: **38751 RODOSTO** (Gr) ex HALLANGER 1973.

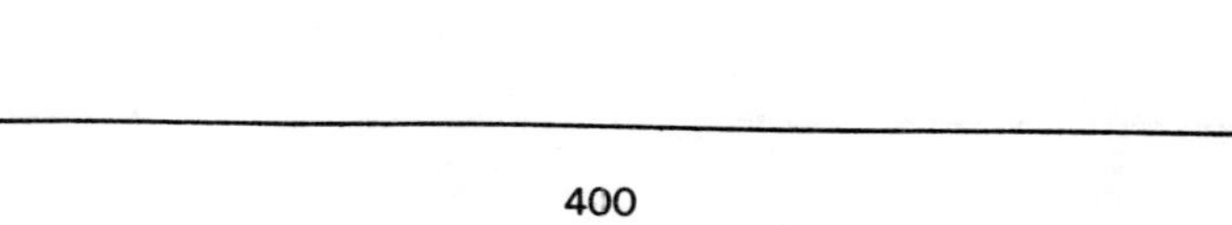

KMK₂FK H123

38760 PAVLOS V. Gr/De 1958; Tk; 18300; 200.13 × 10.36 (656.59 × 33.99); M; 16.5; ex RAINBOW; ex GLOBAL LEADER; ex THOMAS G. CHIMPLES 1977; ex MATHEOS 1972; ex FLOREAL 1968. Sister: **38761 TAMMANNA** (Sr); ex MONACO 1975; ex MAURITIUS 1974; ex MONSEAU 1971.

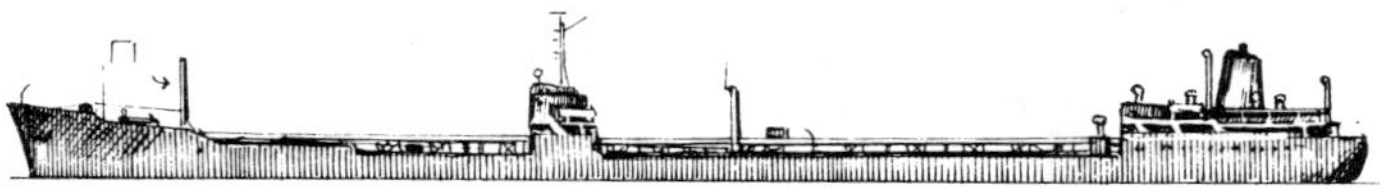

KMK_2FK H123
38770 ZAKYNTHOS. Gr/Sw 1962; Tk; 25200; 213.24 × 11.47 (669.77 × 37.63); T; 17; ex ARIETTA 1978; ex SOYA ANDREA 1967.

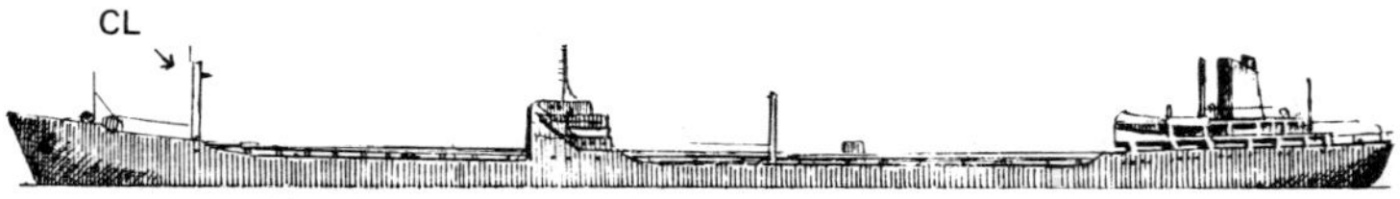

KMK_2FK H123
38780 ADRIATIKI. Gr/No 1963; Tk; 30600; 228.58 × 12.62 (749.93 × 40.23); TSM; 16.5; ex SVERRE REX; ex TANK REX 1978.

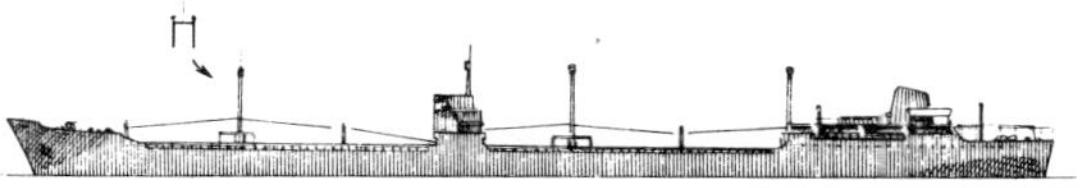

KMK_2FK H123
● **38790 SAINT ETIENNE.** Pa/It 1960; B; 10700; 166.48 × 9.35 (547.83 × 30.68); M; 15.75; ex SAN MARTIN 1970; ex PORTOVADO 1968. Similar (Li flag): **38791 SAINT RAPHAEL** ex PORTOVENERE 1968 **38792 SAINT MARCEL** ex PORTOFINO 1968.

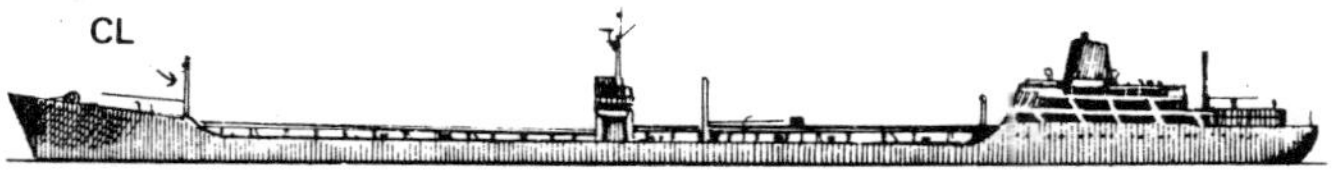

KMK_2FK H13
● **38800 COMMONWEALTH.** Li/It 1958; Tk; 23200; 212.02 × 11.2 (695.6 × 36.75); T; —; ex GRAND COMMONWEALTH 1974; ex CORCO EL TIGRE 1970; ex AGIP RAVENNA 1967.

KMK_2FK H13
38810 COASTAL CALIFORNIA. US/US 1949; Tk; 17900; 191.42 × 10.23 (490.22 × 33.56); T; 16; ex OGDEN YUKON 1976; ex YUKON 1970; ex SEA PIONEER 1968; ex ESSO TAMPA 1964; ex ESSO ZURICH 1962.

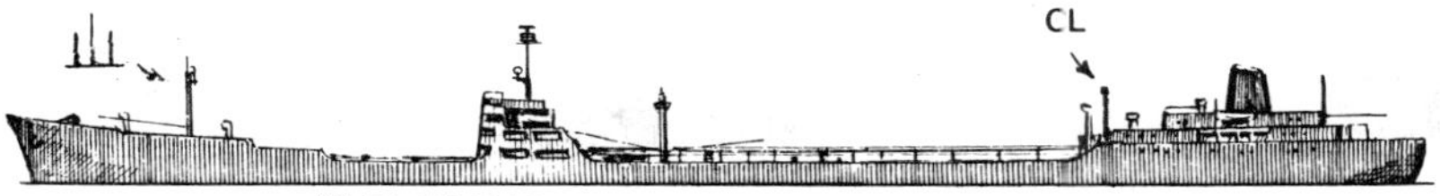

KMK_2FK H13
38820 COVE LEADER. US/US 1959; Tk; 40500; 246.9 × 14.33 (810.04 × 46.71); T; 17.25; ex VANTAGE DEFENDER; ex NATIONAL DEFENDER 1973.

KMK_2FK H13
38830 MONTEBELLO. It/Sw 1963; Tk; 22600; 202.83 × 11.55 (665.45 × 37.89); M; 15.75; ex TANK PRINCESS 1977.

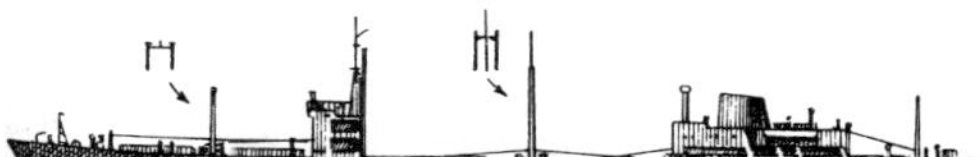

KMK_2FK H13
★**38840 YOUHAO.** RC/FRG 1959; C/HL; 8400; 153.88 × 9.03 (504.86 × 29.63); M; —; ex ETHA RICKMERS 1964.

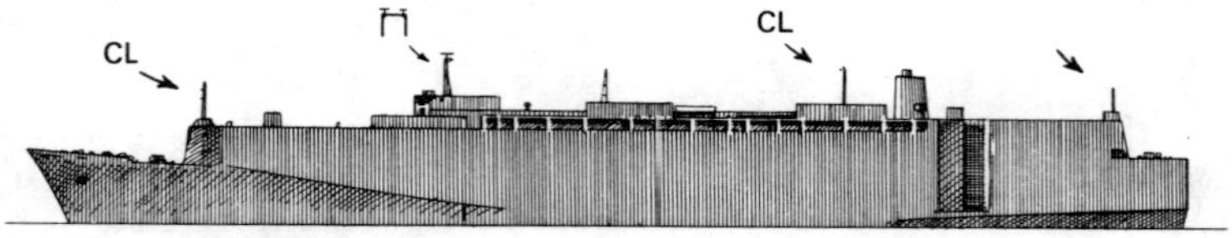

KMK_2FK H 2
38850 JINYU MARU. Ja/Ja 1974; RoVC; 16100; 224.98 × 9.32 (738.12 × 30.58); M; 20.5.

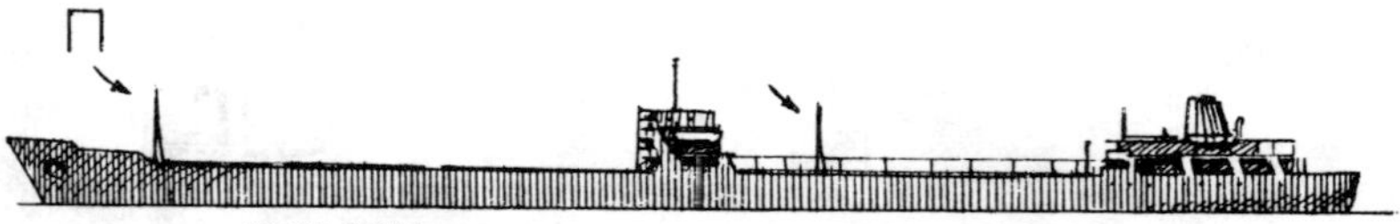

KMK_2F H1
38860 PRESIDENTE DEODORO. Bz/Ja 1960/67; Tk; 29900; 241.05 × 12.26 (791 × 37); T; —; Lengthened and deepened 1967. Sister: **38861 PRESIDENTE FLORIANO** (Bz).

KMK_3F H123
● **38870 VENTURE TEXAS.** Li/Ja 1959; Tk;25000; 217.46 × 11.58 (713.45 × 38); T; —; ex CONOCO TEXAS; ex GEORGE A. DAVIDSON 1977.

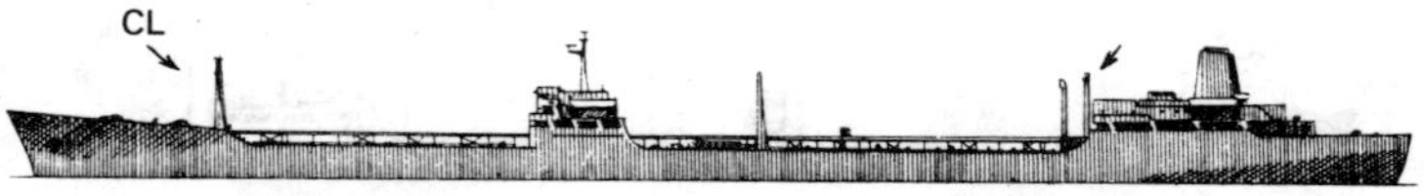

KMK_3F H123
38880 EXXON BOSTON. US/US 1960; Tk; 30700; 225.56 × 12.02 (740 × 39.47); T; 16.5; ex ESSO BOSTON 1973. Sister: **38881 EXXON BALTIMORE** (US) ex ESSO BALTIMORE 1973.

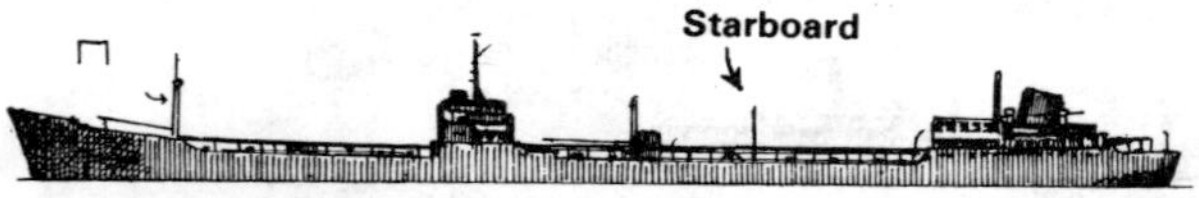

KMK_3F H123
● **38890 MONTAN.** Li/Sw 1959; Tk; 15700; 184.56 × 9.86 (605.51 × 32.35); M; 15.25; ex MONTANA; ex TRAMONTANA; ex MISTRAL 1978; ex OKEANOS 1970.

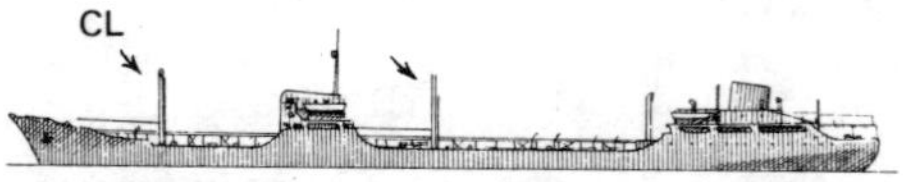

KMK_3FK H123
● **38900 CAMPOVERDE.** Sp/Sp 1958; Tk; 6600; 138.99 × 7.76 (456 × 25.46); M; 13.5. Possible sister: **38901 CAMPOBLANCO** (Sp).

KMK_4F H123
38910 UNIVERSE ADMIRAL. Li/Ja 1957; Tk; 51300; 260.54 × 14.84 (854.79 × 48.69); T; 15.25. Similar: **38911 GEORGE CHAMPION** (Li).

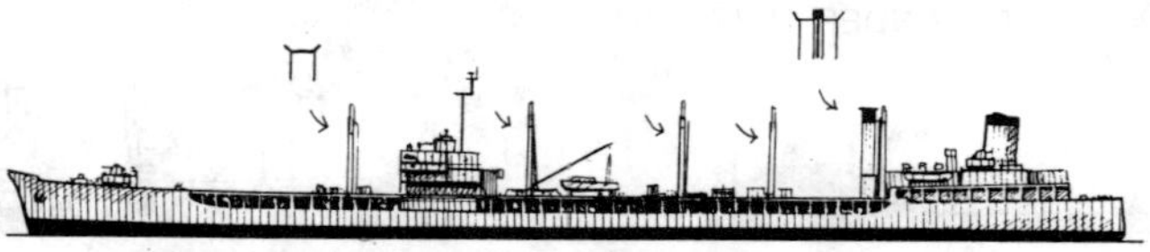

KMK_4F H123
38920 MISPILLION. US/US 1945; RT/FA; 34200 Dspl; 197 × 10.8 (648 × 35.5); TST; 16; Jumboised 'T-3' type. Sisters (US flag): **38921 NAVASOTA 38922 PAWCATUCK 38923 WACCAMAW** Similar: **38924 PASSUMPSIC.**

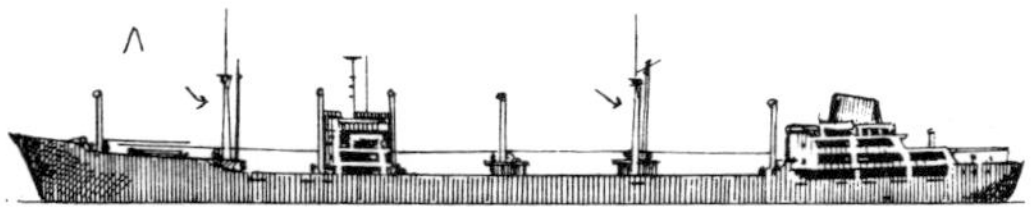

KMK_3MKF H13
38930 ASPASSIA M. Gr/No 1961; C; 9900; 159.72 × 8.1 (524 × 26.57); M; 18; ex MAN FUNG 1980; ex ASMARA 1978. Sisters: **38931 AYUTHIA** (De) **38932 POMALAA** (Ia) ex BORIBANA 1977.

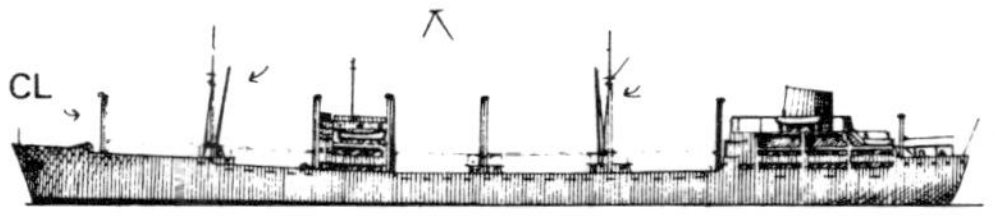

KMK_3MKFK H1
● **38940 ASAHAN.** Ia/De 1959; C; 8700; 151.82 × 8.41 (498.1 × 27.56); M; 17.5; ex BASRA 1977. Sister: **38941 IFEWARA** (Ng) ex BEIRA 1975.

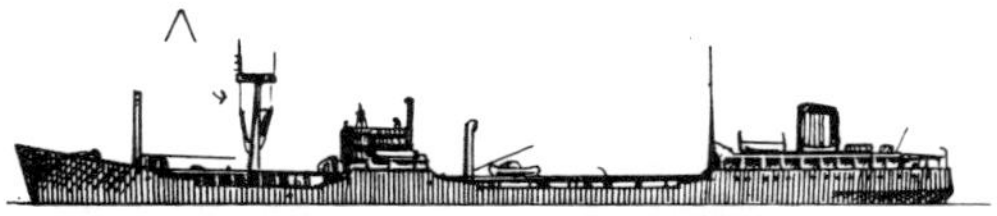

KMK_2MF H123
★**38950 DESNA.** Ru/Ru —; RT/FA; 8200; 136.5 × 7 (448.49 × 22.97); M; —; Converted from 'KAZBEK' class tanker.

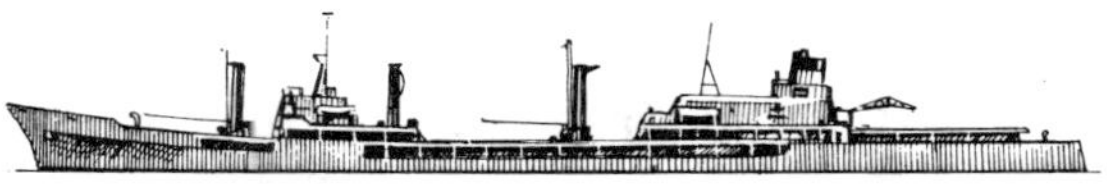

KMK_2MF H123
38960 PROVIDER. Ca/Ca 1963; Rst/FA; 20000; 169.2 × 9.8 (555 × 32); T; 30; 3 helicopters, ranger and flight deck.

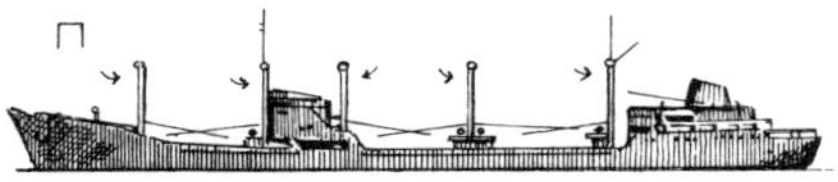

KMK_2MF H13
● **38970 FRANCES.** Fi/Sw 1955; C; 3600/5700; 126.96 × 7.15/8.68 (416.54 × 23.46/28.78); M; 16; ex LYNN 1973; ex FRANCES SALMAN 1971.

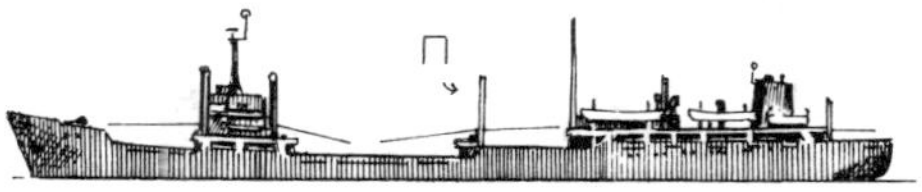

KMK_2MFK H12
38980 KOYO MARU. Ja/Ja 1955; C; 7500; 139.66 × 8.08 (458.2 × 26.51); M; 14.5.

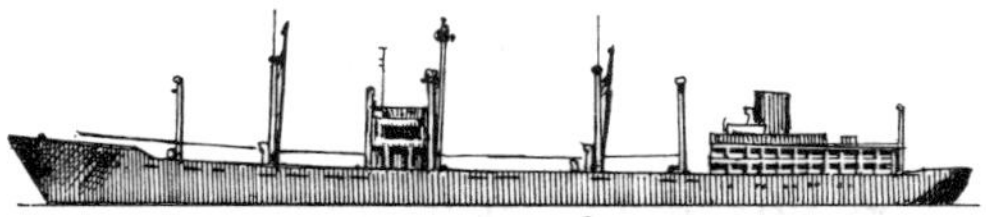

KMK_2MKFK H1
● ★**38990 QUE LIN.** RC/FRG 1954; C; 6900; 155.78 × 8.27 (511.09 × 27.13); M; 17.25; ex GOLDENFELS 1968. Sister: ★**38991 HONG QI 126** (RC) ex JILIN; ex GUTENFELS.

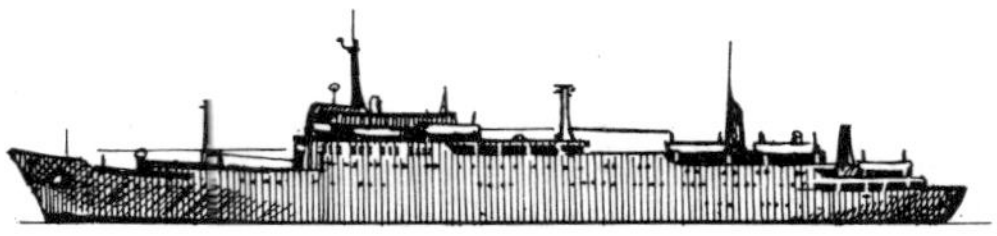

KMKMF H
39000 SAKURA. Ja/Ja 1962; PC; 12500; 157.03 × 8.8 (515.19 × 28.25); M; 17; ex SAKURA MARU 1971.

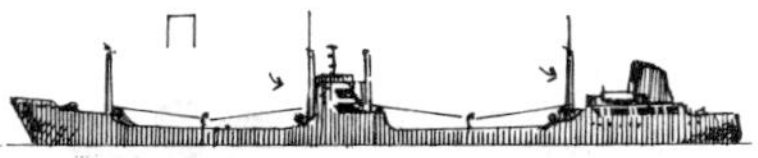

KMKMF H123
39010 CLEOPATRA II. Gr/Fr 1957; C; 4300; 115.93 × 6.2 (380.35 × 20.33); M; 13.5; ex ALFA 1980; ex MOSTAGANEM 1980; ex CAP SIDEROS 1970; ex S.N.A.5 1969.

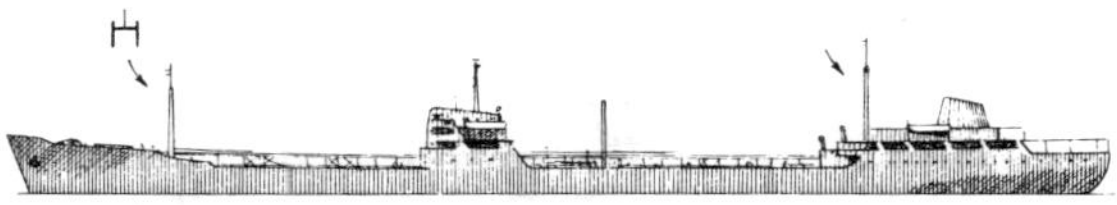

KMKMF H123
39020 EUTERPE. Pa/Fr 1961; Tk; 13400; 175.34 × 9.5 (575.26 × 31); M; 15; ex THALE 1976; ex LACON 1972; ex ATHEN 1968; ex ATHENE 1966.

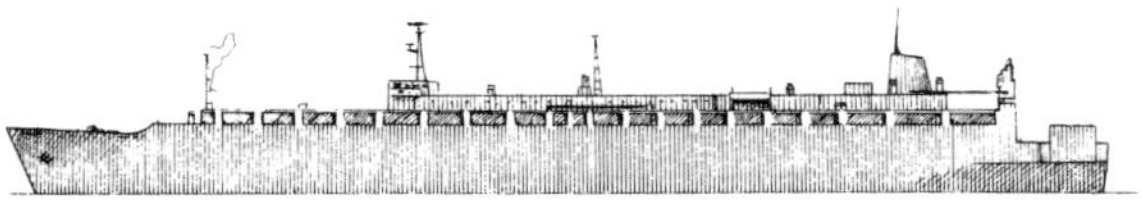

KMKMFC H2
39030 TAMA MARU. Ja/Ja 1972; RoVC; 7000; 174.5 × 7.21 (572.5 × 23.67); M; 18. Sisters (Ja flag): **39031 SAGAMI MARU 39032 SURUGA MARU 39033 TSURUMI MARU.**

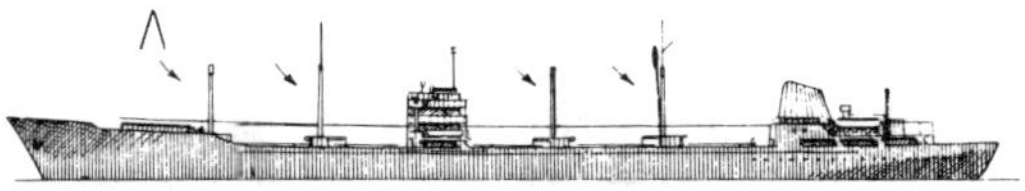

KMKMFK H1
39040 THERMAIKOS. Gr/De 1958; C; 7400/9900; 157.92 × —/9.43 (518.11 × —/30.95); M; —; ex APOLLONIAN 1977; ex DAGFRED 1970; Sisters: **39041 SABIK** (Pa); ex LJUTA 1980; ex RANELLA 1974; ex STOVE WAGGON 1965; ex BELLINA 1962; **39042 MALDIVE PIONEER** (Mv); ex SALAMAT AMBI 1980; ex ENTERPRISE 1975; ex NANCHANG 1973; ex HERVANG 1970; ex AMACITA 1965; Similar: **39043 PANAGIS C** (Gr); ex BRYNJE.

KMKMFK H1
39050 IONIAN SEA. Pa/FRG 1956; C; 9100; 151.42 × 9.09 (496.78 × 29.81); M; 14.5; ex OCEAN REGINA 1973; ex LANCELOT 1963. Sister: **39051 SARONICOS GULF** (Gr) ex MINOAN TRADER 1973; ex AQUILA 1972; ex HEERING CHRISTEL 1967; ex POLARVIND 1964.

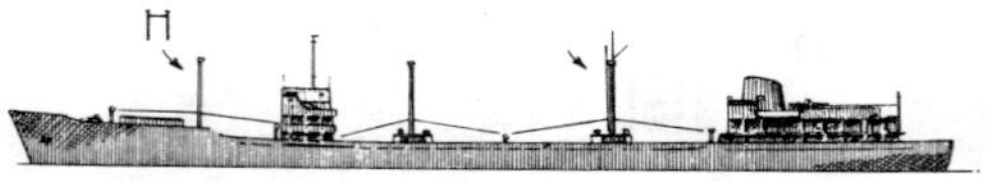

KMKMFK H1
39060 APOSTÓLOS M IV. Gr/FRG 1956; C; 9200; 151.39 × 9.09 (496.69 × 29.82); M; 14; ex HADJI DIMITAR 1980; ex AVIOR 1970; ex BRONNOY 1966.

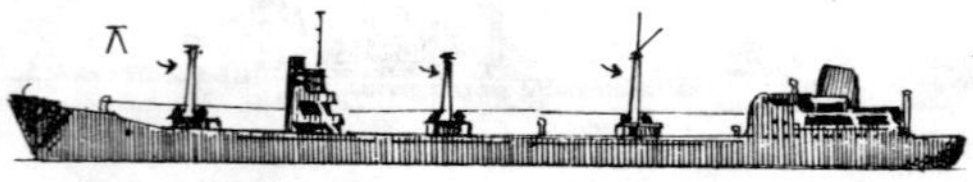

KMKMFK H13
39070 EASTERN MERCHANT. Pa/Sw 1956; C; 9000; 148.27 × 9.2 (486.45 × 30.23); M; 14; ex OHDAE 1980; ex INGWI 1967. Similar: **39071 STATE OF KERALA** (In) ex BERNHARD 1962 **39072 OMALOS** (Gr) ex LENDAS 1977; ex CAMINGOY 1974; ex ANTONIO 1973; ex BELLULLY 1959 **39073 TONG POH** (Sg) ex MARIANNE 1973; ex SUNLEAF 1970; ex SUNVARD 1966.

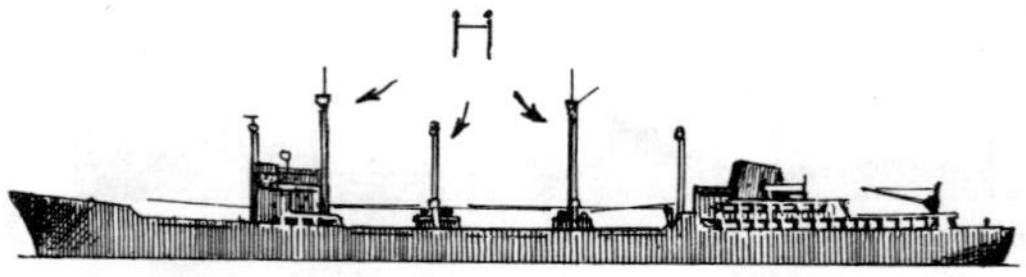

KMKMKFC H1
39080 EURABIA FRIENDSHIP. Le/DDR 1957; CP; 6500/9400; 157.44 × 8.4/9.67 (516.54 × 27.57/31.71); TSM; 15; ex FREUNDSCHAFT 1977; May be others in this class with this sequence. See BERLIN etc. under CKMKMKFC.

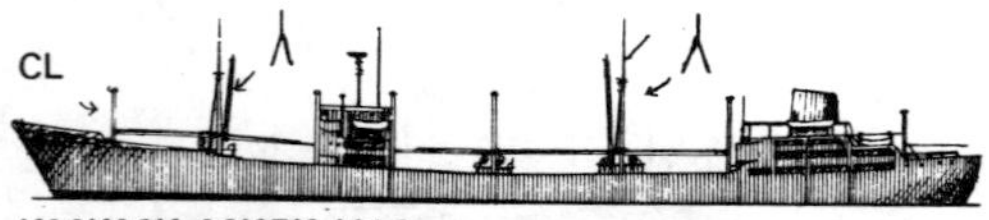

KMKMK$_2$MKFK H13
● **39090 ASAHAN.** Ia/De 1959; C; 8700; 151.82 × 8.41 (498.1 × 27.56); M; 17.5; ex BASRA 1977. Sister: **39091 IFEWARA** (Ng) ex BEIRA 1975.

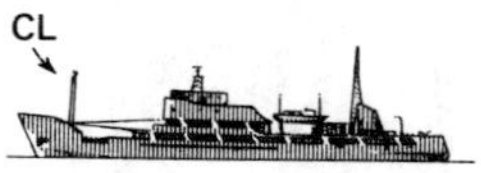

KM$_2$F H1
39100 GAVESHANI. In/Br-In 1964/75; RS; 1600; 67.98 × 3.57 (223.03 × 11.71); TSM; 10; ex HOPPER BARGE No. 2 1975; Converted from dredger 1975.

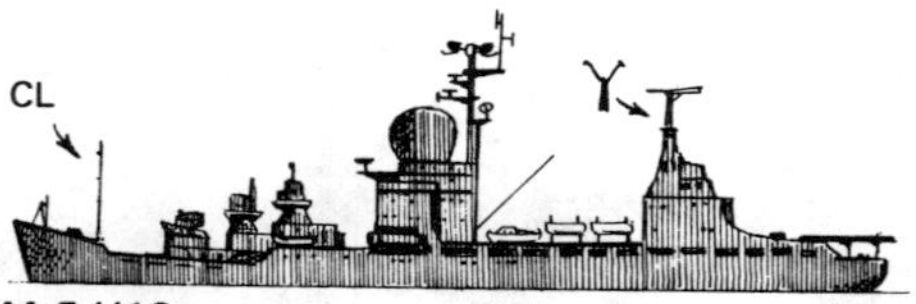

KM$_2$F H12
⋆**39110 CHAZHMA.** Ru/— 1963; Missile Tracking; 5300 Dspl; 132.8 × 6.1 (437 × 20); M; 18; ex DANGARA; Carries 1 helicopter. Similar (Ru flag): ⋆**39111 CHUMIKAN** ex DOLGESCHTSCHELJE ⋆**39112 DESNA.**

KM$_2$F H123
⋆**39120 OLEKMA.** Ru/Fi 1964; RT; 3400; 105.11 × 6.22 (344.85 × 20.41); M; 13.5; Converted from tanker. May be others in this class similarly converted.

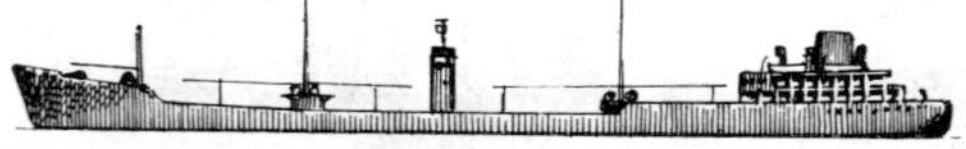

KM$_2$F H13
⋆**39130 BOGDAN.** Bu/Sw 1946; O; 8800; 149 × 8.46 (488.85 × 27.76); M; 13; ex ATLAS 1970; ex RAUNALA 1963; Converted from ore/oil.

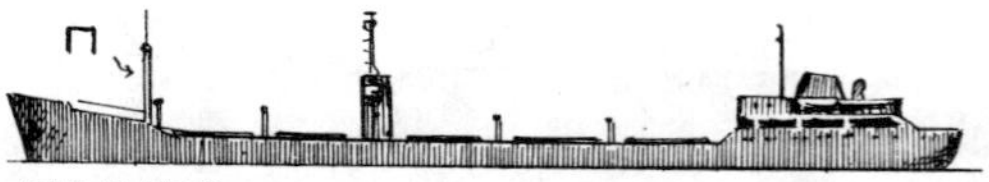

KM$_2$F H13
39140 DAPO ALECOS. Gr/Ne 1958; O; 9000; 153.9 × 8.5 (504.92 × 27.96); M; 12.5; ex BONNYDALE 1976; ex BONITA 1974; ex MESNA 1968.

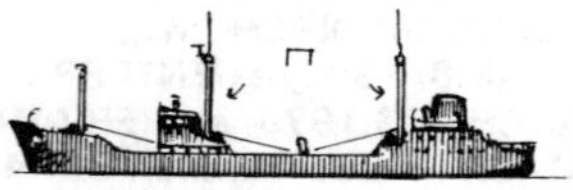

KM$_2$F H13
39150 DON EMILIO. Pa/Ne 1953; C; 1000; 78.87 × 4.32 (258.76 × 14.17); M; 13.5; ex COBAN; ex SEA SAGA 1974; ex TRITO 1968.

KM$_2$F H13
● **39160 CAPRAIA.** It/Br 1932; Tk; 2000; 76.21 × 4.95 (250 × 16.23); R; 9; ex BAY TRANSPORT 1964; ex BRITAMLUBE 1959. Sister: **39161 ELBA** (It) ex ISLAND TRANSPORT 1963; ex BRITAMOIL 1959.

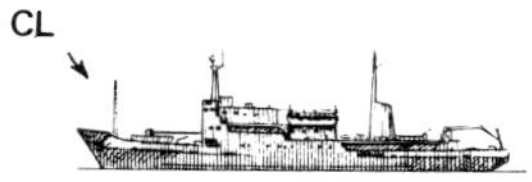

KM_2FC H12

★**39170 PROFESSOR BOGOROV.** Ru/Fi 1976; RS; 1200; 68.76 × 4.21 (225.6 × 13.81); M; 13.5. Sisters (Ru flag): ★**39171 PROFESSOR KURENTSOV** ★**39172 PROFESSOR VODYANITSKIY** ★**39173 FEDOR MATISEN** Possible sister: ★**39174 GEORGIY MAKSIMOV** Similar (different crane & no gantry aft): ★**39175 IVAN KIREYEV.**

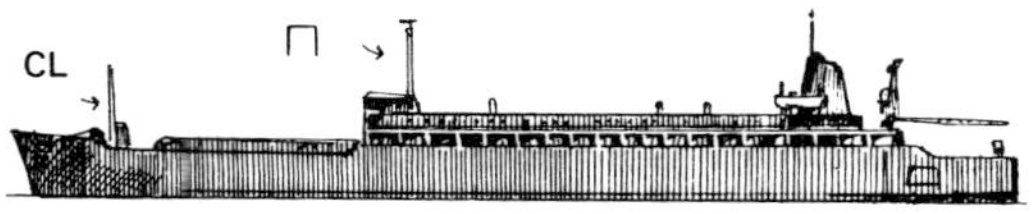

KM_2FC H2

● **39180 CANADA MARU.** Ja/Ja 1971; RoVC; 11500; 161.65 × 6.68 (530.35 × 21.91); M; 18.5.

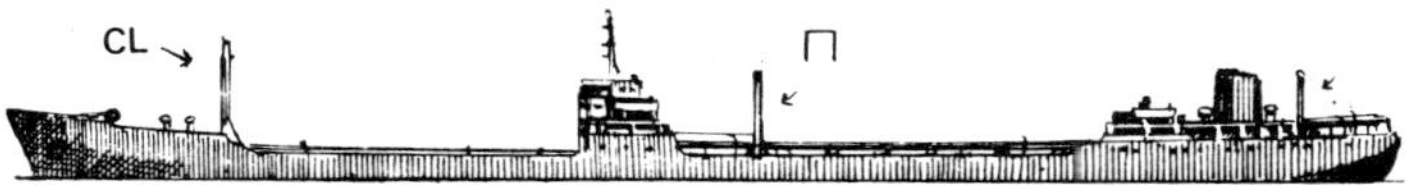

KM_2FK H123

39190 CAROLYN. Li/Ja 1962; Tk; 29400; 218.02 × 11.81 (715.3 × 38.7); M; 16.25; ex YUYO MARU 1976.

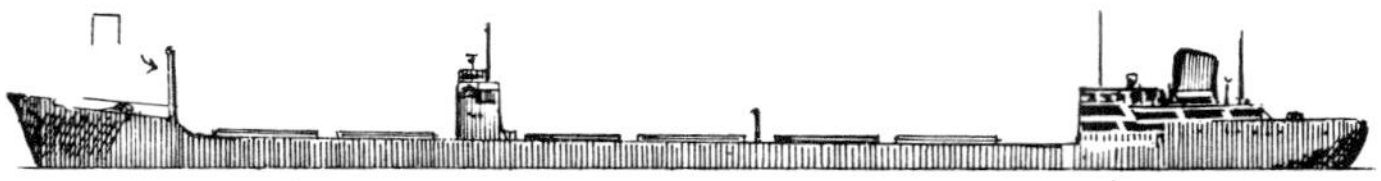

KM_2FK H123

39200 PAN VIGOR. Ko/Ja 1962; O; 29400; 221.04 × 11.43 (725.2 × 37.5); M; 17.25; ex CHESTNUT HEROINE 1980; ex SINGAPURA PERTAMA 1977; ex YUHO MARU 1973.

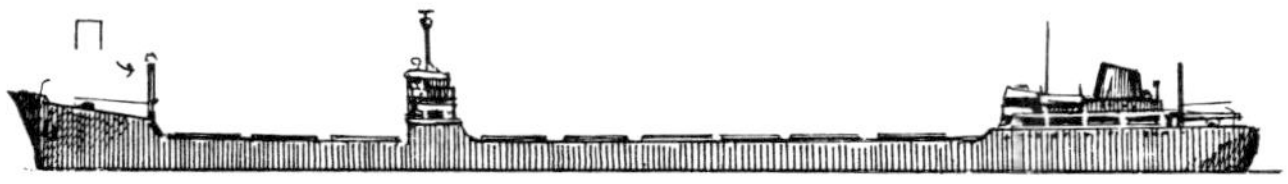

KM_2FK H123

39210 M. EREGLI. Tu/Fr 1962; O; 21200; 197.34 × 10.55 (647.44 × 34.56); M; 15; ex MEKAMBO 1969.

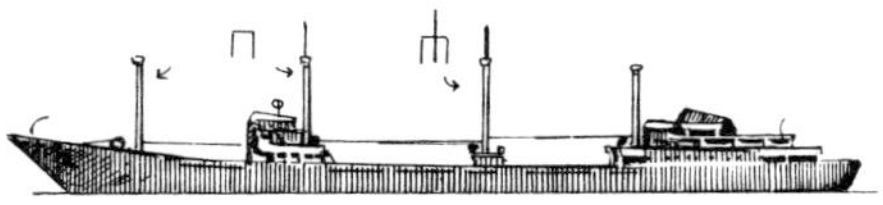

KM_2KF H

39220 CAVACO. Gr/FRG 1953; C; 5300; 132.14 × 7.67 (433.53 × 25.17); D-E; 15; ex HAWKSTONE 1972; ex FALKENSTEIN 1971.

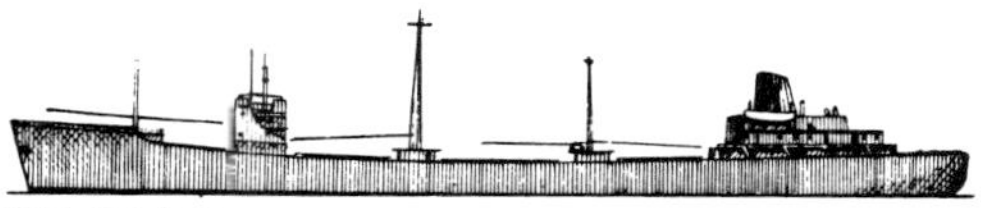

KM_2KF H1

39230 SARFARAZ RAFIQI. Pk/FRG 1966; C; 700/9400; 152.18 × —/9.27 (499.28 × —/30.4); M; 18.5; Launched as SARFRAZ RAFIQI. Sister: **39231 AZIZ BHATTI** (Pk).

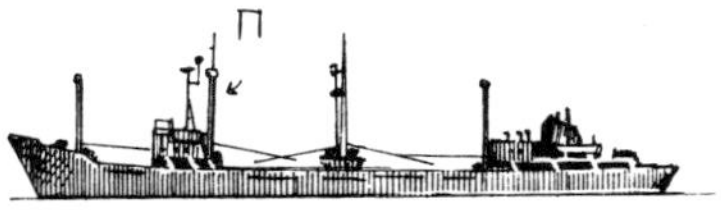

KM_2KF H1

39240 KAPETAN ANDREAS. Pa/FRG 1957; C; 3800; 108.01 × 7.06 (354.36 × 23.16); M; 13.5; ex ALPHARD 1980.

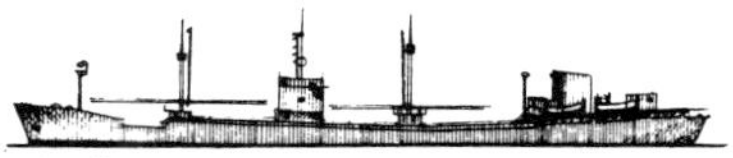

KM_2KF H12

39250 CIRO SECONDO. It/De 1956; C; 2900; 101.78 × 5.99 (333.92 × 19.48); M; 14; ex ALPPILA 1971; ex LENA MARIANE 1968; ex BRETLAND 1964. Similar: **39251 LAGO IZABAL** (Gu) ex SKAGA SIF 1976; ex SKAGA 1973; ex CONCORDIA 1969 **39252 MYRTIA** (Gr) ex CASSIOPEIA 1978; ex CIMBRIA 1969.

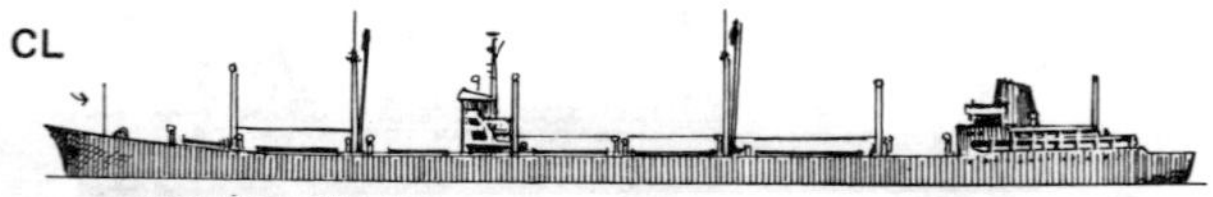

KM_2KMKFK H
39260 LEDEA. Gr/FRG 1963; BC/O; 17900; 182.79 × 10.55 (599.7 × 34.61); M; 16; ex MEDEA 1977. Sister: **39261 SAPHO** (Gr) ex CARMEN 1977.

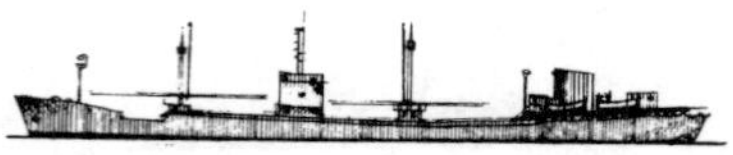

KM_3KF H12
39270 MYRTIA. Gr/De 1963; C; 3500; 110.5 × 6.27 (362.53 × 20.56); M; 14; ex CASIOPEIA 1978; ex CIMBRIA 1969; Strengthened for heavy cargoes. Sister: **39271 LAGO IZABAL** (Gu) ex SKAGA SIF 1976; ex SKAGA 1973; ex CONCORDIA 1967 Similar: **39272 CIRO SECONDO** (It) ex ALPPILA 1971; ex LENA MARIANE 1968; ex BRETLAND 1964.

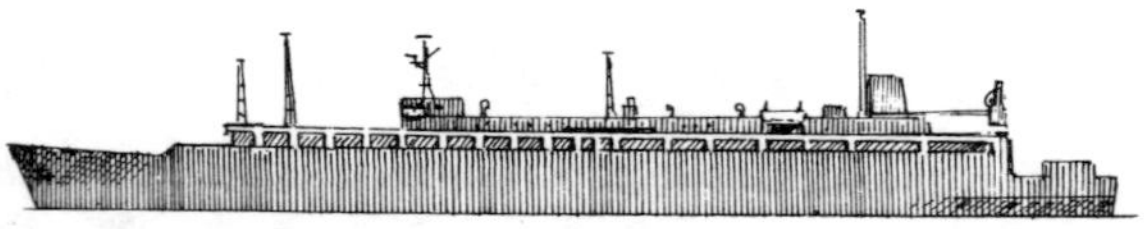

KM_4FC H2
39280 LAUREL. Pa/Ja 1976; C; 6100; 174.5 × 7.2 (572.5 × 23.63); M; 18. Sisters (Li flag): **39281 VIOLET 39282 UNITED SPIRIT.**

MC_2MF H3
⋆**39290 STARITSA.** Ru/—. No further details available.

MCF H123
⋆**39300 POEL.** DDR/DDR 1960; Tk/FA; 600 Dwt; 59.5 × 3.8 (195 × 12.5); M; 14; ex RIEMS; Type **600.** Sister: ⋆**39301 C 37** (DDR) ex HIDDENSEE.

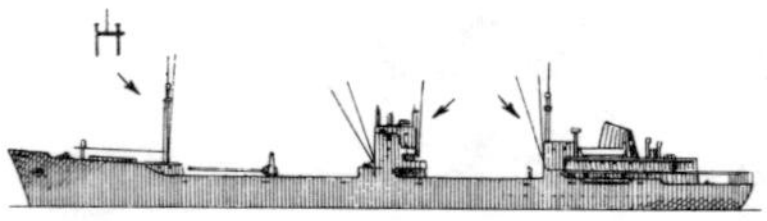

MCK_2MF H1
39310 SOCRATIS. Gr/Fr 1951/57; C/WT; 3200; 115.34 × 5.79 (378.41 × 19); TSM; 14; ex ORANIE 1972; Lengthened 1957. Sister: **39311 CAPRICORN** (Gr) ex PLATON; ex TUNISIE 1972.

$MCMC_2F$ H13
39320 CONNIE. Pi/Br 1954; C; 1700; 85.68 × 4.32 (281.1 × 14.17); M; 11.5; ex HELMA TAYLOR 1973; ex MARIELISA 1970; ex GALLE 1968; ex EL NASSER 1961.

MCMF H1
39330 TSUGARU. Ja/Ja 1955; Cbl/FA; 2150 Dspl; 33.78 × 16 (103 × 4.9); TSM; 13.

MF H
39340 CHRYSANTHY H. Gr/Br 1955; Tk; 315; 45.12 × — (148.03 × —); M; —; ex B.P. HAULIER 1976.

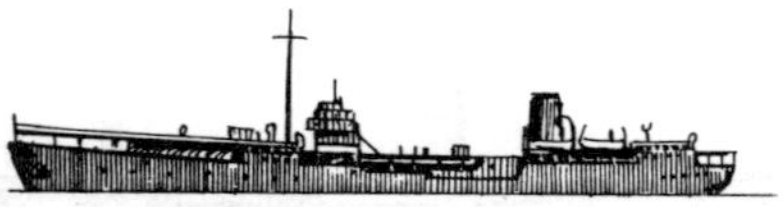

MF H
39350 JALENGI. In/Br 1950; D; 4500; 113.44 × 5.5 (372.18 × 18.04); TSR; 12.

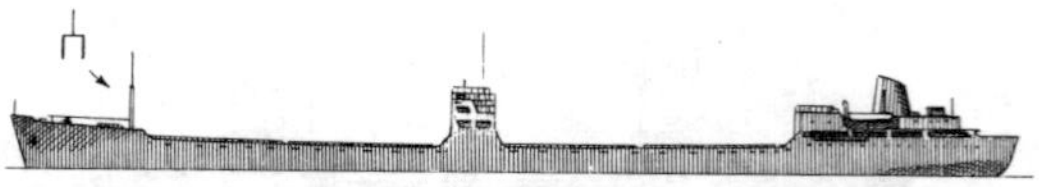

MF H123
39360 VITTORIO GARDELLA. It/Br 1959; O; 10300; 159.87 × 8.55 (524.5 × 28.06); M; 12.5; ex CAPE FRANKLIN 1974.

MF H13
39370 SUNSHINE ISLAND. Gy/Br 1950; MT; 800; 55.89 × 3.6 (183.37 × 11.92); R; 8.5; ex ATHELBROOK 1972.

MF H13
39380 BERESFORD. Br/Ne 1959; Tk; 300; 42.22 × 2.11 (138.52 × 6.92); M; 7.5. Sister: **39381 BACCARAT** (Br).

MF H2
39390 INCAN SUPERIOR. Ca/Ca 1974; RoC/F; 3800; 116.41 × 20.22 (381.92 × 66.34); TSM; 14. Similar: **39391 INCAN ST. LAURENT** (Ca).

MFM H
39400 BHAGIRATHI. In/Br 1957; D; 4700; 113.39 × 5.5 (372.01 × 18.04); TSR; —.

MFM H2

● ⋆**39410 VSEVOLOD BERYEZKIN.** Ru/Ru 1975; RS; 700; 54.87 × 3.66 (180.02 × 12.01); M; 11.75. Sisters (Ru flag): ⋆**39411 VALERIAN VRYVAYEV** ⋆**39412 YAKOV GAKKEL.**

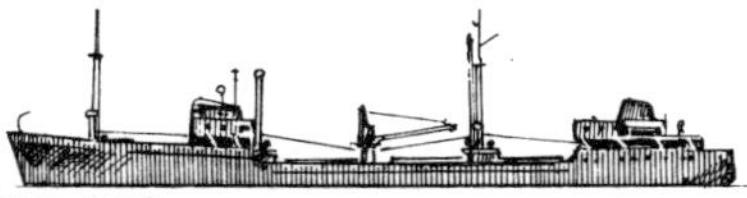

MKCMF H13

● **39440 MELINA TSIRIS.** Cy/FRG 1956; C; 3400; 115.25 × 6.6/7.63 (378.12 × 21.65/25.03); M; 13.5; ex AURIGA 1976; ex ISOLDE 1970.

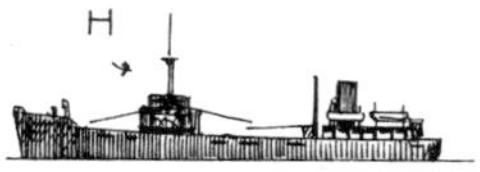

MKF H1

39460 ANTARES. Pa/Ca 1946; C; 1400; 68.33 × 5.04 (224.18 × 16.54); R; 9; ex TA CHUNG 1970; ex HWA LIEN; ex HAI PING 1950; ex HAIYU 1946. Launched as OTTAWA PANDORA. Similar: ⋆**39461 NAN HAI 169** (RC).

MKF H13

39480 CAPO CORSO. It/Br 1948; Tk; 2400; 92.97 × 5.64 (305.02 × 18.50); R; 9; ex WILLIAM 1967; ex IMACOS 1966; ex LINCOLN ELLSWORTH 1956.

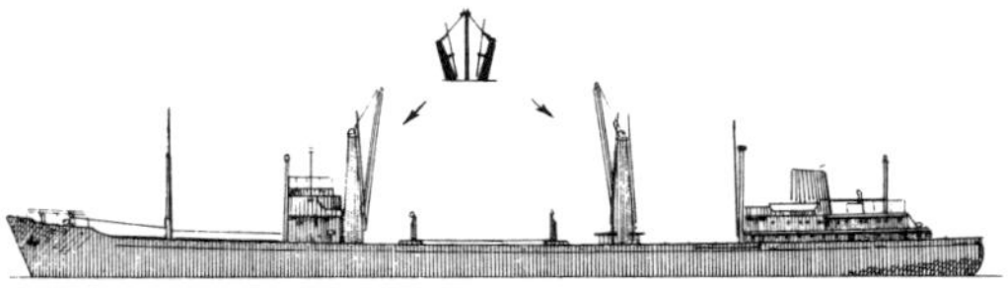

$MK_2C_2K_2FK$ H1

● **39500 UHENFELS.** FRG/FRG 1959/68; C/HL; 10400; 156.65 × 9.02 (513.94 × 29.59); M; 14.5; Rebuilt 1968.

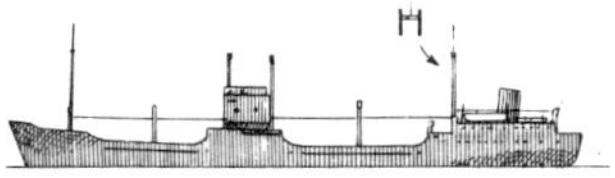

MK_4MF H123

● **39520 CAYMEN TRADER.** Br/No 1950; C; 2100; 91.17 × 5.28 (299.11 × 17.31); M; 10.5; ex MARGRIT 1974; ex ROYAL COMET 1971; ex HOP 1968; ex ASK 1962; ex NORDRAAK 1960.

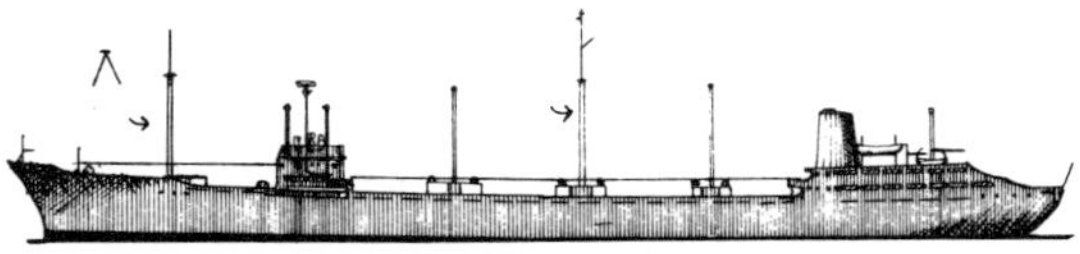

MK_3MKFK H1

● **39540 PIA COSTA.** It/It 1958; C; 10800; 167.8 × 9.45 (550.52 × 31); T; 17. Sister: **39541 MARIA COSTA** (It).

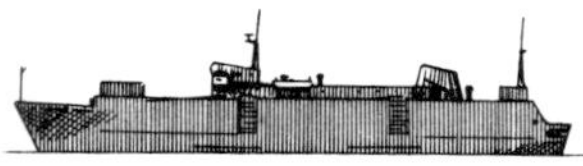

MFM H2

39420 CANABAL. Sp/Sp 1976; V; 1300; 88.02 × 5.18 (288.78 × 16.99); M; 14; Side doors. Sister: **39421 COBRES** (Sp).

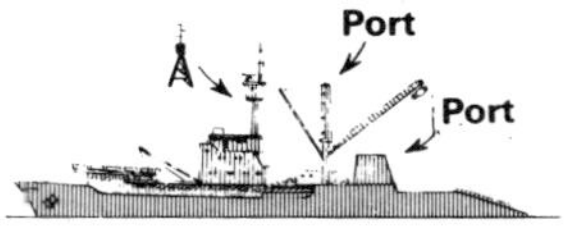

MKF H

● ⋆**39450 RODINA.** Ru/Pd 1978; FF; 1800 Dwt; 85 × 6 (moulded) (278.87 × 19.69); M; 16; Tuna Seiner. Helicopter deck foreward. Further vessels on order for USSR.

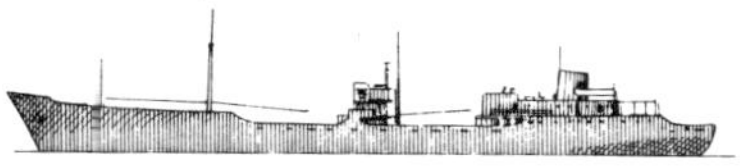

MKF H13

● **39470 LEMPA.** Ho/FRG 1952; R; 3300; 112.58 × 5.73 (369.36 × 18.79); TSM; 14; ex LEITH HILL 1966; ex LEMPA 1959.

MKFM H1

39490 SHIELDHALL. Br/Br 1955; Slu; 1800; 81.69 × 4.06 (268.01 × 13.32); TSR; —

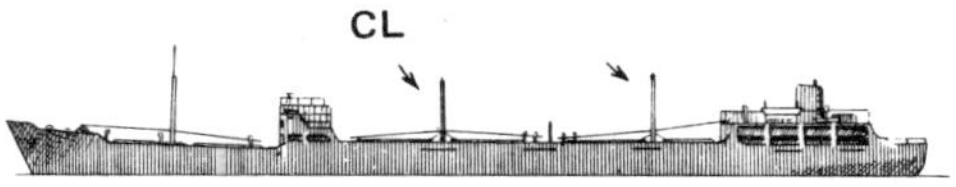

MK_2F H12

39510 VIRGINIA M. Gr/Br 1958; B; 7700; 146.21 × 7 79 (479.69 × 25.56); M; 13; ex GLOXINIA 1977; May be coded MKMF—which see.

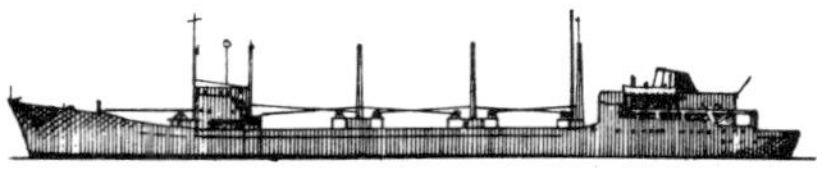

MK_3MF H13

39530 SANTO ANTONIO DO TRIUNFO. Bz/Fi 1960; C; 4000/6400; 126.8 × 6.78/— (416.01 × 22.24/—); M; —; ex TODOS OS SANTOS 1980. Sisters (Bz flag): **39531 ALBERTO MONTEIRO** ex GUANABARA 1980 **39532 TURIACU** (Bz).

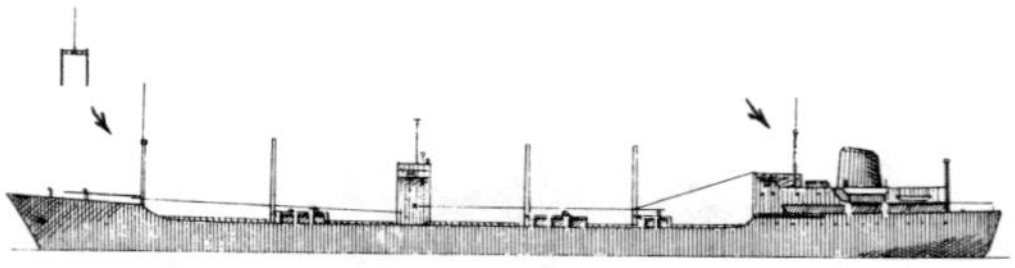

MK_3MFK H13
39550 UNILUCK. Cy/No 1956; B; 10800; 158.45 × 9.19 (519.85 × 30.15); M; 13.75; ex ELTHINA 1975; ex VARANGFJELL 1972.

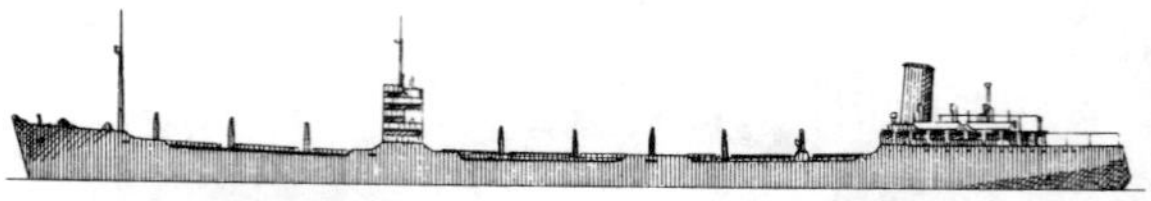

MK_3MK_5FK H123
39560 FLORA. US/US 1948; O; 10900; 177.65 × 10.46 (582.84 × 34.32); T; 16.25; ex FLOR; ex BETHFLOR 1975; ex BALTORE 1960; **'C.5-S-AXI'** type.

MK_2MCF H123
39570 EL FLAMINGO. Br/Br 1950/69; D; 5800; 128.89 × 7.8 (422.87 × 25.6); M; 11; ex BRITISH DEFENDER 1965; Converted from tanker 1969.

MK_2MF H
39580 FARSA 1. Gr/FRG 1951; C; 800; 69.78 × 4.14 (228.94 × 13.58); M; 12; ex SERIFOS 1980; ex MILOS 1 1978; ex LOTHAR 1976; ex HEIMO RECKMANN 1965.

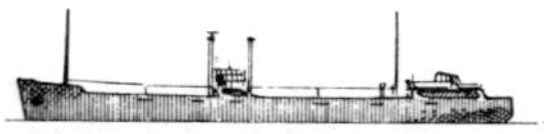

MK_2MF H
39590 FLORIAN. Pa/FRG 1951; C; 900; 78.59 × 4.37 (257.84 × 14.37); M; 11; ex KONSUL I 1977; ex KONSUL SARTORI 1962.

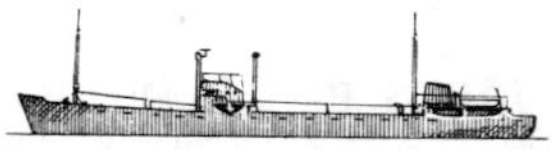

MK_2MF H
39600 ABILITY. Cy/FRG 1951; C; 1000; 82.1 × 4.2 (269.36 × 13.78); M; 12; ex FAETHON 1980; ex PARTHENON 1976; ex NAUTIC 1970; ex BAUMWALL 1967; ex STEINHOFT 1957. Sister: **39601 VENEZIA** (Cy) ex POUNTA 1977; ex ANTONIOS B 1976; ex ODIGITRIA VENTOURI 1973; ex ALEXIA 1966; ex ATLANTA 1963.

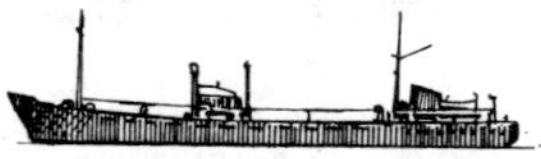

MK_2MF H
39610 UNISON I. Sg/FRG 1955; C; 1600; 76.54 × 5.8 (251.12 × 19.03); M; 12; ex BOTILLA 1973; ex BOTILLA RUSS 1970. Similar: **39611 GEORGIOS G II** (Pa) ex LANCASTER TRADER 1975; ex NOORBEEK 1973; ex NESS 1970 **39612 DENA** (Ho) ex EL WIDAD; ex EHRENFELD 1970.

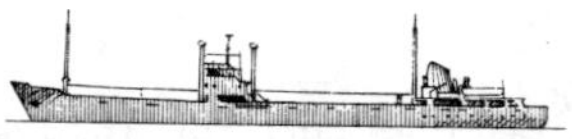

MK_2MF H
39620 COSTAMAR. Br/FRG 1954; C; 1100/1800; 85.55 × 5.16 (280.68 × 16.93); M; 12; ex DORIC MERCHANT 1980; ex FADI 1977; ex OBRESTAD 1973; ex MIRA 1961.

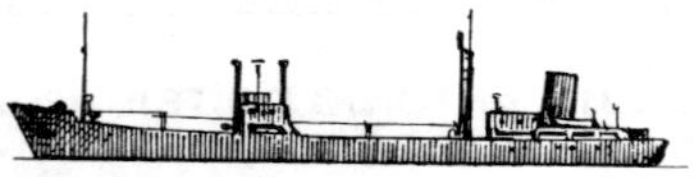

MK_2MF H
39630 ELEISTRIA IV. Cy/FRG 1952; C; 2500; 104.98 × 6.2 (344.42 × 20.34); M; 13; ex ALMAFLORA 1973; ex ALSTERTAL 1966. Sister: **39631 LOON MAU** (Pa) ex UNION KINGS 1975; ex MANCHESTER TRADER 1973; ex WERRATAL 1968.

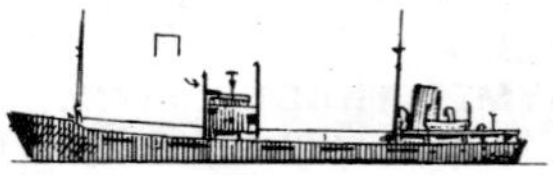

MK_2MF H
39640 DARPO SATU. Ia/Br 1949; C; 1700; 78.47 × 5.3 (257.45 × 17.39); M; 12.5; ex BORRE 1968; Side doors.

MK_2MF H
39650 CEMENTO PUERTO RICO. Pa/Sw 1944; Cem; 1400; 73.39 × 4.54 (240.78 × 14.9); M; 11.5; ex CEMENTIERE 1973; ex SUNNANVIK 1961; ex VIKA I 1959; ex HELGA CORDS 1946. Sister: **39651 LAS MINAS** (Cy) ex PYLIASTRON 1974; ex PAOLA 1971; ex CETI 1969; ex ALTAIR III 1964; ex DIANA 1961.

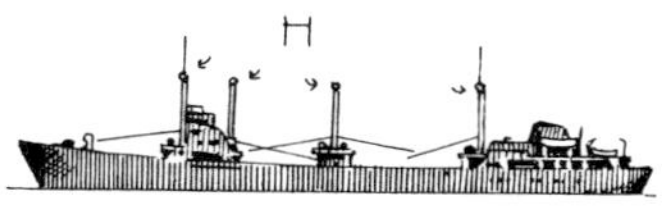

MK_2MF H
★39660 BAIA MARE. Rm/Rm 1965; C; 2100/3100; 100.62 × 5.5/6.58 (330.12 × 18.04/21.59); M; 12.5. Sisters (Rm flag): **★39661 CLUJ ★39662 VICTORIA.**

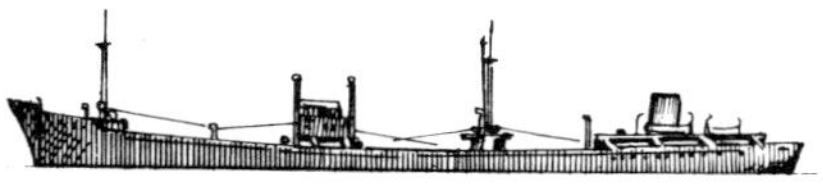

MK_2MF H1
● **39680 KARINA.** Gr/FRG 1956; C; 3200/6000; 126.02 × 6.45/— (413.45 × 21.46/—); M; 14; ex WESERTAL 1967.

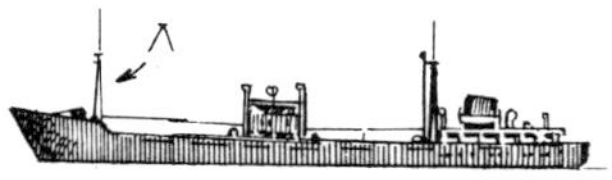

MK_2MF H1
39690 AMALIA. Gr/FRG 1955; C; 1400; 88.85 × 5.34 (281.5 × 17.2); M; 12.5; ex MAKALLA 1977; ex JOHN SCHRODER 1969. Sister: **39691 ELPINIKI K** (Cy) ex MEGALOCHARI 1 1980; ex AGIA MARKELLA 1978; ex ILE SAINTE MARIE 1975; ex CHATEAU LATOUR 1961.

MK_2MF H1
39720 GOLDEN WONDER. Sg/FRG 1952; C; 1500; 87.89 × 5.34 (288.35 × 17.52); M; 12.5; ex VILLE DE MORONDAVA 1973; ex CHATEAU YQUEM 1967; ex JUTTA SCHRODER 1958.

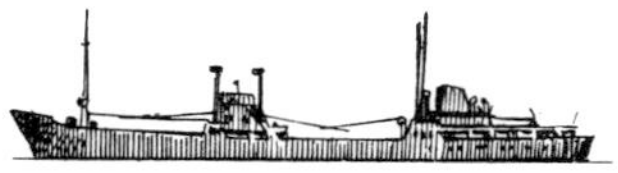

MK_2MF H1
39740 SEBAROK. Sg/FRG 1953; C; 1300; 90.12 × 4.69 (295.67 × 15.39); M; 12; ex DORIS TAYLOR 1977; ex GISELA RUSS 1970. Similar: **39741 BONA TIDE** (Sg) ex DIJKSGRACHT 1974; ex WEST MARCH 1970; ex NANNI RUSS 1969 **39742 SAMULUN** (Sg) ex ANNA TAYLOR 1977; ex ILSE RUSS 1969 **39743 CANALGRANDE** (Pa) ex BLEICHEN 1970 **39744 ARIS V** (Gr) ex SEA AVON 1976; ex CORNISH CHIEFTAN 1975; ex REALENGRACHT 1974; ex BURSTAH 1970.

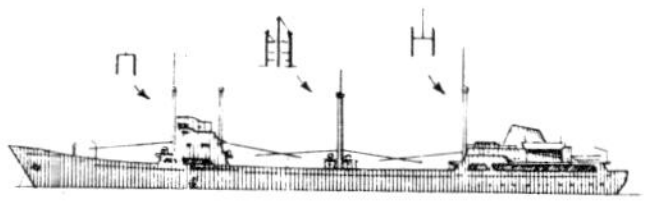

MK_2MF H
★39670 GALATI. Rm/Rm 1960; C; 2100/3100; 100.62 × 5.5/6.59 (330.12 × 18.04/21.62); M; 12.5; Heavy derrick amidships. Sisters: **★39671 SUCEAVA** (Rm) **★39672 BRAILA** (Rm) **39673 ANEMOS** (Gr) ex NIKOLAOS KONTARAS 1973; Launched as NANJI **39674 IVI** (Gr) ex MAGDALINI 1973.

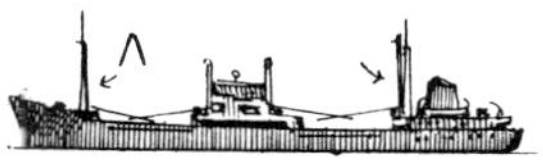

MK_2MF H1
39700 EVER. Sg/FRG 1955; C; 1200/1900; 78.64 × 5.13/6.22 (258 × 16.83/20.41); M; 12; ex GISELA VENNAMANN 1974; ex DON ROBERTO 1965; ex BURKHARD BROHAN 1963.

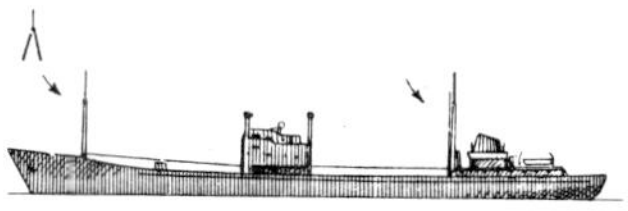

MK_2MF H1
39710 TRANSWORLD NAVIGATOR. Gr/FRG 1957; C; 2400; 95.41 × 6.03 (313.02 × 19.78); M; 12.5; ex ANASTASIA E 1975; ex INSCO JEM 1971.

MK_2MF H1
39730 ASHANTI. Gh/FRG 1957; C; 1300; 93.4 × 4.68 (306.43 × 15.35); M; 12; ex MOON 1977; ex GULF IPSWICH 1977; ex LEIDSEGRACHT 1973; ex HELGA RUSS 1970.

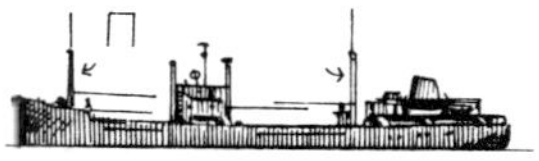

MK_2MF H1
39750 SEA RESOURCE. Pa/FRG 1955/65; C; 1800/2700; 88.7 × 5.78/6.67 (290.01 × 18.96/21.88); M; 14; ex AHMED 1980; ex SEAGULL 1980; ex DUBAI PEARL 1977; ex CARMEN 1974; ex OLHORN 1973; ex NORDERHOLM 1965; Lengthened 1965. Sister: **39751 LEVANT CLIPPER** (Pa) ex ROMAN EDYTHE; ex SUDERHOLM 1974.

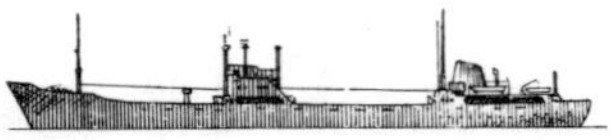

MK_2MF H1
39760 MANAURE. Ve/FRG 1961; C; 1400; 93.4 × 4.67 (306.43 × 15.32); M; 13.5; ex HELENE RUSS 1972. Sister: **39761 EL TAMBO** (Pa) ex CORINTHIAN 1972; ex MARIA RUSS 1970. May be broken up.

MK_2MF H1
39770 HIND-D. Le/FRG 1957; C; 1100; 79.56 × 5.59 (261.02 × 18.34); M; 12.5; ex MELDIN 1979; ex G. PAPPAS 1977; ex GEORGIOS P.A. 1975; ex SOULTANA 1975; ex PRIDE OF CANDIA 1974; ex EDUARD SCHUPP 1971; ex MAJA 1967.

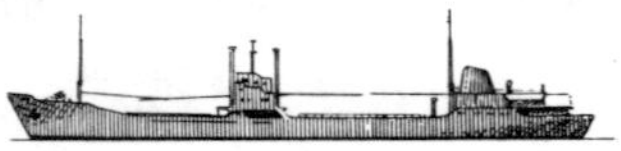

MK_2MF H1
39780 SALEEMA. In/FRG 1957; C; 1400/2300; 93.4 × 4.67/6.07 (306.43 × 15.32/19.91); M; 12; ex ERATO 1971; ex ERIKA BISCHOFF 1962.

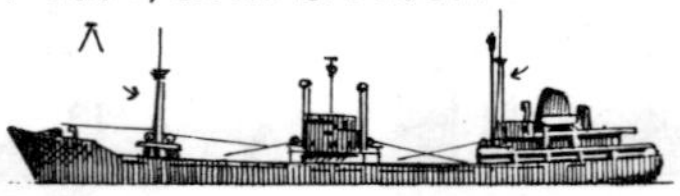

MK_2MF H1
39790 IMAD S. Fr/FRG 1958; C/WT; 2400/3400; 102.01 × 6.1/7.18 (334.68 × 20.01/23.56); M; 14.5; ex VILLE DE PORT LOUIS 1979; ex CHATEAU LAFITE 1969; ex LINDA SCARLETT 1961. Sister: **39791 DIEGO SUAREZ** (Mg) ex CHATEAU MARGAUX 1970; ex FANNY SCARLETT 1960.

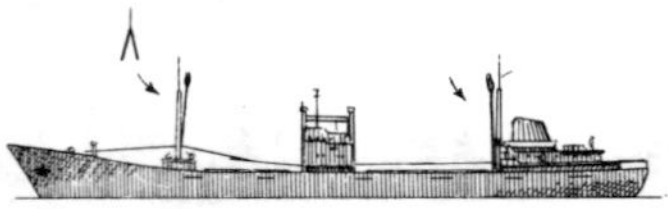

MK_2MF H1
39800 SYNTOMIA. Gr/FRG 1957; C; 2100/3200; 101.96 × 7.01/— (334.51 × 23/—); M; 14.5; ex ERWIN SCHRODER. Sister: **39801 SYMMETRIA** (Gr) ex ERNST SCHRODER.

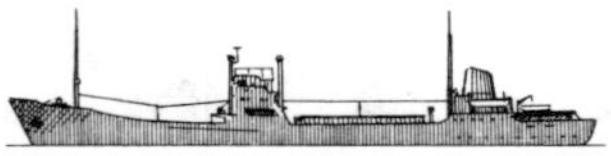

MK_2MF H12
39810 EUSTATHIA. Gr/FRG 1958; C; 1300/2200; 93.38 × 4.67/6.1 (306.36 × 15.32/20.01); M; 12; ex SABINE HOWALDT 1971.

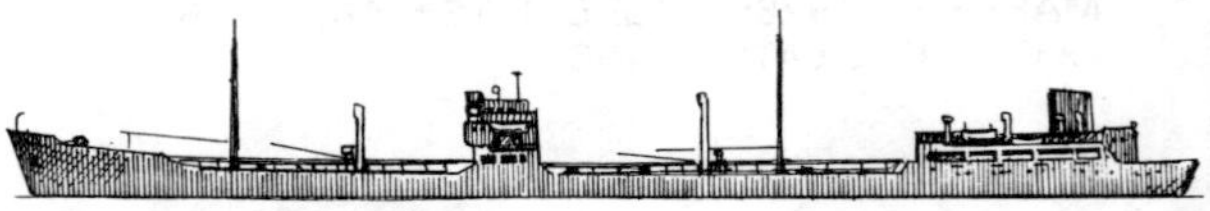

MK_2MF H123
39820 SIROCCA. Fi/Br 1958; Tk; 16700; 187.61 × 9.88 (615.52 × 32.41); M; 13; ex CANTO 1968.

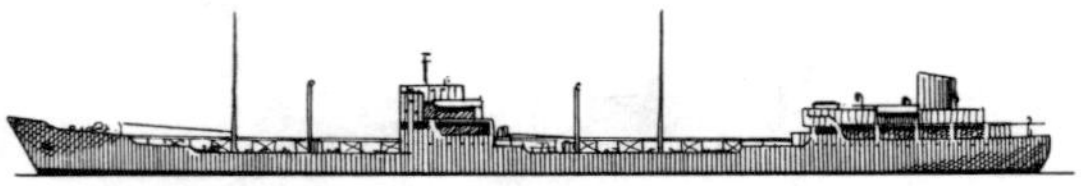

MK_2MF H123
***39830 TELEGONOS.** RC/Br 1951; Tk; 11600; 165.5 × 9.37 (543.01 × 30.8); M; 13.5; ex GAIETY 1970; ex GAUCHITO 1969; ex THORSKOG 1965. May be broken up.

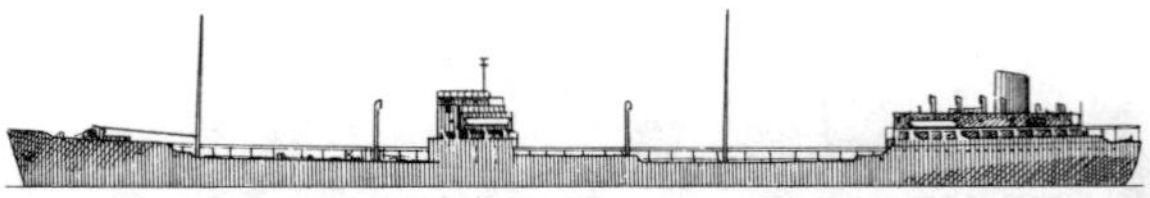

MK_2MF H123
39840 NICOS V. Gr/Br 1949; Tk; 16000; 179.48 × 10.16 (588.85 × 33.33); M; 14; ex BJORNTANGEN 1966; ex FERNCASTLE 1964.

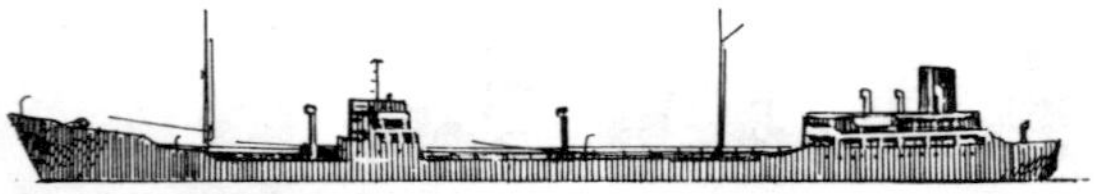

MK_2MF H123
39850 DODONE. Gr/FRG 1954; Tk; 11300; 165.18 × 8.87 (541.93 × 29.1); M; 14; ex VINGA 1970.

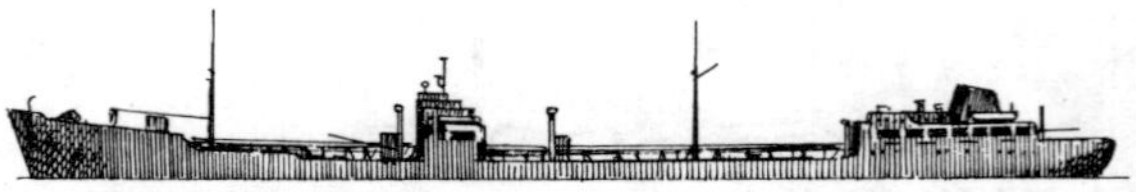

MK_2MF H123
39860 JUAN ALVAREZ. Me/Sw 1955; Tk; 12400; 173.01 × 9.35 (567.67 × 30.68); M; 14.5; ex PRESIDENTE JUAN ALVAREZ 1969; ex PEMEX 66 1966; ex PEGASUS 1966.

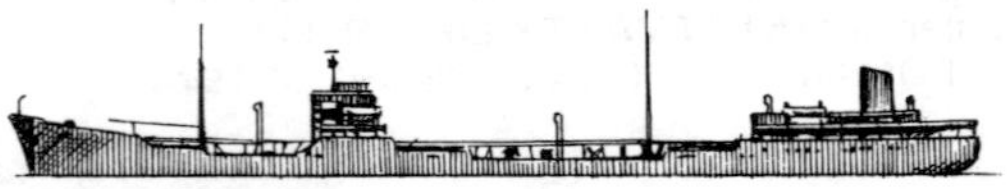

MK_2MF H123
39870 ARALDA. It/Br 1951; Tk; 8800; 150.93 × 8.8 (495.18 × 28.87); M; 12.5; ex CAPTAIN D. GERONTAS 1969; ex STAVIK 1966.

● 39875

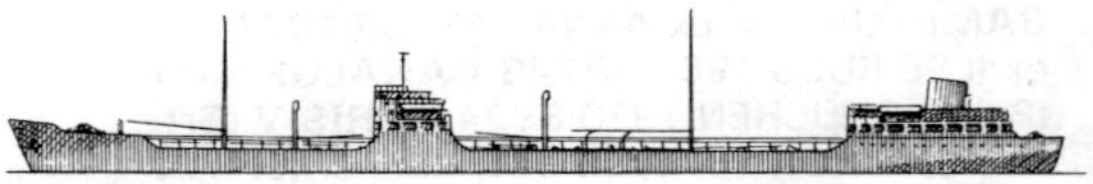

MK_2MF H123
39880 CAPTAIN GREGOS. Gr/Sw 1954; Tk; 10900; 167.57 × 9.2 (549.77 × 30.18); M; 14; ex ARIEGE 1980; ex VALAIS 1972; ex AGHIOS HARALAMPOS 1970; ex JUSTUS WALLER 1966.

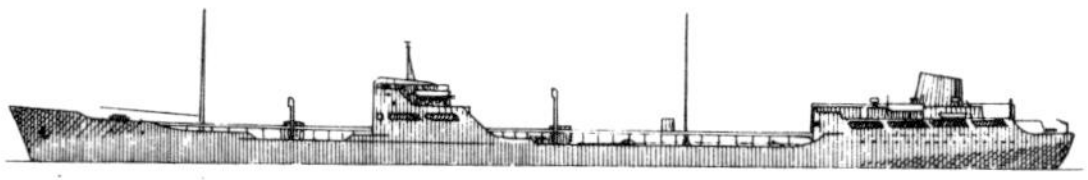

MK_2MF H123
39890 MOLARA. It/Ne 1958; Tk; 12900; 172.78 × 9.72 (566.86 × 31.9); M; 15; ex CIELO AZZURRO 1974; ex TOBRUK 1968; ex NORDHAV 1966. Sisters (Gr flag): **39891 LYDIA P** ex SEATRADER 1979; ex RANDAL 1973; ex STAHOLM 1970; ex TINNES 1968 **39892 THIOS THANASSIS** ex RANJA 1969.

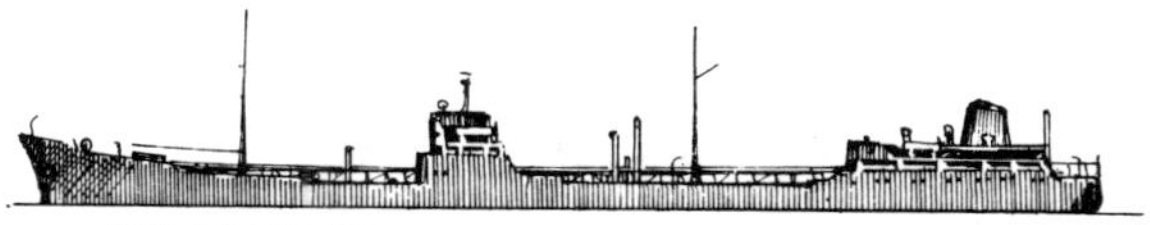

MK_2MF H123
39900 ITHAKI SAILOR. Gr/Br 1959; Tk; 12300; 170.69 × 9.43 (560 × 30.94); M; 14.5; ex ELPETFOIL 1973; ex HAMILTON TRADER 1973.

MK_2MF H123
39910 NIMERTIS. Li/Br 1952; Tk; 11200; 168.87 × 9.21 (554.04 × 30.22); M; 13.5. Sister: **39911 LADY DOROTHY** (Li).

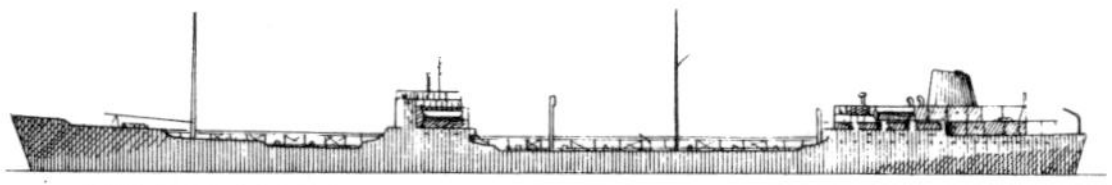

MK_2MF H123
39920 SAINT MARY. Gr/Sw 1956; Tk; 12300; 170.69 × 9.63 (560.01 × 31.59); M; 15; ex RAGNA GORTHON 1974.

MK_2MF H123
● ⋆**39930 DA QING No 410.** RC/Sw 1950; Tk; 5500; 132.62 × 7.9 (435.1 × 25.92); M; —; ex TAIPIENG 1978; ex ANCO SAILOR 1966; ex SANDEFJORD 1964. Sister: **39931 ZENAIDE A** (It) ex SICILTRADER 1970; ex LUISITO 1970; ex ANCO STREAM 1965; ex BUCCANEER 1964.

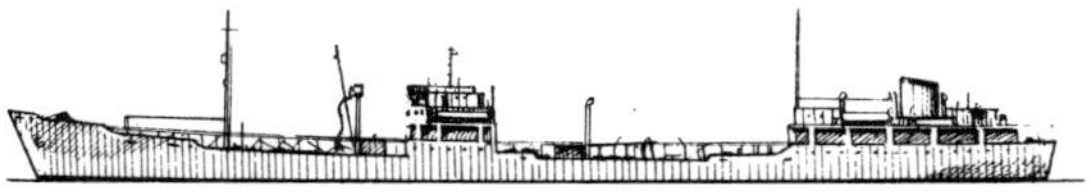

MK_2MF H123
39940 FRANKENLAND. FRG/Br 1950; RT/FA; 11700 Dspl; 167 × 9.1 (521.8 × 37.5); M; 13.5; ex MUNSTERLAND; ex POWELL.

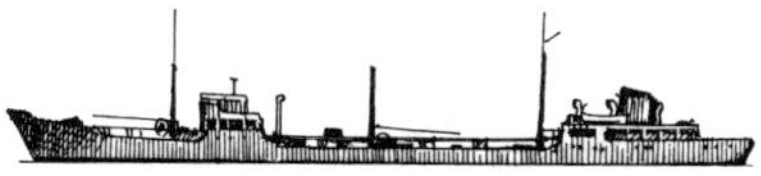

MK_2MF H123
39950 TEIDE. Sp/Sp 1956; RT/FA; 2700 Dspl; 117.5 × 6.2 (385.5 × 20.3); M; 12.

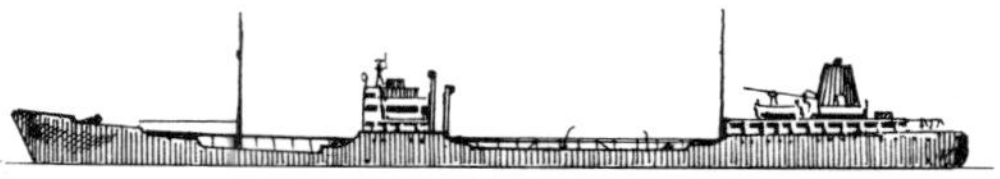

MK_2MF H123
⋆**39960 KLAYPEDA.** Ru/Ru 1954; Tk; 7700; 145.5 × 8.52 (477.36 × 27.95); M; 12.25; **'KAZBEK'** class. Sister: ⋆**39961 ZHDANOV** (Ru).

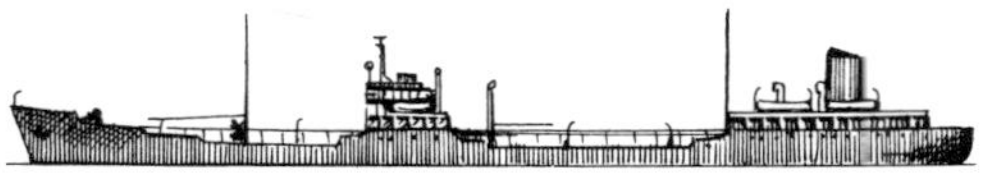

MK_2MF H123
● ⋆**39970 LENINGRAD.** Ru/Ru 1953; Tk; 7700; 145.5 × 8.71 (477.36 × 28.58); M; 12.25; **'KAZBEK'** class. Sisters (Ru flag): ⋆**39971 MAYKOP** ⋆**39972 VOLGODON** ⋆**39973 ASHKHABAD** ⋆**39974 GROZNY** ⋆**39975 KAZBEK** ⋆**39976 KERCH** ⋆**39977 POTI** ⋆**39978 TALLIN** ⋆**39979 CHERNOVTSY** ⋆**39980 FRUNZE** ⋆**39981 GRIGORIY VAKULENCHUK** ⋆**39982 OCHAKOV** ⋆**39983 CHKALOV** ⋆**39984 GRODNO** ⋆**39985 IVANOVO** ⋆**39986 SLAVGOROD** ⋆**39987 CHEBOKSARY** ex ANDREY VISHINSKY 1962 ⋆**39988 VINNITSA** ⋆**39989 ZHITOMIR** ⋆**39990 BUGURUSLAN** ⋆**39991 PETR SHIRSHOV** ⋆**39992 UZHGOROD** ⋆**39993 ELBRUS** ⋆**39994 KOMSOMOLETS UKRAINY** ⋆**39995 TBILISI** ⋆**39996 IZYASLAV** ⋆**39997 KREMENCHUG** ⋆**39998 ROVNO** ⋆**39999 SUMY** ⋆**40000 MOSKALVO** ⋆**40001 MAKHACHKALA** ⋆**40002 SVERDLOVSK** ⋆**40003 KOSTROMA** ⋆**40004 KAUNAS** ⋆**40005 LENINSK** ⋆**40006 MOLODECHNO** ⋆**40007 KOMSOMOL** ⋆**40008 KURSK** ⋆**40009 GELENDZHIK** ex STANISLAV 1974 ⋆**40010 VLADIMIR** ⋆**40011 SAMARKAND** ⋆**40012 DZERZHINSK** The following are operated by the Soviet Navy and others from the list above may be naval manned from time to time
⋆**40013 ALATYR** ⋆**40014 VOLKHOV.**

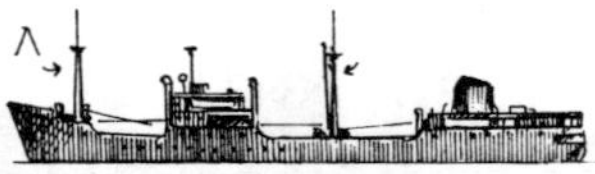

MK_2MF *H123*
40020 KAGOWA. My/Br 1955; C; 2700; 88.32 × 5.34 (289.76 × 17.52); M; 12; ex JACQUES DEL MAR 1971; ex TULAGI 1970.

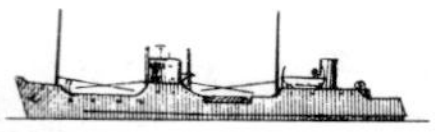

MK_2MF *H123*
40030 SALMIAH COAST. Ku/Br 1946; C; 500; 61.42 × 3.28 (201.51 × 10.76); M; 11; ex KENTISH COAST 1968; ex ULSTER WEAVER 1964; ex JERSEY COAST 1954; ex ULSTER DUCHESS 1946.

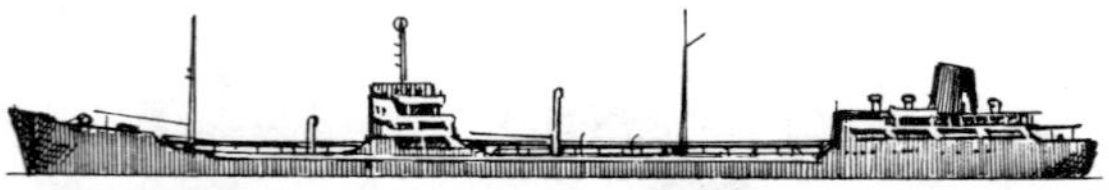

MK_2MF *H13*
40040 ESTRELLA. Fi/Sw 1956; Tk; 12600; 169.81 × 9.54 (557.12 × 31.3); M; 15.25; ex SYNIA 1969.

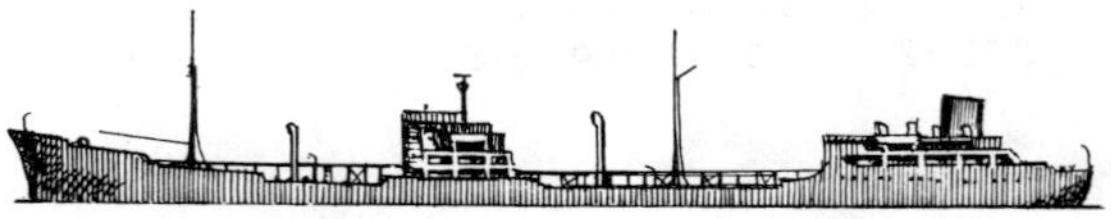

MK_2MF *H13*
40050 SKOPELOS. Gr/Br 1958; Tk; 12500; 170.59 × 9.53 (559.68 × 31.27); M; 14.5; ex TOPLOU BAY; ex PELINEON; ex KONSTANTINOS G. CHIMPLES 1977; ex HUDSON TRADER 1973; ex SPINANGER 1970.

MK_2MF *H13*
★40060 DA QING No15. RC/Br 1952; Tk; 10100; 154.11 × 6.86 (505.61 × 22.51); M; 12; ex SANTA FOURTUNA 1974; ex SANDALWOOD 1962.

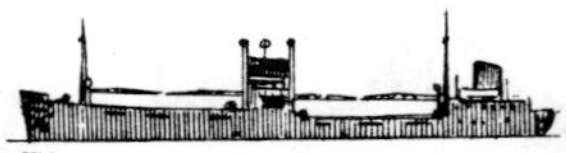

MK_2MF *H13*
40070 CEMENTO PUERTO RICO. Pa/Sw 1944; Cem; 1400; 73.39 × 4.54 (240.78 × 14.9); M; 11.5; ex CEMENTIERE 1973; ex SUNNANVIK 1961; ex VIKA I 1959; ex HELGA CORDS 1946. Sister: **49971 LAS MINAS** (Cy) ex PYLIASTRON 1974; ex PAOLA 1971; ex CETI 1969; ex ALTAIR III 1964; ex DIANA 1961.

MK_2MF *H13*
40080 KARINA. Pa/FRG 1954; C; 1200; 87.33 × 4.6 (286.52 × 15.09); M; 14; ex FELICE 1980; ex REGINA 1976; ex BELEM 1968; ex RADBOD 1957.

MK_2MF *H13*
40090 BLUE SEA. Cy/DDR 1961; C; 1900; 90.1 × 5.69 (295.6 × 18.67); M; 12.5; ex HEINRICH WESCH 1972; ex MARI 1965. Sister: **40091 BLUE SKY** (Cy) ex KIRSTEN WESCH 1972; ex BARI 1964 Similar: **40092 NIUVAKAI** (To) ex WILRI 1963.

MK_2MF *H13*
40100 ABU SIMBEL. Eg/DDR 1960; C; 1900; 85.2 × 5.72 (279.53 × 18.77); M; —; ex MARI 1961. Sister (Eg flag): **40101 BLOUDAN** ex ILRI **40102 HELWAN.**

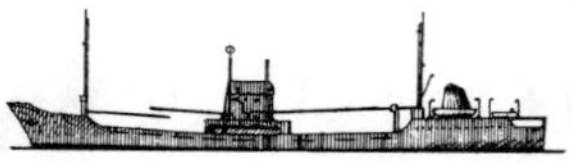

MK_2MF *H13*
40110 GERASIMOS K. Cy/FRG 1954; C; 1200/1900; 86.77 × 4.6/5.7 (284.68 × 15.09/18.7); M; 11.5; ex MARIA FROSO 1975; ex IDDAN 1974; ex MERCATOR 1965.

MK_2MF *H13*
40120 CHERRY CHEPAT. My/Br 1938; C; 700; 61.22 × 4.17 (200.85 × 13.68); TSM; 12; ex SARANG 1970; ex KOPARA 1966.

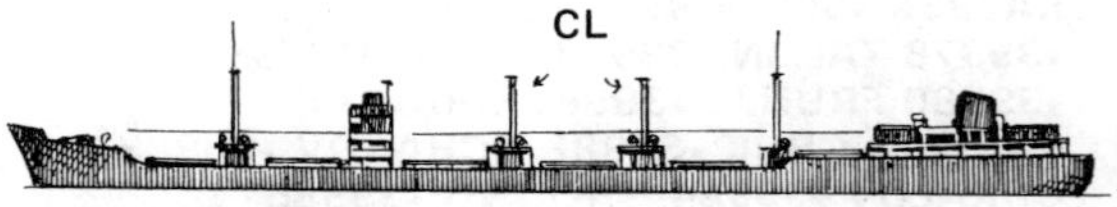

MK_2MF *H13*
40130 NIKOLAOS K. Gr/Br 1959; B; 11700; 170.39 × 8.95 (559.02 × 29.36); M; 14.5; ex LUCKY IMPORTER 1980; ex SUGAR IMPORTER 1976; em ATHELPRINCE 1966. Sisters: **40131 ZEUS** (Gr) ex SUGAR EXPORTER 1976; ex ATHELPRINCESS **40132 TAICHEE** (Pa) ex CRYSTAL SAPPHIRE 1974.

MK_2MF H3
40140 SAN NICOLAS. Ur/FRG 1953; C; 1100/1900; 82.3 × 4.45/5.94 (270.01 × 14.6/19.5); TSM; 12.5; ex HOMBERG 1968.

MK_2MF H3
40150 SOON HENG. Pa/FRG 1951; C; 1100/1800; 86.31 × 4.47/5.94 (283.17 × 14.67/19.49); TSM; 12.5; ex PRINCESS GLORY 1979; ex GOOD GRACE 1978; ex SWIFTHAWK 1976; ex KONIGSAU 1974; ex RUHRORT 1963. Similar: **40151 MARIGOULA G** (Gr) ex PANAGIA 1979; ex HOLSATIA 1969; ex EDMUND HALM 1963.

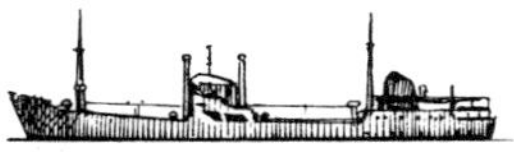

MK_2MF H3
40160 FAHAD. Si/FRG 1953; C; 1300; 74.22 × 5.41 (243.5 × 17.75); M; 12; ex GRACE SAILOR 1978; ex GILETTE 1976; ex GOLFSTRAUM 1966; ex ERIC RECKMANN 1964.

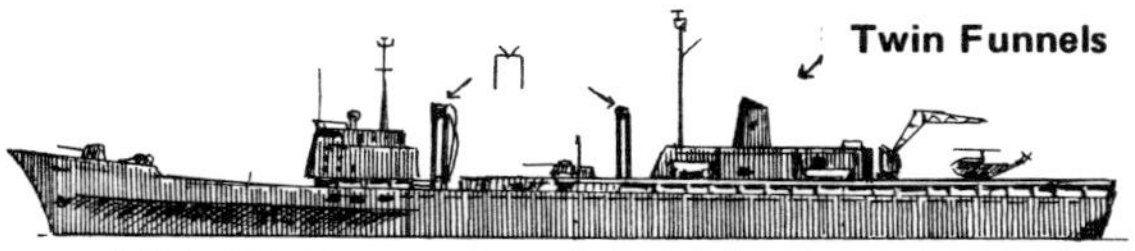

MK_2MFC H
40170 PRESERVER. Ca/Ca 1970; Rst/FA; 24700 Dspl; 172 × 9.1 (564 × 30); T; —; Helicopters. Operated by Royal Canadian Navy. Sister: **40171 PROTECTEUR** (Ca).

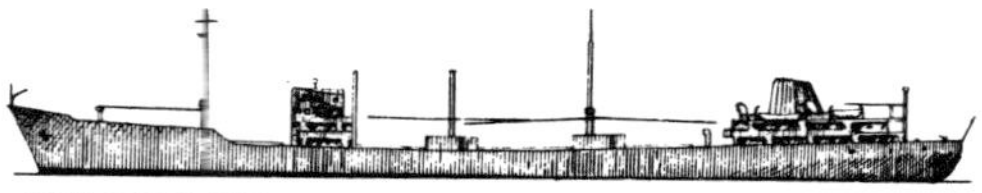

MK_2MFK H1
40180 TONG HAN. Sg/FRG 1956; C; 9200; 151.39 × 9.47 (496.69 × 31.07); M; 15.5; ex ADELFOTIS 1974; ex SANTA MONICA 1967; ex JAROSA 1963.

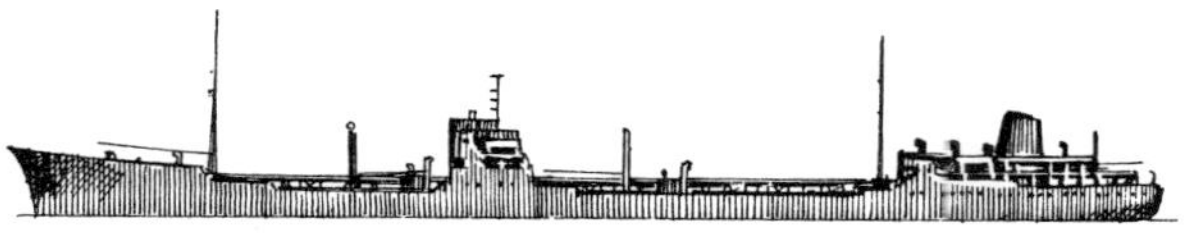

MK_2MFK H123
40190 AGHIOS ERMOLAOS. Pa/No 1956; Tk; 12800; 175.77 × 9.58 (576.67 × 31.43); M; 13.5; ex STOLT CATALINA 1975; ex QUIN DUCHESS 1973; ex TANK DUCHESS 1971

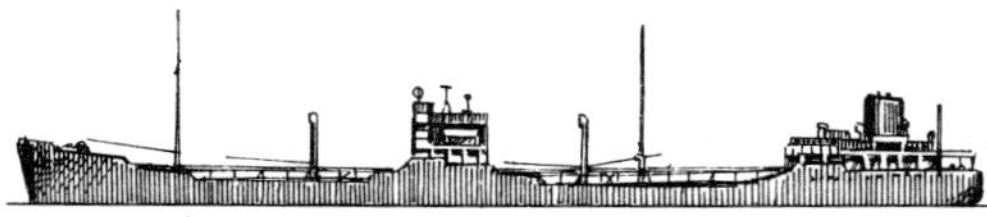

MK_2MFK H123
40200 LAPU LAPU. Pi/Ne 1955; Tk; 9100; 152.74 × 8.33 (501.12 × 27.33); M; 13; ex CAMITIA 1975. Sisters (Ne flag): **40201 CINULIA 40202 CRANIA.**

MK_2MFK H123
40210 LA SAONE. Fr/Fr 1948/61; RT/FA; 24200 Dspl; 160 × 10 (525 × 33); TST; 18; Fitted as a fleet replenishment ship 1961.

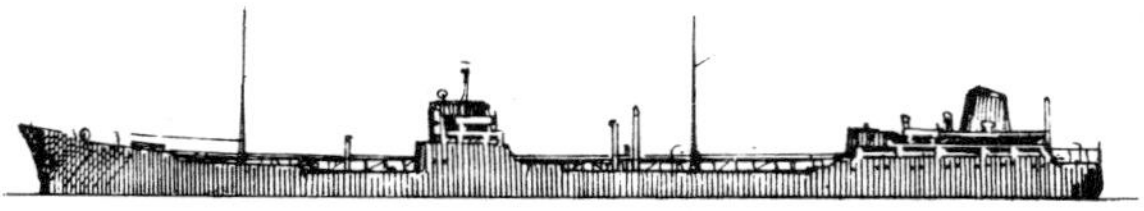

MK_2MFK H13
40220 ITHAKI SAILOR. Gr/Br 1959; Tk; 12300; 170.69 × 9.43 (560 × 30.94); M; 14.5; ex ELPETROIL 1973; ex HAMILTON TRADER 1973.

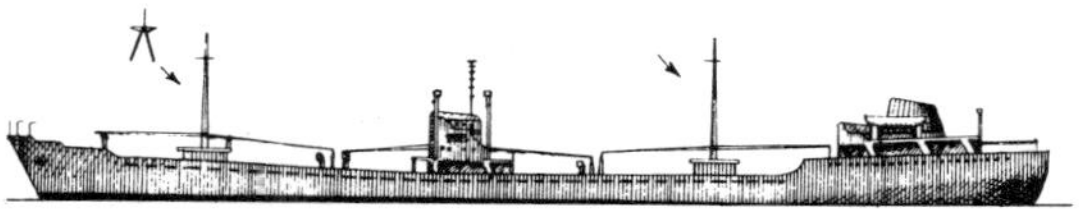

MK_2MFK H13
⋆40230 DRZIC. Ys/Ys 1961; C; 7400/10200; 161.6 × —/9.39 (530.18 × —/30.81); M; 16.

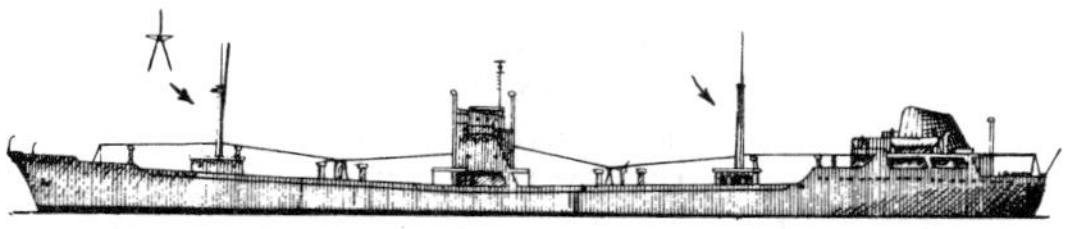

MK_2MFK H13
⋆40240 PLITVICE. Ys/Ys 1964; C; 7500/10500; 166.2 × 8.12/9.11 (545.28 × 26.64/29.89); M; 16. Sister: **⋆40241 KRAGUJEVAC** (Ys).

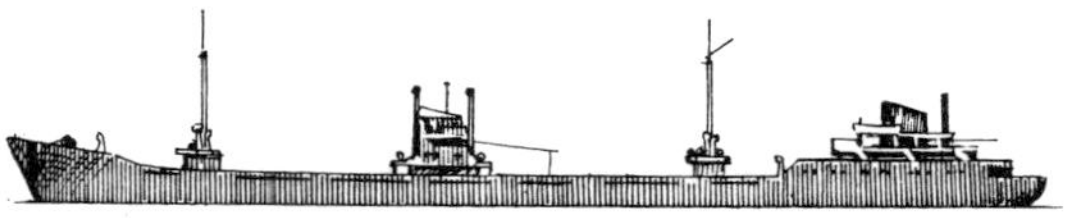

MK_2MFK H13
40250 ARIS. Gr/FRG 1957; C; 6600/9500; 160.53 × 8.05/9.1 (526.67 × 26.41/29.86); M; 14.5; ex ARISTIDIS 1980; ex AMELIE THYSSEN 1972. Sisters: **40251 GELIGA** (Ia) ex RHENANIA 1973 **40252 VISHVA SUDHA** (In) ex WESTFALIA.

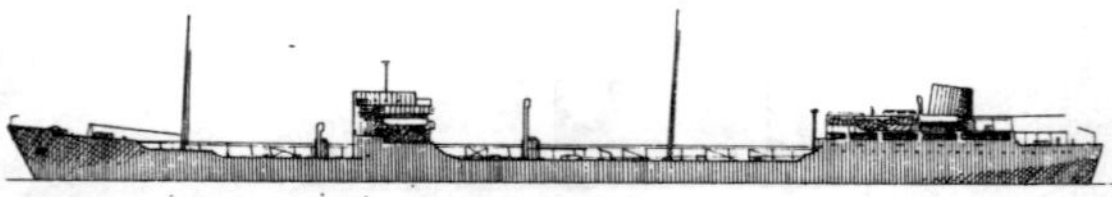

MK_2MKF H123
40260 CAPO MADRE. It/Sw 1953; Tk; 11900; 173.01 × 9.65 (567.62 × 31.66); M; 14.5; ex NORSE LION 1968.

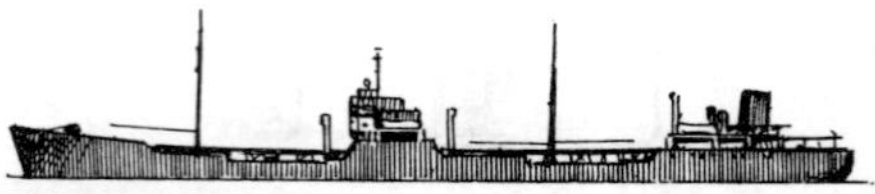

MK_2MKF H123
● **40270 LENTINI.** It/It 1948; Tk; 6300; 140.37 × 7.98 (460.53 × 26.18); M; 13; ex DORDRECT 1961; ex JAN 1954.

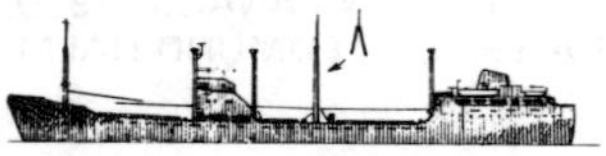

MK_2MKF H13
● **40280 VENTURE SEA.** Cy/FRG 1954; C; 1700/2800; 90.68 × —/6.61 (297.51 × —/21.69); D-E; 12; ex DIONYSSOS 1974; ex MICHRIS 1973; ex CURSA 1970; ex CATHERINE SARTORI 1967; lengthened 1955.

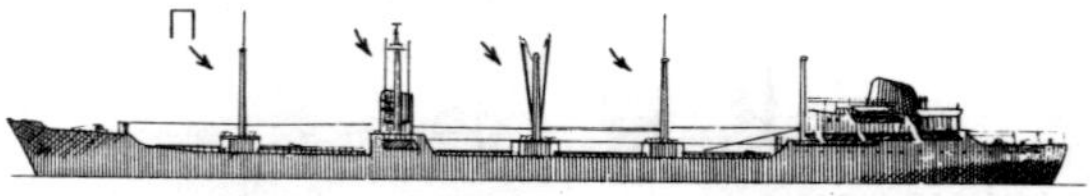

MK_2MKF H13
● **40290 KEHARITOMENI.** Cy/Fr 1958; C; 9000/11800; 169.02 × 8.41/9.55 (554.53 × 27.59/31.33); M; 16; ex CHRISTINA 1; ex LOUIS DELMAS 1976; ex ROCROI 1966. Sister: **40291 CORINTHIAKOS** (Gr) ex ARCADIAN 1977; ex HAWK 1976; ex FONTENOY.

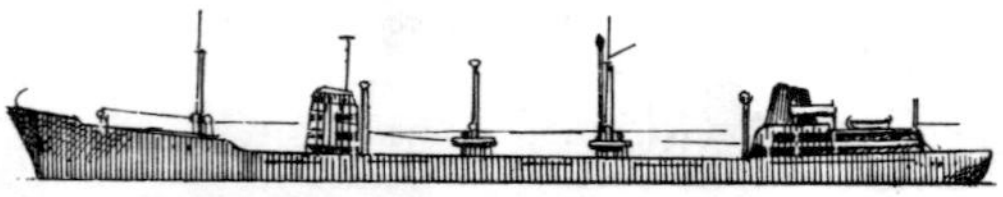

MK_2MKFK H1
● **40300 CAP PALMAS.** FRG/FRG 1957; C; 6600/8900; 151.42 × 8.08/9.09 (496.78 × 26.51/29.82); M; 15.75; ex DAFNE 1969; ex CAP PALMAS 1968; ex BERTIOGA 1958.

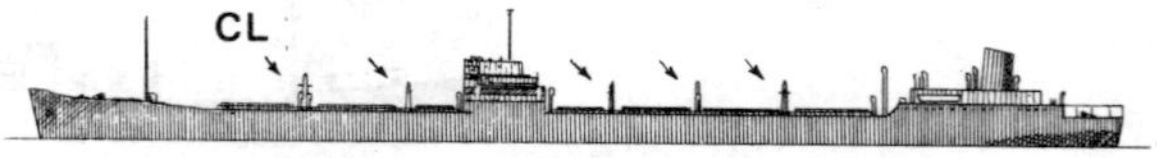

MK_2MK_4F H2
40310 SOPHIA. Pa/US-Ja 1943/59; B; 13500; 174.28 × 10.36 (571.28 × 33.99); T-E; 14.5; ex OVERSEAS PROGRESS 1974; ex GLOBE PROGRESS 1968; ex WORLD CHALLENGER 1961; ex WORLD TREASURE 1959; ex WALLOWA 1956. Lengthened & converted from T-2 tanker 1959.

MKMCF H
40320 BEXLEY. Br/Br 1966; Slu; 2200; 89.87 × 4.06 (294.85 × 13.32); TSM; 12. Sisters (Br flag): **40321 HOUNSLOW 40322 NEWHAM 40323 SIR JOSEPH BAZALGETTE.**

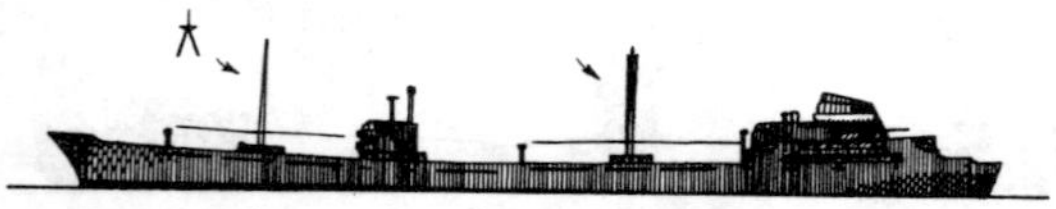

MKMF H
40330 TRINITY HARVEST. Pa/It 1957; C; 9700; 150.58 × 8.96 (494.03 × 28.8); M; 14.5; ex MEGARA.

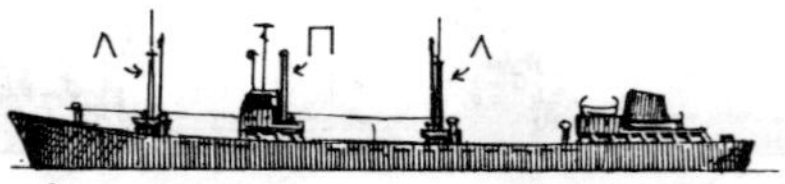

MKMF H
● **40340 DIAKAN MASCOT.** Gr/It 1959; C; 4200; 113.87 × 7.62 (373.59 × 25); M; 15; ex ASKOT 1970. Sisters (may have KP aft): **40341 EASTERN GRAND** (Pa) ex MEDITERRANEAN KLIF 1974; ex CORFU ISLAND 1972; ex SUSAA 1970; ex MARSTENEN 1965; ex BUKKEN 1962; ex MARSTENEN 1960 **40342 YANMAR** (Pa) ex YACU GUAGUA 1980; ex FURKA 1973; ex HELGOLAND 1972; ex MEDICINE HAT 1968; ex ANDERS ROGENAES 1964; ex CONCORDIA ANDERS 1962; ex ANDERS ROGENAES 1960.

MKMF H
40350 ROSA. Pe/Br 1950; C/WT; 800; 69.45 × 4.29 (227.2 × 14.07); M; 12; ex CHRISTINE 1960.

MKMF H1
40360 SHORTHORN EXPRESS. Ne/Ne 1957; LS; 500; 68.56 × 3.57 (224.93 × 11.77); M; 12.5; ex HONTESTROOM 1969. Converted from cargo ship. Sister: **40361 FRISIAN EXPRESS** (Ne) ex VLIESTROOM 1969.

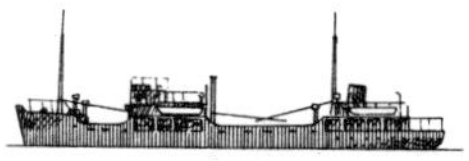

MKMF H1
40390 BREEZE. Pi/Br 1946; C; 2100; 67.02 × 4.9 (222.51 × 16.08); M; 9; ex BENTONG 1966. Sisters: **40391 BRUAS** (My) **40392 ORCHID VENTURE** (Sg) ex BIDOR.

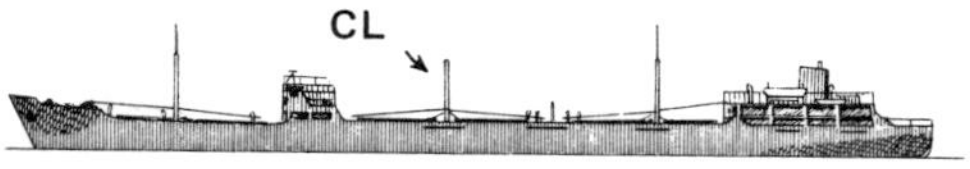

MKMF H1
40400 VIRGINIA M. Gr/Br 1958; B; 7700; 146.21 × 7.79 (479.69 × 25.56); M; 13; ex GLOXINIA 1977.

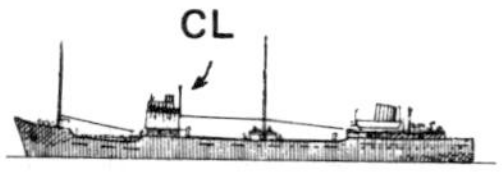

MKMF H12
40420 MARYS KETCH. Br/Br 1957; C; 1500; 73.44 × 4.79 (290.94 × 19.72); M; —; ex ALFRED EVERARD 1978. Similar: **40421 AGHIA MARINA** (Gr) ex SERENITY 1967 **40422 ROBERT KOCH** (Ca) ex GUARDIAN CARRIER 1977; ex ETHEL EVERARD 1963 **40423 RAMONA** (Pa) ex SANGUITY 1978 **40424 IOANNIS** (Cy) ex SELECTIVITY 1975 **40425 CRYSTAL ISLAND** (Pa) ex DESPINA T 1980; ex SIMULARITY 1975 **40426 KING ON** (Pa) ex STABILITY.

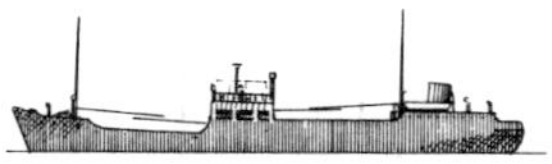

MKMF H12
40450 OPUSO. Ng/Sw 1946; C; 1600; 81.74 × 4.56 (268.18 × 14.96); TSM; 9; ex WARIGI 1968; ex MEXICO 1962; ex TACHIRA 1955; ex CONSUL SARTORI. Sister: **40451 BUENO** (Pa) ex SAN SALVADOR 1973; ex YUCATAN 1970; ex ANZOATEGUI 1955; ex MAYA.

MKMF H
40370 RABUNION IV. Le/Br 1950; LS; 800; 78.47 × 5.29 (257.48 × 17.36); M; 12; ex LAMAYA 1976; ex AGROCORP 1 1974; ex SOFIA 1973; ex BAROK 1971. Side doors. Sister: **40371 DARPO DUA** (la) ex BOLT 1968. These two vessels may now be MK²MF (See DARPO SATU).

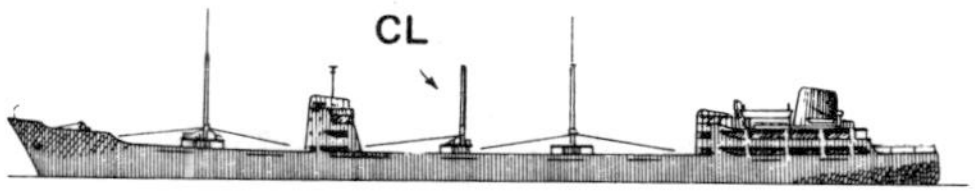

MKMF H1
● **40410 LAMDA.** Li/Br 1959; B; 7900; 148.47 × 7.93 (487.11 × 26.01); M; 14; ex PENNY MICHAELS 1976; ex GRANWOOD 1971.

MKMF H12
40430 MIRONAVE. Bz/Ge 1939; C; 1200; 76.15 × 4.26 (249.84 × 13.98); TSM; 8; ex SAO LEOPOLDO 1965; ex ILA 1952; ex GALTNES 1947; ex EMPIRE CONCLAVE 1946; ex LUNA 1945.

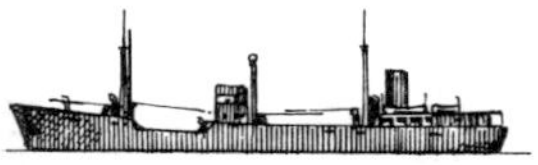

MKMF H12
40440 SLIDRE. Pi/No 1938; C; 1400; 78.64 × 4.92 (258.01 × 16.74); M; 12.5; ex BOMMA 1965.

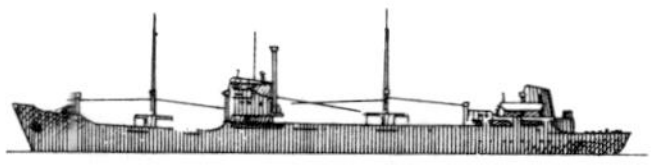

MKMF H12
40460 VARUNA YAMINI. In/FRG 1962; C; 3200; 97.92 × 6.98 (321.26 × 22.9); M; 14.25; ex FIEPKO TEN DOORNKAAT 1972. Sisters: **40461 VARUNA YAN** (In) ex ELLEN KLAUTSCHKE 1972 **40462 MARIA A** (Gr) ex CAROLINE SCHULTE 1978; ex GERTRUD TEN DOORNKAAT 1973.

MKMF H12
40470 SABINE 1. Pa/FRG 1962; C; 2100/3300; 103 × —/6.91 (337.93 × —/22.67); M; 15; ex CITY OF BOCHUM; ex ANNEMARIE KRUGER 1976.

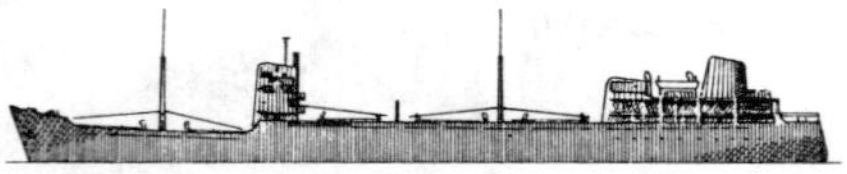

MKMF H12
40490 SIRLAD. Ma/Br 1955; B; 6000; 130.38 × 7.24 (427.76 × 23.75); M; 12; ex KYKLOPS 1980; ex FENI 1979; ex MORCOTE 1977; ex SEBASTIANO 1976; ex DEERWOOD 1969.

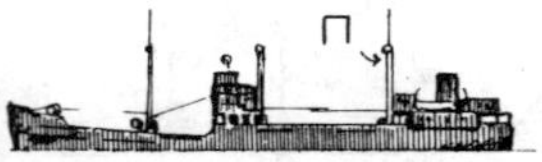

MKMF H12
40510 MERSINI. Cy/Br 1943; C; 1600; 78.9 × 5.32 (258.86 × 17.45); M; 10; ex APOSTOLOS B 1975; ex ERGINA VENTOURI 1972; ex PARALOS 1965; ex EDENWOOD 1960. Shortened 1953.

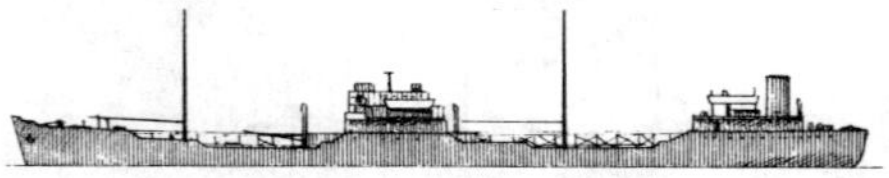

MKMF H123
40530 ASTRACHUBUT. Ar/Br 1949; Tk; 6400; 135.59 × 7.81 (444.85 × 25.62); M; 12; ex CAZADOR.

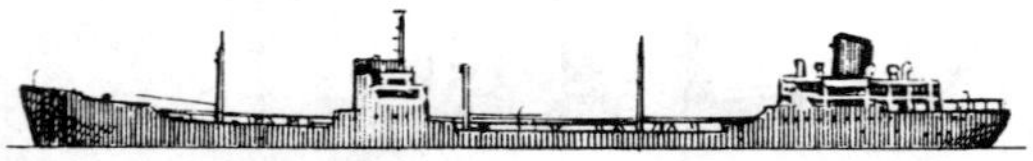

MKMF H123
40550 THERMOPYLAI. Gr/No 1955; Tk; 9000; 156.62 × 8.72 (513.85 × 28.61); M; 13.5; ex ANINA 1978; ex FOSSLAND 1963; ex SLEMDAL 1961.

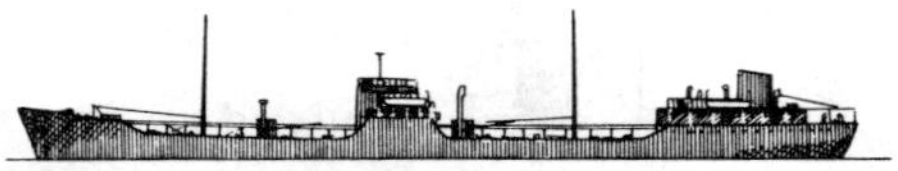

MKMF H123
● ★**40570 DA QING No 410.** RC/Sw 1959; Tk; 5500; 132.62 × 7.9 (435.1 × 25.92); M; —; ex TAIPIENG 1978; ex ANCO SAILOR 1966; ex SANDEFJORD 1964. Sister: **40571 ZENAIDE A** (It) ex SICILTRADER 1970; ex LUISITO 1970; ex ANCO STREAM 1965; ex BUCCANEER 1964.

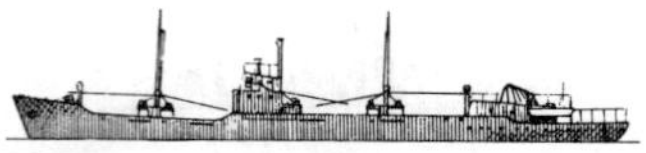

MKMF H12
● **40480 MADINIA.** Gr/FRG 1959; C; 3000; 97.69 × 6.99 (320.51 × 22.93); M; 13.5; ex CLIO 1973; ex ANDRIA 1967; ex CLIO 1965.

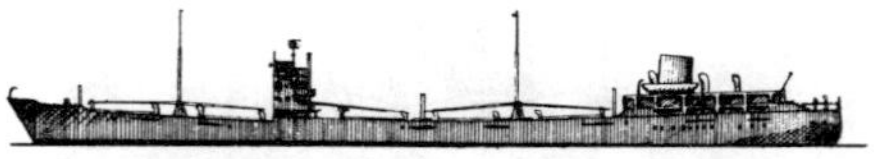

MKMF H12
★**40500 RODOPI.** Bu/Br 1953; C; 6200; 132.44 × 7.18 (434.51 × 23.56); R; 12; ex RUSHWOOD 1962; No longer seagoing.

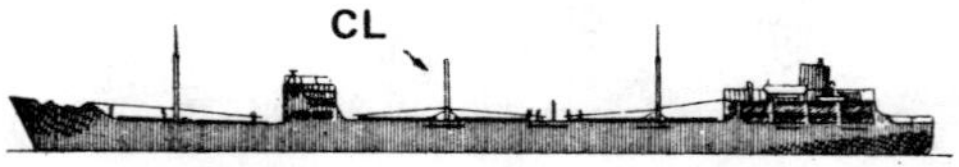

MKMF H12
40520 VIRGINIA M. Gr/Br 1958; B; 7700; 146.21 × 7.79 (479.69 × 25.56); M; 13; ex GLOXINIA 1977.

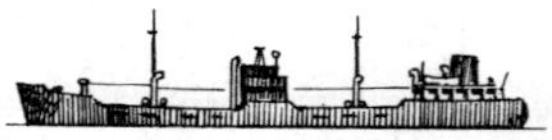

MKMF H123
40540 ASTRO. Cy/No 1952; C; 1600; 78.64 × 5.39 (258.01 × 17.68); M; 10; ex HEROIC JUNIOR 1980; ex DIALA 1973.

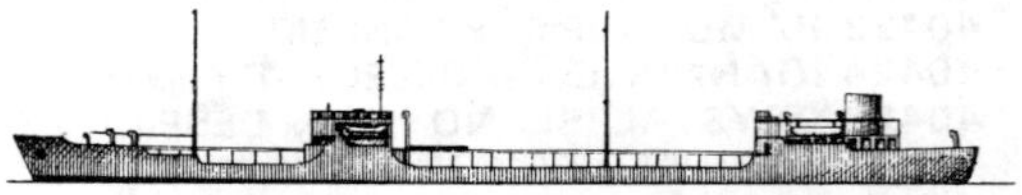

MKMF H123
★**40560 DA QING No 16.** RC/Sw 1952; Tk; 11600; 170.54 × 9.27 (559.51 × 30.41); M; 14; ex BARBRO 1964.

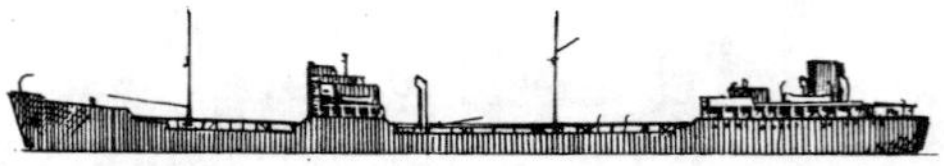

MKMF H123
★**40580 ANTON IVANOV.** Bu/Sw 1945; Tk; 8500; 147.38 × 8.51 (483.53 × 27.92); M; 13; ex MARGIT REUTER 1960; ex KRATOS 1958.

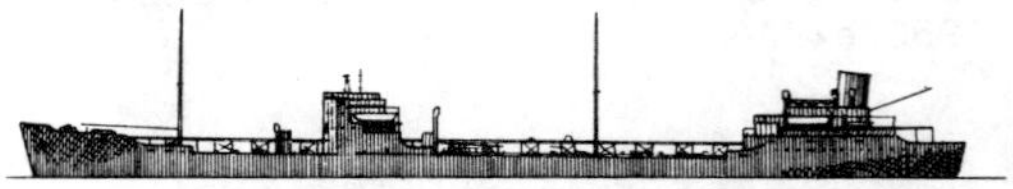

MKMF H123
● ★**40590 COSMOPOLITAN.** RK/De 1952; Tk; 8800; 149.18 × 8.34 (489.44 × 27.36); M; 14; ex BRATTLAND 1968; ex STOLT BRATTLAND 1967; ex BRATTLAND 1963.

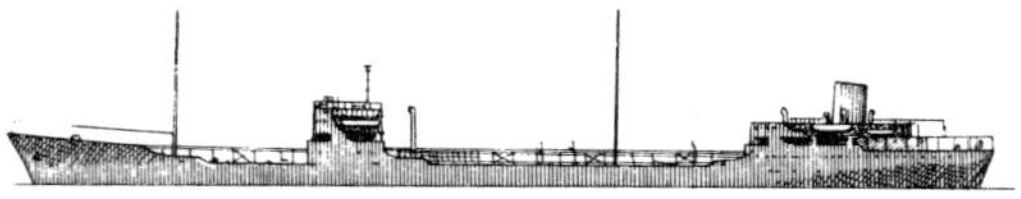

MKMF H123
40600 SALAT. Fr/No 1952; Tk; 8900; 156.37 × 8.74 (513.02 × 28.67); M; 11.5; ex NOEMA II 1969; ex VIVA 1964. Sister: **40601 SELINTI** (It) ex HORNFIGHTER 1968.

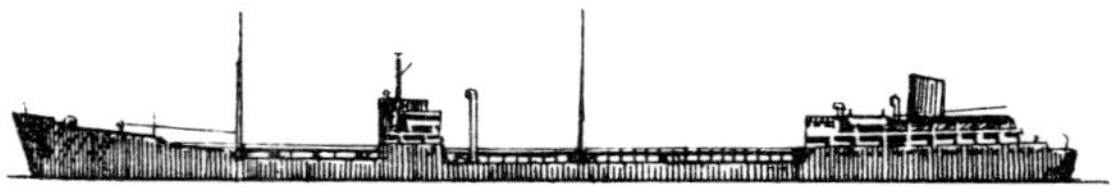

MKMF H123
40610 PETROLINA I. Cy/No 1956; Tk; 11900; 171.53 × 9.34 (562.76 × 30.64); M; 15.5; ex TORE KNUDSEN 1974.

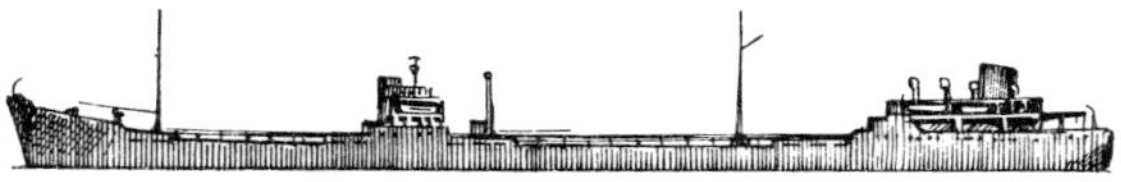

MKMF H123
40620 NISSOS KEFALLINIA. Gr/De 1953; Tk; 9800; 155.51 × 9.08 (510.2 × 29.79); M; 14; ex OCEAN EMPEROR 1973; ex OCEAN SOLICA 1971; ex JUANITA 1968.

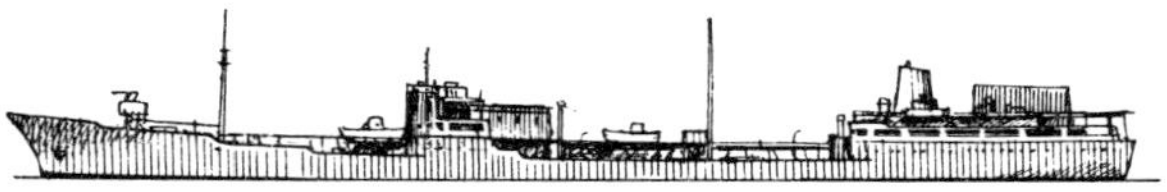

MKMF H123
40640 LA CHARENTE. Fr/No 1957; RT/FA; 2600 Dspl; 179 × 9.3 (587.2 × 30.3); T; 17.5; ex BEAUFORT 1964. Converted from a tanker. Helicopter platform and hangar.

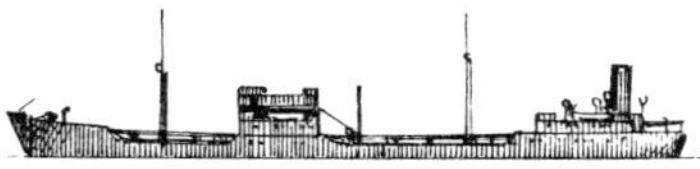

MKMF H123
● **40650 MANTINIA.** Gr/Br 1945; Tk; 3800; 109 × 6.69 (357.61 × 21.95); M; 12; ex MONTMAJOUR 1963; ex BRITISH BUGLER 1957; ex EMPIRE ARROW 1946.

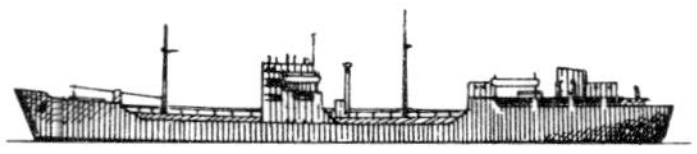

MKMF H123
⋆**40660 SONG LIM.** RK/Fi 1955; Tk; 3100; 105.06 × 6.13 (344.69 × 20.11); M; 15; ex PROGRESS; ex BUNJU 1968; ex DROGOBITZ 1958. Sisters: ⋆**40661 GLORY** (RK) ex SAMBU 1968; ex GUDERMES 1958 ⋆**40662 DA QING No 10** (RC) ex CHIEN SHE 10; ex BESKIDY 1958 ⋆**40663 DA QING No 11** (RC) ex CHIEN SHE 11; ex TATRY 1958 ⋆**40664 LOKBATAN** (Ru).

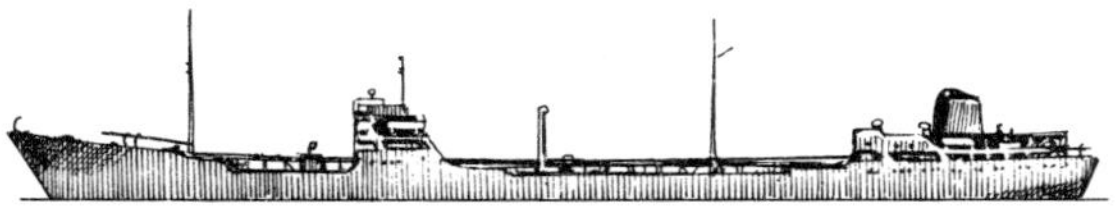

MKMF H123
⋆**40670 DA QING No 35.** RC/No 1958; Tk; 10200; 165.16 × 9.3 (541.86 × 30.51); M; 15; ex NORCLIPPER 1970; ex HORN CLIPPER 1968.

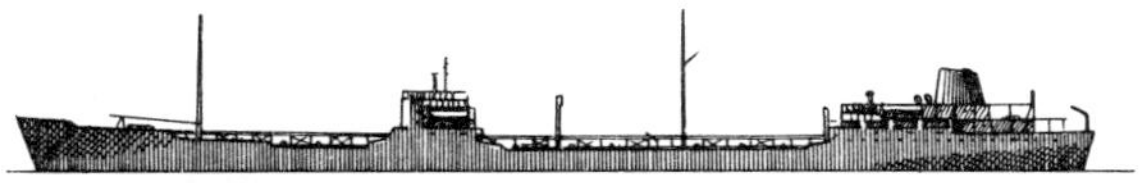

MKMF H123
40680 SAINT MARY. Gr/Sw 1956; Tk; 12300; 170.69 × 9.63 (560.01 × 31.59); M; 15; ex RAGNA GORTHON 1967.

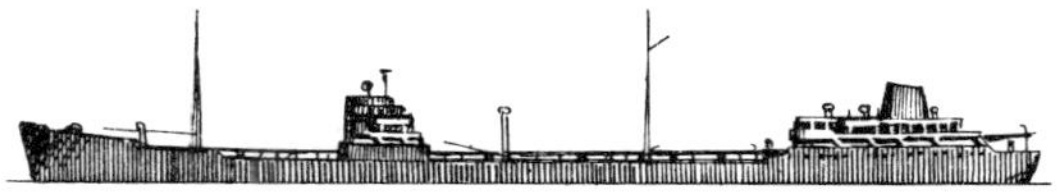

MKMF H123
40690 ETERNITY. Sg/No 1957; Tk; 10300; 161.47 × 9.26 (529.76 × 30.38); M; 14.75; ex SAGA SWALE 1970; ex SKARAAS 1967.

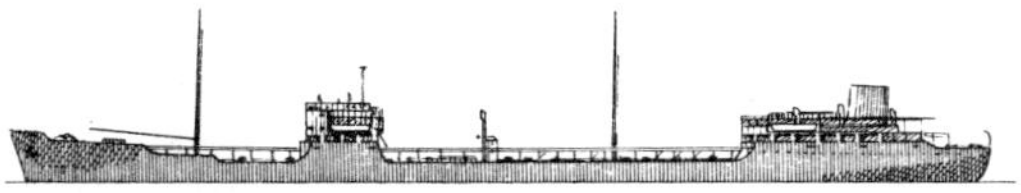

MKMF H123
● **40700 PERMINA 108** Ia/Sw 1950; Tk; 10000; 155.71 × 8.8 (510.86 × 28.88); M; 14; ex SPARTI 1974; ex CONFIDENCE 1969; ex SEA SPRAY 1963; ex WINDWOOD BAY 1960; ex ALCIDES 1957. Similar: **40701 GREEN BAY** (Pa) ex SPLENDOUR 1 1979; ex WALLPORT 1977; ex MERCURY 1977; ex FORTESCUE 1974; ex ATLANTIC TRADER; ex BEL ABETO 1965; ex VESTAN 1965.

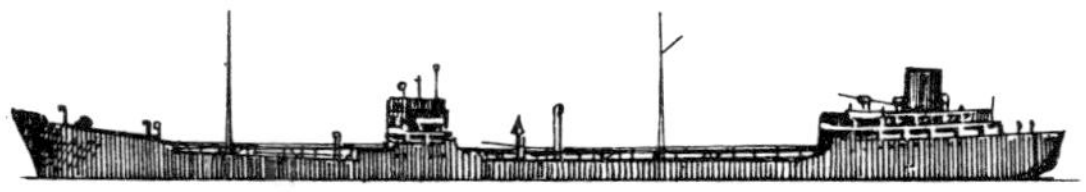

MKMF H123
40710 GOGO RACER. Li/Po 1958; Tk; 11500; 163.76 × 9.08 (537.27 × 29.79); M; 14; ex ERATI.

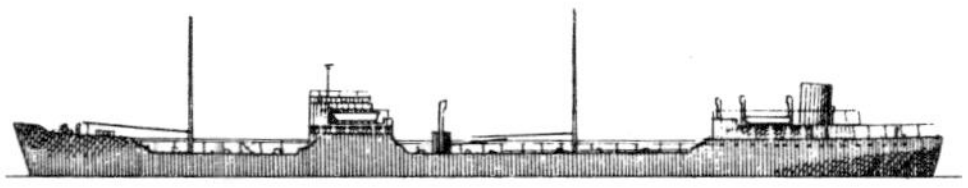

MKMF H123
40720 AMERICANO. It/Sw 1941/45; Tk; 8200; 147.38 × 8.68 (483.53 × 28.98); M; 12.5; ex SIRA 1962; ex SINUS 1949.

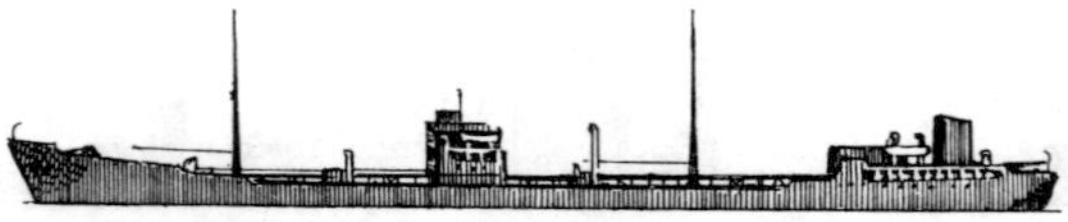

MKMF H123
40730 EVGENIA 1. Pa/Br 1954; Tk; 11200; 164.29 × 9.41 (539.01 × 30.87); M; 13.75; ex EVGENIA 1980; ex DONA EVGENIA 1960. Sister: **40731 DONA MYRTO** (Pa).

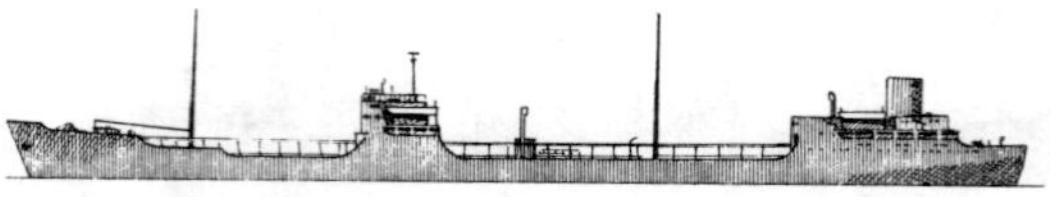

MKMF H123
● **40740 MARIA E.** Gr/Sw 1952; Tk; 10600; 162.54 × 9.11 (533.27 × 29.89); M; 14.5; ex SEABREEZE 1965; ex POLLUX 1960. Similar: **40741 PEDRIN** (It) ex MARIO MARTINI 1974; ex MARIO MARTINI SECONDO 1964; ex SIROCCO 1960.

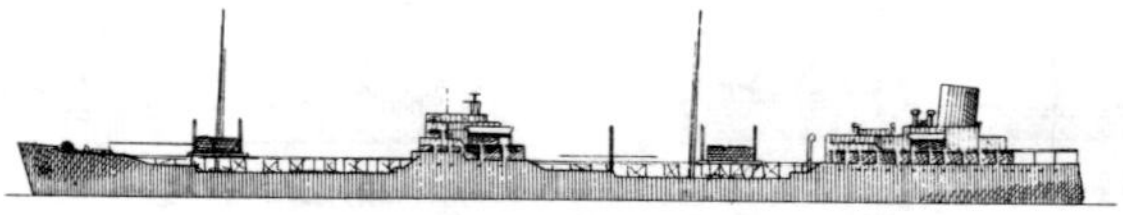

MKMF H123
40750 HALIA. Br/Br 1958; Tk; 11900; 169.4 × 9.35 (555.77 × 30.68); T; 14.5; Fenders on deck for lightening operations. Similar: **40751 PETROLA 11** (Gr) ex PETROLA XI 1976; ex KENIA 1973 **40752 PETROLA 17** (Gr) ex PETROLA XVII 1976; ex PETROLA X 1975; ex KREBSIA 1973 **40753 KYLIX** (Ne).

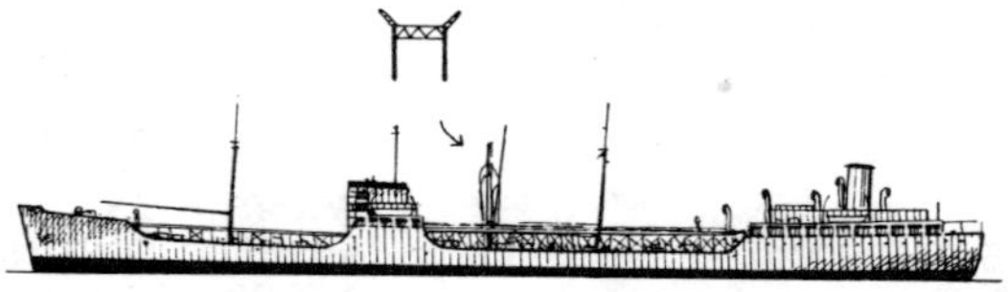

MKMF H123
40760 DACCA. Pk/US 1942/44; RT/FA; 22380 Dspl; 159.7 × 9.4 (523.5 × 30.9); T-E; 15; ex MISSION SANTA CRUZ 1963. Modified T.2 type.

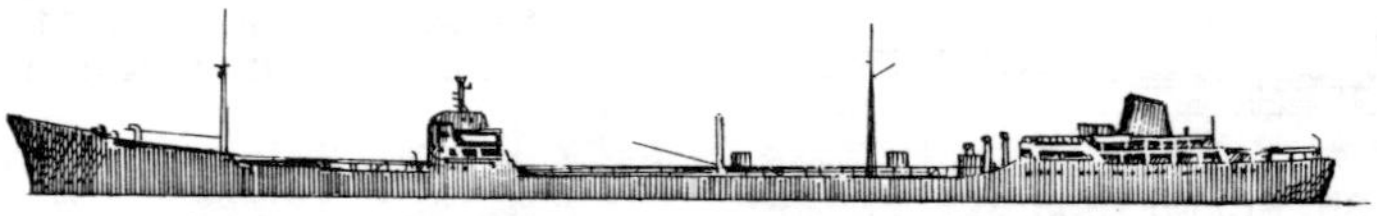

MKMF H123
40770 PALM B. Gr/Sw 1958; Tk; 21500; 212.86 × 11.24 (698.36 × 36.88); TSM; 16.75; ex RONAVILLE 1975; ex THORSVAAG 1965.

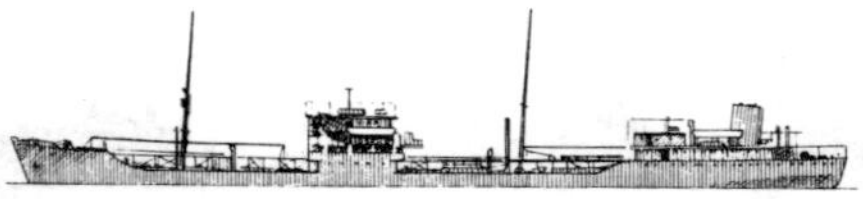

MKMF H123
● **40780 PERMINA 101.** Ia/Br 1952; Tk; 6200; 132.37 × 7.67 (434.28 × 25.16); M; 13; ex BURMAH EMERALD 1963. Sister: **40781 PERMINA 102** (Ia) ex RUBY STAR 1964; ex BURMAH STAR 1962.

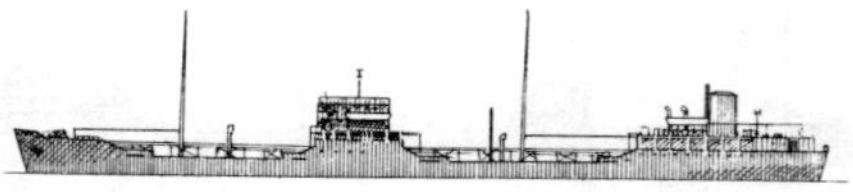

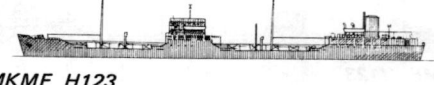

MKMF H123
40790 PALAU. It/Br 1951; Tk; 6100; 128.89 × 7.72 (422.87 × 25.33); M; 11; ex KERKENNAH 1971; ex MAKENI PALM 1967; ex BRITISH ROVER 1961.

MKMF H123
● **40800 PISTIS.** Gr/FRG 1955; Tk; 13600; 180.14 × 9.82 (591.01 × 32.22); M; 15; ex SOPHIA TRANSOCEANIC; ex BORGA 1974.

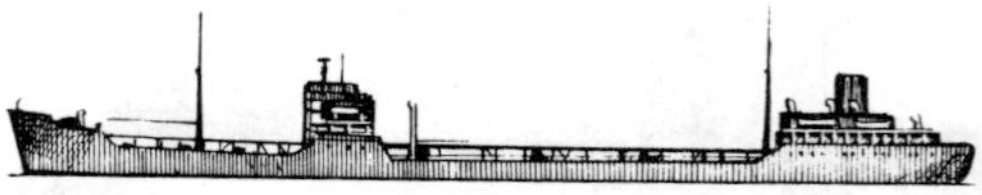

MKMF H123
⋆40810 DA QING No 14. RC/Sw 1945; Tk; 8300; 149.84 × 8.17 (491.6 × 26.8); M; 13; ex CHIEN SHE No 14; ex PIENINY 1961; ex TANKLAND 1957.

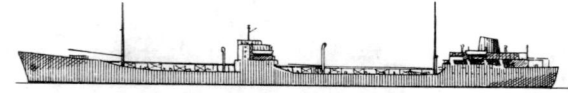

MKMF H123
⋆40820 DA QING No 39. RC/Sw 1958; Tk; 12200; 170.69 × 9.63 (560.01 × 31.59); M; 15; ex ANJA 1971; ex CARL GORTHON 1967.

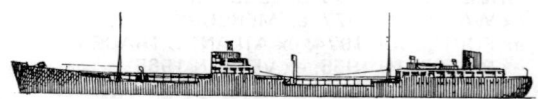

MKMF H123
40830 NIMERTIS. Li/Br 1952; Tk; 11200; 168.87 × 9.21 (554.04 × 30.22); M; 13.5. Sister: **40831 LADY DOROTHY** (Li).

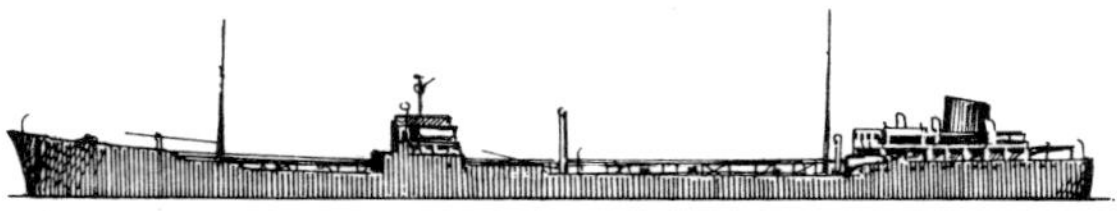

MKMF H123
40840 AL-BAKRY. Si/Ja 1957; Tk; 12600; 170.69 × 9.95 (560.01 × 32.64); M; 14.5; ex LINA CHRISTENSEN 1977; ex MOSTANK 1973. Sister; **40841 ANGELO SCINICARIELLO** (It) ex FRANCESCO CRISPI 1974; ex SKOTLAND 1962.

MKMF H123
40850 ANCAP SEXTO. Ur/FRG 1956; Tk; 2100; 91 57 × 4.52 (300.43 × 14.83); TSR & LPT; 12.

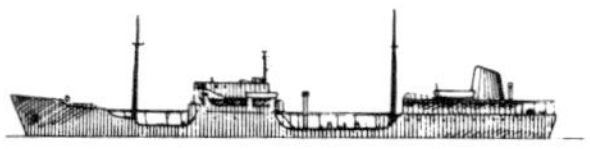

MKMF H123
40860 THITA OLIVA. Gr/Fr 1954; Tk; 2000; 87.53 × 5.2 (287.17 × 17.06); M; 13; ex AGHIA IRINI 1980; ex ANNA FANNY 1971; ex MARCEL MOUNIER 1970.

MKMF H123
40870 LUBNA. Pa/Br 1953; C; 1000; 67.49 × 4.2 (221.42 × 13.78); M; 10.5; ex LITTLE NOTA 1977; ex ARDGLEN 1977; ex KALPOGIORGOS 1977; ex MARIANTHI 1976; ex NENI 1973; ex ARDGLEN 1972.

MKMF H123
● **40880 ELPIS N.** Cy/Br 1956; C; 67.49 × 4.2 (220.44 × 13.78); M; 10.5; ex ELIAS G II; ex YEWMOUNT 1974.

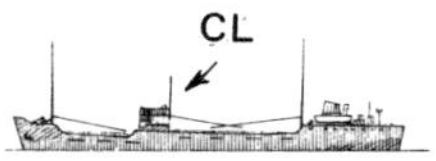

MKMF H123
40890 TEMPESTA. Cy/Br 1956; C; 770; 62.18 × 3.62 (204 × 11.88); M; —; ex CENTURITY 1976.

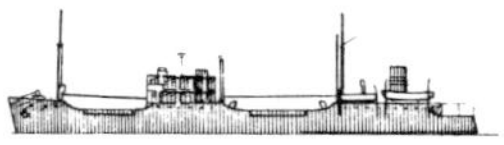

MKMF H123
40900 SINCERE ORIENT. Pa/Br 1937; C; 1000; 74.58 × 4.24 (244.69 × 13.91); TSM; 12; ex VOORLOPER 1968; ex SOFALA 1955.

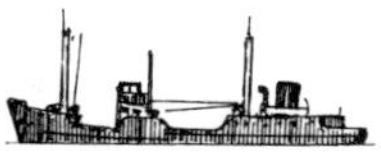

MKMF H123
40910 KIETA. Pp/Au 1948; C; 600; 55.73 × 3.4 (182.84 × 11.15); M; 9; ex EUGOWRA 1969. Similar: **40911 SULTABA** (Pi) ex HELEN J 1967; ex ENFIELD 1965 **40912 DONA LILY** (Pi) ex NUKUMANU 1975; ex WAIBEN 1966; ex ELMORE **40913 MALUKA** (Pp) ex EUROA 1965.

MKMF H123
40920 CAMPONALON. Sp/Sp 1969; Tk; 4600; 123.68 × 6.04 (405.77 × 19.82); M; 16. Sisters (Sp flag): **40921 CAMPODARRO 40922 CAMPOGENIL.**

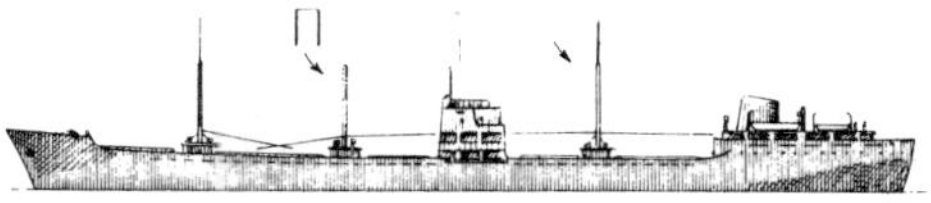

MKMF H13
● **40930 KOSMOS.** Pa/FRG 1953; C; 5800/8400; 144.48 × 7.88/8.56 (474.02 × 25.85/28.08); M; 12; ex DOBROTA ex MARIE 1972; ex SCHWANHEIM 1971.

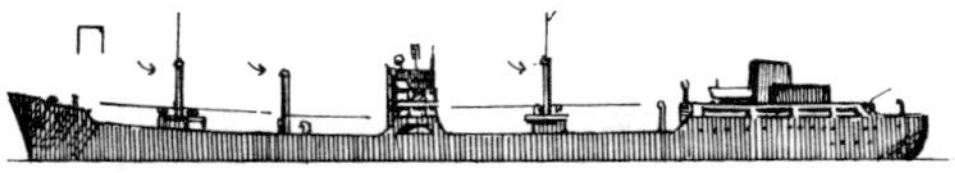

MKMF H13
40940 K.K.S. MUTHOO. Sg/Fr 1957; C; 6500/9000; 146.01 × 8.25/9.17 (479.04 × 27.07/30.09); M; 14.5; ex CAPTAIN D. GREGOS 1980; ex ELIAS XILAS 1973; ex ROLAND 1964.

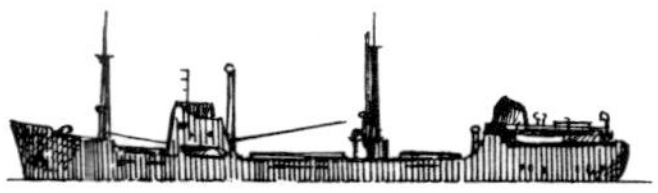

MKMF H13
● **40950 CAPETAN ALECOS MILONAS.** Gr/FRG 1957; C; 1800/2700; 97.77 × 6.76 (320.77 × 22.18); M; 12.5; ex BASTION 1972; ex SKAGATIND 1967; ex LIONEL 1964.

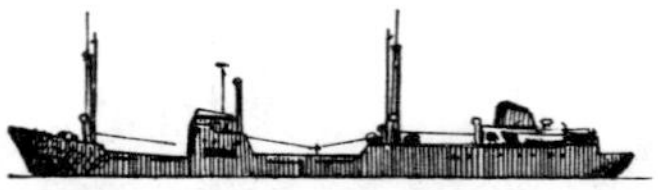

MKMF H13
40960 GIANNAKIS. Gr/FRG 1958; C; 2600; 97.77 × 6.87 (324.05 × 22.54); M; 12; ex KALLIOPE 1971; ex KARL LEONHARDT 1965.

MKMF H13
40970 KIMOLOS. Gr/Ne 1955; Cem; 1600; 85.37 × 4.92 (280.09 × 16.14); M; 11; ex HEKTOR; ex PARGASPORT 1975.

MKMF H13
40980 JUNHOURIYA. Pa/FRG 1952; C; 1000; 67.01 × 4.83 (219.85 × 15.85); M; 11; ex ERIKA HENDRIK FISSER 1975; ex CONCORDIA 1972; ex I.C. ERTEL 1971; ex HOCHMEISTER 1970; ex ERIKA HENDRIK FISSER 1958.

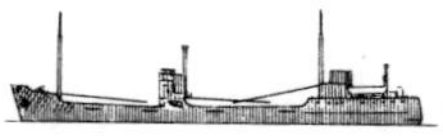

MKMF H13
40990 THE LADY SCOTIA. Me/Br 1952; C; 1200; 65.03 × 3.82 (213.35 × 12.53); M; 11; ex THE LADY GRANIA 1974.

MKMF H13
41000 PISANG RAJA. Ia/Ne 1955; C; 1100/1700; 78.57 × 4.22 (257.78 × 13.85); M; 12; ex SEA EXPRESS 1969; ex SVANEFJELL 1962.

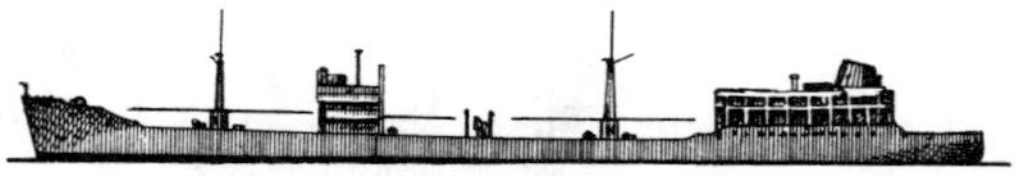

MKMF H13
41010 SWEDE SURPRISE. Gr/Br 1957; C; 10300; 152.89 × 9.74 (501.61 × 31.96); M; 13; ex TOMABI 1976; ex CANTON 1974; ex SANDRA N 1973; ex SALLY 1971; ex ROMANBY 1969. Similar: **41011 FORUM SPIRIT** (Gr) ex ELEFTHEROS: ex EUTHALIA 1974; ex RUSHPOOL 1970.

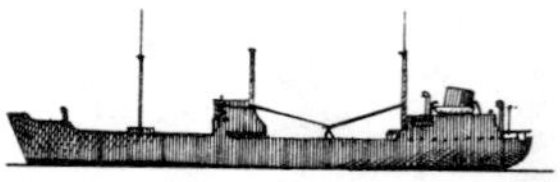

MKMF H13
41020 FEATHER. Cy/Fr 1953; C; 1300; 83.01 × 4.55 (272.34 × 14.93); M; 13; ex TAXIARCHIS 1980; ex AFRICAN EXPRESS 1976; ex ALIKI 1974; ex EVORA 1970; ex AGDAL 1968; ex PONT-AVEN 1965.

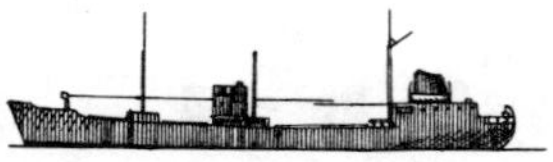

MKMF H13
41030 ORSOLA. It/Ne 1952; C/WT; 1300; 81.49 × 4.42 (267.36 × 14.5); M; 13; ex OUJDA.

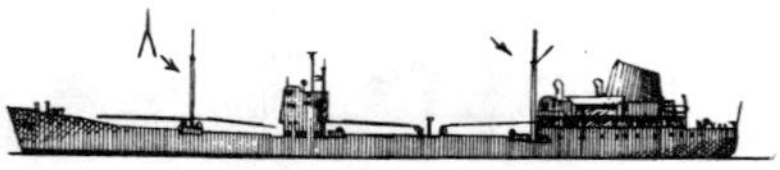

MKMF H13
41040 NAFSIKA L. Gr/Br 1956; O; 3600; 114.99 × 6.33 (377.26 × 20.73); M; —; ex LEON MAZZELLA 1973; ex ANDRE MASSET 1968.

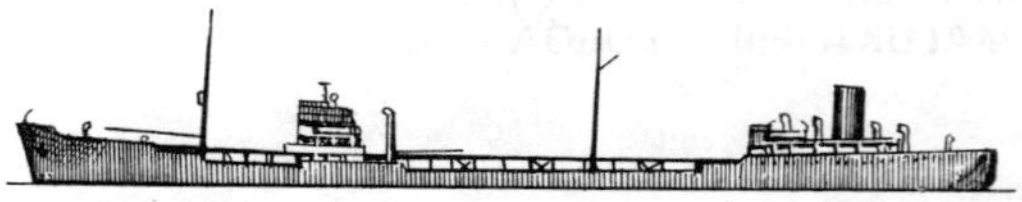

MKMF H13
⋆41050 DA QING No 13. RC/Ge 1937; Tk; 9900; 155.66 × 8.64 (510.7 × 28.35); M; 11.5; ex CHIEN SHE No 13; ex BRAMORA 1961; ex ERLING BROVIG 1946.

MKMF H13
41060 ANCAP SEXTO. Ur/FRG 1956; Tk; 2100; 81.57 × 4.52 (300.43 × 14.83); TSR & LPT; 12.

MKMF H13
41070 RAFFAELLA. Cy/Br 1949; C; 6800; 123.94 × 7.27 (406.69 × 23.85); M; 12.5; ex PHILIPPOPOULIS 1979; ex DOBRI VOINIKOV; ex ALDEBARAN 1970; ex NORDPOL 1964.

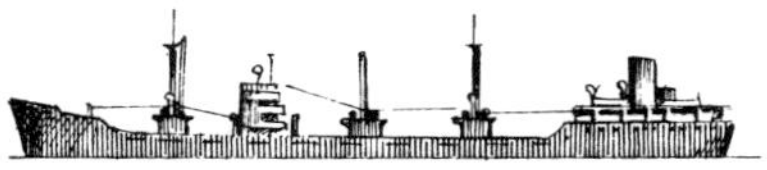

MKMF H13
41080 BUENA FORTUNA. Pa/No 1948; C; 2100/3300; 100.26 × —/5.54 (328.94 × —/18.19); T; 12; ex MITERA ASSIMINA 1971; ex PERSEUS 1969; ex BEMAR 19t9; ex FRAMEGGEN 1956.

MKMF H13
41090 ROBERT M. Br/Hong Kong 1970; Tk/TB; 1600; 85.04 × 4.44 (279 × 14.75); M; 11.75; ex CREE 1977.

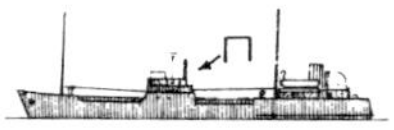

MKMF H2
41100 STAMATA II. Gr/Br 1937; C; 450; 56.95 × 3.34 (186.84 × 10.96); M; 9.5; ex THEODOROS 1976; ex ALLEN COMMODORE 1966; ex GOLDFINCH 1962.

MKMF H23
41110 MERINO. Au/Br 1949/69; FF; 550; 56 × 3.33 (187.01 × 10.93); M; 10; Converted from cargo 1969. May be altered in appearance.

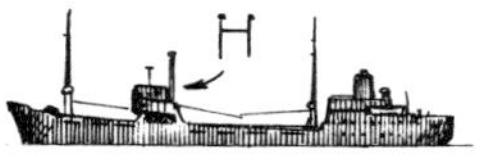

MKMF H3
41120 TELEMAQUE. Gr/FRG 1953; C; 1500; 71.91 × 5.74 (235.93 × 18.83); M; 12; ex POSEIDON 1974; ex ATID 1969; ex FERDINANDSTOR 1963.

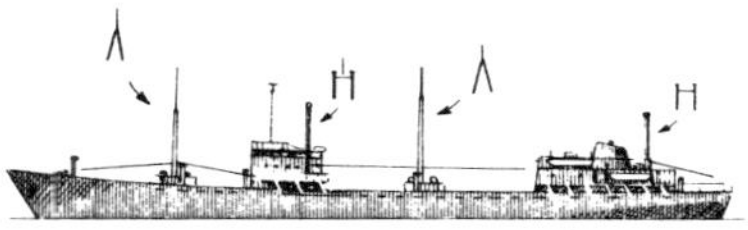

MKMFK H
● **41130 YANMAR.** Pa/It 1960; C; 2700/4200; 113.85 × 6.61/7.62 (373.52 × 21.69/25); M; —; ex YACU GUAGUA 1980; ex FURKA 1973; ex HELGOLAND 1972; ex MEDICINE HAT 1968; ex ANDERS ROGENAES 1964; ex CONCORDIA ANDERS 1962; ex ANDERS ROGENAES 1960. Sisters: **41131 EASTERN GRAND** (Pa) ex MEDITERRANEAN KLIF 1974; ex CORFU ISLAND 1972; ex SUSAA 1970; ex MARSTENEN 1965; ex BUKKEN 1962; ex MARSTENEN 1960 **41132 DIAKAN MASCOT** (Gr) ex ASKOT 1970. (may now be MKMF—which see).

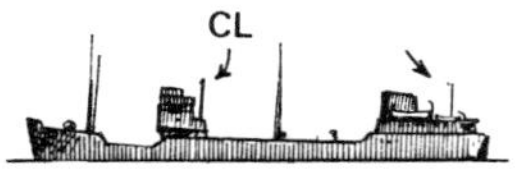

MKMFK H123
41140 AGIOS FANOURIOS V. Gr/Br 1952; C; 1500; 73.41 × 4.92 (240.85 × 16.14); M; 11.5; ex IVY 1976; ex ASTROLAND 1975; ex TOTLAND 1975.

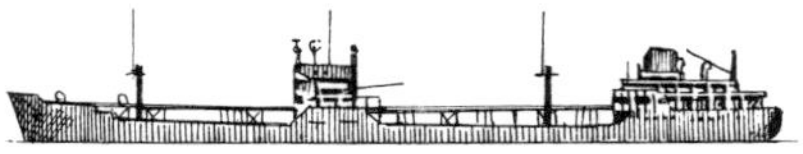

MKMFK H123
⋆41150 OLEG KOSHEVOY. Ru/Ru 1954; Tk; 3700; 123.5 × 4.31 (406.5 × 15.46); TSM; 10.75; Caspian Sea Service. Sisters (Ru flag); **⋆41151 ALEKSEY KRYLOV ⋆41152 IVAN ZEMNUKHOV ⋆41153 LYUBOV SHEVTSOVA ⋆41154 LIZA CHAYKINA ⋆41155 SERGEY TYULENIN ⋆41156 ULYANA GROMOVA.**

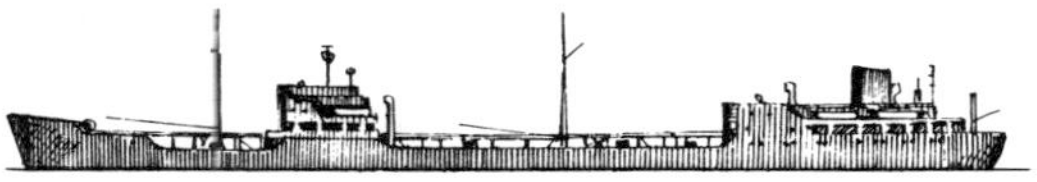

MKMFK H123
● **41160 ISLAS GEORGIAS.** Ar/Sw 1951; Tk; 9900; 157.46 × 8.36 (516.6 × 27.43); TSM; 16. Sister: **41161 ISLAS MALVINAS** (Ar).

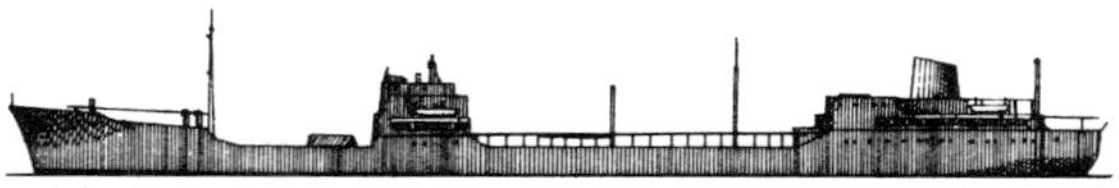

MKMFK H123
● **41170 TEXACO NORTH DAKOTA.** US/US 1953; Tk; 12800; 172.22 × 10.02 (565.03 × 32.87); T; 18.5; ex NORTH DAKOTA 1960.

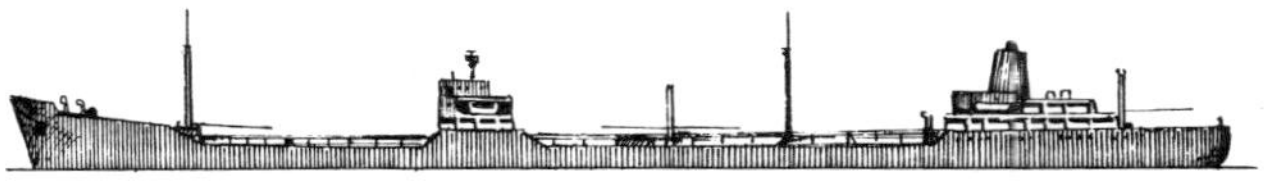

MKMFK H123
41180 TEXACO KENTUCKY. Pa/US 1949; Tk; 17900; 190.38 × 10.55 (624.61 × 34.61); T; 15.75; ex KENTUCKY 1960. Sisters (Pa flag): **41181 TEXACO OHIO** ex OHIO 1961 **41182 TEXACO PENNSYLVANIA** ex PENNSYLVANIA 1960 **41183 TEXACO TEXAS** ex TEXAS 1960.

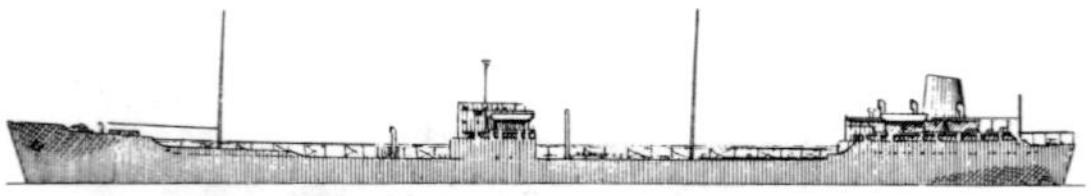

MKMFK H123
41190 CHRISTIANA TRANSOCEANIC. Gr/Br 1956; Tk; 11600; 169.58 × 9.4 (556.36 × 30.84); M; 14.5; ex HADA 1974.

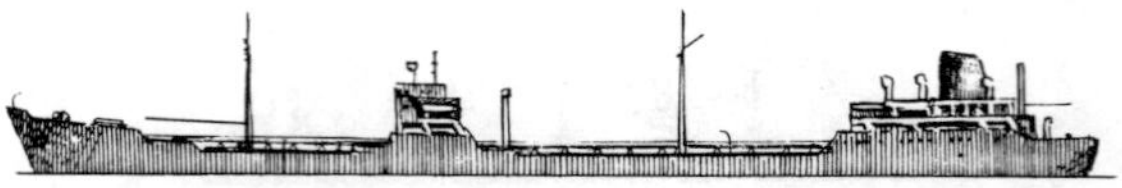

MKMFK H123
41200 WAVE. Li/Sp 1958; Tk; 12700; 172.5 × 9.48 (568.94 × 31.1); M; 14; ex ALINTA 1976; ex ESCOMBRERAS 1973. Possible Sister: **41201 GOGO RAHN** (Pa) ex ALBUERA.

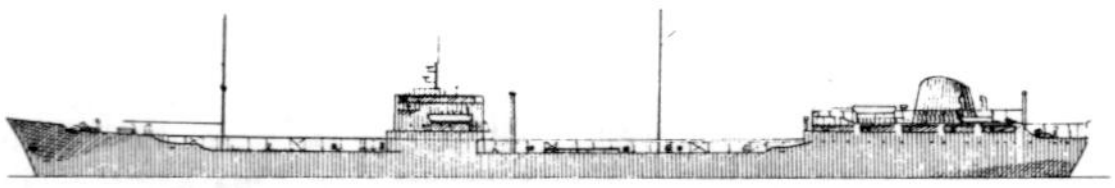

MKMFK H123
41210 ELPIS. Pa/It 1958; Tk; 12200; 169.98 × 9.69 (557.68 × 31.79); M; 15.5; ex ELIAS 1979; ex ANCO ELIAS 1978; ex CARBO COUGAR 1974; ex ANCO GUNVOR 1972; ex SEA SPRING 1972; ex ANCO SPRING 1972; ex DODONA 1964.

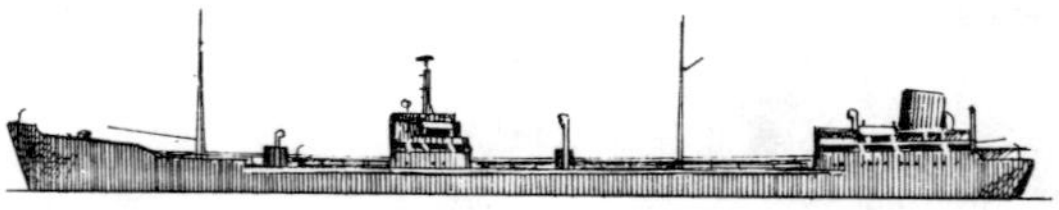

MKMFK H123
41220 YANGOS. Gr/Sw 1957; Tk; 12700; 160.81 × 9.64 (527.59 × 31.63); M; 15.5; ex STOLT YANGOS; ex YANGOS 1972; ex RAILA 1969.

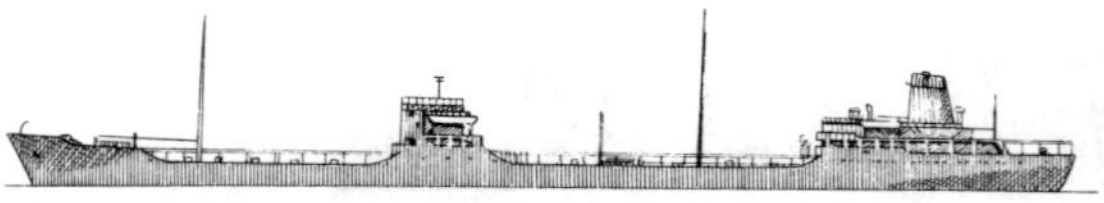

MKMFK H123
41230 DYNAMIC SAILOR. Gr/Br 1958; Tk; 11500; 169.6 × 9.55 (556.43 × 31.33); T; 14.5; ex HUMILARIA 1973.

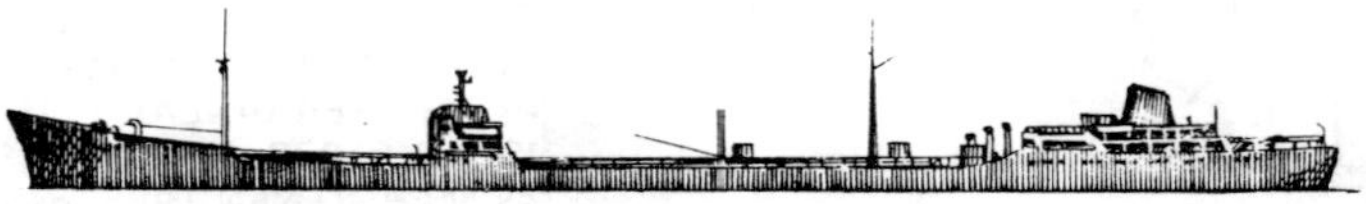

MKMFK H123
41240 PALM B. Gr/Sw 1958; Tk; 21500; 212.86 × 11.24 (698.36 × 36.88); TSM; 16.75; ex RONAVILLE 1975; ex THORSVAAG 1965.

MKMFK H123
41250 SAVVAS. Gr/No 1959; Tk; 20500; 200.95 × 10.9 (659.28 × 35.76); M; 16.5; ex KONGSVANG 1974.

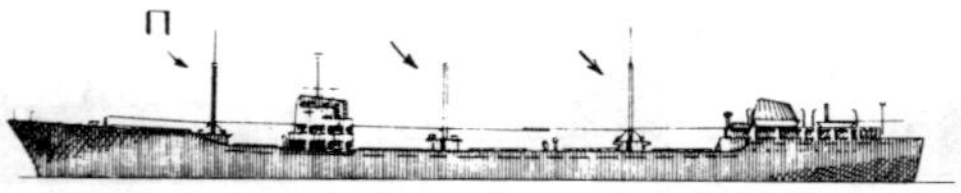

MKMFK H13
● **41260 APJ AKASH.** In/FRG 1954; C; 6300; 144.48 × 7.82 (474.02 × 25.66); M; 13.5; ex HEINRICH HONOLD 1960. Sister: **41261 APJ ANJLI** (In) ex HANS HONOLD 1960.

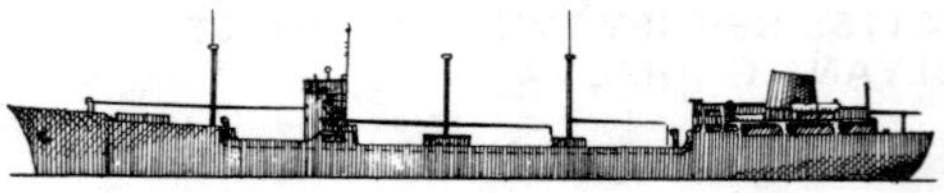

MKMFK H13
41270 TAI SHOU. Tw/Fr 1957; C; 9000; 144.84 × 9.67 (475.2 × 31.73); M; 15; ex ASTWI 1966.

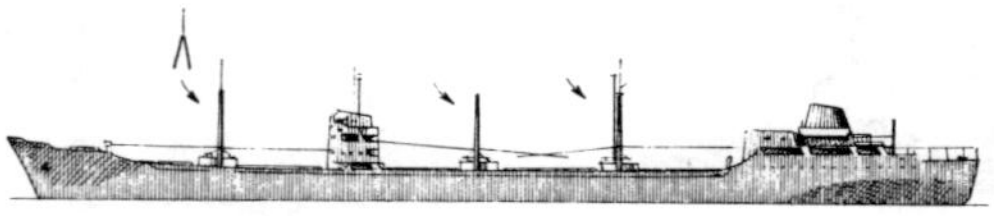

MKMFK H13
41280 ELEISTRIA VIII. Gr/Ys 1959; C; 9200; 153.14 × 9.11 (502.43 × 29.89); M; 13; ex TARIQ 1977; ex SHUGUANG 1965; ex MATANG 1964.

MKMFK H13
41290 EASTERN MERCHANT. Pa/Sw 1956; C; 9000; 148.27 × 9.21 (486.45 × 30.22); M; 14; ex OHDAE 1980; ex INGWI 1967. Similar: **41291 STATE OF KERALA** (In) ex BERNHARD 1962 **41292 OMALOS** (Gr) ex LENDAS 1977; ex CAMINGOY 1974; ex ANTONIO 1973; ex BELLULLY 1959 **41293 TONG POH** (Sg) ex MARIANNE 1973; ex SUNLEAF 1970; ex SUNVARD 1966.

MKMKF H
41300 MAGED. Ly/Hu 1960; C; 1200; 81.92 × 3.09 (268.88 × 10.14); TSM; 11; ex CHRISTINA 1975; ex BADACSONY 1970. Sisters: **41301 AREF** (Ly) ex VITTORIA 1975; ex CSEFEL 1970 **41302 SUNNY L** (Pa) ex ANNAMINA K 1980; ex CARPENTER 1977; ex NINGPO VIOLET 1975; ex DUNAUJVAROS 1974 **41303 BUILDER** (Sg) ex NINGPO LILAC 1975; ex BORSOD 1974 **41304 DECORATOR** (Sg) ex NINGPO ORCHID 1975; ex SZEGED 1974.

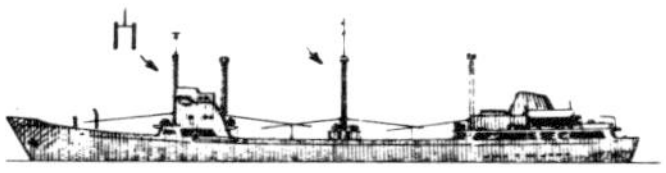

MKMKF H
★41310 ORADEA. Rm/Rm 1963; C; 2100/3100; 100.62 × 5.5/6.59 (330.12 × 18.04/21.62); M; 12.5. Sisters (Rm flag): **★41311 CRAIOVA ★41312 TIMISOARA ★41313 BRASOV ★41313 DEVA ★41315 IASI ★41316 VASLUI ★41317 SIBIU ★41318 BACAU ★41319 TIRGOVISTE ★41320 TIRGU MURES** (RC flag): **★41321 CHANG AN ★41322 HONG QI 150 ★41323 HONG QI 151 ★41324 HONG QI 152 ★41325 HONG QI 153 ★41326 HUAI AN ★41327 ILIA ★41328 XIN AN.**

MKMKF H1
41340 KATERINA K. Cy/Sw 1953; C; 1100; 83.01 × 5.77 (272.34 × 18.93); M; 11.5; ex MAR DEL SUD 1974; ex MEDOV MOROCCO 1974; ex MOROCCO 1970; ex KONG INGE 1967.

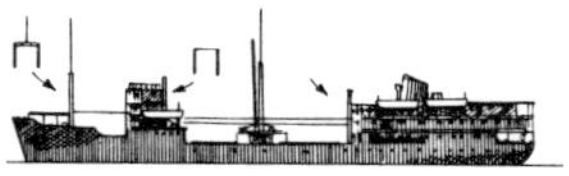

MKMKF H1
● **41350 RAJAH BROOKE.** Sg/Br 1948; PC; 2300; 83.06 × 4.89 (272.51 × 16.04); TSM; 13.

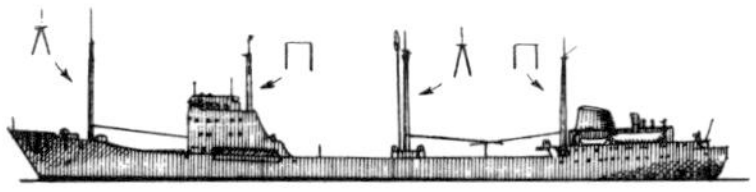

MKMKF H1
41360 MAYA I. Gu/FRG 1958; C; 2600/4000; 114.81 × 6.71/7.69 (376.67 × 22.01/25.23); D-E; 14.5; ex MEDI SEA 1978; ex TIPU 1978; ex MEDI SEA 1977; ex MILDBURG 1971; ex ARCHSUM 1970. Sister: **41361 COBAN** (Gu) ex NORBURG; ex MEDI STAR 1976; ex NORBURG 1971; ex TINNUM 1970.

MKMKF H1
41370 FODELE II. Cy/Br 1957; B; 7700; 144.89 × 7.89 (475.36 × 25.89); M; 13; ex SAN ROBERTO 1974; ex EAST BREEZE 1967; ex HUDSON POINT 1966.

MKMKF H12
41380 GEORGIOS A. Gr/Br 1947; C; 1000; 68.59 × 4.55 (225.03 × 14.93); M; 10.5; ex CICILIANA 1972; ex SEAFORD 1971.

MKMKF H123
41390 SEA BREEZE. Li/No 1961; Tk; 12500; 169.73 × 9.68 (556.86 × 31.76); M; 15; ex VERMONT 1977; ex JONWI 1962; may be spelt **SEABREEZE.** Sister: **41391 FOLIA** (Li) ex STOLT FILIA 1980; ex STOLT ARGOBAY; ex STOLT HAWK 1973; ex OSTHAV 1968.

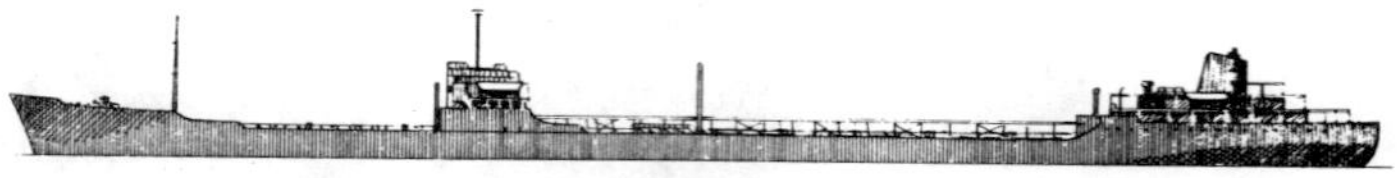

MKMKF H123
41400 GASSI-TOUIL. Ag/Ja 1961; Tk; 25800; 216.42 × 11.6 (710.04 × 38.06); T; 16.75; ex PHILIPPINE SEA 1973.

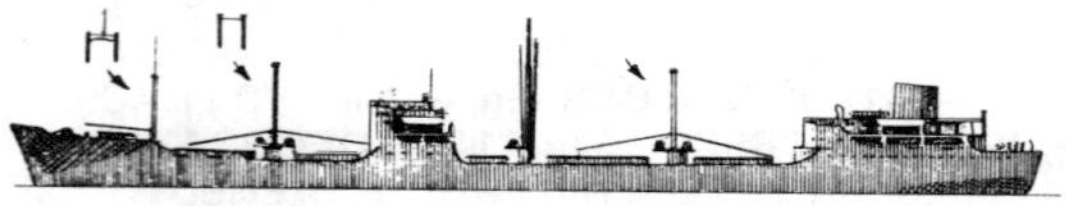

MKMKF H123
★**41410 HONG QI 105.** RC/Sw 1953/61; C; 10400; 162.57 × 8.9 (533.37 × 59.2); M; 14.5; ex NEW NORTH SEA 1975; ex CALYPSO 1972; ex BANNERVALE 1970; ex OCEAN CLIPPER 1960; Converted from tanker 1960.

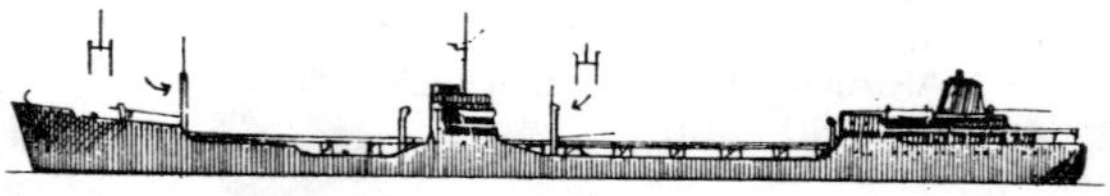

MKMKF H123
41420 VOLUNTAS. It/Sw 1957; Tk; 12400; 170.72 × 9.63 (560.11 × 31.59); M; 14; ex PEPITA 1977. Similar: **41421 STOLT MARGARETA** (Gr) ex ANNIKEN 1974; ex MARGARITA 1961 **41422 EASTERN MARINER** (Tw) **41423 ALEXANDROS** (Cy) ex WILANA 1969 **41424 EGNAZIA** (It) ex POINT LACRE 1973.

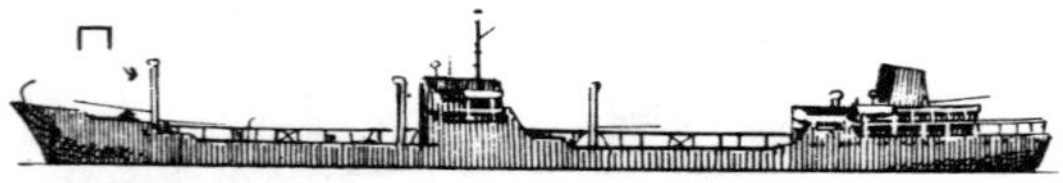

MKMKF H123
41430 POLYVOS. Gr/No 1955; Tk; 10400; 162.29 × 9.31 (532.45 × 30.55); M; 14.5; ex VARVARA 1970. Similar: **41431 CAMELLIA B** (Gr) ex ROSE B; ex VENITA 1974.

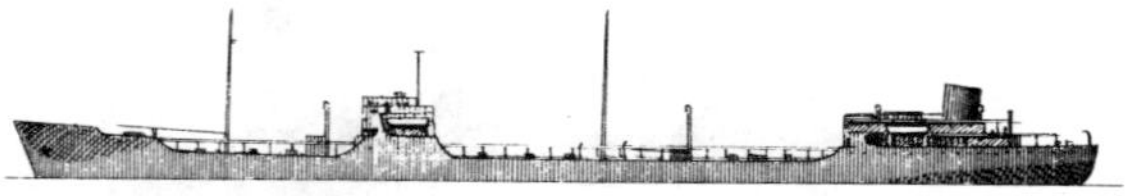

MKMKF H123
● **41440 VALNY.** Pa/Sw 1953; Tk; 11700; 170.49 × 9.26 (559.35 × 30.38); M; 13.5; ex VANESSA 1963.

MKMKF H123
41450 PALAU. It/Br 1951; Tk; 6100; 128.89 × 7.72 (422.87 × 25.33); M; 11; ex KERKENNAH 1971; ex MAKENI PALM 1967; ex BRITISH ROVER 1961.

MKMKF H123
41460 TALLULAH. US/US 1943; Tk/FA; 22400 Dspl.; 159.6 × 9.2 (523.5 × 30); T-E; 15; ex VALLEY FORGE: **'T-2'** type. **'Suamico'** class Sisters (US flag): **41461 MILLICOMA** ex CONASTOGA; ex KINGS MOUNTAIN **41462 SAUGATUCK** ex NEWTON **41463 SCHUYLKILL** ex LOUISBERG.

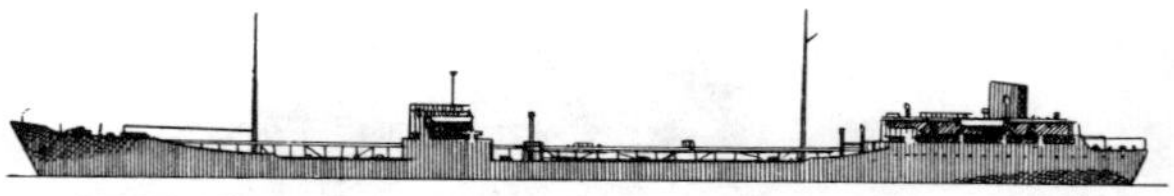

MKMKF H123
● **41470 PISTIS.** Gr/FRG 1955; Tk; 13600; 180.14 × 9.82 (591.01 × 32.22); M; 15; ex SOPHIA TRANSOCEANIC; ex BORGA 1974.

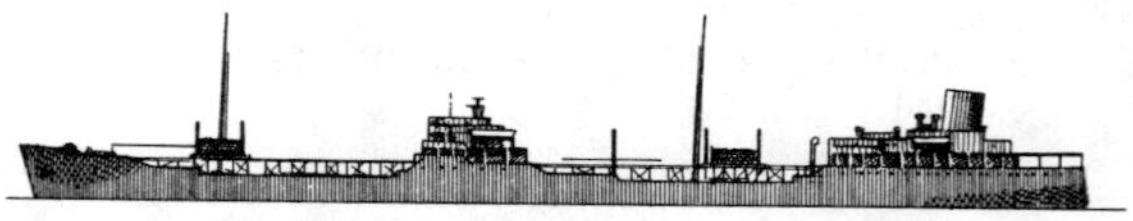

MKMKF H123
41480 HALIA Br/Br 1958; Tk; 11900; 169.4 × 9.35 (555.77 × 30.68); T; 14.5; Fenders on deck for lightening operations. Similar: **41481 PETROLA 11** (Gr) ex PETROLA XI 1976; ex KENIA 1973 **41482 PETROLA 17** (Gr) ex PETROLA XVII 1976; ex PETROLA X 1975; ex KREBSIA 1973 **41483 KYLIX** (Ne).

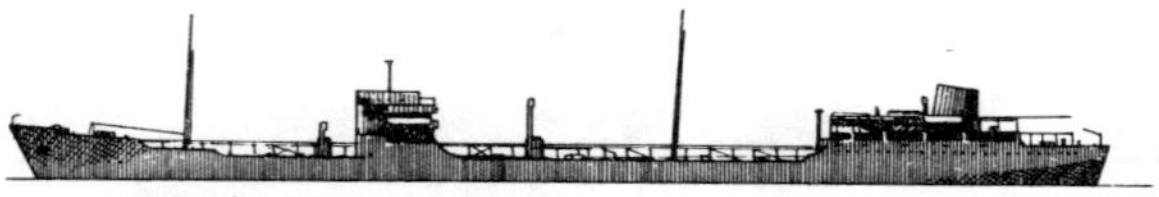

MKMKF H123
41490 CAPO MADRE; It/Sw 1953; Tk; 11900; 173.01 × 9.65 (567.62 × 31.66); M; 14.5; ex NORSE LION 1968.

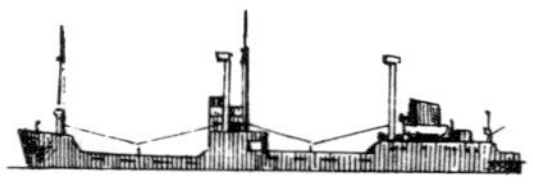

MKMKF H123
41500 SAN DENIS; Gr/Br 1952; C; 1700; 80.78 × 5.23 (265.03 × 17.16); M; 10; ex MARWICK HEAD 1969.

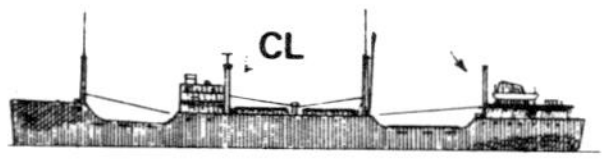

MKMKF H123
● **41510 AKRA AKTION;** Gr/Ne 1957/63; C; 2300; 91.42 × 6.25 (299.93 × 20.51); M; 12.5; ex STEVEN 1969; Lengthened in 1963.

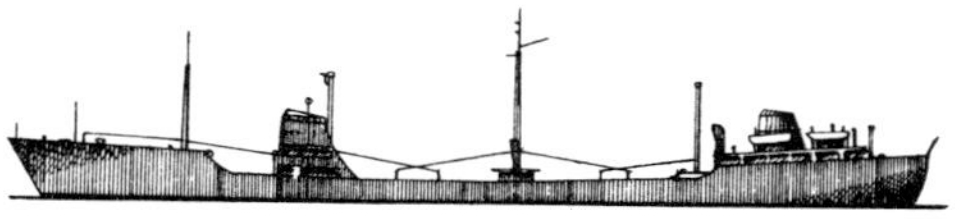

MKMKF H13
41520 AGIOS DIMITROS; Gr/FRG 1955; C; 8500; 146.41 × 9.02 (480.35 × 29.59); M; 14; ex TONY 1977; ex CLEAKI 1972; ex BISCHOFSTOR 1966; May be spelt **AGIOS DEMETRIOS.**

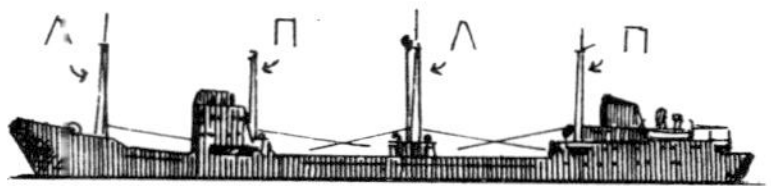

MKMKF H13
41530 MAYA I; Gu/FRG 1958; C; 2600/4000; 114.81 × 671/7.69 (376.67 × 22.01/25.23); D-E; 14.5; ex MEDI SEA 1978; ex TIPU 1978; ex MEDI SEA 1977; ex MILDBURG 1971; ex ARCHSUM 1970. Sister: **41531 COBAN** (Gu) ex NORBURG; ex MEDI STAR 1976; ex NORBURG 1971; ex TINNUM 1970.

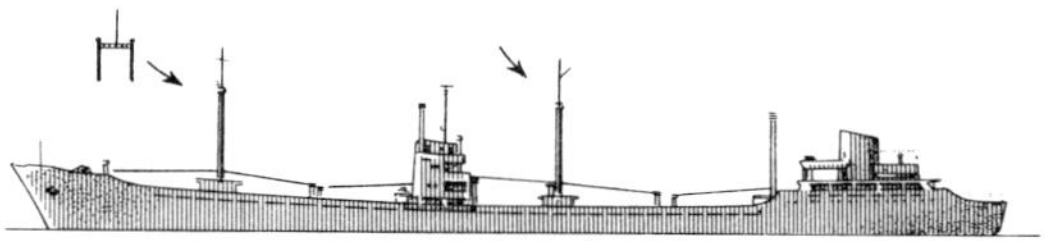

MKMKF H13
41540 IVORY ISLANDS; Pa/FRG 1959; C; 9700; 157.51 × 9.02 (516.77 × 29.59); M; 13.5; ex LINZERTOR 1970.

MKMKFK H1
41550 GEOPOTES VI; Ne/Ne 1963; D; 5100; 101.72 × 7.54; (333.73 × 24.74); TSM; 12.5.

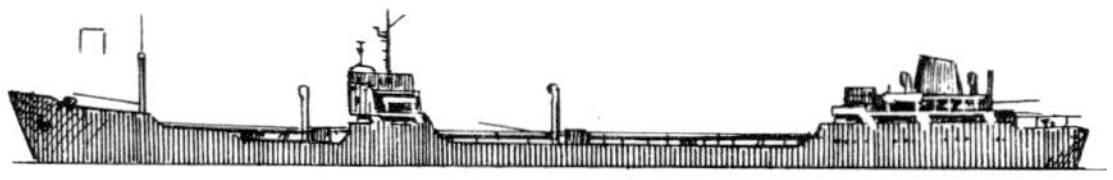

MKMKFK H123
41560 CAMELLIA B; Gr/Sw 1958; Tk; 12000; 169.73 × 9.37 (556.86 × 30.74); M; 14; ex ROSE B 1977; ex VENITA 1974.

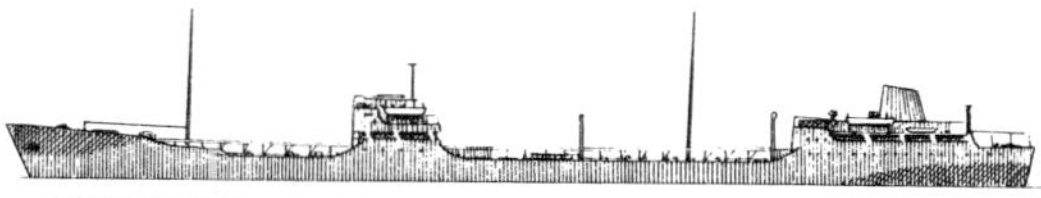

MKMKFK H123
● **41570 STAR.** Li/No 1956; Tk; 10300; 161.47 × 9.27 (529.76 × 30.41); M; 15; ex AKTI 1976; ex TEXACO EUROPE 1969; ex EUROPE 1959.

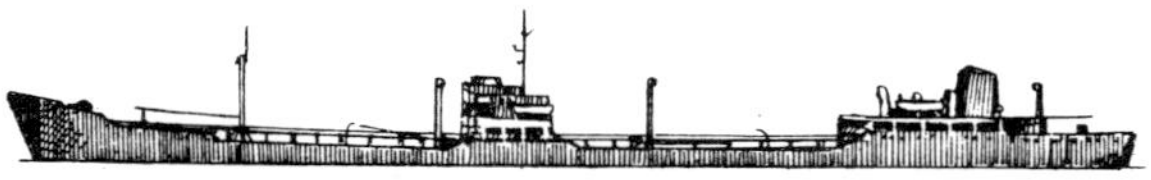

MKMKFK H13
● **41580 ALDERAMINE;** It/It 1954; Tk; 12600; 172.24 × 9.6 (565.1 × 31.5); M; 15. Similar: **41581 ANDROMEDA** (It) **41582 BREZZA** (It) **41583 AURORA** (Cy) ex ATHENIAN AURORA 1980; ex ASTRAL 1975; ex AURORA 1974.

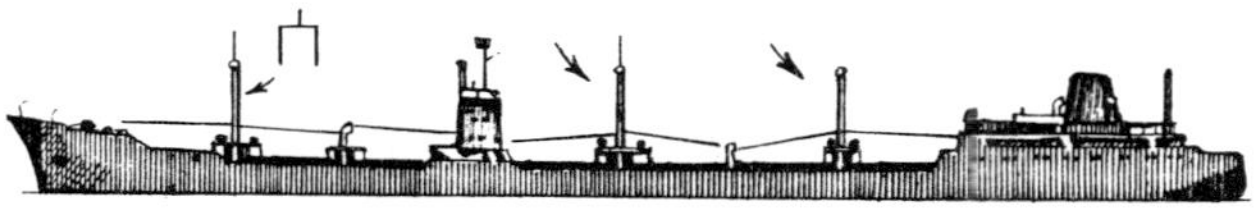

MKMKFK H13
● **41590 ARCHANGELOS;** Gr/Ys 1963; B; 15900; 191.47 × 10.86 (621.18 × 35.63); M; 16; ex ARCHANGEL 1968; ex ARCHANGELOS 1963. Sisters: **41591 ALFITO** (Gr) ex MEANDROS 1980 **41592 THEOFANO LIVANOS** (Gr) Similar: ⋆**41593 HUA TAI** (RC) ex ATLANTIC CHAMPION 1978 **41594 ATLANTIC EAGLE** (Gr) **41695 ATLANTIC STAR** (Gr) **41596 INTERFELICITY** (Gr) ex IAMATIKOS 1980; ex SOUTHERN BREEZE 1973; ex ATLANTIC BREEZE 1972 **41597 EVROS** (Gr) **41598 NESTOS** (Li) **41599 MATHILDE** (Pa) ex THERMOPYLAI; ex KAPETANISSA 1976; ex KALLIOPI PATERAS 1972.

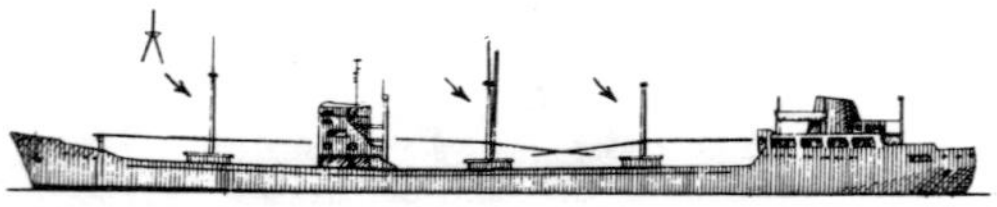

MKMKFK H13
⋆**41610 WU XING;** RC/Ys 1959; C; 7000/9200; 153.09 × 8.19/9.01 (502.26 × 26.87/29.56); M; 15; ex CHOPIN 1979. Sister: ⋆**41611 ZAMENHOF** (Pd).

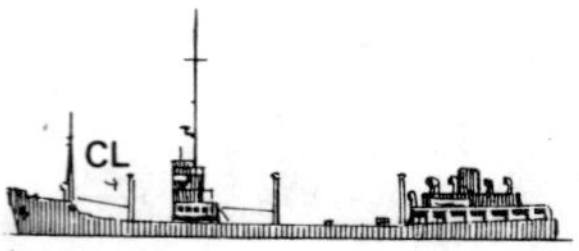

$MKMK_2F$ H123
41620 LSCO PIONEER; Pi/Ja 1955; Tk; 2400; 85.35 × 5.18 (280.02 × 16.99); TSM; 8; ex CALTEX LUZON 1969; ex CALTEX MEDAN 1959. **41621 ZIWAY HAIQ** (Et) ex CHEVRON GORINCHEM 1969; ex CALTEX GORINCHEM 1968; ex CALTEX PADANG 1959 **41622 WITSHUTTLE** i) ex ANNA K 1979; ex CHEVRON DELFZIJL 1977; ex CALTEX DELFZIJL 1968; ex CALTEX SIAK 1959.

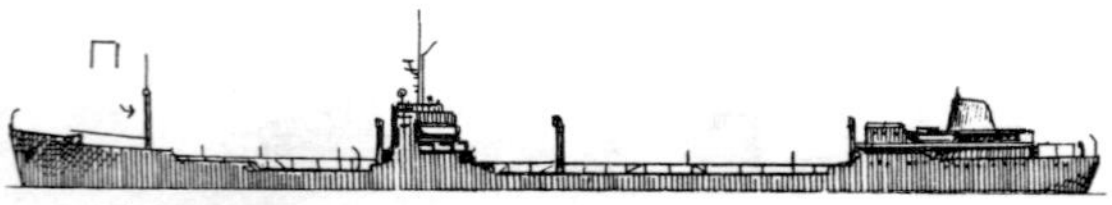

$MKMK_2F$ H123
⋆**41630 PRAHOVA;** Rm/Sw 1957; Tk; 12400; 173.41 × 9.35 (568.93

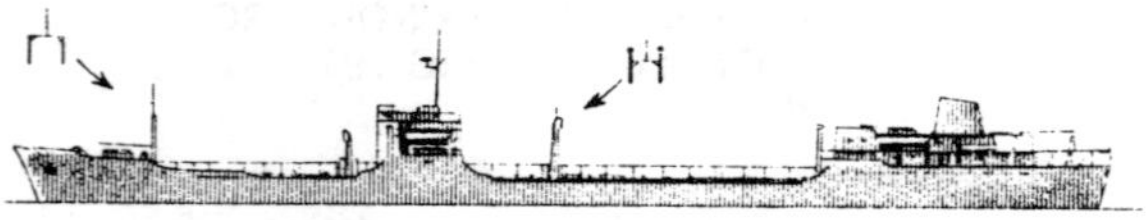

$MKMK_2F$ H123
41640 VASSILIS; Gr/Sw 1958; Tk; 12400; 170.72 × 9.63 (560.1 × 31.59); M; 15; ex LIFJORD 1972; ex ACINA 1961.

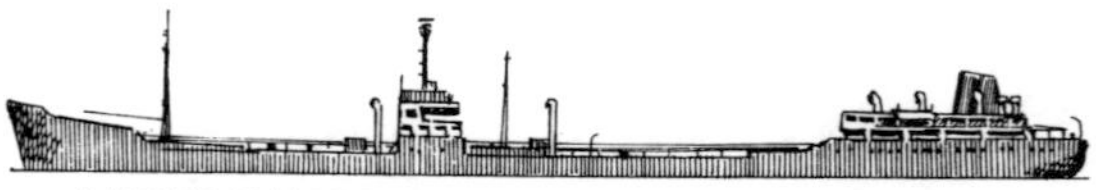

$MKMK_2F$ H123
41650 HARRIET; Pa/Be 1958; Tk; 13500; 170.69 × 9.65 (560.01 × 31.66); M; 14; ex NAT CREST I 1980; ex CALTEX CAPE TOWN 1978; ex WAIKIWI PIONEER 1973; ex ELEFTHEROUPOLS 1972.

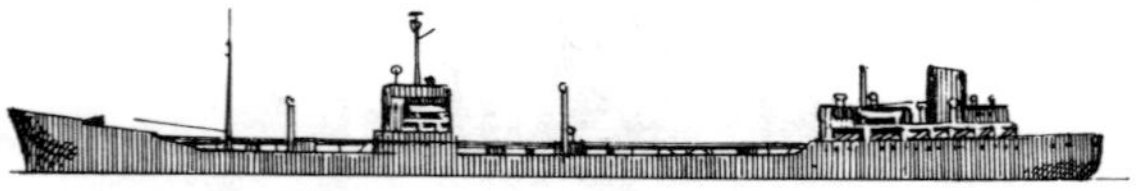

$MKMK_2F$ H123
41660 HALCYON ISLE; Sg/Ne 1956; Tk; 12500; 169.48 × 9.28 (556.04 × 30.45); M; 14.5; ex ALICE 1973; ex IONIC QUEEN 1972; ex KONINGSWAARD 1971.

$MKMK_2F$ H2
41670 POLYTIMI ANDREADIS; Gr/US-Gr 1943/63; B; 14400; 172,37 × 10.1 (565.52 × 33.14); T-E; —; ex FORT NIAGARA 1948; Lengthened and converted from T-2 tanker 1963.

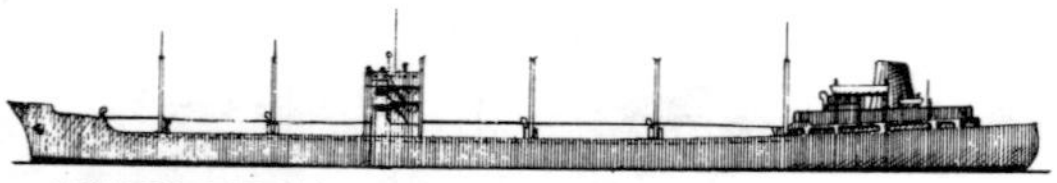

$MKMK_3MF$ H1
41680 CHI TAI; Pa/Ja 1958; B; 12300; 162.52 × 9.48 (533.2 × 31.1); M; 14; ex PAO SHIN 1975; ex ENYO MARU 1971.

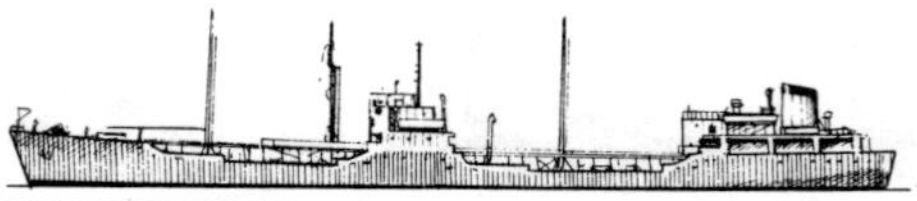

MKMKMF H123
41690 MUNSTERLAND; FRG/It 1947/60; RT/FA; 6200; 141 × 7.8 (461 × 25.8); M; 12.5; ex ANTONIO ZOTTI 1960; Converted from a tanker 1960.

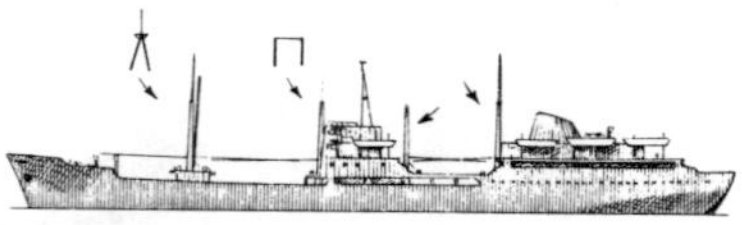

MKMKMF H13
41700 EASTERN RISE; Pa/Fr 1954; F/C; 3700/4600; 115.3 × —/6.12 (378.28 × —/20.54); M; 12.5; ex GALLIENI 1973.

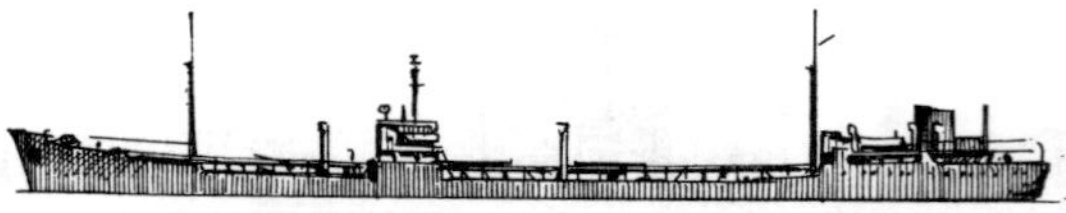

MKMKMFK H123
41710 BAFFIN TRANSPORT; Ca/Br 1955; Tk; 11700; 161.25 × 9.08 (529.04 × 29.79); M; 13; ex CABATERN 1973; ex EUROCHEMIST 1970; ex FOSNA 1967.

MKMKMKFK H13
41720 TABOU; Gr/It 1959; C; 5700/7400; 134.25 × 7.08/8.5 (440.25 × 23.23/27.89); M; 14.5; ex SAINT MARC 1973.

MKMKMFK H13
● **41730 AGIOS NICOLAOS IV;** Pa/FRG 1961; C; 6000; 129.72 × 8.1 (425.59 × 26.57); M; 15; ex SUNNY DANIELLE: ex DAFRA MERCHANT 1976; ex RHEIN 1976.

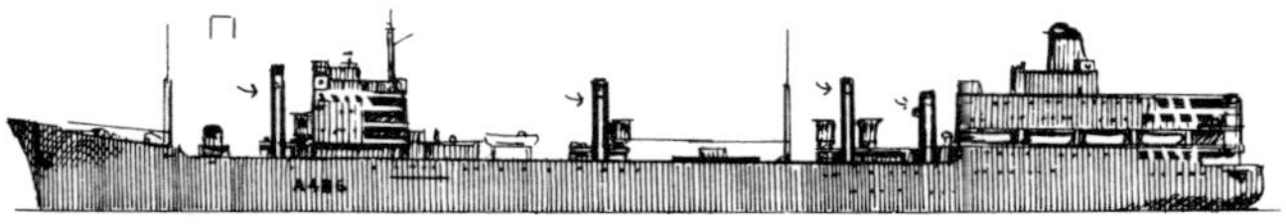

$MKMKMK_2F$ H13

41740 REGENT; Br/Br 1967; Rst/FA; 18000; 195.1 × 8 (640 × 26.1); T; —. Sister: **41741 RESOURCE** (Br).

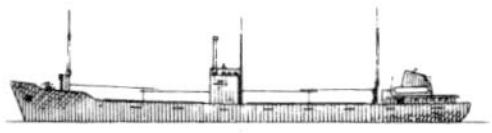

MKM_2F H1

● **41750 TANJA HOLWERDA;** Ne/Ne 1953; C; 500/1000; 73.49 × 3.58/4.32 (241.71 × 11.75/14.17); M; 12.5; ex KROONBORG 1973.

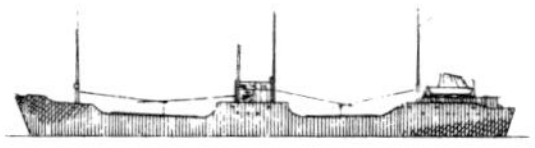

MKM_2F H123

41760 CHRISTINE I; Pa/Ne 1957; C; 1600; 79.43 × 5 (260.6 × 16.4); M; 11; ex BALTICBORG. Sister: **41761 ARGYRO M** (Gr) ex BOTHNIABORG 1980.

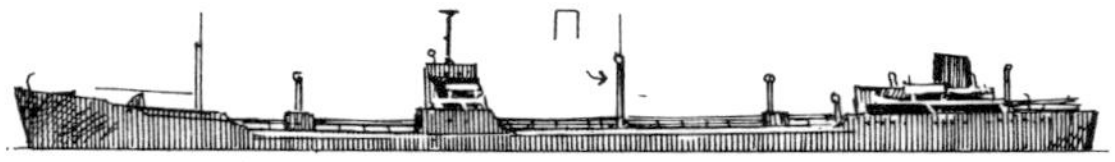

MKM_2KFK H123

41770 CHEMICAL CHALLENGER; Li/Sw 1960; Tk; 12700; 170.03 × 9.7 (557.84 × 31.82); M; 15; ex KAUPANGER 1975.

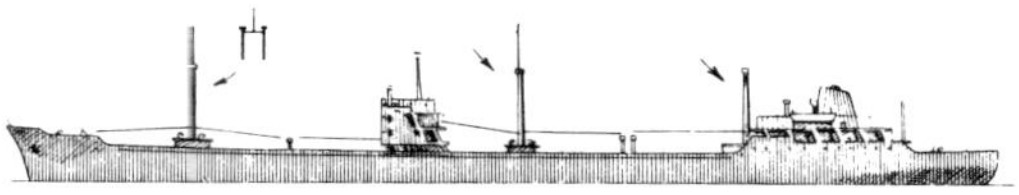

MKM_2KFK H13

● **41780 EIRINI L;** Gr/Ja 1956; C; 10400; 158.2 × 9.4 (519.03 × 38.84); T; 16.5.

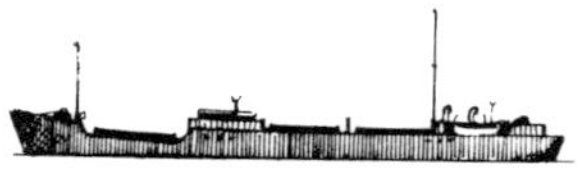

M_2 H12

41790 BLACKWELL POINT; Pa/Br 1951; C; 1800; 82.45 × 5.2 (270.5 × 17.06); M; 11; ex BLACKWALL POINT. Sisters: **41791 GRAINVILLE** (lh) ex BATTERSEA 1980 **41792 CHRISTOFOROS** (Gr) ex EPIC 1976; ex BIRLING 1975; ex THOMAS HARDIE 1968 **41793 GRANITT** (No) ex HORSHAM 1973; ex MURDOCH 1966 **41794 LINERA** (Br) ex LA MOLINERA 1972; ex SANDERSTEAD 1967; ex SAMUEL CLEGG 1967 **41795 FABIO SAVERIO** (It) (deepened 1970); ex CAPITAN ALBERTO 1975; ex BRIGHTLING 1970; ex FALCONER BIRKS 1970 **41796 TITIKA** (Gr) ex KEYNES 1975; ex ACCUM 1967.

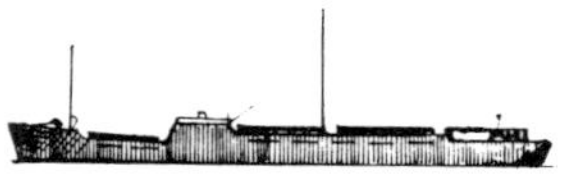

M_2 H12

● **41800 TARRING;** Br/Br 1958; C; 1900; 83.88 × 5.2 (275.2 × 17.09); M; —; ex LAMBETH 1970. Sisters: **41801 TSIMENTION** (Gr) ex KINGSTON 1971 **41802 VASSILIS IV** (Gr) ex MARO; ex CHRIS 1974; ex ACYRO 1972; ex CROYDON 1971 **41803 WORTHY** (Cy) ex WORTHING 1977; ex DULWICH 1970 **41804 ELEISTRIA II** (Gr) ex FULHAM IX 1970.

M_2 H3

41810 BARRIER; Br/Br 1958; Tk; 500; 52.35 × 2.68 (171.75 × 8.79); M; 9.5; ex ULCO 1972.

M_2CFC H

41820 GEOPOTES IX; Ne/Ne 1966; D; 7800; 126.02 × 6.8 (513.45 × 22.31); TSM; 12.5.

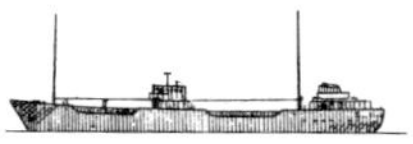

M_2F H

41830 WESTRIDGE; Br/Ne 1951; C; 450; 60.13 × 3.08 (197.28 × 10.1); M; 10; ex ARNOUDSPOLDER 1965.

M_2F H

● **41840 AGIA IRINI I;** Cy/FRG 1952; C; 600; 65.46 × 3.55 (214.76 × 11.64); M; 12; ex AGIA IRENE; ex LURE 1974; ex FRANCES M 1971; ex LURE 1970; ex KANAVELIC 1969; ex ANGLIA 1964; ex JOACHIM HENDRIK FISSER 1959.

M_2F H
41850 ANIS III; Pa/Ne 1948; C; 450; 56.6 × 3.32 (185.7 × 10.9); M; 10; ex SEABREEZE; ex DITA SMITS 1962; ex WESTER-EEMS 1959.

M_2F H
41860 STAR OF MEDINA; Si/Ne 1940; C; 400; 57.3 × 2.82 (188.02 × 9.25); M; 8; ex MOIRA 1966; ex GREENFINCH 1966; ex EMPIRE DAFFODIL 1946; ex CARIBE II 1940.

M_2F H
● **41870 GRIGORIS;** Gr/Br 1946; LS; 800; 57.28 × 3.66 (187.93 × 12); M; 11.5; ex ST CLEMENT 1976.

M_2F H
41880 ISLAND SUPPLIER; Br/Br 1935; C; 650; — —; TSM; 10; ex SOUTHERN STAR 1969; ex FAUVETTE 1963. Sister: **41881 TWILLINGATE** (Ca) ex CORNCRAKE 1967.

M_2F H
41890 YIANNIS DIMAKIS; Gr/Ne 1949; C; 400; 55.43 × 3.03 (181.86 × 9.94); M; 10; ex SWIFT III 1968; ex LOVESTEYN 1966; ex JULIA MARY 1963.

M_2F H
41900 BLACKPOOL; Br/Br 1962; Tk; 530; 52.2 × 2.91 (171.26 × 9.55); M; —; ex UNO 1972. Sister: **41901 BRADFORD** (Br) ex TORO 1972.

M_2F H
⋆**41910 RYSY;** Pd/Ge 1942; Riv/Tk; 760; 61.09 × 4 (200.45 × 13.1); M; 8; ex BLEXEN.

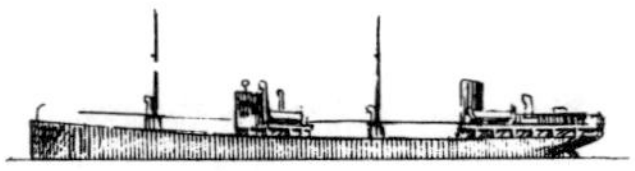

M_2F H
41920 MANSOUR; Si/Ne 1920; C; 2400; 90.84 × 5.94 (298.03 × 19.5); M; 10; ex RAS TANURA 1961; ex SAN MIGUEL 1958.

M_2F H
41930 M.O.P. 225-C; Ar/Br 1950; D; 3400; 105.21 × — (345.18 × —); TSD-E; —.

M_2F H
⋆**41940 DESNA;** Ru/Hu 1944; Riv/C; 2000; 76.33 × 3.1 (250.43 × 10.17); TSM; 10.

M_2F H
41950 MEGAMA; Pa/Ne 1947; C; 1300; 68.59 × 4.83 (225 × 15.9); M; 10; ex BALISA 1967; ex ANDONG 1965; ex ANATA 1965; ex SELAT MADURA 1964; ex BAGAN 1959. Similar: **41951 MESSINA** (Pa) ex BATINA 1967; ex ANNAM 1965; ex ANNA 1965; ex SELAT MAKASSAR 1964; ex BALANIPA 1960 **41952 MESOLO** (Sg) ex MERINDA 1977; ex BABOMA 1967; ex ANGAS 1965; ex ANGORA 1965; ex SELAT BANGKA 1964; ex BANGGAAL 1959 **41953 MELITA** (Pa) ex BALANDA 1967; ex SELAT BALI 1964; ex HOCK HAI 1961; ex HOCK HENG 1951; ex BRATTHEIM 1950 **41954 MESAWA** (Pa) ex MEDDUNO 1969; ex BASONGO 1967; ex ANBAN 1965; ex MOLOPO 1964; ex SELAT SINGKEP 1964; ex NYORA 1963; ex EMPIRE CONIFER 1947; ex ADRIAN 1945 **41955 KING LION** (Sg) ex SAN BLAS 1966; ex BONA 1966; ex SAN BLAS 1965; ex KALI MAS 1964; ex BAKONGAN 1960 **41956 KING BIRD** (Sg) ex SAN MIGUEL 1966; ex CALIBAR 1966; ex SAN MIGUEL 1965; ex BINTANG MAS 1964; ex BATOELA 1960.

M_2F *H*
41960 RAWAS; Ia/Ne 1950; C; 2100; 69.3 × 4.9 (227.36 × 16.09); M; 10; ex ANCON 1965; ex BARUMUN 1959. Similar (Ia flag): **41961 RUPIT** ex TELUK WAP 1968; ex BRAVO 1965; ex BANJOEWANGI 1959 **41962 ENIM** ex TELUK KORIO 1968; ex CELESTIAL 1965; ex BARITO 1959 **41963 KELEKAR** ex TELUK KAMRAU 1968; ex POLLERA 1965; ex BATOEBAHRA 1959.

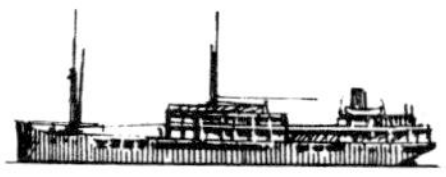

M_2F *H*
41970 TIRTA KARYA; Pa/Ne 1930; C; 1000; 64.67 × 3.07 (212.17 × 10.08); M; 8; ex BAN HO LIONG 1973; ex TOBA 1958.

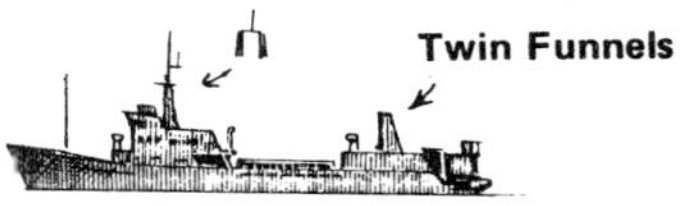

M_2F *H*
● **41980 CAR EXPRESS;** Ne/Ne 1966; RoVC/C/LS; 500; 80.75 × — (264.9 × —); M; 14; ex RIJNSTROOM 1976. Sister: **41981 MEDITERRANEAN EXPRESS** (Ne) ex AMSTELSTROOM 1975.

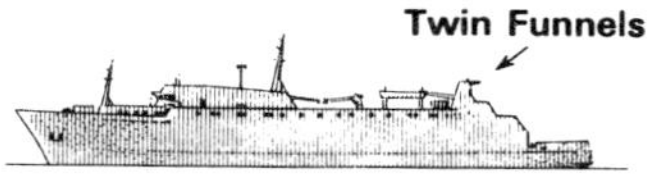

M_2F *H*
41990 AVALO; Pa/No 1968; LS; 1200; 92 × 4.74 (301.84 × 15.55); TSM; 15; ex FEDERAL AVALON 1980; ex SEASPEED TRAILER 1974; ex SKYWAY 1973; ex MANDEVILLE 1970; Converted from Ro/Ro cargo 1980.

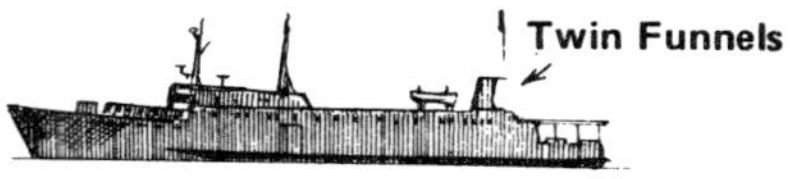

M_2F *H*
● **42000 DAPHNE;** Fr/Fr 1968; RoVC/C; 1200; 92.03 × 4.76 (301.94 × 15.63); TSM; 15; ex BRAVO CONTENDER 1974; ex SEALORD CONTENDER 1969. Sister: **42001 FEDERAL TYNE** (Br) ex FEDERAL BYBLOS 1977; ex SEASPEED FERRY 1975; ex SPEEDWAY 1973; ex CLEARWAY 1970; ex SEALORD CHALLENGER 1969.

M_2F *H*
42010 VIKING IV; No/No 1967; RoC; 1200; 92 × 4.74 (301.84 × 15.54); TSM; 15.

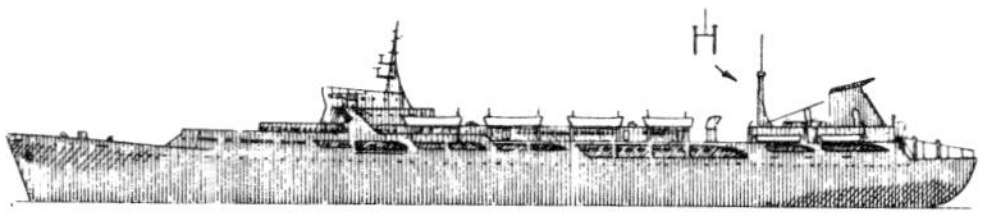

M_2F *H*
42020 KYDON; Gr/Ne 1953/69; RoPCF; 10700; 153.93 × 8.64 (505.02 × 28.34); M; 14.25; ex WIRAKEL 1968; Converted from tanker 1969.

M_2F *H*
42030 GOTH; Br/Br 1974; ST; 1400; 59.75 × 5.34 (196.03 × 17.52); M; —. Sisters (Br flag): **42031 NORSE 42032 ROMAN** Similar: **42033 DANE 42034 PICT 42035 JUNELLA.**

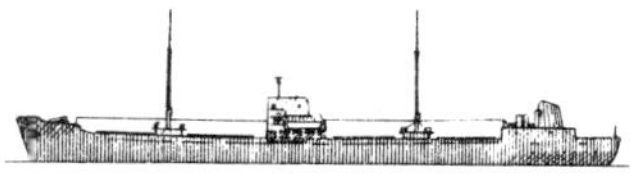

M_2F *H1*
42040 DENIS; Gr/FRG 1942/50; C; 2300; 95.64 × 6.1 (313.68 × 21.55); M; 9; ex CLEOPATRA 1976; ex HEDDERNHEIM 1971; Launched 1942, completed 1950.

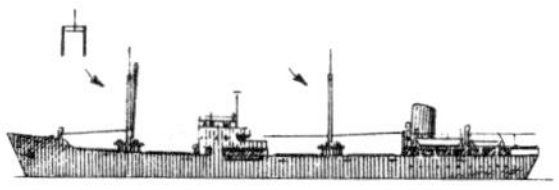

M_2F *H1*
42050 MESSINIA; Cy/No 1948; C; 1400; 84.46 × 5.65 (277.1 × 18.5); M; 10.75; ex BALBLOM 1971.

M_2F *H1*
42060 FRIGO QUEEN; Gr/Ne 1963; C; 500; 78.36 × 3.71 (257.09 × 12.17); T; 16; ex MERES 1976; ex SONJA 1973.

M_2F H1
42070 PELITA DELI: Ia/Pd 1960; C; 700; 65.82 × 3.72 (215.94 × 12.2); M; —; ex MANGGA 1974; **'B-471'** type. Sisters (Ia flag): **42071 NANGKA 42072 DUKUH 42073 DUREN 42074 DJERUK 42075 DEEPA SAKTI** ex LENGKENG 1974 **42076 RAMBUTAN** (Pa flag): **42077 BUILDER II** ex EQUATOR 1977; ex DUWET 1976.

M_2F H1
42090 ATILOLA; Ng/Ne 1958; C; 500; 53.7 × 3.02 (176.18 × 9.94); M; 10; ex ANJOU 1970; ex PRESIDENT E CHALAS 1963.

M_2F H1
42100 ROVENSCA; Pa/Ge 1934; Tk; 700; 53.78 × 3.93 (176.44 × 12.89); M; 8; ex SYLT 1969; ex EMPIRE TEGIDAD 1945; ex SYLT 1945.

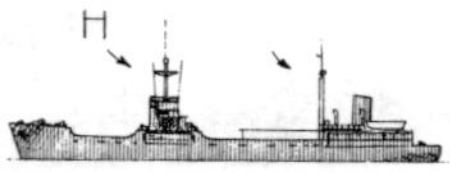

M_2F H1
42110 BANANG; Ia/Br 1946; C; 900; 68.28 × 4.26 (224 × 13.97); M; 9; ex CINDEE 1974; ex KATUL 1967. Similar: ⋆**42111 MIN CHU No 7** (RC) ex HAIYUN 1951; ex OTTAWA PALAT; Also known as **MIN CHU CHI.**

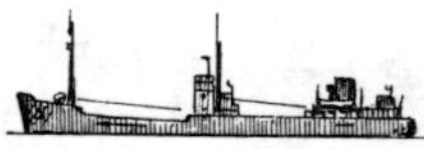

M_2F H12
42120 ROZMARY; Gr/Br 1941; C; 900; 64.32 × 4.11 (211 × 13.48); M; 10; ex LIBYA 1971; ex PEREGRINE 1965; ex EMPIRE SPINNEY 1946.

M_2F H12
42130 ATHANASIOS I; Gr/Br 1938; C; 330; 44.81 × 3.38 (147.01 × 11.09); M; 10; ex KARRI 1967.

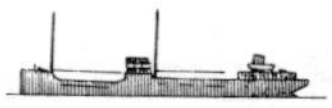

M_2F H12
42140 MORUKA; Pa/Br 1936; C; 370; 43.35 × 4.12 (142.22 × 13.52); M; 8; ex HENRIK 1970; ex KARIN BAHNSEN 1965; ex PUTTE PAN 1962; ex GRANITA 1959; ex BAMBOO 1953.

M_2F H12
42150 FILIPPOS; Gr/Br 1947; C; 420; 45.14 × 3.81 (148.1 × 12.5); M; 12; ex SINERGASIA 1970; ex GEORGE CALLITSIS 1969; ex MONKSVILLE1964; ex EBONY 1958.

M_2F H12
42160 KOTA DJAJA; Ia/Ne 1952; C; 450; 49.64 × 3.26 (162.86 × 10.7); M; 10; ex FEM 1973; ex MYFEM 1969.

M_2F H12
42170 TRISTANIA; SA/Br 1940; FF; 640; 50.02 × 3.98 (164.11 × 13.06); M; —; ex ISOLDA; ex BAY 1952.

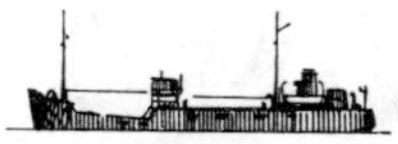

M_2F H12
42180 GEORGIOS VENTOURIS; Gr/Br 1937; C; 470; 51.26 × 3.72 (168.18 × 12.2); M; 9.5; ex HERRIESDALE 1962; ex CROMARTY FIRTH 1957.

M_2F H12
42190 MINO; Gr/Br 1946; C; 860; 58.63 × 4.17 (192.36 × 13.68); M; 10; ex DOMINO RUN; ex DROMINEER 1964; ex KNEBWORTH 1960.

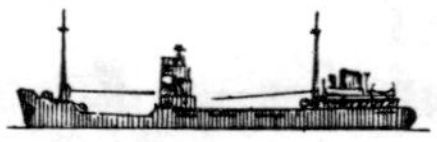

M_2F H12
42200 BAGAS; Ia/Br 1946; C; 960; 63.81 × 4.15 (209.35 × 13.62); M; 10; ex SANDY 1964; ex MALTARA 1967; ex INO 1954.

M_2F H12
42210 AGOI ANARGYROI III: Gr/Br 1950; C; 980; 66.93 × 4.15 (219.59 × 13.62); M; 10.5; ex FIRTH FISHER 1971; ex TURKIS 1954.

M_2F H12
42220 AL AKBER; Pa/Br 1952; C; 1100; 66.12 × 4.23 (216.93 × 13.88); M; 11; ex HOWTH TRADER 1975; ex HAWTHORN 1974; ex HARGLEN 1968; ex IRISH HEATHER 1964.

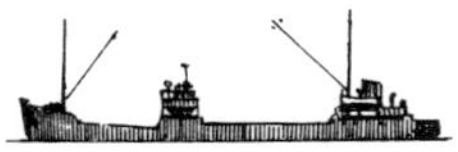

M_2F H12
42230 ANDREAS A. Cy/Ih 1954; C; 1000; 66.45 × 4.33 (218.01 × 14.21); M; 10; ex AL-HASSAN 1976; ex YEWTREE 1974; ex IRISH FERN 1964.

M_2F H12
42240 KAPETAN KOSTANTIS. Gr/Br 1947; C; 500; 55.96 × 3.51 (183.6 × 11.5); M; 10.5g ex AUSTERITY 1967.

M_2F H12
42250 ADINA. Br/Br 1954; C; 600; 55.94 × 3.52 (183.53 × 11.55); M; lg ex SEVERITY 1975. Similar: **42251 ALMY** (Pa) ex SCANDIA III 1978; ex ROWANCRAIG 1976; ex SONORITY.

M_2F H12
42260 MARIAM. Le/Br 1942; C; 520; 52.48 × 3.44 (172.18 × 11.29); M; 9; ex SAINT RULE 1973.

M_2F H12
42270 IOANNIS K. Gr/Br 1931; C; 350; 41.21 × 3.05 (135.2 × 10); M; 8.5; ex GIANKAROS 1971; ex ACTIVITY 1966. Similar; **42271 SKORPIOS** (Gr) ex APRICITY 1965 **42272 STAR I** (Cy) ex SOULA 1976; ex ARIDITY 1966.

M_2F H12
42280 DIMITRIOS A. Gr/Br 1935; C; 410; 43.56 × 2.98 (142.91 × 9.78); M; 10.5; ex ASEITY 1966.

M_2F H12
42290 TATIANGELA. Gr/Ne 1955; C; 420; 54.39 × 3.28 (178.44 × 10.76); M; 10; ex CHARA 1976; ex ZETINA 1974; ex DAMSANES 1974; ex GRINNA 1973; ex VESTA 1969.

M_2F H12
42300 ATILOLA. Ng/Ne 1958; C; 480; 53.7 × 3.02 (176.18 × 9.94); M; 10; ex ANJOU 1970; ex PRESIDENT E. CHALAS 1963.

M_2F H12
42310 JAYA PUTRA II. Ia/Br 1926; C; 950; 62.62 × 3.81 (205.45 × 12.5); M; 10; ex FLORETA 1973; ex KYBRA 1958.

M_2F H12
42320 DARVISH VANANCA. Ir/Fr 1949; C; 380; 51.69 × 3.13 (169.59 × 10.27); M; 10.5; ex SEINE 1967; ex DIJONNAIS 1964. Sister: **42321 SHIRDEL VANANCA** (Ir) ex NORMANDY 1967; ex GATINALS 1954.

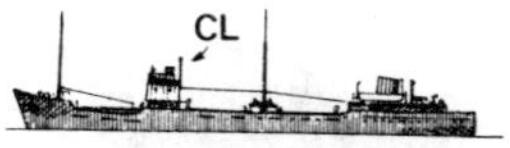

M_2F H12
42330 MARYS KETCH. Br/Br 1957; C; 1500; 73.44 × 4.79 (290.94 × 19.72); M; —; ex ALFRED EVERARD 1978. Similar: **42331 AGHIA MARINA** (Gr) ex SERENITY 1967 **42332 ROBERT KOCH** (Ca) ex GUARDIAN CARRIER 1977; ex ETHEL EVERARD 1963 **42333 RAMONA** (Pa) ex SANGUITY 1978 **42334 IOANNIS** (Cy) ex SELECTIVITY 1975 **42335 CRYSTAL ISLAND** (Pa) ex DESPINA T 1980; ex SIMULARITY 1975 **42336 KING ON** (Pa) ex STABILITY.

M_2F H12
42340 CHRISTINA TH. Gr/Br 1952; C; 1200; 69.68 × 4.6 (228.6 × 15.1); M; 10; ex HUMBERBROOK 1967; ex KYLE OF LOCHALSH 1965; ex BEVERLEY GATE 1958.

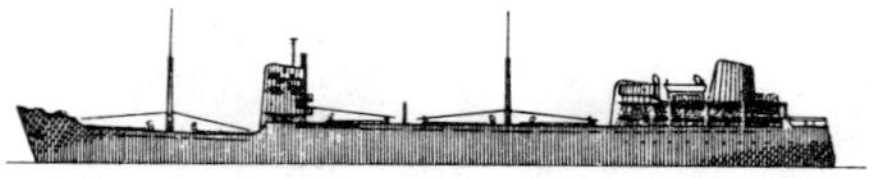

M_2F H12
42350 SIRLAD. Ma/Br 1955; B; 6000; 130.38 × 7.24 (427.76 × 23.75); M; 12; ex KYKLOPS 1980; ex FENI 1979; ex MORCOTE 1977; ex SEBASTIANO 1976; ex DEERWOOD 1969.

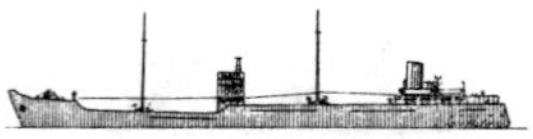

M_2F H12
42360 TAXIARCHIS. Gr/Br 1938; C; 1500; 79.71 × 4.67 (261.52 × 15.32); M; 8; ex PASKALIS 1968; ex EILDON 1966.

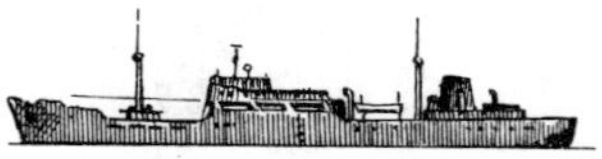

M_2F H12
⋆**42370 HAI FENG.** RC/RC 1960; FFMS; 2500; 86.86 × — (285 × —); M; —.

M_2F H12
42380 MAHDIA. Tn/Fr 1952; C; 1300; 83.01 × 4.68 (272.34 × 15.35); M; 12.75; ex NELEE 1956. Possibly Similar: **42381 TABARKA** (Tn) ex ISEE 1961.

M_2F H12
42390 ALKMINI. Gr/Pd 1923; C; 1200; 73.94 × 4.4 (242.59 × 14.44); M; 9; ex CONSTANTINOS 1969; ex RASK 1967; ex HESNES 1953; ex PAUL L-M RUSS 1947.

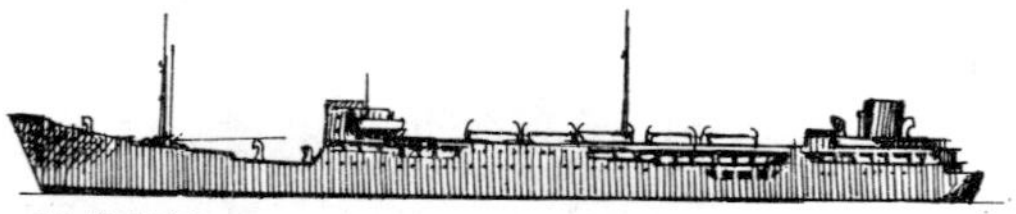

M_2F H12
42400 PHAISTOS. Gr/Sw 1951/65 RoPVF; 8100; 151.29 × 4.6 (496.36 × 15.09; M; 13.5; ex MARIA GORTHON 1963; Converted from tanker 1965.

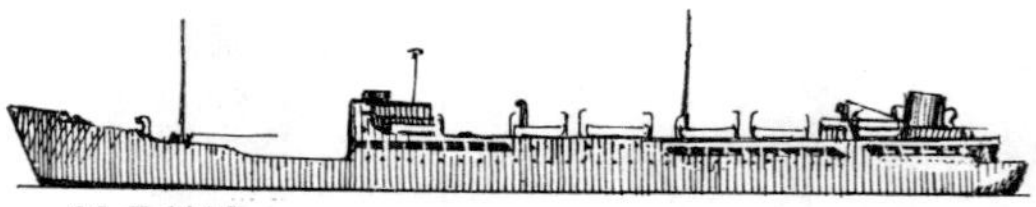

M_2F H12
42410 MINOS. Gr/Sw 1952/66 RoPVF; 9500; 162.57 × 4.9 (533.37 × 16.08); M; 14.75; ex SOYA-MARGARETA 1964; Converted from tanker 1966.

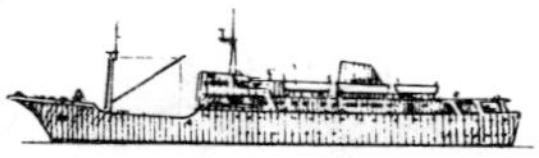

M_2F H12
42420 GRANUAILE. Ih/Br 1970; LT; 2000; 80.68 × 4.01 (264.7 × 13.16); TSM; 13.5.

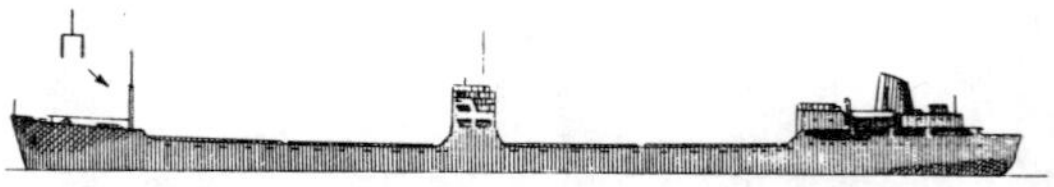

M_2F H123
42430 VITTORIO GARDELLA. It/Br 1959; O; 10300; 159.87 × 8.55 (524.51 × 28.05); M; 12.5; ex CAPE FRANKLIN 1974.

M_2F H123
42440 CLIFF QUAY. Br/Br 1950; C; 3300; 103.31 × 6.1 (338.97 × 20.01); R; 10.5. Similar (taller funnel—no pipe) (It flag): **42441 BRICK NONO** ex DAGNY K 1970; ex DAVID POLLOCK 1967 **42442 BRICK OTTAVO** ex THOMAS GOULDEN 1968 **42443 BRICK UNDICESIMO** ex BOWCOMBE 1971; ex SIR DAVID II 1969 **42444 BRICK DECIMO** ex BRAEMAR 1971; ex SIR FREDERICK JOHN EVANS 1966.

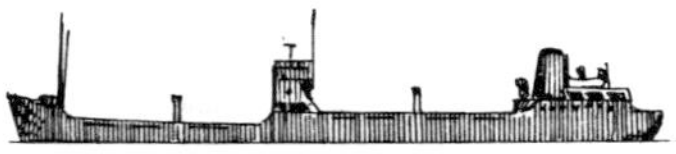

M_2F H123
42450 EAGLE I. Pa/Br 1955; C; 2900; 103.64 × 5.52 (340.03 × 18.11); R; 11.25; ex CHARLES H. MERZ 1977. Sisters: **42451 JAMES ROWAN** (Br) **42452 SIR WILLIAM WALKER** (Br) **42453 FANIS** (Gr) ex SIR JOHNSTONE WRIGHT 1976.

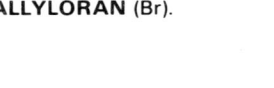

M_2F H123
● **42460 BALLYLESSON.** Br/Br 1958; C; 1300; 76.21 × 4.25 (250.03 × 13.94); M; 11. Sister: **42461 BALLYLORAN** (Br).

M_2F H123
42470 BALLYRORY. Br/Br 1963; C; 1600; 78.03 × 4.62 (256 × 15.16); M; 11.5. Sister: **42471 BALLYRUSH** (Br).

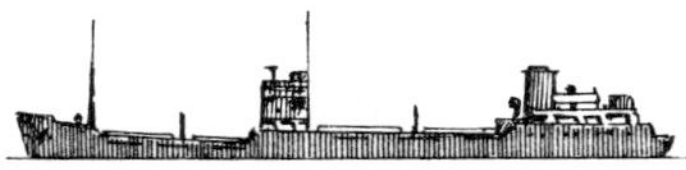

M_2F H123
42480 UGO M. It/Br 1955; C; 3000; 104.86 × 6.06 (344.03 × 19.88); R; 10.25; ex GIOVANNI TRENTO 1977; ex BEARWOOD 1968.

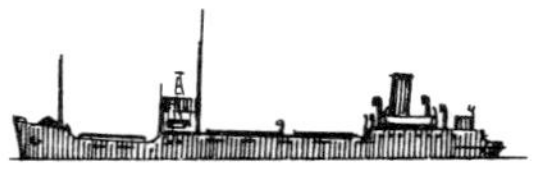

M_2F H123
● **42490 THALASSITRA.** Gr/Br 1955; C; 1300; 77.58 × 4.38 (254.53 × 14.37); M; 10; ex NABULK 1975; ex DYNABULKER 1971; ex BALLYLAGAN 1970; Lengthened 1956.

M_2F H123
42500 MARINE TRANSPORT. Ca/Br 1946; C; 870; 64.17 × 4.12 (210.53 × 13.52); M; 14; ex C. OMER 1972; ex C. OMER MARIE 1967; ex VAUQUELIN 1966 ex CRICHTOUN 1965.

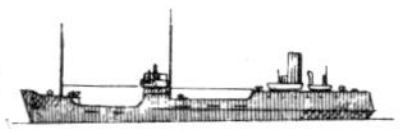

M_2F H123
42510 AGIOS GERASSIMOS. Gr/Br 1948; C; 700; 56.04 × 4.03 (183.86 × 13.22); M; —; ex AGHIOS GERASSIMOS 1976; ex FOULI 1964; ex SPRAYVILLE 1963; ex HAZELFIELD 1959.

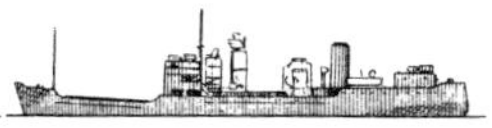

M_2F H123
42520 STAVROS. Gr/Br 1949; Cem; 1400; 71.66 × 4.69 (235.1 × 15.39); R; 9.5; ex TSIMENTAVROS 1974; ex WALCRETE 1966; ex POOLE SOUND 1959; Converted cargo ship. Similar (Cargo ships): **42521 GEORGIOS G** (Gr) ex TRIS IERARCHE 1972; ex SNOWCRETE 1963; ex POOLE QUAY 1959 **42522 MARIA BERLINGIERI** (It) ex SULFACRETE 1962; ex POOLE RIVER. 1959.

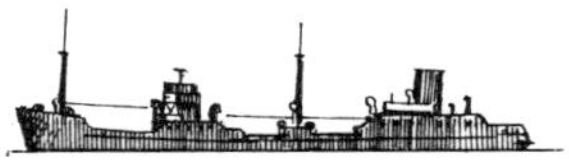

M_2F H123
42530 CUBAHAMA. Pa/Br 1938; C; 1500; 81.36 × 4.09 (266.93 × 13.42); TSM; 13.

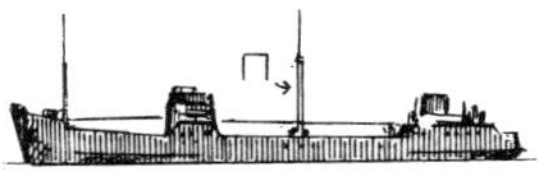

M_2F H123
42540 ZIAD. Le/Br 1949; C; 1000; 80.63 × 3.79 (264.5 × 12.43); M; 12; ex PIERRE RODOLPHE 1973; ex IKARIA 1971; ex BROOKMOUNT 1970; ex LAIRDS BEN 1959.

M_2F H123
42550 ARGOS. Ar/Br 1935; C; 2200; 87.48 × 3.2 (287 × 10.5); TSM; 10. Similar: **42551 AGUILA II** (Ar).

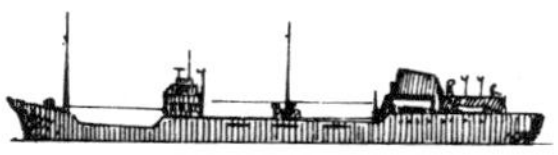

M_2F H123
42560 MARIETTA. Cy/Br 1952; C; 1600; 83.22 × 5.15 (273.03 × 16.9); M; 11.5; ex DIMITRIOS G 1972; ex CARDIFFBROOK 1969.

M_2F H123
42570 ELSA. Cy/Br 1954; C; 1400; 75.65 × 4.63 (248.19 × 15.19); M; 11; ex KAISIS I 1979; ex MALENA 1979; ex SOLON 1971; ex BALMORAL QUEEN 1969; ex PUTNEY 1965; ex BELVEDERE 1965; ex RAMBLER ROSE 1961.

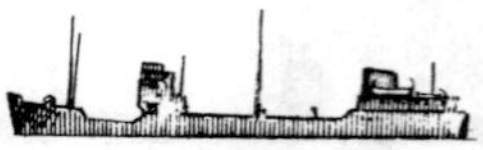

M_2F H123
42580 AGIOS FANOURIOS V. Gr/Br 1952; C; 1500; 73.41 × 4.92 (240.85 × 16.14); M; 11.5; ex IVY 1976; ex ASTROLAND 1975; ex TOTLAND 1975.

M_2F H123
42590 MARYS KETCH. Br/Br 1957; C; 1500; 73.44 × 4.79 (290.94 × 19.72); M; —; ex ALFRED EVERARD 1978. Similar: **42591 AGHIA MARINA** (Gr) ex SERENITY 1967 **42592 ROBERT KOCH** (Ca) ex GUARDIAN CARRIER 1977; ex ETHEL EVERARD 1963 **42593 RAMONA** (Pa) ex SANGUITY 1978 **42594 IOANNIS** (Cy) ex SELECTIVITY 1975 **42595 CRYSTAL ISLAND** (Pa) ex DESPINA T 1980; ex SIMULARITY 1975 **42596 KING ON** (Pa) ex STABILITY.

M_2F H123
42600 LEILA ONE. Le/Br 1957; C; 1000; 64.93 × 4.3 (213.02 × 14.11); M; 10.5; ex FRANCES B 1974; ex BLISWORTH 1971.

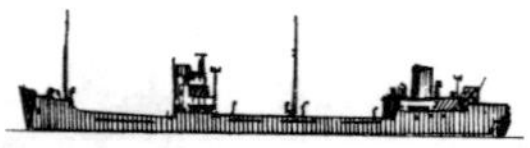

M_2F H123
42610 LUCKY TRADER. Cy/Br 1951; C; 1500; 77.25 × 4.79; (253.45 × 15.72); M; 10.5; ex BALLYROBERT 1977; ex ARDINGLY 1971.

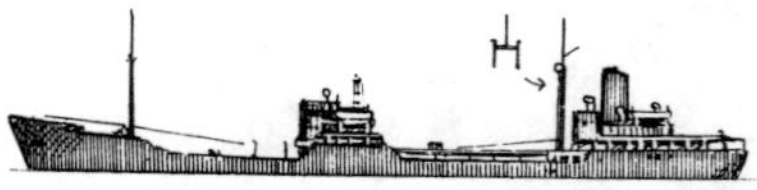

M_2F H123
42620 MICHELEESE. It/Br 1955; Tk; 4300; 117.35 × 6.66 (385 × 21.85); M; —; ex MONTE GRAPPA 1976; ex SECHURA 1968.

M_2F H123
42630 PETRA. It/Fr 1954; Tk; 500; 59.8 × 4.01 (196.19 × 13.16); M; 11; ex S. BIAGIO 1969; ex JOHN-M 1965. Similar: **42631 PETRO BOUSCAT** (Se) ex JUPITER 1968; ex KONNY-M 1965.

M_2F H123
42640 SAHEL. Fr/Fr 1951; Tk/FA; 1400 Dspl; 53.7 × 4.5 (176.2 × 14.5); M; 12.

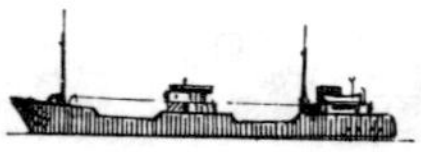

M_2F H123
42650 PEACE. Pa/Ne 1940/73; Rad; 350; 57.31 × 2.84 (188.02 × 9.32); M; 9; ex CITO 1969; ex WESTPOLDER 1960; ex ROLF 1950; Converted cargo ship 1973.

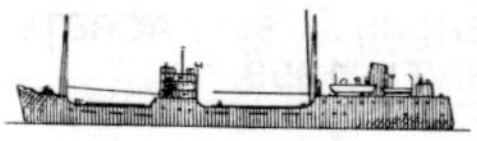

M_2F H123
42660 GLENCOE. Ca/Br 1947; C; 1100; 69.04 × 4.29 (226.51 × 14.07); M; 10.5; ex TEAL 1963.

M_2F H123
42670 PAKPANANG. Th/No 1935; C; 300; 45.73 × 2.31 (150.03 × 7.58); TSM; 11.

M_2F H123
42680 NAIRA. Ia/It 1953; C; 500; 55.33 × 2.93 (181.53 × 9.61); M; 10. Sisters (Ia flag): **42681 NURAGE 42682 PANTAI 42683 NAULI** ex NUKAHA 1959.

M_2F H123
42690 RAJAH SARAWAK. Pa/Ne 1936; C; 450; 50.36 × 3.07 (165.22 × 10.07); M; —; ex KERANDJI 1967; ex KIAN TIONG 1960; ex ROKAN 1958; ex LORENTZ 1954; ex COMORIEN 1953; ex KONINGIN EMMA 1951.

M_2F H123
42700 LANDING. Pa/Br 1957; C; 1800; 79.86 × 4.72 (262 × 15.49); M; 10.5; ex LANCING 1978; Lengthened 1969. Sister: **42701 AGIA ANNA** (Gr) ex SASSA 1980; ex PORTSLADE 1977.

M_2F H123
42710 ABEER DELTA. Eg/Br 1955; C; 1600; 73.77 × 4.81 (242.o3 × 15.78); M; 10.5; ex SALLYWALTER 1980; ex BALLYWALTER; ex STEYNING 1971.

M_2F H123
● **42720 BALLYCASTLE.** Br/Br 1959; C; 1600; 74.73 × 4.86 (245.18 × 15.95); M; 11; ex COWDRAY 1976.

M_2F H123
42730 ZUHAIR. Pa/Br 1955; C; 680; 60.56 × 3.8 (198.69 × 12.47); M; 12; ex GULF PLANET 1976; ex SAINT BLANE 1971.

M_2F H123
42740 AL AKBER. Pa/Br 1952; C; 1100; 66.12 × 4.23 (216.93 × 13.88); M; 11; ex HOWTH TRADER 1975; ex HAWTHORN 1974; ex HARGLEN 1968; ex IRISH HEATHER 1964.

M_2F H123
42750 ANDREAS A. Cy/Ih 1954; C; 1000; 66.45 × 4.33 (218.01 × 14.21); M; 10; ex AL-HASSAN 1976; ex YEWTREE 1974; ex IRISH FERN 1964.

M_2F H123
● **42760 SINGAPORE RAMIN.** Sg/Ne 1956; C; 650; 57.36 × 3.47 (188.19 × 11.38); M; —; ex CHERRY MOLEK 1973; ex ALUGORO I 1968; ex ST. ABBS HEAD 1967.

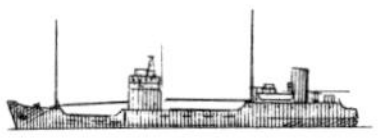

M_2F H123
● **42770 LISSA.** Cy/Br 1952; C; 620; 55.61 × 3.87 (182.45 × 12.7); M; 10.5; ex LADY MCGOWAN 1977.

M_2F H123
42780 ELLI. Gr/Br 1946; C; —; 66.6 × 4.24 (218.5 × 13.91); R; 10; ex SAINT NICHOLAS 1969; ex RUDRY 1966; ex LONDONBROOK 1963.

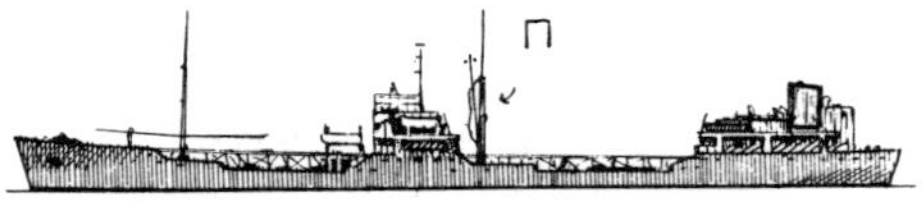

M_2F H123
42790 EMSLAND. FRG/It 1946/60; RT/FA; 6200; 141 × 7.8 (461 × 25.8); M; 12.5; ex ANTONIO ZOTTI 1960; Converted from tanker 1960/61.

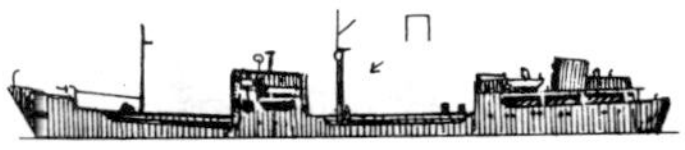

M_2F H123
★**42800 PEVEK.** Ru/Fi 1958; Tk; 3100; 105.11 × 6.13 (344.85 × 20.1); M; 13.5. Sisters (Ru flag): ★**42801 ARTYOM** ★**42802 BALTA** ★**42803 MOZYR** ★**42804 PIRYATIN** ★**42805 VENTSPILS** ★**42806 VILYUYSK** ★**42807 ZOLOTOY ROG** ★**42808 KOKAND.**

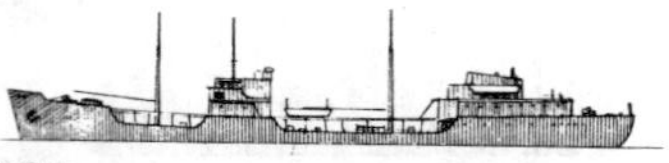

M_2F *H123*

● **42820 LSCO AMIHAN.** Pi/Pa 1945; Tk; 3200; 99.68 × 5.89 (327.03 × 19.32); M; 13; ex AMIHAN 1968; ex DENEB 1967; ex STANVAC SUNDA 1963; ex TANKHAVEN II 1959; ex TANTALLON 1948; **'T-1'** type. Similar: **42821 LSCO CANTHO** (Pi) ex MOBIL BATAAN 1969; ex STANVAC BATAAN 1962; ex STANVAC ALCOR 1961; ex TANKHAVEN I 1959; ex TANNADICE 1948 **42822 LSCO CAMRANH** (Pi) ex MOBIL MICRONESIA 1969; ex CAPELLA 1967; ex STANVAC SUMBA 1963; ex TANKHAVEN III 1959; ex ZENITH 1948; ex TANNAGULL. **42823 PROVIDENCE GETTY** (US) ex TYDOL FLYING A 1958; ex TINSLEY 1948; ex TAROGLE 1945. The following are US Navy and are known as **'PECONIC class'; 42824 RINCON** ex TARLAND **42825 NODAWAY** ex BELRIDGE **42826 PETALUMA** ex RACOON BEND.

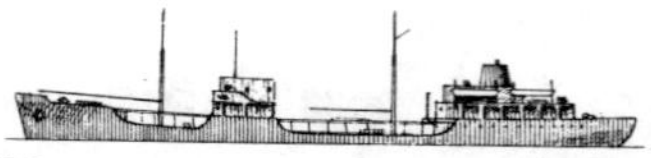

M_2F *H123*

42830 LSCO TRANSASIA. Pi/US 1945; Tk; 3100; 99.12 × 5.9 (325.2 × 19.36); M; 10.5; ex CHEVRON 1970; ex BREA OLINDA 1946; ex TAVERTON 1945.

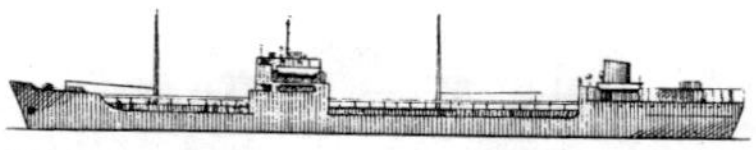

M_2F *H123*

42840 SHOMAR SHAIMA. Si/Br 1954; Ch; 3700; 115.25 × 6.85 (378.12 × 22.47); M; 13; ex GERTRUDE WIENER II 1980; ex SYLPHIDEN 1975; ex NORVEST 1974; Lengthened 1966; Converted Chemical Tanker 1975.

M_2F *H123*

42850 MAGNISI. It/It 1943/48 Tk; 1800; 84.61 × 5.13 (277.59 × 16.83); M; 11; ex YANN ROULLET 1960; ex SATELLITE 1949; Launched 1943. Completed 1948.

M_2F *H123*

42860 PETROLA 20. Gr/No 1949; C; 1600; 78.64 × 5.39 (258 × 17.68); M; 10; ex PETROLA XX 1976; ex MICHAEL S 1976; ex DIVINA 1975.

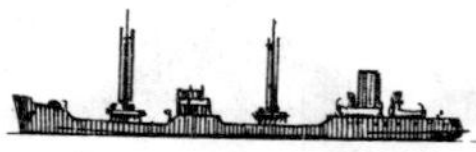

M_2F *H123*

42870 LUCTOR I. Pa/Br 1938; C; 1200; 73.46 × 4.68 (241 × 15.35); M; 10.5; ex UNION BRENDA 1977; ex BRENDA 1968; ex LORINNA 1961.

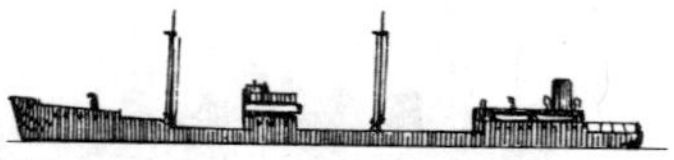

M_2F *H123*

42880 GUALOMA. Pa/Br 1938; C; 2600; 97.95 × 6.44 (321.36 × 21.13); M; 10.5; ex GAMBOMA 1978; ex PADOLA 1966; ex GALULA 1965; ex TONG POH 1964; ex CERION 1956.

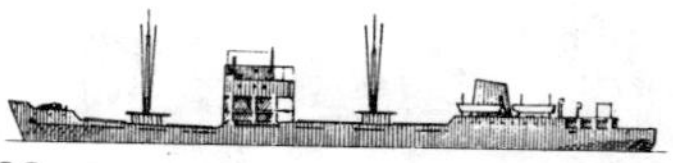

M_2F *H123*

42890 BARU. Cy/Br 1960; C; 3100; 103.33 × 5.94 (339.01 × 19.49); M; 10; ex VENTURER 1977; ex TAFAWA BELEWA 1966.

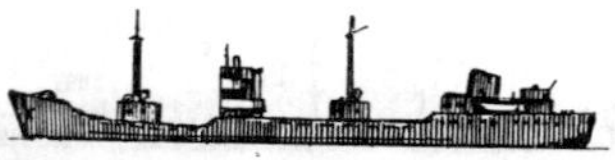

M_2F *H123*

42900 KRITI. Gr/Ne 1954; C; 2000; 90.23 × 5.55 (276.03 × 18.21); M; 13; ex VASILIKI 1977; ex SANTA EIRINI 1974; ex SANTA MARINA 1972; ex NISSOS SKOPELOS 1970; ex PIETER S 1966.

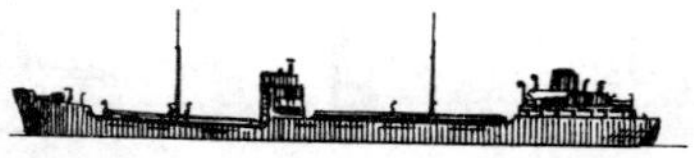

M_2F *H123*

42910 TSIMENTIAS. Pa/Br 1957; C; 3400; 103.33 × 6.17 (339.01 × 20.24); M; —; ex PANAGIA 1977; ex BRENZETT 1976; ex ASTRO VENTURE 1975; ex KAPPA PROGRESS 1974; ex CORSEA 1972.

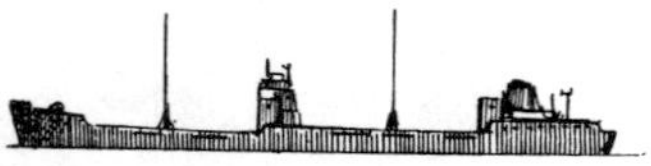

M_2F *H123*

42920 TSIMENTAVROS II. Gr/Br 1950; C; 2700; 95.71 × 6.07 (314 × 19.91); M; 11; ex ANASTASSIOS 1977; ex WATERLAND 1971.

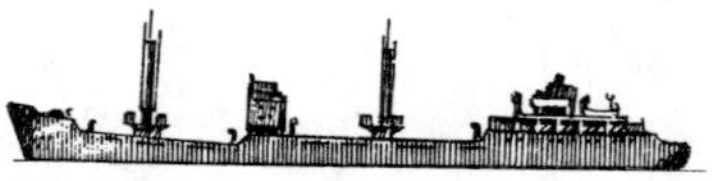

M_2F *H123*

42930 MALDIVE AMITY. Mv/Br 1956; C; 4200; 108.51 × 6.82 (356 × 22.38); M; 12; ex SALINA 1980; ex KOTA BERKAT 1977; ex CENTURY 1974.

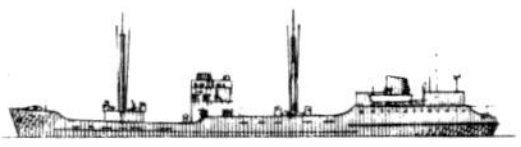

M_2F H123
42940 BONAHOPE. Sg/Br 1952; C; 1400; 77.42 × 4.61 (254 × 15.12); M; 11; ex WAREATEA 1971.

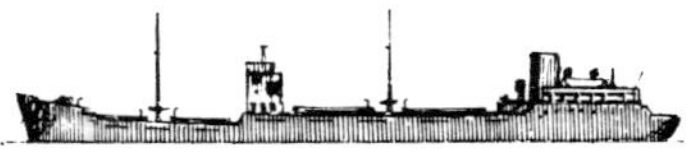

M_2F H123
42950 BRICK DODICESIMO. It/Br 1954; C; 3200; 104.86 × 6.1 (344.03 × 20.05); R; 10.5 ex ARUNDEL 1972.

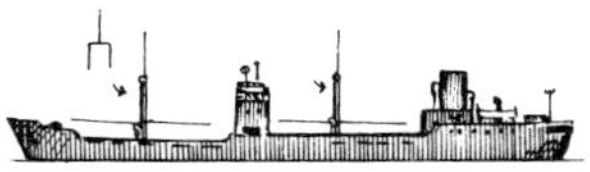

M_2F H123
⋆**42960 SOLDEK.** Pd/Pd 1949; O; 2000; 87 × 5.5 (285.43 × 18.04); R; 9.5; **'B-30'** type. Sisters (Ru flag): **42961 VOLNOVAKHA 42962 GORLOVKA** Similar: **42963 MALAYA ZEMLYA.**

M_2F H123
42970 TAYLAN KALKAVAN. Tu/Br 1945; C; 2000; 85.81 × 5.43 (281.53 × 17.82); R; 9.5; ex ABDULLAH 1976; ex BRAYWOOD 1959; ex EMPIRE VAUXHALL 1946.

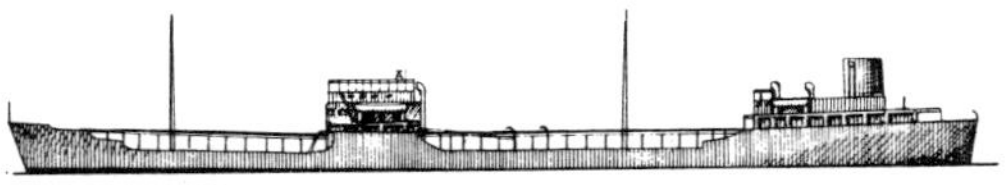

M_2F H123
⋆**42980 DA QING No. 15.** RC/Br 1952; Tk; 10100; 154.11 × 8.86 (505.61 × 29.07); M; 12; ex SANTA FORTUNA 1964; ex SANDALWOOD 1962.

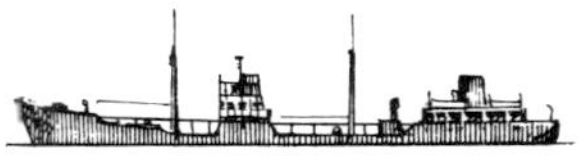

M_2F H123
42990 CAMPOO. Sp/Sp 1955; Tk; 1900; 83.39 × 5.14 (273.59 × 16.86); M; 9.5. Sister: **42991 CAMPROVIN** (Sp).

M_2F H123
43000 PETROLA 1. Gr/Br 1947; Tk; 1000; 67.49 × 3.96 (221.42 × 12.99); R; 9; ex PETROLA I 1976; ex AUTHENTICITY 1966; ex ANIS 1954; ex EMPIRE HARP 1948.

M_2F H123
43010 ISLA LEONES. Ar/No 1934; Tk; 1800; 84.23 × 5.03 (276.35 × 16.5); M; 10; ex EL RIOPLATENSE 1952.

M_2F H123
43020 ASPROPYRGOS. Gr/Br 1946; Tk; 950; 61.42 × 4.1 (201.51 × 13.45); M; 9.5; ex PIREAUS IV 1971; ex AUSTILITY 1969; ex FORRERIA 1951; ex EMPIRE TEDLORA 1947.

M_2F H123
43030 AGIOS GEORGIOS. Gr/Br 1950; Tk; 1200; 70.54 × 4.22 (231.43 × 13.85); M; —; ex ATHENA 1975; ex ATONALITY 1967.

M_2F H123
⋆**43040 PEREDOVIK.** Ru/Ru 1940; Tk; 1900; 83.01 × 5.56 (272.34 × 18.24); M; —.

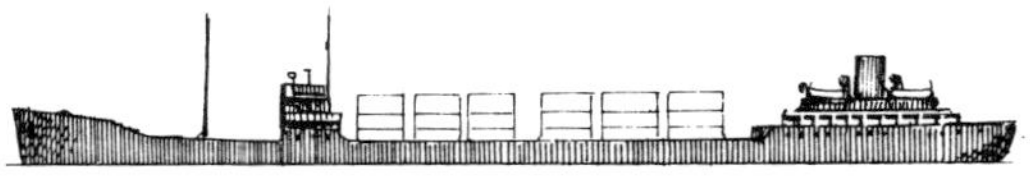

M_2F H123
43050 SEADRIFT. US/US 1942/61 Con/Ch; 9100; 159.57 × 9 (523.52 × 29.53); T-E; 14.5; ex CARBIDE SEADRIFT 1980; ex MICHIGAN SUN 1960; ex WHITE PLAINS 1948; Converted from T-2 tanker 1961. May be broken up.

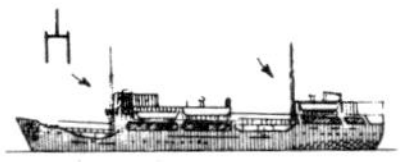

M_2F H123
43060 INTAN. Ia/Ne 1954; C; 700; 58.53 × 2.93 (192.03 × 9.61); M; 9.

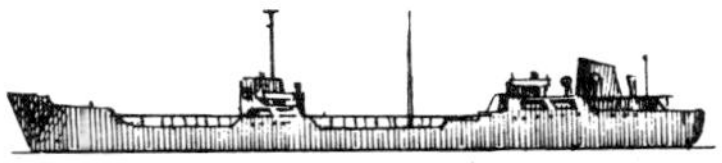

M_2F H123
⋆**43070 CHIEN SHE No. 9.** RC/RC 1960; Tk; 3300; 111.24 × — (361 × —); M; 12.2. Sister: ⋆**43071 CHIEN SHE No. 12** (RC).

M_2F H13
43080 ANINGA. It/FRG 1960; O; 9100; 166.43×9.42 (546.03×30.91); M; 15.5; ex TYNE ORE 1975. Sister: **43081 SEQUOIA** (It) ex QUIJOTE; ex TEES ORE 1975.

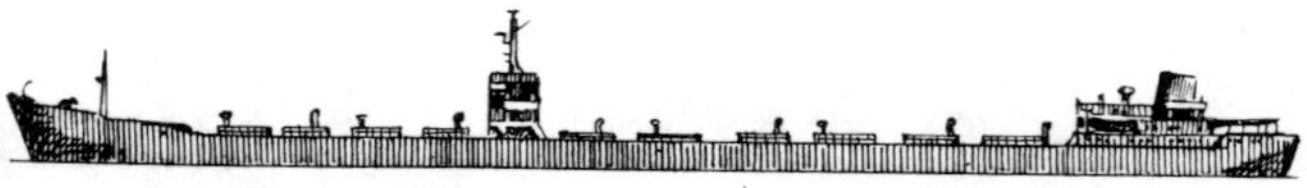

M_2F H13
43090 REGAL STAR. Gr/Ja 1961; B; 23500; 204.12×11.75 (669.69×38.55); M; 16; ex JANECKE 1973; ex JANECKE MAERSK 1965. Sister: **43091 SOTIR** (Gr) ex MARCHEN 1973; ex JESPER MAERSK 1964.

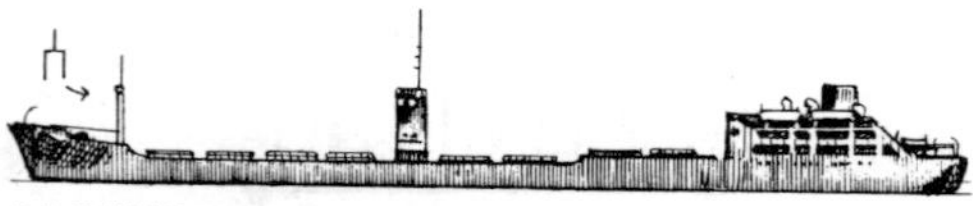

M_2F H13
★43100 MAXHUTTE. DDR/Sw 1955; OO; 8500; 149×8.48 (488.85×27.82); M; 13.5; ex LEDARO 1975; ex VINDAFJORD 1974.

M_2F H13
★43110 ZWICKAU. DDR/Sw 1958; OO; 15600; 181.82×10.04 (595.87×32.91); M; 14; ex VITAFORS 1969. Similar: **43111 FFM VIRIHAURE** (Li) ex VIRIHAURE 1970 **43112 KANARIS** (Gr) ex PAPANICOLIS 1974; ex VITTANGI 1970.

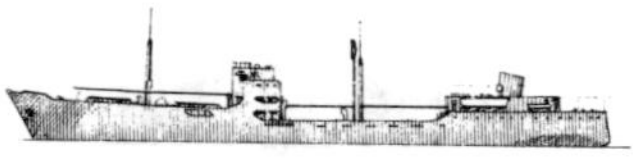

M_2F H13
43120 DONA HELENE. Pi/Fr 1949; C; 2000; 95.41×5.88 (313.02×19.29); M; 13; ex DON ALBERTO 1977; ex ATLAS 1968. Similar: **43121 KOSTAKIS** (Gr) ex ANNOULA 1973; ex TADIA 1968; ex VACCARES 1957; ex CAP COURONNE 1955 **43122 DONA RITA** (Pi) ex MARANIA 1967; ex TAFNA 1964; ex CHEIK **43123 DONA ANGELINA** (Pi) ex VALDOR 1972; ex TOUGOURT 1969 **43124 LAMIA STAR** (Cy) ex PANAGIOTIS V 1976; ex CONCORDE 1971; ex PHRYNE 1969; ex DUNKERQUE 1962; ex KROUMIR 1960 The following is converted to a Fish Factory Mother Ship: **43125 ROSS KELETCHEKIS** (Pa) ex TELL 1966.

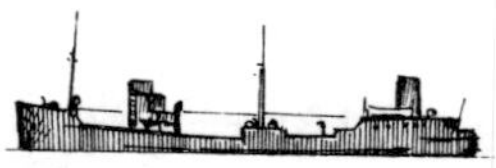

M_2F H13
43130 NEWFOUNDLAND COAST. Br/Br 1934; C; 889; 73.67×4.24 (241.7×13.91); TSM; —; ex BRITISH COAST 1964.

M_2F H13
● **43140 PADJONGE.** Ia/Be 1953; C; 550; 57.31×3.18 (188.02×10.43); M; 9. Sisters (Ia flag): **43141 PAJANGAN 43142 PANEHAN 43143 PAPADO 43144 PASIGI 43145 PALIAT 43146 PAHEPA 43147 PASOSO 43148 PASUDU 43149 KOTA SILAT XII** ex PAILOWA.

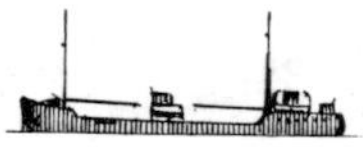

M_2F H13
43160 ANTONELLO. Pa/Ne 1949; C; 450; 48.77×3.48 (160.01×11.42); M; 10; ex ST. PATRICK 1980; ex ASOPI 1975; ex ELIVA 1971; ex DOXA 1970; ex SOMME 1967. Sisters: **43161 RANIA B** (Cy) ex LELIA 1976; ex ANNA MARIA 1974; ex PANAGIOTIS 1974; ex ANNA I 1972; ex NATASA 1972; ex MALTESE TRADER 1971; ex RACHEL PACE 1969; ex GROUVILLE 1969; ex ESCAUT 1965 **★43162 PERNAT** (Ys) ex SILVER TRADER 1974; ex BROOKBANK TRADER 1973; ex MEUSE 1971.

M_2F H13
⋆43170 KOLIMA. Ru/Ge 1936; C/Riv; 1100; 73.67 × 3.11 (241.7 × 10.2); TSM; 10; ex DUISBERG 1946.

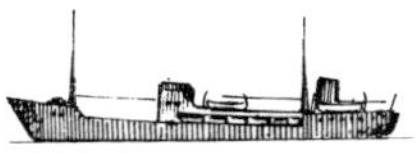

M_2F H13
43190 LALANG. Ia/FRG 1953; C; 520; 57.87 × 3.38 (189.86 × 11.09); M; 10; ex LAGONG 1973. Sisters (Ia flag): **43191 LAIRAN 43192 LAKOR 43193 LAKOTA 43194 LANDU 43195 LAPONDA 43196 LAWAK 43197 LAWANDRA 43198 BIMA** ex LAWIN.

M_2F H13
● **43230 DOMENICO IEVOLI.** It/It 1951; Tk; 1100; 66.32 × 5.39 (217.59 × 17.68); M; 10.5; ex GRAZIA PELLEGRINO 1973.

M_2F H13
43250 ROSARITO. Ec/Sw 1940; Tk; 1300; 78.01 × 4.56 (255.94 × 14.96); M; 12; ex NORDICA 1973; ex SVEA REUTER 1969; ex SOYA VI 1943.

M_2F H13
43270 PERMINA IX. Ia/Ja 1957; Tk; 1600; 72.64 × 5.3 (238.32 × 17.39); M; 12.5; ex KAKUSHIN MARU 1966.

M_2F H13
43290 MURASAKI MARU. Ja/Ja 1954; Tk; 800; 63.51 × 4.8 (208.37 × 15.75); M; 10.5; ex KYOEI MARU No. 3 1961; ex FUKUYO MARU 1955.

M_2F H13
43180 B.G. 1. Br/Ne 1955; Tk; 430; 48.24 × 2.3 (158.27 × 7.55); M; 8.5; ex BLACKFRIARS; ex MOBIL FUEL 1970. Similar (larger): **43181 BUCKINGHAM** (Br) ex BANCO 1972.

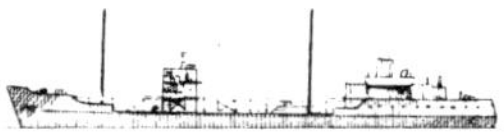

M_2F H13
43210 KYLLINI. Gr/Ge 1935; Tk; 1600; 77.73 × 4.55 (255.02 × 14.93); TSM; 10; ex CAROLINE M 1966; ex THORNOL 1948; ex EMPIRE TEGYIKA 1947; ex LISELOTTE ESSBERGER 1945.

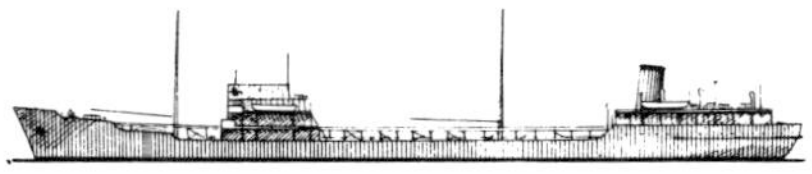

M_2F H13
43220 IMPERIAL SARNIA. Ca/Br 1948/54; Tk; 4900; 124.54 × 6.67 (408.6 × 21.88); T; 12.5.

M_2F H13
⋆43240 GUDERMES. Ru/Ru 1930; Tk; 7100; 132.6 × 7.01 (435.04 × 23); M; 11. Sisters (Ru flag): **⋆43241 TSYURUPA ⋆43242 DROGOBYCH ⋆43243 VKP (b) ⋆43244 AZERBAIJAN.**

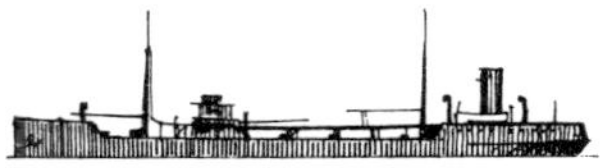

M_2F H13
43260 RAYMOND J BUSHEY. US/US 1938; Tk; 2000; 88.4 × 5.14 (290.03 × 16.86); TSM; 10.5; ex TRAVERSE CITY SOCONY 1962.

M_2F H13
43280 ANTONELLOESSE. It/No 1949; Tk; 1100; 73.21 × 4.64 (240.19 × 15.22); M; 12; ex LUIGIA MONTANARI 1975; ex LUIGIA N. 1960; ex SAPHIR 1956.

M_2F H13
⋆43300 LAMUT. Ru/Ja 1959; FF; 5000; 110.27 × 5.9 (361.78 × 19.36); M; 12.5. Sister: **⋆43301 NIKOLAY ISAYENKO** (Ru).

M_2F *H13*

43310 ACRE. Bz/Ja 1951; Tk; 1800; 85.35 × 4.27 (280.02 × 14.01); M; 10; ex FNP SAO PAULO 1954; ex SALTE 58 1953. Sisters (Bz flag): **43311 PARANA** ex FNP PARANA 1954; ex SALTE 51 1953 **43312 PERNAMBUCO** ex FNP PERNAMBUCO 1954; ex SALTE 52 1953 **43313 RIO GRANDE DO NORTE** ex FNP RIO GRANDE DO NORTE 1954; ex SALTE 54 1953 **43314 RIO GRANDE DO SUL** ex FNP RIO GRANDE DO SUL 1954; ex SALTE 55 1953.

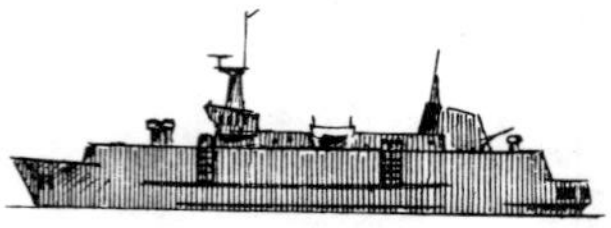

M_2F *H2*

43320 OSHEA EXPRESS. Br/Br 1970; V; 1200; 91.5 × 3.93 (300.2 × 12.89); M; —; ex CLEARWAY; ex SPEEDWAY 1970.

M_2F *H3*

43330 EVDOXIA K. Cy/Br 1949; C; 1000/1550; 78.77 × —/5.21 (258.43 × —/17.09); M; 12.5; ex LAS MINAS 1973; ex SALAMIS 1972; ex ARGOSTOLI II 1970; ex MELROSE 1966.

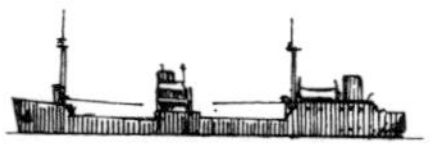

M_2F *H3*

43340 CLYDE. Ca/Br 1950; C; 750; 63.66 × 3.75 (208.86 × 12.3); M; 11.5; ex HIRONDELLE 1966. Similar: **43341 UNITY** (Cy) ex CIKAT 1978; ex SWIFT 1967.

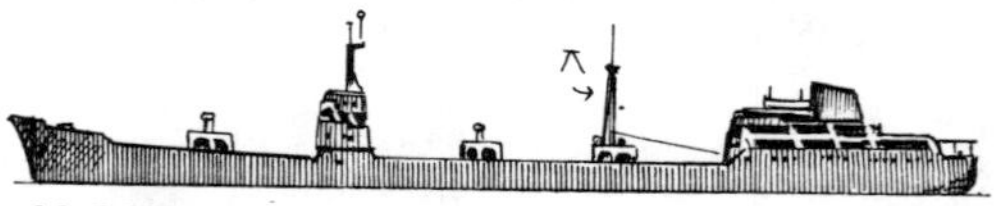

M_2F *H3*

43350 DONA MIRA. Li/Br 1958; C; 9600; 150.81 × 9.48 (494.78 × 31.1); M; 12; ex CHARLTON MIRA 1969.

M_2FC *H1*

43360 SANDERUS. Be/Ne 1968; D; 5000; 103 × — (337.93 × —); TSM; —.

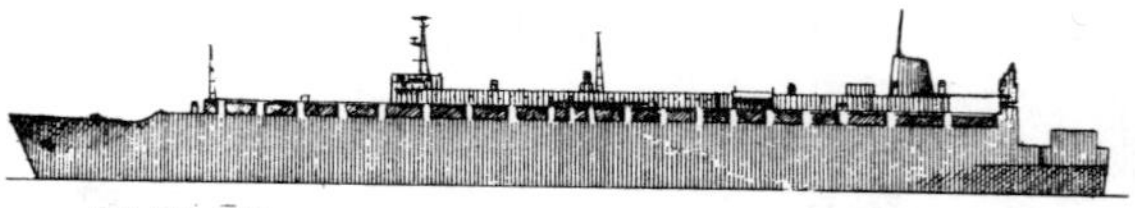

M_2FC *H2*

43370 TAMA MARU. Ja/Ja 1972; RoVC; 7000; 174.5 × 7.21 (572.51 × 23.65); M; 18. Sisters (Ja flag): **43371 SURUGA MARU 43372 SAGAMI MARU 43373 TSURUMI MARU.**

M_2FK *H*

● **43380 TEES BAY.** Br/Ne 1966; D; 2900; 94.49 × 5.67 (310.01 × 18.6); TSM; 12; ex CAP D'ANTIFER 1972; ex TEES BAY 1970.

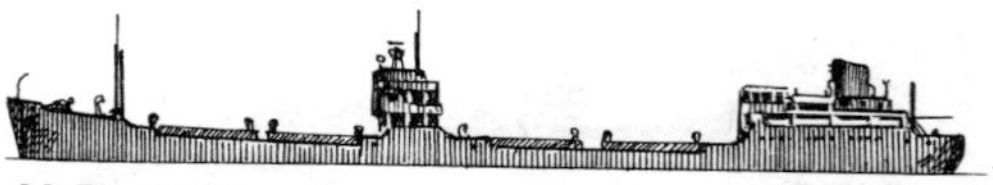

M_2FK *H123*

● **43390 EVPO ARAMIS.** Cy/Br 1957; B; 10800; 153.96 × 8.83 (505.12 × 28.97); M; 12; ex ANTIKLIA; ex RIBBLEHEAD 1972. Sister: **43391 NEMA** (Gr) ex SILVER LAKE 1973; ex RIEVAULX 1973 Similar: **43392 PISOLO** (It) ex NEWLANDS 1975; ex KAPPA UNITY 1974; ex PENNYWORTH 1973.

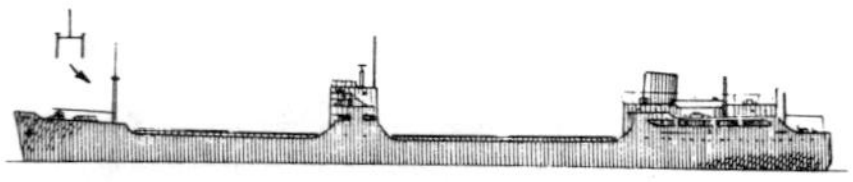

M_2FK *H123*

***43400 BERANE.** Ys/Br 1958; B; 6900; 129.7 × 7.73 (425.52 × 25.36); M; —; ex PHAEDON 1974; ex CLARKEDON 1973.

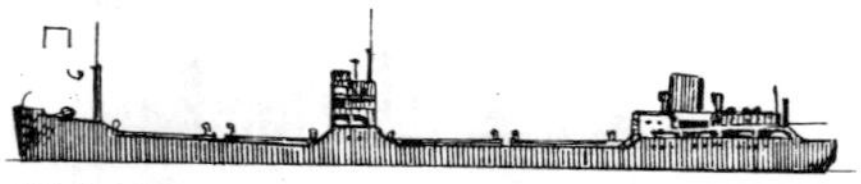

M_2FK *H123*

43410 ALDO CECCONI. It/Br 1953; O; 6600; 130.16 × 7.95 (427.03 × 26.08); R; 11; ex GLEDDOCH 1970.

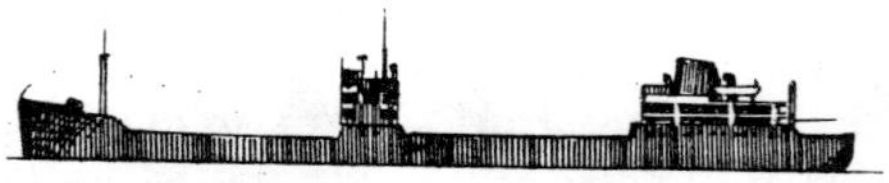

M_2FK *H123*

43420 LSCO TAWI-TAWI. Pi/Br 1960; O; 5300; 130.23 × 7.79 (427.26 × 5.56); M; 11; ex KLAR 1976; ex CRINAN 1974.

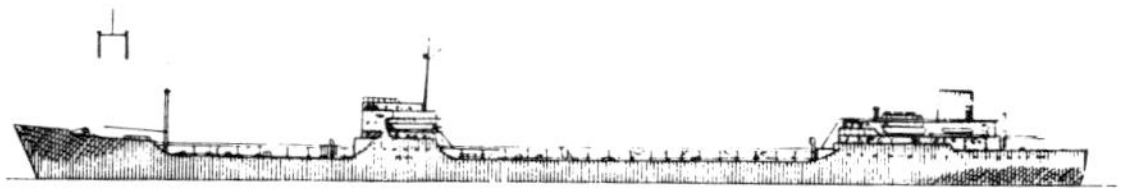

M_2FK H123
43430 ALASKAN TRADER. Gr/Sw 1954 Tk; 11600; 170.52 × 9.54 (559.45 × 31.3); M; 14.5; ex IRENES CHARISMA 1980; ex SWORD; ex HOEGH SWORD 1975.

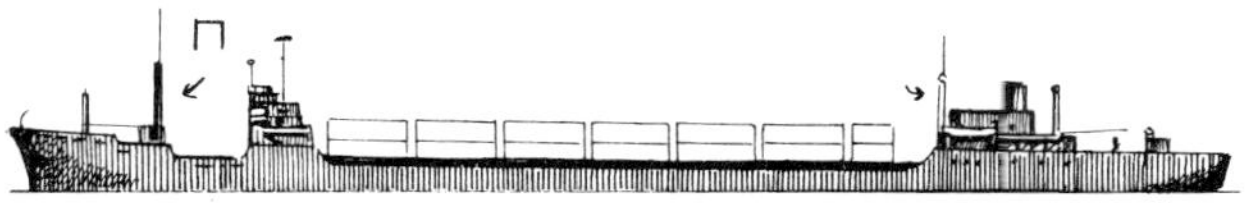

M_2FK H123
● **43440 CALIFORNIAN.** US/US 1946/54/60; C/Con; 13600; 193 × 10.06 (633.2 × 33.01); T; 16.75; ex MOUNT GREYLOCK 1951; Lengthened 1954; Converted from 'C4' cargo to Ore/Oil 1954; Converted from Ore/Oil to Cargo/Container 1960.

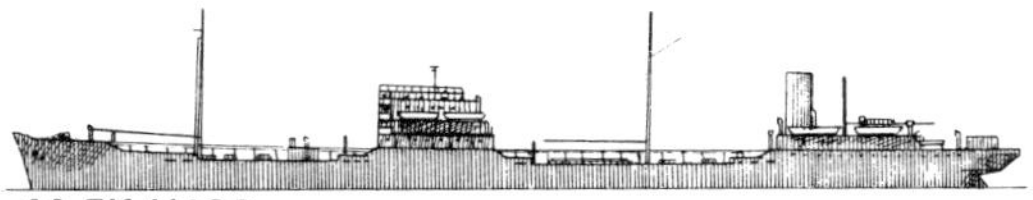

M_2FK H123
43450 13 DE DICIEMBRE. Ar/Ge 1935; Tk; 9500; 159.26 × 7.47 (522.51 × 24.51); R; 12.5.

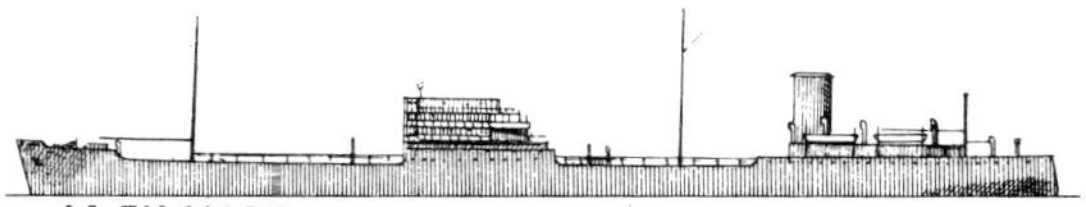

M_2FK H123
43460 SAN JORGE. Ar/Ge 1938; Tk; 10000; 165.34 × 7 79 (542.45 × 25.56); R; 14.

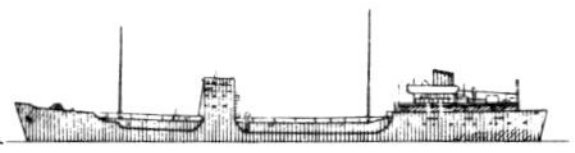

M_2FK H123
43470 VARI. Gr/Br 1954; Tk; 2000; 84.44 × 5.01 (277.03 × 16.44); M; 10; ex ANTERIORITY 1968.

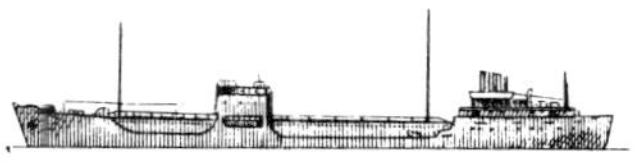

M_2FK H123
43480 KATERINA V. Gr/Br 1958; Tk; 2600; 94.52 × 5.75 (310.1 × 18.86); M; 10; ex ELENI 1973; ex GRIT 1968; At Jeddah May 1978. Being used as an oil storage vessel. Similar: **43481 PETROCLIS** (Gr) ex ASSURITY 1969.

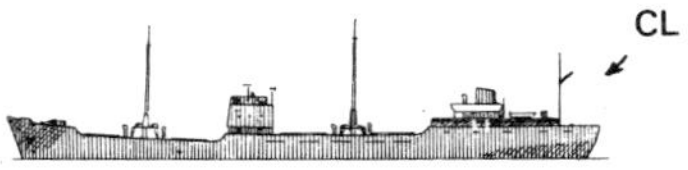

M_2FK H123
● **43490 MYASSAR.** Le/Br 1954; C; 2500; 93.38 × 5.47 (306.36 × 17.95); M; 10; ex MYASSA 1980; ex GEORGINA V. EVERARD 1978. Sister: **43491 ALEXIS G** (Gr) ex EMILIA G. 1975; ex FREDERICK T. EVERARD 1972.

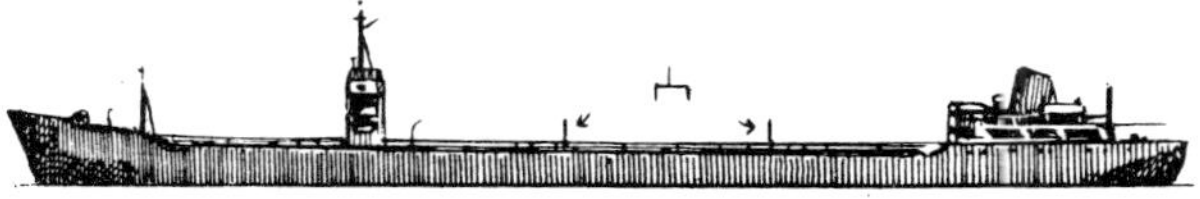

M_2FK H13
43500 CONALCO. Li/FRG 1959; O; 8800; 184.31 × 9.41 (604.69 × 30.87); M; 14.5; ex OLIN 1974. Sisters (Li flag): **43501 REVERE 43502 BURNSIDE** ex MATHIESON 1974.

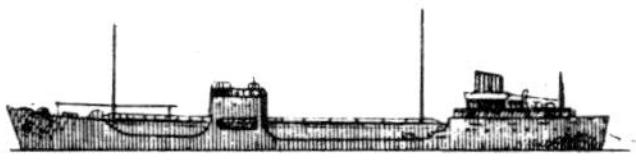

M_2FK H13
43510 KATERINA V. Gr/Br 1958; Tk; 2600; 94.52 × 5.75 (310.1 × 18.86); M; 10; ex ELENI 1973; ex GRIT 1968; At Jeddah May 1978, being used as an oil storage vessel. Similar: **43511 PETROCLIS** (Gr) ex ASSURITY 1969.

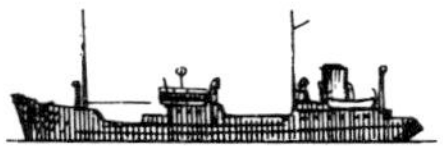

M_2FK H13
★**43520 AMBURAN.** Ru/Ge 1939; Tk; 640; 64.01 × 3.13 (210.01 × 10.27); TSM; 13; ex BERTA 1946.

M_2FK H3
43530 GIOVANNI CEFALU. It/It 1967; ST; 1200; 67.01 × 3.05 (219.85 × 10.01); M; 14; ex STORIONE 1971.

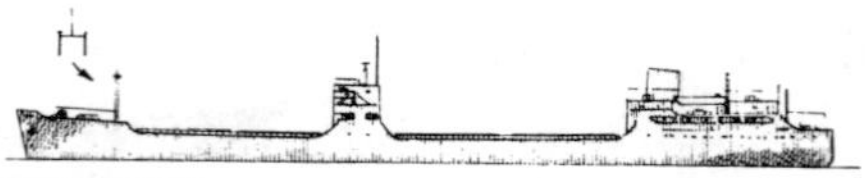

M_2FK_2 H123
⋆**43540 BERANE.** Ys/Br 1958; B; 6900; 129.7 × 7.73 (425.52 × 25.36); M; —; ex PHAEDON 1974; ex CLARKEDON 1973.

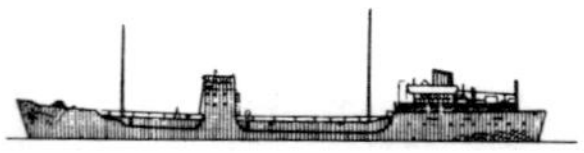

M_2FM H123
● **43550 MYASSAR.** Le/Br 1954; C; 2500; 93.38 × 5.47 (306.36 × 17.95); M; 10; ex MYASSA 1980; ex GEORGINA V. EVERARD 1978. Sister: **43551 ALEXIS G** (Gr) ex EMILIA G 1975; ex FREDERICK T. EVERARD 1972.

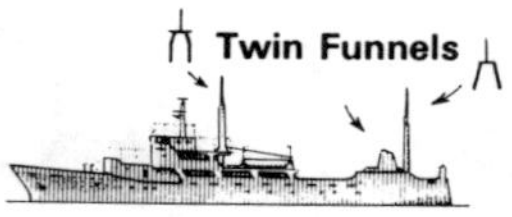

M_2FM H3
43560 GABRIELLA C. It/It 1971; ST; 1300; 70.01 × 4.2 (229.69 × 13.78); M; 15.5. Sister: **43561 MARIA C** (It).

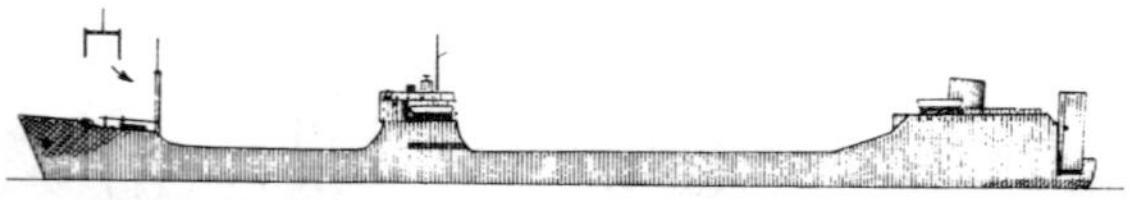

M_2FR H123
● **43570 ELENA.** Cy/Sw 1954/76 RoC; 5400; 170.52 × 6.03 (559.45 × 19.78); M; 16.25; ex DOLPHIN ELENA 1980; ex TABRIZ 1976; ex DAMIANOS 1975; ex TABRIZ 1967; Converted from a tanker 1976.

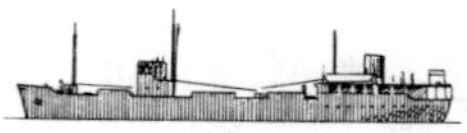

M_2KF H
43580 PANAGIA. Gr/No 1939; C; 870; 68.41 × 4.81 (224.44 × 15.78); M; 11; ex FANEROMINI 1975; ex PELOPS 1972; ex ANDENES 1964. Sister: **43581 SOFIA A** (Gr) ex SOPHIA A 1979; ex PELLINI 1972; ex STAMSUND 1966.

M_2KF H1
43590 GEOPOTES VII. Ne/Ne 1963; D; 4300; 107.63 × 8.04 (353.12 × 26.38); TSM; 12.

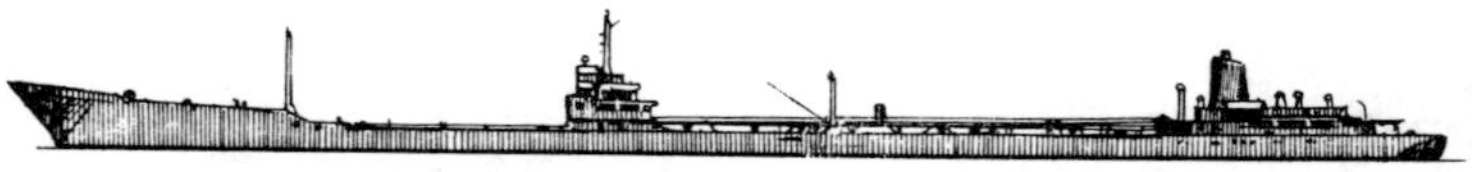

M_2KF H12
● **43600 ANGEL PARK.** Ko/US-Ja 1953/65; Tk; 31300; 233.53 × 11.79 (766.17 × 38.68); T; 12; ex LAS PIEDRAS 1967; Lengthened & deepened 1965.

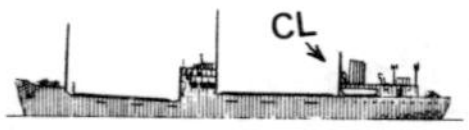

M_2KF H12
43610 THANASSIS. Gr/Br 1949; C; 1100; 68.59 × 4.45 (225.03 × 14.6); M; 10.5; ex TSIMENTEFS 1971; ex DANAE III 1971; ex HENFIELD 1969.

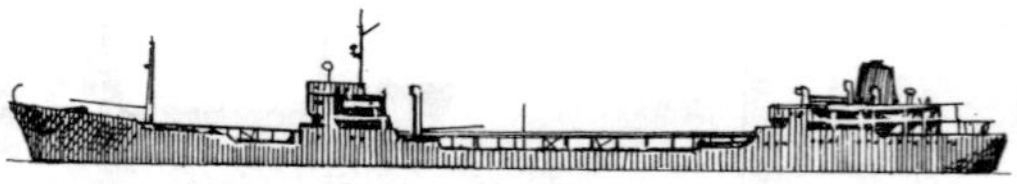

M_2KF H123
43620 THERMOPYLAI II. Gr/No 1955; Tk; 9000; 156.62 × 8.72 (513.85 × 28.61); M; 13.5; ex ANETTE 1978; ex ROBERT STOVE 1963.

M_2KF H123
34630 POLYSTAR. No/Sw 1962; Tk; 12800; 170.67 × 9.74 (559.94 × 31.96); M; 14.5.

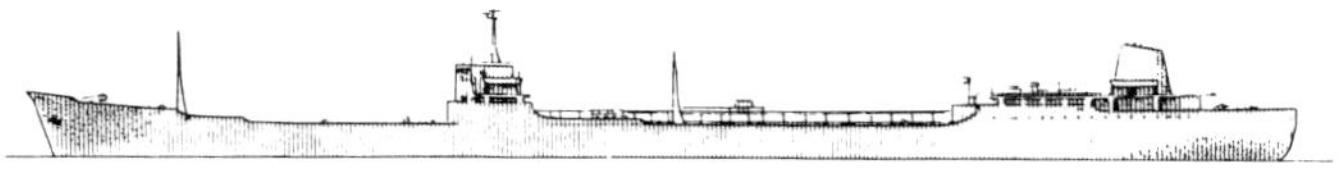

M_2KF H123
43640 THEODEGMON. Gr/Ja 1960; Tk; 19700; 201.53 × 11.07 (661.19 × 36.32); M; 16.5; ex RYUJIN MARU 1973; ex SHINANOGAWA MARU 1970.

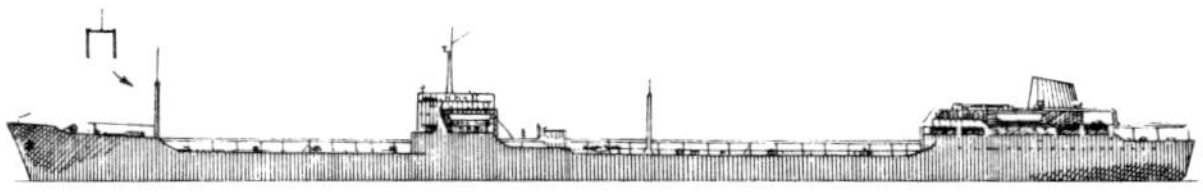

M_2KF H123
● **43650 CLEON.** Gr/Sw 1959; Tk; 16100; 187.71 × 10.48 (615.85 × 34.38); M; 16.5; ex TITUS 1971. Sister (Li flag): **43651 ANTCLIZO** ex TOLUMA 1972 Similar: **43652 GOGO RIVER** ex GRUBE OVE 1977; ex GRUNO OVE 1975; ex POLYDUKE 1974 **43653 TRINITY NAVIGATOR** ex STOLT ZEUS; ex POLYGLORY 1974.

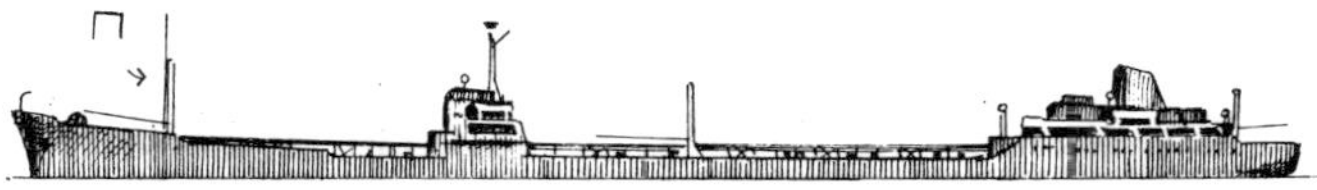

M_2KF H123
43660 PETROLA 32. Gr/FRG 1957; Tk; 22000; 201.17 × 10.93 (660.01 × 35.86); T; —; ex PETROLA XXXII 1976; ex APOLLO XI 1975; ex CAROLINE OETKER 1969.

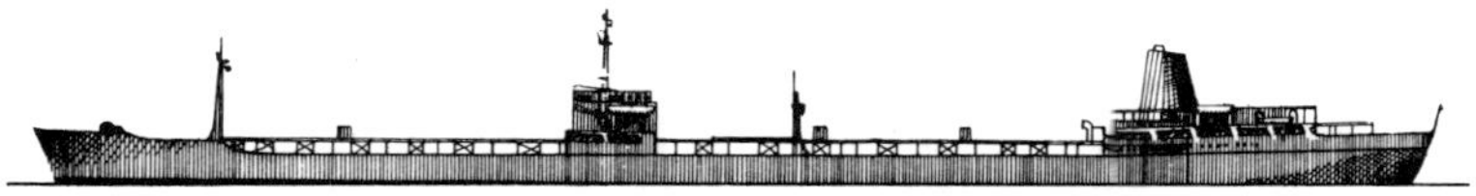

M_2KF H123
● **43670 JENNIFER.** Pa/De 1965; Tk; 33000; 235.11 × 12.27 (771.36 × 40.26); T; 17; ex PRIMA MAERSK 1977.

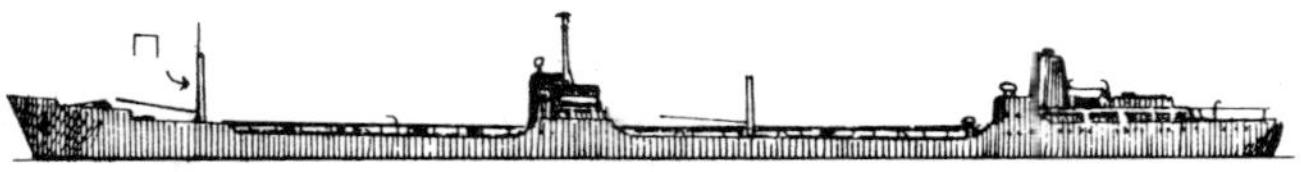

M_2KF H123
43680 ALLEGIANCE. US/US 1956; Tk; 19500; 201.48 × 10.87 (661.02 × 35.66); T; 16.5; ex CITIES SERVICE BALTIMORE 1975. Sister: **43681 BANNER** (US) ex CITIES SERVICE MIAMI 1976.

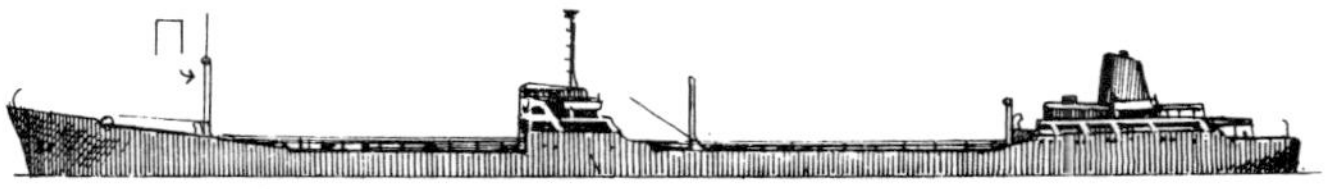

M_2KF H123
43690 TEXACO ROCHESTER. Br/Be 1959; Tk; 22000; 203.16 × 10.98 (666.54 × 36.02); T; 17; ex CALTEX BRISTOL 1968.

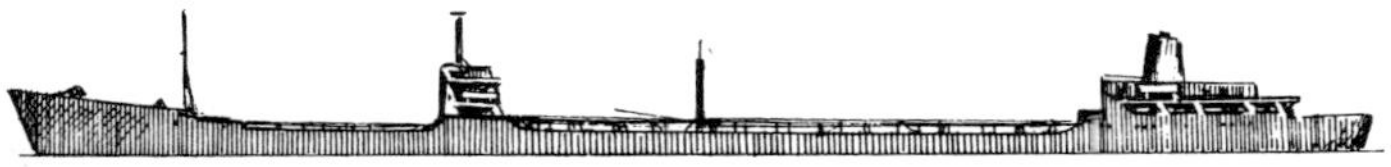

M_2KF H123
● **43700 TEXACO IDAHO.** Pa/Ja 1959; Tk; 25500; 213.77 × 12.09 (701.35 × 39.67); T; 16.5; ex IDAHO 1960. Sister: **43701 TEXACO VIRGINIA** (Pa) ex TEXACO SANTIAGO 1963; ex SANTIAGO 1962.

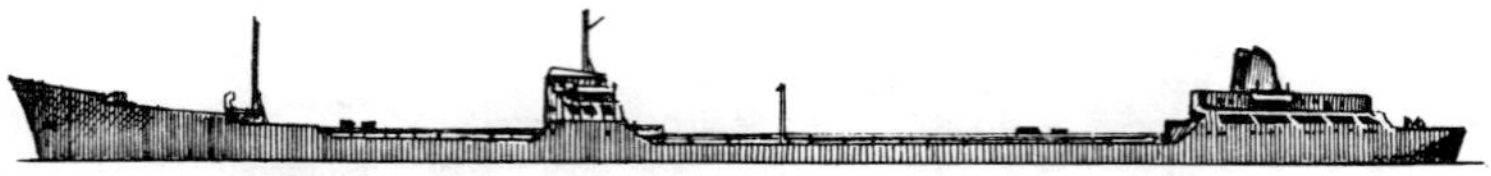

M_2KF H123
43710 TEXACO LIVERPOOL. Br/Br 1962; Tk; 30800; 227.46 × 12.06 (746.26 × 39.57); T; 16; ex REGENT LIVERPOOL 1969.

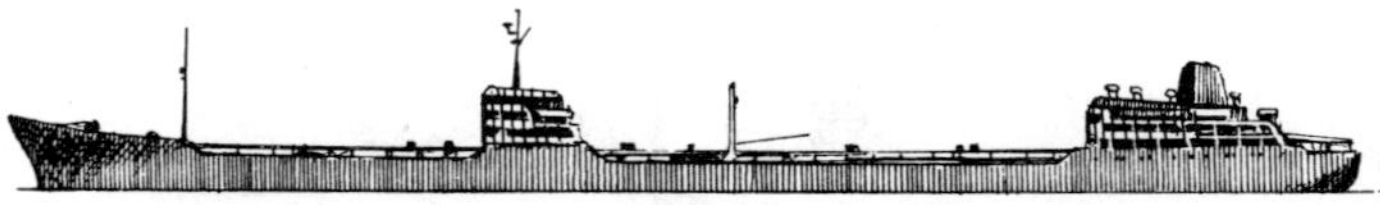

M_2KF H123
43720 PETROMAR MENDOZA. Ar/Ne 1960; Tk; 23600; 211.31 × 11.32 (693.27 × 37.14); T; 17; ex ESSO AMSTERDAM 1970.

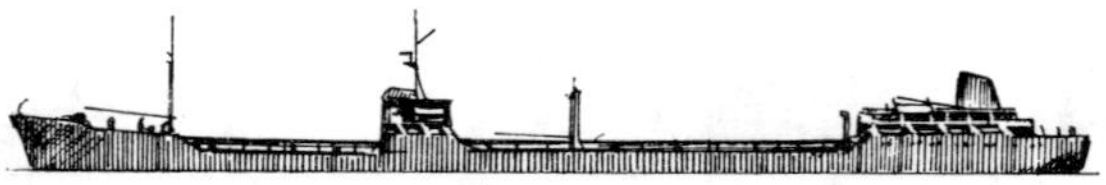

M_2KF H123
43730 PAROS. Gr/Sw 1960; Tk; 12700; 170.01 × 9.73 (557.78 × 31.92); M; 15.5; ex PETER; ex KEF HAWK 1977; ex ASPO 1974; ex AGNETA BILLNER 1972. Sister: ⭑**43731 NANJIANG** (RC) ex GUNILLA BILLNER 1975.

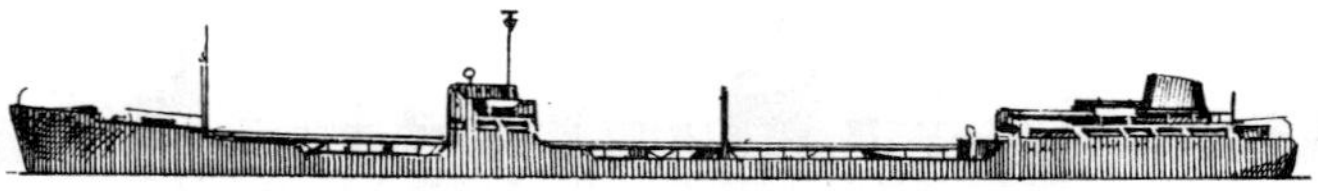

M_2KF H123
43740 NOSTOS. Gr/No 1960; Tk; 21600; 202.7 × 11.15 (665.03 × 36.58); M; 16; ex SUNNY LADY 1977; ex POLARSOL 1972. Sister: **43741 PAYAS** (Tu) ex THORSTRAND 1967.

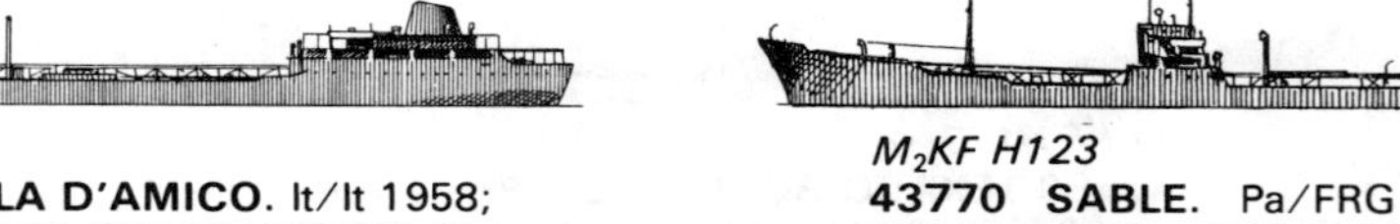

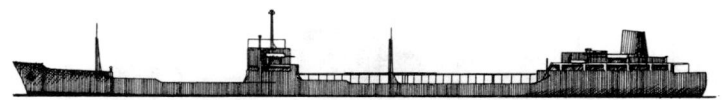

M_2KF H123
43750 HERMINIOS. Po/Ja 1960; Tk; 25400; 216.42 × 11.6 (710.04 × 38.06); T; 17. Sister: **43751 INAGO** (Po).

M_2KF H123
● **43760 GIOVANNELLA D'AMICO.** It/It 1958; Tk; 13000; 169.93 × 9.65 (557.51 × 31.66); M; 15; ex GIOVANNELLA D'AMICO CHEMIST 1972; ex GIOVANNELLA D'AMICO 1965. Sister: **43761 MARINELLA D'AMICO** (It).

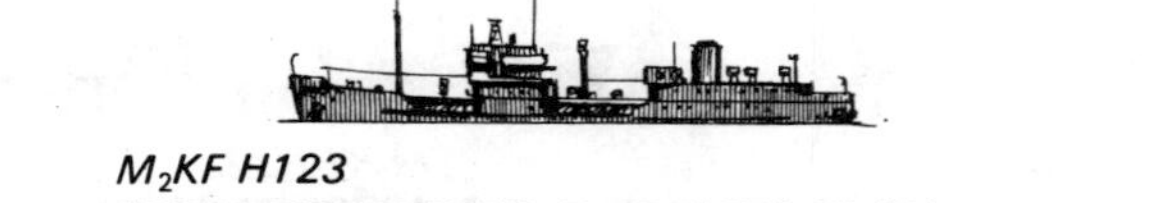

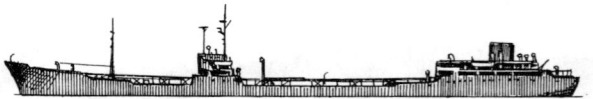

M_2KF H123
43770 SABLE. Pa/FRG 1957; Tk; 13700; 180.14 × 9.82 (591.01 × 32.22); M; 14.5; ex CHERRY BAY; ex HERULV 1978; ex JOHS STOVE 1967.

M_2KF H123
43780 EDDYFIRTH. Br/Br 1954; Tk/FA; 2200; 87.66 × 5.27 (287.6 × 17.29); R; 12.

M_2KF H123
★43790 ARGON. Ru/Fi 1963; Tk; 3400; 105.39 × 6.22 (345.77 × 20.42); M; 14.25. Sisters (Ru flag): **★43791 ALUKSNE ★43792 APE ★43793 AKTASH ★43794 AKSAY ★43795 ABRENE ★43796 AMURSK ★43797 APSHERONSK ★43798 ARAKS ★43799 ANAPKA ★43800 LYUBERTSY ★43801 SINEGORSK ★43802 ALEKSEYEVKA ★43803 ALEKSEYEVSK ★43804 ANIVA ★43805 ALAGIR ★43806 ALEYSK ★43807 ALEKSIN ★43808 ANAPA ★43809 EVENSK ★43810 ABAGUR ★43811 ARDATOV ★43812 DARNITZA ★43813 EREBUS ★43814 INKERMAN ★43815 VOLFRAM ★43816 IMAN ★43817 RADIY ★43818 ABAKAN ★43819 TYUMENNEFT ★43820 YUGLA** (Cu flag): **★43821 CUBA** ex ARTSYZ 1962.

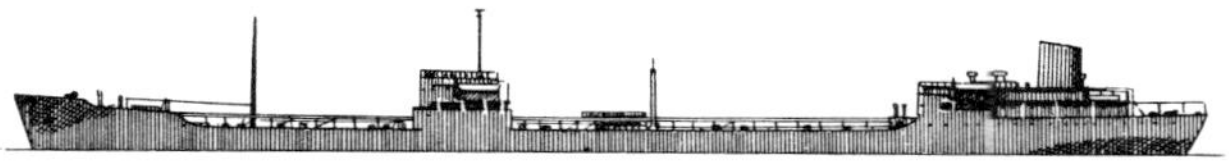

M_2KF H123
43830 FIONA M. Pa/Be 1958; Tk; 16300; 187.36 × 10.38 (614.7 × 34.06); M; 15.75; ex ATHANASIOS 1979; ex PONTUS 1977; ex ARTHUR P 1970; ex HOEGH FOAM 1965.

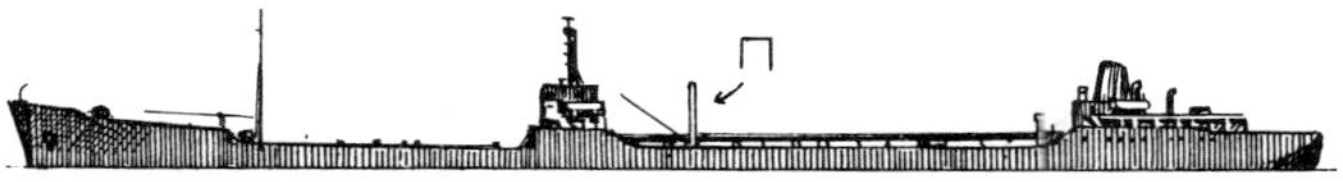

M_2KF H123
43840 AELLO. Li/Ja 1957; Tk; 20700; 206.97 × 11.62 (679.04 × 38.12); T; 16.

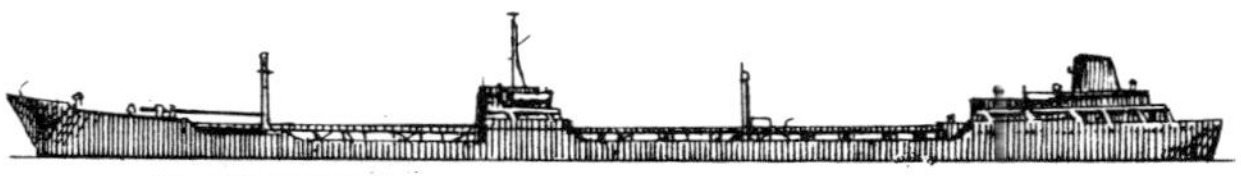

M_2KF H123
43850 PERMINA SAMUDRA V. Li/FRG 1958; Tk; 1600; 189.14 × 10.91 (620.53 × 35.79); M; —; ex LINDOS 1971; ex BENSTREAM 1967; ex RING CHIEF 1964.

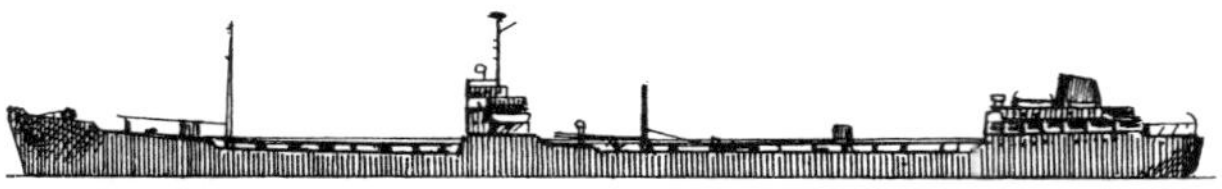

M_2KF H123
43860 GEORGIOS M II. Gr/Sw 1958; Tk. 16600; 187.76 × 10.5 (616.01 × 34.38); M; 16; ex KRONOHOLM 1967; May be broken up.

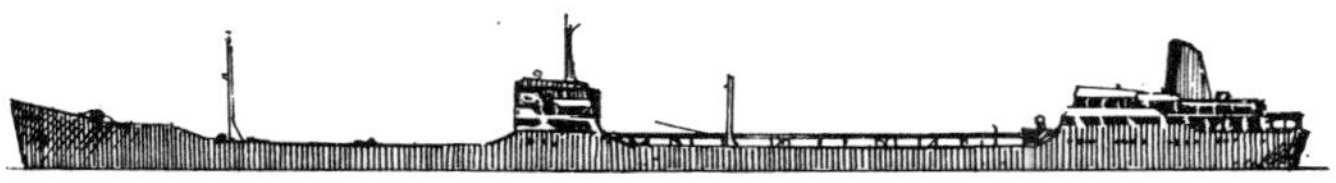

M_2KF H123
43870 EMOULI. Gr/Br 1958; Tk; 20700; 202.67 × 10.99 (664.93 × 36.06); T; 16.25; ex PETROLA 19 1980; ex PETROLA XIX 1976; ex LLANISHEN 1974.

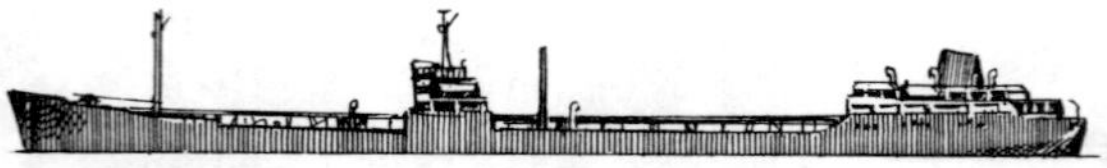

M_2KF H123
43880 PALMIRA ZETA. It/Be 1958; Tk; 12500; 170.69 × 9.65 (560.01 × 31.66); M; 15; ex OCEAN TANKER 1977; ex FINA ALLEMAGNE 1975; ex PURFINA ALLEMAGNE 1960. Similar: **43881 MAR CORRUSCO** (It) ex PROMACHOS 1977.

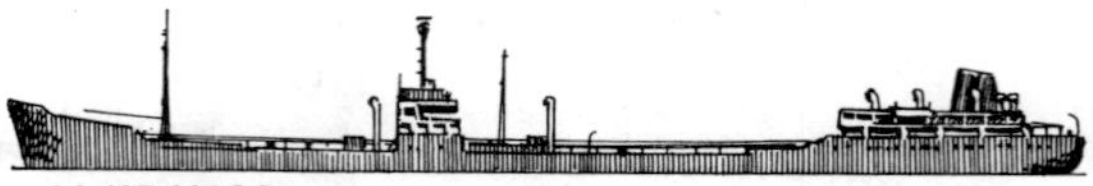

M_2KF H123
43890 HARRIET. Pa/Be 1958; Tk; 13500; 170.69 × 9.65 (560.01 × 31.66); M; 14; ex NAT CREST 1 1980; ex CALTEX CAPE TOWN 1978; ex WAIKIWI PIONEER 1973; ex ELEFTHEROUPOLIS 1972.

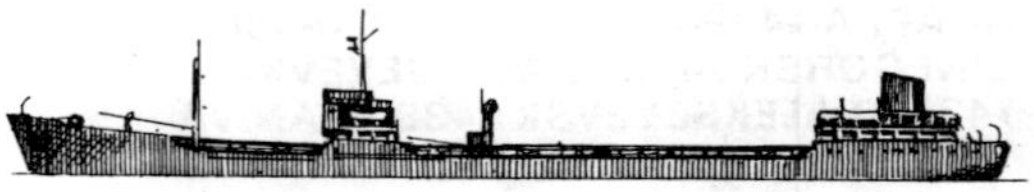

M_2KF H123
● **43900 MIRAMAR.** Gr/No 1956; Tk; 8600; 155.1 × 8.64 (508.86 × 28.35); M; 14; ex ANCO SOUND 1969; ex ANCO STORM 1969; ex BOHEME 1964. Similar: **43901 PIBIMARE PRIMA** (It) ex STOLT FREDDY 1969; ex STOLT NIAGARA 1967; ex FREDDY 1964.

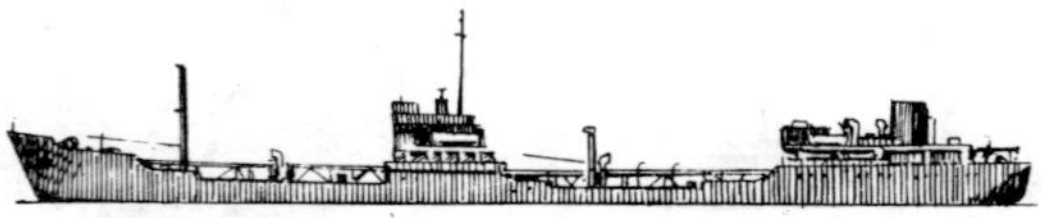

M_2KF H123
43910 LSCO TRIDENT. Pi/Br 1954; Tk; 9500; 157.54 × 8.85 (516.86 × 29.04); M; 12.5; ex LORENZO 1971; ex REGENT ROYAL 1968.

M_2KF H123
43920 COSMOPOLITAN II. Sg/Br 1951; Tk; 8400; 152.46 × 8.41 (500.2 × 27.59); M; 12; ex ASTRAMAR 1971; ex BERNHARD HANSSEN 1960.

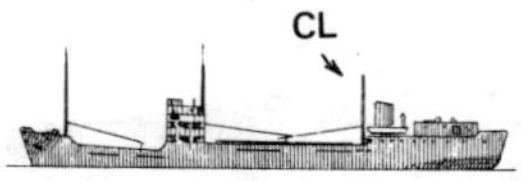

M_2KF H123
43930 HAMEN. No/Br 1949; C; 1400; 76.79 × 4.77 (251.94 × 15.65); M; 10; ex TANDIK 1963; ex POMPEY POWER 1960.

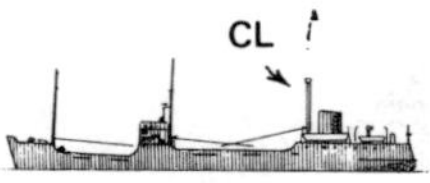

M_2KF H123
43940 MAGDUS. Cy/Br 1949; C; 1000; 65.11 × 4.34 (213.62 × 14.24); M; 10.5; ex BABI 1980; ex IOULIA K 1973; ex MAYFAIR SAPPHIRE 1973; ex SAPPHIRE 1958.

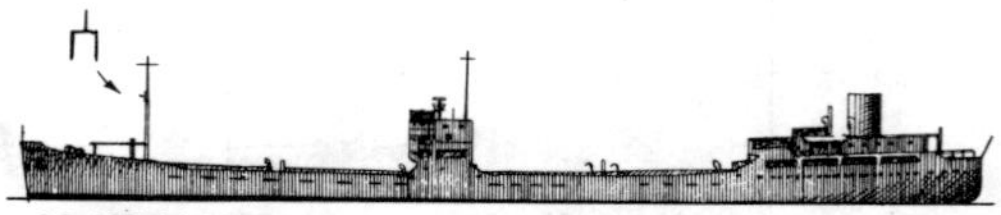

M_2KF H123
● **43950 ALFA CEMENTA.** Gr/Br 1955; O; 7600; 153.93 × 8.57 (505.02 × 28.12); M; 13; ex KATINA 1977; ex DUNADD 1973. Sister: **43951 MARY** (Gr) ex DUNCRAIG 1973.

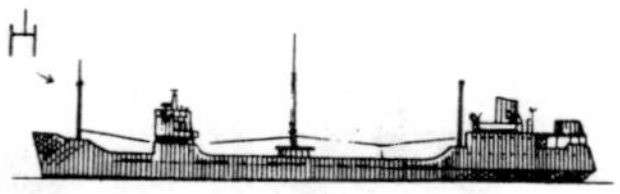

M_2KF H123
43960 NIKITAS. Cy/Fi 1951; C; 2300; 88.5 × 5.18 (290.35 × 16.99); M; 10; ex SANTA PAOLA 1972; ex EMIL BERGER 1969; ex GENOA.

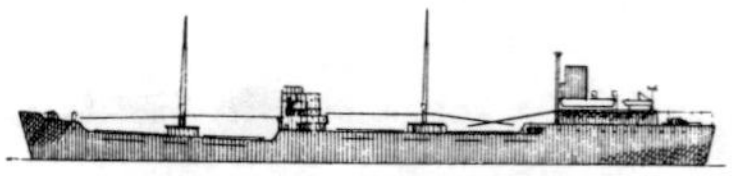

M_2KF H123
43970 DONA ISIDORA. Ch/Br 1949; C; 4100; 109.3 × 6.66 (358.6 × 21.85); R; 10.

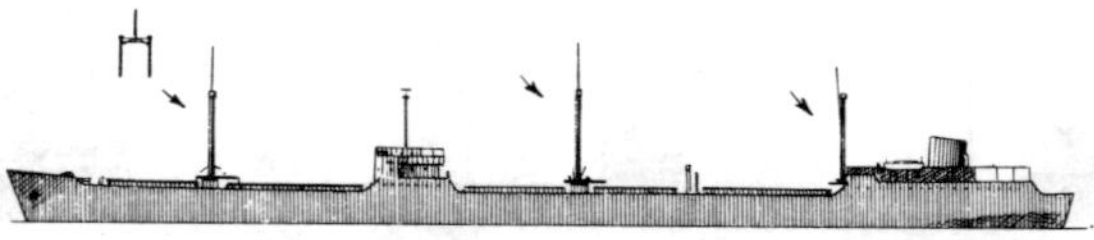

M_2KF H123
43980 PHAEDRA E. Gr/Sw 1954/62; B; 12600; 167.54 × 10.36 (549.67 × 33.99); M; —; ex TRADE CARRIER 1974; ex VERONA 1967. Converted from tanker 1962.

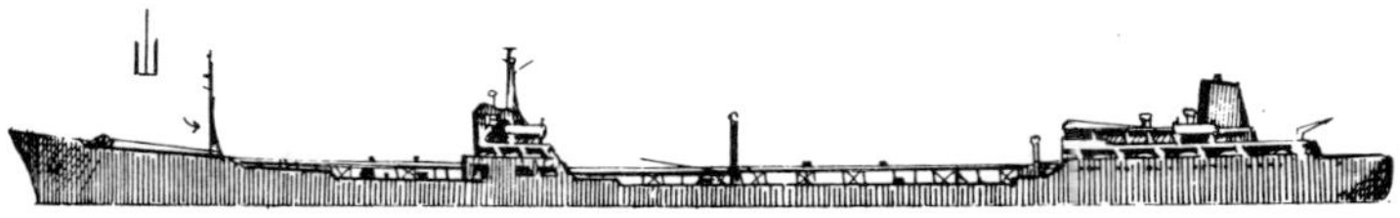

M_2KF $H13$

● **43990 CHEVRON MADRID.** Ne/Be 1961; Tk; 31600; 223.83 × 11.49 (734.35 × 37.7); T; 17; ex CALTEX MADRID 1969. Sister: **43991 CHEVRON NEDERLAND** (Ne) ex CALTEX NEDERLAND 1969 Similar: **43992 TEXACO PLYMOUTH** (Ne) ex CALTEX PLYMOUTH 1968.

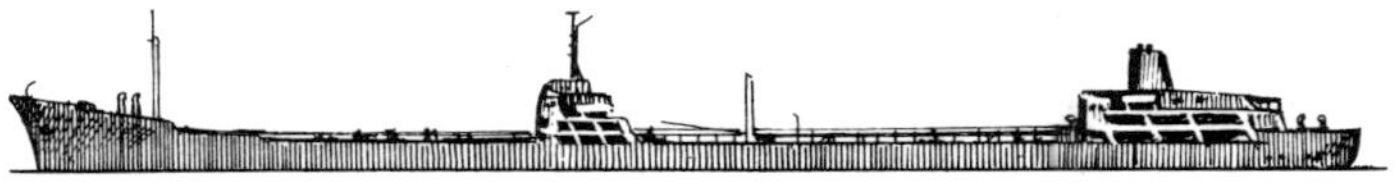

M_2KF $H13$

44000 TEXACO ALASKA. Pa/Sw 1960; Tk; 24100; 213.21 × 11.16 (699.51 × 36.61); T; 16.5. Sister: **44001 TEXAS IOWA** (Pa) ex IOWA 1959.

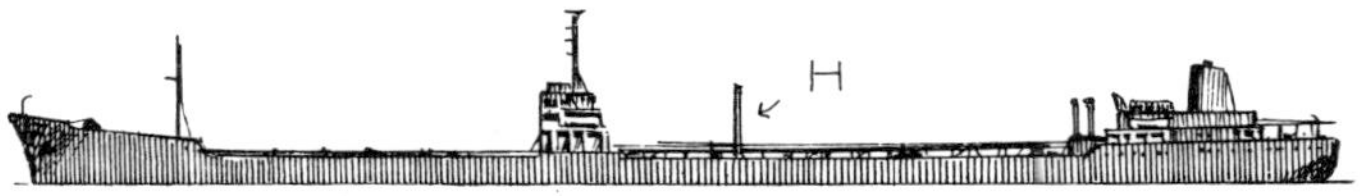

M_2KF $H13$

44010 NEFELI. Li/Ja 1958; Tk; 24300; 211.72 × 10.89 (694.62 × 35.73); T; —. Sister: **44011 KYMO** (Li).

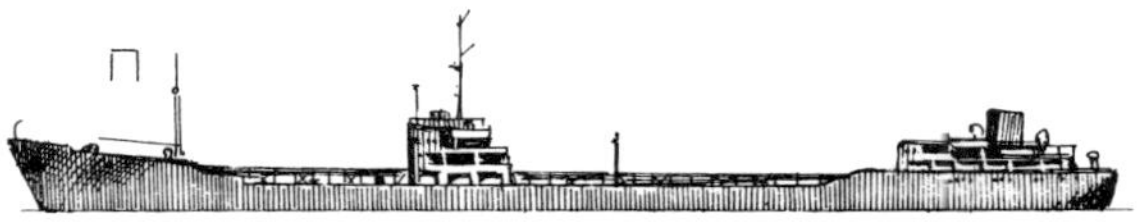

M_2KF $H13$

44020 MIDAS DREAM. Gr/Sw 1956; Tk; 13200; 173.79 × 9.74 (570.18 × 31.96); M; 15; ex MELISITTA 1980; ex LA TURBIE 1971; ex J.M. UGLAND 1969.

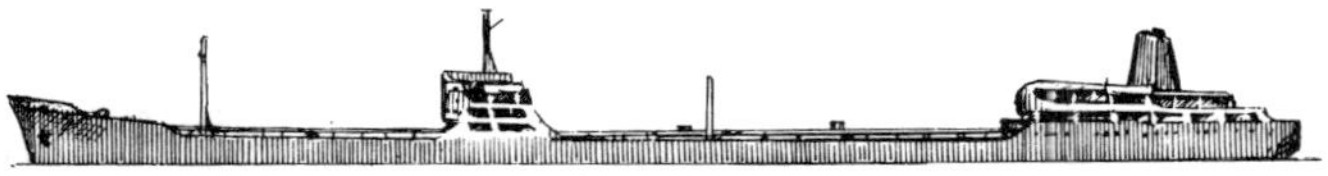

M_2KF $H13$

44030 CHERRY BARON. Sg/Br 1959; Tk; 21600; 202.7 × 10.95 (665.03 × 35.93); T; 15; ex VARICELLA 1976.

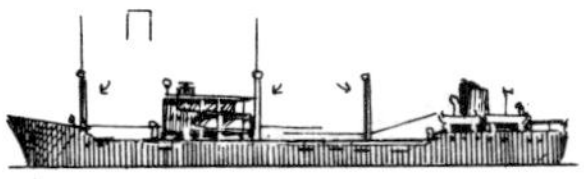

M_2KF $H13$

44040 GOLDEN EASTERN. Sg/Hong Kong 1953; C; 1700; 84.49 × 4.86 (277.2 × 15.94); M; 12; ex SLETHOLM 1972; ex HENDRIK 1964. Sister: **44041 GOLDEN SOURCE** (Sg) ex SLETFJORD 1972; ex HERVAR 1964.

M_2KF $H13$

44060 GEOPOTES 12. Pa/Br 1969; D; 3000; 95 × 5 (311.68 × 16.4); TrSM; 10; ex TRANSMUNDUM II 1974. Sister: **44061 TRANSMUNDUM I** (FRG).

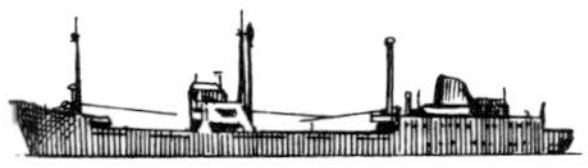

M_2KF $H13$

44050 DELDONA. Pa/FRG 1956; C; 1400; 88.7 × 4.64 (291.01 × 15.19); M; 14.5; ex DORIC ARROW; ex BALTIC ARROW.

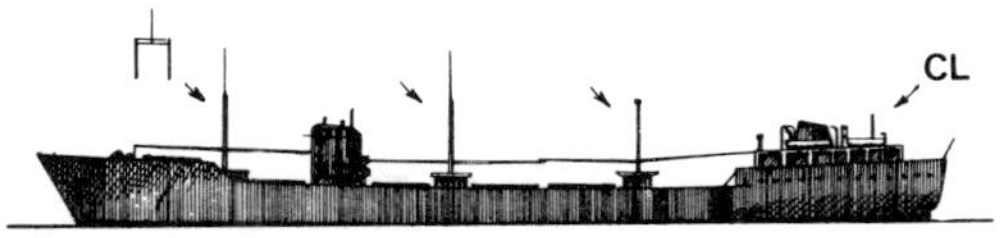

M_2KF $H13$

44070 APJ SUSHMA. In/FRG 1953; C; 6300; 144.48 × 7.8 (474.02 × 25.59); M; 13.5; ex PAUL HONOLD 1961. Sister: **44071 GEORGIOS** (Bz) ex OSTERTOR 1970; ex MARGARETHE HONOLD 1960.

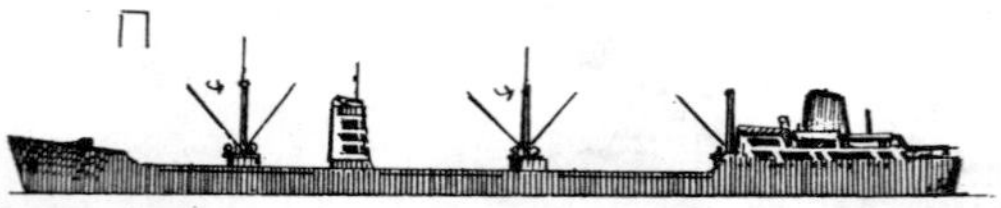

M_2KF H13
● **44080 AEGEAN SEA.** Gr/Fr 1959; B; 9300; 149.38 × 9.15 (490.09 × 30.02); M; 15; ex ASPILOS 1979; ex KEUM MOON 1970; ex ANCORA 1968. Sisters: **44081 WELL SPEEDER** (Pa) ex SAINT CLAIR 1980; ex LALINDA 1976; ex POLARGLIMT **44082 SEALORD 1** (Pa) ex UTVIK 1973; ex AFRICA 1962 **44083 BARRIAN** (Br) ex PERSENK 1980; ex PERSENG; ex ACAMAR 1970; ex DONAU 1968; ex ACAMAR 1966; ex STARCLIPPER 1965; ex ARTHUR STOVE 1962.

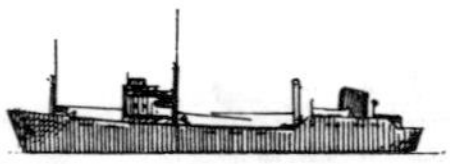

M_2KF H13
44130 KIM GUAN. Pa/Br 1950; C; 1400; 66.6 × 5.06 (218.5 × 16.6); M; 11; ex KING FISH 1969; ex CHOPIN 1966; ex AKASSA 1966; ex CHOPIN 1965; ex RADJA MAS 1964; ex PIADDA 1963.

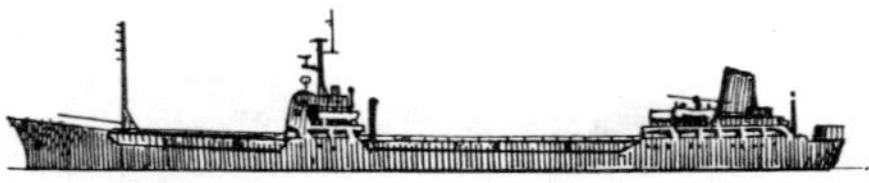

M_2KFK H123
⋆**44140 BATUMI.** Ru/De 1932; Tk; 6600; 129.27 × 8.27 (424.11 × 27.13); M; 11.5; ex BATUM 1939; ex BATUMSKY SOVIET 1934.

M_2KF H13
44090 IVORY ISLANDS. Pa/FRG 1959; C; 7000/9700; 157.46 × 7.86/9.44 (516.6 × 25.78/30.97); M; 13; ex LINZERTOR 1970.

M_2KF H13
⋆**44100 BOLSHEVIK KARAYEV.** Ru/Ru 1959; Tk; 3800; 123.5 × 4.4 (405.18 × 14.44); TSM; 10.5; Caspian Sea Service. Sisters (Ru flag): ⋆**44101 FEDYA GUBANOV** ⋆**44102 PAMYAT 26 KOMISSAROV** ⋆**44103 ALMA-ATA** ⋆**44104 GYURGYAN** ⋆**44104 NEFTECHALA** ⋆**44106 DZHEBRAIL** ⋆**44107 UDZHARY** ⋆**44108 AL PETRI** ⋆**44109 NEBIT DAG** ⋆**44110 NUREK** ⋆**44111 SURAKHANY** ⋆**44112 ORDZHONIKIDZENNEFT** ⋆**44113 SABUNCHI** ⋆**44114 SHIRVANNEFT** ⋆**44115 BUZOVNY** ⋆**44116 DZHORAT** ⋆**44117 MARDAKYANY** ⋆**44118 MASHITAGI** ⋆**44119 KARAKUM KANAL** ⋆**44120 MANGYSHLAK** ⋆**44121 KIROVABAD** ⋆**44122 EMBA** ⋆**44123 NAKHICHEVAN** (wine tanker) ⋆**44124 PORT ILYICH** ⋆**44125 VOLGONEFTGAROZ** ⋆**44126 ZHIGANSK** (RC flag): ⋆**44127 ERMA.**

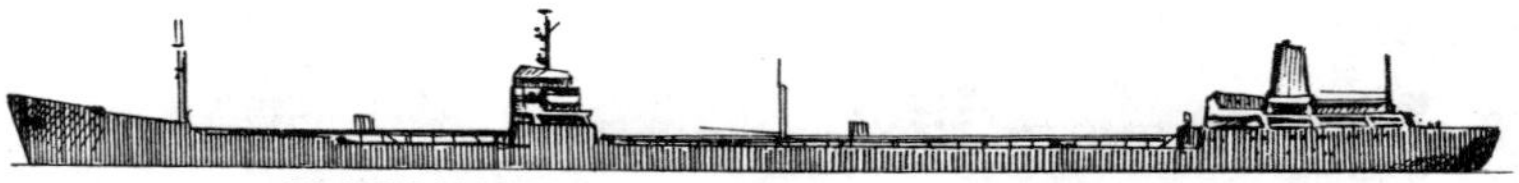

M_2KFK H123
44150 IRINI M. Gr/Sw 1963; Tk; 36500; 236.23 × 12.63 (775.03 × 41.44); T; 17; ex GERD MAERSK 1979.

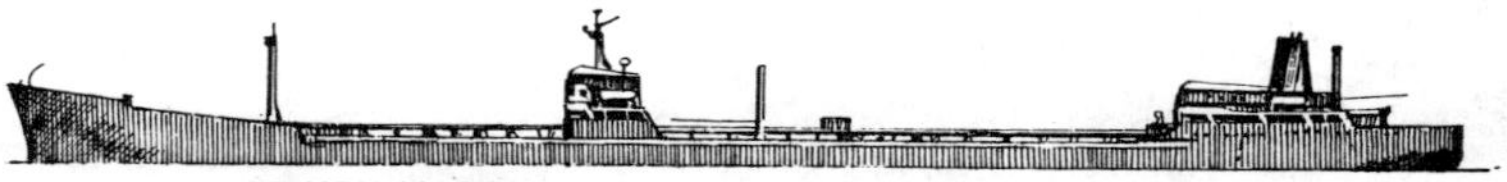

M_2KFK H123
44160 MARIPRIMA. Li/Sw 1961; Tk; 30200; 227.34 × 12.01 (745.87 × 39.4); T; 16.75; ex ESSO STOCKHOLM 1977.

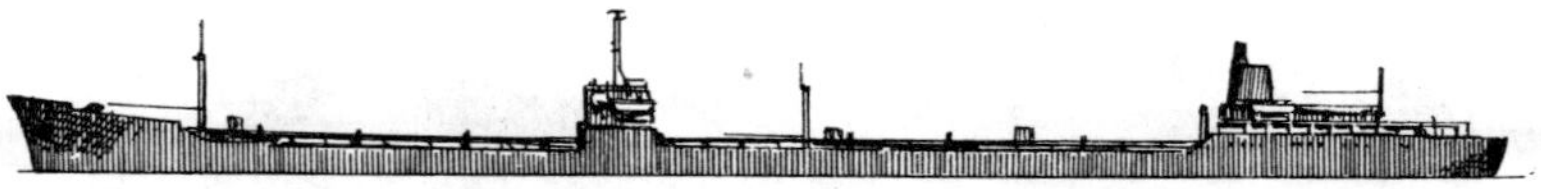

M_2KFK H123
44170 CHERRY PARK. No/Sw 1963; Tk; 35000; 237.27 × 12.69 (778.44 × 41.63); M; 16.5; ex PARK; ex FERNPARK 1977.

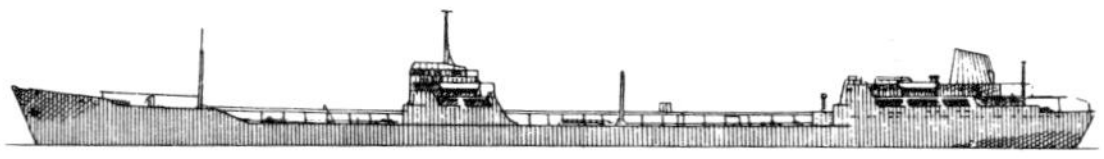

M_2KFK H123
44180 PETROSTAR IV. Si/Sw 1959; Tk; 12600; 170.03 × 9.7 (557.84 × 31.82); M; 14; ex LIDFOLD 1975; ex LIDVARD 1967.

M_2KFK H123
44190 IONIO. It/Sw 1958; Tk; 12700; 170.01 × 9.44 (557.78 × 30.97); M; 15.5; ex BITTERFELD; ex SOUTHERN CLIPPER 1963. Sister: **44191 ATHENIAN HORIZON** (Gr) ex HORIZON 1972; ex ORION 1968; ex FRANS SUELL 1964.

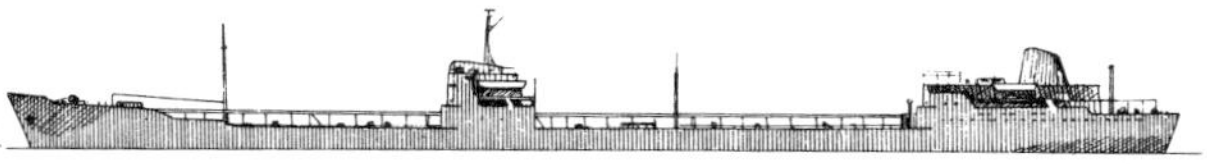

M_2KFK H123
● **44200 ANGELA F.** Gr/Sw 1959; Tk; 15600; 184.87 × 10.19 (606.53 × 33.43); M; —; ex SIRIUS 1967.

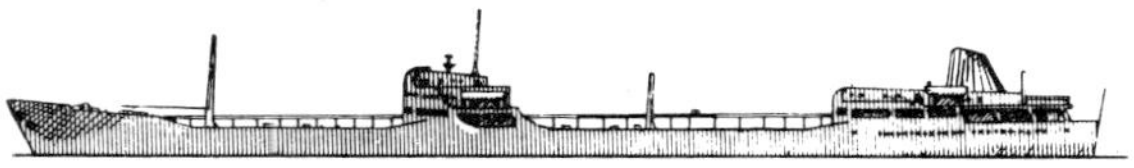

M_2KFK H123
44210 AMASTRA. Br/Br 1958; Tk; 12300; 170.39 × 9.36 (559.02 × 30.71); M; 14.5. Similar: **44211 UJE** (Pa) ex AMORIA **44212 ALINDA** (Br) **44213 ASPRELLA** (Br) **44214 AULICA** (Br) **44215 ACHATINA** (Br) **44216 STONEGATE** (Br).

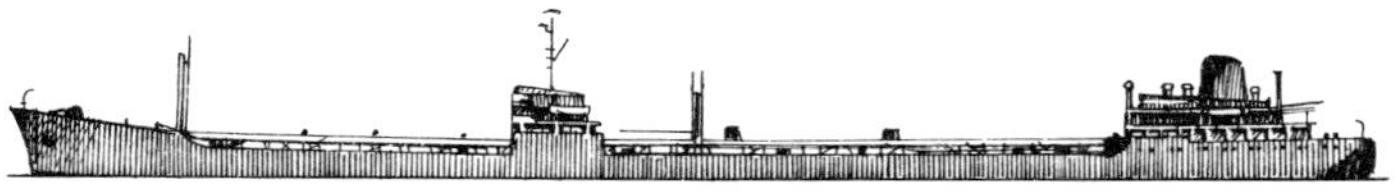

M_2KFK H123
● **44220 PETROMAR ROSARIO.** Ar/FRG 1960; Tk; 22400; 211.23 × 11.33 (693.01 × 37.17); T; 17; ex ESSO NURNBERG. Sister: **44221 PETROMAR CORDOBA** (Ar) ex ESSO HANNOVER 1968.

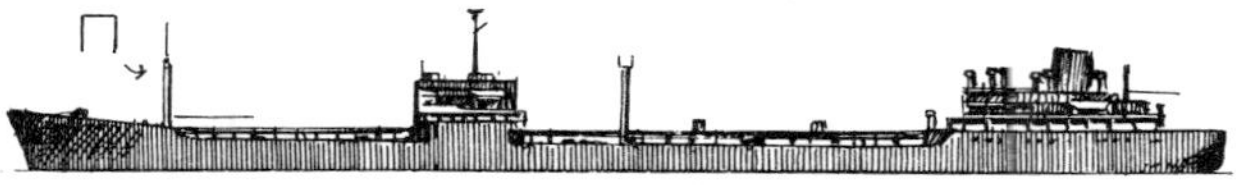

M_2KFK H123
44230 PETROMAR BAHIA BLANCA. Ar/FRG 1955; Tk; 18100; 192.21 × 9.94 (630.61 × 32.61); T; 17; ex ESSO DUSSELDORF 1966.

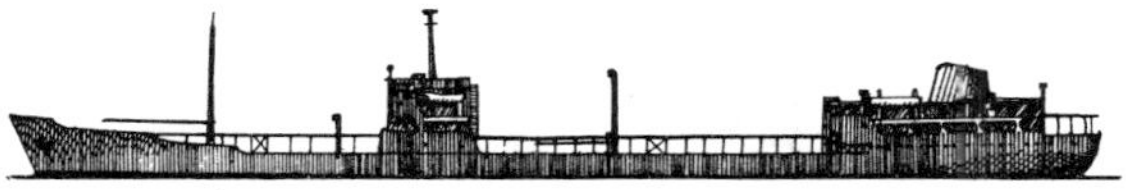

M_2KFK H123
44240 DONGJIANG. Pa/No 1960; Tk; 12800; 170.69 × 9.61 (560.01 × 31.53); M; 14; ex VENTURA 1976; ex LOVDAL 1969.

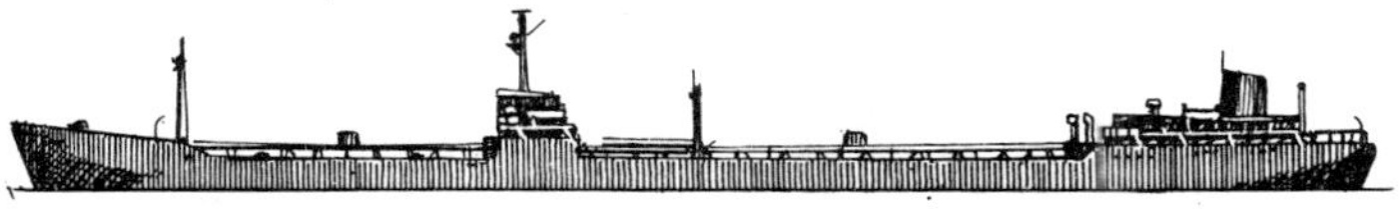

M_2KFK H123
44250 ATHINA. Pa/De 1964; Tk; 21600; 209.15 × 11.27 (686.19 × 36.98); M; 15.5; ex OLUF MAERSK 1980; ex KAREN MAERSK 1978. Sister: **44251 HENNING MAERSK** (De).

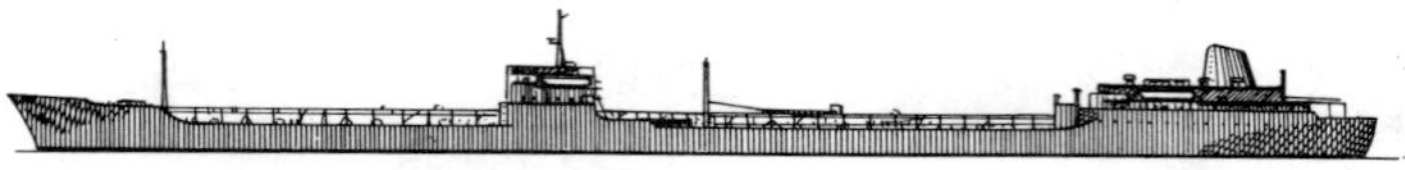

M_2KFK H123
44260 RION. Gr/Sw 1963; Tk; 26400; 215.22 × 11.94 (706.1 × 39.17); M; 15.25. ex POLYCASTLE 1980. Similar: **44261 POLYKARP** (No).

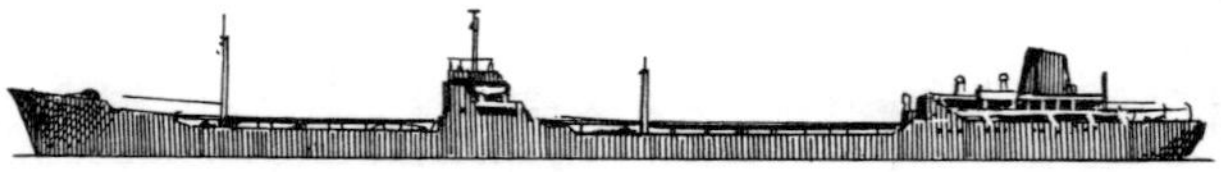

M_2KFK H123
44270 LEFKAS. Gr/Ne 1962; Tk; 16400; 188.83 × 10.35 (619.52 × 33.96); M; 15.75; ex DELIAN APOLLON 1978. Sister (Gr flag): **44271 STYLIS** ex DELIAN SPIRIT 1978 **44272 SAN NIKITAS** ex DELIAN LETO 1978.

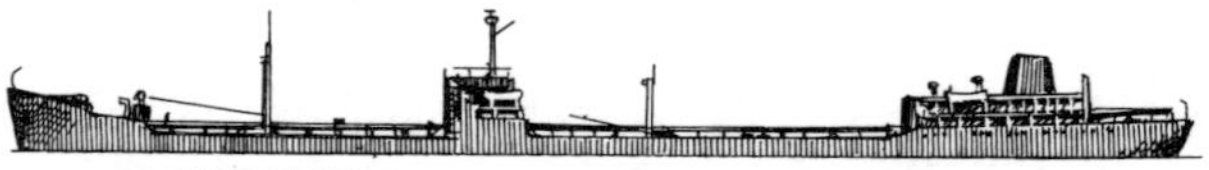

M_2KFK H123
44280 PORT RENARD. Fr/Gr 1961; Tk; 16000; 187.36 × 10.34 (614.7 × 33.92); M; 15; ex YALTON 1974; ex WORLD HOPE 1973.

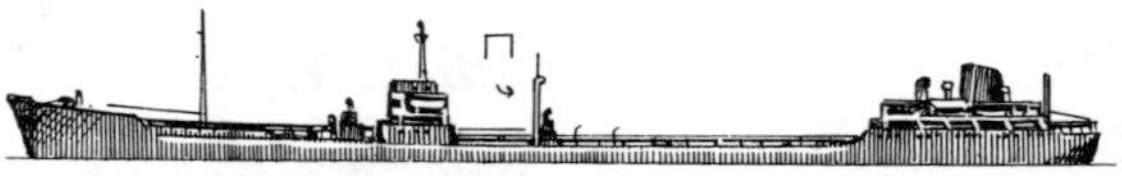

M_2KFK H123
● **44290 TOXOTIS.** Cy/Be 1960; Tk; 12900; 170.75 × 9.65 (560.2 × 31.66); M; 15; ex STOLT ATHENIAN 1976; ex STOLT PROGRESS 1972; ex OLGA NIELSEN 1966.

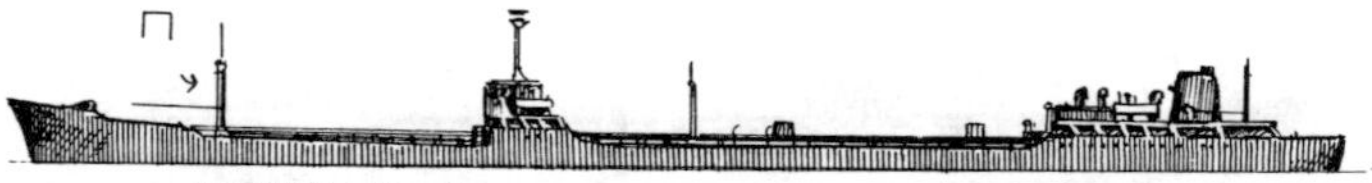

M_2KFK H123
44300 ORIENTAL NAVIGATOR. Li/Ja 1961; Tk; 20900; 207.02 × 10.62 (679.2 × 34.84); M; 15.75; ex YAMATOMI MARU 1970.

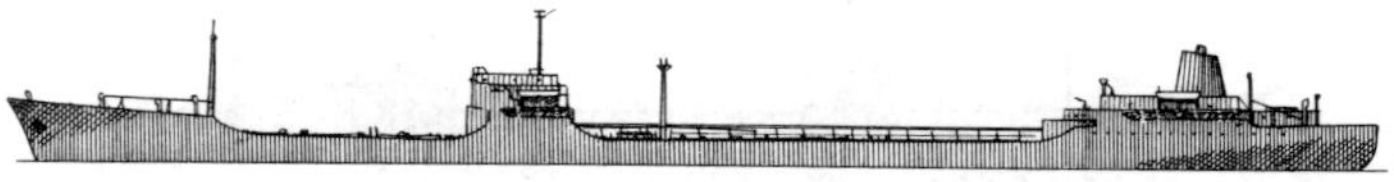

M_2KFK H123
44310 WASHINGTON TRADER. US/US 1959; Tk; 24500; 217.08 × 11.53 (712.2 × 37.83); T; 17; ex THETIS 1975. Sister: **44311 ACHILLES** (US) Possibly Similar: **44312 SOUTHWEST CAPE** (Li) ex G.S. LIVANOS 1973.

M_2KFK H123
● **44320 ASPHALT MERCHANT.** Gr/Sw 1955; Tk; 12300; 169.83 × 9.66 (557.19 × 31.69); T; 15.5; ex YOSEMITE 1978; ex VESPASIAN 1973.

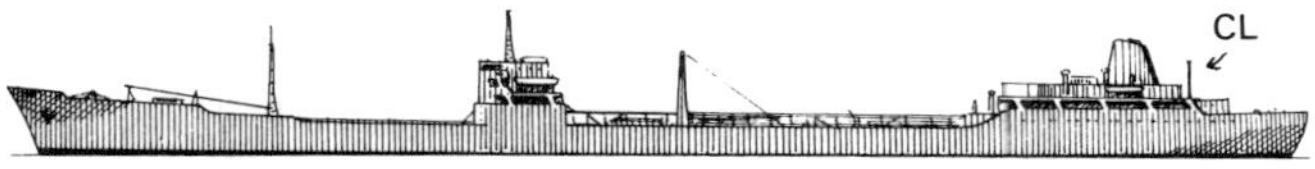

M_2KFK H123
44330 MARLI. Gr/Ja 1959; Tk; 20800; 210.32 × 10.91 (690.03 × 35.79); T; 17; ex EBERLIN 1959.

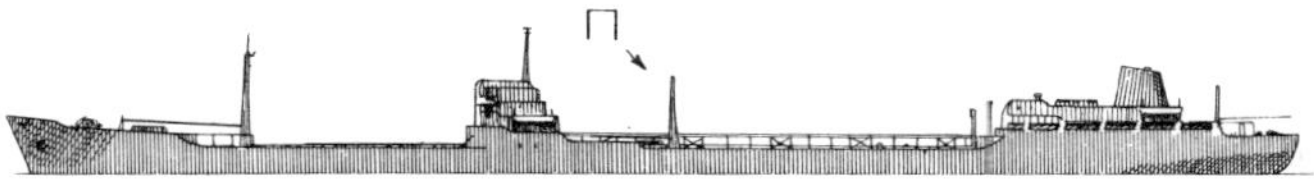

M_2KFK H123
44340 WHITE BEACH. Pa/Ja 1956; Tk; 19800; 203.18 × 10.07 (666.6 × 33.04); T, 16; ex ATHENIAN RUNNER 1975; ex MARIETTA 1972.

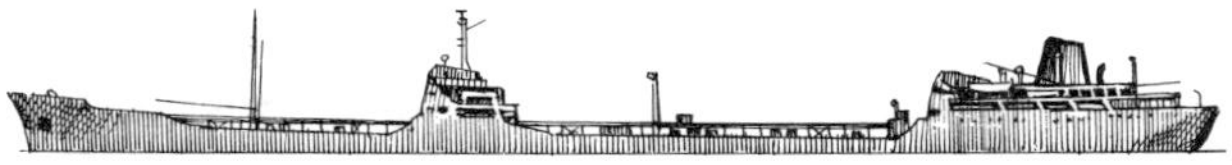

M_2KFK H123
⋆**44350 ADLER.** Ru/Ne 1960; Tk; 15900; 188.3 × 10.3 (617.78 × 33.79); M; 14.75; launched as DELIAN SPIRIT. Sister: ⋆**44351 GARZUF** (Ru).

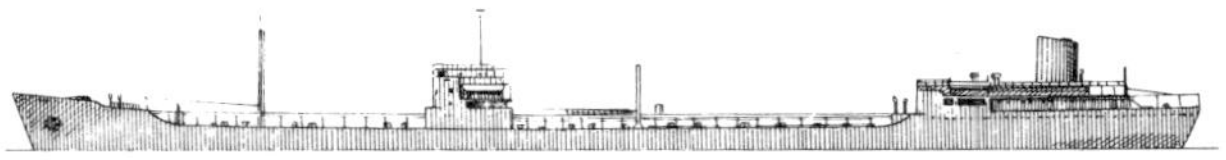

M_2KFK H123
44360 DEMOSTHENES V. Gr/Ne 1958; Tk; 16300; 187.36 × 10.31 (614.7 × 33.83); M: 15; ex NAESS LION 1969.

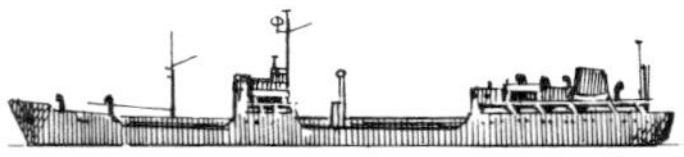

M_2KFK H123
⋆**44370 ELGAVA.** Ru/Sw 1961; Tk; 2900; 104.88 × 6.1 (344.09 × 20.01); M; 14. Sister: ⋆**44371 TUKUMS** (Ru).

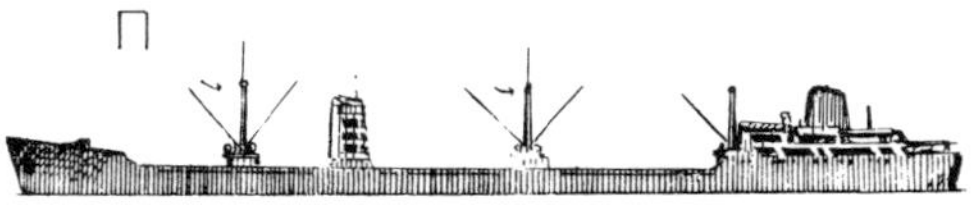

M_2KFK H123
● **44390 AEGEAN SEA.** Gr/Fr 1959; B; 9300; 149.38 × 9.15 (490.09 × 30.02); M; 15; ex ASPILOS 1980; ex KEUM MOON 1970; ex ANCORA 1968. Sisters: **44391 WELL SPEEDER** (Pa) ex SAINT CLAIR 1980; ex LALINDA 1976; ex POLARGLIMT 1970 **44392 SEALORD 1** (Pa) ex UTVIK 1973; ex AFRICA 1962 **44393 BARRIAN** (Br) ex PERSENK 1980; ex PERSENG; ex ACAMAR 1970; ex DONAU 1968; ex ACAMAR 1966; ex STARCLIPPER 1965; ex ARTHUR STOVE 1962.

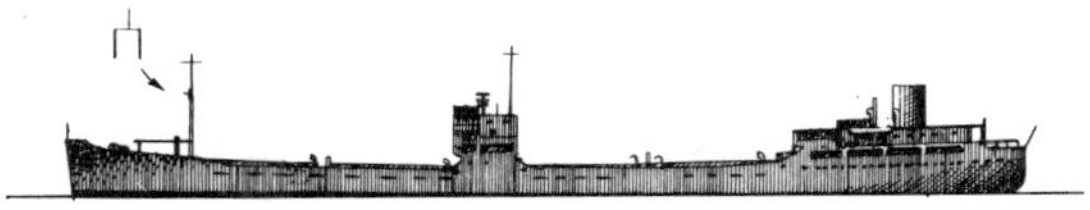

M_2KFK H123
● **44380 ALPHA CEMENTA.** Gr/Br 1955; O; 7600; 153.93 × 8.57 (505.02 × 28.12); M; 13; ex KATINA 1977; ex DUNADD 1973. Sister: **44381 MARY** (Gr) ex DUNCRAIG 1973.

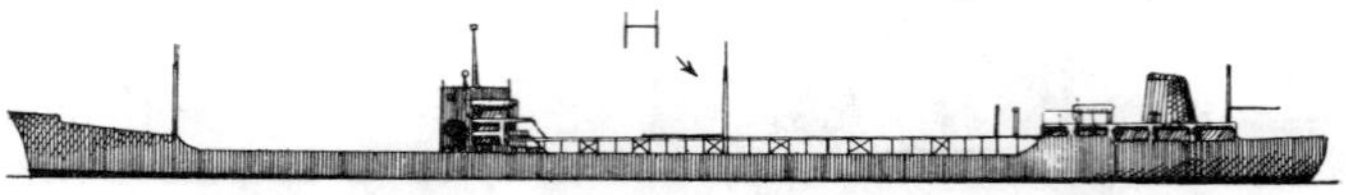

M_2KFK H13
44400 VIKING TRADER. Li/Ja 1960; Tk; 24500; 211.72 × 9.82 (694.62 × 32.22); M; 15.5; ex CURRENT TRADER 1976; ex MIZUSHIMA MARU 1968.

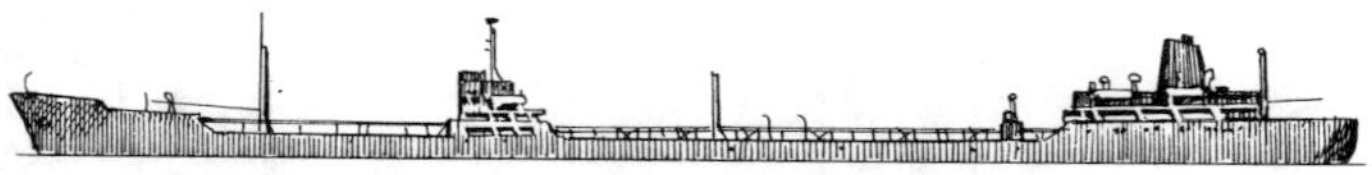

M_2KFK H13
★**44410 DRUZHBA.** Ru/Ja 1960; Tk; 25700; 214.89 × 11.43 (705.02 × 3.75); T; 16.75; launched as the GOLDEN ARROW.

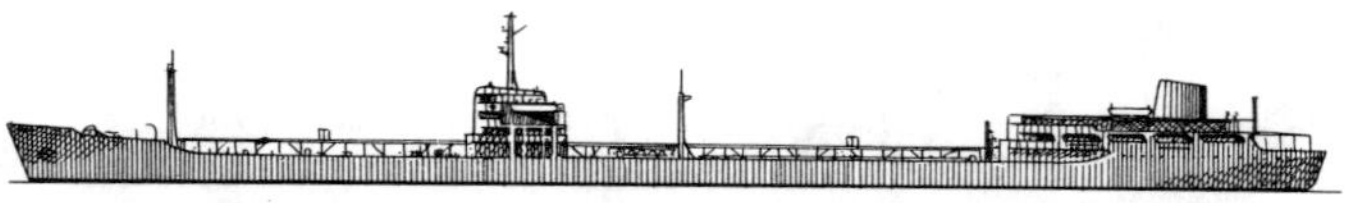

M_2KFK H13
44420 MARIE MAERSK. De/De 1962; Tk; 21600; 209.15 × 10.75 (686.19 × 35.27); M; 15.

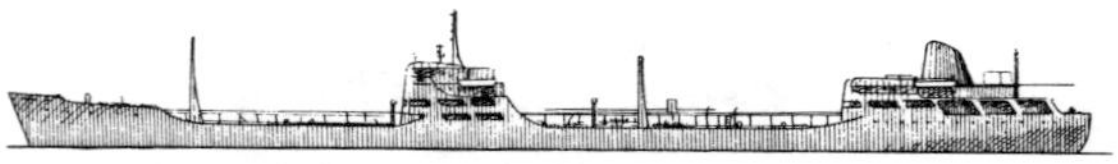

M_2KFK H13
● **44430 PARTULA.** Br/FRG 1959; Tk; 13000; 170.69 × 9.43 (560.01 × 30.94); T; 14.5. Sister: **44431 PALLIUM** (Br).

M_2KFK H13
44440 SORONG. Ia/Ys 1965; RT/FA; 5100 Dwt; 112 × 6.6 (367.4 × 21.6); —; 15.

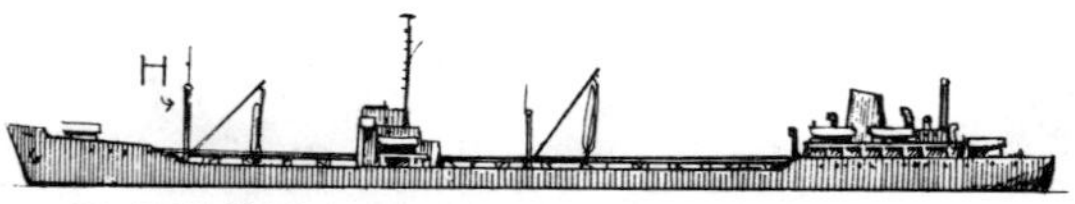

M_2KFK H13
44450 ALMIRANTE JORGE MONTT. Ch/Fr 1956; RT/FA; 17500 Dspl; 167.1 × 9.2 (548 × 30); T; 14.

M_2KFK H13
44460 ANINGA. It/FRG 1960; O; 9100; 166.43 × 9.42 (546.03 × 30.91); M; 15.5; ex TYNE ORE. Sister: **44461 SEQUOIA** (It) ex QUIJOTE; ex TEES ORE 1975.

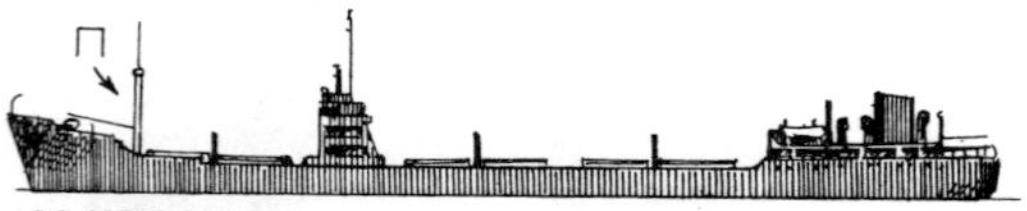

M_2KFK H13
● **44470 SILVER ISLAND.** Gr/Br 1958; O; 8600; 153.75 × 9.13 (504.43 × 29.95); M; 12.25; ex DALHANNA 1973.

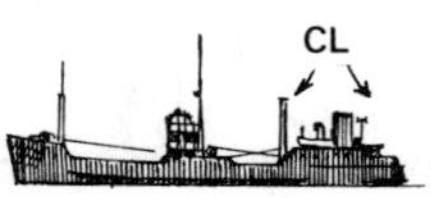

M_2KFK H13
44480 BLUE SKY. Si/Br 1940; C; 700; 63.89 × 4.15 (209.61 × 13.62); M; 11; ex STAR OF IBRAHIM 1973; ex JERSEY COAST 1967; ex MORAY COAST 1954.

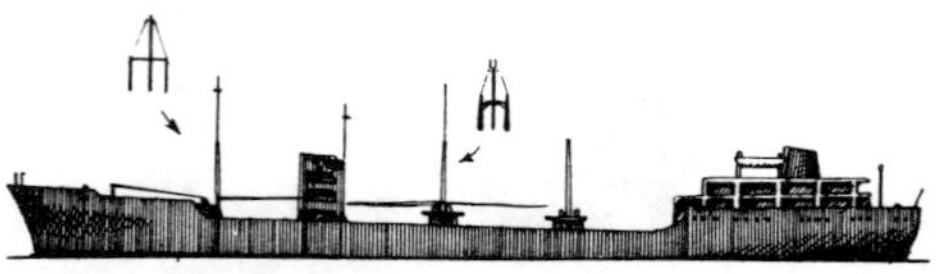

M_2KFK H13
44490 ANDRIOTIS. Gr/Fr 1956; C; 8800; 144.76 × 9.45 (474.93 × 31); M; 14.25; ex GEORGE M EMBIRICOS 1970; ex WAVECREST 1962.

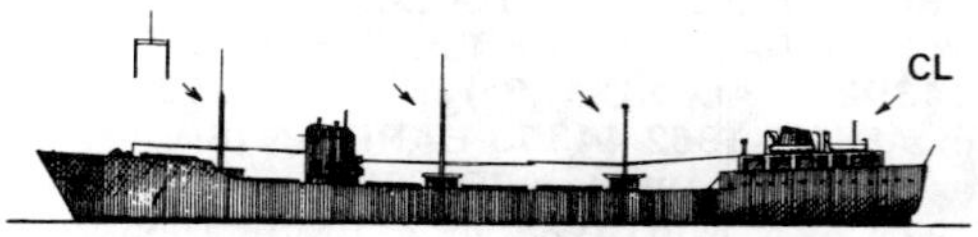

M_2KFK H13
44500 APJ SUSHMA. In/FRG 1953; C; 6300; 144.48 × 7.8 (474.02 × 25.59); M; 13.5; ex PAUL HONOLD 1961. Sister: **44501 GEORGIOS** (Bz) ex OSTERTOR 1970; ex MARGARETHE HONOLD 1960.

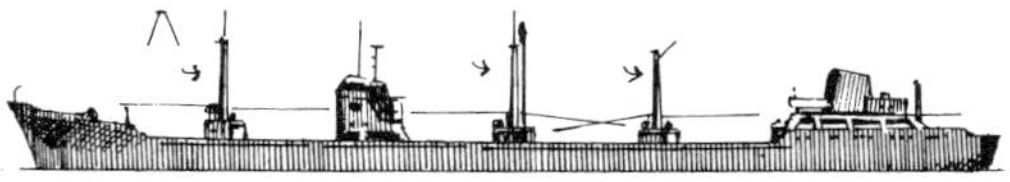

M_2KFK H13
⋆44510 PADEREWSKI. Pd/Ys 1960; C; 7200/9300; 152.81 × 8.05/9.01 (501.35 × 26.41/29.56); M; 15.5. Sisters (Pd flag): **⋆44511 MONIUSZKO ⋆44512 SZYMANOWSKI ⋆44513 NOWOWIEJSKI** (RC flag): **⋆44514 BAO XING** ex WIENIAWSKI 1977.

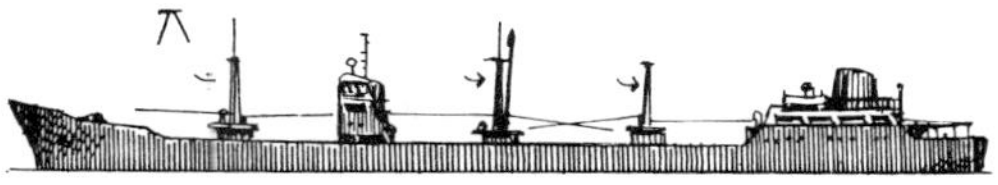

M_2KFK H13
44520 GALLANT EXPRESS. Li/Ya 1958; C; 6700/9000; 153.04 × 8.08/9.26 (502.1 × 26.51/30.38); M; 14.5; ex AKBAR 1974; ex GEORGIA 1969; ex CARINA 1962. Similar: **44521 LEFTERIS II** (Pa) ex KERMAN 1976; ex GERTRUD THERESE 1969; ex WASABORG 1965.

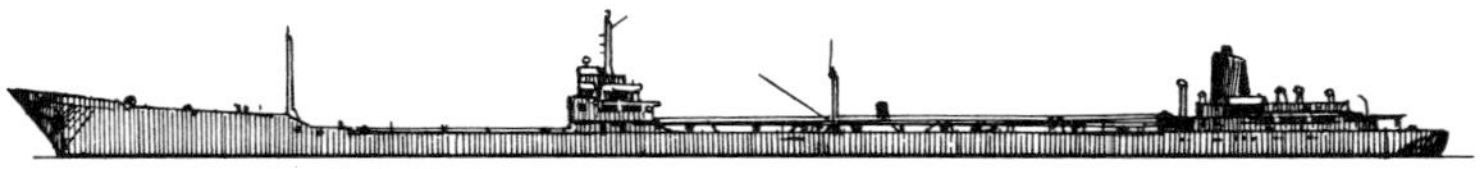

M_2K_2F H12
● **44530 ANGEL PARK.** Ko/US-Ja 1953/65; Tk; 31300; 233.53 × 11.79 (766.17 × 38.68); T; 12; ex LAS PIEDRAS 1967; lengthened & deepened 1965.

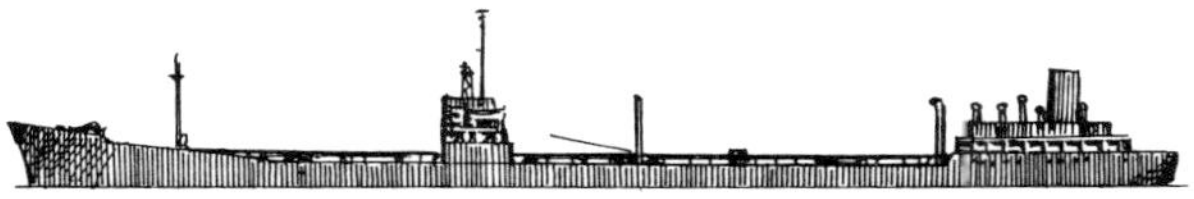

M_2K_2F H12
44540 OBSERVER. US/US 1943/53 Tk; 17600; 181.03 b.p. × 10.19 (593.93 × 33.43); T-E; 13; forward & cargo sections; ex SANTA HELENA 1966; ex WAPELLO 1964; aft section ex TRUSTCO 1966; ex ESSO SHREVEPORT 1962; ex FRONT ROYAL 1948. Joined 1966.

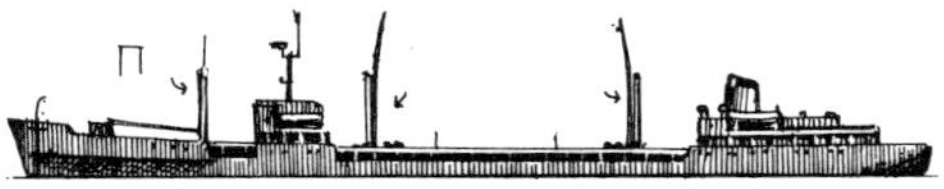

M_2K_2F H123
44550 SAO GABRIEL. Po/Po 1963; RT/FA; 9900; 146 × 8 (479 × 26.2); T; 17.

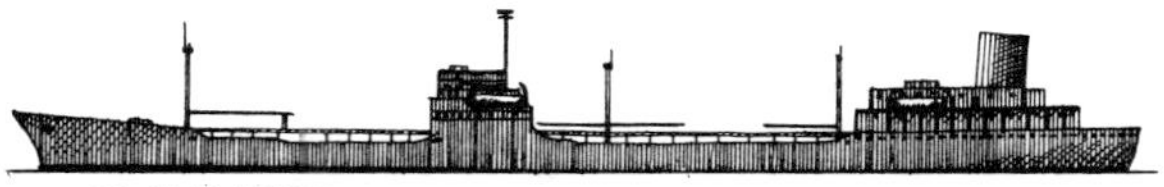

M_2K_2F H123
44560 COVE SPIRIT. US/US 1954; Tk; 16200; 179.08 × 10.45 (587.53 × 34.28); T; 16.75; ex ECLIPSE. Similar (US flag): **44561 MOBILGAS 44562 SOCONY-VACUUM.**

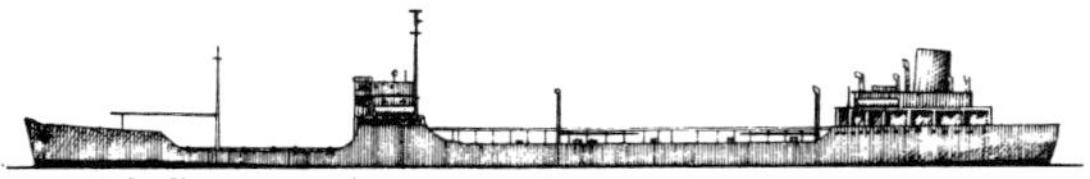

M_2K_2F H123
● **44570 GULFDEER.** US/US 1944/57 Tk; 12600; 168.41 × 9.47 (552.53 × 31.07); T-E; 14.25; ex GULFLAND 1957; ex MOOR'S FIELDS 1948. 'T-2' type. Lengthened. 1957. Sisters (US flag): **44571 GULFLION** ex GULFRAY 1958; ex BUSHY RUN 1947 **44572 GULFTIGER** ex GULFHORN 1958; ex ROXBURY HILL 1947 Similar: **44573 POINT JULIE** ex TEXACO ILLINOIS 1976; ex ILLINOIS 1960; ex SAN PASQUAL 1947 **44574 RED RIVER** ex FORT HOSKINS.

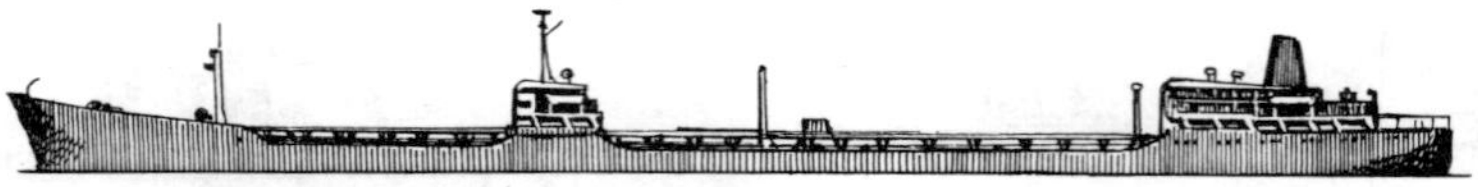

M_2K_2F H123

● **44580 LONG PHOENIX.** No/FRG 1961; Tk; 29700; 225.74 × 12.03 (740.62 × 39.48); M; 16.5; ex ESSO NORWAY 1970; ex NORWAY 1970; ex ESSO NORWAY 1968.

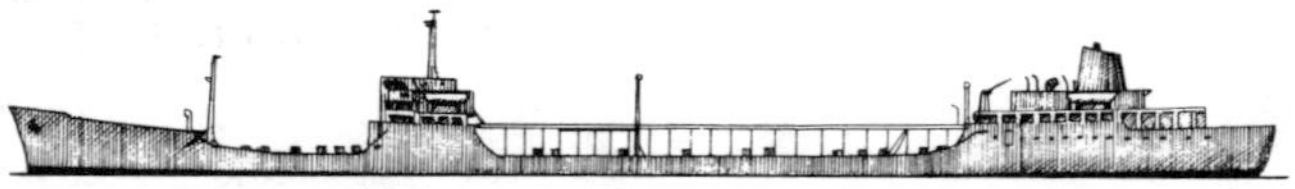

M_2K_2F H123

44590 SANTA PAULA. US/US 1958; Tk; 20100; 201.48 × 10.87 (690.55 × 35.66); T; 16.5; ex HANS ISBRANDTSEN 1971.

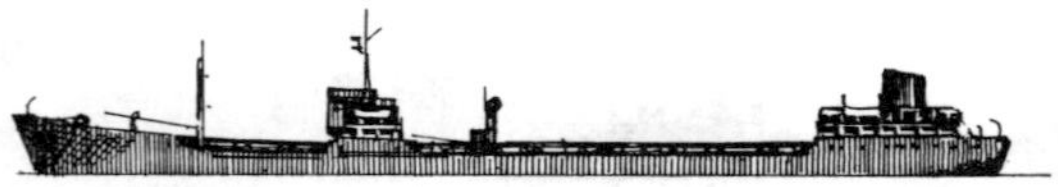

M_2K_2F H123

● **44600 MIRAMAR.** Gr/No 1956; Tk; 8600; 155.1 × 8.64 (508.86 × 28.35); M; 14; ex ANCO SOUND 1969; ex ANCO STORM 1969; ex BOHEME 1964. Similar: **44601 PIBIMARE PRIMA** (It) ex STOLT FREDDY 1969; ex STOLT NIAGARA 1967; ex FREDDY 1964.

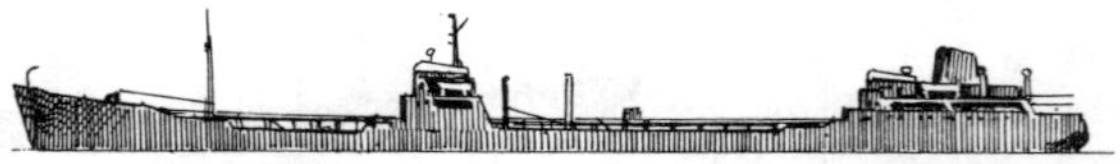

M_2K_2F H123

44610 SAN SALVADOR. Li/Ne 1957; Tk; 12400; 170.69 × 9.48 (560.01 × 31.1); M; 14.5; ex WORLD PEGASUS 1969; ex NAESS FALCON 1964.

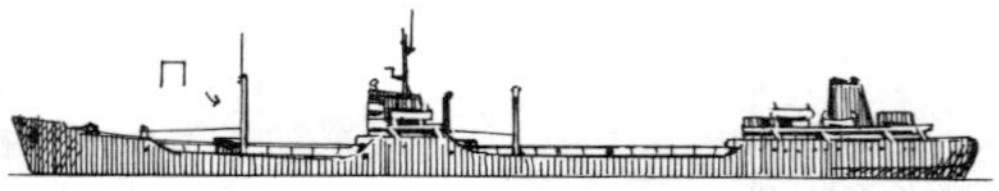

M_2K_2F H123

★44620 YELSK. Ru/Ru 1960; Tk; 7900; 145.5 × 8.69 (477.36 × 28.51); M; —. Sisters (Ru flag): **★44621 EGORYEVSK ★44622 LIEPAYA ★44623 YELNYA ★44624 YESSENTUKI** (Gr flag): **44625 TYR** ex PORT BRIAC; ex SCHWEDT 1968. **44626 ALEXIA** ex LEUNA 1 1981 (Li flag): **44627 ARIS** ex PORT MARIA 1980; ex ZEITZ 1968.

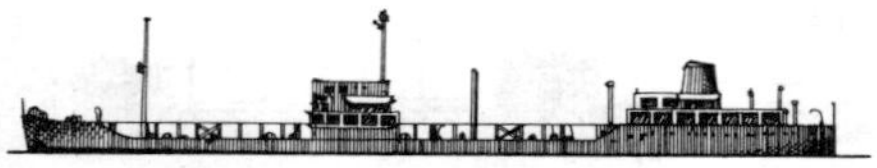

M_2K_2F H123

● **44640 URANUS** Pa/Fr 1957; Tk; 7000; 129.55 × 6.92 (425.03 × 22.7); TSM; —; ex STANVAC LIRIK 1970.

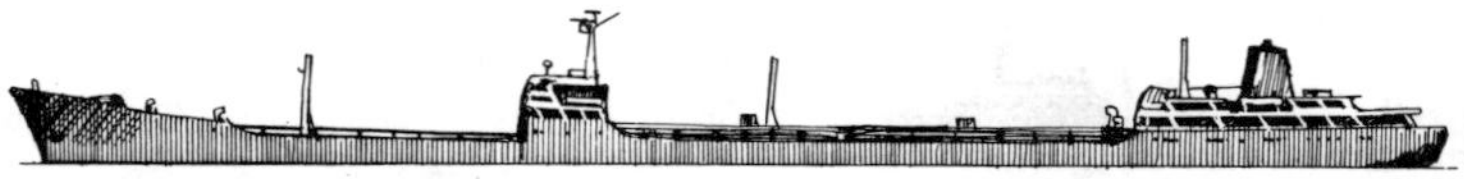

M_2K_2F H123

44650 VENTURE LOUISIANA. Li/Fr 1964; Tk; 32000; 227.52 × 12.29 (746.46 × 40.33); T; 16.5; ex AZAY-LE-RIDEAU.

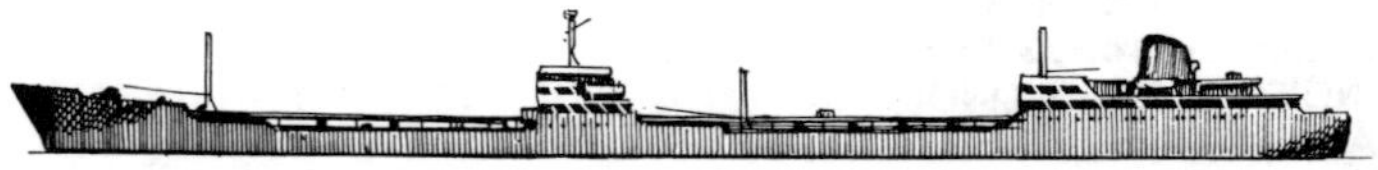

M_2K_2F H123

44660 RALLYTIME 1. Sg/Br 1959; Tk; 25100; 216.49 × 12.33 (710.1 × 40.45); T; 16; ex AGIA TRIAS; ex BRITISH DESTINY 1975.

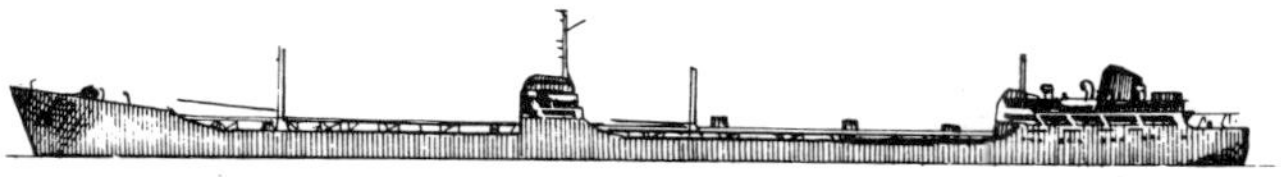

M_2K_2F *H123*
44670 MIDAS TOUCH. Li/Br 1961; Tk; 18600; 196.22 × 10.52 (643.77 × 34.91); M; 15; ex GALAXIAS; ex NORSK DROTT 1968.

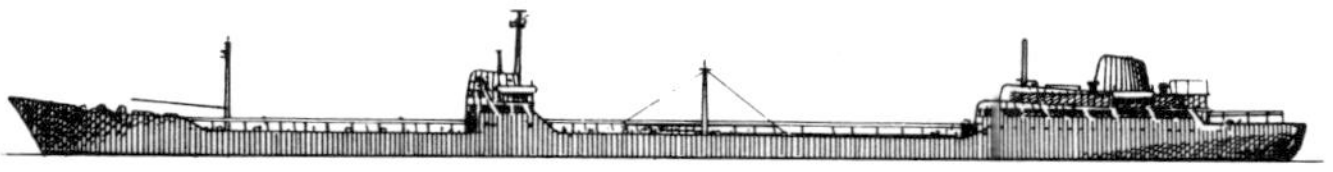

M_2K_2F *H123*
44680 DELESEA. Gr/Fr 1958; Tk; 21300; 206.13 × 11.25 (676.28 × 36.91); T; 17; ex MY ERA 1977; ex ILKON AYA 1972; ex NAESS SEAFARER 1968; ex SOYA-ELISABETH 1961.

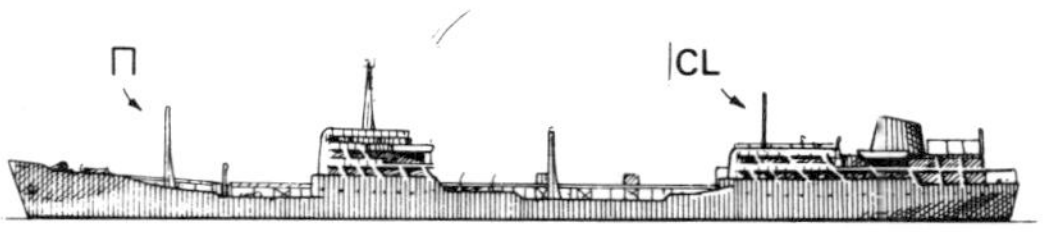

M_2K_2F *H123*
● ★**44690 DA QING 235;** RC/Br 1959; Tk; 10700; 160.18 × 9.16 (525.52 × 30.05); M; 14.5; ex TINGJIANG; ex BRITISH TRUST 1976. Similar: ★**44691 DA QING 136** (RC) ex ZHUJIANG; ex BRITISH FULMAR 1976 **44692 ORIENTAL UNITY** (Li) ex BRITISH CYGNET 1977; ex BP EXPLORER 1969; ex BP ENDEAVOUR 1967; ex BRITISH CYGNET 1964 **44693 ORIENTAL BANKER** (Li) ex ORIENTAL ENDEAVOUR 1977; ex BRITISH CORMORANT 1977 **44694 ORIENTAL PEACE** (Li) ex BRITISH OSPREY 1977 **44695 HANJIANG** (Pa) ex BRITISH GANNET 1976 **44696 SUNJIANG** (Br) ex BRITISH KESTREL 1976 **44697 WENJIANG** (Br) ex BRITISH CURLEW 1976 **44698 NOAH VI** (Ir) ex BRITISH SWIFT 1977 **44699 LOT** (Fr) ex BRITISH ROBIN 1977 **44700 BRITISH GULL** (Br) **44701 PENHORS** (Fr) ex BRITISH MALLARD 1980.

M_2K_2F *H123*
44710 THEOTOKOS; Gr/De 1962; Tk; 24700; 212.12 × 11.74 (695.93 × 38,52); M; 16; ex WATER PRINCE; ex VINCENZIA 1973; ex JETTA DAN 1969.

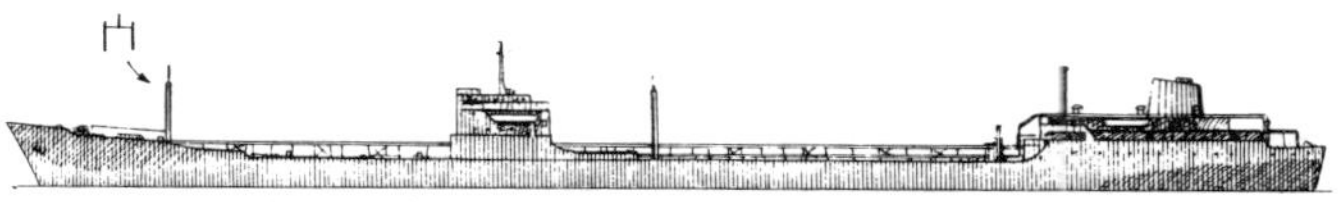

M_2K_2F *H123*
44720 GEORGIOS; Gr/Sw 1960; Tk; 23500; 208.03 × 11.56 (682.51 × 37.93); M; 15; ex HOEGH FULMAR 1968.

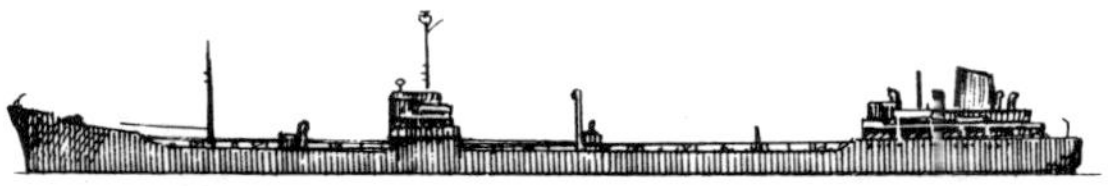

M_2K_2F *H123*
● **44730 CHAPARRAL;** Pa/Ne 1955; Tk; 12500; 169.35 × 9.28 (555.61 × 30.45); M; 14.5; ex CAPTAIN VICTOR 1977; ex DORESTAD 1970.

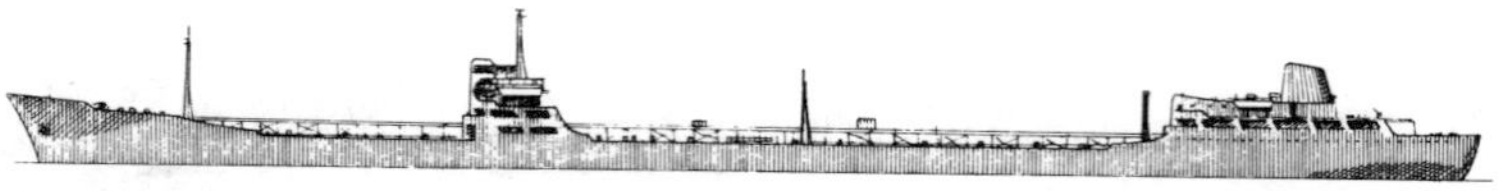

M_2K_2F H13
44740 TEXACO GREENWICH; Br/Ja 1962; Tk; 35700; 232.21 × 12.12 (761.84 × 39.76); T; 15.75; ex CALTEX GREENWICH 1968. Sister: **44741 TEXACO SOUTHAMPTON** (Br) ex CALTEX SOUTHAMPTON 1968 Similar: **44742 TEXACO PLYMOUTH** (Br) ex CALTEX PLYMOUTH 1968.

M_2K_2FK H123
44750 SAN SALVADOR; Li/Ne 1959; Tk; 12400; 170.69 × 9.48 (560.01 × 31.1); M; 14.5; ex WORLD PEGASUS 1969; ex NAESS FALCON 1964.

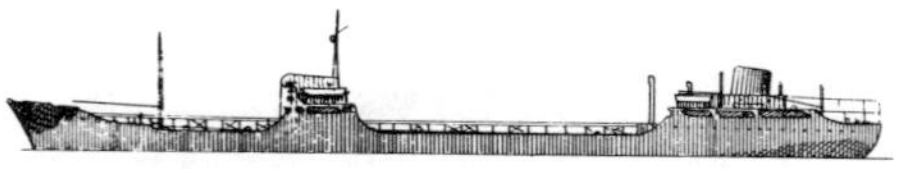

M_2K_2FK H123
● **44760 CAMPOGRIS;** Sp/Sp 1959; Tk; 7100; 139.05 × 7.76 (456.2 × 25.46); M; 13.75. Sister: **44761 CAMPONEGRO** (Sp) Possible Sister: **44762 CAMPOBLANCO** (Sp).

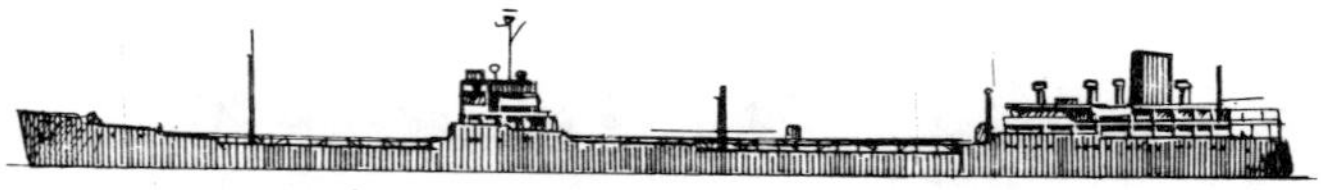

M_2K_2FK H123
● **44770 WASSIMA;** Si/Ne 1957; Tk; 20600; 201.15 × 10.98 (659.94 × 36.02); T; 16.25; ex CHERRY CEARELLE; ex VIVIPARA 1974. Sister: **44771 VOLVULA** (Fr).

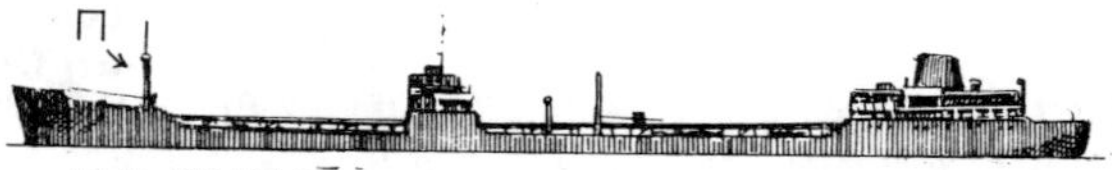

M_2K_2FK H123
44780 POLYSTAR; No/Sw 1962; Tk; 12800; 170.67 × 9.74 (559.94 × 31.96); M; 14.5.

M_2K_2FK H123
44790 RHINO; Gr/FRG 1959; Tk; 12500; 170.69 × 9.68 (560.01 × 31.76); M; 15; ex STOLT RHINO; ex SUNRANA 1973; ex JOHN AUGUSTUS ESSBERGER 1970.

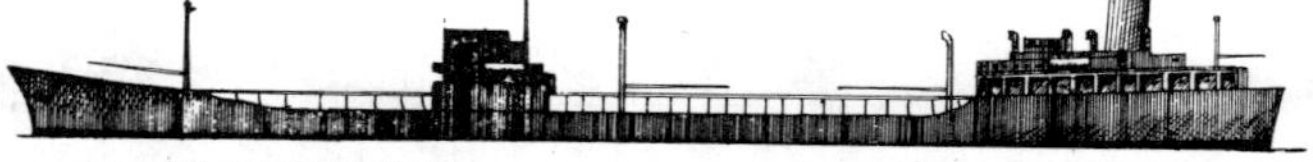

M_2K_2FK H123
44800 THOMAS Q; US/US 1951; Tk; 19500; 201.02 × 10.88 (659.51 × 35.7); T; 16.5; ex ATLANTIC ENGINEER 1970. Sister: **44801 MOUNT NAVIGATOR** (US) ex ATLANTIC NAVIGATOR 1974.

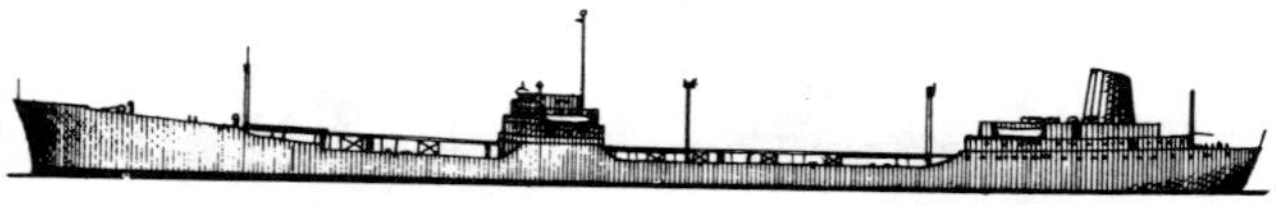

M_2K_2FK H123
44810 DELAWARE SUN; US/US 1953; Tk; 18800; 195.38 × 10.81 (641.01 × 35.47); T; 16.5. Sisters (US flag): **44811 EASTERN SUN 44812 WESTERN SUN 44813 NEW JERSEY SUN.**

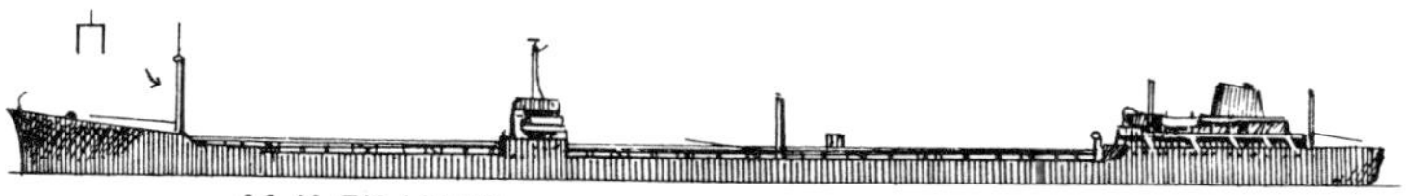

M_2K_2FK H123
44820 CHERRY EARL; Sg/No 1964; Tk; 31800; 228.58 × 12.14 (749.93 × 39.83); M; 15.75; ex ENIGHEDEN 1977; ex THORHILD 1974; ex HARRY BORTHEN 1973.

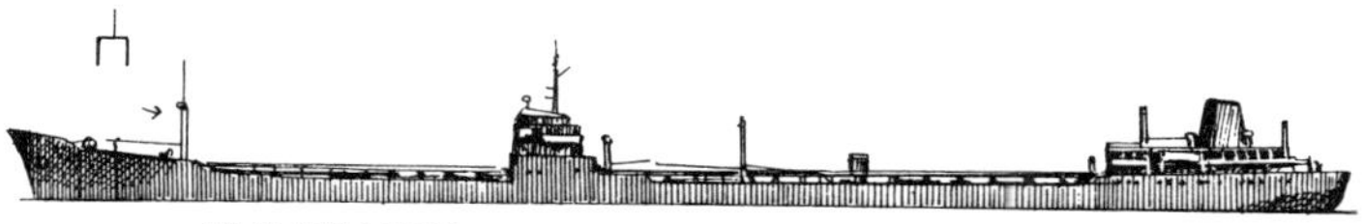

M_2K_2FK H123
44830 ARIADNE E; Cy/Sw 1962; Tk; 25700; 214.87 × 11.65 (704.95 × 38.22); M; 16; ex OKLAHOMA 1974.

M_2K_2FK H123
44840 CAMPORROJO; Sp/Sp 1963; Tk; 7000; 141.79 × 7.76 (465.2 × 25.46); M; 13.7. Sister (Sp flag): **44841 CAMPOGULES** Possible Sisters: **44842 CAMPOCERRADO 44843 CAMPOAZUR 44844 CAMPORRUBIO.**

M_2K_2FK H123
44850 CIELO ROSSO; It/Ne 1959; Tk; 13300; 170.69 × 9.67 (560.01 × 31.73); M; 14.5; ex EIDSFOSS 1968.

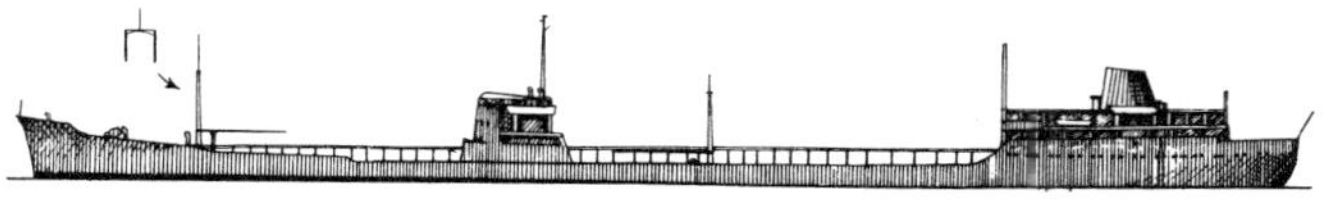

M_2K_2FK H123
44860 GLOBE MARITIMA; Br/FRG 1959; Tk; 22200; 201.28 × 10.9 (660.37 × 35,76); T; —; ex MAGURA 1980; ex SIERRA MARITIMA; ex ST SPYRIDON 1975; ex ACASTA 1968; ex TROLL 1968.

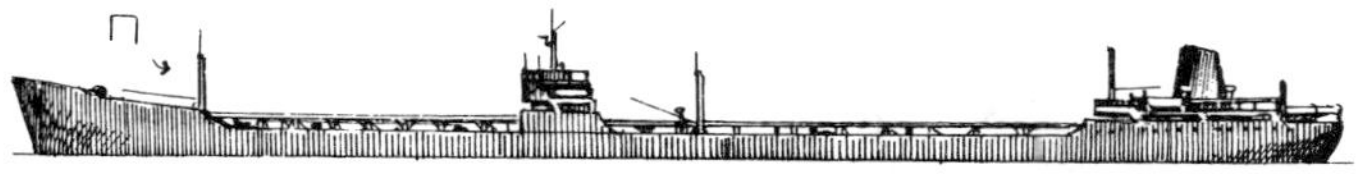

M_2K_2FK H123
44870 SCAPMOUNT; Gr/Sw 1961; Tk; 22000; 208.03 × 11.56 (682.51 × 37.93); M; 16.5; ex MIRFAK 1973; ex TOSCANA 1972.

Similar: ⋆**44871 WOLFEN** (DDR) ex TARIN 1968 **44872 EUGENIA II** (Pa) ex DANA 1974; ex NOTO 1974; ex TORINO 1969.

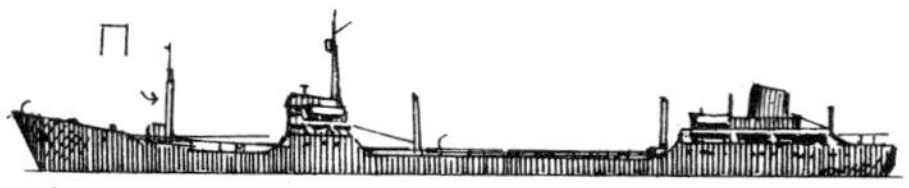

M_2K_2FK H123
44880 CAMPORRASO; Sp/Sp 1962; Tk; 6600; 139.05 × 7.76 (456.2 × 25.46); M; 14. **44881 CAMPORRUBIO** (Sp) Possible Sister: **44882 CAMPOCERRADO** (Sp).

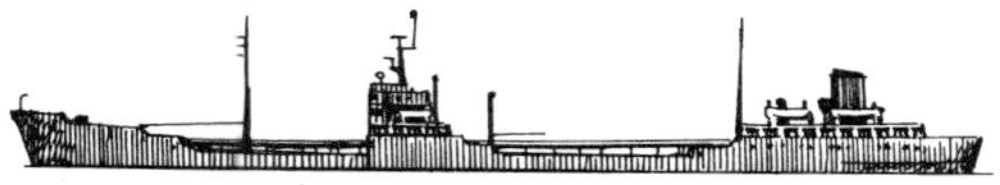

M_2K_2MF H123
⋆**44890 RAVA RUSSKAYA;** Ru/Ru 1960; Tk; 7700; 145.5 × 8.67 (477.36 × 28.44); -m; 12.25; **'KAZBEK'** class. May be others of this class with similar appearance.

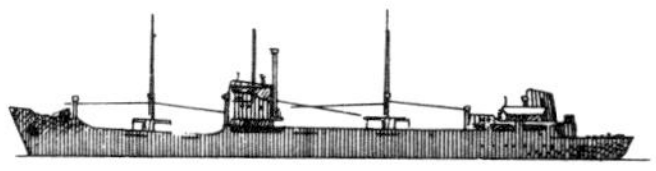

M_2KMF H12
44900 VARUNA YAMINI; In/FRG 1962; C; 3200; 97.92 × 6.98 (321.26 × 22.9); M; 14.25; ex FIEPKO TEN DOORNKAAT 1972. Sisters: **44901 VARUNA YAN** (In) ex ELLEN KLAUTSSCHKE 1972 **44902 MARIA A** (Gr) ex CAROLINE SCHULTE 1978; ex GERTRUD TEN DOORNKAAT 1973.

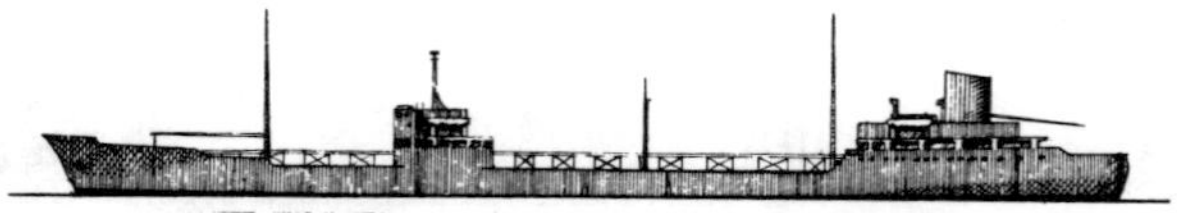

M_2KMF H123
44910 CHERRY JET; Sg/Ja 1956; Tk; 12800; 171.74 × 9.73 (563.45 × 31.92); M; 14.5; ex CONOCO JET; ex CONTINENTAL JET 1967; ex MERCANTILE TRADER 1967; ex URAGA 1966.

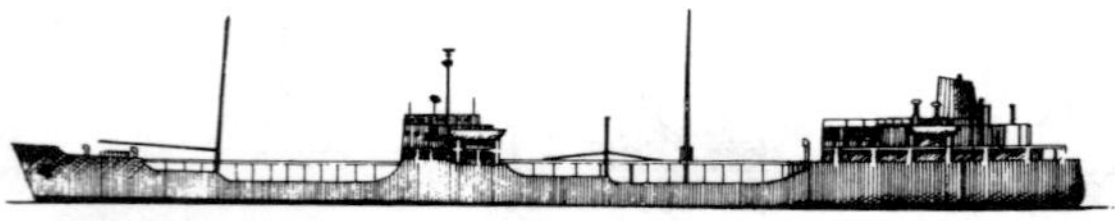

M_2KMF H123
● **44920 BOMIN II;** Sg/Ne 1958; Tk; 12200; 169.4 × 9.37 (555.77 × 30.74); T; 15.5; ex OCEAN TRADER 1974; ex ALKMAAR 1973.

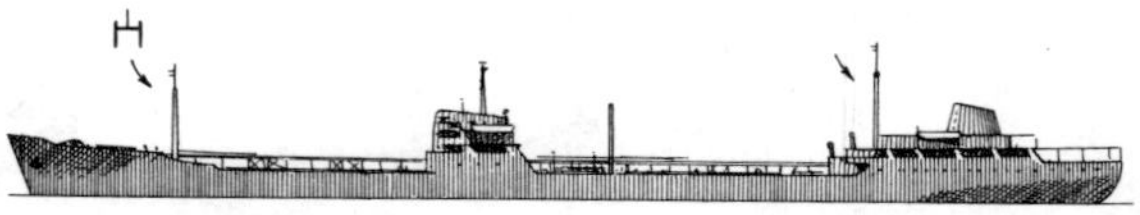

M_2KMF H123
44930 EUTERPE; Pa/Fr 1961; Tk; 13400; 175.34 × 9.5 (575.26 × 31); M; 15; ex THALE 1976; ex LACON 1972; ex ATHEN 1968; ex ATHENE 1966.

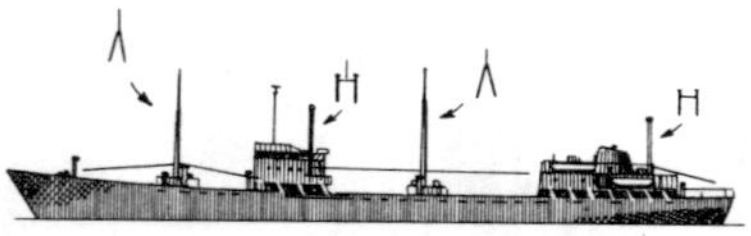

M_2KMFK H
● **44940 YANMAR;** Pa/It 1960; C; 2700/4200; 113.85 × 6.61/7.62 (373.52 × 21.69/25); M; — ; ex YACU GUAGUA 1980; ex FURKA 1973; ex HELGOLAND 1972; ex MEDICINE HAT 1968; ex ANDERS ROGENAES 1964; ex CONCORDIA ANDERS 1962; ex ANDERS ROGENAES 1960. Sisters: **44941 EASTERN GRAND** (PA) ex MEDITERRANEAN KLIF 1974; ex CORFU ISLAND 1972; ex SUSAA 1970; ex MARSTENEN 1965; ex BUKKEN 1962; ex MARSTENEN 1960 **44942 DIAKAN MASCOT** (Gr) ex ASCOT 1970 (may now be MKMF - which see).

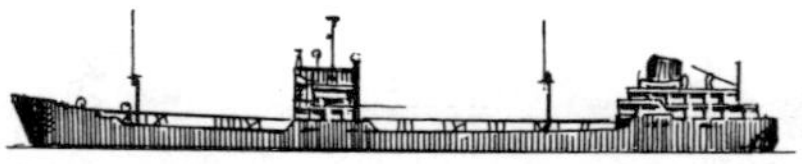

M_2KMFK H123
★44950 OLEG KOSHEVOY; Ru/Ru 1954; Tk; 3700; 123.5 × 4.31 (405.18 × 14.14); TSM; 10.75; Caspian Sea Service. Sisters (Ru flag): **★44951 ALEKSEY KRYLOV ★44952 IVAN ZEMNUKHOV ★44953 LYUBOV SHEVTSOVA ★44954 SERGEY TYULENIN ★44955 ULYANA GROMOVA ★44956 LIZA CHAYKINA.**

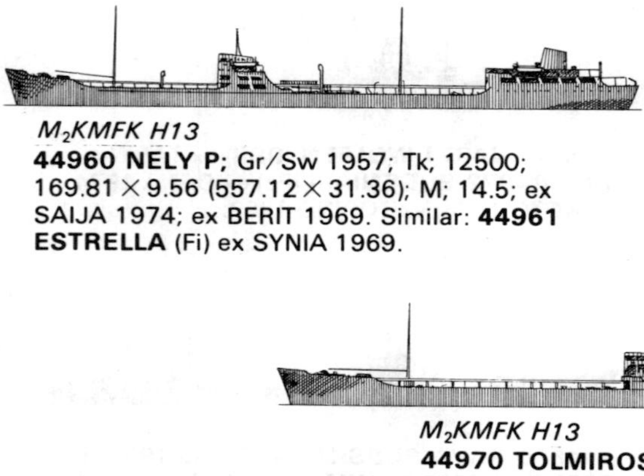

M_2KMFK H13
44960 NELY P; Gr/Sw 1957; Tk; 12500; 169.81 × 9.56 (557.12 × 31.36); M; 14.5; ex SAIJA 1974; ex BERIT 1969. Similar: **44961 ESTRELLA** (Fi) ex SYNIA 1969.

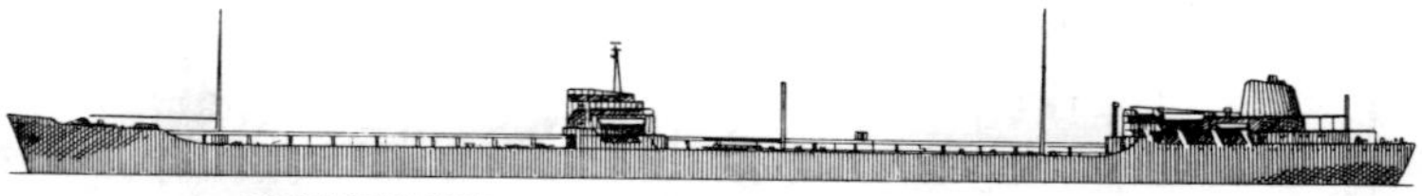

M_2KMFK H13
44970 TOLMIROS; Gr/Br 1963; Tk; 31600; 233.48 × 12.34 (766.01 × 40.49); M; 16.25; ex THEODORA 1975; ex THORSHAMMER 1969.

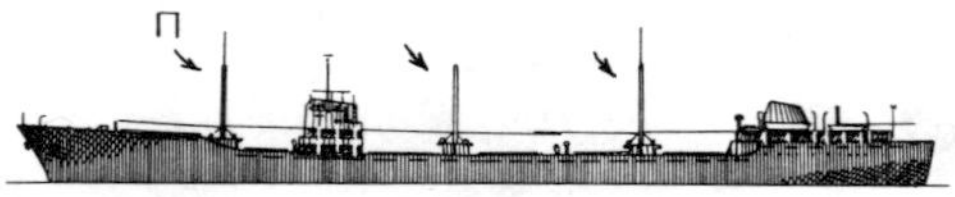

M_2KMFK H13
● **44980 APJ AKASH.** In/FRG 1954; C; 6300; 144.48 × 7.82 (474.02 × 25.66); M; 13.5; ex HEINRICH HONOLD 1960. Sister: **44981 APJ ANJLI** (In) ex HANS HONOLD 1960.

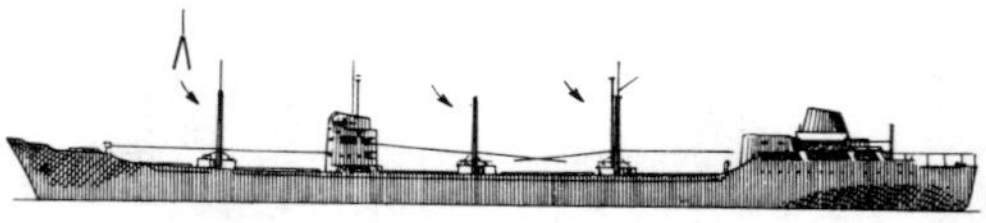

M_2KMFK H13
44990 ELEISTRIA VIII. Gr/Ys 1959; C; 9200; 153.14 × 9.11 (502.43 × 29.89); M; 13; ex TARIQ 1977; ex SHUGUANG 1965; ex MATANG 1964.

M_2KMFK *H13*
45000 EASTERN MERCHANT. Pa/Sw 1956; C; 9000; 148.27 × 9.2 (486.45 × 30.22); M; 14; ex OHDAE 1980; ex INGWI 1967. Similar: **45001 OMALOS** (Gr) ex LENDAS 1977; ex CAMINGOY 1974; ex ANTONIO 1973; ex BELLULLY 1956 **45002 STATE OF KERALA** (In) ex BERNHARD 1962 **45003 TONG POH** (Sg) ex MARIANNE 1973; ex SUNLEAF 1970; ex SUNVARD 1966.

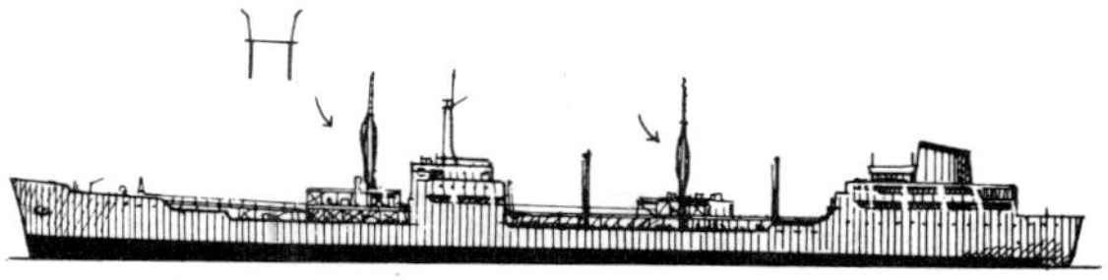

M_2KMFK *H13*
45010 TAFELBERG. SA/De 1959; RT/FA; 12500; 170.6 × — (559.9 × —); M; 15.5; ex ANNAM 1965; Converted from tanker. Now has a helicopter deck (not shown).

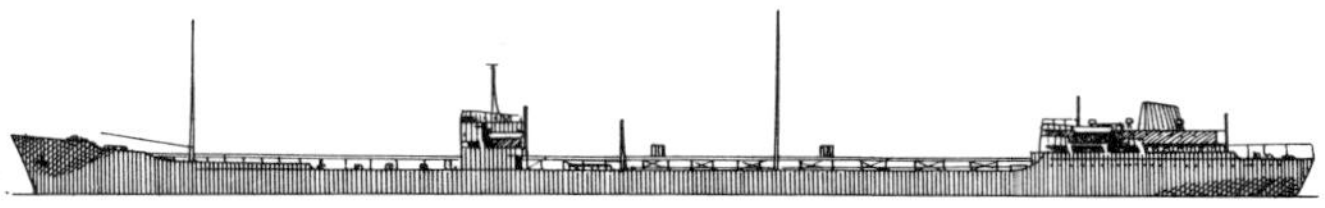

M_2KMKFK *H123*
45020 LITTLE NIKOS. Gr/Sw 1961; Tk; 21900; 209.1 × 11.12 (686.02 × 36.48); M; 16; ex THEODOTI 1977; ex RADNY 1970; May be spelt **LITTLE NICOS.**

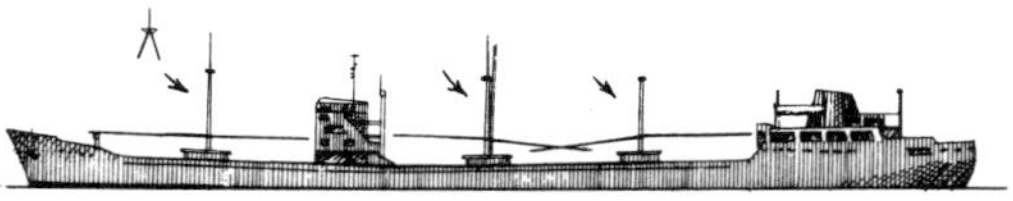

M_2KMKFK *H13*
⋆**45030 CHOPIN.** Pd/Ys 1959; C; 7000/9200; 153.09 × 19/9.01 (502.26 × 26.87/29.56); M; 15. Sister: ⋆**45031 ZAMENHOF** (Pd).

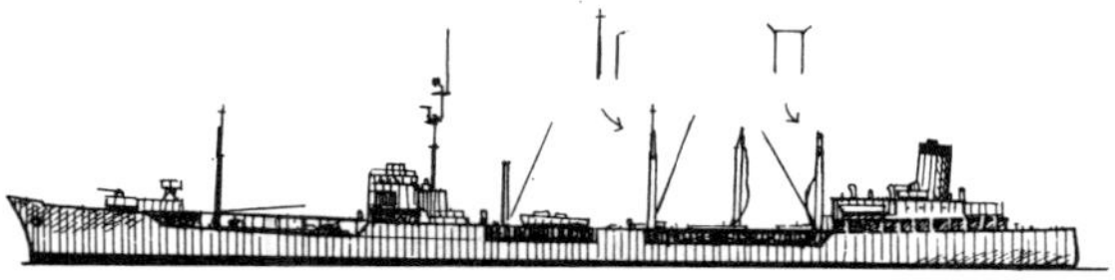

M_2KMK_2F *H123*
45040 MARIAS. US/US 1944; RT/FA; 25500 Dspl; 168 6 × 10.1 (553 × 33); TST; 18; **'CIMARRON'**; class **'T-3'** type; Sister: **45041 TALUGA** (US).

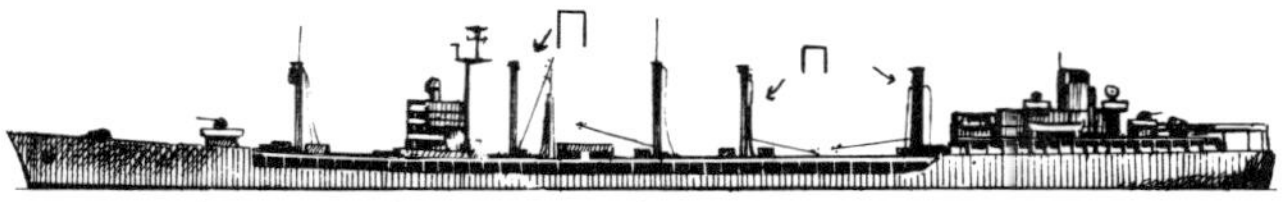

M_2KMK_2F *H13*
45050 NEOSHO. US/US 1954; RT/FA; 38000 Dspl; 199.6 × 10.7 (655.35); TST; 20. Sisters (US flag): **45051 MISSISSINEWA 45052 HASSAYAMPA 45053 KAWISHIWI 45054 TRUCKEE 45055 PONCHATOULA.**

M_3F *H12*
45060 MONIA. Pa/Br 1938; C; 1000; 67.21 × 4.45 (220.51 × 14.6); M; 11; ex ANNE OPEM 1974; ex SIRAVIK 1973; ex STOKKVIK 1970; ex SVELGEN 1964; ex ELEANOR BROOKE 1957.

M_3F *H12*
45070 BINTANG SAMUDRA IV. Ia/Br 1936; C; 660; 55.2 × 3.78 (181.1 × 12.4); M; 9.5; ex BABINDA.

M_3F *H12*
45080 BALABAC. Pi/Br 1933; C; 630; 54.72 × 3.78 (179.53 × 12.4); M; 10; ex BREEZE 1966.

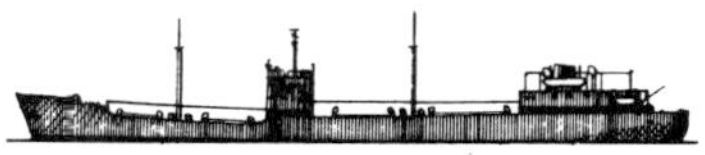

M_3F *H12*
45090 MILOS II. Cy/Br 1959; C; 3800; 105.16 × 6.27 (345.01 × 20.57); M; 11; ex STORRINGTON 1979.

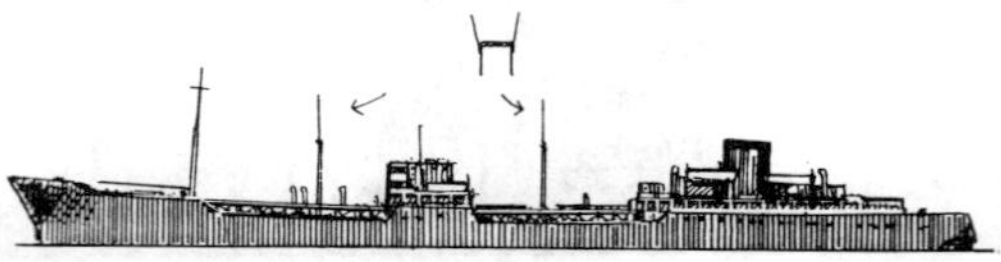

M_3F H123
45100 PUNTA MEDANOS. Ar/Br 1950; RT/FA 16300 Dspl; 153.1 × 8.7 (502 × 28.5); TST; 18.

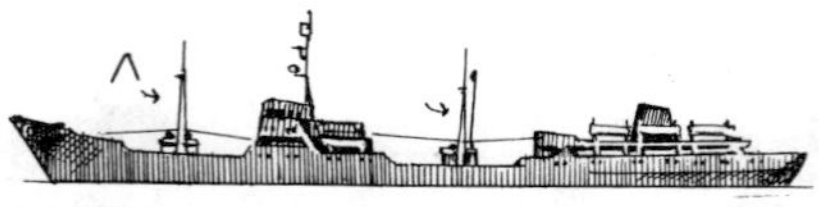

M_3F H123
★45110 KALININGRAD. Ru/Ru 1964; FC; 5500; 130.79 × 6.72 (429.1 × 22.05); D-E; 16.5. Sisters (Ru flag): **★45111 SEVASTOPOL ★45112 SIMFEROPOL ★45113 ARSENYEV ★45114 EGERSHELD ★45115 CHURKIN ★45116 IRKUTSK.**

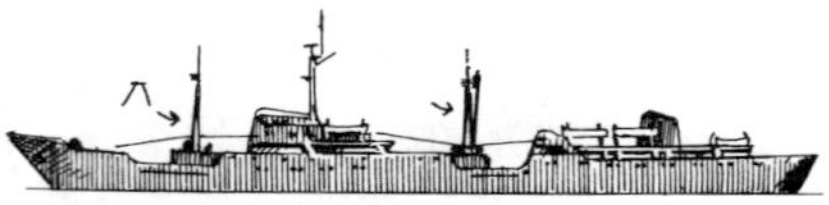

M_3F H123
★45120 YANTARNYY. Ru/Ru 1964; FC; 5500; 130.92 × 6.72 (429.53 × 22.05); D-E; 16.25. Sisters (Ru flag): **★45121 BASHKIR ★45122 AUGUST JAKOBSON ★45123 NIKOLAY ZYSTSTAR** Possible Sisters: **★45124 VOLCHANSK ★45125 VOLOGDA ★45126 KOMISSAR POLUKHIN** ex KAREL 1971 **★45127 KOSMONAUT KOMAROV ★45128 ZABAYKALYE.**

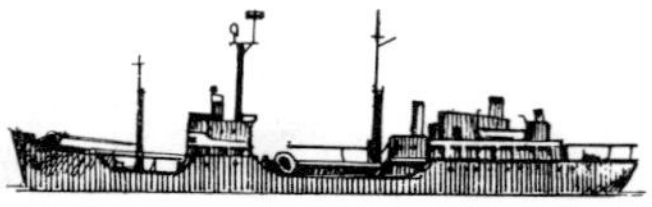

M_3F H123
45140 PUNTA DELGADA. Ar/US 1945; Tk/FA 6100 Dspl; 99.1 × 6.1 (325 × 20); M; 11.5; ex SUGARLAND; ex NATICOKE; **'T-1'** type.

M_3F H123
45150 KIETA. Pp/Ay 1948; C; 600; 55.73 × 3.4 (182.84 × 11.15); M; 9; ex EUGOWRA 1969. Similar: **45151 SULTANA** (Pi) ex HELEN J 1967; ex ENFIELD 1965 **45152 DONA LILY** (Pi) ex NUKUMANU 1975; ex WAIBEN 1966; ex ELMORE **45153 MALUKA** (Pp) ex EUROA 1965 (damaged by stranding).

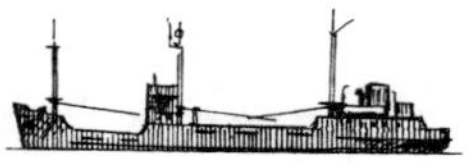

M_3F H123
45160 SCORPION. Pa/Br 1946; C; 1000; 60.04 × 4.34 (226.51 × 14.24); M; 11; ex MARIDAN C; ex LUNAN 1969.

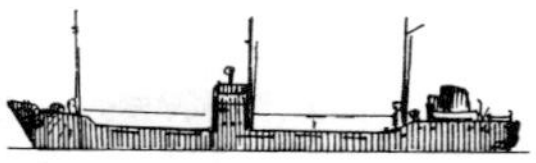

M_3F H123
45170 ATTIKI. Gr/Ne 1961; C; 1400; 81.79 × 4.31 (268.34 × 14.14); M; 13; ex NASSAUBORG 1980; lengthened 1969. Sister: **45171 KATINA C** (Gr) ex PRINSENBORG 1980.

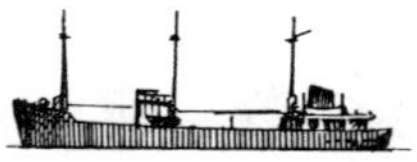

M_3F H123
45180 FRANCO PIERACCINI. It/Ne 1950; C; 500; 64.22 × 3.25 (210.7 × 10.66); M; —; ex EGBERT WAGENBORG 1966.

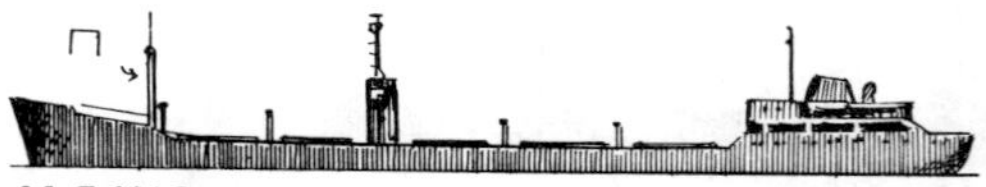

M_3F H13
45190 DAPO ALECOS. Gr/Ne 1958; O; 9000; 153.9 × 8.5 (504.92 × 27.96); M; 12.5; ex BONNYDALE 1976; ex BONITA 1974; ex MESNA 1968.

M_3F H13
● **45200 ARIS VI.** Gr/FRG 1955; C; 1200; 86.72 × 4.59 (284.51 × 1506); M; 14; ex BARROW 1977; ex CORINTHIAN TRADER 1975; ex AGHIOS LAZAROS 1973; ex VILLEGAS 1970. Sisters: **45201 SEAMOON I** (Bh) ex SYLMET 1977; ex PASNI 1973; ex BALTIC COMET 1966. **45202 NIVES** (It) ex VIVES 1970.

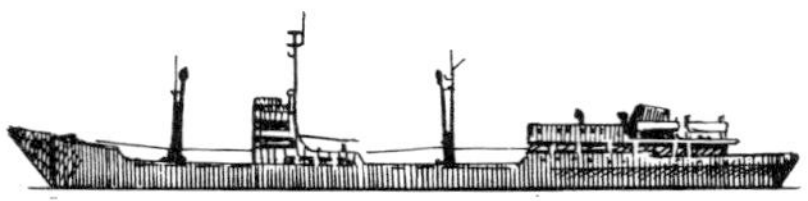

M_3F H13
★**45210 AKTYUBINSK;** Ru/Ru 1956; FC; 5200; 130.92 × 7.49 (429.53 × 24.57); D-E; 17.5. Sisters (RU FLAG): ★**45211 KURGAN** ★**45212 TITANIYA** ex ZELENOGRADSK 1971 ★**45213 TSELINOGRAD** ex AKMOLINSK ★**45214 IVAN STEPANOV** ★**45215 KAMENOGORSK** ★**45216 VLADIVOSTOK** ★**45217 VOLOCHAYEVSK** ★**45218 KRAMATORSK** ★**45219 PRIVOLZHSK** **45220 YAROSLAVL** Similar (cargo ship): ★**45221 KUYBYSHEVGES.**

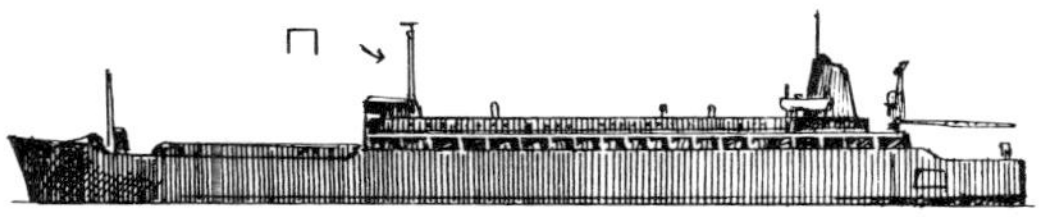

M_3FC H2
● **45230 CANADA MARU;** Ja/Ja 1971; RoVC; 11500; 161.65 × 6.68 (530.35 × 21.92); M; 18.5.

M_3F_2 H123
45240 PUNTA DELGADA; Ar/US 1945; Tk/FA; 6100 Dspl; 99.1 × 6.1 (325 × 20); M; 11.5; ex SUGARLAND; ex NATICOKE; **'T1'** type.

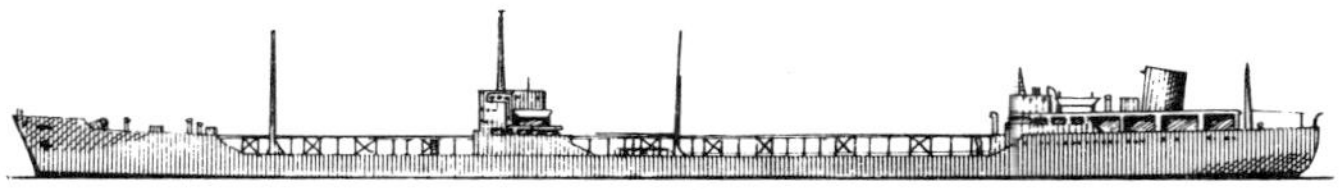

M_3FK H123
45250 CLEO Gr/Ja 1957; Tk; 20900; 206.99 × 10.64 (679.1 × 34.91); M; 15.5; ex YUYO MARU No 8 1973.

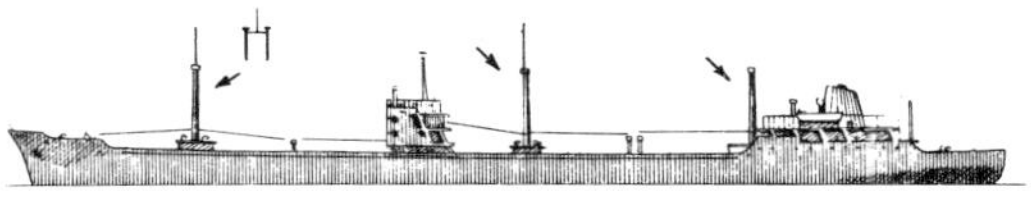

M_3KFK H13
● **45260 EIRINI L;** Gr/Ja 1956; C; 10400; 158.2 × 9.4 (519.03 × 30.84); T; 16.5.

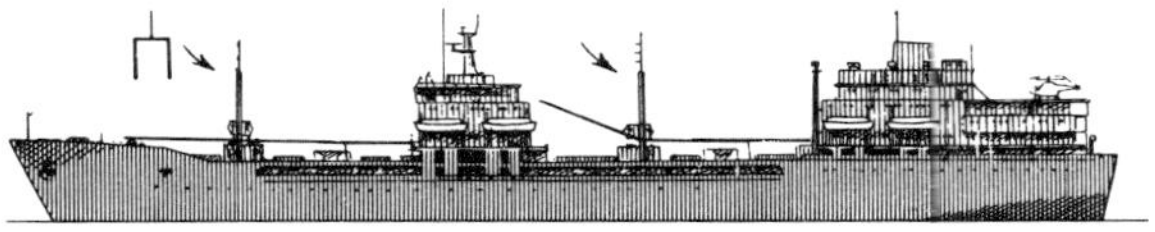

M_3KMF H1
● ★**45270 KONSTITUTSIYA SSSR;** Ru/Pd 1979; FF; 15800; 178.3 × 7.2 (584.97 × 23.62); M; 14.5; **'B-670'** type. Helicopter deck aft. Sisters (Ru flag); ★**45271 RYBAK KAMCHATSKIY** ★**45272 RYBAK PRIMORIYA** ★**45273 RYBAK CHUKOTKI;** 2 more on order.

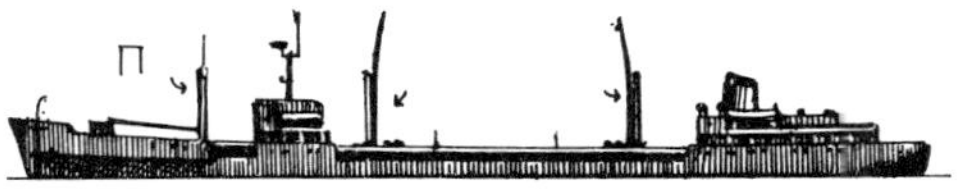

M_4F H123
45280 SAO GABRIEL; Po/Po 1963; RT/FA; 9900; 146 × 8 (479 × 26.2); T; 17.

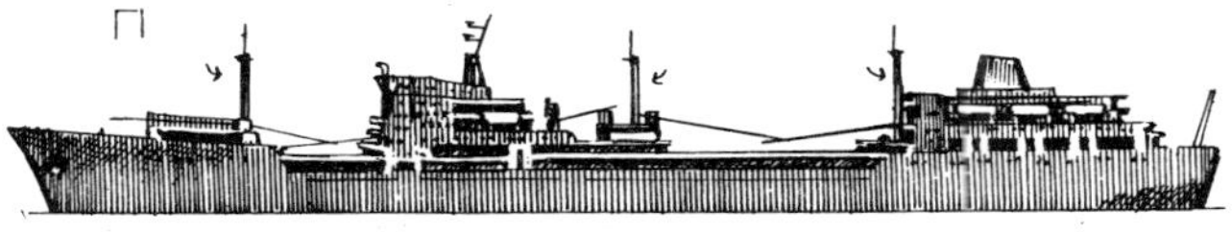

M_4FK H1
★**45290 PYATIDYESYATILYETIYE SSSR;** Ru/Ru 1973; FF; 18500; 197.31 × 8.1 (647.34 × 26.57); M; 14.5; ex POSYET; Also known as **50 LET SSSR.** Sisters (Ru flag): ★**45291 VASILIY CHERNYSHYEV** ★**45292 YEVGENIY LEBEDYEV.**

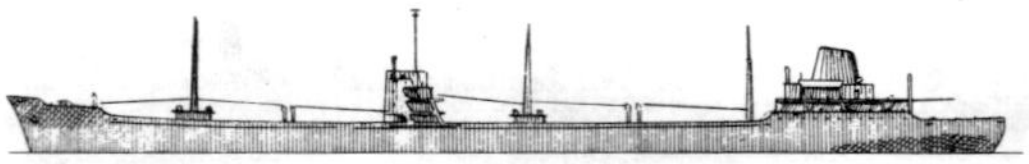

M_4FK H13
45300 AYENI; Gr/Ja 1958; C; 8200/10700; 158.22 × 85/9.44 (519.09 × 27.89/30.97); M; 14.5; ex PANAGHIA THEOSKEPASTI 1980.

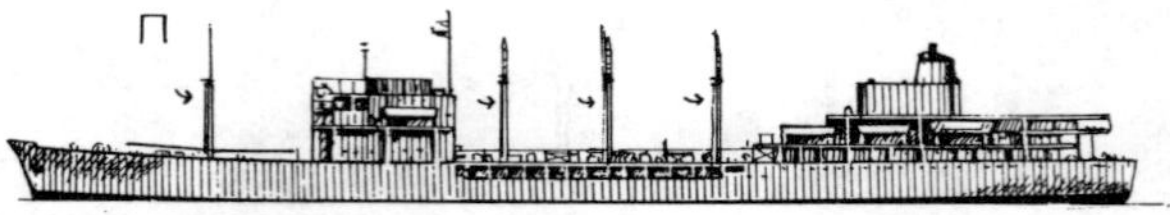

M_5F H123
45310 TIDEPOOL; Br/Br 1963; RT/FA; 14100; 177.91 × 10.28 (583.69 × 33.73); T; 17; Helicopter deck and hangar. Sister: **45311 TIDESPRING** (Br).

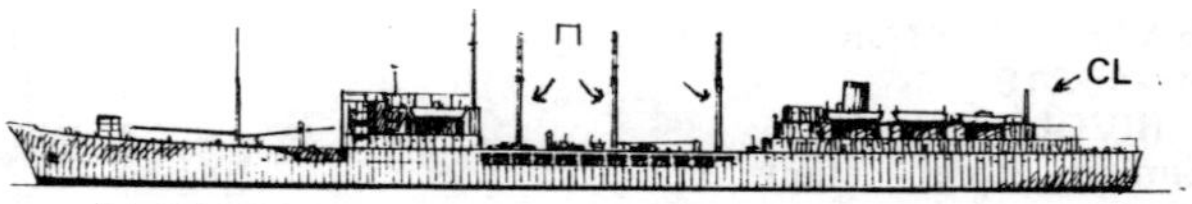

M_5FK H123
45320 SUPPLY; Au/Br 1955; RT/FA; 11200; 177.8 × 9.8 (583 × 32); T; 17.25; ex TIDE AUSTRAL 1962.

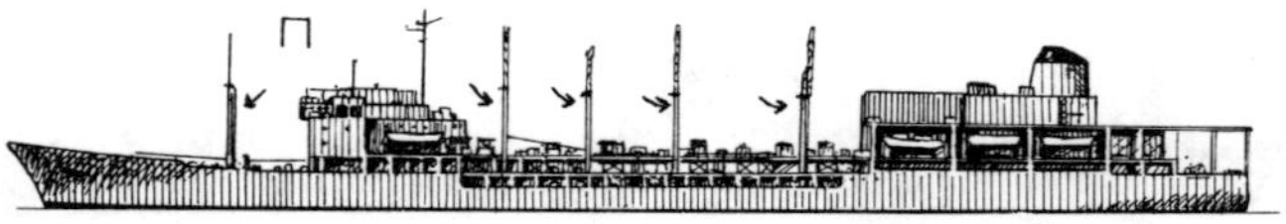

M_6F H13
45330 OLMEDA; Br/Br 1965; RT/FA; 18600; 197.52 × 10.36 (648.03 × 33.99); T; 19; ex OLEANDER 1967; Helicopter deck and hangar. Sisters (Br flag); **45331 OLNA 45332 OLWEN** ex OLYNTHUS 1967.

Profile 4

C_4MF *H1*
45340 CONTI LIBAN. FRG/FRG 1965; C; 1500; 94.01 × 4.67 (308.43 × 15.32); M; 13.5; ex CREMON 1975.

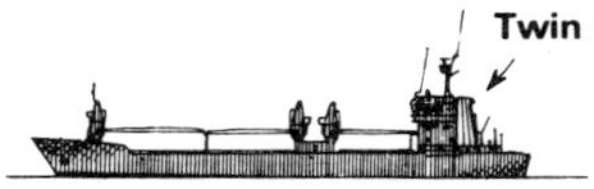

C_3MF *H1*
45410 PACIFIC LADY. Ne/Ne 1977; C; 1200; 80.7 × 5.2 (264.76 × 17.06); M; 15; ex KLIPPER 1980. Sister (Ne flag): **45411 PACIFIC MARCHIONESS** ex KLIPPER II 1980 Similar (single cranes): **45412 PACIFIC QUEEN.**

C_3MF *H1*
45420 HELLA. Be/FRG 1970; C; 2900; 97.24 × 5.2 (319.02 × 17.06); M; 14.5; ex ILSE RUSS 1977.

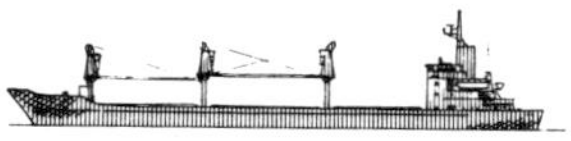

C_3MF *H1*
45430 RIJNBORG. Ne/Ne 1970; C; 1800; 81.79 × 5.18 (268 × 16.99); M; 13. Sister: **45431 SCHELDEBORG** (Ne).

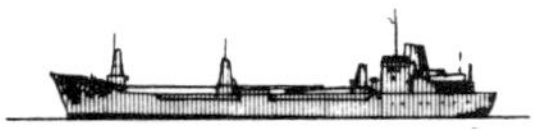

C_3MF *H1*
45440 AGELIKI III. Gr/Sw 1957; C; 500; 71.43 × 3.85 (234.35 × 12.63); M; 12; ex MARIE-AUDE 1978; ex STAFFAN 1969; Launched as PALMA.

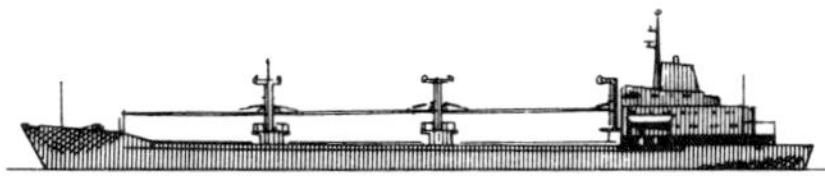

C_3MF *H1*
● **45450 TOLMI.** Gr/FRG 1971; C; 2800/5000; 125.02 × 6.56/7.65 (410.17 × 21.52/25.1); M; 17; ex METTE BEWA 1976; ex CAP MATAPAN 1974. Sisters (Gr flag): **45451 TIMI** ex RIKKE BEWA 1976; ex CAP CARMEL 1974 **45452 CAPE ITEA** ex SAMOS ISLAND; ex CAP ANAMUR 1973.

C_3MC_3MFC *H13*
● ***45350 POLTAVA.** Ru/Ru 1962; C; 9800; 155.68 × 9.09 (510.76 × 29.82); M; 15. Sisters (Ru flag) ***45351 PEREKOP *45352 POLOTSK *45353 NIKOLAYEV *45354 PAVLOVSK *45355 PRIDNEPROVSK *45356 BABUSHKIN *45357 BAKURIANI *45358 BERISLAV *45359 PARTIZANSKAYA ISKRA *45360 KAPITAN VISLOBOKOV *45361 PARTIZANSKAYA SLAVA *45362 BRYANSKIY RABOCHIY *45363 BALASHIKHA *45364 BAYMAK *45365 BELGOROD DNESTROVSKIY *45366 BEREZOVKA *45367 OKTYABRSKAYA *45368 REVOLYUTSIYA** Similar (Hu flag): ***45369 ADY *45370 PETOFI** (Ku flag): **45371 AL ARIDHIAH 45372 AL GURAINIAH 45373 AL KHALIDIAH 45374 AL JABIRIAH 45375 AL MANSOURIAH 45376 AL ODALIAH 45377 AL KADISIAH 45378 AL OMARIAH 45379 AL SABAHIAH 45380 AL FARWANIAH 45381 AL SHIDADIAH 45382 AL SOLAIBIAH 45383 AL SALEHIAH** (Iq flag): **45384 BAGHDAD 45385 BABYLON 45386 BASRAH 45387 SINDBAD** (FRG flag): **45388 POLANA** ex BRUNSKAMP 1968 (Sg flag): **45389 PANGANI** ex BRUNSHAGEN 1969 **45390 WESTGATE** ex PALABORA; ex BRUNSWICK 1968 (Gr flag): **45391 EVGENIA 45392 EFTYHIA 45393 KLAVDIA** ex OAKLAND STAR 1971; ex KLAVDIA 1969 **45394 PEBANE** ex BRUNSHAIN 1971 (In flag): **45395 VISHVA UMANG 45396 VISHVA TARANG 45397 VISHVA ASHA 45398 VISHVA ABHA** (Pk flag): **45399 AL-ABEDIN** (Li flag): **45400 PELINDABA** ex BRUNSHOST 1971 **45401 PONGOLA** ex BRUNSTORF 1972 (Tg flag): **45402 PAYIME** ex PARANGA 1980; ex BRUNSBROCK 1971.

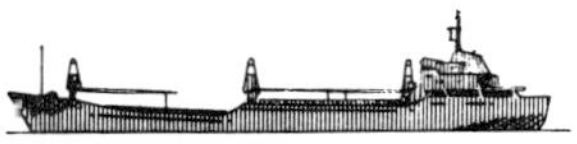

C_3MF *H123*
● **45460 TONY'S LUCK.** Gr/FRG 1966; C; 1600; 85.81 × 5.12 (281.53 × 16.79); M; 12.5; ex ATREUS; ex INGRID RETZLAFF 1974. Sister: **45461 ROSARITA** (Pa) ex NEW HOPE; ex ERICH RETZLAFF 1974.

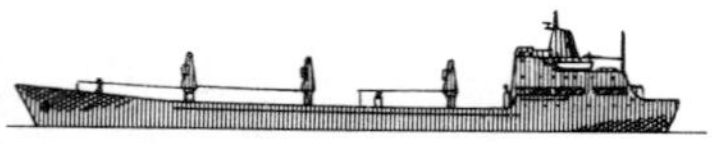

C_3MFK H3
● **45470 GRYNGE.** Sw/No 1965; Ch; 3400; 105.42 × 6.58 (345.87 × 21.59); M; 14; ex BOHUS 1972. Sister: **45471 SUNLUCK** (Cy) ex RUDOLF 1976.

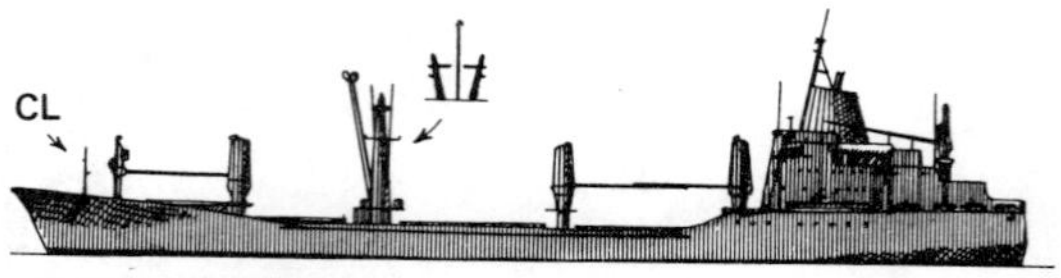

C_2KC_2MFC H13
45480 STRATHMAY. Br/Br 1970; C; 8000/11200; 156.98 × 8.2/9.62 (515.02 × 26.9/31.56); M; 19; ex MANORA 1975. Sisters (Br flag): **45481 STRATHMEIGLE** ex MERKARA 1975 **45482 STRATHMORE** ex MORVADA 1975 **45483 STRATHMUIR** ex MULBERA 1975.

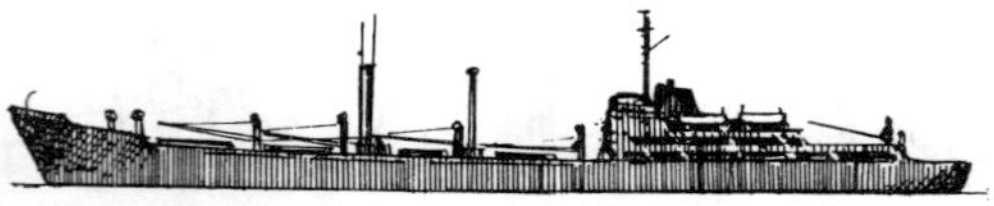

$C_2MCKCMFC$ H1
⋆**45490 KAI HUA.** RC/Sw 1958; C; 6400/10100; 149.36 × —/9.81 (490.03 × —/32.19); M; 15.75; ex GAOYAN 1976; ex ARISTANAX 1973; ex W.R. LUNDGREN 1967.

C_2MF H
45500 AGENOR. FRG/FRG 1964; C; 500; 73 × 3.6 (239.5 × 11.81); M; 13.

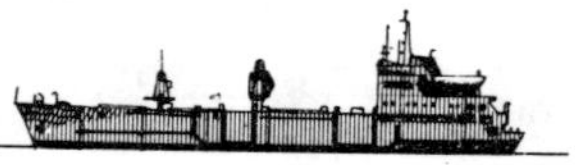

C_2MF H
45510 TYRO. Ne/Ne 1967; C; 1300; 84.23 × 4.49 (276.34 × 14.73); M; 14.

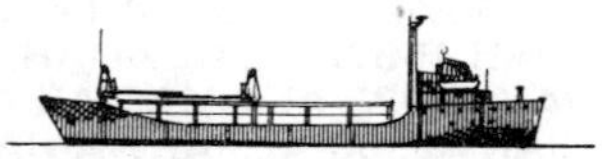

C_2MF H13
45520 ELPIREA. Gr/FRG 1964; C; 1200/1900; 81.23 × 4.83/5.87 (266.5 × 15.85/19.26); M; 13; ex ZEBRAS SUCCESS 1978; ex FREDENHAGEN 1974.

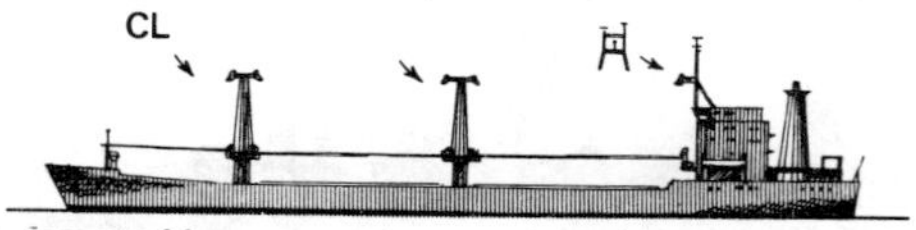

C_2MF H13
45530 SLOMAN NEREUS. FRG/FRG 1977; C; 4400/7400; 129.52 × 6.87/8.06 (424.93 × 22.53/26.44); M; 17; ex TABUCO 1980; ex SLOMAN NEREUS 1980; ex CAROL NEREUS 1980; ex SLOMAN NEREUS 1978; **'CL 10'** type. Sisters (FRG flag): **45531 SLOMAN NAJADE 45532 STUBBENHUK.**

C_2MF H13
⋆**45540 OSKOL** class. Ru/Pd 1963/70; FA; 2500 Dspl; 90 × 4.5 (295.28 × 14.8); TSM; 16.

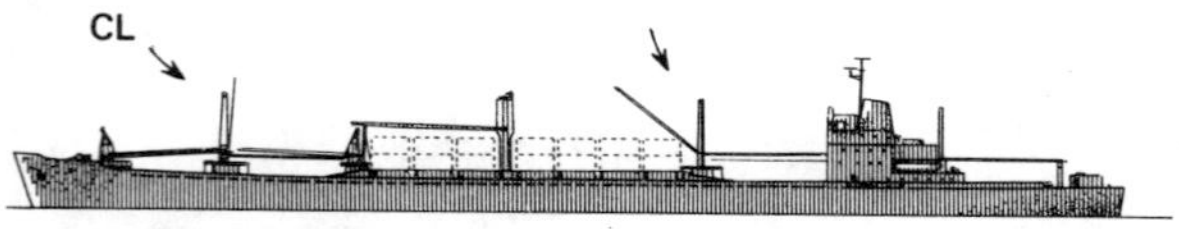

CKC_2KMFK H1
45550 SAINT FRANCOIS. Fr/Br-Po 1970/78; C/Con; 12400; 174.53 × 8.48 (572.6 × 27.82); M; 16; Modified **"SD 14"** type. Lengthened and converted from general cargo. Sister: **4551 ST. PAUL** (Fr).

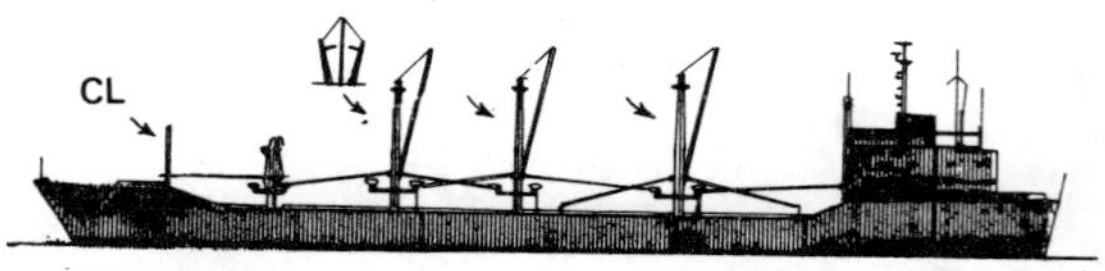

CK_4MF H13
45560 HIGHSEA PROMISE. Sg/FRG 1970; C; 6700/10100; 162.8 × 7.5/8.94 (534.12 × 24.6/29.33); M; 18; ex DALMATIA 1980; ex CONCORD DALMATIA 1978; ex DALMATIA 1977; **'Pioneer'** type.

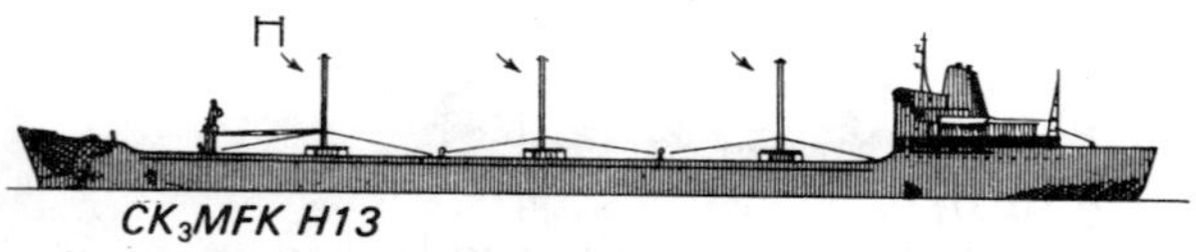

CK_3MFK H13
● **45570 ATLANTIC CHARITY.** Li/Ja 1970; B; 16000; 180.32 × 10.64 (591.6 × 34.9); M; 15.25. Possible Sisters: **45571 ANGEBALTIC** (Gr) ex ATLANTIC CHALLENGE 1981 **45572 TENO** (Ch) ex MINA L. CAMBANIS 1975; ex EAST BREEZE 1969 (May now have a gantry crane).

CKMF H13
45580 IMPERIAL SKEENA. Ca/Ca 1970; Tk; 3000; 91.45 × 5.56 (300.03 × 18.24); TSM; 12.5.

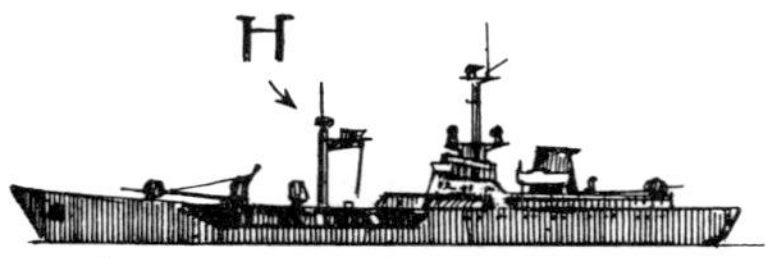

CKMF H13
★**45590 MANYCH.** Ru/Fi 1972; A/Rmt; 7500 Dspl; 115 × 6 (377 × 20). Sister: ★**45591 TAGIL** (Ru).

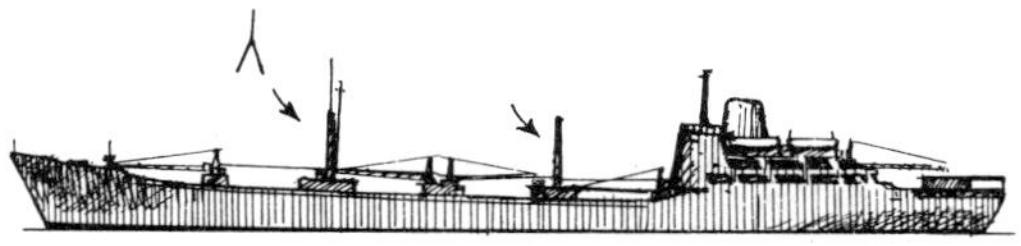

CMC_2KCMFC H13
● **45610 MIRRABOOKA.** Sw/Sw 1961; C; 8200/11300; 156.37 × 8.73/9.47 (513.02 × 28.64/31.06); M; 17.75. Sisters: **45611 POPI** (Gr) ex KLIPPAREN **45612 VENUS DEL MAR** (Ur) ex TEMNAREN.

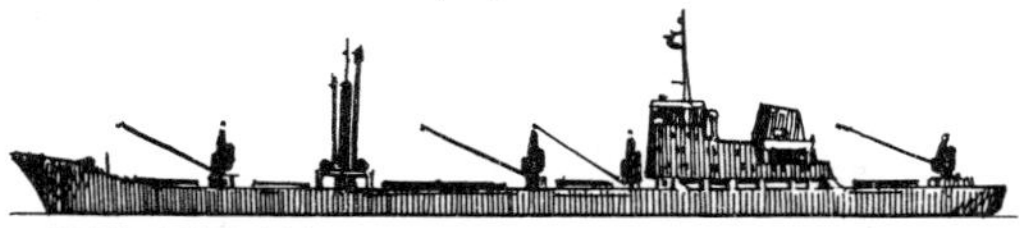

CMC_2MFC H1
★**45630 OLA.** Ru/Ja 1964; C; 11100; 154.77 × 9.59 (507.78 × 31.46); M; 17.25. Sisters (Ru flag): ★**45631 OTRADNOE** ★**45632 OREKHOV** ★**45633 ORSHA** ★**45634 OSTRAGOZHSK.**

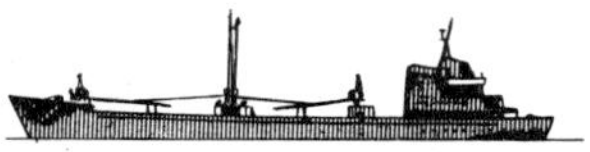

CMCMF H1
45650 BILBARAKAH. Pa/Be 1963; C; 1200/1900; 83.19 × 5.02/6.12 (272.93 × 16.47/20.08); M; 14; ex SOUTHERN ISLES 1979; ex HELMI 1973. Similar: **45651 ARMANDO REVERON** (Ve) ex ALEFANI 1976; ex ALHENA 1974.

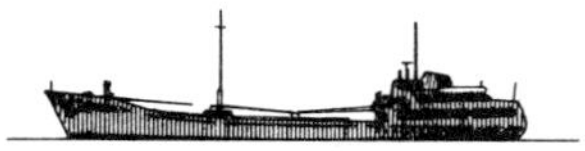

CMCMF H1
45670 MESONGO. Sg/FRG 1952; C; 1600; 76.79 × — (251.93 × —); M; 11.5; ex MELATI 1975; ex INTOMBI 1975; ex HOHENHORN 1964; ex CIANDRA 1961. Sister: **45671 LAUTAN ENAM** (My) ex MENADO 1980; ex INGANE 1977; ex SKAGENHORN 1964; ex COLONIA 1961.

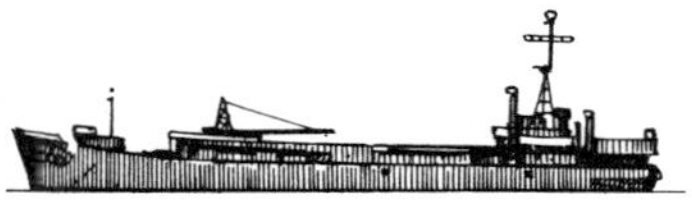

CKMK H
45600 ODIN. FRG/US —; FA/Repair Ship; 3500 Dspl; 100 × 2.8 (328 × 9.2); TSM; 11.5; ex U.S.S. DIOMEDES. Sister: **45601 WOTAN** (FRG) ex U.S.S. ULYSSES.

CMC_2MF H1
45620 SHEARWATER BAY. SA/FRG 1964; C; 800/2000; 83.19 × 3.6/5.39 (272.93 × 11.81/17.68); M; 13.5; ex ZWARTKOPS 1980; ex LOHENGRIN 1969.

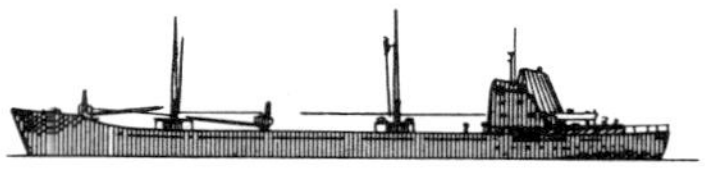

CMCMF H1
45640 HOLSTENLAND. Gr/FRG 1959; C; 2800/4000; 105.92 × 6.72/7.6 (347 × 22.05/24.93); M; 15; ex LINDAUNIS 1974; ex CAP BONAVISTA 1970. Sister: **45641 HOLSTENSAND** (Gr) ex BOKNIS 1974; ex VOLTA SERVICE 1973; ex BOKNIS 1972; ex CAP CASTILLO 1971; ex ISMAILIA 1958.

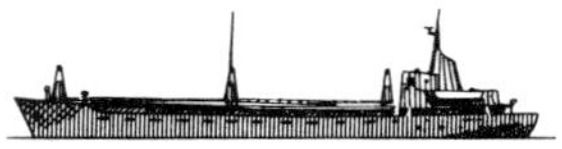

CMCMF H1
45660 SHEARWATER BAY. SA/FRG 1964; C; 800/2000; 83.19 × 3.6/5.39 (272.93 × 11.81/17.68); M; 13.5; ex ZWARTKOPS 1980; ex LOHENGRIN 1969.

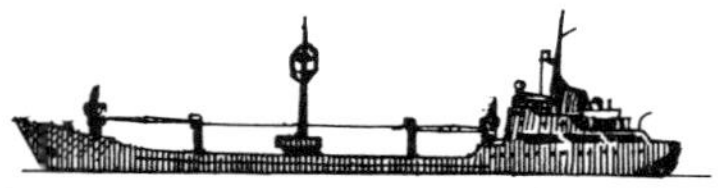

CMCMF H13
★**45680 IZHMALES.** Ru/Fi 1962; C; 2900; 102.32 × 5.91 (335.7 × 19.39); M; 13. Sisters (Ru flag): ★**45681 IRKUTSKLES** ★**45682 IGARKALES** ★**45683 INKURLES** ★**45684 IRBITLES** ★**45685 IRSHALES** ★**45686 IZHEVSKLES** ★**45687 ILMENLES** ★**45688 IRTYSHLES** ★**45689 IZHORALES** ★**45690 ISTRA** ★**45691 PERMLES.**

CMF H
⋆**45700 QSKOL III** type. Ru/Pd 1963/70; FA; 2500 Dspl; 90 × 4.5 (295.28 × 14.8); TSM; 16.

CMF H1
⋆**45710 DORNBUSCH.** DDR/DDR 1965; Cbl/BT; 750; 64 × 3.35 (210 × 11); D-E; 13.5.

CMF H3
⋆**45720 ALLIGATOR III** class. Ru/Ru 1968; A/LC; 4100 Dspl; 113 × 4.4 (371 × 12); TSM; 18.

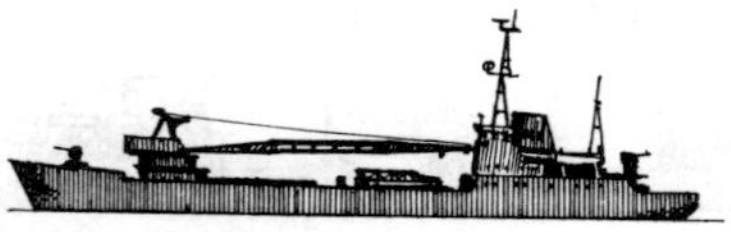

CMFK H13
⋆**45730 AMGA.** Ru/Ru —; A/Missile Support Ship; 6400 Dspl; 102 × 5.8 (361 × 19); M; 18. 1 sister ship.

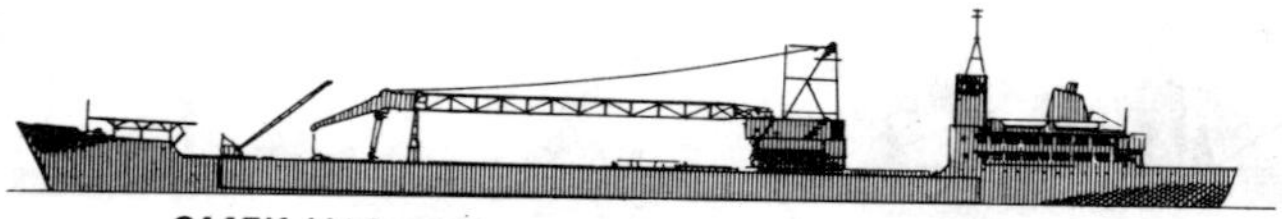

CMFK H13
45740 CHALLENGER I. Li/Ne 1956; CS; 10900; 193.2 × 10.25 (633.86 × 33.63); T; 16; ex CHALLENGER 1970; ex P.G. THULIN; Widened 1970. Converted Ore/Oil Carrier 1970.

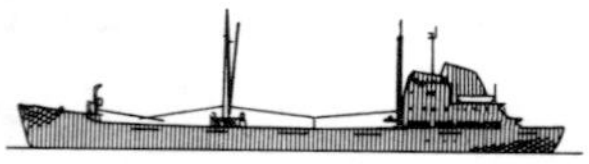

CM_2F H1
45750 KADAS 1. Gh/FRG 1960; C; 1400/2200; 86.39 × 5.02/6.02 (283.43 × 16.47/19.75); M; 13; ex GULF ANGLIA 1977; ex ALKES 1975; ex ALK; Lengthened 1967.

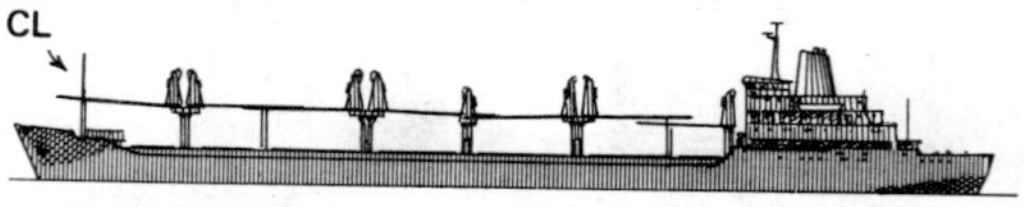

KC_8MF H13
45760 ATLANTA. Fi/Br 1972; C; 8900; 154.9 × 9.17 (508.2 × 30.08); M; 19. Sister: **45761 AURORA** (Fi).

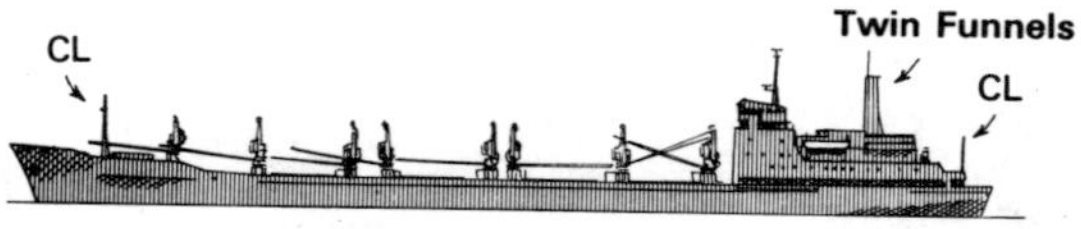

KC_8MFK H1
⋆**45770 PULAWY.** Pd/Sw 1966; C; 7300/10700; 156.17 × 8.36/9.52 (512.37 × 27.42/31.23); M; 19; ex WAITARA 1973; **'Scandia'** type. Sister: **45771 HELLENIC SEAMAN** (Gr) ex KILLARA 1975.

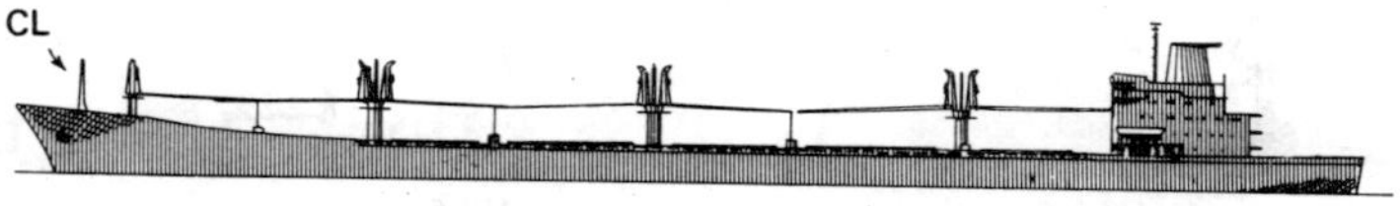

KC_7MF H1
45780 CAST PORPOISE. FRG/FRG 1969; B; 26100; 216.14 × 11.87 (709.12 × 38.94); M; 16; ex E.R. MONTREAL 1978; ex REINHART LORENZ RUSS 1975; Used as a container ship; May have cranes removed.

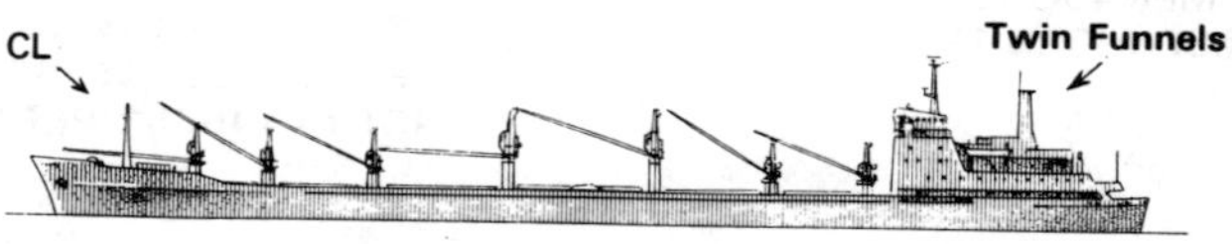

KC_7MF/KC_7MFK H1
● **45790 SAINT JACQUES.** Sw/Sw-Br 1967/71; C/Con; 9400/13100; 178.54 × 8.47/9.51 (585.76 × 27.79/31.2); M; 17.5; ex WOOLAHRA 1978; Lengthened and converted from general cargo 1971. Sister: **45791 SAINT LUC** (Fr) ex TALARAH 1980.

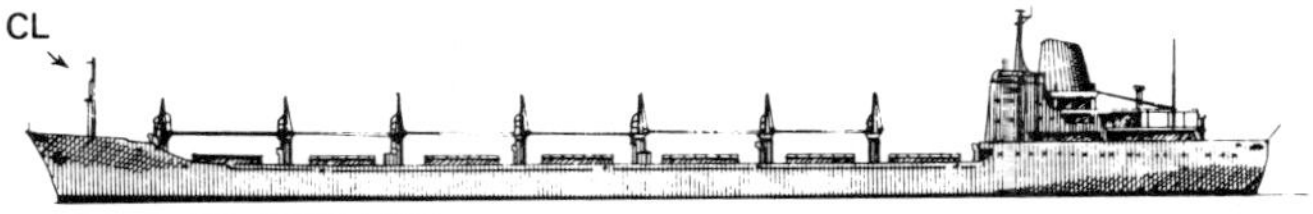

KC$_7$MFK H13
45800 ELOCEAN. Gr/FRG 1965; B; 20500; 196.63 × 11.03 (645.11 × 36.19); M; 15.25; ex STOVE VULCAN 1973.

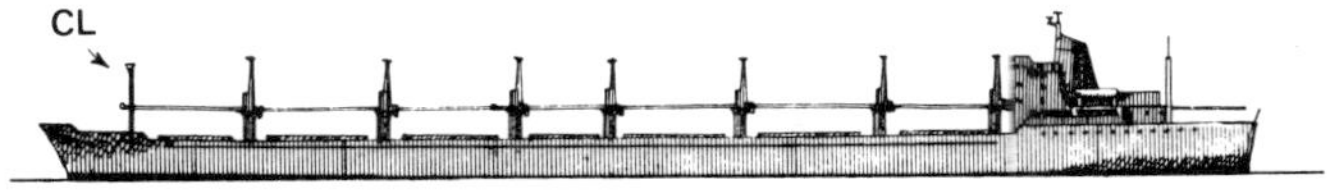

KC$_7$MFK H13
45810 ANDAMAN SEA. Pa/Br 1969; B; 22200; 193.1 × 11.25 (633.53 × 36.91); M; 15.5; ex NORTHAMPTONSHIRE; ex VOLNAY.

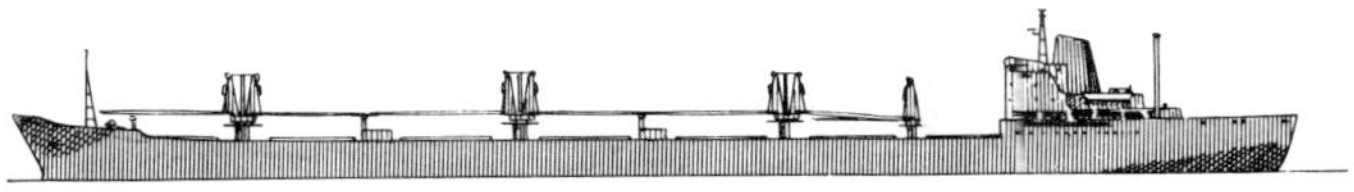

KC$_7$MFK H13
● **45820 ASEAN OBJECTIVE.** Pi/Be 1969; B; 22400; 203.77 × 11.37 (668.53 × 37.3); M; 15.5; ex E.R. SCALDIA.

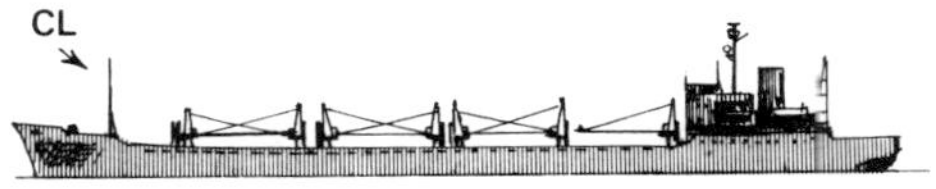

KC$_7$MFK H13
45830 DEKA NAVIGATOR. Gr/Ja 1965; C; 7700; 139.93 × 8.7 (459.08 × 28.54); M; 15.5; ex RIO DE JANEIRO MARU. Sisters: **45831 MATHILDA** (Gr) ex ROSARIO MARU 1980 **45832 CHAR LOONG** (Pa) ex CHEER CETUS 1980; ex RECIFE MARU **45833 CHAR HOONG** (Pa) ex CAPE CETUS; ex RIO GRANDE MARU.

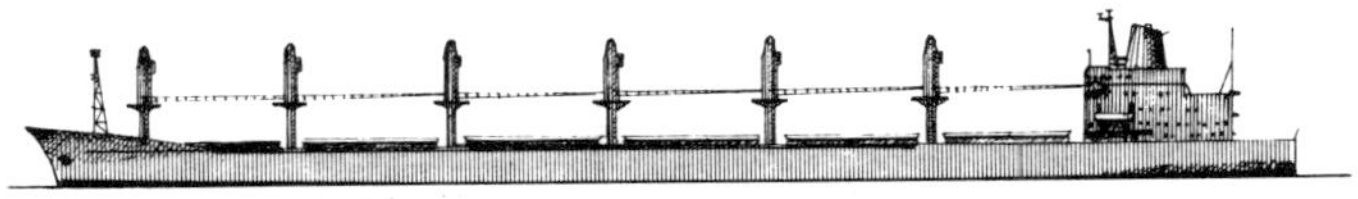

KC$_6$MF H1
45840 WARSCHAU. FRG/FRG 1976; B; 30300; 213.39 × 12.17 (700.09 × 39.93); M; 16. Sisters: **45841 EMMA JOHANNA** (FRG) **45842 DRESDEN** (FRG) **45843 THAMESFIELD** (Br).

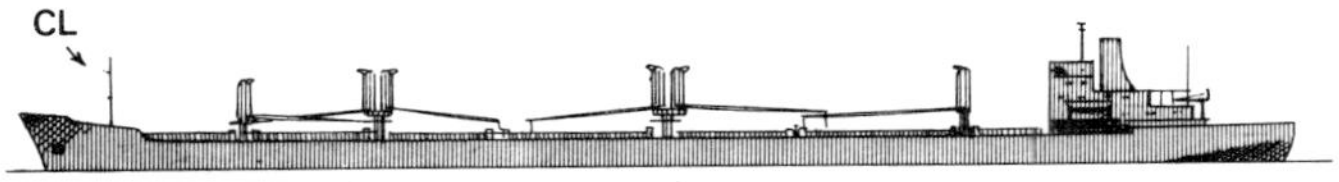

KC$_6$MF H1
45850 BUDAPEST. FRG/FRG 1971; B; 24600; 203.18 × 11.6 (666.6 × 38.06); M; 16. Probably Similar: **45851 PRAG** (FRG).

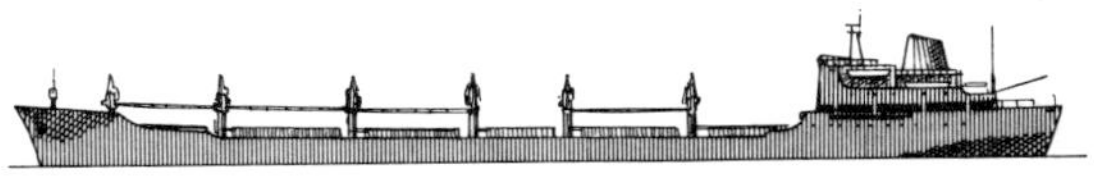

KC$_6$MF H13
● **45860 DESPINA GIAVRIDIS.** Gr/No 1967; B; 11700; 165.64 × 9.31 (543.44 × 30.54); M; 14.5; ex BULK PIONEER 1977. Sisters: **45861 THEODOROS GIAVRIDIS** (Gr) ex BULK EXPLORER 1975 **45862 SUNWARD** (Br) ex REA 1978; ex RINGAR 1972.

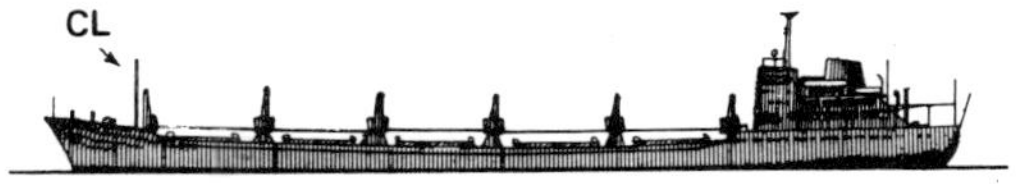

KC$_6$MF H13
45870 SOMERI. Fi/Ja 1956; B; 8200; 144.63 × 8.61 (474.5 × 28.24); M; —; ex JOHN WILSON 1973. Sister: **45871 CARIBBEAN NOSTALGIA** (Pa) ex SANTA MARIA 1978; ex MARKUS 1977; ex CHILEAN NITRATE 1974.

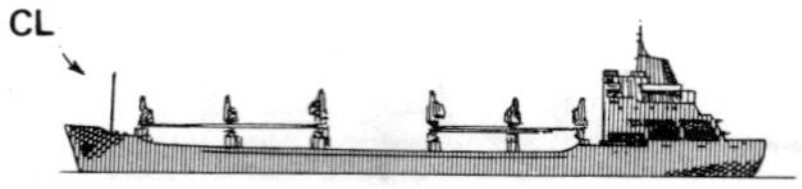

KC_6MF H13

● **45880 NGAPARA.** NZ/Br 1966; C; 4500; 111.89 × 7.16 (367 × 23.49); M; 12.5. Sisters: **45881 NGAHERE** (NZ) **45882 NGAKUTA** (NZ) **45883 KAPETAN ANTONIS** (Gr) ex FLORENTIA 1977; ex NGATORO 1976.

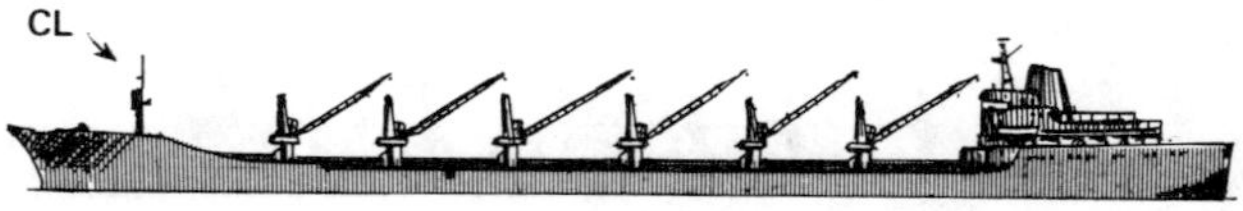

KC_6MF H13

⋆**45890 KUANG HAI.** RC/No 1965; B; 21900; 193.35 × 11.15 (634.35 × 36.58); M; 14.5; ex ROALD JARL 1974.

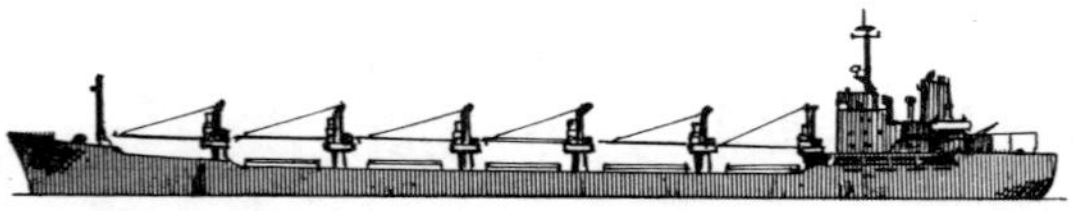

KC_6MF H13

45900 PHILIPPI. Li/Ja 1965; C; 12500; 165.31 × 8.99 (542.36 × 29.49); M; 14; ex WAKO MARU 1975.

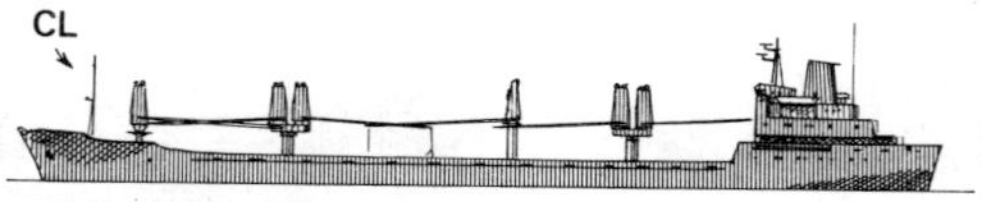

KC_6MF H13

45910 ARIEL. Fi/De 1970; C; 4900/7600; 147.02 × 6.79/7.7 (482.34 × 22.28/25.26); M; 17.5; Lengthened 1974. Sisters (Fi flag): **45911 RHEA 45912 PALLAS.**

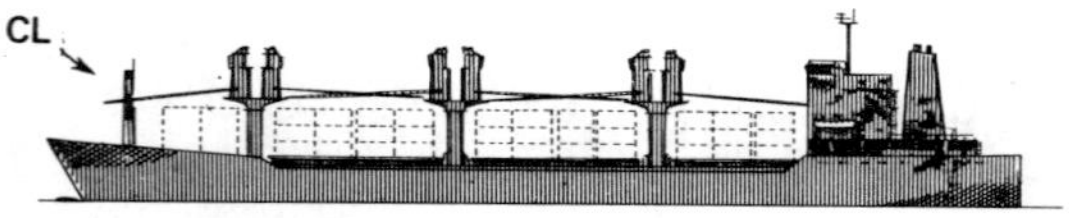

KC_6MF H13

45920 UNIDO. FRG/Ko 1979; C/Con; 13000; 155 × 8.7 (508.5 × 28.54); M; 17. Sister: **45921 AMADO** (FRG).

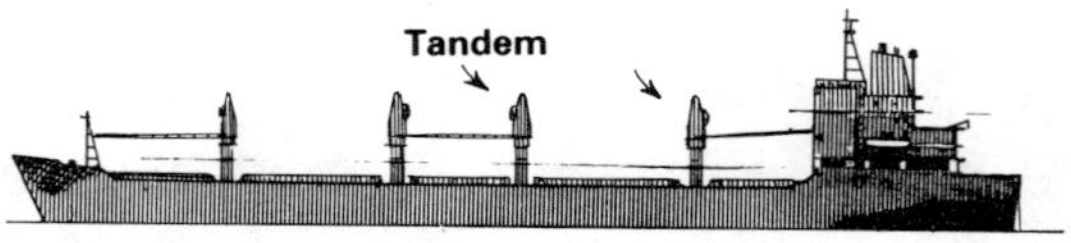

KC_6MF H13

45930 SAMOA. De/De 1978; C; 16200; 159.42 × 10.59 (523.03 × 34.74); M; 16. Sisters (De flag): **45931 SARGODHA 45932 SIMBA 45933 SIENA 45934 SINALOA** (Pk flag): **45935 MAKRAN.**

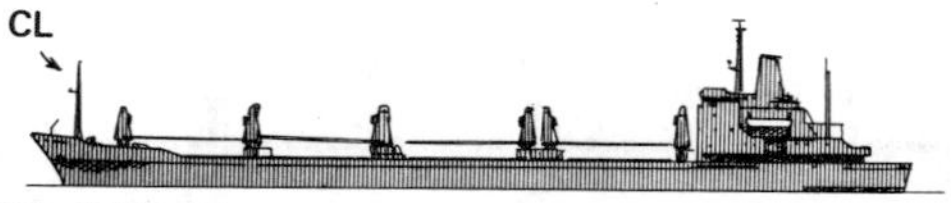

KC_6MFK H1

45940 SUNEMERILLON. Ca/Sw 1969; C; 6000/9600; 140.04 × 7.89/9.52 (459.45 × 25.89/31.23); M; 16.75; ex BORELAND 1979; **'Scandia'** type. Sister: ⋆**45941 YU JIANG** (RC) ex BIRKALAND.

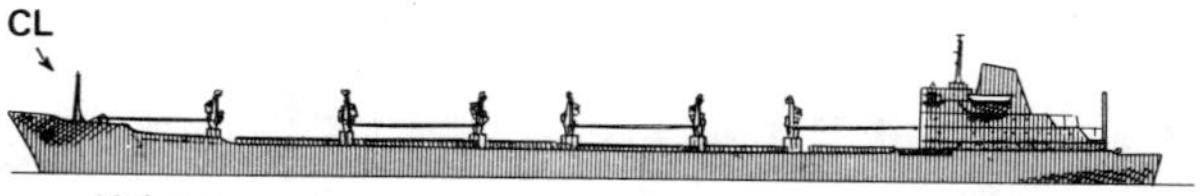

KC_6MFK H1

45950 VITINA. Gr/Br 1975; B; 15000; 183.04 × 10.47 (600.52 × 34.35); M; 15; ex ANNA M 1978; **'B-26'** type. Sister: **45951 KASSOS** (Gr) ex CAMILLA M 1980.

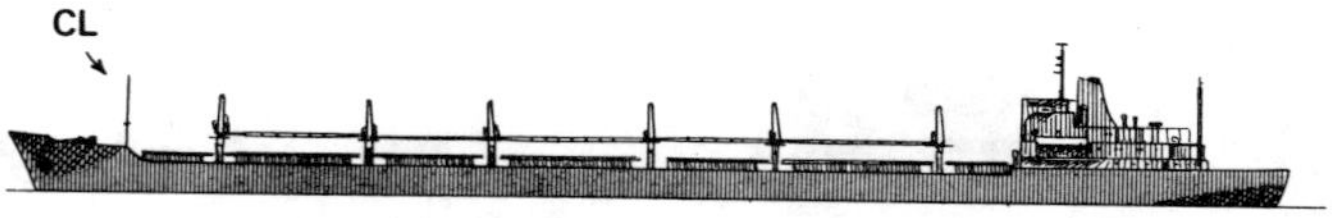

KC_6MFK H1

45960 CHENNAI JAYAM. In/FRG 1965; B; 24400; 203.16 × 11.6 (666.54 × 38.05); M; 14. Sisters (In flag): **45961 CHENNAI OOKKAM 45962 CHENNAI PERUMAI 45963 CHENNAI SADHANAI 45964 CHENNAI SELVAM.**

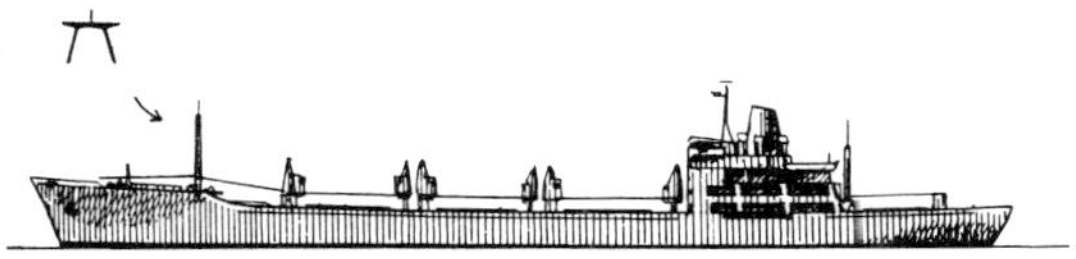

KC_6MFK H1
● **45970 SACRAMENTO MARU.** Ja/Ja 1967; C; 6700; 155.73 × 8.64 (510.92 × 28.34); M; 18.5. Sisters: **45971 HELEN** (Ma) ex ST. LOUIS MARU 1980 **45972 SAN FRANCISCO MARU** (Ja) **45973 SAVANNAH MARU** (Ja).

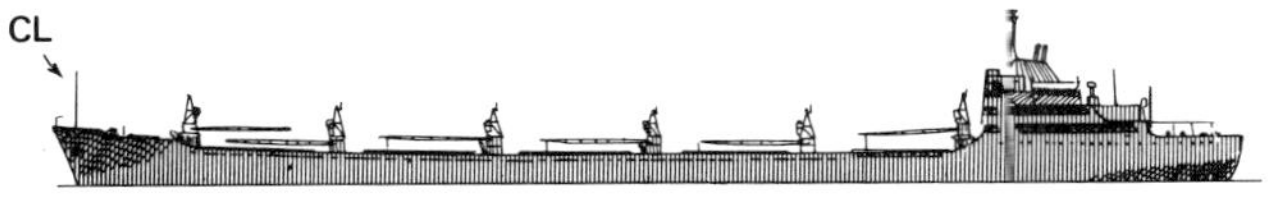

KC_6MFK H13
⋆**45980 QINGHAI.** RC/Br 1962; B; 14500; 188.63 × 9.78 (618.86 × 32.08); M; 15; ex IPANEMA 1973; ex CORCOVADO 1973; ex CHAPEL RIVER 1970. Similar: **45981 ARTADI** (Li) ex CANOPUS 1973; ex PACIFIC PRINCESS 1970.

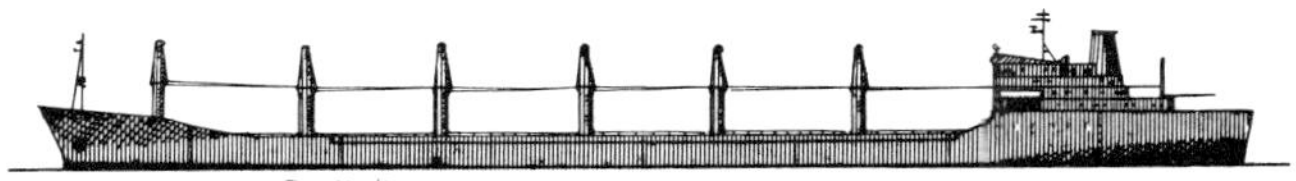

KC_6MFK H13
45990 MELSOMVIK. No/No 1977; B; 23000; 193.45 × 11.77 (634.67 × 38.61); M; —.

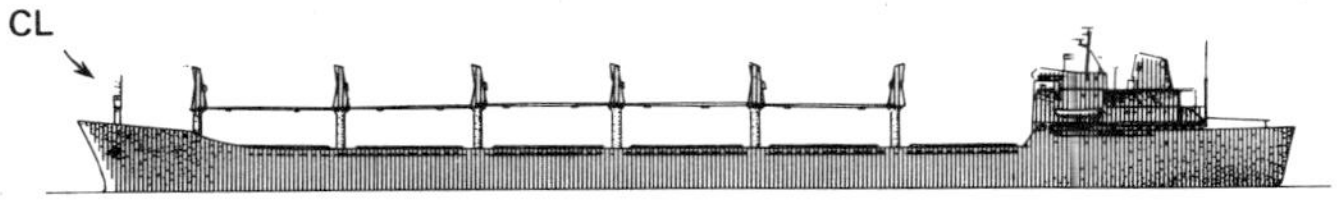

KC_6MFK H13
46000 BELSTAR. No/No 1972; B; 22500; 193.45 × 11.76 (634.68 × 38.58); M; 15. Similar: **46001 ALEPPO** (Sw) **46002 PAN DYNASTY** (Ko) ex BELITA 1977; ex VIATOR 1974 **46003 SKYPTRON** (Gr) ex DOLORES DE PLANDOLIT 1981; ex SANDVAAG 1978 **46004 STOVE CAMPBELL** (No) **46005 STOVE TRANSPORT** (Sw) (RC flag): ⋆**46006 AN HAI** ex SANDAR 1977 ⋆**46007 HU PO HAI** ex BULK PROMOTER 1977 ⋆**46008 JIN HAI** ex RINGSTAD 1977 ⋆**46009 LIULINHAI** ex BELNOR 1977 ⋆**46010 MEI GUI HAI** ex BULK PROSPECTOR 1977.

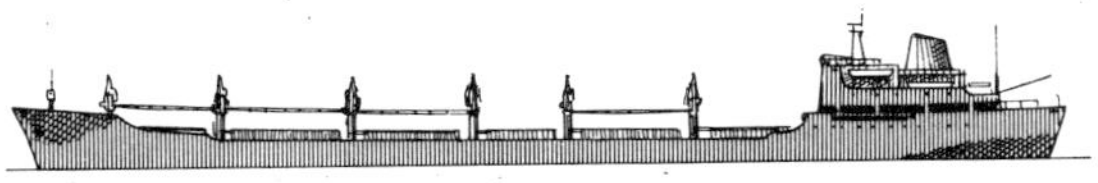

KC_6MFK H13
● **46020 DESPINA GIAVRIDIS.** Gr/No 1967; B; 11700; 165.64 × 9.31 (543.44 × 30.54); M; 14.5; ex BULK PIONEER 1977. Sisters: **46021 THEODOROS GIAVRIDIS** (Gr) ex BULK EXPLORER 1975 **46022 SUNWARD** (Br) ex REA 1978; ex RINGAR 1972.

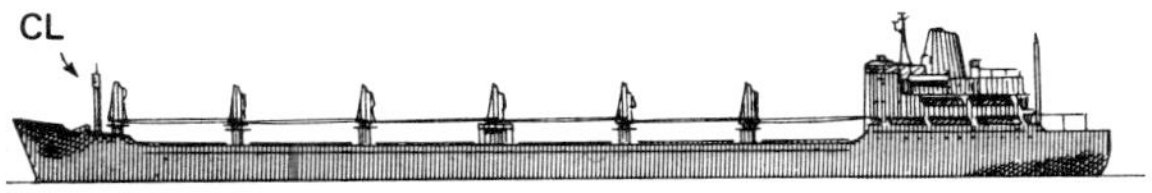

KC_6MFK H13
46030 GINO JULIANO. It/Ja 1967; B; 15700; 174.38 × 10.22 (572.11 × 33.53); M; 15.5; ex ROSS SEA 1978.

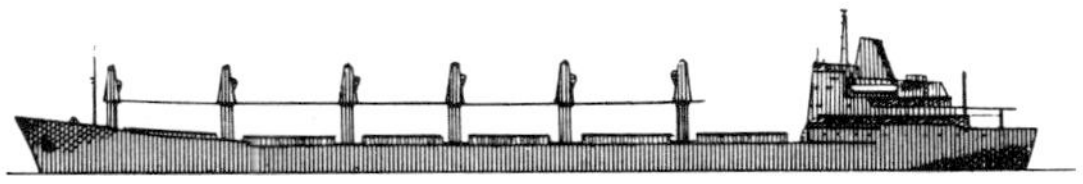

KC_6MFK H13
46040 KIKI YEMELOS. Gr/No 1967; B; 11200; 161.55 × 9.7 (530.02 × 31.82); M; 15.5; ex CAPE CLEAR 1973. Sister: **46041 SATYA SOHAN** (In) ex BARON FORBES 1973.

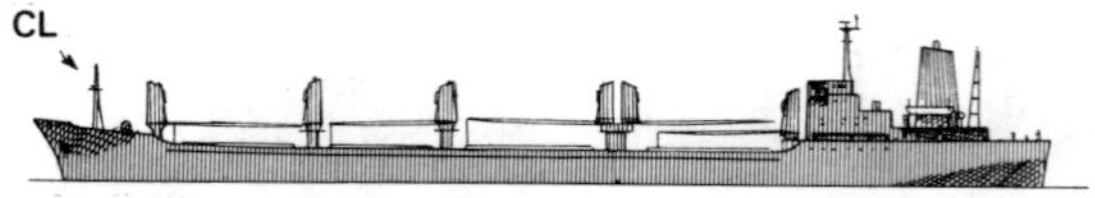

KC_6MFK H13

46050 ASTRA PEAK. Pa/Ja 1976; C; 12800; 161.02 × 10.37 (528.28 × 34.02); M; 17. Sisters (Pa flag): **46051 GLORIA PEAK 46052 PRIMERA PEAK.**

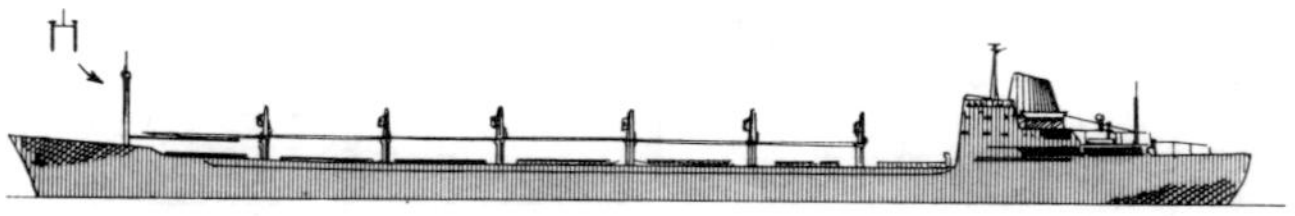

KC_6MFK H13

46060 AL TAJDAR. Li/FRG 1965; B; 20500; 196.55 × 11.03 (644.85 × 36.18); M; 15; ex GERMA; ex CLARO 1974; ex OLAV RINGDAL 1970.

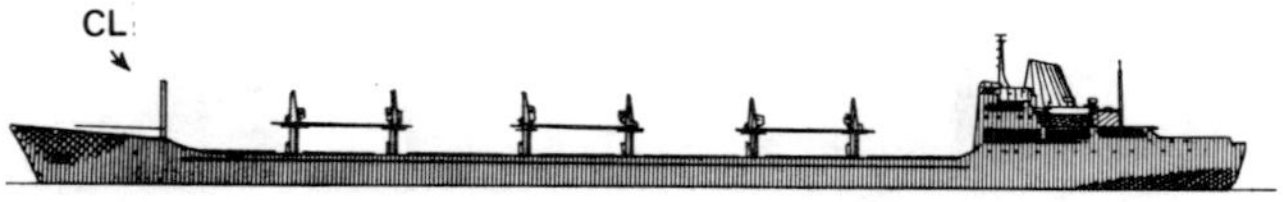

KC_6MFK H13

46070 MARITSA P. LEMOS. Gr/Ys 1972; B; 17500; 196.6 × 10.86 (645.01 × 35.63); M; 15.5. Sister: ⋆**46071 WU SHENG HAI** (RC) ex NICOLAOS PATERAS 1980 Possible sister: **46072 ADRIATIK** (Pa) Similar: ⋆**46073 ZHAO YANG HAI** (RC) ex MERICUNDA ⋆**46074 HERCEGOVINA** (Ys).

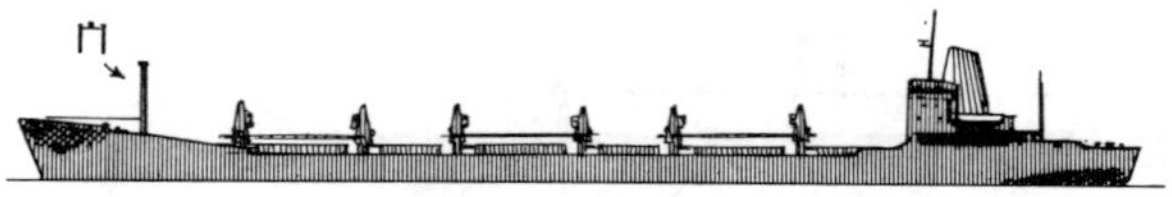

KC_6MFK H13

46080 PANAGIOTIS S. Gr/Sp 1966; C; 1300; 173.31 × 10.26 (568.6 × 33.66); M; 14.5; ex EMILIA LOVERDOS 1975; ex VIZCAYA 1973. Similar: **46081 MONTE ZALAMA** (Gr)-lengthened & may have an extra crane.

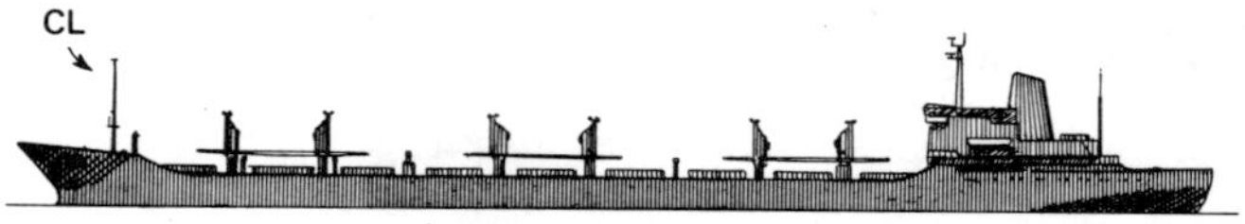

KC_6MFK H13

46090 ON YEUNG. Pa/Ru 1972; B; 23200; 199.9 × 11.23 (655.84 × 36.84); M; 16; ex FIGARO 1978; **'Baltika'** type. Sister: **46091 SAINT ETIENNE** (Li) ex RAVENNA; ex NOPAL RAVENNA 1976; ex STAR RAVENNA 1975 Similar: **46092 ON LEE** (Pa) ex MADAME BUTTERFLY 1978 **46093 AKBAR** (Br) ex TRAVIATA 1977 **46094 WILLIAM** (Sg) ex AUGUST BOLTEN 1977; launched as RENATE Possibly similar: **46095 LUIS BANCHERO** (Pe).

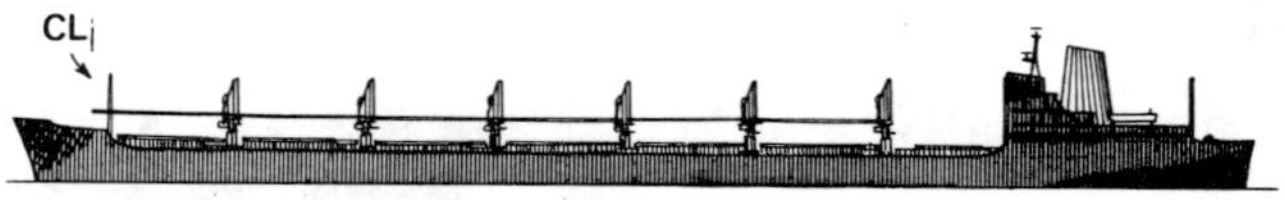

KC_6MFK H13

● **46100 WORLD ARGUS.** Gr/Gr 1973; B; 19500; 193.43 × 11.35 (634.61 × 37.23); M; 15. Similar (Gr flag): **46101 WORLD APOLLO 46102 WORLD ARES 46103 WORLD AJAX 46104 WORLD AGAMEMNON 46105 WORLD ARETUS 46106 WORLD MARINE 46107 DAPHNE 46108 FOTINI 46109 JOANNA 46110 APHRODITE 46111 TARPON SEALANE 46112 MILLY GREGOS** ex SCAPWILL **46113 WORLD AMPHION** (Br flag): **46114 ASIAN ADVENTURESS** ex ALDGATE 1979; ex SCAPDALE 1979 **46115 IRON CUMBERLAND** ex WORLD ACHILLES (Li flag): **46116 WORLD ACHILLES II** Possible sister: **46117 WORLD AEGEUS.** (Gr).

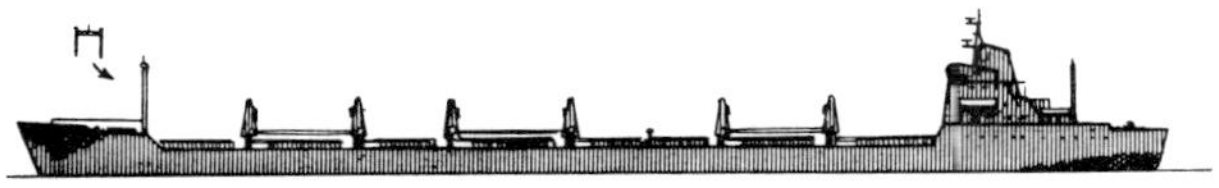

KC_6MFK H13
46120 LUJUA. Sp/Sp 1968; B; 15500; 183.12 × 10.52 (600.78 × 34.51); M; 15. Sisters (Sp flag): **46121 MONTE ZAPOLA 46122 MONTE ZAMBURU 46123 MONTE ZARAYA 46124 SERANTES.**

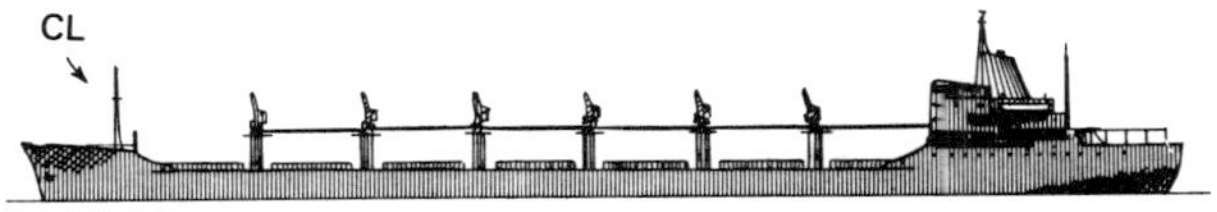

KC_6MFK H13
● **46130 LIBERIAN STATESMAN.** Li/Ne 1964; B; 18300; 183.9 × 11.17 (603.35 × 36.64); M; —; ex PRESIDENT WILLIAM V.S. TUBMAN 1973.

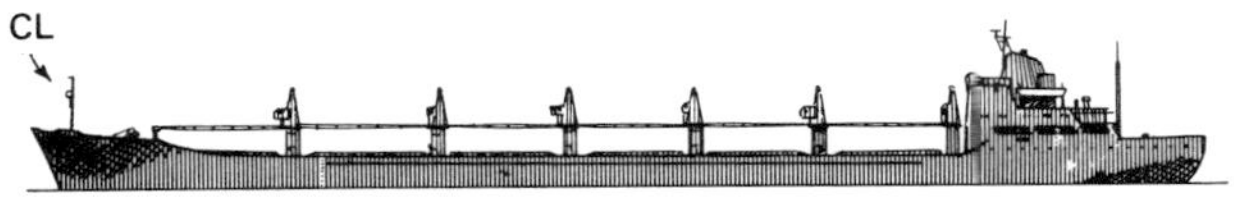

KC_6MFK H13
46140 AMSTELBURCHT. Ne/Ne 1965; B; 16600; 196.42 × 10.91 (611.61 × 35.79); M; 14.5; ex HOLLANDS BURCHT 1977.

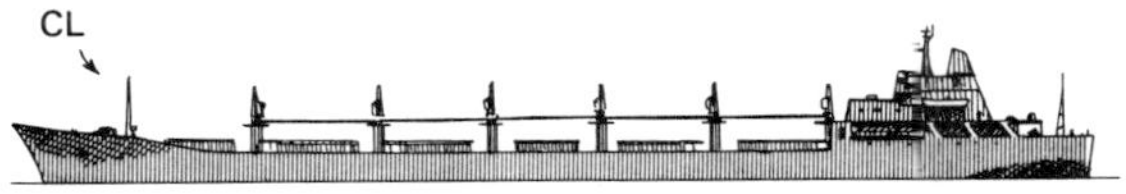

KC_6MFK H13
46150 PELAGOS. Gr/Ja 1967; B; 16000; 171.58 × 10.23 (562.93 × 33.56); M; 15; ex NEPTUNE 1976; ex JEAN 1969.

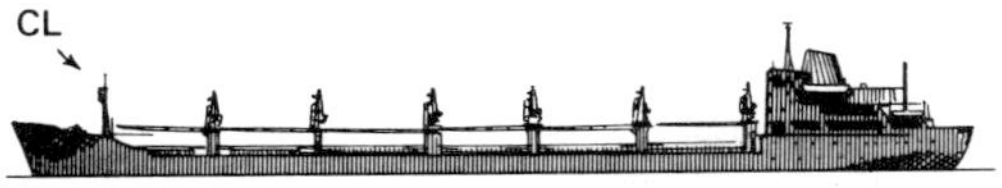

KC_6MFK H13
46160 CORAL. Pa/De 1965; B; 10300; 152.43 × 9.06 (500.09 × 29.72); M; 14.75; ex BELITA 1974.

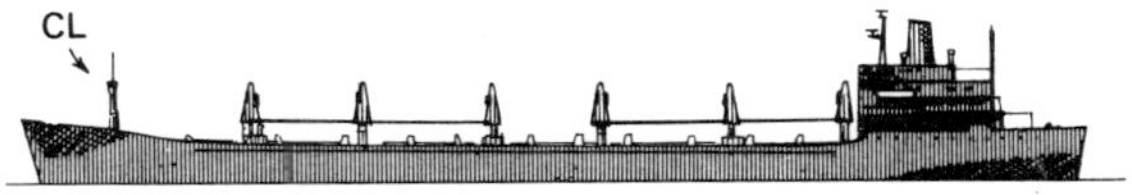

KC_6MFK H13
● **46170 NORSE VIKING.** Br/Sw 1970; B; 14800; 168.99 × 10.27 (554.43 × 33.69); M; 16. Sisters: **46171 PATRICIA** (Gr) ex NORSE CAPTAIN **46172 NORSE RIVER** (Li).

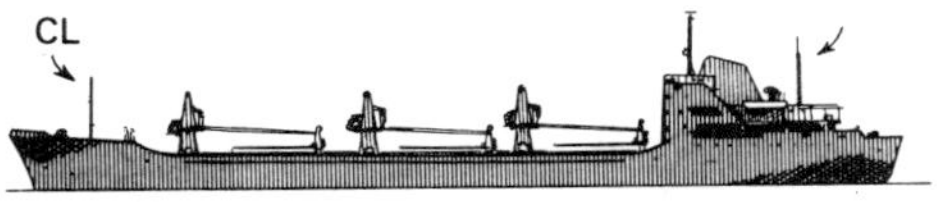

KC_6MFK H13
46180 ATLANTIC EXPRESS. Li/De 1960; C; 5800; 141.54 × 7.87 (464.37 × 25.82); M; 16; ex DOMINO CRYSTAL 1973.

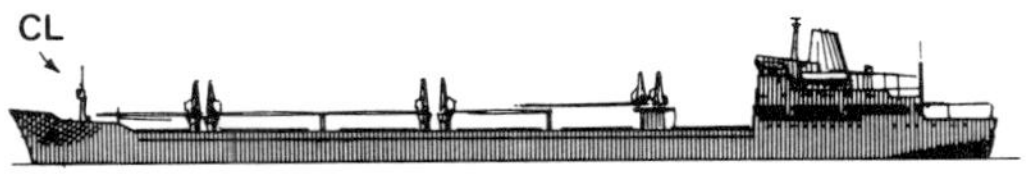

KC_6MFK H13
46190 DEMETRIOS. Gr/Sw 1967; B; 10800; 156.85 × 9.32 (514.6 × 30.57); M; 15; ex ELEFTHEROTRIA; ex BERTIL KARLBOM 1972.

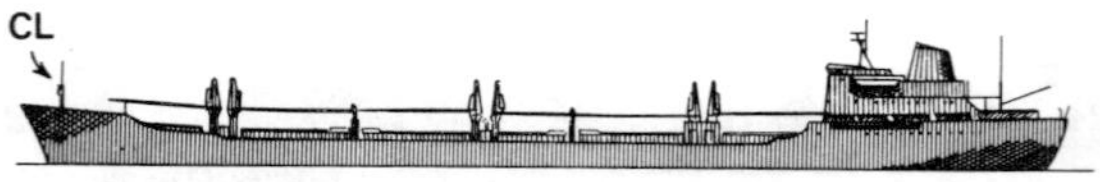

KC_6MFK H13
46200 UNIVERSE CLIPPER. Pa/No 1966; B; 11300; 165.67 × 9.29 (543.53 × 30.48); M; 15; ex TRADITION 1980; ex LAMANT 1975; ex BELCARGO 1973.

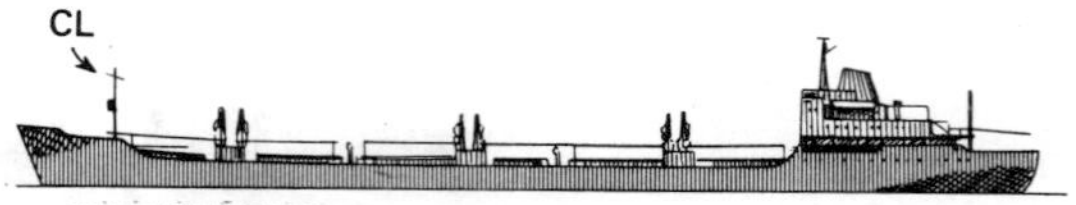

KC_6MFK H13
● **46210 LIN HAI.** RC/FRG 1966; B; 10700; 161.6 × 9.36 (530.18 × 30.7); M; 14.5; ex ATENALIA 1976; ex ALEPPO 1973; Sister: **46211 GOLDEN NICHOLAS** (Gr) ex STOVE CALEDONIA 1972.

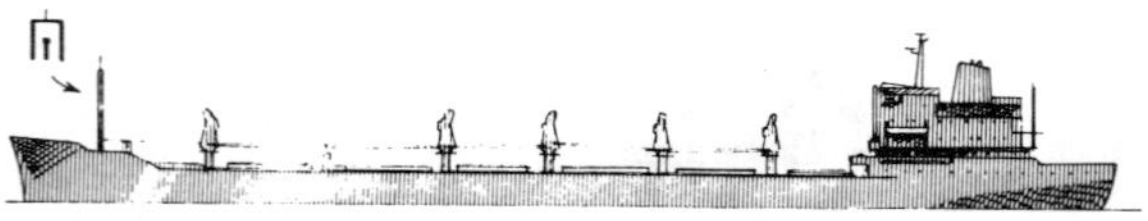

KC_5KMFK H13
46220 VALETTA. No/No 1968; B; 17000; 175.27 × 10.24 (575.03 × 33.59); M; 15.

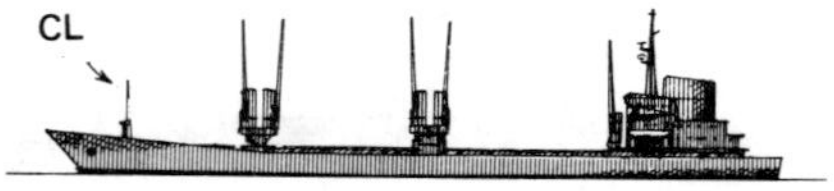

KC_5MF H
46230 WAIGANI EXPRESS. FRG/FRG 1971; C; 5100; 117.2 × 7.53 (384.51 × 24.7); M; 16.5; ex BELLATRIX 1978. Sister: **46231 NIUGINI EXPRESS** (FRG) ex BETEIGUEZE 1978.

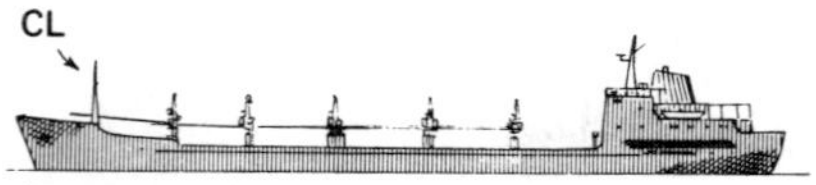

KC_5MF H1
46240 TESABA. Cy/Sp 1964; C; 2700/4300; 121.37 × 6.09/6.95 (398.19 × 19.98/22.8); M; 15; ex VALENCIA 1977; ex HISPANIA 1968. Sisters: **46241 TELINDA** (Cy) ex HANGVING 1977; ex GALLIA 1974 **46242 TEMURA** (Cy) ex INDUSTRIA 1977 **46243 TEMANTA** (Cy) ex BONNIE BAY 1978; ex SCANIA 1973 **46244 GADA** (Eg) ex IKARIA I 1974; ex ITALIA 1974 **46245 SCOL PRESIDENT** (Sw) ex SAGOLAND 1978 ⋆**46246 XINDU** (RC) ex DALMATIA 1976.

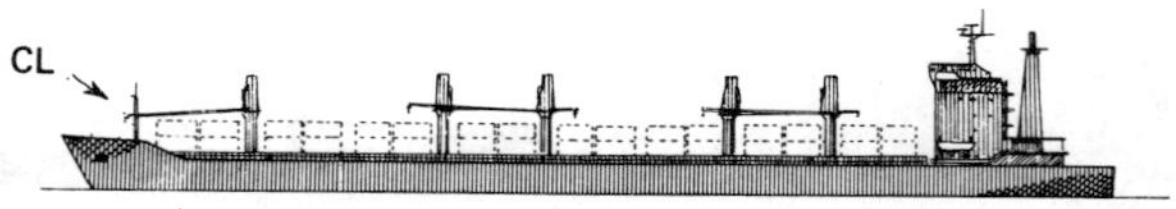

KC_5MF H1
46250 ARABIAN STRENGTH. FRG/FRG 1978; C/Con; 18400; 169.02 × 9.95 (554.53 × 32.64); M; 15; Launched as COLUMBIA. Sisters (FRG flag): **46251 ARABIAN ENDEAVOUR** launched as CALIFORNIA **46252 CALEDONIA.**

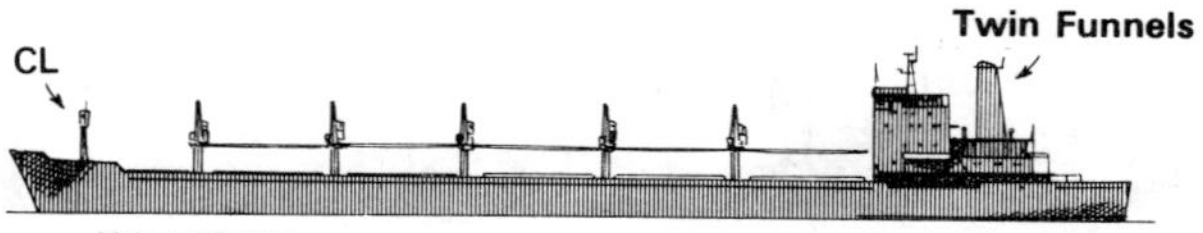

KC_5MF H1
46260 BORGESTAD. No/Ys 1969; B; 18500; 163.02 × 11.09 (534.84 × 36.38); M; 15.5. Sisters: **46261 MILENA** (No) **46262 SILVERMAIN** (Br).

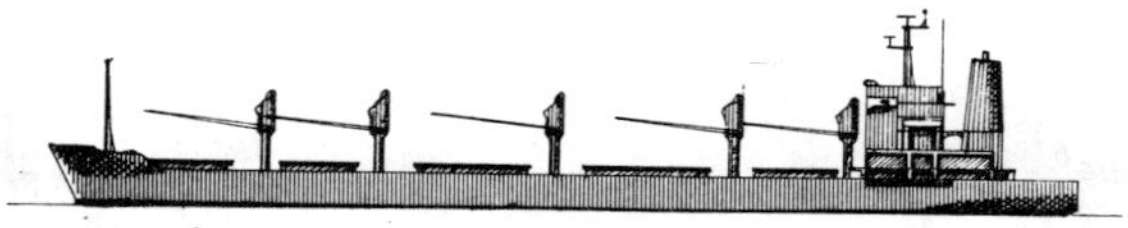

KC_5MF H1
46270 'FRONTIER' type. —/Ja —; C; 14000 approx; 163.8 × 9.15 (537.5 × 30) approx; M; 16.5 approx.

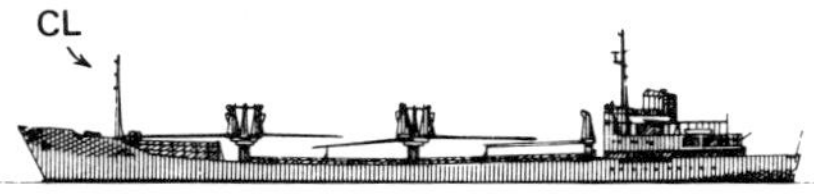

KC_5MF H1
46280 CATHRIN. Pa/FRG 1969; C; 3100/5600; 124.49 × 6.3/7.55 (408.43 × 20.67/24.77); M; 17; ex FRANZISCA DRESCHER 1978; ex WAHELE 1977; ex EDE SOTTORF 1975. Sisters: **46281 TERZIA** (FRG) ex WILLE I 1980; ex COLUMBUS NOUMEA 1978; ex WILLI REITH 1977 **46282 BARBARA LEONHARDT** (Pa) ex WILLE II 1980; ex COLUMBUS TAHITI 1978; ex META REITH 1977.

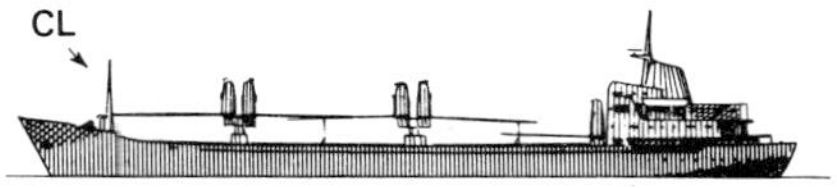

KC_5MF H1
46290 GALILA. Is/FRG 1967; C; 3000/4900; 123.4 × 6.45/7.59 (405 × 21.16/24.9); M; —; launched as CINNAMON BAY.

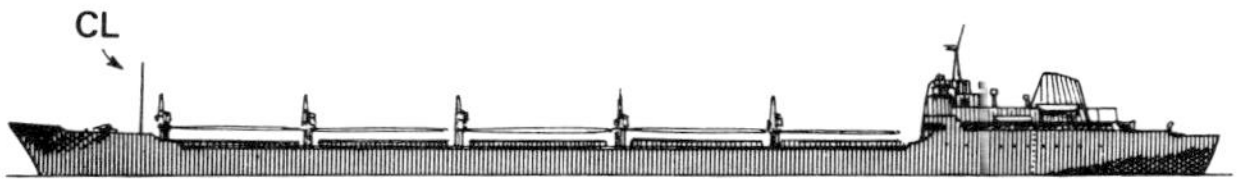

KC_5MF H13
46300 SIMONETTA. It/It 1963; B; 17300; 192.01 × 10.59 (629.95 × 39.74); M; —.

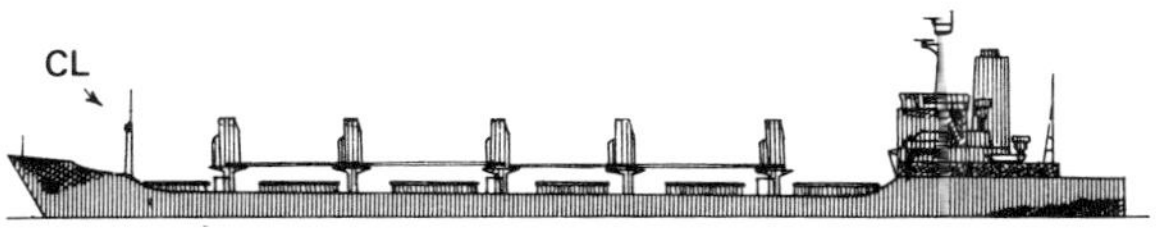

KC_5MF H13
● **46310 BOLNES.** Br/Ja 1976; B; 20100; 177.02 × 11.16 (580.77 × 36.61); M; 15.5. Sisters: **46311 BORGNES** (Br) **64312 BRAVENES** (Li) **46313 BECKNES** (FRG) **46314 BELLNES** (Li) **46315 BEDOUIN BIRKNES** (Li) ex BIRKNES 1977 **46316 BROOKNES** (FRG) **46317 BRISKNES** (Li) **46318 IRON CAPRICORN** (Br) launched as BERGNES.

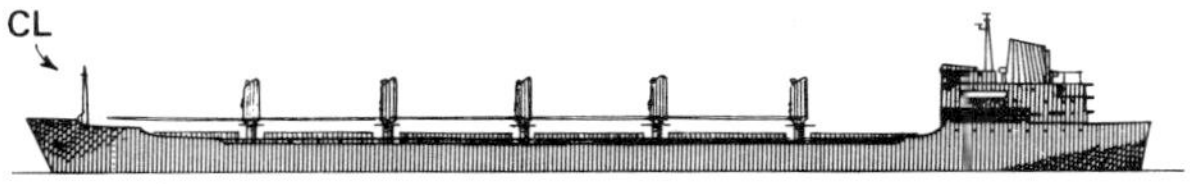

KC_5MF H13
46320 MARINA DI ALIMURI. It/Br 1972; B; 22900; 178.31 × 10.36 (585 × 33.99); M; 15; ex BERNES 1980. Sister: **46321 MARINA DI EQUA** (It) ex BRIMNES.

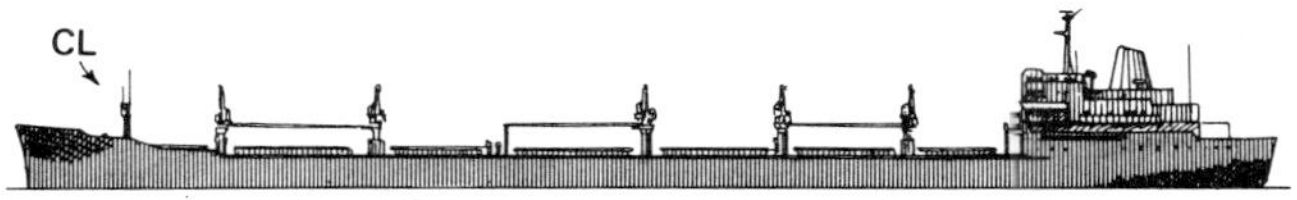

KC_5MF H13
46330 SEALIONET. Pa/Sw 1965; B; 22100; 200.31 × 11.1 (657.19 × 36.42); M; —; ex ROBERT STOVE 1978; ex VESTEROY 1973. Similar: **46331 GOULIAS** (Gr) ex NORBEGA 1977; ex STORMQUEEN 1971 **46332 UNION SPIRIT** (Gr) ex DAGLAND 1973 **46333 GLYFADA FAITH** (Gr) ex NORBROTT **46334 CHI STAR** (Pa) ex AEGIS STORM; ex VINNI 1974 **46335 STALO 2** (Gr) ex ATHOS 1974 ⋆**46336 BAI YUN HAI** (RC) ex AEGIS THUNDER; ex VIGAN 1974 **46337 IRENES SUCCESS** (Gr) ex PETINGO 1974; ex DAGEID 1973; ex VANESSA 1970 ⋆**46338 MING HAI** (RC) ex RUDOLPH OLSEN 1974 ⋆**46339 JIA HAI** (RC) ex PYTHEAS 1977 ⋆**46340 ZHEN RONG HAI** (RC) ex AMAX McGREGOR 1980 ⋆**46341 HENNIGSDORF** (DDR) ex PONTOS 1972.

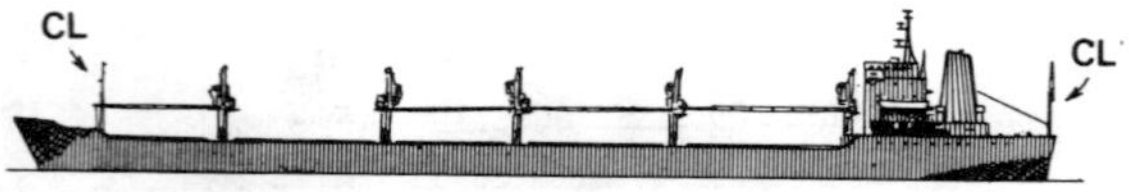

KC_5MF H13
46350 MING JOY. Tw/Ja 1971; B; 16100; 165.56 × 10.42 (543.17 × 34.18); M; 14.5; ex JI MING 1977; ex HAI JUNG 1973; **'26-BC-5'** type. Sisters (Tw flag): **46351 MING LEADER** ex LI MING 1977; ex HAI LO 1973 **46352 MING SHINE** ex SHIN MING 1977; ex HAI CHUAN 1973 Possible sister (Ko flag): **46353 GLOBAL STAR** ex MANNA 1980; ex THAI YUNG 1973.

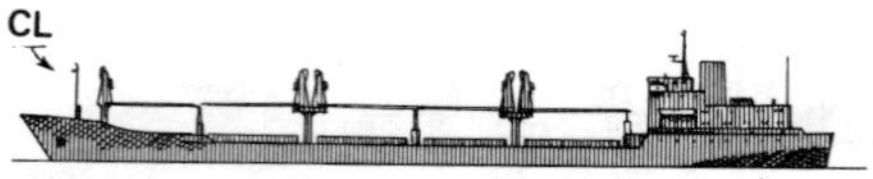

KCMF H13
● **★46360 YAN HE.** RC/Fi 1971; C; 3700/6200; 129.09 × 6.62/7.97 (423.52 × 21.72/26.15); M; 17; ex HERAKLES 1980.

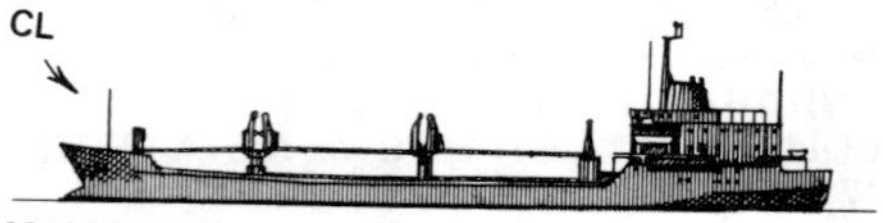

KC_5MF H13
● **★46370 LIEBENWALDE.** DDR/DDR 1977; C; 3500/5700; 120.61 × —/7.83 (395.7 × 25.69); M; 16.75. Sisters (DDR flag): **★46371 CUNEWALDE ★46372 LUCKENWALDE ★46373 SCHONWALDE ★46374 GERINGSWALDE ★46375 MITTENWALDE ★46376 FURSTENWALDE ★46377 EICHWALDE ★46378 RUDOLF DIESEL ★46379 ARENDSEE ★46380 BLANKENSEE ★46381 FLESSENSEE ★46382 MUGGELSEE ★46383 WERBELLINSEE ★46384 KOLPINSEE.**

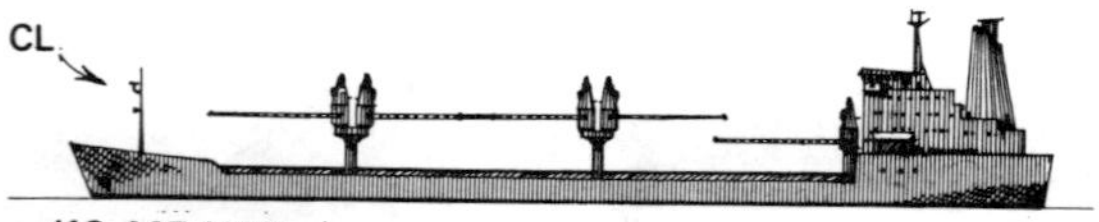

KC_5MF H13
46390 POLLUX. Fi/No 1977; C; 7400/14700; 154.97 × 7.48/9.2 (508.43 × 24.54/30.18); M; 17. Sister: **46391 PATRIA** (Fi).

KC_5MF H13
46400 MILROSS. No/De 1974; B; 30300; 221.75 × 12.09 (727.52 × 39.66); M; 16; ex RODIN 1976; Cranes not shown on drawing as exact positions are not known.

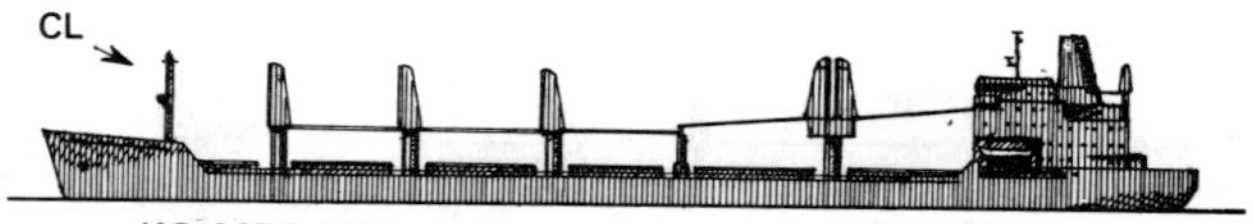

KC_5MFC H13
46410 THULELAND. Sw/Sw 1977; B; 21100; 185.86 × 11.28 (609.77 × 37); M; 16. Sister: **46411 SEATRAIN LONDON** (Sw) ex COLUMBIALAND 1979.

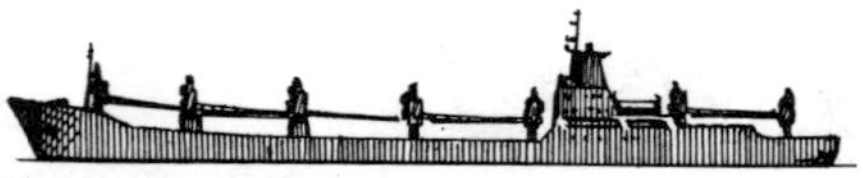

KC_5MFC_2 H13
● **46420 ARGO.** Fi/Fi 1963; C; 3000/5000; 130.97 × 6.21/7.34 (429.69 × 20.37/24); M; 16; Lengthened 1970. Sister: **46421 VIRGO** (Fi).

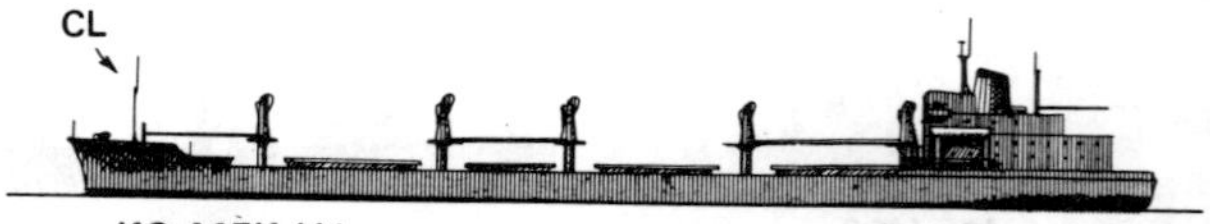

KC_5MFK H1
● **46430 STASIA.** Gr/Br 1970; B; 16600; 173.59 × 9.96 (569.52 × 32.67); M; 15.25; ex VANCOUVER CITY; **'Cardiff'** class Sisters (Br flag): **46431 PORT ALBERNI CITY 46432 PRINCE RUPERT CITY 46433 VICTORIA CITY 46434 FRESNO CITY 46435 TACOMA CITY 46436 NEW WESTMINSTER CITY** Similar: **46437 NORSE PILOT 46438 NORSE MARSHAL 46439 NORSE HERALD 46440 GOLDEN ORIOLE 46441 GOLDEN ANNE** (Ih flag): **46442 IRISH LARCH 46443 IRISH MAPLE 46444 IRISH OAK 46445 IRISH PINE** (RC flag): **★46446 AN DA HAI** ex NORSE TRADER 1977 (De flag): **46447 CAMARA** (Gr flag): **46448 ANASTASIOS** ex CINCHONA 1981.

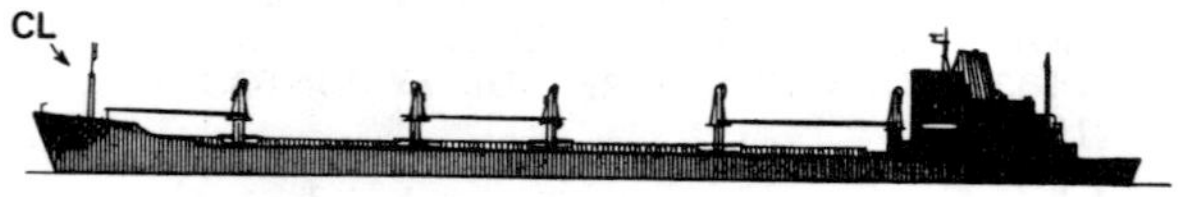

KC_5MFK H1
46460 DONA PAZ. Pi/Br 1977; B; 16200; 175.14 × 9.96 (574.6 × 32.67); M; 15; **'Cardiff'** class Sisters (Pi flag): **46461 DONA MAGDALENA 46462 DONA HORTENCIA II 46463 DON SALVADOR III**

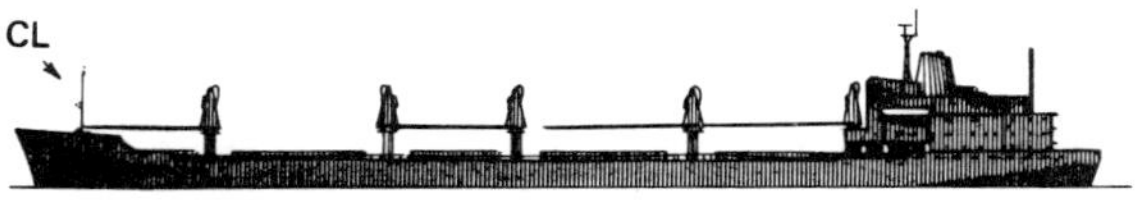

KC$_5$MFK H1
● **46470 ATLAS.** Li/Br 1973; B; 16700; 175.11 × 9.98 (574.5 × 32.74); M; 15.5; ex CHI GRACE; ex HARFLEET. **'Cardiff'** class. Sister: **46471 ANDROMEDA** (Li) ex CHI TRUST 1980; ex HARFLEUR 1979.

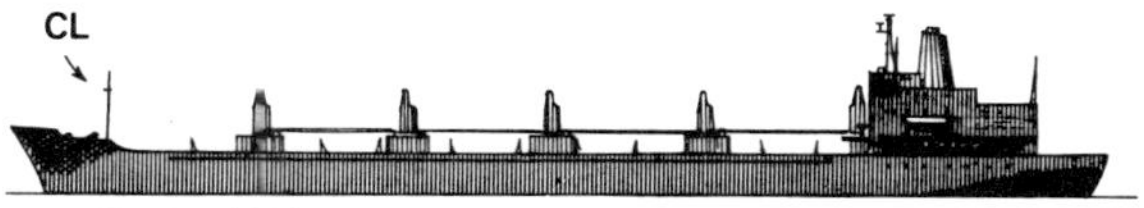

KC$_5$MFK H1
46480 ASIA HUNTER. Li/Ja 1971; B; 17600; 171.25 × 11.02 (561.84 × 36.15); M; 15.

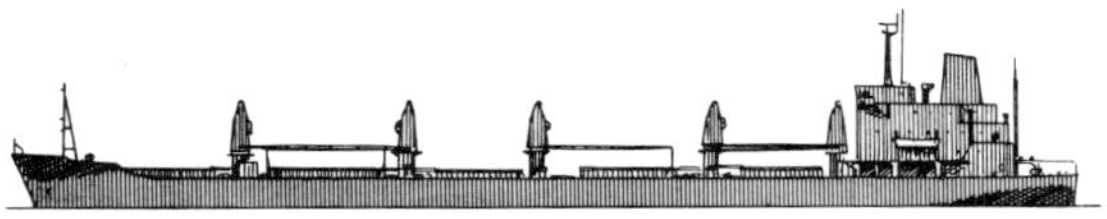

KC$_5$MFK H1
46490 TRITON. Li/Ja 1977; B; 15600; 169.63 × 9.62 (556.53 × 31.56); M; 15.

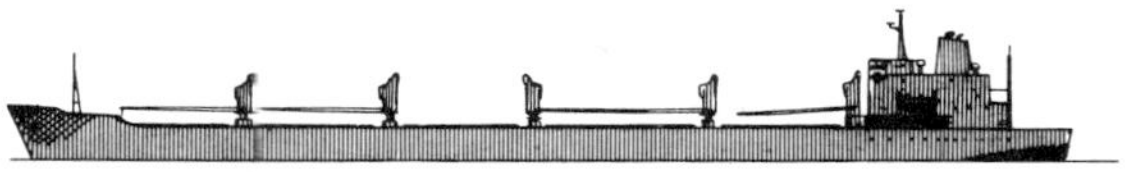

KC$_5$MFK H1
46500 MARINA GRANDE. Gr/Ja 1975; B; 14500; 169.63 × 9.57 (556.52 × 31.39); M; 15.5; ex ASTROS 1980. Sister: **46501 DESERT WIND** (Li).

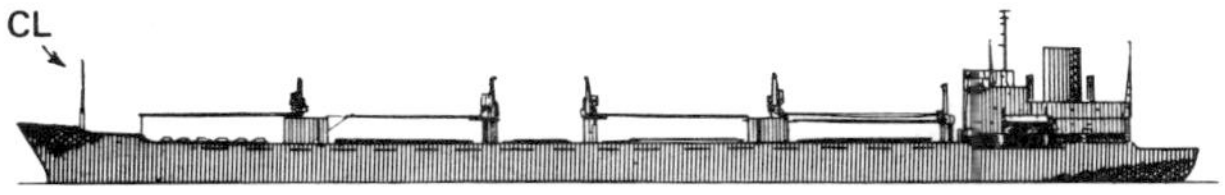

KC$_5$MFK H1
● **46510 TOYOTA MARU No 14.** Ja/Ja 1971; B; 19400; 187 × 10.79 (613.52 × 35.4); M; 14.5. Sister: **46511 VANGUARD ALPHA** (Cy) ex SOYO MARU 1978 Possible Sisters: **46512 TOYOTA MARU No 7** (Ja) **46513 TOYOTA MARU No 8** (Ja) Similar: **46514 TOYOTA MARU No 19** (Ja) **46515 CHIBA** (Li).

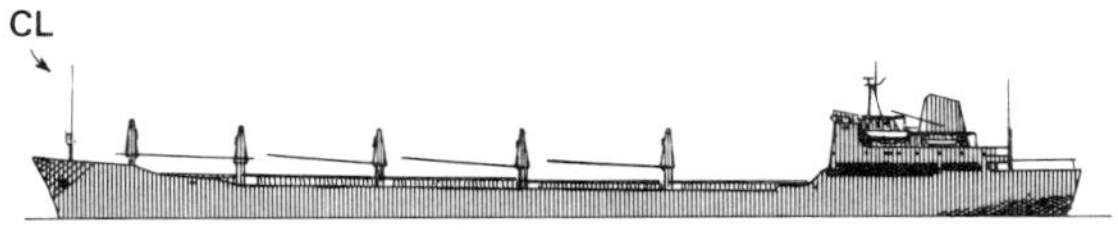

KC$_5$MFK H13
● **46520 SUNNINGDALE.** Sg/No 1969; B; 11300; 165.67 × 9.31 (543.53 × 30.54); M; 15.5; ex STOVE TRADITION. Similar: **46521 ELJIANNI** (Gr) ex MELSOMVIK 1973 **46522 AGIOI VICTORES** (Gr) ex EXPECTATION 1976 **46523 MARIA X** (Gr) ex STOVE OCEAN 1977; ex BELOCEAN 1975 **46524 UNION AUCKLAND** (Br) ex COLUMBIA **46525 DIMITRIS E** (Gr) ex BELBLUE 1975 **46526 GEORGIOS F** (Gr) ex FRIXOS D 1980; ex JAMES STOVE 1973 **46527 CAROLINE** (Pa) ex EASTWIND 1980; ex STOVE SCOTIA 1973 **46528 SANTA POLA** (Gr) ex RINGVARD 1973 ⋆**46529 AN JI HAI** (RC) ex STOVE FRIEND 1977.

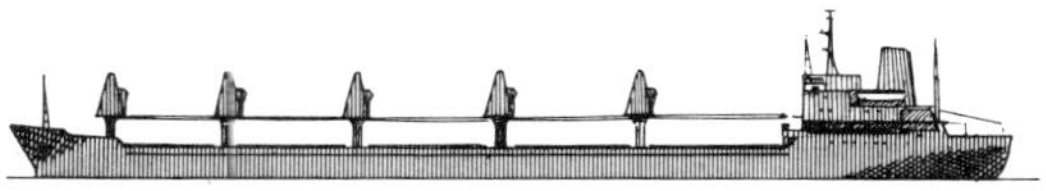

KC$_5$MFK H13
46540 PACIFIC DEFENDER. Li/Ja 1968; B; 12300; 158.5 × 9.18 (520 × 30.12); M; 15.

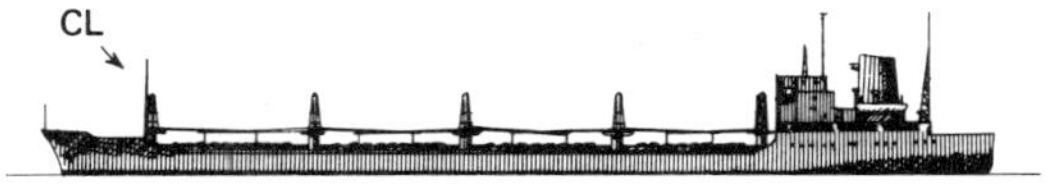

KC$_5$MFK H13
46550 ATLANTICA. Gr/Ja 1964; C; 10300; 150.68 × 9.02 (494.35 × 29.59); M; 14.5; ex ASHBY MARU 1976.

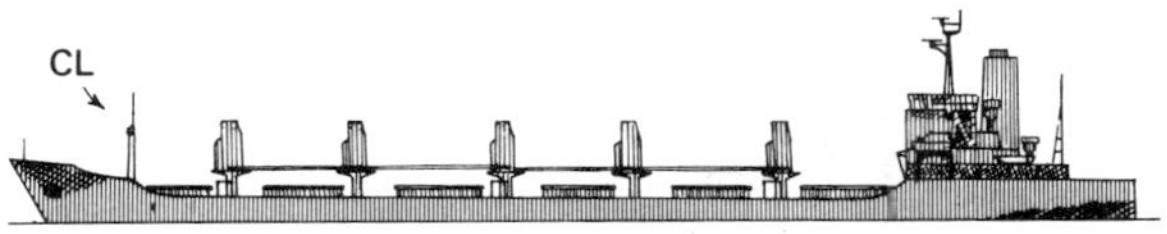

KC$_5$MFK H13
● **46560 BOLNES.** Br/Ja 1976; B; 20100; 177.02 × 11.16 (580.77 × 36.61); M; 15.5. Sisters: **46561 BORGNES** (Br) **46562 BRAVENES** (Li) **46563 BECKNES** (FRG) **46564 BELLNES** (Li) **46565 BEDOUIN BIRKNES** (Li) ex BIRKNES 1977 **46566 BROOKNES** (FRG) **46567 BRISKNES** (Li) **46568 IRON CAPRICORN** (Br) launched as BERGNES

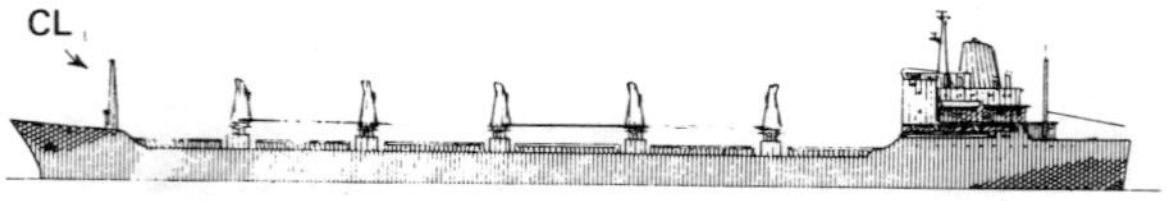

KC_5MFK H13
46580 ACHILLES. Br/Ja 1972; B; 16400; 176.77 × 10.66 (579.95 × 34.97); M; 15.25. Sisters: **46581 AJAX** (Br) **46582 ANCHISES** (Br) **46583 PROTOPOROS** (Gr) ex AGAMEMNON 1978 **46584 SIDERIS** (Li) ex ANTENOR 1978 Similar: **46585 CHLOE** (Gr) ex OCEAN RENTIS 1976; launched as OCEAN RETLA **46586 SHENANDOAH** (Gr) **46587 KENTUCKY HOME** (Gr) **46588 SABIE** (Pa) ex S.A. SABIE ⋆**46589 PRESIDENTE ALLENDE** (Cu) Possibly Similar: **46590 S.A. SKUKUZA** (SA) ex SKUKUZA 1975.

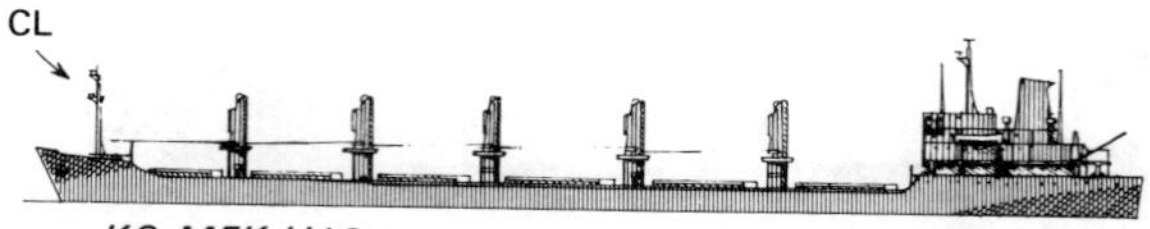

KC_5MFK H13
46600 DONA SOPHIA. Gr/Ja 1978; B; 15200; 172.02 × 10.63 (564.37 × 34.88); M; 17. Probable Sister: **46601 GEORGIS GERONTAS** (Gr).

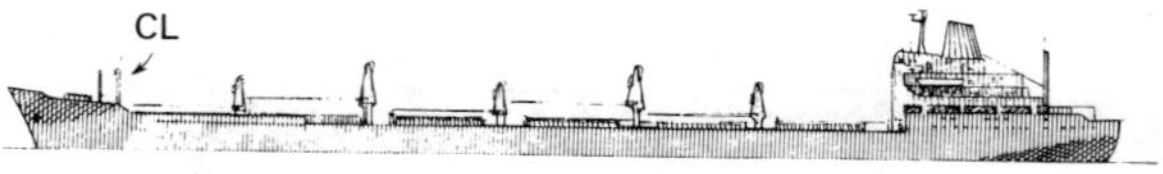

KC_5MFK H13
46610 ALEXANDRA N. In/Sw 1965; B; 16700; 175.88 × 10.43 (577.03 × 34.22); M; 15; ex FALKANGER 1974. Sister: **46611 CHARISMA N** (In) ex FOSSANGER 1974.

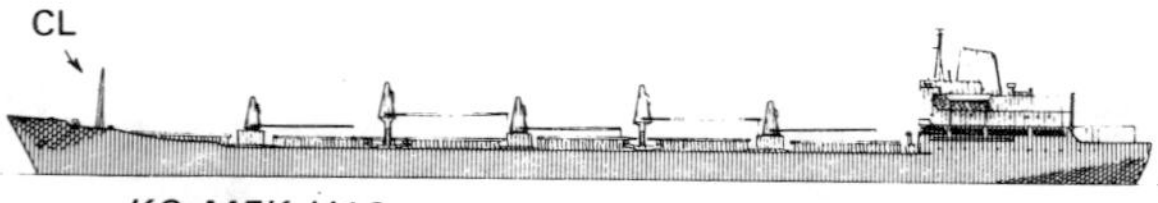

KC_5MFK H13
⋆**46620 YASNOYE.** Ru/No 1967; B; 15800; 180.3 × 10.21 (591.54 × 33.5); M; 15; ex CORNAS; ex TORM GYDA 1977; ex GYDA 1974.

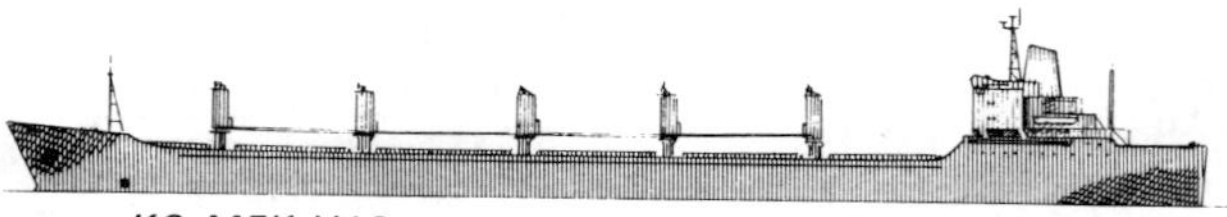

KC_5MFK H13
46630 RUBENS. Br/Be 1976; B; 18000; 190.02 × 10.79 (623.42 × 35.4); M; 15.75.

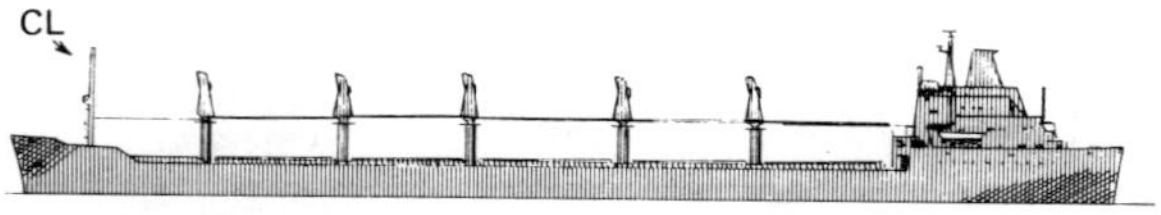

KC_5MFK H13
● **46640 ATHOLL FOREST.** Gr/Sw 1967; B; 17400; 175.22 × 9.88 (574.86 × 32.41); M; 15.5; ex COLUMBIALAND 1976. Sister: **46641 KARAMU FOREST** (Sg) ex VICTORIA 1977 Similar: **46642 KANUKA FOREST** (Sg) ex GIMLELAND 1977 **46643 ASIAN FOREST** (Br) ex CALEDONIAN FOREST 1978; ex VIRGINIA 1976; ex GIMLESKOG 1972.

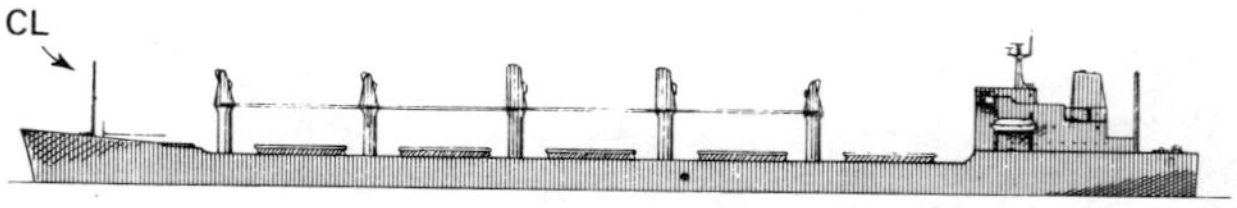

KC_5MFK H13
● **46650 APTMARINER.** Br/Br 1979; B; 18000; 188.75 × 10.66 (619.3 × 34.97); M; 15; ex DEVONBROOK 1980. Sister: **46651 HANDYMARINER** (Br) ex DURHAMBROOK 1980.

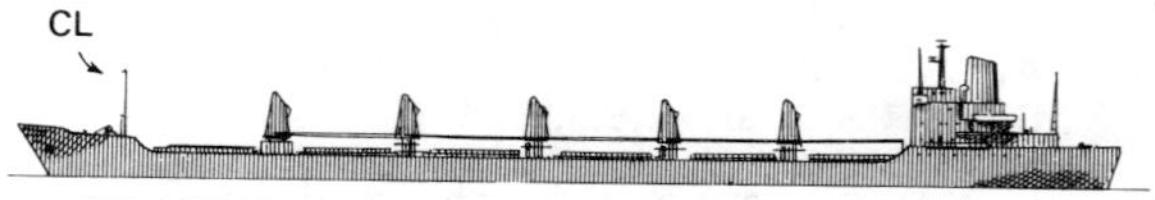

KC_5MFK H13
46660 WAYFARER. Br/Ja 1973; B; 16300; 174.1 × 10.97 (571.19 × 35.99); M; 15.5. Sisters: **46661 WANDERER** (Br) **46662 WARRIOR** (Br) Probably Similar: **46663 PENMARCH** (Fr) **46664 ROSELINE** (Fr).

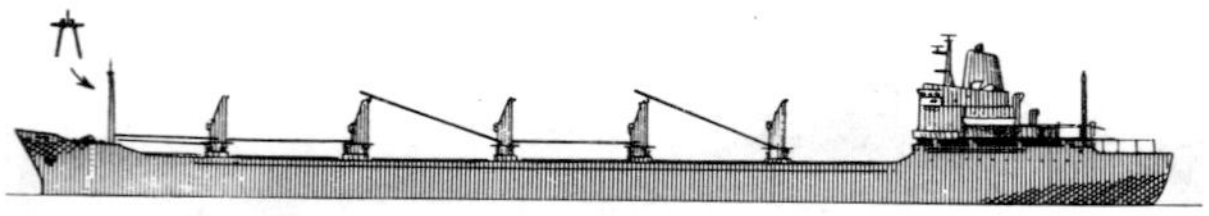

KC_5MFK H13
46670 GEORGIOS XYLAS. Gr/Ja 1970; B; 18600; 182.61 × 10.69 (599.11 × 35.07); M; 16. Sister: **46671 MASTER STEFANOS** (Gr).

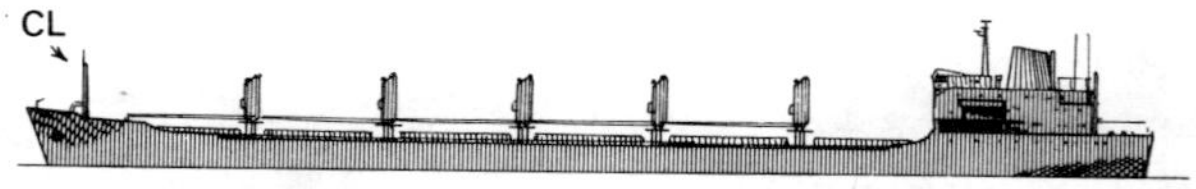

KC_5MFK H13
⋆**46680 FEI CHU HAI.** RC/Br 1973; B; 22900; 178.31 × 10.38 (585.01 × 34.05); M; 15; ex SILVERDON 1978; ex BRAVENES 1973.

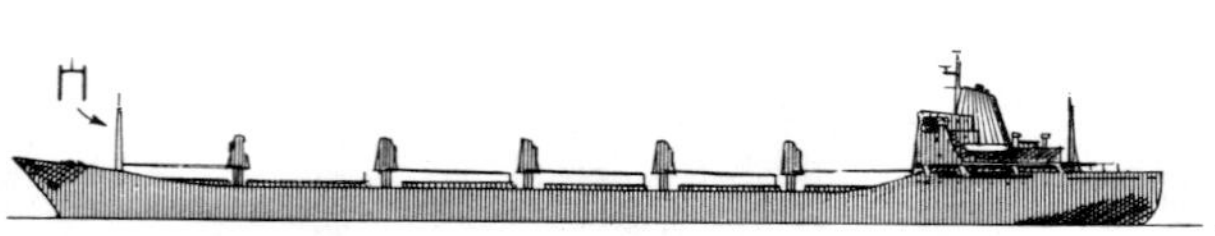

KC_5MFK H13
46690 LARRY L. Gr/Ja 1970; B; 16300; 182 × 10.64 (597.11 × 34.9); M; 14.5. Sisters (Gr flag): **46691 CATHERINE L 46692 GRACE L 46693 PATRICIA L** Similar: **46694 EVY L 46695 MARILYN L.**

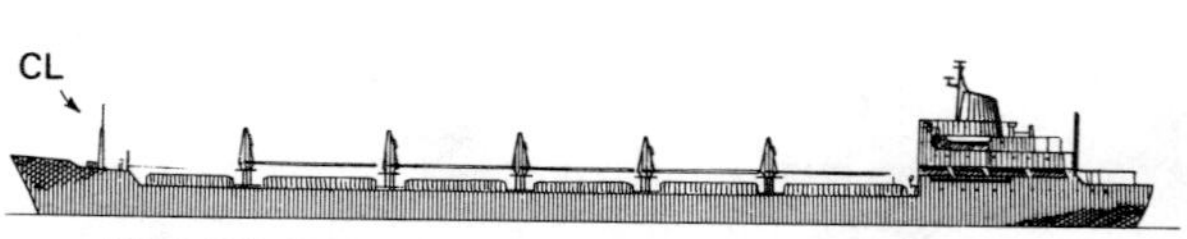

KC_5MFK H13
● **46700 PENERF.** Fr/No 1971; B; 15800; 180.3 × 10.19 (591.53 × 33.43); M; 16. Sisters: **46701 MENHIR** (Li) ex PENHIR **46702 MAGIC SUN** (Li) ex ONDINE.

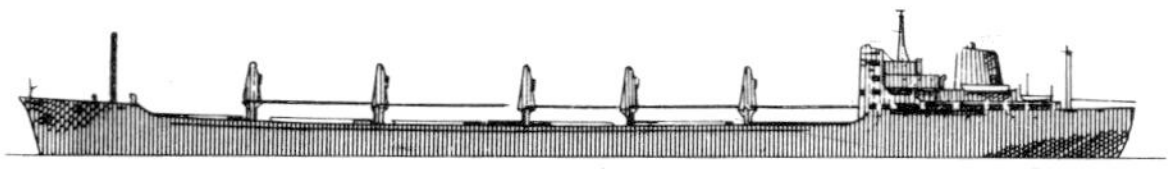

KC_5MFK H13

46710 CAPE STROVILI. Gr/Ja 1958; B; 13700; 173.64 × 10.41 (569.68 × 34.15); M; 15; ex DELPHIC EAGLE 1973; ex PAPHOS 1971. Sister: **46711 CHAVEZ** (Pa) ex PACIFIC CARRIER 1979; ex DELPHIC ORACLE 1969 Similar: **46712 DELPHIC MIRACLE** (Gr).

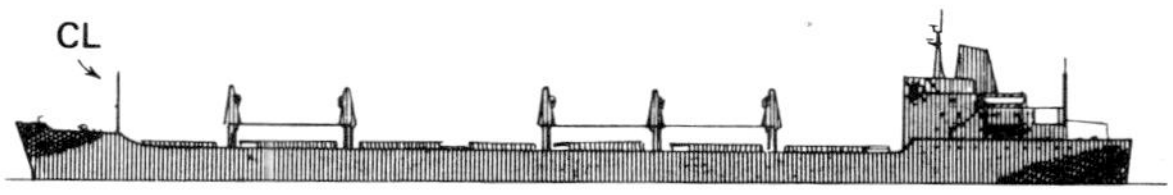

KC_5MFK H13

● **46720 SCOTSPARK.** Br/Br 1969; B; 16800; 176.79 × 10.6 (580 × 34.77); M; 15.25. Sisters: **46721 GLENPARK** (Br) ⋆**46722 YIN SHAN HAI** (RC) ex VANCOUVER ISLAND 1978.

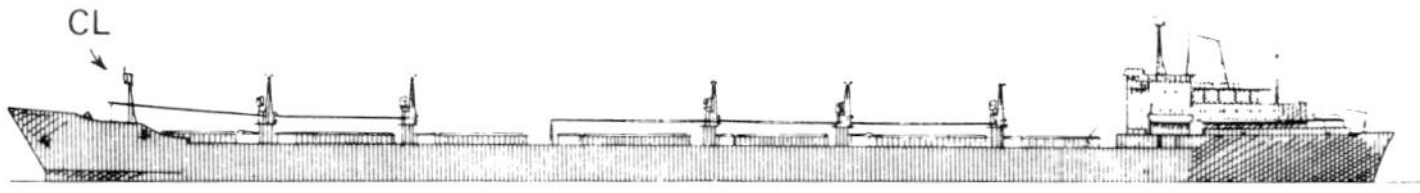

KC_5MFK H13

46730 CAST SEAL. Br/De 1969; B; 29800; 218.85 × 12.1 (718.01 × 39.69); M; 15.5; ex BIANCA 1977; Used as container ship. Cranes may have been removed. Sister: **46731 CAST DOLPHIN** (Br) ex BERIT 1978.

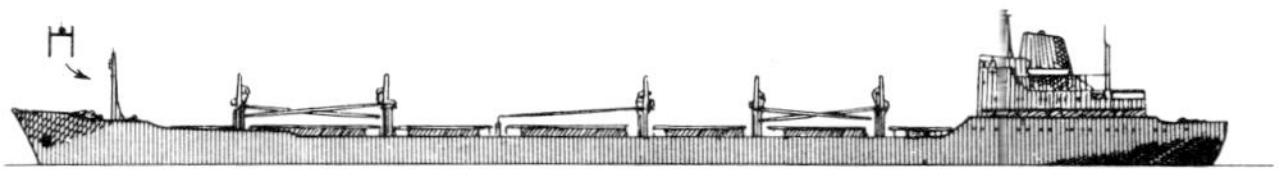

KC_5MFK H13

46740 P.S. PALIOS. Gr/FRG 1963; B; 20300; 192.34 × 10.71 (631.03 × 35.13); M; 15; ex HOLTHORN 1977. Sister: **46741 SEA WALRUS** (Pa) ex MABU 1978; ex FERNWIND 1974.

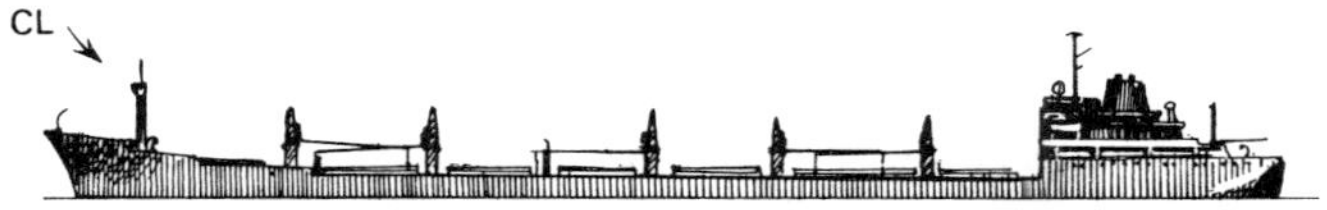

KC_5MFK H13

⋆**46750 BIN HAI.** RC/Sw 1963; B; 20400; 195.13 × 11.02 (640.19 × 36.15); M; 14.75; ex MAI BENTE 1973.

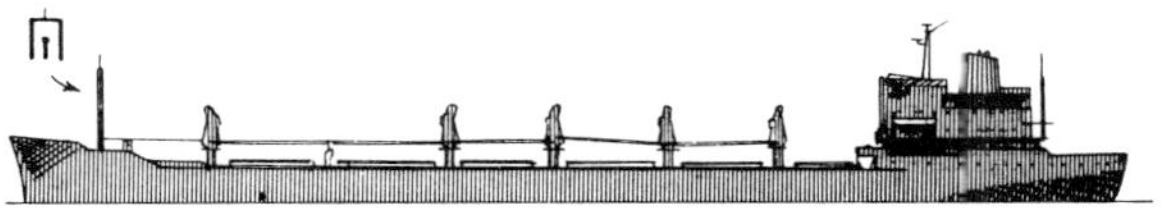

KC_5MFK H13

46760 VALETTA. No/No 1968; B; 17000; 175.27 × 10.24 (575.03 × 33.59); M; 15.

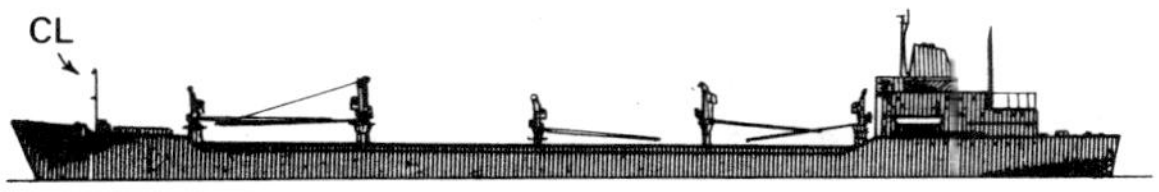

KC_5MFK H13

46770 IBN ABDOUN. Ku/Br 1976; C; 15500; 175.32 × 10.42 (575.19 × 34.18); M; 16; **'KUWAIT'** Class. Sisters (Ku flag): **46771 IBN AL-HAITHAM 46772 IBN BAJJAH 46773 IBN HAZM 46774 IBN SINA 46775 IBN ZUHR 46776 IBN JUBAYR** Similar (Ko flag): **46777 OCEAN ACE 46778 OCEAN BEAUTY 46779 OCEAN CROWN 46780 OCEAN DUKE.**

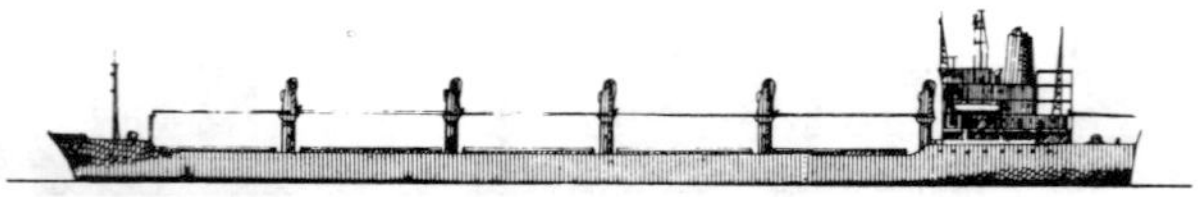

KC_5MFK H13
46790 FORT YALE. Br/Ja 1977; B; 17300; 172.85 × 10.40 (567.09 × 34.12); M; 15.75. Sisters: **46791 FORT KAMLOOPS** (Br) **46792 FORT VICTORIA** (Br).

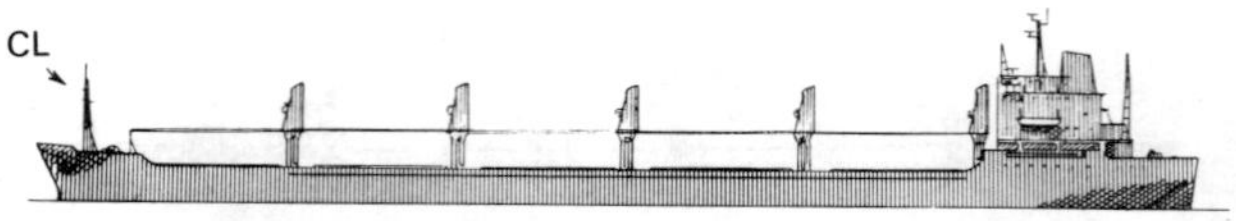

KC_5MFK H13
46800 FORT NELSON. Br/Ja 1975; B; 21900; 184 × 11.06 (603.67 × 36.28); M; 15. Sisters: **46801 FORT CALGARY** (Br) **46802 FORT NANAIMO** (Br) ex LEDA 1980.

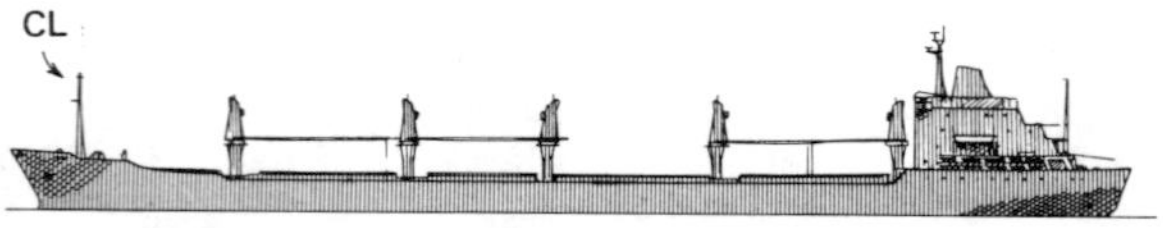

KC_5MFK H13
46810 IRISH CEDAR. Ih/Ja 1977; B; 17300; 176.82 × 10.35 (580.12 × 33.95); M; 15. Sister: **46811 IRISH ROWAN** (Ih).

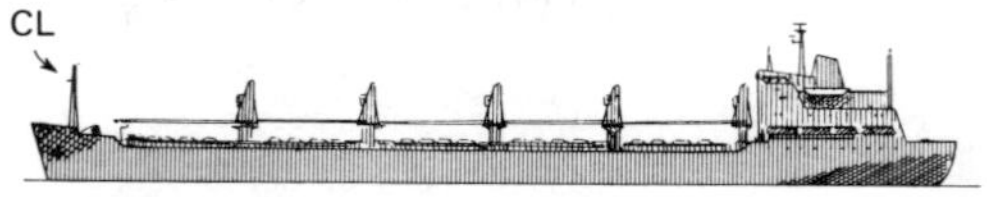

KC_5MFK H13
46820 WILLIAM R ADAMS. Li/Ja 1968; B; 10700; 147.02 × 8.49 (482.34 × 27.85); M; 14.

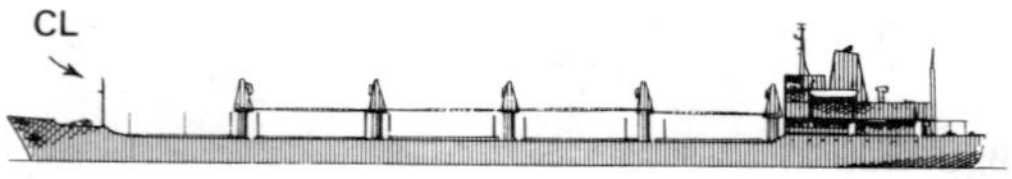

KC_5MFK H13
46830 SONID. Gr/Ja 1968; B; 11700; 156.45 × 9.79 (513.29 × 32.12); M; 14.75; ex RACHEL 1980. Sister: **46831 ANNIKA N** (Gr) ex WORLD VIRTUE 1980.

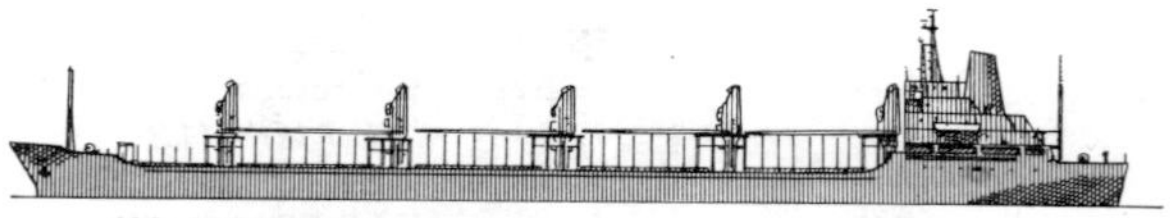

KC_5MFK H13
46840 EASTERN BRIDE. Pa/Ja 1977; B; 16000; 176.89 × 10.34 (580.34 × 33.92); M; 15.

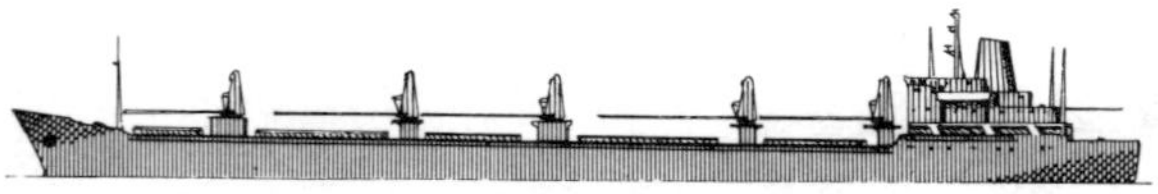

KC_5MFK H13
46850 TOXON. Gr/Ja 1978; B; 16000; 177.04 × 10.41 (580.84 × 34.16); M; 15.5.

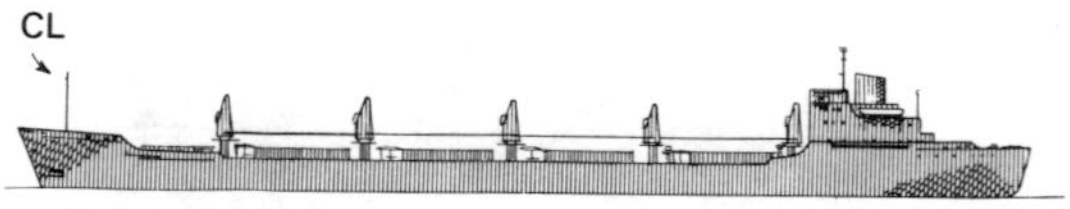

KC_5MFK H13
46860 AMSTELDIEP. Ne/Ne 1970; B; 12600; 160.1 × 9.93 (526.26 × 32.58); M; 14.5; ex PUTTEN 1977. Sister: **46361 AMSTELDREEF** (Ne) ex VOORNE 1977.

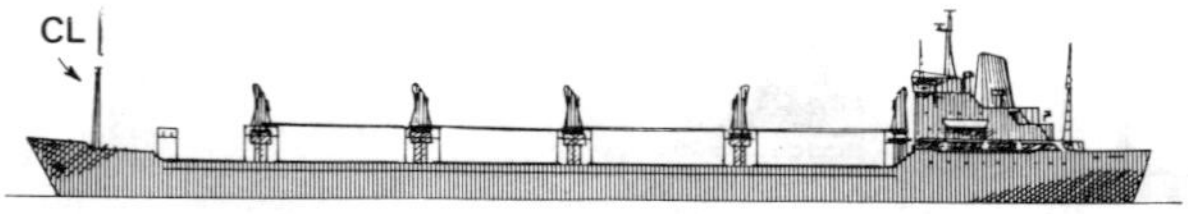

KC_5MFK H13
● **46870 CARDIFF CITY.** Br/Ja 1975; B; 17200; 176.94 × 10.31 (580.51 × 33.82); M; 14.75; ex JADE CITY 1975. Sisters: **46871 DEVON CITY** (Br) launched as PEARL CITY **46872 OPAL CITY** (Li) **46873 STAR EMERALD** (Li) ex EMERALD CITY 1979.

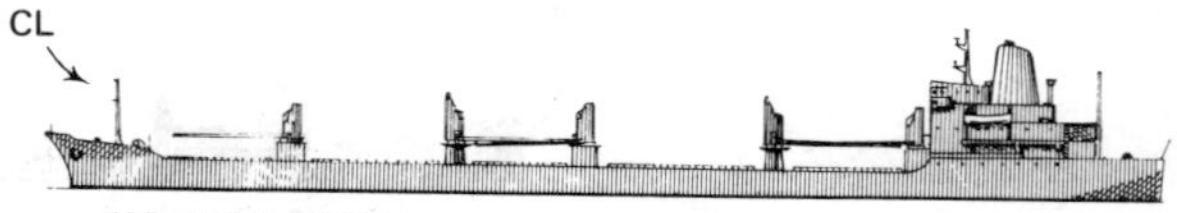

KC_5MFK H13
46880 MARIA G.L. Gr/Ja 1974; B; 15900; 178.49 × 10.42 (585.6 × 34.19); M; 14.75. Sister: **46881 ODYSSEY 10** (Gr) Possible Sister: **46882 KALLIOPE L** (Gr) Similar: **46883 EVER HONOR** (Tw) **46884 SILVER ZEPHYR** (Li) **46885 PACBARON** (Li) **46886 CONTINENTAL CARRIER** (Li) ex PACKING 1980 **46887 PACDUCHESS** (Li) **46888 ORIENT UNION** (Pa) ex GRAND ENTERPRISE 1981 **46889 SEA TRANSPORT** (Li) **46890 ISPARTA** (Tu) **46891 URFA** (Tu) **46892 ISLAND MARINER** (Gr) **46893 LUCY** (Gr) Possibly Similar: **46894 PACBARONESS** (Li) **46895 PACDUKE** (Li).

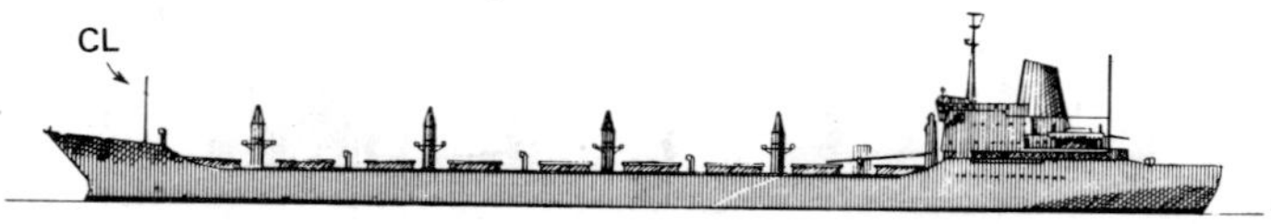

KC_5MFK H13
46900 ARPAD. Tu/Ru 1969; B; 23400; 199.83 × 11.24 (655.61 × 36.87); M; 15.75; ex RIGOLETTO 1976; **'BALTIKA'** type. Similar: **46901 CEBU** (Sg) ex CARE 1980; ex CAROLA P 1979; ex CAROLA REITH 1978 Probably Similar: **46902 NORTRANS VISION** (No) **46903 ON TUNG** (Pa) ex NORTRANS KATHE 1979 **46904 CRESCO** (No) Probable Sister: **46905 LABO** (Sg) ex MARE 1980; ex MAGDALENA 1979; ex MAGDALENA REITH 1978.

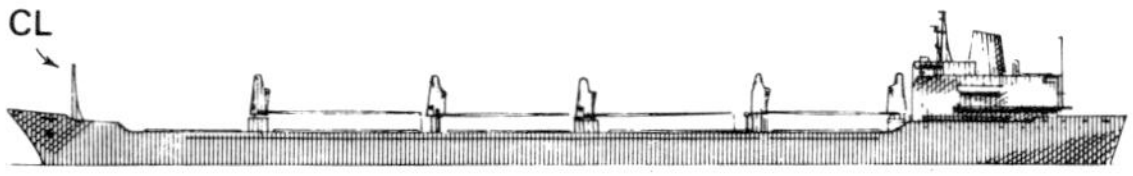

KC_5MFK H13
46910 GEORGIS A GEORGILIS. Gr/Ja 1976; B; 16000; 176.99 × 10.4 (580.67 × 34.12); M; 15.5. Sisters (Gr flag): **46911 ANTONIS P LEMOS 46912 ILENA** Possibly Similar: **46913 IOANNIS MARTINOS 46914 EUROSEA 46915 EUROUNITY.**

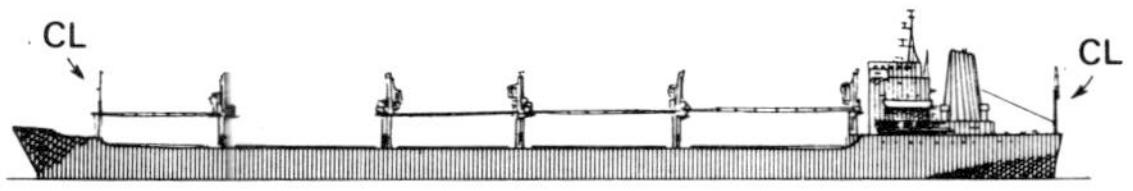

KC_5MFK H13
46920 MING JOY. Tw/Ja 1971; B; 16100; 165.5 × 10.42 (543.17 × 34.18); M; 14.5; ex JI MING 1977; ex HAI JUNG 1973; **'26-BC-5'** type. Sisters: **46921 MING LEADER** (Tw) ex LI MING 1977; ex HI LO 1973 **46922 MING SHINE** (Tw) ex SHIN MING 1977; ex HAI CHUAN 1973 Possible Sister: **46923 GLOBAL STAR** (Ko) ex MANNA 1980; ex THAI YUNG 1973.

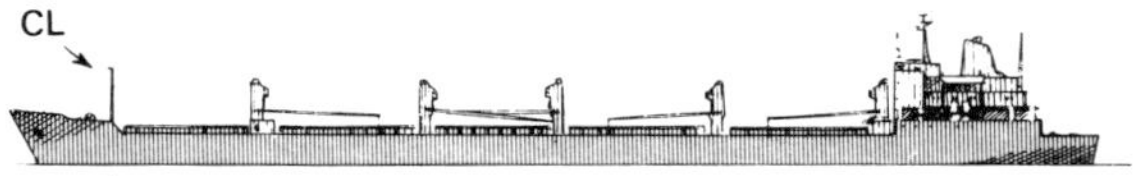

KC_5MFK H13
46930 NEDROMA. Ag/Ja 1978; B; 15900; 172.27 × 10.25 (565.19 × 33.63); M; 16.25. Sister: **46931 NEMEMCHA** (Ag).

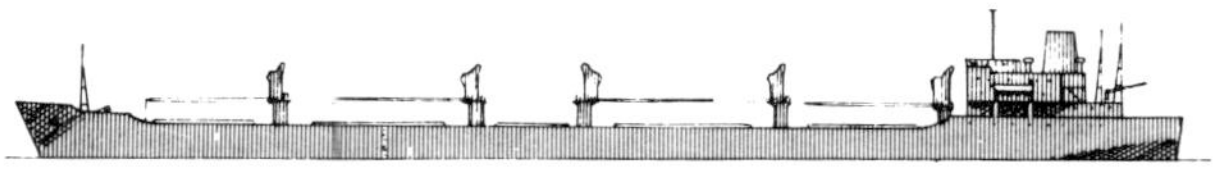

KC_5MFK H13
46940 CRUZEIRO DO SOL. Li/Ja 1975; B; 20600; 185.5 × 10.9 (608.59 × 35.76); M; 15.25. Sisters: **46941 DIAVOLEZZA** (Sd) **46942 ROMANDIE** (Sd) Similar: **46943 NIKEA** (Gr) ex FEDERAL KATSURA 1979 **46944 MONTANA** (Gr) ex FEDERAL HUDSON 1979.

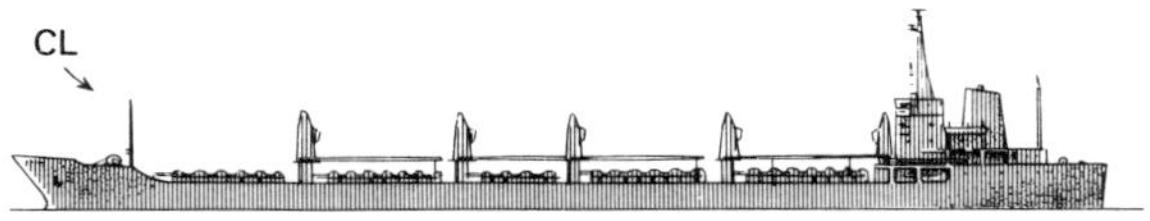

KC_5MFK H13
46950 CELTIC SKY. Pa/Ja 1976; B; 15900; 176.03 × 10.1 (577.53 × 33.14); M; 15; ex SPLENDID ALBATROSS 1980.

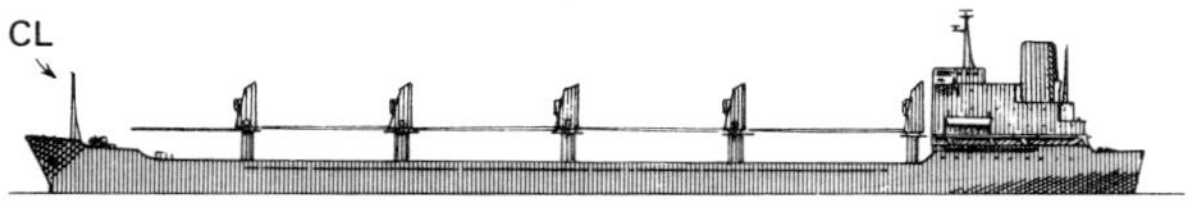

KC_5MFK H13
46960 RIMBA MERANTI. My/Ja 1976; B; 15500; 177.43 × 9.87 (582.12 × 32.38); M; 15. Possible Sister: **46961 RIMBA RAMIN** (My).

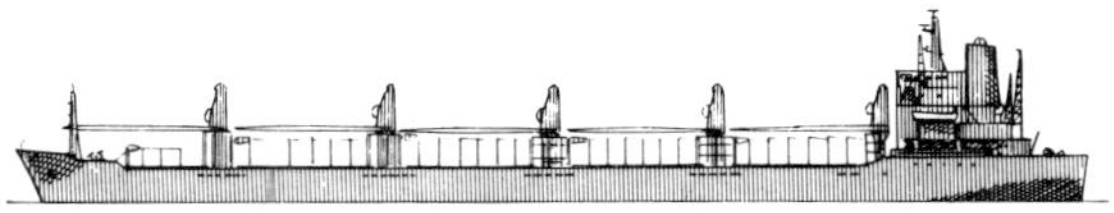

KC_5MFK H13
46970 KAKO MARU. Ja/Ja 1977; B; 16600; 169.58 × 10.3 (556.36 × 33.99); M; 14.75.

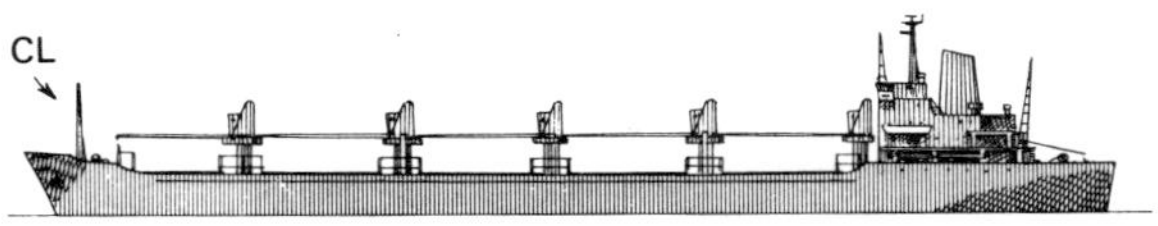

KC_5MFK H13
46980 MICHEL DELMAS. Fr/Ja 1976; B; 16300; 172.5 × 10.35 (565.94 × 33.95); M; 13.

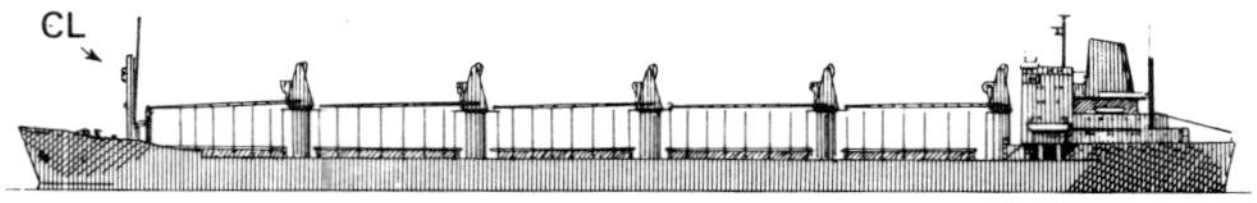

KC_5MFK H13
46990 JAVARA. No/De 1970; B; 25200; 192.06 × 10.12 (630.12 × 33.2); M; 15.5; ex SKOGSTAD 1976. Sisters: **46991 MANNHEIM** (FRG) ex ROLAND BREMEN 1974 **46992 KELKHEIM** (FRG) ex ROLAND KELKHEIM 1971; launched as KELKHEIM Similar: **46993 JANEGA** (No).

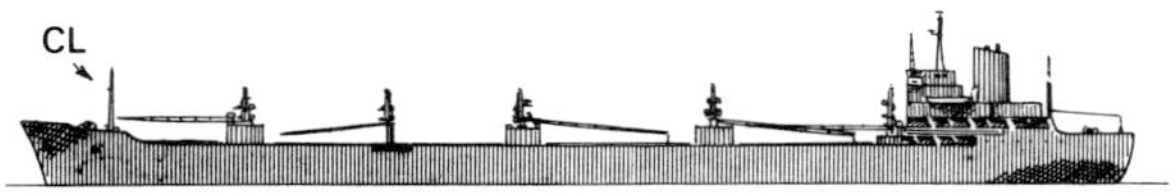

KC_5MFK H13
● **47000 NISSAN MARU.** Ja/Ja 1970; B; 17400; 175.52 × 10.91 (575.85 × 35.79); M; 14.5. Sisters: **47001 KANAGAWA MARU** (Ja) **47002 HIRATSUKA MARU** (Ju) Possible Sister: **47003 TOCHIGI MARU** (Ja).

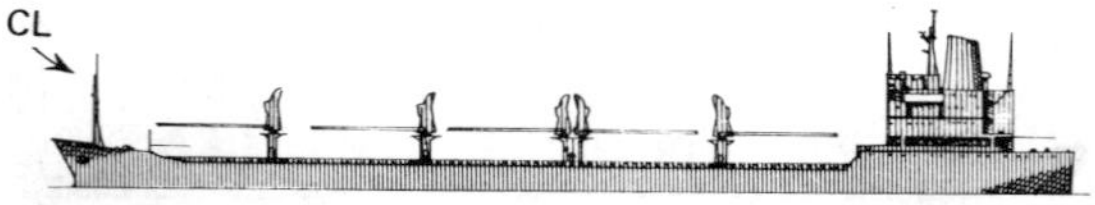

KC$_5$MFK H13
47010 FORT HAMILTON. Br/Ja 1978; B; 14100; 169.9 × 9.79 (527.95 × 32.12); M; 14. Sisters (Br flag): **47011 FORT CARLETON 47012 FORT WALSH.**

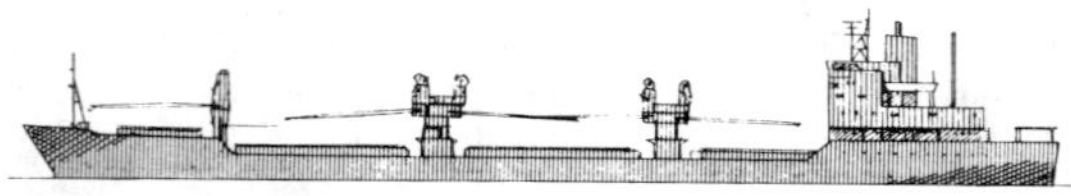

KC$_5$MFK H13
● **47030 E R BRUGGE.** Be/Be 1978; C; 14500; 163.5 × 10.25 (536.5 × 27.5); M; 17. Sister: **47031 CAST WALRUS** (Be) ex E R BRUSSEL; C P HUNTER 1981.

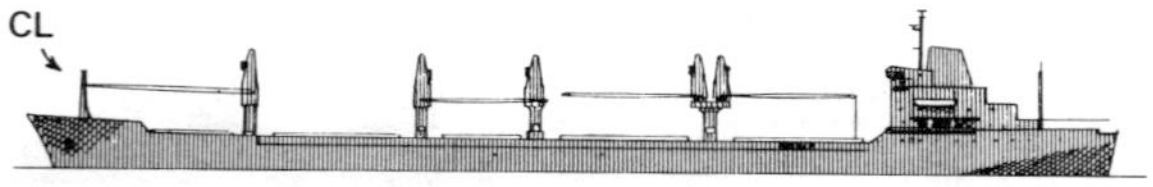

KC$_5$MFK H13
47050 OLIVIA. Bz/Bz 1977; B; 17300; 173.18 × 9.72 (568.17 × 31.89); M; 15.5; **'PRINASA 26/15'** type. Possible Sisters: **47051 ATACAMA** (Ch) **47052 ARAUCO** (Ch) **47053 ALMARIS** (Bz).

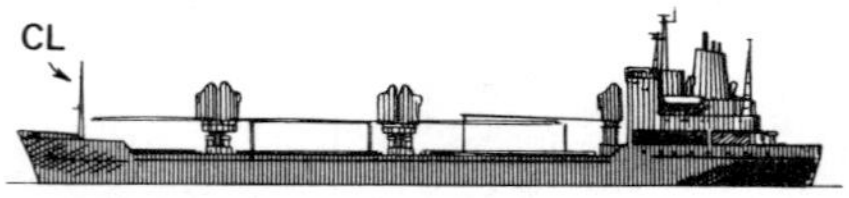

KC$_5$MFK H13
47060 TOZEUR. Tn/Ja 1977; C; 6500; 127.29 × 7.9 (417.62 × 25.92); M; 18. Possible Sister: **47061 EL JEM** (Tn) Possibly Similar: **47062 TOYOFUJI No 2** (Ja).

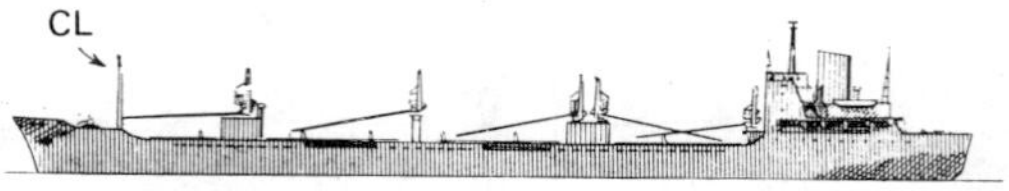

KC$_5$MFK H13
47020 COSMOTOR ACE. Pa/Ja 1968; B; 11200; 152.25 × 8.99 (499.5 × 29.49); M; 14; ex HONMOKU MARU.

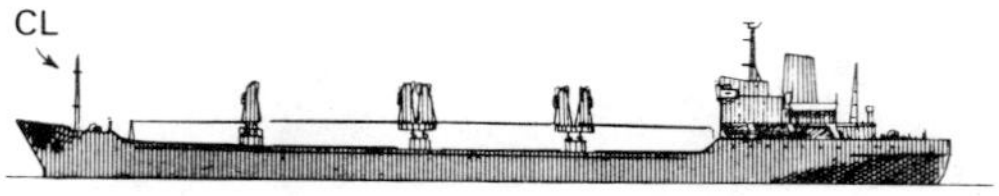

KC$_5$MFK H13
⋆**47040 XIANG CHENG.** RC/Ja 1976; C; 7000/11400; 147.71 × —/9.63 (484.61 × —/31.59); M; 15; ex STAR PROCYON; ex ARISTEIDIS 1977; **'MITSUI - CONCORD 18'** type. Sister: ⋆**47041 RONG CHENG** (RC) ex ARISTOXENOS 1979 Possible Sisters: **47042 JALABALA** (In) ex ARISTONOFOS 1976 **47043 MIZORAM** (In) launched as ARISTOFON ⋆**47044 YUN CHENG** (RC) ex ARISTODIKOS ⋆**47045 TONG CHENG** (RC) ex ARISTONIDAS 1979 **47046 ARUNACHAL PRADESH** (In) launched as ARISTOLAOS **47047 STAR ALCYONE** (Pa) ex ARISTOMACHOS 1976.

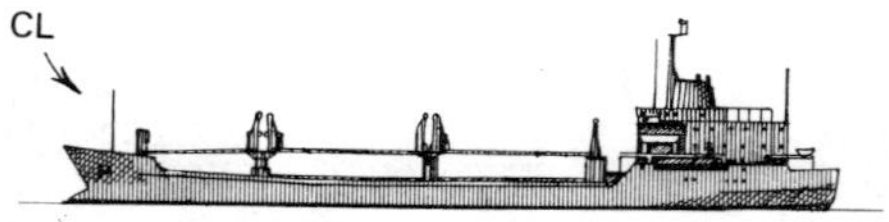

KC$_5$MFK H13
● ⋆**47070 LIEBENWALDE.** DDR/DDR 1977; C; 3500/5700; 120.61 × —/7.83 (395.7 × —/25.69); M; 16.75. Sisters (DDR flag): ⋆**47071 CUNEWALDE** ⋆**47072 LUCKENWALDE** ⋆**47073 SCHONWALDE** ⋆**47074 GERINGSWALDE** ⋆**47075 MITTENWALDE** ⋆**47076 FURSTENWALDE** ⋆**47077 EICHWALDE** ⋆**47078 RUDOLF DIESEL** ⋆**47079 ARENDSEE** ⋆**47080 BLANKENSEE** ⋆**47081 FLEESENSEE** ⋆**47082 MUGGELSEE** ⋆**47083 WERBELLINSEE** ⋆**47084 KOLPINSEE.**

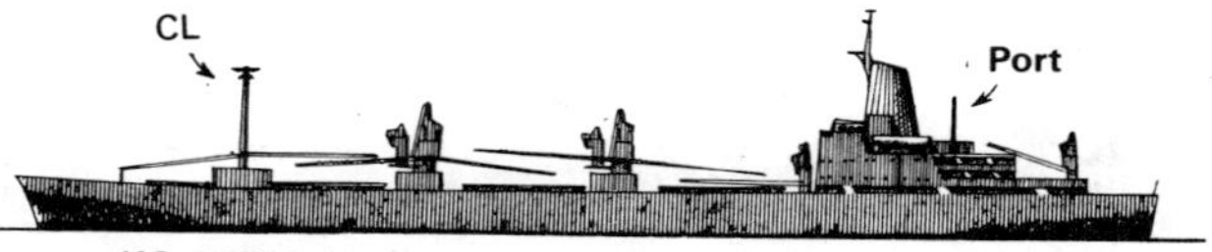

KC$_5$MFKC H
● **47090 GLOBE EXPRESS.** Sg/Br 1970; C; 12800; 182.73 × 9.32 (599.5 × 30.58); M; 21.5; ex BENLAWERS 1978.

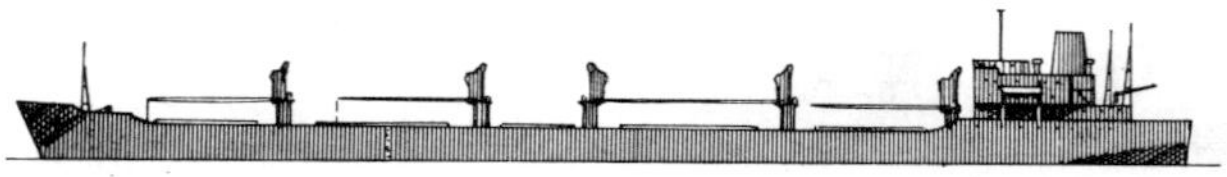

KC$_5$MFK$_2$ H13
47100 CRUZEIRO DO SOL. Li/Ja 1975; B; 20600; 185.5 × 10.9 (608.59 × 35.76); M; 15.25. Sisters: **47101 DIAVOLEZZA** (Sd) **47102 ROMANDIE** (Sd) Similar: **47103 NIKEA** (Gr) ex FEDERAL KATSURA 1979 **47104 MONTANA** (Gr) ex FEDERAL HUDSON 1979.

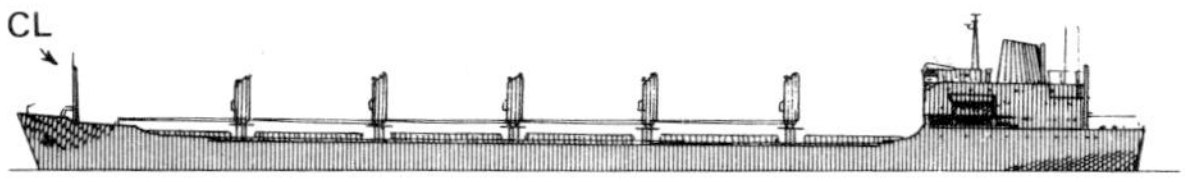

KC_5MFK_2 H13

⋆47110 FEI CHU HAI; RC/Br 1973; B; 22900; 178.31 × 10.38 (585.01 × 34.05); M; 15; ex SILVERDON 1978; ex BRAVENES 1973.

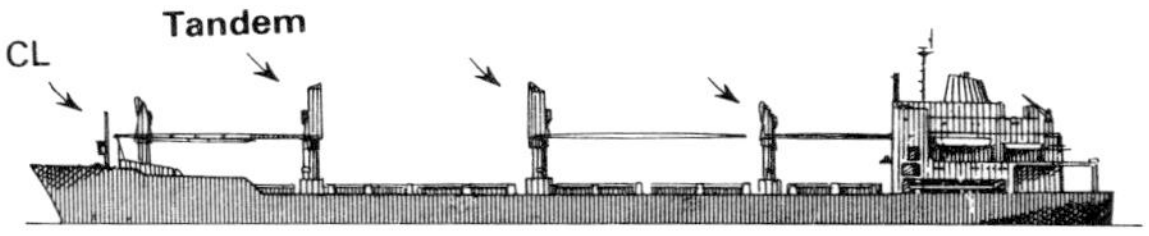

KC_4KMF/KC_4KMFC H1

47130 JOHN BAKKE. No/Ja 1978; C/Con; 16400; 174.02 × 10.15 (570.93 × 33.3); M; 18.25. Sister: **47131 MARIE BAKKE** (No).

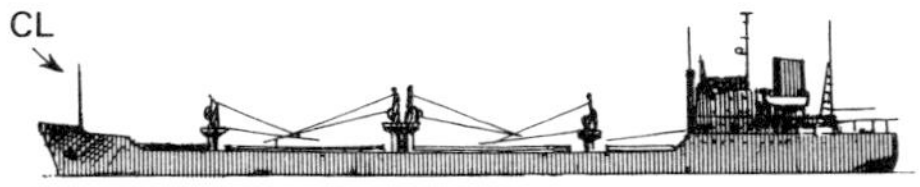

KC_4KMFK H13

47160 CANOPY. Pa/Ja 1967; O; 7400; 135.03 × 7.93 (443 × 26.01); M; 14.5; ex SPENCER MARU 1977.

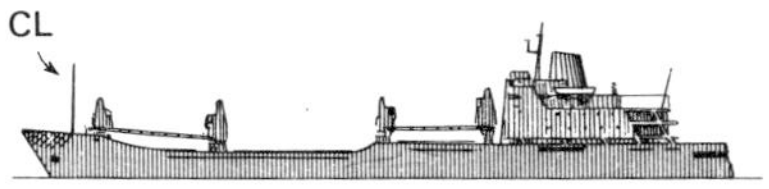

KC_4MF H12

47180 LAUTAN RANI. Sg/Au 1964; RoC; 3000; 113.01 × 5.72 (370.76 × 18.76); TSM; 17; ex SEAWAY QUEEN 1980; Stern door. Sister: **47181 PONTENEGRO** (Gr) ex LUCKY TRADER 1980; ex SENTOSA TRADER 1978; ex SEAWAY KING 1977.

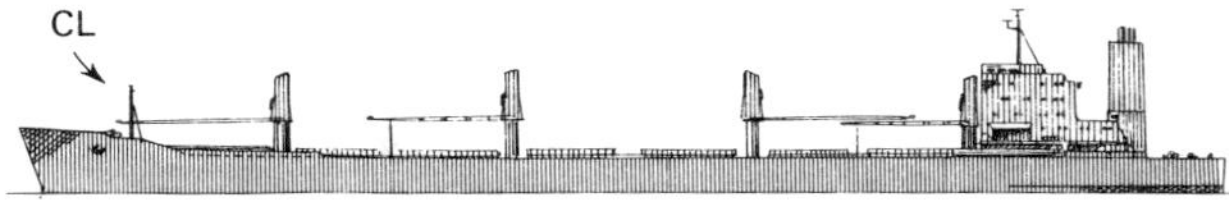

KC_4MF H1

47220 MEERDRECHT. Ne/Sw 1978; B/Con; 26700; 191.4 × 11.33 (627.95 × 37.17); M; —; ex SEATRAIN ROTTERDAM 1980; ex MEERDRECHT 1978; **'COLUMBUS 44'** type. Sisters: **47221 MIJDRECHT** (Ne) ex SEATRAIN AMSTERDAM 1980 ex MIJDRECHT 1978 **47222 ARLBERG** (As) ex STAR ABADAN; ex ARLBERG 1979 **47223 DEVOTION** (Pa) **47224 FRUITION** (Pa) **47225 UNISON** (Pa) **47226 MOORDRECHT** (Ne).

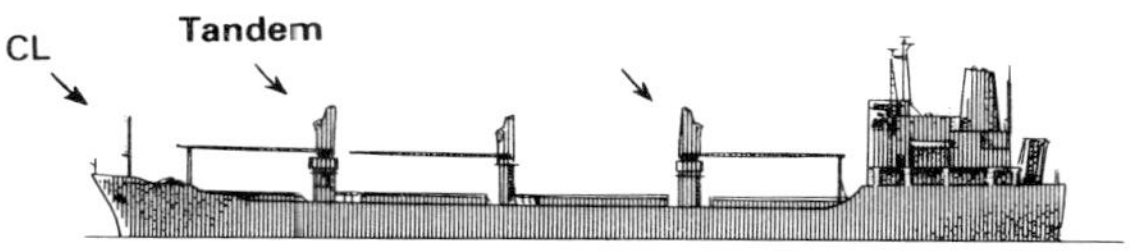

KC_5MFR H13

47120 FIJI MARU; Ja/Ja 1977; C/RoC; 8400; 155.53 × 8.92 (510.27 × 29.27) M; 16.25.

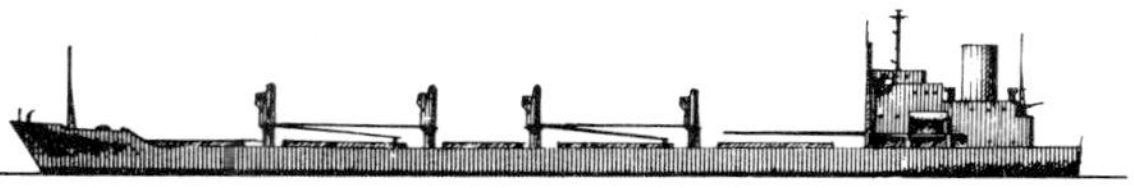

KC_4KMFK H1

47150 MARITIME BRILLIANCE. Li/Ja 1970; B; 15900; 170.52 × 10.06 (559.45 × 33); M; 15. Sisters (Li flag): **47151 MARITIME DOMINION 47152 GOLDEN LOTUS 47153 GOLDEN ORCHID.**

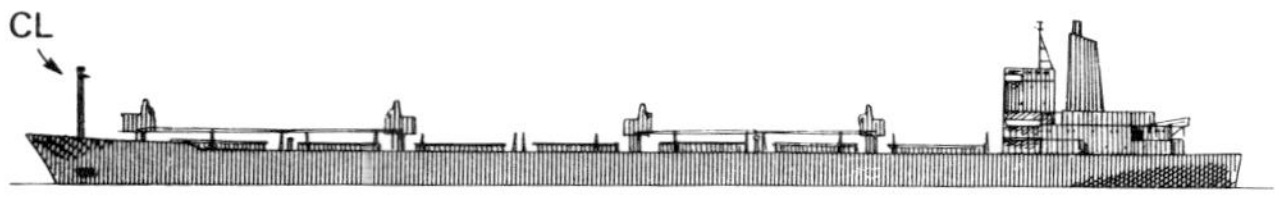

KC_4MF H

⋆47170 MIN YUN HAI. RC/Ih 1968; B; 22200; 192.67 × 11.38 (632.12 × 37.33); M; 15.5; ex PELOPIDAS 1981; ex IRISH ELM.

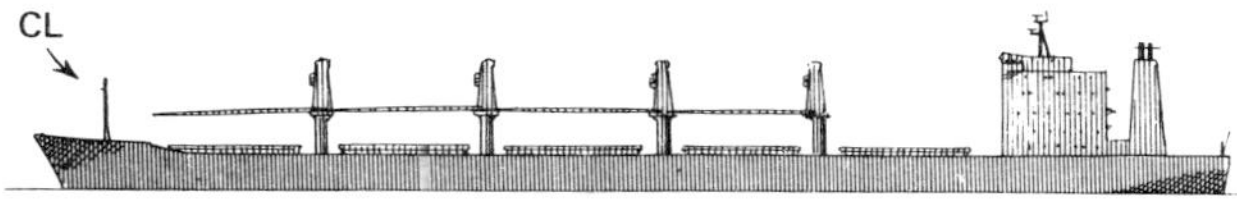

KC_4MF H1

47190 KONTULA. Fi/Fi 1980; B/IB; 19900; 179(BP) × 10.5 (587.27 × 4.92); —.

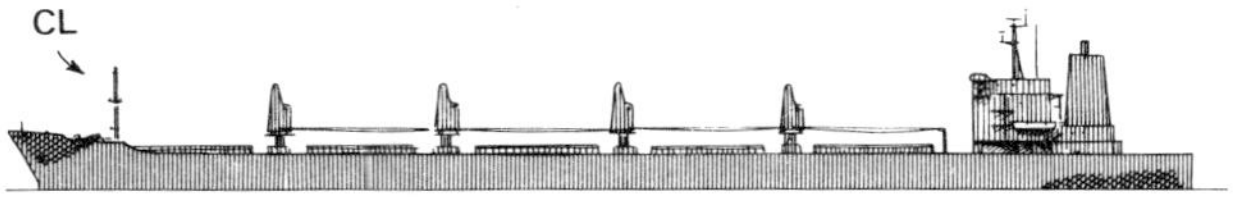

KC_4MF H1

● **47200 RADIANT VENTURE.** Li/Ja 1977; B; 19400; 187.74 × 10.76 (613.51 × 35.3); M; 15.5; **'FUTURE 32'** type. Sisters: Number of cranes may vary. **47201 ROSINA TOPIC** (Li) **47202 SOVEREIGN VENTURE** (Li) **47203 PRIMULA** (FRG) **47204 PRIMAVERA** (FRG) **47205 BISCHOFSTOR** (FRG) **47206 CARLO M** (Li) **47207 ANDROS OCEANIA** (Gr) **47208 MARIA L** (Gr) **47209 FAIRNESS** (Li) **47210 MARIA TOPIC** (Li) **47211 JUNO** (Li) **⋆47212 MOLAT** (Ys) **⋆47213 RUDO** (Ys) Possible Sisters: **47214 COSTIS** (Gr) **⋆47215 GOSPIC** (Ys) Probable Sister (US built): **47216 PRIDE OF TEXAS** (US).

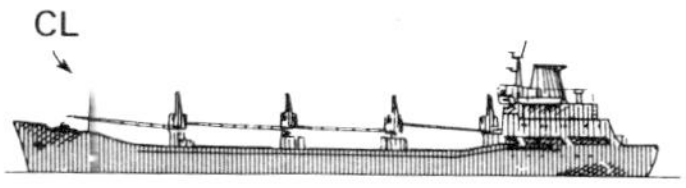

KC_4MF H1

47230 HANGETE. Fi/Fi 1966; C; 4100; 102.11 × 7.58 (335 × 24.86); M; 15; ex NILS GORTHON 1976. Sisters: **47231 ARCTIC** (Sw) ex MARGIT GORTHON 1976 **47232 GREGERSO** (Fi).

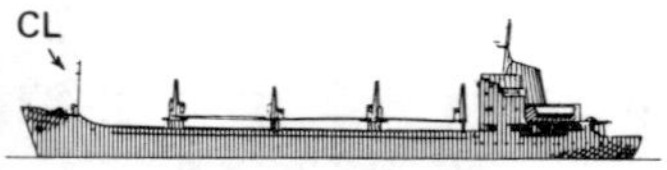

KC_4MF H1
47240 AL SHAN. So/Fi 1960; C; 2000; 96.91 × 5.81 (317.94 × 19.06); M; 13; ex LISA 1975; ex SIMPELE 1973. Sister: **47241 PO SEA** (So) ex SVANO 1975; ex VARJAKKA 1974; ex KAIPOLA 1969.

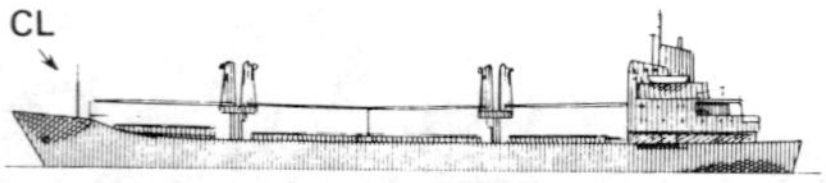

KC_4MF H1
47260 STEFAN DRESCHER. FRG/FRG 1972; C; 3400/6000; 124.52 × 6.59/8.12 (408.53 × 21.62/26.64); M; 17; ex WADAI 1975; ex EDE FOLDENFJORD 1974; ex EDE WITTORF 1973.

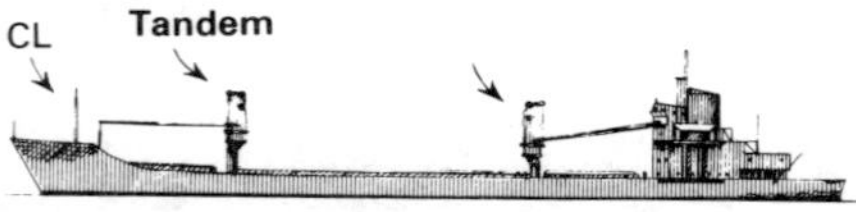

KC_4MF H1
47280 OLIVER DRESCHER. FRG/FRG 1973; C; 3500/6200; 132.52 × 6.5/8 (434.77 × 21,32/26.24); M; 17; ex LLOYD PHILADELPHIA 1980; ex OLIVER DRESCHER 1978; ex EDE SINSTORF 1975. Similar: **47281 LLOYD NEW YORK** (FRG) ex MACAELA DRESCHER 1978.

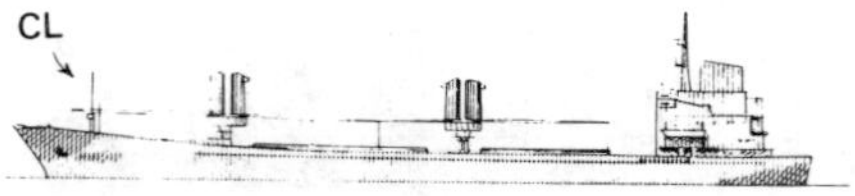

KC_4MF H1
● **47250 KATJANA.** FRG/FRG 1971; C; 3400/5800; 126.83 × 6.51/7.36 (416.1 × 21.35/24.14); M; 16.5. Sister: **47251 STEINDAMM** (FRG) ex MESURADO 1975; ex SAMOS SKY 1974; ex STEINDAMM 1973.

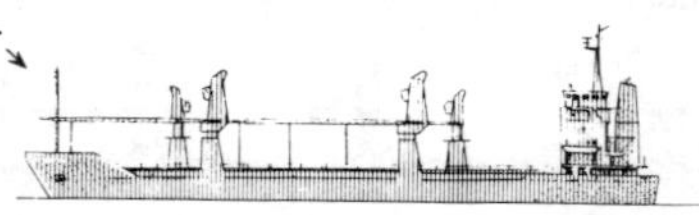

KC_4MF H1
47270 BRITANIA. FRG/FRG 1979; C/Con; 1600/3800; 99.98 × 5.53/— (328 × 18.14/—); M; 15; ex CONTI BRITANIA 1980; Smaller cranes are on starboard side and larger ones on port.

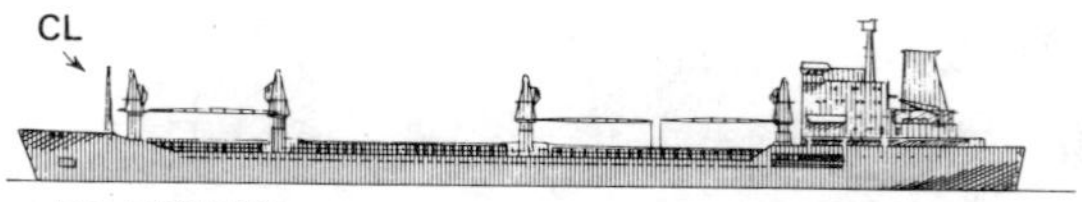

KC_4MF H13
47290 LOTILA. Fi/Sp 1977; B; 6800/12400; 159.21 × 6.87/9.15) (522.34 × 22.53/30.02); M; 16. Sisters (Fi flag): **47291 FINNFIGHTER** ex KAIPOLA 1980 **47292 FINNOCEANIS** ex WALKI 1980 **47293 SALLA** ex WALKI PAPER 1980 **47294 FINNARCTIS 47295 VARJAKKA 47296 POKKINEN.**

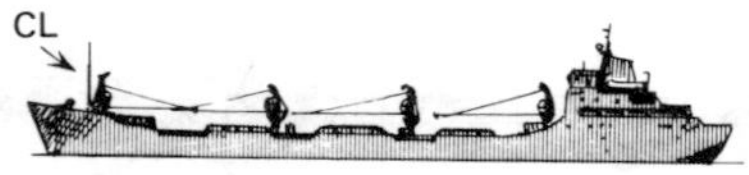

KC_4MF H13
47300 TATAI QUEEN. Gr/Sw 1966; C; 1900; 110.09 × 4.82 (361.19 × 15.81); M; 14.5; ex ANDREW 1980; ex ANDREW SALMAN 1976; Side door. Sister: **47301 TATAI SEA** (Gr) ex MICHAEL 1980; ex MICHAEL SALMAN 1976.

KC_4MF H13
● **47320 ALHALEMI.** Eg/Sp 1971; C; 1200; 87 × 4.87 (285.43 × 15.97); M; 13.5; ex BENIMUSA 1980. Sisters: **47321 BENIMAMET** (Sp) **47322 BENISALEM** (Sp) **47323 ALHAKEM** (Eg) ex BENIAJAN **47324 NIAGA XXXV** (Ia) ex BENIFARAIG 1981 Similar (shorter): **47325 MARIA ZAKELINA S** (Gr) ex BENIMAR 1977 **47326 ALHAMBRA** (Eg) ex BENISA 1978 **47327 BENIALI** (Sp).

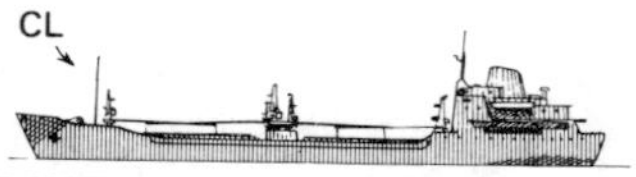

KC_4MF H13
47310 GERMAINE R E. Fr/Sw 1961; C; 1600/2700; 93.81 × 5.07/5.76 (307.77 × 16.63/18.9); M; 13; ex GARM 1975. Similar: **47311 ATLAS** (Fi) ex GRIM 1969.

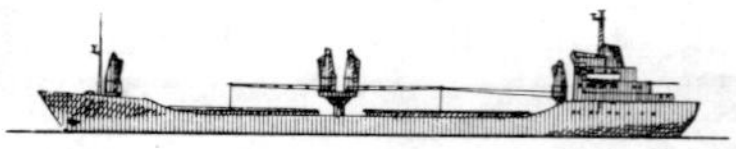

KC_4MF H13
47330 BREMER HORST BISCHOFF. FRG/FRG 1971; C; 1400; 104.63 × 5.04 (343.27 × 16.53); M; 17.

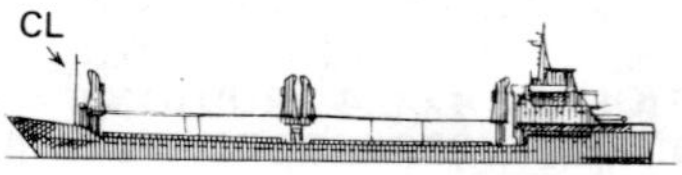

KC_4MF H13
● **47340 PHAEDRA.** Gr/DDR 1971; C; 3200; 104.12 × 5.79 (341.6 × 19); M; 14; ex HANSEATIC. Possible Sister (may have a gantry) **47341 VARDE** (Sw) ex BRUNVARD 1977 Probably Similar: **47342 HILDE** (Pa) ex BRUNHILD 1977.

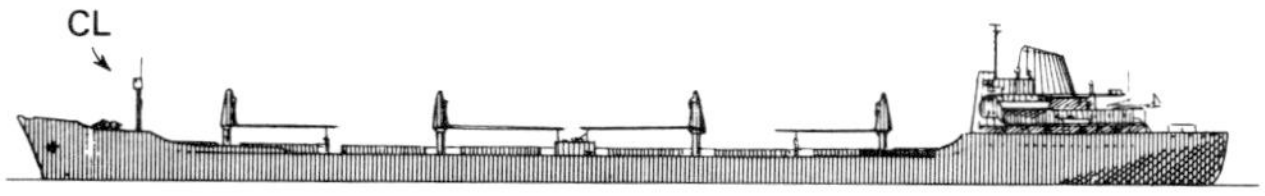

KC_4MF H13
47350 GOOD OCEAN. Gr/FRG 1966; B; 21400; 191.55 × 11.32 (628.45 × 37.14); M; 15.75; ex SOLHOLT 1979.

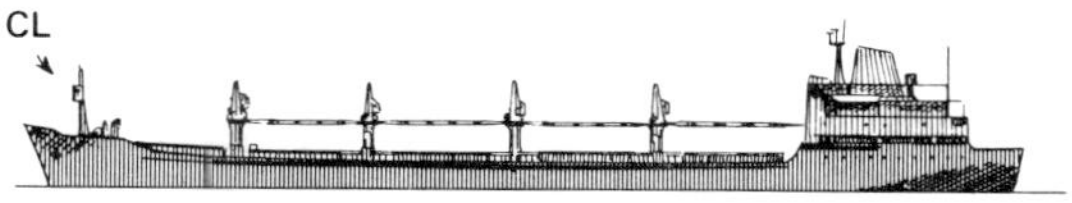

KC_4MF H13
47360 NORITA. No/Br 1970; B; 12600; 158.53 × 9.51 (520.11 × 31.2); M; 15; ex INGEREN 1979.

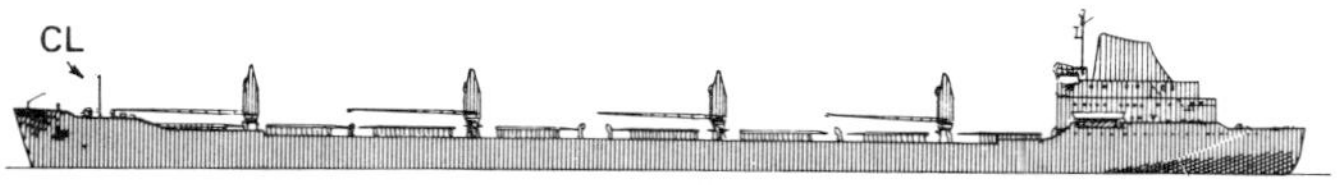

KC_4MF H13
47370 ALTHEA. Gr/Gr 1973; B; 22400; 205.01 × 11.74 (672.6 × 38.51); M; 15.5. Sister: **47371 AKTEA** (Gr).

● 47375

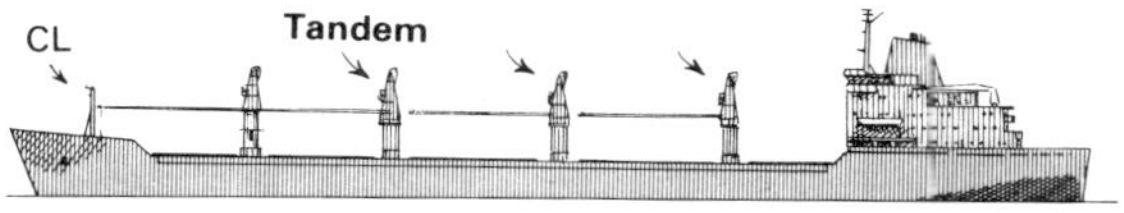

KC_4MF H13
47380 MARCHEN MAERSK. De/De 1974; C/Con; 10400/15900; 170.69 × 9.35/10.27 (560.01 × 30.68/33.69); M; 20.5. Sisters (De flag): **47381 MARGRETHE MAERSK 47382 McKINNEY MAERSK 47383 MATHILDE MAERSK.**

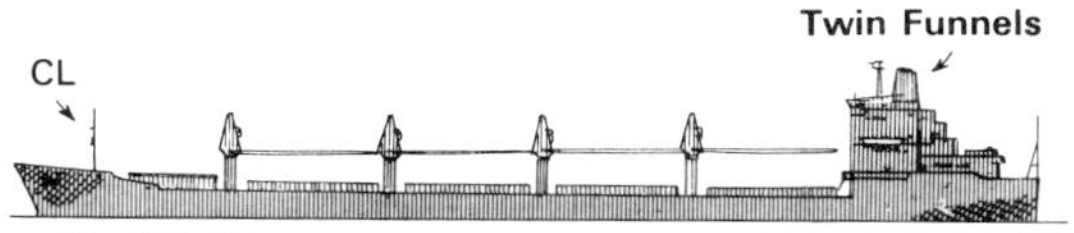

KC_4MF H13
● **47390 HAE YUNG EASTERN.** Ko/No 1970; B; 14500; 162.87 × 10.42 (534.35 × 34.18); M; —; ex BARON ARDROSSAN 1981. Sisters: **47391 BARON WEMYSS** (Br) **47392 CAPE HAWK** (Br) **47393 HAE YUNG GOLD** (Ko) ex CAPE GRAFTON 1980 **47394 CAPE GRENVILLE** (Br) **47395 CAPE HORN** (Br) **47396 CAPE ANTIBES** (gr) ex TEMPLE INN 1979 **47397 SNELAND** (No) **47398 KATERINA E** (Gr) ex WESTOCEAN 1980; ex VESTLAND Similar (lengthened to 188m & may have an extra crane): **47399 FEDERAL ST. CLAIR** (Li) ex BARON INCHCAPE 1977.

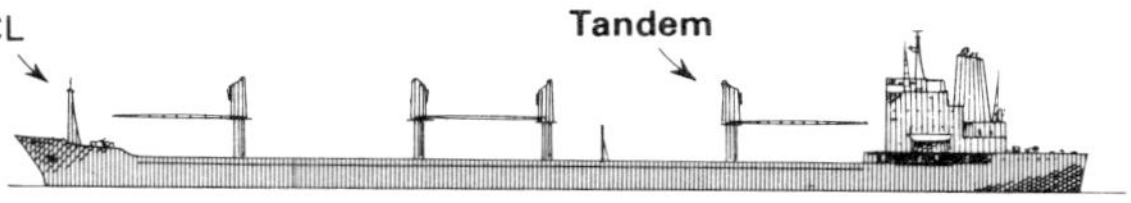

KC_4MF H13
● **47410 MING SPRING.** Tw/Tw 1978; C; 18600; 172.02 × 10.6 (564.37 × 34.78); M; 17. Sisters (Tw flag): **47411 MING SUMMER 47412 MING AUTUMN 47413 MING WINTER.**

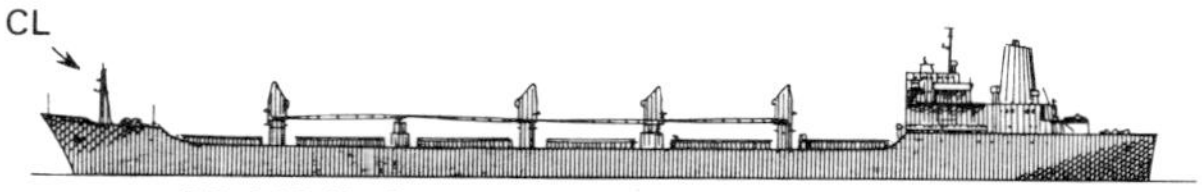

KC_4MF H13
47420 KIELDRECT. Na/Ja 1977; B; 16200; 178.11 × 10.9 (584.35 × 35.76); M; 15.5. Sister: **47421 KATENDRECHT** (NA).

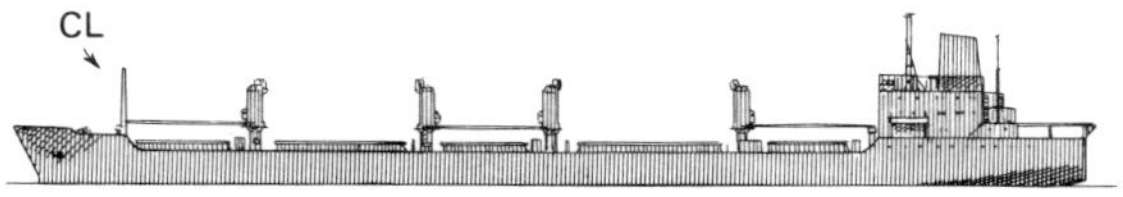

KC_4MF H13
47430 PAGNET. Li/FRG 1976; C; 14600; 171.41 × 10.45 (562.37 × 34.28); M; 16.25; ex PAGNOL 1980 **'Key 26'** type. Sister: **47431 RAIMOL** (Li) ex RAIMU 1980.

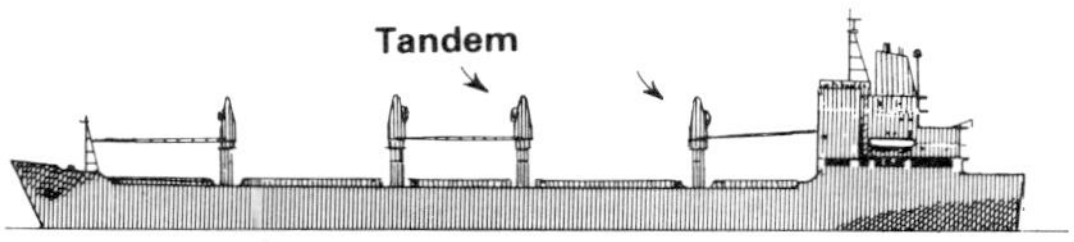

KC_4MF H13
47440 SAMOA. De/De 1978; C; 16200; 159.42 × 10.59 (523.03 × 34.74); M; 16. Sisters (De flag): **47441 SARGODHA 47442 SIMBA 47443 SIENA 47444 SINALOA** (Pk flag): **47445 MAKRAN.**

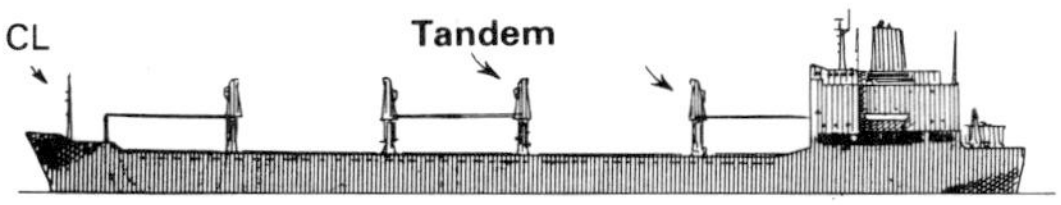

KC_4MF H13
47450 SONGKHLA. De/Ja 1977; B/Con; 16100; 158.02 × 10.59 (518.44 × 34.74); M; 16.25. Sister: **47451 SUMBAWA** (De).

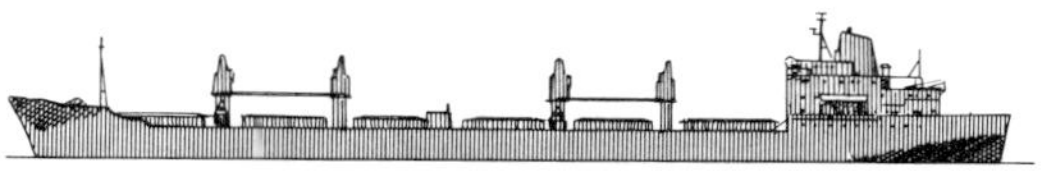

KC_4MF H13
47460 BARON MACLAY. Br/No 1971; B; 13400; 159.21 × 9.76 (522.34 × 32.02); M; 15.

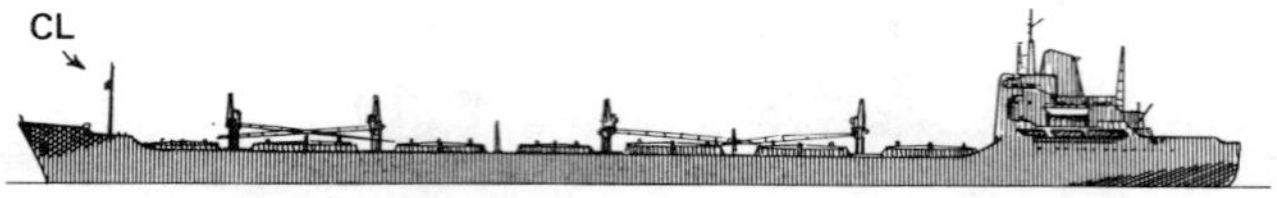

KC_4MF H13
47470 KYRIAKOULA D. LEMOS. Gr/Ja 1966; B; 20500; 194.01 × 11.89 (636.52 × 39.01); M; —.

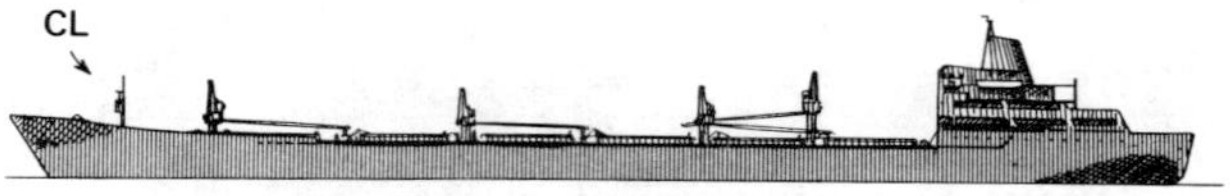

KC_4MF H13
47480 AL TAMMAR. Li/No 1964; B; 17200; 186.82 × 11.22 (612.93 × 36.81); M; 14; ex WESTBULK 1980.

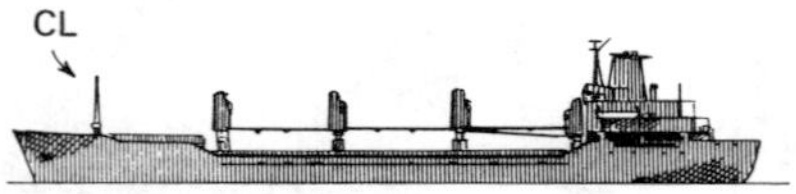

KC_4MF H13
47490 FINNOAK. Fi/Fi 1971; C; 3100/5700; 118.32 × 6.41/7.44 (388.2 × 21.03/24.5); M; 14.75; ex KAIPOLA 1975. Sisters (Fi flag): **47491 FINNKRAFT** ex VALKEOKOSKI 1977 **47492 KOITELI 47493 TUIRA.**

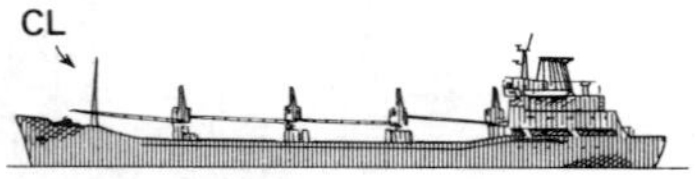

KC_4MF H13
47510 HANGETE. Fi/Fi 1966; C; 4100; 102.11 × 7.58 (335 × 24.86); M; 15; ex NILS GORTHON 1976. Sisters: **47511 ARCTIC** (Sw) ex MARGIT GORTHON 1976 **47512 GREGERSO** (Fi).

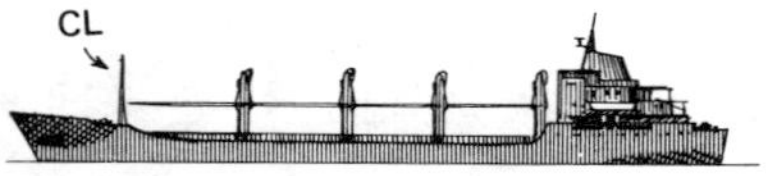

KC_4MF H13
● **47530 CINDERELLA.** Sw/FRG 1968; C; 2600/5000; 113.52 × 6.26/7.51 (372.44 × 20.54/24.64); M; 15.75; ex NIMOS 1977; ex BERKEL 1969.

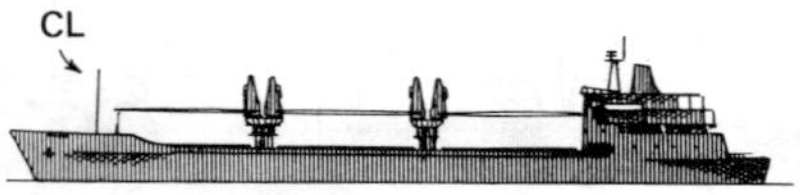

KC_4MF H13
47580 IRON YORK. Au/Au 1973; C; 6350; 119.69 × 7.71 (392.68 × 25.29); M; 16; ex CAPE YORK 1975. Sister: **47581 IRON ARNHEM** (Au) ex CAPE ARNHEM 1975.

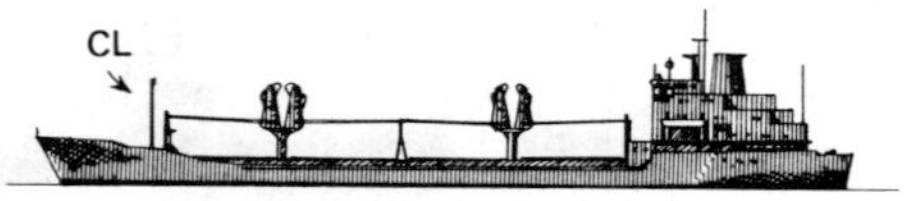

KC_4MF H13
47590 FINNPINE. Fi/Fi 1971; C; 3900/6600; 129.39 × 6.43/8.07 (424.51 × 21.1/24.48); M; 17.25. Sisters (Fi flag): **47591 FINNALPINO 47592 FINNTRADER 47593 FINNWOOD.**

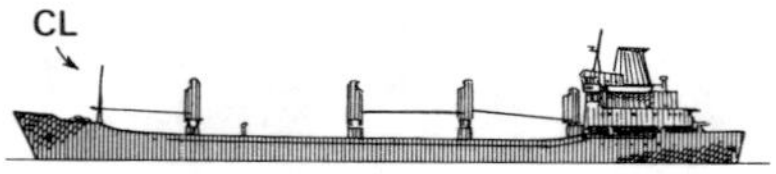

KC_4MF H13
47500 GERMUNDO. Fi/Fl 1969; C; 4500; 116.01 × 7.41 (380.61 × 24.31); M; 15.

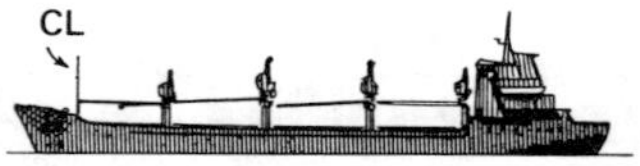

KC_4MF H13
47520 ALCA. Fi/Sw 1967; C; 1600/2900; 93.81 × 5.08/6.6 (307.77 × 16.66/21.65); M; 14. Sisters (Fi flag): **47521 DORIS 47522 HAMNO**

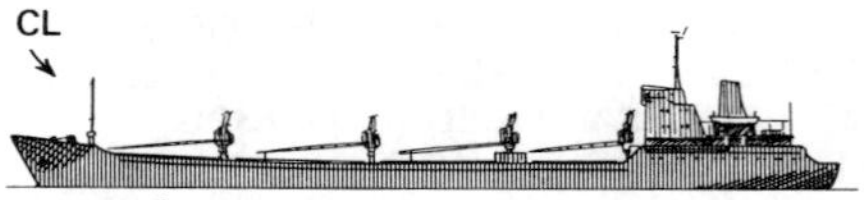

KC_4MF H13
● **⋆47540 RADAUTI.** Rm/Rm 1974; C; 4400/6300; 130.77 × 6.6/8.1 (429.04 × 21.65/26.57); M; 15.75. Sisters (Rm flag): **⋆47541 FAGET ⋆47542 FIERBINTI ⋆47543 FILIDARA ⋆47544 CALIMANESTI ⋆47545 FAUREI ⋆47546 FAGARAS ⋆47547 BUSTENI ⋆47548 TELEORMAN ⋆47549 FIRIZA ⋆47550 BIHOR ⋆47551 OLANESTI ⋆47552 FILIASI ⋆47553 SATU MARE ⋆47554 ODORHEI ⋆47555 SIMERIA ⋆47556 GORJ ⋆47557 FRUNZANESTI ⋆47558 FRASINET ⋆47559 FELIX ⋆47560 DOLJ ⋆47561 CACIULATA ⋆47562 FIENI ⋆47563 RUPEA ⋆47564 HATEG ⋆47565 ORAVITA ⋆47566 GOVORA ⋆47567 FUNDULEA** (Bu flag): **⋆47568 SEFAN KARADJA ⋆47569 ZAHARI STOIANOV.**

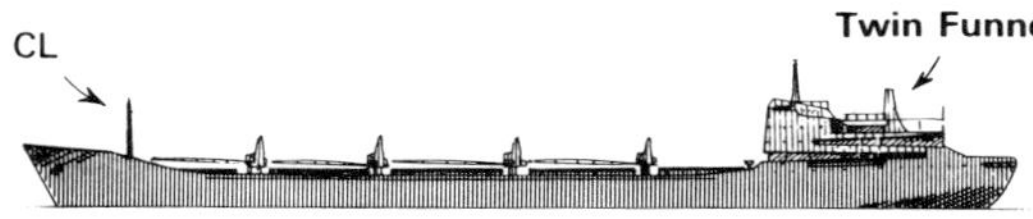

KC_4MF H13
47600 HILTONA. Pa/Pd 1966; C; 7500/10700; 156.34 × 8.13/8.89 (512.93 × 26.67/29.17); M; 15.5; ex WLOKNIARZ 1980 **'B-512'** type. Sister: ⋆**47601 GORNIK** (Pd) Possible Sister: **47602 ELEISTRIA** (Gr) ex METALOWIEC 1980. (May have cranes removed).

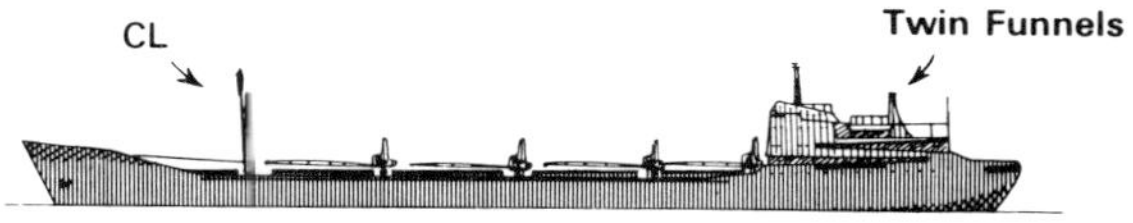

KC_4MF H13
⋆**47610 TRANSPORTOWIEC.** Pd/Pd 1964; C; 7500/10600; 155.76 × 8.13/8.9 (511.02 × 26.67/29.2); M; 14.25; **'B 512'** type. Sister: ⋆**47611 HUTNIK** (Pd) Possibly Similar: ⋆**47612 CHEMIK** (Pd) ⋆**47613 ENERGETYK** (Pd) (may not have cranes).

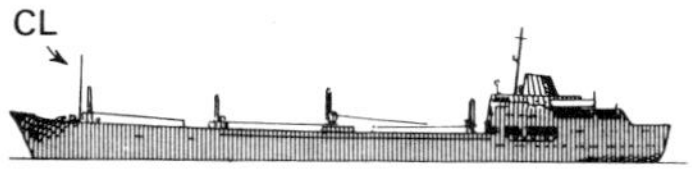

KC_4MF H3
47620 VIKI-LAM. Gr/Sw 1957; C; 2500/4000; 105.29 × 5.87/6.48 (345.44 × 19.26/21.26); M; 12.75; ex NEVA 1971.

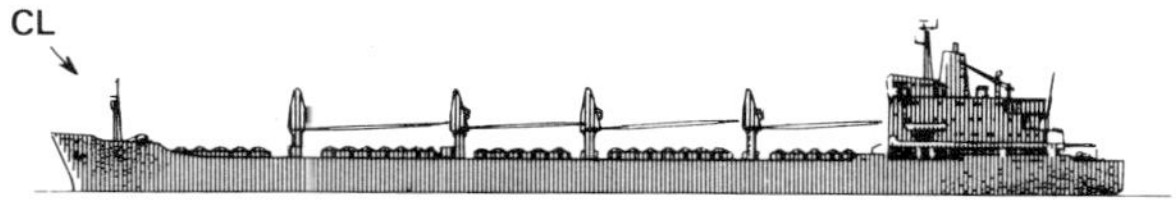

KC_4MFC H1
47630 MOSRIVER. No/Ja 1976; B; 17900; 169.98 × 10.26 (557.68 × 33.66); M; 15. **47631 MOSLAKE** (No).

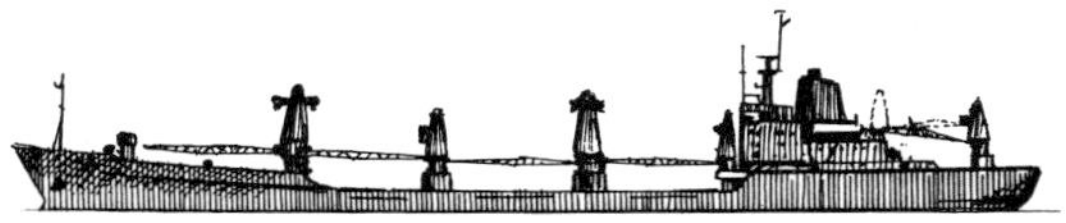

KC_4MFC H13
47640 NEDLLOYD NAGASAKI. Ne/Ne 1972; C; 12100; 155.9.7 (543 × 32); M; 121; ex STRAAT NAGASAKI 1977. Sisters (Ne flag): **47641 NEDLLOYD NAGOYA** ex STRAAT NAGOYA **47642 NEDLLOYD NAPIER** ex STRAAT NAPIER **47643 NEDLLOYD NASSAU** ex STRAAT NASSAU.

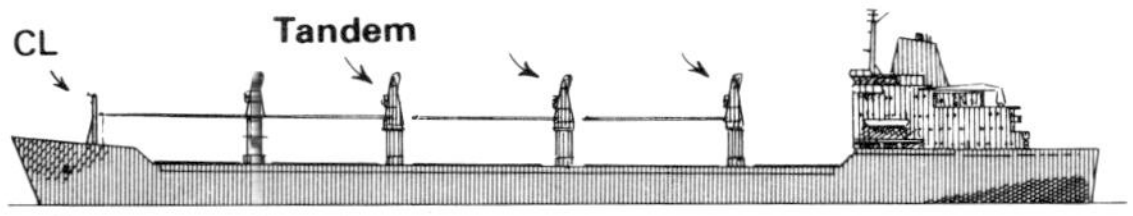

KC_4MFC H13
47650 MARCHEN MAERSK. De/De 1974; C/Con; 10400/15900; 170.69 × 9.34/10.27 (560.01 × 30.68/33.69); M; 20.5. Sisters (De flag): **47651 MARGRETHE MAERSK 47652 MCKINNEY MAERSK 47653 MATHILDE MAERSK.**

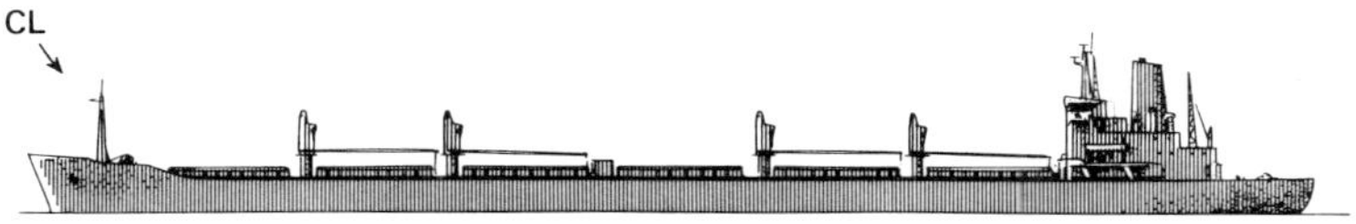

KC_4MFK H1
47660 PACIFIC MASTER. Pa/Ja 1976; B; 30300; 222.99 × 12.32 (731.59 × 40.42); M; 14.5. Possible Sister: **47661 NEW APOLLO** (Li).

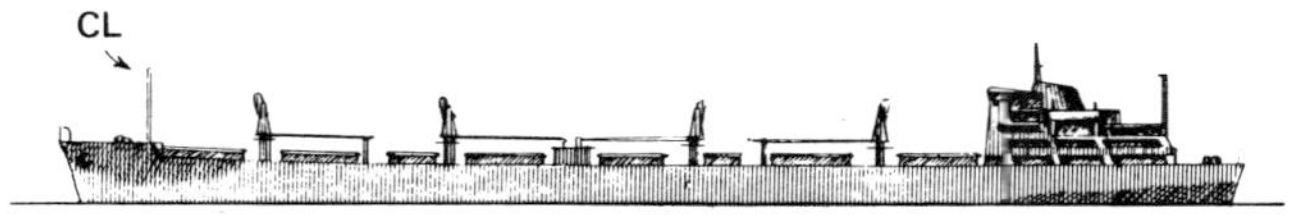

KC_4MFK H1
47670 FAIR WIND. Gr/Br 1964; B; 17600; 188.07 × 10.57 (617.03 × 34.68) M; 14.5; ex ALEXANDRA ex BENHIANT 1978; ex CRAMOND 1977; ex BENHIANT 1975; ex WEARFIELD 1973.

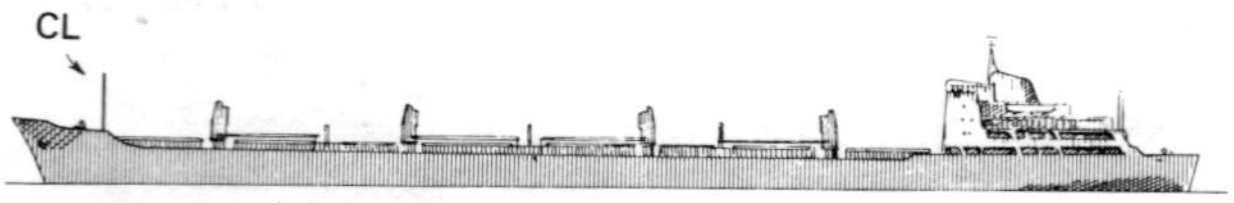

KC_4MFK H1
47680 MARGARITA. Gr/Br 1966; B; 18100; 188.07 × 11.02 (617.03 × 36.15); M; 15; ex MARGARITA CHANDRIS 1977. Probable Sister: **47681 MARI CHANDRIS** (Gr).

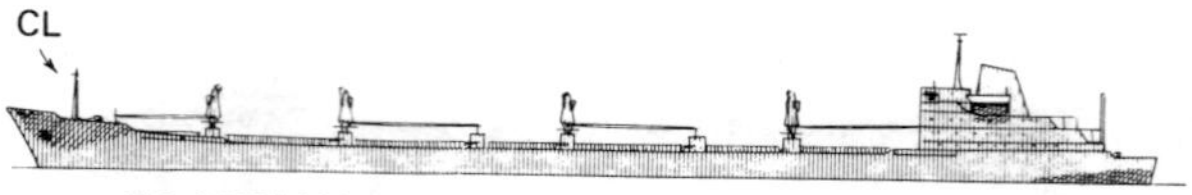

KC_4MFK H1
47690 LONDON BARON. Br/Br 1977; B; 15800; 183.04 × 10.71 (600.5 × 35.14); M; 15; **'B-26'** type. Sisters (Br flag): **47691 LONDON EARL 47692 LONDON VISCOUNT.**

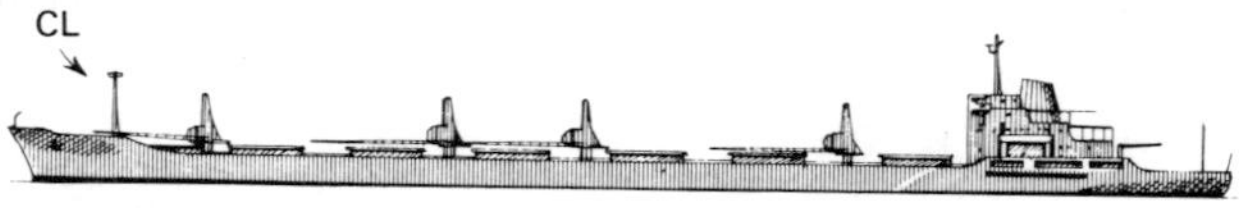

KC_4MFK H1
47700 DAMODAR TANABE. In/Ys 1969; B; 24573; 193.11 × 11.88 (635.51 × 38.97); M; 15.75; Cranes travel athwartships. Sister: **47701 DAMODAR TASAKA** (In).

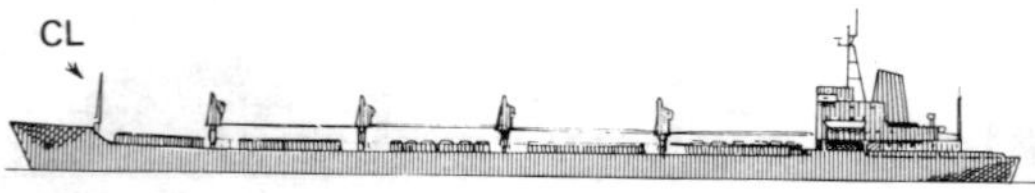

KC_4MFK H1
⋆**47710 DUBROVNIK.** Ys/Sp 1971; B; 14700; 164.85 × 10.17 (540.85 × 33.37); M; 13.5; launched as MAGDALENA DEL MAR. Sister: **47711 MAGDALENA DEL MAR** (Sp).

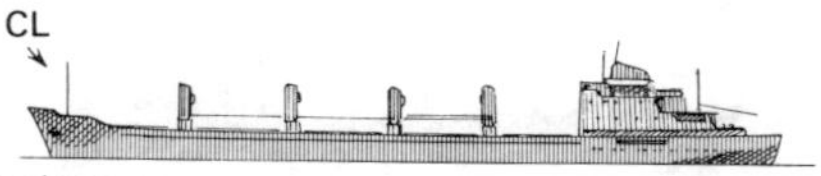

KC_4MFK H1
47720 SPYROS V. Gr/Sp 1964; C; 3200/5000; 119.26 × 6.4/7.32 (391.27 × 21/24.02; M; —; ex HESPERUS 1980; ex AKERA 1964; lengthened 1971.

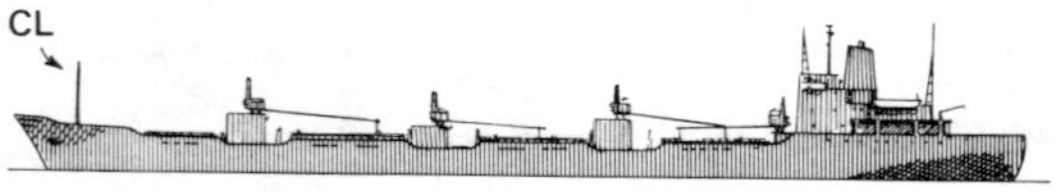

KC_4MFK H13
47730 PIONEER No 1. Ja/Ja 1968; B/Vehicles; 12400; 159.04 × 9.55 (521.78 × 31.33); M; 14.5; ex TOYOTA MARU No 1 1979. Sister (Ja flag): **47731 PIONEER No 2** ex TOYOTA MARU No 2 1973 **47732 PIONEER No 3** (Ja) ex TOYOTA MARU No 3.

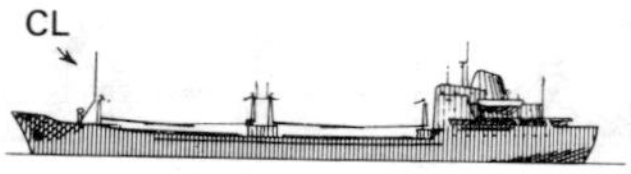

KC_4MFK H13
47740 NANOULA. Pa/De 1963; C; 1600/2700; 93.88 × 5.07/6.37 (307.68 × (307.68 × 16.63/20.9); M; 13.5; ex TAMARIS; ex FINNROVER 1973; ex NINA 1971.

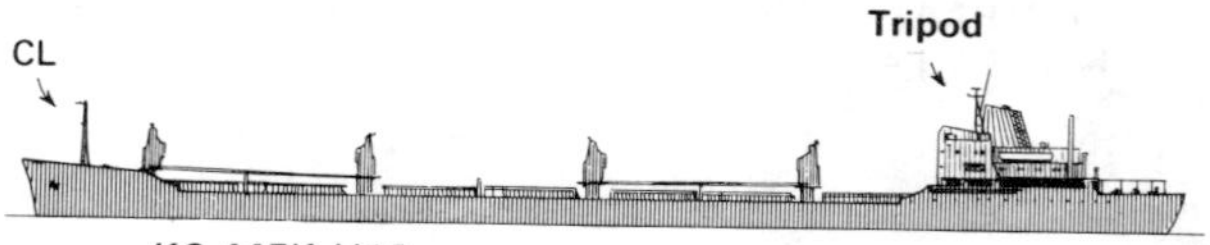

KC_4MFK H13
47750 KEFALONIA SUN. Gr/Ih 1966; B; 18800; 183.93 × 11.17 (603.45 × 36.65); M; 15.5; ex SEA CREST 1980; ex NEW ADVENTURE 1973. Similar: **47751 AMSTELPARK** (Ne) **47752 AMSTELLAAN** (NA) Similar (may have no cranes) **47753 DHALIT** (Is) ex WAVE CREST 1977; ex NEW FRONTIERS 1973; ex MAAS 1965. Similar (mast from funnel): **47754 ELIAS K** (Pa) ex SAMOS GLORY; ex JAMES BENEDICT 1972.

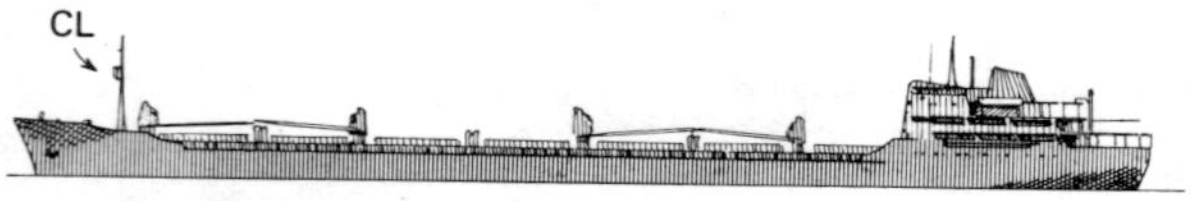

KC_4MFK H13
47760 OCEAN PEGASUS. Gr/Ne 1961; B; 16600; 180.6 × 10.8 (592.52 × 35.43); M; 14.5; ex SKAUVANN 1965.

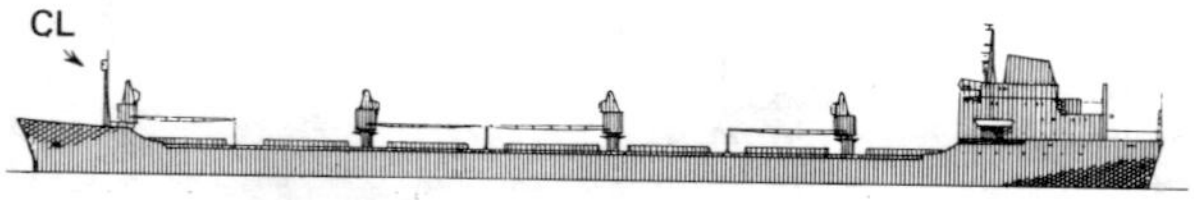

KC_4MFK H13
47770 PRACTICIAN. Br/Br 1972; B; 20100; 180.96 × 11.23 (593.7 × 36.84); M; 15; ex LETCHWORTH 1978. Sisters (Br flag): **47771 HUMANIST** ex NAWORTH 1978 **47772 PROGRESSIST** ex OAKWORTH 1978.

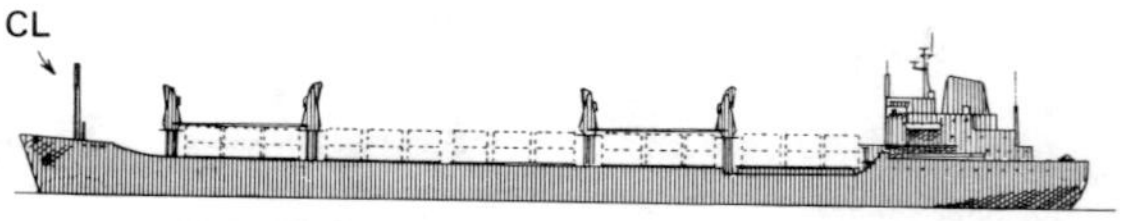

KC_4MFK H13
● **47780 ADVARA.** Br/Br 1970; C/Con; 17600; 175.27 × 9.88 (575.03 × 32.41); M; 15.25; ex KYOTO FOREST 1975; converted from bulk carrier & shortened 1975.

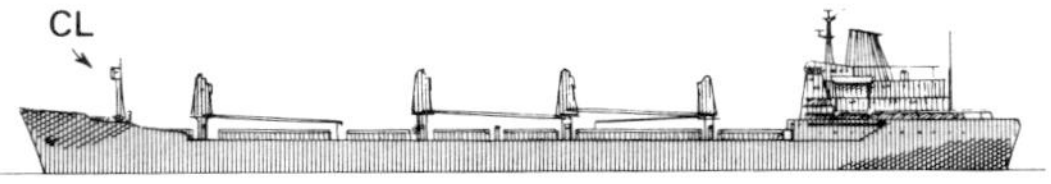

KC_4MFK H13
47790 KOTKANIEMI. Fi/Fi 1968; B; 12100; 158.32×9.59 (519.42×31.46); M; 14.5.

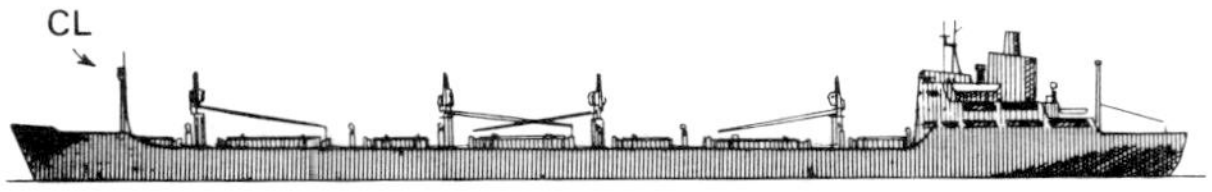

KC_4MFK H13
47800 ALARIC. Br/FRG 1963; B; 17500; 186.16×9.71 (610.76×31.86); M; 15; ex MENKAR 1979; ex TOSCA 1977; ex DONAU 1968.

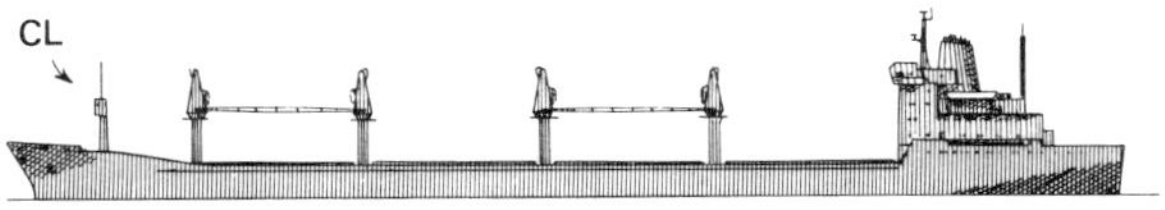

KC_4MFK H13
47810 PEGASUS TIMBER. Ko/DDR 1972; B/Con; 16200; 176.16×10.11 (579.59×33.17); M; 15.5; ex FOOCHOW 1980; ex BELLA COOLA 1977. Sisters: **47811 ARCTIC WASA** (Sw) **47812 GALAPAGOS** (Li) ex BALTIC WASA **47813 ORKNEY** (Li) ex CELTIC WASA 1979 **47814 TASMANIA** (Li) ex DELPHIC WASA 1980 **47815 SALAMIS** (Li) ex GOTHIC WASA 1980 **47816 FINNTIMBER** (Fi) **47817 SYLVO** (No) Possible Sisters: ⋆**47818 JENA** (DDR) **47819 ARIA** (Gr) **47820 ARIADNE** (Gr).

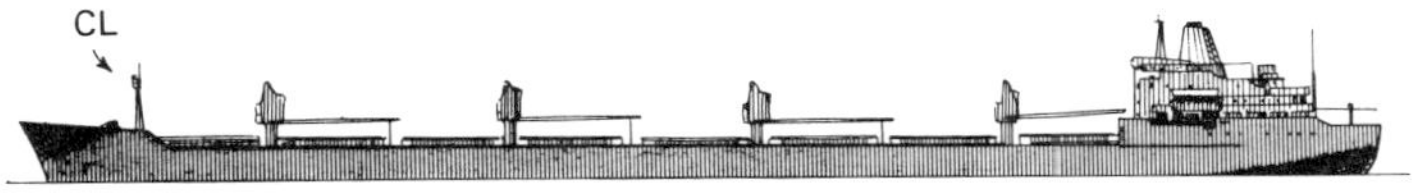

KC_4MFK H13
47830 NORWEGIAN SEA. Li/No 1969; B; 19300; 216.14×10.99 (709.12×36.06); M; 16; ex BENFRI 1978; ex ANDWI 1974. Similar: **47831 BERING SEA** (Pa) ex NANFRI 1978 **47832 CASPIAN SEA** (Pa) ex LORFRI 1978; ex DOBERG 1975; ex ROLWI 1974.

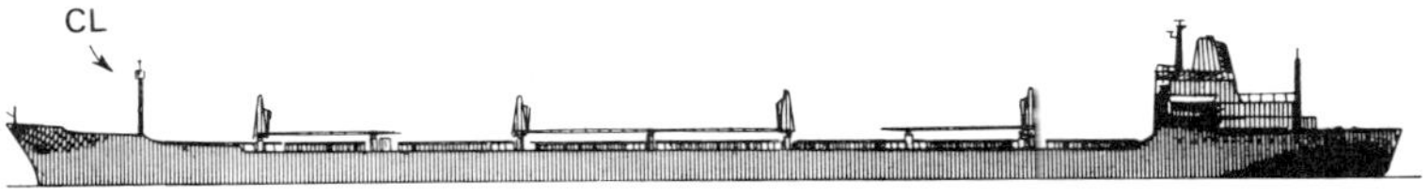

KC_4MFK H13
47840 PROSO. Gr/Ja 1968; B; 34600; 235.52×13.74 (772.7×45.08); M; —.

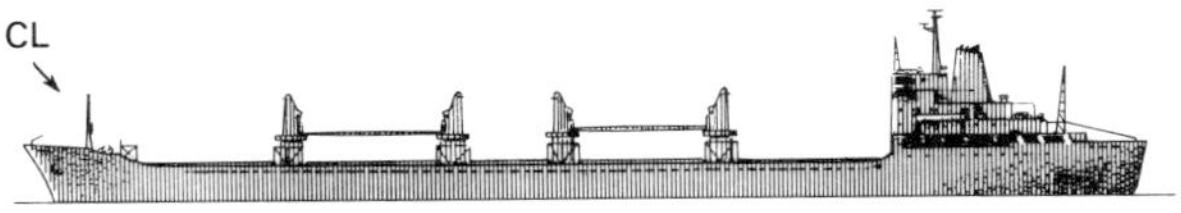

KC_4MFK H13
47850 MARE ITALICO. It/Ja 1974; B; 17200; 178.39×10.65 (585.27×34.94); M; 15.5; ex ACEDRELAS 1980; ex CEDRELA 1980.

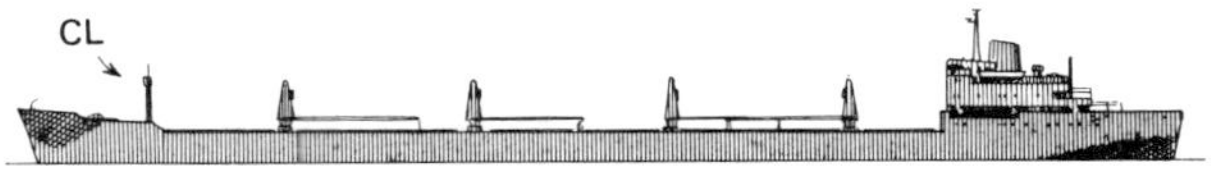

KC_4MFK H13
47860 ALKYON. Gr/Sw 1968; B; 17400; 185.12×10.22 (607.35×33.53); M; 16; ex JARL R. TRAPP.

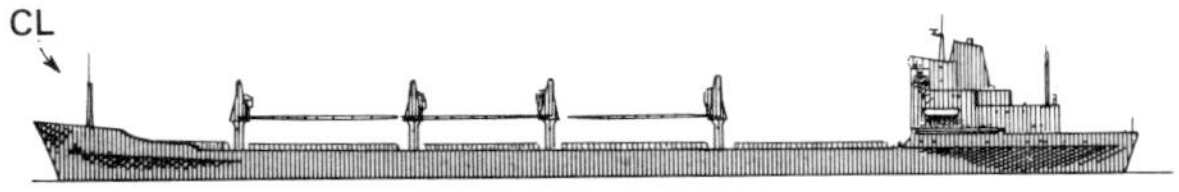

KC_4MFK H13
47870 CAPE ORTEGAL. Br/Br 1976; B; 16600; 175.11×10.14 (574.51×33.27); M; 15; **'Cardiff'** class. Sister (Br flag): **47871 CAPE RODNEY** Similar: **47872 BARON NAPIER 47873 BARON PENTLAND.**

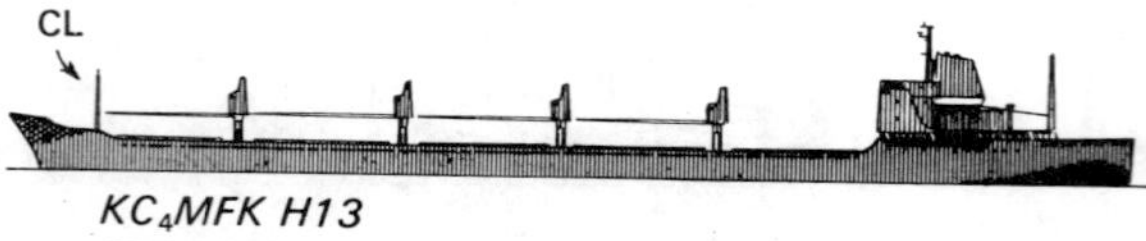

KC_4MFK H13
47880 STAR CAPELLA. Gr/Ja 1973; B; 14700; 177.96 × 10.69 (583.86 × 35.07); M; 15. Possible Sisters: **47881 STAR CASTOR** (Gr) **47882 STAR UNITED** (Pa) ex STAR NESTOR, 1980 **47883 RATNA VANDANA** (In) ex STAR LILY 1977 **47884 IRON KERRY** (Br) ex STAR KERRY 1975 **47885 IRON KESTREL** (Br) ex STAR KESTREL 1975.

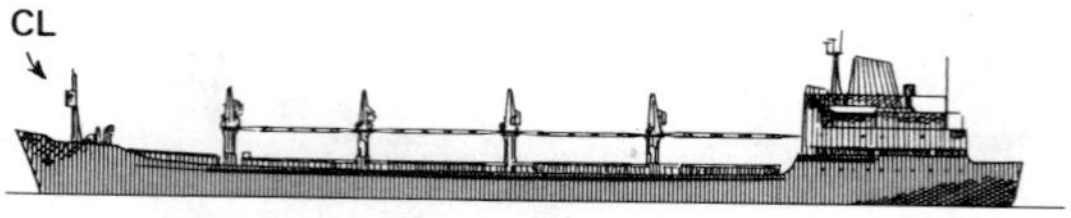

KC_4MFK H13
47890 NORITA. No/Br 1970; B; 12600; 158.53 × 9.51 (520.11 × 31.2); M; 15; ex INGEREN 1979.

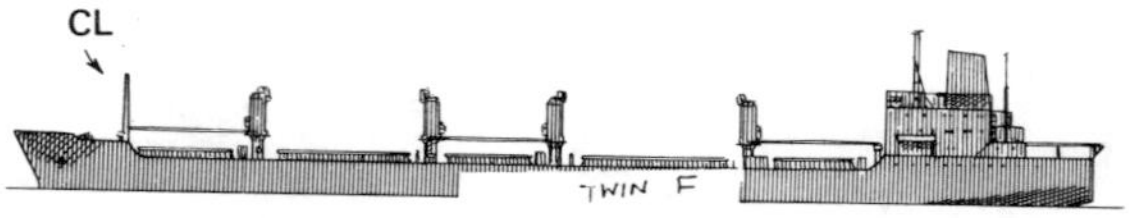

47900 PAGNET. Li/FRG 1976; C; 14600; 171.41 × 10.45 (562.37 × 34.28); M; 16.25; ex PAGNOL 1980 **'Key 26'** type Sister: **47901 RAIMOL** (Li) ex RAIMU 1980.

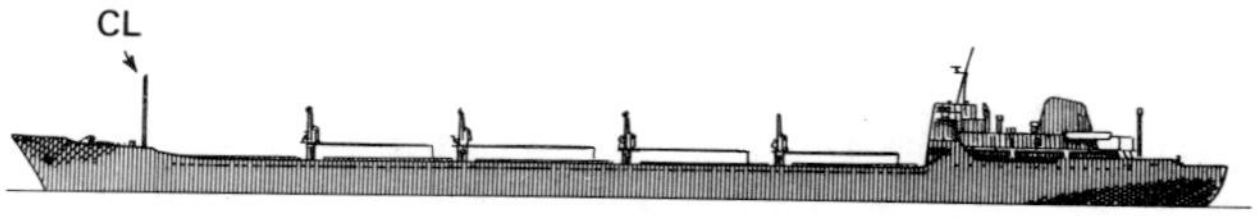

KC_4MFK H13
47910 NAI CAROLINA. It/It 1963; B; 17200; 192.03 × 10.59 (630 × 34.74); M; 15.5; ex CAROLINA LOLLI-GHETTI 1974; ex LERICI SECONDA 1969. Similar: ⋆**47911 GUI HAI** (RC) ex ADRIATIC SEA 1976; ex ANGELO SCINICARIELLO 1973.

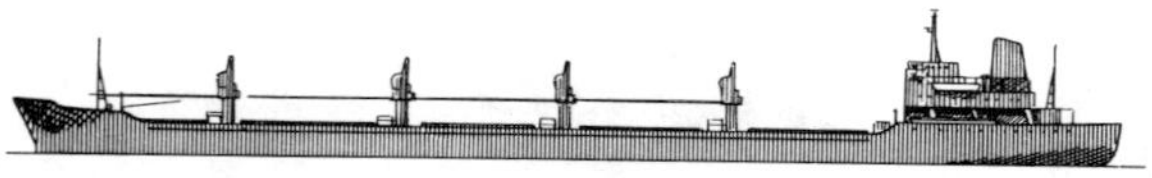

KC_4MFK H13
47920 RIO PLATA. Gr/Ja 1970; B; 13900; 174.5 × 9.92 (572.5 × 32.54); M; 14.75; ex OCEAN NAVIGATOR; ex COSMOS FOMALHAUT 1979. Sisters (Li flag): **47921 ASIA HAWK 47922 ASIA SWALLOW.**

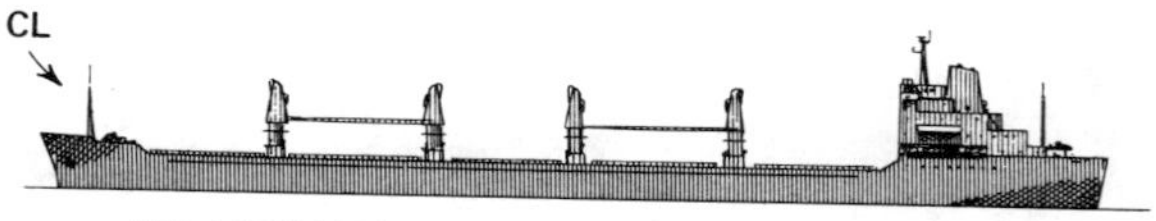

KC_4MFK H13
● **47930 FLORA C.** Gr/Ja 1978; B; 15400; 169 × 9.72 (556.43 × 31.89); M; 16. Sisters (Gr flag): **47931 JOHN C 47932 SOPHIE C** Possible Sisters: **47933 DESERT PRINCE 47934 DESERT QUEEN.**

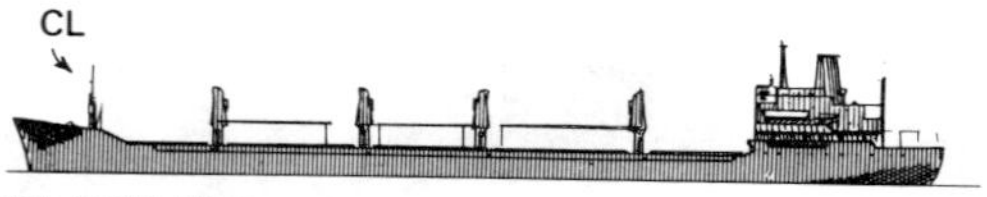

KC_4MFK H13
47940 TURGUT GUNERI. Tu/Sw 1969; B; 9900; 147.55 × 8.94 (484.09 × 29.33); M; 15; ex GARDEN SUN 1977; ex GERVALLA 1973.

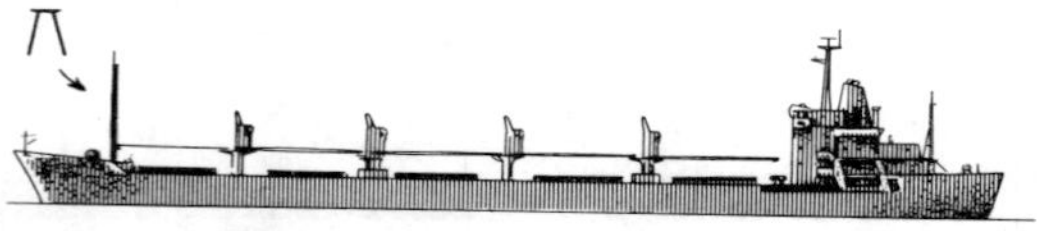

KC_4MFK H13
47950 MOUNT ATHOS. Gr/Ja 1977; B; 12500; 155.71 × 9.9 (510.86 × 32.48); M; 17.5; ex SACHSENHAUSEN 1978. Sisters (Gr flag): **47951 GOLDEN TRADER 47952 GOLDEN CHALLENGER 47953 GOLDEN POLYDINAMOS 47954 ALKMAN** ex GOLDEN POLYKLEITOS.

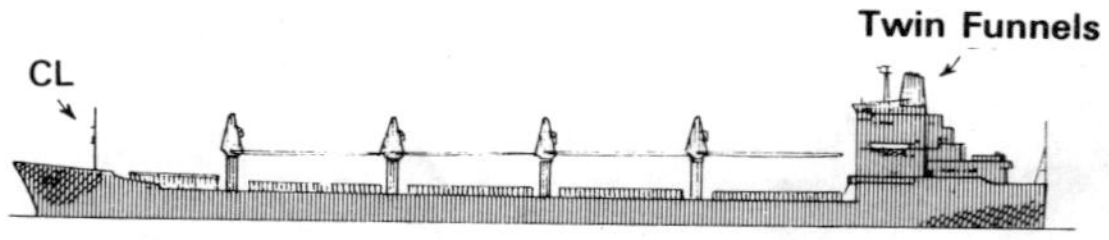

KC_4MFK H13
● **47960 HAE YUNG EASTERN.** Ko/No 1970; B; 14500; 162.87 × 10.42 (534.35 × 34.18); M; —; ex BARON ARDOSSAN 1981. Sisters: **47961 BARON WEMYSS** (Br) **47962 CAPE HAWK** (Br) **47963 HAE YUNG GOLD** (Ko) ex CAPE GRAFTON 1980 **47964 CAPE GRENVILLE** (Br) **47965 CAPE HORN** (Br) **47966 CAPE ANTIBES** (Gr) ex TEMPLE INN 1979 **47967 SNELAND** (No) **47968 KATERINA E** (Gr) ex WESTOCEAN 1980; ex VESTLAND Similar (lengthened to 188m & may have an extra crane): **47969 FEDERAL ST. CLAIR** (Li) ex BARON INCHCAPE 1977.

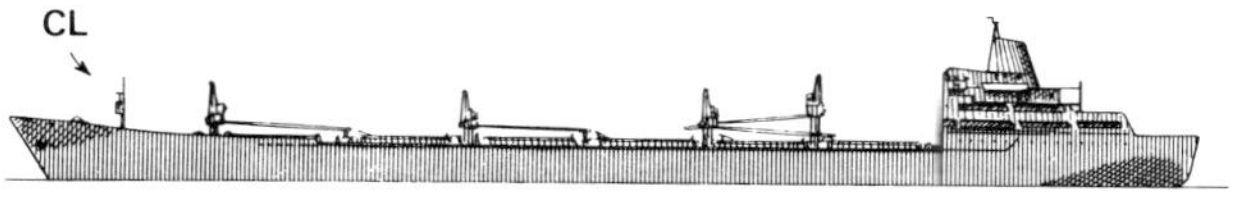

KC_4MFK H13
47980 AL TAMMAR. Li/No 1964; B; 17200; 186.82 × 11.22 (612.93 × 36.81); M; 14; ex WESTBULK 1980.

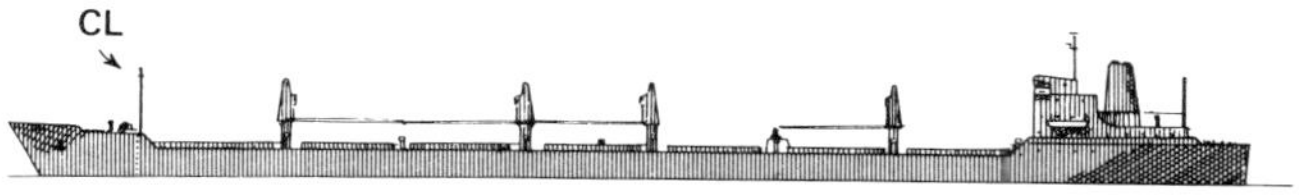

KC_4MFK H13
47990 GALEA. Sp/Sp 1974; B; 19900; 196.02 × 11.15 (643.1 × 36.58); M; 15. Possible Sister (may be gearless) **47991 RIVIERA** (Li) ex FADURA.

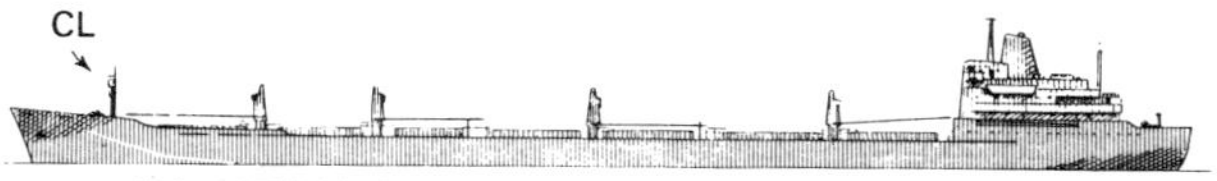

KC_4MFK H13
48000 WAH SHUN. Li/No 1966; B; 18200; 187.o3 × 11.26 (613.62 × 36.9); M; 16.5; ex ITEL VOLANS 1980; ex AMAX TRADER 1976; ex SKAUSUND 1974. Sister (may have 7 cranes): ⋆**48001 WEI HAI** (RC) ex FRUEN 1973; ex LYSLAND 1970.

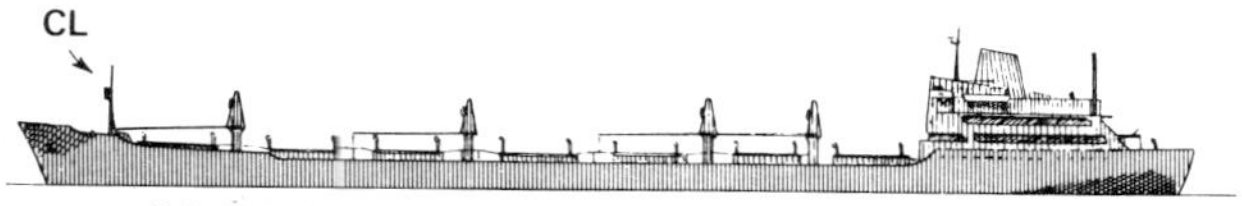

KC_4MFK H13
⋆**48010 LING LONG HAI.** RC/No 1963; B; 18800; 185.66 × 11.2 (609.12 × 36.75); M; 14.5; ex NORBU.

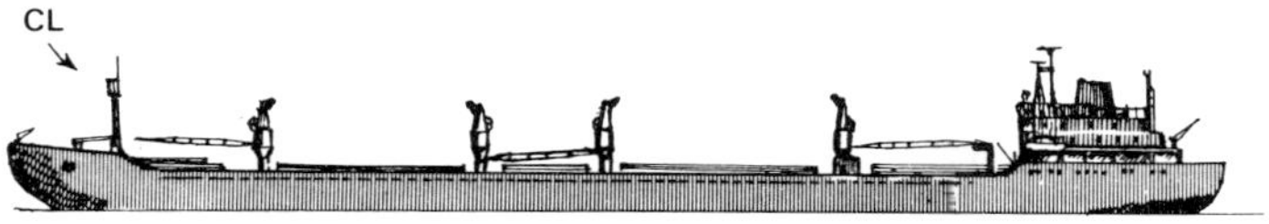

KC_4MFK H13
48020 ARCTIC. Ca/Ca 1978; B/IB 19400; 209.51 × 10.97 (687.37 × 35.99); M; 15.5.

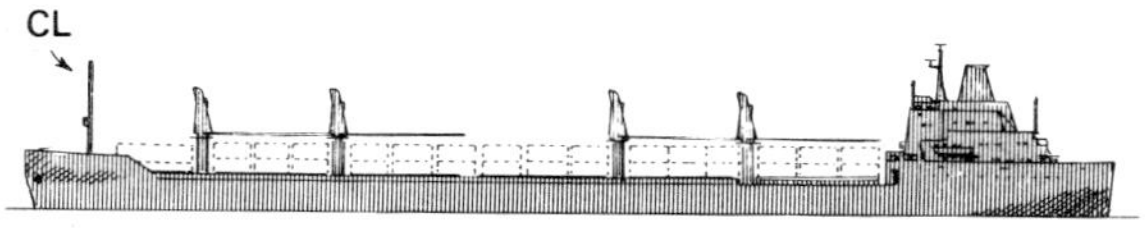

KC_4MFK H13
48030 ANDROS. Br/Sw 1968; C/Con; 17400; 172.22 × 9.9 (565.03 × 32.48); M; 16; ex FERMLAND 1975; converted from bulk carrier 1975.

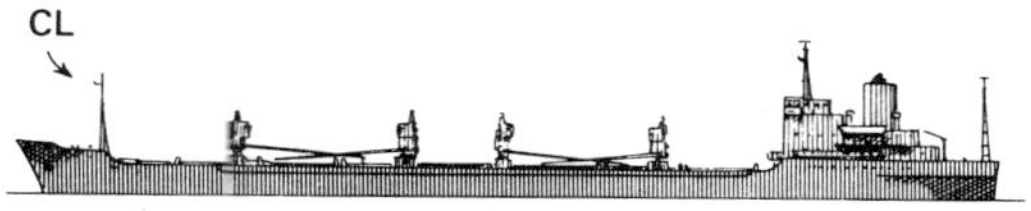

KC_4MFK H13
48040 ASIA MORALITY. Li/Ja 1971; B; 10400; 155.48 × 9.9 (510.1 × 32.48); M; 15.25. Sisters (Li flag): **48041 ASIA FLAMINGO 48042 ASIA GOLD 48043 ASIA LOYALTY.**

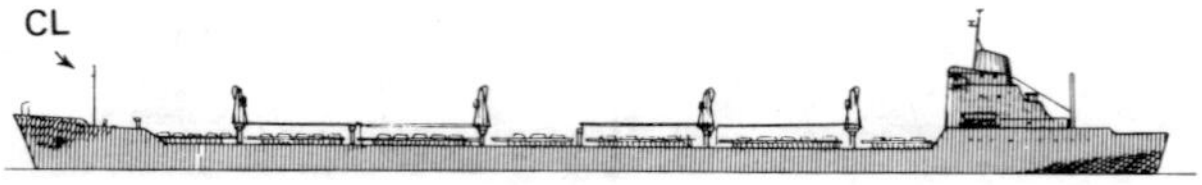

KC_4MFK H13
● **48050 JAG SHAKTI.** In/Sp 1972; B; 15500; 182.84 × 10.55 (599.88 × 34.61); M; 15.5; ex CUNARD CARAVEL 1974. **'Euskalduna 27'** type. Sisters: **48051 JAG SHANTI** In) ex CUNARD CAMPAIGNER 1974 **48052 AENEAS** (Br) ex CUNARD CARRIER 1978 **48053 CHIEFTAIN** (Pa) ex CUNARD CHIEFTAIN 1978 **48054 EL CHAMPION** (Pi) ex CUNARD CHAMPION 1978 **48055 IONIAN CARRIER** (Gr) ex CUNARD CALAMANDA 1978 **48056 OLYMPIC HISTORY** (Gr) ex CUNARD CARRONADE 1978 **48057 OLYMPIC HARMONY** (Li) ex CUNARD CAVALIER 1978 Similar: **48058 COBETAS** (Sp) Possibly Similar: **48059 DEUSTO** (Sp) **48060 LAURENTINE** (Fr) **48061 PENMEN** (Fr).

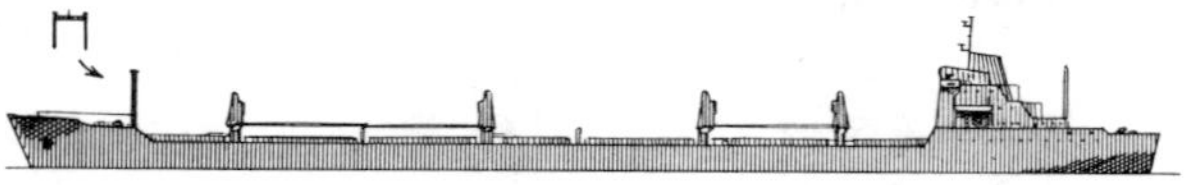

KC_4MFK H13
48070 BANDERAS. Sp/Sp 1970; B; 15600; 183.12 × 10.51 (600.79 × 34.48); M; 14. Sister: **48071 LEKEITIO** (Sp).

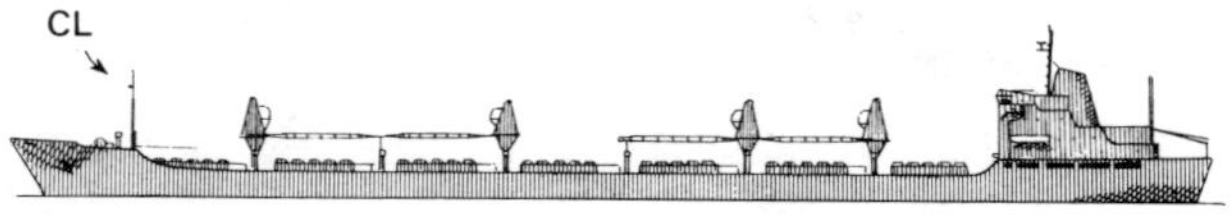

KC_4MFK H13
48080 KARA. Fi/Sp 1977; B; 17000; 181.11 × 10.65 (594.19 × 34.94); M; 15$ Sisters (Fi flag): **48081 KELO 48082 PAMELA 48083 PETER 48084 PUHOS** Similar (larger): **48085 ALTANO 48086 CALDERETA 48087 FINNBEAVER** ex PASSAD 1978; ex MATAI 1978 **48088 FINNFURY** ex MONSON 1978; ex FORANO 1978 **48089 PAMINA** ex KAUKO **48090 LITA 48091 NAN FUNG 48092 PAMPERO 48093 PATRICIA** (Pa flag): **48094 VITALITY** ex LEVANTE.

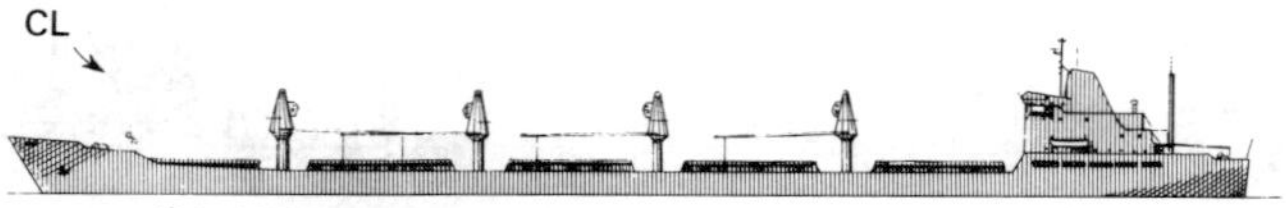

KC_4MFK H13
● **48100 CORDIALITY.** Pa/Sp 1979; B; 19800; 197.6 × 11.11 (648.3 × 36.45); M; 15.1 ex ANGELA PANDO 1980. Sister: **48101 MARCOPLATA** (Sp) Possible Sister: **48102 SOKORRI** (Sp).

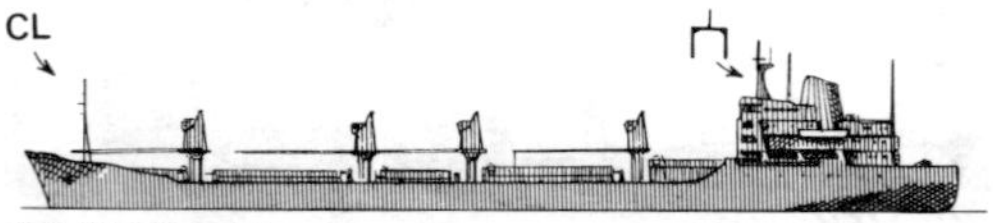

KC_4MFK H13
48110 CLYMENIA. Fr/Ja 1968; B; 10700; 147.5 × 9.09 (483.93 × 29.82); M; 16.5; **'Sanoyasu 16BC5'** type Sister: **48111 PETRAIA** (Fr).

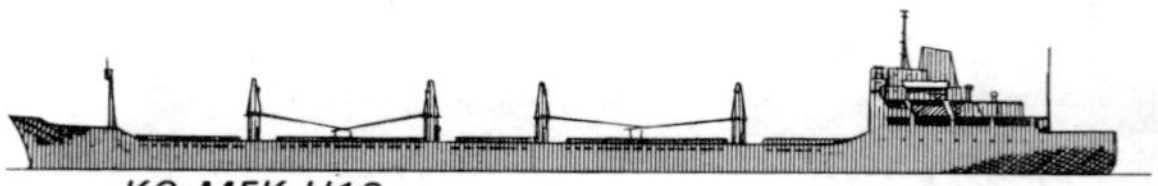

KC_4MFK H13
48120 GLYFADA SUN. Gr/Ja 1965; C; 16400; 175.98 × 10.31 (577.36 × 33.83); M; 16.75; ex STAR TARO 1980.

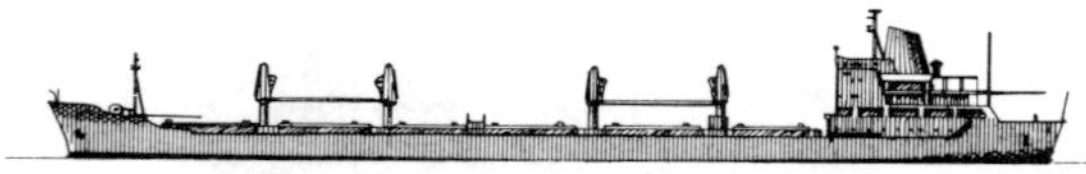

KC_4MFK H13
48130 ANTIGONI. Gr/No 1968; B; 13600; 160.86 × 9.78 (527.76 × 32.00); M; 15.5; ex STIRLING RANGE; ex BARON CAWDOR 1975.

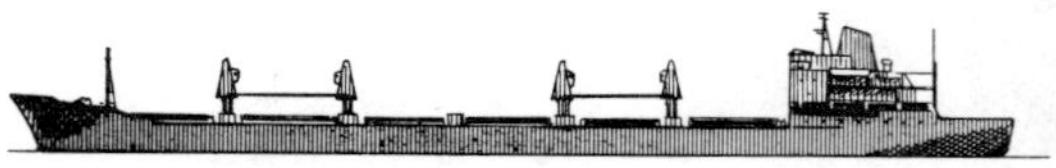

KC_4MFK H13
48140 CAPTAIN NICOLAS. Gr/No 1968; B; 13600; 160.86 × 9.78 (527.76 × 32.09); M; 16; ex CAPE SABLE 1978. Sister: **48141 CHANDA** (In) ex CAPE WRATH 1976.

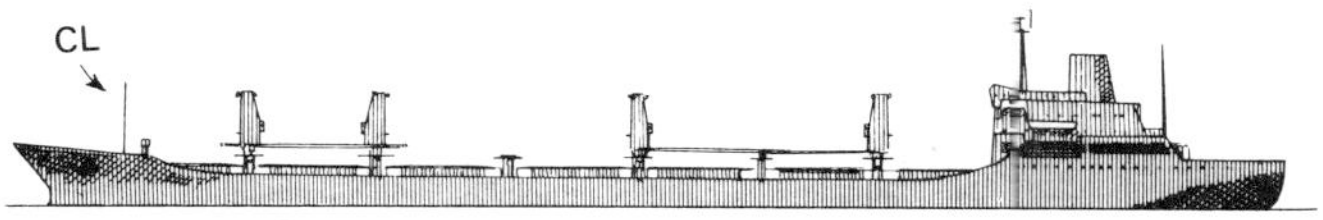

KC_4MFK H13

● **48150 ARIETTA GREGOS.** Gr/Br 1973; B; 23700; 201.3 × 11.23 (660.43 × 36.84); M; 15; ex TROPWIND. Sister: **48151 KARIN VATIS** (Gr) ex TROPWAVE Similar (different type of cranes): **48152 AMSTELVLIET** (Ne) **48153 AMSTELVAART** (Ne) **48154 AMSTELVOORN** (Ne).

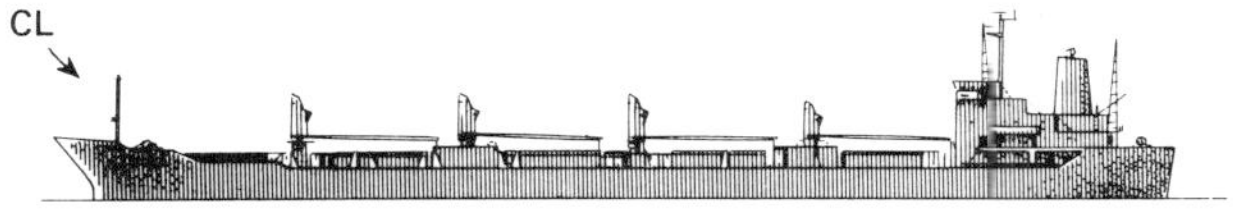

KC_4MFK H13

48160 TOSHU MARU. Ja/Ja 1976; BC; 20200; 178.87 × 11.12 (586.84 × 36.48); M; 15.5.

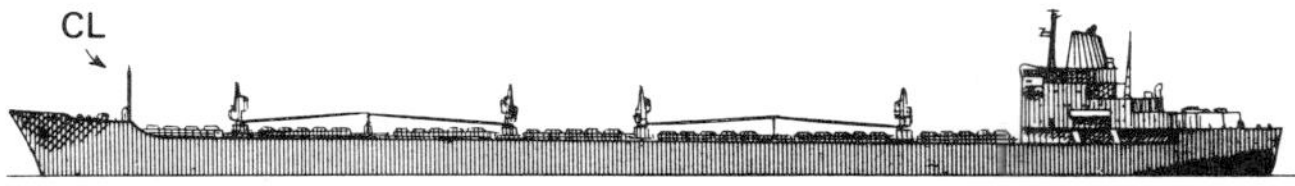

KC_4MFK H13

48170 AQUACHARM. Li/Ja 1968; B; 25200; 202.72 × 12.27 (665.09 × 40.26); M; 15.5. Similar: **48171 AQUAFAITH** (Li) **48172 AQUAGLORY** (Li) **48173 AQUAGRACE** (Li) **48174 AQUAJOY** (Li) **48175 CARRAS** (Gr) **48176 M.G. TSANGARIS** (Gr) Possibly Similar (may not have cranes) **48177 AQUAGEM** (Li) **48178 LUCENDRO** (Li) ex AQUABELLE.

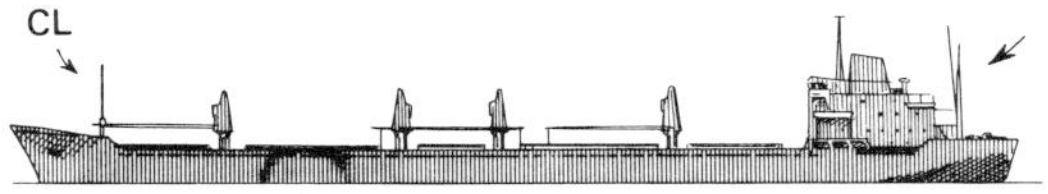

KC_4MFK H13

● **48180 AEGIS MAJESTIC.** Gr/Sp 1974; C; 12500; 159.01 × 9.77 (521.68 × 32,05); M; —; **'SANTA FE 77'** type. Sisters (Gr flag): **48181 AEGIS ATHENIC 48182 AEGIS ATOMIC 48183 AEGIS BALTIC 48184 AEGIS BRITANNIC 48185 AEGIS COSMIC 48186 AEGIS DORIC 48187 AEGIS DYNAMIC 48188 AEGIS HARMONIC 48189 AEGIS HISPANIC 48190 AEGIS IONIC 48191 AEGIS LOGIC 48192 AEGIS LYRIC 48193 AEGIS MAGIC 48194 AEGIS MYSTIC 48195 AEGIS PRACTIC 48196 AEGIS SONIC 48197 AEGIS TOPIC.**

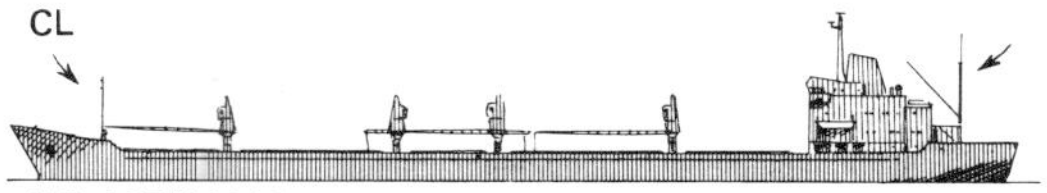

KC_4MFK H13

48200 KAVO MATAPAS. Gr/Sp 1977; C; 8700/12700; 159.01 × —/9.77 (521.68 × —/32.05); M; 15.5; ex MISHREF; **'SANTA FE 77'** type. Sister: **48201 KAVO PEIRATIS** (Gr) ex JUMAIRAH 1978.

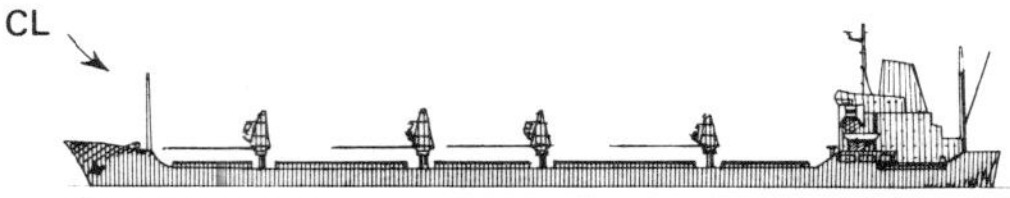

KC_4MFK H13

⋆**48210 PINA DEL AGUA;** Cu/Sp 1977; C; 9500 approx.; 148.06 × 8.96 (485.76 × 29.4); M; 15.5; ex ANGEL PEREZ; **'CARTAGO'** class. Probable Sisters: **48211 ELENA PEREZ** (Sp) ⋆**48212 LAS COLORADAS** (Cu) ex ALVARO PEREZ 1979 ⋆**48213 PALMA MOCHA** (Cu) ex RAMON PEREZ 1980 ⋆**48214 ALEGRIA DE PIO** (Cu) ex GABRIEL PEREZ 1980 **48215 ALVARO PEREZ** (Sp).

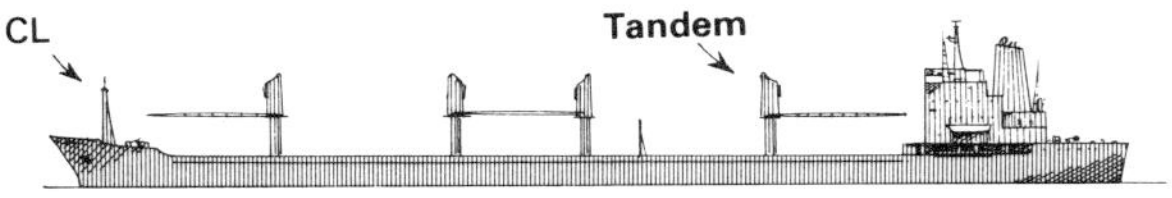

KC_4MFK H13

● **48220 MING SPRING.** Tw/Tw 1978; C; 18600; 172.02 × 10.6 (564.37 × 34.78); M; 17. Sisters (Tw flag): **48221 MING SUMMER 48222 MING AUTUMN 48223 MING WINTER.**

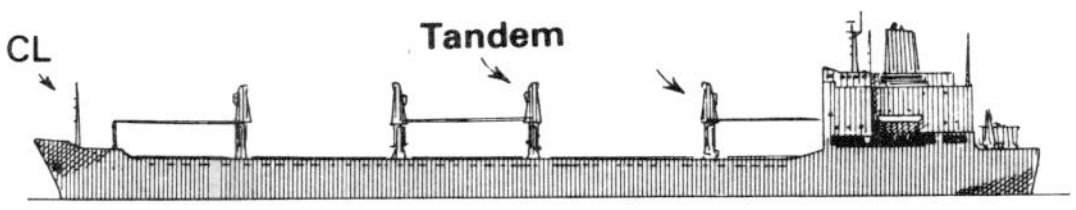

KC_4MFK H13

48230 SONGKHLA. De/Ja 1977; B/Con; 16100; 158.02 × 10.59 (518.44 × 34.74); M; 16.25. Sister: **48231 SUMBAWA** (De).

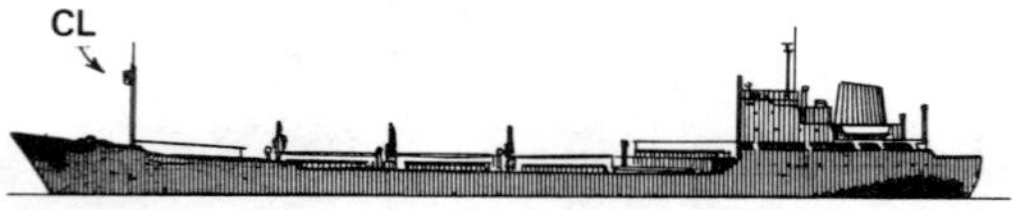

KC_4MFK H13
48240 ARGOLICOS GULF; Gr/FRG 1960; B; 9900; 153.8 × 9.4 (504.6 × 30.84); M; 14; ex FARO 1974; KP against bridge front possibly removed and crane added. Sister: **48241 MIA** (Pa) ex OCEAN GOLD 1980; ex BALTO 1974.

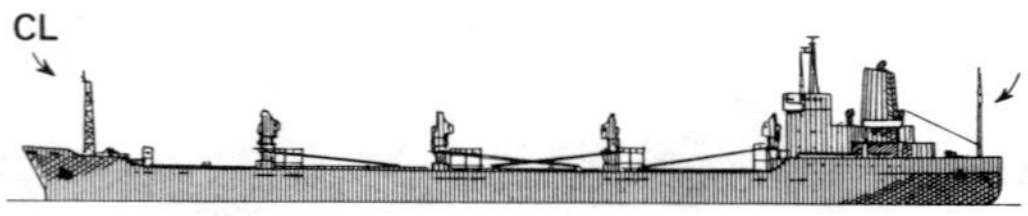

KC_4MFK H13
48270 KOREAN PEARL; Pa/Ja 1970; B; 11800; 155.05 × 9.14 (508.7 × 29.99); M; 14.75; ex WOKO MARU 1975.

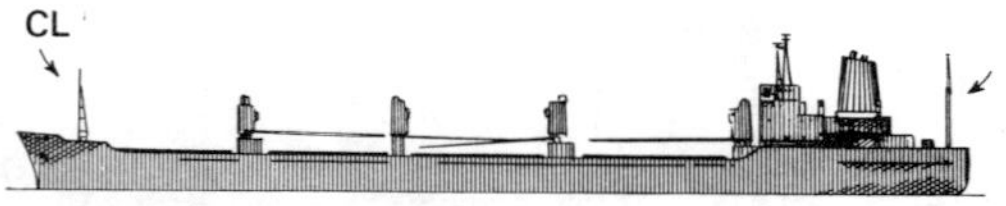

KC_4MFK H13
48290 INACHUS STAR; Li/Ja 1972; B; 11000; 150.12 × 9.73 (492.52 × 31.92); M; 14.5; ex AMAZON MARU 1975.

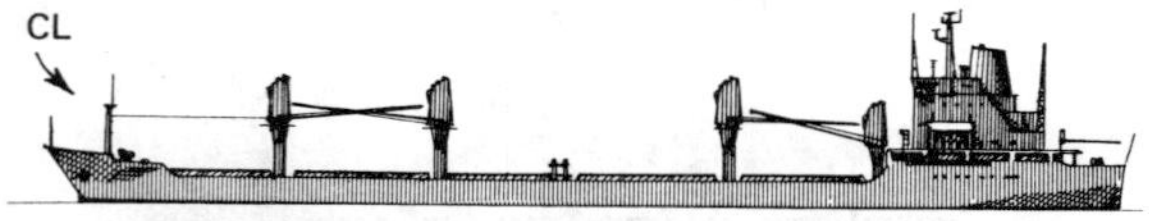

KC_4MFK H13
● **48300 WELLPARK;** Br/Ja 1977; B; 18622; 170.01 × 10.21 (557.77 × 33.5); M; 15.5. Sisters (Br flag): **48301 STAR BAY** (Br) ex CLARKSPEY 1978 **48302 TRONGATE.**

KC_4MFK H13
● **48320 AYESHA;** Cy/Fr 1962; B; 14600; 178.06 × 9.49 (584.19 × 31.14); M; 14.5; ex MARIVERDA; ex SOPHIA COLOCOTRONI 1978; ex HOEGH TRAVELLER 1967. Possible Sister: **48321 ARETHOUSA** (Li) ex MOORDRECHT 1978; ex FRUEN 1969; ex HOEGH TRANSPORTER 1965; (may have only 2 cranes).

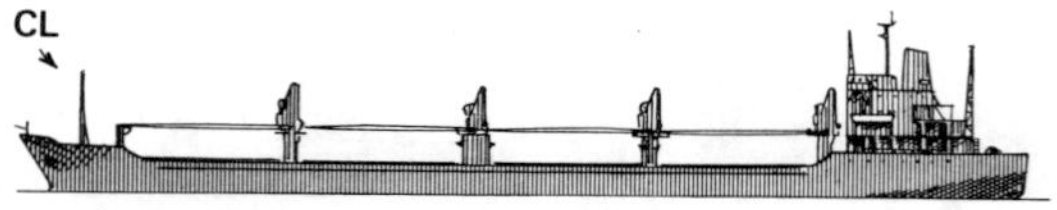

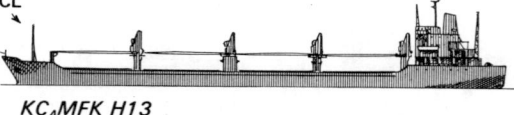

KC_4MFK H13
48250 SEIYEI MARU; Ja/Ja 1977; B; 14300; 160.03 × 9.92 (525.03 × 32.55); M; 14.5.

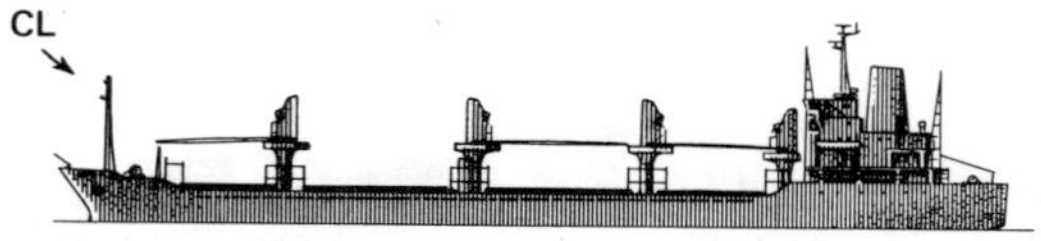

KC_4MFK H13
48260 ANDRE DELMAS; Fr/Ja 1976; B; 14600; 156.01 × 10.35; (511.84 × 33.96); M; 15.5. Probable Sister (may have kingposts): **48261 LUCIEN DELMAS** (Fr).

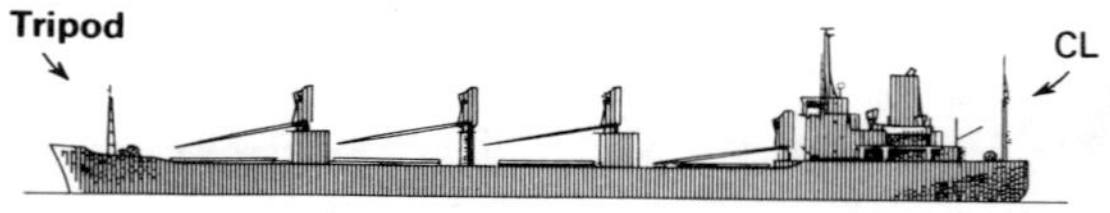

KC_4MFK H13
48280 KINKO MARU; Ja/Ja 1970; B; 12300; 155.1 × 9.19; (508.86 × 30.15); M; 14.75. Probable Sisters: **48281 KANESHIZU MARU** (Ja) **48282 KIKUKO MARU** (Ja) **48283 ELEUROPA** (Gr) ex KANEKIYO MARU 1973.

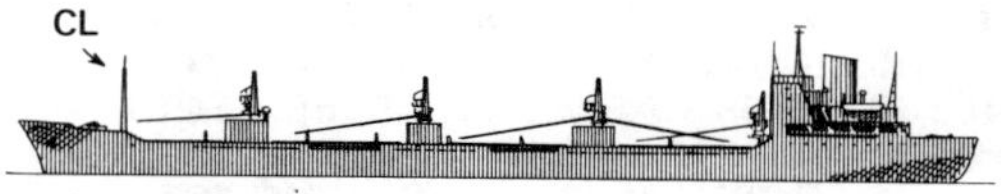

KC_4MFK H13
48310 ALMAZ; Gr/Ja 1965; C/V; 10500; 152.25 × 8.99 (499.51 × 29.5); M; 14.25; ex YUKONA 1981; ex NISSAN No 1 1979; ex OPPAMA 1974. Similar: **48311 BLUEBIRD** (Ja) **48312 EUROTRANSPORT** (Gr) ex HO SHIN 1977; ex ZAMA MARU 1975.

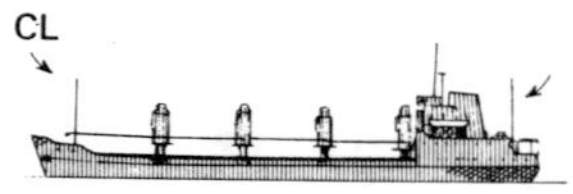

KC_4MFK H13
48330 MALDIVE SWIFT; Mv/Au 1961; C; 2000; 78.42 × 4.97 (257.28 × 16.31); M; 11; ex WILLIAM HOLYMAN 1976.

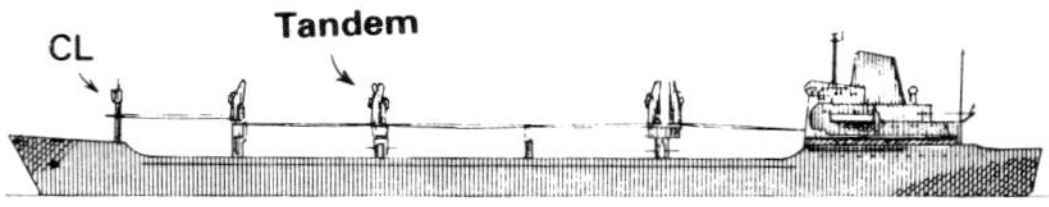

KC_4MFK H13
48340 KASSANDRA; Pa/FRG 1969; B; 14300; 163.56 × 10.03 (536.61 × 32.91); M; 16; ex TELLUS 1980; ex EVAMO 1978. Sisters (No flag): **48341 DICTO 48342 SPERO.**

KC_4MFK H13
48350 SIAM VENTURE; Li/Ja 1972; B; 7300; 130 × 8.3 (426.51 × 27.23); M; 14.

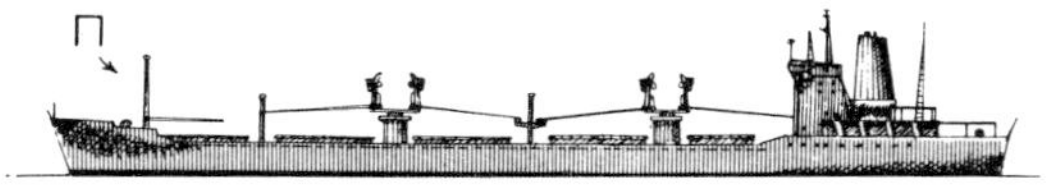

KC_4MFK H13
48360 JAMAICA FAREWELL; Li/Ja 1975; C; 13500; 161.6 × 9.93 (530.18 × 32.58); M; 15.5; **'HITACHI UT-20'** type. Sister: **48361 MARI BOEING** (Li).

KC_4MFK H13
● **48370 CORRIENTES II;** Ar/Sp 1977; C; 12600; 159.01 × 9.76 (521.69 × 32.02); M; 16; **'SANTA FE 77'** type. Sisters (Ar flag): **48371 CHACO 48372 ENTRE RIOS II 48373 FORMOSA 48374 RIO NEGRO II 48375 SANTA CRUZ II 48376 TIERRA DEL FUEGO II 48377 MISIONES II.**

KC_4MFKC H13
48380 PENTA; Li/Ja 1969; R; 5000; 135 × 7.1 (443 × 23.2); M; 17; ex AOTEAROA 1972.

●
48383

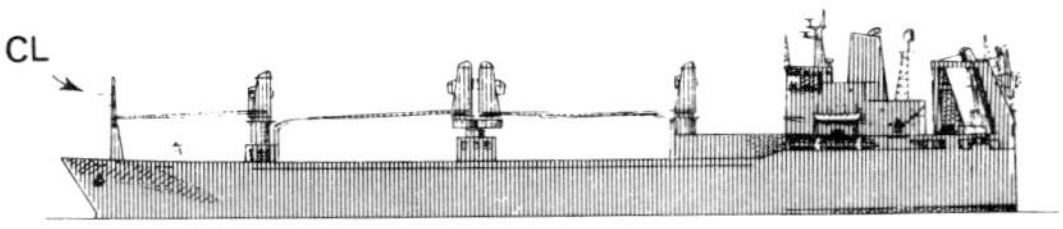

KC_4MFKR H3
48390 SEKI ROKAKO; Ja/Ja 1979; Con/RoC; 17400; 152 × 9.08 (498.7 × 29.79); M; 17; Quarter ramp. Sister: **48391 SEKI ROKEL** (Ja).

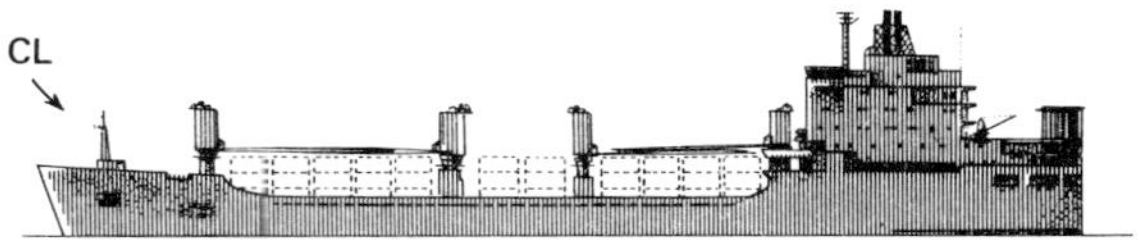

KC_4MFR H13
48400 DEGAS; Fr/Fr 1977; RoC/Con; 13900; 163.79 × 10.74 (537.36 × 35.23); M; 20.75; Stern door/ramp. Sisters (Fr flag): **48401 CEZANNE 48402 RENOIR 48403 MONET 48404 GAUGUIN 48405 UTRILLO.**

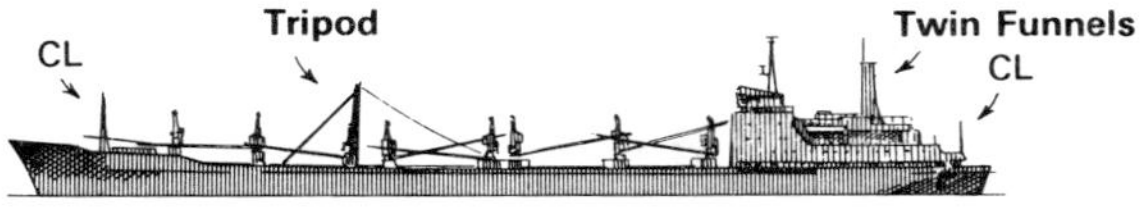

KC_3KC_5MFK H1
⋆**48410 PULAWY;** Pd/Sw 1966; C; 7300/10700; 156.17 × 8.36/9.52 (512.37 × 27.43/31.23); M; 19; ex WAITARA 1973; **'SCANDIA'** type. Sheerlegs are not permanent. Sister: **48411 HELLENIC SEAMAN** (Gr) ex KILLARA 1975.

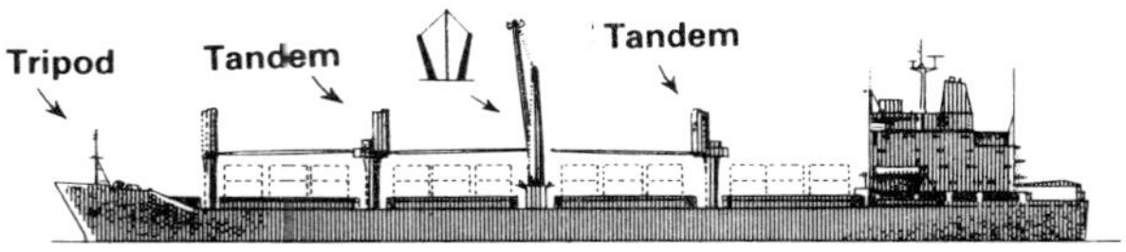

KC_3KC_2MF H1
● **48420 VILLE D'ANVERS;** Fr/No 1977; C; 16500; 171.41 × 10.55 (562.37 × 34.61); M; 17.5. Sisters: **48421 VILLE DE BORDEAUX** (Fr) ex SEATRAIN WEST POINT 1979; ex VILLE DE BORDEAU **48422 NARA** (Fr) **48423 NAUSICAA** (Fr) **48424 CONCORDIA STAR** (No).

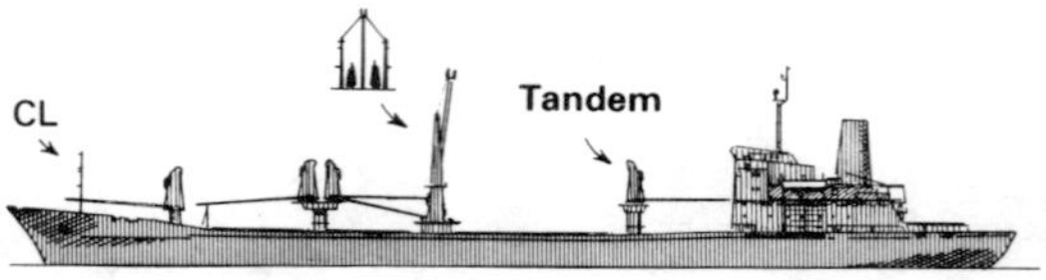

KC_3KCMF H1

● *48430 **IVAN ZAGUBANSKI**; Bu/Ru 1975; C; 11800; 162.31 × 9.17 (532.51 × 30.09); M; 18; **'DNEPR'** type. Sisters (Bu flag): ***48431 CHRISTO BOTEV *48432 GOTZE DELCHEV *48433 LUBEN KARAVELOV *48434 KAPITAN PETKO VOLVODA *48435 VASIL LEVSKY** (Ru flag): ***48436 GRIGORIY PETRENKO *48437 NIKITA MITCHENKO *48438 PETR DUTOV *48439 IVAN SHEPETKOV *48440 IVAN MOSKALENKO *48441 GEROI PANFILOVTSY *48442 VASILY KLOCHKOV *48443 NIKOLAY ANANYEV *48444 NIKOLAY MAKSIMOV *48445 PETR YEMTSOV *48446 YAKOV BONDARENKO *48447 SOVIETSKIYE PROFSOYUZY** (Ys flag): ***48448 ADMIRAL PURISIC *48449 HEROJ PAIC *48450 HEROJ KOSTA STAMENKOVIC *48451 HEROJ SENJANOVIC** (Rm flag): ***48452 ZALAU** (Cu flag): ***48453 JOSE ANTONIO ECHEVERRIA *48454 JULIO ANTONIO MELLA *48455 30 DE NOVIEMBRE *48456 XI FESTIVAL** (Br flag): **48457 LYCAON 48458 LAERTES** (FRG flag): **48459 SANTA ELENA.** (Hu flag) ***48460 VOROSMARTY**

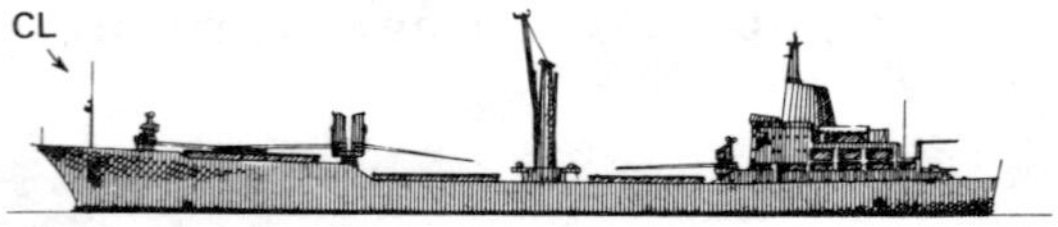

KC_3KCMF H13

48470 HALLA PILOT; Ko/Br 1970; C; 6700/10000; 154.13 × 8.17/9.62 (505.68 × 26.8/31.56); M; 17; ex STRATHCARROL; ex ASKA 1975. Sister: **48471 HALLA PRIDE** (Ko) ex STRATHCARRON; ex AMRA 1976.

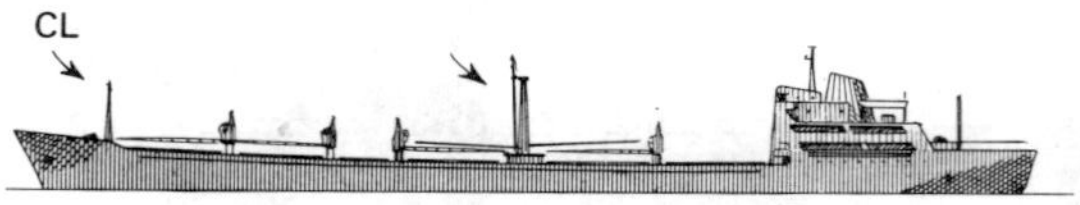

KC_3KCMFK H13

***48480 SINAIA;** Rm/Br 1966; C; 10800; 162.46 × 9.38 (533 × 30.77); M; 18.25. Sister: ***48481 PREDEAL.**

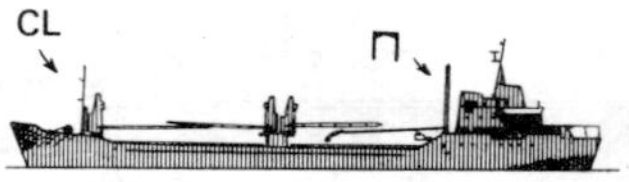

KC_3KMF H13

48490 ARGIRO; Cy/Br 1967; C; 1500; 93.88 × 5.08 (308 × 16.66); M; 13; ex ALDEBARAN II 1980; ex CITY OF ATHENS 1977; ex SALMO 1974. Sisters: **48491 GRACECHURCH** (Br) ex CITY OF SPARTA 1977; ex SORRENTO 1974 **48492 PYRGOS STAR** (Gr) ex CITY OF CORINTH 1978; ex SALERNO 1975 Similar: **48493 KOTA JADE** (Sg) ex CITY OF VALETTA; ex ATHENIAN.

KC_3KMF H13

● **48500 CAP PINEDE;** Fr/No 1957; C; 1500; 88.65 × 5.44 (290.85 × 17.85); M; —; ex BREDA 1975. Similar: **48501 RAY** (Pa) ex PERAMA 1976; ex VATNASUND 1972; ex BRABANT 1972.

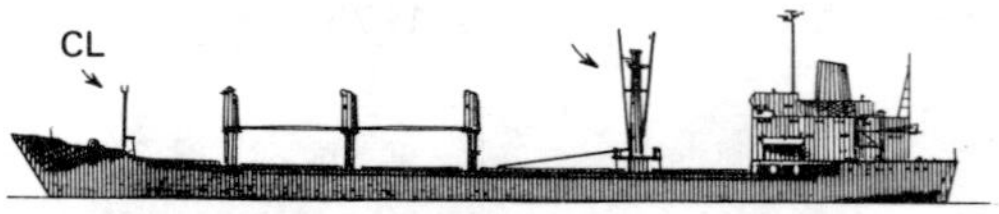

KC_3KMF/KC_3KMFK H13

● **48510 CITY OF WINCHESTER;** Br/FRG 1976; C; 7700/10800; 150.65 × 8.03/9.35 (494.26 × 26.35/30.68); M; 16; **'BREMEN PROGRESS'** type (Series A). Sisters (Br flag): **48512 CITY OF CANTERBURY 48513 CITY OF YORK.**

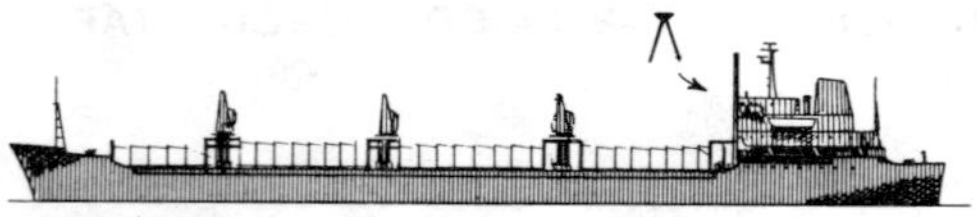

KC_3KMFK H13

48520 SHANTA ROHAN; In/Ja 1969; B; 10300; 148.37 × 8.98 (486.79 × 29.46); M; 15; ex FORT ST JOHN 1980; ex PACIFIC LOGGER 1977.

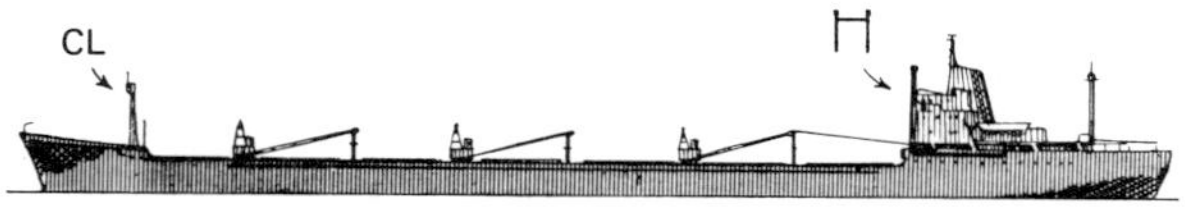

KC_3KMFK H13
48530 SARONIS; Gr/Be 1962; B; 13700; 182.96 × 10.08 (600.26 × 33.07); M; 15.5; ex GEORGIOS A 1981; ex PATIGNIES 1974.

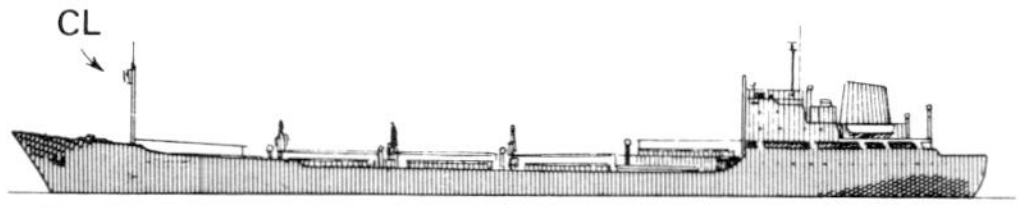

KC_3KMFK H13
48540 ARGOLICOS GULF; Gr/FRG 1960; B; 9900; 153.8 × 9.4 (504.6 × 30.84); M; 14; ex FARO 1974; KP against bridge front possibly removed & 4th crane added. Sister: **48541 MIA** (Pa) ex OCEAN GOLD 1980; ex BALTO 1974.

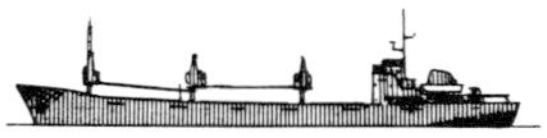

KC_3MF H
● **48550 SAN GEORGE;** Gr/No 1964; C; 800; 79.18 × 4.11 (259.78 × 13.48); M; 12.5; ex POTOS BEACH 1977; ex DOCTOR GEORGE 1976; ex SPAARNESTROOM 1975.

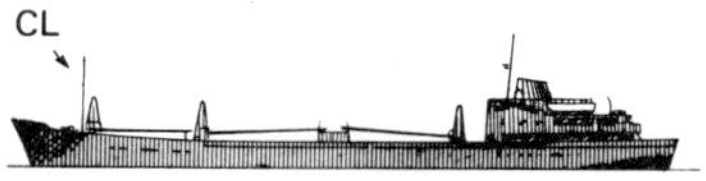

KC_3MF H
48560 INGA; Gr/Sw 1958; C; 2400/3900; 105.29 × 5.87/6.48 (345.44 × 19.26/21.26); M; 12.5.

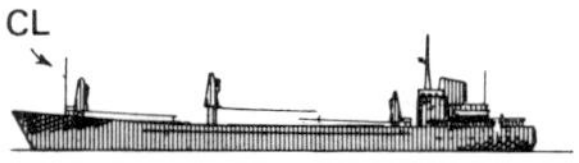

KC_3MF H
48570 GRIPEN; Sw/Sw 1964; C; 600; 83.55 × 3.67 (274.11 × 12.04); M; 12; ex ASPEN 1970.

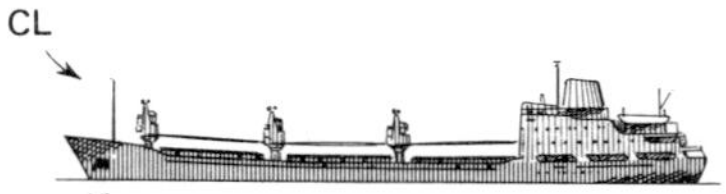

KC_3MF H1
48580 GELINDA; Pa/FRG 1960; C; 3600; 99.7 × 6.74 (327.1 × 22.11); M; 13.5; ex CARMENCITA 1980; ex FINNROSE 1974; ex LOVISA 1971; ex DAN 1968.

KC_3MF H1
48590 CHANTALA FORTUNE; Br/No 1967; C; 1400; 75.85 × 6.05 (248.85 × 19.85); M; 14; ex LORENA; ex LORENA HORN 1970.

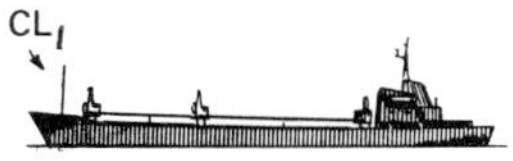

KC_3MF H1
48600 FLORA; FRG/FRG 1966; C; 800/1400; 73.34 × 4.01/5.38 (240.62 × 13.16/17.65); M; 12.5. Sisters: **48601 FAUNA** (Cy) **48602 FORTUNA I** (Cy) ex FORTUNA 1978 Similar: **48603 ARION** (FRG) **48604 ASTARTE** (It) **48605 REWI** (FRG) ex ACHILLES 1978.

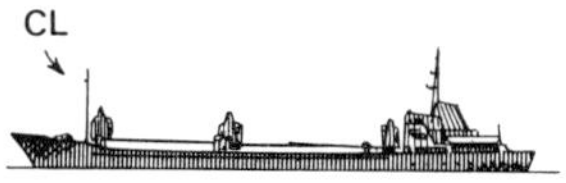

KC_3MF H1
48610 SAN REMO; Sp/Sp 1967; C; 1000/1600; 82.53 × 5.98/7.04 (270.76 × 19.62/23.09); M; 16.25.

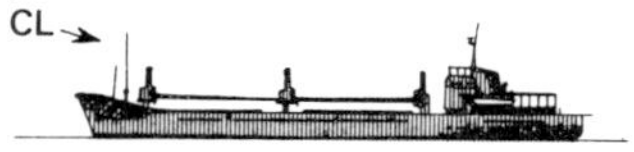

KC_3MF H1
***48620 USTRINE;** Ys/FRG 1960; C; 900/1600; 80.17 × —/5.64 (263.02 × —/18.5); M; 13; ex BALTIC SPRITE 1974.

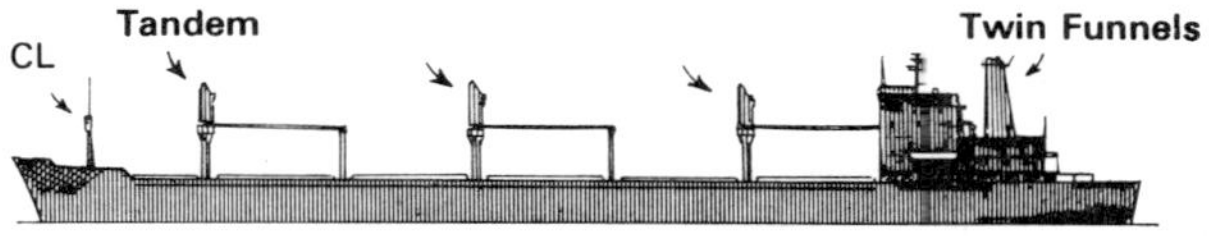

KC_3MF H1
● **48630 SILVERFJORD;** Br/Ys 1971; B; 20700; 179 × 11.09 (587.27 × 36.38); M; 16; ex JYTTE ENGHOLM 1973; ex SILVERFJORD 1971.

Sisters: **48631 BLUE MASTER** (No) **48632 TAURUS** (Fi) ex NORBETH 1978.

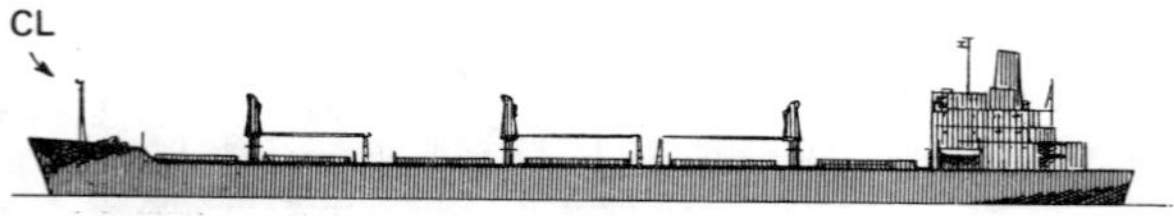

KC_3MF H1
48640 EURO PRINCESS; Li/Ne 1972; B; 15900; 175.5 × 10.25 (575.78 × 33.63); M; 15.75; ex PEGASUS 1976. Sister: **48641 DASHAKI** (Li) ex OCEAN CORACLE 1980; ex OCEAN COURAGE 1979; ex ANDROMED 1977; ex ANDROMEDA 1976.

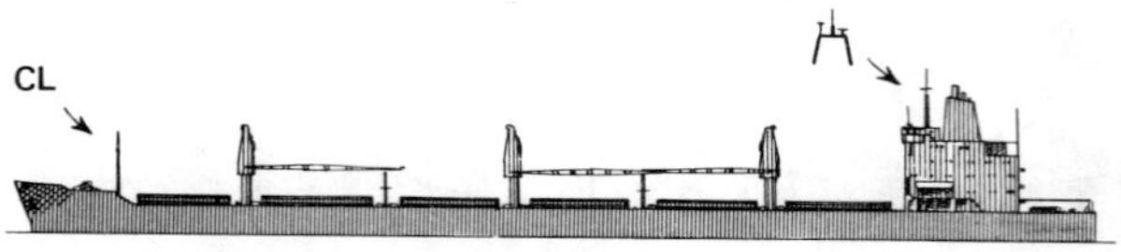

KC_3MF H1
48650 TORM HERDIS; De/De 1977; B; 25600; 182.99 × 11 (600.4 × 36.1); M; 15. Sisters (De flag): **48651 TORM HELVIG 48652 TORM HILDA 48653 TORM HELENE.**

KC_3MF H1
⋆48660 KOPALNIA GRZYBOW. Pd/Sp 1972; B; 9200; 145.01 × 8.36 (475.75 × 27.43); M; 16. Sister: **⋆48661 KOPALNIA MACHOW** (Pd).

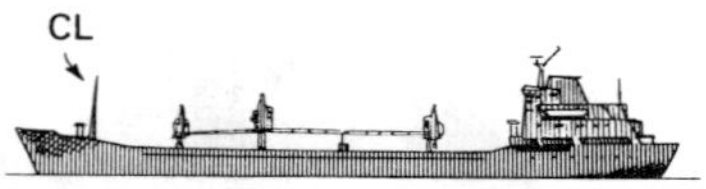

KC_3MF H1
48670 HOELIEN. Sg/Fi 1965; C; 2100/3300; 105.29 × 5.51/; ex CLIO 1980; ex NEFERTARI 1979; ex CLIO 1978; Lengthened 1970. Side doors. Sister: **48671 FENNIA** (Fi).

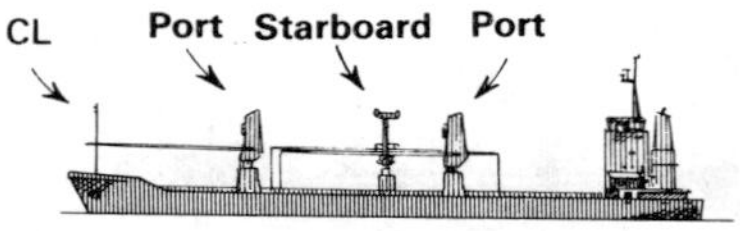

KC_3MF H1
48680 MARTINIQUE. FRG/FRG 1978; C; 1600/4000; 101.01 × /5.53 (328.12 × 18.14); M; 15; ex BLUE BELL 1980; ex CONTI BELGICA 1980.

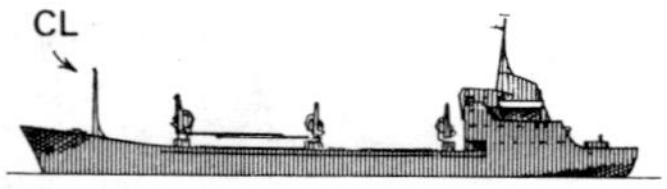

KC_3MF H1
● **48690 BALTIC VENTURE.** Br/Br 1965; C/V; 1800; 97.9 × 5.5 (321.2 × 18.05); M; 14; ex MELVILLE VENTURE 1981; ex BALTIC VENTURE 1980.

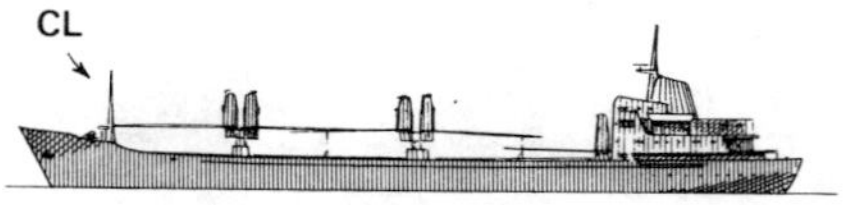

KC_3MF H1
48700 GALILA. Is/FRG 1967; C; 3000/4900; 123.4 × 6.45/7.59 (405 × 21.16/24.9); M; —; Launched as CINNAMON BAY.

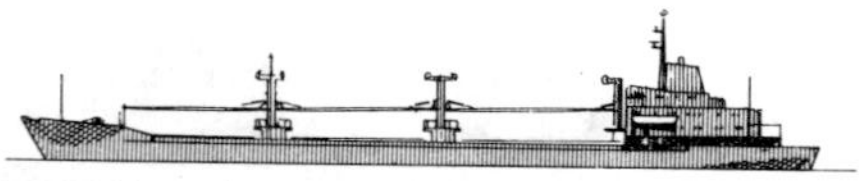

KC_3MF H1
● **48710 TOLMI.** Gr/FRG 1971; C; 2800/5000; 125.02 × 6.5/7.65 (410.17 × 21.52/25.1); M; 17; ex METTE BEWA 1976; ex CAP MATAPAN 1974. Sisters (Gr flag): **48711 TIMI** ex RIKKE BEWA 1976; ex CAP CARMEL 1974 **48712 CAPE ITEA** ex SAMOS ISLAND; ex CAP ANAMUR 1973.

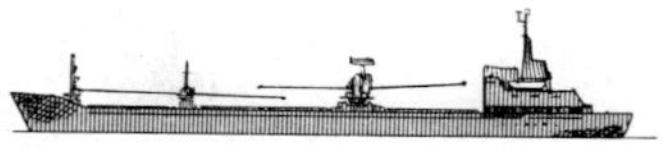

KC_3MF H123
● **48720 TONY'S LUCK.** Gr/FRG 1966; C; 1600; 85.81 × 5.12 (281.53 × 16.79); M; 12.5; ex ATEUS 1980; ex INGRID RETZLAFF 1974. Sister: **48721 ROSARITA** (Pa) ex NEW HOPE; ex ERICH RETZLAFF 1974.

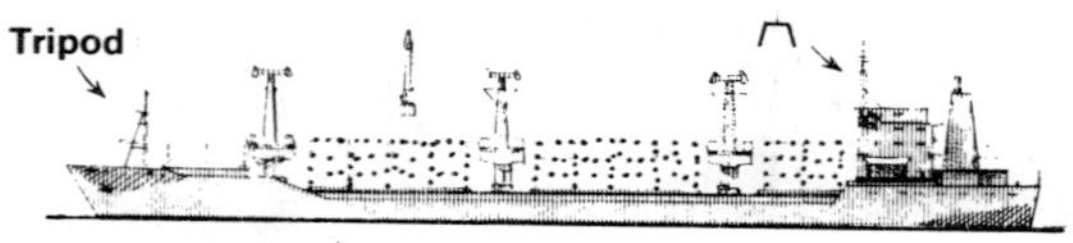

KC_3MF H13
● **48730 CAROL MERCUR.** FRG/FRG 1979; C/Con; 5800/9500; 154.05 × 8.14/7.16 (505.41 × 26.7/23.49); M; 17.5; ex SLOMAN MERCUR 1979; Cranes can rotate and are probably stowed in the position shown in the inset. Sister: **48731 SLOMAN MIRA** (FRG).

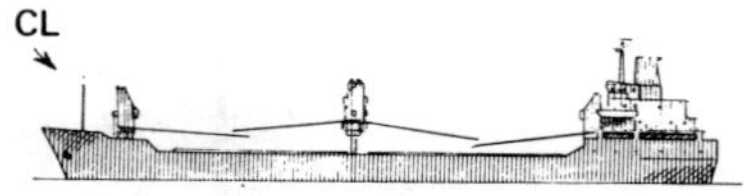

KC_3MF H13
48740 FINNMASTER. Fi/No 1972; C; 2100/4000; 106.61 × 5.47/7.08 (349.77 × 17.95/23.23); M; —.

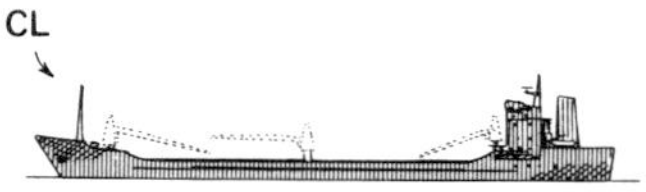

KC$_3$MF H13
48750 LESLIE GAULT. Br/Br 1977; C; 1600; 91.52 × 5.16 (300.26 × 16.93); M; 12.5; Deck cranes may be removed. Sisters (Br flag): **48751 CERINTHUS 48752 GALLIC FJORD 48753 MARKINCH.**

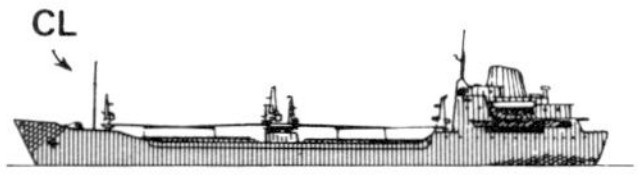

KC$_3$MF H13
48760 GERMAINE R.E. Fr/Sw 1961; C; 1600/2700; 93.81 × 5.07/5.76 (307.77 × 16.63/18.9); M; 13; ex GARM 1975. Similar: **48761 ATLAS** (Fi) ex GRIM 1969.

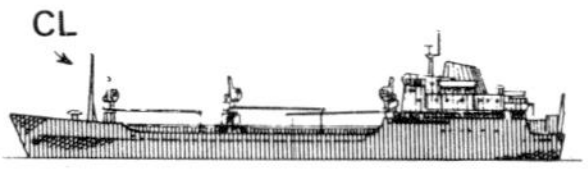

KC$_3$MF H13
⋆**48770 RISNJAK.** Ys/Fi 1967; RoC; 18800/3300; 100.01 × 5.56/6.22 (328.11 × 18.24/20.41); M; 15; ex BORE VI 1974; Stern door. Sister: **48771 AFROS** (Gr) ex BORE V 1977.

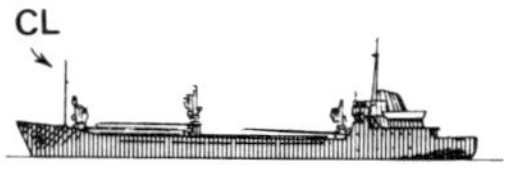

KC$_3$MF H13
48780 SUDURLAND. Ic/Fi 1964; C; 500/1100; 73.21 × 3.65/4.99 (240.19 × 11.97/16.39); M; 12; ex TAVI 1974. Probable Sister: **48781 LOKKY** (It) ex ELKAS 1979; ex NORMANNBAY 1977; ex LOKKI 1973.

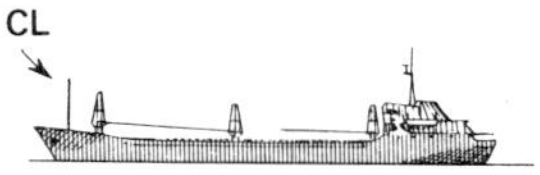

KC$_3$MF H13
48790 MOKSTEIN. No/FRG 1966; C; 500/1200; 73.61 × 3.6/5.25 (241.5 × 11.81/17.22); M; 12.5; ex HENRIETTE R. 1974.

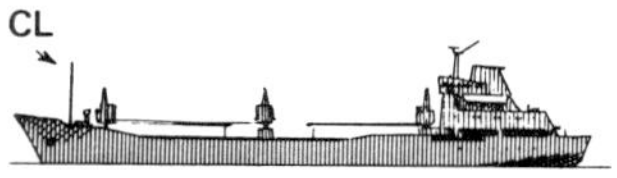

KC$_3$MF H13
48800 AURIGA. Gr/Fi 1967; C; 2800; 91.55 × 5.42/6.52 (300.36 × 17.78/21.39); M; 13.5.

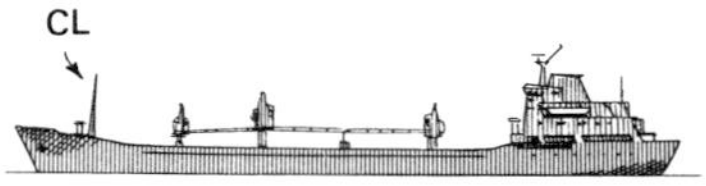

KC$_3$MF H13
48810 HOELIEN. Sg/Fi 1965; C; 2100/3300; 105.29 × 5.51/6.54 (345.44 × 18.08/21.46); M; 14.5; ex CLIO 1980; ex NEFERTARI 1979; ex CLIO 1978; Lengthened 1970; side doors. Sister: **48811 FENNIA** (Fi).

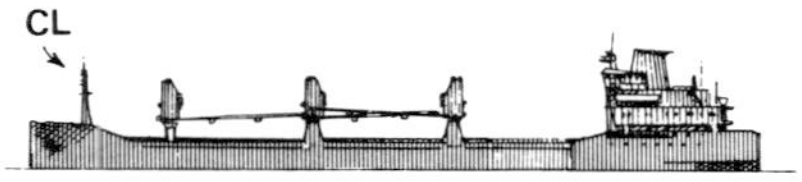

KC$_3$MF H13
● **48820 MARIA GORTHON.** Sw/Fi 1970; C; 3000/5600; 144.31 × 5.79/8.08 (375 × 18.99/28.47); M; 15; Lengthened 1975. Sisters: **48821 ADA GORTHON** (Sw) **48822 FEDERAL PIONEER** (Ca) ex CARL GORTHON 1980.

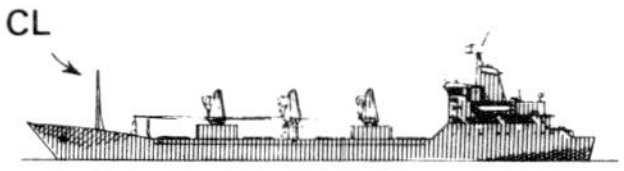

KC$_3$MF H13
48830 PUERTO CADIZ. Sp/Sp 1979; R; 1400; 90.4 × 5.11 (296.6 × 16.77); M; 14. Sisters (Sp flag): **48831 FERO CADIZ 48832 MAR CADIZ.**

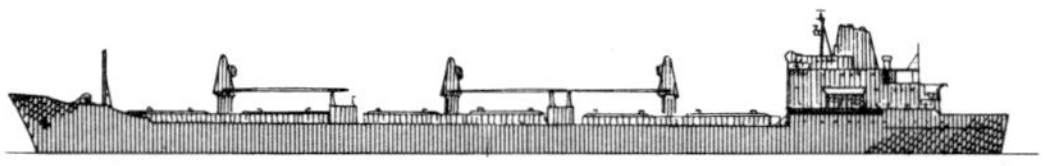

KC$_3$MF H13
48840 LEILA. Cy/No 1969; B; 13500; 160.86 × 9.97 (527.76 × 32.71); M; 15; ex SOLITAIRE 1978; ex TEMPLE ARCH 1977. Sister: **48841 BAYBRIDGE** (Li) ex FREEDOM A.S. 1980; ex CAPE YORK 1979.

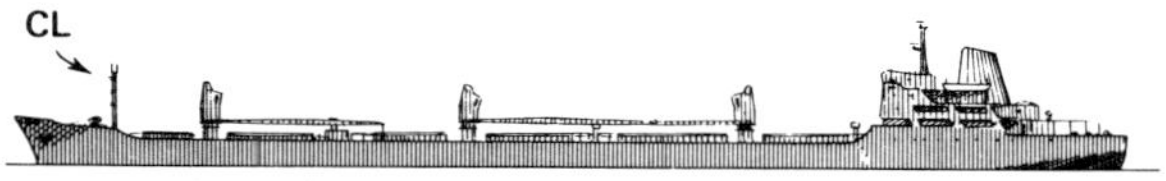

KC$_3$MF H13
48850 SANTISTA. Bz/Bz 1973; B; 13800; 176.41 × 10.08 (578.77 × 33.07); M; 14.5.

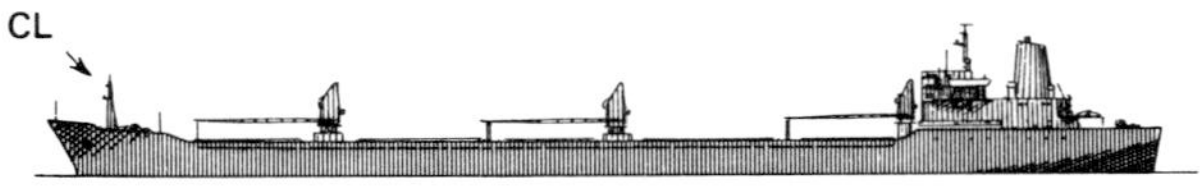

KC$_3$MF H13
48860 LAVINIA V. Li/Ja 1977; B; 15900; 178.21 × 10.92 (584.68 × 35.83); M; 15.5. Sisters (Li flag): **48861 FELICIA V 48862 PATRICIA V.**

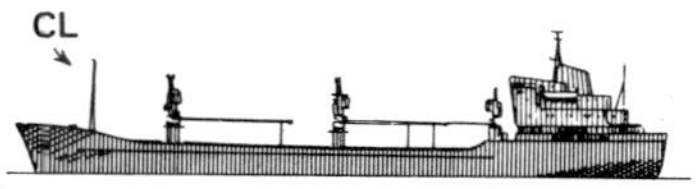

KC$_3$MF H13
48870 BALTIC VALIANT. Br/FRG 1970; RoC; 2100; 103.43 × 5.94 (339.33 × 19.49); M; —; Stern door.

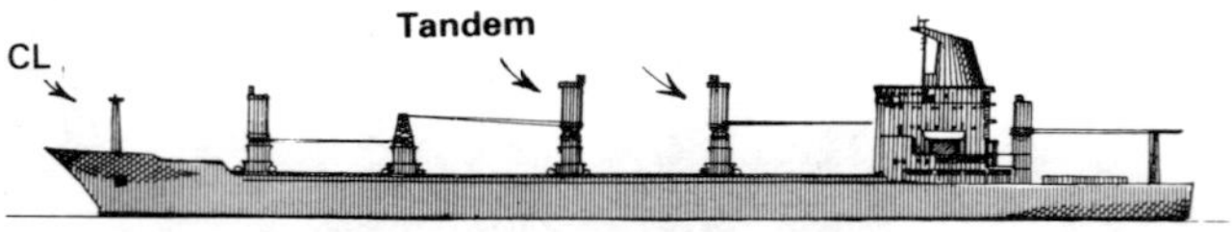

KC_3MFC H1
48880 HELENE DELMAS. Fr/Fr 1978; Con; 18900; 188.63 × 11.42 (618.86 × 37.47); M; 20. Sisters (Fr flag): **48881 IRMA DELMAS 48882 LUCIE DELMAS 48883 MARIE DELMAS.**

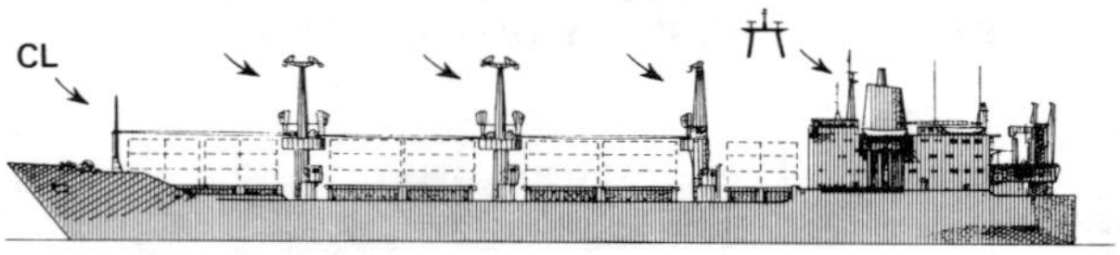

KC_3MFCR H13
48920 ELEO MAERSK. De/De 1979; RoC/Con/C; 13700/21800; 182.95 × 9.76/11.85 (597.9 × 32.02/38.88); M; 18.5; Stern quarter ramp; **'Caroliner'** type. Sisters (De flag): **48921 EMMA MAERSK 48922 EMILIE MAERSK 48923 ELISABETH MAERSK 48924 ESTELLE MAERSK 48925 EVELYN MAERSK.**

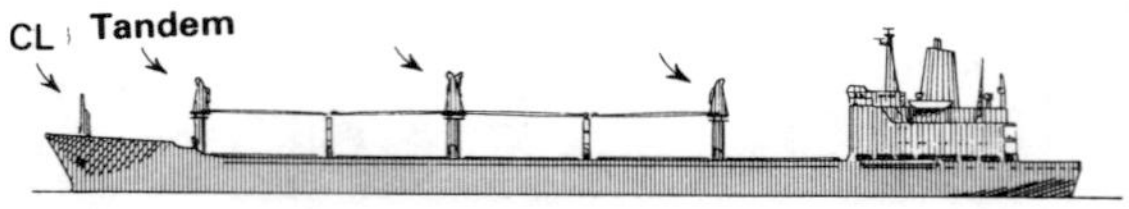

KC_3MFC H1
48890 VAN DYCK. Be/Ja 1977; B/Con; 15000; 164.12 × 10.01 (538.45 × 32.84); M; 16.5. Sister: **48891 QUELLIN** (Be).

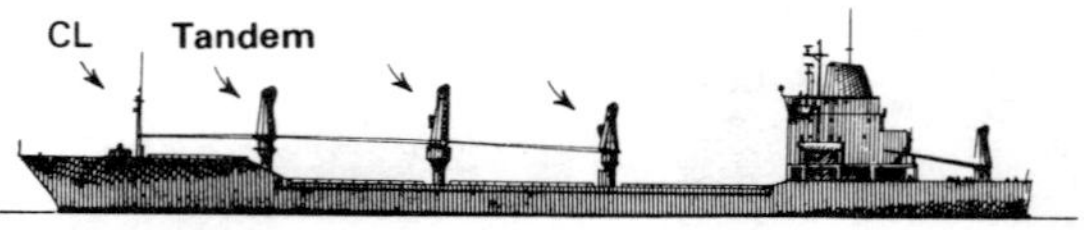

KC_3MFC H13
48900 LA PALLICE. Fr/Ca 1975; C; 6600/11500; 160.15 × 10.05 (525.43 × 32.97); M; 18; **'Marindus'** class. Sisters (Fr flag): **48901 LA ROCHELLE 48902 POITIERS 48903 ROCHEFORT 48904 ROYAN 48905 TOURS** (Ag flag): **48906 BABOR 48907 BIBAN** (Ia flag): **48908 SUHADIWARNO PANANG** ex AMSTELSTROOM 1980; ex MARINDUS MONTREAL 1979; ex ARISTANDROS **48909 L. JALABERT BONTANG** ex AMSTELSTRAAT 1980; ex MARINDUS SOREL 1979; ex ARISTEIDUS **48910 PALEMBANG** ex AMSTELSTRAND 1980; ex MARINDUS TRACY 1979; ex ARISTARCHOS

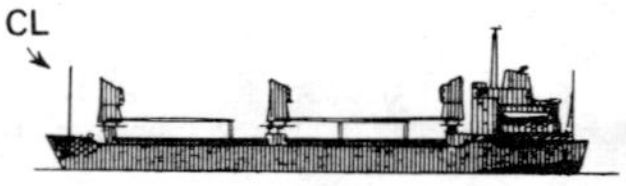

KC_3MFK H
48930 BUNGA SETAWAR. My/Ja 1976; C; 1800/3000; 86.01 × 6.06/6.39 (282.18 × 19.88/20.96); M; 12.5. Sisters (My flag): **48931 BUNGA MAS 48932 BUNGA BINDANG** Probable sister: **48933 BUNGA GELANG.**

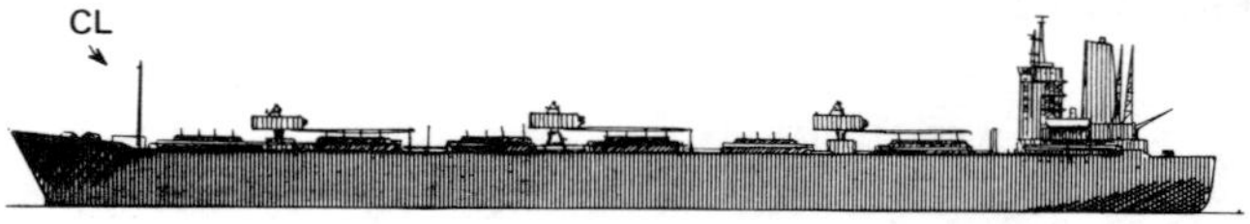

KC_3MFK H
48940 TOHOKU MARU. Ja/Ja 1971; BWC; 34800; 197.01 × 10.99 (646.35 × 36.08); M; 13.5. Similar: **48941 TAIKAI MARU** (Ja) **48942 KASUGAI MARU** (Ja) **48943 SENDAI** (Pa) **48944 NEW INDEPENDENCE** (Li) **48945 PACIFIC VENTURE** (Li) **48946 SUNNY STATE** (Li) **48947 SCANSILVA** (Li) **48948 OJI MARU No 1** (Ja) **48949 SCANSPRUCE** (Li) Similar: **48950 EHIME MARU** (Ja)-cranes on travelling gantries **48951 PRINCE OF TOKYO** (Li)-large bins by hatches 2, 4 & 6.

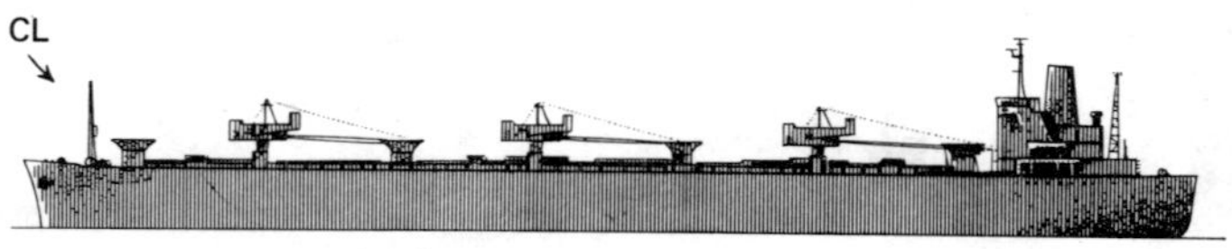

KC_3MFK H
48960 WORLD WOOD. Li/Ja 1974; BWC; 37000; 205.44 × 11.3; (674.02 × 37.07); M; 13.5. Possibly similar (Li flag): **48961 ORIENTAL TAIO 48962 UNIVERSAL TAIO.**

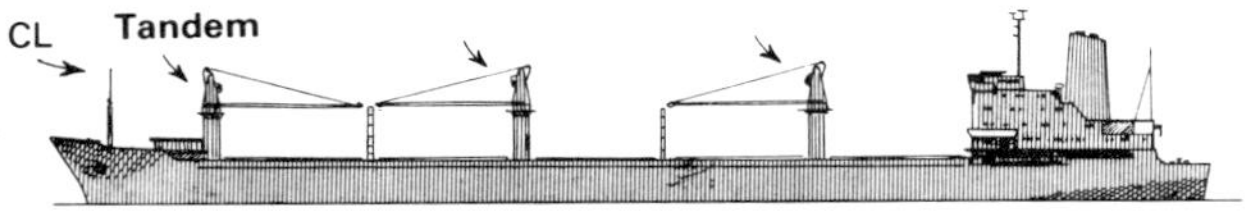

KC_3MFK H1

48970 ARCTIC TROLL. Br/Ys 1971; B; 22200; 183.32 × 11.37 (601.44 × 37.3); M; 15.75. Sisters: **48971 TROLL LAKE** (Br) **48972 TROLL PARK** (Br) **48973 CIELO DI GENOVA** (It) ex TROLL RIVER 1980 (Converted to container ship 1977).

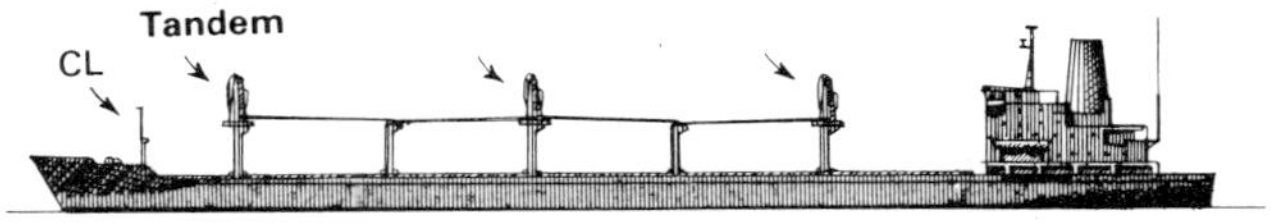

KC_3MFK H1

● **48980 TROLL FOREST.** No/No 1970; B; 20200; 187.43 × 10.76 (614.93 × 35.3); M; 15.75.

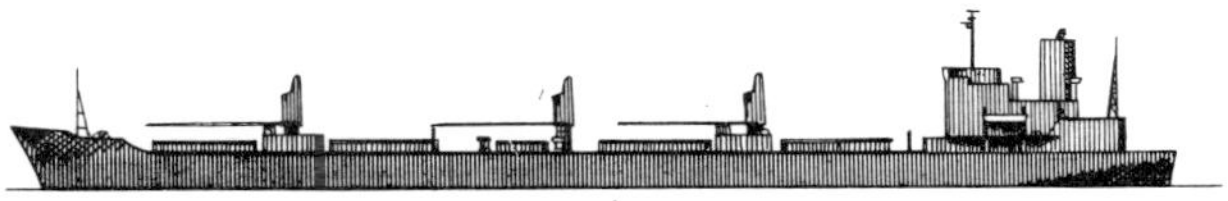

KC_3MFK H1

48990 WORLD FINANCE. Li/Ja 1974; B; 20500; 184.97 × 11.34 (606.85 × 37.2); M; 14.75. Sisters (Li flag): **48991 STREAM BOLLARD 48992 STREAM DOLPHIN 48993 STREAM HAWSER 48994 STREAM RUDDER** Similar: **48995 ASIA HERON 48996 ASIA INDUSTRY.**

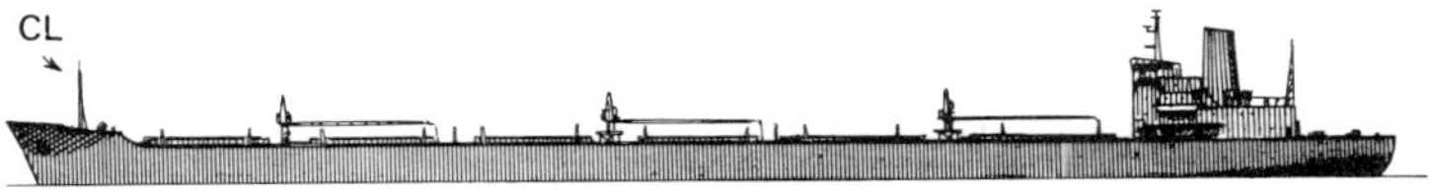

KC_3MFK H1

49000 HOHKOKUSAN MARU. Ja/Ja 1969; B; 34100; 222.99 × 11.84 (731.59 × 38.84); M; 14.5.

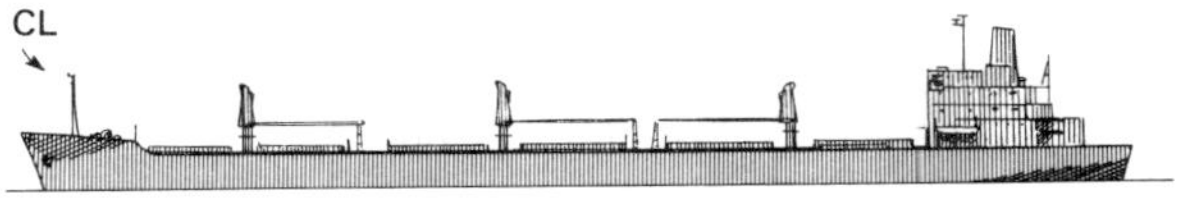

KC_3MFK H1

49010 EURO PRINCESS. Li/Ne 1972; B; 15900; 175.5 × 10.25 (575.78 × 33.63); M; 15.75; ex PEGASUS 1976. Sister: **49011 DASHAKI** (Br) ex OCEAN CORACLE 1980; ex OCEAN COURAGE 1979; ex ANDROMED 1977; ex ANDROMED 1976.

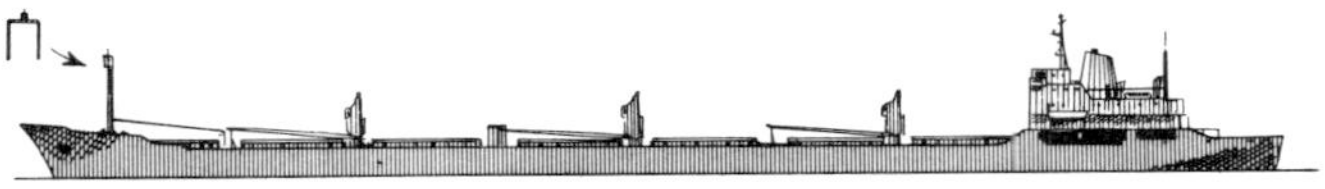

KC_3MFK H1

⋆**49020 SISAK.** Ys/Ys 1967; B; 23700; 201.02 × 11.5 (659.51 × 37.73); M; 15.

●
49021

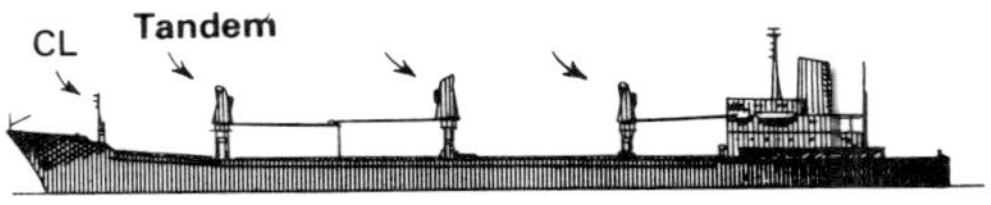

KC_3MFK H1

49030 IRAN REZVAN. Ir/FRG 1976; C; 10200; 149.79 × 9.26 (488.85 × 30.38); M; 16.5; ex ARYA RASTAKHIZ 1980; **'36-L'** type. Sisters (Ir flag): **49031 IRAN MEEZAN** ex ARYA SOROOSH **49032 IRAN SOKAN** ex IRAN NAVID 1980; ex ARYA NAVID 1980 **49033 IRAN BORHAN** ex ARYA GOHAR 1980 **49034 IRAN EHSAN** ex ARYA AKHTAR 1980; ex ARISTAIOS 1975 **49035 IRAN VOJDAN** ex IRAN KAY 1980; ex ARYA KAY 1980; launched as ARISTONIDAS **49036 IRAN JENAN** ex ARYA NEDA 1980; launched as ARISTOLAOS **49037 IRAN BAYAN** ex ARYA SEPAND 1980; ex ARISTONIMOS 1975.

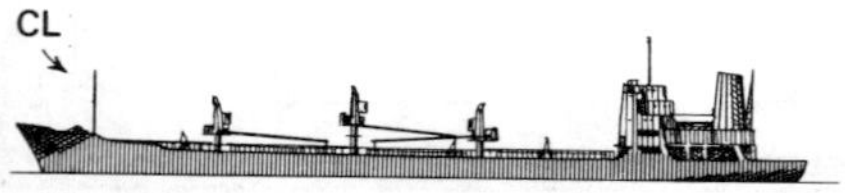

KC_3MFK H1
⋆49040 PIRIN. Bu/Ja 1965; B; 6100; 126.02 × 7.6 (413.45 × 24.93); M; 13. Sisters (Bu flag): **⋆49041 SREDNA GORA ⋆49042 STARA PLANINA ⋆49043 STRADJA.**

KC_3MFK H13
49050 FINA. Ch/FRG 1952; C; 1000; 68.28 × 4.88 (224.5 × 16); M; —; May be out of service.

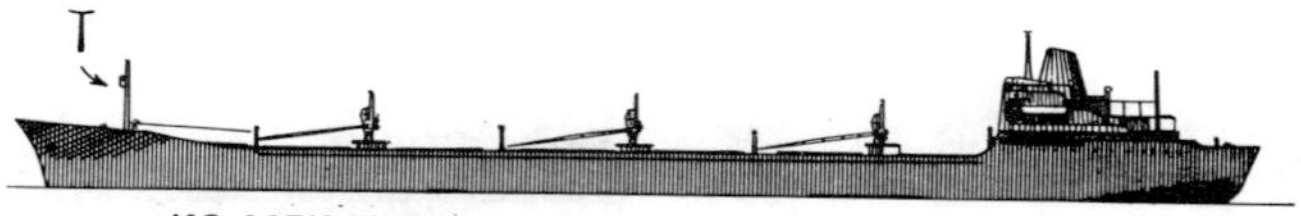

KC_3MFK H13
49060 AKAD. Tu/Sw 1966; B; 21600; 196.91 × 11.33 (646 × 37.17); M; 15.5; ex SANGSTAD 1975.

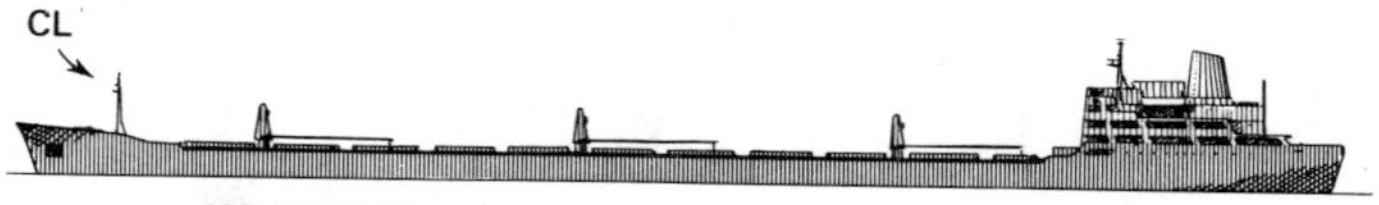

KC_3MFK H13
49070 H 1070. Br/Ca 1966; OO; 21200; 210.47 × 10.95 (690.52 × 35.93); T; 15.5.

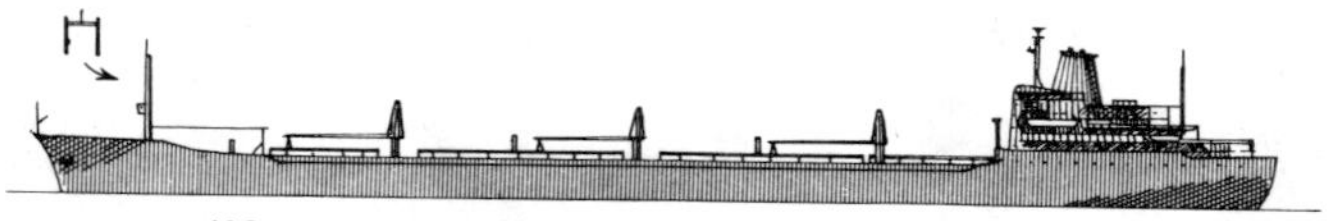

KC_3MFK H13
49080 ON DING. Pa/Sw 1966; B; 20700; 196.32 × 10.88 (644.09 × 35.69); M; 16.25; ex ORANIA.

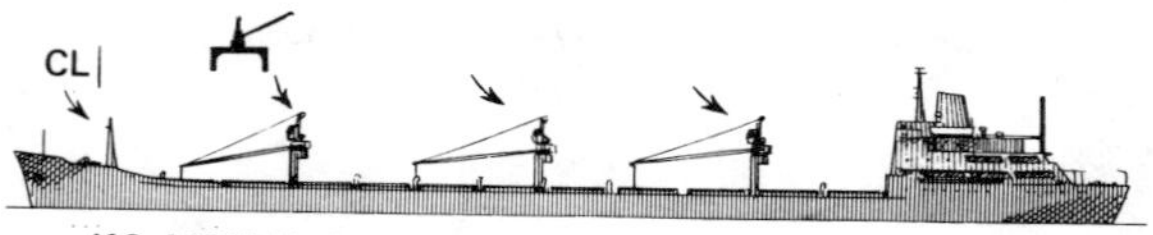

KC_3MFK H13
49090 TASMAN SEA. Pa/Sw 1962; B; 16400; 178.09 × 10.48 (584.28 × 34.38); M; 15; ex THERESIE 1973; Cranes may be on travelling gantries.

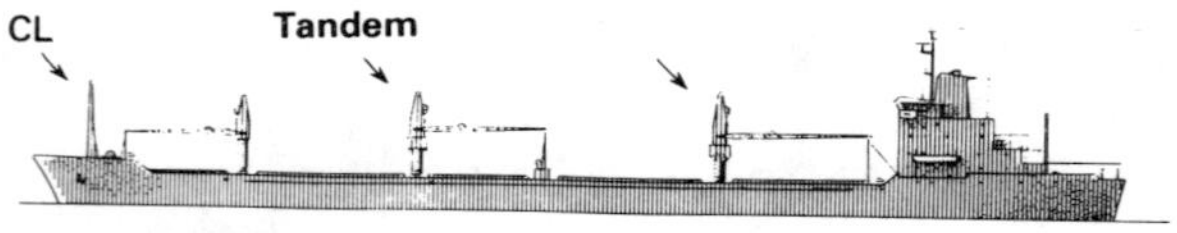

KC_3MFK H13
● **49110 ALEXANDROS G. TSAVLIRIS.** Gr/Bz 1978; B; 15700; 173.18 × 9.72 (568.17 × 31.89); M; 15.5; **'Prinasa 26/15'** type. Sister: **49111 CLAIRE A. TSAVLIRIS** (Gr) Possible sister: **49112 ANASTASIA** (Li).

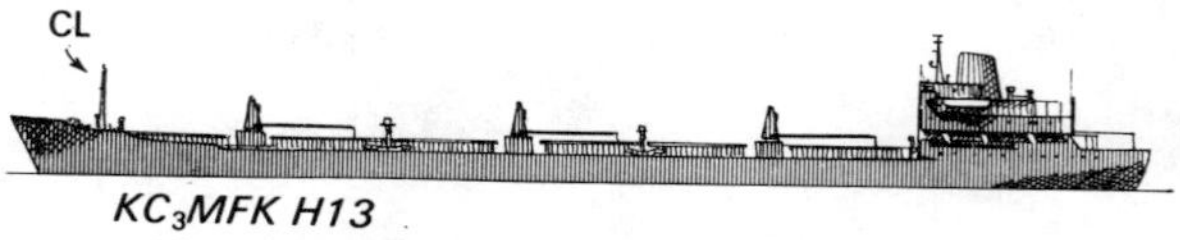

KC_3MFK H13
⋆49100 YASENYEVO. Ru/No 1967; B; 15800; 180.3 × 10.21 (591.54 × 33.5); M; 15.5; ex GIGONDAS 1980; ex TORM RAGNHILD 1977; ex RAGNHILD 1974. Similar: **⋆49101 YAGOTIN** (Ru) ex JULIENAS 1980 Probably similar: **49102 SIFNOS** (Gr) ex TORM ASLAUG 1978; ex ASLAUG 1974 **49103 TORM KRISTINA** (De) ex KRISTINA 1974 Possibly similar (may have 6 cranes): **49104 AETOLIA** (Gr) ex TORM GERD; ex GERD 1979.

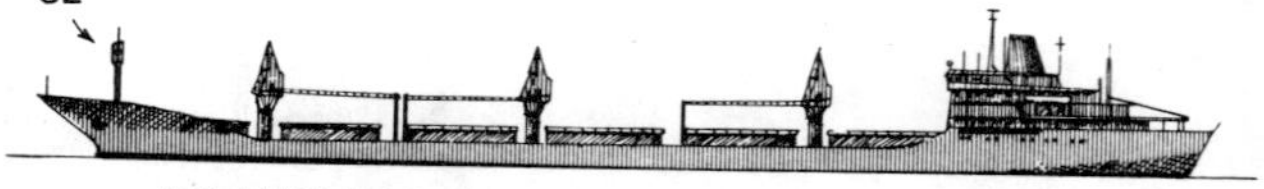

KC_3MFK H13
49120 AZTECA. Me/Pd 1969; B; 16000; 186.01 × 10.57 (610.27 × 34.68); M; 15.5; **'B-449'** type.

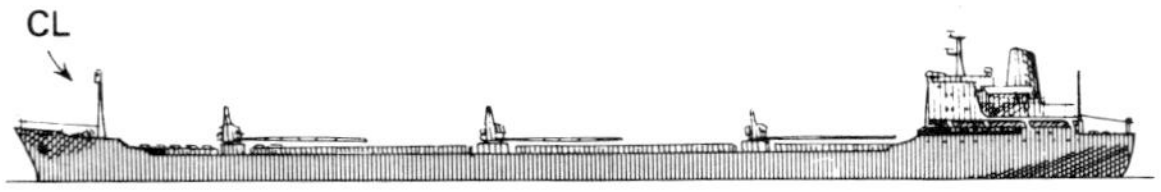

KC_3MFK H13
★49130 YING GE HAI. RC/Ja 1967; B; 15600; 178.01 × 10.17 (584.02 × 33.37); M; 15; ex NORMANDIET 1977. Similar: **49131 TURKIYE** (Tu) ex HIMMERLAND 1977.

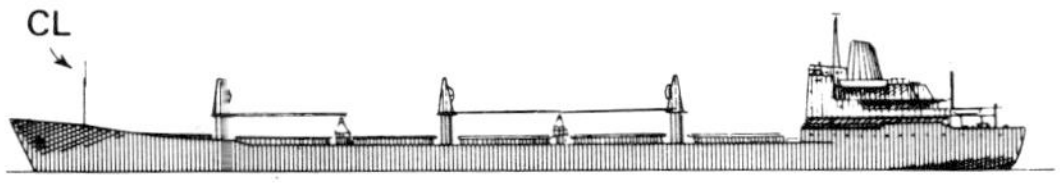

KC_3MFK H13
49140 BENNEVIS. Br/No 1968; B; 12700; 161.55 × 9.7 (530 × 31.82); M; 16; ex BARON DUNMORE 1977.

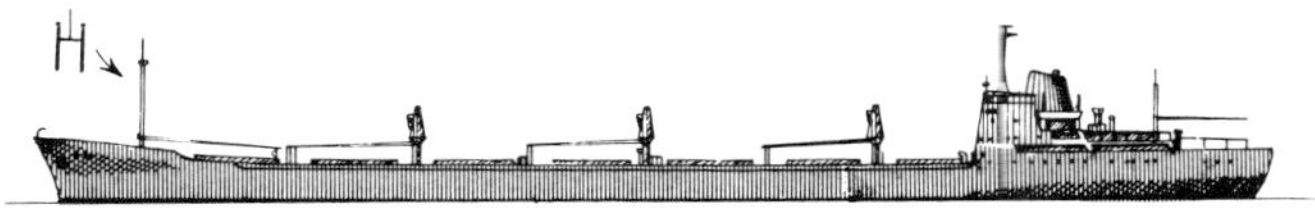

KC_3MFK H13
49150 HADJANNA. Gr/FRG 1965; B; 18000; 196.63 × 11.04 (645.11 × 36.22); M; —; ex AMICA 1974. Similar (RC flag): **★49151 GUANG HAI** ex ANGELIC PROTECTOR 1975; ex AINO 1968 **★49152 QIONG HAI** ex ARICA 1974.

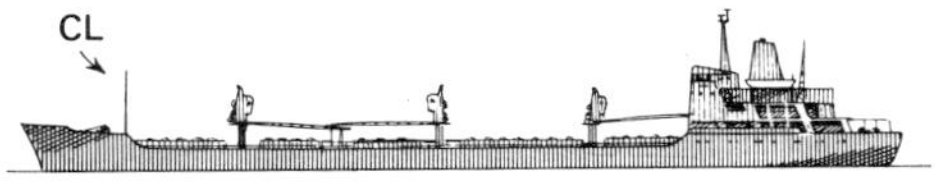

KC_3MFK H13
★49160 BUZLUDJA. Bu/Ja 1968; B; 9100; 139.83 × 9.26 (458.75 × 30.38); M; 15. Sisters (Bu flag): **★49161 MURGASH ★49162 LUDOGORETZ ★49163 OBORISHTE.**

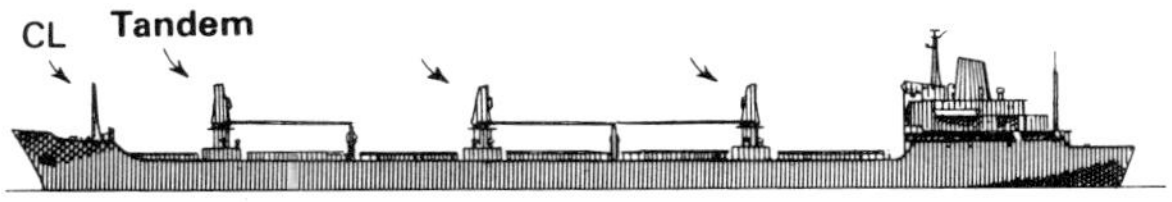

KC_3MFK H13
49170 NORDKAP. De/Ja 1975; B/Con; 19600; 179.03 × 10.97 (587.37 × 35.99); M; 15. Sisters (De flag): **49171 NORDPOL 49172 NORDTRAMP 49173 NORDKYN 49174 NORDHVAL.**

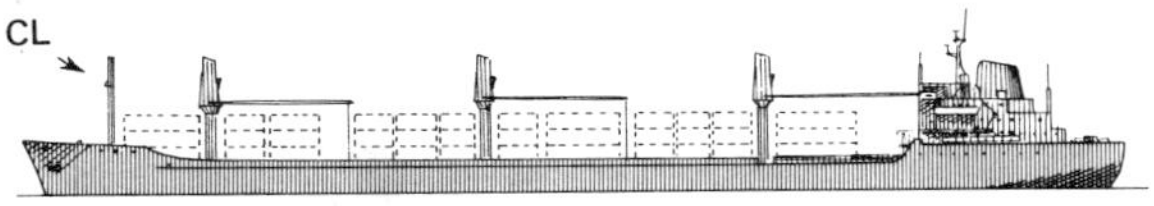

KC_3MFK H13
● **49180 VANCOUVER FOREST.** Br/Br 1969/77; Con; 17700; 175.27 × 9.91 (575.03 × 32.51); M; 15.5; Converted from Bulk Carrier 1977. Sister: **49181 WILLINE TOYO** (Br) ex HAVRAIS 1980; ex CONON FOREST.

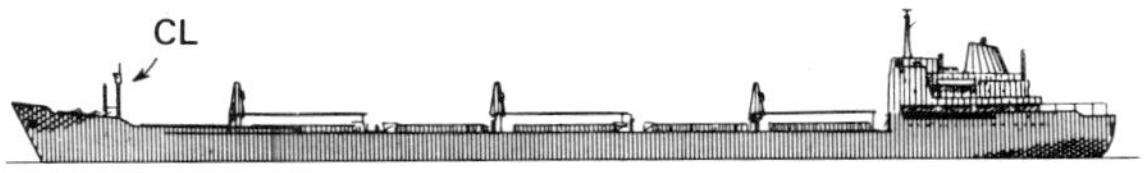

KC_3MFK H13
49190 GEORGIAN GLORY. Gr/Sw 1962; B; 16600; 175.88 × 11 (577.03 × 36.06); M; 14.5; ex SIGHAUG 1966. Sister: **49191 EUROPEAN MASTER** (Gr) ex CESTOS BAY 1980; ex PANTOKRATOR 1979; ex PAN 1972; ex THEOLOGOS 1970; ex SIGANKA 1966.

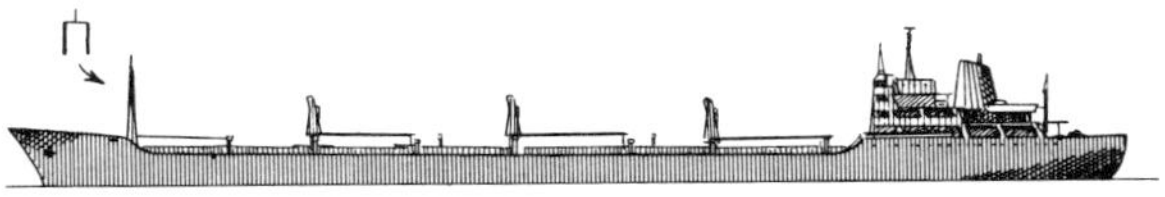

KC_3MFK H13
49200 RIO ZAIRE. Po/Ja 1960; B; 14300; 177.02 × 9.59 (580.77 × 31.46); M; 16.25.

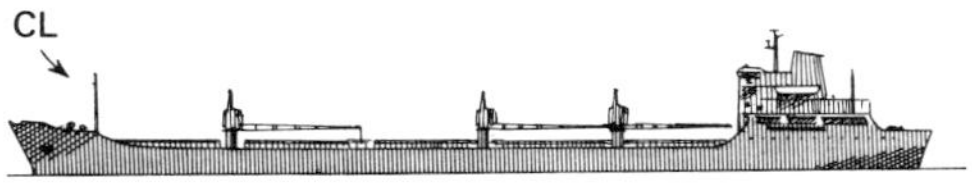

KC_3MFK H13
★49210 KOPALNIA PIASECZNO. Pd/Sp 1971; B; 9100; 146.72 × 8.27 (481.36 × 27.13); M; 15.5. Sister: **★49211 KOPALNIA JEZIORKO** (Pd).

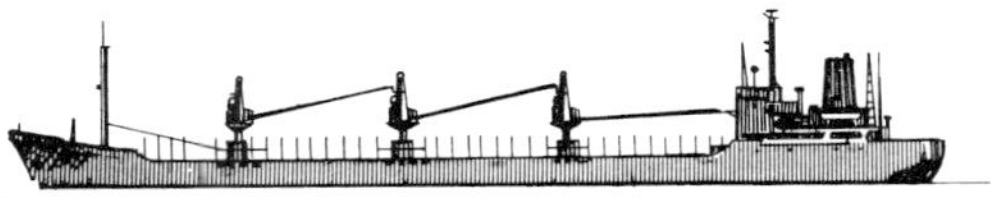

KC_3MFK H13
49220 IRENES FRIENDSHIP. Gr/Ja 1965; C; 8900; 147.02 × 8.61 (482.34 × 28.25); M; 15; ex WAKAMIYASAN MARU 1977. Sisters: **49221 ORIENT TRUST** (Pa) ex WAKAOSAN MARU 1978 **49222 ORIENT PINE** (Pa) ex WAKATAKESAN MARU 1974 **49223 IOANNIS** (Gr) ex WAKANESAN MARU 1979 **49224 MARESOL** (Li) ex WAKASUGISAN MARU 1979.

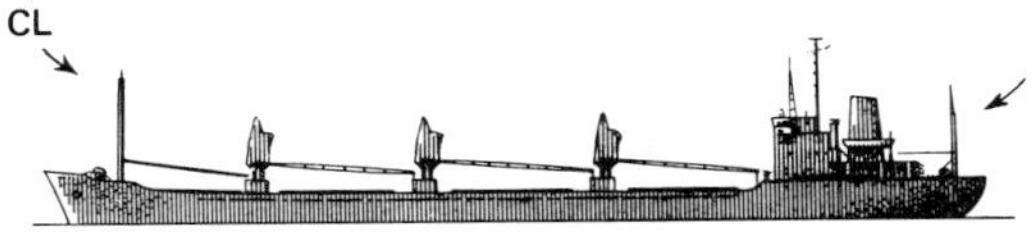

KC_3MFK H13
49230 KANEYOSHI MARU. Ja/Ja 1969; C; 10000; 148.93 × 8.89; (488.62 × 29.17); M; 14.

KC$_3$MFK H13
★49240 KISHINEV. Ru/Ru 1968; C(Sea/River); 3600; 123.53 × 4.5 (405.28 × 14.76); TSM; 11.75. Sisters (Ru flag): **★49241 ALEKSANDR POKALCHUK ★49242 GORKOVSKAYA KOMSOMOLIYA ★49243 NIKOLAY SHCHETININ** ex BUOR-KHAYA 1980 **★49244 PETR GUTCHENKO ★49245 SHURA BURLACHENKO ★49246 GORNYAK ★49247 HELME ★49248 MUOSTAKH ★49249 SERGEY BURYACHEK.**

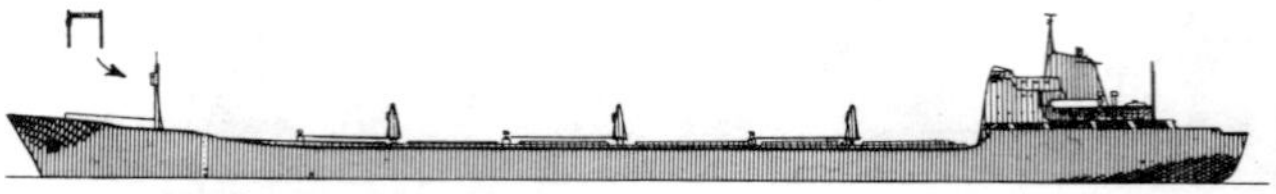

KC$_3$MFK H13
49260 DIMITRIS L.F. Gr/Ys 1963; B; 17700; 196.5 × 10.86 (644.68 × 35.63); M; 16; ex ALIDA GORTHON 1974.

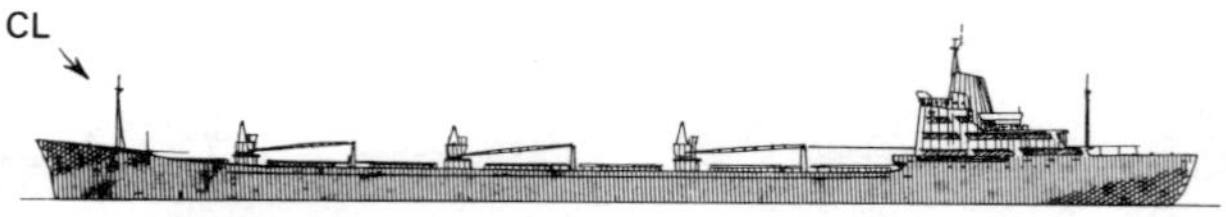

KC$_3$MFK H13
49270 MAIROULA. Gr/Be 1963; B; 14200; 183.22 × 10.42 (601.12 × 34.19); M; 15; ex IRENE S. LEMOS 1973.

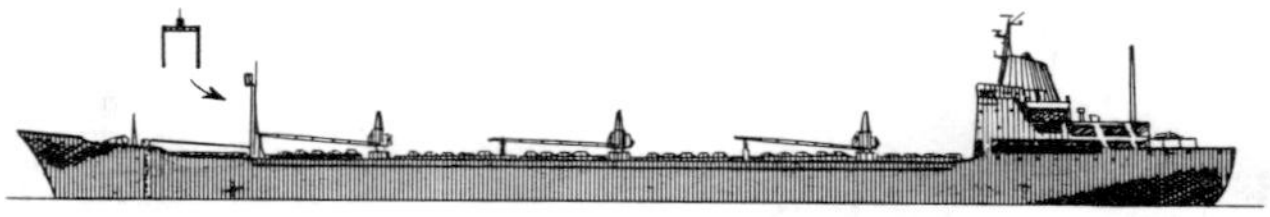

KC$_3$MFK H13
● **49280 ANNITSA L.** Gr/Ja 1965; B; 19500; 193.02 × 11.17 (633.26 × 36.64); M; —. Sisters: **49281 CAPTAIN GEORGE L** (Gr) Similar: **49282 WAH HING** (Li) ex ITEL CARINA 1980; ex CHRISTINA II 1973 **49283 WAH FAT** (Li) ex ITEL PEGASUS 1980; ex GENIE 1973 **49284 ITEL TAURUS** (Li) ex MARINA 1973.

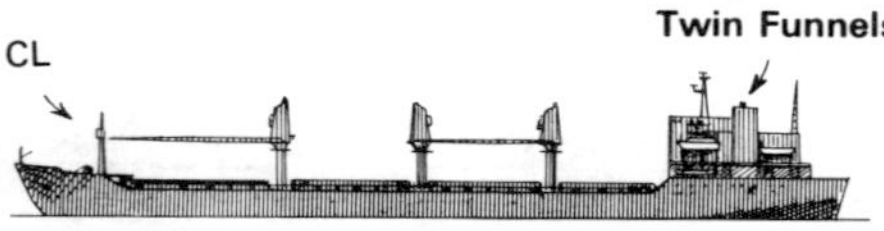

KC$_3$MFK H13
49290 FRINES. Li/Ja 1978; C; 8100; 134.52 × 8.67 (441.34 × 28.44); M; 14.75. Sister: **49291 FINNSNES** (Li).

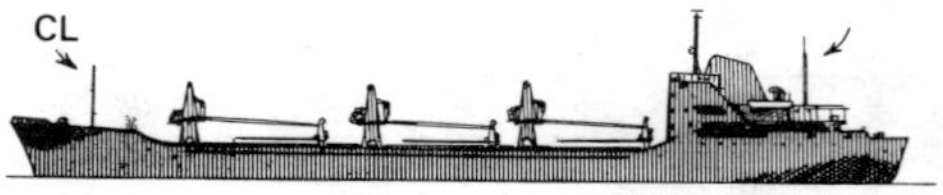

KC$_3$MFK H13
49300 ATLANTIC EXPRESS. Li/De 1960; C; 5800; 141.54 × 7.87 (464.37 × 25.82); M; 16; ex DOMINO CRYSTAL 1973.

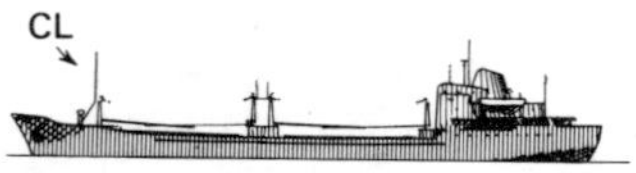

KC$_3$MFK H13
49310 NANOULA. Pa/De 1963; C; 1600/2700; 93.78 × 5.07/6.37 (307.68 × 16.63/20.9); M; 13.5; ex TAMARIS; ex FINNROVER 1973; ex NINA 1971.

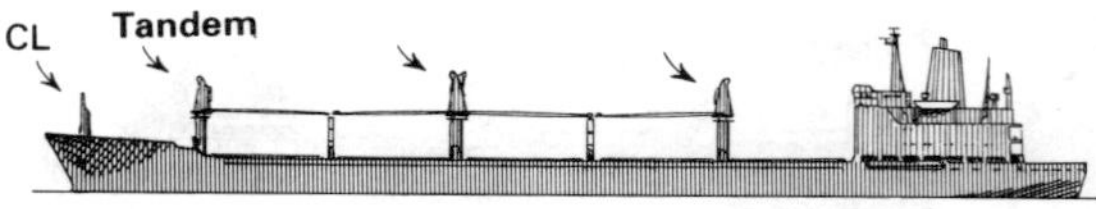

KC$_3$MFKC H1
49320 VAN DYCK. Be/Ja 1977; B/Con; 15000; 164.12 × 10.01 (538.45 × 32.84); M; 16.5. Sister: **49321 QUELLIN** (Be).

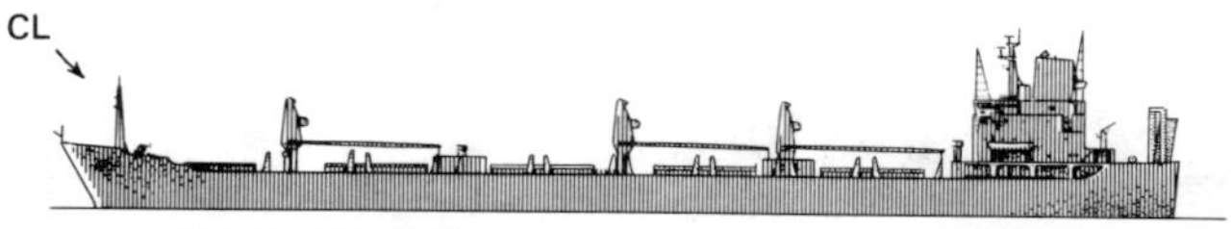

KC$_3$MFKR H13
49330 MEIHOU MARU. Ja/Ja 1978; B/RoVC; 26200; 184.72 × 12; (606.04 × 39.37); M; 15; Stern quarter ramp. Sister: **49331 NIPPOU MARU** (Ja).

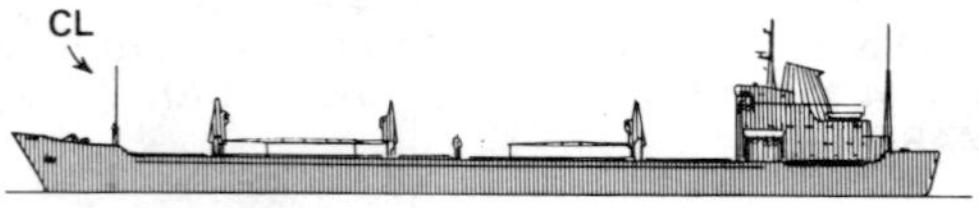

KC$_3$MFM H13
49340 MED VICTORY. Gr/Sp 1973; C; 7800/11400; 147.02 × —/9.9 (482.35 × —/32.48); M; 15.5; ex IRENE 1981; **'Santa Fe'** type.

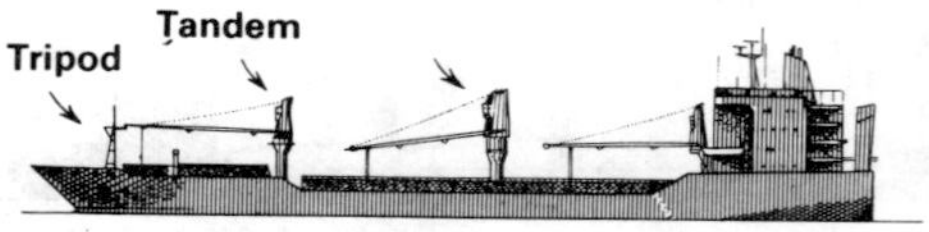

KC$_3$MFR H13
49350 WHITE NILE. Su/Ne 1979; RoC/Con/C/HL; 9100; 132.9 × 9.4 (436 × 30.84); M; 16; Slewing stern ramp; **'Hamlet-Multiflex'** type. Sister: **49351 BLUE NILE** (Su).

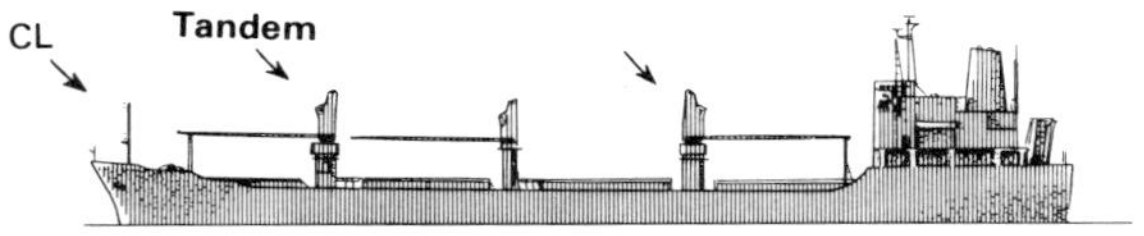

KC_3MFR H13
49360 FIJI MARU. Ja/Ja 1977; C/RoC; 8400; 155.53 × 8.92; (510.27 × 29.27); M; 16.25.

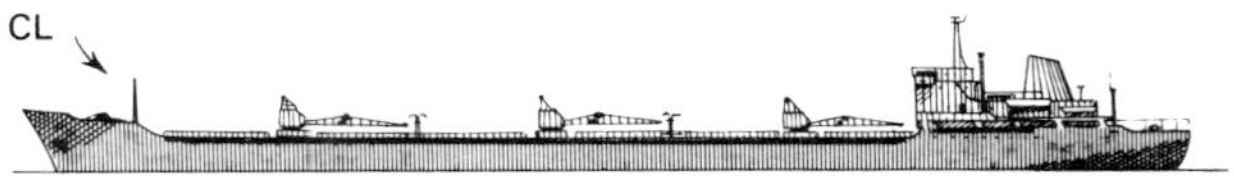

KC_3MKFK H13
● **49370 SOUTH WIND.** Gr/It 1963; B; 16000; 185.25 × 9.84 (607.78 × 32.28); M; 16.25; ex TRANSOCEANICA ELENA 1980. Sister: **49371 CANMAR CARRIER** (Ca) ex TRANSOCENICA GIOVANNA 1976.

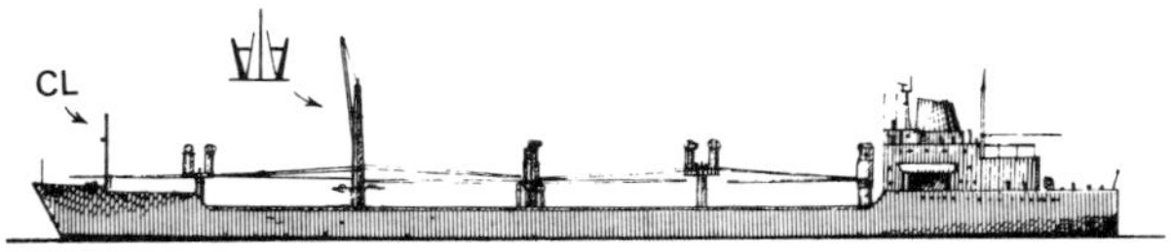

KC_2KC_4MFK H13
49380 IBN SHUHAID. Ku/Ko 1977; C; 11100/15400; 175.32 × —/10.4 (575.2 × —/34.12); M; 16; **'Kuwait'** class. Sisters (Ku flag): (some Br built). **49381 IBN AL-ATHEER 49382 IBN AL-NAFEES 49383 IBN AL-MOATAZ 49384 IBN ALBEITAR 49385 IBN ASAKIR 49386 IBN BASSAM 49387 IBN BATTOTAH 49388 IBN DURAID 49389 IBN HAYYAN 49390 IBN KHALDOON 49391 IBN KHALLIKAN 49392 IBN MALIK 49393 IBN QUTAIBAH 49394 IBN RUSHD 49395 IBN TUFAIL 49396 IBN YOUNUS 49397 AL SALIMIAH 49398 AL MUBARAKIAH 49399 AL YAMAMAH 49400 AL FUJAIRAH 49401 AL MUHARRAQ 49402 AL RAYYAN 49403 AHMAD AL-FATEH 49404 ARAFAT 49405 DANAH 49406 FATHULKHAIR 49407 HIJAZ 49408 JILFAR 49409 QAROUH 49410 KUBBAR 49411 SALAH ALDEEN 49412 THEEKAR 49413 TABUK.**

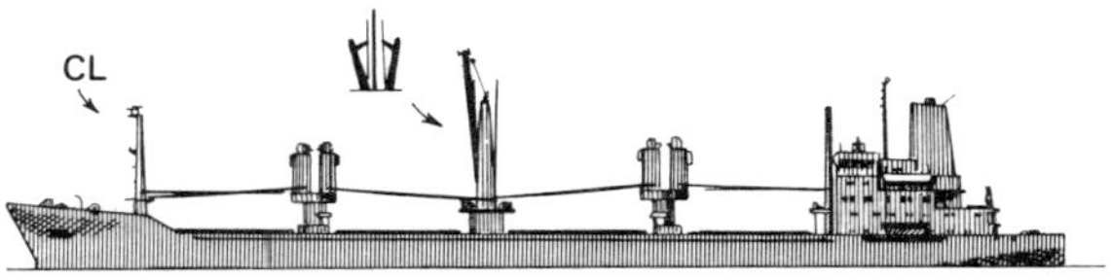

KC_2KC_2KMF H1
49420 NEDLLOYD BAHRAIN. Ne/Ne 1978; C; 13200; 173.03 × 10 (567.68 × 32.81); M; 17. Sisters (Ne flag): **49421 NEDLLOYD BALTIMORE 49422 NEDLLOYD BANGKOK 49423 NEDLLOYD BARCELONA.**

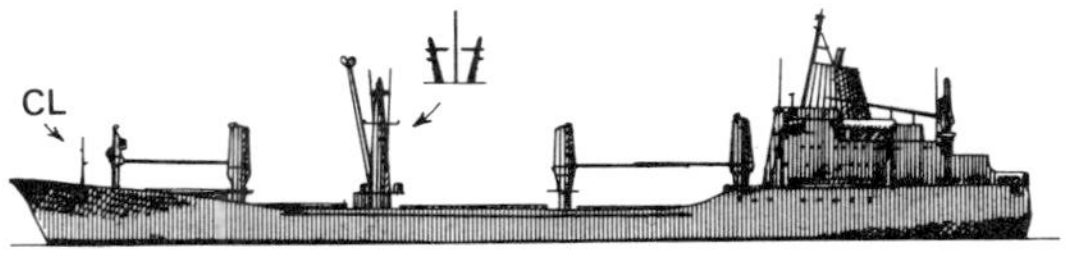

KC_2KC_2MFC H13
49430 STRATHMAY. Br/Br 1970; C; 8000/11200; 156.98 × 8.2/9.62 (515.02 × 26.9/31.56); M; 19; ex MANORA 1975. Sisters (Br flag): **49431 STRATHMEIGLE** ex MERKARA 1975 **49432 STRATHMORE** ex MORVADA 1975 **49433 STRATHMUIR** ex MULBERA 1975.

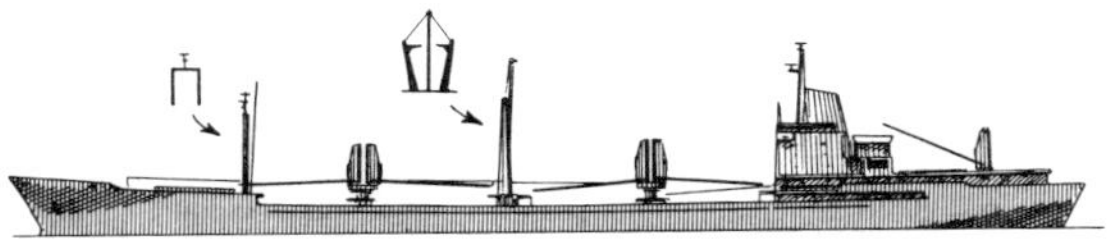

KC_2KC_2MFC H13
49440 VILLE DE VALENCE. Fr/Fr 1972; C; 8100/12600; 171.2 × 8.43/9.71 (561.68 × 27/66/31.86); M; 20. Sister: **49441 VILLE DE GENES** (Fr).

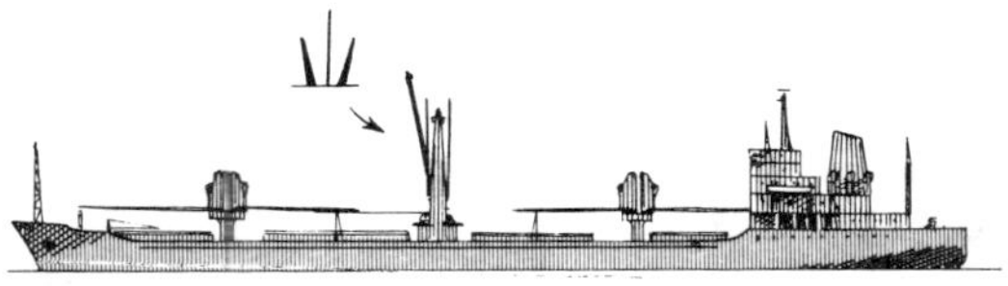

KC_2KC_2MFK H13
49450 KSAR ETTIR. Ag/Ja 1977; C; 12800; 156.11 × 9.9 (512.77 × 32.48); M; 15. Sisters (Ag flag): **49451 KSAR CHELLALA 49452 KSAR EL BOUKHARI.**

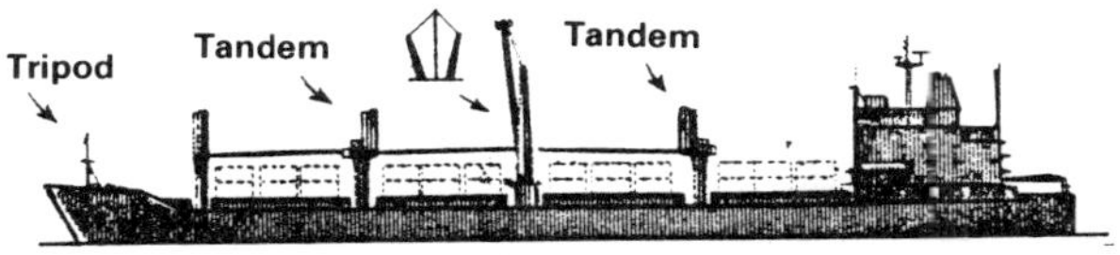

KC_2KCKMF H1
● **49460 VILLE D'ANVERS.** Fr/No 1977; C; 16500; 171.41 × 10.55 (562.37 × 34.61); M; 17.5. Sisters: **46461 VILLE DE BORDEAUX** (Fr) ex SEATRAIN WEST POINT 1979; ex VILLE DE BORDEAUX 1978 **49462 NARA** (Fr) **49463 NAUSICAA** (Fr) **49464 CONCORDIA STAR** (No).

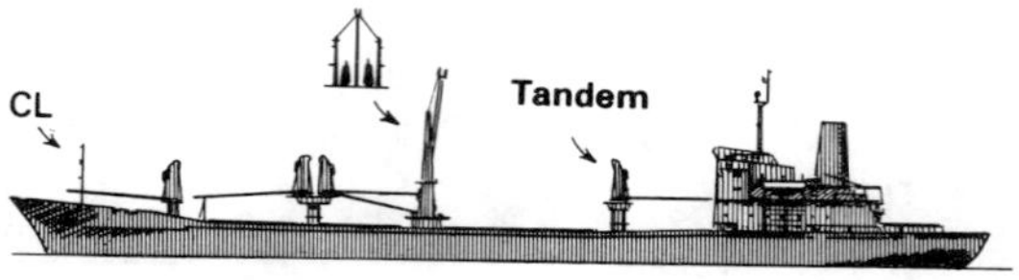

KC_2KCMF H1
★49470 IVAN ZAGUBANSKI Bu/Ru 1975; C; 11800; 162.31 × 9.17 (532.51 × 30.09); M; 18; **'Dnepr'** type. Sisters (Bu flag): **★49471 CHRISTO BOTEV ★49472 GOTZE DELCHEV ★49473 LUBEN KARAVELOV ★49474 KAPITAN PETKO VOIVODA ★49475 VASIL LEVSKY** (Ru flag): **★49476 GRIGORIY PETRENKO ★49477 NIKITA MITCHENKO ★49478 PETR DUTOV ★49479 IVAN SHEPETKOV ★49480 IVAN MUSKALENKO ★49481 GEROI PANFILOVTSY ★49482 VASILY KLOCHKOV ★49483 NIKOLAY ANANYEV ★49484 NIKOLAY MAKSIMOV ★49485 PETR YEMTSOV ★49486 YAKOV BONDARENKO ★49487 SOVIETSKIYE PROFSOYUZY** (Ys flag): **★49488 ADMIRAL PURISIC 49489 HEROJ PAIC ★49490 HEROJ KOSTA STAMENKOVIC ★49491 HEROJ SENJANOVIC** (Rm flag): **★49492 ZALAU** (Cu flag): **★49493 JOSE ANTONIO ECHEVERRIA ★49494 JULIO ANTONIO MELLA ★49495 30 DE NOVIEMBRE ★49496 XI FESTIVAL** (Br flag): **49497 LYCAON 49498 LAERTES** (FRG flag): **49499 SANTA ELENA.** (Hu flag) **★49500 VOROSMARTY**

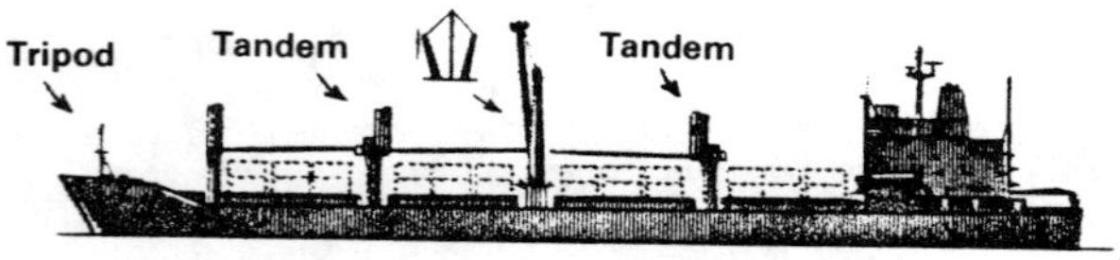

KC_2KCMF H1
49510 VILLE D'ANVERS. Fr/No 1977; C; 16500; 171.41 × 10.55 (562.37 × 34.61); M; 17.5. Sisters: **49511 VILLE DE BORDEAUX** (Fr) ex SEATRAIN WEST POINT 1979; ex VILLE DE BORDEAUX 1978 **49512 NARA** (Fr) **49513 NAUSICAA** (Fr) **49514 CONCORDIA STAR** (No).

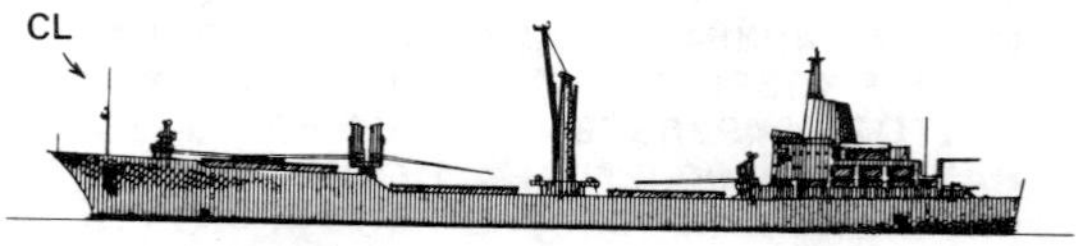

KC_2KCMF H13
49520 HALLA PILOT. Ko/Br 1970; C; 6700/10000; 154.13 × 8.17/9.62 (505.68 × 26.8/31.56); M; 17; ex STRATHCARROL; ex ASKA 1975. Sister: **49521 HALLA PRIDE** (Ko) ex STRATHCARRON; ex AMRA 1976.

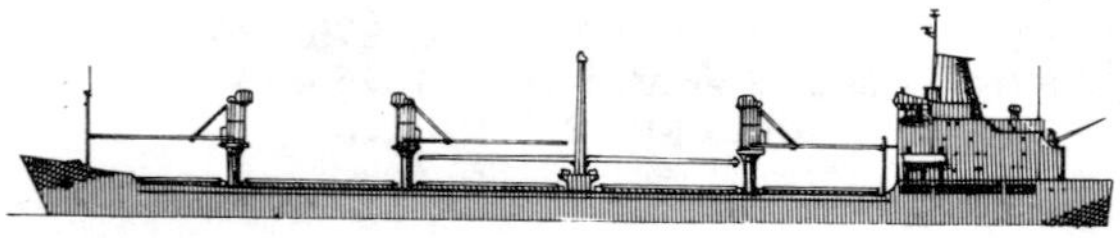

KC_2KCMF H13
49530 VILLE DE BREST. Fr/Sp 1978; C/Con; 16500; 173.01 × 10.5 (567.62 × 34.45); M; 17.5; Stulcken derrick amidships. Sisters (Fr flag): **49531 VILLE DE REIMS 49532 VILLE DE ROUEN.**

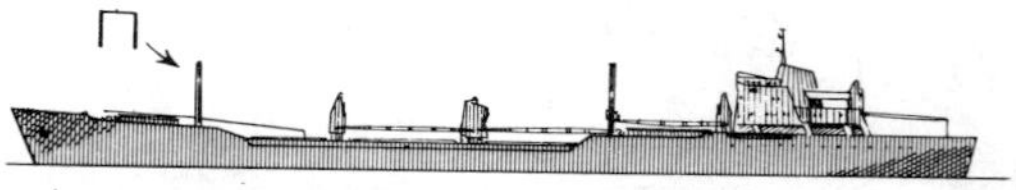

KC_2KCMFC H13
● **49540 HYDRA.** Gr/Br 1966; C; 8300; 153.04 × 8.78 (502.1 × 28.81); M; 17.5; ex BIOKOVO 1980; ex MANCHESTER PORT 1971.

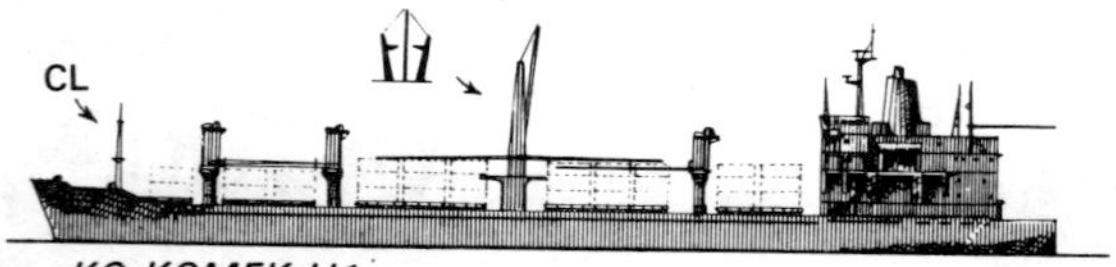

KC_2KCMFK H1
49550 EIFFEL. Fr/Ja 1977; C/Con; 16600; 163.02 × 10 (534.84 × 32.81); M; 18. Sisters (Fr flag): **49551 HAUSSMANN 49552 MANSART 49553 SOUFFLOT.**

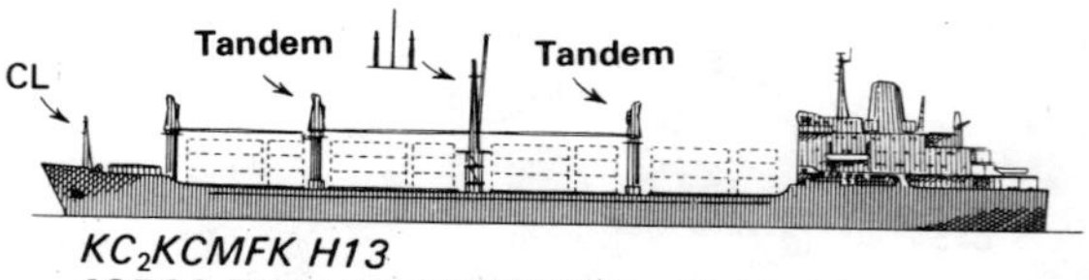

KC_2KCMFK H13
49560 THALASSINI MANA. Gr/Ja 1977; C/Con; 14500; 165 × 10.48 (451.34 × 34.38); M; 18.5; ex AMERIKA; ex ARABIAN LEADER; ex AMERIKA 1978. Sister: **49561 THALASSINI KYRA** (Gr) ex NIGERIA; ex ARABIAN PROGRESS; ex NIGERIA 1978.

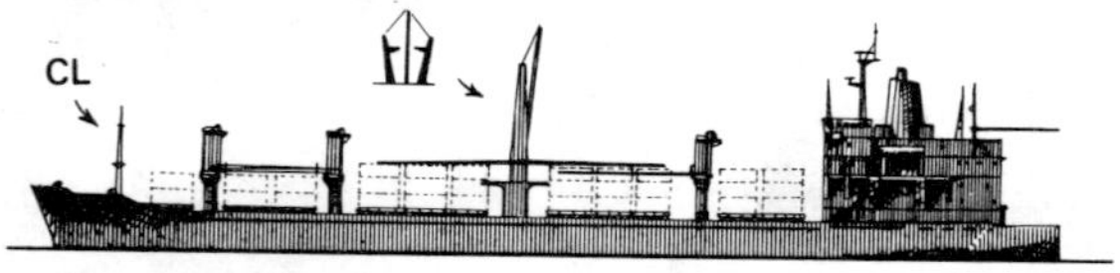

$KC_2KCMFKC$ H1
49570 EIFFEL. Fr/Ja 1977; C/Con; 16600; 163.02 × 10 (534.84 × 32.81); M; 18. Sisters (Fr flag): **49571 HAUSSMANN 49572 MANSART 49573 SOUFFLOT.**

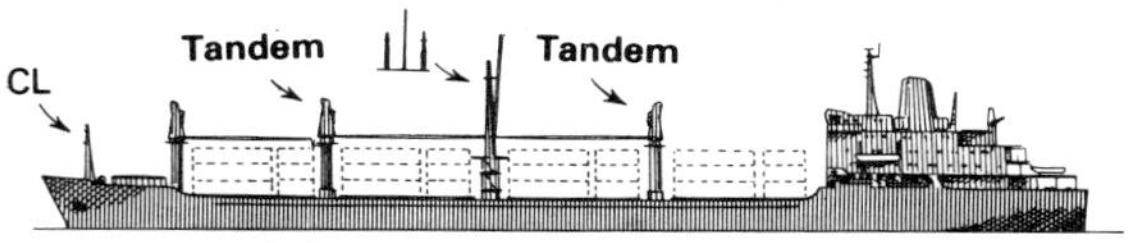

KC$_2$KCMFKC H13
49580 THALASSINI MANA. Gr/Ja 1977; C/Con; 14500; 165 × 10.48 (451.34 × 34.38); M; 18.5; ex AMERIKA; ex ARABIAN LEADER; ex AMERIKA 1978. Sister: **49581 THALASSINI KYRA** (Gr) ex NIGERIA; ex ARABIAN PROGRESS; ex NIGERIA 1978.

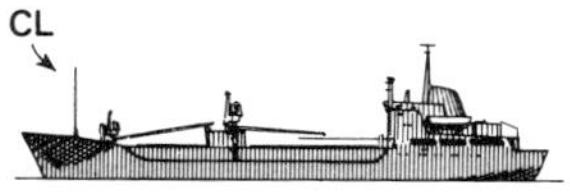

KC$_2$KMF H
49590 VILLABLANCA. Sp/Sp 1965; C; 2300; 83.67 × 5.42 (274.51 × 17.78); M; 13; ex ASTENE 94 1967; launched as BRETAGNE. Sisters (Sp flag): **49591 VILLAFRANCA** ex ASTENE 97 1968 **49592 VILLAFRIA** ex ASTENE 96 1968 **49593 VILLAVERDE** ex ASTENE 95 1968.

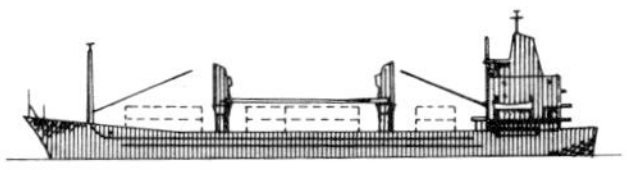

KC$_2$KMF H
49600 AMERICA. US/US 1979; Con/C/R; 2000 Dwt; 90.07 × 4.5 (295.5 × 14.76); M; 13.75. Sisters (US flag): **49601 AMAZONIA 49602 ANTILLIA.**

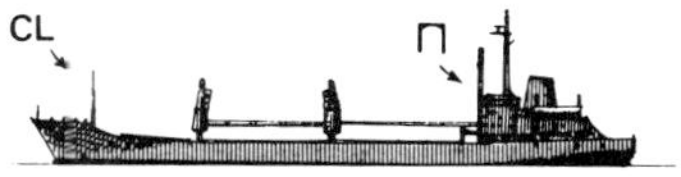

KC$_2$KMF H1
49610 KRIS MELELA. My/SA 1969; C; 2100/3100; 95.71 × 5.67/6.55 (314.01 × 18.6/21.49); M; 13.5; ex TUGELA 1980. Sister: **49611 KRIS MADURA** (My) ex PONGOLA 1980.

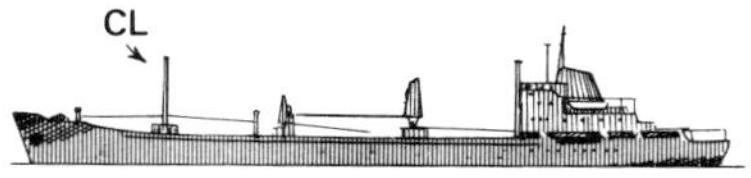

KC$_2$KMF H1
49620 EAST RAINBOW. Pa/Sw 1961; C; 4500; 114 × 7.34 (374.02 × 24.08); M; 15; ex TESIRA; ex MAJ RAGNE 1973. Possible Sister: **49621 AKRA SIGRI** (Gr) ex BIRGIT RAGNE 1976.

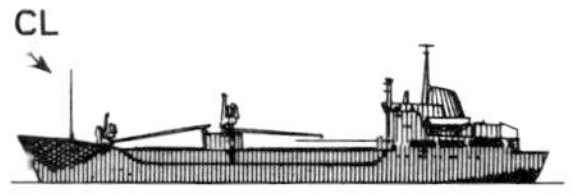

KC$_2$KMF H13
49630 VILLABLANCA. Sp/Sp 1965; C; 2300; 83.67 × 5.42 (274.51 × 17.78); M; 13; ex ASTENE 94 1967; launched as BRETAGNE. Sisters (Sp flag): **49631 VILLAFRANCA** ex ASTENE 97 1968 **49632 VILLAFRIA** ex ASTENE 96 1968 **49633 VILLAVERDE** ex ASTENE 95 1968.

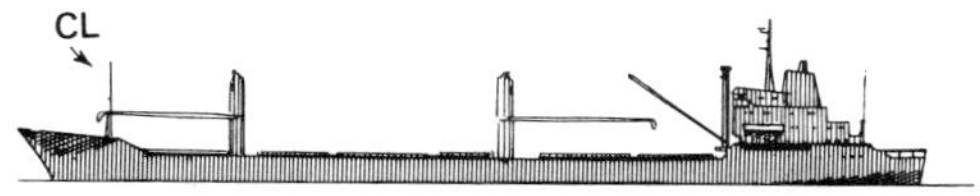

KC$_2$KMF H13
● **49640 TRISTAN.** FRG/FRG 1974; C; 8400; 143.85 × 8.31 (471.99 × 27.26); M; 18; ex COLUMBUS CARIBIC 1980; launched as TRISTAN. Sisters (FRG flag): **49641 RIENZI** ex BAVARIA SINGAPORE 1980; ex COLUMBUS CAPRICORN 1980 launched as RIENZI **49642 COLUMBUS COROMANDEL** launched as SENTA.

KC$_2$KMF H13
● **49650 ALIMAR.** Br/Sw 1963; B; 11300; 152.56 × 9.16 (500.52 × 30.05); M; 14.5; ex KARMALU 1979; ex SANTA CLAUS 1976; ex KANANGOORA 1973.

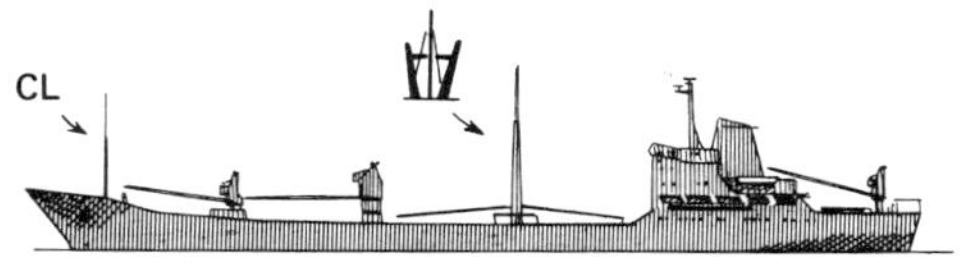

KC$_2$KMFC H13
49660 LLOYD HUMAITA. Bz/Bz 1976; C; 5600/7700; 142.02 × 7.67 (465.95 × 25.16); M; 18. Sisters (Bz flag): **49661 LLOYD CUIABA 49662 LLOYD MARABA 49663 LLOYD ALTAMIRA 49664 LLOYD SANTAREM.**

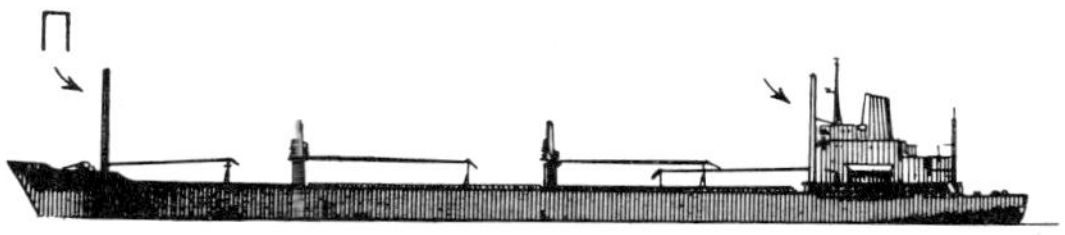

KC$_2$KMFK H1
● **49670 PRINCESS AURORA.** Li/Ja 1968; B; 15700; 162.01 × 10.61 (531.53 × 34.81); M; 15. Sisters: **49671 MARITIME ALLIANCE** (Pa) **49672 TAIHO** (Li) ex SNOW WHITE 1980.

KC_2KMFK H13
49680 ABUQIR. Eg/Ja 1976; C; 4700; 114.33 × 7.25 (375.1 × 23.79); M; 16.75. Sisters (Eg flag): **49681 ALMANDARAH 49682 ALMOUNTAZAH 1 49683 MARYUT.**

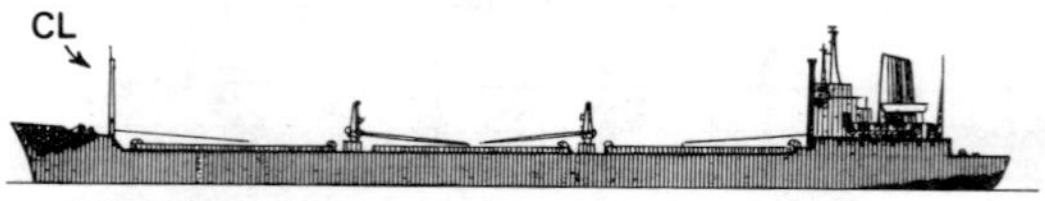

KC_2KMFK H13
49690 SANTA MONICA 1. Pa/Ja 1969; O; 12100; 158.6 × 8.99 (520.34 × 29.49); M; 14; ex SAGANOSEKI MARU 1974.

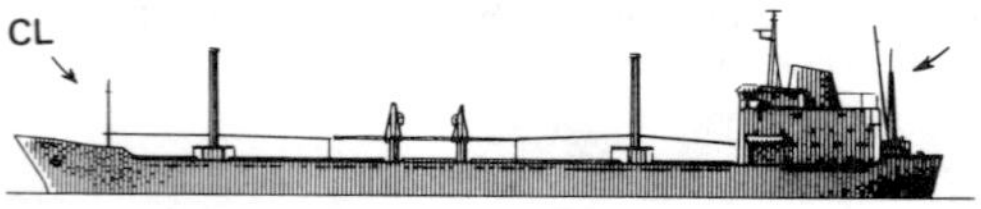

KC_2KMFK H13
● **49700 RATNA MANORAMA.** In/Sp 1973; C; 11200; 147.02 × 9.81 (482.35 × 32.19); M; 15.5; **'Santa Fe'** type. Sister: **49701 RATNA KIRTI** (In).

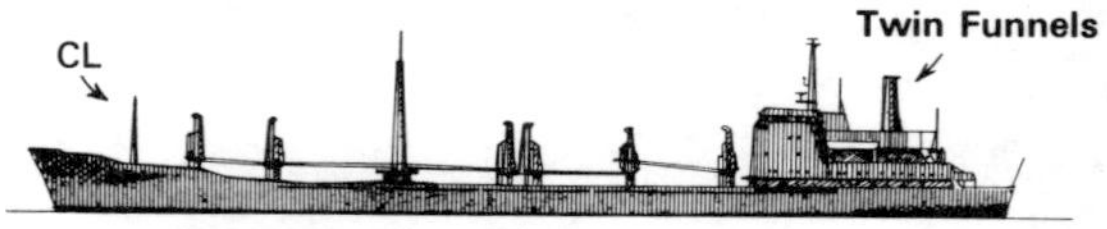

KC_2MC_4MF H1
49710 BANGLAR MITA. Bh/Sw 1966; C; 7300/10700; 156.14 × 8.4/9.51 (512.27 × 27.56/31.2); M; 19; ex HOKKAIDO 1977. Sisters: **49711 BANGLAR MAAN** (Bh) ex HIRADO 1977 **49712 HALLBORG** (Li) ex HAKONE **49713 SIFNOS** (Gr) ex HONDO.

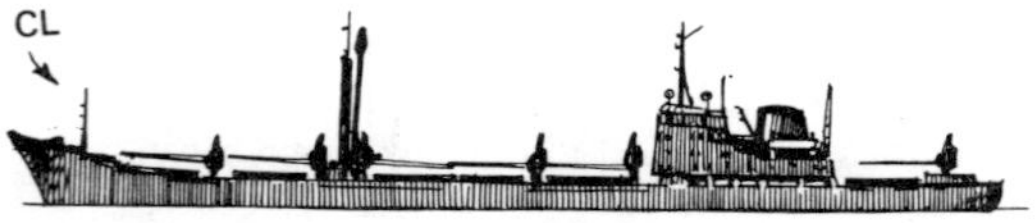

KC_2MC_3MFC H1
★49720 OMSK. Ru/Ja 1961; C; 7500/10900; 155 × 9.6 (509 × 31.5); M; 17. Sisters (Ru flag): **★49721 OKHOTSK ★49722 ORENBURG.**

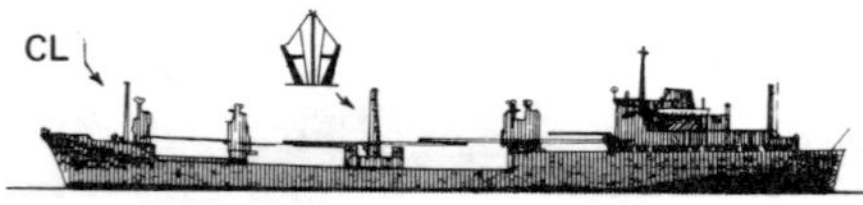

KC_2MC_2MFK H13
49730 BANGPRA-IN. Sg/Sw 1966; C; 3500/5800; 127.4 × 8.2 (418 × 26.9); M; 16; ex TRADER. Sister: **49731 BANGPLEE** (Sg) ex LINGUIST.

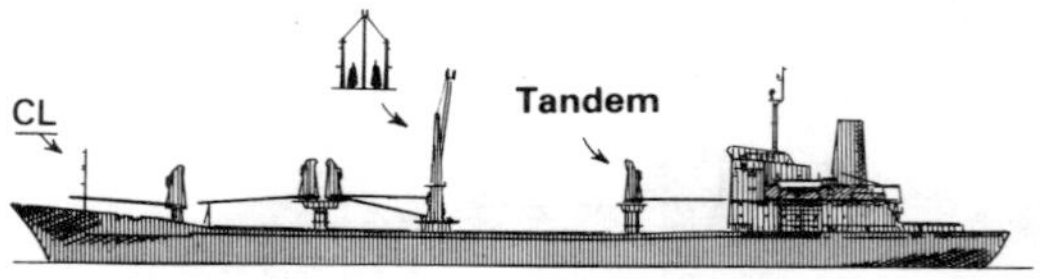

KC_2MCMF H1
● **49740 IVAN ZAGUBANSKI.** Bu/Ru 1975; C; 11800; 162.31 × 9.17 (532.51 × 30.09); M; 18.; **'Dnepr'** type. Sisters (Bu flag): **★49741 CHRISTO BOTEV ★49742 GOTZE DELCHEV ★49743 LUBEN KARAVELOV ★49744 KAPITAN PETKO VOIVODA ★49745 VASIL LEVSKY** (Ru flag): **★49746 GRIGORIY PETRENKO ★49747 NIKITA MITCHENKO ★49748 PETR DUTOV ★49749 IVAN SHEPETKOV ★49750 IVAN MOSKALENKO ★49751 GEROI PANFILOVTSY ★49752 VASILY KLOCHKOV ★49753 NIKOLAY ANANYEV ★49754 NIKOLAY MAKSIMOV ★49755 PETR YEMTSOV ★49756 YAKOV BONDARENKO ★49757 SOVIETSKIYE PROFSOYUZY** (Ys flag): **★49758 ADMIRAL PURISIC ★49759 HEROJ PAIC ★49760 HEROJ KOSTA STAMENKOVIC ★49761 HEROJ SENJANOVIC** (Rm flag): **★49762 ZALAU** (Cu flag): **★49763 JOSE ANTONIO ECHEVERRIA ★49764 JULIO ANTONIO MELLA ★49765 30 DE NOVIEMBRE ★49766 XI FESTIVAL** (Br flag): **49767 LYCAON 49768 LAERTES** (FRG flag): **49769 SANTA ELENA.** (Hu flag) **★49770 VOROSMARTY**

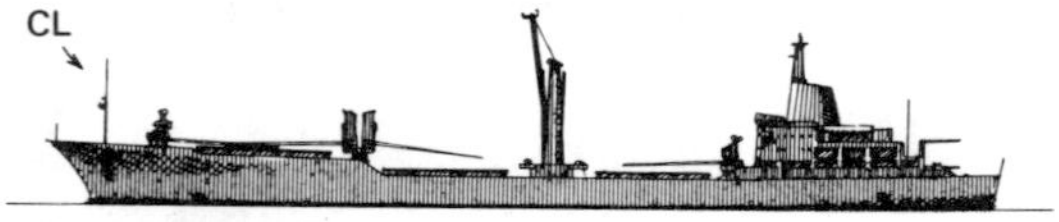

KC_2MCMF H13
49775 HALLA PILOT; Ko/Br 1970; C; 6700/10000; 154.13 × 8.17/9.62 (505.68 × 26.8/31.56); M; 17; ex STRATHCARROL; ex ASKA 1975. Sister: **49776 HALLA PRIDE** (Ko) ex STRATHCARRON; ex AMRA 1976.

KC_2MF H
49790 AGENOR; FRG/FRG 1964; C; 500; 73 × 3.6 (239.5 × 11.81); M; 13.

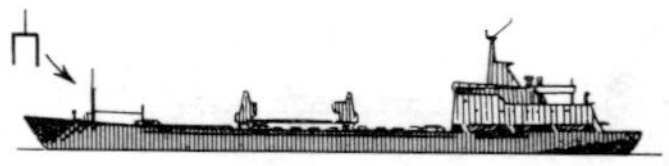

KC_2MF H
49800 PLANTA DE BETANIA; Co/Sp 1971; C; 2400; 96.93 × 3.86 (318.01 × 12.66); TSM; 12. Sisters (Co flag): **49801 PLANTA DE MAMONAL 49802 SALINA DE MANAURE.**

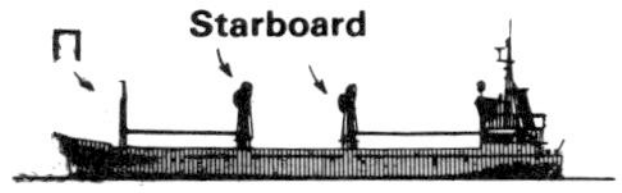

KC_2MF H

● **49810 LELIEGRACHT;** Ne/Ja 1976; C; 1600; 80.22 × 5.98 (263.19 × 19.62); M; 13.5. Sisters (Ne flag): **49811 LEIDSEGRACHT 49812 LIJNBAANSGRACHT 49813 LINDENGRACHT 49814 LAURIERGRACHT 49815 LOOIESGRACHT 49816 RAAMGRACHT 49817 REALENGRACHT 49818 REGULIERSGRACHT 49819 RIJPGRACHT 49820 RINGGRACHT 49821 ROZENGRACHT 49822 SCHIPPERSGRACHT 49823 SINGELGRACHT 49824 SPIEGELGRACHT 49825 STADIONGRACHT** ex SELIBA 1978.

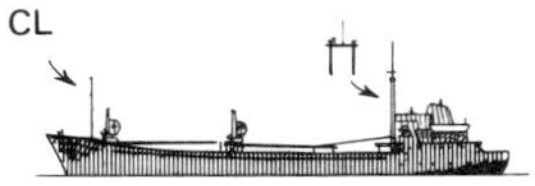

KC_2MF H1

● **49850 PELINA;** Gr/Fi 1961; C; 500/1100; 73.21 × 3.65/5 (240.19 × 11.97/16.4); M; 11.5; ex VILKA 1972. Sisters: **49851 ARAB ALRIYAD** (Si) ex GULF OMAN 1974; ex KURKI 1971 **49852 ARAB NAJAD** (Si) ex GULF MAZOON 1974; ex SOTKA 1971 **49853 ELISSAR** (Sy) ex BALTIC SEA 1977; ex MORSO 1974; ex ANCYLUS II 1972; ex TIIRA 1971.

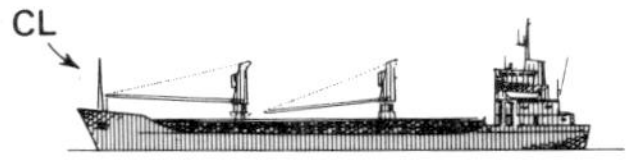

KC_2MF H1

49880 AROS ATHENE; FRG/FRG 1976; C/Con; 1000; 81.41 × 5.04 (267.09 × 16.54); M; —; ex ELBSTROM 1979; Travelling cranes. Sister: **49881 HOVE** (FRG).

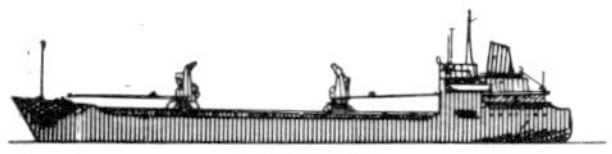

KC_2MF H1

● **49900 ESTEBOGEN;** FRG/FRG 1972; C/Con; 1000; 88.5 × 5.28 (290.35 × 17.32); M; 14; ex SCOL UNIT; ex ESTEBOGEN 1975. Sisters (FRG flag): **49901 SCOL PROGRESS 49902 SCOL SPIRIT 49903 BALTICA** ex SCOL HUNTER 1977; ex BALTICA 1976 Similar: **49904 JORK** ex SCOL VALIANT 1977; ex JORK 1975.

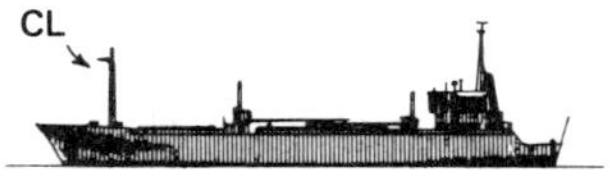

KC_2MF H

49830 LEE SHARON; Pa/No 1966; C; 1300; 83.47 × 4.64 (273.85 × 15.22); M; 14.5; ex BRILLIANT 1976. Similar: **49831 CYRUS** (Le) ex BRETAGNE 1976; (converted to livestock carrier).

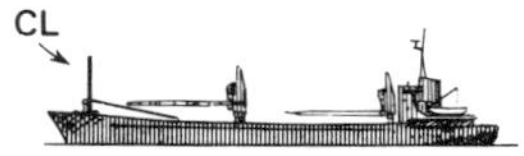

KC_2MF H

49840 ATLANTIC SEA; Ne/FRG 1965; C; 500; 72.07 × 3.71 (236.45 × 12.17); M; 12; ex OKDINE 1978; ex NORDFELD 1974; ex FRYKEN 1971.

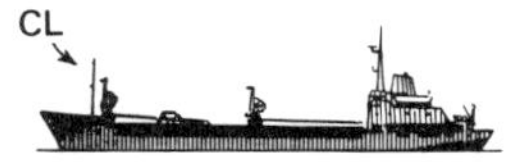

KC_2MF H1

49860 LABORE; Fi/Fi 1965; C; 500/1300; 72.14 × 3.54/5.46 (236.68 × 11.61/17.91); M; 12.5; ex BORE XI 1972. Sisters: **49861 KARE** (Fi) ex BORE IV 1972 **49862 MEDWAY** (PA) ex OBRESTAD 1978; ex BORE VIII 1973.

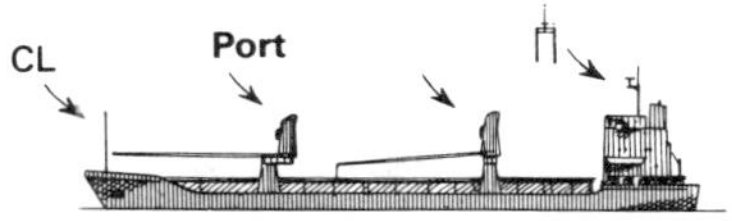

KC_2MF H1

49870 WESTERMOOR; FRG/FRG 1977; Con; 1600; 97.54 × 5.39 (320.01 × 17.68); M; 14. Sister: **49871 NEERLANDIA** (FRG) ex KAREN OLTMANN.

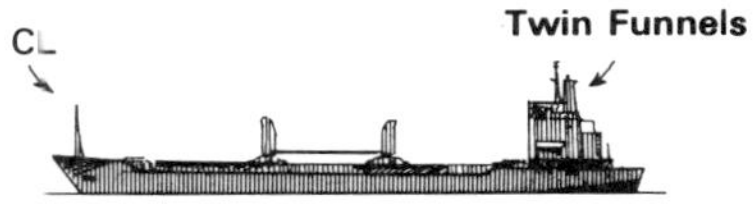

KC_2MF H1

49890 JOHN WULFF; FRG/FRG 1977; C; 1600; 93.53 × 6.06 (306.86 × 19.88); M; 14.5; Travelling cranes. Sister: **49891 HILDEGARD WULFF** (FRG).

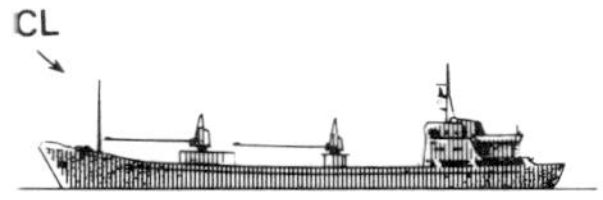

KC_2MF H1

49910 SIERRA LUCENA; Sp/Sp 1967; R; 1600; 83.47 × 5.01; (273.85 × 16.44); M; 16. Sister: **49911 SIERRA LUNA** (Sp).

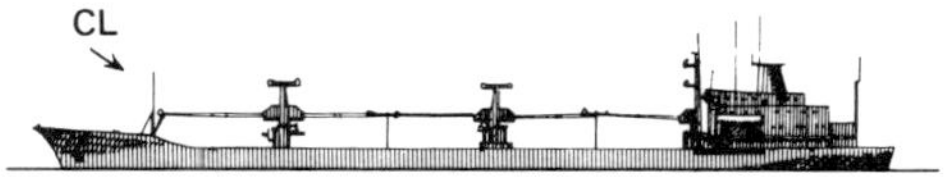

KC_2MF H1

49920 NADINA; Gr/FRG 1970; C; 3500/5900; 136.81 × 6.47/7.51 (448.85 × 21.23/24.64); M; 15.5; ex BARBARELLA 1978. Possible Sister: **49921 STINTFANG** (FRG) ex BIANCA 1973; Launched as STINTFANG.

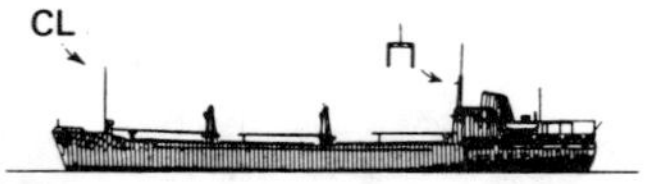

KC_2MF H1
49930 MARIKA; Gr/No 1962; C; 1500; 86.01 × 4.69 (282.19 × 15.39); M; 14.5; ex ARNES 1969; Launched as ALBERTINA. Sister: **49931 PIREAS** (Gr) ex DENEB 1969; Launched as FREDRIKA.

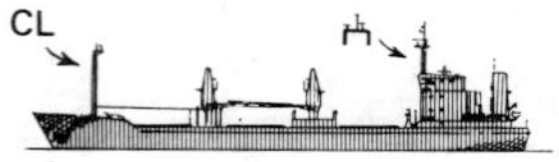

KC_2MF H1
49940 PACIFIC PRINCESS; Ne/Ne 1979; R; 1400; 80.7 × 5.42 (264.76 × 17.78); M; 14.5.

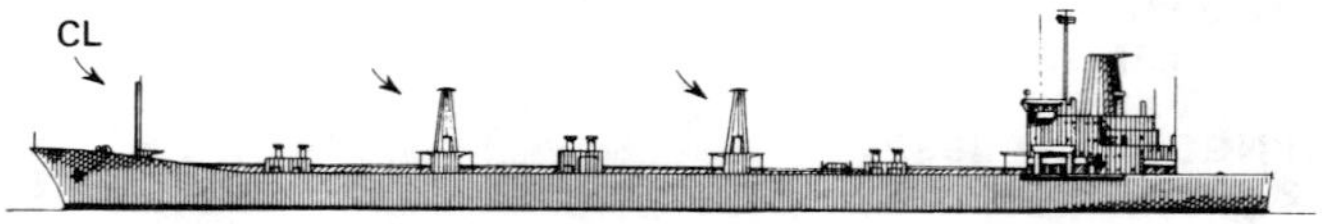

KC_2MF H1
49950 ERIKA BOLTEN; FRG/FRG 1973; BC; 20300; 196.32 × 10.9 (644.09 × 35.76); M; 18. Sister: **49951 NATALIE BOLTEN** (FRG).

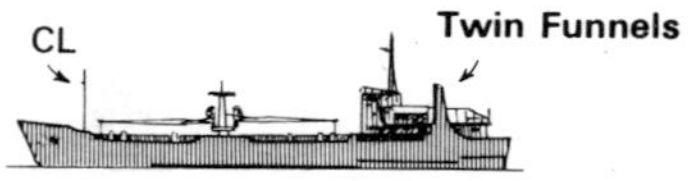

KC_2MF H1
49960 ZEJTUN; Ma/FRG 1967; RoC; 1000; 78.03 × 4.29 (256 × 14.07); M; —; ex TAOS 1974; ex WASA 1973; Bow and stern doors. Sister: **49961 ALPILLES** (Fr) ex HANSA 1972.

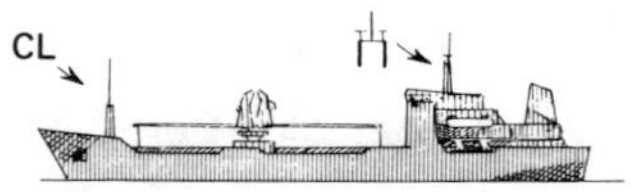

KC_2MF H1
49970 MAGNUS JENSEN. De/De 1979; C; 2400; 95.51 × 5.3 (313.35 × 17.39); M; 14.5.

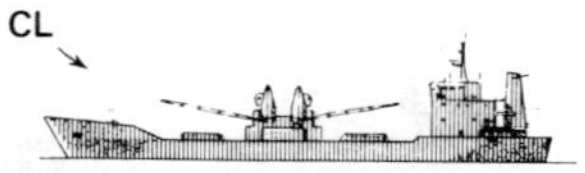

KC_2MF H1
49980 ICE STAR. De/De 1979; R; 1000; 80.20 × 4.71 (263.12 × 15.45); M; 14.7; side door.

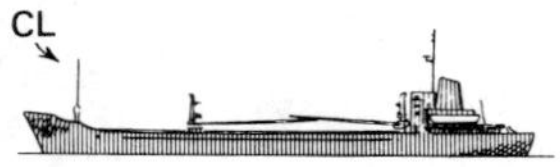

KC_2MF H1
49990 LA PAIX. Le/Ne 1963; C; 600; 81.03 × 3.83 (265.85 × 12.57); M; 12; ex EDDA 1980. Lengthened 1969. Sister: **49991 PLAYA DE EZARO** (Sp) ex CEDAR GLORY 1980; ex VEGA 1978 Similar (Unlengthened): **49992 STAVROS H** (Cy) ex ASK 1977 **49993 AL SALAM 1** (Le) ex LA PAIX 1978; ex EMBLA 1977.

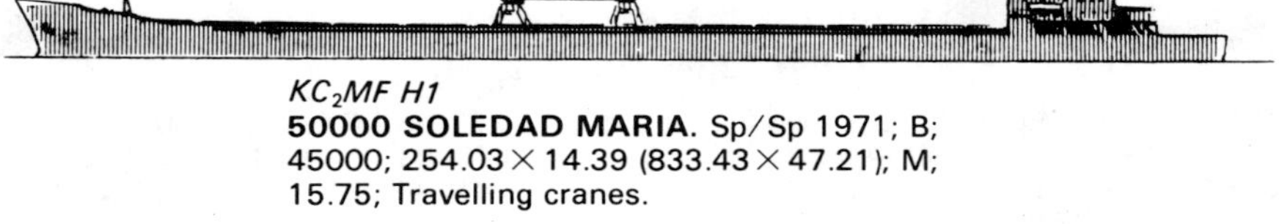

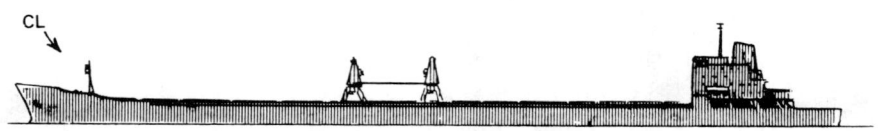

KC_2MF H1
50000 SOLEDAD MARIA. Sp/Sp 1971; B; 45000; 254.03 × 14.39 (833.43 × 47.21); M; 15.75; Travelling cranes.

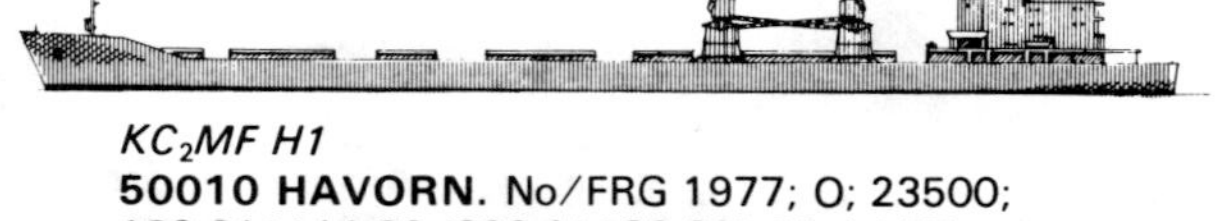

KC_2MF H1
50010 HAVORN. No/FRG 1977; O; 23500; 182.91 × 11.89 (600.1 × 39.01); M; 14.75; Travelling cranes. Sisters (No flag): **50011 HAVFALK 50012 HAVJO.**

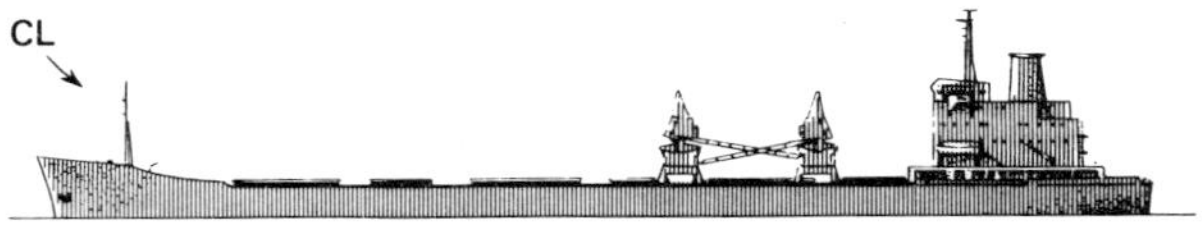

KC_2MF H1
50020 BETH. No/Pd 1978; B; 22100; 176.59 × 11.51 (579.36 × 37.76); M; 16; **"B515"** type. Travelling cranes. Sisters (No flag): **50021 BARDU 50022 BARRY 50023 BAUCHI 50024 BAVANG 50025 BERGO.**

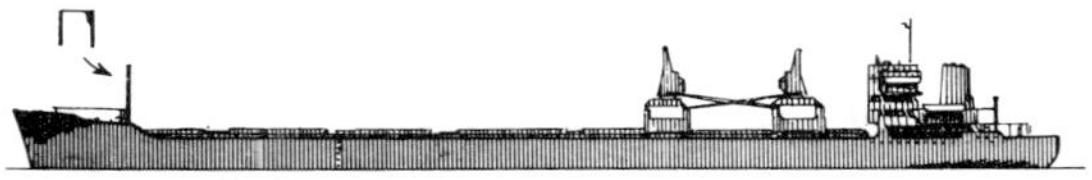

KC_2MF H1
50030 ARABIAN LULUAH. Pa/Sw-FRG 1954/62 B; 13600; 166 × 10.35 (544.62 × 33.96); M; 14; ex HAVJARL 1974. Aft section 1954. Forward & cargo section 1962. Converted from tanker. Travelling cranes.

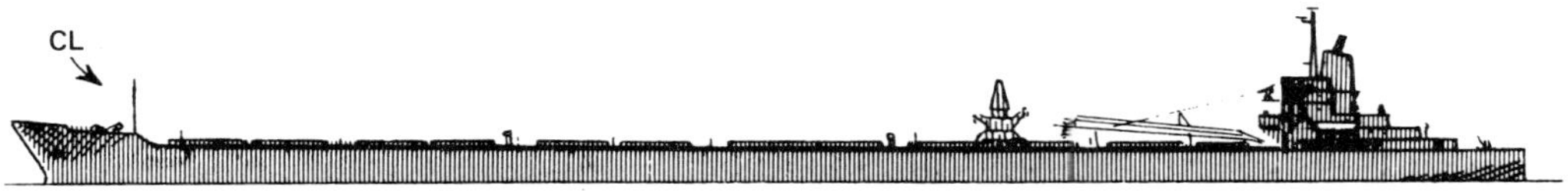

KC_2MF H1
50040 KURE. Li/Ja 1971; B; 76000; 303.82 × 17.45 (996.78 × 57.25); T; 15.5; ex UNIVERSE KURE 1980; launched as CEDROS PACIFIC. Travelling cranes.

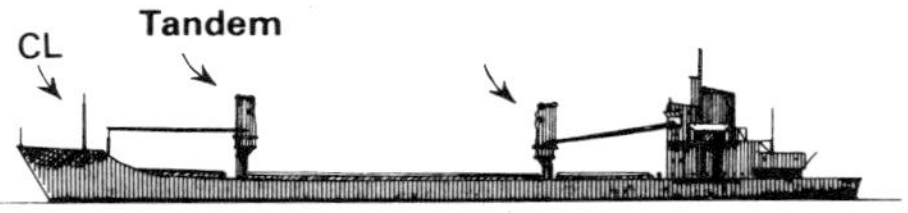

KC_2MF H1
● **50050 OLIVER DRESCHER.** FRG/FRG 1973; C; 3500/6200; 132.52 × 6.5/8 (434.77 × 21.32/26.24); M; 17; ex LLOYD PHILADELPHIA 1980; ex OLIVER DRESCHER 1978; ex EDE SINSTORF 1975. Similar: **50051 LLOYD NEW YORK** (FRG) ex MACAELA DRESCHER 1978.

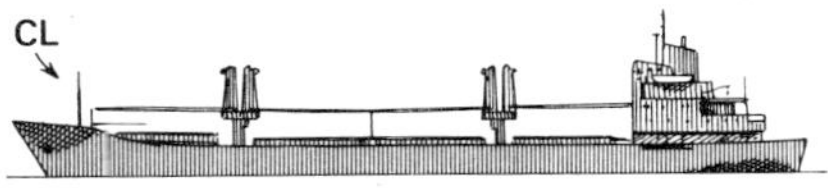

KC_2MF H1
50060 STEFAN DRESCHER. FRG/FRG 1972; C; 3400/6000; 124.52 × 6.59/8.12 (408.53 × 21.62/26.64); M; 17; ex WADAI 1975; ex EDE FOLDENFJORD 1974; ex EDE WITTORF 1973.

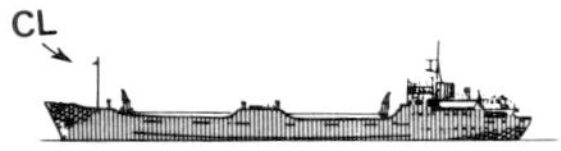

KC_2MF H123
● **50070 COSTAS.** Gr/Ne 1960; R; 800; 77.32 × 4.02 (253.67 × 13.19); M; 11.5; ex MARKAB II 1979; ex MARKAB 1969.

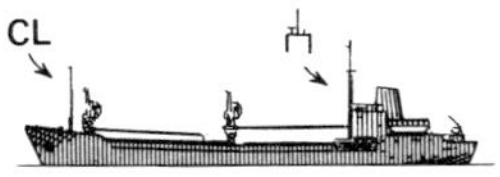

KC_2MF H13
● **50080 BORELLA.** Fi/Fi 1963; C; 500/1300; 71.73 × 3.53/5.44 (235.33 × 11.58/17.85); M; 12.5; ex BORE VII 1971. Sister (Pa flag): **50081 MADIMAR** (Pa) ex SAGA 1977; ex BORINA 1973; ex BORE X 1972.

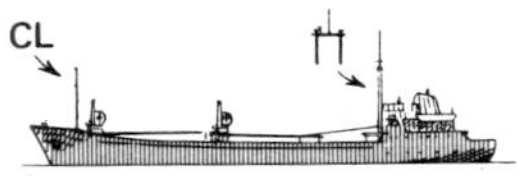

KC_2MF H13
50090 PELINA. Gr/Fi 1961; C; 500/1100; 73.21 × 3.55/5 (240.19 × 11.97/16.4); M; 11.5; ex VILKA 1972. Sisters: **50091 ARAB ALRIYAD** (Si) ex GULF OMAN 1974; ex KURKI 1971 **50092 ARAB NAJAD** (Si) ex GULF MAZOON 1974; ex SOTKA 1971 **50093 ELISSAR** (Sy) ex BALTIC SEA 1977; ex MORSO 1974; ex ANCYLUS 1972; ex TIIRA 1971.

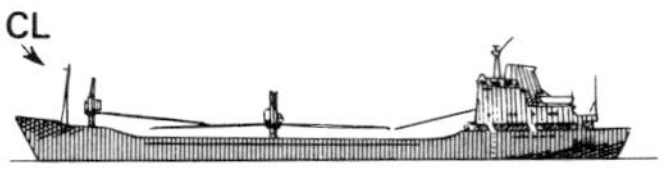

KC_2MF H13
50100 TIAN SHAN. Pa/Fi 1965; C; 1800/3000; 96.91 × 5.4/6.57 (317.95 × 17.72/21.56); M; 13; ex FINNREEL 1977; ex ANNIKA 1971.

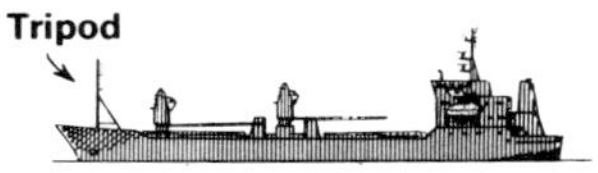

KC_2MF H13
50110 NORCAN. No/No 1979; R/RoC; 1200; 79.44 × 5.12 (260.63 × 16.8); M; 14.

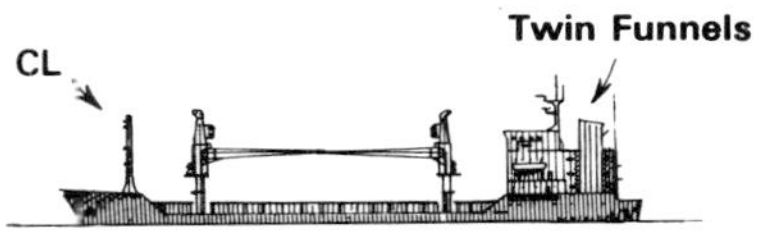

KC_2MF H13
50120 ALTNES. No/No 1978; C; 3000; 92.03 × 6.4 (301.94 × 21); M; 13.5 Probable Sisters (No flag): **50121 GARNES 50122 KORSNES 50123 VIGNES.**

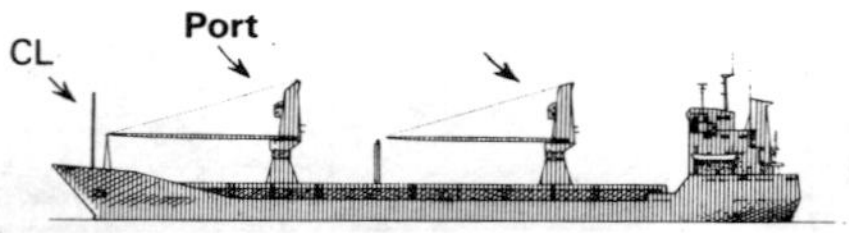

KC_2MF H13

● **50130 KARTHAGO.** FRG/FRG 1979; C; 1600/3200; 104.5 × 5.45/6.65 (342.85 × 17.88/21.82); M; 14.25; ex MATTHIAS CLAUDIUS 1979.

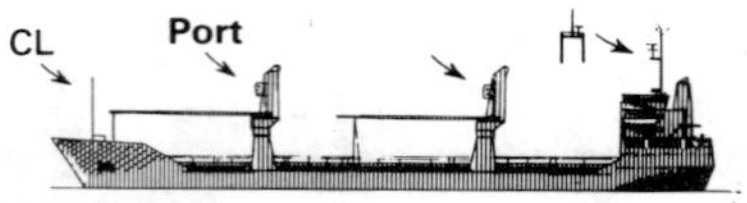

KC_2MF H13

50140 KAHIRA. FRG/FRG 1978; C/Con; 1600/3200; 104.76 × 5.58/— (343.7 × 18.31/—); M; 15; launched as HANSETOR. Sisters (FRG flag): **50141 KALYMNOS** ex OSTEBAY 1979 **50142 KARAMAN** ex HANSADAM 1979 **50143 REGULUS.**

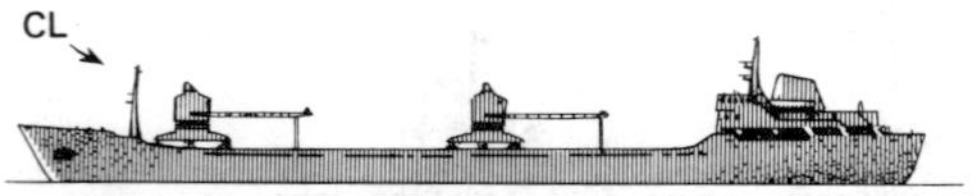

KC_2MF H13

50150 CABOT. Ca/Ca 1965; C; 6000; 143.54 × 7.21 (470.93 × 23.65); M; —; Travelling cranes. Sister: **50151 CHIMO** (Ca).

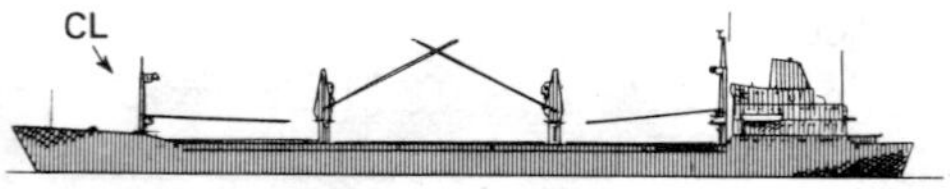

KC_2MF H13

50160 CAPE FREELS. Li/FRG 1972; C; 3400/6000; 142.73 × 6.5/7.68 (468.27 × 21.32/25.2); M; 16.5 ex FLEETHORN 1974. Sister: **50161 ROSA ROTH** (Cy) ex CAPE BRETON 1978; ex SANDHORN 1973.

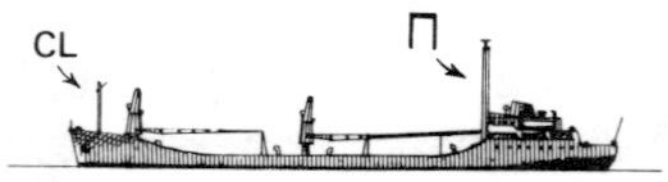

KC_2MF H13

50170 MALLING. Br/Br 1970; C; 1600; 85.91 × 5.31 (281.86 × 17.42); M; 12.5. Sister: **50171 FERRING** (Br).

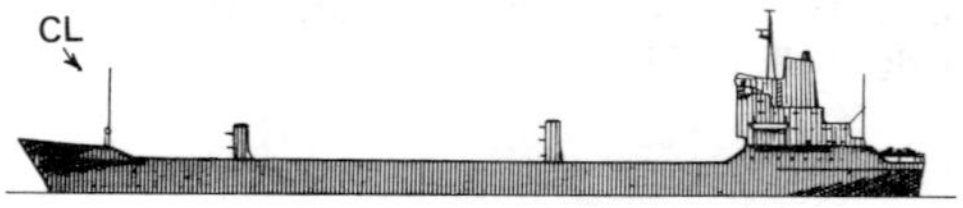

KC_2MF H13

50180 ANEMOS. Gr/FRG 1976; Con; 8400; 143.82 × 8.32 (471.85 × 27.3); M; 18.25. Sister: **50181 PELAGOS** (Gr).

KC_2MF H13

50190 MARGARETHA SMITS. Ne/Ne 1976; C; 1600; 84.21 × 6.32 (276.8 × 20.73); Travelling cranes. Sister (Ne flag): **50191 MARIJKE SMITS** Probable Sisters: **50192 MAKIRI SMITS 50193 MARIA SMITS 50194 MARINUS SMITS.**

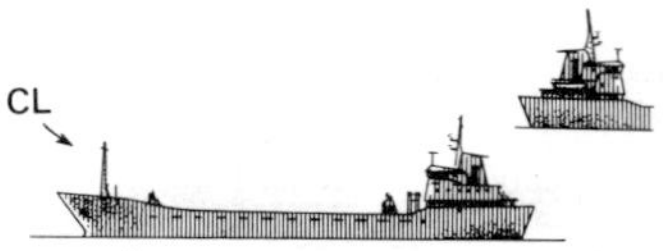

KC_2MF H13

● **50200 URRIDAFOSS.** Ic/De 1971; C; 500; 76.61 × 3.47 (251.35 × 11.38); M; 12; ex MERC EUROPA 1974; Travelling cranes. Starboard side of superstructure differs (see inset). Sisters: **50201 ASMAA** (Mo) ex MERC PHOENECIA 1977 **50202 ECO SADO** (Po) ex MERC ASIA 1973 **50203 ECO TEJO** (Po) ex MERC CONTINENTAL 1973 **50204 GRUNDARFOSS** (Ic) ex MERC AUSTRALIA 1974 **50205 NEXUS** (Pa) ex ALBERT S 1978; ex NORDSEE 1977; ex MERC GROENLANDIA 1974.

KC_2MF H13

50210 RIO BESAYA. Sp/Sp 1967; C; 1000/1700; 86.24 × —/5.02 (282.94 × —/16.47); M; 13.5. Sister: **50211 BAIA DE SAO BRAS** (Pa) ex RIO NANSA 1971 Probably similar: **50212 TREVINCA** (Sp).

KC_2MF H13

50220 HANIA T. Pa/Fi 1965; C; 500/1700; 75.42 × 3.56/5.41 (247.44 × 11.68/17.75); M; 13.75; ex CAPELLA 1980. Side doors. **50221 NORDGARD** (Fi) ex CANOPUS 1980.

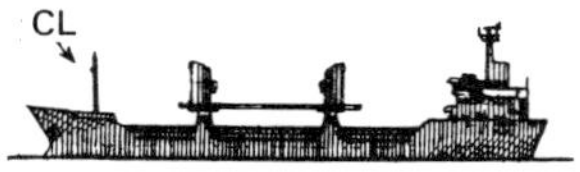

KC_2MF *H13*

● **50230 JAN TAVENIER.** Ne/Ne 1977; C; 1600; 82.71 × 5.99 (271.36 × 19.65); M; 13.

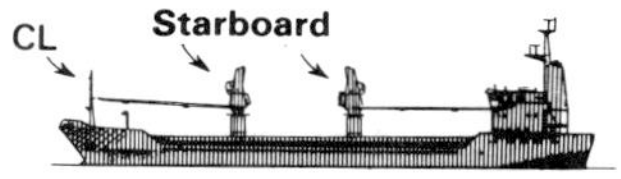

KC_2MF *H13*

50240 DELFBORG. Ne/Ne 1978; C; 3700; 83.06 × 7.8 (272.5 × 25.59); M; 13.

KC_2MF *H13*

50250 VISTEN. Ne/Ne 1977; C; 3200; 83.88 × 7.62 (275.2 × 34.99); M; 13.

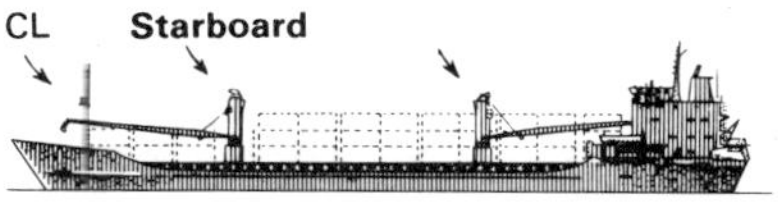

KC_2MF *H13*

● **50260 BERNHARD S.** FRG/FRG 1978; C/Con; 2700/5200; 117.2 × 7.7/—; (384.5 × 25.26/—); M; 16.

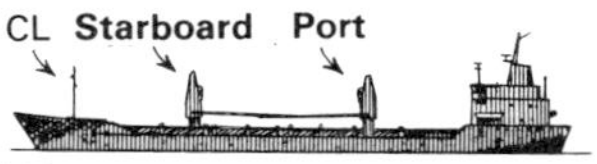

KC_2MF *H13*

50270 JUNIOR LILIAN. De/Ne 1976; C; 1600; 93 × 5.59 (305.12 × 18.34); M; 13.

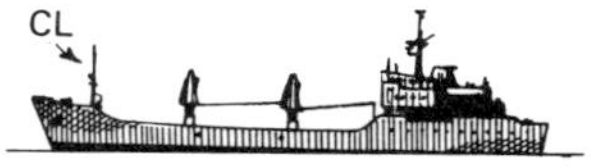

KC_2MF *H13*

⋆**50280 SOVETSKIY VOIN.** Ru/Ru 1968; C; 1700; 82 × 5.43 (269.03 × 17.82); M; 12.75. Sisters (Ru flag): ⋆**50281 KONSTANTIN SHESTAKOV** ⋆**50282 ALEKSANDR PANKRATOV** ⋆**50283 ARSENIY MOSKVIN** ⋆**50284 EVGENIY NIKONOV** ⋆**50285 KONSTANTIN SAVELYEV** ⋆**50286 ANDREY IVANOV** ⋆**50287 EVGENIY ONUFRIEV** ⋆**50288 JAKOV KUNDER** ⋆**50289 KONSTANTIN KORSHUNOV** ⋆**50290 NARVSKAYA ZASTAVA** ⋆**50291 VYBORGSKAYA STORONA** ⋆**50292 LENINGRADSKIY OPOLCHENETS** ⋆**50293 LENINGRADSKIY PARTIZAN** ⋆**50294 SOVETSKIY POGRANICHNIK** ⋆**50295 ALEKSANDR MIROSHNIKOV** ⋆**50296 NIKOLAY EMELYANOV** ⋆**50297 SOVIETSKIY MORYAK** ⋆**50298 VYACHESLAV DENISOV** ⋆**50299 YAKOV REZNICHENKO.**

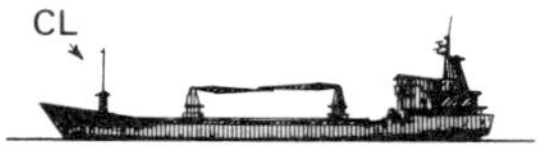

KC_2MF *H13*

50310 PEP STAR. De/De 1977; C; 500/1400; 71.91 × 3.76/5.67 (235.93 × 12.34); M; 13. Sisters (De flag): **50311 PEP SUN 50312 PEP SPICA 50313 PEP SIRIUS.**

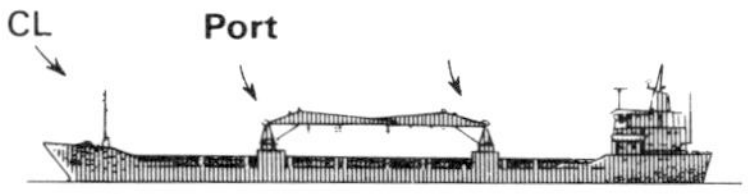

KC_2MF *H13*

50320 JUNIOR LONGO. De/Ne-De 1974/79; Con/HL; 2000; 106.43 × 5.45; (349.18 × 17.88); M; approx 13.5; ex JUNIOR LILO 1979; converted from cargo 1979.

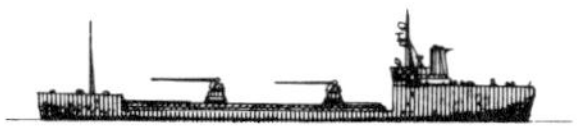

KC_2MF *H13*

● **50330 ESTHER SILVANA.** De/De 1975; C; 1400; 78.77 × 5.06 (258.43 × 16.6); M; 12.5; ex ESTHER BECH 1978. Travelling Cranes. Sisters: **50331 LOUISE BRAVO** (De) **50332 SOFIE BRAVO** (Sg) ex LEILA BECH **50333 OLGA BRAVO** (Sg) ex ANNA MARIE BECH 1978 Probable Sister: **50334 SUSAN MAC** (De) ex SUSAN SILVANA 1980.

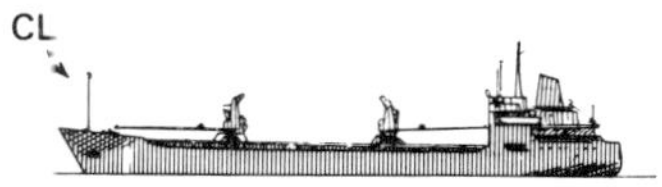

KC_2MF *H13*

● **50340 ESTEBOGEN.** FRG/FRG 1972; C/Con; 1000; 88.5 × 5.28 (290.35 × 17.32); M; 14; ex SCOL UNIT; ex ESTEBOGEN 1975. Sisters (FRG flag): **50341 SCOL PROGRESS 50342 SCOL SPIRIT 50343 BALTICA** ex SCOL HUNTER 1977; ex BALTICA 1976 Similar: **50344 JORK** ex SCOL VALIANT 1977; ex JORK 1975.

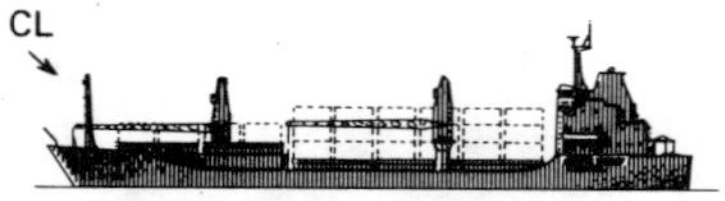

KC_2MF H13
50350 BUNGA PENAGA. My/Ja 1979; Con; 3900; 102.4 × 6.2; (335.96 × 20.34); M; 14.6. Sister: **50351 BUNGA DAHLIA** (My).

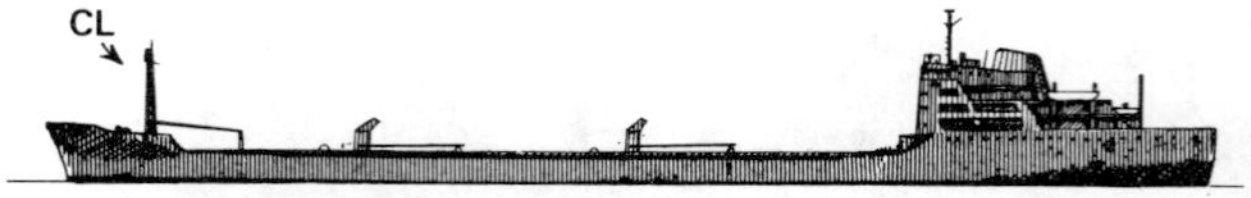

KC_2MF H13
50360 IRENES SINCERITY. Cy/Fr 1959; OO 1800; 185.99 × 9.75 (601.2 × 31.99); M; 15; ex FREE LANCER 1974; ex JUNIN 1971; ex LENS 1969.

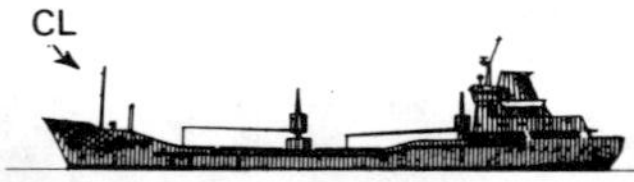

KC_2MF H13
50370 ALTAIR. Ne/Fi 1966; C; 1600/2800; 91.55 × 5.41/6.52 (300.36 × 17.75/21.4); M; 14. Sister: **50371 ALGENIB** (FRG).

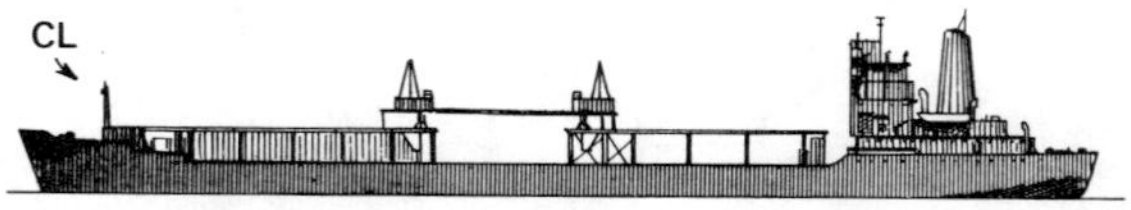

KC_2MF H13
50380 PUERTO RICO. US/US 1944/67; RoC; 8000; 170.67 × 8.25 (559.94 × 27.07); T-E; 16; ex SEATRAIN PUERTO RICO 1977; ex FRUITVALE HILLS 1967; ex MISSION SAN LUIS OBISPO 1966. Converted from various T-2 tankers. Sisters (US flag): **50381 CAROLINA** ex SEATRAIN CAROLINA 1978; ex MISSION SANTA BARBARA 1966 **50382 FLORIDA** ex SEATRAIN FLORIDA 1978; ex PAMANSET 1968 **50383 MAINE** ex SEATRAINE MAINE 1978; ex OHIO 1967; ex MISSION SAN JOSE 1966; ex MERCURY 1967; ex MISSION SAN JUAN 1966; ex MAINE 1967; ex TOMAHAWK 1966 **50384 MARYLAND** ex SEATRAIN MARYLAND 1978; ex SAN JACINTO 1965; ex MISSION SAN CARLOS 1966 **50385 OHIO** ex SEATRAIN OHIO 1978; ex MISSION SAN DIEGO 1967; ex MAINE 1967; ex TOMAHAWK 1966; ex OHIO 1967; ex MISSION SAN JOSE 1966.

50390 SIR BEDIVERE. Br/Br 1967; P/RoC/FA; 4500; 126.02 × 3.98 (413.45 × 13.06); TSM; 17.25. Sisters (Br flag): **50391 SIR LANCELOT 50392 SIR GALAHAD 50393 SIR GERAINT 50394 SIR PERCIVAL 50395 SIR TRISTRAM.**

KC_2MF H13
50400 CAPO MELE. It/Fr 1969; O; 12500; 151.97 × 9.9 (498.59 × 32.48); M; 16; ex LA CORDILLERA 1974; ex ALAIN L.D. 1973. Travelling cranes. Sister: **50401 DORIC CARRIER** (Gr) ex ROBERT L.D.

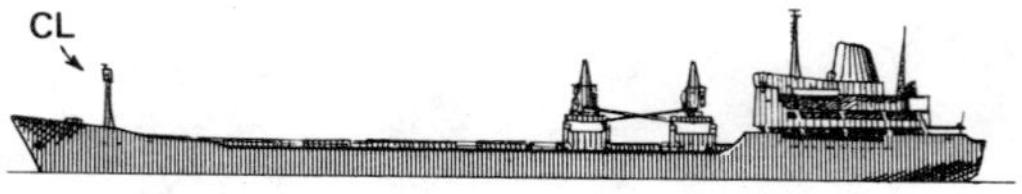

KC_2MF H13
50410 BAGRU. No/Ja 1967; B; 13300; 153.93 × 10.25 (505.02 × 33.63); M; 15.5; Travelling cranes. Sisters (No flag): **50411 BAHMA 50412 BANGOR 50413 BANI 50414 BIAKH 50415 HAVFRU 50416 HAVMANN** Similar (aft KP alongside funnel on Port Side) (Br flag) **50417 MOMBAKA** ex FINNA 1980.

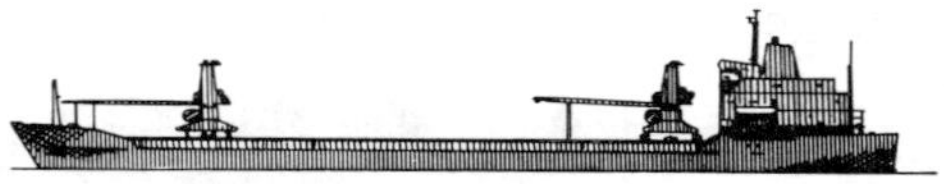

KC_2MF H13
50420 PETRA CROWN. Sd/FRG 1975; C/Con; 7700; 143.82 × 7.54 (471.85 × 24.74); M; 15.5; ex MALOJA; ex SKOTLAND; Travelling cranes. Sister: **50421 CALANDA** (Sd) ex VINLAND; ex MAERSK TEMPO 1978; ex VINLAND 1977.

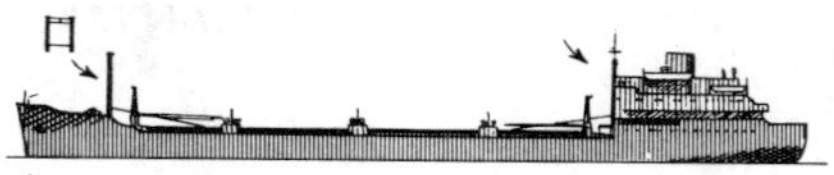

KC_2MF H13
★**50430 LE DU.** RC/Sw 1961; C; 4500/6700; 125.02 × 6.75/8.53 (410.17 × 22.15/27.99); M; 15; ex HUSARO 1976. Travelling cranes. Sister: **50431 TIUNA** (Ve) ex SEGERO 1976.

KC_2MF H13
***50440 MARLOW.** DDR/DDR 1971; C/Con; 300; 57.87 × 3.68 (189.86 × 12.07); M; 12; **'Boizenburg'** type Sisters (DDR flag): ***50441 HAGENOW *50442 MILTZOW *50443 MIROW *50444 NEUBOKOW *50445 RAKOW *50446 SATOW *50447 SEMLOW *50448 TORGELOW *50449 ZUROW *50450 ZUSSOW.**

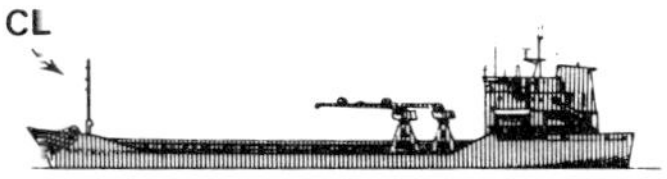

KC_2MF H13
***50460 BOLESLAWIEC.** Pd/Br 1979; B; 3000; 95 × 6.08 (311.68 × 19.95); M; 12.25; Travelling cranes. Sisters (Pd flag): ***50461 CHORZOW *50462 WYSZKOW *50463 MLAWA *50464 GNIEZNO II *50465 SIERADZ *50466 BYTOM *50467 ZGORZELEC *50468 KOSCIERZYNA *50469 LOMZA *50470 WIELUN** Some of these vessels may not have cranes.

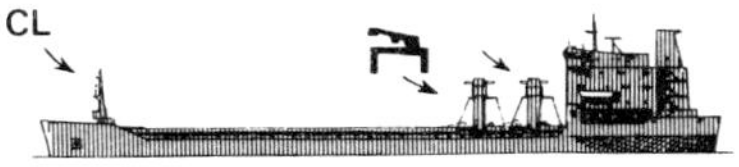

KC_2MF H13
50480 BOXY. Sw/Sw 1978; B/TC 6200; 121 × 7.62 (396.98 × 25); M; 14.6; Travelling cranes. The jibs are normally stowed athwartships as shown. Sister: **50481 DANIA** (Sw).

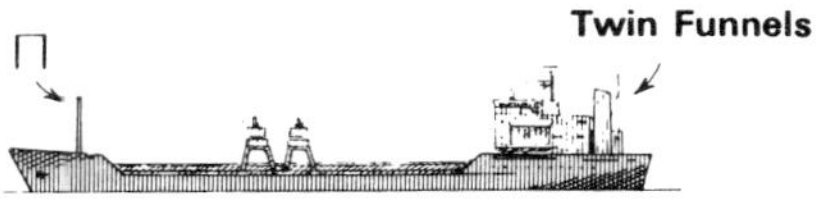

KC_2MF H13
50490 SANDGATE. Br/Br 1976; C; 3700; 102.04 × 6.93 (334.78 × 22.74); M; 14; Travelling cranes. Sisters (Br flag): **50491 SOUTHGATE 50492 SALTERSGATE** ex GREEN PARK 1977. (May not have cranes).

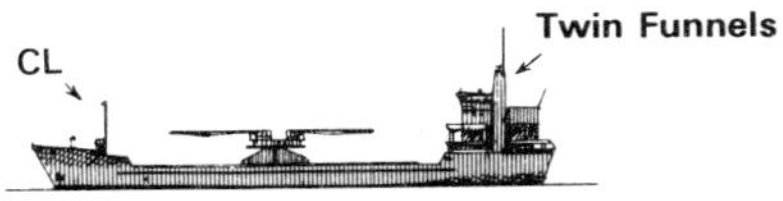

KC_2MF H13
50500 ALIDA SMITS. Ne/Ne 1978; C; 3500; 86.62 × 8.38 (274.34 × 27.49); M; —; Sisters (Ne flag): **50501 ANDREA SMITS 50502 ANGELA SMITS 50503 AMANDA SMITS 50504 ANITA SMITS 50505 ALSYTA SMITS.**

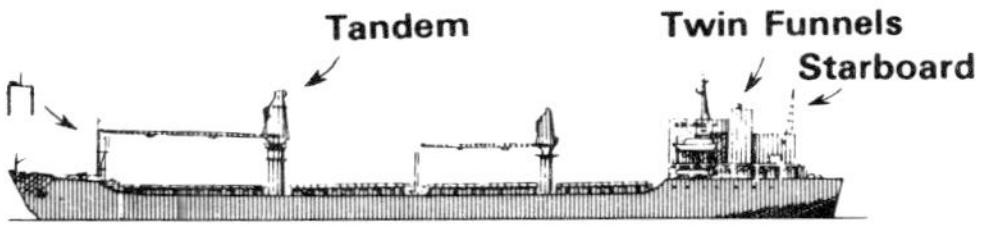

KC_2MF H13
50510 FARNES. Li/Ja 1978; C; 8100; 134.52 × 8.67 (441.34 × 28.44); M; 14.75. Probable Sister: **50511 FIRMNES** (Li).

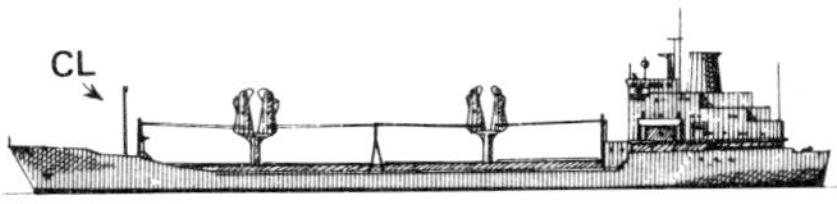

KC_2MF H13
50520 FINNPINE. Fi/Fi 1971; C; 3900/6600; 129.39 × 6.43/8.07 (424.51 × 21.1/24.48); M; 17.25. Sisters (Fi flag): **50521 FINNALPINO 50522 FINNTRADER 50523 FINNWOOD.**

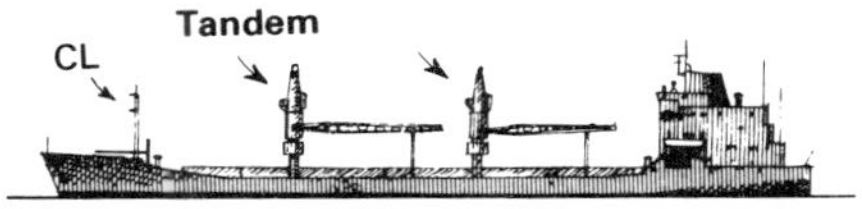

KC_2MF H13
50530 A.C. CROSBIE. Ca/Br 1972; C/Con; 7100; 122.31 × 8.1 (402.92 × 26.57); M; 15; ex IDA LUNDRIGAN 1976. Sister: **50531 OCEAN CHALLENGE** (Gr) ex GOMBA CHALLENGE 1980; ex SIMONBURN 1979; ex CITY OF PRETORIA 1977; ex RIA JEAN McMURTRY 1976.

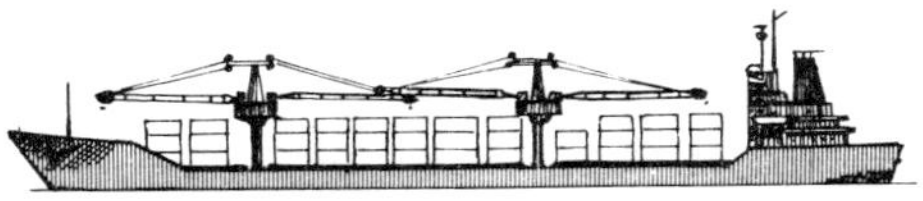

KC_2MF H13
● **50540 LLOYD BALTIMORE.** FRG/FRG 1978; C/Con; 7500; 140.6 × 7.9 (461.29 × 25.92); M; 16; ex CORINNA DRESCHER 1979.

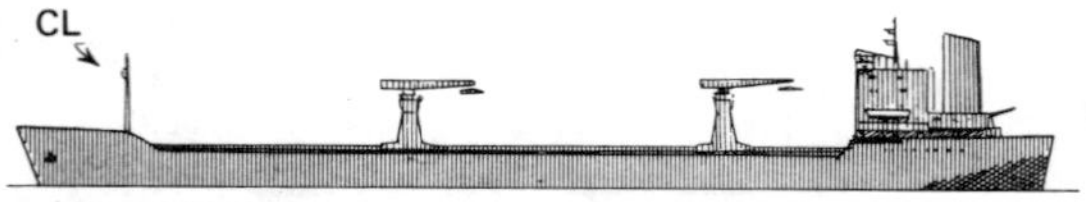

KC_2MF H13
50550 ANTARES. Fi/Ko 1978; B; 13000; 163.96 × 8.65 (537.93 × 28.38); M; 15.75; ex CHASE ONE 1979; ex ANTARES 1978. Travelling cranes. **'HD16F'** type. Sisters (Fi flag): **50551 ALDEBARAN** ex KHALIJ ENTERPRISE 1978 **50552 ATALAYA** ex CHASE TWO 1979; ex ATALAYA 1978 **50553 ASTREA** ex CHASE FOUR 1979; ex ASTREA 1978 **50554 ANDERSO** ex CHASE THREE 1979; ex ANDERSO 1978.

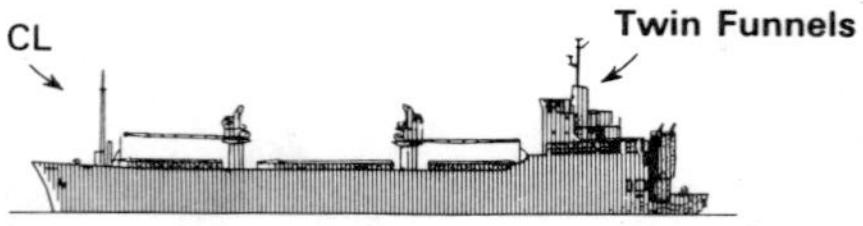

KC_2MF H3
50560 WILCON 1. Pi/Ja 1970; RoC/C; 2200; 107.42 × 5.38 (352.43 × 17.65); M; 14.75; ex HOKUTO MARU 1978; Port and starboard quarter ramps.

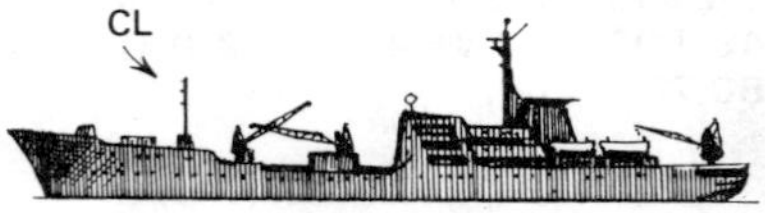

KC_2MFC H1
⋆**50570 'AMUR'** class.Ru/Ru 1969; A/Repairs; 6400 Dspl; 115 × 5.5 (377 × 18); TSM; 18. 14 ships in class and 1 building.

KC_2MFC H13
● **50590 DORRIT CLAUSEN.** De/No 1965; LS; 8000; 164.45 × 8.15 (539.53 × 26.74); M; 20.75; ex ANCONA 1976. Converted from cargo ship 1977.

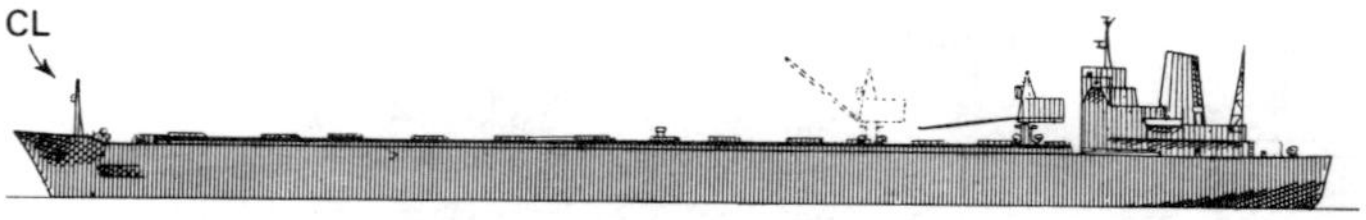

KC_2MFK H
● **50600 NEGO TRIABUNNA.** Li/Ja 1971; B; 32100; 209.02 × 10.99 (685.76 × 36.05); M; 15.75. Travelling cranes. Sister: **50601 SILVICULTURE** (Li).

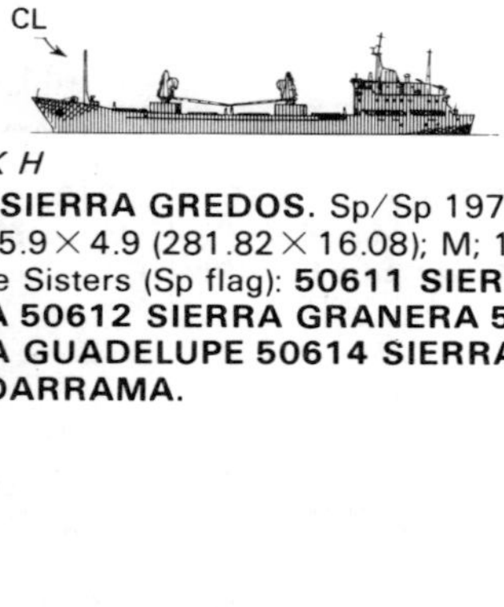

KC_2MFK H
50610 SIERRA GREDOS. Sp/Sp 1979; R; 1200; 85.9 × 4.9 (281.82 × 16.08); M; 14.4. Probable Sisters (Sp flag): **50611 SIERRA GRANA 50612 SIERRA GRANERA 50613 SIERRA GUADELUPE 50614 SIERRA GUARDARRAMA.**

KC_2MFK H1
50620 NADINA. Gr/FRG 1970; C; 3500/5900; 136.81 × 6.47/7.51 (448.85 × 21.23/24.64); M; 15.5; ex BARBARELLA 1970. Possible Sister: **50621 STINTFANG** (FRG) ex BIANCA 1973; launched as STINTFANG.

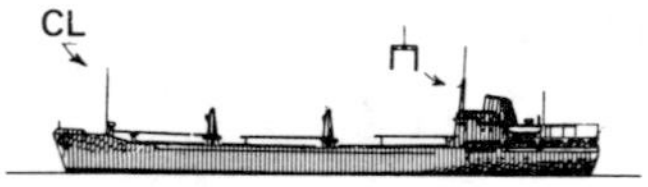

KC_2MFK H1
50630 MARIKA. Gr/No 1962; C; 1500; 86.01 × 4.69 (282.19 × 15.39); M; 14.5; ex ARNEB 1969; Launched as ALBERTINA. Sister: **50631 PIREAS** Gr) ex DENEB 1969; launched as FREDRIKA.

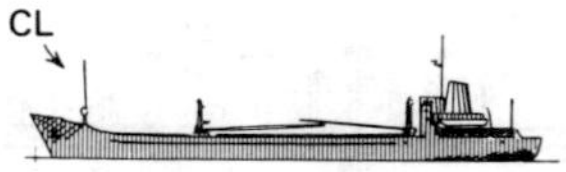

KC_2MFK H1
50640 PLAYA DE EZARO. Sp/Ne 1963; C; 600; 81.03 × 3.83 (265.85 × 12.57); M; 12; ex CEDAR GLORY 1980; ex VEGA 1978. Lengthened 1969.

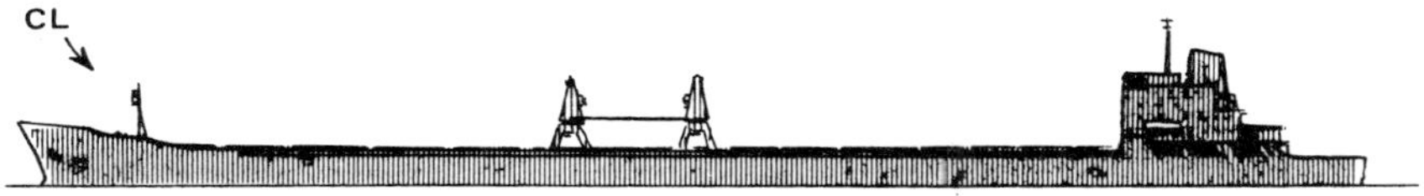

KC_2MFK H1
● **50650 SOLEDAD MARIA.** Sp/Sp 1971; B; 45000; 254.03 × 14.39 (833.43 × 47.21); M; 15.75; Travelling cranes.

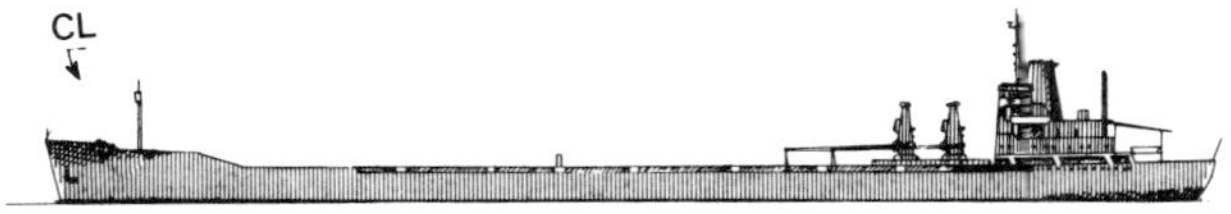

KC_2MFK H1
● **50660 FIDELIO.** Sw/Sw 1966; B/V; 18800; 185.66 × 10.71 (609.12 × 35.13); M; 15; ex CITADEL 1976. Travelling cranes. Sisters: **50661 PHILIPPINE ORCHID** (Pi) ex HUAL ORCHID 1980; ex ANDREAS U 1979 **50662 FALSTAFF** (Sw) ex DAPHNE 1977 **50663 HUAL JASMINE** (No) ex JOHAN U 1979 **50664 HUAL ROSAL** (No) ex AXEL U 1979.

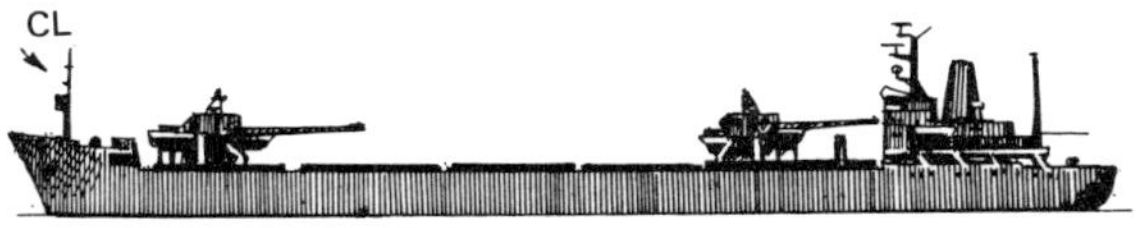

KC_2MFK H1
*__50670 GRIGORIY ALEKSEEV.__ Ru/Ja 1974; BWC; 18400; 169.45 × 9.88 (555.94 × 32.41); M; 14.5; Travelling cranes. Sister: ***50671 PAVEL RYBIN** (Ru).

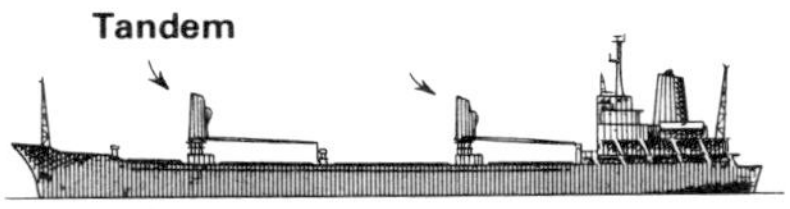

KC_2MFK H1
50700 RASELTIN. Eg/Ja 1976; C; 5800; 119.06 × 7.45 (390.61 × 24.44); M; 14.5. Sisters (Eg flag): **50701 ALANFUSHI 50702 ALCHATBY 50703 ALIBRAHIMIYA.**

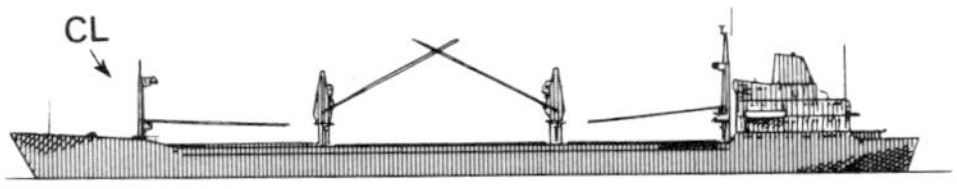

KC_2MFK H13
50710 CAPE FREELS. Li/FRG 1972; C; 3400/6000; 142.73 × 6.5/7.68 (468.27 × 21.32/25.2); M; 16; ex FLEETHORN 1974. Sister: **50711 ROSA ROTH** (Cy) ex CAPE BRETON 1978; ex SANDHORN 1973.

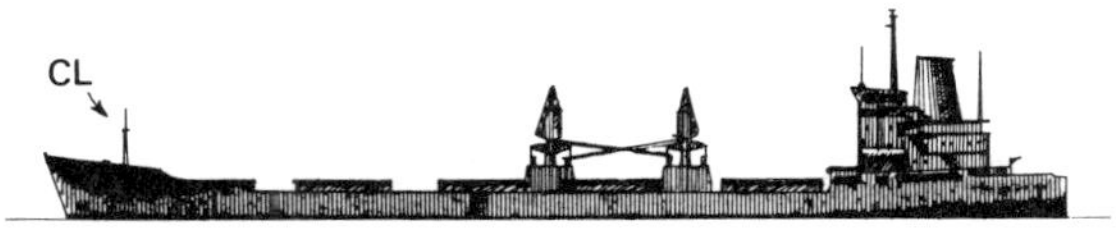

KC_2MFK H1
● **50680 HAVBJORN.** No/Pd 1971; B; 18000; 163.2 × 10.99 (535.43 × 36.05); M; 15; Travelling cranes. **'B-523'** type. Sisters (No flag): **50681 HAVKATT 50682 HAVTROLL 50683 BAJKA 50684 BAKAR 50685 BALAO 50686 BANTA 50687 BARO 50688 BARWA 50689 BERGLJOT 50690 BLIX 50691 STAVERN 50692 TRYM.**

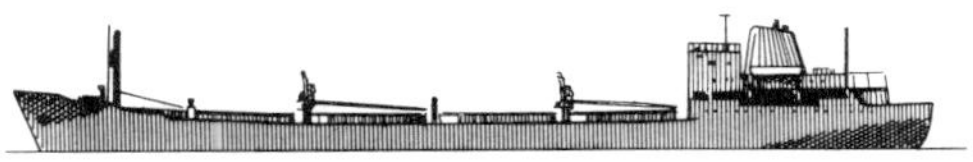

KC_2MFK H13
50720 MERITA. Fi/No 1963; B; 9900; 146.31 × 9.61 (480.02 × 30.05); M; 14.5; ex ANATINA 1971.

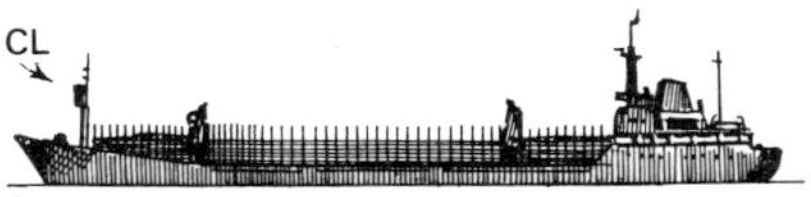

KC_2MFK H13
***50730 SOVIETSKAYA YAKUTIYA;** Ru/Ru 1972; C(Sea/River); 3600; 123.53 × 4.5 (405.28 × 14.76); TSM; 11.75. Sisters: ***50731 AFANASIY BOGATYREV *50732 FYODOR POPOV *50733 YAKUB KOLAS *50734 IVAN STROD *50735 KONSTANTIN ZASLONOV *50736 KOZELSK *50737 KHUDOZHNIK KUINDZHA *50738 YANKA KUPALA *50739 FIZULI *50740 VAGIF *50741 VASILIY YAN *50742 AVETIK ISAAKYAN *50743 BERDY KERBABAYEV *50744 BULUNKHAN *50745 KIGILYAKH *50746 ANDREY KIZHEVATOV *50747 DMITRIY KANTEMIR *50748 KHUDOZHNIK PLASTOV *50749 SERGEY GRITSEVETS *50750 FYODOR OKHLOPOV *50751 MIKAIL MUSHFIK *50752 KOMANDARM GAY *50753 ISIDOR BARAKHOV *50754 ILYA SELVINSKIY *50755 MAKSIM AMMOSOV *50756 NIKOLAY ZAZOLOTSKIY *50757 NIZAMI *50758 PLATON OYUNSKIY *50759 OGNYAN NAYDOV *50760 ASHUG ALEKSER *50761 DZHAFER DZHABARLY *50762 KOSTA KHETAGUROV.**

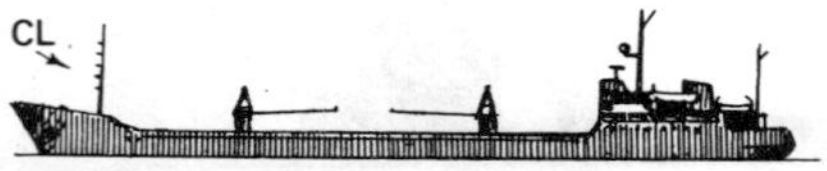

KC_2MFK H13
⋆50770 BAKU; Ru/Ru 1959; C; 3400; 120.02 × 4.4 (393.77 × 14.44); TSM; 11.5; **'CASPIAN-VOLGO-BALT'** type. Sisters (Ru flag): **⋆50771 INZHENIER BELOV ⋆50772 AGDAM ⋆50773 AKSTAFA ⋆50774 GEOKCHAY ⋆50775 MURGAB ⋆50776 SHAMKHOR ⋆50777 ASTARA ⋆50778 SALYANY ⋆50779 YANGI-YUL ⋆50780 KASPIY ⋆50781 HIMKI ⋆50782 SABIRABAD ⋆50783 HOROL ⋆50784 KUBATLY ⋆50785 NAVASHINO ⋆50786 SAATLY ⋆50787 ZANGELAN ⋆50788 SANGAR** ex HASAVJURT.

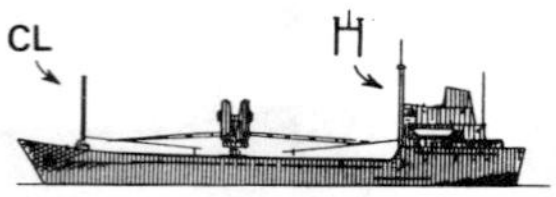

KC_2MFK H13
50800 HVASSAFELL; Ic/FRG 1971; C; 900/1800; 80.17 × 4.07/5.87 (263.02 × 13.36/19.25); M; 14. Similar: **50801 SKAFTAFELL** (Ic).

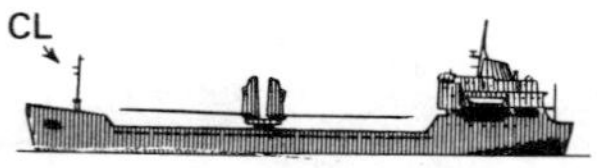

KC_2MFK H13
● **50810 EOS;** Sw/Sw 1972; C; 1600/2500; 87.03 × 5.89/6.83 (285.53 × 19.32/22.4); M; 12.5. Probable Sisters (Sw flag): **50811 ANNIKA** ex SKOGCELL FORESTER 1978 **50812 VESTANHAV.**

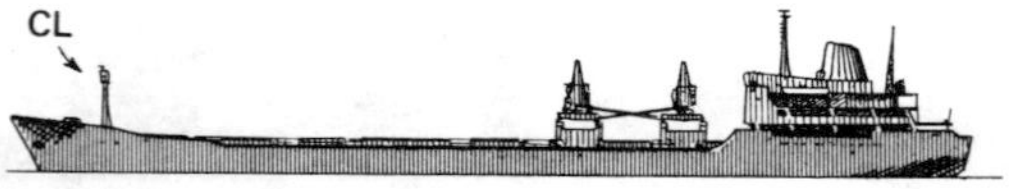

KC_2MFK H13
50820 BAGRU; No/Ja 1967; B; 13300; 153.93 × 10.25 (505.02 × 33.63); M; 15.5; Travelling cranes. Sisters (No flag): **50821 BAHMA 50822 BANGOR 50823 BANI 50824 BIAKH 50825 HAVFRU 50826 HAVMANN** Similar (aft KP alongside funnel on Port Side) (Br flag) **50827 MOMBAKA** ex FINNA 1980.

KC_2MFK H13
50830 CAPO MELE; It/Fr 1969; O; 12500; 151.97 × 9.9 (498.59 × 32.48); M; 16; ex LA CORDILLERA 1974; ex ALAIN L D 1973; Travelling cranes. Sister: **50831 DORIC CARRIER** (Gr) ex ROBERT L D.

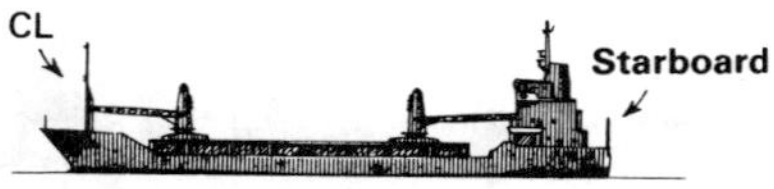

KC_2MFK H13
50840 DOLLART; FRG/FRG 1976; C; 1000/2900; 91.09 × 4.8/6.91 (298.85 × 15.75/22.67); M; 14.5; Travelling cranes. Sisters (FRG flag): **50841 JAN WILHELM 50842 OSTEREMS.**

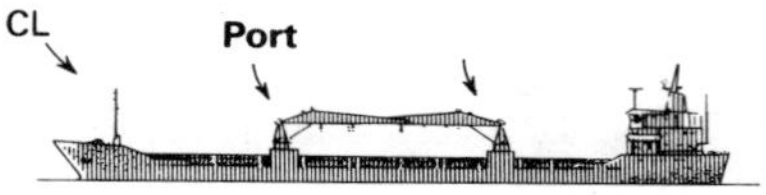

KC_2MFK H13
50850 JUNIOR LONGO; De/Ne-Ne 1974/79; Con/HL; 2000; 106.43 × 5.45; (349.18 × 17.88); M; approx 13.5; ex JUNIOR LILO 1979; Converted from cargo 1979.

KC_2MFK H13
50860 ANDERS; Sw/Sw 1971; C; 1600; 87.03 × 4.96 (285.53 × 16.27); M; 12; Cranes may have been removed.

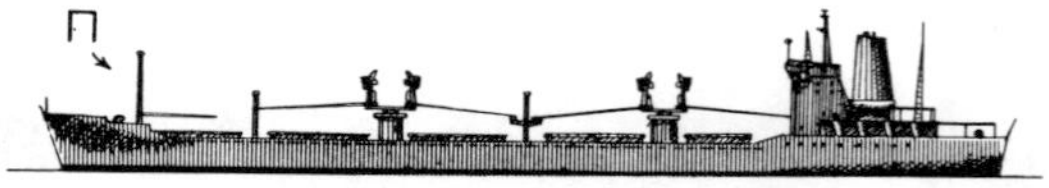

KC_2MFK H13
50870 JAMAICA FAREWELL. Li/Ja 1975; C; 13500; 161.6 × 9.93 (530.18 × 32.58); M; 15.5; **'Hitachi UT-20'** type. Sister: **50871 MARI BOEING** (Li).

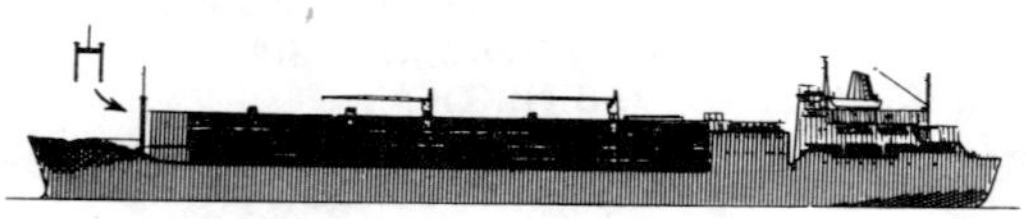

KC_2MFK H13
50880 CLARA CLAUSEN. De/No 1966; LS; 5900; 154.59 × 6.74 (507.19 × 22.11); M; 15; ex MAPLE 1976; ex SUNMAPLE 1969; Converted bulk carrier.

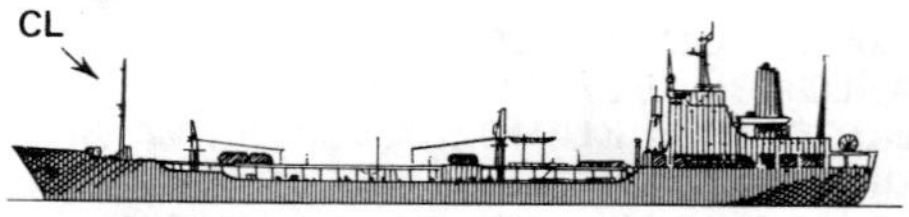

KC_2MFK H13
50890 JAPAN TUNA No 2. Ja/Ja 1979; Sply/Hospital; 6500; 128.38 × 8.2 (421.19 × 26.9); M; 15.7.

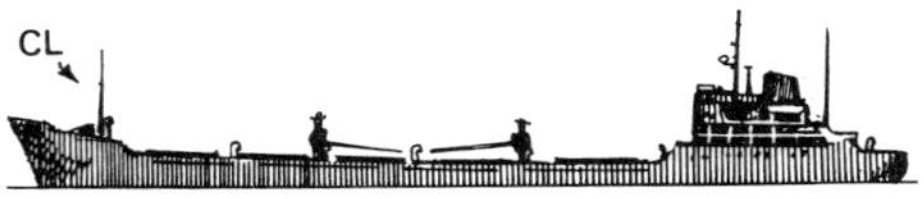

KC$_2$MFM H13
⋆**50900 DOLMATOVO.** Ru/DDR 1960; B; 6800; 139.5 × 8 (457.68 × 26.25); M; 14.25.

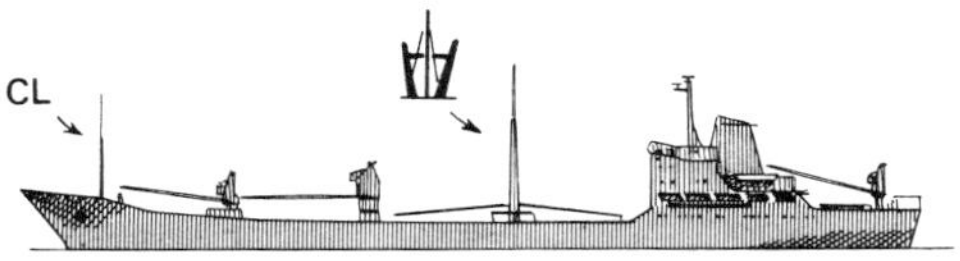

KC$_2$M$_2$FC H13
50930 LLOYD HUMAITA. Bz/Bz 1976; C; 5600/7700; 142.02 × 7.67 (465.95 × 25.16); M; 18. Sisters (Bz flag): **50931 LLOYD CUIABA 50932 LLOYD MARABA 50933 LLOYD ALTAMIRA 50934 LLOYD SANTAREM.**

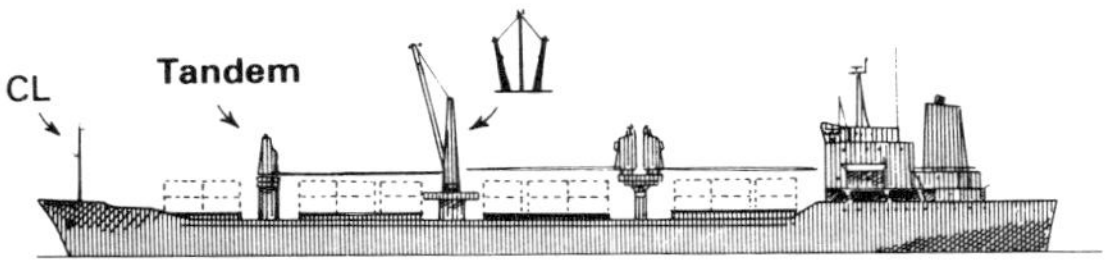

KCKC$_2$MF H13
50980 TABORA. FRG/Ja 1977; C; 13700; 161.53 × 10 (529.95 × 32.8); M; 16.25; **'UC-20'** type. Sister: **50981 TAGAMA** (FRG).

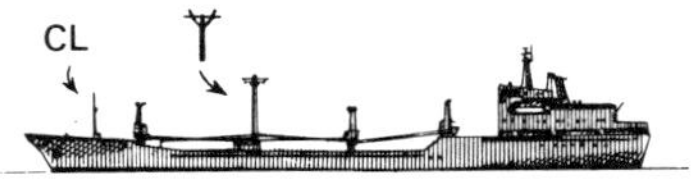

KCKC$_2$MF H13
50990 MARIANNE. Li/FRG 1968; C; 3100/5100; 119.97 × 6.45/7.6 (393.6 × 21.16/24.93); M; 16.5. Sister: ⋆**50991 QIAN TANG JIANG** (RC) ex MADELEINE 1977.

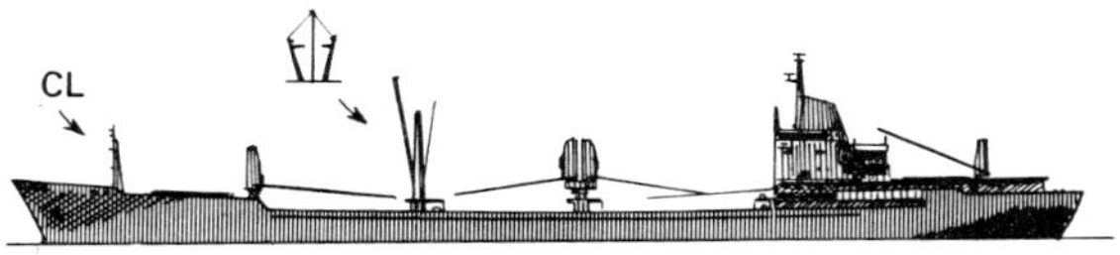

KCKC$_2$MFC H13
51000 VILLE DE MARSEILLE. Fr/Fr 1974; C; 12600; 171.02 × 9.7 (561.08 × 31.82); M; 20. Sisters (Fr flag): **51001 VILLE DE NANTES 51002 VILLE DE STRASBOURG.**

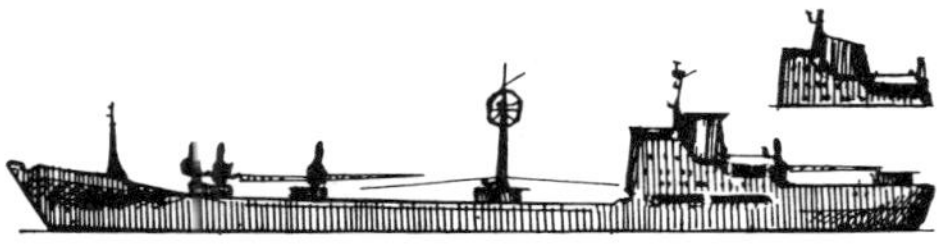

KC$_2$M$_2$FC H13
⋆**50910 KASIMOV.** Ru/Fi 1962; C; 9300; 147 × 9.1 (482 × 30); M; 15.35. Sisters (Ru flag): ⋆**50911 KALININABAD** ⋆**50912 KANEV** ⋆**50913 KARACHAJEVO-CHERKESSIJA** ⋆**50914 KASPIJSK** ⋆**50915 KIMOVSK** ⋆**50916 KOVROV** ⋆**50917 KRASNOUFIMSK** Similar: ⋆**50918 KRASNOGRAD.**

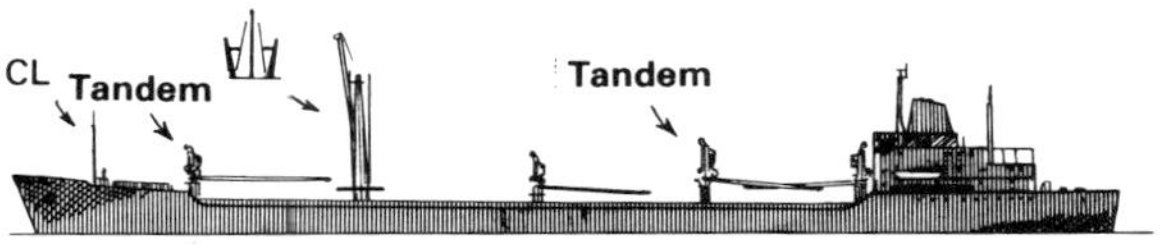

KCKC$_3$MFK H13
50940 IBN SHUHAID. Ku/Ko 1977; C; 11100/15400; 175.32 × —/10.4 (575.2 × —/34.12); M; 16; **'Kuwait'** class Sisters (Ku flag): (Some Br built). **50941 IBN AL-ATHEER 50942 IBN AL-NAFEES 50943 IBN AL-MOATHAZ 50944 IBN ALBEITAR 50945 IBN ASAKIR 50946 IBN BASSAM 50947 IBN BATTOTAH 50948 IBN DURAID 50949 IBN HAYYAN 50950 IBN KHALDOON 50951 IBN KHALLIKAN 50952 IBN MALIK 50953 IBN QUTAIBAH 50954 IBN RUSHD 50955 IBN TUFAIL 50956 IBN YOUNUS 50957 AL SALIMIAH 50958 AL MUBARAKIAH 50959 AL YAMAMAH 50960 AL FUJAIRAH 50961 AL MUHARRAQ 50962 AL RAYYAN 50963 AHMAD AL-FATEH 50964 ARAFAT 50965 DANAH 50966 FATHULKHAIR 50967 HIJAZ 50968 JILFAR 50969 QAROUH 50970 KUBBAR 50971 SALAH ALDEEN 50972 THEEKAR 50973 TABUK.**

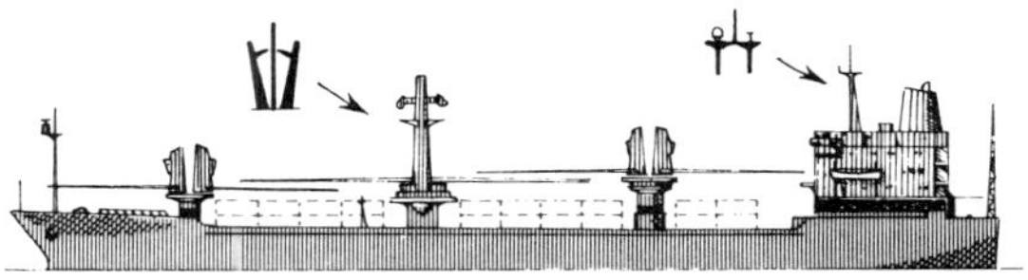

KCKC$_2$MFK H13
51010 WAKANAMI MARU. Ja/Ja 1978; C/Con/HL; 14500; 162.52 × 10.45 (533.2 × 34.28); M; 18. Sister: **51011 WAKAMIZU MARU** (Ja) Similar (second pair of cranes on travelling gantry, heavier KP foreward): **51012 WAKAGIKU MARU 51013 WAKATAKE MARU.**

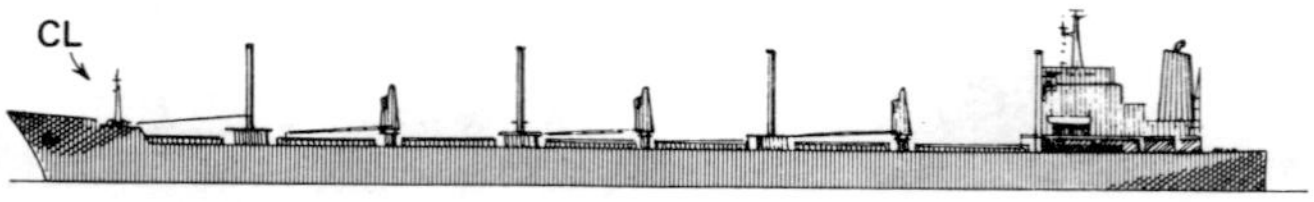

KCKCKCKMFK H1
51020 BUNKO MARU. Ja/Ja 1976; C; 30700; 215.02 × 12.4 (705.45 × 40.68); M; 14.75; **'Hi-bulk 50'** type.

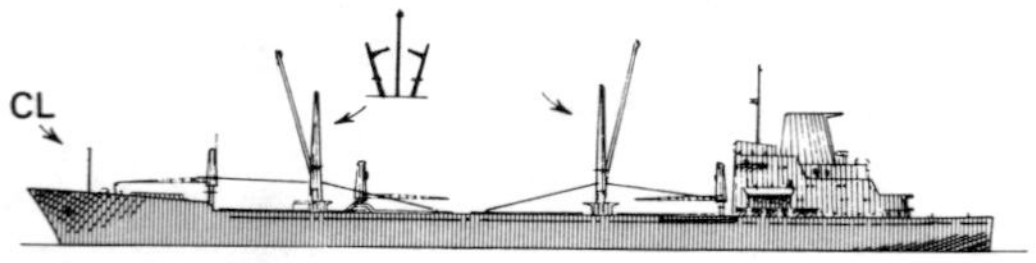

KCKCKCMF H1
● **51030 LONE STAR.** Sg/FRG 1970; C/HL; 7500/10600; 153.27 × 9.06/10.12 (502.85 × 29.72/33.2); M; 20; ex STEINFELS 1980. Sisters: **51031 EMILIA S** (Pa) ex STERNENFELS 1980 **51032 FRANCESCA** (Pa) ex STOCKENFELS 1980 **51033 MANILA** (Pi) ex STOLZENFELS 1980 Probable sisters: **51034 ZAMBOANGA** (Pi) ex STRAHLENFELS 1980 **51035 TORM AMERICA** (Sg) ex GOLDENFELS 1980; ex ATLANTICA MONTREAL 1976; ex GOLDENFELS 1972 **51036 TORM AFRICA** (Sg) ex DENEB 1981; ex GUTENFELS; ex ATLANTICA NEW YORK 1973; ex GUTENFELS.

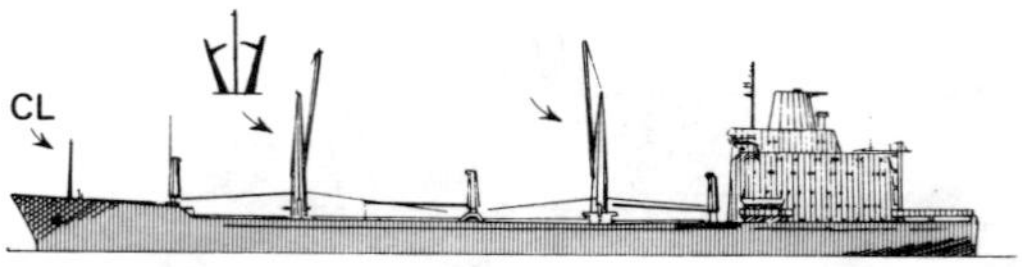

KCKCKCMF H1
51040 IBERIA. FRG/FRG 1972; C/HL/TS; 8000/11200; 153.24 × 9.06/10.07 (502.75 × 29.72/33.2); M; 20; ex STURMFELS 1980.

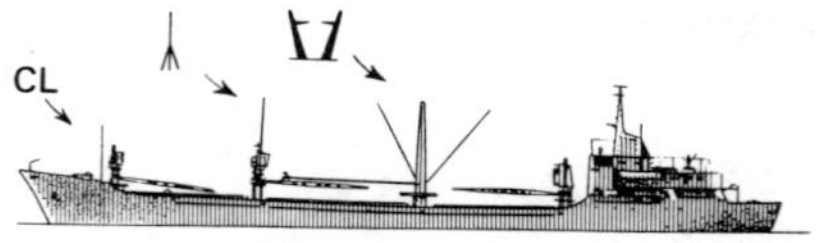

KCKCKCMF H13
51050 BOA ESPERANCA. Bz/Bz 1969; C; 4300/5400; 121.04 × —/7.7; (397.11 × —/25.26); M; 16. Probable sisters (may have kingpost aft): **51051 AMAZONIA** (Bz) **51052 PEDRO TEIXEIRA** (Bz).

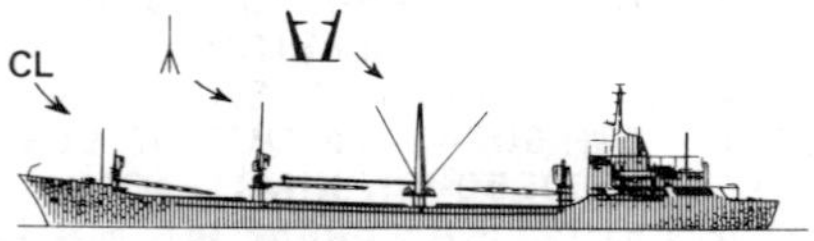

KCKCKCMFK H13
51060 MARCOS SOUZA DANTAS. Bz/Bz 1969; C; 4300/5400; 121.04 × —/7.7; (397.11 × —/25.26); M; 16.

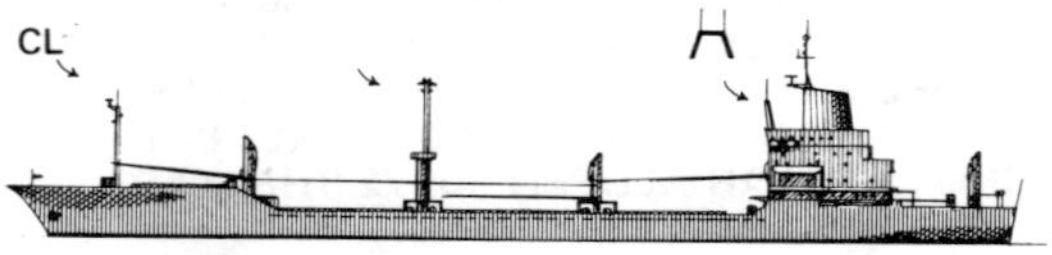

KCKCKMFC H13
51070 CREUSE. Fr/Ca 1973; C; 11800; 159.01 × 8.18 (521.68 × 26.83); M; 18.5; **'Marindus'** type. Sisters (Fr flag): **51071 COTES DU NORD 51072 CORREZE 51073 CANTAL 51074 CALVADOS** (Ar flag): **51075 PUNTA MALVINA** ex FRONTENAC **51076 PUNTA BRAVA** ex JOLIETTE.

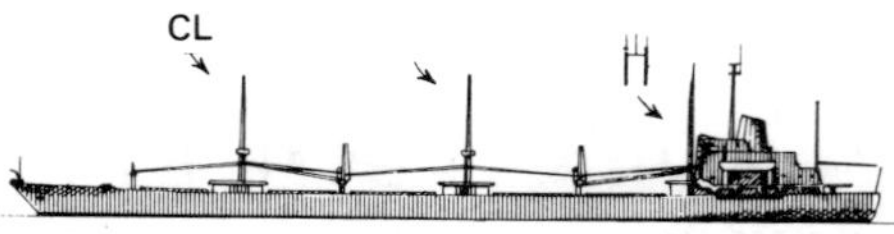

KCKCKMFK H
51080 NEDLLOYD TALBOT. Ne/Ja 1967; C; 9300; 137.78 × 9.05 (452.03 × 29.69); M; 14.5; ex STRAAT TALBOT 1977; ex OCEAN PRIMA 1970. Sisters: **51081 NEDLLOYD TAURANGA** (Ne) ex STRAAT TAURANGA 1977; ex PIPAT SAMUT 1970; launched as OCEAN UNITY **51082 MAHAKIRAN** (In) ex JAG RAVI 1980; ex GREEN WALRUS 1971 **51083 JAG REKHA** (In) ex PURPLE DOLPHIN 1971 **51084 SIGI SIGI** (Ia) ex OCEAN UNITY 1977 **51085 MUHUTI** (Ia) ex SEA DOLPHIN 1977; ex PICHAI SAMUT 1971 ⋆**51086 TIAN TAI SHAN** (RC) ex OCEAN PROSPER ⋆**51087 YUN TAI SHAN** RC) ex OCEAN PROGRESS.

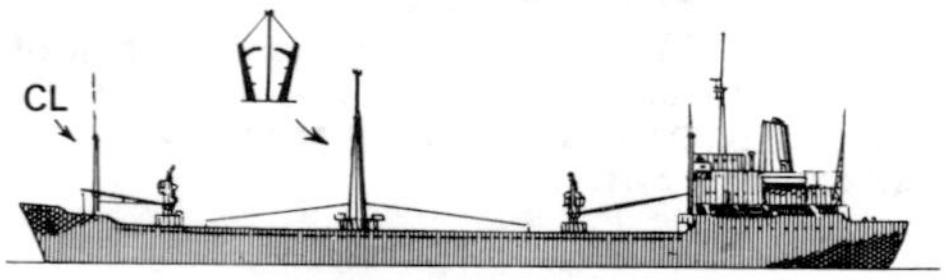

KCKCKMFK H13
51090 BOIN. Ko/Ja 1970; C; 8400; 140.06 × 8.99 (459.51 × 29.49); M; 15.5; ex CLINTONA 1980; ex YAMASHIGE MARU 1980. Sister: **51091 YANNIS** (Gr) ex NIISHIGE MARU.

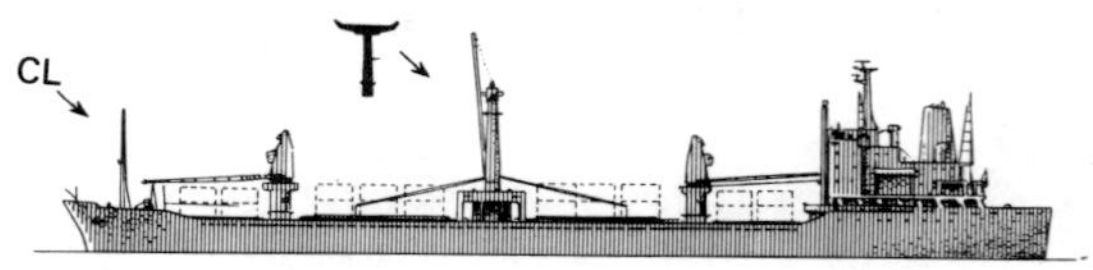

KCKCKMFK H13
● **51100 YOUNG SPORTSMAN.** Pa/Ja 1979; C; 11500; 156.53 × 9.1; (513.55 × 29.86); M; 15.4; ex VAN OCEAN 1980. Sister: **51101 VAN ENTERPRISE** (Pa) Possibly similar: **51102 VAN HAWK** (Li).

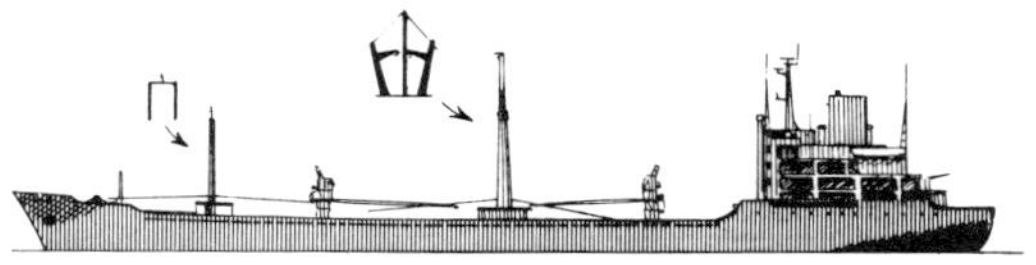

KCKCKMFK H13
51110 JESBON. Ko/Ja 1971; C; 9500; 155.56 × 9.3 (510.36 × 30.51); M; 16.75; ex NICHIWA MARU. Sisters: **51111 PACIFIC** (Li) ex NICHIBU MARU 1980 **51112 MONIMBO** (Ni) ex PALM ISLANDS 1980 Probable sister: **51113 SHINKAWA MARU** (Ja).

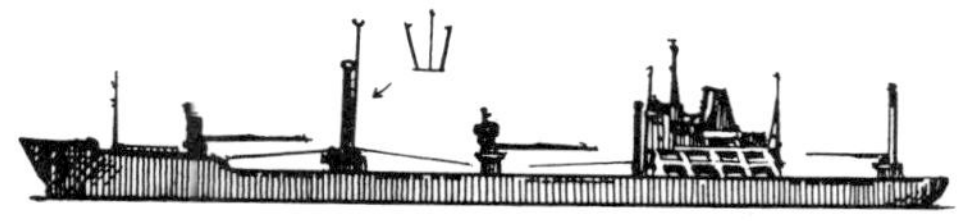

KCKCKMFK$_2$ H1
51120 JAPAN CAOBO. Li/Ja 1970; C; 8500; 148.75 × 8.73 (488.02 × 28.64); M; 15.75. Sister: **51121 JAPAN CANELA** (Li).

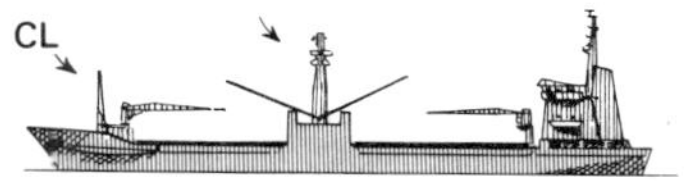

KCKCMF H1
51130 PEP CORAL. De/De 1977; C; 1600; 98.96 × 5.73 (324.67 × 18.79); M; 13. Possible sisters (De flag): **51131 PEP COMET 51132 PEP ICE.**

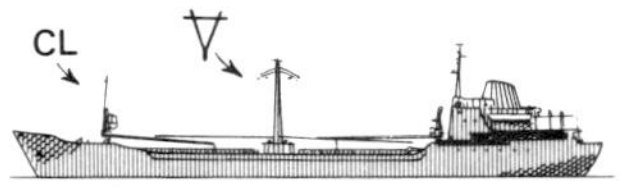

KCKCMF H13
51140 HUDSON VENTURE. Ca/Sw 1964; C; 1600/2800; 93.81 × 5.07/5.76 (307.77 × 16.63/18.9); M; 13.75; ex SILVA 1980; ex GONDUL 1971. Similar: **51141 ASTA** (Fi).

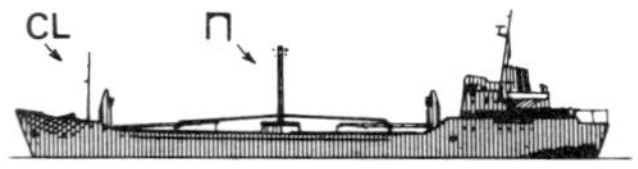

KCKCMF H13
51150 CITY OF TEMA; Gh/Br 1968; C; 1500; 93.88 × 5 08 (308 × 16.67); M; 13; ex CITY OF PATRAS 1978; ex SILVIO 1974. Sister: **51151 REZEKI** (Ia) ex CITY OF ANKARA 1978; ex SANGRO 1974.

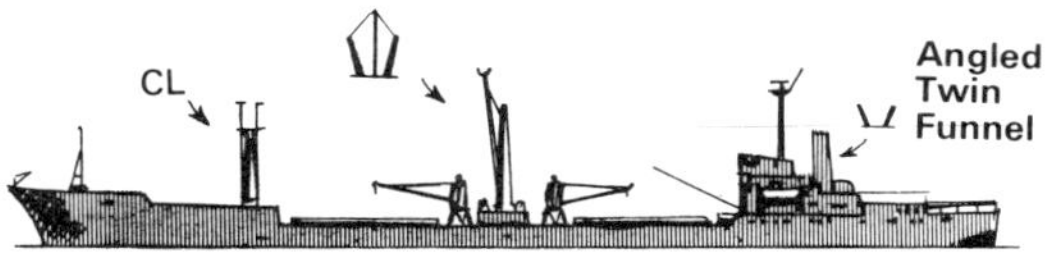

KCKCMF H13
51160 IRAN MEEAD; Ir/Be 1970; C; 12000; 160.51 × 9.79 (526.6 × 32.12) M 16.5; ex ARYA GAM 1980; Travelling cranes. Sisters (Ir flag): **51161 IRAN MEELAD** ex ARYA NUR **51162 IRAN ABAD** ex ARYA TAJ **51163 IRAN ERSHAD** ex ARYA TAB **51164 IRAN JAHAD** ex ARYA PAS.

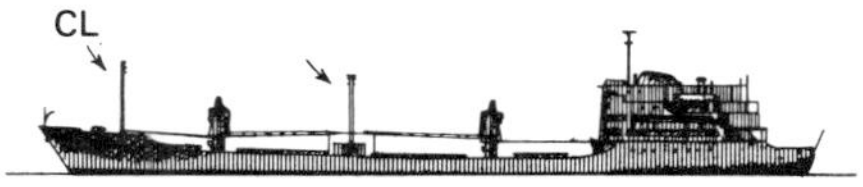

KCKCMF H13
● **51170 KATY;** Pa/Br 1963; C; 5400; 122.84 × 7.3 (403.02 × 23.95); M; 15.25; ex BOOKER VANGUARD. Sister: **51171 AL AMIRAH** (Qt) ex BOOKER VIKING 1980.

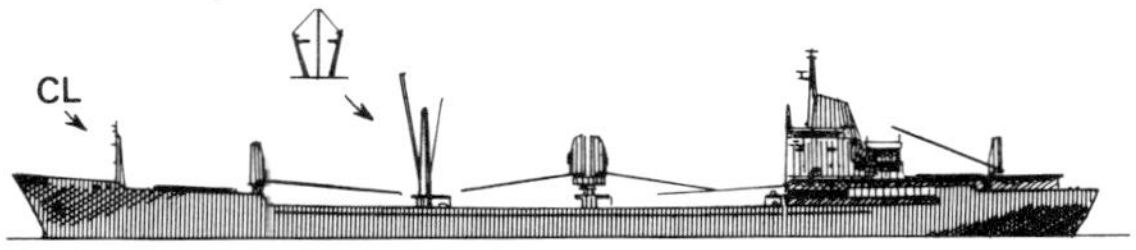

KCKCMFC H13
51180 VILLE DE MARSEILLE; Fr/Fr 1974; C; 12600; 171.02 × 9.7 (561.08 × 31.82); M; 20. Sisters (Fr flag): **51181 VILLE DE NANTES 51182 VILLE DE STRASBOURG.**

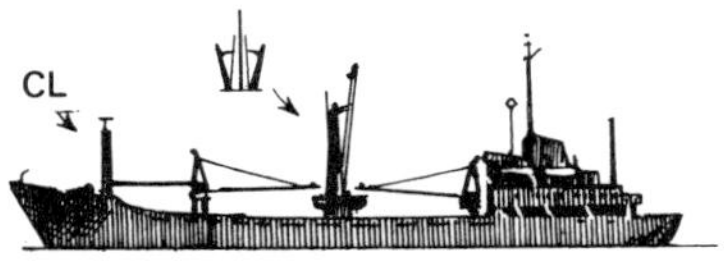

KCKCMFK H1
51190 LOS TEQUES; Pa/Br 1972; C; 2700; 105.16 × 6.26 (345.01 × 20.54); M; 15.5; ex MAKARIA. Sister: **51191 SIBONEY** (Pa) ex MELITA.

KCKCMFK H13
51200 PENNY; US/US 1943/64; C; 11400; 159.39 × 10 (522.93 × 32.8); T; —; ex PENN 1978; ex PENNMAR 1976; ex GENERAL G.O. SQUIER 1964; Converted Passenger/Troopship.

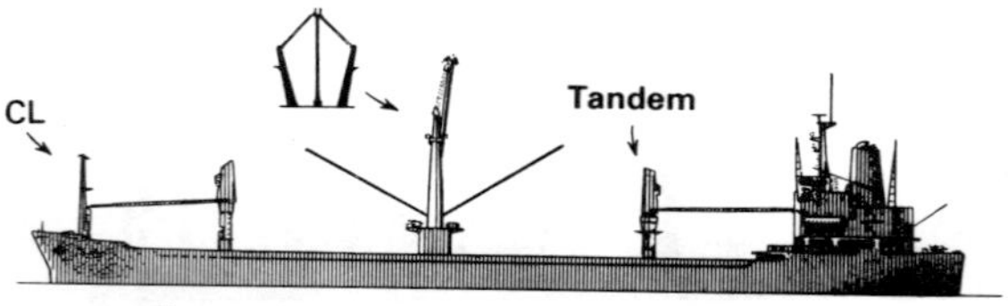

KCKCMFK H13
51210 ALTAI MARU; Ja/Ja 1979; C/HL; 16000; 166.12 × 10.39; (545 × 34.09); M; 16. Sister: **51211 HIMALAYA MARU** (Ja).

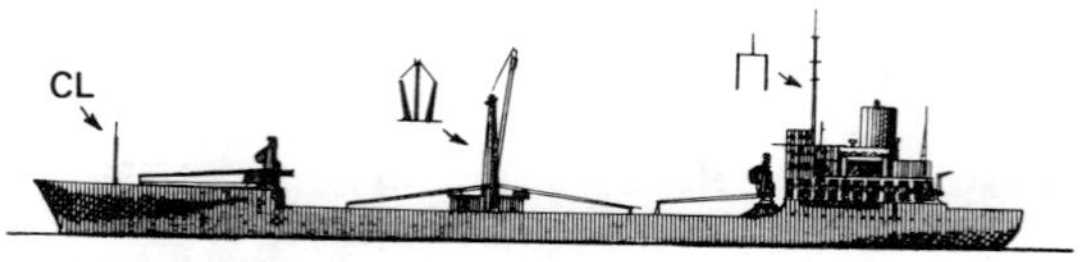

KCKCMFK H13
51220 WAKAUME MARU; Ja/Ja 1970; C/HL; 9900; 156.55 × 9.02 (513.61 × 29.59); M; 16.75.

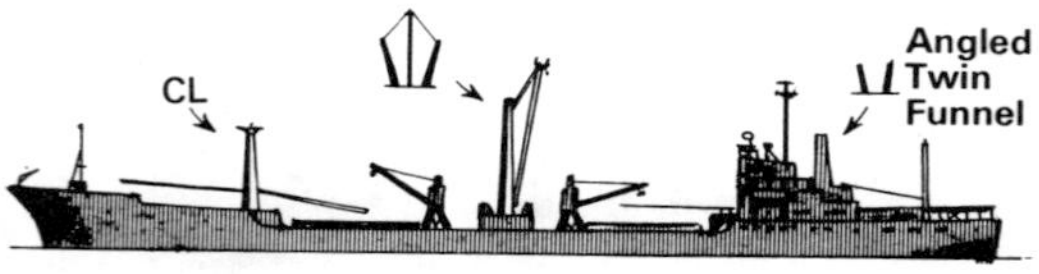

KCKCMFK H13
51230 IRAN NAHAD; Ir/Be 1970; C; 12100; 160.51 × 9.79 (526.6 × 32.12); M; 19; ex ARYA NAZ 1980; Travelling cranes.

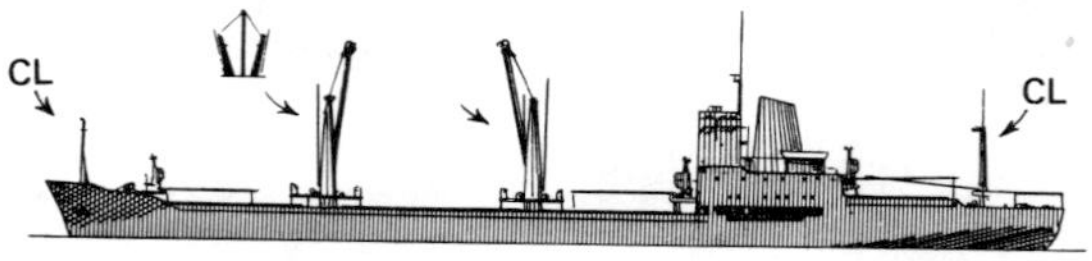

KCK$_2$CMFCK H13
51240 CRAFTSMAN; Br/Br 1972; C/HL; 6700/10200; 162.01 × 8.01/9.36 (531.52 × 26.28/30.7); M; 17.

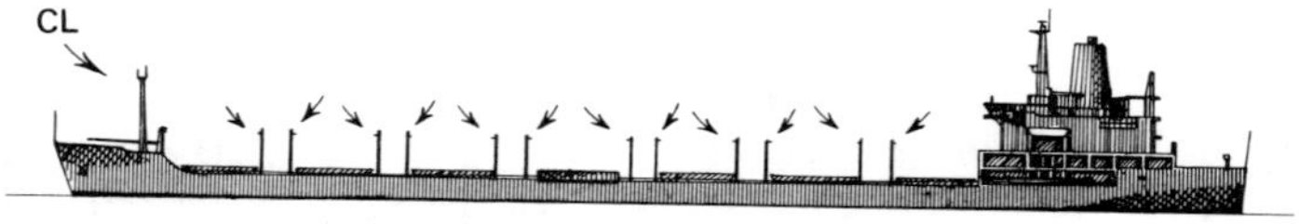

KCK$_{12}$MFC H13
51250 IRON CARPENTARIA; Au/Au 1977; B; 25900; 202.72 × 12.52 (665.09 × 41.07); GT; 15. Sister: **51251 IRON CURTIS** (Au).

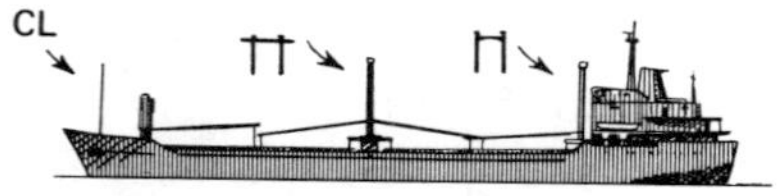

KCK$_2$MF H13
⋆**51260 KWIDZYN;** Pd/Pd 1974; C; 2800; 106.38 × 5.68 (349.02 × 18.64); M; 14; **'B-472'** type. Sisters (Pd flag): ⋆**51261 LEBORK** ⋆**51262 WEJHEROWO.**

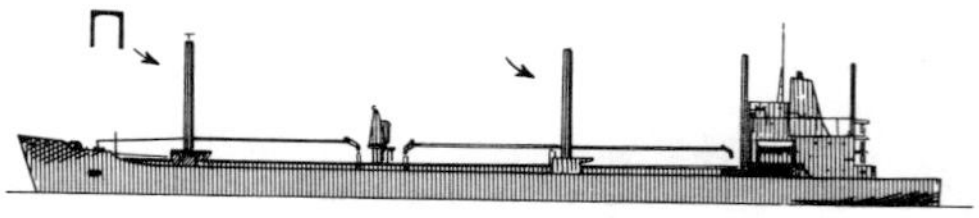

KCK$_2$MFK H1
51270 GOLD ALISA; Br/Br 1973; C; 7800/11900; 147.2 × 8.59/10.02 (482.93 × 28.18/32.87); M; —; ex ALISA 1980; **'CLYDE'** class. Sisters (Br flag): **51271 GOLD HILLA** ex HILLA **51272 GOLD ORLI** EX ORLI **51273 GOLD VARDA** ex VARDA.

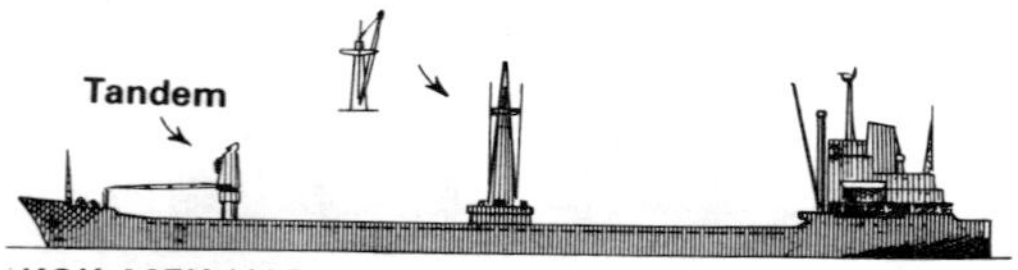

KCK$_2$MFK H13
● **51280 KASUGA MARU;** Ja/Ja 1976; C/HL; 11800; 154.41 × 9.58 (506.59 × 31.43); M; 15. Similar (larger): **51281 KATORI MARU** (Ja).

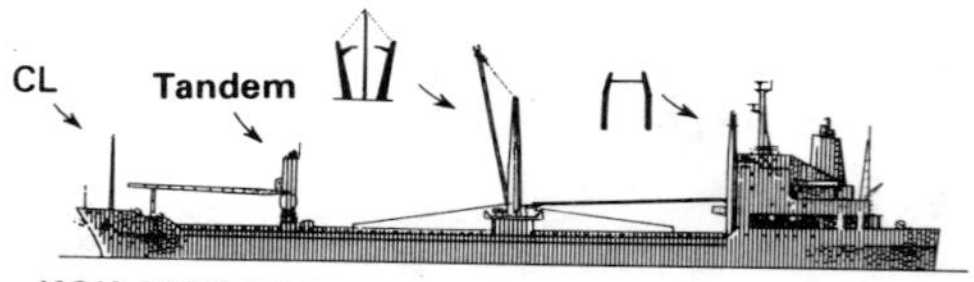

KCK$_2$MFK H13
51290 BIZERTE; Tn/Ja 1979; C/B; 7800; 137.31 × 7; (450.49 × 22.97); M; approx 15; Designed for the transportation of phosphate rock. Sister: **51291 KAIROUAN** (Tn).

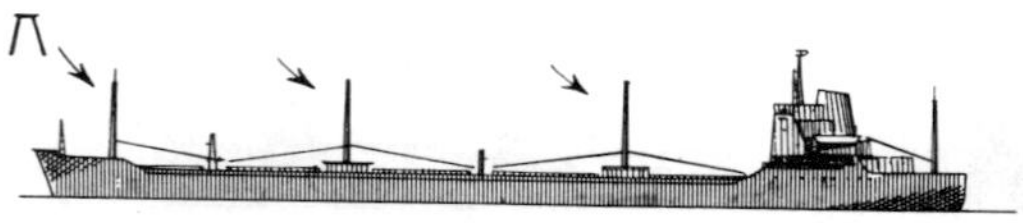

KCK$_2$MFK H13
51300 SAN JOHN; Gr/Ja 1967; B; 10300; 147.53 × 9.07 (484.02 × 29.76); M; 15; ex GRAND JUSTICE 1980.

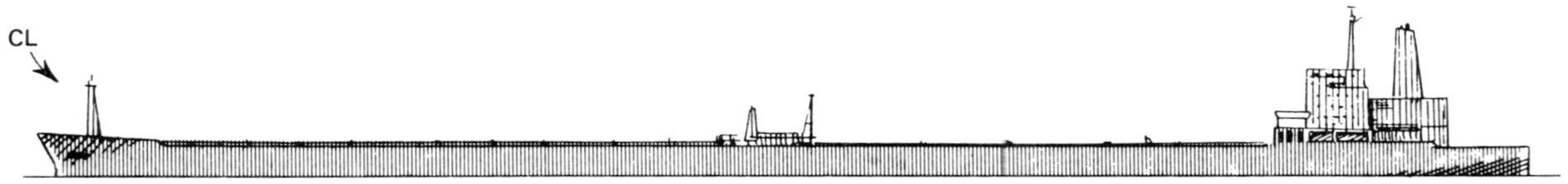

KCKMF H
51310 LAGENA; FRG/FRG 1974; Tk; 162000; 351.49 × 22.38 (1153.18 × 73.43); T; —. Sisters (FRG flag): **51311 LIOTINA 51312 LOTTIA.**

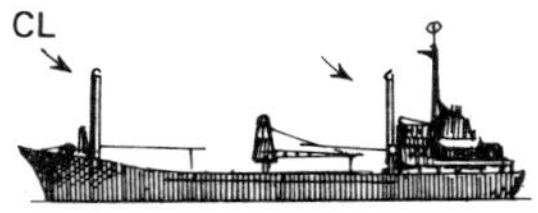

KCKMF H
51320 LAXA; Ic/FRG 1967; C; 1000; 79.51 × 4.42 (260.85 × 14.5); M; 13; ex SIMONE 1975; ex ROLANDSECK 1973.

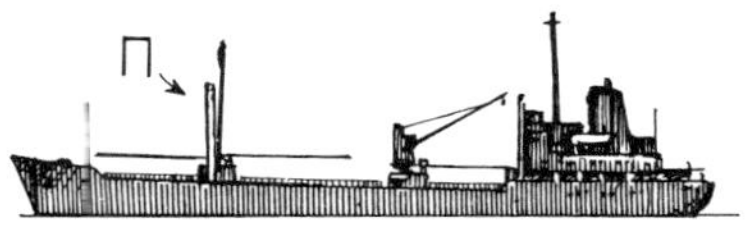

KCKMF H
51330 MING YOUTH; Tw/Tw 1969; C; 3700; 107.04 × 7.08 (351.18 × 23.23); M; 14.5; ex YU MING 1977; ex HAI LI 1973.

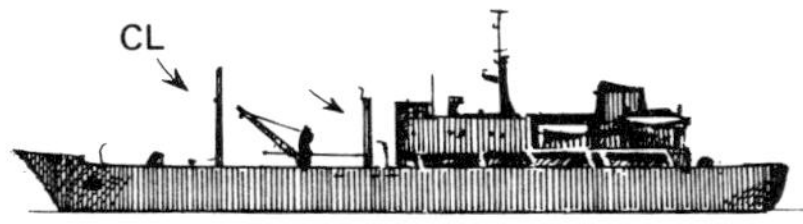

KCKMF H
51340 WHITEHEAD; Br/Br 1971; A/Trials ship; 3000 Dspl; 88.8 × 5.2 (291.34 × 17); M; 15.5.

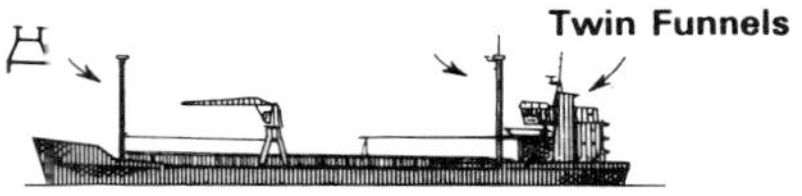

KCKMF H1
51350 AMULET; De/De 1975; C; 1600; 94.39 × 5.77 (309.67 × 18.93); M; 13; Travelling cranes. Sisters (De flag): **51351 TALISMAN 51352 CHARM.**

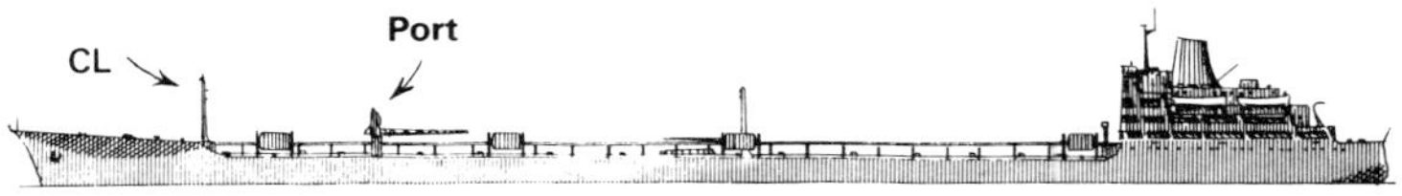

KCKMF H13
51360 ESSO CARDIFF; Br/Ne 1963; Tk; 31700; 226.5 × 11.95 (743.11 × 39.21); T; 17; Used as a Lightening Tanker.

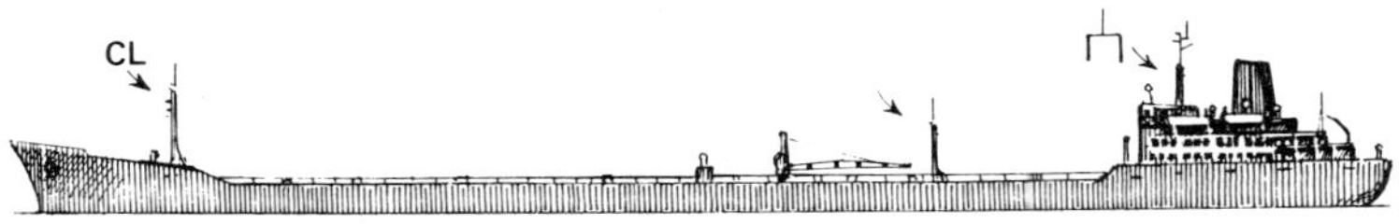

KCKMF H13
● **51370 AL-SABBIYAH;** Ku/Ja 1965; Tk; 35800; 231.5 × 12.55 (759.51 × 41.17); T; —. Sister: **51371 WARBAH.**

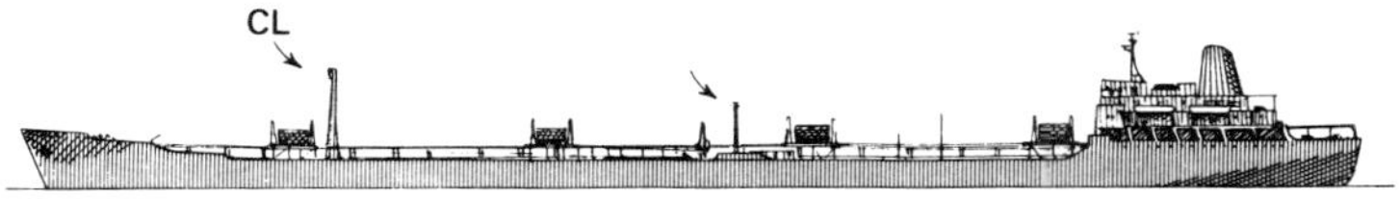

KCKMF H13
51380 BRITISH DRAGOON; Br/Br 1963; Tk; 31100; 221.39 × 12.58 (726.34 × 41.27); T; 15.5; Used as a Lightening Tanker.

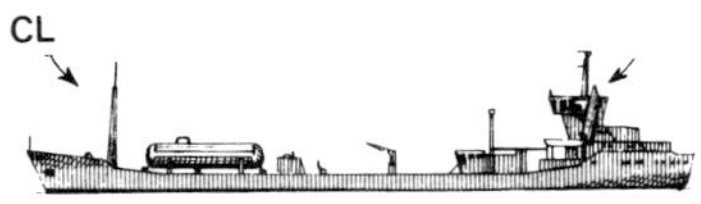

KCKMF H13
51390 SUVARNABHUMI; Th/Br 1969; Ch/LPG/Tk; 3100; 106.13 × 4.65 (348.19 × 15.26); TSM; 11.

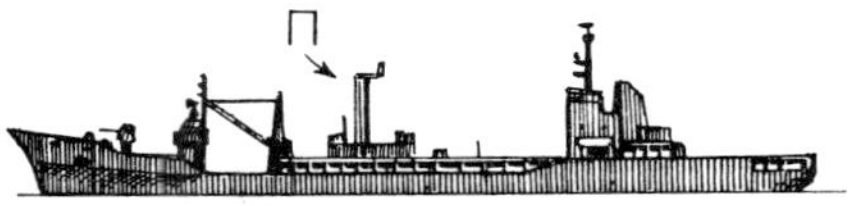

KCKMF H13
51400 STROMBOLI; It/It 1975; A/Rmt; 8700 Dspl; 123 × 6.5 (403.54 × 21.32); M; 20. Sister: **51401 VESUVIO** (It).

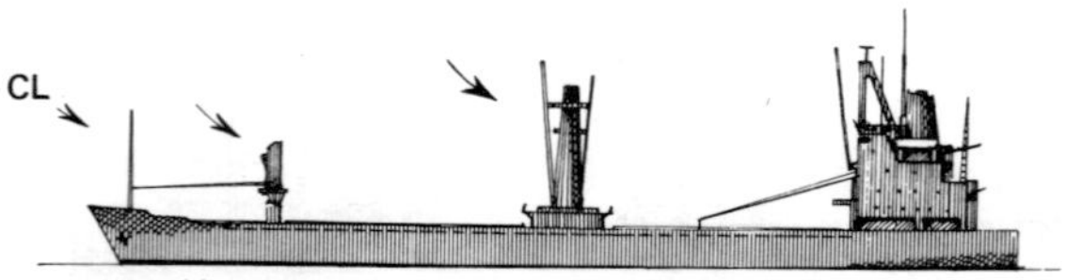

KCKMFK H1
51420 MALACCA MARU; Ja/Ja 1978; C/HL; 15900; 157.03 × 9.5 (515.19 × 31.17); M; 15.5.

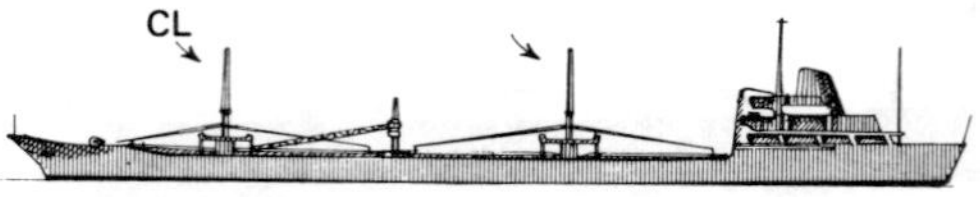

KCKMFK H13
★**51430 LIAN HUA CHENG;** RC/Ja 1969; C; 10300; 152.16 × 9.47 (495.93 × 31.06); M; 15.25; ex YGUAZU 1977; **'MM-14'** type. Sister: ★**51431 HONG GU CHENG** (RC) ex OCEAN SAILOR 1977; ex NILS AMELON 1975.

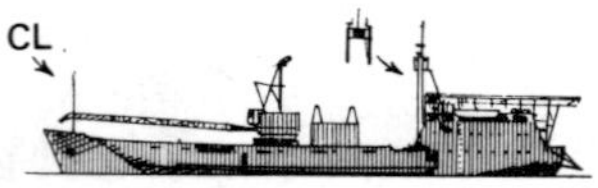

KCM H3
51440 INSTALLER I; Li/Ne 1960; BT; 1800; 81.9 × 5.32 (268.7 × 17.45); M; 13; ex SKADI 1970; Converted from general cargo & shortened 1969. Helicopter platform aft.

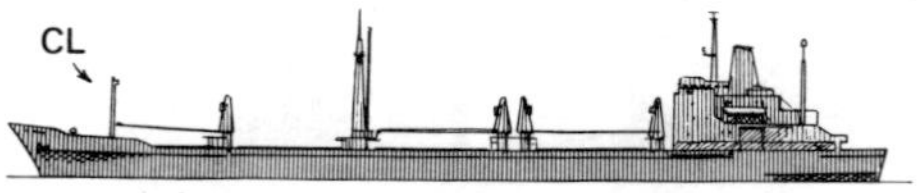

KCMC$_3$MFK H1
51450 SEAFALCON; Sg/Sw 1969; C; 6200/9600; 140.04 × 7.89/9.53 (459.45 × 25.88/31.26); M; 16.5; ex ISFAHAN; **'SCANDIA'** type. Sister: ★**51451 TONG BAI SHAN** (RC) ex TURTLE BAY; ex INDUS 1979.

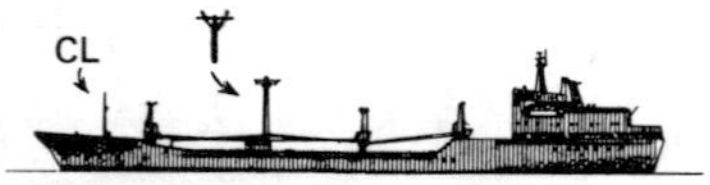

KCMC$_2$MF H13
51460 MARIANNE; Li/FRG 1968; C; 3100/5100; 119.97 × 6.45/7.6 (393.6 × 21.16/24.93); M; 16.5. Sister: ★**51461 QIAN TANG JIANG** (RC) ex MADELEINE 1977.

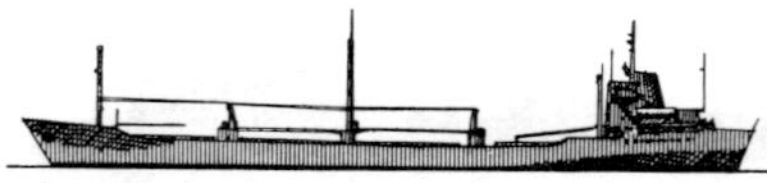

KCMCKMFK H13
51470 BOOKER VULCAN; Br/Pd 1968; C; 2200/4100; 116.52 × 5.73/— (382.28 × 18.79/—); M; 14; ex SEAHAWK 1974; ex CONCORDIA STAR 1970; ex SEA VIKING 1969; ex SEAHAWK 1968; **'B-448'** type.

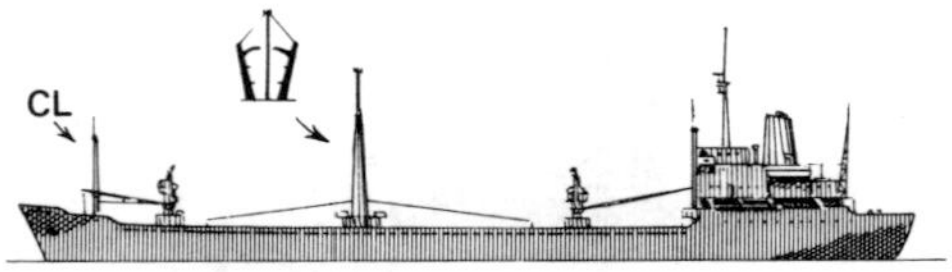

KCMCKMFK H13
51480 BOIN; Ko/Ja 1970; C; 8400; 140.06 × 8.99 (459.51 × 29.49); M; 15.5; ex CLINTONA 1980; ex YAMASHIGE MARU 1980. Sister: **51481 YANNIS** (Gr) ex NIISHIGE MARU.

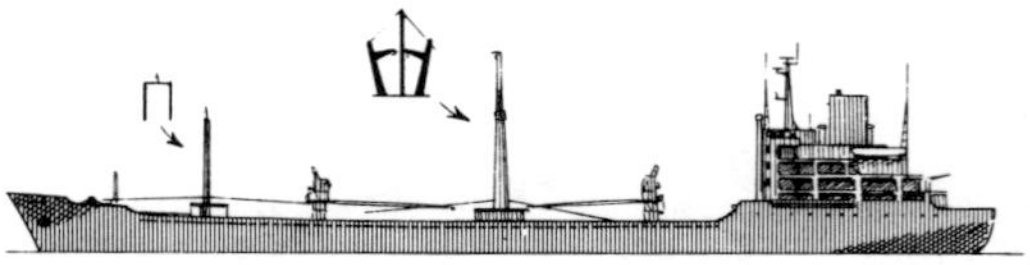

KCMCKMFK H13
51490 JESBON; Ko/Ja 1971; C; 9500; 155.56 × 9.3 (510.36 × 30.51); M; 16.75; ex NICHIWA MARU. Sisters: **51491 PACIFIC** (Li) ex NICHIBU MARU 1980 **51492 MONIMBO** (Ni) ex PALM ISLANDS 1980 Probable Sister: **51493 SHINKAWA MARU** (Ja).

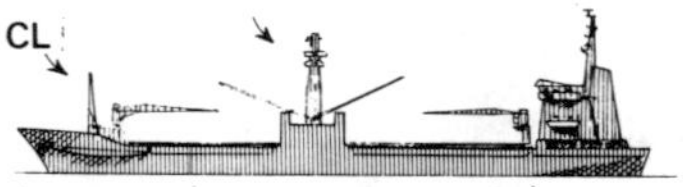

KCMCMF H1
51500 PEP CORAL; De/De 1977; C; 1600; 98.96 × 5.73 (324.67 × 18.79); M; 13. Possible Sisters (De flag): **51501 PEP COMET 51502 PEP ICE.**

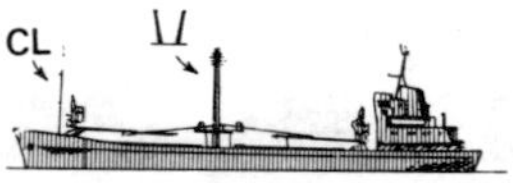

KCMCMF H1
51510 BALTIC VIKING; Br/FRG 1967; C; 700/1600; 74.53 × 4.09/5.17 (244.52 × 13.41/16.96); M; 14.

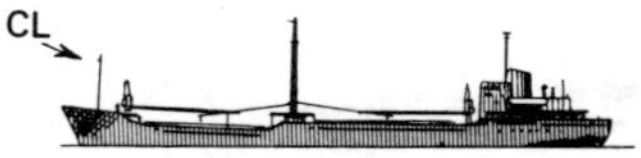

KCMCMF H123
51520 GIAMAICA; It/FRG 1960; C; 1600; 87.08 × 4.98 (285.7 × 16.34); M; 12.5; ex CAPTAIN GIGETTO 1975; ex INDAL RETZLAFF 1972; ex INDAL 1965.

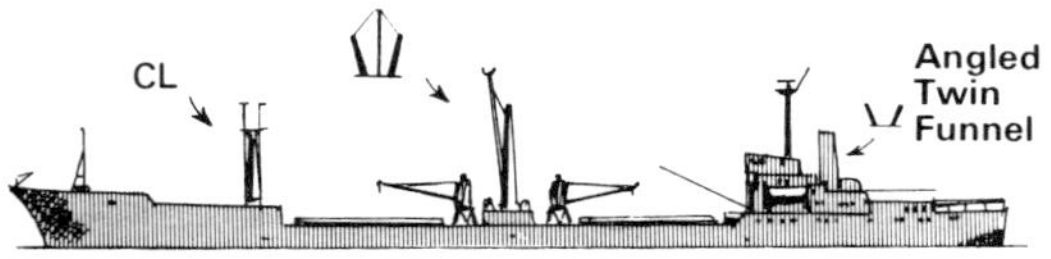

KCMCMF H13
51530 IRAN MEEAD; Ir/Be 1970; C; 12000; 149.79 × 9.26 (491.44 × 30.38); M; 16.5; ex ARYA GAM 1980. Sisters (Ir flag): **51531 IRAN ABAD** ex ARYA TAJ 1980 **51532 IRAN MEELAD** ex ARYA NUR 1980 **51533 IRAN ERSHAD** ex ARYA TAB 1980 **51534 IRAN JAHAD** ex ARYA PAS.

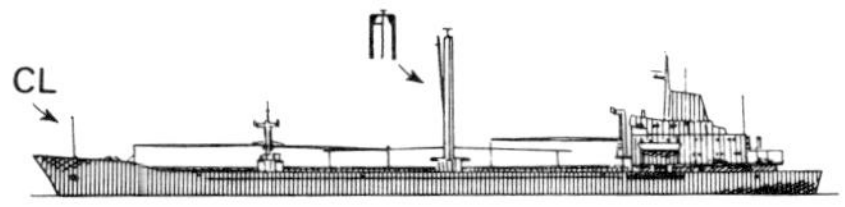

KCMCMFK H1
● **51540 CAP SERRAT;** Sg/FRG 1970; C; 2800/5000; 125.02 × 6.56/7.64 (410.17 × 21.52/25.06); M; 17. Sisters: **51541 ANDRA** (Pa) ex MARHEIKE; ex EASTERN RIVER 1975; ex CAP SUNION 1974 **51542 AMAZONIA** (Pe) ex MISTRAL DEL NORTE 1981; ex CAP SIDERO 1976 **51543 NORDBAY** (Sg) ex CAP SARAY 1976.

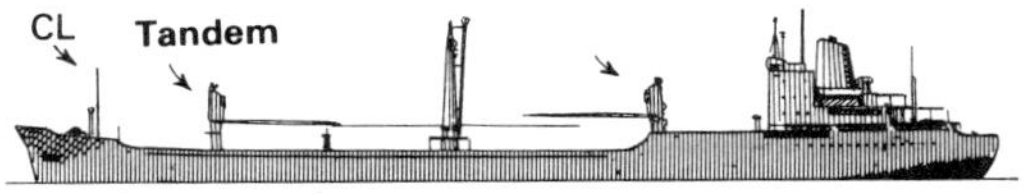

KCMCMFK H13
51550 GOLDEN TOGO; Li/No 1970; C; 11500; 155.53 × 9.4 (510.26 × 30.84); M; 17; ex ARIADNE 1980; ex NORLANDA 1978. Sister: ⋆**51551 GAN JIANG** (RC) ex NORBELLA.

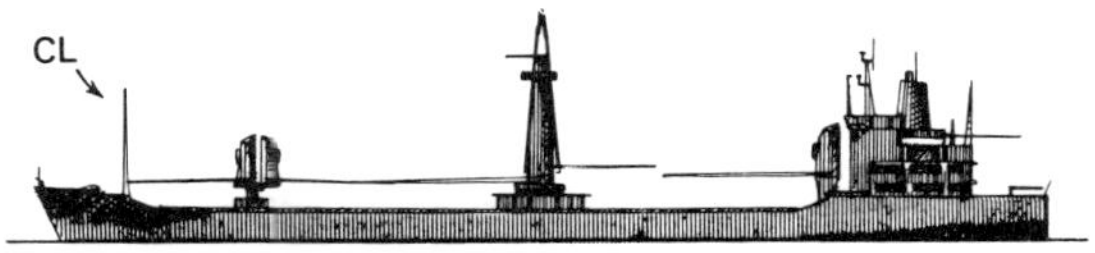

KCMCMFK H13
51560 ATLAS MARU; Ja/Ja 1978; C/HL; 15100; 161.02 × 9.5 (528.28 × 31.16); M; 15.25. Sister: **51561 ANDES MARU** (Ja).

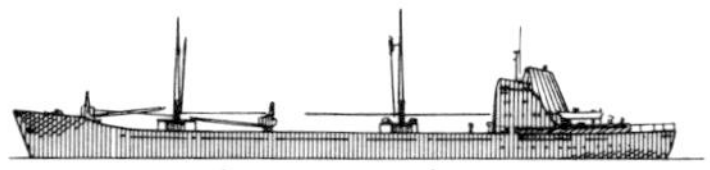

KCMCM$_2$F H1
51580 HOLSTENLAND; Gr/FRG 1959; C; 2800/4000; 105.92 × 6.72/7.6 (347 × 22.05/24.93); M; 15; ex LINDAUNIS 1974; ex CAP BONAVISTA 1970. Sister: **51581 HOLSTENSAND** (Gr) ex BOKNIS 1974; ex VOLTA SERVICE 1973; ex BOKNIS 1972; ex CAP CASTILLO 1971; ex ISMAILIA 1958.

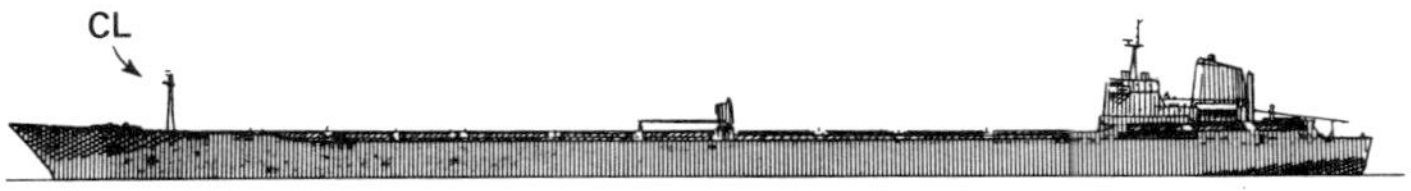

KCMF H
51590 NAI LUISA; It/It 1969; OBO; 26200; 216.42 × 12.45 (710 × 40.85); M; 15.5; ex LUISA LOLLI GHETTI 1974.

KCMF H
● **51600 SCANDINAVIAN EXPRESS;** Sg/No 1965; C; 500/1500; 72.73 × 3.55/4.61 (238.62 × 11.65/15.12); M; 13.25; ex BASTANT 1976.

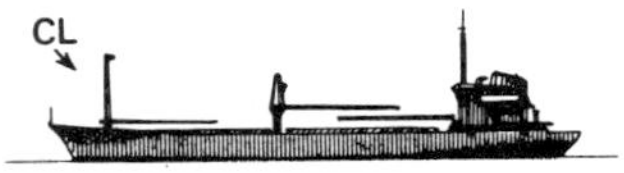

KCMF H
51610 BAMMEN; Sw/FRG 1968; C; 700/1600; 83.9 × 3.71/4.61 (275.26 × 12.17/15.12); M; 12.5; ex SOMMEN 1980; Lengthened 1973. Sister: **51611 SKAGERN** (Sw).

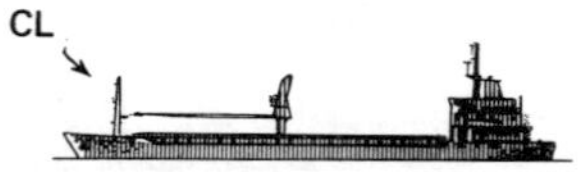

KCMF H

● **51620 DALSLAND;** FRG/Ja 1977; C; 1000; 75.47 × 4.77; (247.6 × 15.65); M; 12.5. Sister: **51621 GOTALAND** (FRG) Possible Sisters (FRG flag) (some, or all, may not have crane - see BARKENKOPPEL etc under KMF): **51622 ALAND 51623 ALSTERBERG 51624 BOBERG 51625 MESSBERG 51626 SYBILLE 51627 VAERMLAND 51628 OELAND 51629 LANGELAND.**

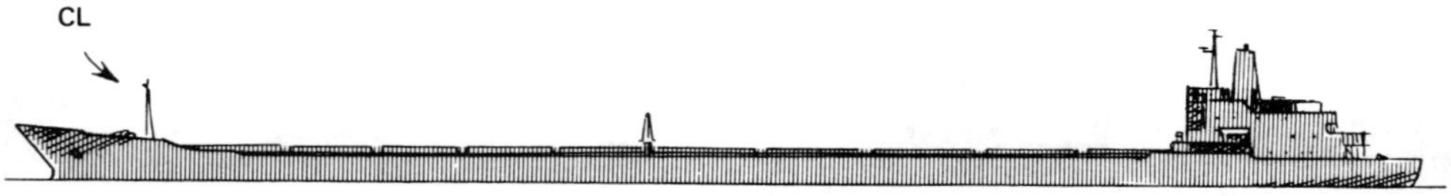

KCMF H1

● **51630 TRANSOCEANICA MARIO;** It/It 1973; OO; 72400; 297.21 × 16.18 (975.1 × 53.08); T; 16.5. Similar: **51631 MARILENA** (Gr) ex OMBRINA; ex GIOIA PATRIZIA; ex MASANO 1974 **51632 LAURA PRIMA** (It) **51633 IRON TRANSPORTER** (Li) ex LILY PRIMA Possibly Similar: **51634 AGIOS IOANNIS** (Gr) ex NAI ANNALISA; ex ANNALISA LOLLI GHETTI 1974 **51635 NAI MARIA AMELIA** (It) ex MARIA AMELIA LOLLI GHETTI 1974 **51636 ELIOS** (It) **51637 BRASILIA** (It) **51638 ARETUSA** (It) **51639 WEST WONORI** (Pa) ex OCEAN DOLPHIN 1979; ex ERNESTO FASSIO.

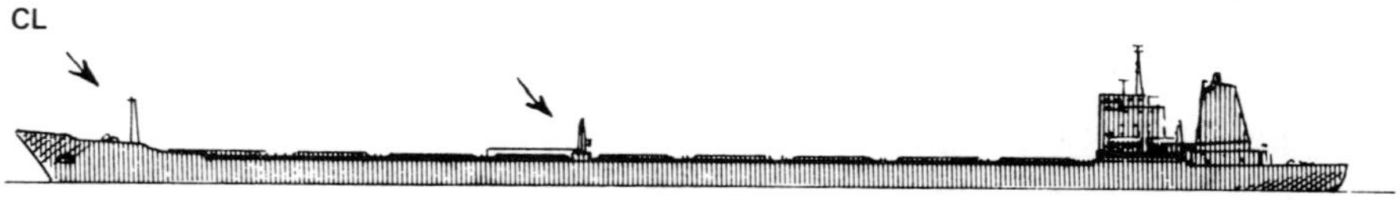

KCMF H1

51650 MARCONA TRANSPORTER; Li/It 1968; OO; 48500; 260.1 × 15.2 (853.35 × 49.87); M; —; ex ROSS SOUND 1973; ex RIVALTA 1971. Possible Sister: **51651 ASTAKOS** (Li) ex HASTINGS 1977; ex ROSS POINT 1975; ex VITTORIO VALLETTA 1971.

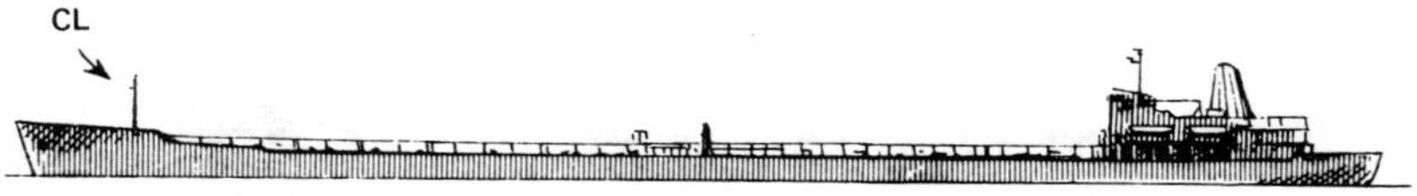

KCMF H1

51660 BRITISH COMMERCE; Br/Br 1965; Tk; 37800; 248.65 × 12.91 (815.78 × 42.35); M; 15.5. Sisters: **51661 BRITISH COMMODORE** (Br) **51662 BRITISH CENTAUR** (Br) **51663 HALCYON MED** (Gr) ex BRITISH CAPTAIN 1976.

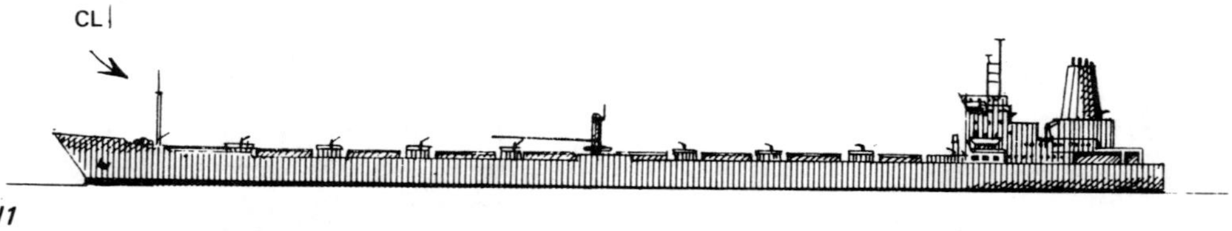

KCMF H1

51670 CHEYENNE; Li/FRG 1977; BO; 68800; 273.26 × 16.38 (896.52 × 53.74); M; 15.75; ex SAGGAT 1978. Sister: **51671 CAYUGA** (Li) ex SUORVA 1978.

KCMF H1
51680 TAURUS; Gr/Fi 1977; Tk; 18700; 171.35 × 11.38 (562.17 × 37.34); M; 16.25; ex MESSINIAKI AKTI. Sisters: **51681 GERD MAERSK** (De) ex MESSINIAKI ANATOLI **51682 VEGA** (Gr) ex MESSINIAKI AVGI **51683 CARUAO** (Ve) launched as MESSINIAKI AVRA **51684 PARIATA** (Ve) launched as MESSINIAKI AKTIDA.

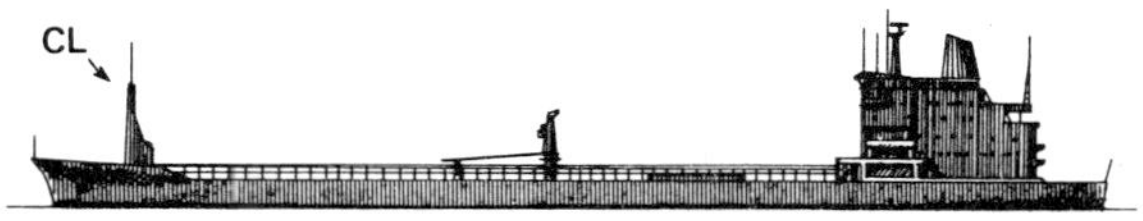

KCMF H1
51690 FULGUR; Li/No 1974; Tk; 19300; 170.69 × 11.37 (560 × 37.3); M; 15.5. Sisters (Li flag): **51691 FELANIA 51692 FELIPES 51693 FICUS 51694 FLAMMULINA 51695 FOSSARUS 51696 FUSUS.**

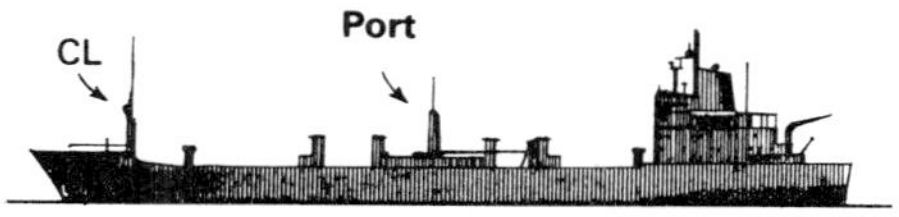

KCMF H1
51700 HUMBER ARM; Li/FRG 1976; RoC; 3700; 130.03 × 6.68 (426.6 × 21.92); M; 16; Side door. Sister: **51701 CORNER BROOK** (Li).

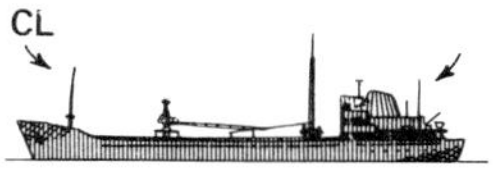

KCMF H1
51710 AL OSMAN. Le/Ne 1965; C; 500; 71.99 × 3.82 (236.18 × 12.53); M; 12.75; ex ZEEBURGH 1979.

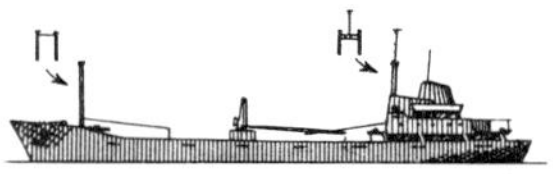

KCMF H1
51720 TATAI. Gr/FRG 1965; C; 1100/1900; 83.04 × 4.77/6.14 (272.44 × 15.65/20.14); M; 14; ex NEPTUNE HERCULES; ex ANGLIAN 1975; ex NEPTUNE HERCULES 1974; ex HERCULES 1972.

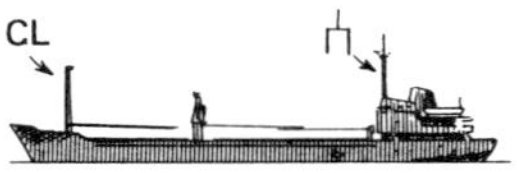

KCMF H1
51730 MANGEN. Ne/Ne 1969; C; 600/1500; 77.65 × 4.14/5.83 (254.75 × 13.58/19.12); M; 12. Sister: **51731 WADDENZEE** (Ne) ex UNDEN.

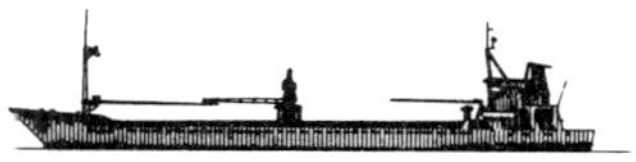

KCMF H1
● **51740 MERCANDIAN PRINCE.** De/De 1977; C; 1600; 96.53 × 5.64 (316.69 × 18.51); M; 12.25; **'Commander'** class. Sisters: **51741 POLYDORUS** (Ne) ex MERCANDIAN ADMIRAL **51742 CASABLANCA** (FRG) ex MERCANDIAN AMBASSADOR 1980 **51743 SEVILLA** (FRG) ex MERCANDIAN COMMANDER 1980 **51744 MERCANDIAN QUEEN** (De).

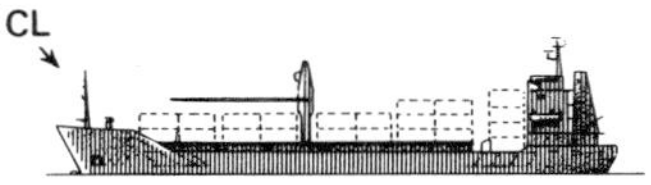

KCMF H1
51750 BELGICA. FRG/FRG 1980; C/Con; 1000; 89. × 4.59; (291.99 × 15.06); M; 13.2; ex HEIDKAMP 1980.

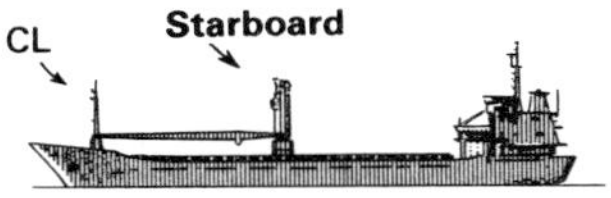

KCMF H1
51760 CHRISTA THIELEMANN. FRG/FRG 1979; C/Con; 1000; 86.2 × 4.87; M; approx. 13.7.

KCMF H1
51770 RUGARD. FRG/FRG 1977; C; 900; 78.01 × 4.85 (255.94 × 15.91); M; 13.5. Similar: **51771 SCHWANECK** (FRG).

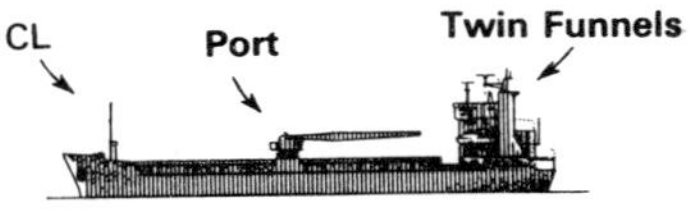

KCMF H1
● **51780 GERMA TARA.** No/Sg 1978; C/B/Con; 1600/3300; 81 × 5.75/—; (265.75 × 18.86/—); M; 13.5; The crane may not be fitted. This could also apply to any, or all, of the sisters. See GERMA KARMA under KMF. Sisters: **51781 GERMA FONDAL** (No) **51782 GERMA FOREST** (Ma) **51783 GERMA FRAM** (No) **51784 GERMA LINA** (No) ex LINA 1980 **51785 GERMA LIONEL** (No) ex LIONEL 1979 **51786 GERMA PRIDE** (No) **51787 GERMA TEAM** (No) Probable sister: **51788 KATAWA** (Sg).

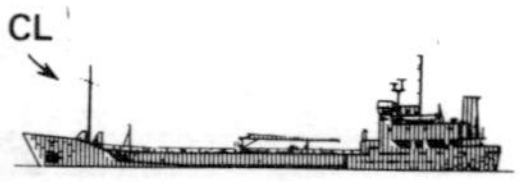

KCMF H1
51800 STAPAFELL. Ic/FRG 1979; Tk; 1400; 75.74 × 4.79; (248.49 × 15.72); M; 13.5.

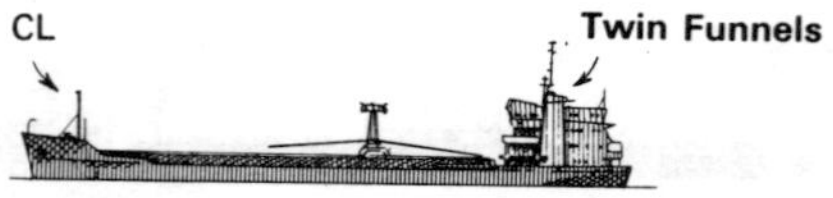

KCMF H1
51810 VILLIERS. FRG/Po 1972; C/Con; 3900; 46.6 × — (316.93 × —); M; 13; ex ELISABETH FISSER 1979; Travelling cranes. Sisters: **51811 BAUCIS** (Cy) ex ALICE BOLTEN 1973 **51812 BOCA TABLA** (NA) ex IMELA FISSER 1973.

KCMF H1
51820 ZEJTUN. Ma/FRG 1967; RoC; 1000; 78.03 × 4.29 (256 × 14.07); M; —; ex TAOS 1974; ex WASA 1973; Bow and stern doors. Sister: **51821 ALPILLES** (Fr) ex HANSA 1972.

KCMF H1
51830 REDSEA EXPRESS. Pa/Br 1969; Pal; 700; 75.32 × 3.4 (247.11 × 11.15); TSM; 13.75; ex DANGELD 1977; 2 side doors.

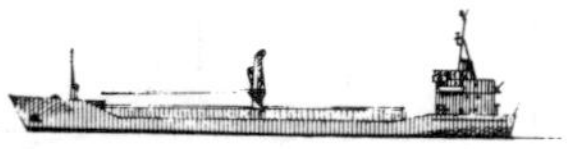

KCMF H1
51840 NORLAND. FRG/FRG 1977; C; 1000; 80.7 × — (264.76 × —); M; 13.5.

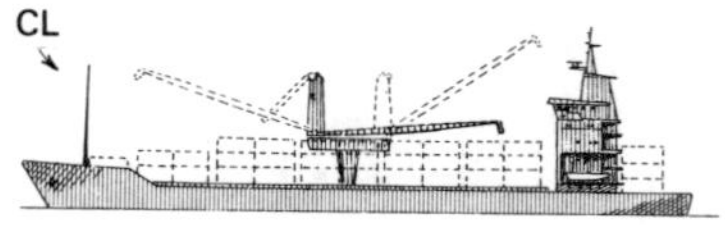

KCMF H1
51850 ASD HEKTOR. Sg/Gr 1977; C/Con; 2000; 106.2 × 5.02 (348.43 × 16.47); TSM; 16.

KCMF H1
● **51860 ASEAN PIONEER.** Pa/Sg 1975; C; 1600; 69.07 × 4.23 (226.6 × 13.87); TSM; 9. Sisters (Pa flag): **51861 ASEAN PROSPERITY 51862 ASEAN VENTURE 51863 OCEAN LEADER** ex ASEAN LEADER 1980 **51864 OCEAN PROGRESS** ex ASEAN PROGRESS 1980 **51865 OCEAN PROMOTER** ex ASEAN PROMOTER 1980 **51866 OCEAN CHALLENGER** ex ASEAN CHALLENGER 1980.

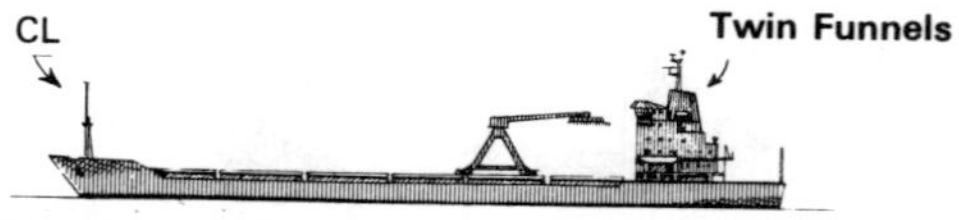

KCMF H1
51870 CONTRACT MARINER. Sg/Ja 1976; Con; 1600/4200; 117.46 × 4.93/6.49 (385.36 × 16.17/21.29); M; 16.25; ex ZEPATLANTIC 1978; ex GULF PIONEER 1978; launched as ZEPATLANTIC; Travelling cranes. Sisters (Sg flag): **51871 CONTRACT CARRIER** ex ZEPBALTIC 1978; ex DAFRA NORTHSEA **51872 CONTRACT TRADER** ex ZEPPACIFIC 1978; ex DAFRA RED SEA 1978; ex GULF TRADER 1977; launched as ZEP PACIFIC.

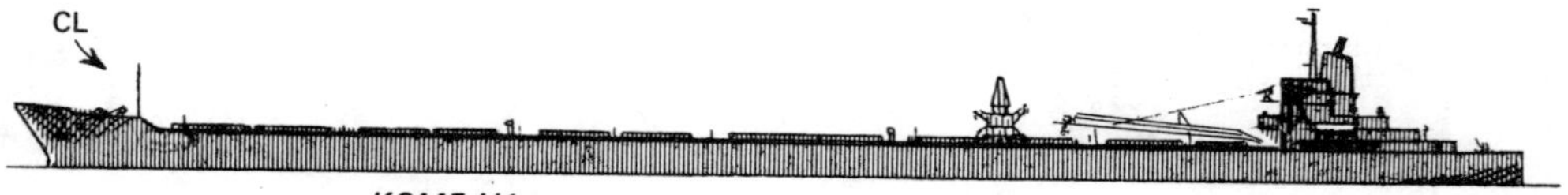

KCMF H1
● **51880 UNIVERSE KURE.** Li/Ja 1971; B; 76000; 303.82 × 17.45 (996.78 × 57.25); T; 15.5; launched as CEDROS PACIFIC; Travelling cranes.

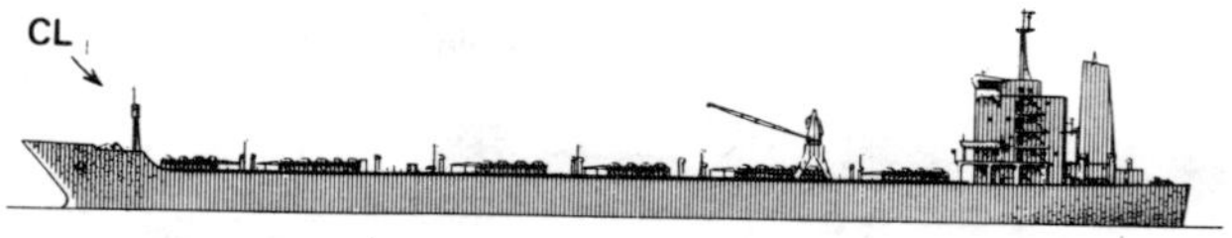

KCMF H1
● **51890 BAROJA.** Sp/Sp 1979; B/Cem; 22500; 186.65 × 9.75; (612.37 × 31.99); M; approx. 15; Travelling crane. Sister: **51891 UNAMUNO** (Sp).

●
51895

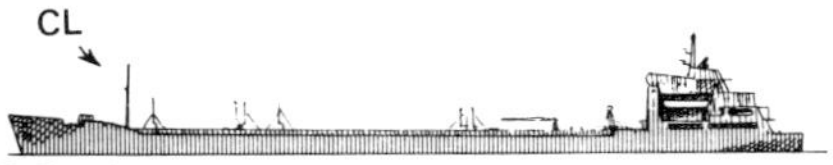

KCMF H1
● **51900 MARINA.** Sw/Sw 1972; Tk/Ch; 5800; 126.12 × 7.2 (413.78 × 23.6); M; 14.25. Sisters (Sw flag): **51901 MARIA 51902 MARIANN.**

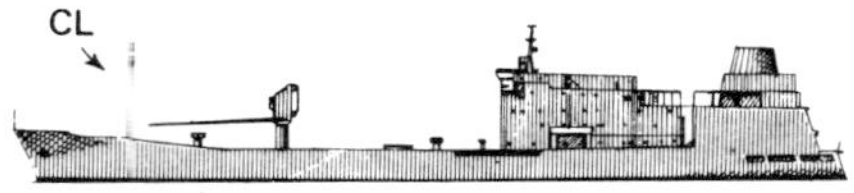

KCMF H1
51910 SEAWAY PRINCE. Au/Au 1975; RoC; 4200; 132.44 × 6.42 (434.51 × 21.06); TSGT; 18; Stern door/ramp. Sister: **51911 SEAWAY PRINCESS** (Au).

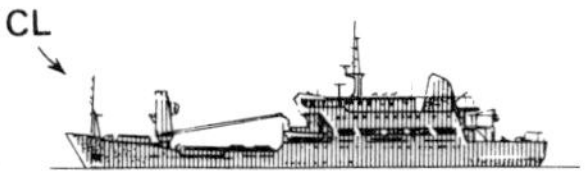

KCMF H12
51920 RELUME. Br/Br 1979; BT; 1600; 75.94 × 3.75; (249.15 × 12.3); TSM; —; Bow thruster.

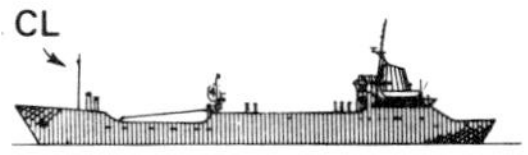

KCMF H12
51930 PEZZATA ROSA. It/No 1964; C; 500; 75.8 × 3.77 (248.68 × 12.37); M; 12.25; ex PIRHOLM 1979; ex NEDERLANDIA 1976.

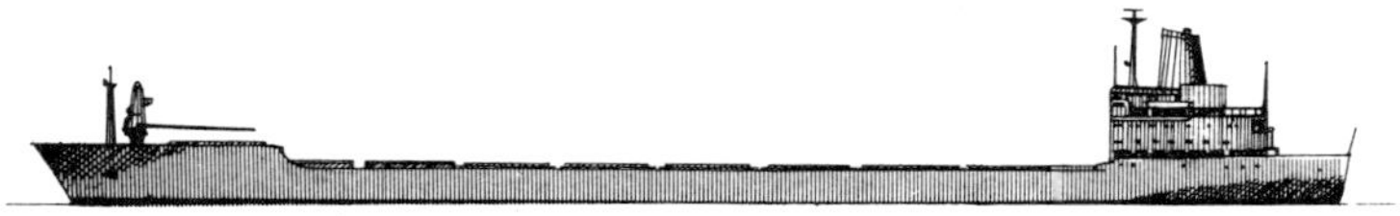

KCMF H13
51940 ACT 3. Br/FRG 1971; Con; 23800; 217.25 × 10.52 (712.76 × 34.51); T; 22.5. Sisters (Br flag): **51941 ACT 4 51942 ACT 5 51943 AUSTRALIAN EXPORTER.**

KCMF H13
51950 ANAHUAC II. Me/Sp 1969; Cem; 5300; 120.12 × 7.03 (394.09 × 23.06); TSM; —.

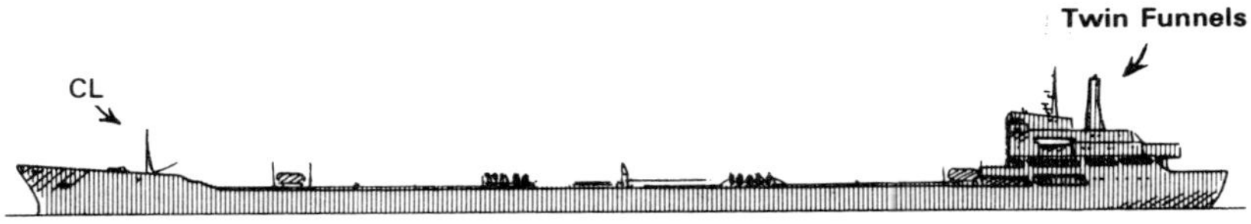

KCMF H13
51960 DRUPA. Br/FRG 1966; Tk; 39800 243.8 × 13.25 (799.87 × 43.47); T; 14; Fenders on upper deck are on port side.

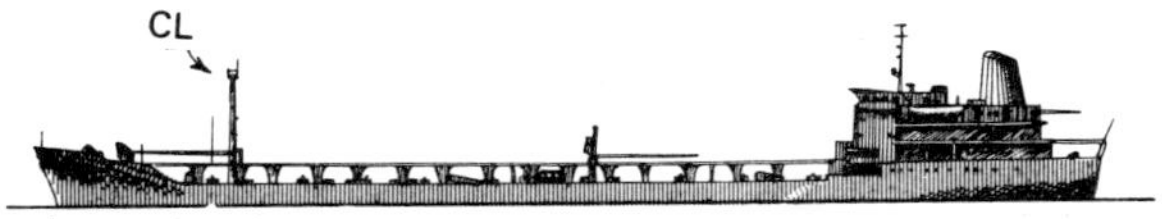

KCMF H13
● **51970 BRITISH LIBERTY.** Br/Sw 1968; Tk; 15100; 169.63 × 9.55 (556.52 × 31.33); M; 16. Similar (Br flag): **51971 BRITISH LOYALTY 51972 BRITISH SECURITY 51973 BRITISH TENACITY 51974 BRITISH UNITY 51975 BRITISH FIDELITY.**

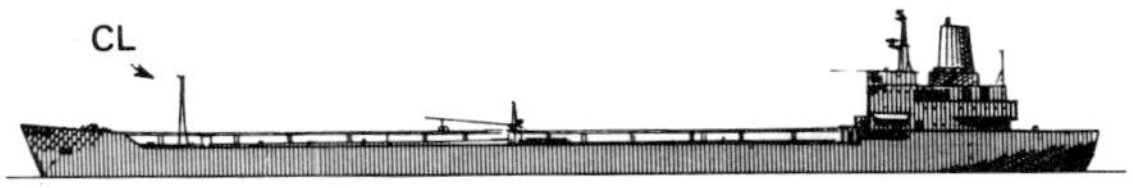

KCMF H13
51980 CELLANA. Au/Au 1968; Tk; 16000; 171.02 × 9.78 (561.09 × 32.08); M; 14.5.

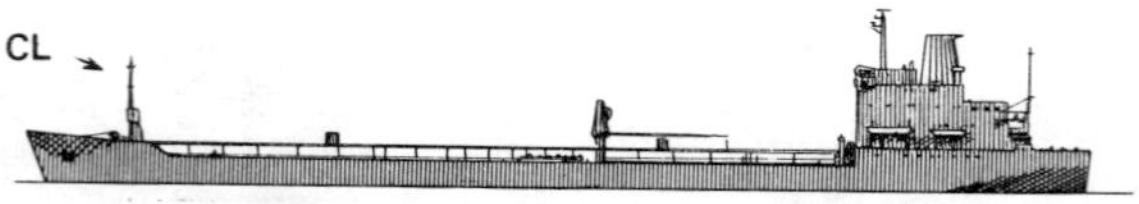

KCMF H13
51985 NORSK BARDE. No/No 1976; Tk; 18000; 168.76 × 10.9 (553.67 × 35.76); M; 16.

KCMF H13
⋆**52000 MARLOW.** DDR/DDR 1971; C/Con; 300; 57.87 × 3.68 (189.86 × 12.07); M; 12; **'Boizenburg'** type. Sisters (DDR flag): ⋆**52001 HAGENOW** ⋆**52002 MILTZOW** ⋆**52003 MIROW** ⋆**52004 NEUBOKOW** ⋆**52006 RAKOW** ⋆**52007 SATOW** ⋆**52008 SEMLOW** ⋆**52009 TORGELOW** ⋆**52010 ZUROW** ⋆**52011 ZUSSOW.**

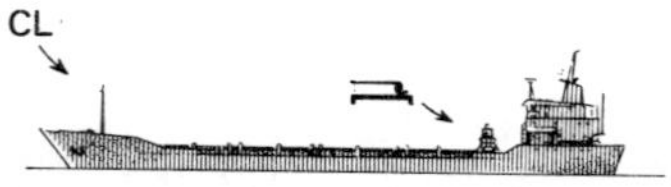

KCMF H13
52040 JUNIOR LOTTE. De/DNe 1975; C; 1600; 93 × 5.58 (305.12 × 18.31); M; 13; Travelling crane.

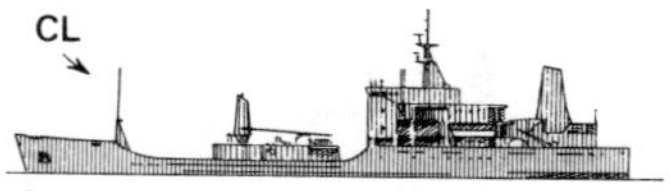

KCMF H13
52060 GOLIATH. Au/Au 1978; Cem; 3400; 95.03 × 5.8 (311.78 × 19.03); M; 14.

KCMF H13
52080 STAPAFELL. Ic/FRG 1979; Tk; 1400; 75.74 × 4.79; (248.49 × 15.72); M; 13.5.

KCMF H13
52100 BINTANG BOLONG. Gm/No 1976; C; 1600; 63.71 × 6.59 (209.02 × 21.62); M; 12; ex JANADA 1978; Travelling crane.

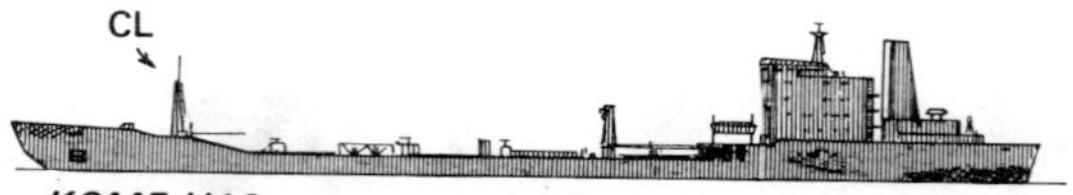

KCMF H13
● **51990 LUNNI.** Fi/FRG 1976; Tk/'B; 11000; 162.01 × 9.5 (531.52 × 31.16); M; 14.5; Sisters (Fi flag): **51991 SOTKA;51992 TIIRA; 51993 UIKKU.**

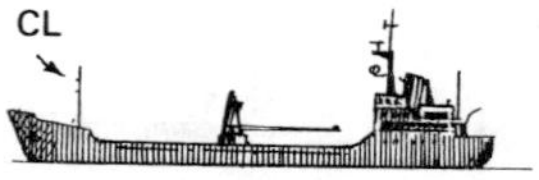

KCMF H13
⋆**52020 BALKHASH.** Ru/Ru 1969; C; 1100; 72.12 × 4.63 (236.61 × 15.19); M; 11; Sisters (Ru flag): ⋆**52021 BAKHCHISARAY;** ⋆**52022 BELOMORYE.**

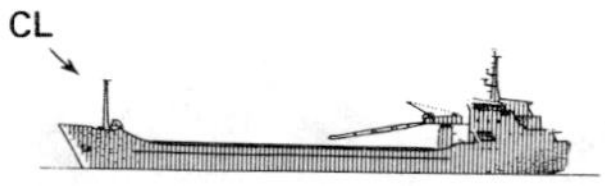

KCMF H13
52030 NOORDLAND. Ne/Ne 1977; C; 1600; 81.44 × 4.78; (267.2 × 15.68); M; 11.5.

KCMF H13
52050 AL SULTANA. O/Ne 1975; FA/Spt; 1400 Dspl; 65.4 × 4.2 (214.56 × 13.77); M; 11.

KCMF H13
⋆**52070 BUNA.** DDR/Ne 1979; Ch; 1800; 73.46 × 4.91; (241 × 16.11); M; 13. Sister: ⋆**52071 SCHKOPAU** (DDR) (may be spelt **ZSCHJOPAU).**

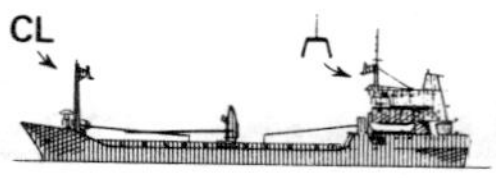

KCMF H13
52090 BALDER B. De/De 1974; C; 500/1400; 71.48 × 3.76/5.68 (234.51 × 12.34/18.63); M; 12; ex LYKKE BEWA 1978. Sisters: **52091 KOERIER** (Pa) ex LITA BEWA 1978 **52092 HAVSO** (Sw) ex KARIN BEWA 1976 Possible sister: **52093 NIAGA XX** (Ia) ex NINA BEWA 1978.

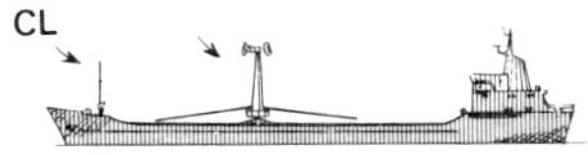

KCMF H13
52110 KIRSTEN SMITS. Ne/De 1976; C; 1600; 84.31 × 6.32 (276.6 × 20.73); M; 13; Travelling crane. Probable sister: **52111 MARINUS SMITS** (Ne).

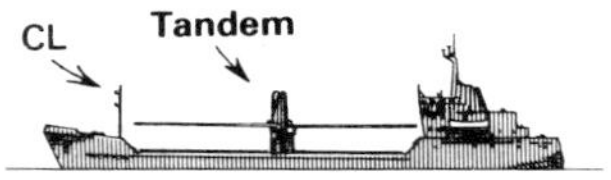

KCMF H13
52120 ANNETTE. Ne/Ne 1976; C; 1600; 81.92 × 6.05 (268.77 × 19.85); M; 12.

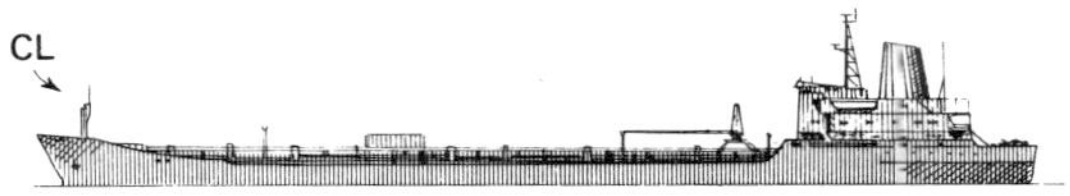

KCMF H13
52130 STOLT NORNESS. Li/Be 1970; Tk; 11100; 158.58 × 9.47 (520.27 × 31.67); M; 15.5; Travelling crane. Sisters (Li flag): **52131 STOLT CROWN 52132 STOLT CASTLE 52133 STOLT SYDNESS.**

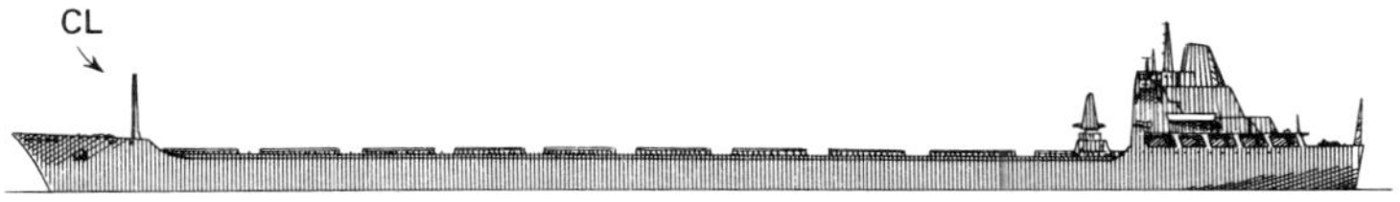

KCMF H13
52140 ORIENT ENTERPRISE. Li/Ja 1968; B; 35500; 223.96 × 13.7 (734.78 × 44.94); M; 15; ex PROMETHEUS; Travelling crane. Possible sisters (Gr flag): **52141 AFOVOS 52142 THEOGENNITOR** ex AGAMEMNON.

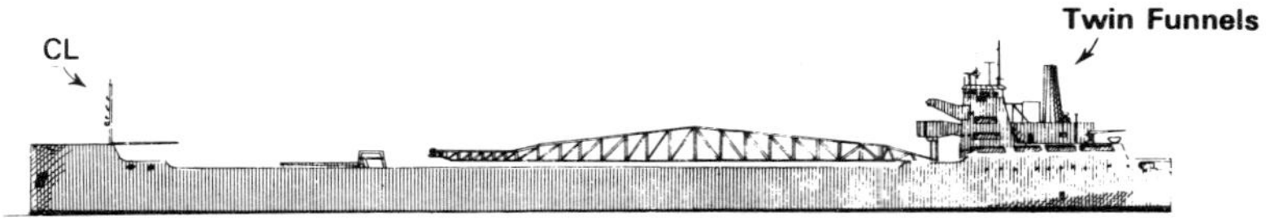

KCMF H13
52150 CANADIAN PROGRESS. Ca/Ca 1968; B; 21400; 222.51 × 8.73 (730 × 28.64); M; 14.5.

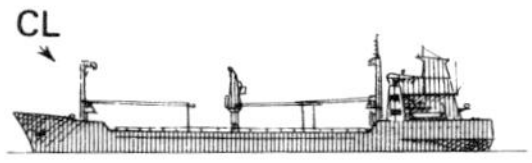

KCMF H13
● **52160 SCHOONEBEEK.** Ne/Ne 1973; C; 1600; 77.09 × 5.81 (252.92 × 19.06); M; 12.5; ex AERDENHOUT 1975. Sister: **52161 AZORES STAR** (Cy) ex GROESBEEK 1980 Probable sisters (Ne flag): **52162 WIIDSWAL** ex SAMBEEK 1980 **52163 SCHOUWENBANK** ex WEDLOOPER 1980.

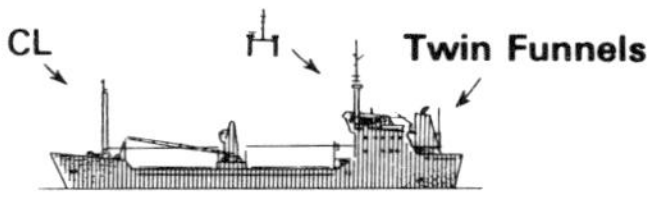

KCMF H13
52170 ATLANTIC. Ne/Ne 1979; R; 1000/1600; 66 × 5.16/5.63; (216.54 × 16.93/18.47); M; 12. Sisters (Ne flag): **52171 BALTIC 52172 CELTIC.**

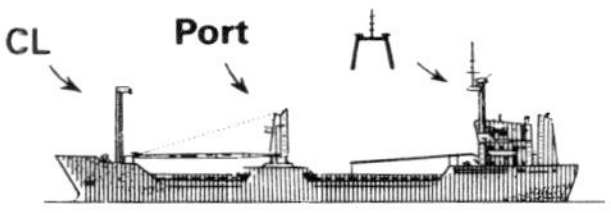

KCMF H13
52180 NESTOR. Ne/Ne 1979; C/Con; 1600/3000; 82.78 × 5.93/7.39; (271.59 × 19.46/24.25); M; approx. 12.5. Sisters (Ne flag): **52181 MENTOR 52182 STENTOR.**

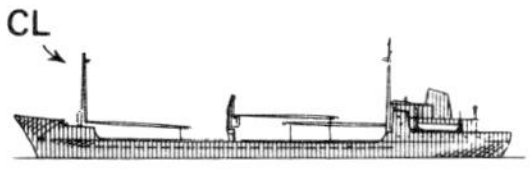

KCMF H13
52190 NIAGA XXVIII. Ia/Ne 1970; C; 1500; 78.75 × 5.84 (258.37 × 19.16); M; 12; ex HOLLAND; ex HEERENGRACHT 1979; ex HILVARENBEEK 1973. Sister: **52191 NIAGA XXXII** (Ia) ex NOORDWAL 1980.

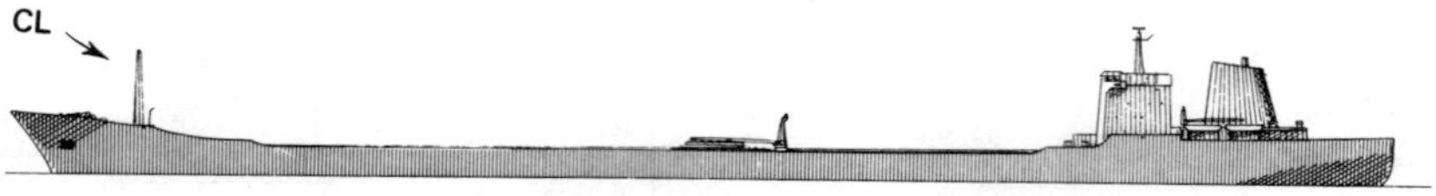

KCMF H13

● **52200 GUNGNIR 1.** Pa/It 1966; Tk; 48500; 253.6 × 13.32 (832.02 × 43.7); M; 16.25; ex NAI GIUSEPPINA; ex GIUSEPPINA LOLLI GHETTI 1974; ex ROSS LAKE 1972; ex FORT ST. CATHERINE 1971. Sister: **52201 ELIZABETH II** (Pa) ex MARGARET SIMONE 1980; ex PETRA 1973; ex WARWICK FORT 197 Similar (It flag): **52202 SARISSOLA** ex CLAUDIO R 1979 **52203 OMBRINA** ex MONICA R 1979 **52204 SCRIVIA** ex ANDREA LEOPOLDO Similar (Bulk/Oil): **52205 CIELO BIANCO** (It) ex HERMES 1972; ex SANTA VALERIA 1971 **52206 SHINWA** (In) ex DAYA PARVATI; ex ROSS HEAD 1977.

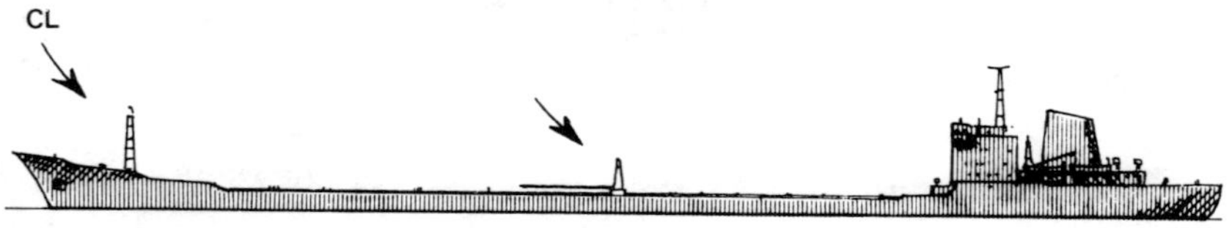

KCMF H13

● **52210 SANTA CRISTINA PRIMA.** It/It 1966; Tk; 48700; 253.6 × 13.29 (832.02 × 43.6); M; —. Sisters (It flag): **52211 SANTA ANNA PRIMA 52212 SANTA AUGUSTA.**

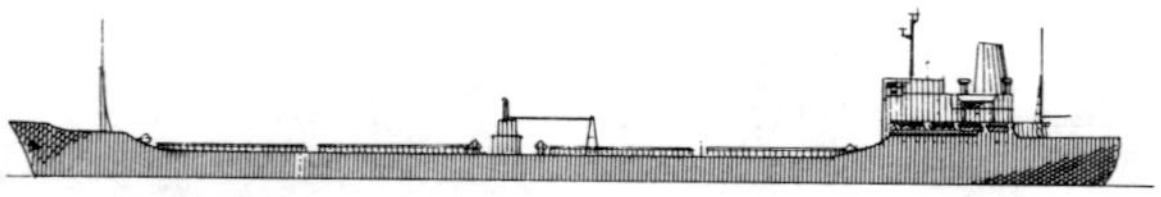

KCMF H13

52220 NIKKEI MARU No 3. Ja/Ja 1969; O; 17900; 175.04 × 11 (574.28 × 36.09); M; 14.25.

KCMF H13

● **52230 SVEALAND.** FRG/FRG 1970; C; 1000; 87.61 × 5.29 (287.43 × 17.35); M; 14.5; ex CONTI SYRIA 1980; ex SVEALAND 1979; ex HELGA RUSS 1979; ex SVEALAND 1977; ex ROYAL ENTERPRISE 1975; launched as SVEALAND.

KCMF H13

52240 TAKARI I. Ia/FRG 1966; C; 2300; 94.9 × 5.26 (311.35 × 17.26); M; 12.5. Sisters (Ia flag): **52241 TAKARI II 52242 TAKARI III 52243 TAKARI IV 52244 TAKARI V 52245 TAKARI VI 52246 TAKARI VII 52247 TAKARI VIII.**

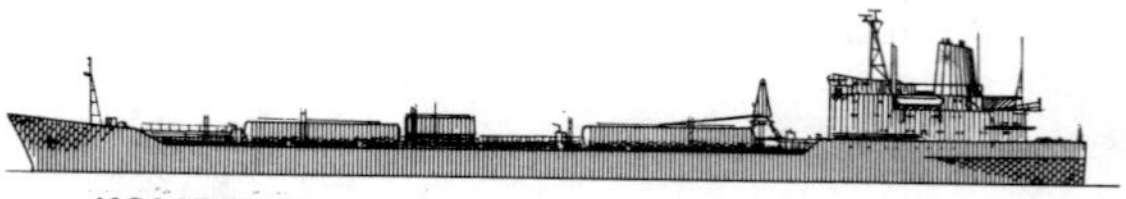

KCMF H13

52250 QUITAUNA. Bz/Be 1975; Ch; 14300; 170.72 × 10.21 (560.1 × 33.49); Travelling crane. Sister: **52251 QUIXADA** (Bz).

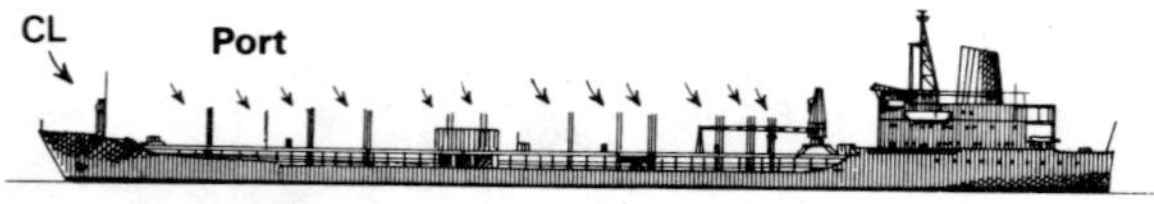

KCMF H13

52260 STOLT SHEAF. Li/Be 1972; Tk/Ch; 14600; 170.72 × 10.54 (560.1 × 34.58); M; 13.75; Travelling crane. Sisters: **52261 STOLT BOEL** (Li) **52262 STOLT LLANDAFF** (Br).

● 52265

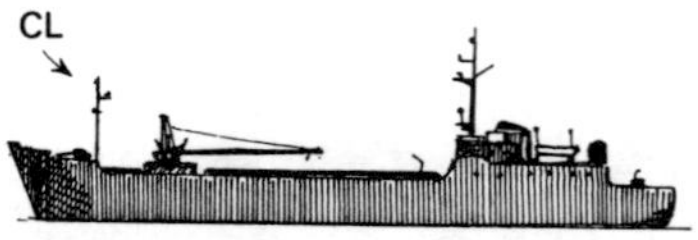

KCMF H13

***52270 URAL.** Ru/Ru —; A/Spt. Nuclear; 4000 Dspl; 103 × 6 (337.92 × 19.68); M; —.

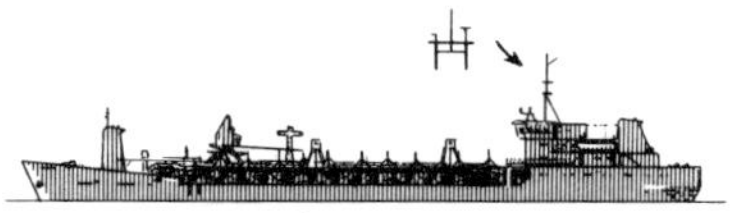

KCMF H13

52280 BOA VISTA 1. Bz/Ne 1977; D; 5500; 107.52 × 7.49; (352.76 × 24.57); TSM; 12. Sister: **52281 MACAPA** (Bz).

● 52285

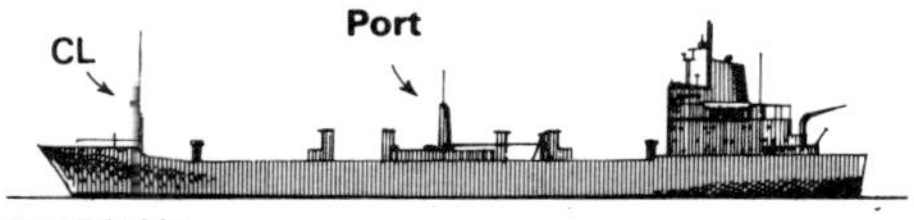

KCMFC H1

52290 HUMBER ARM. Li/FRG 1976; RoC; 3700; 130.03 × 6.68 (426.6 × 21.92); M; 16; Side docr. Sister: **52291 CORNER BROOK** (Li).

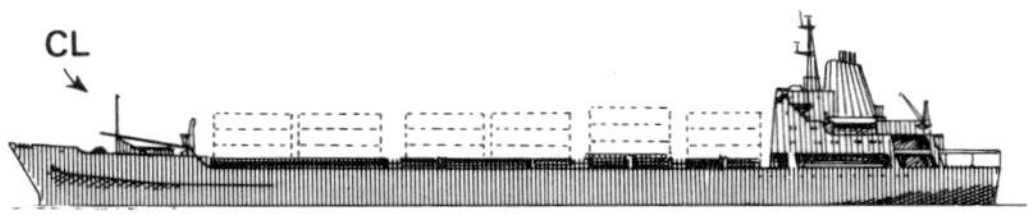

KCMFC H1

52300 COVADONGA. Sp/Au 1969; Con; 12800; 156.67 × 9.17 (514 × 30.08); M; 17.5; ex CP HUNTER 1981; ex SEATRAIN GALVESTON 1980; ex TRANS EUROPA 1979; ex CHESHIRE VENTURE 1979; ex TRANS EUROPA 1978; ex KANIMBLA 1976. Sister: **52301 GUADALUPE 1** (Sp) ex SEATRAIN TEXAS 1979; ex TRANS AMERICA 1979; ex CHESHIRE ENDEAVOUR 1979; ex TRANS AMERICA 1978; ex MANOORA 1976.

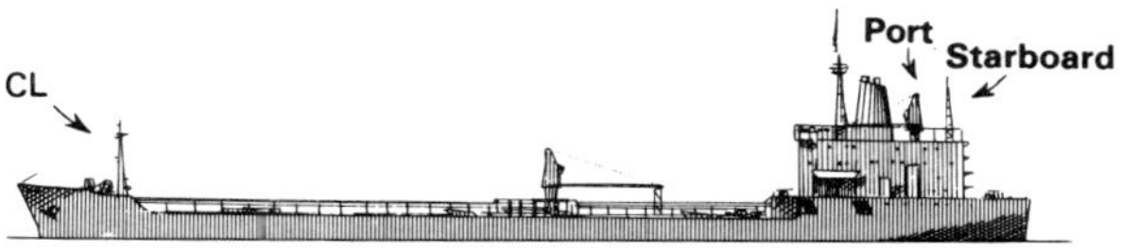

KCMFCK H13

52310 EBURNA. Br/Ja 1979; Tk; 19800; 170 × 11.04 (557.74 × 36.22); M; 14.1. Sisters (Br flag): **52311 ERVILIA 52312 EUPLECTA 52313 EBALINA.**

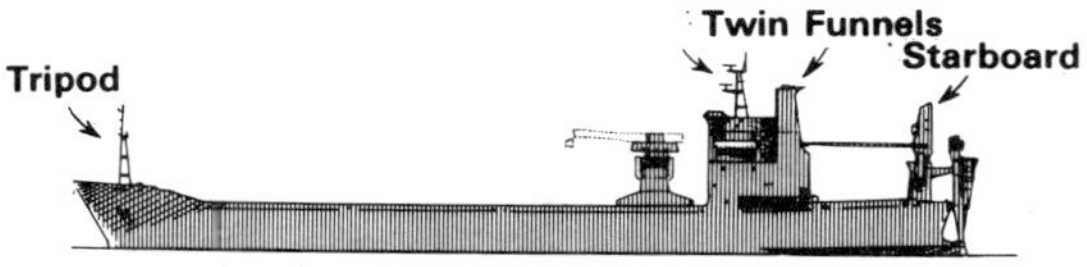

KCMFCP H1

⋆**52320 LEDENICE.** Ys/Ys 1979; RoC/Con/C; 5600; 144.4 × 6.5 (473.75 × 21.33); M; 17.9; Travelling gantry (with slewing deck crane). Stern slewing ramp. Probable sister: ⋆**52321 BRIBIR** (Ys).

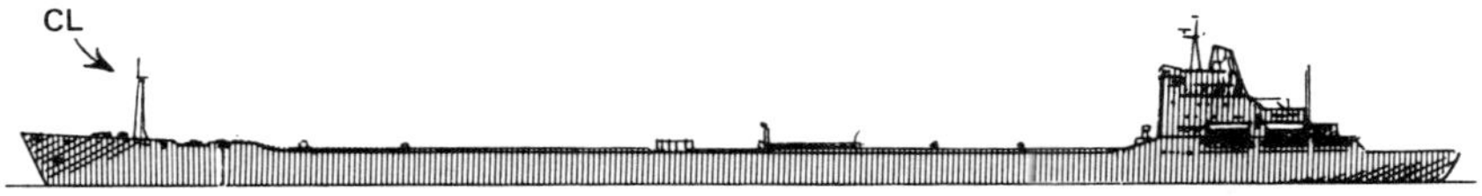

KCMFK H

52330 FINA BELGIQUE. Fr/Fr 1966; Tk; 48200; 250.02 × 12.75 (820.27 × 41.83); M; 16.

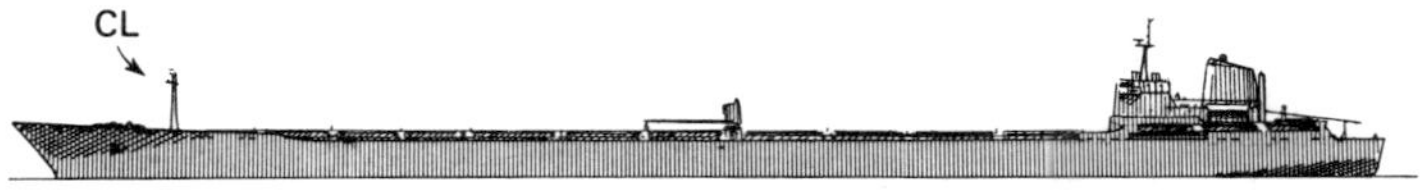

KCMFK H

52340 NAI LUISA. It/It 1970; OBO; 28700; 216.42 × 12.45 (710 × 40.85); M; 15.5; ex LUISA LOLLI GHETTI 1974.

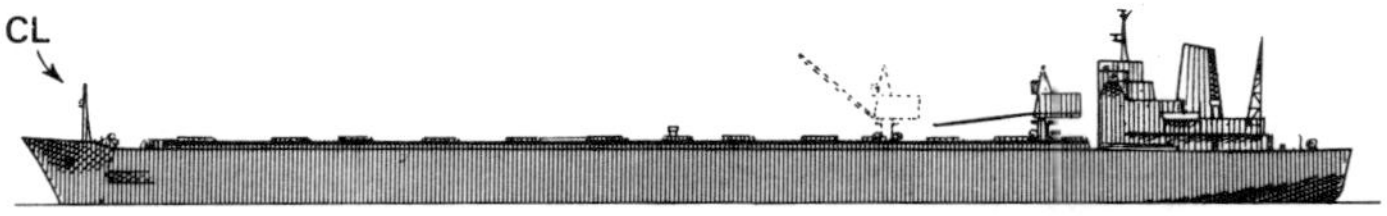

KCMFK H

● **52350 NEGO TRIABUNNA.** Li/Ja 1971; B; 32100; 209.02 × 10.99 (685.76 × 36.05); M; 15.75; Travelling cranes. Sister: **52351 SILVICULTURE** (Li).

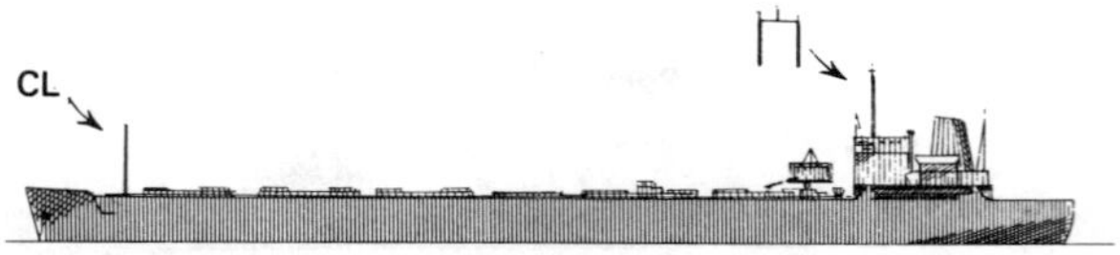

KCMFK H

● **52360 GOLDEN STATE.** Li/Ja 1964; B; 17400; 174.02 × 9.92 (570.93 × 32.55); M; 13.5; ex KURE MARU 1976; Travelling crane. Similar: **52361 BLUE STAR** (Ko) ex HONSHU MARU 1978 **52362 SUNWAY** (Pa) ex MARUSUMI MARU 1978 **52363 HIRO MARU** (Ja).

KCMFK H1

52370 AL OSMAN. Le/Ne 1965; C; 500; 71.99 × 3.82 (236.18 × 12.53); M; 12.75; ex ZEEBURGH 1979.

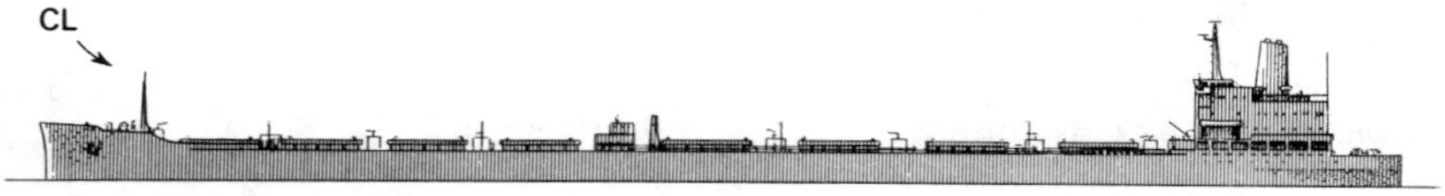

KCMFK H1

52380 MOSEL ORE. Li/Sw 1969; OO; 58800; 253.02 × 15.13 (830.12 × 49.64); M; 15; ex BARON VENTURE 1980; ex PAJALA 1978. Sister: **52381 SAAR ORE** (Li) ex UNITED VENTURE; ex PORJUS 1978; ex FLOWERGATE 1974.

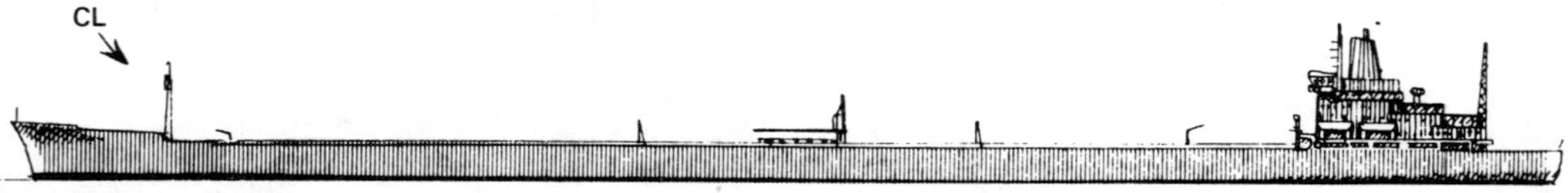

KCMFK H1

● **52390 AL BADIAH.** Ku/Ja 1970; Tk; 107400; 325.33 × 18.99 (1067.35 × 62.3); T; —.

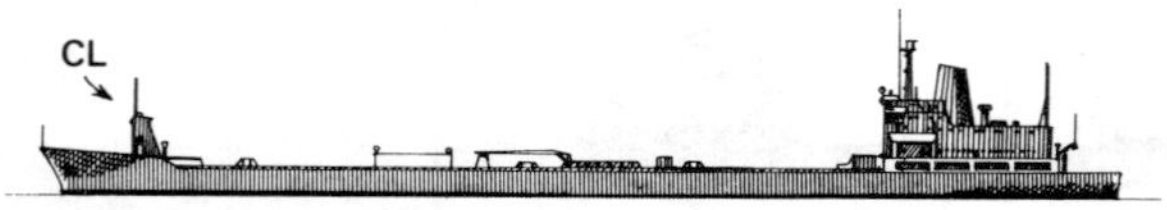

KCMFK H1

52400 FJORDSHELL. No/No 1973; Tk; 18600; 170.69 × 11.37 (560 × 37.3); M; 16.

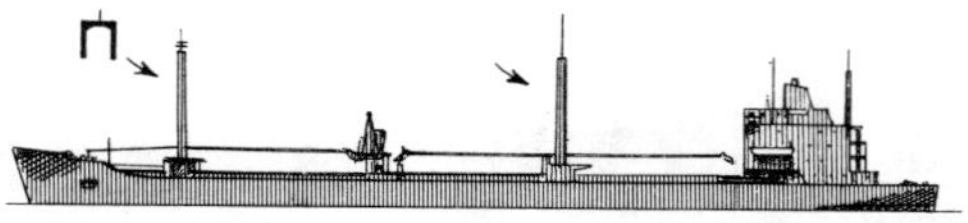

KCMFK H1

52410 AGIOS NIKOLAS. Gr/Br 1971; C; 7500/11900; 147.2 × 6.76/10 (482.93 × 22.18/32.81); M; 18.75; ex SIG RAGNE; **'Clyde'** class. Sisters (Li flag): **52411 SAMJOHN GOVERNOR 52412 SAMJOHN PIONEER.**

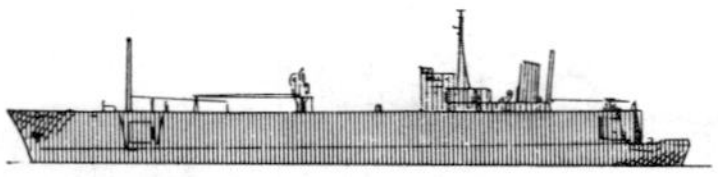

KCMFK H1

52420 HOKUO MARU. Ja/Ja 1969; RoC; 2400; 107.7 × 4.49 (353.34 × 14.73); TSM; 14.75.

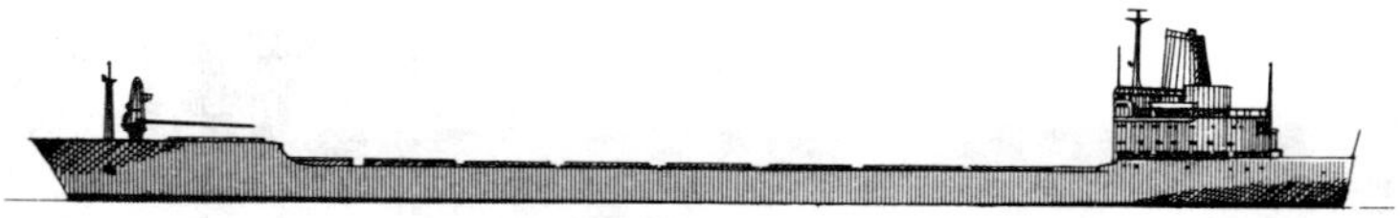

KCMFK H13

52430 ACT 3. Br/FRG 1971; Con; 23800; 217.25 × 10.52 (712.76 × 34.51); T; 22.5. Sisters (Br flag): **52431 ACT 4 52432 ACT 5 52433 AUSTRALIAN EXPORTER.**

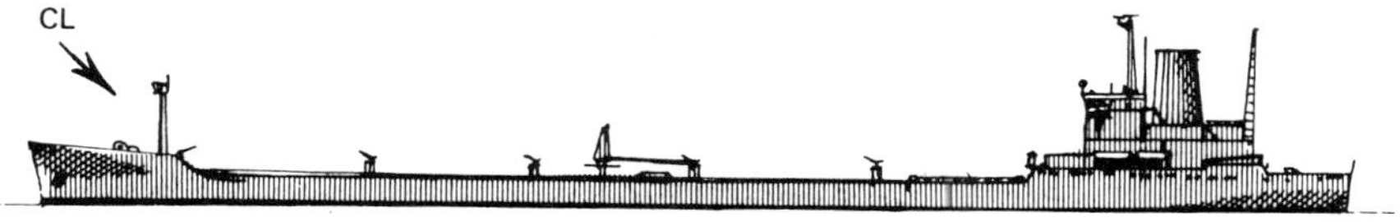

KCMFK H13

★**52440 KHAN ASPARUKH.** Bu/Bu 1976; Tk; 59900; 244.48 × 15.5 (802.1 × 50.85); M; 14.5. Probable Sister: **52441 OLYMPIC STAR** (Li) ex KHAN KRUN.

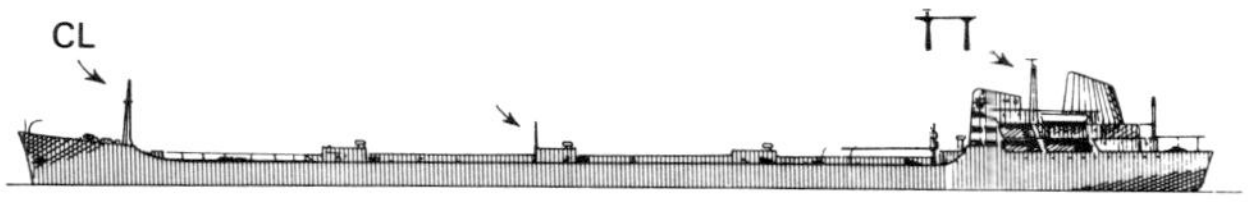

KCMFK H13

52450 NORDIC LOUISIANA. Br/Br 1964; Sulphur Carrier; 18600; 188.98 × 10.35 (620.01 × 33.96); M; 16; ex NAESS LOUISIANA 1973. Sister: **52451 NORDIC TEXAS** (Br) ex NAESS TEXAS.

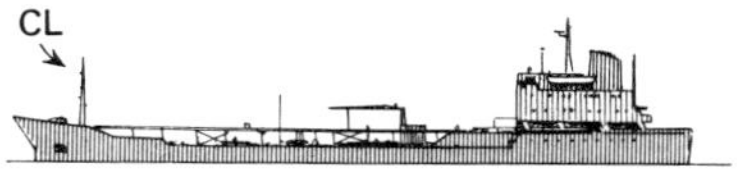

KCMFK H13

52460 ETTORE. It/No 1974; Tk; 4500; 107.93 × 8.08 (354.1 × 26.51); M; 14; ex JOARCTIC 1978. Sisters: **52461 HUMBOLT** (No) ex JOALASKA 1978 **52462 TANIT** (Gr) ex ESSI ATLANTIC; ex JOATLANTIC 1978.

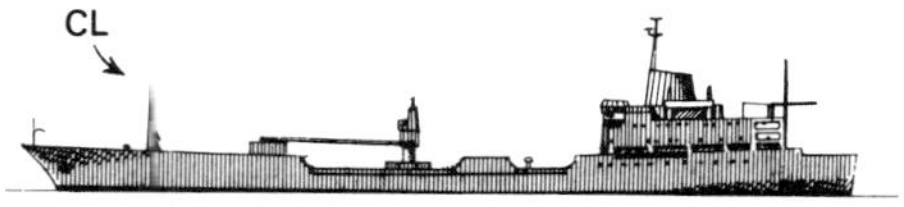

KCMFK H13

52470 VENDEE. Br/Br 1972; C; 6100; 132.29 × 7.34 (434.02 × 24.08); M; 18; ex ZAIDA 1975. Sister: **52471 VOSGES** (Br) ex ZAIRA 1975.

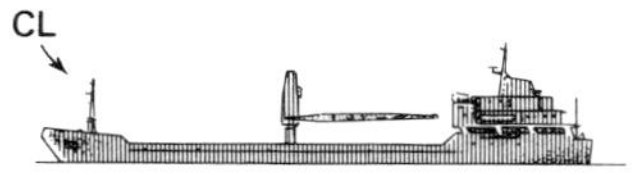

KCMFK H13

52480 KRISTINA. Sw/Sw 1970; C/Con; 1600; 87.03 × 4.96; (285.53 × 16.27); M; 12; ex ALICE 1973.

KCMFK H13

52490 HOKUSEI MARU. Ja/Ja 1959; C; 4600; 117.23 × 6.81 (384.61 × 22.34); M; 12.25; Travelling cranes.

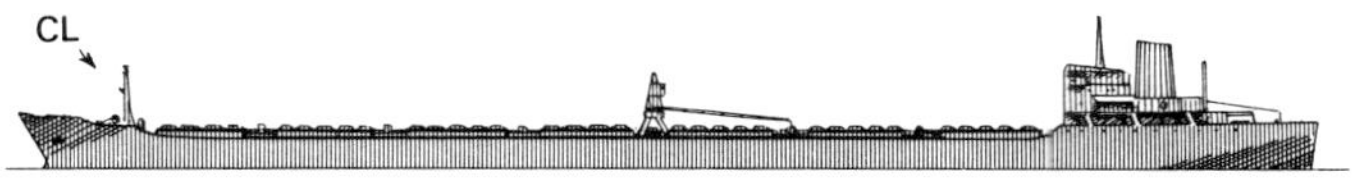

KCMFK H13

52500 ARALAR. Sp/Sp 1971; B; 29300; 206.86 × 13.35 (678.67 × 43.79); M; 16; Travelling crane. Similar: **52501 PILAR MARIA** (Sp).

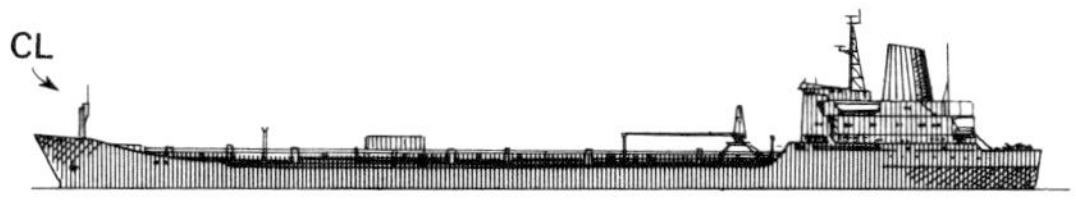

KCMFK H13

52510 STOLT NORNESS. Li/Be 1970; Tk; 11100; 158.58 × 9.47 (520.27 × 31.67); M; 15.5; Travelling crane. Sisters (Li flag): **52511 STOLT CROWN 52512 STOLT CASTLE 52513 STOLT SYDNESS.**

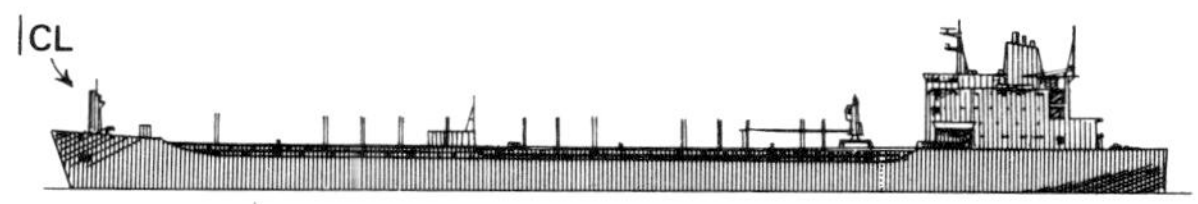

KCMFK H13

52520 STOLT PRIDE. Li/Fr 1976; Tk; 12500; 170.69 × 9.68 (560 × 31.76); M; 15; Travelling crane. Probable Sisters (Li flag): **52521 STOLT SPIRIT 52522 STOLT SINCERITY 52523 STOLT INTEGRITY 52524 STOLT TENACITY 52525 STOLT LOYALTY 52526 STOLT EXCELLENCE.**

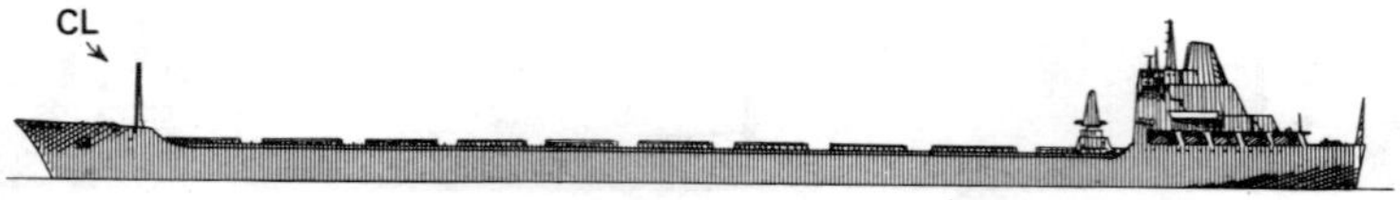

KCMFK H13
52530 ORIENT ENTERPRISE. Li/Ja 1968; B; 35500; 223.96 × 13.7 (734.78 × 44.94); M; 15; ex PROMETHEUS; Travelling crane. Possible Sisters: **52531 THEOGENNITOR** (Gr) ex AGAMEMNON **52532 AFOVOS** (Gr).

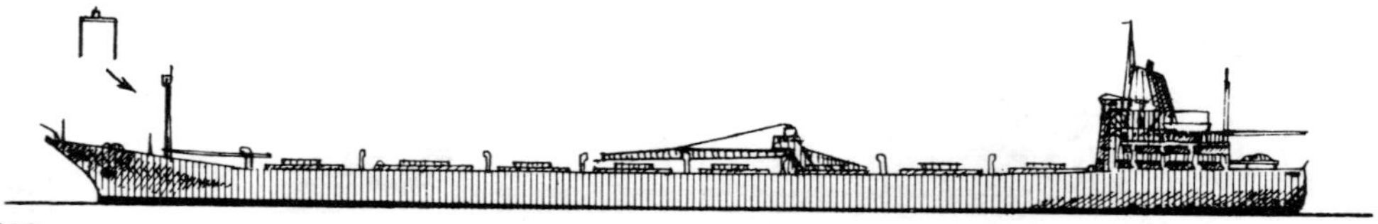

KCMFK H13
52540 MARCONA CONVEYOR. Li/Ja 1967; B; 32600; 259.75 × 13.58 (852.19 × 44.55); M; 16.25; ex ARAGONITE ISLANDER 1973; ex FOTINI L 1971.

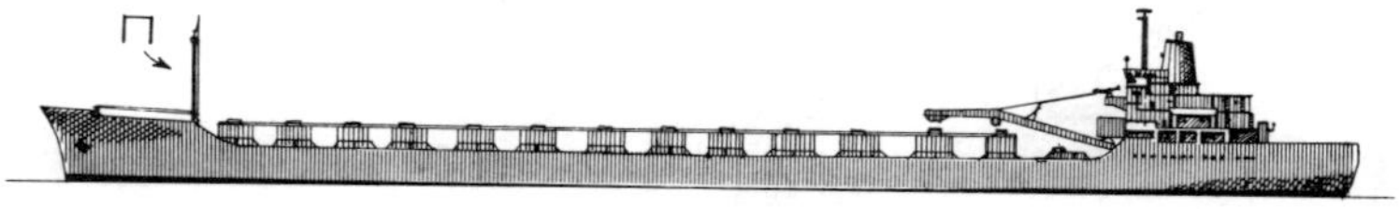

KCMFK H13
52550 DAVID P. REYNOLDS. Li/FRG 1970; B; 28600; 226.7 × 12.79 (743.76 × 41.96); T; 16.

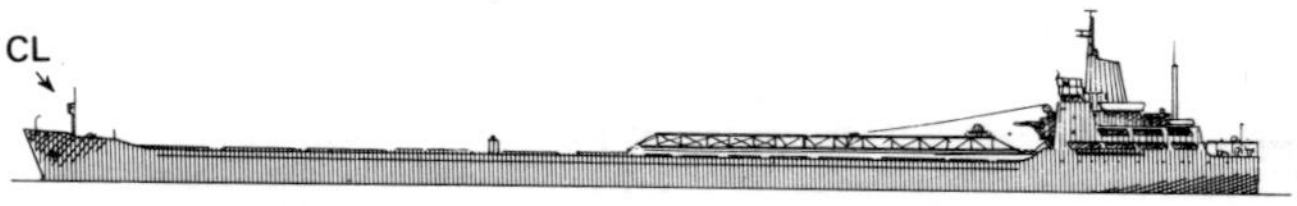

KCMFK H13
52560 ALGOSEA. Ca/Br 1970; B; 13100; 195.94 × 9.54 (642.85 × 31.29); M; 15; ex BROOKNES 1976. Lengthened 1976.

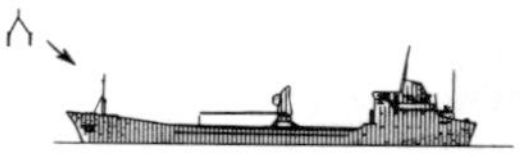

KCMFK H13
52570 FREYFAXI. Ic/No 1966; Cem; 1000; 65.03 × 4 (213.35 × 13.12); M; 12; launched as FAXI; Travelling crane.

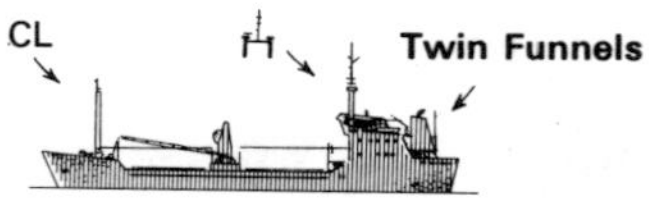

KCMFK H13
52580 ATLANTIC. Ne/Ne 1979; R; 1000/1600; 66 × 5.16/5.63 (216.54 × 16.93/18.47); M; 12;. Sisters: **52581 BALTIC** (Ne) **52582 CELTIC** (Ne).

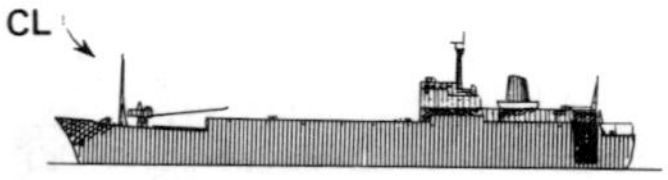

KCMFK H2
52590 KOYO MARU. Ja/Ja 1970; RoC; 2000; 92 × 4.91 (301.84 × 16.11); M; 14.

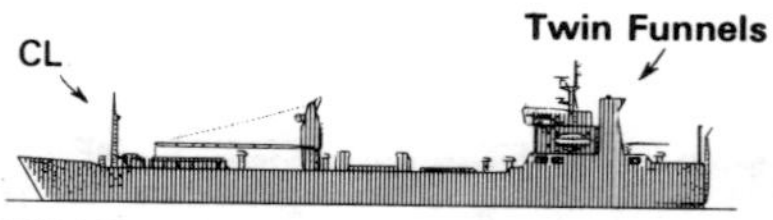

KCMFK H3
52600 ASTREA. No/No 1979; RoC/Con; 1600; 109 × 4.79 (357.61 × 15.72); M; 17; Stern ramp. Side door on starboard side.

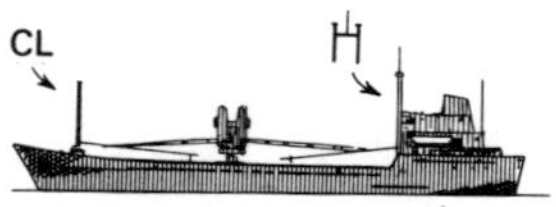

KCMFK H3
52610 HVASSAFELL. Ic/FRG 1971; C; 900/1800; 80.17 × 4.07/5.87 (263.02 × 13.36/19.25); M; 14. Possible Sister: **52611 SKAFTAFELL** (Ic).

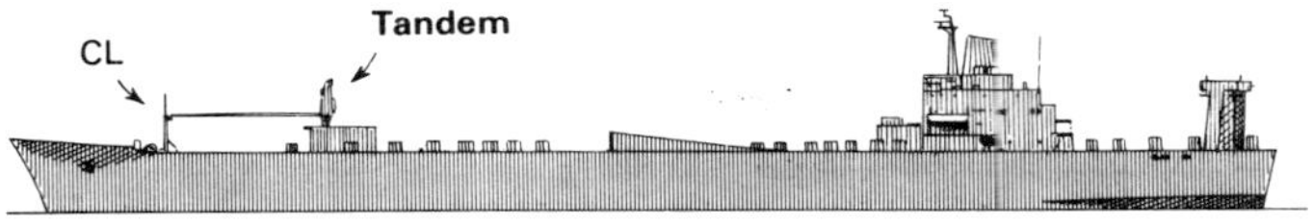

KCMFR H

● **52620 TYSON LYKES.** US/US 1976; RoC; 13200; 208.72 × 9.8 (684.77 × 32.15); T; 23; ex MAINE 1979; Quarter door/ramp. Sisters (US flag): **52521 CHARLES LYKES** ex NEVADA 1979 **52622 ILLINOIS 52623 JUPITER** (US Navy) ex LIPSCOMB LYKES 1980.

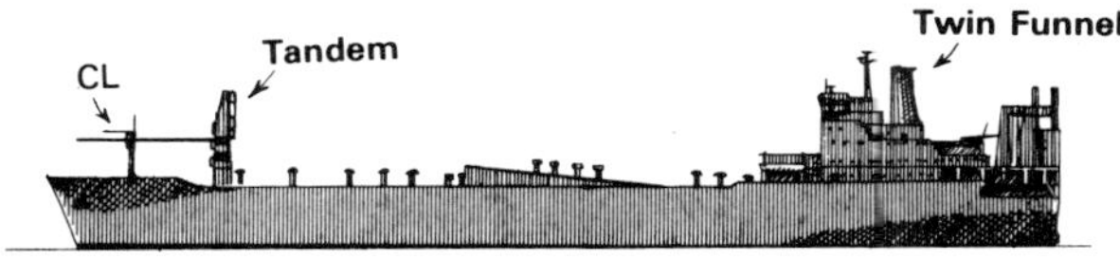

KCMFR H

52630 PARALLA. Sw/Sw 1971; RoC; 13400; 199.02 × 9.59 (652.95 × 31.46); M; 21; stern doors. Sisters: **52631 ALLUNGA** (Au) **52632 DILKARA** (Br).

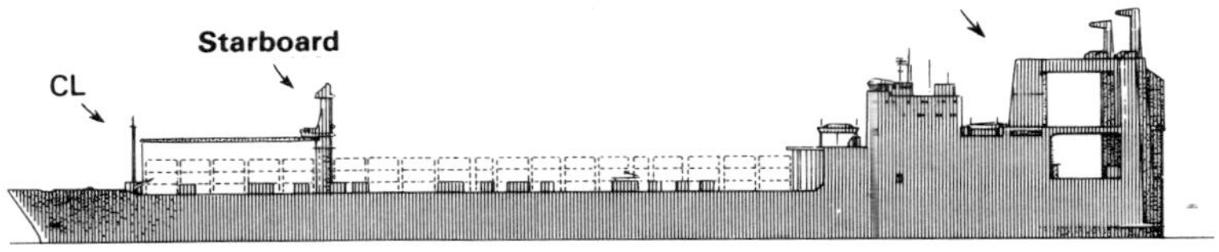

KCMFR H3

52640 BARBER TONSBERG. No/No 1979; RoC/Con; 22100; 228.5 × 10.8 (749.67 × 35.43); M; 22; Starboard quarter ramp. Sister: **52641 BARBER TAIF** (No) Similar (Ja built. Differences include funnel shape, design of crane etc.): **52642 BARBER NARA** (Sw) **52643 BARBER PRIAM** (Br) **52644 BARBER PERSEUS** (Br) **52645 BARBER TOBA** (No).

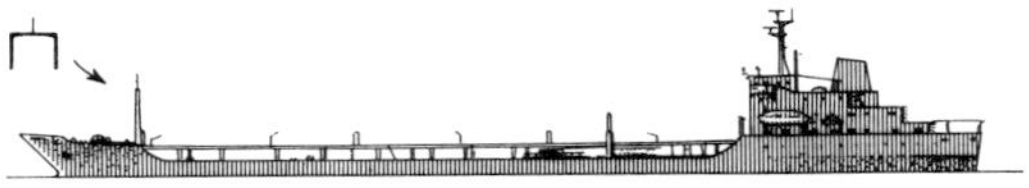

KCMKF H13

52650 LIBERTADOR SAN MARTIN. Ar/Ar 1979; Tk; 10000; 153 × 8.24 (501.97 × 27.03); M; 15. Sisters (Ar flag) **52651 INGENIERO VILLA 52652 MINISTRO EXCURRA** (also reported as MINISTRO EZCURRA).

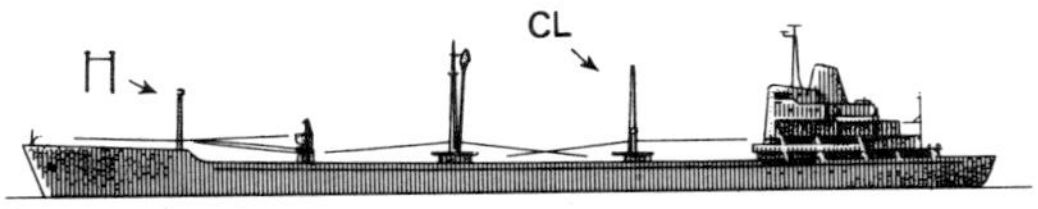

KCMKMFK H1

52680 TARBELA. Pk/FRG 1968; C; 7000/9000; 153.88 × -/9.27 (504.86 × -/30.41); M; —. Sisters (Pk flag): **52681 KAPTAI 52682 WARSAK.**

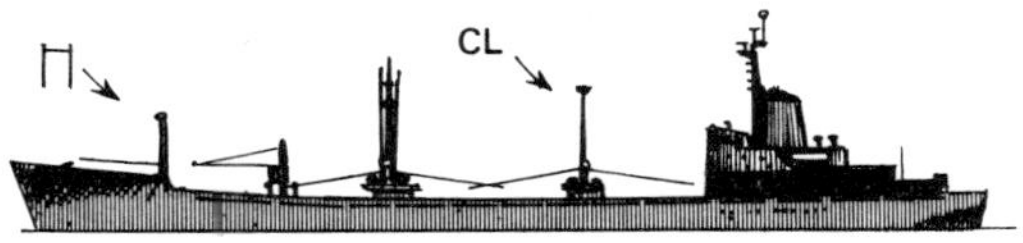

KCMKF H13

52660 ILO. Pe/Pe 1972; C; 8600; 153.88 × 9.39 (504.86 × 30.81); M; 19.5; Naval service. Sister: **52661 RIMAC** (Pe).

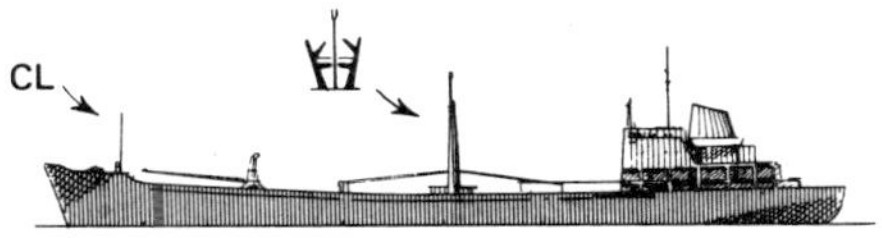

KCMKF H13

52670 ADHARA. Pa/FRG 1962; C/HL; 5500; 127.11 × 7.78 (417.03 × 25.52); M; 15.75; ex ASTIR I; ex NAXOS TRADER 1978; ex EVI A 1977; ex PACIFIC 1972; ex TRIPOLI 1969; ex AXENFELS 1965; Travelling crane. Sister: **52671 MYOMA YWA** (Bm) ex ALTENFELS 1969.

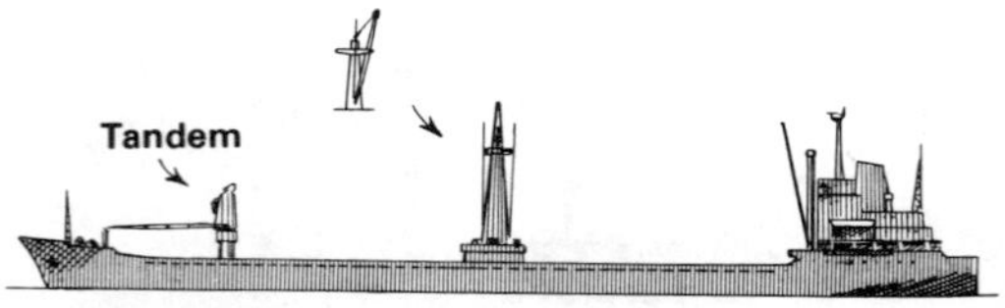

KCMKMFK H13
52690 KASUGA MARU. Ja/Ja 1976; B; 11800; 145.9 × 9.5 (478.67 × 31.16); M; 15. Similar (larger): **52691 KATORI MARU.** (Ja)

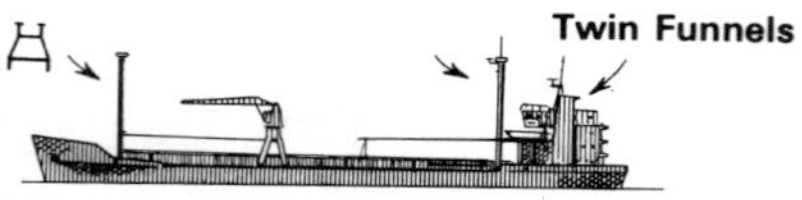

KCM$_2$F H1
52700 AMULET. De/De 1975; C; 1600; 94.39 × 5.77 (309.67 × 18.93); M; 13; Travelling cranes. Sisters (De flag): **52701 TALISMAN 52702 CHARM.**

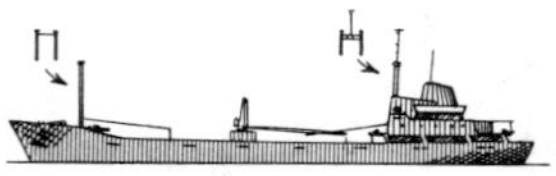

KCM$_2$F H1
● **52710 NEPTUN HERCULES.** No/FRG 1965; C; 1100/1900; 83.04 × 4.77/6.14 (272.44 × 15.66)20.14); M; 14; ex ANGLIAN 1975; ex NEPTUN HERCULES 1974; ex HERCULES 1972.

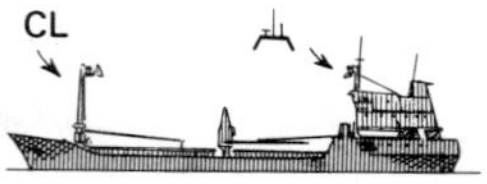

KCM$_2$F H13
52720 COMBI TRADER. Ne/De 1975; C; 1400; 71.48 × 5.74 234.51 × 18.83); M; 12; ex OCEAN COAST 1975. Similar: **52721 RIJNHAVEN** (Ne); launched as JANNE.

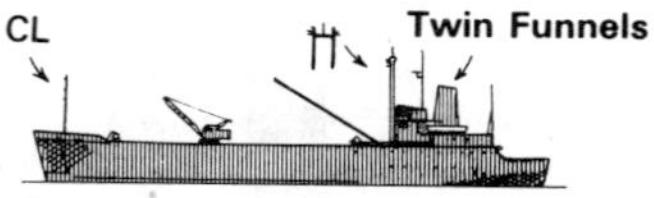

KCM$_2$FK H
● **52730 MARITIME RESOURCE.** Sg/Ja 1966; RoC/LC; 3600; 78.49 × 4.37 (257.51 × 14.33); TSM; 10.5; ex OMAN VENTURE 1978; ex COSMOS 1975; Bow doors.

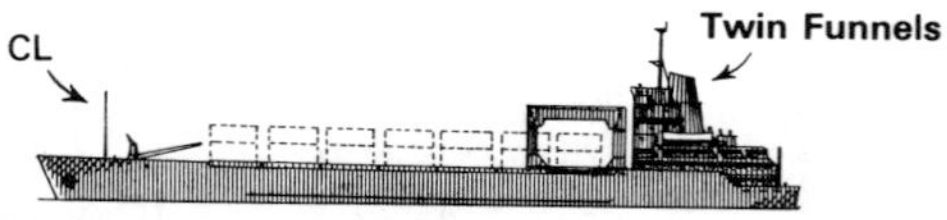

KCNMF H1
52740 FRANK H. BROWN. Ca/Ca 1965; Con; 8000; 120.12 × 6.12 (394.09 × 20.08); TSM; —; May be converted to a barge.

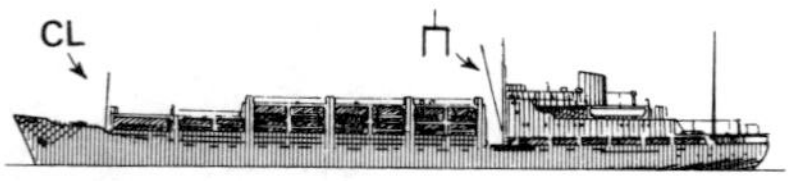

KFM H1
52750 MERINO EXPRESS. Li/Ne 1960; LS; 2400/3400; 119.49 × 5.68/6.41 (392.03 × 18.64/21.03); M; 16; ex CAP FARINA 1976; ex CARIBBEAN EXPRESS 1974; ex KREON 1973. Converted from cargo ship 1976.

KFM H1
52760 APOLLO. Br/Br 1954/68; C; 1300; 84.82 × 4.17 (278.28 × 13.68); M; 10.5; Lengthened 1968. Sister: **52761 AGELIKI III** (Gr) ex ECHO 1980.

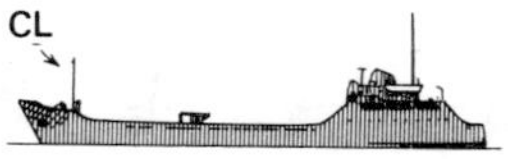

KFM H13
● **52770 SIRIUS.** Cy/Br 1959; C; 1100; 74.48 × 4.03 (244.36 × 13.22); M; 12; ex STAR 1977; ex ORWELL QUAY 1976; ex GULF SEA 1975; ex LEEDS 1972. Sister: **52771 GULF COAST** (Cy) ex WAKEFIELD Similar: **52772 DIMITRIS** (Gr) ex DIMITRIOS 1980; ex ALOUETTE 1978; ex STORK 1976; ex HARROGATE 1972. **52773 VICTORY** (Gr) ex JEAN R 1980; ex RAVEN 1977; ex SELBY 1973.

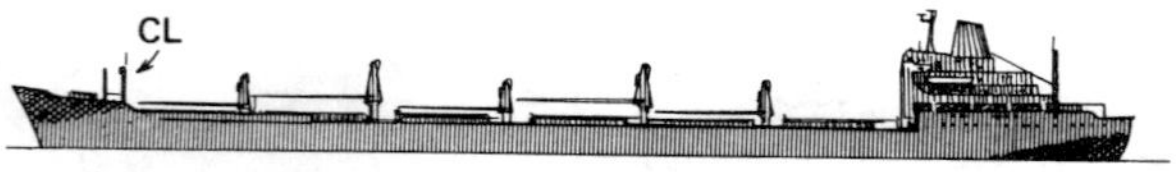

K$_2$C$_5$MFK H13
52780 ALEXANDRA N. In/Sw 1965; B; 16700; 175.88 × 10.43 (577.03 × 34.22); M; 15; ex FALKANGER 1974. Sister: **52781 CHARISMA N** (In) ex FOSSANGER 1974.

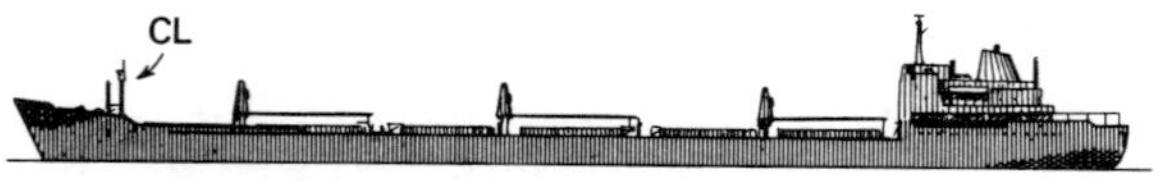

K$_2$C$_3$MFK H13
52790 GEORGIAN GLORY. Gr/Sw 1962; B; 16600; 175.88 × 11 (577.03 × 36.09); M; 14.5; ex SIGHAUG 1966. Sister: **52791 EUROPEAN MASTER** (Gr) ex CESTOS BAY 1980; ex PANTOKRATOR 1979; ex PAN 1972; ex THEOLOGOS 1970; ex SIGANKA 1966.

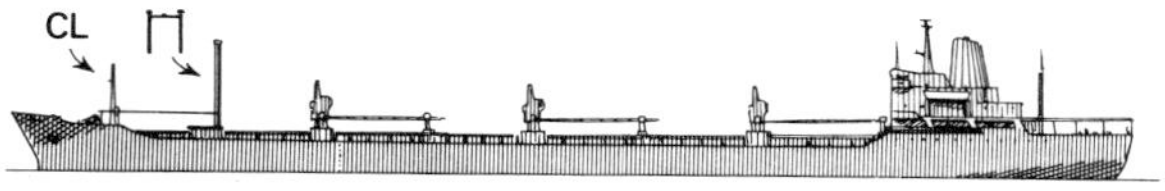

K_2C_3MFK H13

52800 CONTINENTAL SHIPPER. Li/Ja 1968; B; 15500; 178.14 × 10.27 (584.45 × 33.69); M; 15.5. Sister: **52801 CONTINENTAL PIONEER** (Li).

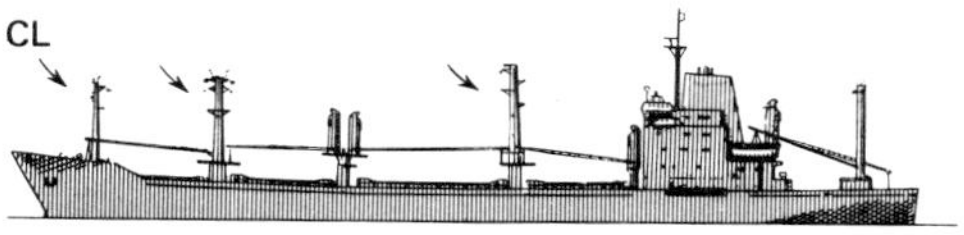

$K_2C_2KCMFCK$ H1

52820 ALDABI. Ne/Ne 1977; C/Con; 9800; 143.06 × 4.49 (469.36 × 14.73); M; 16.25. Sisters (Ne flag): **52821 ALHENA 52822 ALNATI 52823 ALPHACCA.**

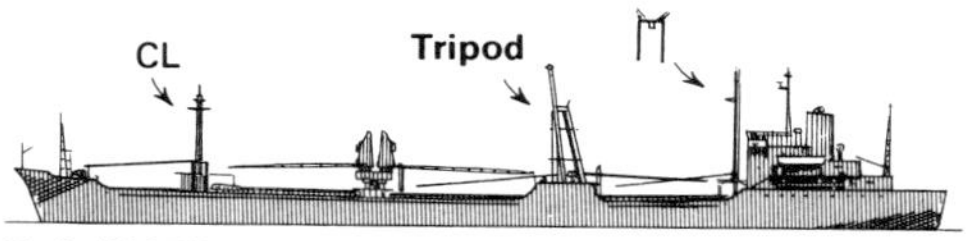

K_2C_2KMFK H13

⋆**52830 YAN SHAN.** RC/Ja 1976; C; 11300; 148.01 × 9.5 (485.6 × 31.17); M; 15; ex ALOHA 1980.

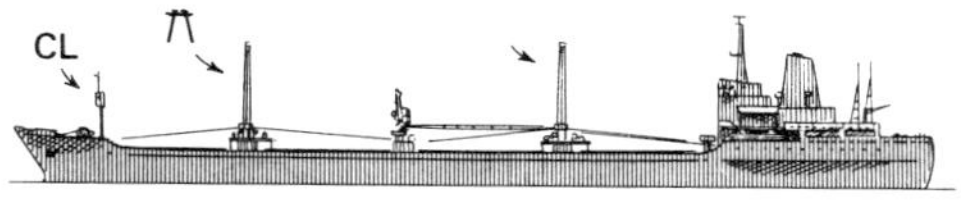

K_2C_2KMFK H13

● **52850 RANENFJORD.** No/Ja 1971; C; 6500/10100; 145.7 × 8.01/9.27 (478.02 × 26.28/30.41); M; 16; **'Concord'** type. Possible Sister-: **52851 LYNGENFJORD** (No).

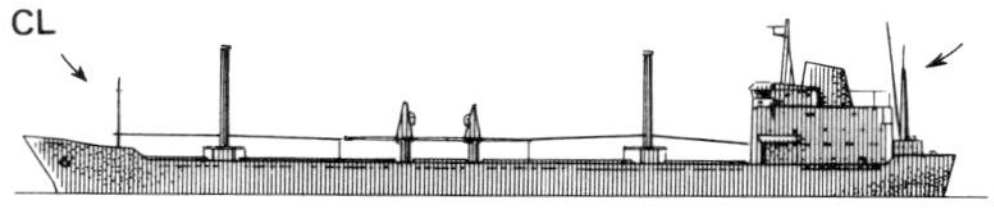

K_2C_2KMFK H13

● **52860 RATNA MANORAMA.** In/Sp 1973; C; 11200; 147.02 × 9.81 (482.35 × 32.19); M; 15.5; **'SANTA FE'** type. Sister: **52861 RATNA KIRTI** (In) launched as AEGIS GRACE.

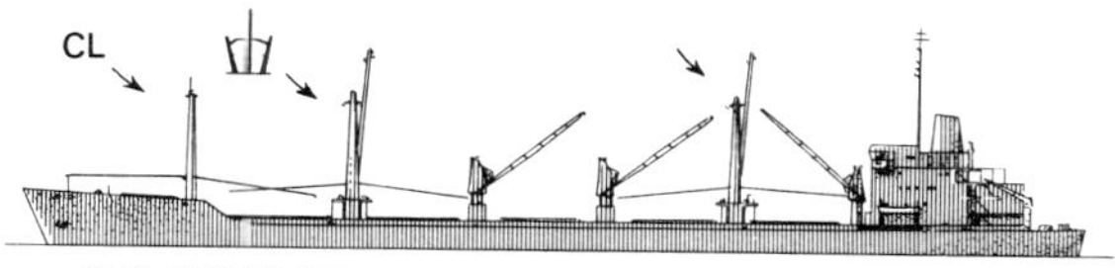

K_2C_2KCMF H1

52810 BERTRAM RICKMERS. FRG/FRG-FRG 1970/79; C/Con; 10000/14400; 170.7 × 10.68/9.87 (560.04 × 35.04/32.38); M; 17.5; ex LEVERKUSEN (Forebody). Hull is made up using forebody of Leverkusen. Sister: **52811 RENEE RICKMERS** (FRG) ex LUDWIGSHAFEN (Forebody).

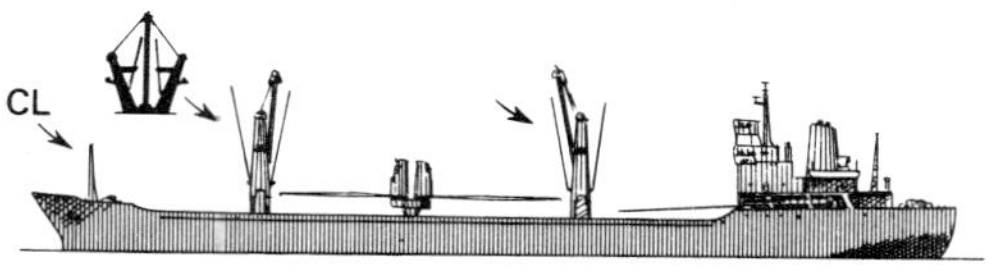

K_2C_2KMFK H13

● **52840 TRIFELS.** FRG/Ja 1974; C/HL; 6900/11600; 147.71 × 8.08/9.63 (484.61 × 26.51/31.59); M; 18.5; ex ARISTOGENIS 1975. Converted from 'Mitsui-Concord' type cargo vessel.

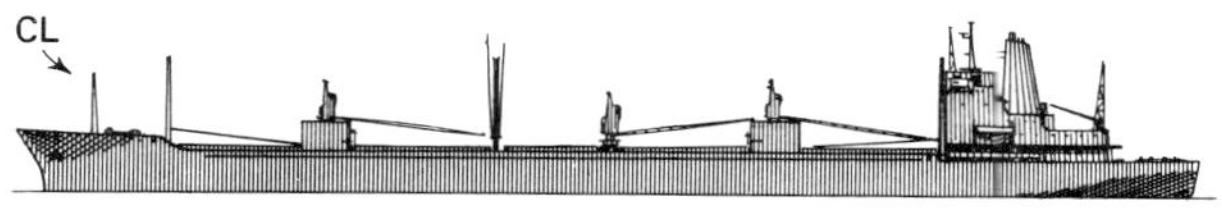

K_2CKC_2KMFK H1

52870 TOYOTA MARU No 16. Ja/Ja 1971; BC; 23200; 187.51 × 12.12 (615.19 × 39.76); M; 14.5. Probable Sister: **52871 TOYOTA MARU No 17** (Ja) Possible Sister: **52872 SHUNYO MARU** (Ja).

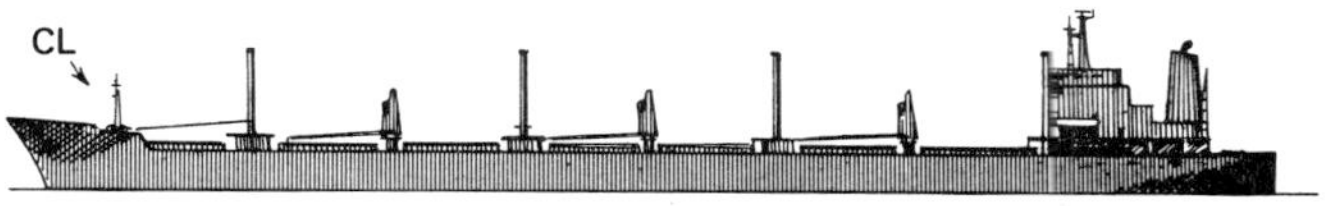

$K_2CKCKCKMFK$ H3

52880 BUNKO MARU. Ja/Ja 1976; B; 30700; 215.02 × 12.4 (705.45 × 40.68); M; 14.75; **'Hi-Bulk-50'** type.

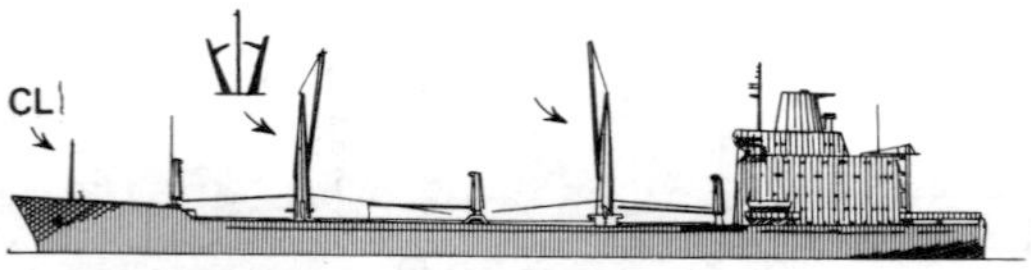

$K_2CKCKCMF$ H1
52890 IBERIA. FRG/FRG 1972; C/HL/TS; 8000/11200; 153.24 × 9.06/10.07 (502.75 × 29.72/33.2); M; 20; ex STURMFELS 1980.

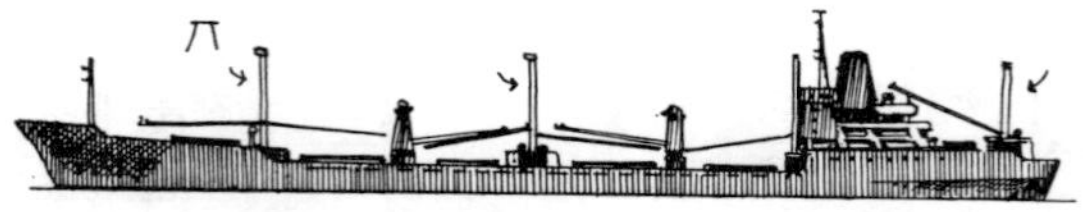

$K_2CKCKMFK$ H13
52900 NEDLLOYD KEMBLA. Ne/Ja 1971; C; 7900/12400; 162 × 10.4 (533 × 34); M; 17. Sisters (Superstructure may vary slightly) (Ne flag): **52901 NEDLLOYD KIMBERLEY 52902 NEDLLOYD KINGSTON 52903 NEDLLOYD KYOTO 52904 NEDLLOYD KATWIJK.**

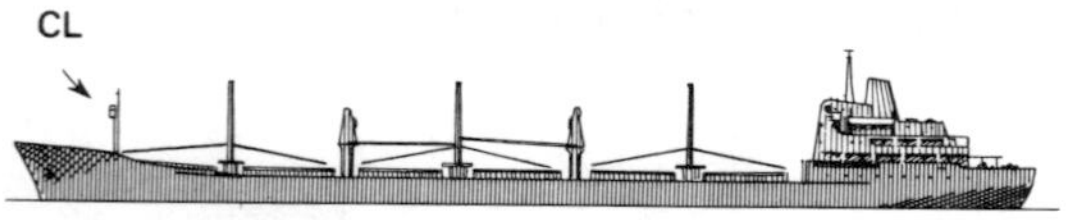

$K_2CKCKMF$ H13
52910 GUNGNIR V. Pa/No 1963; B; 12800; 162.16 × 9.7 (532.02 × 31.82); M; 15; ex SUNRAY ex TONTO 1964.

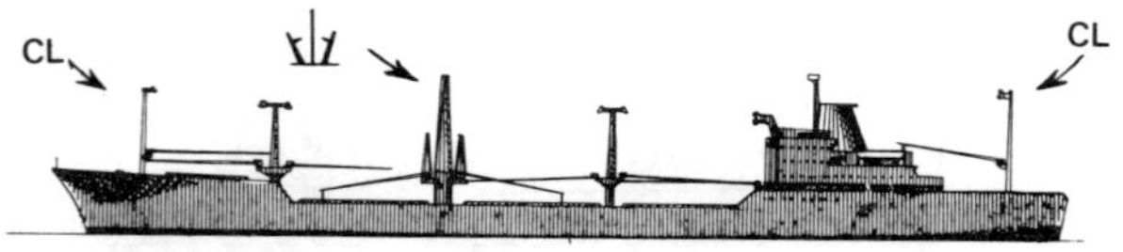

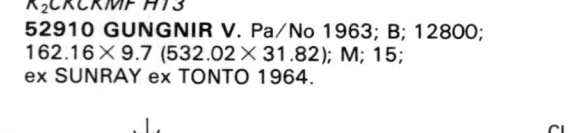

$K_2CKCKMFK$ H13
52920 STRATHEDEN. Br/Pd 1977; C/HL; 12600; 169.83 × 9.76 (557.18 × 32.02); M; 18. **'B-466'** type. Sisters (Br flag): **52921 STRATHELGIN 52922 STRATHERROL 52923 STRATHESK 52924 STRATHETTRICK 52925 STRATHEWE.**

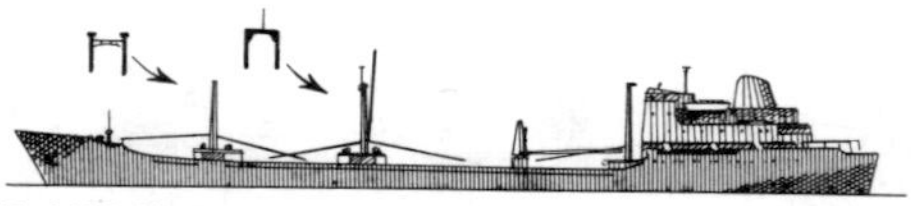

K_2CKF H13
52930 KITHNOS. Pa/No 1962; C; 4800/7400; 137.14 × 7.3/8.69 (449.93 × 23.95/28.51); M; 15.5; ex VINGAHOLM 1975; ex FELIS 1967.

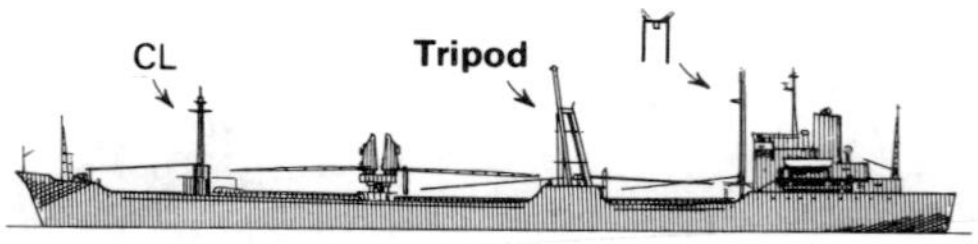

K_2CK_2MFK H123
★**52940 YAN SHAN.** RC/Ja 1976; C; 11300; 148.01 × 9.5 (485.6 × 31.17); M; 15; ex ALOHA 1980.

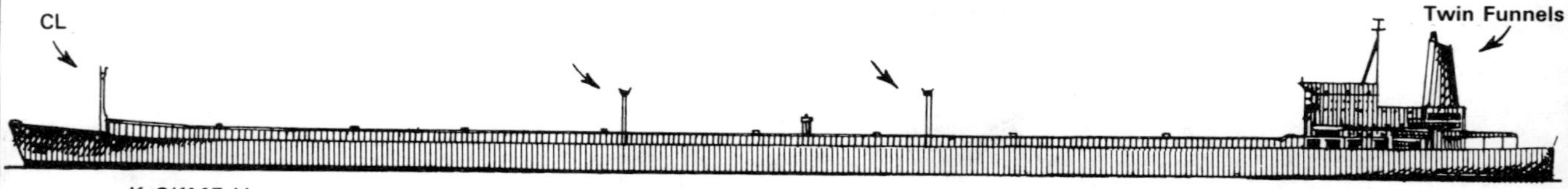

K_2CKMF H
52950 BATILLUS. Fr/Fr 1976; Tk; 273600; 414.21 × 28.5 (1358.96 × 93.5); TST; 16. Sisters (Fr flag): **52951 BELLAMYA 52952 PIERRE GUILLAUMAT 52953 PRAIRIAL.**

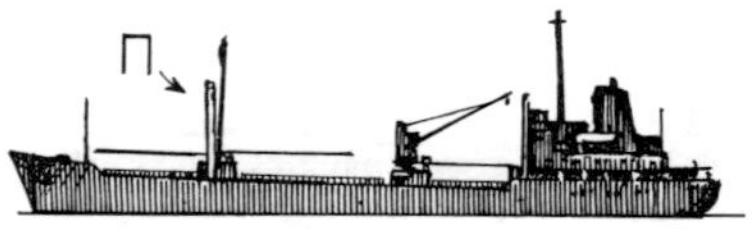

K_2CKMF H
52960 MING YOUTH. Tw/Tw 1969; C; 3700; 107.04 × 7.08 (351.18 × 23.23); M; 14.5; ex YU MING 1977; ex HAI LI 1973.

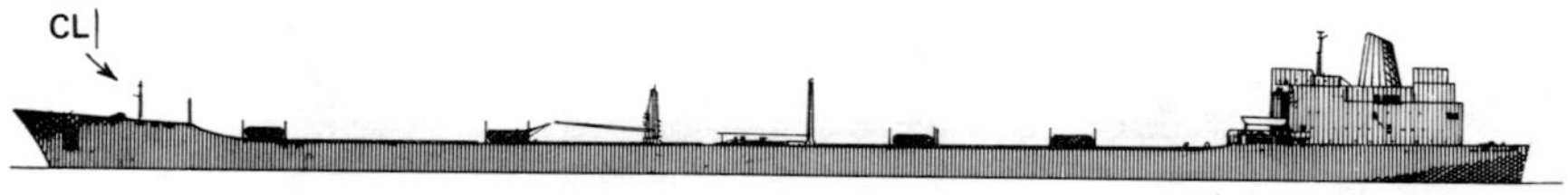

K_2CKMF H1
52970 NATICINA. Br/De 1967; Tk; 60700; 265.18 × 14.95 (870 × 49.05); M; 15; Used for lightening.

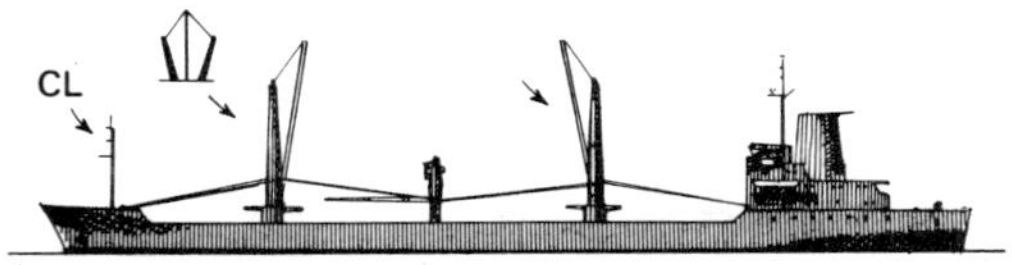

K_2CKMF H13

● **52980 BARENBELS.** Gr/FRG 1976; C/HL; 7400/11800; 149.16 × 8.1/9.6 (489.37 × 26.57/31.5); M; 16; ex BARENFELS 1980. Sister: **52981 HISPANIA** (FRG) ex BRAUENFELS 1980.

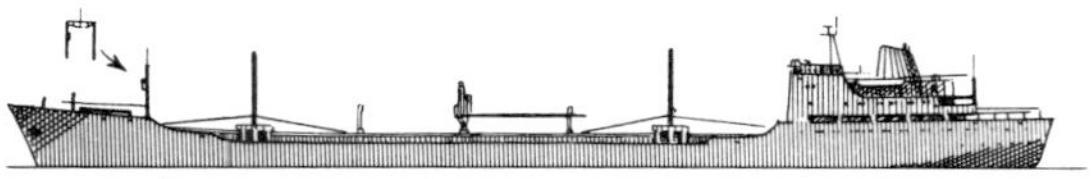

K_2CKMF H13

52990 PABLO V. Ag/No 1962; C; 12600; 166.48 × 10.19 (546.19 × 33.43); M; 13.5; ex VENABU 1974.

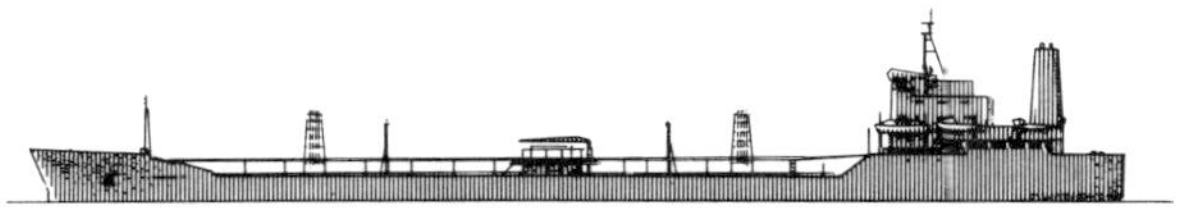

K_2CKMF H13

53000 IVER HERON. No/No 1979; Ch; 19800; 173.7 × 10.5 (569.88 × 34.45); M; approx. 14.5.

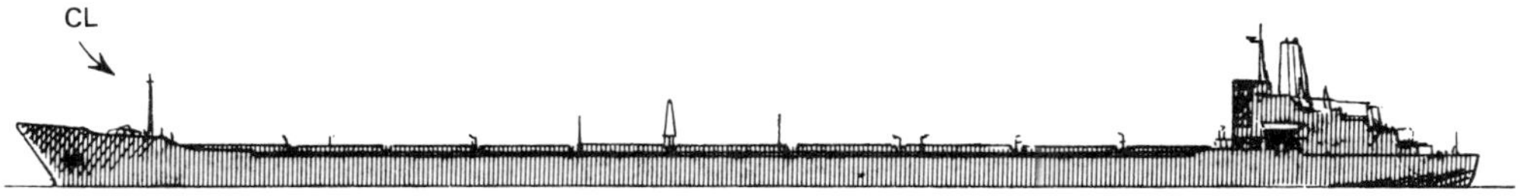

K_2CKMFC H1

53010 MARILENA. Gr/It 1971; OO; 72300; 297.21 × 16.48 (975.1 × 54.07); T; 16.5; ex OMBRINA; ex GIOIA PATRIZIA; ex MASANO 1974.

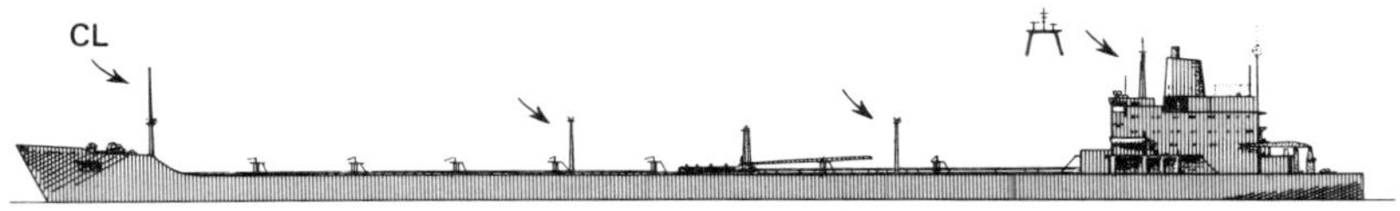

K_2CKMFC H1

53020 NORA MAERSK. De/De 1977; Tk; 39200; 247.25 × 13.17 (811.2 × 43.21); M; 16.5. Sisters (De flag): **53021 NELE MAERSK 53022 NELLY MAERSK 53023 NICOLAI MAERSK 53024 NICOLINE MAERSK 53025 NIELS MAERSK.**

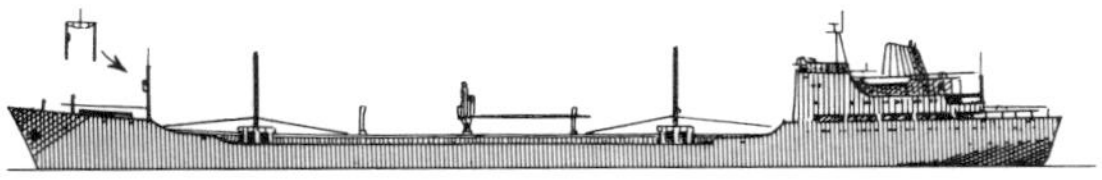

K_2CKMFK H13

53030 PABLO V. Ag/No 1962; C; 12600; 166.48 × 10.19 (546.19 × 33.43); M; 13.5; ex VENABU 1974.

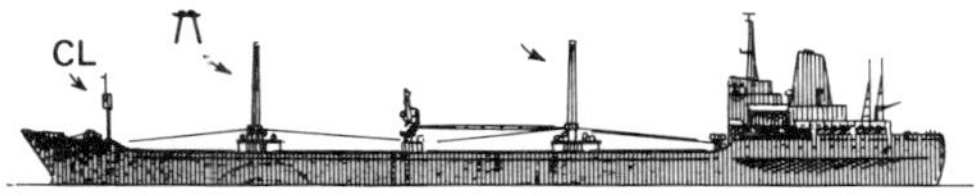

K_2CKMFK H1

● **53040 RANENFJORD.** No/Ja 1971; C; 6500/10100; 145.7 × 8.01/9.27 (478.02 × 26.28/30.41); M; 16; **'Concord'** type. Possible s ster: **53041 LYNGENFJORD** (No).

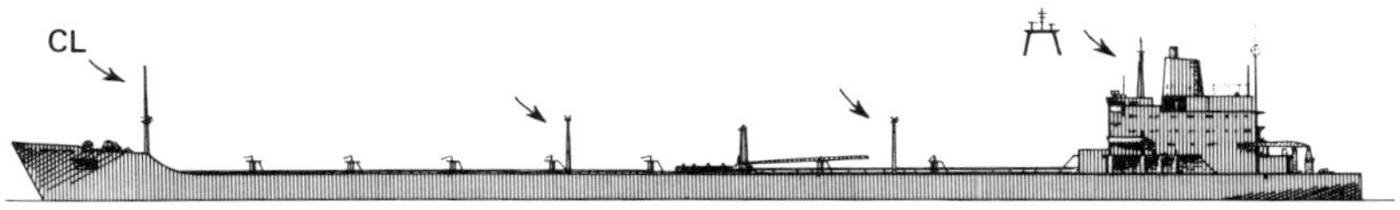

K_2CKMFK H13

53050 NORA MAERSK. De/De 1977; Tk; 39200; 247.25 × 13.17 (811.2 × 43.21); M; 16.5. Sisters (De flag): **53051 NELE MAERSK 53052 NELLY MAERSK 53053 NICOLAI MAERSK 53054 NICOLINE MAERSK 53055 NIELS MAERSK.**

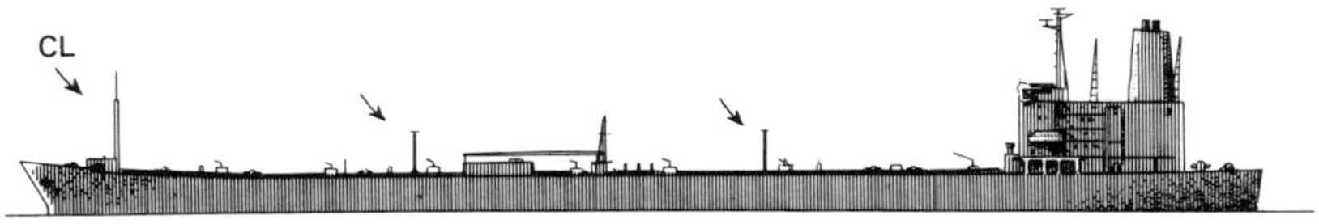

$K_2CKMKF/K_2CKMKFK$ H

53060 AMPOL SAREL. Au/Ja 1979; Tk; 65100; 243 × 13.74 (797.24 × 45.08); M; 15.6.

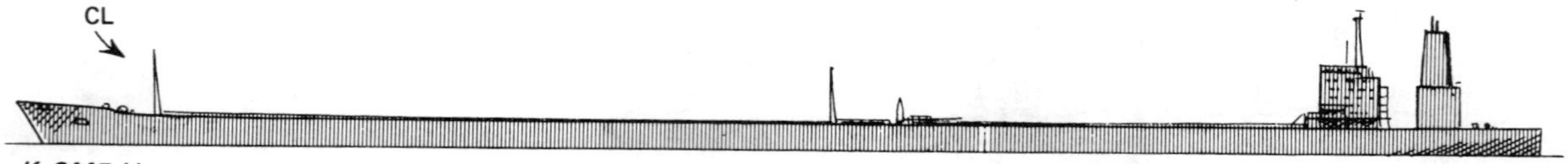

K_2CMF H

● **53070 LINGA.** Br/De 1975; Tk; 160400; 354.57 × 23.83 (1163.29 × 78.18); T; 15.75. Sisters (Br flag): **53071 LIMATULA 53072 LIPARUS 53073 LIMNEA 53074 LIMOPSIS 53075 LYRIA.**

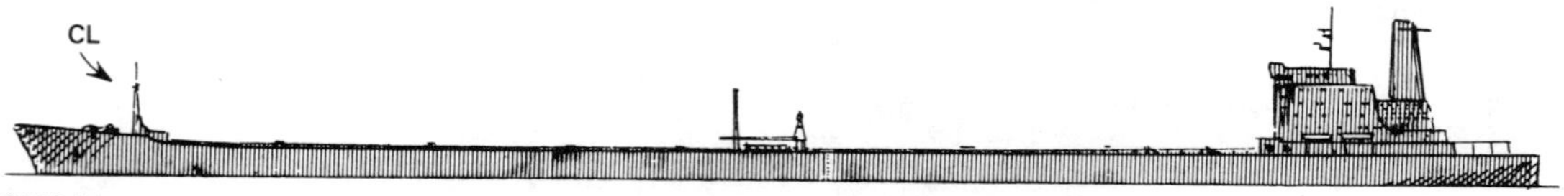

K_2CMF H

53080 MYRTEA. Fr/Fr 1970; Tk; 105400; 324.72 × 18.99 (1065.35 × 62.3); T; 16. Sister: **53081 MIRALDA** (Fr).

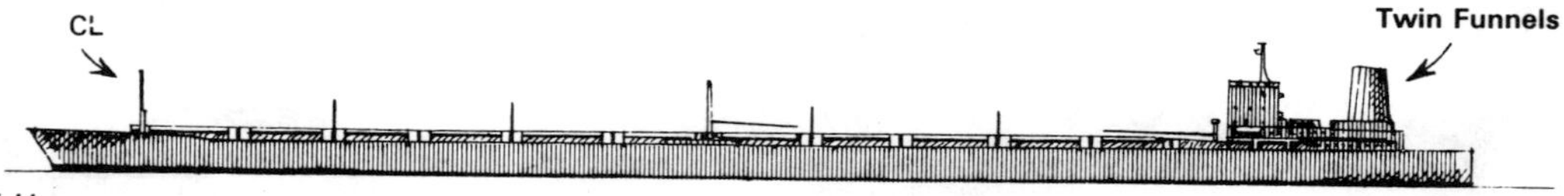

K_2CMF H

53090 CAST FULMAR. Br/Br 1973; OBO; 86100; 291.85 × 18.22 (975.51 × 59.78); M; 15.5; ex NORDIC CRUSADER 1980; ex NAESS CRUSADER 1974. Sister: **53091 CAST HERON** (Br) ex NORDIC CHIEFTAIN 1980.

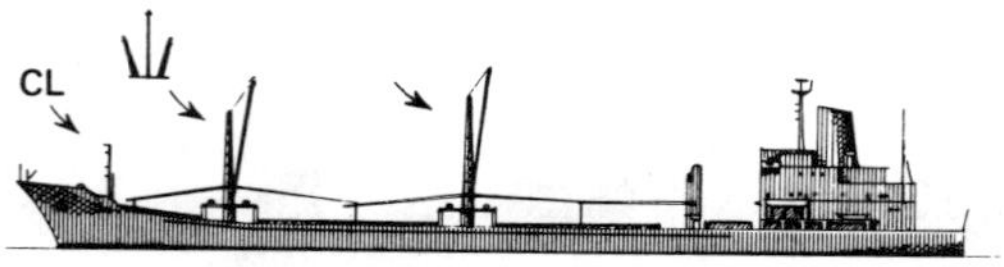

K_2CMF H

53100 MENDOZA. Ar/FRG 1977; C; 7200/10200; 149.82 × 9.09/9.25 (491.54 × 29.82/30.35); M; 16.5; **'36-L'** type. Sisters (Ar flag): **53101 CATAMARCA II 53102 LA RIOJA 53103 SAN JUAN 53104 SAN LUIS.**

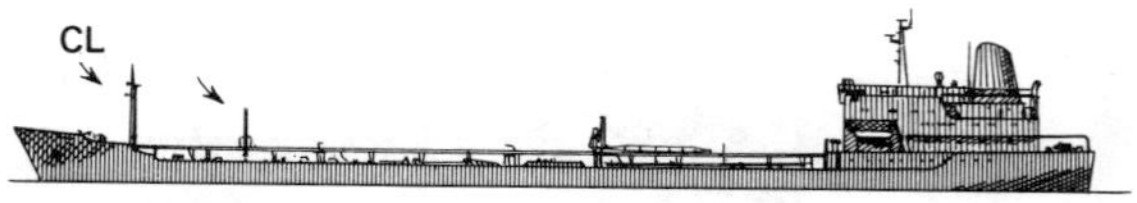

K_2CMF

53110 KUAKA. NZ/Sw 1975; Tk; 16200; 171.46 × 9.58 (562.53 × 31.43); M; 16. Sister: **53111 KOTUKU** (NZ).

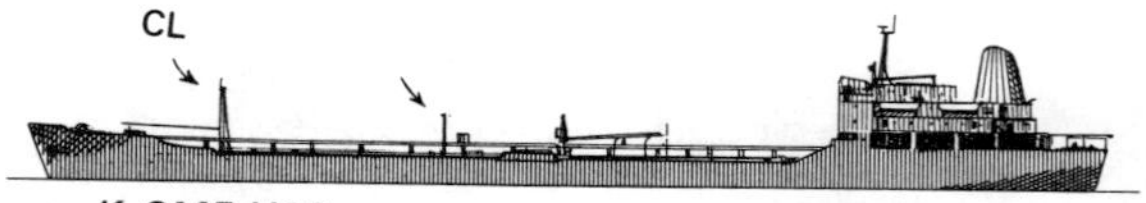

K_2CMF H13

● **53120 BRITISH HOLLY.** Br/Br 1965; Tk; 13300; 171 × 9.47 (561 × 31.07); M; 14.5. Similar (Br flag): **53121 BRITISH BEECH 53122 BRITISH HAWTHORN 53123 BRITISH HAZEL 53124 BRITISH IVY 53125 BRITISH LAUREL 53126 BRITISH MAPLE 53127 BRITISH POPLAR 53128 BRITISH VINE 53129 BRITISH WILLOW.**

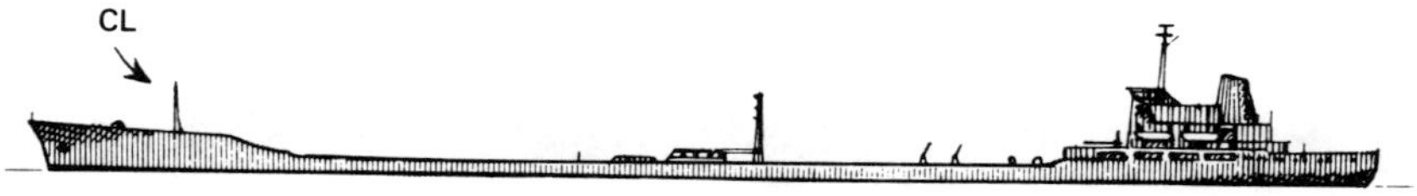

K_2CMF H13

● **53140 DIONE.** NA/Ne 1967; Tk; 39100; 243.85 × 13.37 (800.03 × 43.86); M; —. Sisters: **53141 DOSINA** (NA) **53142 DIADEMA** (NA) **53143 TAKIS E** (Gr) ex DILOMA 1981 Similar: **52144 DONOVANIA** (Br) **53145 SIAM** (Th) ex DORCASIA 1977 Possible sisters (NA flag): **53146 DALLIA 53147 DAPHNE.**

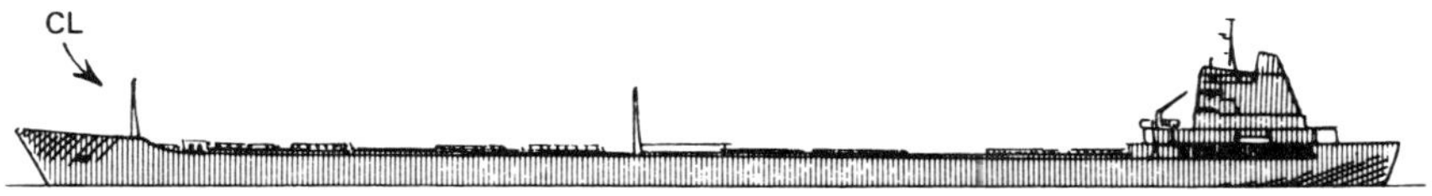

K_2CMF H13

53150 ATHENIC. Gr/Ja 1967; OO; 36700 Ore/ 48700 Oil; 254.26 × 13.31 (834.19 × 43.67); M; —. Sisters (Gr flag): **53151 GLORIC 53152 PLATONIC** Similar (tankers): **53153 ATOMIC** (Gr) **53154 DORIC** (Li) **53155 HARMONIC** (Gr) **53156 IONIC** (Gr) **53157 TROPIC** (Gr)

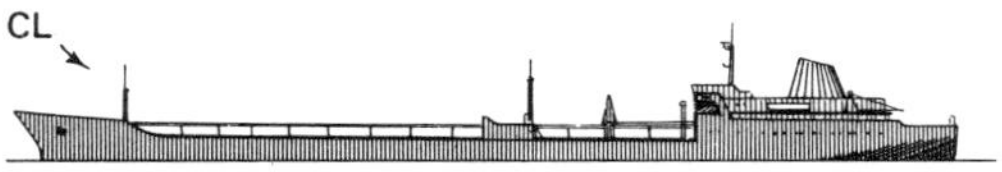

K_2CMF H13

⋆53160 MANGYSHLAK. Ru/Ru 1969; Tk; 8400; 150.02 × 8 (492 × 26.25); M; 13.5. Sisters (Ru flag): **⋆53161 GENERAL ASLANOV ⋆53162 GENERAL BABAYAN ⋆53163 KAFUR MAMEDOV ⋆53164 NIKIFOR ROGOV ⋆53165 RUKHULLA AKHUNDOV**

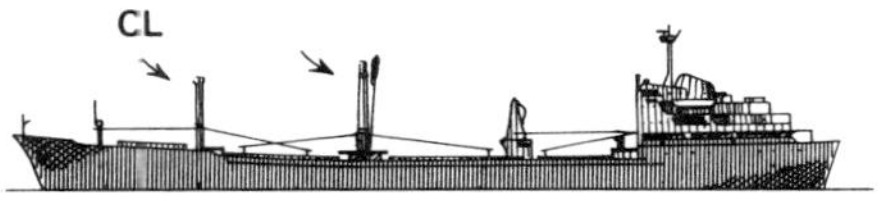

K_2CMF H13

53170 AKRA RION. Gr/Sw 1962; C; 4200/6500; 130.69 × 7.47/7.89 (428.77 × 24.51); M; 15; ex NOPAL LUNA 1980; ex HAVDHEM 1967. Sister: **53171 AKRA TENARON** (Gr) ex NOPAL TELLUS 1980; ex STERNO 1967.

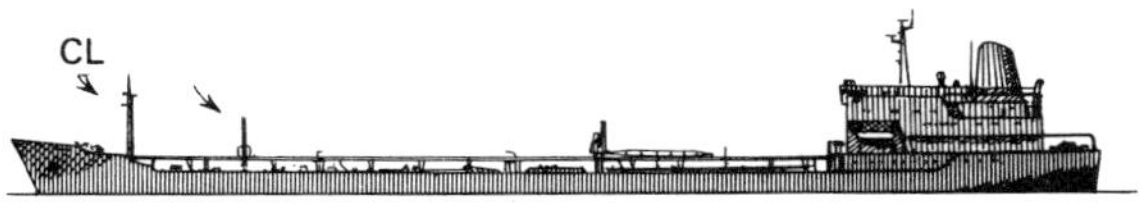

K_2CMFC H13

53180 KUAKA. NZ/Sw 1975; Tk; 16200; 171.46 × 9.58 (562.53 × 31.43); M; 16. Sister: **53181 KOTUKU** (NZ).

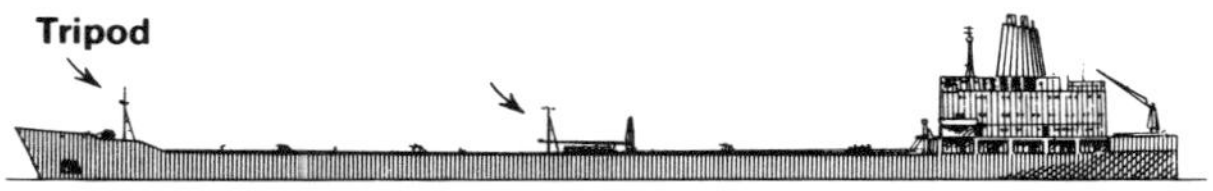

K_2CMFC H13

53190 JAKOB MAERSK. De/No 1976; Tk; 33100; 211.82 × 12.78 (694.95 × 41.93); M; 17. Sisters (De flag): **53191 JANE MAERSK 53192 JESSIE MAERSK 53193 JEPPESEN MAERSK 53194 JESPER MAERSK.**

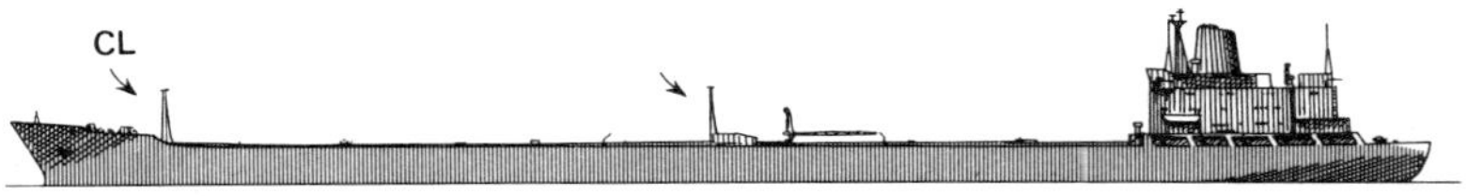

K_2CMFK H1

53200 ROBERT MILLER. Au/Au 1974; Tk; 37700; 239.28 × 13.14 (785.04 × 43.11); M; 16.5.

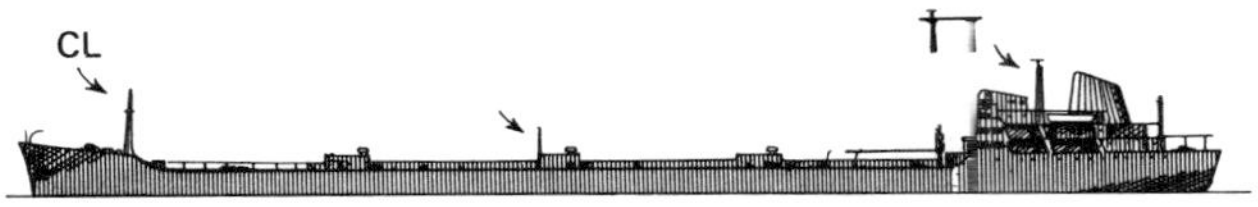

K_2CMFK H13

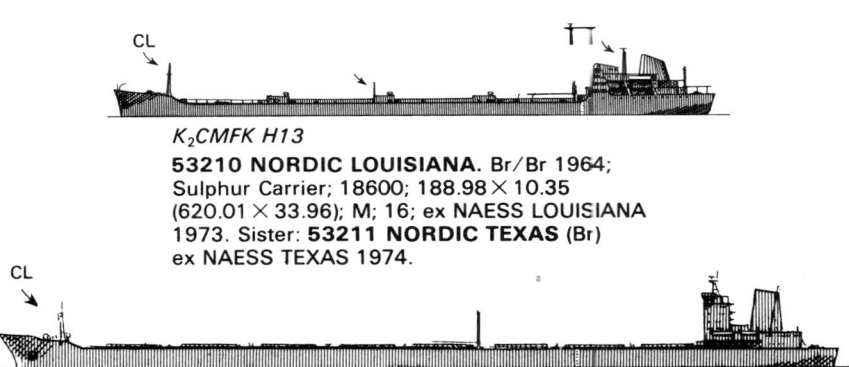

53210 NORDIC LOUISIANA. Br/Br 1964; Sulphur Carrier; 18600; 188.98 × 10.35 (620.01 × 33.96); M; 16; ex NAESS LOUISIANA 1973. Sister: **53211 NORDIC TEXAS** (Br) ex NAESS TEXAS 1974.

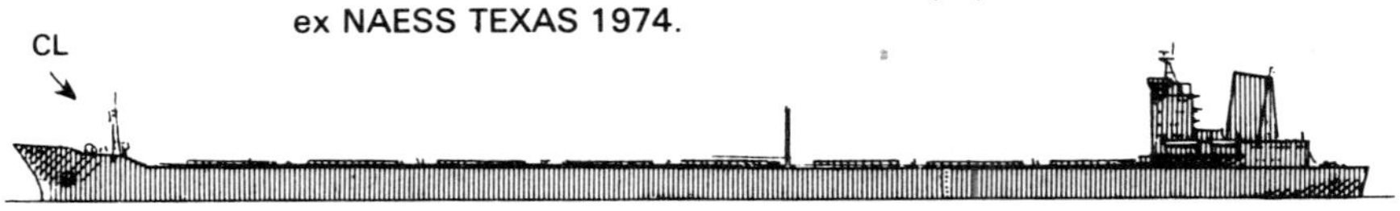

K_2F H1

53220 BELLARY. In/Ys 1970; OO; 45800; 256.62 × 14.98 (841.93 × 49.15); M; —. Sisters (In flag): **53221 BARAUNI 53222 BAILADILA.**

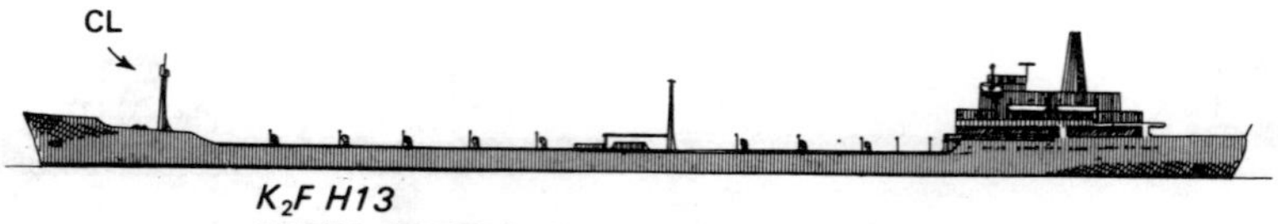

K_2F H13
53230 ONOBA. Ne/Ne 1962; Tk; 31100; 228.02 × 12.2 (748.1 × 40.03); T; —.

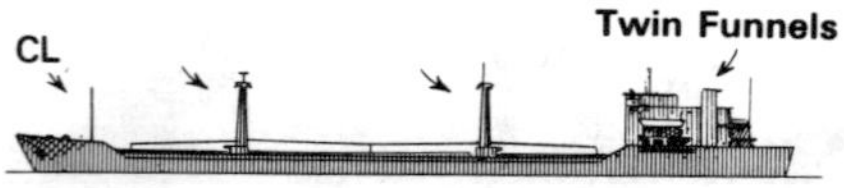

K_2F H13
53240 TAMMO. Fi/FRG 1972; C; 4900; 123.27 × 6.85 (404.43 × 22.47); M; 13.5; ex FALKNES 1979.

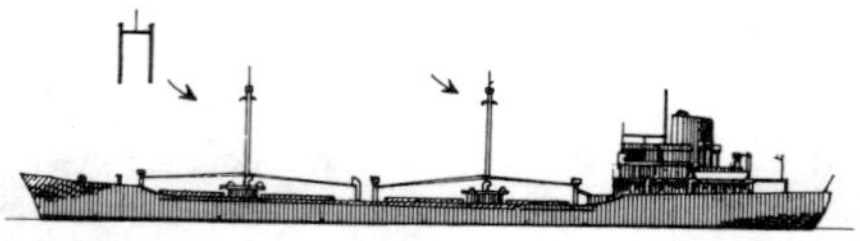

K_2F H13
53250 VALENTINA P. Gr/FRG 1954; C; 5500; 127.62 × 7.06 (418.7 × 23.16); T; 10.5; ex MARKUS 1973; ex AUNGTHITSA 1964.

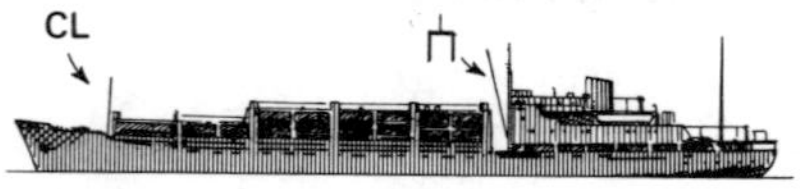

K_2FM H1
53260 MERINO EXPRESS. Li/Ne 1960/76; LS; 2400/3400; 119.49 × 5.68/6.41 (392.03 × 18.64/21.03); M; 16; ex CAP FARINA 1976; ex CARIBBEAN EXPRESS 1974; ex KREON 1973; Converted from cargo 1976.

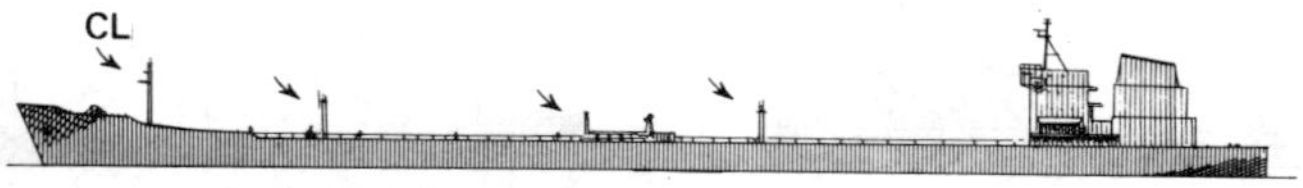

K_3CKMF H1
53270 CHEVRON WASHINGTON. US/US 1976; Tk; 16900; 198.13 × 11.35 (650.03 × 37.24); GT; 15. Sisters (US flag): **53271 CHEVRON COLORADO 53272 CHEVRON LOUISIANA 53273 CHEVRON OREGON 53274 CHEVRON ARIZONA.**

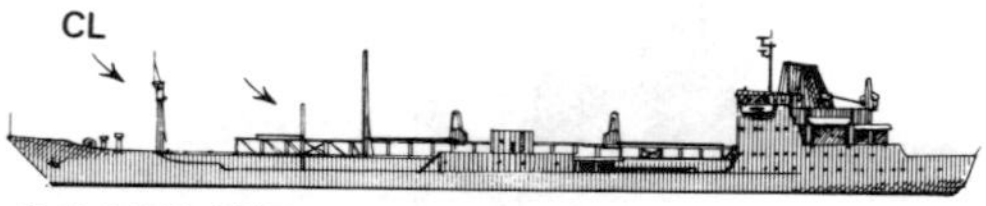

K_3C_2MFC H13
53280 GAMBHIRA. Br/Sp 1969; LGC; 11500; 153.2 × 8.52 (502.69 × 27.96); M; 16.5; ex BUTANAVAL 1973; ex BUTANUEVE 1971.

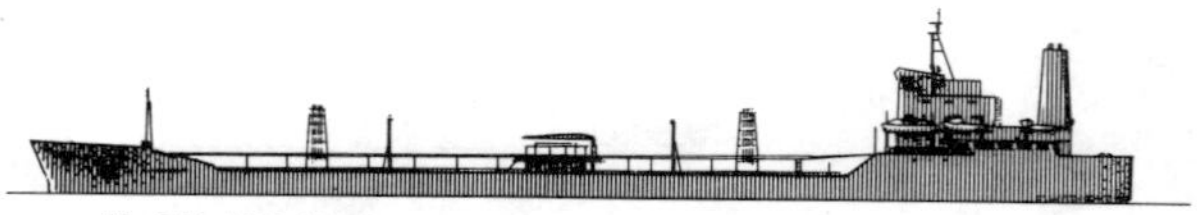

K_3CK_2MF H13
53290 IVER HERON. No/No 1979; Ch; 19800; 173.7 × 10.5 (569.88 × 34.45); M; approx. 14.5.

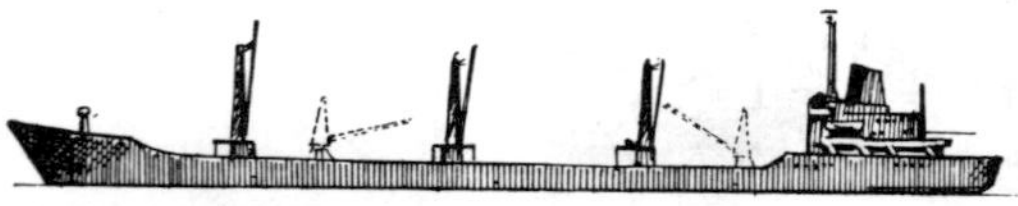

K_3CKMFK H13
● **⋆53300 GUANGHE.** RC/FRG 1972; C; 7200/11100; 154.87 × 8.31/9.78 (508.1 × 27.26/32.09); M; 18.5; ex LUTZ JACOB 1973. Travelling crane. Sisters (Cu flag): **⋆53301 ABEL SANTAMARIA** ex SULA 1975; ex URSULA JACOB 1974 **⋆53302 FRANK PAIS** ex NATE 1975; ex RENATE JACOB 1974.

K_3CKMFK H13
53310 OSCO LINEA. Ne/Sw 1975; Ch; 21300; 171.81 × 11.85 (563.68 × 38.88); M; 16; ex OSCO SAILOR. Sisters: **53311 OSCO SPIRIT** (No) **53312 OSCO SIERRA** (Li) ex CARBO SIERRA 1976 **53313 OSCO STRIPE** (No) ex CARBO STRIPE 1975.

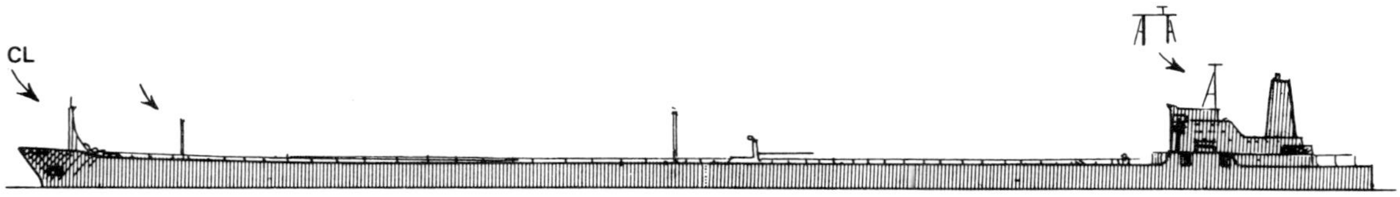

K_3CMF H1

● **53320 LATONA.** Fr/Fr 1973; Tk; 138500; 343.04×21.36 (1125.46×70.08); T; 15.5. Sisters: **53321 LEDA** (Fr) **53322 LUCINA** (Fr) **53323 LATIRUS** (Ne) **53324 LATIA** (Ne) **53325 LABIOSA.** (Br)

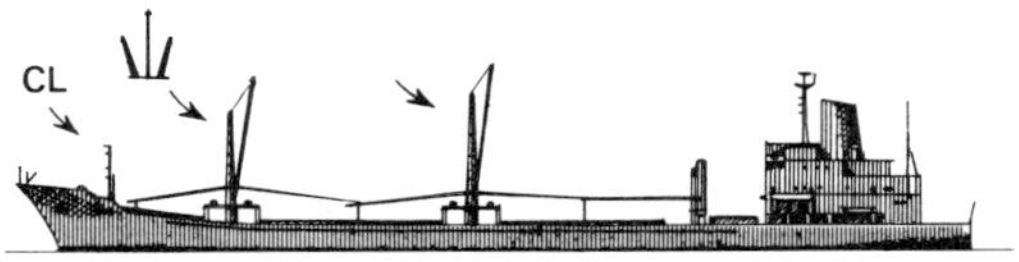

K_3CMF H

53330 MENDOZA. Ar/FRG 1977; C; 7200/10200; 149.82×9.09/9.25 (491.54×29.82/30.35); M; 16.5; **'36-L'** type. Sisters (Ar flag): **53331 CATAMARCA II 53332 LA RIOJA 53333 SAN JUAN 53334 SAN LUIS.**

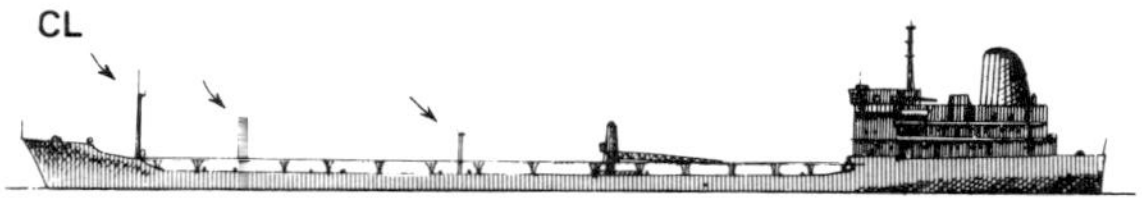

K_3CKMF H13

53340 BRITISH DART. Br/Sw 1972; Tk; 15700; 171.46×9.58 (562.53×31.43); M; 15.5; Similar (Br flag): **53341 BRITISH AVON 53342 BRITISH ESK 53343 BRITISH FORTH 53344 BRITISH HUMBER 53345 BRITISH KENNET 53346 BRITISH SPEY 53347 BRITISH TAMAR 53348 BRITISH TAY 53349 BRITISH TEST 53350 BRITISH TRENT 53351 BRITISH TWEED 53352 BRITISH WYE** (Ir flag): **53353 MARUN** ex BRITISH SEVERN 1976 **53354 MINAB** ex BRITISH FAL 1976 **53355 MOKRAN** ex BRITISH NEATH 1976.

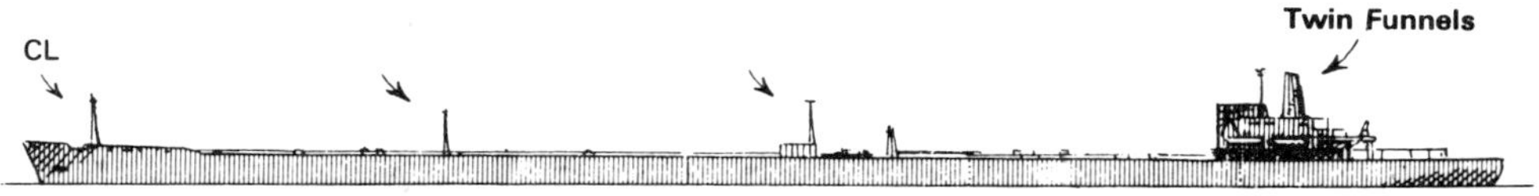

K_3CMFC H

53360 ATLAS 1. Tu/Fr 1969; Tk; 79800; 288.53×16 (946.62×52.49); M; 16; ex FRIMAIRE 1980. Probable Sister: **53361 OBERNAI** (Fr).

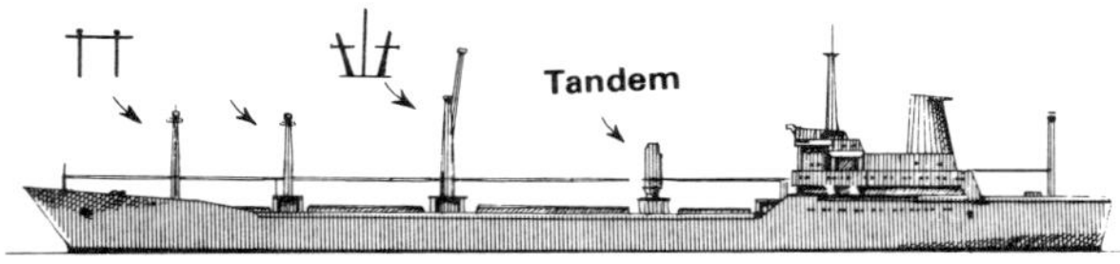

K_3CMFK H13

● **53370 CIUDAD DE POPAYAN.** Co/Pd 1976; C; 11700/16100; 180.7×8.7/9.67 (592.85×28.54/31.73); M; 21; **'B-464'** type. Sisters (Co flag): **53371 CIUDAD DE NEIVA 53372 CIUDAD DE SANTA MARTA** Similar (**B-469** type): **53373 CIUDAD DE ARMENIA 53374 CIUDAD DE PASTO 53375 CIUDAD DE QUITO.**

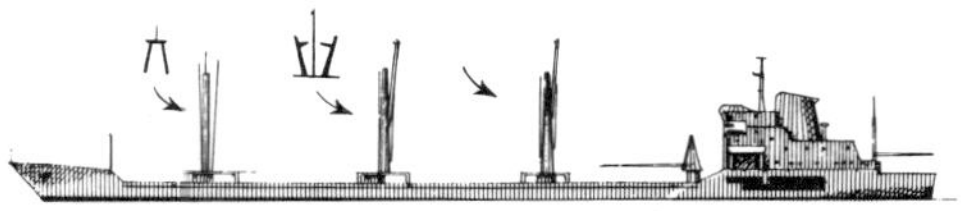

K_3CMFK H13

53380 NORTHWIND. Li/Sp 1970; B; 11300; 147.02×9.93 (482.35×32.58); M; 16; **'Santa Fe'** type. Sisters (Li flag): **53381 SOUTHWIND 53382 WESTWIND.**

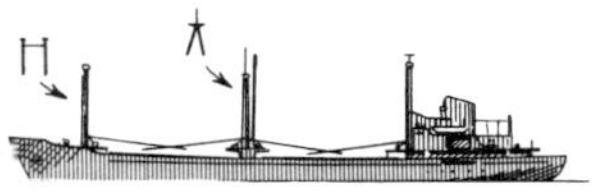

K_3F H1

53390 AYAN 1. Tu/FRG 1967; C; 1800; 88.45×5.22 (290.19×17.13); M; 14; ex HIMNO 1 1980; ex CAP HERO 1977; ex SCOMBER 1977; ex HIPPO SAILOR 1976; ex MARIE REITH 1975. Sisters: **53391 NANO K** (Gr) ex HIPPO LADY 1977; ex PERCA 1977; ex HIPPO LADY 1976; ex SUSANNE REITH 1974. **53392 EME** (Sg) ex EMIL P 1978; ex EMIL REITH 1978. Possible Sister: **53393 CRESTENA** (Gr) ex RAJA 1977; ex HIPPO CARRIER 1976; ex ELISABETH REITH 1975.

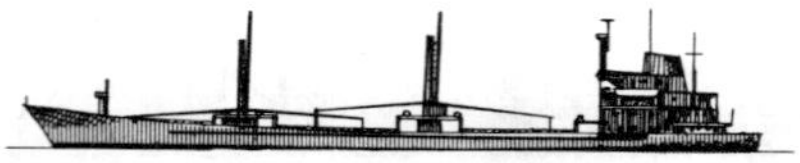

K_3F H

● **53400 MEJEAN III.** Fr/FRG 1969; C; 2800/4800; 116.8 × 6.52/7.53 (383.2 × 21.39/24.7); M; 15.5; ex NORDWELLE 1977. **'Trampco'** type. **53401 NORDKAP** (Sg) **53402 DIAMOND SUN** (gr) ex NORDWOGE 1980 **53403 NORDSTRAND** (Sg) **53404 DRUCILLA U** (Li) ex CARLO PORR 1976 **53405 ILLERBERG** (Cy) ex HAMBURGER SENATOR 1978 **53406 HEKTOR** (Cy) ex PARZIVAL 1972 **53407 ACHILL** (Cy) ex LOHENGRIN 1974 **53408 CAP BRETON** (FRG) launched as SONNHOLM **53409 ISAR** (FRG) ex CAP VINCENT 1972; launched as ISAR **53410 ANTJE SCHULTE** (Pa) **53411 JUDITH SCHULTE** (Br) **53412 GEORG KURZ** (Pa) ex EASTERN LAKE 1977; ex HAMBURGER FLEET 1975 **53413 TECONA** (Cy) ex PROMINENT 1; ex SCOL PROMINENT 1977; ex EASTERN BRIDGE 1974; ex CAPE HENRY 1974; ex HINRICH WITT 1972 **53414 MARIANNE ROTH** (Cy) ex CAPE RAY 1978; ex HAMBURGER DOM 1974. **53415 RIDGE** (SA) **53416 VERGE** (SA) Similar (Stulcken derricks) **53417 TERENGA** (FRG) ex BACHUE 1981; ex DOROTHEA BOLTEN 1978 **53418 PAMPERO** (FRG) ex NOPAL PAMPERO 1977; ex SCHIROKKO 1975 **53419 TAIFUN** (FRG).

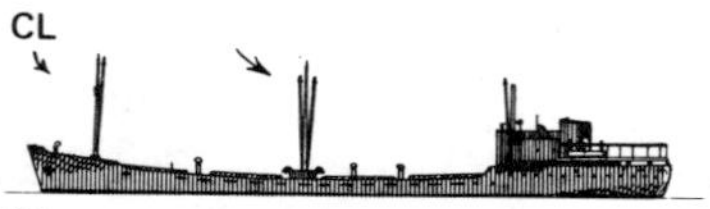

K_3F H13

● **53460 MALEA.** Pa/Br 1953; C; 3800; 108.69 × 6.66 (356.59 × 21.86); M; 11; ex MISTRAL 1977; ex BUSHWOOD 1971; ex LONGFELLOW 1961.

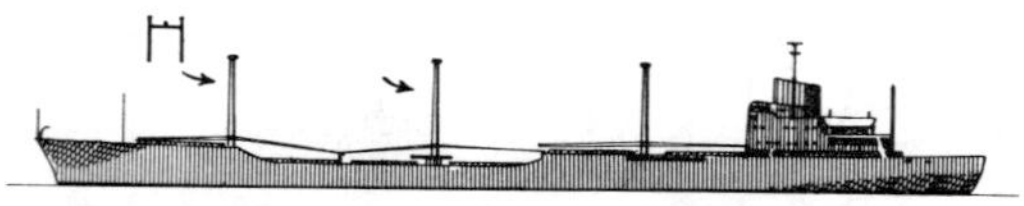

K_3FK H13

53480 CONSTANCIA. Pa/FRG 1961; C; 8500/11200; 151.21 × 9.06/9.9 (496.1 × 29.72/32.48); M; 15.5; ex CONSTANTIA.

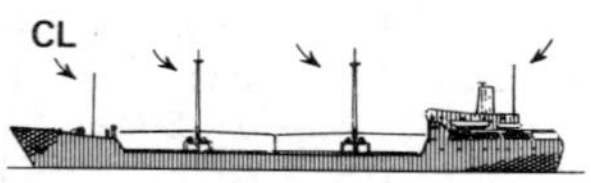

K_3FK H13

● **53490 TROUP HEAD.** Br/Ne 1971; C; 1600; 87.61 × 5.37 (287.43 × 17.62); M; 12. Sister: **53491 TOD HEAD** (Br).

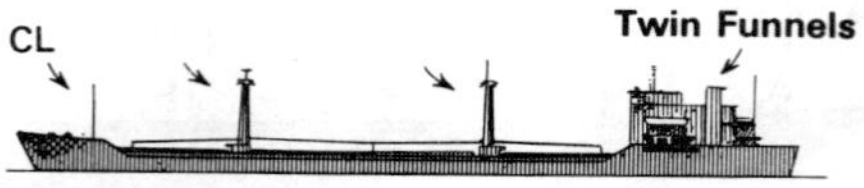

K_3F H13

53430 TAMMO. Fi/FRG 1972; C; 4900; 123.27 × 6.85 (404.43 × 22.47); M; 13.5; ex FALKNES.

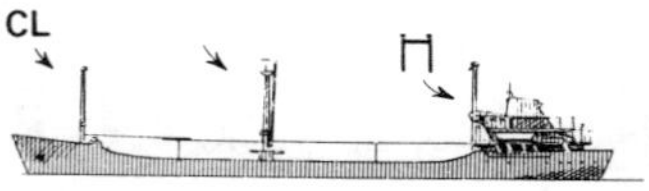

K_3F H13

● *__53440 MIKULIC OREB.__* Ys/FRG 1970; C; 2000; 95.28 × 5.53 (312.6 × 18.14); M; 14.5; ex BALTRUMERSAND 1980. Sister: ***53441 MARKO TASILO** (Ys) ex BORKUMERSAND 1980 Similar: **53442 MELLUMERSAND** (FRG).

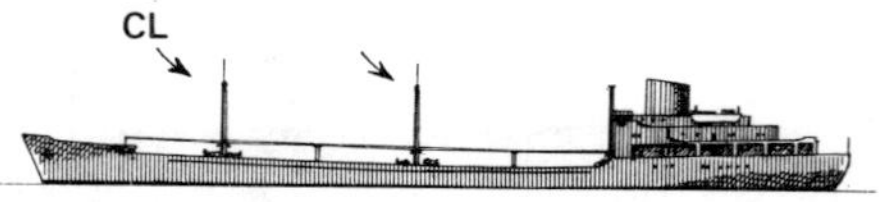

K_3F H13

53450 OMEGA LEROS. Gr/Br 1960; C; 5800; 131.53 × 7.84 (431.53 × 25.71); M; 15.5; ex ELMINER 1980; ex VALLILA 1976; ex SUGAR CARRIER 1969.

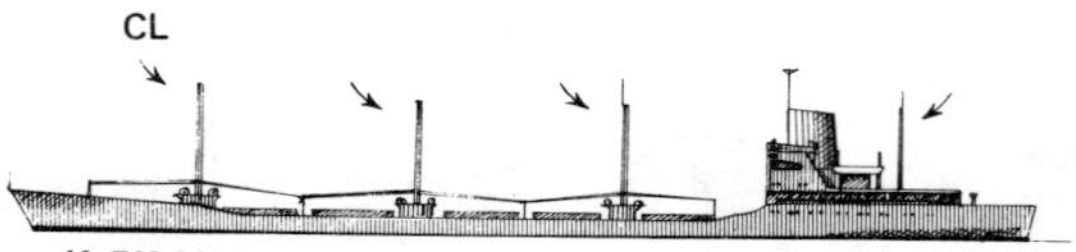

K_3FK H13

53470 FAIR ISLAND. Pa/FRG 1960; C; 12000; 162.44 × 9.92 (532.94 × 32.55); M; 15.5; ex GAROUFALIA 1980; ex KONSUL SCHULTE 1972. Sister: **53471 CHIOS MERCHANT** (Gr) ex SCAPHILL; ex MATHILDE BOLTEN 1970.

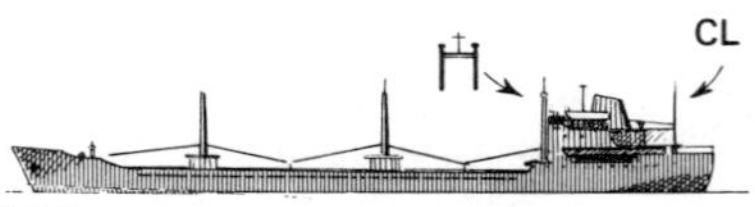

K_3FK H13

● **53500 JOYEID.** Li/No 1966; C; 2500; 111.33 × 6.33 (365.26 × 20.77); M; 13; ex EILERT RINDE 1974. Sisters: **53501 JUSTEID** (Li) ex OLE RINDE 1974 **53502 DON ALEJO** (Pa) ex FOSSUM 1977.

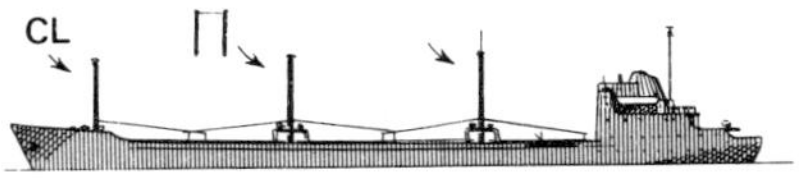

K_3FM H13
● **53510 HARIS.** Gr/No 1965; C; 5000; 119.39×8.1 (391.7×26.57); M; 13; ex DIAKAN GRACE 1977; ex DINAR 1973.

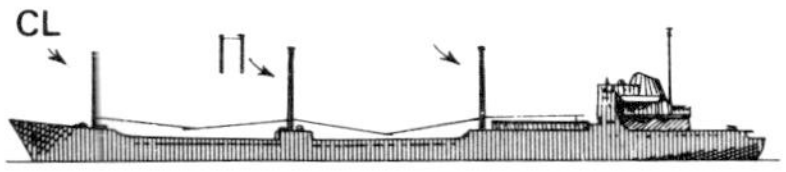

K_3FM H13
53520 MYRTIA V. Gr/No 1967; C; 5100; 119.39×8.23 (391.7×27); M; 13; ex AGRABELE 1980; ex DISKOS 1978.

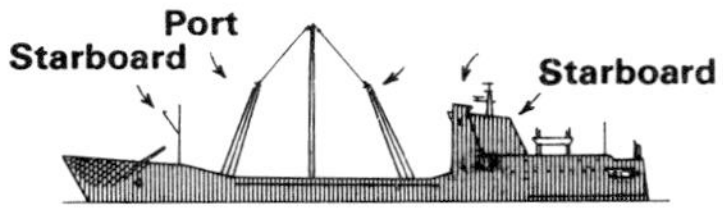

K_3FM H13
53530 STARMAN AMERICA. Br/Br 1974; RoC/HL; 1600/2500; 93.63×4.13/- (307.19×13.55/—); TSM; 12; ex STARMAN 1977.

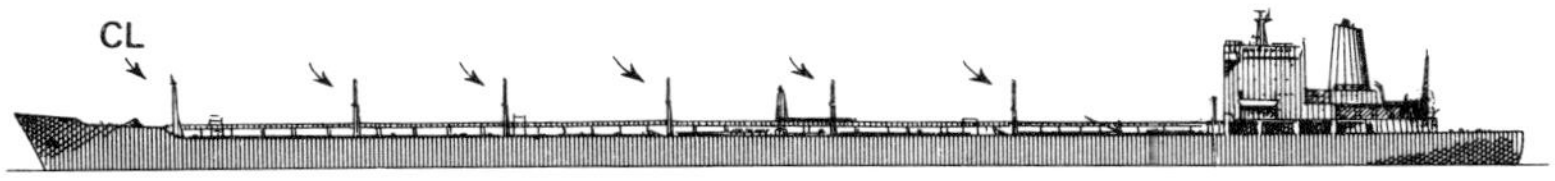

K_4CK_2MFK H1
53540 ARTHUR PHILLIP. Au/Au 1974; Tk; 37200; 239.28×13.16 (785.04×43.18); M; 16.

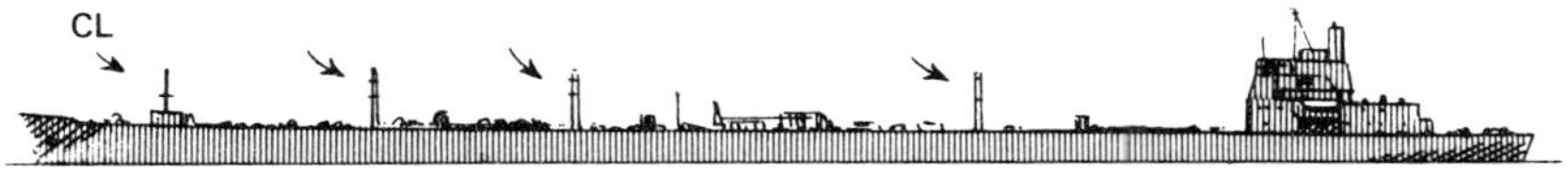

K_4CKMF H
53550 EXXON SAN FRANCISCO. US/US 1969; Tk; 38100; 146.84×12.6 (809.84×41.34); T; 17.5; ex ESSO SAN FRANCISCO 1973. Sisters (US flag): **53551 EXXON BATON ROUGE** ex ESSO BATON ROUGE 1973 **53552 EXXON PHILADELPHIA** ex ESSO PHILADELPHIA 1973.

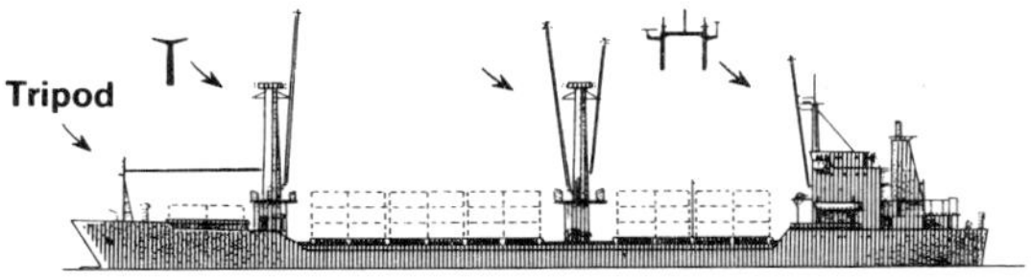

K_4F H13
53560 TIELBANK. FRG/FRG 1978; C/Con; 9300; 151.03×8.13 (495.51×26.67); M; 17; ex CAROLINA; modified **"CL 10"** type. Sister: **53561 TESTBANK** (FRG) ex CHARLOTTA.

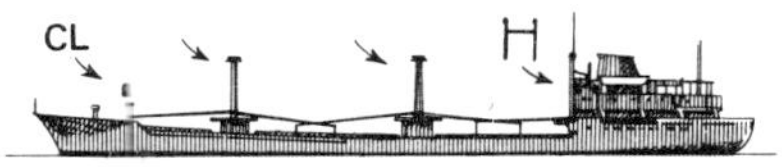

K_4FK H13
53570 ISMENE. Gr/DDR 1968; C; 4200; 114.74×6.48 (376.44×21.26); M; 14; ex FLEUR; ex JOPRIMA 1971.

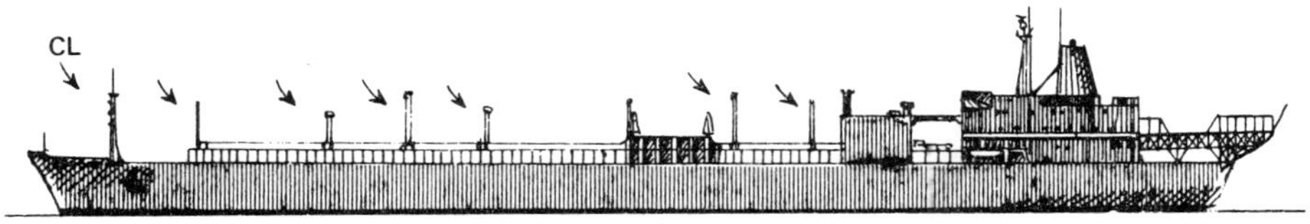

$K_5C_2K_3MF$ H
53580 GADINIA. Br/Fr 1972; LGC; 48700; 256.7×11.53 (842.2×37.83); T; 18.25. Sisters (Br flag): **53581 GADILA 53582 GARI 53583 GASTRANA 53584 GEOMITRA 53585 GENOTA 53586 GOULDIA**

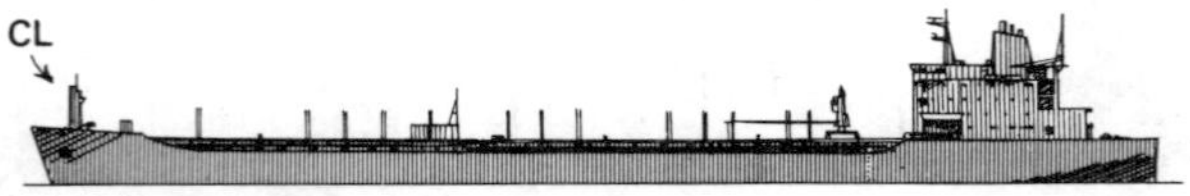

$K_{12}CMFK$
53590 STOLT PRIDE. Li/Fr 1976; Ch; 12500; 170.69 × 9.68 (560 × 31.76); M; 15; Travelling crane. Probable Sisters (Li flag): **53591 STOLT SPIRIT 53592 STOLT SINCERITY 53593 STOLT INTEGRITY 53594 STOLT TENACITY 53595 STOLT LOYALTY 53596 STOLT EXCELLENCE.**

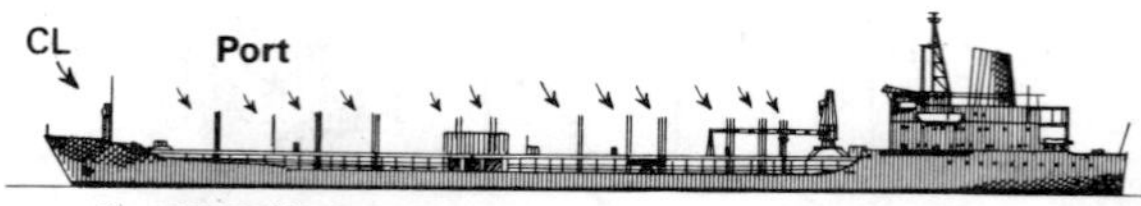

$K_{13}CMF\ H13$
53600 STOLT SHEAF. Li/Be 1972; Tk/Ch; 14600; 170.72 × 10.54 (560.1 × 34.58); M; 13.75; Travelling crane. Sisters: **53601 STOLT BOEL** (Li) **53602 STOLT LLANDAFF** (Br).

$K_{13}MF\ H13$
● **53610 SUNNY BABY.** No/No 1965; LGC; 1400; 71.18 × 5.51 (233.53 × 18.08); M; 12.5; ex KINGS STAR 1970; Converted cargo ship 1971. Sister: **53611 SUNNY BOY** (No) ex TERESA 1970.

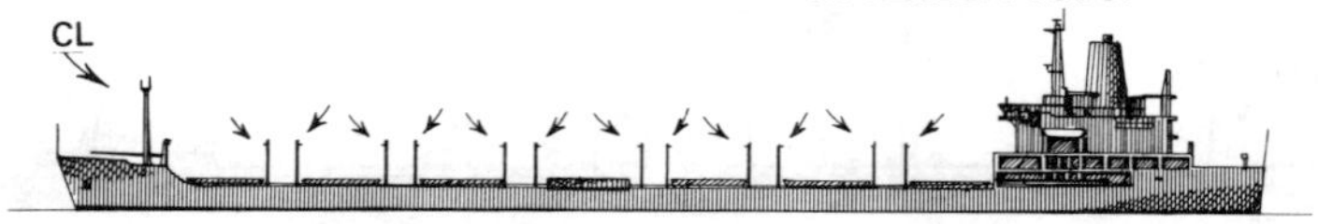

$K_{13}MFC\ H13$
53620 IRON CARPENTARIA. Au/Au 1977; B; 25900; 202.7 × 12.52 (665.03 × 41.08); GT; 15. Sister: **53621 IRON CURTIS** (Au).

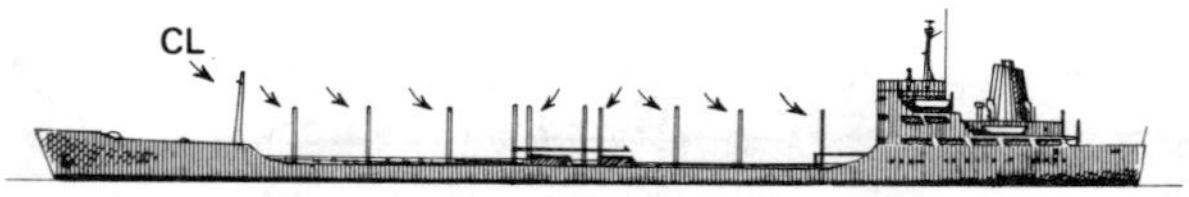

$K_{11}MF\ H13$
53630 ALCHEMIST. Li/US-FRG 1944/61; LGC/Tk; 13000; 175.9 × 9.12 (577.1 × 29.92); T; 14; ex PINNACLES 1961. Lengthened, widened & converted from tanker 1961.

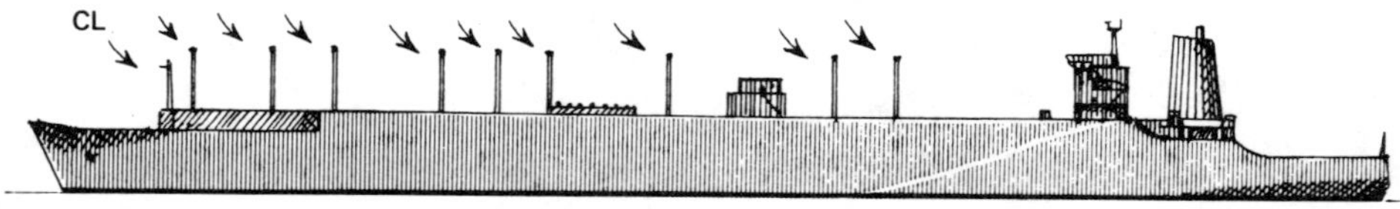

$K_{10}MF\ H1/H2$
● **63640 EL PASO PAUL KAYSER.** Li/FRG 1975; LGC; 66800; 280.6 × 11.18 (920.6 × 36.68); T; 20.5. Sisters: **53641 EL PASO CONSOLIDATED** (Li) **53642 EL PASO SONATRACH** (Li) **53643 EDOUARD L.D.**(Fr).

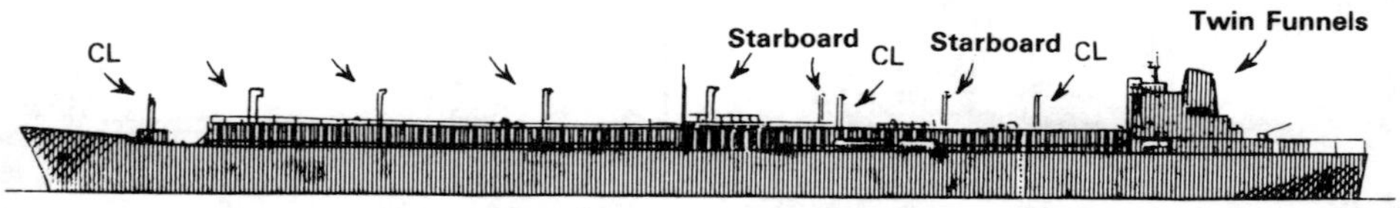

$K_9MF\ H$
53650 BEN FRANKLIN. Fr/Fr 1973; LGC: 80100; 272.78 × 11.1 (894.95 × 36.42); T; 19. Sister: **53651 MOSTEFA BEN BOULAID** (Ag).

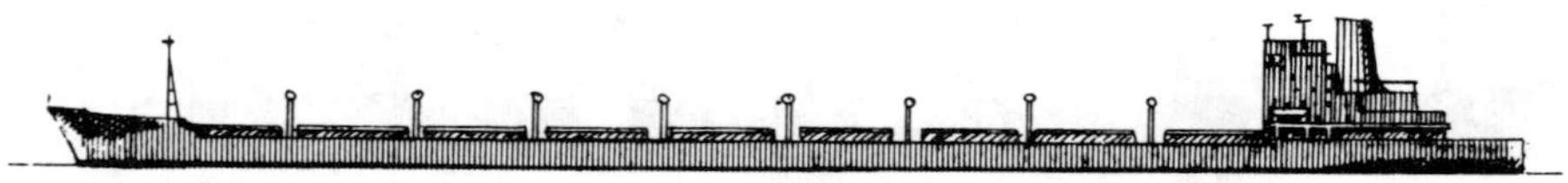

$K_9MF\ H1$
● **53660 ITALMARE.** It/It 1974; B; 43800; 259.01 × 14.05 (849.77 × 46.1); M; 16. Sisters (It flag): **53661 MARE LIGURE 53662 MARE TIRRENO.**

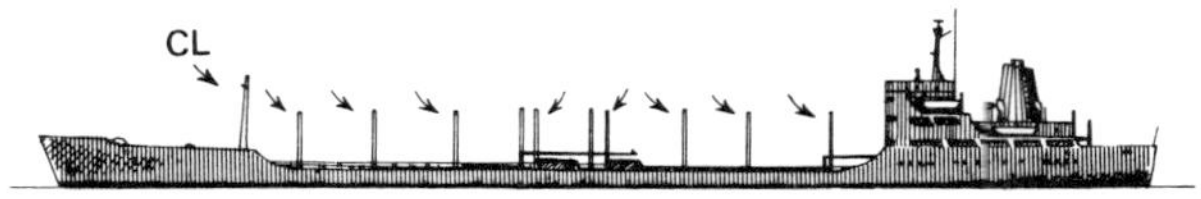

K_9MF H13
53670 ALCHEMIST. Li/US-FRG 1944/61; LGC/Tk; 13000; 175.9 × 9.12 (577.1 × 29.92); T; 14; ex PINNACLES 1961. Lengthened, widened & converted from tanker 1961.

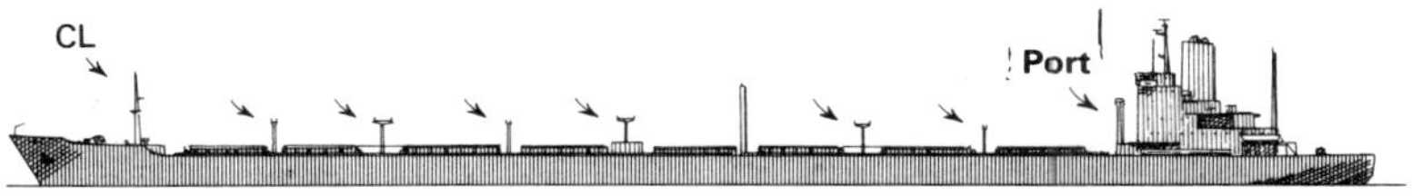

K_9MFK H1
● **53680 DONAU MARU.** Ja/Ja 1969; 00; 45200; 239.02 × 13.34 (784.19 × 43.77); M; 15.5. Sisters: **53681 VOLGA MARU** (Ja) **53682 CASPIAN TRADER** (Li) ex CASPIA MARU 1971 **53683 MOSTUN SANKO** (No) **53684 REGENT PIMPERNEL** (Li) ex KIEV MARU 1972 **53685 SPRING ODESSA** (Sg) ex ODESSA MARU 1972. Similar: **53686 CAUCASUS MARU** (Ja) **53687 EASTERN HAZEL** (Li).

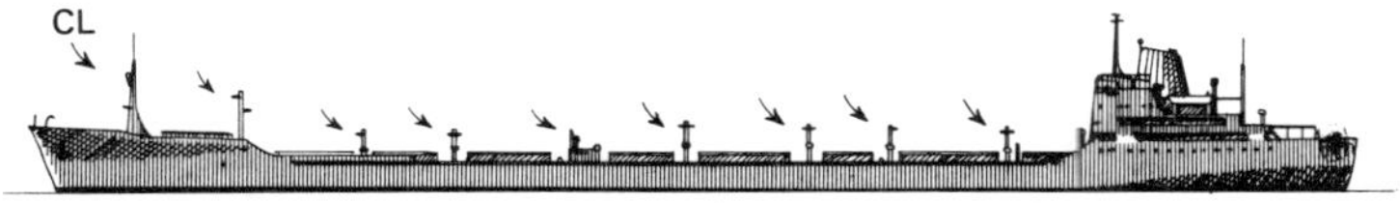

K_9MFK H13
53700 ARCHANGELOS III. Gr/FRG 1963; B; 22800; 217.99 × 11.59 (715.19 × 38.02; M; 15; ex NAESS LIBERTY 1974. Sister: **53701 PYTHEUS** (Gr) ex RUBYCORN 1980; ex FRIGGA 1973 Similar: **53702 TRADE LIGHT** (Gr) ex BALDUR 1978.

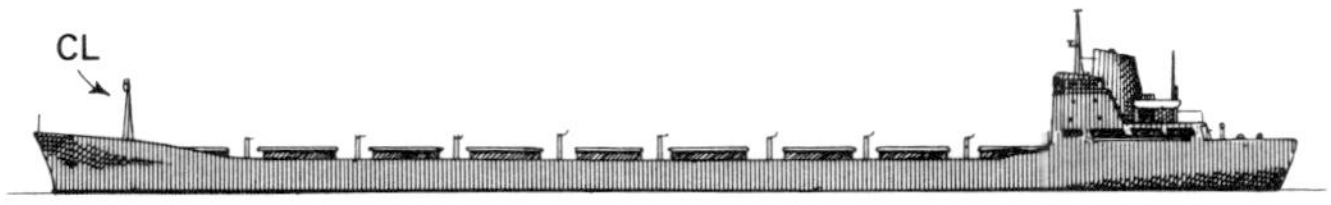

K_9MFK H13
53710 LABRADOR CURRENT. Li/FRG 1962; B; 17700; 200.01 × 9.81 (656.2 × 32.19); M; 16; ex VULKAN 1972. Similar (Li flag): **53711 CHRISTOFFER OLDENDORFF 53712 HENNING OLDENDORFF.**

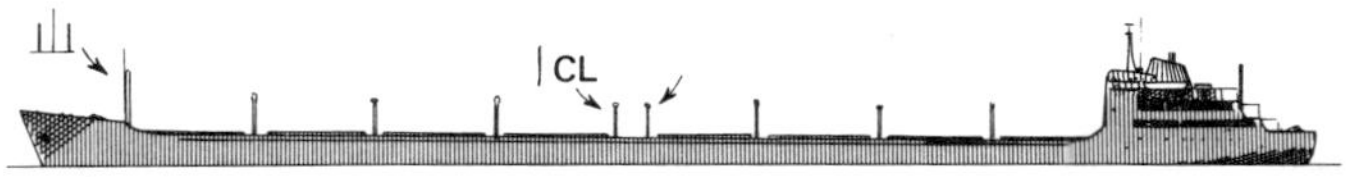

K_9MFK H13
53720 MEZADA. Is/FRG 1960; B; 19200; 206.1 × 10.88 (876.18 × 35.7); M; —; Lengthened 1965. Sister: **53721 ELAT** (Is) Similar: **53722 TIMNA** (Is).

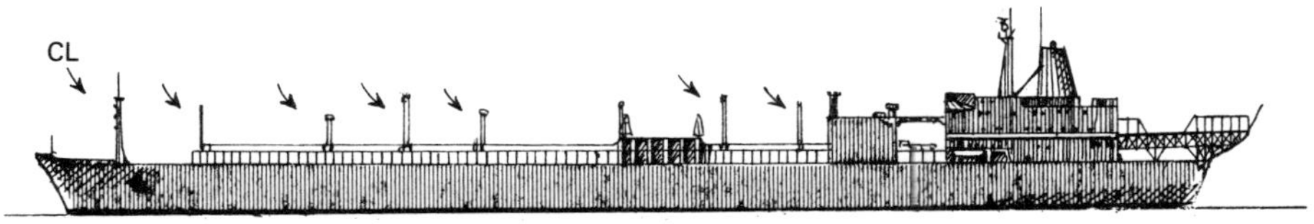

K_8MF H
53730 GADINIA. Br/Fr 1972; LGC; 48700; 256.7 × 11.53 (842.2 × 37.83); T; 18.25. Sisters (Br flag): **53731 GADILA 53732 GARI 53733 GASTRANA 53734 GEOMITRA 53735 GENOTA 53736 GOULDIA.**

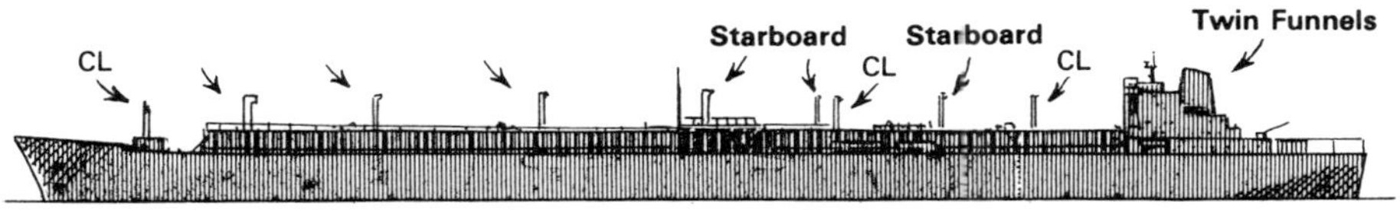

K_8MF H
53740 BEN FRANKLIN. Fr/Fr 1973; LGC; 80100; 272.78 × 11.1 (894.95 × 36.42); T; 19. Sister: **53741 MOSTEFA BEN BOULAID** (Ag).

K_8MF H1
● **53750 ULTRAGAS.** Pa/No 1959; LGC; 1100; 74.81 × 4.3 (245.44 × 14.11); M; 13; ex NORRO; Converted from cargo 1969.

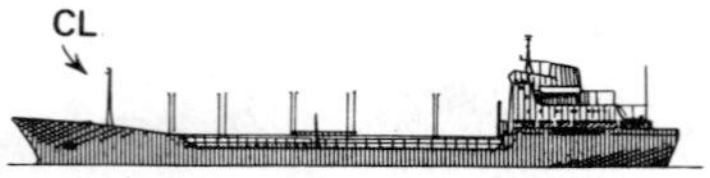

K_8MF H13
53760 OMANIAH. Ku/FRG 1971; Ch; 2900; 106.03 × 6.43 (347.87 × 21.1); M; 14.5; ex OPOBO 1980; ex TERKOL 1972.

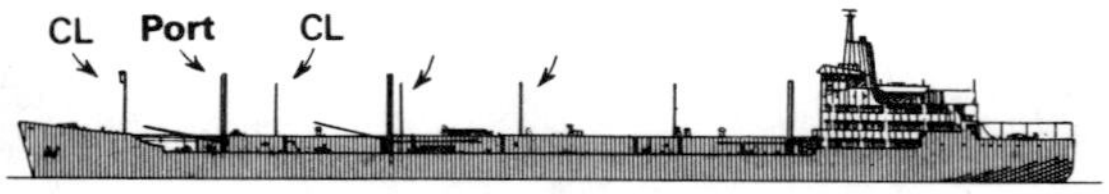

K_8MF H13
53770 HARRY C. WEBB. Li/Ne 1965; Tk/Ch; 11900; 167.65 × 9.52 (550 × 31.24); T; 16.5.

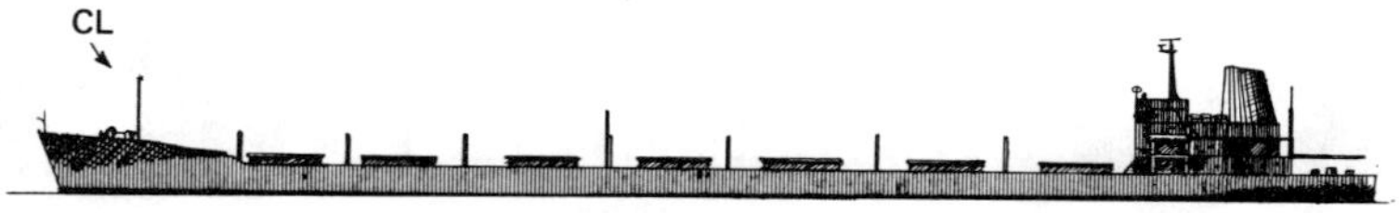

K_8MFK H1
53780 THETIS. Gr/Br 1974; B; 35600; 228.05 × 14.03 (748.2 × 46.03); M; 15. Sisters (Gr flag): **53781 MELETE 53782 NAIAD.**

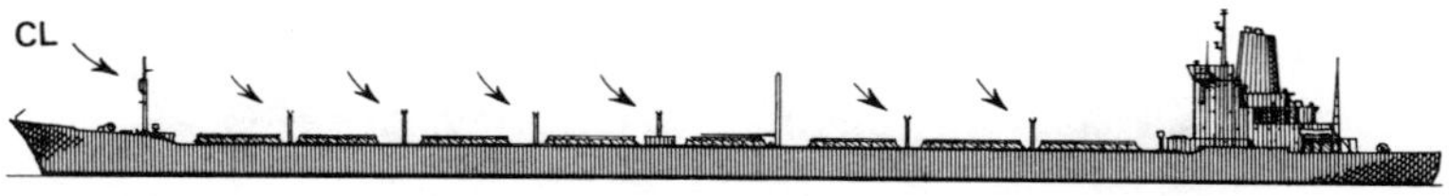

K_8MFK H1
● **53790 ARMAND HAMMER.** Li/Ja 1967; OO; 43900; 232.49 × 13.13 (762.76 × 43.08); M; 15.5; ex MARGARET C. MOSHER 1968.

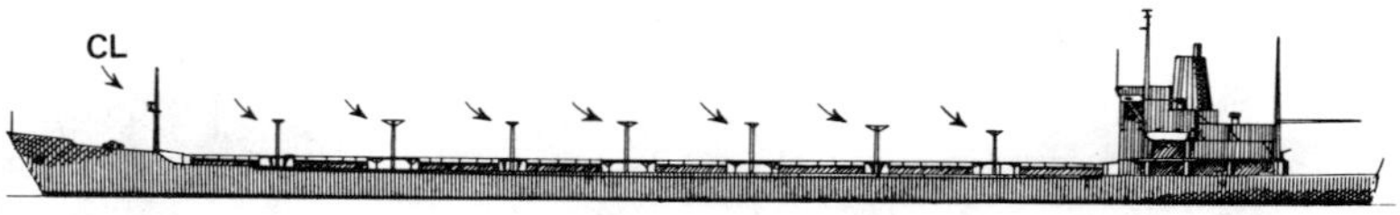

K_8MFK H1
⋆**53800 BAO QING HAI.** RC/Ja 1971; O; 45800; 239.07 × 14.36 (784.35 × 47.11); M; 15.5; ex MOSLANE 1978. Sister: **53801 MOSBROOK** (Br).

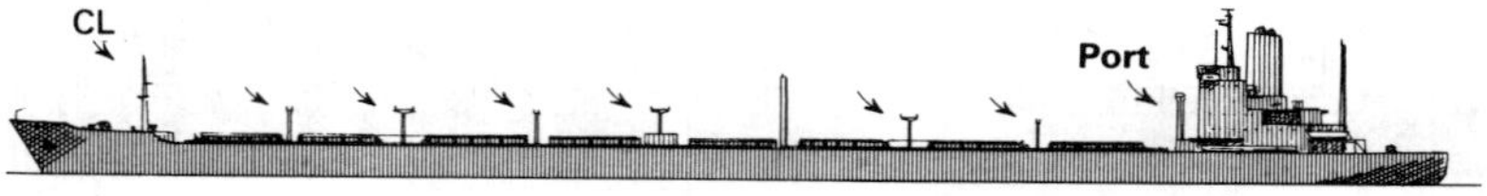

K_8MFK H1
● **53810 DONAU MARU.** Ja/Ja 1969; OO; 45200; 239.02 × 13.34 (784.19 × 43.77); M; 15.5. Sisters: **53811 VOLGA MARU** (Ja) **53812 CASPIAN TRADER** (Li) ex CASPIA MARU 1971 **53813 MOSTUN SANKO** (No) **53814 REGENT PIMPERNEL** (Li) ex KIEV MARU 1972 **53815 SPRING ODESSA** (Sg) ex ODESSA MARU 1972;Similar: **53816 CAUCASUS MARU** (Ja) **53817 EASTERN HAZEL** (Li).

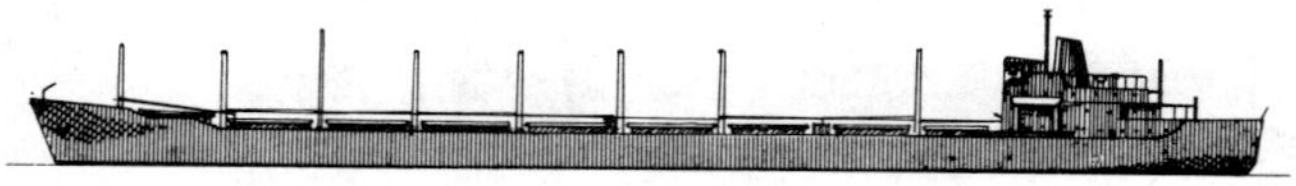

K_8MFK H13
53820 JAGAT NETA. In/FRG 1965; B; 22500; 194.67 × 10.89 (638.68 × 35.73); Sister: **53821 JAGAT VIJETA** (In).

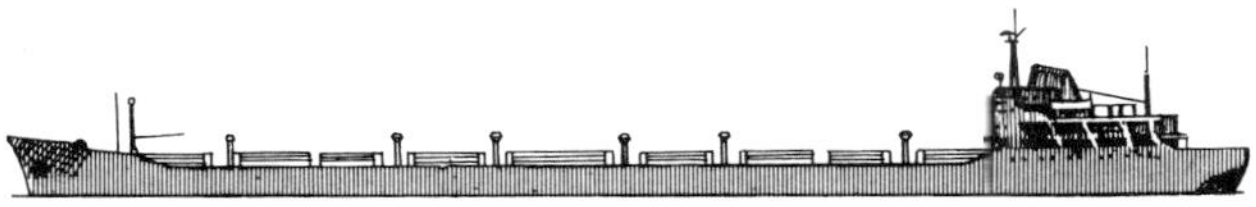

K_8MFK H13
53830 AVEDAT. Is/It 1964; B; 23500; 195.99 × 10.67 (643.01 × 35.01); M; 16. Sister: **53831 EN GEDI** (Is).

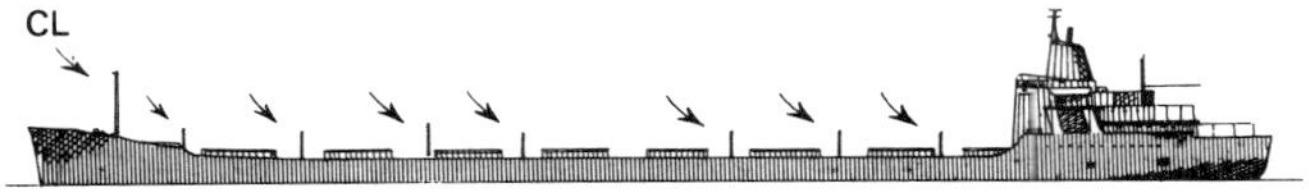

K_8MFK H13
53840 DRYS. Gr/Br 1965; B; 20200; 196.7 × 11.65 (645.34 × 38.22); M; 15; ex OAKWOOD 1971.

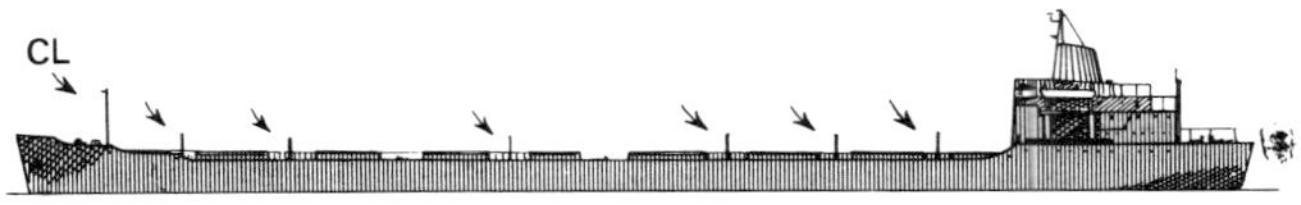

K_8MFK H13
53850 GENERAL M. MAKLEFF. Is/Br 1965; B; 22200; 196.76 × 11.65 (645.54 × 38.22); M; 16.5; ex OCEAN VALOUR, 1980; ex ST. PROVIDENCE 1976; ex SNEHOLT 1973; ex TOWER BRIDGE 1970; launched as SILVERHOW.

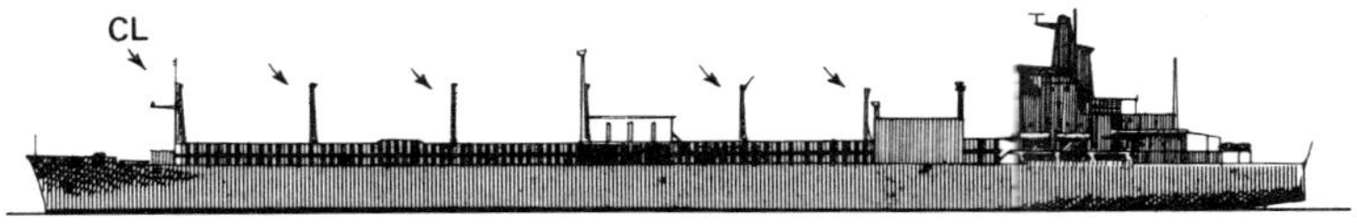

K_7MF H
53860 DESCARTES. Fr/Fr 1971; LGC; 32700; 220.02 × 9.2 (721.85 × 30.18); T; 17.

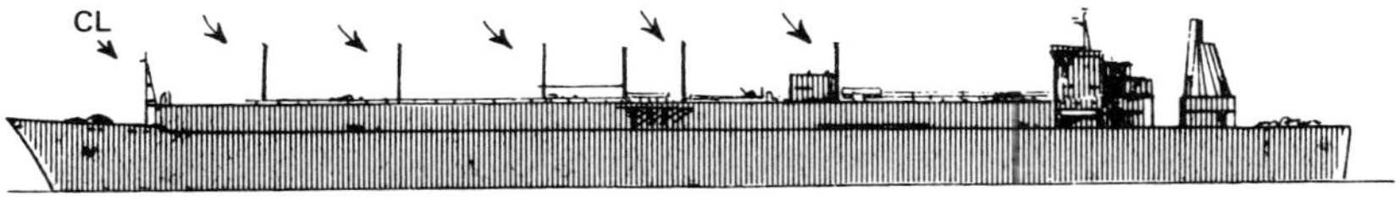

K_7MF H
53870 POLAR ALASKA. Li/Sw 1969; LGC; 44100; 243.34 × 10.04 (798.36 × 32.94); T; 18.25. Sister: **53871 ARCTIC TOKYO** (Li).

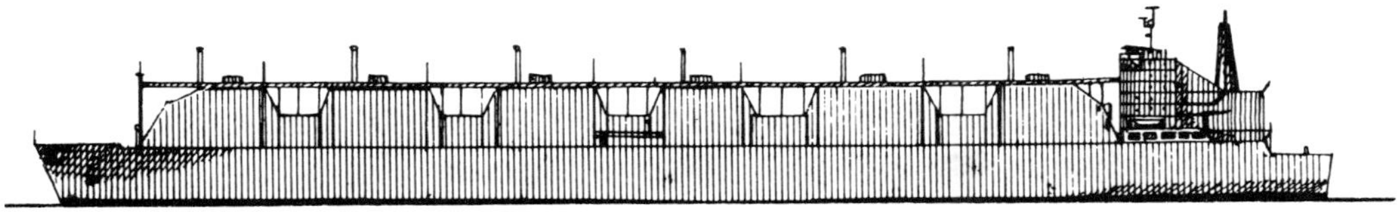

K_7MF H
53880 KHANNUR. Li/No 1977; LGC; 85000; 293.76 × 11.7 (963.78 × 38.39); T; 19.75. Similar (Li flag): **53881 HILLI 53882 GIMI**.

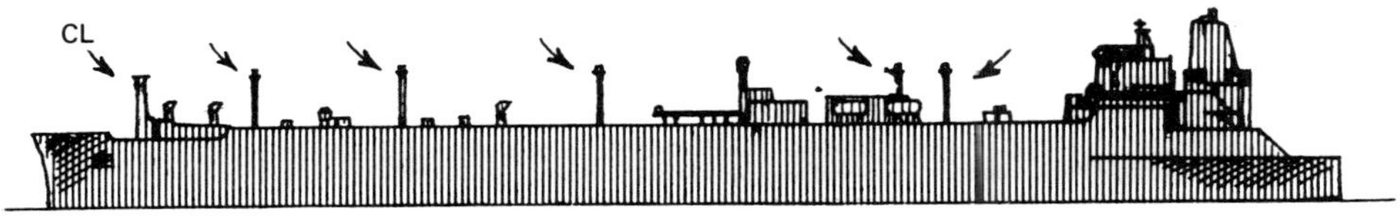

K_7MF H1
53890 GASTOR. Pa/Fr 1976; LGC; 68200; 275.01 × 12.9 (902.26 × 42.32); T; 19. Sister: **53891 NESTOR** (Pa).

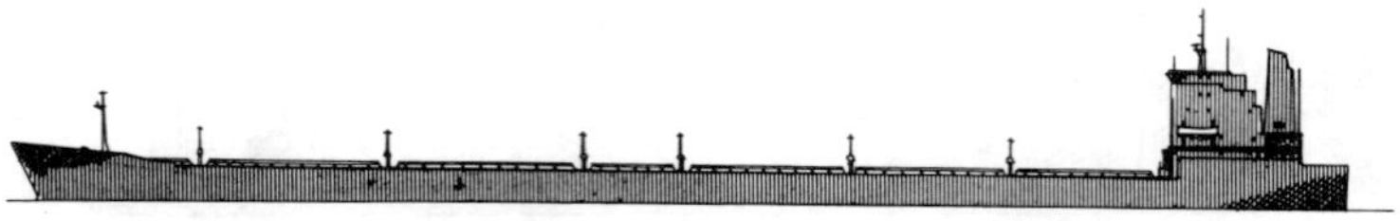

K_7MF H13

● **53900 FEDERAL CLYDE.** Li/Ko 1978; B; 22000; 222.51 × 9.7 (730 × 31.82); M; 14. Sisters (Li flag): **53901 FEDERAL CALUMET 53902 FEDERAL RHINE 53903 FEDERAL SCHELDE.**

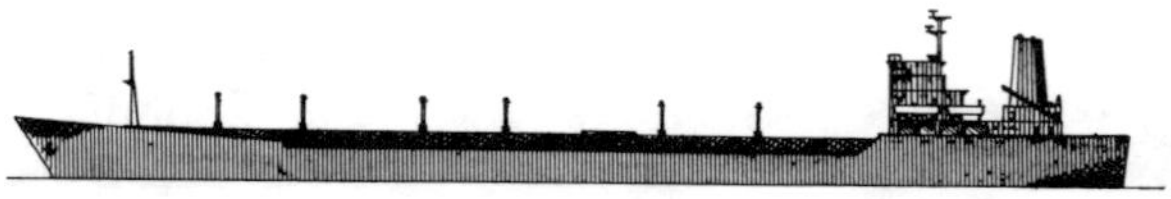

K_7MF H13

53910 STOLT FALCON. Li/Ko 1978; Ch; 21000; 173.64 × 11.58 (569.69 × 37.99); M; 15.5; ex STOLT SEOUL. Probable Sisters (Li flag): **53911 STOLT OSPREY** ex STOLT BUSAN **53912 STOLT HAWK** ex STOLT INCHON **53913 STOLT HERON** ex STOLT YOSU **53914 STOLT CONDOR** ex STOLT OKPO 1979 **53915 STOLT EAGLE** ex STOLT ULSAN 1979.

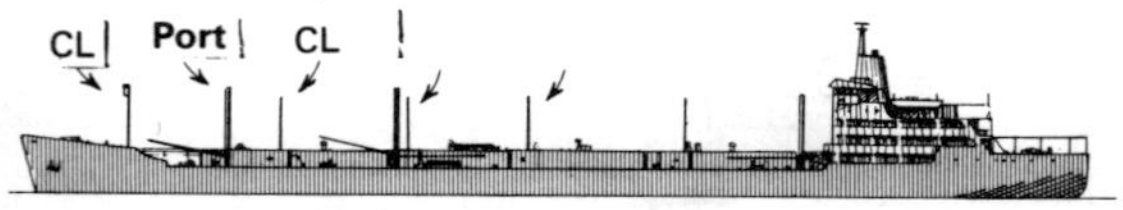

K_7MF H13

53920 HARRY C. WEBB. Li/Ne 1965; Tk/Ch; 11900; 167.65 × 9.52 (550 × 31.24); T; 16.5.

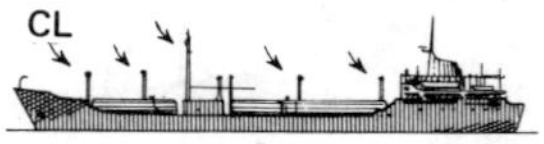

K_7MF H13

53930 AMCO 1. Pa/Fr 1965; LGC; 1800; 80.88 × 3.61 (265.35 × 11.84); M; 14.25; ex SORINE THOLSTRUP 1980; ex NIELS HENRIK ABEL 1970. Similar: **53931 S.G. THOLSTRUP** (De) ex GAZELLE 1970.

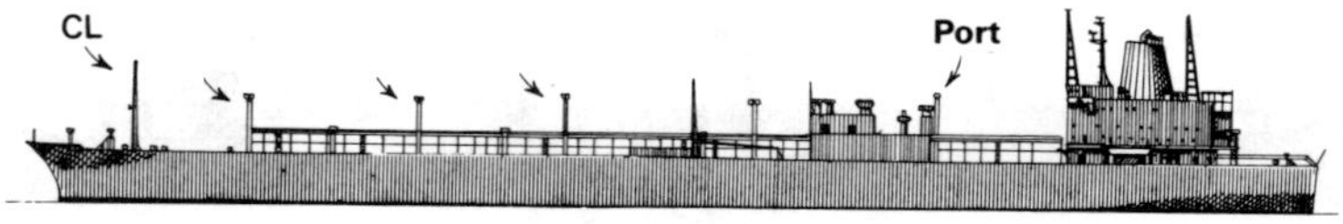

K_7MFK H

53940 SUN RIVER. Ja/Ja 1974; LGC; 45600; 224.01 × 11.89 (734.94 × 39.01); M; 16. Similar (Li flag): **53941 WORLD CONCORD 53942 WORLD CREATION 53943 WORLD VIGOUR.**

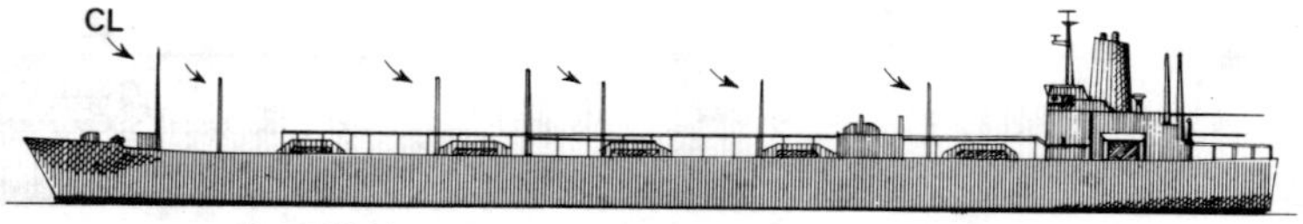

K_7MFK H

53950 PIONEER LOUISE. Li/Ja 1976; LGC; 42300; 228.02 × 12.05 (748.1 × 39.53); M; 15.75.

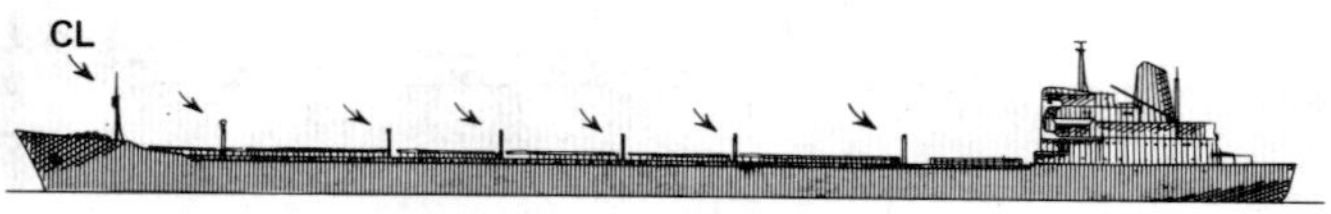

K_7MFK H1

53960 OTTO LEONHARDT. FRG/FRG 1967; B; 23400; 202.34 × 11.27 (663.85 × 36.98); M; 16.

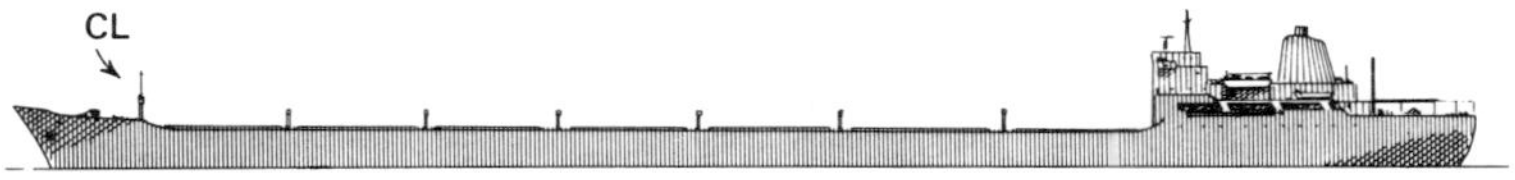

K_7MFK H13
53970 MARALUNGA. It/It 1962; B; 26400; 229.74 × 11.7 (753.74 × 38.39); M; 16; ex MARIA AMELIA LOLLI GHETTI 1966; Lengthened 1968. Sister: **53971 EDERA** (It).

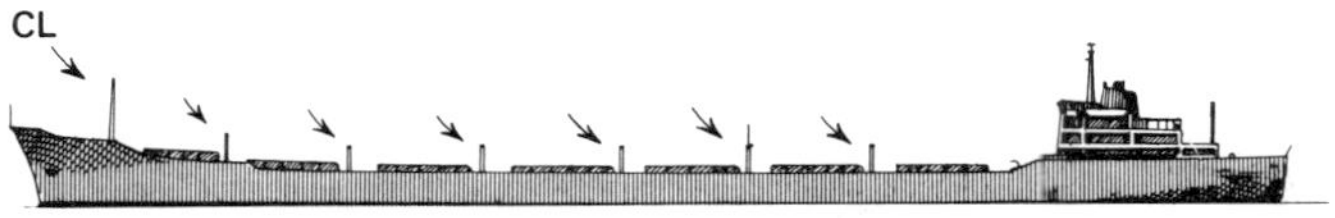

K_7MFK H13
● **53980 SUZANNE.** Gr/Br 1965; B; 21500; 201.78 × 11.18 (662.01 × 36.68); M; 15; ex GARTHNEWYDD 1972; ex CLUDEN 1972.

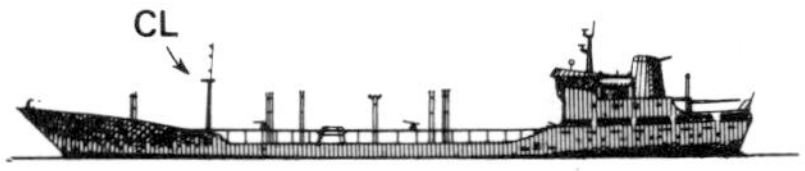

K_7MFK
53990 PERTUSOLA. It/It 1975; Tk; 4000; 117.66 × 7.32 (386.02 × 24.02); M; 15.5. Sister: **53991 PUGLIOLA** (It).

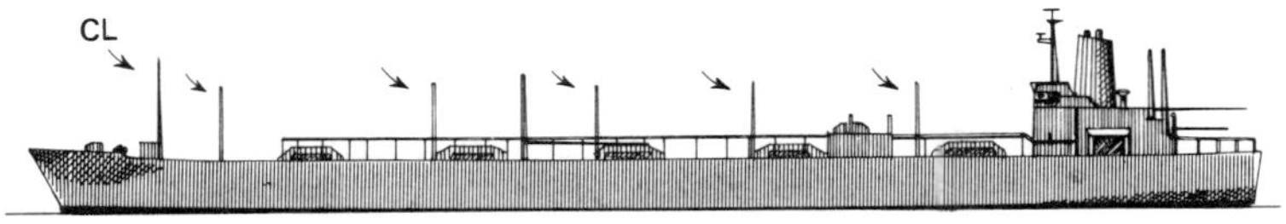

K_7MFK_2 H
54000 PIONEER LOUISE. Li/Ja 1976; LGC; 42300; 228.02 × 12.05 (748.1 × 39.53); M; 15.75.

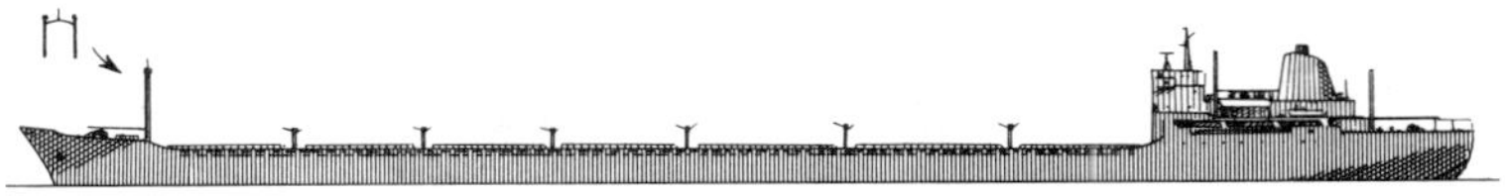

K_7MKFK H13
54010 CENTAURO. It/It 1962; B; 26400; 229.75 × 11.73 (753.77 × 38.48); M; 15; Lengthened 1967. Sisters (It flag): **54011 POSEIDON 54012 VOLONTA** ex MARIO Z 1978; launched as URSA MAJOR Possibly similar: **54013 GALASSIA.**

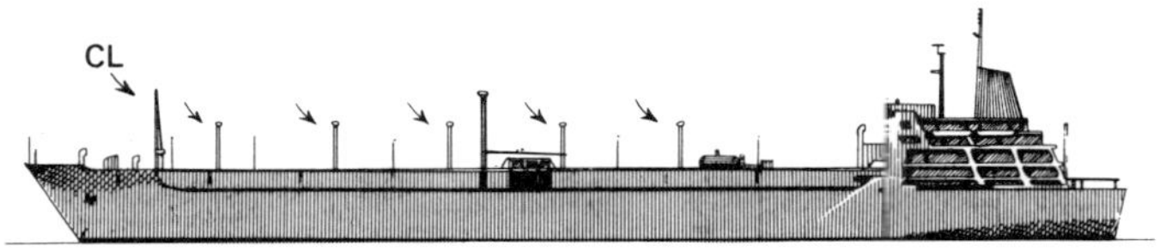

K_7M_2FK H1
54020 HASSI R'MEL. Ag/Fr 1971; LGC; 31400; 200.01 × 8.5 (656.2 × 27.89); T; 16.

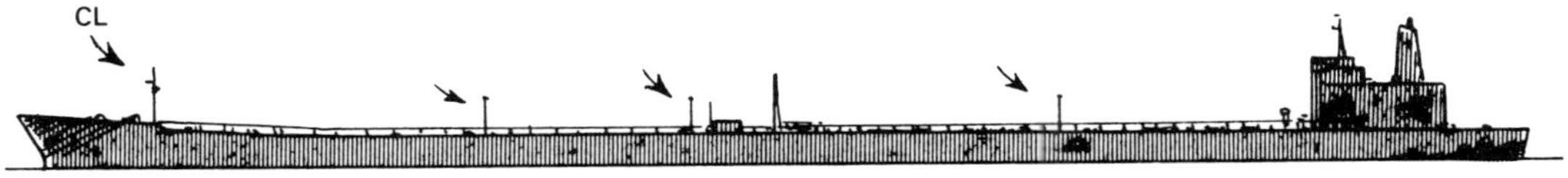

K_6MF H
● **54030 WORLD BRIGADIER.** Pa/Ja 1974; Tk; 105200; 319.31 × 19.53 (1047.6 × 64.07); T; 16.5. Similar: **54031 WORLD AZALEA** (Pa) **54032 WORLD COMET** (Pa) **54033 WORLD EMPIRE** (Pa) **54034 TACTIC** (Gr) **54035 MANHATTAN KING** (Li) Possible sisters: **54036 WORLD PHILIPPINES** (Pa) **54037 WORLD SOVEREIGN** (Pa).

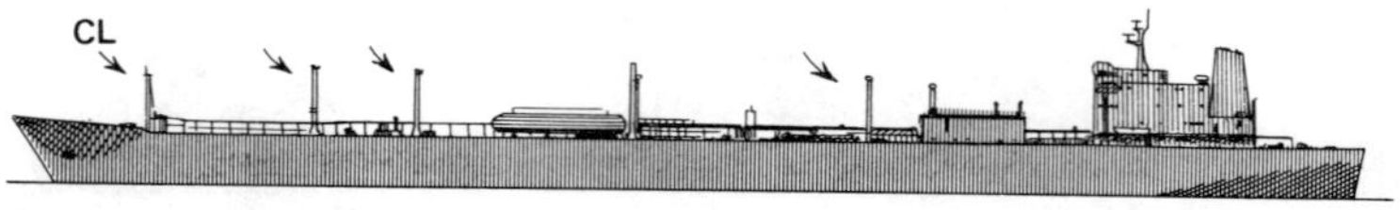

K_6MF H

54040 MONGE. Fr/Fr 1977; LGC; 43700; 231.12 × 13.55 (758.27 × 44.46); M; 20. Probable Sister: **54041 GAS ENTERPRISE** (Br) ex RAZI 1980 Similar (Ku flag): **54042 GAS AL-AHMADI 54043 GAS AL-BURGAN 54044 GAS AL-KUWAIT 54045 GAS AL-MINAGISH.**

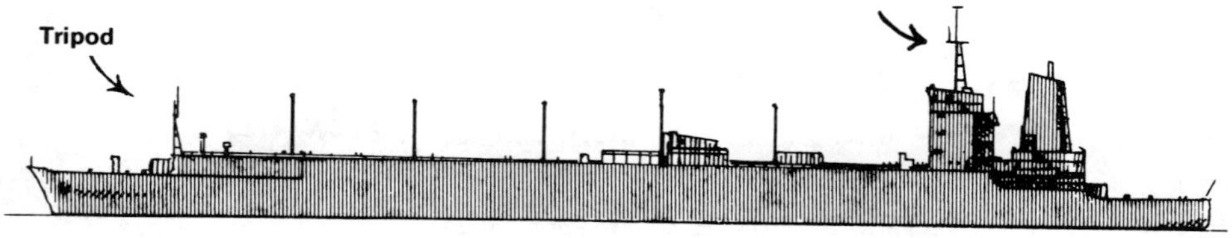

K_6MF H

54050 METHANIA. Be/Be 1978; LGC; 78100; 280.02 × 11.23 (918.7 × 36.84); T; 19.

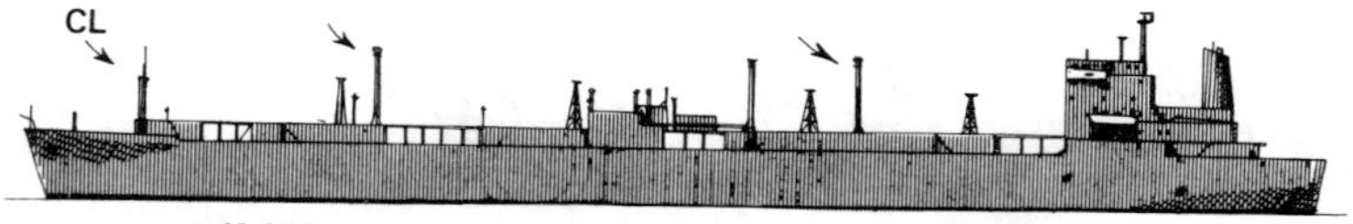

K_6MF H

54060 STAFFORDSHIRE. Li/Fr 1977; LGC; 41700; 226.32 × 13.03 (742.52 × 42.75); M; 17.

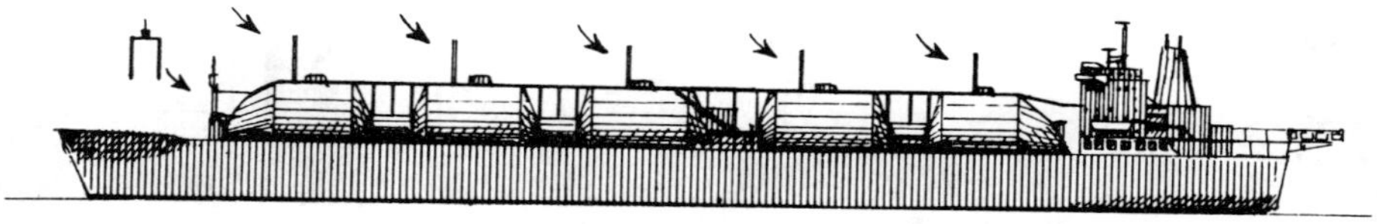

K_6MF H

54070 POLLENGER. Br/No 1974; LGC; 76500; 261.4 × 10.5 (857.6 × 34.45); T; 19.5; ex LNG CHALLENGER 1979.

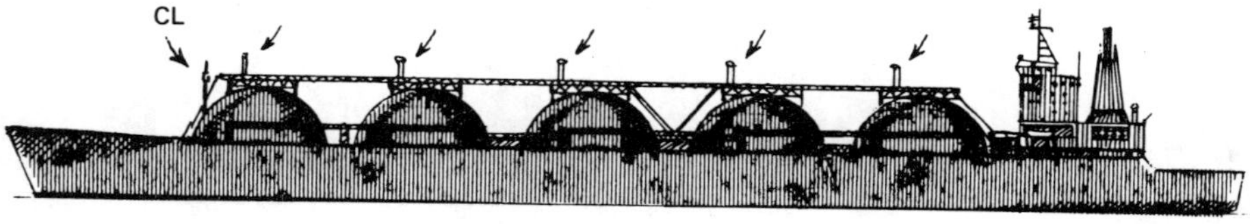

K_6MF H

54080 HOEGH GANDRIA. No/FRG 1977; LGC; 95700; 287.54 × 11.52 (943.37 × 37.8); T; 20. Sister: **54081 GOLAR FREEZE** (No).

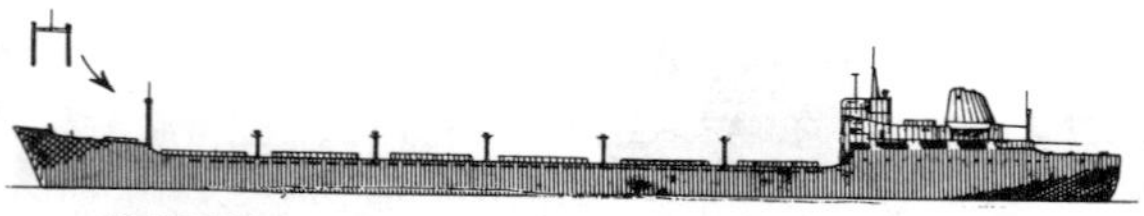

K_6MF H1

54090 GOLFO DI PALERMO. It/It 1960; B; 12900; 174.91 × 9.99 (573.85 × 32.78); M; —.

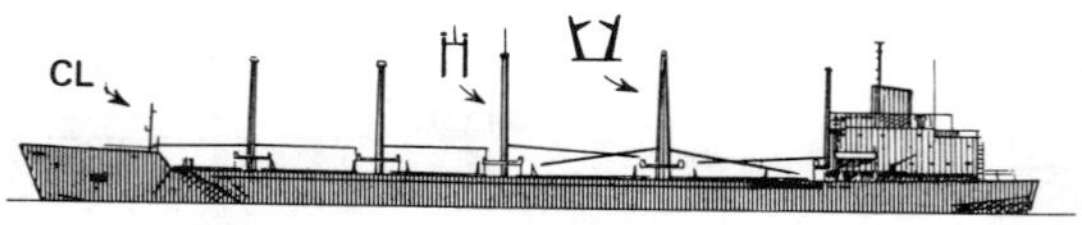

K_6MF H1

54100 ANANGEL HARMONY. Gr/FRG 1968; B; 12300; 162.19 × 10.36 (532.12 × 33.99); M; 16.5; ex NORMANNIA 1980. **'PIONEER'** type.

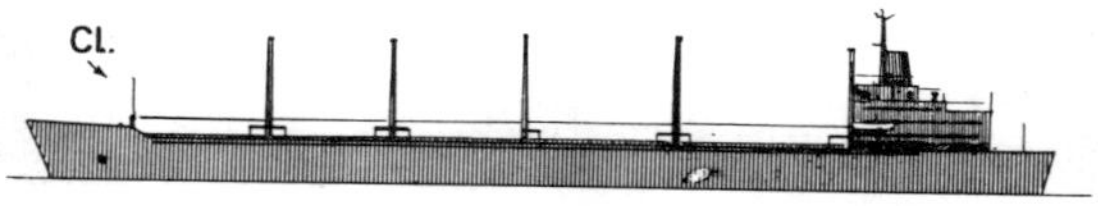

K_6MF H1

54110 JAG DARSHAN. In/FRG 1969; C; 13300; 162.21 × 10.38 (532.19 × 34.06); M; 16.5; **'PIONEER'** type. Sisters (In flag): **54111 JAG DEESH 54112 JAG DHARMA 54113 JAG DHIR 54114 JAG DOOT 54115 JAGAT PRIYA 54116 DAMODAR GANGA 54117 INDIAN GLORY 54118 INDIAN GRACE 54119 VEER VARUNA** ex JAG DEV 1978.

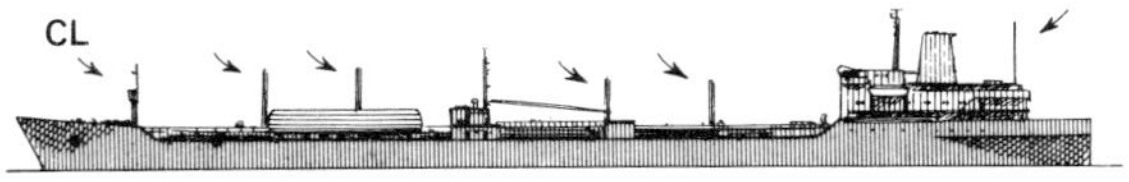

K_6MF H1
54130 BOW FORTUNE. No/Pd 1975; Ch; 17100; 170.52 × 11.08 (559.45 × 36.35); M; 17; **'B-76'** type. Sisters (No flag): **54131 BOW SEA 54132 BOW SKY 54133 BOW SPRING 54134 BOW STAR 54135 BOW SUN 54136 BRIMANGER 54137 NORDANGER 54138 PORSANGER 54139 RISANGER 54140 SPINANGER 54141 TORVANGER.**

K_6MF H13
● **54150 LADY AUGUSTA.** It/Br 1970; Tk/Ch; 1800; 86.87 × 5.44 (285 × 17.85); M; 13; ex STAINLESS WARRIOR 1976. Sister: **54151 SILWON** (It) ex STAINLESS DUKE 1978.

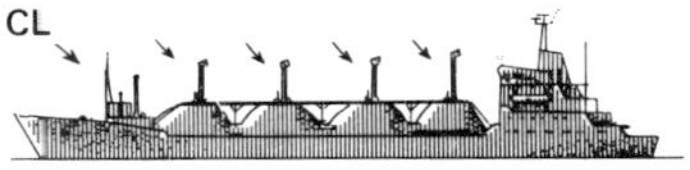

K_6MF H13
54160 SANT JORDI. Sp/Sp 1973/76; LGC; 5500; 109.86 × 5.75 (360.43 × 18.86); M; 15; Launched 1973. Completed 1976.

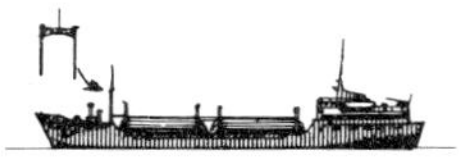

K_6MF H13
54170 CELIA. Sg/Fr 1963; LGC; 1200; 62.03 × 4.27 (203.51 × 14.01); M; 12; ex CELSIUS 1976.

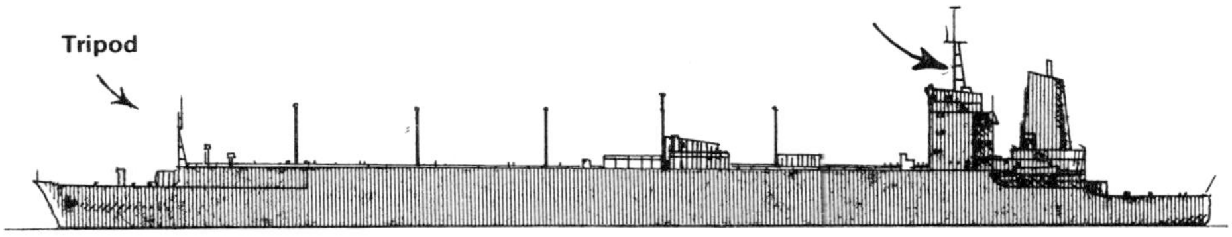

K_6MF H2
54180 METHANIA. Be/Be 1978; 78100; 280.02 × 11.23 (918.7 × 36.84); T; 19.

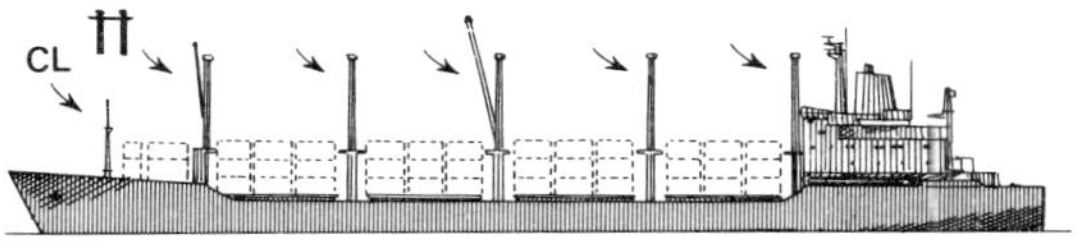

K_6MF H2
● **54190 BARBER MENELAUS.** Br/Ja 1977; C; 10400/16000; 164.62 × 10.62 (540.1 × 34.84); M; 18; ex MENELAUS 1980; **'MP-20'** type. Sisters (Br flag): **54191 BARBER MEMNON** ex MEMNON 1980 **54192 BARBER MENESTHEUS** ex MENESTHEUS 1980 **54193 MELAMPUS 54194 MARON** (Br built) **54195 MENTOR 54196 MYRMIDON** (Br built).

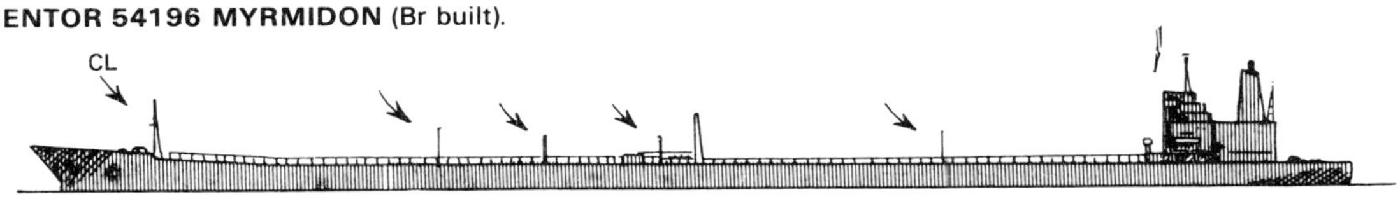

K_6MFK H
54200 WAKO MARU. Ja/Ja 1975; Tk; 116400; 319.92 × 1966 (1049.61 × 64.5); T; 16.5.

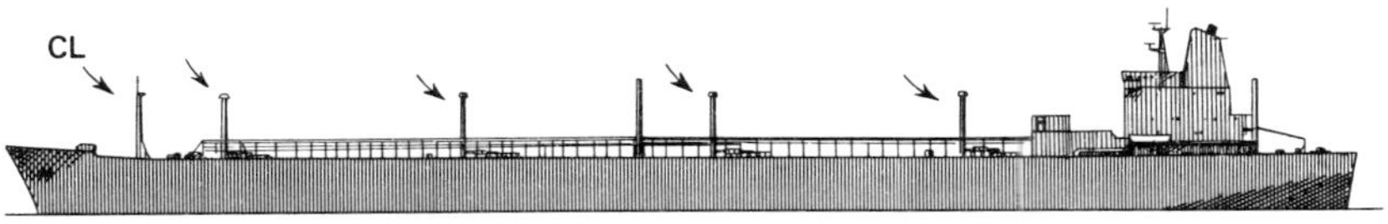

K_6MFK H
54210 ESSO WESTERNPORT. Li/Fr 1977; LGC; 54100; 255.13 × 12.6 (837.04 × 41.34); M; 16.75.

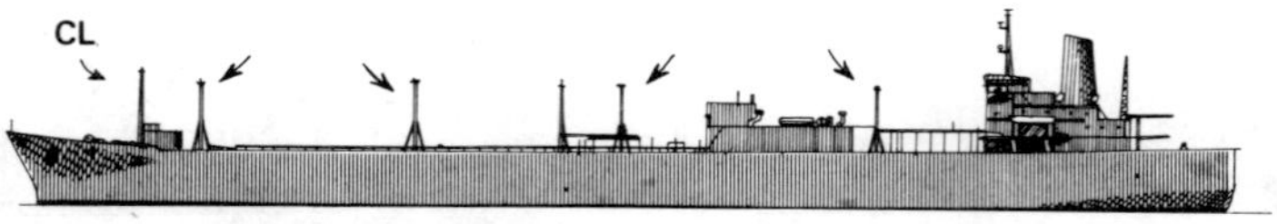

K_6MFK H
54220 IZUMISAN MARU. Ja/Ja 1970; LGC; 38900; 215.09 × 11.01 (705.67 × 36.12); M; 16.

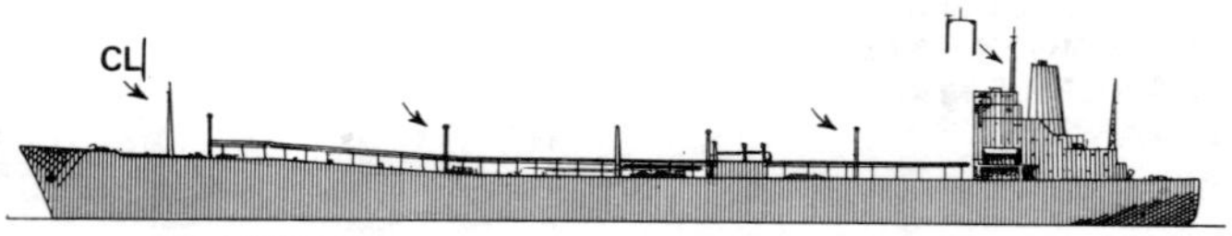

K_6MFK H
54230 TATSUNO MARU. Ja/Ja 1967; LGC; 31100; 202.11 × 11.81 (663.09 × 38.75); M; 15.5.

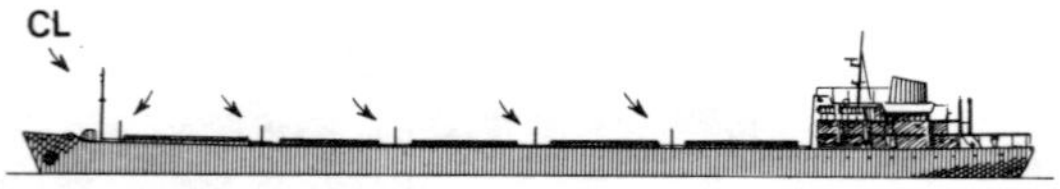

K_6MFK H
54240 WANDERER. Li/Sw-Ja 1953/64; B; 10200; 160.38 × 8.15 (526.18 × 26.74); M; —; Aft section built Sweden 1953. Forward & cargo section built Japan 1964. Sister: **54241 WAYFARER** (Li).

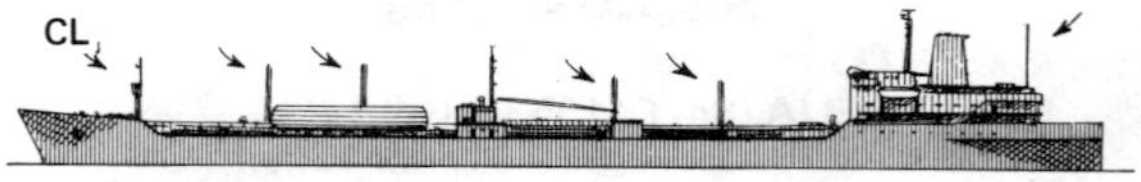

K_6MFK H13
54250 BOW FORTUNE. No/Pd 1975; Ch; 17100; 170.52 × 11.08 (559.45 × 36.35); M; 17; **'B-76'** type. Sisters (No flag): **54251 BOW SEA 54252 BOW SKY 54253 BOW SPRING 54254 BOW STAR 54255 BOW SUN 54256 BRIMANGER 54257 NORDANGER 54258 PORSANGER 54259 RISANGER 54260 SPINANGER 54261 TORVANGER**

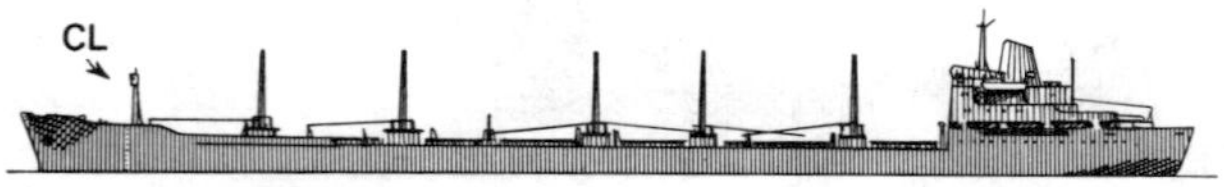

K_6MFK H13
● **54270 KINGSNORTH.** Gr/Sw 1964; B; 15600; 185.25 × 9.82 (607.78 × 32.22); M; 15; ex GRIMLAND 1973.

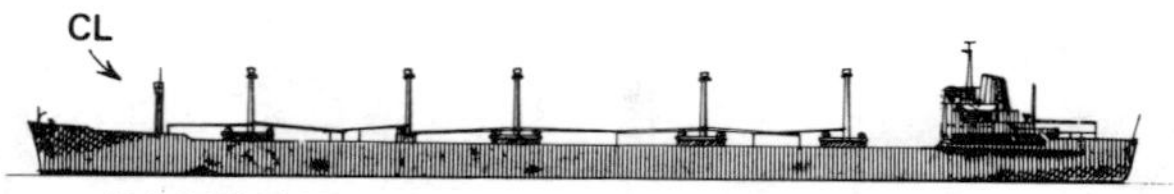

K_6MFK H13
54280 SAMOS. Gr/Sw 1966; B; 17200; 185.25 × 9.82 (607.78 × 32.22); M; —; ex DESPINA C 1968.

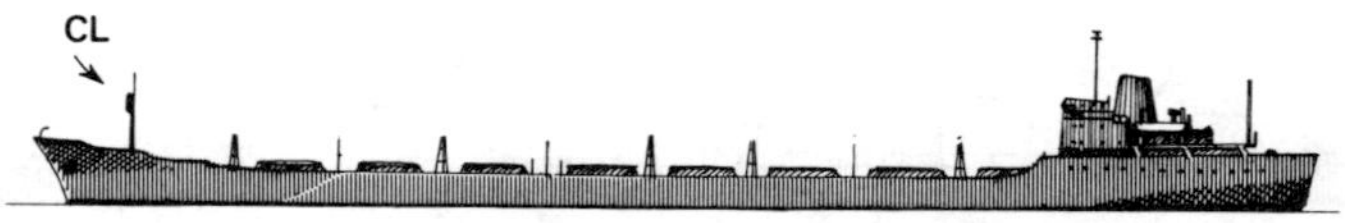

K_6MFK H13
54290 SUNRISE. Li/FRG 1963; B; 23000; 214.18 × 11.66 (702.69 × 38.26); M; 15; ex SKYLINE 1980; ex LEROS 1978; ex SPLENDID HONOUR 1977; ex DELPHINA 1974. Sister: ⋆**54291 TIAN SHUI HAI** (RC) ex DORADO 1979.

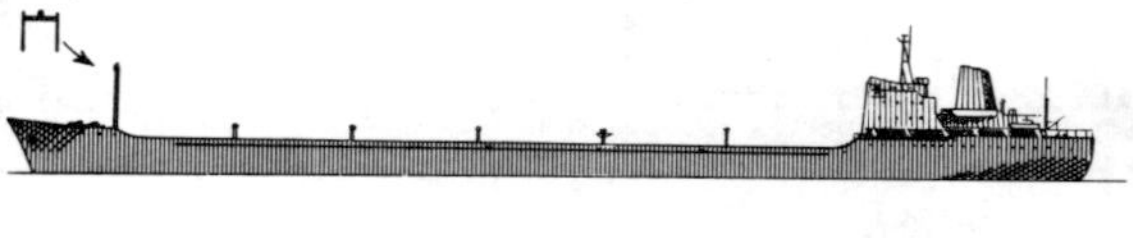

K_6MFK H13
● **54300 NICOLE I.** Pa/Be 1959; B; 10700; 172.22 × 9.7 (565.03 × 31.82); M; 14.5; ex PHANTOM 1980; ex HUMBER 1977; ex ANTONAKI 1974; ex MARLY II 1973; Lengthened 1968. Sisters: **54301 MARGARITA** (Gr) ex GEORGIOS C 1980; ex TIELRODE 1974; ex TAMISE 1966 ⋆**54302 CALBE** (DDR) ex MARLY I 1965.

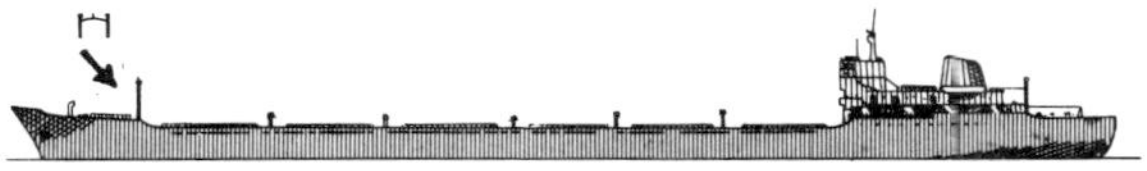

K_6MFK H13
54310 TITO CAMPANELLA. It/It 1962; B; 13300; 175.27 × 10.28 (575.03 × 33.73); M; 13.75.

K_6MFK H13
● **54320 DON MANUEL.** Gr/Br 1961; O; 9300; 162.95 × 9.06 (534.61 × 29.72); M; 12; ex FINNAMORE MEADOW 1977.

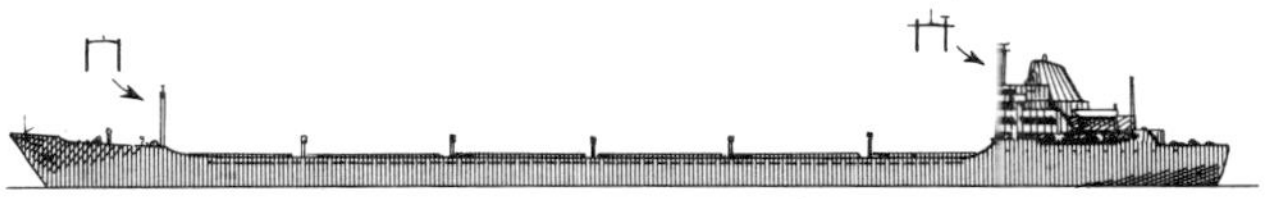

K_6MFK H13
54330 FIESTA I. Pa/It 1962; B; 16000; 193.66 × 10.39 (635.37 × 34.09); M; —; ex FENICE 1977.

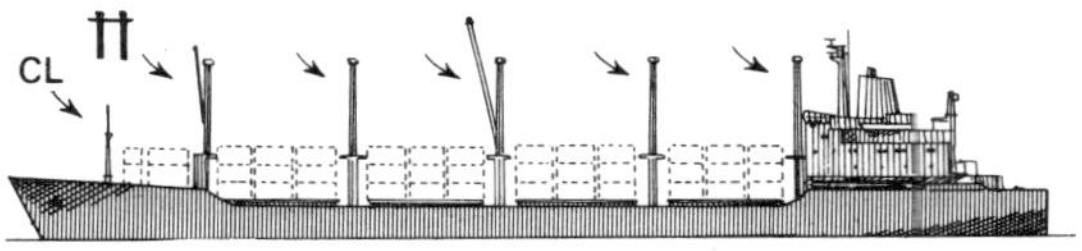

K_6MFKC H13
● **54340 BARBER MENELAUS.** Br/Ja 1977; C; 10400/16000; 164.62 × 10.62 (540.1 × 34.84); M; 18; ex MENELAUS 1980; **'MP-20** type. Sisters (Br flag): **54341 BARBER MEMNON** ex MEMNON 1980 **54342 BARBER MENESTHEUS** ex MENESTHEUS 1980 **54343 MELAMPUS 54344 MARON** (Br built) **54345 MENTOR 54346 MYRMIDON** (Br built).

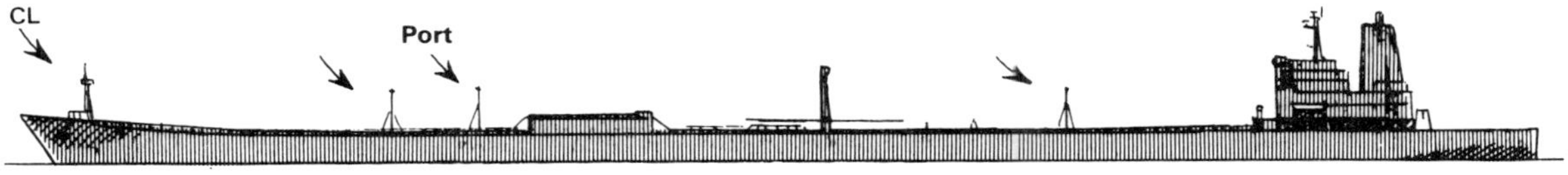

K_5MF H
54350 THORSHOLM. No/Ja 1973; Tk; 140000; 342.91 × 21.78 (1125.03 × 71.46); M; 14.75. Sister: **54351 THORSAGA** (No).

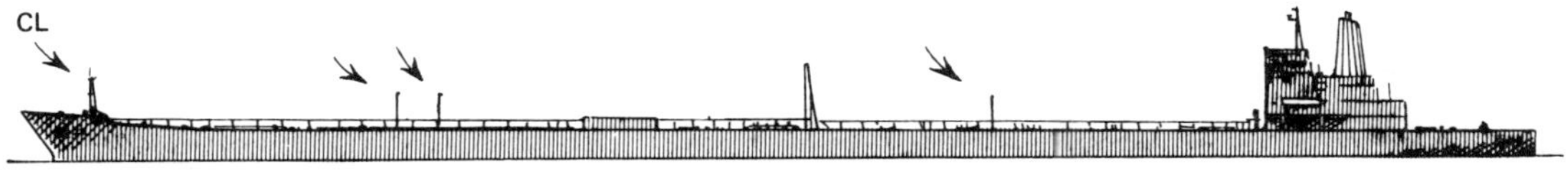

K_5MF H
54360 WORLD DUKE. Pa/Ja 1975; Tk; 11400; 324.01 × 20.03 (1063.03 × 65.68); T; 16.5.

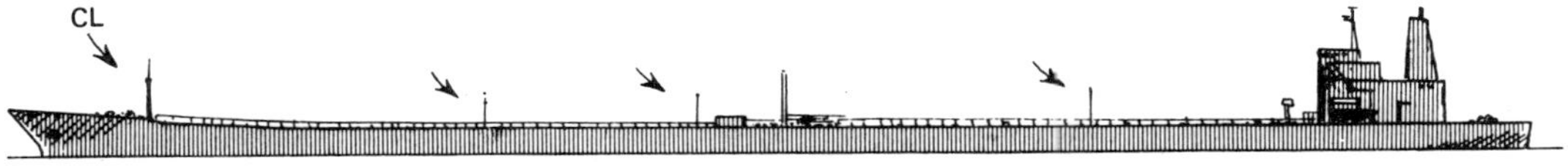

K_5MF H
54370 JAPAN VIOLET. Ja/Ja 1974; Tk; 116300; 319.95 × 19.66 (1049.7 × 64.5); T; 16.25; Launched as WORLD CONSUL. Similar: **54371 ENERGY GROWTH** (Li).

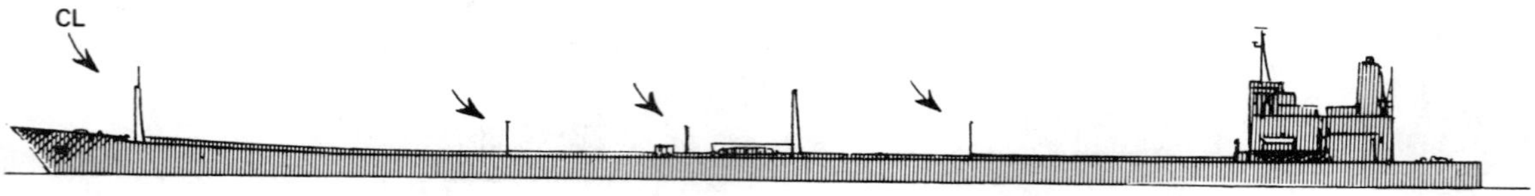

K_5MF H

54380 SAINT MARCET. Li/Ja 1974; Tk; 122900; 340.8 × 21.07 (1118.11 × 69.13); T; 15.5. Sisters (Li flag): **54381 PRIMROSE 54382 VENTURE EUROPE** ex CONOCO EUROPE 1978 Probable Sister: **54383 VENTURE CANADA** ex CONOCO CANADA Possible Sister: **54384 WORLD CANADA.**

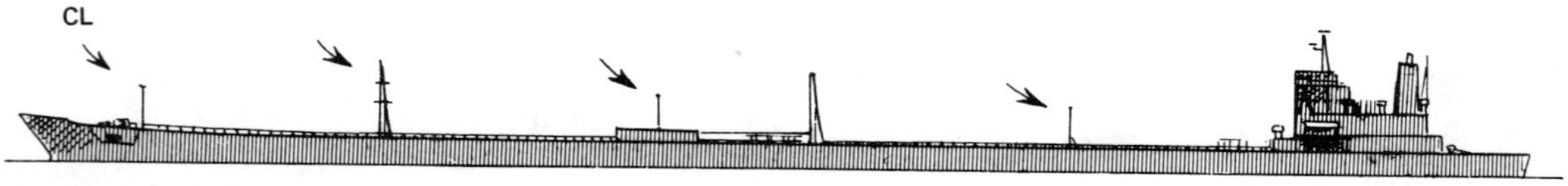

K_5MF H

54390 RESOLUTE. Li/Ja 1973; Tk; 152300; 340.01 × 24.68 (1115.52 × 80.97); T; 15.5; ex VENOIL 1980. Sister: **54391 ALEXANDER THE GREAT** (Gr) ex VENPET 1980.

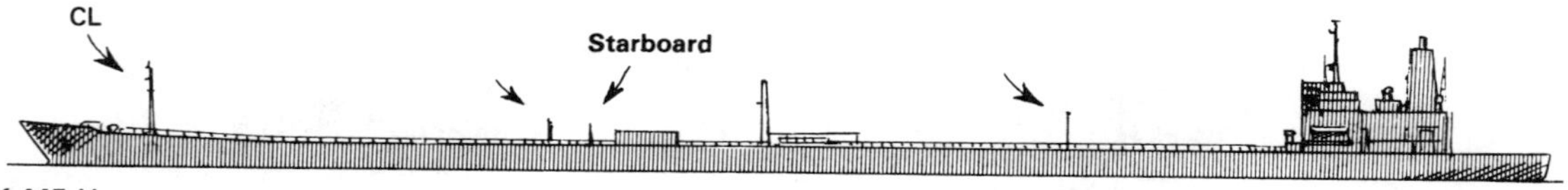

K_5MF H

54400 WORLD BERMUDA. Li/Ja 1974; Tk; 117800; 336.99 × 21.05 (1105.61 × 69.06); T; 16; Launched as WORLD MONARCH.

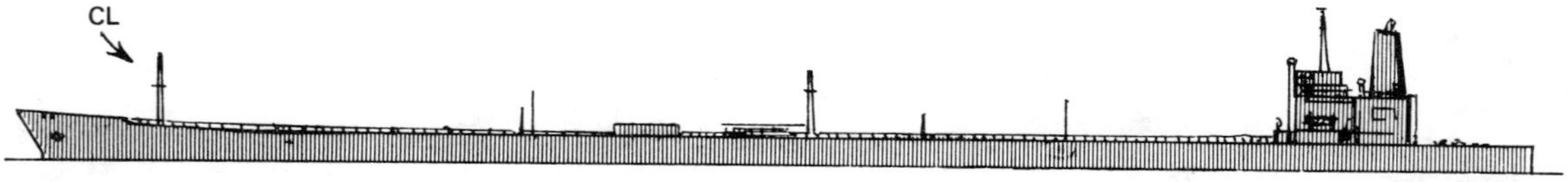

K_5MF H

● **54410 LAUREL.** Li/Ja 1972; Tk; 117200; 336.36 × 20.29 (1103.54 × 66.57); T; 16.75; ex UNIVERSE PIONEER 1980. Similar (Li flag): **54411 UNIVERSE BURMAH 54412 UNIVERSE EXPLORER 54413 ACADIA** ex UNIVERSE GUARDIAN 1980 **54414 PECONIC** ex UNIVERSE MARINER 1980 **54415 MOSELLE** ex UNIVERSE MONITOR 1980 **54416 MENANTIC** ex UNIVERSE RANGER 1980 **54417 HAMLET** ex UNIVERSE SENTINEL 1980 **54418 ARISTOTLE S ONASSIS** ex UNIVERSE FRONTIER 1977 (Pa flag): **54419 TEXACO CARIBBEAN 54420 TEXACO VERAGUAS.**

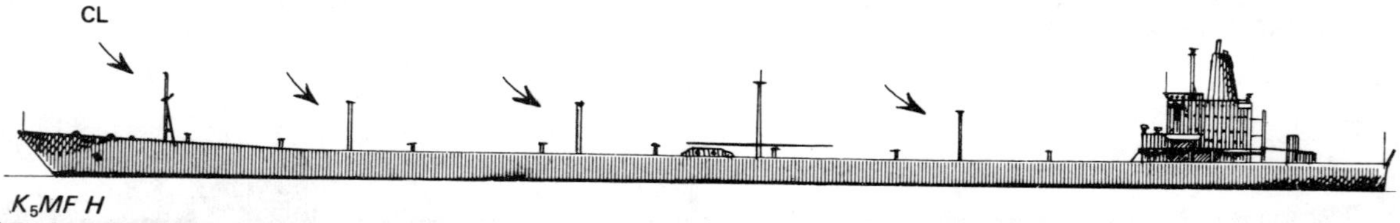

K_5MF H

● **54430 RAS MAERSK.** De/De 1973; Tk; 143100; 347.18 × 22.22 (1139.04 × 72.9); T; 15. Sisters: **54431 ROBERT MAERSK** (De) **54432 ROMO MAERSK** (De) **54433 REGINA MAERSK** (De) **54434 ADELE** (Li) ex RASMINE MAERSK 1973 **54435 TEXACO IRELAND** (Pa) ex ROY MAERSK 1976 **54436 TEXACO NEDERLAND** (Pa) ex ROSA MAERSK 1975 **54437 TEXACO BRASIL** (Pa) ex RICHARD MAERSK 1975.

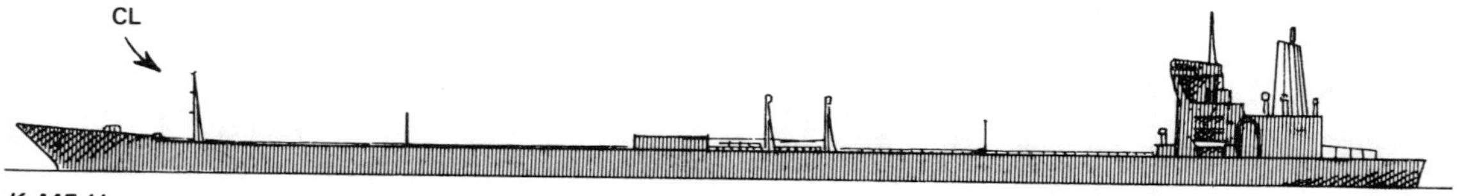

K_5MF H

54440 OKINOSHIMA MARU. Ja/Ja 1970; Tk; 130900; 337.5 × 19.74 (1107.28 × 64.76); T; 15.5. Possibly Similar: **54441 TAKAMIYA MARU** (Ja).

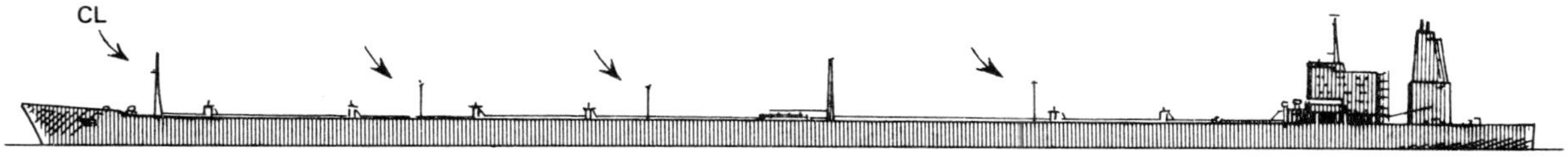

K_5MF H

54450 KIRSTEN MAERSK. De/De 1975; Tk; 167200; 370.47 × 22.46 (1215.45 × 73.69); T; 15.75. Similar (De flag): **54451 KARAMA MAERSK 54452 KAREN MAERSK 54453 KAROLINE MAERSK 54454 KATE MAERSK 54455 KATRINE MAERSK 54456 KRISTINE MAERSK.**

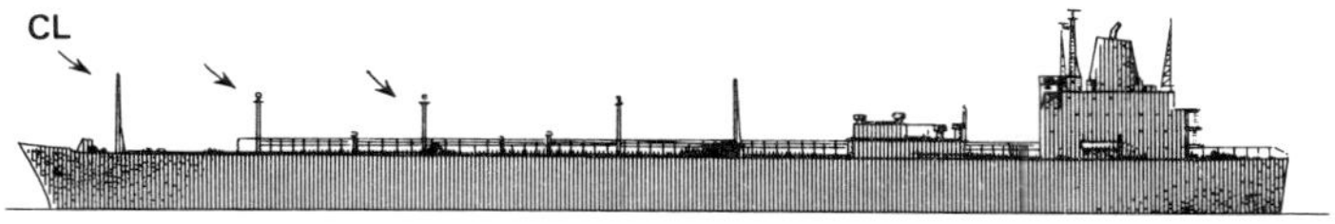

K_5MF H

● **54460 BRIDGESTONE MARU V.** Ja/Ja 1969; LGC; 40900; 210.52 × 12.2 (690.68 × 40.03); M; 14.75.

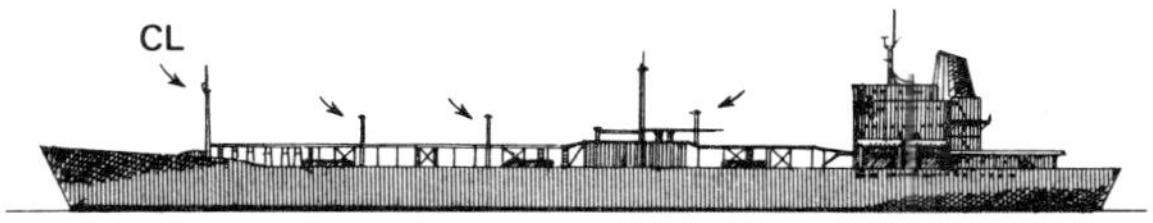

K_5MF H1

54470 MUNDOGAS EUROPE. No/Fr 1968; LGC; 16500; 171.1 × 9.03 (561.35 × 29.63); M; 17; ex FERNWIND 1979; ex KRISTIAN BIRKLAND 1975. Sisters: **54471 DISCARIA** (Li) ex FERNVALLEY 1979; ex CYPRESS 1973 **54472 MUNDOGAS PACIFIC** (No) ex FERNWOOD 1979; ex GAS MASTER 1974.

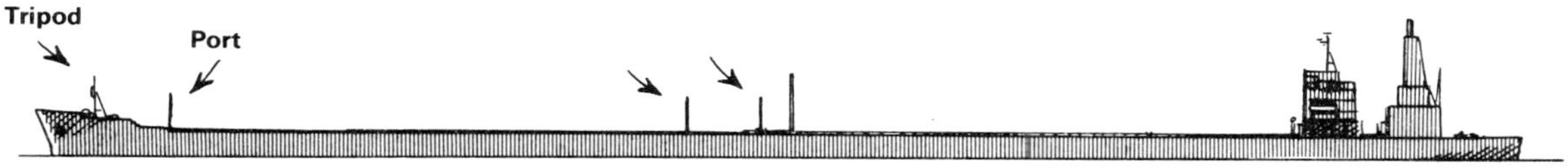

K_5MF H1

54480 LONDON PRIDE. Br/Sw 1971; Tk; 125300; 340.52 × 20.08 (1117.19 × 65.88); T; —

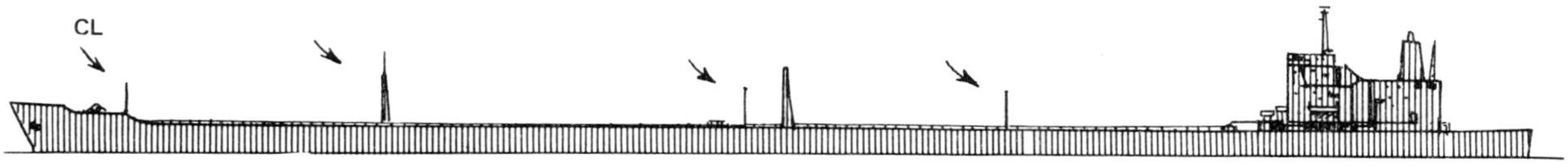

K_5MF H1

54490 AIKO MARU. Ja/Ja 1976; Tk; 209800; 365.87 × 22.9 (1200.36 × 75.13); T; 15.75. Sisters: **54491 JINKO MARU** (Ja) **54492 AL REKKAH** (Ku) Possibly Similar: **54493 CHEVRON SOUTH AMERICA** (Li) **54494 CHEVRON NORTH AMERICA** (Li).

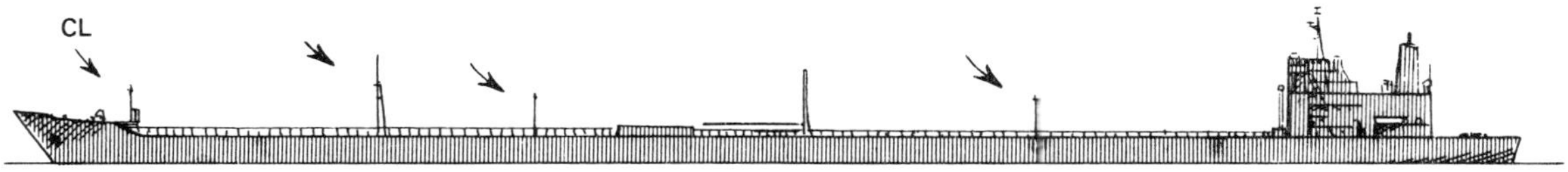

K_5MF H1

54500 NEPTUNE WORLD. Li/Ja 1973; Tk; 105800; 320.89 × 19.85 (1052.79 × 65.12); T; 15.75. Sister: **54501 WORLD PROGRESS** (Li) Possibly Similar: **54502 WORLD CITY** (Li).

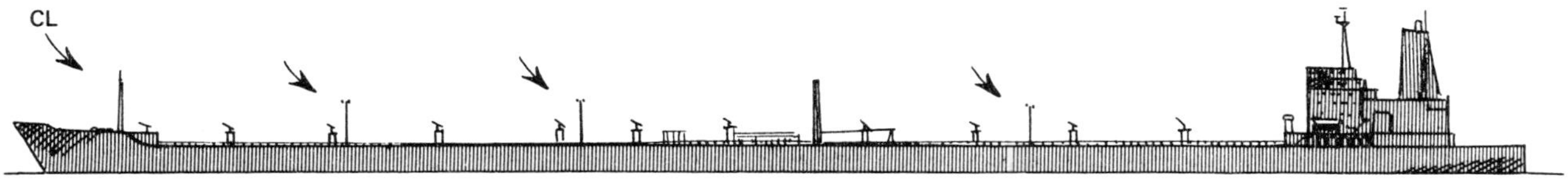

K_5MF H1

54510 ESSO DEUTSCHLAND. FRG/Ja 1976; Tk; 203900; 378.01 × 22.98 (1240.19 × 75.39); T; 15.75. Probable Sister: **54511 HILDA KNUDSEN** (No) Possibly Similar: **54512 CORAGGIO** (It) **54513 ROBINSON** (Li) ex GOLAR PATRICIA.

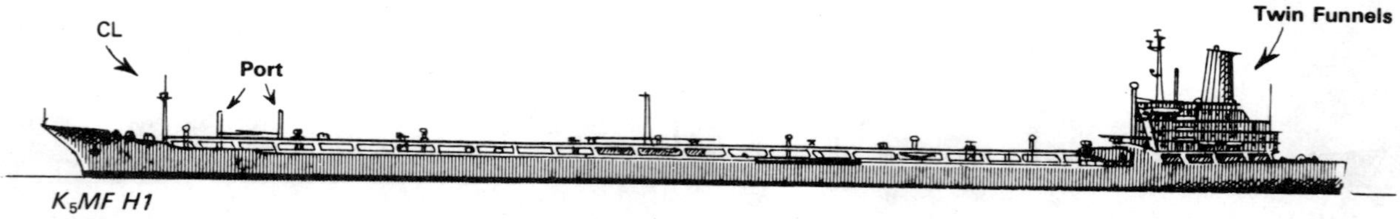

K_5MF H1

54520 ARTEAGA. Sp/Sp 1972; Tk; 163800; 347.94 × 24.82 (1141.54 × 81.43); TST; 14.5. Sister: **54521 BUTRON** (Sp) Similar (Ko flag): **54522 OCEAN PARK 54523 CHUN WOO.**

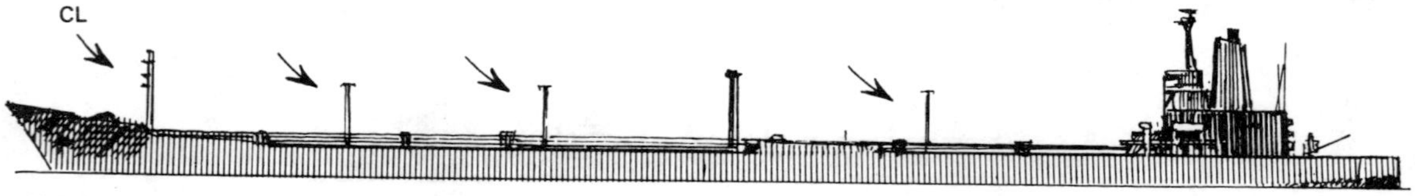

K_5MF H1

54530 ESSO HONOLULU. Li/Ja 1974; Tk; 133000; 343.01 × 22.05 (1125.36 × 72.34); T; 16.25. Sisters (Li flag): **54531 ESSO BILBAO 54532 ESSO OSAKA.**

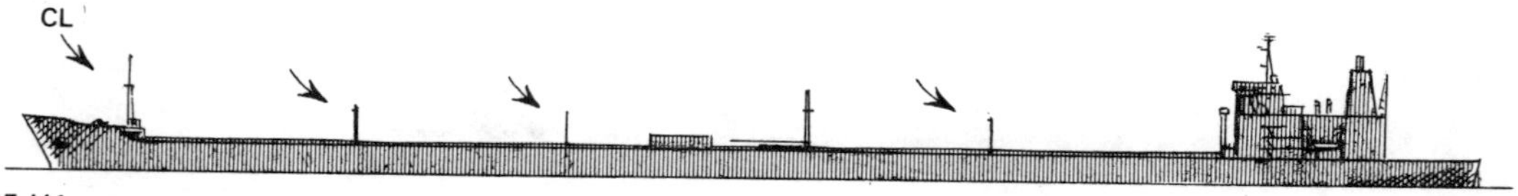

K_5MF H1

54540 SHINKO MARU. Ja/Ja 1972; Tk; 117600; 321.85 × 19.81 (1055.94 × 64.99); T; 15.75. Sisters (Ja flag): **54541 KOKKO MARU 54542 KYOKKO MARU 54543 MEIKO MARU** Similar: **54544 AMUR MARU 54545 JAPAN ADONIS 54546 TOTTORI MARU.**

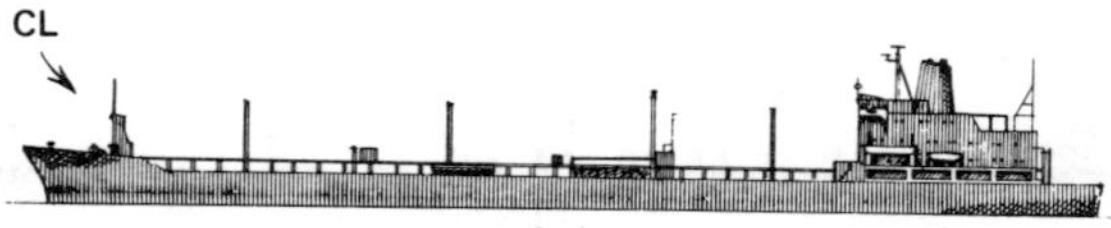

K_5MF H1

54550 NYHOLT. No/Fi 1975; Ch; 17900; 170.72 × 11.37 (560.1 × 37.3); M; 16.25. Sisters (No flag): **54551 NYHORN 54552 BOW FAGUS 54553 BOW FLOWER.**

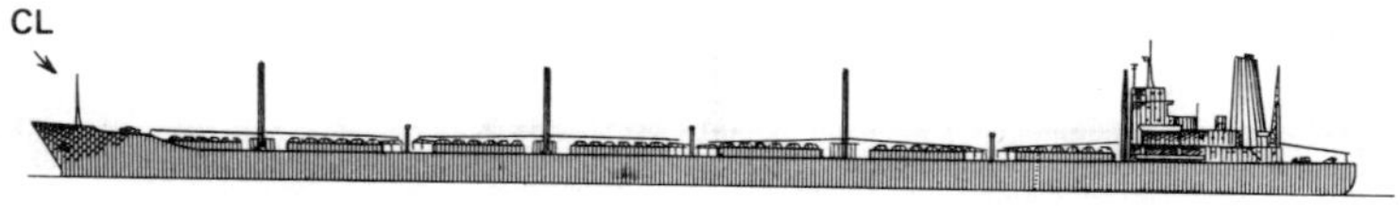

K_5MFK H

● **54560 EVELYN.** Li/Ja 1971; C; 30300; 225 × 12.46 (738.19 × 40.88); M; 14.75. Sisters: **54561 IVORY** (Li) **54562 PEACE VENTURE** (Li) **54563 WORLD VANGUARD** (Li) **54564 VELA** (Li) **54565 STAMY** (Gr) **54566 NORMAN VENTURE** (Sg) ex JAGUAR.

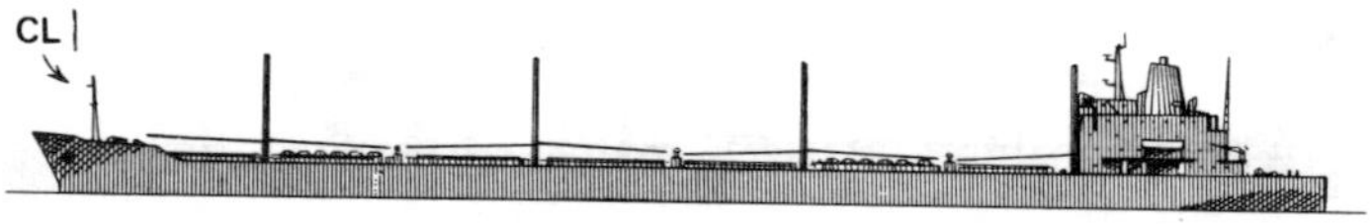

K_5MFK H

54570 CHOKO MARU. Ja/Ja 1970; B; 32000; 208.01 × 11.73 (682.45 × 38.48); M; 14.75. Similar (Li flag): **54571 MEXICAN GULF 54572 SPRAY DERRICK 54573 UNIONA** ex Y.S. VENTURE.

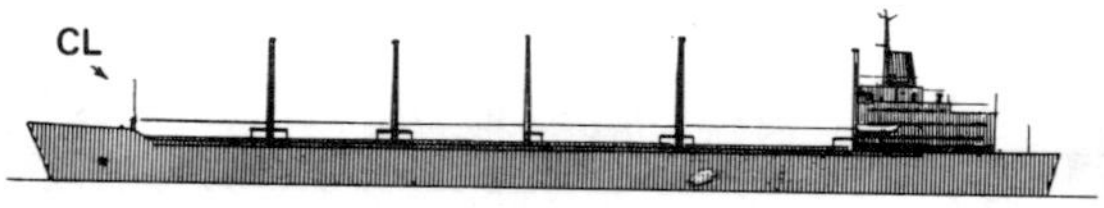

K_5MF H1

54580 JAG DARSHAN. In/FRG 1969; C; 13300; 162.21 × 10.38 (532.19 × 34.06); M; 16.5; **'PIONEER'** type. Sisters (In flag): **54581 JAG DEESH 54582 JAG DHARMA 54583 JAG DHIR 54584 JAG DOOT 54585 JAGAT PRIYA 54586 DAMODAR GANGA 54587 INDIAN GLORY 54588 INDIAN GRACE 54589 VEER VARUNA** ex JAG DEV 1978.

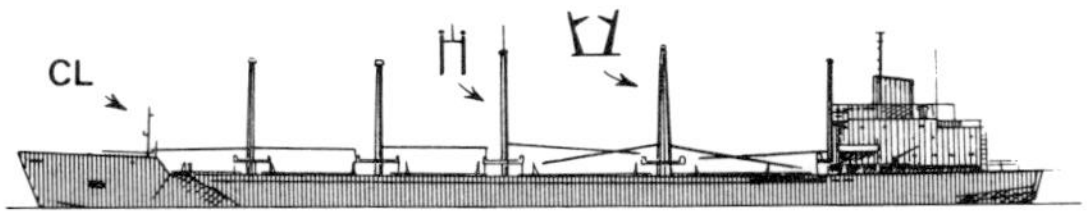

K_5MF H1

54600 ANANGEL HARMONY. Gr/FRG 1968; B; 12300; 162.19 × 10.36 (532.12 × 33.99); ex NORMANNIA 1980; **'PIONEER'** type.

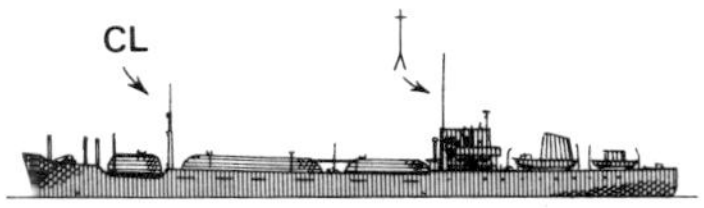

K_5MF H12

54610 SOCRATES. Pa/Fr 1954/61; LGC; 1100; 73.11 × 4.17 (239.86 × 13.68); M; 10; ex MARCELIN BERTHELOT 1968; ex CANTENAC 1961; Converted from cargo 1961.

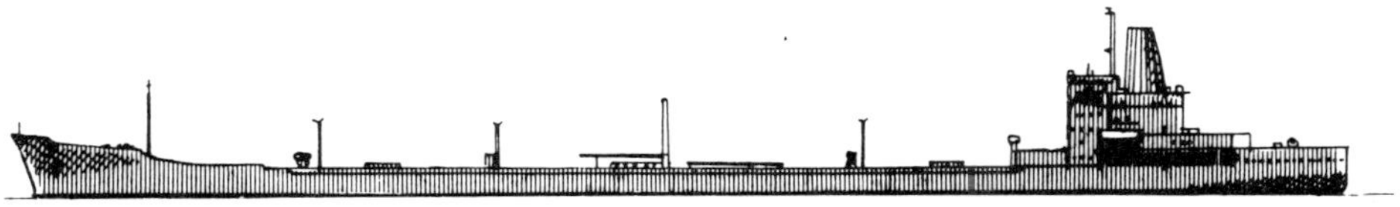

K_5MF H13

54620 ESSO ABERDEEN. Br/Ja 1967; Tk; 59300; 276.51 × 14.87 (907.19 × 48.79); T; 17; ex IMPERIAL OTTAWA 1978.

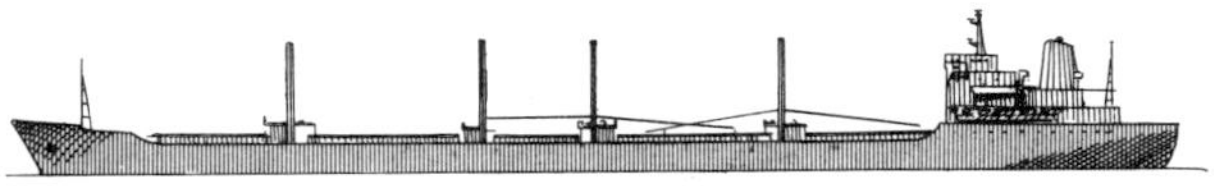

K_5MF H13

● **54630 MARITIME ACE.** Pa/Ja 1971; B; 19700; 185.5 × 11.15 (608.6 × 36.58); M; 14.75. Sisters (Pa flag): **54631 MARITIME CHALLENGE 54632 MARITIME FORTUNE 54633 MARITIME JUSTICE 54634 MARITIME TRADER 54635 MARITIME UNITY** (Li flag): **54636 MARITIME HARMONY 54637 EASTERN HORNET 54638 EASTERN JADE** ex MARQUEE 1980; ex EASTERN JADE 1979 **54639 EASTERN LILAC 54640 EASTERN TREASURE 54650 GOLDEN DAISY 54651 GOLDEN DOLPHIN 54652 WORLD RUBY** (My flag): **54653 BUNGA CHEMPAKA** Similar (Br flag): **54654 ERRADALE.**

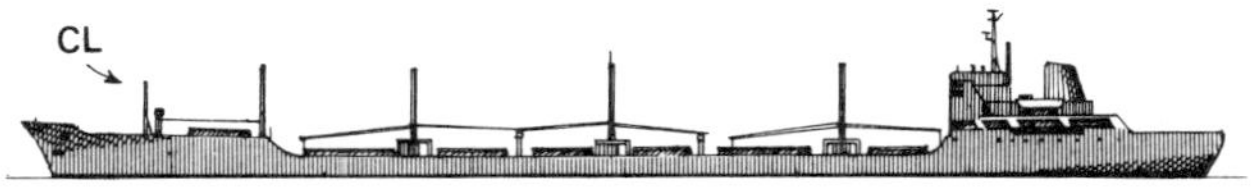

K_5MF H13

● **54660 MARE FELICE.** It/It 1966; B; 16000; 190.48 × 10.61 (624.93 × 34.81); M; —. Sisters (It flag): **54661 MARE PLACIDO 54662 MARE SERENO 54663 MARE TRANQUILLO.**

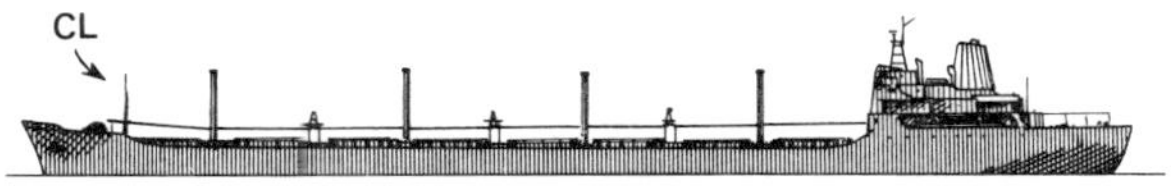

K_5MF H13

● **54670 FALCONERA.** Gr/Ja 1960; B; 13800; 176.31 × 9.94 (578.44 × 32.61); T; —. Sisters (Gr flag): **54671 KEA 54672 PAROS 54673 PHOLEGANDROS 54674 SIFNOS.**

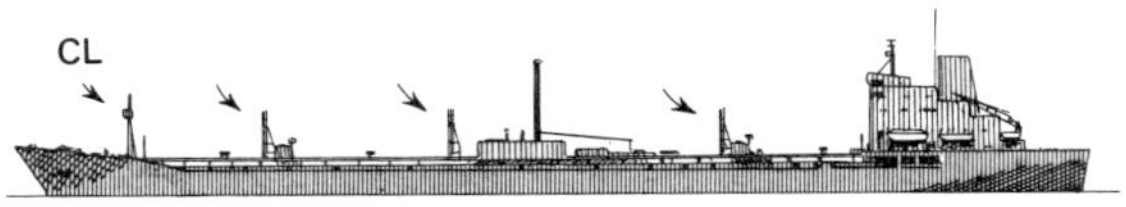

K_5MF H13

54680 CHAC. Me/No 1976; Ch; 17600; 170.72 × 10.01 (560.1 × 32.84); M; 15.5; ex FOSSANGER 1977. Sister: **54681 BACAB** (Me) ex BOW CLIPPER 1977.

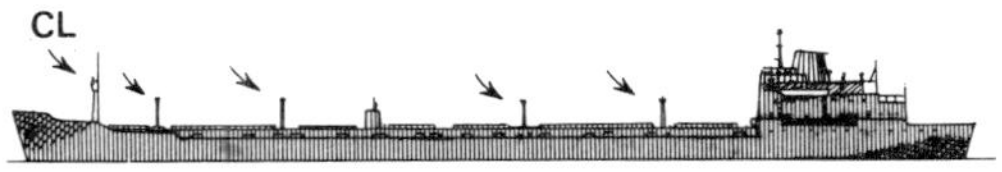

K_5MF H13

54690 KIMOLIAKI AIGLI; Gr/Sw 1962; B; 10800; 152.56 × 9.16 (500.52 × 30.05); M; 14.25; ex OINOUSSIAN CAPTAIN 1981; ex FALSTER 1972. Sister: **★54691 DING HAI** (RC) ex SUCCESSOR 1974; ex MATUMBA 1969.

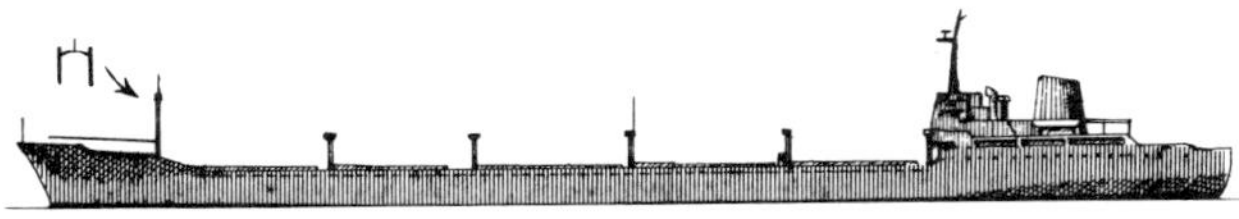

K_5MF H13

● **54700 POLINNIA.** It/It 1962; B; 17300; 192.03 × 10.61 (630.02 × 34.81); M; 16. Sisters (It flag): **54701 MASSIMO PRIMO 54702 UMBERTO D'AMATO** ex PEPPINA D'AMATO 1978; ex DONATELLA 1978.

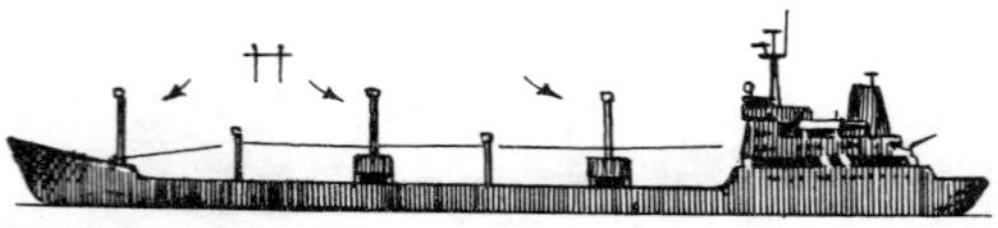

K_5MF H13
⋆**54710 NIKOLAY NOVIKOV.** Ru/Pd 1973; B/TC; 10200; 150.27 × 8.69 (493.01 × 28.51); M; 15; **'B-436'** type. Sisters: ⋆**54711 IVAN SYRYKH** ⋆**54712 VLADIMIR MORDVINOV** ⋆**54713 VLADIMIR TIMOFEYEV** The following are **'B-540'** type: ⋆**54714 KAPITAN MOCHALOV** ⋆**54715 KAPITAN BAKANOV** ⋆**54716 KAPITAN KIRIY** ⋆**54717 KONSTANTIN PETROVSKIY** ⋆**54718 MEKHANIK GORDYENKO** ⋆**54719 VLAS NICHKOV** ⋆**54720 KAPITAN DUBLITSKIY** ⋆**54721 KAPITAN MILOVZOROV** ⋆**54722 KAPITAN SAMOYLENKO** ⋆**54723 PETR SMIDOVICH** ⋆**54724 VASILIY MUSINSKIY** ⋆**54725 KAPITAN BURMAKIN** ⋆**54726 KAPITAN GLAZACHYEV** ⋆**54727 KAPITAN VASILYEVSKIY** ⋆**54728 KAPITAN ZAMYATIN** ⋆**54729 YURIY SAVINOV** ⋆**54730 BOTSMAN MOSHKOV** ⋆**54731 FEDOR VARAKSIN** ⋆**54732 KAPITAN SHEVCHENKO** ⋆**54733 KAPITAN LYUBCHENKO** ⋆**54734 PETR STRELKOV.**

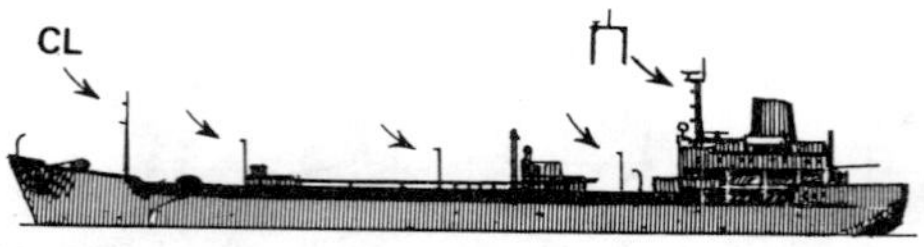

K_5MF H13
54740 CLERK-MAXWELL. Br/Br 1966; LGC; 8300; 140.67 × 8.25 (461.52 × 27.07); M; 17. Similar: **54741 MARIANO ESCOBEDO** (Me).

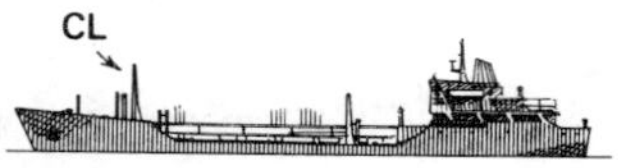

K_5MF H13
54750 MULTITANK BADENIA. Pa/No 1971; Tk; 1600; 91.22 × 5.53 (299.28 × 18.14); M; 13; ex MARK 1974. Sisters: **54751 MULTITANK HAMMONIA** (Cy) ex MULTITANK RHENANIA **54752 MULTITANK WESTFALIA** (Pa) ex SEAMARK 1974; May now be broken up following casualty.

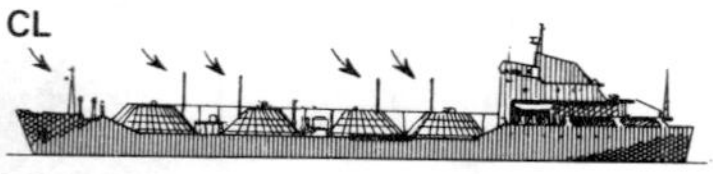

K_5MF H13
54760 EUCLIDE. It/Fr 1971; LGC; 5100; 107.02 × 6.09 (351.12 × 19.98); M; 15.5; ex EUCLIDES 1976.

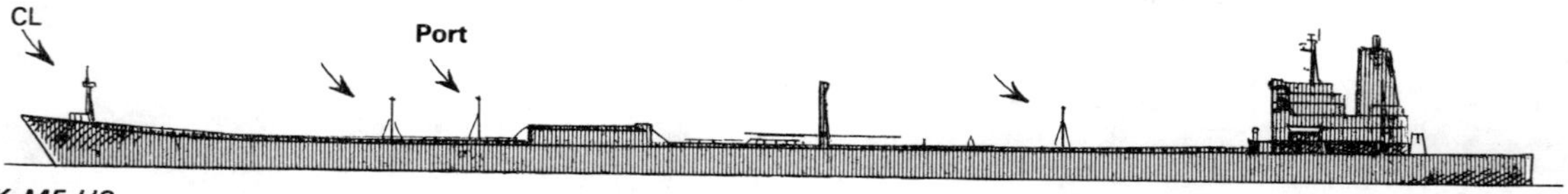

K_5MF H2
54770 THORSHOLM. No/Ja 1973; Tk; 140000; 342.91 × 21.78 (1125.03 × 71.46); M; 14.75. Sister: **54771 THORSAGA** (No).

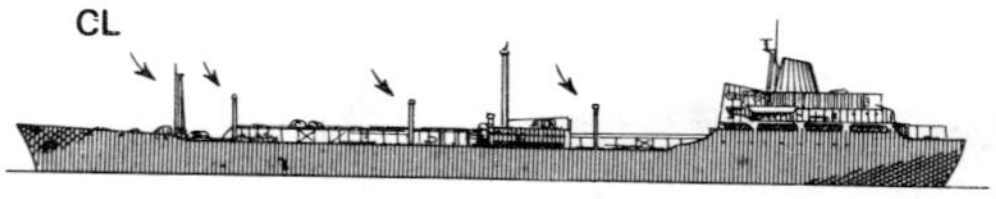

K_5MF H3
54780 LUIGI CASALE. It/It 1966; LGC; 10900; 150.48 × 8.86 (493.7 × 29.06); M; 16; ex CAPELLA 1973; ex FRANKLIN 1967; ex CAPELLA 1967; Launched as BENJAMIN FRANKLIN. Sister: **54781 PYTHAGORE** (Pa) ex ARQUIMEDES 1975.

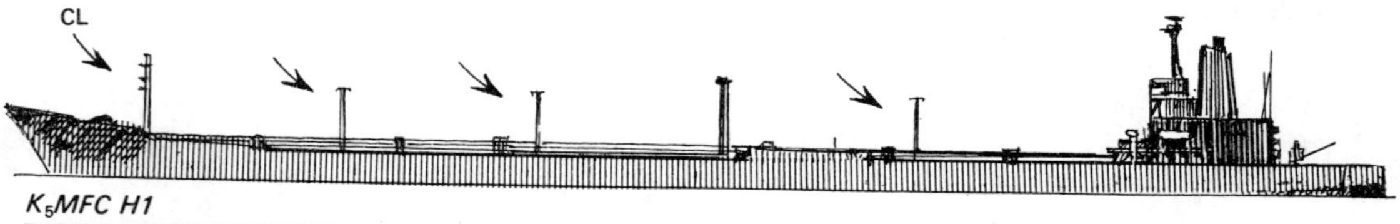

K_5MFC H1
54790 ESSO HONOLULU. Li/Ja 1974; Tk; 133000; 343.01 × 22.05 (1125.36 × 72.34); T; 16.25. Sisters (Li flag): **54791 ESSO BILBAO 54792 ESSO OSAKA.**

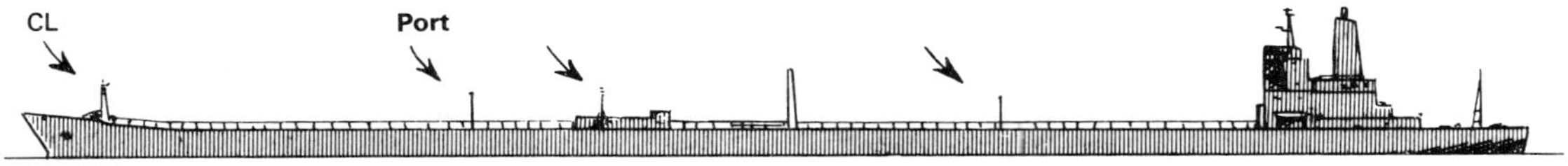

K_5MFK H
54800 YOKO MARU. Ja/Ja 1975; Tk; 135100; 331.5 × 20.55 (1087.6 × 67.42); T; 16.25; ex BARBARA T SHAHEEN 1976. Similar: **54801 JAPAN COSMOS** (Ja) **54802 MOBIL SWIFT** (Li) ex TAKAKURASAN MARU 1978.

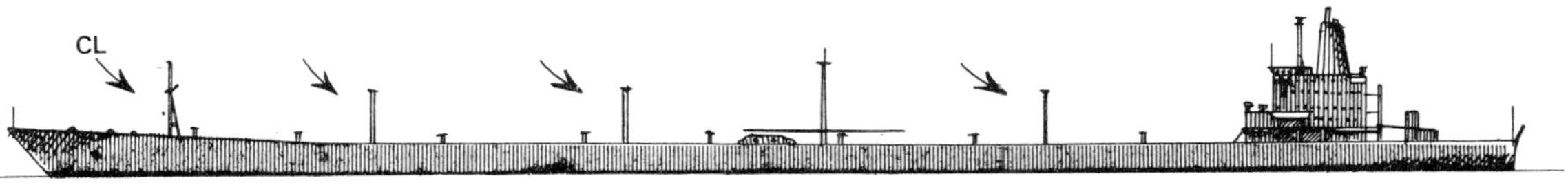

K_5MFK H
● **54810 RAS MAERSK.** De/De 1973; Tk; 143100; 347.18 × 22.22 (1139.04 × 72.9); T; 15. Sisters: **54811 ROBERT MAERSK** (De) **54812 ROMO MAERSK** (De) **54813 REGINA MAERSK** (De) **54814 ADELE** (Li) ex RASMINE MAERSK 1973 **54815 TEXACO IRELAND** (Pa) ex ROY MAERSK 1976 **54816 TEXACO NEDERLAND** (Pa) ex ROSA MAERSK 1975 **54817 TEXACO BRASIL** (Pa) ex RICHARD MAERSK 1975.

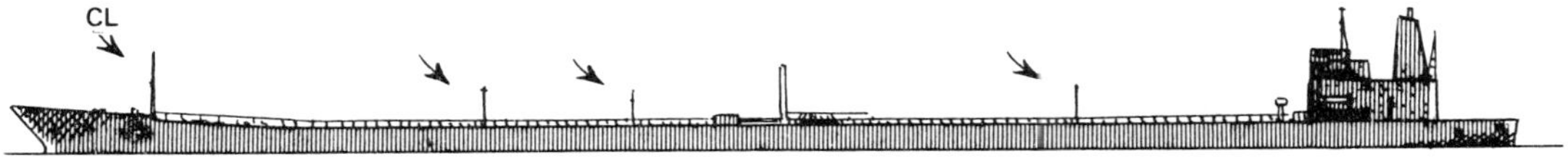

K_5MFK H
54820 ENERGY GROWTH. Li/Ja 1974; Tk; 105700; 319.92 × 19.66 (1049.61 × 64.5); T; 16.

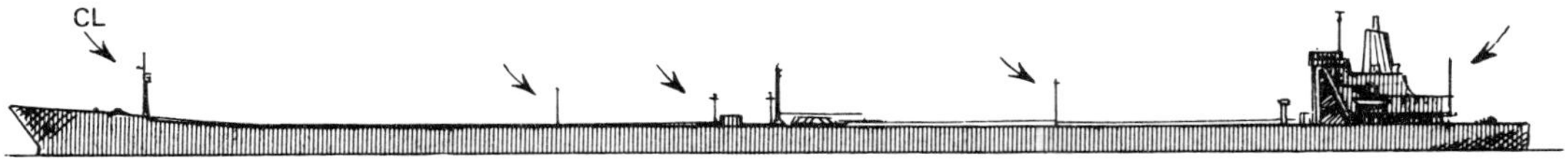

K_5MFK H
54830 TOHO MARU. Ja/Ja 1972; Tk; 115900; 319.34 × 19.5 (1047.7 × 63.98); T; 16.5.

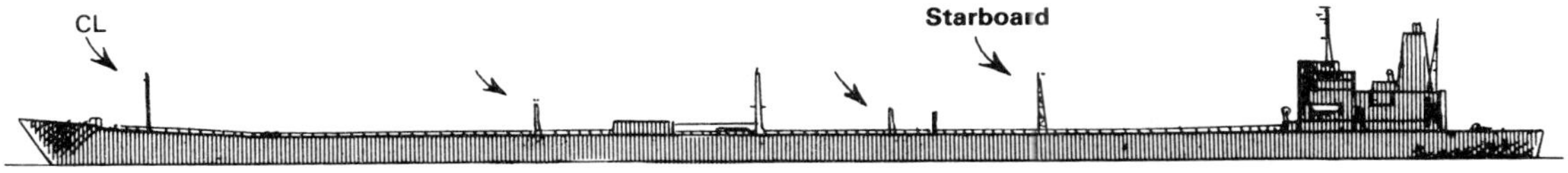

K_5MFK H
54840 TOKUYAMA MARU. Ja/Ja 1975; Tk; 136100; 337.07 × 19.94 (1105.87 × 65.42); T; 16.25.

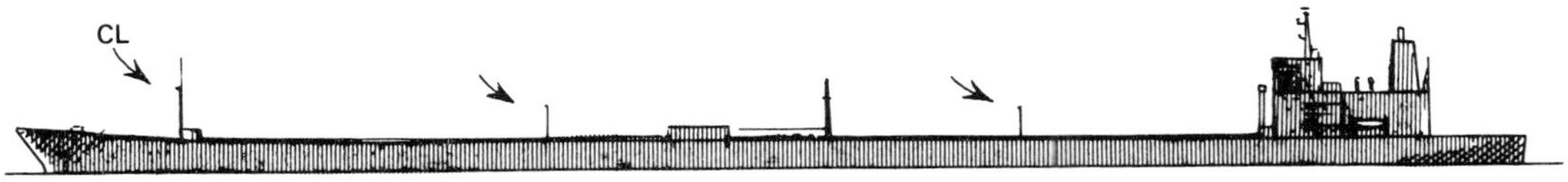

K_5MFK H
54850 TAKASE MARU. Ja/Ja 1970; Tk; 111700; 319.74 × 74.19 (1049.02 × 62.34); T; 16. Similar: **54851 WORLD MITSUBISHI** (Li) **54852 TAKOAKA MARU** (Ja).

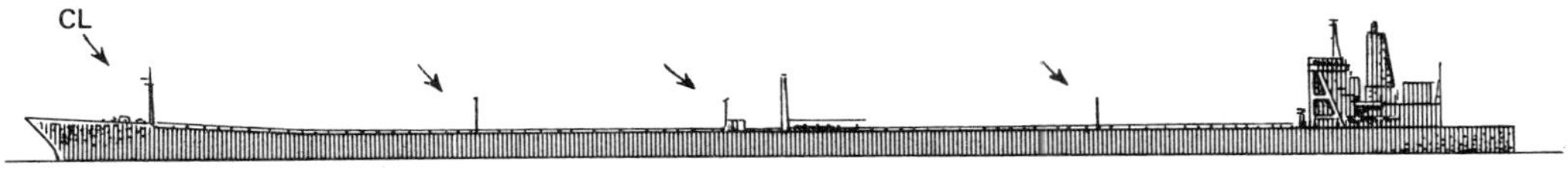

K_5MFK H
54860 WORLD EMPIRE. Pa/Ja 1972; Tk; 105100; 319.31 × 19.53 (1047.6 × 64.07); T; 16.

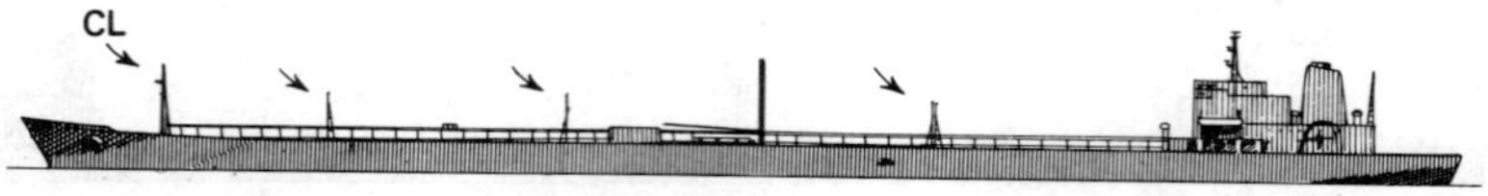

K_5MFK H

★54870 MESTA. Bu/Ja 1974; Tk; 46800; 237.01 × 12.92 (777.59 × 42.39); M; 16.5. Sister: **★54871 OSAM** (Bu).

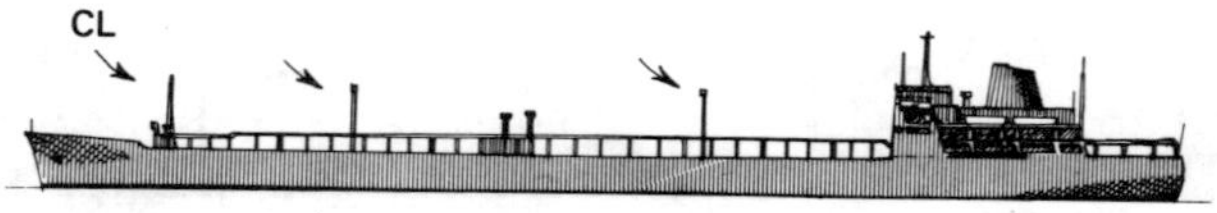

K_5MFK H

54880 PETRON GASUL; Pi/Ja 1962; LGC; 17800; 183.72 × 10.54 (602.76 × 34.58); M; 18.5; ex CONTANK BRIDGESTONE 1980; ex BRIDGESTONE MULTINA 1978; ex BRIDGESTONE MARU 1971; In use as a storage vessel.

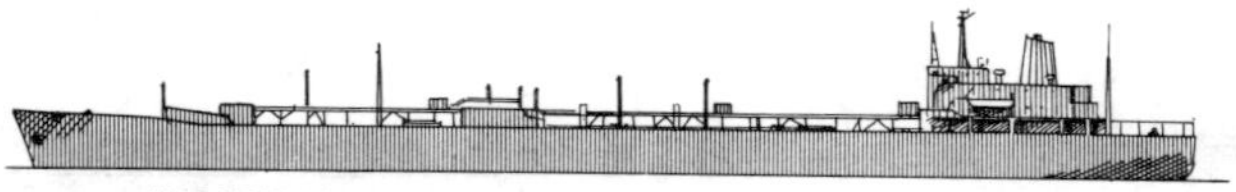

K_5MFK H

54890 YAMAHIDE MARU. Ja/Ja 1977; LGC; 24500; 187.48 × 10.52 (615.1 × 34.51); M; 15.

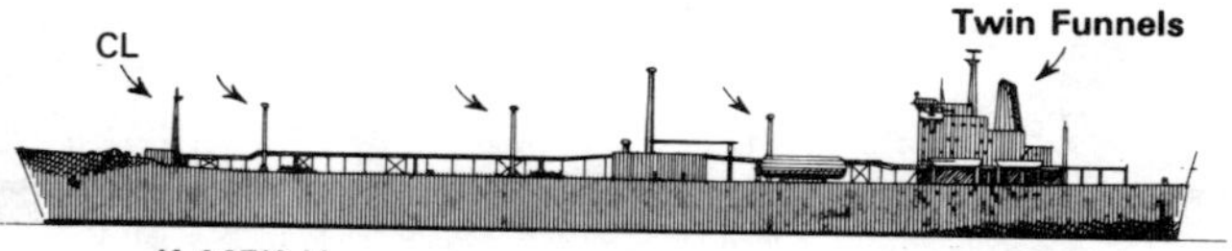

K_5MFK H

● **54900 GAY LUSSAC.** Pa/Fr 1969; LGC; 23800; 197.52 × 9.91 (648.03 × 32.51); M; 16.5. Sister: **54901 CAVENDISH** (Br).

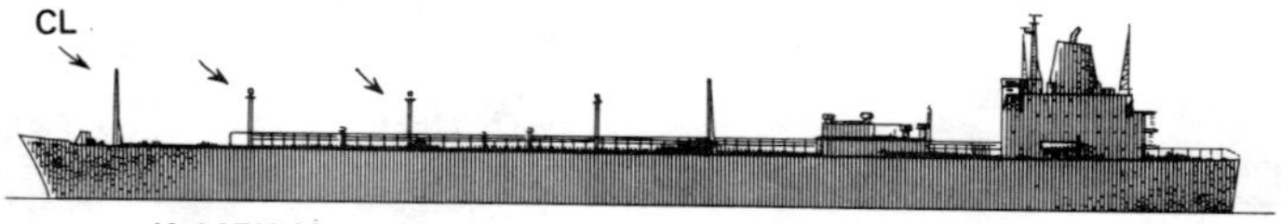

K_5MFK H

54910 BRIDGESTONE MARU V. Ja/Ja 1969; LGC; 41000; 210.52 × 12.2 (690.68 × 40.03); M; 14.75.

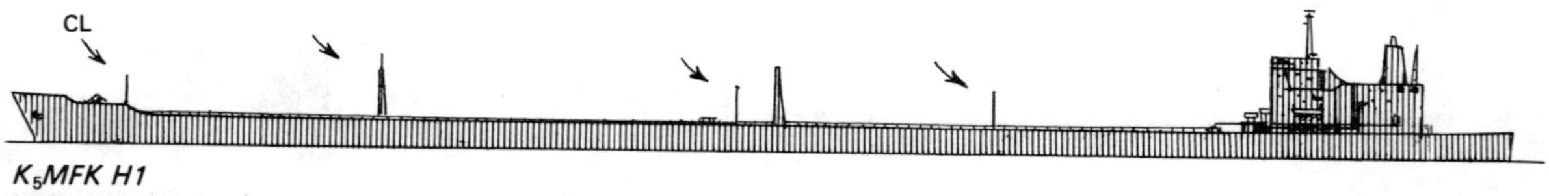

K_5MFK H1

54920 AIKO MARU. Ja/Ja 1976; Tk; 209800; 365.87 × 22.9 (1200.36 × 75.13); T; 15.75. Sisters: **54921 JINKO MARU** (Ja) **54922 AL REKKAH** (Ku) Possibly Similar: **54923 CHEVRON SOUTH AMERICA** (Li) **54924 CHEVRON NORTH AMERICA** (Li).

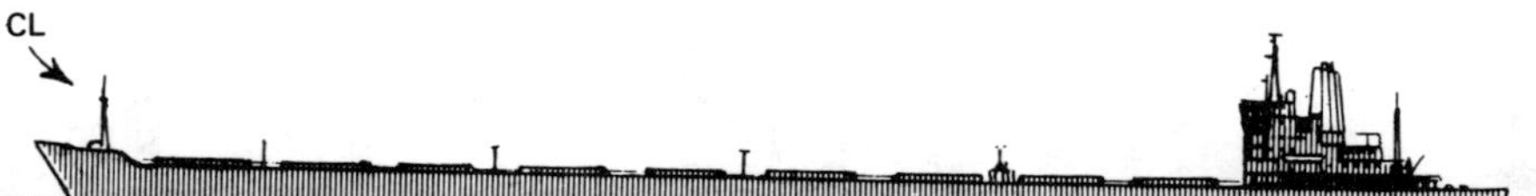

K_5MFK H1

54930 ERSKINE BRIDGE. Br/Ja 1973; B; 65900; 261.02 × 16.5 (856.36 × 54.13); M; 15. Sister: **54931 LAKE ALMANOR** (Li) ex SEVERN BRIDGE 1976 Similar: **54932 TAGELUS** (Ne) ex STIRLING BRIDGE 1979.

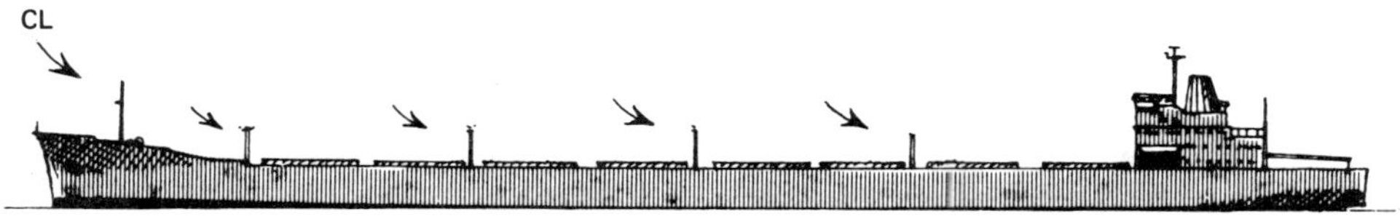

K5MFK H1
54940 CARSTEN RUSS. FRG/FRG 1971; B; 74500; 282.23 × 16.42 (925.95 × 53.87); M; 15.75. Sister: **54941 JACOB RUSS** (FRG) Similar: **54942 FUERTE VENTURA** (FRG) ex STADT BREMEN 1979.

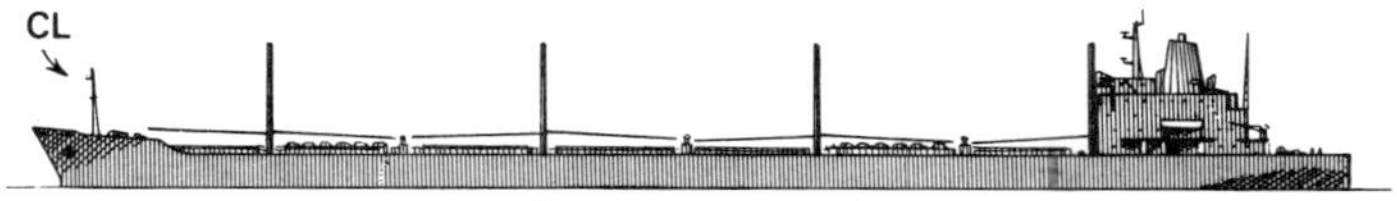

K5MFK H1
54950 CHOKO MARU. Ja/Ja 1970; B; 32000; 208.01 × 11.73 (682.45 × 38.48); M; 14.75. Similar (Li flag): **54951 MEXICAN GULF 54952 SPRAY DERRICK 54953 UNIONA** ex Y.S. VENTURE.

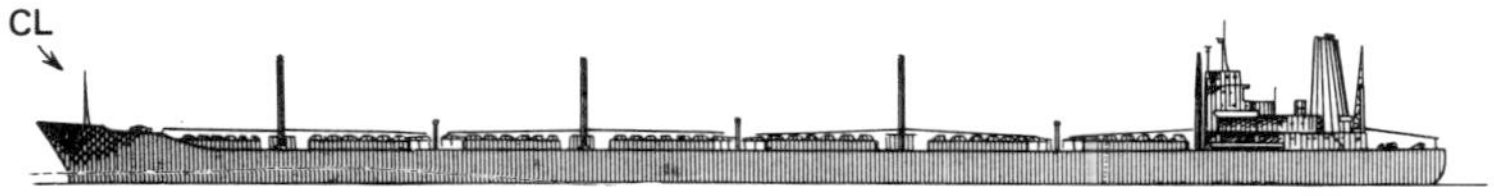

K5MFK H1
● **54960 EVELYN.** Li/Ja 1971; C; 30300; 225 × 12.46 (738.19 × 40.88); M; 14.75. Sisters: **54961 IVORY** (Li) **54962 PEACE VENTURE** (Li) **54963 WORLD VANGUARD** (Li) **54964 VELA** (Li) **54965 STAMY** (Gr) **54966 NORMAN VENTURE** (Sg) ex JAGUAR.

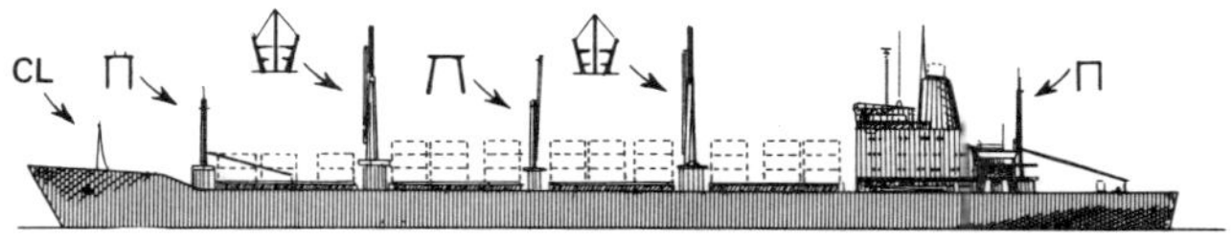

K5MFK H1
⋆**54970 JOZEF CONRAD KORZENIOWSKI.** Pd/Pd 1978; C/Con; 17600 190.28 × 9.55 (624.28 × 31.33); M; 25; **'B-467'** type. Sisters (Pd flag): **54971 ADAM MICKIEWICZ 54972 GENERAL FR. KLEEBERG** 1 further vessel under construction.

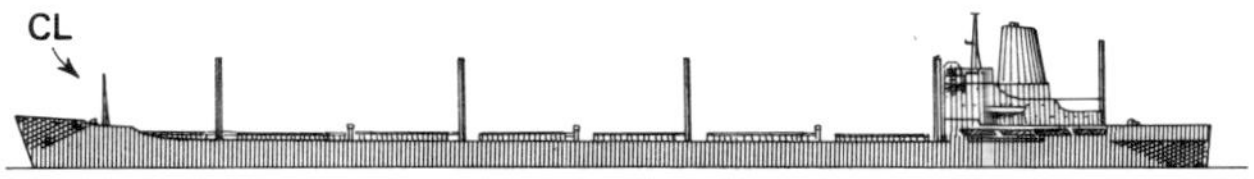

K5MFK H1
54980 WORLD NAVIGATOR. Li/Ja 1967; B; 22800; 190.02 × 12.27 (623.43 × 40.26); M; 15. Sisters (Li flag): **54981 WORLD NEGOTIATOR; 54982 WORLD NEWS; 54983 WORLD NOBILITY; 54984 WORLD NOMAD.** Some may not be fitted with cargo gear. See WORLD NEIGHBOUR.

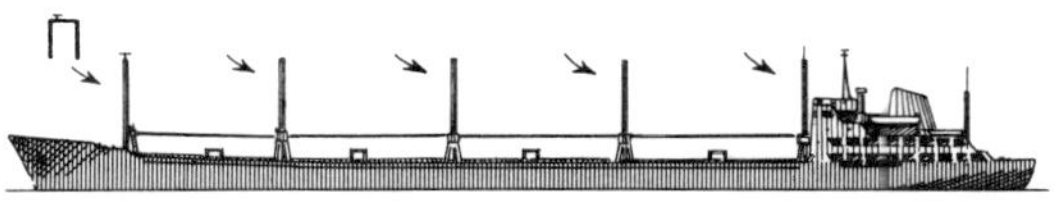

K5MFK H1
54990 PENN HILLS. Sg/Fr 1960; B; 12800; 162.57 × 9.17 (533.37 × 30.08); M; 14.25; ex MONARCH 1977; ex JULIEN DELMAS 1976; ex OPPELIA 1968.

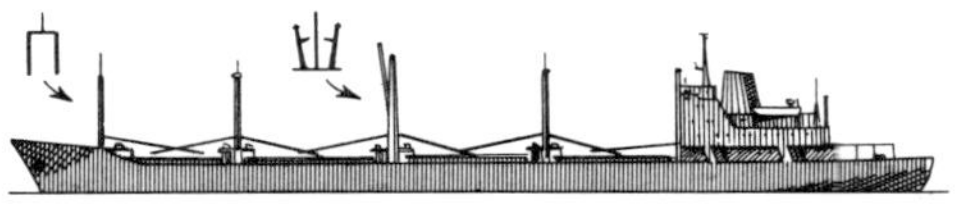

K5MFK H1
55000 DIANA. Bz/Bz 1968; C; 6900; 145.52 × 8.75 (477.43 × 28.71); M; 17; ex BAGE 1968. Probable Sister: **55001 CORINA** (Bz) ex CURVELO 1968.

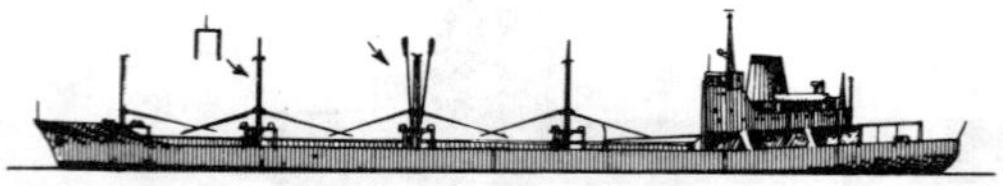

K_5MFK H

● **55010 PRESIDENTE KENNEDY.** Bz/Bz 1965; C; 6900/9100; 145.5 × 7.94/8.75 (477.36 × 26.05/28.7); M; 15.5. Sisters: **55011 ALMIRANTE GRACA ARANHA** (Bz) **55012 EL MEXICANO** (Me) **55013 PUEBLA** (Me) Similar: **55014 BUARQUE** (Bz) **55015 ROMEO BRAGA** (Bz).

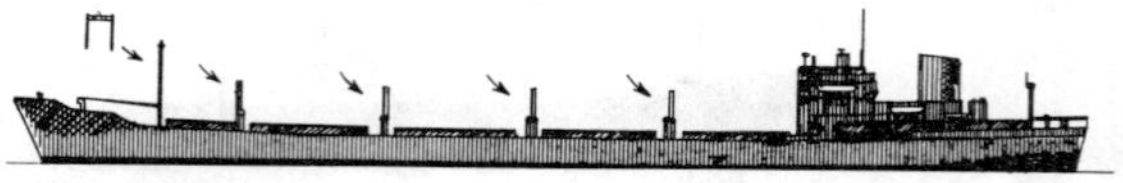

K_5MFK H1

55020 FIVI. Cy/Sw 1950; B; 13100; 169.78 × 9.82 (557.02 × 32.22); M; 14.5; ex ASTYANAX 1980; ex SLIEDRECHT 1974; Converted tanker 1960.

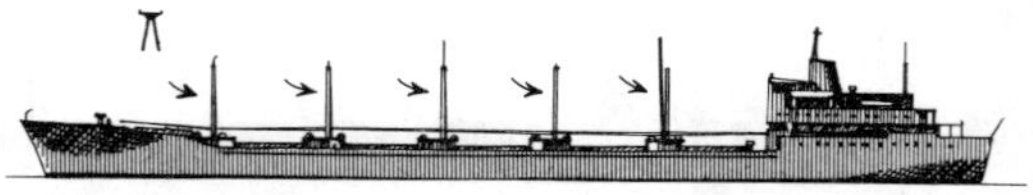

K_5MFK H13

55030 TRITON. Gr/Sw 1963; C; 11100; 154.84 × 9.48 (508 × 31.1); M; —; ex SWAZI MAIDEN 1979; ex TRITON 1978; ex JAG ANAND 1976; ex CEDAR 1968. Similar: **55031 UNION DARWIN** (Pa) ex OSWEGO TAPPER 1980; ex SUNSHINE STATE 1972; ex VIKARA 1969 **55032 LEDA** (Gr) ex GEIRA 1978; ex SUNGEIRA 1972; ex GEIRA 1969 **55033 IRAN HOJJAT** (Ir) ex ARYA FAR 1980; ex ARYA PEY 1973; ex VINSTRA 1969.

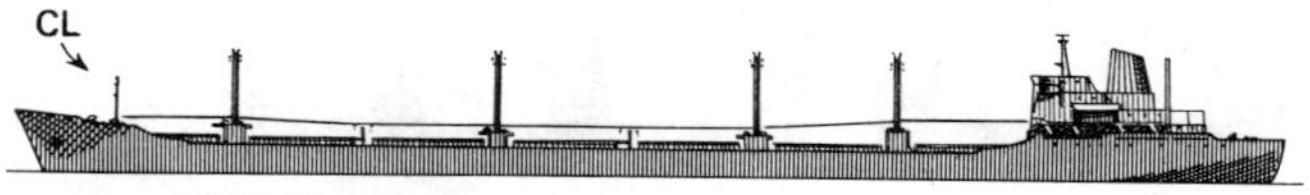

K_5MFK H13

● **55040 GRECIAN LEGEND.** Li/Br 1969; B; 23000; 201.78 × 11.61 (662 × 38.09); M; 15. Sister: **55041 GRECIAN SPIRIT** (Li).

K_5MFK H13

55050 HAR CARMEL. Is/Br 1965; B; 22000; 196.76 × 11.73 (645.54 × 38.48); M; 14; ex HAR CARMEL I 1973; ex SHEAF MOUNT 1972.

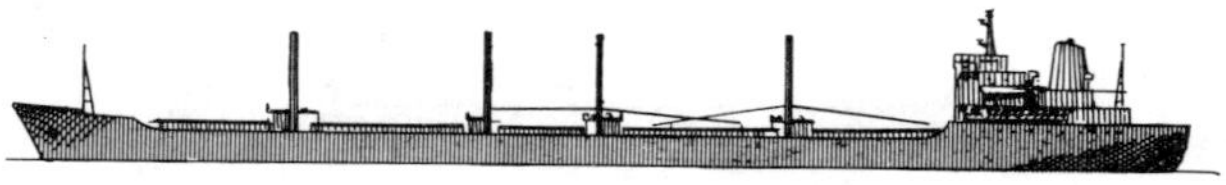

K_5MFK H13

● **55060 MARITIME ACE.** Pa/Ja 1971; B; 19700; 185.5 × 11.15 (608.6 × 36.58); M; 14.75. Sisters (Pa flag): **55061 MARITIME CHALLENGE 55062 MARITIME FORTUNE 55063 MARITIME JUSTICE 55064 MARITIME TRADER 55065 MARITIME UNITY** (Li flag): **55066 MARITIME HARMONY 55067 EASTERN HORNET 55068 EASTERN JADE** ex MARQUEE 1980; ex EASTERN JADE 1979 **55069 EASTERN LILAC 55070 EASTERN TREASURE 55071 GOLDEN DAISY 55072 GOLDEN DOLPHIN 55073 WORLD RUBY** (My flag): **55074 BUNGA CHEMPAKA** Similar (Br flag): **55075 ERRADALE.**

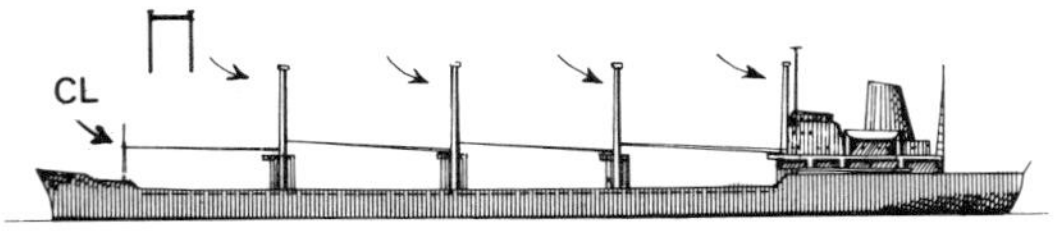

K_5MFK H13
55080 ALICAMPOS. Gr/Ja 1968; B; 11400; 156.17 × 9.53 (512.37 × 31.27); M; 15; ex MARITIME QUEEN 1980; **'HITACHI STANDARD 18'** type. Sister: **55081 MARITIME PIONEER** (Pa).

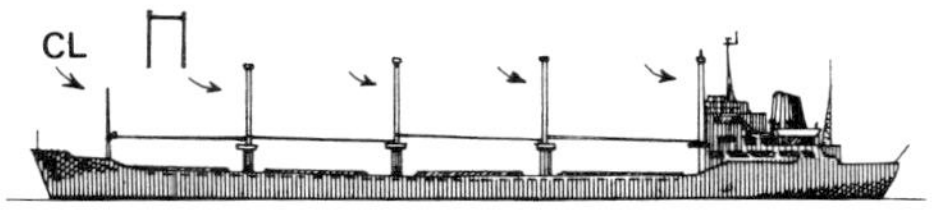

K_5MFK H13
55090 AIGEORGIS. Gr/Ja 1964; C; 8100; 137.52 × 8.31 (451.18 × 27.26); M; 14.5; ex SOLOMON CAREER 1980; ex YAMATADA MARU 1976.

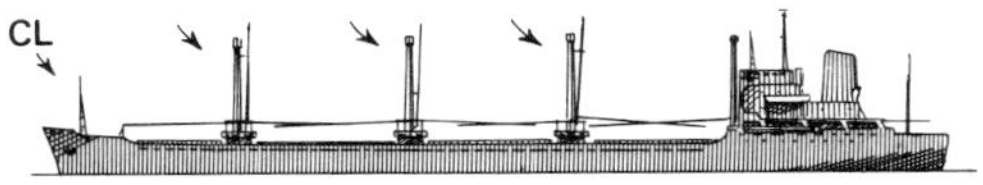

K_5MFK H13
55100 LISANA. Li/Ja 1968; B; 9400; 143.68 × 8.99 (472 × 29.5); M; 14.5. Similar: **55101 ENATON** (Gr) ex MARITIME LEADER 1979 **55102 MARIA XILAS** (Gr) ex EASTERN UNION 1971.

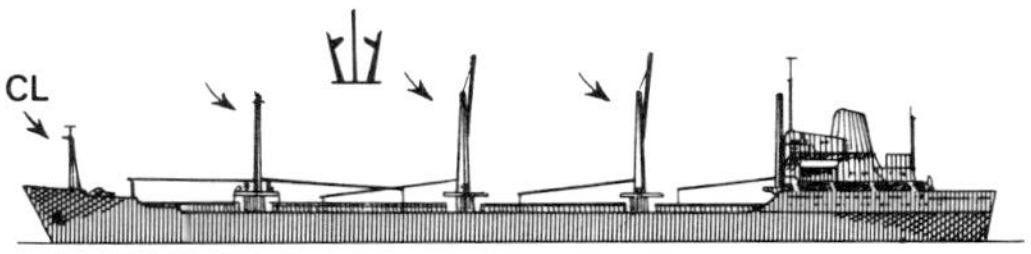

K_5MFK H13
● **55110 MAERSK PINTO.** FRG/FRG 1971; C; 7600/10900; 154.87 × 8.66/9.79 (508.1 × 28.41/32.12); M; 18.5; ex MAERSK MANGO 1978; ex LUISE LEONHARDT 1975.

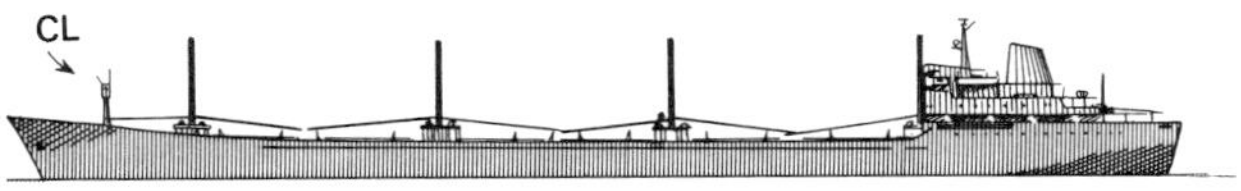

K_5MFK H13
55120 NORSE TRANSPORTER. Tu/No 1966; B; 16900; 190.79 × 10.12 (625.95 × 33.2); M; 17.5.

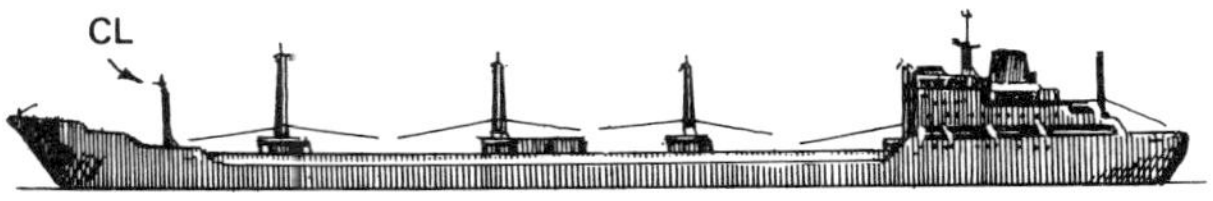

K_5MFK H13
⋆**55130 KARSKOYE MORE;** Ru/Fr 1972; FC; 18300; 186.8 × 7.75 (612.86 × 25.43); M; 19. Sister: ⋆**55131 OKHOTSKOYE MORE** (Ru).

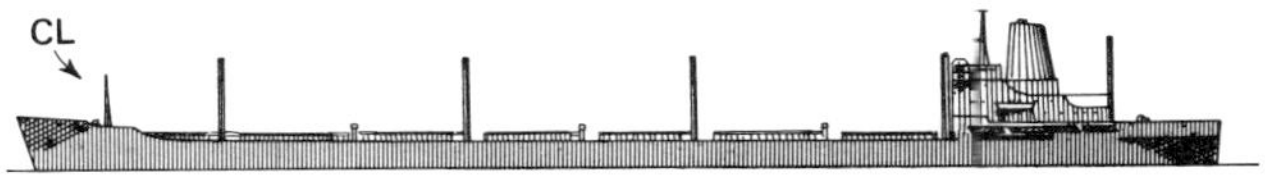

K_5MFK H13
55140 WORLD NAVIGATOR. Li/Ja 1967; B; 22800; 190.02 × 12.27 (623.43 × 40.26); M; 15. Sisters: **55141 WORLD NEGOTIATOR** (Li) **55142 WORLD NEWS** (Li) **55143 WORLD NOBILITY** (Li) **55144 WORLD NOMAD** (Li) Some may not be fitted with cargo gear. See WORLD NEIGHBOUR.

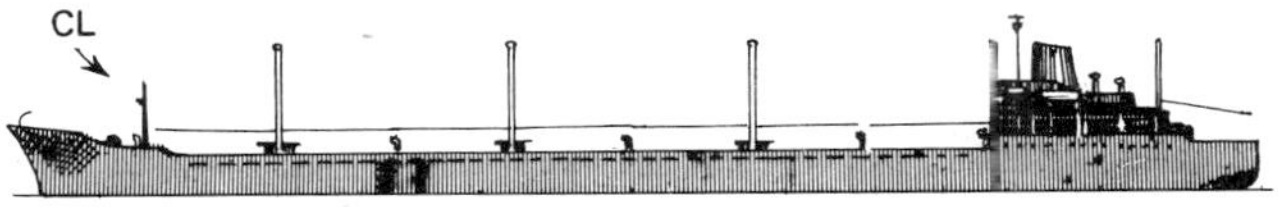

K_5MFK H13
55150 MARATHA PROGRESS. In/FRG 1964; B; 22200; 197.97 × 11.29 (649.51 × 37.04); M; 15.

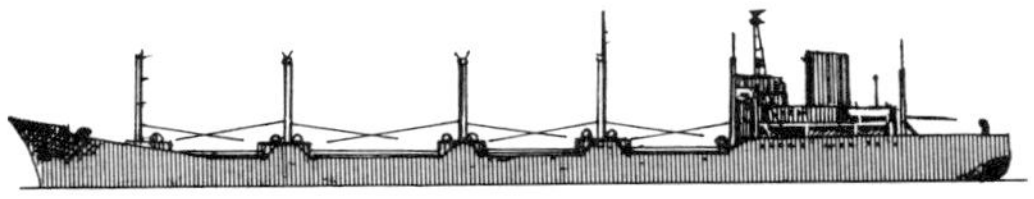

K_5MFK H13
55160 PAPACAROLOS. Gr/Ja 1959; O; 10200; 156.11 × 8.54 (512.17 × 28.02); M; 13; ex TOMIURA MARU 1975.

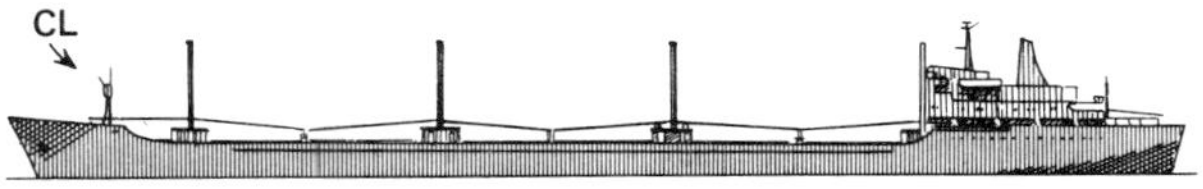

K_5MFK H13
55170 IAPETOS. Sg/No 1963; B; 16300; 186.52 × 10.78 (611.94 × 35.37); M; 17; ex TURICUM; ex IVORY STAR 1975; ex JAROSA 1972.

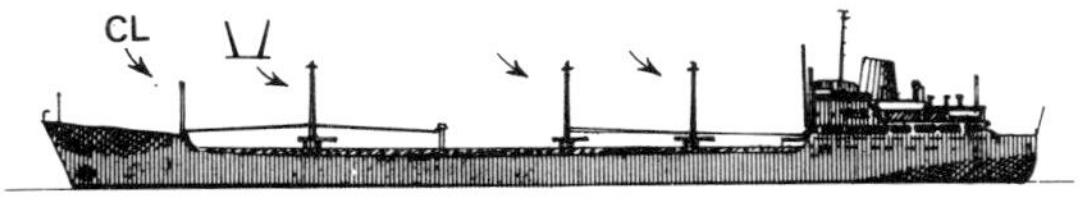

K_5MFK H13
55180 RAMIN. Ia/FRG 1960; B; 10400; 157.69 × 9.21 (517.36 × 30.22); M; 14; ex DINA 1975; ex ALTERANI 1967.

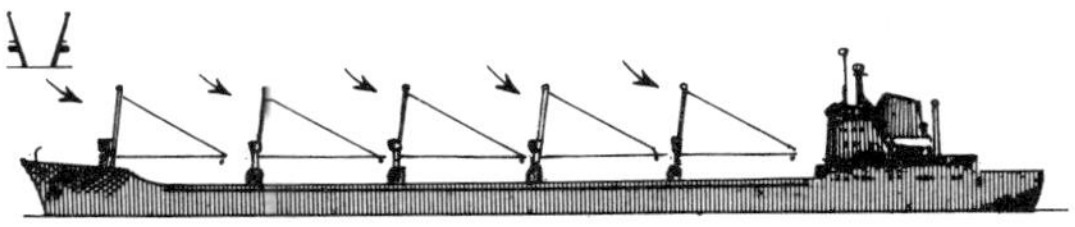

K_5MFK H13
55190 DAPHNA. Cy/FRG 1963; C; 11600; 160.03 × 8.7 (525.03 × 28.54); M; —; ex MIRETA 1980; ex VESPERA 1979; ex HELENA I 1979; ex IVAN DELMAS 1976; ex TIHA 1970.

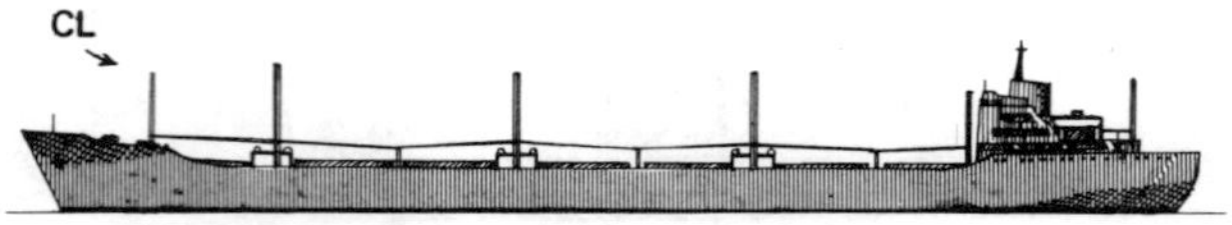

K_5MFK H13
55200 EPTA DAFNES. Gr/Br 1964; B; 16300; 186.09 × 10.85 (610.53 × 35.6); M; —; ex ANTHONY 1981; ex GRAIGWERDD 1974. Sister: **55201 GLOBAL SUN** (Ko) ex GRAIGFFION.

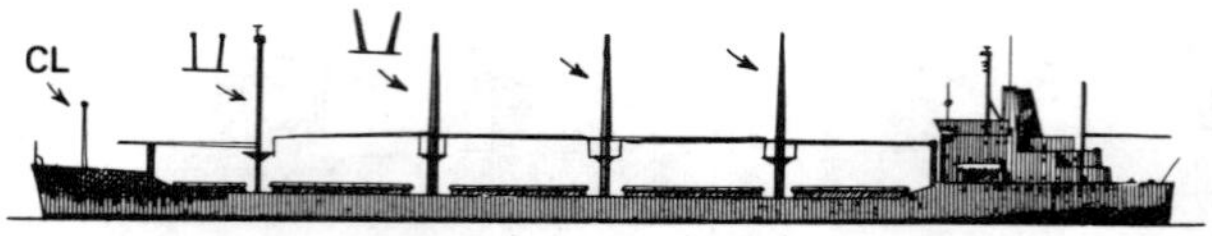

K_5MFK H13
● **55210 CAPETAN MANOLIS HAZIMANOLIS.** Li/Ne 1973; B/Con; 18100; 181.67 × 11.24 (596.03 × 36.88); M; 16; ex HAMBURGER WAPPEN 1977; Converted from bulk carrier 1978. Sister: **55211 OCEAN TRADER** (Sg) ex BARENDRECHT 1980; ex ARABIAN UNITY; ex BARENDRECHT 1978; ex HAMBURGER FLAGGE 1978.

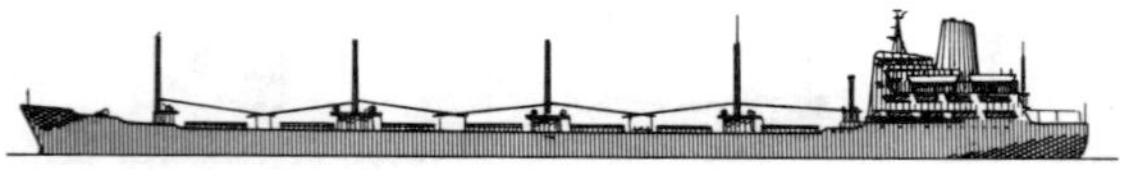

K_5MFK H13
55220 BHASKARA. In/Ja 1965; OO; 15500; 169.02 × 9.63 (554.53 × 31.6); M; 14.5; ex BHASKARA JAYANTI 1973. Sisters: **55221 CHANAKYA** (In) ex CHANAKYA JAYANTI 1974 **55222 LEELAVATI** (In) ex LEELAVATI JAYANTI 1974.

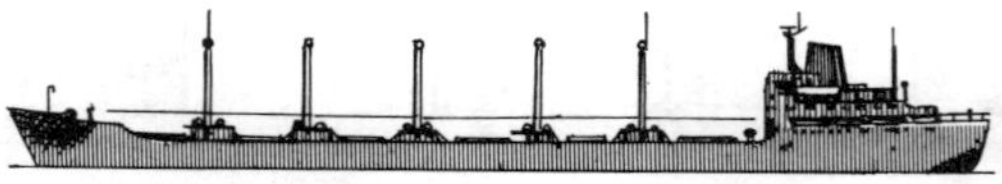

K_5MFK H13
55230 TAI TUNG. Tw/Ja 1964; C; 10700/11100; 155.25 × 8.92/9.45 (509.35 × 29.27/31); M; 15; ex OCEAN ENDURANCE 1973; ex STEEL ENGINEER 1971; ex BLUE MASTER 1969.

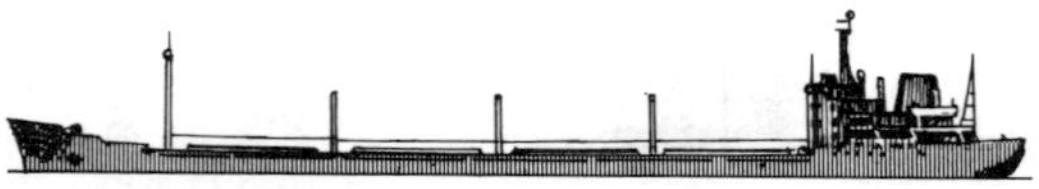

K_5MFK H13
55240 LAWTONA. Pa/Ja 1960; O; 12300; 161.5 × 8.94 (529.86 × 29.33); M; 13; ex YOSHU MARU 1978; ex YAMAHIRO MARU 1961.

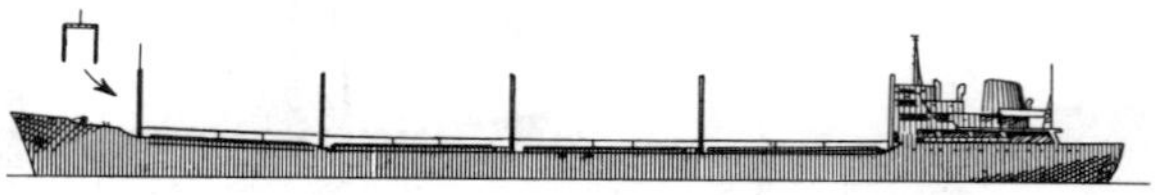

K_5MFK H13
55250 SUNNY TRADER. Pa/Ja 1962; O; 15600; 176.84 × 9.83 (580.18 × 32.25); M; 13.25; ex KOTOURA MARU 1971.

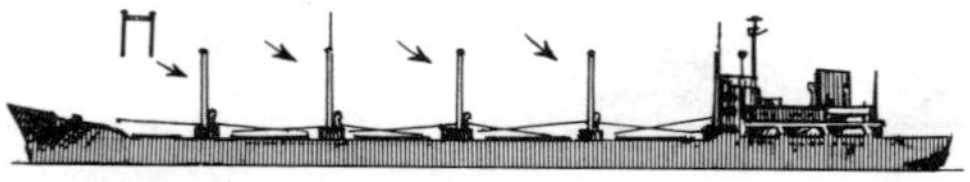

K_5MFK H13
55260 NOBLE FIVE. Pa/Ja 1959; B; 9000; 148.52 × 9.04 (487.27 × 29.66); M; 13.5; ex ARCHANGELOS MICHAIL 1980; ex KOKUSAI MARU 1970.

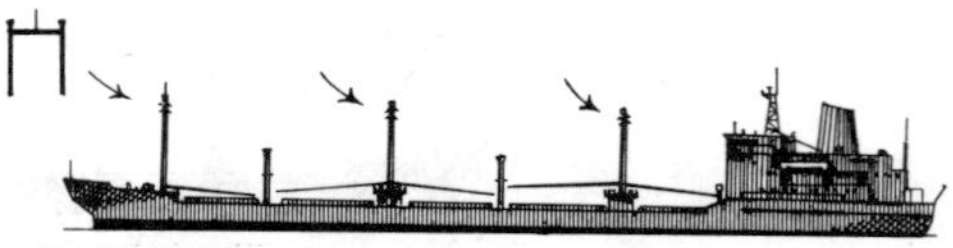

K_5MFK H13
⋆**55270 KRAS.** Ys/Ys 1968; B; 8600; 138.46 × 9 (454.27 × 29.53); M; 13.

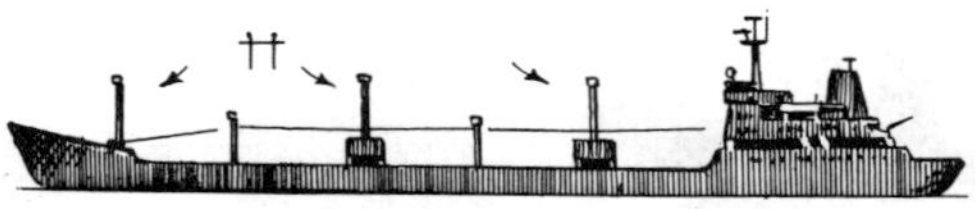

K_5MFK H13
⋆**55280 NIKOLAY NOVIKOV.** Ru/Pd 1973; B/TC; 10200; 150.27 × 8.69 (493.01 × 28.51); M; 15; **'B-436'** type. Sisters: ⋆**55281 IVAN SYRYKH** ⋆**55282 VLADIMIR MORDVINOV** ⋆**55283 VLADIMIR TIMOFEYEV** The following are **'B-540'** type ⋆**55284 KAPITAN MOCHALOV** ⋆**55285 KAPITAN BAKANOV** ⋆**55286 KAPITAN KIRIY** ⋆**55287 KONSTANTIN PETROVSKIY** ⋆**55288 MEKHANIK GORDYENKO** ⋆**55289 VLAS NICHKOV** ⋆**55290 KAPITAN DUBLITSKIY** ⋆**55291 KAPITAN MILOVZOROV** ⋆**55292 KAPITAN SAMOYLENKO** ⋆**55293 PETR SMIDOVICH** ⋆**55294 VASILIY MUSINSKIY** ⋆**55295 KAPITAN BURMAKIN** ⋆**55296 KAPITAN GLAZACHYEV** ⋆**55297 KAPITAN VASILYEVSKIY** ⋆**55298 KAPITAN ZAMYATIN** ⋆**55299 YURIY SAVINOV** ⋆**55300 BOTSMAN MOSHKOV** ⋆**55301 FEDOR VARAKSIN** ⋆**55302 KAPITAN SHEVCHENKO** ⋆**55303 KAPITAN LYUBCHENKO** ⋆**55304 PETR STRELKOV.**

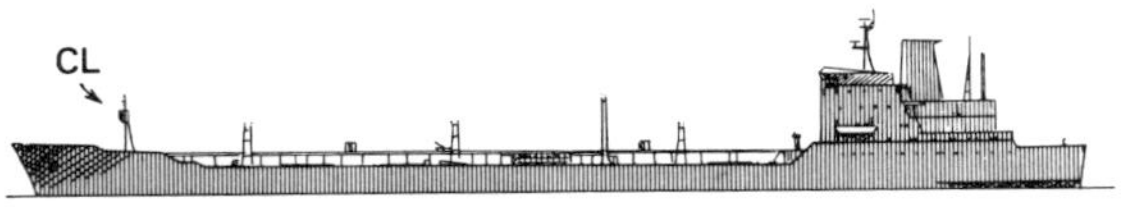

K_5MFK H13
55310 SOFIE. Sw/Sw 1974; Tk; 18300; 170.77 × 10.97 (560.27 × 35.99); M; 15.5. Sisters: **55311 SONJA** (Sw) **55312 RABIGH BAY I** (Gr) ex SUSANNE 1980 Similar: ⋆**55313 TATRY** (Pd) ⋆**55314 KARKONOSZE** (Pd) ⋆**55315 PIENINY II** (Pd) **55316 BEJAIA** (Ag); Launched as MESSINIAKI PROODOS **55317 BETHIOUA** (Ag); Launched as MESSINIAKI DOXA Possible Sister: **55318 SELMA** (Sw).

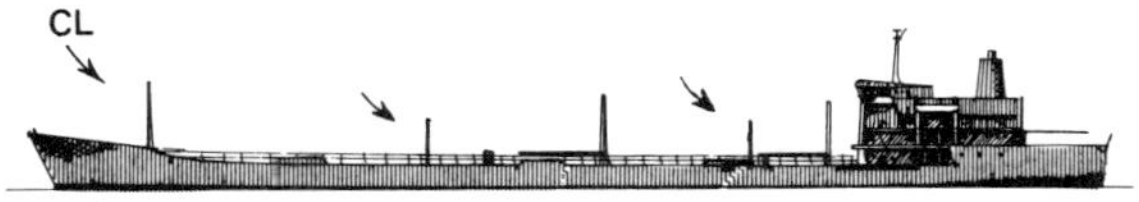

K_5MFK H13
● **55320 STOLT LION.** Br/Br 1971; Tk/Ch; 16500; 170.82 × 9.91 (560.43 × 32,51); M; 14.75.

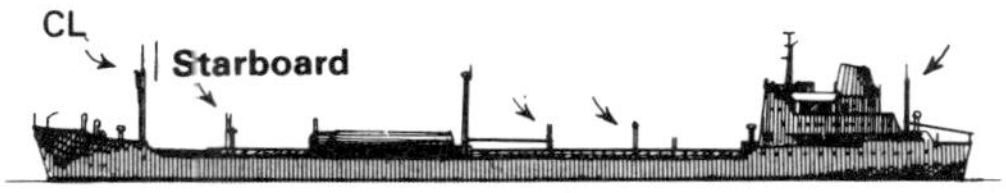

K_5MFK H13
55330 CANSO TRANSPORT. Ca/No 1967; Tk/Ch; 9400; 149.41 × 9.02 (490.19 × 29.59); M; 16; ex LONN. Sister: **55331 COASTAL TRANSPORT** (Ca) ex BIRK.

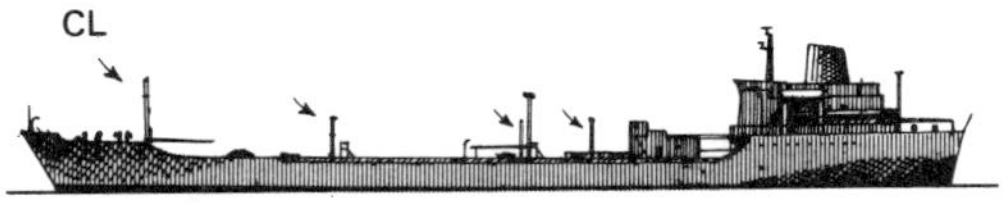

K_5MFK H13
55340 WILTSHIRE. Br/Br 1968; LGC; 10000; 151.7 × 8.23 (497.7 × 27); M; 16.

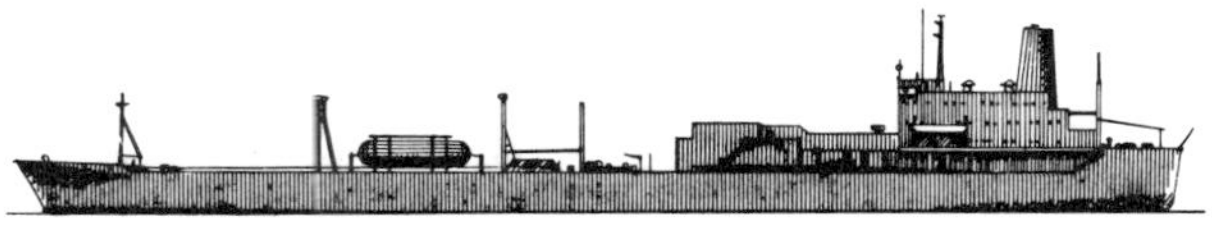

K_5MFK H13
55350 DANIAN GAS. Li/Sw 1969; LGC; 18000; 184.74 × 9.7 (606.1 × 31.82); M; 17; ex RELIANCE GAS 1977; ex AMY MULTINA 1977; ex PHILLIPS ARKANSAS 1971.

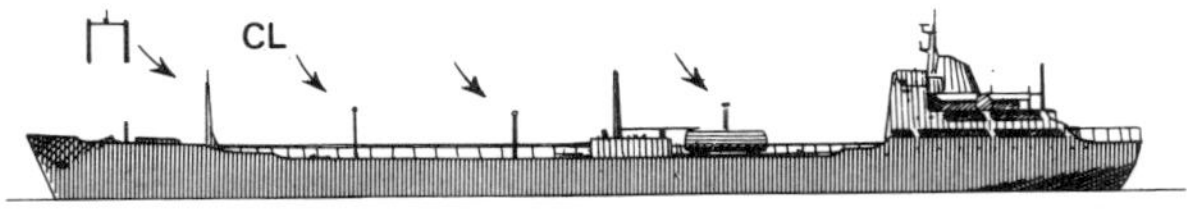

K_5MFK H13
55360 ISFONN. No/Fr 1967; LGC; 15000; 177.2 × 7.72 (581.36 × 25.33); M; 16.

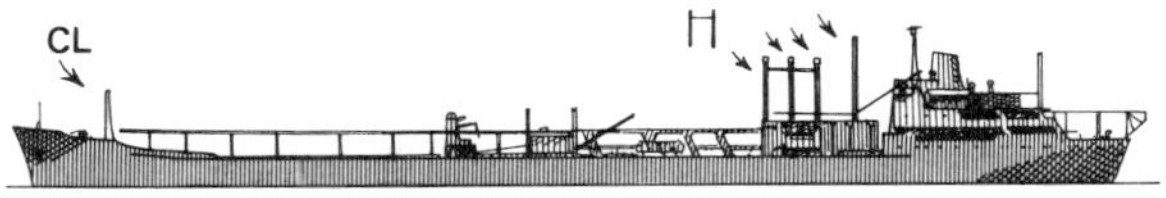

K_5MFK H13
55370 HARVEST TRADER. Pa/Sw 1962; FF; 17600; 178.09 × 10.9 (584.28 × 35.76); M; 15.25; ex INTERPECHE 1980; ex MARINE HARVESTER 1979; ex NORGLOBAL 1978; ex KRATOS 1970; Converted from ore carrier 1970.

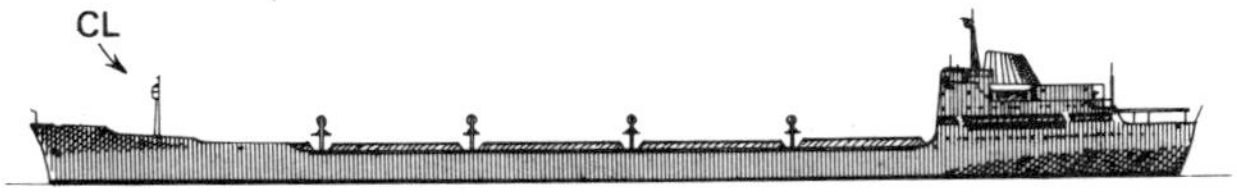

K_5MFK H13
55380 SIRENA. Li/No 1963; O; 18800; 184.16 × 10.55 (604.2 × 34.61); M; 13; ex VIVITA 1977. Sister: **55381 VIDA** (Li) ex LIVANITA 1978 Similar: **55382 BEATRICE** (Li) ex SENORITA 1977 **55383 HERA** (Li) ex ANGELITA 1978.

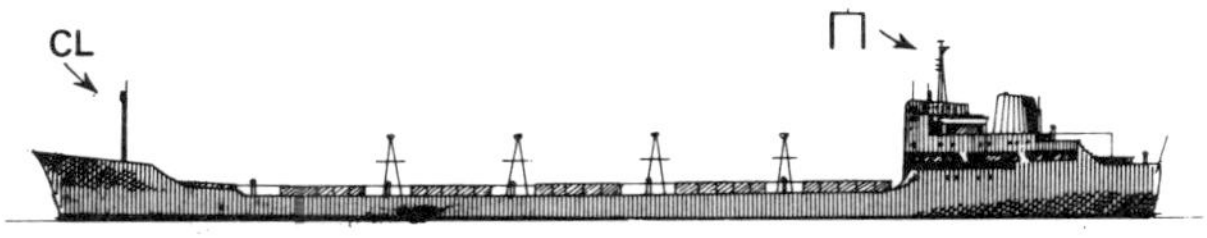

K_5MFK H13
55390 REGAL SKY. Gr/FRG 1963; B; 14700; 179.38 × 10.93 (588.52 × 35.86); M; 14; ex LANCING 1973.

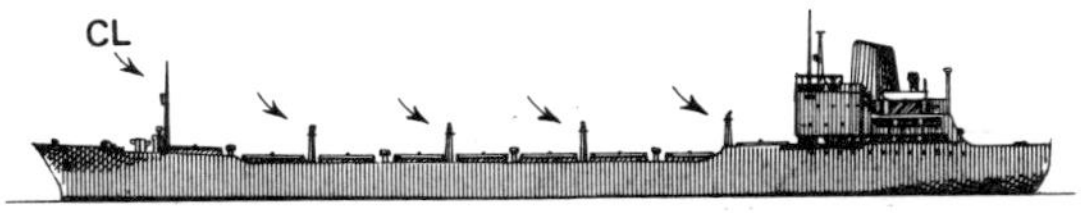

K_4MFK H13
55400 JAGAT MOHINI. In/FRG 1958; B; 12200; 160.97 × 9.39 (528.12 × 30.8); M; 14; ex RHEINSTAHL 1969. Sister: **55401 JAGAT SWAMINI** (In) ex OTTO SPRINGORUM 1971.

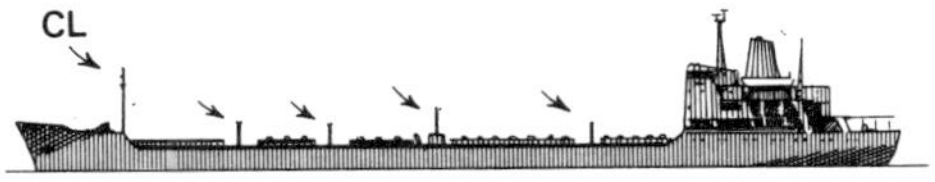

K_5MFK H13
⋆**55410 MUSALA;** Bu/Ja 1967; B; 9100; 139.83 × 9.26 (458.76 × 30.38); M; 14. Sisters: ⋆**55411 RUEN** (Bu) ⋆**55412 VEJEN** (Bu).

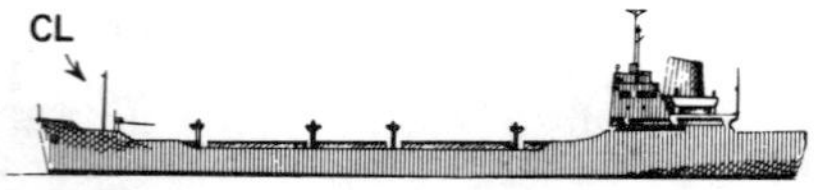

K_5MFK H13
55420 TONY. Gr/FRG 1962; B; 6200; 121.34 × 8.51 (398.1 × 27.92); M; 13; ex ATLAS 1979; ex ECKENHEIM 1974. Sister: **55421 ATLANTIS** (Gr) ex LANGELSHEIM 1974.

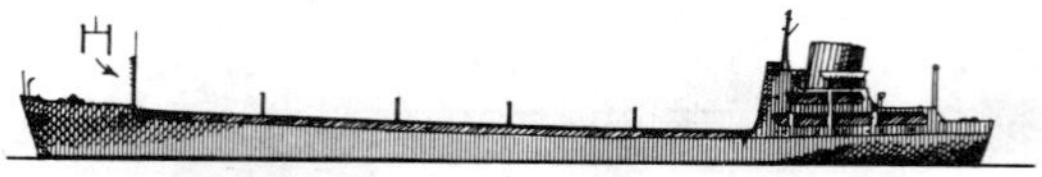

K_5MFK H13
55430 DUGLASIA. It/Br 1958; O; 9700; 153.96 × 8.85 (505.12 × 29.04); M; 12; ex WELCOME 1976; ex EDENMORE 1975. Sister: **55431 CAPITAN ALBERTO** (It) ex SAGAMORE 1975.

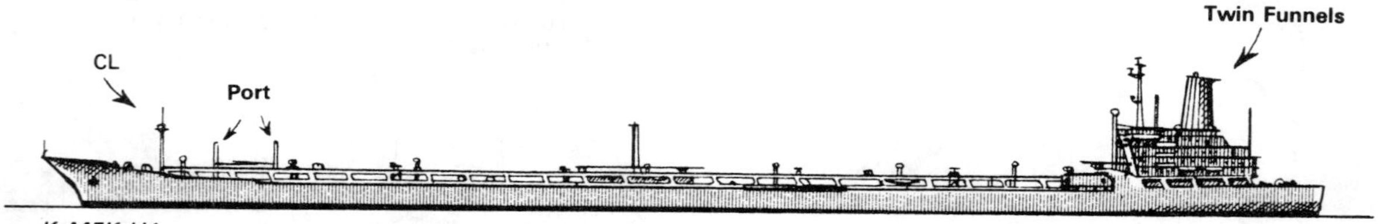

K_5MFK H1
55440 ARTEAGA. Sp/Sp 1972; Tk; 163800; 347.94 × 24.82 (1141.54 × 81.43); TST; 14.5. Sister: **55441 BUTRON** (Sp) Similar: **55442 OCEAN PARK** (Ko) **55443 CHUN WOO** (Ko).

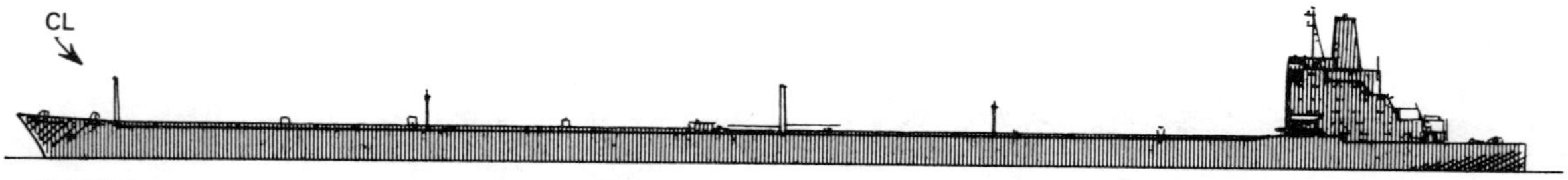

K_4MF H
55450 ESSO NORTHUMBRIA. Br/Br 1970; Tk; 126500; 348.47 × 19.98 (1143.27 × 65.55); T; 15.75. Sisters: **55451 ESSO HIBERNIA** (Br) **55452 ESSO ULIDIA** (Br) Similar: **55453 ESSO COPENHAGEN** (Li) **55454 ESSO SKANDIA** (Li).

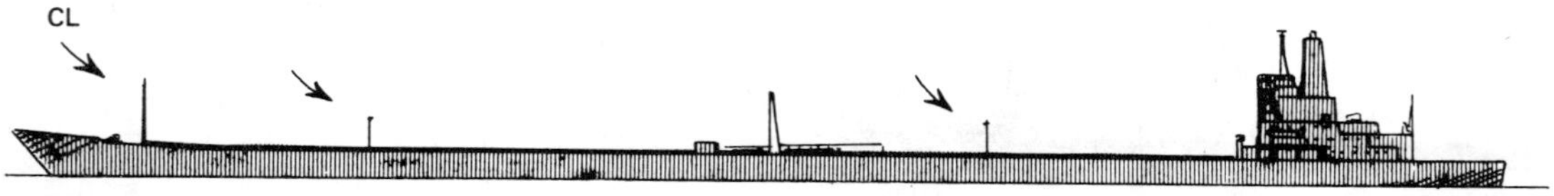

K_4MF H
● **55460 JAPAN LUPINUS.** Ja/Ja 1972; Tk; 120500; 324.01 × 19.47 (1063.02 × 63.88); T; 15.75. Sister: **55461 JAPAN CARNATION** (Ja) Similar: **55462 WORLD ADMIRAL** (Li) **55463 WORLD AMBASSADOR** (Li) **55464 KHARK** (Ir).

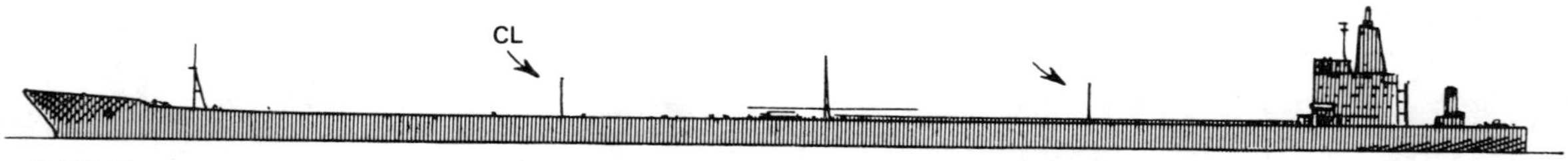

K_4MF H
55470 ANTONIOS G. Li/De 1973; Tk; 129700; 347.23 × 22.22 (1139.21 × 72.9); T; 16. ex RANIA CHANDRIS 1976. Similar: **55471 TORILL KNUDSEN** (Li).

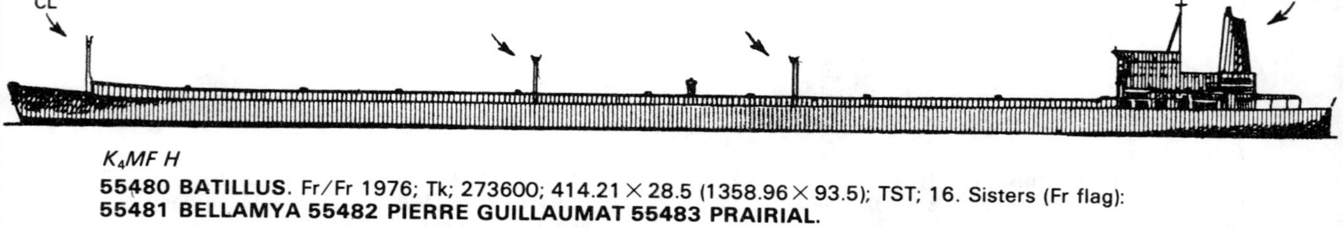

K_4MF H
55480 BATILLUS. Fr/Fr 1976; Tk; 273600; 414.21 × 28.5 (1358.96 × 93.5); TST; 16. Sisters (Fr flag): **55481 BELLAMYA 55482 PIERRE GUILLAUMAT 55483 PRAIRIAL.**

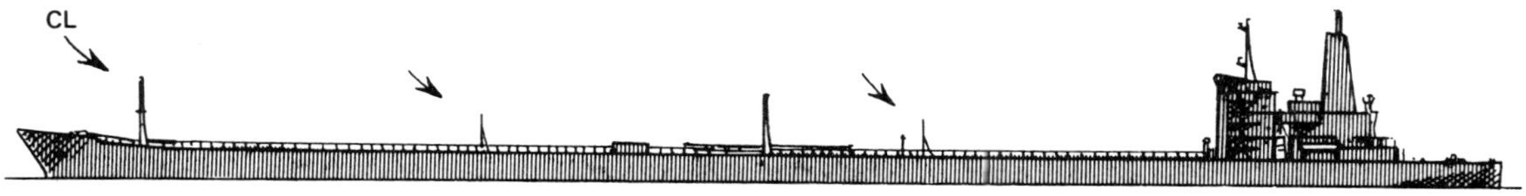

K_4MF H

55490 MAASBREE. Ne/Ja 1973; Tk; 135400; 337.07 × 21.05 (1105.87 × 69.06); T; 16; ex SINDE 1973.

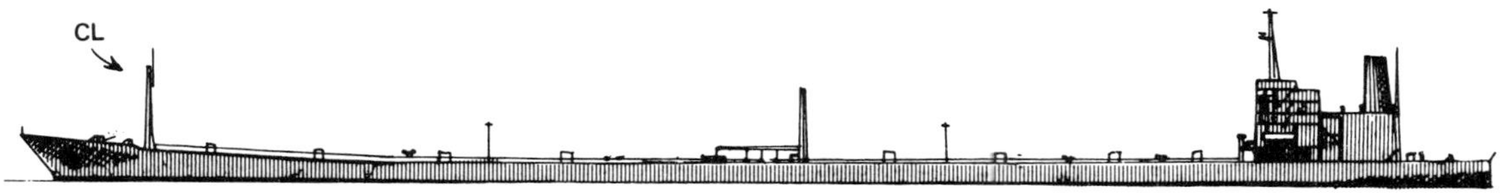

K_4MF H

55500 OGDEN SUNGARI. Li/Ja 1975; Tk; 124100; 338.87 × 21.01 (1111.78 × 68.93); T; 16. Similar: **55501 MOSCLIFF** (No).

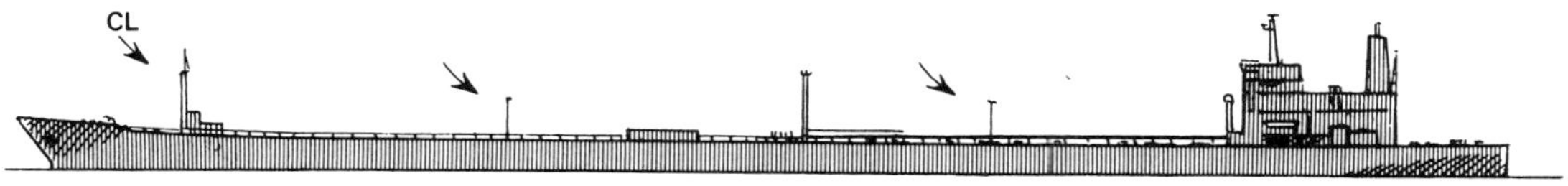

K_4MF H

55510 TOWADA MARU. Ja/Ja 1970; Tk; 111600; 319.74 × 19 (1046.02 × 62.34); T; 16.

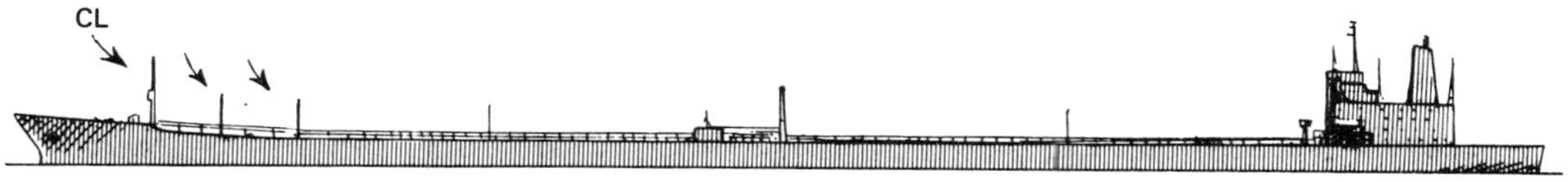

K_4MF H

55520 TAKASAKA MARU. Ja/Ja 1976; Tk; 116500; 319.95 × 19.74 (1049.7 × 64.76); T; 15.25.

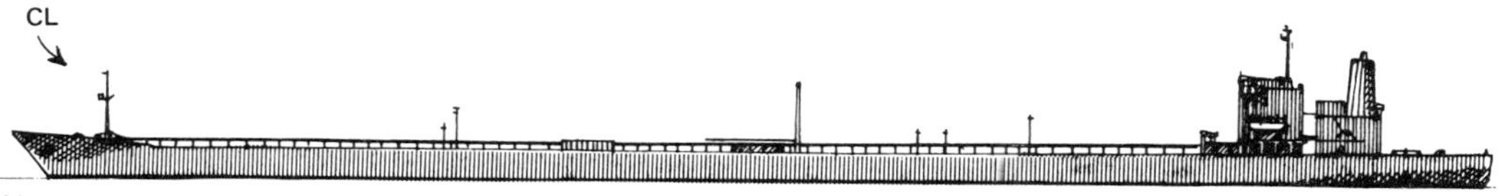

K_4MF H

55530 GRESHAM. Li/Ja 1975; Tk; 104400; 317 × 20.79 (1040.03 × 68.21); T; 16. Probable Sister: **55531 LOMBARD** (Li).

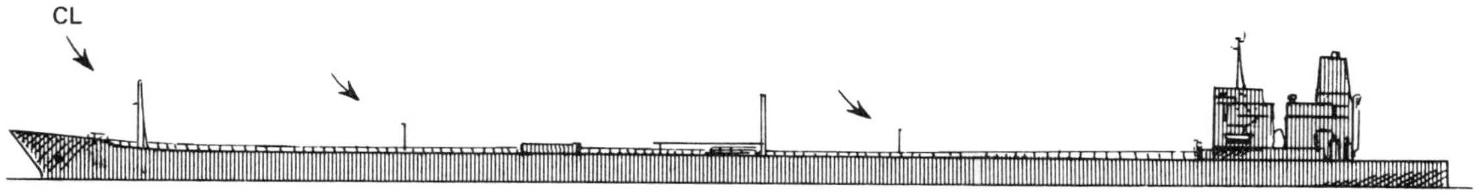

K_4MF H

55540 CAIRU. Bz/Ja 1974; Tk; 129400; 337.09 × 21.62 (1105.94 × 70.93); T; 15.75. Sister: **55541 VIDAL DE NEGREIROS** (Bz).

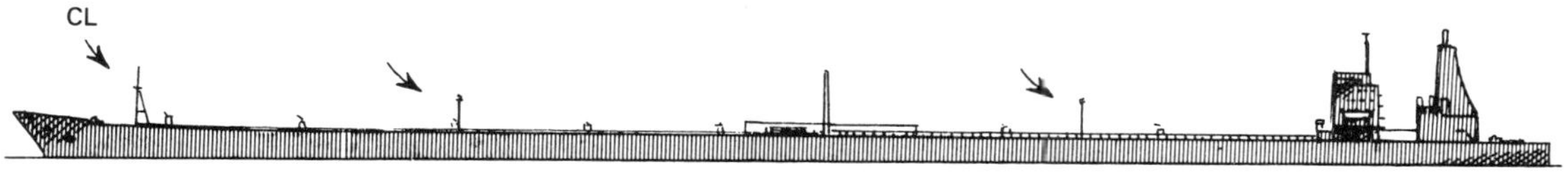

K_4MF H

55550 ARIETTA. Gr/De 1972; Tk; 129300; 347.51 × 22.32 (1140.12 × 73.23); T; —; ex ARIETTA LIVANOS 1979. Sister: **55551 EUGENIE LIVANOS** (Li).

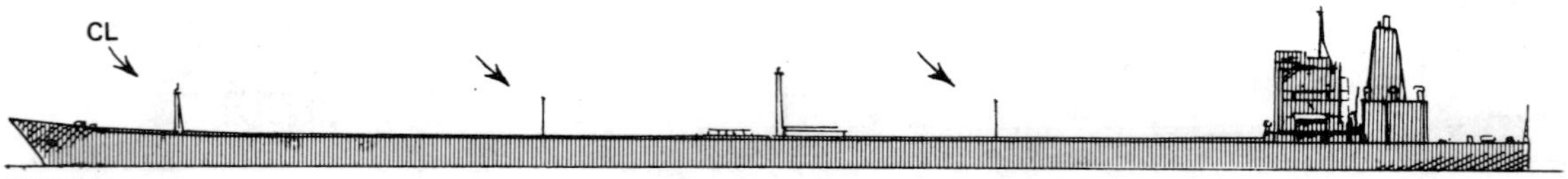

K_4MF H
55560 PROSPERITY. Li/Ko 1974; Tk; 124700; 344.43 × 20.77 (1130.02 × 68.14); T; 16; ex ATLANTIC BARON 1977. Sister: **55561 KOREA SUN** (Ko) launched as ATLANTIC BARONESS Possible Sisters: **55562 KOREA STAR** (Ko) **55563 KOREA BANNER** (Ko) **55564 CATTLEYA** (Li).

K_4MF H
55570 EXXON SAN FRANCISCO. US/US 1969; Tk; 38100; 246.84 × 12.6 (809.84 × 41.34); T; 17.5; ex ESSO SAN FRANCISCO 1973. Sisters: **55571 EXXON BATON ROUGE** (US) ex ESSO BATON ROUGE 1973 **55572 EXXON PHILADELPHIA** (US) ex ESSO PHILADELPHIA 1973.

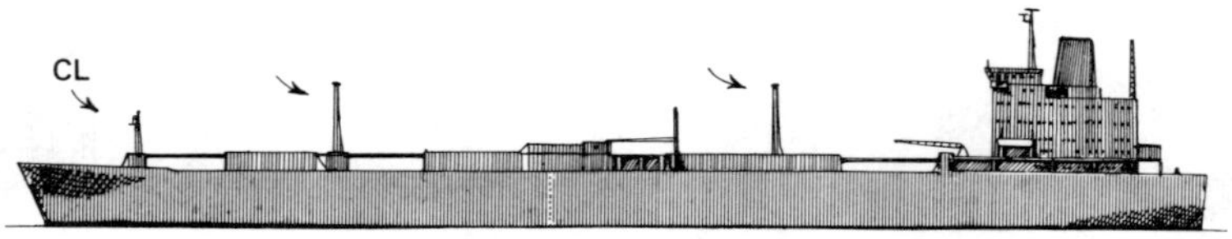

K_4MF H
55580 BLUE OCEAN. Li/Pd 1976; LGC; 48500; 229.32 × 12.7 (752.36 × 41.67); M; 17.25; ex HOEGH SWALLOW; **'B-550'** type. **55581 HOEGH SWIFT** (No)—being used as a storage vessel. **55582 HOEGH SWORD** (No).

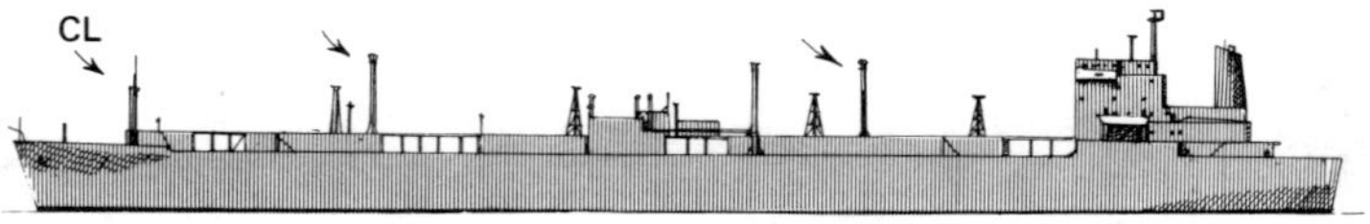

K_4MF H
55590 STAFFORDSHIRE. Li/Fr 1977; LGC; 41700; 226.32 × 13.03 (742.52 × 42.75); M; 17.

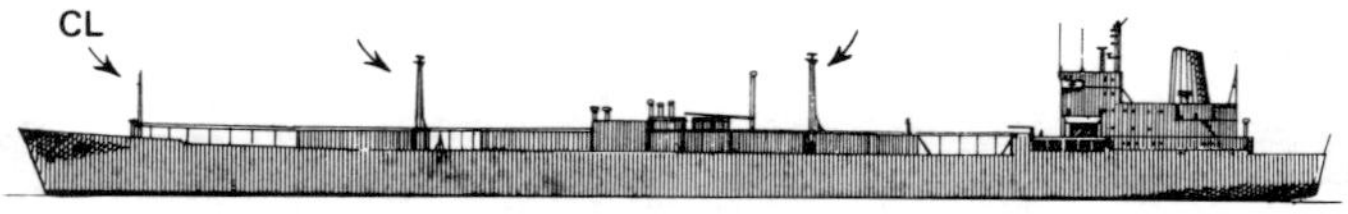

K_4MF H
55600 HAMPSHIRE. Br/Fr 1974; LGC;32100; 207.08 × 11.28 (679.43 × 37.01); M; 17.5. Sister: **55601 DEVONSHIRE** (Br).

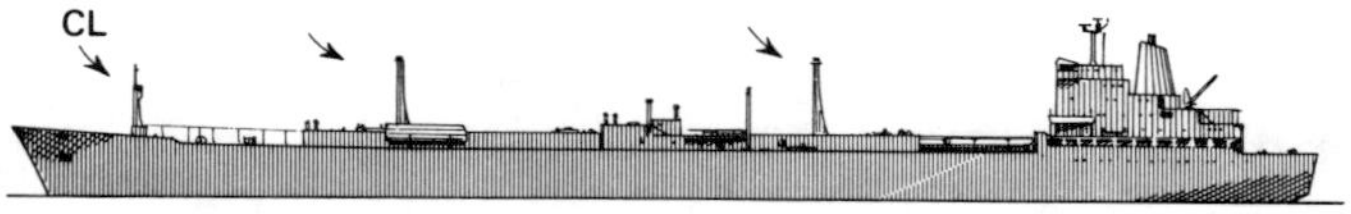

K_4MF H
55610 MUNDOGAS AMERICA. US/No 1972; LGC; 32200; 207.07 × 11.32 (679.36 × 37.14); M; 17.5 ex GARMULA.

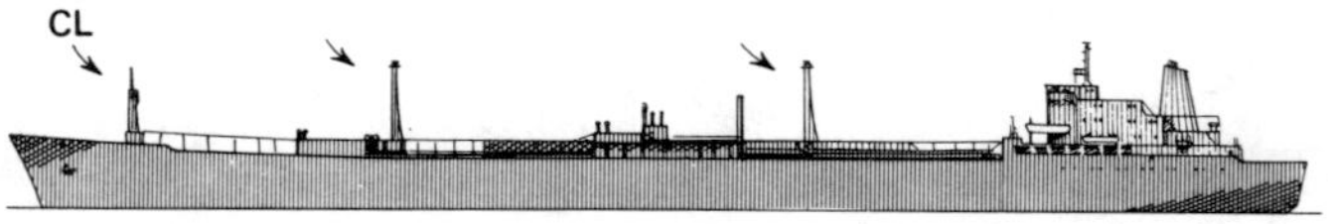

K_4MF H
55620 HOEGH SKEAN. No/No 1971; LGC/Tk; 31900; 207.07 × 11.32 (679.36 × 37.14); M; 18; ex HOEGH MULTINA 1977.

K_4MF H

55630 ESSO BREGA. It/It 1969; LGC; 30400; 207.73 × 9.17 (681.53 × 30.09); T; —. Sisters: **55631 ESSO LIGURIA** (It) **55632 ESSO PORTOVENERE** (It) **55633 LAIETA** (Sp).

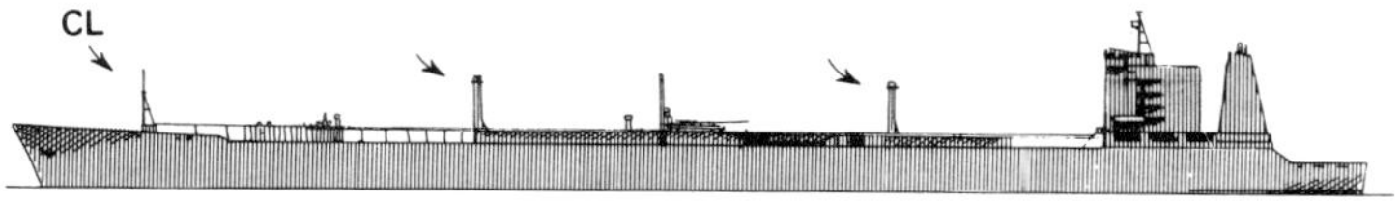

K_4MF H

● **55640 GAS RISING SUN.** Ja/Fi 1978; LGC; 45000; 223 × 13 (731.63 × 42.65); M; 16.7. Sisters (No flag): **55641 BERGE SISU 55642 BERGE SISAR 55643 BERGE SAGA** (Li flag): **55644 GOLAR FROST.**

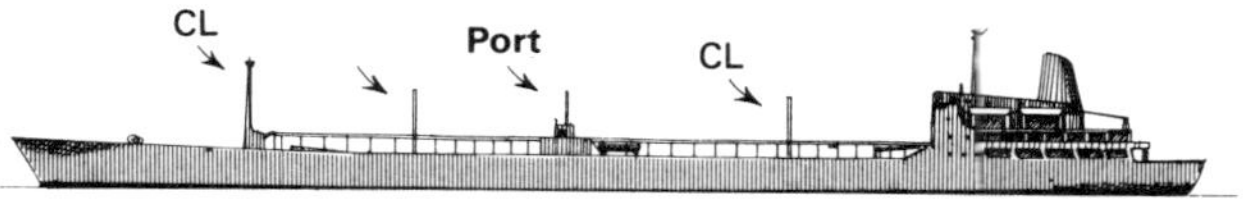

K_4MF H

55650 METHANE PRINCESS. Br/Br 1964; LGC; 21900; 189.31 × 10.7 (621.1 × 35.1); T; 17.25. Sister: **55651 METHANE PROGRESS** (Br).

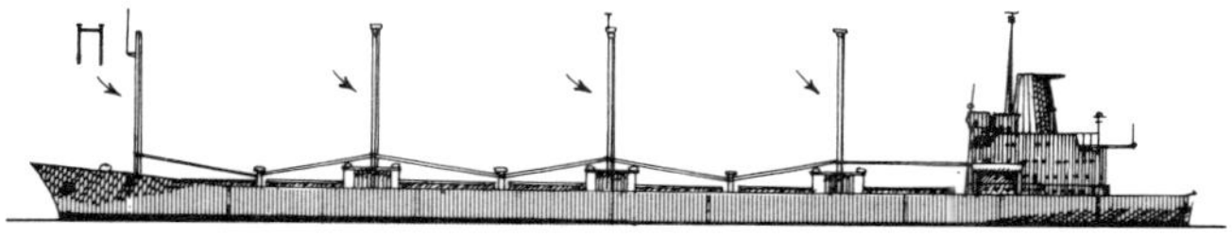

K_4MF H

55660 PROTECTOR ALPHA. Cy/FRG 1970; B; 20400; 196.32 × 10.9 (644.09 × 35.76); M; 16.5; ex SHANGRI LA 1981; ex ELISABETH BOLTEN 1979. Sisters (FRG flag): **55661 CELEBES** ex EVELYN BOLTEN 1980 **55662 MARIANNE BOLTEN** ex HERMANN SCHULTE 1978.

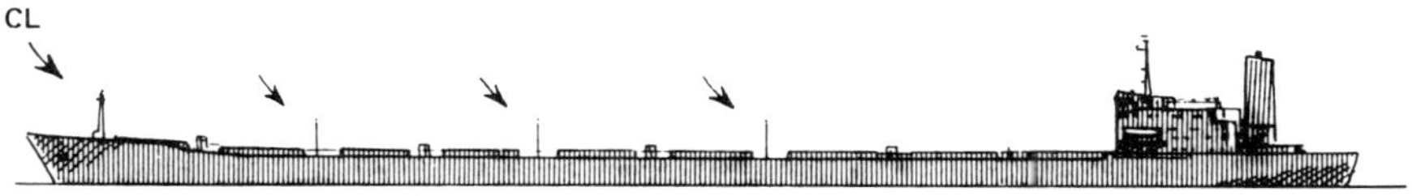

K_4MF H

55670 GOLDEN CAMEO. Li/FRG 1974; B; 44700; 260.79 × 14.2 (855.61 × 46.59); M; 16.5; ex MALMLAND 1978. Sister: ★**55671 MIAN ZHU HAI** RC) ex THALASSIN I AVRA 1980; ex FERROLAND 1978.

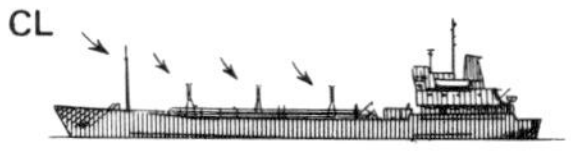

K_4MF H

55680 SOLVENT EXPLORER. Br/FRG 1974; Ch; 1500; 77.12 × 4.78 (253.02 × 15.68); M; 12; ex ESSBERGER PILOT 1977. Sister: **55681 SOLVENT VENTURER** (Br) ex ESSBERGER PIONEER 1977.

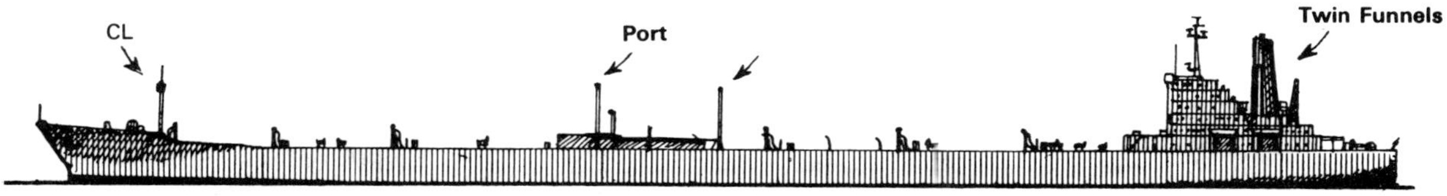

K_4MF H1

● **55690 UNIVERSE IRELAND.** Li/Ja 1968; Tk; 149600; 345.3 × 24.82 (1132.87 × 81.43); TST; 15. Sisters: **55691 JUBAYL** (Si) ex AVIN OIL SAFKIA 1980; ex UNIVERSE JAPAN 1980 **55692 AVIN OIL GERANI** (Gr) ex UNIVERSE KUWAIT 1980.

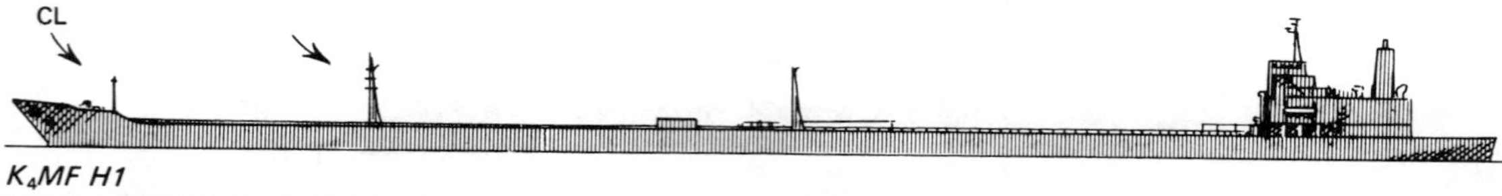

K_4MF H1

55700 CHEVRON NAGASAKI. Li/Ja 1974; Tk; 118100; 338.64 × 20.56 (1111.1 × 67.4); T; 15.25. Sisters (Li flag): **55701 CHEVRON PERTH 55702 CHEVRON FELUY 55703 CHARLES PIGOTT** Possible Sisters: **55704 CHEVRON COPENHAGEN 55705 CHEVRON EDINBURGH 55706 OTTO N. MILLER 55707 L.W. FUNKHAUSER 55708 C.W. KITTO** Similar (Pa flag): **55709 TEXACO ITALIA 55710 TEXACO JAPAN.**

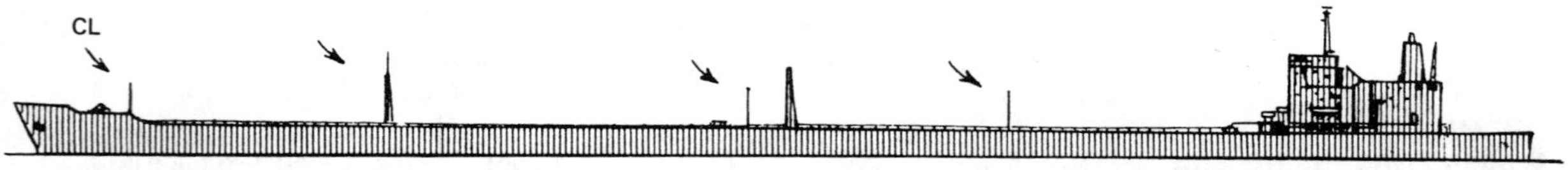

K_4MF H1

55720 AIKO MARU. Ja/Ja 1976; Tk; 209800; 365.87 × 22.9 (1200.36 × 75.13); T; 15.75. Sisters: **55721 JINKO MARU** (Ja) **55722 AL REKKAH** (Ku) Possibly Similar: **55723 CHEVRON SOUTH AMERICA** (Li) **55724 CHEVRON NORTH AMERICA** (Li).

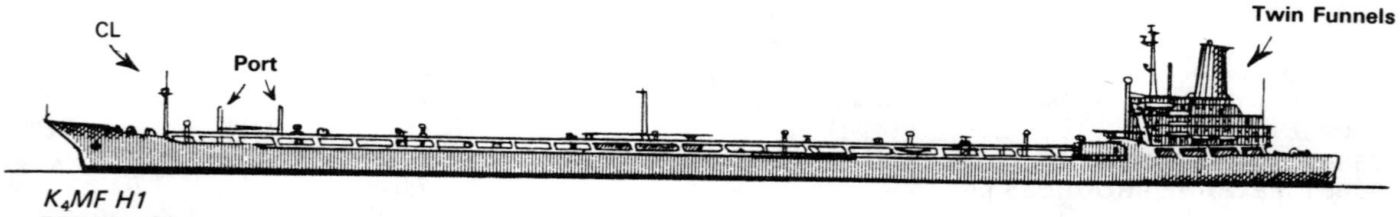

K_4MF H1

55730 ARTEAGA. Sp/Sp 1972; Tk; 163800; 347.94 × 24.82 (1141.54 × 81.43); TST; 14.5. Sister: **55731 BUTRON** (Sp) Similar (Ko flag): **55732 OCEAN PARK 55733 CHUN WOO.**

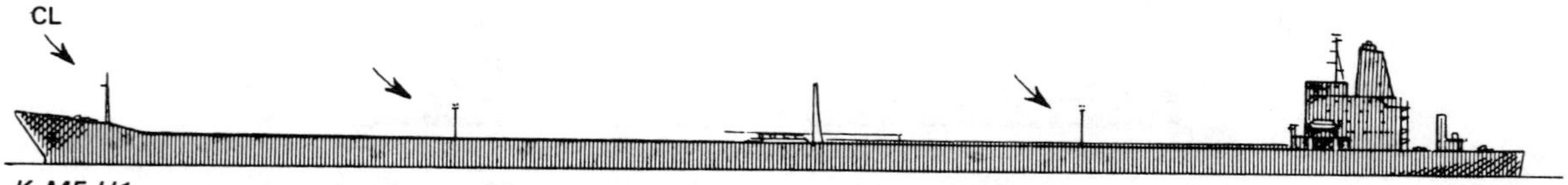

K_4MF H1

55740 TEXACO DENMARK. Br/De 1970; Tk; 125400; 345.02 × 20.11 (1131.96 × 65.98); T; 15.5. Sisters: **55741 TEXACO NORWAY** (Br) **55742 SIPCA DAMMAM** (Si) ex TEXACO COPENHAGEN 1979.

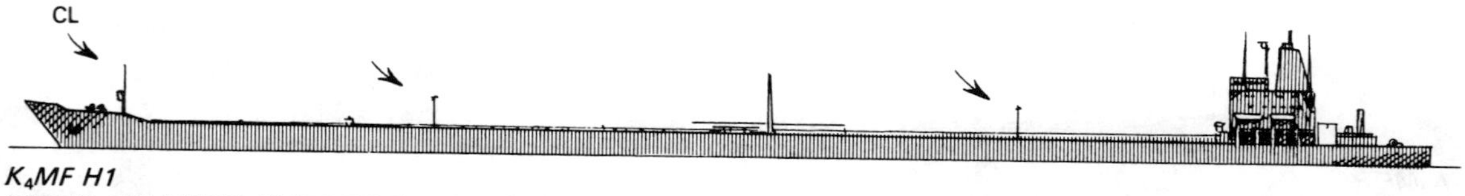

K_4MF H1

● **55750 ATLANTIC EMPOROR.** Li/De 1974; Tk; 128400; 347.23 × 22.32 (1139.21 × 73.23); T; 15.5.

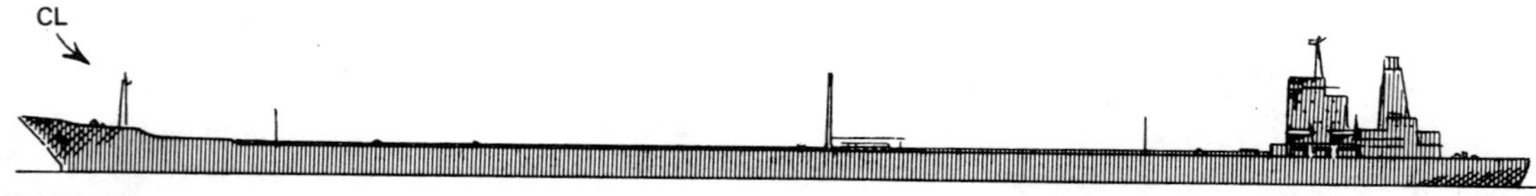

K_4MF H1

● **55760 SIRENIA.** Pa/It 1970; Tk; 115900; 329.73 × 19.91 (1081.79 × 65.32); T; —; ex CATERINA M. Sister (Could be K^2MF): **55761 FLYING CLOUD** (Li) ex ANITA MONTI.

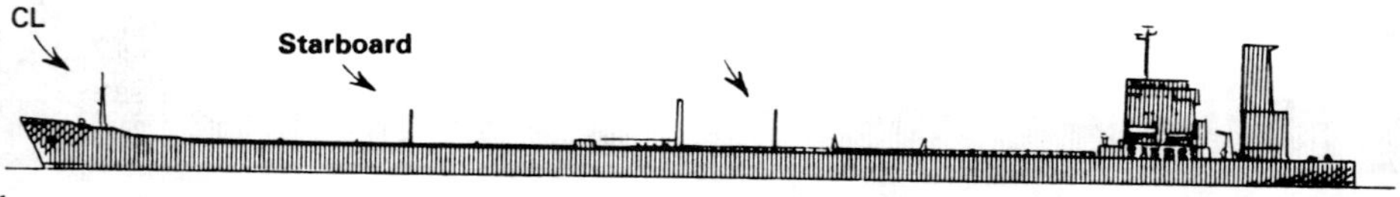

K_4MF H1

55770 LONDON ENTERPRISE. Br/Sw 1974; Tk; 74400; 270.01 × 17.07 (885.86 × 56); M; 16.25. Sisters: **55771 LONDON GLORY** (Br) **55772 OVERSEAS ARGONAUT** (Br) **55773 N'TCHENGUE** (Ga).

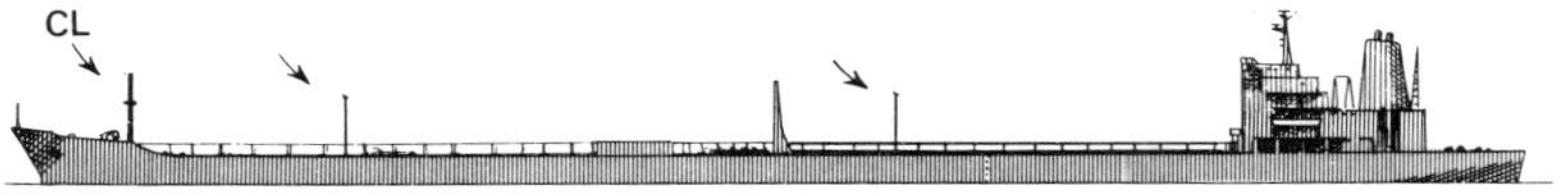

K_4MF H1
⋆**55780 BANAT.** Rm/Ja 1975; Tk; 46900; 242.12×13.61 (794.36×44.65); M; 15.75. Sisters (Rm flag): ⋆**55781 CRISANA** ⋆**55782 DACIA** ⋆**55783 MUNTENIA.**

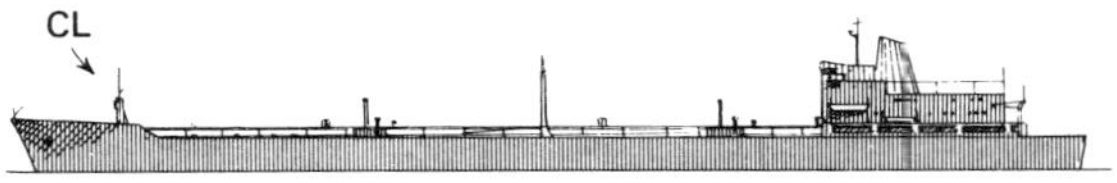

K_4MF H1
55790 CIELO DI NAPOLI. It/No 1970; Ch; 18700; 170.67×11.37 (559.94×37.3); M; 15.5; ex TEAM ASTWI 1979; launched as ASTWI. Sisters: **55791 HADA** (No) ex TEAM CASTOR **55792 SOLVIKEN** (No) ex TEAM POLLUX **55793 MYKONOS** (Li) ex TEAM AUGWI 1979 **55794 MYRTEA** (Li) ex TEAM HILWI 1979.

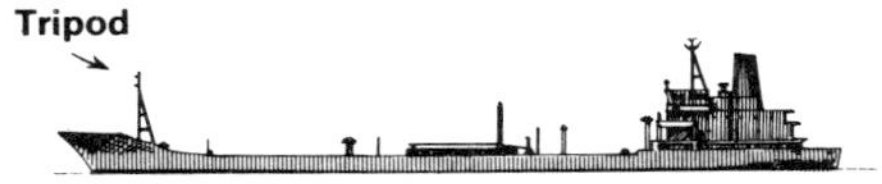

K_4MF H1
55800 FRAMNAS. Sw/Sw 1972/73; Bitumen/Oil Carrier; 4300; 122.84×5.74 (403.02×18.83); M; 14.25; Launched 1972, lengthened and completed 1973.

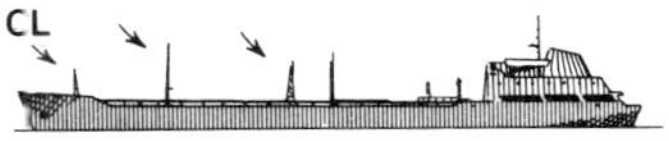

K_4MF H1
55810 OTARU. Sw/Sw 1969; Tk/Ch; 2700, 99.01×9 36 (324.84×30.71); M; 12.5.

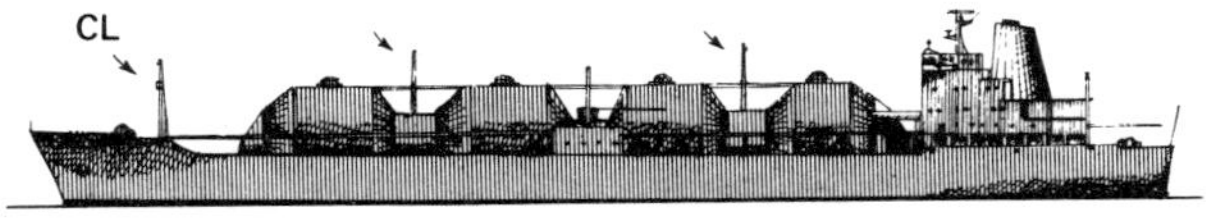

K_4MF H1
55820 CENTURY. No/No 1975; 27100; 181.54×9.42 (595.6×30.91); M; 19; ex LUCIAN 1980; Converted from Gas Turbine 1980. Similar: **55821 VENATOR** (No).

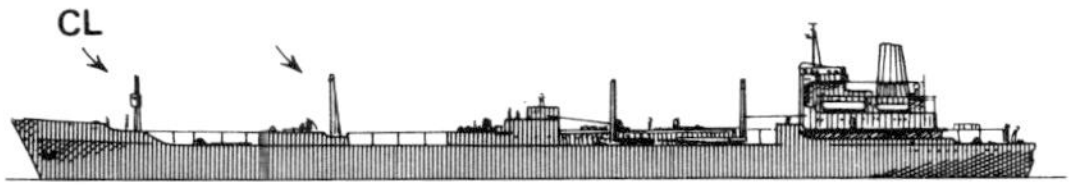

K_4MF H1
55830 MUNDOGAS RIO. No/No 1967; LGC; 13200; 162.57×9.52 (533.37×31.23); M; 17.

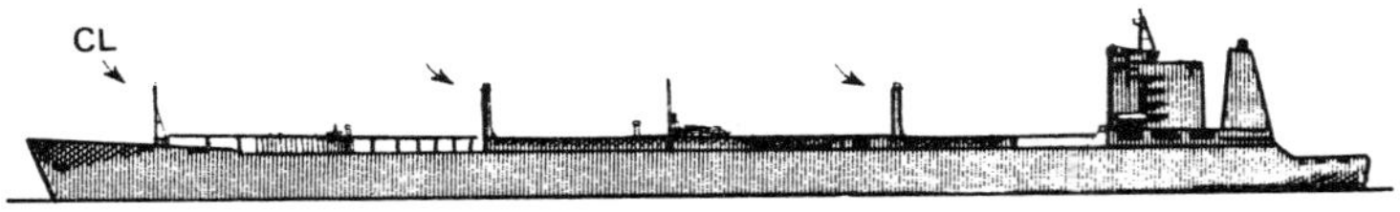

K_4MF H1
● **55840 GAS RISING SUN.** Ja/Fi 1978; LGC; 45000; 223×13 (732.63×42.65); M; 16.7. Sisters (No. flag): **55841 BERGE SISU 55842 BERGE SISAR 55843 BERGE SAGA** (Li flag): **55844 GOLAR FROST.**

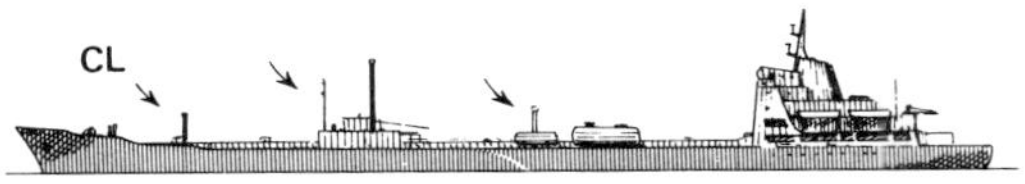

K_4MF H1
55850 CAPO OVEST. It/Fr 1967; LGC; 10800; 154.51×7.7 (506.92×25.26); M; 16; ex MARIOTTE 1976; ex AEOLOS 1968; Could be spelt **CAPO VEST**

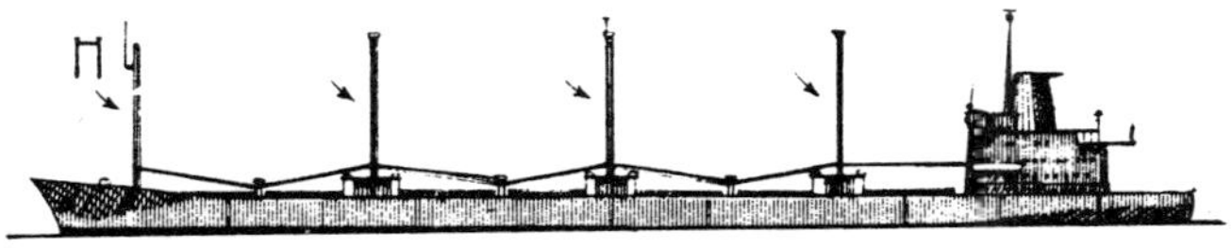

K_4MF H1
55860 PROTECTOR ALPHA. Cy/FRG 1970; B; 20400; 196.32×10.9 (644.09×35.76); M; 16.5; ex SHANGRI LA 1981; ex ELISABETH BOLTEN 1979. Sisters (FRG flag): **55861 CELEBES** ex EVELYN BOLTEN 1980 **55862 MARIANNE BOLTEN** ex HERMANN SCHULTE 1978.

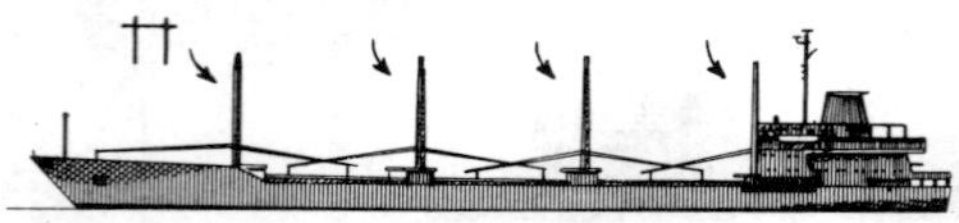

K_4MF H1
55870 SHONGA. Br/Pd 1973; C/Con; 5700/9200; 145.73 × 7.04/8.4 (478.12 × 23.1/27.56); M; 16.5. **'B-430'** type Sisters: **55871 SHERBRO** (Br) **55872 APAPA PALM** (Br) ex SCHAUENBURG 1977 **55873 MEXICO** (Li) ex HASSELBURG 1980; ex HOEGH APAPA 1979; ex APAPA PALM 1977; ex HASSELBURG 1976 **55874 MONSUN** (FRG) ex SAPELE 1979; ex MONSUN 1976. **55875 RIVER HADEJIA** (Ng).

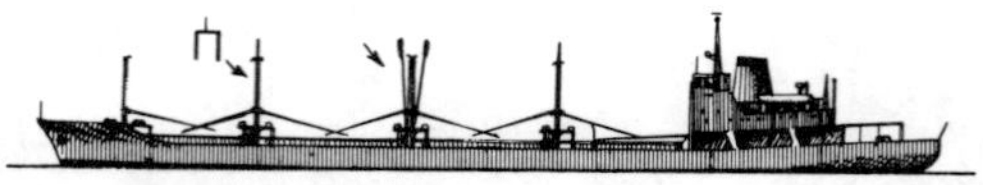

K_4MF H1
● **55880 PRESIDENTE KENNEDY.** Bz/Bz 1965; C; 6900/9100; 145.5 × 7.94/8.75 (477.36 × 26.05/28.7); M; 15.5. Sisters: **55881 ALMIRANTE GRACA ARANHA** (Bz) **55882 EL MEXICANO** (Me) **55883 PUEBLA** (Me) Similar: **55884 BUARQUE** (Bz) **55885 ROMEO BRAGA** (Bz).

K_4MF H1
55890 WAIAL. Si/FRG 1968; Tk; 500; 64.9 × 3.75 (212.93 × 12.3); M; 12; ex BILL ROBERTS 1981. Sisters: **55891 MAGID** (Si) ex HARRY LEWIS 1981 (being used as bunkering vessel) **55892 SUSANNA** (Fa) ex PEDER LYSGAARD 1981.

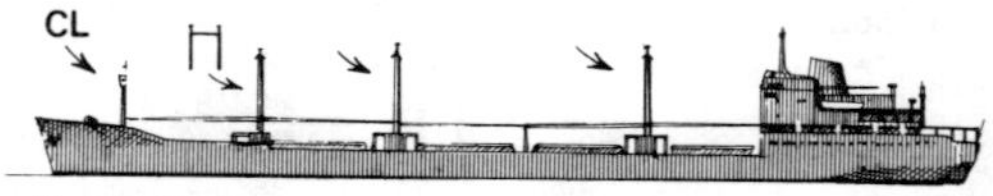

K_4MF H13
55900 STROFADES. Gr/Sw 1962; B; 9000; 149.76 × 8.97 (491.34 × 29.43); M; 13.5; ex DELFIN 1972; ex SONATA 1968.

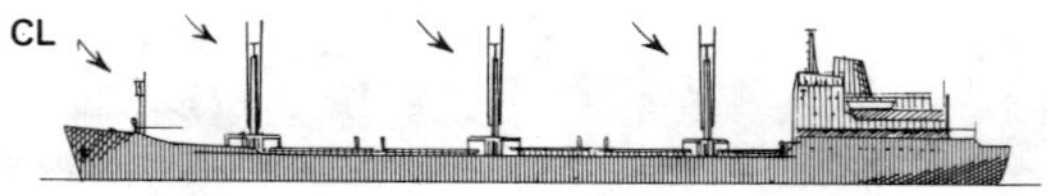

K_4MF H13
55910 ANTON STJEPOV. Ma/Sw 1962; B; 10900; 149.99 × 9.55 (492.09 × 31.33); M; 14; ex BELLAMI 1976.

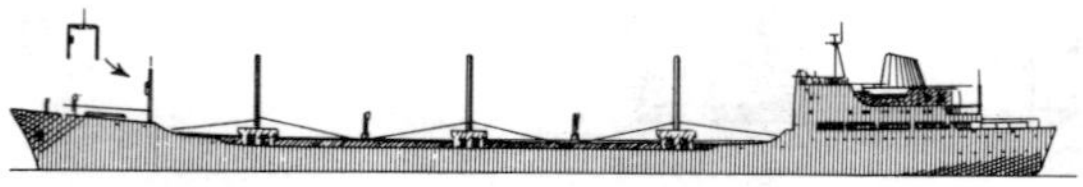

K_4MF H13
55920 MIHALIOS XILAS. Gr/No 1961; B; 12700; 166.48 × 10.21 (546.19 × 33.5); M; 15; ex GREY MASTER 1970. Sister: **55921 NEW SULU SEA** (A) ex SULU SEA 1976; ex GJENDEFJELL 1972 ex ANGELINE 1968.

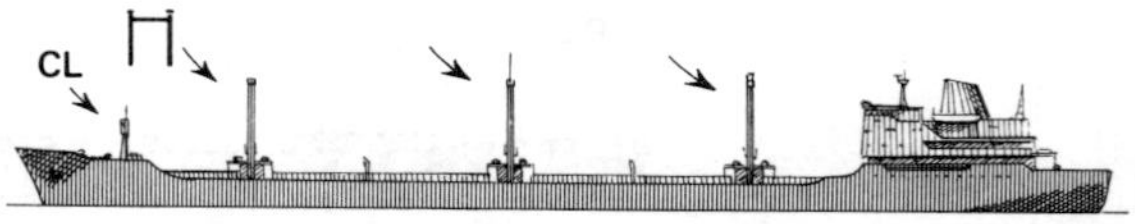

K_4MF H13
⋆55930 BAI YUN HAI. RC/Ys 1967; B; 13800; 174.05 × 9.02 (571.03 × 29.59); M; ex SUNIMA 1977.

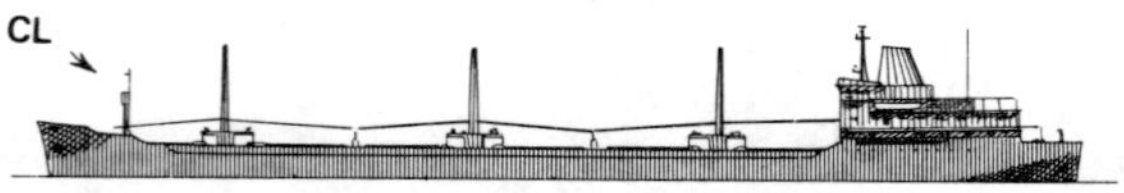

K_4MF H13
55940 PSILI. Gr/No 1965; B; 12400; 165.08 × 10.42 (541.6 × 34.19); M; 16; ex WILFRED 1977.

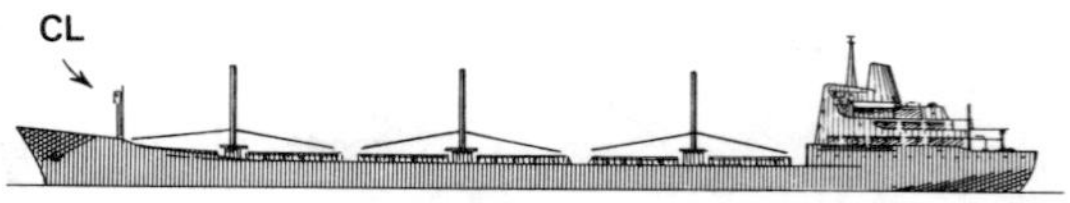

K_4MF H13
⋆55950 CHANG HAI. RC/No 1964; B; 12800; 162.16 × 9.7 (532 × 31.8); M; 14.5; ex BRIS 1974. Sisters: **55951 TRAKYA** (Tu) ex ISCELU 1981; ex POLARLAND 1977. **55952 VALHALL** (No).

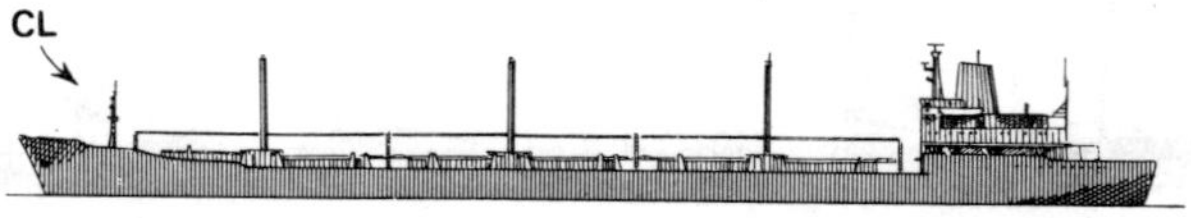

K_4MF H13
● **55960 BELLA MAERSK.** De/No 1969; B; 15900; 180.32 × 10.21 (591.6 × 33.5); M; —. Sister: **55961 BRIGIT MAERSK** (De) Similar: **55962 MAERSK COMMANDER** (Br) **55963 MAERSK CADET** (Br) **55964 DANILA** (Li) ex MAERSK CAPTAIN **55965 IRENES ZEST** (Li) ex GOLDEN MISTRAL 1980; ex HOEGH MISTRAL 1978 **55966 GLYFADA** (Gr) ex GOLDEN MINERVA 1980; ex HOEGH MINERVA 1978 **55967 GOLDEN MIRANDA** (Li) ex HOEGH MIRANDA 1978 **55968 IRENES ZEAL** (Gr) ex LEAL 1980; ex BELHUDSON 1976; launched as BELVENI.

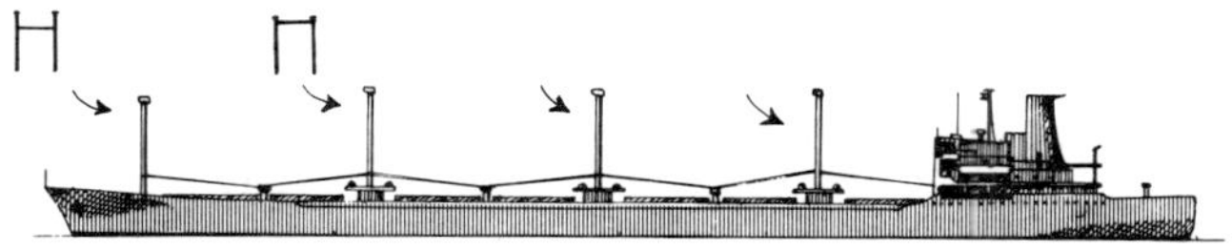

K_4MF H13

55980 WANDA. Gr/FRG 1966; B; 15600; 189.92 × 9.89 (623.1 × 32.45); M; 17; ex WESER 1980.

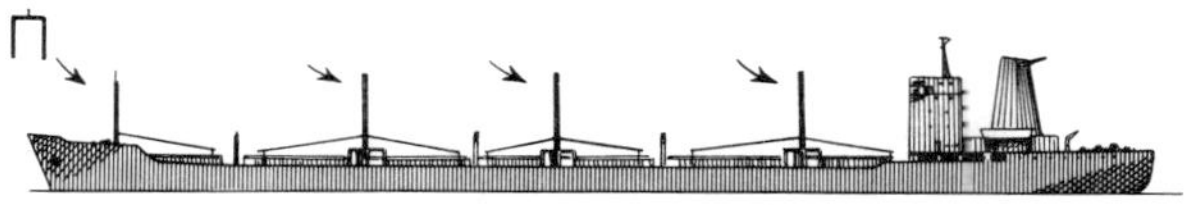

K_4MF H13

55990 MARINA DI CASSANO. It/It 1968; B; 14800; 178.44 × 10.12 (585.43 × 33.2); M; 15.5; ex KYUNGJU 1978. Sister: **55991 HANYANG** (Ko) Similar (Ys flag): **★55992 DRAVA ★55993 KIDRIC B ★55994 KRAIGHER B.**

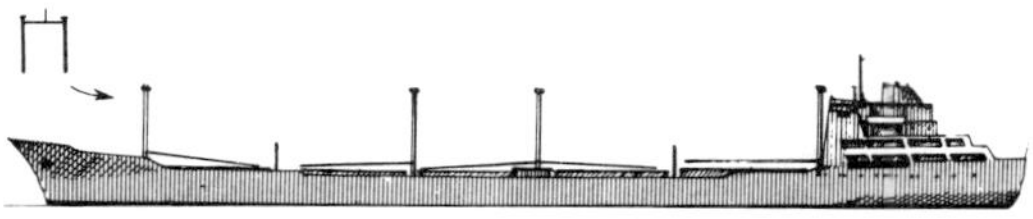

K_4MF H13

56000 THANIC . Gr/Br 1961/66; B; 9500; 161.47 × 7.89 (529.76 × 25.89); M; 12.5; ex CARIBBEAN MEMORIES 1980; ex THANIC 1980; ex CARIBBEAN MEMORIES 1980; ex BOOKER VENTURE 1978. Lengthened 1966.

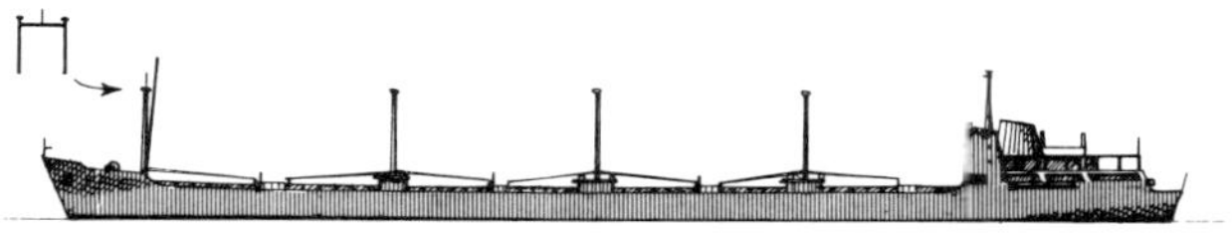

K_4MF H13

56010 IXIA. Br/Br 1964; B; 15900; 181.36 × 10.52 (595.01 × 34.51); M; 14.5.

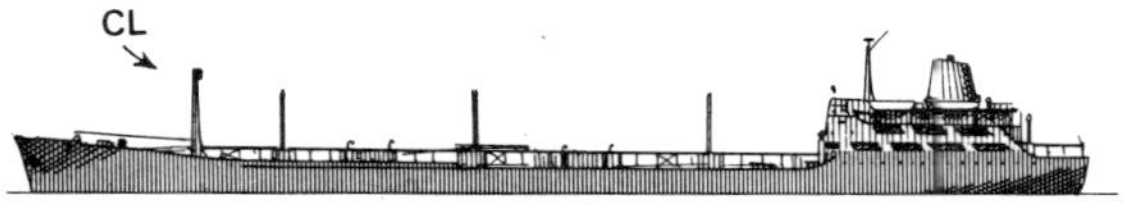

K_4MF H13

56020 HAROLD H. JAQUET. Li/Sw 1958; Ch; 9800; 170.69 × 9.45 (560 × 31); T; 15.25; ex ARCTIC 1964; ex MELINE 1963; Converted oil tanker.

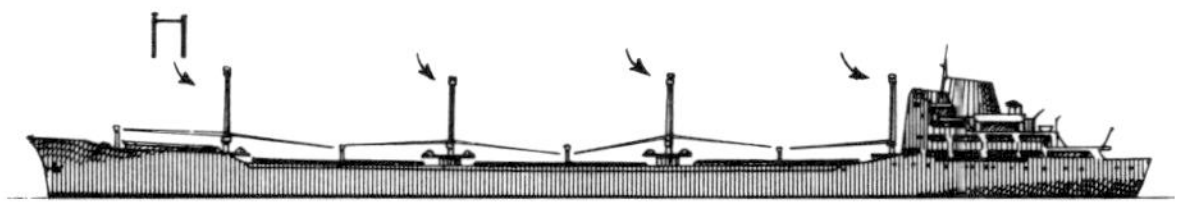

K_4MF H13

● **56030 ORIENTAL ENVOYS.** Li/Sp 1965; B; 15200; 177.5 × 9.89 (582.35 × 32.45); M; 16; launched as SANTA POLA. Sister: **56031 ECLAIR** (Gr) ex SANTA ALICIA 1979.

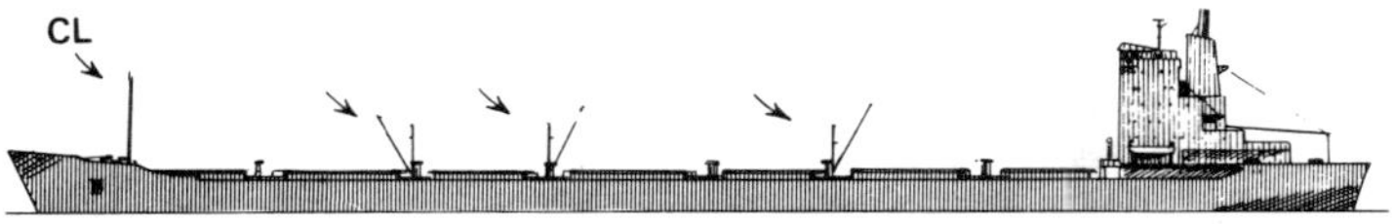

K_4MF H13

56040 BANDAK. No/De 1974; B; 30300; 221.75 × 12.09 (727.53 × 39.67); M; 16; ex MILLES 1976.

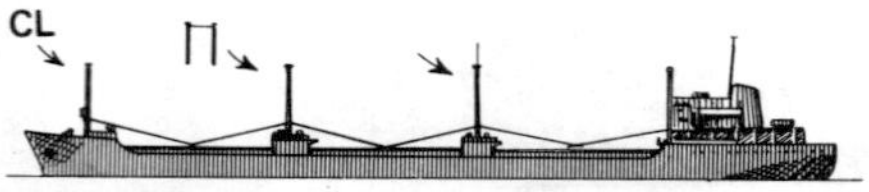

K_4MF H13
56050 ELIZA. Sg/No 1969; C; 6200; 128.28 × 8.48 (420.87 × 27.82); M; 13; ex DIMONA 1978. Sister: **56051 ALEXANDRA T** (Gr) ex ALEXANDROS T; ex DIAGARA.

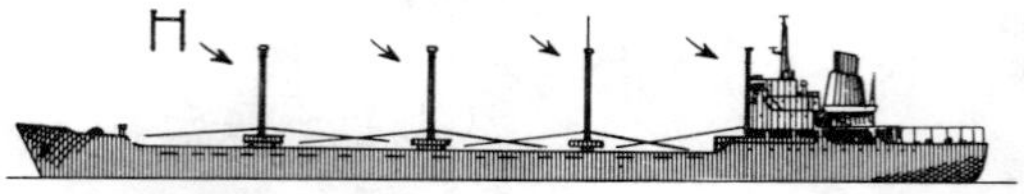

K_4MF H13
56060 MARITIME STAR. Li/Ja 1963; B; 9800; 153.52 × 9.18 (503.67 × 30.12); M; 14.5; ex DONA VIVIANA 1969.

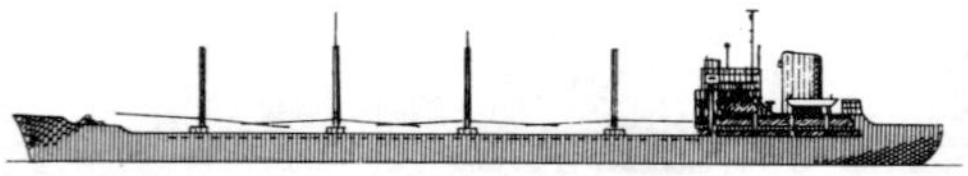

K_4MF H13
56070 KANDA. Pa/Ja 1957; C; 8300; 147.12 × 8.6 (482.68 × 28.22); M; 13.5; ex ASIA TAIMO 1976; ex TENZAN MARU 1973.

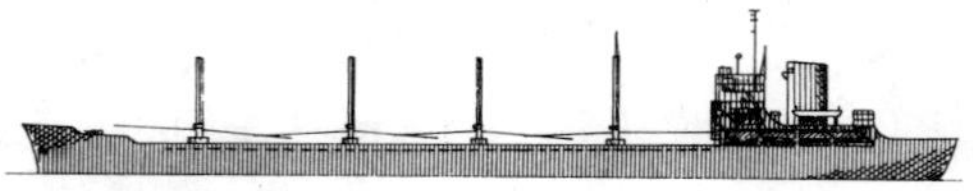

K_4MF H13
56080 KONPIRA. Sg/Ja 1958; C; 8500; 148.14 × 8.69 (486.02 × 28.51); M; 13; ex CHOZAN MARU 1973.

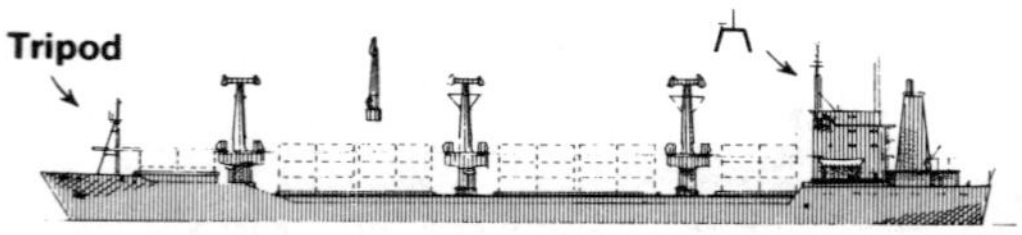

K_4MF H13
56090 SLOMAN MERCUR. FRG/FRG 1979; C/Con; 9600; 154.05 × 7.16/8.14 (505.41 × 23.49/26.7); M; 17.75; ex CAROL MERCUR; ex SLOMAN MERCUR 1979; Cranes can rotate and are probably stowed in the position shown in the inset. Sister: **56091 SLOMAN MIRA** (FRG).

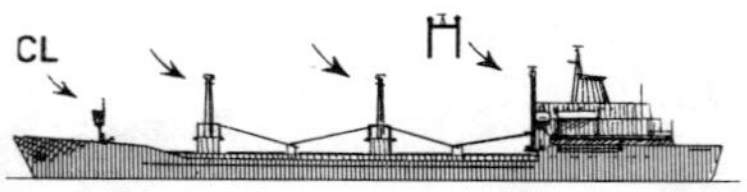

K_4MF H13
56100 LA MINERA. Bz/FRG 1969; C; 4200; 112.83 × 6.9 (370.18 × 22.64); M; 13.75; ex FOSSHEIM 1978.

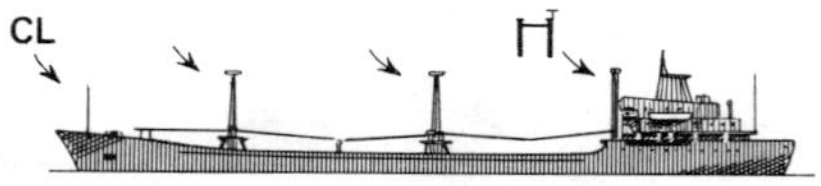

K_4MF H13
● **56110 JOHN M.** Pa/FRG 1970; C; 4000; 117 × 6.61 (383.86 × 21.69); M; 15; ex JOHN M REHDER. Sister: **56111 ALFRED REHDER** (FRG) Similar: **56112 LEO SCHRODER** (FRG) **56113 LUTZ SCHRODER** (FRG).

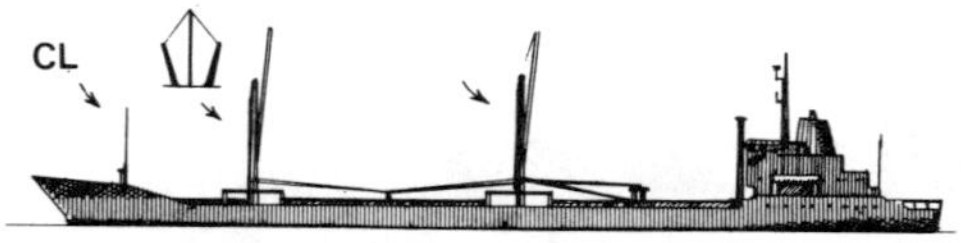

K_4MF H13
56120 EDITA. Pa/FRG 1972; C; 5000/8300; 143.8 × 7.07/8.33 (471.78 × 23.19/27.33); M; 18; ex EDITH HOWALDT RUSS 1980; ex CAMBRIDGE 1976; ex EDITH HOWALDT RUSS 1975; launched as EDITH HOWALDT. Sisters: **56121 COLUMBUS CALIFORNIA** (FRG) ex RHEINGOLD 1973 **56122 WALKURE** (FRG) ex BAVARIA TRIESTE 1980; ex COLUMBUS CANADA 1980; launched as WALKURE.

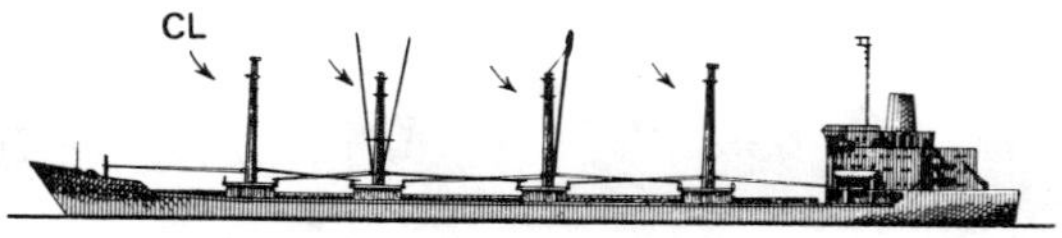

K_4MF H13
56130 FLAVIA. FRG/FRG 1977; C; 7600/11000; 157.38 × 8.07/9.28 (516.34 × 26.48/30.45); M; 16; **BREMEN PROGRESS "B"** type.

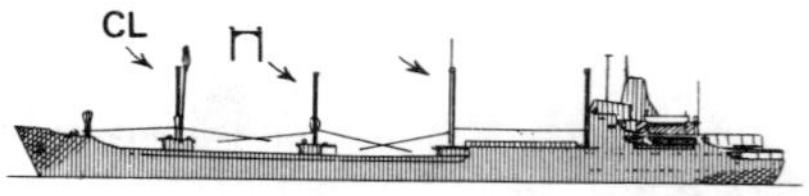

K_4MF H13
● ⋆**56140 ALTMARK.** DDR/Fi 1959; C; 2700/4600; 121.52 × 6.1/7.67 (398.69 × 20.01/25.16); M; —; ex INGE TOFT 1964.

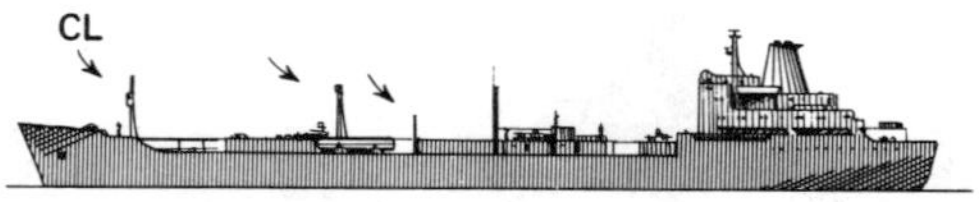

K_4MF H13
56150 HAVIS. No/No 1970; LGC; 11200; 146.77 × 10.61 (481.53 × 34.81); M; 17.

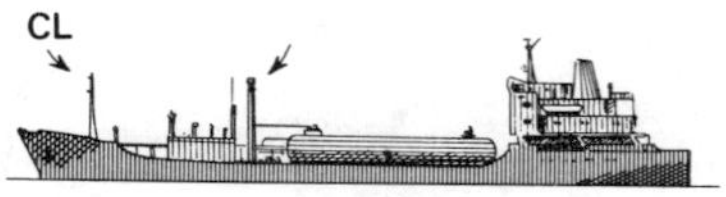

K_4MF H13
56160 TORDENSKIOLD. No/No 1971; LGC/Ch; 3500; 106.05 × 6.45 (347.93 × 21.16); M; 15. Similar: **56161 ROALD AMUNDSEN** (No).

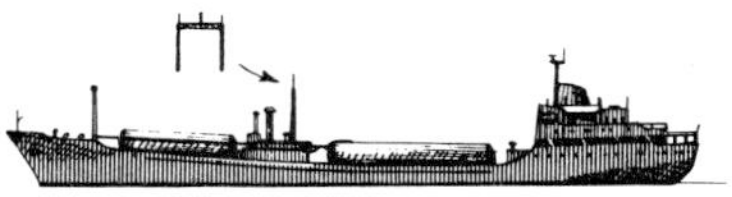

K_4MF H13
56170 GAZ PIONEER. Pa/Fr 1965; LGC; 4200; 110.85 × 6.67 (363.68 × 21.88); M; 13.5; ex FROSTFONN 1978. Sisters: **56171 GAZ UNITY** (Pa) ex NORDFONN **56172 GAZ MED** (Gr) ex GEROLAMO GARDANO 1980; ex SYDFONN 1972.

● 56185

K_4MF H13
56200 ODET. Fr/FRG 1975; WT; 16000; 90.1 × 5.72 (295.6 × 18.77); M; 13.5. Sister: **56201 RHONE** (Sd).

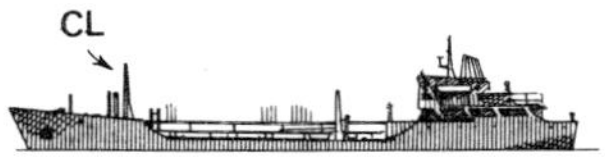

K_4MF H13
56210 MULTITANK BADENIA. Pa/No 1971; Tk; 1600; 91.22 × 5.53 (299.28 × 18.14); M; 13; ex MARK 1974. Sisters: **56211 MULTITANK HAMMONIA** (Cy) ex MULTITANK RHENANIA **56212 MULTITANK WESTFALIA** (Pa) ex SEAMARK 1974; may now be broken up following casualty.

K_4MF H13
56240 BANDIM. Po/Po 1968; LGC; 1800; 82.71 × 4.65 (271.36 × 15.26); M; 13. Sister: **56241 CIDLA** (Po).

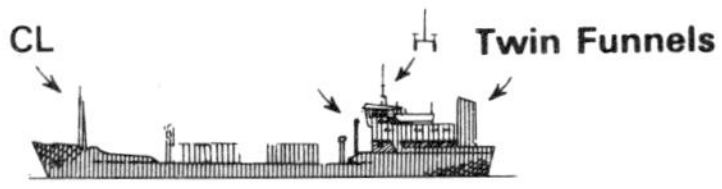

K_4MF H13
56260 PROOF SPIRIT. Li/Ne 1975; Ch; 1500; 73.46 × 6.15 (241.01 × 20.18); M; 12.5. Sister: **56261 PROOF TRADER** (Li).

K_4MF H13
56180 PRESIDENT DELCOURT. Fr/Fr 1972; Ch; 6000; 125.46 × 7.75 (411.61 × 25.43); M; 17.

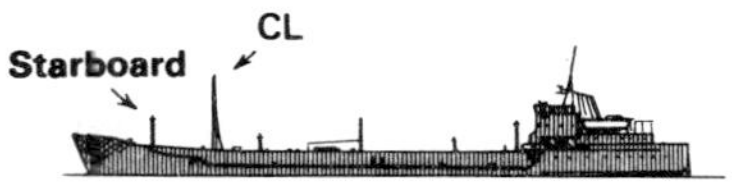

K_4MF H13
56190 TEXACO WARRIOR. Ca/Br 1970; Tk; 3300; 98.3 × 6.55 (322.51 × 21.49); M; 12.75; ex ANTERIORITY 1975; ex THUNTANK 6 1972. Sister: **56191 EKFJORD** (Sw) ex AMITY 1977; ex POINTE DE TOULINGUET 1976; ex AMITY 1975; ex THUNTANK 5 1972.

K_4MF H13
56220 THUNTANK 7. Sw/Sw 1967; LGC; 1200; 72.95 × 5.17 (239.34 × 16.96); M; 12.5; ex THUNGAS 1975; ex THUNGAS 1 1974; ex PORSGRUNN 1974.

K_4MF H13
56230 ABDOUL AZIZ SY. Se/Fr 1964; C; 500; 57.71 × 3.51 (189.34 × 11.52); M; 11; ex PYTHAGORE 1975; Drawing is before conversion from LGC. Coding and appearance may have altered.

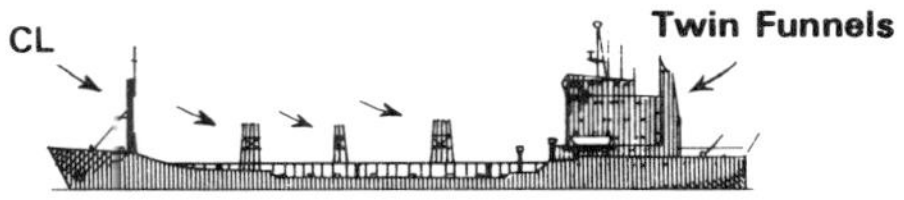

K_4MF H13
● **56250 ALCHIMIST LAUSANNE.** Li/FRG 1974; Ch; 3900; 109 × 8.54 (357.61 × 28.02); M; 14.5. Sisters: **56251 CHEMIST LUTETIA** (Li) **56252 QUIMICO LISBOA** (Pa) **56253 QUIMICO LEIXOES** (Po) **56254 CHIMISTE SAYID** (Mo).

K_4MF H13
★**56270 DUBNA.** Ru/Fi 1974; RT; 6000; 130 × 7.19 (426.51 × 23.59); M; 16. Sisters (Ru flag): ★**56271 IRKUT** ★**56272 PECHENGA** ★**56273 SVENTA.**

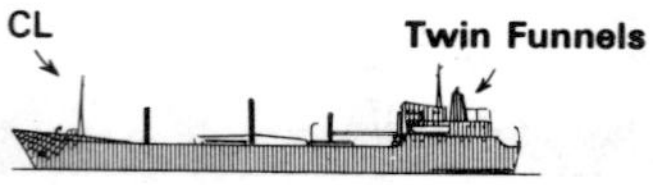

K_4MF H3
● **56280 BIFROST.** Ic/FRG 1968; RoC; 1000; 81.01 × 5.06 (265.78 × 16.6); M; 14.5; ex NIOLON 1977; ex ARKTOS 1974.

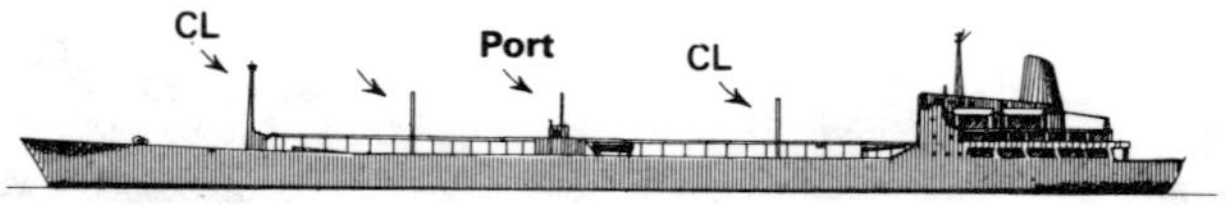

K_4MFC H
56290 METHANE PRINCESS. Br/Br 1964; LGC; 21900; 189.31 × 10.7 (621.1 × 35.1); T; 17.25. Sister: **56291 METHANE PROGRESS** (Br).

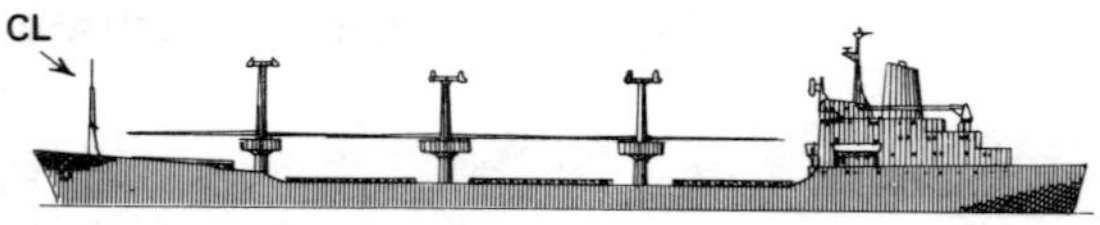

K_4MFC H13
56300 IRAN SHAMS. Ir/Ja 1978; C/Con; 14400; 166.61 × 10.52 (546.62 × 34.51); M; 18; ex ARYA SHAMS 1980. Sisters (Ir flag): **56301 IRAN EMAMAT** ex ARYA JAHAN 1980 **56302 IRAN KEYHAN** ex ARYA KEYHAN 1980 **56303 IRAN SEPEHR** ex ARYA SEPEHR 1980 **56304 IRAN SHAHAB** ex ARYA SHAHAB 1980.

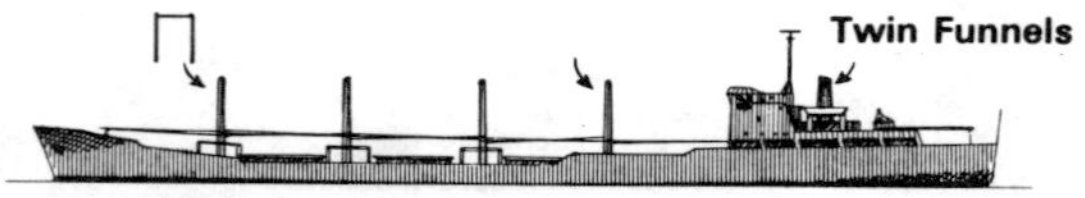

K_4MFC H13
● ★**56310 YANG CHUN.** RC/Br 1963; C; 5500/8200; 153.07 × —/8.83 (502.2 × 28.97); M; 17; ex BER SEA 1974; ex MANCHESTER COMMERCE 1970. Sisters: **56311 EDESSA** (Gr) ex KOREAN CHALLENGER 1978; ex MANCHESTER RENOWN 1971 **56312 ONE WEST No. 8** (Ko) ex KOREAN WINNER 1978; ex MANCHESTER CITY 1971.

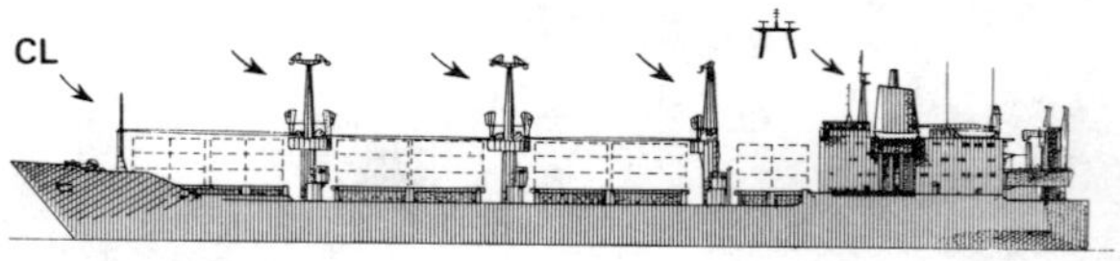

K_4MFCR H13
56320 ELEO MAERSK. De/De 1979; RoC/Con/C/HL; 13700/21800; 182.95 × 9.76/11.85 (597.9 × 32.02/38.88); M; 18.5; Stern quarter ramp. **'Caroliner'** type. Sisters (De flag): **56321 EMMA MAERSK 56322 EMILIE MAERSK 56323 ELISABETH MAERSK 56324 ESTELLE MAERSK 56325 EVELYN MAERSK.**

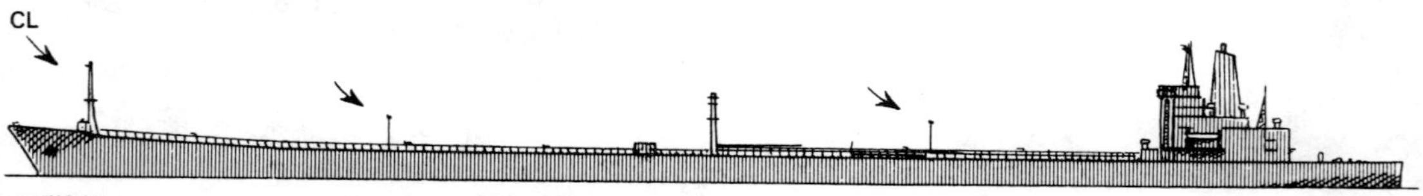

K_4MFK H
56330 KINKO MARU. Ja/Ja 1971; Tk; 129200; 331.53 × 20.53 (1087.7 × 67.36); T; 15.75.

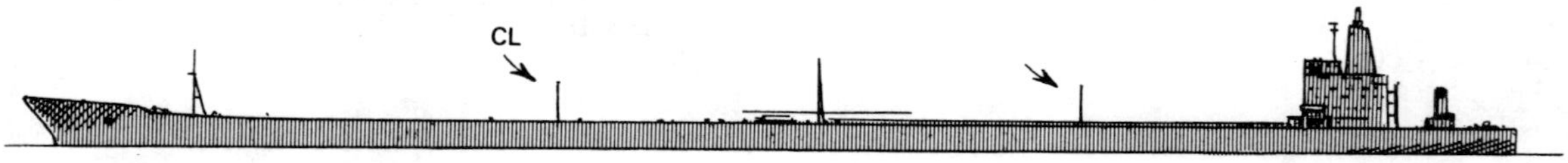

K_4MFK H
56340 ANTONIOS G. Li/De 1973; Tk; 129700; 347.23 × 22.22 (1139.21 × 72.9); T; 16; ex RANIA CHANDRIS 1976. Similar: **56341 TORILL KNUDSEN** (No).

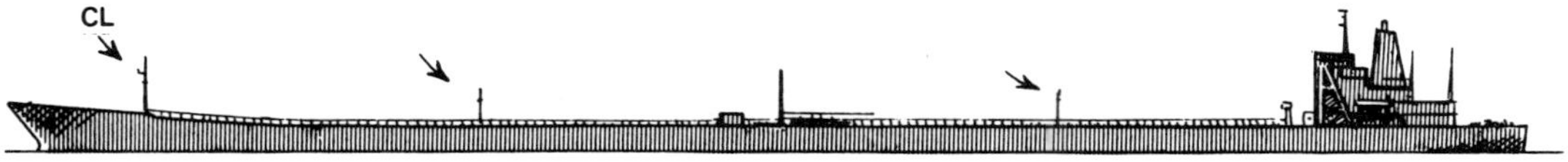

K_4MFK H

56350 JAPAN ORCHID. Ja/Ja 1971; Tk; 116100; 318.83 × 19.51 (1046.03 × 64.01); T; 16.25. Similar: **56351 HARMONY VENTURE** (Li) **56352 TIVOLI** (Ja) **56353 WORLD ENDEAVOUR** (Li) ex ASUKAGAWA MARU 1977 **56354 WORLD SAGA** (Li) ex UJIGAWA MARU 1977.

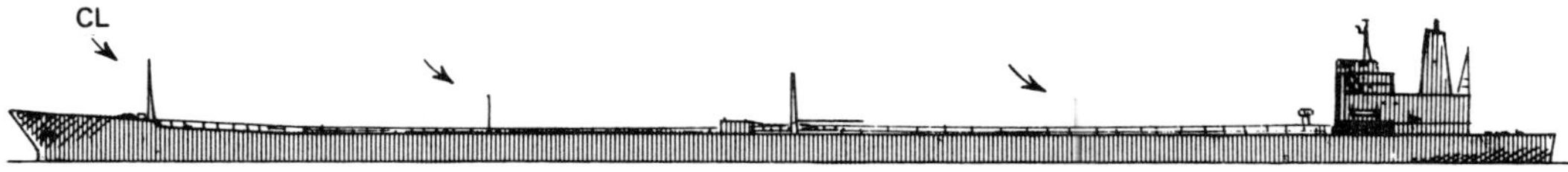

K_4MFK H

56360 FUJIKAWA MARU. Ja/Ja 1975; Tk; 116800; 319.95 × 19.66 (1049.7 × 64.5); T; 16.75.

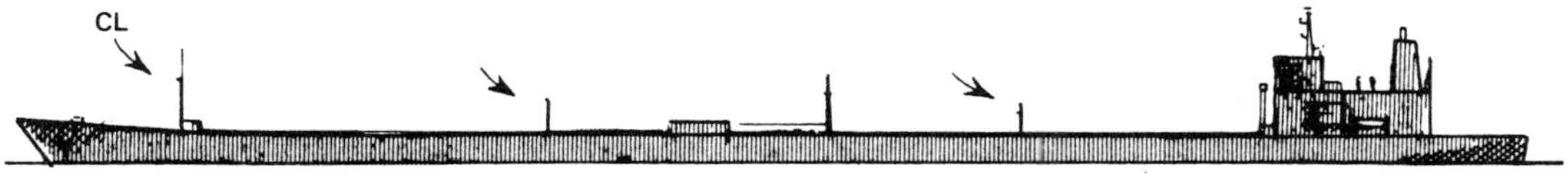

K_4MFK H

56370 TAKASE MARU. Ja/Ja 1970; Tk; 111700; 319.74 × 74.19 (1049.02 × 62.34); T; 16. Similar: **56371 WORLD MITSUBISHI** (Li) **56372 TAKOAKA MARU** (Ja).

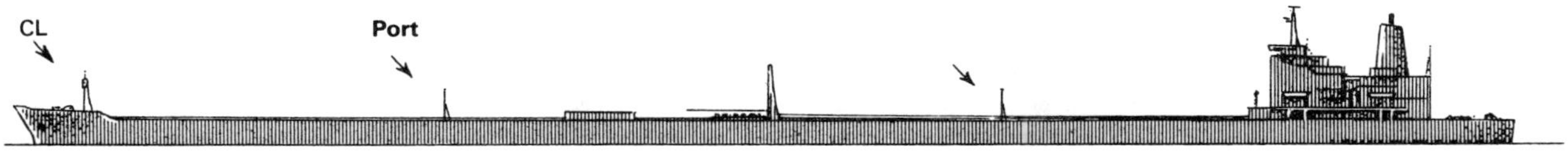

K_4MFK H

56380 BERGE EMPEROR. No/Ja 1975; Tk; 211400; 391.83 × 22.63 (1285.5 × 74.25); T; 15.5. Sister: **56381 BERGE EMPRESS** (No).

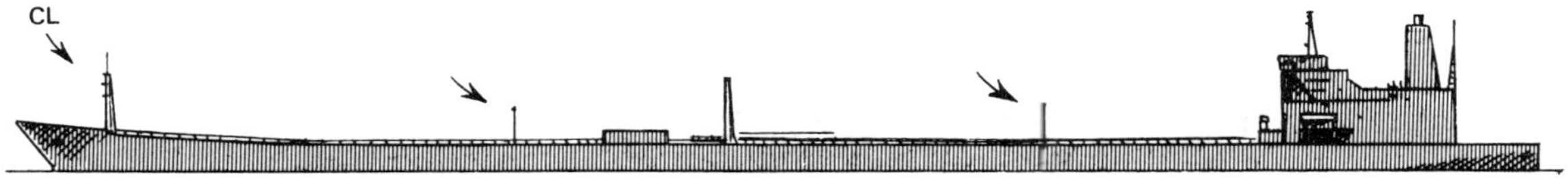

K_4MFK H

56390 IKUYO MARU. Ja/Ja 1972; Tk; 128700; 341.13 × 20.04 (1119.19 × 65.75); T; 15.5.

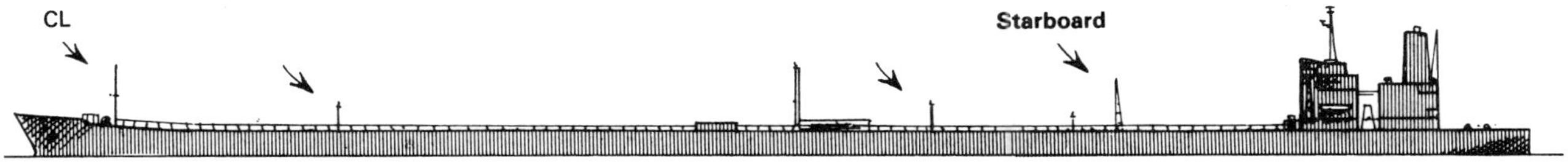

K_4MFK H

56400 ESSO CARIBBEAN. Li/Ja 1976; Tk; 177300; 378.39 × 22.27 (1241.44 × 73.06); T; 15.25; ex ANDROS PETROS 1977. Sisters: **56401 BURMAH ENDEAVOUR** (Br) **56402 BURMAH ENTERPRISE** (Br) **56403 ESSO MEDITERRANEAN** (Li) ex HOMERIC 1977 Similar: **56404 ANDROS CHRYSSI** (Li).

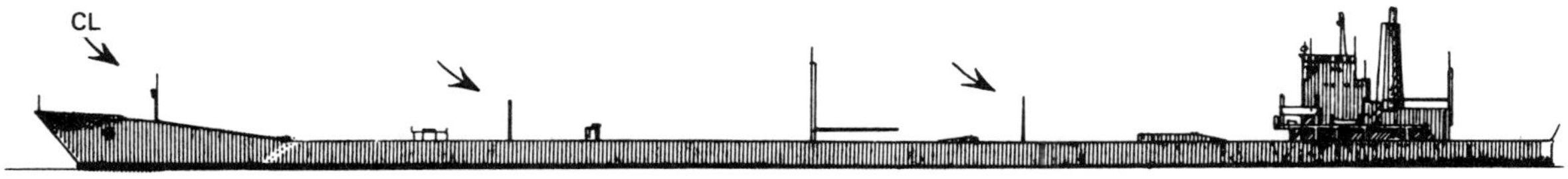

K_4MFK H

56410 FABIAN. No/No 1972; Tk; 140500; 347.84 × 22.14 (1114.21 × 72.64); T; 15.5. Sisters (No flag); **56411 JULIAN 56412 VESPASIAN** Possibly similar (no short uprights on deck): **56413 BEAUMONT 56414 BEAURIVAGE** Similar: **56415 CYPRIAN 56416 SIR CHARLES HAMBRO 56417 NORBORN** ex SONGA 1971 **56418 NORBRIGHT** ex RADNY 1977.

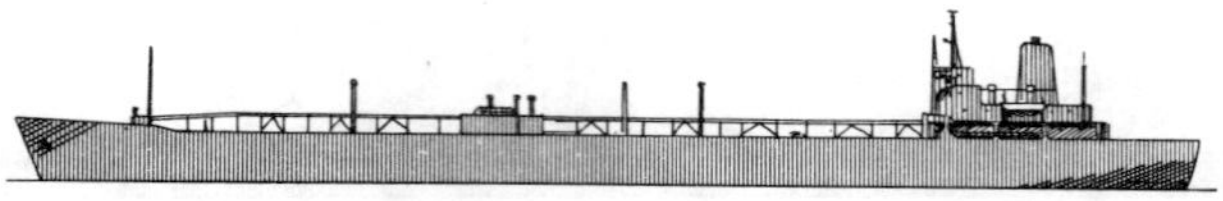

K_4MFK H
● **56420 GRAND REXTAR.** Li/Ja 1984; LGC; 21500; 187.51 × 10.49 (615.19 × 34.42); M; 15; ex BRIDGESTONE MARU II 1974.

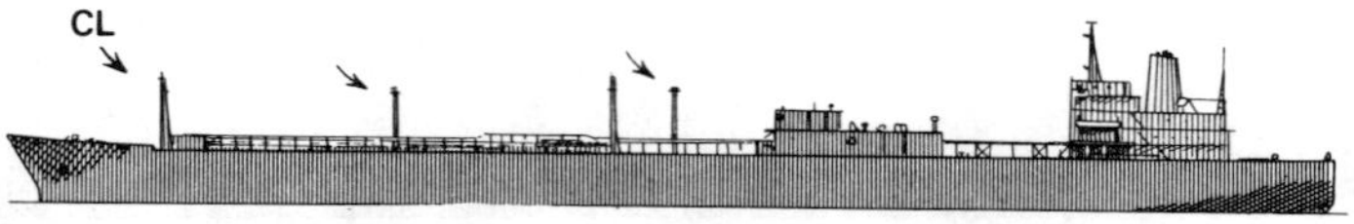

K_4MFK H
56430 TOKUHO MARU. Ja/Ja 1973; LGC; 39100; 215.07 × 11.14 (705.61 × 36.55); M; 16.

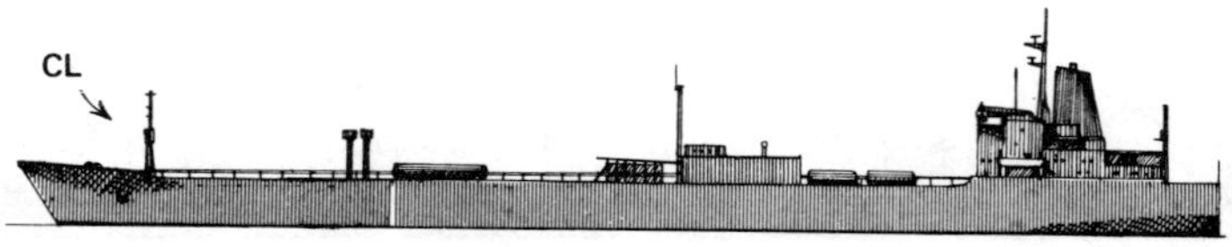

K_4MFK H
56440 SANDRINA. Pa/Fr 1973; LGC; 34300; 216.47 × 11.02 (710.2 × 36.15); M; 17.5; ex ATLANTE 1980; ex PROVIDENCE MULTINA ex DORSETOWN 1973. Sisters: **56441 STENA OCEANICA** (Br) ex MANDRILL 1980; ex MALMROS MULTINA 1979; ex DOVERTOWN 1974 **56442 ANTILLA BAY** (NA) Similar: **56443 REYNOSA** (Me) **56444 MONTERREY** (Me).

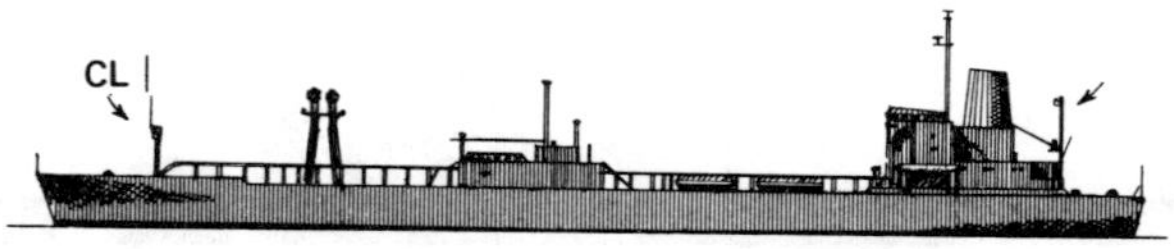

K_4MFK H
56450 ANTILLA CAPE. NA/FRG 1968; LGC; 19700; 173.84 × 10.26 (570.34 × 33.66); M; 17.5.

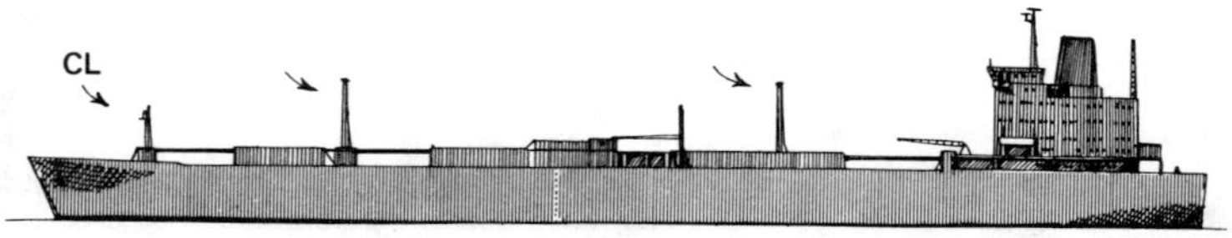

K_4MFK H
56460 BLUE OCEAN. Li/Pd 1976; LGC; 48500; 229.32 × 12.7 (752.36 × 41.67); M; 17.25; ex HOEGH SWALLOW; **'B-550'** type. Sisters (No flag): **56461 HOEGH SWIFT** being used as a storage vessel **56462 HOEGH SWORD.**

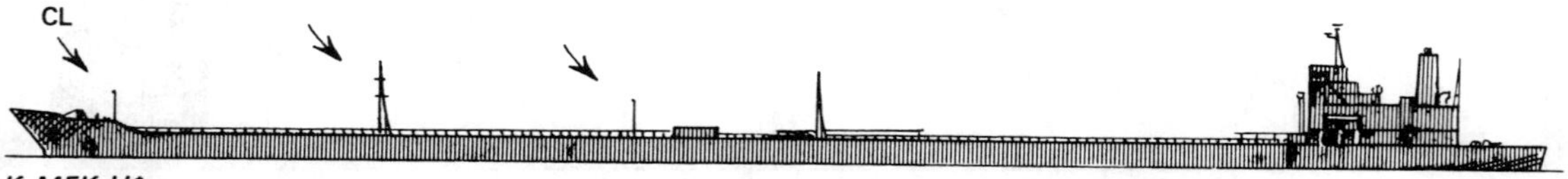

K_4MFK H1
56470 GRAND BRILLIANCE. Li/Ja 1975; Tk; 118200; 338.62 × 20.4 (1110.96 × 67.25); T; 15. Sister: **56471 GRAND ALLIANCE** (Li) Possible sister: **56472 GRAND CONCORDANCE** (Li).

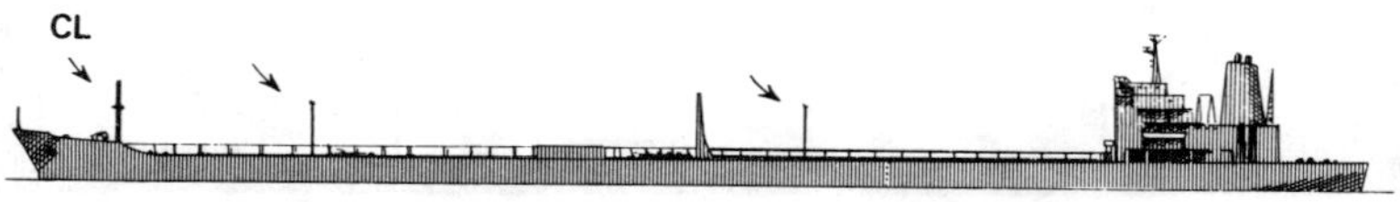

K_4MFK H1
⋆**56480 BANAT.** Rm/Ja 1975; Tk; 46900; 242.12 × 13.61 (794.36 × 44.65); M; 15.75. Sisters (Rm flag): ⋆**56481 CRISANA 56482 DACIA** ⋆**56483 MUNTENIA.**

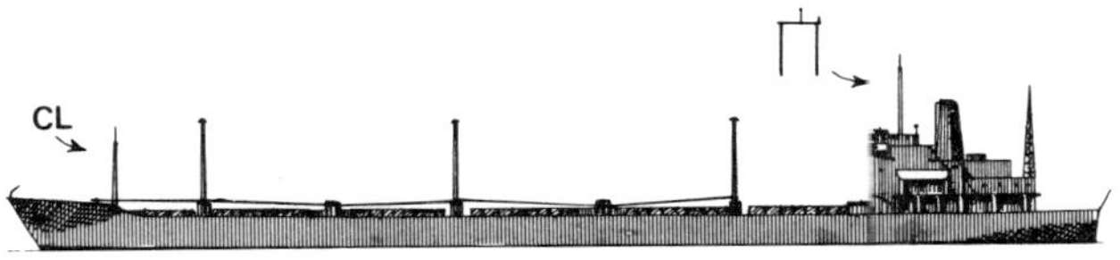

K_4MFK H1
56490 EAGLE GLORY. Pa/Ja 1969; B; 23500; 193.5 × 11.4 (634.97 × 37.4); M; 14.25.

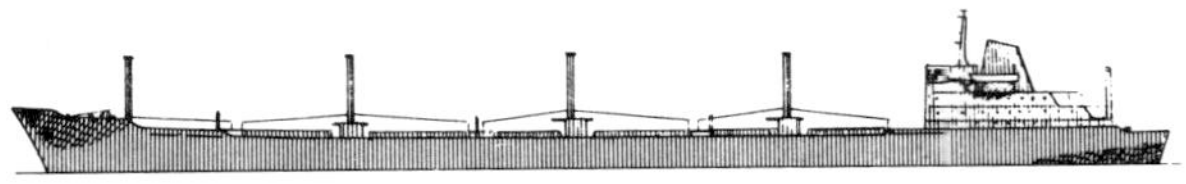

K_4MFK H1
56500 SEAKITTIE. Br/Br 1975; B; 15900; 183.04 × 10.47 (600.53 × 34.35); M; 15.5; ex CAIRNSMORE 1978; **'B-26'** type. Sisters: **56501 LYNTON GRANGE** (Br) **56502 UPWEY GRANGE** (Br) **56503 LEON.** (Gr) Possible sister: **56504 RIGHTEOUS** (Li).

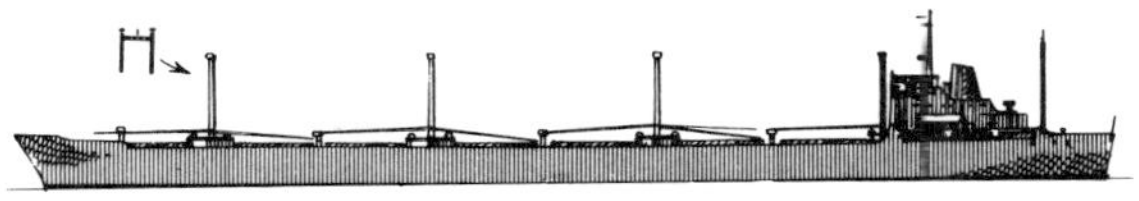

K_4MFK H1
56510 NESTOR. Gr/Ys 1968; B; 25800; 205.8 × 11.93 (675.2 × 39.14); M; —; ex ARCHONTAS 1973.

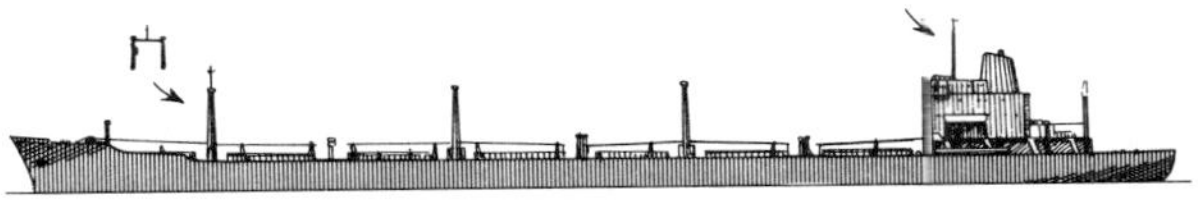

K_4MFK H1
56520 ERITHIANI. Gr/Ja 1968; B; 19700; 184.36 × 11.17 (604.86 × 36.65); M; 15.25; ex SOUTH GLORY 1981; ex JANOVA 1978. Sister: **56521 ELAFI** (Gr) ex SANDEFJORD 1974 Similar (mast from funnel): **56522 ARIETTA** (Gr) ex JAPANA 1978; ex NOPAL JAPANA 1976; ex JAPANA 1974 **56523 JONNI** (Gr) ex JANITA 1978 **56524 HAUNDOY** (Pe) ex KATE N.L. 1980; launched as WORLD CENTENARY.

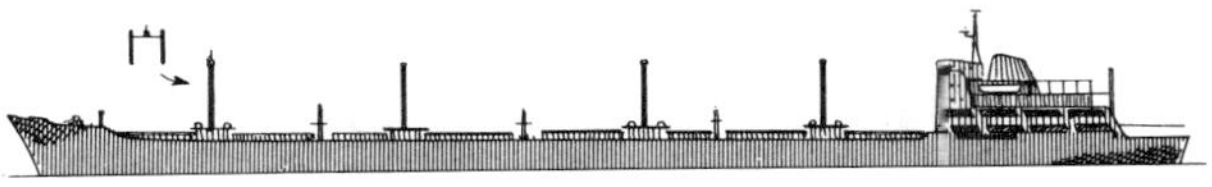

K_4MFK H1
56530 MARGIO. Li/Br 1965; B; 17200; 188.07 × 10.86 (617.03 × 35.63); M; 14; ex BARON INVERFORTH 1969.

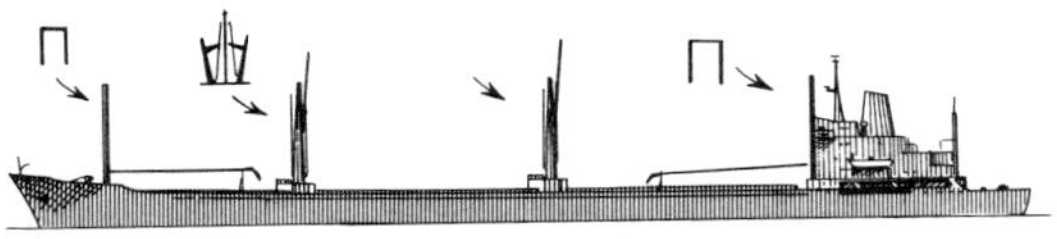

K_4MFK H1
56540 EASTERN WISEMAN. Li/Ja 1972; B; 15500; 162.01 × 10.64 (531.53 × 34.91); M; 14.5.

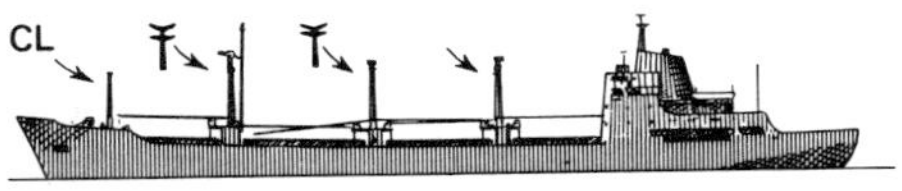

K_4MFK H1
56560 PALM TRADER. Gr/Br 1963; C; 5100; 133.13 × 7.49 (436.78 × 24.57); M; 16.5; ex BEROONA 1978; ex MEDIA 1971. Sister: **56561 RICE TRADER** (Gr) ex WAMBIRI; ex STASHIP 1 1973; ex PARTHIA 1971.

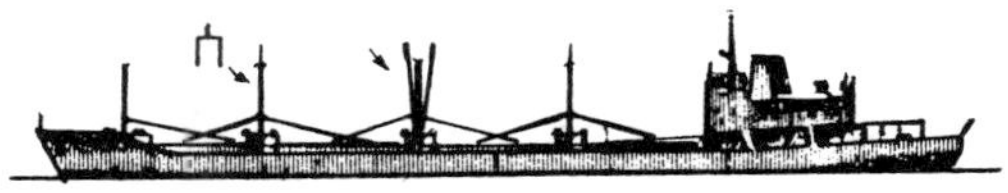

K_4MFK H1
● **56550 PRESIDENTE KENNEDY.** Bz/Bz 1965; C; 6900/9100; 145.5 × 7.94/8.75 (477.36 × 26.05/28.7); M; 15.5. Sisters: **56551 ALMIRANTE GRACA ARANHA** (Bz) **56552 EL MEXICANO** (Me) **56553 PUEBLA** (Me) Similar: **56554 BUARQUE** (Bz) **56555 ROMEO BRAGA** (Bz).

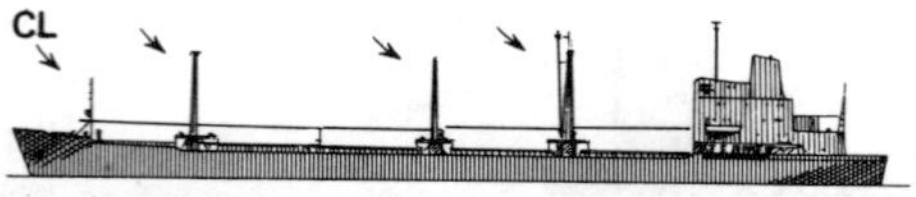

K_4MFK H1
56570 MARLY. Li/FRG 1976; C; 9500; 139.58 × 9.17 (457.94 × 30.09); M; 16; ex SUSANNE 1979; **'German Liberty'** type.

● 56575

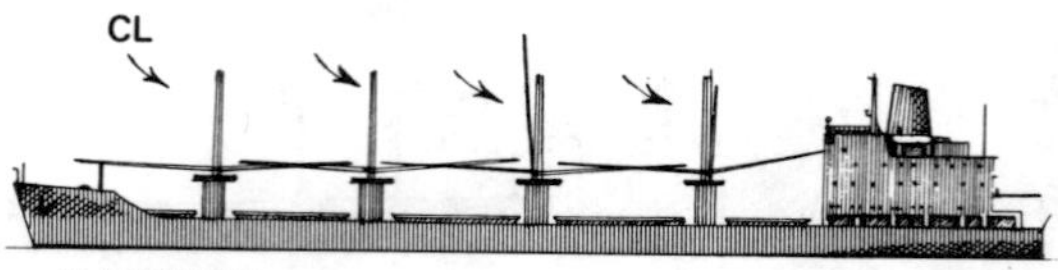

K_4MFK H1
56580 OROYA. Br/Br 1978; C; 9000/14100; 163.15 × 9.68 (535.27 × 31.76); M; 16.5. Sister: **56581 OROPESA** (Br).

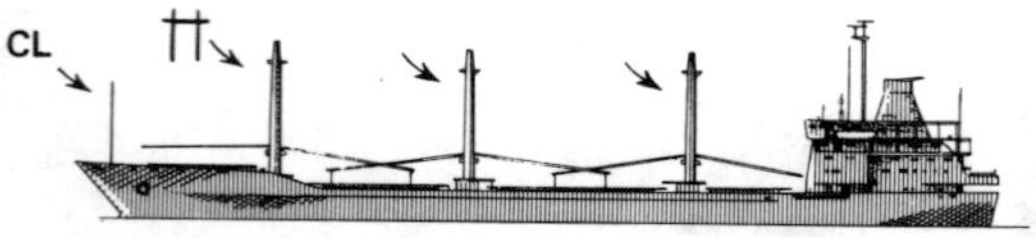

K_4MFK H1
● **56590 SOKOTO.** Br/Pd 1979; C/Con; 9100; 145.85 × 7.65 (478.5 × 25.1); M; 16.8; **'B-430'** type. Sisters: **56591 SEKONDI** (Br) **56592 SAPELE** (Br) **56593 GUATEMALA** (Li) **56594 HOEGH APAPA** (Li) ex HONDURAS 1980 **56595 COSTA RICA** (FRG).

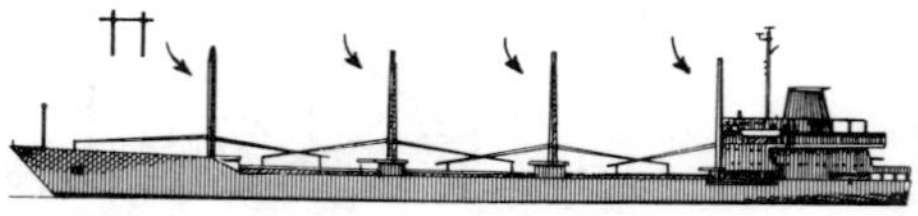

K_4MFK H1
56600 SHONGA. Br/Pd 1973; C/Con; 5700/9200; 145.73 × 7.04/8.4 (478.12 × 23.1/27.56); M; 16.5; **'B-430'** type. Sisters: **56601 SHERBRO** (Br) **56602 APAPA PALM** (Br) ex SCHAUENBURG 1977 **56603 MEXICO** (Li) ex HASSELBURG 1980; ex HOEGH APAPA 1979; ex APAPA PALM 1977; ex HASSELBURG 1976 **56604 MONSUN** (FRG) ex SAPELE 1979; ex MONSUN 1976 **56605 RIVER HADEJIA** (Ng).

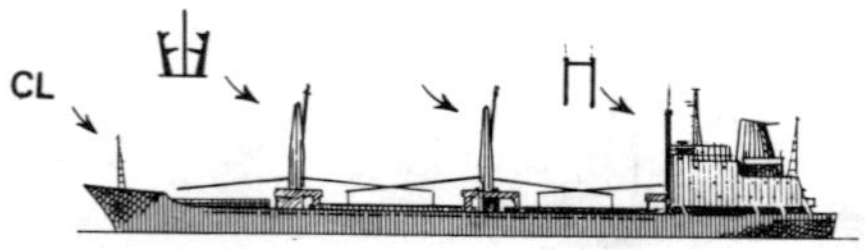

K_4MFK H1
56610 LAURIE U. Li/Ja 1977; C; 6200; 119.41 × 7.41 (391.77 × 24.31); M; 16. Sister: **56611 MARIA U** (Li).

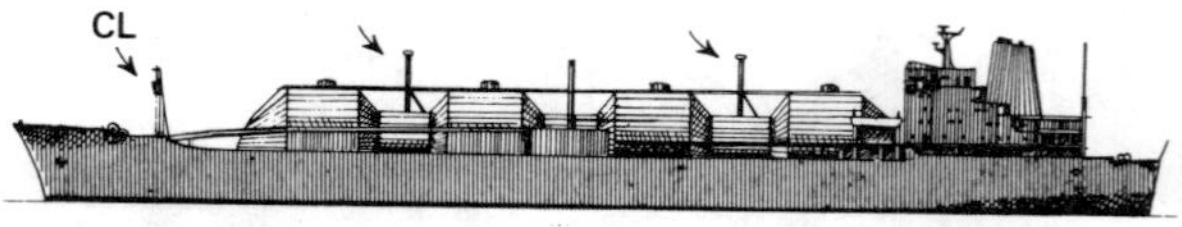

K_4MFK H1
56620 VENATOR. No/No 1973; LGC; 27300; 181.54 × 9.42 (595.6 × 30.91); M; 20; Converted from gas turbine 1980. Sister: **56621 CENTURY** (No) ex LUCIAN 1980.

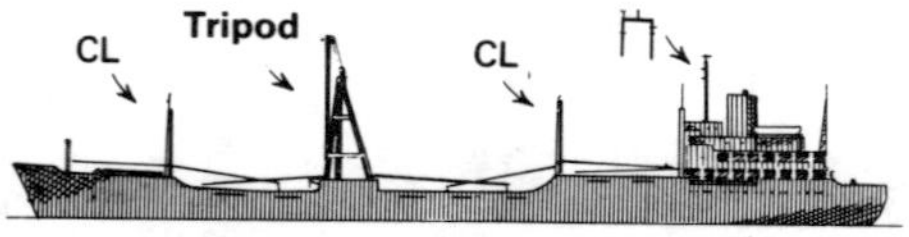

K_4MFK H123
56630 WAKAMATSU MARU. Ja/Ja 1967; C/HL; 7800; 138.51 × 8.48 (454.43 × 27.82); M; 15.25. Similar (Ja flag): **56631 WAKAURA MARU 56632 WAKAKUSA MARU.**

● 56636

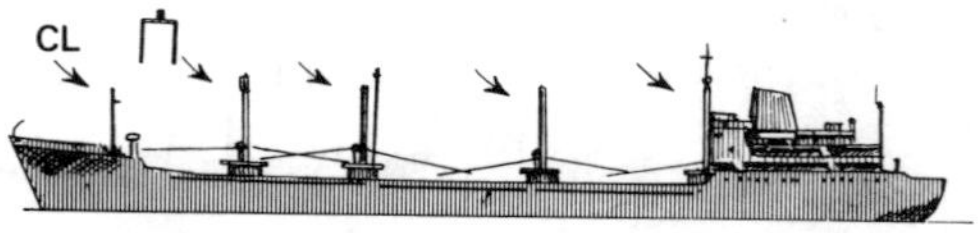

K_4MFK H13
56640 SANDVIKEN. Fi/Sw 1962; C; 7200/9300; 148.47 × 8.21/9.25 (487.1 × 26.9/30.3); M; —.

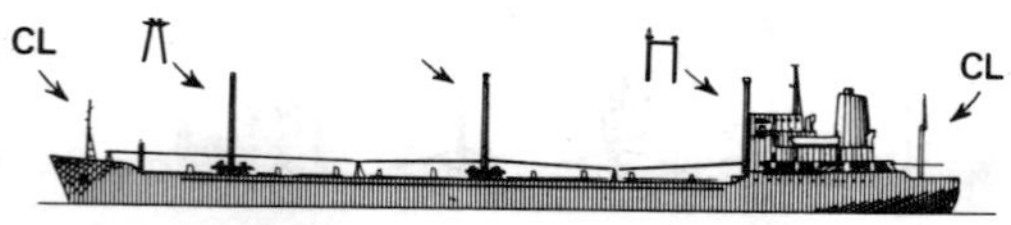

K_4MFK H13
56650 HOLY. Li/Ja 1971; B; 9400; 147.53 × 9.31 (484 × 30.5); M; 15; **'16 BC 5'** type. Possible sister: **56651 EASTERN MARINER** (Li).

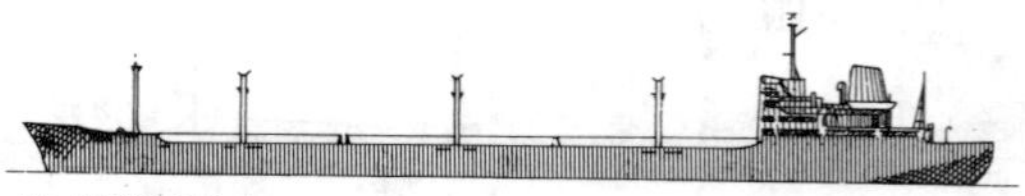

K_4MFK H13
56660 CHEER MAY. Pa/Ja 1959; O; 9900; 154.11 × 8.54 (505.61 × 28.02); M; 13; ex TIEN SHIN 1977; ex NITTEI MARU 1975.

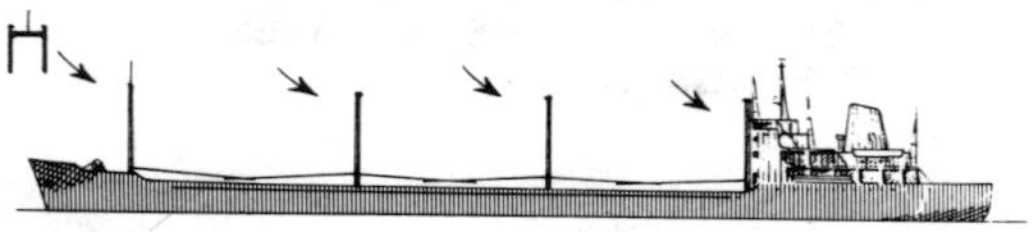

K_4MFK H13
● **56670 UNITED FAITH.** Pa/Ja 1959; O; 10300; 152.71 × 8.55 (501.02 × 28.05); M; 13.5; ex KAGOSHIMA MARU 1972.

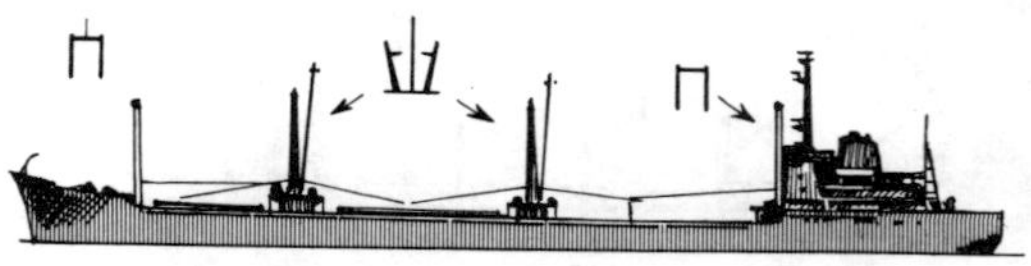

K_4MFK H13
56680 PACIFIC ERA. Li/Ja 1971; B; 15100; 160.99 × 10.79 (528.2 × 35.4); M; 14.5. Sister: **56681 PACIFIC SAGA** (Li).

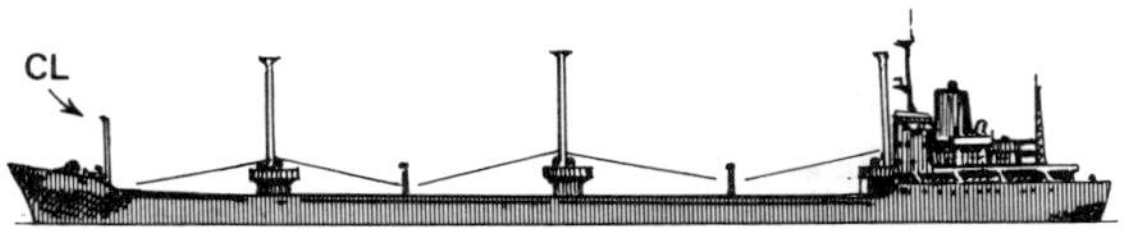

K_4MFK *H13*
56690 ISLAND ARCHON. Li/Ja 1971; B; 15700; 174.71 × 10.31 (573.2 × 33.8); M; 15.5. Sister: ★**56691 YI NING HAI** (RC) ex ISLAND SUN 1978.

● 56695

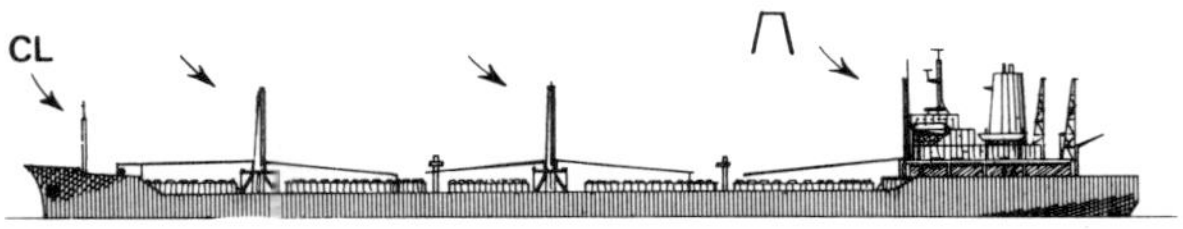

K_4MFK *H13*
56700 ASIA FIDELITY. Pa/Ja 1971; B; 15700; 174.53 × 10.19 (572.6 × 33.43); M; 15.

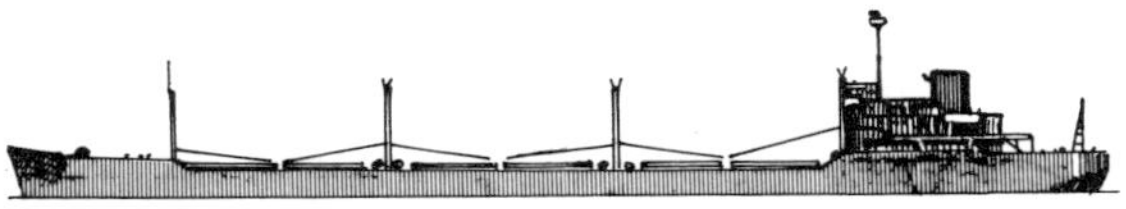

K_4MFK *H13*
56710 CEMENT CARRIER. Sg/Ja 1961; B; 13700; 174.07 × 9.48 (571.1 × 31.1); M; 13.5; ex GRAND APOLLO 1980; ex CHIYOKAWA MARU 1972.

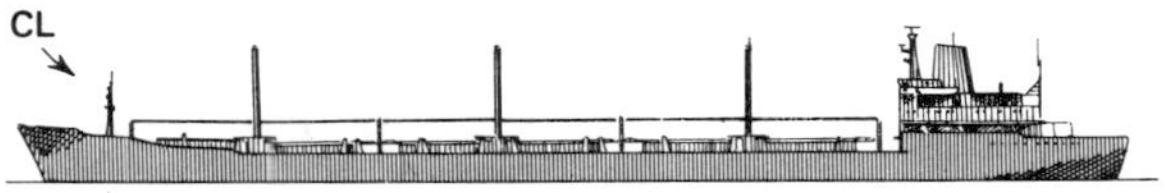

K_4MFK *H13*
● **56720 BELLA MAERSK.** De/No 1969; B; 15900; 180.32 × 10.21 (591.6 × 33.5); M; —. Sister: **56721 BRIGIT MAERSK** (De) Similar: **56722 MAERSK COMMANDER** (Br) **56723 MAERSK CADET** (Br) **56724 DANILA** (Li) ex MAERSK CAPTAIN **56725 IRENES ZEST** (Li) ex GOLDEN MISTRAL 1980; ex HOEGH MISTRAL 1978 **56726 GLYFADA** (Gr) ex GOLDEN MINERVA 1980; ex HOEGH MINERVA 1978 **56727 GOLDEN MIRANDA** (Li) ex HOEGH MIRANDA 1977 **56728 IRENES ZEAL** (Gr) ex LEAL 1980; ex BELHUDSON 1976; launched as BELVENI.

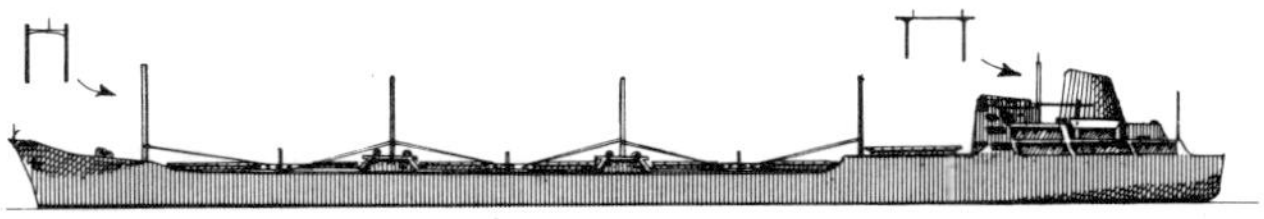

K_4MFK *H13*
56740 SEACALF. Pa/Br 1965; B; 21400; 192.03 × 10.75 (630 × 35.3); M; 15.5; ex PRODROMOS 1978; ex SIMONBURN 1972.

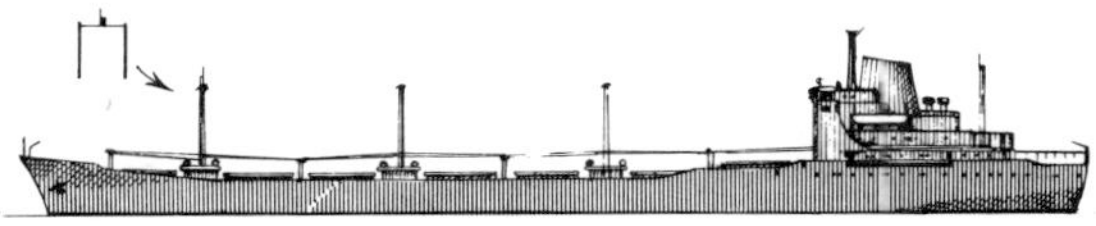

K_4MFK *H13*
56750 ATLAS CHALLENGER. Ko/Sw 1962; B; 12200; 169.17 × 9.7 (555.02 × 31.82); M; 15.75; ex RONACASTLE 1972; ex CAP RONA 1972; ex RONACASTLE 1965. Sisters: **56751 ARIEL** (Gr) ex THORSODD 1970 **56752 ARISTIDES** (Gr) ex HAFNIA 1975 **56753 UNITED SKY** (Sg) ex EASTERN ROSE 1980; ex AEGIS FURY 1979; ex ARIEL 1970 **56754 MARAZUL 1** (Pa) ex GLYFADA SUMMER; ex NORSE LADY 1973.

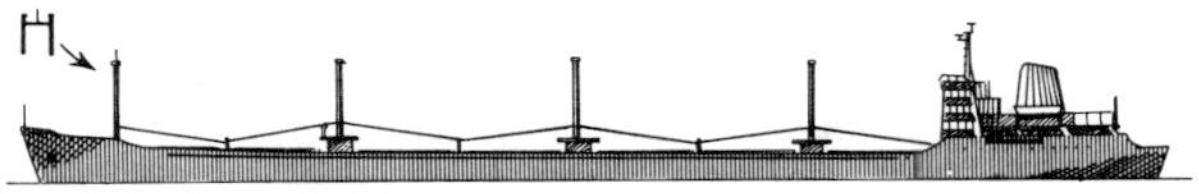

K_4MFK *H13*
56760 ZINNIA. Br/Br 1968; B; 16100; 182.2 × 10.64 (597.77 × 34.91); M; 14.5.

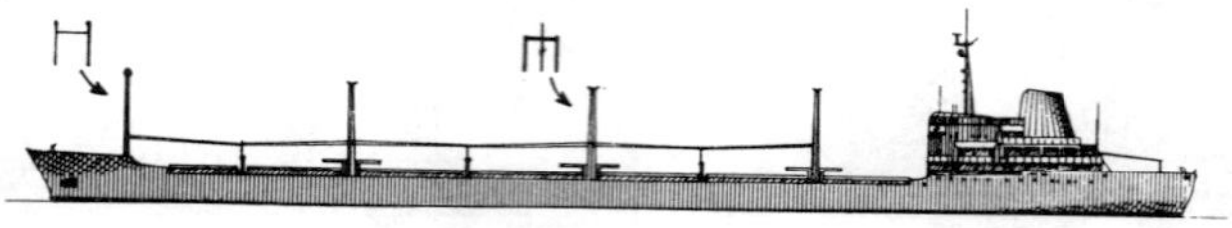

K_4MFK H13
56770 PACIFIC SKOU. De/FRG 1968; B; 15800; 186.93×10.59 (613.3×34.7); M; 17. Sister: **56771 ATLANTIC SKOU** (De).

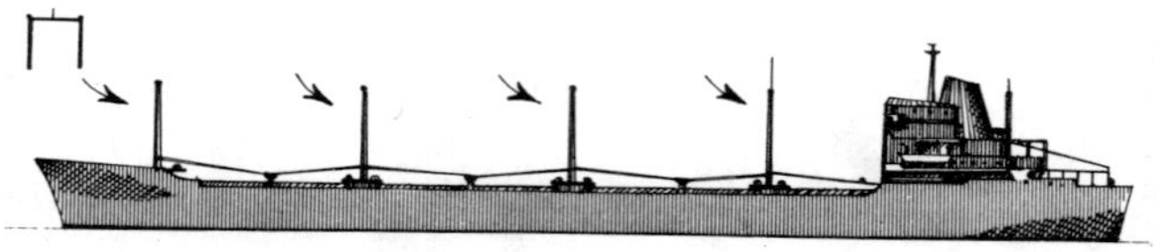

K_4MFK H13
56780 SANCHI. In/Ys 1968; B; 23400; 193.5×11.58 (635.1×38); M; 14.25. Sisters (In flag): **56781 AJANTA 56782 NALANDA.**

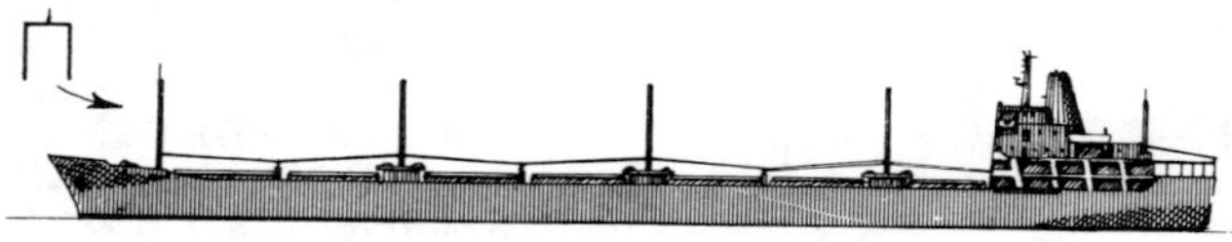

K_4MFK H13
56790 GRECIAN TEMPLE. Li/Ja 1966; B; 23600; 191.01×11.7 (626.67×38.4); M; 15; ex RESPLENDENT 1970. Sisters (Gr flag): **56791 CAPETAN TASSOS 56792 ANASTASSIA.**

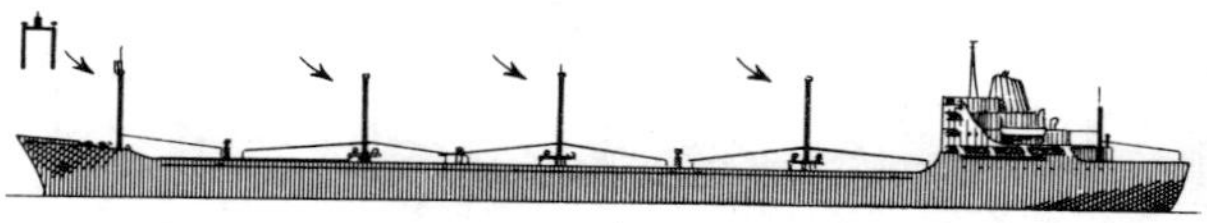

K_4MFK H13
56800 LEONIDAS Z. CAMBANIS. Gr/Ja 1965; B; 15700; 186.01×10.68 (610.3×35); M; 17.

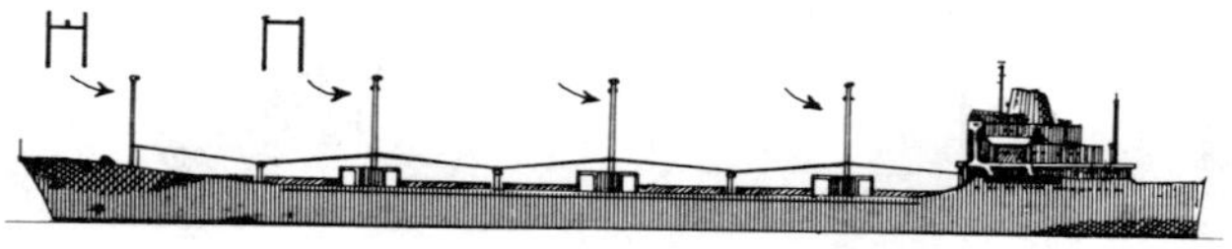

K_4MFK H13
56810 SINGAPORE CAR. Sg/FRG 1963; B; 15300; 189.9×9.88 (623.03×32.41); M; 17.25; ex CAPTAIN JUAN FONSECA 1980; ex FRIENDLY ISLANDS 1979; ex JOHANN SCHULTE 1974.

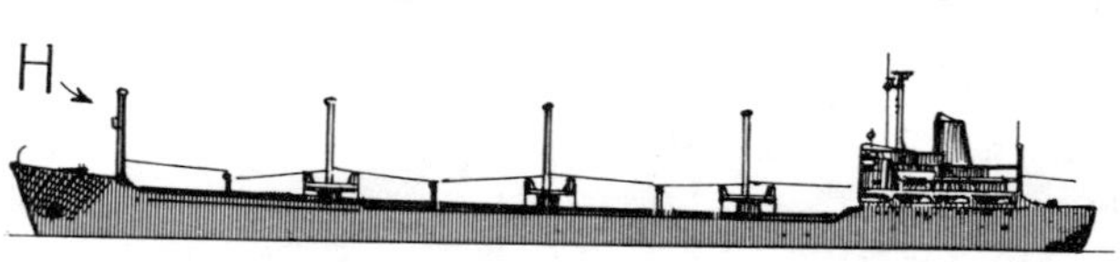

K_4MFK H13
56820 CAPTAIN VENIAMIS. Gr/FRG 1967; B; 15700; 186.9×10.55 (613.2×34.6); M; 17; ex GEORG RUSS 1980; ex NORDSTERN 1975. Sister: **56821 LUTETIAN** (Pa) ex MARGARETHE BOLTEN 1979; ex STADT WOLFSBURG 1978.

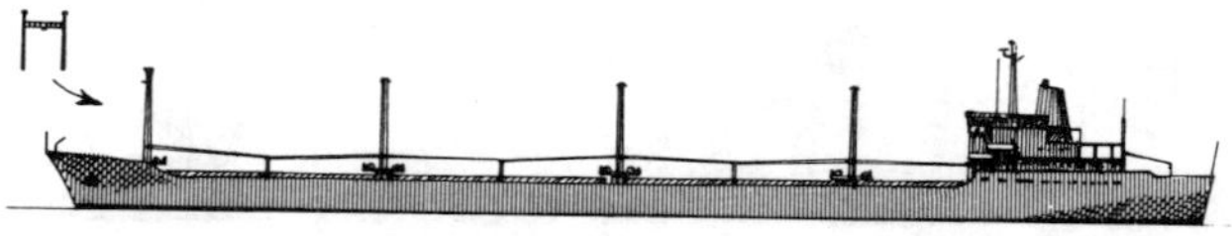

K_4MFK H13
56830 DRAKE SEA. Pa/FRG 1968; B; 15000; 186.9×9.89 (613.19×32.45); M; 17; ex BELGRANO 1978.

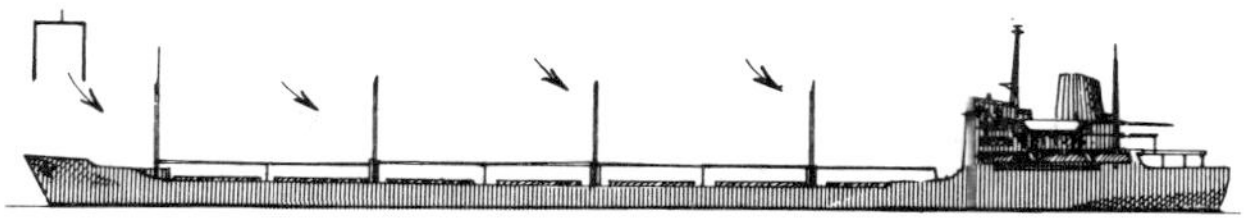

K_4MFK H13
56840 BHARATA. In/Ja 1963; B; 21300; 191.12 × 10.97 (627.03 × 35.99); M; 12.5; ex BHARATA JAYANTI 1974. Sisters (In flag): **56841 DEVARAYA** ex DEVARAYA JAYANTI 1974 **56842 KANISHKA** ex KANISHKA JAYANTI 1974 **56843 LAXMI** ex AKBAR JAYANTI 1974 **56844 PARVATI** ex GOTAMA JAYANTI 1975 **56845 SAMUDRAGUPTA** ex SAMUDRAGUPTA JAYANTI 1975 **56846 SHAHJEHAN** ex SHAHJEHAN JAYANTI 1974.

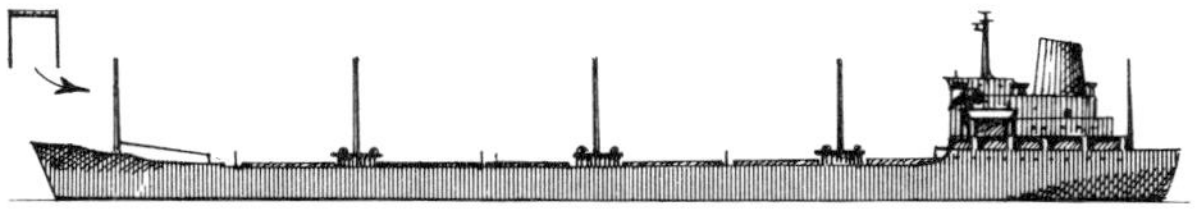

K_4MFK H13
★**56850 HUA HAI.** RC/Br 1964; B; 16400; 182.43 × 9.93 (598.52 × 32.58); M; 15.5; ex CHINA SEA 1976; ex SILKSWORTH 1972.

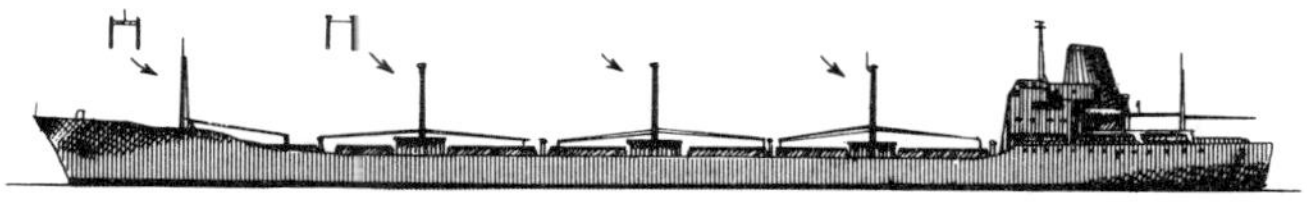

K_4MFK H13
56860 MOUNT OTHRYS. Gr/Ys 1968; B; 18800; 199.63 × 10.85 (199.63 × 35.6); M; 15.5; ex WELSH MINSTREL 1978. Sisters: ★**56861 JIN ZHOU HAI** (RC) ex DORIC ARROW 1980 **56862 HELLAS IN ETERNITY** (Gr) **56863 APOLLON** (Gr).

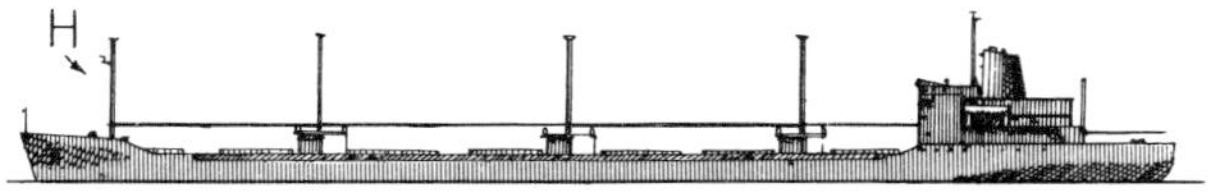

K_4MFK H13
56870 BERKSHIRE. Br/Br 1970; B; 19100; 182.58 × 10.67 (599.01 × 35.01); M; 16. Sisters: **56871 CHESHIRE** (Br) **56872 GEORGIOS TSAKIROGLOU** (Gr) ex OXFORDSHIRE 1978.

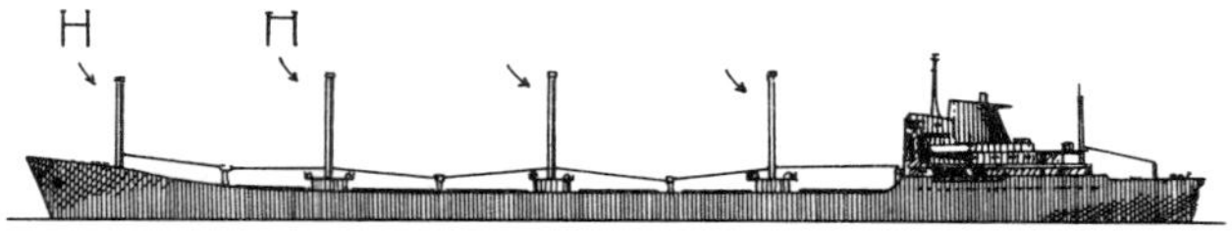

K_4MFK H13
★**56880 BEI HAI.** RC/FRG 1963; B; 15500; 190.13 × 9.88 (623.8 × 32.4); M; 17.5; ex MARGARETHE BOLTEN 1974. Sister: ★**56881 FU JIN HAI** (RC) ex MARIE LUISE BOLTEN 1978.

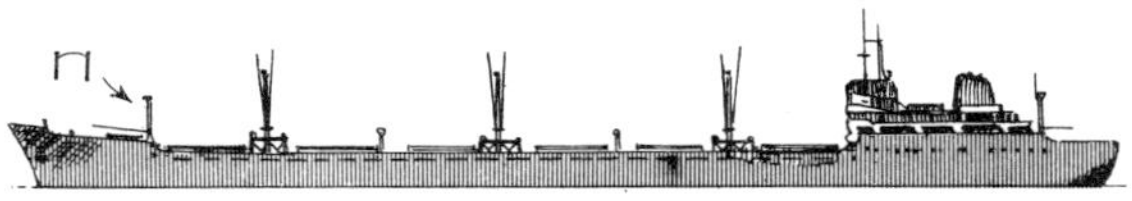

K_4MFK H13
56890 KOSTAS MELAS. Pa/It 1961; B; 13300; 175.24 × 10.27 (574.9 × 33.7); M; —; ex LUCIANA DELLA GATTA; ex BONASSOLA.

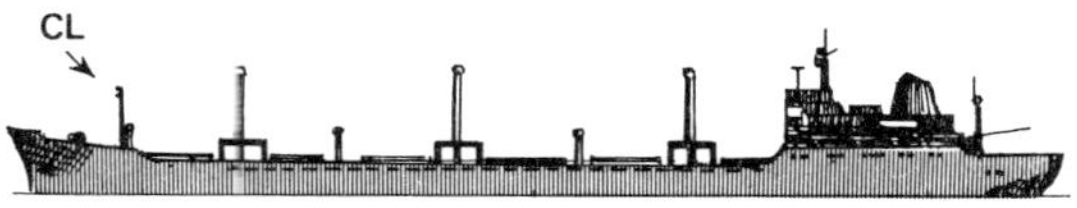

K_4MFK H13
56900 WEST RIVER. Li/It 1962; C; 10900; 166.45 × 9.519 (546.1 × 31.2); M; 14.

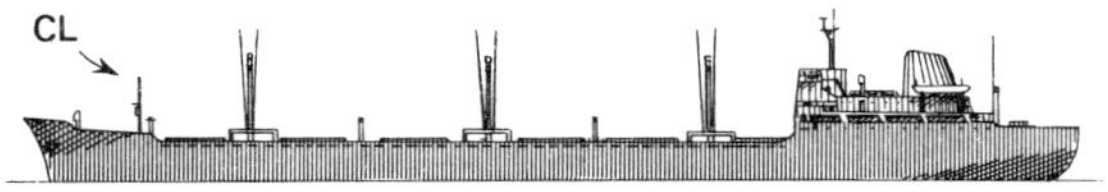

K_4MFK H13
56910 PANARMA. Pa/It 1957; C; 10200; 165.51 × 8.75 (543.01 × 28.71); M; 14.5; ex HERMOSA 1979.

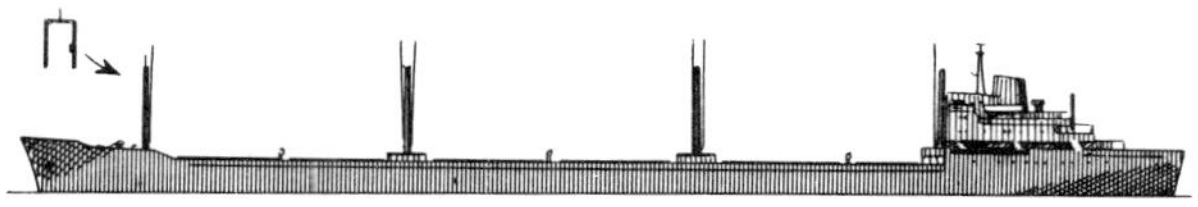

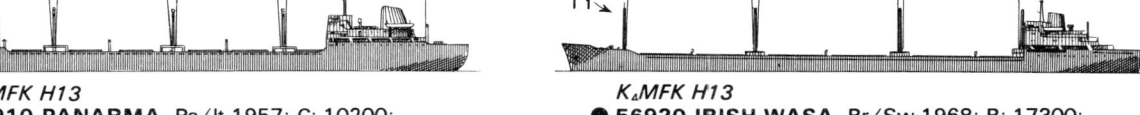

K_4MFK H13
● **56920 IRISH WASA.** Br/Sw 1968; B; 17300; 185.17 × 10.23 (607.5 × 33.6); M; 16; ex NORDIC WASA 1977; ex LISA BRODIN 1971.

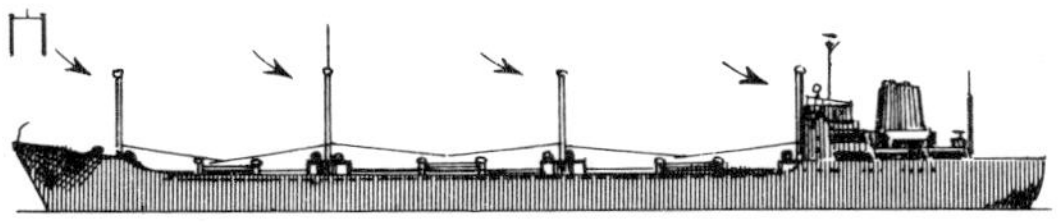

K_4MFK H13
56930 DOBROTA. Ma/Ja 1960; B; 11100; 161.96 × 9.21 (531.4 × 30.21); M; 14.75; ex ROSINA TOPIC. Sister: **56931 LJUTA** (Ma) ex SERAFIN TOPIC 1979.

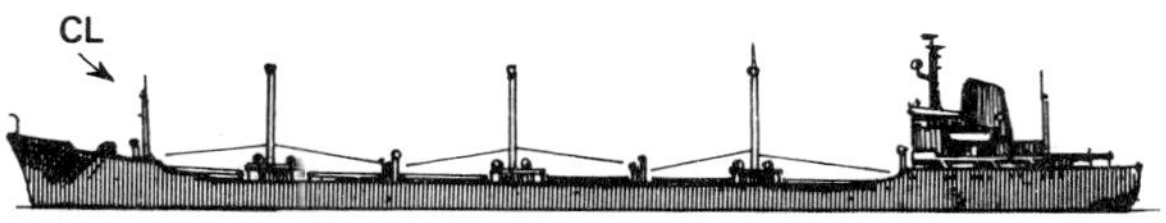

K_4MFK H13
56940 JOANA. Gr/Ja 1969; B; 15900; 178.01 × 10.57 (584 × 34.7); M; 16.

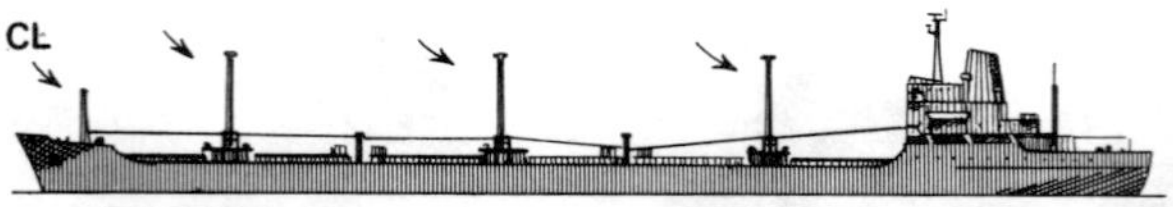

K_4MFK H13
56950 JILL CORD. De/Ja 1973; B; 19600; 179.03 × 10.96 (587.4 × 36); M; 15.25.

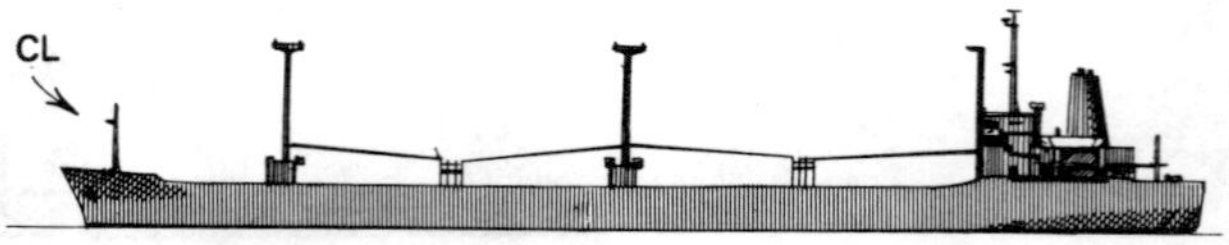

K_4MFK H13
56960 SPLENDID HOPE. Pa/Ja 1974; B; 16800; 181.52 × 10.06 (592.26 × 34.74); M; 15; ex SEIHO MARU 1978.

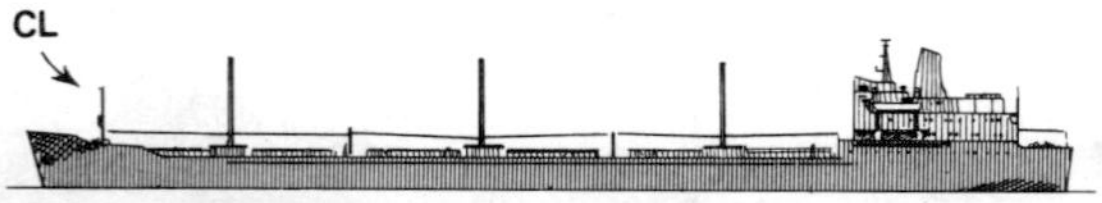

K_4MFK H13
● **56970 IRENES FANTASY.** Gr/No 1968; B; 13400; 165.03 × 9.82 (541.44 × 32.22); M; 16; ex AVENTICUM; ex IVORY NEPTUNE 1976; ex JANNETTA 1974. Similar: **56971 AUSTRAL** (Pa) ex JAWAGA 1977 **56972 CARA** (Gr) ex JACARA 1976 **56973 SEMI** (Gr) ex JALANTA 1977.

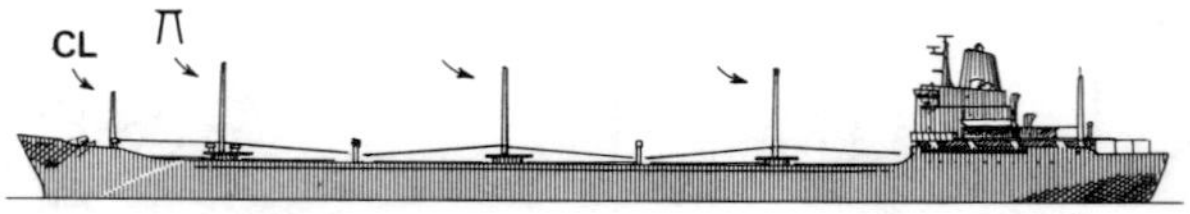

K_4MFK H13
56980 AGIA ERINI II. Gr/Ja 1970; B; 18600; 182.61 × 10.63 (599.11 × 34.88); M; 16. Sisters: **56981 FOSO** (Gr) **56982 PUFFIN PRIDE** (Gr) ex CINDY 1980 **56983 SILVAPLANA** (Li) Similar: **56984 GEORGIS PROIS** (Gr) **56985 MARGARITE** (Gr) **56986 CAPETAN COSTIS 1** (Gr) **56987 KIKA** (Gr) ex KAREN 1980 **56988 CHARALAMBOS F** (Gr) ex MARY S 1980 **56989 EFPLOIA** (Gr) **56990 KATERINA** (Li) ex SCOTSTOUN 1980; ex FORESTLAND 1975; ex RUBY 1969 **56991 JAY DURGA** (In) ex RIO ELL 1980; ex RUBY 1975 ⋆**56992 YONG FENG HAI** (RC) ex COSTAS FRANGOS 1978 ⋆**56993 JIA YU HAI** (RC) ex LORINA 1978.

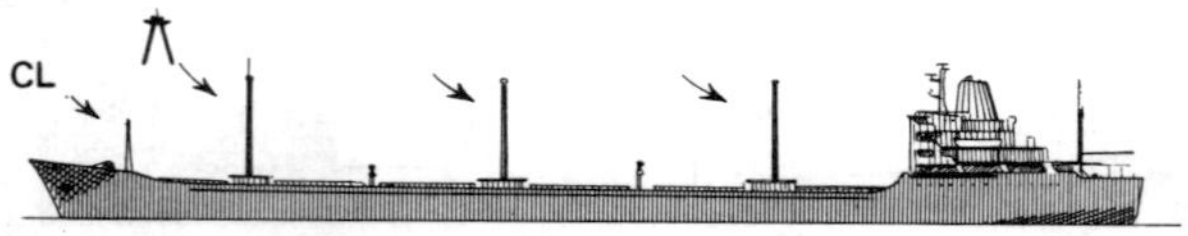

K_4MFK H13
⋆**57000 ZHIHAI.** RC/Ja 1968; B; 15400; 176.61 × 10.06 (579.43 × 33.01); M; 17; ex AURORA II 1976. Similar: **57001 AGIOS NIKOLAOS III** (Gr) **57002 GEORGE S. EMBIRICOS** (Gr) **57003 MAISTROS** (Li).

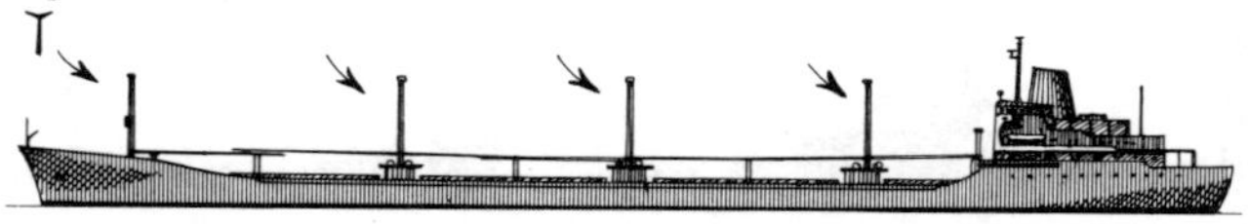

K_4MFK H13
⋆**57010 YUN HAI.** RC/Sw 1963; B; 20100; 196.32 × 10.88 (644.09 × 35.7); M; —; ex ANDAMAN SEA 1974; ex ROBERT STOVE 1973. Sister: **57011 DONA ELVIRA** (Pa) ex GAUSDAL 1978.

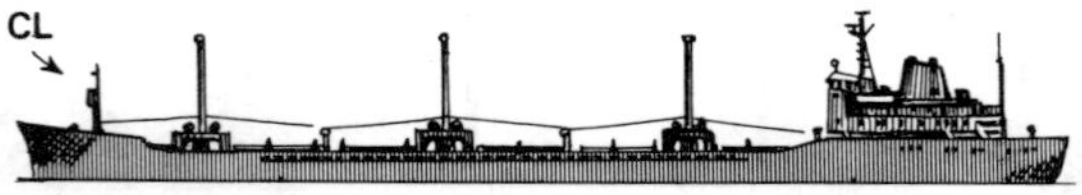

K_4MFK H13
● **57020 MITERA ITENA.** Gr/No 1967; B; 13600; 166.12 × 10.36 (545 × 34); M; 15; ex SPARTO 1980; ex VINGNES 1977. Sister: **57021 SUNRIVER** (Li) ex DAGRUN 1976.

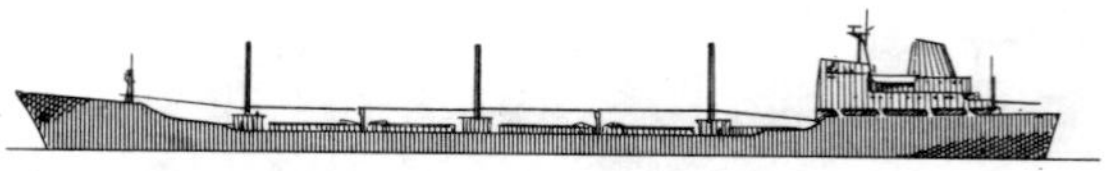

K_4MFK H13
57030 SEMELI. Gr/No 1963; B; 11200; 164.83 × 9.18 (540.78 × 30.12); -m; 14; ex MAREVA A S; ex MESNA 1973; ex AXEL B LORENTZEN 1969.

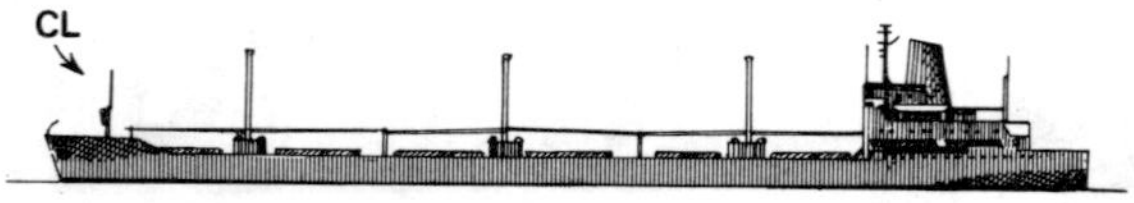

K_4MFK H13
57040 NIHON ALPHA. Cy/No 1965; B; 13500; 164.9 × 10.02 (541 × 32.9); M; 15.5; ex FERNGROVE 1978. Sister: **57041 INICIATIVA** (Pa) ex AALSUM 1978; ex FERNLEAF 1973 Similar: **57042 BASTION ALPHA** (Cy) ex BUSSUM 1980; ex FERNGULF 1974.

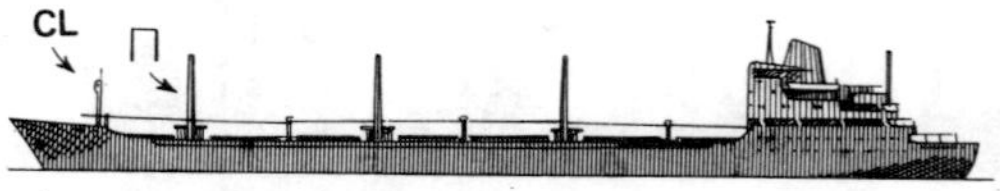

K_4MFK H13
57050 NAOUSSA. Gr/FRG 1962; B; 11000; 152.58 × 10.3 (500.6 × 33.8); M; 14.5; ex MARIA P LEMOS; ex FERDER 1970.

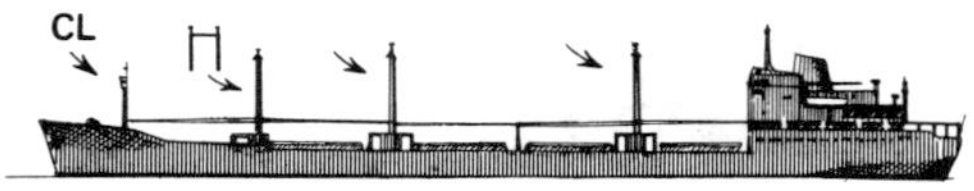

K_4MFK H13
57060 STROFADES. Gr/Sw 1962; B; 9000; 149.76 × 8.97 (491.34 × 29.43); M; 13.5; ex DELFIN 1972; ex SONATA 1968.

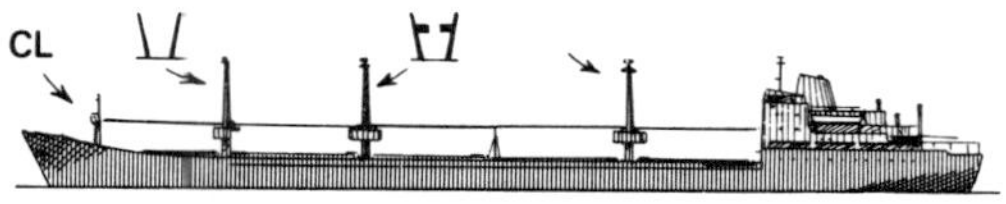

K_4MFK H13
57070 UJUNG RAJA. Ia/Sw 1960; B; 8890; 152,46 × 8.72 (500.2 × 28.6); M; 14; ex SALUNAKA 1978; ex DJIBA 1976; ex BONITA 1966.

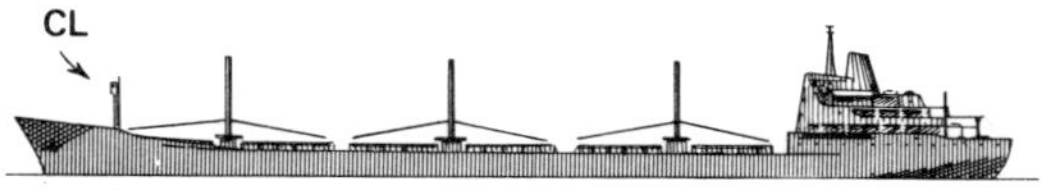

K_4MFK H13
⋆57080 CHANG HAI. RC/No 1964; B; 12800; 162.16 × 9.7 (532 × 31.8); M; 14.5; ex BRIS 1974. Sisters: **57081 TRAKYA** (Tu) ex ISCELU 1981; ex POLARLAND 1977 **57082 VALHALL** (No).

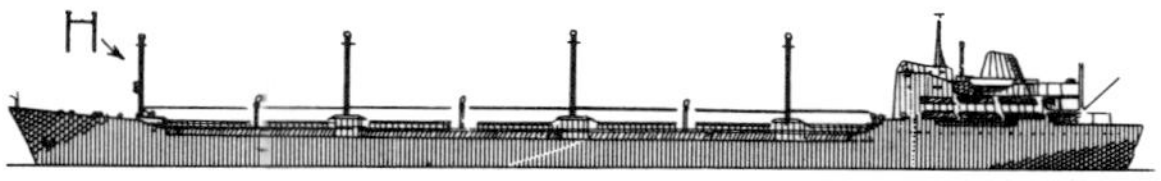

K_4MFK H13
57090 ORIENT HORIZON. Li/Ne 1961; B; 15300; 180.63 × 10.78 (592.6 × 35.4); M; 14; ex NEW HORIZON; ex VENI 1968.

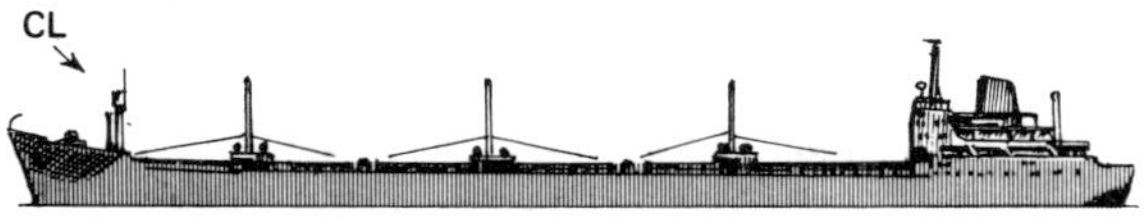

K_4MFK H13
57100 KEHREA. Gr/Sw 1961; B; 15000; 175.88 × 10.96 (577 × 36); M; 15; ex WINDSOR CARRIER 1973; ex SCANDIA CLIPPER 1972. Similar: **57101 LEFTHERO** (Gr) ex CRETAN LIBERTY 1977; ex CONWELL 1974; ex ERLING H SAMUELSEN 1971.

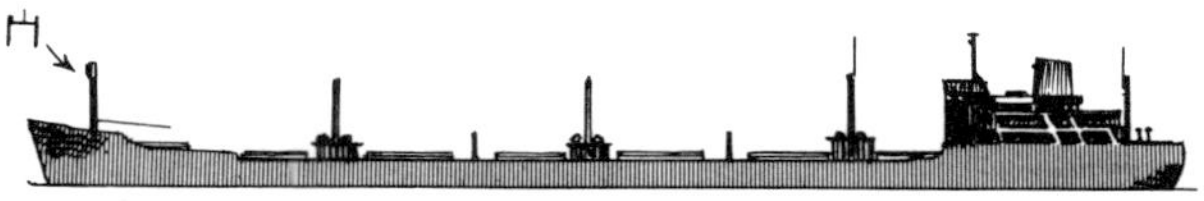

K_4MFK H13
⋆57110 HONG QI 303. RC/Br 1963; B; 16500; 182.43 × 10.52 (598.52 × 34.51); M; 15; ex DAN HAI 1980; ex KOLLFINN 1974.

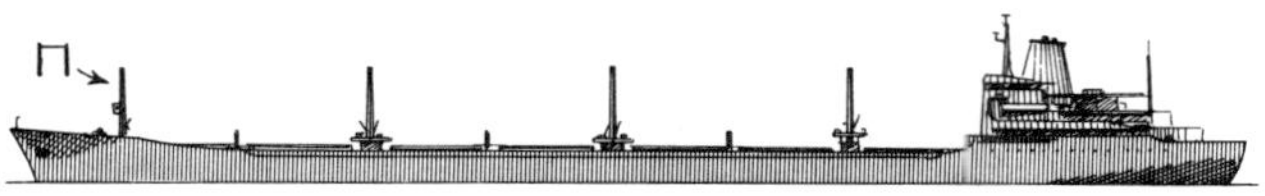

K_4MFK H13
57120 AEGNOUSSIOTIS. Gr/Sw 1966; B; 20500; 196.32 × 10.89 (644.09 × 35.73); M; 15.75; ex KOLLGEIR 1975.

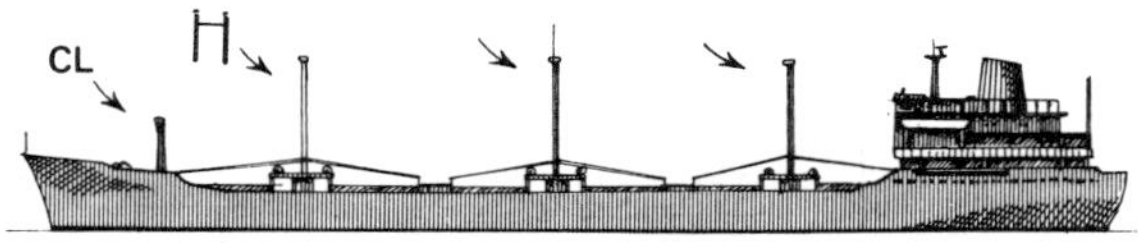

K_4MFK H13
57130 EVANGELISTRIA. Gr/Ys 1967; B; 12800; 174.05 × 9.14 (571.03 × 29.99); M; 15.5; ex AVONFIELD 1976; Launched as BJORN STANGE.

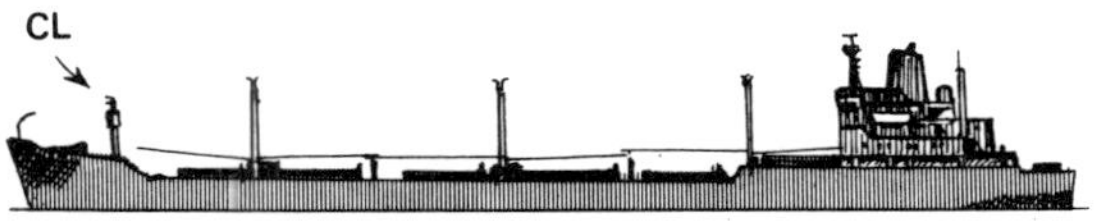

K_4MFK H13
57140 LONG CHARITY. No/FRG 1969; B; 14100; 169.02 × 10.12 (554.5 × 33.2); M; 16. Sisters: **57141 DAYSPRING** (Pa) ex FERNFIELD 1978 **57142 OINOUSSAI ALPHA** (Cy) ex FERNDALE 1978 **57142 WINSUM** (Ne) ex FERNSIDE 1977.

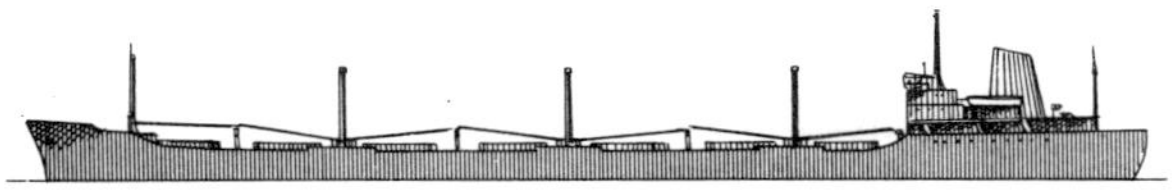

K_4MFK H13
57150 GLYFADA BREEZE. Gr/Ja 1965; B; 17400; 176.71 × 10.71 (579.76 × 35.14); M; 14; ex ORIENTAL MERCHANT; ex ROSELLO 1977.

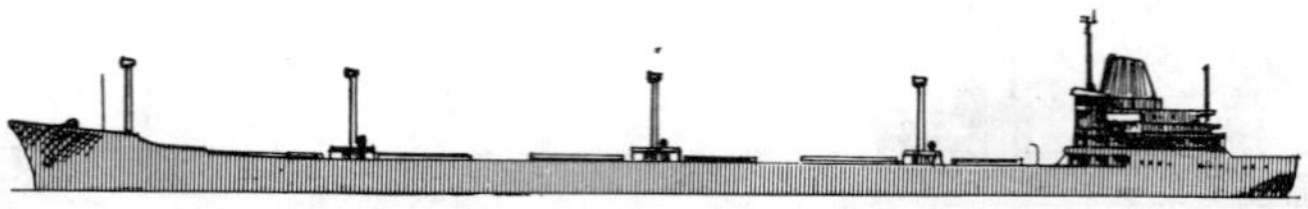

K_4MFK H13
57160 EASTPORT. Gr/Br 1967; B; 27000; 203.66×12.04 (668.18×39.5); M; 15.25; ex INDIAN CITY 1977. Sister: **57161 ORIENT CORAL** (Li) ex OLMECA 1980; ex ATLANTIC 1979; ex ATLANTIC CITY 1976.

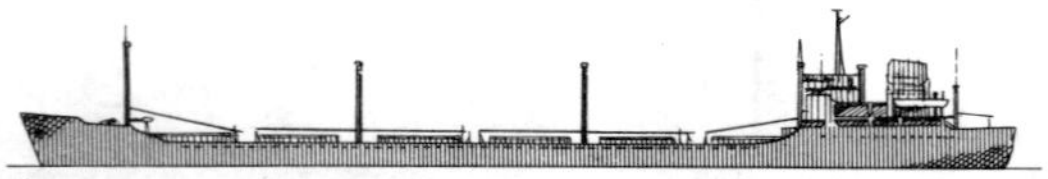

K_4MFK H13
57170 MESSINIAKOS GULF. Gr/Ja 1960; B; 11700; 157.61×9.07 (517.09×29.76); M; 13.25; ex YASHIWOSAN MARU 1975.

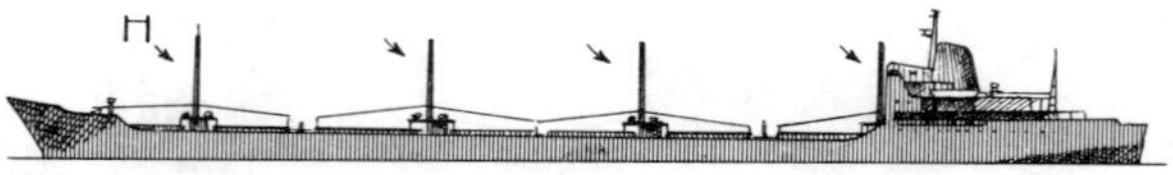

K_4MFK H13
57180 ATLANTIC HERO. Gr/Ja 1969; B; 16200; 180.8×10.69 (593.18×35.07); M; 15. Sisters (Gr flag): **57181 ATLANTIC HAWK 57182 ATLANTIC HELMSMAN 57183 ATLANTIC HERITAGE 57184 ATLANTIC HORIZON 57185 ALIAKMON 57186 CHRYSANTHI G L 57187 GLAFKOS 57188 ATHINA ZAFIRAKIS 57189 VOMAR** ex MARIAVOYAZIDES 1976 **57190 IOANNIS ZAFIRAKIS 57191 ANTAIOS 57192 DIAS** (RC flag): ⋆**57193 HENG CHUN HAI** ex GOLDEN RIVER; ex VENTHISIKIMI 1978 (Pa flag): **57194 IRISH SEA** ex DIMITROS CRITICOS 1980.

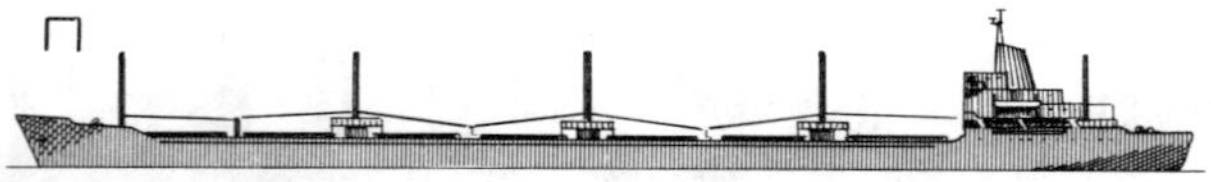

K_4MFK H13
⋆**57200 DAGONYS.** Ru/Br 1971; B; 18600; 186.11×10.83 (610.6×35.53); M; 14; ex CUMBRIA 1980.

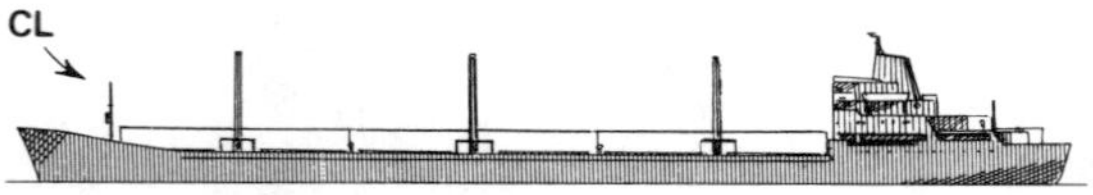

K_4MFK H13
57210 ATLAS COUNSELLOR. Ko/No 1963; B; 12800; 168.43×9.44 (552.59×30.97); M; 14.5; ex JARABELLA 1972.

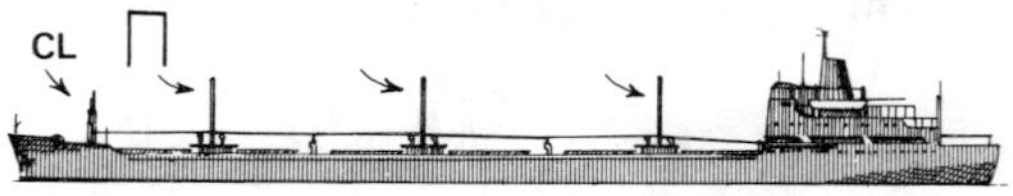

K_4MFK H13
● **57220 LADY VICTORIA.** Pa/Sw 1964; B; 11000; 155.45×9.2 (510×30.2); M; 15; ex NEGO VICTORIA 1975.

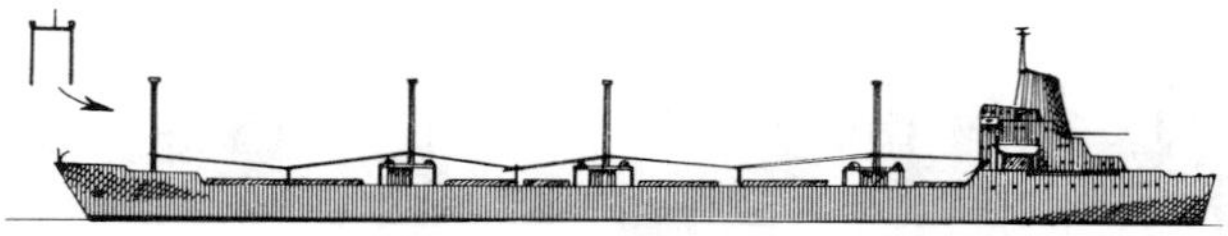

K_4MFK H13
57230 IONIO. Gr/Sp 1970; B; 15400; 183.12×10.58 (600.79×34.71); M; 14; ex AEGIS DESTINY. Sisters: **57231 AEGIS BRAVERY** (Gr) **57232 AEGIS PROGRESS** (gr) **57233 SHANTA SHIBANI** (In) ex AEGIS KINGDOM **57234 BETIS** (Sg) ex ARENAL 1975 **57235 MACARENA** (Sg) ex TRIANA 1975 **57236 ERZURUM** (Tu) **57237 ERDEMIR** (Tu) **57238 OLYMPIC HOPE** (Gr) ex GRAIGAUR 1978; ex TORRE DEL ORO 1975.

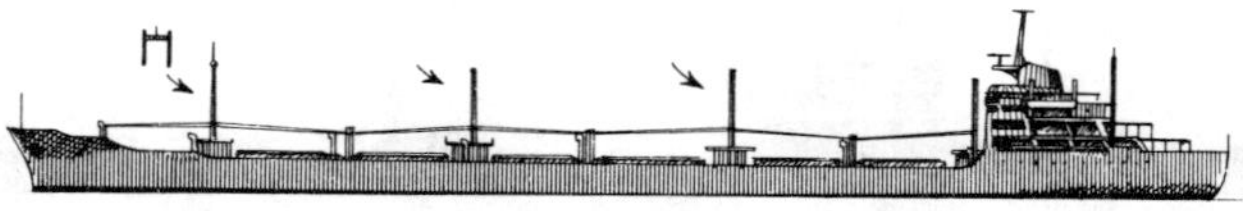

K_4MFK H13
57240 ATLANTIC HOPE. Li/Fr 1965; B; 18400; 193.5×10.94 (634.84×35.9); M; 15.

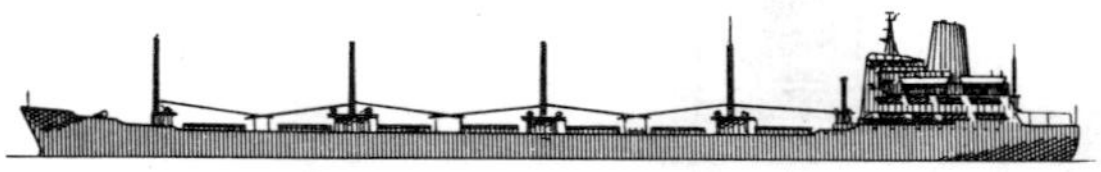

K_4MFK H13
57250 BHASKARA. In/Ja 1965; 00; 15500; 169.02×9.63 (554.53×31.6); M; 14.5; ex BHASKARA JAYANTI 1973. Sisters (In flag): **57251 CHANAKYA** ex CHANAKYA JAYANTI 1974 **57252 LEELAVATI** ex LEELAVATI JAYANTI 1974.

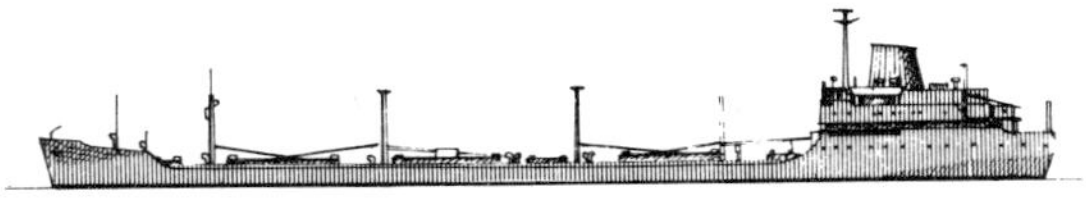

K_4MFK H13

● **57260 OCEAN TRITON.** Gr/Sw 1963; B; 11900; 163.23 × 9.38 (535.53 × 30.77); M; 15.5; ex TROJA 1970.

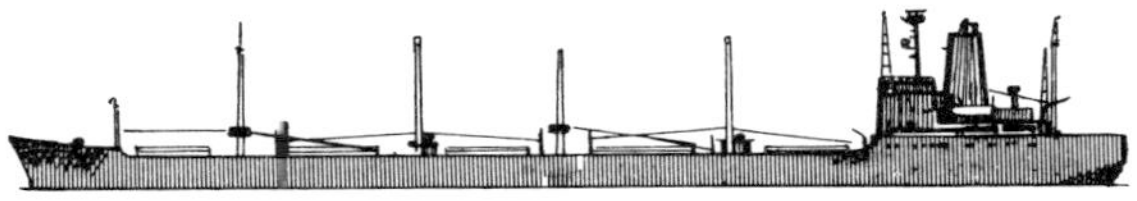

K_4MFK H13

57270 C.K. APOLLO. Li/Ja 1967; B; 14800; 175.32 × 10.1 (575.2 × 33.14); M; 15; ex GOLAR ARROW 1975. Sister: **57271 ADELFOTIS** (Gr) ex GOLAR BOW 1975.

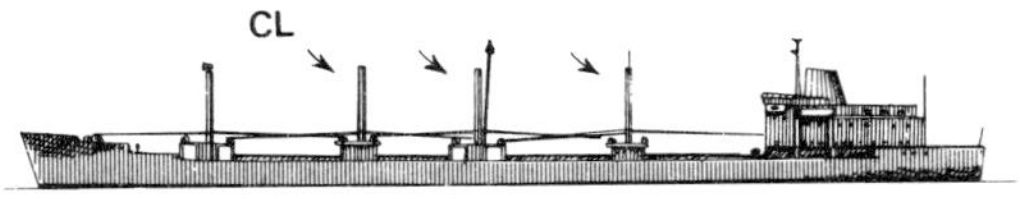

K_4MFK H13

57280 JADE STAR. Pa/Br 1968; C; 10600; 152.25 × 9.11 (499.5 × 29.9); M; 16; ex WELSH CITY 1977. Sister-: **57281 NEPTUNE STAR** (Pa) ex CORNISH CITY 1977.

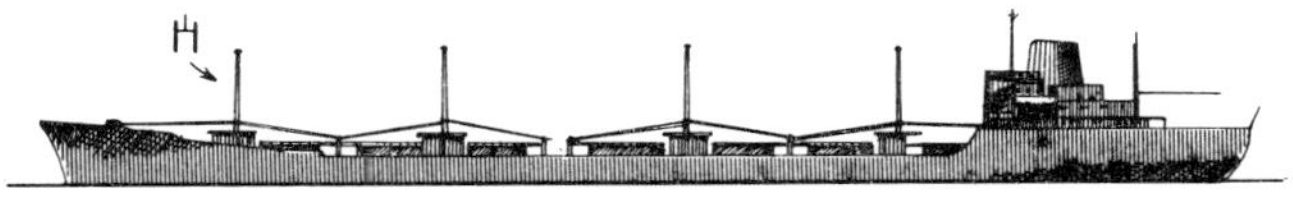

K_4MFK H13

57290 CAPTAIN DEMOSTHENES. Gr/FRG 1965; B; 19000; 191.32 × 11.3 (627.69 × 3707); M; 14.

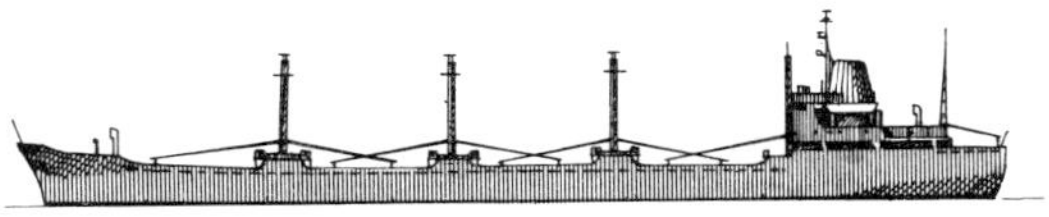

K_4MFK H13

57300 ORIENTAL VENUS. Li/Fr 1963; C; 10800; 160.03 × 9.5 (525 × 31.2); M; 16.25.

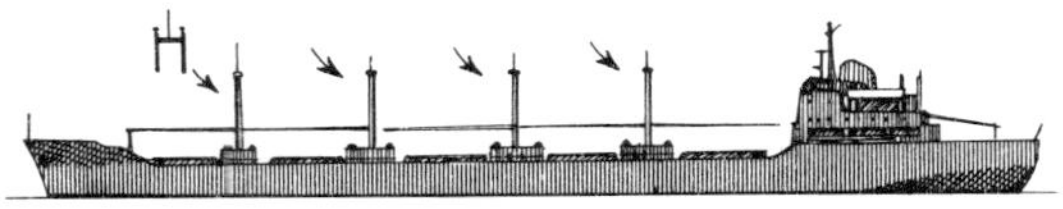

K_4MFK H13

57310 MAJESTIC. Gr/Ja 1965; B; 10600; 156.72 × 9.29 (514.2 × 30.5);.M; —; ex MAXIM 1976. Possibly Similar: **57311 SILVER SHELTON** (Li).

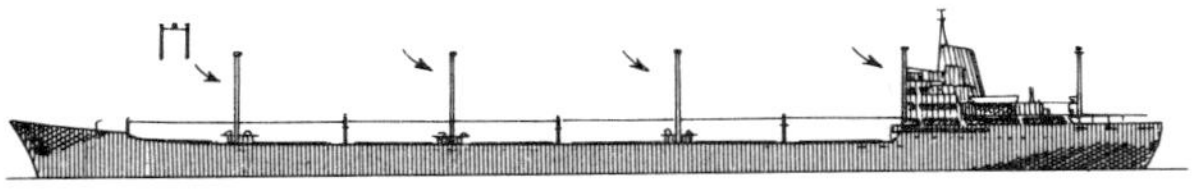

K_4MFK H13

57320 TASIA. Gr/Be 1962; B; 14200; 182.25 × 10.4 (597.9 × 34.1); M; 15; ex KONSTANTIA ex NTINA J. PATERA 1973. Sister: **57321 ORIENT VENTURE** (Sg) ex AEGIS KUDU 1979; ex AJAX 1973; ex THALASSOPOROS 1972.

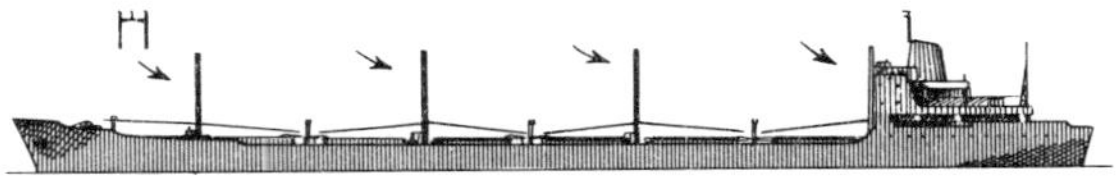

K_4MFK H13

57330 EPTA VELI. Gr/Ja 1966; B; 16300; 174.76 × 10.95 (573.36 × 35.93); M; 14.5; ex CORONA 1980; ex COROPUNA 1979; ex NORTH BREEZE 1974. Sister: **57331 NEWHAVEN** (Li) ex GLYNTAF 1971; launched as EAST BREEZE.

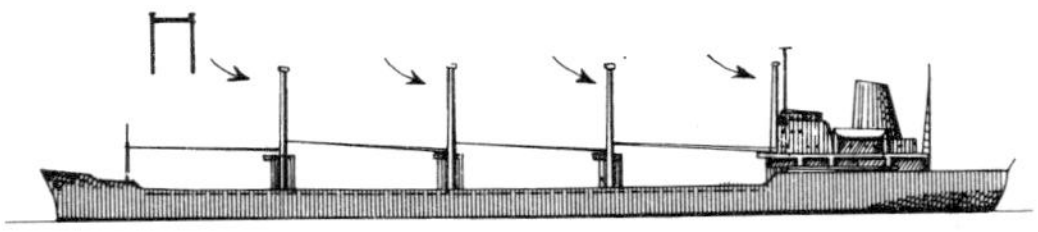

K_4MFK H13

57340 ALICAMPOS. Gr/Ja 1968; B; 14400; 156.17 × 9.53 (512.37 × 31.27); M; 15; ex MARITIME QUEEN 1980; **'Hitachi Standard 18'** type. Sister: **57341 MARITIME PIONEER** (Pa).

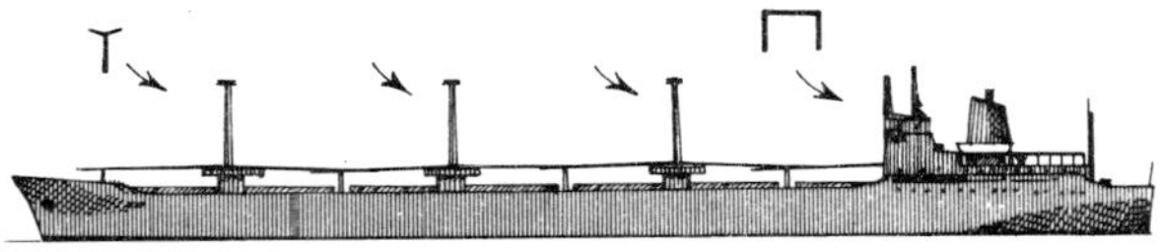

K_4MFK H13

57350 AL-TAHA. Li/Br 1970; B; 14700; 182.89 × 10.15 (600.03 × 33.3); M; —; ex COUNTY CLARE 1974; **'B-25'** type. Sister: **57351 YERUPAJA** (Pe) ex STAR HELENE 1974; ex HELENE 1973.

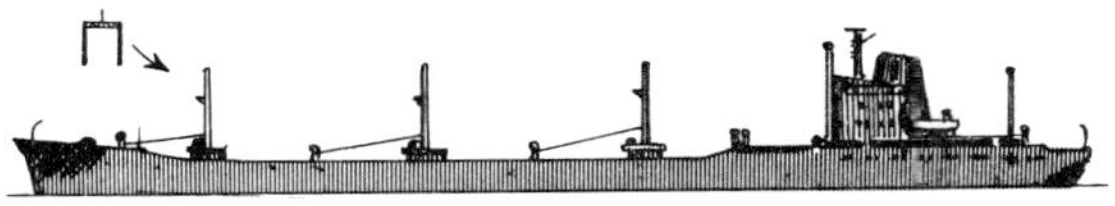

K_4MFK H13

57360 AMETHYSTOS. Li/Bz 1968; B; 13100; 169.2 × 9.68 (555.12 × 31.76); M; 15; ex DOCELAGO; ex ANTONIO FERRAZ 1970. Slsters (Bz flag): **57361 DOCEPRAIA** ex JAYME MAIA 1970 **57362 SONIA** ex DOCEGOLFO 1977; ex AMANNOON CAMARA 1970. These vessels may be K_2MFK.

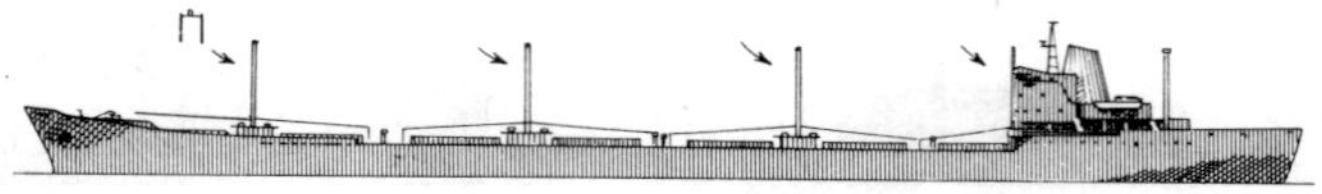

K_4MFK H13
⋆**57370 LONG HAI;** RC/Be 1968; B; 25000; 203.77 × 11.48 (668.54 × 37.66); M; —; ex AGIOI VICTORES 1974. Sister: ⋆**57371 PING HAI** (RC) ex IOANNIS N PATERAS 1974.

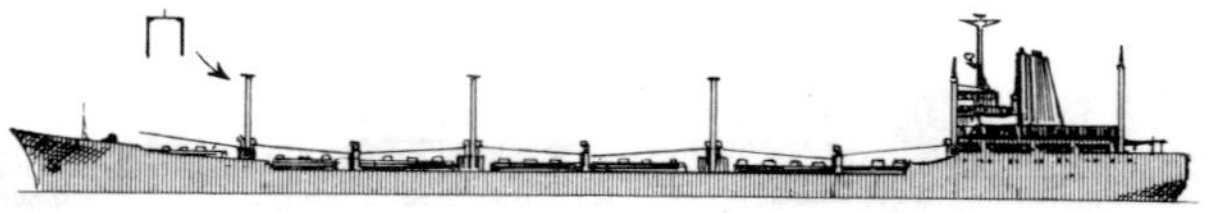

K_4MFK H13
57380 KEFALONIA LIGHT; Gr/Ja 1967; B; 23100; 185.02 × 11.78 (607.02 × 38.65); M; 15; ex EASTERN FREEDOM 1980. Sisters: **57381 NIOBE** (Gr) ex EASTERN MERIT 1980 **57382 TARPON SENTINEL** (Gr) ex EREDINE 1974 **57383 SAM SOO** (Pa) ex GRINDA 1980; ex WORLD GEMINI.

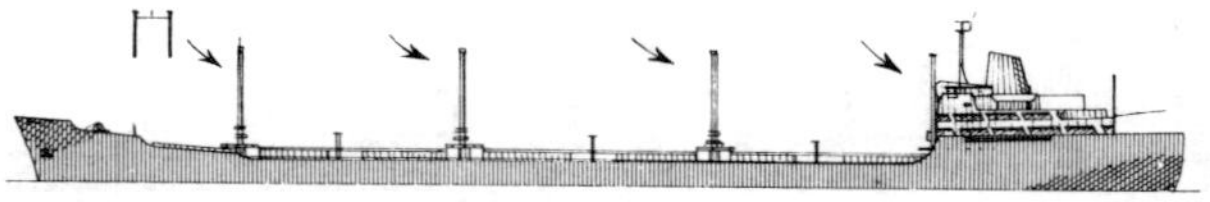

⋆**57390 DONG HAI;** RC/Br 1965; B; 17000; 184.59 × 10.22 (605.61 × 33.53); M; —; ex THEOMANA 1973; ex RILEY 1968.

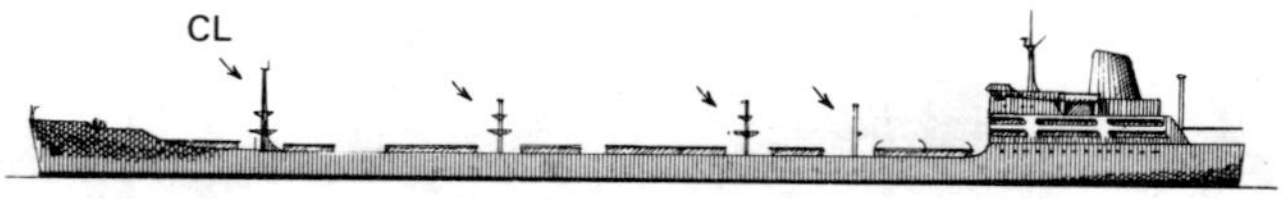

K_4MFK H13
57400 TAI LIENG; Tw/Br 1965; B; 21350; 192.03 × 11.09 (630 × 36.4); M; 14.75; ex TAI LIEN 1976; ex OCEAN SKIPPER 1974; ex MOUNTPARK 1974.

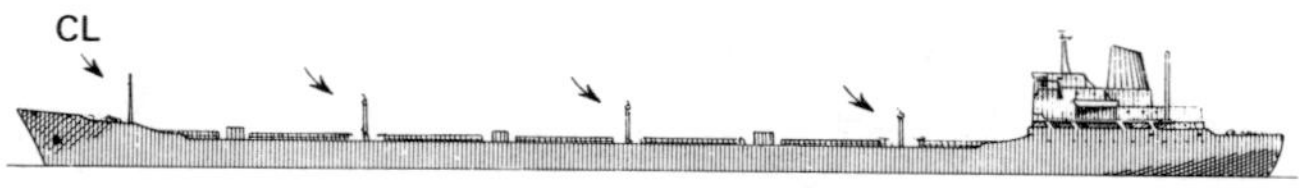

K_4MFK H13
57410 DUNSTER GRANGE; Br/Br 1967; B; 24000; 201.78 × 11.62 (662 × 38.12); M; 15; ex CLYDE BRIDGE 1977.

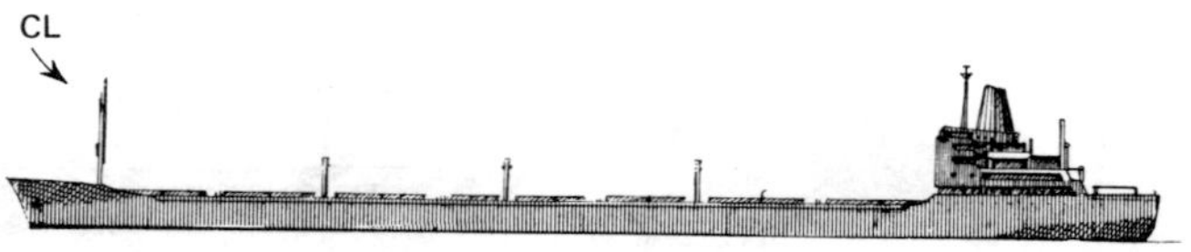

K_4MFK H13
57420 TEL-AVIV; Is/FRG 1963; B; 20300; 200.18 × 10.36 (656.76 × 34); M; 15.5. Sister: **57421 ARAD** (Is).

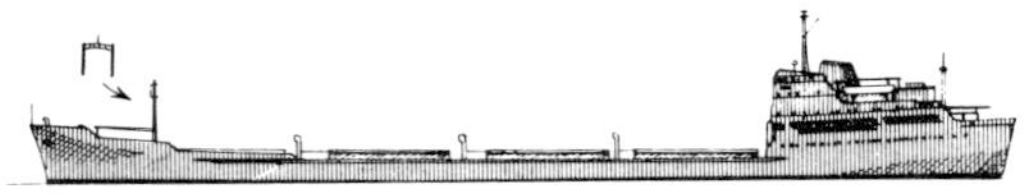

K_4MFK *H13*
57430 MARTHA ELLE; Pa/Sw 1959; O; 8600; 157.13 × 8.88 (515.52 × 29.13); M; 12.5; ex AMAX MINER 1980; ex FALCONDALE 1976; ex FAVORITA 1973. Similar: **57431 GALINI** (Gr) ex CARMENDALE 1980; ex CARMENCITA 1975 **57432 DAPO ANTIKLIA** (Gr) ex EVINDALE 1978; ex EVITA **57433 MAREDALE** (Li) ex MARGARITA 1973.

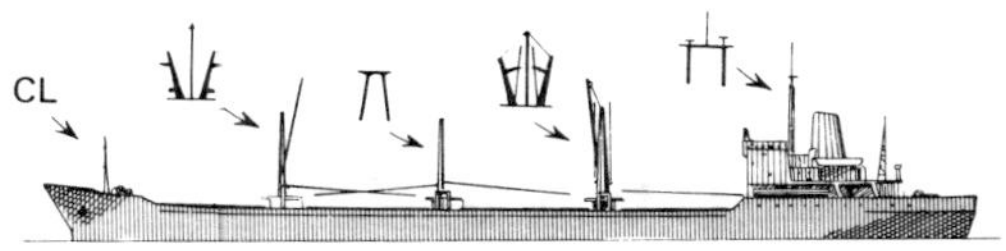

K_4MFK *H13*
⋆57440 VELENJE; Ys/Ja 1976; C/HL; 7400/11900; 147.71 × 9.63 (484.61 × 31.59); M; 16; **'MITSUI-CONCORD 18'** type. Sisters (Ys flag): **⋆57441 MARIBOR ⋆57442 KRANJ ⋆57443 CELJE ⋆57444 KAMNIK.**

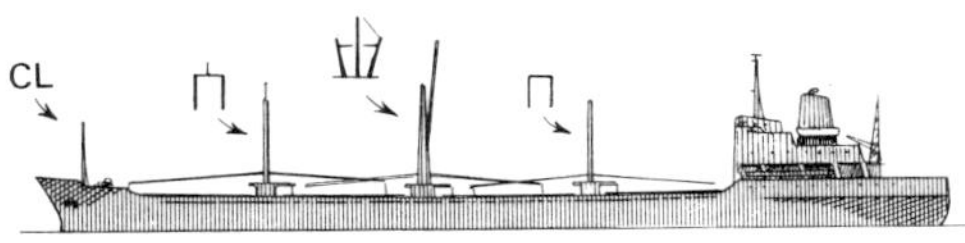

K_4MFK *H13*
⋆57450 LONG CHUAN JIANG; RC/Ja 1971; C; 6600/10200; 147.7 × 8.02/9.1 (478 × 26.31/29.8); M; 17; ex HEELSUM 1978; **'MITSUI-CONCORD 15'** type. Sister: **⋆57451 JIN CHENG JIANG** (RC) ex LEERSUM 1977.

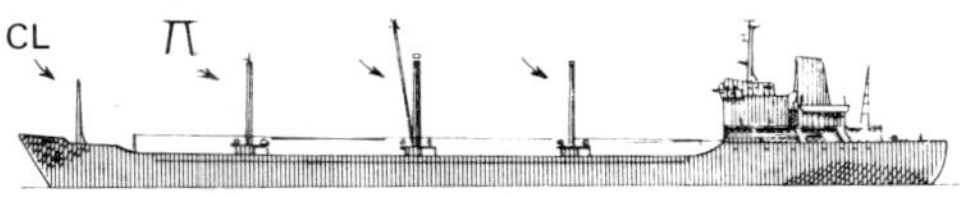

K_4MFK *H13*
57460 INDIAN PRESTIGE; In/Ja 1971; C; 12000; 147.71 × 9.63 (484.61 × 31.59); M; 15; ex ARISTAGORAS 1974; **'MITSUI-CONCORD 18'** type. Sisters (In flag): **57461 INDIAN PROGRESS** ex ARISTODIMOS 1974 **57462 INDIAN PROSPERITY** ex IOANNA 1975 Similar (heavy lift, fitted with Stulcken derricks): **57463 TRAUTENBELS** (Gr) ex TRAUTENFELS 1980; ex EHRENFELS 1976; ex ARISTOKLEIDIS 1975.

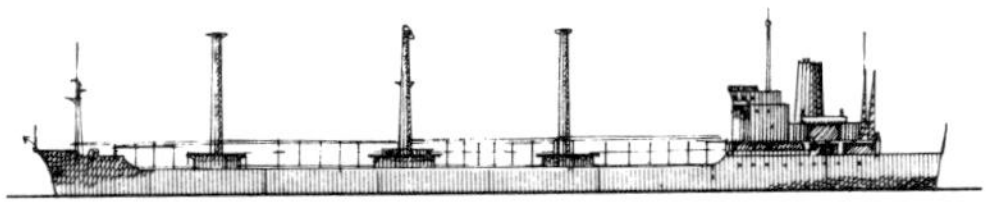

K_4MFK *H13*
57470 IRENES EMERALD; Gr/Ja 1977; B; 10200; 144 × 8.87 (472.4 × 29.1); M; 14.25; ex PACIFIC EMERALD 1980; ex MONTMARTRE 1980. Sister: **57471 IRENES SAPPHIRE** (Gr) ex ATLANTIC EMERALD 1980; ex MONTPARNASSE 1980.

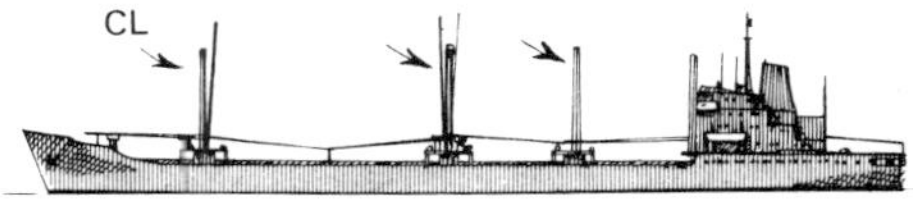

K_4MFK *H13*
57480 ALPINA; Sd/FRG 1970; C; 6900/9600; 139.76 × 8.22/9.19 (458.53 × 26.97/30.15); M; 16; **'GERMAN LIBERTY'** type. Possible Sister: **57481 ASCONA** (Sd).

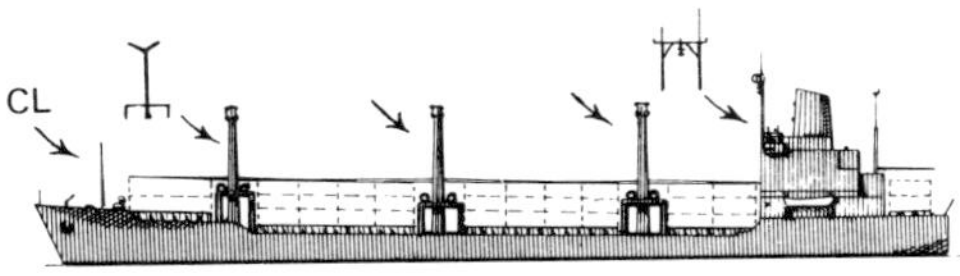

K_4MFK *H13*
57490 HOLSTENSAILOR; FRG/FRG 1978; C; 8700; 146.01 × 8.16 (479.04 × 26.77); M; 18; **'KEY 12'** type. Sisters (FRG flag): **57491 HOLSTENCLIPPER** ex SEAWAY CLIPPER 1980; ex HOLSTENCLIPPER **57492 HOLSTENTRADER.**

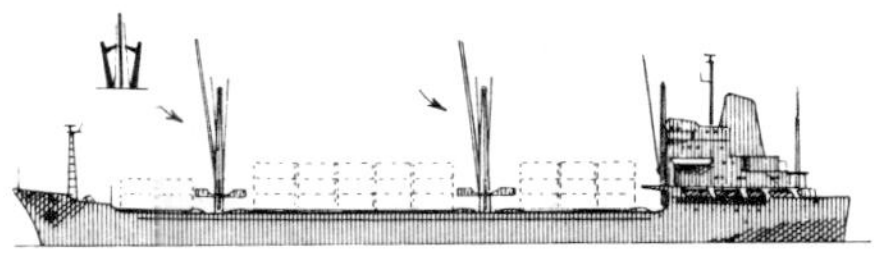

K_4MFK *H13*
● **57500 BIANKA LEONHARDT;** Pa/Ja 1977; C; 8500; 133.2 × 8.83 (437.01 × 28.97); M; 16.75. Sister: **57501 BRITTA LEONHARDT** (Pa) ex BRITTA 1980; ex BRITTA LEONHARDT 1977.

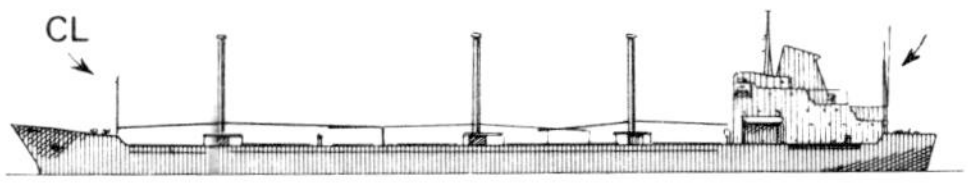

K_4MFK *H13*
57510 GOOD WIND; Gr/Sp 1970; C; 11300; 147.02 × 9.87 (482.34 × 32.4); M; 16; ex GOOD HELMSMAN 1978; ex DAVID, MARQUESS OF MILFORD HAVEN 1973; **'SANTA-FE'** type. Sister: **57511 PANAGIA MYRTIDIOTISSA** (Gr) ex JOCELYNE 1980.

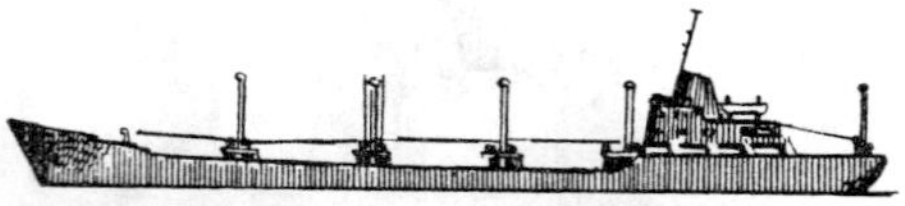

K_4MFK H13
57520 JULIO REGIS; Bz/Bz 1964; C; 6200/8300; 142 × 8.2/— (466 × 27/—); M; 18.5. Possibly (Bz flag) (some have stulcken derricks): **57521 CELESTINO 57522 PETROPOLIS** ex LAJES 1968 **57523 CARLOS BORGES** ex NAVEM PIRATINI 1971; launched as MIDOSI **57524 GONCALO** ex CAMPOS 1968.

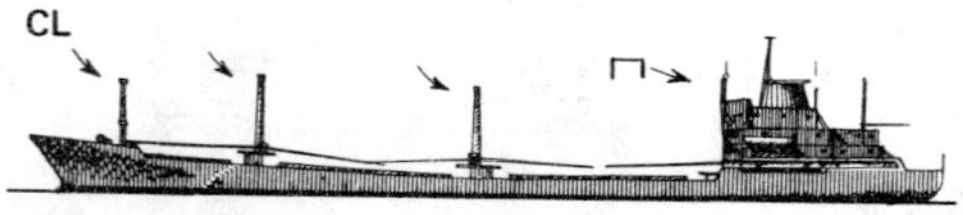

K_4MFK H13
● **57550 HELENE PRESTHUS.** No/FRG 1970; C/Con; 5100/7900; 146.23 × 8.89 (479.76 × 29.17); M; —; ex BRITTENBURG 1981; ex EASTERN STREET 1977; ex LLOYD NEW YORK 1975; ex HAMBURGER DAMM 1973; ex TASCO 1971; Launched as HAMBURGER DAMM; **'NEPTUN'** type. Similar: **57551 SPETSES ISLAND** (Gr) ex DAFRA TRADER 1978; ex LLOYD PHILADELPHIA 1975; ex HAMBURGER WALL 1973; ex SPARREHOLM 1971; ex HAMBURGER WALL 1970 **57552 BOOKER CHALLENGE** (Br) ex SOL MICHEL; ex LLOYD COPENHAGUE 1976; ex SOL MICHEL 1972 **57553 BOOKER CRUSADE** (Br) ex SOL NEPTUN; ex WOLFGANG RUSS 1977; ex SOL NEPTUN 1976 **57554 ANNA PRESTHUS** (No ex SWEDRU 1978; ex ANNA PRESTHUS 1976 **57555 FREEDEBURG** (FRG) ex LLOYD ESTOCOLMO 1978; Launched as FREEDEBURG **57556 ROLAND PACIFIC** (FRG) ex MUGGENBURG; ex LLOYD JACKSONVILLE 1979; ex MUGGENBURG 1975 **57557 BOOKER COURAGE** (Br) ex BRAGELAND 1980 **57558 BALTICLAND** (Sw) **57559 BARDALAND** (Sw)

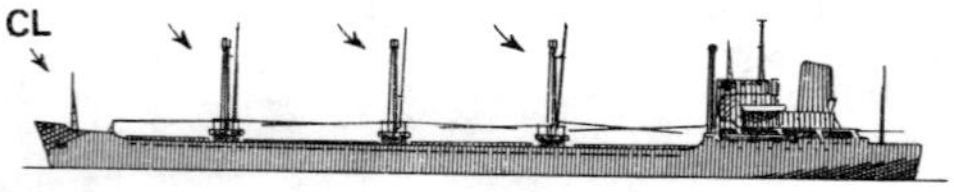

K_4MFK H13
57590 LISANA. Li/Ja 1968; B; 9400; 143.68 × 8.99 (472 × 29.5); M; 14.5. Similar: **57591 ENATON** (Gr) ex MARITIME LEADER 1979 **57592 MARIA XILAS** (Gr) ex EASTERN UNION 1971.

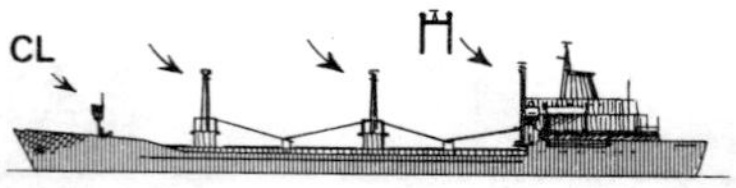

K_4MFK H13
57530 LA MINERA. Bz/FRG 1969; C; 4200; 112.83 × 6.9 (370.18 × 22.64); M; 13.75; ex FOSSHEIM 1978.

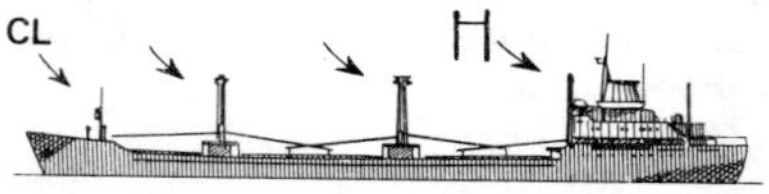

K_4MFK H13
57540 HESPERIA. Fi/DDR 1968; C; 4200; 114.71 × 6.48 (376.35 × 21.26); M; 14.5; ex JORUNA 1969. Sisters: **★57541 BOLGRAD** (Ru) ex McDERMOTT; ex BOLINA 1979; ex JOTINA 1977; Launched as SIGYN **★57542 BORISLAV** (Ru) ex JANE AUSTEN 1980; ex ROSELINA 1978; ex JOSELIN 1977 **57543 LORETTA** (Gr) ex ATTU; ex JOULLA 1975.

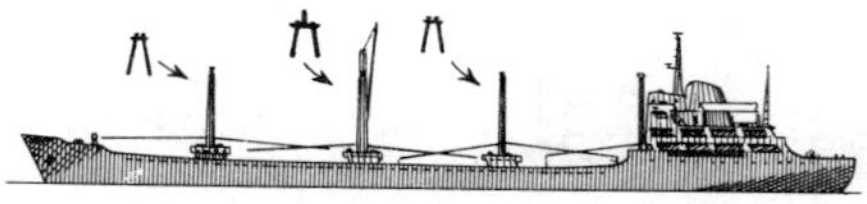

K_4MFK H13
57570 IRENE. Pi/Ja 1966; C; 7100; 131.93 × 7.6 (432.8 × 24.9); M; 15.

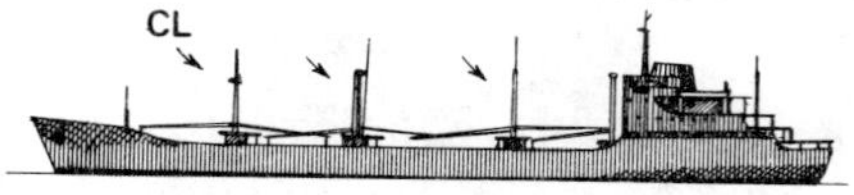

K_4MFK H13
57580 AL KAHERAH; Eg/Sw 1961; C; 4100/5900; 126.93 × 6.81/8.14 (416.44 × 22.34/26.71); M; 16.25; ex SEAHORSE 1975; ex CONCORDIA SEAHORSE 1975; ex SEAHORSE 1972; ex SUNSEAHORSE 1972; ex SEAHORSE 1963.

K_4MFK H13
57600 ANITA. Gr/Ja 1976; C; 5000; 117.61 × 7.3 (385.8 × 23.9); M; 16. Sisters (Sg flag): **57601 NORDHEIM 57602 NORDFELS 57603 NORDHOLM 57604 NORDMARK 57605 SINGAPURA** ex RAUTE 1979 **57606 BAYU** ex RHOMBUS 1979 **57607 KIRSTEN WESCH** (Cy flag): **57608 HELEN SCHULTE 57609 JOHANNA SCHULTE** (Gr flag): **57610 KAREN** (Li flag): **57611 CORAL VOLANS 57612 RAINBOW VOLANS** (Pa flag): **57613 NEPTUNE VOLANS.**

● 57614

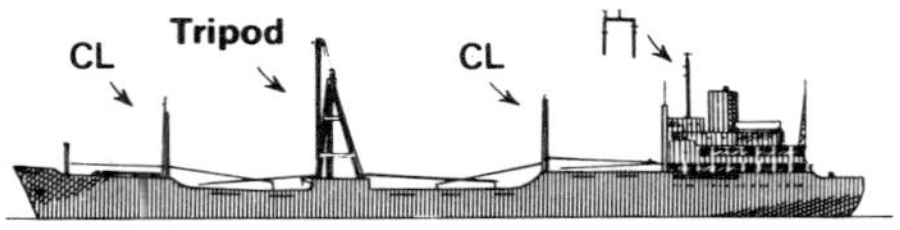

K_4MFK H13
57620 WAKAMATSU MARU. Ja/Ja 1967; C/HL; 7800; 138.51 × 8.48 (454.43 × 27.82); M; 15.25. Similar: **57621 WAKAURA MARU** (Ja) **57622 WAKAKUSA MARU** (Ja).

● 57625

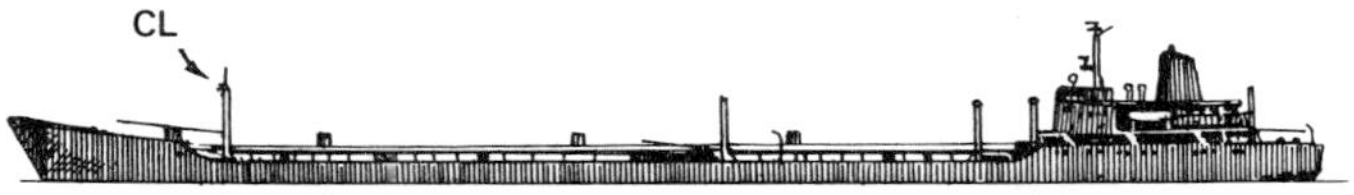

K_4MFK H13
★57630 LIVNY. Ru/Ja 1963; Tk; 22500; 207.04 × 11.11 (679.27 × 36.45); M; 17.25. Sisters (Ru flag): **★57631 LOZOVAYA ★57632 LENINAKAN ★57633 LYUDINOVO** Possible Sister: **★57634 LENKORAN ★57635 LISICHANSK ★57636 LYUBOTIN**

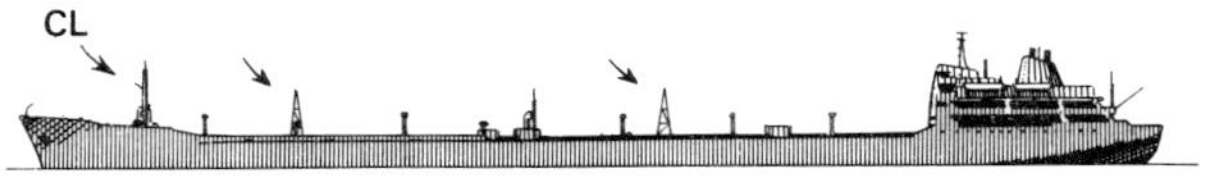

K_4MFK H13
57640 FFM-VIRIS. Li/Sw 1959/71 Tk/Ch; 15200; 181.62 × 10.36 (595.87 × 33.99); M; 14.5; ex VIRIS 1971; Converted from OO 1971.

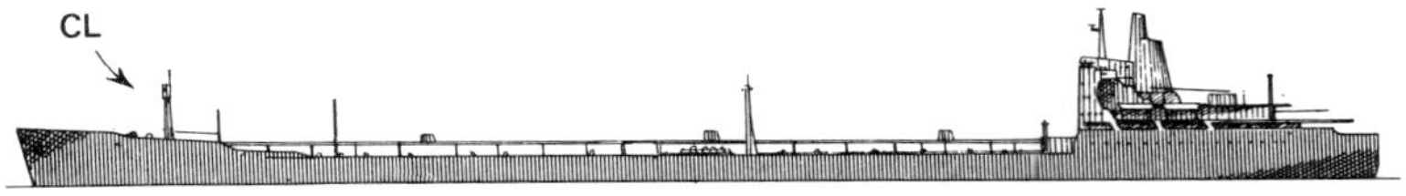

K_4MFK H13
57650 COSMAS. Gr/Sw 1964; Tk; 35400; 236.23 × 12.64 (775.03 × 41.47); M; 16.5; ex BURMAH OPAL 1978; ex JONWI 1972.

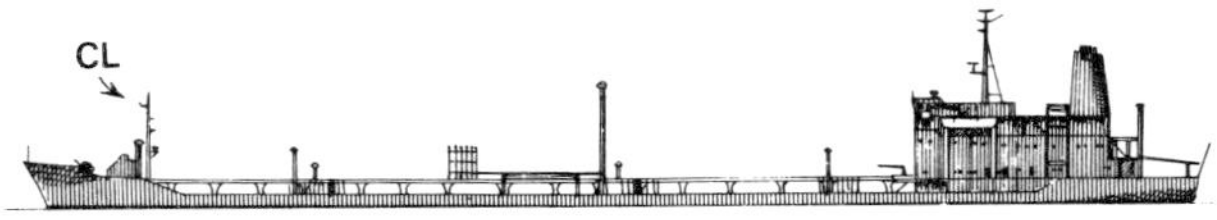

K_4MFK H13
57660 STOLT SEA. Li/FRG 1970; Tk; 14600; 169.6 × 9.56 (556.4 × 31.4); M; 16.25; ex ANCO SEA 1973. Sisters: **57661 STOLT SPAN** (Li) ex ANCO SPAN 1973 **57662 STOLT SPUR** (Li) ex ANCO SPUR 1973 **57663 STOLT SURF** (Li) ex ANCO VILLE **57664 IVER SWAN** (No) ex ANCO SWAN 1976.

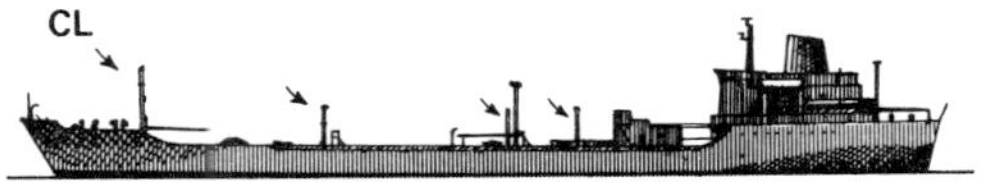

K_4MFK H13
57670 WILTSHIRE. Br/Br 1968; LGC; 10000; 151.7 × 8.23 (497.7 × 27); M; 16.

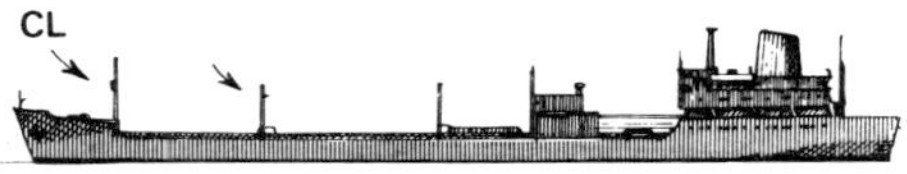

K_4MFK H13
57680 GAS PILOT. Li/Br 1968; LGC; 8200; 140.49 × 8.17 (461 × 26.8); M; 16.5; ex GAS LION.

K_4MFK H13
★57690 MING HU. RC/Ja 1974; Tk; 5100; 110.24 × 7.88 (361.68 × 25.85); M; 13.5; ex POINTE DE TALLAGRIP 1976; ex OLAU THOR 1975.

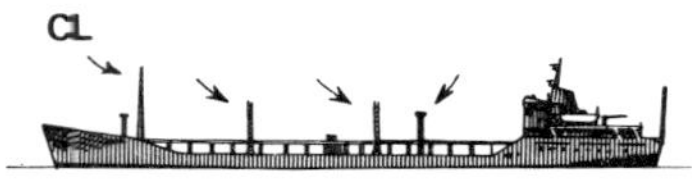

K_4MFK H13
57700 PASS OF BALMAHA. Br/Br 1975; Ch; 2500; 97.52 × 6.2 (319.95 × 20.35); M; 15. Similar: **57701 PASS OF BRANDER** (Br).

K_4MFK H13

57710 SHINRYO ETHYLENE MARU. Ja/Ja 1971; LGC; 980; 63.1 × 3.7 (207 × 12.1); M; 11.

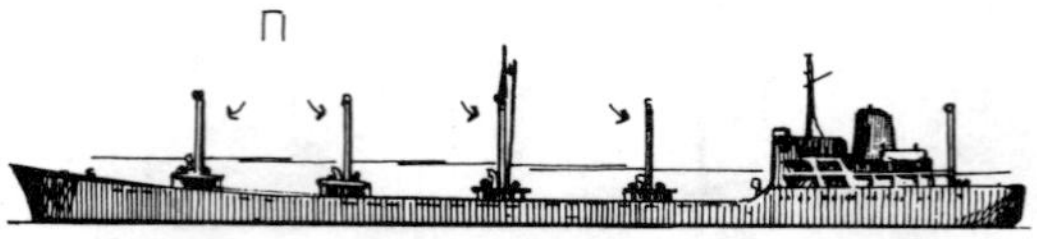

K_4MFK H3

⋆**57720 KAI PING.** RC/Ja 1961; C; 8300/10700; 156.19 × —/9.48 (512.43 × —/31.1); M; 15; ex OCEANIC 1973. Sister: **57721 SUPREME FIVE** (Pa) ex CORINTHIC 1981 Similar: **57722 TROVATORE** (Br) ex ATHINA B 1977; ex FAY 1976; ex LEONIDAS VOYAZIDES 1976. ex WORLD JAPONICA 1965.

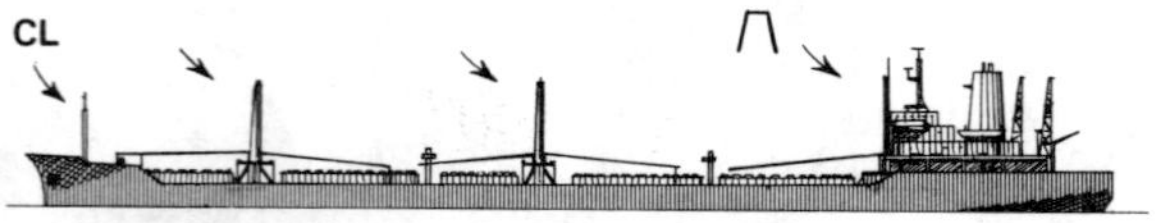

K_4MFK_2 H13

57730 ASIA FIDELITY. Pa/Ja 1971; B; 15700; 174.53 × 10.19 (572.6 × 33.43); M; 15.

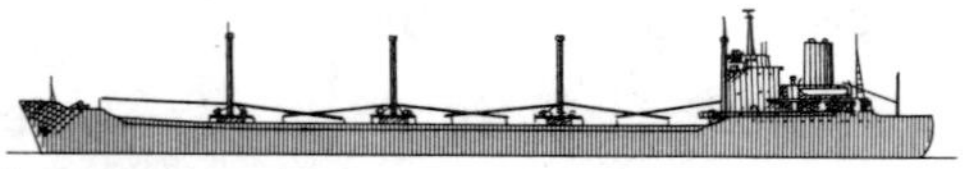

K_4MFK_2 H13

57740 MIDAS APOLLO. Li/Ja 1964; C; 9000; 144.63 × 8.76 (474.51 × 28.74); M; 14.5; ex KYOKKO MARU 1972.

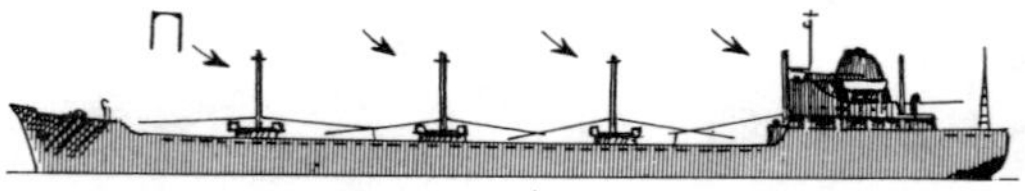

K_4MFK_2 H13

57750 AGELOS MICHAEL. Li/Ja 1964; B; 9800; 152.51 × 9.58 (500.4 × 31.4); M; 14.5; ex WORLD YURI 1973.

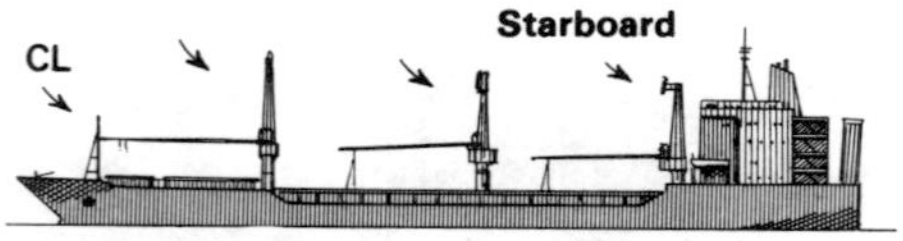

K_4MFR H13

● ⋆**57760 HAU GIANG.** Vn/De 1977; RoC; 9700; 132.92 × 9.4 (436.09 × 30.84); M; 15; Launched as HAMLET ALICE; **'HAMLET-MULTIFLEX'** type. Sisters: **57761 HAMLET ARABIA** (De) **57762 HAMLET SAUDIA** (De) ⋆**57763 NEN JIANG** (RC) ex NOPAL AUDREY 1978 ⋆**57764 IZVESTIYA** (Ru) **57765 KIMBERLEY** (Au) ⋆**57766 KNUD JESPERSEN** (Ru) ex ALEKSEY STAKHANOV.

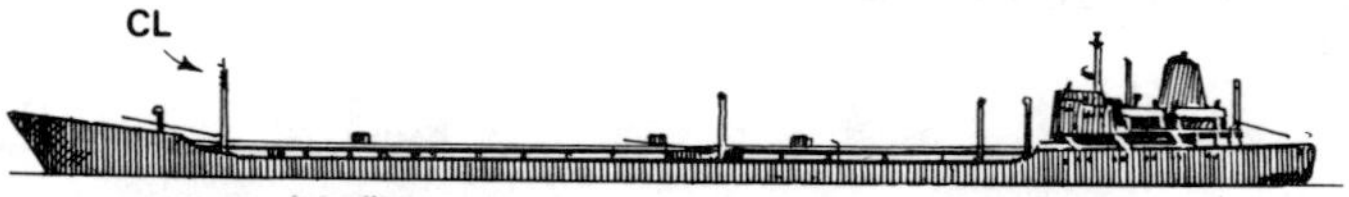

K_4MKFK H13

⋆**57770 LENINABAD.** Ru/Ja 1964; Tk; 23100; 207.04 × 11.11 (679.27 × 36.45); M; 16.5. Sister: ⋆**57771 LUTSK** (Ru).

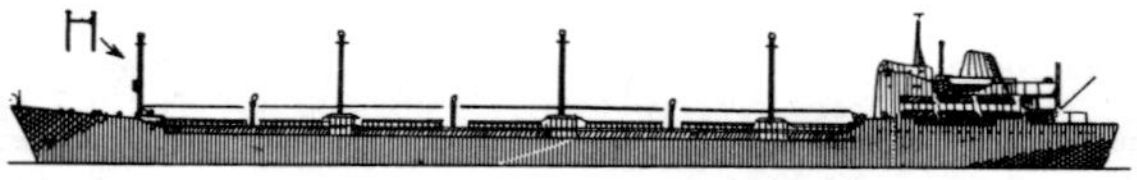

K_4MKFK H13

57780 ORIENT HORIZON. Li/Ne 1961; B; 15300; 180.63 × 10.78 (592.6 × 35.4); M; 14; ex NEW HORIZON; ex VENI 1968.

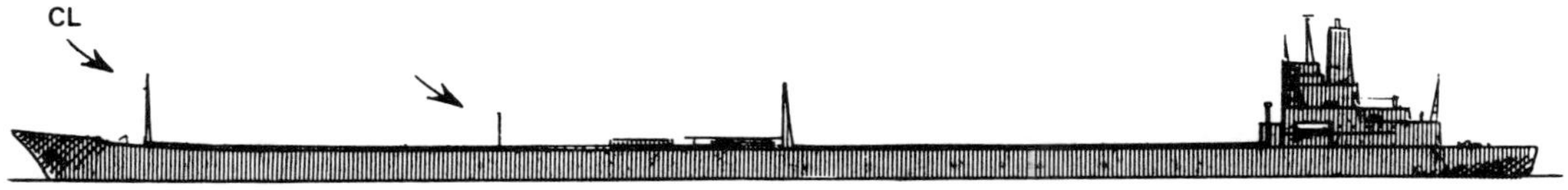

K_3MF H

57790 SHUNKO MARU. Ja/Ja 1974; Tk; 120500; 324.01 × 19.43 (1063.02 × 63.75); T; 15.75. Similar: **57791 HOKO MARU** (Ja).

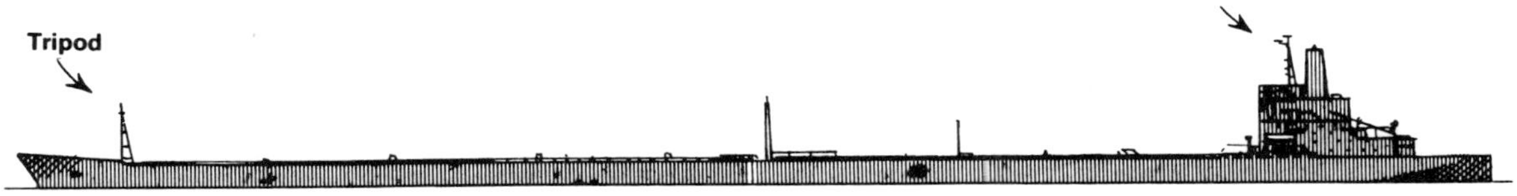

K_3MF H

● **57800 ESSO SCOTIA.** Br/FRG 1969; Tk; 127150; 347.81 × 19.95 (1141.1 × 65.4); T; 16. Similar: **57801 ESSO CALEDONIA** (Br) **57802 ESSO CAMBRIA** (Br) **57803 ESSO COPENHAGEN** (Li) **57804 ESSO EUROPA** (FRG) **57805 ESSO NEDERLAND** (NA) **57806 ESSO SKANDIA** (Li) **57807 ESSO EUROPOORT** (NA) **57808 ESSO BONAIRE** (NA) **57809 ESSO SABA** (NA) **57810 ESSO BONN** (FRG) **57811 ESSO WILHELMSHAVEN** (Li) **57812 ESSO FLANDRE** (Fr) ex ESSO ROTTERDAM 1978 **57813 STALAND** (No).

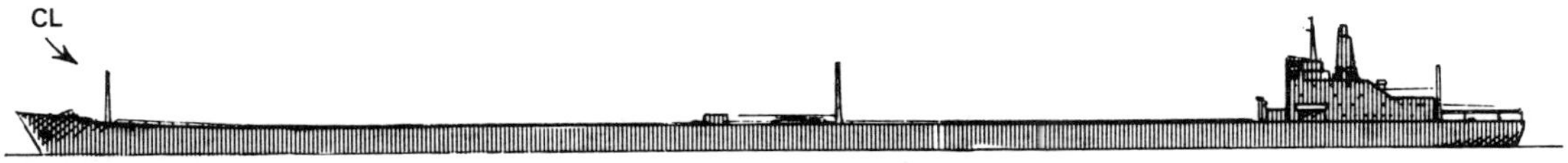

K_3MF H

● **57820 OLYMPIC BOND.** Li/Ja 1972; Tk; 126000; 331 × 22.02 (1085.96 × 72.24); T; 15.5.

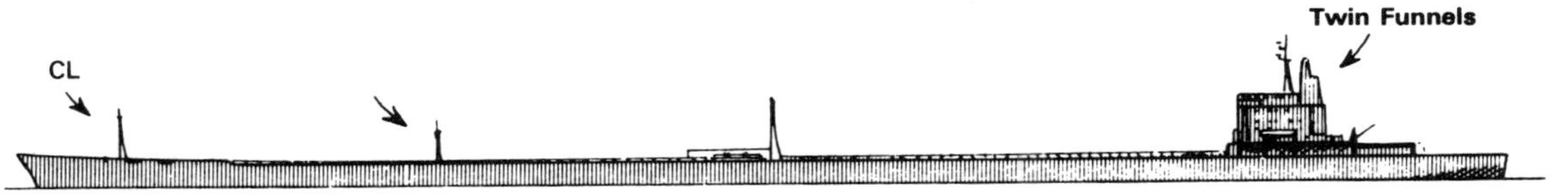

K_3MF H

57830 ALSACE. Fr/Fr 1975; Tk; 118700; 334.12 × 20.34 (1096.19 × 66.73); T; 15.5. Possibly Similar: **57831 AQUITANE** (Fr) **57832 BRUMAIRE** (Fr) **57833 NORMANDIE** (Fr).

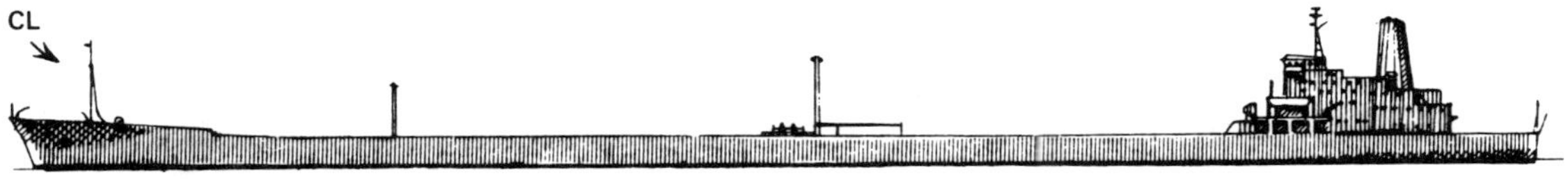

K_3MF H

57840 AVIN OIL LEADER. Gr/FRG 1969; Tk; 104610; 325.33 × 18.98 (1067.4 × 62.3); T; 15.5; ex SIPCA JUBAIL; ex SIPCA II 1978; ex TEXACO HAMBURG 1978. Sisters: **57841 VENUS** (Gr) ex SIPCA DAREEN; ex SIPCA I 1978; ex TEXACO FRANKFURT 1978 **57842 KIMBERLY** (Li) ex OLYMPIC SKY; ex TEXACO NORTH AMERICA 1977.

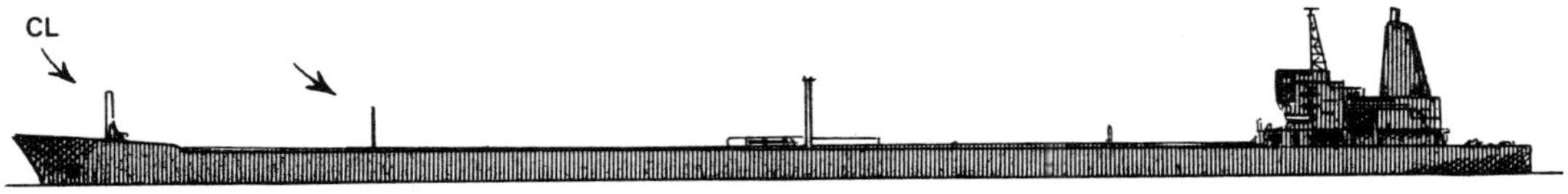

K_3MF H

57850 BRITISH PRIDE. Br/Fr 1973; Tk; 111980; 329.62 × 19.41 (1081.4 × 63.66); T; 15.5.

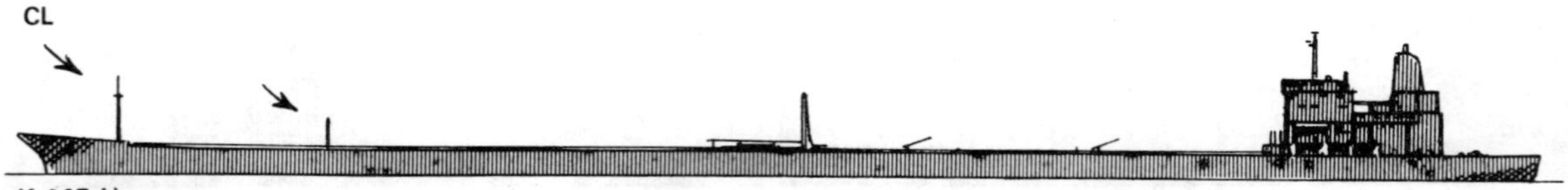

K_3MF H

57860 BRITISH PROMISE. Br/Ne 1974; Tk; 131400; 344.41 × 19.95 (1129.95 × 65.45); T; 16. Sister: **57861 BRITISH PATIENCE** (Br).

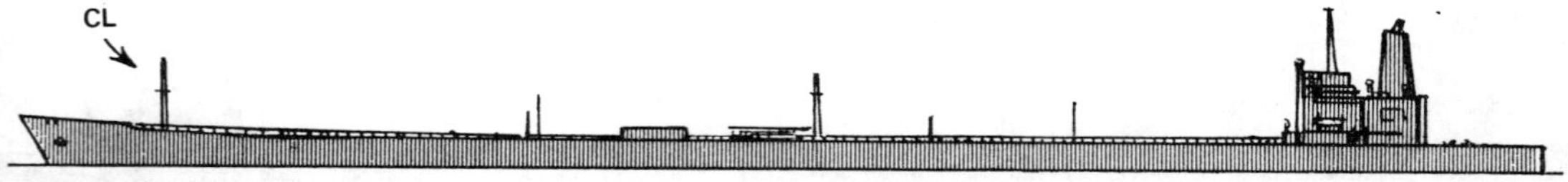

K_3MF H

● **57870 LAUREL.** Li/Ja 1972; Tk; 117200; 336.36 × 20.29 (1103.54 × 66.57); T; 16.75; ex UNIVERSE PIONEER 1980. Similar (Li flag): **57871 UNIVERSE BURMAH 57872 UNIVERSE EXPLORER 57873 ACADIA** ex UNIVERSE GUARDIAN 1980 **57874 PECONIC** ex UNIVERSE MARINER 1980 **57875 MOSELLE** ex UNIVERSE MONITOR 1980 **57876 MENANTIC** ex UNIVERSE RANGER 1980 **57877 HAMLET** ex UNIVERSE SENTINEL 1980 **57878 ARISTOTLE S ONASSIS** ex UNIVERSE FRONTIER 1977 (Pa flag): **57879 TEXACO CARIBBEAN 57880 TEXACO VERAGUAS.**

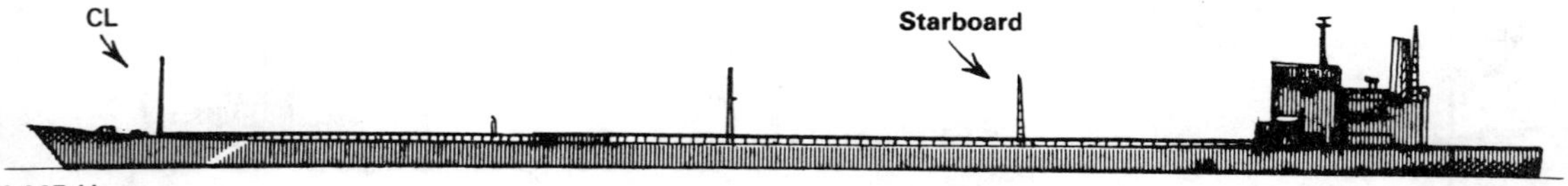

K_3MF H

57890 VENTURE AMERICA. Li/Ja 1973; Tk; 119700; 337.12 × 21.01 (1106.04 × 68.93); T; 16; ex CONOCO AMERICA 1978. Possibly Similar: **57891 VENTURE INDEPENDENCE** (Li) ex CONOCO INDEPENDENCE 1978.

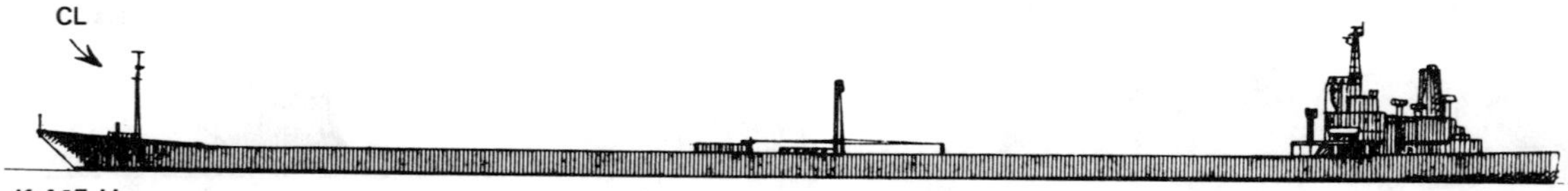

K_3MF H

57900 PAUL L FAHRNEY. Li/Ja 1971; Tk; 118860; 337.5 × 20.49 (1107.3 × 67.2); T; 15.5. Sister: **57901 J.R. GREY** (Li) Similar: **57902 UNITED OVERSEAS I** (Li).

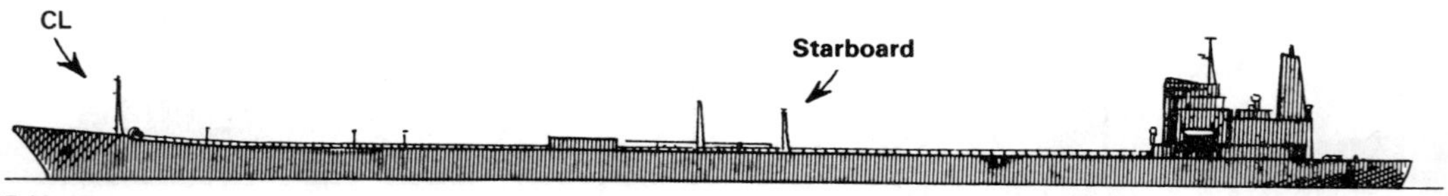

K_3MF H

57910 OHSHIMA MARU. Ja/Ja 1971; Tk; 116830; 317.03 × 20.04 (1040.1 × 65.7); T; 16.5.

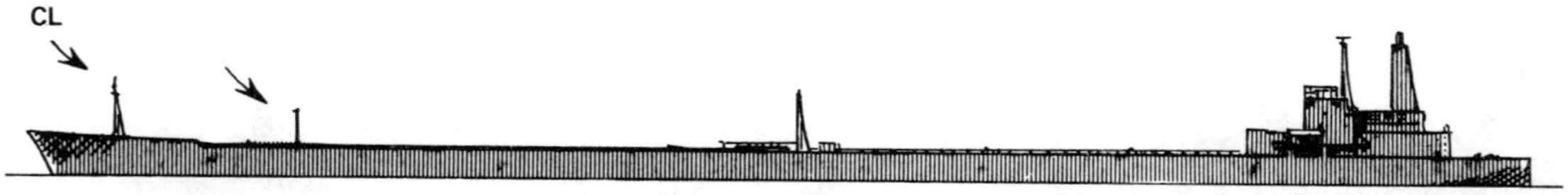

K_3MF H

57920 AL QASIM. Li/Ne 1970; Tk; 92000; 325.33 × 18.98 (1067.36 × 62.27); T; 16; ex MOBIL RAVEN 1977; ex BERGEMASTER 1976; ex MARTICIA 1976. Similar: **57921 SOLON** (Li) ex MOBIL TERN 1979; ex BERGECAPTAIN 1976; ex MYSELLA 1976.

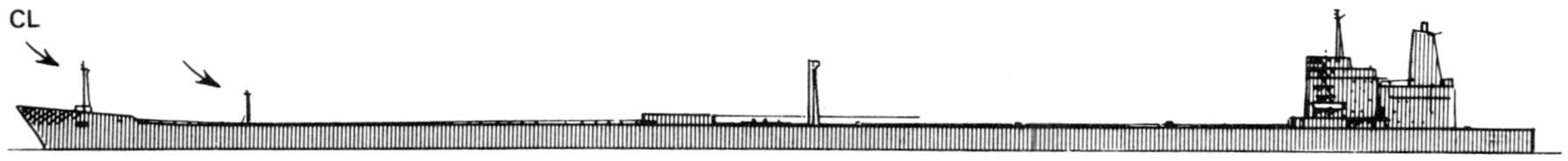

K_3MF H

57930 LACONICA. NA/Ja 1975; Tk; 159600; 343.62 × 22.37 (1127.36 × 73.39); T; 15.25. Sisters: **57931 LANISTES** (Br) **57932 LITIOPA** (Br).

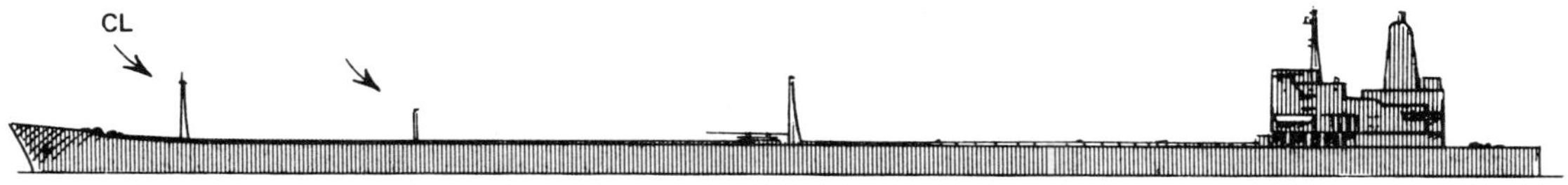

K_3MF H

57940 BRITISH RENOWN. Br/Ja 1974; Tk; 133000; 338.64 × 20.66 (1111.02 × 67.78); T; 14.5. Possible sisters (Br flag): **57941 BRITISH NORNESS; 57942 BRITISH RANGER; 57943 BRITISH RELIANCE; 57944 BRITISH RESOLUTION; 57945 BRITISH RESOURCE** (motor ship) **57946 BRITISH TRIDENT;** Similar (Fr flag); **57947 CHAMBORD; 57948 CHAUMONT; 57949 CHENONCEAUX; 57950 CHINON.**

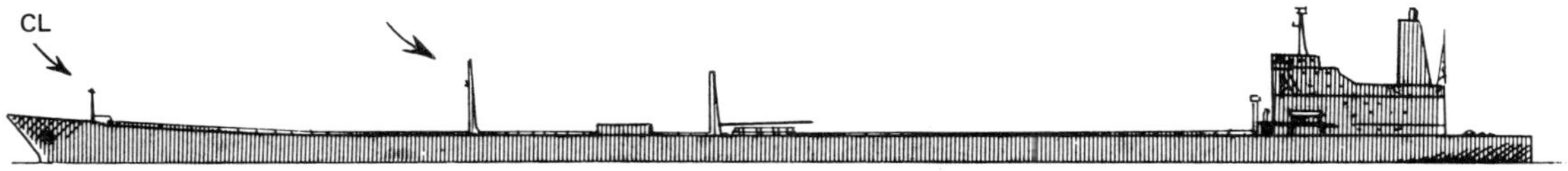

K_3MF H

57960 MUNETAMA MARU. Ja/Ja 1973; Tk; 128800; 341.11 × 20.04 (1119.13 × 65.75); T; 15.25.

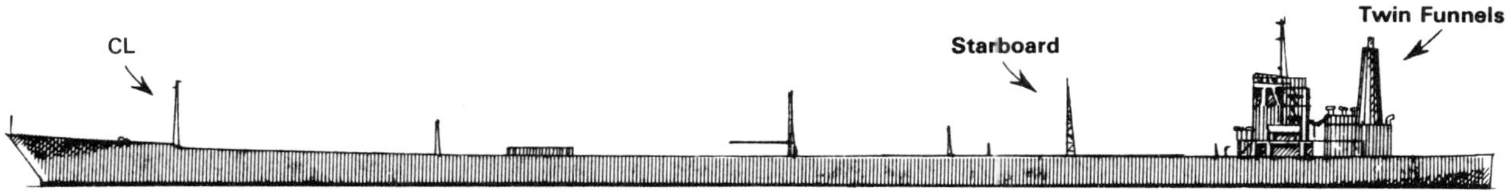

K_3MF H

57970 GLOBTIK TOKYO. Br/Ja 1973; Tk; 238230; 378.88 × 28.2 (1243 × 92.5); T; 15. Sisters: **57971 GLOBTIK LONDON** (Br) **57972 NISSEI MARU** (Ja) Similar: **57973 NISSEKI MARU** (Ja).

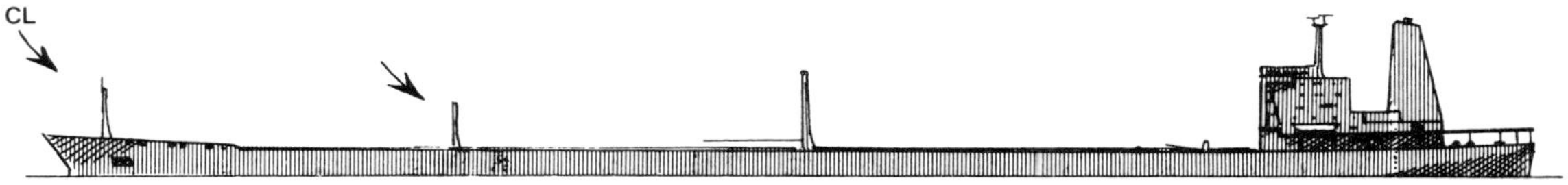

K_3MF H

57980 BRISSAC. Fr/Fr 1976; Tk; 117900; 334.12 × 20.34 (1096.19 × 66.73); T; 15.5.

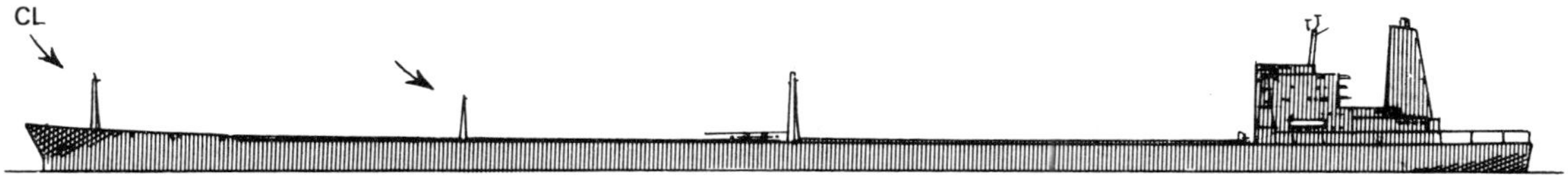

K_3MF H

● **57990 BLOIS.** Fr/Fr 1970; Tk; 118400; 334.02 × 20.34 (1095.9 × 66.7); T; 15.5. Sister: **57991 BEAUGENCY** (Fr).

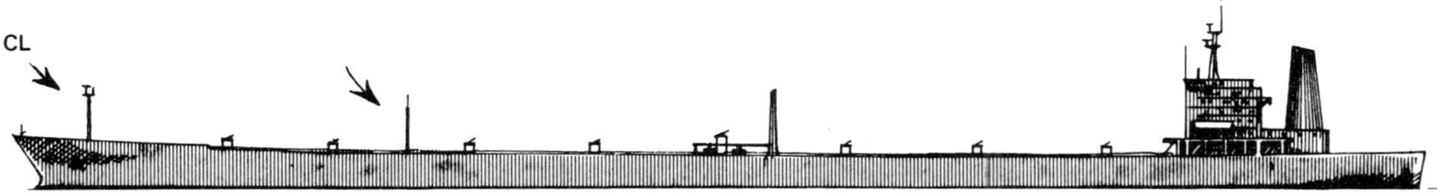

K_3MF H

58000 AL RAWDATAIN. Ku/Fr 1976; Tk; 162200; 352.76 × 22.5 (1157.3 × 73.8); T; 15.5.

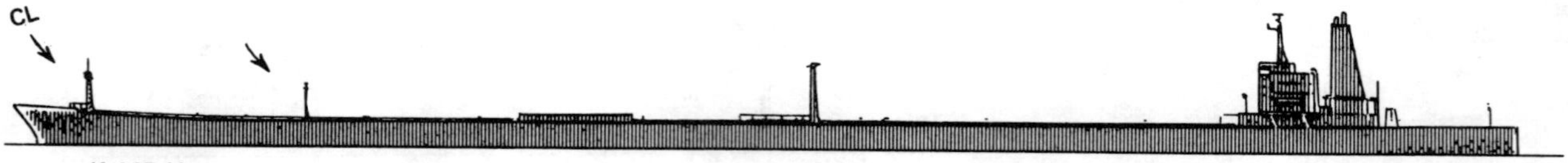

K_3MF H
58010 BERGE DUKE. No/Ja 1973; Tk; 139800; 342.91 × 21.78 (1125.03 × 71.8); M; 15.5. Sisters (No. flag): **58011 BERGE SEPTIMUS 58012 BERGE LORD.**

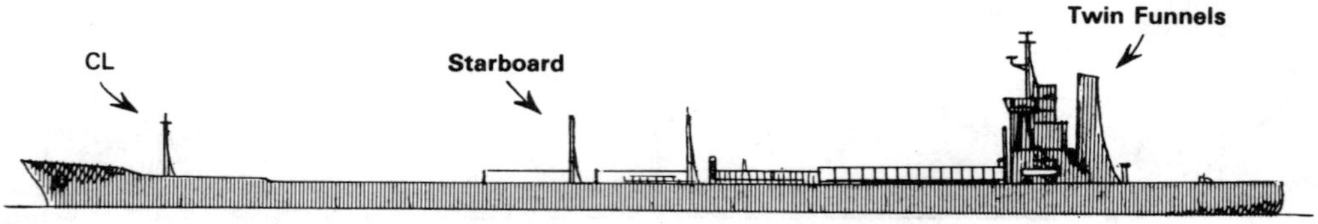

K_3MF H
● **58020 BADR.** Si/Ja 1968; Tk; 81700; 293.02 × 16.1 (961.35 × 52.82); M; 16; ex TOHKOHSAN MARU 1975.

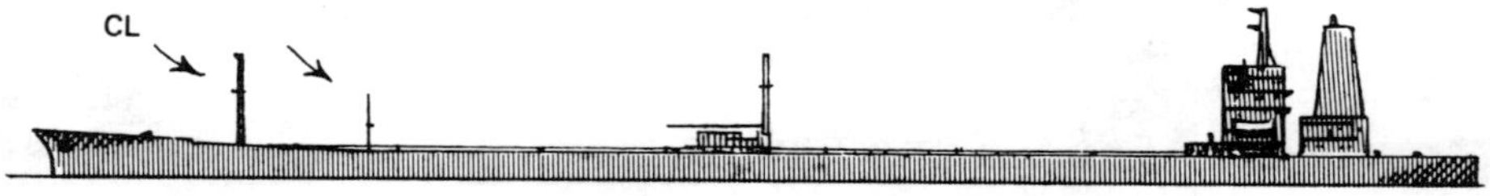

K_3MF H
58030 ATIGUN PASS. US/US 1977; Tk; 74300; 276.16 × 17.47 (906.04 × 57.32); T; 14. Sisters (US flag): **58031 BROOKS RANGE 58032 KEYSTONE CANYON 58033 THOMPSON PASS.**

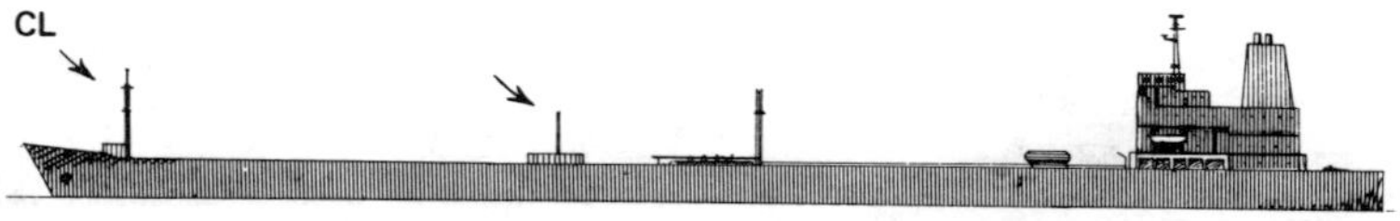

K_3MF H
● **58040 NORDIC FAITH.** Br/Ja 1978; Tk; 55500; 231 × 12.11 (757.87 × 39.73); M; 16.5. Sister: **58041 NORDIC SPIRIT** (Br).

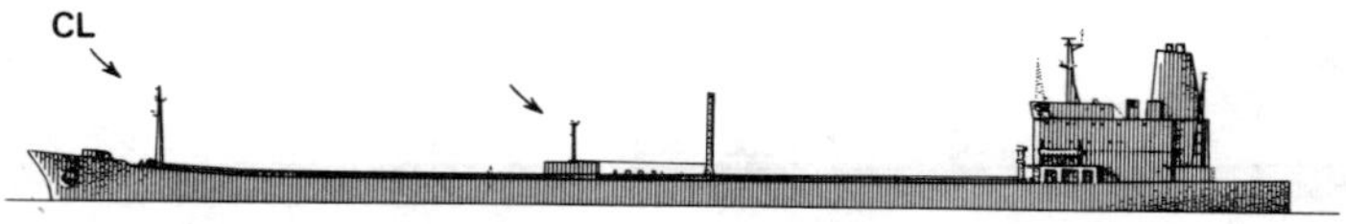

K_3MF H
58050 SAIRYU MARU. Ja/Ja 1978; Tk; 34900; 209.51 × 12.08 (687.37 × 39.63); M; 15.

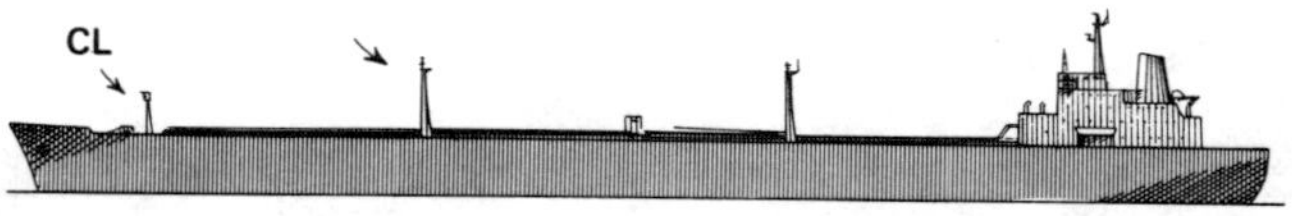

K_3MF H
58060 KAZUTAMA MARU. Ja/Ja 1967; LGC; 34500; 200.11 × 10.5 (656.5 × 34.4); M; 15.5.

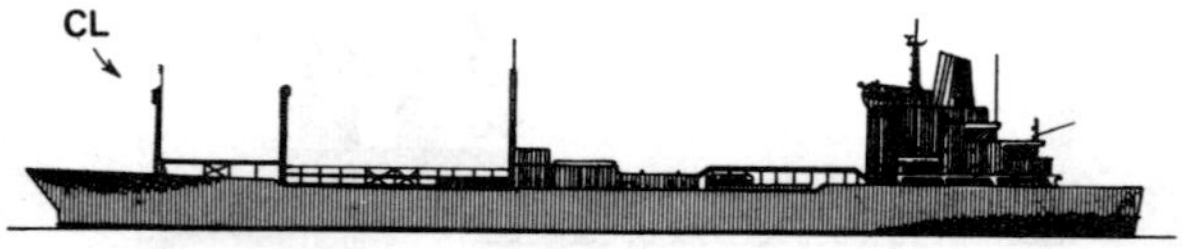

K_3MF H
58070 GAMBADA. Br/Br 1973; LGC; 21360; 177.86 × 10.02 (583.5 × 32.9); M; 16.25. Sister: **58071 GAZANA** (Br).

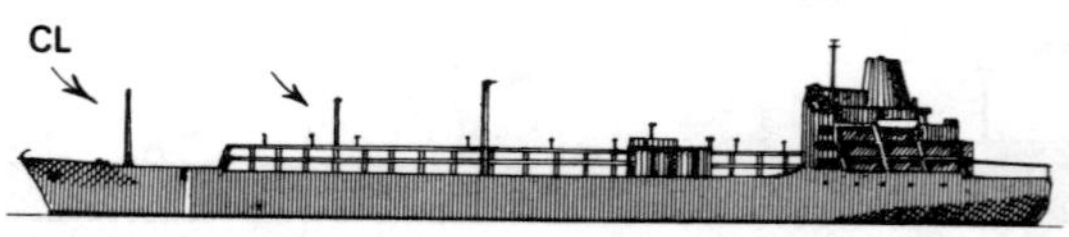

K_3MF H
58080 M. P. GRACE. Li/Ja 1967; LGC; 13500; 162.8 × 8.4 (534.12 × 27.56); M; 16.

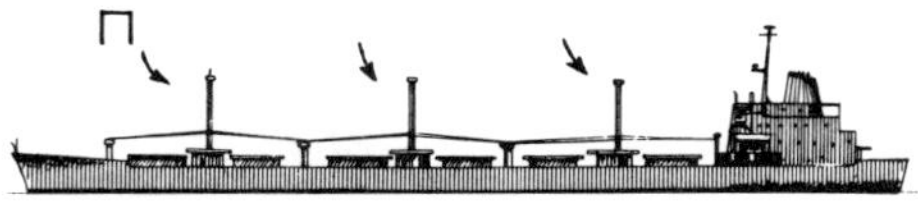

K_3MF H

58090 'FREEDOM' type. Gr/Ja 1967; C; 11000; 141.76×8.77 (465.1×28.8); M; 14.5; Later ships are K_3MFK. Some of the following have taller funnels (Gr flag): **58091 KHIAN CAPTAIN 58092 KHIAN ENGINEER 58093 KHIAN HILL 58094 KHIAN ISLAND 58095 KHIAN SAILOR 58096 KHIAN SEA 58097 KHIAN STAR 58098 KHIAN SUN 58099 KHIAN WAVE 58100 KHIAN ZEPHYR.**

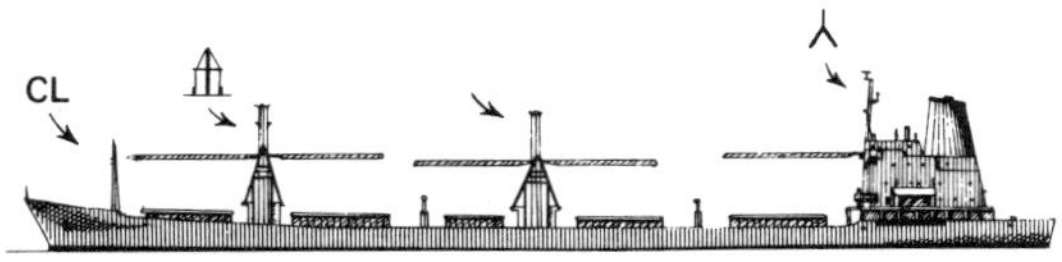

K_3MF H

● **58140 'FORTUNE'** type. —/Ja 1971 onwards; B; 13160; 164.34×9.87 (539.2×32.4); M; 14.5. Sisters (Gr flag): **58141 ACROPOLIS 58142 AKRITAS 58143 ALKYONIS 58144 AMILLA 58145 ANANGEL GLORY 58146 ANANGEL HONOUR 58147 ANANGEL HOPE 58148 ANANGEL LIBERTY 58149 ANANGEL PROSPERITY 58150 ANANGEL TRIUMPH 58151 ANANGEL WISDOM 58152 ANDROS MENTOR 58153 ARETI 58154 ASTERION 58155 ASTIR 58156 ATTICA 58157 CHERRY FLOWER 58158 EVIMERIA 58159 LOUCAS N 58160 MARIA N 58161 PISTIS 58162 SANTORINI 58163 SEA TIGER 58164 TUAREG** ex THEANO Possible sisters: **58165 ANANGEL FORTUNE 58166 ANANGEL HAPPINESS 58167 ANANGEL PEACE 58168 ARION 58169 ATREUS 58170 CHERRY** Sisters (Li flag): **58171 AKADEMOS 58172 AL SADIQ** ex ZUIHO **58173 AL SALAAM 58174 AL SAMAD 58175 AL SAMIE 58176 ANDROS TRANSPORT 58177 CAROLINE P** ex VERA VENTURE **58178 FORTUNE LEADER 58179 PACGLORY 58180 UNILUCK** Probable sisters: **58181 OHTORI 58182 SHUN OH 58183 UNIQUE FORTUNE 58184 YULSAN POSEIDON** ex RYUHO Sisters (Pa flag): **58185 BENIGNITY 58186 HONESTY** Probable sister: **58187 JOLLITY** ex EVERJUST 1980 Sisters (Pi flag): **58188 TRANSOCEAN TRANSPORT II** ex TRADEWIND WEST 1977 **58189 VALOR 58190 ORONMONTE** ex EVERRAY 1980 **58191 RIA LUNA** ex TRADEWIND EAST (Tu flag): **58192 KOCAELI 1** (Ja flag): **58193 ATHOL** (Cu flag): **★58194 XIII CONGRESO** ex UNIASIA (Ys flag): **★58195 DUGI OTOK ★58196 NIN ★58197 NOVIGRAD ★58198 RAVNI KOTARI.**

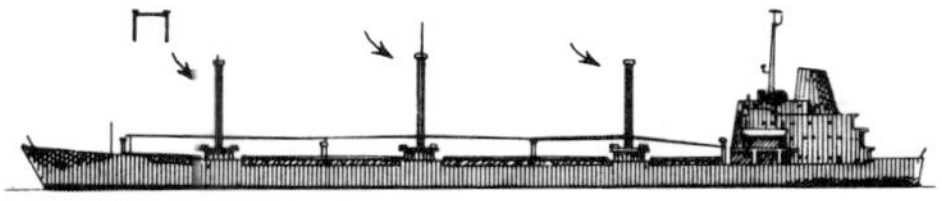

K_3MF H

● **58110 'FREEDOM-HISPANIA'** type. —/Sp and Ar 1968 onwards; C; 9900; 143.69×9.29 (471.42×30.48); M; 15.5. Sisters (Ar flag): **58111 MARBONITA 58112 MARLINDA** (Ch flag): **58113 AYSEN 58114 LAGO HUALAIHUE 58115 LAGO LANALHUE 58116 LAGO LLANQUIHUE 58117 LAGO MAIHUE 58118 LAGO PUYEHUE** (Gr flag): **58119 SANTO EVAN** ex SOLANO 1980 **58120 GOOD FRIEND** ex VIRPAZAR 1973 **58121 THEOHARIS** ex TIVANO 1975 (Li flag): **58122 EASTERN PIONEER** ex CIGOITIA 1980 **58123 ALTAJ** ex AIBOA 1975 (Sg flag): **58124 GREZ** ex ELIANNE 1979 (Pa flag): **58125 MUTAN CAREER** ex ANCUD 1980 **58126 FAJAR** ex LAGO RINIHUE 1980 (It flag): **58127 NONNA RAFFAELLA** ex SANTA KATARINA ex ARCADIA BERLIN 1976; launched as VIRPAZAR (Ys flag): **★58128 GETALDIC ★58129 GUNDULIC ★58130 IVO VOJNOVIC ★58131 KOLASIN ★58132 MAVRO VETRANIC.**

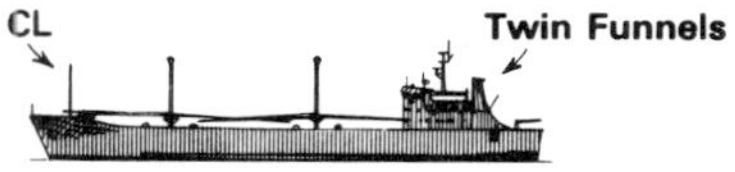

K_3MF H

58210 PASSAT. FRG/FRG 1965; C; 1000; 81.84×5.1 (268.5×16.7); M; 11.

K_3MF H

58220 VISKO REEFER. Fi/FRG 1966; R; 500/1200; 75.57×3.81/5.02 (247.93×12.5/16.47); M; 15; ex KEPPO 1975.

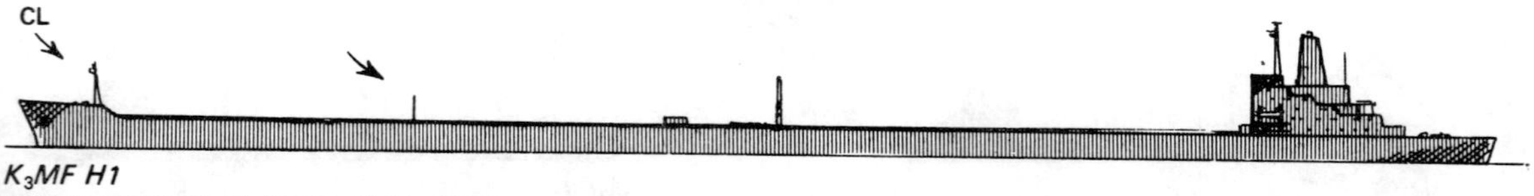

K_3MF H1

58230 TROPICAL LION. Li/Br 1972; Tk; 125300; 345.5 × 20.07 (1133.5 × 65.85); T; 15.5; ex LONDON LION 1978. Sisters: **58231 WINDSOR LION** (Br) **58232 THERMIDOR** (Fr) ex OPPORTUNITY;launched as TYNE PRIDE **58233 EVERETT F. WELLS** (Pa) Similar: **58234 WORLD UNICORN** (Br).

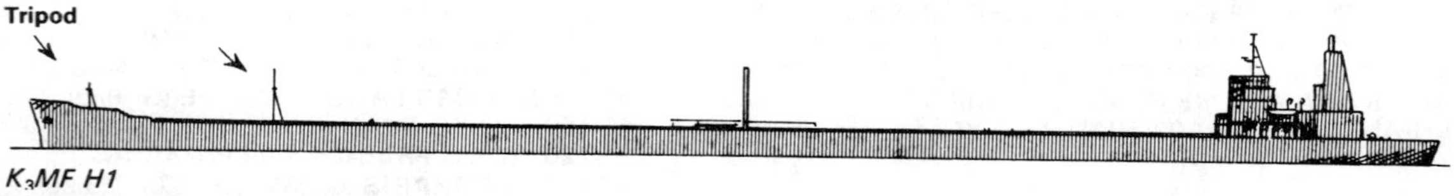

K_3MF H1

58240 CHEVRON BRUSSELS. Li/Sw 1972; Tk; 122800; 340.52 × 20.07 (1117.19 × 65.85); T; 16. Sister: **58241 CHEVRON LONDON** (Li).

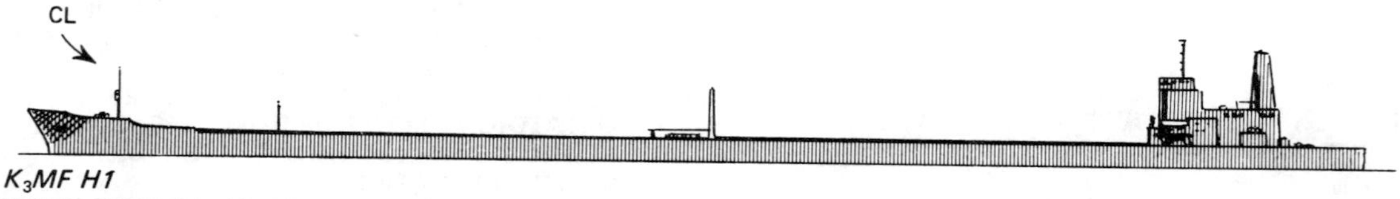

K_3MF H1

58250 TEXACO AMSTERDAM. No/Ne 1971; Tk; 116200; 330.03 × 19.91 (1082.78 × 65.32); T; 16. Sister (may be K_2MF): **58251 TEXACO PANAMA** (Pa).

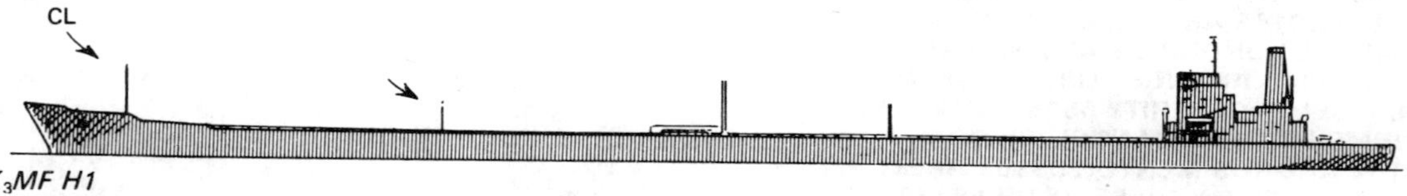

K_3MF H1

58260 FINA BRITANNIA. Fr/Ne 1971; Tk; 116000; 329.68 × 19.85 (1081.63 × 65.12); T; 16.

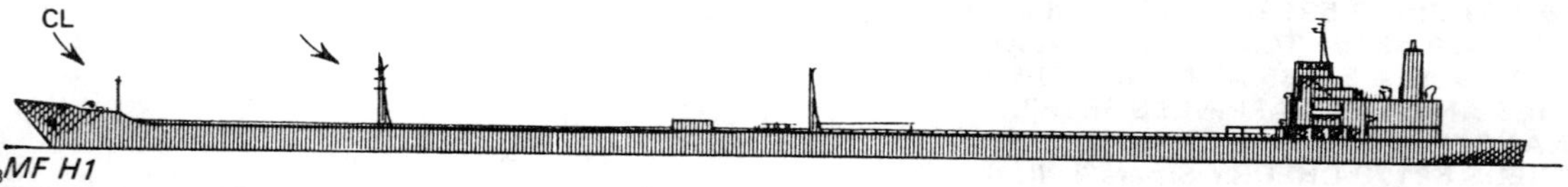

K_3MF H1

58270 CHEVRON NAGASAKI. Li/Ja 1974; Tk; 118100; 338.64 × 20.56 (1111.1 × 67.4); T; 15.25. Sisters (Li flag): **58271 CHEVRON PERTH 58272 CHEVRON FELUY 58273 CHARLES PIGOTT** Possible sisters: **58274 CHEVRON COPENHAGEN 58275 CHEVRON EDINBURGH 58276 OTTO N. MILLER 58277 L. W. FUNKHAUSER 58278 C. W. KITTO** Similar: **58279 TEXACO ITALIA 58280 TEXACO JAPAN.**

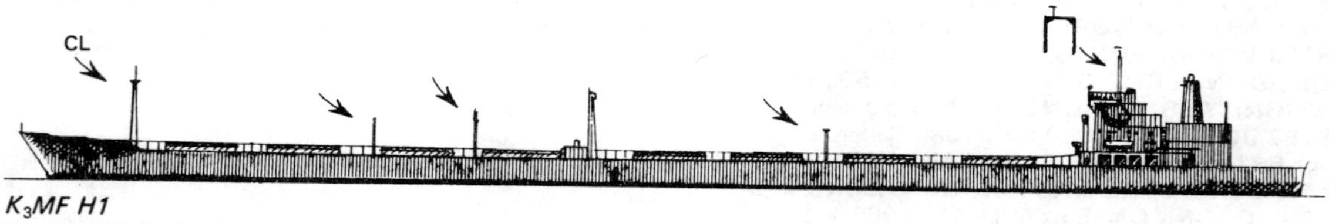

K_3MF H1

● **58290 CAST NARWHAL.** Br/Ja 1972; OO; 132300; 335.67 × 20.62 (1101.28 × 67.65); T; 15.75; ex NORDIC CONQUEROR 1980; ex NAESS AMBASSADOR 1974. Sister: **58291 LAUDERDALE** (Br).

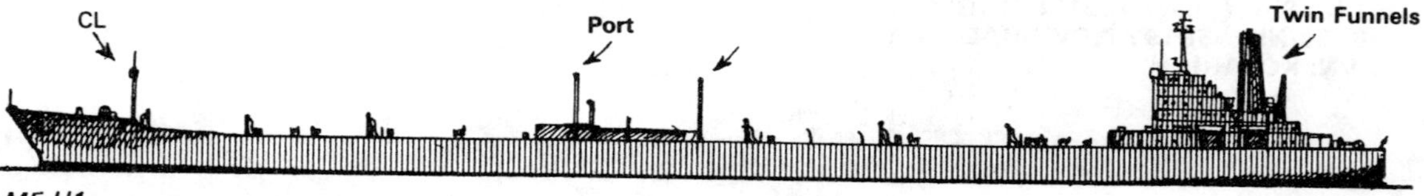

K_3MF H1

● **58300 UNIVERSE IRELAND.** Li/Ja 1968; Tk; 149600; 345.3 × 24.82 (1132.87 × 81.43); TST; 15. Sisters: **58301 JUBAYL** (Si) ex AVIN OIL SAFKIA 1980; ex UNIVERSE JAPAN 1980 **58302 AVIN OIL GERANI** (Gr) ex UNIVERSE KUWAIT 1980.

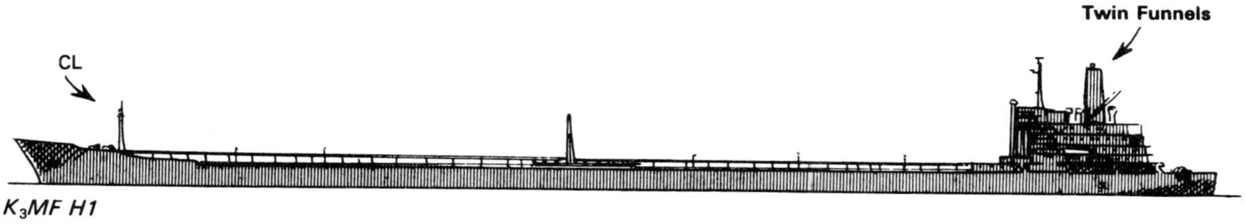

K_3MF H1

58310 DALMA. Li/Sp 1975; Tk; 124200; 349.82 × 20.19 (1147.7 × 66.24). TSM; 16.5; launched as AFRAN ODYSSEY. Similar: **58311 AL ANDALAS** (Ku) Possibly similar: **58312 SANTA MARIA** (Sp) launched as LA SANTA MARIA.

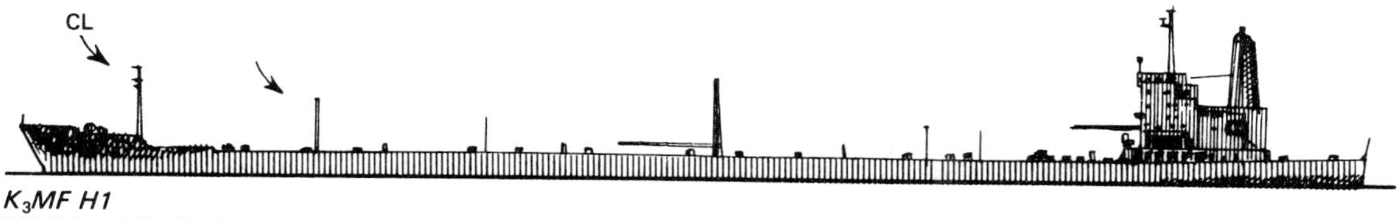

K_3MF H1

58320 BRITISH RESPECT. Br/Ja 1974; Tk; 136600; 336.03 × 21.21 (1102.5 × 69.6); T; 17.

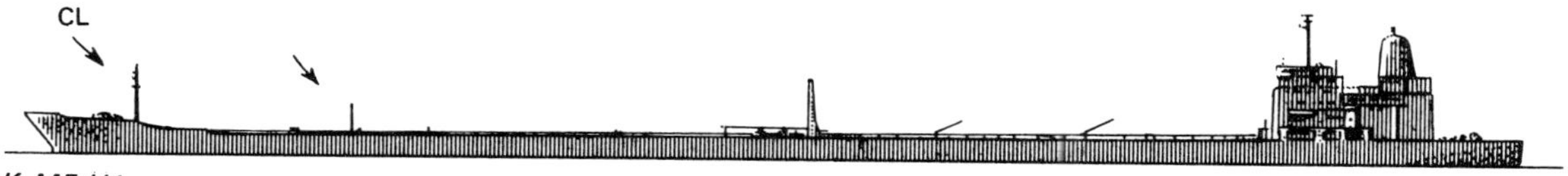

K_3MF H1

58330 BRITISH PROGRESS. Br/Ne 1973; Tk; 117500; 330.01 × 19.9 (1082.71 × 65.29); T; 16. Sister: **58331 BRITISH PURPOSE** (Br).

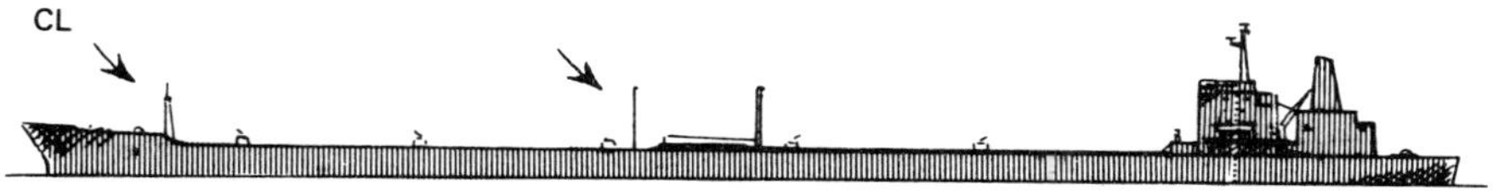

K_3MF H1

58340 OLYMPIC SPLENDOUR. Gr/Br 1976; Tk; 66300; 260.33 × 15.18 (854.1 × 49.8); M; 16; ex GEROI SEVASTOPOLYA launched as KYRA LYNN. Sisters: **58341 ARTEMIS GAROFALIDIS** (Gr) ex GEROI NOVOROSSIYSKA launched as INTEROCEANIC I **58342 AFRAN EQUATOR** (Li) ex GEROI KERCHI; ex INTEROCEANIC II launched as ROBCAP VI Similar: **58343 YORKSHIRE** (Br).

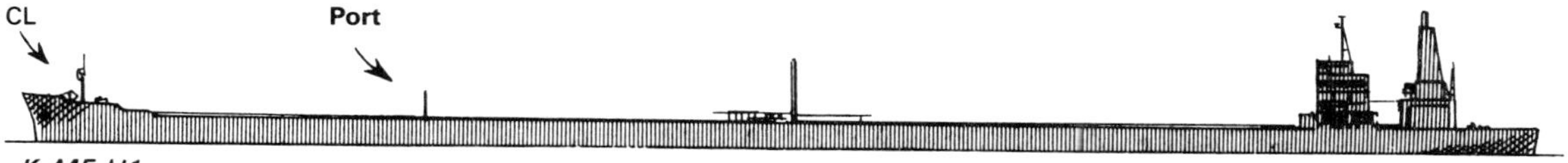

K_3MF H1

● **58350 JATULI.** Fi/Sw 1971; Tk; 125400; 340.06 × 20.07 (1115.68 × 65.85); T; 15.75; ex GORDIAN; ex HUDSON FRIENDSHIP 1976. Sister: **58351 GRATIAN** (No) ex HUDSON VENTURE 1976 Similar: **58352 SEA SCOUT** (Sw) **58353 SEA SWIFT** (Sw).

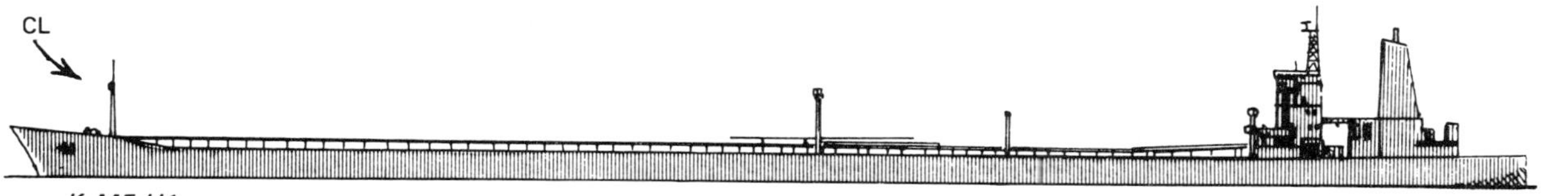

K_3MF H1

58360 BONN. FRG/FRG 1976; Tk; 188700; 370.24 × 22.59 (1214.7 × 74.1); T; 16; **'EUROPA'** type. Sisters: **58361 BREMEN** (Li) ex VASSILIKI COLOCOTRONIS 1976 **58362 BERLIN** (Li) ex IOANNIS COLOCOTRONIS 1976 **58363 BRAZILIAN HOPE** (Li) launched as WORLD GIANT **58364 SHAT-AL ARAB** (Iq) **58365 WAHRAN** (Ag).

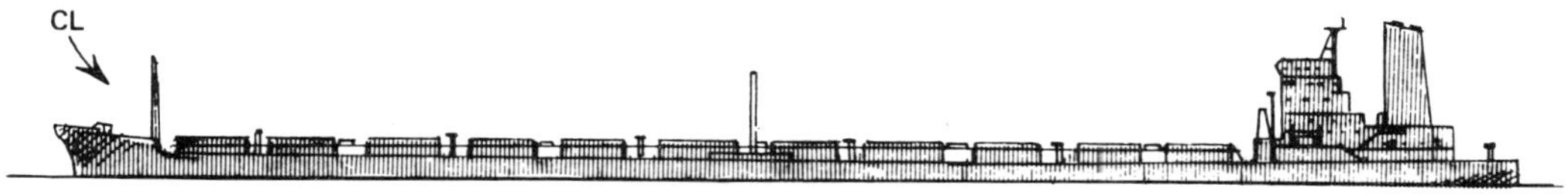

K_3MF H1

58370 RECIFE. Li/Fr 1974; OBO; 76400; 299.25 × 17.6 (981.79 × 57.74); M; 16. Sister: **58371 YEMANJA** (Li).

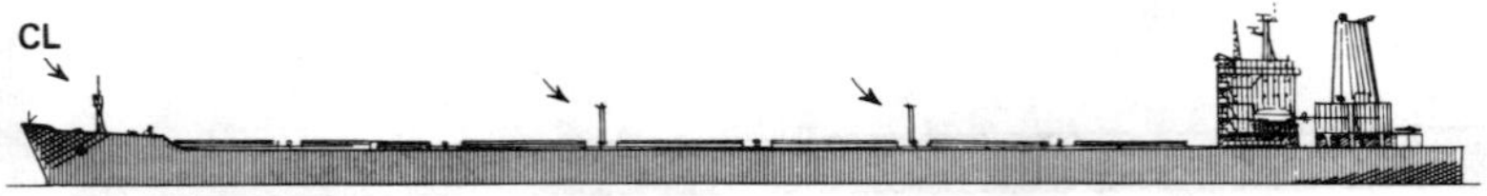

K_3MF H1

58380 THALASSINI EFHI. Gr/Ja 1976; B; 42300; 239.05 × 14 (784.28 × 45.93); M; 15.2; ex IKAN BAWAL 1980; ex THORSDRAKE 1979.

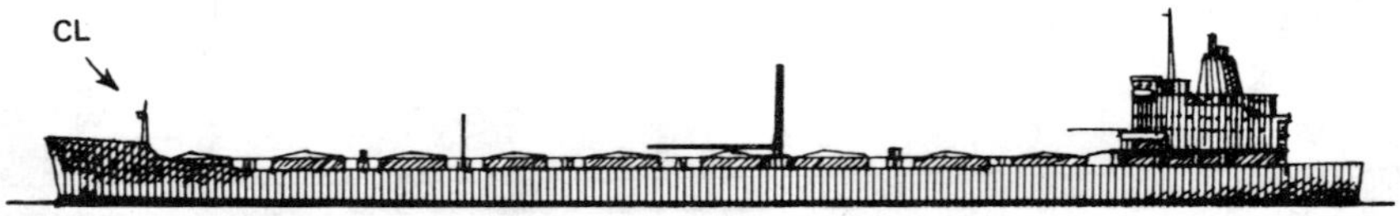

K_3MF H1

58390 JOREK COMBINER. No/Pd 1976; OBO; 66370; 245.02 × 16 (803.9 × 52.5); M; 16; **'B-525'** type. Sister: **58391 ISABELLE** (Li) ex KUTWO VENTURE; ex JOREK CONTENDER 1978; ex JOHAN REKSTEN 1977.

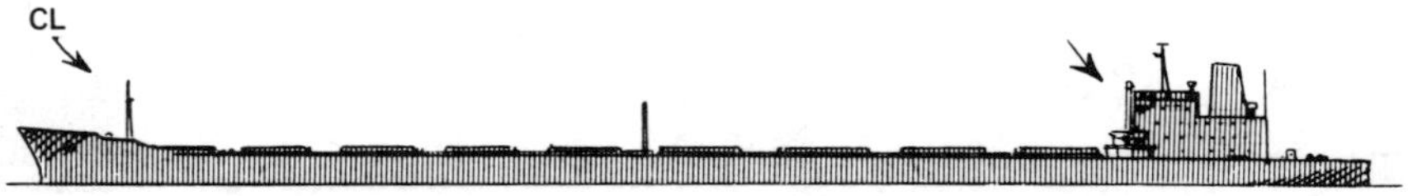

K_3MF H1

● **58400 CAST OSPREY.** Br/Sw 1972; OBO; 56300; 256.04 × 15.08 (840.03 × 49.48); M; 15.75; ex ANGLIA TEAM. Sisters (Br flag): **58401 CAST SKUA** ex NORVEGIA TEAM **58402 CAST GANNET** ex SUECIA TEAM **58403 LONDON TEAM 58404 SCANDIA TEAM 58405 SEVONIA TEAM** (In flag): **58406 WALCHAND.**

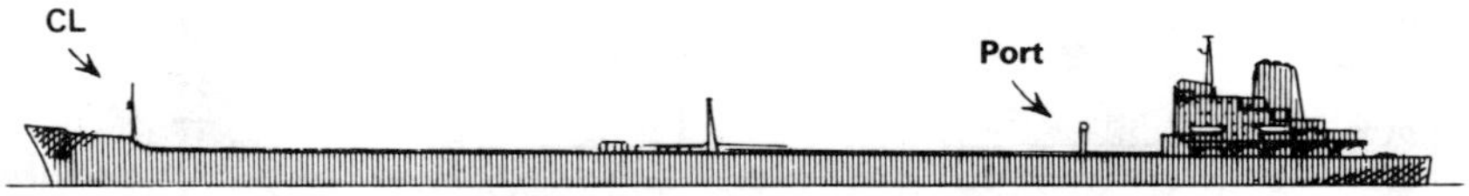

K_3MF H1

58410 MARIAM. Gr/Ja 1966; Tk; 48500; 248.42 × 13.65 (815.03 × 44.78); M; —; ex MORGEDAL 1978; ex MORNING LIGHT 1976; ex PEMBROKE TRADER 1972. Similar: **58411 IRINIO** (Pa) ex SKAUGUM 1976.

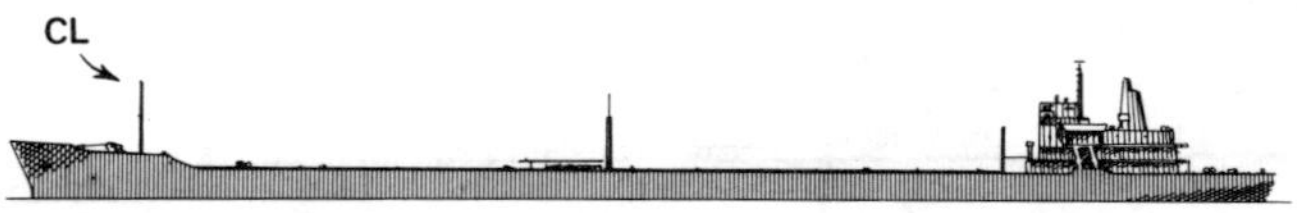

K_3MF H1

58420 OGDEN CHARGER. US/US 1969; Tk; 20900; 201.23 × 11.17 (660.2 × 36.65); T; 16; ex EAGLE CHARGER. Sisters (US flag): **58421 OGDEN LEADER** ex EAGLE LEADER **58422 OVERSEAS ALICE 58423 OVERSEAS VALDEZ** ex OVERSEAS AUDREY 1971 **58424 OVERSEAS VIVIAN** Possible sisters: **58425 OGDEN CHAMPION** ex PENN CHAMPION 1974 **58426 OGDEN WABASH 58427 OGDEN WILLAMETTE 58428 SPIRIT OF LIBERTY.**

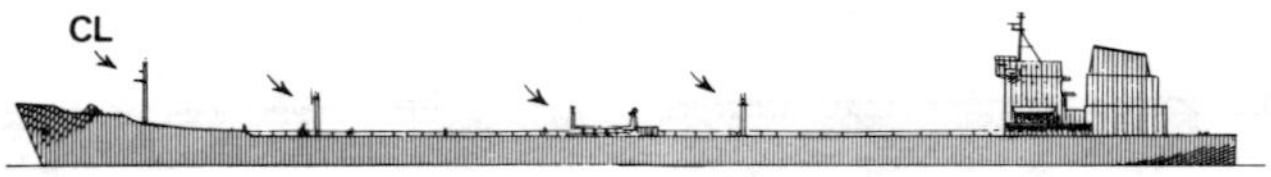

K_3MF H1

58430 CHEVRON WASHINGTON. US/US 1976; Tk; 16900; 198.13 × 11.35 (650.03 × 37.24); GT; 15. Sisters (US flag): **58431 CHEVRON COLORADO 58432 CHEVRON LOUISIANA 58433 CHEVRON OREGON 58434 CHEVRON ARIZONA.**

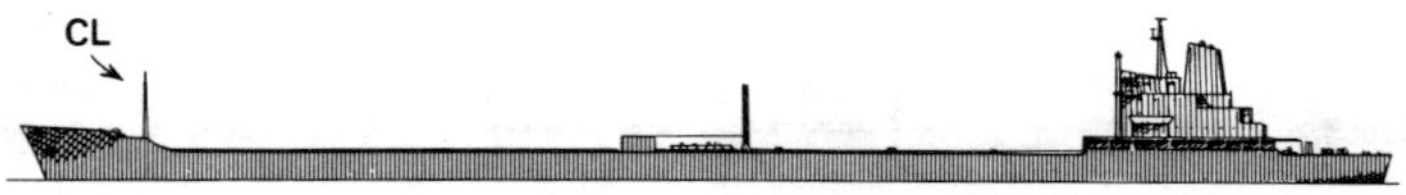

K_3MF H1

● **58440 ZAPATA PATRIOT.** US/US 1975; Tk; 21600; 216.8 × 10.52 (711.29 × 34.51); M; 16. Sisters (US flag): **58441 ZAPATA COURIER 58442 ZAPATA RANGER 58443 ZAPATA ROVER.**

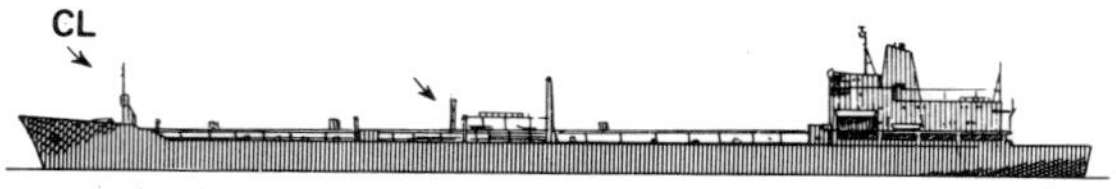

K_3MF H1
58450 BORGA. No/No 1973; Ch; 18700; 170.62 × 11.37 (559.78 × 37.3); M; 16; ex TEAM VESTA.

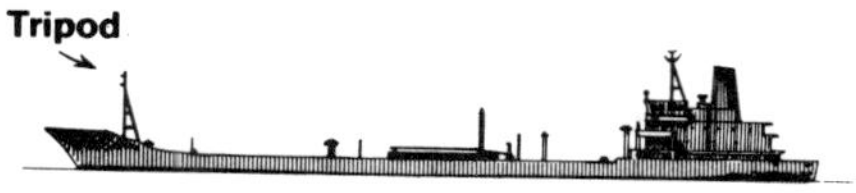

K_3MF H1
58460 FRAMNAS. Sw/Sw 1972/73; Bitumen/Oil carrier; 4300; 122.84 × 5.74 (403.02 × 18.83); M; 14.25; launched 1972, lengthened and completed 1973.

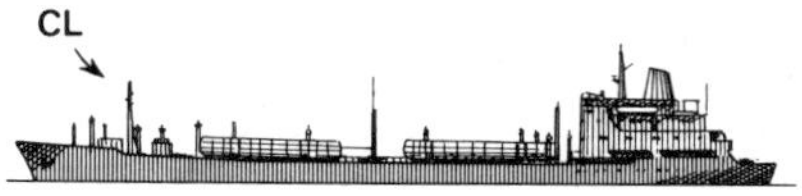

K_3MF H1
58470 JO ROGN. No/No 1970; Tk; 5500/6700; 120.83 × 8.55/9.06 (396.42 × 28.05/29.72); M; 14.5; ex BOW ROGN 1980. Similar (No flag): **58471 JO GRAN** ex BOW GRAN 1980 **58472 JO LIND** ex BOW LIND 1980.

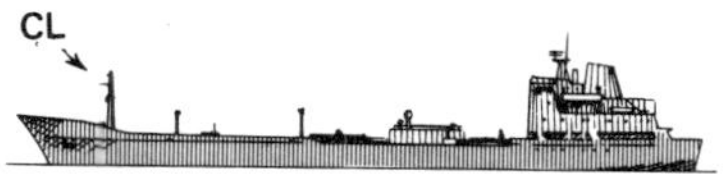

K_3MF H1
58480 BENGHAZI. Ag/FRG 1978; LGC; 4600; 108.8 × 7.5 (356.96 × 24.61); M; 16.6.

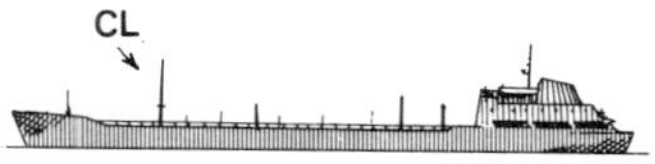

K_3MF H1
58490 OTELIA. Sw/Sw 1969; Tk; 2700; 98.94 × 6.43 (324.61 × 21.1); M; 12. Sisters: **58491 OTTAWA** (Sw) **58492 KHALIJIAH** (Ku) ex OTELLO 1978 Similar: **58493 OTARU** (Sw) **58494 WOTONI** (Ma) ex OTONI 1977.

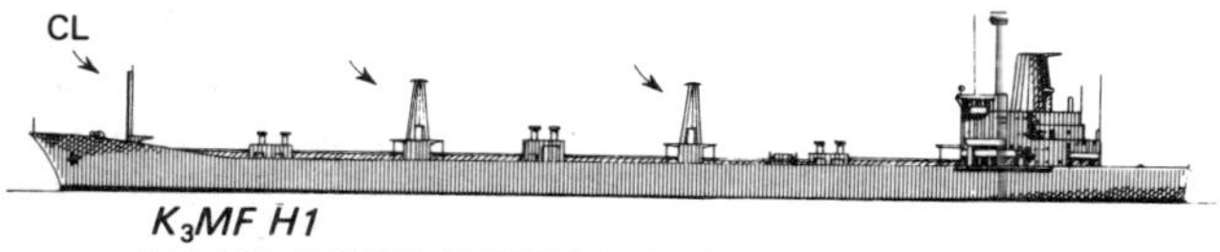

K_3MF H1
58500 ERIKA BOLTEN. FRG/FRG 1973; BC; 20300; 196.32 × 10.9 (644.1 × 35.8); M; 18. Sister: **58501 NATALIE BOLTEN.**

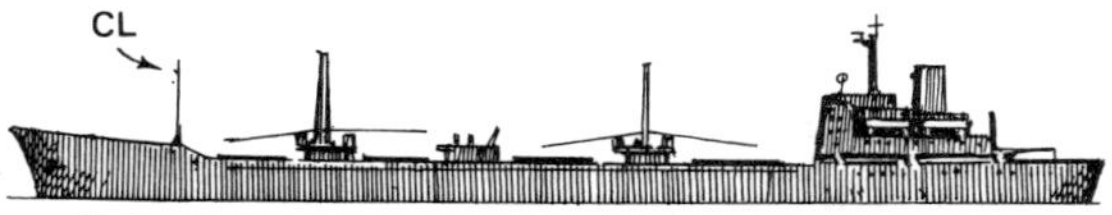

K_3MF H1
⋆58510 PYATIDYESYATILYETIYE SSSR Ru/Ru 1973; FC; 13100; 172.12 × 8.1 (564.7 × 26.57); M; 19; Also known as **50 LET SSSR.** Sisters (Ru flag): **⋆58511 BERINGOV PROLIV ⋆58512 IRBENSKIY PROLIV ⋆58513 PROLIV LAPERUZA ⋆58514 PROLIV SANNIKOVO ⋆58515 PROLIV VILKITSKOGO ⋆58516 XXV SYEZD KPSS.**

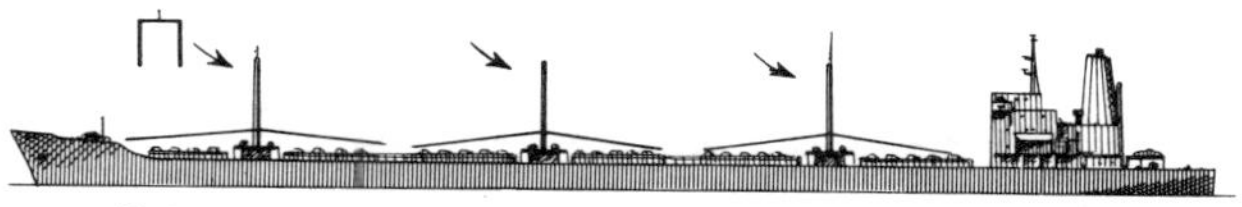

K_3MF H1
58520 WEST JINORIWON. Pa/Ja 1972; B; 24600; 194.01 × 11.44 (636.52 × 37.53); M; 14.75; ex INVERALMOND 1980.

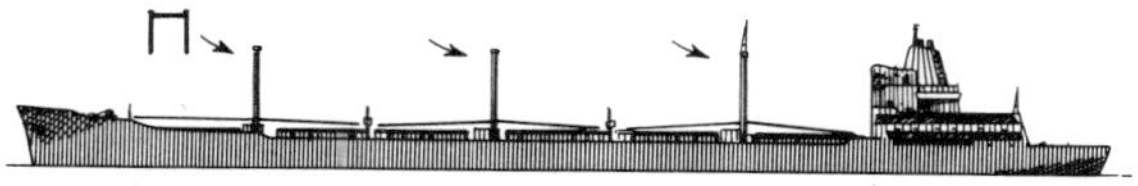

K_3MF H1
58530 GEORGIOS. Gr/Ja 1966; B; 15800; 173.51 × 10.11 (569.26 × 33.17); M; 14.5; ex FINNISH WASA; ex GENERAL AGUINALDO 1973.

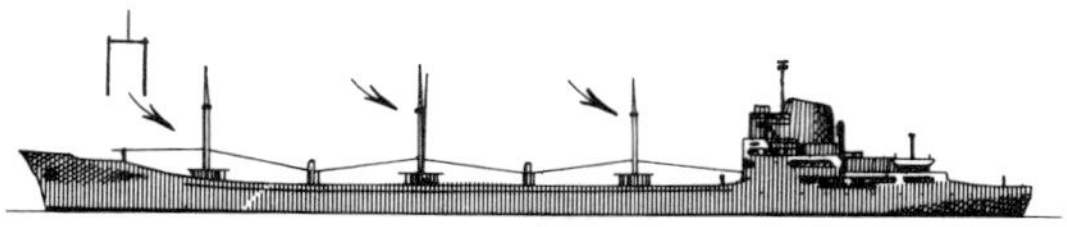

K_3MF H1
58540 ORIENTAL TRADER. Li/Ja 1956; C; 10200; 159.9 × 9.57 (524.61 × 31.4); M; —; ex PACIFIC PIONEER 1960.

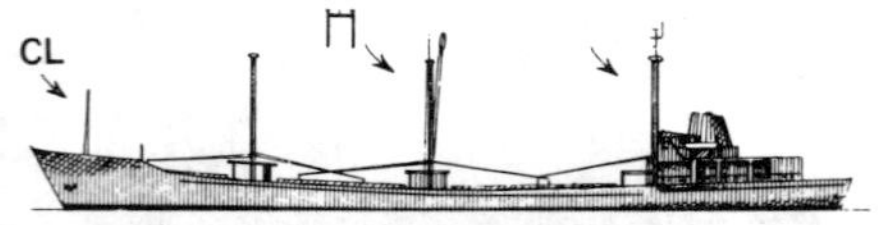

K_3MF H1
58550 HELENE ROTH. Cy/FRG 1969; C; 3310/5560; 124.49 × 6.4/8 (408.4 × 21/26.2); M; 17. Sisters: **58551 ERIKA NABER** (FRG) ex ERIKA SCHULTE 1978 **58552 CARBET** (Fr) ex GUNTHER SCHULTE 1976; ex WAMERU 1976; ex GUNTHER SCHULTE 1975 **58553 CARIMARE** (Fr) ex WANGONI 1976; ex AUGUSTE SCHULTE 1975.

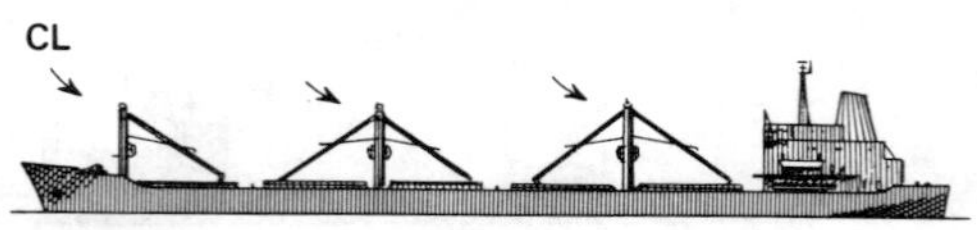

K_3MF H1
● **58560 'FREEDOM' MARK II** type. —/Ja 1977 onwards; C; 11000; 137 (bp) × 9.45 (449.48 × 31); M; 13.5; Also licensed to be built in Brazil. Sisters (Li flag): **58561 AL AHAD** (Gr flag): **58565 ANTIOPI 58567 ALTIS 58568 ANTHOS 58569 ATHLON 58570 AVLIS 58571 ALKMINI 58572 AMAZON 58573 ARAN 58574 EFDIM HOPE 58575 EFDIM JUNIOR** ex AL AWAL 1979 **58576 GHIKAS 58577 MILOS ISLAND 58578 NEMEA 58579 PELLA 58580 SUNCARIBE** ex ANANGEL SKY 1979 **58581 SUNGUAJIRA** ex ANANGEL VICTORY **58582 SUNARAWAK** ex ANANGEL APOLLO 1979 (Bs flag): **58583 YORKTOWN** ex AL ALEEM.

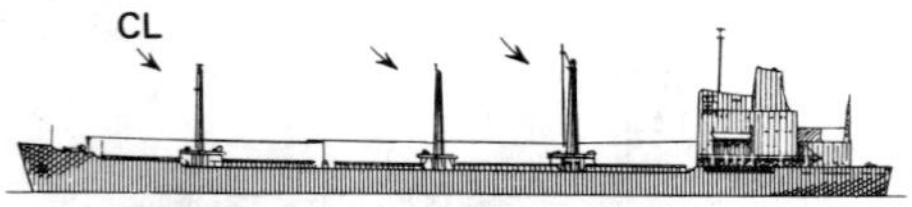

K_3MF H1
⋆**58590 ZHONG TIAO SHAN.** RC/FRG 1970; C; 6600/9300; 139.58 × (9.19 (457.94 × —/30.15); M; 16; ex ATLANTIS 1978; **'German Liberty'** type. Sisters: ⋆**58591 HAN YIN** (RC) ex OKEANIS 1974 ⋆**58592 XIN AN JIANG** (RC) ex OCTAVIA 1977 ⋆**58593 FENG HUANG SHAN** (RC) ex IA 1978; ex NIRIIS 1974 **58594 ALTAVIA** (FRG) **58595 NOVIA** (FRG) **58596 LONTUE** (Ch) ex MEGALOPOLIS 1976.

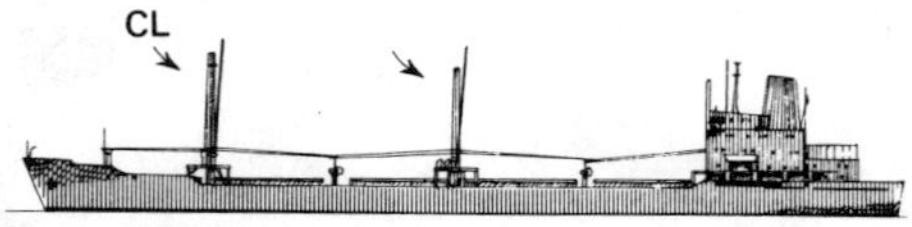

K_3MF H1
● **58600 ATLANTIC CURRENT.** Li/FRG 1968; C; 6350/9000; 139.73 × —/9.02 (458.4 × —/29.6); M; —; ex DIRK MITTMAN 1971; ex SUNDIRK 1971; ex DIRK MITTMAN 1969; **'German Liberty'** type. Similar: **58601 JOSEF STEWING** (FRG) ex VIGRAFJORD 1977; ex JOSEF STEWING 1976; ex RHEINFELS 1970; launched as JOSEF STEWING **58602 GOLDEN GHANA** (Pa) ex SLOMAN SENIOR ⋆**58603 SHI JING SHAN** (RC) ex SAXONIA 1977; ex SUNSAXONIA 1971 **58604 PETRADI** (Gr) ex PITRIA 1980 Possibly similar: **58605 GOLDEN CAMEROON** (Pa) ex MINERVA 1980 **58606 ATTIKA HOPE** (Gr) ex SUNHOPE 1976; ex ATTIKA HOPE 1973 **58607 RIZCUN HONG KONG** (Br) ex PITRIA STAR 1980.

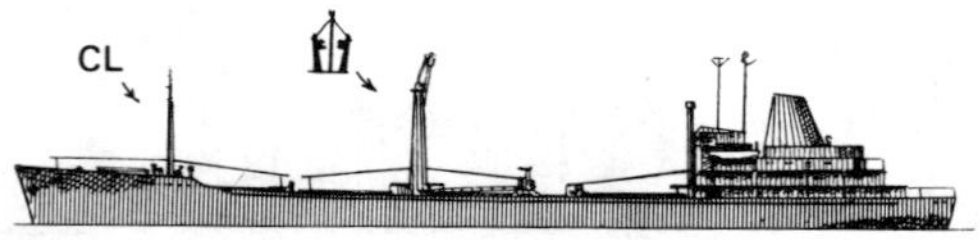

K_3MF H1
●⋆**58610 DA LONG TIAN.** RC/Ja 1966; C/HL; 7010/9450; 152.25 × 8.31/9.48 (499.5 × 27.2/31.1); M; 19; ex CROSTAFELS 1978. Sisters: ⋆**58611 DA HONG QIAO** (RC) ex KYBFELS 1979 ⋆**58612 WU YI SHAN** (RC) ex BIRKENFELS 1978 ⋆**58613 DA QING SHAN** (RC) ex SCHONFELS **58614 FALKENFELS** (Gr) **58615 HOHENFELS** (Gr).

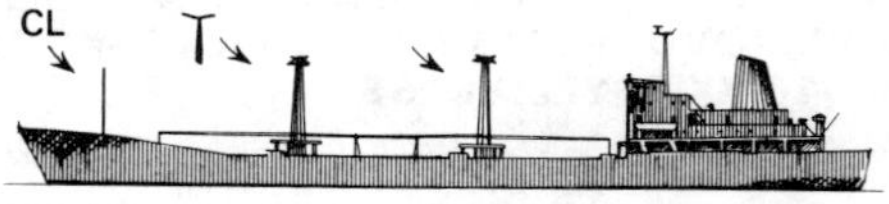

K_3MF H1
58620 BAMSA DAN. De/De 1973; R; 5000; 135.11 × 7.62 (443.3 × 25); M; 17.

K_3MF H1
● **58630 STOCKHORN.** Sd/FRG 1966; C; 1000; 71.61 × 4.98 (234.94 × 16.34); M; 11.5; ex UTHOERN 1976; ex UTHORN 1972.

K_3MF H1
58640 ADRIANA. Ne/Sw 1965; C; 800/1500; 72.47 × 3.6/5.02 (237.8 × 11.8/16.5); M; 11.5; ex KLARENBEEK 1976; ex SILVA 1971.

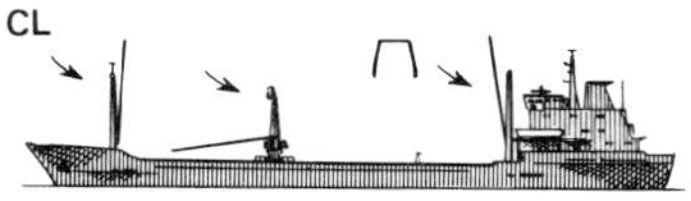

K_3MF H1
58650 MARLENE S. FRG/FRG 1977; C; 1600/3800; 102.88 × 5.11/7.29 (337.53 × 16.76/23.92); M; 15.

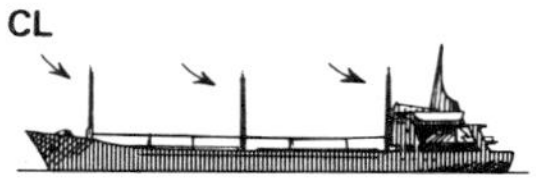

K_3MF H1
58660 CONTI MISR. Pa/FRG 1966; C; 1600; 74.76 × 5.99 (245.3 × 19.6); M; 13.5; ex TROJAN PRINCE 1974; ex DANERIVER 1973; ex PER BASSE 1972; ex LOCKFLETHERSAND 1972.

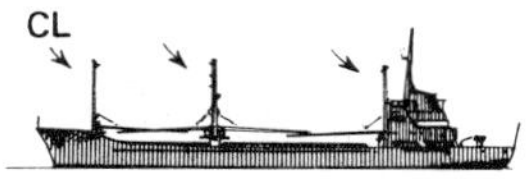

K_3MF H1
58670 NOTRE DAME D'AFRIQUE. Fr/Ne 1967; Wine Carrier; 500; 76.38 × 4.29 (250.59 × 14.07); M; 14; ex KHARSIS 1976.

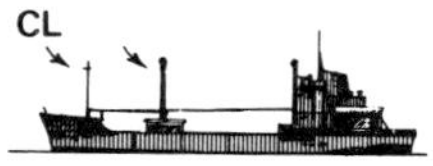

K_3MF H1
58680 INARAN. Ia/No 1977; C; 650; 59.92 × 3.65 (196.6 × 12); M; —. Sisters (Ia flag): **58681 INABUKWA 58682 IKAGURI 58683 ISABELA 58684 ILOSANGI.**

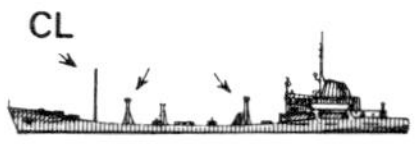

K_3MF H1
58690 WAIAL. Si/FRG 1968; Tk; 500; 64.9 × 3.75 (212.93 × 12.3); M; 12; ex BILL ROBERTS 1981. Sisters: **58691 MAGID** (Si) ex HARRY LEWIS 1981 (being used as bunkering vessel) **58692 SUSANNA** (Fa) ex PEDER LYSGAARD 1981.

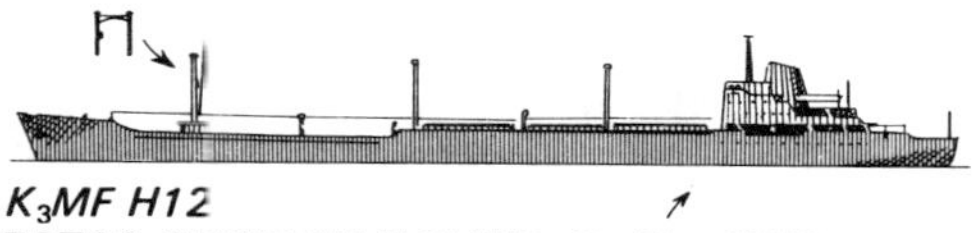

K_3MF H12
● **58700 SKYRIAN ROVER.** Gr/Sw 1958; 1958; 8600; 148.7 × 8.81 (487.86 × 28.9); M; 15.25; ex SKYRIAN SPIRIT 1980; ex LEFTERIS 1980; ex SUNRIVER 1974.

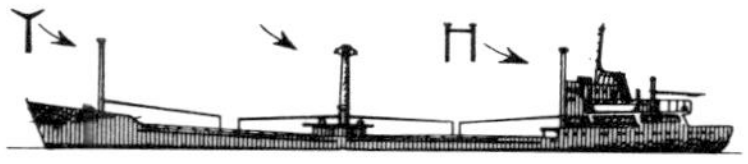

K_3MF H123
● **58710 MOKHA.** Sg/DDR 1967; C; 2600/4000; 112.1 × 7.17 (367.78 × 23.52); M; 13.5; ex EURABIA SPRING 1978; ex CLARI 1975; ex KARLSBURG 1970; ex CLAUDIA MARIA 1967. Sister: **58711 LE ROVE** (Fr) ex SCOL INDEPENDENT 1975; ex GERMANICA 1975; ex WILRI 1975; ex GERMANIC 1974; ex WILRI 1974; ex ATLANTA 1973 Similar: **58712 IRENES SUN** (Gr) ex BLOCKLAND 1977; ex JIRI 1969; ex HOEGH JIRI 1968; ex JIRI 1966 **58713 IRENES SEA** (Gr) ex WERDERLAND 1977; ex WILRI 1969; ex HOEGH WILRI 1969; ex WILRI 1967 **58714 CONTI ALMANIA** (FRG) ex GRIMSNIS 1975; ex HEIN JENEVELT 1970; ex BARI 1968 **58715 EURABIA PROGRESS** (Le) ex CLAUDIA MARIA 1975 **58716 DUBURG** (FRG) ex BILSTEIN 1978; ex CONTI SYRIA 1978; ex ANTONY 1977; ex BILSTEIN 1975; ex HOEGH SUSANN 1968; launched as SUSAN VON BARGEN.

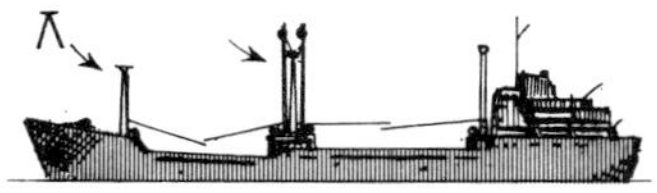

K_3MF H123
58720 BLUE SPIRIT. Cy/DDR 1964; C; 2800; 97.57 × 6.63 (320 × 21.75); M; 13; ex EGON WESCH 1973; ex JIRI 1965.

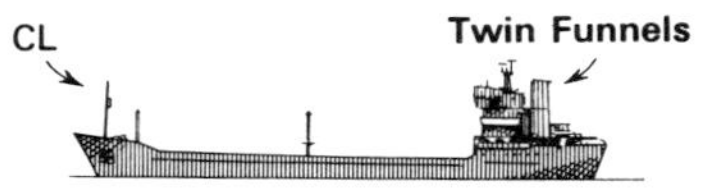

K_3MF H13
★**58730 NIEWIADOW.** Pd/Pd 1978; C; 1600; 84.18 × 5.73 (276.18 × 18.8); M; 14; Launched as RAN; **'B-431'** type. Sister: ★**58731 LIPSK N/BIEBRZA** (Pd).

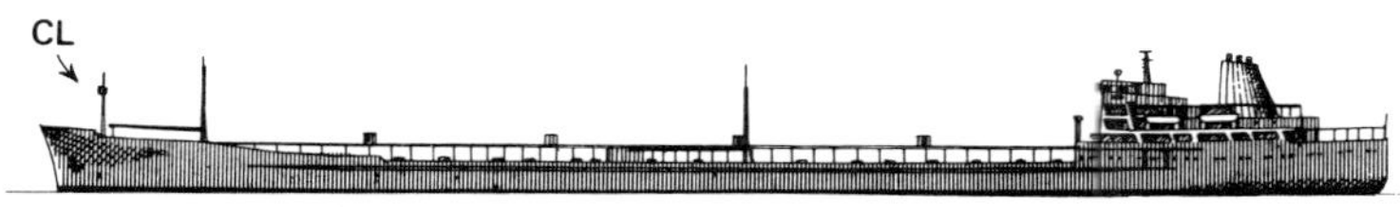

K_3MF H13
58740 PANOCEANIC FAME. Gr/Ne 1964; Tk; 33600; 223.73 × 12.21 (734.02 × 40.06); M; 15.5; ex BURMAH GEM 1976; ex MOSLI 1974.

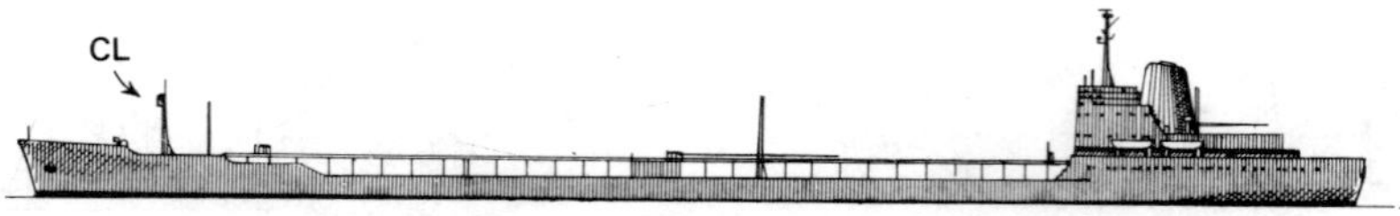

K_3MF H13
58750 ARMONIKOS. Gr/Sw 1963; Tk; 36800; 236.33 × 12.63 (775.36 × 41.44); M; 17.25; ex VESTALIS 1975.

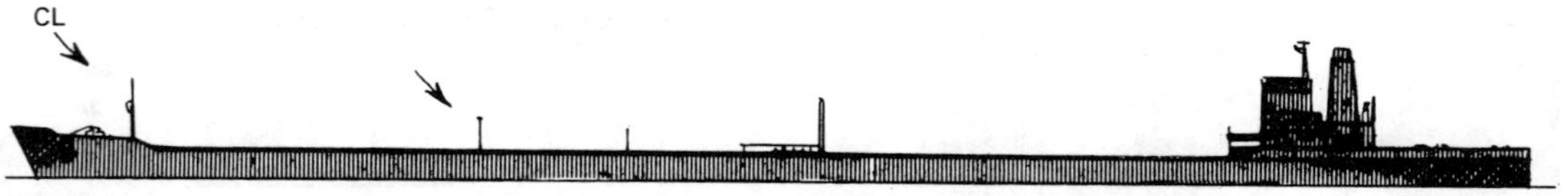

K_3MF H13
58760 FLEURTJE. NA/No 1970; Tk; 109600; 327.72 × 20.42 (1075.2 × 66.99); T; 15; ex HUMBOLDT 1980.

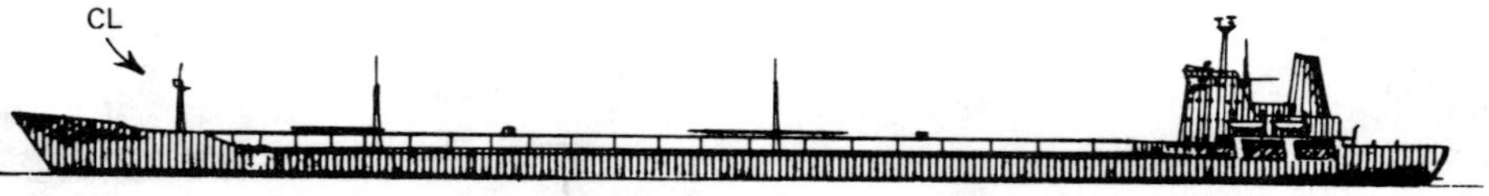

K_3MF H13
● **58770 AFRAN MERIDIAN.** Li/Sp 1968; Tk; 53800; 269.35 × 14.07 (883.69 × 46.16); M; 16.25; ex LA RABIDA 1980. Sister: **58771 MONTESA** (Sp) Similar: **58772 MUNATONES** (Sp) **58773 LA NINA** (Sp).

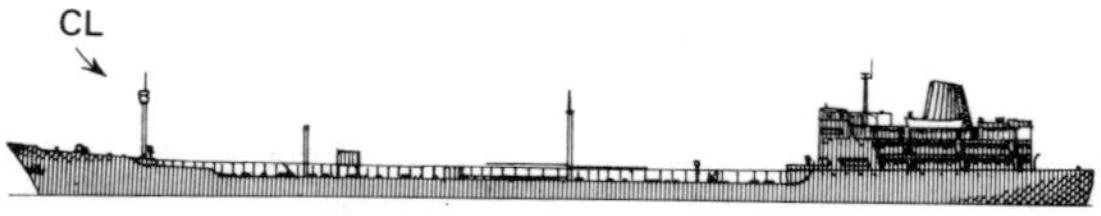

K_3MF H13
58780 MASTER JOHN. Gr/Ja 1962; Tk; 12200; 171 × 9.46 (561.02 × 31.04); T; 16.5; ex BELGULF ENTERPRISE 1976.

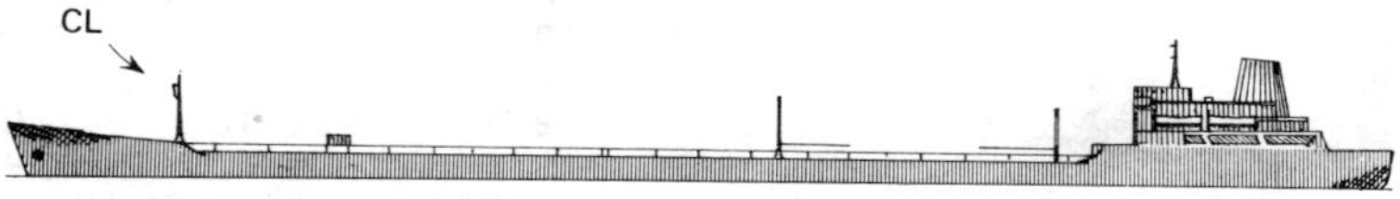

K_3MF H13
58790 YEOTA E. Gr/No 1964; Tk; 34800; 236.23 × 12.84 (775.03 × 42.13); M; 16; ex WOODBURN 1979; ex HALCYON LOCH 1974; ex SIBEAU 1973; ex BEAU 1972.

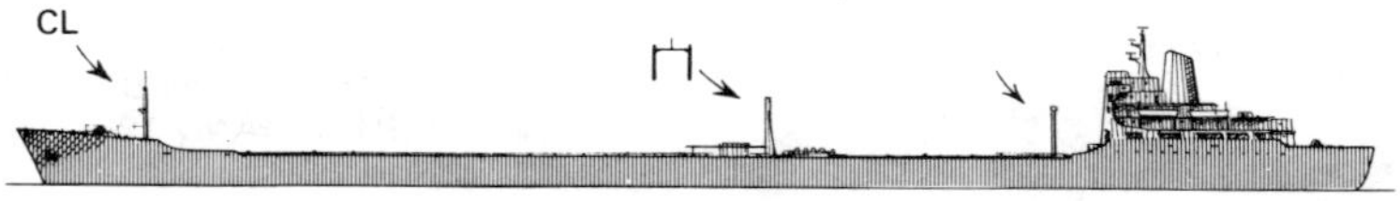

K_3MF H13
58800 GARGI. In/Ja 1964; Tk; 34700; 229.95 × 12.03 (754.43 × 39.47); M; 16.5; ex VIKRAM JAYANTI 1974.

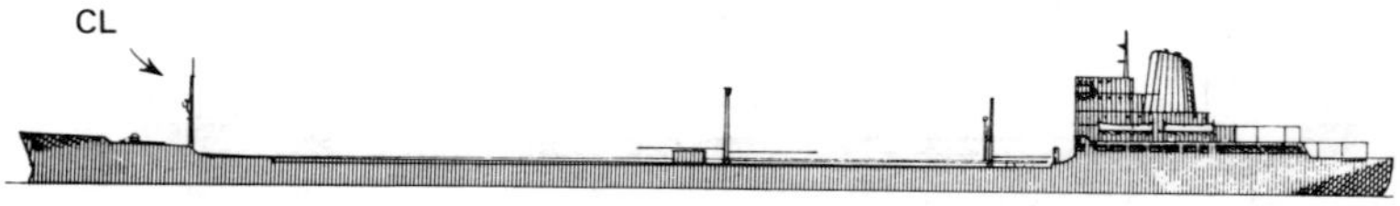

K_3MF H13
58810 FRANCES HAMMER. Li/Ja 1965; Tk; 34900; 236.2 × 12.85 (774.93 × 42.16); M; 16; ex SAMUEL B. MOSHER 1969. Sister: **58811 JULIUS HAMMER** (Li) ex RUSSELL H. GREEN 1977.

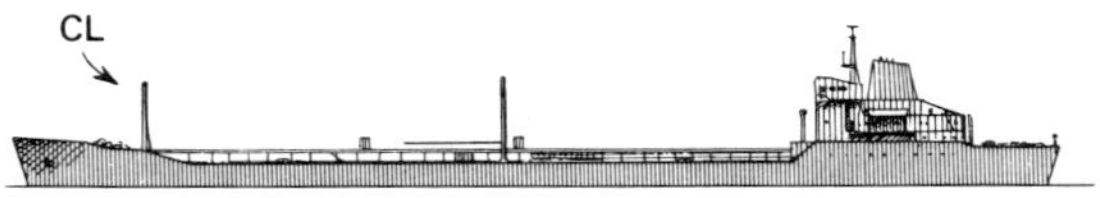

K_3MF H13
58820 ESSO MERSEY. Br/Br 1972; Tk; 12300; 166.5 × 9.21 (546.26 × 30.22); M; 15.5. Sisters (Br flag): **58821 ESSO CLYDE 58822 ESSO SEVERN.**

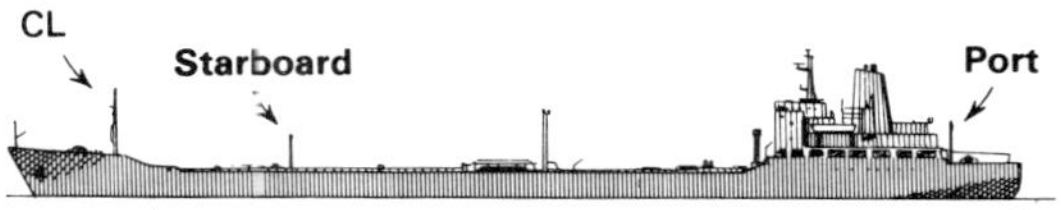

K_3MF H13
58830 ESSO PORT JEROME. Fr/Ja 1972; Tk; 12800; 161.02 × 9.76 (528.28 × 32.02); M; 15; ex ESSO KUMAMOTO 1980; **'22 Type';** Some others in this class may have this sequence.

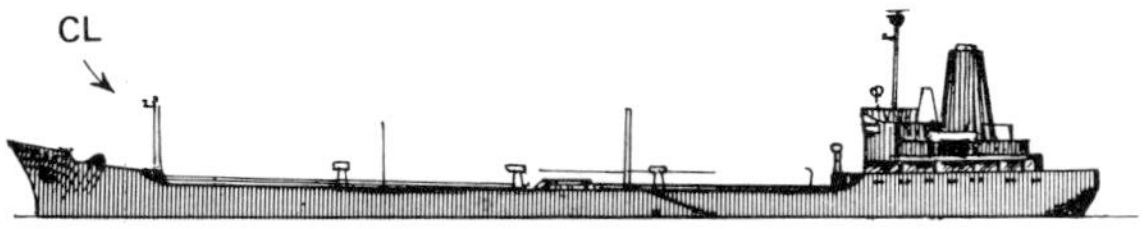

K_3MF H13
58840 ESSO BANGKOK. Pa/Ja 1968; Tk; 13000; 170.08 × 9.41 (558 × 30.87); M; 14.5. Sisters (Pa flag): **58841 ESSO BOMBAY 58842 ESSO PORT DICKSON 58843 ESSO YOKOHAMA 58844 ESSO KOBE 58845 ESSO INTERAMERICA 58846 ESSO KARACHI 58847 ESSO MALACCA 58848 ESSO NAGASAKI** (Li flag): **58849 ESSO KURE 58850 ESSO BATAAN 58851 ESSO CHITTAGONG 58852 ESSO HUMBER** ex ESSO PENANG 1978.

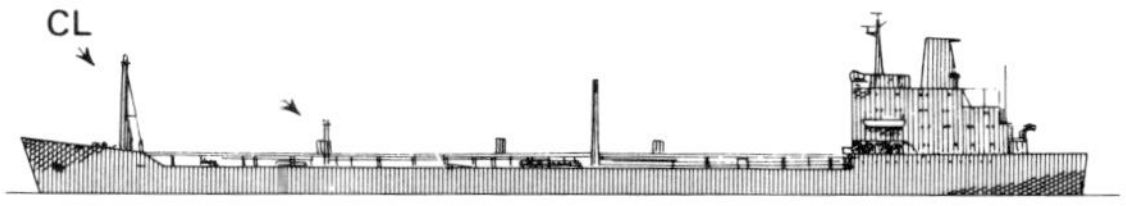

K_3MF H13
58860 ARDMAY. Br/FRG 1975; Tk; 168.76 × 10.9 (553.67 × 36.76); M; 16. Sister: **58861 ARDMORE** (Br).

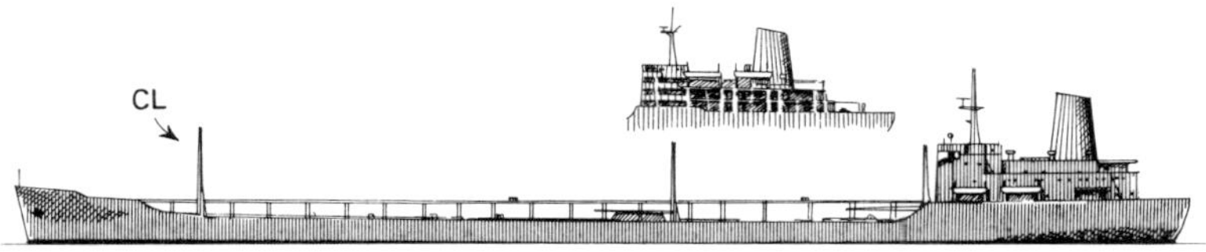

K_3MF H13
58870 ANANGEL FRIENDSHIP. Gr/Br 1965; Tk; 35300; 236.46 × 13.22 (775.79 × 43.37); M; 16.25; ex OPAWA 1974. Similar (See inset): **58871 ANANGEL PRUDENCE** (Gr) ex ORISSA 1974.

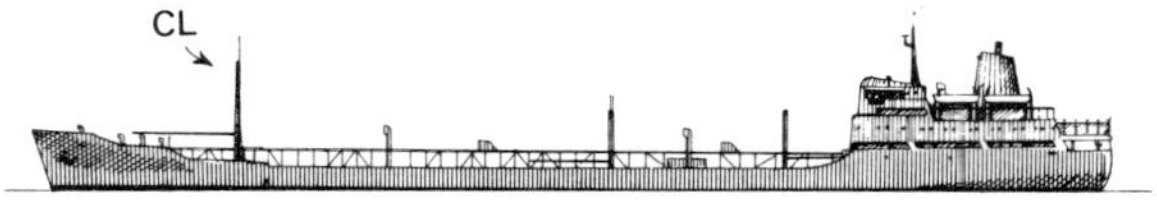

K_3MF H13
58880 ERNE. Br/Br 1962; Tk; 13700; 170.62 × 9.47 (559.78 × 31.07); T; 14.5.

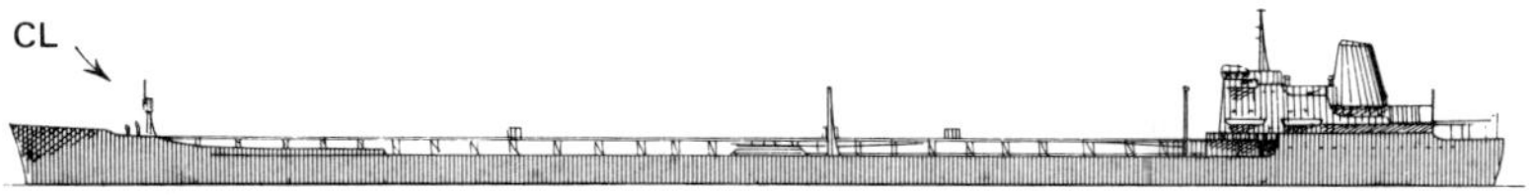

K_3MF H13
58890 FOTINI. Gr/Sw 1965; Tk; 41000; 239.28 × 12.74 (785.04 × 41.8); M; 17; ex TANK REGINA 1970. Similar: **★58891 YU HU** (RC) ex VANJA 1975 **58892 AURELIA** (Li) ex VELMA 1972.

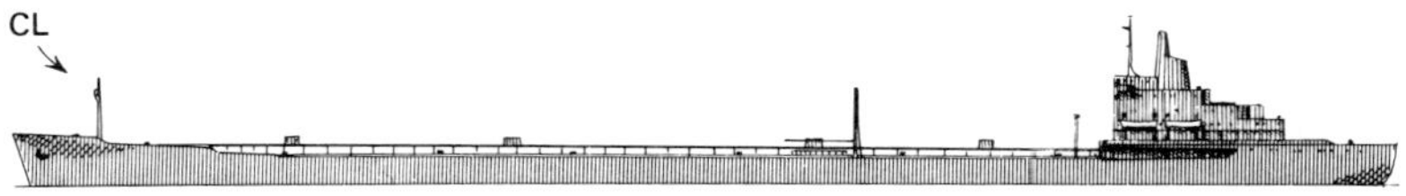

K_3MF H13
58900 NIRITOS. Gr/Sw 1964; Tk; 42100; 243.87 × 13.06 (800.1 × 42.85); M; 16; ex SCHWARZHEIDE 1980; ex SOVEREIGN CLIPPER 1970.

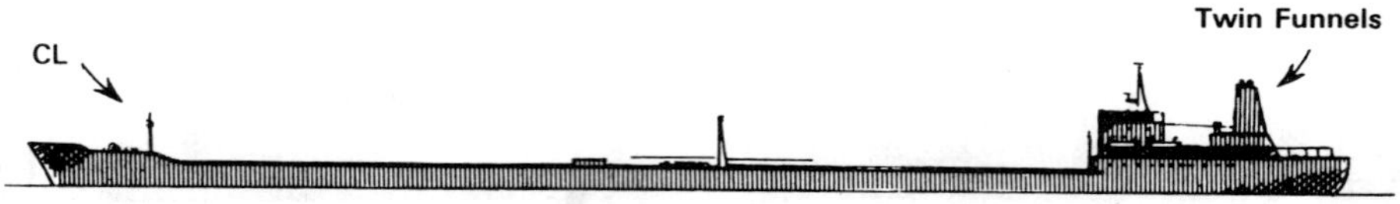

K_3MF H13
● **58910 MOBIL WESER.** FRG/Ja 1967; Tk; 49200; 263.51 × 14.63 (864.53 × 47.99); M; 16; ex AL BILAD; ex BERGE SIGVAL 1975. Similar (No flag): **58911 CIS BROVIG 58912 VIVITA** ex BERGEVIK 1978.

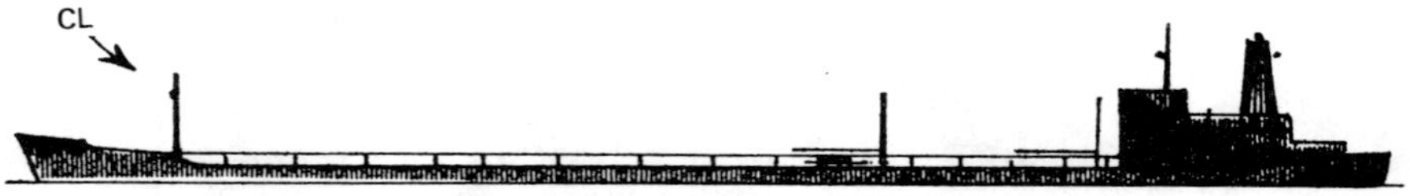

K_3MF H13
58920 UDANG NATUNA. Li/Br 1964; Tk; 51800; 259.47 × 14.7 (851.28 × 48.23); T; 16.5; ex OTTAWA 1978; This vessel has been converted to an offshore support ship, permanently moored off the Indonesian coast.

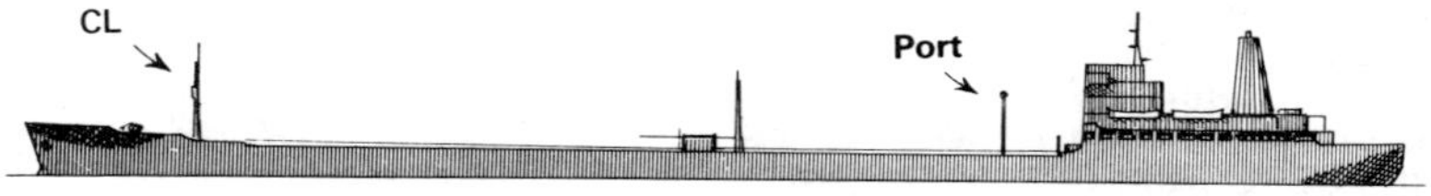

K_3MF H13
58930 MARIA ISABELLA. Gr/Ja 1964; Tk; 33100; 236.23 × 9.35 (775.03 × 30.68); T; —. Sisters (Li flag): **58931 CONSTANTINE 58932 WORLD EULOGY** ex EUGENIE 1977; Launched as WORLD INHERITOR.

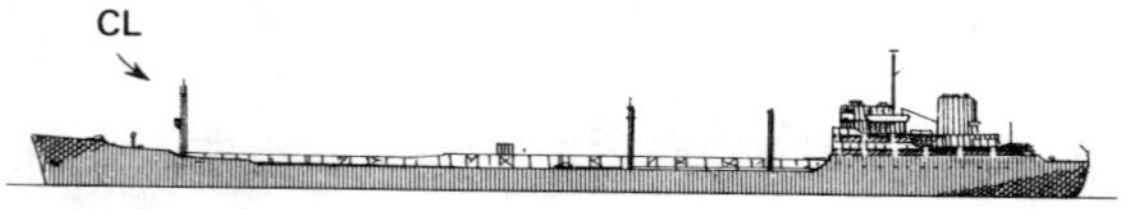

K_3MF H13
58940 CIRON. Fr/Br 1960; Tk; 12500; 167.47 × 9.54 (549.44 × 31.3); M; 15; ex RED SEA VENTURE 1980; ex POLLO 1977; ex MOBIL APEX 1969.

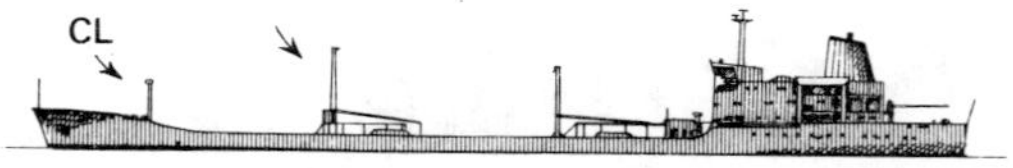

K_3MF H13
58950 MATADI PALM. Br/Br 1970; Tk; 8900; 147.83 × 8.55 (485 × 28.05); M; 15.

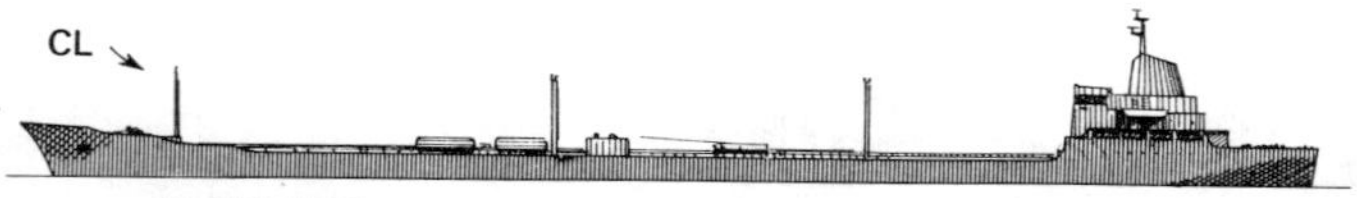

K_3MF H13
58960 MARINE CHEMIST. US/US 1970; Tk/Ch; 20200; 204.93 × 11.05 (672.34 × 36.25); T; 16.5.

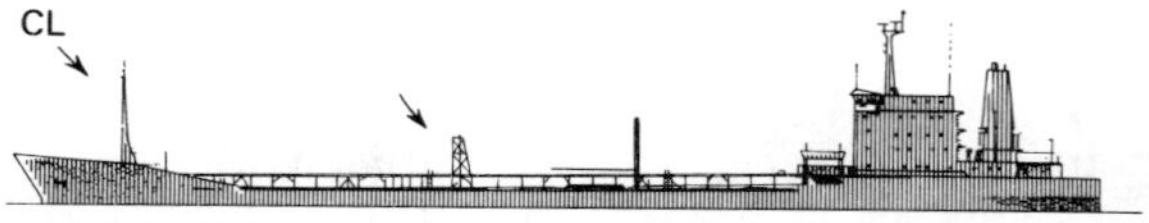

K_3MF H13
58970 IBN ROCHD. Mo/Ne 1977; Ch; 13500; 172.29 × 10.5 (565.26 × 34.45); M; 17. Sister: **58971 IBN ALBANNA** Sisters (Norwegian built): **58972 IBN OTMAN 58973 IBN SINA.**

K_3MF H13
58980 PRESIDENT DELCOURT. Fr/Fr 1972; Ch; 6000; 125.46 × 7.75 (411.61 × 25.43); M; 17.

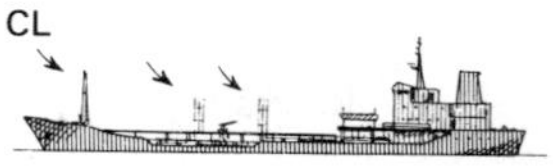

K_3MF H13
58990 STELLAMAN. Br/Br 1976; Ch; 1500; 79.51 × 5.27 (260.86 × 17.29); M; 13.75. Sister: **58991 MARSMAN** (Br).

K_3MF H13
59000 CENTAURMAN. Br/Br 1976; Ch; 2500; 89.18 × 5.9 (292.59 × 19.36); M; 13.5. Sister: **59001 VEGAMAN** (Br).

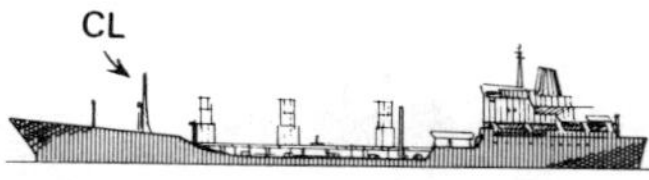

K_3MF H13
59010 LA BAHIA. Br/No 1972; Ch; 1600; 100.72 × 5.89 (330.45 × 19.32); M; 16; ex WAVEMARK 1974. Sister: **59011 LA FALDA** (Br) ex SUNMARK 1974.

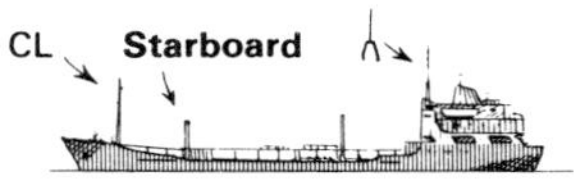

K_3MF H13
59020 ISLAND JESTER. Pa/No 1964; Tk/Ch; 1200; 76.03 × 4.6 (249.44 × 15.09); M; 11.5; ex WINBLOW 1978; ex SIREGLEN 1970; ex RUBICON 1968.

K_3MF H13
59030 DEVON CURLEW. Br/Sp 1969; Ch; 800; 68.18 × 3.96 (223.69 × 12.99); M; 12.5; ex FENOL. Sisters: **59031 DORSET FULMAR** (Br) ex FORMOL 1979 **59032 THITA STAINLESS** (Gr) ex METANOL 1974.

K_3MF H13
59040 ELOISEID. Br/Br 1969; Ch; 1600; 91.45 × 4.93 (300.03 × 16.17); M; 13; ex SILVEREID 1975.

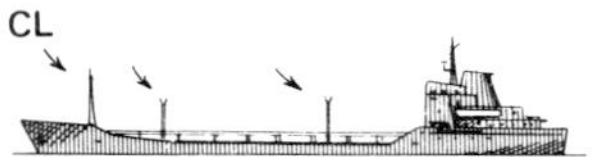

K_3MF H13
59050 ALCHIMIST LUBECK. Cy/FRG 1970; Ch; 1600; 87.03 × 5.1 (285.53 × 16.73); M; 12.5. Possible sister: **59051 ALCHIMIST FLENSBURG** (Cy) ex CHEMATHENE 1980; ex ALCHIMIST FLENSBURG 1979.

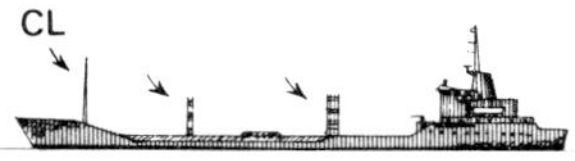

K_3MF H13
59060 ASTRAMAN. Br/Br 1973; Ch; 1600; 87.41 × 5.5 (286.78 × 18.04); M; 14. Sister: **59061 POLARISMAN** (Br).

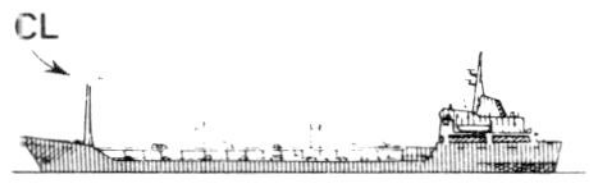

K_3MF H13
59070 ALCHIMIST ROTTERDAM. Cy/Sw 1973; Ch; 1600; 85.86 × 5.4 (281.69 × 17.72); M; 13.5; ex CHEMAPHRODITE 1980; ex ALCHIMIST MARATHON 1979; ex ALCHIMIST ROTTERDAM 1978; ex CHIMISTE NANTES 1977. Sisters (Sg flag): **59071 MULTITANK FRISIA** ex OFRISIA 1974; ex FRISIA 1973; ex MONSUN 1972 **59072 MULTITANK HOLSATIA** ex HOLSATIA 1974 Possibly similar (Fr flag): **59073 POINTE DU ROC 59074 POINTE DU VAN** ex POINTE DE PENHARN.

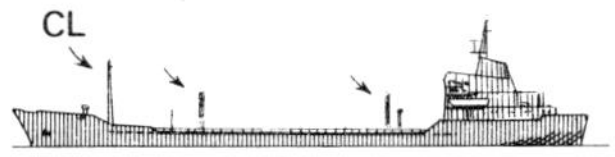

K_3MF H13
59080 CAPT. F. GAIGNEROT. Pa/Ne 1974; Ch; 1600; 90.76 × 5.49 (297.77 × 18.01); M; 14. Sister: **59081 RHIN** (Sd)—type WT/Ch.

K_3MF H13
59090 ODET. Fr/FRG 1975; WT; 1600; 90.1 × 5.72 (295.6 × 18.77); M; 13.5. Sister: **59091 RHONE** (Sd).

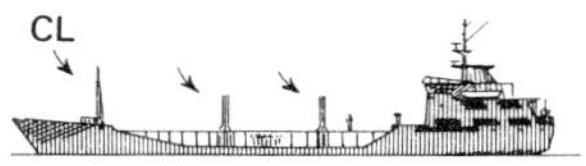

K_3MF H13
59100 MARE NOVUM. Ne/No 1977; Ch; 1600; 83.01 × 5.91 (272.34 × 19.4); M; 13. Sisters (Ne flag): **59101 MARE BONUM 59102 MARE MAGNUM.**

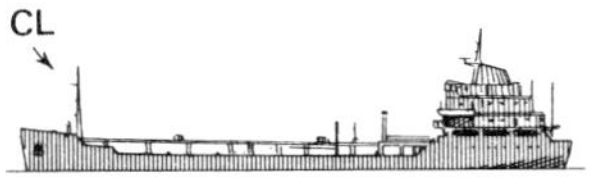

K_3MF H13
59110 THUNTANK I. Sw/Sw 1973; Ch; 3700; 107.19 × 6.7 (351.67 × 21.98); M; 12.

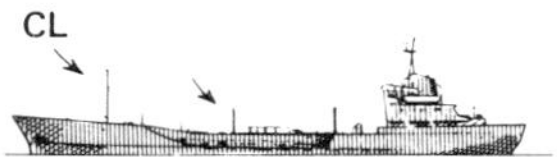

K_3MF H13
59120 LUDWIG. FRG/FRG 1969; Tk; 1200; 81.11 × 4.97 (266.11 × 16.31); M; 12.

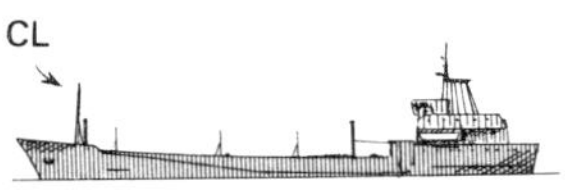

K_3MF H13
59130 SELMA. Mo/No 1972; Ch; 1600; 82.71 × 6.37 (271.36 × 20.9); M; 12.5; ex POINTE DE LERVILY 1944; ex BRAS 1974.

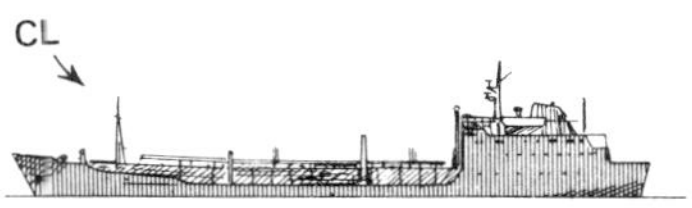

K_3MF H13
● **59140 ONE STAR.** Sg/No 1965; Tk; 3000; 100.87 × 6.1 (330.94 × 19.95); M; 12.5; ex LOTOS 1974. Sisters: **59141 ONE SKY** (Sg) ex LIANA 1975 **59142 BETACRUX** (It) ex HAENSEL 1977; ex HASSEL 1975.

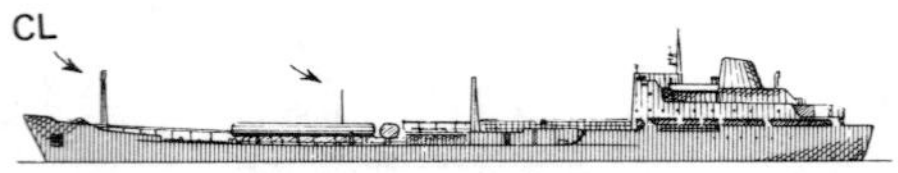

K_3MF H13
59150 PETRO SOULAC. Fr/Sw 1963; LGC/Tk; 6200; 134.73 × 6.97 (442.03 × 22.87); M; 14; ex SULFO 1975; ex SELJE 1973.

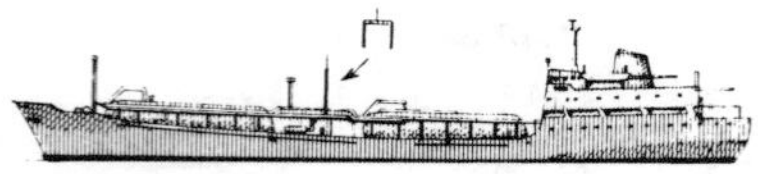

K_3MF H13
59160 HUMBOLDT. Br/Fr 1968; LGC; 5200; 116.9 × 6.5 (383.53 × 21.33); M; 17. Similar: **59161 BERGA** (Ag) ex PASCAL 1970 **59162 LAVOISIER** (Ar).

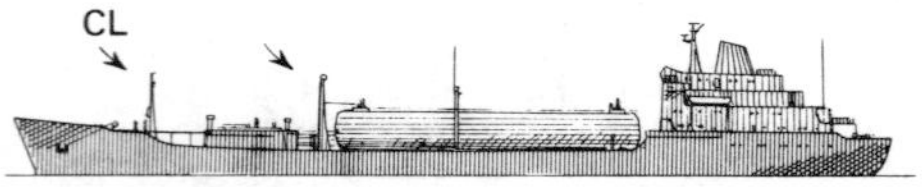

K_3MF H13
59170 VESTRI. No/No 1971; LGC; 9000; 138.72 × 9.23 (455.12 × 30.28); M; 17.

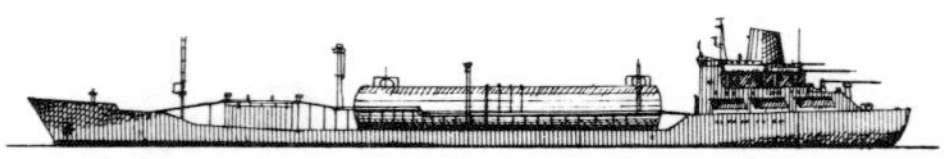

K_3MF H13
59180 HERA. No/No 1977; LGC; 9100; 138.72 × 11.04 (455.12 × 36.22); M; 17.75. Sister: **59181 HEROS** (No).

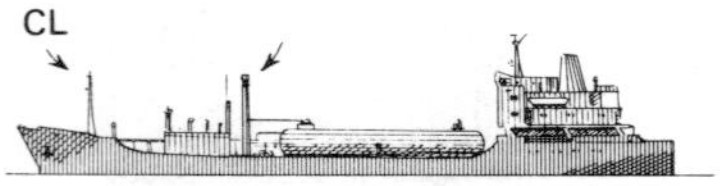

K_3MF H13
59190 TORDENSKIOLD. No/No 1971; LGC/Ch; 3500; 106.05 × 6.45 (347.93 × 21.16); M; 15. Similar: **59191 ROALD ADMUNDSEN** (No).

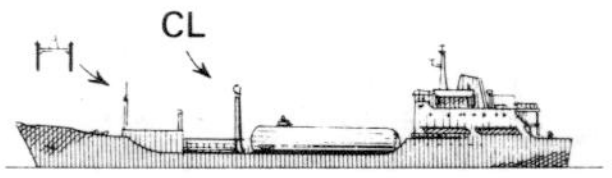

K_3MF H13
59200 LEIV EIRIKSSON. No/No 1971; LGC; 2500; 88.14 × 6.38 (289.17 × 20.93); M; 13.

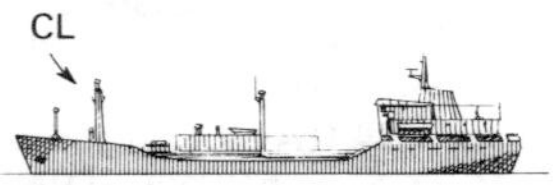

K_3MF H13
59210 NIELS HENRIK ABEL. No/Ne 1973; LGC; 1600; 79.48 × 6.04 (260.76 × 19.82); M; 13.5; launched as ANITA. Sister: **59211 SIGURD JORSALFAR** (No).

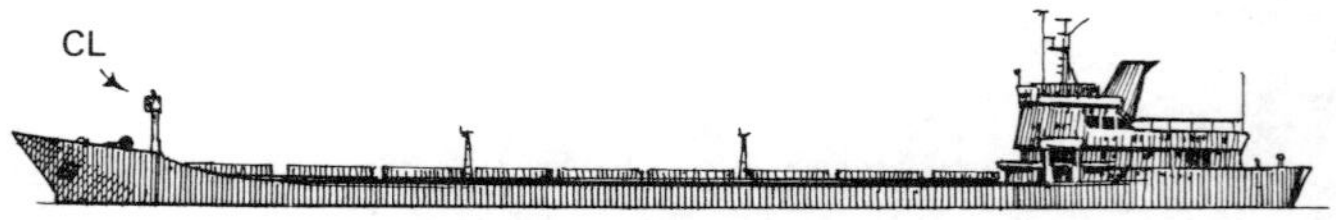

K_3MF H13
⋆59220 FILIPP MAKHARADZE. Ru/Pd 1972; B; 20300; 198.71 × 10.68 (651.93 × 35.03); M; 15; **'B-447'** type. Sisters (Ru flag): **⋆59221 NIKO NIKOLADZE ⋆59222 MIKHA TSKHAKAYA** (Pd flag): **⋆59223 CZWARTACY AL ⋆59224 OBRONCY POCZTY ⋆59225 POWSTANIEC SLASKI ⋆59226 SIEKIERKI ⋆59227 TOBRUK.**

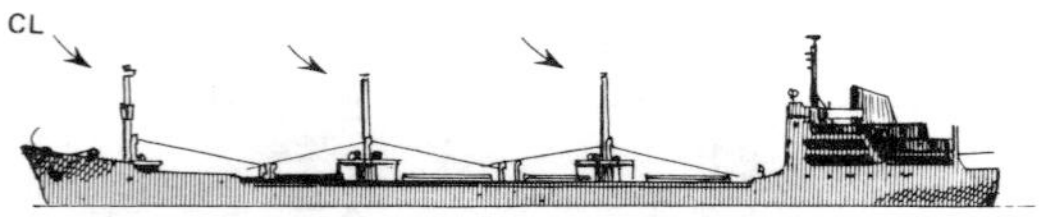

K_3MF H13
59230 ATHINA. Gr/Br 1963; B; 10800; 152.56 × 8.66 (500.52 × 28.4); M; 14.5; ex SIMANDOU 1980.

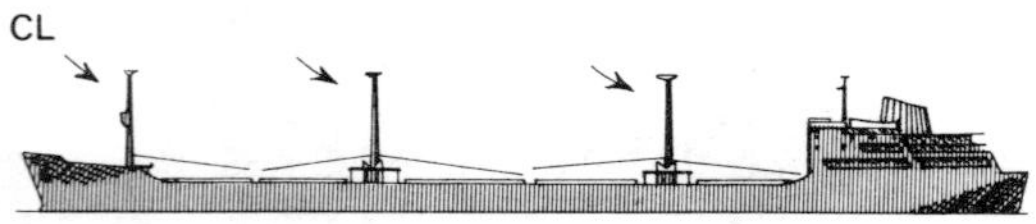

K_3MF H13
59240 OCEAN SOVEREIGN. Li/Br 1966; B; 11100; 158.5 × 8.99 (520.01 × 29.49); M; 14; ex BOLNES 1972.

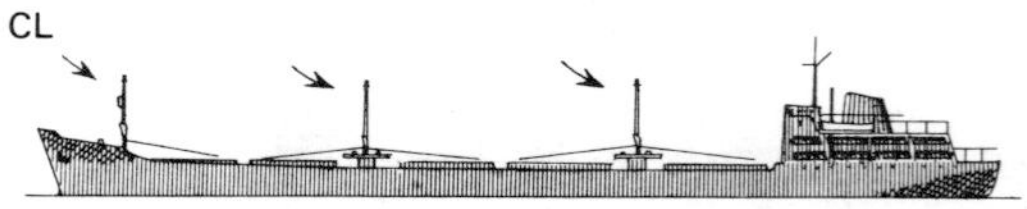

K_3MF H13
59250 KIAN AN. Li/Br 1962; B; 9900; 152.56 × 8.66 (500.52 × 28.41); M; 14.75; ex BERNES 1972. Sister: **59251 APILIOTIS** (Li) ex BRIMNES 1970 Similar: **59252 ELPIDA** (Gr) ex GRANTON 1978; ex BINSNES 1970.

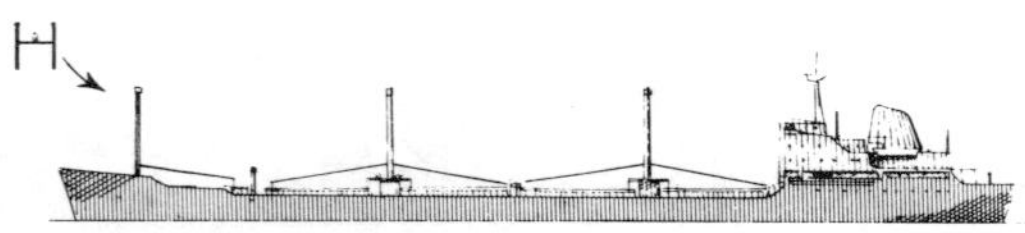

K_3MF H13
● **59260 CAPTAIN PAPPIS.** Gr/FRG 1961; B; 9400; 151.19 × 9.21 (496.03 × 30.22); M; 14.75; ex OGOOUE 1976; ex DRACULA 1973; ex RINGULV 1969. Sister: **59261 SILVERCORN** (Li) ex JAGONA 1973.

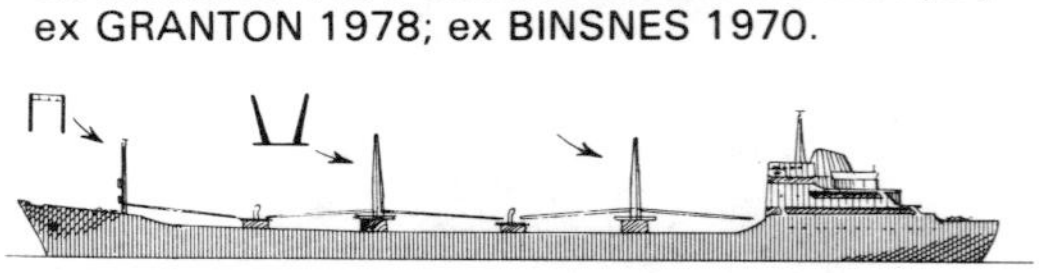

K_3MF H13
59270 CASSANDRA. Li/FRG 1959; C; 9500; 157.82 × 9.24 (517.78 × 30.32); M; 14.5; ex DELOS; ex JESSIE STOVE 1968.

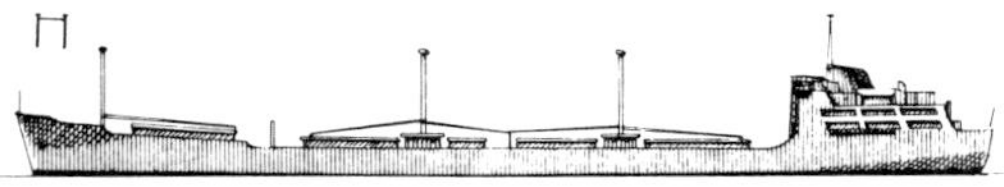

K_3MF H13
59280 ROZEL BAY. Pa/Br 1962; B; 10700; 154.67 × 9.02 (507.48 × 29.59); M; 14; ex FEDERAL SALSO 1978; ex FEDERAL TYNE 1971; ex SCOTTISH TRADER 1968.

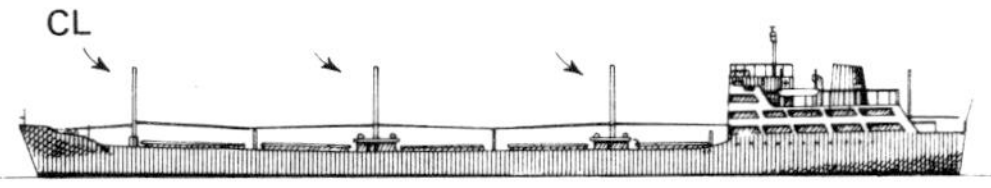

K_3MF H13
59300 SEA RANGER. Gr/Br 1959; B; 10100; 158.05 × 9.68 (518.54 × 31.76); M; 14.25; ex WANDBY 1972.

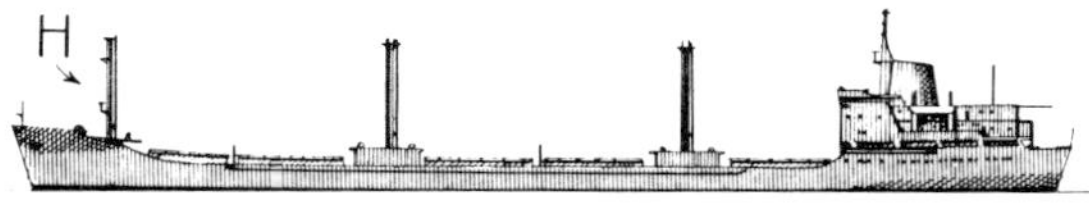

K_3MF H13
59290 SOUNION. Gr/Br 1968; B; 13900; 167.65 × 9.58 (550.03 × 31.43); M; 15.5; ex SUGAR CRYSTAL. Sister: **59291 CAPE AVANTI DUE** (Gr) ex SUGAR PRODUCER. Similar (centre line kingposts): **59292 KEFALONIA WIND** (Gr) ex SUGAR TRANSPORTER **59293 KEFALONIA STAR** (Gr) ex SUGAR REFINER.

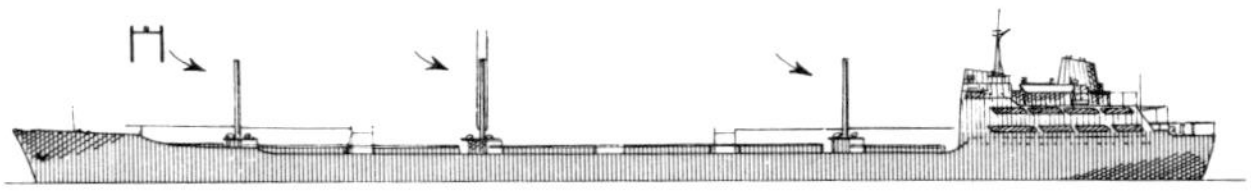

K_3MF H13
59310 CASPIANA. Gr/No 1959; B; 15300; 190.66 × 10.87 (625.52 × 35.66); M; 14.5; ex THEOMITOR 111 1976; ex GAUCHO CRUZ 1970; ex HILWI 1969; lengthened 1965. Sister: **59311 ANNA** (Gr) ex GERWI 1972.

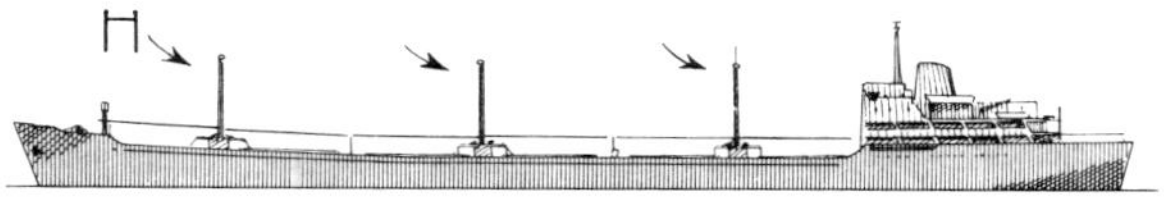

K_3MF H13
59320 TIVAT. Ma/Br 1963; B; 9900; 163.53 × 9.2 (536.5 × 30.18); M; 14; ex JEAN; ex ELEOUSSA 1976; ex ATHENOULA 1972; ex BELISLAND 1970. Sister: **59321 MERCUR** (Gr) ex AGNI; ex GRIGOROUSSA 1976; ex KEHARITOMENI 1972; ex RINGWOOD 1969.

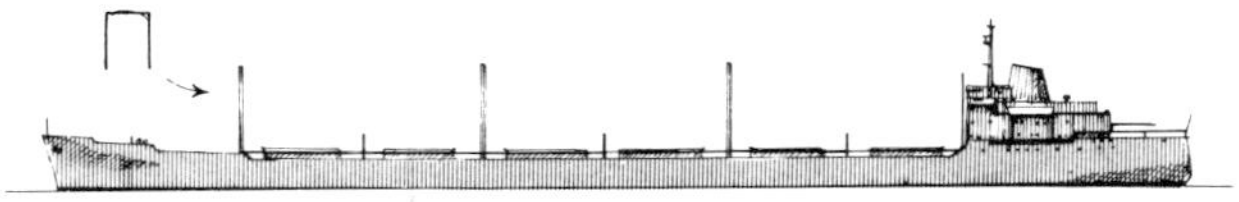

K_3MF H13
⋆59330 KANG HAI. RC/Br 1956; B; 18100; 182.81 × 10.95 (599.77 × 32.93); M; 15; ex BENVORLICH 1976; ex RIBERA 1973.

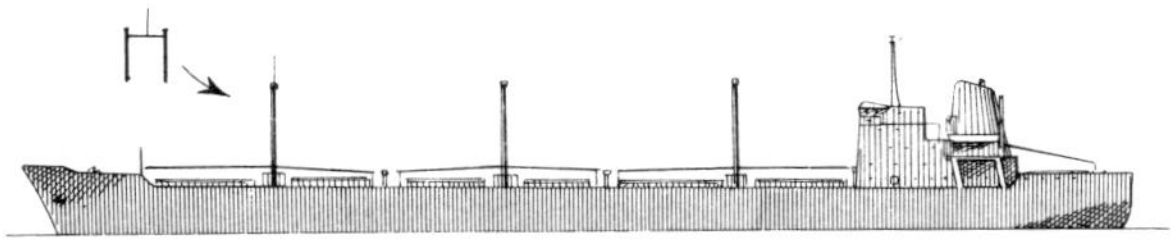

K_3MF H13
59360 OGDEN EXPORTER. Li/Ja 1966; B; 15600; 175.6 × 10.78 (576.12 × 35.37); M; 15; ex ORIENTAL EXPORTER 1970. Sister: **59361 OGDEN IMPORTER** (Li) ex ORIENTAL IMPORTER 1970.

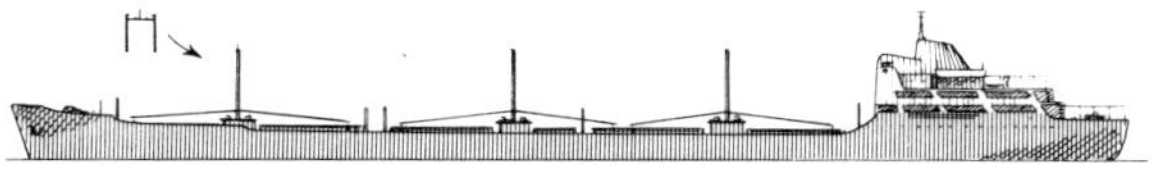

K_3MF H13
59370 MANIA. Gr/Br 1963; B; 13500; 177.71 × 9.6 (583.04 × 31.5); M; 14.5; ex POLLUX 1980; ex ASSIOS 1978; ex HOMER 1970; ex MIDDLESEX TRADER 1969. Similar: **59371 CORAJE** (Ur) ex SATURN; ex SURREY TRADER 1970.

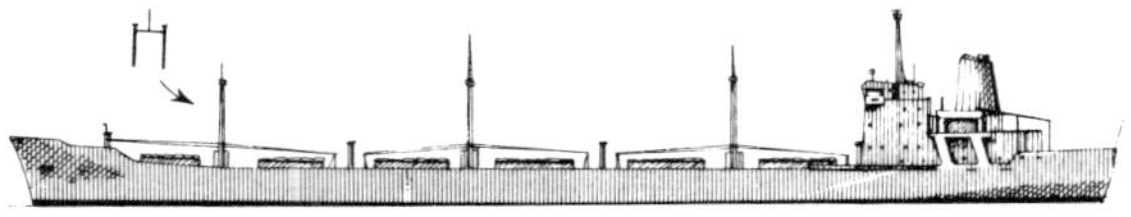

K_3MF H13
59340 OLYMPIC PALM. Li/Ja 1965; B; 15600; 175.6 × 10.88 (576.12 × 35.7); M; 16.25. Sisters (Li flag): **59341 OLYMPIC PEARL 59342 OLYMPIC PEGASUS 59343 OLYMPIC PHAETHON 59344 OLYMPIC PIONEER** Similar (longer poop): **59345 OLYMPIC PEACE 59346 OLYMPIC POWER 59347 OLYMPIC PRESTIGE 59348 OLYMPIC PRIDE 59349 OLYMPIC PROGRESS** (Gr) **59350 ALBION** (Gr) ex NORTH ATLANTIC VALOUR 1975; ex ALBION 1973 **59351 MARYLISA** (Gr) **59352 WINSTON** (Gr) ex ZITA 1977 **59353 AMSTELBRINK** (Ne) ex HOLLANDS BRINK 1977.

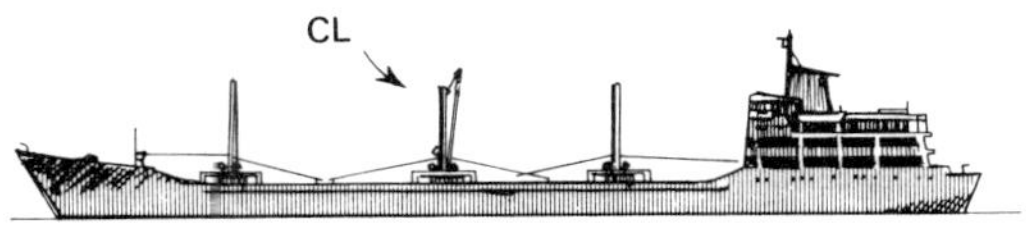

K_3MF H13
59380 ORIENT TRADER. Pa/Ne 1961; C; 9500; 151 49 × 9.2 (497.01 × 30.18); M; —; ex LIMARI; ex TROLLGAR 1970.

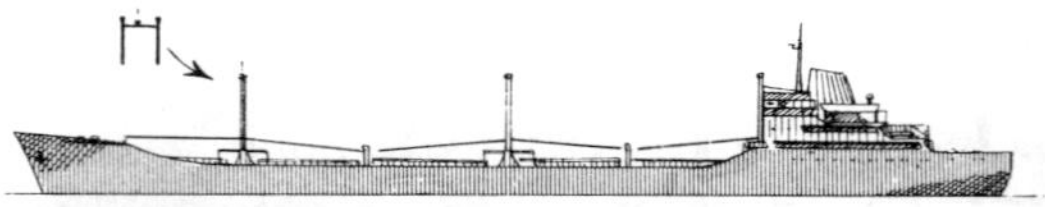

K_3MF H13
59390 GREGOS. Gr/FRG 1959; B; 9200; 157.82 × 9.68 (517.78 × 31.76); M; 14.25; ex OSTRIA 1975; ex BULK TRADER 1972. Sister: **59391 RASAMALA** (la) ex DAPHNIS 1975; ex HAVKATT 1969.

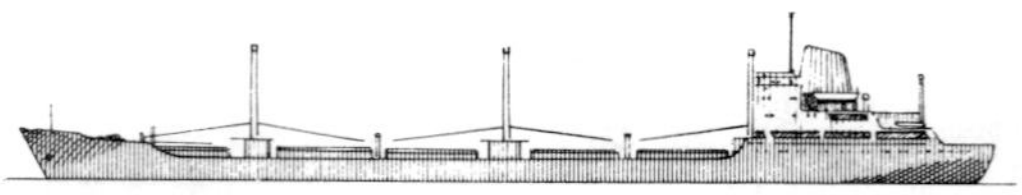

K_3MF H13
59400 BIJELA. Ma/FRG 1963; B; 9500; 153.98 × 9.13 (503.18 × 29.95); M; 13.5; ex RIGEL 1977; ex SPLENDID BREEZE 1977; ex EXECUTIVE TRADER 1974; ex BERNHARD 1973.

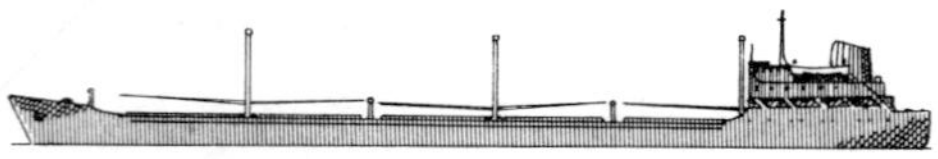

K_3MF H13
59410 MALDIVE PLEDGE. Mv/Br 1960; C; 9100; 145.62 × 9.35 (477.76 × 30.68); M; 13.5; ex VALIANT 1981; ex SANTA CRUZ 1972; ex LA LAGUNA 1965.

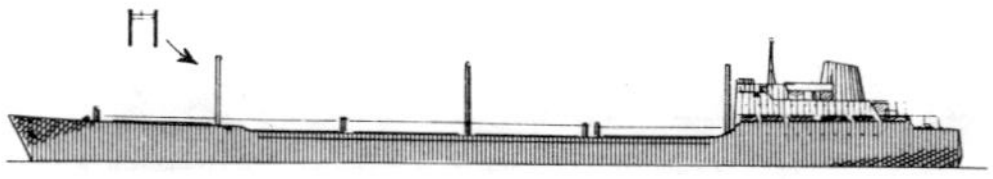

K_3MF H13
● **59420 FISKARDO.** Gr/Br 1959; C; 7500/10000; 150.53 × —/9.47 (493.86 × —/31.07); M; 14; ex JAPAN AUTO A. 1980; ex FALMOUTH 1979; ex LA LOMA 1969.

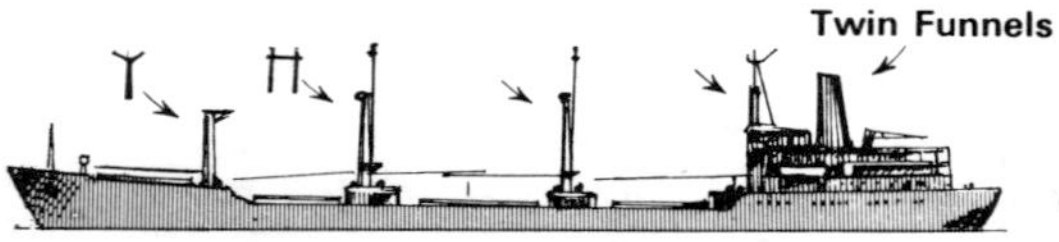

K_3MF H13
59430 KUDU. It/Sp 1972; C; 11600; 154.64 × 10.37 (507.35 × 34.02); M; 18; ex AQUAMARIN 1972. Sisters: **59431 GHERENUK** (It) launched as TOPAS **59432 GIOACCHINO LAURO** (It) launched as TURKIS **59433 ANIELLO** (Pa) ex JOGOO 1980; ex TURMALIN 1978.

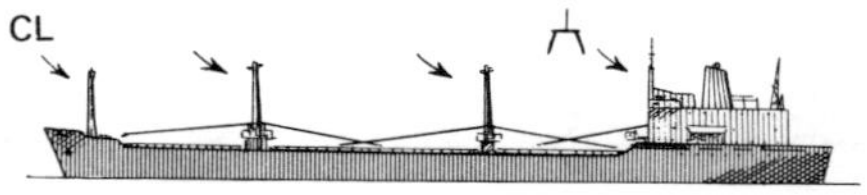

K_3MF H13
59440 ROEBUCK. Br/Ko 1976; B; 6800; 125 × 7.56 (410.1 × 24.8); M; 14.25. Sisters (Br flag): **59441 RAVENSWOOD 59442 RIVERINA**

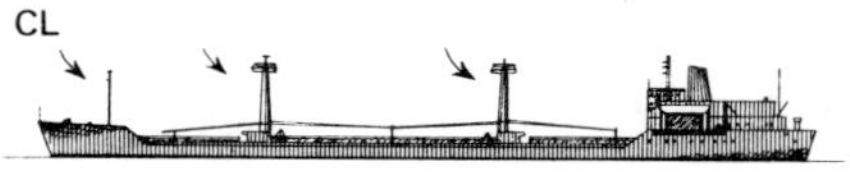

K_3MF H13
● **59450 FIDUCIA.** Pa/FRG 1972; C; 4900; 123.32 × 6.85 (404.59 × 22.47); M; 13.25; ex FURUNES 1980. Sister: **59451 FJORDNES** (No).

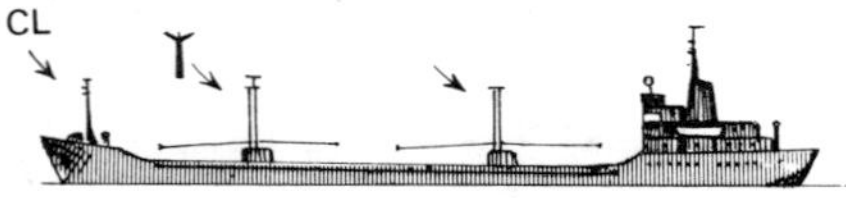

K_3MF H13
● **59460 FOSSNES.** No/FRG 1970; C; 4800; 123.25 × 6.99 (404.36 × 22.93); M; 13.5; ex MIDIBOY 1977; ex BRINKNES 1973; lengthened 1974. Sister: **59461 GENERAL LIM** (Pi) ex FJELLNES 1980; ex JENNES 1977; ex MIDIGIRL 1976; ex JENNES 1974.

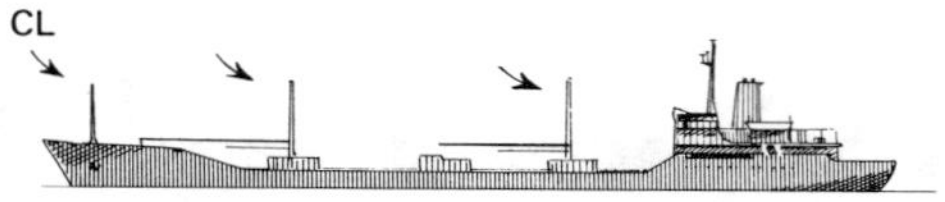

K_3MF H13
59470 ELBIA. Pa/FRG 1978; Cem; 7000; 135.01 × 8.02 (442.95 × 26.31); M; —. Similar (Pa flag): **59471 ASPIA 59472 FLORIA.**

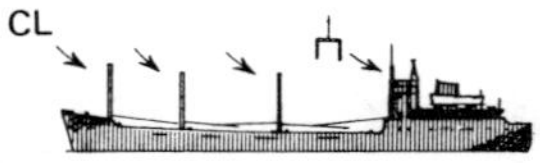

K_3MF H13
● **59480 AZELIA.** Cy/Br 1954; C; 1200; 78.14 × 4.24 (256.36 × 13.91); M; 12; ex VENTURE 1974; ex CHESHIRE COAST 1971; ex SPARTAN PRINCE 1971; ex CHESHIRE COAST 1967; ex MALABAR 1967; ex CHESHIRE COAST 1967.

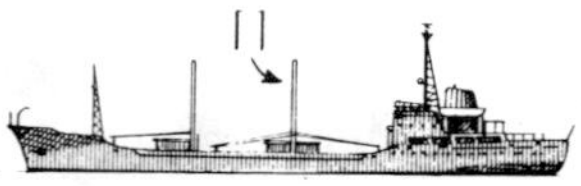

K_3MF H13
59490 PECHEUR BRETON. Fr/Ne 1961; C; 1000; 88.4 × 4.1 (290.03 × 13.45); M; 15; ex LJOSAFOSS 1972; ex ECHO 1969.

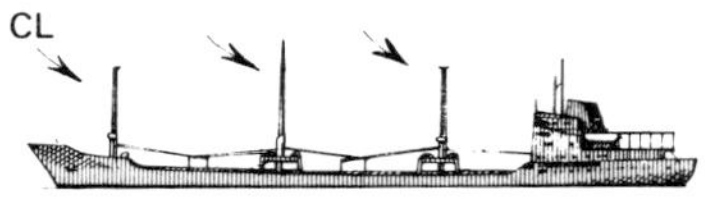

K_3MF H13
59500 LUANA. Pa/FRG 1965; C; 3200; 106.63 × 6.99 (349.84 × 22.93); M; 13.5; ex MAXI PORR 1980.

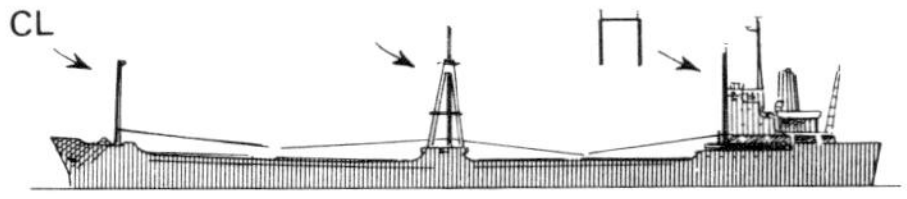

K_3MF H13
59520 SEIYO MARU. Ja/Ja 1971; C/HL; 7000; 131.81 × 8.23 (262.5 × 26); M; 14. Sister: **50521 SAKURA MARU** (Ja) Probable sister: **59522 FORUM STAR** (Gr) ex TACHIBANA MARU.

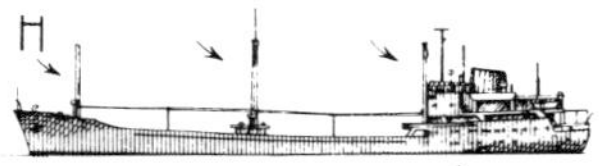

K_3MF H13
● **59540 REEM 1.** Gr/Ne 1971; C; 3000; 91.45 × 7.18 (300.03 × 23.56); M; 13.5; ex RAHA 1980; ex NELLY MAERSK 1976. Sister: **59541 ATLAS RIVER** (Gr) ex NIELS MAERSK 1976.

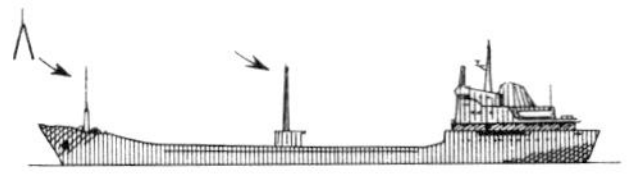

K_3MF H13
59560 ELEFSIS. Gr/Fi 1962; C; 1900; 85.81 × 5.39 (281.53 × 17.68); M; 13; ex LADY SABINA 1979; ex CECLONA 1974; ex PIRJO 1970.

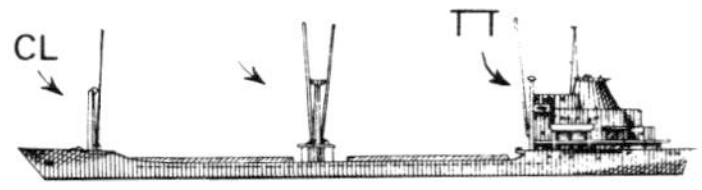

K_3MF H13
59580 OKEANIS. Gr/Gr 1973; C; 3700; 107.52 × 6.69 (352.76 × 21.95); M; 14.5. Sister: **59581 TITHIS** (Gr).

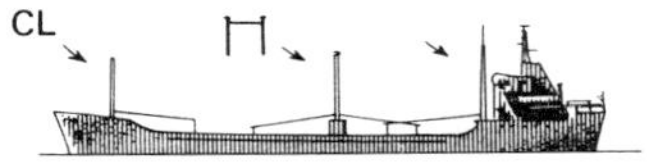

K_3MF H13
● ⭑**59600 POTIRNA.** Ys/Pd 1967; C; 1500; 87.58 × 4.81 (287.34 × 15.78); M; 12; ex NORMANNSUND; ex GDYNIA 1976; Lengthened 1970; **'B-459'** type. Sisters: ⭑**59601 PERNA** (Ys) ex NORMANNBAY; ex CAROLINE 1975; ex GERMA LORD 1973 ⭑**59602 POPLAT** (Ys) ex NORMANNVAAG; ex JOSEFINE 1976; ex GEISHA 1975 **59603 JADE** (Br) ex FONDAL 1974; ex GDANSK 1973 Similar (not lengthened): **59604 CAREBEKA VI** (Ne) ex LIONEL.

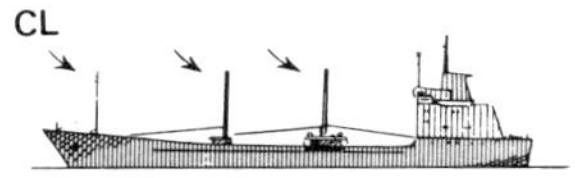

K_3MF H13
59510 GROOTSAND. Cy/FRG 1978; R; 1600; 78.11 × 5.75 (256.27 × 18.86); M; 14. Sisters (Cy flag): **59511 WITTSAND 59512 YORKSAND 59513 KNIEPSAND** (Sd flag): **59514 BASILEA 59515 TURICIA.**

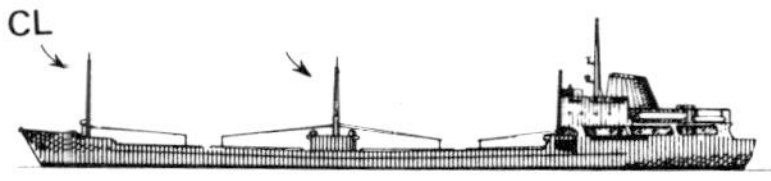

K_3MF H13
59530 INGERSEKS. No/Sw 1958; C; 5000; 117.63 × 7.57 (385.93 × 24.84); M; 13.

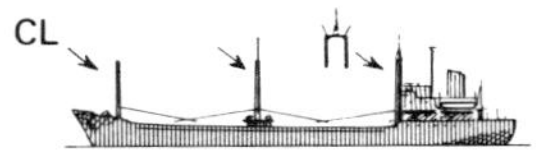

K_3MF H13
59550 TAI LAI. Tw/Ja 1962; C; 1000; 69.73 × 4.59 (228.76 × 15.06); M; 11; ex YAMATSUNE MARU 1969.

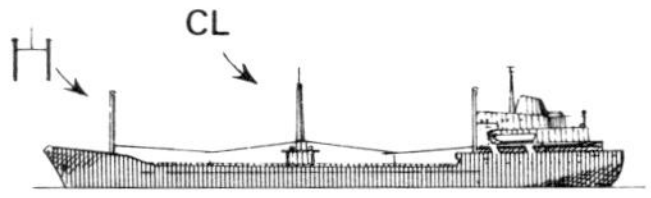

K_3MF H13
59570 LESLIE. Gr/FRG 1965; C; 2400; 92.06 × 5.6 (302.03 × 18.37); M; 13; ex ANNA REHDER 1973. Sister: ⭑**59571 KRKA** (Ys) ex MATTHIAS REHDER 1974.

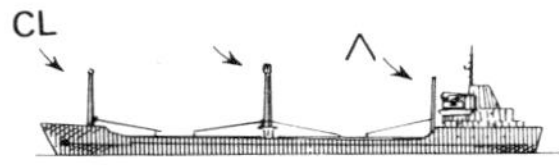

K_3MF H13
59590 ARGO PIONEER. Gr/Gr 1976; C; 1600; 79.99 × 5.34 (262.43 × 17.52); M; 13.5. Sisters (Gr flag): **59591 ARGO CHALLENGE 59592 ARGO FAITH 59593 ARGO GLORY 59594 ARGO HOPE 59595 ARGO SPIRIT 59596 ARGO VALOUR.**

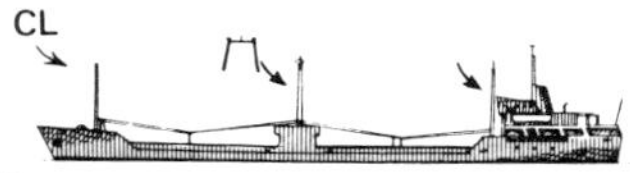

K_3MF H13
59610 ROMMY. Pa/Pd 1972; C; 2000; 93.73 × 5.57 (307.51 × 18.27); M; 13; ex ENID 1977; **'B-431'** type. Sisters: **59611 HILDEGARD** (Pa) ex MILDRED 1977 **59612 CUPID** (No) **59613 ELDRID** (No) **59614 GUDRID** (No) **59615 SIGRID** (No).

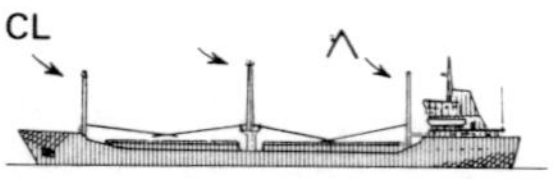

K_3MF H13
59620 BREEHORN. Ne/No 1971; C; 1600; 80.02 × 5.32 (262.53 × 17.45); M; 13; ex LYSHAV 1975. Sister: **59621 BREEHELLE** (Ne) ex ANGELIKA LEHMANN 1973 Similar: **59622 GALLIC MINCH** (Br) ex TORNES 1974 **59623 MONARCH** (Br) ex MORNES 1974 **59624 BREEHOEK** (Ne) ex BLANKENBURG 1976 **59625 DELTA** (FRG) **59626 ZUIDWAL** (Ne) ex KALMARVIND **59627 STAVRAKIS II** (Gr) ex KARIN LEHMANN 1980 **59628 MAIK PRIMO** (It) ex RUDOLF KURZ 1981.

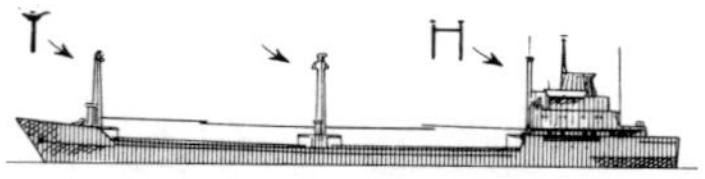

K_3MF H13
★**59650 KLOSTERFELDE.** DDR/DDR 1972; C; 3100; 104.91 × 6.39 (344.19 × 20.97); M; 14.5. Sisters (DDR flag): ★**59651 NEUHAUSEN** ★**59652 RADEBERG.**

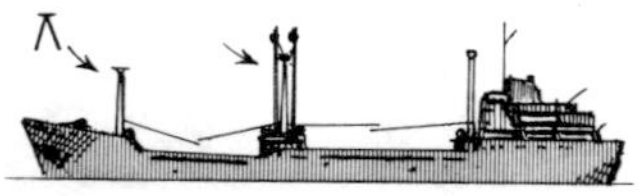

K_3MF H13
59660 BLUE SPIRIT. Cy/DDR 1964; C; 2800; 97.57 × 6.63 (320 × 21.75); M; 13; ex EGON WESCH 1973; ex JIRI 1965.

K_3MF H13
59670 EDY 1. Le/FRG 1965; C; 500/1000; 68.59 × 4.02/5.13 (225.03 × 13.19/16.83); M; 12; ex BIERUM; ex HILDA ECKHARDT 1971. Probable Sister: **59671 MUKALLA** (Ye) ex RENATE S 1974; ex GOLZWARDERSAND 1972.

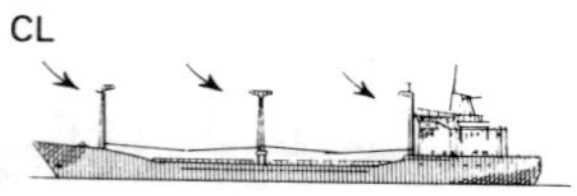

K_3MF H13
59630 LAURA. Gr/Ne 1965; C; 1600; 81.79 × 4.97 (268.34 × 16.31); M; 13.5; ex BREEVECHT; ex KAREN WINTHER 1971. Sister: **59631 MELINA** (Gr) ex BREEVEERTIEN; ex EVA WINTHER 1971.

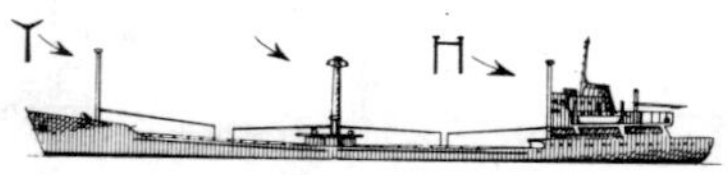

K_3MF H13
● **59640 MOKHA.** Sg/DDR 1967; C; 2600/4000; 112.1 × 7.17 (367.78 × 23.52); M; 13.5; ex EURABIA SPRING 1978; ex CLARI 1975; ex KARLSBURG 1970; ex CLAUDIA MARIA 1967. Sister: **59641 LE ROVE** (Fr) ex SCOL INDEPENDENT 1975; ex GERMANICA 1975; ex WILRI 1975; ex GERMANIC 1974; ex WILRI 1974; ex ATLANTA 1973 Similar: **59642 IRENES SUN** (Gr) ex BLCOKLAND 1977; ex JIRI 1969; ex HOEGH JIRI 1968; ex JIRI 1966 **59643 IRENES SEA** (Gr) ex WERDERLAND 1977; ex WILRI 1969; ex HOEGH WILRI 1969; ex WILRI 1967 **59644 CONTI ALMANIA** (FRG) ex GRIMSNIS 1975; ex HEIN JENEVELT 1970; ex BARI 1968 **59645 EURABIA PROGRESS** (Le) ex CLAUDIA MARIA 1975 **59646 DUBURG** (FRG) ex BILSTEIN 1978; ex CONTI SYRIA 1978; ex ANTONY 1977; ex BILSTEIN 1975; ex HOEGH SUSANN 1968; launched as SUSAN VON BARGEN.

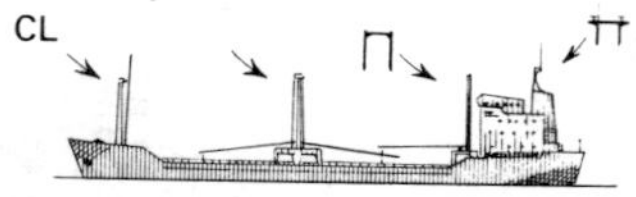

K_3MF H13
59680 ALAMAK. Ne/Ne 1978; C; 3400; 83.52 × 8.2 (274.02 × 26.9); M; 12.5.

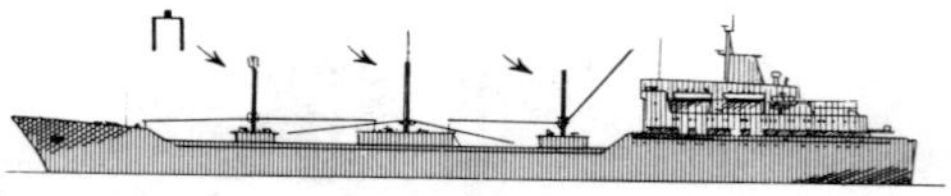

K_3MF H13
★**59690 ZULAWY.** Pd/Pd 1974; FC; 8100; 151.31 × 7.4 (496.42 × 24.28); M; 19. **'B 68'** type. Sisters (Pd flag): ★**59691 KASZUBY II** (Pd) ★**59692 WINETA** (Pd).

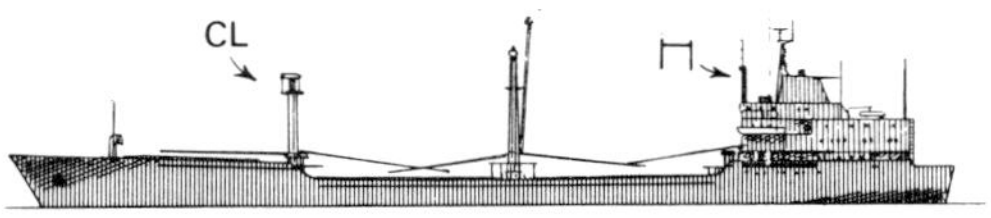

K_3MF H13
● **59700 DOUCE FRANCE.** Fr/FRG 1977; C; 6600/9800; 150.17 × 7.7/9.07 (492.68 × 25.26/29.76); M; 17; ex BARBARELLA; ex HOEGH APAPA; ex CLAUDIA MARIA; **'Neptun'** type. Similar: **59701 CAM BUBINGA** (Cn) launched as IVORY URANUS **59702 CAM DOUSSIE** (Cn) **59703 IRON BARON** (Br) **59704 IVORY TELLUS** (Sg) **59705 VESTLAND** (No) **59706 SOL LAILA** (No) **59707 SOL TULLA** (No).

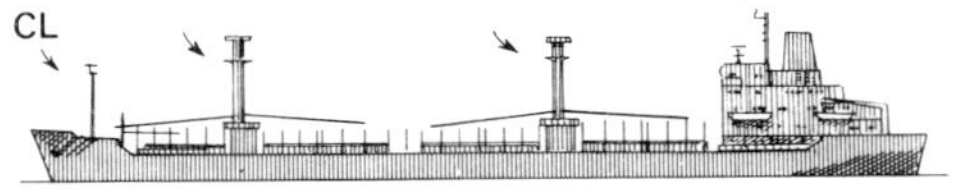

K_3MF H13
59740 FLORENZ. FRG/FRG 1977; C; 10000; 142.07 × 9.06 (466.11 × 29.72); M; 14.5; **'Modified German Liberty'** type. Sisters (FRG flag): **59741 WILLIAM SHAKESPEARE 59742 TOLEDO.**

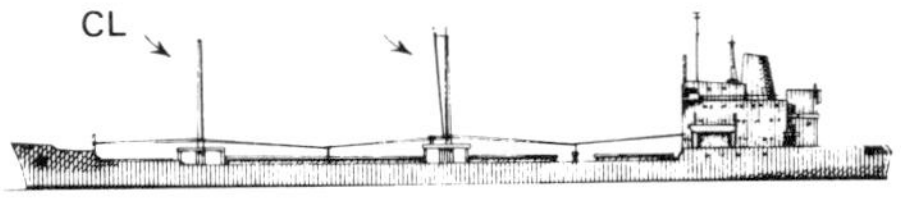

K_3MF H13
59750 LINA FISSER. FRG/FRG 1971; C; 6700/9500; 139.76 × 8.23/9.18 (458.53 × 27/30.12); M; 16; ex SUNLINA 1980; Launched as LINA FISSER; **'German Liberty'** type. Similar: **59752 SUNVREELAND** (FRG); Launched as CARL FISSER **59753 HEIDE LEONHARDT** (FRG); ex FINN HEIDE 1970 **59754 KLAUS LEONHARDT** (FRG) **59755 CASON** (Pa); ex FINN LEONHARDT 1980; ex WOLFGANG RUSS 1978; ex FINN LEONHARDT 1978 **59756 MARITA LEONHARDT** (FRG); ex ALTENFELS 1970; Launched as MARITA LEONHARDT **59757 ALPAMAYO** (Pe); ex MARTHA FISSER 1980; ex SUNBADEN 1978; ex MARTHA FISSER 1974; ex SUNBADEN 1973 **59758 PETRADI** (Gr); ex PITRIA 1980 **59759 RIZCUN HONG KONG** (Br); ex PITRIA STAR 1980.

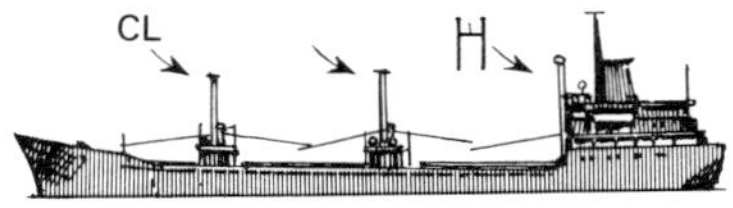

K_3MF H13
59790 LINDO. No/No 1972; C; 4200; 112.83 × 6.89 (370.18 × 22.6); M; 13.75.

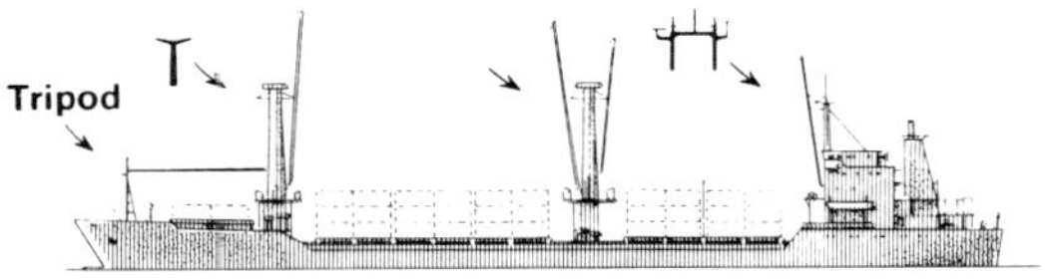

● 59710

K_3MF H13
59720 TIELBANK. FRG/FRG 1978; C/Con; 9300; 151.03 × 8.13 (495.51 × 26.67); M; 17; ex CAROLINA; **Modified "CL 10"** type. Sister: **59721 TESTBANK** (FRG) ex CHARLOTTA.

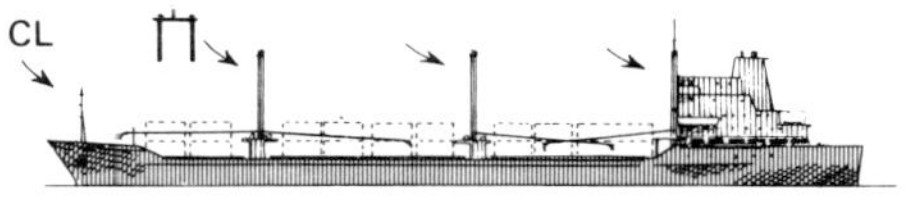

K_3MF H13
● **59730 ESTEBLICK.** Sg/Ja 1978; C; 6400; 129.32 × 7.83 (424.3 × 25.7); M; 15; ex B.M.I. EXPORTER 1978. Similar (Pa flag): **59731 ATALANTA II** ex ATALANTA **59732 GERMANIC 59733 IMPALA** Probably Similar: **59734 ADRIA I** (Pa); ex NAXOS I 1979; ex RENATE WUNSCHE 1978; ex NORDWELLE 1977 **59735 HILDA WESCH** (Cy); Launched as BLUE SOVEREIGN.

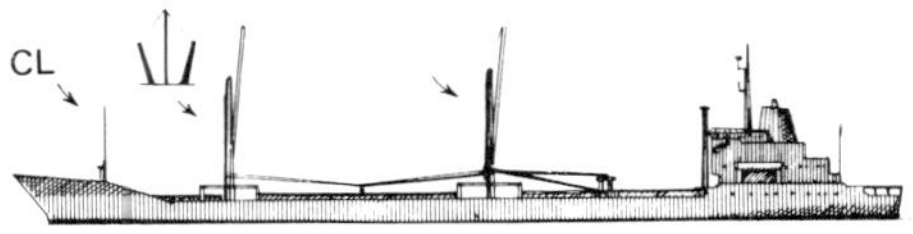

K_3MF H13
59770 EDITA. Pa/FRG 1972; C; 5000/8300; 143.8 × 7.07/8.33 (471.78 × 23.19/27.33); M; 18; ex EDITH HOWALDT RUSS 1980; ex CAMBRIDGE 1976; ex EDITH HOWALDT RUSS 1975; Launched as EDITH HOWALDT. Sisters: **59771 COLUMBUS CALIFORNIA** (FRG); ex RHEINGOLD 1973 **59772 WALKURE** (FRG); ex BAVARIA TRIESTE 1980; ex COLUMBUS CANADA 1980; Launched as WALKURE.

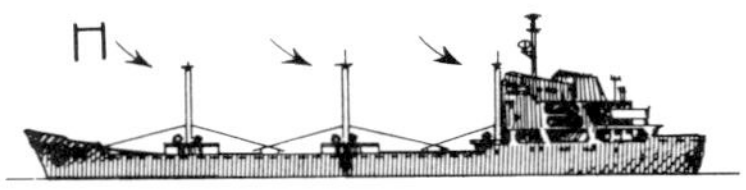

K_3MF H13
59780 SARI BUDI. Ia/Ja 1961; C; 4200; 108.82 × 6.52 (357.02 × 21.39); M; —; ex GUNUNG GUNTUR 1978. Sisters: **59781 MIRA PERMATA** (Ia); ex GUNUNG KERINTJI 1978 **59782 RANTIH GUMALA** (Ia); ex GUNUNG TAMBORA 1978.

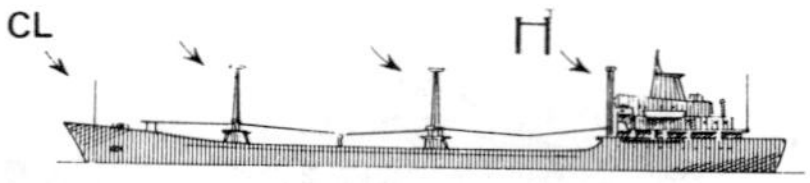

K_3MF H13
● **59800 JOHN M.** Pa/FRG 1970; C; 4000; 117 × 6.61 (383.86 × 21.69); M; 15; ex JOHN M REHDER. Sister: **59801 ALFRED REHDER** (FRG) Similar: **59802 LEO SCHRODER** (FRG) **59803 LUTZ SCHRODER** (FRG).

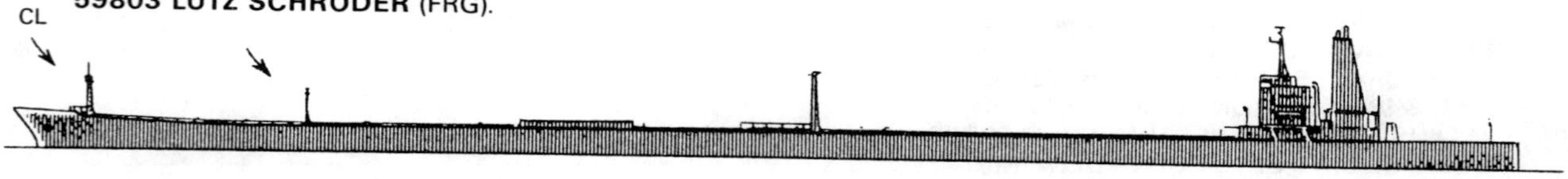

K_3MF H2
59810 BERGE DUKE. No/Ja 1973; Tk; 139800; 342.91 × 21.78 (1125.03 × 71.8); M; 15.5. Sisters (No flag): **59811 BERGE SEPTIMUS 59812 BERGE LORD.**

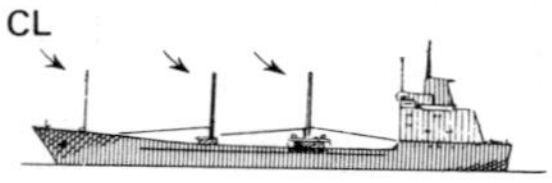

K_3MF H3
59820 GROOTSAND. Cy/FRG 1978; R; 1600; 78.11 × 5.75 (256.27 × 18.86); M; 14. Sisters (Cy flag): **59821 WITTSAND 59822 YORKSAND 59823 KNIEPSAND** (Sd flag): **59824 BASILEA 59825 TURICIA.**

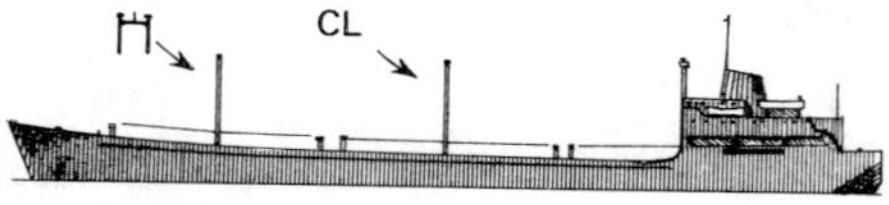

K_3MF H3
59830 CYCLOPUS. Gr/Fr 1957; C; 9100; 138.33 × 8.89 (453.84 × 29.17); M; 14; ex MAESTRALE 1980; ex LILY M 1978; ex LOUIS L. D. 1970.

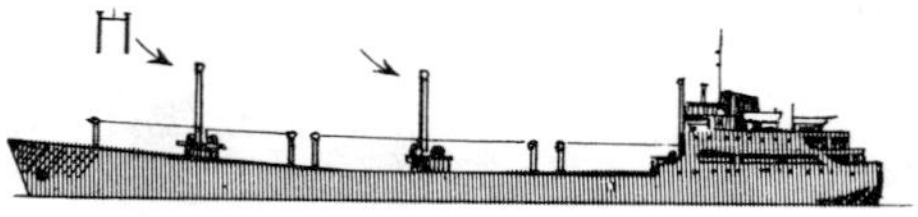

K_3MF H3
59840 MARIANNINA. Gr/Sp 1958; C; 6400; 138.41 × 9.49 (454.1 × 31.14); M; 14; ex LA SELVA 1967.

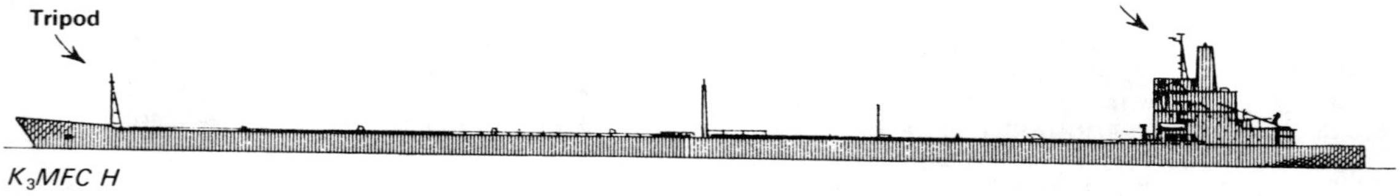

K_3MFC H
● **59850 ESSO SCOTIA.** Br/FRG 1969; Tk; 127150; 347.81 × 19.95 (1141.1 × 65.4); T; 16. Similar: **59851 ESSO CALEDONIA** (Br) **59852 ESSO CAMBRIA** (Br) **59853 ESSO COPENHAGEN** (Li) **59854 ESSO EUROPA** (FRG) **59855 ESSO NEDERLAND** (NA) **59856 ESSO SKANDIA** (Li) **59857 ESSO EUROPOORT** (Na) **59858 ESSO BONAIRE** (NA) **59859 ESSO SABA** (NA) **59860 ESSO BONN** (FRG) **59861 ESSO WILHELMSHAVEN** (Li) **59862 ESSO FLANDRE** (Fr); ex ESSO ROTTERDAM 1978 **59863 STALAND** (No).

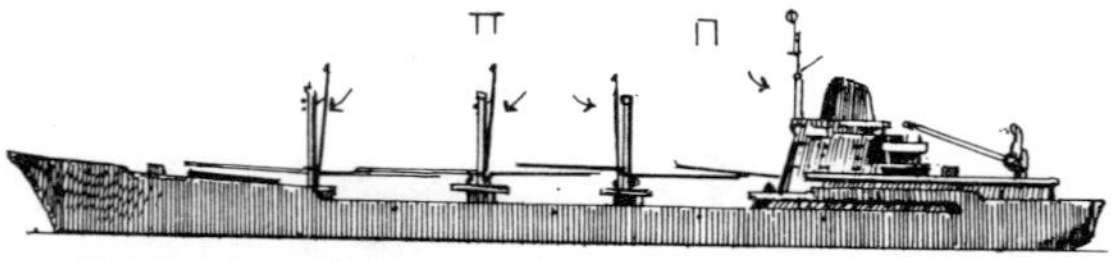

K_3MFC H13
● **59870 LEONCE VIELJEUX.** Fr/Fr 1970; C; 7900/12500; 171 × 7.7/9.7 (561 × 25.6/32); M; 19. Sisters (Fr flag): **59871 CHRISTIAN VIELJEUX 59872 GEORGES VIELJEUX 59873 PIERRE VIELJEUX 59874 THORON;** ex ERIC VIELJEUX Possibly Similar: **59875 PATRICK VIELJEUX 59876 TAJ;** ex STEPHANE VIELJEUX 1978.

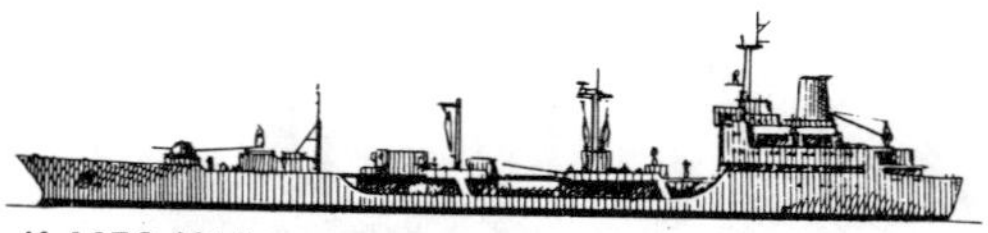

K_3MFC H13
⋆59880 BORIS CHILIKIN. Ru/Ru 1971; Rmt; 23400 Dspl; 162 × 8.6 (532 × 28.1); MS; 16.5. Similar (Ru flag): **⋆59881 DNESTR ⋆59882 GENRIK GASANOV ⋆59883 IVAN BUBNOV ⋆59884 VLADIMIR KOLECHITSKY.**

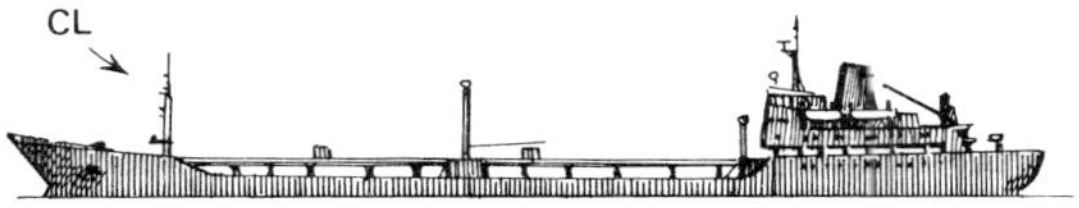

K_3MFC H13
⋆59890 VELIKIY OKTYABR. Ru/Ru 1967; Tk; 11000; 162.31 × 8.93 (532.51 × 29.3); M; 16.25. Sisters (Ru flag): **⋆59891 POBYEDA OKTYABRYA ⋆59892 TSEZAR KUNIKOV ⋆59893 NIKOLAY SIPYAGIN ⋆59894 KERCH ⋆59895 EYZHENS BERGS ⋆59896 KONSTANTIN TSIOLKOVSKIY ⋆59897 GENERAL BAGRATION ⋆59898 ZAKHARIY PALIASHVILI ⋆59899 FRIDRIKH TSANDER ⋆59900 VASILIY KIKVIDZE** (Bu flag): **⋆59901 MARITZA ⋆59902 REZVAYA ⋆59903 VELEKA** (Cu flag): **⋆59904 9 DE ABRIL ⋆59905 7 DE NOVIEMBRE** (In flag): **59906 BHAGAT SINGH 59907 SAROJINI NAIDU 59908 VISVES VARAYA.**

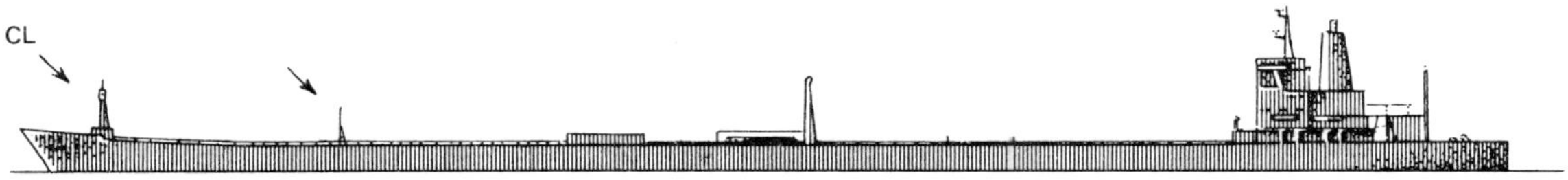

K_3MFK H
59910 AMOCO SEAFARER. Li/Ja 19744; Tk; 140200; 331.53 × 20.6 (1087.7 × 67.59); M; 16; ex POLYBRITANNIA 1979.

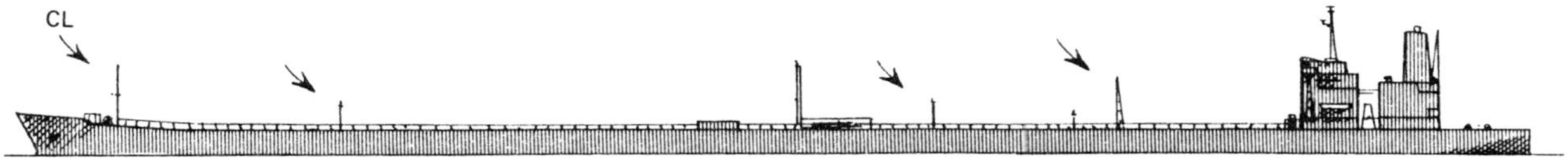

K_3MFK H
59920 ESSO CARIBBEAN. Li/Ja 1976; Tk; 177300; 378.39 × 22.27 (1241.44 × 73.06); T; 15.25; ex ANDROS PETROS 1977. Sisters: **59921 BURMAH ENDEAVOUR** (Br) **59922 BURMAH ENTERPRISE** (Br) **59923 ESSO MEDITERRANEAN** (Li); ex HOMERIC 1977 Similar: **59924 ANDROS CHRYSSI** (Li) **59925 ETHNIC** (Li) **59926 SUNSHINE LEADER** (Li).

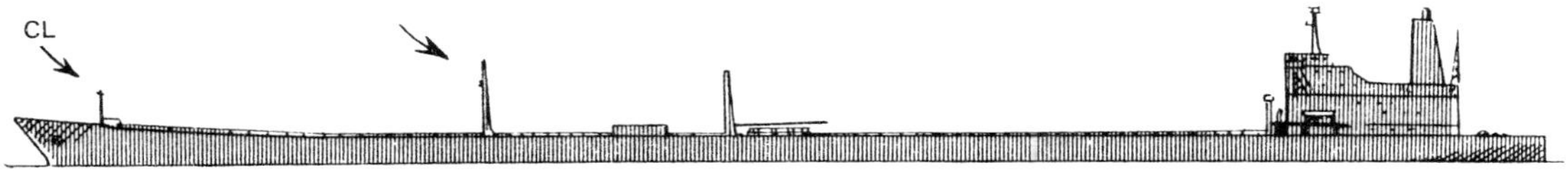

K_3MFK H
59930 MUNETAMA MARU. Ja/Ja 1973; Tk; 128800; 341.11 × 20.04 (1119.13 × 65.75); T; 15.25.

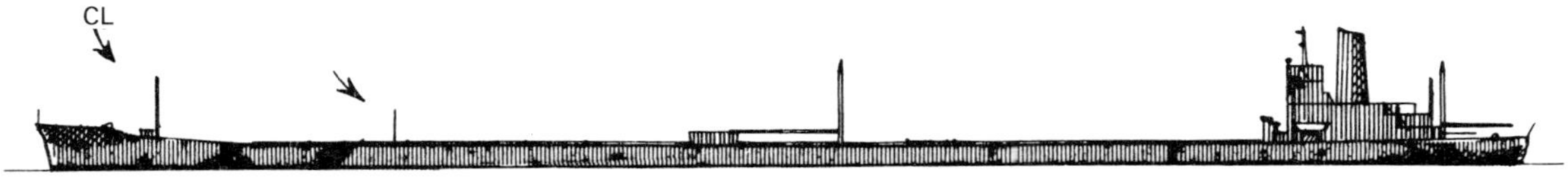

K_3MFK H
59940 OGDEN NELSON. Li/Ja 1972; Tk; 124400; 331 × 22.02 (1085.96 × 72.24); T; 15.5. Sisters (Li flag): **59941 COALINGA** ex IOANNIS CHANDRIS 1976 Similar (Li flag): **59942 WORLD CROWN 59943 WESTERN LION 59944 SOUTHERN LION 59945 NORTHERN LION 59946 EASTERN LION.**

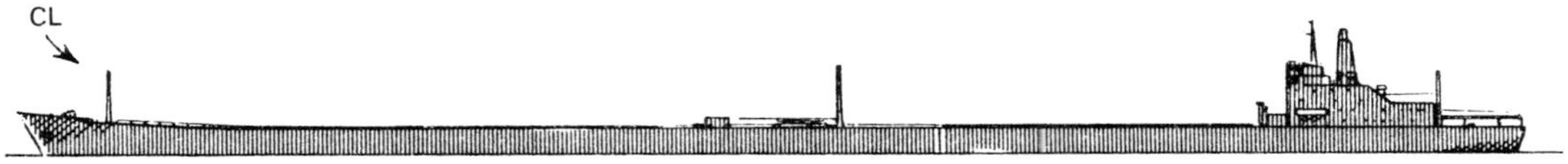

K_3MFK H
59950 OLYMPIC BOND. Li/Ja 1972; Tk; 12600; 331 × 22.02 (1085.96 × 72.24); T; 15.5.

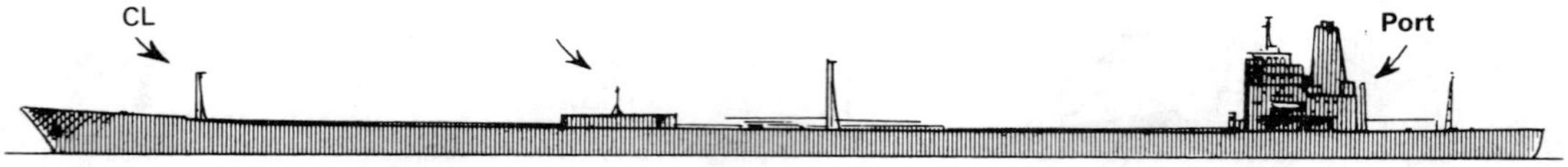

K_3MFK H
59960 MEITAI MARU. Ja/Ja 1974; Tk; 123900; 324.01 × 19.51 (1063.03 × 64.01); M; 16.

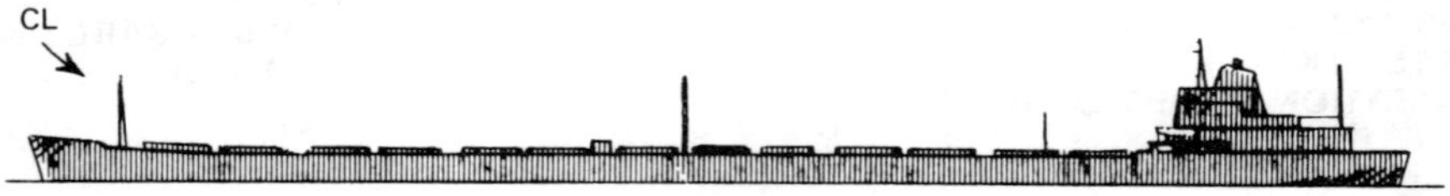

K_3MFK H
59970 NORMAN PACIFIC. Sg/Ys 1971; OBO; 42200; 252.36 × 14.78 (827.95 × 48.49); M; 16; ex CAPETAN CARRAS.

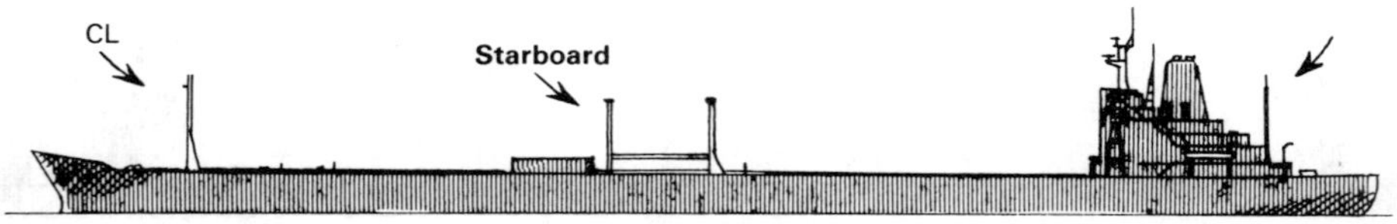

K_3MFK H
59980 VENTURE BRITAIN. Li/Ja 1970; Tk; 63400; 274.02 × 17.03 (899.02 × 55.87); M; 15.25; ex OCEAN CHAMPION 1981; ex SEIKO MARU 1976.

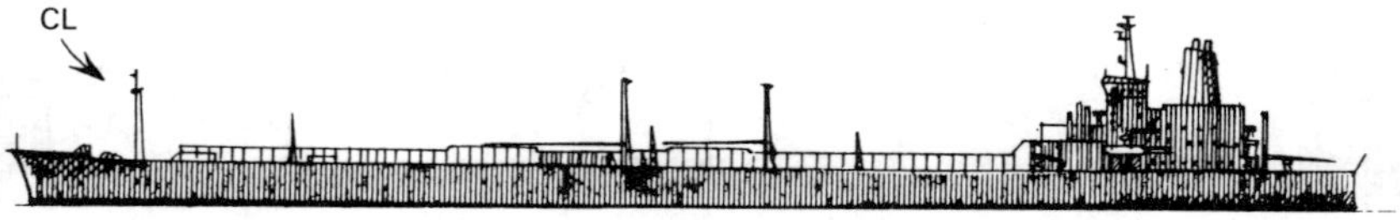

K_3MFK H
59990 ESSO FUJI. Pa/Ja 1972; LGC; 55900; 246.01 × 13.08 (807.12 × 42.91); M; 15.5.

K_3MFK H
60000 PETRON GASUL. Pi/Ja 1962; LGC; 17800; 183.72 × 10.54 (602.76 × 34.58); M; 18.5; ex CONTANK BRIDGESTONE 1980; ex BRIDGESTONE MULTINA 1978; ex BRIDGESTONE MARU 1971; In use as a storage vessel.

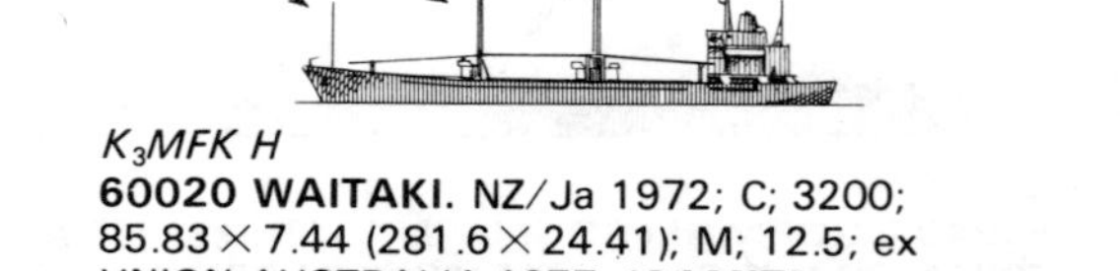

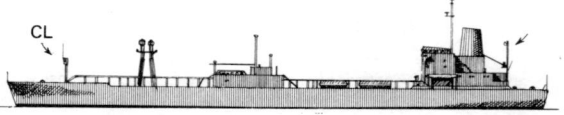

K_3MFK H
60010 ANTILLA CAPE. NA/FRG 1968; LGC; 19700; 173.84 × 10.26 (570.34 × 33.66); M; 17.5.

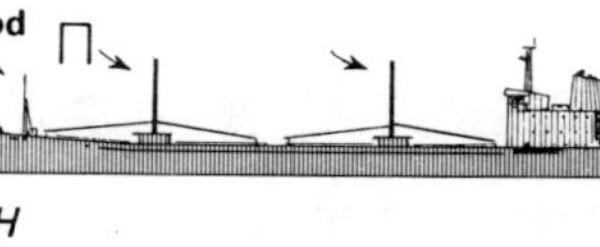

K_3MFK H
60020 WAITAKI. NZ/Ja 1972; C; 3200; 85.83 × 7.44 (281.6 × 24.41); M; 12.5; ex UNION AUSTRALIA 1977; **'CAMIT'** type. Sisters: **60021 DUNEDIN** (NZ) ex UNION NEW ZEALAND 1978 **60022 ARNON** (Is) ex UNION TRANS TASMAN 1977.

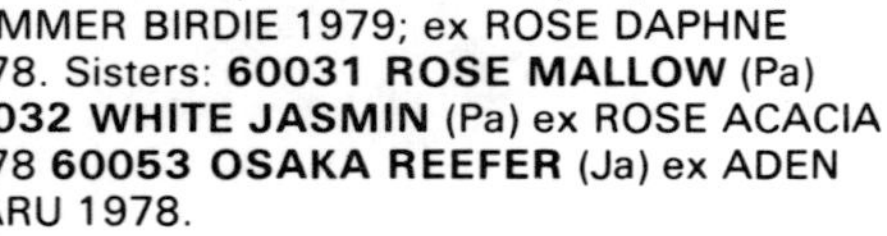

K_3MFK H
60030 OCEAN SKY. Ko/Ja 1975; C; 3700; 131.48 × 6.99 (431.36 × 22.93); M; 17.75; ex SUMMER BIRDIE 1979; ex ROSE DAPHNE 1978. Sisters: **60031 ROSE MALLOW** (Pa) **60032 WHITE JASMIN** (Pa) ex ROSE ACACIA 1978 **60053 OSAKA REEFER** (Ja) ex ADEN MARU 1978.

K_3MFK H
60040 EITOKU MARU. Ja/Ja 1971; C; 3500; 127.41 × 7.07 (418.01 × 23.2); M; 20.5. Similar: **60041 NITTOKU MARU** (Ja).

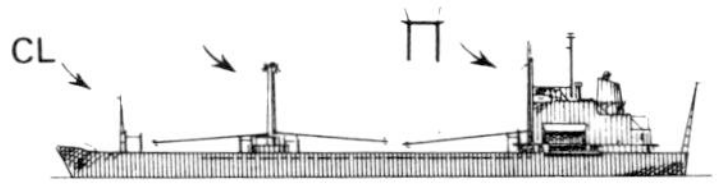

K_3MFK H
60050 MASBON. Li/Ja 1975; C; 4800; 102.16 × 6.02 (335.17 × 19.75); TSM; 12. Sisters (Li flag): **60051 MINAROSA 60052 MINADOR 60053 MASLUCK.**

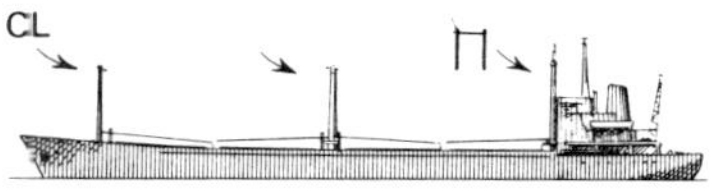

K_3MFK H
60060 UNITY. Li/Ja 1973; C; 3700; 108.01 × 7.7 (354.36 × 25.26); M; 12.25.

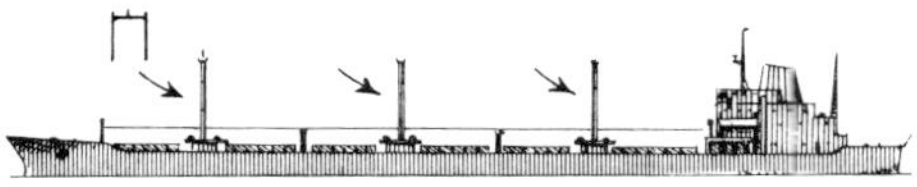

K_3MFK H
● **60070 'FREEDOM'** type. —/Ja & Sg 1968-; C; 8000 approx; 142.3 × 9.06 (466.86 × 29.72); M; 14.5; Some ships under K_3MF. Some later ships have HL. Sisters (Gr flag): **60071 ACRITAS 60072 ADAMAS 60073 AEOLOS 60074 AGAPI 60075 AGATHON 60076 AGENOR 60077 AMYNTAS 60078 ANNOULA 60079 ANTHEMIOS 60080 AQUAMARINE 60081 ARAMIS 60082 ARGOS 60083 ARIS 60084 ARISTARCHOS 60085 ARISTEUS 60086 ASSOMATOS** ex PROSPERITY **60087 ATHOS 60088 BARAHONA** ex MARIGO YEMELOS 1980 **60089 COMET 60090 CAPE KENNEDY 60091 CAPE MONTEREY** ex KASTRAKI **60092 DELOS** ex ACROPOLIS 1978 **60093 DIMOS HALCOUSSIS 60094 EFTHITIS 60095 ELPIS 60096 EPIMELIA 60097 EPOS 60098 EVNIA 60099 FREE WAVE 60100 FRINTON 60101 FRONISIS 60102 GEORGIOS MATSAS 60103 GEORGIOS PARAVALOS 60104 LACON** ex SPARTA **60105 LARA S** ex SHARPEVILLE 1980 **60106 LIPS** ex STAR OF KUWAIT **60107 LYDIA** ex WISTARIA PURPLE **60108 MARABOU 60109 MARIGO 60110 MELITON 60111 NATA 60112 NAXOS** ex ATHENS **60113 OCEANIS 60114 PATMOS** ex PACQUEEN 1979 **60115 PELLEAS 60116 POUNENTES** ex SHAMALY **60117 PROSPATHIA 60118 RELIANT 60119 SANTO FORTUNE 60120 SANTO PIONEER 60121 SATURNIA** ex POMPOSA 1975 **60122 SEA BIRD 60123 SEA FALCON 60124 SEA TIDE 60125 SILVER ATHENS 60126 SITHONIA 60127 TELFAIR CHALLENGER** ex ESTINA 1980 **60128 TETI N 60129 TINTOS** ex DELPHI **60130 TITIKA HALCOUSSI 60131 UNITY 60132 YANNIS HALCOUSSIS** Probable Sisters: **60140 AKRATA 60141 LEONIS HALCOUSSIS 60142 SEA STAR 60143 THASSOS ISLAND** Sisters (Li flag): **60150 AL RAKEEB 60151 AL RASHED 60152 AL RAZAK 60153 ALEA** ex NEPTUNE SAKURA 1974 **60154 ARKANDROS 60155 CONSTANCE 60156 EMERALD 60157 ENDURANCE EXPRESS 60158 ENDURANCE FRIENDSHIP 60159 LUCK WAVE 60160 MESIS** ex KUWAIT HORIZON **60161 MICHALIS 60162 MILOS ISLAND 60163 NEGO MAY** ex VOLTA FRIENDSHIP **60164 PACPRINCE 60165 PACPRINCESS 60166 POLA 60167 POMPOSA** ex UNILION; ex LIJA **60168 POTENZA 60169 POZEGA 60170 SOROKOS** ex DAWN OF KUWAIT **60171 SOUTHERN FRIENDSHIP** ex BOUNTEOUS **60172 TELFAIR LEADER** ex HERMINA 1980 **60173 UNION EXPANSION** Probable Sisters: **60175 AL RAHIM** ex CONCORDIA GLORY 1980; ex AL RAHIM **60176 AL RAHMAN 60177 AL RAZIQ 60178 AL REDHA 60179 TELFAIR PIONEER** Sisters (Pa flag): **60185 LONG BEACH 60186 OAKLAND 60187 REGINA S** Probable Sisters: **60188 DUTEOUS 60189 SPACIOUS** Sisters (Sg flag): **60200 HIGHSEA PRIDE** ex WISTARIA MARBLE 1979 **60201 NEPTUNE CYPRINE 60202 NEPTUNE IOLITE 60203 NEPTUNE IRIS 60204 NEPTUNE KIKU 60205 NEPTUNE PERIDOT 60206 NEPTUNE RUBY 60207 NEPTUNE SARDONYX 60208 NEPTUNE SPINEL 60209 NEPTUNE TOURMALINE 60210 NEPTUNE TURQUOISE 60211 WISTARIA CORAL 60212 WISTARIA PEARL** (Ta flag): **★60215 RAVU** ex SEA HORSE (Cy flag): **60220 ADVENTURE** ex CARNIVAL VENTURE 1980 (In flag): **60230 INDIAN FAITH 60231 INDIAN FAME** ex PERICLES HALCOUSSIS **60232 INDIAN FORTUNE** ex LEONIS HALCOUSSIS **60234 INDIAN FRATERNITY 60235 INDIAN FREEDOM** (RC flag): **★60240 JIA LING JIANG** ex ARAN **★60241 LAN CAN JIANG** ex ZOGRAFNIA Y 1977 **★60242 QUI JIANG** ex SEA SWAN 1980 **★60243 SONG HUA JIANG** ex EVIE **★60244 XUAN CHENG** ex THEODOROS A.S. **★60245 WU JIANG** ex SEA EAGLE 1980 Similar - Taiwan built & flag: **60250 GLORIOUS TRADER 60251 SINCERE TRADER.**

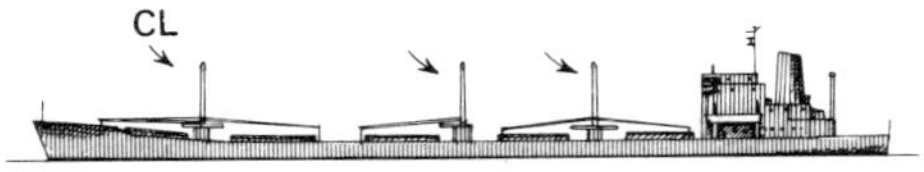

K_3MFK H
60260 FATHER PANOS. Gr/Br 1968; C; 6200/9300; 140.87 × —/8.58 (462.17 × —/28.15); M; 14.25; ex SHEAF CREST 1974.

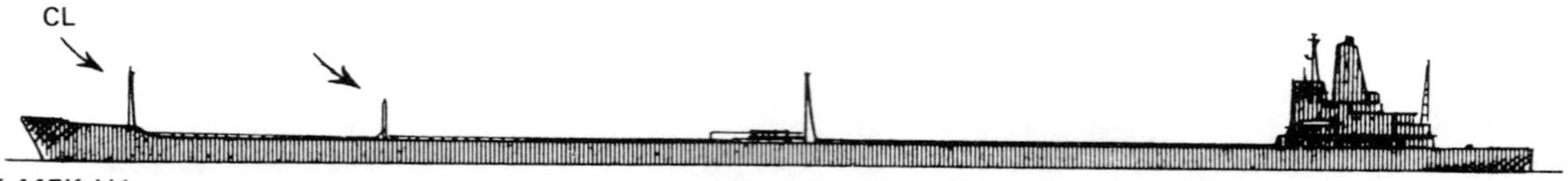

K_3MFK *H1*

● **60270 BRITISH PIONEER.** Br/Ja 1971; Tk; 112700; 324.21 × 19.65 (1063.68 × 64.47); T; 16. Possibly Similar (may be K^2MF): **60271 BRITISH SCIENTIST** (Br) **60272 SHOUSH** (Ir) ex BRITISH SURVEYOR 1976.

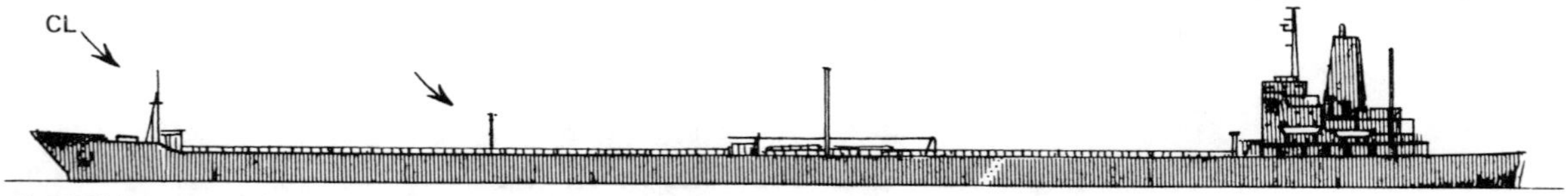

K_3MFK *H1*

60280 JALINGA. No/Ja 1970; Tk- 128300; 338.13 × 20.89 (1109.35 × 68.54); T; 15.5. Sisters (No flag): **60281 JAMUNDA 60282 JARABELLA 60283 JASTELLA** Similar: **60284 VIOLANDO** (Li) ex VIOLANDO N. GOULANDRIS 1978.

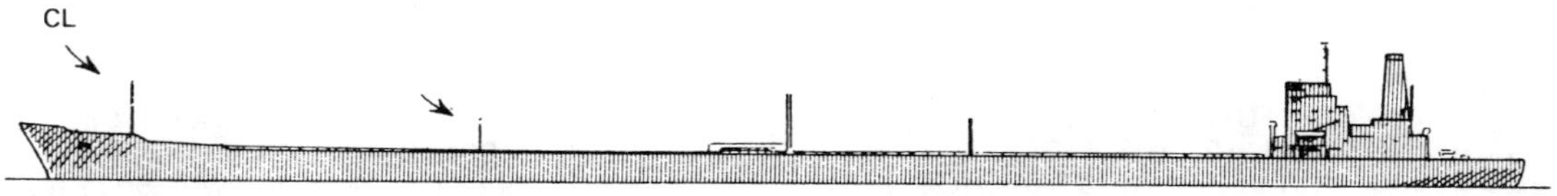

K_3MFK *H1*

60290 FINA BRITANNIA. Fr/Ne 1971; Tk; 116000; 329.68 × 19.85 (1081.63 × 65.12); T; 16.

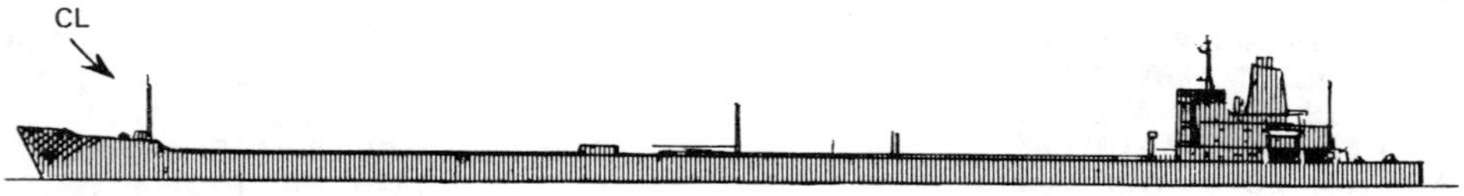

K_3MFK *H1*

60300 AMOCO CAIRO. Li/Ja 1975; Tk; 76500; 280.02 × 15.24 (918.7 × 50); M; 15.25. Sisters: **60301 AMOCO WHITING** (Li) ex AMOCO TEHRAN 1980 **60302 AMOCO TRINIDAD.**

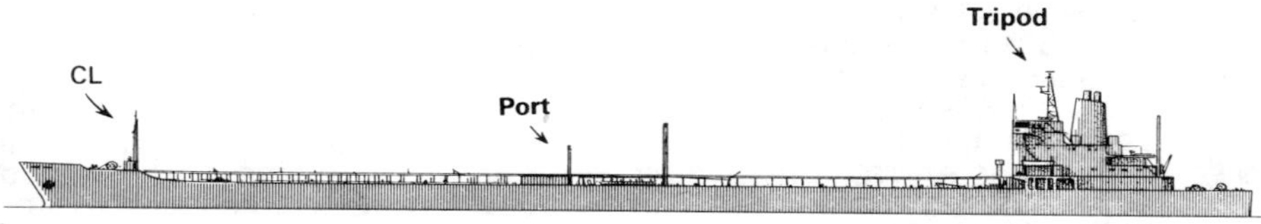

K_3MFK *H1*

● **60310 GREY WARRIOR.** Br/Ja 1976; Tk; 84600; 280.42 × 15.24 (920.01 × 50) M; 15.25.

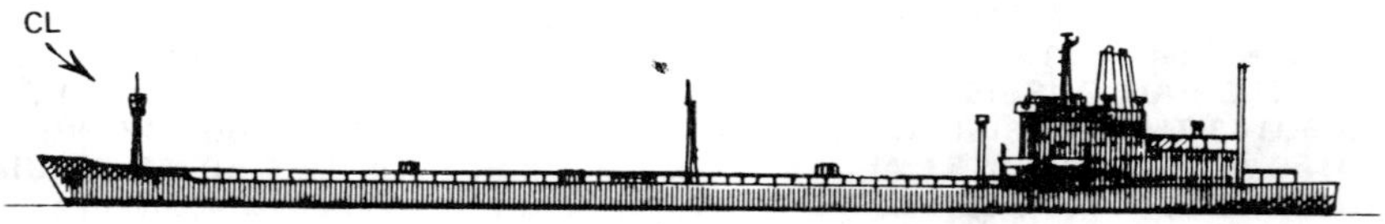

K_3MFK *H1*

60320 BARIS. No/Ja 1966; Tk; 45000; 243.85 × 13.42 (800.03 × 44.03); M; 16.25; ex MOSPRINCE 1980. Similar: **60321 GRADIENT ENERGY** (Li) ex MOSDUKE 1978.

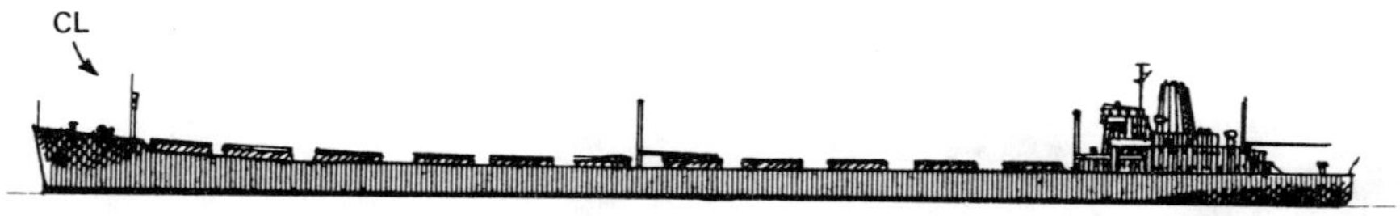

K_3MFK *H1*

60330 SANTAMAR. Pe/FRG 1965; OBO; 38000; 250.07 × 13.68 (820.44 × 44.88); M; —; ex NORDIC NAVIGATOR 1979; ex NAESS NORSEMAN 1974.

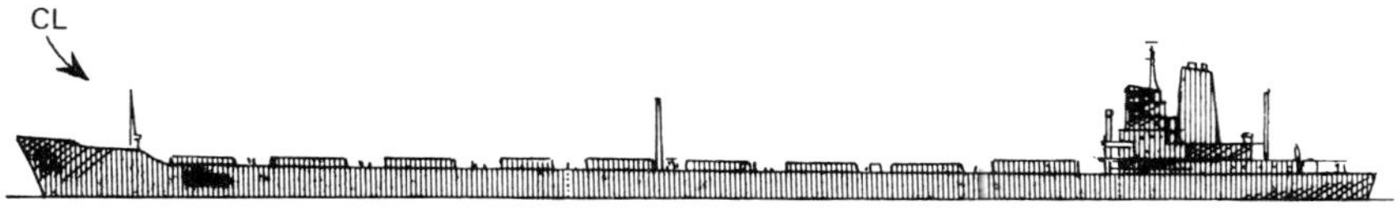

K_3MFK H1
60340 MOZART. Li/Ja 1969; OBO; 43500; 254.52 × 14.01 (835.04 × 45.96); M; 15.5.

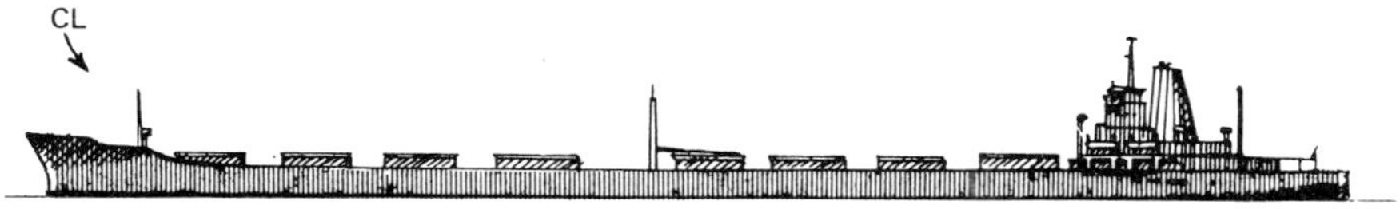

K_3MFK H1
60350 BALBINA. Li/Ja 1969; OBO; 43400; 254.52 × 14.02 (835.04 × 46); M; 14.75.

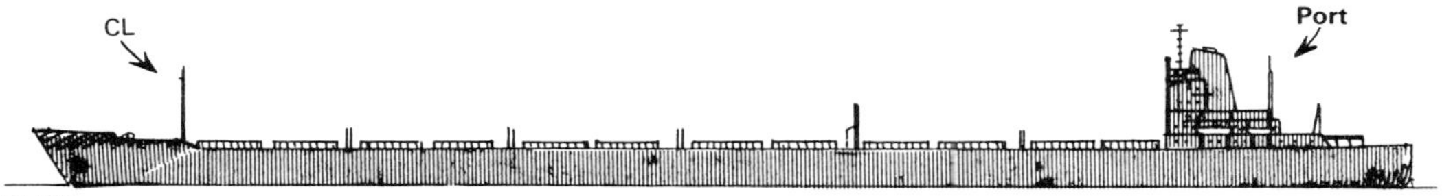

K_3MFK H1
60360 CEDROS. Li/Ja 1966; BO; 85900; 303.51 × 18.97 (995.77 × 62.24); T; 15.

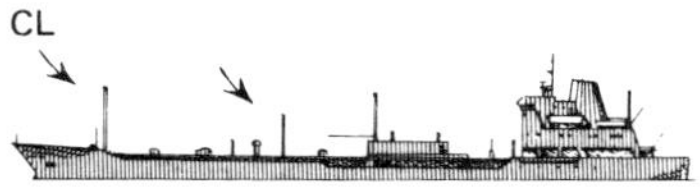

K_3MFK H1
60370 DELTAGAS. FRG/FRG 1975; LGC; 4300; 106.41 × 7.44 (349.11 × 24.41); M; 16.5. Possible Sisters: **60371 EPSILONGAS** (FRG) **60372 CORAL ISIS** (NA).

K_3MFK H1
60380 THALASSINI EFHI. Gr/Ja 1976; B; 42300; 239.05 × 14 (784.28 × 45.93); M; 15.2; ex IKAN BAWAL 1980; ex THORSDRAKE 1979.

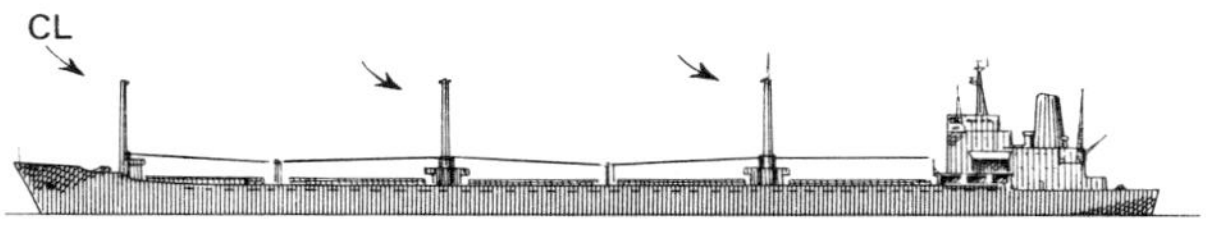

K_3MFK H1
60390 CHIEFTAIN BULKER. Li/Ja 1977; B; 19500; 182.23 × 11.28 (597.87 × 37.01); M; 14.75. Sisters: (Li flag): **60391 CAVALIER BULKER 60392 CENTURION BULKER 60393 CONQUEROR BULKER.**

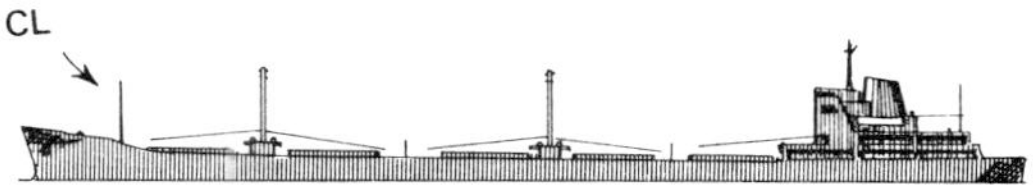

K_3MFK H1
60400 MENELAOS. Gr/Br 1969; B; 12700; 160.03 × 9.15 (525.03 × 30.02); M; 15.5; ex FEDERAL LAKES 1980. Sister: **60401 MICHALIS** (Gr) ex FEDERAL SEAWAY 1980; ex SIMSMETAL 1972.

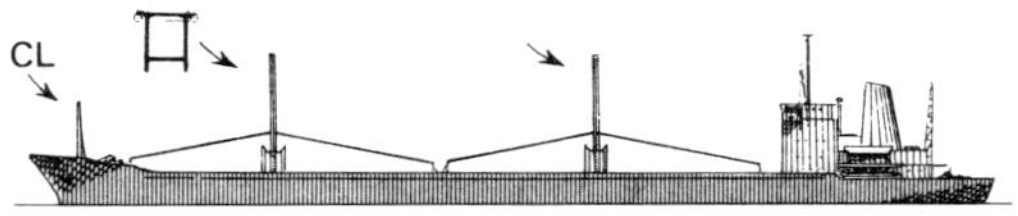

K_3MFK H1
60410 ELAFINA. Gr/Ja 1973; B; 15000; 154.11 × 10.52 (505.61 × 34.51); M; 15.5; ex TRANS RUBY 1973.

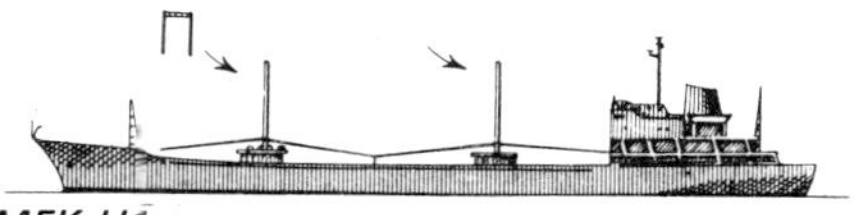

K_3MFK H1
60420 OCEAN DYNAMIC. Pa/Ja 1975; C; 3600; 124.08 × 6.92 (407.08 × 22.7); M; 17.5. Sister: **60421 OCEAN FRESH** (Pa).

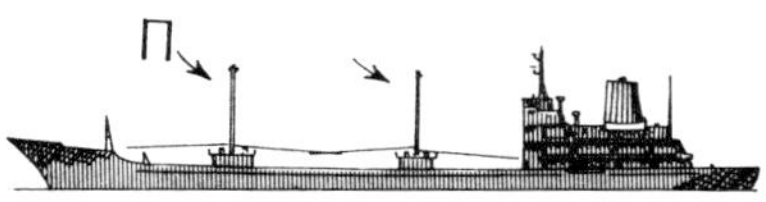

K_3MFK H1
60430 SATSUKI MARU. Ja/Ja 1973; R; 4400; 117.02 × 6.68 (383.92 × 21.92); M; 17.

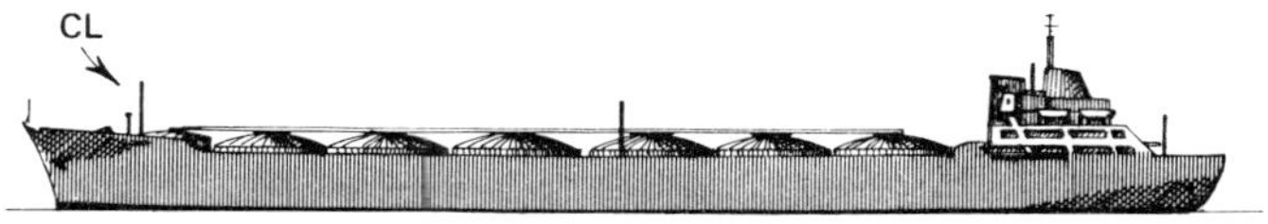

K_3MFK H1
60440 JULES VERNE. Fr/Fr 1965; LGC; 22300; 201.02 × 7.53 (659.51 × 24.7); T; 17.

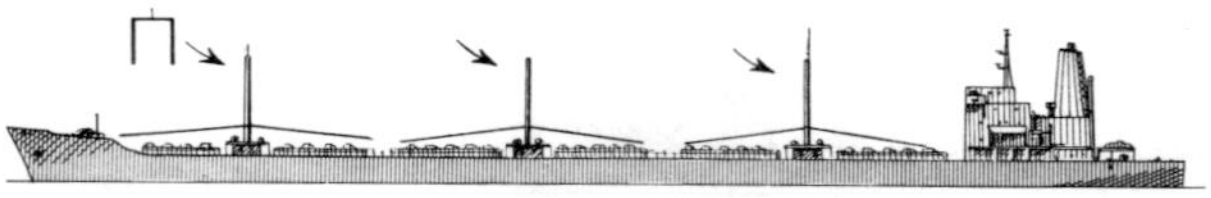

K_3MFK H1
60450 WEST JINORIWON. Pa/Ja 1972; B; 24600; 194.01 × 11.44 (636.52 × 37.53); M; 14.75; ex INVERALMOND 1980.

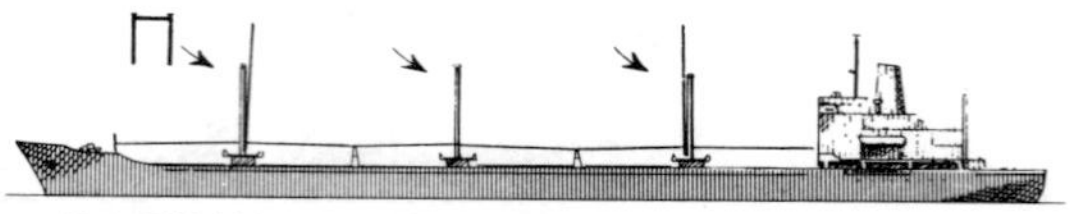

K_3MFK H1
60460 SEAFOX. Pa/Ja 1970; B; 13400; 163.51 × 9.63 (536.45 × 31.59); M; 16.5.

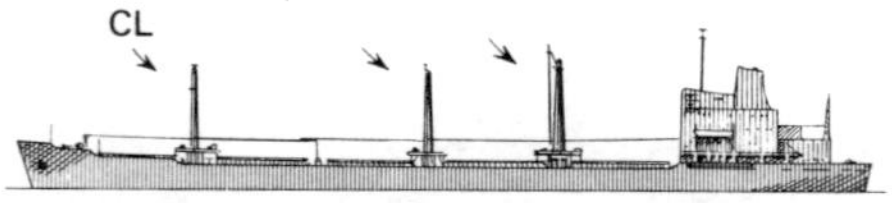

K_3MFK H1
⋆60470 ZHONG TIAO SHAN. RC/FRG 1970; C; 6600/9300; 139.58 × —/9.19 (457.94 × —/30.15); M; 16; ex ATLANTIS 1978; **'German Liberty'** type. Sisters: **⋆60471 HAN YIN** (RC) ex OKEANIS 1974 **⋆60472 XIN AN JIANG** (RC) ex OCTAVIA 1977 **⋆60473 FENG HUANG SHAN** (RC) ex IA 1978; ex NIRIIS 1974. **60474 ALTAVIA** (FRG) **60475 NOVIA** (FRG) **60476 LONTUE** (Ch) ex MEGALOPOLIS 1976.

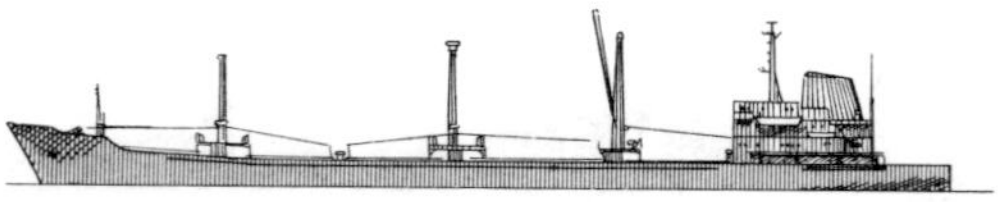

K_3MFK H1
60480 ARGOLIKOS. Gr/FRG 1977; C; 7200/10000; 149.82 × 8.18/9.26 (491.53 × 26.84/30.38); M; 16.5; **'36-L'** type. Probable Sister: **60481 ARISTAGELOS** (Li) **60482 ARISTANAX** (Gr).

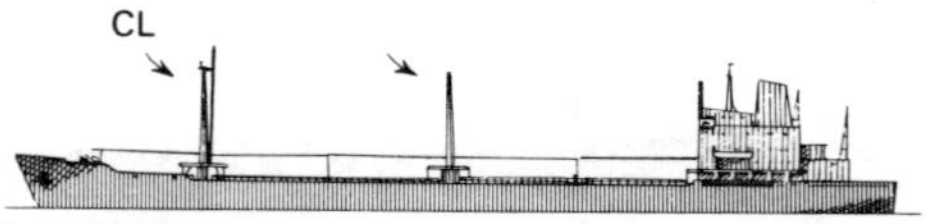

K_3MFK H1
60490 AEGIS SPIRIT. Gr/FRG 1970; C; 9200; 139.58 × 9.02 (457.94 × 29.59); M; 15; **'German Liberty'** type. Sisters: **60491 AEGIS FAITH** (Gr) **60492 AEGIS PIONEER** (Gr) **60493 AEGIS PRIDE** (Gr) **60494 ROBERTO** (Pa) ex PAULA HOWALDT RUSS 1979 Possibly similar: **60495 GOLDEN CAMEROON** (Pa) ex MINERVA 1979.

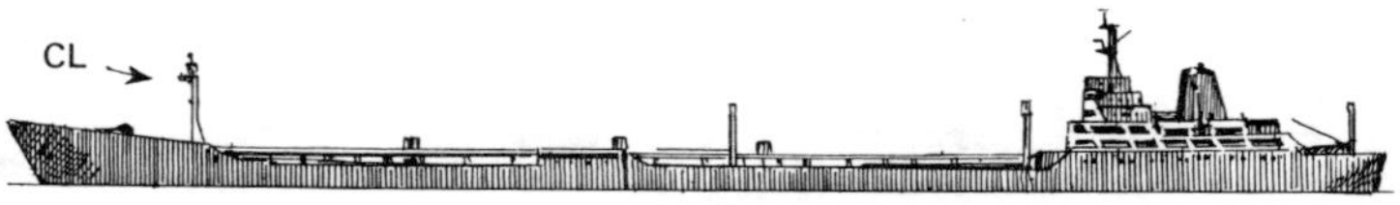

K_3MFK H123
⋆60500 GIUSEPPE VERDI. Ru/It 1964; Tk; 30300; 227.9 × 12.14 (747.7 × 39.83); M; 16; May be spelt **DZHUZEPPE VERDI.** Sisters (Ru flag): **⋆60501 GALILEO GALILEI** (Ru) **⋆60502 RAPHAEL** (Ru) may be spelt **RAFAEL.**

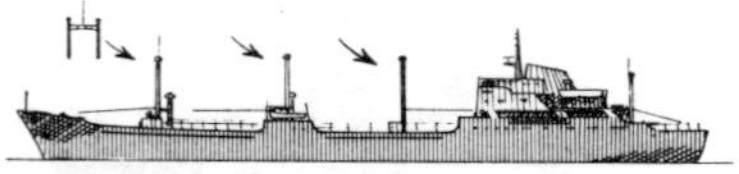

K_3MFK H123
60510 SHABELLE. Gr/Ys-FRG 1964/65; LS; 2900; 109.18 × 6.04 (358.2 × 19.82); M; 15; ex DONA CLAUSEN 1980; Launched Ys 1964. Lengthened & completed FRG 1965. Sister: **60511 AL-KUWAIT** (Ku) launched as DAGMAR CLAUSEN.

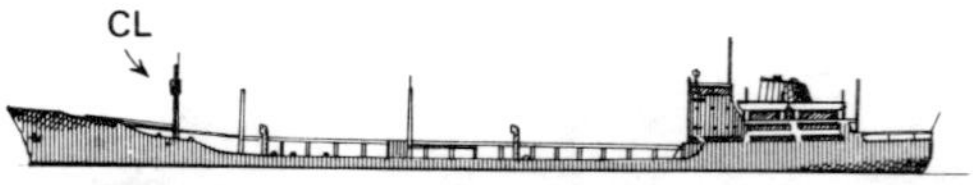

K_3MFK H13
60520 YU KONG. Ko/No 1961; Tk; 8300; 146.31 × 8.37 (480.02 × 27.46); M; 14.5; ex HUSVIK 1969.

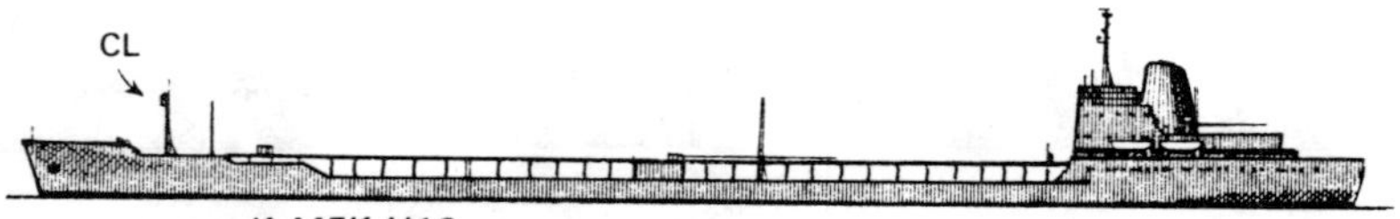

K_3MFK H13
60530 ARMONIKOS. Gr/Sw 1963; Tk; 36800; 236.33 × 12.63 (775.36 × 41.44); M; 17.25; ex VESTALIS 1975.

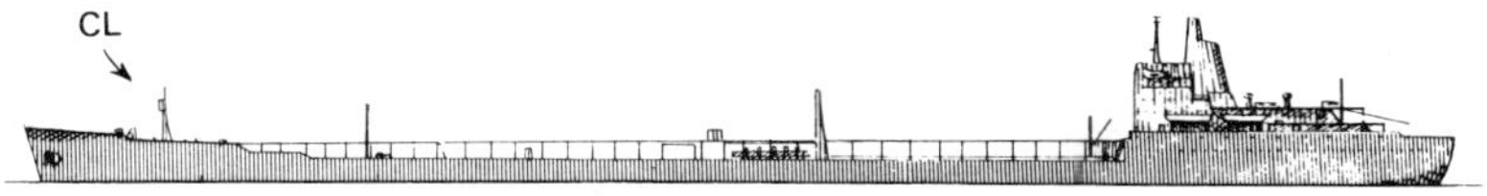

K_3MFK H13

● **60540 ZACHARIA T.** Gr/Sw 1965; Tk; 34500; 236.25 × 12.66 (775.1 × 41.54); M; 17; ex ZACHARIA TSIRLIS 1979; ex PATRIOTIC COLOCOTRONIS 1976; ex TANK COUNTESS 1969. Sister: **60541 DEVALI 1** (Li) ex AURORE 1978.

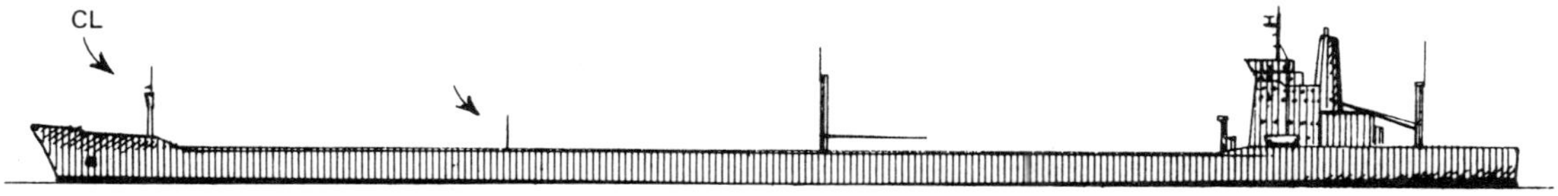

K_3MFK H13

60550 KONG HAAKON VII. No/No 1969; Tk; 109400; 327.72 × 20.42 (1075.2 × 66.99); T; 16. Sisters (No flag): **60551 AURELIAN 60552 HADRIAN 60553 NERVA 60554 OCTAVIAN.**

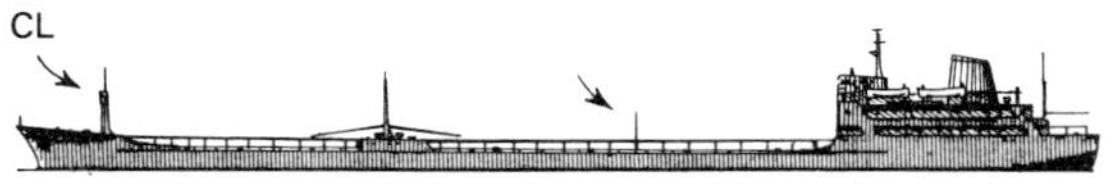

K_3MFK H13

60560 GLOBE NOVA. Li/No 1964; Tk/LGC; 13500; 169.78 × 9.6 (557.02 × 31.5); M; 15.75; ex GRANHEIM 1978.

● 60565

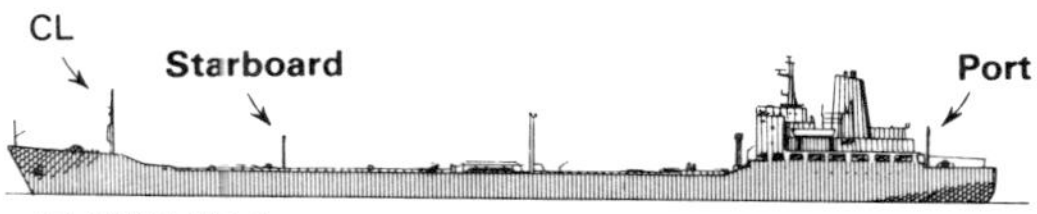

K_3MFK H13

60570 ESSO PORT JEROME. Fr/Ja 1972; Tk; 12800; 161.02 × 9.76 (528.28 × 32.02); M; 15; ex ESSO KUMAMOTO 1980; **'22'** type. Some others in this class may have this sequence.

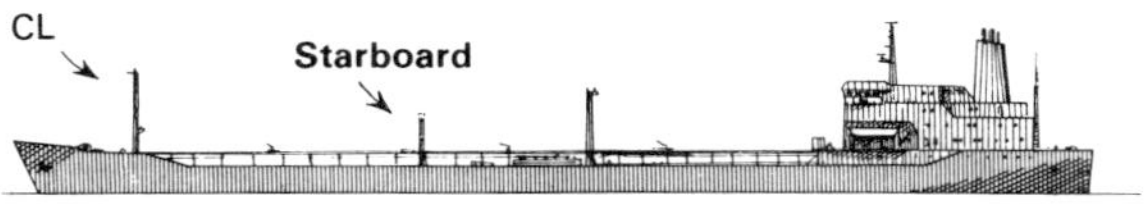

K_3MFK H13

60580 JUPITER. Li/Sw 1975; Tk; 18300; 170.77 × 11.35 (560.27 × 37.24); M; 16. Sisters: **60581 MERCURY** (Li) **60582 NEZLA** (Ag) ex SCAPTRUST 1976 **60583 HAOUD L'HAMRA** (Ag) ex SCAPMARINER 1976.

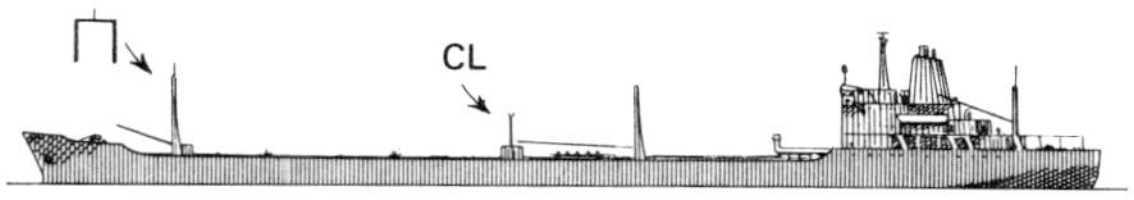

K_3MFK H13

● **60590 STAKARA.** Gr/Ja 1970; Tk; 17500; 170.82 × 11.01 (560.43 × 36.12); M; 16. Sisters (Gr flag): **60591 STABENKO 60592 STAMENIS 60593 STAWANDA 60594 MESSINIAKI AIGLI 60595 MESSINIAKI ARETI 60596 MESSINIAKI ANAGENNISIS 60597 MESSINIAKI BERGEN 60598 MESSINIAKI GI 60599 MESSINIAKI IDEA 60600 MESSINIAKI MINDE 60601 MESSINIAKI ORMI 60602 MESSINIAKI PARADIS 60603 MESSINIAKI PNOI 60604 MESSINIAKI CHARA 60605 MESSINIAKI THEA** (Li flag): **60606 MESSINIAKI LAMPSIS 60607 MESSINIAKI TIMI.**

K_3MFK H13

60610 BUNGA KESUMBA. My/Ja 1975; Tk; 19000; 170.01 × 11.15 (557.78 × 36.58); M; 15.25. Sisters (My flag): **60611 BUNGA SELASIH 60612 BUNGA SEPANG.**

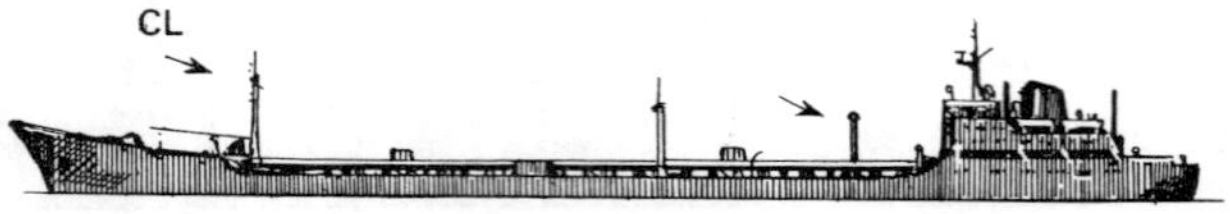

K_3MFK H13

★60620 DAUGAVPILS. Ru/Ys 1965; Tk; 15100; 186.21 × 9.84 (610.93 × 32.28); M; 17. Sisters (Ru flag): **★60621 GRIGORIY ACHKANOV ★60622 SPLIT ★60623 GORI ★60624 VASILIY PORIK ★60625 GENERAL ZHDANOV ★60626 MARSHAL BIRYUZOV ★60627 OLEKO DUNDICH ★60628 PETR ALEKSEYEV ★60629 BORZHOMI ★60630 GENERAL KARBYSHEV ★60631 DMITRIY ZHLOBA ★60632 NIKOLOZ BARATASHVILI ★60633 ERIFAN KOVITYUKH ★60634 MITROFAN SEDIN ★60635 MOS SHOVGENOV ★60636 STEPAN VOSTRETSOV ★60637 PYATIDYESYATILYETIYE SOVETSKOY GRUZII** Also known as **50 LETIYE SOVETSKOY GRUZII ★60638 PAVEL DYBENKO ★60639 REZEKNE ★60640 RIJEKA ★60641 GENERAL BOCHAROV ★60642 GENERAL KRAVTSOV ★60643 GENERAL SHKODUNOVICH ★60644 NIKOLAY PODVOSKIY** (Ag flag): **★60645 SKIKDA** ex KUTAISI 1974 **★60646 ARZEW** ex BATUMI 1974.

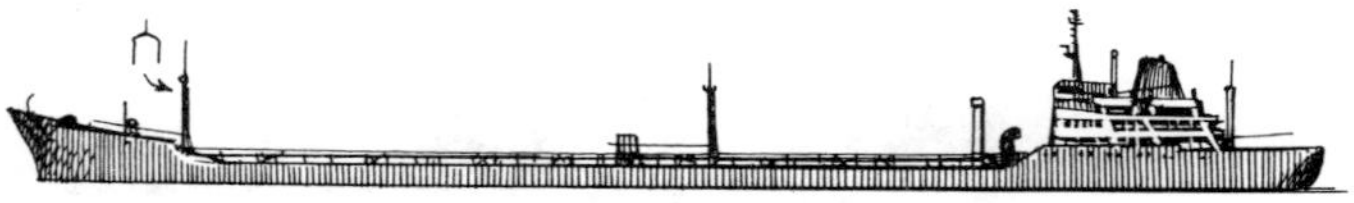

K_3MFK H13

★60660 LUGANSK. Ru/Ja 1962; Tk; 22100; 207.02 × 11.08 (679.2 × 36.35); M; 16.5. Sisters (Ru flag): **★60661 LEBEDIN ★60662 LIKHOSLAVL ★60663 LUBNY ★60664 LENINO ★60665 LYUBLINO ★60666 LYUBERTSY ★60667 LUKHOVITSY** (May be spelt **LUHOVITSY**).

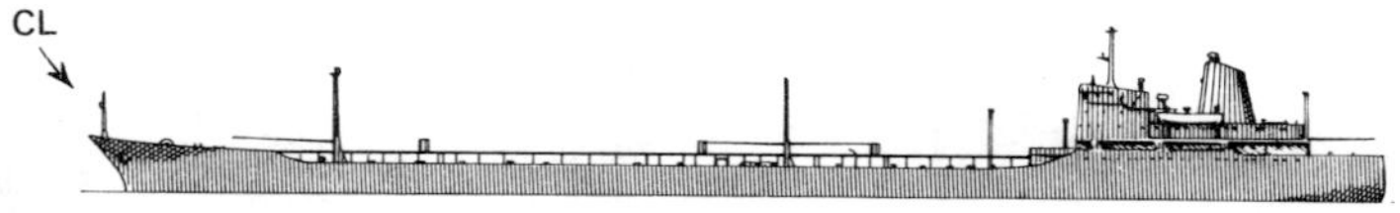

K_3MFK H13

★60670 LISICHANSK. Ru/Ru 1962; Tk; 23100; 207.04 × 11.11 (679.27 × 36.45); M; 16.5; Sisters (Ru flag): **★60671 LENKORAN ★60672 LYUBOTIN.**

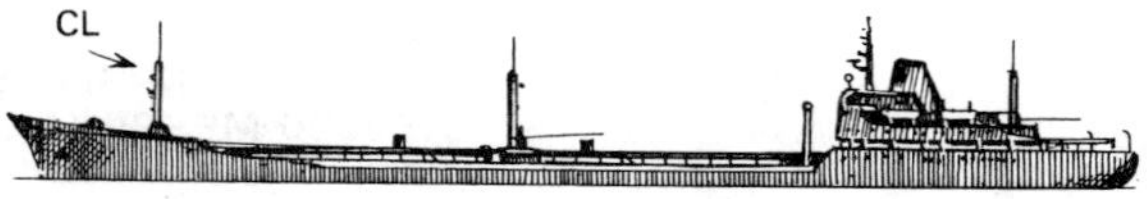

K_3MFK H13

★60680 INTERNATSIONAL. Ru/Pd 1968; Tk; 14200; 177.27 × 9.37 (581.59 × 30.74); M; 16 **'B-72' type** Sisters (Ru flag): **★60681 DRUZHBA ★60682 NARODOV ★60683 ISKRA ★60684 LENINSKOE ZNAMYA ★60685 NAKHODKA ★60686 PROLETARSKAYA POBEDA ★60687 PAMYAT LENINA ★60688 PETR STUCHKA ★60689 ZAVYETY ILYICHA.**

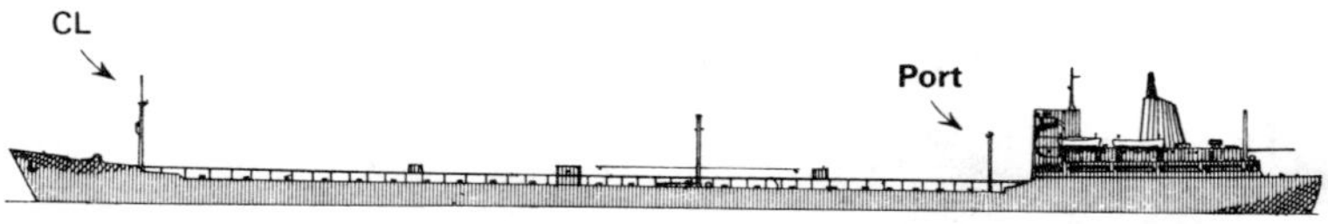

K_3MFK H13

60700 MARIBELLA. Li/Ja 1964; Tk; 38600; 237.8 × 12.7 (780.18 × 41.67); T; 16; ex POLAR LION 1978; ex MOSQUEEN 1975. Sister: **60701 VENTURE OKLAHOMA** (Li) ex TURBINIA 1978; ex ANDKING 1978; ex MOSKING 1976.

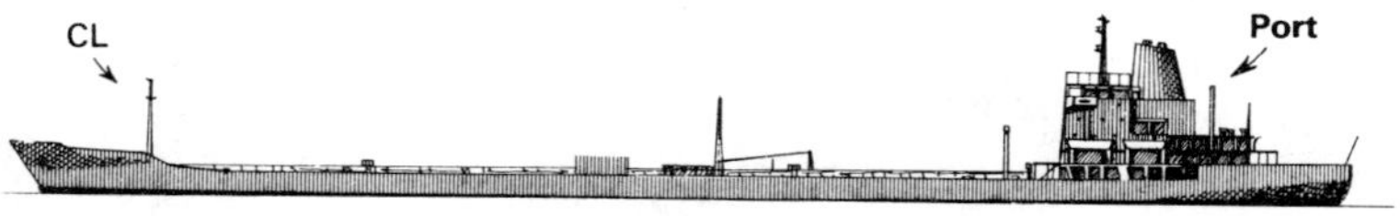

K_3MFK H13

60710 LORD MOUNT STEPHEN. Br/Ja 1966; Tk; 41500; 231.02 × 13.13 (757.94 × 43.08); M; 16.25. Sister: **60711 LORD STRATHCONA** (Br).

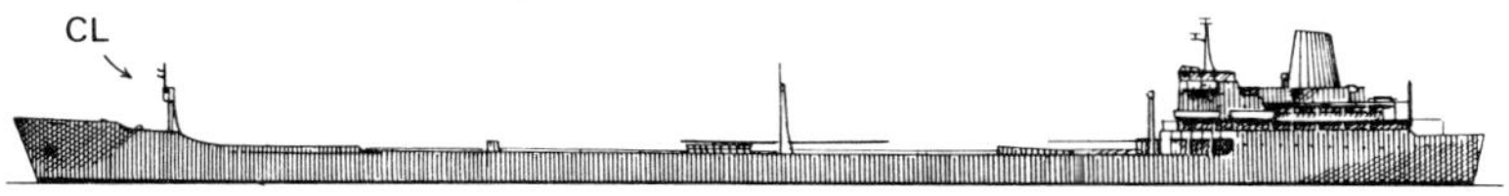

K_3MFK H13
★**60720 TAI HU.** RC/Sw 1965; Tk; 41000; 239.28 × 12.74 (785.04 × 41.8); M; 16; ex BEAUREGARD 1974. Sisters: **60721 KATHERINE ALEXANDRA** (Gr) ex BEAUFORT 1978 ★**60722 GAO HU** (RC) ex BEAUMONT 1974 ★**60723 BAO HU** (RC) ex JOHN KNUDSEN Similar: ★**60724 DA QING NO 252** (RC) ex ZHEN HU 1978; ex ANNA KNUDSEN 1975 ★**60725 STRUMA** (Bu) ex THELMA 1972 **60726 FOTINI** (Gr) ex JANE STOVE 1973; ex TANK REGINA 1970 **60727 ALNAIR II** (Li) ex IDDI 1977 **60728 BURMAH SPAR** (Li) ex SAGA SKY 1974 **60729 KWAI** (Sg) ex AXEL BROSTROM Similar (higher superstructure) **60730 VIGNEMALE** (Fr) ex BOURGOGNE 1975; ex NYHOLM 1969.

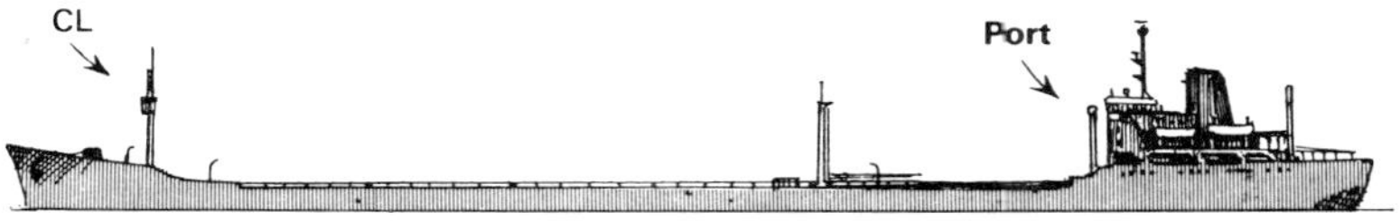

K_3MFK H13
60740 DIANE. Li/Ja 1965; Tk; 35900; 236.2 × 12.38 (774.93 × 40.62); M; 16.5. Sister: **60741 LEOPARDIS** (Pa) ex LEON 1979.

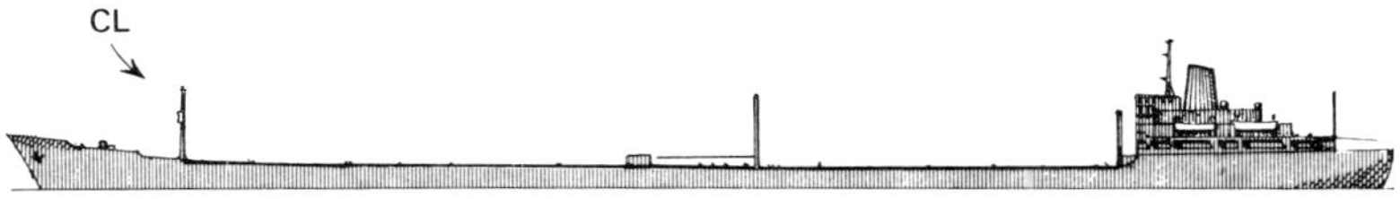

K_3MFK H13
60750 ORIENTAL CONFIDENCE. Li/Ja 1966; Tk; 42700; 243.82 × 13.28 (799.93 × 43.57); M; 16.25; ex PACIFIC GLORY 1972.

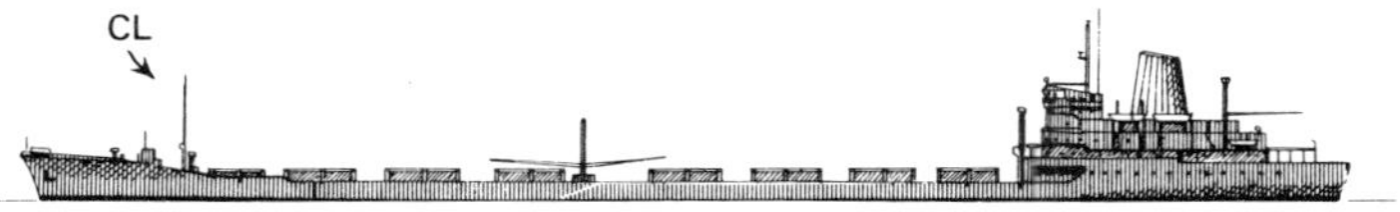

K_3MFK H13
● **60760 TRADE ENDEAVOR.** Gr/FRG 1961; OO; 16600 (ore) 24500 (oil); 210.29 × 11.06 (689.93 × 36.29); T; 15.75; ex ELISABETH ENTZ 1971.

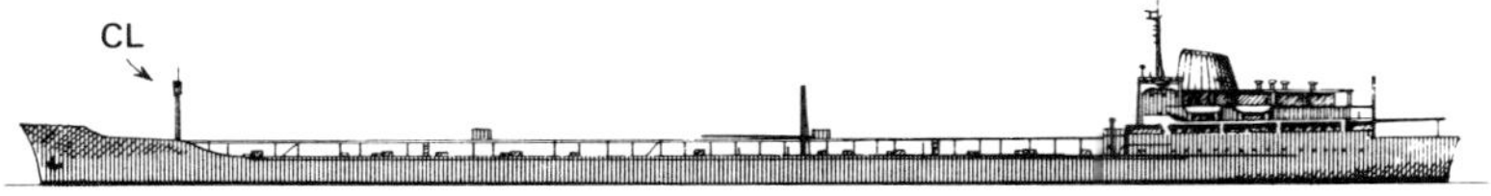

K_3MFK H13
60770 HASSAN B. Pa/Sw 1964; Tk; 35400; 236.13 × 12.82 (774.71 × 42.06); M; 16; ex ATHELKING 1977. Sister: **60771 KIMOLOS** (Gr) ex WILL ADAMS 1980; ex ATHELREGENT 1977.

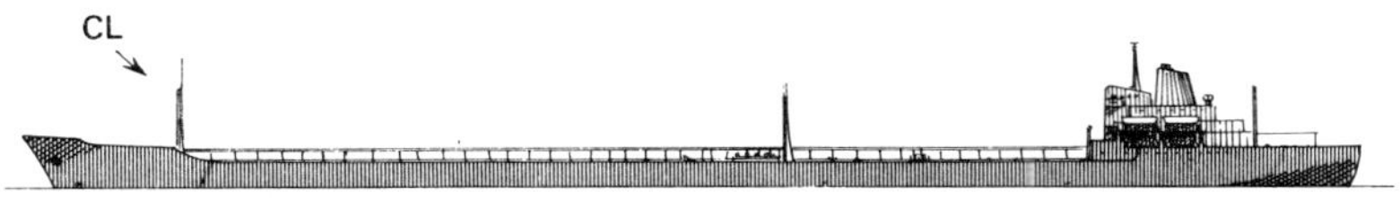

K_3MFK H13
60780 TRADE FORTITUDE. Gr/Ja 1963; Tk; 31200; 235.62 × 12.57 (773.03 × 41.24); M; 17.25; ex MAGNA 1972.

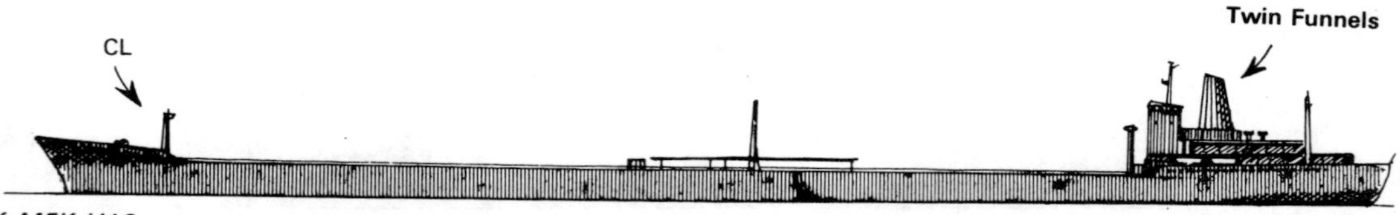

K_3MFK H13

● **60790 ENERGY ENDURANCE.** Li/Ja 1967; Tk; 103200; 324.72 × 18.64 (1065.35 × 61.15); M; 15.75; ex BERGEHUS. Sister: **60791 BERGE COMMANDER** (No).

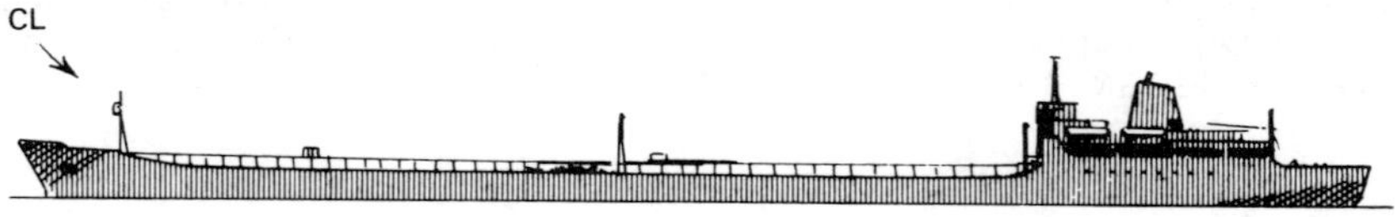

K_3MFK H13

⋆**60800 LUTZKENDORF.** DDR/No 1965; Tk; 46400; 249.03 × 13.38 (817.03 × 43.9); M; 16; ex SONJA 1974.

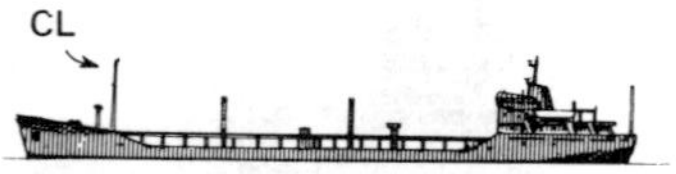

K_3MFK H13

60810 PASS OF BRANDER. Br/Br 1975; Ch; 2500; 97.52 × 6.2 (329.95 × 20.35); M; 15. Similar: **60811 PASS OF BALMAHA** (Br).

K_3MFK H13

60820 AL KHLOOD. Si/FRG 1973; Ch; 4500; 113.14 × 7.41 (371.19 × 24.31); M; 14; ex SILVERPELERIN 1980.

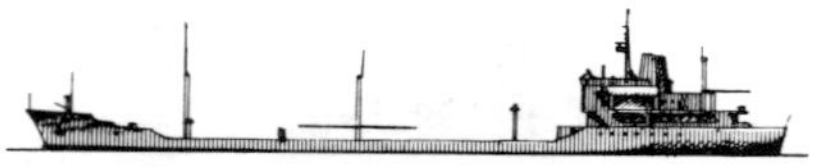

K_3MFK H13

60830 UM EL FAROUD. Ly/Br 1969; Ch; 3100; 109.56 × 6.41 (359.45 × 21.03); M; 14; ex SEAFALCON 1973. Sister: **60831 STORNA** (Li) ex SEATERN 1975.

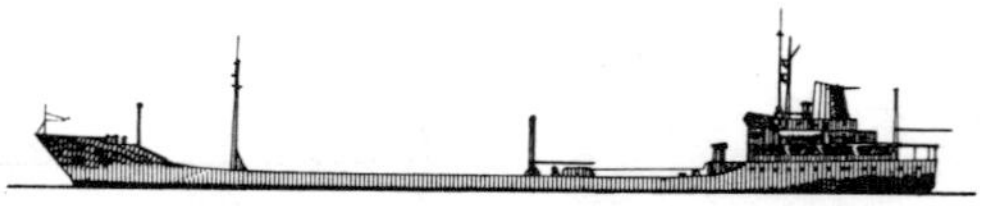

K_3MFK H13

60840 PERMINA 109. Ia/It 1973; Tk; 7700; 140.21 × 7.9 (460.01 × 25.92); M; 15; ex DONNA GABRIELLA 1974. Sister: **60841 ELISA d'ALESIO** (It) ex DONNA MARIELLA.

K_3MFK H13

60850 PRESIDENT DELCOURT. Fr/Fr 1972; Ch; 6000; 125.46 × 7.75 (411.61 × 25.43); M; 17.

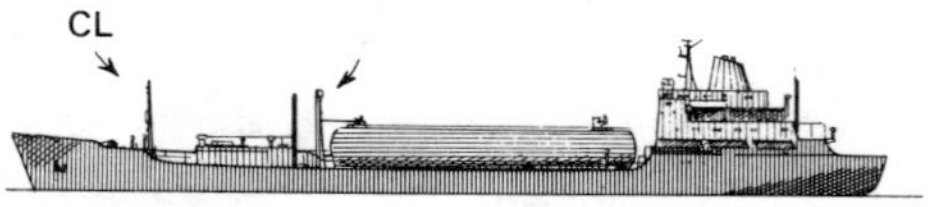

K_3MFK H13

60860 INGE MAERSK. De/No 1972; LGC/Ch; 9200; 138.74 × 9.21 (455.18 × 30.22); M; 17. Sister: **60861 FERNWAVE** (Li) Similar (smaller) (No flag): **60862 HARDANGER 60863 BOW ELM** (No) Similar (later built): **60864 SOFIE MAERSK** (De) **60865 SINE MAERSK** (De) **60866 HESPERUS** (No) ex FERNBROOK 1978.

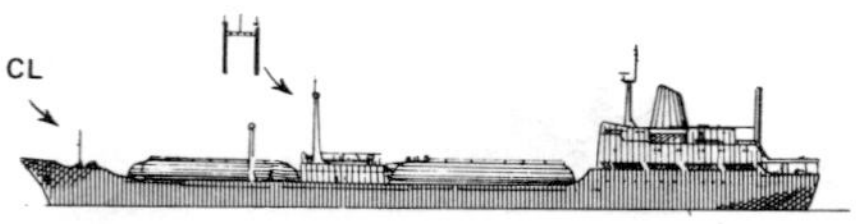

K_3MFK H13

60870 BERNARDO HOUSSAY. Ar/Fr 1969; LGC; 6900; 126.22 × 7.32 (414.11 × 24.02); M; 16; ex BARFONN 1979.

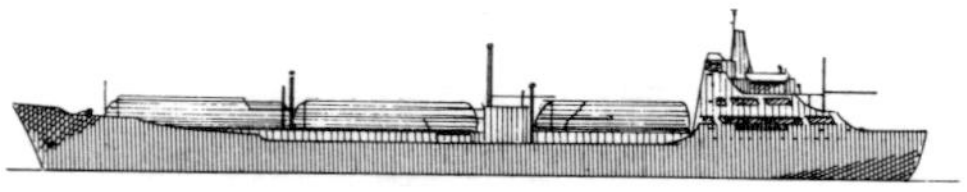

K_3MFK H13

● **60880 ANG PANGARAP.** Li/Fr 1963/65; LGC; 8000; 145.01 × 8.38 (475.75 × 27.49); M; 15; ex RYE GAS; ex CRYSTAL 1977; ex CAP MARTIN 1975; ex SAVOIE 1965; Converted from ore carrier 1965.

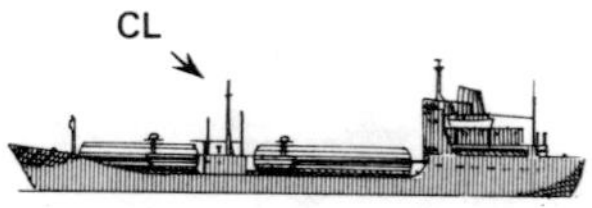

K_3MFK H13

60890 GAZ PROGRESS. Pa/No 1966; LGC; 2700; 90.56 × 6.03 (297.11 × 19.78); M; 12.25; ex CORAL OBELIA 1979; ex ARCTIC PROPANE 1971.

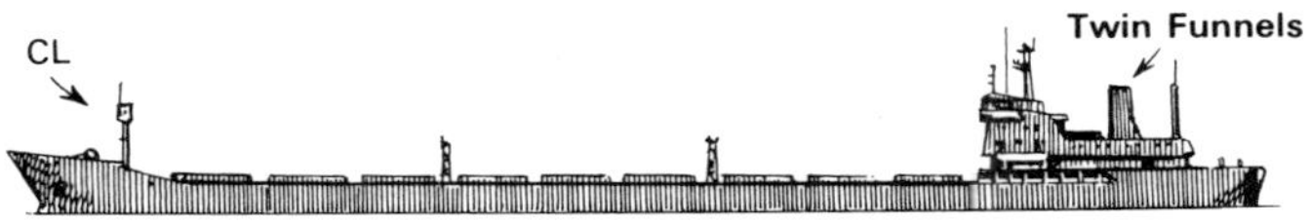

K_3MFK H13
⋆**60900 GEORGIY LEONIDZE.** Ru/Pd 1974; B; 20300; 202.34 × 10.64 (663.85 × 34.91); M; 15; **'B 447'** type. Sister: ⋆**60901 GENERAL LESELIDZE** (Ru).

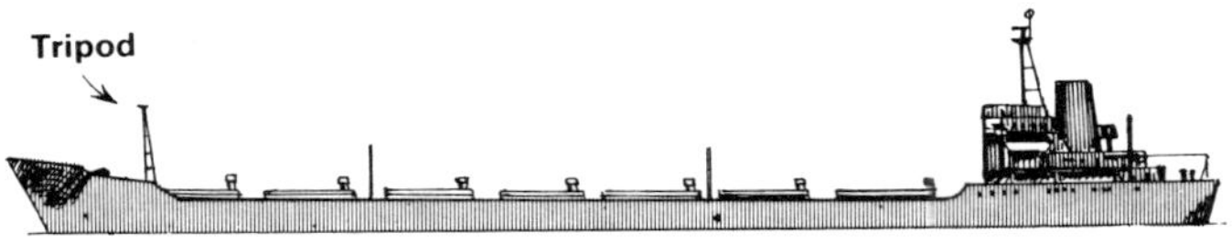

K_3MFK H13
● **60910 KING CHARLES.** Br/Sp 1974; B; 30300; 206.76 × 13.28 (678.35 × 43.57); M; 15.25. Similar: **60911 GARTHNEWYDD** (Br).

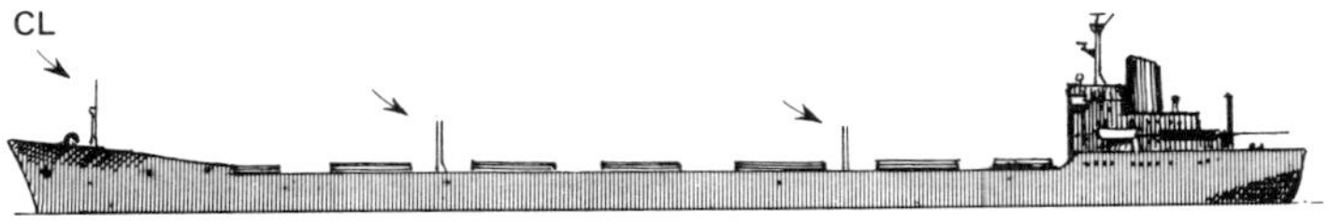

K_3MFK H13
60920 LEDA. Gr/Br 1968; B; 28900; 218.35 × 12.56 (716.37 × 41.21); M; 15.5; ex RIPON GRANGE 1980; ex OROTAVA 1979; ex OROTAVA BRIDGE 1974; ex OROTAVA 1969.

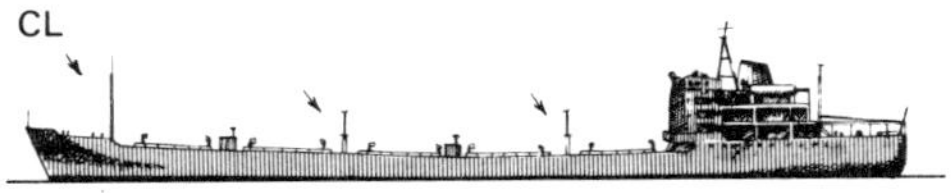

K_3MFK H13
● **60930 GUNGNIR V.** Pa/Au 1957; B; 7300; 142.7 × 8.3 (468.18 × 27.23); M; 11.75; ex LAKE; ex LAKE BOGA 1978. Sisters: **60931 AL TOOS** (Li) ex LAKE SORELL 1980 **60932 AL TASLIM** (Sg) ex LAKE MACQUAIRE 1978.

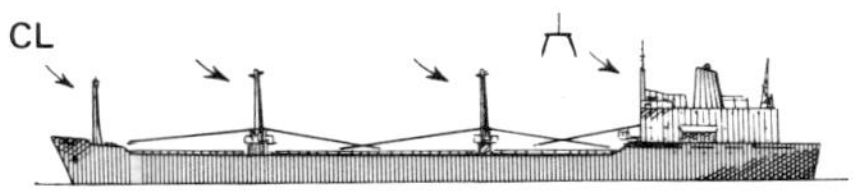

K_3MFK H13
60940 ROEBUCK. Br/Ko 1976; B; 6800; 125 × 7.56 (410.1 × 24.8); M; 14.25. Sisters (Br flag): **60941 RAVENSWOOD 60942 RIVERINA** (Br).

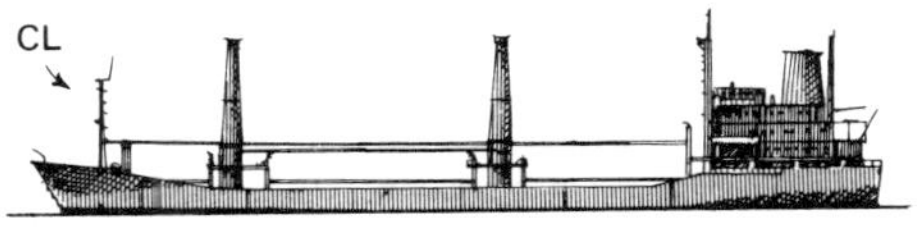

K_3MFK H13
● **60950 GHADAMES.** Ag/Ja 1977; C; 8600; 136.38 × 8.33 (447.44 × 27.33); M; 18; ex JENNY PORR 1977. Sisters: **60951 KITTY PORR** (Sg) **60952 KASSANTINA** (Ly) Possible Sisters: **60953 HENRIETTE SCHULTE** (FRG) **60954 LLOYD VIRGINIA** (Cy) ex WILHELM SCHULTE 1980; ex CONCORDIA HAWK 1980; ex WILHELM SCHULTE 1979 **60955 RENATE SCHULTE** (FRG) Similar: **60956 REGINA** (Sd).

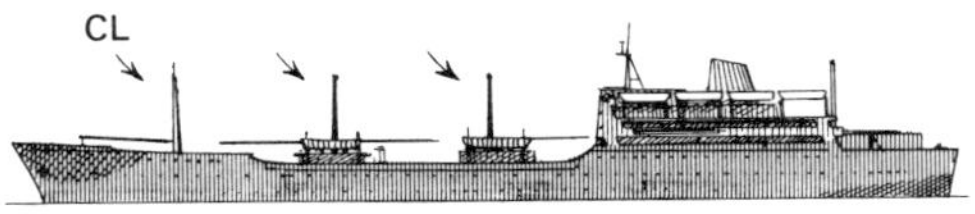

K_3MFK H13
60960 AKBAR. In/No 1971; P/C; 8300; 149.51 × 7.71 (490.52 × 25.29); M; 18.5.

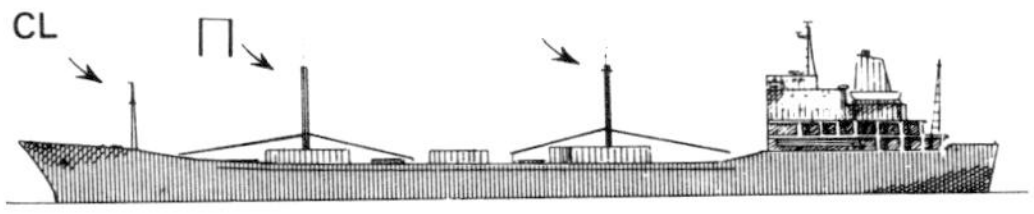

K_3MFK H13
60970 TAISEI MARU No 98. Ja/Ja 1977; FC; 9700; 155 × 8.22 (508.53 × 26.97); M; 19.

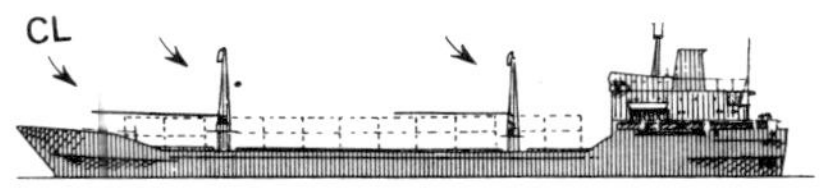

K_3MFK H13
60980 URANUS I. FRG/FRG 1977; C/Con; 3600/6700; 131.71 × 6.35/8.03 (432.12 × 20.83/26.35); M; 15.25; ex DIPLOMAT 1978; ex URANUS 1977.

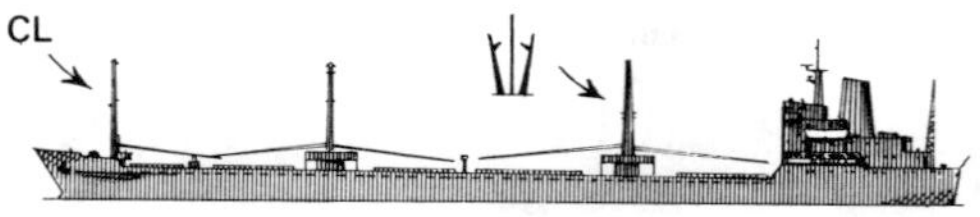

K₃MFK H13
60990 TARPON SANTIAGO. Gr/Ja 1978; C/HL; 7500/11600; 146.01 × —/9.51 (479.04 × —/31.2); M; 14.5.

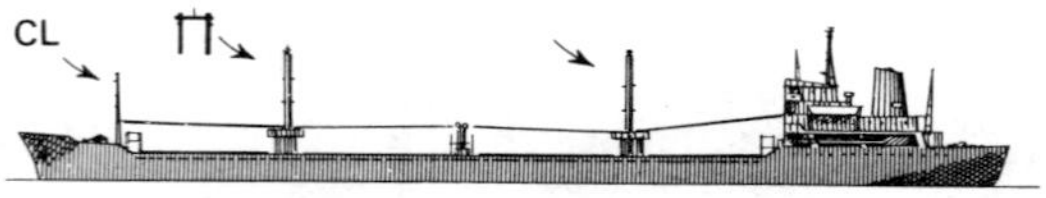

K₃MFK H13
● **61010 SANAGA.** Sg/Ja 1971; B; 12100; 156.17 × 9.29 (512.37 × 30.48); M; 15; ex WOERMANN SANAGA 1976. Sisters: **61011 HUDSON DEEP** (Sg) ex WOERMANN SASSANDRA **61012 THEANO** (Gr) ex WOERMANN UBANGI 1980 **61013 SANKURU** (Pa) ex WOERMANN SANKURU 1976 **61014 SWAKOP** (Sg) ex MARITIME COURIER 1978; ex SWAKOP 1976 **61015 ZAMBESI** (Pa) ex MARITIME TRANSPORTER 1978; ex WOERMANN SAMBESI 1976 **61016 SAN PEDRO** (Pa) launched as WOERMANN SAN PEDRO Similar: **61017 MARITIME VICTOR** (Pa) **61018 TRANSOCEAN RAM** (Pi) ex VAN WARRIOR 1980 **61019 ANGEATLANTIC** (Gr) ex VAN HAWK **61020 CALYPSO N** (Gr) ex MARINER 1978; ex EASTERN CHERRY 1980 **61021 STEPHANOS** (Gr) ex MERLIN 1980; ex EASTERN MARY **61022 WORLD HERCULES** (Ja) **61023 ZINI** (Gr) **61024 GEORTINA** (Gr) Possibly Similar: **61025 ISLAND SKY** (Li) **61026 ANGEARCTIC** (Gr) ex WORLD CHAMPION **61027 UNITED PRIDE** (Li) ex WORLD PRIDE 1981 **61028 GOLDEN EXPLORER** (Li) **61029 GOLDEN PIONEER** (Li) Similar (Ko built): **61030 PAN KOREA** (Ko) Possibly Similar (Ko built): **61031 KOREAN PRIDE** (Li) **61032 KOREAN FIR** (Li) **61033 CATHERINE ANN** (Li) ex GLORY RIVER 1980 **61034 REBECCA ELYSE** (Li) ex GREAT RIVER 1980 **61035 AKTION** (Gr) **61036 ALKAIOS** (Gr).

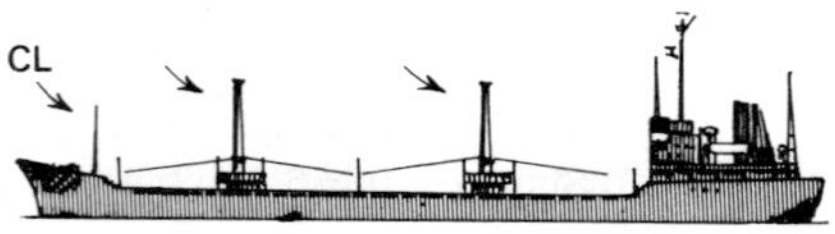

K₃MFK H13
● **61070 ORIENT FISHER.** Pa/Ja 1974; Cem; 6600; 127.77 × 8.25 (419.19 × 27.07); M; 13.25; ex UNION AMSTERDAM 1980; ex ORIENTAL VICTORY 1977. Sisters: ⋆**61071 QINLING** (RC) ex MYOKEN MARU 1975 **61072 HAND LOONG** (Pa) **61073 HAND FORTUNE** (Pa) Possible Sisters: **61074 CHERRYFIELD** (Li) **61075 SEVEN DAFFODIL** (Pa) ex GEORGIA MERRY 1978; ex SUN DENEB 1977 **61076 JELAU** (Pa) ex AKITAKA MARU 1978 **61077 EVANGELOS D** (Pa) ex SUN SIRIUS; ex KORYU MARU 1975 **61078 GOLDEN DRAGON** (Pa) **61079 SHUWA MARU** (Ja) **61080 HAUDA BEAUTY** (Cy) ex YANCEY **61081 SUN ORION** (Pa) **61082 HILARY B** (Sg) ex BLUE JUPITER 1977 **61083 NATIONAL STEEL FOUR** (Pi) ex YU-LIN 1978 **61084 SWEELEAN** (Ja) ex LUSTY 1979.

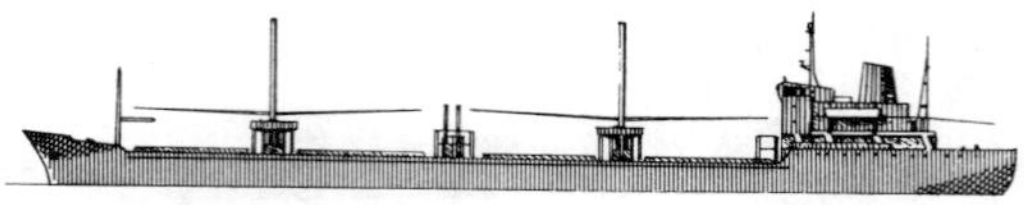

K₃MFK H13
61000 ROSANA. Gr/Ja 1978; B; 11300; 156.24 × 9.5 (512.6 × 31.17); M; 15.5. Pssibly Similar: **61001 YOUNG STATESMAN** (Li) **61002 PROVIDENCE** (Ja).

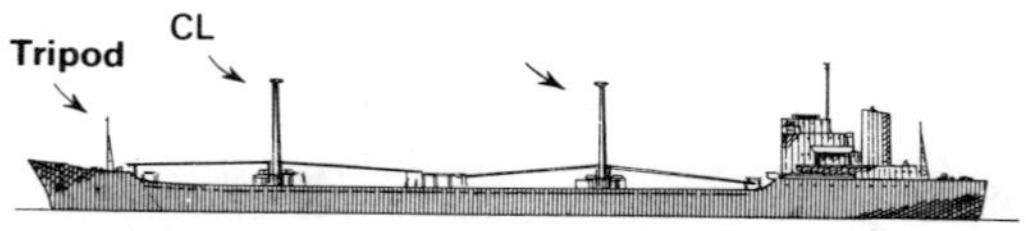

K₃MFK H13
61040 ARCHIMEDES. Gr/Ja 1970; B; 10500; 154.34 × 9.18 (506.36 × 30.12); M; 15; ex HAE DUCK No 3 1980; ex FEDERAL YODO 1979. Sister: **61041 ALMAR** (Gr) ex FEDERAL MACKENZIE.

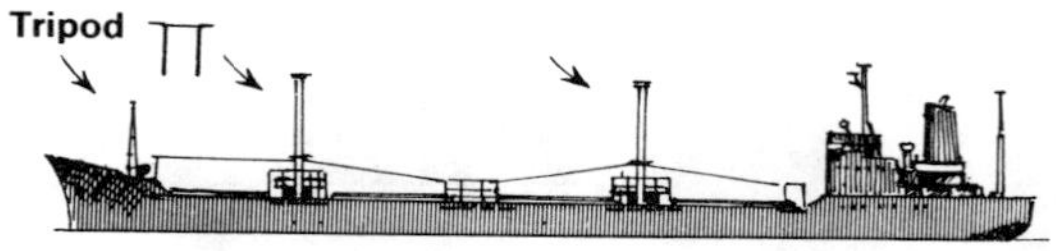

● 61045

K₃MFK H13
61050 IRENES ECSTACY. Gr/Ja 1969; B; 10300; 154.05 × 9.19 (505.41 × 30.15); M; 14.75; ex MIDAS ARROW; ex NAGATO MARU 1971. Sister: **61051 NIKOS N** (Gr) ex DONA JUANA 1979; ex RETLADAWN 1979; ex OVERSEAS NAVIGATOR 1975; ex HAIKO MARU 1973 Possible Sisters: **61052 NIKOLAOS A** (Gr) ex MIDAS PRINCE; ex ORIENTAL PRINCE 1971; ex YAMATO MARU 1970 **61053 MIDAS RHEIN** (Li) ex RHEIN MARU 1972 **61054 MONTROSE** (Li).

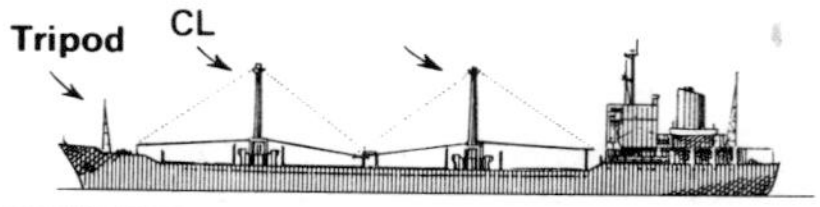

● 61055

K₃MFK H13
61060 GOMASA. Gr/Ja 1971; C; 4700; 114.2 × 7.04 (374.67 × 23.1); M; 13; ex KISSHU MARU 1975. Possible Sisters: **61061 PETRELO** (Pa) ex TOFUKU MARU 1977 **61062 ZIRIA** (Gr) ex TOJU MARU 1975.

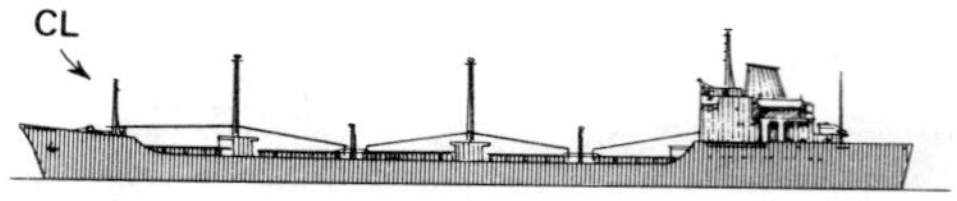

K₃MFK H13
⋆**61090 KOPALNIA MOSZCZENICA.** Pd/De 1968; B; 8400; 141.71 × 8.2 (464.93 × 26.9); M; 15.25. Sisters (Pd flag): ⋆**61091 KOPALNIA KLEOFAS** ⋆**61092 KOPALNIA MARCEL** ⋆**61093 KOPALNIA SOSNICA** ⋆**61094 KOPALNIA SZCZYGLOWICE** ⋆**61096 KOPALNIA WIREK** ⋆**61096 GLIWICE II.**

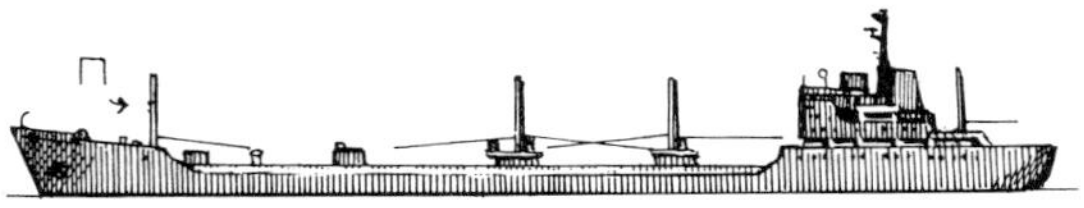

K_3MFK H13
⋆**61100 RIZHSKIY ZALIV**. Ru/Fr 1969; FC; 12900; 164.62 × 7.01 (540.09 × 23); M; 17.5. Sisters (Ru flag): ⋆**61101 AMURSKIY ZALIV** ⋆**61102 BOTNICHESKIY ZALIV** ⋆**61103 DVINSKIY ZALIV** ⋆**61104 FINSKIY ZALIV** ⋆**61105 KANDALAKSHSKIY ZALIV** ⋆**61106 NARVSKIY ZALIV** ⋆**61107 ONEZHSKIY ZALIV** ⋆**61108 TAGANROGSKIY ZALIV** ⋆**61109 USSURIYSKIY ZALIV**.

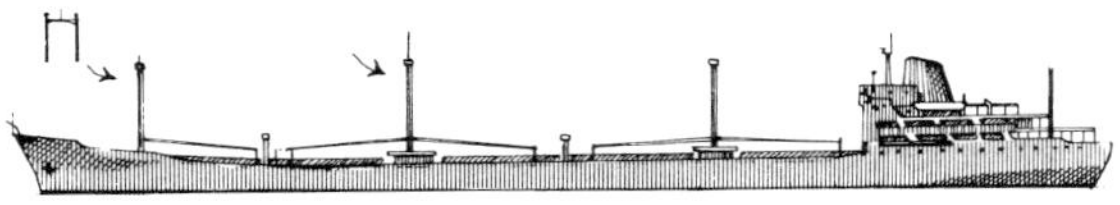

K_3MFK H13
61140 EOLIA. It/It 1964; B; 10600; 160.1 9.6 (525.26 × 31.5); M; 16. Probably similar: **61141 ILICE** (It) **61142 ORFEO** (It).

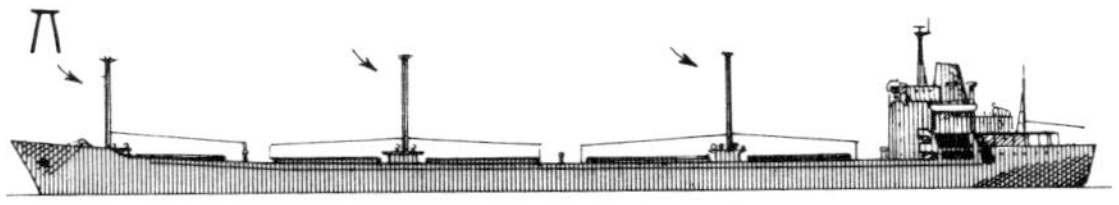

K_3MFK H13
61160 GOLDEN TENNYO. Gr/Ja 1977; B; 14500; 172.27 × 9.78 (565.19 × 32.09); M; 15. Sisters (Gr flag): **61161 GOLDEN CHASE 61162 GOLDEN HORIZON 61163 GOLDEN PANAGIA 61164 GOLDEN SHIMIZU 61165 POLYTROPOS** Similar: **61166 GOLDEN CHARIOT 61167 GOLDEN CROWN 61168 GOLDEN SPEAR 61169 GOLDEN SWORD**.

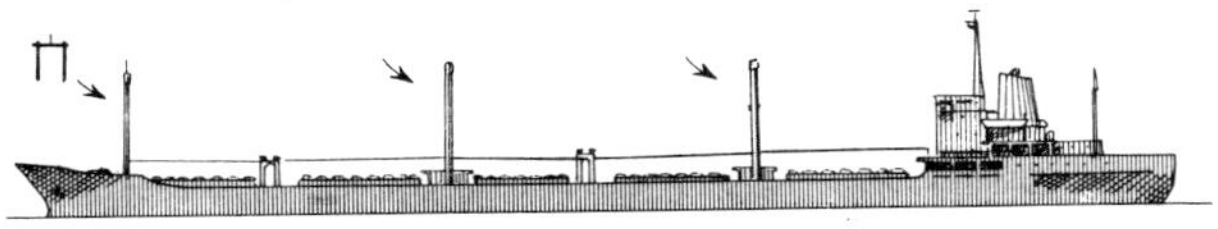

K_3MFK H13
● **61190 TOXOTIS**. Gr/Ja 1974; B; 19200; 182.2 × 10.92 (597.77 × 35.83); M; 16. Sisters: **61191 DIDYMI** (Gr) **61192 HYDROMOS** (Gr) **61193 ZYGOS** (Gr) Similar: ⋆**61194 NOVA GORICA** (Ys) **61195 BUFFALO** (Ko) ex CORAL ARCADIA 1978; ex CASCADE MARU 1973 Possibly Similar: **61196 MAMMOTH FIR** (Li) **61197 MOMMOTH PINE** (Li) **61198 CISSUS**(Li) ex ZINNIA 1975 **61199 STADION** (Li) **61200 TROPHY** (Pa).

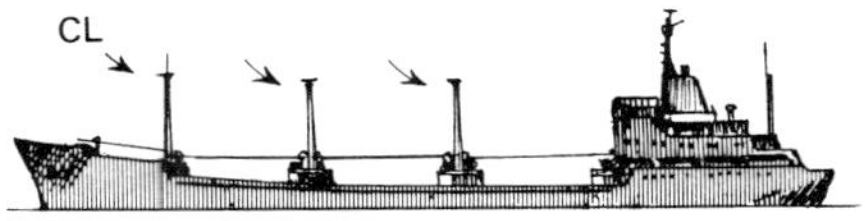

K_3MFK H13
61120 DIAMOND. Li/Ys 1967; C; 5400; 128.96 × 7.42 (423.1 × 24.34); M; —; ex TAMAR 1971. Sister: **61121 RIMON** (Is) ex OPAL 1973; ex RIMON 1970.

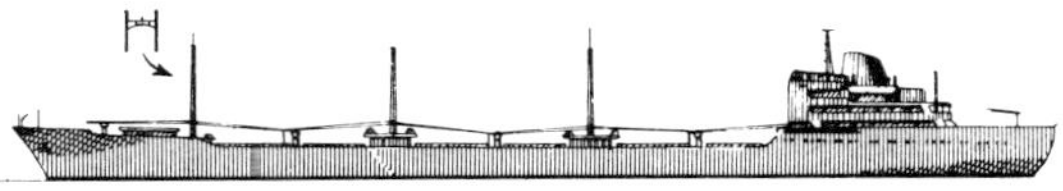

K_3MFK H13
61130 AGNIC II. Gr/FRG 1963; B; 12300; 165.51 × 10.01 (543.01 × 32.84); M; —; ex SKYLARK 1978; ex RIVIERA 1969.

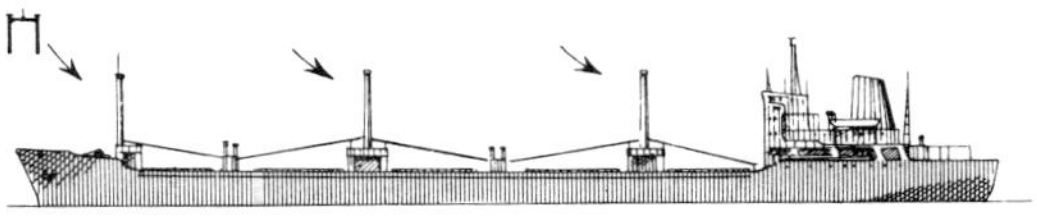

K_3MFK H13
61150 ELEFTHERIOS. Gr/Ja 1966; B; 11300; 156.01 × 9.48 (511.8 × 31.1); M; 15; ex HUDSON BAY; ex TRANSOCEAN TRANSPORT 1977; **'Hitachi Standard 19'** type. Sisters: **61151 FIFTH AVENUE** (Gr) **61152 CORONIA** (Gr) **61153 ALKYONIA** (Gr) **61154 ANDROMACHI** (Gr) ex WILSHIRE BOULEVARD 1976 **61155 ORESTIA** (Gr) **61156 SEA PIONEER** (Li) **61157 ANTIOCHA** (Gr) **61158 OLYNTHIA** (Gr).

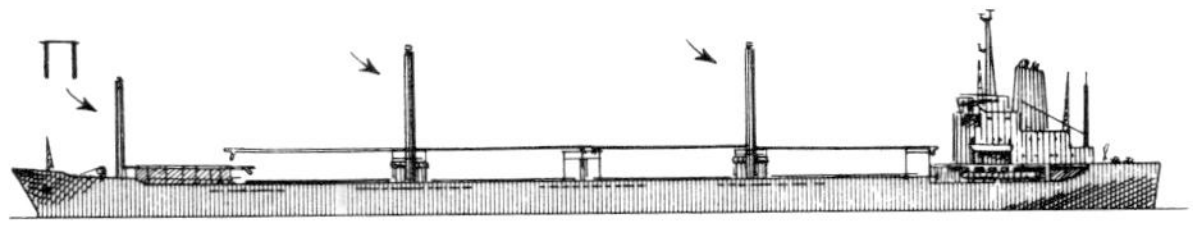

K_3MFK H13
61180 FEDERAL FRASER. Li/Ja 1977; B; 22400; 183.67 × 12 (602.59 × 39.37); M; 15.5. Sister: **61181 FEDERAL SUMIDA** (Li) Similar: **61182 SEINE MARU** (Ja) **61183 THAMES MARU** (Ja) **61184 RHEIN MARU** (Ja) Possibly Similar: **61185 SUIKO MARU** (Ja).

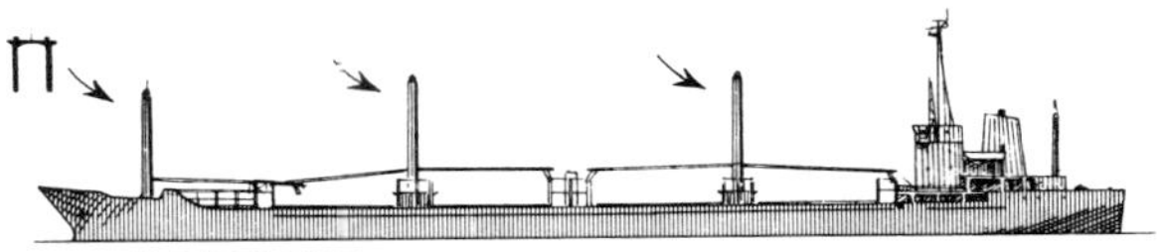

K_3MFK H13
61210 LUCENT STAR. Li/Ja 1977; B; 15400; 175.8 × 9.6 (576.77 × 31.5); M; 14.5. Sisters (Li flag): **61211 BRILLIANT STAR 61212 RADIANT STAR 61213 SHINING STAR 61214 WORLD CANDOUR 61215 WORLD PROBITY** Probable Sisters - may have cranes: **61216 MORNING GLORY 61217 RED ARROW**.

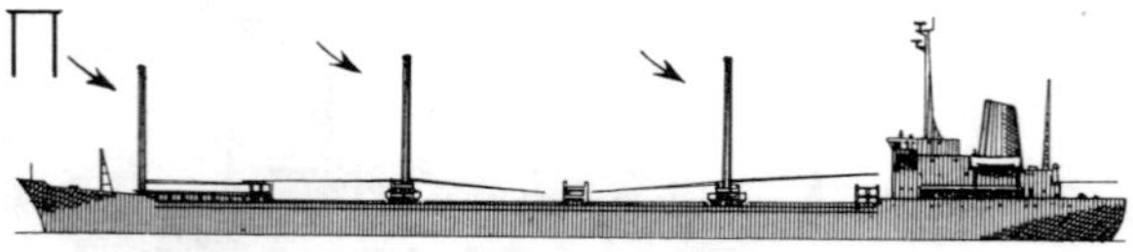

K_3MFK H13
● **61220 OINOUSSIAN DESTINY.** Gr/Ja 1979; B; 19300; 179.91 × 11.26 (590.26 × 36.94); M; 15. Sisters (Gr flag): **61221 OINOUSSIAN FRIENDSHIP 61222 OINOUSSIAN LEADERSHIP 61223 OINOUSSIAN PRESTIGE 61224 OINOUSSIAN VIRTUE.**

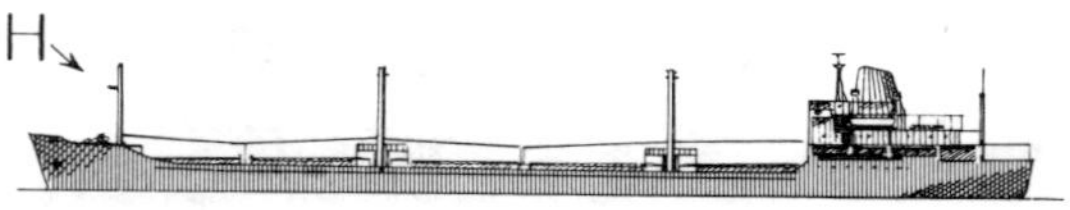

K_3MFK H13
61260 PRABHU SATRAM. In/Br 1969; B; 12300; 158.5 × 9.26 (520.01 × 30.38); M; 14.75; ex ERISORT 1977; ex WORLD PRESIDENT 1974. Sisters: **61261 ANADRIA** (Br) ex ERIBOLL 1977; ex WORLD HONG KONG 1973 **61262 ARGONAVI** (Br) ex SIGANTO A S 1980; ex ERISKAY 1978.

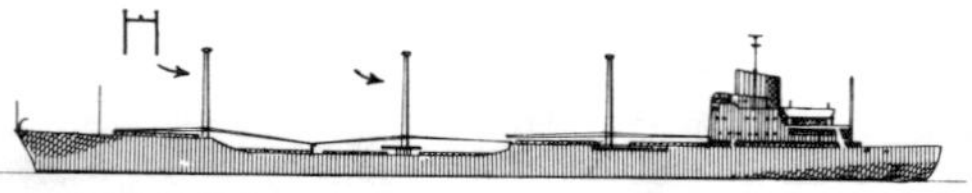

K_3MFK H13
61280 CONSTANCIA. Pa/FRG 1961; C; 8500/11200; 151.21 × 9.06/9.9 (496.1 × 29.72/32.48); M; 15.5; ex CONSTANTIA.

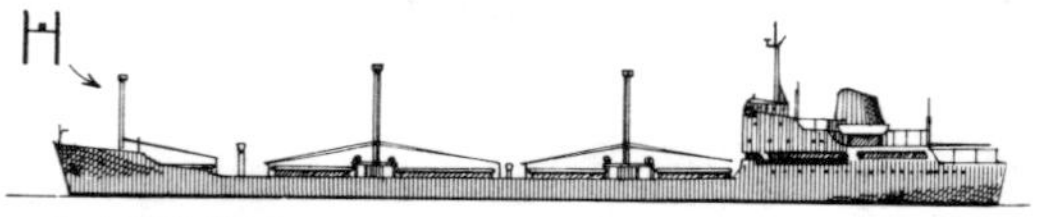

K_3MFK H13
● **61300 CHRISTINA C.** Gr/FRG 1961; C; 10400; 151.19 × 8.98 (496.03 × 29.46); M; 14.75; ex BREIM 1977; ex FRUEN 1965. Similar: **61301 CAPTAIN PAPPIS** (Gr) ex OGOOUE 1976; ex DRACULA 1973; ex RINGULV 1969 **61302 GOLD CORAL** (Gr) ex GOLDCORN 1979; ex JAVARA 1973 **61303 SILVERCORN** (Li) ex JAGONA 1973.

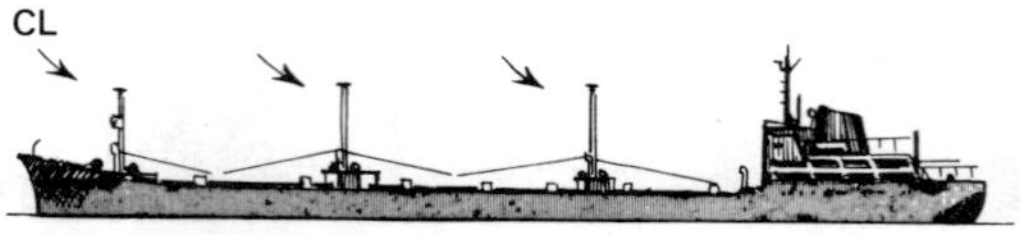

K_3MFK H13
● **61230 MARCOS M F.** Gr/Br 1962; B; 10000; 152.56 × 8.94 (500.52 × 29.33); M; 14; ex BRUNES 1969.

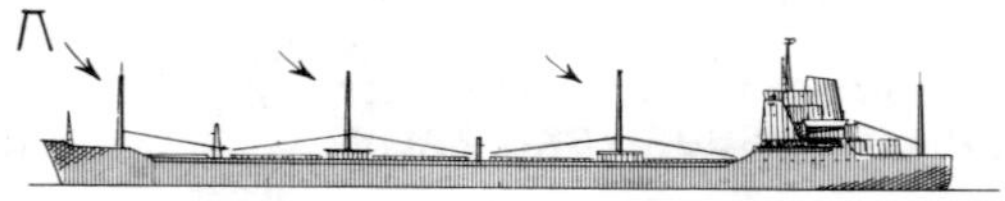

K_3MFK H13
61250 SAN JOHN. Gr/Ja 1967; B; 10300; 147.53 × 9.07 (484.02 × 29.76); M; 15; ex GRAND JUSTICE 1980.

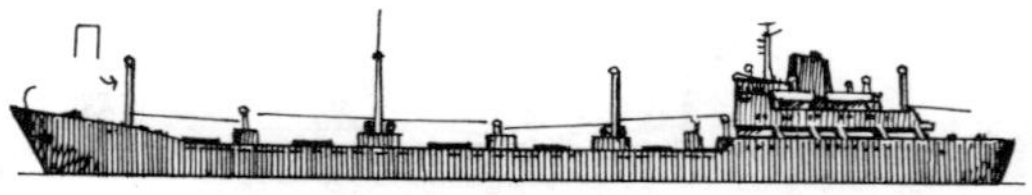

K_3MFK H13
⋆**61270 PRIBOY.** Ru/Sw 1964; FC; 10900; 156.93 × 7.4 (514.86 × 24.28); M; 18.25. Sisters (Ru flag): ⋆**61271 KARL LINNE** ⋆**61272 KHIBINSKIE GORY** ⋆**61273 KRYMSKIE GORY** ⋆**61274 LENINSKIYE GORY** ⋆**61275 URALJSKIE GORY.**

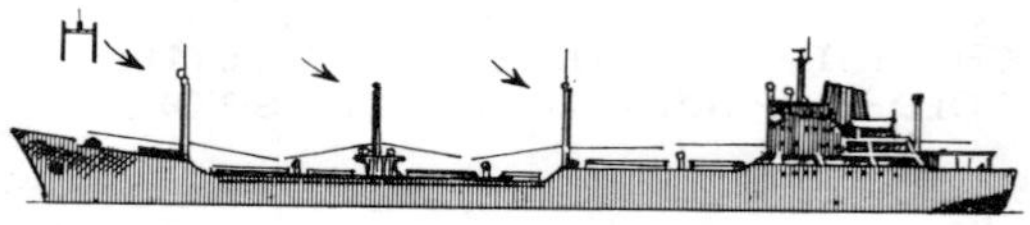

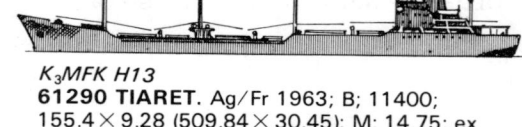

K_3MFK H13
61290 TIARET. Ag/Fr 1963; B; 11400; 155.4 × 9.28 (509.84 × 30.45); M; 14.75; ex ARTHUR STOVE 1972. Similar: **61291 CAPE KAMARI** (Gr) ex KOSTOS M 1978; ex JOHS STOVE 1973; ex BRISSAC 1969 **61292 ALKOR** (Gr) ex TIMUR ENDURANCE 1980; ex LITA 1974; ex SNELAND 1972.

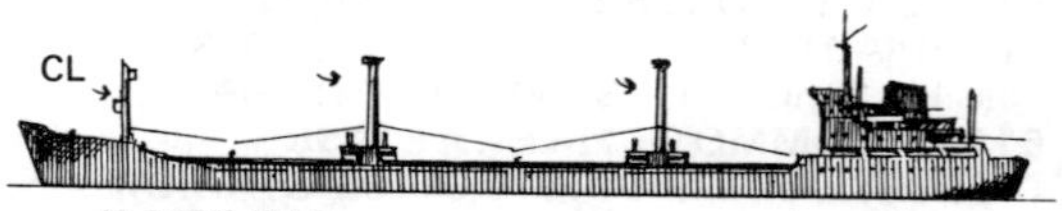

K_3MFK H13
⋆**61310 JING HAI.** RC/Br 1968; B; 12400; 159.06 × 9.47 (521.85 × 31.07); M; 14.75; ex BAYNES 1973. Sisters: **61311 ALBAFORTH** (Gr) ex SILVERFORTH 1978; ex BELLNES 1974 **61312 MARIA LEMOS** (Gr) ex CAPTAIN PANDELIS S LYRAS 1975; ex BIRKNES 1973 **61313 SATYA PADAM** (In) ex BORGNES 1973.

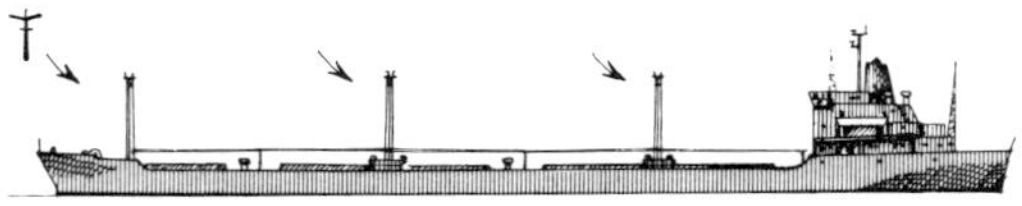

K_3MFK H13
● **61320 SWIFTNES**. Br/Ja 1972; B; 1300; 155.53 × 9.84 (510.27 × 32.28); M; 15.5. Sisters (Br flag): **61321 SALTNES 61322 SEALNES 61323 SPRAYNES 61324 SHARPNES 61325 SURENES**.

K_3MFK H13
61330 SOUNION. Gr/Br 1968; B; 13900; 167.65 × 9.58 (550.03 × 31.43); M; 15.5; ex SUGAR CRYSTAL. Sister: **61331 CAPE AVANTI DUE** (Gr) ex SUGAR PRODUCER Similar (centre line kingposts): **61332 KEFALONIA WIND** (Gr) ex SUGAR TRANSPORTER **61333 KEFALONIA STAR** (Gr) ex SUGAR REFINER.

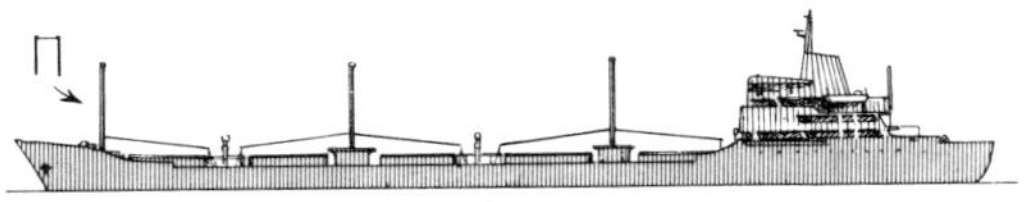

K_3MFK H13
61340 SALAMIS. Gr/Ne 1963; B; 9600; 153.7 × 8.94 (504.27 × 29.33); M; 15; ex CANADIAN FARMER 1980; ex SALAMIS 1976; ex IRISH PLANE 1976. Sister: **61341 PARALOS** (Gr) ex IRISH CEDAR 1976.

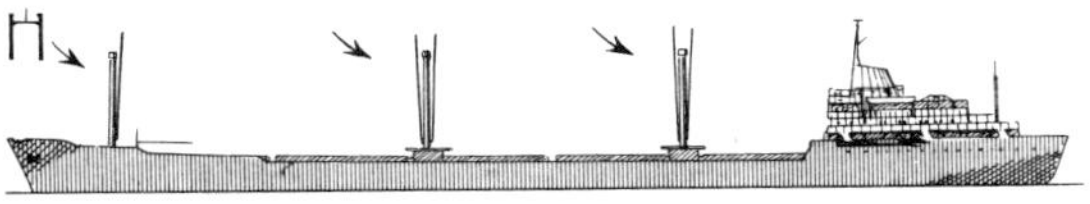

K_3MFK H13
61350 ESPERANZA. Gr/Sw 1963; B; 12800; 167.65 × 10.02 (550.03 × 32.87); M; 15; ex SCOTTISH WASA 1978; ex SCANDIC WASA 1977; ex EVA BRODIN 1971.

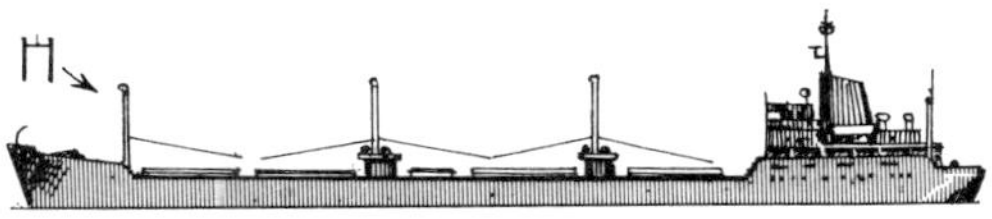

K_3MFK H13
61360 LUGANO. Pa/Br 1968; B; 11100; 154.67 × 9 02 (507.48 × 29.6); M; 14; ex TAMWORTH 1978.

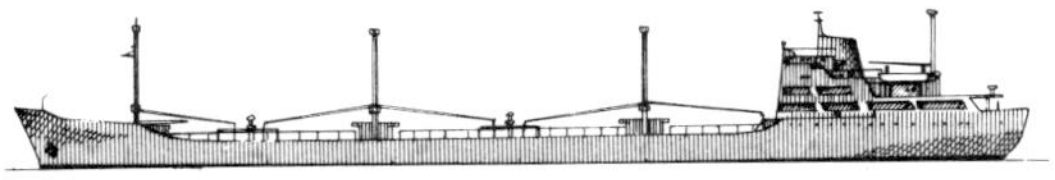

K_3MFK H13
61370 TAI JOHN. Tw/No 1961; B; 11300; 159.65 × 9.75 (523.79 × 31.99); M; 14.5; ex POLYROVER 1968.

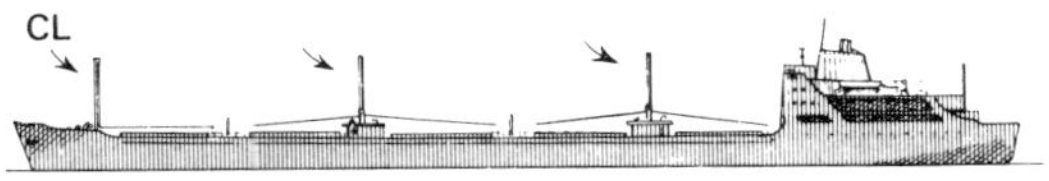

K_3MFK H13
61380 EKTON. Gr/Br 1962; B; 11400; 159.11 × 9.55 (522.01 × 31.33); M; 15; ex BRIDGEPOOL 1975.

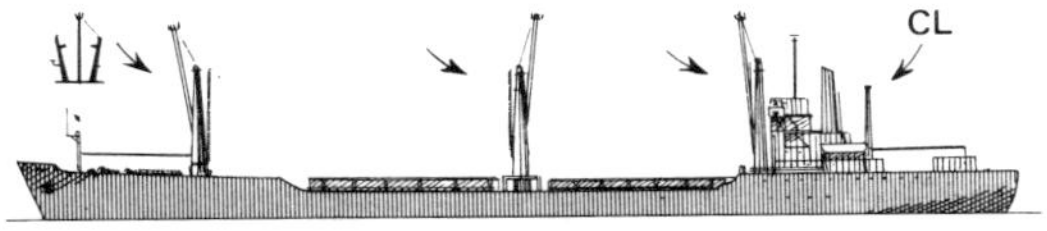

K_3MFK H13
61390 TRANSCOLUMBIA. US/US 1945; C/HL; 12400; 158.5 × 9.88 (520.01 × 32.42); T; 17; ex MARINE LYNX 1967; Converted passenger/troopship. Sister: **61391 TRANSCOLORADO** (US) ex MARINE ADDER 1967.

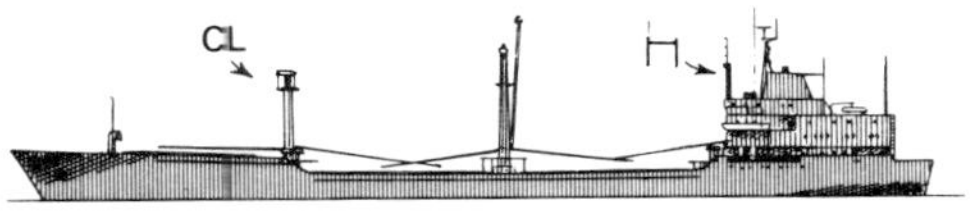

K_3MFK H13
● **61400 DOUCE FRANCE**. Fr/FRG 1977; C; 6600/9800; 150.17 × 7.7/9.07 (492.68 × 25.26/29.76); M; 17; ex BARBARELLA; ex HOEGH APAPA; ex CLAUDIA MARIA; **'Neptun'** type. Similar: **61401 CAM BUBINGA** (Cn) launched as IVORY URANUS **61402 CAM DOUSSIE** (Cn) **61403 IRON BARON** (Br) **61404 IVORY TELLUS** (Sg) **61405 VESTLAND** (No) **61406 SOL LAILA** (No) **61407 SOL TULLA** (No).

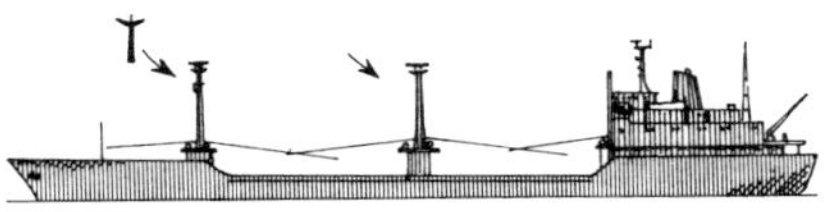

K_3MFK H13
● **61410 OSLOFJORD**. No/Ja 1977; C; 8100; 144 × 8.22 (472.44 × 26.97); M; 16.5. Sister: **61411 BERGENSFJORD** (No) Possibly similar: **61412 TANAFJORD** (No).

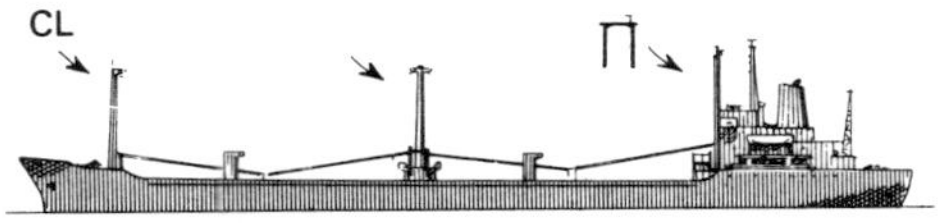

K_3MFK H13
61420 CAMPHOR. Ja/Ja 1977; B; 9600; 141.97 × 9.1 (465.78 × 29.86); M; 14. Similar: **61421 SEA ZEPHYR** (Pa) ex SEIZAN MARU 1977.

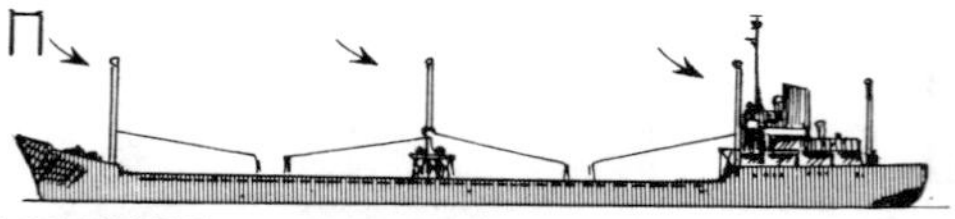

K_3MFK H13
61430 SEA LINDEN. Pa/Ja 1971; B; 9500; 147.2 × 9.09 (482.94 × 29.82); M; 14.5; ex SKYLINE 1978.

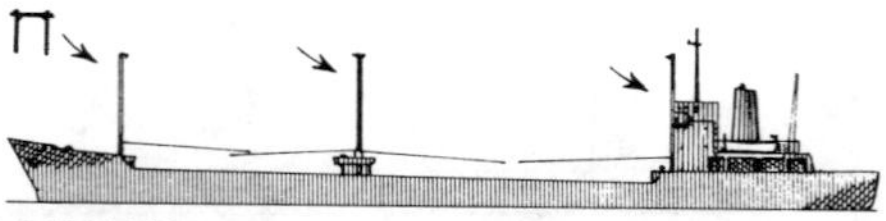

K_3MFK H13
● **61440 SEISHIN MARU.** Ja/Ja 1974; C; 9100; 138.41 × 9.01 (454.1 × 29.56); M; 14.25. Possibly similar: **61441 CAPETAN GIORGIS Z** (G) ex WASHINGTON RAINBOW; ex SEIRAN MARU 1976 **61442 ANANGEL DILIGENCE** (Gr) ex SHINTO MARU 1976 **61443 SEA TRIUMPH** (Li) ex SEITEN MARU 1977 **61444 GRAND FELICITY** (Pa).

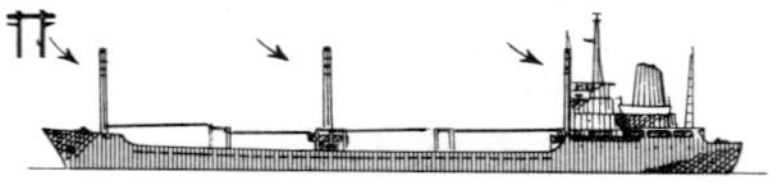

K_3MFK H13
61450 DONA AMALIA. Pi/Ja 1970; C; 3900; 111 × 6.7 (364.17 × 21.98); M; 13. Sister: **61451 DON AMBROSIO** (Pi).

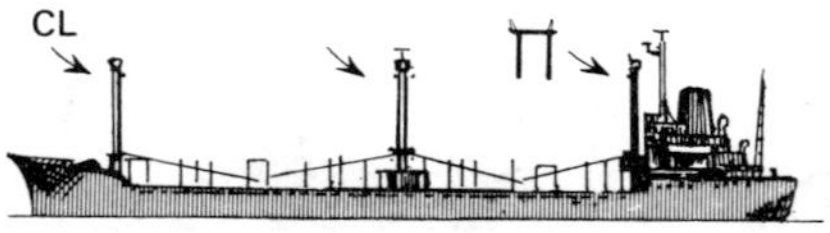

K_3MFK H13
● **61460 PAMELA.** Pa/Ja 1971; C; 5000; 124.31 × 7.52 (407.84 × 24.67); M; 13.75; ex HOSHO MARU 1980. Similar (Pa flag): **61461 MILANGO** ex MARUGAME MARU 1980 **61462 SEA DYNAMICS** ex SEAWARD; ex REJOICE 1976; ex SEIWA MARU 1976 Probably similar: **61463 HIGASHIKAWA MARU** (Ja) **61464 MARY K** (Gr) ex KOYO MARU 1979 **61465 CHRISTOS K** (Gr) ex CEREZA 1980; ex CHOKEI MARU 1976 **61466 SUMMER LIGHT** (Gr) ex IRENES HARMONY 1981; ex SUMIHO MARU 1977 **61467 VANGUARD 8** (Pa) ex SOMARIA 1978; ex KYOWA MARU No 8 1978.

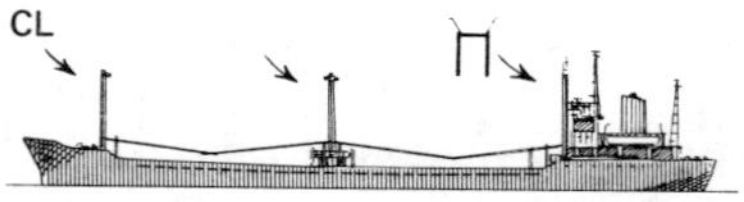

K_3MFK H13
● **⋆61470 JIN GANG LIN.** RC/Ja 1974; C; 4200; 109.05 × 7.01 (357.78 × 23); M; 14.5; ex QIN FEN 22 1980; ex GULF PRESIDENT 1978. Probable sisters: **⋆61471 NAN GUAN LING** (RC) ex QIN FEN 21 1980 **61472 TRES MAR** (Pa) **61473 GARZA OCEAN** (Pa) **61474 MARIGOLD** (Pa) ex ABS 1980; ex BUNGALOW 1978; ex EMPRISE 1976; ex SENKO MARU 1976 **61475 BERDIKARI** (Ia) ex MAY BREEZE **61476 KAPUAS** (Pa) ex SUN SALVIA 1977 **61477 TONG MYUNG No 5** (Ko) ex SEA BLOOM 1979; ex OCEAN STAR No 1 1975 **61478 ANGELITA** (Pa) ex KYONAN MARU 1976 **61479 CHUN UNG** (Pa) ex SANRYO MARU 1976 **61480 HOYU MARU** (Ja) ex SANYO MARU 1975.

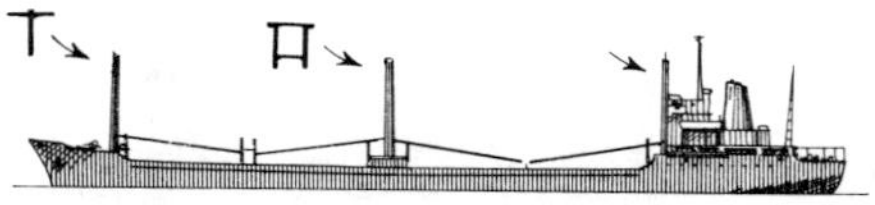

K_3MFK H13
61490 CANIS MAJOR. Pa/Ja 1973; C; 6600; 129.06 × 7.98 (423.43 × 26.18); M; 13.5; ex LUXURIANT. Possibly similar: **61491 SHINPO MARU** (Ja).

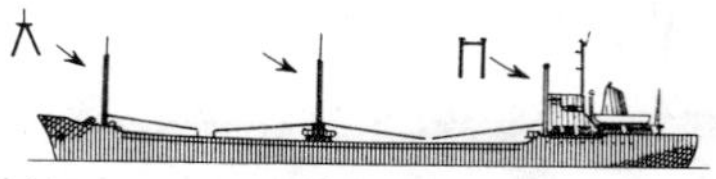

K_3MFK H13
61500 TAIWAN MAHOGANY. Pa/Ja 1964; C; 3600; 105.29 × 6.25 (345.44 × 20.5); M; 12; ex SEIJUN MARU 1972; ex JUNSHO MARU 1969.

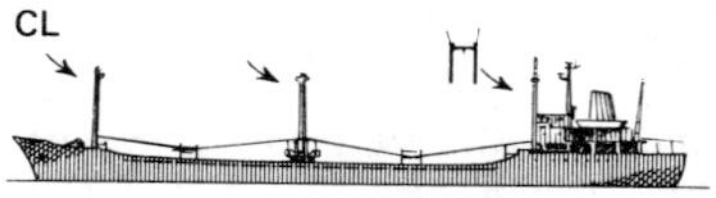

K_3MFK H13
61510 SRI KANDI. Pa/Ja 1975; C; 3400; 106.46 × 6.6 (349.28 × 21.65); M; 12.5; ex MUSASHI 1980.

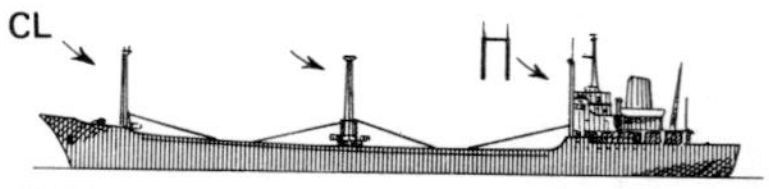

K_3MFK H13
61520 TAIHO. Tw/Ja 1970; C; 4000; 110.98 × 6.66 (364.11 × 21.85); M; 12.5.

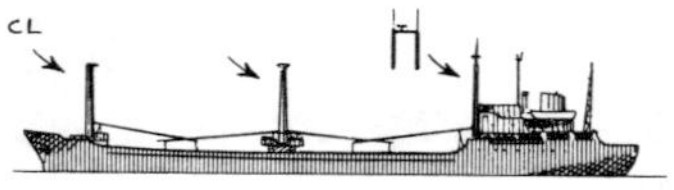

K_3MFK H13
61530 CENTRAL CRUISER. Tw/Ja 1970; C; 3000; 97.39 × 6.38 (319.52 × 20.93); M; 12.5.

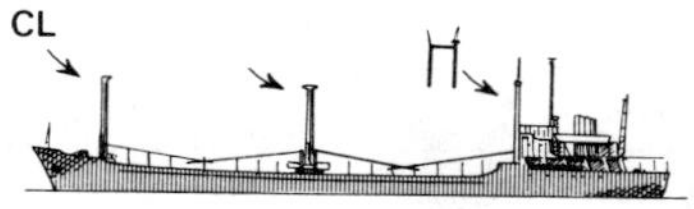

K_3MFK H13
61540 NAN A. Tw/Ja 1972; C; 3300; 100.87 × 6.71 (330.94 × 22.01); M; 12.5.

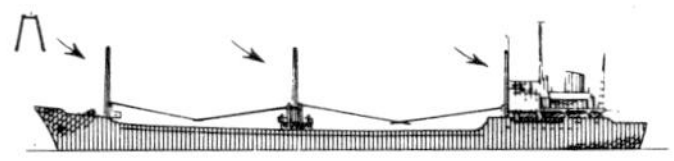

K_3MFK H13
61550 CHANG CHUN. Tw/Ja 1969; C; 3000; 97.21 × 6.38 (318.93 × 20.93); M; 13. Possibly similar: **61551 CHUN JIN** (Pa) ex SHINNAN MARU 1973 **61552 HUNG MING** (Tw) ex TA HO 1978; ex ICHIZAN UNZEN 1971 **61553 TARAKAN MARU** (Ja) ex HASHIHAMA MARU 1972.

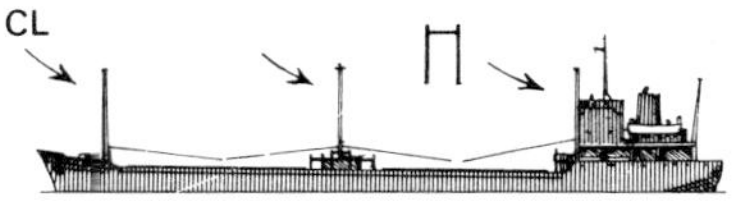

K_3MFK H13
61560 VIRGINIA RHEA. Pa/Ja 1977; C; 4200; 107.35 × 6.75 (353.84 × 22.15); M; 12; ex KASUGA 1980. Sisters (Pa flag): **61561 BELA KOSMO 61562 BELA ROZO** Possible sisters: **61563 ANDHIKA ADIRAJA 61564 ADHIGUNA DHARMA.**

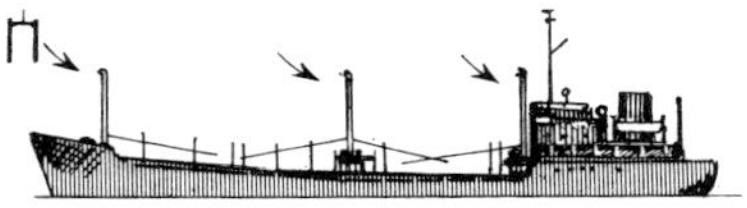

K_3MFK H13
● **61570 YUNG LEE.** Pa/Ja 1965; C; 3700; 109.94 × 6.66 (360.7 × 21.85); M; 13; ex SHINSEI MARU No 7 1973. Possible sisters (Ko flag): **61571 HAI MOON** ex KIZUGAWA MARU 1973 **61572 NAMYANG BAY** ex WALSONG 1976.

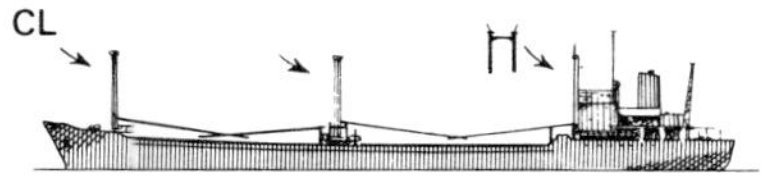

K_3MFK H13
61580 RAINBOW STAR. Pa/Ja 1975; C; 4400; 109.99 × 6.91 (360.86 × 22.67); M; 13.5; ex SUN CROCUS 1980. Probable sister: **61581 ROSE BAY** (Pa) ex SUN BEGONIA 1980.

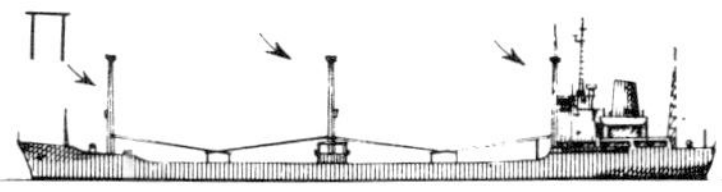

K_3MFK H13
61590 SUNGLOW. Pa/Ja 1970; C; 4100; 110.5 × 6.86 (362.53 × 22.51); M; 12.75; ex LUCID 1978; ex URSA No 1 1973; ex RYUSEI MARU 1973.

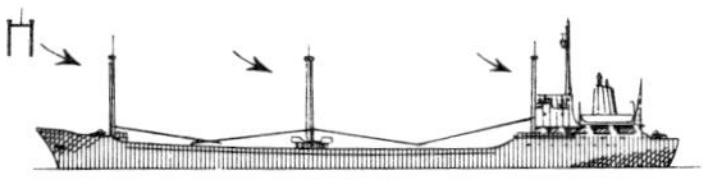

K_3MFK H13
61600 AIKATERINE K. Gr/Ja 1967; C; 3000; 101.96 × 6.63 (334.51 × 21.75); M; 14.5; ex WAKATOMI 1977; ex BINGO MARU 1974.

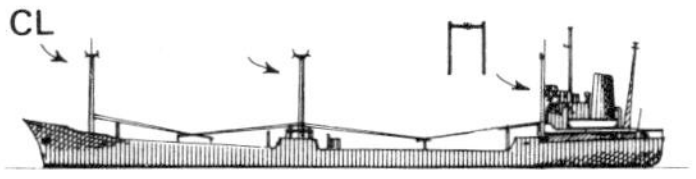

K_3MFK H13
● **61610 TAKASAGO MARU No 12.** Ja/Ja 1971; C; 3000; 101.12 × 6.81 (331.76 × 22.34); M; 12.5. Possible sisters: **61611 EASTERN DRAGON** (Ko) ex TORYU MARU 1976 **61612 GOLD STATE** (Pa) ex PACIFIC ECHO 1976; ex TOSHIN MARU 1975 **61613 PAPILIONA** (Li) ex TOKO MARU 1976 **61614 ALA WAI** (Pa) ex HAPPY REX 1980; ex ASIAN PARK 1976; ex TOKEI MARU No 2 1974 **61615 MOGES AGATHIS** (Ia) ex UMIYAMA MARU 1975 **61616 YAMATO MARU** (Ja) **61617 SUN ISLAND** (Ja) ex UMESHIMA MARU 1977 **61618 SANVASS** (Pa) ex TAIYO MARU 1978 **61619 SHINKO MARU** (Ja) **61620 ASIAN PALM** (Pa) ex SHINGEN MARU 1976 **61621 NANSHIN MARU** (Ja) **61622 SEIZAN MARU** (Ja) **61623 DONG SAN** (Ko) ex MAYA MARU 1980 **61624 ROBIN** (Pa) ex RUNNA 1980; ex MASAHARU MARU 1974 **61625 GOLD MARINE** (Pa) ex GREEN RAY 1977; ex KUWANA MARU 1975 **61626 ALEXANDRA** (Pi) ex KUCHING 1976 **61627 TEMA** (Pa) ex GEPPO MARU 1973 **61628 FOUNTAIN AZALEA** (Pa) ex KODAI MARU 1974 **61629 FORTUNE MARINER** (Pa) ex KINRIKI MARU No 21 1978 **61630 TINI P** (Gr) ex KAIRYU MARU 1976 **61631 FAR EAST VANGUARD** (Pa) ex HOSO MARU 1980 **61632 BRIGHT SKY** (Gr) ex KOYO MARU 1976 **61633 DON PABLO** (Pi) ex BONANZA 1980; ex OCEAN BETELGUESE 1978; ex DOUN MARU 1976 **61634 DONG AH** (Ko) ex OSHIMA MARU 1973 **61635 PRONAOS** (Pa) ex RAMBUT 1978; ex EIMEI MARU 1977 **61636 DAE YANG** (Ko) ex SHOYO MARU 1973 **61637 AMAGI MARU** (Ja).

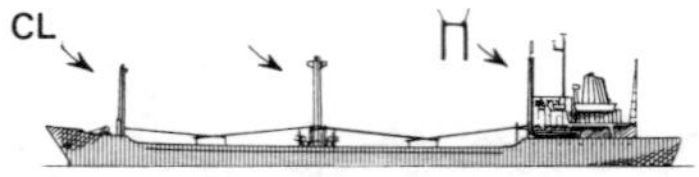

K_3MFK *H13*

● **61640 BO CHURN.** Ko/Ja 1970; C; 3200; 101.05 × 6.61 (331.53 × 21.69); M; 12.75; ex CALAMUS 1978; ex GULF GALLANT 1977; ex KOBE MARU No 7 1975. Possible sisters: **61641 KAISEI MARU** (Ja) **61642 AKIHIRO MARU** (Ja) **61643 WAHYUNI** (Ia) ex KAMELLIA 1977; ex AKIYOSHI MARU 1974 **61644 GOLDEN HARVEST** (Pa) ex KOKAI MARU 1977; Launched as KENYO MARU **61645 SANKO MARU** (Ja) **61646 HELIOS MARU** (Ja) ex SHINWA MARU 1975 **61647 ASIA SPICA** (Pa) ex SHOSHIN MARU 1980 **61648 RADIANT MED** (Gr) ex SHUSEI MARU 1977 **61649 YAETT 1** (Pa) ex SHINYO MARU 1973 **61650 ORIENTAL ANTELOPE** (Pa) ex ZUIRYU MARU 1974 **61651 DAYAKA TIGA** (Ia) ex KOBE MARU 1974 **61652 IKUTA MARU** (Ja) **61653 RIMBA DUA** (Ia) ex HANDSENG 1977; ex SHUNYO MARU 1971 **61654 RAINBOW** (Ja) ex HORYU MARU 1975 **61655 CHAMNARN SAMUT** (Th) ex HOEI MARU 1976 **61656 FLAMINGO** (Pa) ex KOWA MARU 1979 **61657 PAKALONG SERAYA** (Ia) ex ORIENTAL LION 1974; ex ULTRAMAR 1973; ex ROKKO MARU 1972 **61658 LILAC ACE** (Pa) ex REIYO MARU 1978 **61659 MOUNT PALMA** (Pa) ex PALMA 1980; ex KNIGHT 1976; ex SHUHO MARU 1975 **61660 BASCA** (Pa) ex KOKAI MARU 1976.

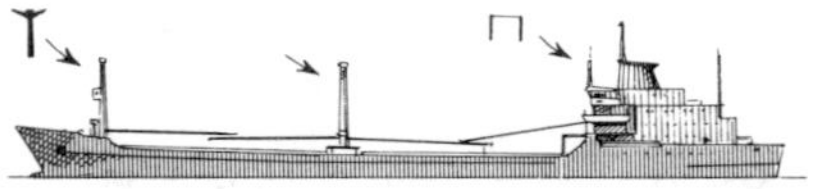

K_3MFK *H13*

● **61700 BELLEA.** Sg/DDR 1973; C; 5900; 121.75 × 7.73 (399.44 × 25.36); M; 15.5; ex SPLIT 1978; ex JOBELLA 1977. Possible sisters: **61701 BRUNLA** (Sg) **61702 BRUNHORN** (Sg) **61703 CLYMENE** (Br) ex BARBIZON; ex OYAPOK 1978; ex JOCARE 1977 **61704 ARC MINOS** (Gr) ex BOUGIVAL; ex BOCHICA 1978; Launched as JODEW **61705 CHARLOTTE BASTIAN** (Pa) ex JOADA 1978 **61706 PIRKKOLA** (Fi) ex SAVONIA 1980; ex HETLAND RANGER 1978; ex HANSA 1974 **61707 MOUTSAINA** (Gr) ★**61708 HETTSTEDT** (DDR) ex JOBEBE 1977 ★**61709 BURG** (DDR) ex JOBOY 1977 ★**61710 AKEN** (DDR) ★**61711 FREITAL** (DDR) ★**61712 KOTHEN** (DDR).

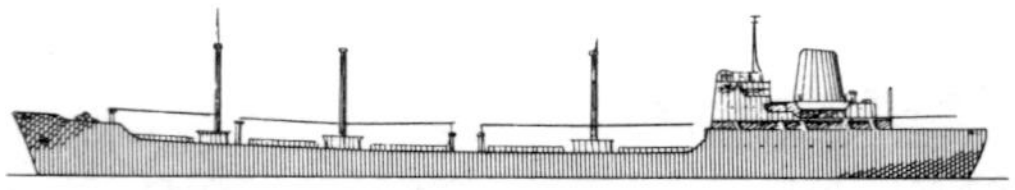

K_3MFK *H13*

61730 ALHAJA MAMA BAKARE. Pa/Ja 1957; C; 10300; 154.84 × 9.36 (508.01 × 30.71); T; —; ex THARROS 1977. Similar: **61731 DUPE BAKARE** (Pa) ex RYTHME 1977.

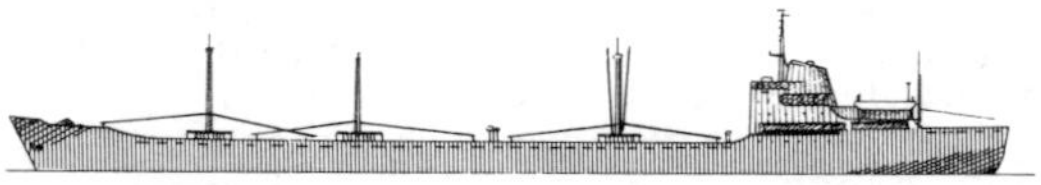

K_3MFK *H13*

61740 DJATIPURA. Ia/Ja 1961; C; 9900; 157.03 × 9.02 (515.19 × 29.59); M; 15; ex SOUTH BREEZE 1976.

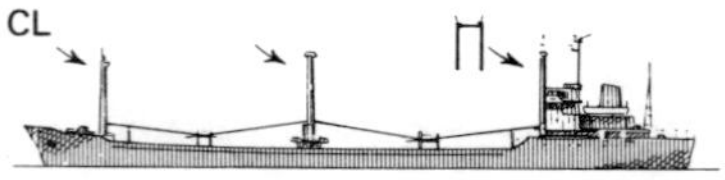

K_3MFK *H13*

61670 WOOSTER KING. Pa/Ja 1974; C; 3500; 106.28 × 6.58 (348.69 × 21.59); M; 12.5.

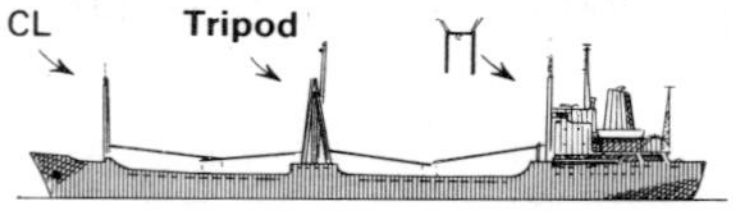

K_3MFK *H13*

61680 BOSWICK. Li/Ja 1975; C/HL; 3800; 106.46 × 7.11 (349.28 × 23.33); M; 16. Sister: **61681 ALDRICH** (Li).

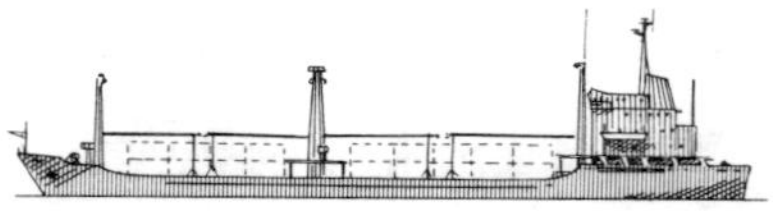

K_3MFK *H13*

61690 CAP BAITAR. FRG/Ja 1977; C; 4600; 118.01 × 6.96 (387.17 × 22.84); M; 14.5; ex MAX BASTIAN 1977. Sister: **61691 CAP BIZERTA** (FRG) ex INGA BASTIAN 1977.

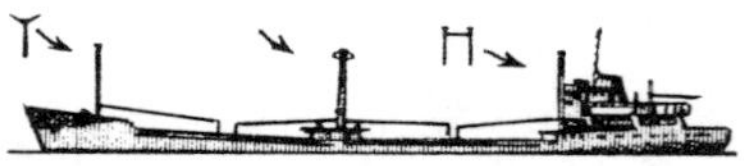

K_3MFK *H13*

● **61720 MOKHA.** Sg/DDR 1967; C; 2600/4000; 112.1 × 7.17 (367.78 × 23.52); M; 13.5; ex EURABIA SPRING 1978; ex CLARI 1975; ex KARLSBURG 1970; ex CLAUDIA MARIA 1967. Sister: **61721 LE ROVE** (Fr) ex SCOL INDEPENDENT 1975; ex GERMANICA 1975; ex WILRI 1975; ex GERMANIC 1974; ex WILRI 1974; ex ATLANTA 1973 Similar: **61722 IRENES SUN** (Gr) ex BLOCKLAND 1977; ex JIRI 1969; ex HOEGH JIRI 1968; ex JIRI 1966 **61723 IRENES SEA** (Gr) ex WERDERLAND 1977; ex WILRI 1969; ex HOEGH WILRI 1969; ex WILRI 1967 **61724 CONTI ALMANIA** (FRG) ex GRIMSNIS 1975; ex HEIN JENEVELT 1970; ex BARI 1968 **61725 EURABIA PROGRESS** (Le) ex CLAUDIA MARIA 1975 **61726 DUBURG** (FRG) ex BILSTEIN 1978; ex CONTI SYRIA 1978; ex ANTONY 1977; ex BILSTEIN 1975; ex HOEGH SUSANN 1968; Launched as SUSAN VON BARGEN.

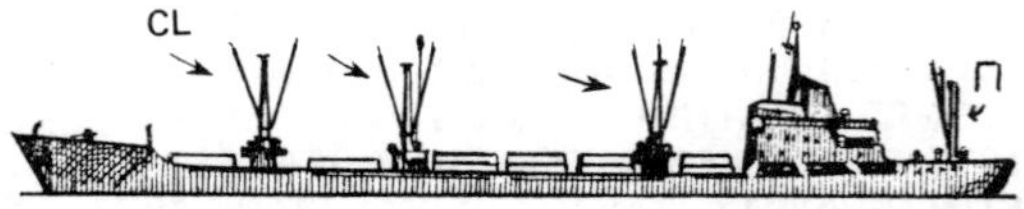

K_3MFK *H13*

● **61750 ESHKOL.** Is/Fr 1964; C; 4900/7700; 159 × 6.7/7.9 (522 × 22/30.1); M; 17.5; Lengthened 1971. Sisters: **61751 ETROG** (Is) **61752 ROGET** (Pa) ex YAFO 1980; ex DOLLY 1979; ex YAFO 1979. **61753 GIANT PILOT** (Pa) ex GOLD PILOT 1978; ex HADAR 1977.

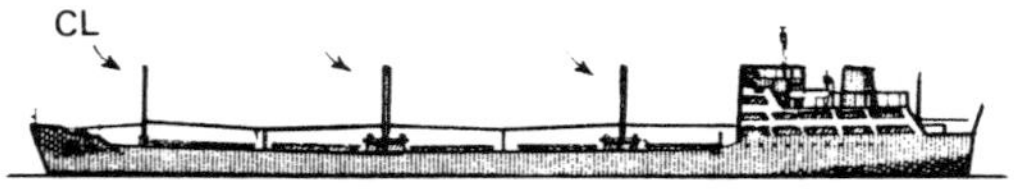

K_3MFK H13
61760 SEA RANGER. Gr/Br 1959; B; 10100; 158.05 × 9.68 (518.54 × 31.76); M; 14.25; ex WANDBY 1972.

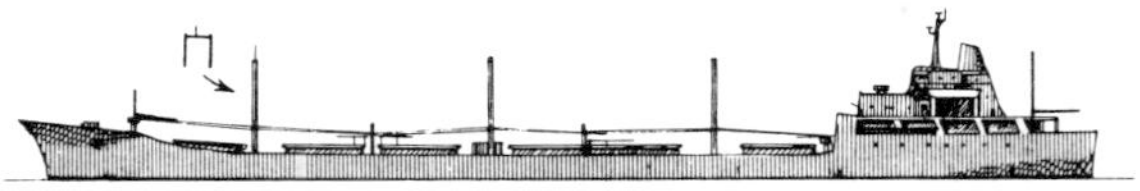

K_3MFK H13
61770 ARCHIMEDES. Gr/Ja 1966; B; 16100; 171.33 × 10.23 (562.11 × 33.56); M; 15; **'ALGONQUIN II'** type. Sisters (Gr flag): **61771 APOLLONIUS 61772 CAPETAN PSARROS 61773 CAPETAN RAHIOTIS** ex CAPETAN YEMELOS 1975.

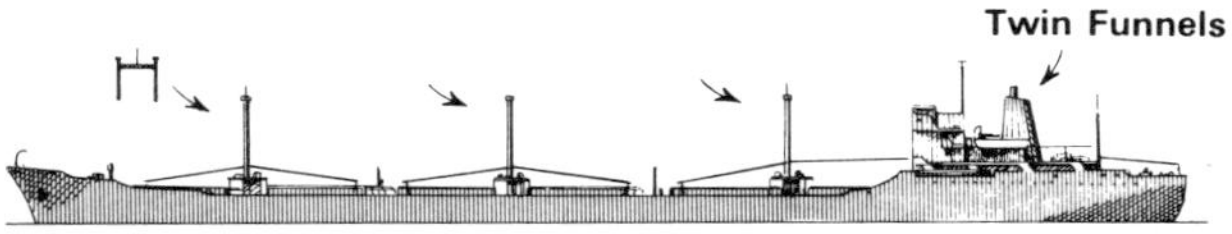

K_3MFK H13
⋆61780 BANIJA. Ys/Ys 1966; B; 16900; 187.03 × 10.74 (613.62 × 35.24); M; 16. Sister: **61781 BOSANKA** (Ys).

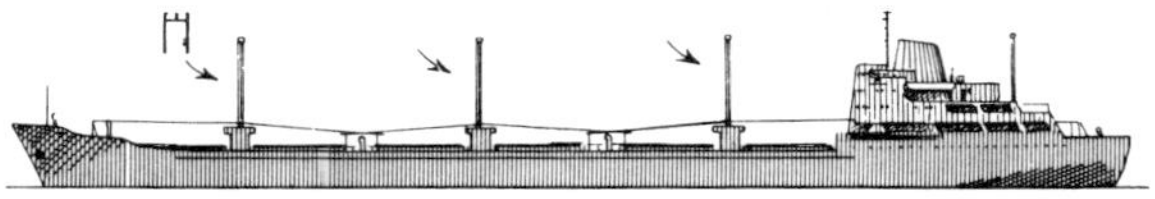

K_3MFK H13
61790 KRONOS. Gr/Sw 1962; C; 12100; 157.92 × 9.25 (518.11 × 30.35); M; 14; ex GLYFADA MILU 1981; ex BREVIK 1978.

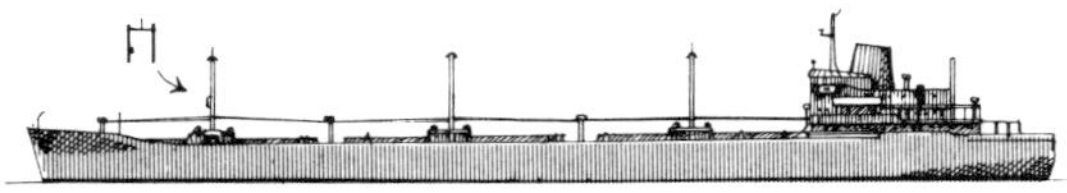

K_3MFK H13
61800 SEMIRA. Gr/Sw 1965; B; 11900; 165.06 × 10.05 (541.54 × 32.97); M; 17; ex CESIRA 1980; ex NORSE CARRIER 1976. Similar (taller funnel): **61801 REGAL SCOUT** (Pa) ex MARY STOVE 1974.

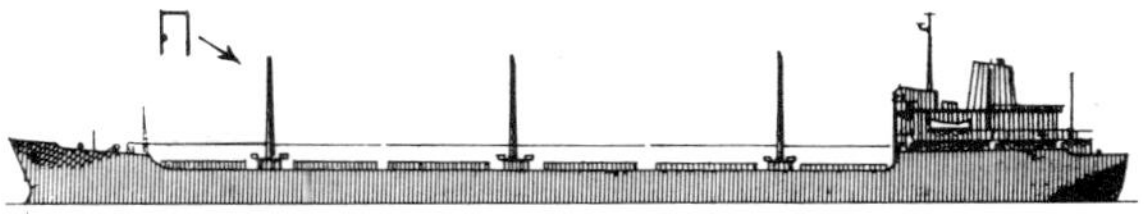

K_3MFK H13
61810 STAR CARRIER. Ko/Ja 1967; B; 16200; 178.52 × 10.39 (585.7 × 34.09); M; 15.5; ex VALIANT RACER 1978; ex HOEGH MUSKETEER 1974. Similar: **61811 PAN PACIFIC** (Ko) ex HOEGH MARLIN 1974 **61812 AVON** (Gr) ex HOEGH MERCHANT 1974 **61813 BARRY** (Gr) ex HOEGH MERIT 1974 **⋆61814 YANG ZONG HAI** (RC) ex SOUTHERN RUBY 1978; ex HOEGH MALLARD 1974.

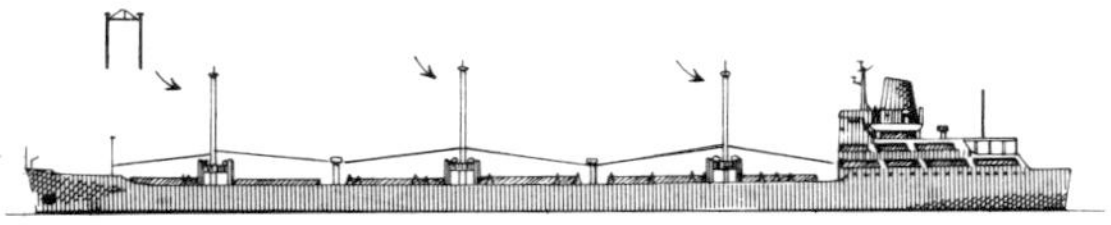

K_3MFK H13
61820 GLYFADA MIMI. Gr/No 1965; B; 12900; 164.9 × 10.18 (541.01 × 33.4); M; 15; ex BELMAR 1978; ex HOEGH BELMAR 1971; ex BELMAR 1970.

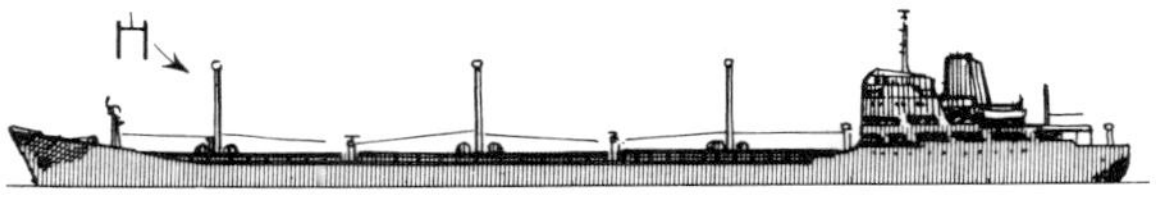

K_3MFK H13
61830 SOHANLAL. Sg/Ja 1960; B; 14300; 177.02 × 9.73 (580.77 × 31.92); T; 15.5; ex LINDA 1978.

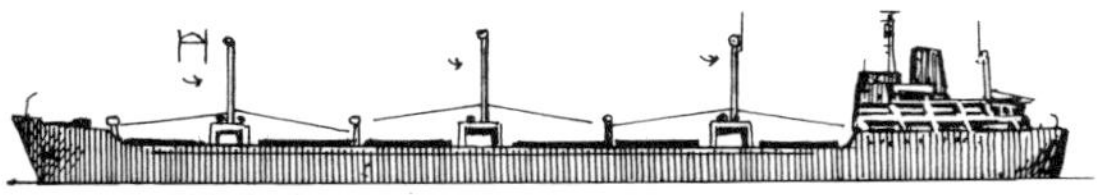

K_3MFK H13
⋆61840 YAKHROMA. Ru/No 1967; B; 1300; 166.45 × 10.17 (546.1 × 33.37); M; 15.5; ex FARMAND 1973. Sister: **61841 UNION PRIDE** (Gr) ex BLANCA 1972.

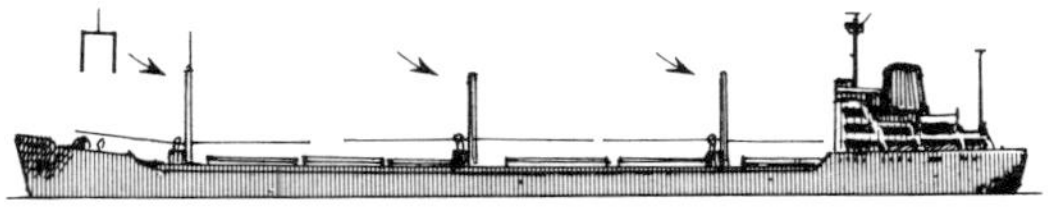

K_3MFK H13
61850 OCEAN PROSPECT. Pa/Ja 1961; B; 1200; 160 × 9.17 (524.93 × 30.09); M; 14.25; ex LUNA 1976; ex TETSUKUNI MARU 1974.

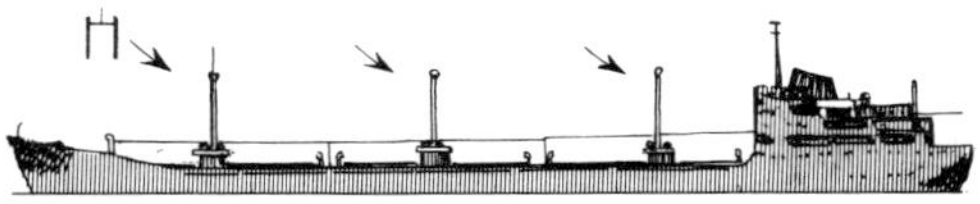

K_3MFK H13
61860 ERGINA I. Pa/De 1961; B; 10300; 152.43 × 9.36 (500.1 × 30.71); M; 13.5; ex BYZANTION 1978; ex PARASKEVI YEMELOS 1973; ex MOGEN 1971; ex STOVE TRANSPORT 1969. Similar: **61861 TETIEN** (Gr) ex ROBERT KABELAC 1972.

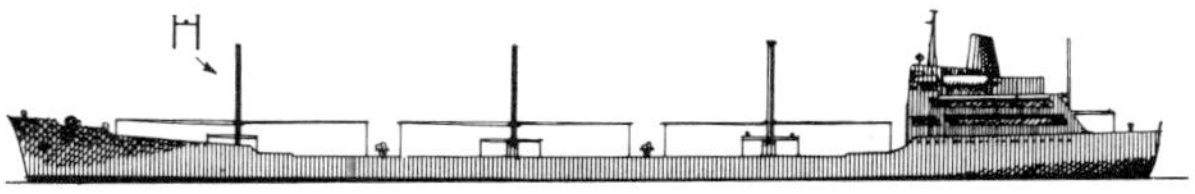

K_3MFK H13
61870 BASIL III. Gr/No 1965; B; 18500; 185.63 × 11.18 (609.02 × 36.68); M; 15.5. Sister: **61871 TRITON C** (Gr) ex AEGEAN TRITON 1980.

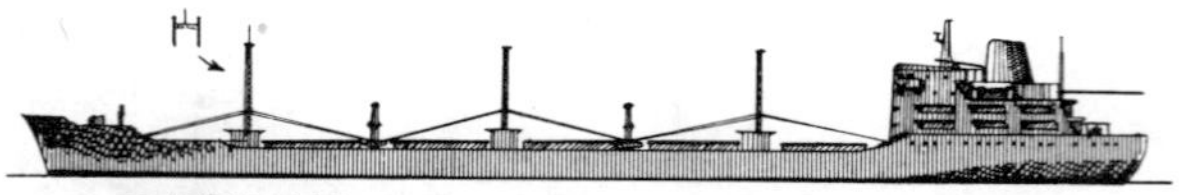

K_3MFK H13
61880 GRECIAN FLAME. Gr/Fr 1962; B; 15400; 178.24 × 10.02 (584.78 × 32.87); M; 15. Sisters: **61881 KING NESTOR** (Gr) **61882 URANIA C** (Gr) **61883 PETROS V** (Gr) ex MARINA GRANDE; ex CAPE MARINA 1969; ex MARINA GRANDE 1966 ⋆**61884 ZHEN HAI** (RC) ex TIMOR SEA 1974; ex DESTREHAN 1972 ⋆**61885 ZHU HAI** (RC) ex CERAM SEA 1973; ex VICTORIA I 1972; ex VICTORIA 1968.

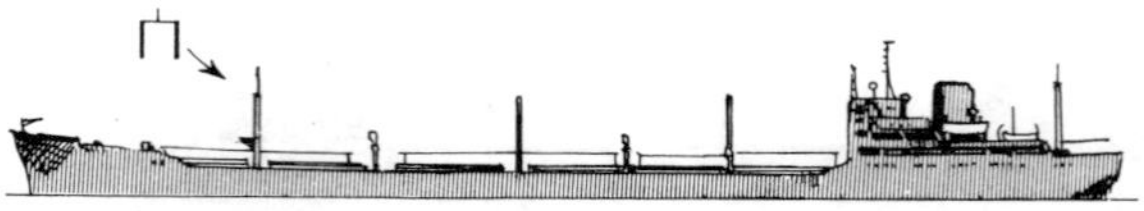

K_3MFK H13
● **61890 DELPHIC SKY.** Gr/Ja 1963; B; 13900; 176.87 × 10.42 (580.28 × 34.19); M; 15.5.

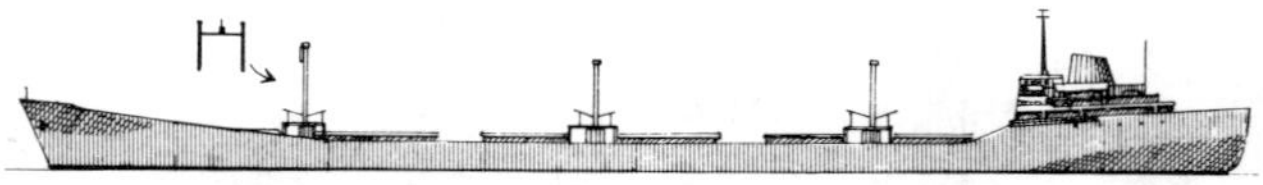

K_3MFK H13
61900 MARINA. It/Br 1964; B; 17800; 194.7 × 10.4 (638.78 × 34.12); M; 15; ex CHIKUMA 1976; ex WILKAWA 1974; ex AUSTRALIAN CITY 1969. Sister: **61901 CHIYODA** (Gr) ex EASTERN CITY 1970.

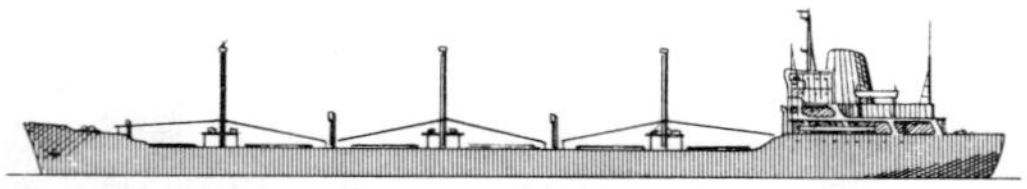

K_3MFK H13
61910 PEGASOS. Gr/Ja 1966; B; 12400; 155 × 9.17 (508.53 × 30.09); M; 14.5; ex GALISSA 1980; ex SYRA 1976; ex DONA CORAZON 1972.

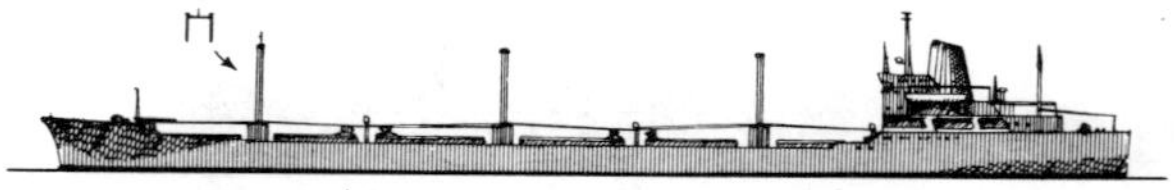

K_3MFK H13
61920 SATYA KAMAL. In/Ja 1967; B; 16500; 173.67 × 10.94 (569.78 × 35.89); M; 15.5; ex WORLD UNION 1973.

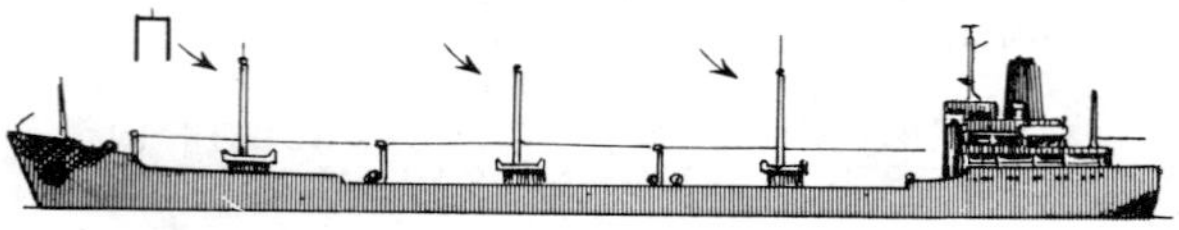

K_3MFK H13
61930 JELA TOPIC. Li/Ja 1967; C; 16700; 181.31 × 10.17 (594.85 × 33.37); M; 15.

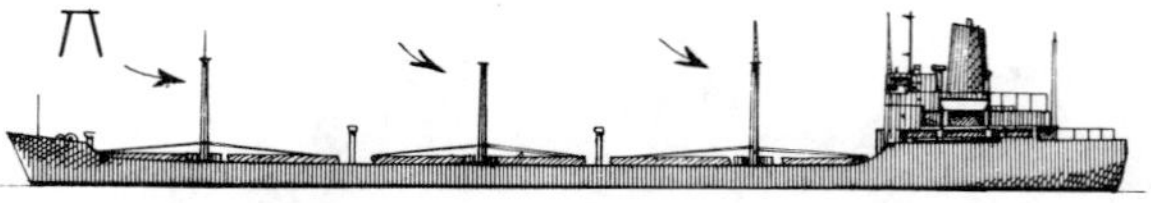

K_3MFK H13
61940 MARATHA ENVOY. Br/Ja 1968; B; 16500; 176.79 × 10.5 (580.02 × 34.45); M; 17.

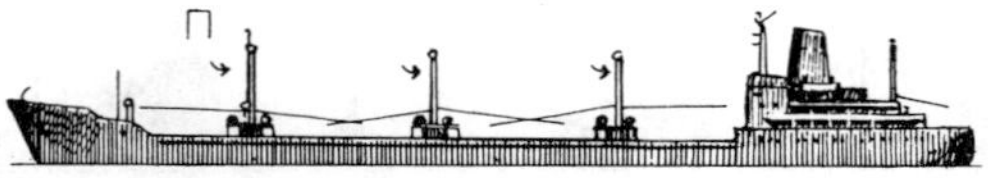

K_3MFK H13
⋆**61950 CONG HUA.** RC/Sw 1962; C; 6700/9000; 148.62 × 8.54/9.32 (487.6 × 28.02/30.58); M; 15.75; ex VAASA LEADER 1973.

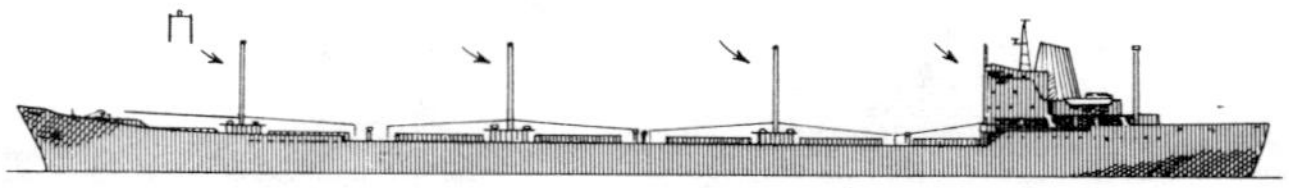

K_3MFK H13
⋆**61960 LONG HAI.** RC/Be 1968; B; 25000; 203.77 × 11.48 (668.54 × 37.66); M; —; ex AGIOI VICTORES 1974. Sister: ⋆**61961 PING HAI** (RC) ex IOANNIS N. PATERAS 1974.

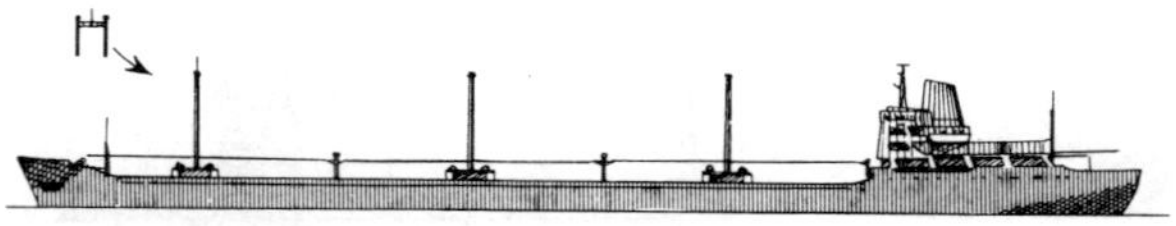

K_3MFK H13
61970 AGIOS CONSTANTINOS. Gr/Ja 1965; B; 14300; 179.1 × 10.14 (587.6 × 33.27); M; —; ex MEGALOHARI II 1981.

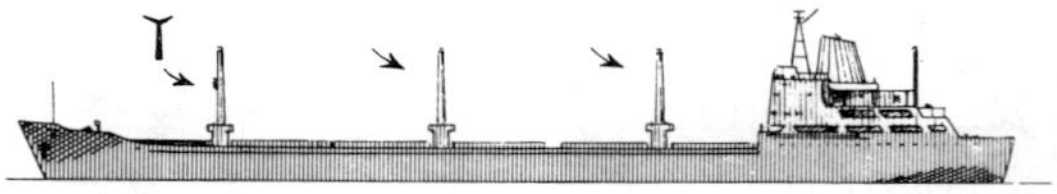

K_3MFK H13
61980 SETIF. Ag/Sw 1963; B; 12100; 157.99 × 9.71 (518.38 × 31.86); M; 14.5; ex EVINA 1971; ex SAGA SAILOR 1968; ex FARLAND 1967.

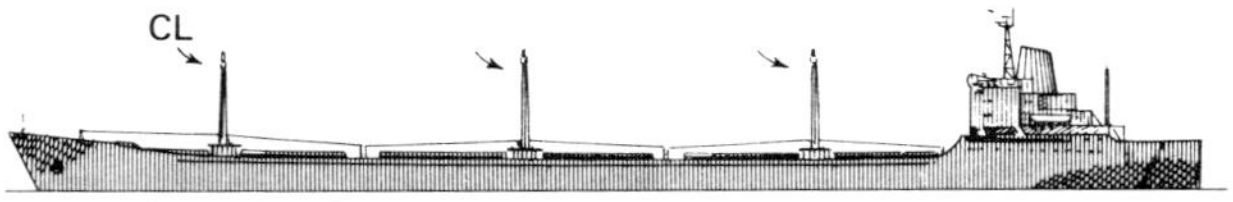

K_3MFK H13
61990 EKTOR. Gr/Be 1970; B; 16300; 190.02 × 10.81 (623.43 × 35.47); M; 15. Sisters: **61991 ERMIS** (Gr) **61992 GAREFOWL** (Br) ex ROSSETTI 1978 **61993 REYNOLDS** (Br).

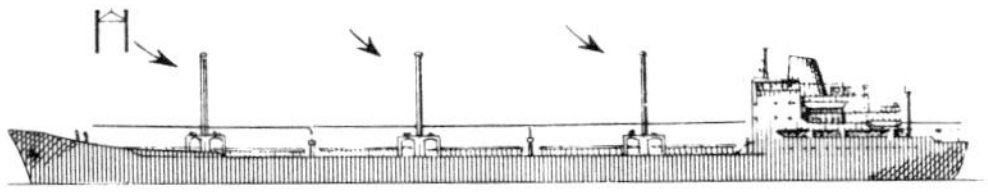

K_3MFK H13
62010 MARATHON LAKE. Gr/No 1962; B; 8900; 152.48 × 8.99 (500.26 × 29.49); M; 13.5; ex PTOLEMAIS 1979; ex JEANINE 1972; ex BELTANA 1968. Sisters: **62011 MATHIOS** (Gr) ex POLYFYTON 1978; ex MARITA 1972 **62012 NAGOS** (Li) ex ARGO MASTER 1977; ex GERNIC 1970; ex MORGANA 1967.

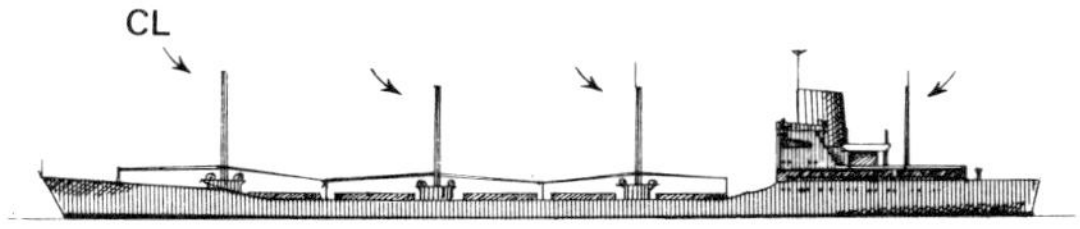

K_3MFK H13
62050 FAIR ISLAND. Pa/FRG 1960; C; 1200; 162.44 × 9.92 (532.94 × 32.55); M; 15.5; ex GAROUFALIA 1980; ex KONSUL SCHULTE 1972. Sister: **62051 SCAPHILL** (Gr) ex MATHILDE BOLTEN 1970.

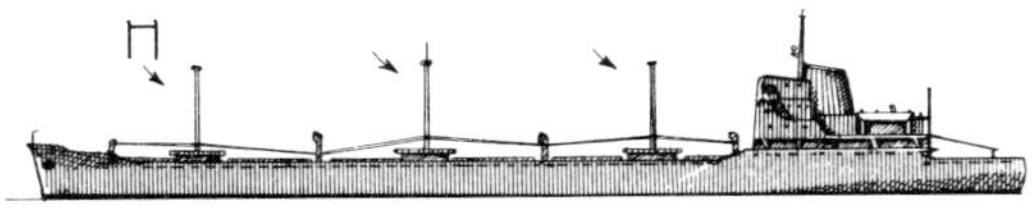

K_3MFK H13
⋆62060 KOSOVO. Ys/Ja 1959; C; 8000/10600; 158.25 × —/9.7 (519.19 × —/31.82); M; 15. Sister: **⋆62061 PIRAN** (Ys).

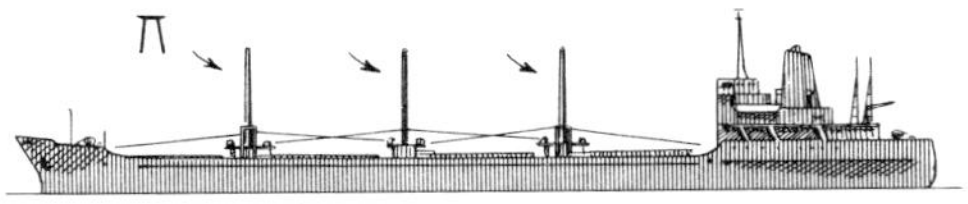

K_3MFK H13
62080 PROTOKLITOS. Gr/Ja 1968; C; 6200/9900; 145.7 × 7.92/9.27 (478.02 × 25.98/30.41); M; 15.5; ex SILJA DAN 1975; ex SYLVIA CORD 1973; **'MITSUI CONCORD'** type. Sister: **⋆62081 FU PING** (RC) ex MARGARET CORD 1977.

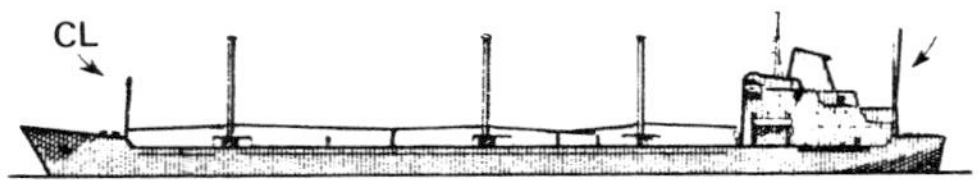

K_3MFK H13
62000 GOOD WIND. Gr/Sp 1970; C; 11300; 147.02 × 9.87 (482.34 × 32.4); M; 16; ex GOOD HELMSMAN 1978; ex DAVID, MARQUESS OF MILFORD HAVEN 1973; **'Santa-Fe'** type. Sister: **62001 PANAGIA MYRTIDIOTISSA** (Gr) ex JOCELYNE 1980.

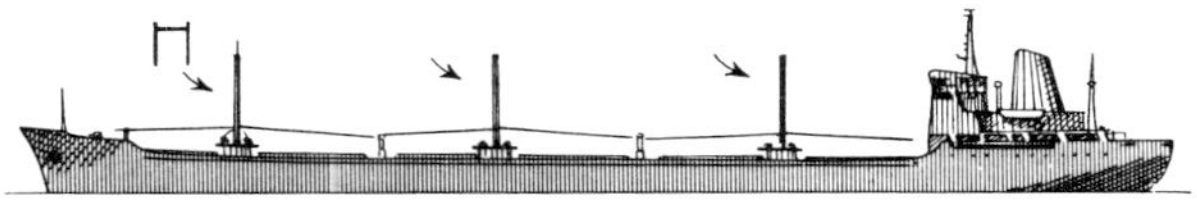

K_3MFK H13
● **62020 POLLY**. Li/Tw 1977; B; 17900; 181.31 × 10.28 (594.85 × 33.73); M; 15. Sister: **62021 ROSSANA** (Li) ex JULIANA 1980 Similar: **62022 CAMERONA** (Li) **62023 IRENE** (Tw) **⋆62024 BUDVA** (Ys) Launched as PACIFIC ENDEAVOUR Possible similar (Tw flag): **62025 ALLY 62026 ANITA 62027 CHRISTINA 62028 EVER RELIANCE 62029 HARRIET 62030 JEANNIE 62031 MING BELLE 62032 TAI SHING 62033 VIRTUOUS** (Li flag): **62034 LUCINA 62035 SILVER CLIPPER** (Gr flag): **62036 TAUROS** (Pa flag): **62037 HARMONY SEA** ex JUSTINA 1980 (Pe flag): **62038 SALCANTAY** ex RIGHTEOUS 1973.

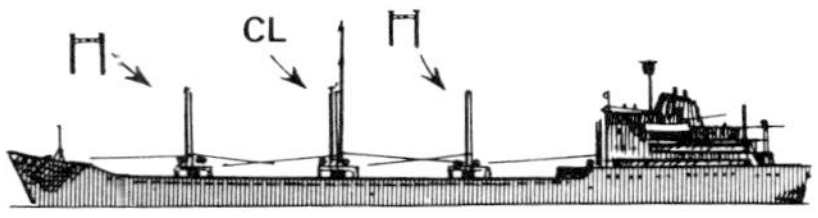

K_3MFK H13
62070 LORD BYRON. Gr/Sp 1964; C; 4200/6500; 127.23 × 6.96/8.34 (417.42 × 22.83/27.36); M; —; ex NORTH STAR 1973; ex ALEX 1972.

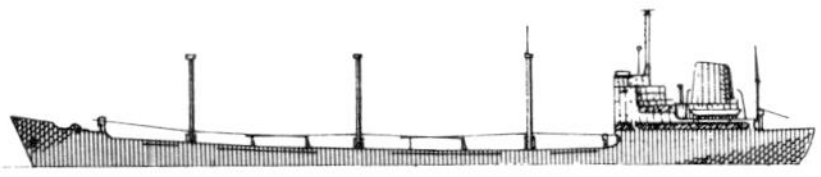

K_3MFK H13
62090 AN LEE. Pa/Ja 1958; C; 5500; 126.02 × 7.49 (413.45 × 24.57); M; 12.5; ex GOLDEN WOOD 1973; ex NICHIEI MARU 1971.

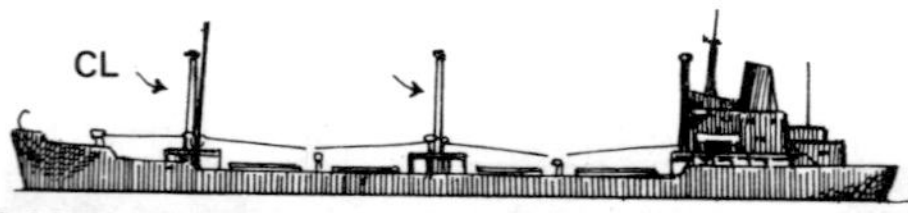

K_3MFK H13
★62100 HUA YIN. RC/FRG 1969; C; 6700/9400; 139.45 × —/9.2 (457.51 × —/30.18); M; 15.5; ex JENS JOST 1974; **'German Liberty'** type. Similar: **62101 SUNFRANCIS** (Pa) Launched as FRANCISKA FISSER **62102 FRANZ XAVER KOGEL** (Pa) ex OLGA JACOB 1976 **62103 ELISABETH ROTH** (FRC) **62104 BERTHA FISSER** (FRG) ex SUNCAPRI 1973 Launched as BERTHA FISSER **★62105 PING DING SHAN** (RC) ex KLAUS SCHOKE 1981; ex NYANGA; ex KLAUS SCHOKE; ex VERENA WIARDS 1972 **62106 FJORD MASTER** (Pa).

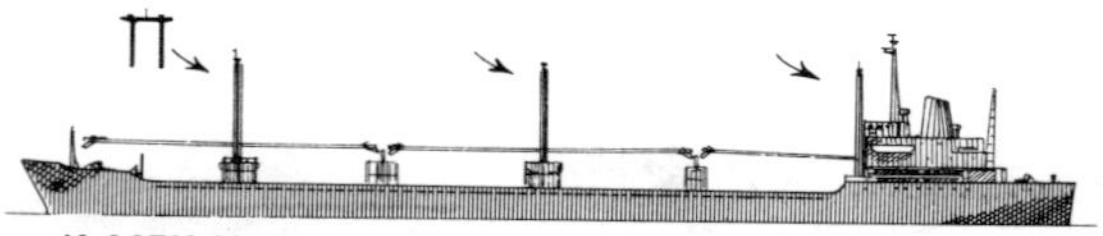

K_3MFK H13
62130 FRANK DELMAS. Fr/Ja 1975; B; 16700; 167.16 × 13.08 (548.43 × 42.91); M; 17.5.

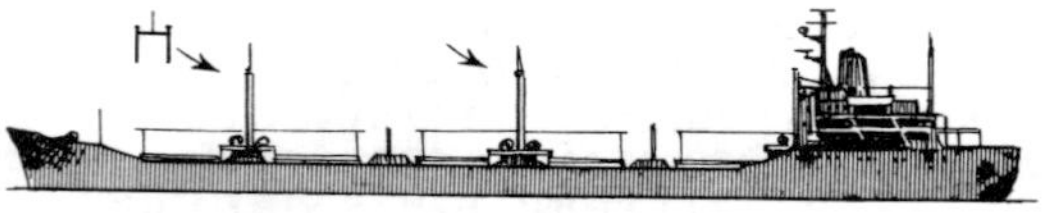

K_3MFK H13
62150 MARCALAN. Gr/Ja 1968; B; 14800; 159.01 × 10.65 (521.69 × 34.94); M; 15.5; ex VERDALA 1978; ex SHROPSHIRE 1977; ex VERDALA 1975.

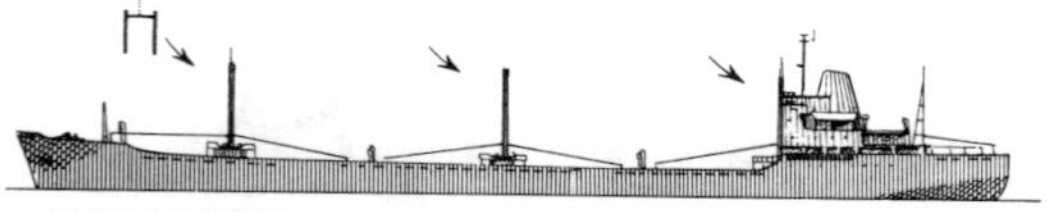

K_3MFK H13
62170 ARCADIAN SKY. Gr/Ja 1965; B; 12200; 157.54 × 9.62 (516.86 × 31.56); M; 14.5; ex EASTERN KIKU. Sister: **62171 ARCADIAN FAITH** (Gr) ex WORLD HARMONY.

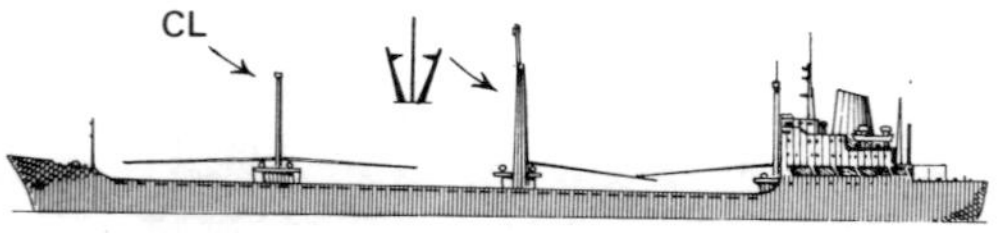

K_3MFK H13
★62190 DACHENG. RC/Ja 1973; C/HL; 6900/10700; 154.95 × —/9.08 (508.37 × —/29.79); M; 16.25. Sister: **★62191 DATIAN** (RC).

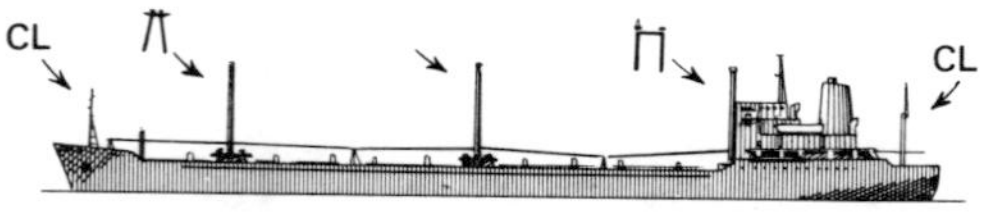

K_3MFK H13
62210 HOLY. Li/Ja 1971; B; 9400; 147.53 × 9.31 (484 × 30.3); M; 15; **'16 BC 5'** type. Possible sister: **62211 EASTERN MARINER** (Li).

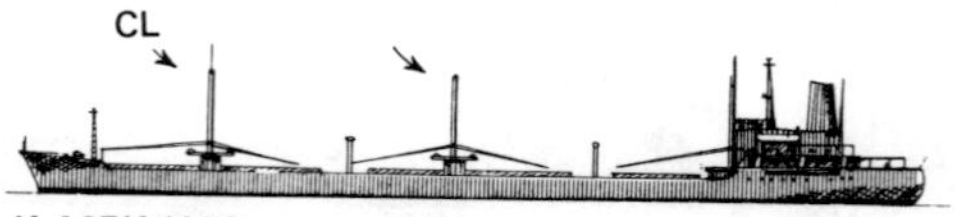

K_3MFK H13
62110 LEIDENSCHAFT. Li/Ja 1972; C; 6900/10000; 145.01 × —/9.08 (475.75 × —/29.79); M; 14.5; **'UT-15'** type. Sister: **62111 LIECHTENSTEIN** (Li).

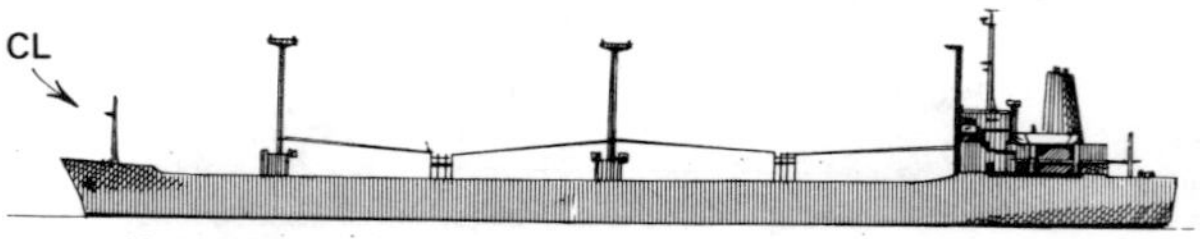

K_3MFK H13
62120 SPLENDID HOPE. Pa/Ja 1974; B; 16800; 181.52 × 10.06 (592.26 × 34.74); M; 15; ex SEIHO MARU 1978.

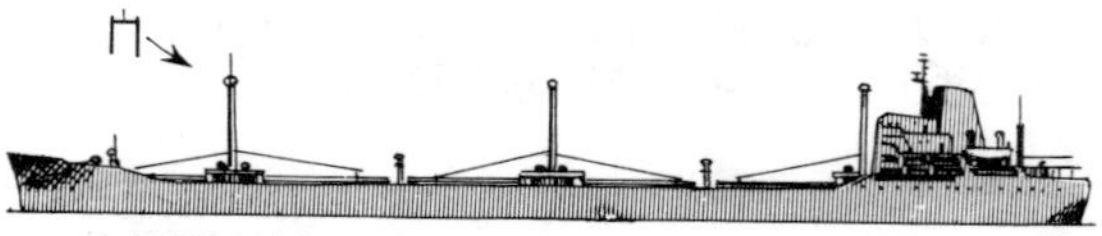

K_3MFK H13
● **62140 ANDROS.** Gr/Ja 1965; B; 15400; 178.19 × 9.83 (584.61 × 32.25); M; 15. Sisters (Gr flag): **62141 ANTIGUA 62142 PHAEDRA 62143 TOKYO OLYMPICS.**

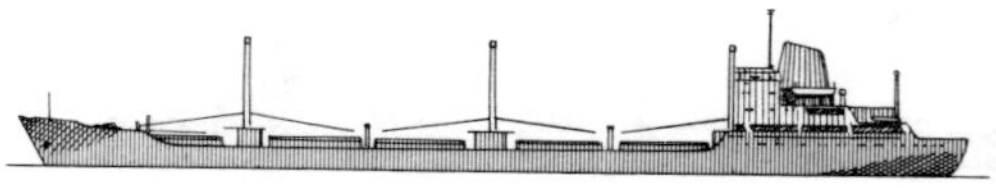

K_3MFK H13
62160 BIJELA. Ma/FRG 1963; B; 9500; 153.98 × 9.13 (505.18 × 29.95); M; 13.5; ex RIGEL 1977; ex SPLENDID BREEZE 1977; ex EXECUTIVE TRADER 1974; ex BERNHARD 1973; After kingpost may be removed.

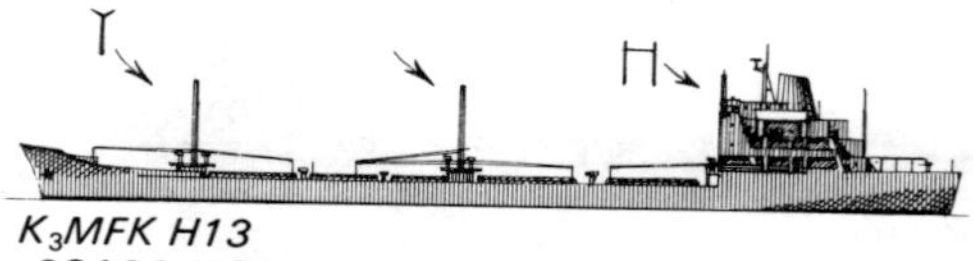

K_3MFK H13
★62180 KOPER. Ys/Be 1967; B; 9100; 149.41 × 8.59 (490.19 × 28.18); M; 12. Sister: **★62181 KRPAN** (Ys).

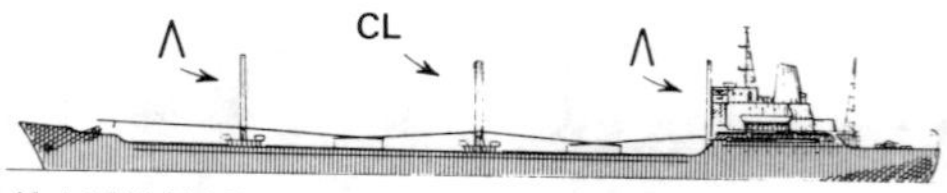

K_3MFK H13
62200 OKPO PEARL. Ko/Ja 1969; B; 10100; 146.01 × 9.35 (479.04 × 30.68); M; 14.5; ex CRESTA IV 1980; ex KUSUNOKI MARU 1977.

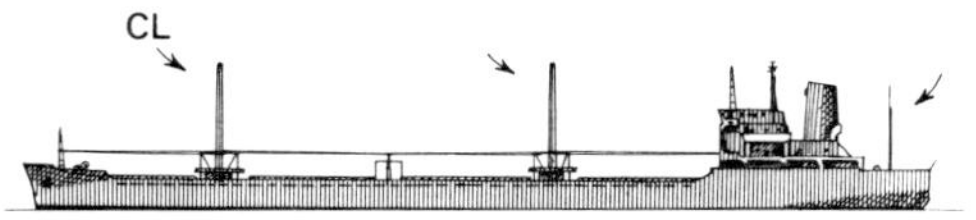

K_3MFK H13
62220 UNION WISDOM. Li/Ja 1969; B; 10000; 143.54 × 9.16 (470.93 × 30.05); M; 15. Sisters: **62221 CAPTAIN LEMOS** (Gr) ex UNION FRIENDSHIP 1976 **62222 EVER FAITH** (Tw) **62223 RENACIMIENTO** (Pa) ex COSMOS ELTANIN 1977 Possible sisters: **62224 PETERSBERG** (Li) ex VICTORIA 1980; ex GEORGIANA 1979 **62225 KOSTAR** (Ko) ex KATRINA 1978 **62226 MYUNG JIN** (Ko) ex PEARL VENTURE 1978.

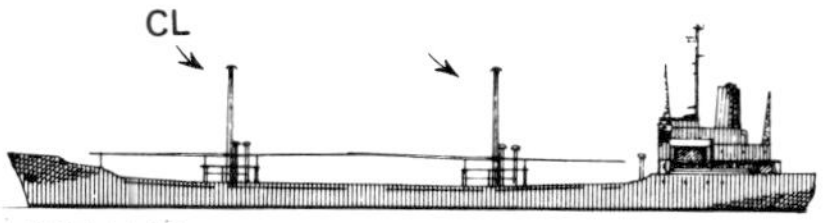

K_3MFK H13
● **62230 MERZARIO ASIA.** Sg/Ja 1976; C; 7400; 127.79 × 8.05 (419.26 × 26.41); M; 13.25; ex ZEPSEA 1980; ex GULF UNITY 1978; ex ZEPSEA 1977. Sisters: **62231 LILY VENTURE** (Li) **62232 OCEAN ACE (Ja)** Possibly similar: **62233 SINGAPORE MERCHANT** (Sg) ex ACE AMERICA 1979; ex ZEPHAWK 1978.

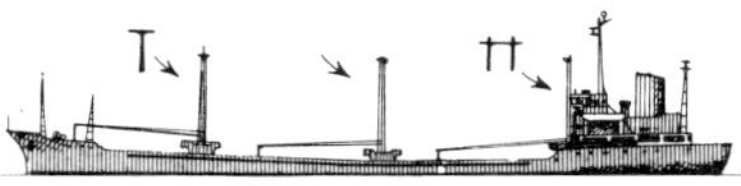

K_3MFK H13
● **62240 ANITA.** Gr/Ja 1976; C; 5000; 117.61 × 7.3 (385.8 × 23.9); M; 16. Sisters: **62241 KAREN** (Gr) **62242 HELEN SCHULTE** (Cy) **62243 JOANNA SCHULTE** (Cy) **62244 NORDHEIM** (Sg) **62245 NORDFELS** (Sg) **62246 NORDHOLM** (Sg) **62247 NORDMARK** (Sg) **62248 SINGAPURA** (Sg) ex RAUTE 1979 **62249 BAYU** (Sg) ex RHOMBUS 1979 **62250 RIO EXPLORER** (Li) **62251 KIRSTEN WESCH** (Sg) **62252 CORAL VOLANS** (Li) **62253 RAINBOW VOLANS** (Li) **62254 NEPTUNE VOLIANS** (Li).

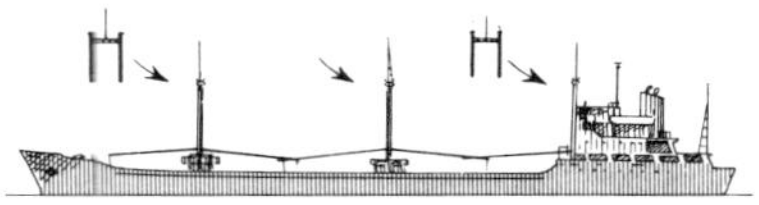

K_3MFK H13
62260 RINA. Pa/Ja 1966; C; 4500; 113.59 × 6.85 (372.67 × 22.47); M; 15.5; ex KONG KIM 1980; ex FOH KIM 1978.

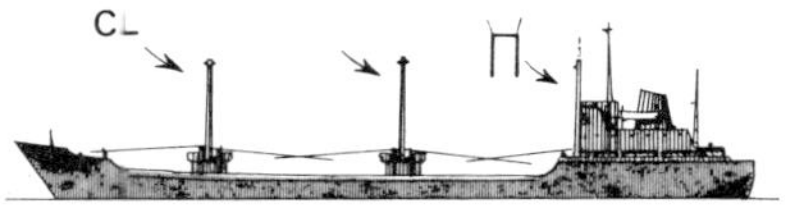

K_3MFK H13
62270 HSIEH YUNG. Tw/Ja 1969; C; 5000; 117.05 × 7.43 (384.02 × 24.38); M; 13. Possible sisters: **62271 LUNG YUNG** (Tw) **62272 MUI KIM** (Br).

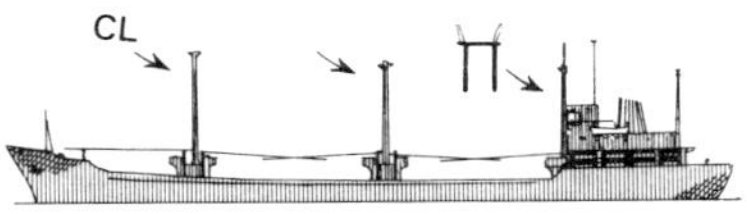

K_3MFK H13
62280 CAPIRA. Pa/Ja 1976; C; 5700; 116.06 × 7.62 (380.77 × 24.99); M; 12.5; ex KOYO MARU 1980; ex HAPPUSAN MARU.

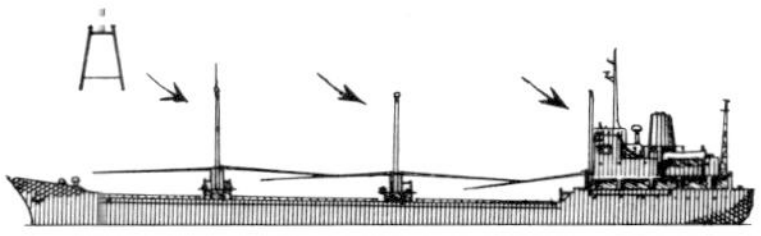

K_3MFK H13
62290 JOHN P. Gr/Ja 1968; C; 4700; 117.46 × 6.91 (385.37 × 22.67); M; 13; ex KWONG FUNG 1980; ex WAH FEI 1974; ex SHINPO MARU 1971.

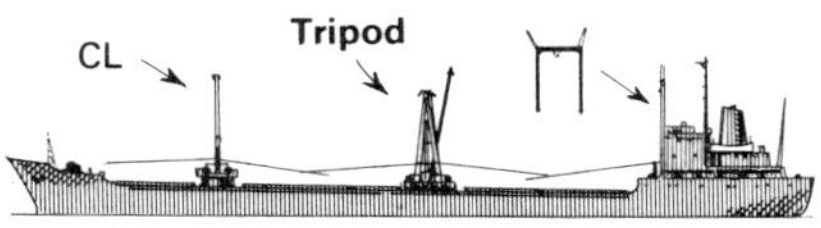

K_3MFK H13
● **62300 JESAMINE.** Pa/Ja 1973; C; 6100; 126.04 × 7.85 (413.52 × 25.75); M; 14; ex JASMINE 1978. Possibly similar: **62301 KATSURA MARU** (Ja).

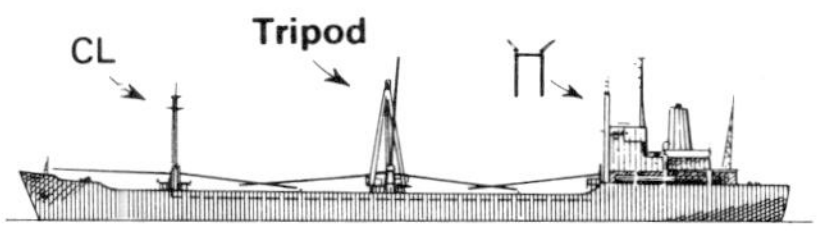

K_3MFK H13
62310 KAMO MARU. Ja/Ja 1970; C/HL; 5600; 122.05 × 7.7 (400.43 × 25.26); M; 13.5. Probable sister: **62311 BRIGHT MOON** (Pa) ex KYOKYU MARU 1978 Possible sister: **62312 KITANO MARU** (Ja).

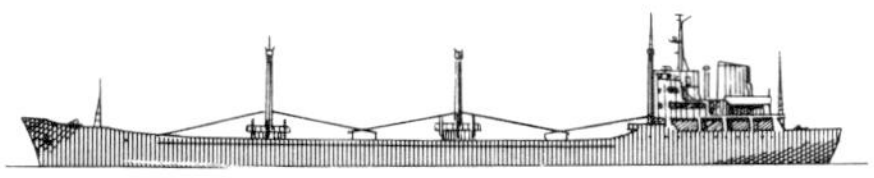

K_3MFK H13
● **62320 EUROLOGGER.** Gr/Ja 1965; C; 6700; 130.1 × 7.99 (426.83 × 26.2); M; 13; ex THEORIS 1974; ex KOYO MARU 1972.

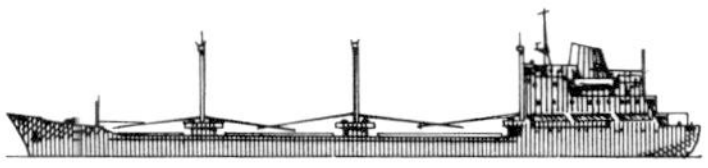

K_3MFK H13
● **62330 INDIA.** Pa/Ja 1967; C; 4000; 109.58 × 6.53 (359.5 × 21.42); M; 14.5; ex ILE GRANDE 1978; ex STAV VIKING 1975; ex STAVBORG 1967.

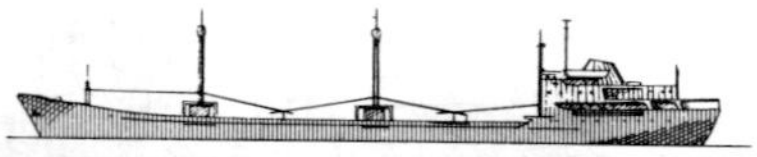

K_3MFK H13
62340 MARKINA. Pa/Sp 1965; C; 3700; 111.69 × 6.09 (366.44 × 20); M; 12.75; ex MAURINE K 1980; ex HANNAH BLUMENTHAL 1975; ex PINTO 1969.

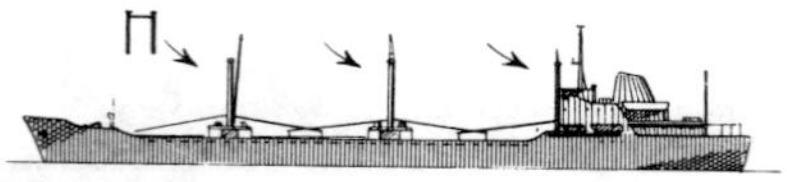

K_3MFK H13
62350 ATLANTIC SKY. Gr/Bz 1962; C; 3900/5400; 115.3 × —/6.32 (378.28 × —/20.73); M; 12; ex VOLTA REDONDA 1978. Sisters: **62351 SUNNY MED** (Li) ex CIDADE DE BELEM 1970 **62352 LONDRINA** (Bz) **62353 MARILIA** (Bz).

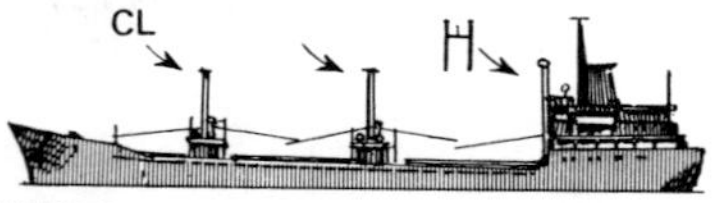

K_3MFK H13
62360 LINDO. No/No 1972; C; 4200; 112.83 × 6.89 (370.18 × 22.6); M; 13.75.

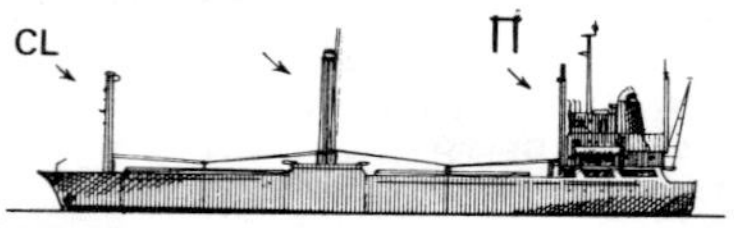

K_3MFK H2
62370 EBN JUBAIR. Ly/Ja 1976; C; 3500/6200; 105.7 × 7.5/7.62 (346.78 × 24.61/25); M; 13. Sister: **62371 EBN BATUTA** (Ly).

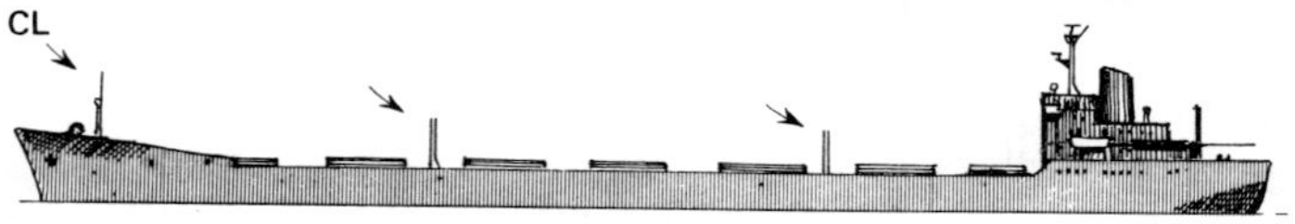

K_3MFK H3
62380 LEDA. Gr/Br 1968; B; 28900; 218.35 × 12.56 (716.37 × 41.21); M; 14.5; ex RIPON GRANGE 1980; ex OROTAVA 1978; ex OROTAVA BRIDGE 1974; ex OROTAVA 1969.

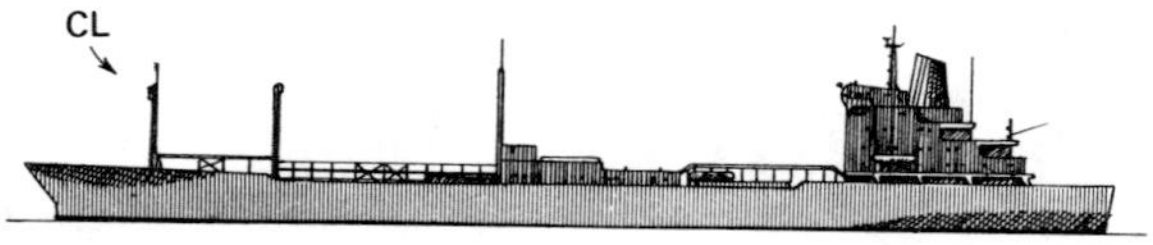

K_3MFKC H
62390 GAMBADA. Br/Br 1973; LGC; 21360; 177.86 × 10.02 (583.5 × 32.9); M; 16.25. Sister: **62391 GAZANA** (Br).

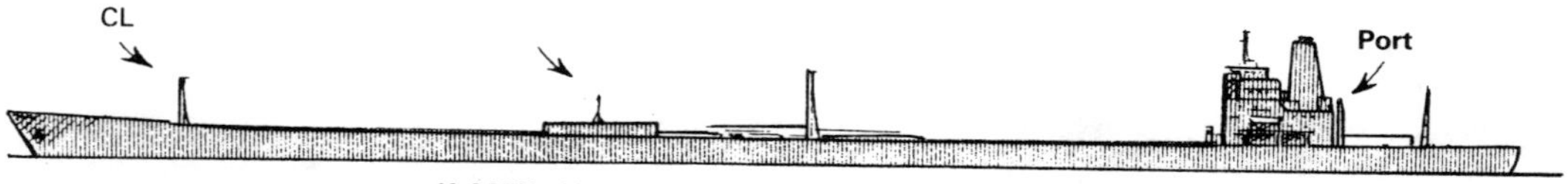

K_3MFK_2 H
62400 MEITAI MARU. Ja/Ja 1974; Tk; 123900; 324.01 × 19.51 (1063.03 × 64.01); M; 16.

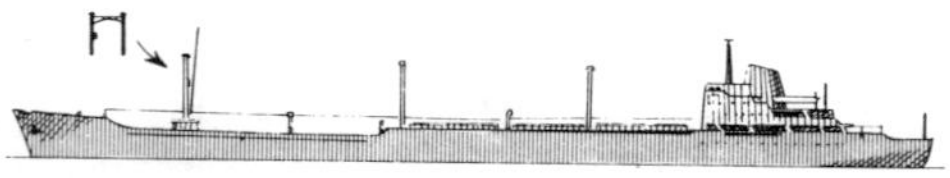

K_3MFK_2 H12
● **62410 SKYRIAN ROVER.** Gr/Sw 1958; 1958; 8600; 148.7 × 8.81 (487.86 × 28.9); M; 15.25; ex SKYRIAN SPIRIT 1980; ex LEFTERIS 1980; ex SUNRIVER 1974.

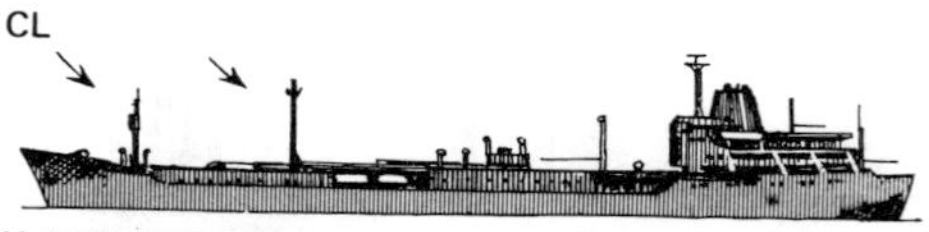

K_3MFK_2 H123
● **62420 JOULE.** Br/No 1965; LGC; 8700; 141.33 × 9.52 (463.68 × 31.23); M; 16; ex HAVGAS 1974. Sister: **62421 HAVFROST** (No).

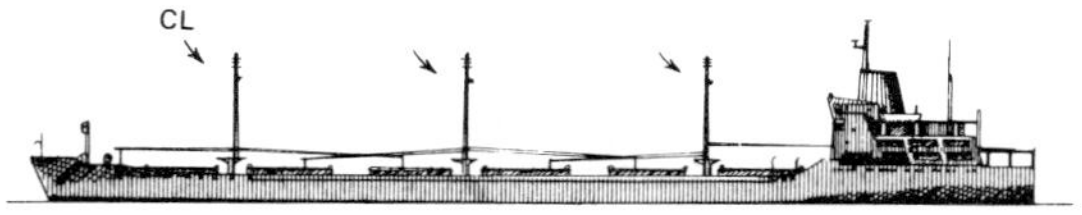

K_3MFK_2 H13

● **62430 MINORIES LUCK.** Gr/Br 1969; B; 13100; 158.5 × 9.54 (520.01 × 31.3); M; 15; ex BRENDA 1980; ex KATHY C 1978; ex BRUNES 1975. Sisters: **62431 BROTHER STAR** (Pa) ex EFTHALIA 1980; ex MANOS SAVE 1979; ex JANET C 1978; ex BRISKNES 1974; ex AQUILA 1971 **62432 BULKNES** (Br) **62433 WESTBON** (Ko) ex BAUGNES 1980 **62434 KAMPOS** (Gr) ex BLIDNES 1980 **62435 TOPAZ** (Pa) ex CHIOS PILOT 1980; ex ARGO CLYDE; ex SILVERCLYDE 1979; ex BAKNES 1974 **62436 CHIOS CAPTAIN** (Li) ex ARGO TWEED; ex SILVERTWEED 1979; ex BINSNES 1974.

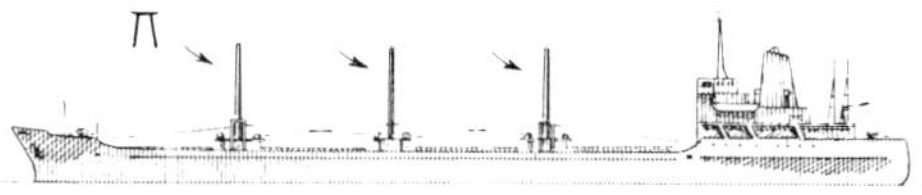

K_3MFK_2 H13

62440 PROTOKLITOS. Gr/Ja 1968; C; 6200/9900; 145.7 × 7.92/9.27 (478.02 × 25.98/30.41); M; 15.5; ex SILJA DAN 1975; ex SYLVIA CORD 1973; **'MITSUI - CONCORD''** type. Sister: ★**62441 FU PING** (RC) ex MARGARET CORD 1977.

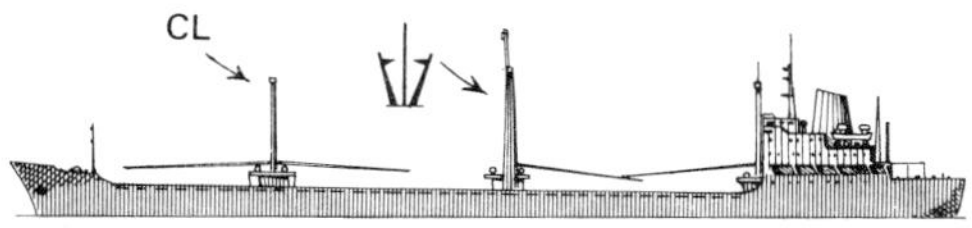

K_3MFK_2 H13

★**62450 DACHENG.** RC/Ja 1973; C/HL; 6900/10700; 154.95 × —/9.08 (508.37 × —/29.79); M; 16.25. Sister: ★**62451 DATIAN** (RC).

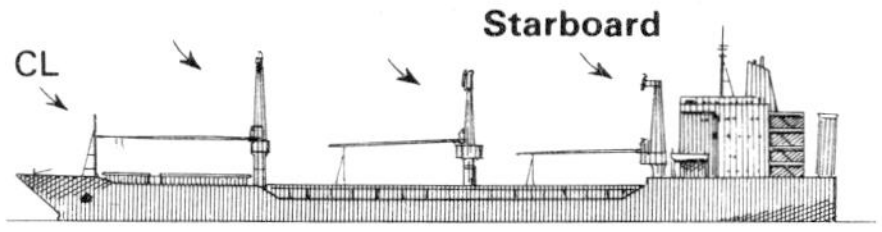

K_3MFR H13

● ★**62480 HAU GIANG.** Vn/De 1977; RoC; 9700; 132.92 × 9.4 (436.09 × 30.84); M; 15; Launched as HAMLET ALICE: **'HAMLET - MULTIFLEX'** type. Sisters: **62481 HAMLET ARABIA** (De) **62482 HAMLET SAUDIA** (De) ★**62483 NEN JIANG** (RC) ex NOPAL AUDREY 1978 ★**62484 IZVESTIYA** (Ru) **62485 KIMBERLEY** (Au) ★**62486 KNUD JESPERSEN** (Ru) ex ALEKSEY STAKHANOV.

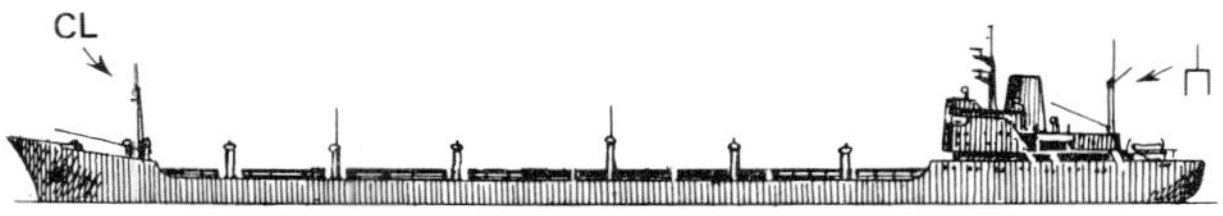

K_3MFM H13

★**62460 ZVENIGOROD.** Ru/Pd 1967; B; 16000; 187.15 × 9.54 (614 × 31.29); M; 15.5; **'B 470'** type. Sisters (Ru flag): ★**62461 ZAPOROZHYE** ★**62462 ZAKARPATYE** ★**62463 ZADONSK** ★**62464 ZARECHENSK** ★**62465 ZLATOUST** ★**62466 ZORINSK** (Pd flag): ★**62467 ZIEMIA KRAKOWSKA** ★**62468 ZIEMIA LUBELSKA** ★**62469 ZAGLEBIE MIEDZIOWE.**

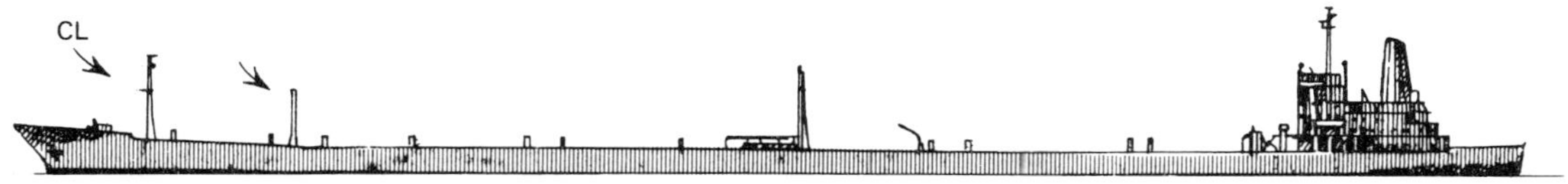

K_3MKF H

● **62490 BRITISH EXPLORER.** Br/Ja 1970; Tk; 108500; 326.02 × 18.9 (1069.62 × 62.01); T; 15.25. Sisters: **62491 SOUTH FOUNDATION** (Li) ex BRITISH PROSPECTOR **62492 SIVAND** (Ir) ex BRITISH NAVIGATOR 1976.

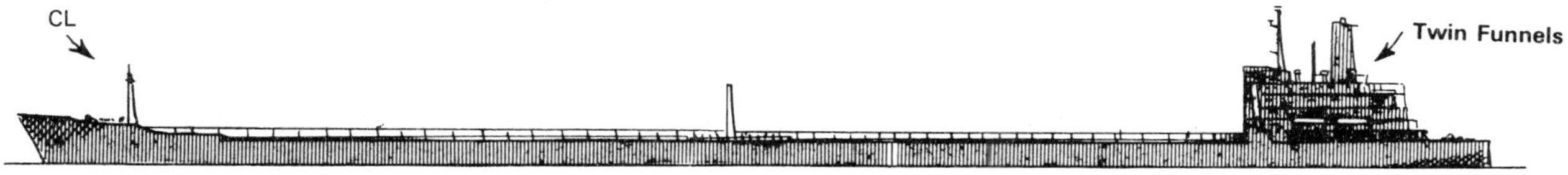

K_3MKF H1

62500 AL ANDALUS. Ku/Sp 1975; Tk; 191000; 362.57 × 26.09 (1189.5 × 85.6); TST; 14.5. Probable Sister: **62501 SANTA MARIA** (Sp) Launched as LA SANTA MARIA.

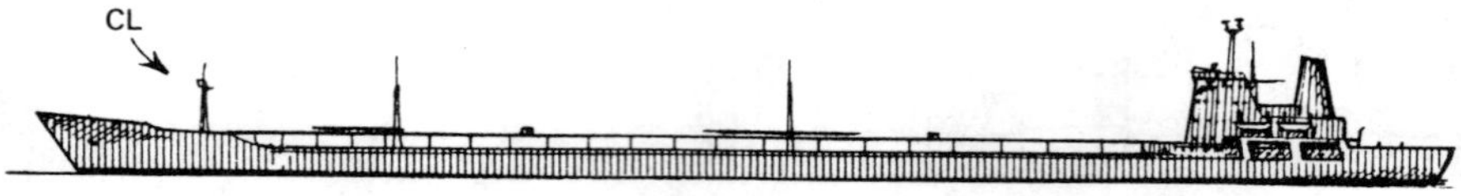

K_3MKF H

● **62510 AFRAN MERIDIAN.** Li/Sp 1968; Tk; 53800; 269.35 × 14.07 (883.69 × 46.16); M; 16.25; ex LA RABIDA 1980. Sister: **62511 MONTESA** (Sp) Similar: **62512 MUNATONES** (Sp) **62513 LA NINA** (Sp).

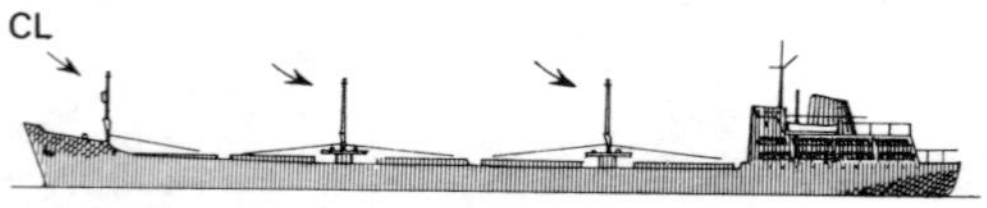

K_3MKF H13

62520 KIAN AN. Li/Br 1962; B; 9900; 152.56 × 8.66 (500.52 × 28.41); M; 14.75; ex BERNES 1972. Sister: **62521 APILIOTIS** (Li) ex BRIMNES 1970 Similar: **62522 ELPIDA** (Gr) ex GRANTON 1978; ex BINSNES 1970.

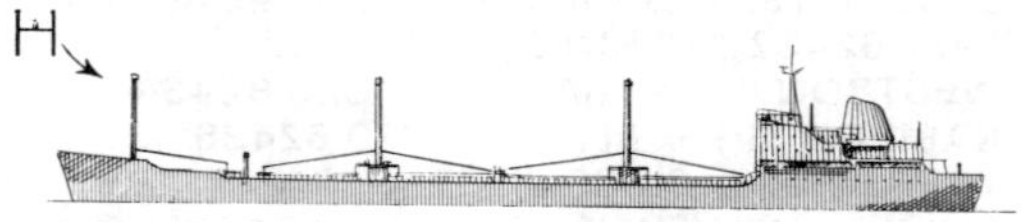

K_3MKF H13

● **62530 CAPTAIN PAPPIS.** Gr/FRG 1961; B; 9400; 151.19 × 9.21 (496.03 × 30.22); M; 14.75; ex OGOOUE 1976; ex DRACULA 1973; ex RINGULV 1969. Sister: **62531 SILVERCORN** (Li) ex JAGONA 1973.

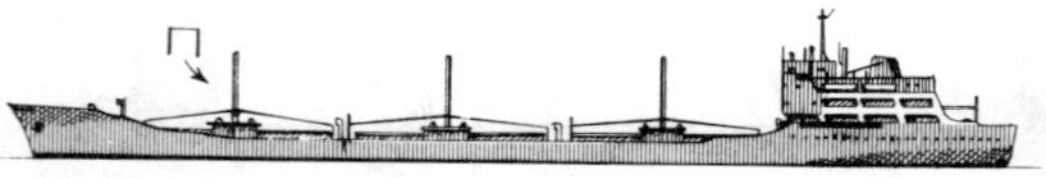

K_3MKF H13

62540 MARTIS. Gr/Br 1961; C; 11900; 161.63 × 9.64 (530.28 × 31.63); M; 13.5; ex ARC 1980; ex MARCO BOTZARIS 1976; ex VIRANA 1967.

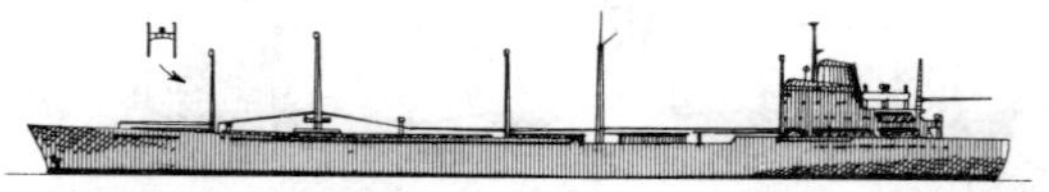

K_3MKFK H

62550 EVANGELOS LEMOS. Cy/FRG 1960; C/V; 14600; 174.56 × 10.11 (572.7 × 33.17); M; 14.75; ex CARL TRAUTWEIN 1975; Lengthened & deepened 1966. Sister: **62551 ELIAS ANGELAKOS** (Cy) ex EMMA JOHANNA 1976.

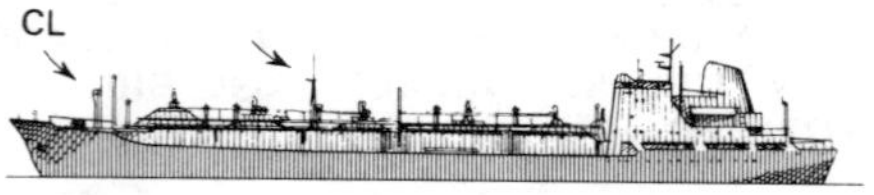

K_3MKFK H1

62560 MUNDOGAS BRASILIA. Li/No 1961; LGC/Tk; 8500; 131.4 × 8.32 (431.1 × 27.3); M; 15.

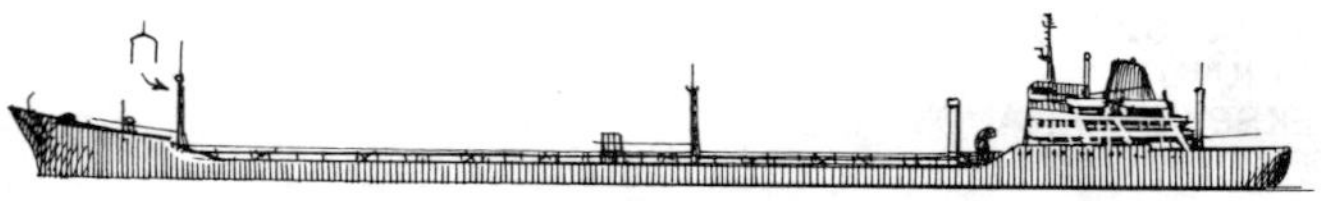

K_3MKFK H13

★**62570 LUGANSK.** Ru/Ja 1962; Tk; 22100; 207.02 × 11.08 (679.2 × 36.35); M; 16.5. Sisters (Ru flag): ★**62571 LEBEDIN** ★**62572 LIKHOSLAVL** ★**62573 LUBNY** ★**62574 LENINO** ★**62575 LYUBLINO** ★**62576 LYUBERTSY** ★**62577 LUKHOVITSY** (may be spelt **LUHOVITSY**).

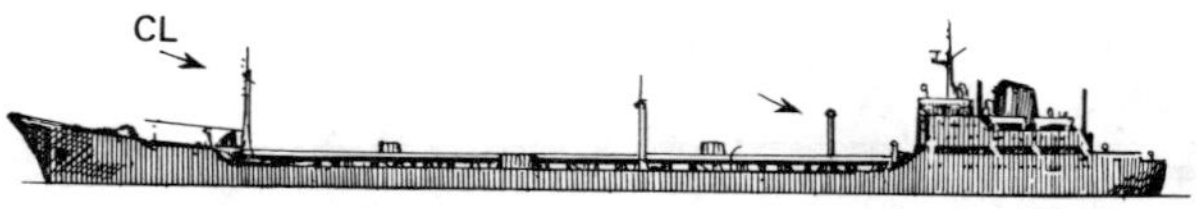

K_3MKFK H13

★**62580 DAUGAVPILS.** Ru/Yu 1965; Tk; 15100; 186.21 × 9.84 (610.93 × 32.28); M; 17. Sisters (Ru flag): ★**62581 GRIGORIY ACHKANOV** ★**62582 SPLIT** ★**62583 GORI** ★**62584 VASILIY PORIK** ★**62585 GENERAL ZHDANOV** ★**62586 MARSHAL BIRYUZOV** ★**62587 OLEKO DUNDICH** ★**62588 PETR ALEKSEYEV** ★**62589 BORZHOMI** ★**62590 GENERAL KARBYSHEV** ★**62591 DMITRIY ZHLOBA** ★**62592 NIKOLOZ BARATASHVILI** ★**62593 EPIFAN KOVTYUKH** ★**62594 MITROFAN SEDIN** ★**62595 MOS SHOVGENOV** ★**62596 STEPAN VOSTRETSOV** ★**62597 PYATIDYESYATILYETIYE SOVETSKOY GRUZII** (also known as **50 LETIYE SOVETSKOY GRUZII**) ★**62598 PAVEL DYBENKO** ★**62599 REZEKNE** ★**62600 RIJEKA** ★**62601 GENERAL BOCHAROV** ★**62602 GENERAL KRAVTSOV** ★**62603 GENERAL SHKODUNOVICH** ★**62604 NIKOLAY PODVOYSKIY** (Ag flag): **62605 SKIKDA** ex KUTAISI 1974 **62606 ARZEW** ex BATUMI 1974.

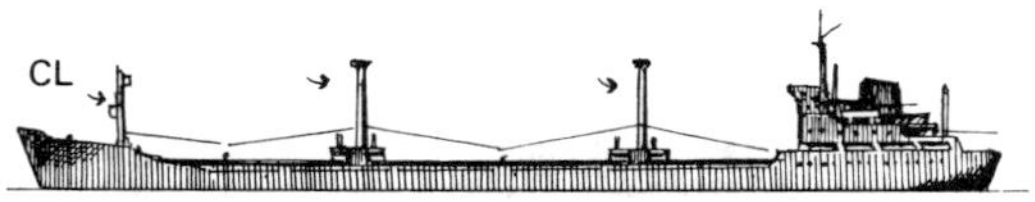

K_3MKFK H13

★**62610 JING HAI.** RC/Br 1968; B; 12400; 159.06 × 9.47 (521.85 × 31.07); M; 14.75; ex BAYNES 1973. Sisters: **62611 ALBAFORTH** (Gr) ex SILVERFORTH 1978; ex BELLNES 1974 **62612 MARIA LEMOS** (Gr) ex CAPTAIN PANDELIS S LEMOS 1975; ex BIRKNES 1973 **62613 SATYA PADAM** (In) ex BORGNES 1973.

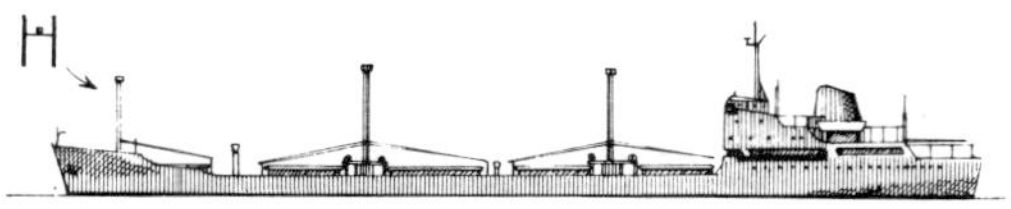

K_3MKFK H13

● **62620 CHRISTINA C.** Gr/FRG 1961; C; 10400; 151.19 × 8.98 (496.03 × 29.46); M; 14.75; ex BREIM 1977; ex FRUEN 1965. Similar: **62621 CAPTAIN PAPPIS** (Gr) ex OGOOUE 1976; ex DRACULA 1973; ex RINGULV 1969 **62622 GOLD CORAL** (Gr) ex GOLDCORN 1979; ex JAVARA 1973 **62623 SILVERCORN** (Li) ex JAGONA 1973.

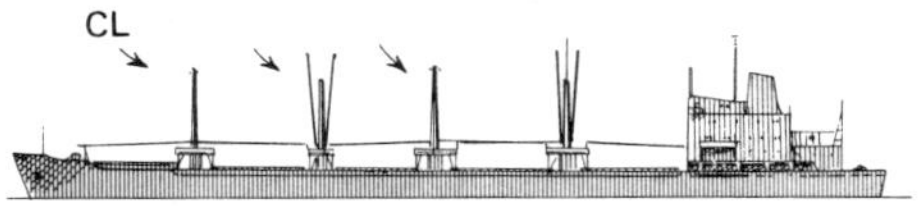

K_3MKMF H1

62630 NEDLLOYD NIGER. Ne/FRG 1971; C; 6500; 139.55 × 9.19 (457.84 × 30.15); M; 15.5; **'GERMAN LIBERTY'** type.

K_3MKMF H13

62640 GOGO RANGER. Li/Sw 1958; Tk; 12500; 170.57 × 9.58 (559.61 × 31.43); M; 15; ex POST RANGER 1977; ex ANCO STRIPE 1971; ex ANCO BERGLJOT 1969; ex BERGLJOT 1964.

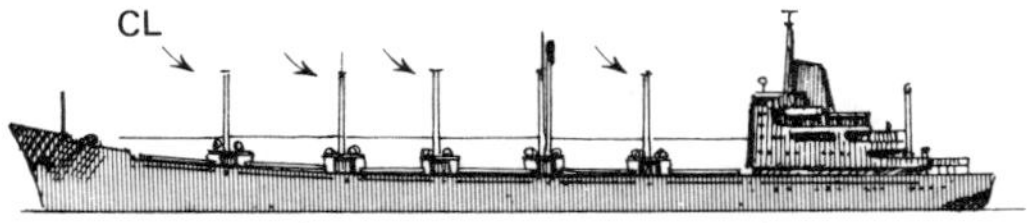

K_3MKMFK H1

62650 SELAS. Gr/Ne 1963; C; 8300/10900; 154.13 × 8.59/9.91 (505.68 × 28.18/32.51); M; 15; ex JAG ASHA 1976; ex DAGEID 1967.

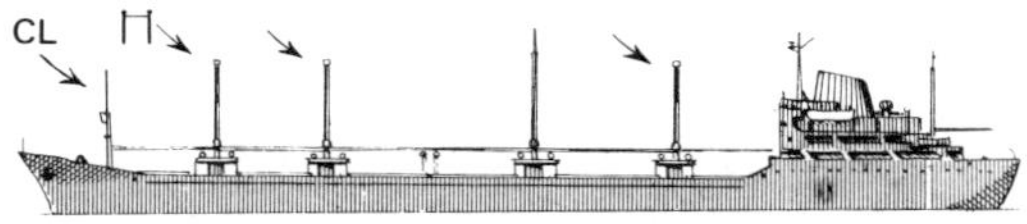

K_3MKMFK H13

62660 NOVO REDONDO. Po/De 1963; C; 10900; 158.25 × 9.51 (519.19 × 31.2); M; 16.25; ex FERNCAPE 1970.

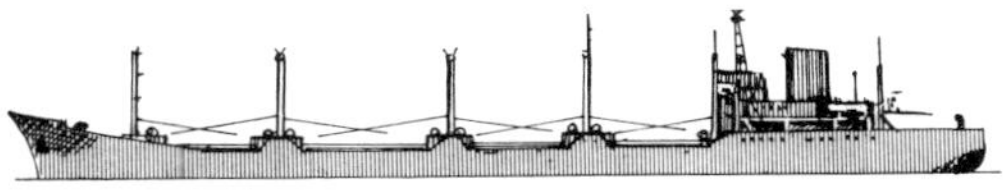

K_3MKMFK H13

62670 PAPACAROLOS. Gr/Ja 1959; O; 10200; 156.11 × 8.54 (512.17 × 28.02); M; 13; ex TOMIURA MARU 1975.

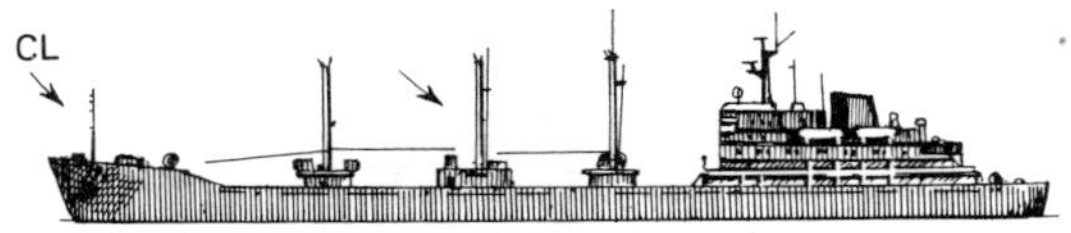

K_3M_2F H1

★**62680 KARL LIEBKNECHT.** Ru/DDR 1970; FC; 11900; 155 × 7.79 (508.53 × 25.58); M; 17.25; **'POLAR'** type. Similar (Ru flag): ★**62681 ERNST THALMANN** ★**62682 OTTO GROTEVOHL** ★**62683 WILHELM PIECK** ★**62684 ROSA LUXEMBURG** ★**62685 FRITZ HECKERT** ★**62686 MATHIAS THESEN** ★**62687 ANTANAS SNECHKUS**; Launched as IGNALINA ★**62688 DIMANT** ★**62689 LAZURNYY BEREG** ★**62690 SOLNECHNYY BEREG** ★**62691 YANTARNIY BEREG** ★**62692 IZUMRUDNYY BEREG** ★**62693 GRANITNYY BEREG** ★**62694 SKALISTYY BEREG** ★**62695 ZHEMCHUYNYY BEREG** (Rm flag): ★**62696 POLAR III** ★**62697 POLAR IV** ★**62698 POLAR V** ★**62699 POLAR VI** Possibly Similar (DRR flag): ★**62700 LICHTENHAGEN.**

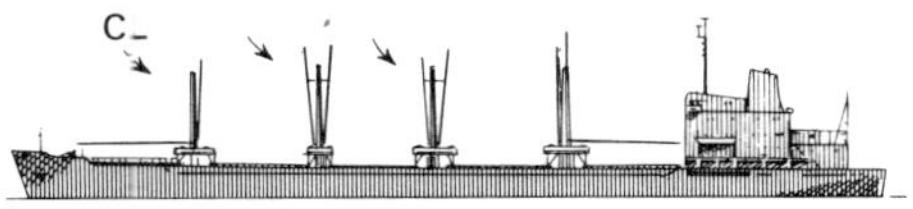

K_3M_2F H1

62710 LUMUMBA. Zr/FRG 1974; C; 6600/9400; 139.55 × —/9.17 (457.84 × —/30.09); M; 16; **'German Liberty'** type. Sisters (Zr flag): **62711 BANDUNDU 62712 BUKAVU 62713 KISANGANI 62714 MBANDAKA 62715 MBUJI-MAYI.**

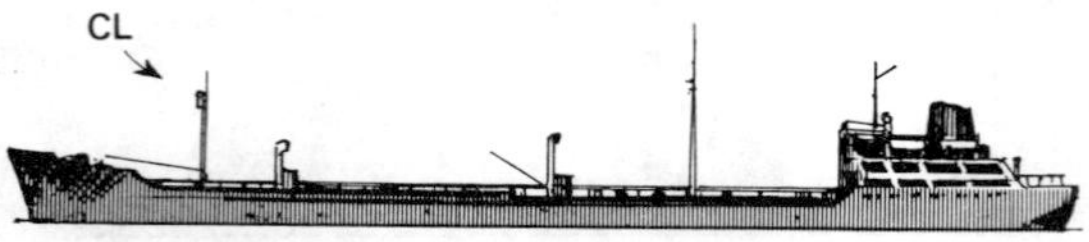

K_3M_2F H13
62720 THASSOS. Gr/Sw 1958; Tk; 12400; 169.7×9.57 (556.75×31.4); M; 14.75; ex PACIFICA 1978; ex STOLT PACIFIC 1975; ex STOLT SILDRA 1972; ex SILDRA 1964; ex SIGNE INGELSSON 1964.

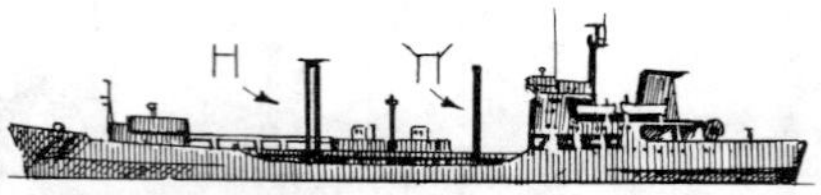

K_3M_2F H13
★62730 DUBNA. Ru/Fi 1974; RT; 6000; 130×7.19 (426.51×23.59); M; 16. Sisters (Ru flag): **★62731 IRKUT ★62732 PECHENGA ★62733 SVENTA.**

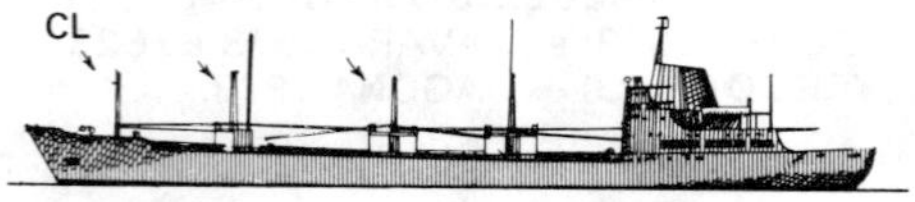

K_3M_2FK H1
62740 SISAL TRADER. Gr/Br 1964; C; 5400/7600; 139.25×7.62/7.74 (456.86×25/25.39); M; 16.5; ex MERCHANT; ex SCYTHIA 1969. Sisters: **62741 STEEL TRADER** (Gr) ex SCHOLAR; ex SAMARIA 1970 **62742 SRI KAILASH** (In) ex NEPTUNE AMBER 1977; ex SCOTIA 1970.

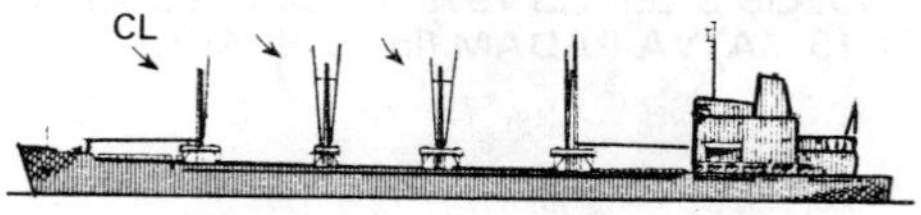

K_3M_2FK H1
62750 LUMUMBA. Zr/FRG 1974; C; 6600/9400; 139.55×—/9.17 (457.84×—/30.09); M; 16; **'German Liberty'** type. Sisters (Zr flag): **62751 BANDUNDU 62752 BUKAVU 62753 KISANGANI 62754 MBANDAKA 62755 MBUJI-MAYI.**

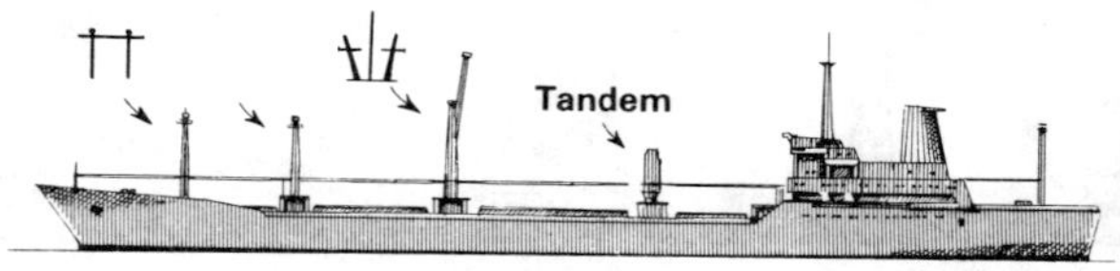

K_2MCMFK H13
● **62760 CIUDAD DE POPAYAN.** Co/Pd 1976; C; 117.00/16100; 180.7×8.7/9.67 (592.85×28.54/31.73); M; 21; **'B-464'** type. Sisters (Co flag): **62761 CIUDAD DE NENA 62762 CIUDAD DE SANTA MARTA** Similar (B-469 type): **62763 CIUDAD DE ARMENIA 62764 CIUDAD DE PASTO 62765 CIUDAD DE QUITO.**

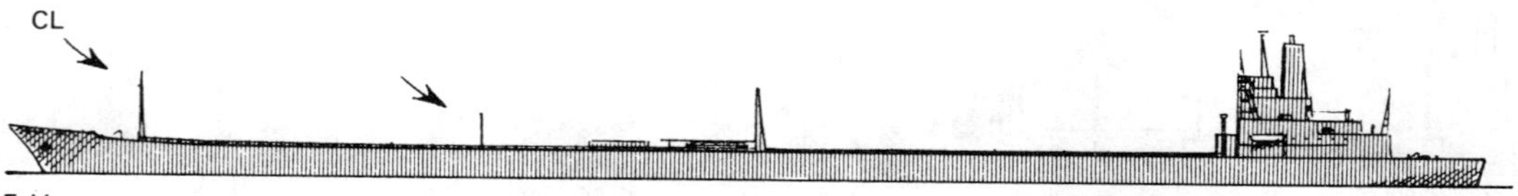

K_2MF H
62770 SHUNKO MARU. Ja/Ja 1974; Tk; 120500; 324.01×19.43 (1063.02×63.73); T; 15.75. Similar: **62771 HOKO MARU** (Ja).

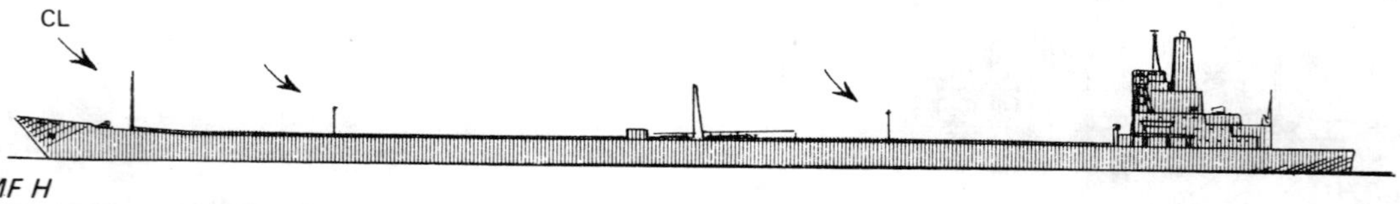

K_2MF H
62780 JAPIN LUPINUS. Ja/Ja 1972; Tk; 120500; 324.01×19.47 (1063.02×63.88); T; 15.75. Sister: **62781 JAPAN CARNATION** (Ja) Similar: **62782 WORLD ADMIRAL** (Li) **62783 WORLD AMBASSADOR** (Li) **62784 KHARK** (Ir).

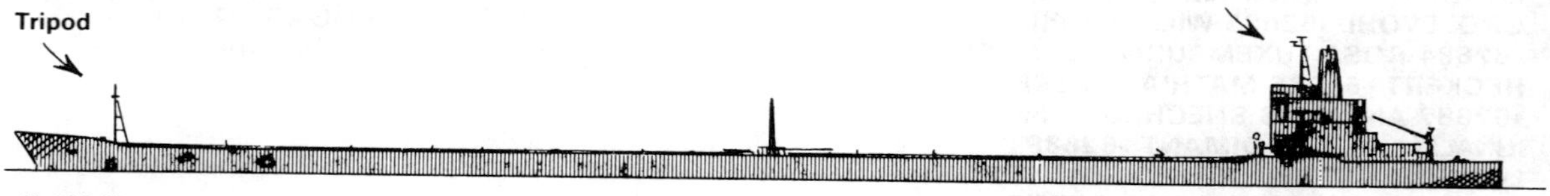

K_2MF H
62790 MELPO LEMOS. Li/FRG 1971; Tk; 113800; 347.81×19.96 (1141.1×65.55); T; 16. Sisters: **62791 CHRYSANTHY M LEMOS** (Li) **62792 IRENE LEMOS** (Li) **62793 MICHAEL C LEMOS** (Gr).

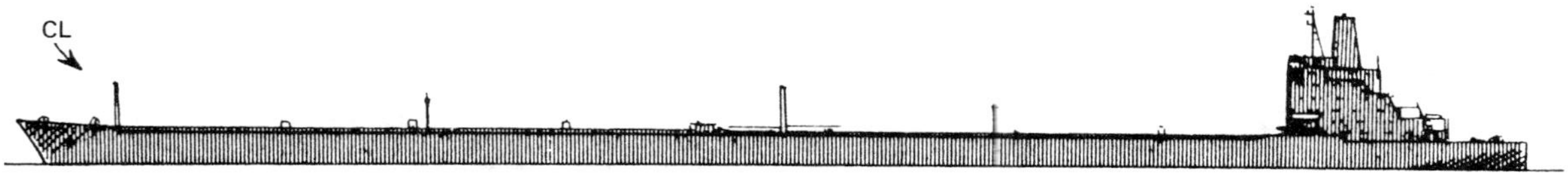

K_2MF H
62800 ESSO NORTHUMBRIA. Br/Br 1970; Tk; 126500; 348.47 × 19.98; (1143.27 × 65.55); T; 15.75. Sisters: **62801 ESSO HIBERNIA** (Br) **62802 ESSO ULIDIA** (Br) Similar: **62803 ESSO SKANDIA** (Li) **62804 ESSO COPENHAGEN** (Li) **62805 ESSO BRETAGNE** (Fr) **62806 ESSO PROVENCE** (Fr).

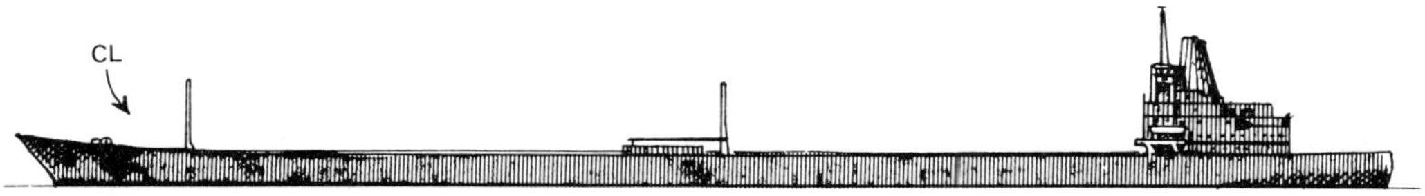

K_2MF H
62810 TOKYO MARU. Ja/Ja 1966; Tk; 94400; 306.51 × 16.5 (1005.61 × 54.13); T; 16; Converted to a loading tanker and equipped with fenders on deck.

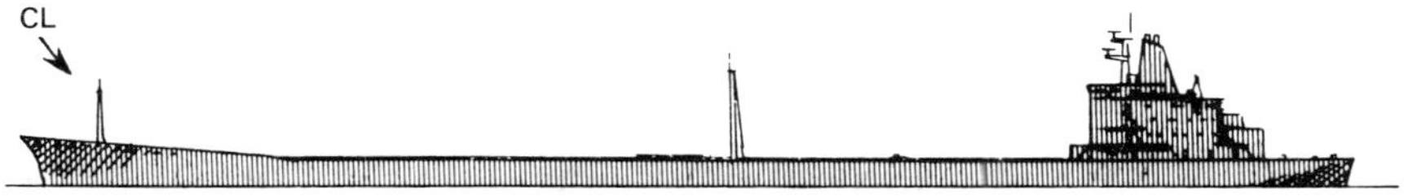

K_2MF H
62820 ST VINCENT. Sg/Fr 1976; Tk; 44500; 250.53 × 14.25 (820.96 × 46.75); M; 16. Sisters: **62821 ST MARCOS** (Sg) ex DOMINANT 1977 **62822 TOURAINE** (Fr) ex CHANGI STAR 1980; ex ST RAPHAEL 1977; ex ADAMANT 1977.

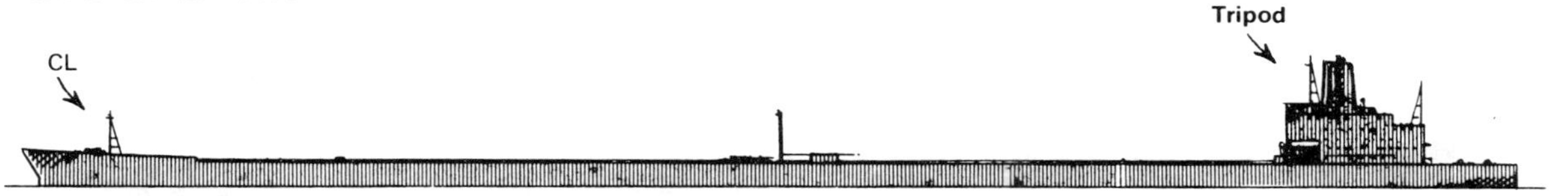

K_2MF H
● **62830 LEPTON.** Li/Ne 1975; Tk; 155300; 352.61 × 22.35 (1156.86 × 73.33); T; —. Possibly Similar: **62831 LEMBULUS** (Br).

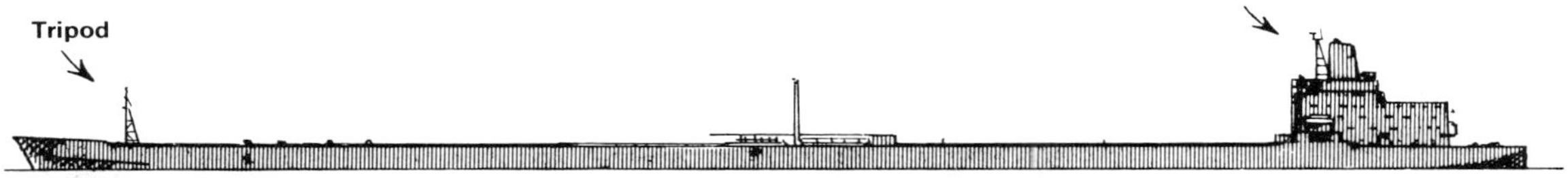

K_2MF H
62840 ESSO NORMANDIE. Fr/Fr 1974; Tk; 137600; 343.04 × 21.06 (1125.46 × 69.09); T; 16. Sisters: **62841 ESSO PICARDIE** (Fr) **62842 ESSO AFRICA** (Li).

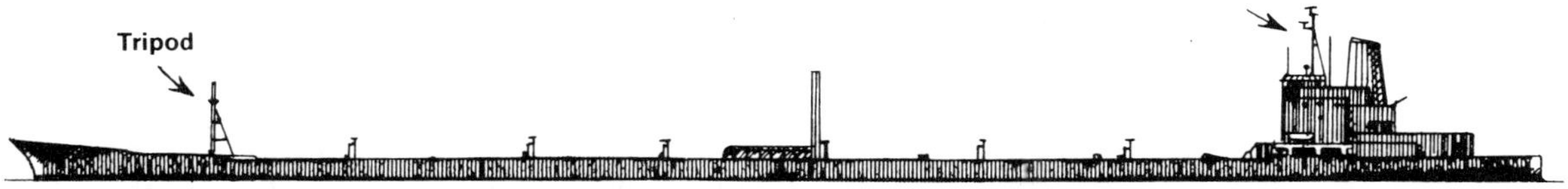

K_2MF H
62850 AGIP SICILIA. It/It 1972; Tk; 126100; 348.32 × 20.02 (1142.78 × 65.68); M; 16. Sisters (It flag): **62851 AGIP SARDEGNA 62852 PARAGGI** ex SANT' AMBROGIO 1978 **62853 NIRVANA** ex OCEANIA 1977 Possible Sisters: **62854 AGIP ABRUZZO 62855 AGIP CAMPANIA 62856 AGIP LAZIO 62857 AGIP MARCHE 62858 NAI MARIO PERRONE 62859 NAI DI STEFANO 62860 NAI MATTEINI 62861 NAI ROCCO PIAGGIO 62862 PRIMAROSA 62863 RITINA 62864 VOLERE.**

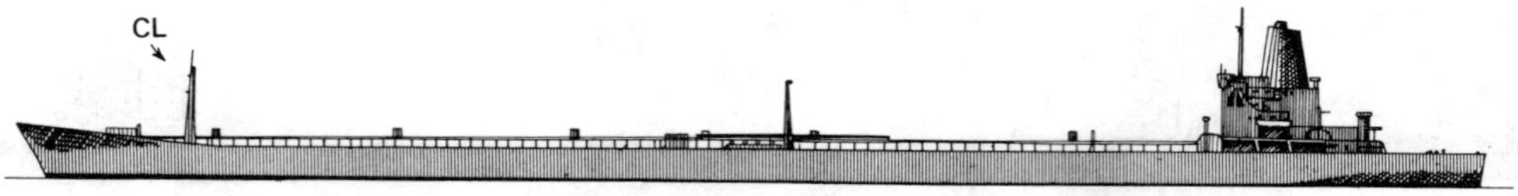

K_2MF H

62870 KYPROS. Gr/Ja 1969; Tk; 120000; 324.29× 19.3 (1063.94× 63.32); T; 16; ex ARDTARAIG 1979. Sisters (Li flag): **62871 ELPIDA** ex ARDLUI 1981 **62872 PERCH** ex PAULA; ex ARDVAR.

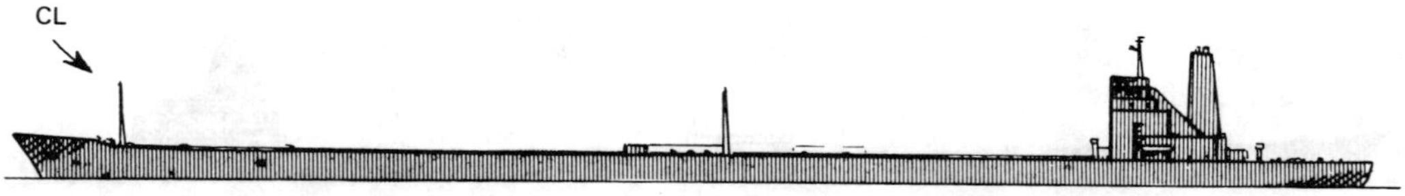

K_2MF H

62880 GOLDEN MARINER. Ja/Ja 1969; Tk; 93500; 305.7× 16.99 (1002.95× 55.75); M; 15.75; ex NIKKO MARU 1980.

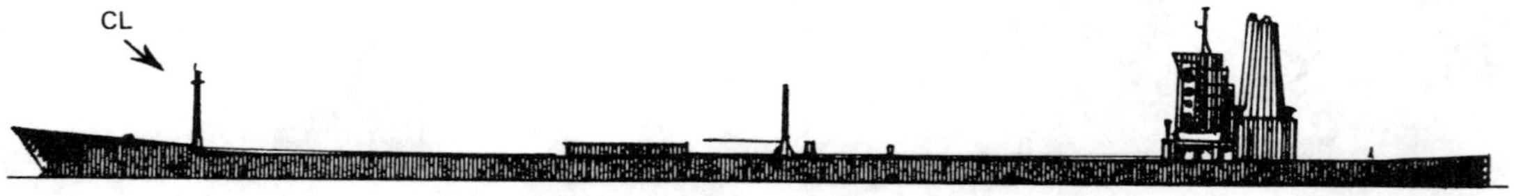

K_2MF H

62890 MOBIL KESTREL. Li/Ja 1970; Tk; 104400; 324.01 × 19 (1063.02× 62.34); M; 15.75; ex MITSUMINESAN MARU 1977.

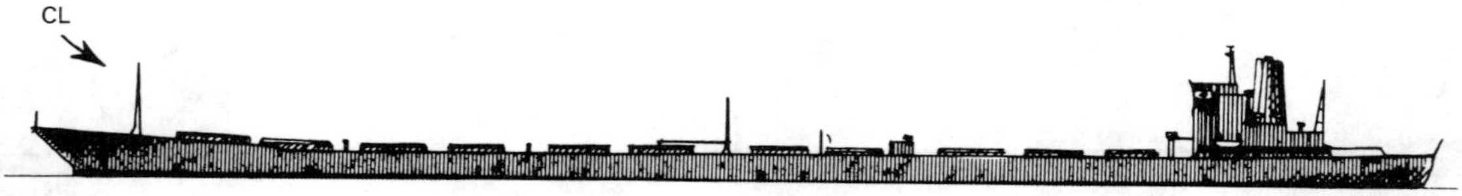

K_2MF H

62900 TANTALUS. Br/Ja 1972; 00; 120800; 327.82× 19.1 (1075.53× 62.66); T; 15.5. Similar: **62901 TSURUMI MARU** (Ja) **62902 WORLD ERA** (Li) ex JARL MALMROS 1979 **62903 WORLD LADY** (Li) ex TARTAR 1978 Similar (larger): **62904 DOCECANYON** (Li).

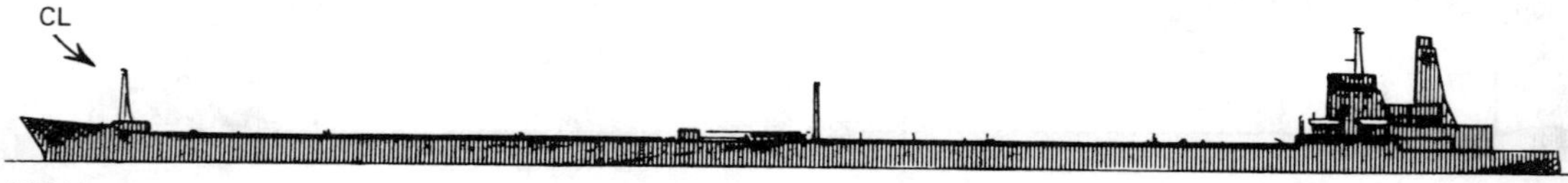

K_2MF H

● **62910 OLYMPIC ACTION.** Li/Ja 1970; Tk; 98600; 329.88× 19.42 (1082.28× 63.71); T; 15.5. Sisters (Li flag): **62911 OLYMPIC ANTHEM 62912 OLYMPIC ASPIRATION 62913 OLYMPIC AVENGER.**

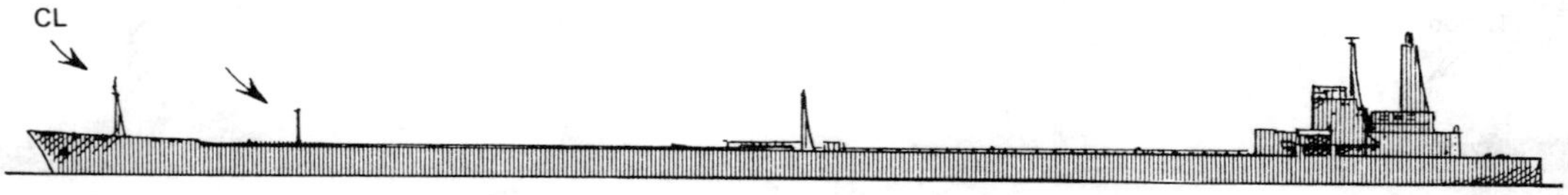

K_2MF H

62920 AL QASIM. Li/Ne 1970; Tk; 92000; 325.33× 18.98 (1067.36× 62.27); T; 16; ex MOBIL RAVEN 1977; ex BERGEMASTER 1976; ex MARTICIA 1976. Similar: **62921 SOLON** (Li) ex MOBIL TERN 1979; ex BERGE CAPTAIN 1976; ex MYSELLA 1976.

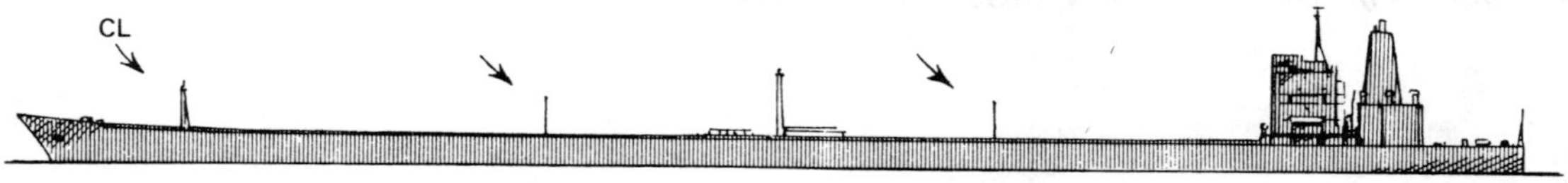

K_2MF H

62940 PROSPERITY. Li/Ko 1974; Tk; 124700; 344.43× 20.77 (1130.02× 68.14); T; 16; ex ATLANTIC BARON 1977. Sister: **62941 KOREA SUN** (Ko) launched as ATLANTIC BARONESS Possible Sisters: **62942 KOREA STAR** (Ko) **62943 KOREA BANNER** (Ko) **62944 CATTLEYA** (Li)

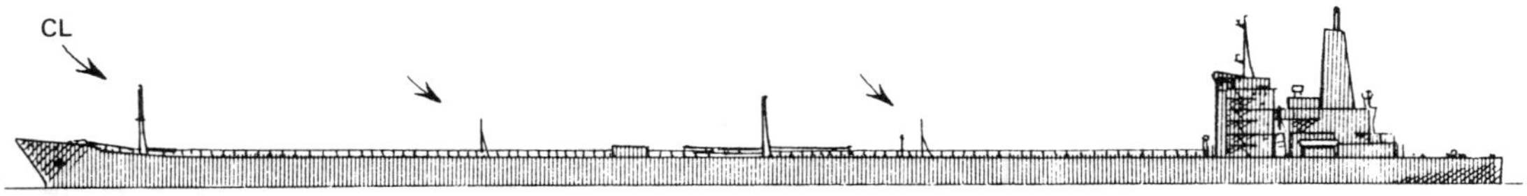

K_2MF H
62950 MAASBREE. Ne/Ja 1973; Tk; 135400; 337.07 × 21.05 (1105.87 × 69.06); T; 16; ex SINDE 1973.

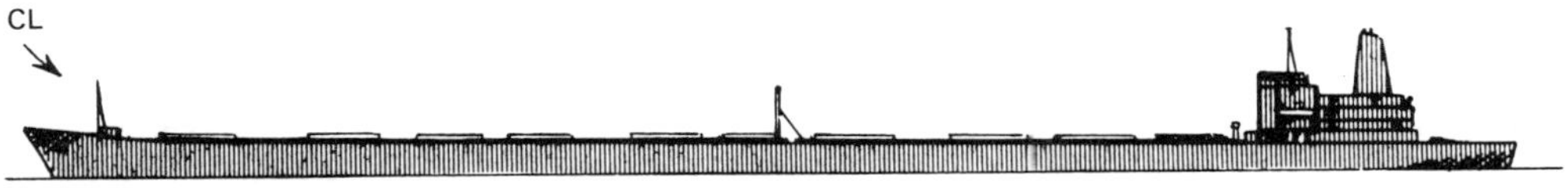

K_2MF H
62960 ASIATIC. Gr/Ja 1971; OBO; 70500; 290.99 × 17.03 (953 × 55.87); T; 16.5. Sisters (Gr flag): **62961 SYMPHONIC 62962 CLASSIC 62963 AUTHENTIC.**

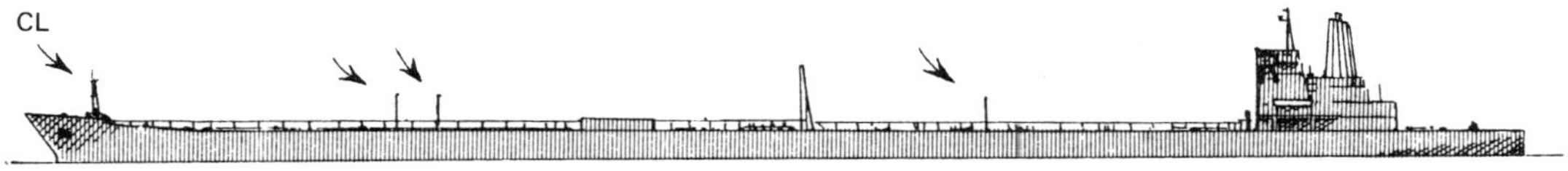

K_2MF H
62970 WORLD DUKE. Pa/Ja 1975; Tk; 111400; 324.01 × 20.03 (1063.03 × 65.68); T; 16.5.

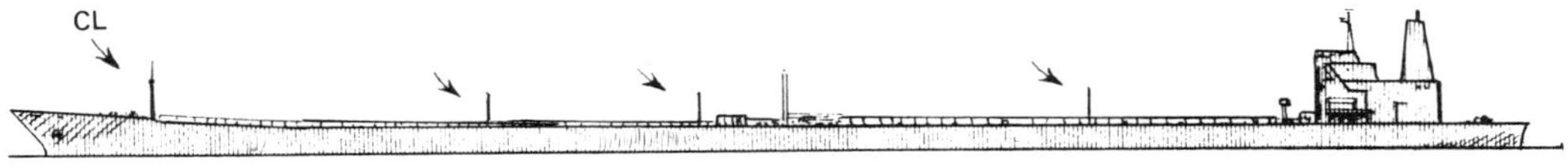

K_2MF H
62980 JAPAN VIOLET. Ja/Ja 1974; Tk; 116300; 319.95 × 19.66 (1049.7 × 64.5); T; 16.25; launched as CONSUL. Similar: **62981 ENERGY GROWTH** (Li).

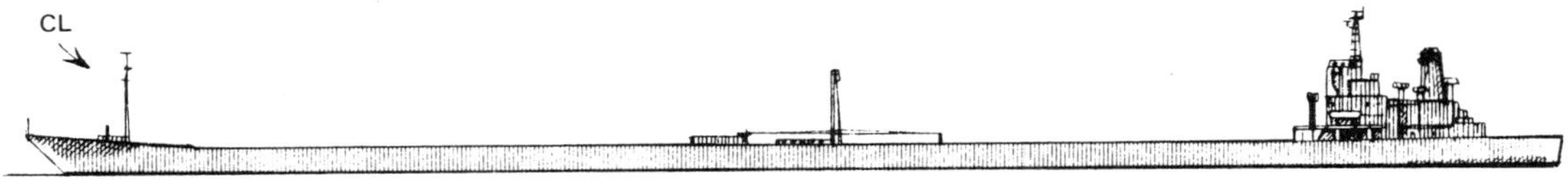

K_2MF H
62990 PAUL L. FAHRNEY. Li/Ja 1971; Tk; 118860; 337.5 × 20.49 (1107.3 × 67.2); T; 15.5. Sister: **62991 J.R. GREY** (Li) Similar: **62992 UNITED OVERSEAS 1** (Li).

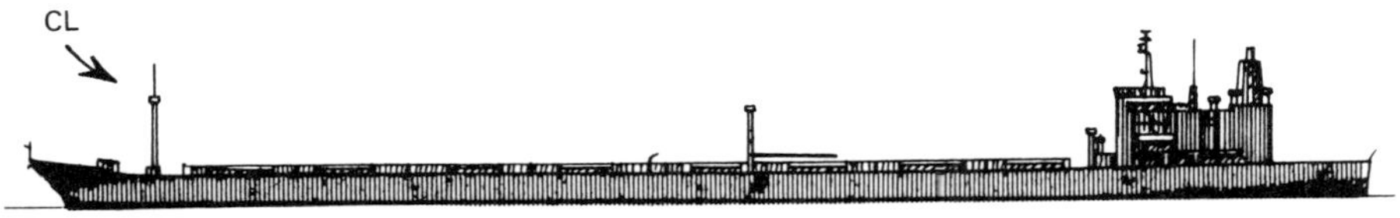

K_2MF H
● **63000 CYPRESS KING.** Sg/Ja 1972; 00; 95000; 295.03 × 17.5 (967.95 × 57.42); T; 16; launched as TAIKO MARU.

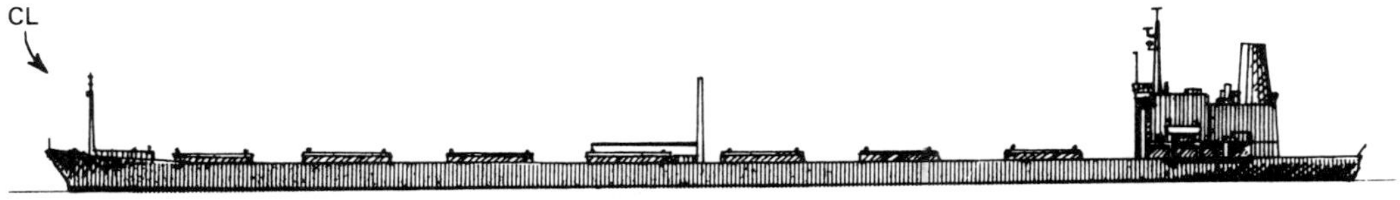

K_2MF H
63010 HAMPTON MARU. Ja/Ja 1971; OBO; 95900; 297.01 × 17.62 (974.44 × 57.81); T; 15.5. Sister: **63011 PACIFIC MARU** (Ja).

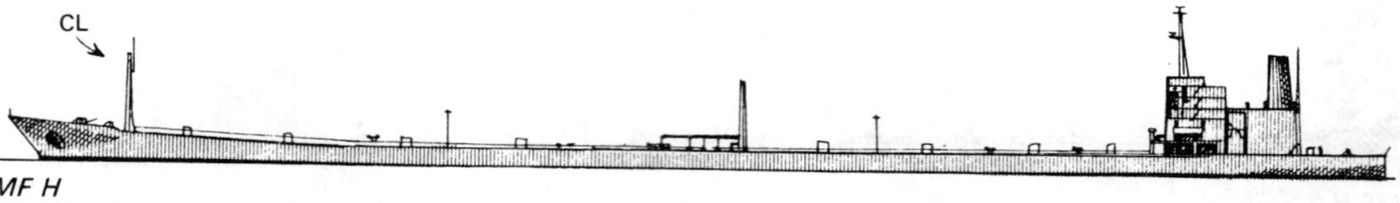

K_2MF H

63020 OGDEN SUNGARI. Li/Ja 1975; Tk; 124100; 338.87 × 21.01 (1111.78 × 68.93); T; 16. Similar: **63021 MOSCLIFF** (No).

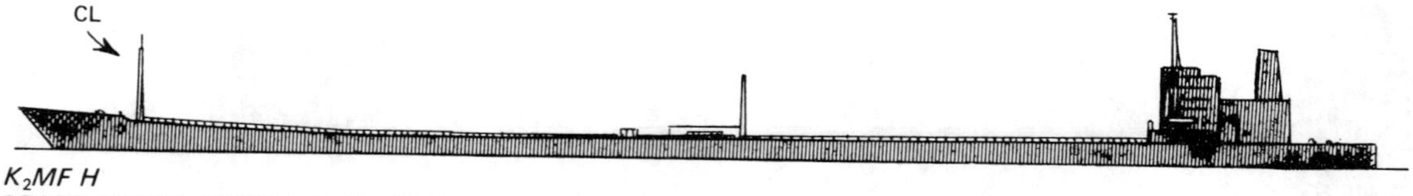

K_2MF H

63030 SAUDI GLORY. Li/Ja 1974; Tk; 122300; 340.8 × 21.07 (118.11 × 69.13); T; 16.25; ex MOBIL MARINER 1974. Sisters: **63031 AL HARAMAIN** (Li) launched as MOBIL SUPPLIER **63032 ATHOS** (Fr) **63033 D'ARTAGNAN** (Fr) **63034 MOBIL FALCON** (Li).

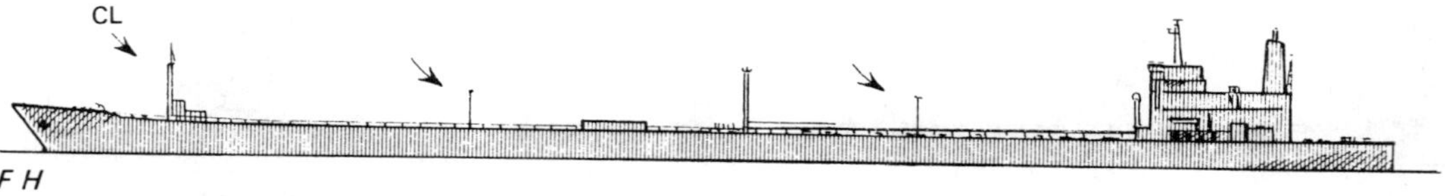

K_2MF H

63040 TOWADA MARU. Ja/Ja 1970; Tk; 111600; 319.74 × 19 (1049.02 × 62.34); T; 16.

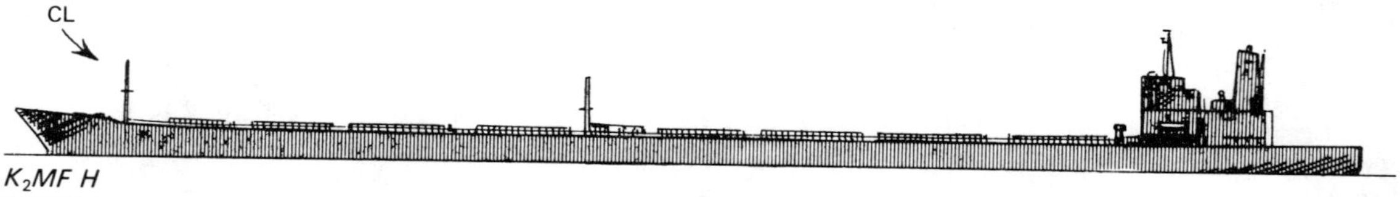

K_2MF H

63050 USA MARU. Ja/Ja 1972; 00; 142200; 337.02 × 21.02 (1105.71 × 68.96); T; 16.

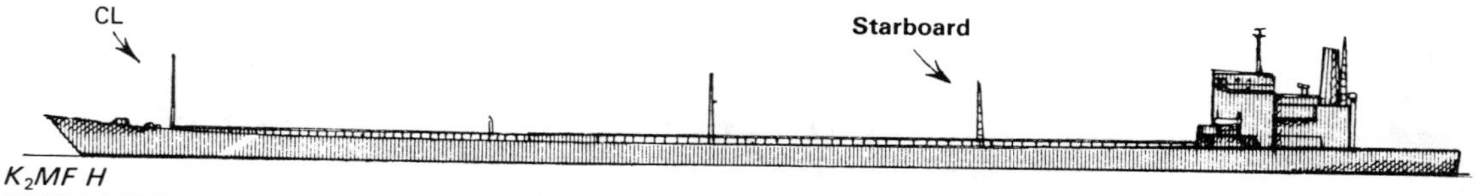

K_2MF H

63060 VENTURE AMERICA. Li/Ja 1973; Tk; 119700; 337.12 × 21.01 (1106.04 × 68.93); T; 16; ex CONOCO AMERICA 1978. Possibly Similar: **63061 VENTURE INDEPENDENCE** (Li) ex CONOCO INDEPENDENCE 1978.

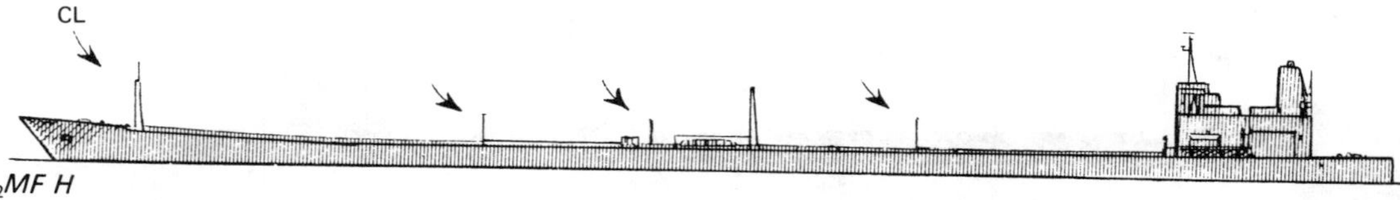

K_2MF H

63070 SAINT MARCET. Li/Ja 1974; Tk; 122900; 340.8 × 21.07 (1118.11 × 69.13); T; 15.5. Sisters (Li flag): **63071 PRIMROSE 63072 VENTURE EUROPE** ex CONOCO EUROPE Probable Sister: **63073 VENTURE CANADA** ex CONOCO CANADA **63074 WORLD CANADA.**

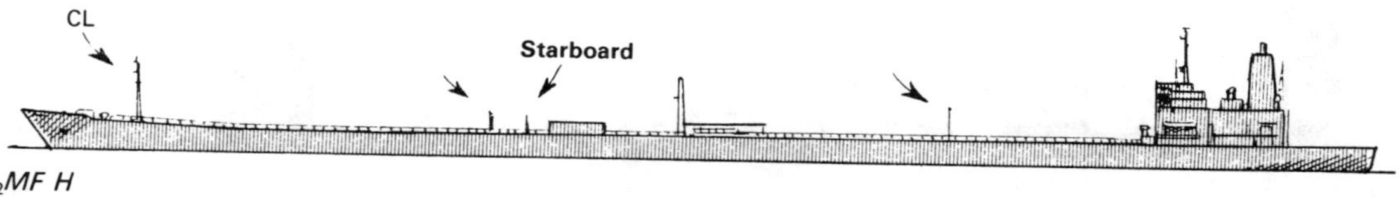

K_2MF H

63080 WORLD BERMUDA. Li/Ja 1974; Tk; 117800; 336.99 × 21.05 (1105.61 × 69.06); T; 16; launched as WORLD MONARCH.

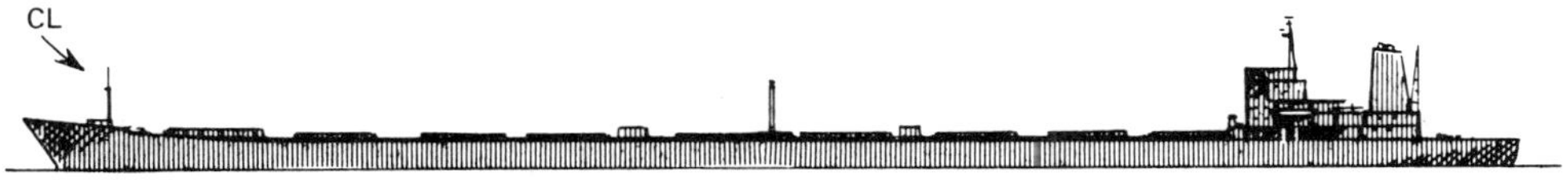

K_2MF H

63090 LAUREL WREATH. Li/Ja 1975; BO; 27300; 286.65 × 22 (940.45 × 72.18); M; 15.5.

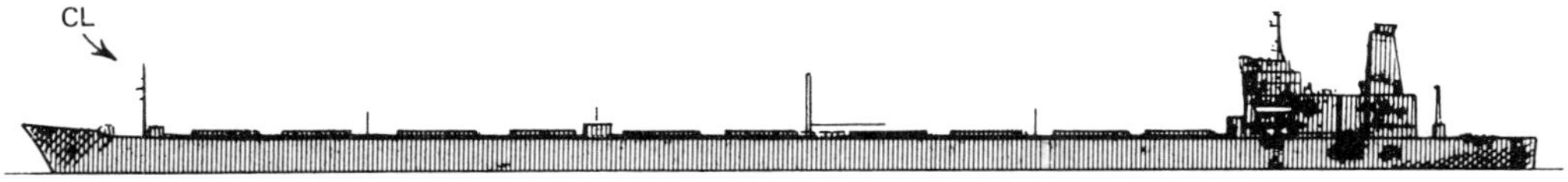

K_2MF H

63100 AMAZON MARU. Ja/Ja 1973; OO; 89500; 300.01 × 16.99 (984.28 × 55.74); M; 16; ex SANKO ROBIN 1980. Sister: **63101 TRIPHAROS** (Li) Similar: **63102 WAKAZURA MARU** (Ja) **63103 YAMAZURA MARU** (Ja) **63104 ZUIHO MARU** (Ja) **63105 LARINA** (Li).

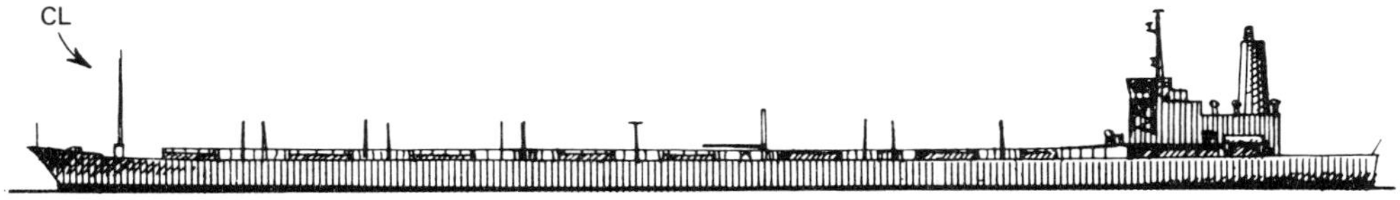

K_2MF H

63110 GOLDEN CLOVER. Li/Ja 1971; OBO; 89100; 295.03 × 17.45 (967.95 × 57.25); T; 16. Sisters (Li flag): **63111 GOLDEN TULIP 63112 WORLD SPLENDOUR** Possibly Similar: **63113 EASTERN SPIRIT.**

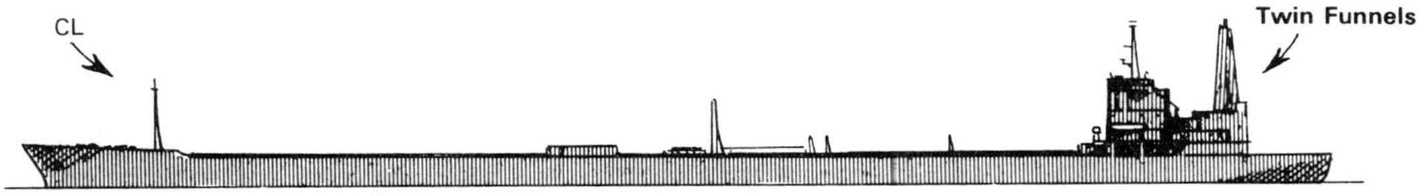

K_2MF H

63120 KAIMON MARU. Ja/Ja 1968; Tk; 95600; 300.24 × 18.01 (985.04 × 59.09); T; 15.75.

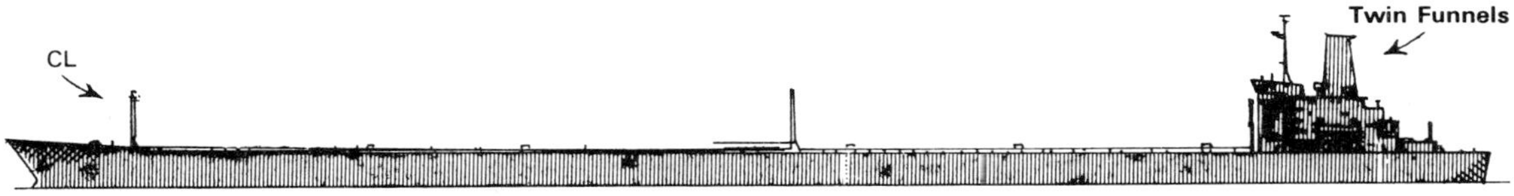

K_2MF H

● **63130 CARTHAGO-NOVA.** Sp/Sp 1976; Tk; 136400; 344.33 × 20.1 (1129.69 × 65.94); T; 15.5. Similar: **63131 TEXACO LONDON** (Br) **63132 TEXACO SOUTH AMERICA** (Pa).

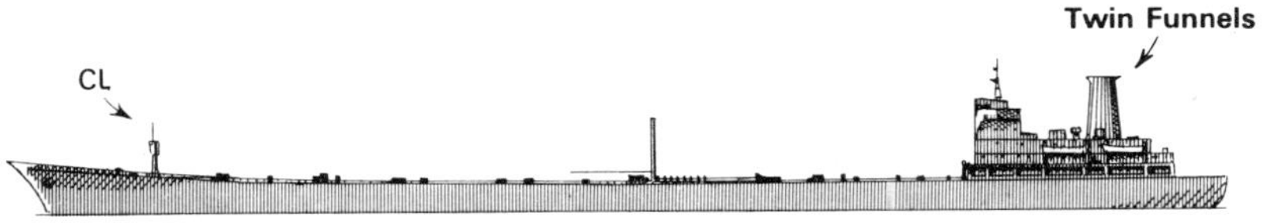

K_2MF H

63140 ASIAN GLORY. Li/Sp 1967; Tk; 33600; 245.32 × 12.85 (804.86 × 42.16); M; 17; ex JUAN DE AUSTRIA 1979.

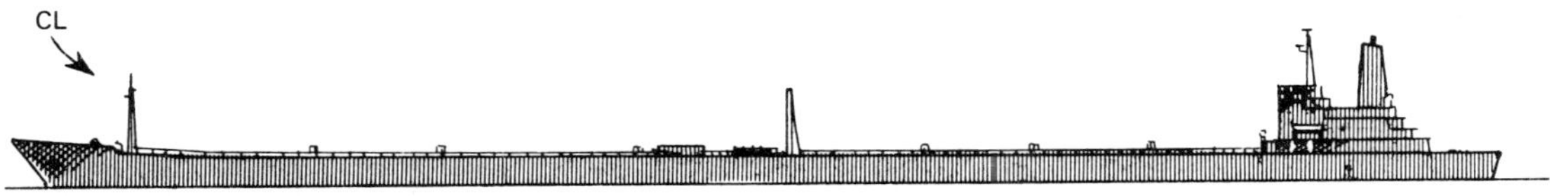

K_2MF H

63150 JAMES E. O'BRIEN. Br/Ja 1969; Tk; 109500; 326.32 × 18.97 (1070.6 × 62.24); T; 15.25. Probable Sister: **63151 E. HORNSBY WASSON** (Br).

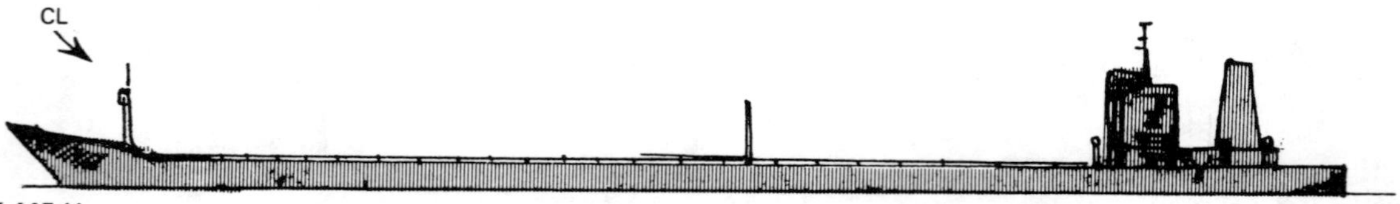

K_2MF H

63160 ARAGON. Sp/Sp 1976; Tk; 122600; 321.55 × 20.35 (1054.95 × 66.77); M; 15.25. Sister: **63161 GIBRALTAR** (Sp).

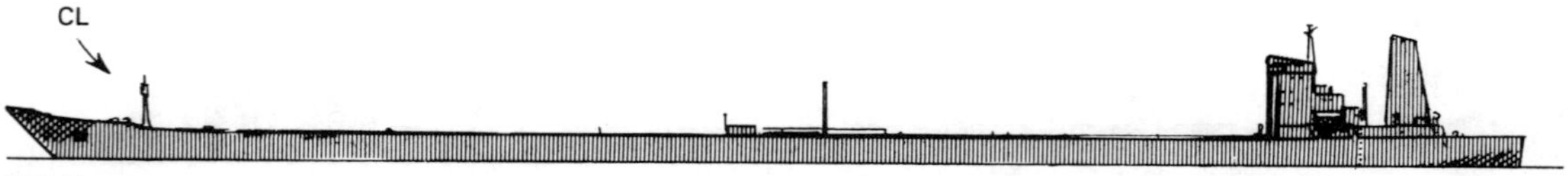

K_2MF H

63170 BARCELONA. Sp/Sp 1973; Tk; 122800; 334.02 × 19.81 (1095.87 × 64.99); M; 16.5. Similar (Li flag): **63171 AMOCO EUROPA 63172 AMOCO MILFORD HAVEN 63173 AMOCO SINGAPORE 63174 AMOCO CHICAGO.**

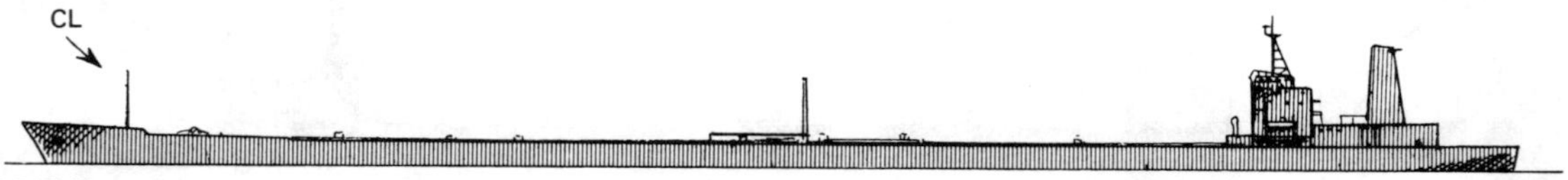

K_2MF H

● **63180 SAGITTA.** Li/FRG 1971; Tk; 109700; 325.99 × 20.65 (1069.52 × 67.75); T; 15.5.

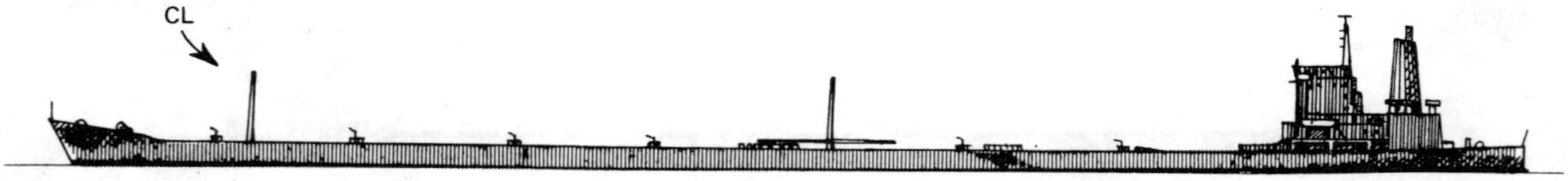

K_2MF H

63190 NORDIC CLANSMAN. Br/Br 1974; Tk; 138700; 344.43 × 20.77 (1130.02 × 68.14); T; 15.5; Aft section launched as NAESS SCOTSMAN. Sisters: **63191 CAST RORQUAL** (Br) ex NORDIC COMMANDER 1980 **63192 WORLD SCORE** (Li) after section launched as CARTSDYKE GLEN **63193 WORLD SCHOLAR** (Li).

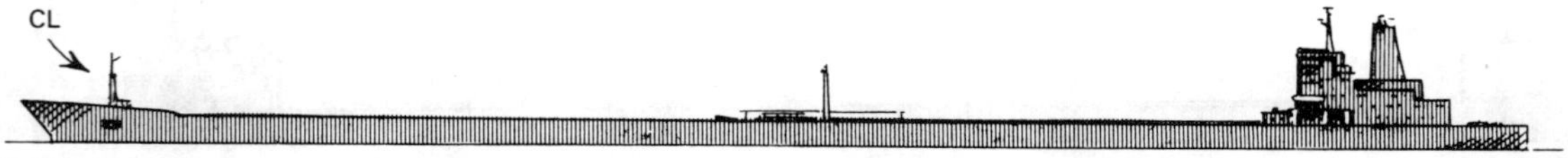

K_2MF H

63200 ANGELIKI G. Gr/De 1969; Tk; 90900; 329.09 × 19.8 (1079.7 × 64.96); T; 16; ex EVGENIA CHANDRIS 1976.

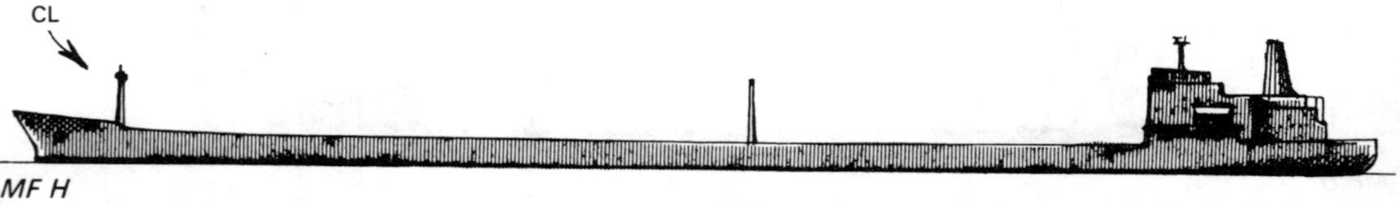

K_2MF H

63210 HERMIONE. Fr/Fr 1971; Tk; 111800; 329.8 × 19.41 (1082.02 × 63.68); T; 15.

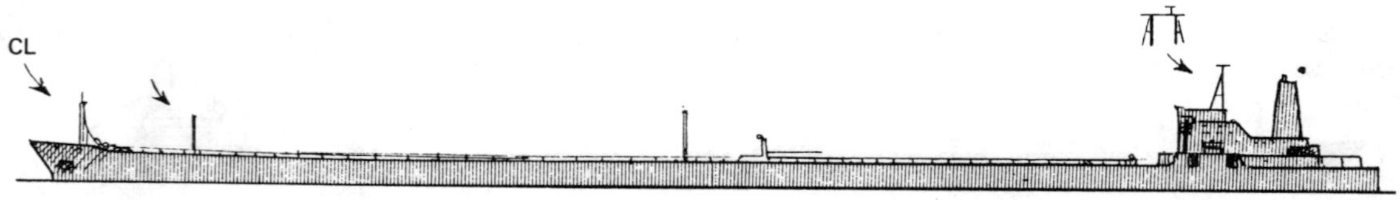

K_2MF H

● **63220 LATONA.** Fr/Fr 1973; Tk; 138500; 343.04 × 21.36 (1125.46 × 70.08); T; 15.5. Sisters (Fr flag): **63221 LEDA 63222 LUCINA** (Br flag): **63223 LATIRUS 63224 LATIA 63225 LABIOSA.**

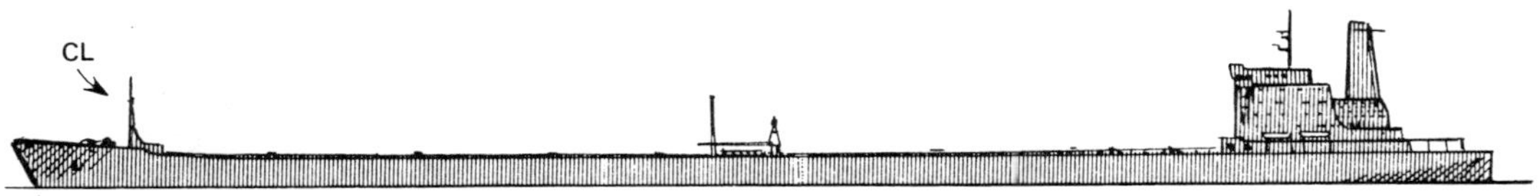

K_2MF H
63230 MYRTEA. Fr/Fr 1970; Tk; 105400; 324.72 × 18.99 (1065.35 × 62.3); T; 16. Sister: **63231 MIRALDA** (Fr).

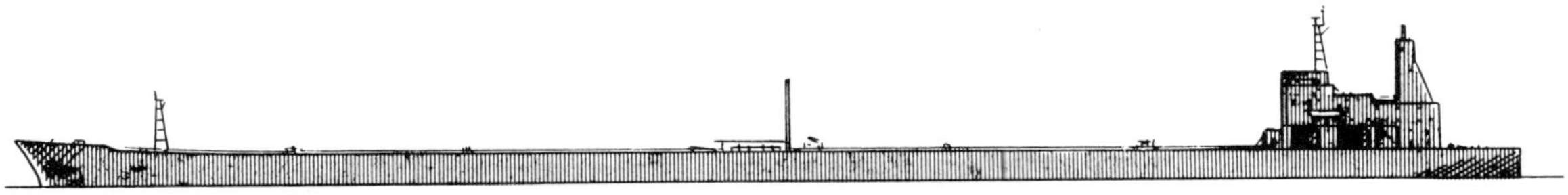

K_2MF H
63240 SAPHIR. Fr/Fr 1973; Tk; 138200; 343.04 × 21.36 (1125.46 × 70.08); T; 16. Sister: **63241 ISEULT** (Fr).

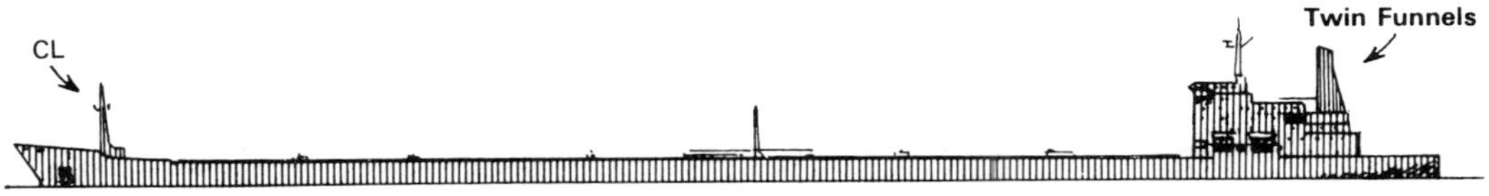

K_2MF H
● **63250 RUBIS.** Fr/Fr 1971; Tk; 112000; 329.88 × 19.41 (1082.28 × 63.68); T; 16. Sister: **63251 EMERAUDE** (Fr).

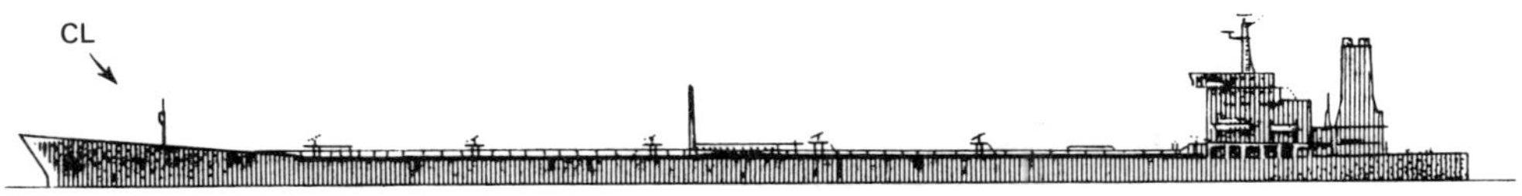

K_2MF H
63260 SOMMERSTAD. No/Fi 1977; Tk; 75000; 285.02 × 15.5 (935.1 × 50.85); M; 16.5. Sisters (No flag): **63261 SANGSTAD 63262 SILJESTAD 63263 SOLSTAD.**

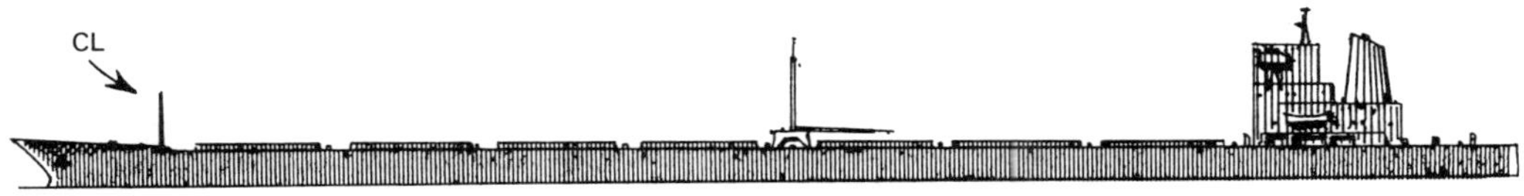

K_2MF H
63270 ARAFURA MARU. Ja/Ja 1972; 00; 96700; 311.82 × 18.04 (1023.03 × 59.19); M; 15.25. Sister: **63271 ADRIA MARU** (Ja).

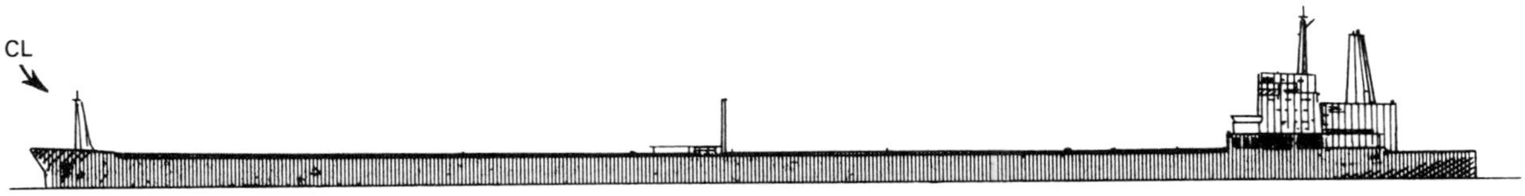

K_2MF H
63280 AL RAFIDAIN. Iq/FRG 1975; Tk; 16200; 351.44 × 22.38 (1153.02 × 73.43); T; 15.75; ex BELFRI 1976. Sister: **63281 AMICA** (No) Possible Similar: **63282 AJDABYA** (Ly).

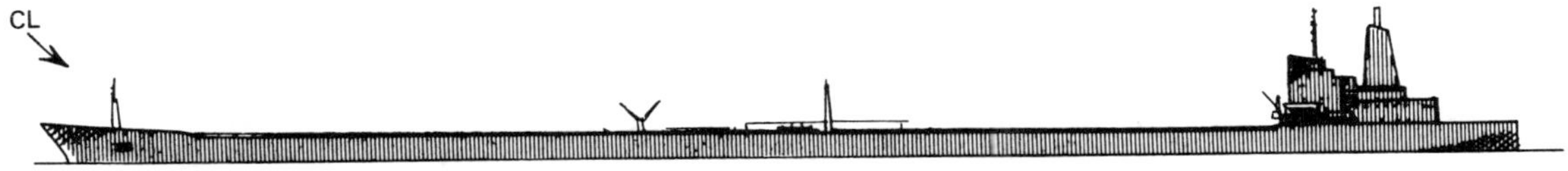

K_2MF H
63290 MARINULA. NA/Sw 1968; Tk; 99100; 328.3 × 18.99 (1077.13 × 62.3); T; 16; The cranes amidships may have been removed.

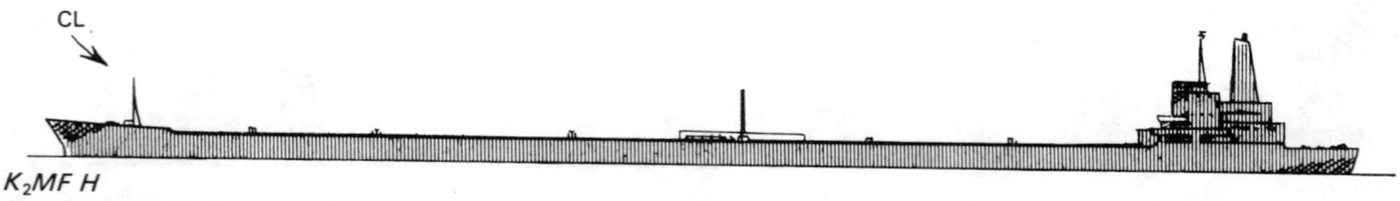

K_2MF H

● **63300 MEDORA.** Br/Ja 1968; Tk; 105300; 325.03 × 18.96 (1066.37 × 62.2); T; 16.25; Converted to floating storage unit 1980. Probably altered in appearance. Similar: **63301 META** (NA) **63302 MYTILUS** NA) **63303 MACOMA** (NA) **63304 KOREAN DONGHAE II** (Ko) ex JARMONA; ex ANDROS TANKER 1976; ex MANGELIA 1975.

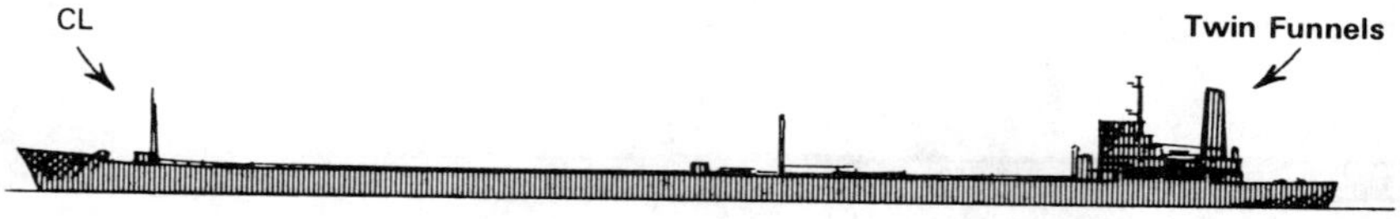

K_2MF H

● **63310 BIYO MARU.** Ja/Ja 1964; Tk; 49100; 244.51 × 14.45 (802.2 × 47.41); M; 15.5.

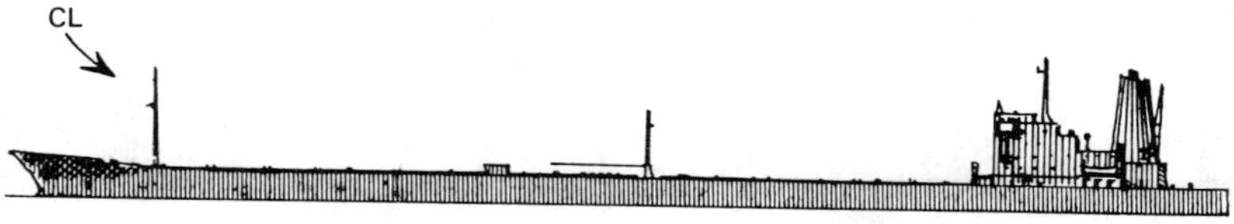

K_2MF H

63320 GARYVILLE. Li/Ja 1972; Tk; 65600; 274.94 × 17.32 (902.03 × 56.82); M; 15.75; ex FAIRFIELD 1977. Sister: **63321 ORIENTAL PHOENIX** (Li).

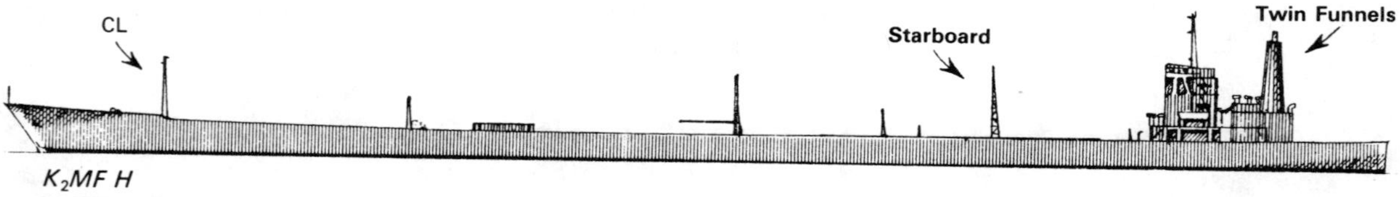

K_2MF H

63330 GLOBTIK TOKYO. Br/Ja 1973; Tk; 238230; 378.88 × 28.2 (1243 × 92.5); T; 15. Sisters: **63331 GLOBTIK LONDON** (Br) **63332 NISSEI MARU** (Ja) Similar: **63333 NISSEKI MARU** (Ja).

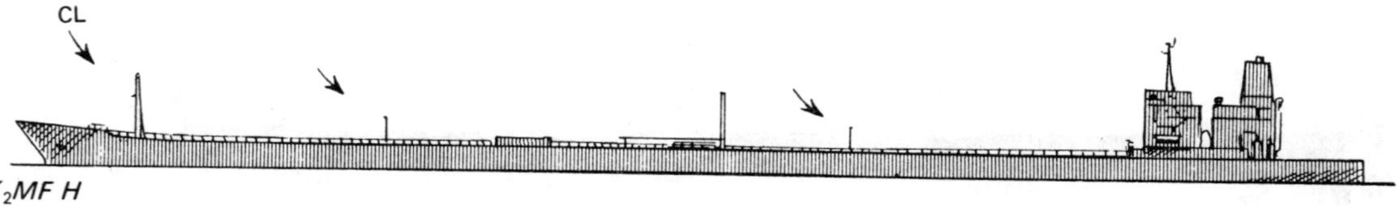

K_2MF H

63340 CAIRU. Bz/Ja 1974; Tk; 129400; 337.09 × 21.62 (1105.94 × 70.93); T; 15.75. Sister: **63341 VIDAL DE NEGREIROS** (Bz).

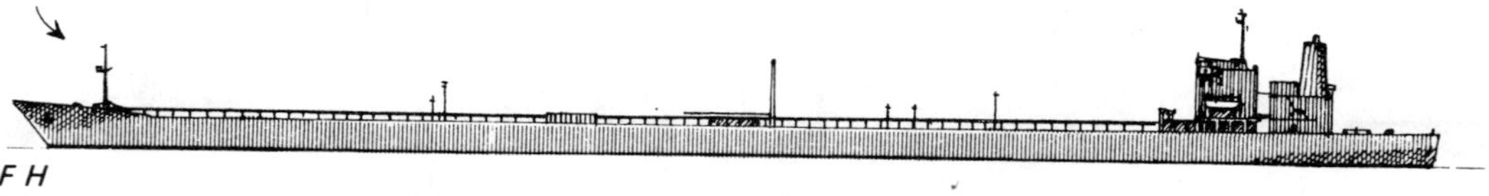

K_2MF H

63350 GRESHAM. Li/Ja 1975; Tk; 104400; 317 × 20.79 (1040.03 × 68.21); T; 16. Probable Sister: **63351 LOMBARD** (Li).

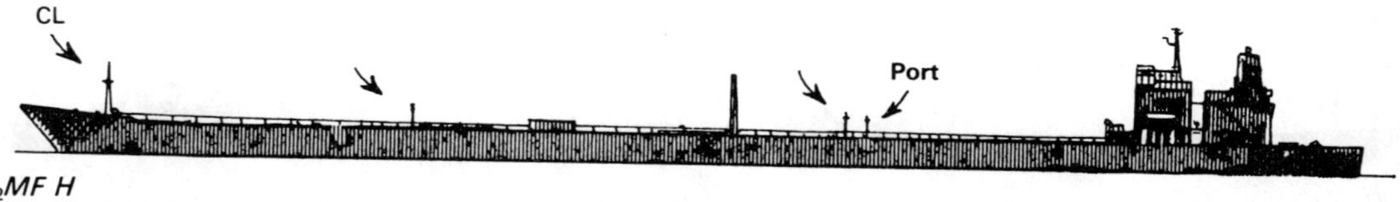

K_2MF H

63360 AZARPAD. Ir/Ja 1975; Tk; 122000; 317 × 20.78 (1040.68 × 68.18); T; 16. Similar: **63361 GEKKO MARU** (Ja) ex GOLDEN DAFFODIL 1980 **63362 EISHO MARU** (Ja) **63363 WORLD DIPLOMAT** (Li).

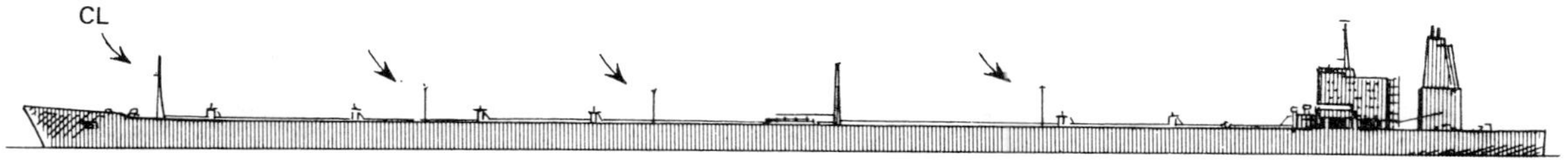

K_2MF H
63370 KIRSTEN MAERSK. De/De 1975; Tk; 167200; 370.47 × 22.46 (1215.45 × 73.69); T; 15.75. Similar (De flag): **63371 KARAMA MAERSK 63372 KAREN MAERSK 63373 KAROLINE MAERSK 63374 KATE MAERSK 63375 KATRINE MAERSK 63376 KRISTINE MAERSK.**

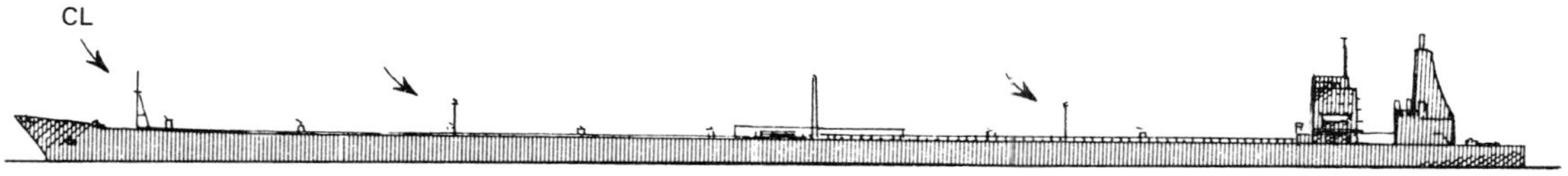

K_2MF H
63380 ARIETTA. Gr/De 1972; Tk; 129300; 347.51 × 22.32 (1140.12 × 73.23); T; —; ex ARIETTA LIVANOS 1979. Sister: **63381 EUGENIE LIVANOS** (Li).

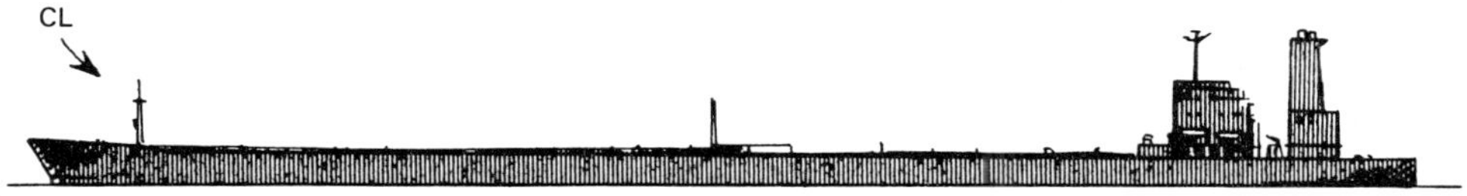

K_2MF H
● **63390 AMURIYAH.** Iq/Sw 1977; Tk; 81200; 285.02 × 17.15 (935.11 × 56.27); M; 16.25. Sisters: **63391 ALMUSTANSIRIYAH** (Iq) **63392 ALQADISIAH** (Iq) **63393 PERSEUS** (Li) **63394 MESSINIAKI FISIS** (Li) **63395 MESSINIAKI FRONTIS** (Li) **63396 ELFWAIHAT** (Ly) **63397 ELGURDABIA** (Ly) **63398 BRALANTA** (No) **63399 JOHNAKI** (Gr) ex ESTHEL 1980 **63400 LIMOUSIN** (Fr) **63401 THALASSINI DOXA** (Gr) **63402 WILNORA** (No) ex THALASSINI NIKI 1979.

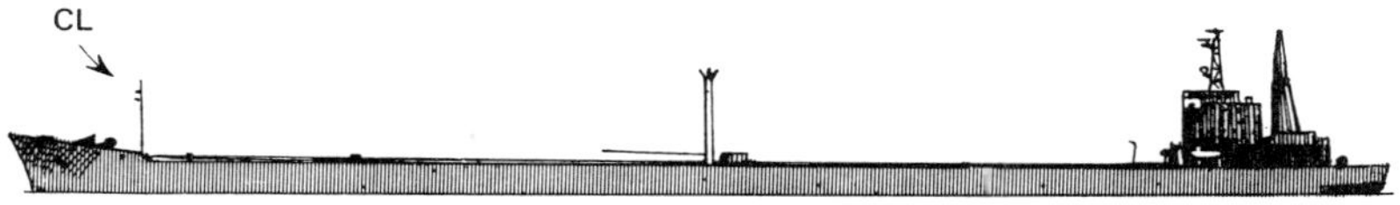

K_2MF H
63410 AMERICA SUN. US/US 1969; Tk; 37300; 249.33 × 13.29 (818.01 × 43.6); T; 16.5. Sister: **63411 GLACIER BAY** (US) ex JOSEPH D. POTTS 1977 Probable Sisters: **63412 SOHIO INTREPID** (US) **63413 SOHIO RESOLUTE** (US) Similar (larger): **63414 MOBIL ARCTIC** (US).

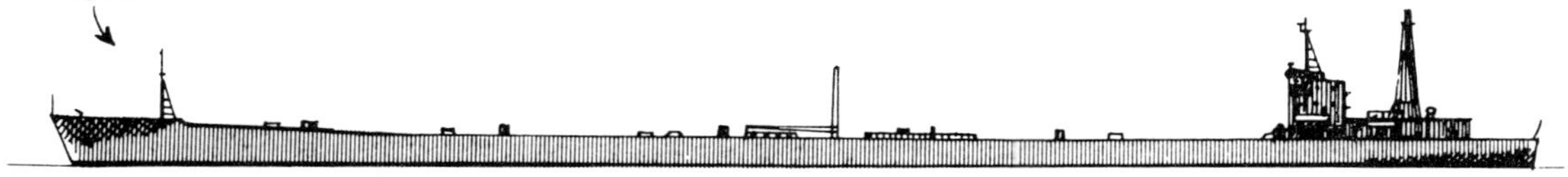

K_2MF H
63420 FAUST. FRG/FRG 1973; Tk; 120800; 326.02 × 20.65 (1069.62 × 67.75); T; 15.5. Sisters: **63421 MINERVA** (FRG) **63422 EGMOND** (Li) **63423 SANKO STRESA** (Li) **63424 SCHLESWIG-HOLSTEIN** (Pa) Possible Sisters: **63425 NIEDERSACHSEN** (FRG) **63426 VICTORIA** (FRG) **63427 WESTFALEN** (FRG) **63428 WILHELMINE ESSBERGER** (FRG) **63429 SANKO CREST** (Li) **63430 HAVDROTT** (No).

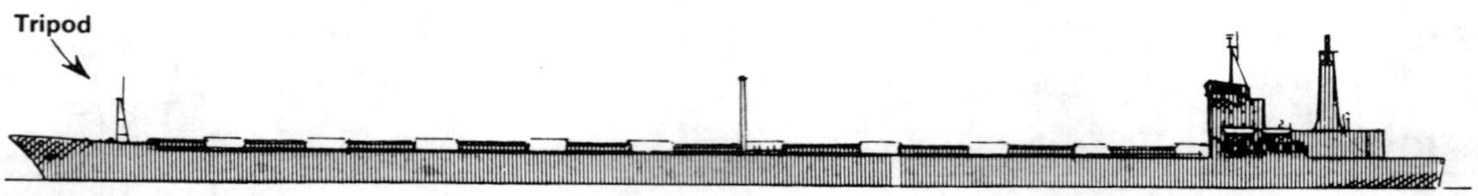

K_2MF H'

63440 WORLD RECOVERY. Li/FRG 1973; 00; 126000; 327.74 × 20.5 (1075.26 × 67.26); T; 15.5; ex HAVKONG 1976. Sister: **63441 KONKAR DINOS** (Gr) ex FALKEFJELL 1976.

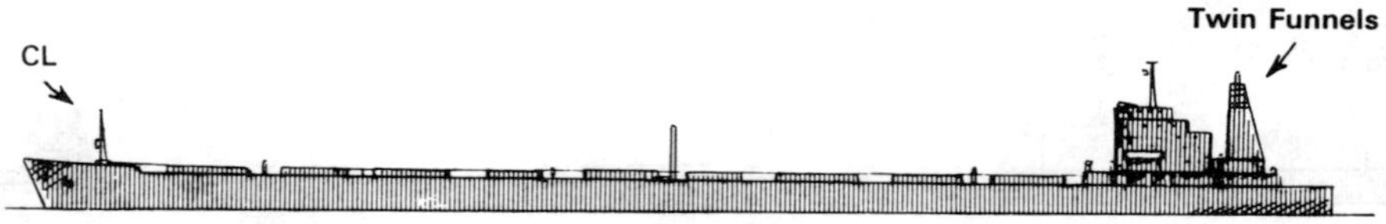

K_2MF H

● **63450 SAUDA.** It/Sw 1974; OBO; 61500; 256.85 × 17.07 (842.68 × 56); M; 15.25. Sisters: **63451 OSLO** (It) **63452 BRITANNIA TEAM** (Br) ex ANGELIC BLESSING 1978 **63453 GOTHIA TEAM** (Br) ex ANGELIC HARMONY 1978 **63454 MOHAWK** (Li) ex NORDIC SKY 1980; ex ANGELIC SKY 1977 **63455 BJORGHOLM** (No) **63456 HAVPRINS** (No) **63457 JAG LAXMI** (In) **63458 JAG LEELA** (In) **63459 MAHARISHI DAYANAND** (In) **63460 MAHARISHI KARVE** (In).

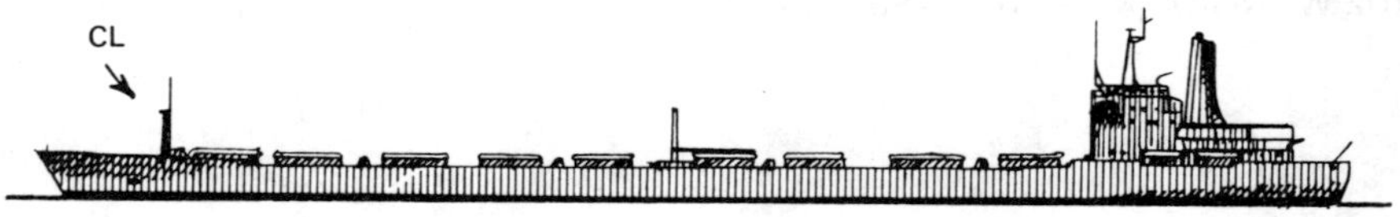

K_2MF H

63470 AMALIA II. Gr/Fr 1967; OBO; 51600; 250.86 × 14.54 (823.03 × 47.7); M; 15; ex JACQUES CARTIER 1978.

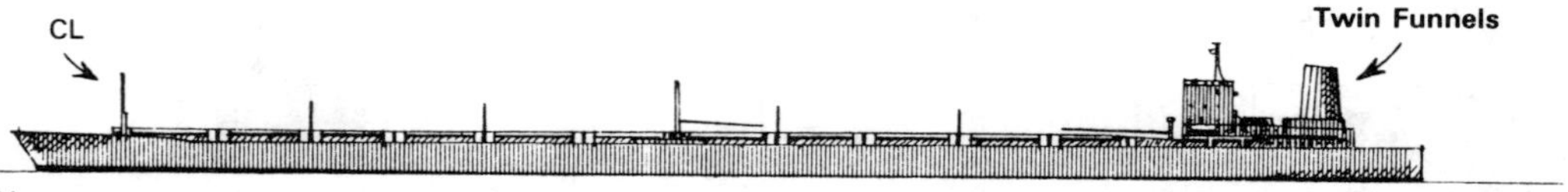

K_2MF H

63480 CAST FULMAR. Br/Br 1973; OBO; 86100; 291.85 × 18.22 (975.51 × 59.78); M; 15.5; ex NORDIC CRUSADER 1980; ex NAESS CRUSADER 1974. Similar: **63481 CAST HERON** (Br) ex NORDIC CHIEFTAIN 1980.

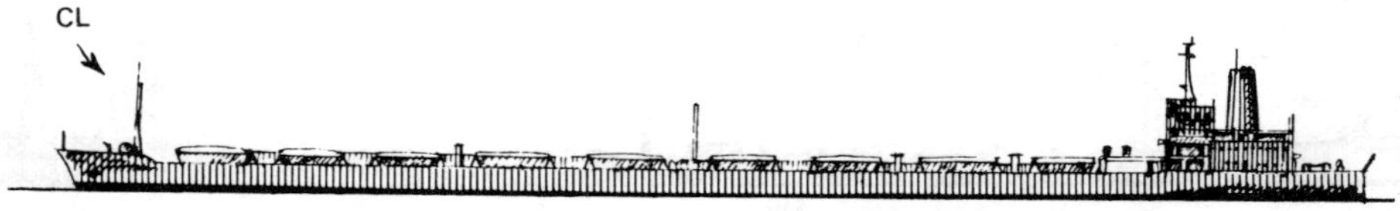

K_2MF H

63490 LAKE ARROWHEAD. Li/Br 1971; OBO; 77300; 294.19 × 18.44 (965.19 × 60.5); M; 15.5; ex FURNESS BRIDGE 1977. Sister: **63491 TYNE BRIDGE** (It) Similar: **63492 SIR ALEXANDER GLEN** (Br) **63493 CAST KITTIWAKE** (Br) ex NORDIC CHALLENGER; ex SIR JOHN HUNTER **63494 MERCURIO** (It) ex SUNSHINE 1980; ex ENGLISH BRIDGE 1979.

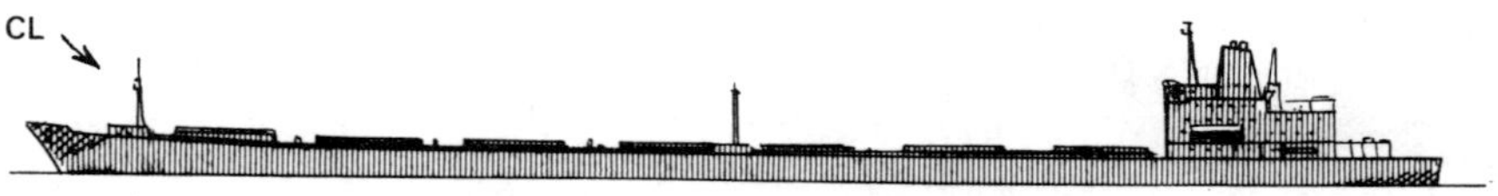

K_2MF H

63500 HOEGH RAINBOW. No/Ja 1970; OBO; 57500; 250.05 × 15.52 (820.37 × 50.92); M; 15.5. Sisters: **63501 HOEGH ROVER** (No) **63502 VEGA SEAL** (Br) ex HOEGH ROBIN 1978 Similar: **63503 HOEGH RIDER** (No).

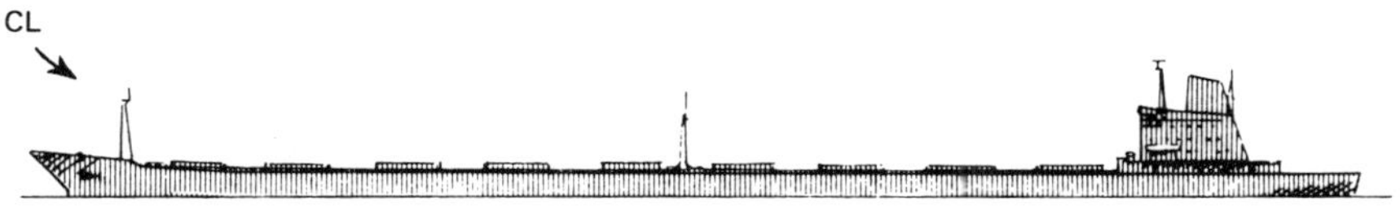

K_2MF H

63510 BELOBO. No/FRG 1974; OBO; 42800; 253.63×14.24 (832.12×46.72); M; 15. Sisters: **63511 TAI CHEUNG** (Br) ex OBO DUKE 1980 **63512 SIBOSIX** (No) ex JARMINA 1980. (Being used as storage vessel at Singapore).

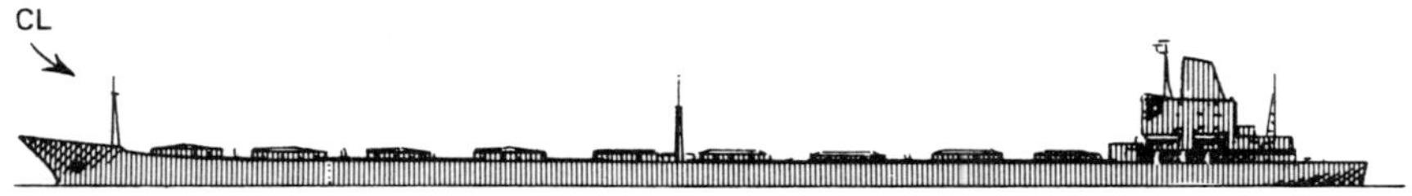

K_2MF H

63520 SAXONIA. FRG/FRG 1973; OBO; 42400; 253.68×14.23 (832.28×46.69); M; 15.25; ex MERCEDES.

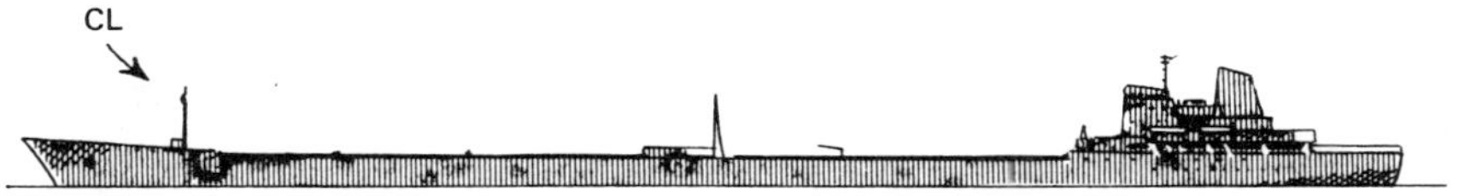

K_2MF H

63530 FINA NORVEGE. Be/Be 1965/67; Tk; 39500; 249.26×12.54 (817.78×41.14); M; 17; Aft section 1965, Forward and cargo sections 1967.

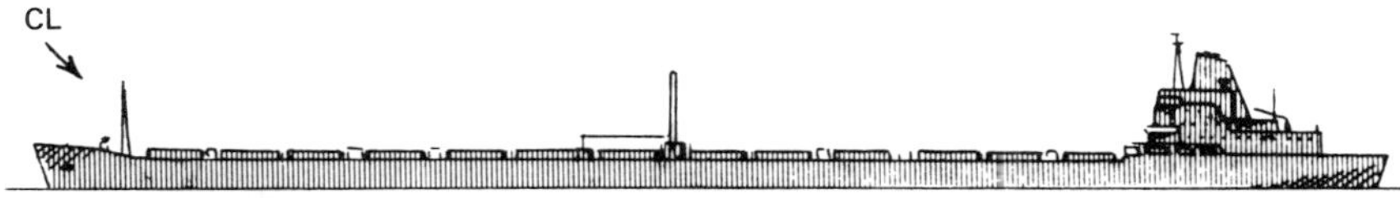

K_2MF H

63540 ARCHONTISSA KATINGO. Gr/Ys 1972; BO; 42300; 252.38×14.82 (828.02×48.62); M; 15. Sister: **63541 SIBOTEM** (Li) ex TRANSUD III; ex DIAMANTIS PATERAS 1979. Possible Similar: **63542 NORMAN ATLANTIC** (Sg) ex ANNITSA CARRAS.

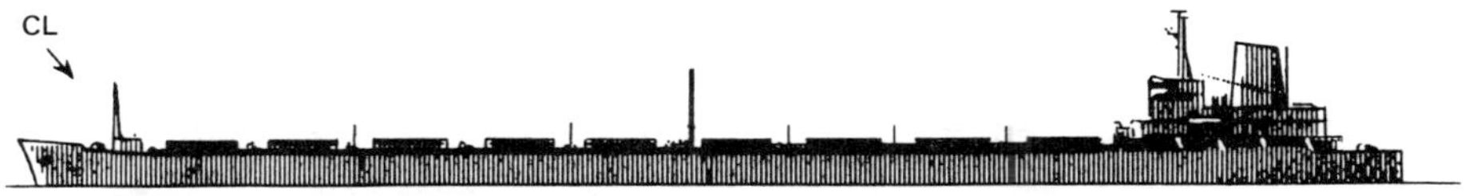

K_2MF H

63550 LAKE MENDOCINO. Li/Ja 1971; OBO; 71600; 266.02×18.1 (872.77×59.38); M; 15.5; ex AVON BRIDGE 1976. Sisters (Br flag): **63551 CAST PETREL** ex EDEN BRIDGE **63552 CAST GULL** ex SILVER BRIDGE **63553 CAST PUFFIN** ex ENTERPRISE TRANSPORTER; ex AUSTRALIAN BRIDGE 1978.

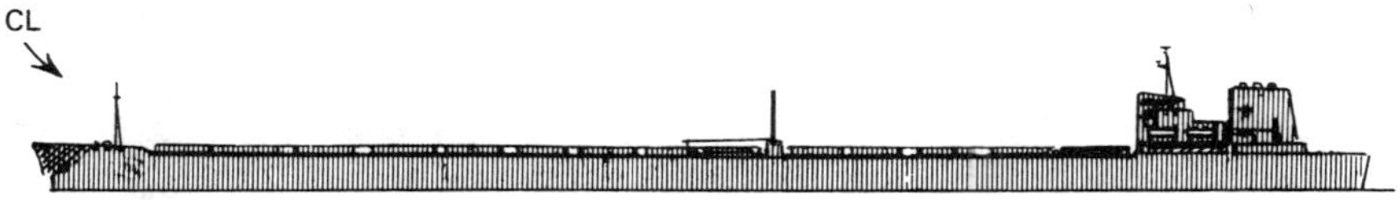

K_2MF H

63560 MOTILAL NEHRU. In/Ys 1973; OBO; 62900; 254.52×16.87 (835.04×55.35); M; 16. Sister (In flag): **63561 ABUL KALAN AZAD** Possibly Similar: **63562 VALLABHBHAI PATEL 63563 VALLATHOL.**

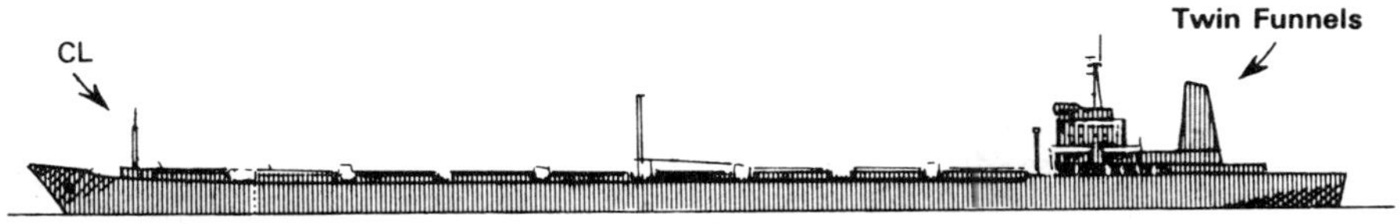

K_2MF H

★63570 BORIS BUTOMA. Ru/Ru 1978; BO; 63200; 258.22×15.65 (847.17×51.34); M; 15; ex OKTYABRSK. Sisters (Ru flag): **★63571 AKADEMIK KRYLOV ★63572 AKADEMIK PAVLOV ★63573 AKADEMIK SECHENOV ★63574 NIKOLAY ZHUKOVSKIY.**

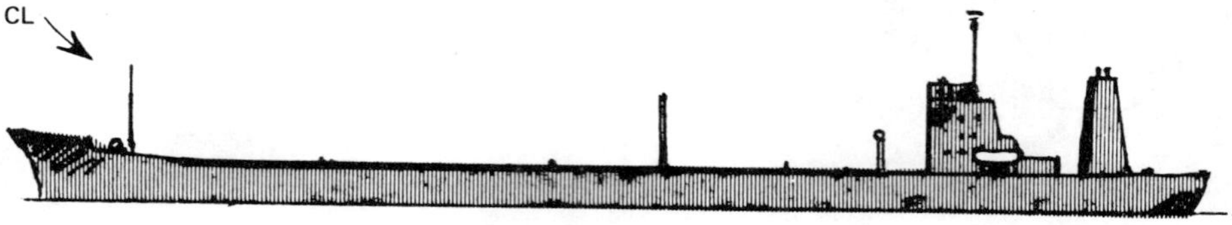

K_2MF H

63580 KYRNICOS E. Gr/Ja 1966; Tk; 74400; 273.77 × 15.9 (898.19 × 52.16); M; 16; ex MOBIL ALADDIN 1980; ex ISUZUGAWA MARU 1977. Kingpost abreast funnel. Similar: **63581 TRADE INDEPENDENCE** (Gr) ex KINOKAWA MARU 1976 **63582 MOBIL LIGHT** (Li) ex IZUMIGAWA MARU 1976 Similar (larger): **63583 ATLANTIC PROGRESS** (Gr) ex KIHO MARU.

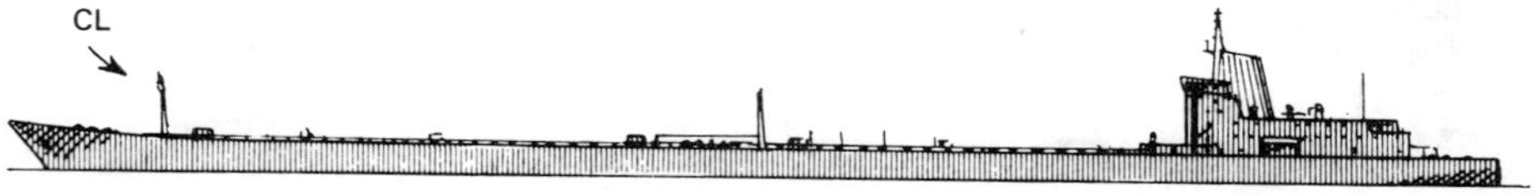

K_2MF H

63590 NICOS I. VARDINOYANNIS. Gr/Br 1971; Tk; 65300; 274.4 × 16.96 (900.26 × 55.64); M; 16; ex GOLD STAR 1973. Sister: **63591 IDEFIX** (Li) ex NORDIC ENTERPRISE 1976; ex NAESS ENTERPRISE 1974 Possible Sister: **63592 KING STAR** (Ko).

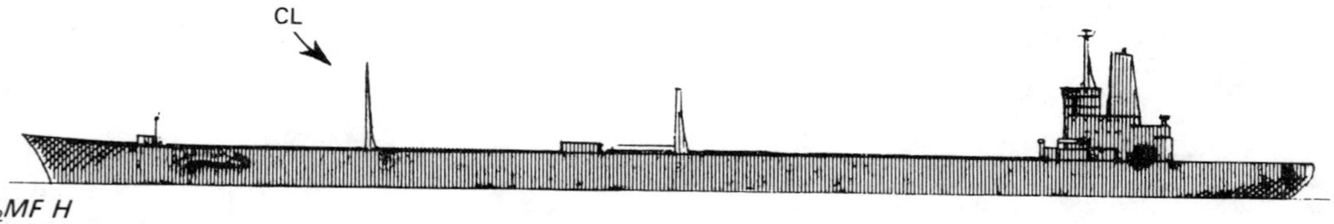

K_2MF H

63600 GLAROS. Gr/Ja 1968; Tk; 90900; 312.73 × 17.4 (1026 × 57.09); T; 16; ex HIEN MARU 1976.

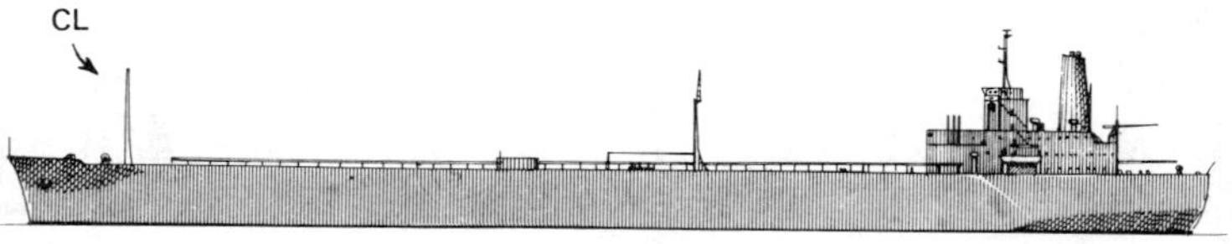

K_2MF H

63610 YUSHO. Li/Ja 1971; LGC; 47800; 227.03 × 11.51 (744.85 × 37.76); M; 15.75; ex YUSHO MARU 1978.

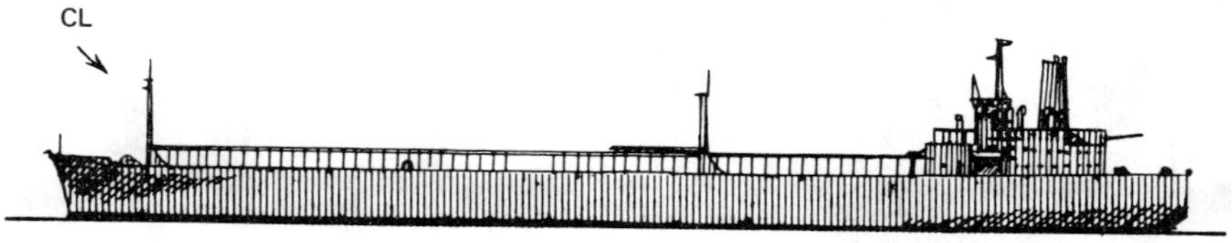

K_2MF H

63620 PALACE TOKYO. Ja/Ja 1974; LGC; 64400; 246.11 × 12.7 (807.45 × 41.67); M; 16.5.

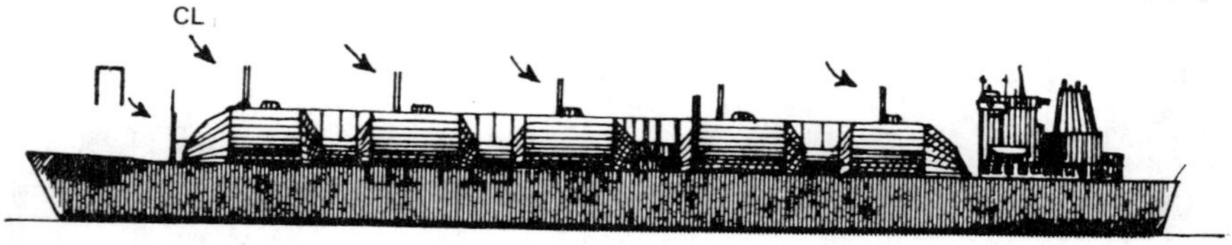

K_2MF H

63630 NORMAN LADY. Br/No 1973; LGC; 76400; 249.51 × 10.62 (818.6 × 34.84); T; 19.

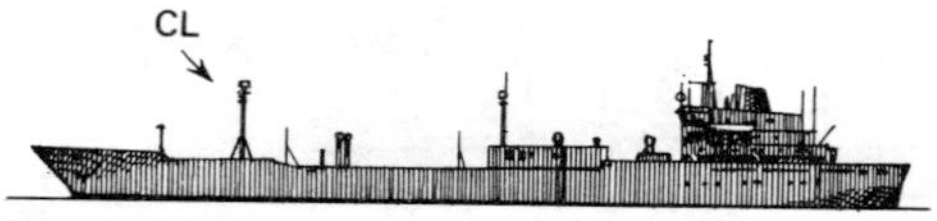

K_2MF H

***63640 YURMALA.** Ru/FRG 1976; LGC; 9100; 139.71 × 8.22 (458.37 × 26.97); M; 16.25. Sisters (Ru flag): ***63641 BOLDURI** ***63642 DUBULTY** ***63643 DZINTARI** ***63644 LIELUPE** ***63645 MAYORI.**

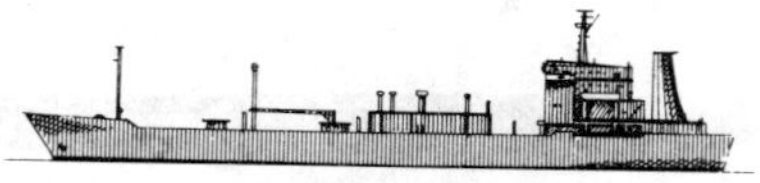

K_2MF H

63650 CHEMTRANS WEGA. FRG/FRG 1977; LGC; 7000; 112.76 × 7.5 (369.59 × 24.61); M; 15; ex BAVARIA MULTINA 1978.

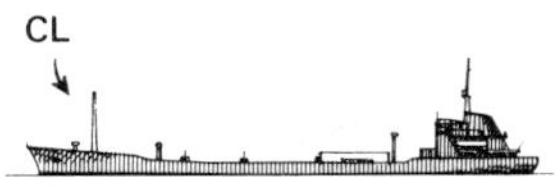

K_2MF H
63660 OLIVER. FRG/FRG 1970; Tk; 1300; 81.59 × 5.2 (267.68 × 17.06); M; 12.5.

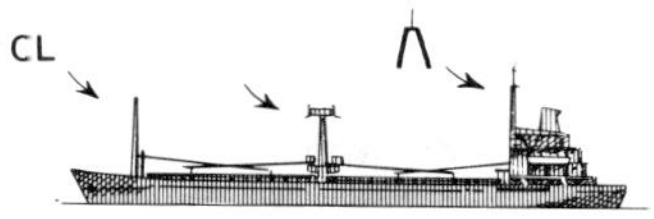

K_2MF H
63670 DENIZATI. Tu/Tu 1978; C; 1600; 87.7 × 6 (287.73 × 19.69); M; 15.

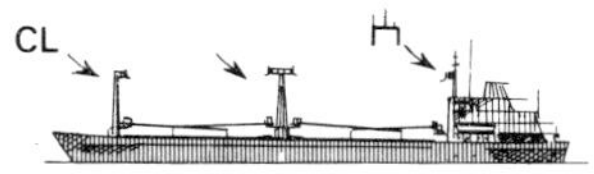

K_2MF H
● **63680 ALEDREESI.** Iq/FRG 1976; C; 1600; 81.62 × 6.1 (267.78 × 20.1); M; 12.5. Sisters (Iq flag): **63681 ALZAWRAA 63682 ALKHANSAA 63683 ZANOOBIA** Similar: **63684 ROSA DANIA** (De) **63685 MERCANDIAN SUN** (De) ⋆**63686 LIAN JIANG** (RC) ex CALABAR 1979; ex ANNETT BENTSEN 1978 ⋆**63687 HUAN JIANG** (RC) ex SUSANN BENTSEN **63688 PEP ATLANTIC** (De) ex ALICE STEEN 1980; ex BALTIC SEA; ex ALICE STEEN 1979; ex BALTIC SEA 1977; ex ALICE STEEN 1977 **63689 EGE MELTEMI** (Tu) ex MERCANDIAN SEA 1976 **63690 MERCANDIAN SKY** (De) Possibly Similar: **63691 GERT STAERKE** (De).

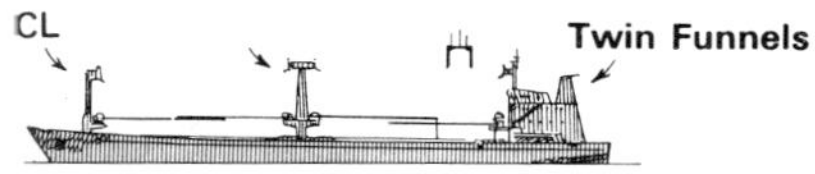

K_2MF H
63700 MERCANDIAN MOON. De/FRG 1977; C; 1600; 93.3 × 6.04 (306.1 × 19.82); M; 12.5. Probable Sister: **63701 MERCANDIAN STAR** (De).

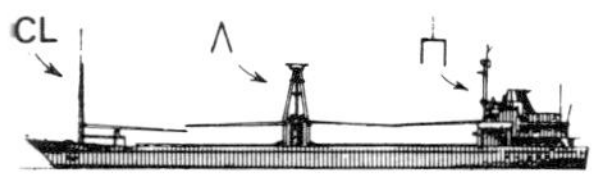

K_2MF H
⋆**63710 XI JIANG.** RC/FRG 1974; C/HL; 1600; 89.74 × 6.04 (294.42 × 19.82); M; 13; ex VERA BENTSEN. Similar: **63711 ABIRIBA** (Li) ex BIRGITTE B 1980; ex BIRGITTE BENTSEN 1978; ex WIVI BEWA 1977 **63712 HANNATU** (Li) ex GERDA B 1980; ex GERDA BENTSEN 1978; ex CONNY BEWA 1977 **63713 ARWAD** (Sy) ex VIGGO SCAN 1975 **63714 HEAVY SCAN** (De) ⋆**63715 KUTINA** (Ys) ex SUPER SCAN 1979.

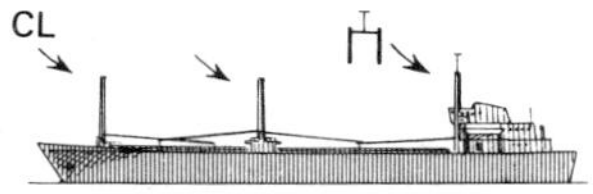

K_2MF H
63720 BRAGA. No/No 1970; RoC; 1500; 87.03 × 6.15 (285.53 × 20.18); M; 14.75; Side doors. Sister: **63721 BISMILLAH** (No).

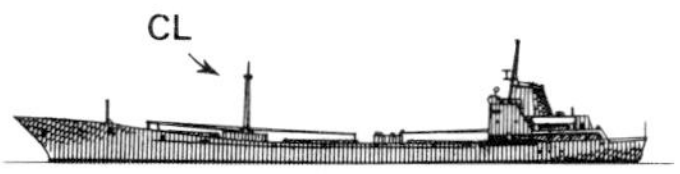

K_2MF H
⋆**63730 GAN QUAN.** RC/Fr 1970; C; 2000; 100.44 × 6.2 (329.53 × 20.34); M; —; ex SIRARA 1980. Sister: **63731 ALMIRANTE** (Ho) ex EA 1979.

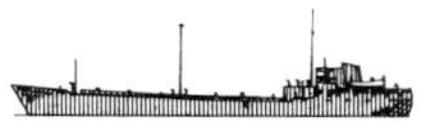

K_2MF H
● **63740 CRYOMAR.** It/Ne 1955/64; LGC; 1000; 63.23 × 3.77 (207.45 × 12.37); M; 12.25; ex CAPO CERVO 1972; ex ABBAS 1968; ex BROUGHTY 1963; Converted from general cargo 1964.

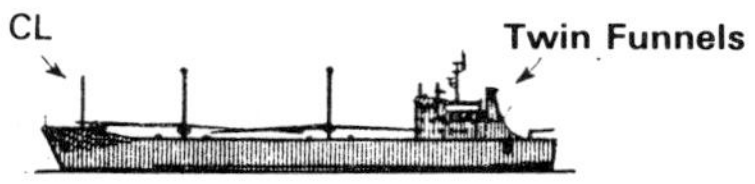

K_2MF H
63750 PASSAT. FRG/FRG 1965; C; 1000; 81.84 × 5.1 (268.5 × 16.7); M; 11.

K_2MF H
63760 SHINJU MARU. Ja/Ja 1969; RoC; 2200; 95.41 × 6 (313.02 × 19.69); M; 14; Stern doors.

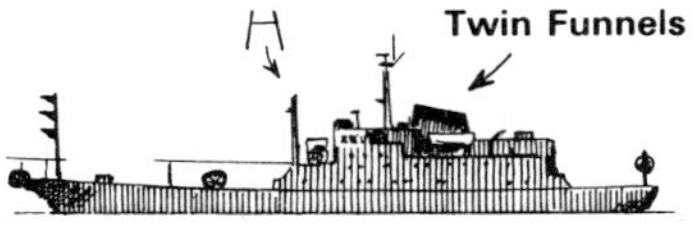

K_2MF H
63770 NEWTON. Br/Br 1976; A/Trials ship; 3900 Dspl; 98.6 × 5.7 (324 × 18.5); D-E; 15; Also serves as cable layer.

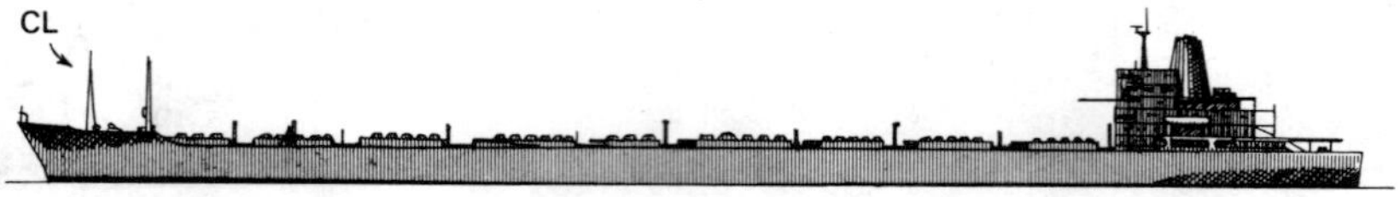

K_2MF H1
63780 FORT FRASER. Br/Ja 1967; B; 42400; 251.49 × 13.6 (825.09 × 44.61); M; 16; ex ALCYONE 1980; ex FERNIE 1979.

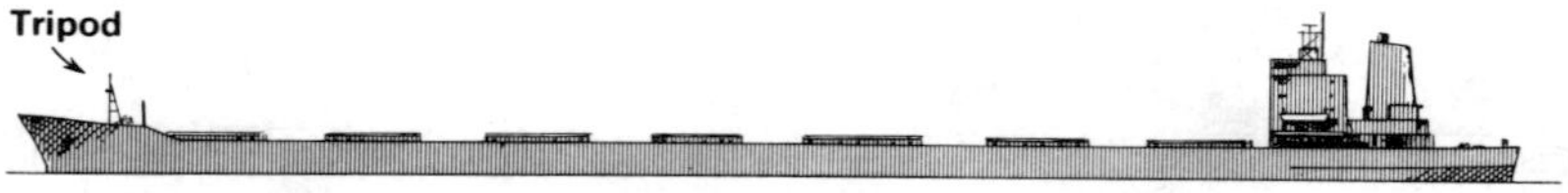

K_2MF H1
63790 EEKLO. Be/Be 1978; B; 38500; 242.02 × 13.83 (794 × 45.37); M; 16.

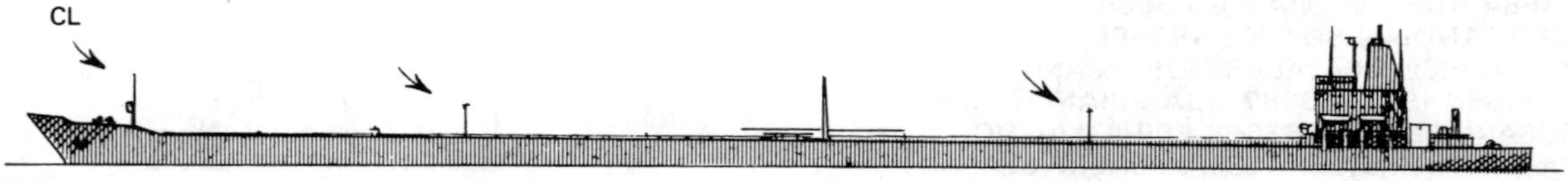

K_2MF H1
63800 ATLANTIC EMPEROR. Li/De 1974; Tk; 128400; 347.23 × 22.32 (1139.21 × 73.23); T; 15.5.

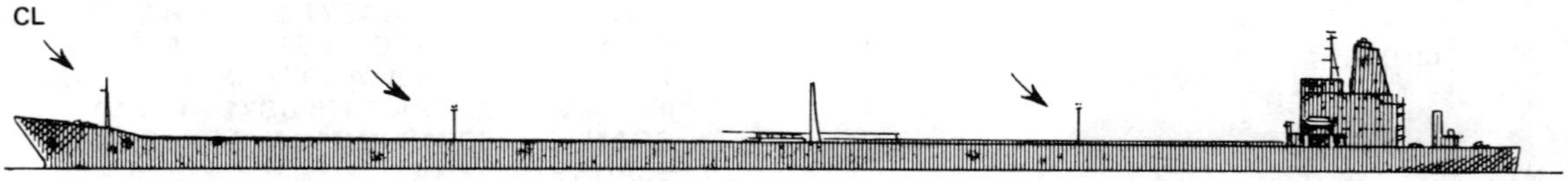

K_2MF H1
63810 TEXACO DENMARK. Br/De 1970; Tk; 125400; 345.02 × 20.11 (1131.96 × 65.98); T; 15.5. Sisters: **63811 TEXACO NORWAY** (Br) **63812 SIPCA DAMMAM** (Si) ex TEXACO COPENHAGEN 1979.

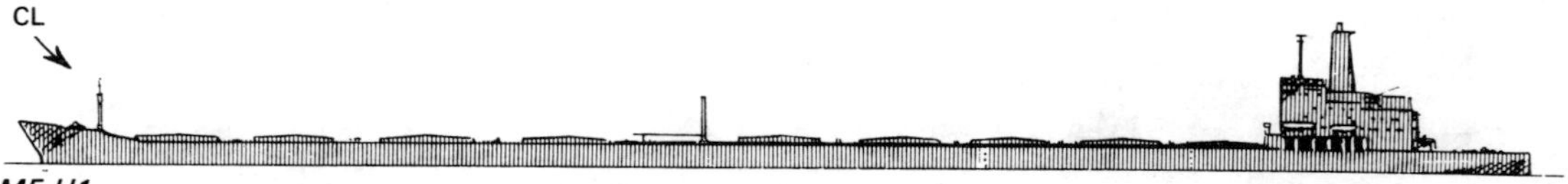

K_2MF H1
63820 RIMULA. Br/Sw 1974; OO; 117200; 332.77 × 20.51 (1091.76 × 67.29); T; 16; ex AMBROSIANA 1980; ex RINDA 1974. Sisters: **63821 RAPANA** (Br) ex SAN GIUSTO 1980; ex RUNA 1973 **63822 RUHR ORE** (Li) ex SYSLA.

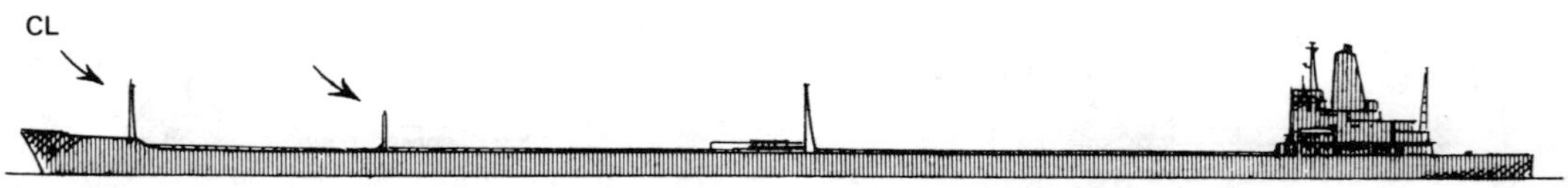

K_2MF H1
● **63830 BRITISH PIONEER.** Br/Ja 1971; Tk; 112700; 324.21 × 19.65 (1063.68 × 64.47); T; 16. Possible Sisters: **63831 SHOUSH** (Ir) ex BRITISH SURVEYOR 1978 **63832 BRITISH SCIENTIST** (Br).

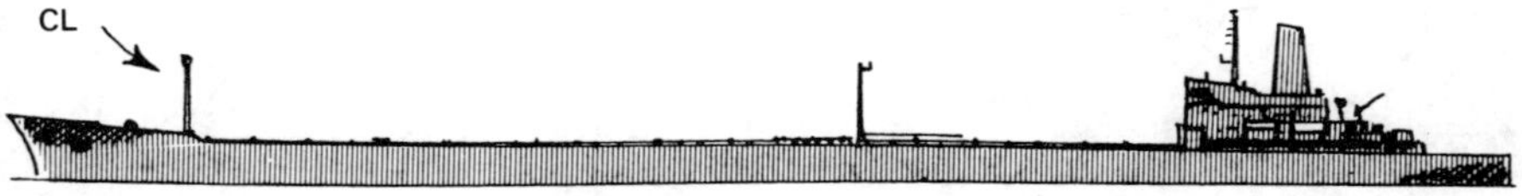

K_2MF H1
63840 AVIN OIL TRADER. Gr/Sw 1968; Tk; 51100; 277.05 × 14.72 (908.95 × 48.29); M; 16; ex ALEXANDROS M 1979; ex FRUEN 1975; ex SOLSTAD 1973.

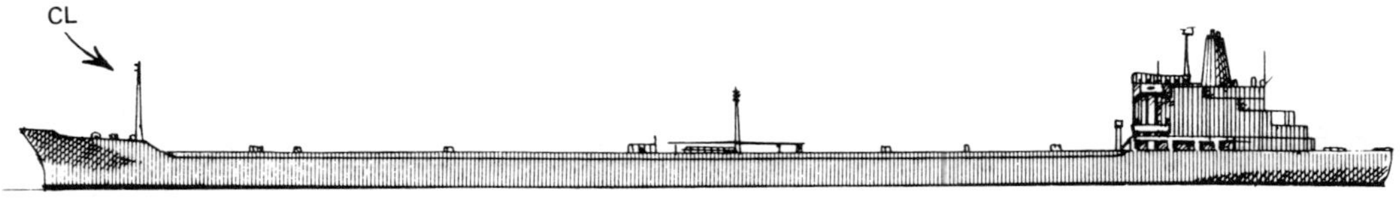

K_2MF H1
63850 HONAM RUBY. LI/Ja 1970; Tk; 99000; 327.01 × 19.61 (1027.87 × 64.34); T; 16.5; ex GOLAR NICHU 1980. Sister: **63851 GOLAR ROBIN** (Li) Similar: **63852 GOLAR KANTO** (Li) **63853 GOLAR KANSAI** (Li) **63854 KOREA DONGHAE** (Ko) ex ELISABETH KNUDSEN Possibly Similar: **63855 HONAM TOPAZ** (Li) ex FERNMOUNT 1978.

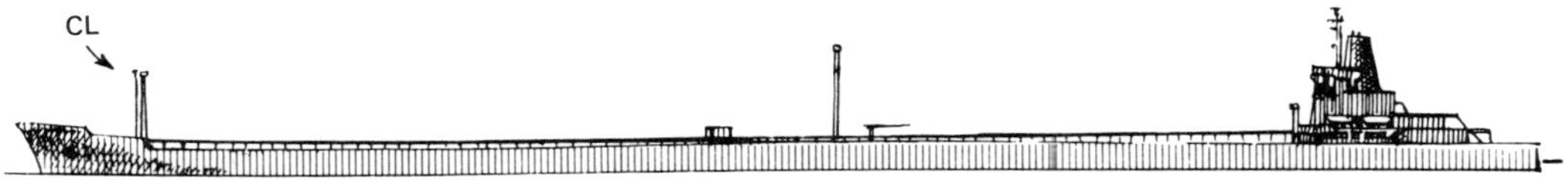

K_2MF H1
● **63860 MOBIL PINNACLE.** Br/Ja 1970; Tk; 112700; 326.02 × 54.13 (1069.62 × 54.13); T; 18.75. Sisters (Li flag): **63861 MOBIL PRIDE 63862 MOBIL PROGRESS 63863 MOBIL PETROLEUM.**

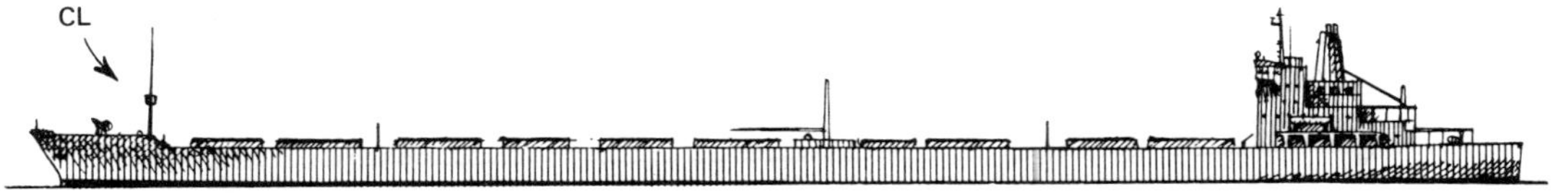

K_2MF H1
63870 HOEGH HOOD. No/Ja 1973; OO; 129000; 326.04 × 20.49 (1069.68 × 67.22); T; 15.5. Sisters: **63871 HOEGH HILL** (No) **63872 WORLD TRUTH** (Li) ex LA LOMA 1978.

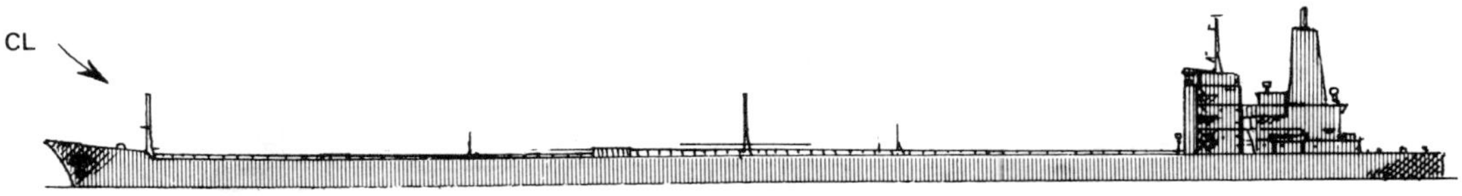

K_2MF H1
63880 SPYROS A LEMOS. Gr/Ja 1972; Tk; 103300; 322.99 × 19.73 (1059.6 × 64.73); T; 16.25; ex GONDWANA. Sister: **63881 PHOINIKAS** (Gr) ex EASTERN PROSPECTOR; ex KULU.

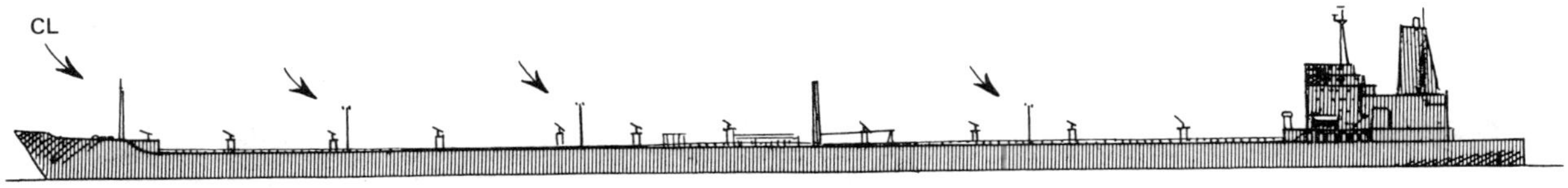

K_2MF H1
63890 ESSO DEUTSCHLAND. FRG/Ja 1976; Tk; 203900; 378.01 × 22.98 (1240.19 × 75.39); T; 15.75. Probable Sister: **63891 HILDA KNUDSEN** (No) Possibly Similar: **63892 CORRAGIO** (It) **63893 ROBINSON** (Li) ex GOLAR PATRICIA.

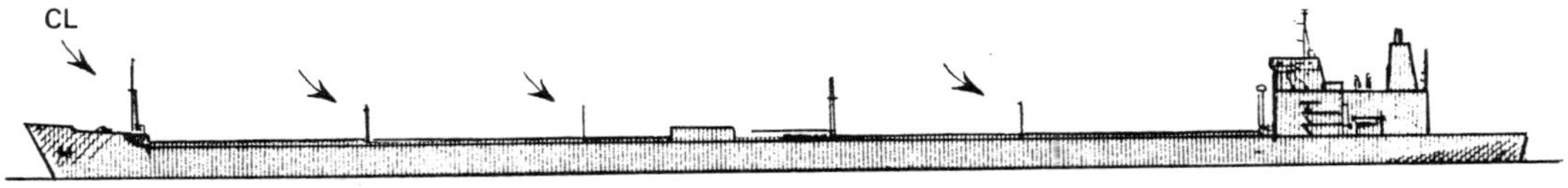

K_2MF H1
63900 SHINKO MARU. Ja/Ja 1972; Tk; 117600; 321.85 × 19.81 (1055.94 × 64.99); T; 15.75. Sisters (Ja flag): **63901 KOKKO MARU 63902 KYOKKO MARU 63903 MEIKO MARU** Similar: **63904 AMUR MARU 63905 JAPAN ADONIS 63906 TOTTORI MARU.**

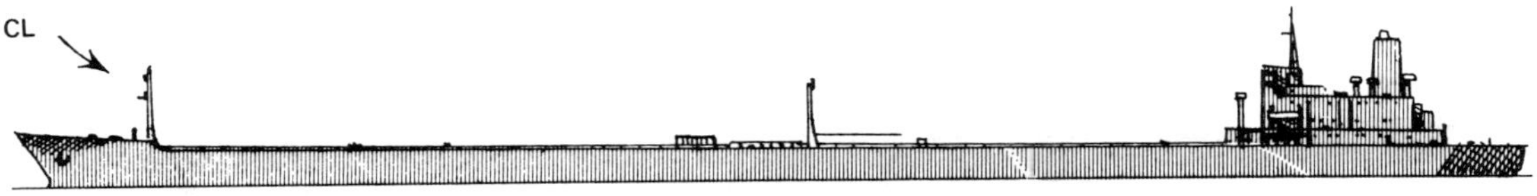

K_2MF H1
63910 GEORGE M KELLER. Li/Ja 1972; Tk; 118300; 337.5 × 20.52 (1107.28 × 67.32); T; 15.75. Sister: **63911 HOWARD W BELL** (Li).

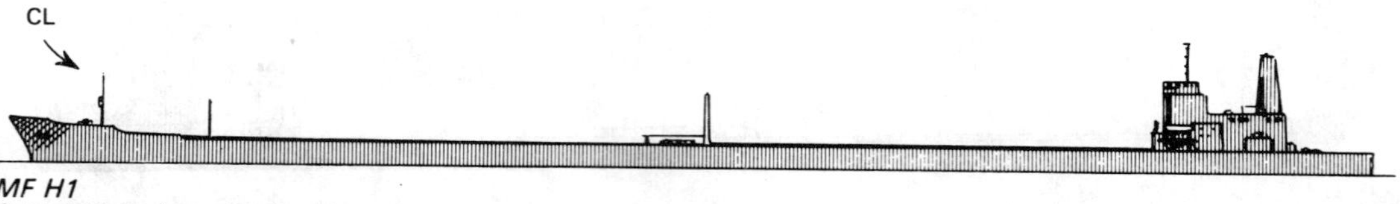

K_2MF H1
63920 TEXACO PANAMA. Pa/Ne 1972; Tk; 107300; 329.6 × 19.91 (1081.36 × 65.32); T; 16. Similar: **63921 TEXACO AMSTERDAM** (Pa).

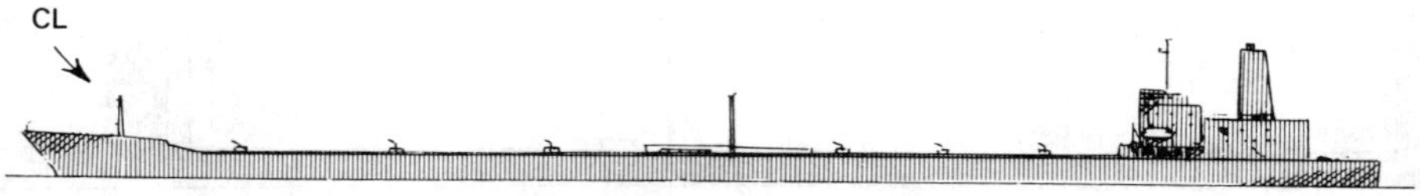

K_2MF H1
63930 SOUTH ANGELA. Li/Bz 1977; Tk; 65100; 271.66 × 15.01 (891.27 × 49.24); M; —; ex BOCAINA. Sisters: **63931 SOUTH VIVIEN** (Li) ex BEBERIBE **63932 BRAGANCA** (Bz).

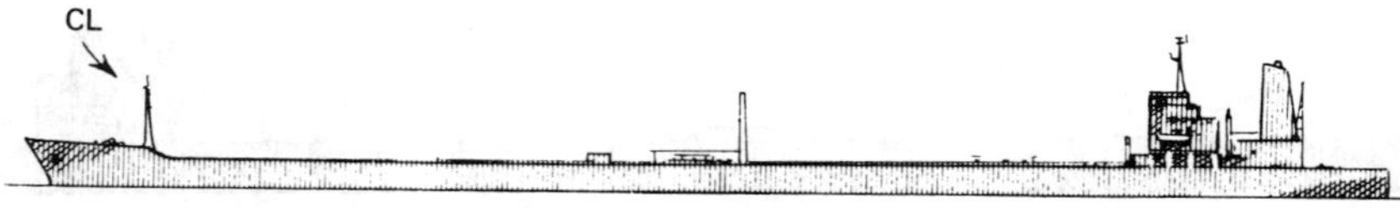

K_2MF H1
63940 GOLDEN SUNRAY. Sg/Ja 1974; Tk; 48900; 241.51 × 14.14 (792.35 × 46.39); M; 16.5. Probable Sister: **63941 CANADIAN OWL** (Sg).

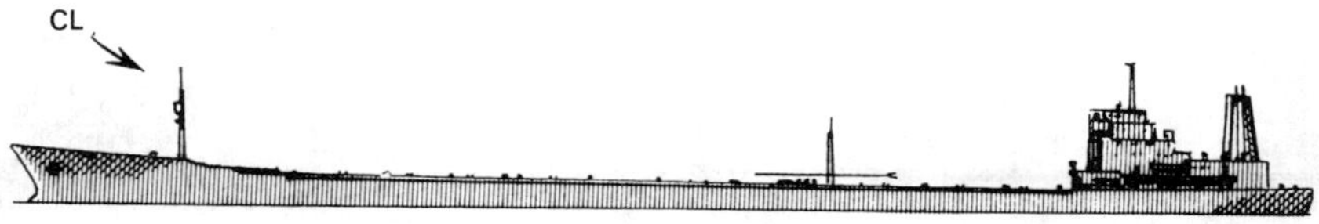

K_2MF H1
63950 KAVO MALEAS. Gr/Ja 1966; Tk; 54000; 258.99 × 15.62 (849.7 × 51.24); T; —; ex GOLAR LIZ 1976.

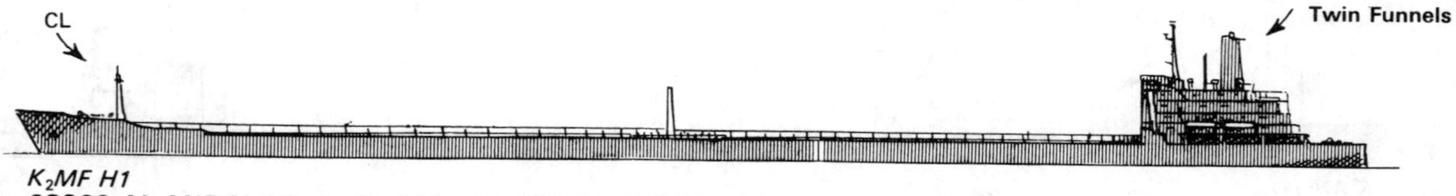

K_2MF H1
63960 AL ANDALUS. Ku/Sp 1975; Tk; 191000; 362.57 × 26.09 (1189.5 × 85.6); TST; 14.5. Probable Sister: **63961 SANTA MARIA** (Sp); Launched as LA SANTA MARIA Similar: **63962 DALMA** (Li); Launched as AFRAN ODYSSEY.

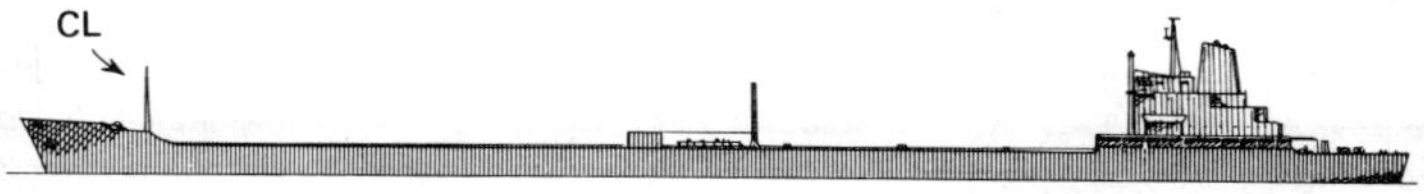

K_2MF H1
● **63970 ZAPATA PATRIOT.** US/US 1975; Tk; 21600; 216.8 × 10.52 (711.29 × 34.51); M; 16. Sisters (US flag): **63971 ZAPATA COURIER 63972 ZAPATA RANGER 63973 ZAPATA ROVER.**

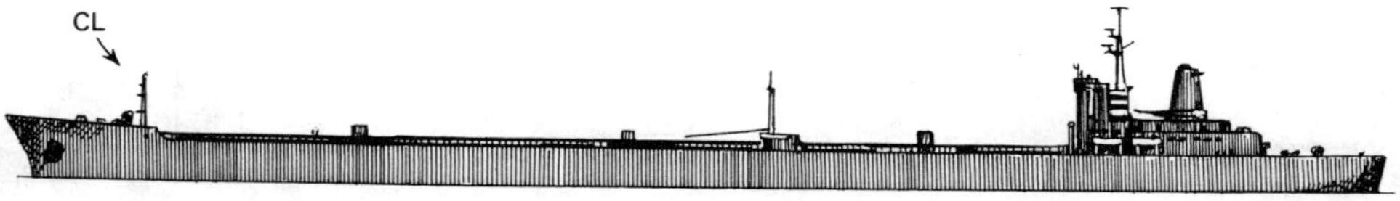

K_2MF H1
★63980 KRYM. Ru/Ru 1975; Tk; 88700; 295.05 × 17 (968.01 × 55.77); T; 17. Sisters (Ru flag): **★63981 KUBAN ★63982 KAVKAZ ★63983 KUZBASS ★63984 KRIVBASS** Possible Sister: **★63985 SOVETSKAYA NEFT.**

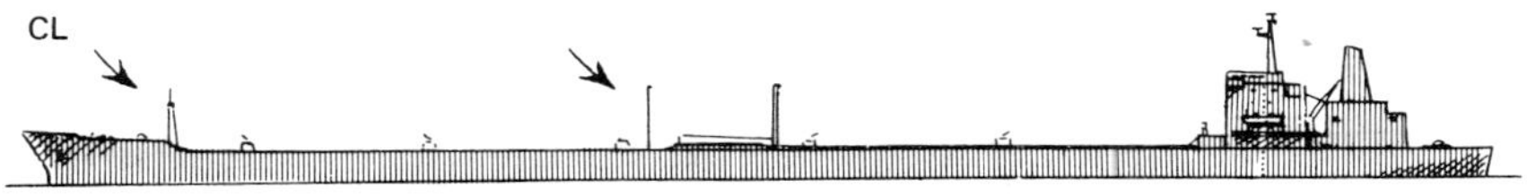

K_2MF H1

63990 OLYMPIC SPLENDOUR. Gr/Br 1976; Tk; 66300; 260.33 × 15.18 (854.1 × 49.8); M; 16; ex GEROI SEVASTOPOLYA; Launched as KYRA LYNN. Sisters: **63991 ARTEMIS GAROFALIDIS** (Gr) ex GEROI NOVOROSSIYSKA; Launched as INTEROCEANIC I **63992 AFRAN EQUATOR** (Li) ex GEROI KERCHI; ex INTEROCEANIC II; Launched as ROBCAP VI Similar: **63993 YORKSHIRE** (Br).

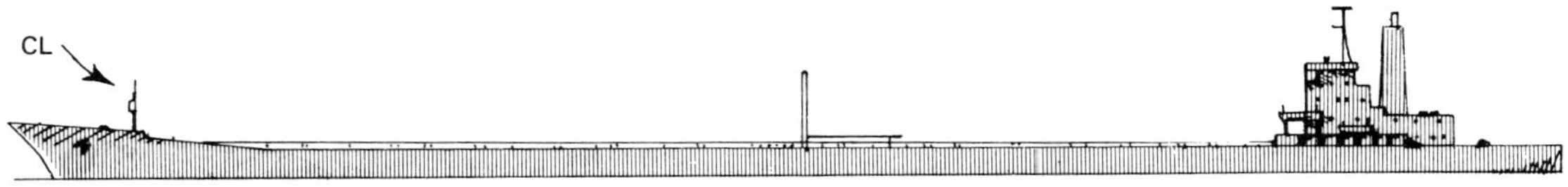

K_2MF H1

64000 TIGRE. No/No 1974; Tk; 140300; 347.84 × 22.14 (1141.2 × 72.63); T; 15.5.

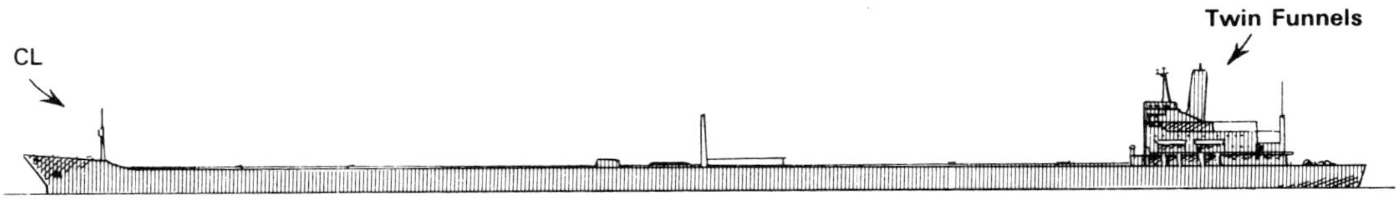

K_2MF H1

64010 THORSHAMMER. No/Sw 1969; Tk; 113700; 324.98 × 20.44 (1066.21 × 67.06); T; 15.75. Sisters: **64011 NORSE KING** (No) **64012 NORSE QUEEN** (No) **64013 PHILLIPS ENTERPRISE** (Li) ex KOLLBJORG **64014 SYLVANIA** (Li) ex MARGA; ex MARGARET ONSTAD 1978 Probable Sisters (No flag): **64015 ADNA 64016 NORSEMAN 64017 POLYVICTORIA 64018 REGINA** Similar (single funnel): **64019 HOEGH LAUREL** (No) ex OSTHAV.

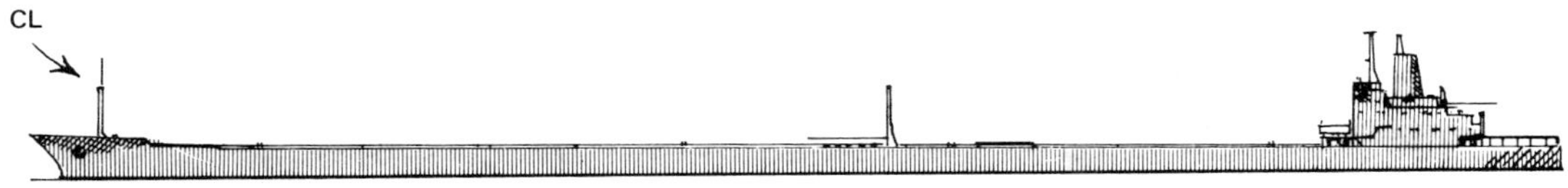

K_2MF H1

64020 NORBEGA. No/Sw 1971; Tk; 113500; 332.24 × 20.65 (1090 × 67.74); T; 16; ex SYNIA 1977.

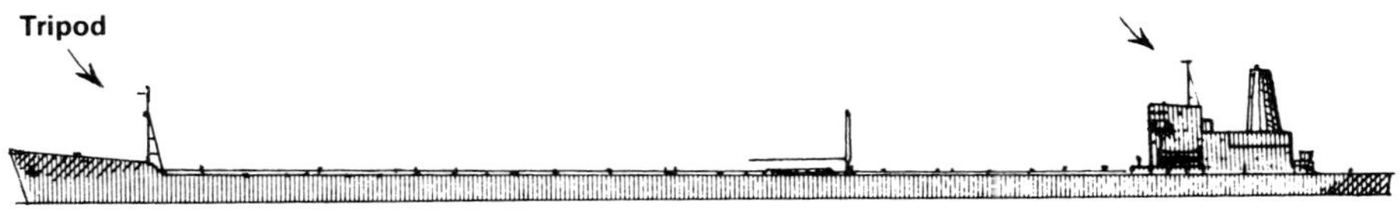

K_2MF H1

64030 SEA ANTWERP. Li/FRG 1970; Tk; 73000; 285.53 × 17.07 (936.78 × 56); T; 16; ex CLAVIGER 1980; ex CLAVIGO 1979.

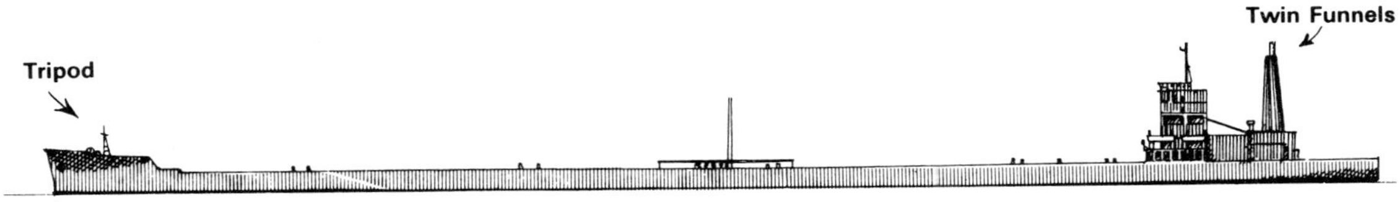

K_2MF H1

● **64040 JADE.** Fr/Sw 1970; Tk; 126400; 340.52 × 20.04 (1117.19 × 65.74); T; 15.

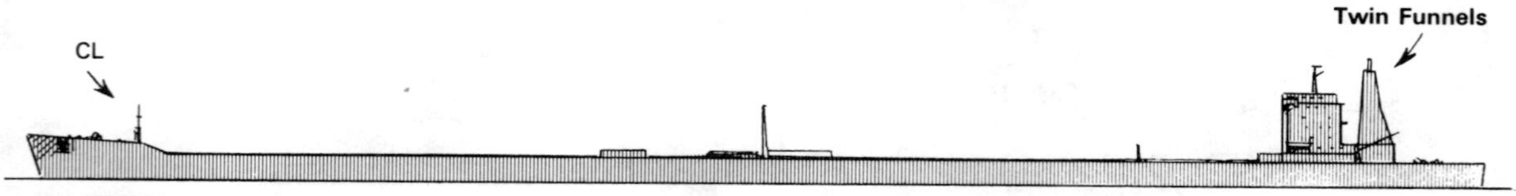

K_2MF H1
64050 NANNY. Sw/Sw 1978; Tk; 245100; 364.02 × 25.07 (1194.29 × 82.25); TST; 16.

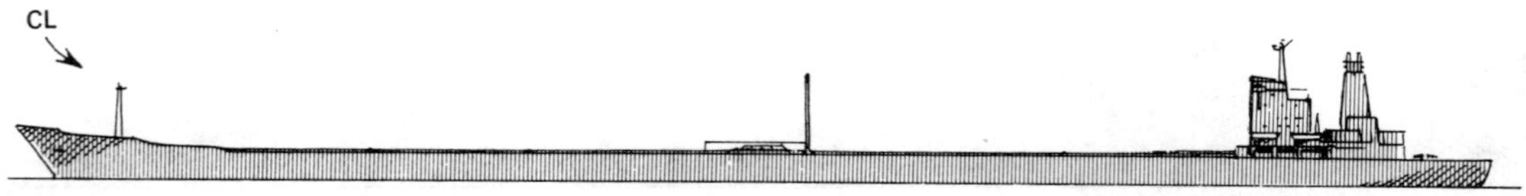

K_2MF H1
● **64060 MOBIL RAVEN.** Li/It 1971; Tk; 116600; 329.73 × 19.9 (1081.79 × 65.28); T; 16; ex PORTHOS; ex SAN GIUSTO 1972. Sister: **64061 ANNA I. ANGELICOUSSI** (Gr) ex SANTA ROSALIA 1980. The following may be K_4MF—which see. **64062 FLYING CLOUD** (Li) ex ANITA MONTI **64063 SIRENIA** (Pa) ex CATERINA M.

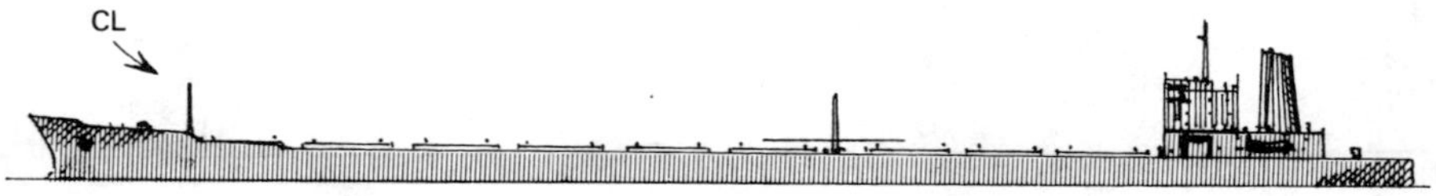

K_2MF H1
64070 ULTRASEA. US/US 1973; OBO; 39800; 272.04 × 13.97 (892.51 × 45.83); T; 16.5. Sister: **64071 ULTRAMAR** (US).

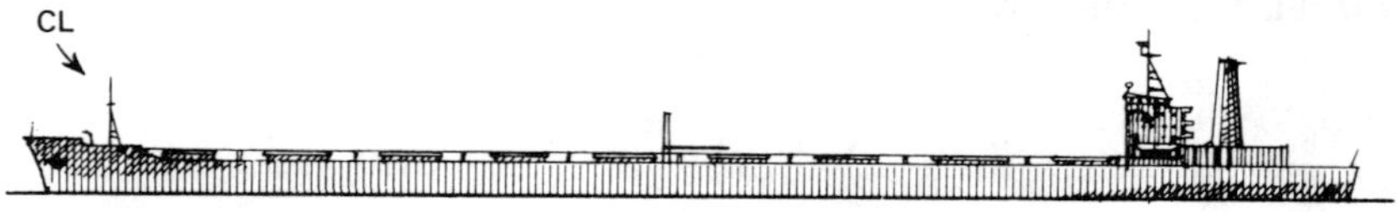

K_2MF H1
● **64080 TATIANA.** Gr/FRG 1970; OBO; 73500; 280.07 × 16.61 (918.86 × 54.49); T; 15.75; ex POLARBRIS 1978. Similar: **64081 IRFON** (Br) Possibly Similar: **64082 ALEXANDRA DYO** (Pa) ex AL QASIM 1981; ex JOHN AUGUSTUS ESSBERGER 1978.

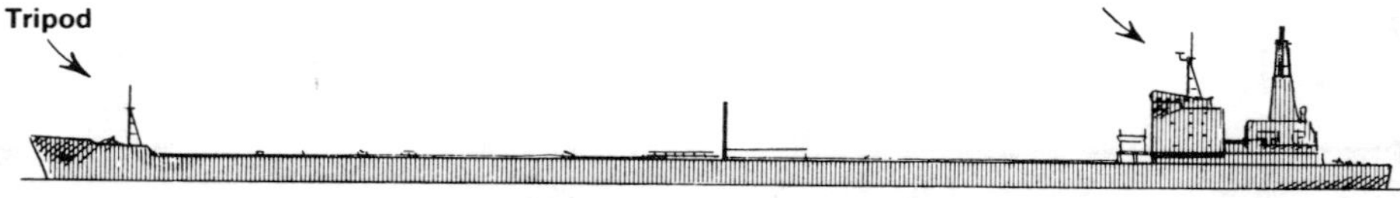

K_2MF H1
★**64090 KASPROWY WIERCH.** Pd/FRG 1974; Tk; 70700; 283.9 × 15.73 (931.43 × 51.61); T; 15.5. Sisters (Pd flag): ★**64091 GIEWONT II** ★**64092 RYSY II** Possibly Similar: **64093 BADEN** (FRG) **64094 BAYERN** (FRG) **64095 DONA MARGARO** (Pa) ex HEINRICH ESSBERGER 1979.

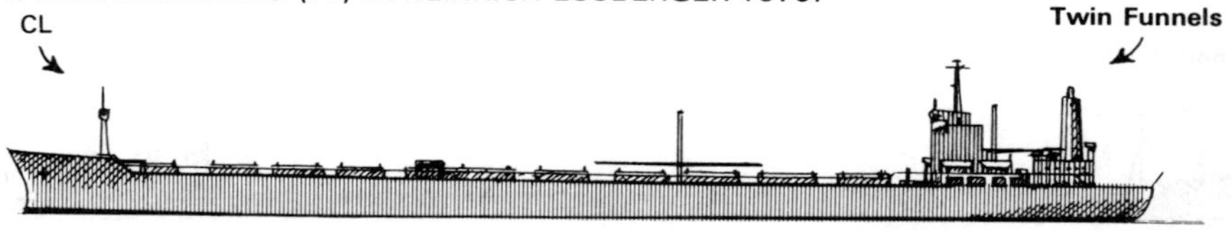

K_2MF H1
64100 BANGLAR NOOR. Bh/Ja 1967; OO; 55800; 252.1 × 14.45 (827.1 × 47.41); M; 15.75; ex VESTAN 1977. Sister: **64101 SKYROS** (Gr) ex APACHE 1979; ex IVORY SUN 1978; ex FERNSTAR 1973.

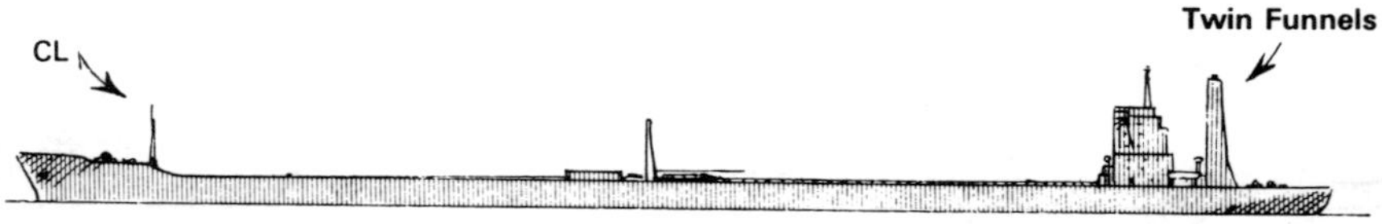

K_2MF H1
64110 YANBU. Li/Ja 1966; Tk; 51400; 258.53 × 15.01 (848.19 × 49.24); M; 15.5; ex MOBIL ARROW 1978; ex SHIN OSAKA MARU 1977.

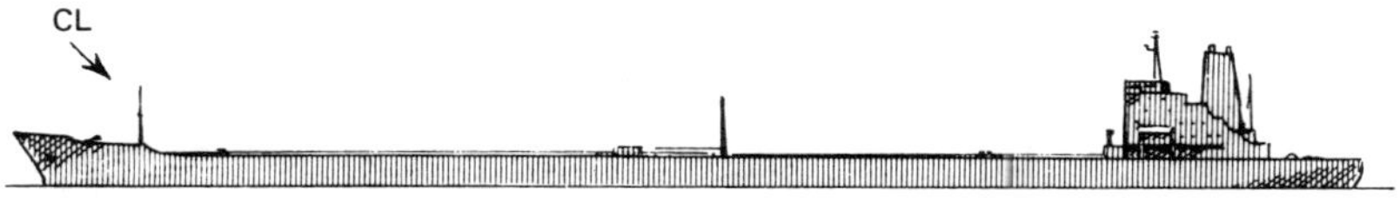

K_2MF *H1*

64120 KURUSHIMA MARU. Ja/Ja 1973; Tk; 44800; 245.98 × 13.27 (807.02 × 43.53); M; 15.5. Sisters (Sg flag): **64121 VIRGINIA LILY 64122 VIRGINIA STAR.**

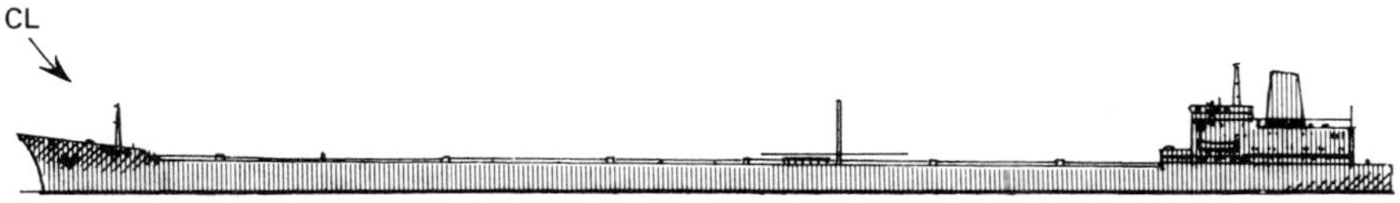

K_2MF *H1*

64130 HAMILTON LOPES. Bz/No 1969; Tk; 62600; 271.66 × 15 (891.27 × 49.21); M; 16. Sister: **64131 HORTA BARBOSA** (Bz).

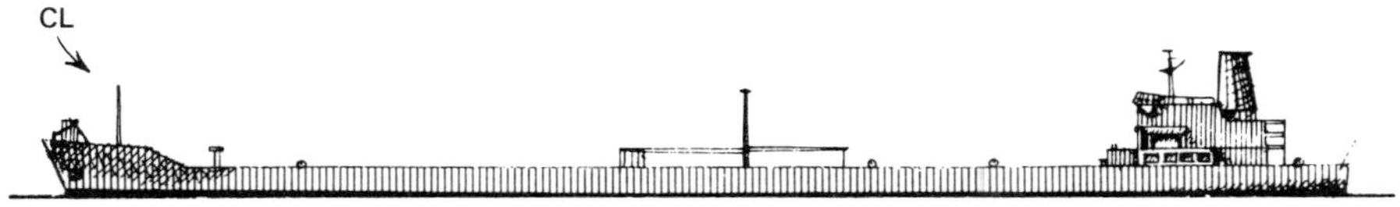

K_2MF *H1*

64140 POLYTRADER. No/Sw 1978; Tk (offshore loading); 65200; 263.71 × 16.77 (865.19 × 55.02); M; 16. Sister: **64141 POLYTRAVELLER** (No) Similar: **64142 HERVANG** (No) **64143 GEORGIA** (No) **64144 WANGLI** (No) **64145 WANGSKOG** (No) **64146 WANGKOLL** (No) **64147 BURMAH LEGACY** (Li) ex FAGERJELL 1979 **64148 CREDO** (No) ex RONACASTLE 1979 **64149 CURRO** (No)—may be K^{2}MFK **64150 AFRAN WAVE** (Li) ex WIND ENDEAVOUR 1977 **65151 GERINA** (No).

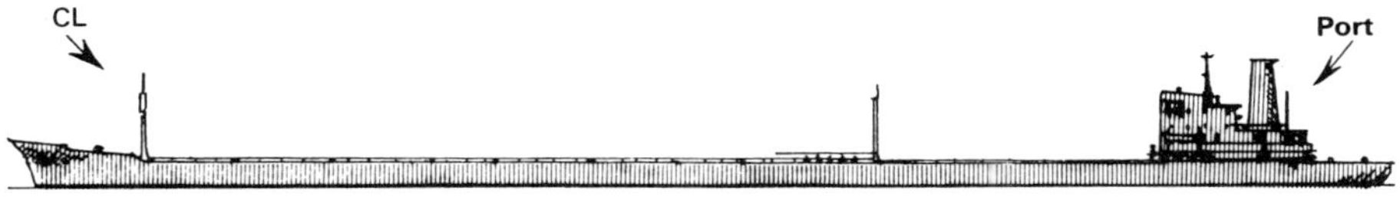

K_2MF *H1*

64160 ALABAMA GETTY. Li/Sw 1971; Tk; 63200; 284.13 × 16.7 (932.18 × 54.79); M; 16; ex CURRO 1976. Sister: **64161 JUANITA** (No)

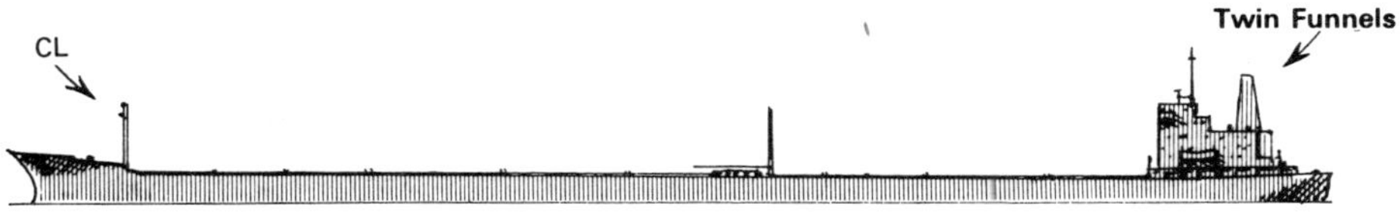

K_2MF *H1*

● **64170 TIHAMA.** Si/Fr 1970; Tk; 68400; 274.33 × 15.46 (900.03 × 50.72); T; 15.5 ex GILDA 1980.

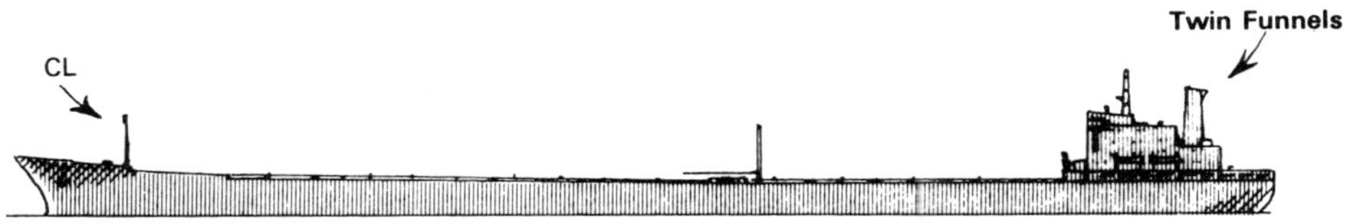

K_2MF *H1*

64180 GEORGES. Gr/Fr 1968; Tk; 60000; 275.01 × 15.08 (902.26 × 49.47); M; 16.5; ex DAUPHINE 1980. Sister: **64181 TRANSUD IV** (Li) ex SAINTONGE.

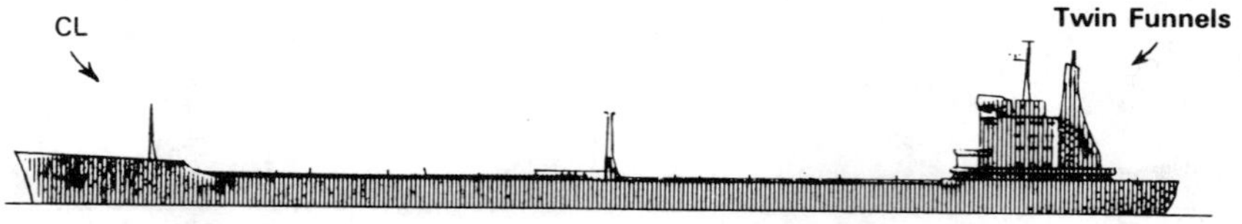

K_2MF H1
64190 DIALA. FRG/FRG 1966; Tk; 39400; 243.77 × 13.08 (799.77 × 42.91); T; 15.5.

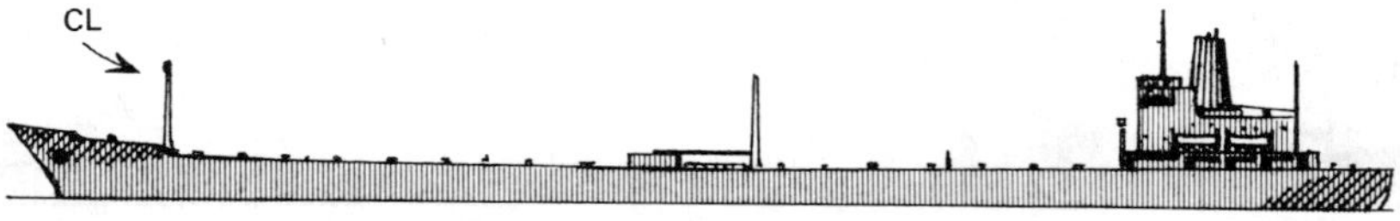

K_2MF H1
64200 VOO SHEE. Tw/Ja 1969; Tk; 52400; 253.04 × 15.57 (830.18 × 51.08); M; 16.5. Sisters (Some Tw built): **64201 HSIEN YUAN** (Tw) **64202 SHEN NON** (Tw) **64203 YU TSAO** (Tw) **64204 FORTUNE** (Li) **64205 GLORY** (Li) **64206 AFRAN ENERGY** (Li)

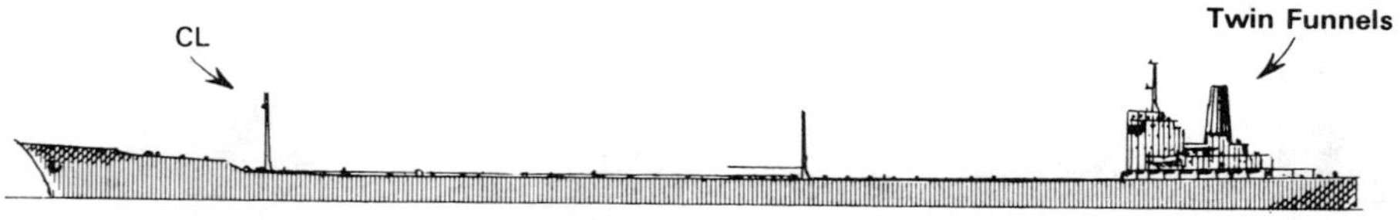

K_2MF H1
● **64210 AL WASEL.** Db/Fr 1968; Tk; 67900; 274.33 × 15.49 (900 × 50.52); T; 16; ex TRADE JUSTICE 1978; ex MONTSOREAU 1976. Now converted to oil storage barge.

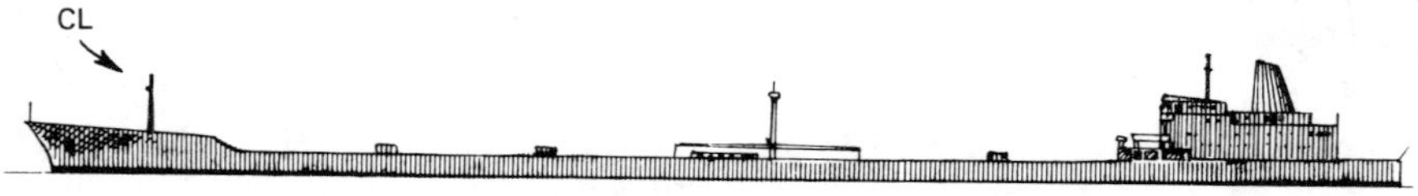

K_2MF H1
64220 NARICA. FRG/Br 1967; Tk; 59900; 264.9 × 14.91 (869.09 × 48.91); M; 14.5. Sister: **64221 NACELLA** (FRG) Similar: **64222 NEVERITA** (FRG).

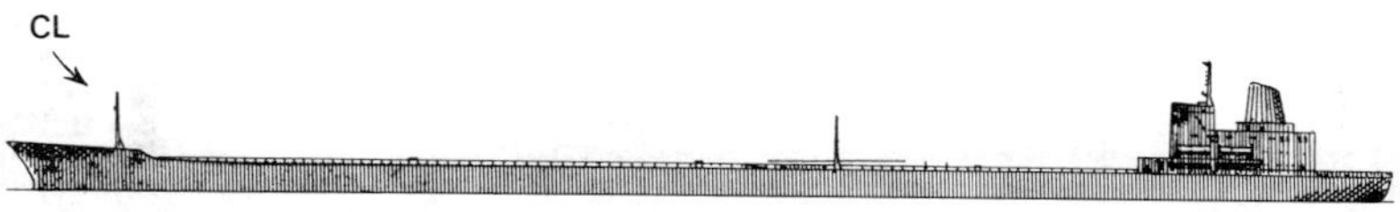

K_2MF H1
64230 DONAX. Br/Br 1966; Tk; 41400; 243.85 × 13.12 (800.03 × 43.04); M; 15.5.

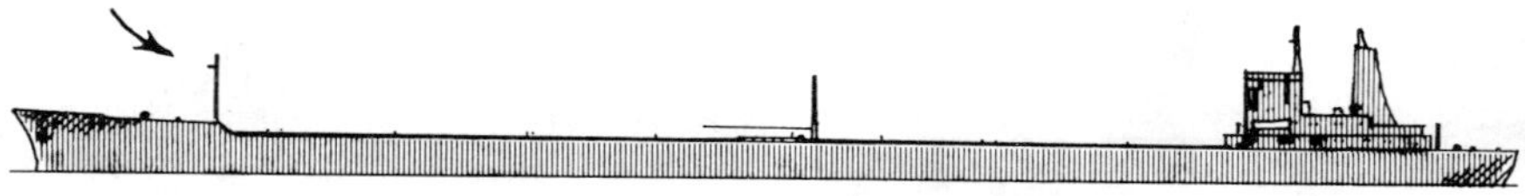

K_2MF H1
64240 ARCO JUNEAU. US/US 1974; Tk; 57700; 269.15 × 15.77 (883.03 × 51.73); T; 16.75. Sisters (US flag): **64241 ARCO ANCHORAGE 64242 ARCO FAIRBANKS 64243 OVERSEAS JUNEAU.**

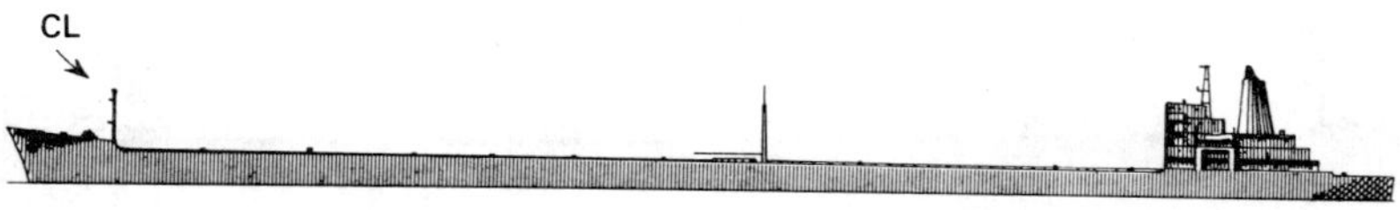

K_2MF H1
64250 ARCO PRUDHOE BAY. US/US 1971; Tk; 35600; 246.9 × 13.18 (810.04 × 43.24); T; 15.5. Sister: **64251 ARCO SAG RIVER** (US) Probable sister: **64252 SANSINENA II** (US) Similar (US flag): **64253 CHEVRON CALIFORNIA 64254 CHEVRON HAWAII 64255 CHEVRON MISSISSIPPI** Probably similar (US flag): **64256 OVERSEAS ALASKA 64257 OVERSEAS ARCTIC**

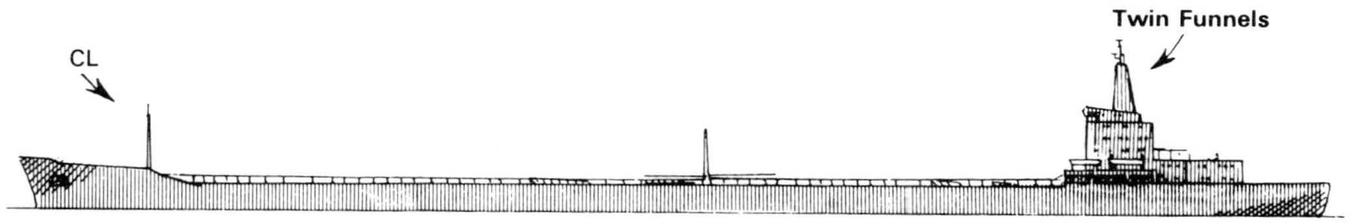

K_2MF H1

● **65260 MYRINA.** FRG/Br 1968 Tk; 95800; 320.05 × 17.68 (1050.03 × 58.01); T; 16.

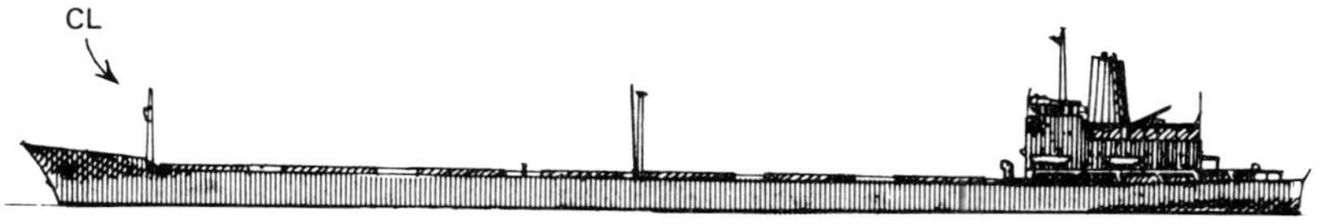

K_2MF H1

64270 HOEGH RANGER. No/Ja 1966; OBO; 42100; 242.5 × 13.69 (795.6 × 44.91); M; 15.5. Sister: **64271 BYZANTION** (Gr) ex VEGA STINGRAY; ex HOEGH RAY 1978.

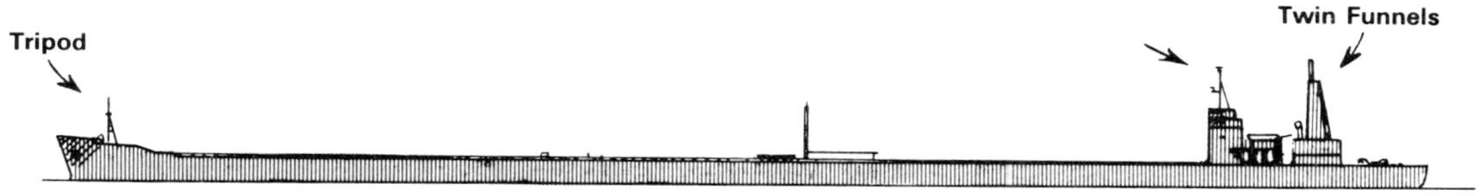

K_2MF H1

64280 JOHN A. McCONE. Li/Sw 1969; Tk; 97000; 316.09 × 19.01 (1037.04 × 62.36); T; 15.5. Sister: **64281 H.J. HAYNES** (Li).

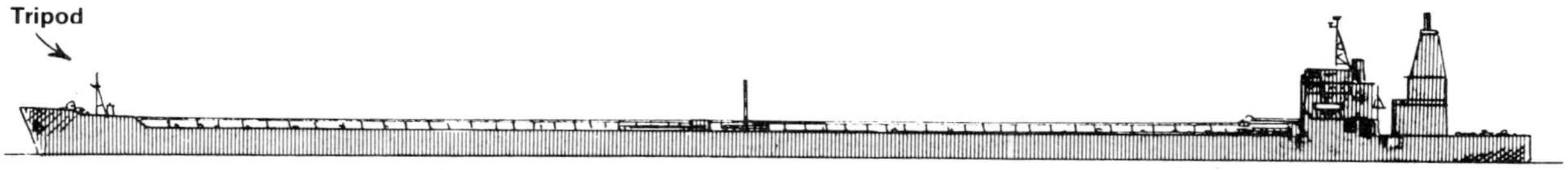

K_2MF H1

● **64290 SEA SAINT.** Sw/Sw 1974; Tk; 178500; 362.75 × 22.32 (1190.1 × 73.22); T; 15.5. Sisters (Sw flag): **64291 SEA SAGA 64292 SEA SERENADE 64293 SEA SCAPE 64294 SEA SONG** (Li flag): **64295 WORLD SYMPHONY** ex SEA SYMPHONY **64296 LONDON TRADER** ex SEA STRATUS 1978 (Gr flag): **64297 TINA 64298 STAVROS G.L.** (No flag): **64299 VANJA 64300 VELA 64301 WIND EAGLE 64302 WIND ENTERPRISE 64303 WIND ESCORT.**

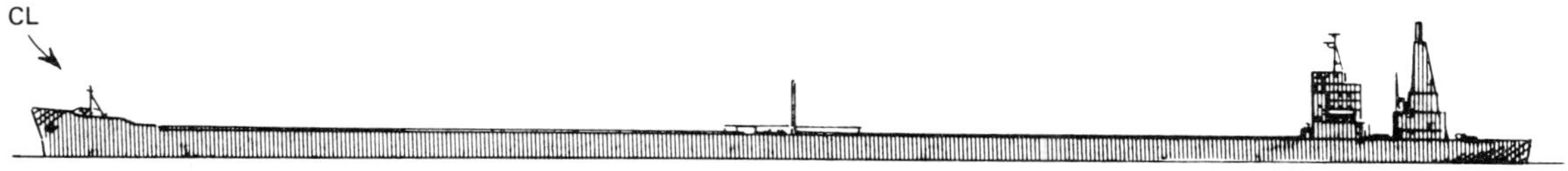

K_2MF H1

● **64310 JARLI.** Fi/Sw 1972; Tk; 125400; 340.52 × 20.07 (1117.1 × 65.8); T; 16; ex SEA SOLDIER. Similar: **64311 SEA SCOUT** (Sw) **64312 SEA SWIFT** (Sw) **64313 JURMO** (Fi) ex SEA SPLENDOUR **64314 CABRITE** (Li) ex SEA SERPENT **64315 SAINT LUCIA** (Li) ex SEA SWAN **64316 ATHENE (No) 64317 ANDRES BONIFACIO** (Pi) ex WORLD JOY 1980; ex BOLETTE 1980; ex DAGHILD **64318 ATLANTIC SUN** (Li) **64319 WORLD SUN** (Li) ex PACIFIC SUN **64320 ESSO DALRIADA** (Br) **64321 ESSO DEMETIA** (Br) **64322 LONDON PRIDE** (Br) **64323 TURQUOISE** (Fr).

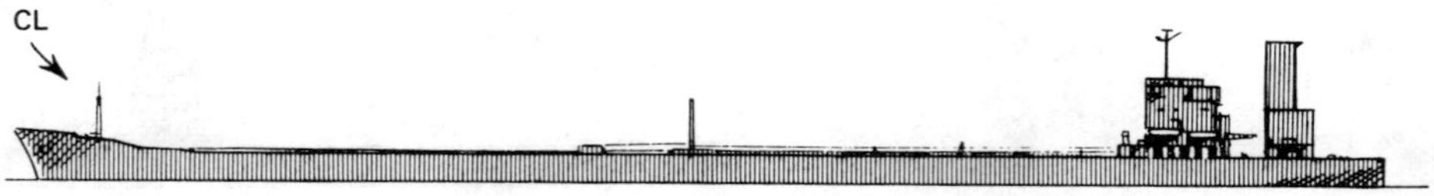

K_2MF H1
64330 ARAMIS. Fr/Sw 1974; Tk; 74100; 270.09×17.06 (886.12×55.97); M; 16; ex SYDHAV 1980. Sisters: **64331 JARICHA** (Li) ex WISA **64332 JAGRANDA** (No) ex PELLOS 1979 **64333 JARITA** (No) ex AINO 1979 **64334 IN-SAFRA** (Ag) ex EMMA FERNSTROM 1976 **64335 IN-AMENAS** (Ag) ex TEAKWOOD 1975 **64336 INTISAR** (Ly) launched as MISTRAL Similar (larger): **64337 ARCHONTAS** (Gr) **64338 MESSINIAKI FILIA** (Li) **64339 MESSINIAKI FLOGA** (Li)—may be H.

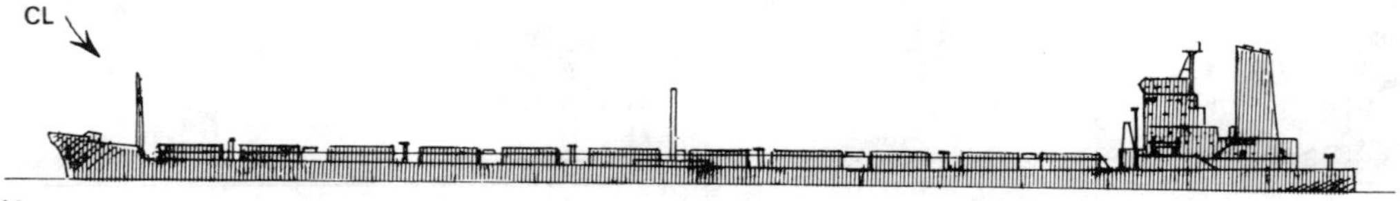

K_2MF H1
64350 RECIFE. Li/Fr 1974; OBO; 76400; 299.25×17.6 (981.79×57.74); M; 16. Sister: **64351 YEMANJA** (Li).

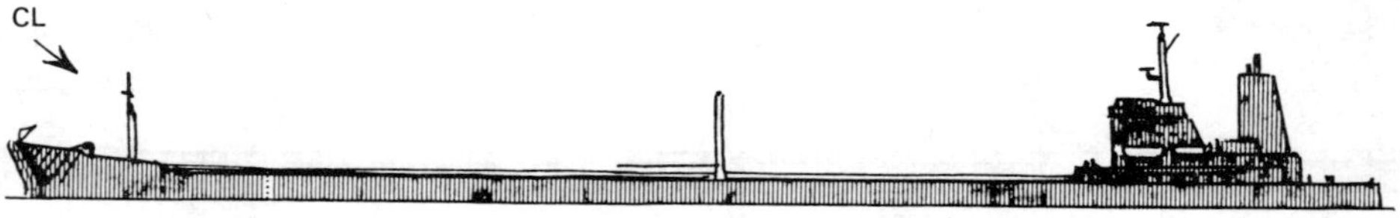

K_2MF H1
64360 AL AIN. Li/Sw 1974; Tk; 68400; 280.07×16.71 (918.86×54.82); M; 16; ex ORATOR 1977. Sisters: **64361 NOGA** (Li) ex IBNU 1977 **64362 HOUSTON GETTY** (Li) **64363 EVITA** (No) **64364 KOLLBRIS** (No) **64365 MARIANNA VII** (Gr) ex KOLLSKEG 1981 **64366 JOHS STOVE** (No) ex GORM 1977 **64367 SEA BREEZE** (No) **64368 JEROM** (Li) ex GINA 1978 **64369 JONNY** (Fi) **64370 CAMARGUE** (Fr) **64371 RABIGH BAY 3** (Gr) ex ERIKA **64372 POITOU** (Fr) **64373 SOLOGNE** (Fr).

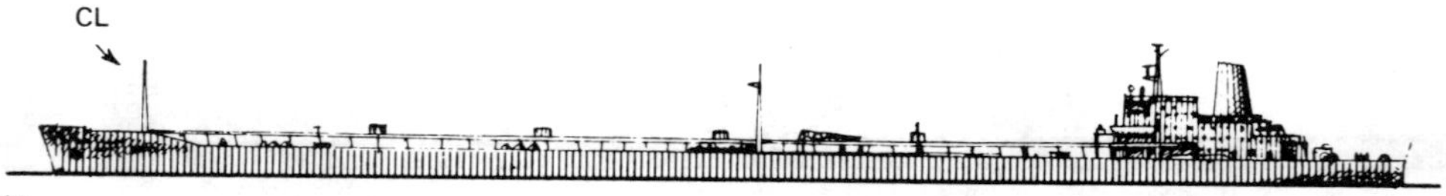

K_2MF H1
● **64380 TULSA GETTY.** Li/Sw 1971; Tk; 69200; 280.07×16.17 (918.86×53.05); M; 15.5; ex MARKLAND 1977. Sister: **64381 NORTHIA** (Br) ex OCEANIC RENOWN 1980; ex KRONOLAND 1979.

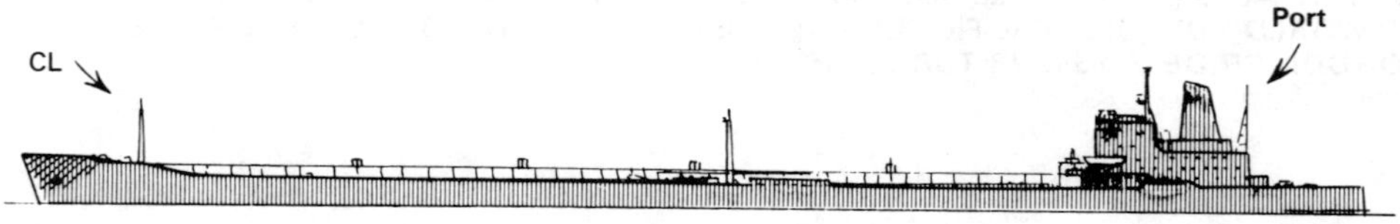

K_2MF H1
64390 MARAO. Po/Sw-Po 1972/73 Tk; 69300; 280.09×16.7 (918.9×54.8); M; 15.5; Forward section built Portugal 1972; aft section built Sweden 1973. Sisters (Po flag): **64391 MAROFA 64392 MONTEMURO.**

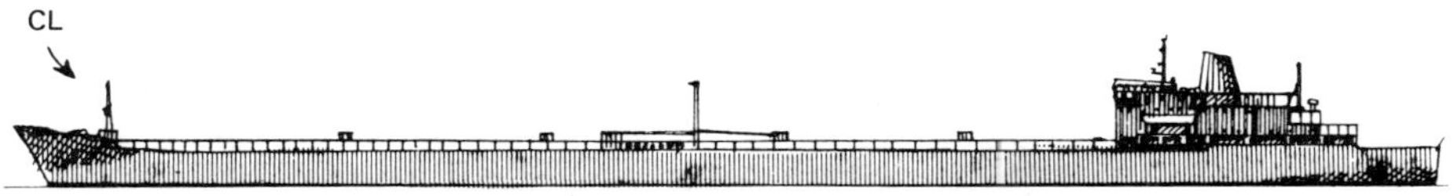

K_2MF H1
64400 PERA. Gr/Sw 1967; Tk; 57800; 277.02 × 14.72 (908.86 × 48.29); M; 16; ex KUNGALAND 1976.

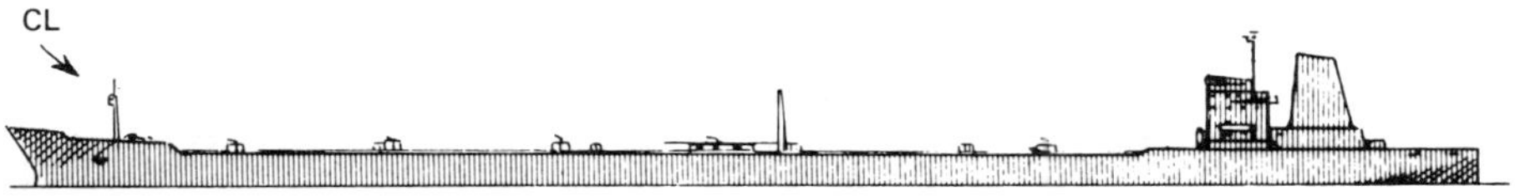

K_2MF H1
64410 FRIESLAND. FRG/FRG 1974; Tk; 65200; 272.27 × 16.51 (893.27 × 54.17); M; 17; launched as TITUREL. Probable sister: **64411 ESSO ORIENT** (Pa) ex SVEA MARINA 1978.

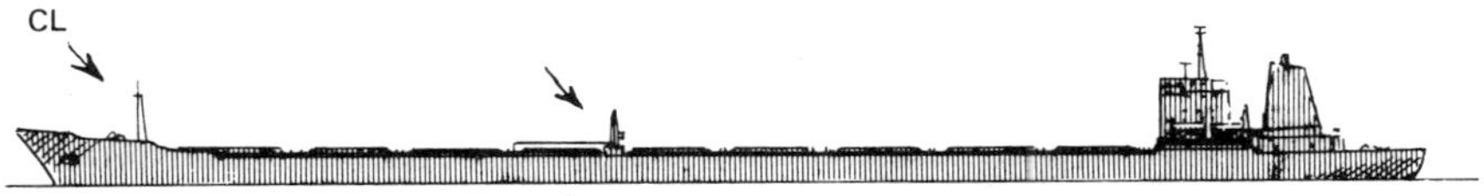

K_2MF H1
64420 MARCONA TRANSPORTER. Li/It 1968; OO; 48500; 260.1 × 15.2 (853.34 × 49.86); M; 16; ex ROSS SOUND 1973; ex RIVALTA 1971. Probable sister: **64421 ASTAKOS** (Li) ex HASTINGS 1977; ex ROSS POINT 1975; ex VITTORIO VALLETTA 1971.

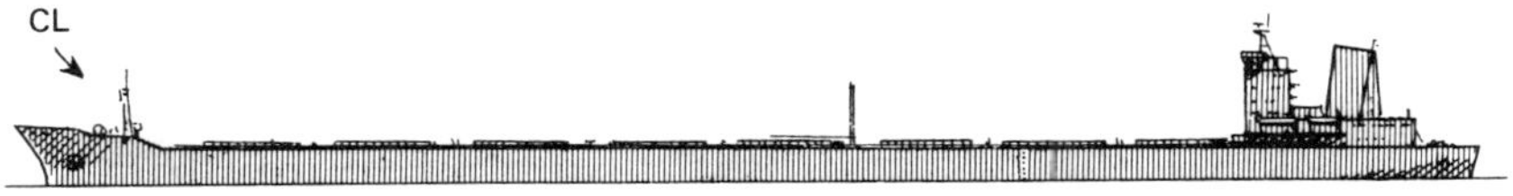

K_2MF H1
64430 BELLARY. In/Ys 1970; OO; 45800; 256.62 × 14.98 (841.93 × 49.15); M; —. Sisters (In flag): **64431 BAILADILA 64432 BARAUNI.**

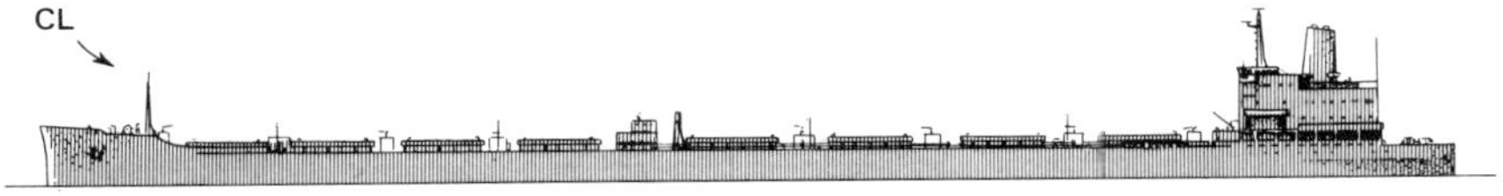

K_2MF H1
64440 MOSEL ORE. Li/Sw 1969; OO; 58800; 253.02 × 15.13 (830.12 × 49.64); M; 15; ex BARON VENTURE 1980; ex PAJALA 1978. Sister: **64441 SAAR ORE** (Li) ex UNITED VENTURE; ex PORJUS 1978; ex FLOWERGATE 1974.

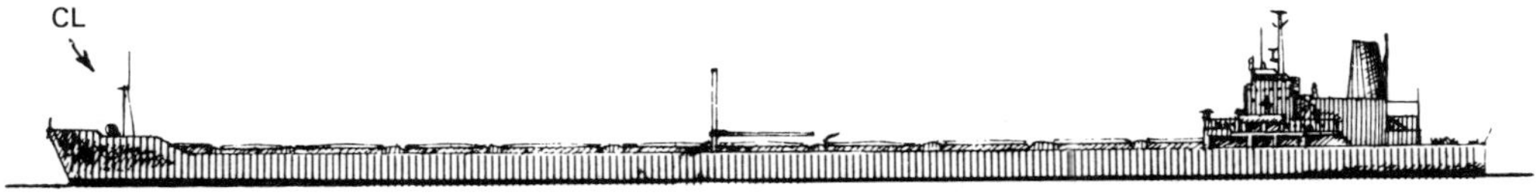

K_2MF H1
64450 LAKE TAHOE. Li/Sw 1972; OBO; 80000; 291.7 × 16.3 (957.02 × 53.47); M; 16; ex KOLL 1976.

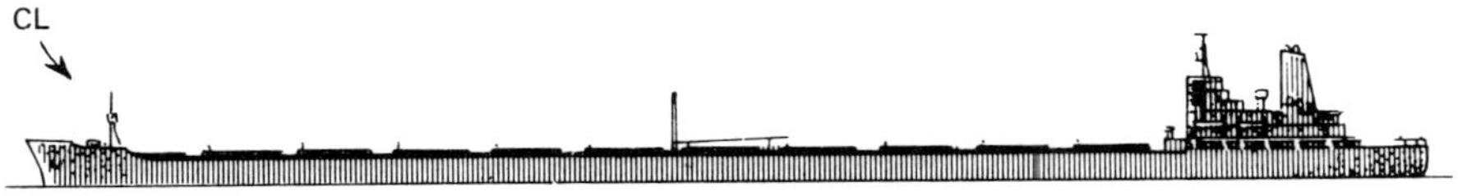

K_2MF H1
64460 LAFUMINA. Li/Ja 1968; OBO; 48600; 261.53 × 13.32 (858.03 × 43.7); M; 16; ex TEHERAN.

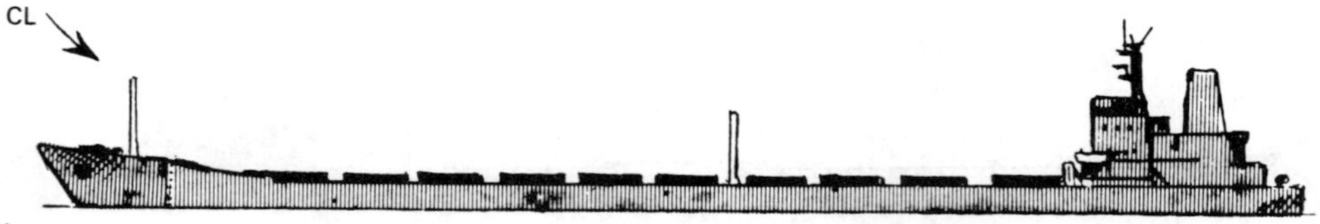

K_2MF H1

● **64470 ATLANTIC SPLENDOUR.** Br/Sw 1970; OBO; 83000; 302.98 × 16.94 (994.02 × 55.57); M; 16.5; ex MUIRFIELD 1978; ex TIBETAN 1972. Sister: **64471 DASHWOOD** (Br) ex RESOLUTE; ex TURCOMAN 1978.

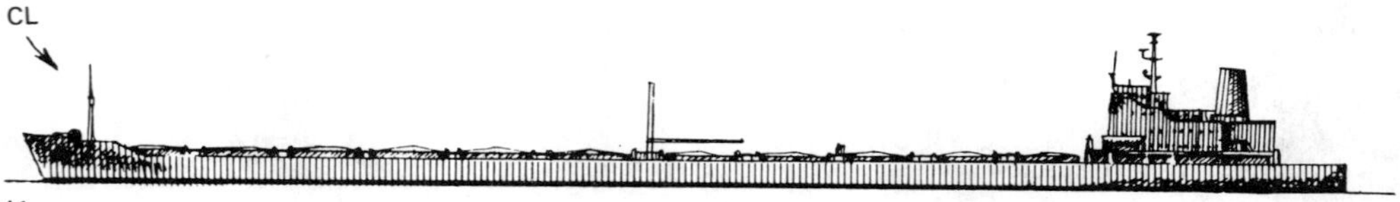

K_2MF H1

64480 KILDARE. Br/Sw 1972; OBO; 83700; 291.65 × 17.01 (956.85 × 55.8); M; 16.25. Sister: **64481 CAST CORMORANT** (Br) ex NORDIC CLIPPER 1980.

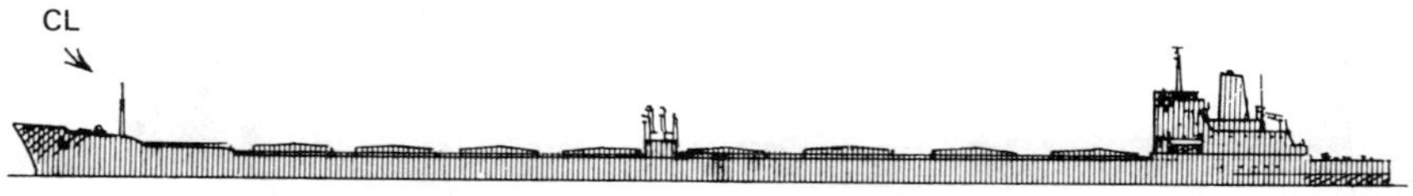

K_2MF H1

64490 ATLANTIC BOUNTY. Li/Sw 1971; OBO; 55600; 256.55 × 15.11 (841.7 × 49.57); M; 16; ex DALSLAND 1980; ex ERIC K. FERNSTROM 1978. Sister: **64491 ATLANTIC ENDEAVOUR** (Li) ex FUJISAN 1978 Similar (larger KP amidships) **64492 SILVERLAND** (Sw) ex A.K. Fernstrom 1977.

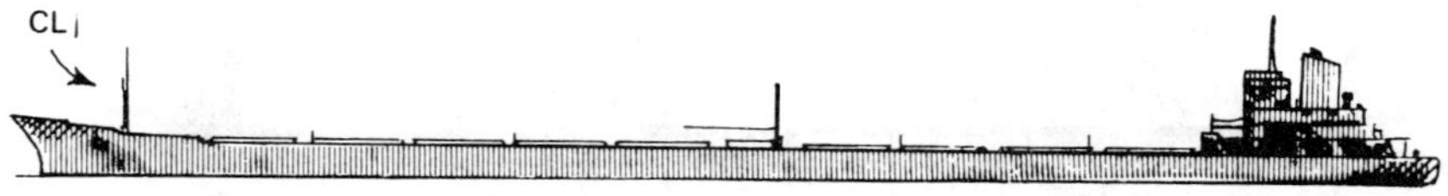

K_2MF H1

64500 NAVIOS CRUSADER. Li/Sw 1972; OBO; 54800; 256.52 × 15.11 (841.6 × 49.57); M; 15.75; ex DAGFRED 1977. Similar (No flag): **64501 VARVARA 64502 VISCAYA.**

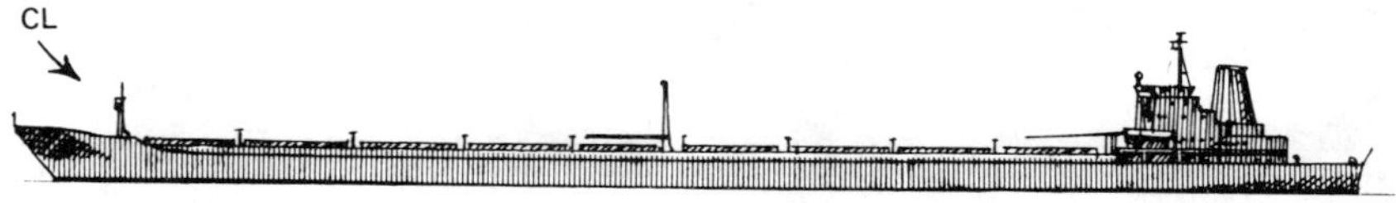

K_2MF H1

● **64510 PALOMA DEL MAR.** Sp/Sp 1972; OBO; 65100; 263.99 × 16.68 (866.1 × 54.72); M; 16. Sisters: **64511 ELISABETH** (Li) ex EULALIA DEL MAR 1981 **64512 FILATRA LEGACY** (Gr) launched as SPIRIT OF PHOENIX **65413 VICTORIA VENTURE** (Li) ex SNESTAD 1978.

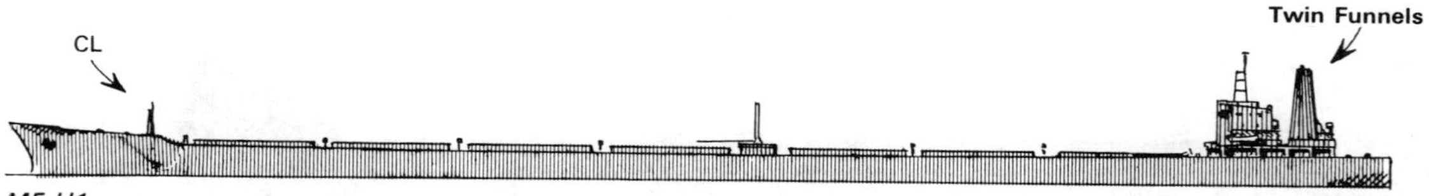

K_2MF H1

64520 BRAZILIAN WEALTH. Li/Ys 1973; OO; 141800; 335.03 × 21.99 (1099.17 × 72.14); TSM; 16.5; ex TARFALA 1978. Sister: **64521 RHINE ORE** (Li) ex TORNE 1979 Similar: **64522 MARY R. KOCH** (Li).

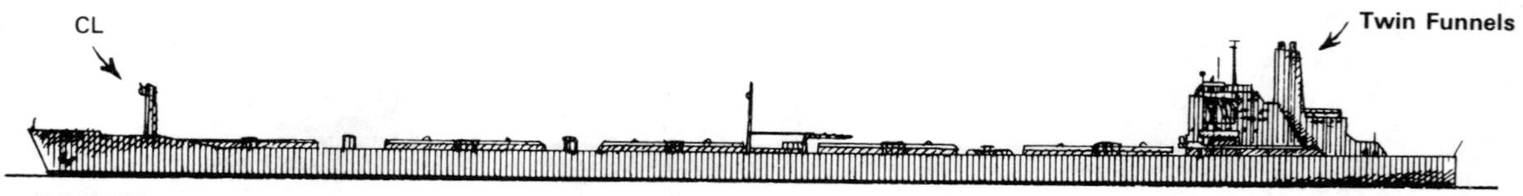

K_2MF H1

64530 WORLD GALA. Li/Sw 1973; OO; 152000; 338.16 × 21.69 (1109.44 × 71.16); M; 15.25; ex SVEALAND 1978.

K_2MF H1
64540 SIBOEN. No/Sw 1968; OBO; 44300; 258.66 × 13.73 (848.62 × 45.04); M; 15.75. Sisters: **64541 SIBOTO** (Li) **64542 SIBOTRE** (No).

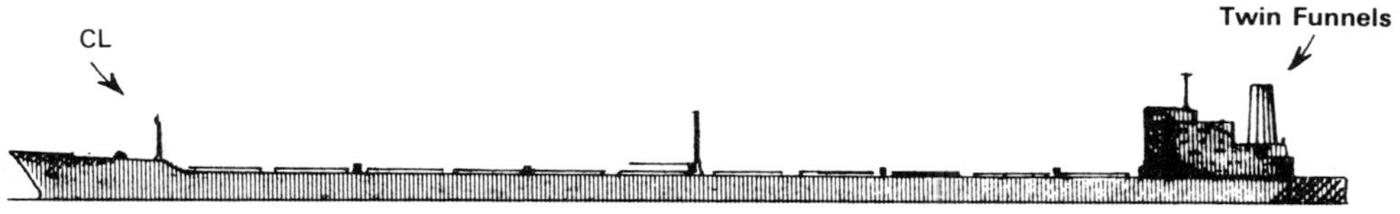

K_2MF H1
64550 BERGEBONDE. No/Sw-Sp 1973; OBO; 84200; 291.68 × 17.01 (956.96 × 55.77); M; 16.5; ex ATLAND 1976; Aft section built Sweden; forward section built Spain. Sister: **64551 BERGE ODEL** (No) ex LAPPLAND 1976.

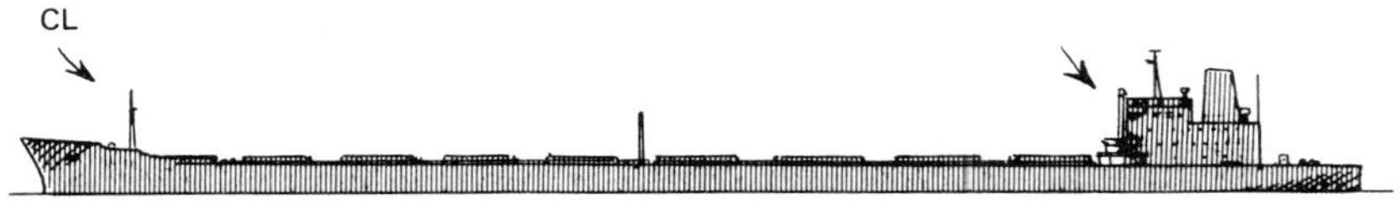

K_2MF H1
● **64560 CAST OSPREY.** Br/Sw 1972; OBO; 56300; 256.04 × 15.08 (840.03 × 49.48); M; 15.75; ex ANGLIA TEAM. Sisters (Br flag): **64561 CAST SKUA** ex NORVEGIA TEAM **64562 CAST GANNET** ex SUECIA TEAM **64563 LONDON TEAM 64564 SCANDIA TEAM 64565 SEVONIA TEAM** (In flag): **64566 WALCHAND.**

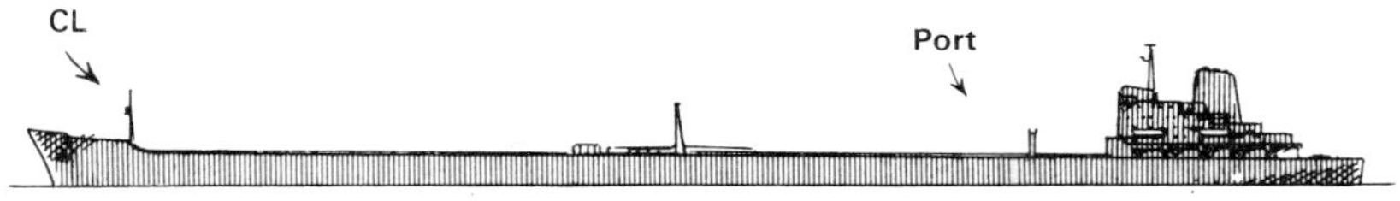

K_2MF H1
64570 MARIAM. Gr/Ja 1966; Tk; 48500; 248.42 × 13.65 (815.03 × 44.78) M; —; ex MORGEDAL 1978; ex MORNING LIGHT 1976; ex PEMBROKE TRADER 1972. Similar: **64571 IRINIO** (Pa) ex SKAUGUM 1976.

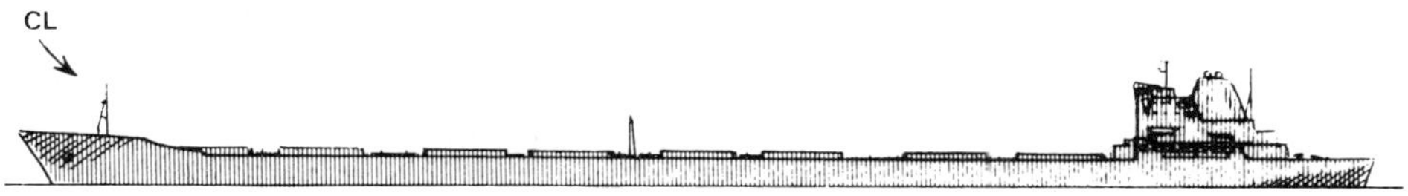

K_2MF H1
64580 ANCORA. No/No 1973; OO; 71300; 282 × 17 (925.19 × 55.77); M; 16. Sisters (No flag): **64581 ACINA 64582 SANDEFJORD.**

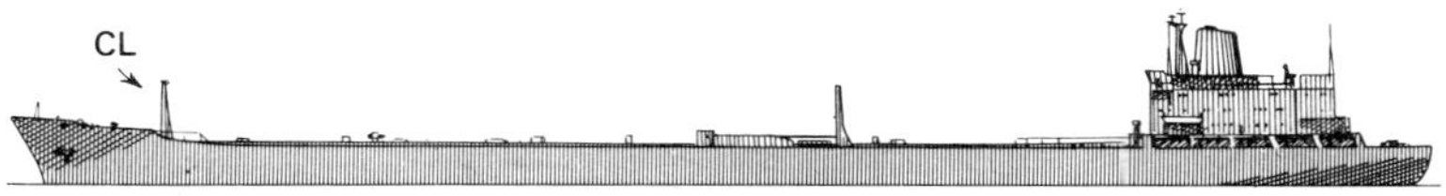

K_2MF H1
64590 AMANDA MILLER. Au/Au 1971; Tk; 39100; 239.28 × 13.17 (785.04 × 43.21); M; 16.5.

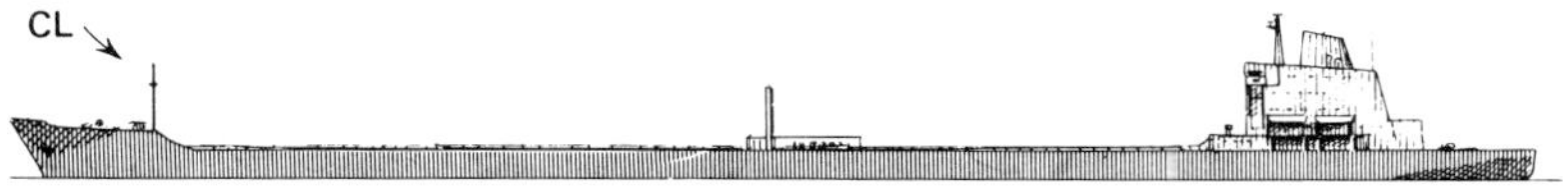

K_2MF H1
64600 CAPO EMMA. It/It 1967; Tk; 48500; 243.85 × 14.21 (800.03 × 46.62); M; —; ex MARE AEGEUM 1978; ex PETROLSADE 1973.

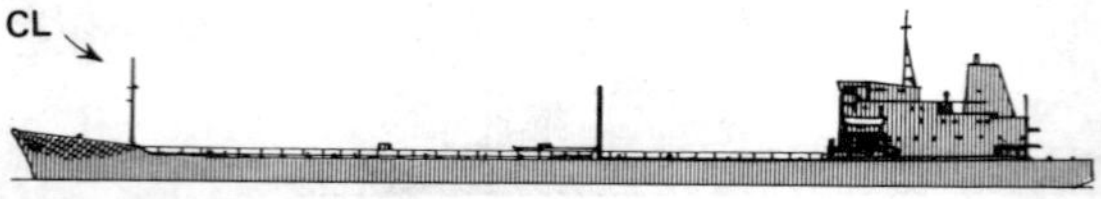

K_2MF H1
64610 DONA OURANIA. Gr/FRG 1971; Tk; 17800; 170.69 × 10.82 (560.01 × 35.5); M; 15.5; ex ST. JACOBI 1979. Sisters: **64611 SENTOSA BAY** (Sg) ex EBERHART ESSBERGER **64612 RAFFLES BAY** (Sg) ex ROLAND ESSBERGER 1979 **64613 DONA EVGENIA** (Gr) ex ST. KATHARINEN 1978.

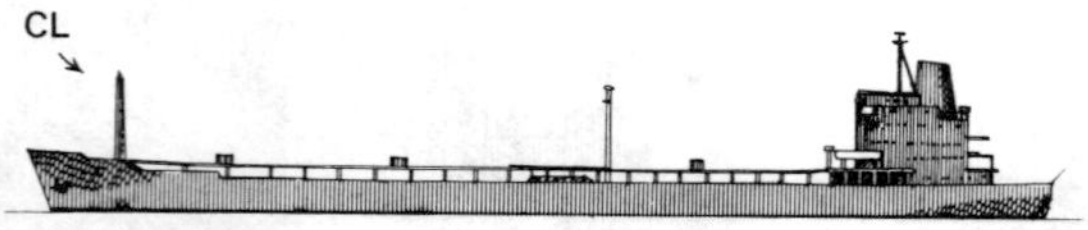

K_2MF H1
64640 MELTEMI. Gr/FRG 1976; Tk; 24700; 193.02 × 11.65 (633.26 × 38.22); M; 16; ex TAIFUN 1978. **'Key 40'** type. Sisters: **64641 LOIDA** (Gr) ex ST. GEORGE 1980; ex LADY CLIO 1977. **64642 ST. CLEMENS** (FRG).

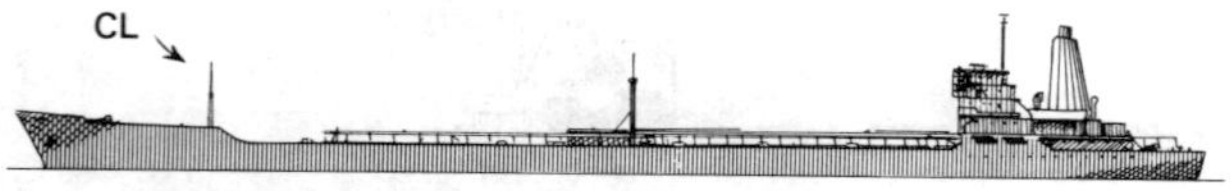

K_2MF H1
64660 MARINE EAGLE. US/US 1944/69; LGC; 15900; 187.38 × 10.08 (516.33 × 33.07); T-E; 14.5; ex PARKERSBURG 1968; ex ESSO PARKERSBURG 1956; ex FORT CORNWALLIS 1946; converted from "T2" tanker and lengthened 1969.

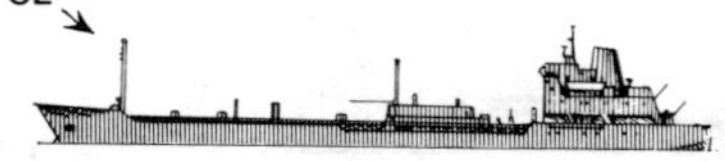

K_2MF H1
● **64680 GAMMAGAS.** FRG/FRG 1972; LGC; 4300; 106.41 × 7.26 (349.11 × 23.8); M; 15.5. Possibly similar: **64681 DELTAGAS** (FRG) **64682 EPSILONGAS** (FRG) **64683 CORAL ISIS** (NA).

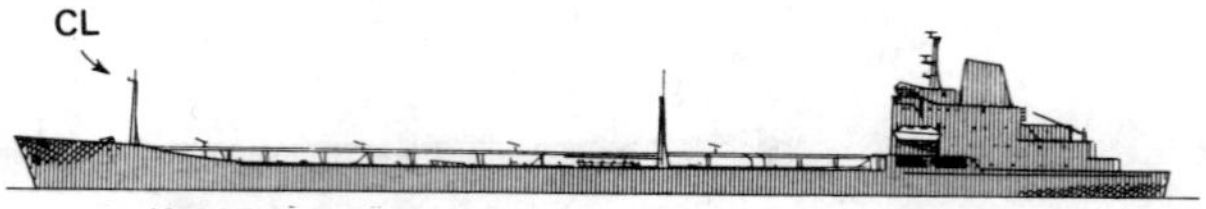

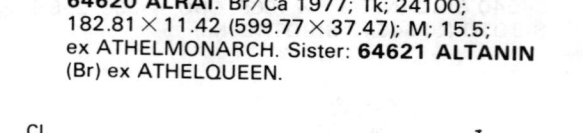

K_2MF H1
64620 ALRAI. Br/Ca 1977; Tk; 24100; 182.81 × 11.42 (599.77 × 37.47); M; 15.5; ex ATHELMONARCH. Sister: **64621 ALTANIN** (Br) ex ATHELQUEEN.

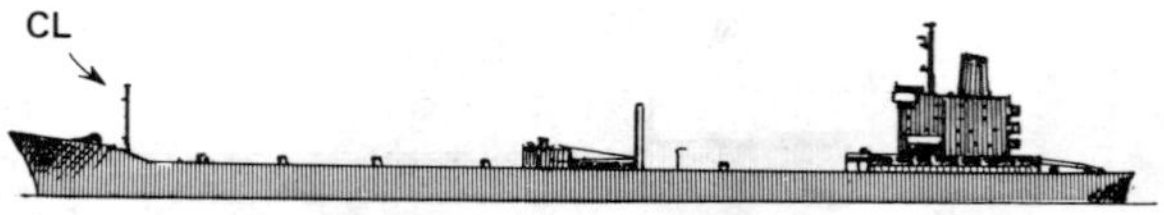

K_2MF H1
64630 SEALIFT ANTARCTIC. US/US 1975; Tk; 17200; 178.92 × 10.54 (587 × 34.58); M; 16; operated commercially for the US Military Sealift Command. Sisters (US flag): **64631 SEALIFT ARABIAN SEA 64632 SEALIFT ARCTIC 64633 SEALIFT ATLANTIC 64634 SEALIFT CARIBBEAN 64635 SEALIFT CHINA SEA 64636 SEALIFT INDIAN OCEAN 64637 SEALIFT MEDITERRANEAN 64638 SEALIFT PACIFIC.**

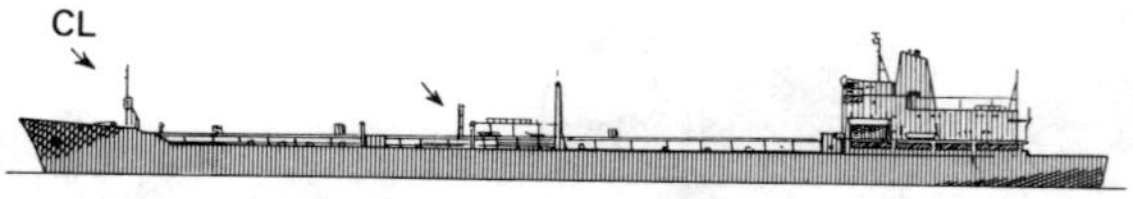

K_2MF H1
64650 BORGA. No/No 1973; Ch; 18700; 170.62 × 11.37 (559.78 × 37.3); M; 16; ex TEAM VESTA. Similar: **64651 CIELO DI NAPOLI** (It) ex TEAM ASTWI 1979; launched as ASTWI **64652 HADA** (No) ex TEAM CASTOR **64653 SOLVIKEN** (No) ex TEAM POLLUX **64654 MYKONOS** (Li) ex TEAM AUGWI 1979 **64655 MYRTEA** (Li) ex TEAM HILWI 1979.

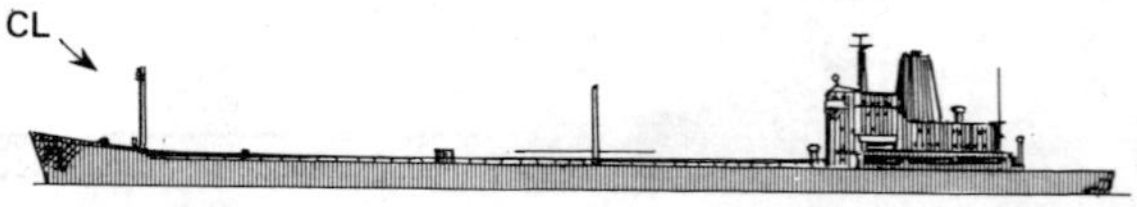

K_2MF H1
64670 MOBIL ENGINEER. Li/No 1973; Tk; 18800; 170.69 × 11.33 (560 × 37.17); M; 15.75. Sister: **64671 MOBIL NAVIGATOR** (Li).

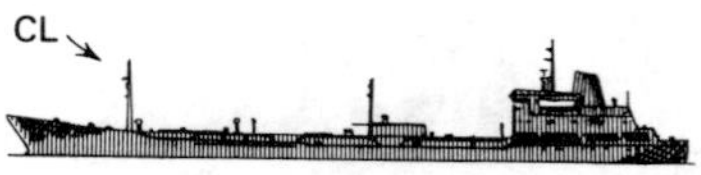

K_2MF H1
64690 FRITZ HABER. FRG/FRG 1971; LGC; 4300; 106.41 × 7.27 (349.11 × 23.85); M; 16; ex IRENE 1974.

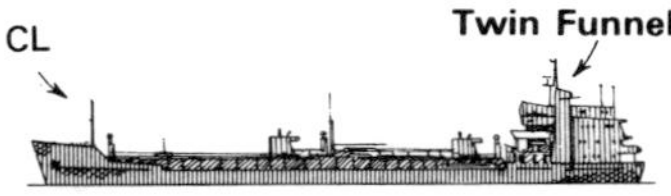

K_2MF H1
64700 OSWEGO STAR. Li/Ne 1972; Ch; 4000; 96.88 × 7.49 (317.84 × 24.57); M; 13; ex SILVER EIRIK 1977.

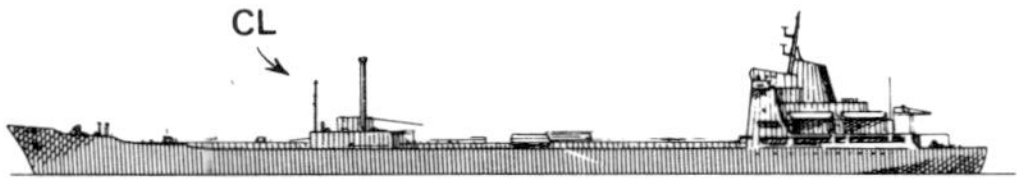

K_2MF H1
64710 GALILEO. Ch/Fr 1967; LGC; 9900; 154.51 × 7.65 (506.92 × 25.09); M; 17.5; ex ZENON 1974; ex CERONS 1971; ex AEOLOS II 1968.

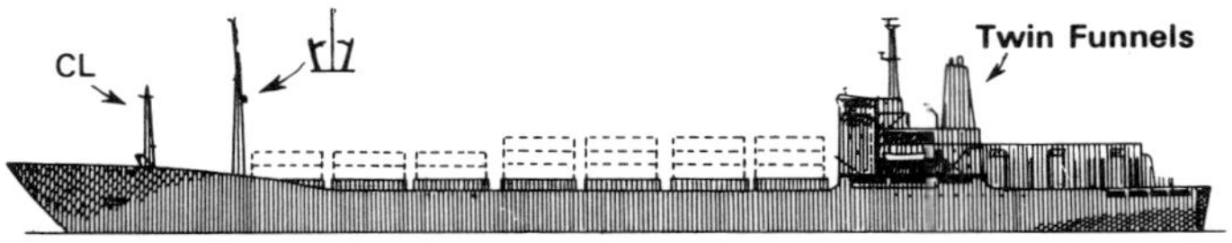

K_2MF H1
64720 AMERICANA. It/It 1974; Con/V; 22200; 208 × 10.3 (683 × 34.1); T; 23.5; Side door on port side. Sister: **64721 ITALICA** (It).

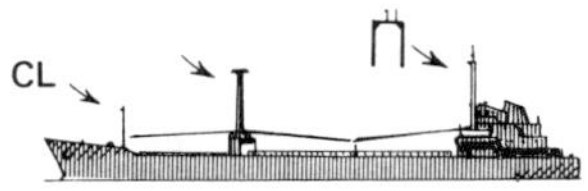

K_2MF H1
64730 DWEJRA II. Ma/Ne 1969; C; 1000; 84.26 × 5.11 (276.44 × 16.77); M; —; ex ASD IRIS 1976; ex IRIS 1973.

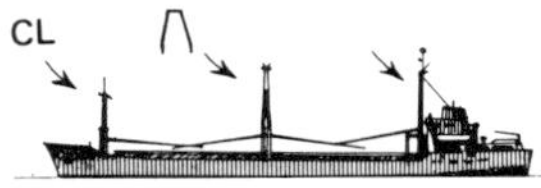

K_2MF H1
● **64740 ANNELISE OLTMANN.** FRG/No 1972; C; 1000; 77.09 × 5.1 (252.92 × 16.73); M; 14. Sisters (Pa flag): **64741 ESTEFLUT 64742 ESTETAL**

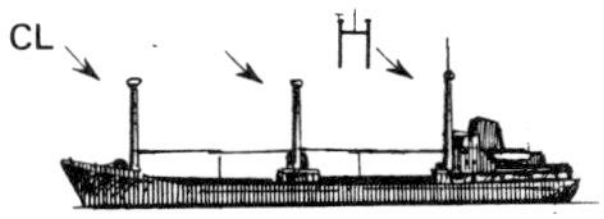

K_2MF H1
64750 ITALIAN EXPRESS. Sg/FRG 1964; C; 955/1590; 83.72 × 4.52/5.89 (274.67 × 14.82/19.32); M; 14; ex THESEE 1977.

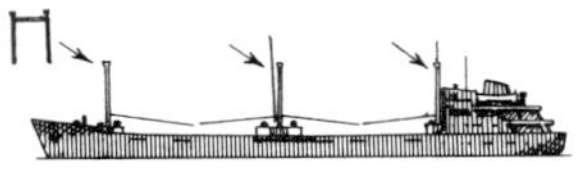

K_2MF H1
● **64760 FADEL.** Cy/FRG 1953; C; 1300; 83.37 × 5.25 (273.52 × 17.22); M; 12; ex TEMAYA 1978; ex AMMERLAND 1972; ex CALDAS 1967; ex FALKENBURG 1962; ex SANKT MARIEN 1962.

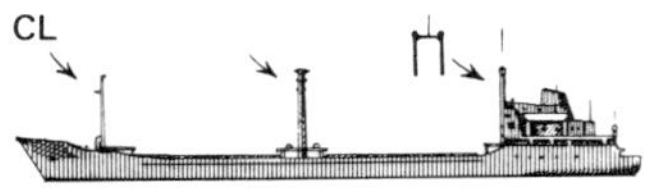

K_2MF H1
● **64770 MAERSK MONDO.** Li/FRG 1969; Con; 1600; 99.22 × 5.36 (325.5 × 17.58); M; 14.5; ex MONDO 1975; ex BEAVERMONDO 1971; Launched as MONDO. Sister: **64771 MAERSK RANDO** (Li) ex RANDO 1975; ex BEAVERRANDO 1971; Launched as RANDO.

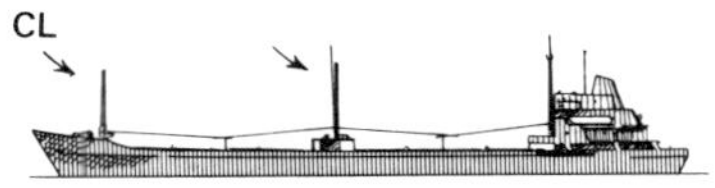

K_2MF H1
64780 HARTFORD EXPRESS. FRG/FRG 1970; C; 1500/3300; 103.38 × 4.78/6.37 (339.17 × 15.68/20.89); M; 15.5; Launched as PETER WEHR.

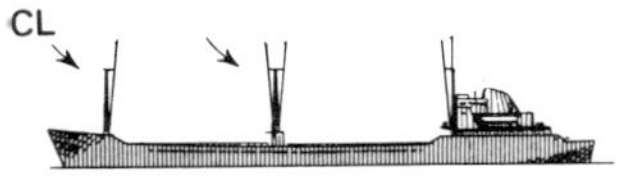

K_2MF H1
64790 STIRLINGBROOK. Br/Br 1970; C; 1600; 86.34 × 5.03 (283.27 × 16.5); M; 12. Sister (Br flag): **64791 SOLENTBROOK 64792 SOMERSETBROOK 64793 SURREYBROOK 64794 SUSSEXBROOK.**

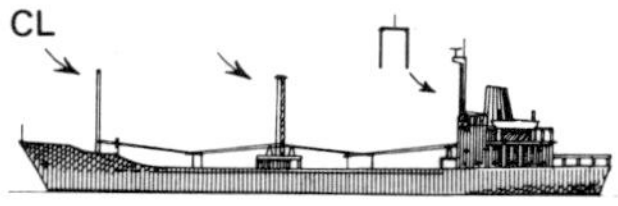

K_2MF H1
64800 FENCHURCH. Br/Br 1968; C; 1500; 94.24 × 5.01 (309.19 × 16.44); M; 13; ex CITY OF ISTANBUL 1978; ex MEDITERRANIAN 1974.

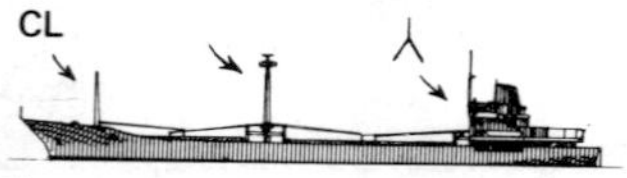

K_2MF H1
★64810 MAN CHENG. RC/FRG 1975; C; 1600; 91.47 × 6.12 (300 × 20); M; 15; ex LINDINGER LIGHT 1979. Sisters (RC flag): **★64811 XIONG ER SHAN** ex LINDINGER KARAT 1978 **★64812 KUAN CHENG** ex LINDINGER IVORY 1978 **★64813 TIAN LI SHAN** ex LINDINGER JADE 1978 **★64814 YA CHENG** ex LINDINGER NIMBUS 1978 **★64815 HAI CHENG** ex LINDINGER MOONSTONE 1978 **★64816 LI CHENG** ex LINDINGER SILVER 1978 (De flag): **64817 LEIF STAERKE** ex LINDINGER TOPAZ 1979 Possible Sisters (RC flag): **★64818 HE LAN SHAN** ex LINDINGER OPAL 1978 **★64819 SHI ZUI SHAN** ex LINDINGER QUETZAL 1978

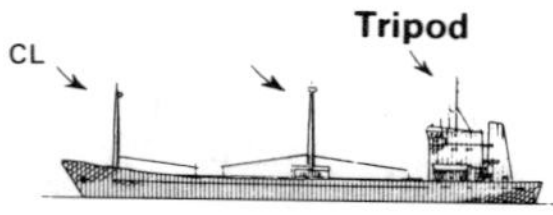

K_2MF H1
● **64850 MIRA.** FRG/Ne 1974; C; 800; 76 × 4.45 (249.34 × 14.6); M; 11; ex AMIGO EXPRESS 1975. Similar (De flag). **64851 KASPAR SIF 64852 JETTE SIF 64853 ANN SANDVED 64854 CHRIS ISA** ex BALTON 1975 **64855 RIKKE ISA 64856 HERMAN SIF** ex GERDA LONBORG 1977 **64857 OTTO DANIELSEN** ex EGYPTIAN; launched as OTTO DANIELSEN **64858 WINNI HELLESKOV 64859 AMIGO FORTUNA** (Ne flag). **64860 SWIFT 64861 NIELSE DANIELSEN** ex AMIGO DEFENDER 1978 Possible similar (De flag). **64862 INGE DANIELSEN** ex TROJAN PRINCE 1977; launched as INGE DANIELSEN **64863 KETTY DANIELSEN** ex AMIGO EXPRESS 1978 **64864 ERIK SIF 64865 GRETE SIF 64866 FRELLSEN HILLE** ex HILLE FRELLSEN 1980 (Fa flag). **64867 RUNATINDUR** ex LOTTE SCHEEL 1976.

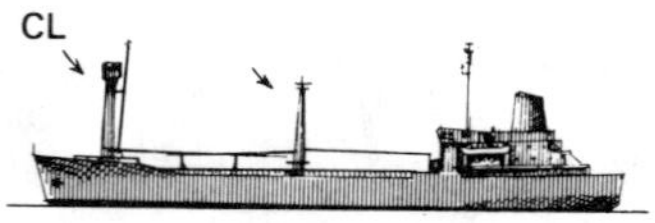

K_2MF H1
64900 LINDA DAN. De/De 1973; C; 3300; 93.93 × 7.36 (308.16 × 24.14); M; 14.75. Sister: **64901 GRONLAND** (De).

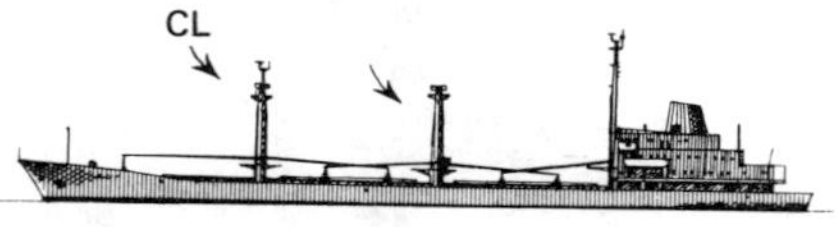

K_2MF H1
64920 TRIUMPH ORIENT. De/FRG 1972; C; 3000/5200; 125 × 6.61/7.64 (410.1 × 21.69/25.07); M; 17.25; ex EMMA JEBSEN. Sister. **64921 SIGNAL** (Pa) ex HEINRICH JESSEN.

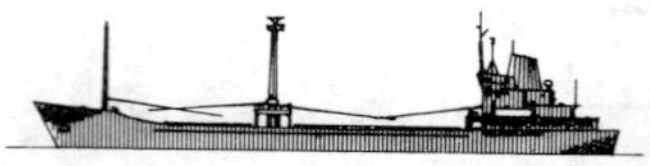

K_2MF H1
64830 EIDER. FRG/FRG 1978; C; 1600; 91.47 × 6.2 (300.1 × 20.34); M; 13. Sister: **64831 HEVER** (FRG).

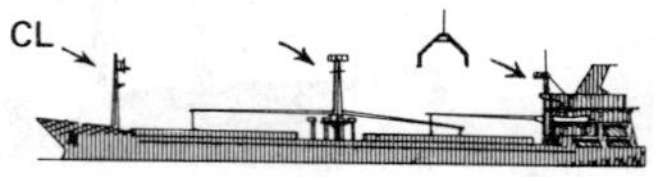

K_2MF H1
64840 MERCANDIAN ATLANTIC. De/De 1977; C; 1700/3300; 96.53 × —/6.8 (316.69 × —/22.3); M; 14. Sister. **64841 MERCANDIAN PACIFIC** (De).

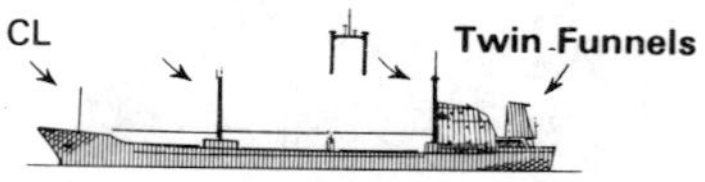

K_2MF H1
64870 JAN WILLEM. Ne/Ne 1977; R; 1200; 83.93 × 5.3 (275.36 × 17.38); M; 14. Sisters (Ne flag). **64871 CALAFIA 64872 CASABLANCA 64873 LAURA CHRISTINA 64874 INCA 64875 MAYA 64876 MAGDALENA 64877 MATHILDA.**

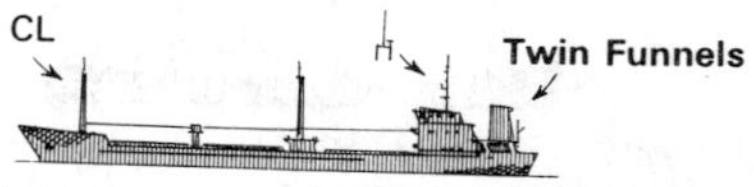

K_2MF H1
64880 OCEANIC. Ne/Ne 1977; R; 1150; 82.73 × 5.01 (271.42 × 16.43); M; 13. Probable sister: **64881 ICELANDIC** (Ne).

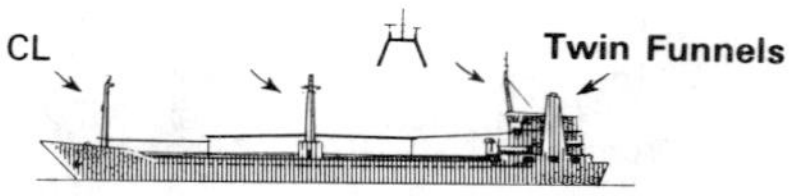

K_2MF H1
64890 KAREN WINTHER. De/De 1977; C; 1600; 96.53 × 5.64 (316.69 × 18.5); M; 12.5.

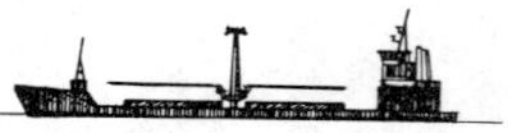

K_2MF H1
● **64910 ASEAN PIONEER.** Pa/Sg 1975; C; 1600; 69.07 × 4.23 (226.6 × 13.87); TSM; 9. Sisters (Pa flag). **64911 ASEAN PROSPERITY 64912 ASEAN VENTURE 64913 OCEAN LEADER** ex ASEAN LEADER 1980 **64914 OCEAN PROGRESS** ex ASEAN PROGRESS 1980 **64915 OCEAN PROMOTER** ex ASEAN PROMOTER 1980 **64916 OCEAN CHALLENGER** ex ASEAN CHALLENGER 1980.

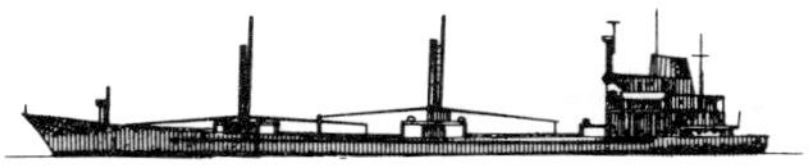

K_2MF H1
● **64930 MEJEAN III.** Fr/FRG 1969; C; 2800/4800; 116.8 × 6.52/7.53 (383.2 × 21.39/24.7); M; 15.5; ex NORDWELLE 1977; **'TRAMPCO'** type. Sisters. **64931 NORDKAP** (Sg) **64932 DIAMOND SUN** (Gr) ex NORDWOGE 1980 **64933 NORDSTRAND** (FRG) **64934 DRUCILLA U** (Li) ex CARLO PORR 1976 **64935 ILLERBERG** (Cy) ex HAMBURGER SENATOR 1978 **64936 HEKTOR** (Cy) ex PARZIVAL 1972 **64937 ACHILL** (Cy) ex LOHENGRIN 1974 **64938 CAP BRETON** (FRG) launched as SONNHOLM **64939 ISAR** (FRG) ex CAP VINCENT 1972; launched as ISAR **64940 ANTJE SCHULTE** (Pa) **64941 JUDITH SCHULTE** (Br) **64942 GEORG KURZ** (Pa) ex EASTERN LAKE 1977; ex HAMBURGER FLEET 1975 **64943 TECONA** (Cy) ex PROMINENT 1; ex SCOL PROMINENT 1977; ex EASTERN BRIDGE 1974; ex CAPE HENRY 1974; ex HINRICH WITT 1972 **64944 MARIANNE ROTH** (Cy) ex CAPE RAY 1978; ex HAMBURGER DOM 1974 **64945 RIDGE** (SA) **64946 VERGE** (SA) Similar (Stulcken derricks). **64947 TERENGA** (FRG) ex BACHUE 1981; ex DOROTHEA BOLTEN 1978 **64948 PAMPERO** (FRG) ex NOPAL PAMPERO 1977; ex SCHIROKKO 1975 **64949 TAIFUN** (FRG).

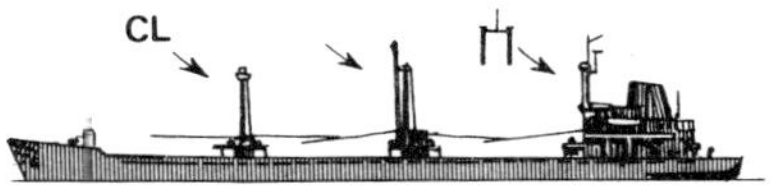

K_2MF H1
● **64960 IBN ROCHD.** Ag/FRG 1973; C; 2800/4800; 116.69 × 6.51/7.52 (328.84 × 21.36/24.67); M; 15.75; **'TRAMPCO'** type. Sisters (Ag flag). **64961 IBN BADIS 64962 IBN BATOUTA 64963 IBN SIRAJ 64964 AURES 64965 DJORF 64966 DJURDJURA 64967 EDOUGH 64968 OUARSENIS 64969 IBN KHALDOUN II 64970 IBN SINA II** Some of these sisters are 10m longer than the name ship.

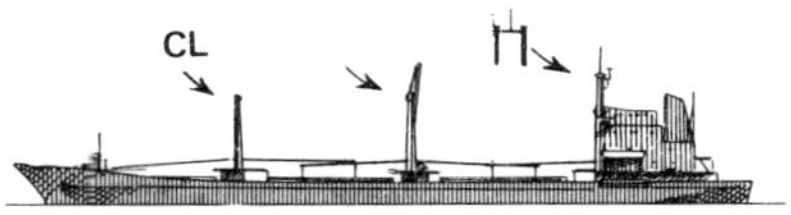

K_2MF H1
64980 FLENSAU. FRG/FRG 1978; C; 5000; 116.64 × 7.52 (382.68 × 24.67); M; 15.25. Sister. **64981 KRUSAU** (FRG).

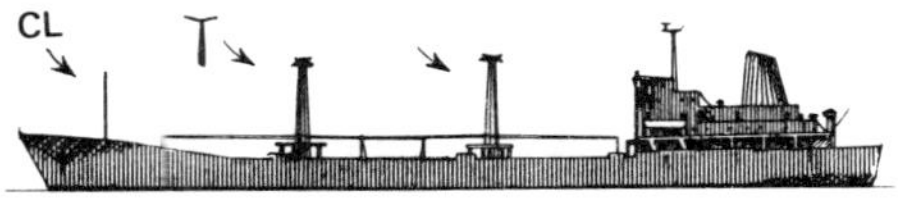

K_2MF H1
64990 BAMSA DAN. De/De 1973; R; 5000; 135.11 × 7.62 (443.3 × 25); M; 17.

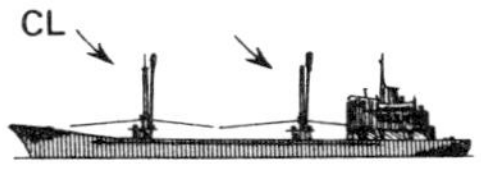

K_2MF H1
65000 IBN JUBAIR. Eg/Sp 1970; C; 650/1200; 72.7 × 5.19 (238.5 × 16.96); M; —; ex ATLAN ESMERALDA 1974. Sister. **65001 IBN KORRA** (Eg) ex ATLAN RUBI 1975 Possibly similar. **65002 LUR-TXORI** (Sp) ex JADE 1975; ex LIAN 1974 **65003 UR-TXORI** (Sp) ex TOPACIO 1976; ex LIAN DOS 1973.

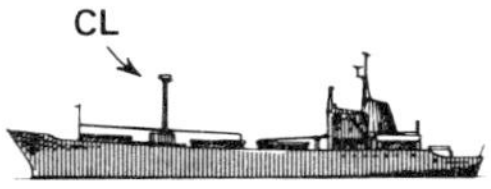

K_2MF H1
65010 ADRIATIC. Ne/Fr 1968; R; 500/1200; 75.55 × 4.02/5.11 (247.86 × 13.18/16.76); M; 15; ex JOFRIGO 1975. Sisters. **65011 REEFER GIULIA** (It) ex ATLANTIDE; ex JOQUITA 1975 **65012 GRIPO** (Fi) ex EVOFRIO 1976; ex JO-RIVKA 1974 **65013 TOA MOANA** (NZ) ex JOGELA 1974.

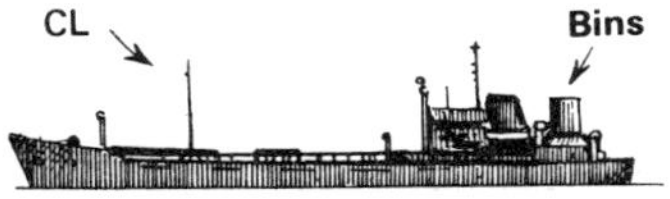

K_2MF H1
65020 VULCANUS. Sg/FRG 1956; Waste-incinerator ship; 3100; 101.96 × 6.07 (334.51 × 19.91); M; 12; ex ERICH SCHRODER 1972; Converted from general cargo vessel.

K_2MF H12
65030 ALPRO. Sp/Sp 1957; C; 700; 61.07 × 3.9 (200.36 × 12.79); M; 12; ex MIRENCHU 1968.

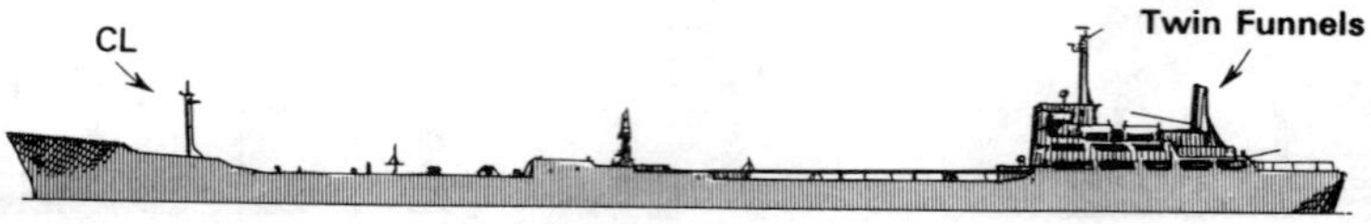

K_2MF H123
65040 AGIP TRIESTE. It/It 1964; Tk; 30400; 228.61 × 12.14 (750.03 × 39.83); M; 17.

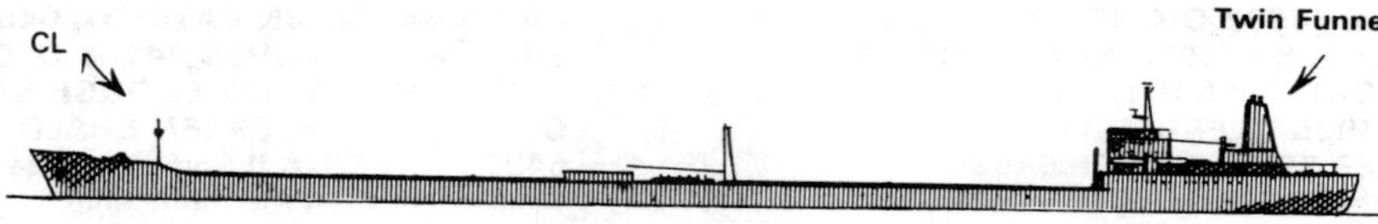

K_2MF H123
65050 VIVITA. No/Ja 1969; Tk; 54300; 263.51 × 14.73 (864.53 × 48.32); M; —; ex BERGEVIK 1978.

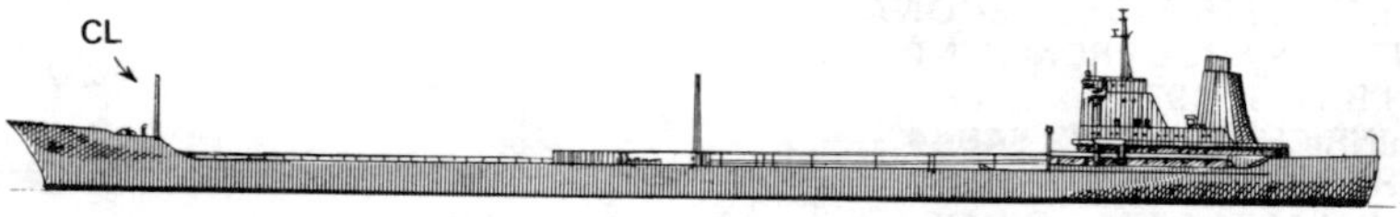

K_2MF H123
65060 ORIENTAL EXPLORER. Li/FRG 1965; Tk; 38900; 235.67 × 13.12 (773.19 × 43.04); M; 17.25; ex AUDACIOUS 1977; ex ST. PAULS 1974; ex ST. NIKOLAI 1973. Sisters. **65061 AIKATERINA** (Gr) ex ATLANTIC CONQUEROR 1980; ex COURAGEOUS COLOCOTRONIS 1977; ex ST. PETRI 1972 **65062 OCEANIC WINNER** (Li) ex CHAMPION COLOCOTRONIS 1977; ex ST. MICHAELIS 1972.

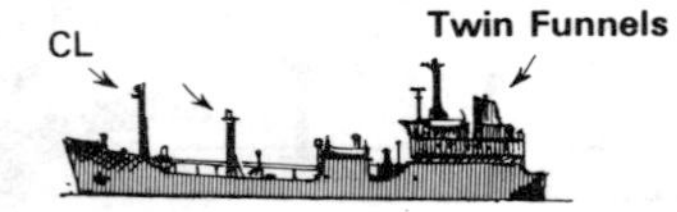

K_2MF H123
65070 HEMINA. No/No 1977; LGC; 2000; 75.72 × 5.5 (248.42 × 18.04); M; 13. Sister. **65071 HESTIA** (No).

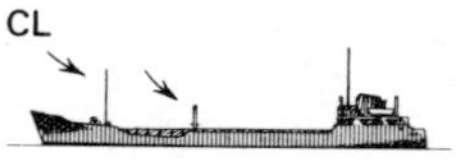

K_2MF H123
65080 ALEX G. Gr/Br 1959; C; 860; 62.69 × 3.76 (205.67 × 12.33); M; 10.5; ex QUIESCENCE 1975.

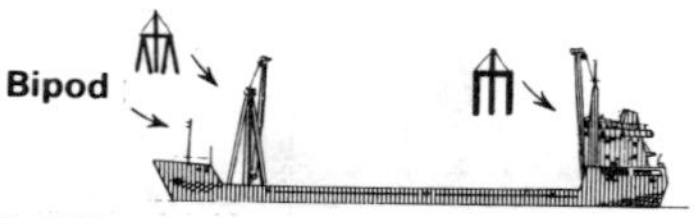

K_2MF H13
65090 ENAK. Ne/Ne 1979; HL/C; 1600; 81.45 × 4.9 (267.22 × 16.08); M; 12.75; Kingpost in well has six legs and is on a travelling gantry. Sisters (Ne flag). **65091 ELGER** travelling KP. may not be fitted **65092 ELDIR.**

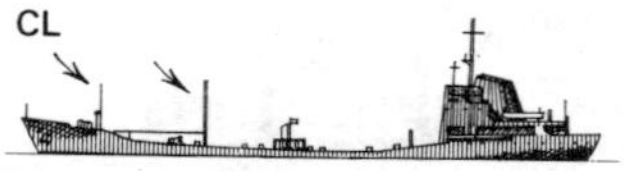

K_2MF H13
65100 GRANVIK. Fi/Fi 1961; Cem; 1600; 90.84 × 4.95 (298.03 × 16.24); M; 12.5.

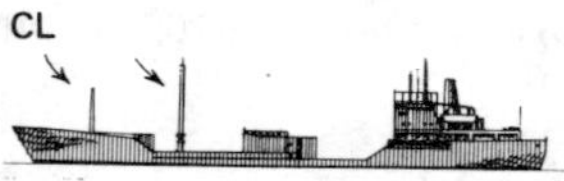

K_2MF H13
65110 CEMBULK. No/FRG 1973; Cem; 2200; 84.89 × 5.8 (278.51 × 19.03); M; 14.

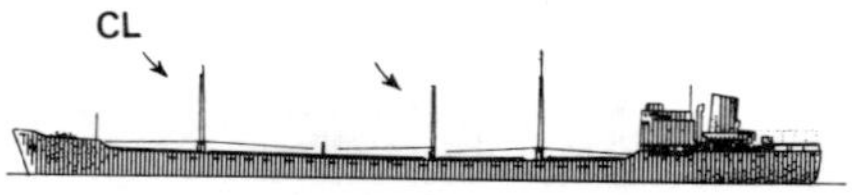

K_2MF H13
65120 OMEGA PATMOS. Gr/Br 1959; C; 5300; 126.24 × 6.92 (414.17 × 22.7); M; 12.5; ex JEVINGTON 1980; ex MACAULAY 1968; lengthened 1964.

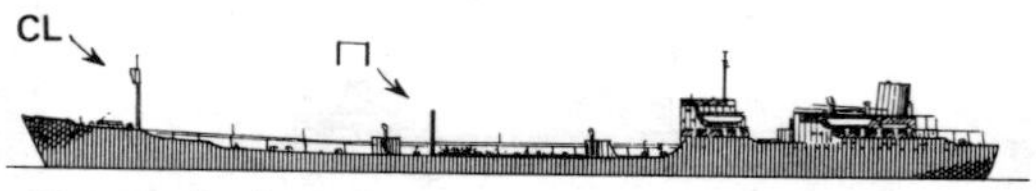

K_2MF H13
65130 NOTUS. Mg/Sw 1950; Tk; 8900; 154.57 × 8.33 (507.12 × 27.33); M; 14; ex VEZO 1974; ex NOTUS 1972; ex AURELIAN 1969; Lengthened 1965.

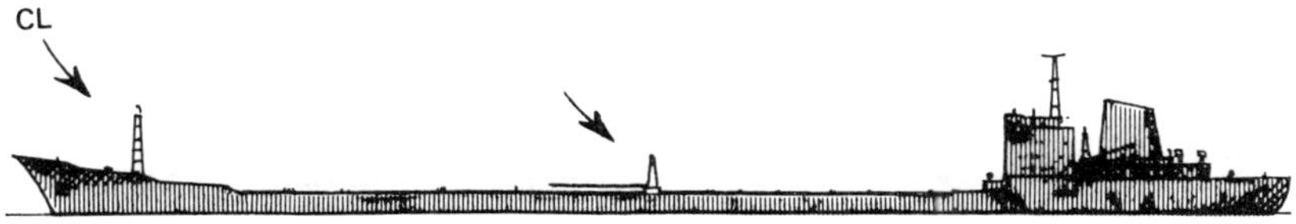

K_2MF H13

● **65140 SANTA CRISTINA PRIMA.** It/It 1966; Tk; 48700; 253.6 × 13.29 (832.02 × 43.6); M; —. Sisters (It flag). **65141 SANTA ANNA PRIMA 65142 SANTA AUGUSTA.**

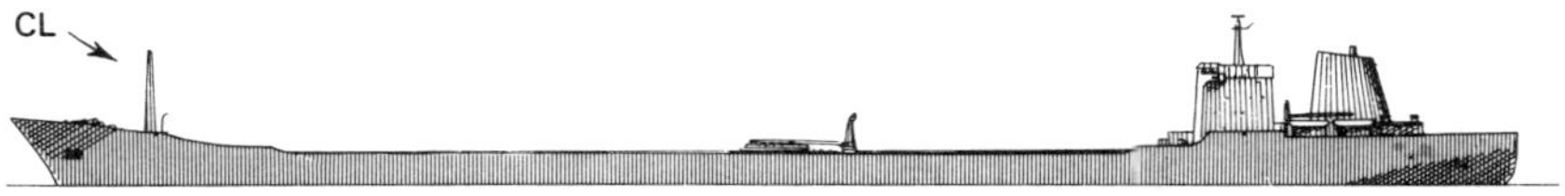

K_2MF H13

● **65150 GUNGNIR 1.** Pa/It 1966; Tk; 48500; 253.6 × 13.32 (832.02 × 43.7); M; 16.25; ex NAI GIUSEPPINA; ex GIUSEPPINA LOLLI GHETTI 1974; ex ROSS LAKE 1972; ex FORT ST. CATHERINE 1971. Sister: **65151 ELIZABETH II** (Pa) ex MARGARET SIMONE 1980; ex PETRA 1973; ex WARWICK FORT 1971. Similar: **65152 SARISSOLA** (It) ex CLAUDIO R 1979 **65153 OMBRINA** (It) ex MONICA R 1979 **65154 SCRIVIA** (It) ex ANDREA LEOPOLDO Similar: (Bulk/Oil) **65155 CIELO BIANCO** (It) ex HERMES 1972; ex SANTA VALERIA 1971 **65156 SHINWA** (In) ex DAYA PARVATI; ex ROSS HEAD 1977

K_2MF H13

65160 LUNNI. Fi/FRG 1976; Tk/IB; 11000; 162.01 × 9.5 (531.52 × 31.16); M; 14.5. Sisters (Fi flag): **65161 SOTKA 65162 TIIRA 65163 UIKKU.**

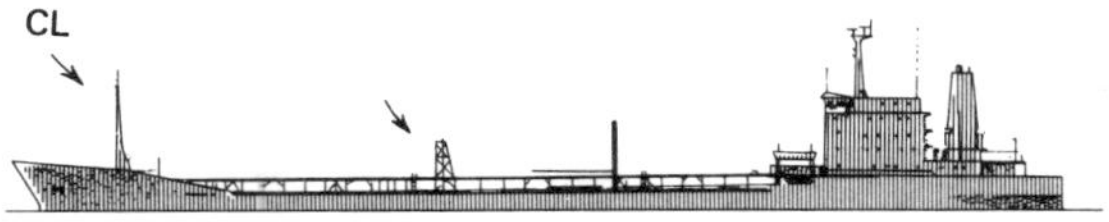

K_2MF H13

65170 IBN ROCHD. Mo/Ne 1977; Ch; 13500; 172.29 × 10.5 (565.26 × 34.45); M; 17. Sister (Mo flag): **65171 IBN ALBANNA** Sisters (Norwegian built): **65172 IBN OTMAN 65173 IBN SINA.**

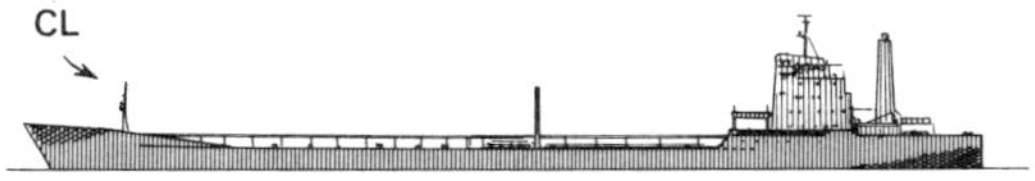

K_2MF H13

65180 SANGATTA/PERMINA 1015. Ia/No 1975; Tk/Ch; 9500; 152.3 × 8.97 (499.67 × 29.43); M; 16.5. Sister: **65181 KLAMONO/PERMINA 1016** (Ia).

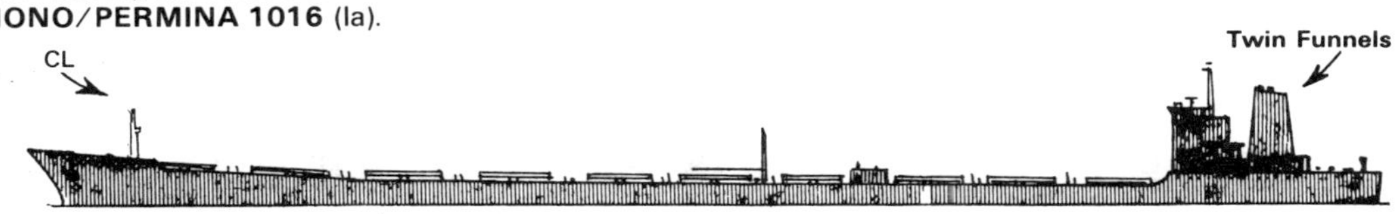

K_2MF H13

65190 BERGE BRIONI. No/Ys 1973; OO; 117400; 314 × 20.42 (1030.18 × 66.99); TSM; 16. Sister: **65191 BERGE ADRIA** (No).

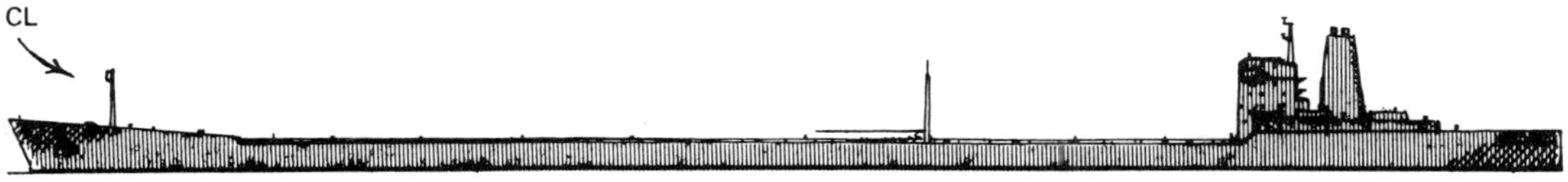

K_2MF H13

65200 NORBIRD. No/No 1971; Tk; 109500; 327.72 × 20.35 (1075.2 × 66.77); T; 16; ex RAILA 1977. Sister (No flag): **65201 NORBAY** ex RANJA 1977 Possibly similar: **65202 BEAUMARIS 65203 AURELIAN.**

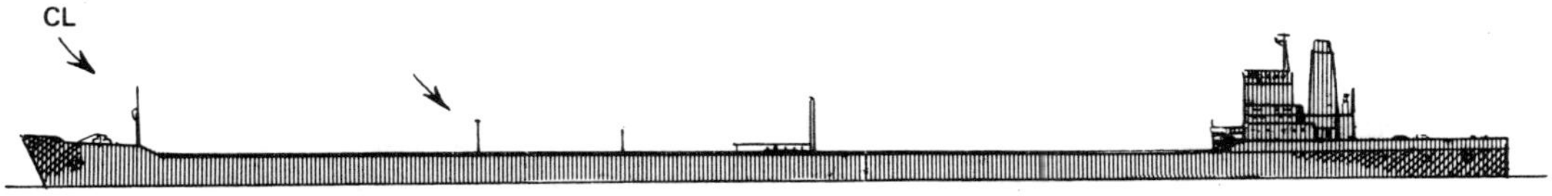

K_2MF H13

65210 FLEURTJE. NA/No 1970; Tk; 109600; 327.72 × ×20.42 (1075.2 × 67); T; 15; ex HUMBOLDT 1980.

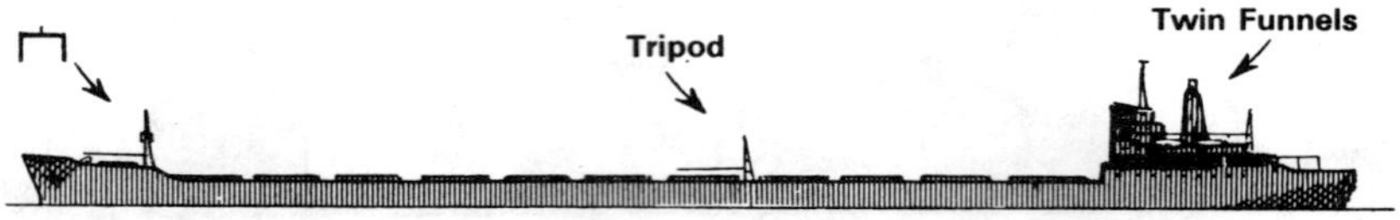

K_2MF H13
65220 INAYAMA. No/Ja 1964; OO; 48100; 249.99 × 13.74 (820.18 × 45.08); M; 16. Similar (Li flag): **65221 SHIGEO NAGANO 65222 MARSHALL CLARK.**

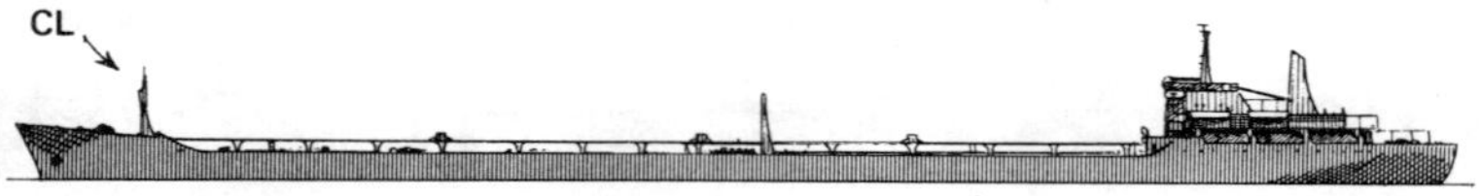

K_2MF H13
65230 OLYMPIC CHIVALRY. Li/FRG 1964; Tk; 30600; 235.08 × 12.36 (771.26 × 40.55); T; —. Sister: **65231 OLYMPIC CHARIOT** (Li).

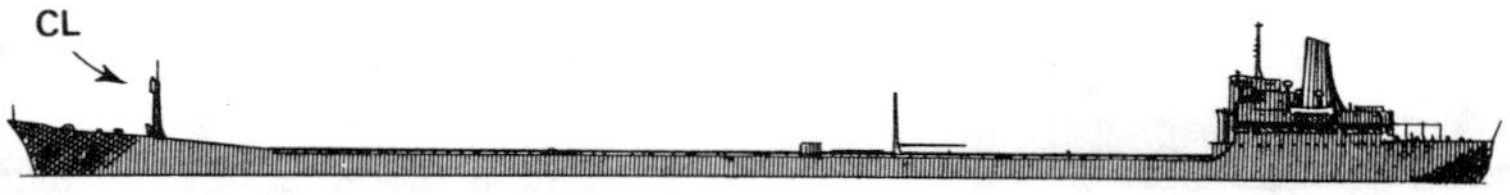

K_2MF H13
65240 OLYMPIC GRACE. Li/Ja 1965; Tk; 32400; 234.58 × 12.88 (769.62 × 42.26); T; 16.5. Sisters (Li flag): **65241 OLYMPIC GATE 65242 OLYMPIC GAMES.**

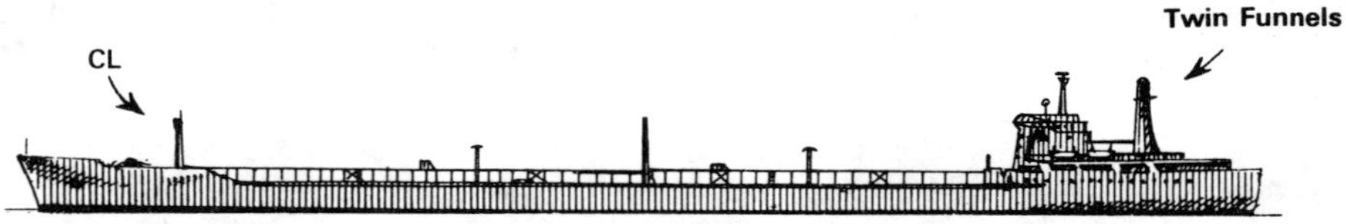

K_2MF H13
● **65250 SAINT NICHOLAS.** Li/Fr 1964; Tk; 47500; 265.18 × 14.9 (870.01 × 48.88); T; —; ex OLYMPIC FREEDOM 1980.

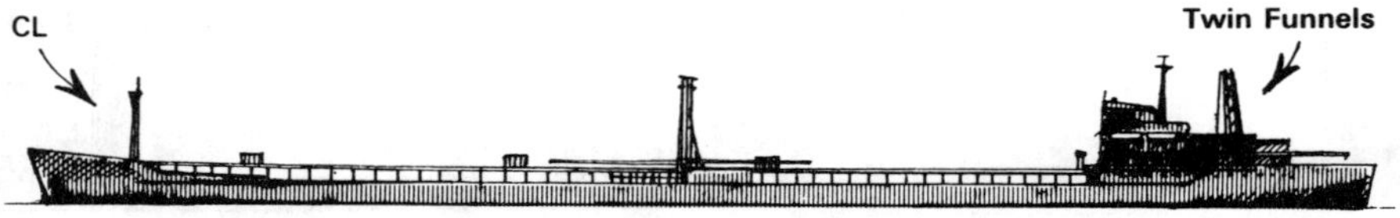

K_2MF H13
65260 ALMIZAR. Li/FRG-Ja 1964/71; Tk; 51600; 268.92 × 14.63 (882.28 × 47.99); T; —; Aft section built Hamburg 1964; forward section built Yokohama 1971. Lengthened 1971.

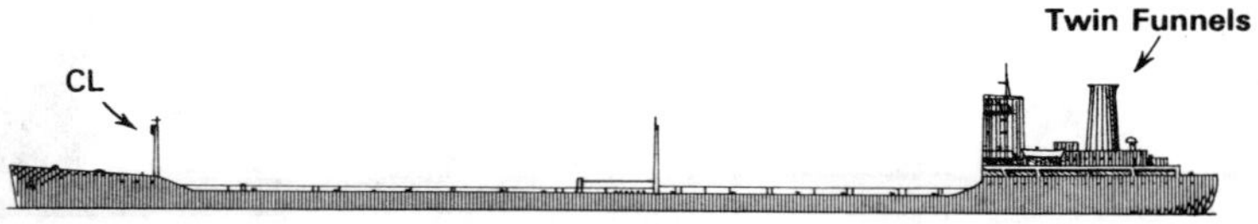

K_2MF H13
65270 CALATRAVA. Sp/Sp 1965; Tk; 29200; 224.64 × 12.48 (737 × 40.94); M; 17.

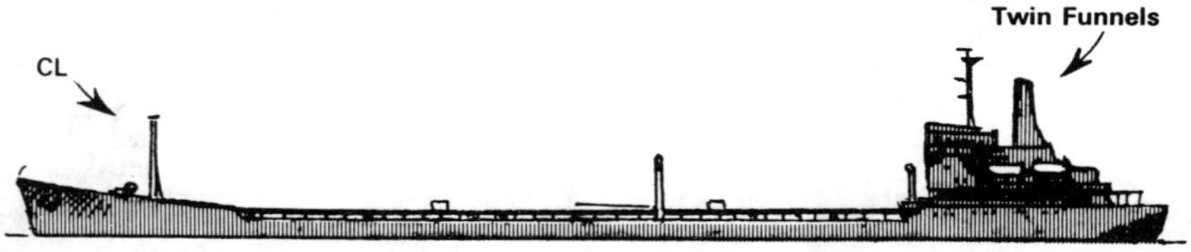

K_2MF H13
● **65280 PETROLA 26.** Gr/Ne 1963; Tk; 53100; 262.62 × 14.46 (861.61 × 47.44); T; —; ex PETROLA XXVI 1976; ex PETROLA XX 1975; ex ESSO DEN HAAG 1975.

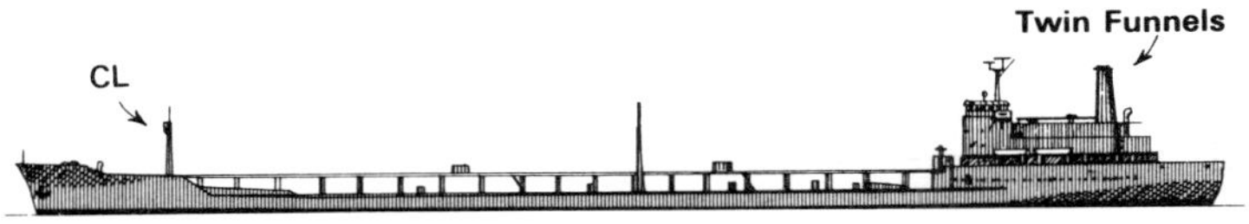

K_2MF H13
★65290 DA QING 250. RC/Sw 1964; Tk; 29000; 220.78 × 11.93 (724.34 × 39.14); M; 16; ex WUHU 1976; ex ANMAJ 1975; ex BELMAJ 1971.

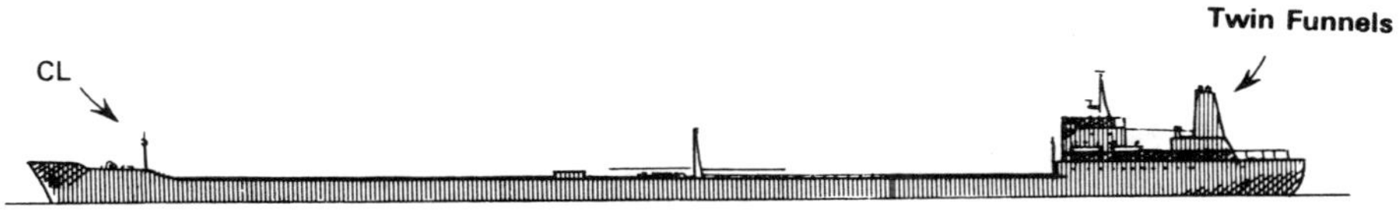

K_2MF H13
● **65300 MOBIL WESER.** FRG/Ja 1967; Tk; 49200; 263.51 × 14.63 (864.53 × 47.99); M; 16; ex AL BILAD; ex BERGE SIGVAL 1975. Similar (No flag): **65301 CIS BROVIG 65302 VIVITA** ex BERGEVIK 1978.

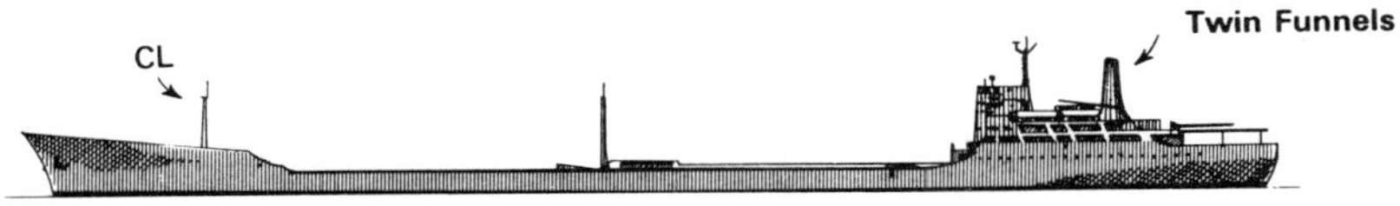

K_2MF H13
65310 AGIP ANCONA. It/It 1963; Tk; 31300; 229.17 × 12.3 (751.87 × 40.35); M; 16.5. Sister (It flag): **65311 AGIP GENOVA.**

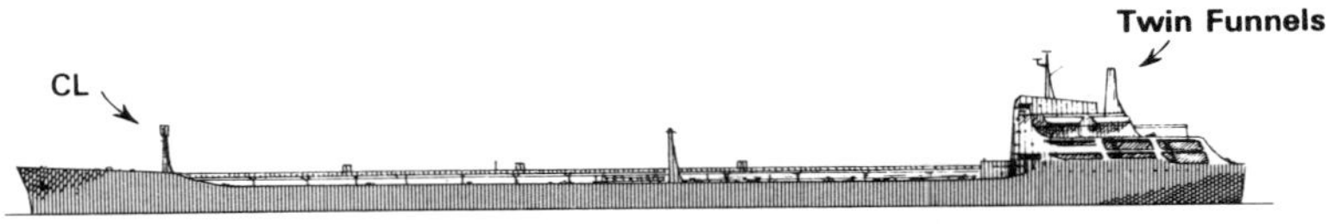

K_2MF H13
65320 OLIVA. FRG/FRG 1963; Tk; 33100; 225.58 × 11.68 (740.09 × 38.32); T; 15.5.

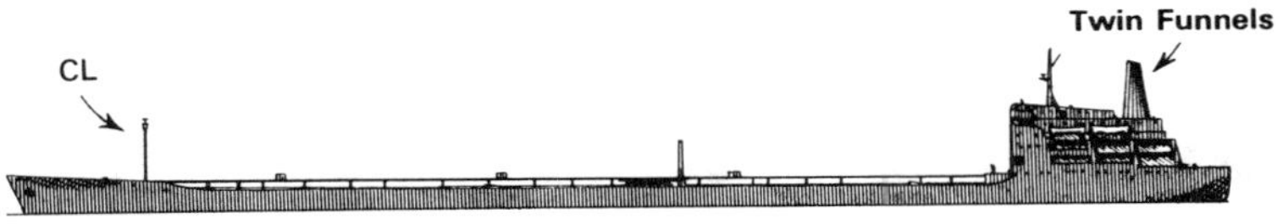

K_2MF H13
65330 OPALIA. Br/Br 1963; Tk; 31700; 228.02 × 12.24 (748.08 × 40.16); T; —.

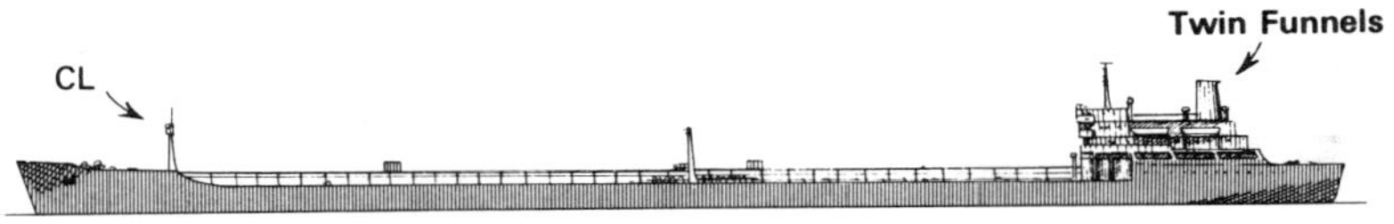

K_2MF H13
65340 FADI B. Pa/No 1965; Tk; 31600; 236.2 × 12.33 (774.93 × 40.45); M; 16.25; ex GIMLE 1976.

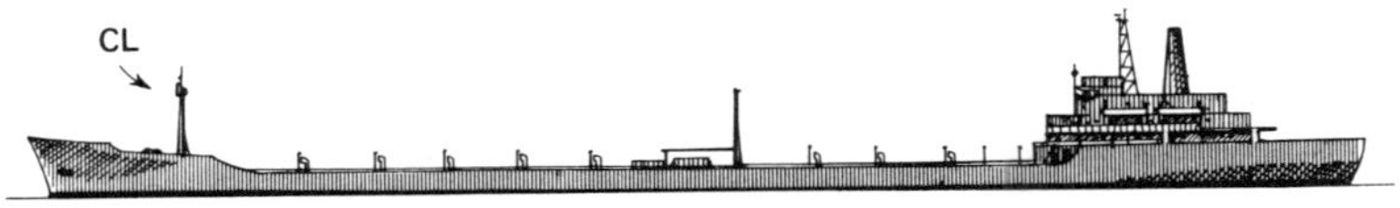

K_2MF H13
65350 EPTANISSOS. Gr/Ne 1963; Tk; 31100; 231.5 × 11.83 (759.51 × 38.81); T; 16.5; ex DOELWIJK 1978.

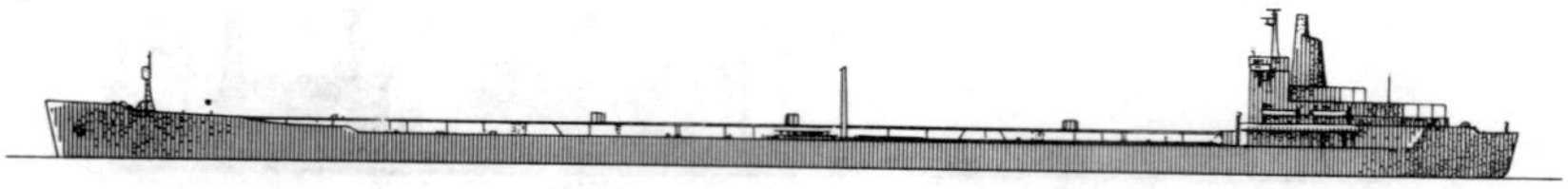

K_2MF H13
65360 SAINT SPYRIDON. Gr/Sw 1965; Tk; 39000; 243.85 × 13.16 (800.03 × 43.17); M; —; ex HISTORIC COLOCOTRONIS 1978; ex HOEGH LANCE 1969. Similar: **65361 SEA VALIANT** (Li) ex CORAL SEA 1971; ex EJNAR THORSEN 1970 **65362 NIRITOS** (Gr) ex SCHWARZHEIDE 1980; ex SOVEREIGN CLIPPER 1970.

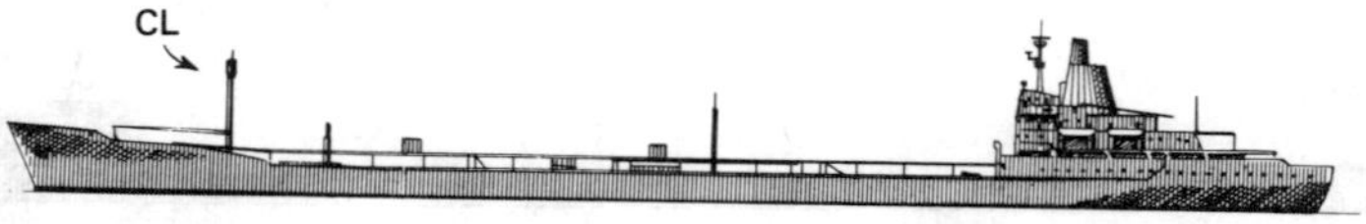

K_2MF H13
65370 RALLYTIME II. Sg/Sw 1966; Tk; 25700; 213.21 × 11.67 (699.51 × 38.29); M; 16.75; ex SCAPNORD: ex HELFRID BILLNER 1976.

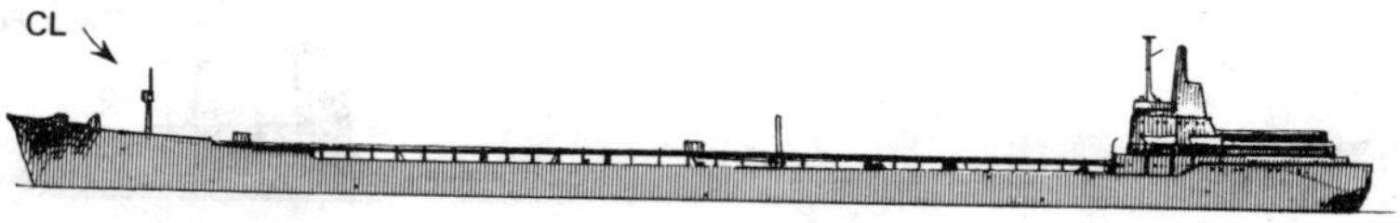

K_2MF H13
65380 FARMER. Pa/Sw 1963; Tk; 36900; 236.28 × 12.64 (775.2 × 41.47); T; —; ex POLARVIK 1978.

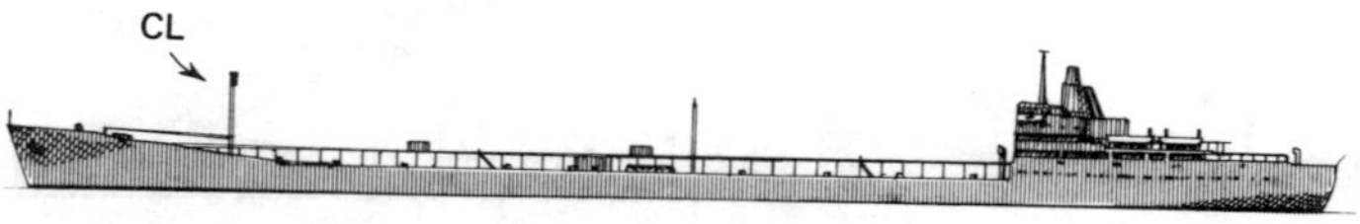

K_2MF H13
65390 BARCOLA. Li/Sw 1963; Tk; 25300; 213.21 × 11.67 (699.21 × 38.28); M; 16; ex OKTANIA 1973.

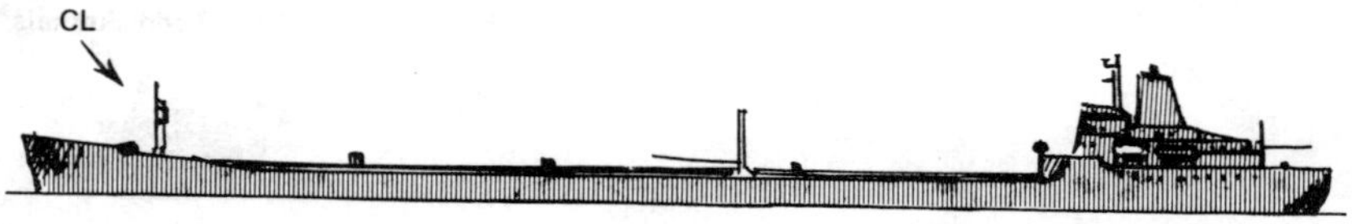

K_2MF H13
65400 SINOIA. Li/Br 1966; Tk; 51200; 259.47 × 14.88 (851.28 × 48.82); T; 17; ex CLEMENTINA 1977; ex CLEMENTINE CHURCHILL 1973. Similar: ★**65401 ON SUNG** (RK) ex GALLANT SEAHORSE; ex VALENTINIAN 1972 **65402 THISTLE VENTURE** (Gr) ex JARITA 1977; ex GRATIAN 1972.

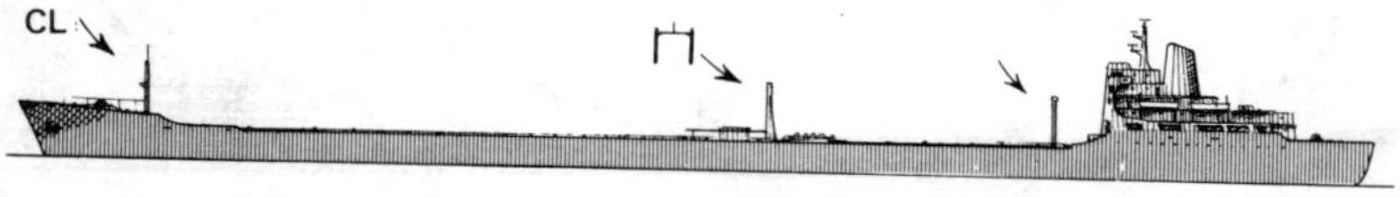

K_2MF H13
65410 GARGI. In/Ja 1964; Tk; 34700; 229.95 × 12.03 (754.43 × 39.47); M; 16.5; ex VIKRAM JAYANTI 1974.

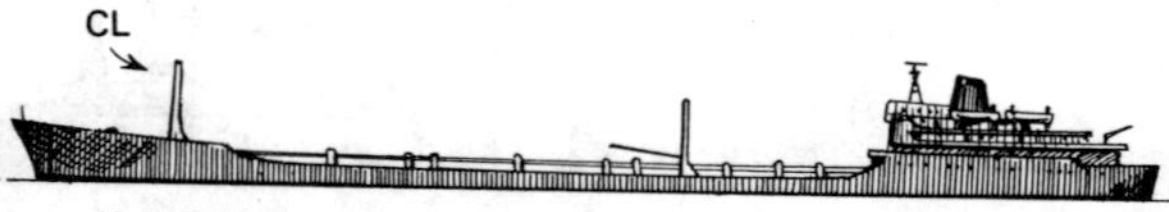

K_2MF H13
65420 GIULIANA 1. Pa/Sp 1968; Tk; 15100; 184 × 10.1 (606 × 33); M; 15; ex SUNNIAO; ex STOLT HERON 1974; ex TUNACO 1970.

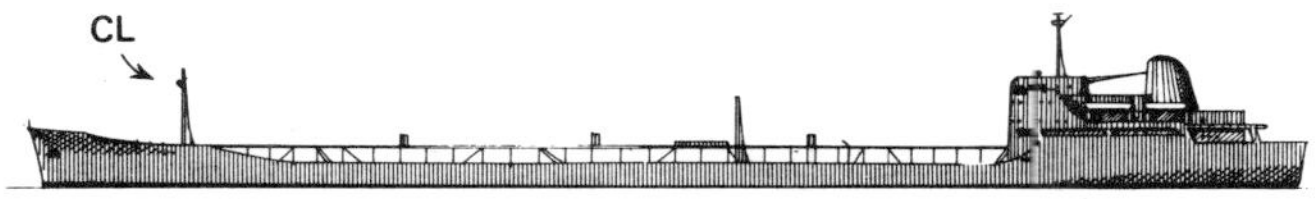

K_2MF H13
65430 VITREA. Ne/Ne 1962; Tk; 21900; 202.75 × 10.56 (665.19 × 34.64); T; 15.

K_2MF H13
65440 ESTRELLA PATAGONICA. Ar/Br 1962; Tk; 24400; 202.65 × 11.24 (664.86 × 36.88); T; —; ex VOLUTA 1970.

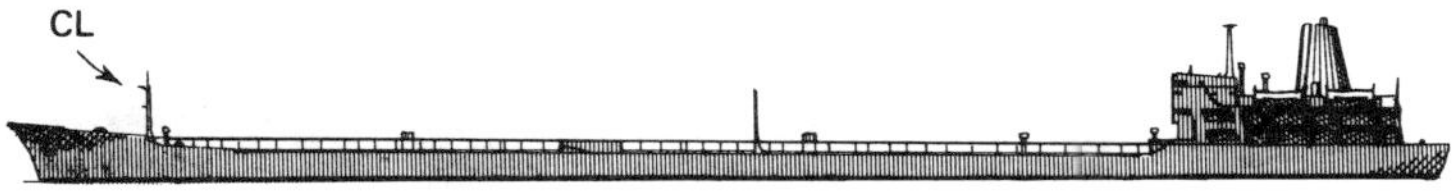

K_2MF H13
● **65450 WILLIAM LARIMER MELLON.** Li/Ja 1965; Tk; 29700; 229.52 × 12 (753.02 × 39.37); T; —. Similar (Li flag): **65451 RALPH O. RHOADES.**

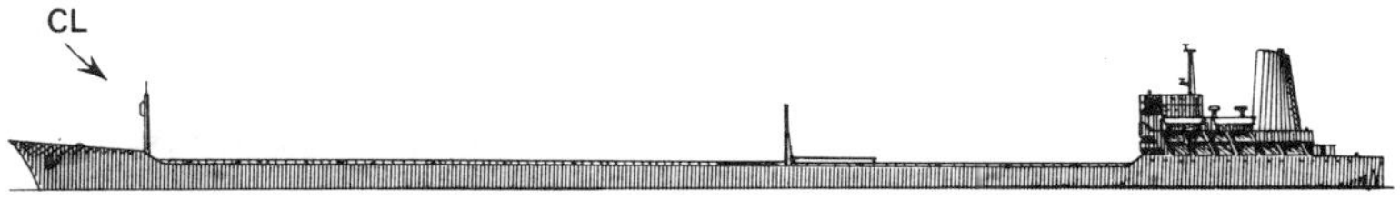

K_2MF H13
65460 EKATERINI. Gr/Ja 1965; Tk; 40000; 237.32 × 12.22 (778.61 × 40.09); T; 16; ex JOHN C. PAPPAS 1970. Sister: **65461 ALECOS M** (Gr) ex VASILIKI 1980; ex THOMAS A. PAPPAS 1970.

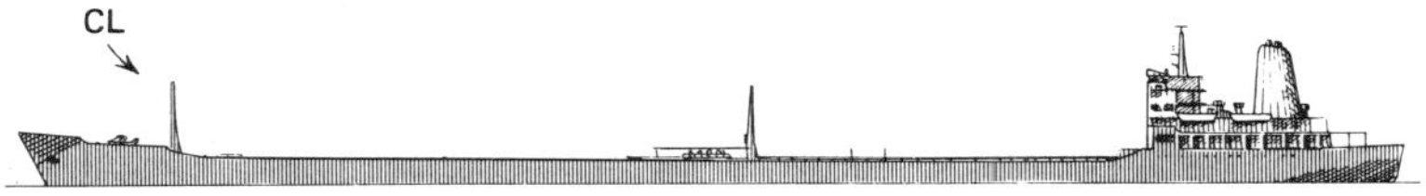

K_2MF H13
● **65470 SANTA MARINA.** Li/Ja 1964; Tk; 31800; 236.18 × 12.69 (774.87 × 41.63); M; 15. Similar: **65471 DEA MARIS** (Li) **65472 SPIROS** (Gr) ex TRYSBEJ 1969; ex CARIB TRADER 1968.

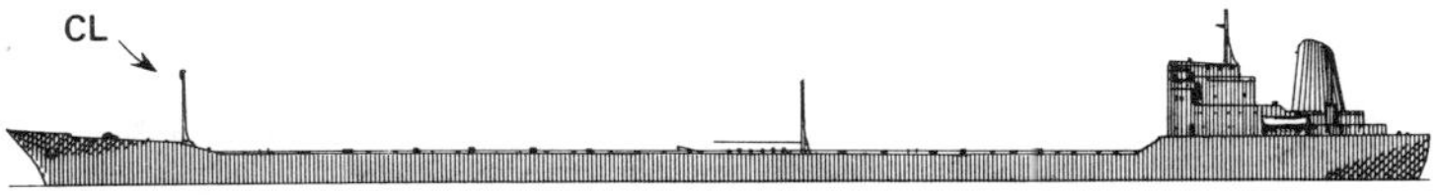

K_2MF H13
65480 LEONIDAS. Li/Sp 1966; Tk; 29300; 227.77 × 12.35 (747.28 × 40.52); T; —; ex SARDINERO 1974.

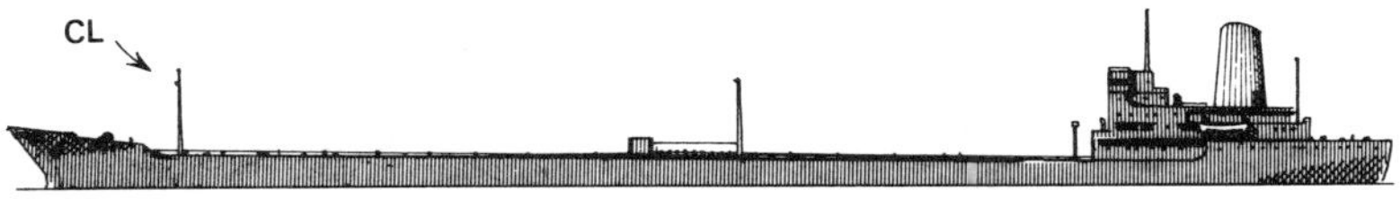

K_2MF H13
● **65490 FAIRFIELD ARCHER.** Li/Ja 1964; Tk; 37300; 242.98 × 11.99 (797.12 × 39.34); M; 15.25; ex FAIRFIELD COPA 1979; ex ASIA MARU No2 1973.

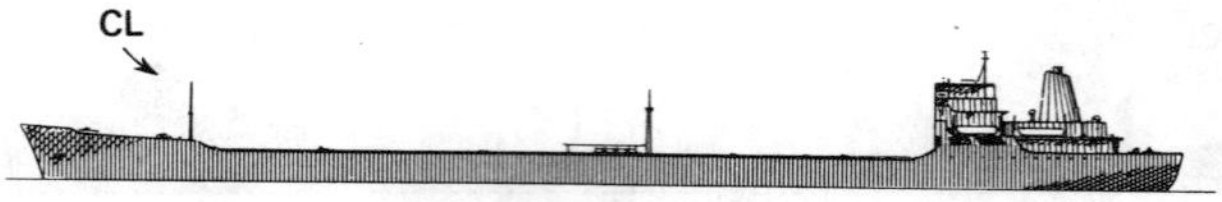

K_2MF H13
65500 VIRGO. US/US 1943/61; Tk; 13900; 184.41 × 9.92 (605.01 × 32.54); T-E; 14.5; ex HESS PETROL 1976; ex EVANS CREEK 1955; Forward and aft sections built 1943; Cargo section built 1961; Lengthened, widened and deepened 1961 from 'T.2' tankers. Sisters (US flag): **65501 CAPRICORN** ex BUNKER 1977; ex HESS BUNKER 1977; ex POWDER RIVER 1955 **65502 COVE EXPLORER** ex MOUNT EXPLORER 1978; ex WILLIAM J. FIELDS 1975; ex THALIA 1971; ex HESS DIESEL 1966; ex W.E. DOWNING 1953; ex HUNTINGDON HILLS 1948 **65503 PISCES** ex HESS REFINER 1976; ex ESSO WORCESTER 1961; ex MULTNOMAH 1947.

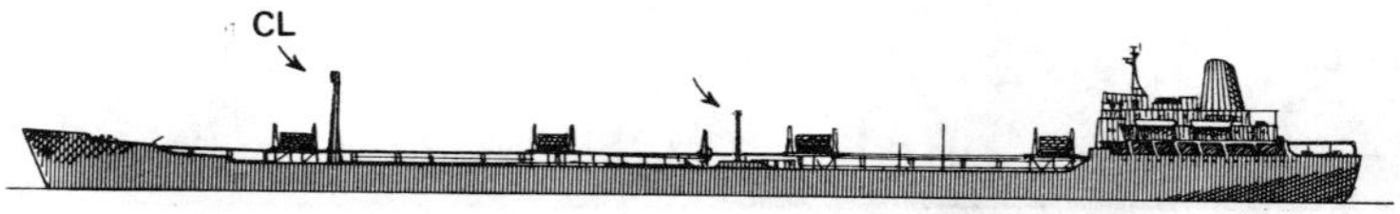

K_2MF H13
65510 BRITISH DRAGOON. Br/Br 1963; Tk; 31100; 221.39 × 12.58 (726.34 × 41.27); T; 15.5; Used as lightening tanker.

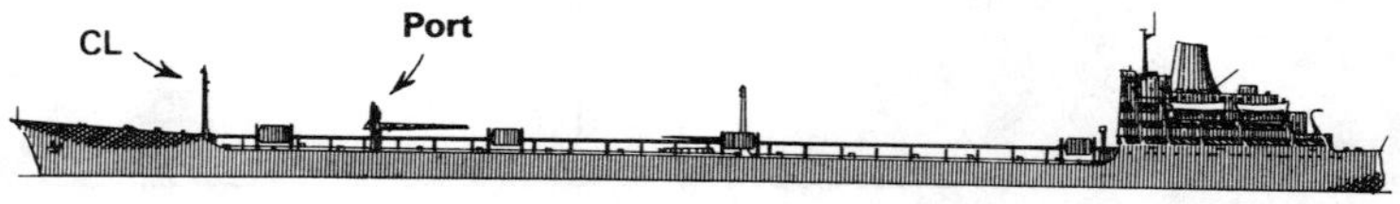

K_2MF H13
65520 ESSO CARDIFF. Br/Ne 1963; Tk; 31700; 226.5 × 11.95 (743.11 × 39.21); T; 17; Used as lightening tanker.

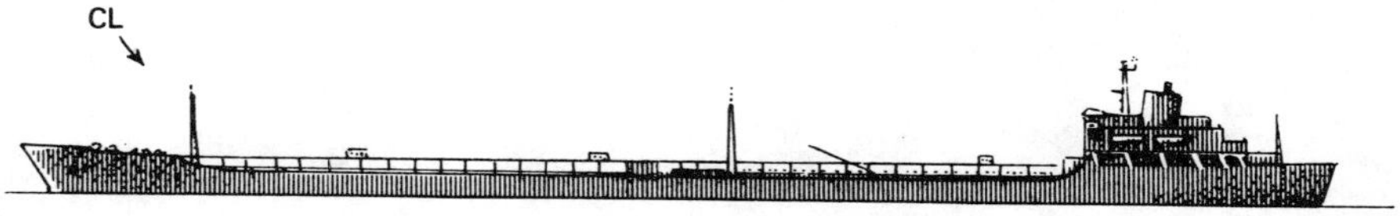

K_2MF H13
65530 KAVO SPATHI. Gr/Ja 1965; Tk; 44000; 254.57 × 13.54 (824.61 × 44.49); T; 17; ex MOBIL LIBYA 1977.

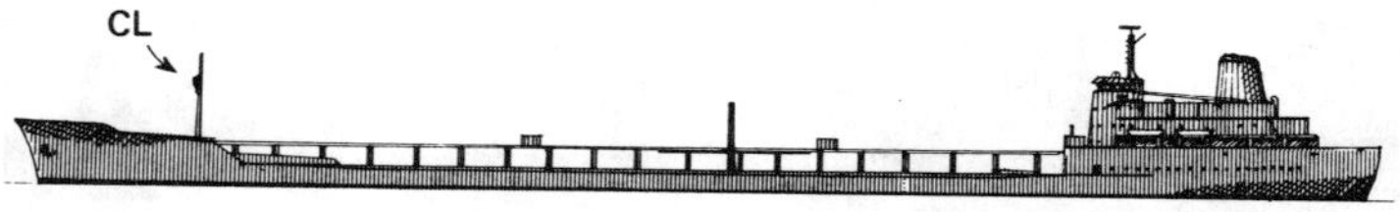

K_2MF H13
⋆65540 CHANG HU. RC/Sw 1965; Tk; 28900; 221.14 × 12.05 (725.52 × 39.53); M; 15; ex ANNE 1975; ex ACINA 1971. Sister: **65541 AL MALAZ** (Si) ex SERRA TRADER 1978; ex OSCO SURF 1975; ex SAGA SURF 1975; ex BIRGITTA FERNSTROM 1972.

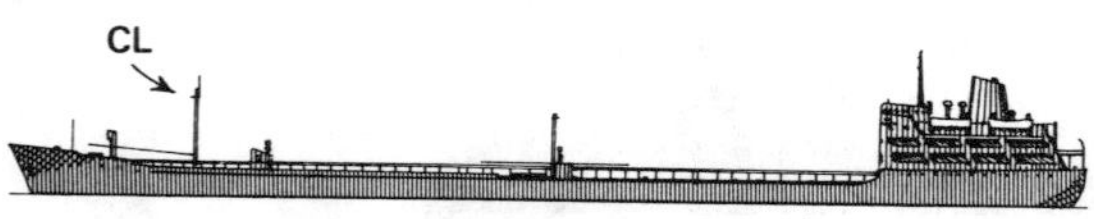

K_2MF H13
65550 DOLPHIN II. Gr/Sw 1959; Tk; 12700; 169.81 × 9.57 (557.11 × 31.38); M; 15; ex VIBEKE 1978. Similar: **⋆65551 DA QING No41** (RC) ex ANELLA 1972; ex OSCAR GORTHON 1971; ex VINSTRA Similar (asphalt tanker): **65552 VIBIT** (No).

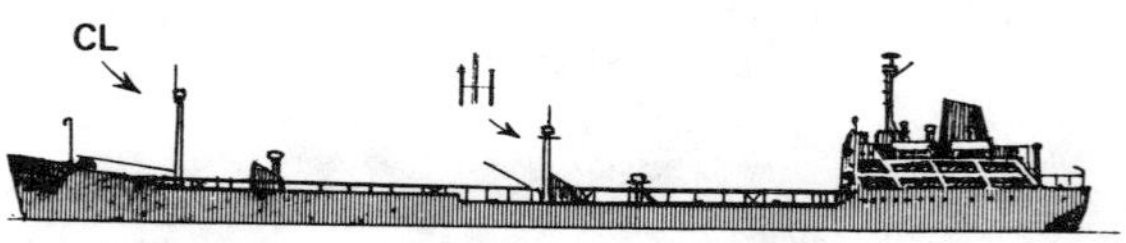

K_2MF H13
65560 ANCO GLORY. Gr/Sw 1958; Tk; 12700; 169.81 × 9.55 (557.11 × 31.33); M; 16; ex APOLLONIAN GLORY 1974; ex ANCO STAR 1973; ex SAGA STAR 1965; ex TERNOY 1962; Probably a total loss.

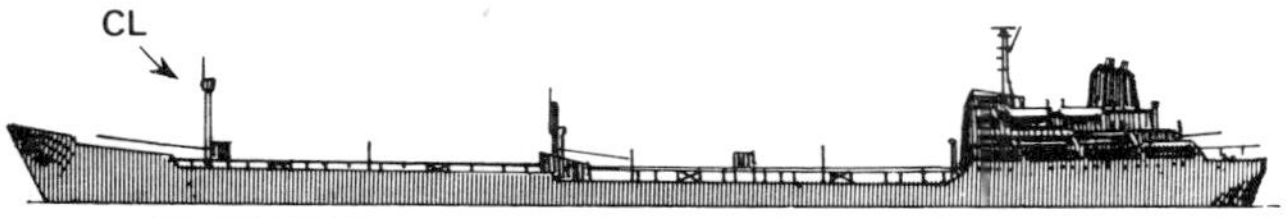

K_2MF H13
65570 NINFEA. It/Sw 1958; Tk; 19500; 198.15 × 10.85 (650.1 × 35.6); M; 15.25; ex INGER KNUDSEN 1970.

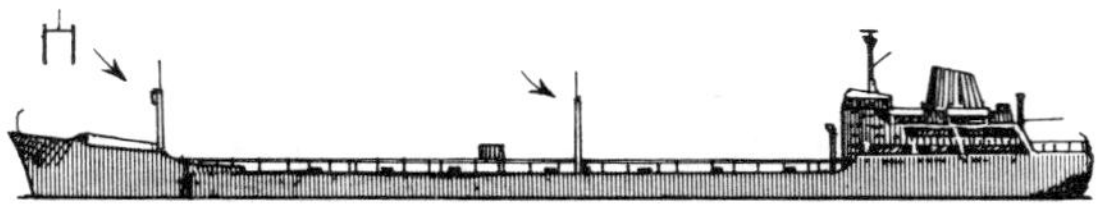

K_2MF H13
65580 LAKE KATYA. Gr/No 1961; Tk; 13000; 169.7 × 9.67 (556.76 × 31.73); M; 15; ex IVER SWIFT 1978; ex ANCO SWIFT 1976; ex SKOGAAS 1964.

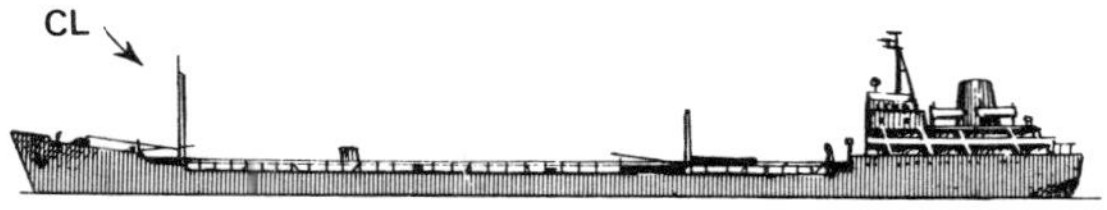

K_2MF H13
65590 STOLT VIKING. Li/Br 1962; Tk; 13300; 172.27 × 10.11 (565.19 × 33.17); M; 14.5; ex STOLT TIGER 1974; ex STOLT ABADESA 1973; ex ABADESA 1969.

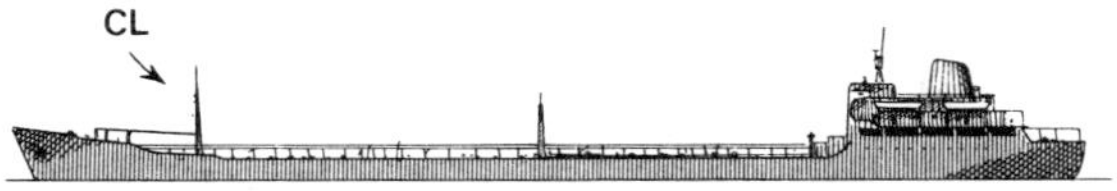

K_2MF H13
65600 VICTORY. Gr/Sw 1960; Tk; 12500; 170.57 × 9.58 (559.61 × 31.43); M; 14.5; ex STOLT VICTOR 1977; ex STOLT BRALI 1974; ex BRALI 1969.

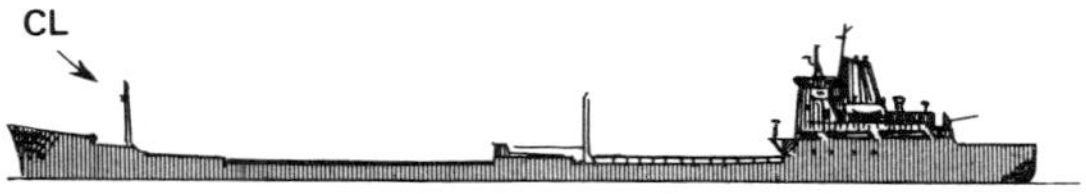

K_2MF H13
65610 ESSO MILFORD HAVEN. Br/Sw 1968; Tk; 10900; 162.67 × 8.54 (533.69 × 28.02); M; 16.75. Sister (Br flag): **65611 ESSO FAWLEY.**

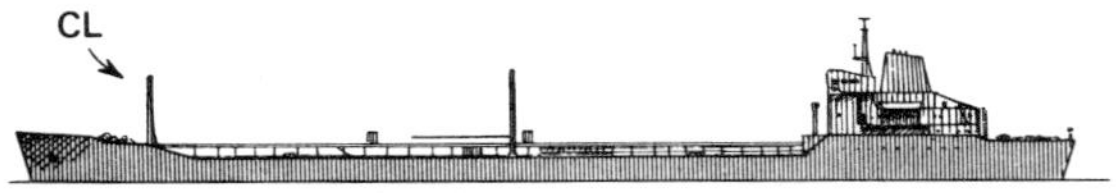

K_2MF H13
65620 ESSO MERSEY. Br/Br 1972; Tk; 12300; 166.5 × 9.21 (546.26 × 30.22); M; 15.5. Sisters (Br flag): **65621 ESSO CLYDE 65622 ESSO SEVERN.**

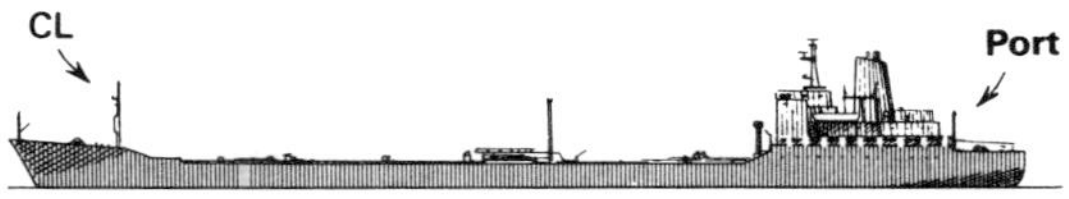

K_2MF H13
● **65630 PETROMAR BAHIA BLANCA II.** Bz/Ja 1974; Tk; 12800; 161.02 × 9.81 (528.28 × 32.19); M; 15; ex ESSO MUKAISHIMA 1978. Sisters: **65631 PETROMAR CAMPANA II** (Bz) ex ESSO BAYBAY 1978 **65632 ESSO NAGOYA** (Li) **65633 ESSO BRISBANE** (Li) **65634 ESSO GUAM** (Li) **65635 ESSO ALBANY** (Li) **65636 ESSO CALLUNDA** (De) **65637 ESSO HAFNIA** (De) Similar (also under K_3MF). **65638 ESSO PORT JEROME** (Fr) ex ESSO KUMAMOTO 1980.

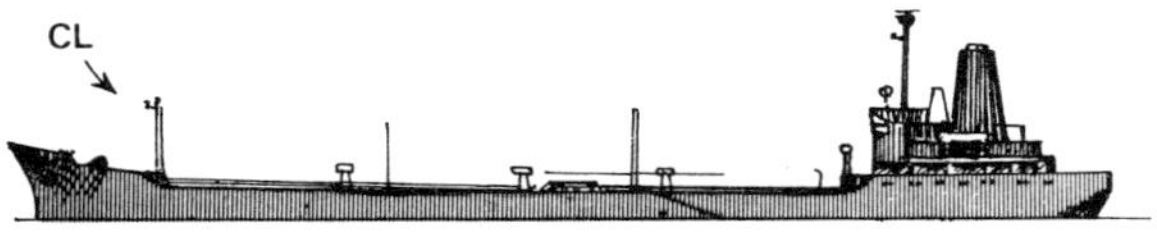

K_2MF H13
65650 ESSO BANGKOK. Pa/Ja 1968; Tk; 13000; 170.08 × 9.41 (558 × 30.87); M; 14.5. Sisters (Pa flag): **65651 ESSO BOMBAY 65652 ESSO PORT DICKSON 65653 ESSO YOKOHAMA 65654 ESSO KOBE 65655 ESSO INTERAMERICA 65656 ESSO KARACHI 65657 ESSO MALACCA 65658 ESSO NAGASAKI** (Li flag): **65659 ESSO KURE 65660 ESSO BATAAN 65661 ESSO CHITTAGONG 65662 ESSO HUMBER** (Br) ex ESSO PENANG 1978.

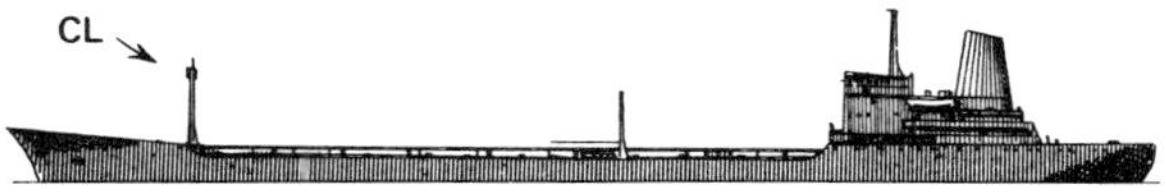

K_2MF H13
65670 TEXACO BRUSSELS. Br/Ne 1968; Tk; 14900; 180.22 × 10.33 (591.27 × 33.89); T; 18. Sisters (Br flag): **65671 TEXACO GHENT 65672 TEXACO ROTTERDAM.**

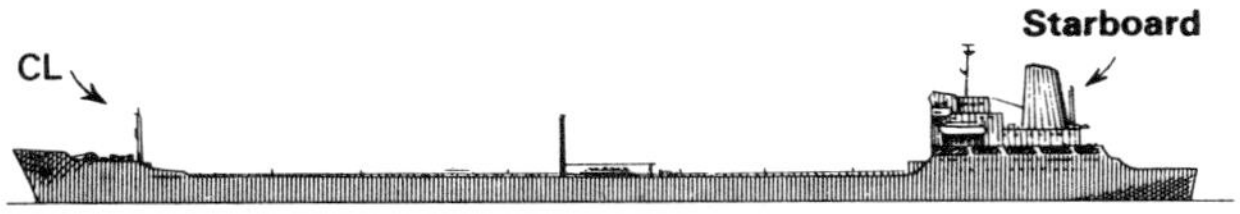

K_2MF H13
65680 ESSO HALIFAX. Li/Ca 1973; Tk; 18800; 187.76 × 10.42 (616 × 34.19); M; 15. Sisters (Li flag): **65681 ESSO MONTREAL 65682 ESSO SAINT JOHN.**

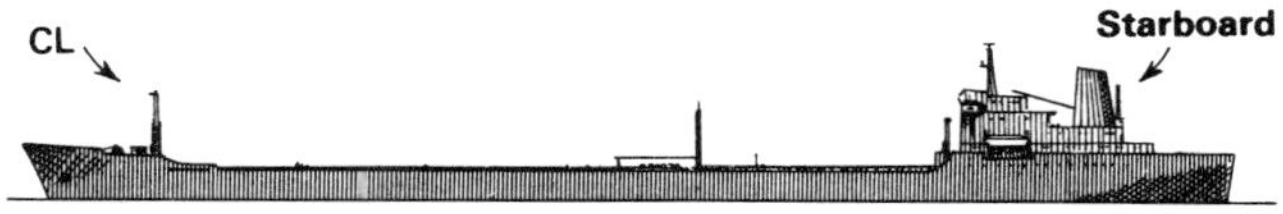

K_2MF H13
● **65690 ESSO EVERETT.** Li/Ca 1975; Tk; 21600; 191.57 × 11.25 (628.51 × 36.91); M; 15.5. Sisters (Li flag): **65691 ESSO PROVIDENCE 65692 ESSO SAINT PETERSBURG 65693 ESSO TORONTO** Possible sisters (Ca flag). **65694 IRVING ARCTIC 65695 IRVING ESKIMO.**

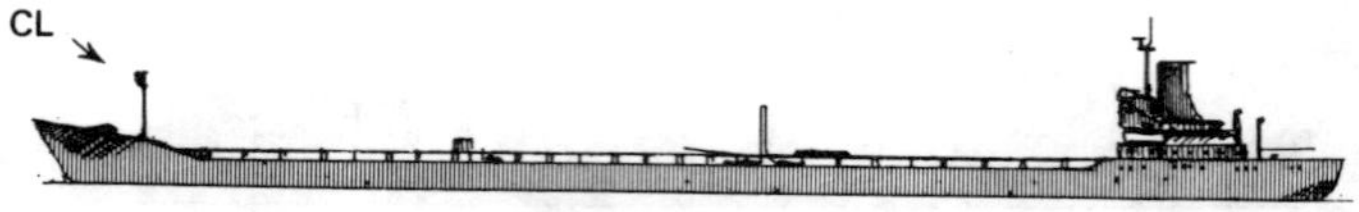

K_2MF H13
65700 CAMPEADOR. Sp/Sp 1969; Tk; 20500; 209.02 × 10.73 (685.76 × 35.2); M; 16.5. Sister: **65701 CAMPOMAYOR** (Sp).

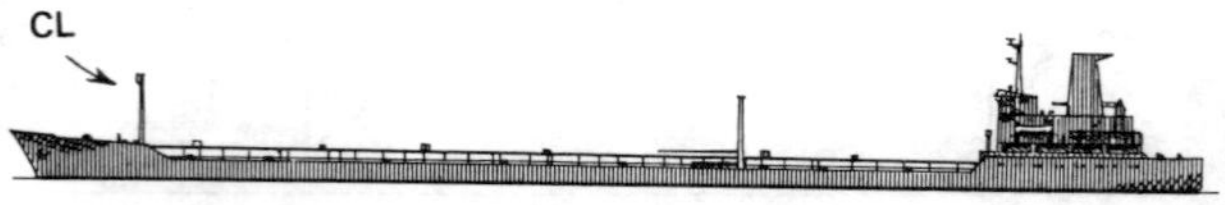

K_2MF H13
65710 OKTURUS. Sw/Ne 1973; Tk; 17900; 188.2 × 10.36 (617.45 × 33.99); M; 15. Sister: **65711 OKTAVIUS** (Sw).

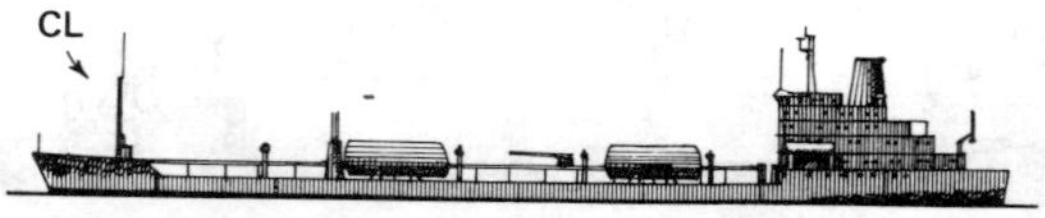

K_2MF H13
65720 ANCO CHALLENGER. Br/No 1972; Tk/Ch; 16000; 165.08 × 9.94 (541.6 × 32.61); M; 15.5; ex POST CHALLENGER 1979. Sisters (Br flag): **65721 ANCO CHAMPION** ex POST CHAMPION 1979 **65722 ANCO CHARGER** ex POST CHARGER 1979 **65723 ANCO CHASER** ex POST CHASER 1980 **65724 ANCO ENDEAVOUR** ex POST ENDEAVOUR 1977 **65725 ANCO ENTERPRISE** ex POST ENTERPRISE 1978 (Fr flag): **65726 ANCO ENTENTE** ex POST ENTENTE 1978 **65727 ANCO ENERGIE** ex POST ENERGIE 1978.

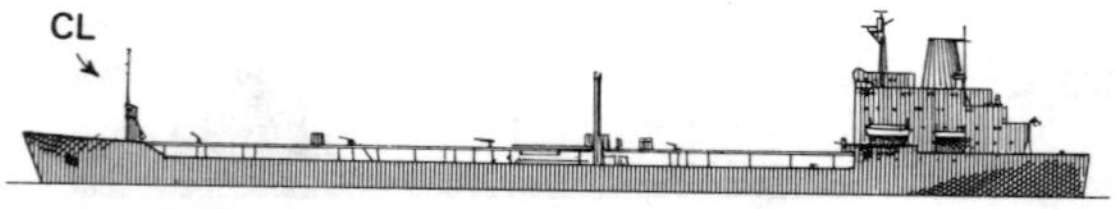

K_2MF H13
65730 TEXACO BERGEN. No/No 1977; Tk; 18400; 168.79 × 11.16 (553.77 × 36.61); M; 16. Sisters (No flag): **65731 TEXACO BALTIC 65732 TEXACO STOCKHOLM.**

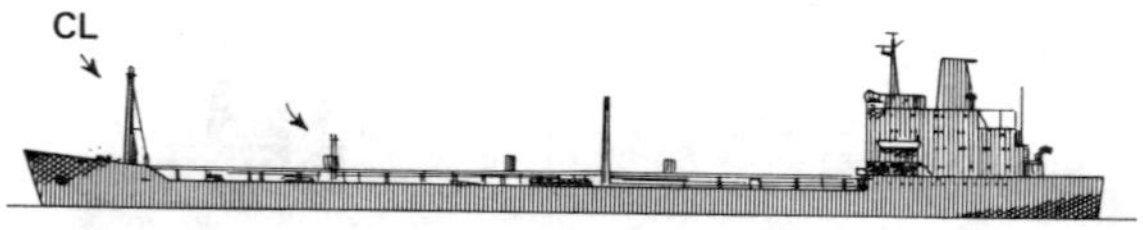

K_2MF H13
65740 ARDMAY. Br/FRG 1975; Tk; 19100; 168.76 × 10.9 (553.67 × 35.76); M; 16. Sister: **65741 ARDMORE** (Br).

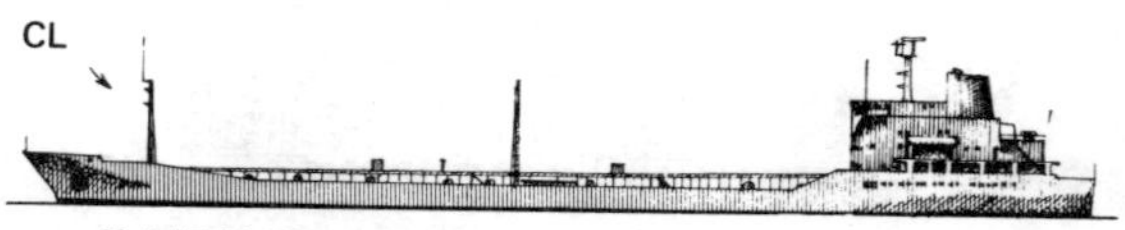

K_2MF H13
● **65750 MOBIL MARKETER.** Li/Fi 1974; Tk; 18300; 170.49 × 11.06 (559.35 × 36.29); M; 15. Sisters: **65751 MOBIL PRODUCER** (Li) **65752 MOBIL REFINER** (SA) **65753 PAOLA** (Fi).

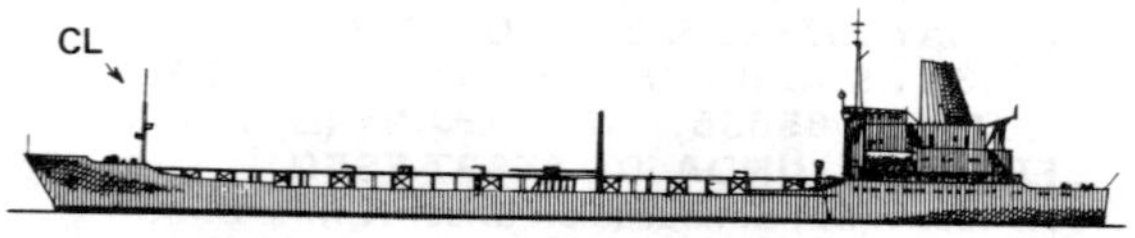

K_2MF H13
● **65760 GLOBE COMET.** FRG/FRG 1972; Tk; 17600; 172.04 × 10.68 (564.43 × 35.04); M; 15.5; ex THOR ASGARD. Sisters (Li flag): **65761 SALLY I** ex AMISIA 1973; launched as P.C.I. **65762 SALLY II.**

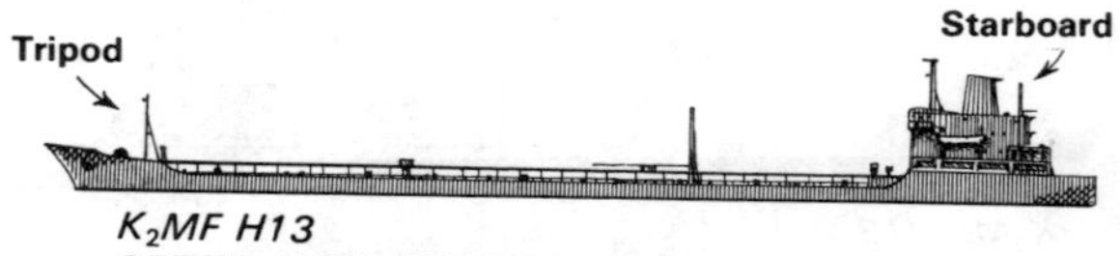

K_2MF H13
65770 JUBILEE VENTURE. Li/Sp 1972; Tk; 14800; 170.01 × 9.8 (557.78 × 32.15); M; —; ex POST ROVER 1976.

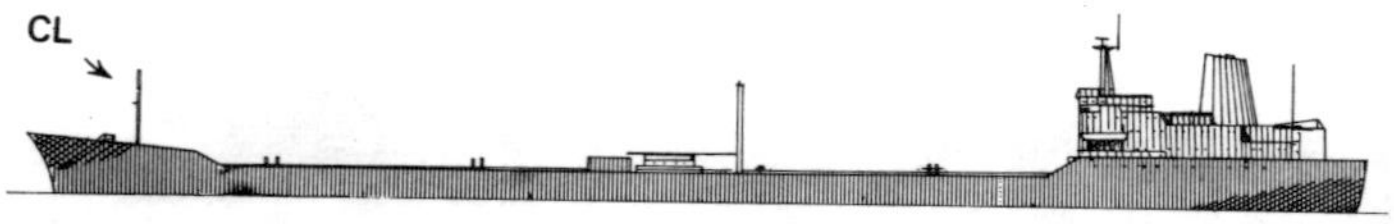

K_2MF H13
65780 CYCLOPS. Br/Ne 1975; Tk; 32600; 210.32 × 12.41 (690.01 × 40.71); M; 16.75. Sister: **65781 CLYTONEUS** (Br) Probable sister: **65782 RAIKO MARU** (Ja) ex SANKO TRUST 1979; launched as HELLESPONT ARGOSY.

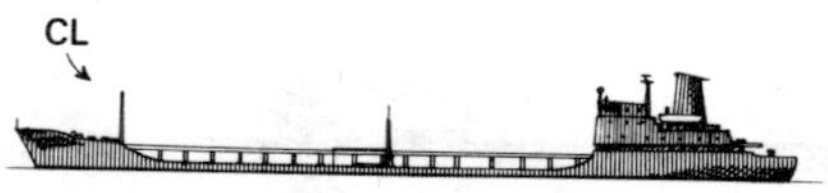

K_2MF H13
65790 CAMPONAVIA. Sp/Sp 1973; Tk; 4200; 123.68 × 6.03 (405.77 × 19.78); M; 13. Sister: **65791 CAMPOMINO** (Sp).

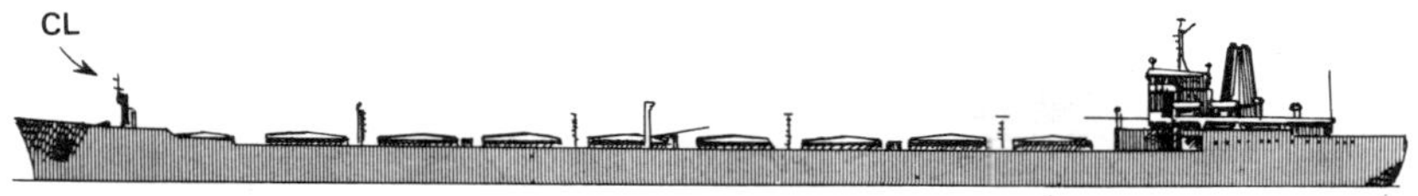

K_2MF H13
65800 VENTURE ITALIA. Li/Sw 1967; OBO; 39700; 258.66 × 13.27 (848.62 × 43.55); M; 16; ex CONOCO ITALIA 1978; ex RINDA 1972. Sister: **65801 DELAWARE** (Li) ex RANGER 1973; ex RUNA 1972.

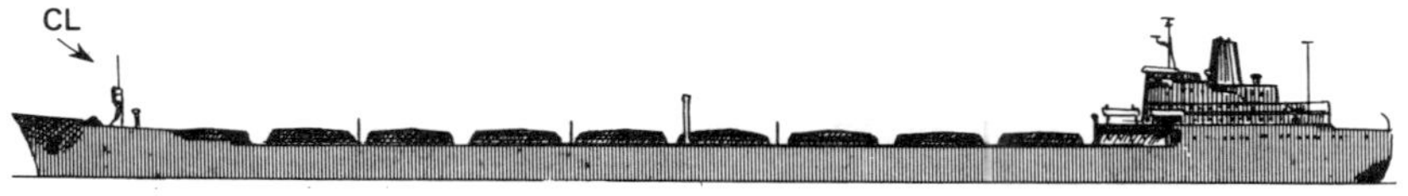

K_2MF H13
65810 FALCON BAY. Li/Sw 1967; OBO; 44500; 258.66 × 13.47 (848.62 × 44.19); M; 16.5; ex MOSPOINT 1979; ex VITORIA 1976.

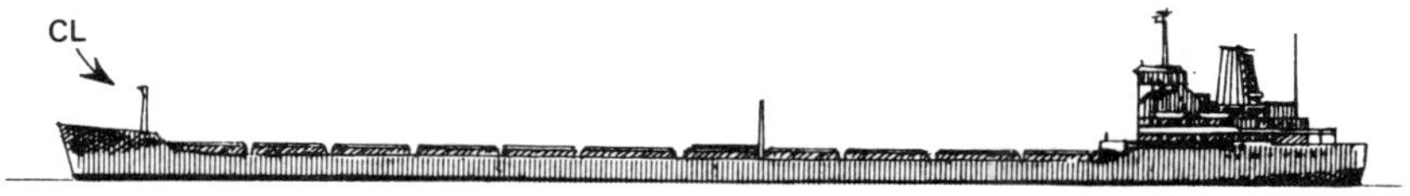

K_2MF H13
● **65820 ASEAN MISSION.** Pi/No 1968; OBO; 42500; 243.85 × 13.93 (800 × 45.7); M; 16.5; ex BJORGFJELL. Sisters: **65821 ASEAN MISSION** (Pi) ex BJORGHAV 1979 **65822 ASEAN LIBERTY** (Pi) ex BRALI 1978; ex HAVMOY 1975 **65823 M. EFES** (Tu) ex BANTRY 1978; ex HAVTOR 1975.

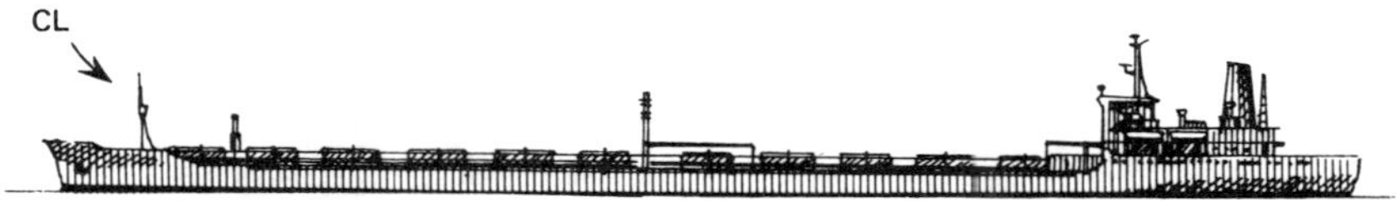

K_2MF H13
65830 RIO SUN. Li/Ja 1967; OBO; 42500; 250.96 × 13.98 (823.36 × 45.87); M; 16; ex TOKYO 1977. Sister: **65831 GARBIS** (Li) ex CANTO 1975; ex VESTFOLD 1971.

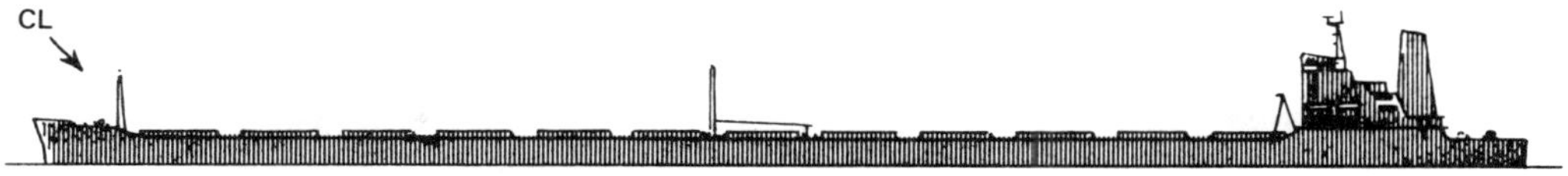

K_2MF H13
65840 CETRA CENTAURUS. Fr/Fr 1972; OO; 88100; 299.27 × 18.31 (981.86 × 60.07); M; 15.

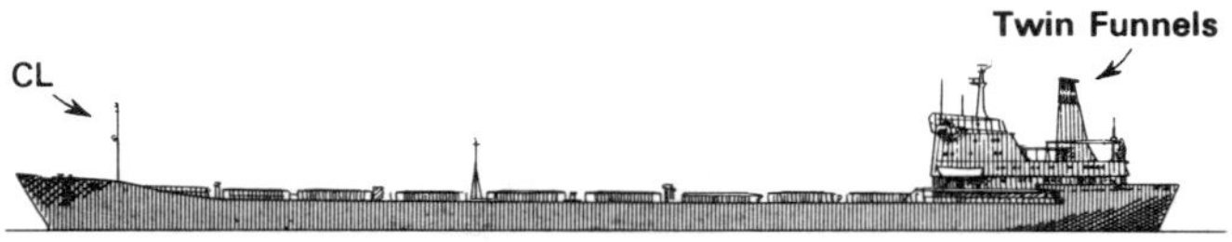

K_2MF H13
★**65850 FELIKS DZIERZYNSKI.** Pd/Pd 1978; B; 20300; 198.18 × 11 (650.2 × 36.09); M; 15.2; **'B-517'** type. Sisters (Pd flag): ★**65851 WALKA MLODYCH** ★**65852 UNIWERSYTET SLASKI.**

K_2MF H13
65860 AGUA GRANDE. Bz/De 1961; Tk; 8000; approx 154.11 × 7.17 (505.61 × 23.52); M; 13; Lengthened 1972. Note: drawing shows vessel before lengthening. Sisters (Bz flag): **65861 ARATU 65862 CANDEIAS 65863 ITAPARICA 65864 POJUCA 65865 TAQUIPE.**

K_2MF $H13$

65870 MARAJO. Bz/Ja 1968; FA/Tk; 10500 Dwt; 134.4 × 7.3 (440.7 × 24); M; 13.5.

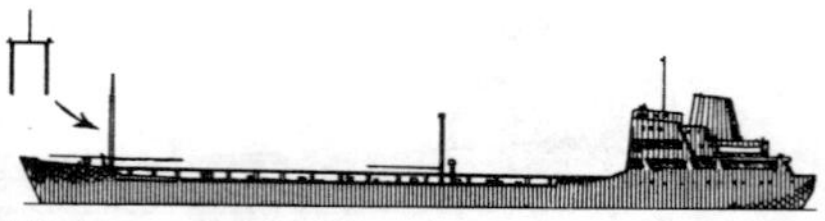

K_2MF $H13$

65880 EDOUARD SIMARD. Ca/Ca 1961/78; Tk; 5100; 125.71 × 6.85 (412.43 × 22.47); M; 12; ex J. EDOUARD SIMARD 1967; New forward section added 1978.

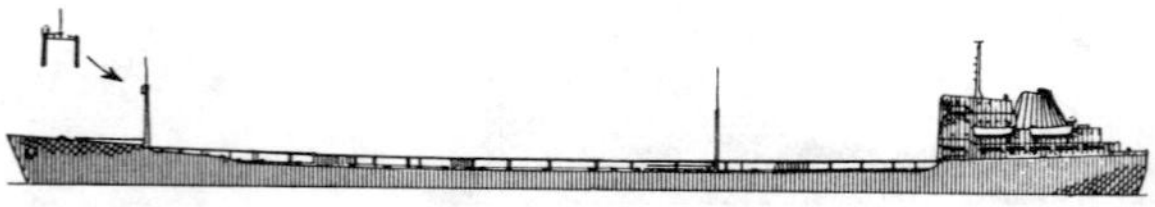

K_2MF $H13$

65890 TEXACO BOGOTA. No/Sw 1960; Tk; 13600; 181.67 × 9.57 (596.03 × 31.38); M; 14.5; Lengthened and converted 1968.

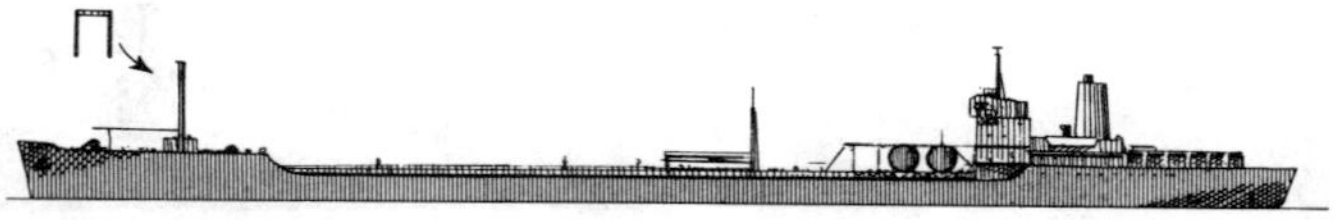

K_2MF $H13$

65900 ALASKAN. US/US 1944/69; Tk; 15200; 202.7 × 10.43 (665.02 × 34.21); T; 17; ex CLENDENIN 1969; ex HAVEN 1945; ex MARINE HAWK; Forward and aft sections built 1944; Cargo section built 1969. Converted from hospital ship 1969; Lengthened 1969.

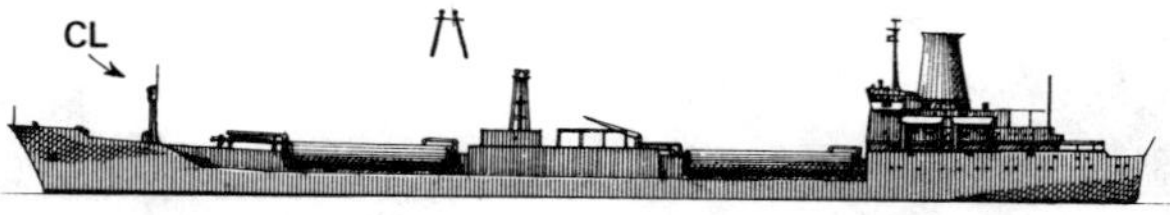

K_2MF $H13$

65910 PETROGAS I. Si/Sw 1964; LGC; 18000; 180.58 × 10.61 (592.45 × 34.8); M; 16; ex CASSIE HILL 1979; ex NORFOLK MULTINA 1978; ex PAUL ENDACOTT 1973.

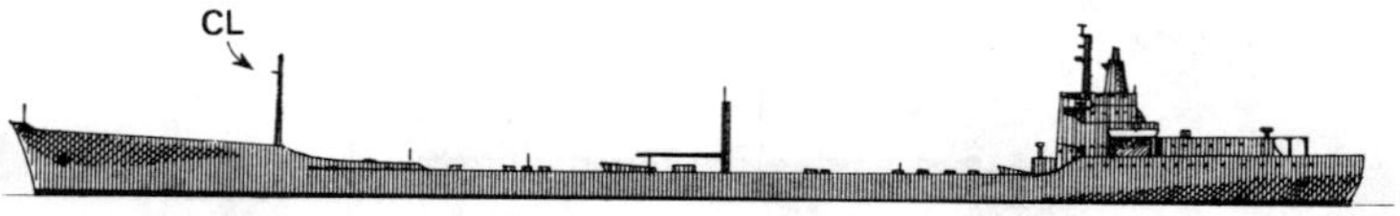

K_2MF $H13$

● **65920 SINCLAIR TEXAS.** US/US 1963; Tk; 27500; 224.44 × 12.13 (735.69 × 39.79); T; 16.5.

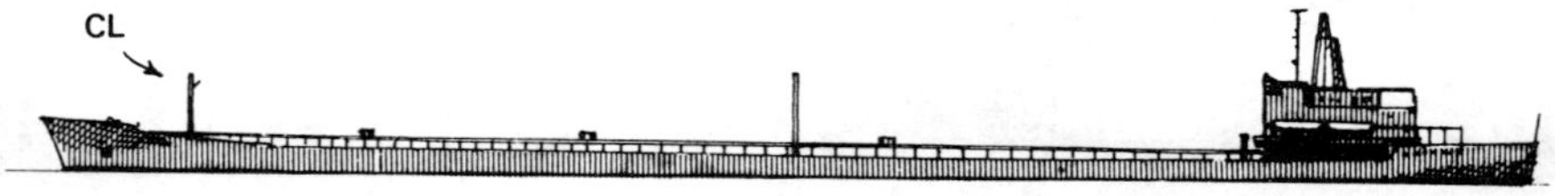

K_2MF $H13$

65930 STROFADES. Gr/De 1966; Tk; 52700; 263.48 × 14 (864.43 × 45.93); T; 17; ex A.P. MOLLER 1980. Similar (Br flag): **65931 MAERSK BUCHAN** ex ELISABETH MAERSK **65932 MAERSK ANGUS** ex EVELYN MAERSK.

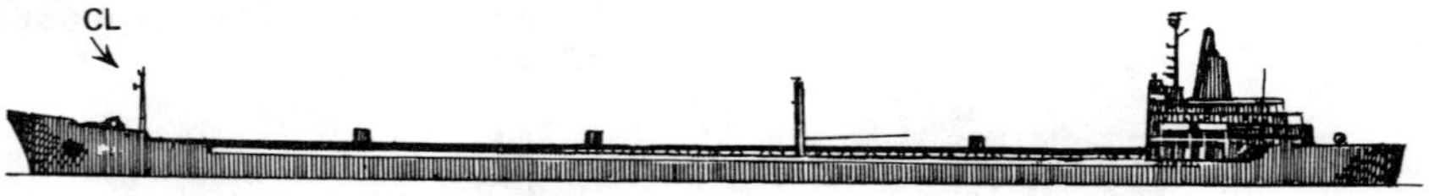

K_2MF $H13$

65940 CONCORDE. Gr/De 1966; Tk; 42600; 261.83 × 13.49 (859.02 × 44.26); T; 16.75; ex MOZDOK; ex JOSEPHINE 1976; ex JANE MAERSK 1975.

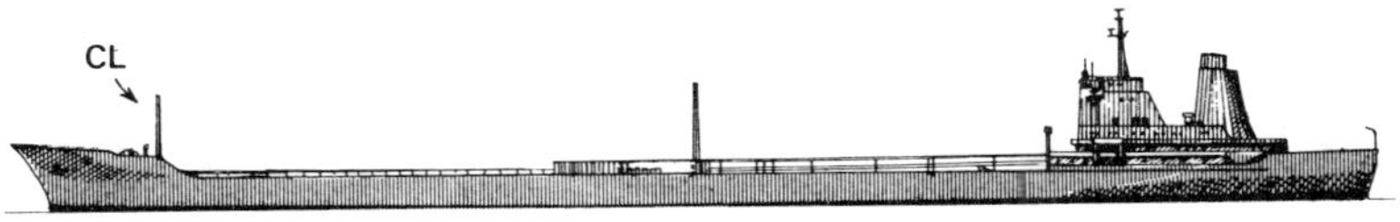

K_2MF H13
65950 ORIENTAL EXPLORER. Li/FRG 1965; Tk; 38900; 235.67 × 13.12 (773.19 × 43.04); M; 17.25; ex AUDACIOUS 1977; ex ST PAULS 1974; ex ST NIKOLAI 1973. Sisters: **65951 AIKATERINA** (Gr) ex ATLANTIC CONQUEROR 1980; ex COURAGEOUS COLOCOTRONIS 1977; ex ST PETRI 1972 **65952 OCEANIC WINNER** (Li) ex CHAMPION COLOCOTRONIS 1977; ex ST MICHAELIS 1972.

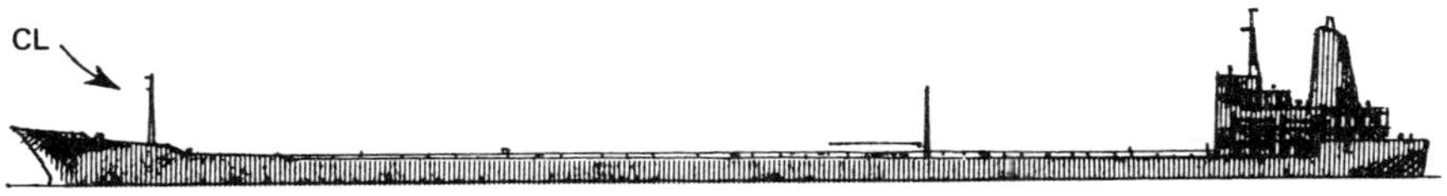

K_2MF H13
● **65960 GATOOMA.** Li/Sp 1969; Tk; 51800; 267.62 × 13.94 (878.02 × 45.73); T; 16.5; ex PABLO GARNICA. Probable Sister: **65961 SANTANDER** (Sp).

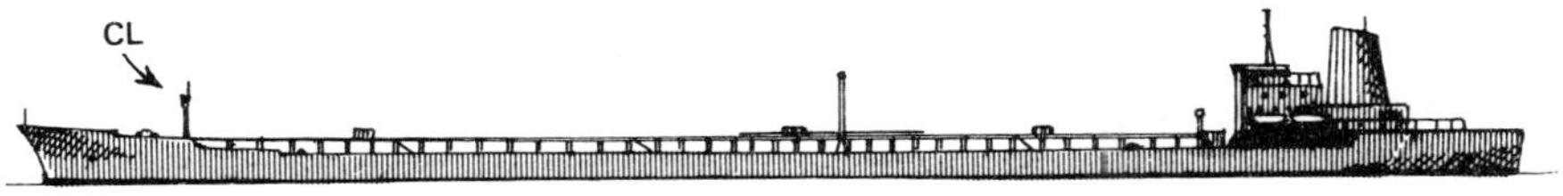

K_2MF H13
65970 SAFINA SAUDIA. Si/Sp 1968; Tk; 51400; 265.69 × 13.94 (871.69 × 45.73); M; 17; ex ZARAGOZA 1980. Similar: **65971 HAWAIIAN SEA** (Li) ex HAGENSEE 1977; ex BAMBERG 1973 **65972 CERVANA** (It) ex JOLE FASSIO 1977; ex LOYOLA 1971 **65973 ALENDALE** (Li) ex MARITIME LAWYER 1979; ex OLDENFELD 1976; ex ARNSBERG 1973; Launched as PETRO ZULIA **65974 CEUTA** (Sp) **65975 MOSTOLES** (Sp) Possibly Similar: **65976 OCEAN VICTORY** (Gr) ex DORA 1976 Possibly Similar (larger): **65977 ORDUNA** (Sp).

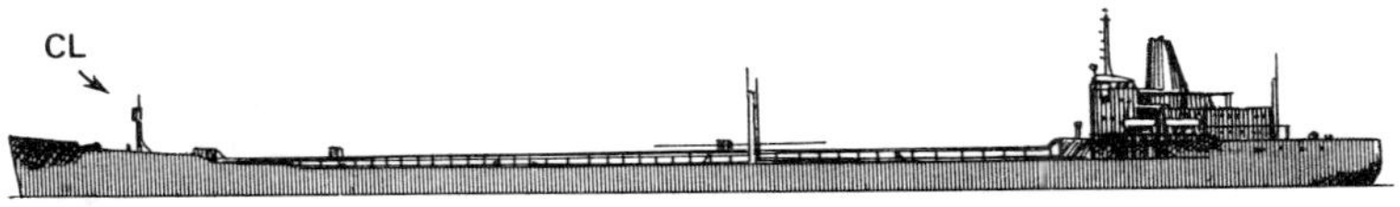

K_2MF H13
65990 DESPINA A L. Gr/Sw 1965; Tk; 32700; 236.38 × 12.64 (775.52 × 41.47); T; 17.25; ex LUCIAN 1973. Sister: **65991 ADAMANTIOS** (Gr) ex CHIOS ISLAND 1977; ex BOTANY BAY 1975; ex CYPRIAN 1973.

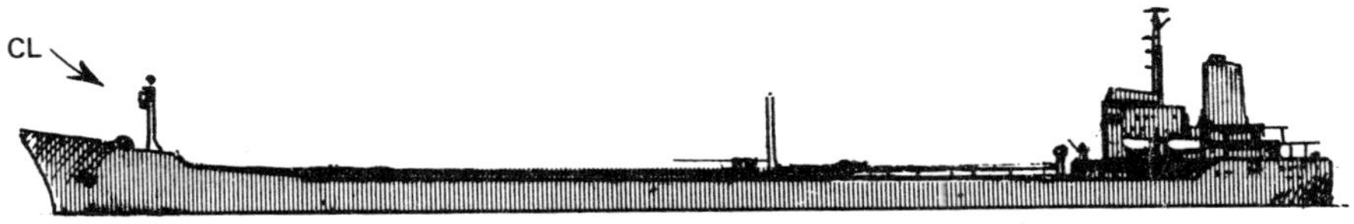

K_2MF H13
66000 JILL. Li/De 1966; Tk; 45400; 265.72 × 13.95 (871.78 × 45.77); M; 16.75; ex FERNCREST 1977.

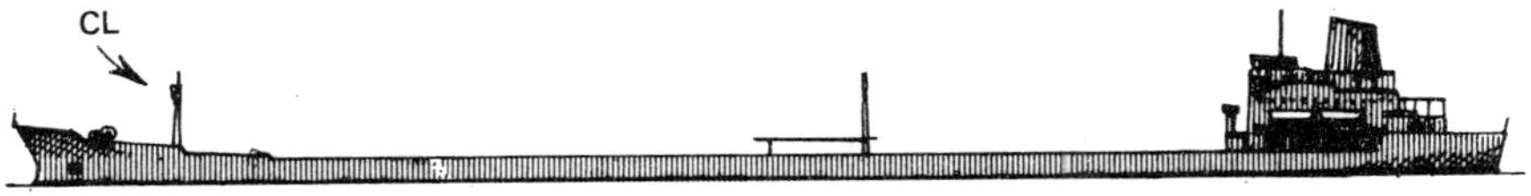

K_2MF H13
● **66010 AFRAN TIDE.** Li/De 1966; Tk; 45300; 265.69 × 13.94 (871.68 × 45.73); M; 16.25; ex ELI MAERSK 1977.

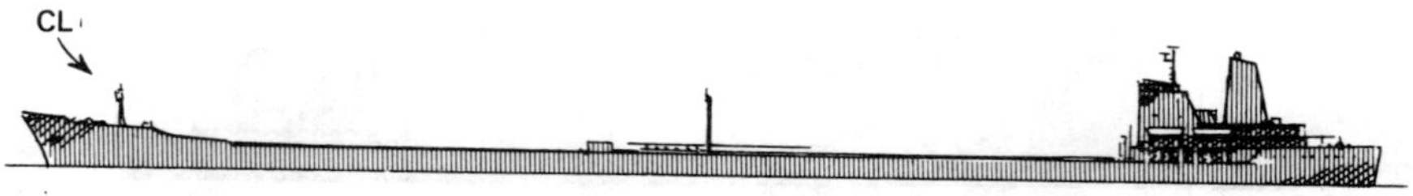

K_2MF *H13*

66020 FANARI. Li/De 1967; Tk; 52700; 265.74 × 13.95 (773.43 × 45.76); M; 16.25; ex NORDHAV 1975. Similar: **66021 YPAPANTI** (Li) ex AFRAN COAST 1980; ex STAVIK 1976; ex PERMINA III 1976; ex PERMINA I 1972; ex STAVIK 1972.

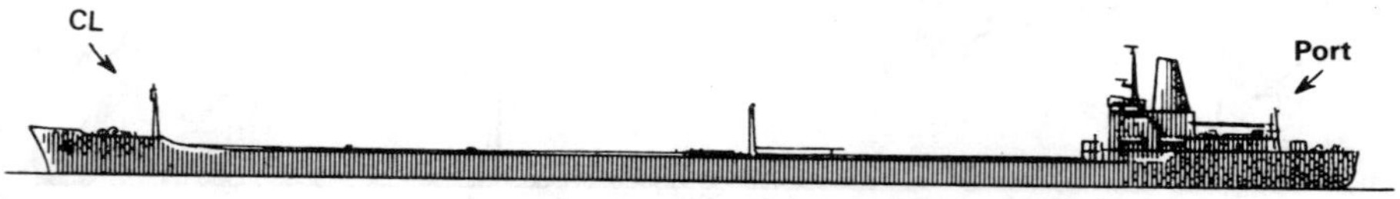

K_2MF *H13*

66030 LILY H. Gr/Sw 1967; Tk; 48700; 265.13 × 14.66 (869.85 × 48.1); M; 16.5; ex MOBIL RADIANT; ex CERNO 1976; ex STIKLESTAD 1973.

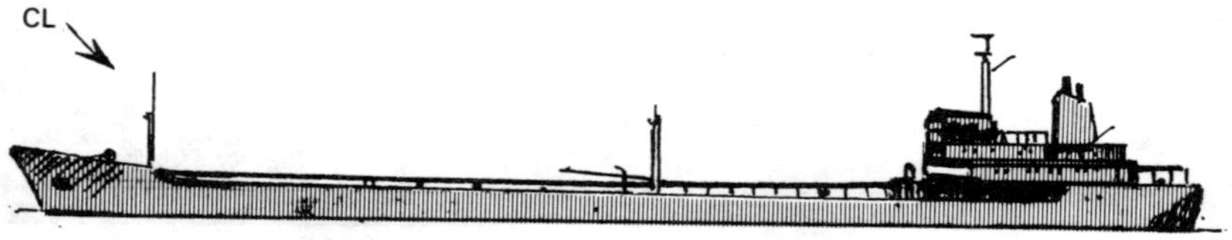

K_2MF *H13*

66040 MYTILENE. Li/FRG 1967; Tk; 44700; 253.12 × 12.27 (830.45 × 40.26); M; 16.5; ex HELGA ESSBERGER 1979.

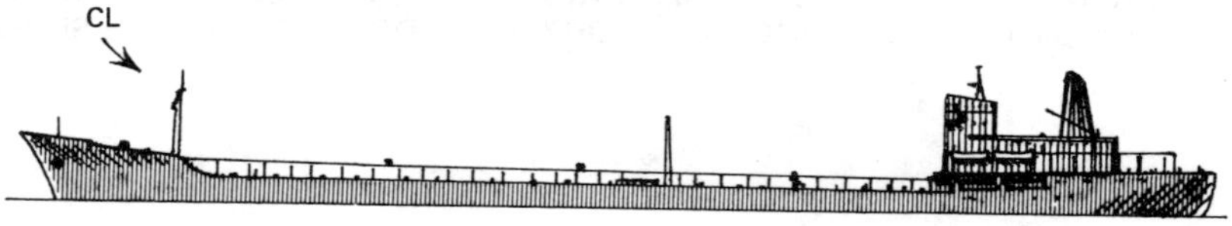

K_2MF *H13*

66050 MARIA. Gr/FRG 1965; Tk; 42100; 249.11 × 13.77 (817.29 × 45.18); T; 17; ex GENERAL COLOCOTRONIS 1977; ex BARBRO 1969. Similar: **66051 ERAWAN** (Pa) ex TRADE RESOLVE 1980; ex KATINGO COLOCOTRONIS 1979; ex HOEGH LAUREL 1973.

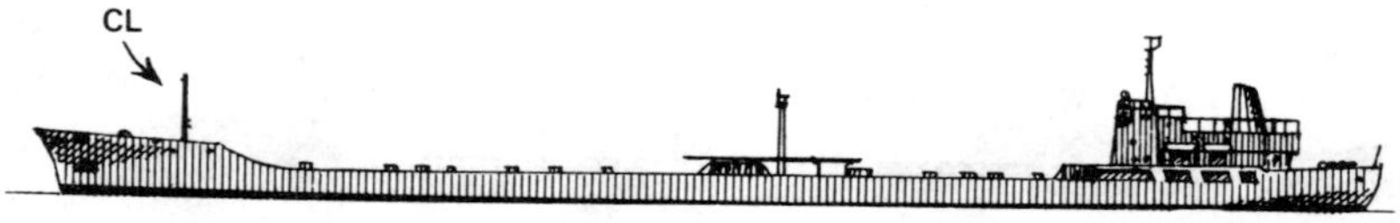

K_2MF *H13*

66060 NEDI. Gr/Br 1965; Tk; 35300; 243.72 × 13.23 (799.61 × 43.41); M; —; ex AEOLUS 1977; ex NORTH SANDS 1970. Similar: **66061 MENA** (Th) ex DONACILLA 1976 **66062 CATALUNYA** (Li) ex PHILIPPINE STAR 1980; ex DAPHNELLA 1976.

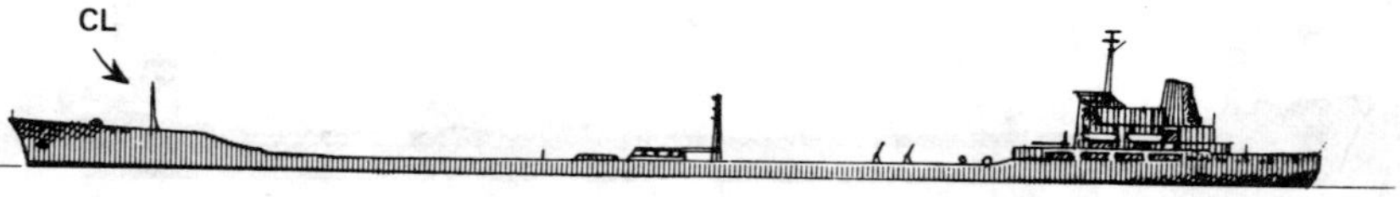

K_2MF *H13*

● **66070 DIONE.** Na/Ne 1967; Tk; 39100; 243.85 × 13.37 (800.03 × 43.86); M; —. Sisters: **66071 DOSINA** (NA) **66072 DIADEMA** (NA) **66073 TAKIS E** (Gr) ex DILOMA 1981 Similar: **66074 DONOVANIA** (Br) **66075 SIAM** (Th) ex DORCASIA 1977 Possible Sister: **66076 DALLIA** (NA) **66077 DAPHNE** (NA).

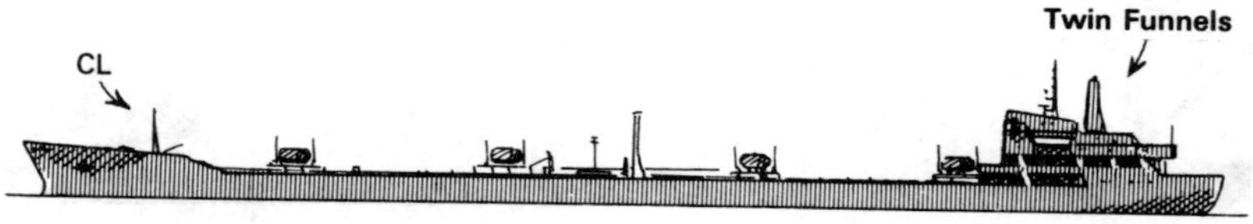

K_2MF *H13*

66080 DARINA. Br/FRG 1966; Tk; 39800; 243.8 × 13.32 (799.87 × 43.7); T; 14.25; Used as lightening tanker. Fenders on deck.

K_2MF H13
66090 ESSO ZURICH. Pa/Ja 1965; Tk; 37300; 243.85 × 12.75 (800.03 × 41.83); M; 15.5. Sisters (Pa flag): **66091 ESSO PHILIPPINES 66092 EXXON HOUSTON** ex ESSO HOUSTON 1973 **66093 EXXON NEW ORLEANS** ex ESSO NEW ORLEANS 1973.

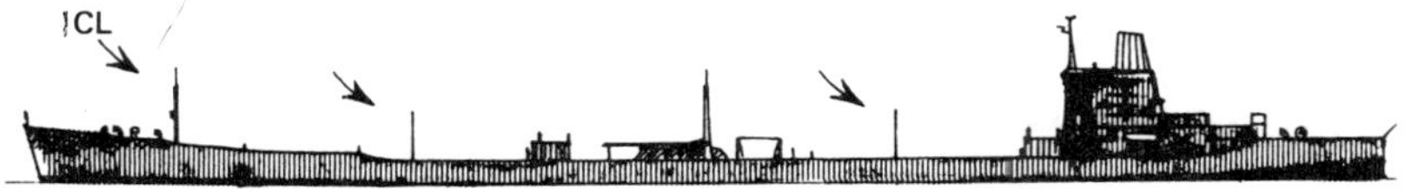

K_2MF H13
66100 ESSO ANTWERP. Br/No 1967; Tk; 42100; 246.59 × 12.7 (809.02 × 41.67); M; 17. Sister: **66101 ESSO CASTELLON** (Pa).

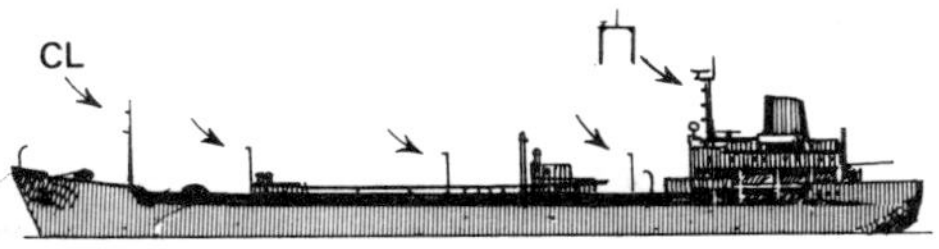

K_2MF H13
66110 CLERK-MAXWELL. Br/Br 1966; LGC; 8300; 140.67 × 8.25 (461.52 × 27.07); M; 17. Similar: **66111 MARIANO ESCOBEDO** (Me).

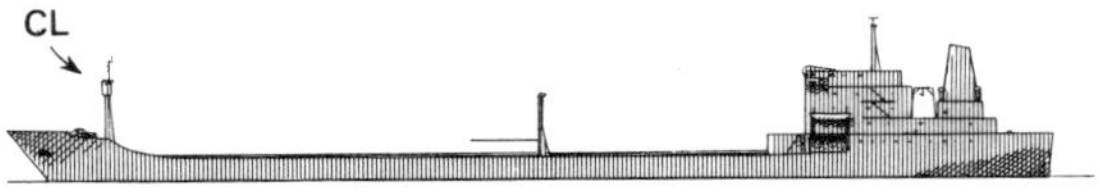

K_2MF H13
66130 CAMPONUBLA. Sp/Sp 1979; Tk; 14900; 166 × 9.25 (544.62 × 30.35); M; 14.87; May be named **CAMPONUBIA.** Sister: **66131 CAMPEON** (Sp).

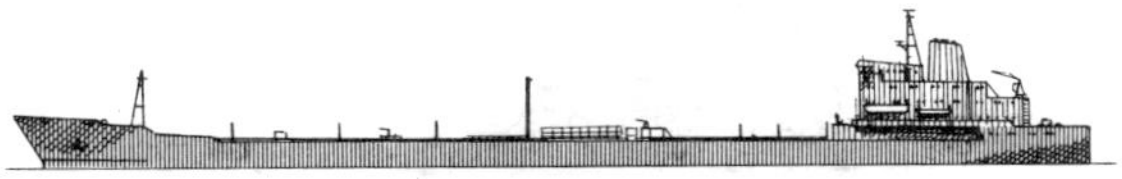

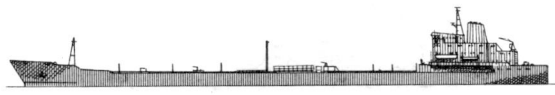

K_2MF H13
66150 OSCO SAGONA. No/No 1976; Tk/Ch; 18600; 170.31 × 9.91 (558.76 × 32.51); M; 15.25; ex SAGONA 1980. Possibly Similar (No flag): **66151 VINCITA 66152 VENTURA.**

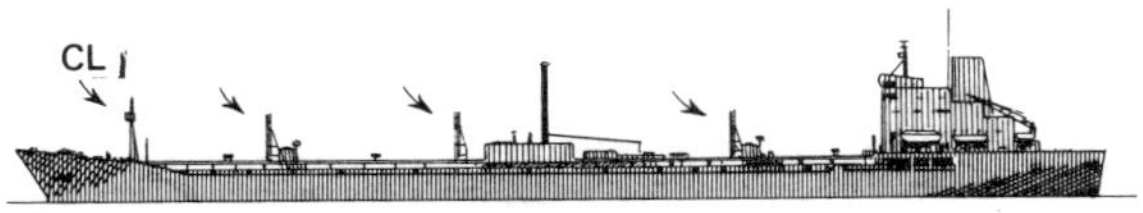

K_2MF H13
66160 CHAC. Me/No 1976; Ch; 17600; 170.72 × 10 (560.1 × 32.8); M; 15.5; ex FOSSANGER 1977. Sister: **66161 BACAB** (Me) ex BOW CLIPPER 1977.

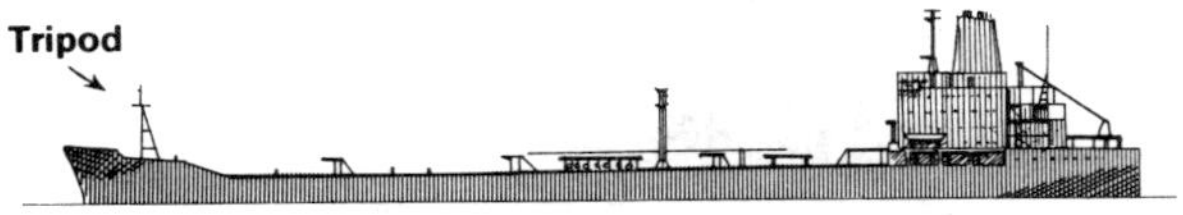

K_2MF H13
● **66180 GUDRUN MAERSK.** De/No 1973; Tk; 19900; 170.54 × 11.75 (559.51 × 38.55); M; 15.5. Sisters: **66181 GJERTRUD MAERSK** (De) **66182 GRETE MAERSK** (De) **66183 TITIPOR** (Gr) ex GUNVOR MAERSK 1980.

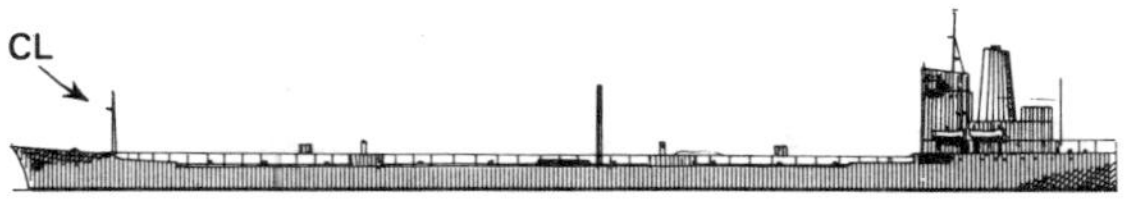

K_2MF H13
66120 PALUDINA. Br/Ne 1968; TB/Tk; 15400; 157.17 × 10.11 (574.7 × 33.17); M; 15.25; ex URSHALIM 1973. Similar: **66121 POMELLA** (Br) ex HORAMA 1974; Launched as NORDVARD.

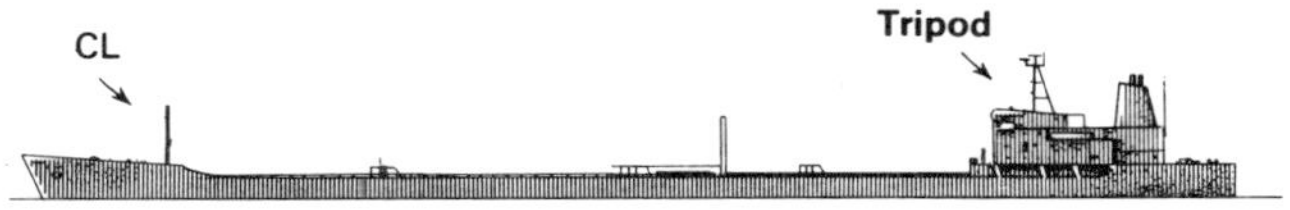

K_2MF H13
66140 AQUARIUS. Br/Br 1972; Tk; 19900; 192.01 × 10.38 (629.95 × 34.05); M; 16; ex NEWBURN 1980; ex AFGHANISTAN; ex JOSEPH R SMALLWOOD 1975. Sisters: **66141 STRAIT OF CANSO** (Br) **66142 SIMONBURN** (Br) ex KURDISTAN; ex FRANK D MOORES 1976 Probable Sister: **66143 AMOKURA** (NZ) ex HINDUSTAN 1978.

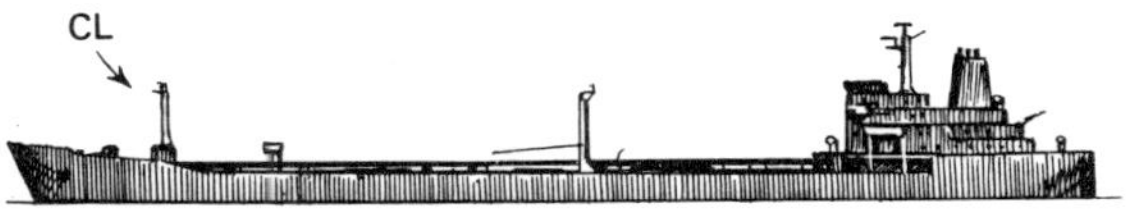

K_2MF H13
★**66170 MAYKOP.** Ru/Br 1975; Tk; 19600; 171 × 11.3 (562 × 37); M; 15; Launched as HELENA K. Sisters (Ru flag): ★**66171 GROZNYY;** Launched as ROBKAP I ★**66172 APSHERON;** Launched as ROBKAP II ★**66173 MAKHACHKALA;** Launched as ROBKAP III ★**66174 GUDERMES;** Launched as ROBKAP IV (Ve flag): **66175 LAGOVEN QUIRIQUIRE 66176 LAGOVEN SANTA RITA.**

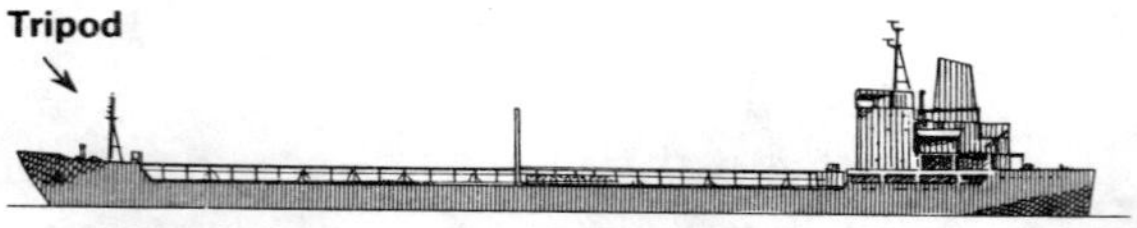

K_2MF H13
66190 PREMUDA ROSA. It/It 1974/76; Tk; 18000; 170.69 × 10.95 (560 × 35.95); M; 16.5; Launched 1974. Completed 1976. Sisters: **66191 PREMUDA BIANCA** (It) **66192 BUFFALO** (SA) (Ar flag - some have fenders on deck): **66193 CAMPO DURAN 66194 CANADON SECO 66195 MEDANITO 66196 PUERTO ROSALES** Possibly Similar (It flag): **66197 AGIP GELA 66198 AGIP RAVENNA 66199 CIELO DI ROMA 66200 CIELO DI SALERNO.**

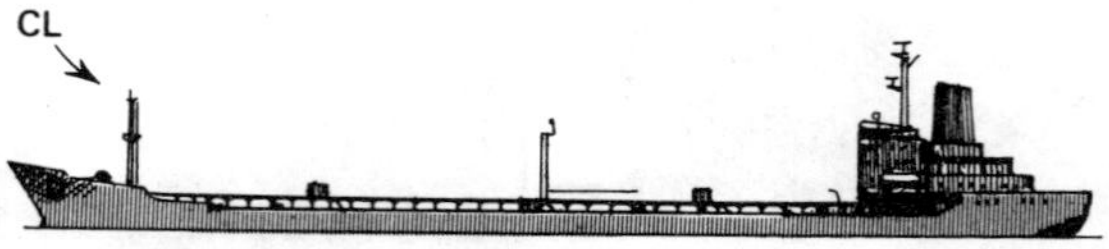

K_2MF H13
66210 CONASTOGA. Li/It 1972; Tk; 17500; 171.61 × 10.93 (563.02 × 35.86); M; 16. Probable Sisters: **66211 CORSICANA** (It) **66212 SACHEM** (Br) **66213 SATUCKET** (Br) Possible Sisters: **66214 INDEPENDENCIA I** (Ve); Launched as INDEPENDENCIA **66215 INDEPENDENCIA II** (Ve).

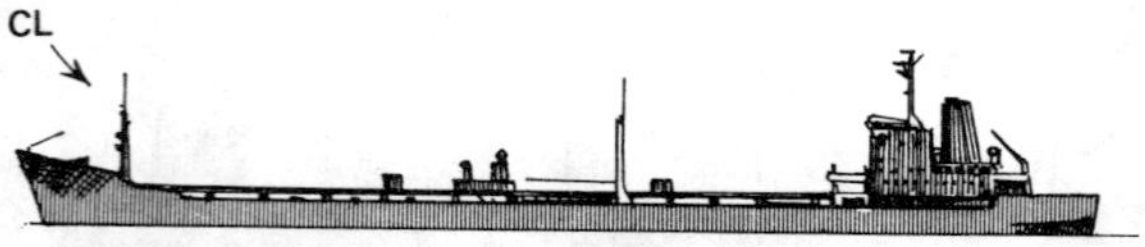

K_2MF H13
● **66220 NITSA.** Gr/Sw 1971; Tk; 16400; 170.97 × 10.21 (560.93 × 33.5); M; 15.25. Sisters (Gr flag): **66221 CEPHEUS 66222 CYGNUS.**

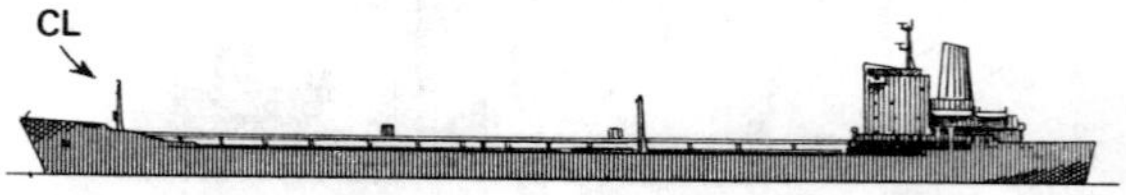

K_2MF H13
66230 OSCO TAMPIMEX EAGLE. Br/Sw 1977; Tk; 18500; 170.97 × 11.36 (560.93 × 37.27); M; 15; ex TAMPIMEX EAGLE 1980; ex NORDIC AURORA. Sister: **66231 LADY EMA** (Gr) ex BERA 1981; ex NORDIC BREEZE.

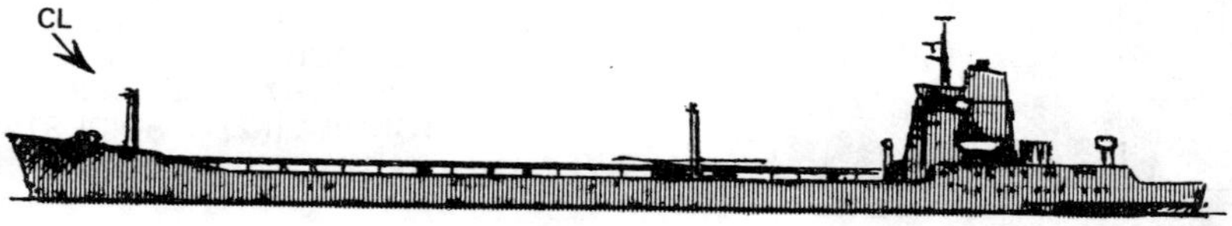

K_2MF H13
66240 POLYS. Gr/Ja 1965; Tk; 40300; 243.85 × 13.04 (800 × 42.78); M; 15; ex BERRY 1976; ex BOLETTE 1970.

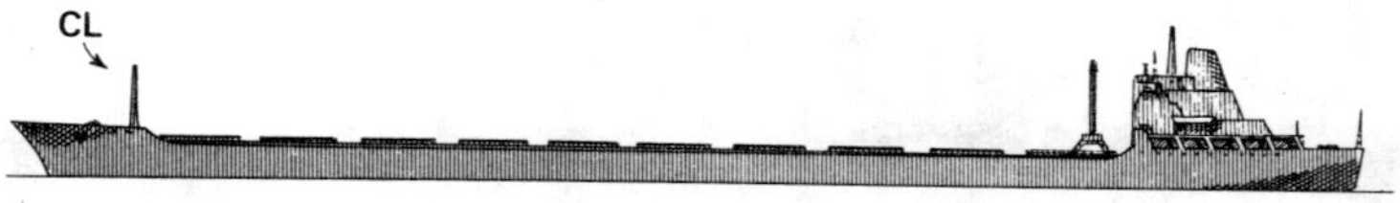

K_2MF H13
66250 HOPECLIPPER. Br/Ja 1967; B; 35300; 223.96 × 13.7 (734.78 × 44.95); M; 15.5; ex CAPTAIN W D CARGILL 1977; Kingposts on travelling gantry.

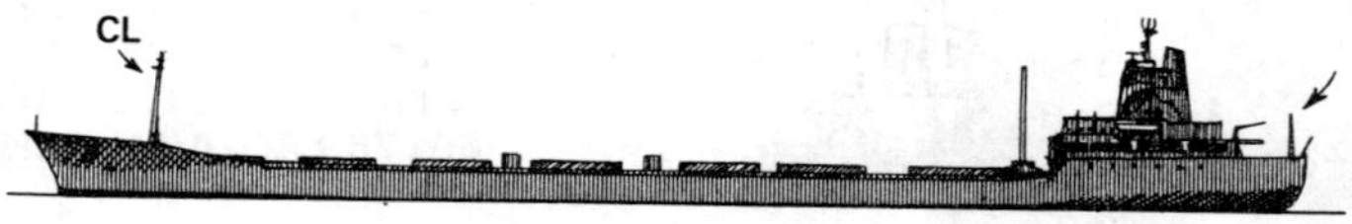

K_2MF H13
66260 ACHILLEUS. Gr/Ja 1965; B; 21500; 195.84 × 10.62 (642.51 × 34.84); M; 15; Kingposts on travelling gantry. Sister: **66261 EPHESTOS** (Gr).

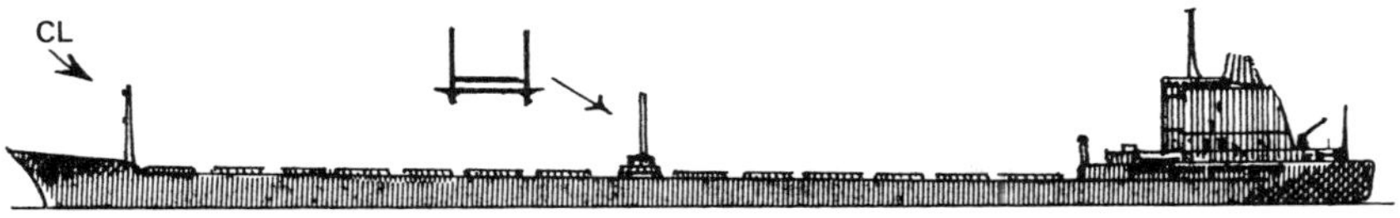

K_2MF H13
66270 METHODIC. Li/Ja 1966; OBO; 39600; 257.87 × 12.35 (846.03 × 40.52); M; —; ex MELODIC 1974; Kingposts on travelling gantry. Sister: **66271 MYTHIC** (Li) Probable Sister: **66272 LORENZO HALCOUSSI** (Li) ex ARCTIC 1971.

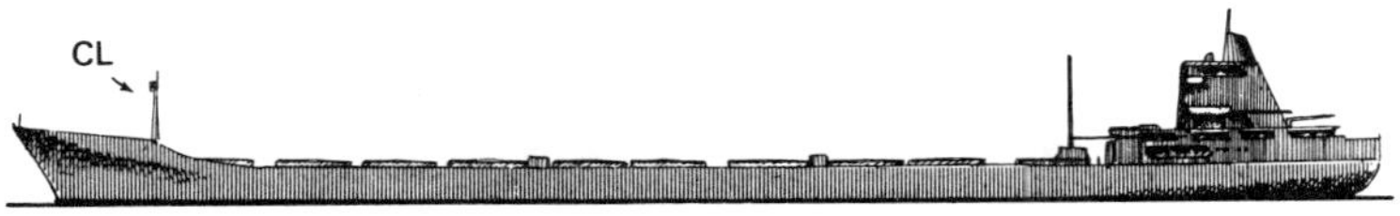

K_2MF H13
66280 LIRYC. Li/Ja 1964; B; 29400; 227.03 × 12.2 (744.85 × 40.03); T; 16; Kingposts on travelling gantry. Sister: **66281 HEROIC** (Li).

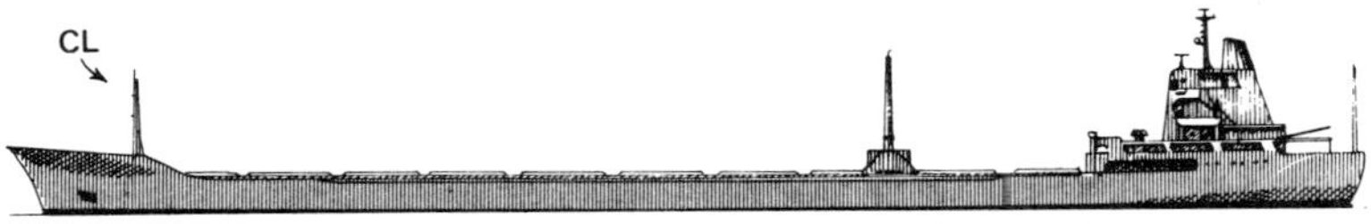

K_2MF H13
66290 POETIC. Li/Ja 1966; OO; 33300; 240.7 × 12.64 (789.7 × 41.47); T; 16; Kingposts on travelling gantry. Sister: **66291 SCENIC** (Li).

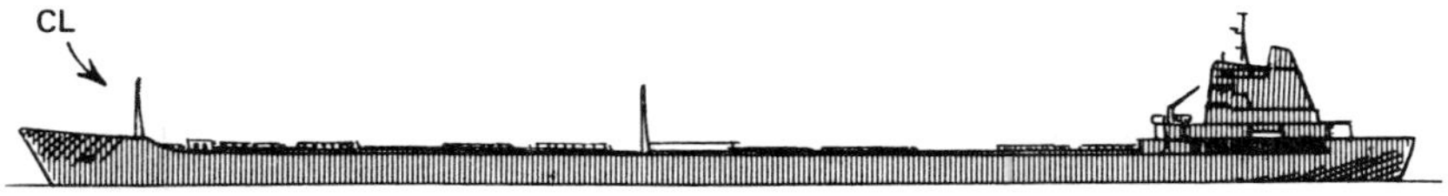

K_2MF H13
66300 ATHENIC. Gr/Ja 1967; OO; 36700 ORE 48700 OIL; 254.26 × 13.31 (834.18 × 43.67); M; —. Sisters (Gr flag): **66301 GLORIC 66302 PLATONIC** Similar (tankers): **66303 ATOMIC 66304 HARMONIC 66305 IONIC 66306 TROPIC** (Li flag): **66307 DORIC.**

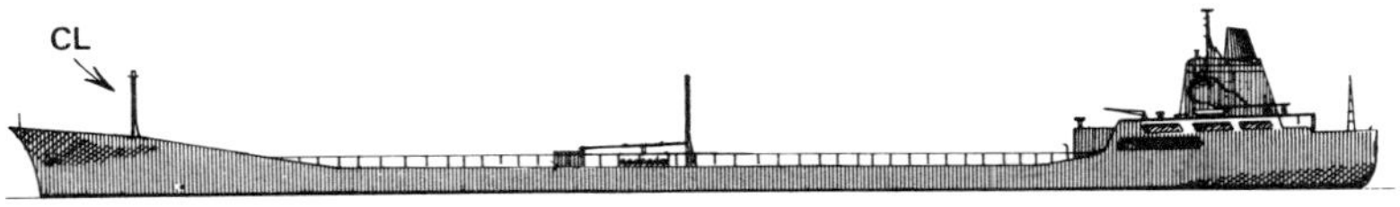

K_2MF H13
66310 LACONIC. Gr/Ja 1965; Tk; 34200; 241.1 × 14.72 (791.01 × 48.29); T; 17. Sister: **66311 MAJESTIC** (Gr) Probable Sister (may be HI): **66312 PACIFIC** (Li).

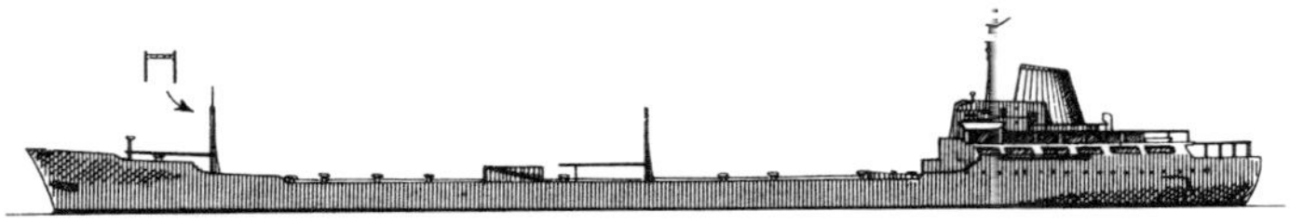

K_2MF H13
66320 RAFFAELE CAFIERO. It/It 1962; Tk; 24400; 210.52 × 11.55 (690.68 × 37.9); M; 17.5.

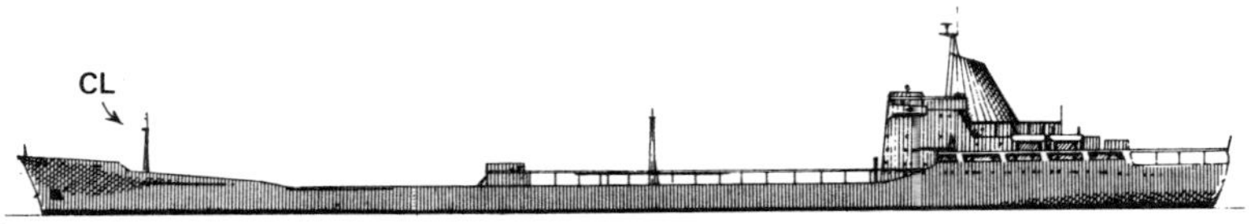

K_2MF H13
● **66330 TECALLI.** Pa/Fr 1964; Tk; 36300; 236.02 × 12.19 (774.34 × 39.99); T; 16; ex ALEXANDRA; ex TOURAINE 1978.

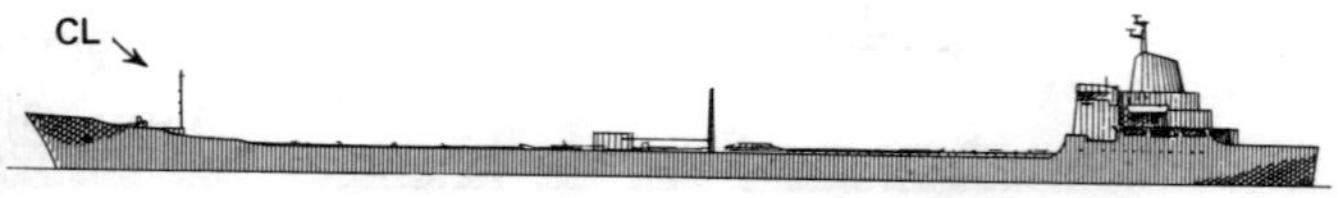

K_2MF H13

66340 COLUMBIA. US/US 1971; Tk; 20800; 204.93 × 11.04 (672.34 × 36.22); M; 16.25; ex FALCON LADY 1976; Chartered to Military Sealift Command. Sisters (US flag): **66341 HUDSON** ex FALCON PRINCESS 1976 **66342 NECHES** ex FALCON DUCHESS 1976 **66343 SUSQUEHANNA** ex FALCON COUNTESS 1976.

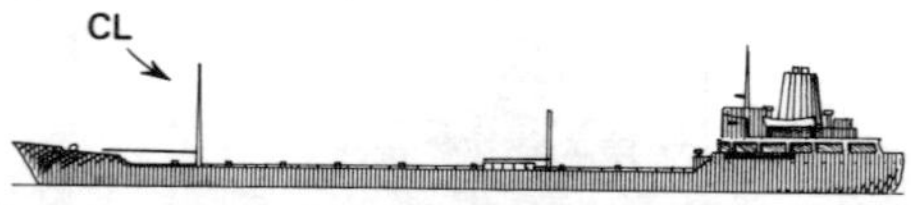

K_2MF H13

● **66350 BRUCE BALI.** Li/Ja 1971; Tk; 9200; 141.26 × 9 (463.45 × 29.53); M; 14.5; ex GOLAR BALI 1978. Sisters (Li flag): **66351 BRUCE BAWGAN** ex GOLAR BAWGAN 1978 **66352 BRUCE BINTAN** ex GOLAR BINTAN 1978 **66353 BRUCE BUATAN** ex GOLAR BUATAN 1978 **66354 BRUCE SURABAYA** ex GOLAR SURABAYA 1978 (Ia flag): **66355 PERMINA XXVII** ex BRUCE SABANG 1978; ex GOLAR SABANG 1978 **66356 PERMINA XXX** ex BRUCE SIGLI 1980; ex GOLAR SIGLI 1978 **66357 PERMINA XXXI** ex BRUCE PADANG 1980; ex INDOTANK 1978.

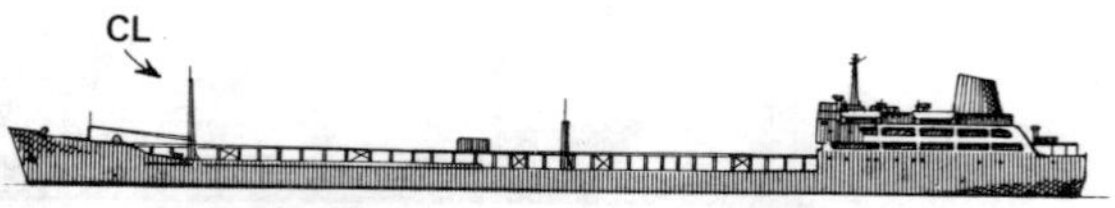

K_2MF H13

66360 DOLPHIN OLIVIA. Cy/Sw 1960; Tk; 12800; 169.81 × 9.61 (557.12 × 31.53); M; 15; ex BRACONDA 1978.

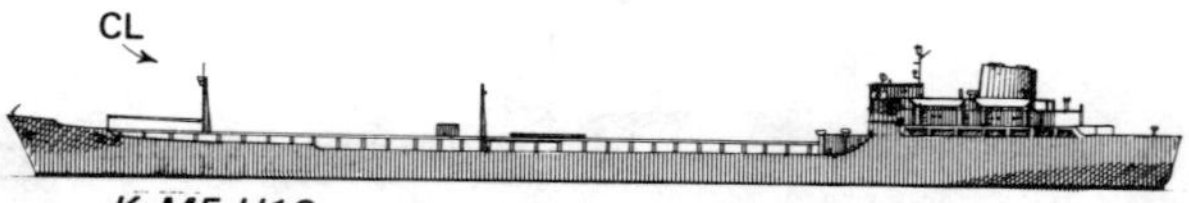

K_2MF H13

66370 EPIROS. Li/Sw 1960; Tk; 15400; 186.09 × 10.33 (610.53 × 33.89); M; 15.5; ex THOMAS B KIMBALL 1972.

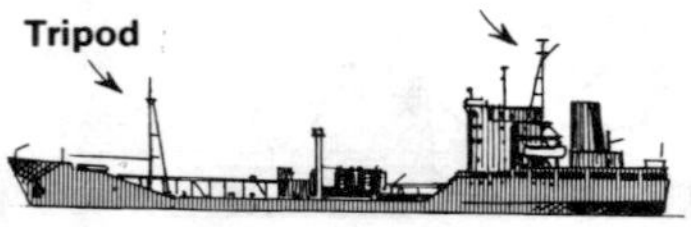

K_2MF H13

● ★**66380 KALININGRADNEFT.** Ru/Fi 1978; RT/Tk; 4500; 115.53 × 6.5 (379.04 × 21.33); M; 16. Sisters (Ru flag): ★**66381 OKHANEFT** ★**66382 GALVYE** ★**66383 KALININGRADSKIY-NEFTYANIK** ★**66384 MYSSAYEH** ★**66385 SARYCH** ★**66386 UST-KARSK** ★**66387 UST-KUT** ★**66388 VESYEGONSK** ★**66389 VIDNOYE.**

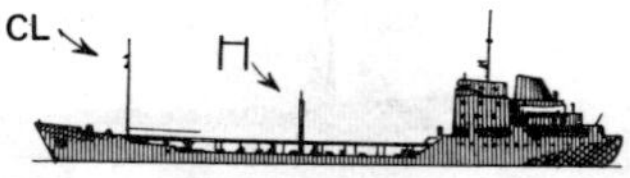

K_2MF H13

66400 REEM B. Pa/Fi 1960; Tk; 2700; 92.11 × 6.27 (302.2 × 20.57); M; 13.5; ex ESSO FENNIA 1976.

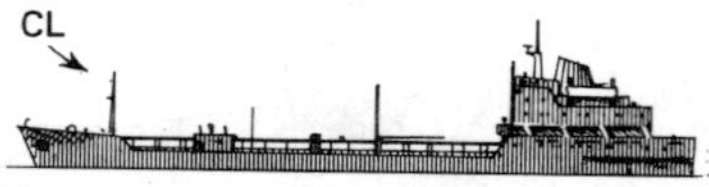

K_2MF H13

● **66410 KYRGO.** Br/Br 1970; Ch/Tk; 4600; 106.99 × 7.34 (351.02 × 24.08)) M; 14. ex SILVERHARRIER 1980.

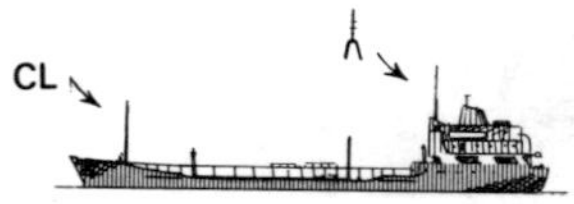

K_2MF H13

66420 TARNFORS. Sw/No 1965; Tk; 1200; 76.03 × 4.6 (249.44 × 15.09); M; 11.5; ex WINJONA 1975; ex RUBISTREAM 1968.

K_2MF H13

66430 ONCU. Tu/Tu 1969; Tk; 3300; 111.56 × 5.88 (366.01 × 19.29); M; —; lengthened 1971.

K_2MF H13

66440 ESSO TENBY. Br/Br 1970; Tk; 2200; 91.42 × 5.9 (299.93 × 19.36); M; —.

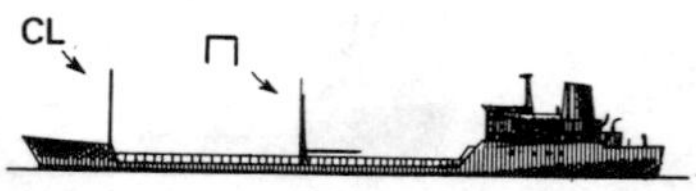

K_2MF H13

66450 PORT TUDY. Fr/Br 1969; Tk; 3100; 101.73 × 6.57 (333.76 × 21.56); M; 14.

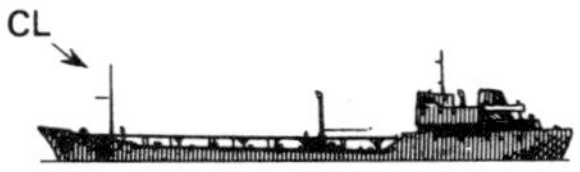

K_2MF H13
66460 MARK VII. Gr/Ne 1958; Tk; 1700; 83.57 × 5.24 (274.18 × 17.19); M; 12; ex AIRISMAA 1977.

K_2MF H13
66470 ALLURITY. Br/Ne 1969; Tk; 700; 73.97 × 3.96 (242.68 × 12.99); M; 12. Sister: **66471 ACTIVITY** (Br).

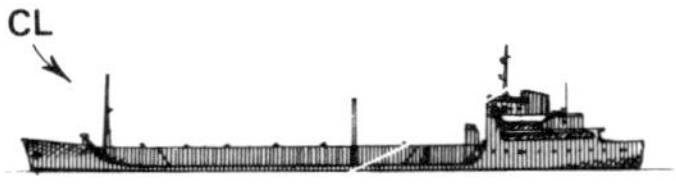

K_2MF H13
66480 GIMONE. Fr/Fr 1969; Tk; 3400; 100.03 × 5.61 (328.18 × 18.41); TSM; 11.75.

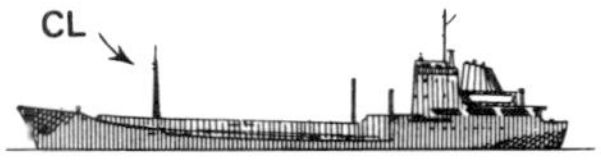

K_2MF H13
66490 RATHOWEN. Ih/Sw 1965; Tk; 2250; 86.75 × 5.79 (284.6 × 19); M; 12; ex BELLONA 1974; ex LUNA 1974. Similar: (One less deck on superstructure) **66491 WENA** (Ma) ex LENA 1977 Similar: **66492 LANA** (Sw) **66493 SIDON** (Gr) ex BELLONA 1978; ex LISA 1975 Possible similar: **66494 BELLONA** (Sw) ex STELLA ATLANTIC 1978.

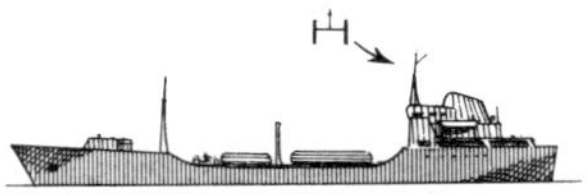

K_2MF H13
66500 MELROSE. Br/FRG 1971; LGC; 2000; 86.95 × 6.12 (285.27 × 20.08); M; 14.

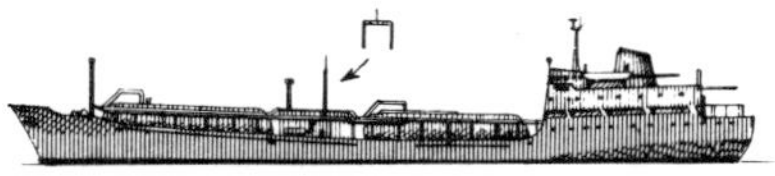

K_2MF H13
66510 HUMBOLDT. Br/Fr 1968; LGC; 5200; 116.9 × 6.5 (383.53 × 21.32); M; 15. Similar: **66511 BERGA** (Ag) ex PASCAL 1970 **66512 LAVOISIER** (Ar).

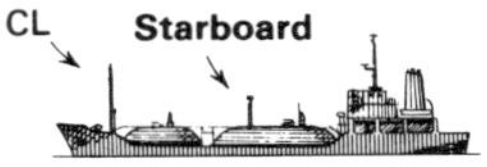

K_2MF H13
66520 KYOSEKI MARU No 3. Ja/Ja 1977; LGC; 1000; 65.28 × 4.56 (214.17 × 14.96); M; 12.5.

K_2MF H13
66530 SANKYO ETHYLENE MARU. Ja/Ja 1974; LGC; 1600; 65.54 × 4.12 (215.03 × 13.52); M; 11.25.

K_2MF H13
66540 KEPLERO. It/FRG 1968; LGC; 1600; 77.78 × 4.65 (255.18 × 15.26); M; 14; ex JOHANN KEPLER 1979; ex KAP ROLAND 1974.

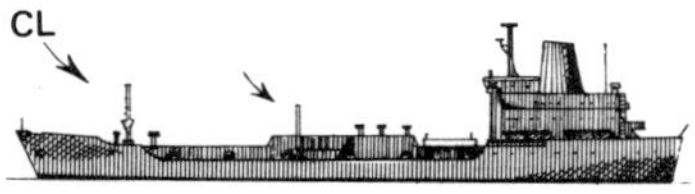

K_2MF H13
66550 NESTEGAS. Fi/No 1973; LGC; 4400; 105.01 × 7.06 (344.52 × 23.16); M; 14.75.

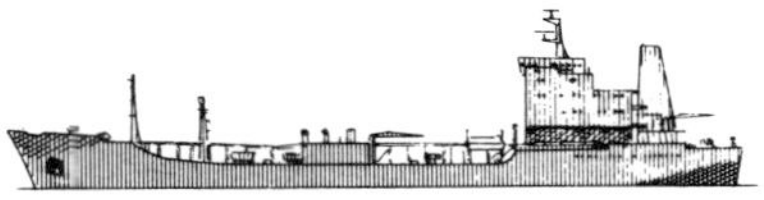

K_2MF H13
66560 NESTEFOX. Fi/No 1977; LGC; 6800; 116.54 × 7.81 (382.35 × 25.62); M; 15.25.

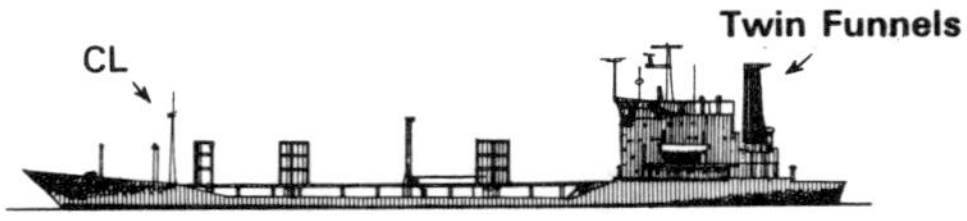

K_2MF H13
66570 THORALBE. Pa/No 1973; Ch; 4800; 129.85 × 7 (426.01 × 22.97); M; 16. Sisters (Pa flag): **66571 THORHEIDE 66572 THORDRACHE 66573 THORODLAND** Possibly similar: **66574 THORHAMER 66575 THORHAVEN.**

● 66577

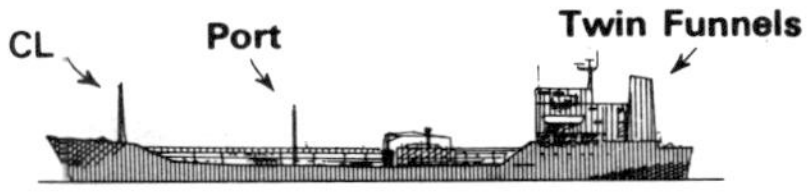

K_2MF H13
66580 AL GHASSANI. Mo/No 1977; LGC; 4100; 102.06 × 7.4 (334.84 × 24.27); M; 14.75.

K_2MF H13
66590 ANNA BROERE. Ne/FRG 1976; Ch; 1600; 82.5×5.74 (270.66×18.83); M; 13.5.

K_2MF H13
66610 BENVENUE. Br/Ne 1974; Ch; 1600; 30.78×5.38 (265.02×17.65); M; 12.75. Sisters (Br flag): **66611 BENCLEUCH 66612 BENMACDHUI.**

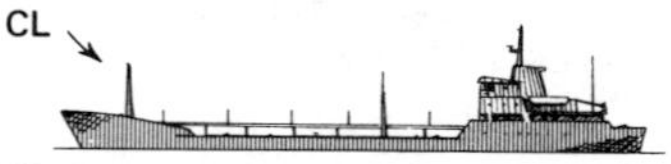

K_2MF H13
66630 MOBIL LUBCHEM. Br/Sp 1973; Tk/Ch; 2100; 93.33×5.36 (306.2×17.59); M; 12.75.

K_2MF H13
66650 GUN. Li/No 1973; Ch; 1600; 82.76×6.06 (271.52×19.88); M; 13; ex STELLA NOVA 1980; ex JOY SAPHIR 1978; ex BOW SAPHIR 1978. Sister: **66651 BIMBO** (Pa) ex ALECTO; ex BOW ALECTO 1978. Possibly similar: **66652 JO SAILOR** (No) ex JOY SAILOR 1980; ex BOW SAILOR 1978.

K_2MF H13
66680 ANDINE. No/No 1965; Tk; 900; 71.05×5.16 (233.1×16.93); M; 12; ex MODENA 1978; ex THUNTANK I.

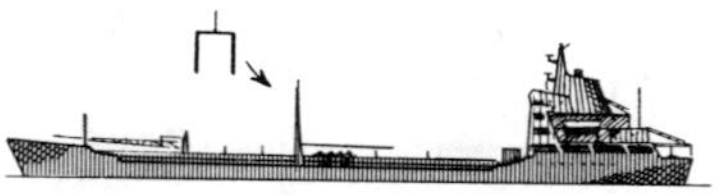

K_2MF H13
66700 PYTHEAS. Mn/It 1972; Tk; 3300; 108.51×4.7 (356×15.42);TSM; 11.5. Sister: **66701 EUTHYMENES** (Fr).

K_2MF H13
66600 DUTCH GLORY. Ne/Ne 1975; Ch; 1400; 80.24×5.42 (263.25×17.78); M; 13.5. Sister: **66601 DUTCH MASTER** (Ne) Possibly similar: **66602 CORRIE BROERE** (Ne).

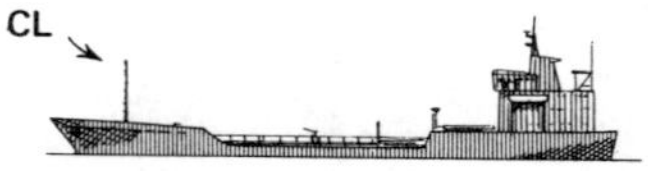

K_2MF H13
66620 ISMARA. Ag/FRG 1978; Tk/WT; 2000; 87.76×5.72 (287.93×18.77); M; 13.5. Sisters (Ag flag): **66621 DAHRA 66622 ZACCAR.**

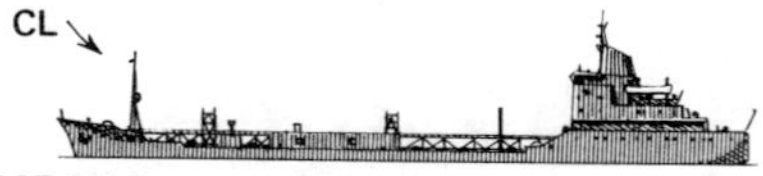

● 66635

K_2MF H13
● **66640 SILVEREAGLE.** Br/Br 1970; Ch; 4100; 108.08×7.32 (354.59×24.02); M; 13.75. Similar (lengthened & may be altered): **66641 SILVEROSPREY** (Br).

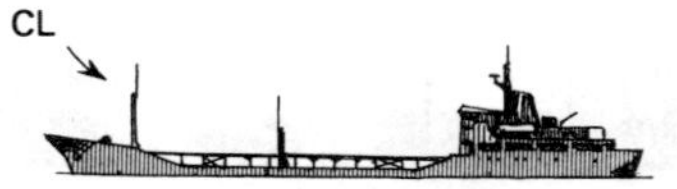

K_2MF H13
66660 PETROSTAR V. Si/FRG 1969; Tk; 2000; 93.91×5.68 (308.1×18.64); M; 12.5; ex SOLHEIM 1976. Sister: **66661 PETROSTAR VI** (Si) ex SOLSTREIF 1976.

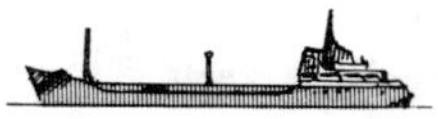

K_2MF H13
66670 BRAENNAREN. Sw/FRG 1965; Tk; 660; 61.63×3.58 (202.21×11.75); M; 11; ex INDIO 1972. Swedish Navy.

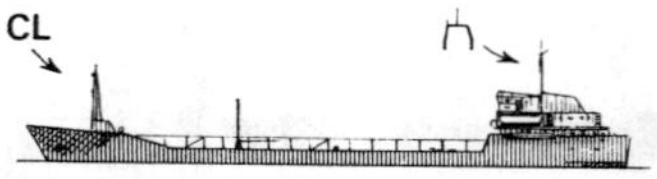

K_2MF H13
66690 VINGASJO. Sw/FRG 1972; Tk; 2000; 96.12×5.96 (315.35×19.55); M; 12; ex TARNSJO 1980.

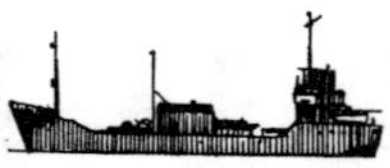

K_2MF H13
66710 SENKAKU MARU. Ja/Ja 1971; LGC; 800; 57×3.51 (187×11.52); M; 10.75. Possible sisters (Ja flag): **66711 SHOKAKU MARU 66712 TONEN ETHLENE MARU.**

K_2MF H13
66720 KINGSABBEY. Br/Br 1966; LGC; 700; 56.7 × 3.43 (186.02 × 11.25); M; 11.5; ex RUDI M 1980; ex TEVIOT.

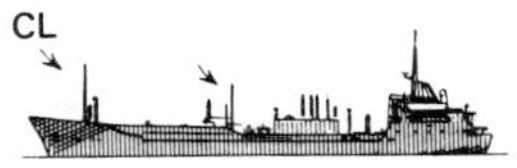

K_2MF H13
● **66730 SUNNY BABY.** No/No 1965; LGC; 1400; 71.18 × 5.51 (233.53 × 18.08); M; 12.5; ex KINGS STAR 1970. Converted cargo ship 1971. Sister: **66731 SUNNY BOY** (No) ex TERESA 1970.

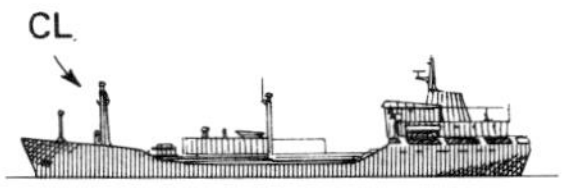

K_2MF H13
66740 NIELS HENRIK ABEL. No/Ne 1973; LGC; 1600; 79.48 × 6.04 (260.76 × 19.82); M; 13.5; launched as ANITA. Sister: **66741 SIGURD JORSALFAR** (No).

K_2MF H13
66750 FORT POINT. Br/Ne 1968; C; 4400; 110.42 × 6.85 (362.27 × 22.47); M; 12.5; ex DUNVEGAN HEAD 1977. Sister: **66751 BEACON POINT** (Br) ex DUNCANSBY HEAD 1977.

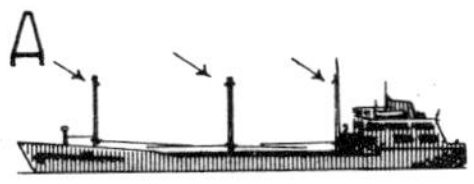

K_2MF H13
66760 SPES. No/De 1971; C; 500; 70.67 × 3.6 (231.86 × 11.81); M; 12; ex METTE BRAVO 1980; ex KIRSTEN BECH 1975; ex CAPTAIN MAGELLAN 1975; ex KIRSTEN BECH 1973.

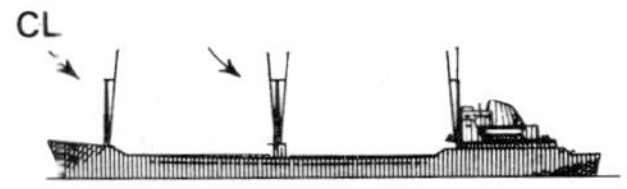

K_2MF H13
66770 STIRLINGBROOK. Br/Br 1970; C; 1600; 86.34 × 5.03 (283.27 × 16.5); M; 12. Sisters (Br flag): **66771 SOLENTBROOK 66772 SOMERSETBROOK 66773 SURREYBROOK 66774 SUSSEXBROOK.**

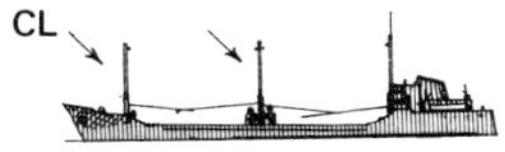

K_2MF H13
66780 ACTUALITY. Br/Br 1966; C; 700; 68.23 × 3.72 (223.85 × 12.1); M; —.

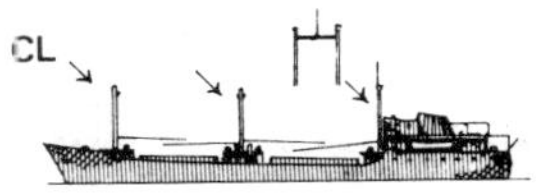

K_2MF H13
66790 ANTARES. Ne/FRG 1966; C; 1300; 73.61 × 5.28 (241.5 × 17.32); M; 12.5; ex DANESEA 1973; ex ANTARES I 1971; ex TANTZEN 1967.

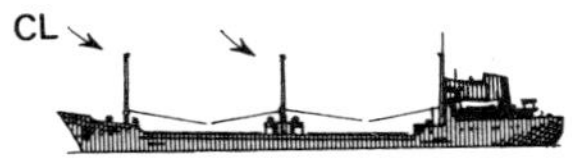

K_2MF H13
66800 ARUNTO. No/DDR 1966; C; 1200; 78.59 × 5.06 (257.84 × 16.6); M; 11.5; ex BRUNTO 1970. Similar: **66801 AVANT** (No) ex BLUE LADY 1974; ex BRUNETTE 1971 **66802 ANGLO** (No) ex JANJA 1974; ex RECTO 1971 **66803 CAREBEKA I** (Ne) ex HANSEATIC 1970 **66804 NORDON** (Sw) ex BLUE MOON 1973; ex BRUNITA 1972 **66805 HOLMON** (Sw) ex AKO 1972 **66806 LE GOELO** (Fr) ex JANNE 1974; ex JOBELLA 1970 **66807 ANTONIO M** (It) ex RETHYMNON 1978; ex JOCEFA 1969 **66808 RIBICONE** (It) ex BENTE SLEIRE 1977; ex FAGERTIND 1976; ex STOKKTIND 1073 **66809 TIBANIA** (It) ex TIBANA 1978; ex JOSUSAN 1970 **66810 DOMENICO PALUMBRO** (It) ex DOUCE FRANCE 1978; ex HANSEAT 1970 **66811 MAIK** (It) ex ALTAIR 1976; ex FRO 1974 **66812 ELVIRA** (It) ex HEEMSKERK 1978; ex HANSA 1970.

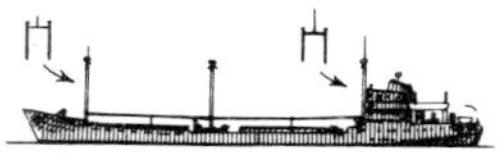

K_2MF H13
66820 EDGAR JOURDAIN. Ca/Ca 1956; C; 1000/1500; 73.26 × 2.79/4.97 (240.34 × 9.15/16.31); M; —; ex GEORGE CROSBIE 1976; ex PIERRE RADISSON 1972; ex MONTCLAIR 1961.

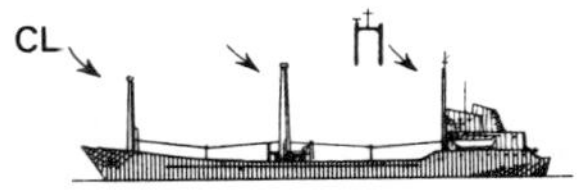

K_2MF H13
66830 NIAGA XXIV. Ia/FRG 1969; C; 700/1500; 75.49 × 4.22/6 (247.6 × 13.84/19.68); M; 14; ex BILBAO ex INGER 1973; ex TRURO 1971; launched as BELE. Sister: **66831 ELDVIK** (Ic) ex HEIDI 1975; ex TASSO 1971.

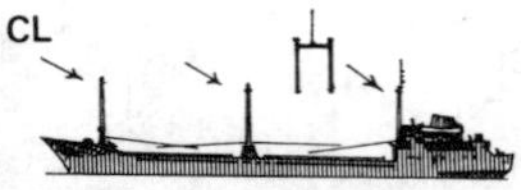

K_2MF H13
66840 JAN. Ne/Ne 1966; C; 500/1100; 73.06 × 3.84/4.27 (239.7 × 12.6/14); M; 12.5. Sisters (Hu built): **66841 DIEGO DE BLASIO** (It) ex AMARI; ex JOERKA 1975 **66842 PELTI** (Gr) ex GABRIELLE 1980; ex RODON 1979; ex JODONNA 1976.

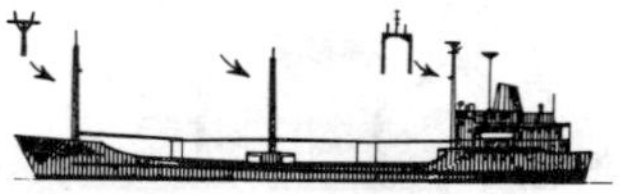

K_2MF H13
66870 COLOMBO VENTURE. Pa/FRG 1970; C; 1700/3300; 100.56 × 5.47/6.76 (329.92 × 17.94/22.17); M; 15.25; ex ASHDOD Sister: **66871 APUS** (Is).

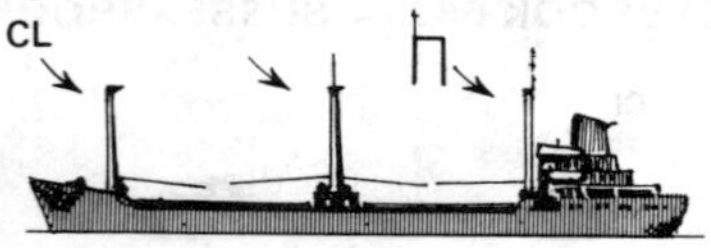

K_2MF H13
66890 FAITH. Sg/Ne 1971; C; 1600/3000; 103.51 × 5.14/6.52 (339.51 × 16.86/21.39); M; 15; ex CHESHIRE FAITH 1979; ex OSTERFEHN 1978. Sister: **66891 GANVIE** (Bi) ex FAROS 1978; launched as WESTERFEHN.

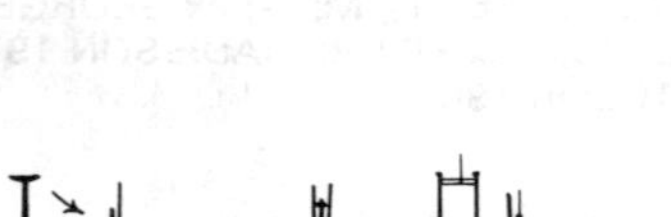

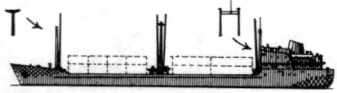

K_2MF H13
● **66900 ILHA DE SAO MIGUEL.** Po/FRG 1970; Con; 2900; 102.42 × 6.24 (336.02 × 20.47); M; —; ex ANJA 1980; ex CHESHIRE CHALLENGE; ex ANJA 1974; launched as NORDERFEHN. Sister: **66901 PACIFIC** (FRG).

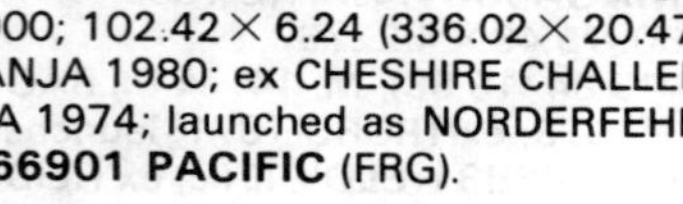

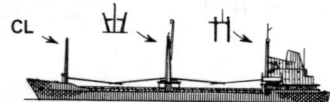

K_2MF H13
66920 NORTHRIDGE. Br/FRG 1973; C/HL; 1600; 96.45 × 5.19 (316.44 × 17.03); M; 14.5; ex CAIRNGORM 1977; converted from general cargo.

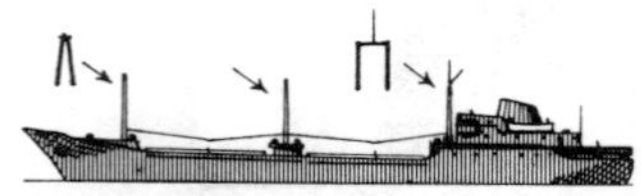

K_2MF H13
66850 GAVILAN. Pa/De 1965; C; 1700/2400; 95.61 × 5.59/6.58 (313.68 × 18.34/21.59); M; 14; ex REYKJAFOSS 1980. Sister: **66851 LEFKAS** (Cy) ex SKOGAFOSS 1980.

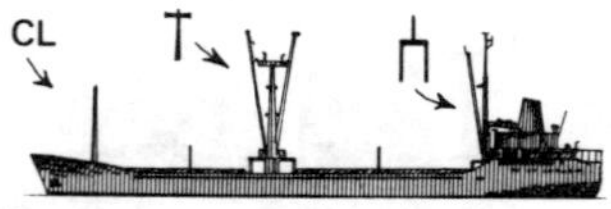

K_2MF H13
● **66860 GOTHIA.** FRG/FRG 1970; C; 1000; 90.81 × 4.77 (297.93 × 15.65); M; 14; launched as TAURUS.

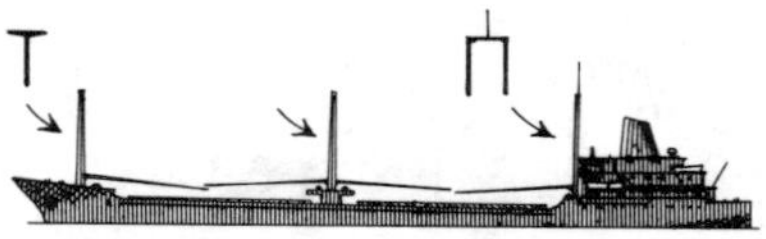

K_2MF H13
66880 AL HODEIDAH. Li/FRG 1970; C; 1900/3900; 113.77 × 6.48 (373.26 × 21.26); M; 15; ex CAROLINA 1978. Lengthened 1973. Similar (lengthened): **66881 FORUM NIUGINI** (Pp) ex AROSIA 1980 Similar (unlengthened): **66882 BURDIGALA** (Fr) ex ARCASEA 1980; ex ISABELLA 1976 **66883 AMANDA 1** (As) ex ANNY 1977; ex AMANDA 1 1976; ex AMANDA 1972; launched as SUDERFEHN **66884 AL BATTANI** (Eg) ex BIRTA ANDREA 1977; ex ANDREA 1977; launched as BIRTA ANDREA **66885 RIGI** (Pa) ex ANITA-ADELE 1980; ex CHESHIRE RESOLVE 1978; ex ANITA 1976; launched as ANITA-ADELE **66886 HEINRICH WESCH** (FRG) ex MASCAREIGNES; ex WESER DISPATCHER.

K_2MF H13
66910 HIRMA. No/No 1978; C; 800/1600; 79.46 × 5.35 (260.7 × 17.55); M; 14.

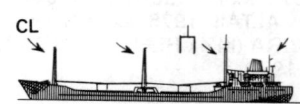

K_2MF H13
66930 ZEIDA. Mo/Sp 1971; C; 700/1600; 84.82 × —/5.67 (278.28 × —/18.6); M; 11; ex VILYA 1975. Sisters: **66931 ZERHOUN** (Mo) ex NENYA 1975 **66932 CELTIC VENTURE** (Br) ex MONKCHESTER 1978; ex WAYNEGATE 1976 Similar (Ne built): **66933 MARIA MONICA** (It) ex MONICA 1976.

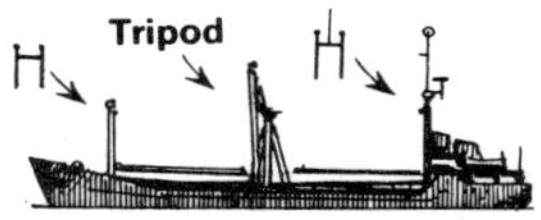

K_2MF H13
66940 AMALI. Si/Ne 1961; C/HL; 600/1200; 80.7× —/4.76 (264.76× —/15.61); M; —; ex AMAL 1980; ex BELLATRIX 1 1977; ex BELLATRIX 1974; launched as MARIJKE IRENE. Lengthened & widened 1970.

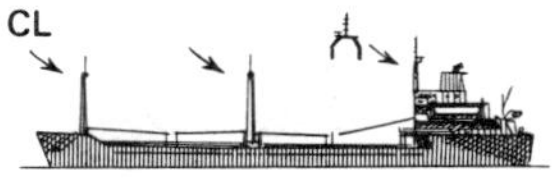

K_2MF H13
66970 BREEKANT. Ne/No 1972; C; 1600; 79.91×5.28 (262.17×17.32); M; 14; ex KEIZERSGRACHT 1979; ex MINI SUN 1973. Sisters: **66971 BREEKADE** (Ne) ex MINI CLOUD 1978 **66972 CEBO MOON** (Sg) ex MINI MOON 1979 **66973 EERBEEK** (Ne) ex MINI SKY 1974 **66974 STROMBEEK** (Ne) ex MINI STAR 1973.

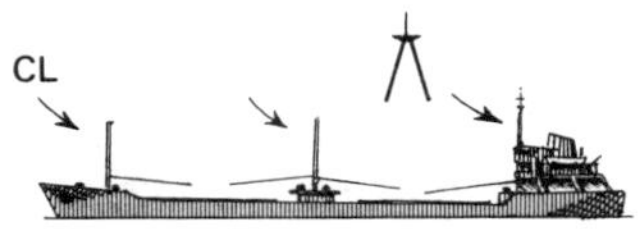

K_2MF H13
66990 MARIANN. FRG/Ma 1972; C; 1600; 91.37×5.12 (299.77×16.8); M; 14. Sister: **66991 THERESE** (Cy).

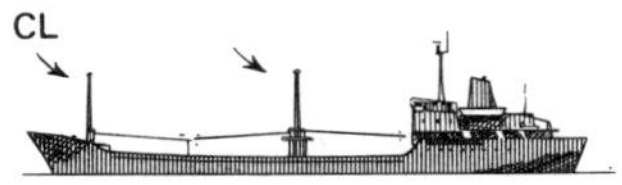

K_2MF H13
★67010 ANTON GUBARYEV. Ru/Rm 1974; C; 1200/2100; 88.75×4.15/5.2 (291.17×13.62/17.06); M; 13. Sisters (Ru flag): **★67011 DZHEMS BANKOVICH ★67012 GRISHA PODOBEDOV ★67013 KHENDRIK KUYVAS ★67014 LIDA DEMESH ★67015 MALDIS SKREYA ★67016 MARAT KOZLOV ★67017 NADE RIBAKOVAYTE ★67018 NYURA KIZHEVATOVA ★67019 PECHORA ★67020 PETYA KOVALYENKO ★67021 PETYA SHITIKOV ★67022 PINEGA ★67023 RICHARDAS BUKAUSKAS ★67024 TANYA KARPINSKAYA ★67025 TURGAY ★67026 VALYA KURAKINA ★67027 VANYA KOVALYEV ★67028 VASHA GORDIYENKO ★67029 VASYA STABROVSKIY ★67030 VASYA KURKA ★67031 VITYA NOVITSKIY ★67032 YUNYY PARTIZAN.**

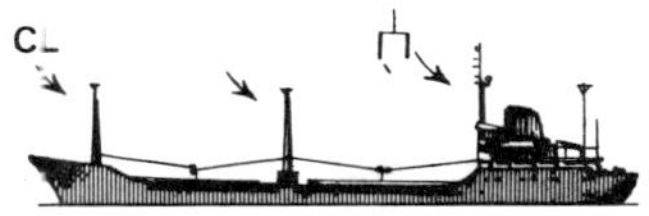

K_2MF H13
★66950 KAPRIJE. Ys/FRG 1968; C; 2600; 95.81×6.36 (314.34×20.87); M; 12.25; ex LEKNES 1978. Sisters (Ys flag): **★66951 BOSUT** ex RAKNES 1977 **★66952 CIKOLO** ex TINNES 1978 **★66953 ROGOZNICA** ex VIGSNES 1978 (It flag): **66954 MARIA DORMIO** ex TELNES 1979 **66955 PIETRO** ex ALTNES 1978 **66956 BEATRICE** ex KORSNES 1977 **66957 VISPY** ex GARNES 1978 (No flag): **66958 ISNES** ex FRINES 1977; ex FRITRE 1973.

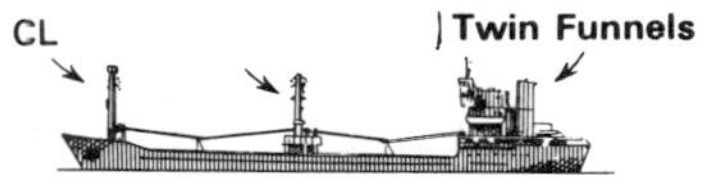

K_2MF H13
★66980 JAROSLAW. Pd/Pd 1979; C; 1600; 84×5.65 (275.59×18.54); M; 14; Probably **'B-431'** type.

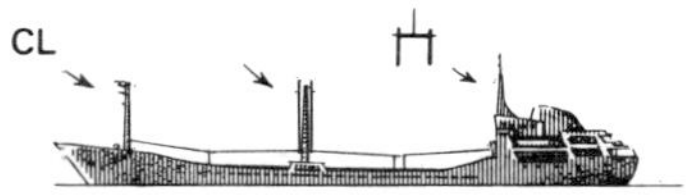

K_2MF H13
● **67000 BECKUMERSAND.** FRG/FRG 1970; C; 1000/2000; 92.21×4.54/5.99 (302.52×14.89/19.65); M; 15.5. Sister: **67001 BOSTONSAND** (FRG) **67002 BURHAVERSAND** (FRG) **67003 STOLLHAMMERSAND** (FRG) **67004 ANDY'S PRIDE** (Sg) ex LEO PRIDE 1980; ex MAROCSAND 1977 **67005 SEEFELDERSAND** (FRG)—May have KP amidships removed.

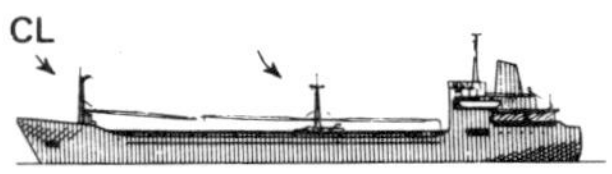

K_2MF H13
● **67040 SVEALAND.** FRG/FRG 1970; C; 1000; 87.61×5.29 (287.43×17.35); M; 14.5; ex CONTI SYRIA 1980; ex SVEALAND 1980; ex HELGA RUSS 1979; ex SVEALAND 1977; ex ROYAL ENTERPRISE 1975; launched as SVEALAND.

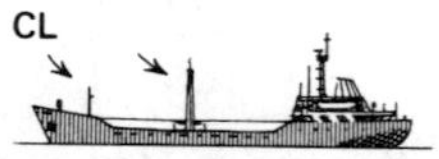

K_2MF H13
● ⋆**67050 HAJNOWKA.** Pd/Pd 1971; C; 800; 59.82 × 4.2 (196.26 × 13.78); M; 11.5. **"B457"** type. Sisters (Pd flag): ⋆**67051 BARLINEK** ⋆**67052 RUCIANE.**

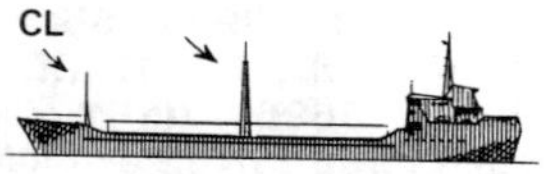

K_2MF H13
67070 FRISIAN TRADER. Ne/Ne 1976; C; 1600; 79.81 × 5.44 261.84 × 17.85); M; 13.

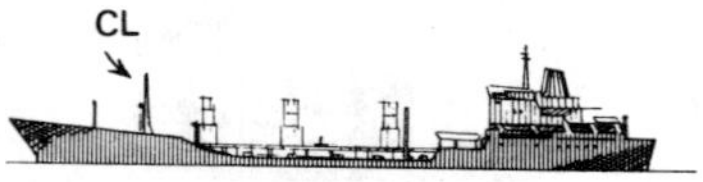

K_2MF H13
67090 LA BAHIA. Br/No 1972; Ch; 1600; 100.72 × 5.89 (330.45 × 19.32); M; 16; ex WAVEMARK 1974. Sister: **67091 LA FALDA** (Br) ex SUNMARK 1974.

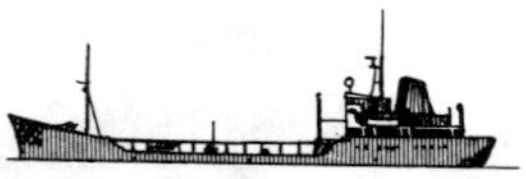

K_2MF H13
67110 MANITOU. FRG/FRG 1968; Tk; 1000; 76.92 × 4.67 (252.36 × 15.32); M; 12. Sisters (FRG flag): **67111 WINNETOU 67112 YUMA.**

K_2MF H13
67130 TORA. No/Ne 1968; Tk; 500; 72.98 × 3.57 (239.44 × 11.71); M; 12.

K_2MF H13
67150 BOREA. Pa/Sw 1971; Tk; 1600; 86.42 × 5.26 (283.53 × 17.26); M; 12.

K_2MF H13
67170 ESSI BALTIC. No/No 1977; TB/Ch; 1500; 69.73 × 5.4 (228.77 × 17.72); M; 11.5; ex JOHOT 1979. Sister: **67171 ESSI CORAL** (No) ex JOHERO 1979.

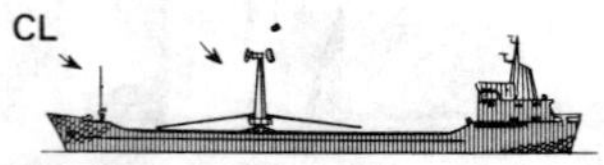

K_2MF H13
67060 KIRSTEN SMITS. Ne/De 1976; C; 1600; 84.31 × 6.32 (276.6 × 20.73); M; 13. Probable sister: **67061 MARINUS SMITS** (Ne).

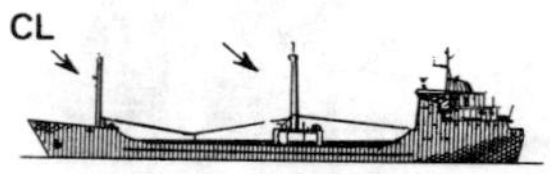

K_2MF H13
67080 HOOP. Ne/Ne 1978; C; 1500; 78.67 × 5.04 (258.1 × 16.54); M; 12.

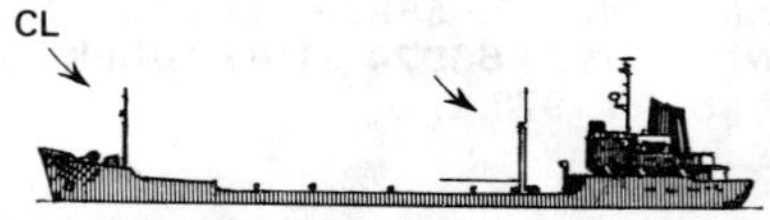

K_2MF H13
67100 DANGULF MAERSK. De/De 1965; Tk; 3900; 112.68 × 6.1 (369.68 × 20.01); M; 13.5. Sister: **67101 SVENGULF MAERSK** (De).

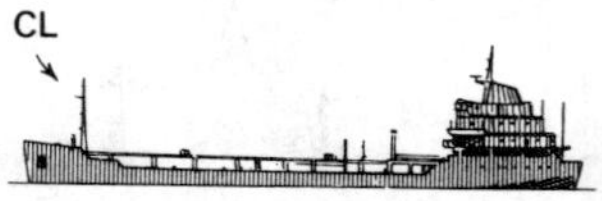

K_2MF H13
67120 THUNTANK 1. Sw/Sw 1973; Ch; 3700; 107.19 × 6.7 (351.67 × 21.98); M; 12.

K_2MF H13
67140 CAMPOTEJAR. Sp/Sp 1967; Tk; 1800; 76.91 × 5.13 (261.18 × 16.83); M; 14. Sisters (Sp flag): **67141 CAMPOSALINAS 67142 CAMPOLONGO.**

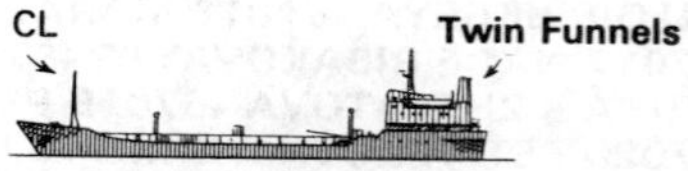

K_2MF H13
67160 HECHT V. FRG/Sw 1970; Tk; 1100; 75.29 × 3.51 (247.01 × 11.52); M; 12.5; ex TRANSTANK 1972; ex CONTANK LUBECK 1972. Similar: **67161 THUNTANK 10** (Sw) ex CREDO 1974.

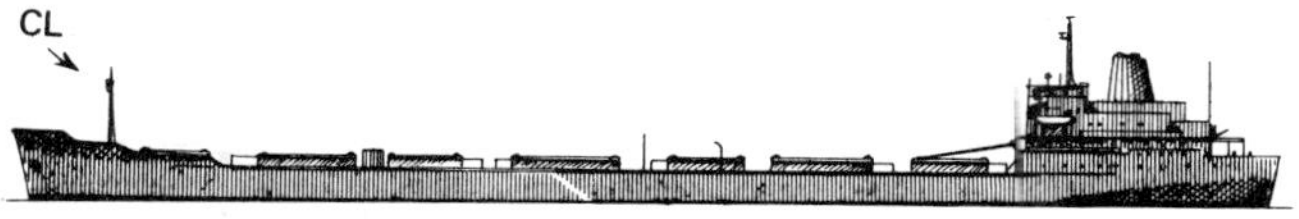

K_2MF H13
67180 OCEAN GIRL. Li/Sw 1968; B; 22700; 200.24 × 11.17 (656.96 × 36.65); M; 15.5; ex GRETA THULIN.

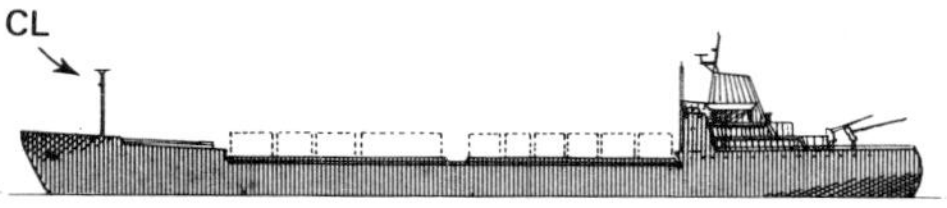

K_2MF H13
67190 NEW PENGUIN. Sg/Br 1965; Con; 6800; 141.94 × 8.09 (465.68 × 26.54); M; 15; ex ALALANTA 1980; ex ZIM ATALANTA 1980; ex ATALANTA; ex C. P. AMBASSADOR 1974; ex BEAVEROAK 1970; Converted from general cargo 1969. Lengthened 1970.

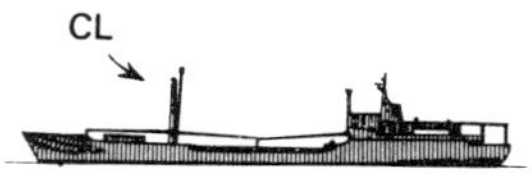

K_2MF H13
67200 CHESLEY A. CROSBIE. Ca/Ca 1964; R; 2000; 77.12 × 5.12 (253.02 × 16.78); M; 13.5; Helicopter deck aft. Sister: **67201 TERRA NOVA** (Ca) ex SIR JOHN CROSBIE 1980.

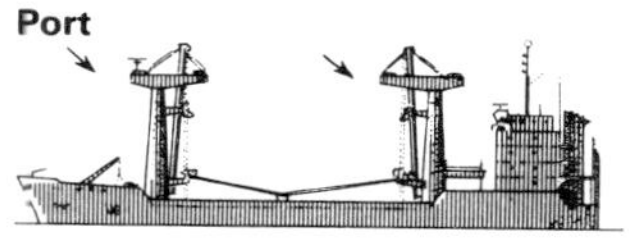

K_2MF H13
67210 STAHLECK. FRG/FRG 1977; RoC/HL; 3500; 91.5 × 5.17 (300.2 × 16.96); TSM; 13.5. Similar (US flag): **67211 JOHN HENRY 67212 PAUL BUNYAN.**

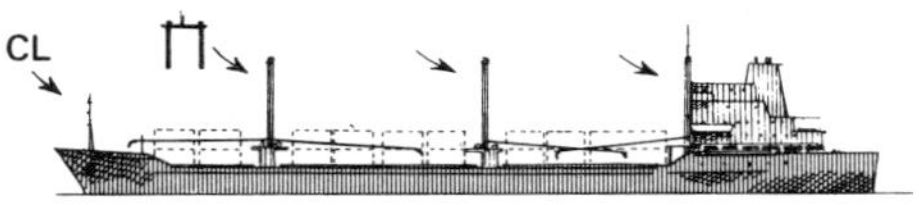

K_2MF H13
● **67220 ESTEBLICK.** Sg/Ja 1978; C; 6400; 129.32 × 7.83 (424.3 × 25.7); M; 15; ex B M I EXPORTER 1978. Similar: **67221 ATALANTA II** (Pa) ex ATALANTA **67222 GERMANIC** (Pa) **67223 IMPALA** (Pa) Probably Similar: **67224 ADRIA 1** (Pa) ex NAXOS I 1979; ex RENATE WUNSCHE 1978; ex NORDWELLE 1977 **67225 HILDA WESCH** (Cy); Launched as BLUE SOVEREIGN.

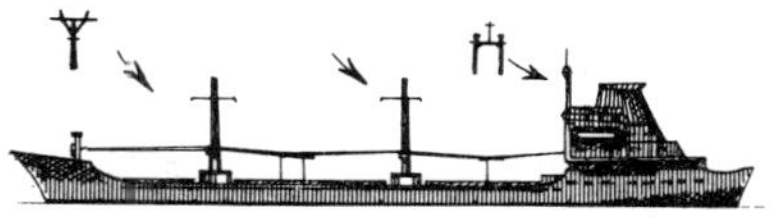

K_2MF H13
⋆67230 FU SHUN CHENG. RC/FRG 1969; C; 3400/5400; 117.35 × 6.68/7.06 (385.01 × 21.92/23.16); M; 17; ex JORG KRUGER 1981; ex CAPARNAUTI 1975; ex JORG KRUGER 1974. Sister: **⋆67231 PING XIANG CHENG** (RC) ex BRITTA KRUGER 1977.

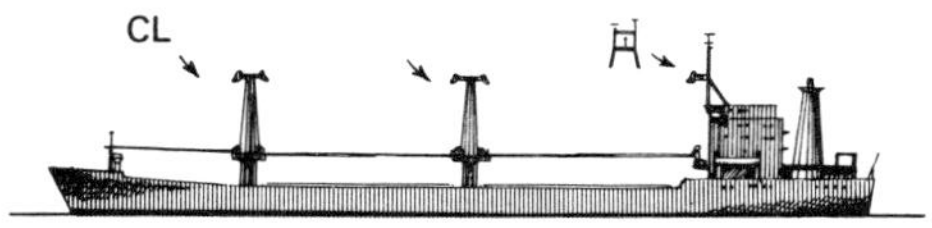

K_2MF H13
67240 SLOMAN NEREUS. FRG/FRG 1977; C; 4400/7400; 129.52 × 6.81/8.06 (424.93 × 22.34/26.44); M; 16.75; ex TABUCO 1980; ex SLOMAN NEREUS 1980; ex CAROL NEREUS 1980; ex SLOMAN NEREUS 1978; **'CL-10'** type. Sisters (FRG flag): **67241 SLOMAN NAJADE 67242 STUBBENHUK.**

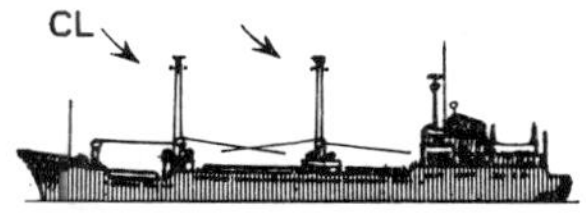

K_2MF H13
67250 KRANTOR. Gr/Ne 1964; C; 1400/2300; 87.89 × —/6.31 (288.35 × —/20.7); M; 13; ex ASTRA 1980; ex RAHEL 1978. Sister: **67251 BRANT POINT** (Br) ex ORAN 1978; ex DEVORA 1978.

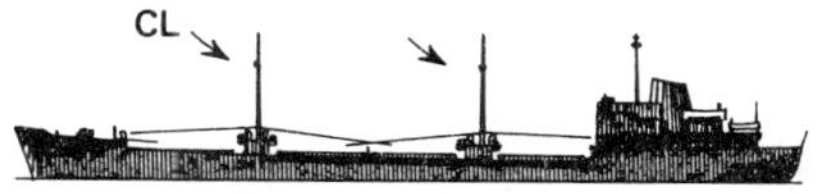

K_2MF H13
67260 THOROLD. Ca/Br 1962; B; 5700; 125.05 × 7.58 (410.27 × 24.87); M; —; ex GOSFORTH 1972.

K_2MF H13
67270 DAYAKA DUA. Ia/Ia 1965; C; 3300; 100.89 × 6.35 (331.— × 20.83); M; 12; ex MIURA MARU 1972.

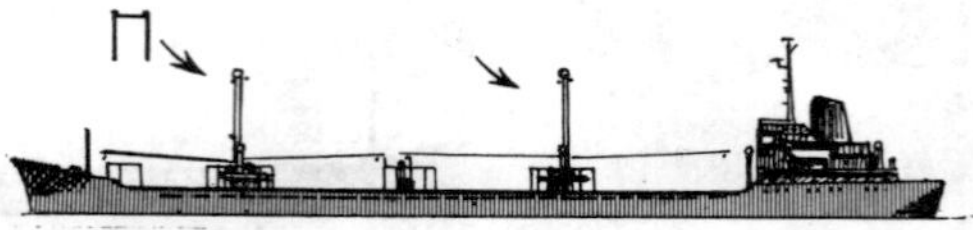

K_2MF H13
67280 GOLDEN VENTURE. Li/Ja 1971; B; 10100; 148.42 × 8.99 (486.94 × 29.49); M; 14.75. Possibly Similar (some may have deck cranes): **67281 FIDES** (Li) **67282 HSING MAY** (Li) ex NATIONA 1980 **67283 BETTY** (Gr) ex SAMMI No I 1981 **67284 SINCERE No 3** (Li) **67285 HARNGJIN** (Ko) ex DAISHOWA VENTURE 1978.

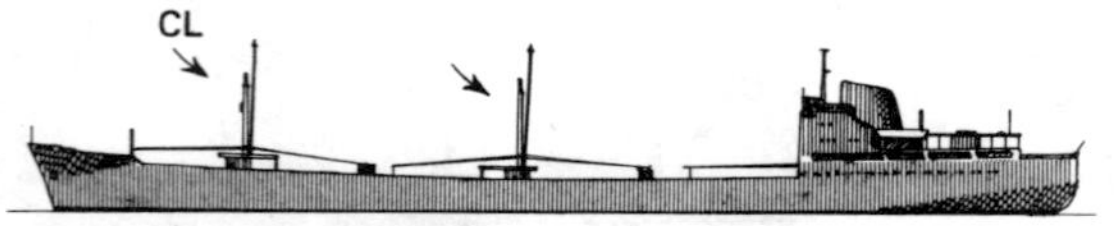

K_2MF H13
67290 JALATARANG. In/Br 1963; C; 8800/12100; 164.57 × 8.48/9.51 (539.93 × 27.82/31.2); M; 15; ex BENTE BROVIG 1969.

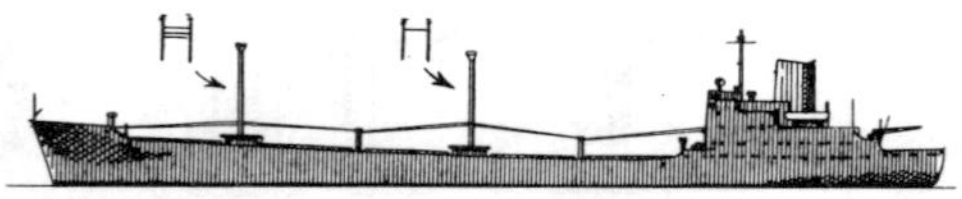

K_2MF H13
67300 AGIOS NECTARIOS. Gr/FRG 1958; C; 6700/9100; 145.35 × 8.3/9.4 (476.87 × 27.23/30.83); M; 13.25; ex SAN JOHN 1973; ex HINDUSTAN 1968.

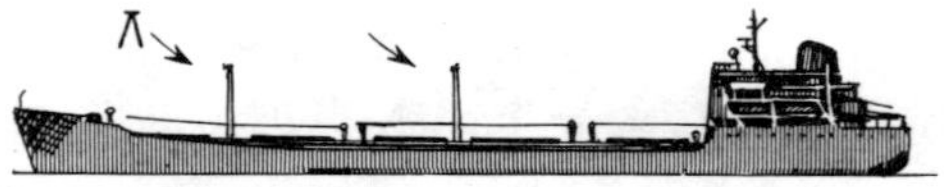

K_2MF H13
67310 NICOLAOS CH. Gr/Fr 1960; C; 6900/9400; 141.18 × 8.4/9.56 (463.19 × 27.56/31.36); M; —; ex APOSTOLOS M III 1980; ex KAVO GROSSOS 1979; ex TRIAENA 1974; ex LAMBROS M FATSIS 1972; ex LA HORTENSIA 1968. Similar: **⋆67311 GEORGI BENKOVSKI** (Bu) ex LA ESTANCIA 1963 Similar (with goalposts): **67312 DIRPHYS II** (Gr) ex ARMONIA 1980.

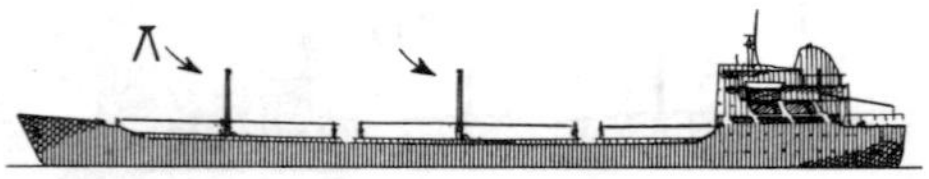

K_2MF H13
67320 THEOTOKOS. Gr/Fr 1961; C; 7000/9400; 141.18 × —/9.56 (463.19 × —/31.36); M; 14; ex STAR FLOWER; ex DAHLIA 1978. Sister: **67321 DESPINA** (Gr) ex STAR FISH; ex NURITH 1978.

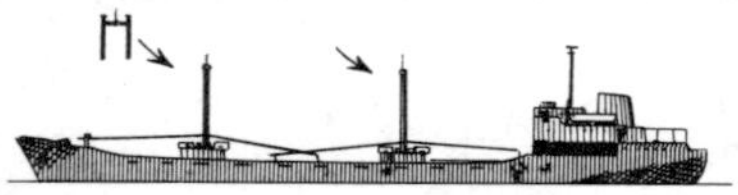

K_2MF H13
67330 KAI YUNG. Tw/Ja 1963; C; 4000; 109.71 × 6.51 (359.94 × 21.36); M; 12; ex YIN KIM 1973. Similar: **67331 SINGAPORE VOYAGER** (Sg) ex MOCK HWA 1980; ex TOSHO MARU 1971.

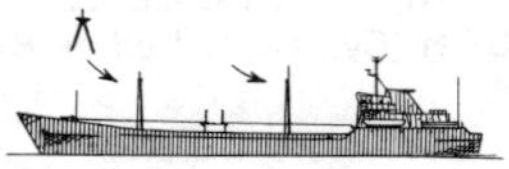

K_2MF H13
⋆67340 BATALLA DE STA. CLARA. Cu/Fi 1975; R; 500/1300; 74.12 × —/4.71 (243.18 × —/15.45); M; 14. Sister: **⋆67341 BATALLA DE YAGUAJAY** (Cu).

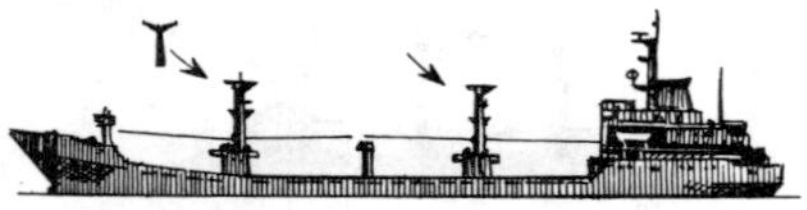

K_2MF H13
⋆67350 ROSTOK. Ru/DDR 1973; C; 2900/4500; 117.79 × 5.8/6.92 (386.45 × 19.03/22.7); M; 16.5; **"POSEIDON"** class. Sisters (Ru flag): **⋆67351 CHITA ⋆67352 KHASAN ⋆67353 NOVOCHERKASSK ⋆67354 RYSHKANY ⋆67355 RUSHANY ⋆67356 RUDNYY ⋆67357 ROMNY ⋆67358 RUBEZHNOYE ⋆67359 RZHEV ⋆67360 RAKHOV ⋆67361 REUTOV ⋆67362 RATNO ⋆67363 RADOMYSHI ⋆67364 RYAZAN ⋆67365 ROSLAVL ⋆67366 RYBINSK ⋆67367 MAGO.**

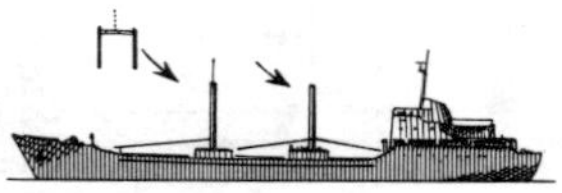

K_2MF H13
● **67380 HORUS.** Sp/Sp 1969; R; 1800; 84 × 5 (275.59 × 16.4); M; —.

K_2MF H13
67390 SHELL CRAFTSMAN. Br/Br 1968; Tk; 1500; 75.95 × 4.67 (249.18 × 15.32); M; 14.5; ex ARDROSSAN 1979.

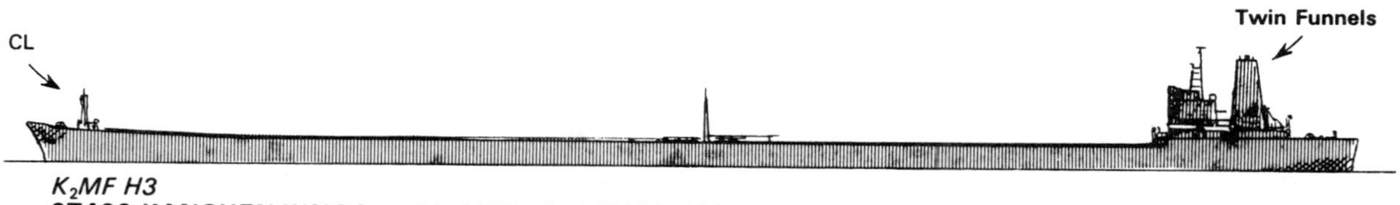

K_2MF H3
67400 KANCHENJUNGA. In/Ys 1975; Tk; 140000; 332.39 × 21.79 (1090.52 × 71.49); TSM; 17. Sister: **67401 KOYALI** (In) Probable Sister: **67402 OLOIBIRI** (Ng).

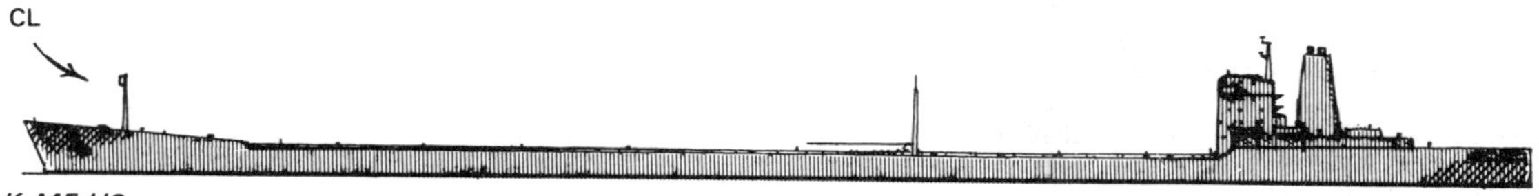

K_2MF H3
67410 NORBIRD. No/No 1971; Tk; 109500; 327.72 × 20.35 (1075.2 × 66.77); T; 16; ex RAILA 1977. Sister (No flag): **67411 NORBAY** ex RANJA 1977 Possibly Similar: **67412 BEAUMARIS 67413 AURELIAN.**

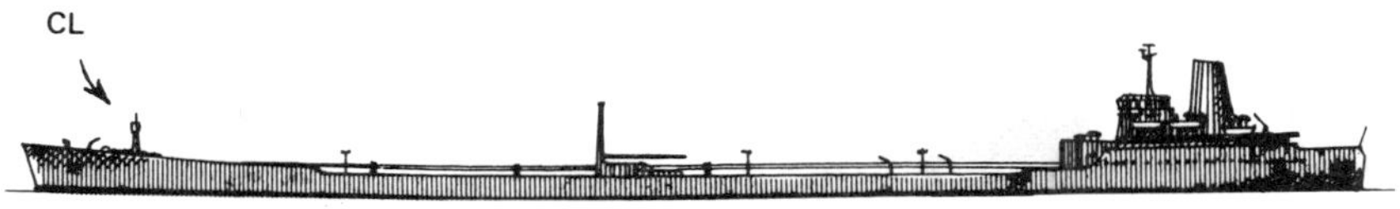

K_2MF H3
67420 FINNY. Fi/Sw 1967; Tk; 52900; 258.53 × 15.29 (848.19 × 50.16); M; 16; ex SYMRA 1975. Sister **67421 FANNY** (Fi) ex RUTH 1975.

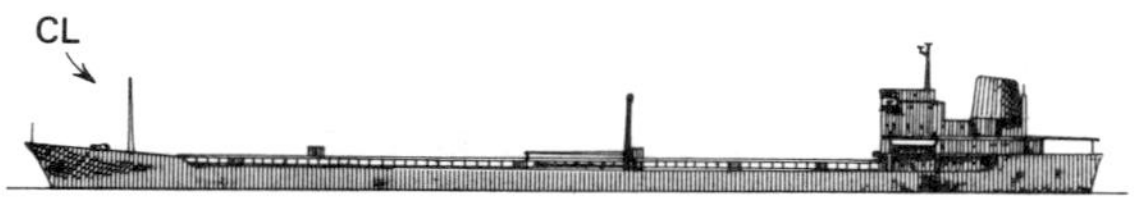

K_2MF H3
67430 SAUCON. Li/Br 1969; Tk; 14800; 169.78 × 9.75 (557.02 × 31.99); M; 15.5; ex LAURELWOOD 1975. Sisters: **67431 SHABONEE** (Br) ex SEA GRIFFIN 1974 **67432 NAND KAVITA** (In) ex CAPTAIN X KYRIAKOU 1980; ex DAFNI C 1978; ex HOLLYWOOD 1977.

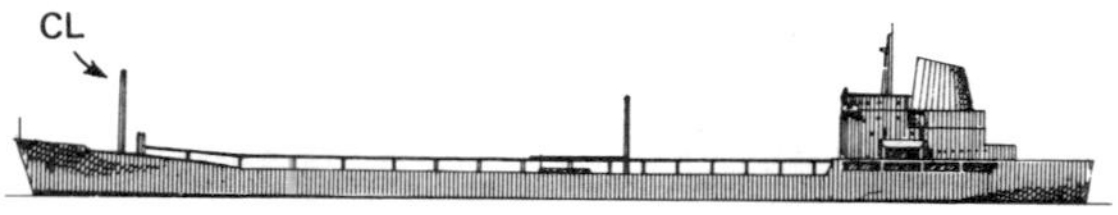

K_2MF H3
67440 BALDER LONDON. Br/Br 1975; Tk; 19000; 170.69 × 11.83 (560 × 38.81); M; 16.25; ex HUDSON PROGRESS; **'STAT 32'** type.

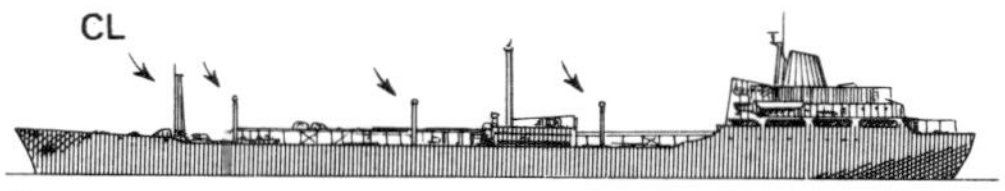

K_2MF H3
67450 LUIGI CASALE. It/It 1966; LGC; 10900; 150.48 × 8.86 (493.7 × 29.06); M; 16; ex CAPELLA 1973; ex FRANKLIN 1967; ex CAPELLA 1967; Launched as BENJAMIN FRANKLIN. Sister: **67451 PYTHAGORE** (Pa) ex ARQUIMEDES 1975.

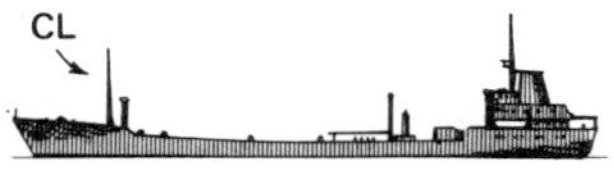

K_2MF H3
67460 BRAS. No/No 1976; Ch; 2000; 92.79 × 6.8 (304.43 × 22.31); M; 13. Sister (No flag): **67461 BRAVUR** Similar: **67462 BRAGD.**

K_2MF H3
67470 DANISH ARROW. De/De 1976; LGC; 500; 66.5 × 3.27 (218.17 × 10.71); M; 12.5. Sister: **67471 DANISH DART** (De).

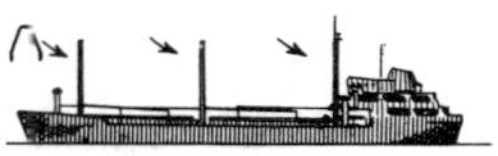

K_2MF H3
● **67480 LILLGAARD.** Fi/De 1970; C; 500; 70.77 × 3.66 (232.19 × 12.01); M; —; ex GERDA BECH 1973. Similar: **67481 INGE BECH** (De) **67482 SPES** (No) ex METTE BRAVO 1980; ex KIRSTEN BECH 1975; ex CAPTAIN MAGELLAN 1975; ex KIRSTEN BECH 1973.

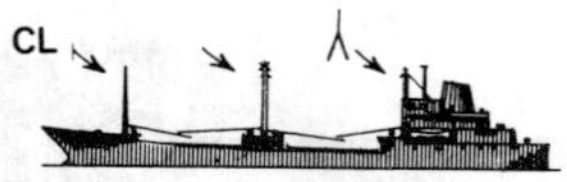

K_2MF H3

● **67490 MORESBY CHIEF.** Pp/FRG 1972; C; 900/1600; 81.01 × 4.4/5.49 (265.78 × 14.43/18.01); M; 13; ex PETRA; ex LINDINGER BRILLIANT 1978. Sisters: **67491 ANCHANA** (Sg) ex LINDINGER EMERALD 1977 **67492 ATLANTISCH** (Ne) ex LINDINGER FACET 1978 **67493 ZARKA** (Qt) ex MERCANDIAN CAIX 1980; ex LINDINGER CORAL 1978 **67494 MOR** (Br) ex LINDINGER AMBER 1978 **67495 SANTO ANTAO** (CV) ex LINDINGER DIAMOND 1977 Possible Sisters: **67496 ILHA DE COMO** (CV) ex LINDINGER HYACINTH 1978 **67497 NAUTILUS** (Ne) ex LINDINGER GOLD 1978.

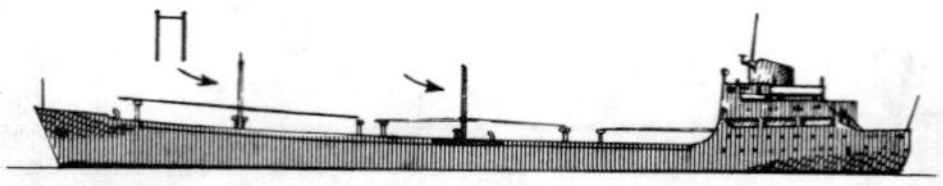

K_2MF H3

67500 GLORY. Pa/Fr 1956; C; 9200; 138.39 × 8.46 (454.04 × 27.76); M; 13; ex PANAIOT HITOV 1980; ex SAPPHIRE 1970; ex LA PRADERA 1965.

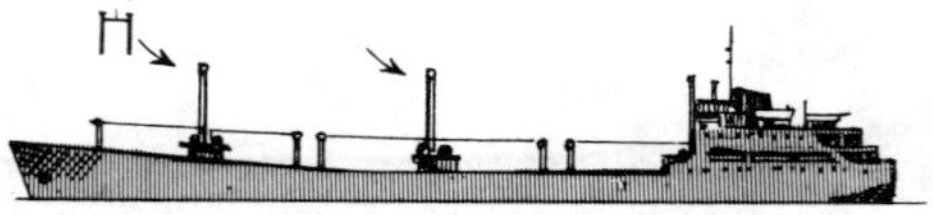

K_2MF H3

67510 MARIANNINA. Gr/Sp 1958; C; 6400; 138.41 × 9.49 (454.1 × 31.14); M; 14; ex LA SELVA 1967.

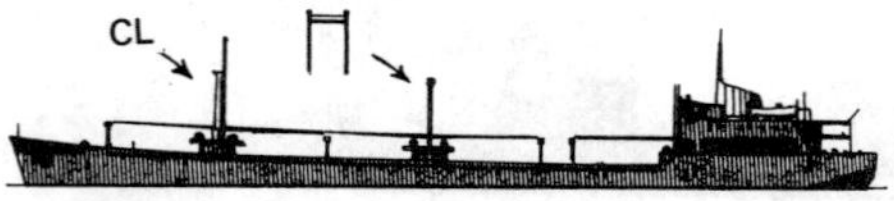

K_2MF H3

● **67520 HWA CHU.** Sg/Fr 1957; C; 6600/9100; 152 × —/9.01 (498.69 × —/29.56); M; 14; ex STEENWIJK 1968.

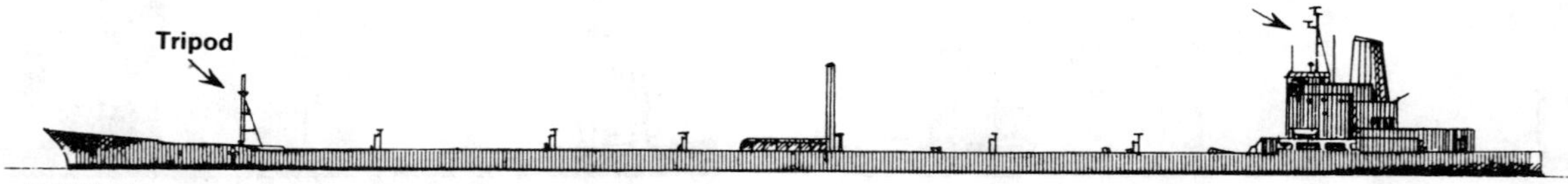

K_2MF H

67530 AGIP SICILIA. It/It 1972; Tk; 126100; 348.32 × 20.02 (1142.78 × 65.68); M; 16. Sisters (It flag): **67531 AGIP SARDEGNA 67532 PARAGGI** ex SANT' AMBROGIO 1978 **67533 NIRVANA** ex OCEANIA 1979 Possible Sisters: **67534 AGIP ABRUZZO 67535 AGIP CAMPANIA 67536 AGIP LAZIO 67537 AGIP MARCHE 67538 NAI MARIO PERRONE 67539 NAI DI STEFANO 67540 NAI MATTEINI 67541 NAI ROCCO PIAGGIO 67542 PRIMAROSA 67543 RITINA 67544 VOLERE**

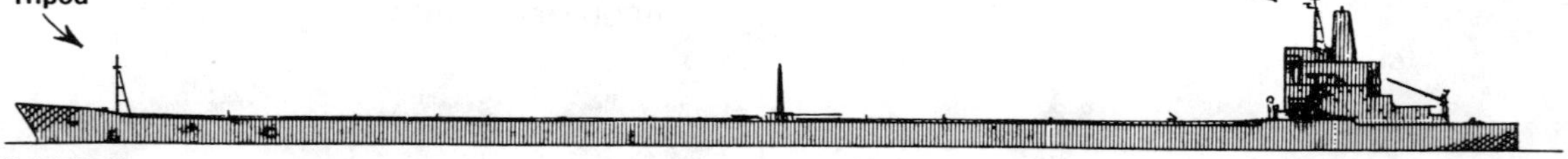

K_2MFC H

67550 MELPO LEMOS. Li/FRG 1971; Tk; 113800; 347.81 × 19.96 (1141.1 × 65.55); T; 16. Sisters: **67551 CHRYSANTHY M LEMOS** (Li) **67552 IRENE LEMOS** (Li) **67553 MICHAEL C LEMOS** (Gr).

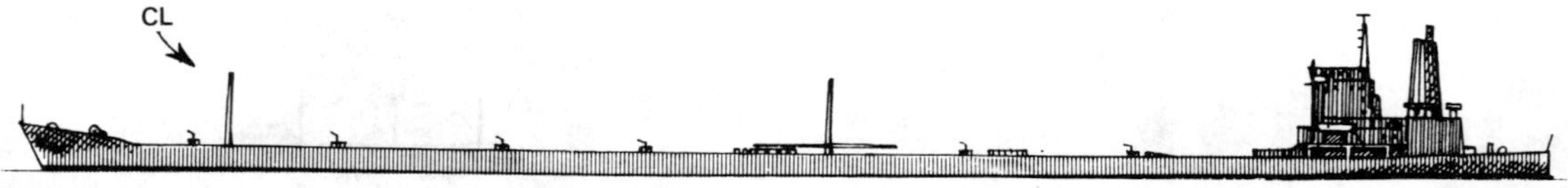

K_2MFC H

67560 NORDIC CLANSMAN. Br/Br 1974; Tk; 138700; 344.43 × 20.77 (1130.02 × 68.14); T; 15.5; Aft section launched as NAESS SCOTSMAN. Sisters: **67561 CAST RORQUAL** (Br) ex NORDIC COMMANDER 1980 **67562 WORLD SCORE** (Li); Aft section launched as CARTSDYKE GLEN **67563 WORLD SCHOLAR** (Li).

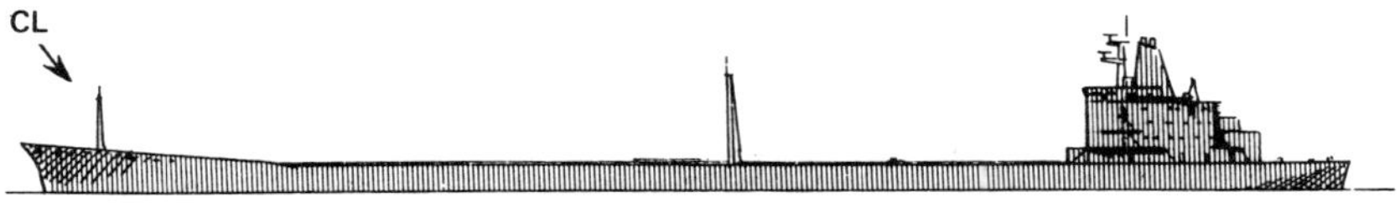

K_2MFC H
67570 ST VINCENT. Sg/Fr 1976; Tk; 44500; 250.53 × 14.25 (820.96 × 46.75); M; 16. Sisters: **67571 ST MARCOS** (Sg) ex DOMINANT 1977 **67572 TOURAINE** (Fr) ex CHANGI STAR 1980; ex ST RAPHAEL 1977; ex ADAMANT 1977.

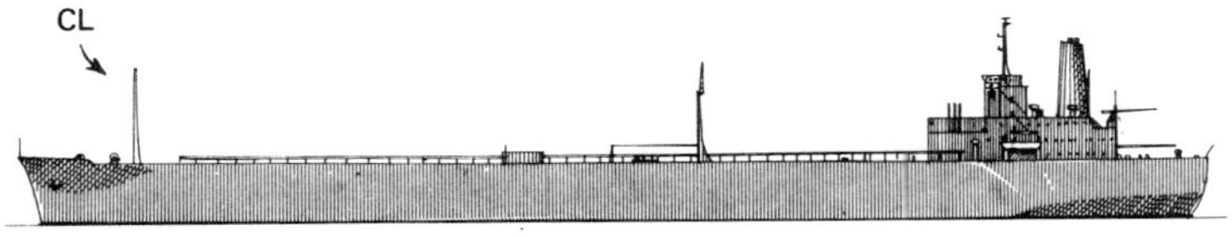

K_2MFC H
67580 YUSHO. Li/Ja 1971; LGC; 47800; 227.03 × 11.51 (744.85 × 37.76); M; 15.75; ex YUSHO MARU 1978.

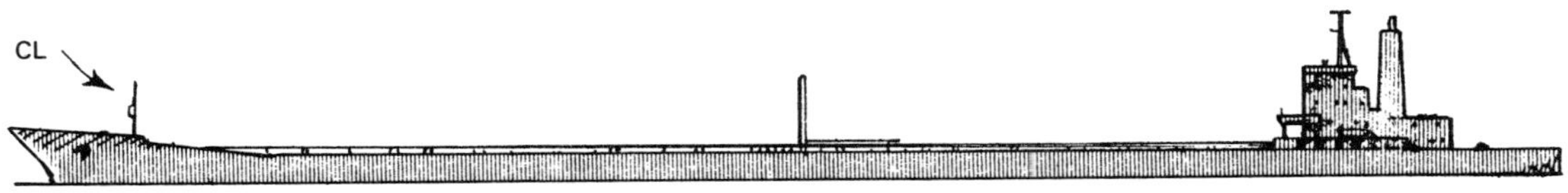

K_2MFC H1
67590 TIGRE. No/No 1974; Tk; 140300; 347.84 × 22.14 (1141.2 × 72.63); T; 15.5.

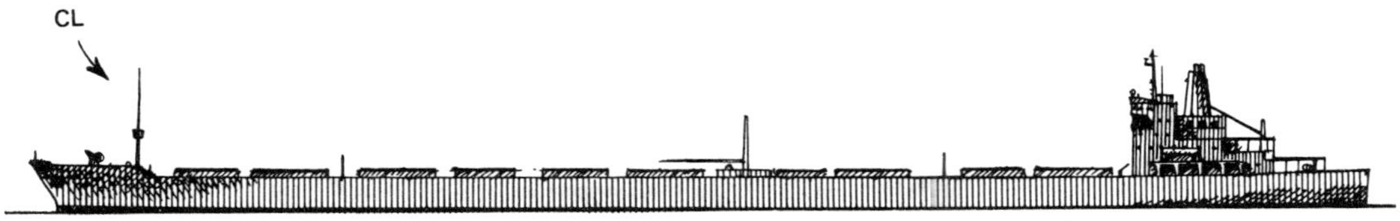

K_2MFC H
67600 HOEGH HOOD. No/Ja 1973; OO; 129000; 326.04 × 20.49 (1069.68 × 67.22); T; 15.5. Sisters: **67601 HOEGH HILL** (No) **67602 WORLD TRUTH** (Li) ex LA LOMA 1978.

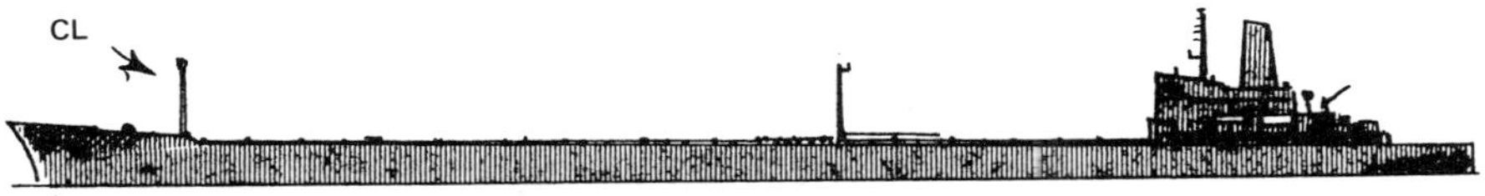

K_2MFC H1
67610 AVIN OIL TRADER. Gr/Sw 1968; Tk; 51100; 277.05 × 14.72 (908.95 × 48.24); M; 16; ex ALEXANDROS M 1979; ex FRUEN 1975; ex SOLSTAD 1973.

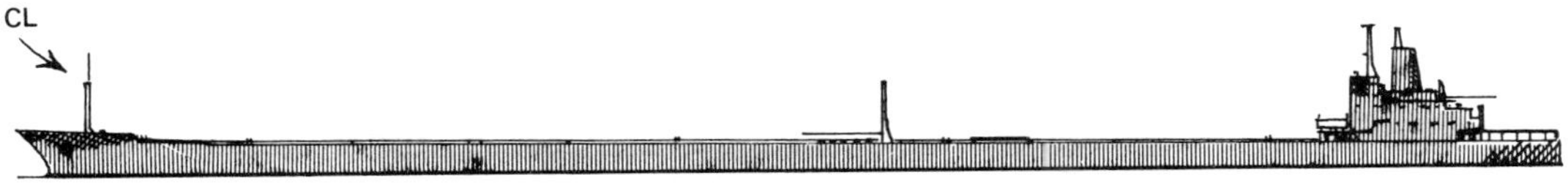

K_2MFC H1
67620 NORBEGA. No/Sw 1971; Tk; 113500; 332.24 × 20.65 (1090 × 67.74); T; 16; ex SYNIA 1977.

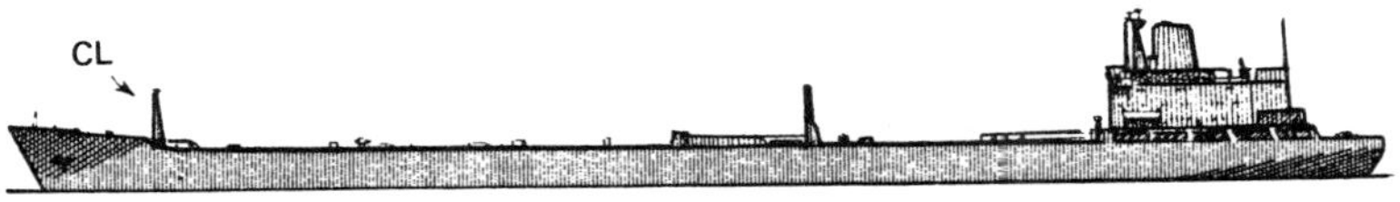

K_2MFC H1
67630 AMANDA MILLER. Au/Au 1971; Tk; 39100; 239.28 × 13.17 (785.04 × 43.21); M; 16.5.

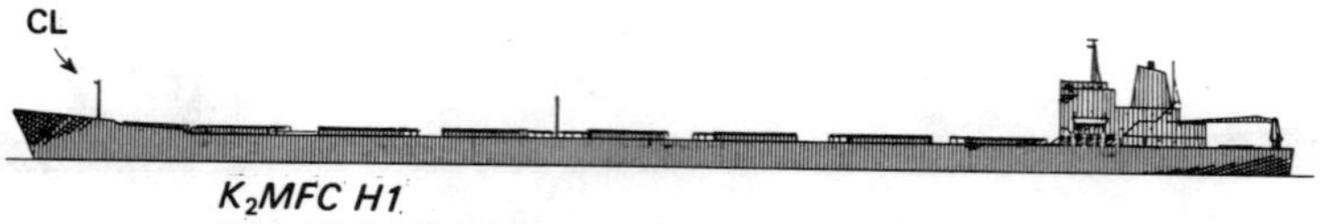

K_2MFC *H1*

67640 BENHOPE. Br/Br 1978; B; 39100; 228.12 × 14.02 (748.42 × 45.99); M; 15.

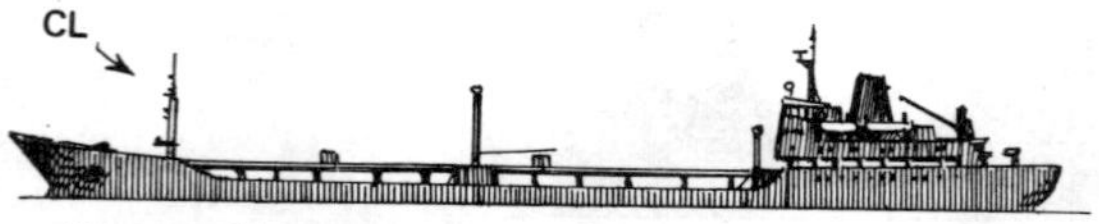

K_2MFC *H13*

★**67650 VELIKIY OKTYABR.** Ru/Ru 1967; Tk; 11000; 162.31 × 8.93 (532.51 × 29.3); M; 16.25. Sisters (Ru flag): ★**67651 POBYEDA OKTYABRYA** ★**67652 TSEZAR KUNIKOV** ★**67653 NIKOLAY SIPYAGIN** ★**67654 KERCH** ★**67655 EYZHEN BERG** ★**67656 KONSTANTIN TSIOLKOVSKIY** ★**67657 GENERAL BAGRATION** ★**67558 ZAKHARIY PALIASHVILI** ★**67659 FRIDRIKH TSANDER** ★**67660 VASILIY KIKVIDZE** (Bu flag): ★**67661 MARITZA** ★**67662 REZVAYA** ★**67663 VELEKA** (Cu flag): ★**67664 9 DE ABRIL** ★**67665 7 DE NOVIEMBRE** (In flag): **67666 BHAGAT SINGH 67667 SAROJINI NAIDU. 67668 VISVESVARAYA.**

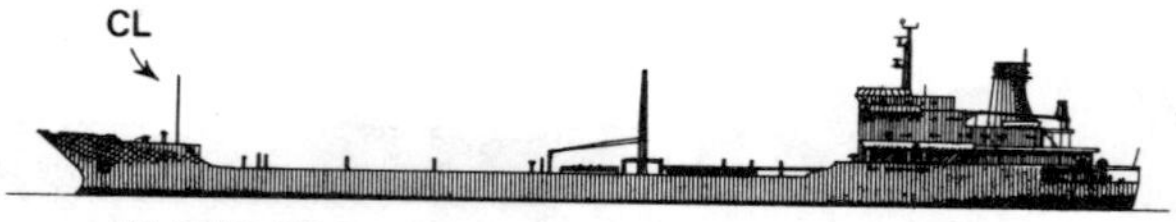

K_2MFC *H13*

● ★**67680 KOMANDARM FEDKO.** Ru/Ru 1976; Tk; 18500; 178.49 × 10.4 (585.6 × 34.12); M; 15.25. Sisters (Ru flag): ★**67681 GENERAL MERKVILADZE** ★**67682 KHERSON** ★**67683 VSEVELOD KOCHETOV.**

K_2MFC *H13*

★**67690 FELIKS DZIERZYNSKI.** Pd/Pd 1978; B; 20300; 198.18 × 11 (650.2 × 36.09); M; 15.2; **'B-517'** type. Sisters (Pd flag): ★**67691 WALKA MLODYCH** ★**67692 UNIWERSYTET SLASKI.**

K_2MFC *H13*

67700 OKTURUS. Sw/Ne 1973; Tk; 17900; 188.2 × 10.36 (617.45 × 33.99); M; 15. Sister: **67701 OKTAVIUS** (Sw).

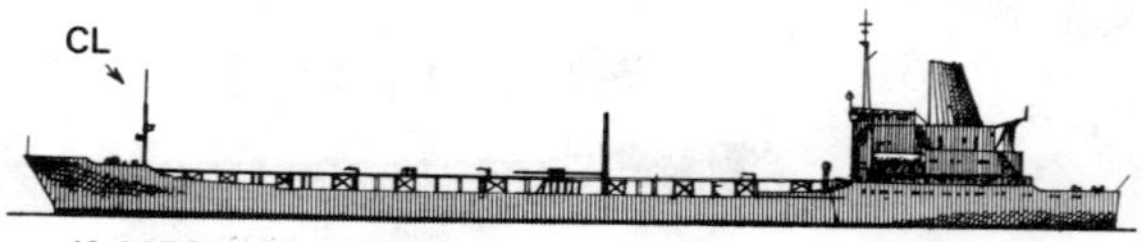

K_2MFC *H13*

67710 GLOBE. FRG/FRG 1972; Tk; 17600; 172.04 × 10.68 (564.43 × 35.04); M; 15.5; ex THOR ASGARD. Sisters (Li flag): **67711 SALLY I** ex AMISIA 1973; Launched as P. C. I **67712 SALLY II.**

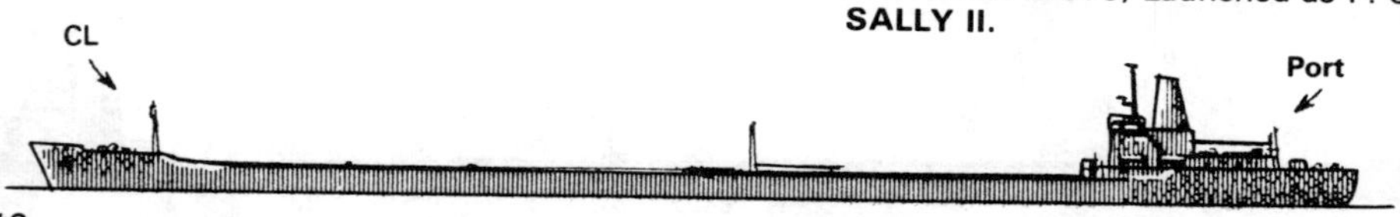

K_2MFC *H13*

67720 LILY H. Gr/Sw 1967; Tk; 48700; 265.13 × 14.66 (869.85 × 48.1); M; 16.5; ex MOBIL RADIANT; ex CERNO 1976; ex STIKLESTAD 1973.

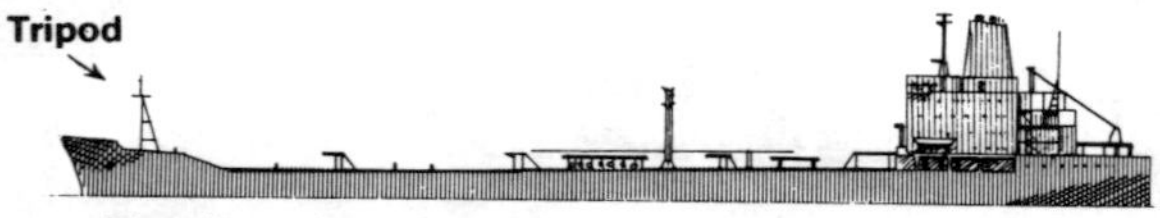

K_2MFC *H13*

● **67730 GUDRUN MAERSK.** De/No 1973; Tk; 19900; 170.54 × 11.75 (559.51 × 38.55); M; 15.5. Sisters: **67731 GJERTRUD MAERSK** (De) **67732 GRETE MAERSK** (De) **67733 TITIPOR** (Gr) ex GUNVOR MAERSK 1980.

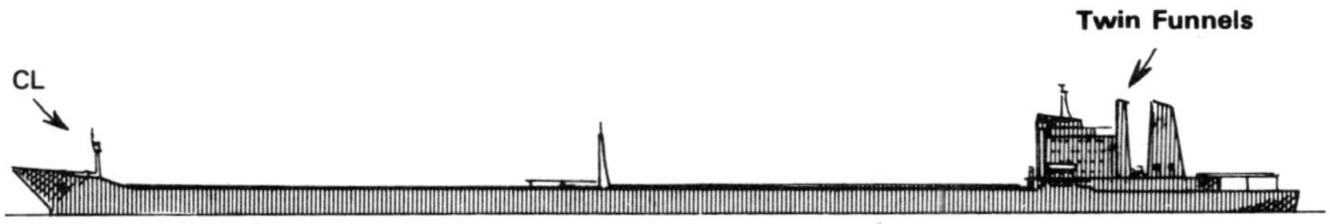

K_2MFF H1

● **67740 VENTURE ESPANA.** Li/Sp 1972; Tk; 58300; 279.31 × 15.26 (916.37 × 50.06); M; 16; ex CONOCO ESPANA 1978; Being used as a storage vessel at Dubai. Sister: **67741 AL AHOOD** (Li) ex VENTURE BRITANNIA 1980.

K_2MFF H1

67750 VULCANUS. Sg/FRG 1956; Incinerator ship; 3100; 101.96 × 6.07 (334.51 × 19.91); M; 12; ex ERICH SCHRODER 1972; Converted from general cargo.

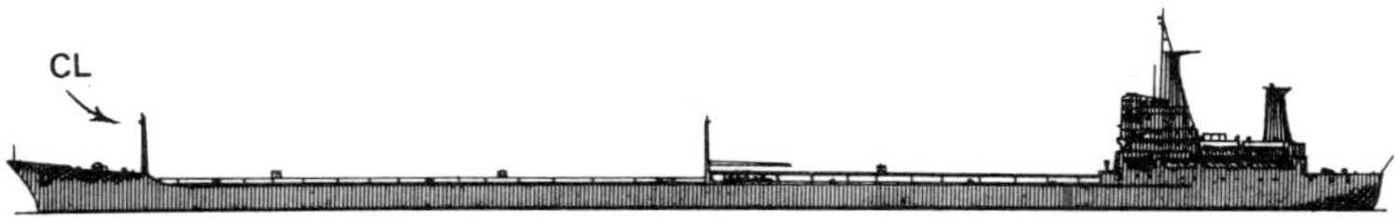

K_2MFF H13

67760 ASTORIA. Gr/Ja 1964; Tk; 33800; 229.65 × 12.33 (753.44 × 40.45); M; 17; ex SELMA DAN 1976. Similar: **67761 BORLA** (Li) ex BOMI 1980; ex SAMOS STAR 1979; ex TANJA DAN 1976.

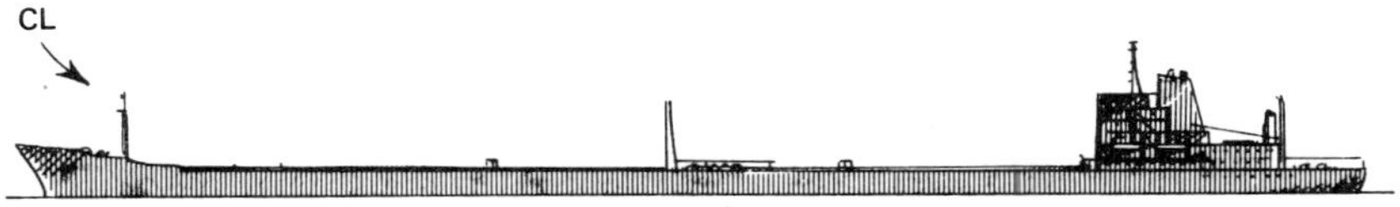

K_2MFFK H1

67770 JAWAHARLAL NEHRU. In/Ys 1969; Tk; 48400; 256.85 × 14.05 (842.68 × 46.09); M; 15.5; Has small twin "funnels" near after kingposts.

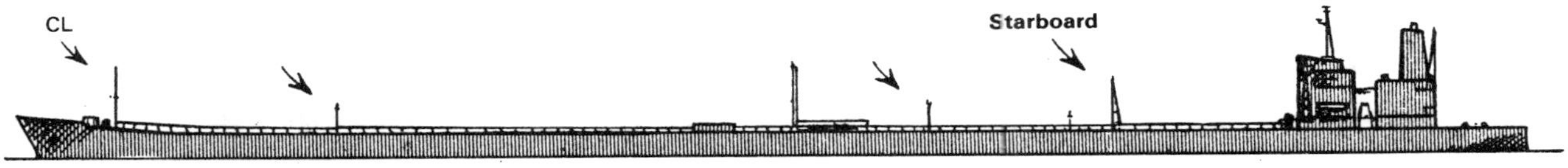

K_2MFK H

67780 ESSO CARIBBEAN. Li/Ja 1976; Tk; 177300; 378.39 × 22.27 (1241.44 × 73.06); T; 15.25; ex ANDROS PETROS 1977. Sisters: **67781 BURMAH ENDEAVOUR** (Br) **67782 BURMAH ENTERPRISE** (Br) **67783 ESSO MEDITERRANEAN** (Li) ex HOMERIC 1977 Similar: **67784 ANDROS CHRYSSI** (Li) **67785 ETHNIC** (Li) **67786 SUNSHINE LEADER** (Li) **67787 ISE MARU** (Ja).

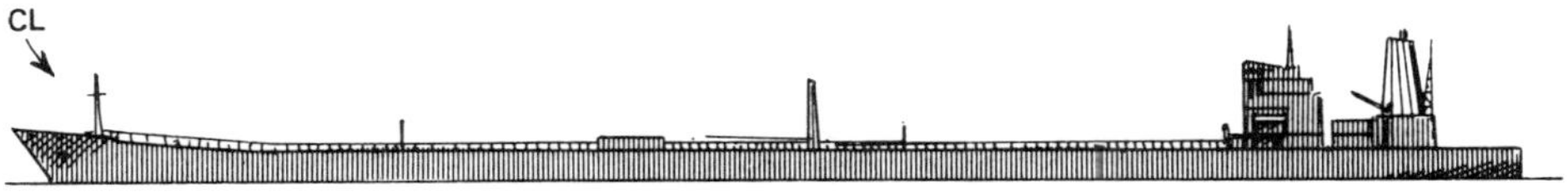

K_2MFK H

67800 GAZIANTEP. Tu/Ja 1974; Tk; 79800; 286.52 × 16.84 (940.03 × 55.25); M; 15.5.

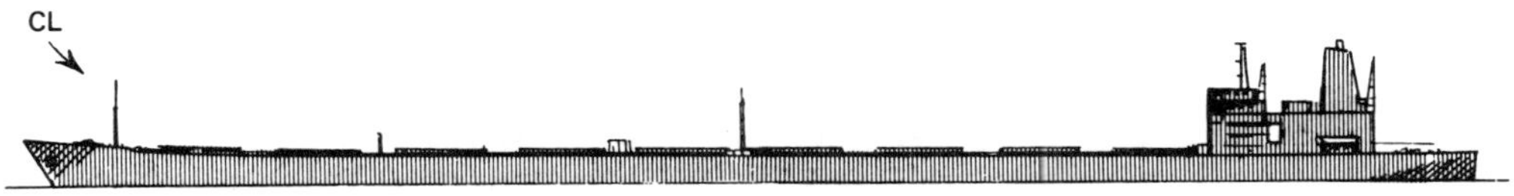

K_2MFK H

67810 NIPPON MARU No 3. Ja/Ja 1971; OO; 89500; 305.01 × 17.47 (1000.69 × 57.32); T; 16.25.

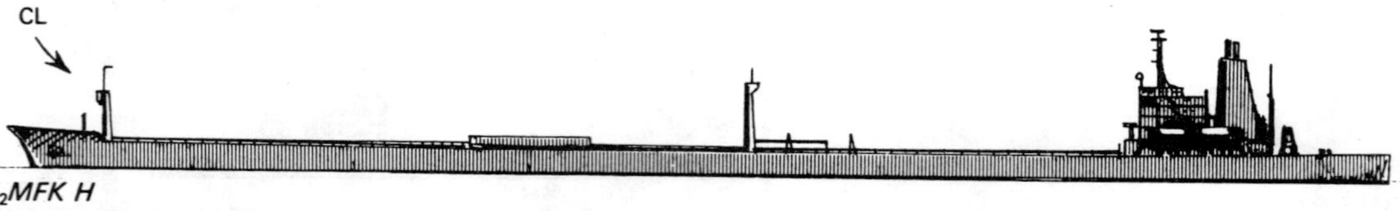

K_2MFK H

67820 BERGE KING. No/Ja 1970; Tk; 140000; 342.91 × 21.78 (1125.03 × 71.46); M; 15. Sisters (No flag): **67821 BERGE QUEEN 67822 BERGE PRINCE 67823 BERGE PRINCESS**

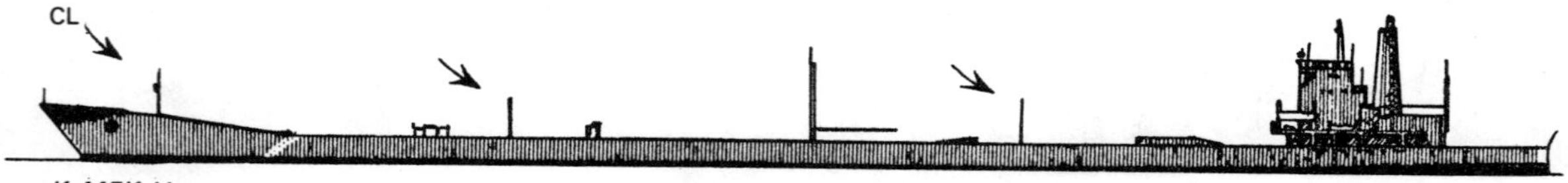

K_2MFK H

67830 FABIAN. No/No 1972; Tk; 140500; 347.84 × 22.14 (1141.21 × 72.64); T; 15.5. Sisters (No flag): **67831 JULIAN 67832 VESPASIAN** Possibly similar (no short uprights on deck) **67833 BEAUMONT 67834 BEAURIVAGE** Similar: **67835 CYPRIAN 67836 SIR CHARLES HAMBRO 67837 NORBORN** ex SONGA 1971 **67838 NORBRIGHT** ex RADNY 1977.

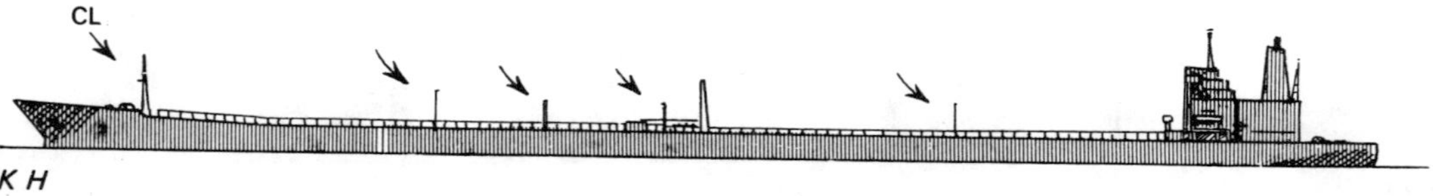

K_2MFK H

67840 WAKO MARU. Ja/Ja 1975; Tk; 116400; 319.92 × 19.66 (1049.61 × 64.5); T; 16.5.

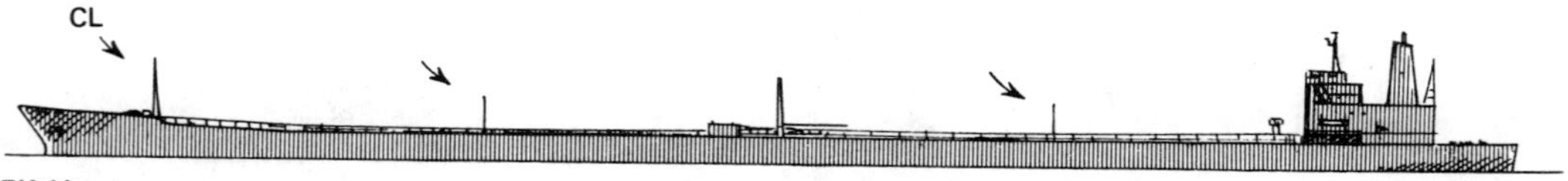

K_2MFK H

67850 FUJIKAWA MARU. Ja/Ja 1975; Tk; 116800; 319.95 × 19.66 (1049.7 × 64.5); T; 16.75.

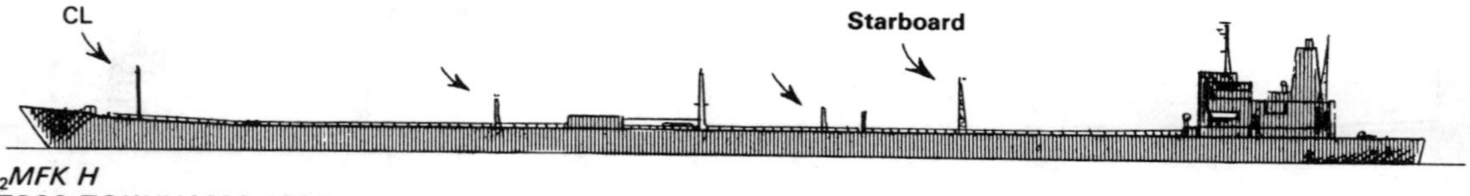

K_2MFK H

67860 TOKUYAMA MARU. Ja/Ja 1975; Tk; 136100; 337.07 × 19.94 (1105.87 × 65.42); T; 16.25.

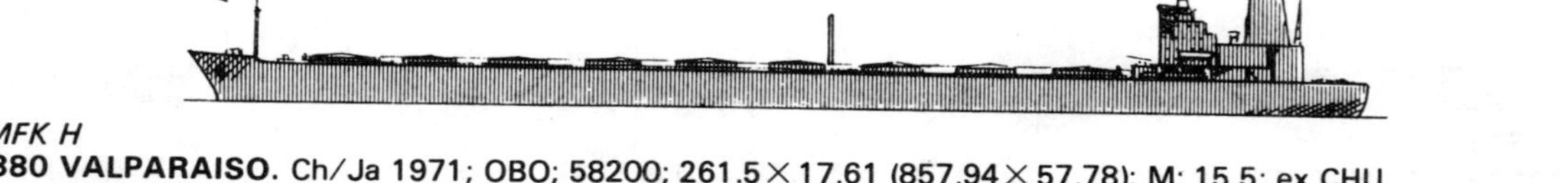

K_2MFK H

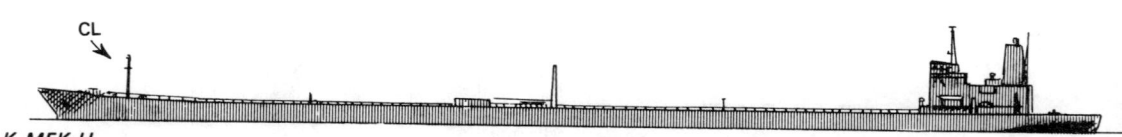

67870 ANDES MARU. Ja/Ja 1974; Tk; 135600; 337.02 × 21.03 (1105.7 × 68.1); T; 16.

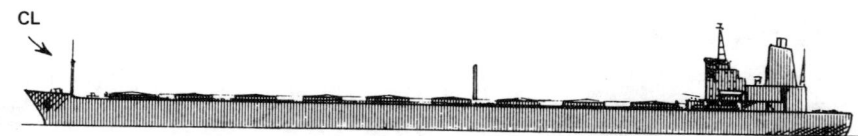

K_2MFK H

67880 VALPARAISO. Ch/Ja 1971; OBO; 58200; 261.5 × 17.61 (857.94 × 57.78); M; 15.5; ex CHU FUJINO.

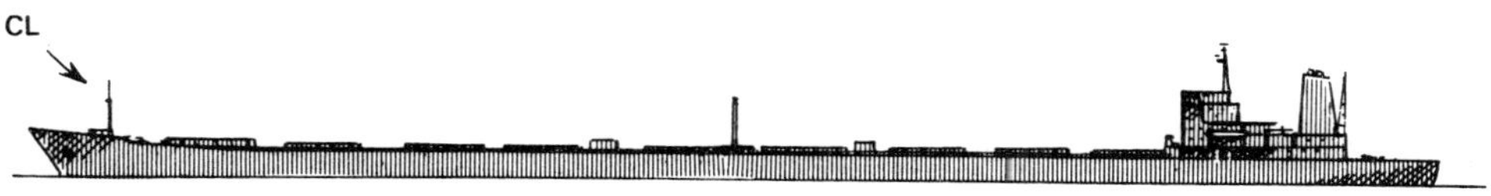

K_2MFK H
67890 LAUREL WREATH. Li/Ja 1975; BO; 72300; 286.65 × 22 (940.45 × 72.18); M; 15.5.

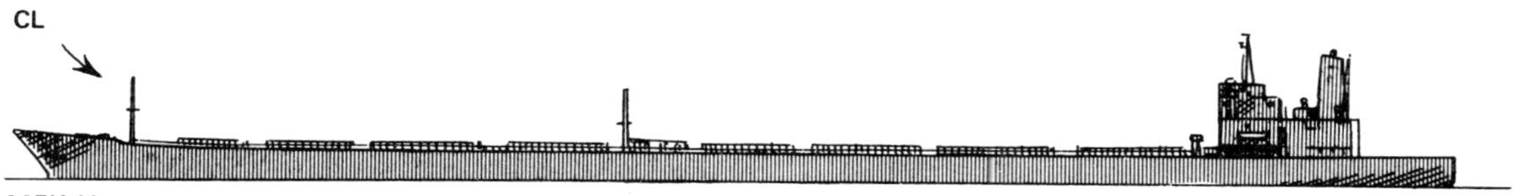

K_2MFK H
67900 USA MARU. Ja/Ja 1972; OO; 14200; 337.02 × 21.02 (1105.71 × 68.96); T; 16.

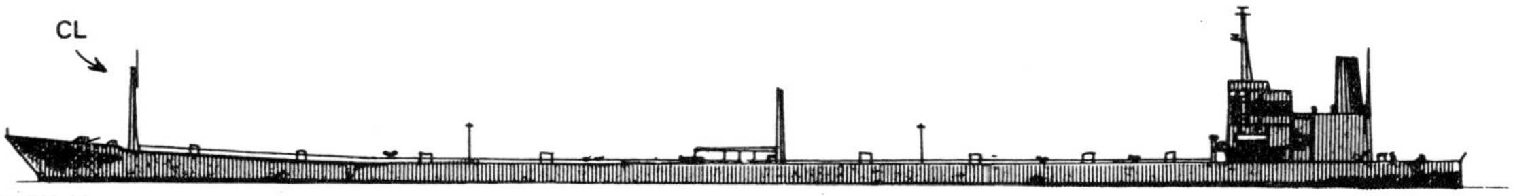

K_2MFK H
67910 OGDEN SUNGARI. Li/Ja 1975; Tk; 124100; 338.87 × 21.01 (1111.78 × 68.93); T; 16. Similar: **67911 MOSCLIFF** (No) **67912 SAINT MARCET** (Li).

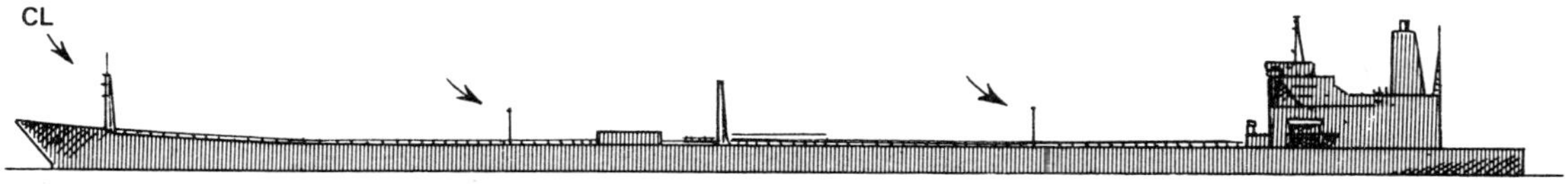

K_2MFK H
67920 IKUYO MARU. Ja/Ja 1972; Tk; 128700; 341.13 × 20.04 (1119.19 × 65.75); T; 15.5.

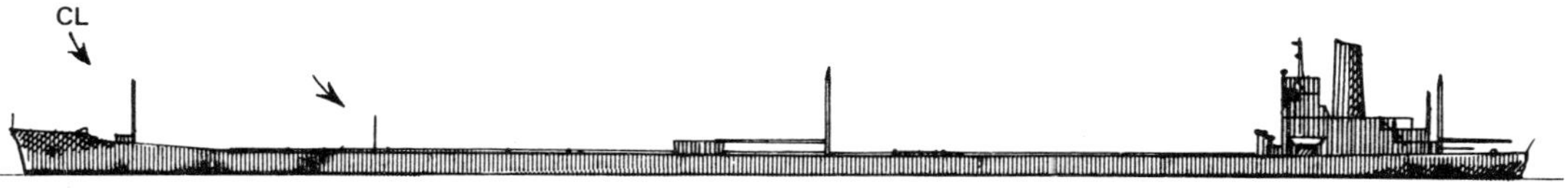

K_2MFK H
67930 OGDEN NELSON. Li/Ja 1972; Tk; 12400; 331 × 22.02 (1085.96 × 72.24); T; 15.5. Sister: **67931 COALINGA** (Li) ex IOANNIS CHANDRIS 1976 Similar (Li flag): **67932 WORLD CROWN 67933 WESTERN LION 67934 SOUTHERN LION 67935 NORTHERN LION 67936 EASTERN LION.**

K_2MFK H
● **67940 CONCORDIA.** Li/Ja 1976; Tk; 61100; 265.62 × 16.78 (871.46 × 55.05); M; 15.5. Sisters (Li flag): **67941 ANIA. 67942 NORTHERN STAR 67943 RUTH 67944 SHIRLEY** Similar: **67945 MESOLOGI** (Gr) **67946 MONEMVASIA** (Gr) **67947 AFRAN STREAM** (Li) ex MANTINIA 1977.

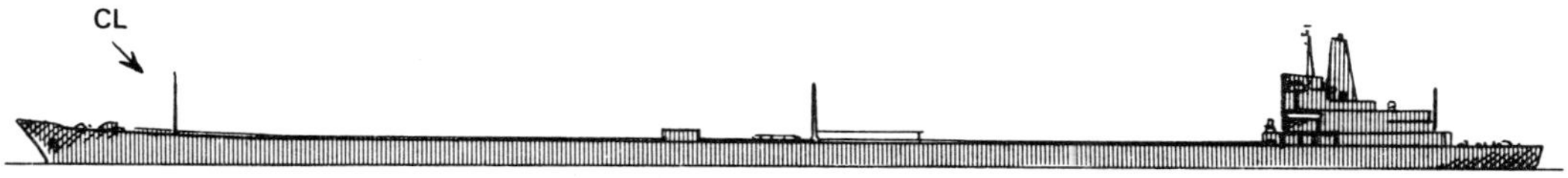

K_2MFK H
67960 HERCULES. Li/Ja 1971; Tk; 99800; 322.61 × 19.4 (1058.43 × 63.65); T; —. Sister: **67961 JUMBO PIONEER** (Li) ex AQUARIUS 1972.

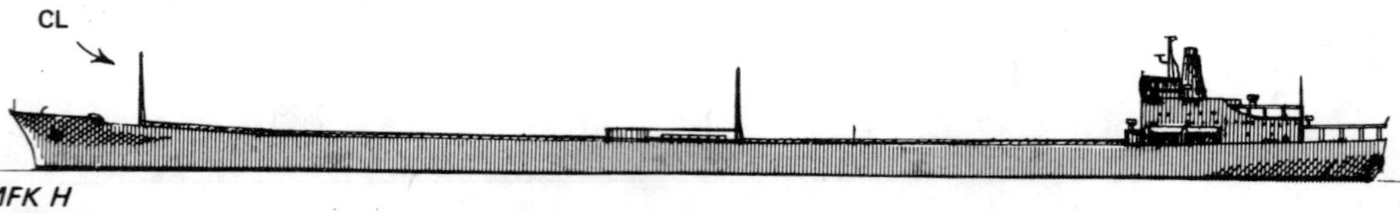

K_2MFK H

● **67970 OLYMPIC ALLIANCE.** Li/Ja 1970; Tk; 97200; 324.47 × 19.39 (1064.53 × 63.62) T; 15.5. Sister: **67971 OLYMPIC ACCORD** (Li).

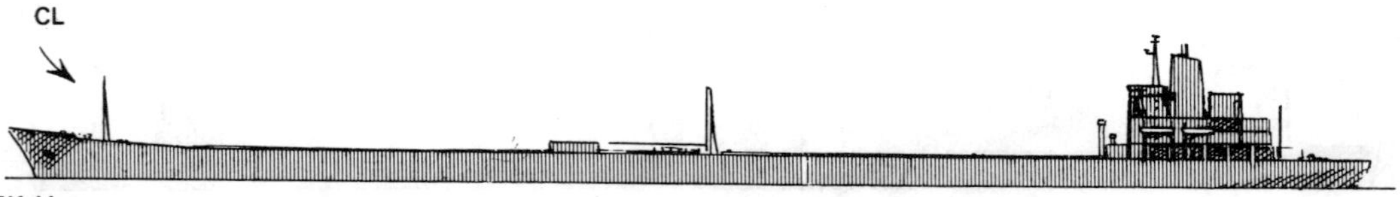

K_2MFK H

67980 WORLD BARONESS. Li/Ja 1971; Tk; 104100; 320 × 20.11 (1049.87 × 65.98); T; 16.

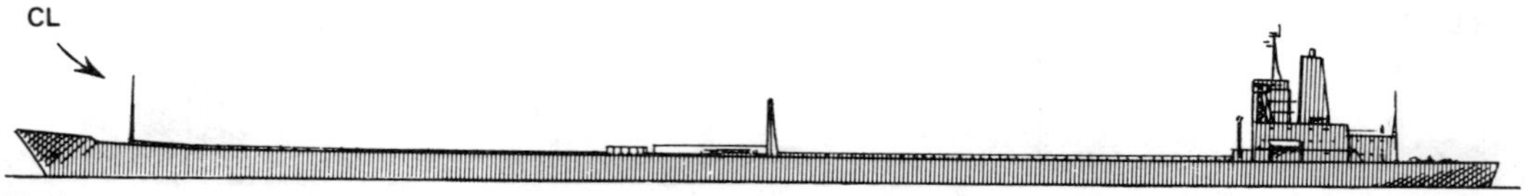

K_2MFK H

● **67990 NICHIO MARU.** Ja/Ja 1972; Tk; 120300; 324.01 × 19.36 (1063.02 × 63.52); T; 15.5. Similar: **67991 EIKO MARU** (Ja) **67992 WORLD PRESTIGE** (Li) ex SANKOLAKE 1976.

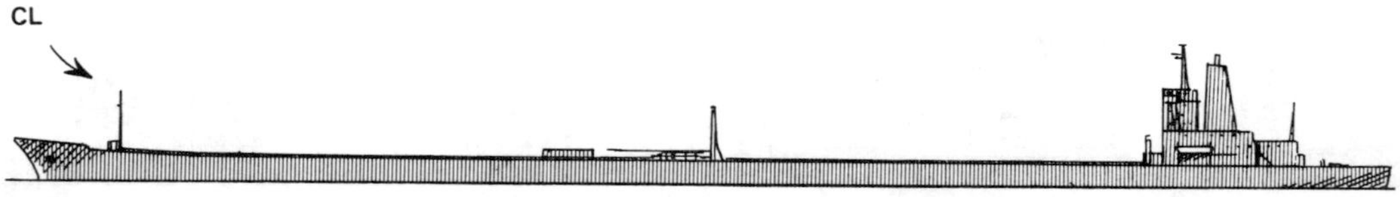

K_2MFK H

68000 SHIN-EN MARU. Ja/Ja 1971; Tk; 120300; 324.01 × 19 (1063.02 × 62.34); T; 15.25.

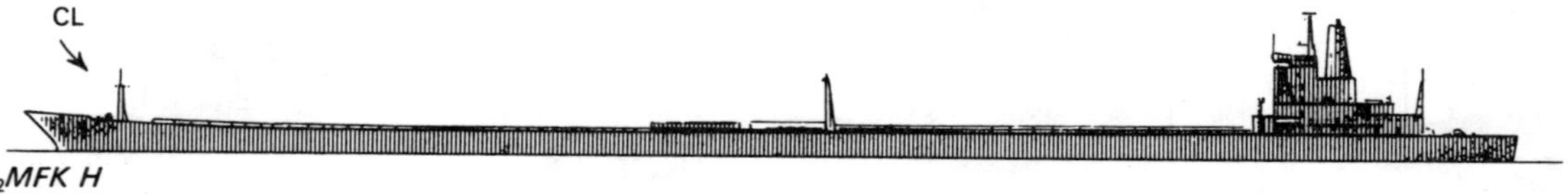

K_2MFK H

68010 KASHIMASAN MARU. Ja/Ja 1973; Tk; 120700; 324.01 × 19.46 (1063.02 × 63.85); T; 15.25.

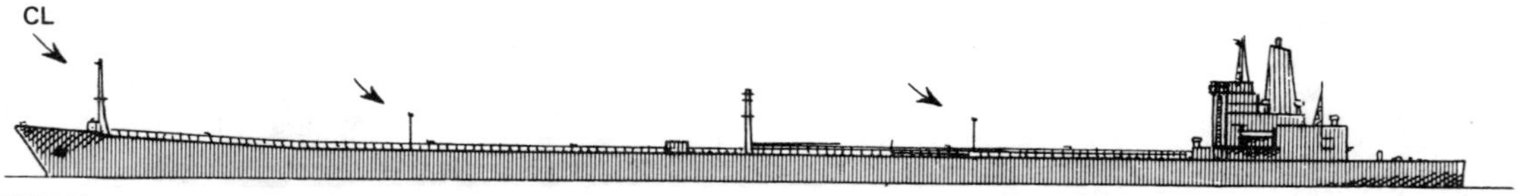

K_2MFK H

68020 KINKO MARU. Ja/Ja 1971; Tk; 12900; 331.53 × 20.53 (1087.7 × 67.36); T; 15.75.

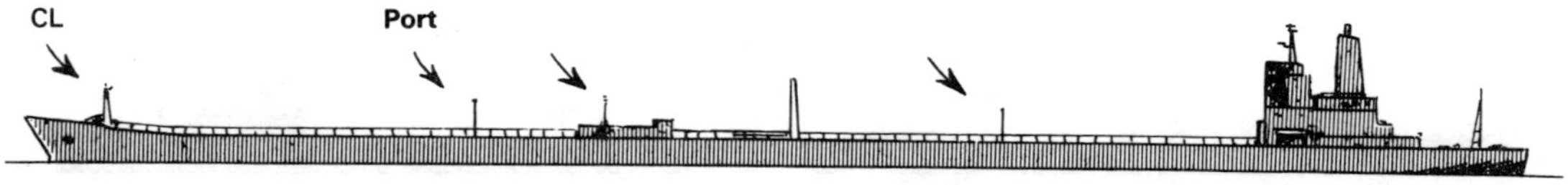

K_2MFK H

68030 YOKO MARU. Ja/Ja 1975; Tk; 135100; 331.5 × 20.55 (1087.6 × 67.42); T; 16.25; ex BARBARA T. SHAHEEN 1976. Similar: **68031 JAPAN COSMOS** (Ja) **68032 MOBIL SWIFT** (Li) ex TAKAKURASAN MARU 1978.

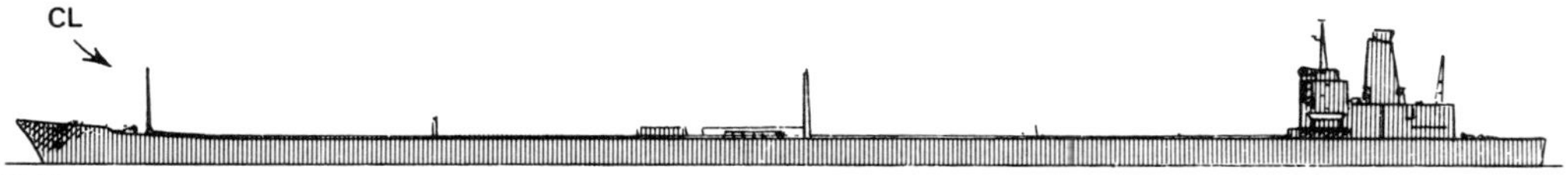

K_2MFK H
68040 HONAM PEARL. Li/Ja 1974; Tk; 83800; 314.99 × 18.91 (1033.43 × 62.04); M; 15.5. Possible sister: **68041 HONAM JADE** (Li).

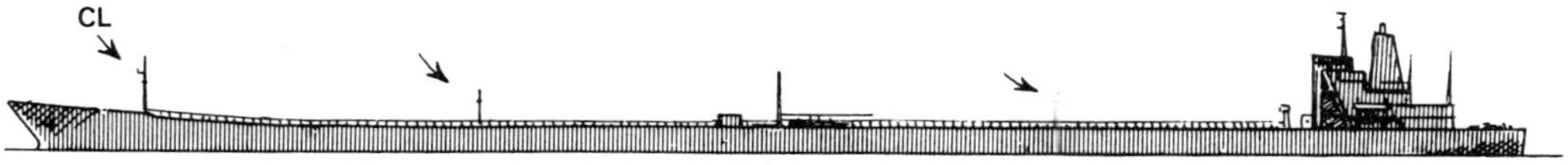

K_2MFK H
68050 JAPAN ORCHID. Ja/Ja 1971; Tk; 116100; 318.83 × 19.51 (1046.03 × 64.01); T; 16.25. Similar (Li flag): **68051 HARMONY VENTURE 68052 TIVOLI 68053 WORLD ENDEAVOUR** ex ASUKAGAWA MARU 1977 **68054 WORLD SAGA** ex UJIGAWA MARU 1977.

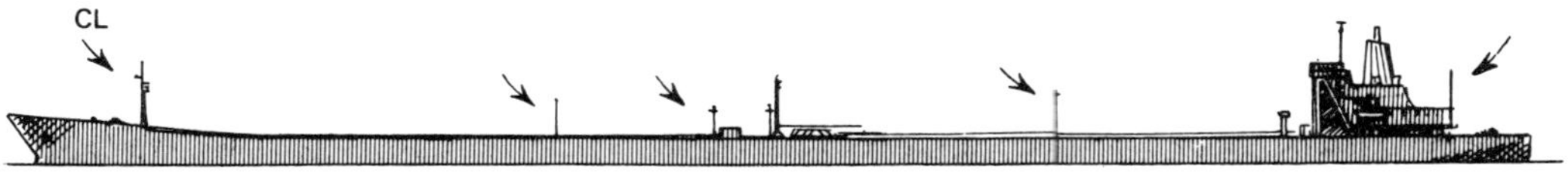

K_2MFK H
68060 TOHO MARU. Ja/Ja 1972; Tk; 115900; 319.34 × 19.5 (1047 × 63.98); T; 16.5.

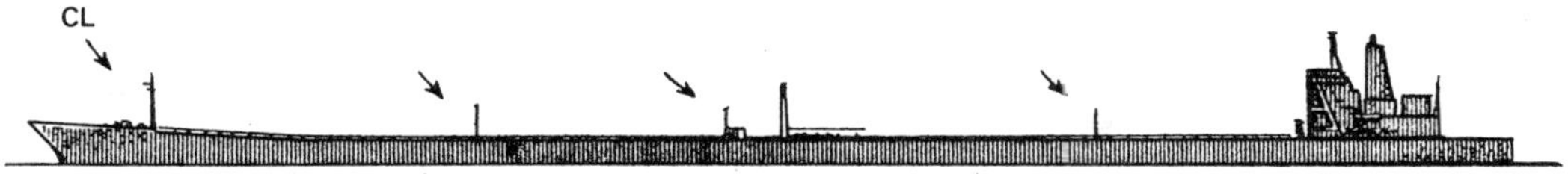

K_2MFK H
68070 WORLD EMPIRE. Pa/Ja 1972; Tk; 105100; 319.31 × 19.53 (1047.6 × 64.07); T; 16.

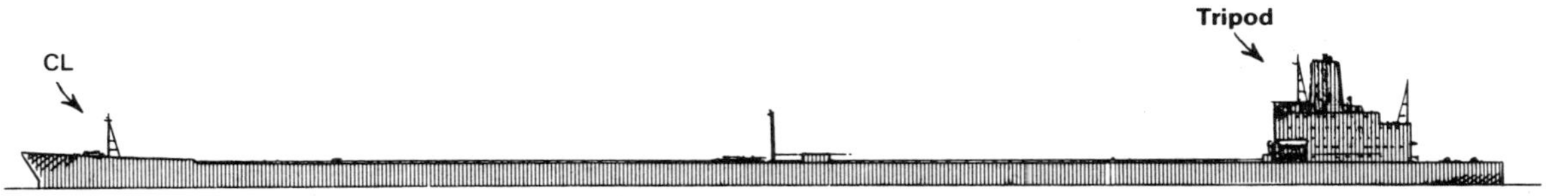

K_2MFK H
● **68080 LEPTON.** Li/Ne 1975; Tk; 155300; 352.61 × 22.35 (1156.86 × 73.33); T; —. Possible similar: **68081 LEMBULUS** (Br).

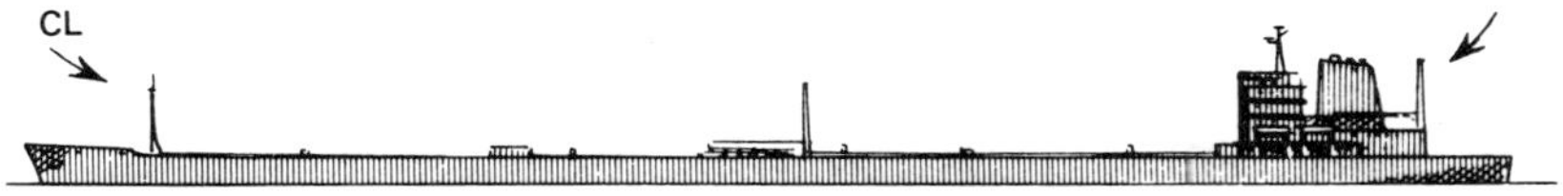

K_2MFK H
68090 RAJENDRA PRASAD. In/Ys 1975; Tk; 63500; 248.39 × 16.51 (814.93 × 54.17); M; 15. Probable sister: **68091 ZAKIR HUSSAIN** (In).

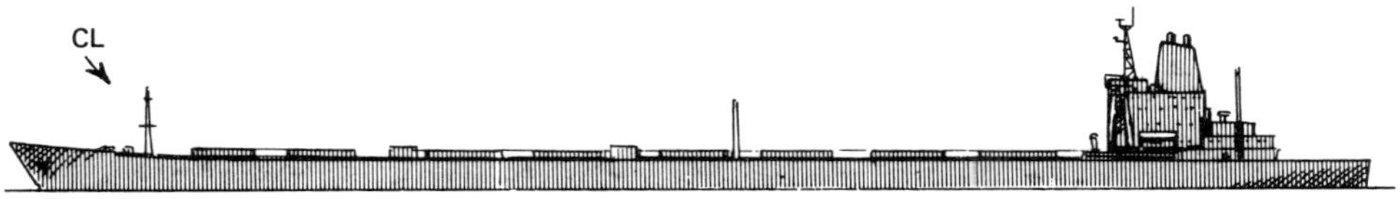

K_2MFK H
68100 CHAMPAGNE. Fr/Ja 1975; OO; 93900; 295.03 × 17.9 (967.95 × 58.72); M; 16.5. Similar: **68101 CETRA VELA** (Fr) **68102 BUNGA MAWAR** (My) **68103 GARDEN GREEN** (Li) launched as HENRY J. KAISER.

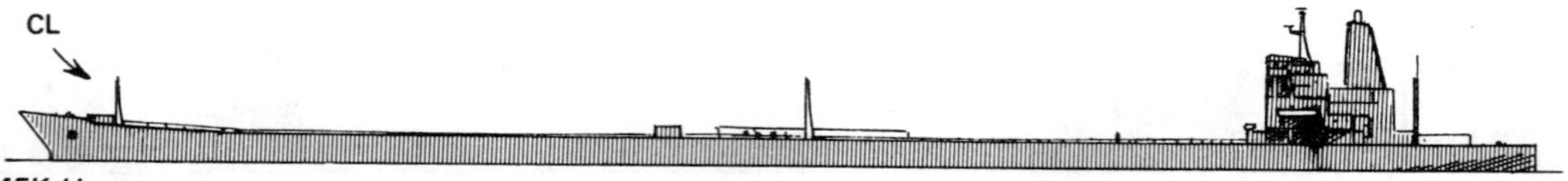

K_2MFK H

68110 WORLD HAPPINESS. Li/Ja 1971; Tk; 102326; 324.19 × 19.62 (1063.62 × 64.37); T; 17. Sister: **68111 WORLD HORIZON** (Li).

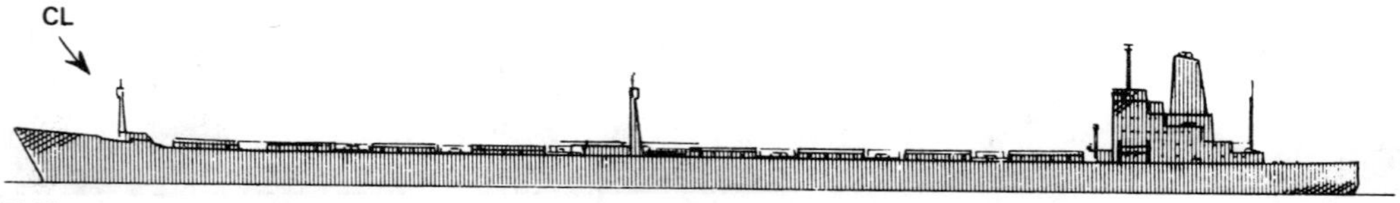

K_2MFK H

68120 POLYSAGA. No/Ja 1970; OO; 95400; 307.83 × 17.37 (1009.94 × 56.99); M; 16.5.

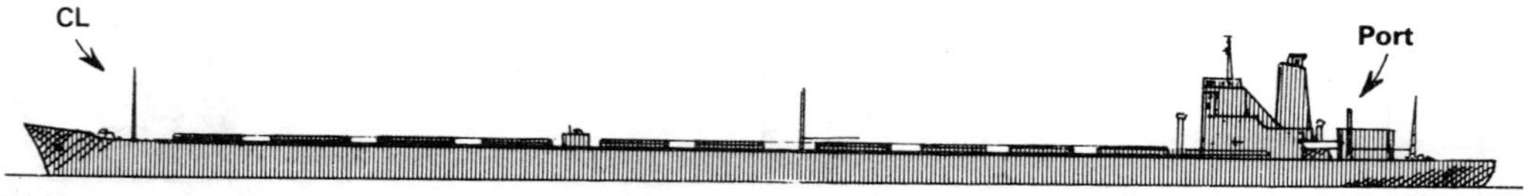

K_2MFK H

68130 WORLD GUARD. Li/Ja 1971; OBO; 85800; 314.21 × 17.13 (1030.87 × 56.2); M; 16. Sister: **68131 WORLD CHALLENGER** (Li).

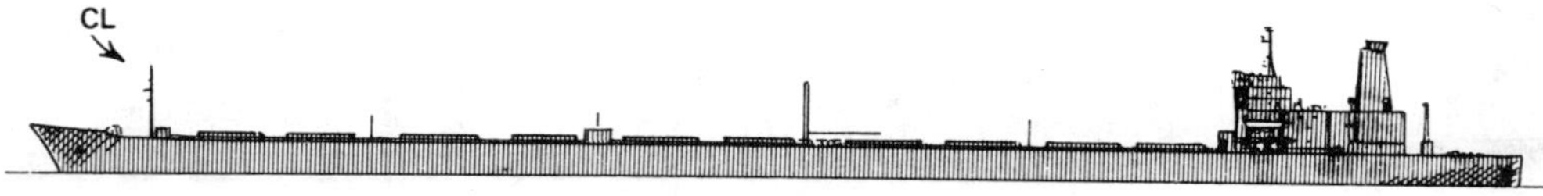

K_2MFK H

68140 AMAZON MARU. Ja/Ja 1973; OO; 89500; 300.01 × 16.99 (984.28 × 55.74); M; 16; ex SANKO ROBIN 1980. Sister: **68141 TRIPHAROS** (Li) Similar: **68142 WAKAZURA MARU** (Ja) **68143 YAMAZURA MARU** (Ja) **68144 ZUIHO MARU** (Ja) **68145 LARINA** (Li).

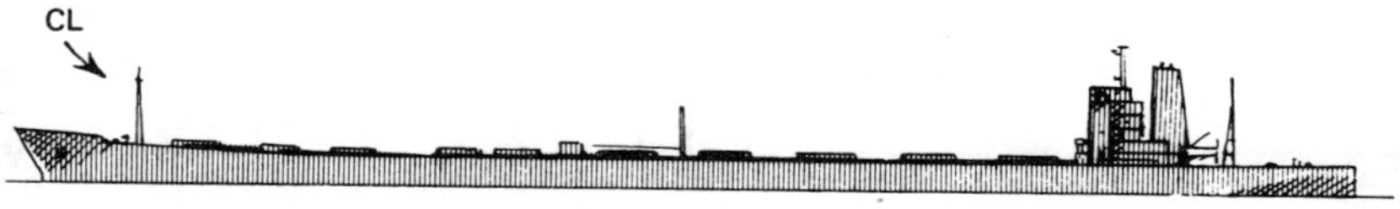

K_2MFK H

● ⋆**68150 SHUANG FENG HAI.** RC/Ja 1968; OO; 55500; 252.64 × 15.01 (828.87 × 49.25); M; 15.25; ex KOHFUKUSAN MARU 1978. Probable sister: **68151 FUKUYAMA MARU** (Ja) Similar (funnel on housing): **68152 EASTERN GIANT** (Li).

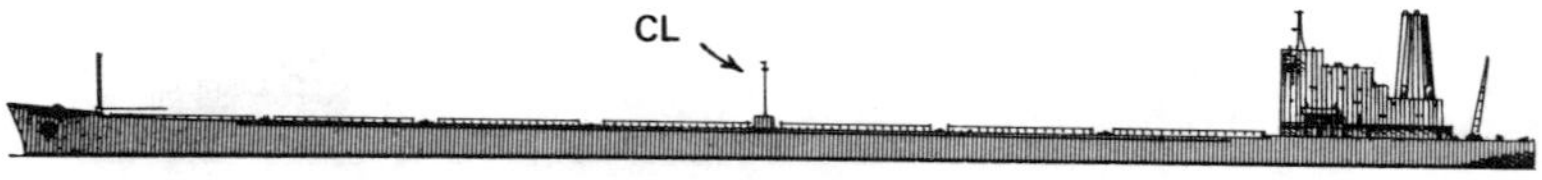

K_2MFK H

68160 SLURRY EXPRESS. Li/Ja 1978; B (Sand); 48500; 240.52 × 17.04 (821.92 × 55.91); M; 14.25.

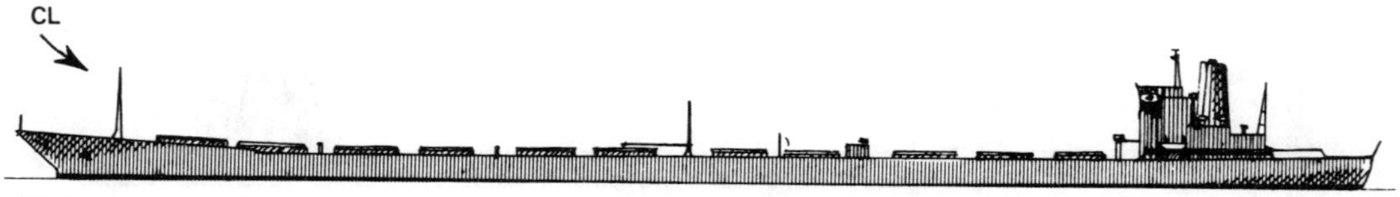

K_2MFK H

68170 TANTALUS. Br/Ja 1972; OO; 120800; 327.82 × 19.1 (1075.53 × 62.66); T; 15.5. Similar: **68171 TSURUMI MARU** (Ja) **68172 WORLD ERA** (Li) ex JARL MALMROS 1979 **68173 WORLD LADY** (Li) ex TARTAR 1978 Similar (larger): **68174 DOCECANYON** (Li).

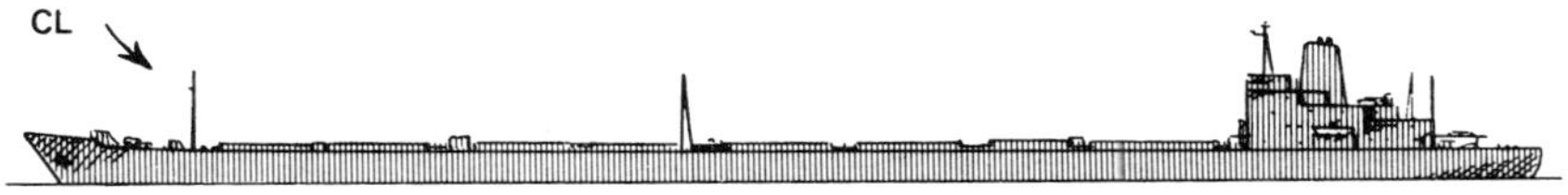

K_2MFK H
68180 DOCEMAR. Bz/Ja 1970; OO; 61900; 258.02 × 15.7 (846.52 × 51.51); M; 15.5.

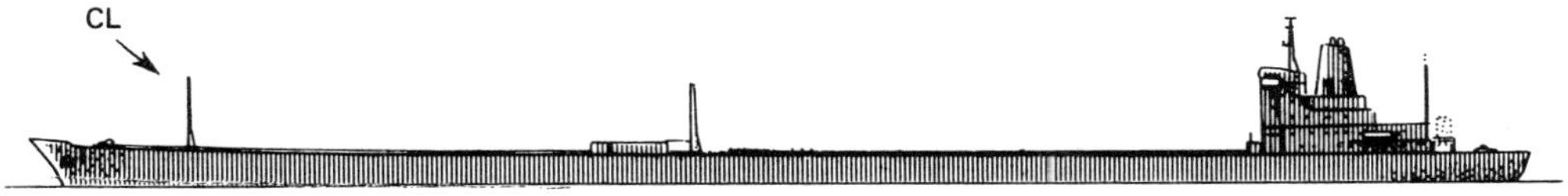

K_2MFK H
68190 JINGU MARU. Ja/Ja 1968; Tk; 73300; 294 × 17.03 (964.57 × 55.87); M; 14.5.

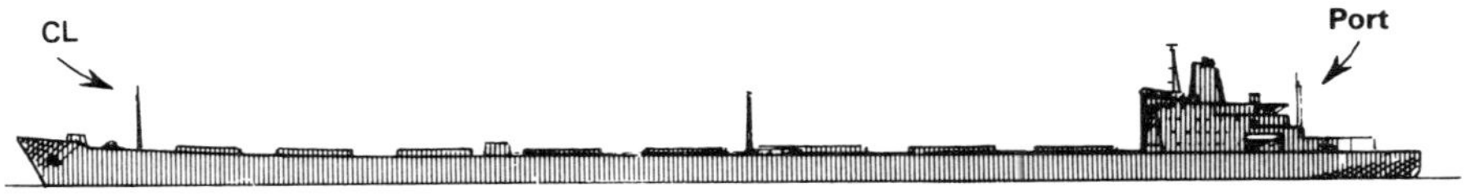

K_2MFK H
● **68200 DOCEPOLO.** Bz/Bz 1975; OO; 72400; 273.52 × 16.12 (897.37 × 52.89); M; 16. Sister (Ja built): **68201 DOCEBAY** (Li) Probable sisters (Bz flag): **68202 DOCECORAL 68203 JAPURA 68204 JARI 68205 JOINVILLE 68206 JURUA 68207 JURUPEMA.**

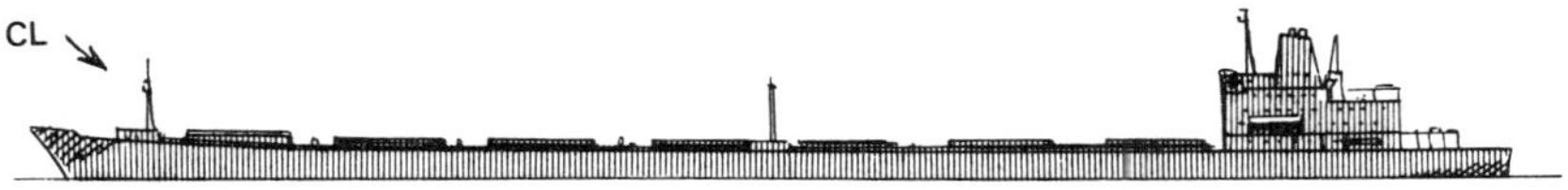

K_2MFK H
68220 HOEGH RAINBOW. No/Ja 1970; OBO; 57500; 250.05 × 15.52 (820.37 × 50.92); M; 15.5. Sisters: **68221 HOEGH ROVER** (No) **68222 VEGA SEAL** (Br) ex HOEGH ROBIN 1978 Similar: **68223 HOEGH RIDER** (No).

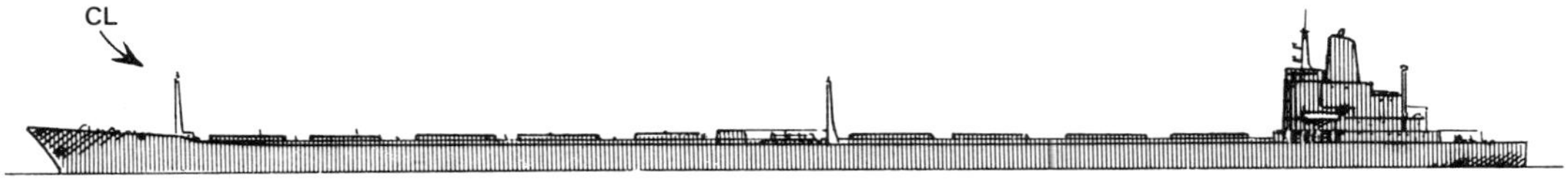

K_2MFK H
● **68230 ANDROS ANTARES.** Li/Ja 1973; OO; Ore 57900/Oil 115100; 323.63 × 20.49 (1061.78 × 67.22); T; 15. Sisters (Li flag): **68231 ANDROS ARIES 68232 ANDROS ATLAS** Similar (tankers): **68233 ANDROS MASTER 68234 ANDROS TITAN.**

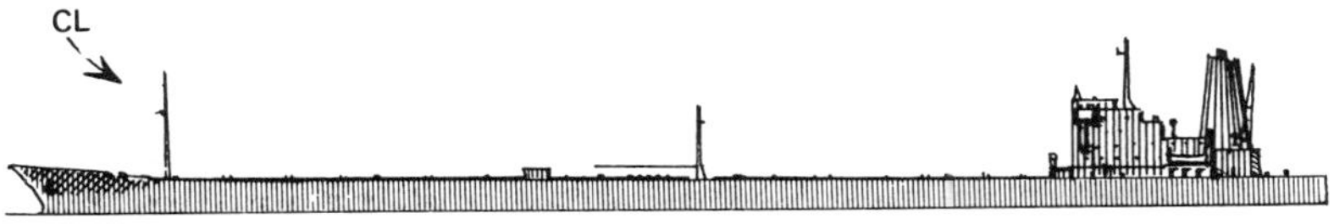

K_2MFK H
68240 GARYVILLE. Li/Ja 1972; Tk; 65600; 274.94 × 17.32 (902.03 × 56.82); M; 15.75; ex FAIRFIELD 1977. Sister: **28241 ORIENTAL PHOENIX** (Li).

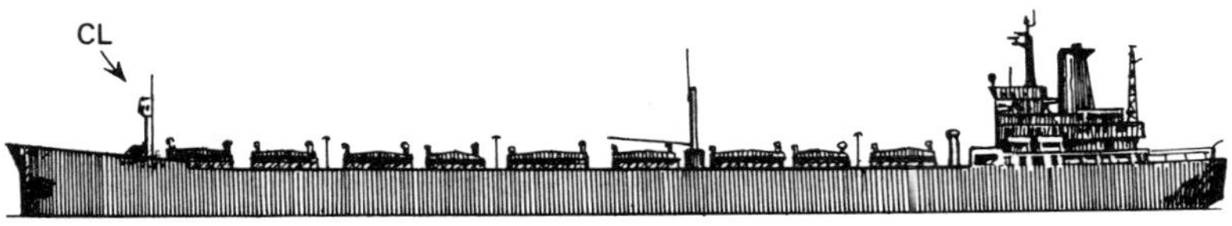

K_2MFK H
★68250 MARSHAL BUDENYY. Ru/Pd 1975; BO; 59600; 245.52 × 16 (805.51 × 52.49); M; 16; **"B524"** type. Sisters (Ru flag): **★68251 MARSHALL KONYEV ★68252 MARSHAL ROKOSSOVSKIY ★68253 MARSHAL ZHUKHOV.**

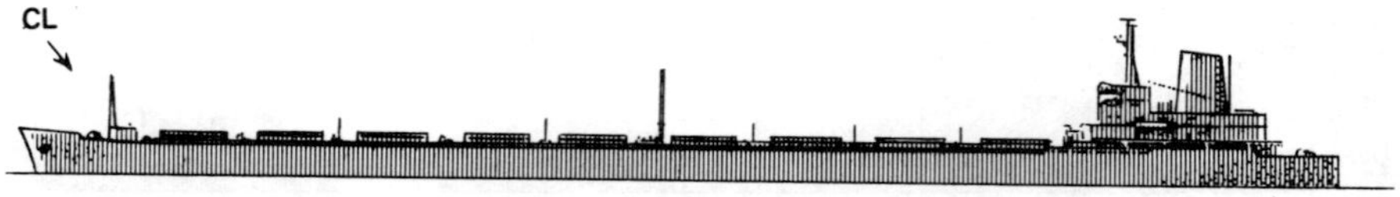

K_2MFK *H*

68260 LAKE MENDOCINO. Li/Ja 1971; OBO; 71600; 266.02 × 18.1 (872.77 × 59.38); M; 15.5; ex AVON BRIDGE 1976. Sisters: **68261 CAST PETREL** (Br) ex EDEN BRIDGE **68262 CAST GULL** (Br) ex SILVER BRIDGE **68263 CAST PUFFIN** (Br) ex ENTERPRISE TRANSPORTER; ex AUSTRALIAN BRIDGE 1978.

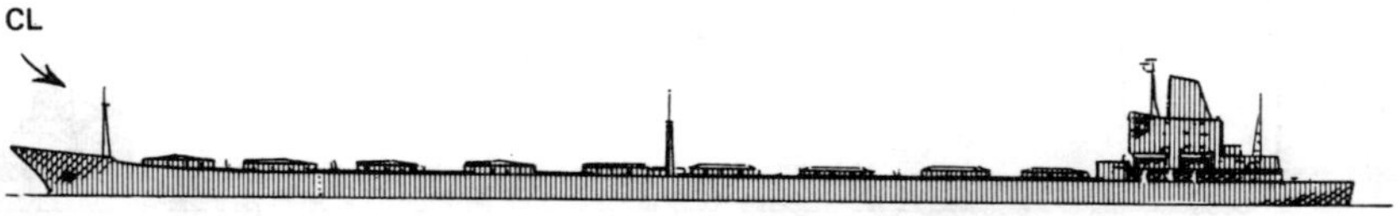

K_2MFK *H*

68270 SAXONIA. FRG/FRG 1973; OBO; 42400; 253.68 × 14.23 (832.28 × 46.69); M; 15.25; ex MERCEDES.

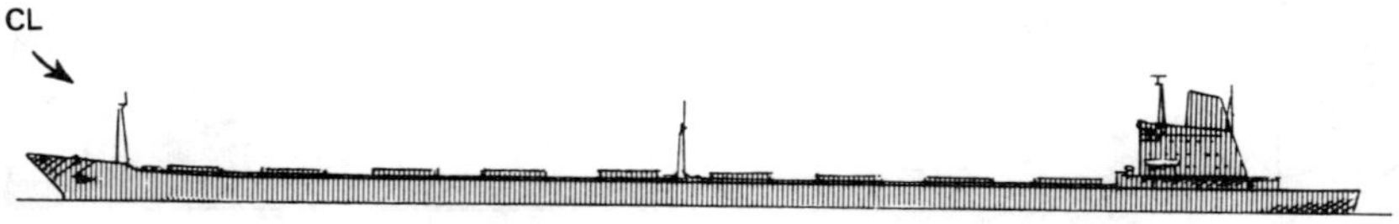

K_2MFK *H*

68280 BELOBO. No/FRG 1974; OBO; 42800; 253.63 × 14.24 (832.12 × 46.72); M; 15. Sisters: **68281 TAI CHEUNG** (Br) ex OBO DUKE 1980 **68282 SIBOSIX** (No) ex JARMINA 1980; (being used as storage vessel at Singapore).

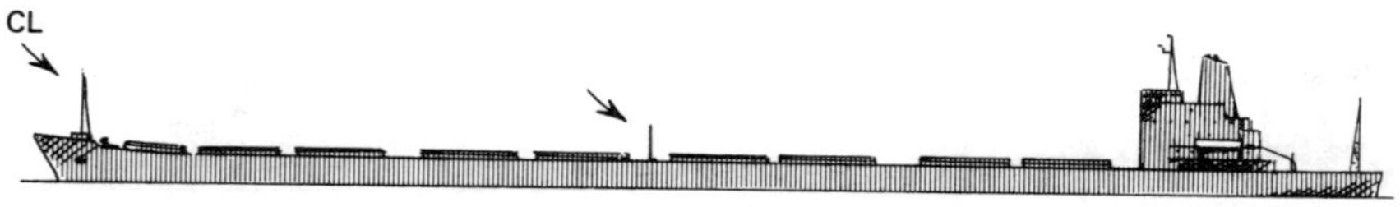

K_2MFK *H*

68290 BROCKMAN. Li/Ja 1974; O; 33900; 259.39 × 16.13 (851.02 × 52.92); M; 15. Sisters (Li flag): **68291 MARRA MAMBA 68292 SEVEN TEAM** ex SEVENSEAS CONQUEROR 1979.

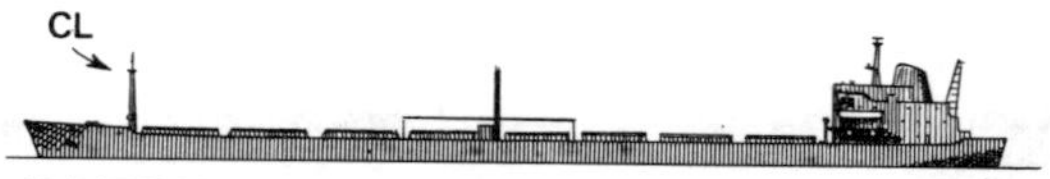

K_2MFK *H*

68300 CARCHESTER. Br/Ja 1967; B; 9900; 155.73 × 8.1 (510.93 × 26.57); M; 15.75.

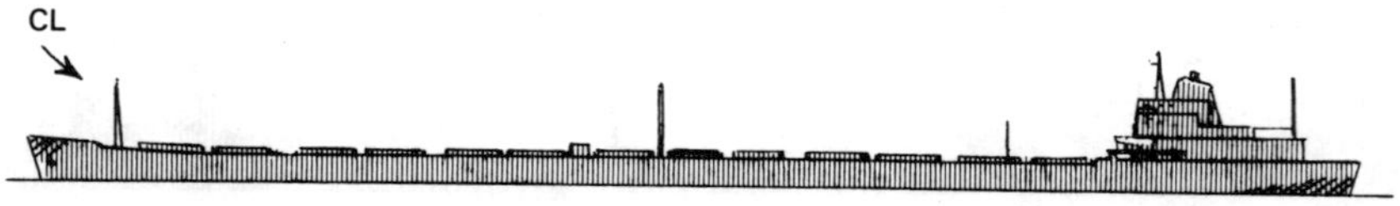

K_2MFK *H*

68310 NORMAN PACIFIC. Sg/Ys 1971; OBO; 42200; 252.36 × 14.78 (827.95 × 48.49); M; 16; ex CAPETAN CARRAS.

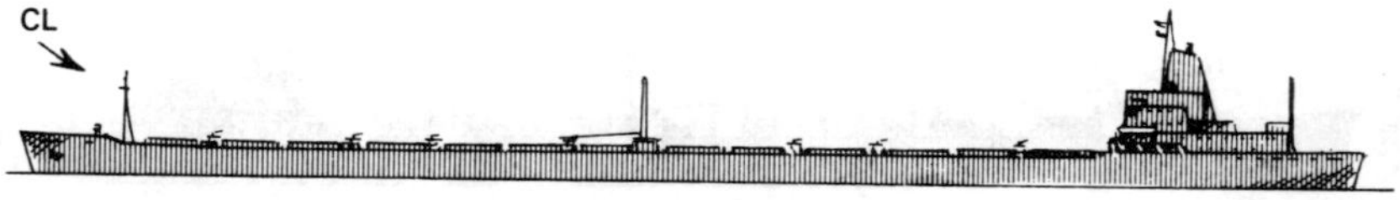

K_2MFK *H*

● **68320 SENECA.** Li/Ys 1975; OBO; 42000; 252.86 × 14.81 (829.59 × 48.59); M; 14.5; ex EXCOMM MERCHANT 1980. Sister: **68321 SEQUOIA** (Li) ex EXCOMM MARINER 1980 Possible sister: **68322 CARLANTIC** (li) Similar: **68323 CARBAY** (Li) **68324 CARCAPE** (Li) **68325 CARISLE** (Br).

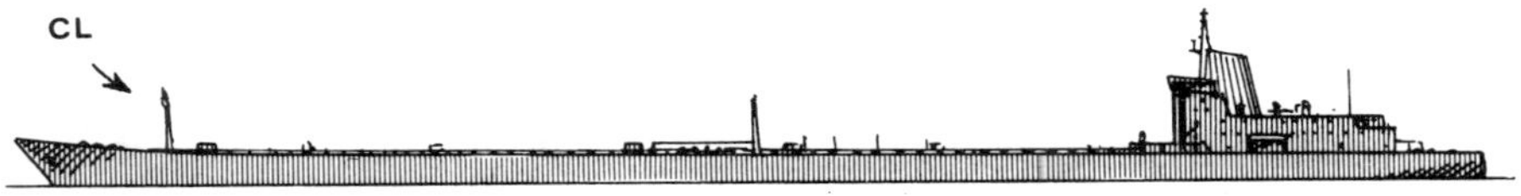

K_2MFK H
68330 NICOS I. VARDINOYANNIS. Gr/Br 1971; Tk; 65300; 274.4 × 16.96 (900.26 × 55.64); M; 16; ex GOLD STAR 1973. Sister: **68331 IDEFIX** (Li) ex NORDIC ENTERPRISE 1976; ex NAESS ENTERPRISE 1974 Possible sister: **68332 KING STAR** (Ko).

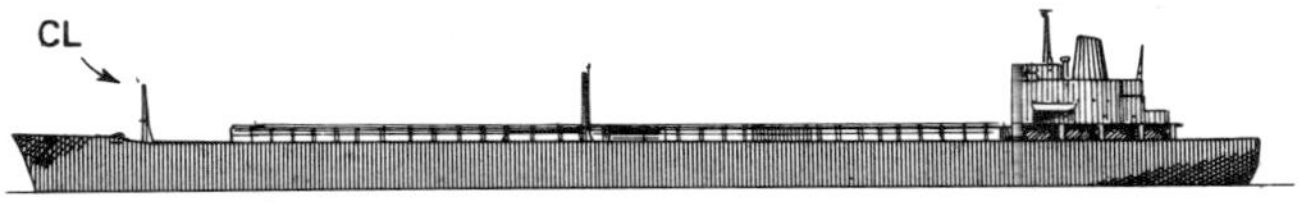

K_2MFK H
68340 JOYAMA MARU. Ja/Ja 1965; LGC; 29500; 198.03 × 11.02 (649.7 × 36.15); M; 15.75.

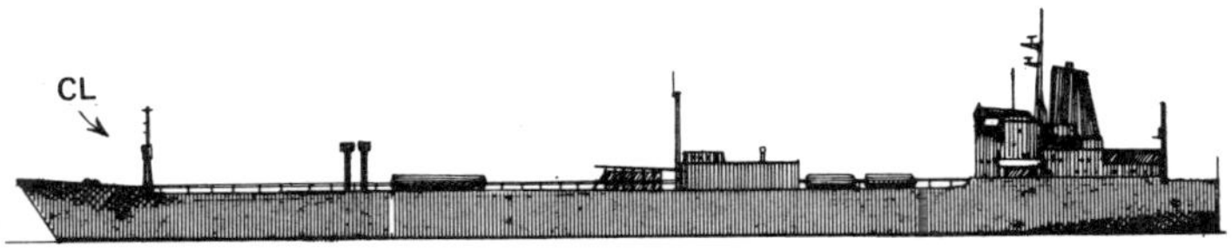

K_2MFK H
68350 SANDRINA. Pa/Fr 1973; LGC; 34300; 216.47 × 11.02 (710.2 × 36.15); M; 17.5; ex ATLANTE 1980; ex PROVIDENCE MULTINA; ex DORSETOWN 1973. Sisters: **68351 STENA OCEANICA** (Br) ex MANDRILL 1980; ex MALMROS MULTINA 1979; ex DOVERTOWN 1974 **68352 ANTILLA BAY** (NA) Similar: **68353 REYNOSA** (Me) **68354 MONTERREY** (Me).

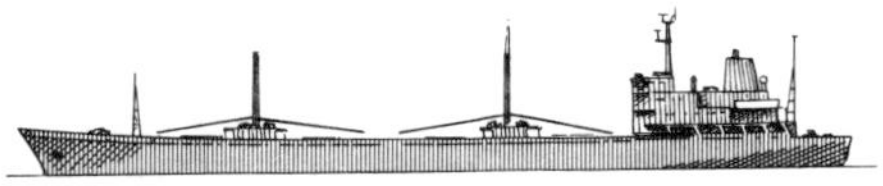

K_2MFK H
68360 OCEAN SKY. Ko/Ja 1975; C; 3700; 131.48 × 6.99 (431.36 × 22.93); M; 17.75; ex SUMMER BIRDIE 1979; ex ROSE DAPHNE 1978. Sisters: **68361 ROSE MALLOW** (Pa) **68362 WHITE JASMIN** (Pa) ex ROSE ACACIA 1978 **68363 OSAKA REEFER** (Ja) ex ADEN MARU 1978.

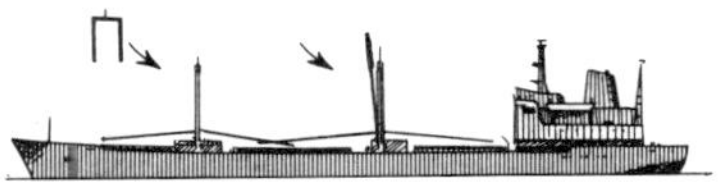

K_2MFK H
68370 UNION EVERGREEN. Tw/Tw 1968; C; 3600; 106.99 × 7.12 (351.02 × 23.36); M; 14.5.

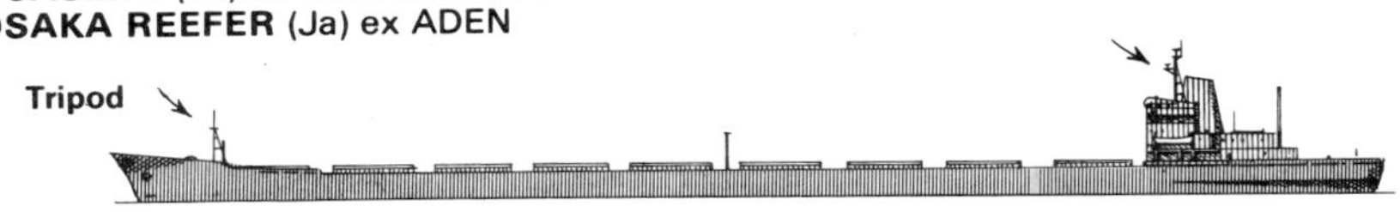

K_2MFK H1
68390 E.R. BRABANTIA. Be/Be 1971; B; 36800; 234.75 × 13.2 (770.18 × 43.31); M; 15. Sisters: **68391 ASEAN GREATNESS** (Pi) ex E.R. ANTVERPIA **68392 JAGAT SAMRAT** (In) Possibly similar: **68393 MARATHA MELODY** (In) **68394 MARATHA MARINER** (In).

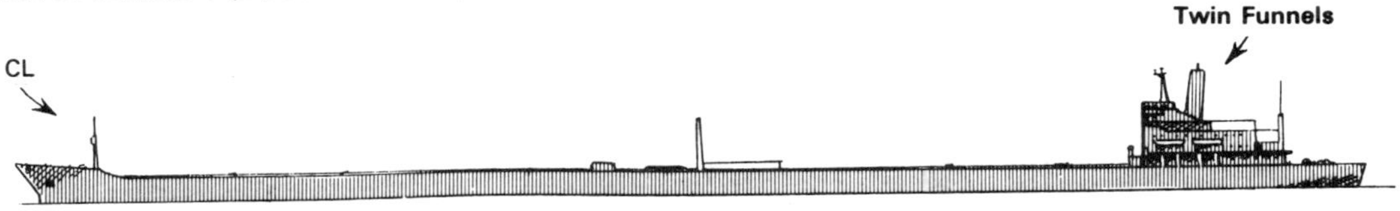

K_2MFK H1
68400 THORSHAMMER. No/Sw 1969; Tk; 113700; 324.98 × 20.44 (1066.21 × 67.06); T; 15.75. Sisters: **68401 NORSE KING** (No) **68402 NORSE QUEEN** (No) **68403 PHILLIPS ENTERPRISE** (Li) ex KOLLBJORG **68404 SYLVANIA** (Li) ex MARGA; ex MARGARET ONSTAD 1978 Probable sisters: **68405 ADNA** (No) **68406 NORSEMAN** (No) **68407 POLYVICTORIA** (No) **68408 REGINA** (No) Similar (single funnel): **68409 HOEGH LAUREL** (No) ex OSTHAV.

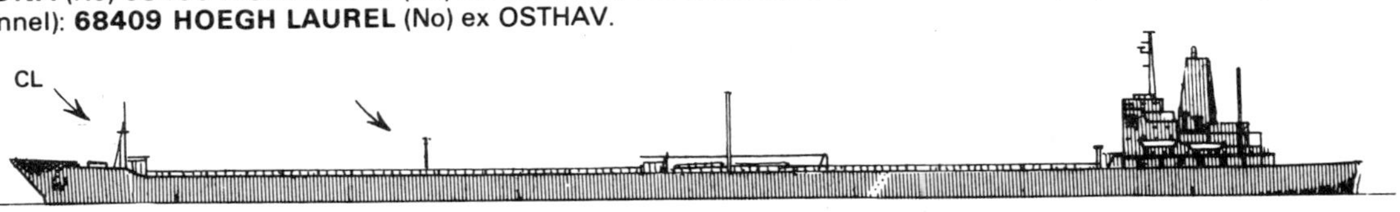

K_2MFK H1
68420 JALINGA. No/Ja 1970; Tk; 128300; 338.13 × 20.89 (1109.35 × 68.54); T; 15. Sisters (No flag): **68421 JAMUNDA 68422 JARABELLA 68423 JASTELLA** Similar (Li flag): **68424 VIOLANDO** ex VIOLANDO N. GOULANDRIS 1978.

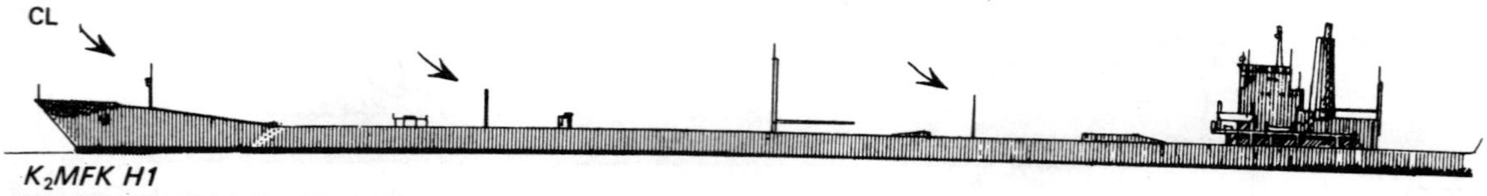

K_2MFK *H1*

68430 FABIAN. No/No 1972; Tk; 140500; 347.84 × 22.14 (1141.21 × 72.64); T; 15.5. Sisters (No flag): **68431 JULIAN 68432 VESPASIAN** Possibly similar (no short uprights on deck) **68433 BEAUMONT 68434 BEAURIVAGE** Similar: **68435 CYPRIAN 68436 SIR CHARLES HAMBRO 68437 NORBORN** ex SONGA 1971 **68438 NORBRIGHT** ex RADNY 1977.

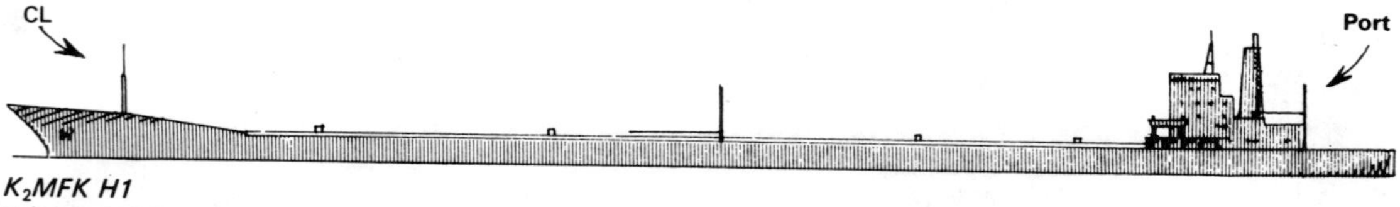

K_2MFK *H1*

68450 LICORNE OCEANE. Li/No 1975; Tk; 137900; 347. × 22.01 (1138.45 × 72.21); T; 15.5.

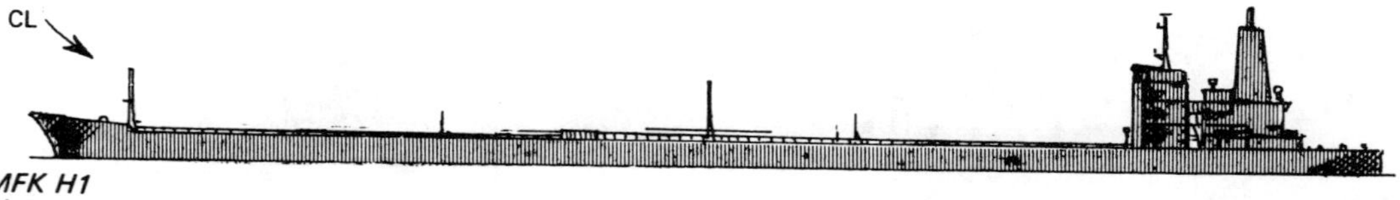

K_2MFK *H1*

68460 SPYROS A. LEMOS. Gr/Ja 1972; Tk; 103300; 322.99 × 19.73 (1059.6 × 64.73); T; 16.25; ex GONDWANA. Sister: **68461 PHOINIKAS** (Gr) ex EASTERN PROSPECTOR; ex KULU.

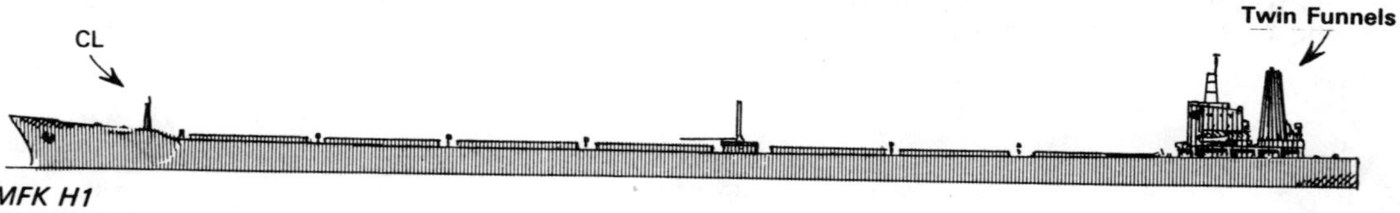

K_2MFK *H1*

68470 BRAZILIAN WEALTH. Li/Ys 1973; OO; 141800; 335.03 × 21.99 (1099.17 × 72.14); TSM; 16.5; ex TARFALA 1978. Sister: **68471 RHINE ORE** (Li) ex TORNE 1979 Similar: **68472 MARY R. KOCH** (Li).

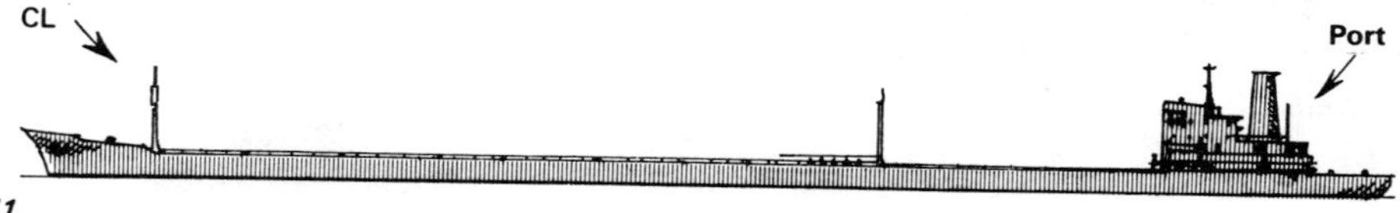

K_2MFK *H1*

68480 ALABAMA GETTY. Li/Sw 1971; Tk; 63200; 284.13 × 16.7 (932.18 × 54.74); M; 16; ex CURRO 1976. Sister: **68481 JUANITA** (No).

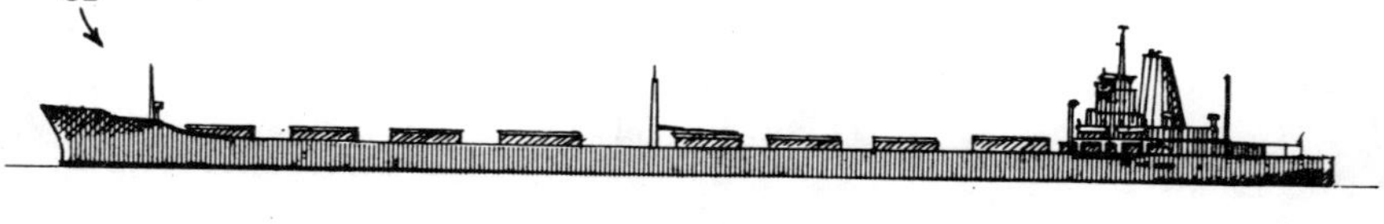

K_2MFK *H1*

68490 BALBINA. Li/Ja 1967; OBO; 43400; 254.52 × 14.02 (835.04 × 46); M; 14.75.

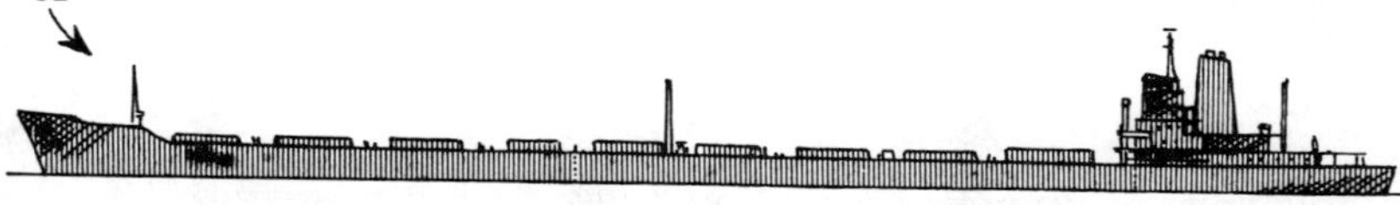

K_2MFK *H1*

68500 MOZART. Li/Ja 1969; OBO; 43500; 254.52 × 14.01 (835.04 × 45.96); M; 15.5.

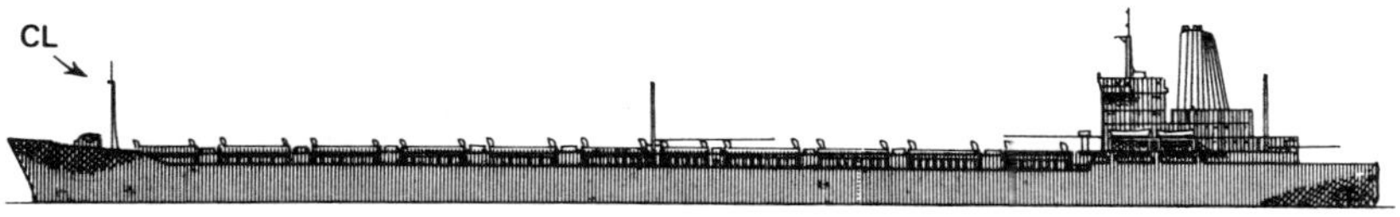

K_2MFK H1
68510 ROYAL LYNX. Pa/Ja 1966; OBO; 38100; 250.86 × 13.75 (823.03 × 45.11); M; 16; ex CELEBRATION VENTURE 1980; ex ERIDGE 1978. Similar (Smaller funnels): **68511 ENDURANCE** (Li) ex SABRINA; ex GRAFTON 1978 **68512 TRADE OCEAN** (Gr) ex HEYTHROP 1978.

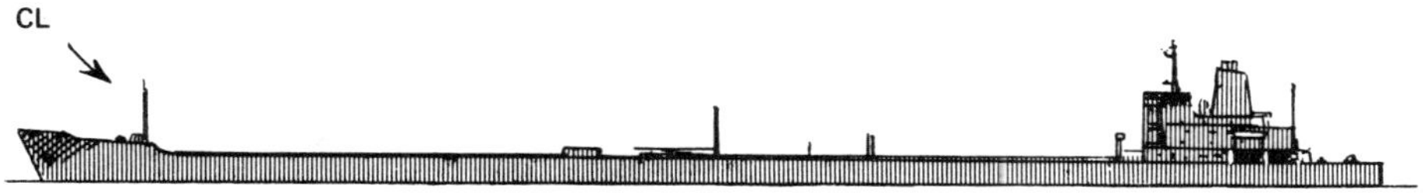

K_2MFK H1
68520 AMOCO CAIRO. Li/Ja 1975; Tk; 76500; 280.02 × 15.24 (918.7 × 50); M; 15.25. Sisters: **68521 AMOCO WHITING** (Li) ex AMOCO TEHRAN 1980 **68522 AMOCO TRINIDAD.**

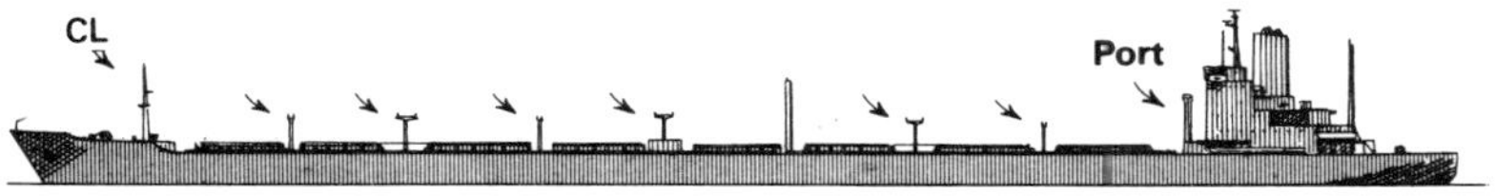

K_2MFK H1
● **68530 DONAU MARU.** Ja/Ja 1969; OO; 45200; 239.02 × 13.34 (784.19 × 43.77); M; 15.5. Sisters: **68531 VOLGA MARU** (Ja) **68532 CASPIAN TRADER** (Li) ex CASPI MARU 1971 **68533 MOSTUN SANKO** (No) **68534 REGENT PIMPERNEL** (Li) ex KIEV MARU 1972 **68535 SPRING ODESSA** (Sg) ex ODESSA MARU 1972 Similar: **68536 CAUCASUS MARU** (Ja) **68537 EASTERN HAZEL** (Li).

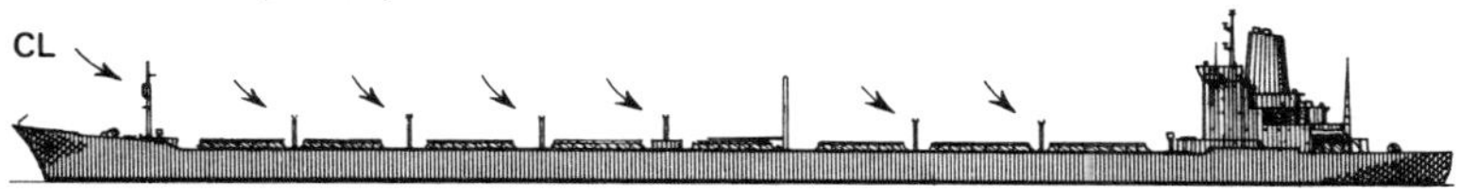

K_2MFK H1
● **68550 ARMAND HAMMER.** Li/Ja 1967; OO; 43900; 232.49 × 13.13 (762.76 × 43.08); M; 15.5; ex MARGARET C. MOSHER 1968.

●
68551

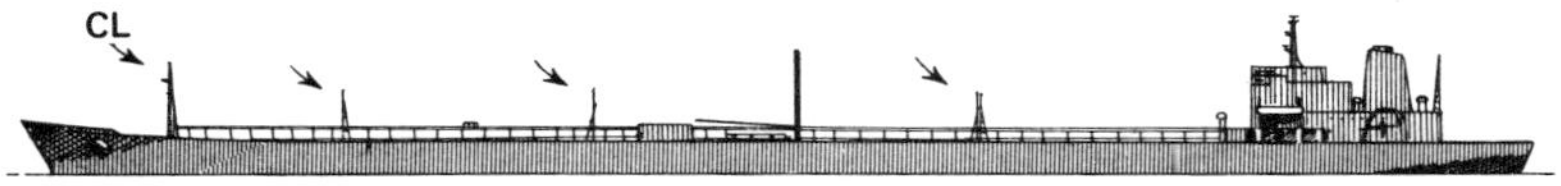

K_2MFK H1
⋆**68560 MESTA.** Bu/Ja 1974; Tk; 46800; 237.01 × 12.92 (777.59 × 42.39); M; 16.5. Sister: ⋆**68561 OSAM** (Bu).

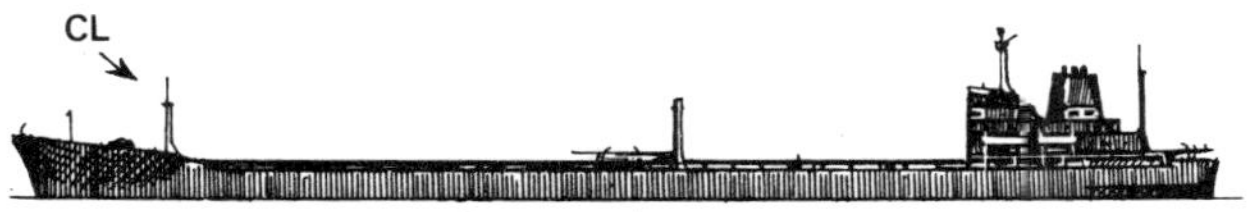

K_2MFK H1
68570 PETROSHIP A. Li/Ys 1975; Tk; 25000; 197.64 × 11.7 (648.43 × 38.39); M; 16.5. Sister: **68571 PETROSHIP B** (Li).

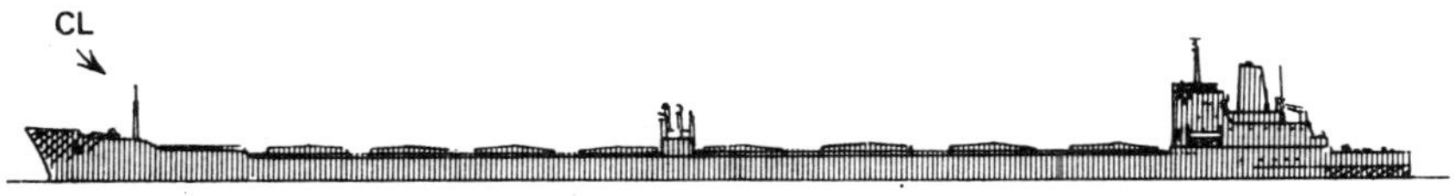

K_2MFK H1
68580 ATLANTIC BOUNTY. Li/Sw 1971; OBO; 55600; 256.55 × 15.11 (841.7 × 49.57); M; 16; ex DALSLAND 1980; ex ERIC K. FERNSTROM 1978. Sister: **68581 ATLANTIC ENDEAVOUR** (Li) ex FUJISAN 1978 Similar (larger KP amidships): **68582 SILVERLAND** (Sw) ex A.K. FERNSTROM 1977.

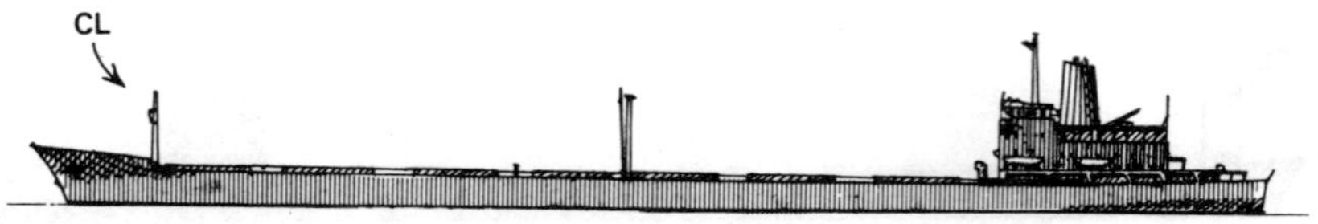

K_2MFK H1
68590 HOEGH RANGER. No/Ja 1966; OBO; 42100; 242.5 × 13.69 (795.6 × 44.91); M; 15.5. Sister: **68591 BYZANTION** (Gr) ex VEGA STINGRAY; HOEGH RAY.

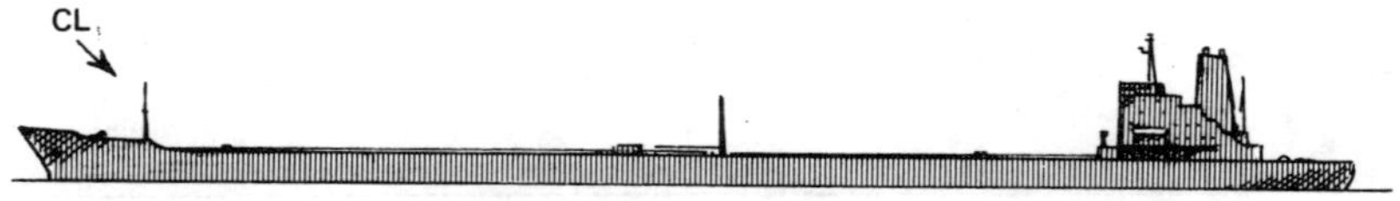

K_2MFK H1
68600 KURUSHIMA MARU. Ja/Ja 1973; Tk; 44800; 245.98 × 13.27 (807.02 × 45.53); M; 15.5. Sisters (Sg flag): **68601 VIRGINIA LILY 68602 VIRGINIA STAR.**

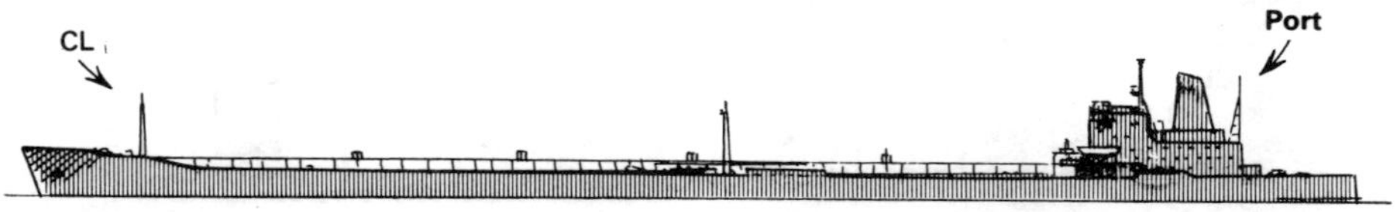

K_2MFK H1
68610 MARAO. Po/Sw-Po; 1972/73; Tk; 69300; 280.09 × 16.7 (918.9 × 54.8); M; 15.5; Foreward section built Portugal 1972—aft section built Sweden 1973. Sisters (Po flag): **68611 MAROFA 68612 MONTEMURO.**

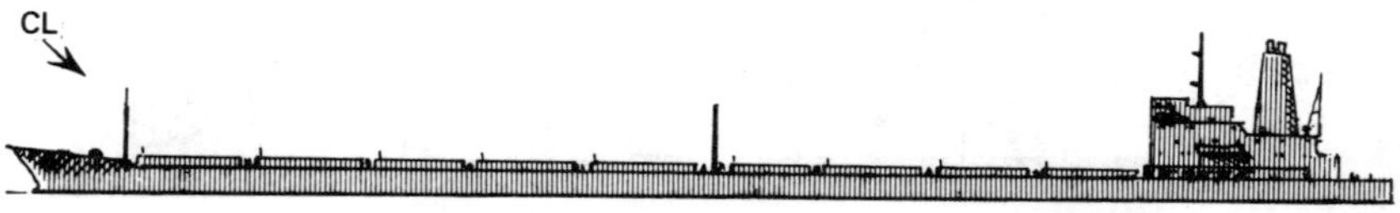

K_2MFK H1
68620 PENTELI. Gr/Ja 1972; OBO; 57800; 261.02 × 15.85 (856.36 × 52); M; 16; ex AEGEAN ISLAND 1980. Sister: **68621 NEMEA** (Li) ex AEGEAN WAVE 1980 Probable sister: **68622 AEGEAN SEA** (Li).

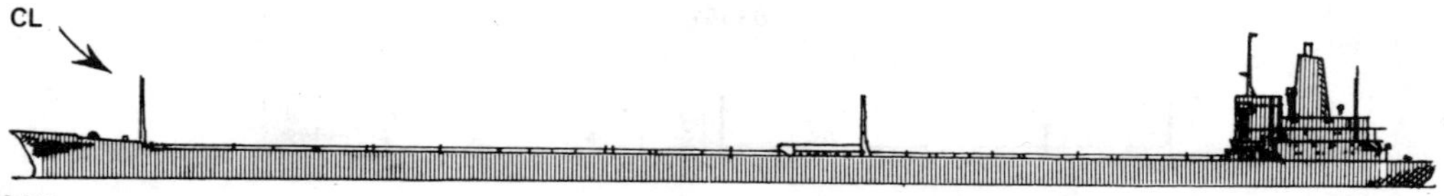

K_2MFK H1
68630 MOBIL TERN. Li/Ja 1970; Tk; 88300; 315.02 × 19.32 (1033.53 × 63.39); T; 16; ex AL ROWDAH 1979.

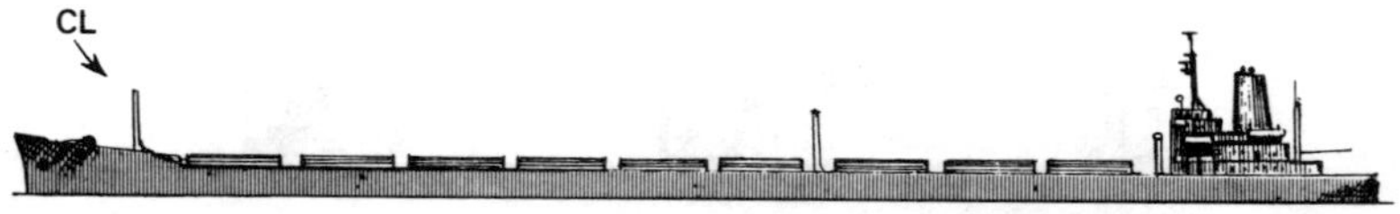

K_2MFK H1
68640 THYELLA. Li/Ja 1966; OO; 19400 (Ore) 40900 (Oil); 242.02 × 13.68 (794.03 × 44.88); M; 16. Sister: **68641 TORNADO** (Gr).

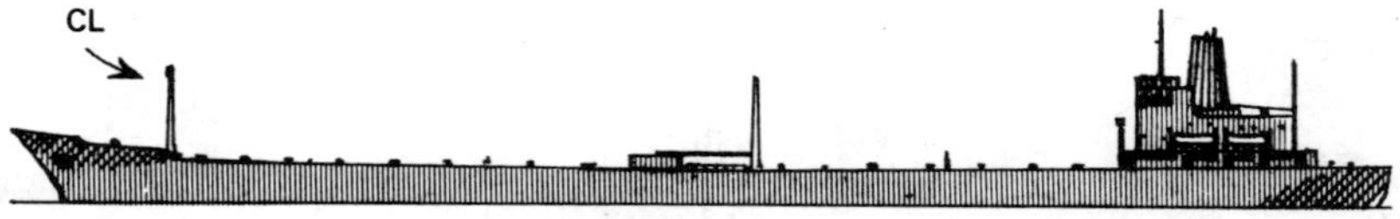

K_2MFK H1
68650 VOO SHEE. Tw/Ja 1969; Tk; 52400; 253.04 × 15.57 (830.18 × 51.08); M; 16.5. Sisters (some Tw built): **68651 HSIEN YUAN** (Tw) **68652 SHEN NON** (Tw) **68653 YU TSAO** (Tw) **68654 FORTUNE** (Li) **68655 GLORY** (Li) **68656 AFRAN ENERGY** (Li).

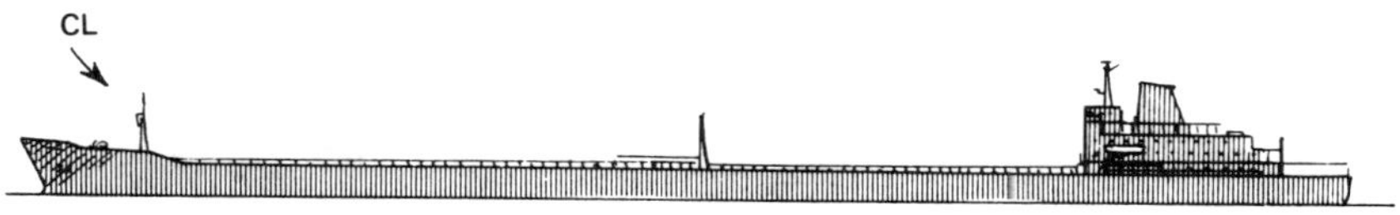

K_2MFK H1
68660 BONNY. Fi/Sw 1969; Tk; 51500; 255.25 × 14.38 (837.43 × 47.18); M; 16. Sister: **68661 PEGNY** (Fi).

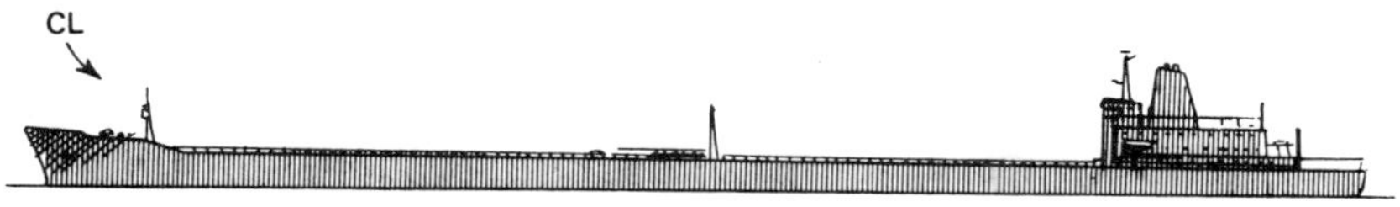

K_2MFK H1
68670 AFRAN LEEWARD. Li/Sw 1972; Tk; 50400; 255.25 × 14.38 (837.46 × 47.18); M; 16.5; ex EVITA DAN 1978; ex EVINA 1976. Possible sister: **68671 SEA ROVER** (Sg) ex RONA RIVER 1978.

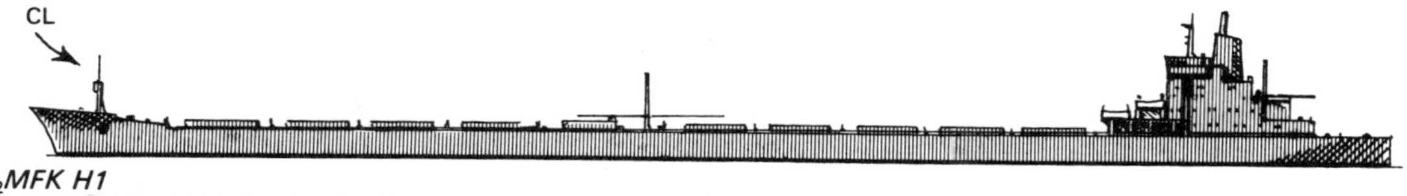

K_2MFK H1
68680 ALVA BAY. Br/Sw 1973; OO; 120700; 332.57 × 20.65 (1091.11 × 67.75); T; 16. Sister: **68681 ALVA SEA** (Br)—motor ship.

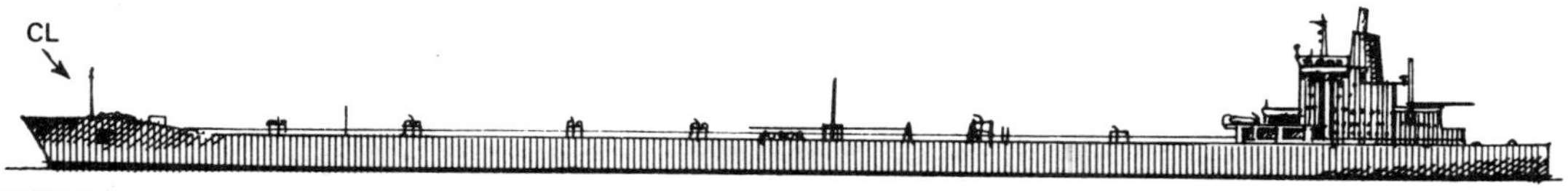

K_2MFK H1
● **68690 BRALI.** No/Sw 1969; Tk; 113500; 332.24 × 20.68 (1090.03 × 67.85); T; 16; ex VENI 1980. Sisters: **68691 AL SAUDIA** (Si) ex ALVA STAR 1980 **68692 ILE DE LA CITE** (Li) **68693 BUENA SUERTE** (Gr) ex BRITA ONSTAD 1979 Probable sister: **68694 THORSHAVET** (No).

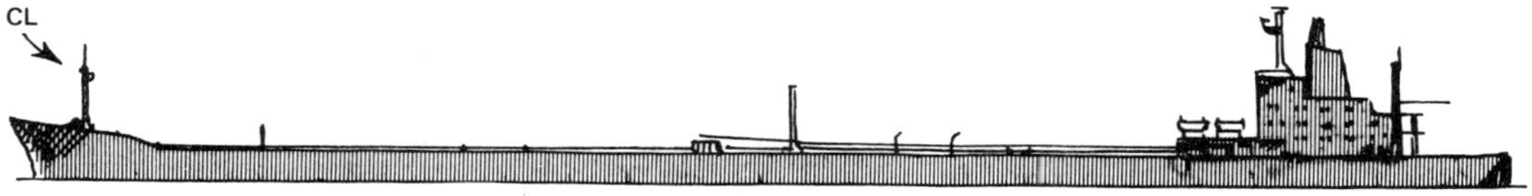

K_2MFK H1
68700 MOBIL CONDOR. Li/Sw 1970; Tk; 104600; 332.32 × 20.66 (1090.29 × 67.78); T; —; ex TITAN 1975. Sister: **68701 ENERGY PROSPERITY** (Li) ex HALCYON THE GREAT 1974 Similar: **68702 TRAJAN** (No) ex CORONA.

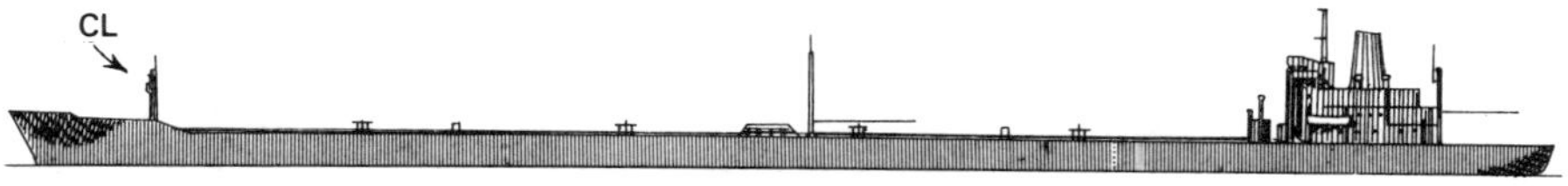

K_2MFK H1
68710 OCEANUS. Sw/Sw 1969; Tk; 67500; 281.44 × 16.7 (923.36 × 54.79); M; 16.

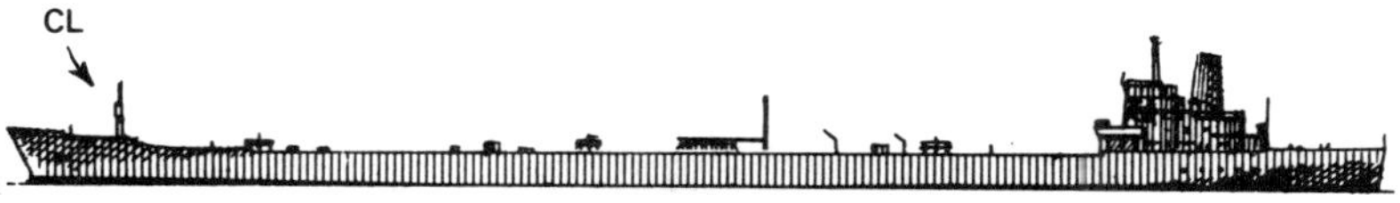

K_2MFK H1
68720 TASSIA. Gr/Sw 1969; Tk; 64000; 272.24 × 16.28 (893.18 × 53.41); M; 16; ex NEW STAR.

K_2MFK H1
68730 DORIOS. Li/Sw 1967; Tk; 43200; 258.02 × 13.5 (846.52 × 44.29); M; 16; ex PAPPAS THESSALONIKI 1970. Sisters (Li flag): **68731 MEGAS** ex BESSIE A. PAPPAS 1970 **68732 ZOE** ex KATHERINE A. PAPPAS 1970 Similar: **68733 MARILIA** ex BEAUVAL 1978.

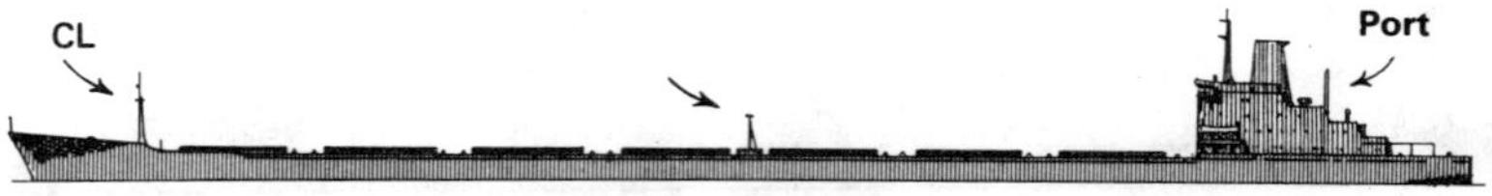

K_2MFK H1
68740 CATHAY SEATRADE. Li/Sw 1973; B; 35500; 224.06 × 13.1 (735.1 × 42.98); M; 16; ex LILI BILLNER 1978.

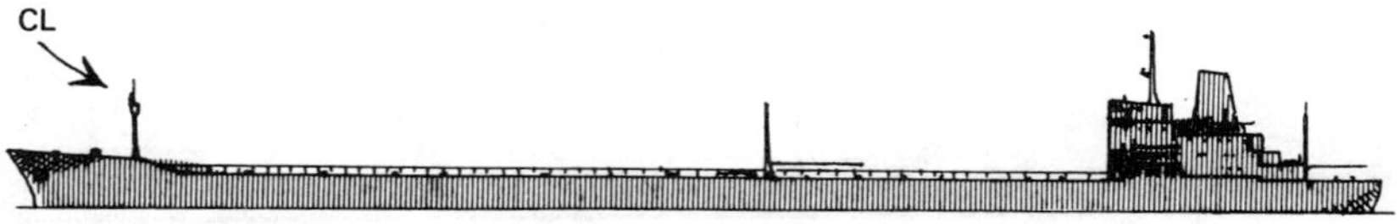

K_2MFK H1
68750 THEONYMPHOS. Gr/Sw 1968; Tk; 44900; 255.33 × 14.38 (837.7 × 47.18); M; 16; ex WANGSTAR 1979; ex FOLDSTAR 1978; ex WANGSTAR 1976; ex ARTEMIS 1974.

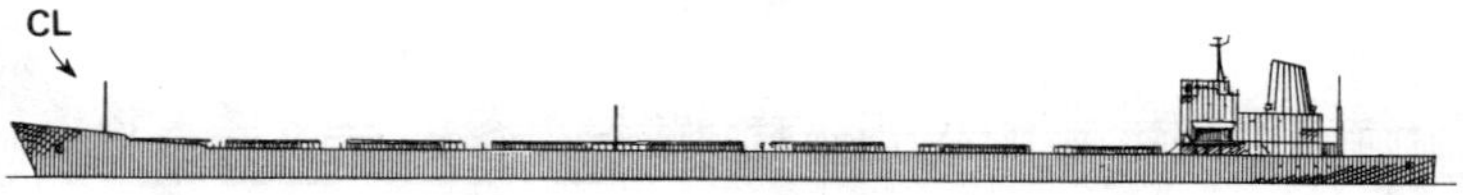

K_2MFK H1
⋆68760 JADRAN. Ys/Br 1976; B; 38500; 228.12 × 14.03 (748.43 × 46.03); M; 15. Sisters (Ys flag): **⋆68761 KORDUN ⋆68762 KOSMAJ ⋆68763 ORJEN ⋆68764 SUTJESKA.**

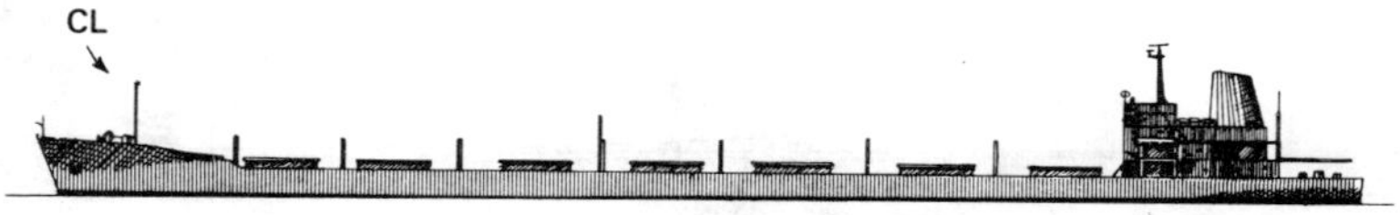

K_2MFK H1
68770 THETIS. Gr/Br 1974; B; 35500; 228.05 × 14.03 (748.2 × 46.03); M; 15. Sisters (Gr flag): **68771 MELETE 68772 NAIAD.**

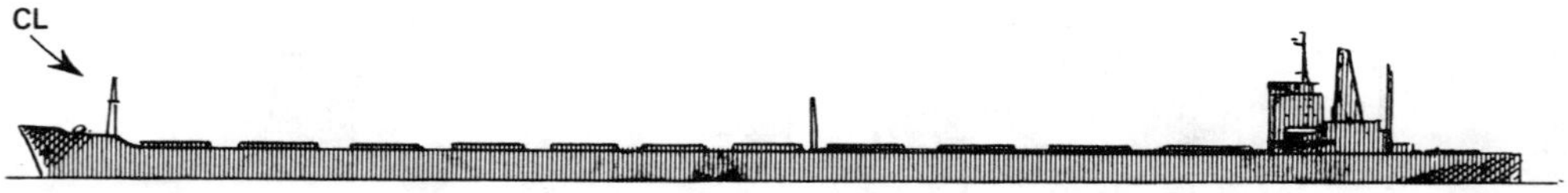

K_2MFK H1
68780 RHETORIC. Li/Ja 1971; OBO; 77000; 303.51 × 18.25 (995.76 × 59.88); T; 15.75. Sister: **68781 ROMANTIC** (Li).

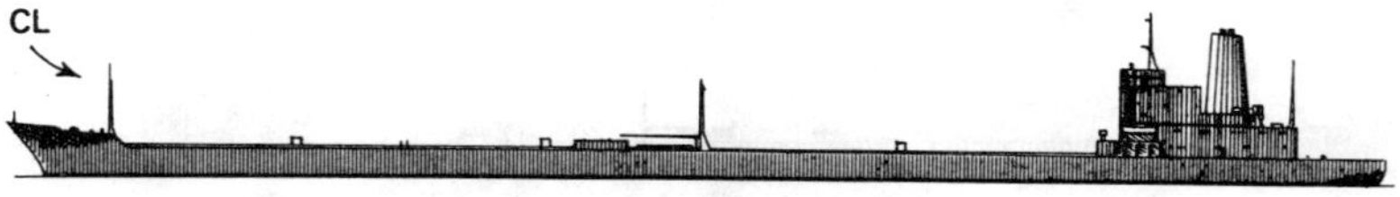

K_2MFK H1
68790 AMOCO VOYAGER. Li/Ja 1973; Tk; 35300; 239.3 × 13.24 (785.1 × 43.44); M; 16; ex NAVARCHOS MIAOULIS 1977. Similar: **68791 LYNDA** (Li).

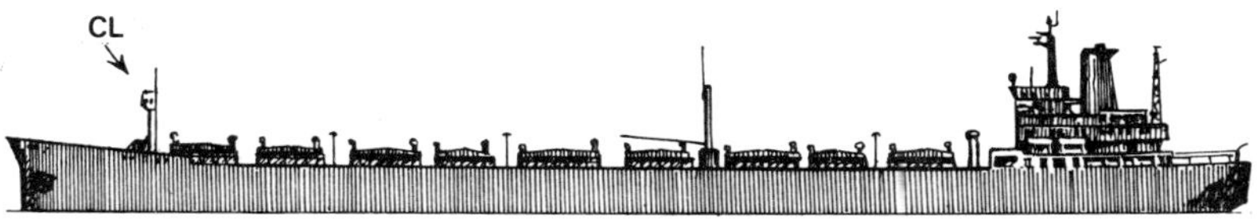

K_2MFK H1
★**68800 MARSHAL BUDENYY.** Ru/Pd 1975; OBO; 59600; 245.52 × 16 (805.51 × 52.49); M; 16; **"B524"** type. Sisters (Ru flag): ★**68801 MARSHAL KONYEV** ★**68802 MARSHAL ROKOSSOVSKIY** ★**68803 MARSHAL ZHUKHOV.**

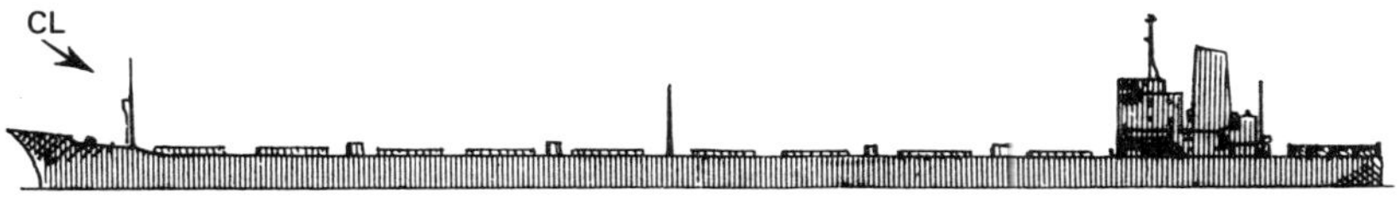

K_2MFK H1
68810 POINT CLEAR. Li/Ja 1972; OBO; 57100; 264.35 × 14.63 (867.29 × 48); M; 16; Helicopter deck aft. Similar: **68811 NAVIOS COURIER** (Li) ex ROSS ISLE **68812 VERGO** (Gr).

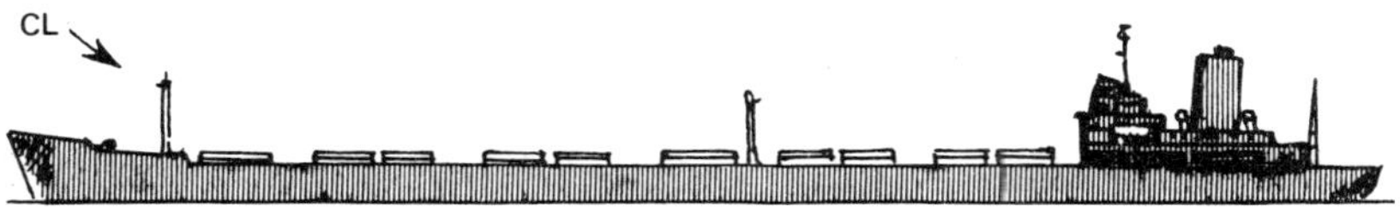

K_2MFK H1
68820 MOBIL ENERGY. Br/Sw-Ja 1962/71; OBO; 42600; 252.64 × 13.22 (828.87 × 43.37); T; 15.75; Converted from tanker 1971.

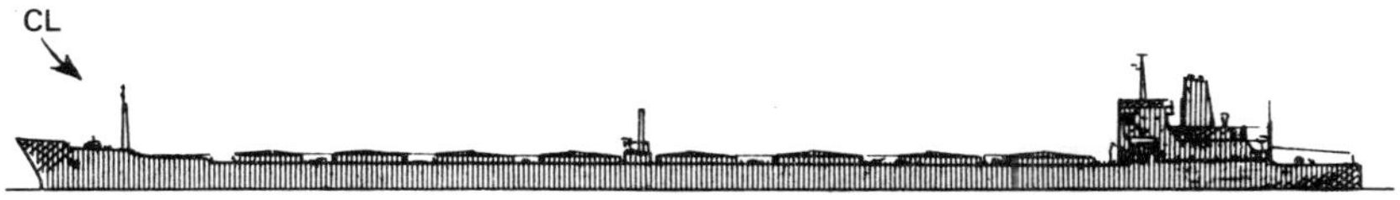

K_2MFK H1
68830 LAKE BERRYESSA. Li/Sw 1972; OBO; 51400; 256.55 × 15.11 (841.7 × 49.57); M; 16; ex ARIADNE 1976. Sister: **68831 JAG LAADKI** (In) ex ATHEL LAADKI 1977; ex JAG LAADKI 1974.

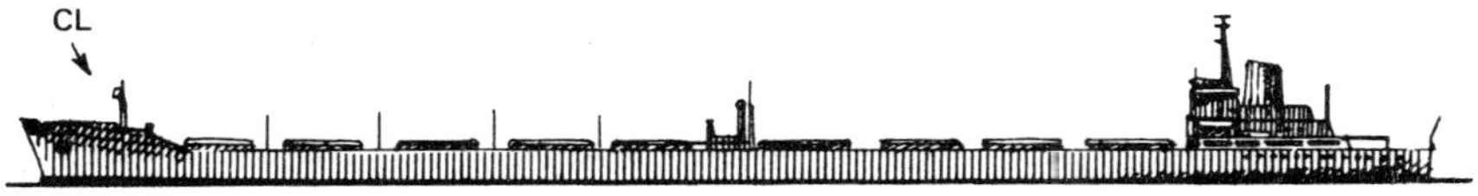

K_2MFK H1
● **68840 VARENNA.** No/Sw 1970; OBO; 55000; 256.52 × 15.11 (841.6 × 49.57); M; 15.5. Similar: **68841 CAST TERN** (Br) ex THISTLE STAR; ex SPYROS A. LEMOS 1978; ex VIANNA 1976 **68842 VANESSA** (No).

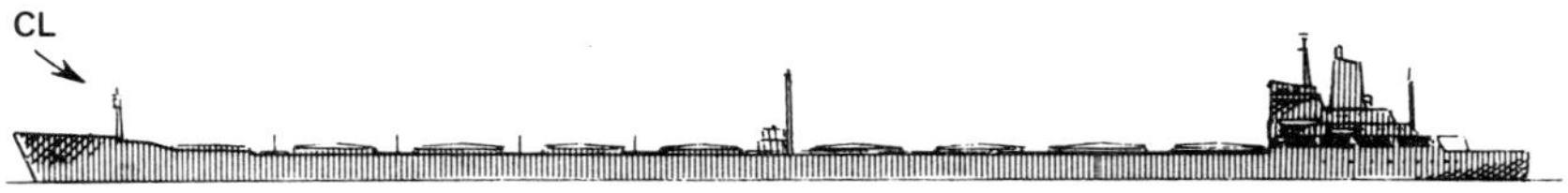

K_2MFK H1
68850 LAKE SHASTA. Li/Sw 1973; OBO; 54800; 256.47 × 15.11 (841.44 × 49.57); M; 16; ex APHRODITE 1976. Similar: **68851 OBO QUEEN** (No) **68852 MIHALIS** (Gr) ex KONGSHAV 1978.

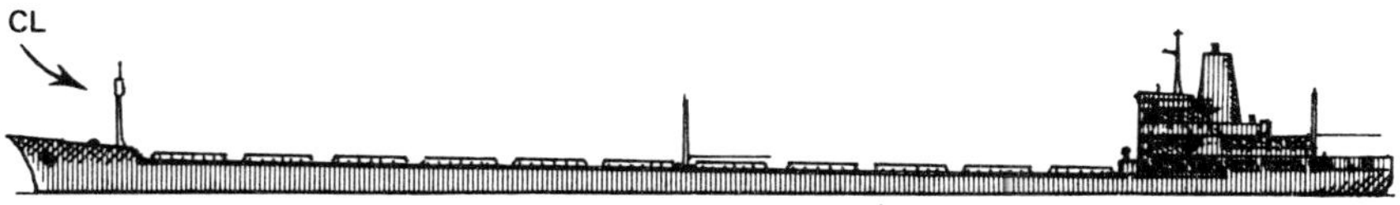

K_2MFK H1
68860 MARITIME HAWK. Pa/Ja 1968; OBO; 60500; 265.23 × 15.47 (870.18 × 50.75); T; 15.5; ex JACOB MALMROS 1977. Sister: **68861 MARITIME EAGLE** (Pa) ex FRANS MALMROS 1977.

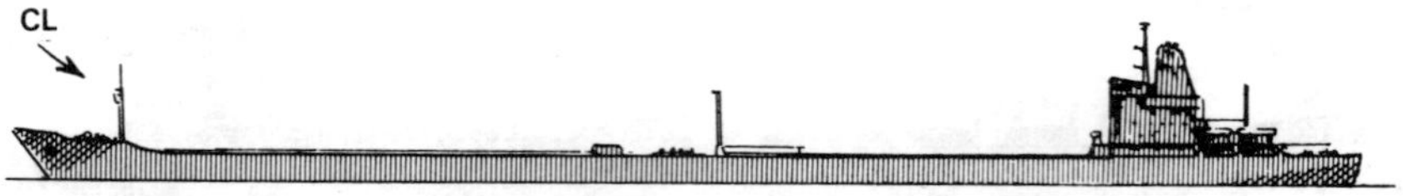

K_2MFK H1
★**68870 HEINERSDORF.** DDR/Ja 1968; Tk; 47000; 256.01 × 13.33 (839.93 × 43.73); M; 16; ex ATLANTIC MARCHIONESS 1974. Sister: **68871 ATLANTIC MARQUESS** (Li) Similar: **68872 ATLANTIC PRINCESS** (Gr).

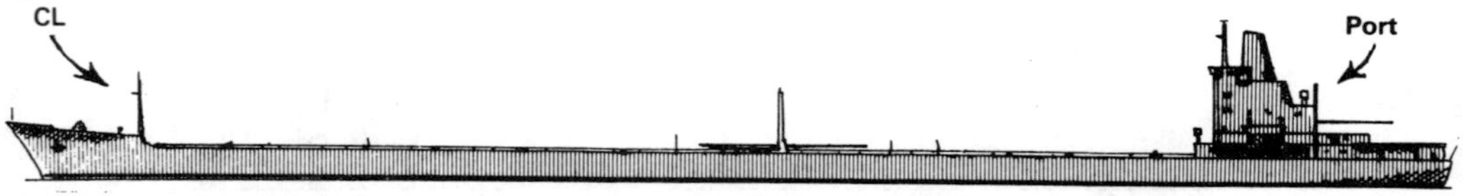

K_2MFK H1
68880 CASTLETON. Br/Ja 1973; Tk; 113200; 325.76 × 20.5 (1068.77 × 67.26); T; 14.75.

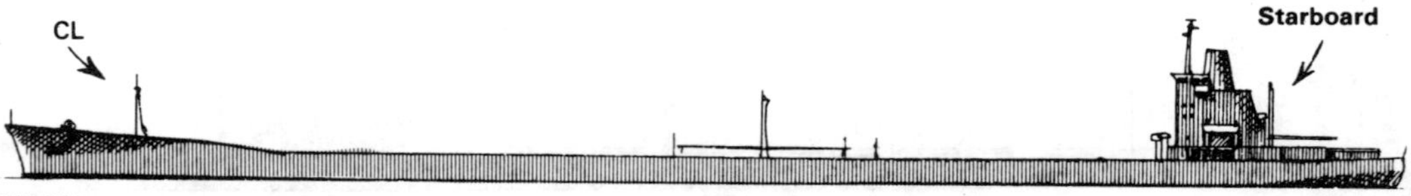

K_2MFK H1
68890 PHILIP OF MACEDON. Gr/Ja 1970; Tk; 113100; 325.26 × 18.9 (1067.13 × 62.01); T; 15.75; ex CARNEGIE 1979; ex BOXFORD 1973.

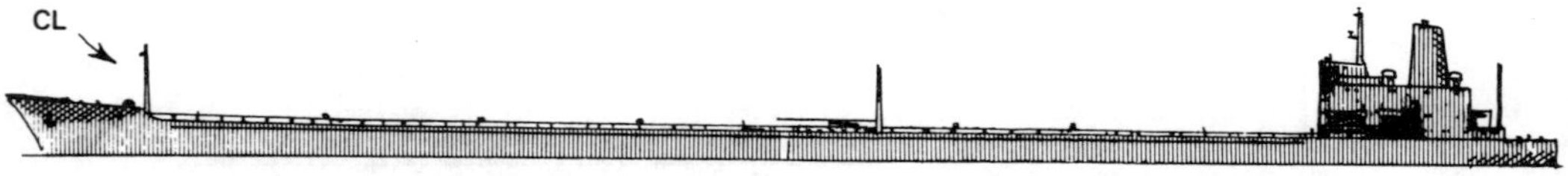

K_2MFK H1
68900 WORLD CHIEF. Li/Ja 1969; Tk; 98500; 329.73 × 19.5 (1081.79 × 63.98); T; 16.75.

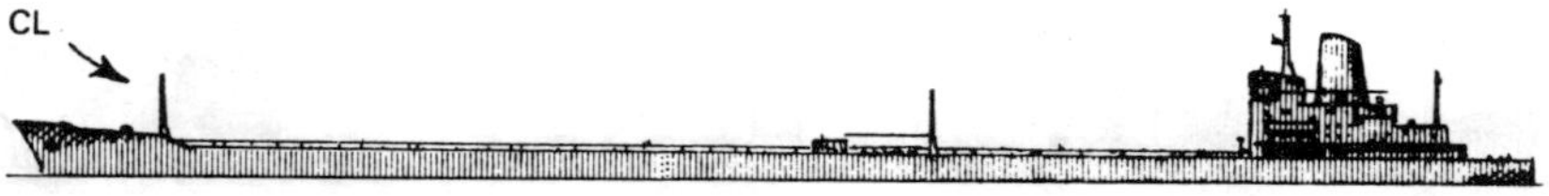

K_2MFK H1
68910 WORLD KINDNESS. Li/Ja 1969; Tk; 41500; 257.49 × 13.37 (844.78 × 43.86); M; 17. Sister: **68911 WORLD KNOWLEDGE** (Li).

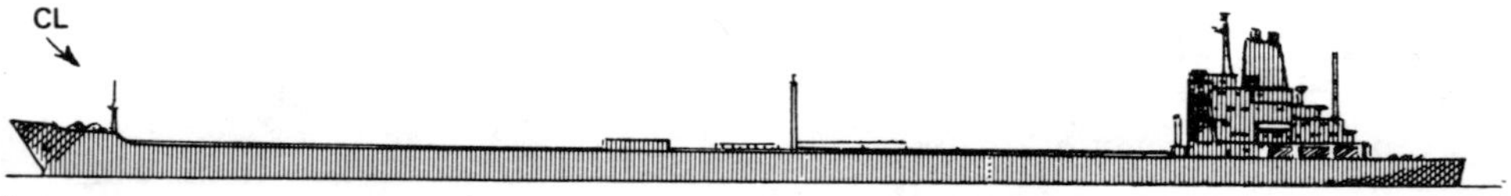

K_2MFK H1
★**68920 ZAWRAT.** Pd/Ja 1975; Tk; 81200; 293 × 15.29 (961.29 × 50.16); M; 16.25. Sisters (Pd flag): ★**68921 CZANTORIA** ★**68922 SOKOLICA.**

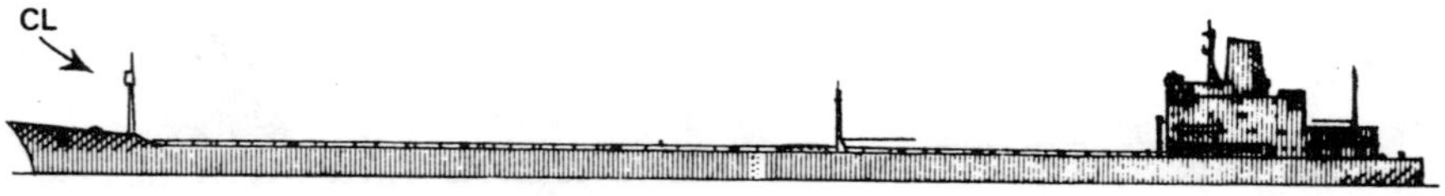

K_2MFK H1
68930 PETROSTAR XV. Si/Ja 1966; Tk; 48200; 271.03 × 14.19 (889.21 × 46.56); M; 16.25; ex WORLD STANDARD 1980.

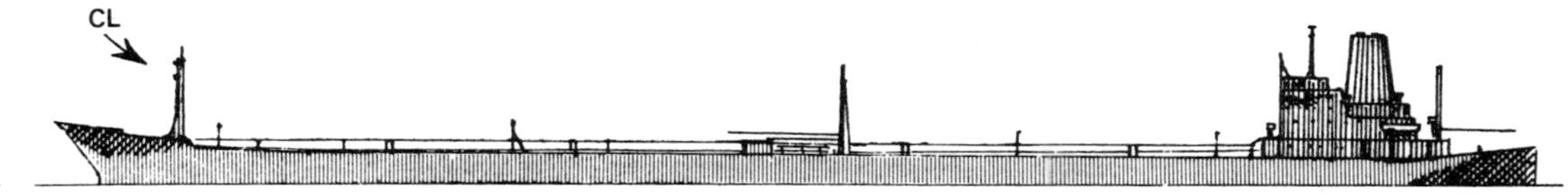

K_2MFK H1
68940 T. G. SHAUGNESSY. Br/Ja 1971; Tk; 133700; 338.11 × 20.58 (1109.28 × 67.52); M; 15.5. Sister: **68941 PORT HAWKESBURY** (Br) Similar: **68942 I. D. SINCLAIR** (Br).

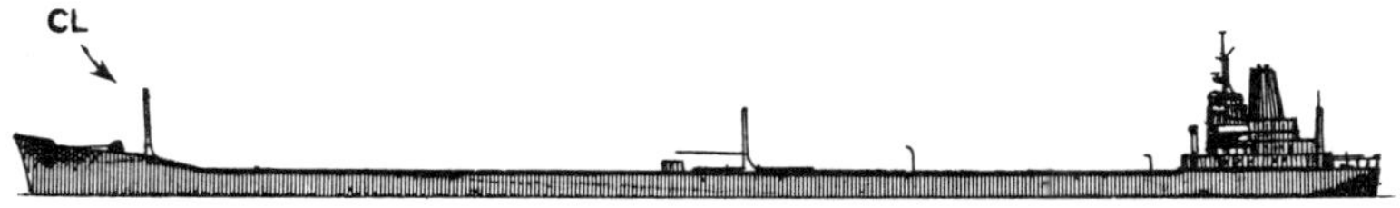

K_2MFK H1
68950 EVANTHIA. Gr/Ja 1966; Tk; 38300; 239.12 × 13.49 (784.51 × 44.26); M; —. Sister: **68951 JOHN** (Gr) ex JOHN P. GOULANDRIS 1980.

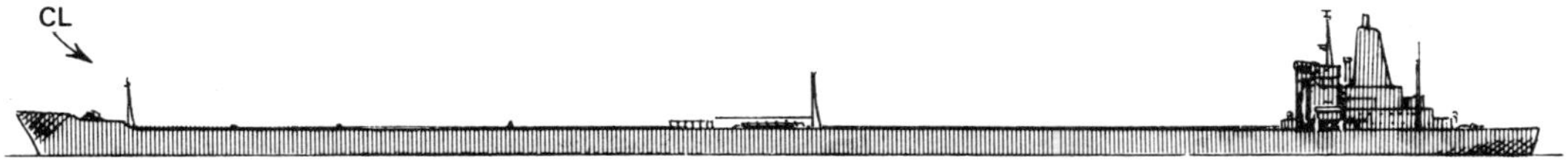

K_2MFK H1
68960 FULTON. Sg/Ja 1972; Tk; 106000; 328.61 × 20.45 (1078.12 × 67.09); T; 15.25; ex ATHINA 1980; ex ATHINA S. NIARCHOS 1979; In use as a storage vessel at Singapore.

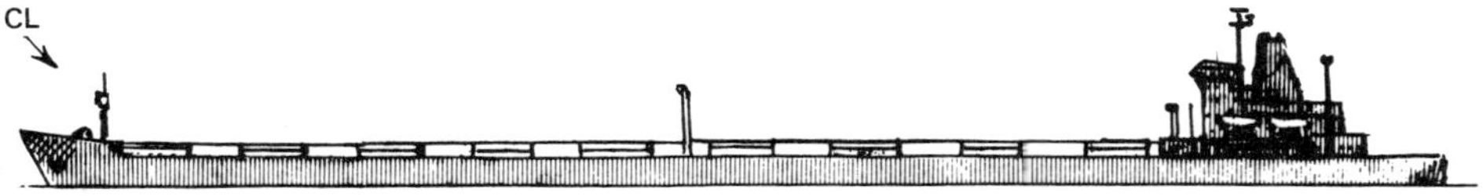

K_2MFK H1
68970 LYRA. It/FRG 1970; OBO; 84200; 293.2 × 17.44 (961.94 × 57.22); M; 16; ex NAI MARCUS 1980; ex MARCUS LOLLI—GHETTI 1974; ex TARIM 1972.

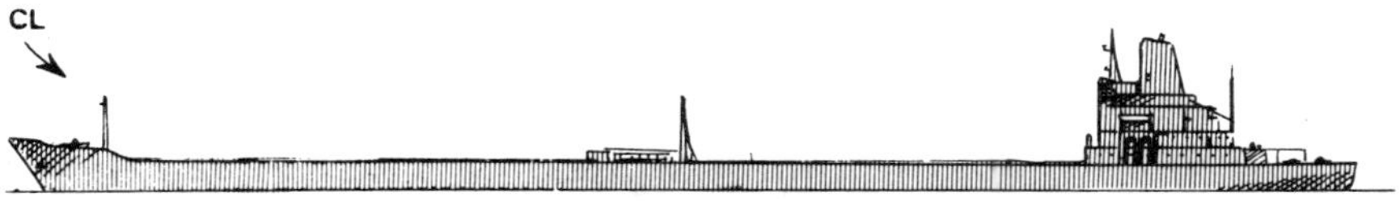

K_2MFK H1
68980 ALLEGRO. Li/Ja 1967; Tk; 46400; 266.02 × 14.2 (872.77 × 46.59); T; —. Sister: **68981 FIDELIO** (Li) Similar (lower superstructure & taller funnel): **68982 PETROS** (Li) ex PETROS J. GOULANDRIS **68983 CHRYSSI** (Li) ex CHRYSSI P. GOULANDRIS 1980.

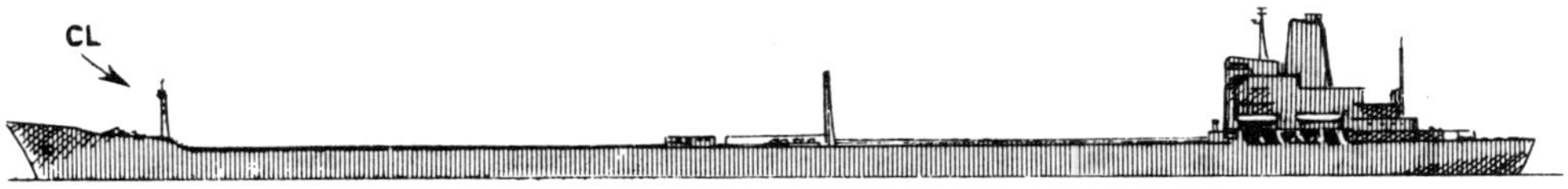

K_2MFK H1
● **68990 NICHOLAS.** Li/Ja 1968; Tk; 86500; 303 × 18.52 (994.09 × 60.76); T; 15.5; ex NICHOLAS J. GOULANDRIS 1978.

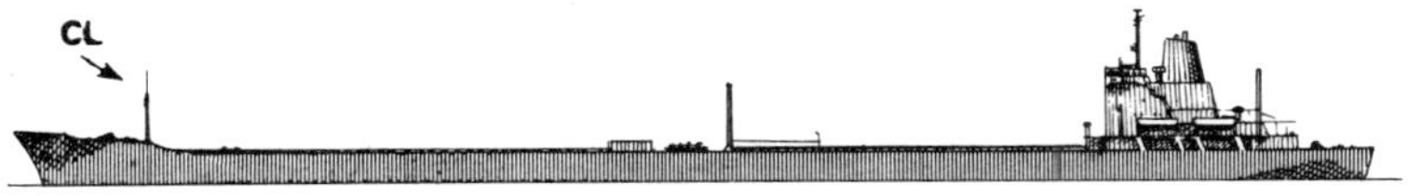

K_2MFK H1
69000 SPES. Pa/Ja 1968; Tk; 37900; 231.66 × 13.38 (760.04 × 43.9); M; 16.

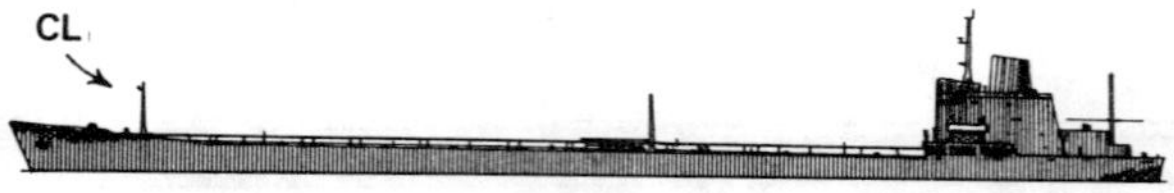

K_2MFK H1
69010 CIUDAD DE BARRANCABERMEJA. Co/Ca 1975; Tk; 23700; 182.89 × 11.42 (600.03 × 37.47); M; 15; ex LUCELLUM 1978. Sister: **69011 LUCERNA** (Br) Possibly similar (Li flag): **69012 OGDEN OTTAWA 69013 OGDEN SAGUENAY.**

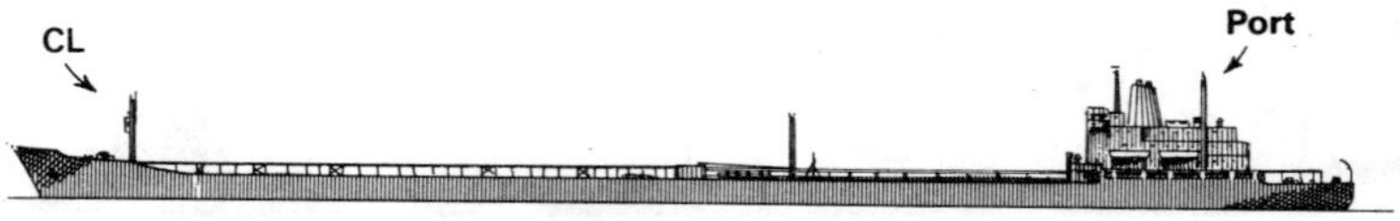

K_2MFK H1
⋆69020 RADE KONCAR. Ys/Ja 1967; Tk; 36300; 226.52 × 12.79 (743.18 × 41.96); M; 16.5. Sisters (Ys flag): **⋆69021 JORDAN NIKOLOV ⋆69022 MILOS MATIJEVIC ⋆69023 SLAVISA VAJNER.**

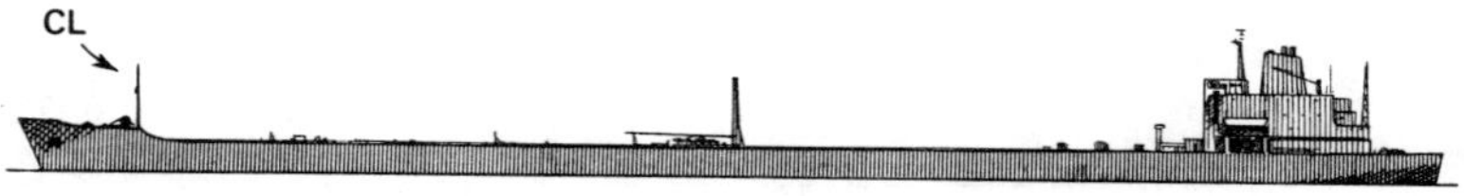

K_2MFK H1
69030 ALAMO. Li/Ja 1978; Tk; 33100; 238.01 × 12.16 (780.87 × 39.9); M; 15.

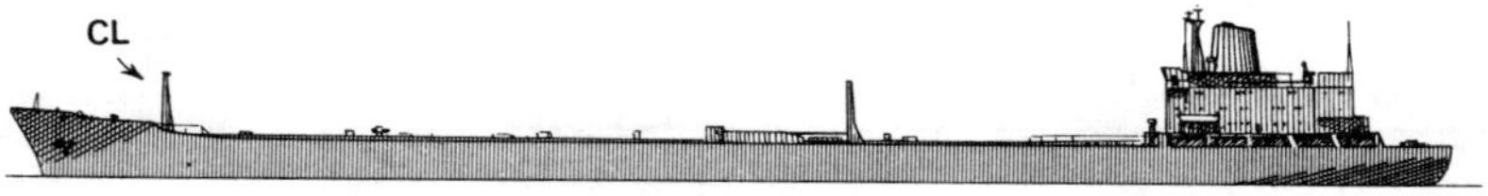

K_2MFK H1
69040 AMANDA MILLER. Au/Au 1971; Tk; 39100; 239.28 × 13.17 (785.04 × 43.21); M; 16.5.

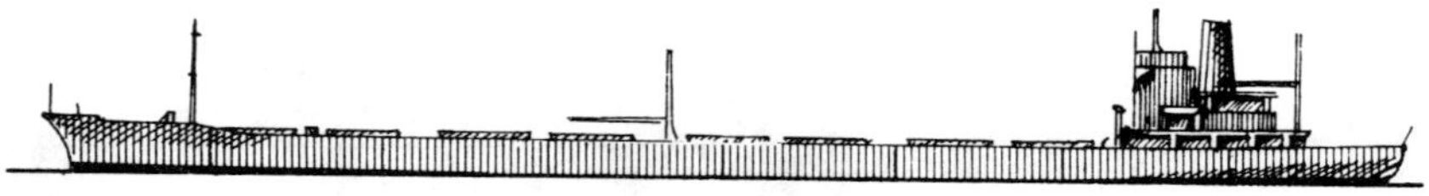

K_2MFK H1
69050 BRAZILIAN FRIENDSHIP. Li/Tw 1977; OO; 48900; 253.02 × 15.15 (830.12 × 49.7); M; 15.5.

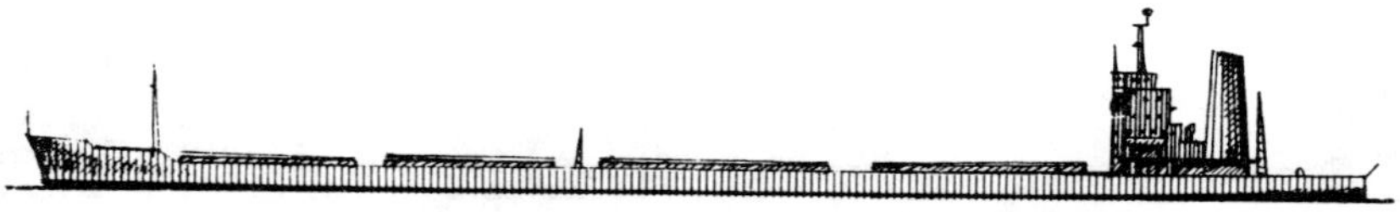

K_2MFK H1
69060 KAKOGAWA MARU. Ja/Ja 1970; O; 43600; 250.02 × 13.31 (820.28 × 43.67); M; 15.25.

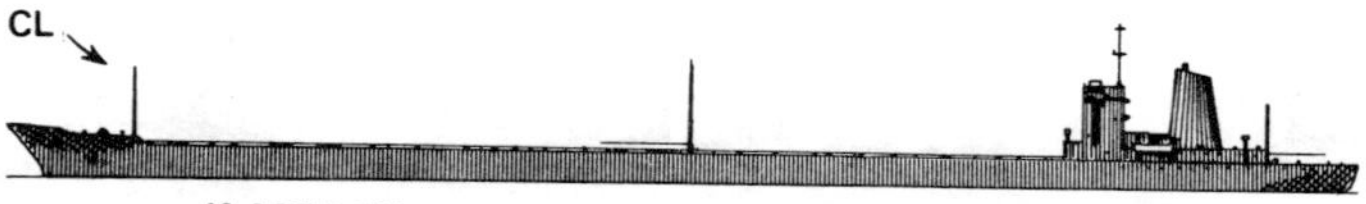

K_2MFK H1
69070 PRINKIPOS. Li/Ja 1964; Tk; 27400; 213.01 × 14.3 (698.85 × 46.92); M; 16; ex CONOCO LIBYA 1976; ex CONTINENTAL C. 1978.

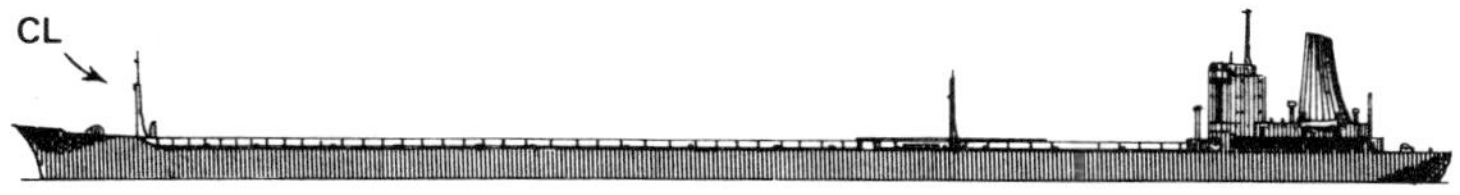

K_2MFK H1
69080 BUENA ESPERANZA. Gr/Ja 1964; Tk; 32700; 225 × 12.38 (738.19 × 40.62); M; 16; ex JARELSA.

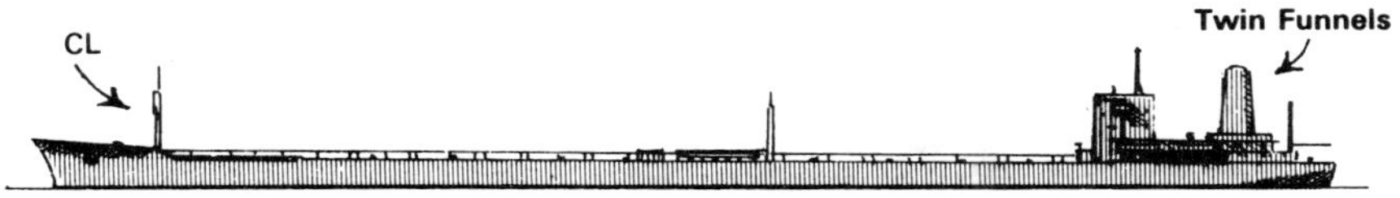

K_2MFK H1
69090 OCEANIC ENERGY. Li/Sw 1967; Tk; 47000; 253.47 × 13.06 (831.59 × 42.85); M; 16.5; ex H.M. WRANGELL 1978.

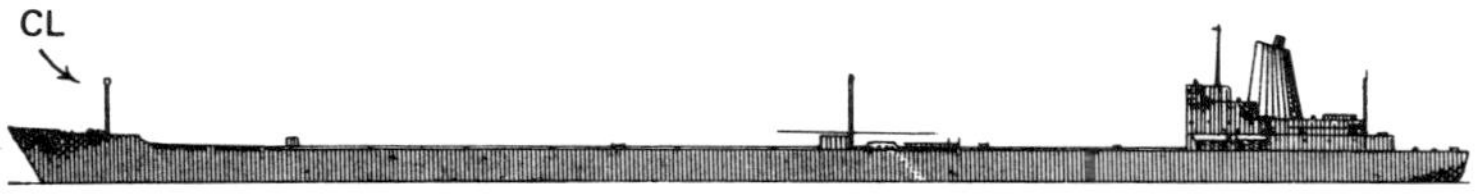

K_2MFK H1
● **69100 TULA.** Me/FRG 1966; Tk; 35900; 230.31 × 11.61 (755.61 × 38.09); T; 16.75; ex FORTUNA 1978. Sister: **69101 TULUM** (Me) ex UNION 1978.

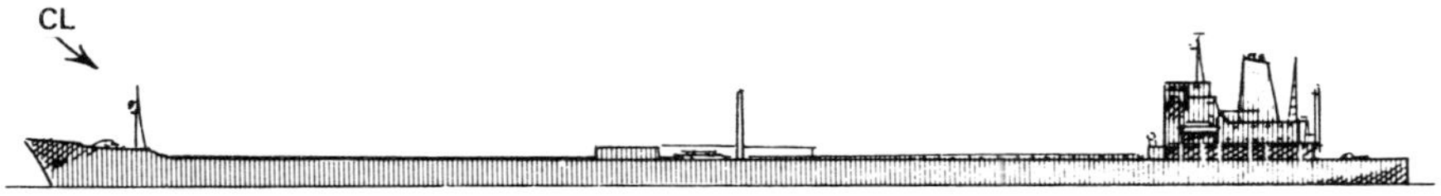

K_2MFK H1
69110 IN-NAHALA. Ag/Ja 1975; Tk; 71900; 266. × 16.99 (872.7 × 55.74); M; 15.75; ex POLARTANK 1976. Possibly similar: **69111 HALUL** (Qt) launched as NORTH MONARCH **69112 JANE STOVE** (No) **69113 UMM SHAIF** (Ab) launched as VINCENZIA.

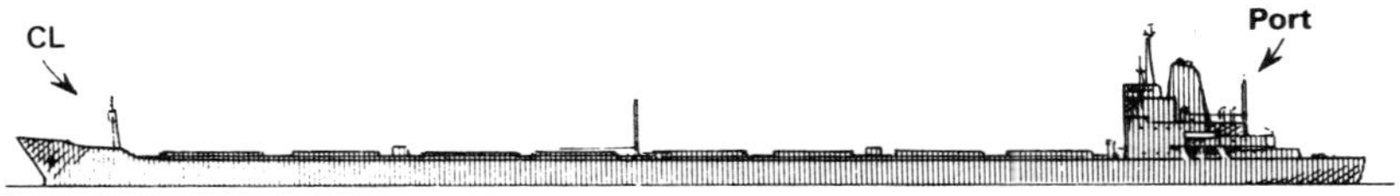

K_2MFK H1
● **69120 JAPAN WISTERIA.** Ja/Ja 1967; OO; 56300; 253.02 × 14.48 (830.12 × 47.51); M; 15.25. Sister: **69121 MINERAL TRANSPORTER** (Be) ex WHITE ROSE 1980; ex JAPAN LILAC 1977 Similar: **69122 OCEAN VENTURE** (Li) ex ORIENTAL TITAN 1973; ex DAIKO MARU 1971 **69123 ELMINA** (Gr) ex JAPAN MAGNOLIA **69124 JIZAN CEMENT** (Si) ex TSUGARU MARU 1979 Possibly similar: **69125 FIRST VENTURE** (Li) ex ORIENTAL NATION 1973; ex KOKKO MARU 1971 **69126 TSURUSAKI MARU** (Ja) **69127 DR. D.K. SAMY** (Li) ex KAIKO MARU 1972.

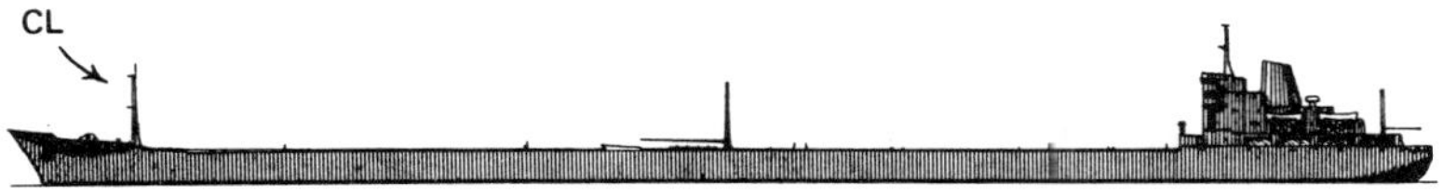

K_2MFK H1
69140 KRITI STAR. Gr/Ca 1973; Tk; 42500; 239.25 × 13 (784.94 × 43.77); M; 16. Sisters (Gr flag): **69141 KRITI LAND 69142 KRITI WAVE.**

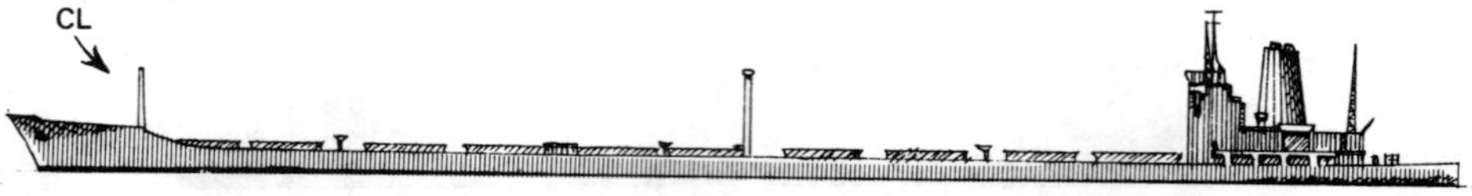

K_2MFK H1
69150 OHTSUKAWA MARU. Ja/Ja 1972; OO; 87100; 289.01 × 17.96 (948.2 × 58.92); M; 15.5.

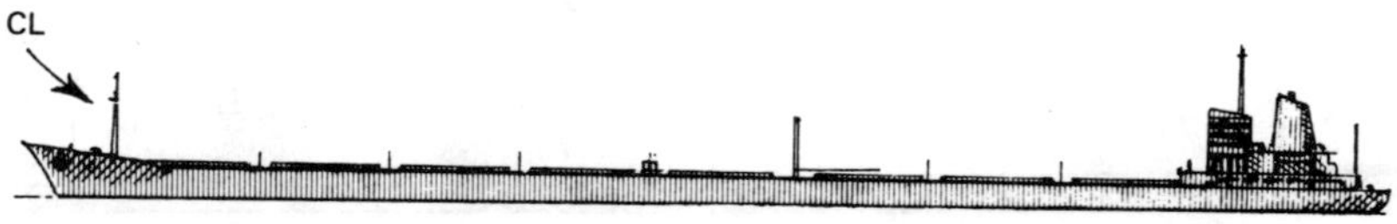

K_2MFK H1
69160 OKLAHOMA GETTY. Li/Fr-Ja 1957/69; OO; 44300; 248.67 × 13.26 (815.85 × 43.5); T; 16; Converted from tanker 1969. Similar (bulk/oil): **69161 MASSACHUSETTS GETTY** (Li) **69162 PENNSYLVANIA GETTY** (Li).

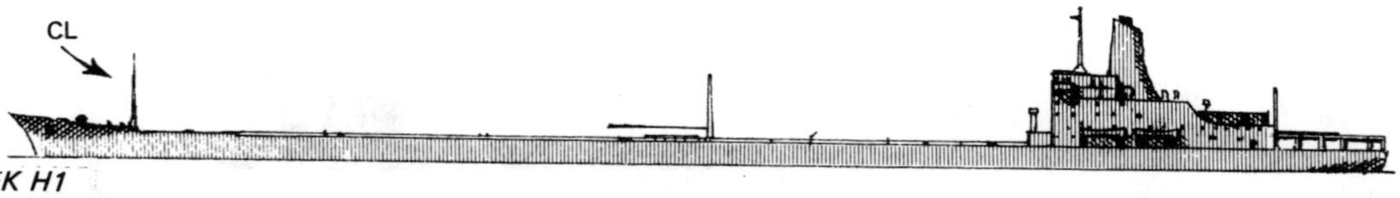

K_2MFK H1
● **69170 OLYMPIC ARCHER.** Li/Ja 1970; Tk; 96700; 322.99 × 19.35 (1059.68 × 63.48); T; 15.5. Sister: **69171 OLYMPIC ARROW** (Li).

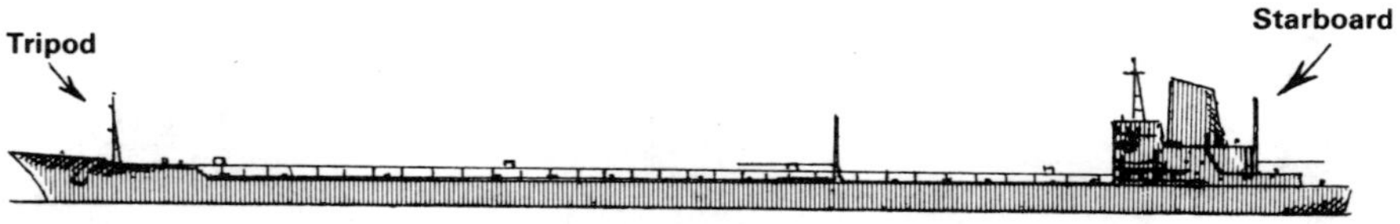

K_2MFK H1
69180 ANNA XYLA. Gr/Sp 1971; Tk; 23800; 206.76 × 11.95 (678.35 × 39.21); M; 15; ex PATIANNA 1980; ex HALCYON SKIES 1974. Similar (Ly flag): **69181 MARSA EL HARIGA 69182 SERIR.**

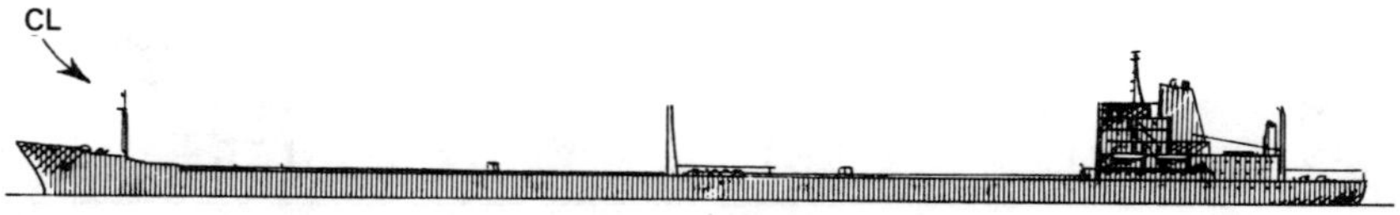

K_2MFK H1
69190 JAWAHARLAL NEHRU. In/Ys 1969; Tk; 48400; 256.85 × 14.05 (842.68 × 46.09); M; 15.5; Has small twin "Funnels" near after kingposts.

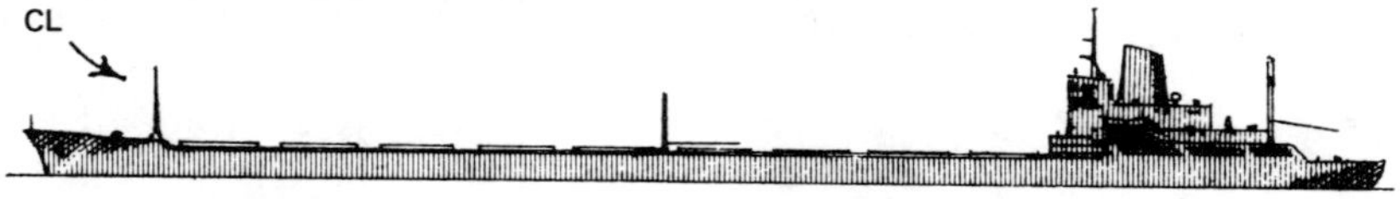

K_2MFK H1
69200 SPEY BRIDGE. Br/Ja 1969; OBO; 66100; 259.01 × 15.89 (849.77 × 52.13); M; 16. Sister: **69201 OCEANIC VICTORY** (Li) ex OCEAN BRIDGE 1978.

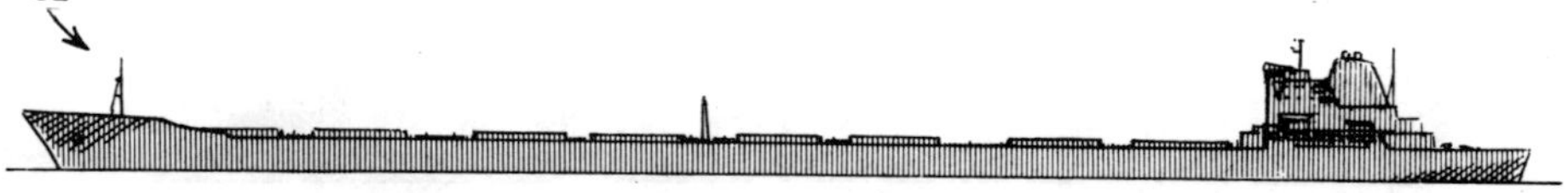

K_2MFK H1
69210 ANCORA. No/No 1973; OO; 71300; 282 × 17 (925.19 × 55.77); M; 16. Sisters (No flag): **69211 ACINA 69212 SANDEFJORD.**

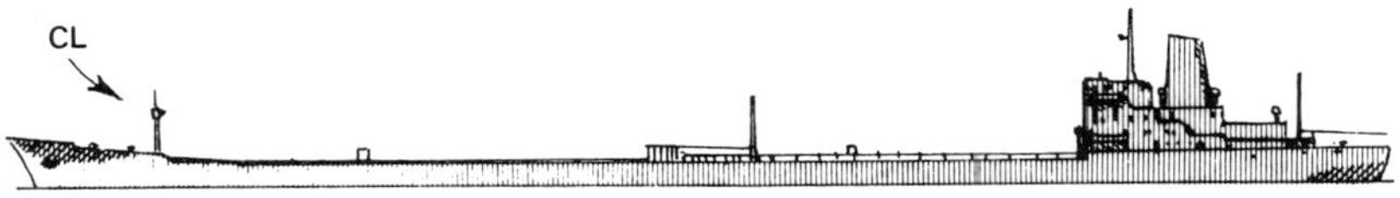

K_2MFK H1
69220 ATLANTIC TRADER. Li/Sw 1969; Tk; 44000; 257.67 × 13.5 (845.37 × 44.29); M; 16.5; ex TIDE CROWN; launched as BUTANGA.

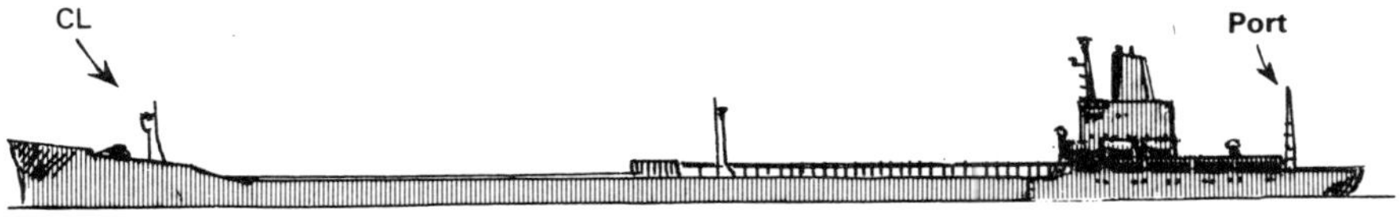

K_2MFK H1
69230 PHILIPPE NOIR. Gr/Ja 1967; Tk; 54500; 271.28 × 14.26 (890.03 × 46.78); M; 16.5; ex PEGGY O; ex THORSHOV 1978. Sisters: **69231 EIRAMA** (Br) ex THORSHOVDI 1979 **69232 PALMYRA** (Li) ex CALEO 1976; ex THORSKOG 1973.

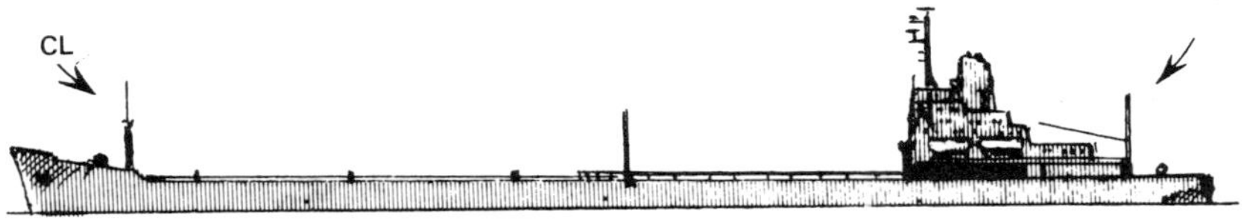

K_2MFK H1
69240 EASTERN MOBILITY. Li/Ja 1968; Tk; 41800; 257.51 × 13.46 (844.85 × 44.16); M; —; ex WORLD MOBILITY 1972. Similar (Li flag): **69241 LACONIAN** ex WORLD CENTENARY 1973.

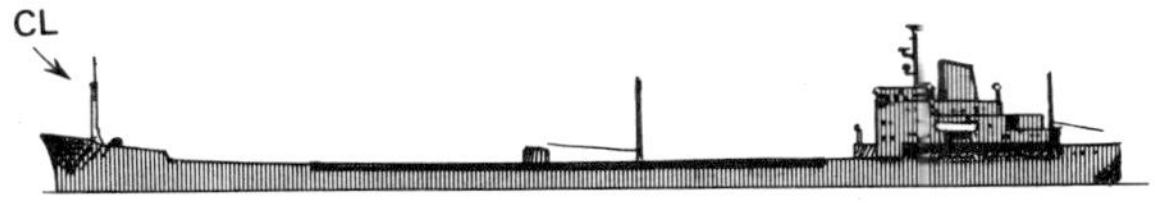

K_2MFK H1
69250 SEABORNE. Li/Ja 1973; Tk; 15000; 171.02 × 10.71 (561.09 × 35.14); M; 15. Sisters (Li flag): **69251 SEASERVICE 69252 SEASTAR** Possibly similar: **69253 CYS INTEGRITY** (Li) **69254 KOREA SUNNYHILL** (Ko) ex CYS HOPE 1980.

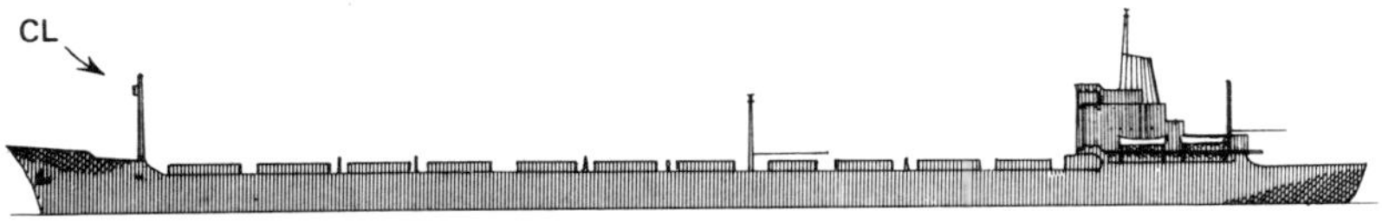

K_2MFK H1
69260 MARCONA TRADER. Li/Ja 1966; OBO; 39600; 248.42 × 12.56 (815.03 × 41.21); M; 15.5; ex JUAN TRADER 1973.

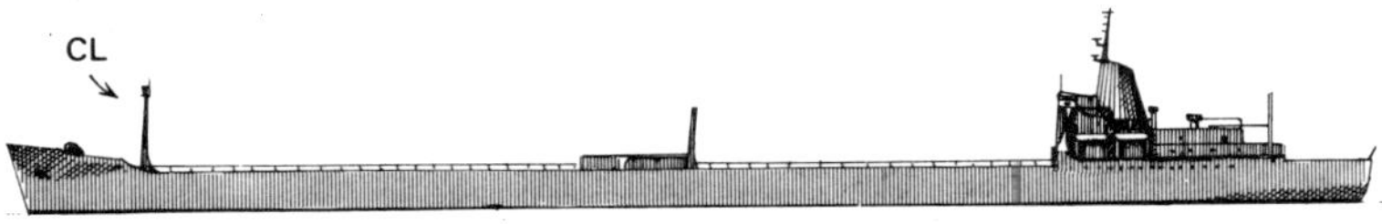

K_2MFK H1
69270 WORLD FIELD. Gr/Br 1965; Tk; 32700; 236.07 × 12.64 (774.51 × 41.47); M; 16; ex EDENFIELD 1978; ex DEWDALE 1977; ex EDENFIELD 1967.

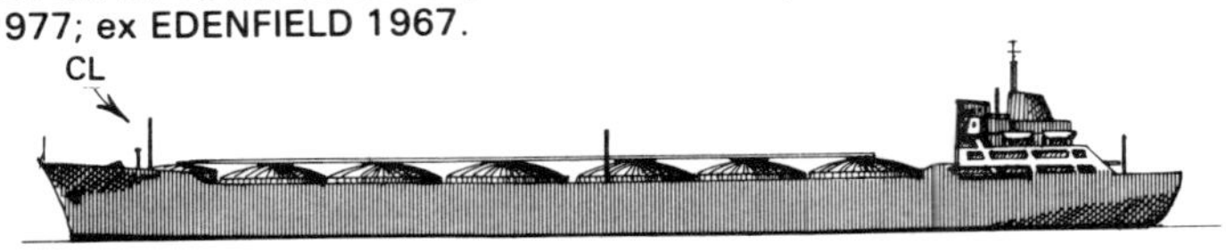

K_2MFK H1
69280 JULES VERNE. Fr/Fr 1965; LGC; 22300; 201.02 × 7.53 (659.51 × 24.7); T; 17.

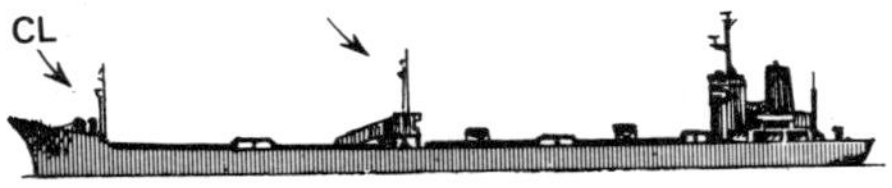

K_2MFK H1
69290 KIMITSU MARU. Ja/Ja 1971; O; 8000; 136.18 × 8.28 (446.78 × 27.17); M; 13; Limestone carrier. **69291 KIMITETSU MARU** (Ja).

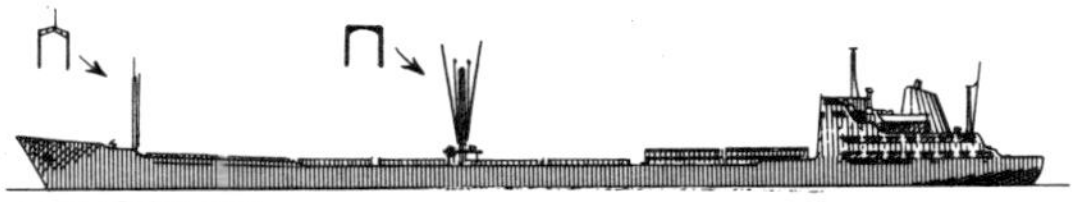

K_2MFK H1
69300 LIKE ONE. Pa/Fr 1959; O; 10300; 164.42 × 9.86 (539.44 × 32.35); M; 14.5; ex VILLE DE MEXICO 1975; ex JAQUES D'ANGLEJAN U.N.1 1969.

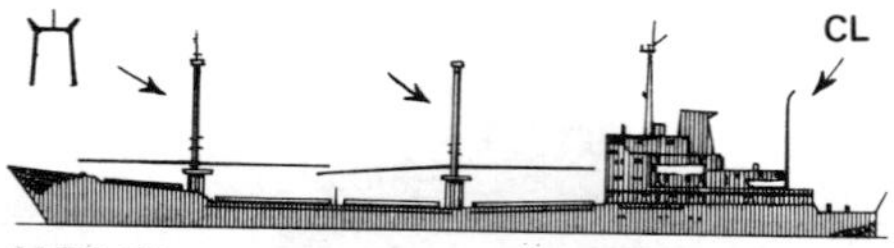

K_2MFK H1
69310 YONA B. Sg/Ru 1977; C; 6500; 136.81 × 7.49 (448.85 × 24.57); M; —; ex NOPAL YONA 1978. **'UNIVERSAL'** type. Sisters (Sg flag): **69311 CAMILLE B** ex CAMILLE 1978; ex NOPAL CAMILLE 1978 (Ru flag): ***69312 NIKOLAY ZHUKHOV *69313 NIKOLAY MOROZOV *69314 GRIGORIY KOVALCHUK *69315 KONSTANTIN ZANKOV *69316 VASILIY BYELOKONYENKO *69317 VITALIY KRUCHINA *69318 IVAN KOROTEYEV *69319 MIKHAIL STENKO *69320 NIKOLAY SHCHUKIN *69321 PETR STAROSTIN *69322 ANDRIAN GONCHAROV *69323 INZHENIER YAMBURENKO.**

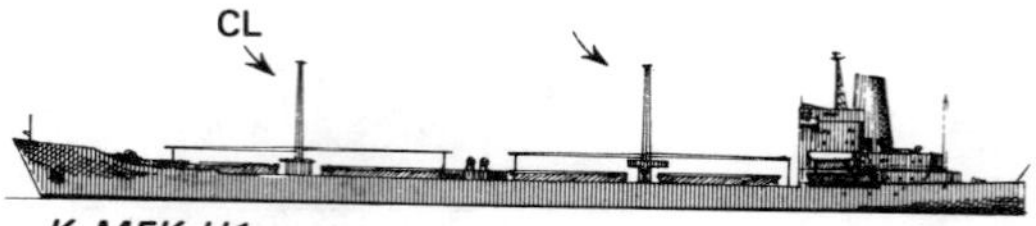

K_2MFK H1
69330 MARINA DEL CANTONE. It/Be 1969; C; 13000; 160.03 × 9.88 (525.03 × 32.41); M; 15.5; ex ZELZATE. Sisters: **69331 TEMA** (Li) ex CHARLEROI 1980 **69332 ANTOFAGASTA** (Pa) ex CHERTAL 1981 **69333 BRAINPOWER** (Pa) ex BELVAL 1978.

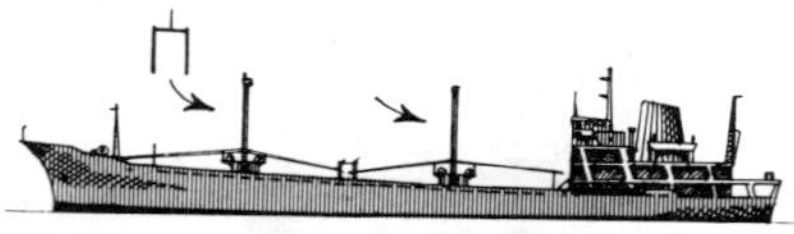

K_2MFK H1
69340 DAITOKU MARU No 31. Ja/Ja 1974; C/R; 3000; 120.53 × 6.96 (395.44 × 22.83); M; 17.5.

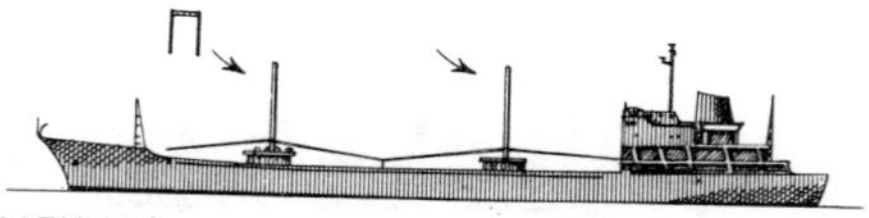

K_2MFK H1
69350 OCEAN DYNAMIC. Pa/Ja 1975; C; 3600; 124.08 × 6.92 (407.08 × 22.7); M; 17.5. Sister: **69351 OCEAN FRESH** (Pa).

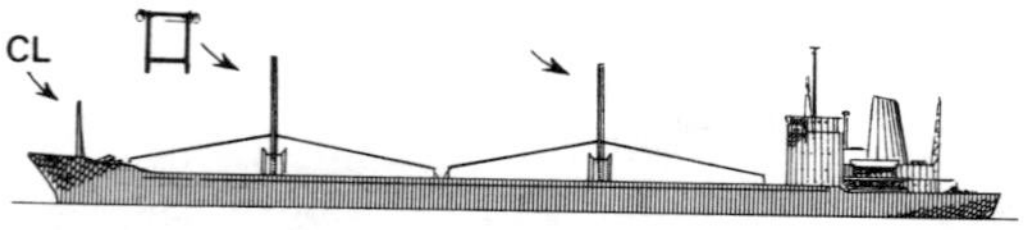

K_2MFK H1
69360 ELAFINA. Gr/Ja 1973; B; 15000; 154.11 × 10.52 (505.61 × 34.51); M; 15.5; ex TRANS RUBY 1973.

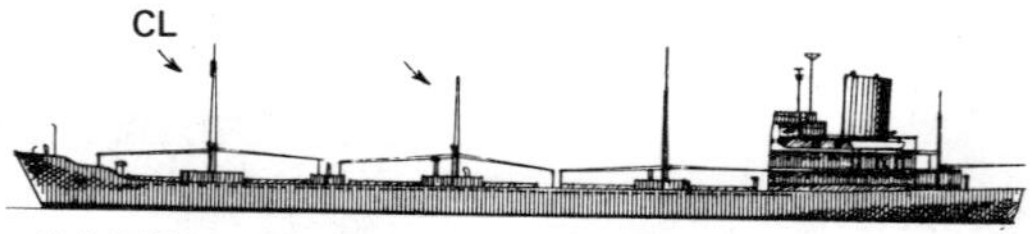

K_2MFK H1
● **69370 TINA LENTOUDIS.** Gr/FRG 1961; C; 9300/11800; 159.44 × 9.83/10.22 (523.1 × 32.25/33.53); M; 15.25; ex WIENERTOR 1976.

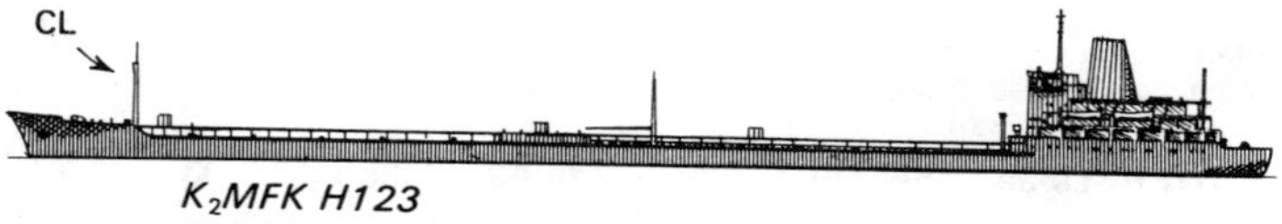

K_2MFK H123
69380 CHERRY NES. Sg/Sw 1960; Tk; 28200; 217.81 × 12.27 (714.6 × 40.26); M; 16.25; ex KATARINA 1978.

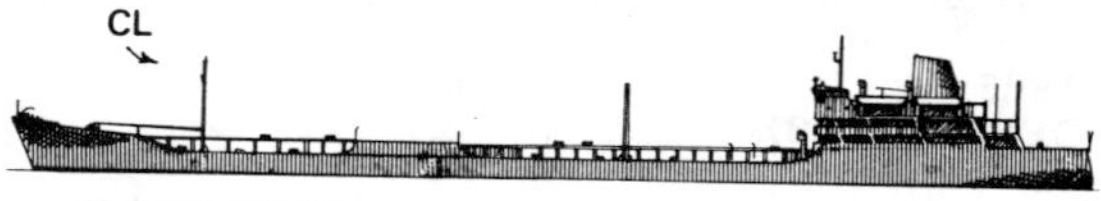

K_2MFK H123
● **69390 ANATOLI.** Gr/Br 1962; Tk; 12400; 170.47 × 9.44 (559.28 × 30.97); M; 15; ex LUCIGEN 1975.

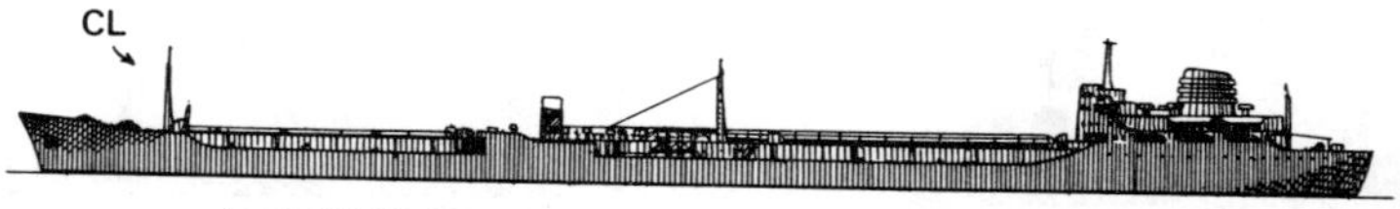

K_2MFK H123
69400 CONTOVELLO. Li/Ja 1961; LGC/Tk; 30100; 221.47 × 11.84 (726.61 × 38.85); M; 16; ex GREAT CRANE 1980; ex GOHSHU MARU 1973.

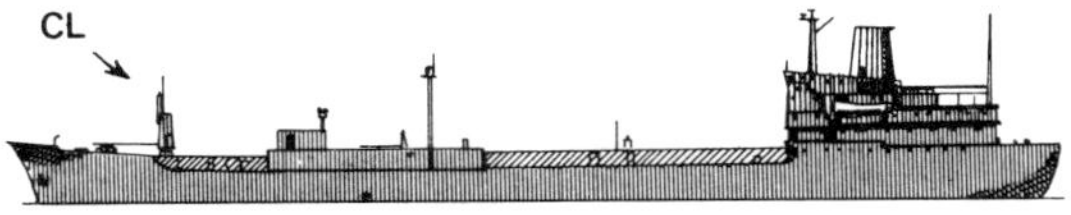

K_2MFK H123
69410 KATRISA. Gr/FRG 1968; LGC; 13100; 166.15 × 9.22 (545.11 × 30.25); M; 16.5; ex TRINA MULTINA 1977; ex ROLAND 1974.

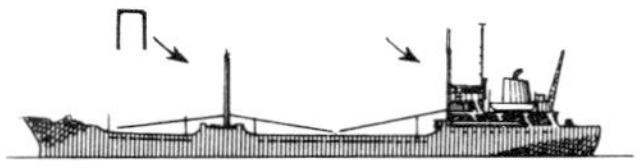

K_2MFK H123
● **69420 SENG KONG No 1**.. Pa/Ja 1969; C; 2100; 91.9 × 5.82 (301.51 × 19.09); M; 13; ex MARUKICHI MARU No 3 1976. Possible sisters: **69421 HORNED OWL** (Pa) ex MEISHO MARU 1976 **69422 KYOHO MARU** (Ja) **69423 LIM GLORY** (Pa) ex SHOREI MARU.

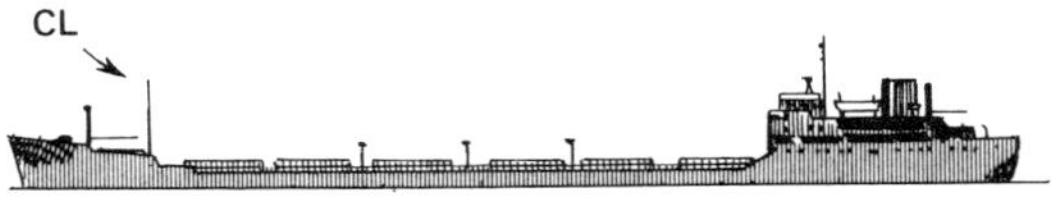

K_2MFK H13
69430 DANUBE. Cy/Br 1960; O; 12600; 160.03 × 9.01 (525.03 × 29.56); M; 12; ex PUERTO MADRYN 1977; ex SILVERSHORE 1975; ex ALDERSGATE 1969. Sister: **69431 CAPITANO FRANCO V** (It) ex NICOLAS C 1976; ex BEECHWOOD 1975; ex BISHOPSGATE 1969 Similar (smaller): **69432 STENIES** (Gr) ex TORNADO 1977; ex SHEAF FIELD 1969.

K_2MFK H13
● **69440 KAPPA VICTORY**. Gr/Br 1958; O; 10900; 153.45 × 8.55 (503.44 × 28.05); M; 12.5; ex CHERRYWOOD 1973; ex SILVERCRAG 1969.

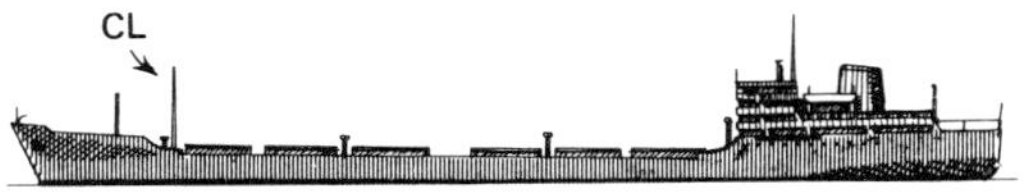

K_2MFK H13
69450 EVA. Gr/Br 1959; O; 11900; 156.11 × 9.01 (512.17 × 29.56); M; 12; ex BAMBURGH CASTLE 1976. Similar: **69451 DAPO TRADER** (Sg) ex CHEVIOT 1977 ⋆**69452 BONG SAN** (RK) ex COSMOS TRADERS 1980; ex LINDISFARNE 1975 **69453 PARNASSOS** (Gr) ex LONGSTONE 1975.

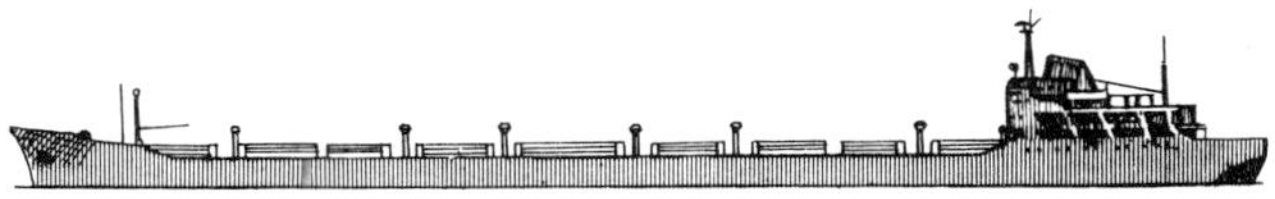

K_2MFK H13
69460 AVEDAT. Is/It 1964; B; 23500; 195.99 × 10.67 (643.01 × 35.01); M; 16. Sister: **69461 EN GEDI** (Is).

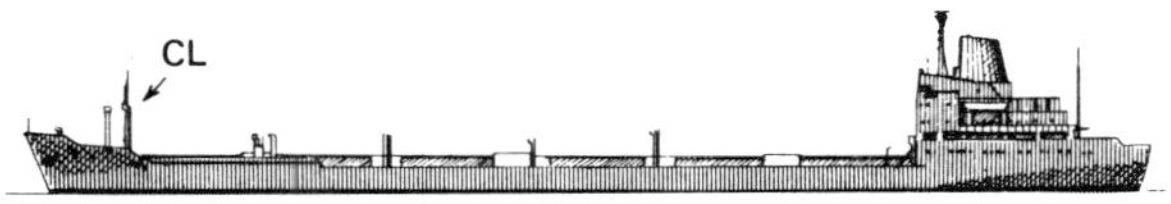

K_2MFK H13
69470 ORION. Gr/Sw 1963; B; 14600; 175.88 × 10.83 (577.03 × 35.53); M; 14.5.

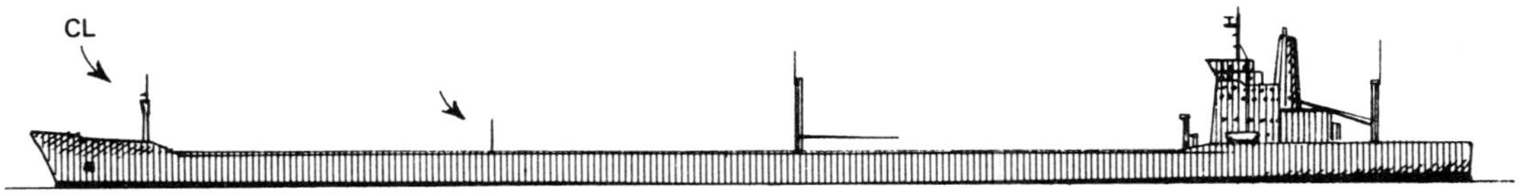

K_2MFK H13
69480 KONG HAAKON VII. No/No 1969; Tk; 109400; 327.72 × 20.42 (1075.2 × 66.99); T; 16. Sisters (No flag): **69481 AURELIAN 69482 HADRIAN 69483 NERVA 69484 OCTAVIAN**.

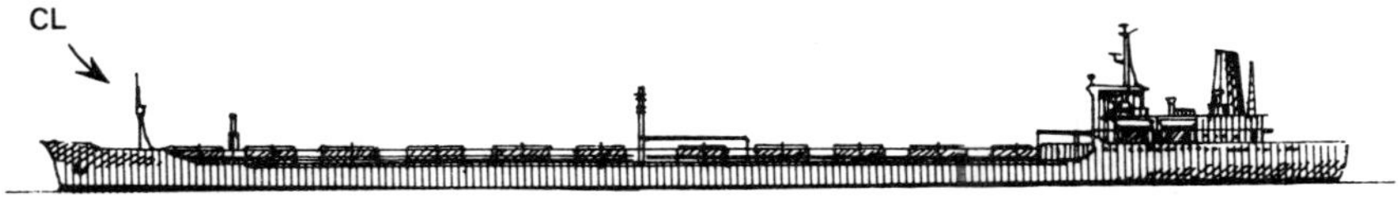

K_2MFK H13
69490 RIO SUN. Li/Ja 1967; OBO; 42500; 250.96 × 13.98 (823.36 × 45.87); M; 16; ex TOKYO 1977. Sister: **69491 GARBIS** (Li) ex CANTO 1975; ex VESTFOLD 1971.

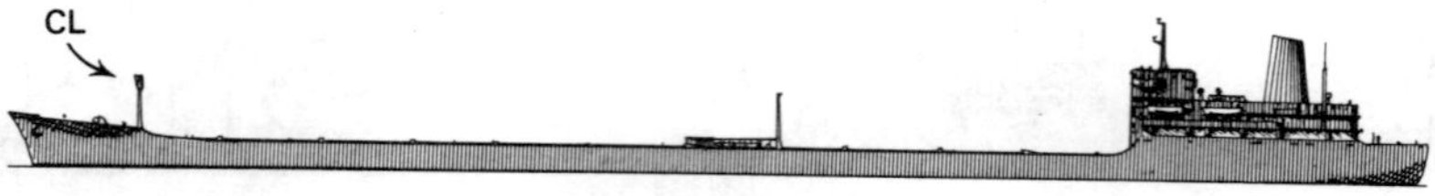

K_2MFK H13
69500 MARIZINA. Gr/Sw 1967; Tk; 40100; 244.89 × 13.69 (803.44 × 44.91); M; 16.75; ex NORSE MOUNTAIN 1973.

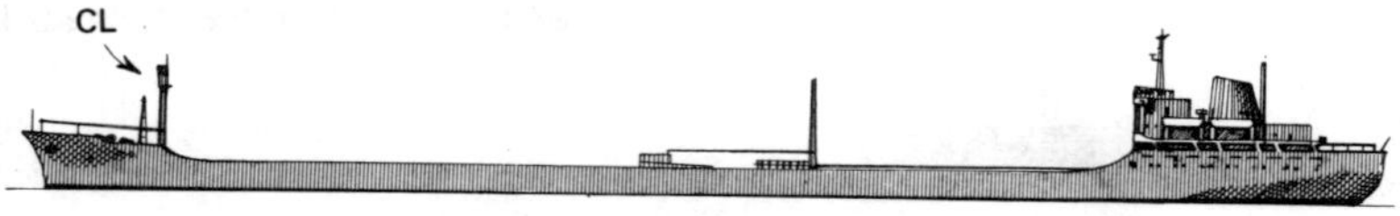

K_2MFK H13
69510 EFYRA. Li/Ja 1965; Tk; 35400; 238.03 × 12.77 (780.94 × 41.9); M; 15.5.
Sister: **69511 EVDORI** (Li).

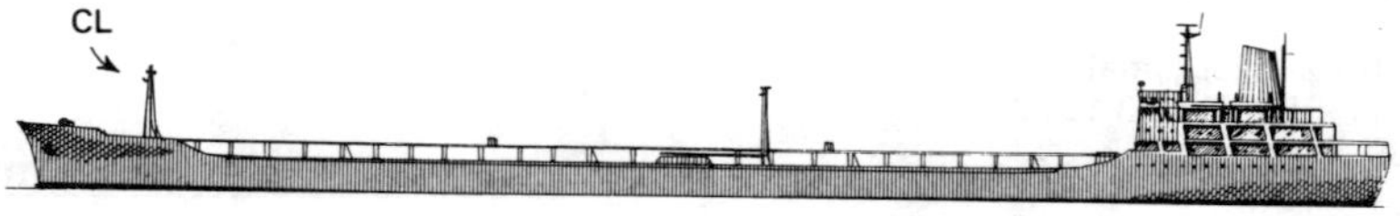

K_2MFK H13
69520 RAS TANURA. Si/Br 1965; Tk; 37700; 237.68 × 12.83 (779.79 × 42.09); T; 16; ex YANNIS V 1976; ex PYRROS V 1976; ex SPECTRA J 1975; ex PYRROS V 1971; ex LARISTAN 1970.

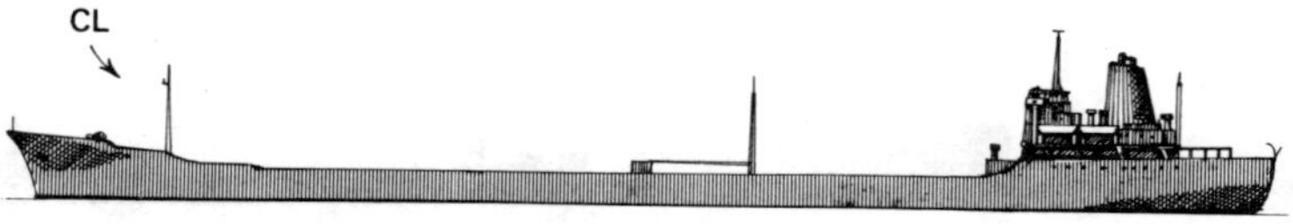

K_2MFK H13
69530 KING CADMUS. Gr/Ja 1964; Tk; 33400; 228.71 × 12.41 (750.36 × 40.75); M; 15.75.

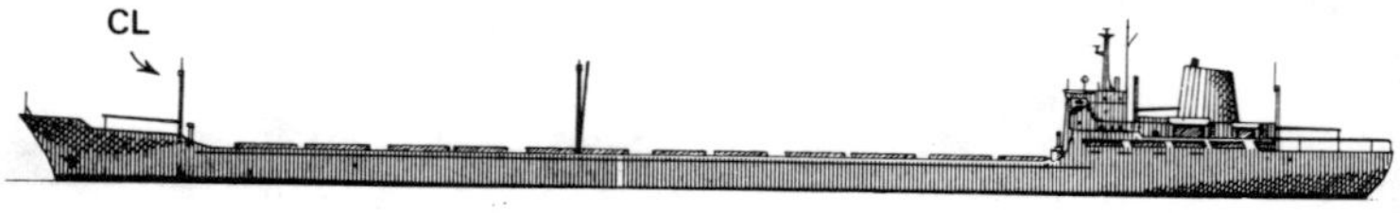

K_2MFK H13
69540 AMBRONIA It/It 1965; OO; 28600; 229.45 × 12.41 (752.79 × 40.72); M; —.
Sister: **69541 ASPRA** (It).

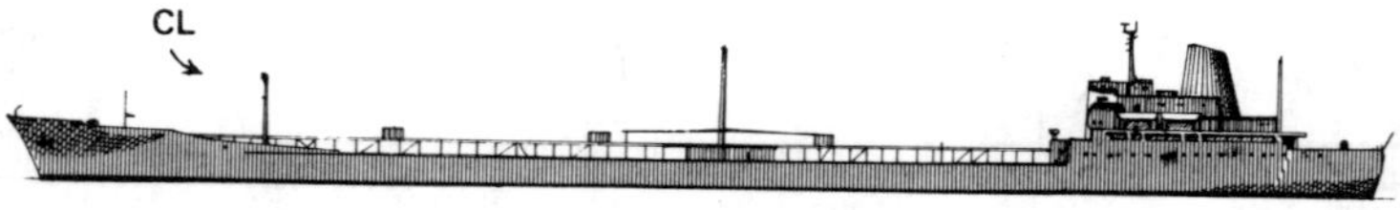

K_2MFK H13
69550 BONAIRE CROSS. Li/Ne 1963; Tk; 31200; 227.77 × 12.4 (797.28 × 40.68); T; 15.25; ex SOUTHERN CROSS 1980; ex AVEDRECHT 1976.

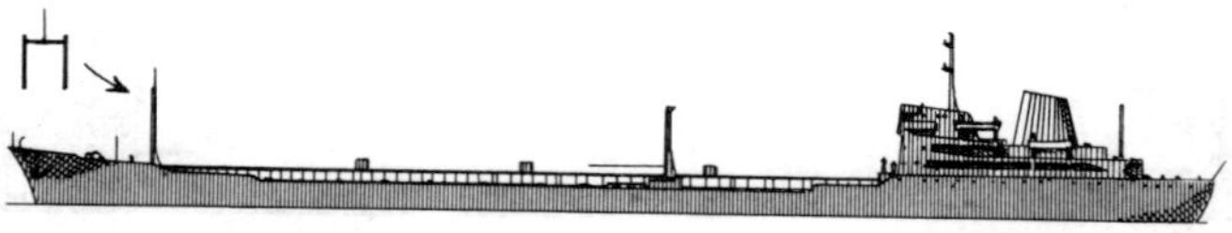

K_2MFK H13
69560 SCAPTRADE. Gr/Ne 1960; Tk; 21200; 202.62 × 10.83 (664.76 × 35.53); M; 16.5; ex BARENDRECHT 1975.

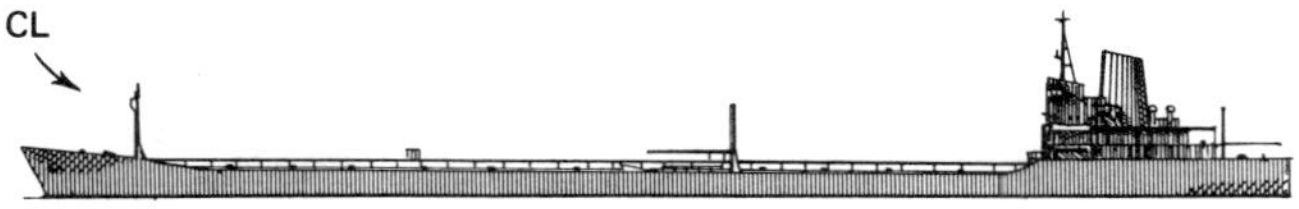

K_2MFK H13
69570 BABA GURGUR. Iq/Sp 1973; Tk: 21400; 201.02 × 10.96 (659.51 × 35.96); M; 16. Sisters (Iq flag): **69571 AIN ZALAH 69572 BUZURGAN 69573 JAMBUR 69574 KHANAQUIN 69575 KIRKUK 69576 RUMAILA.**

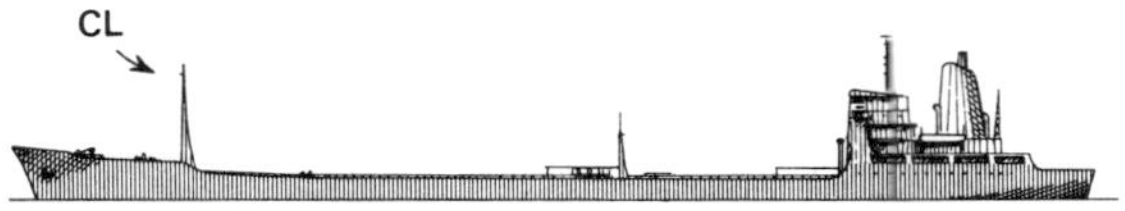

K_2MFK H13
● **69590 TEXACO MELBOURNE.** Br/US-Ja 1945/67; Tk; 13900; 172.4 × 10 (565.62 × 32.81); T-E; 13.25; ex CALTEX MELBOURNE 1967; ex VICTORY LOAN 1951; Lengthened & converted from 'T-2' tanker 1967. Sisters: **69591 TEXACO WELLINGTON** (Br) ex CALTEX WELLINGTON 1968; ex PAULUS HOOK 1952 **69592 CHEVRON THE HAGUE** (Ne) ex CALTEX THE HAGUE 1967; ex BOONESBOROUGH 1950 **69593 TEXACO BOMBAY** (Br) ex CALTEX BOMBAY 1968; ex CASTLES WOODS 1951 **69594 TEXACO ROME** (Br) ex CALTEX ROME 1968; ex SIDELING HILL 1953 **69595 TEXACO KANSAS** (US) ex GREENPOINT 1960; ex CROWN POINT 1955 **69596 TEXACO NEW JERSEY** (US) ex NEW JERSEY 1961; ex LAKE ERIE 1947.

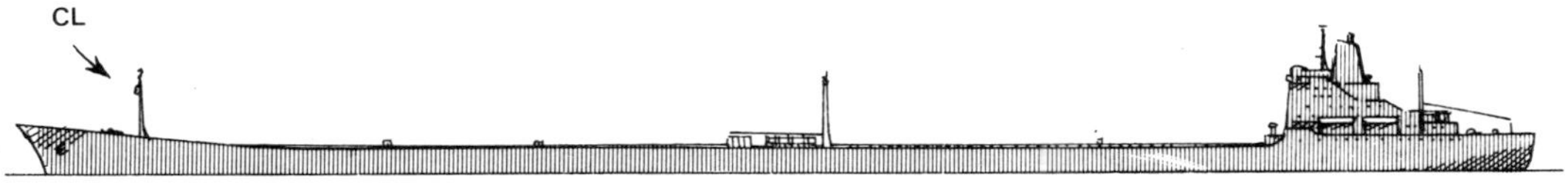

K_2MFK H13
● **69610 ENERGY EVOLUTION.** Li/Ja 1969; Tk; 98900; 326.02 × 19.34 (1069.62 × 63.45); T; 16. Sisters (Li flag): **69611 ENERGY GREATION 69612 ENERGY GENERATION 69613 ENERGY MOBILITY 69614 ENERGY PRODUCTION 69615 ENERGY RESOURCE 69616 ENERGY VITALITY** Similar: **69617 WORLD VICTORIA 69618 WORLD DUCHESS 69619 WORLD GENERAL.**

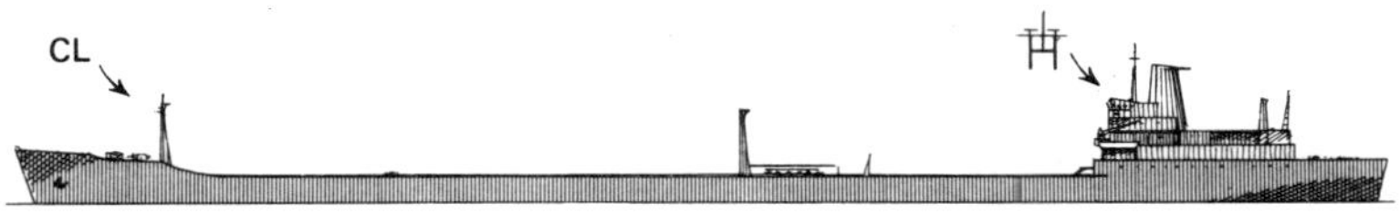

K_2MFK H13
69630 HALKI. Gr/Ja 1966; Tk; 41100; 240.57 × 12.73 (789.27 × 41.65); M; 16.5; ex KINNA DAN 1977.

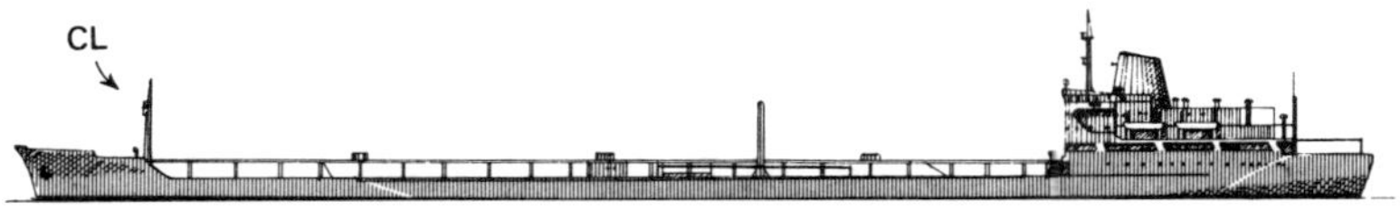

K_2MFK H13
★**69640 LING HU.** RC/Sw 1965; Tk; 33100; 236.1 × 12.68 (774.61 × 41.6); M; 16; ex KISMET II 1975; ex MINORU 1972.

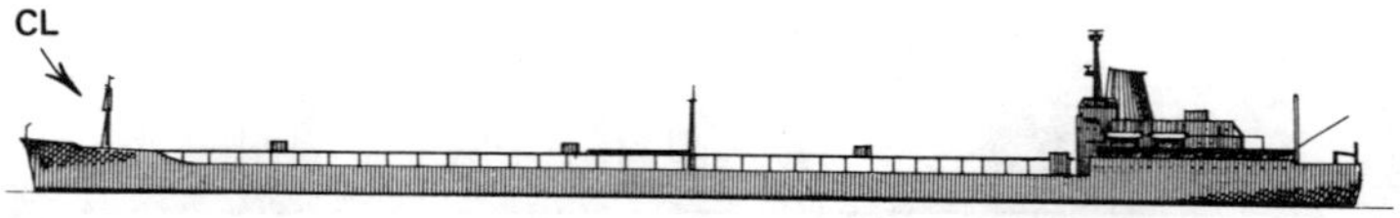

K_2MFK H13
69650 LA FLECHE. Li/Sw 1964; Tk; 26200; 216.36 × 12.16 (709.84 × 39.9); M; 16.5; ex TARTAR 1969. Similar (larger): **69651 ACTIUM** (Gr) ex CAPTO 1975; ex TIBETAN 1968.

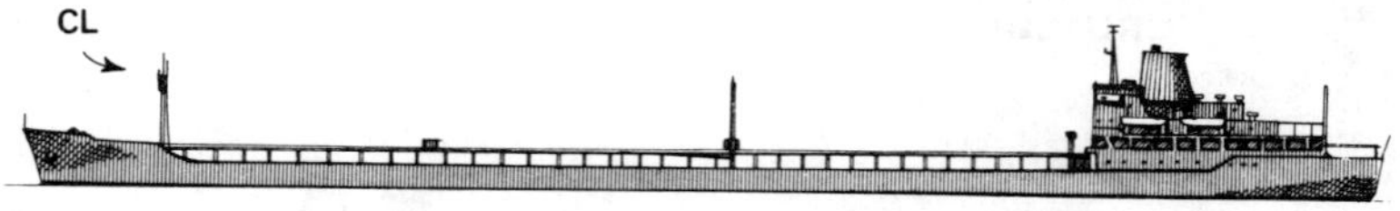

K_2MFK H13
69660 RIVA 1. Pa/Sw 1965; Tk; 31700; 236.51 × 12.32 (775.95 × 40.78); M; 16; ex MAJESTIC COLOCOTRONIS ex FAGERFJELL 1969. Similar: **69661 LUNAMAR** (Pe) ex ATLAS EXPLORER 1980; ex KRISTINA 1976; ex TURCOMAN 1968 Similar (tall pipe from funnel): **69662 THANASSIS A** (Gr) ex DYNAMIC COLOCOTRONIS 1979; ex BJORGHOLM 1968.

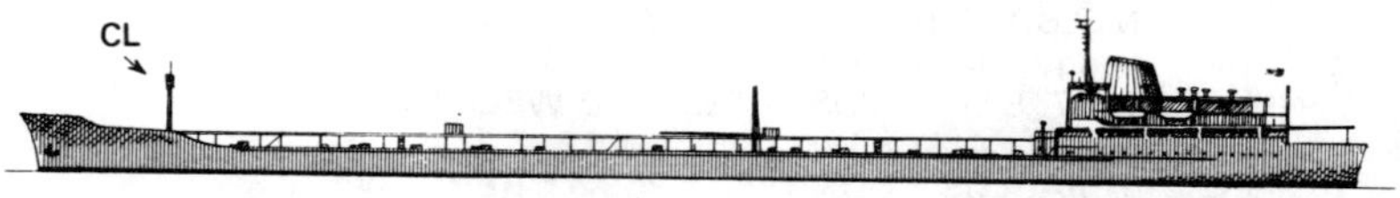

K_2MFK H13
69670 HASSAN B. Pa/Sw 1964; Tk; 35400; 236.13 × 12.82 (774.71 × 42.06); M; 16; ex ATHELKING 1977. Sister: **69671 KIMOLOS** (Gr) ex WILL ADAMS 1980; ex ATHELREGENT 1977.

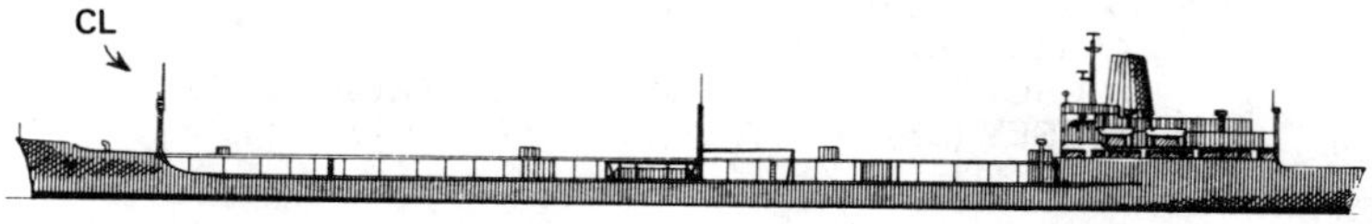

K_2MFK H13
69680 SILVER LADY. Li/Sw 1966; Tk; 33700; 236.68 × 12.75 (776.51 × 41.83); M; 17; ex OKLAND 1977.

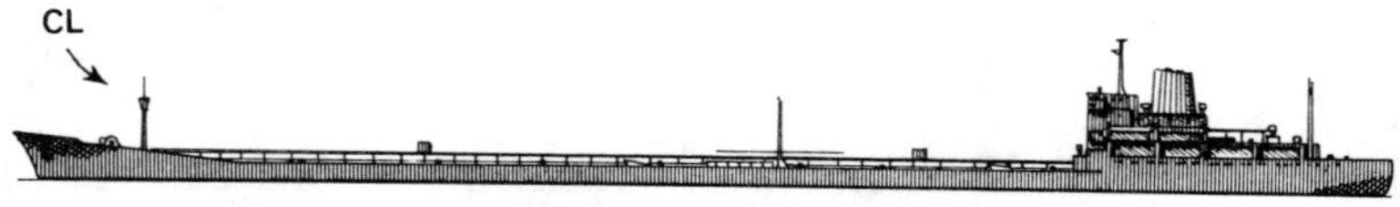

K_2MFK H13
69690 LANGEAIS. Fr/Ja 1965; Tk; 41200; 237.73 × 12.78 (779.95 × 41.93); M; 16; ex THORSHEIMER 1971. Similar: **69691 SUSAN** (Li) ex TAMARITA 1977; ex THORSTAR 1972.

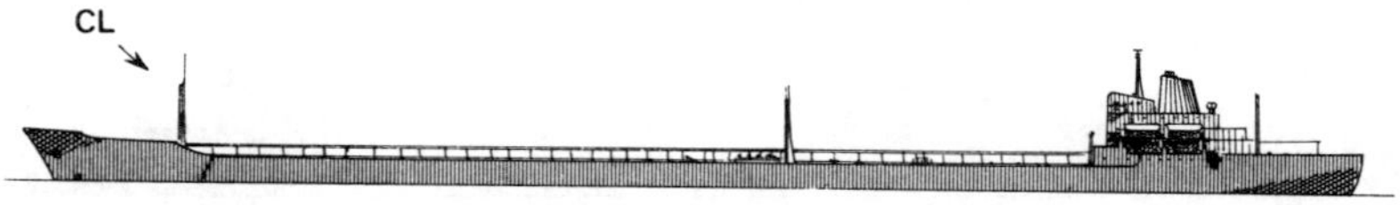

K_2MFK H13
69700 TRADE FORTITUDE. Gr/Ja 1963; Tk; 31200; 235.62 × 12.57 (773.03 × 41.24); M; 17.25; ex MAGNA 1972.

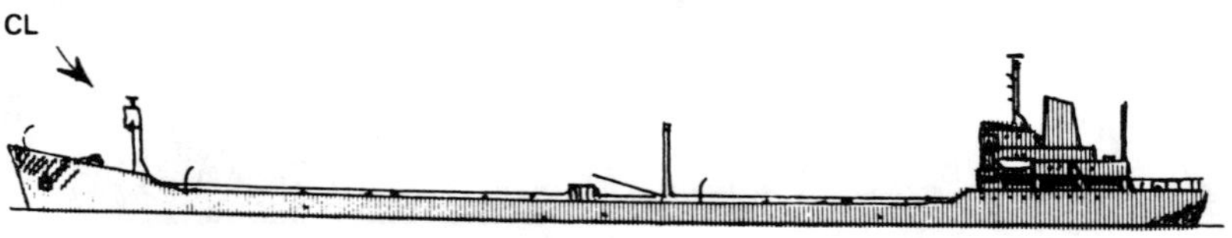

K_2MFK H13
● **69710 OLYMPIC GARLAND.** Li/Ja 1965; Tk; 38600; 246.82 × 12.76 (809.78 × 41.96); M; 16.75. Sisters (Li flag): **69611 OLYMPIC GLORY 69712 OLYMPIC GOAL.**

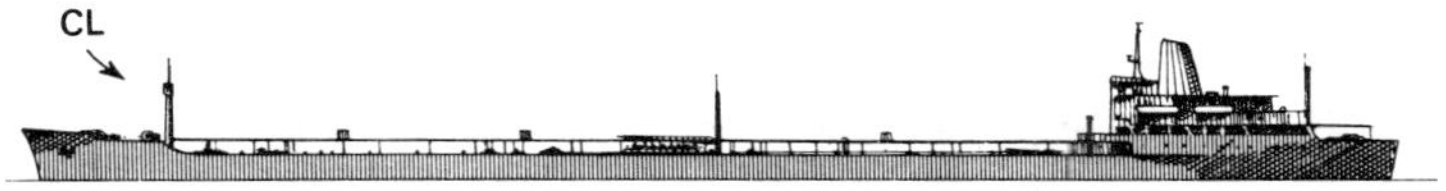

K_2MFK H13
★**69720 GRIMMEN.** DDR/Sw 1966; Tk; 28700; 217.81 × 12.16 (714.6 × 39.9); M; 16.5; ex SEA BREEZE 1974.

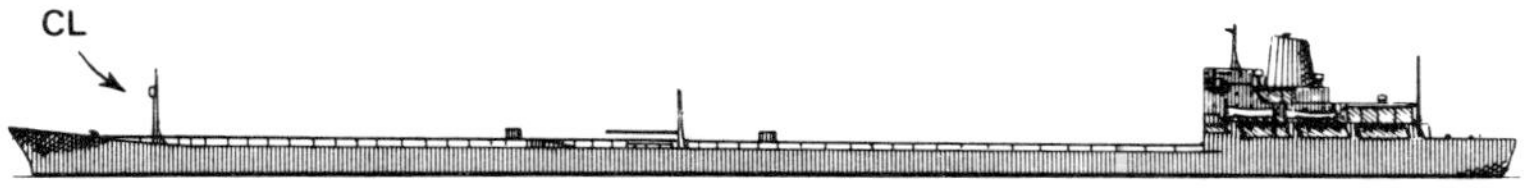

K_2MFK H13
69730 APHRODITE B. Gr/Ja 1965; Tk; 37100; 239.28 × 12.66 (785.04 × 41.53); M; 15.5; ex ILLUSTRIOUS COLOCOTRONIS 1979; ex MOSTER 1972.

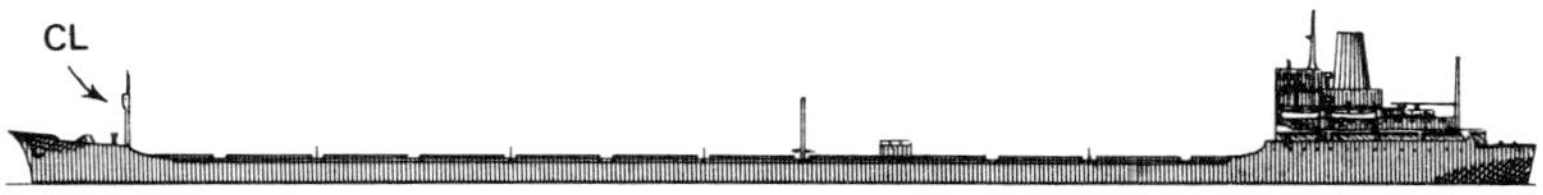

K_2MFK H13
● **69740 MISTRAL.** Li/Ja 1965; OO; 37400; 243.21 × 12 (797.93 × 39.37); M; 16.25; ex RAUTAS 1977.

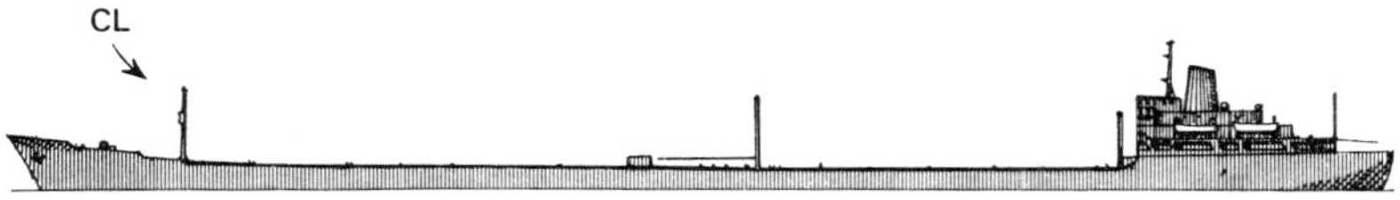

K_2MFK H13
69750 ORIENTAL CONFIDENCE. Li/Ja 1966; Tk; 42700; 243.82 × 13.28 (799.93 × 43.57); M; 16.25; ex PACIFIC GLORY 1972.

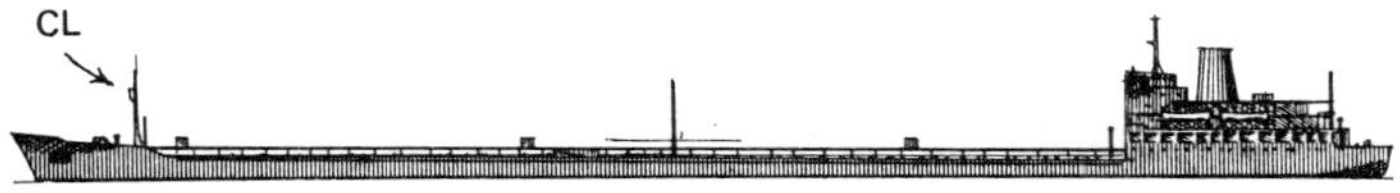

K_2MFK H13
69760 YANXILAS. Gr/Sw 1965; Tk; 28900; 217.81 × 12.16 (714.6 × 39.9); M; 16; ex POLYCOMMANDER 1970.

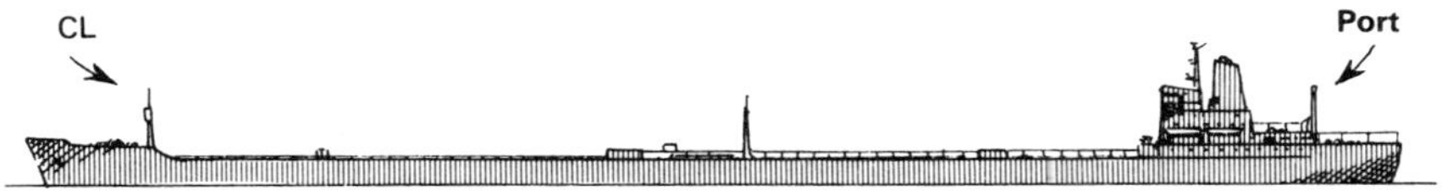

K_2MFK H13
69770 SKYRON II. Li/Ja 1967; Tk; 45100; 258.17 × 14.05 (847.01 × 46.1); M; 16; ex CARPO 1975; ex POLYMONARCH 1972.

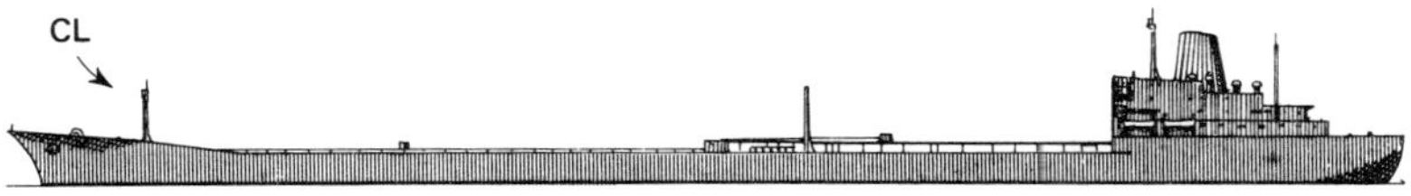

K_2MFK H13
69780 LEVANT. Li/Ja 1967; Tk; 37900; 243.85 × 13.3 (800.03 × 43.64); M; 16; ex GIMLEVANG 1978.

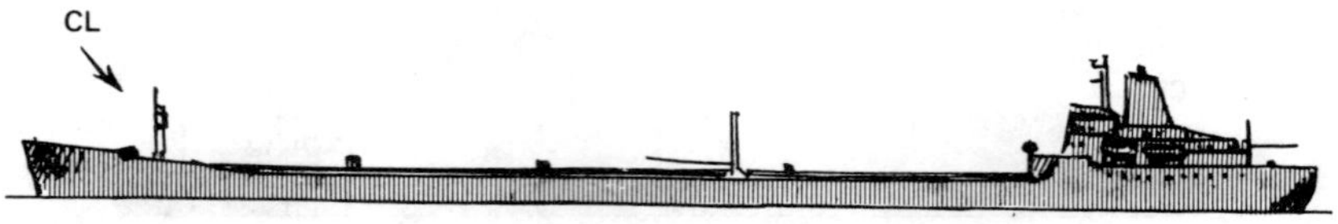

K_2MFK H13
69790 SINOIA. Li/Br 1966; Tk; 51200; 259.47 × 14.88 (851.28 × 48.82); T; 17; ex CLEMENTINA 1977; ex CLEMENTINE CHURCHILL 1973. Similar: ⋆**69791 ON SUNG** (RK) ex GALLANT SEAHORSE; ex VALENTINIAN 1972 **69792 THISTLE VENTURE** (Gr) ex JARITA 1977; ex GRATIAN 1972.

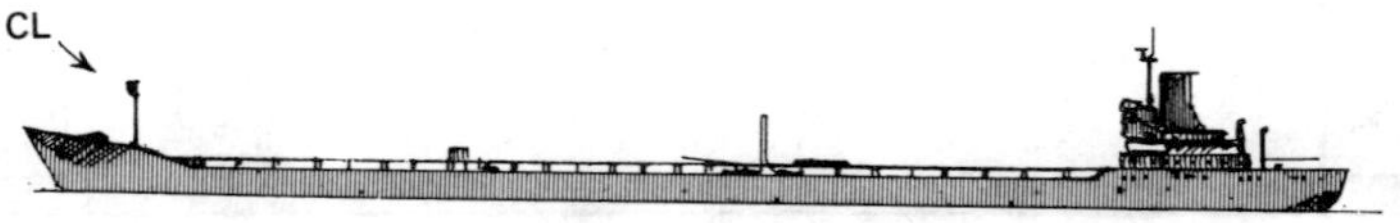

K_2MFK H13
69800 CAMPEADOR. Sp/Sp 1969; Tk; 20500; 209.02 × 10.73 (685.76 × 35.2); M; 16.5. Sister: **69801 CAMPOMAYOR** (Sp).

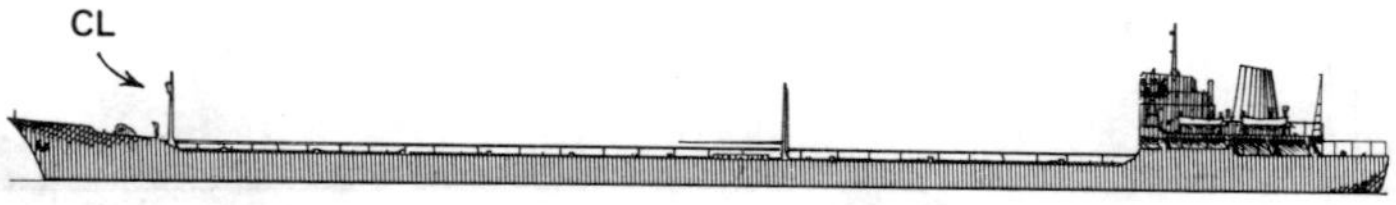

K_2MFK H13
69810 LAJPAT RAI. In/Ja 1965; Tk; 28800; 217.51 × 11.16 (713.62 × 36.61); M; —.

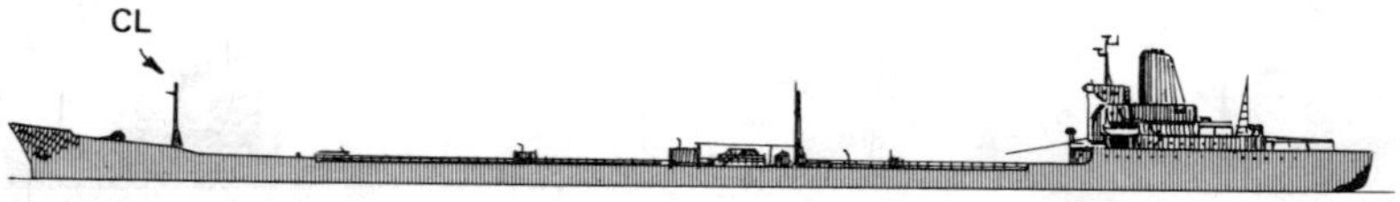

K_2MFK H13
69820 AMOCO BRISBANE. Li/Ja 1968; Tk; 35500; 240.55 × 12.76 (789.21 × 41.86); M; 16. Sisters (Li flag): **69821 AMOCO BALTIMORE 69822 AMOCO CREMONA 69823 AMOCO YORKTOWN.**

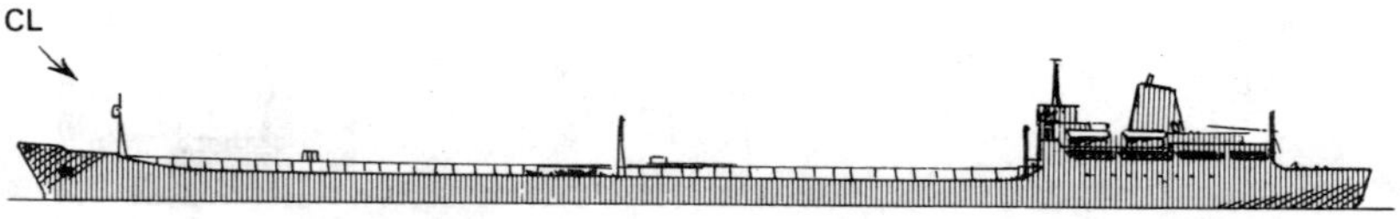

K_2MFK H13
⋆**69830 LUTZKENDORF.** DDR/No 1965; Tk; 46400; 249.03 × 13.38 (817.03 × 43.9); M; 16; ex SONJA 1974.

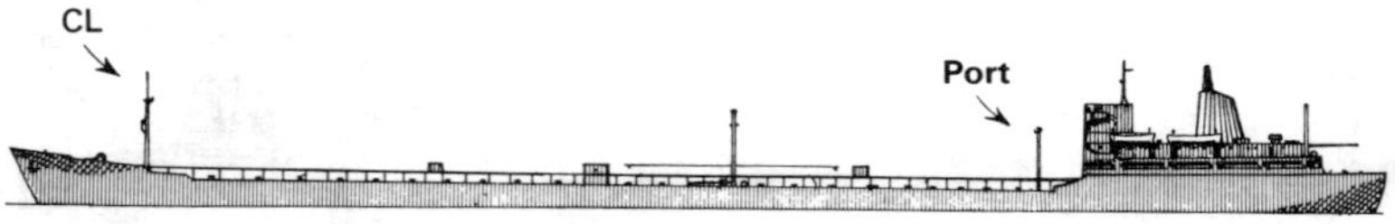

K_2MFK H13
69840 MARIBELLA. Li/Ja 1964; Tk; 38600; 237.8 × 12.7 (780.18 × 41.67); T; 16; ex POLAR LION 1978; ex MOSQUEEN 1975. Sister: **69841 VENTURE OKLAHOMA** (Li) ex TURBINIA 1978; ex ANDKING 1978; ex MOSKING 1976.

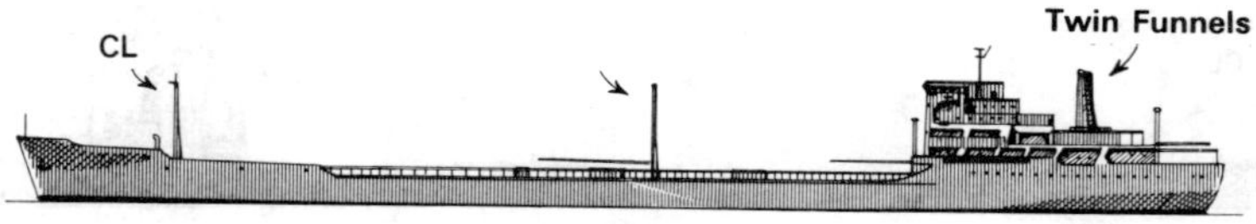

K_2MFK H13
69850 RIGEL. Fr/Fr 1960; Tk; 30800; 224.64 × 11.6 (737.76 × 38.o6); M; 16.25. Sister: **69851 TRATUS** (Li) ex STRATUS 1978; ex POLAIRE 1972.

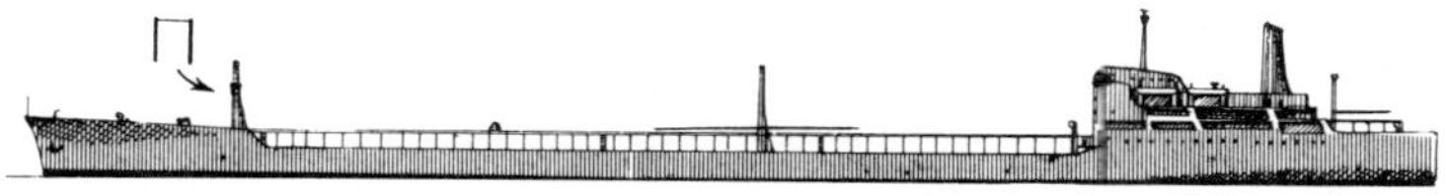

K_2MFK H13
● **69860 CHERRY LORD.** Sg/FRG 1962; Tk; 32800; 225.58 × 12.39 (740.09 × 40.65); T; 16; ex JAWACHTA 1976. Sisters: **69861 CATAMARCA** (Ar) ex ASOPOS 1974; ex KOBERG 1972; ex JALINGA 1967 **69862 CITIALI** (Me) ex ELEKTRA 1980; ex TOXON 1976; ex ARIETTA VENIZELOS 1972; ex JALTA 1969.

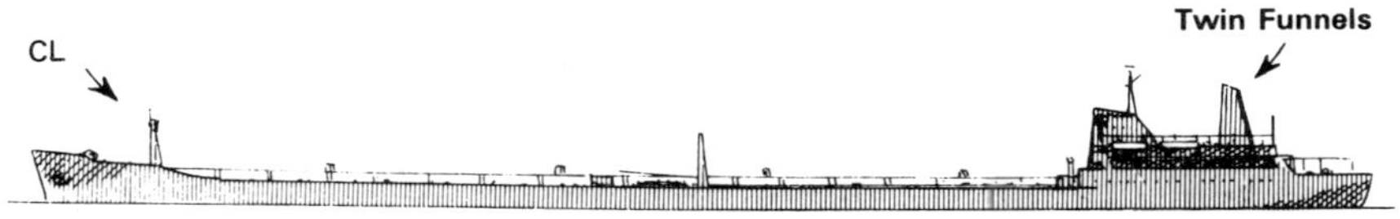

K_2MFK H13
⋆**69870 DAN HU.** RC/No 1963; Tk; 52700; 264.78 × 14.73 (868.7 × 48.33); M; —; ex BERGE BERGESEN 1975. Sister: **69871 HUGO** (Fi) ex BERGELAND 1975.

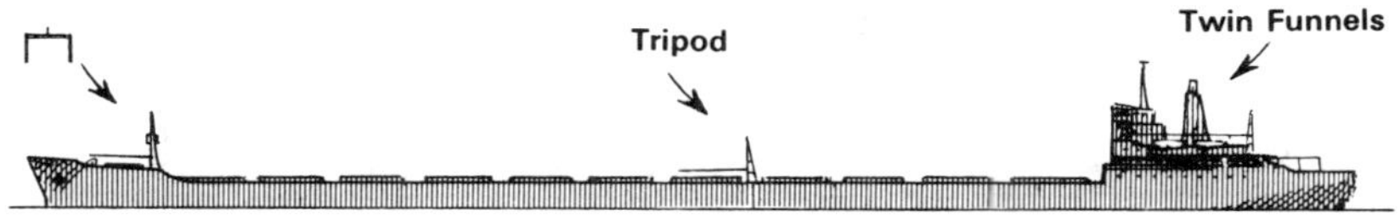

K_2MFK H13
69880 INAYAMA. No/Ja 1964; OO; 48100; 249.99 × 13.74 (820.18 × 45.08); M; 16. Similar (Li flag): **69881 SHIGEO NAGANO 69882 MARSHALL CLARK.**

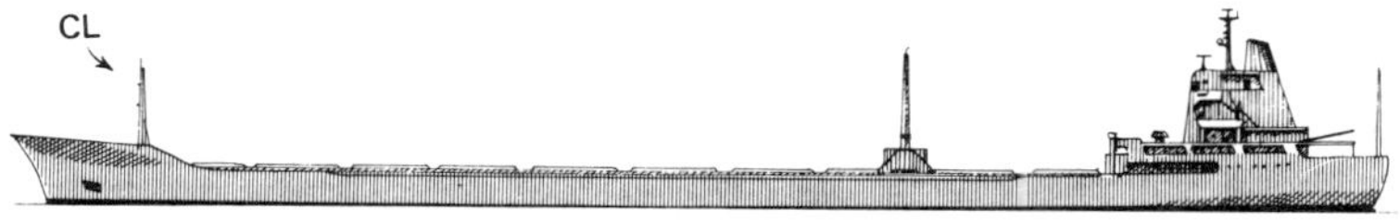

K_2MFK H13
69890 POETIC. Li/Ja 1966; OO; 33300; 240.7 × 12.64 (789.7 × 41.47); T 16; kingposts on travelling gantry. Sister: **69891 SCENIC** (Li).

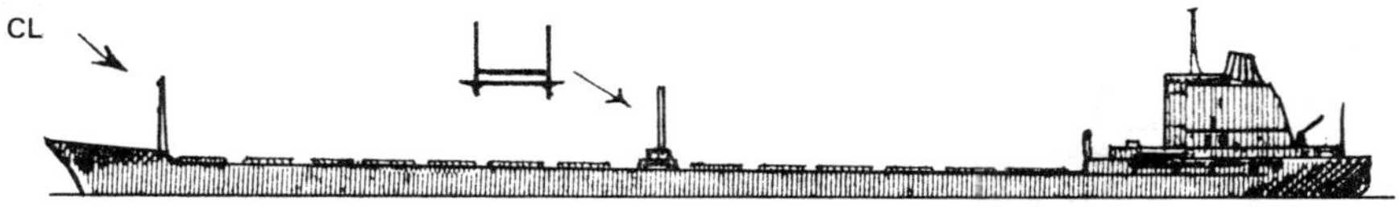

K_2MFK H13
69900 METHODIC. Li/Ja 1966; OBO; 39600; 257.87 × 12.35 (846.03 × 40.52); M; —; ex MELODIC 1974; Kingposts on travelling gantry. Sister: **69901 MYTHIC** (Li) Probable sister: **69902 LORENZO HALCOUSSI** (Li) ex ARCTIC 1971.

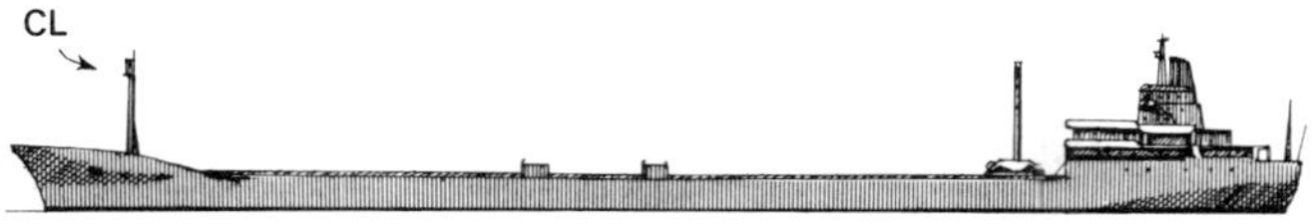

K_2MFK H13
69910 GIANNIS N. Gr/Ja 1965; B; 21400; 204.71 × 10.62 (671.62 × 34.84); M; 15.75; ex PENTAS; Kingposts on travelling gantry.

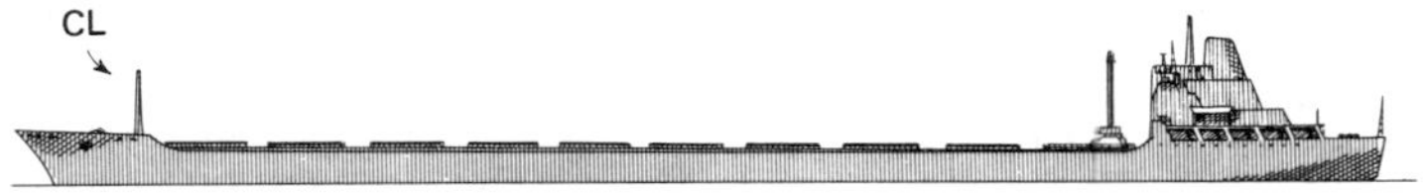

K_2MFK H13
69920 HOPECLIPPER. Br/Ja 1967; B; 35300; 223.96 × 13.7 (734.78 × 44.95); M; 15.5; ex CAPTAIN W.D. CARGILL 1977; Kingpost on travelling gantry.

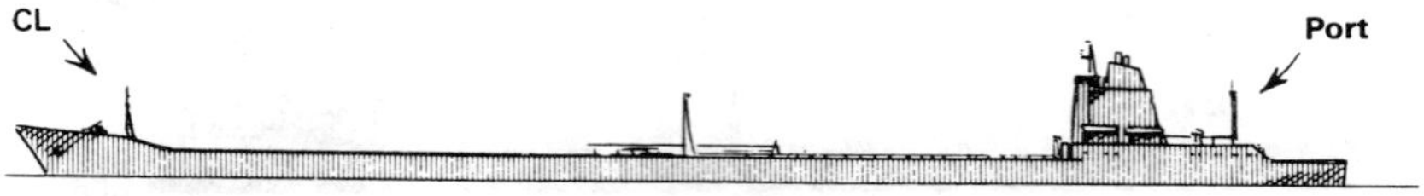

K_2MFK H13
69930 CORINTHIAN. Li/Ja 1967; Tk; 43100; 246.9×13.55 (810.04×44.46); M; 16; ex BLANKENBERG 1973.

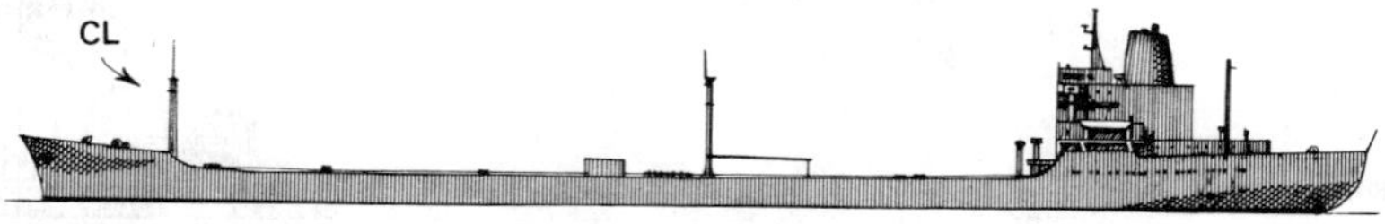

K_2MFK H13
69940 PELOPIDAS. Gr/Ja 1965; Tk; 34400; 238.51×12.19 (782.51×39.99); M; 15.75; ex GALVA 1976; ex HEIWA MARU 1972. Sister: **69941 THEODOHOS** (Gr) ex TAMA MARU 1976.

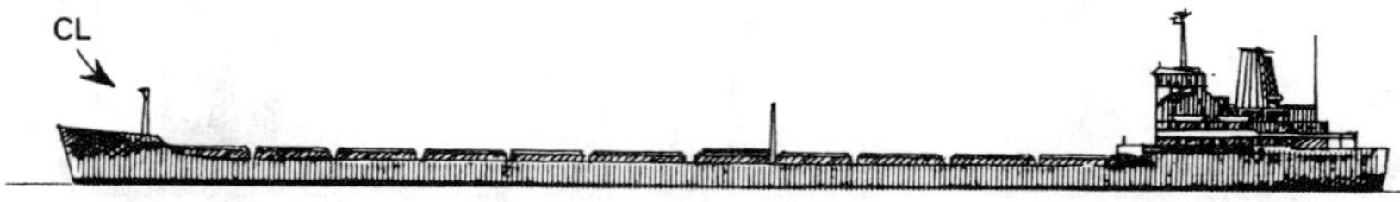

K_2MFK H13
● **69950 ASEAN KNOWLEDGE.** Pi/No 1968; OBO; 42500; 243.85×13.93 (800×45.7); M; 16.5; ex BJORGFJELL. Sisters: **69951 ASEAN MISSION** (Pi) ex BJORGHAV 1979 **69952 ASEAN LIBERTY** (Pi) ex BRALI 1978; ex HAVMOY 1975 **69953 M. EFES** (Tu) ex BANTRY 1978; ex HAVTOR 1975.

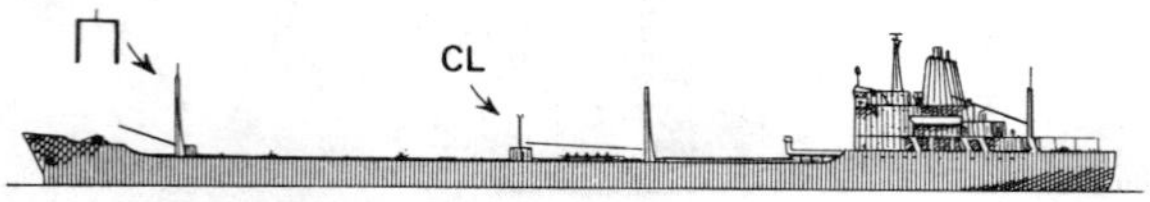

K_2MFK H13
● **69960 STAKARA.** Gr/Ja 1970; Tk; 17500; 170.82×11.01 (560.43×36.12); M; 16. Sisters (Gr flag): **69961 STABENKO 69962 STAMENIS 69963 STAWANDA 69964 MESSINIAKI AIGLI 69965 MESSINIAKI ARETI 69966 MESSINIAKI ANAGENNISIS 69967 MESSINIAKI BERGEN 69968 MESSINIAKI GI 69969 MESSINIAKI IDEA 69970 MESSINIAKI MINDE 69971 MESSINIAKI ORMI 69972 MESSINIAKI PARADIS 69973 MESSINIAKI PNOI 69974 MESSINIAKI CHARA 69975 MESSINIAKI THEA** (Li flag): **69976 MESSINIAKI LAMPSIS 69977 MESSINIAKI TIMI.**

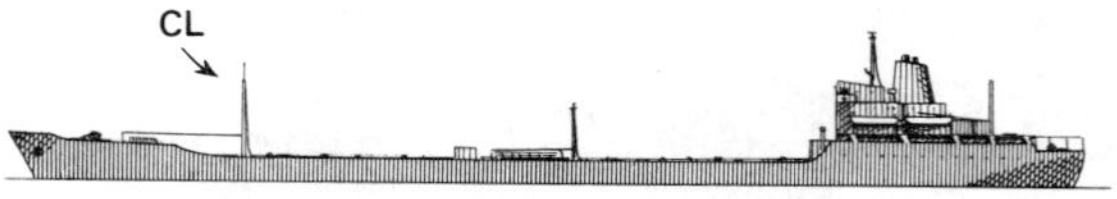

K_2MFK H13
69990 BENITO JUAREZ. Me/Ja 1968; Tk; 12800; 170.75×9.47 (560.2×31.07); M; 15.5. Sisters (Me flag): **69991 ALVARO OBREGON 69992 FRANCISCO I MADERO 69993 MELCHOR OCAMPO 69994 PLAN DE AYALA 69995 PLAN DE AYUTLA 69996 JOSE MARIA MORELOS 69997 PLAN DE GUADELUPE** Possibly similar: **69998 PLAN DE SAN LUIS.**

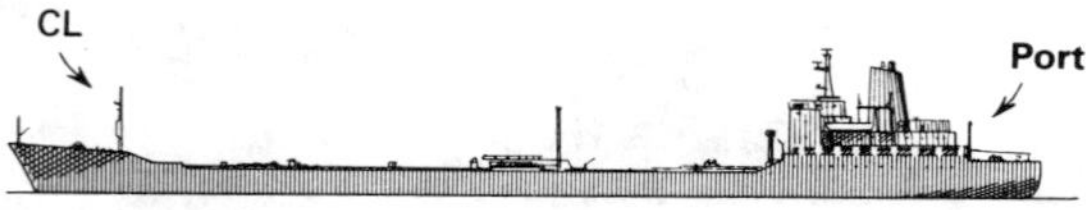

K_2MFK H13
● **70000 PETROMAR BAHIA BLANCA II.** Bz/Ja 1974; Tk; 12800; 161.02×9.81 (528.28×32.19); M; 15; ex ESSO MUKAISHIMA 1978. Sisters: **70001 PETROMAR CAMPANA II** (Bz) ex ESSO BAYWAY 1978 (Li flag): **70002 ESSO NAGOYA 70003 ESSO BRISBANE 70004 ESSO GUAM 70005 ESSO ALBANY** (De flag): **70006 ESSO CALLUNDA 70007 ESSO HAFNIA** Similar (also under K_3MF): **70008 ESSO PORT JEROME** (Fr) ex ESSO KUMAMOTO 1980.

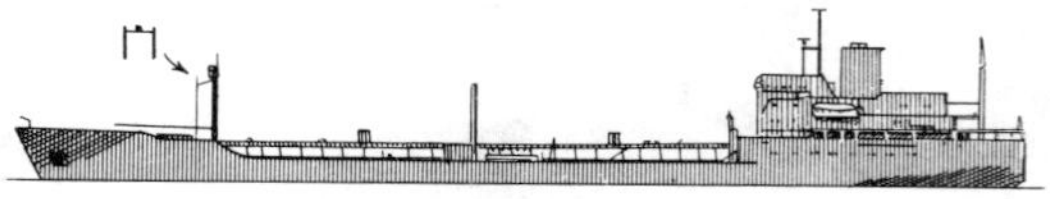

K_2MFK H13
⋆70020 SAMOTLOR. Ru/Fi 1975; Tk/IB; 12200; 160×9.17 (524.93×30.09); M; 16.25. Sisters (Ru flag): **⋆70021 URENGOY ⋆70022 BEREZOVO ⋆70023 GORNOPRAVDINSK ⋆70024 NADYM ⋆70025 NIZHNEVARTOVSK ⋆70026 SAMBURG ⋆70027 USINSK ⋆70028 BAM ⋆70029 VILYUYSK ⋆70030 LENINSK-KUZNETSKIY ⋆70031 KAMENSK-URALSKIY ⋆70032 YENISEYSK ⋆70033 IGRIM.**

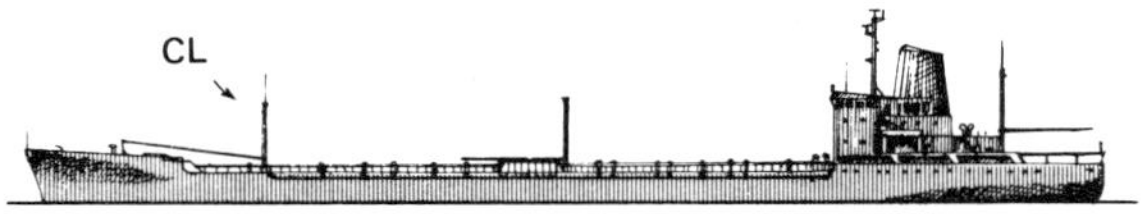

K_2MFK H13
70040 MANUEL AVILA COMACHO. Me/Ne 1973; Tk; 14700; 170.69 × 9.48 (560.01 × 31.1); M; —. Sisters (Me flag): **70041 INDEPENDENCIA 70042 REFORMA 70043 REVOLUCION 70044 MARIANO MOCTEZUMA 70045 FRANCISCO J MUGICA.**

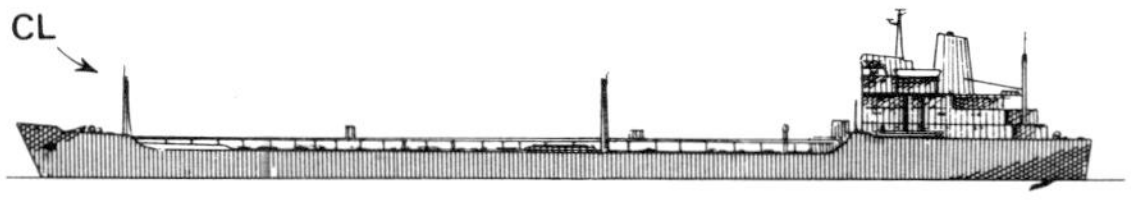

K_2MFK H13
● **70050 BELGULF MERCURY.** Be/Ko 1974; Tk; 14300; 171.05 × 9.99 (561.19 × 32.78); M; 15.5; ex AFRAN MERCURY 1977. Sisters (Li flag): **70051 GLOBE VENUS** ex AFRAN VENUS 1978 **70052 GLOBE CONSTELLATION** ex AFRAN CONSTELLATION 1978 **70053 GLOBE GALAXY** ex KOREA GALAXY 1978 Probably Similar (larger): **70054 AFRAN JUPITER 70055 AFRAN NEPTUNE 70056 GOLDEN CANARY** ex GOLDEN CRANE 1978 **70057 GOLDEN CAPE;** Launched as SWEET BRIAR Similar (lower boat deck etc): **70058 PRIMA** (Li)

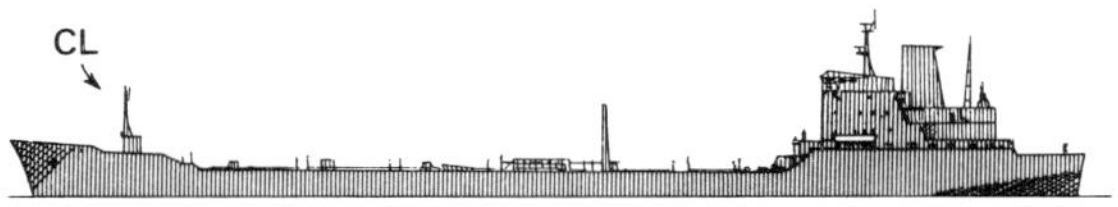

K_2MFK H13
70060 BEJAIA. Ag/Sw 1977; Tk; 18000; 170.72 × 10.97 (560.1 × 39.99); M; 13.5; Launched as MESSINIAKI PROODOS. Sister: **70061 BETHIOUA** (Ag); Launched as MESSINIAKI DOXA Similar: **70062 SONJA** (Sw) **70063 RABIGH BAY I** (Gr) ex SUSANNE 1980 **⋆70064 TATRY** (Pd) **⋆70065 KARKONOSZE** (Pd) **⋆70066 PIENINY II** (Pd) Possible Sister: **70067 SELMA** (Sw).

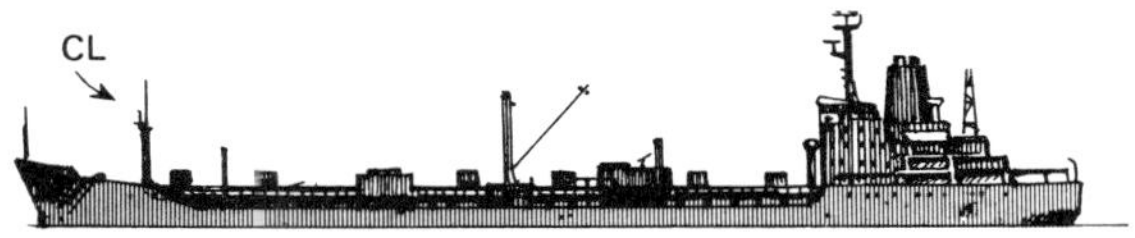

K_2MFK H13
70070 BUNGA KESUMBA. My/Ja 1975; Tk; 19000; 170.01 × 11.15 (557.78 × 36.58); M; 15.25. Sisters: **70071 BUNGA SELASIH** (My) **70072 BUNGA SEPANG** (My).

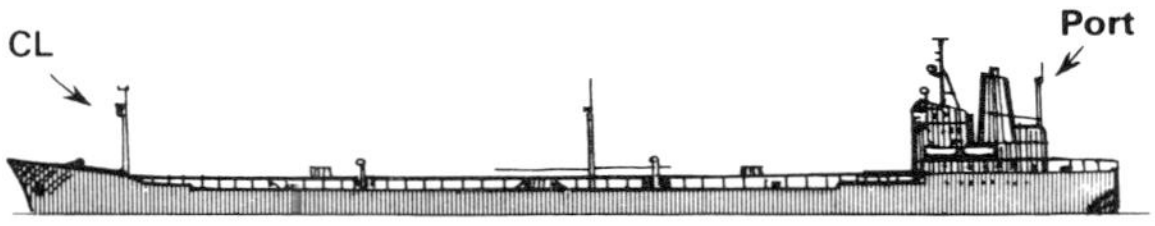

K_2MFK H13
70080 POMELLA. Br/Ne 1967; Tk; 15800; 175.17 × 10.11 (574.7 × 33.17); M; 15; ex HORAMA 1974; Launched as NORDVARD. Sister (may be K_2MF, which see): **70081 PALUDINA** (Br) ex URSHALIM 1973.

K_2MFK H13
● **70090 ANCO EMPRESS.** Br/Sw 1971; Tk; 15400; 169.7 × 9.69 (556.76 × 31.79); M; 16. Sisters (Br flag): **70091 ANCO PRINCESS 70092 ANCO SCEPTRE 70093 ANCO SOVEREIGN 70094 ANCO STANE 70095 ANCO TEMPLAR.**

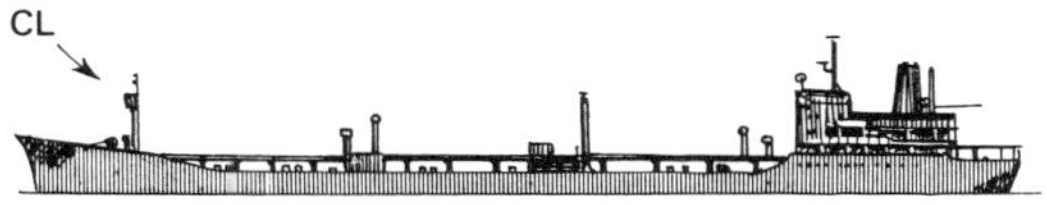

K_2MFK H13
70100 TARN. Fr/Sw 1968; Tk; 11100; 160.13 × 9.15 (525.36 × 30.02); M; 16; ex ANCO DUCHESS 1978. Sisters: **70101 LAKE ANETTE** (No) ex ANCO DUKE 1980 **70102 JAG JYOTI** (In) ex ANCO JYOTI 1977; ex JAG JYOTI 1974; ex ANCO KNIGHT 1972; ex ATHELKNIGHT 1970.

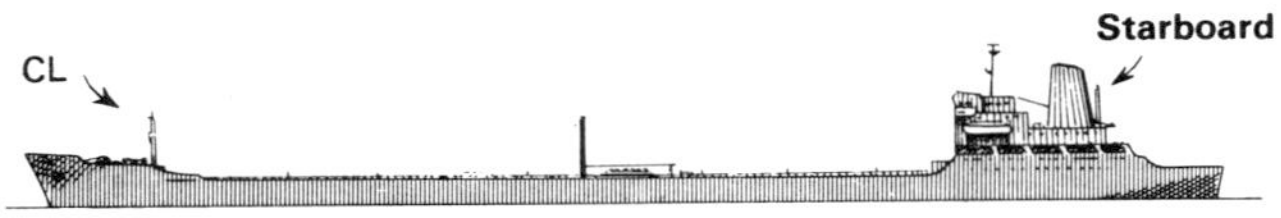

K_2MFK H13
70110 ESSO HALIFAX. Li/Ca 1973; Tk; 18800; 187.76 × 10.42 (616 × 34.19); M; 15. Sisters (Li flag): **70111 ESSO MONTREAL 70112 ESSO SAINT JOHN.**

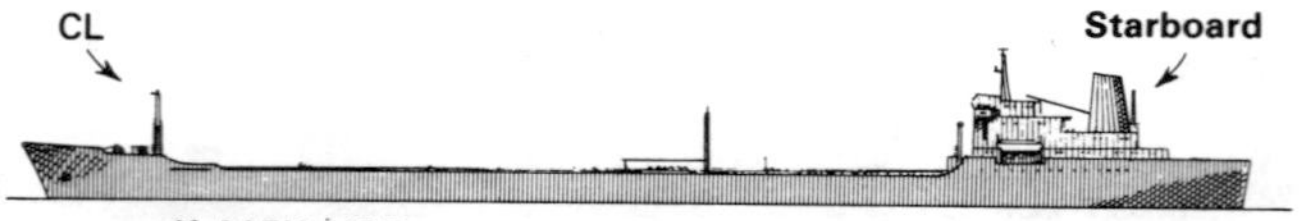

K_2MFK H13
● **70120 ESSO EVERETT.** Li/Ca 1975; Tk; 21600; 191.57 × 11.25 (628.51 × 36.91); M; 15.5. Sisters (Li flag): **70121 ESSO PROVIDENCE 70122 ESSO SAINT PETERSBURG 70123 ESSO TORONTO** Possible Sisters (Ca flag): **70124 IRVING ARCTIC 70125 IRVING ESKIMO.**

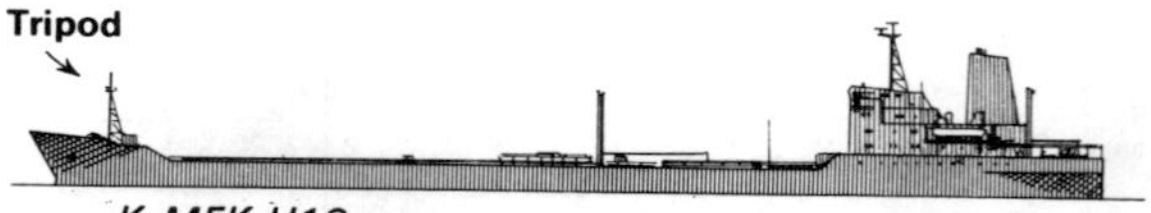

K_2MFK H13
70130 MAASKADE. Be/Be 1975; Tk/Ch; 18300; 170.69 × 11.41 (560 × 37.43); M; 15.75. Sisters (Be flag): **70131 MAASKANT 70132 MAASKERK 70133 MAASKROON** Possibly Similar: **70134 MANDO V** (Gr) **70135 MARIANNA** (Gr) **70136 ESSO BAHAMAS** (Li) ex TETHYS 1972 **70137 ESSO NASSAU** (Li).

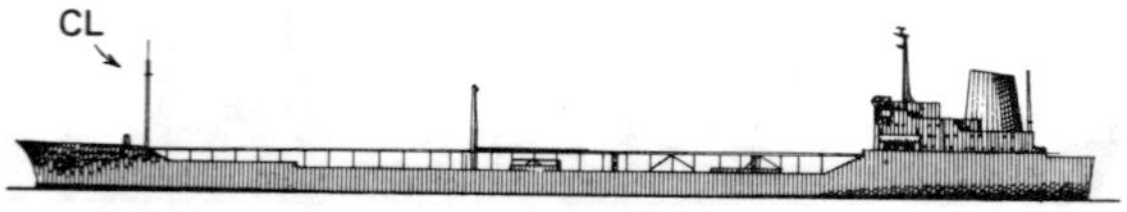

K_2MFK H13
70150 G A WALKER. Br/Ne 1973; Tk; 18700; 170.69 × 11 (560.01 × 36.09); M; 15. Sisters (Br flag): **70151 R A EMERSON 70152 W A MATHER 70153 FORT COULOGNE 70154 FORT EDMONTON 70155 FORT KIPP 70156 FORT MACLEOD 70157 FORT STEELE.**

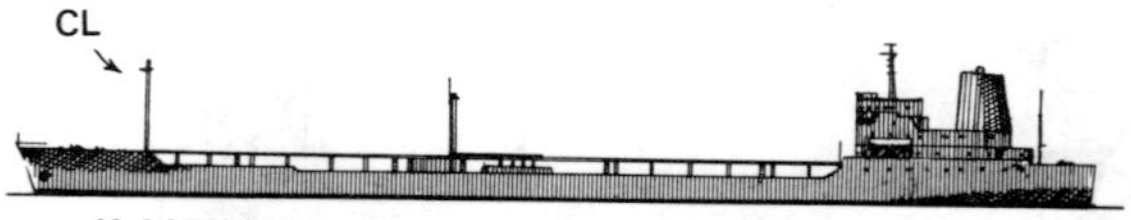

K_2MFK H13
● **70160 WORLD PROMISE.** Gr/Gr 1974; Tk; 18300; 170.62 × 11.02 (559.78 × 36.15); M; 15. Sisters: **70161 WORLD PROTECTOR** (Gr) Launched as WORLD PROSPECTOR **70162 WORLD PROVIDER** (Gr) **70163 OLYMPIC DREAM** (Gr) ex WORLD PROSPECT 1975 **70164 FAILAKA** (No) ex TEAM SINMAR; ex TEAM GERWI 1976.

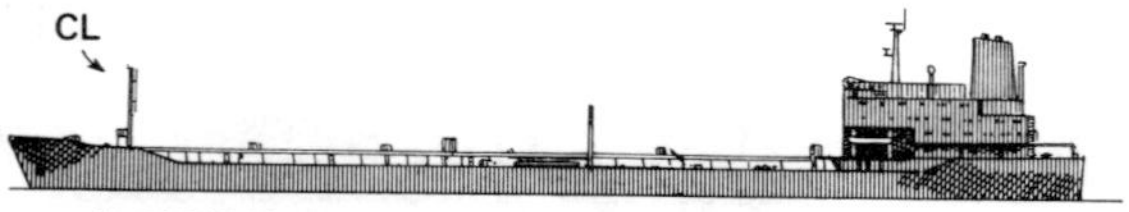

K_2MFK H13
70170 INLAND. Sw/Sw 1977; Tk/Ch; 18200; 170.72 × 11.33 (560.1 × 37.17); M; 16. Sisters (Sw flag): **70171 BROLAND 70172 ATLAND.**

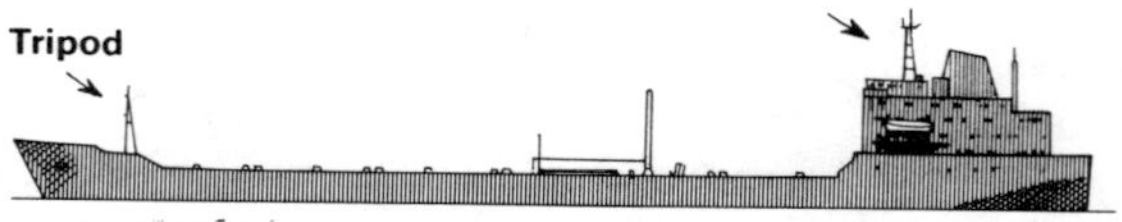

K_2MFK H13
70180 PASADENA. De/De 1976; Tk; 20500; 170.69 × 11.3 (560.01 × 37.07); M; 15.5. Sisters (De flag): **70181 PANAMA 70182 PARANAGUA 70183 PATAGONIA.**

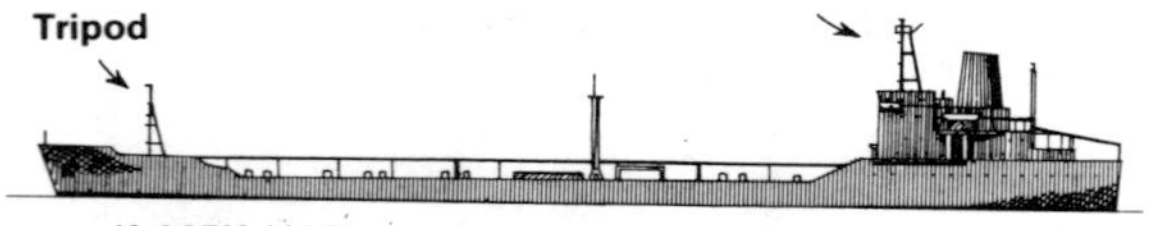

K_2MFK H13
70190 NEPTUNE ARIES. Sg/De 1974; Tk; 16400; 170.69 × 10.42 (560.01 × 34.19); M; 15. Sister: **70191 NEPTUNE ORION** (Sg).

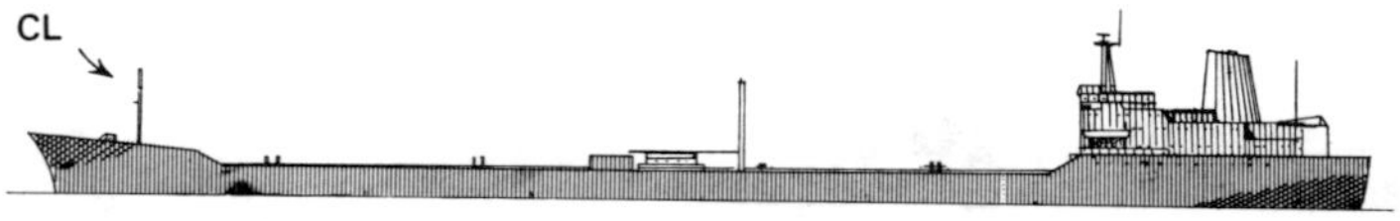

K_2MFK H13
70200 CYCLOPS. Br/Ne 1975; Tk; 32600; 210.32 × 12.41 (690.01 × 40.71); M; 16.75. Sister: **70201 CLYTONEUS** (Br) Probable Sister: **70202 RAIKO MARU** (Ja) ex SANKO TRUST 1979; Launched as HELLESPONT ARGOSY.

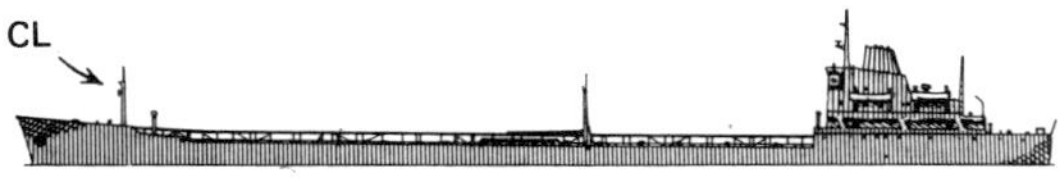

K_2MFK H13
70210 ESSO SLAGEN. No/Sw 1968; Tk; 11000; 162.67 × 8.87 (533.69 × 29.1); M; 16.25.

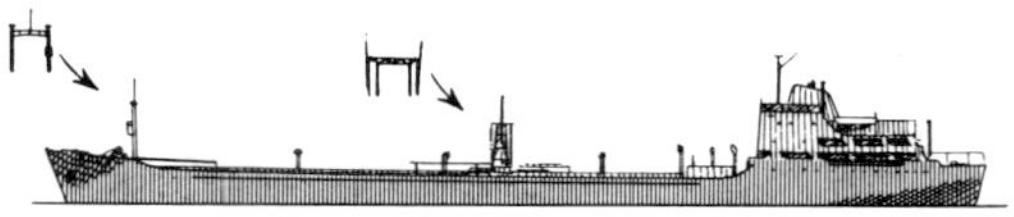

K_2MFK H13
70220 ESSI KARI. No/Sw 1956/65; Tk; 10700; 149.36 × 9.38 (490.03 × 30.77); M; 13.5; ex ARJEPLOG 1965; Converted from ore carrier 1965.

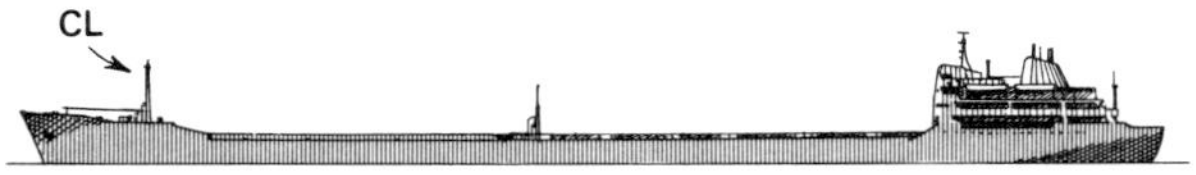

K_2MFK H13
⋆**70230 AUE.** DDR/Sw 1959; OO; 15800; 181.62 × 9.99 (595.87 × 32.78); M; 14.5; ex VIRTALA 1969.

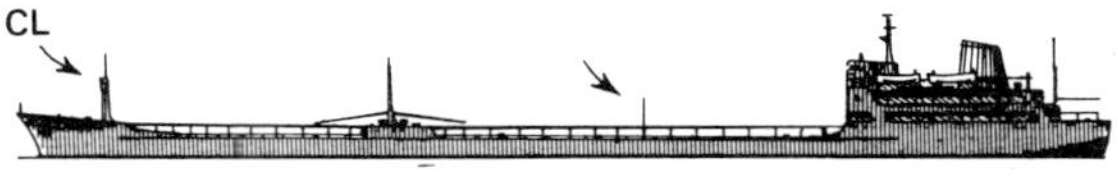

K_2MFK H13
70240 GLOBE NOVA. Li/No 1964; Tk/LGC; 13500; 169.78 × 9.6 (557.02 × 31.5); M; 15.75; ex GRANHEIM 1978.

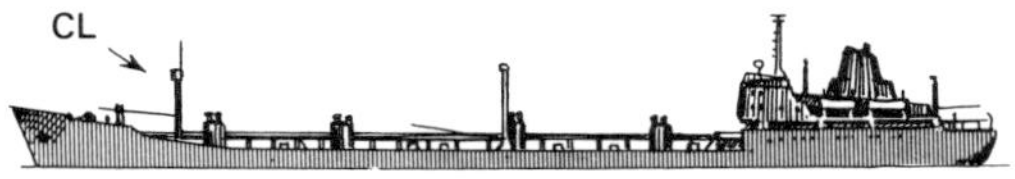

K_2MFK H13
70250 CHELSEA PIONEER. Pa/No 1961; Tk; 8800; 155.02 × 8.8 (508.6 × 28.87); M; 16; ex ACRON C 1980; ex ARGENPUMA 1979; ex POST RUNNER 1977; ex SAGA STATE 1970; ex ANCO STATE 1967; ex BEREAN 1964.

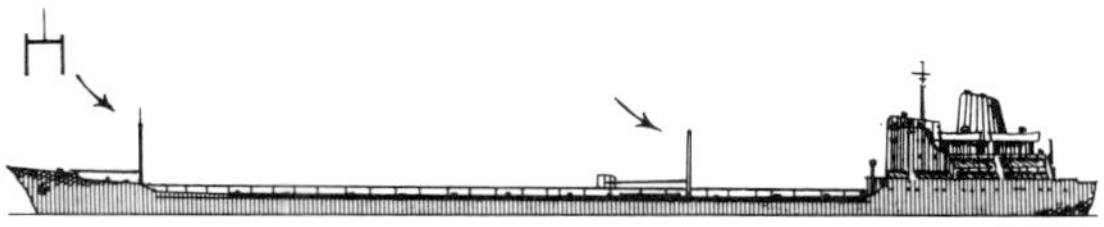

K_2MFK H13
● **70260 LAKE ANJA.** No/No 1963; Tk; 13000; 169.75 × 9.4 (556.92 × 30.84); M; 16; ex GIMLEKOLLEN 1977; ex GARD 1963. Sister: **70261 GUNDA BROVIG** (No) ex OLYMP 1968 Probably Similar: **70262 ANTONIO D'ALESSIO** (It) ex ERGINA I 1977; ex ANNA ODLAND 1975.

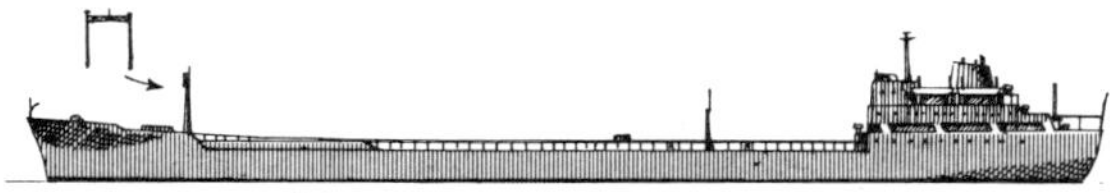

K_2MFK H13
70270 LAKE ANIARA. Li/Sw 1962; Tk; 12800; 170.62 × 9.7 (559.78 × 31.82); M; 15.5; ex ANIARA 1977; ex ADA GORTHON 1971.

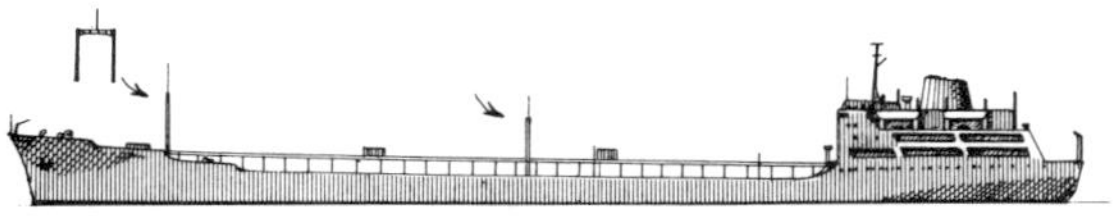

K_2MFK H13
70280 ESTRELLA ANTARTICA. Ar/No 1962; Tk; 13000; 169.7 × 9.68 (556.76 × 31.76); M; 14.5; ex FLEETTRADER 1979; ex HERSTEIN 1978; ex LANDVARD 1969.

K_2MFK H13
⋆**70290 DA QING No 38.** RC/No 1962; Tk; 8800; 152.41 × 8.46 (500.03 × 27.76); M; 14; ex DANSBORG 1970; ex KINDVIK 1969.

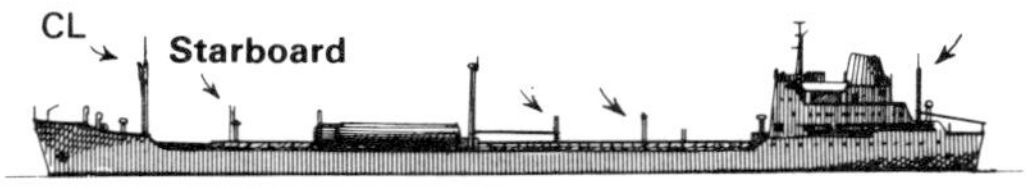

K_2MFK H13
70300 CANSO TRANSPORT. Ca/No 1967; Tk/Ch; 9400; 149.41 × 9.02 (490.19 × 29.59); M; 16; ex LONN. Sister: **70301 COASTAL TRANSPORT** (Ca) ex BIRK.

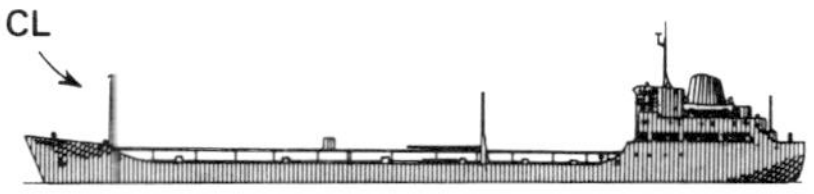

K_2MFK H13
70310 MONTELEON. Sp/Sp 1969; Tk; 5200; 123.37 × 7.32 (404.76 × 24.02); M; —.

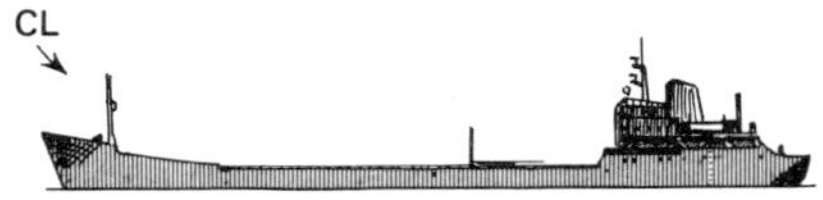

K_2MFK H13
70320 UNGAVA TRANSPORT. Ca/No 1959/71; Tk; 4700; 122.97 × 7.11 (403.44 × 23.33); M; 13; ex TOMMY WIBORG 1974; ex VARANGNES 1970; Converted from ore/oil 1971.

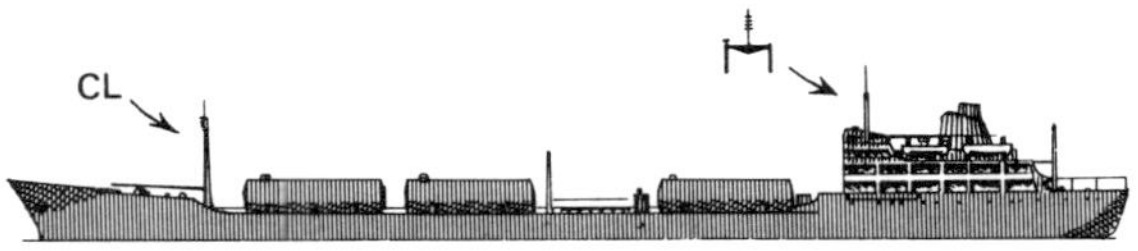

K_2MFK H13
70330 MAYA FARBER. Pa/No 1960; Ch; 13300; 176.18 × 9.59 (578.02 × 31.46); M; 14.5; ex BJORGHEIM 1978; ex LYSEFJELL 1972; Converted from tanker 1970.

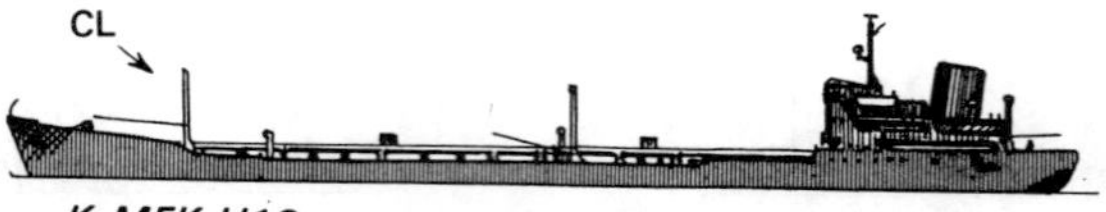

K_2MFK H13
70340 LLAIMA. Ch/Br 1960; Tk; 12500; 170.47 × 9.48 (559.28 × 31.1); M; 14.5; ex STOLT STUART 1976; ex STUART PRINCE 1971. Sister: **70341 STELLA AZZURRA** (It) ex STOLTA 1977; ex STOLT TUDOR 1975; ex TUDOR PRINCE 1971.

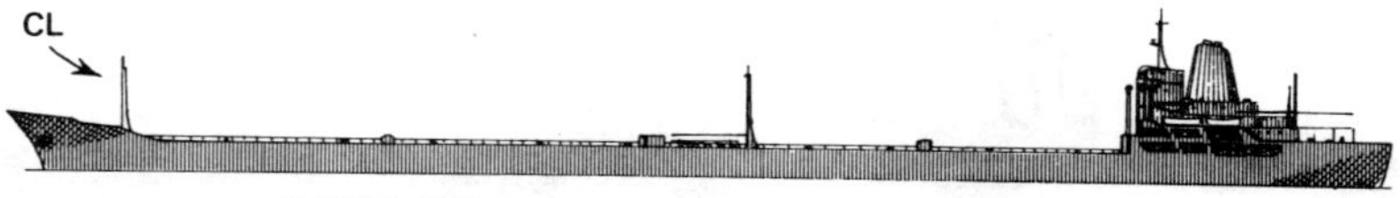

K_2MFK H13
70350 MILOS. Li/Ja 1964; Tk; 37300; 242.02 × 13.37 (794.03 × 43.86); M; 16.5.

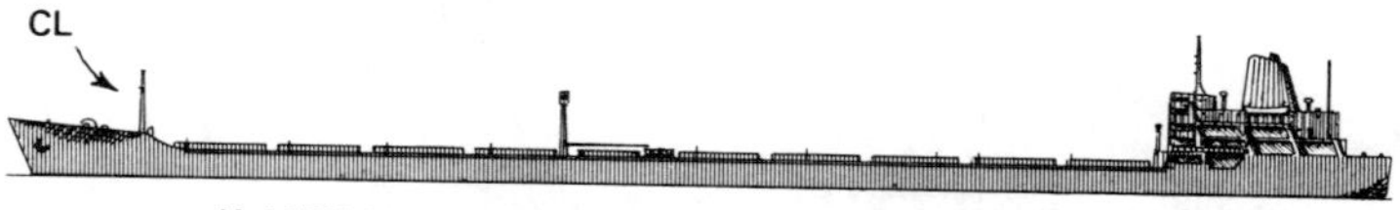

K_2MFK H13
70360 ATHENA. Li/Ja 1964; OO; 30700 (oil) 16700 (ore); 224.29 × 12.08 (735.86 × 39.63); T; —; ex SANTA FE PIONEER 1968. Sister: **70361 DAPHNE** (Li) ex SANTA FE EXPLORER 1968.

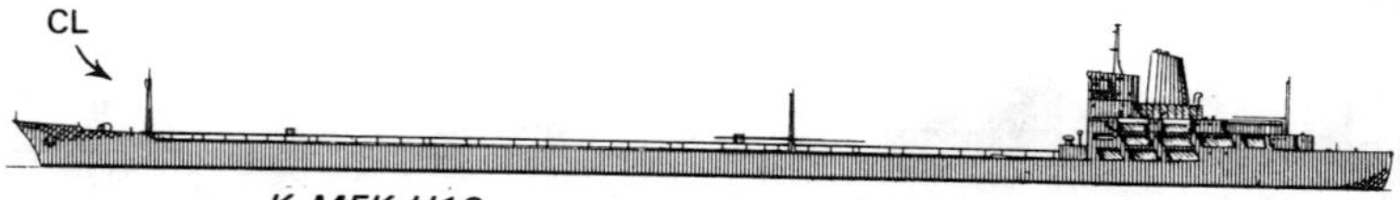

K_2MFK H13
70370 ARHON. Li/Ja 1966; Tk; 30600; 236.23 × 12.48 (775.03 × 40.94); M; 17; ex MOORGATE QUEEN 1977; ex VASSOS GEORGIADIS 1976; ex KONGSHOLM 1973.

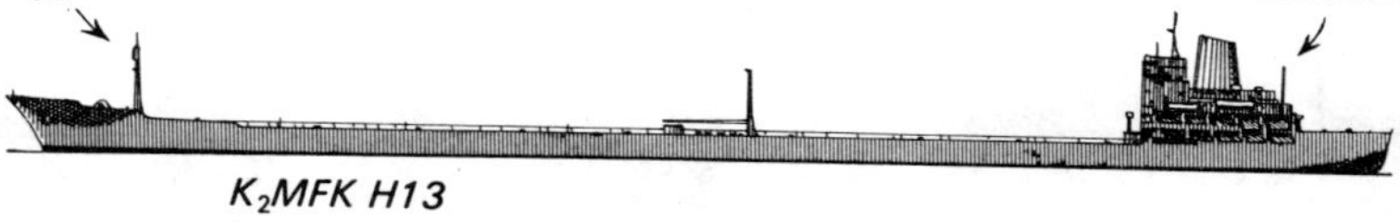

K_2MFK H13
70380 CHARALAMBOS. Gr/Ja 1966; Tk; 31100; 235.01 × 12.22 (771.03 × 40.09); M; 16.25; ex WORLD LEADER 1980.

K_2MFK H13
70390 PRINCESS ANNE-MARIE. Gr/Ja 1964; Tk; 34700; 235.47 × 12.32 (772.54 × 40.42); T; —. Sister: **70391 LAMYRA** (Li) ex NICHOLAS J GOULANDRIS 1968.

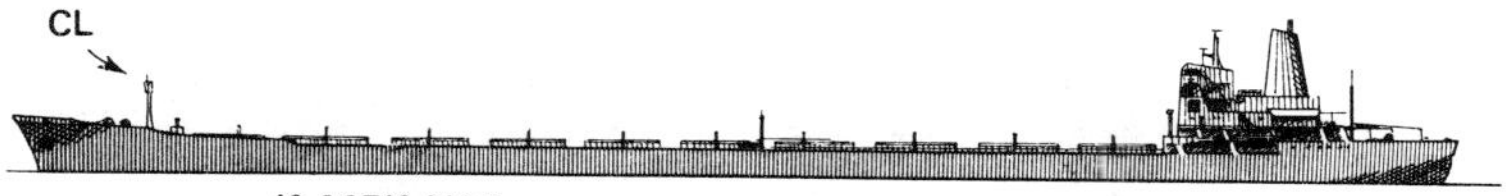

K_2MFK H13
70400 ANEMOS. Gr/Ja 1963; OO; 23300 (ore) 33000 (oil); 230.66 × 12.16 (756.76 × 39.9); T; —. Sisters: **70401 ASTRAPI** (Gr) **70402 VRONTI** (Gr).

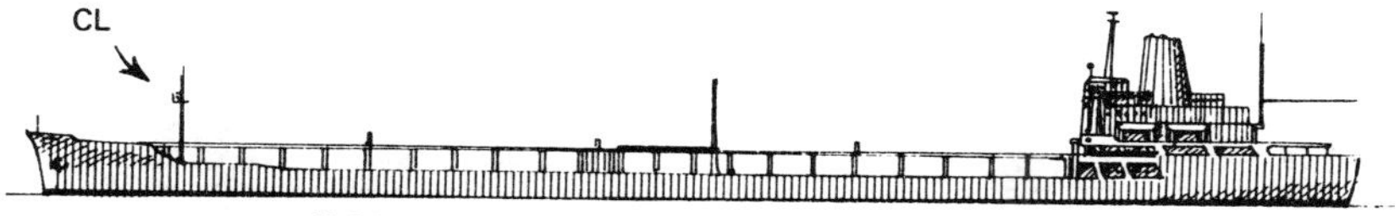

K_2MFK H13
70410 SUNG-UN No 2. Li/Ja 1964; Tk; 44500; 249.16 × 13.47 (817.45 × 44.19); M; 16; ex FERNMANOR 1977; Lengthened 1968.

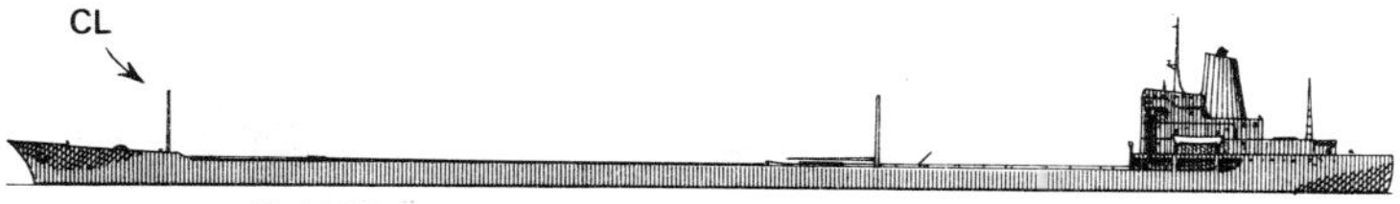

K_2MFK H13
70420 BEAUFORT MARINER. Li/Ja 1965; Tk; 31000; 230 × 12.36 (754.59 × 40.55); T; —; ex ARCO COLOMBIA; ex SINCLAIR COLOMBIA 1970.

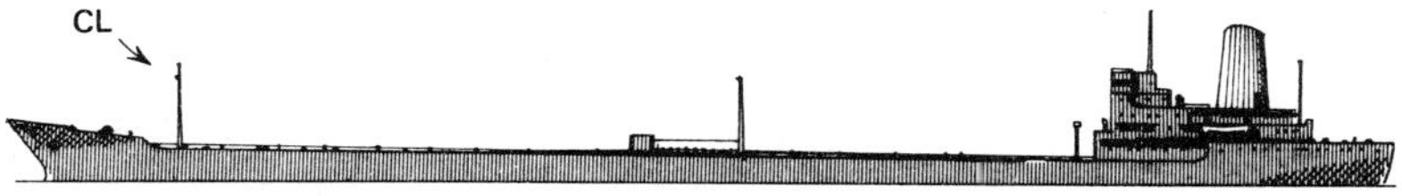

K_2MFK H13
● **70430 FAIRFIELD ARCHER.** Li/Ja 1964; Tk; 37300; 242.98 × 11.99 (797.12 × 39$34); M; 15.25; ex FAIRFIELD COPA 1979; ex ASIA MARU No 2 1973.

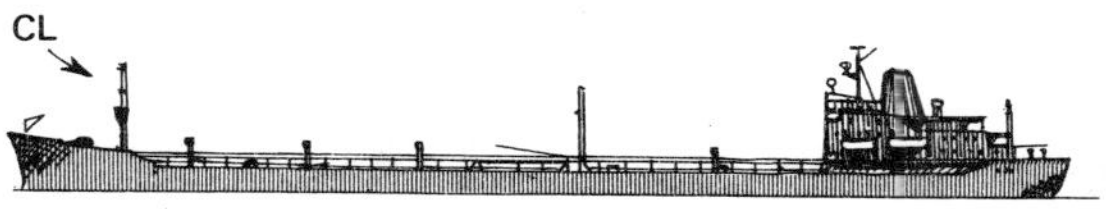

K_2MFK H13
70440 DOLORES. Ch/No 1967; Tk; 14500; 169.02 × 9.53 (554.53 × 31.27); M; 16.5; ex IVER STREAM; ex SAGA STREAM 1977; ex ANCO STREAM 1973.

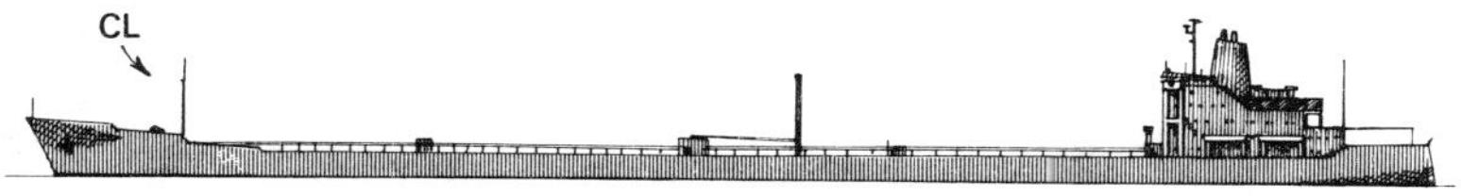

K_2MFK H13
70450 ULFSBORG. Li/Ja 1966; Tk; 34700; 236.23 × 12.61 (775.03 × 41.37); M; 15.5; ex EASTERN QUEEN; ex WORLD QUEEN 1972.

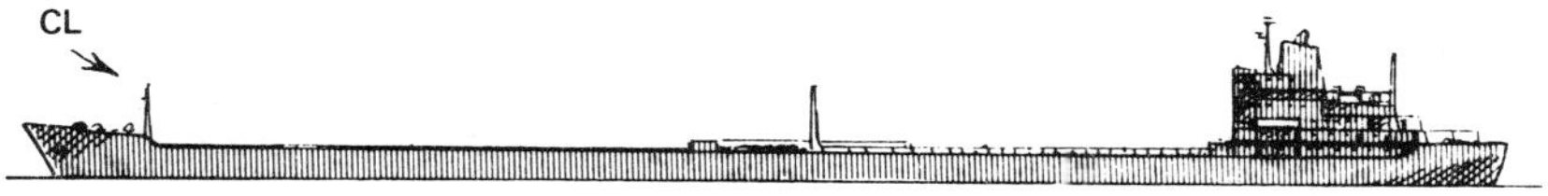

K_2MFK H13
70460 AVRA. Gr/Ja 1967; Tk; 44500; 250.12 × 14.05 (820.6 × 46.1); T; —; ex CALLIOPI CARRAS 1978. Sister: **70461 ARTEMIS** (Gr) ex ATHINA CARRAS 1978 Similar: **70462 LETO** (Gr) ex M.J. CARRAS 1978 **70463 ASTRAEA** (Li) ex ALEXANDRA CARRAS 1978 **70464 DIONE** (Li) ex IOANNIS CARRAS 1978 **70465 WILLIAM DAMPIER** (Au) ex IOLCOS; ex FOTINI CARRAS 1978.

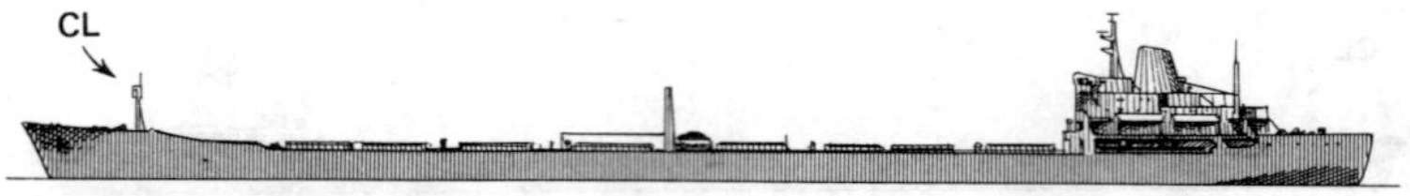

K_2MFK H13
● **70470 CALEDONIA.** Li/Ja 1967; OO; 34500; 228.51 × 12.68 (749.7 × 41.6); M; 16.25. Sister: **70471 MAKEDONIA STAR** (Li) ex MAKEDONIA 1981.

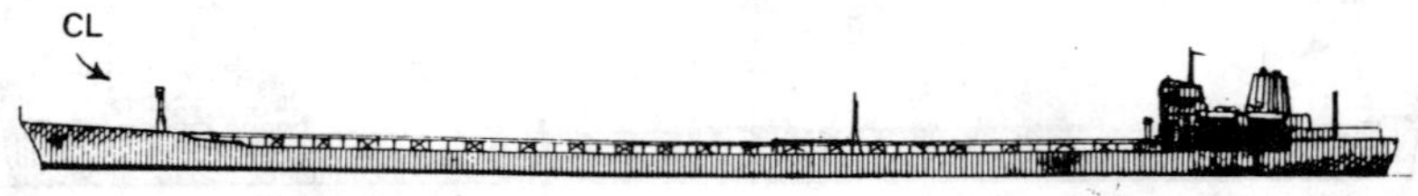

K_2MFK H13
70480 ALNAJDI. Si/Ja 1964; Tk; 42300; 243.52 × 12.96 (798.95 × 42.52); M; 15.5; ex DERWENTDALE 1975; ex HALCYON BREEZE 1967.

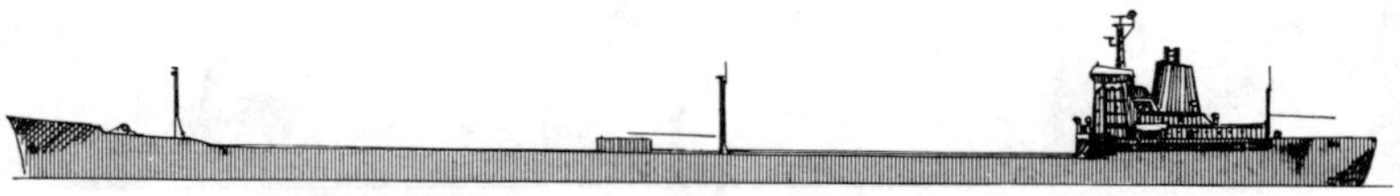

K_2MFK H13
● **70490 YUYO MARU No 2.** Ja/Ja 1966; Tk; 38900; 238.59 × 11.99 (782.78 × 39.34); M; 15.5.

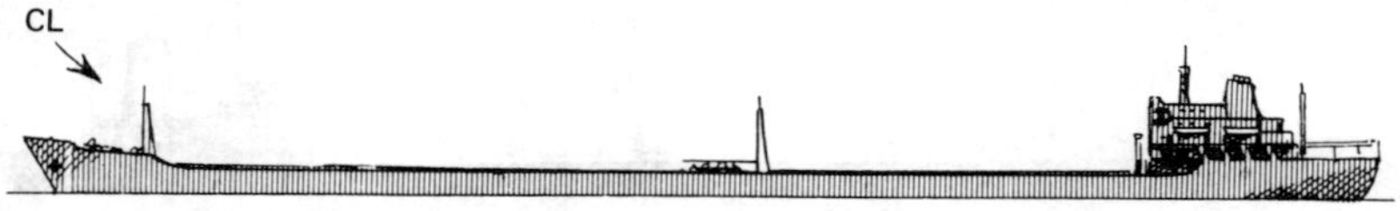

K_2MFK H13
70500 PETROLA 31. Gr/Ja 1966; Tk; 43400; 246.49 × 13.83 (808.69 × 45.37); M; 16; ex PETROLA XXXI 1976; ex HELLAS 1975; ex HENRIETTA LATSI 1973.

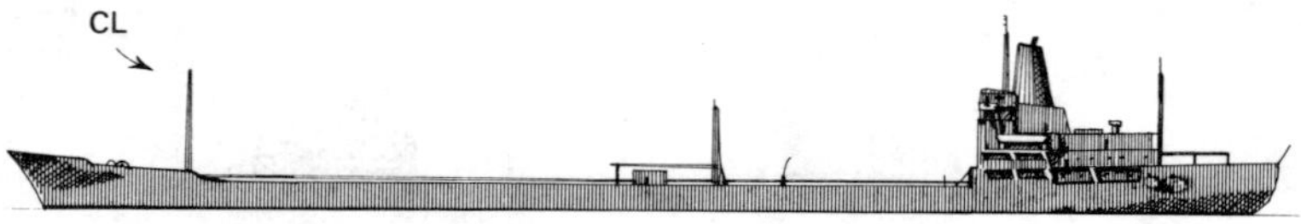

K_2MFK H13
70510 GHIONA. Gr/Ja 1963; Tk; 30600; 225.03 × 12.24 (738.29 × 40.16); T; —. Sisters (Gr flag): **70511 GHERANIA 70512 GHERESTOS.**

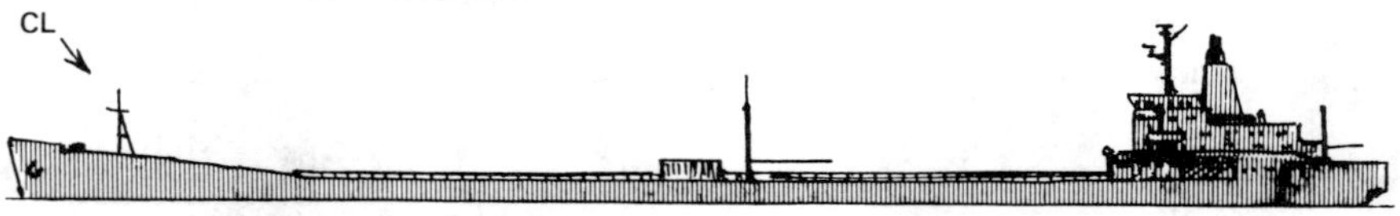

K_2MFK H13
70520 COASTAL SPIRIT. Li/Sw 1966; Tk; 60900; 265.56 × 16.51 (871.26 × 54.17); T; 17; ex SEA SPIRIT 1977. Similar: **70521 SAFINA SALAMAH** (Si) ex SEVEN SEAS 1976.

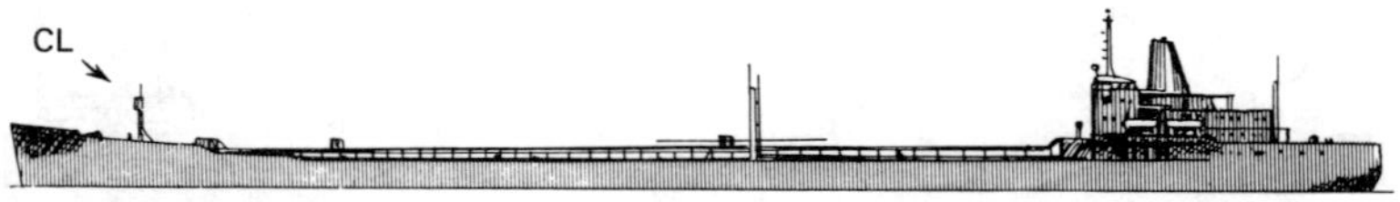

K_2MFK H13
70530 DESPINA A.L. Gr/Sw 1965; Tk; 32700; 236.38 × 12.64 (775.52 × 41.47); T; 17.25; ex LUCIAN 1973. Sister: **70531 ADAMANTIOS** (Gr) ex CHIOS ISLAND 1977; ex BOTANY BAY 1975; ex CYPRIAN 1973.

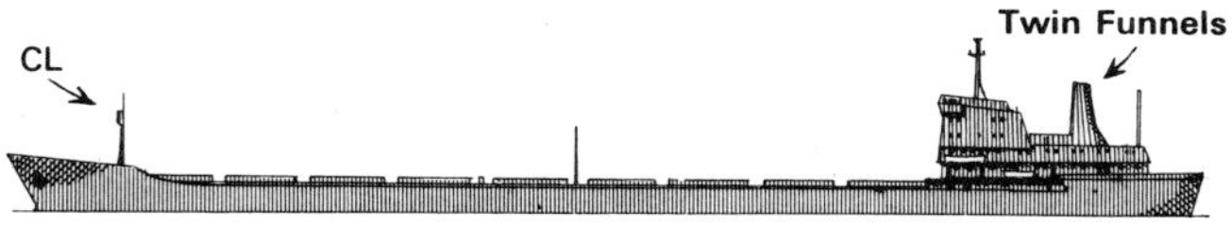

K_2MFK H13
★70540 SYN PULKU. Pd/Pd 1974; B; 20600; 199.17 × 10.63 (653.44 × 34.88); M; 15.25; **'B 447'** type. Sisters (Pd flag): **★70541 CEDYNIA ★70542 MIROSLAWIEC ★70543 NARWIK II ★70544 POWSTANIEC WIELKOPOLSKI ★70545 STUDZIANKI.**

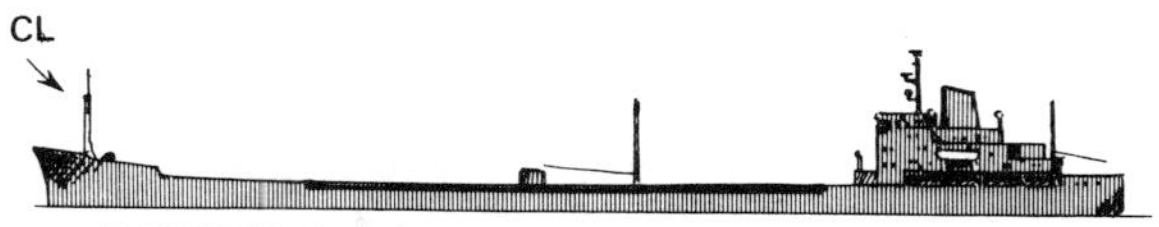

K_2MFK H13
70550 SEABORNE. Li/Ja 1973; Tk; 15000; 171.02 × 10.71 (561.09 × 35.14); M; 15. Sisters: **70551 SEASERVICE** (Li) **70552 SEASTAR** (Li) Possibly similar: **70553 CYS INTEGRITY** (Li) **70554 KOREA SUNNYHILL** (Ko) ex CYS HOPE 1980.

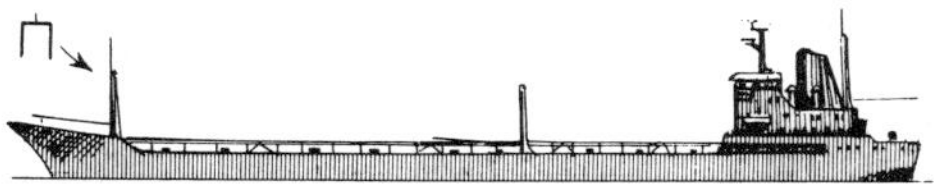

K_2MFK H13
70560 IRATI. Bz/Ys 1970; Tk; 9700; 142.53 × 7.32 (467.62 × 14.02); M; 13.5. Sisters (Bz flag): **70561 IPANEMA 70562 ITORORO.**

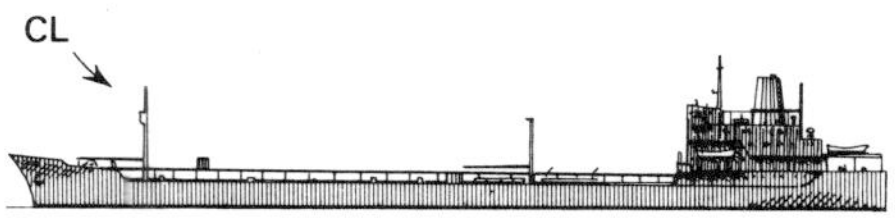

K_2MFK H13
70570 PERMINA XXIX. Ia/Sw 1971; Tk; 9400; 139.3 × 9.2 (457.02 × 30.18); M; 15.5; ex BRUCE SOVERINO 1980. Sister: **70571 BRUCE TORRES** (Li).

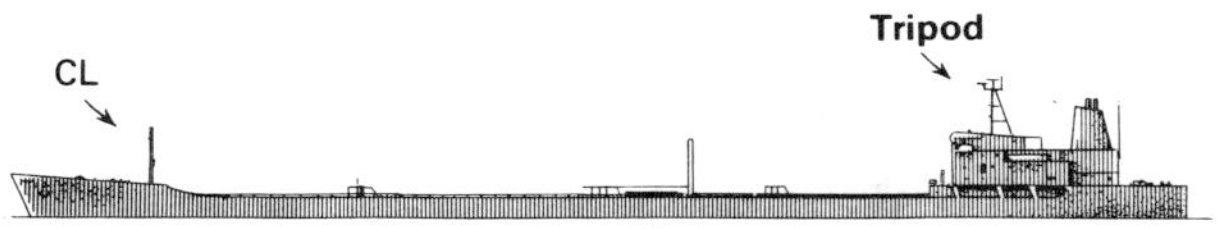

K_2MFK H13
70580 AQUARIUS. Br/Br 1972; Tk; 19900; 192.01 × 10.38 (629.95 × 34.05); M; 16; ex NEWBURN 1980; ex AFGHANISTAN; ex JOSEPH R. SMALLWOOD 1975. Sisters: **70581 STRAIT OF CANSO** (Br) **70582 SIMONBURN** (Br) ex KURDISTAN; ex FRANK D. MOORES 1976 Probable sister: **70583 AMOKURA** (NZ) ex HINDUSTAN 1978.

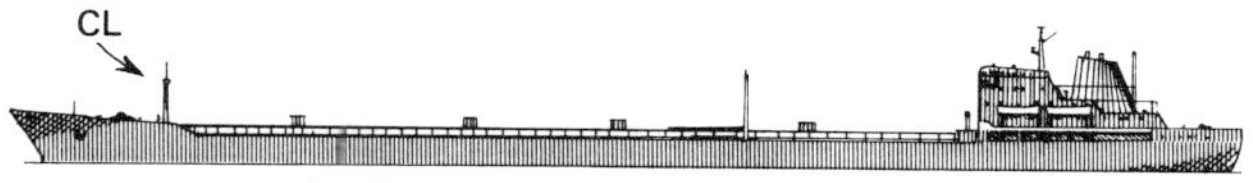

K_2MFK H13
● **★70590 MATE ZALKA.** Ru/Ys 1976; Tk; 27700; 195 × 12.2 (639.76 × 40.03); M; 17. Sisters (Ru flag): **★70591 ANTONIO GRAMSCI ★70592 PABLO NERUDA ★70593 DAVID SIQUEIROS 70594 VIKTORIO CODOVILLA ★70595 JACQUES DUCLOS ★70596 JOHN REED ★70597 JOSE MARTI ★70598 PAUL ROBESON ★70599 KLEMENT GOTTWALD ★70600 SUKHE BATOR.**

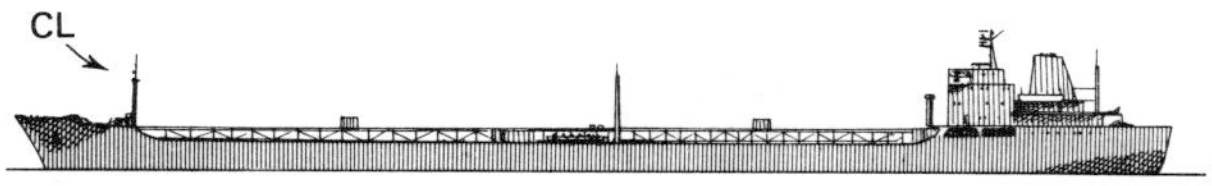

K_2MFK H13
★70610 KUTAISI. Ru/Ys 1976; Tk; 15700; 182.99 × 10 (600.36 × 32.81); M; 17. Sister (Ru flag): **★70611 SUKHUMI.**

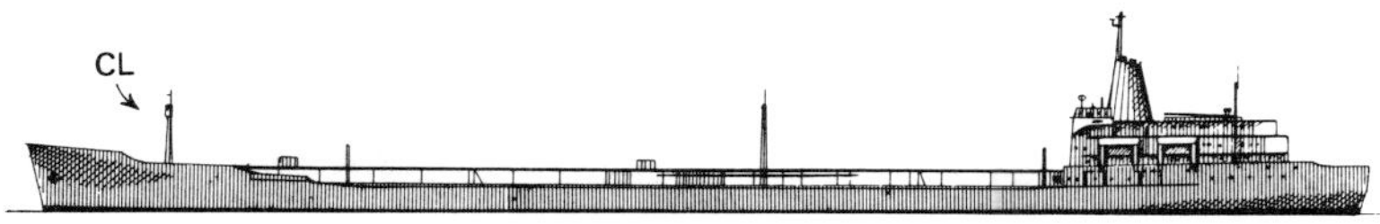

K_2MFK H13
70620 KYNOSSOURA. Gr/Sw 1964; Tk; 30600; 236.23 × 12.42 (775.03 × 40.75); M; 15.5; ex ORIENTAL DISCOVERER 1981; ex DEFIANT COLOCOTRONIS 1977; ex BRUSE JARL 1969.

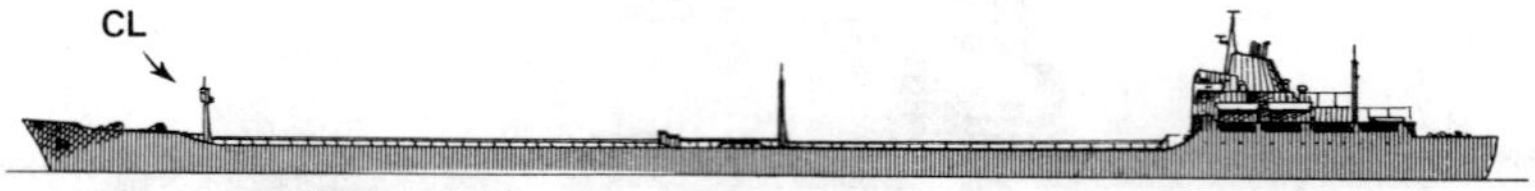

K_2MFK H13
70630 STERLING. Li/Ja 1966; Tk; 30700; 234.02 × 11.86 (767.78 × 38.91); M; 15.75.

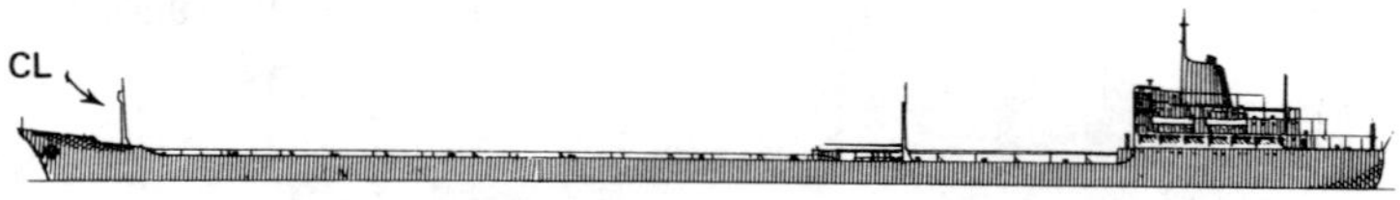

K_2MFK H13
70640 MICHAEL. Li/Ja 1965; Tk; 28300; 222.51 × 11.96 (730.02 × 39.24); M; —; ex MICHAEL J. GOULANDRIS 1978. Sisters (Li flag): **70641 ARGOLIS 70642 TRIPOLIS.**

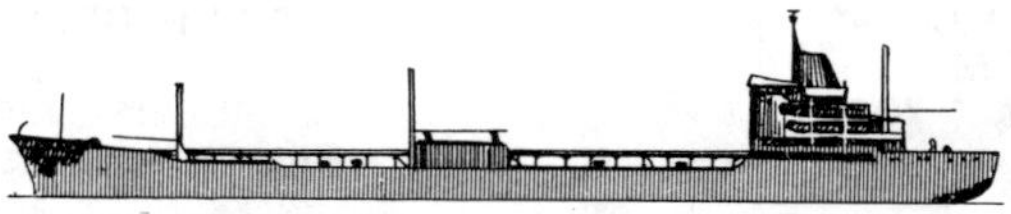

K_2MFK H13
70650 WILLIAM R. GRACE. Li/Ne 1964; LGC; 10000; 156.47 × 7.51 (513.35 × 24.64); M; 17. Sister: **70651 JOSEPH P. GRACE** (Li).

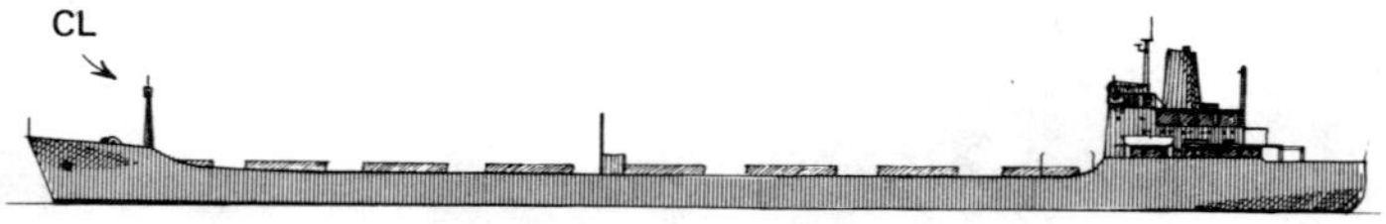

K_2MFK H13
70660 CANADIAN HIGHLANDER. Ca/Br 1967; B; 29300; 213.39 × 12.68 (700.1 × 41.6); M; 15; ex CAPE BRETON HIGHLANDER 1980; ex THORSDRAKE 1975.

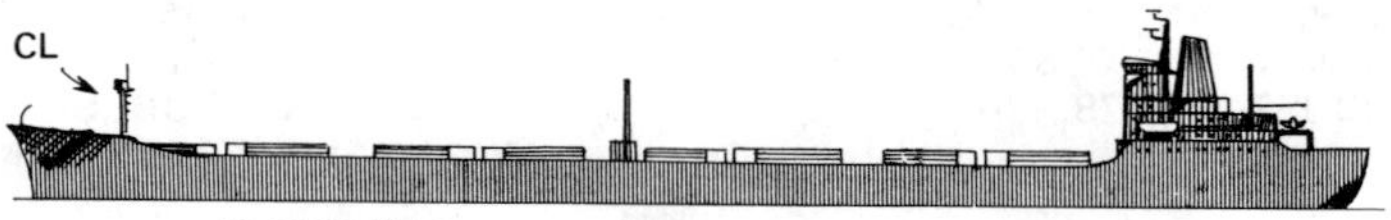

K_2MFK H13
70670 IRENES RHAPSODY. Gr/Br 1967; B; 29300; 213.37 × 12.75 (700.03 × 41.83); M; 15.75; ex MEDIOLANUM; ex HAMLET 1972.

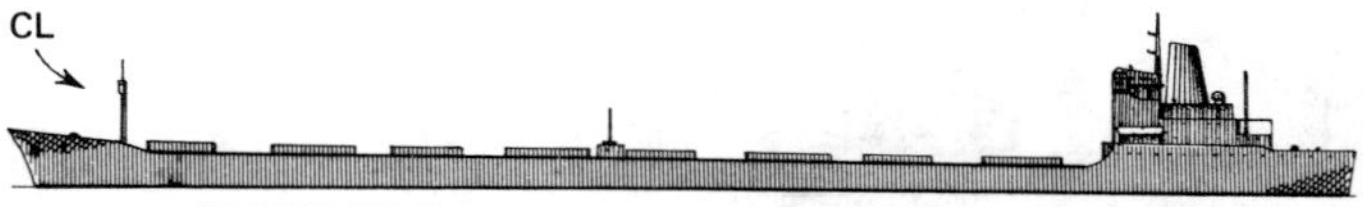

K_2MFK H13
70680 EVANGELIA C. Gr/Br 1967; B; 29400; 213.37 × 12.75 (700.32 × 41.83); M; 15; ex POLYFREEDOM 1978. Sister: **70681 PAN WESTERN** (Gr) ex NORSEMAN 1975.

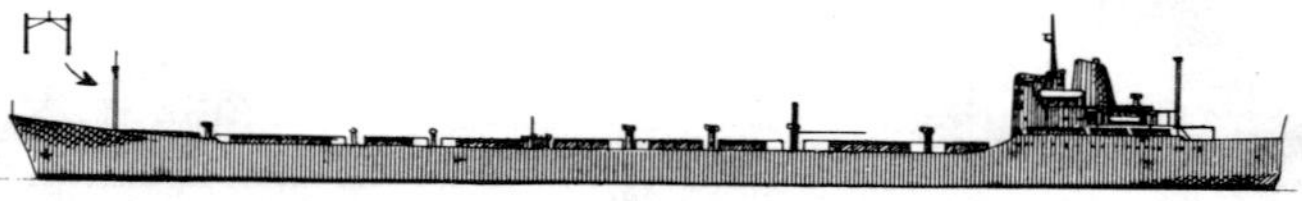

K_2MFK H13
70690 ADOLF LEONHARDT. Li/FRG 1964; B; 18600; 201.66 × 11.53 (661.6 × 37.83); M; 15.

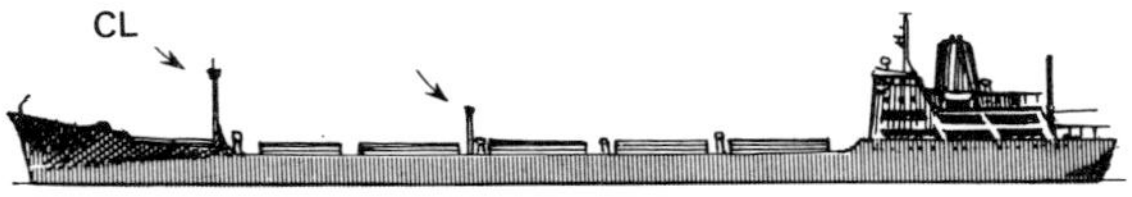

K_2MFK H13
70700 GLAFKI. Li/Fr 1964; B; 15200; 178.24 × 9.46 (584.78 × 31.04); M; —.

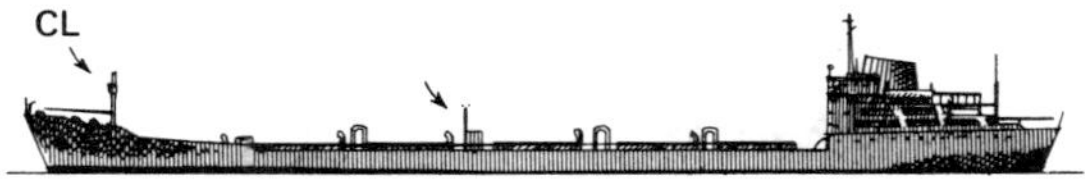

K_2MFK H13
● **70710 PROVIDENCE.** Pa/De 1959; B; 12000; 174.73 × 9.53 (573.26 × 31.27); M; 15.

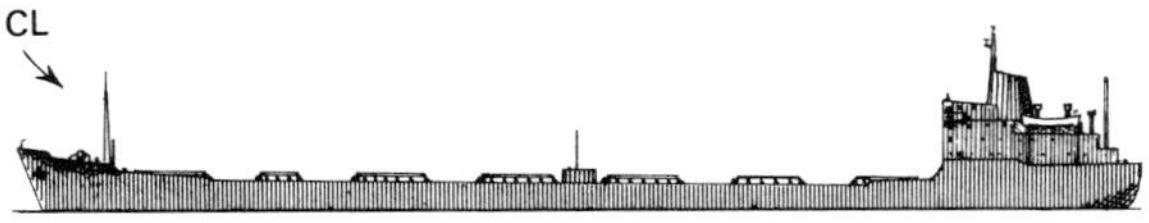

K_2MFK H13
70720 NEW FUTURE. Pa/Br 1968; B; 14000; 177.71 × 9.85 (583.04 × 32.32); M; 14.5; ex VANCOUVER TRADER ex ESSEX TRADER 1971.

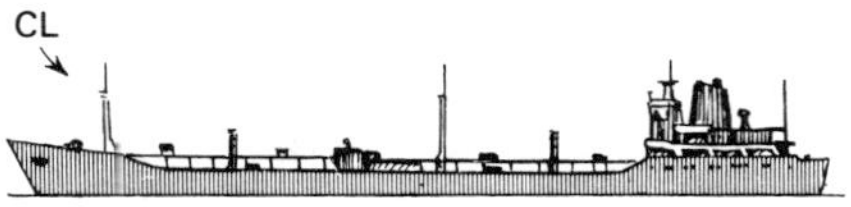

K_2MFK H13
70730 DOAN TRANSPORT. Ca/Br 1972; Tk; 6800; 131.37 × 8.39 (431 × 27.53) ex JON RAMSOY 1975.

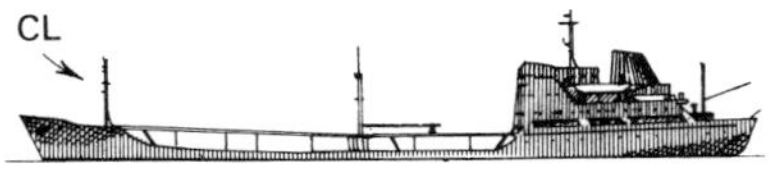

K_2MFK H13
★70740 KAPITAN SHVETSOV. Ru/Bu 1973; Tk; 4200; 116.08 × 6.69 (381 × 21.95); M; 14. Sisters (Ru flag): **★70741 DROGOBYCH ★70742 KAPITAN IZOTOV ★70743 INZHEHIER AGEYEV ★70744 KAPITAN GRIBIN ★70745 KAPITAN MAKATSARIYA ★70746 FORE MOSULISHVILI ★70747 KAPITAN DYACHUK ★70748 KAPITAN DOTSYENKO ★70749 KAPITAN KOBETS ★70750 KAPITAN NEVEZHKIN** (No flag): **70751 SLORA 70752 SLAGEN** Similar (larger) (No flag): **70753 SLETTA 70754 SLITAN 70755 SLENSVIK.**

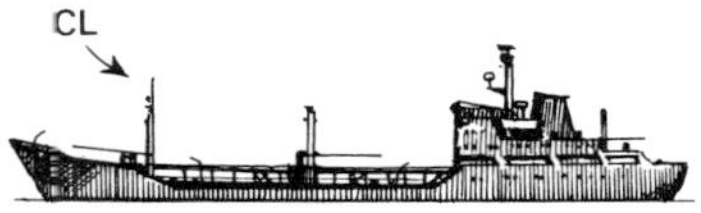

K_2MFK H13
★70760 ALTAY. Ru/Fi 1967; Tk; 3500; 106.15 × 6.74 (348.26 × 22.11); M; 13.25. Sisters (Some have bipod masts foreward—Ru flag): **★70761 AKTAU ★70762 AKTYUBINSK ★70763 AMGUN ★70764 ADYGENI ★70765 ANAKLIYA ★70766 AYKHAL ★70767 AKHALTSIKHE ★70768 ARARAT ★70769 AUTSE ★70770 AYNAZHI ★70771 AYON ★70772 ANTARES ★70773 AUSEKLIS ★70774 ABAVA ★70775 ANYUY ★70776 ASPINDZA ★70777 KOLA ★70778 KHERSONES ★70779 RAUMA ★70780 YELNYA ★70781 BIRYUZA ★70782 OMSK ★70783 YEGORLIK ★70784 YUGANSK ★70785 ZHALGIRIS ★70786 ZUGDIDI ★70787 SURGUTNEFT ★70788 ILIM ★70789 NEFTEGORSK ★70790 TARKHANKUT ★70791 DEBRECEN ★70792 NEFTEKAMSK ★70793 RUMBALA ★70794 SAKHALINNEFT ★70795 SIBIRNEFT**

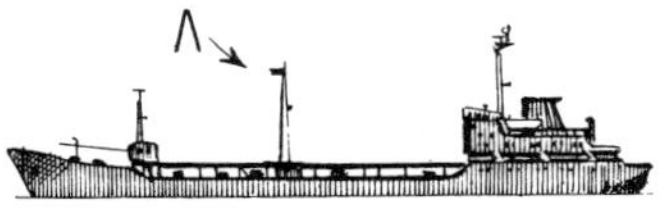

K_2MFK H13
★70810 PRUT. Ru/Fi 1971; RT; 3700; 106.08 × 6.5 (348.03 × 21.33); M; 14; Converted from oil tanker. Sister: **★70811 IZHORA** (Ru) May be others of the ALTAY class similarly converted.

K_2MFK H13
70820 ESSO PURFLEET. Br/Br 1967; Tk; 2800; 98.61 × 5.87 (323.52 × 19.26); M; 12.

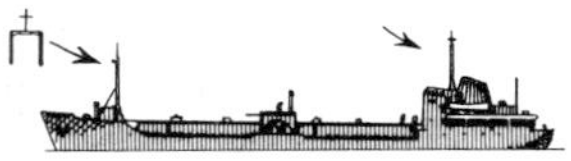

K_2MFK H13
70830 BUTATRES. Sp/Sp 1965; LGC; 1500; 80.8 × 4.93 (265.09 × 16.17); M; —. Sister: **70831 BUTACUATRO** (Sp).

K_2MFK H13
70840 AL KHLOOD. Si/FRG 1973; Ch; 4500; 113.14 × 7.41 (371.19 × 24.31); M; 14; ex SILVERPELERIN 1980.

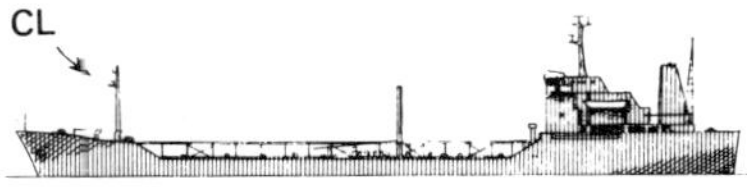

K_2MFK H13
70850 MASSA. Mo/Ja 1978; Tk; 4500; 114.8 × 6.6 (376.64 × 21.65); M; 13.

K_2MFK H13
70860 ELENI V. Gr/No 1964; Tk; 1900; 86.24 × 5.67 (282.94 × 18.6); M; 12.25; ex LIBRA; ex PANGLOBAL UNITY 1977; ex SEADRAKE 1972; ex SOLGLIMT 1970.

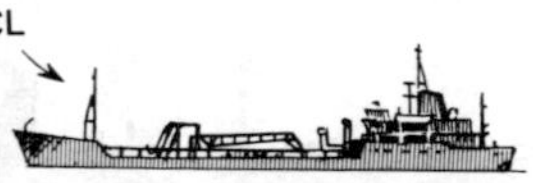

K_2MFK H13
70880 B.P. JOUSTER. Br/Br 1972; Tk; 1600; 78.95 × 4.74 (259.02 × 15.55); M; 12; ex SWANSEA 1976. Sister: **70881 SHELL EXPLORER** (Br) ex DUNDEE 1979 Similar: **70882 SHELL DIRECTOR** (Br) ex CAERNARVON 1979 **70883 SHELL SUPPLIER** (Br) ex PLYMOUTH 1979.

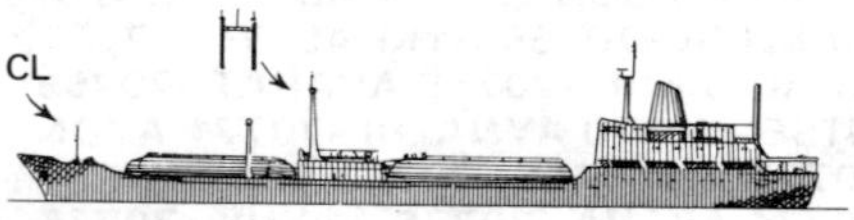

K_2MFK H13
● **70910 BARFONN.** No/Fr 1969; LGC; 6900; 126.22 × 7.32 (414.11 × 24.02); M; 16.

K_2MFK H13
70920 SENKO MARU. Ja/Ja 1971; Ch; 1000; 68.03 × 4.01 (223.2 × 13.16); M; 12. Probable sister: **70921 OGISHIMA MARU** (Ja) Possibly similar (LGC) **70922 KOSHIN MARU No 3.** (Ja).

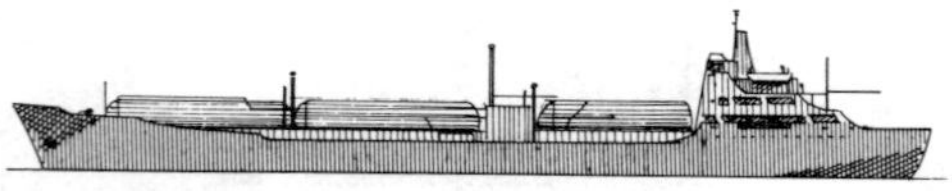

K_2MFK H13
● **70940 ANG PANGARAP.** Li/Fr 1963/65; LGC; 8000; 145.01 × 8.38 (475.75 × 27.49); M; 15; ex RYE GAS; ex CRYSTAL 1977; ex CAP MARTIN 1975; ex SAVOIE 1965; Converted from ore carrier 1965.

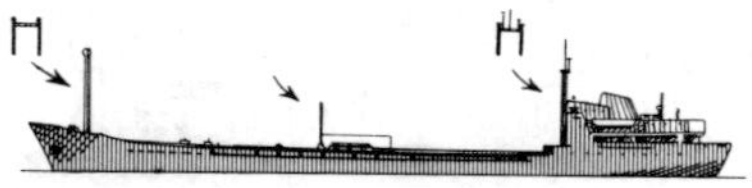

K_2MFK H13
70960 ASHURST. Br/Sp 1964/72 Tk; 3500; 102.49 × 6.29 (336.25 × 20.64); M; 12.5; ex FINSE 1972; Converted from cargo 1972.

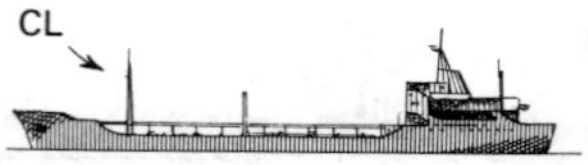

K_2MFK H13
70870 PETROSTAR III. Si/Br 1968; Tk; 1900; 86.21 × 5.67 (282.84 × 18.6); M; 12; ex NETTE THERESA 1974; ex PRECIOSA 1972.

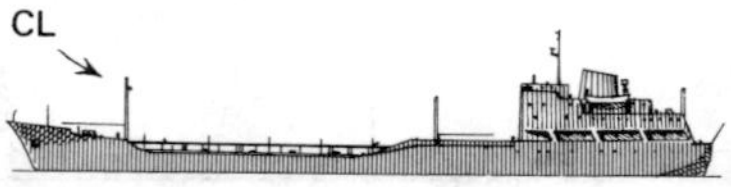

K_2MFK H13
70890 NAESBORG. De/Br 1966; Tk; 3700; 111.74 × 7.32 (366.6 × 24.02); M; 16; ex SEA TRANSPORT 1977; ex OLAV MARK 1971. Sister: **70891 BAILU** (So) ex OLAV LEIF 1972.

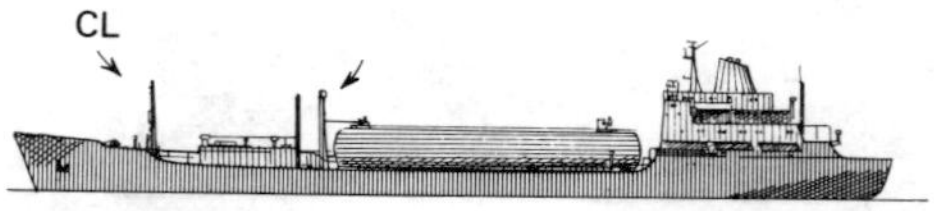

K_2MFK H13
70900 INGE MAERSK. De/No 1972; LGC/Ch; 9200; 138.74 × 9.21 (455.18 × 30.22); M; 17. Sister: **70901 FERNWAVE** (No) Similar (smaller): **70902 HARDANGER** (No) **70903 BOW ELM** (No) Similar (later built): **70904 SOFIE MAERSK** (De) **70905 SINE MAERSK** (De) **70906 HESPERUS** (No) ex FERNBROOK 1978.

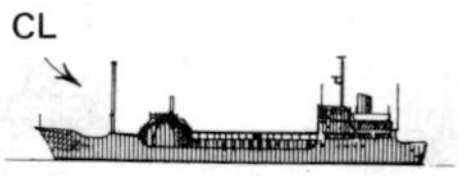

K_2MFK H13
70930 SANKYO ETHYLENE MARU. Ja/Ja 1974; LGC; 1600; 65.54 × 4.12 (215.03 × 13.52); M; 11.25.

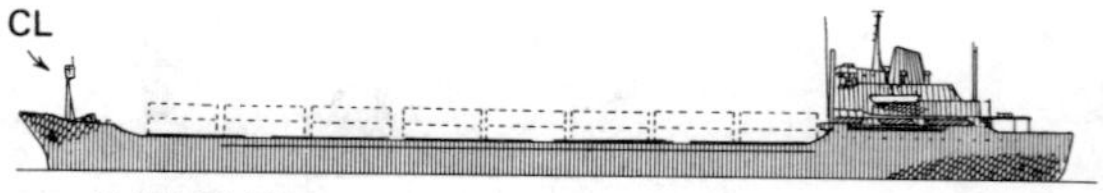

K_2MFK H13
70950 HICKORY. Li/Ja 1968; B/Con; 17100; 167.01 × 10.67 (547.93 × 35.01); M; 15.5; ex STAR MOSTANGEN 1978; ex MOSTANGEN 1975; Converted from bulk carrier 1969. Sisters: **70951 GREAT COSMOS** (Pa) ex GEORGES CHR. LEMOS 1980; ex MOSENGEN 1975 **70952 BERJAYA** (Sg) ex MOSBAY 1978 **70953 SENTOSA** (Sg) ex MOSGULF 1979.

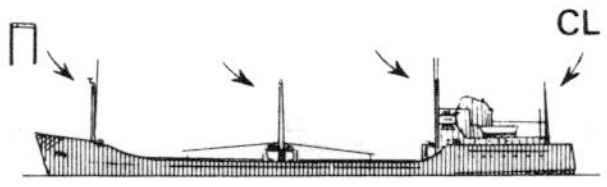

K_2MFK H13
70970 ETHEL EVERARD. Br/Br 1966; C; 1600; 85.1 × 5.1 (279.2 × 16.73); M; 11.

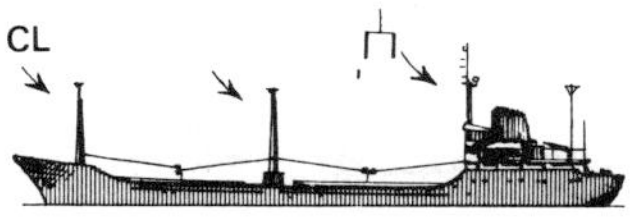

K_2MFK H13
⋆**70990 KAPRIJE.** Ys/FRG 1968; C; 2600; 95.81 × 6.36 (314.34 × 20.87); M; 12.25; ex LEKNES 1978. Sisters (Ys flag): ⋆**70991 BOSUT** ex RAKNES 1977 ⋆**70992 CIKOLO** ex TINNES 1978 ⋆**70993 ROGOZNICA** ex VIGSNES 1978 (It flag): **70994 MARIA DORMIO** ex TELNES 1979 **70995 PIETRO** ex ALTNES 1978 **70996 BEATRICE** ex KORSNES 1977 **70997 VISPY** ex GARNES 1978 (No flag): **70998 ISNES** ex FRINES 1977; ex FRITRE 1973.

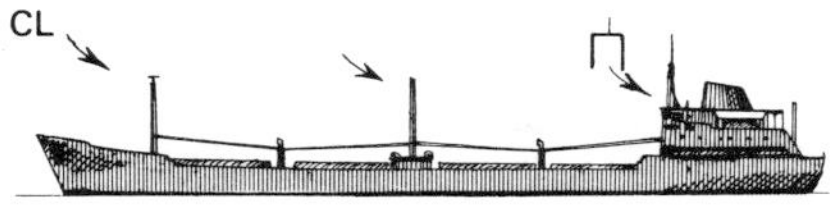

K_2MFK H13
⋆**71020 KRAPANJ.** Ys/Br 1967; C; 4900; 123.81 × 7.1 (406.2 × 23.29); M; 14; ex LYMINGE 1975.

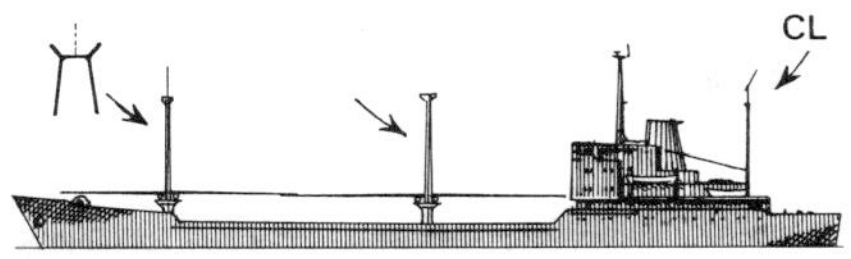

K_2MFK H13
● ⋆**71040 PIONER MOSKVY.** Ru/Ru 1973; C/Con; 4800; 130.31 × 7.36 (428 × 24.15); M; 15.5. Sisters (Ru flag): ⋆**71041 PIONER ARKHANGELSKA** ⋆**71042 PIONER SAKHALINA** ⋆**71043 PIONER YUZHNO SAKHALINSKA** ⋆**71044 PIONER CHUKOTKI** ⋆**71045 PIONER KHOLMSKA** ⋆**71046 PIONER ONEGI** ⋆**71047 PIONER ESTONII** ⋆**71048 PIONER KAMCHATKI** ⋆**71049 PIONER ROSSI** ⋆**71050 PIONER BURYATII** ⋆**71051 PIONER LITVY** ⋆**71052 PIONER SEVERODVINSKA** ⋆**71053 PIONER SLAVYANKI** ⋆**71054 PIONER AYKUTII** ⋆**71055 PIONER BELORUSSII** ⋆**71056 PIONER KARELII** ⋆**71057 PIONER KAZAKHSTANA** ⋆**71058 PIONER KIRGIZII 71059 PIONER MOLDAVII** ⋆**71060 PIONER UZBEKISTANA.**

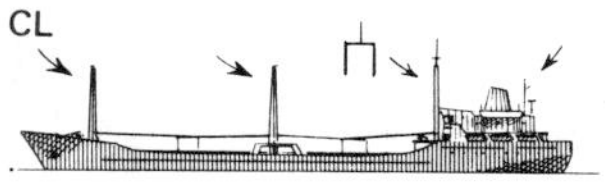

K_2MFK H13
70980 ZEIDA. Mo/Sp 1971; C; 700/1600; 84.82 × —/5.67 (278.28 × —/18.6); M; 11; ex VILYA 1975. Sisters: **70981 ZERHOUN** (Mo) ex NENYA 1975 **70982 CELTIC VENTURE** (Br) ex MONKCHESTER 1978; ex WAYNEGATE 1976 Similar (Ne built): **70983 MARIA MONICA** (It) ex MONICA 1976.

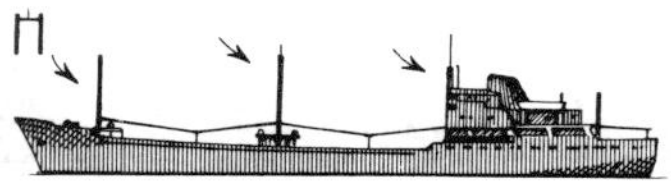

K_2MFK H13
⋆**71010 KORCULA.** Ys/Ys 1968; C; 2100; 102.14 × 5.67 (335.1 × 18.6); M; 14.5.

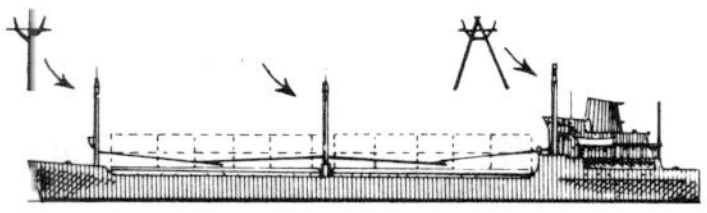

K_2MFK H13
● **71030 BREST.** Sg/Rm 1975; C; 5000; 105.97 × 8.24 (347.67 × 27.03); M; 15.5; ex CYPRESS ex BOW EK. Sisters: **71031 BEBEDOURO** (Sg) ex OAK 1979; ex BOW OAK 1978 **71032 FELLOWSHIP** (De) launched as FRENDO-FELLOWSHIP **71033 MEMBERSHIP** (De) ex FRENDO-MEMBERSHIP 1976 **71034 PARTNERSHIP** (De) ex FRENDO PARTNERSHIP 1977; ex PARTNERSHIP 1975; launched as FRENDO-PARTNERSHIP.

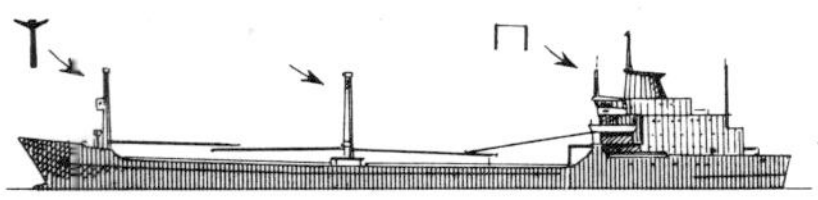

K_2MFK H13
● **71070 BELLEA.** Sg/DDR 1973; C; 5900; 121.75 × 7.73 (399.44 × 25.36); M; 15.5; ex SPLIT 1978; ex JOBELLA 1977. Possible sisters: **71071 BRUNLA** (Sg) **71072 BRUNHORN** (Sg) **71073 CLYMENE** (Br) ex BARBIZON; ex OYAPOK 1978; ex JOCARE 1977 **71074 ARC MINOS** (Gr) ex BOUGIVAL; ex BOCHICA 1978; launched as JODEW **71075 CHARLOTTE BASTIAN** (Pa) ex JOADA 1978 **71076 PIRKKOLA** (Fi) ex SAVONIA 1980; ex HETLAND RANGER 1978; ex HANSA 1974 **71077 MOUTSAINA** (Gr) ⋆**71078 HETTSTEDT** (DDR) ex JOBEBE 1977 ⋆**71079 BURG** (DDR) ex JOBOY 1977 ⋆**71080 AKEN** (DDR) ⋆**71081 FREITAL** (DDR) ⋆**71082 KOTHEN** (DDR).

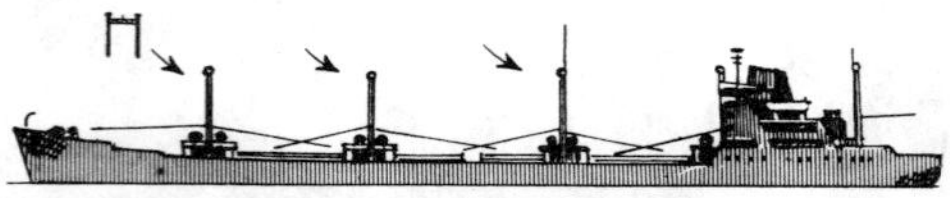

K_2MFK H13
71090 VISHVA KAUSHAL. In/Ys 1966; B; 9700; 146.01 × 8.66 (479.04 × 28.41); M; 13.5. Sisters (In flag): **71091 VISHVA PREM** ex VISHVA TILAK 1973 **71092 VISHVA VIJAY 71093 LOK SEVAK.**

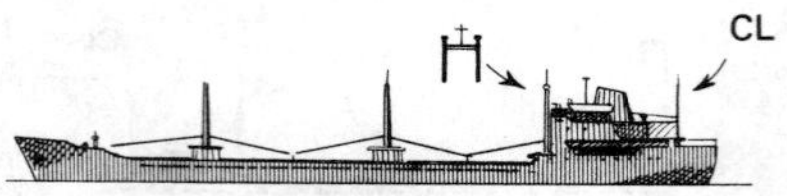

K_2MFK H13
● **71100 JOYEID.** Li/No 1966; C; 2500; 111.33 × 6.33 (365.26 × 20.77); M; 13; ex EILERT RINDE 1974. Sisters: **71101 JUSTEID** (Li) ex OLE RINDE 1974 **71102 DON ALEJO** (Pa) ex FOSSUM 1977.

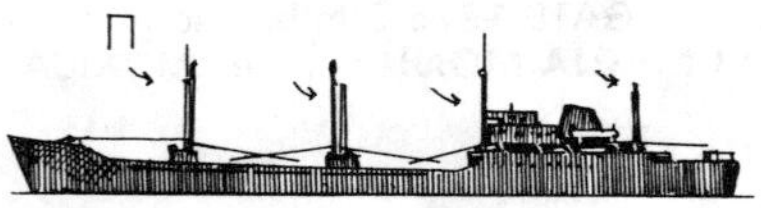

K_2MFK H13
71110 ELAZIG. Tu/No 1960; C; 4800; 116.29 × 6.45/7.93 (381.53 × 21.16/26.02); M; —; ex MAROSA 1960.

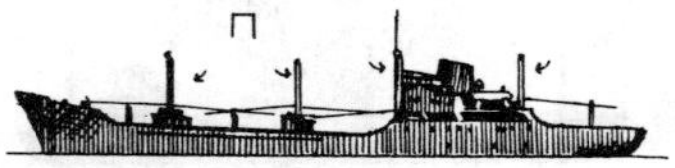

K_2MFK H13
71120 ISORA. Sp/Sp 1967; C; 1600; 96.68 × 5.67 (317.19 × 18.6); M; —; ex LAGO SAN MAURICIO 1975.

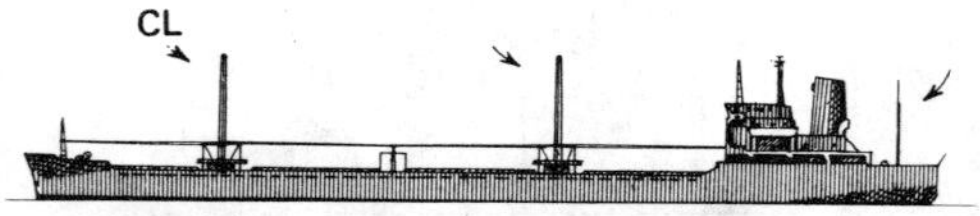

K_2MFK H13
71130 UNION WISDOM. Li/Ja 1969; B; 10000; 143.54 × 9.16 (470.93 × 30.05); M; 15. Sisters: **71131 CAPTAIN LEMOS** (Gr) ex UNION FRIENDSHIP 1976 **71132 EVER FAITH** (Tw) **71133 RENACIMIENTO** (Pa) ex COSMOS ELTANIN 1977 Possible sisters: **71134 PETERSBERG** (Li) ex VICTORIA 1980; ex GEORGIANA 1979 **71135 KOSTAR** (Ko) ex KATRINA 1978 **71136 MYUNG JIN** (Ko) ex PEARL VENTURE 1978.

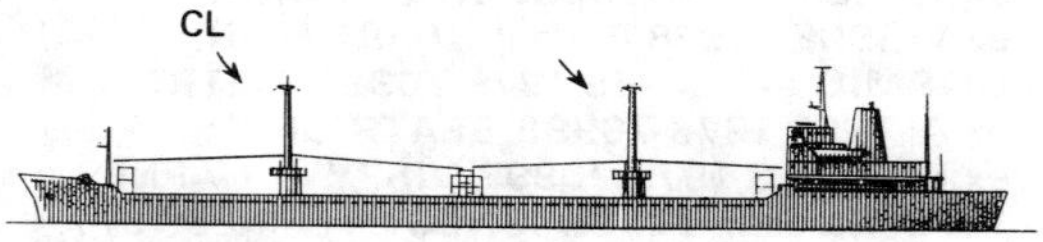

K_2MFK H13
● **71140 MARKOS N.** Gr/Ja 1969; B; 11400; 156.17 × 9.54 (512.37 × 31.3); M; 15; ex UNITED BRIGHTNESS 1981; ex ASIA BRIGHTNESS 1980. Sister: **71141 ASIA GRACE** (Li).

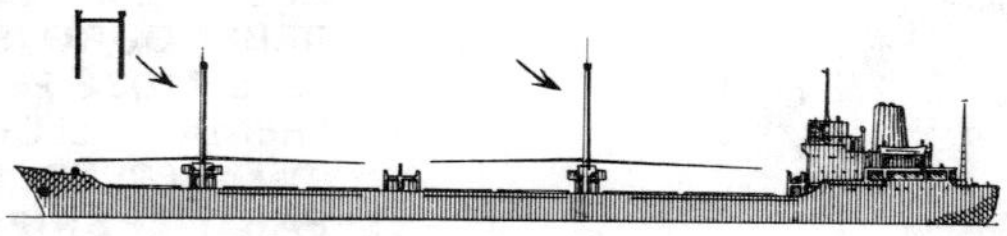

K_2MFK H13
71150 PACIFIC QUEEN. Ja/Ja 1968; B; 10700; 154.18 × 8.76 (505.84 × 28.74); M; 14.75; ex PACIFIC ARES 1975; ex TAJIMA MARU 1974; ex SHOKU MARU 1968. Similar: **71151 GOLDENROD** (Li) ex ORIENTAL LIGHT 1973; ex SHINKO MARU 1971 Similar (centre line KP instead of Goalposts): **71152 EVERGREEN** (Pa) ex KOHO MARU 1972 **71153 AUGUST MOON** (Pa) ex WAKAOSAN MARU 1972 possibly similar: **71154 MIDAS SEINE** (Li) ex SEINE MARU 1972 **71155 REIHO MARU** (Ja) **71156 VAN UNION** (Li) ⋆**71157 KOCEVJE** (Ys) ex PIONEER MERCHANT 1975; ex TANBA MARU 1973 **71158 KENAN MARU** (Ja) **71159 KOH EUN** (Ko) ex NEW ZEALANDERS 1977; ex KOSHO MARU 1973.

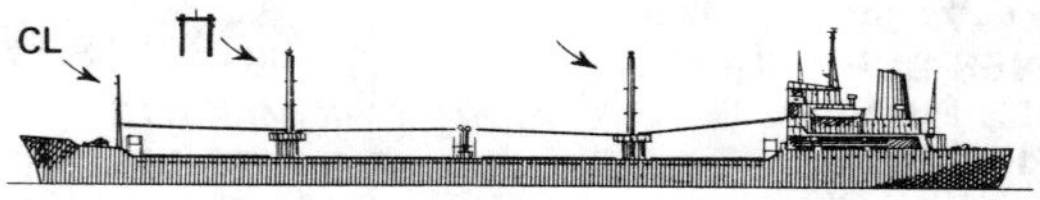

K_2MFK H13
● **71170 SANAGA.** Sg/Ja 1971; B; 12100; 156.17 × 9.29 (512.37 × 30.48); M; 15; ex WOERMANN SANAGA 1976. Sisters: **71171 HUDSON DEEP** (Sg) ex WOERMANN SASSANDRA **71172 THEANO** (Gr) ex WOERMANN UBANGI 1980 **71173 SANKURU** (Pa) ex WOERMANN SANKURU 1976 **71174 SWAKOP** (Sg) ex MARITIME COURIER 1978; ex SWAKOP 1976 **71175 ZAMBESI** (Pa) ex MARITIME TRANSPORTER 1978; ex WOERMANN SAMBESI 1976 **71176 SAN PEDRO** (Pa) launched as WOERMANN SAN PEDRO Similar: **71177 MARITIME VICTOR** (Pa) **71178 TRANSOCEAN RAM** (Pi) ex VAN WARRIOR 1980 **71179 ANGEATLANTIC** (Gr) ex VAN HAWK **71180 CALYPSO N** (Gr) ex MARINER 1978; ex EASTERN CHERRY 1980 **71181 STEPHANOS** (Gr) ex MERLIN 1980; ex EASTERN MARY **71182 WORLD HERCULES** (Ja) **71183 ZINI** (Gr) **71184 GEORTINA** (Gr) Possibly similar: **71185 ISLAND SKY** (Li) **71186 ANGEARCTIC** (Gr) ex WORLD CHAMPION **71187 UNITED PRIDE** (Li) ex WORLD PRIDE 1981 **71188 GOLDEN EXPLORER** (Li) **71189 GOLDEN PIONEER** (Li) Similar (Ko built): **71190 PAN KOREA** (Ko) Possibly similar (Ko built) **71191 KOREAN PRIDE** (Li) **71192 KOREAN FIR** (Li) **71193 CATHERINE ANN** (Li) ex GLORY RIVER 1980 **71194 REBECCA ELYSE** (Li) ex GREAT RIVER 1980 **71195 AKTION** (Gr) **71196 ALKAIOS** (Gr).

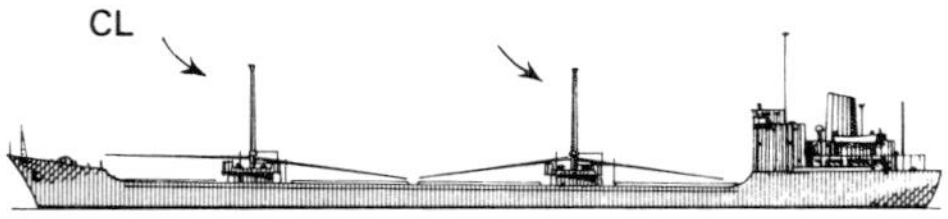

K_2MFK H13
71200 DALMAR. Sg/Ja 1966; B; 9400; 147.02 × 8.71 (482.35 × 28.58); M; 14.5; ex WOERMANN NYANGA 1974; ex MERIDIAN 1969.

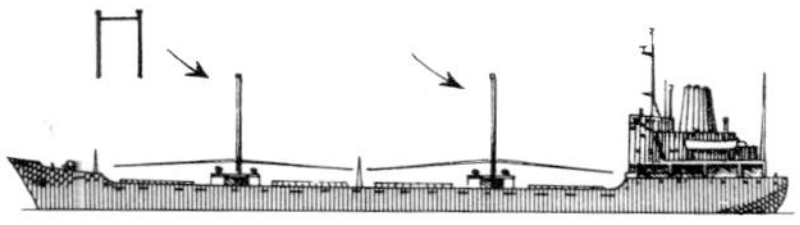

K_2MFK H13
71210 SILVER FERN. Pa/Ja 1968; C; 5000; 123.81 × 7.09 (406.2 × 23.26); M; 16; ex JAPAN KOWHAI 1972.

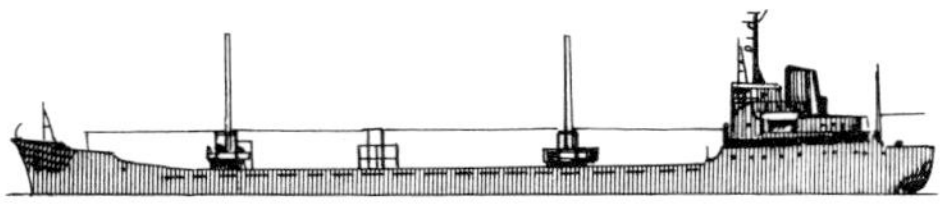

K_2MFK H13
● **71220 EASTERN ACE.** Li/Ja 1969; B; 9800; 145.65 × 9.11 (477.85 × 29.89); M; 16.5. Sisters: **71221 EVER SPLENDOR** (Tw) ex EVER SUCCESS 1973 **71222 CAPE MUSTANG** (Li) ex MUSTANG; ex WORLD PELAGIC 1978.

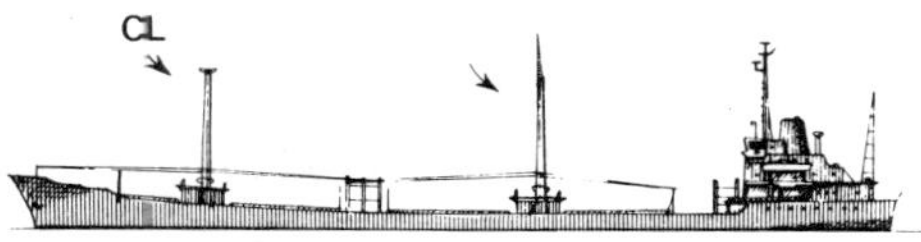

K_2MFK H13
71230 KYOTEN MARU. Ja/Ja 1970; C/TC; 8500; 141.28 × 8.84 (463.52 × 29); M; 14.5. Sister: **71231 KYOSEI MARU** (Ja).

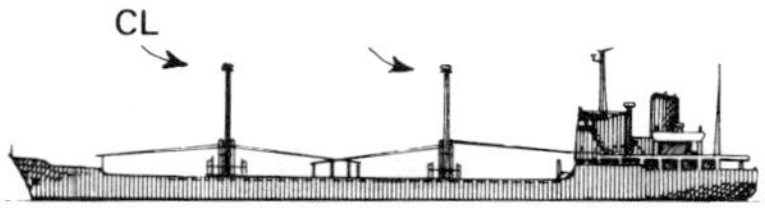

K_2MFK H13
● **71240 WOO YANG.** Ko/Ja 1971; C; 5900; 127.97 × 7.54 (419.85 × 24.74); M; 13.5; ex SSANG YONG No 333 1976; ex TENSA MARU 1974.

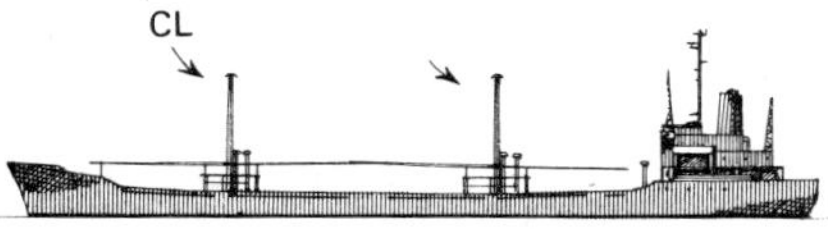

K_2MFK H13
● **71250 MERZARIO ASIA.** Sg/Ja 1976; C; 7400; 127.79 × 8.05 (419.26 × 26.41); M; 13.25; ex ZEPSEA 1980; ex GULF UNITY 1978; ex ZEPSEA 1977. Sisters: **71251 LILY VENTURE** (Li) **71252 OCEAN ACE** (Ja) Possibly similar: **71253 SINGAPORE MERCHANT** (Sg) ex ACE AMERICA 1979; ex ZEPHAWK 1978.

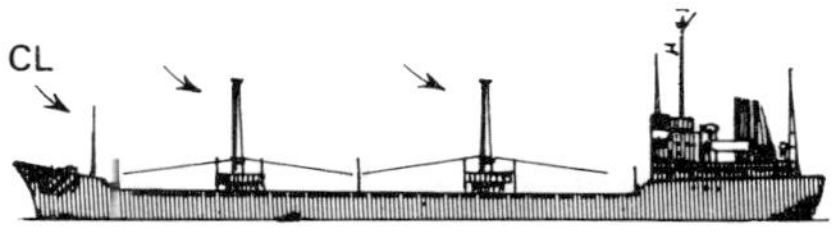

K_2MFK H13
71260 ORIENT FISHER. Pa/Ja 1974; Cem; 6600; 127.77 × 8.25 (419.19 × 27.07); M; 13.25; ex UNION AMSTERDAM 1980; ex ORIENTAL VICTORY 1977. Sisters: ★**71261 QINLING** (RC) ex MYOKEN MARU 1975 **71262 HAND LOONG** (Pa) **71263 HAND FORTUNE** (Pa) Possible sisters: **71264 CHERRYFIELD** (Li) **71265 SEVEN DAFFODIL** (Pa) ex GEORGIA MERRY 1978; ex SUN DENEB 1977 **71266 JELAU** (Pa) ex AKITAKA MARU 1978 **71267 EVANGELOS D** (Pa) ex SUN SIRIUS; ex KORYU MARU 1975 **71268 GOLDEN DRAGON** (Pa) **71269 SHUWA MARU** (Ja) **71270 HAUDA BEAUTY** (Cy) ex YANCEY **71271 SUN ORION** (Pa) **71272 HILARY B** (Sg) ex BLUE JUPITER 1977 **71273 NATIONAL STEEL FOUR** (Pi) ex YU-KIN 1978 **71274 SWEE LEAN** (Ja) ex LUSTY 1979.

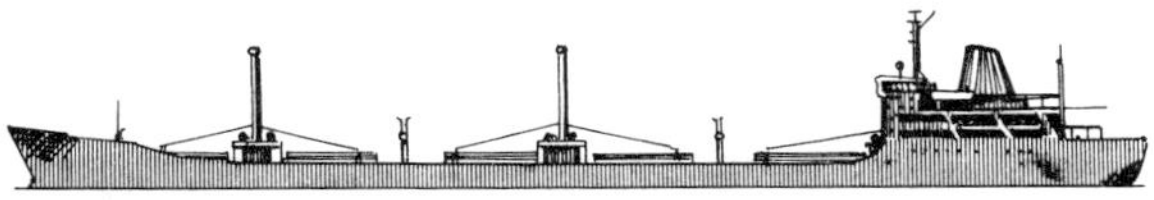

K_2MFK H13
71280 SAINT NICOLAS. Gr/Ja 1966; B; 16200; 180.02 × 9.87 (590.62 × 32.38); M; —.

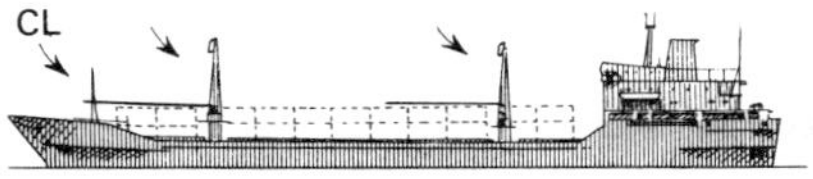

K_2MFK H13
71290 URANUS 1. FRG/FRG 1977; C/Con; 3600/6700; 131.71 × 6.35/—.03 (432.12 × 20.83/6.35); M; 15.25; ex DIPLOMAT 1978; ex URANUS 1977.

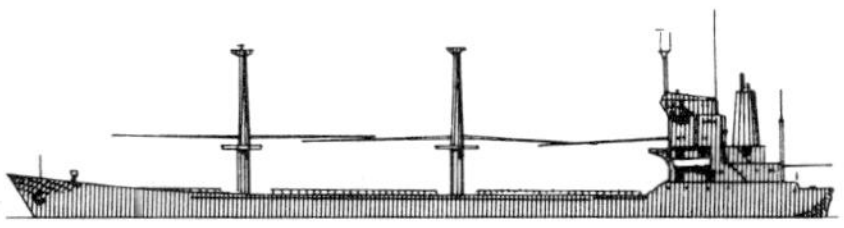

K_2MFK H13
71300 HODO. Tg/FRG 1978; C; 7600; 133.81 × 8.25 (439.01 × 27.07); M; 15. Sisters: **71301 PIC D'AGOU** (Tg) **71302 MAW-LA-MYAING** (Bm) **71303 SIT-TWAY** (Bm).

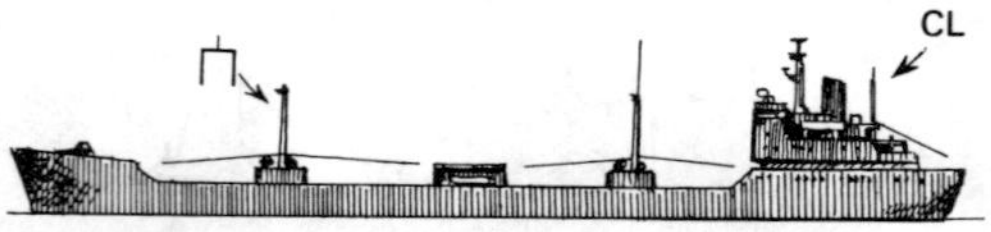

K_2MFK H13
★**71310 OSTROV RUSSKIY.** Ru/Sw 1969; FC; 9800; 150.55 × 7.47 (494 × 24.51); M; 18.25. Sisters (Ru flag): ★**71311 OSTROV ATLASOVA** ★**71312 OSTROV BERINGA** ★**71313 OSTROV KARAKINSKIY** ★**71314 OSTROV KOTLIN** ★**71315 OSTROV LISYANSKOGO** ★**71316 OSTROV LITKE** ★**71317 OSTROV MEDNYY** ★**71318 OSTROV SHMIDTA** ★**71319 OSTROV SHOKALSKOGO** ★**71320 OSTROV SIBIRYAKOVA** ★**71321 OSTROV USHAKOVA.**

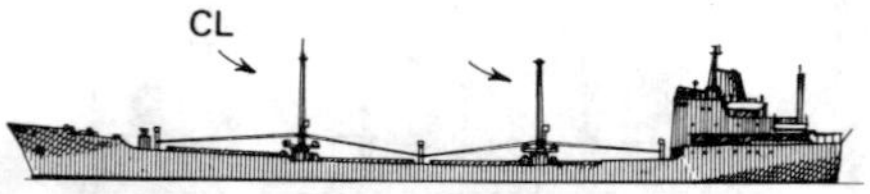

K_2MFK H13
71350 OMEGA RHODOS. Gr/Fr 1960; O; 6000; 132.52 × 7.56 (434.78 × 24.8); M; 16.5; ex PENCHATEAU 1980; ex AEQUATOR 1980; ex QUEEN OF AMPELOS 1978; ex PENCHATEAU 1974.

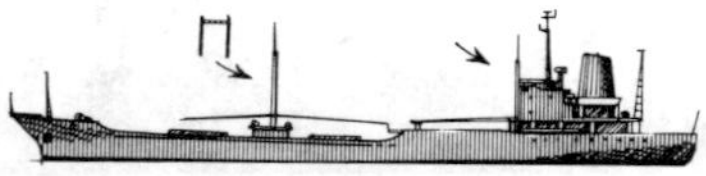

K_2MFK H13
71380 NIPPONHAM MARU No 1. Ja/Ja 1972; R; 2900; 109.02 × 6.73 (357.68 × 22.08); M; 16.5. Probably similar: **71381 DAIRYO MARU** (Ja).

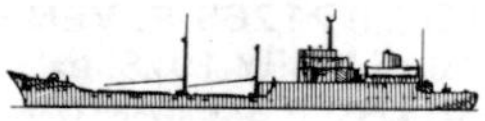

K_2MFK H13
71390 KANO REEFER. Pa/Ja 1960/73; C/R; 1200; 74.25 × 4.75 (243.6 × 15.58); M; 12; ex KYOEI MARU 1978; ex AZUMA MARU No 21 1973; Converted from trawler 1973.

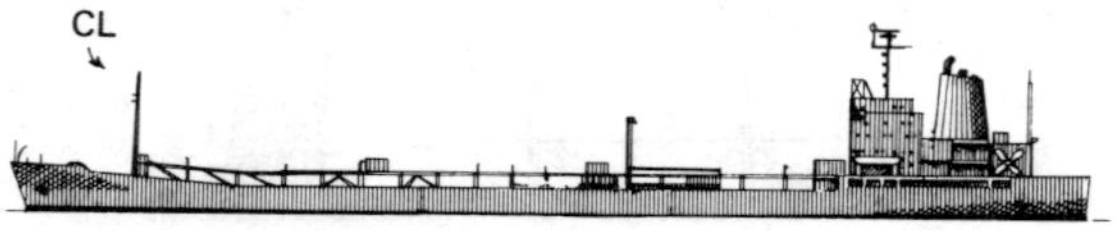

K_2MFK H3
71410 DIRK JACOB. FRG/Ne 1976; Tk; 19500; 170.69 × 11.85 (560.06 × 38.88); M; 16. Sisters (FRG flag): **71411 GERTRUD JACOB 71412 ERIKA JACOB** launched as PROTAN MAAS.

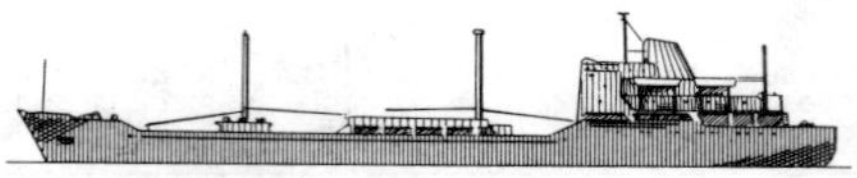

K_2MFK H13
★**71330 BAEK DU SAN.** RK/Ne 1965; FC; 7200; 130.33 × — (427.59 × —); M; —; May also be known as **TOP VAN WITTE BERG.**

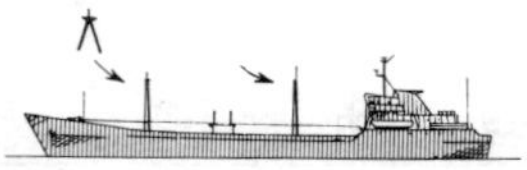

K_2MFK H13
★**71340 BATALLA DE STA. CLARA.** Cu/Fi 1975; R; 500/1300; 74.12 × —/4.71 (243.18 × —/15.45); M; 14. Sister: ★**71341 BATALLA DE YAGUAJAY** (Cu).

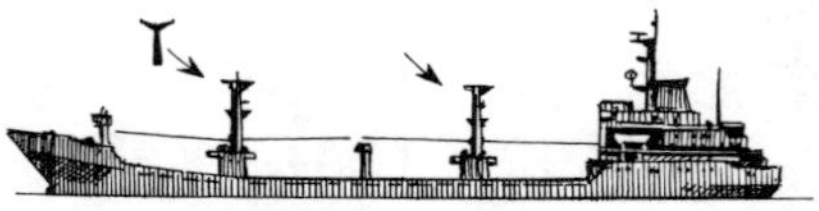

K_2MFK H13
★**71360 ROSTOK.** Ru/DDR 1973; C; 2900/4500; 117.79 × 5.8/6.92 (386.45 × 19.03/22.7); M; 16.5; **'POSEIDON'** class. Sisters (Ru flag): ★**71361 CHITA** ★**71362 KHASAN** ★**71363 MAGO** ★**71364 NOVOCHERKASSK** ★**71365 RYSHKANY** ★**71366 RUSHANY** ★**71367 RUDNYY** ★**71368 ROMNY** ★**71369 RUBEZHNOYE** ★**71370 RZHEV** ★**71371 RAKHOV** ★**71372 REUTOV** ★**71373 RATNO** ★**71374 RADOMYSHI** ★**71375 RYAZAN** ★**71376 ROSLAVL** ★**71377 RYBINSK.**

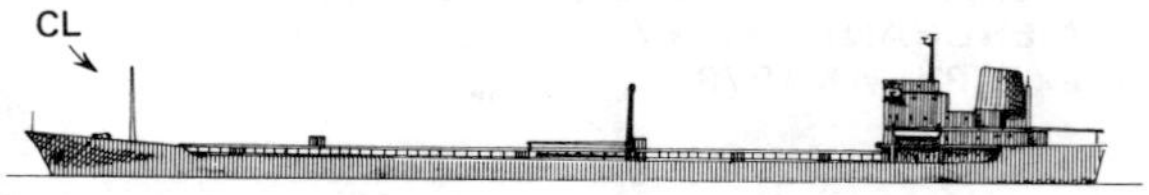

K_2MFK H3
71400 SAUCON. Li/Br 1969; Tk; 14800; 169.78 × 9.75 (557.02 × 31.99); M; 15.5; ex LAURELWOOD 1975. Sisters: **71401 SHABONEE** (Br) ex SEA GRIFFIN 1974 **71402 NAND KAVITA** (In) ex CAPTAIN X. KYRIAKOU 1980; ex DAFNI C 1978; ex HOLLYWOOD 1977.

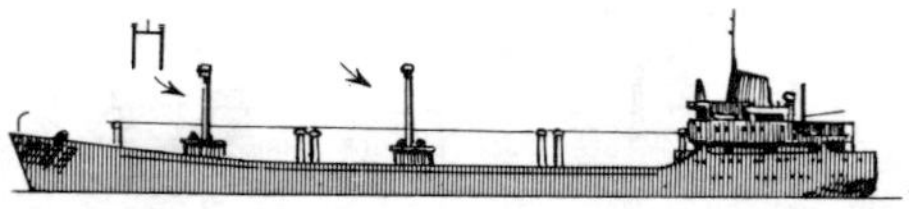

K_2MFK H3
71420 ORIENTAL STAR. Pa/Fr 1957; C; 9200; 138.39 × 9.49 (454.05 × 31.14); M; 14.

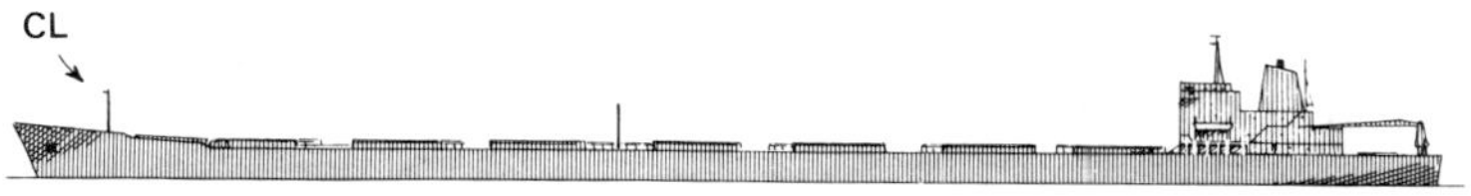

K_2MFKC H1
71430 BENHOPE. Br/Br 1978; B; 39100; 228.12 × 14.02 (748.42 × 45.99); M; 15.

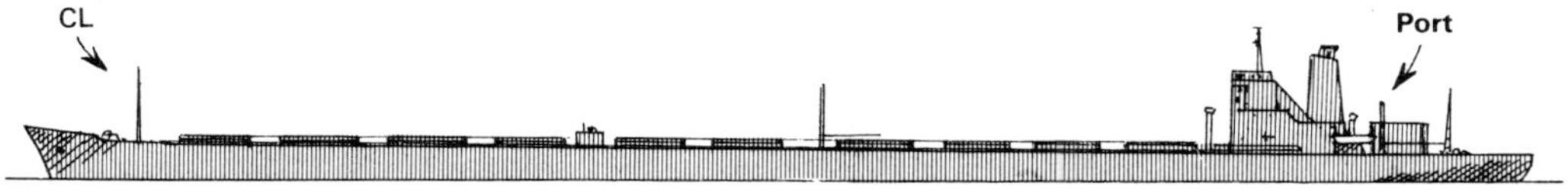

K_2MFK_2 H
71440 WORLD GUARD. Li/Ja 1971; OBO; 85800; 314.21 × 17.13 (1030.87 × 56.2); M; 16. Sister: **71441 WORLD CHALLENGER** (Li).

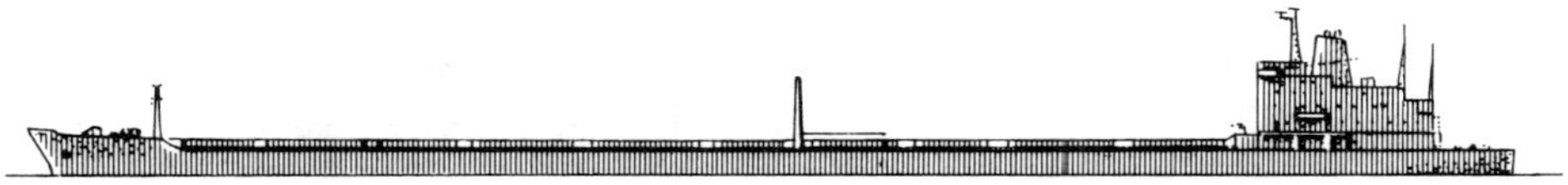

K_2MFK_2 H1
71450 BRAZILIAN VITORIA. Li/Ja 1977; OO; 69300; 273.24 × 16.39 (896.46 × 53.77); M; 15.25. Probable sister: **71451 BRAZILIAN TRADER** (Li).

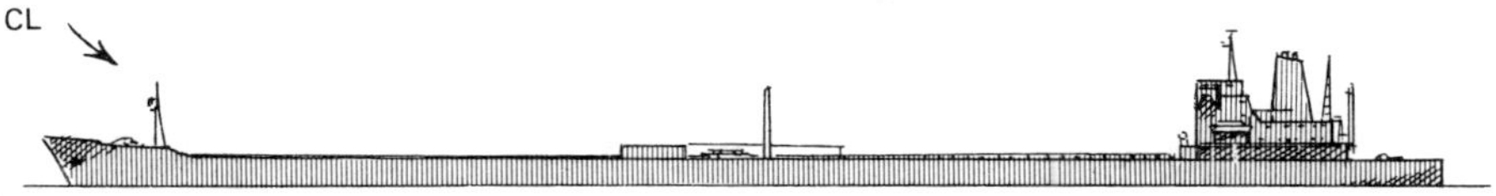

K_2MFK_2 H1
71460 IN-NAHALA. Ag/Ja 1975; Tk; 71900; 266 × 16.99 (872.7 × 55.74); M; 15.75; ex POLARTANK 1976. Possibly similar: **71461 HALUL** (Qt) launched as NORTH MONARCH **71462 JANE STOVE** (No) **71463 UMM SHAIF** (Ag) launched as VINCENZIA.

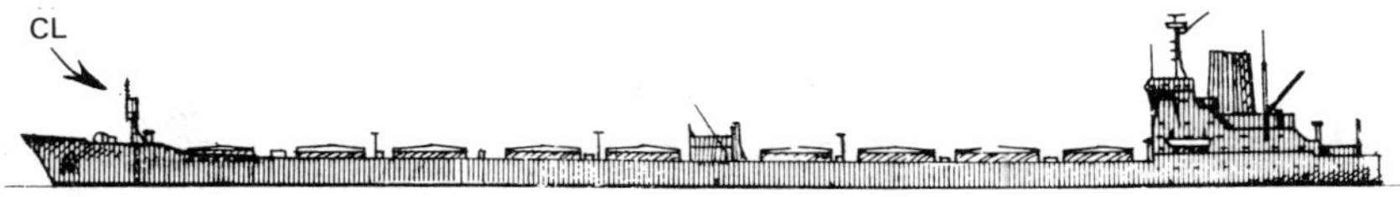

K_2MFK_2 H1
71470 THALASSINI TYHI. Gr/Sw 1968; OBO; 48800; 256.52 × 14.44 (841.6 × 47.38); M; 15.25; ex OBO PRINCE 1978. Similar: **71471 NAVIOS CHALLENGER** (Li) ex THORFRID 1978.

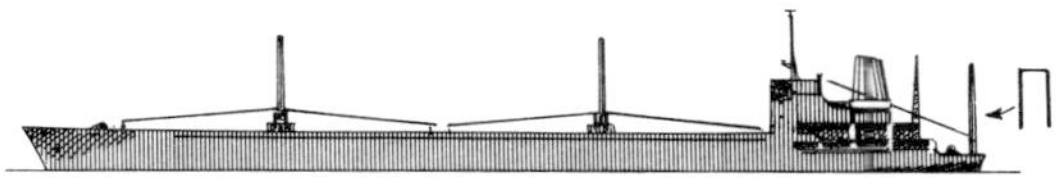

K_2MFK_2 H1
71480 EASTERN GRACE. Pa/Ja 1973; C; 17100; 153.24 × 10.52 (502.76 × 34.51); M; 14.5; ex SHINYO MARU. Probably similar (Vehicle carrier): **71481 EUROCARRIER** (Gr) ex TOKUSHO MARU 1976.

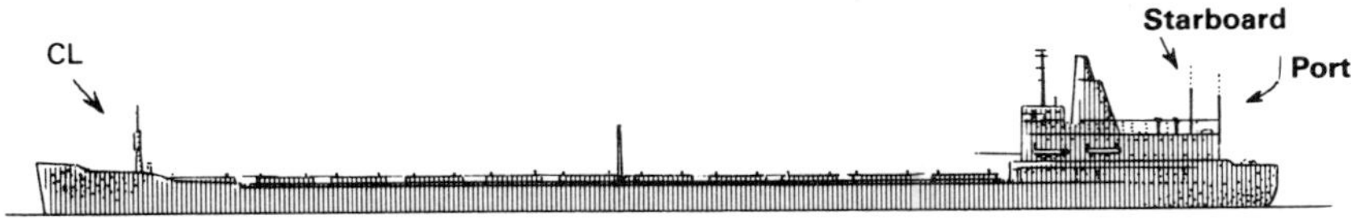

K_2MFK_2 H13
● **71490 GOOD CHAMPION.** Cy/Sw 1967; OBO; 38500; 243.85 × 13.81 (800.03 × 45.31); M; 16.5; ex SAINT CHRIS; ex BJORN RAGNE 1978. Sister: **71491 LA LIBERTAD** (Pe) ex BALDER ALVAR;ex AIMEE 1977.

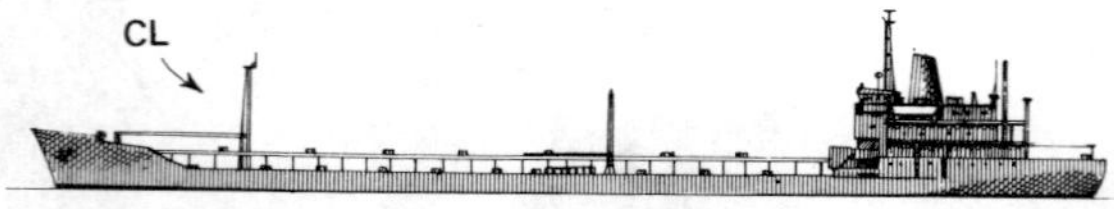

K_2MFK_2 H13
71500 AL HOFUF. Si/Sw 1968; Tk; 14900; 169.63 × 9.55 (556.53 × 31.33); M; 14.75; ex LUSTROUS 1977. Sisters: **71501 AL KHAFJI** (Si) ex LUMINOUS 1977 **71502 AL DAMMAM 1** (Si) ex LUMEN 1977 **71503 LUMIERE** (Br) **71504 LUMINETTA** (Br).

● 71505

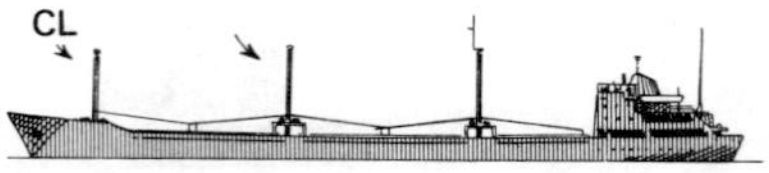

K_2MFM H1
71510 ALITHIA. Gr/No 1962; C; 5000; 116.29 × 8.1 (381.53 × 26.57); M; 13; ex DIAKAN TRUTH 1977; ex DIANET 1974.

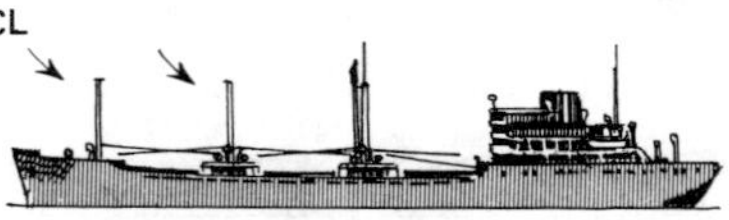

K_2MFM H13
● **71520 SENEGAL.** Pa/Ne 1953; C; 4600; 112.45 × 6.48 (368.93 × 21.26); M; 13.5; ex SENEGALKUST 1971; ex VAN SPILBERGEN 1956.

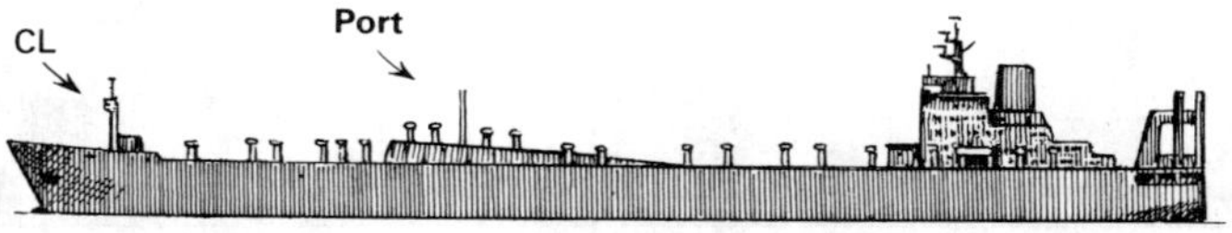

K_2MFR H
● ⋆**71530 MAGNITOGORSK.** Ru/Fi 1975; RoC; 15300; 205.8 × 9.7 (675.2 × 31.82); M; 22; Stern door and angled ramp. Sister: ⋆**71531 KOMSOMOLSK** (Ru) Similar: ⋆**71532 ANATOLIY VASILYEV** (Ru).

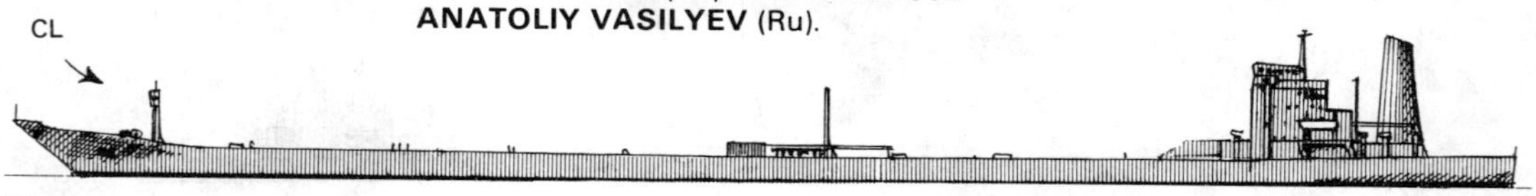

K_2MKF H
71540 AMOCO SINGAPORE. Li/Sp 1973; Tk; 109700; 334.02 × 19.94 (1095.87 × 65.42); M; 15.25. Sisters: **71541 AMOCO EUROPA** (Li) **71542 AMOCO MILFORD HAVEN** (Li) Similar: **71543 AMOCO CHICAGO** (Li) **71544 BARCELONA** (Sp).

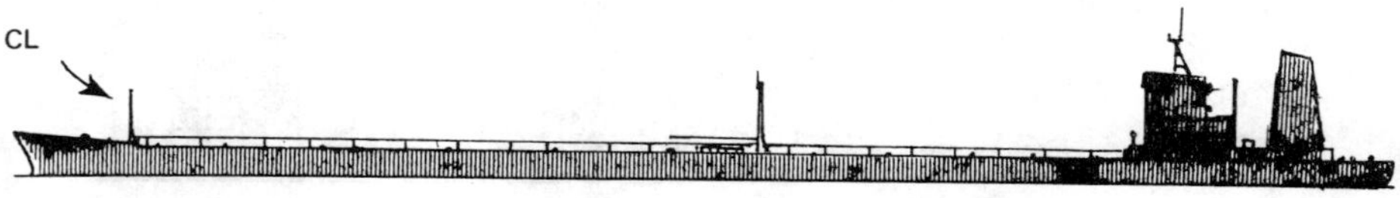

K_2MKF H
71550 MALAGA. Sp/Sp 1969; Tk; 80300; 288.02 × 17.25 (944.95 × 56.59); M; 16.5. Sisters: **71551 ALCAZAR** (Sp) **71552 OCEAN LION** (Li).

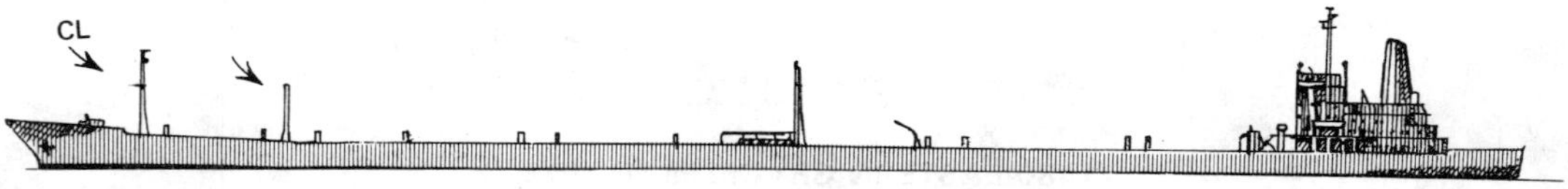

K_2MKF H
● **71560 BRITISH EXPLORER.** Br/Ja 1970; Tk; 108500; 326.02 × 18.9 (1069.62 × 62.01); T; 15.25. Sisters: **71561 SOUTH FOUNDATION** (Li) ex BRITISH PROSPECTOR **71562 SIVAND** (Ir) ex BRITISH NAVIGATOR 1976.

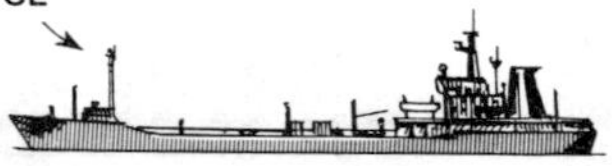

K_2MKF H
71570 TOPPEN. Sw/FRG 1973; Ch; 2200; 109.99 × 5.77 (360.86 × 5.77); M; 13.5; ex SIOUX; lengthened 1977. Sister: **71571 TEDDE** (Sw) ex UNKAS.

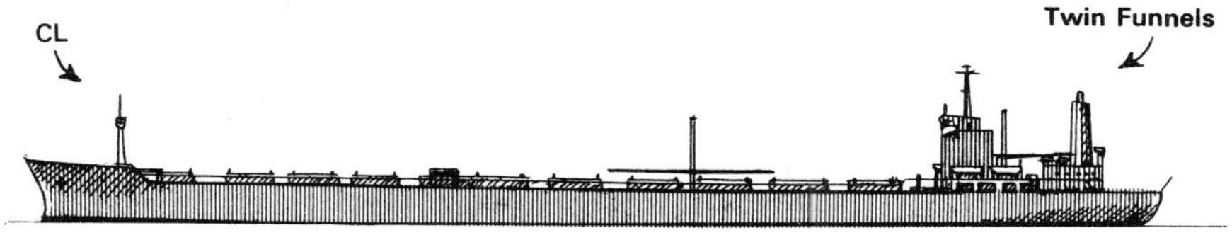

K_2MKF H1
71580 BANGLAR NOOR. Bh/Ja 1967; OO; 55800; 252.1 × 14.45 (827.1 × 47.41); M; 15.75; ex VESTAN 1977. Sister: **71581 SKYROS** (Gr) ex APACHE 1979; ex IVORY SUN 1978; ex FERNSTAR 1973.

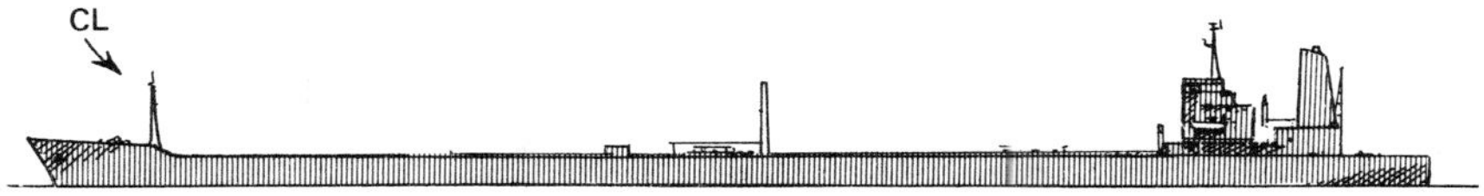

K_2MKF H1
71590 GOLDEN SUNRAY. Sg/Ja 1974; Tk; 48900; 241.51 × 14.14 (792.35 × 46.39); M; 16.5. Probable sister: **71591 CANADIAN OWL** (Sg).

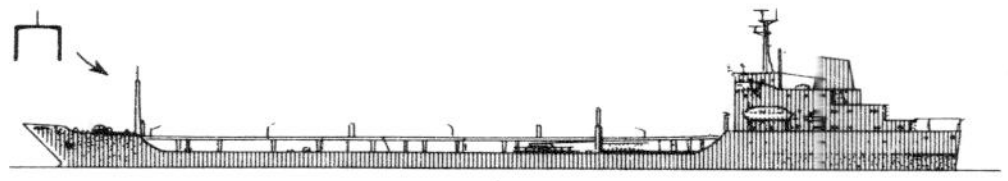

K_2MKF H13
71600 LIBERTADOR SAN MARTIN. Ar/Ar 1979; Tk; 10000; 153 × 8.24 (501.97 × 27.03); M; 15. Sisters(Ar flag): **71601 INGENIERO VILLA 71602 MINISTRO EXCURRA** (also reported as **MINISTRO EZCURRA**).

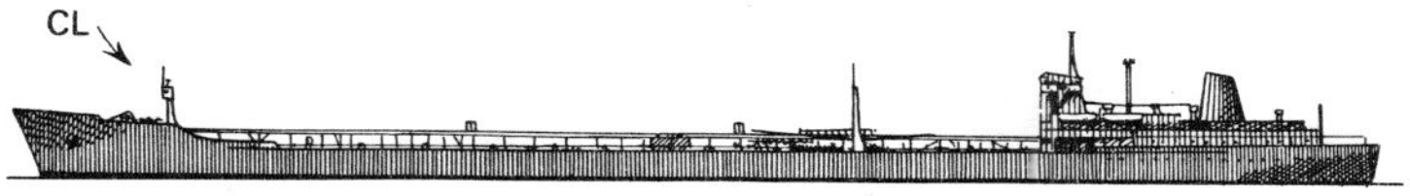

K_2MKFK H1
★**71610 HONG HU.** RC/Sw 1965; Tk; 29900; 223.45 × 12.64 (733.1 × 41.47); M; 16.5; ex BRALINDA 1974.

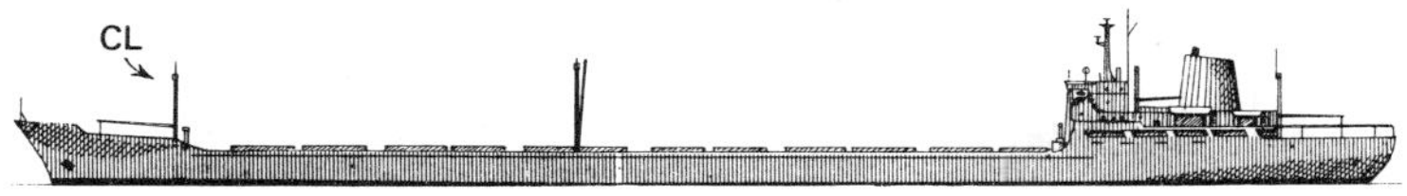

K_2MKFK H13
71620 AMBRONIA. It/It 1965; OO; 28600; 229.45 × 12.41 (752.79 × 40.72); M; —. Sister: **71620 ASPRA** (It).

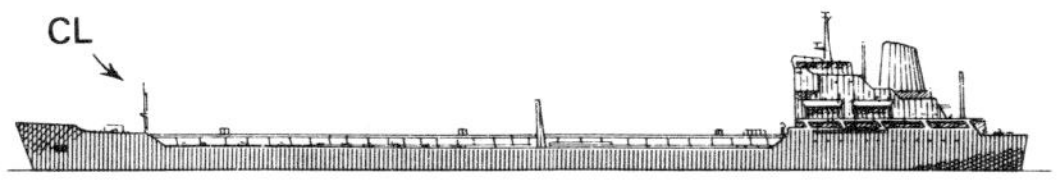

K_2MKFK H13
71630 KOLANDIA. In/Ys 1976; Tk; 15000; 159.75 × 10.79 (524.11 × 35.4); M; 15. Sisters (In flag): **71631 AUROBINDO 71632 DADABHAI NAOROJI 71633 JAINARAYAN VYAS 71634 RAFI AHMED KIDWAI.**

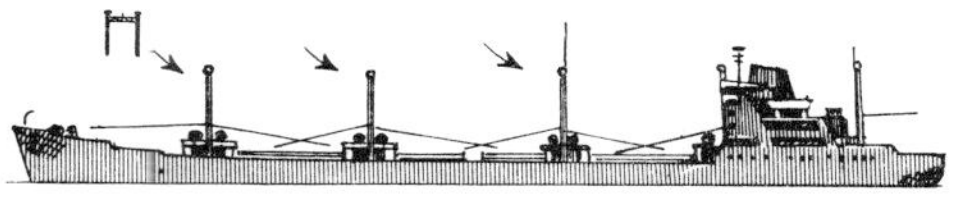

K_2MKFK H13
71640 VISHVA KAUSHAL. In/Ys 1966; B; 9700; 146.01 × 8.66 (479.04 × 28.41); M; 13.5. Sisters (In flag): **71641 VISHVA PREM** ex VISHVA TILAK 1973 **71642 VISHVA VIJAY 71643 LOK SEVAK.**

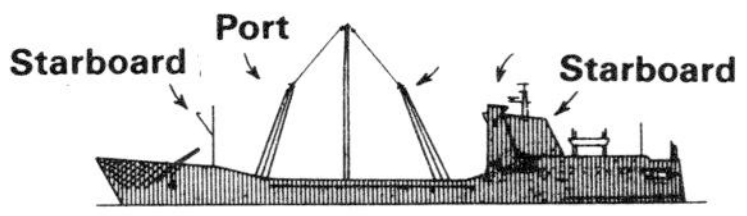

K_2MKFM H13
71650 STARMAN AMERICA. Br/Br 1974; RoC/HL; 1600/2500; 93.63 × 4.13/— (307.19 × 13.55/—); TSM; 12; ex STARMAN 1977.

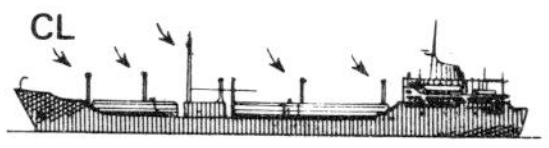

K_2MK_4MF H13
71660 AMCO 1. Pa/Fr 1965; LGC; 1800; 80.88 × 3.61 (265.35 × 11.84); M; 14.25; ex SORINE THOLSTRUP 1980 ex NIELS HENRIK ABEL 1970. Similar: **71661 S. G. THOLSTRUP** (De) ex GAZELLE 1970.

K_2MK_3MFK H13
***71670 LENINSKIY LUCH.** Ru/Ja 1964; FC; 5000; 115.02 × 5.6 (377 × 18.37); M; 14. Sisters (Ru flag): ***71671 KRASNYY LUCH *71672 SOLNECHNYY LUCH *71673 YARKIY LUCH *71674 SVETLYY LUCH.**

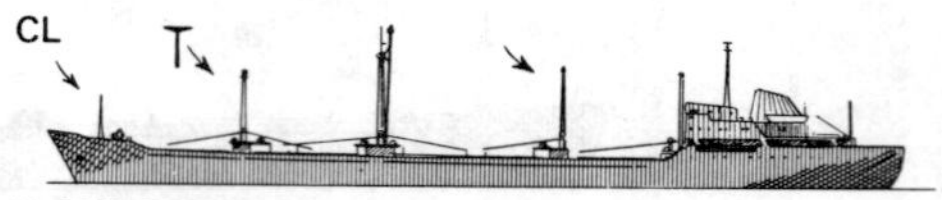

K_2MK_2MF H13
***71680 PRIGNITZ.** DDR/Ne 1967; C; 4200/6100; 135.79 × 6.67/7.61 (446 × 21.88/24.97); M; 17. Sisters (DDR flag): ***71681 FLAMING *71682 EICHSFELD.**

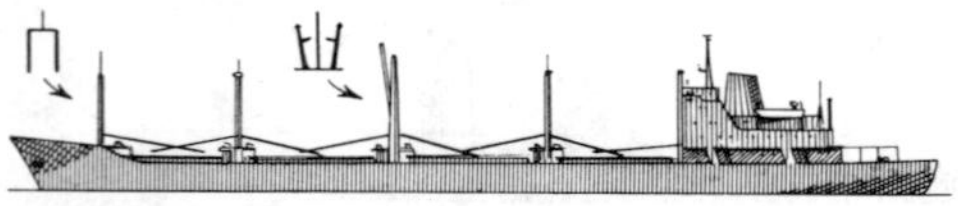

K_2MK_2MFK H1
71690 DIANA. Bz/Bz 1968; C; 6900; 145.52 × 8.75 (477.43 × 28.71); M; 17; ex BAGE 1968. Probable sister: **71691 CORINA** (Bz) ex CURVELO 1968.

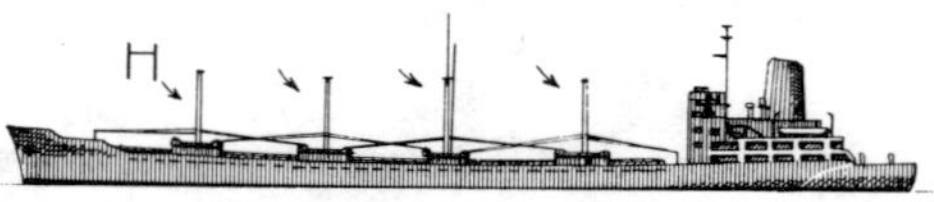

K_2MKMF H1
71700 GOLDEN SEAGULL. Gr/Ja 1960; C; 8800; 144 × 8.83 (472.44 × 28.97); M; 13.25; ex SANTA CONSTANCE 1975.

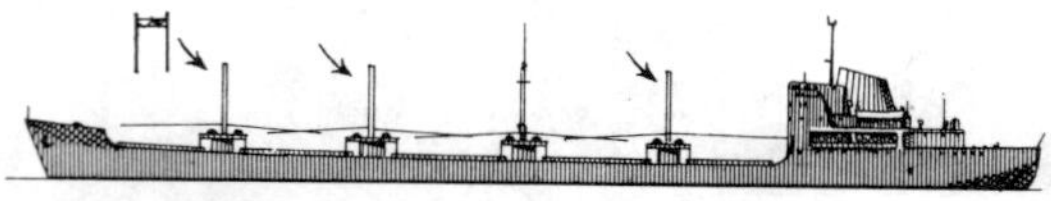

K_2MKMF H13
71710 ANNITA. Gr/Br 1964; C; 11100; 159.49 × 9.9 (523.26 × 32.48); M; 16; ex EXMOOR 1978; ex MELBROOK 1972.

K_2MKMF H13
● ***71720 ALTMARK.** DDR/Fi 1959; C; 2700/4600; 121.52 × 6.1/7.67 (398.69 × 20.01/25.16); M; —; ex INGE TOFT 1964.

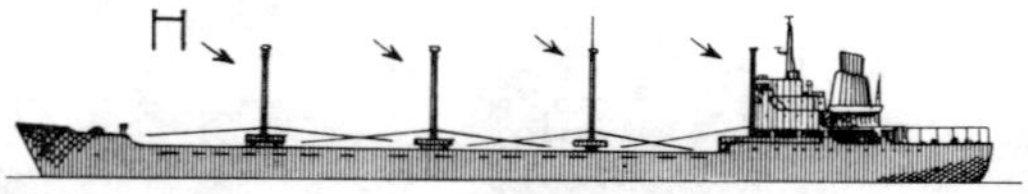

K_2MKMF H13
71730 MARITIME STAR. Li/Ja 1963; B; 9800; 153.52 × 9.18 (503.67 × 30.12); M; 14.5; ex DONA VIVIANA 1969.

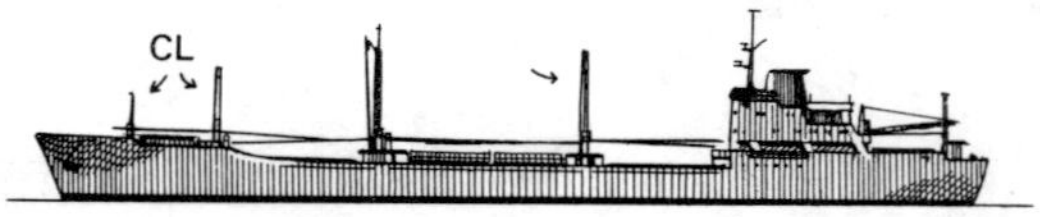

$K_2MKMFCK$ H13
● **71740 FERNANDOEVERETT.** Li/Fi 1964/69; C/Con; 8700; 152 × 8.6 (500 × 28.7); M; 16; ex FINNHAWK; ex MALTESHOLM 1976; Converted from cargo and lengthened 1969. Sisters: **71741 CORDILLERA** (Pa) ex FINNARROW; ex VASAHOLM 1976 **71742 CORRAL** (Pa) ex MAH 1980; ex FINN-ENSO 1979 **71743 CONDOR** (Ch) ex PALLADIA 1980; ex FINNMAID 1979 **71744 POYANG** (Br) ex ASIAN EXPORTER 1975; ex FINNBOSTON 1973; ex FINNENSO 1964.

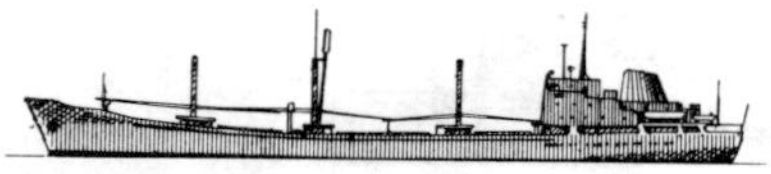

K_2MKMFK H1
***71750 RHON.** DDR/Sw 1960; C; 2700/4300; 114.33 × —/7.19 (375 × —/23.59); M; 14.5; ex BINDAL 1964.

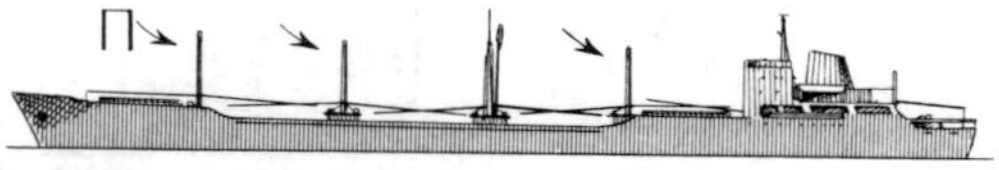

K_2MKMFK H13
● **71760 CELIA.** Pa/Ja 1962; C; 9300; 152.43 × 8.12 (500.1 × 26.64); M; 17.5; ex ANETTE MAERSK 1980. Possibly similar: **71761 EMILIA UNO** (Pa) ex HENRIETTE MAERSK 1980.

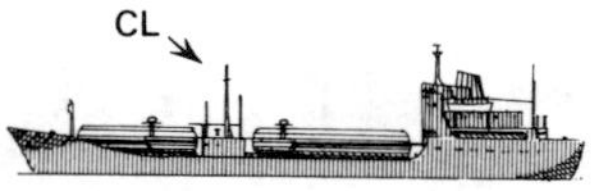

K_2MKMFK H13
71770 GAZ PROGRESS. Pa/No 1966; LGC; 2700; 90.56 × 6.03 (297.11 × 19.78); M; 12.25; ex CORAL OBELIA 1979; ex ARCTIC PROPANE 1971.

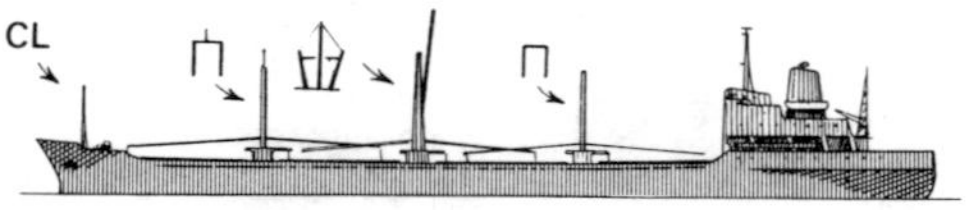

K_2MKMFK H13
***71780 LONG CHUAN JIANG.** RC/Ja 1971; C; 6600/10200; 145.7 × 8.02/9.1 (478 × 26.31/29.8); M; 17; ex HEELSUM 1978; **'MITSUI-CONCORD 15'** type. Sister: ***71781 JIN CHENG JIANG** (RC) ex LEERSUM 1977.

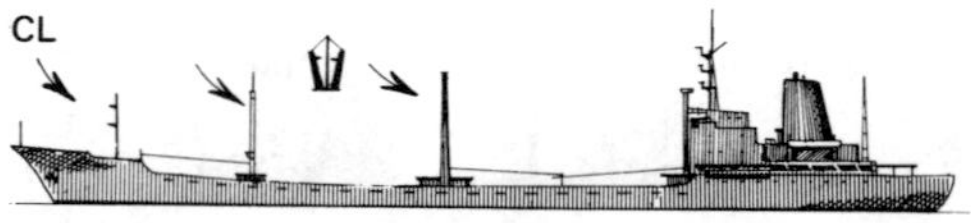

K_2MKMFK H13
71790 NILE MARU. Ja/Ja 1970; C/HL; 10100; 148.52 × 8.99 (487.27 × 29.49); M; 15.

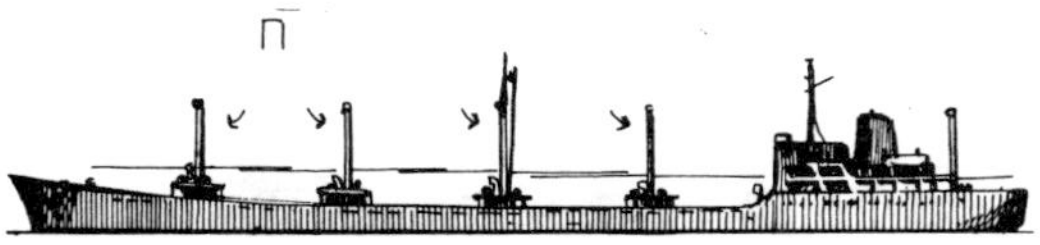

K_2MKMFK H13
⋆71800 KAI PING. RC/Ja 1961; C; 8300/10700; 156.19 × —/9.48 (512.43 × —/31.1); M; 15; ex OCEANIC 1973. Sister: **71801 SUPREME FIVE** (Pa) ex CORINTHIC 1981 Similar: **71802 TROVATORE** (Br) ex ATHINA B 1977; ex FAY 1976; ex LEONIDAS VOYAZIDES 1976; ex WORLD JAPONICA 1965.

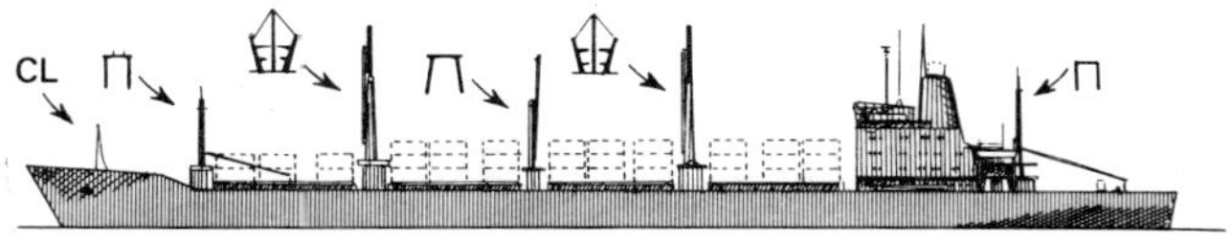

K_2MKM_2FK H1
⋆71810 JOZEF CONRAD KORZENIOWSKI. Pd/Pd 1978; C/Con; 17600; 190.28 × 9.55 (624.28 × 31.33); M; 25; **'B-467'** type. Sisters (Pd flag): **71811 ADAM MICKIEWICZ 71812 GENERAL KLEEBERG** 1 further vessel under construction.

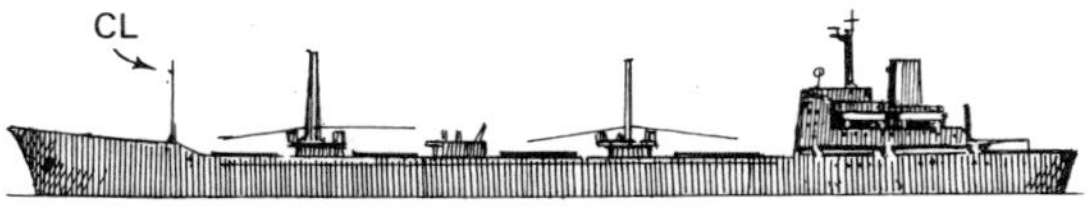

K_2M_2F H1
⋆71820 50 LET SSSR. Ru/Ru 1973; FC; 13100; 172.12 × 8.1 (564.7 × 26.57); M; 19; also known as **PYATIDYESYATILYETIYE S.S.S.R.** Sisters (Ru flag): **⋆71821 BERINGOV PROLIV ⋆71822 IRBENSKIY PROLIV ⋆71823 PROLIV LAPERUZA ⋆71824 PROLIV SANNIKOVO ⋆71825 PROLIV VILKITSKOGO ⋆71826 XXV SYEZD KPSS.**

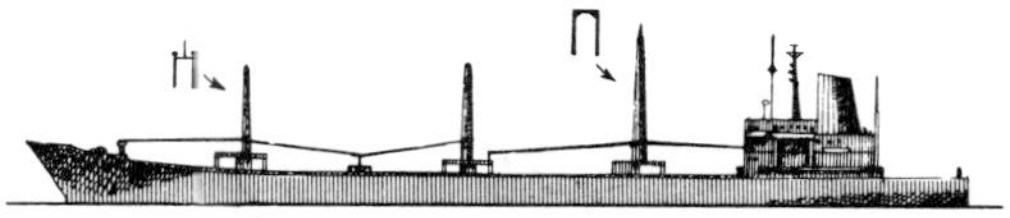

K_2M_2F H1
● **71840 LUISE BORNHOFEN.** FRG/FRG 1976; C; 6800/9800; 149.82 × 8.18/9.28 (491.54 × 26.84/30.45); M; 16.5; **'36-L'** type. Similar (some have 5-deck superstructure): **71841 CAROLINE OLDENDORFF** (Pa) ex BREDA 1973; ex CAROLINE OLDENDORFF 1972 **71842 HUGO OLDENDORFF** (Pa) **71843 GERDT OLDENDORFF** (Pa) ex BENNEKOM 1974; ex GERDT OLDENDORFF 1972 **71844 ELISABETH OLDENDORFF** (Pa) ex BAARN 1974; ex ELISABETH OLDENDORFF 1972 **71845 GRETKE OLDENDORFF** (Pa) **71846 MARIA OLDENDORFF** (Pa) ex BARNEVELD 1975; ex MARIA OLDENDORFF 1972 **71847 ALMUT BORNHOFEN** (FRG) **71848 KARIN BORNHOFEN** (FRG) **71849 CHARLOTTE KOGEL** (FRG) **71850 ANDALUSIA** (FRG) ex ELISABETH SCHULTE 1977 **71851 SUSANNE VINNEN** (FRG) ex CONCORDIA MOON 1980; ex SUSANNE VINNEN 1979; ex ELISE SCHULTE 1978 **71852 ALIKI I. P.** (Gr) **⋆71853 DA SHA PING** (RC) ex TARPON SEAWAY 1978 **⋆71854 DA SHI ZHAI** (RC) ex TARPON SANDS 1978 **⋆71855 JIN JIANG** (RC) ex AQUITANIA 1981; ex ILSE SCHULTE 1977 **⋆71856 MU DAN JIANG** (RC) ex CAPE MAGDALENA 1977; ex HEDI WIARDS 1972 **⋆71857 BOLESLAW PRUS** (Pd) **⋆71858 LEOPOLD STAFF** (Pd) The following may be similar (190ton derrick): **71859 SARONIKOS** (Gr).

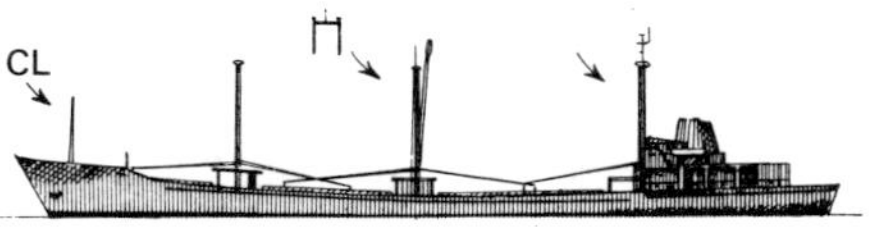

K_2M_2F H1
71870 HELENE ROTH. Cy/FRG 1969; C; 3300/5600; 124.49 × 6.4/8 (408.4 × 21/26.2); M; 17. Sisters: **71871 ERIKA NABER** (FRG) ex ERIKA SCHULTE 1978 **71872 CARBET** (Fr) ex GUNTHER SCHULTE 1976; ex WAMERU 1976; ex GUNTHER SCHULTE 1975 **71873 CARIMARE** (Fr) ex WANGONI 1976; ex AUGUSTE SCHULTE 1975.

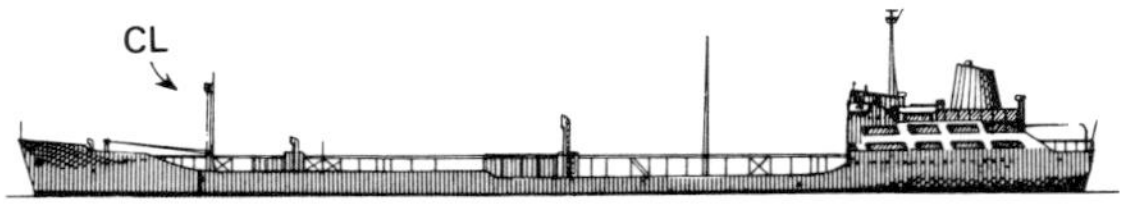

K_2M_2F H13
71880 LIONELLO L. It/Sw 1957; Tk; 12600; 169.81 × 9.58 (557.12 × 31.43); M; 15.25; ex CHEMICAL MARKETER 1978; ex VINCITA 1973; ex SEVEN SKIES 1965; ex HARRY R. TRAPP 1959.

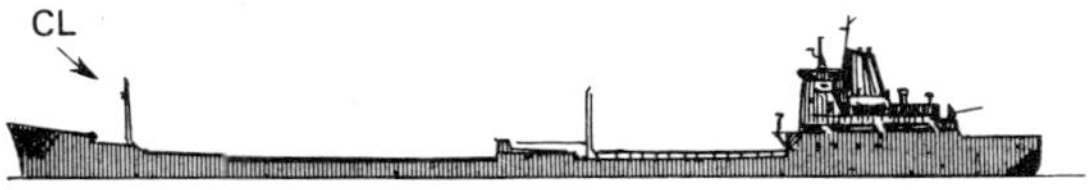

K_2M_2F H13
71890 ESSO MILFORD HAVEN. Br/Sw 1968; Tk; 10900; 162.67 × 8.54 (533.69 × 28.02); M; 16.75. Sister: **71891 ESSO FAWLEY** (Br).

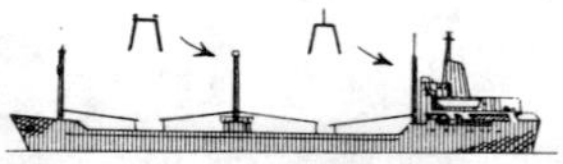

K_2M_2F H13
71900 SIG. No/Pd 1973; C; 1600; 84.18 × 5.3 (276.18 × 17.39); M; 13.75; **'B-431'** type. Sisters (No flag): **71901 ASK 71902 EIR 71903 EVA 71904 FRO 71905 HOP 71906 LYSPOL 71907 SOKNATUN 71908 STAVSUND** launched as LIONEL (Ma flag): **71909 WEST BAY** ex GERMA GIRL **71910 WEST CLIFF** ex GERMA GLORIA **71911 WEST REEF** ex GERMA STAR **71912 WEST END** ex GERMA GRACIA (It flag): **71913 CANOVA** ex LOG 1978 **71914 SINNI** ex RAN 1978; ex PAN 1975 (DDR flag): ⋆**71915 ARTERN** ex GRONG 1973 ⋆**71916 COSWIG** ex GARLI 1973.

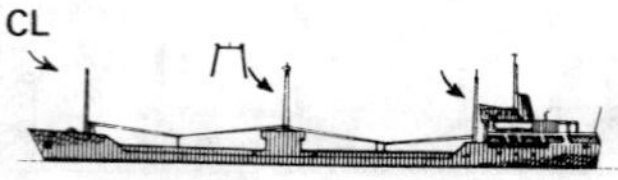

K_2M_2F H13
71920 ROMMY. Pa/Pd 1972; C; 2000; 93.73 × 5.57 (307.51 × 18.27); M; 13; ex ENID 1977; **'B-431'** type. Sisters: **71921 HILDEGARD** (Pa) ex MILDRED 1977 **71922 CUPID** (No) **71923 ELDRID** (No) **71924 GUDRID** (No) **71925 SIGRID** (No).

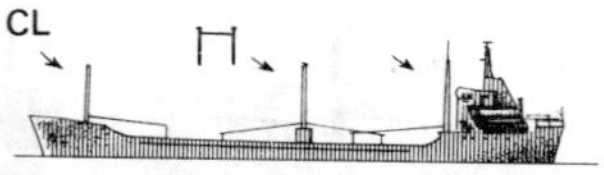

K_2M_2F H13
● ⋆**71930 POTIRNA.** Ys/Pd 1967; C; 1500; 87.58 × 4.81 (287.34 × 15.78); M; 12; ex NORMANNSUND; ex GDYNIA 1976; Lengthened 1970; **'B-459'** type. Sisters: ⋆**71931 PERNA** (Ys) ex NORMANNBAY; ex CAROLINE 1975; ex GERMA LORD 1973 ⋆**71932 POPLAT** (Ys) ex NORMANNVAAG; ex JOSEFINE 1976; ex GEISHA 1975 **71933 JADE** (Br) ex FONDAL 1974; ex GDANSK 1973 Similar (not lengthened): **71934 CAREBEKA VI** (Ne) ex LIONEL.

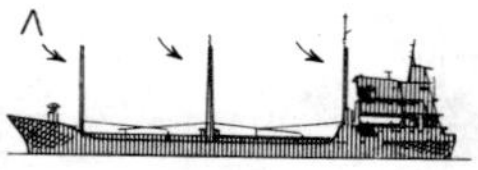

K_2M_2F H13
● **71940 HORSA.** No/De 1971; C; 500/1400; 71.48 × 3.76/5.67 (234.51 × 12.34/18.6); M; 12; ex ALICE BEWA 1976. Sister: **71941 NIAGA XXVI** (Ia) ex PEP OCEAN; ex CHRIS LION 1974 Possible sister: **71942 PHOENIX TRADER** (Br) ex PHOENIX 1979; ex KIS BEWA 1976 Similar (lengthened): **71943 WAKENITZ** (FRG) ex METTE CHRISTENSEN 1976.

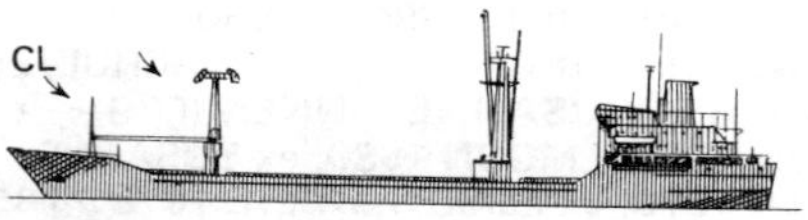

K_2M_2F H13
71950 SCILLA. FRG/FRG 1977; C/Con; 3600/6700; 131.6 × 6.36/8.03 (431.76 × 20.87/26.35); M; 16.

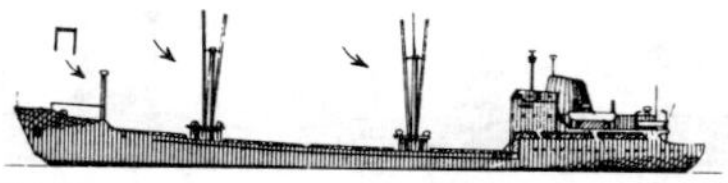

K_2M_2F H13
71960 OUTOKUMPU. Fi/Fi 1958; O; 3800; 110.19 × 6.4 (361.52 × 21); M; 13.

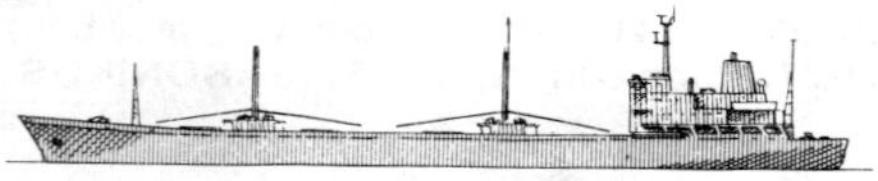

K_2M_2FK H
71970 OCEAN SKY. Ko/Ja 1975; C; 3700; 131.48 × 6.99 (431.36 × 22.93); M; 17.75; ex SUMMER BIRDIE 1979; ex ROSE DAPHNE 1978. Sisters: **71971 ROSE MALLOW** (Pa) **71972 WHITE JASMINE** (Pa) ex ROSE ACACIA 1978 **71973 OSAKA REEFER** (Ja) ex ADEN MARU 1978.

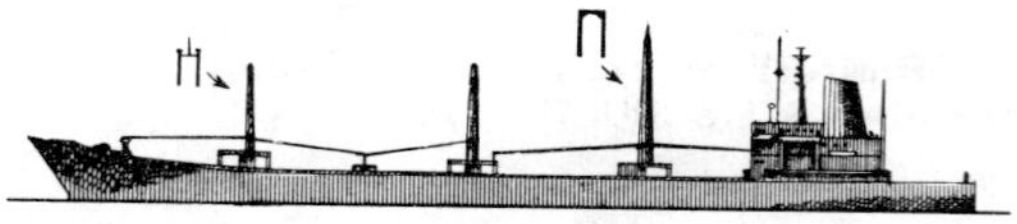

K_2M_2FK H1
71980 LUISE BORNHOFEN. FRG/FRG 1976; C; 6800/9800; 149.82 × 8.18/9.28 (491.54 × 26.84/30.45); M; 16.5; **'36-L'** type. Similar: ⋆**71981 MU DAN JIANG** (RC) ex CAPE MAGDALENA 1977; ex HEDI WIARDS 1972 May be others of this type with this sequence.

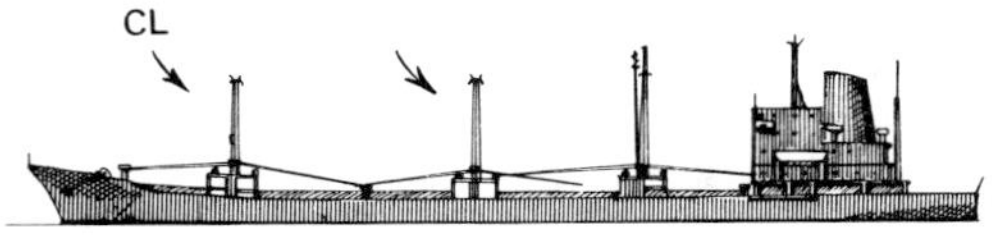

K_2M_2FK *H1*
● ⋆**71990 JUN LIANG CHENG.** RC/FRG 1970; C; 7100/1000; 150.15 × 8.31/9.27 (492.62 × 27.26/30.41); M; 16; ex ARABONNE 1977; **'36-L'** type. Sisters: **71991 ARAGRACE** (No) **71992 BAARN** (Ne) ex ARALUCK 1976; launched as APPIAN **71993 BREDA** (Ne) ex GORDIAN 1976 **71994 JOSEFA** (Br) ex TRAJAN 1976 ⋆**71995 ARBERIA** (Al) ex ARAPRIDE 1978.

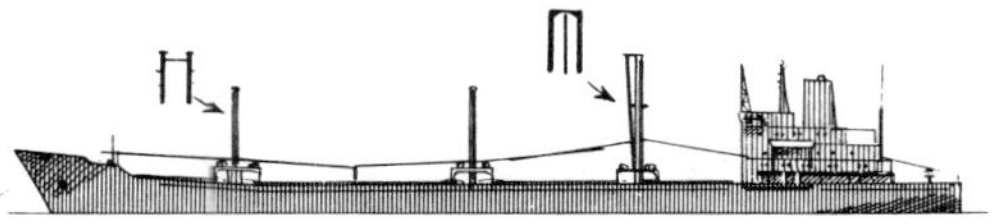

K_2M_2FK *H1*
72000 HILDESHEIM. FRG/FRG 1977; C; 9800; 149.82 × 9.25 (491.54 × 30.35); M; 16.5; **'36-L'** type. Sisters (FRG flag): **72001 RUDESHEIM 72002 INGELHEIM 72003 RUSSELSHEIM 72004 HEIDENHEIM 72005 UNTERTURKHEIM.**

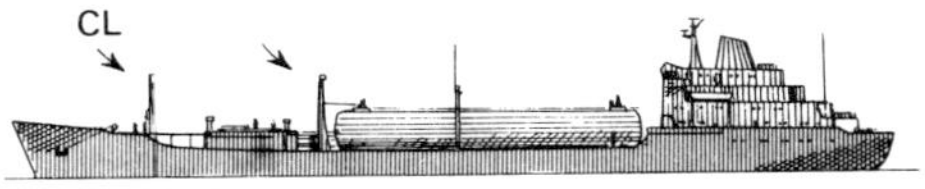

K_2M_2FK *H13*
72010 VESTRI. No/No 1971; LGC; 9000; 138.72 × 9.23 (455.12 × 30.28); M; 17.

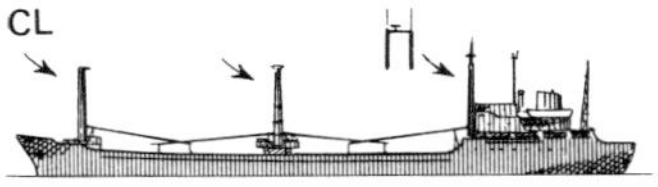

K_2M_2FK *H13*
72030 CENTRAL CRUISER. Tw/Ja 1970; C; 3000; 97.39 × 6.38 (319.52 × 20.93); M; 12.5.

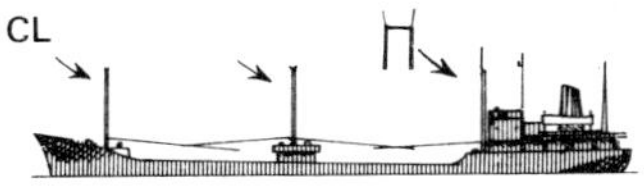

K_2M_2FK *H13*
72050 CARRIE. Cy/Ja 1966; C; 2800; 94.8 × 6.15 (311.02 × 20.18); M; 12; ex LION 1980; ex ASPA 1980; ex STEELY CARRIER 1974; ex KYONAN MARU 1971. Similar: **72051 GIORGOS K** (Gr) ex BLUE BILL 1979; ex MAY PLUM 1977; ex NORTHERN STAR 1976; ex KYOKEI MARU 1972 Probably Similar: **72052 RIMBA DUA** (Ia) ex HANDSENG 1977; ex SHUNYO MARU 1971.

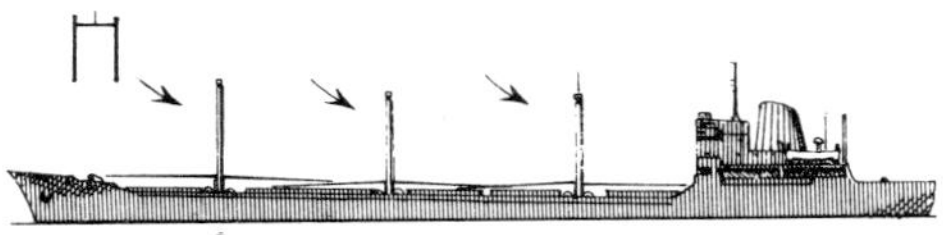

K_2M_2FK *H13*
72070 TRIA. Gr/Ja 1957; C; 8500; 145.75 × 8.69 (478.18 × 28.5); M; 15; ex SILVER WAVE 1980; ex SHUNMEI MARU 1971.

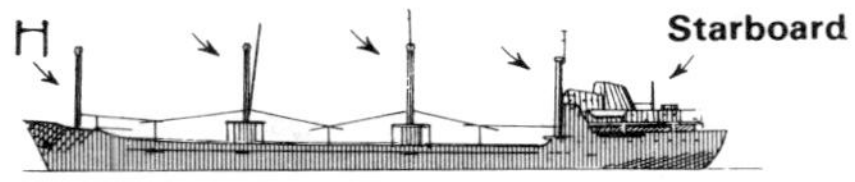

K_2M_2FK *H13*
72020 GUAYANA. Ve/Sp 1963; C; 3500; 111.61 × 6.1 (366.17 × 20); M; 12; ex ARGO 1963.

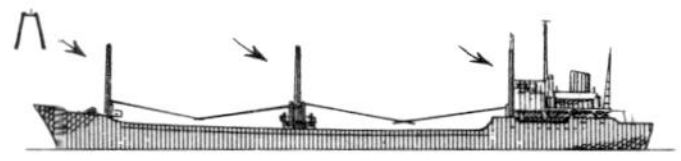

K_2M_2FK *H13*
72040 CHANG CHUN. Tw/Ja 1969; C; 3000; 97.21 × 6.38 (318.93 × 20.93); M; 13. Possibly Similar: **72041 CHUN JIN** (Pa) ex SHINNAN MARU 1973 **72042 HUNG MING** (Tw) ex TA HO 1978; ex ICHIZAN UNZEN 1971 **72043 TARAKAN MARU** (Ja) ex HASHIHAMA Maru 1972.

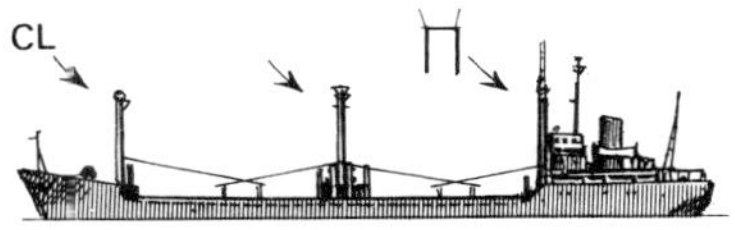

K_2M_2FK *H13*
72060 EKMAN. Pa/Ja 1970; C; 4000; 110.7 × 6.66 (363.19 × 21.85); M; 12; ex LILIA 1978. Sister: **72061 SIGMA** (Li) ex LAGUNA 1978 Possibly Similar: **72062 SARUNTA I** (Pa) ex YUSHIN MARU 1972 **72063 YUNAM No 9** (Pa) ex BINEKA No 4 1980; ex YUFUKU MARU 1976.

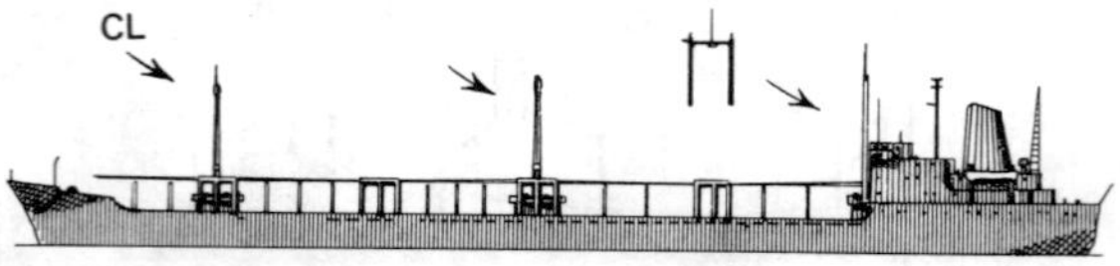

K_2M_2FK H13
72080 EASTERN FORTUNE. Li/Ja 1968; B; 13300; 172.02 × 9.63 (564.37 × 31.59); M; 14.25; ex JAPAN AZALEA 1973. Similar: **72081 DEKKA CONCORD** (Gr) ex MIPO 1980; ex WAYWAY 1978 **72082 ALEXANDRA DYO** (Gr) ex MAGENTA 1980; ex HALO 1979.

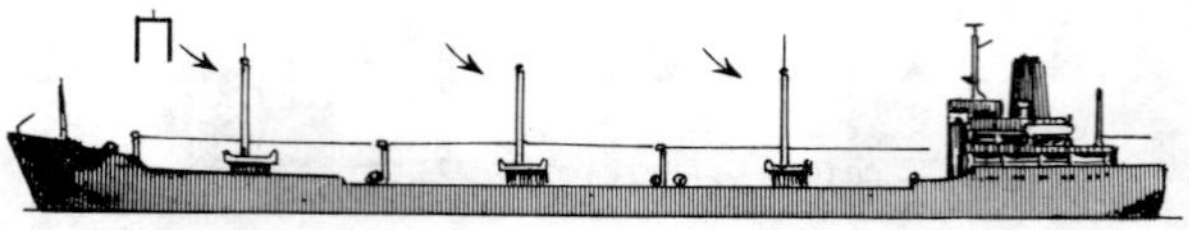

K_2M_2FK H13
72090 JELA TOPIC. Li/Ja 1967; C; 16700; 181.31 × 10.17 (594.85 × 33.37); M; 15.

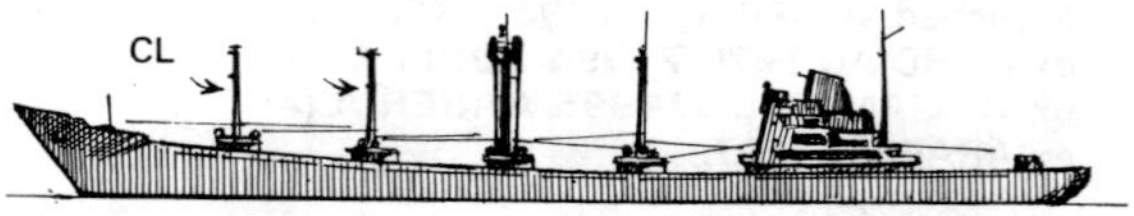

K_2M_2FM H1
72100 GOOD HERALD. Gr/Ne 1960; C; 7200; 162.85 × 8.21 (534.28 × 26.94); M; 17; ex GAASTERDYK 1978. Similar: **72101 HELLENIC SKY** (Gr) ex GREBBEDYK 1974 **72102 HELLENIC GRACE** (Gr) ex GORREDYK 1974 **72103 H CAPELO** (Po) ex MOERDYK 1973.

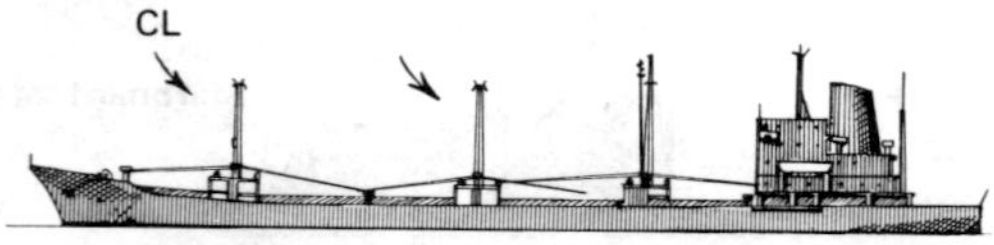

K_2M_2FM H1
⋆**72110 JUN LIANG CHENG.** RC/FRG 1970; C; 7100/10000; 150.15 × 8.31/9.27 (492.62 × 27.26/30.41); M; 16; ex ARABONNE 1977; **'36-L'** type. Sisters: **72111 ARAGRACE** (No) **72112 BAARN** (Ne) ex ARALUCK 1976; Launched as APPIAN **72113 BREDA** (Ne) ex GORDIAN 1976 **72114 JOSEFA** (Br) ex TRAHAN 1976 ⋆**72115 ARBERIA** (Al) ex ARAPRIDE 1978.

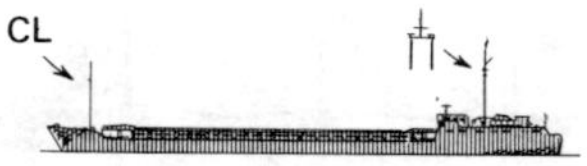

KM H13
● **72120 ERIKA BOJEN.** FRG/FRG 1978; C(sea/river); 500; 81.62 × 3.28 (267.78 × 10.76); M; 11; Hinged masts. Sister (FRG flag): **72121 KONIGSEE** Similar (poop extends to stern): **72122 ALEXANDER** Similar (higher bridge): **72123 LARISSASEE** Probably Similar: **72124 HUBERNA.**

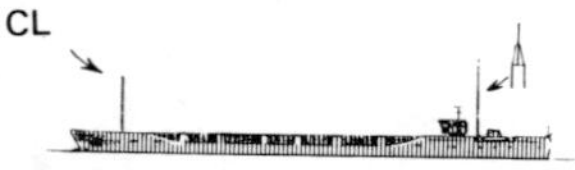

KM H13
72130 CONDOR. FRG/FRG 1978; C(sea/river); 900; 73.11 × 3.4 (239.86 × 11.15); M; 11; Masts hinge.

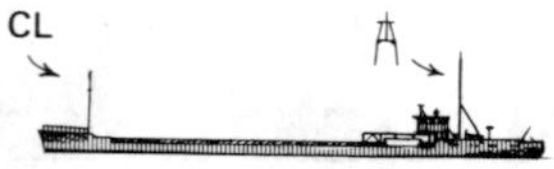

KM H13
72140 CARGO - LINER I. FRG/Ne 1973; C(sea/river); 900; 80.02 × 3.18 (262.53 × 10.43); M; 10; Masts & bridge can be lowered. Sisters (FRG flag): **72141 CARGO - LINER II 72142 CARGO - LINER III 72143 CARGO - LINER IV 72144 CARGO - LINER V 72145 CARGO - LINER VI.**

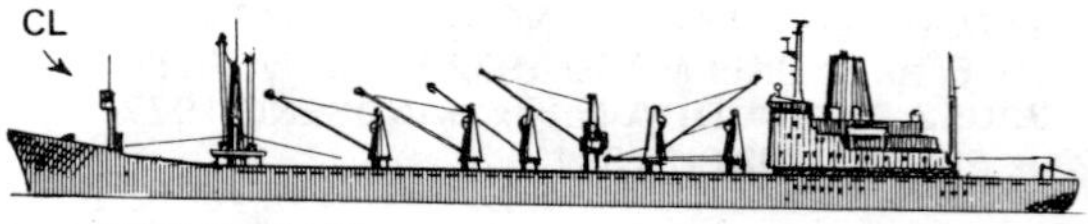

KMC_6MFK H1
72150 MALLECO. Ch/Ja 1967; C; 8800/12500; 168.26 × 9.08/10.18 (552.03 × 29.79/33.4); M; 21.5; ex NEW DAWN 1980; ex TALABOT 1979; Side door. Sisters: **72151 TAIKO** (No) **72152 SOUTHERN DIAMOND** (Li) ex TAIMYR 1981 **72153 MAULE** (Ch) ex NEW SUN 1980; ex TAMANO 1979; ex TRINIDAD 1978.

KMC$_5$MFK H1
72160 HALLDOR. Pa/Ja 1968; C; 5500/8300; 138.06 × 7.72/8.42 (452.95 × 25.33/27.62); M; 16.25; ex TYR 1980. Sister: **72161 HALLVARD** (Pa) ex TORO 1980.

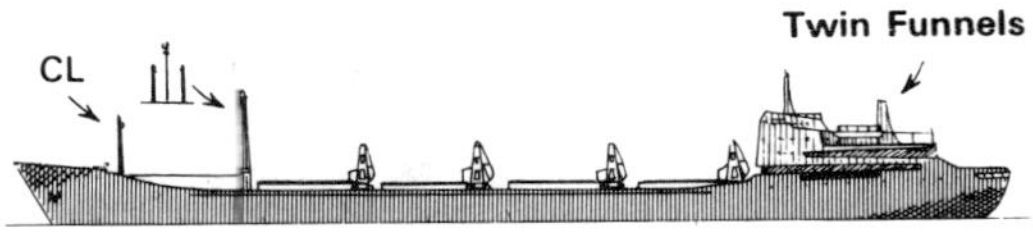

KMC$_4$MF H13
● **72170 LAODIKI.** Gr/Pd 1964; C/B; 10300; 159.59 × 8.14/8.85 (523.59 × 26.71/29.04); M; —; ex CAPE BLANCO 1978; ex REPUBLIKA 1973; **'B-512'** type. Sisters (some may have cranes removed): ⋆**72171 BRNO** (Cz) ⋆**72172 ZEUNG SAN** (RK) ex KOLEJARZ 1980 **72173 ELEISTRIA 1** (Gr) ex STOCZNIOWIEC.

KMC$_4$MFC H13
72180 NEDLLOYD WISSEKERK. Ne/Ne 1967; C; 7400/10700; 166.6 × 7.8/9.6 (546 × 25.6/31.6); M; 20; ex WISSEKERK 1977. Sisters (Ne flag): **72181 NEDLLOYD WAALEKERK** ex WAALEKERK 1977 **72182 NEDLLOYD WESTERKERK** ex WESTERKERK 1977 **72183 NEDLLOYD WILLEMSKERK** ex WILLEMSKERK 1977.

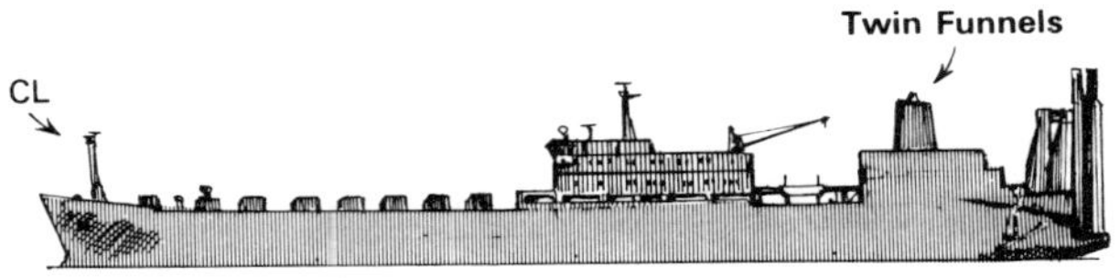

KMCFR H3
72190 IRON MONARCH. Au/Au 1973; RoC; 10600; 179.33 × 8.87 (588.35 × 29.1); GT; 20.5; Stern and side doors. Sister: **72191 IRON DUKE** (Au).

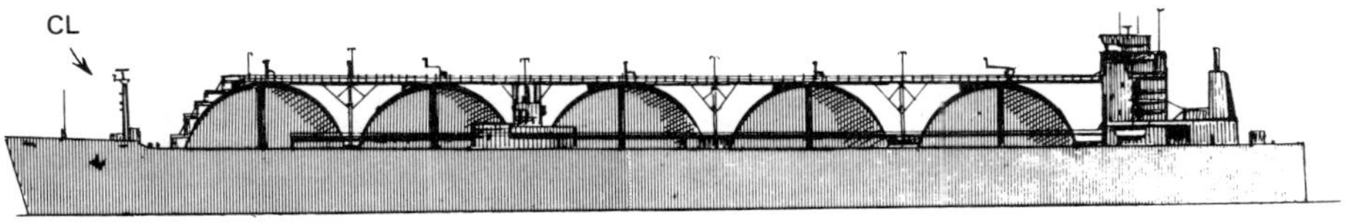

KMF H
72200 LNG AQUARIUS. US/US 1977; LGC; 83100; 285.3 × 11.51 (936.02 × 37.76); T; 20.5. Sisters (US flag): **72201 LNG ARIES 72202 LNG CAPRICORN 72203 LNG GEMINI 72204 LNG LEO 72205 LNG LIBRA 72206 LNG TAURUS 72207 LNG VIRGO 72208 LAKE CHARLES 72209 LOUISIANA.**

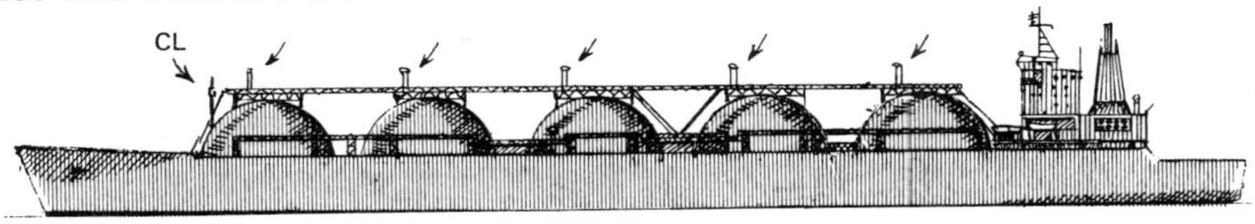

KMF H
72210 HOEGH GANDRIA. No/FRG 1977; LGC; 95700; 287.54 × 11.52 (943.37 × 37.8); T; 20. Sister: **72211 GOLAR FREEZE** (No).

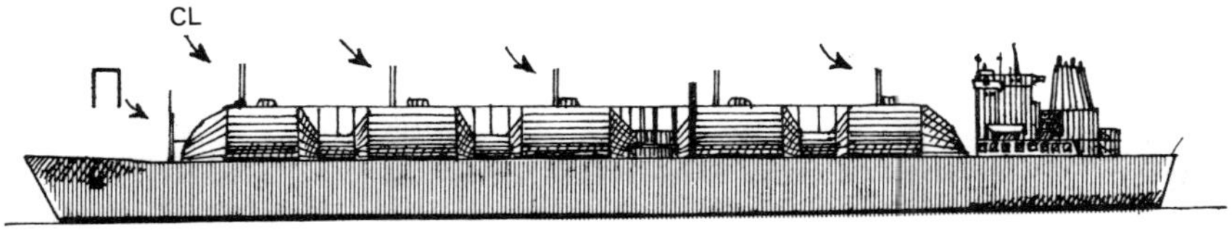

KMF H
72220 NORMAN LADY. Br/No 1973; LGC; 76400; 249.51 × 10.62 (818.6 × 34.84); T; 19. Similar: **72221 POLLENGER** (Br) ex LNG CHALLENGER 1979.

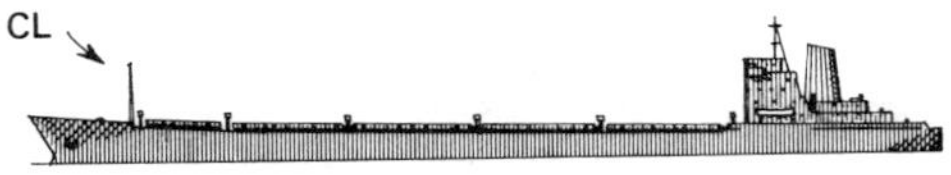

KMF H
72230 FORUM PRIDE. Gr/Sp 1970; B; 11800; 144.96 × 9.6 (475.59 × 31.5); M; 14; ex ASTURIAS 1981. Sister: **72231 JOVELLANOS** (Sp).

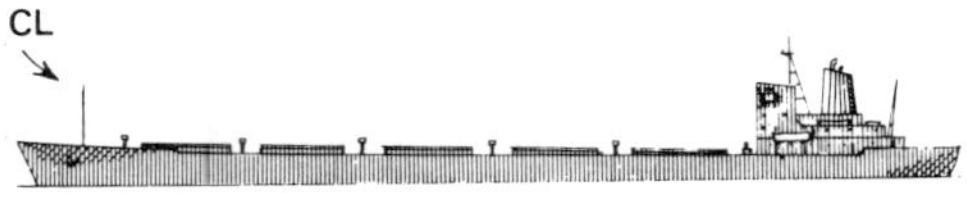

KMF H
● **72240 LLARANES.** Sp/Sp 1971; B; 12900; 148.72 × 10.34 (487.93 × 33.92); M; 15. Similar (taller funnel): **72241 TRASONA** (Sp).

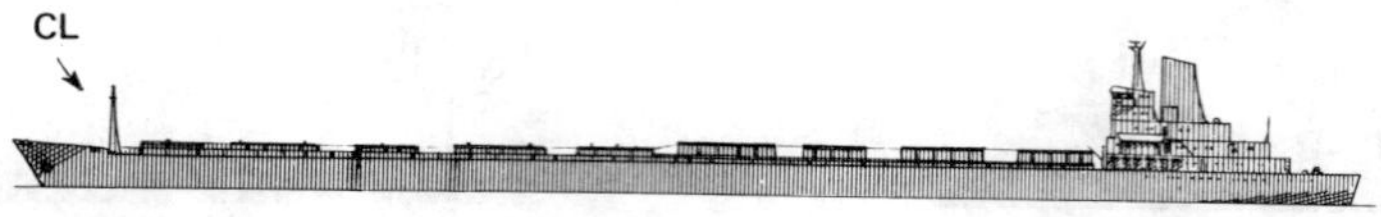

KMF H
72250 BERNHARD OLDENDORFF. Pa/FRG 1967; B; 30500; 213.88 × 12.18; (701.71 × 39.96); M; 15.5; Sister: **72251 HARMEN OLDENDORFF** (Pa).

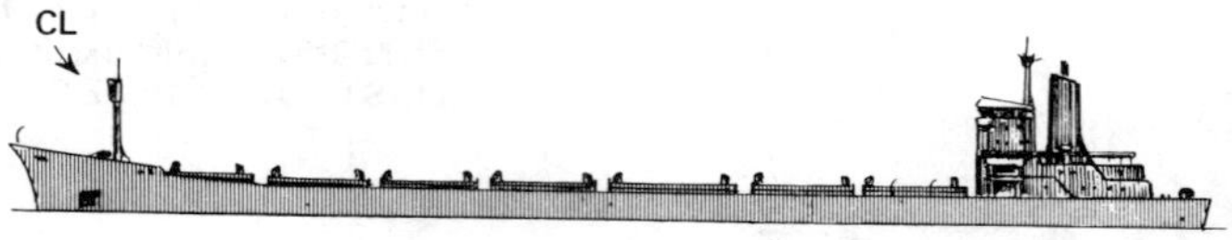

KMF H
72260 M. ISTANBUL K. Tu/Ne 1967; B; 28500; 205.49 × 11.99 (674.18 × 39.34); M; 15; ex LONDON BRIDGE 1977. Sister: **72261 ALKEOS C** (Gr) ex YAUZA 1980;ex FORTH BRIDGE 1978.

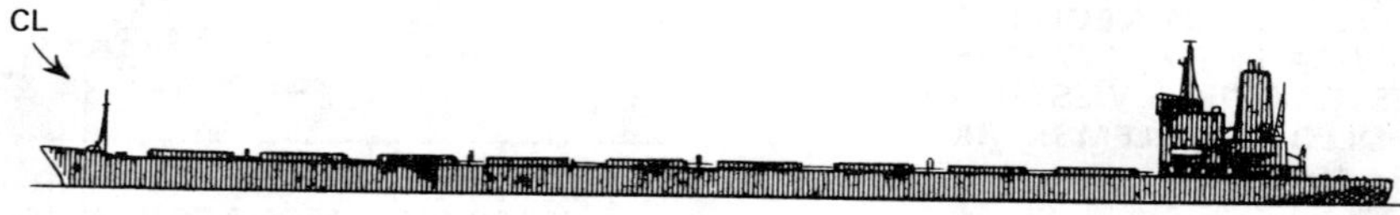

KMF H
72270 MEYNELL. Br/Ja 1973; B; 69900; 261.02 × 17.58 (856.36 × 57.68); M; 15.5. Sister: **72271 NORDIC PATRIOT** (Br) ex NAESS PATRIOT 1974.

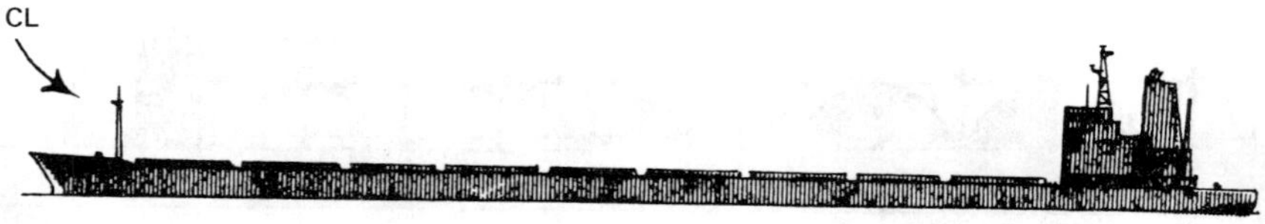

KMF H
72280 GOOD LEADER. Gr/Ja 1973; B; 59200; 261.02 × 17.62 (856.36 × 57.81); M; 14.75; ex ELWOOD MEAD 1974. Sister: **72281 TRENTWOOD** (Sg).

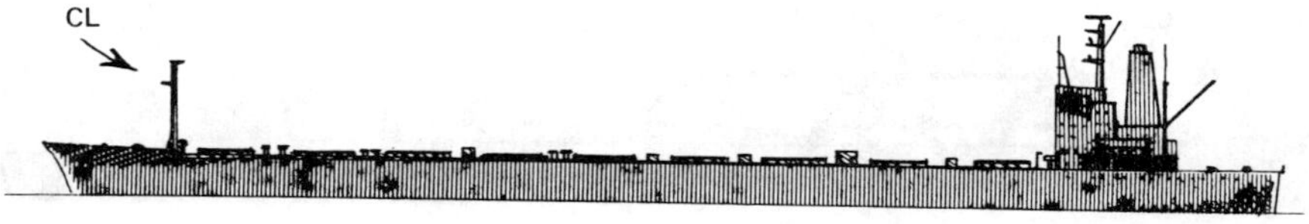

KMF H
72290 D. C. COLEMAN. Br/Ja 1974; B; 69900; 260 × 16.79 (853.02 × 55.09); M; 15. Sisters (Br flag): **72291 E. W. BEATTY 72292 W. M. NEAL 72293 OCEANIC CREST.**

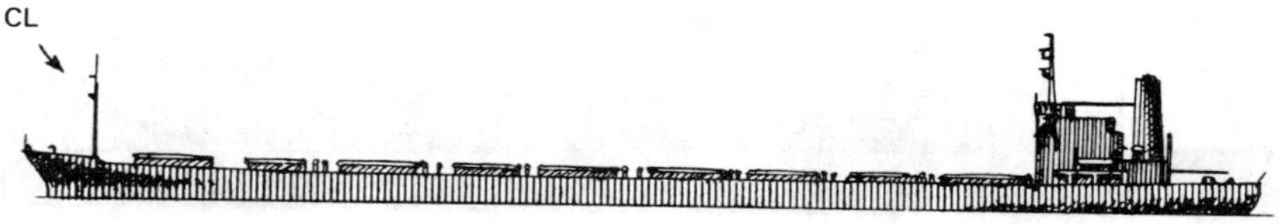

KMF H
72300 KATORI MARU. Ja/Ja 1973; B; 65300; 257.03 × 16.93 (843.27 × 55.54); M; 15.5.

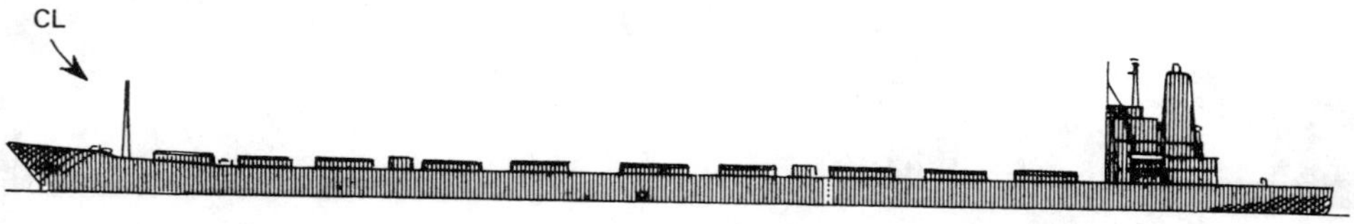

KMF H
72310 KOHSHO MARU. Ja/Ja 1972; O; 87400; 295 × 17.01 (967.85 × 55.81); M; 15.25.

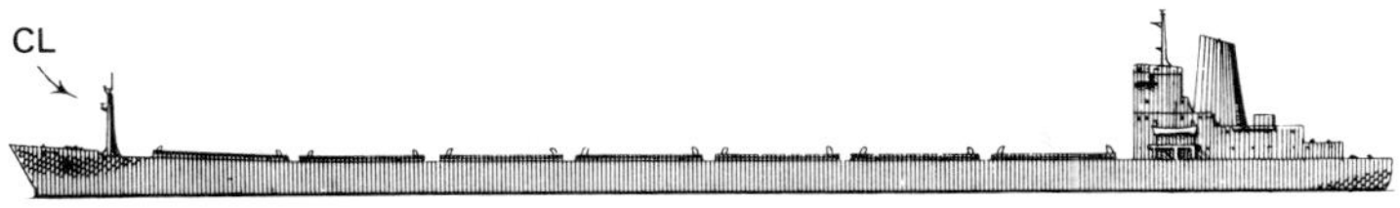

KMF H
72320 BONTRADER. Br/Br 1970; B; 35900; 224.04 × 12.52 (735.04 × 41.08); M; 15.25; ex AMORGOS 1980; ex SYDNEY BRIDGE 1978.

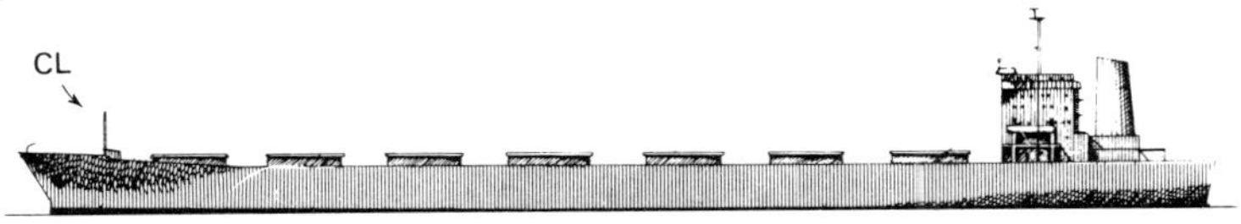

KMF H
● **72330 MAERSK NEPTUN.** Li/De 1975; B; 35700; 219.56 × 12.5 (720.34 × 41.01); M; 15.75; ex CALEDONIA. Sisters: **72331 MAERSK TRITON** (Li) ex CALABRIA **72332 BONNIEWAY** (Br) **72333 CAUSEWAY** (Br) **72334 BENLEDI** (Br) ex ROS CASTLE 1980; launched as SHEAF CREST **72335 SPECIALIST** (Br) **72336 STRATEGIST** (Br) **72337 PORT QUEBEC** (Br) **72338 PORT VANCOUVER** (Br) **72339 EREDINE** (Br) **72340 ATLANTIS** (Gr) ex HAMLET BEATRICE **72341 MALACCA** (De) **72342 MORELIA** (De) **72343 JAPANA** (Li) ex EASTERN CITY.

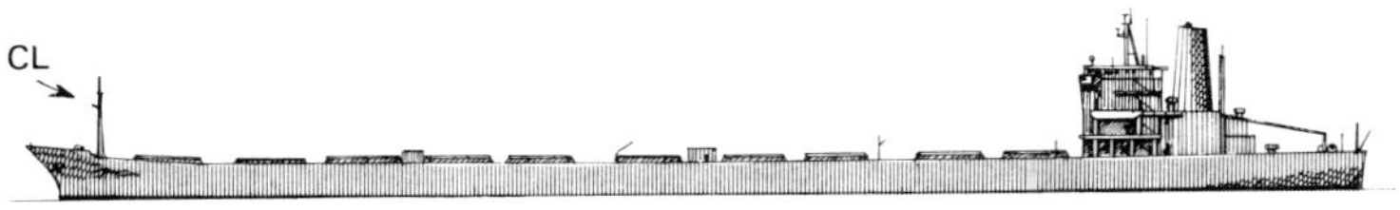

KMF H
72350 ZEEBRUGGE. Be/Be 1974; B; 37700; 224.01 × 13.09 (734.94 × 42.95); M; 15.5. Sisters (Be flag): **72351 MARTHA 72352 KYOTO 72353 YAFFA 72354 RUTH** Possible sisters (In flag): **72355 MARATHA MARINER 72356 MARATHA MELODY** Possibly similar (larger): **72357 ARGOSY PACIFIC** (Br) **72358 LEON & PIERRE C** (Be).

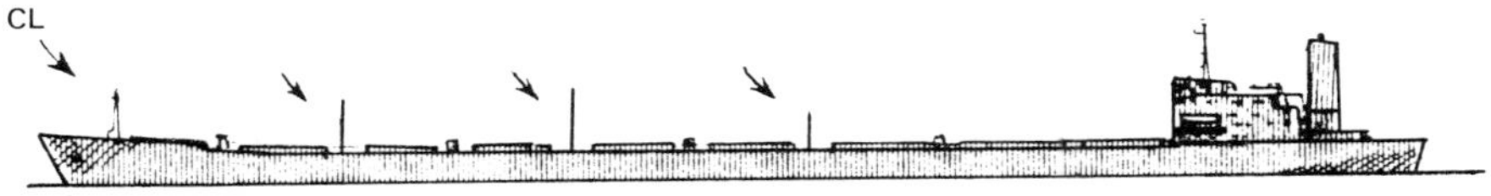

KMF H
72370 GOLDEN CAMEO. Li/FRG 1974; B; 44700; 260.79 × 14.2 (855.61 × 46.59); M; 16.5; ex MALMLAND 1978. Sister: ★**72371 MIAN ZHU HAI** (RC) ex THALASSINI AVRA 1980; ex FERROLAND 1978.

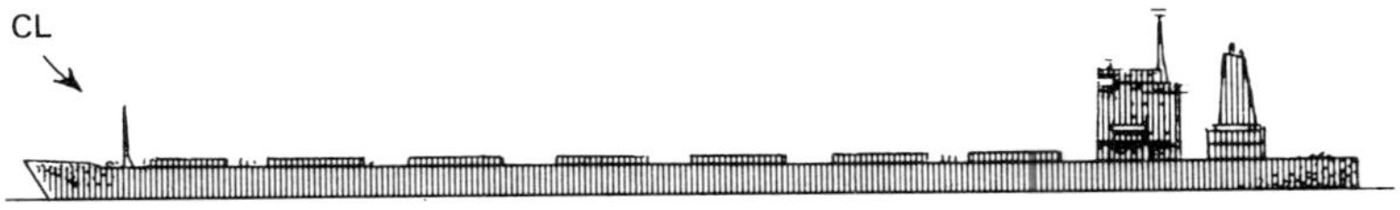

KMF H
72380 IRENA DAN. De/Ih 1977; B; 39400; 225.61 × 14.09 (740.19 × 46.23); M; 16.

● 72383

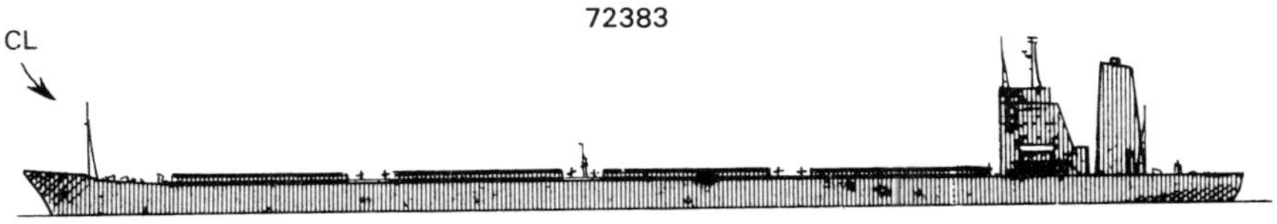

KMF H
72390 NIIHATA MARU. Ja/Ja 1970; O; 62200; 261.02 × 15.71 (856.36 × 51.54); M; 14.75.

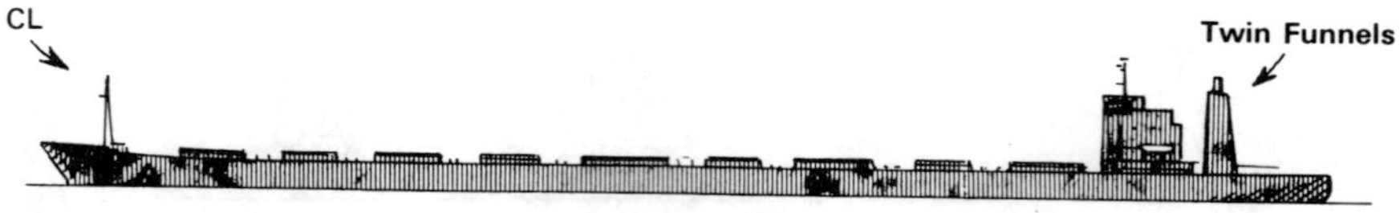

KMF H
72400 KASHIMA MARU. Ja/Ja 1970; B; 65300; 256.01 × 16.92 (839.93 × 55.51); M; 15.25.

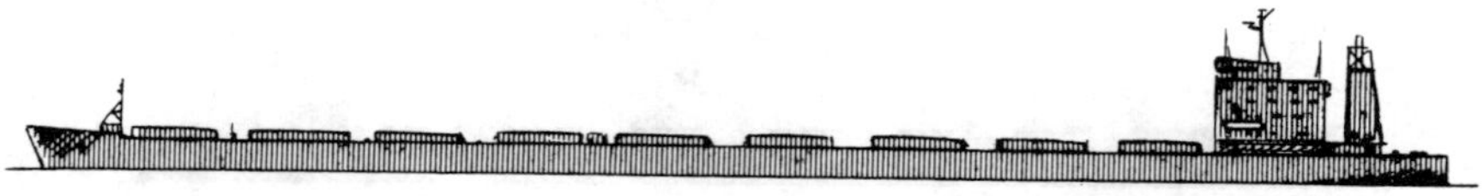

KMF H
72410 AUSTRALIAN PIONEER. Au/Sw 1976; B; 64900; 267.6 × 16.45 (877.95 × 53.97); M; 15.75. Sister: **72411 AUSTRALIAN PURPOSE** (Au) Similar (lower superstructure): **72412 MONTCALM** (Fr) **72413 PENCHATEAU** (Fr) **72414 TARCOOLA** (No) **72415 TONGALA** (No).

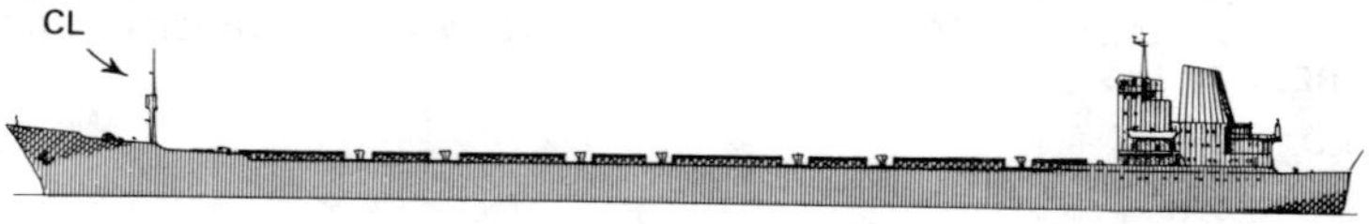

KMF H
72420 MERAKLIS. Gr/FRG 1975; B; 28100; 227.24 × 12.57 (745.54 × 41.24); M; 16. Sisters (Gr flag): **72421 MARQUISE 72422 MINOS 72423 MISTER MICHAEL.**

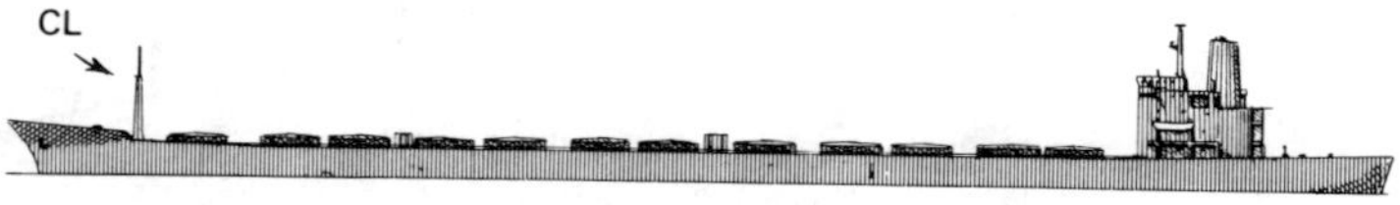

KMF H
● **72430 SCHERPENDRECHT.** NA/Ja 1974; B; 38600; 223.98 × 13.59 (734.84 × 44.59); M; 14.75. Sister: **72431 SLIEDRECHT** (NA) Possibly similar: **72432 ZWIJNDRECHT** (NA) Similar: **72433 AMAK** (Li) ex HAMPTON BAY 1977 **72434 OGDEN AMAZON** (Li) **72435 ROBERTS BANK** (Sg).

KMF H
72440 GOLDEN FLAG. FRG/FRG 1973; B; 43500; 255.91 × 14.2 (839.6 × 46.59); M; 16; ex PROSERPINA 1981. Sister: **72441 PROPONTIS** (FRG).

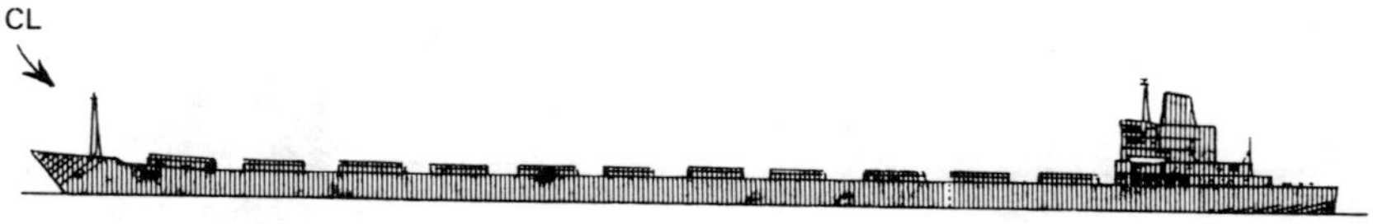

KMF H
72450 EMMA OLDENDORFF. FRG/FRG 1969; B; 37600; 251.01 × 12.52 (823.52 × 41.08); M; 15.5. Sister: **72451 ECKERT OLDENDORFF** (FRG).

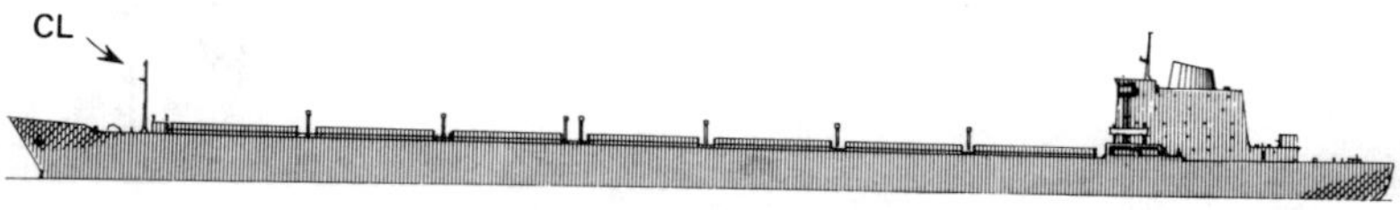

KMF H
72460 SANTAGATA. It/It 1967; B; 39700; 243.85 × 13.01 (800.03 × 42.68); M; —. Sister: **72461 SORRENTO** (It).

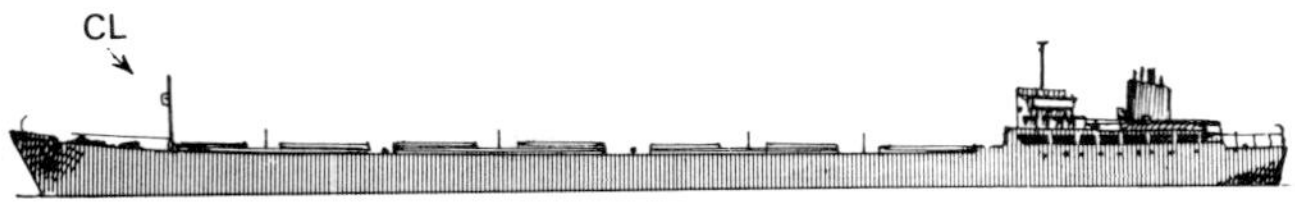

KMF H
72470 CAPIRONA. Pe/Br 1951/62; B; 17200; 202.44 × 9.77 (664.17 × 32.05); M; —; ex NESTOR 1972; ex RONDEFJELL 1968; Converted from a tanker, lengthened and deepened 1962.

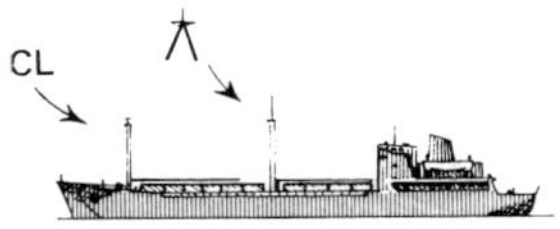

KMF H
● **72490 AEGEAN STAR.** Gr/Sw 1965; RoC; 500/1700; 75.57 × 3.4/5.11 (247.93 × 11.15/16.77); M; 12; ex ALPHA TRANSPORTER 1980; ex RORO NEWFOUNDLAND 1975; ex APOLLO NEWFOUNDLAND 1972; ex BESS 1971; Bow door & ramp. Similar (Bi-pods): **72491 SINNO M.E.** (Le) ex JEANNE R.E.; ex OBERON 1972 **72492 SUNSETTER** (Br) ex CIUDAD DE LEON 1980; ex LEON 1975; ex RORO NEW BRUNSWICK 1975; ex APOLLO NEW BRUNSWICK 1972; ex ANIARA 1971 **72493 AEGEAN POLYVOS** (Gr) ex ALPHA CARRIER 1980; ex NOPAL SEA 1975; ex SERGEL 1973; ex ELEKTRA 1972.

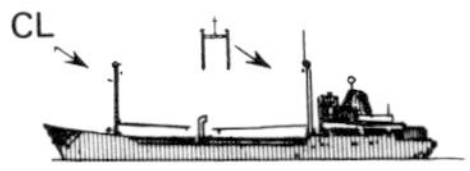

KMF H
⋆**72510 INA.** Pd/Pd 1958; C; 500; 59.85 × 3.41 (196.36 × 11.19); M; 9; **'B-51'** type. Sisters: ⋆**72511 KRUTYNIA** (Pd) ⋆**72512 NER** (Pd) ⋆**72513 SOLA** (Pd) **72514 KRISGAIL** (Fi) ex ORLA 1980.

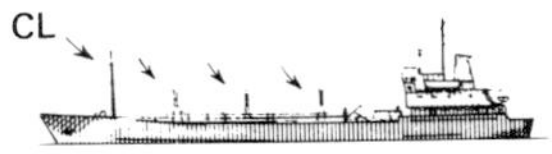

KMF H
72530 SOLVENT EXPLORER. Br/FRG 1974; Ch; 1500; 77.12 × 4.78 (253.02 × 15.68); M; 12; ex ESSBERGER PILOT 1977. Sister: **72531 SOLVENT VENTURER** (Br) ex ESSBERGER PIONEER 1977.

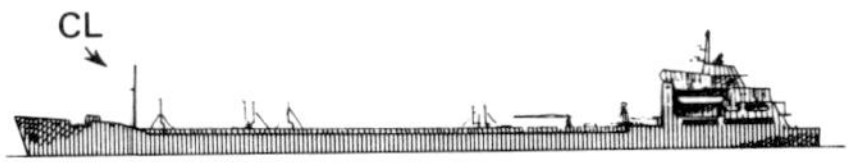

KMF H
● **72550 MARINA.** Sw/Sw 1972; Tk/Ch; 5800; 126.12 × 7.2 (413.78 × 23.6); M; 14.25. Sisters (Sw flag): **72551 MARIA 72552 MARIANN.**

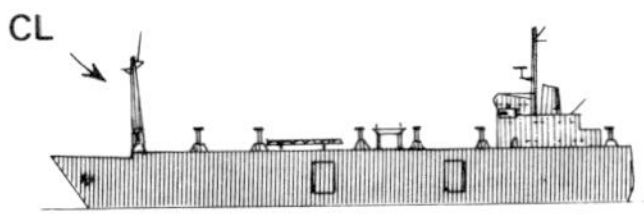

KMF H
72570 RAMSGATE. FRG/FRG 1973; RoC; 800; 92.56 × 3.87 (303.67 × 12.7); M; 14; Stern and side doors.

KMF H
72480 HOUSTON. US/US 1944/67; Con; 11600; 159.57 × 9.56 (523.52 × 31.36); T-E; 16; ex MISSION CARMEL 1968; Converted from a 'T-2' tanker. Sister: **72481 JACKSONVILLE** (US) ex MISSION SOLANO 1968. Similar: **72482 TAMPA** (US) ex MISSION DOLORES 1969.

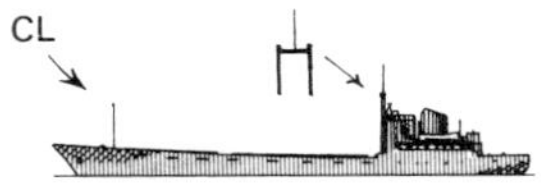

KMF H
● **72500 ALEXANDRA K. II.** Gr/Be 1950; C; 840/1400; 75.29 × 4.6/4.7 (247.01 × 15.09/15.42); M; 12.5; ex OWENBAWN 1976; ex LADY SANCHIA 1968; ex ALFONSO 1966.

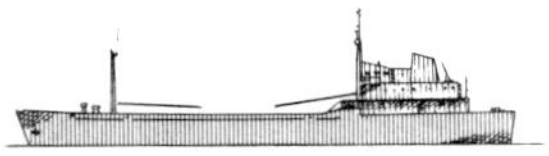

KMF H
72520 ANTINEA. Fr/Fr 1973; RoC; 500; 78.87 × 4.22 (258.76 × 13.85); M; 15; Stern door. Similar (larger): **72521 ANAHITA** (Fr).

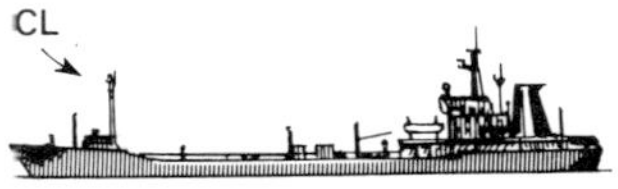

KMF H
72540 TOPPEN. Sw/FRG 1973; Ch; 2200; 109.99 × 5.77 (360.86 × 5.77); M; 13.5; ex SIOUX lengthened 1977. Sister: **72541 TEDDE** (Sw) ex UNKAS.

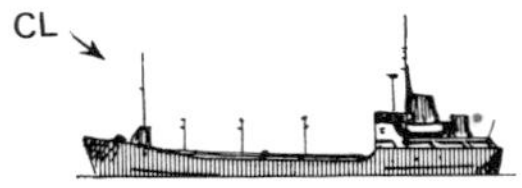

KMF H
72560 AMALIE ESSBERGER. FRG/FRG 1972; Ch; 1000; 69.32 × 4.66 (227.43 × 15.29); M; 12. Similar (larger): **72561 EDITH ESSBERGER** (FRG).

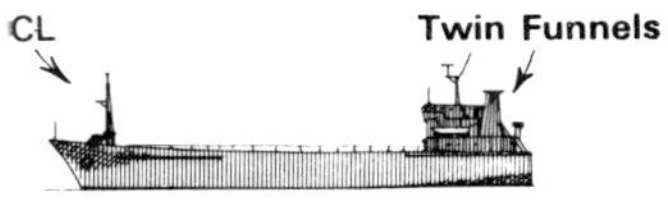

KMF H
● **72580 ANTARES.** FRG/FRG 1967; RoC; 500; 76.43 × 4.22 (250.75 × 13.85);; M; 14.5; Stern door. Sister: **72581 ARNEB** (FRG).

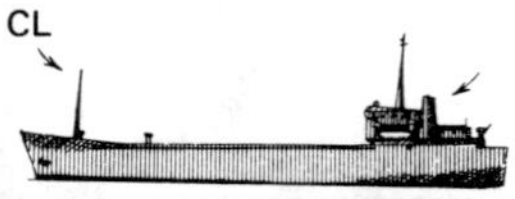

KMF H
72590 MONTE D'ORO. Fr/FRG 1970; RoC; 500; 77.98 × 3.86 (255.84 × 12.66); M; 14.

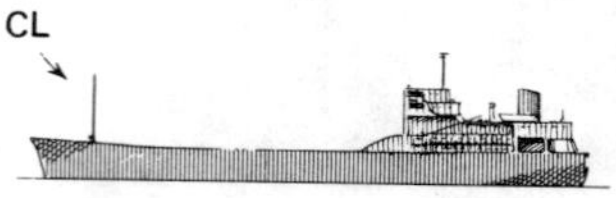

KMF H
72600 PRINCE MARU No 2. Ja/Ja 1964; RoC; 2800; 88.55 × 4.5 (290.52 × 14.76); M; 13.

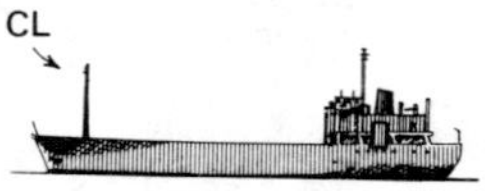

KMF H
72610 TOCHO MARU. Ja/Ja 1962; V; 1400; 68.1 × 3.1 (223.43 × 10.17); M; 10.75.

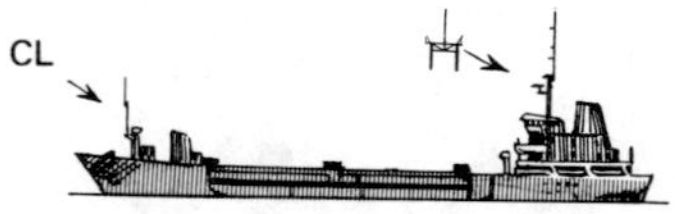

KMF H
72620 ROCKY GIANT. Ne/Ne-Ne 1972/78; Self-discharging stone carrier; 2600; 91.37 × — (299.77 × —); M; —; ex GRETE NIELSEN 1978; Converted from cargo ship & widened 1978. Bow & stern thrust propellors.

KMF H
● **72630 GENEVE.** Li/Ja 1971; C/B; 3000; 85.83 × 7.45 (281.59 × 24.44); M; 11; **'Camit'** type. Sisters (Li flag): **72631 AMSTERDAM 72632 HAMBURG 72633 GHENT 72634 SAINT NAZAIRE 72635 TARAGONA** (NA flag): **72636 EARLY BIRD ex SETE 1973.**

KMF H
72650 PAOLINO. Ho/Br 1954/69; C/Con; 1000; 78.03 × 4.26 (256 × 13.98); M; 12; ex LANCASHIRE COAST 1980; ex TROJAN PRINCE 1969; ex LANCASHIRE COAST 1968; Converted from General Cargo 1969.

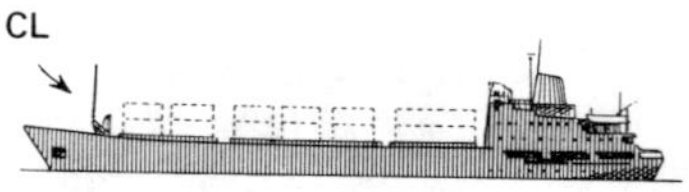

KMF H
72660 KATRINA. Fi/FRG 1958/70; Con; 3900; 98.46 × 7.25 (323.03 × 23.79); M; 13.5; ex NEVA 1969; ex FENJA DAN 1967; Converted from cargo 1970.

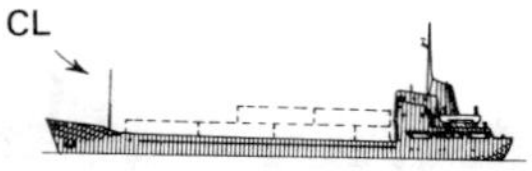

KMF H
72670 ECO DOURO. Po/FRG 1968; Con; 500; 73.51 × 3.66 (241.17 × 12.01); M; 13.25; ex CRAIGAVAD 1973.

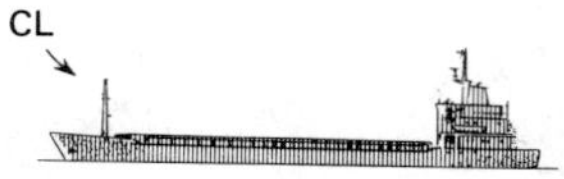

KMF H
● **72680 BARKENKOPPEL.** FRG/Ja 1976; C/Con; 1000; approx. 74 × 4.77 (242.78 × 15.65); M; 12; ex NORDHOLM 1979. Sisters (FRG flag): **72681 SIGGEN 72682 SANDERSKOPPEL** Possible sisters (some, or all, may have crane—see Dalsland etc under KCMF): **72683 OELAND 72684 LANGELAND 72685 ALAND 72686 ALSTERBERG 72687 BOBERG 72688 MESSBERG 72689 SYBILLE 72690 VAERMLAND.**

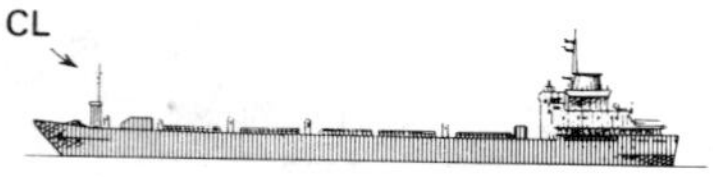

KMF H
72700 PACIFIC FISHER. Br/DDR 1970; C; 3600; 103 × 5.8 (337.93 × 19.03); M; 13; ex JOPULP 1975; Carries Nuclear Waste. Converted from General Cargo 1978.

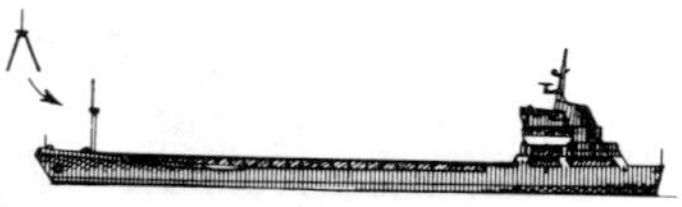

KMF H
72710 KILKENNY. Ih/Ih 1973; Con; 1500; 99.6 × 4.43 (326.77 × 14.53); M; 15. Sister: **72711 WICKLOW** (Ih).

KMF H
72720 THE LADY PATRICIA. Br/Br 1962/74; C/WT; 1300; 64.93 × 4.59 (213.02 × 15.06); M; 11; Modernised 1974.

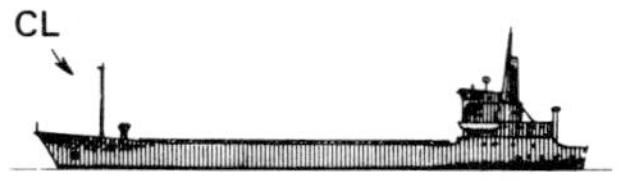

KMF H
72730 BALTIC OSPREY. Br/FRG 1972; Con; 1000; 88.3 × 4.35 (289.7 × 14.27); M; 14; ex ATLANTIC VISCOUNT 1977; ex NAD PRINCE 1975; ex KALKGRUND 1974. Similar (probably with shorter funnel): **72731 STOLLER GRUND** (FRG).

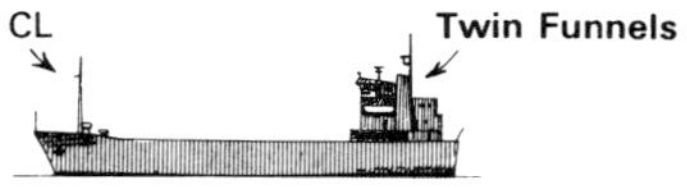

KMF H
72770 HENRY STAHL. FRG/FRG 1973; RoC; 700; 79.41 × 4.24 (260.53 × 13.91); M; 12.5; Lengthened 1975. Stern door.

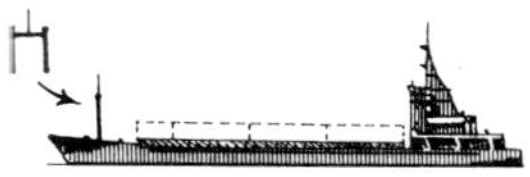

KMF H
72740 BISCAYNE SEA. NA/Sp 1972; Con; 700; 74.71 × 4.24 (245.11 × 13.91); M; 12.5; ex KERRY 1978; ex ASTILUZU 201 1972. Sister: **72741 BISCAYNE SKY** (NA) ex SLIGO 1978; ex ASTILUZU 200 1971.

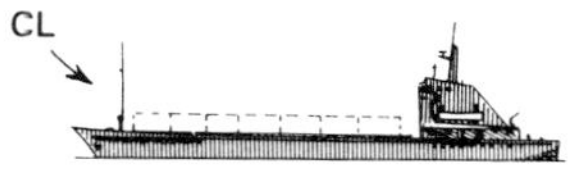

KMF H
● **72750 MINIFOREST.** Fi/FRG 1972; C/Con; 500; 78.14 × 4.13 (256.36 × 13.55); M; 13; ex ILSE WULFF. Similar (FRG flag): **72751 ARA** launched as SCHWARZENBERG **72752 ARNIS 72753 GAZELLE 72754 FUCHSBERG** ex CARIBOU 1972; launched as FUCHSBERG **72755 JENNY GRAEBE** ex HEIDBERG 1978; ex SKEPPSBRON 1972; launched as HEIDBERG **72756 JORN GRAEBE** ex FALKENBERG 1978; ex VELAZCUEZ 1973; launched as FALKENBERG **72757 GERDA GRAEBE** ex SLOTTSBRON 1975; launched as RIEKSBRON **72758 MARIA GRAEBE** ex KUNGSBRON 1973; launched as MARIA GRAEBE **72759 ANNE CATHARINA 72760 HELENE GRAEBE** ex SEEBERG 1978; ex STROMBRON 1973; launched as SEEBERG **72761 GABRIELLA.**

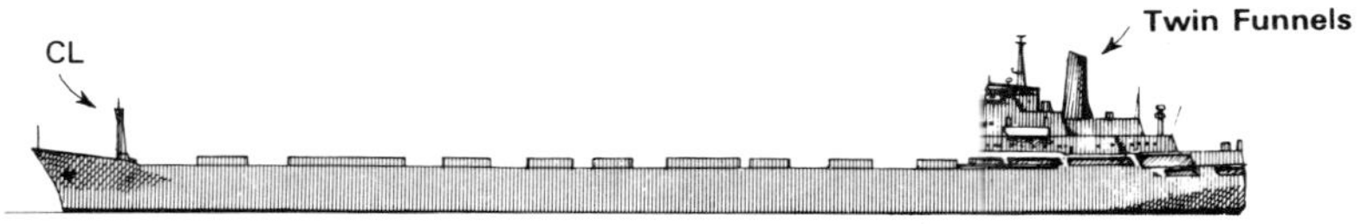

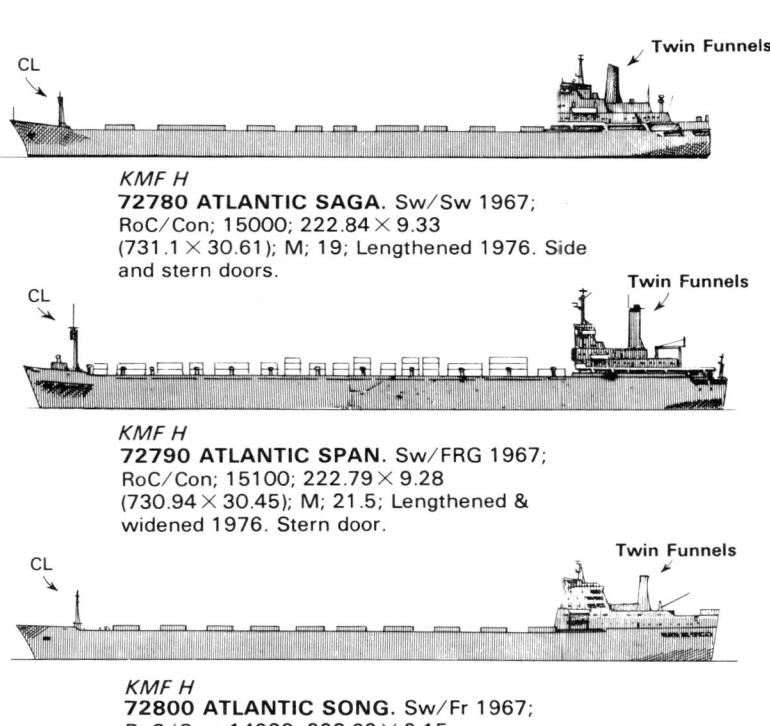

KMF H
72780 ATLANTIC SAGA. Sw/Sw 1967; RoC/Con; 15000; 222.84 × 9.33 (731.1 × 30.61); M; 19; Lengthened 1976. Side and stern doors.

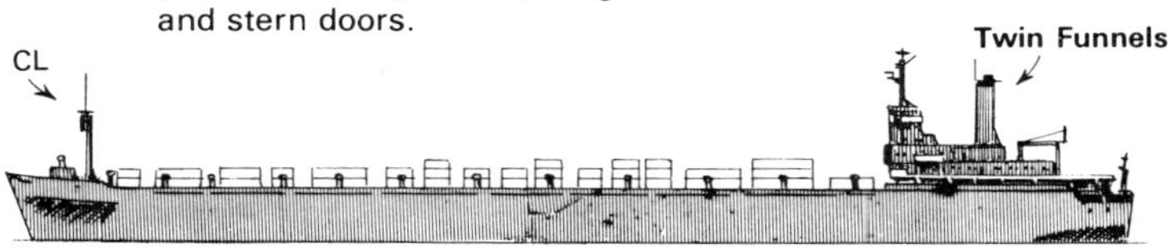

KMF H
72790 ATLANTIC SPAN. Sw/FRG 1967; RoC/Con; 15100; 222.79 × 9.28 (730.94 × 30.45); M; 21.5; Lengthened & widened 1976. Stern door.

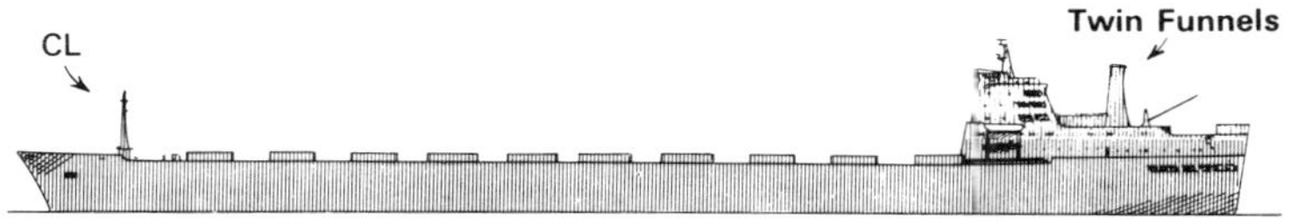

KMF H
72800 ATLANTIC SONG. Sw/Fr 1967; RoC/Con; 14900; 223.02 × 9.15 (731.69 × 30.02); M; 21.5; Lengthened 1976. Stern door. Sister: **72801 ATLANTIC STAR** (Ne).

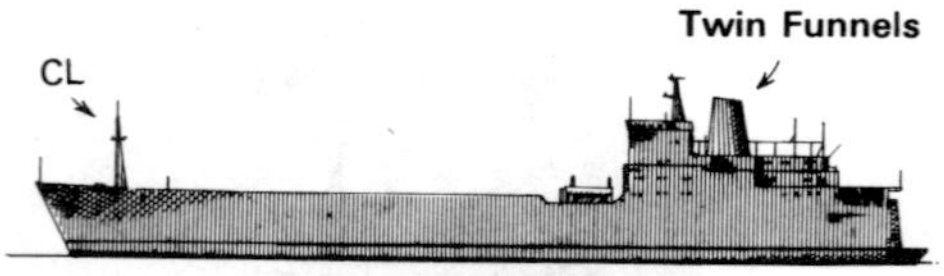

KMF H
72810 LYSAGHT ENTERPRISE. Au/Au 1973; RoC; 7600; 168.05 × 7.7 (551.34 × 25.26); M; 18; Lengthened 1977. Drawing before lengthening. Stern door. Sister: **72811 LYSAGHT ENDEAVOUR** (Au).

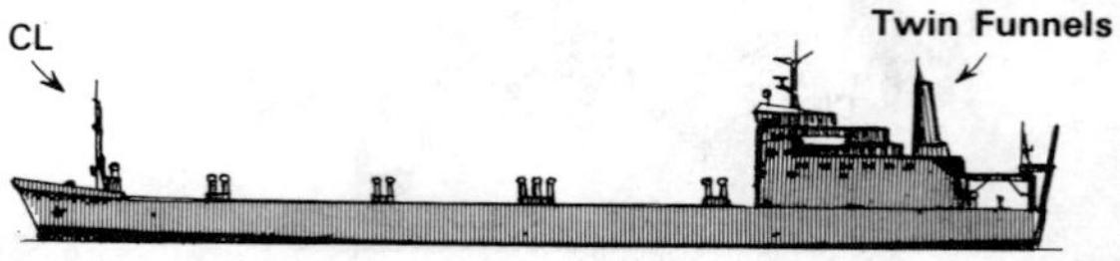

KMF H
72820 KAPRIFOL. Sw/Sw 1977; RoC/Con; 5500; 162.11 × 6.6 (531.86 × 21.65); M; 17.25; Stern door/ramp. Sisters (Sw flag): **72821 VALLMO 72822 LINNE** (Funnel variations).

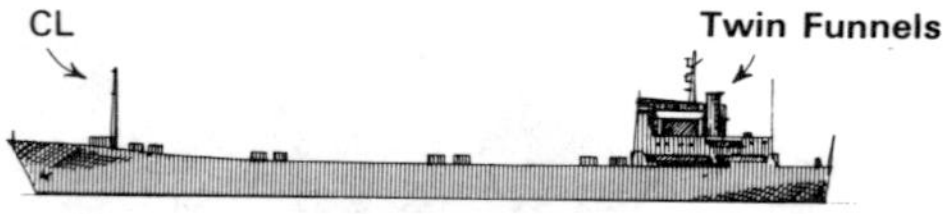

KMF H
72830 VALERIE. Br/Sw 1972; RoC; 3400; 130.71 × 6.74 (428.84 × 22.11); M; 14.75; Stern & side doors. Sisters: **72831 TRANSCON** (Li) ex VALLANN **72832 SAINT SERVAN** (Fr) ex ALPHA MARINER 1978; ex SAINT SERVAN 1977; ex VALLMO 1975.

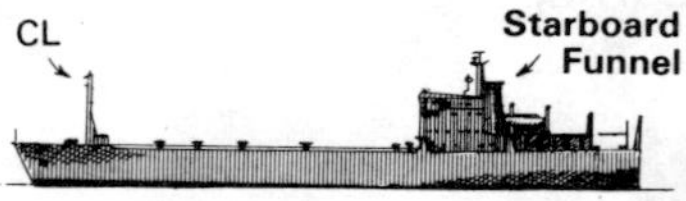

KMF H
● **72840 IGGESUND.** Sw/FRG 1974; RoC; 1600; 99.7 × 4.98 (327.1 × 16.34); M; 15; Stern door/ramps. Sister (Sw flag): **72841 BRAVIK** Similar (larger): **72842 MODO GORTHON 72843 MERZARIO OLIMPIA** ex KALMARSUND 1977.

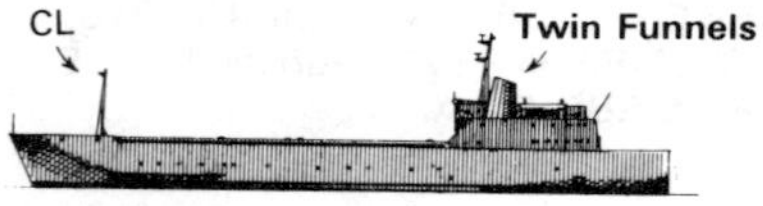

KMF H
72850 TRANSCONTAINER 1. Fr/Fr 1968; RoC/P/Con; 2800; 104.02 × 4.7 (341.27 × 15.42); TSM; 16.

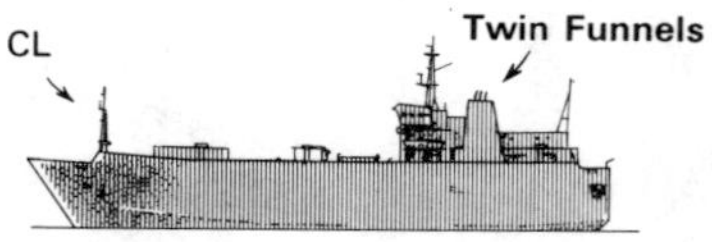

KMF H
72860 FREDENHAGEN. FRG/Ne 1977; RoC; 1000; 89.34 × 4.23 (293.11 × 13.88); M; 13.75; Bow door/ramp. Stern door/ramp. Side door/ramp.

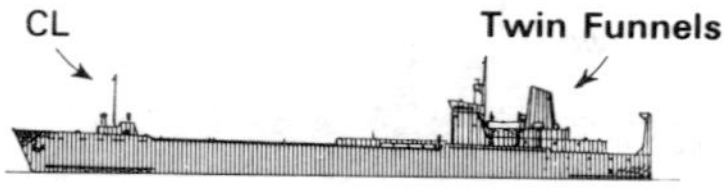

KMF H
72870 MARY HOLYMAN. Br/Ne —; RoC; 2600; 101.2 × 5.18 (332.02 × 16.99); M; 15; Stern door.

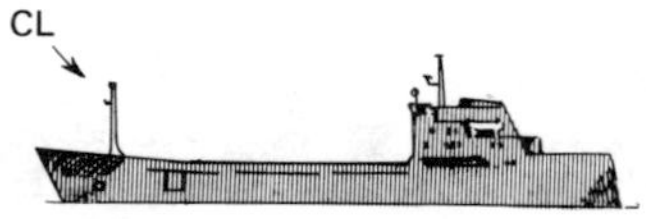

KMF H
72880 RAAD. Si/Fr 1969; RoC/WT; 2100; 99.68 × 4.5 (327.03 × 14.76); TSM; 15.5; ex MONTE CINTO 1980; Stern door.

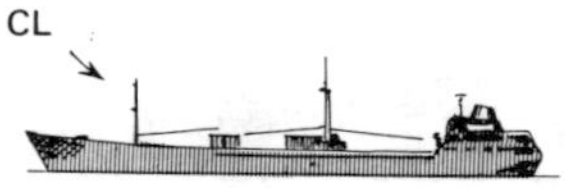

KMF H
72890 BASTO. Fi/No 1968; C; 1200; 81.44 × 3.8/5.02 (267.19 × 12.47/16.47); M; 16; ex FRIO TRADER 1973.
Sister: **72891 BORGO** (Fi) ex FRIO CARRIER 1973.

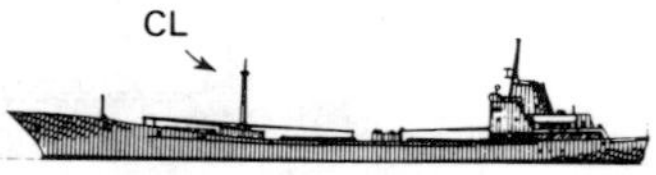

KMF H
⋆72900 GAN QUAN. RC/Fr 1970; C; 2000; 100.44 × 6.2 (329.53 × 20.34); M; —; ex SIRARA 1980. Sister: **72901 ALMIRANTE** (Ho) ex EA 1979.

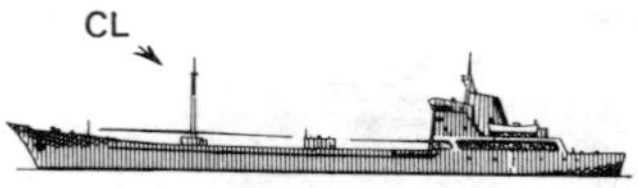

KMF H
72910 GOOD ISLANDER. Gr/Fr 1968; R; 1800; 97.01 × 6.22 (318.27 × 20.41); M; —; ex SELENA 1980; ex REEFERJO 1978; ex BARRAD FOAM 1975.

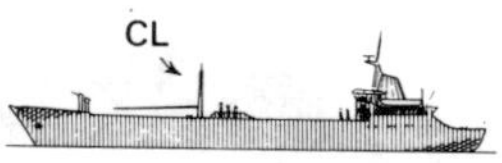

KMF H
72920 LEO. No/No 1965; C; 500; 75.72 × 2.59 (248.43 × 8.5); M; 13; ex TOR BRABANTIA 1971; ex BRABANTIA 1971; Side door. Sister: **72921 LIDROTT** (No) ex HAUKELI 1979; ex TOR FLANDRIA 1972; ex FLANDRIA 1971.

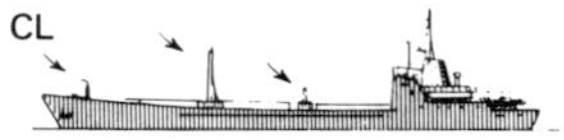

KMF H
72930 VISKO REEFER. Fi/FRG 1966; R; 500/1200; 75.57×3.81/5.02 (247.93×12.5/16.47); M; 15; ex KEPPO 1975.

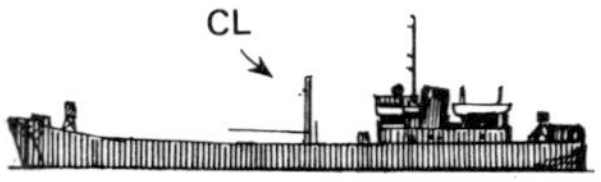

KMF H
72940 ATSUMI. Ja/Ja 1972; A/LST; 1500 Dspl; 89×2.6 (292.8×5); TSM; 14; Japanese Defence Force. Sisters (Ja flag): **72941 MOTOBU 72942 NEMURO.**

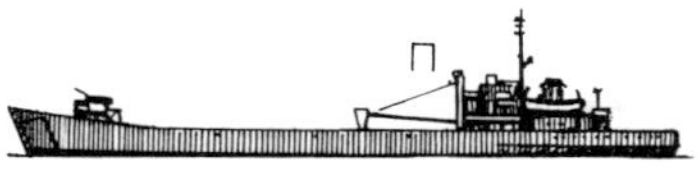

KMF H
72950 MAGAR. In/Br —; LC; 5000 Dspl; 106×3.4 (348×11.2); TSR; 13; ex H.M.S. AVENGER; Indian Navy.

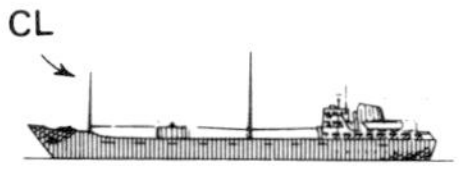

KMF H1
72960 FRUCUBA. Cu/Fr 1956; R; 900; 64.62×4.51 (212.01×14.8); M; 12.5; ex ICE BIRD 1957. Sisters: **72961 AGIOS GEORGIOS** (Gr) ex SEA CHALLENGE 1973; ex ICE FLOWER 1968; ex ATLANTIC FLOWER 1966; ex ICE FLOWER 1965 **72962 SOL REEFER** (Br) ex ICE PEARL 1966; ex ATLANTIC PRINCESS 1966; ex ICE PEARL 1965.

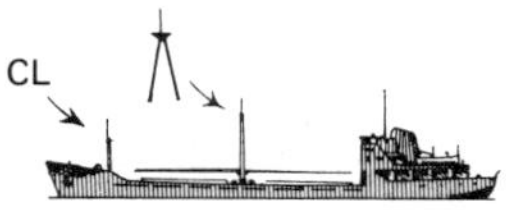

KMF H1
72970 NICE KATHRINE. Pa/Be 1957; C; 1100; 70.72×4.85 (232.02×15.91); M; 13; ex LONE WOLF 1980; ex JASON 1976.

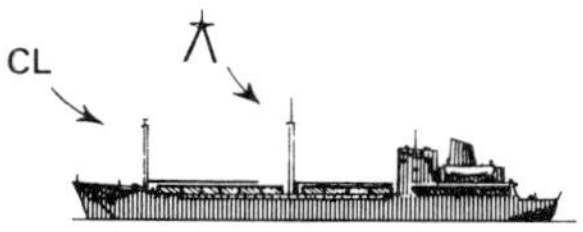

KMF H1
● **72980 AEGEAN STAR.** Gr/Sw 1965; RoC; 500/1700; 75.57×3.4/5.11 (247.93×11.15/16.77); M; 12; ex ALPHA TRANSPORTER 1980; ex RORO NEWFOUNDLAND 1975; ex APOLLO NEWFOUNDLAND 1972; ex BESS 1971; Bow door & ramp. Similar (Bi-pods): **72981 SINNO M.E.** (Le) ex JEANNE R.E.; ex OBERON 1972 **72982 SUNSETTER** (Br) ex CIUDAD DE LEON 1980; ex LEON 1975; ex RORO NEW BRUNSWICK 1975; ex APOLLO NEW BRUNSWICK 1972; ex ANIARA 1971 **72983 AEGEAN POLYVOS** (Gr) ex ALPHA CARRIER 1980; ex NOPAL SEA 1975; ex SERGEL 1973; ex ELEKTRA 1972.

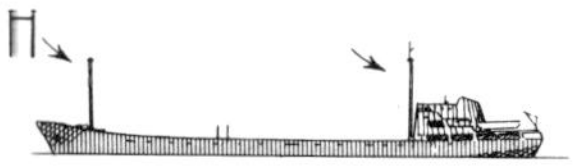

KMF H1
72990 BRISE II. Cy/FRG 1957; C; 1000; 80.22×5 (263.19×16.4); M; 11.5; ex DORA REITH 1968; ex DINKLAGE 1964; Lengthened & deepened 1968. Sister: **72991 LARYMNA** (Gr) ex GOTLAND 1975; ex NORDLANDER 1968; ex ANNE REITH 1968; ex ASSEN 1964 Similar (unlengthened): **72992 SEELAND** (Cy) ex GRETHE REITH 1969; ex BEROLINA 1964.

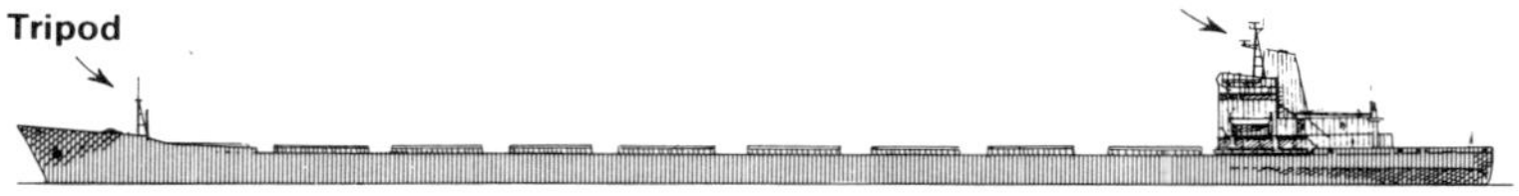

KMF H1
73000 MINERAL MARCHIENNE. Be/Be 1973; B; 35900; 234.8×13.27 (770.34×43.54); M; 16. Sister: **73001 MINERAL ALEGRIA** (Be) Possible sister: **73002 BELGIUM** (Be) ex MINERAL BELGIUM.

KMF H1
73010 HELEN. Be/Be 1978; B/Con; 24100; 199.02×11.05 (652.95×36.25); M; 16. Sister: **73011 DELORIS** (Be).

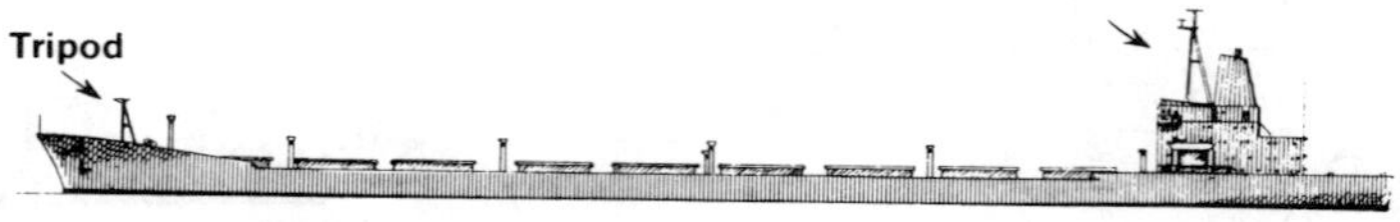

KMF H1

73020 MEISTERSINGER. FRG/FRG 1973; B; 28300; 215.53 × 12.55 (707.12 × 41.17); M; 15. Sisters (FRG flag): **73021 ADRIANO 73022 HANS SACHS 73023 TANNHAUSER** ex PARNASSOS 1980; ex TANNHAUSER 1975 Possibly similar: **73024 WIEN 73025 WERA JACOB.**

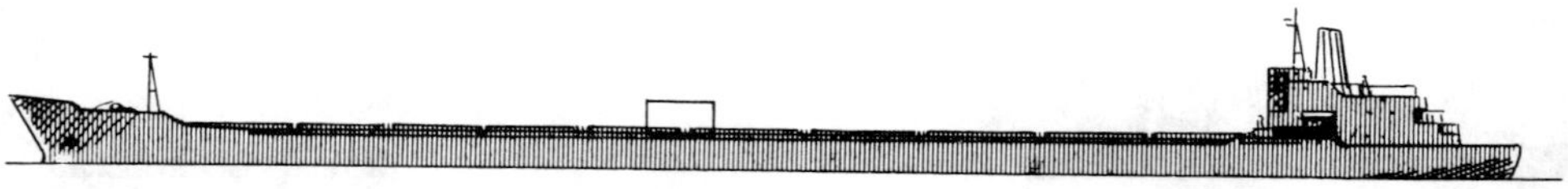

KMF H1

73030 ERMINIA PRIMA. It/It 1973; OO; 72700; 297.29 × 16.48 (975.36 × 54.07); T; 16.5. Probable sister: **73031 WISTERIA** (Ja) ex ERACLIDE; ex IGARA 1974.

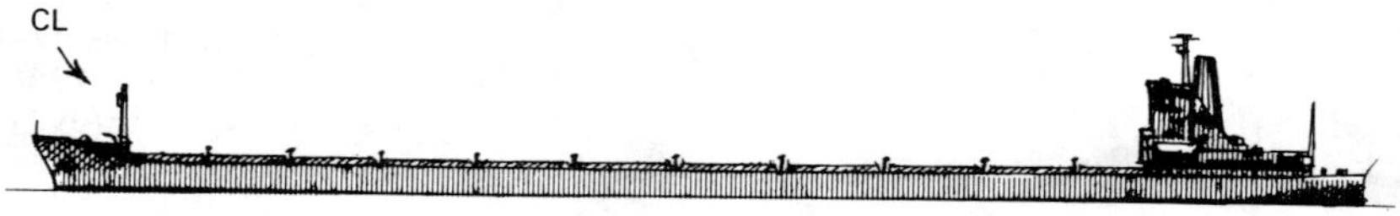

KMF H1

73040 IRON SIRIUS. Br/Ja 1967; B; 57300; 250.07 × 14.94 (820.44 × 49.02); M; 14.75; ex CHELSEA BRIDGE 1973; ex SIGSILVER 1971.

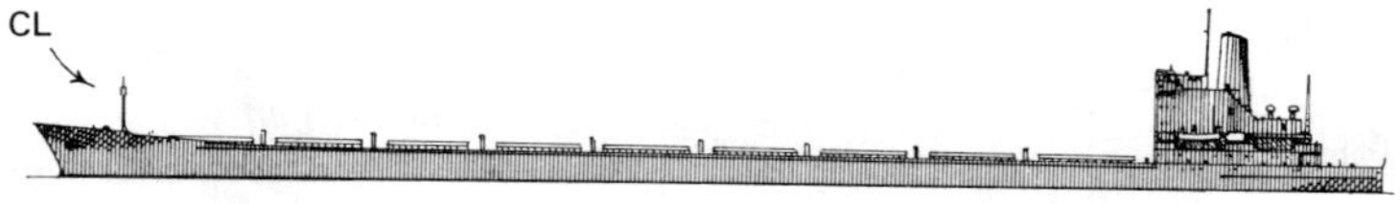

KMF H1

73050 REBECCA. Li/Ja 1967; B; 37600; 224.01 × 13.95 (734.94 × 45.77); M; 16; ex BERGE SIGWALDO 1972; ex SIGWALDO 1970.

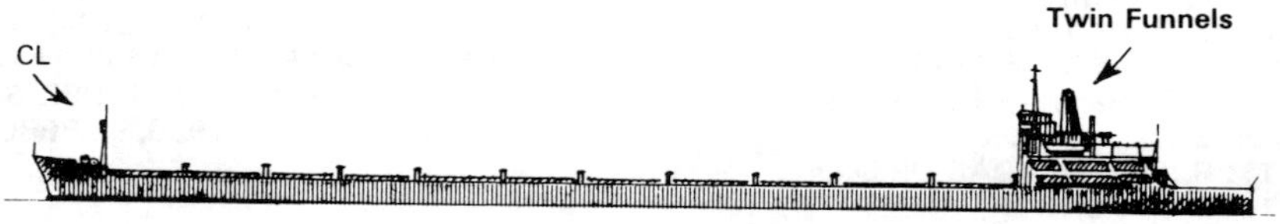

KMF H1

73060 THEOMANA. Gr/Ja 1965; B; 40500; 250.02 × 13.73 (820.28 × 45.05); M; 18; ex SUSANNE SCHULTE 1976; ex SIGTINA 1970.

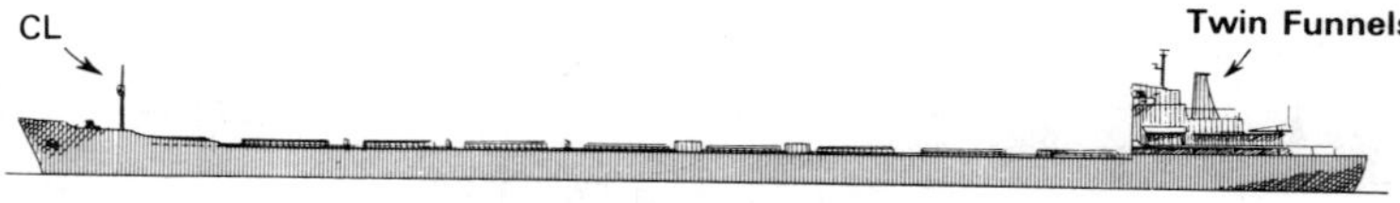

KMF H1

73070 NACIONAL MONCHIQUE. Pa/FRG 1967; B; 31000; 229.09 × 12.56 (751.61 × 41.21); M; 15.25; ex BRUSSELS 1980; ex BRUSSEL 1978.

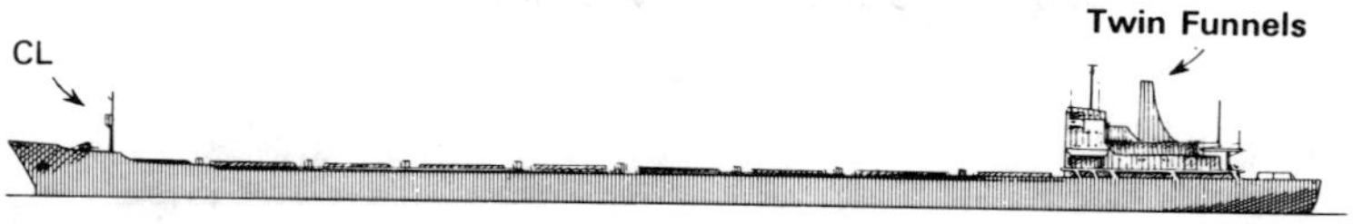

KMF H1

73080 DAMODAR GENERAL T.J. PARK. In/FRG 1974; B; 31300; 229.12 × 12.57 (751.71 × 41.24); M; 15.25. Sister: **73081 JALVALLABH** (In).

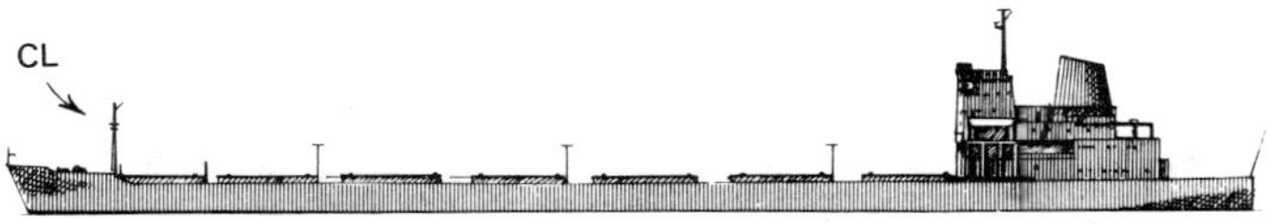

KMF H1

● **73090 GAUCHO MOREIRA.** Ar/De 1966; B; 27100; 212.22 × 11.82 (896 26 × 38.78); M; 15.75; ex LAURA 1978; ex LAURA MAERSK 1978. Similar: **73091 OLKAS** (Ar) ex ST. ASIMI 1978; ex LAUST MAERSK 1971.

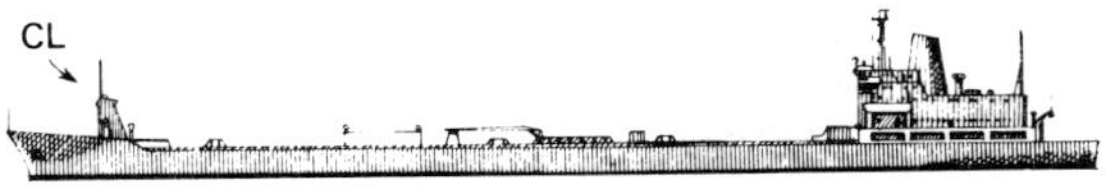

KMF H1

73100 FJORDSHELL. No/No 1973; Tk; 18600; 170.69 × 11.37 (560 × 37.3); M; 16.

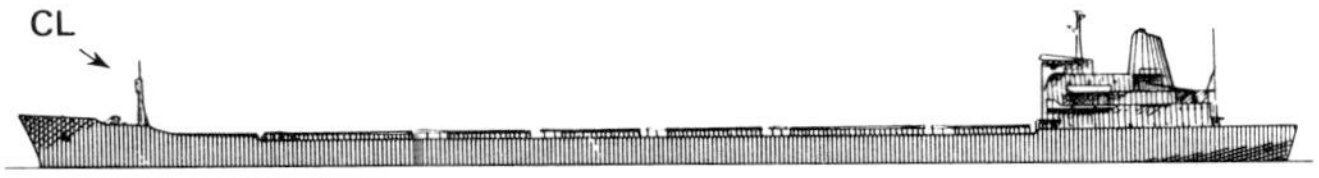

KMF H1

73110 ALEXANDER STAR. Pa/FRG 1967; B; 23700; 202.11 × 10.82 (663.09 × 35.5); M; 16; ex STEENDORP 1978; ex SOGNEFJELL 1975. Sister: **73111 OCEAN JADE** (Pa) ex OMEGA 1978; ex IRONGATE 1978; ex HOLTEFJELL 1975 Similar (converted to container ship): **73112 ALTAIR** (Gr) ex CAST OTTER 1980; ex DOVREFJELL 1977.

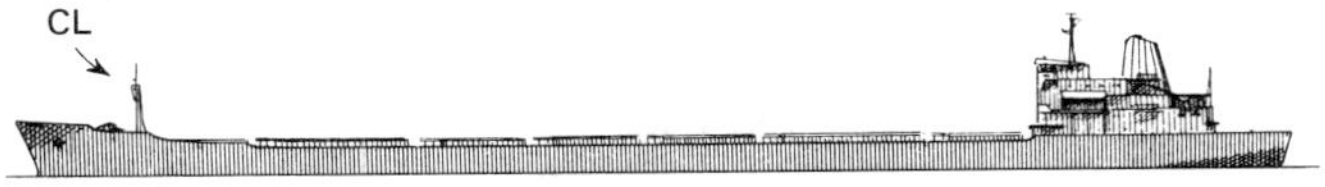

KMF H1

73120 IRENE PATERAS. Gr/FRG 1966; B; 23700; 202.11 × 10.82 (663.09 × 35.5); M; 16; ex NOREFJELL 1977. Similar: **73121 RIO NUNEZ** (Li) ex FILEFJELL 1976.

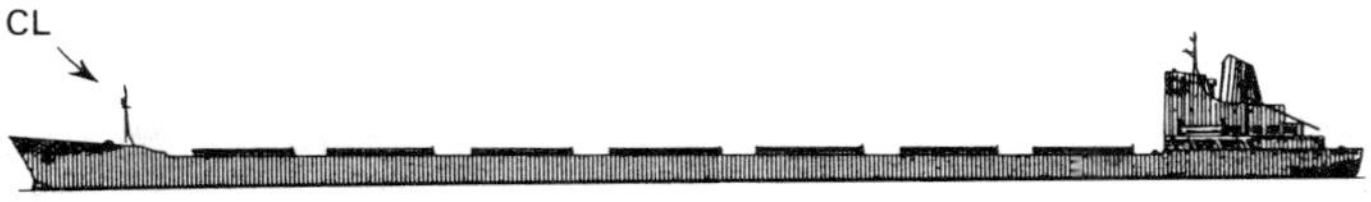

KMF H1

73130 CASTILLO DE LA MOTA. Sp/Sp 1971; B; 29600; 212.78 × 12.28 (698.1 × 40.29); M; 17; KP abreast funnel.

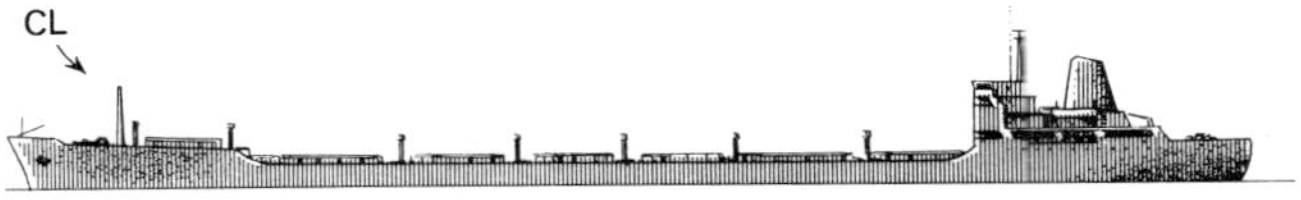

KMF H1

⋆**73140 ZIEMIA KIELECKA.** Pd/It 1969; B; 15700; 195.97 × 10.59 (642.95 × 34.74); M; 15. Sister: ⋆**73141 ZIEMIA KOSZALINSKA** (Pd).

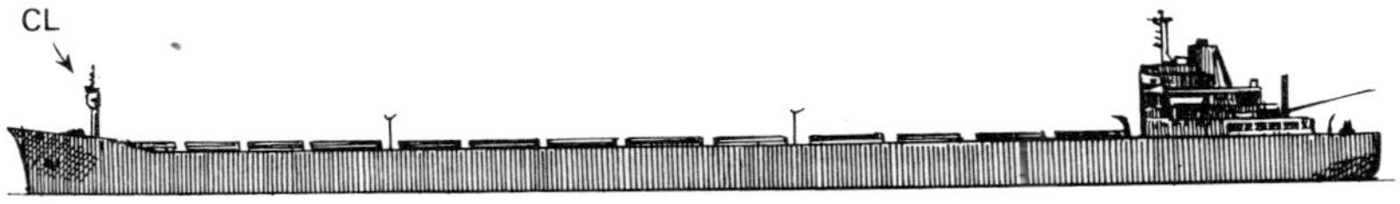

KMF H1

73150 AEOLOS C. Gr/Br 1966; B; 40800; 249.94 × — (820.01 × —); M; 15; ex YALTA; ex BERGE SIGLION 1973; ex SIGLION 1971.

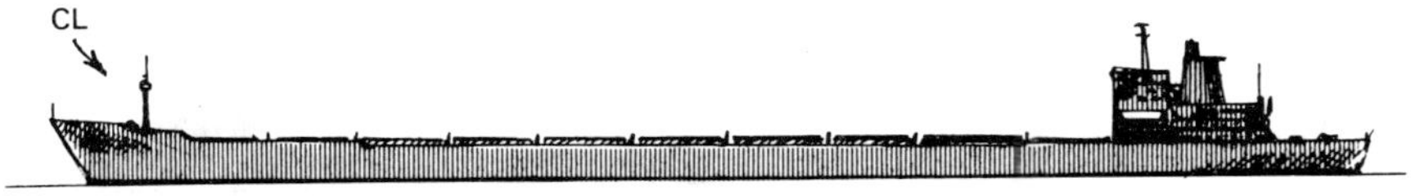

KMF H1

73160 AEGIR. FRG/FRG 1968; B; 45800; 254.9 × 13.75 (836.29 × 45.11); M; 16. Sister: **73161 BRAGE** (FRG).

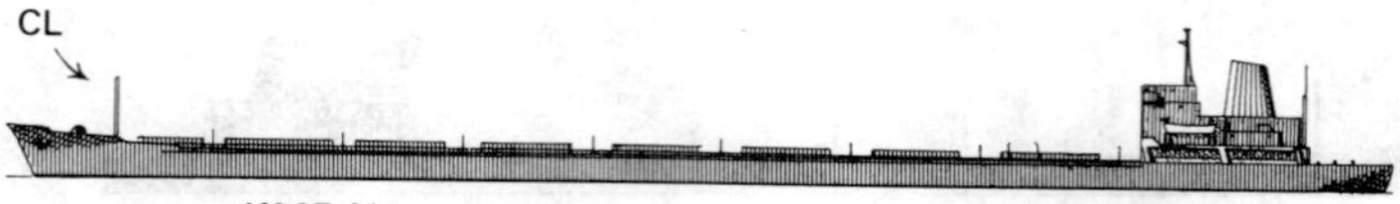

KMF H1

● **73170 AMBER PACIFIC.** Br/Br 1969; B; 31400; 220.99 × 12.62 (725.03 × 41.4); M; 15. Sister: **73171 GOLDEN ENTERPRISE** (Li) ex AUGUST PACIFIC.

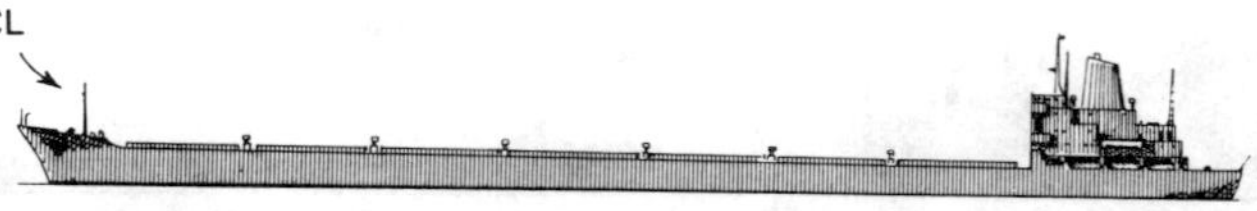

KMF H1

73180 SHOZEN MARU. Ja/Ja 1966; B; 24000; 193.4 × 10.59 (634.51 × 34.74); M; 15.

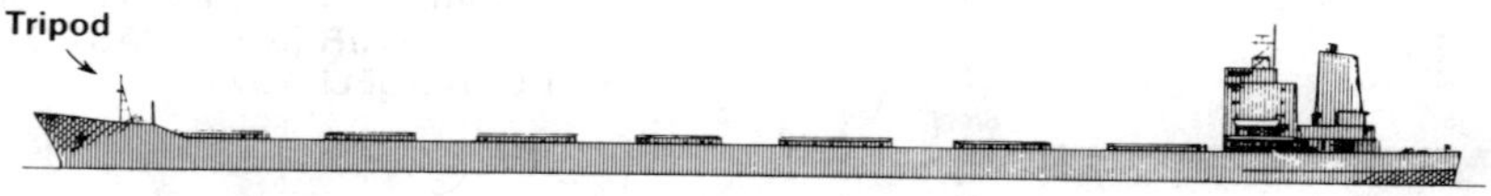

KMF H1

73190 EEKLO. Be/Be 1978; B; 38500; 242.02 × 13.83 (794.03 × 45.37); M; 16.

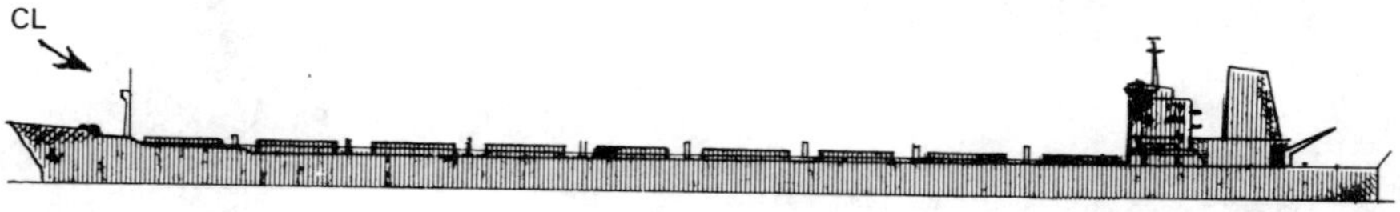

KMF H1

● **73200 YOU ARE MY SUNSHINE.** Li/FRG 1976; B; 64100; 272.32 × 16.08 (893.44 × 52.76); M; 16; ex FERNSEA 1981. Sisters: **73201 FARLAND** (Br) ex NAWALA 1980; ex NAWADA; ex FERNBAY **73202 ESTELLE J** (Pa) ex FERNHILL 1981 **73203 ENDEAVOR** (Li) ex SEALANE; ex FERNLANE 1978 **73204 PAN YOUNG** (Pa) ex SEALEAF 1980; ex FERNLEAF 1978.

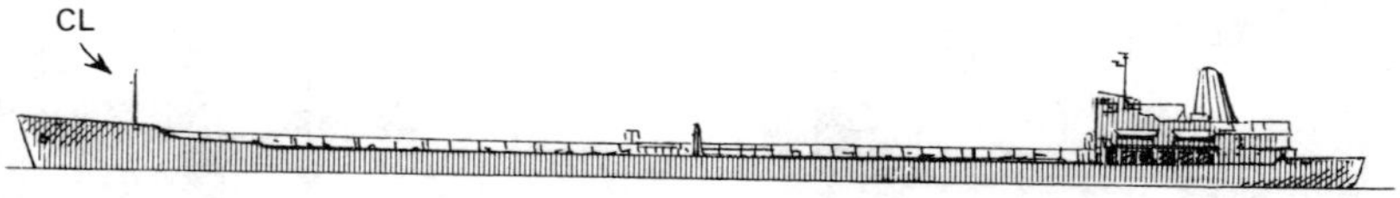

KMF H1

73210 BRITISH COMMERCE. Br/Br 1965; Tk; 37800; 248.65 × 12.91 (815.78 × 42.35); M; 15.5. Sisters: **73211 BRITISH COMMODORE** (Br) **73212 BRITISH CENTAUR** (Br) **73213 HALCYON MED** (Gr) ex BRITISH CAPTAIN 1976.

KMF H1

● **73220 NAVIOS PATRIOT.** Li/De 1967; B; 38600; 255.63 × 14.03 (838.68 × 46.03); M; 16.75; ex LEISE MAERSK 1976. Sister: **73221 NAVIOS PIONEER** (Li) ex LOUIS MAERSK 1976.

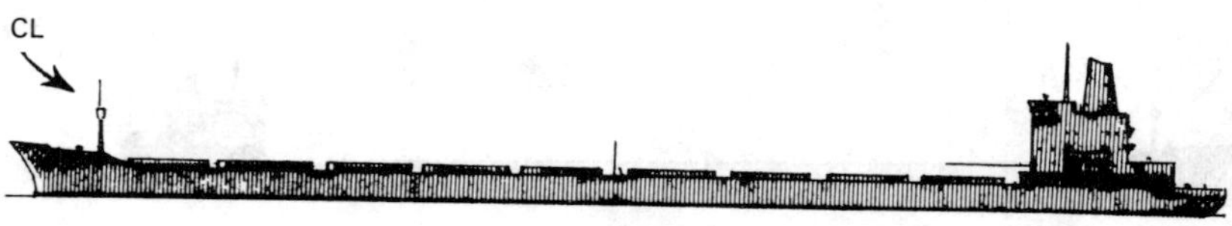

KMF H1

73230 KING GEORGE. Br/Sp 1975; B; 43700; 256.22 × 14.42 (840.62 × 47.31); M; 15.75. Sister: **73231 KING WILLIAM** (Br).

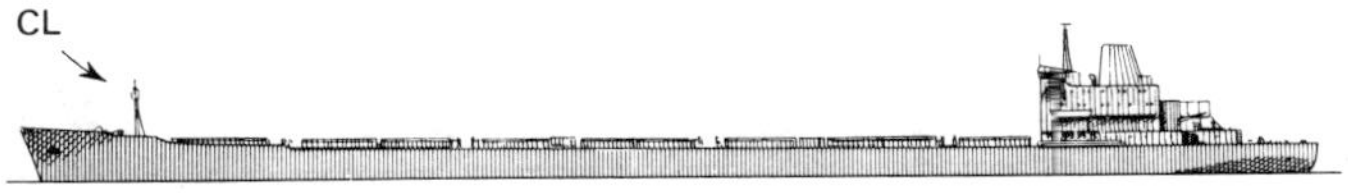

KMF H1
73240 DOCEDELTA. Bz/Bz 1974; B; 24600; 205.49 × 12.42 (674.18 × 40.75); M; 15.5.

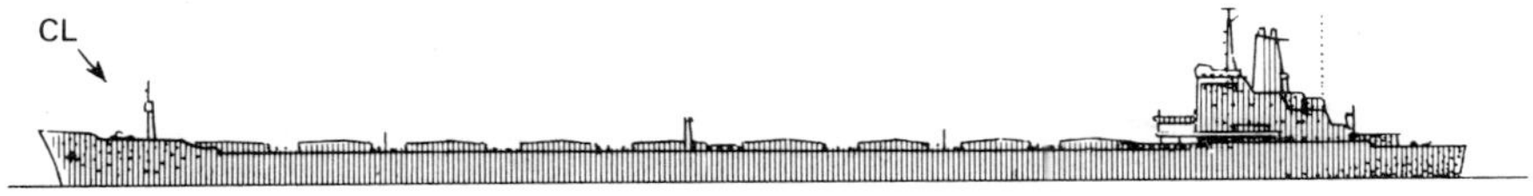

KMF H1
73250 SIBOEN. No/Sw 1968; OBO; 44300; 258.66 × 13.73 (848.62 × 45.04); M; 15.75. Sisters: **73251 SIBOTO** (Li) **73252 SIBOTRE** (No).

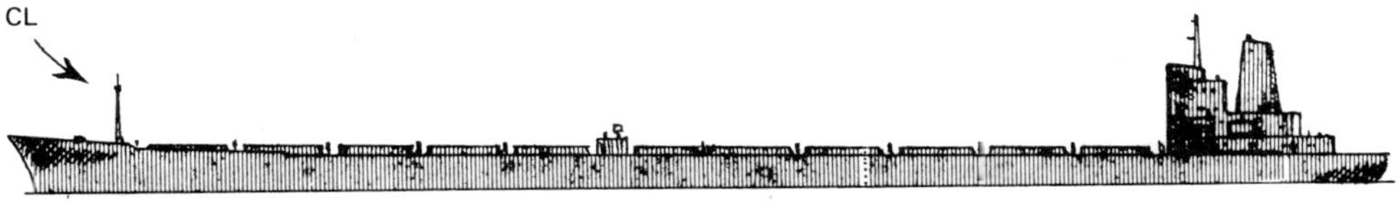

KMF H1
73260 WIDAR. FRG/FRG 1971; B; 79000; 303.16 × 16.53 (994.62 × 54.23); M; 16.25. Sisters (FRG flag): **73261 HERMOD 73262 THOR.**

KMF H1
73270 YAMATO. Li/Br 1968; B; 35400; 246.59 × 14.47 (809.02 × 47.47); M; 16; ex HAR ADDIR 1975. Sisters (Li flag): **73271 CHIHAYA** ex HAR SAGGI 1970 **73272 MISAKA** ex MOUNT KATHERINA 1974 **73273 MOUNT EDEN.**

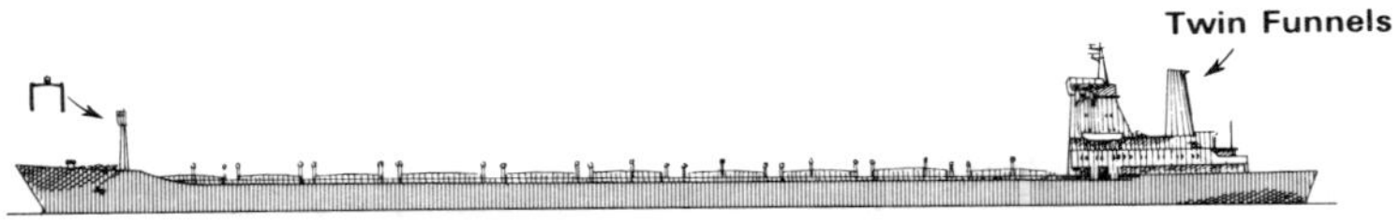

KMF H1
⋆73280 MANIFEST LIPCOWY. Pd/Pd 1970; B; 32800; 218.42 × 12.4 (716.6 × 40.68); M; 15.25; **'B-521'** type.

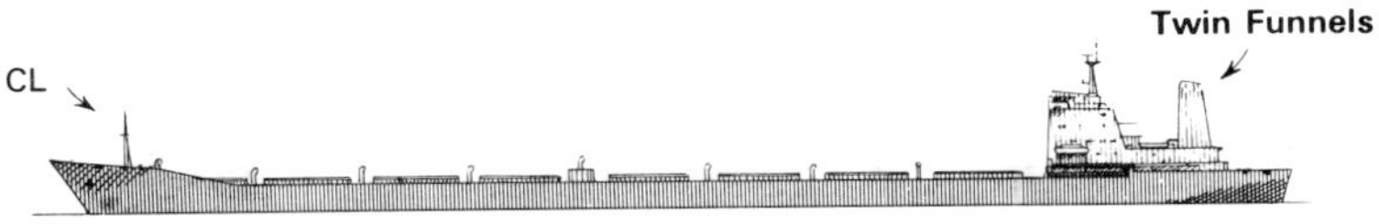

KMF H1
⋆73290 ZOYA KOSMODEMYANSKAYA. Ru/Ru 1973; B; 30100; 215.37 × 11.73 (706.59 × 38.48); M; 15.7. Sisters (Ru flag): **⋆73291 ALEKSANDR MATROSOV ⋆73292 ION SOLTYS ⋆73293 IZGUTTY AYTYKOV ⋆73294 PARFENTIY GRECHANYY ⋆73295 UNAN AVETISYAN** Similar (Bu flag): **⋆73296 BULGARIA ⋆73297 RODINA.**

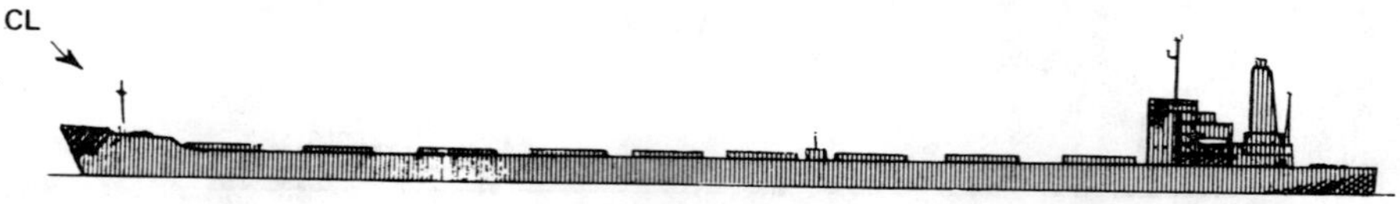

KMF H1

73310 PACIFIC JASMIN. Li/Ja 1976; B; 44700; 266.99 × 16.54 (875.95 × 54.27); M; 16.

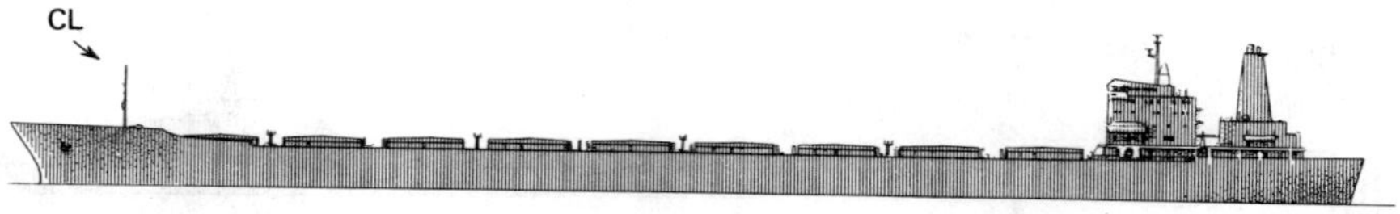

KMF H1

73320 STOVE TRADER. Sw/Fi 1976; B; 60000; 265.6 × 15.39 (871.39 × 50.49); M; 14.5; ex HORN CRUSADER.

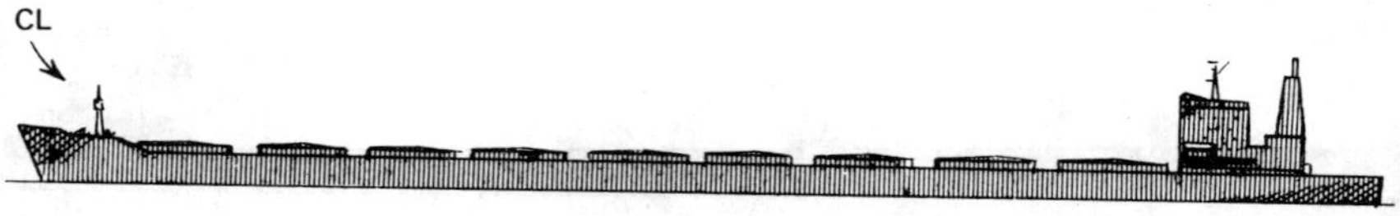

KMF H1

73330 POLYCRUSADER. No/Sw 1977; B; 63100; 253.65 × 15.91 (832.19 × 52.2); M; 16. Sister: **73331 ABBEY** (Br) ex ANDWI 1979.

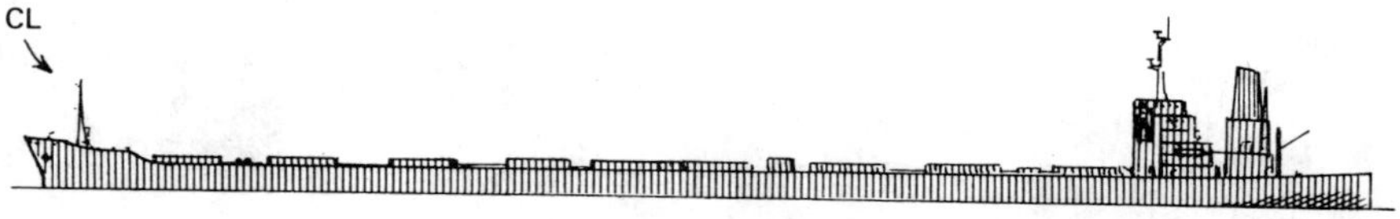

KMF H1

73340 AFRICA MARU. Ja/Ja 1977; O; 74900; 267.01 × 16.6 (876.02 × 54.46); M; 14.75. Possible sister: **73341 OCEANIA MARU** (Ja).

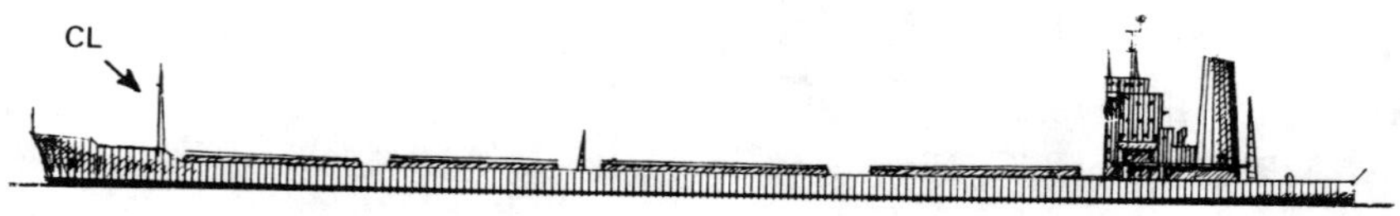

KMF H1

73350 KAKOGAWA MARU. Ja/Ja 1970; O; 43600; 250.02 × 13.31 (820.28 × 46.67); M; 15.25.

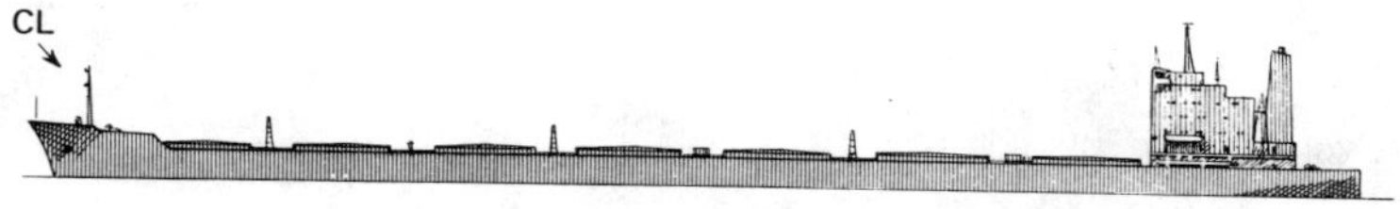

KMF H1

73360 IKAN BILIS. Sg/Ja 1977; B; 36200; 224.54 × 12.45 (736.68 × 40.85); M; 15.25. Sisters: **73361 EASTERN RIVER** (Li) ex PEARL CASTLE 1978 **73362 SALVATORE d'AMICO** (It) ex PACIFIC CROWN; ex PEARL CROWN 1978 **73363 SOUTH SKY** (Li) ex ENGLISH WASA 1978 **73364 ARIAKE** (Li) launched as PEARL CITADEL **73365 CO-OP GRAIN** (Li) launched as SONETTE **73366 NYON** (Sd) ex ITEL POLARIS; ex PEARL CORONA 1978 Possible sister: **73367 SOUTH RAINBOW** (Li) Similar: **73368 CO-OP GRAIN II** (Li) ex ARGO EXPLORER **73369 YAMAHIRO MARU** (Ja) ex ARGO ENTERPRISE.

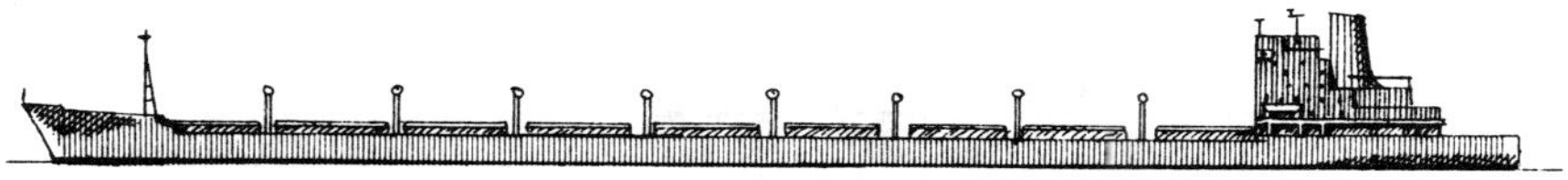

KMF H1

73380 ITALMARE. It/It 1974; B; 43800; 259.01 × 14.05 (849.77 × 46.1); M; 16. Sisters (It flag): **73381 MARE LIGURE 73382 MARE TIRRENO 73383 URSA MAJOR 73384 CAPRICORNUS 73385 DRACO 73386 DELPHINUS 73387 PERSEUS** (Pa flag): **73388 AMUNDSEN SEA** (Pa) ex SEXTUM 1979 Probable sister: **73389 LUPUS** (It).

● 73335

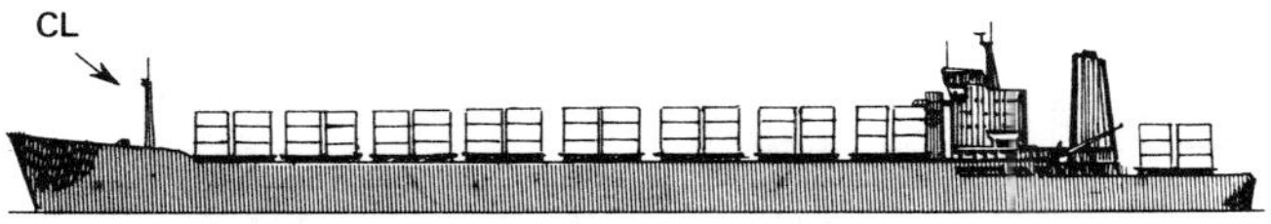

KMF H1

73400 CARIBIA EXPRESS. FRG/Pd 1976; Con; 27900; 203.99 × 10 (669.26 × 32.81); M; 22; **'B-463'** type. Sisters: **73401 CORDILLERA EXPRESS** (FRG) **73402 ALLEMANIA EXPRESS** (FRG) **73403 AMERICA EXPRESS** (FRG) **73404 ADVISER** (Br) **73405 ASTRONOMER** (Br) **73406 CARAIBE** (Fr) **73407 HOLLANDIA** (Ne) **73408 AUTHOR** (Br).

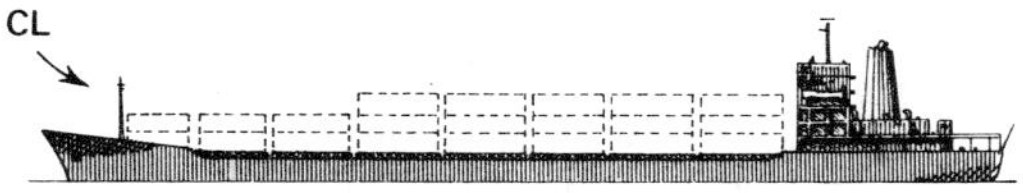

KMF H1

73420 BALTIMORE. US/US 1944/45/67/70; Con; 10900; 151.59 × 9.17 (497.34 × 30.09); T-E; —; Aft section ex ROANOKE 1970; ex ESSO ROANOKE 1956. Forward section ex BALTIMORE 1970; ex MARINE CARDINAL 1965. Converted from 'C4' type cargo & 'T-2' type tanker.

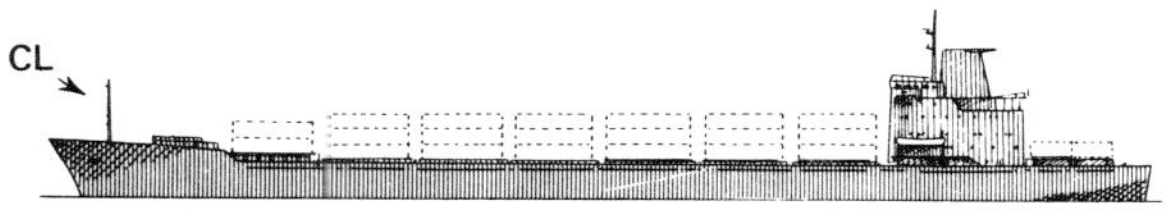

KMF H1

73430 PRINCESS JADE. Pa/FRG 1971; Con; 13100; 174.86 × 9.9 (573.69 × 32.48); M; 20; ex ACANDI; ex ATLANTICA GENOVA 1976; ex GRUENFELS 1971; lengthened 1974. Sister: **73431 RUHR EXPRESS** (Pa) ex GEYERFELS 1980; ex SEATRAIN BREMEN; ex SEATRAIN VALLEY FORGE 1979; ex ATLANTIC LIVORNO 1977; launched as GEYERFELS.

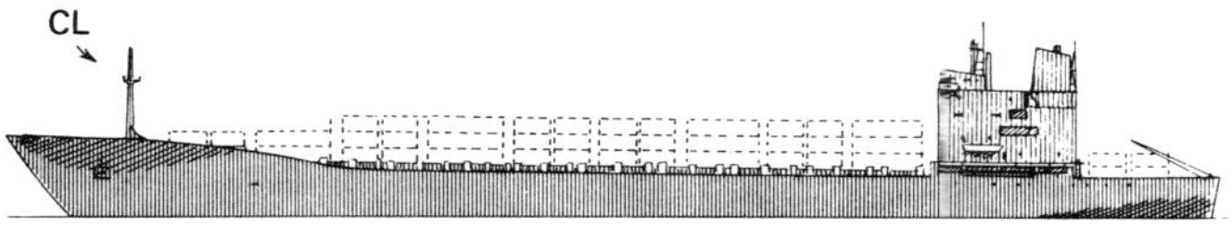

KMF H1

● **73440 KOREAN JUPITER.** Ko/Fr 1975; Con; 21300; 208.19 × 9.27 (683.04 × 30.4); T; 23.5; ex ORIENTAL FINANCIER 1978. Sisters: **73441 ORIENTAL EXECUTIVE** (Li) **73442 ORIENTAL RESEARCHER** (Li) **73443 ORIENTAL STATESMAN** (Li) **73444 CHEVALIER VALBELLE** (Fr) Similar (lengthened): **73445 CHEVALIER ROZE** (Fr) **73446 CHEVALIER PAUL** (Fr) **73447 MERCATOR** (Be).

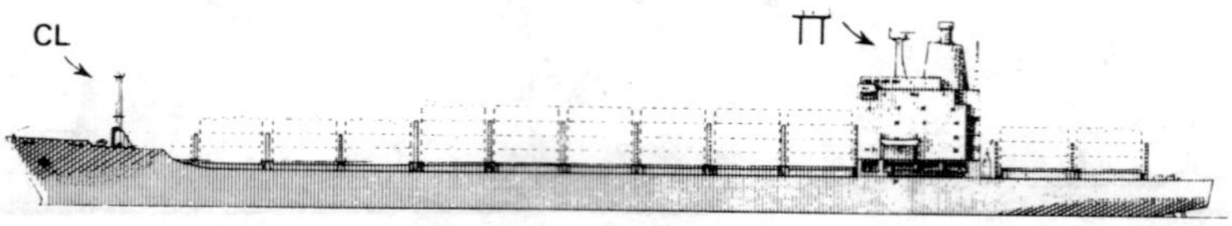

KMF H1

73460 SEA-LAND PATRIOT. US/Ja 1980; Con; 24900; 226.96 × 10 (744.62 × 32.81); M; 22. Sisters (US flag): **73461 SEA-LAND DEFENDER 73462 SEA-LAND DEVELOPER 73463 SEA-LAND EXPLORER 73464 SEA-LAND INDEPENDENCE 73465 SEA-LAND LIBERATOR 73466 SEA-LAND EXPRESS 73467 SEA-LAND VOYAGER 73468 SEA-LAND FREEDOM 73469 SEA-LAND MARINER 73470 SEA-LAND ENDURANCE 73471 SEA-LAND INNOVATOR.**

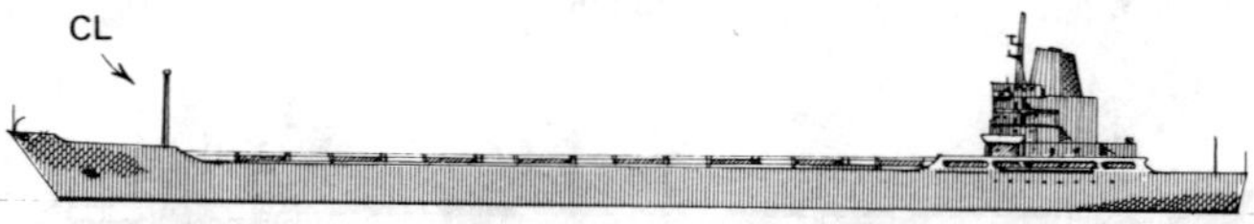

KMF H1

● **73480 ORIENTAL LEADER.** Li/Fr 1971; Con; 22600; 234.5 × 9.68 (769.36 × 31.76); M; 22.25; Lengthened 1976. Similar: **73481 ORIENTAL EDUCATOR** (Li) ex ATLANTIC PHOENIX 1975; Launched as ORIENTAL EDUCATOR **73482 ORIENTAL COMMANDER** (Li) ex PACIFIC PHOENIX 1975; Launched as ORIENTAL COMMANDER **73483 KOREAN LEADER** (Ko) ex ORIENTAL CHEVALIER 1975.

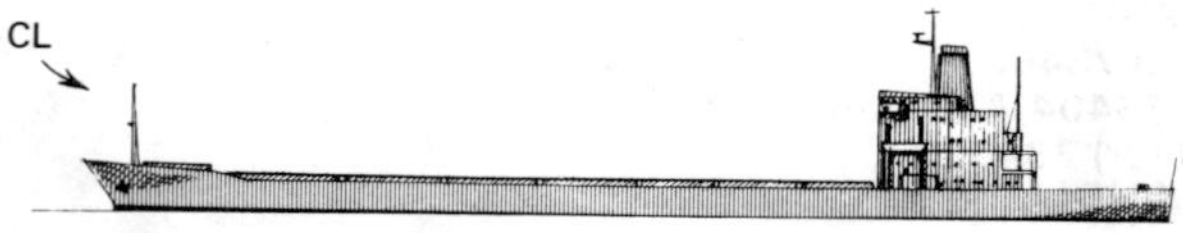

KMF H1

● **73490 SEATRAIN PRINCETON.** FRG/Ne 1972; Con; 13300; 172.52 × 7.2 (566 × 23.62); M; 21; ex PLUVIUS 1977. Sister: **73491 KOREAN LOADER** (Pa) ex SEATRAIN LEXINGTON 1980; ex PLUTOS 1977.

KMF H1

73500 OCEAN CONTAINER. Pa/Br 1968; Con; 12000; 161.47 × 8.26 (529.76 × 27.1); M; 19.5; ex MANCHESTER CHALLENGE 1979. Sisters (Pa flag): **73501 PACIFIC CONTAINER** ex MANCHESTER COURAGE 1979 (Br flag) **73502 MANCHESTER CONCORDE 73503 MANCHESTER CRUSADE 73504 MANCHESTER RENOWN** ex ASIAN RENOWN 1979; ex MANCHESTER RENOWN 1974 **73505 MANCHESTER REWARD** ex ASIAN REWARD 1979; ex MANCHESTER REWARD.

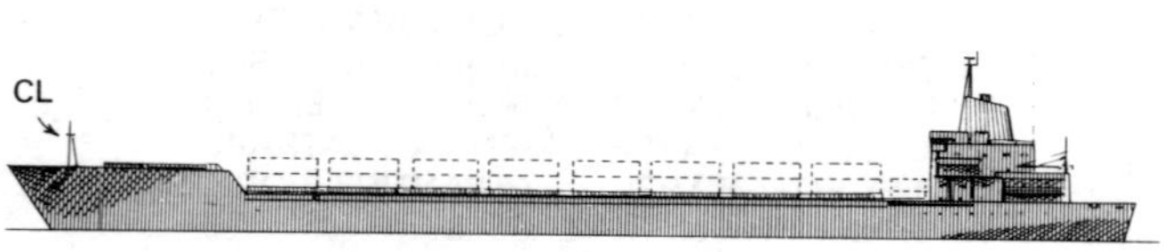

KMF H1

● **73510 WESER EXPRESS.** FRG/FRG 1968; Con; 17100; 201.12 × — (659.84 × —); M; 20; Lengthened 1973. Sister (FRG flag): **73511 MOSEL EXPRESS** Similar (taller funnels): **73512 ALSTER EXPRESS 73513 ELBE EXPRESS** Similar (unlengthened): **73514 MAIN EXPRESS** ex ORIENTAL IMPORTER 1976; ex MAIN EXPRESS 1973 **73515 RHEIN EXPRESS** ex ORIENTAL EXPORTER 1976; ex RHEIN EXPRESS 1973.

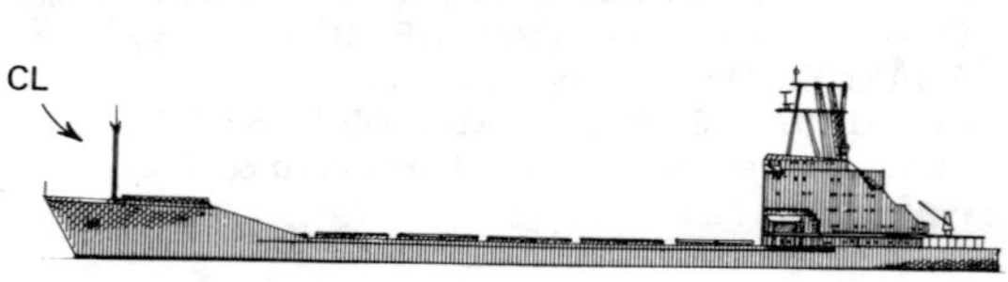

KMF H1

73520 COLUMBUS VICTORIA. FRG/FRG 1976; Con; 14200; 161.02 × 9.42 (528.28 × 30.91); M; 19. Sisters (FRG flag): **73521 COLUMBUS VIRGINIA 73522 COLUMBUS WELLINGTON.**

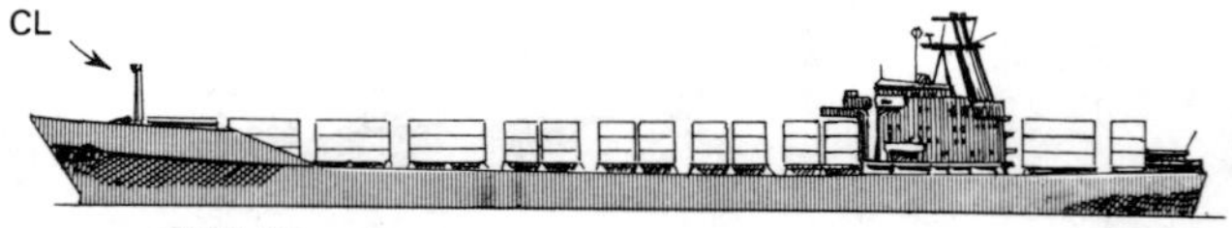

KMF H1

73530 COLUMBUS AUSTRALIA. FRG/FRG 1971; Con; 19100; 193.94 × 10.85 (636.29 × 35.6); T; 22. Sisters (FRG flag): **73531 COLUMBUS AMERICA 73532 COLUMBUS NEW ZEALAND.**

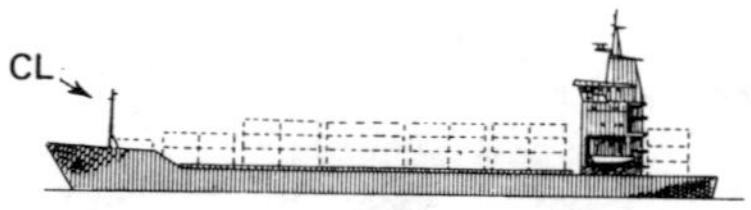

KMF H1

73540 METEOR II. Sg/Gr 1977; Con; 2000; 106.23 × 3 (348.52 × 9.84); M; —. Possible Sister: **73541 METEOR I** (Sg).

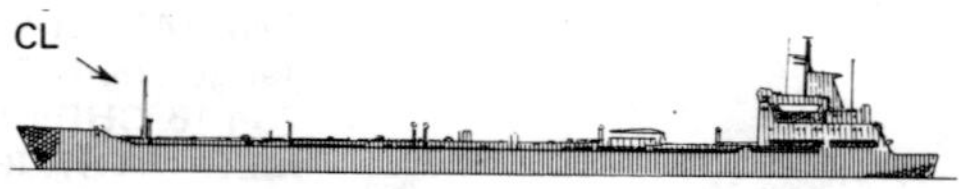

KMF H1

⋆**73550 TARNOBRZEG.** Pd/Sw 1973; Ch; 7000; 146.11 × 7.61 (479.36 × 24.97); M; 14.5. Sisters (Pd flag): ⋆**73551 PROFESOR K BOHDANOWICZ** ⋆**73552 SIARKOPOL** ⋆**73553 ZAGLEBIE SIARKOWE.**

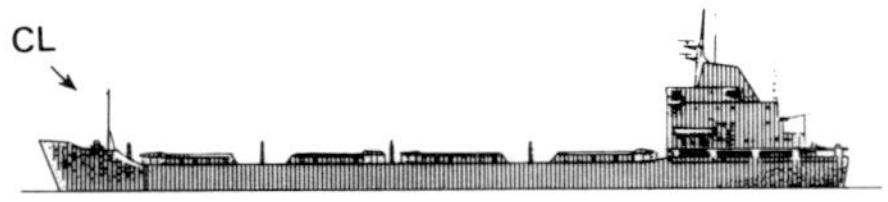

KMF H1
73560 GARRISON POINT. Br/Br 1977; C; 8000; 127.44×8.12 (418.11×26.64); M; 13.

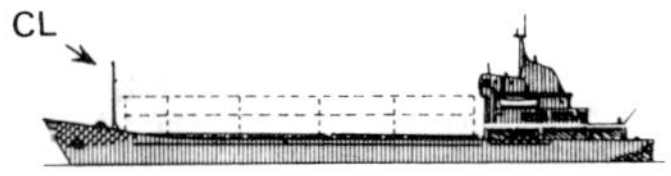

KMF H1
73570 DROR II. Is/Ne 1969; Con; 2900; 95.61×4 85 (313.68×15.91); M; 15; ex DEROR II; ex VILLE D'ORIENT; ex HOPE 1977; ex HOPE ISLE 1974. Sister: **73571 HEHALUZ II** (Is) ex SALLY; ex SALLY ISLE 1974.

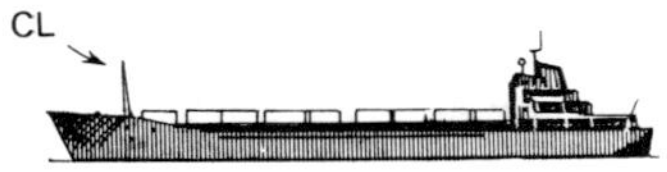

KMF H1
73580 RODRIGUES CABRILHO. Po/FRG 1969; Con; 2800; 95.59× — (313.62× —); M; 15; ex EAGLE 1972; ex SEETRANS 1972; ex ELLEN ISLE 1972. Similar: **73581 MAURICIO DE OLIVEIRA** (Po) ex CONTRANS 1972; ex WESER ISLE 1972.

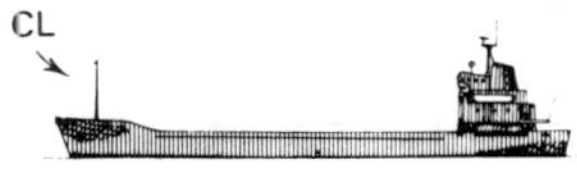

KMF H1
73590 KORMORAN I. Pa/FRG 1969; Con; —; 82.1×3.82 (269.36×12.53); M; 15; ex KORMORAN 1977; ex KORMORAN ISLE 1972.

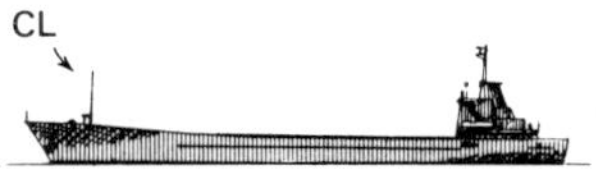

KMF H1
73600 EKENES. Ne/FRG 1968; C/Con; 1000; 86.75×4.55 (284.61×14.93); M; 14.5; ex THEANO; ex BARBEL BOLTEN 1973. Sister: **73601 HERMIA** (FRG) ex MARIETTA BOLTEN 1974.

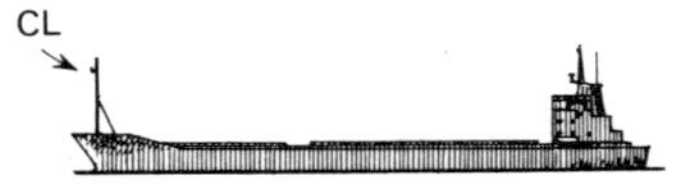

KMF H1
73610 COMMODORE ENTERPRISE. Br/Br 1977; C/Con; 1200; 95.18×4.87 (312.27×15.98); M; 13.

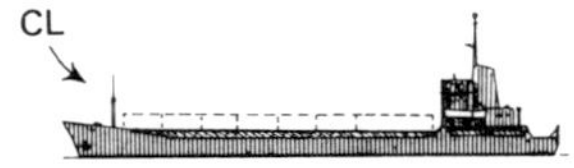

KMF H1
● **73620 CRAIGABOY.** FRG/Ne 1971; C/Con; 700; 76.82×4 (252.03×13.12); M; 13.5; ex RUBIN 1972. Sister: **73621 NASSAU I** (FRG) ex NASSAU 1978; ex KIELER FORDE 1972; ex CRAIGAVON 1972; Launched as KIELER FORDE.

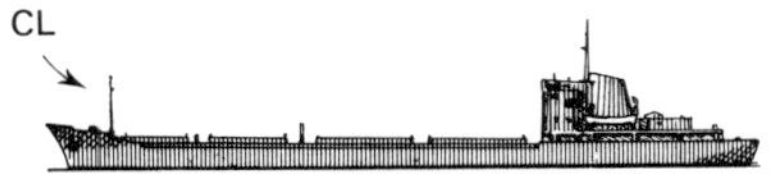

KMF H1
73630 DOLPHIN POINT. Br/Br 1965; C; 4800; 112.76×7.32 (369.95×24.02); M; 12; ex CORCHESTER 1977.

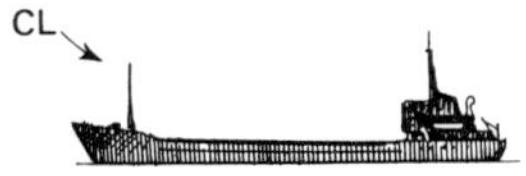

KMF H1
73640 ISABEL. Ne/Ne 1972; C/Con; 1400; 71.28×4.97 (233.86×16.31); M; 12. Probable Sisters (Ne flag): **73641 INGER 73642 IRINA.**

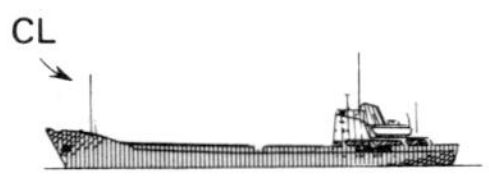

KMF H1
● **⋆73650 SKRZAT.** Pd/Pd 1961; Con; 500/1000; 65.84×3.7/— (216.01×12.14/—); M; 11.5; Converted from **'B-57'** type cargo ship. Sister: **⋆73651 SYRENKA** (Pd) Similar (lengthened): **⋆73652 WILA** (Pa) May be others of this class similarly lengthened - see KRASNAL etc.

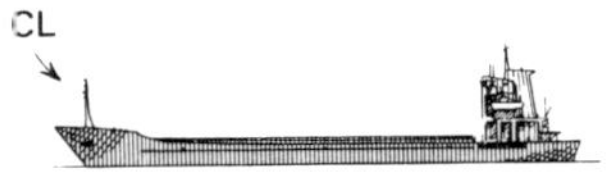

KMF H1
73660 VOLINE. FRG/FRG 1976; C/Con; 1000; 83.52×4.96 (274.02×16.27); M; 14.

KMF H1
73670 HEJO. FRG/FRG 1976; C/Con; 1000; 84.26×4.96 (276.44×16.27); M; 14. Sister: **73671 BOKELNBURG** (FRG) ex BOURGOGNE 1978; ex BOKELNBURG 1975 Similar (smaller): **73672 HUSUM** (FRG).

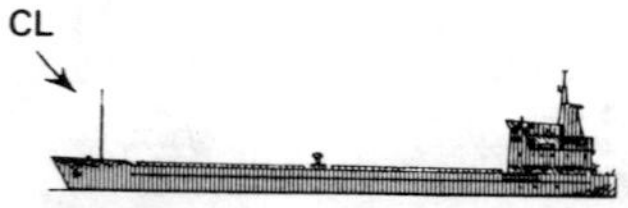

KMF H1
73680 SPECIALITY. Br/Br 1977; C; 1600; 89.67 × 6.04 (294.19 × 19.82); M; 12.5. Possible Sisters (may be geared like SINGULARITY - see MCMF): (Br flag): **73681 STABILITY 73682 JACK WHARTON.**

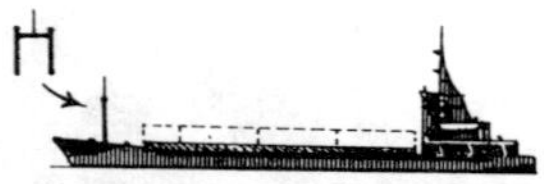

KMF H1
73700 BISCAYNE SEA. NA/Sp 1972; Con; 700; 74.71 × 4.24 (245.11 × 13.91); M; 12.5; ex KERRY 1978; ex ASTILUZU 201 1972. Sister: **73701 BISCAYNE SKY** (NA) ex SLIGO 1978; ex ASTILUZU 200 1971.

KMF H1
73720 REGINE. FRG/FRG 1976; Con; 1600; 93.53 × 6.08 (306.86 × 19.88); M; 14.5. Sisters: **73721 JAN** (FRG) **73722 ZIM NORTHLAND** (Pa) ex NORDIC 1980 **73723 WIELAND** (FRG) ex STRATHSPEY 1980; ex WIELAND 1978 **73724 TRITON I** (FRG) ex CONTSHIP THREE 1979; ex TRITON 1977 Similar: **73725 DIANA** (FRG).

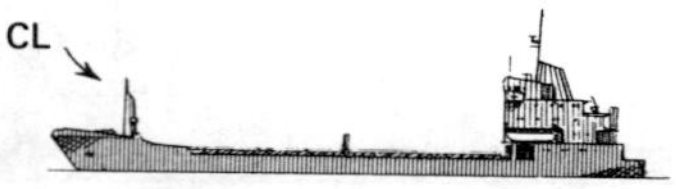

KMF H1
● **73690 TRIMAR GUY.** Pa/FRG 1971; C/Con; 1500; 94.01 × 5.6 (308.43 × 18.37); ex MARECLOUD 1980; ex SCANTRAIN; Launched as INO J.

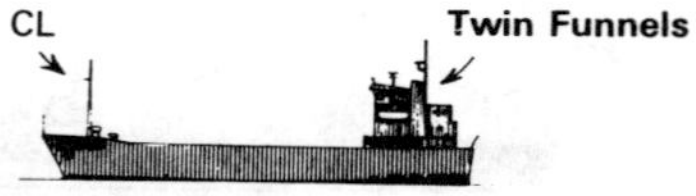

KMF H1
73710 HENRY STAHL. FRG/FRG 1973; RoC; 700; 79.41 × 4.24 (260.53 × 13.91); M; 12.5; Lengthened 1975. Stern door.

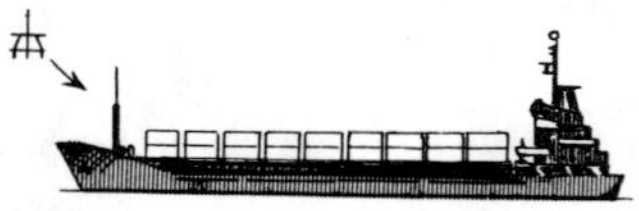

KMF H1
● **73730 SHAIKAH AL QURAICHI.** FRG/As 1972; C/Con; 1000; 90.4 × 4.64 (296.59 × 15.22); M; 14.5; ex ATLANTIC KING 1978; ex NAD KING 1975; ex KORNEUBURG 1972. Sisters (FRG flag): **73731 ATLANTIC EARL** ex MONARCH 1975; ex HAINBURG 1972 **73732 ATLANTIC COUNT** ex SALZBURG 1974 **73733 ATLANTIC BARON** ex KATHARINA 1974 **73734 ILE DE FRANCE** ex ROSWITHA 1978 **73735 STUART PRINCE** ex ATLANTIC DUKE 1977; ex JOACHIM 1975.

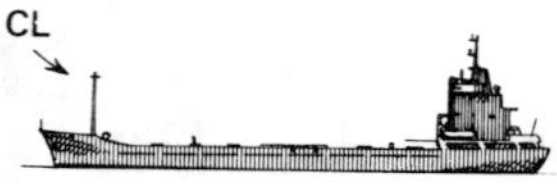

KMF H1
● **73740 RANE.** Ne/Ne 1970; Con; 1100; 81.64 × 5.03 (267.85 × 16.5); M; —. Sisters: **73741 DANIA** (De) ex RING (Spanish built) **73742 BRAGE** (Ne).

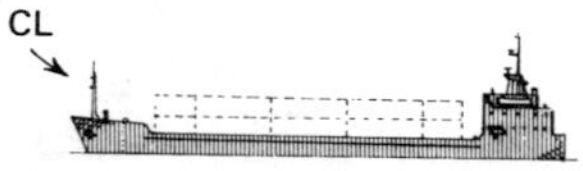

KMF H1
73760 CRAIGANTLET. Cy/F; 1972; Con; 800; 77.98 × 4.16 (255.84 × 13.65); M; 15. Sister: **73761 CRAIGWOOD** (Cy).

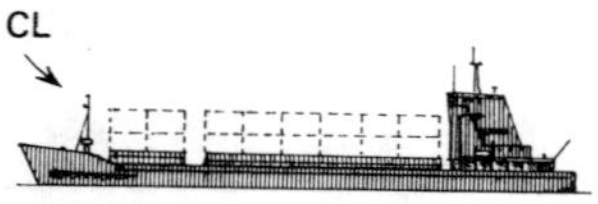

KMF H1
● **73790 NORDWIND.** FRG/FRG 1976; C/Con; 900; 87 × 4.73 (285.43 × 15.52); M; 13.25. Sisters (FRG flag): **73791 BRIGITTE GRAEBE 73792 LUBECA** Similar: **73793 SPAROS** ex INKA 1979 **73794 ALITA** Probably Similar: **73795 BARBARA-BRITT 73796 BARBARA-CHRIS 73797 LINDAUNIS.**

KMF H1
73750 LADY M.A. CROSBIE. Ca/Br 1966/77; Con; 4000; 118.73 × 6.5 (389.53 × 21.33); M; 14.75; ex CORTES 1978; ex BALTIC VANGUARD 1977; Converted from cargo & lengthened 1977.

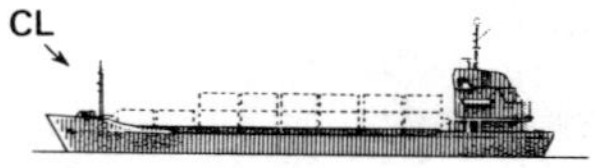

KMF H1
73770 BELL ROVER. Ih/Ja 1976; Con/C; 500/1600; 80.02 × 3.32/3.77 (262.53 × 10.89/12.37); M; 13.75. Sisters (Ih flag): **73771 BELL RACER 73772 BELL RAIDER 73773 BELL RANGER 73774 BELL REBEL 73775 BELL RULER 73776 BELL RENOWN 73777 BELL RELIANT 73778 BELL RESOLVE 73779 BELL RIVAL**

KMF H1
73810 GARZA. Pa/Ne 1969; C/Con; 1000; 70.57 × 3.52 (231.53 × 11.55); M; 12.5; ex GEESTDUIN 1976. Sister: **73811 CARAVELLE** (Pa) ex GEESTROOM 1976.

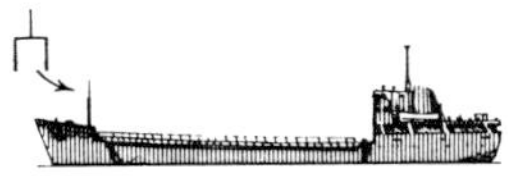

KMF H1
73820 PIETER WINSEMIUS. Ne/Ne 1959; HL/C; 700; 73.87 × 3.72 (242.36 × 12.2); M; 11.5; Lengthened 1961. Widened & converted from cargo 1968. Sister: **73821 ANK WINSEMIUS** (Ne).

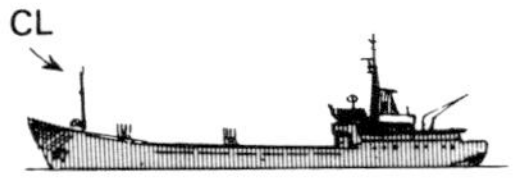

KMF H1
73830 BASALT. FRG/Hu 1970; C; 1500; 76.41 × 5.31 (250.69 × 17.42); M; 11.5; Lengthened 1975. Sisters: **73831 DIORIT** (FRG) **73832 DIABAS** (FRG) **73833 GABBRO** (FRG) **73834 GRANIT** (Sg) Similar (fitted with satellite communication dome): **73835 DOLOMIT** (FRG).

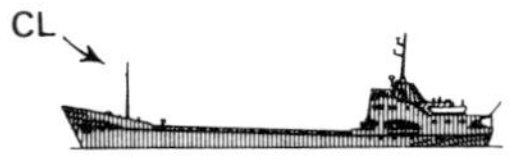

KMF H1
***73840 ANDRZWJ BOROWY.** Pd/Pd 1963; Con; 1200; 69.04 × 4.45 (226.51 × 14.6); M; 11.5; **'B-458'** type. Converted from cargo. May be others of this type similarly converted.

KMF H1
73850 ANTXON MARI. Sp/Sp 1976; C; 700; 63.91 × 3.96 (209.68 × 12.99); M; 12.

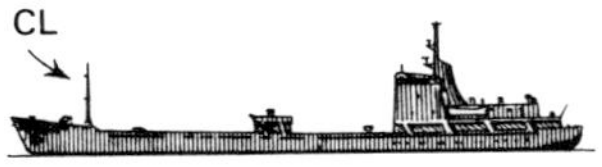

KMF H1
73860 MALARVIK. Sw/F; 1965; Cem; 2200; 90.33 × 5.77 (296.36 × 18.93); M; —. Sister: **73861 VASTANVIK** (Sw).

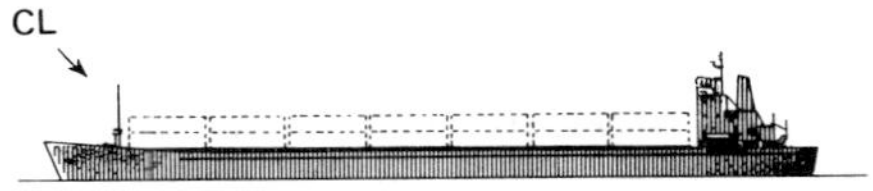

KMF H1
73870 ATLANTIC SWAN. Sg/Ne 1969; Con; 1400; 121.54 × 3.8 (398.75 × 12.47); M; 14.5; ex ASD BLACK SWAN 1978; ex ATLANTIC SWAN 1976; Lengthened 1976.

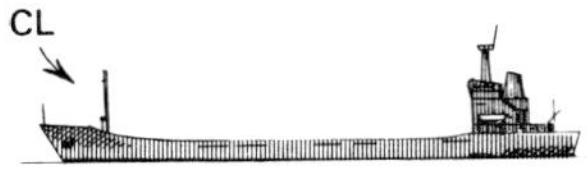

KMF H1
● **73880 CITY OF MILAN.** Br/Ne 1969; Con; 1600; 85.32 × 4.71 (279.92 × 15.45); M; 16; ex MINHO 1974; **'HUSTLER'** class. Sisters: **73881 CAPE HUSTLER** (Br) ex CITY OF LISBON 1980; ex TAGUS 1974 **73882 ECO GUADIANA** (Pa) ex CITY OF OPORTO 1980; ex TORMES 1974 **73883 CITY OF FLORENCE** (Br) ex TUA 1974 **73884 CITY OF GENOA** (Br) ex TAMEGA 1974 **73885 ATLANTIC CLIPPER** (Br) ex TIBER 1979; ex CITY OF NAPLES 1979; ex TIBER 1974 **73886 ATLANTIC RESOLUTE** (Br) ex CITY OF VENICE 1980; ex MONDEGO 1974 **73887 HUSTLER CHEYENNE** (Br) ex ISBRIT 1976; ex ENGLAND 1974 **73888 ATLANTIC INTREPID** (Br) ex TRONTO 1980; ex CITY OF LA SPEZIA; ex TRONTO 1974.

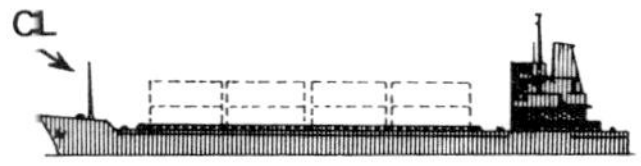

KMF H1
● **73900 SAGITTA.** FRG/FRG 1973; C/Con; 1000; 93.2 × 4.88 (305.77 × 16.01); M; 15. Sisters (FRG flag): **73901 WIKING 73902 ELBE 73903 WESER** Similar: **73904 MANCHESTER FAITH** ex FRANCOP 1978; ex MANCHESTER FAITH 1977; ex FRANCOP 1976.

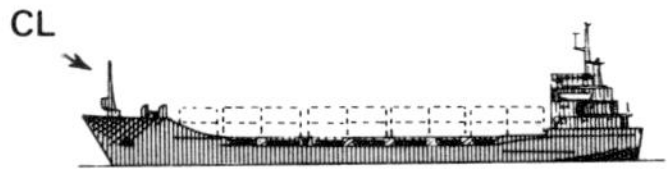

KMF H1
73910 THUNAR. FRG/FRG 1979; Con; 1000; 88.65 × 4.88 (290.85 × 16.01); M; —; **'Sietas type 81'.** Sisters (FRG flag): **73911 WOTAN 73912 NORDSEE 73913 ATLANTIS.**

KMF H1
73920 OUEZZANE. Mo/FRG 1976; C/Con; 1600; 93.38 × 5.56 (307.02 × 18.24); M; 14.5. Sisters (Mo flag): **73921 OUARZAZATE 73922 OUIRGANE.**

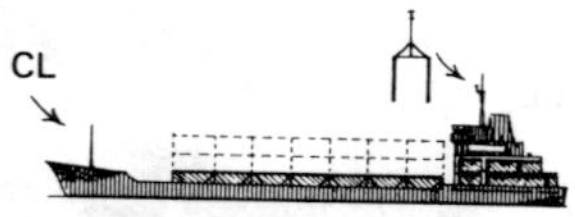

KMF H1
73940 VANTAGE. FRG/FRG 1974; C/Con; 1000; 81.41 × 4.91 (267.09 × 16.11); M; 13.5; ex BELL VANTAGE 1978. Similar (FRG flag): **73941 OSTECLIPPER** ex NIC CLIPPER 1979; ex OSTECLIPPER 1978 **73942 CANOPUS 73943 ODIN 73944 NIC TRADER** ex OSTELAND 1978; ex THUNAR 1976; ex OSTELAND 1974 **73945 NAVIGIA** ex DONAR 1979 **73946 PATRIA** ex AMERICAN COMANCHE 1978 **73947 AMERICAN CHEROKEE;** Launched as NAUTILUS **73948 BRITTA I** ex AMERICAN CHEYENNE 1979; ex BRITT 1977 **73949 BOURGOGNE** ex KOMET I 1978; ex SARACEN PRINCE 1976; Launched as KOMET **73950 YANKEE CLIPPER** ex LAPPLAND 1980; ex MANCHESTER FALCON 1976; Launched as LAPPLAND **73951 ANNA BECKER** ex KILLARNEY 1980; ex ANNA BECKER 1977; ex SCOL ENTERPRISE 1977; Launched as ANNA BECKER **73952 AROS OLYMPIC** ex UTE WULFF 1980; ex GALWAY 1980; ex UTTE WULFF 1977; ex AMERICAN APACHE 1977; Launched as UTTE WULFF **73953 OSTERHEIDE 73954 JAN KARS 73955 FALKENSTEIN 73956 PASSAT 73957 SEEVETAL 73958 ORION 73959 IBESCA PORTUGAL;** Launched as NIEDERMEHNEN **73960 PARNASS** (Br flag): **73961 MELTON CHALLENGER** Similar (large funnel - Fi flag): **73962 TAJAMI** ex RIE BRES 1980.

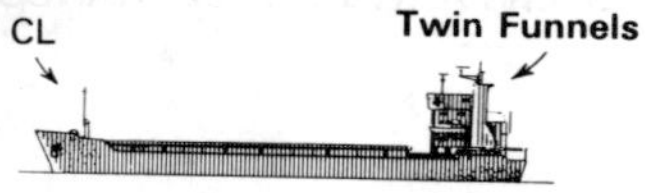

KMF H1
● **74000 GERMA KARMA.** No/Sg 1979; C/B/Con; 1600/3300; 81 × 5.75/— (265.75 × 18.86/—); M; 13.5; There are probably others in this class with this sequence—see GERMA TARA etc under KCMF.

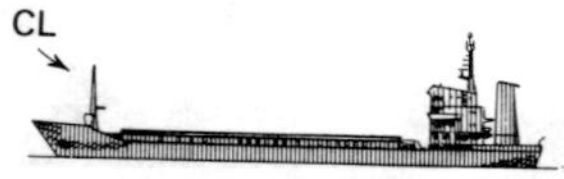

KMF H1
74010 DELTA. FRG/FRG 1978; Con; 1000; 82.02 × 4.9 (269.09 × 16.08); M;

● 74015

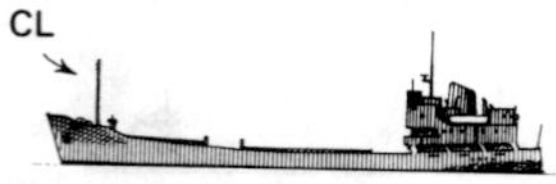

KMF H1
73930 NEWFOUNDLAND CONTAINER. Ca/Br 1962/72; Con; 1500; 78.64 × 5.04 (258.01 × 16.54); M; 13; ex ROE DEER 1977; ex NORBRAE 1974; ex BUFFALO 1972; Converted from cargo 1972. Sister: **73931 FLAMINGO** (Sn) ex NORBANK 1980; ex BISON 1971.

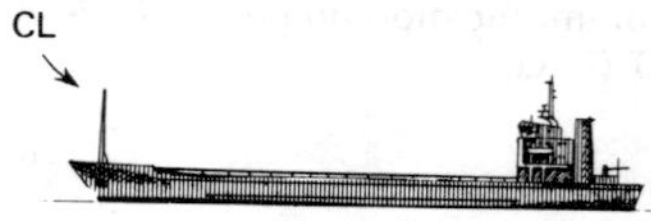

KMF H1
73970 KATHE JOHANNA. FRG/FRG 1976; C/Con; 1600; 100.28 × 5.56 (329 × 18.24); M; 14; ex MANCHESTER TRADER 1979; ex KATHE JOHANNA 1978.

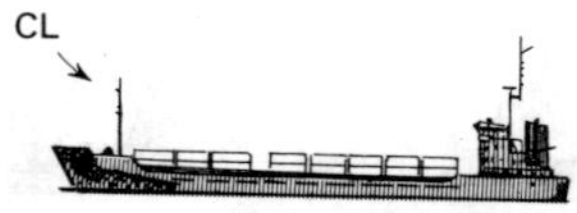

KMF H1
73980 SERTAN. Ne/Ne 1978; Con/C; 1300; 81.84 × 5.65 (268.5 × 18.54); M; 12.75. Sister: **73981 MIDSLAND** (Ne).

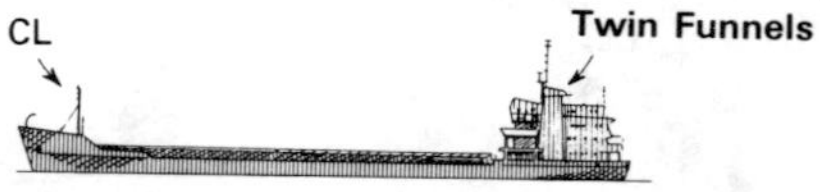

KMF H1
73990 CHRISTIANE SCHULTE. Cy/Ne 1972; C; 3900; 96.68 × 7.11 (317.19 × 23.33); M; 13. Similar (some may have travelling crane - see VILLIERS): **73991 PHILEMON** (Cy) ex CARLOTA BOLTEN 1973 **73992 ANGELICA SCHULTE** (Cy) ex ESTHER BOLTEN 1974 **73993 ARTEMIS** (Gr) ex SUSAN MILLER **73994 VENTUS** (Cy) ex ERIKA FISSER **73995 NEGAM** (Sg) ex OTTO PORR 1978.

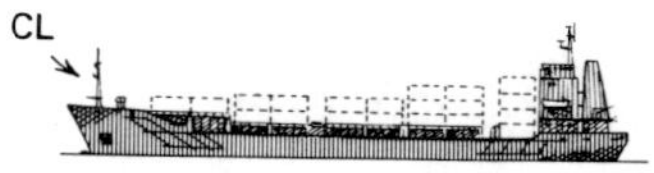

KMF H1
74020 DONAR. FRG/FRG 1979; Con; 1000; 89 × 4.95 (292 × 16.24); M; 13 (max); Sisters (FRG flag): **74021 THIASSI; 74022 ALGERIA;** ex HALDEM 1980; **74023 ESPANA;** ex STEMWEDE 1980; Possible sister (may have deck crane): **74024 LUSITANIA;** ex WESTERFELDE 1980.

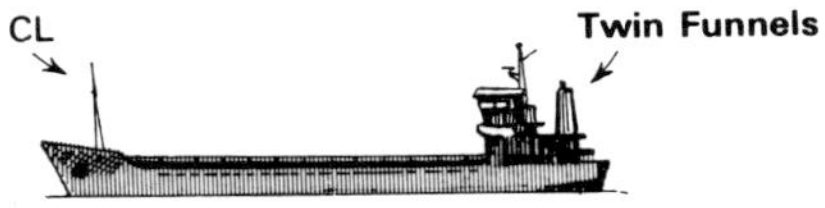

KMF H1
● **74030 ANNIKA.** FRG/Ne 1974; C; 1000; 87.89 × 4.85 (288.35 × 15.91); M; 14.

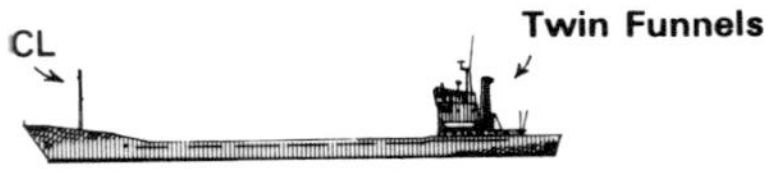

KMF H1
74040 ALFA. Gr/Ne 1971; Con; 1600; 85.93 × 4.9 (281.92 × 16.08); M; 16; ex SOLDIER PRINCE; ex SAILOR PRINCE 1977; ex PENNINE PRINCE 1972.

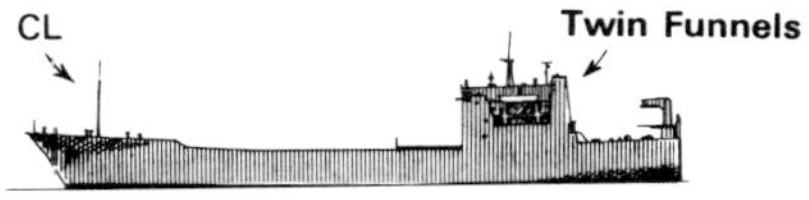

KMF H1
● **74050 ARISTEOS.** Gr/Br 1971; RoC; 3700; 117.48 × 6.32 (385.43 × 20.73); TSM; 17.5; ex CARIBBEAN PROGRESS; ex IRANIAN PROGRESS 1976; ex CARIBBEAN PROGRESS 1975; May be spelt **ARISTAIOS;** Stern door; Sisters (FRG built): **74051 ARISTEFS** (Gr); ex CARIBBEAN ENDEAVOUR.

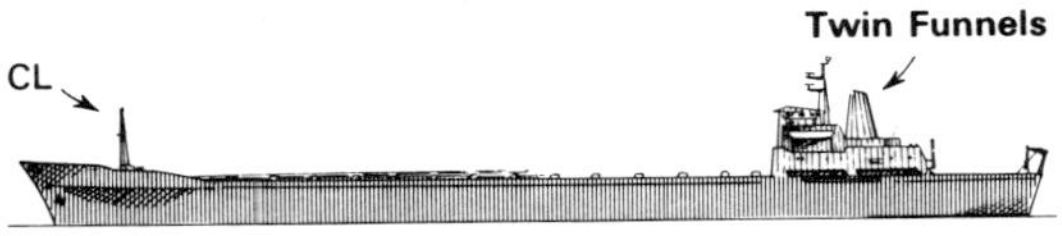

KMF H1
74060 ATLANTIC PREMIER. Sw/Fi 1972; RoC/Con; 11000; 162.36 × 7.22 (532.68 × 23.69); TSM; 17; ex MONT ROYAL 1978; Stern door/ramp; Lengthened and converted 1978; Sister: **74061 ATLANTIC PRELUDE** (Sw); ex MONTMORENCY 1978.

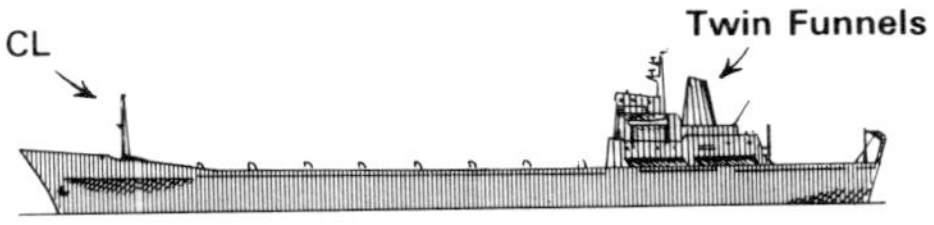

KMF H1
74070 BORE MOON. Fi/Fi 1972; RoC; 4200; 135.01 × 6.65 (442.95 × 21.82); TSM; 17.5; ex MONT LOUIS 1979; Stern door/ramp.

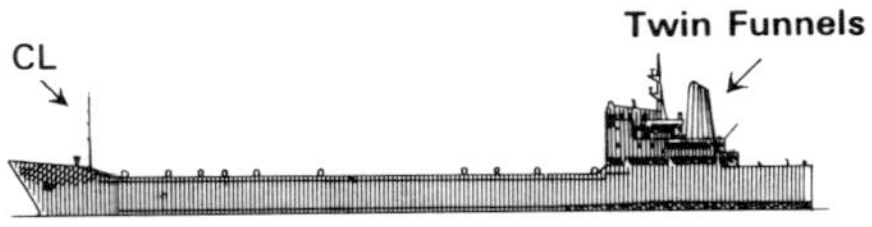

KMF H1
74080 OCEAN LINK. Sw/Sp 1972; RoC; 3400; 127.23 × 6.4 (417.42 × 21); TSM; 17.5; ex FRAGARIA 1980; Lengthened 1975; Side and stern doors; Sister: **74081 FOREST LINK** (Sw); ex STELLARIA 1980.

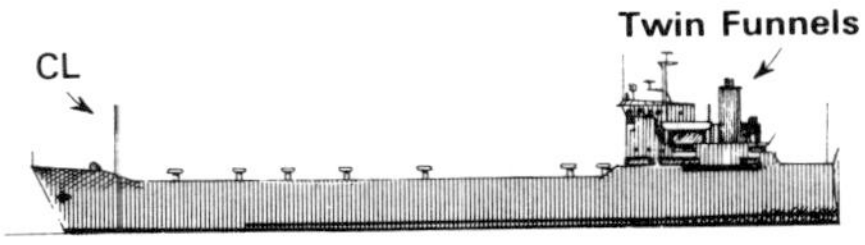

KMF H1
74090 MANAURE VI. Ve/Ne 1972; RoC; 3400; 127.26 × 6.4 (417.52 × 21); TSM; 17.5; ex MERZARIO SAUDIA 1978; ex IRANIAN PROSPERITY 1976; ex NIKE 1975; launched as CORA; Stern and side doors; Sister: **74091 MANAURE V** (Ve); ex KRATOS 1978.

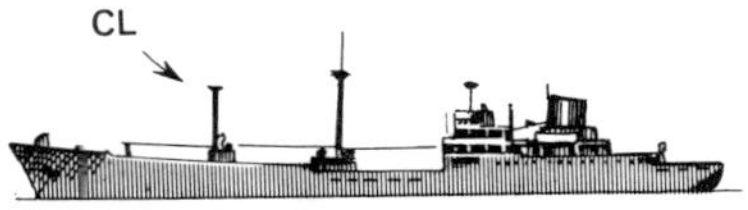

KMF H1
74100 REEFER STAR. Si/FRG 1954; R; 3500; 114.99 × 6.57 (377.26 × 21.56); M; 15; ex NIKOLAOS 1980; ex KETTY 1979; ex ARAGON 1973.

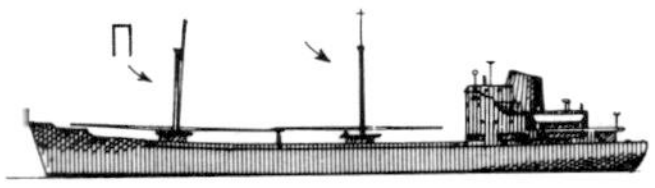

KMF H1
74110 PARTHENON. Gr/Fi 1956; C; 2000; 97.85 × 5.82 (321.03 × 19.09); M; 13; ex RED SKY 1977; ex FINNKRAFT 1973.

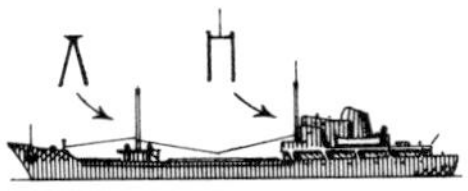

KMF H1
74120 STRAY DOG. Pa/Ne 1960; C; 500; 70.36 × 3.71 (230.84 × 12.17); M; 11.5; ex ROYKSUND 1977; ex KARMSUND 1972; ex KONG SIGURD 1969; ex BORE IX 1965; ex KUURTANES 1962.

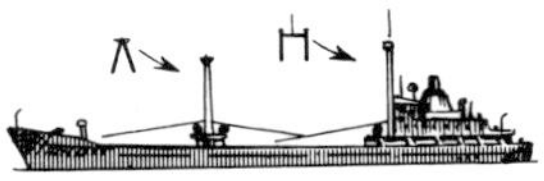

KMF H1
● ⋆**74130 TITOV VELES.** Ys/Sp 1962; C; 1500/2300; 85.45 × 5.28/6.02 (280.35 × 17.32/19.75); M; 12.5; ex TERICA 1966.

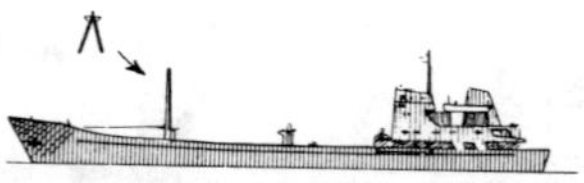

KMF H1

● ⋆**74140 NALECZOW.** Pd/Rm 1970; C; 1200/200; 85.88 × 4.5/5.1 (281.76 × 14.76/73); M; 14; Others of this class may be similarly modified—See BUSKO ZDROJ; Sisters (Pd flag): ⋆**74141 SWINOUJSIE;** ⋆**74142 SWIERADOW ZDROJ.**

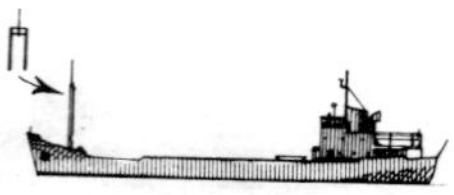

KMF H12

74150 ISVANIA. Pa/De 1938; C; 1000; 65.94 × 4.38 (216.3 × 14.37); M; 10; ex SVANO 1971; ex FRYKEN 1961.

KMF H12

74160 SOCRATES. Pa/FRG 1954; LGC; 1100; 73.11 × 4.17 (239.86 × 13.68); M; 10; ex MARCELIN BERTHELOT 1968; ex CANTENAC 1961; Converted from cargo 1961.

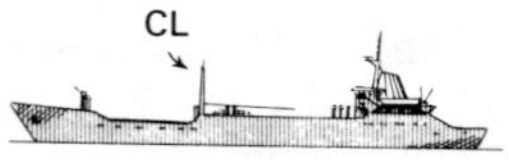

KMF H12

● **74170 FRATERN.** No/No 1966; C; 500; 75.75 × 3.76 (248.52 × 12.34); M; 13.5; ex MERCUR 1980; ex FRATERNIA 1971; Side doors; Sisters: **74171 KVIKSHOLM** (No); ex DANIA 1976; **74172 PEZZATA ROSA** (It); ex PIRHOLM 1979; ex NERLANDIA 1976; Similar: **74173 IRIS** (No); ex HELENIA 1969.

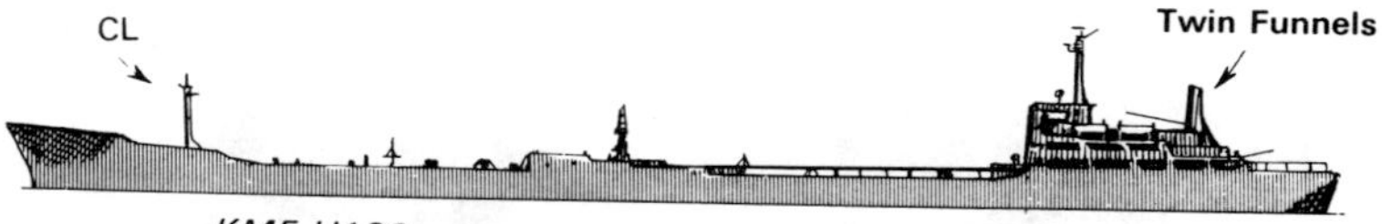

KMF H123

74180 AGIP TRIESTE. It/It 1964; Tk; 30400; 228.61 × 12.14 (750.03 × 39.83); M; 17.

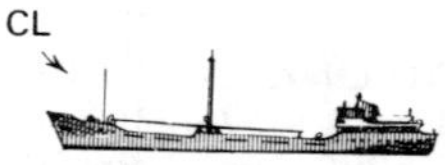

KMF H123

74190 ALFONSO CUARTO. Sp/Sp 1960; C; 700; 62.26 × 4.02 (204.27 × 13.19); M; 11.5.

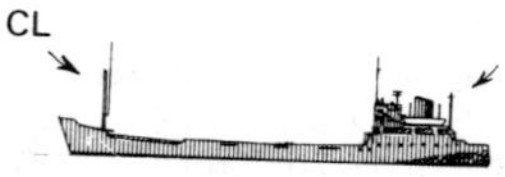

KMF H123

● **74200 CONISTER.** Br/Br 1955; C/Con; 900; 68.2 × 4.59 (223.75 × 15.06); M; 11.5; ex SPANIEL 1973; ex BRENTFIELD 1959; Sister: **74201 TAURUS III** (Cy); ex POINTER 1975; ex BIRCHFIELD 1959.

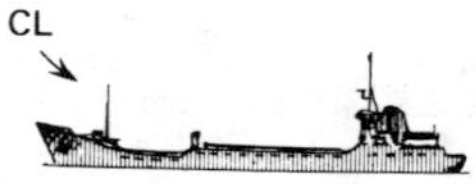

KMF H123

● **74210 CRESCENCE.** Br/Br 1965; C; 1000; 67.32 × 3.82 (220.87 × 12.53); M; 12.

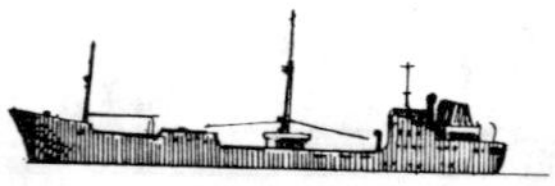

KMF H123

⋆**74220 PEI CHING No 1.** RC/Fr 1957; R; 1200; 74.2 × 4.6 (243.44 × 15.09); M; —; ex ICE PRINCESS 1961; Sister: **74221 FRIGORA** (Br).

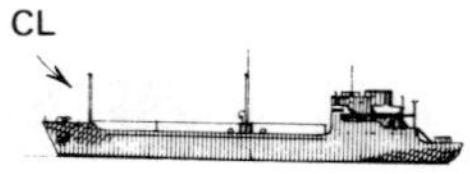

KMF H13

74230 LITORAL SANTAFECINO. Ar/US 1948; C; 1100; 66.51 × — (218.21 × —); TSM; —; ex 941 1969; ex M.O.P. 941 1958; Probable Sister: **74231 KARINA RIO GRANDE** (Ar); ex KARINA 1971; ex 942 1968; ex M.O.P. 942 1958.

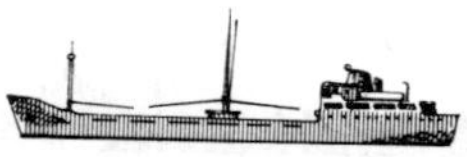

KMF H13

⋆**74240 TEUTA.** Al/It 1960; C; 1100; 72.42 × 4.77 (237.6 × 15.65); M; 11.75.

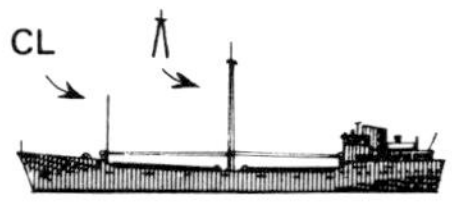

KMF H13
74250 ORGEO. Pa/Be 1953; C; 900; 67.11 × 4.47 (220.18 × 14.67); M; 12; ex ARDENNE 1975; ex MARIE-FLORE 1974.

KMF H13
74260 ANABELA. Cy/Sp 1956; C; 700; 67.85 × 3.86 (222.6 × 12.66); M; 13; ex BALKAN UNITY 1978; ex BAYREN 1977; ex AMELIA DE ASPE 1968; ex ASTENE PRIMERO 1962; Sister: **74261 MAGALI** (Cy); ex PAULA DE ASPE 1965; ex ASTENE SEGUNDO 1962.

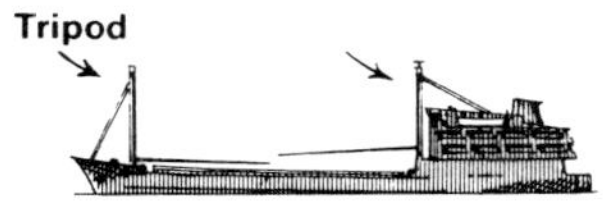

KMF H13
74270 STOKKSUND. No/No 1974; C/HL; 1600; 79.66 × 5.32 (261.35 × 17.45); M; 15.

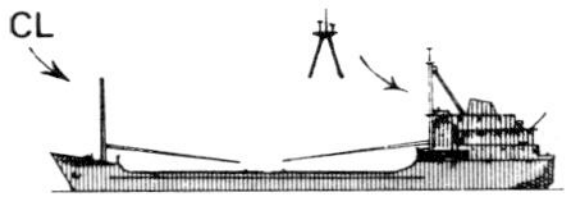

KMF H13
74280 VROUWE ALIDA. Ne/Ne 1976; C; 1500; 78.67 × 5.03 (258.1 × 16.5); M; 11.5.

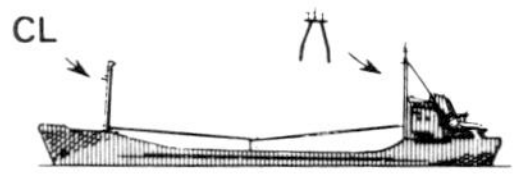

KMF H13
74290 MARITTA JOHANNA. Ne/Ne 1978; C; 1600; 73 (bp) × 5.45 (239.5 (bp) × 17.88); M; 12.5.

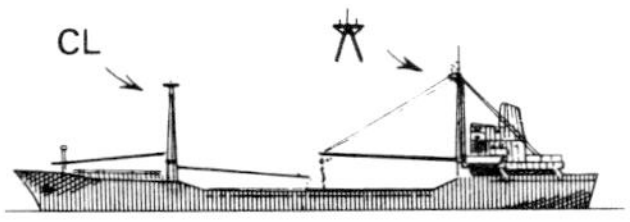

KMF H13
74300 LIFT-ON. Li/De 1977; C/HL; 1600; 97.06 × 5.91 (318.44 × 19.39); M; 14.5; ex LIFTON 1980.

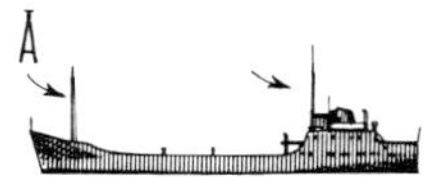

KMF H13
74310 NADIA 1. Le/Br 1962; C; 900; 61.96 × 4 3 (203.28 × 14.11); M; 12.5; ex PORTMARNOCK 1980; ex SHEVRELL 1973; ex WIRRAL COAST 1972.

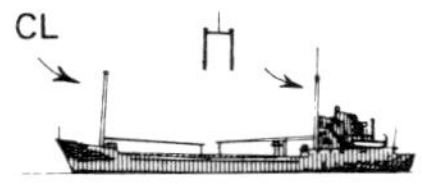

KMF H13
74320 OROSI. CR/Sp 1965; C/R; 800; 56.24 × 4.2 (184.5 × 13.78); M; 11; ex SIERRA ESPUNA 1977; Sisters: **74321 ARENAL** (CR); ex SIERRA ESCUDO 1977; **74322 AL DHAID STAR** (Sh); ex SIERRA ESTRELLA 1980.

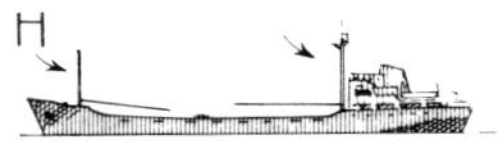

KMF H13
74330 NIKA. Gr/FRG 1958; C; 1000; 71.73 × 4.68 (235.33 × 15.35); M; 10; ex LEON 1980; ex SUNRAY 1979; ex ELDVIK 1975; ex GRJOETY 1970; ex SUSANNA 1967; ex SUSANNE REITH.

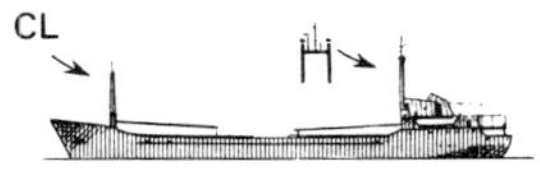

KMF H13
74340 CHRISTINA CLAUSEN. Sg/FRG 1966; LS; 600; 72.85 × — (239.01 × —); M; 11; ex ARMIK 1978; ex ESBERN SNARE 1973; Converted from cargo; Vessel shown before conversion.

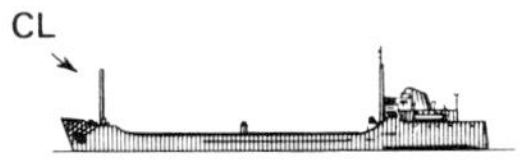

KMF H13
74350 APRICITY. Br/Br 1967; C; 700; 68.23 × 3.72 (223.85 × 12.2); M; —.

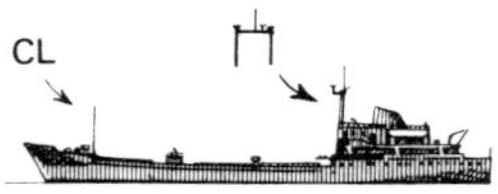

KMF H13
74360 BULK TRADER. Cy/Hu 1964; C; 1600; 84.44 × 4.93 (277.03 × 16.17); M; 12.5; ex PRIMROSE 1980; ex GYRAM 1974; ex PAULINE 1973; ex PATRICIA X 1972; ex SAGAFJELL 1971; May be others of this class similarly altered—see MMF.

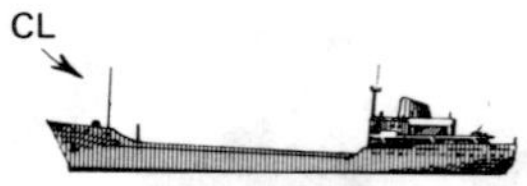

KMF H13
74370 GRACE BONNY II. Cy/Hu 1968; C; 1200; 74.81 × 4.99 (245.44 × 16.37); M; 11.75; ex DE GELE TULP 1978; ex PETRO AQUAMARINE 1973; ex PETRO COCO 1971; Sisters: **74371 DE RODE TULP** (NA); ex PETRO RUBY 1973; ex PETRO PRINCE 1971; **74372 DE WITTE TULP** (NA); ex GIOVANNI TRICOLI 1978; ex SOKNAVIK 1977; ex PETRO DUKE 1972; Similar (converted to bulk starch carrier; Large housing in well etc): **74373 RESURGENCE** (Br); ex DE PAARSE TULP 1974; ex PETRO TOPAZ 1973; ex PETRO QUEEN 1971.

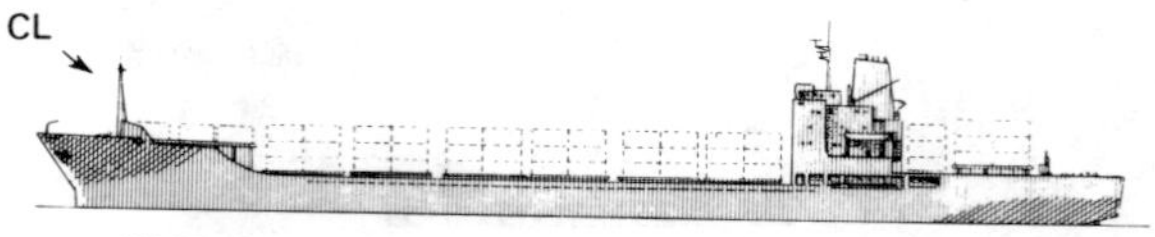

KMF H13
● **74380 SEATRAIN ORISKANY.** Li/Ja 1979; Con; 13800; 177.03 × 10.13 (383.96 × 33.23); M; 19; Sisters: **74381 SEATRAIN BENNINGTON** (FRG); **74382 SEATRAIN CHESAPEAKE** (Li); **74383 SEATRAIN YORKTOWN** (Li); **74384 SEATRAIN INDEPENDENCE** (Li); **74385 TFL JEFFERSON** (Br); ex SEATRAIN SARATOGA 1980.

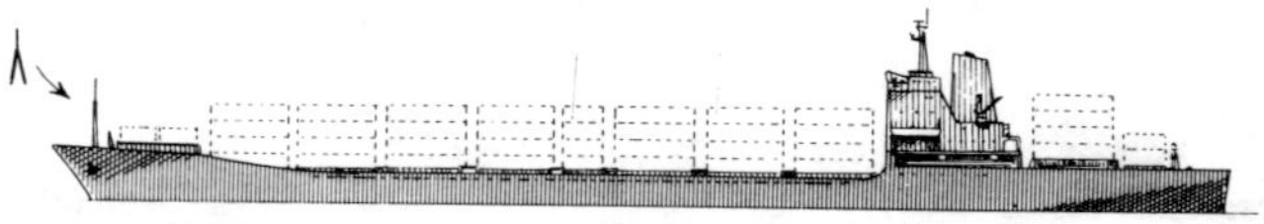

KMF H13
74390 EVER VALIANT. Pa/Ja 1977; Con; 14400; 186.75 × 10.02 (612.7 × 32.87); M; 22; Similar (Pa flag): **74391 EVER VICTORY; 74392 EVER VOYAGER; 74393 EVER VIGOR; 74394 EVER VITAL;** Possibly similar: **74395 EVER VALOR; 74396 EVER VALUE.**

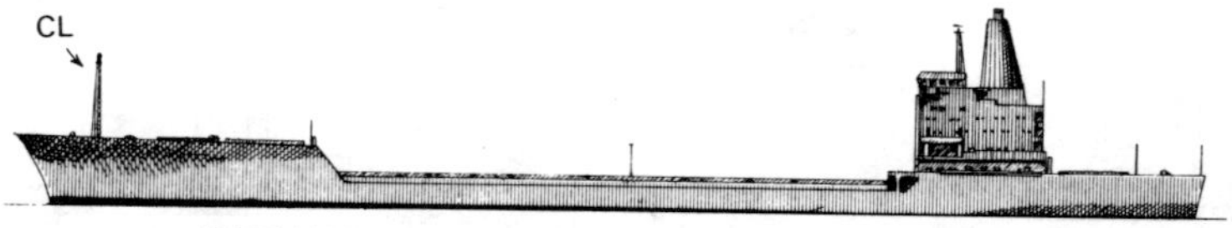

KMF H13
74410 SYDNEY EXPRESS. FRG/FRG 1970; Con; 27400; 226.47 × 11.56 (743 × 37.93); T; 21.5; Sister (Ne built): **74411 NEDLLOYD TASMAN** (Ne); ex ABEL TASMAN 1977; Similar (It built): **74412 LLOYDIANA** (It).

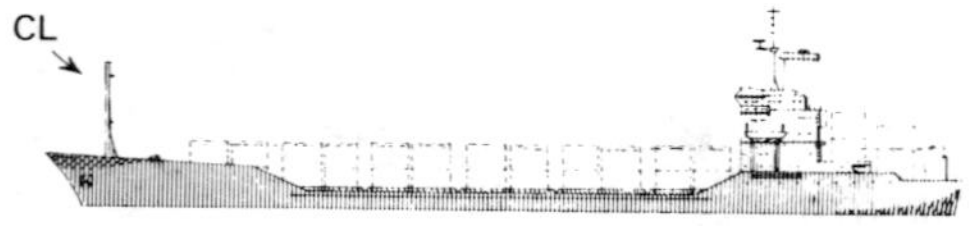

KMF H13
● **74420 NEW ENGLAND HUNTER.** Li/Ne 1971; Con; 6700; 144.94 × 7.62 (475.52 × 25); M; 22; ex FIERY CROSS ISLE 1973; Sisters: **74421 GRAND HAVEN** (Li); ex NEW ENGLAND TRAPPER 1980; ex LORD OF THE ISLE 1973; **74422 WIBKE** (Gr); ex SPINDRIFT: ex ATLANTICA MILANO 1977; ex NEW ENGLAND SCOUT 1976; ex SPINDRIFT ISLE 1973.

● 74435

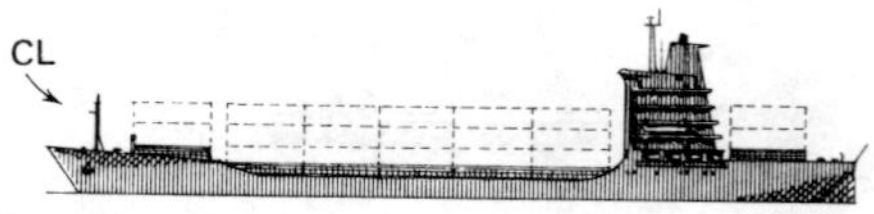

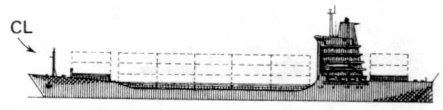

KMF H13
74430 VISURGIS. As/FRG 1971; Con; 6000; 128.43 × 8.07 (421.36 × 26.48); M; 18.

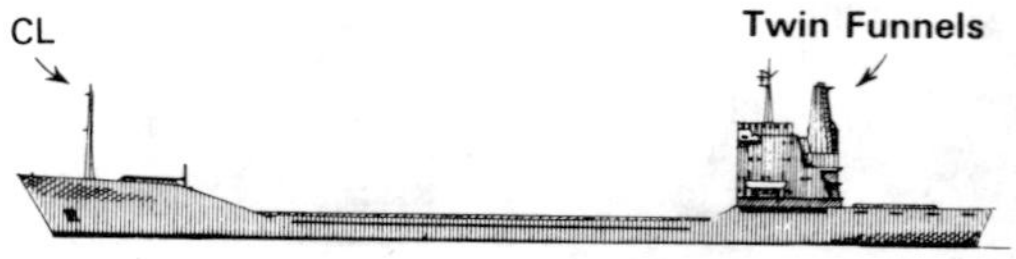

KMF H13
⋆**74440 HRELJIN.** Ys/FRG 1977; Con; 8100; 153.88 × 8.59 (504.86 × 28.18); M; 18.5; Sister: ⋆**74441 SUSAK** (Ys).

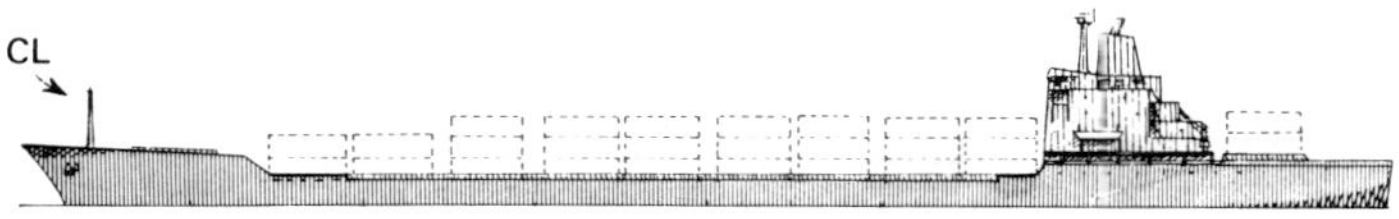

KMF H13
74450 ZIM MONTREAL. Li/FRG 1973; Con; 23100; 218.6 × 11.51 (717.19 × 37.76); T; 23.5; Sister: **74451 ZIM HONG KONG** (Is).

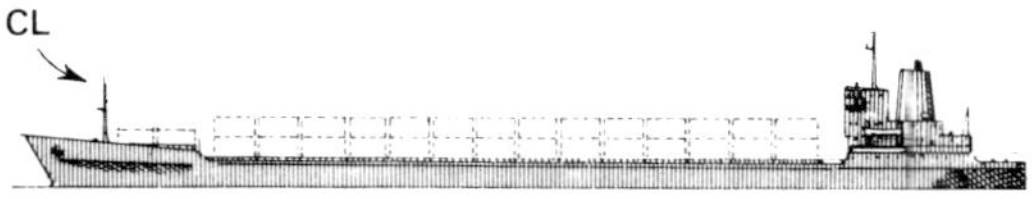

KMF H13
● **74460 SEATRAIN ITALY.** Pa/FRG 1976; Con; 9100; 159.01 × 8.26 (521.69 × 27.1); M; 17.5; ex SOVEREIGN EXPRESS 1977; Sister: **74461 SOVEREIGN ACCORD** (Ja).

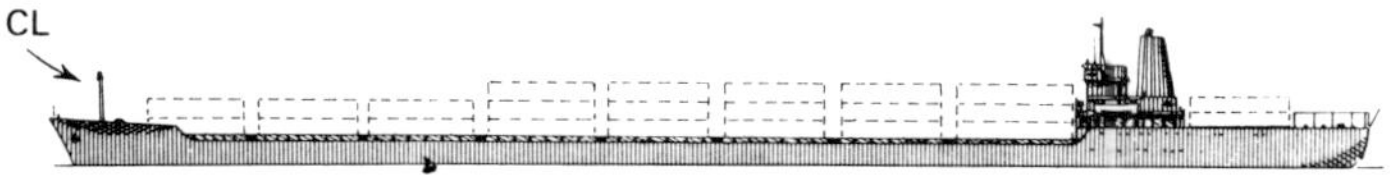

KMF H13
● **74470 BORINQUEN.** US/US 1945/66; Con; 17200; 208.77 × 9.19 (684.94 × 30.15); T; 17; ex TRENTON 1975; ex MARINE FALCON 1966; Converted from 'C-4' type general cargo; Lengthened and deepened 1966; Similar (some lengthened—US flag): **74471 LONG BEACH;** ex MARINE FLASHER 1966; **74472 OAKLAND;** ex MARINE TIGER 1966; **74473 PANAMA;** ex MARINE JUMPER 1966; **74474 SAN JUAN;** ex CHICAGO 1975; ex GENERAL C. H. MUIR 1969; **74475 PHILADELPHIA;** ex GENERAL A. W. BREWSTER 1968; **74476 HUMACAO;** ex BROOKLYN 1975; ex GENERAL C. C. BALLOU 1968; **74477 GUAYAMA;** ex NEW ORLEANS 1975; ex GENERAL E. T. COLLINS 1969; **74478 CHARLESTON;** ex MARINE SHARK 1968.

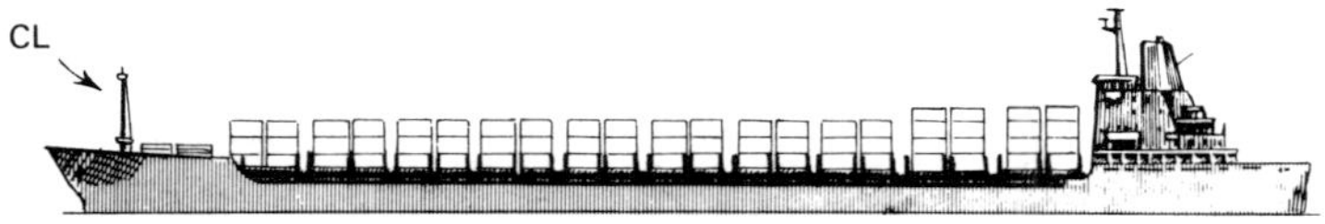

KMF H13
74490 MELBOURNE EXPRESS. FRG/FFG 1970; Con; 25600; 217.91 × 11.51 (714.93 × 37.76); T; 21.5.

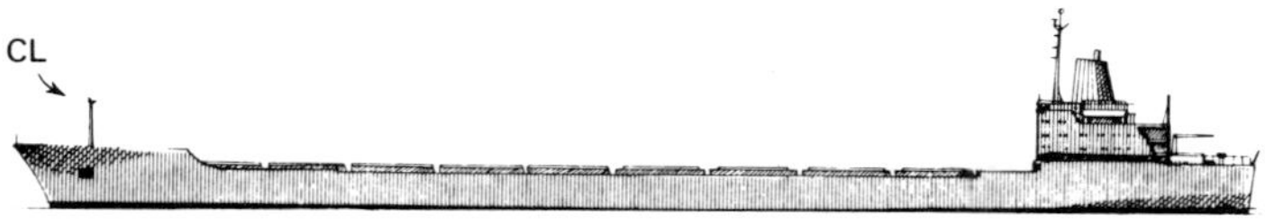

KMF H13
74500 ACT 1. Br/FRG 1969; Con; 24800; 217.25 × 10.83 (712.76 × 35.53); T; 22; Sisters (Br flag): **74501 ACT 2; 74502 AUSTRALIAN ENDEAVOUR** launched as ACT 3; Similar: **74503 ACT 6.**

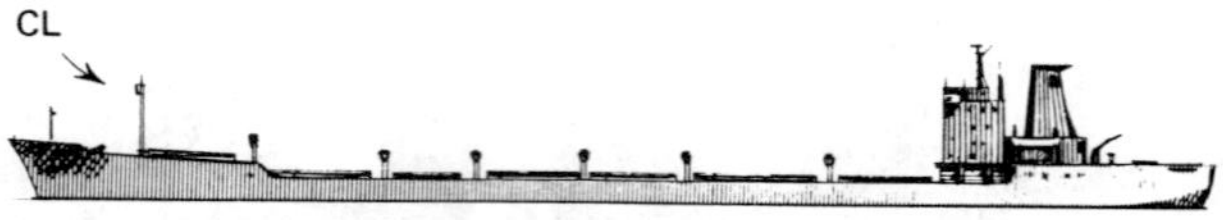

KMF H13
★**74510 BANJA LUKA.** Ys/It 1968; B; 16000; 190.48 × 10.59 (624.93 × 34.74); M; 15.5; Sister: ★**74511 BARANJA** (Ys).

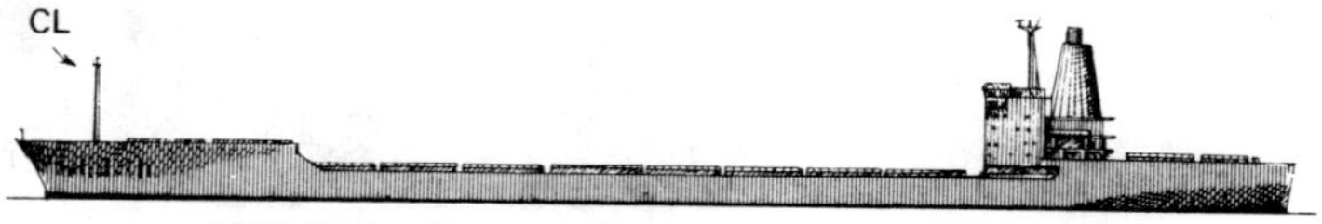

KMF H13
● **74520 DART CANADA.** Br/FRG 1978; Con; 26700; 218.6 × 11.77 (717.19 × 38.62); M; 23.

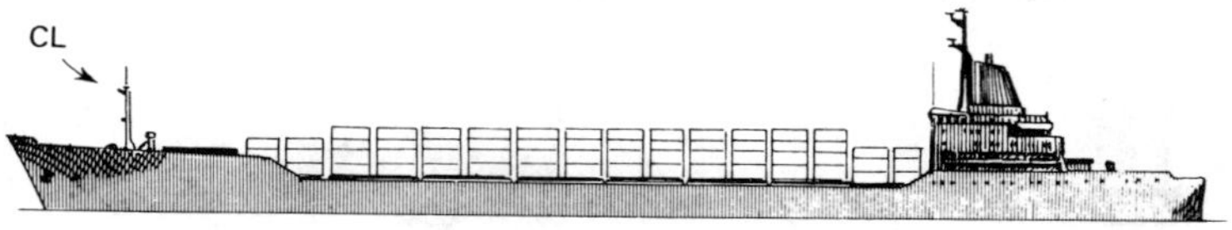

KMF H13
74530 KANGOUROU. Fr/Fr 1970; Con; 26500; 227.95 × 10.69 (747.87 × 35.07); T; 21.5.

KMF H13
★**74540 FILIPP MAKHARADZE.** Ru/Pd 1972; B; 20300; 198.71 × 10.68 (651.93 × 35.03); M; 15 **B-447 type.** Sisters (Ru flag): ★**74541 NIKO NIKOLADZE;** ★**74541 NIKO NIKOLADZE;** ★**74542 MIKHA TSKHAKAYA;** (Pd flag): ★**74543 CZWARTACY AL;** ★**74544 OBRONCY POCZTY;** ★**74545 POWSTANIEC SLASKI;**★**74546 SIEKIERKI;** ★**74547 TOBRUK.**

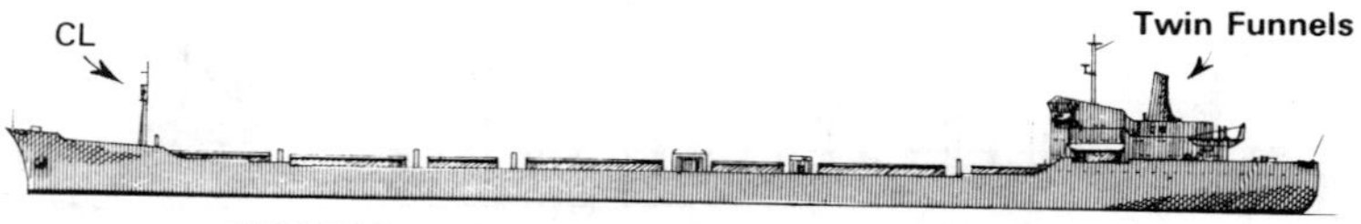

KMF H13
74560 ORIENT VENTURE. Li/FRG 1965; B; 26500; 227.11 × 10.53 (745.11 × 34.55); ex ESCHERSHEIM 1980; lengthened 1968. Sister: **74561 BORNHEIM** (FRG).

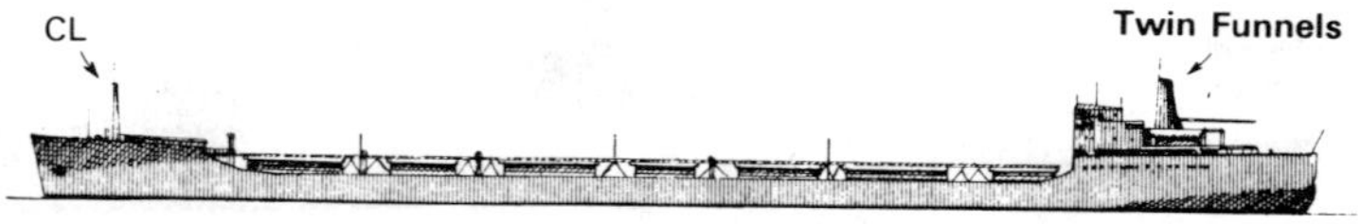

KMF H13
74570 ONESSILUS. Pa/FRG 1963; B; 24700; 214.66 × 10.47 (704.27 × 34.35); M; 15; ex STRASSBURG.

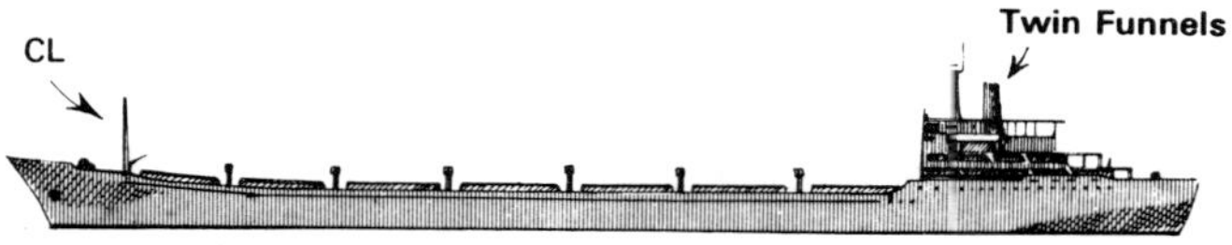

KMF H13
74580 NAI ASSIA. It/It 1965; B; 18100; 201 × 10.53 (659.45 × 34.55); M; 17; ex DRIN 1974.

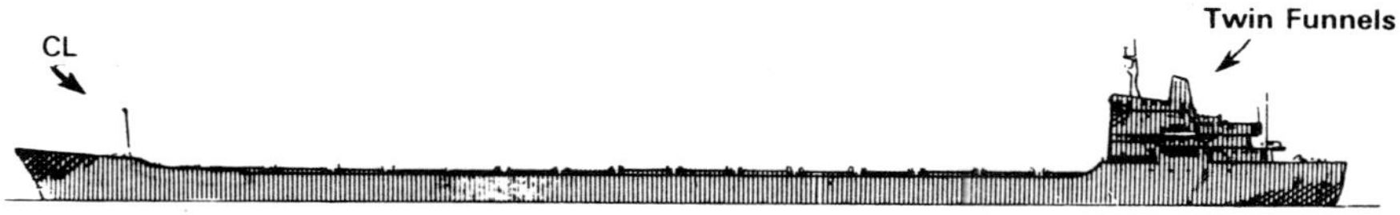

KMF H13
74590 ANASTASIA L. Gr/Fr 1967; B; 53400; 264.24 × 13.72 (866.93 × 45.01); M; 14.5; ex CETRA COLUMBA 1978.

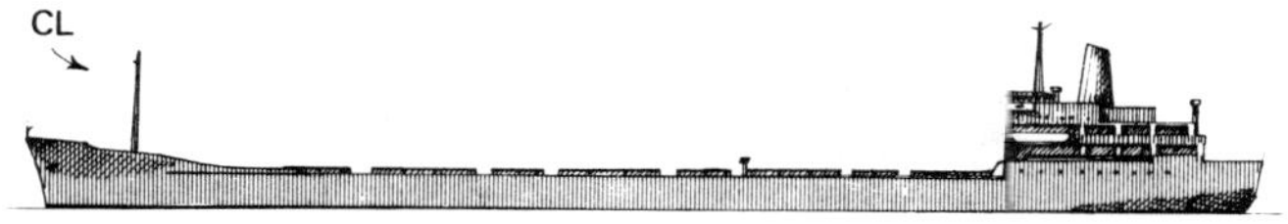

KMF H13
74600 YIANNIS. Pa/Sw 1964; O; 24800; 199.88 × 11.37 (655.77 × 37.3); M; 15.75; ex YASNAYA POLYANA 1980; ex LAIDAURE 1978; Sister: **74601 ELA MANA MOU** (Pa); ex YAKUTSK 1980; ex LAPONIA 1978.

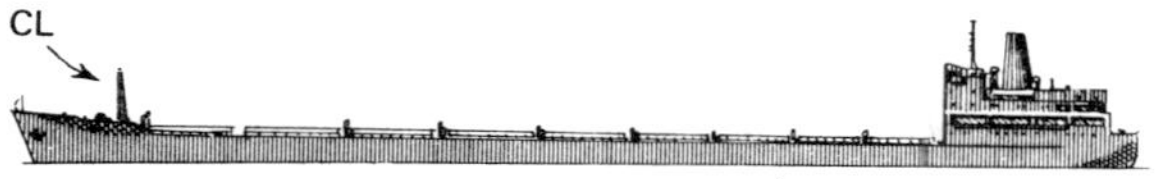

KMF H13
74610 POLYXENI. Gr/Sw 1962; O; 18000; 178.09 × 10.9 (584.28 × 35.76); M; 14.25; ex LUOSSA 1977.

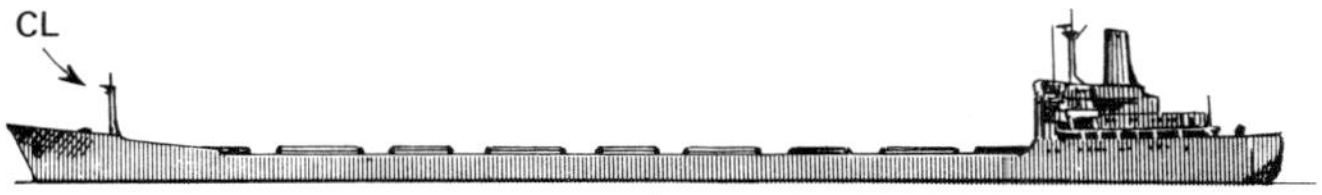

KMF H13
74620 TETE OLDENDORFF. Pa/FRG 1967; B; 22400; 201.66 × 11.53 (661.61 × 37.83); M; 16; Sister: **74621 RIXTA OLDENDORFF** (Sg); Similar **74622 SAVOY DEAN** (Li); ex BUNTENTOR 1980.

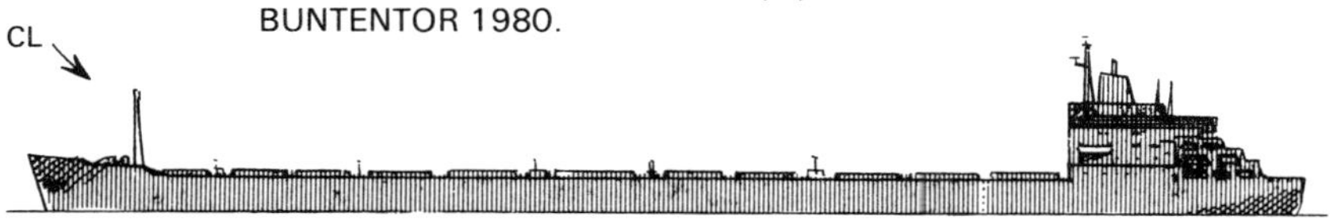

KMF H13
74630 CURTIS CAPRICORN. Br/Au 1972; B; 48900; 255.43 × 15.14 (838.02 × 49.67); T; —; ex CLUTHA CAPRICORN 1977.

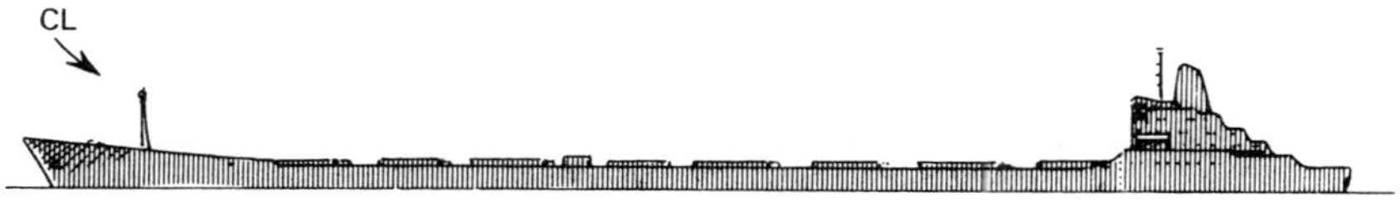

KMF H13
74640 PROTEKTOR. FRG/FRG 1967; B; 43200; 253.02 × 13.67 (830.12 × 44.85); M; 15; ex URSULA SCHULTE 1978.

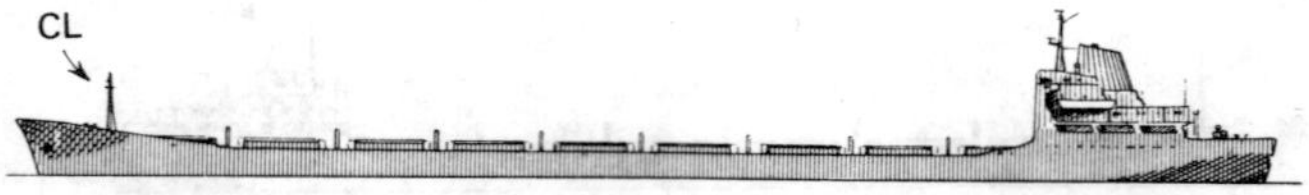

KMF H13
74650 HELENA OLDENDORFF. Li/FRG 1965; B; 19300; 200.13 × 11.5 (656.59 × 37.73); M; 15.25; Sister: **74651 REGINA OLDENDORFF** (Li).

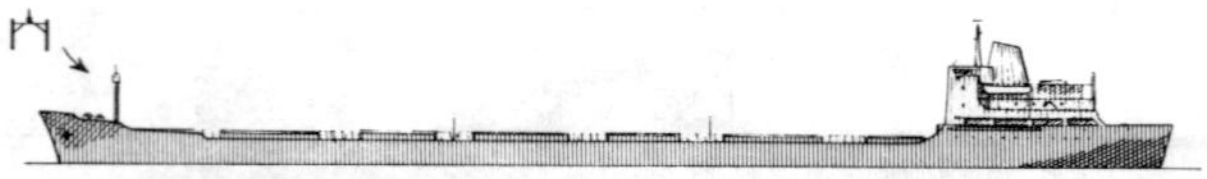

KMF H13
★74660 ZIEMIA BYDGOSKA. Pd/Br 1967; B; 15700; 179.51 × 9.91 (588.94 × 32.51); M; 15; Sister: **★74661 ZIEMIA MAZOWIECKA** (Pd).

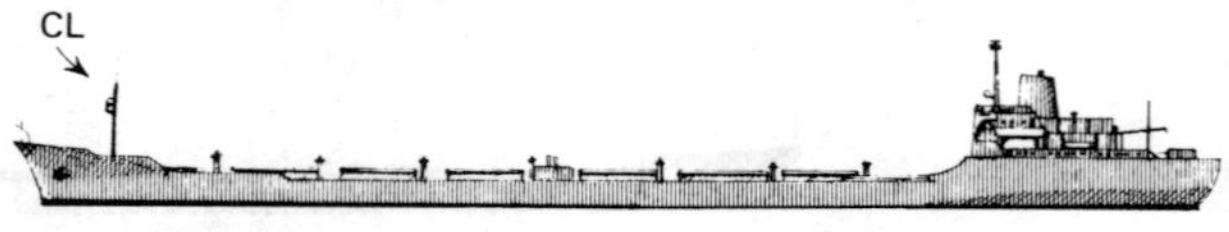

KMF H13
● **74670 ARCADIAN SEA.** Gr/FRG 1965; B; 21000; 191.27 × 11.32 (627.53 × 37.14); M; 15.25; ex ASTRAMARINA 1980; ex TORM HELVIG 1975; ex HELVIG 1974; Sisters: **74671 ASTRADIEGO** (Ar); ex TORM HERDIS 1975; ex HERDIS 1974; **74672 TRADE MASTER** (Gr); ex OCEAN MASTER 1977; **74673 ODYSSEUS** (Ar); ex TYROL 1978; ex FERNGLEN 1975.

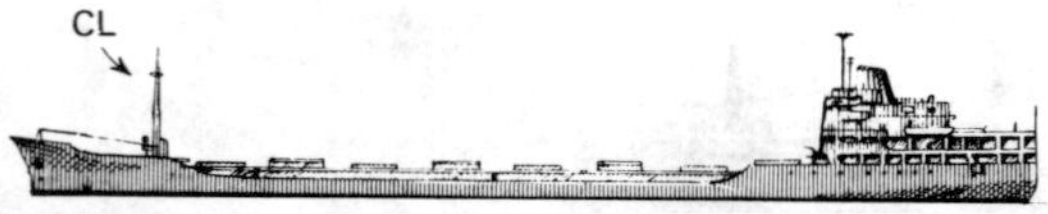

KMF H13
74680 LOUISE. Pa/Sw 1957; B; 10900; 162.97 × 9.32 (534.68 × 30.58); T; 17.

KMF H13
74690 AL TAWWAB. Sg/Br 1962; O; 18800; 185.33 × 9.86 (608.04 × 32.35); M; 12; ex CAPE HOWE 1978.

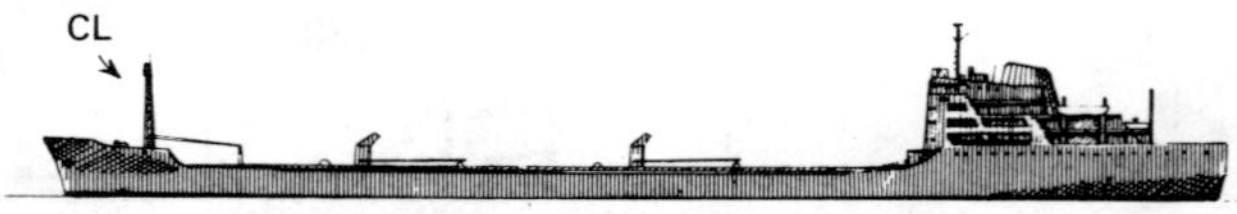

KMF H13
74700 IRENES SINCERITY. Gr/Fr 1959; OO; 17900; 185.99 × 9.75 (610.2 × 31.99); M; 15; ex FREE LANCER 1974; ex JUNIN 1971; ex LENS 1969; Similar: **74701 JALTIPAN** (Gr); ex ARNE PRESTHUS 1974; ex LONGWY 1970.

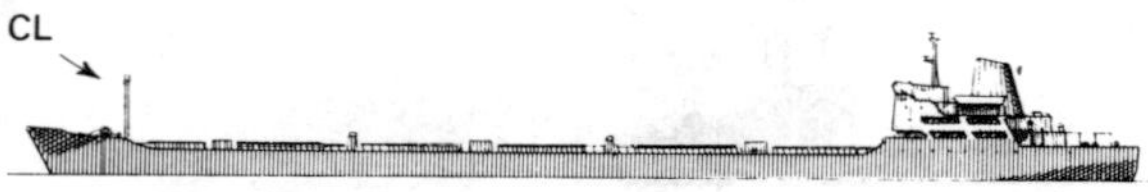

KMF H13
74710 FROTANORTE. Bz/Bz 1969; B; 13800; 176.41 × 10.09 (578.77 × 33.1); M; 14.5; Sister: **74711 FROTASUL** (Bz); Probably similar: **74712 FROTALESTE** (Bz); **74713 FROTAOESTE** (Bz); **74714 OMNIUM PRIDE** (Li).

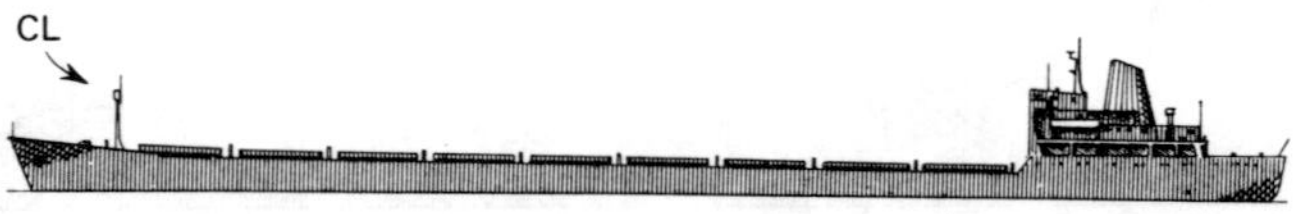

KMF H13
74720 DIETRICH OLDENDORFF. Li/FRG 1965; B; 19400; 201.73 × 11.53 (661.84 × 37.83); M; 15.25.

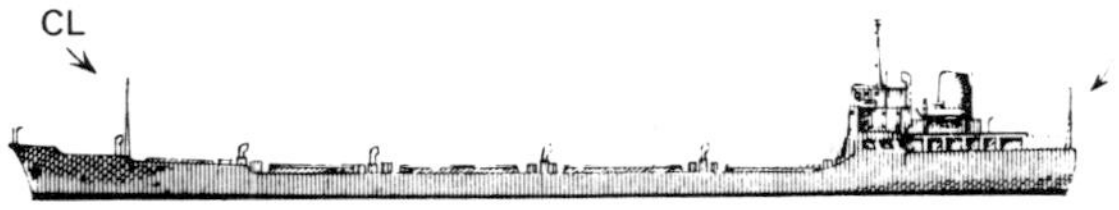

KMF H13
74730 AGIA ANASTASIA. Gr/Ja 1959; C; 12300; 169.17 × 9.53 (555.02 × 31.27); M; 15.5; Similar: **74731 MENITES** (Gr); ex SAAS FEE 1977; ex BUTTERFLY 1972.

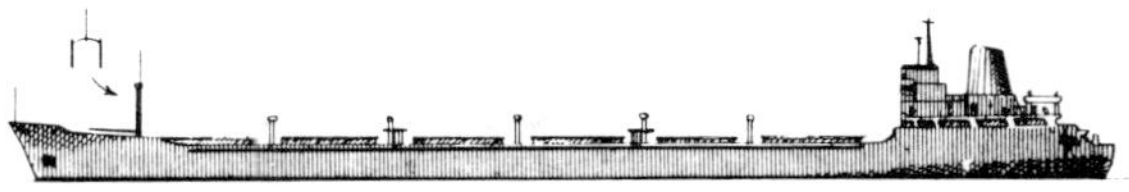

KMF H13
74740 PALLADE. It/It 1959; B; 12600; 174.71 × 9.88 (573.2 × 32.41); M; 15.

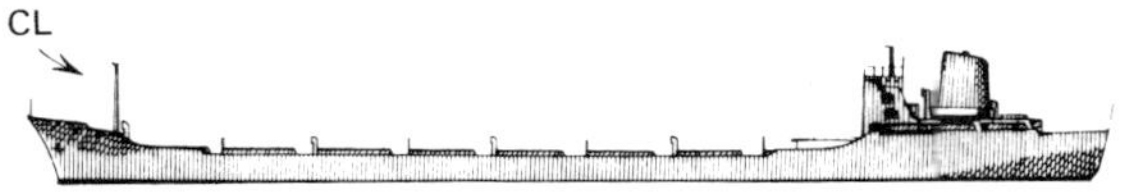

KMF H13
74750 MEDCEMENT CARRIER. Gr/Br 1962; B/Cem; 11900; 170.9 × 10.12 (560.7 × 33.2); M; 14.25; ex ATLANTIC CARRIER 1977; ex WORLD EXPLORER 1972; Converted from bulk 1972.

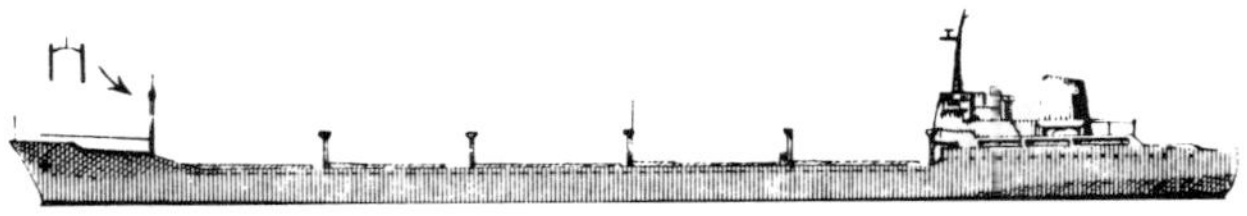

KMF H13
● **74760 POLINNIA.** It/It 1962; B; 17300; 192.03 × 10.61 (630.02 × 34.81); M; 16; Sisters (It flag): **74761 MASSIMO PRIMO; 74762 UMBERTO D'AMATO:** ex PEPPINO D'AMATO 1978; ex DONATELLA 1978.

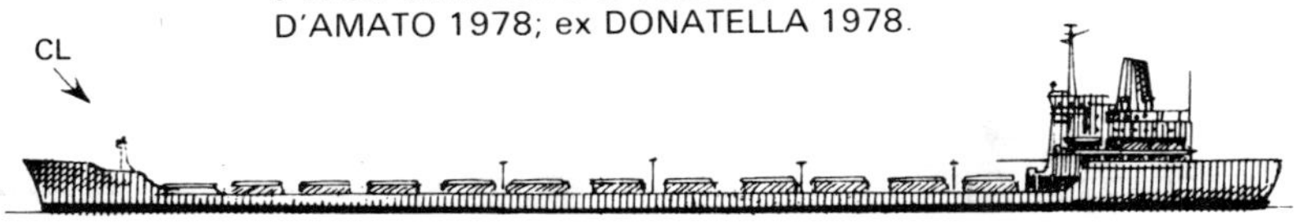

KMF H13
74770 NIMBA. Li/SW 1966; O; 44000; 243.85 × 12.26 (800.03 × 40.22); M; 16.25; ex NUOLJA 1974; Sister: **74771 ALIANZA** (Ar); ex NIKKALA 1978.

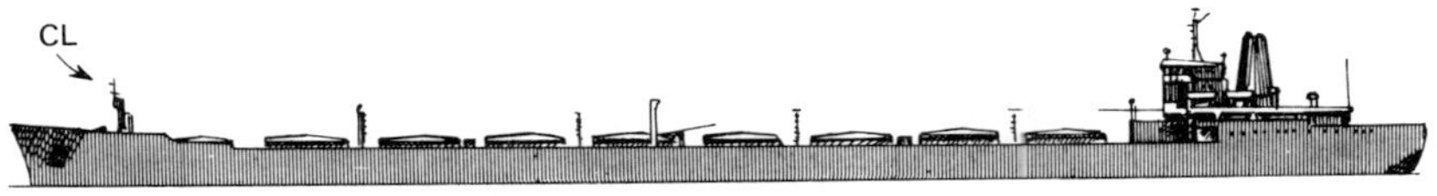

KMF H13
74780 VENTURE ITALIA. Li/Sw 1967; OBO; 39700; 258.36 × 13.27 (848.62 × 43.54); M; 16; ex CONOCO ITALIA 1978; ex RINDA 1972; Sister: **74781 DELAWARE** (Li); ex RANGER 1973; ex RUNA 1972.

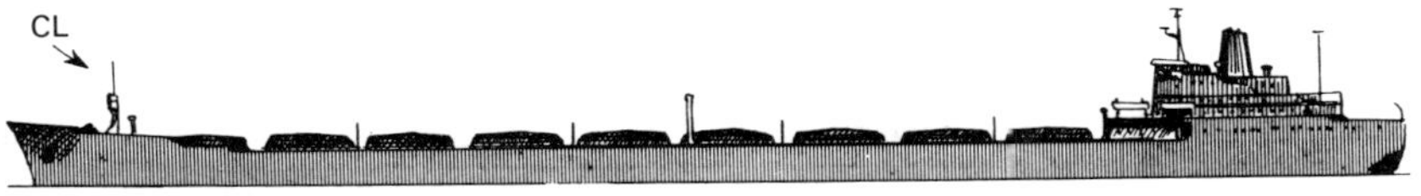

KMF H13
74790 FALCON BAY. Li/Sw 1967; OBO; 44500; 258.66 × 13.47 (848.62 × 44.19); M; 16.5; ex MOSPOINT 1978; ex VITORIA 1976.

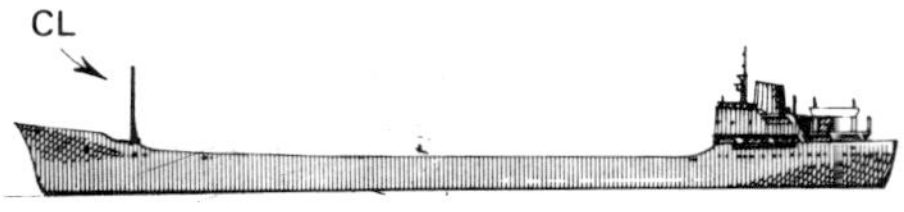

KMF H13
74800 FORT ST. LOUIS. Ca/Ca 1965; C; 5900; 142.14 × 7.21 (466.34 × 23.65); M; —.

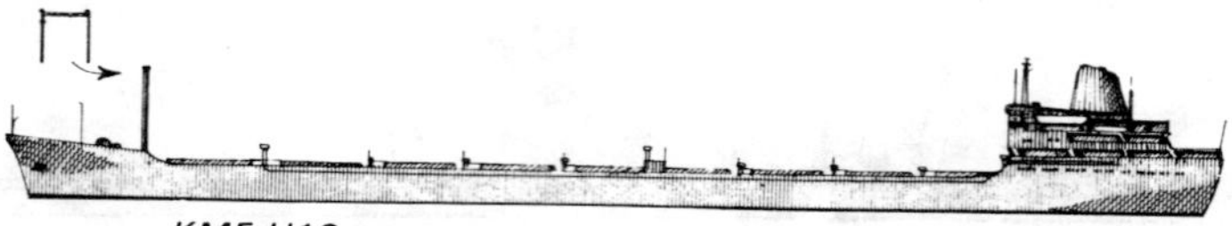

KMF H13
74810 OCEAN LADY. Pa/FRG 1963; B; 25400; 215.91 × 11.13 (708.37 × 36.52); M; 14.5; ex KIMPO 1981; ex BANDAK 1973.

KMF H13
⋆**74820 THALE.** DDR/FRG 1960; B; 14500; 171.79 × 10.28 (563.62 × 33.73); M; 14.75; ex H. L. LORENTZEN 1964.

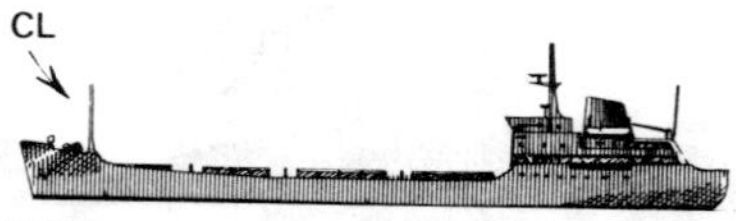

KMF H13
74830 CASTLE POINT. Br/Br 1965; C; 5600; 112.68 × 9.09 (369.69 × 29.82); M; 13.5; ex HUDSON LIGHT 1976.

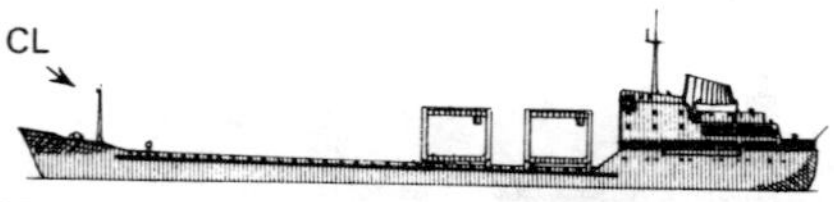

KMF H13
74840 ISLAND CONTAINER. Pa/Au 1964; Con; 5700; 126.17 × 7.62 (413.94 × 25); M; 16; ex KOORINGA: May have two travelling gantries.

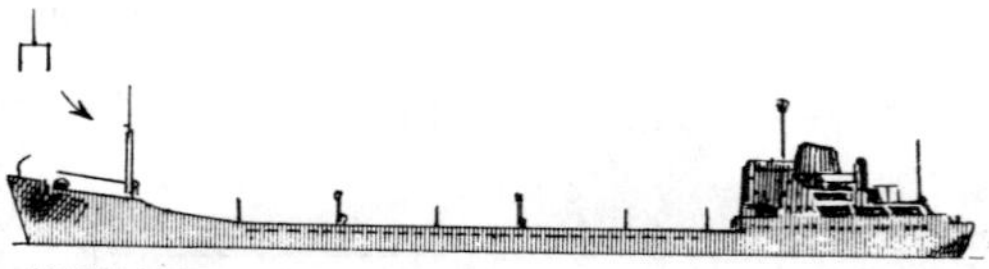

KMF H13
74850 MALESSINA. Gr/No 1958; O; 10600; 153.93 × 9.19 (505.02 × 30.15); M; 11.75; ex GOOD TRAINER 1975; ex NORDLAND 1972.

KMF H13
74860 HONG KONG EXPRESS. Pa/FRG 1956/69; Con; 6600; 137.45 × 6.54 (450.95 × 21.46); M; 14; ex LILAC 1980; ex KARIN-ELISE 1973; ex HOTHER ISLE 1973; ex CHRISTIANE 1968; Converted from cargo 1969.

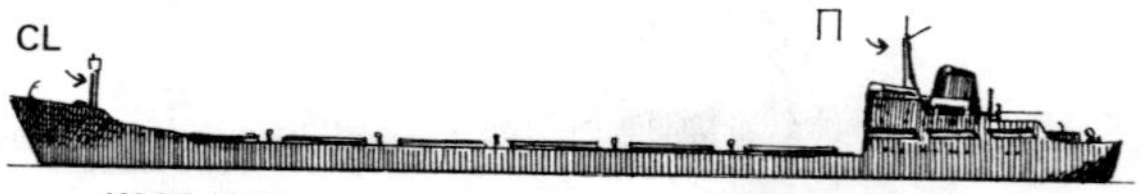

KMF H13
⋆**74870 HUAI HAI.** RC/FRG 1962; B; 14800; 179.38 × 10.92 (588.52 × 35.83); M; 14; ex GEORGIOS A GEORGILIS 1974; ex BENEDICTE 1969; Similar: ⋆**74871 HUANG HAI** (RC); ex AMUNDSEN SEA 1975; ex ANTONIS P LEMOS 1974; ex BEATRICE 1969.

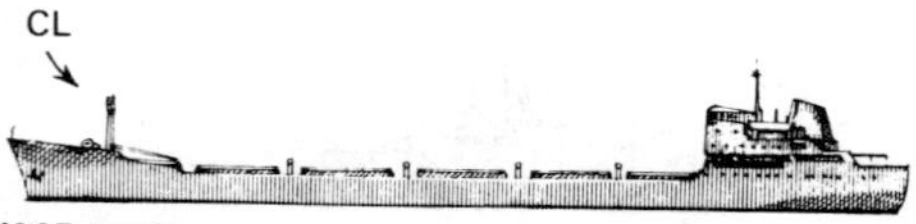

KMF H13
74880 ALIKI. Gr/FRG 1959; B; 13000; 171.79 × 10.55 (563.62 × 34.61); M; 14; ex JARILLA 1977.

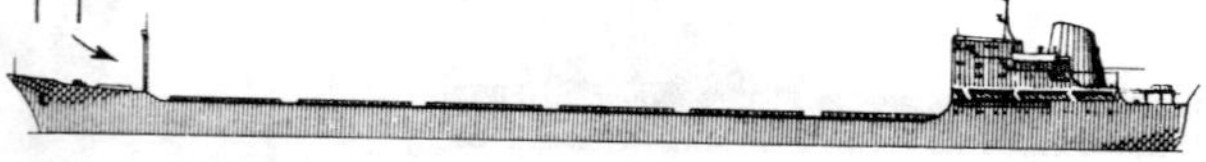

KMF H13
74890 ROSYTH. Sg/FRG 1961; O; 17400; 184.41 × 9.77 (605.02 × 32.05); M; 13.75; ex NORITA 1977; ex FILEFJELL 1967.

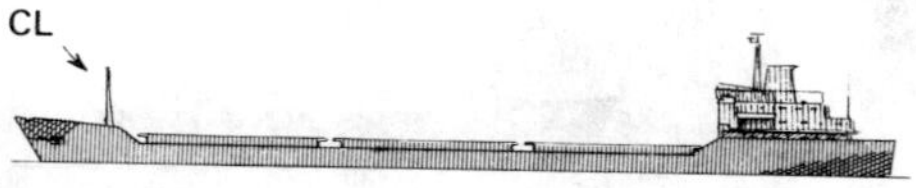

KMF H13
74900 RAUTARUUKKI. Fi/FRG 1976; B; 7400; 143.31 × 7.57 (470.18 × 24.84); M; 15.25; Sister: **74901 KUURTANES** (Fi); Possibly similar: **74902 MINI ORBIT** (No).

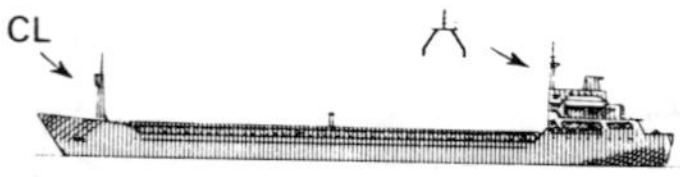

KMF H13
74910 MINI STAR. No/No 1978; C; 1600/3400; 100.84 × —/5.05 (330.84 × —/16.57); M; 13.25; Deck is strengthened to allow a gantry crane to be fitted; Sister: **74911 MINI SUN** (No).

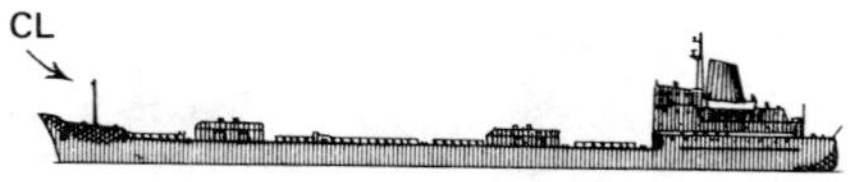

KMF H13
74920 ALBRIGHT PIONEER. Br/Br 1968; Ch; 6800; 125.81 × 8.88 (412.76 × 29.13); M; 14.5; Similar: **74921 ALBRIGHT EXPLORER** (Br).

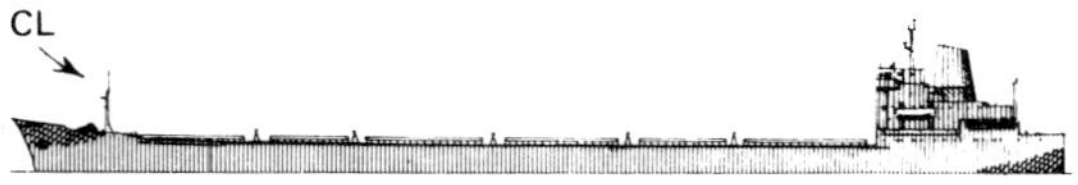

KMF H13
74930 CAPE RACE. Br/No 1971; B; 14900; 165.21 × 10.22 (542.03 × 33.53); M; 15; Sister: **74931 BARON BELHAVEN** (Br).

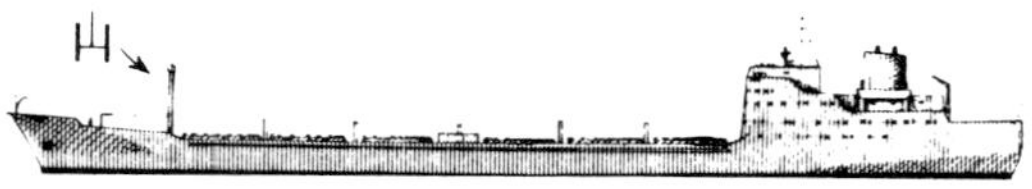

KMF H13
● **74940 LEVANTINO**. Pa/Br 1957; O; 8600; 160.28 × 8.76 (525.85 × 28.74); M; 11.5; ex AFGHANISTAN 1972; Similar: **74941 ASPIDOFOROS** (Fr); ex IRON HORSE 1970; **74942 JEANNIE** (Gr); ex SCOTTISH WASA 1977; ex IRON CROWN 1971; **74943 MAHINDA** (Pa); ex IRON BARQUE 1970; **74944 ONORATO** (It); ex NINO 1969; ex IRON AGE 1968; **74945 SIROCO** (Li); ex IRON ORE 1969.

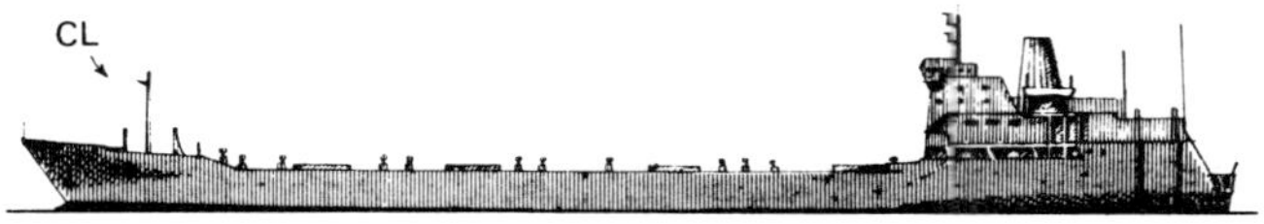

KMF H13
74950 GRAND ENCOUNTER. Pa/Ca 1972; RoC; 16400; 208.19 × 9.3 (683.04 × 30.51); TSM; 19; ex LAURENTIAN FOREST 1980; Sister: **74951 AVON FOREST** (Br).

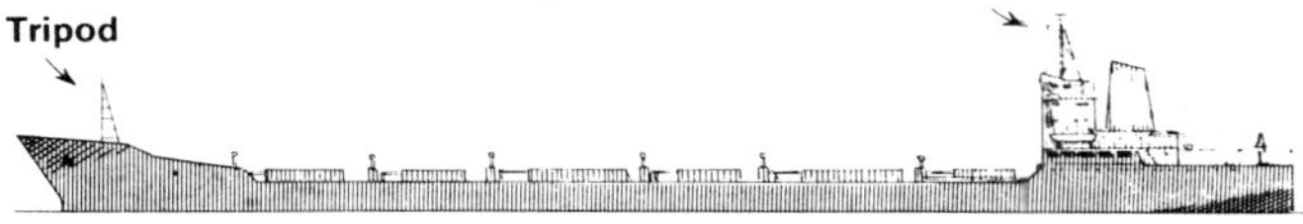

KMF H13
74960 RIO VERDE. Bz/Bz 1977; B; 21700; 193.86 × 10.9 (636.02 × 35.76); M; 16; Sister: **74961 RIO NEGRO** (Bz); Possible sisters: **74962 RIO BRANCO** (Bz); **74963 RIO GRANDE** (Bz); Possibly similar (may have cargo gear): **74964 MULHEIM** (FRG); **74965 GOLDEN RIO** (Li); ex WEINHEIM 1979.

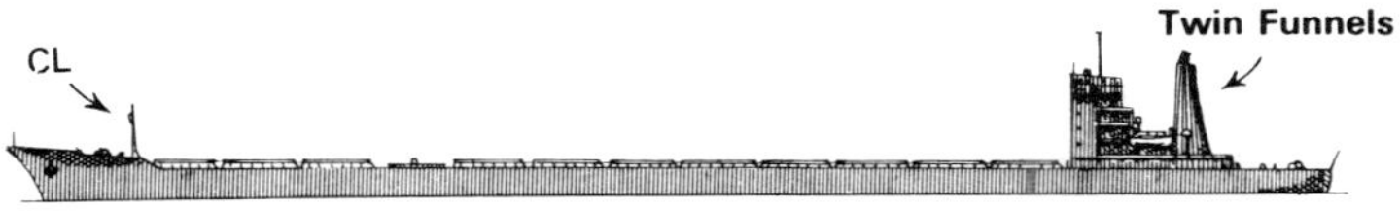

KMF H13
74970 ONOE MARU. Ja/Ja 1963; O; 29500; 214.51 × 11.5 (703.77 × 37.73); M; 14.75.

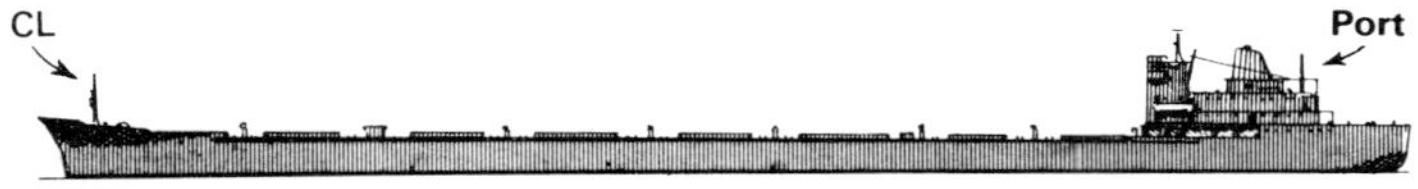

KMF H13
74980 ORIENT HARMONY. Li/Br 1967; B; 29500; 215.96 × 12.43 (708.53 × 40.78); M; 16.75; ex GAUCHO GUEMES ex MARDULCE II; ex FERNSPRING; Probable sister: **74981 WELFARE** (Gr); ex PILIO 1980; ex FERNRIVER 1978.

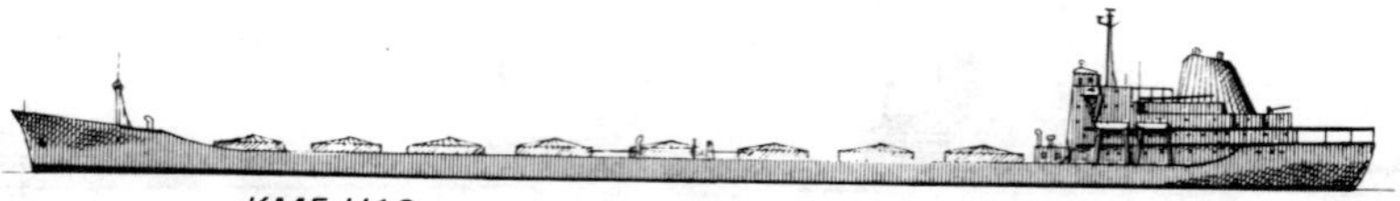

KMF H13
74990 BREEZE. Pa/FRG 1964; OO; 35100; 235.64 × 12.52 (773.1 × 41.08); M; 15; ex HOWARD SMITH 1979; ex HOEGH HELM 1969.

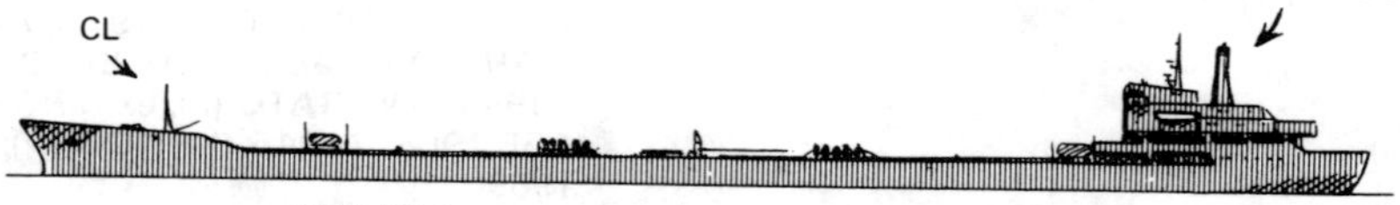

KMF H13
75000 DRUPA. Br/FRG 1966; Tk; 39800; 243.8 × 13.25 (799.87 × 43.47); T; 15; Fenders on upper deck are on port side.

KMF H13
75010 LYRA. Gr/Fr 1967; B; 41900; 254.52 × 13.49 (835.04 × 44.26); M; 16; ex CETRA LYRA; Sister: **75011 CARINA** (Gr); ex CETRA CARINA.

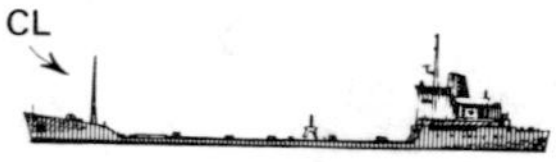

KMF H13
75020 RUDDERMAN. Br/Br 1968; Tk; 1600; 83.52 × 5.15 (274.02 × 16.9); M; 12.

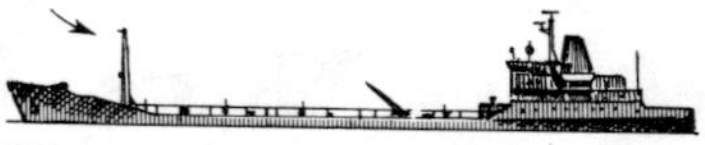

KMF H13
75030 VINGAVAG. Sw/Fi 1973; Tk; 3800; 107.32 × 6.62 (352.1 × 21.72); M; 14; ex TARNVAG 1980; ex VUOSAARI 1978; Probably similar: **75031 TEBOSTAR** (Fi).

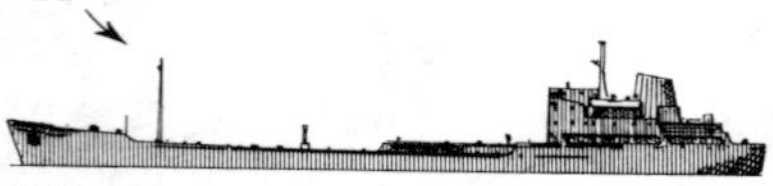

KMF H13
75040 SAVE. Fr/Sw 1962; Tk; 4500; 118.78 × 6.86 (389.7 × 22.5); M; 14; ex ALOR STAR 1972; ex ROGN 1968.

KMF H13
75050 ALBAY HAKKI BURAK. Tu/Tu 1964; FA/Tk; 3800 Dspl; 83.7 × 5.5 (275 × 18); D—E; 16.

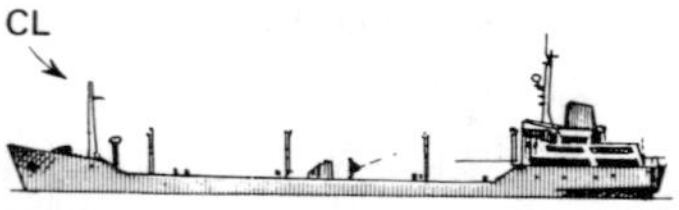

KMF H13
75060 BILLESBORG. De/De 1970; Tk/Ch; 1400; 107.32 × 5.21 (352.1 × 17.09); M; 12; Lengthened 1974; Sister: **75061 BRATTINGSBORG** (De).

KMF H13
75070 ASPERITY. Br/Ne 1967; Tk/Ch; 700; 71.86 × 3.84 (235.76 × 12.6); M; 12; Similar (smaller): **75071 AUTHORITY** (Br).

KMF H13
75080 ROCHE'S POINT. Br/FRG 1968; Tk/Ch; 1600; 94.32 × 5.3 (309.45 × 17.39); M; 15; ex SAMOS FORTUNE 1980; ex THORHAGEN 1973.

●
75085

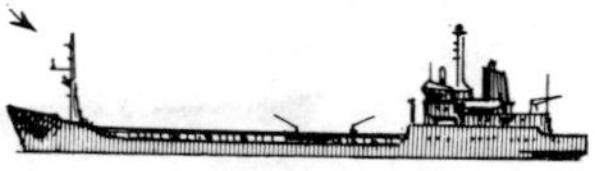

KMF H13
75090 ESSO INVERNESS. Br/Br 1971; Tk; 2200; 91.42 × 5.9 (299.93 × 19.36); M; 13; Sister: **75091 ESSO PENZANCE** (Br).

KMF H13
75100 SAND SAPPHIRE. Br/Br 1963/75; D; 900; 61.88 × 3.83 (203.02 × 12.57); M; 11; ex CY—THREESOME 1974; ex PASS OF GLENOGLE 1973; Converted from tanker 1975.

KMF H13
75110 DEVON CURLEW. Br/Sp 1969; Ch; 800; 68.18 × 3.96 (223.69 × 12.99); M; 12.5; ex FENOL. Sisters: **75111 DORSET FULMAR** (Br); ex FORMOL 1979; **75112 THITA STAINLESS** (Gr); ex METANOL 1974.

KMF H13
75120 ELOISEID. Br/Br 1969; Ch; 1600; 91.45 × 4.93 (300.03 × 16.17); M; 13; ex SILVEREID 1975.

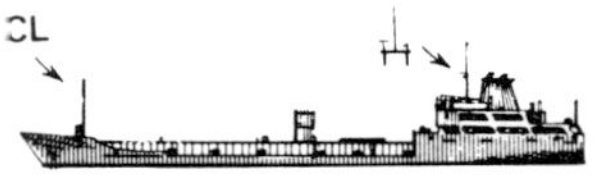

KMF H13
75130 BENVENUE. Br/Ne 1974; Ch; 1600; 80.78 × 5.38 (265.02 × 17.65); M; 12.75; Sisters (Br flag): **75131 BENCLEUCH; 75132 BENMACHDHUI.**

KMF H13
75140 UNICORN DANIEL. Li/FRG 1968; Tk; 600; 69.5 × 4.32 (228.02 × 14.17); M; 12.5; ex BOBODI 1977; Similar (smaller and with lower superstructure etc): **75141 UNICORN MICHAEL** (Br); ex ONABI 1977.

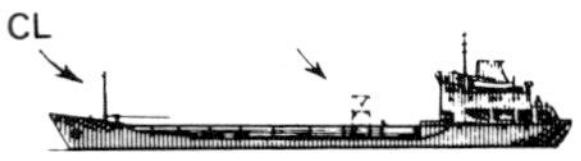

KMF H13
75150 DUTCH GLORY. Ne/Ne 1975; Ch; 1400; 80.24 × 5.42 (263.25 × 17.78); M; 13.5; Sister: **75151 DUTCH MASTER** (Ne); Possibly similar: **75152 CORRIE BROERE** (Ne).

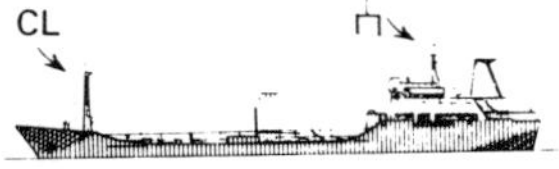

KMF H13
75160 ANNA BROERE. Ne/FRG 1976; Ch; 1600; 82.5 × 5.74 (270.66 × 18.83); M; 13.5.

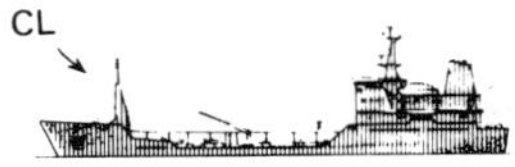

KMF H13
⋆**75170 BUNA.** DDR/Ne 1979; Ch; 1800; 73.46 × 4.91 (241.01 × 16.11); M; 13; Sister: ⋆**75171 SCHKOPAU** (DDR) (may be spelt **ZSCHOPAU**).

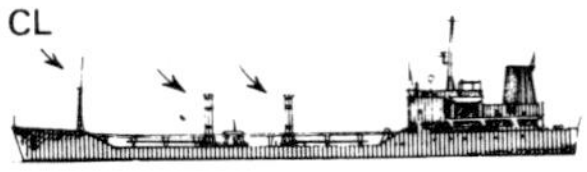

KMF H13
75180 CENTAURMAN. Br/Br 1976; Ch; 2500; 89.18 × 5.9 (292.59 × 19.36); M; 13.5; Sister: **75181 VEGAMAN** (Br).

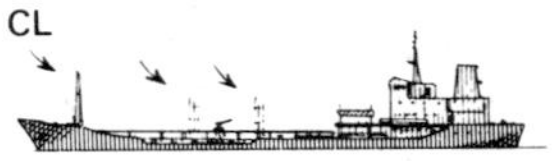

KMF H13
75190 STELLAMAN. Br/Br 1976; Ch; 1500; 79.51 × 5.27 (260.26 × 17.29); M; 13.75; Sister: **75191 MARSMAN** (Br).

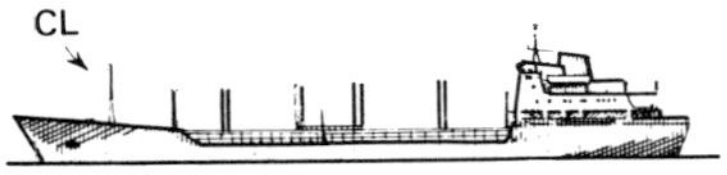

KMF H13
75200 OMANIAH. Ku/FRG 1971; Ch; 2900; 106.03 × 6.43 (347.87 × 21.1); M; 14.5; ex OPOBO 1980; ex TERKOL 1972.

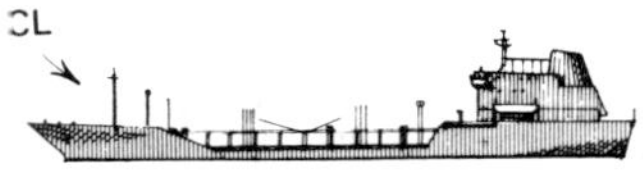

KMF H13
75210 LA COLINA. Br/No 1976; Ch; 1600; 96.02 × 5.47 (315.03 × 17.95); M; 13.75; Sister: **75211 LA PRADERA** (Br).

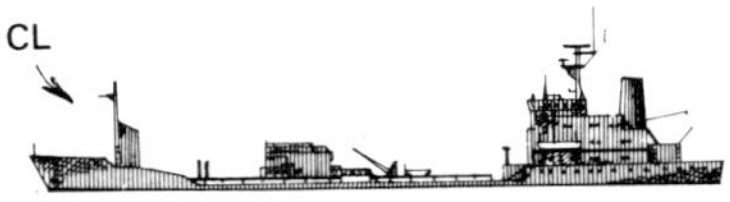

KMF H13
75220 KIISLA. Fi/Fi 1974; Tk; 3900; 109.33 × 6.59 (358.69 × 21.62); M; 14.

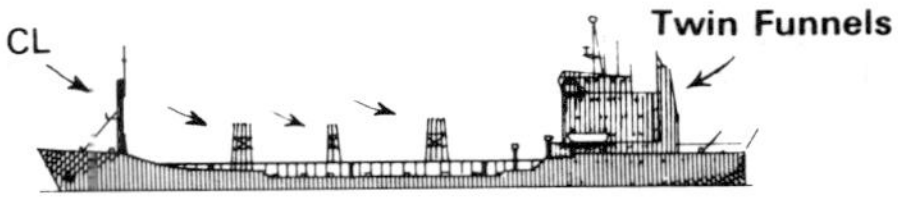

KMF H13
● **75230 ALCHIMIST LAUSANNE.** Li/FRG 1974; Ch; 3900; 109 × 8.54 (357.61 × 28.02); M; 14.5; Sisters: **75231 CHEMIST LUTETIA** (Li); **75232 QUIMICO LISBOA** (Pa); **75233 QUIMICO LEIXOES** (Po); **75234 CHIMISTE SAYID** (Mo).

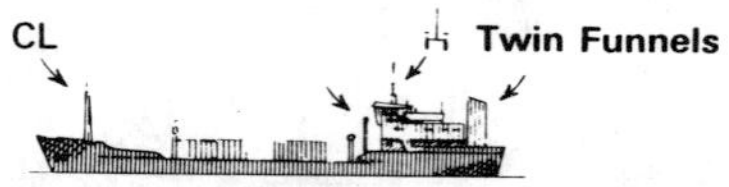

KMF H13
75240 PROOF SPIRIT. Li/Ne 1975; Ch; 1500; 73.46 × 6.15 (241.01 × 20.18); M; 12.5; Sister: **75241 PROOF TRADER** (Li).

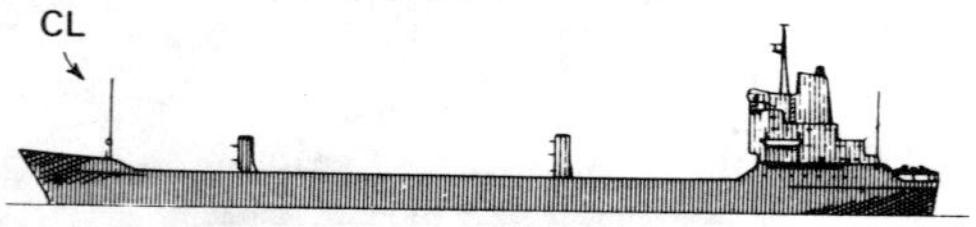

KMF H13
75260 ANEMOS. Gr/FRG 1976; Con; 8400; 143.82 × 8.32 (471.85 × 27.3); M; 18.25; Sister: **75261 PELAGOS** (Gr); Similar (probably has no 'towers' on deck): **75262 HERMES 1** (Pa).

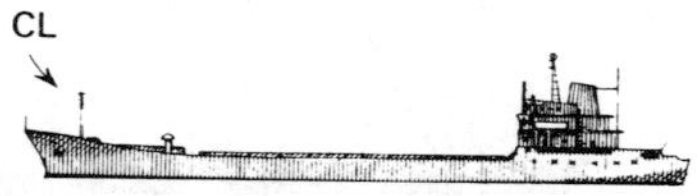

KMF H13
● ★**75280 EUROBRIDGE PIONIR.** Ys/FRG 1973; Con; 4000; 118.88 × 6.4 (390.03 × 21); M; 15.5; ex PIONIR 1978; ex MARITIME CHAMP 1974; Sister: **75281 SUN FLOWER** (Ko); ex MARITIME ACE 1973.

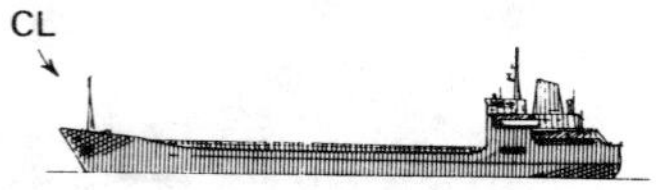

KMF H13
● **75290 HEINO.** FRG/FRG 1971; C/Con; 1000; 88.5 × 5.28 (290.35 × 17.32); M; 14; ex SCOL VENTURE 1976; ex BALTIC UNIT; ex HEINO 1971; Similar (some may have deck cranes) (FRG flag): **75291 IBESCA ALGERIA;** ex IBESCA ESPANA 1978; ex TWIEHAUSEN 1977; **75292 IBESCA BELGICA;** ex IBESCA BRITANNIA 1978; ex LUBBECKE 1977; **75293 NORRSUNDET;** ex URSA 1977; **75294 FRAUKE;** ex COMAR II 1974; ex FRAUKE 1972; **75295 MARGRET;** ex MARGRET KNUPPEL 1976; ex PINTO 1973; ex HANNES KNUPPEL 1973; **75296 BOMBERG;** ex ROXANE KERSTEN 1980; ex BOMBERG; **75297 NAUTIC.**

KMF H13
★**75320 BOLTENHAGEN.** DDR/DDR 1970; C/Con; 300; 57.79 × 3.68 (189.6 × 12.07); M; 12; Sisters (DDR flag): ★**75321 DIERHAGEN;** ★**75322 NIENHAGEN;** ★**75323 TRINWILLERSHAGEN;** (Ru flag): ★**75324 F. GAYLIS; (or FRITSIS GAYLIS);** ex JOCON; launched as NIENHAGEN; ★**75325 V. KUCHER;** ex JOBOX

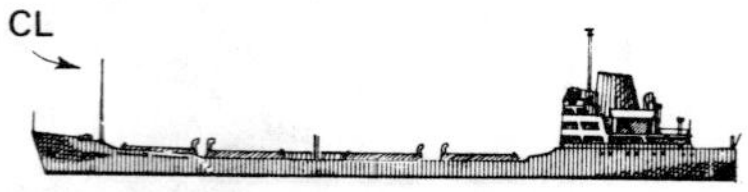

KMF H13
75250 CYMBELINE. Br/Br 1966; C; 5600; 112.78 × 7.64 (370.01 × 25.66); M; —; ex DALEWOOD 1974; Similar: **75251 OSWESTRY GRANGE** (Br); ex CHELWOOD 1974.

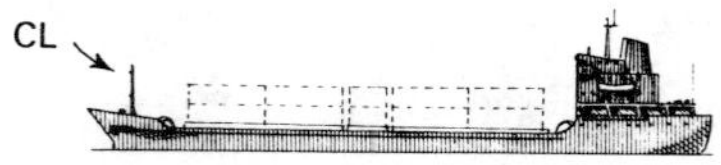

KMF H13
75270 ESLA. Sp/Sp 1977; C/Con; 3300; 99.73 × 6.9 (327.2 × 22.64); M; 14; ex GABRIELA DE PEREZ 1980; ex ZIM ATLANTIC 1978; launched as GABRIELA DE PEREZ; Sister: **75271 TAJO** (Sp); ex MARIA DE LAS ANGUSTIAS 1980; ex ZIM IBERIA 1979; ex MARIA DE LAS ANGUSTIAS 1976; Possibly similar (may have deck cranes): **75272 AVE** (Sp); **75273 TERMANCIA** (Sp); **75274 GALIA** (Sp); ex CHIEF ABULE; launched as GALIA.

KMF H13
75310 PACIFIC COURIER. Li/FRG 1969; C/Con; 2200; 94.98 × 5.72 (311.61 × 18.77); M; —; ex BLUHM 1; ex IDA BLUMENTHAL 1979; ex IDA ISLE 1972; launched as IDA BLUMENTHAL; Sister: **75311 PACIFIC CONVOY** (Li); ex JOHANN BLUMENTHAL 1979; ex GRETCHEN ISLE 1972; ex JOHANN ISLE 1969; launched as JOHANN BLUMENTHAL.

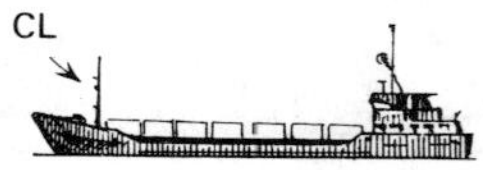

KMF H13
★**75330 FRITSIS ROSIN.** Ru/DDR 1971; C/Con; 500; 71.07 × 3.68 (233.17 × 12.07); M; 12; Sisters (Ru flag): ★**75331 GLEB SEDIN;** (DDR flag): ★**75332 WARIN;** ★**75333 BANSIN;** ★**75334 TESSIN;** ★**75335 KROPELIN;** ★**75336 RECHLIN.**

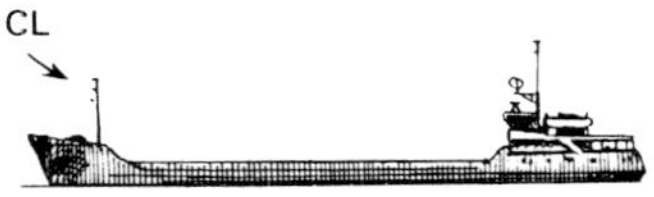

KMF H13
★75350 'BALTIYSKIY' type. Ru/Ru 1962 onwards, C(sea/river); 1900; 95.61 × 3.26 (313.68 × 10.7); TSM; 10; Most of this class of over 70 ships have the sequence KMFK—which see; Funnel heights vary; Among vessels known to be KMF (Ru flag): **★75351 KILIYA; ★75352 VLAS CHUBAR; ★75353 GOROKHOVETS.**

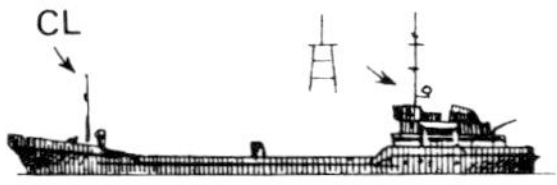

KMF H13
● **★75360 'LADOGA'** type. Ru/Fi 1972 onwards; C(sea/river); 1600; 81.01 × 4.01 (265.78 × 13.16); TSM; 12 approx; Sisters (Ru flag): **★75361 LADOGA 1; ★75362 LADOGA 2; ★75363 LADOGA 3; ★75364 LADOGA 4; ★75365 LADOGA 5; ★75366 LADOGA 6; ★75367 LADOGA 7; ★75368 LADOGA 9;** (Fi flag): **75369 NORPPA;** ex LADOGA 8 1974.

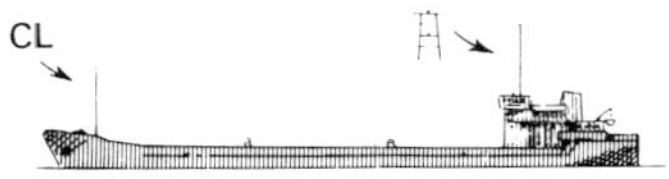

KMF H13
★75380 BALTIYSKIY 101. Ru/Fi 1978; C/Con(sea/river); 2000; 95 × 4 (311.68 × 13.12); TSM; 11.5; Hinged masts; Sisters (Ru flag): **★75381 BALTIYSKIY 102; ★75382 BALTIYSKIY 103; ★75383 BALTIYSKIY 104; ★75384 BALTIYSKIY 105; ★75385 BALTIYSKIY 106; ★75386 BALTIYSKIY 107; ★75387 BALTIYSKIY 108; ★75388 BALTIYSKIY 109; ★75389 BALTIYSKIY 110; ★75390 BALTIYSKIY 111.**

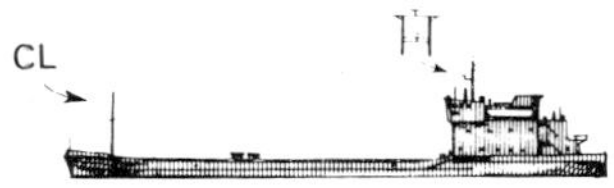

KMF H13
★75400 SAYMENSKIY KANAL. Ru/Fi 1978; C(sea/river); 1600; 81.01 × 4 (265.78 × 13.12); TSM; 12; ex LADOGA 10 1980; Sisters (Ru flag): **★75401 LADOGA 11; ★75402 LADOGA 12; ★75403 LADOGA 13; ★75404 LADOGA 14; ★75405 LADOGA 15; ★75406 LADOGA 16; ★75407 LADOGA 17; ★75408 LADOGA 18; ★75409 LADOGA 19; ★75410 LADOGA 20.**

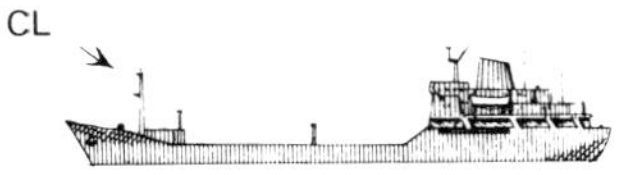

KMF H13
75420 TYYSTERNIEMI. Fi/Fr 1967; Ch; 2000; 87 × 5.97 (285.43 × 19.59); M; 13.75.

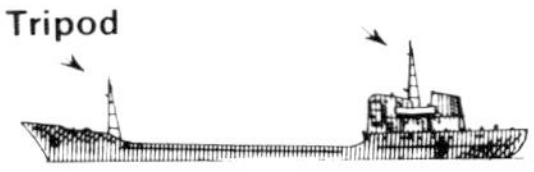

KMF H13
75430 ORAN. Pa/Ne 1960; C/Con; 500/1100; 79.08 × 3.68/4.9 (259.45 × 12.07/16.08); M; 14.5; ex BRIGITTE 1979; ex FREIA 1976; ex HAGNO

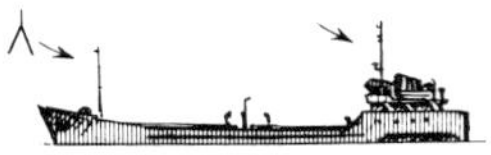

KMF H13
75440 EMINENCE. Br/Br 1969; C; 1000; 67.67 × 4.22 (222.01 × 13.85); M; 10.5; Similar (lower poop, pole masts): **75441 SENTENCE** (Br).

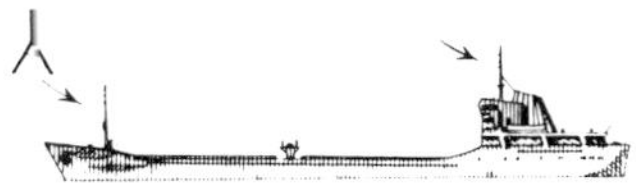

KMF H13
75450 FRED EVERARD. Br/Br 1972; C; 1600; 91.14 × 5.14 (299.02 × 16.86); M; 12.75; Sisters (Br flag): **75451 SAGACITY; 75452 SERENITY; 75453 SUMMITY; 75454 SUPERIORITY; 75455 SUAVITY;** Similar: **75456 EILDON: 75457 ETTRICK;** Similar (extended poop & forecastle): **75458 MARTINDYKE; 75459 MAIRI EVERARD.**

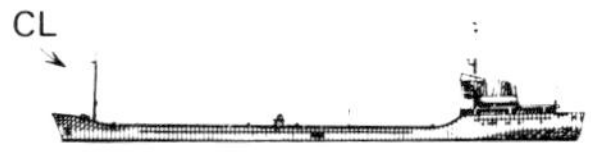

KMF H13
75470 SECURITY. Br/Br 1971; C; 1600; 85.02 × 5.07 (278.94 × 16.63); M; 13; Sister: **75471 SINCERITY** (Br).

KMF H13
75480 HYDE PARK. Br/Ne 1974; C; 1600; 83.5 × 5.13 (273.95 × 16.83); M; 12; ex SYON PARK 1974; Sister: **75481 MISHNISH** (Br); Similar: **75482 BALLYKERN** (Br); ex BAXTERGATE 1980; **75483 COTINGA** (Br); **75484 ATLANTIC SUN** (Ne); ex OKKO BOSMA 1978.

KMF H13
75490 STAR VENUS. Gr/Ne 1978; C; 1000; 71.38 × 4.53 (234.19 × 14.86); M; —.

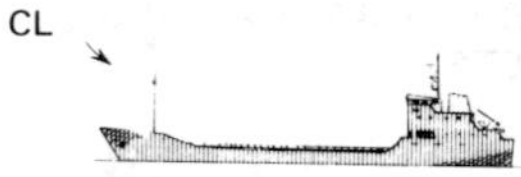

KMF H13
● **75500 PAULINA BRINKMAN.** Ne/Ne 1975; C; 1000; 65.82 × 4.3 (215.94 × 14.11); M; —; Sisters (Ne flag): **75501 ALLIANCE; 75502 CALYPSO; 75503 DOGGERSBANK; 75504 ELS TEEKMAN; 75505 EMMAPLEIN; 75506 HUGO BRINKMAN; 75507 FLEVO; 75508 KARIN; 75509 MARJAN; 75510 PAVONIS.**

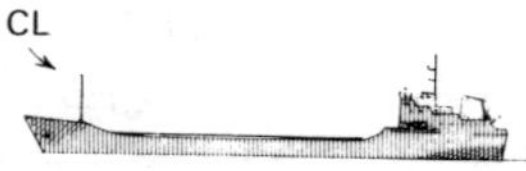

KMF H13
● **75520 MERAK.** Ne/Ne 1976; C; 1400; 76.41 × 4.83 (250.69 × 15.85); M; 13.

KMF H13
75530 NORRBOTTEN. Ne/Ne 1977; C; 1600; 80.22 × 5.55 (263.19 × 18.21); M; 13.25; launched as MALLARSEE; Sisters (Ne flag): **75531 BOTTENVIKKEN;** launched as DELTASEE; **75532 KARLSVIK;** ex ERIESEE 1977.

KMF H13
75540 SYLVIA ALPHA. Ne/Ne 1977; C; 1600; 81.72 × 5.5 (268.11 × 04); M; 12.5; Sisters (Ne flag): **75541 SYLVIA BETA; 75542 SYLVIA DELTA; 75543 SYLVIA EPSILON; 75544 SYLVIA GAMMA; 75545 SYLVIA OMEGA.**

KMF H13
75550 MATHILDE. Ne/Ne 1977; C; 1600; 75.11 × 5.37 (246.42 × 17.62); M; 12.

KMF H13
75560 ALTAPPEN. Ne/Ne 1978; C; 1600; 80.68 × 5.12 (264.7 × 16.8); M; 12; Sisters (Ne flag): **75561 SILVIA; 75562 SUSANNA.**

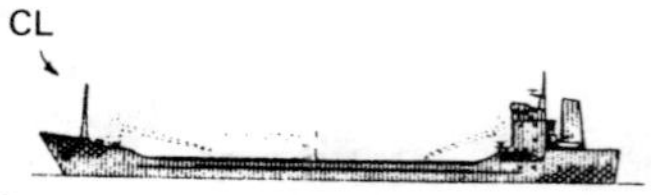

KMF H13
75570 LESLIE GAULT. Br/Br 1977; C; 1600; 91.52 × 5.16 (300.26 × 16.93); M; 12.5; May have deck cranes; Sisters (Br flag): **75571 CERINTHUS; 75572 GALLIC FJORD; 75573 MARKINCH.**

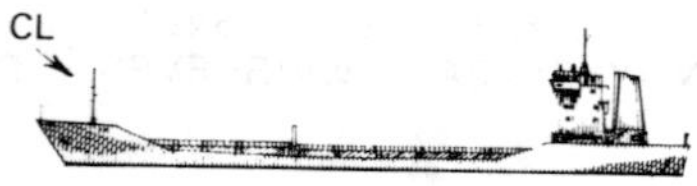

KMF H13
● **75580 CITY OF PLYMOUTH.** Br/Br 1978; Con; 1600; 104.17 × 5.56 (341.77 × 18.24); M; 14.5; **'AS—300'** type; Sisters (Br flag): **75581 CITY OF PERTH; 75582 CITY OF HARTLEPOOL; 75583 CITY OF IPSWICH; 75584 CITY OF OXFORD;** Similar (smaller funnels): **75585 CROWN PRINCE; 75586 ROYAL PRINCE.**

KMF H13
75600 BREEZAND. Ne/FRG 1975; C; 1600; 79.51 × 5.55 (260.86 × 18.21); M; 12.5; Sisters (Br flag): **75601 CAIRNCARRIER; 75602 CAIRNFREIGHTER; 75603 CAIRNLEADER.**

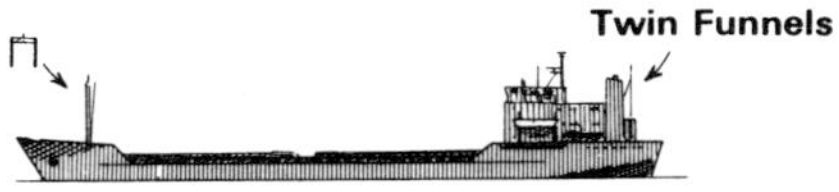

KMF H13
● **75610 SELNES.** Ic/Br 1975; C/B; 3600; 102.01 × 6.83 (334.68 × 22.41); M; 14; ex RISNES; Sisters (Br flag): **75611 RINGNES; 75612 ROCKNES; 75613 ROLLNES; 75614 SALTERSGATE;** ex GREEN PARK 1977; (may now have cranes).

KMF H13
⋆**75640 KESSULAID.** Ru/Tu 1972; RoC; 1000; 80.22 × 4.15 (263.19 × 13.62); M; 13; ex WOTAN 1975; Stern door; Similar (Ru flag): ⋆**75641 MANILAID;** ex THUNAR 1975; ⋆**75642 SUURLAID;** ex DONAR 1975; Similar (FRG built—Ru flag): ⋆**75643 HEINLAID;** ex YMIR 1974; ex FREJ 1972; launched as YMIR; ⋆**75644 VIIRELAID;** ex THIASSI 1974; ex IRISH TRADER 1972; launched as THIASSI.

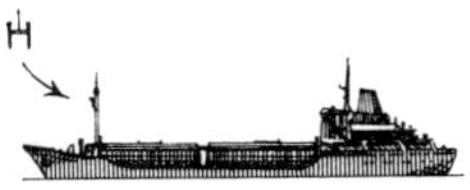

KMF H13
75680 CLAUDE. Pa/FRG 1967; LGC; 1200; 67.67 × 5.03 (222.01 × 16.5); M; 12; Similar (Pa flag): **75681 BRIGITTA;** ex LIGUR 1973; **75682 SUNNY FELLOW;** ex LIBRA 1973.

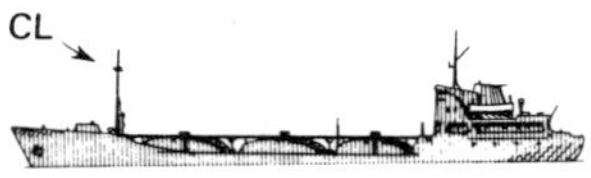

KMF H13
75690 ESSO FLAME. Fi/Fi 1966; LGC/Tk; 1000; 74.53 × 4.08 (244.52 × 13.39); M; 12.

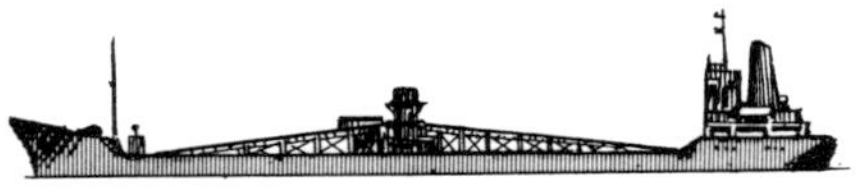

KMF H13
75710 CHIKUMA MARU. Ja/Ja 1970; Cem; 6400; 131.5 × 7.82 (431.43 × 25.66); M; 12.75.

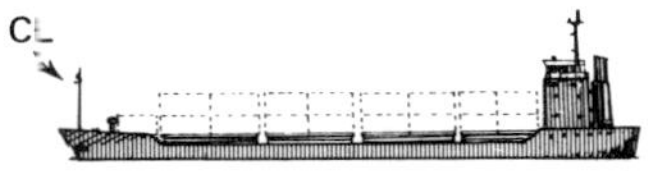

KMF H13
75620 SUDWIND. FRG/FRG 1978; C/Con; 500; 79.23 × 3.5 (259.94 × 11.48); M; 12.5; Sisters (FRG flag): **75621 DETLEF SCHMIDT; 75622 EIDER; 75623 MAJA—M; 75624 ST. ANTONIUS.**

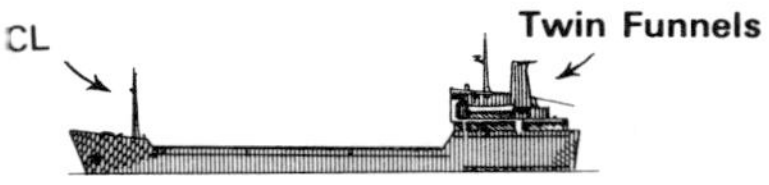

KMF H13
75630 ROF BEAVER. Br/FRG 1971; RoC; 1000; 80.7 × 4.14 (264.76 × 13.58); M; 14; ex HELGA 1 1975; ex BIBIANA 1973; ex MONARCH FAME 1972; ex IRISH FAME 1971; ex BIBIANA 1971; Stern door.

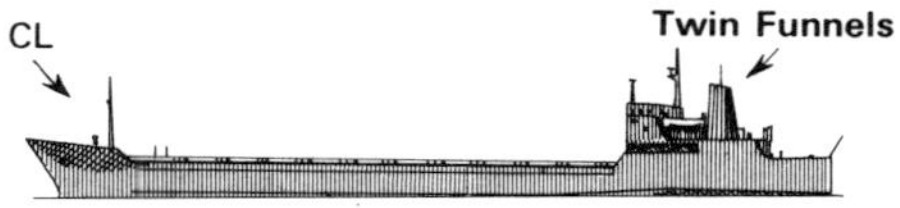

KMF H13
75650 DELLYS. Ag/Sp 1974; RoC; 1600; 107 × 4.85 (351.05 × 15.91); TSM; 18; Sisters (Ag flag): **75651 COLLO; 75652 TENES.**

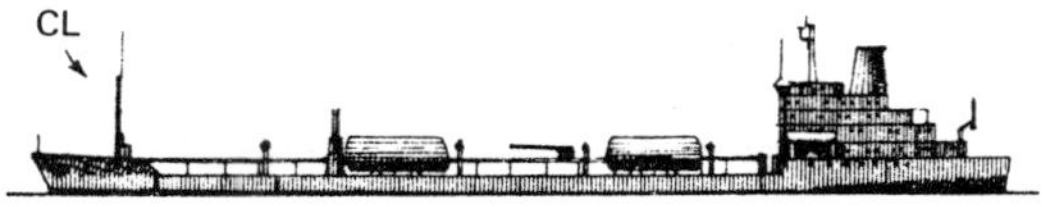

KMF H13
75660 ANCO CHALLENGER. Br/No 1972; Tk/Ch; 16000; 165.08 × 9.94 (541.6 × 32.61); M; 15.5; ex POST CHALLENGER 1979; Sisters (Br flag): **75661 ANCO CHAMPION;** ex POST CHAMPION 1979; **75662 ANCO CHARGER;** ex POST CHARGER 1979; **75663 ANCO CHASER;** ex POST CHASER 1980; **75664 ANCO ENDEAVOUR;** ex POST ENDEAVOUR 1977; **75665 ANCO ENTERPRISE;** ex POST ENTERPRISE 1978; (Fr flag): **75666 ANCO ENTENTE;** ex POST ENTENTE 1978; **75667 ANCO ENERGIE;** ex POST ENERGIE 1978.

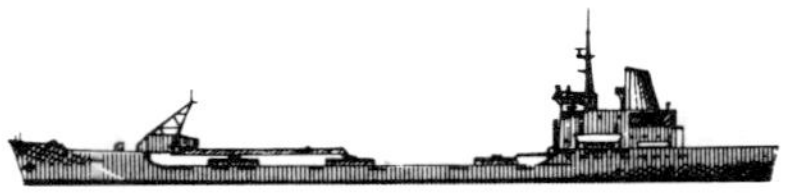

KMF H13
75700 ANAHUAC II. Me/Sp 1969; Cem; 5300; 120.12 × 7.03 (394.09 × 23.06); TSM; —.

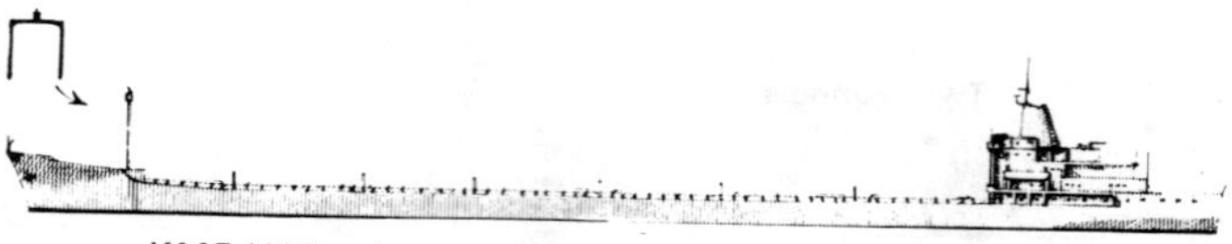

KMF H13
★75720 VITKOVICE. Cz/Br 1966; B; 24300; 209.91 × 11.56 (688 × 37.93); M; —.

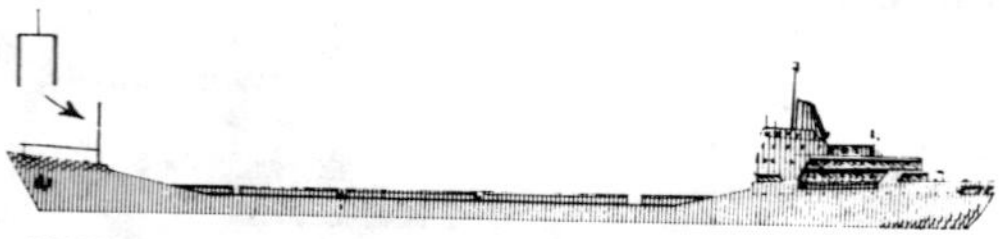

KMF H13
★75730 ZAGLEBIE DABROWSKIE. Pd/Pd 1967; B; 11000; 156.37 × 9.51 (513.02 × 31.2); M; 15.5; **'B—520'** type; Sisters (Pd flag): **★75731 DOLNY SLASK; ★75732 GORNY SLASK; ★75733 PODHALE; ★75734 KUJARWY; ★75735 BIESZCZADY.**

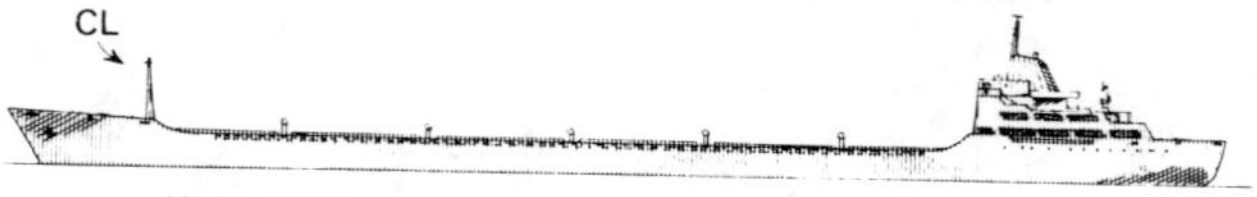

KMF H13
75740 FIDES. It/It 1964; B; 16100; 193.63 × 10.35 (635.27 × 33.96); M; 16.

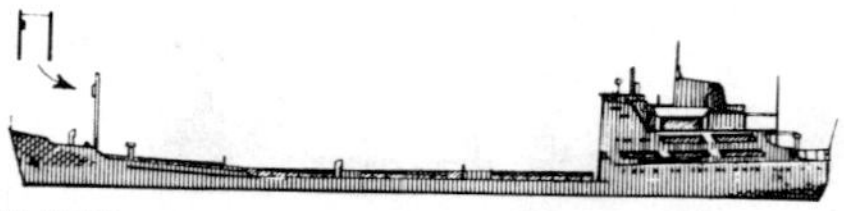

KMF H13
75750 SUNNY. Pa/Nc 1959; O; 6900; 130.16 × 7.86 (427.03 × 25.79); M; 11.5; ex SUNNY PRINCE 1977; ex ARABELLA 1974.

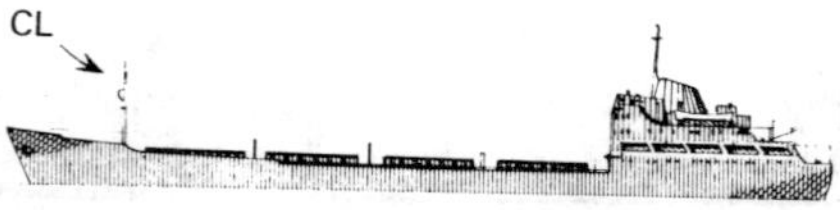

KMF H13
75760 LUIGI GARDELLA. It/No 1959; O; 6500; 130.16 × 7.88 (427.03 × 25.85); M; —; ex GEORGE 1971.

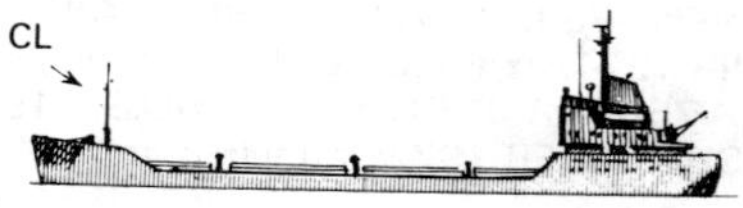

KMF H13
● **★75770 TARNOW.** Pd/Pd 1970; O; 3800; 108.77 × 6.86 (356.86 × 22.51); M; 14; **'B-447'** type. Sisters: **★75771 KEDZIERZYN** (Pd); **★NOWY SACZ** (Pd); **★75773 EUGENIE COTTON** (Pd).

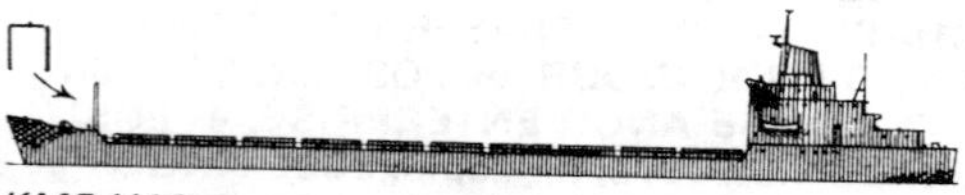

KMF H13
75780 GYPSUM KING. Br/Ca 1975; B; 12800; 150.81 × 9.25 (494.78 × 30.35); T; 15; Sister: **75781 GYPSUM BARON** (Br).

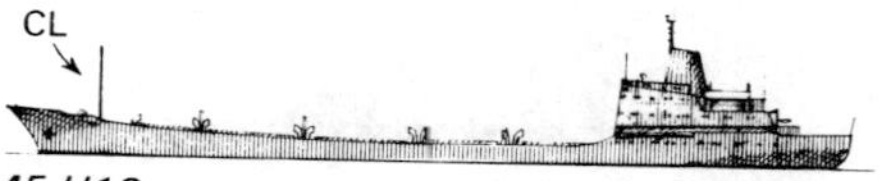

KMF H13
● **★75790 VERILA.** Bu/Bu 1969; B; 7800; 134.02 × 7.48 (439.7 × 24.54); M; 13; Sisters: **★75791 VESLETS** (Bu); **★75792 VIDEN** (Bu); **75793 EIRA** (Fi).

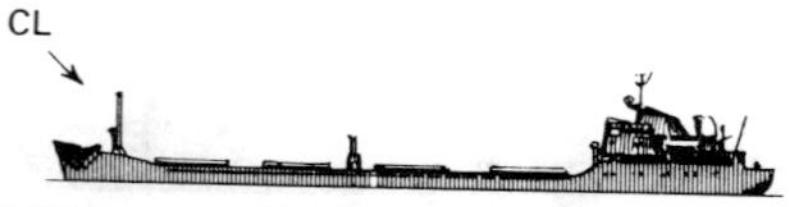

KMF H13
75800 FORT POINT. Br/Ne 1968; C; 4400; 110.42 × 6.85 (362.27 × 22.47); M; 12.5; ex DUNVEGAN HEAD 1977; Sister: **75801 BEACON POINT** (Br); ex DUNCANSBY HEAD 1976.

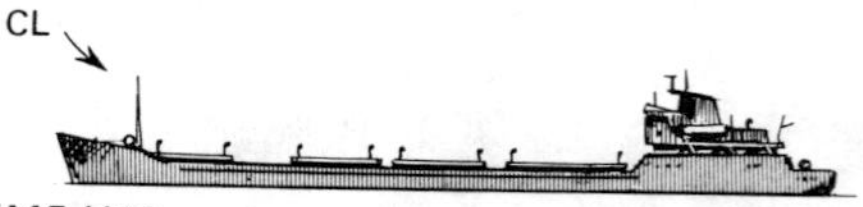

KMF H13
75810 WILMINGTON. Br/Br 1969; B; 5700; 124.96 × 7.71 (410.01 × 25.3); M; 13.

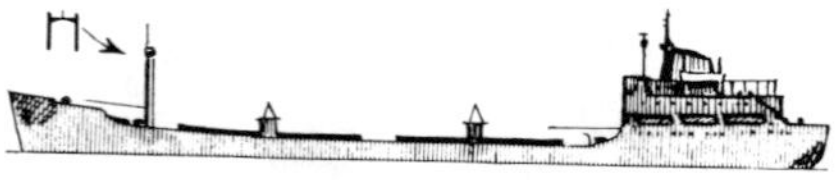

KMF H13
★75820 SUTOMORE. Ys/Fr 1958; O; 6100; 130.16 × 7.67 (427 × 25.16); M; 13; ex LA COLINA 1974.

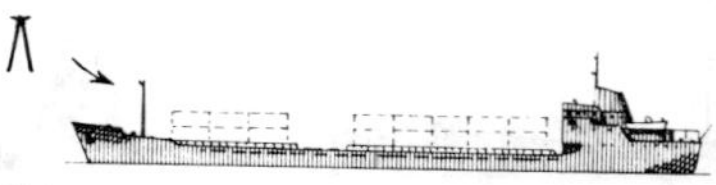

KMF H13
75830 VALANI. Cy/Br 1968; Con; 1600; 98.48 × 4.85 (323.1 × 15.91); M; 16; ex CERVANTES: converted from cargo & lengthened 1970; Sister: **75831 CONTMAR** (Pa); ex CHURRUCA.

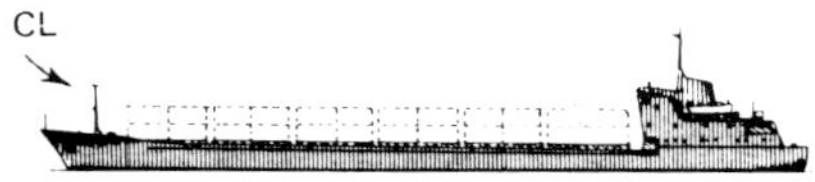

KMF H13
75840 LADY M.A.CROSBIE. Ca/Br 1966; Con; 400; 118.73 × 6.5 (389.53 × 21.33); M; 14.75; ex CORTES 1978; ex BALTIC VANGUARD 1977; Converted from cargo 1977.

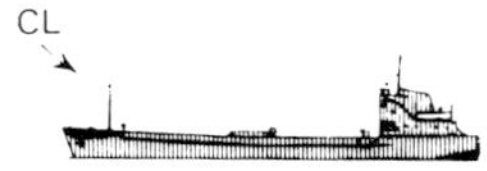

KMF H13
75850 THE LADY PATRICIA. Br/Br 1962; C/Tk; 1300; 64.93 × 4.59 (213.02 × 15.06); M; 11; Modernised 1974.

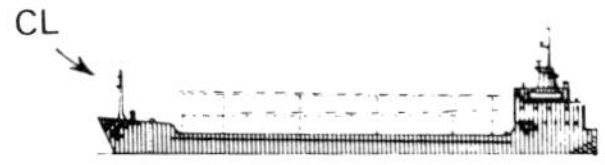

KMF H13
75860 CRAIGANTLET. FRG/Fi 1972; Con; 800; 77.98 × 4.16 (255.84 × 13.65); M; 15; Sister: **75861 CRAIGWOOD**(FRG).

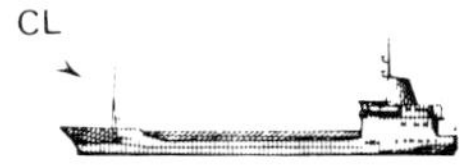

KMF H13
75870 HILARY WESTON. Br/Ne 1974; B; 1600; M; 11; ex FRENDO HOPE 1976; Sisters:(Br flag): **75871 CAROLINE WESTON;** ex FRENDO GRACE; **75872 BARBARA WESTON;** ex FRENDO PRIDE 1976; **75873 GRETCHEN WESTON;** ex FRENDO STAR; **75874 LOUISE WESTON;** ex FRENDO FAITH 1976; **75875 WENDY WESTON;** ex FRENDO SPIRIT 1976; Similar (some Gr. Build): **75876 ANNA DRENT** (Ne); **75877 CHANTENAY** (Fr); **75878 AGIOS SPYRIDON** (Gr); launched as FRENDO VENTURE; Similar (lengthened): **75879 CARIB**(Cy); ex FRENDO CARIB 1977; ex FRENDO UNITED 1976; **75880 NORNED THOR** (Ne); ex HOLBERG 1979; ex ATLANTIC PROGRESS 1977.

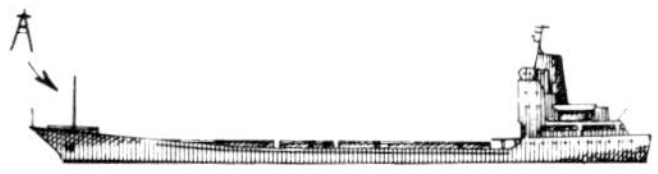

KMF H13
● **75890 KATHLEEN.** Li/Sp 1970; Con; 3200; 99.73 × 6.37 (327.2 × 20.9); M; 14.5; ex FORTUNA 1975; ex MANCHESTER MERIT 1972; ex MANCHESTER MERITO 1970; launched as CATALINA DEL MAR; Similar: **75891 BOX TRADER** (Gr); ex FRONTIER: **75892 PROGRESS** (Sg); ex VILLE D'ORIENT 1980; ex PROGRESS 1979; ex CHESHIRE PROGRESS; ex STADT ELSFLETH 1976; launched as MAGDALENA DEL MAR.

KMF H13
● **75900 MANCHESTER ZEAL.** Br/Br 1973; Con; 2500/5300; 112.1 × 5.74/6.38 (367.78 × 18.8/20.93); M; 15.5; ex CARGO ZEAL 1976; ex MANCHESTER ZEAL 1975; Sister: **75901 VILLE D'ORIENT** (Fr); ex MANCHESTER VIGOUR 1980; ex CARGO VIGOUR 1976; ex MANCHESTER VIGOUR 1975.

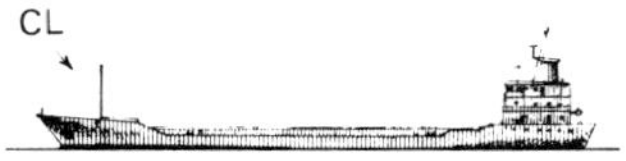

KMF H13
● **75910 LONDONBROOK.** Br/Ne 1975; C; 1600; 93.6 × 5.64 (307.09 × 18.5); M; 13; ex TOWERSTREAM 1979; ex LONDON BOOK 1977; Sister (Br flag): **75911 LANCASTERBROOK;** ex CHELSEASTREAM; ex LEICESTERBROOK 1977; **75912 LINCOLNBROOK;** Similar (De flag): **75913 JUNIOR LONE**; **75914 HELGE FOLMER**; **75915 JUNIOR LOTTE** (small travelling crane).

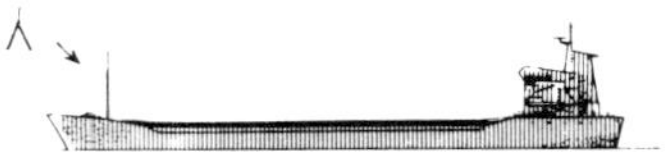

KMF H13
● **75920 BIRLING.** Br/Br 1977; C; 1600; 91.22 × 5.45 (299 × 17.88); M; 14; Sister: **75921 EMERALD** (Br).

KMF H13
75930 WHITEGATE. Br/Ne 1972; C; 1600; 87.46 × 5.45 (286.94 × 17.88); M; 12; Sisters: **75931 MOIDART** (Br); **75932 MINGARY** (Br); **75933 REGENT'S PARK** (Br); Possible sisters: **75934 HIGHGATE** (Br); **75935 BONA FE** (Fi); ex NORRSTAL 1977.

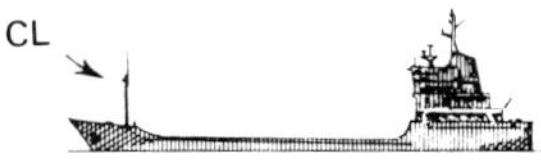

KMF H13
75940 OSTETURM. FRG/Ne 1971; C; 1000; 71.43 × 4.49 (234.35 × 14.73); M; 12.

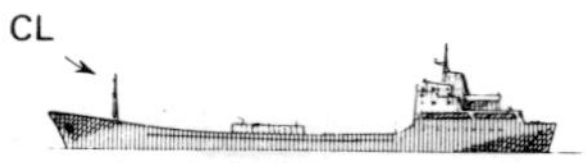

KMF H13
★75950 COMANDANTE VILO ACUNA. Cu/Sp 1977; Cem; 1800; 81.46 × 5.11 (267.26 × 16.77); M; 12.

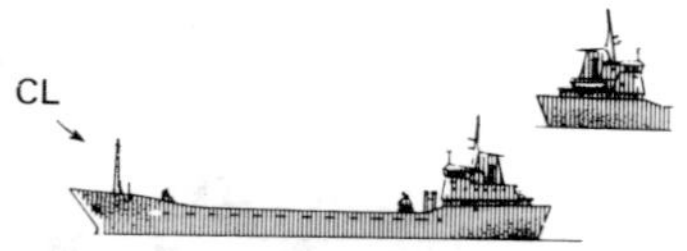

KMF H13
● **75970 URRIDAFOSS.** Ic/De 1971; C; 500; 76.61 × 3.47 (251.35 × 11.38); M; 12; ex MERC EUROPA 1974; Travelling cranes. Starboard side of superstructure differs—see inset; Sisters: **75971 ASMAA** (Mo) ex MERC PHOENECIA 1977; **75972 ECO SADO** (Po) ex MERC ASIA 1973; **75973 ECO TEJO** (Po) ex MERC CONTINENTAL 1973; **75974 GRUNDARFOSS** (Ic) ex MERC AUSTRALIA 1974; **75975 NEXUS** (Pa) ex ALBERT S 1978; ex NORDSEE 1977; ex MERC GROENLANDIA 1974.

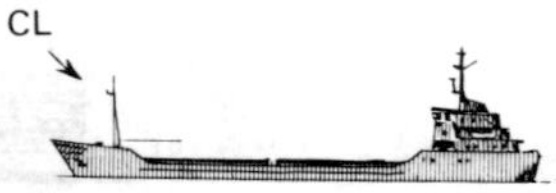

KMF H13
75990 VANDA. Ne/Ne 1974; C; 1500; 78.77 × 5.02 (258.43 × 16.47); Sister: **75991 VICTORY** (Ne); Similar: **75992 VANESSA** (Ne).

KMF H13
76010 KORTENAER. Ne/Pd 1968; C; 1500; 82.17 × 4.89 (269.59 × 16.04); M; —; ex HOVIN 1971; **'B-459'** type.

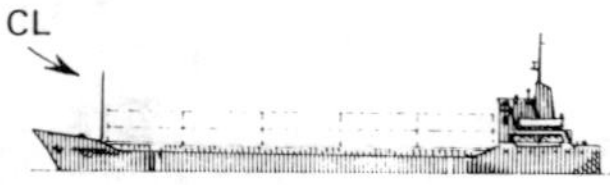

KMF H13
76030 CARMEN DEL MAR. Sp/Sp 1970; Con; 2800; 88.22 × 5 (289.44 × 16.4); M; 12; ex ISLA DEL MEDITERRANEO 1974; Sisters: **76031 ISLA DEL ATLANTICO** (Sp); **76032 MING CHUN** (Tw); ex ECHUCA 1976; launched as ARDAN.

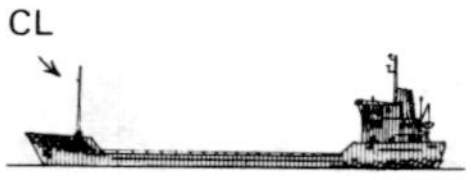

KMF H13
76050 PROCYON. Ne/Ne 1977; C; 1400; 66.53 × 5.2 (218.27 × 17.06); M; 11.

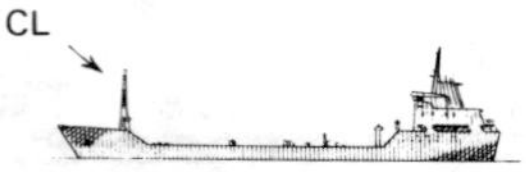

KMF H13
★75960 JUAN DE DIOS FRAGA MORENA. Cu/De 1970; Tk/AT; 500; 70.67 × 3.39 (231.86 × 11.12); M; 12; ex CHARLOTTENBORG 1974; Sister: **★75961 ELPEDIO BEROVIDES** (Cu); ex CHRISTIANSBORG 1976; Similar: **75962 ISLAND KING** (Pa); ex AGGERSBORG.

KMF H13
75980 VALZELL. Ih/Ih 1976; C; 1000; 61.52 × 4.78 (201.84 × 15.68); M; 11; Sister: **75981 SERENELL** (Ih).

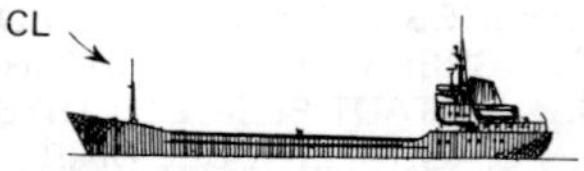

KMF H13
76000 TUVANA. Ne/Ne 1972; C; 1400; 78.01 × 4.92 (255.94 × 16.14); M; —.

KMF H13
● **76020 VISCOUNT.** Ne/Ne 1976; C; 1000; 65.84 × 4.29 (216.01 × 14.07); M; 13; Probable sister: **76021 VELOX** (Ne).

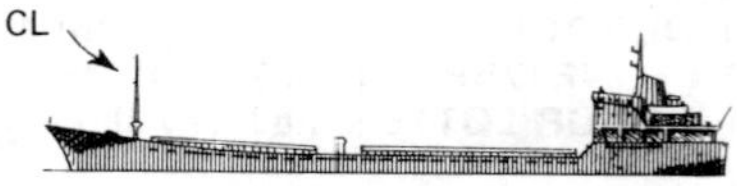

KMF H13
76040 MINA COTO. Sp/Sp 1972; C; 3800; 108.21 × 6.62 (355.02 × 21.72); M; 13.25; Sister: **76041 MINA ENTREGO** (Sp).

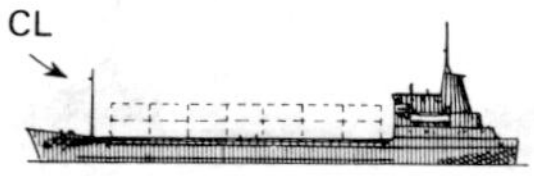

KMF H13
76060 PACIFIC DESPATCHER. Li/FRG 1968; Con; 1500; 78.06 × 3.62 (256.1 × 11.88); M; —; ex KILDARE 1974.

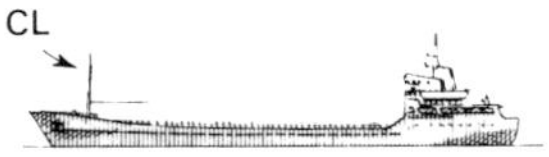

KMF H13
76070 EXTRAMAR NORTE. Sp/Sp 1976; C; 1200; 77.02 × 4.52 (252.69 × 14.83); M; 11; Sister (Sp flag): **76071 EXTRAMAR ESTE:** Probable sisters: **76072 EXTRAMAR OESTE; 76073 EXTRAMAR SUR;** Possible sisters: **76074 CATALINA DEL MAR; 76075 MARIONA DEL MAR.**

KMF H13
76080 MYRIAM DEL TORO. Sp/Sp 1972; C/Con; 800; 61.65 × — (202.26 × —); M; 11.5; Sisters (Sp flag): **76081 BEGONA DEL MAR; 76082 JOSE ESQUIVEL; 76083 SANTURIO; 76084 LOLA DEL MAR; 76085 PILAR DEL MAR; 76086 SOMIO;** Possible sisters: **76087 JUAN CARLOS TORO**(Sp); **76088 NORTHUMBRIA ROSE**(Br); ex KIELDER STAG 1978; ex BEGONA DE ASTOBIZA 1975; Similar (smaller): **76089 ASTONDO**(Sp); **76090 MOUNTCREST**(Br) ex ANZORAS 1976; **76091 CAPECREST**(Br) ex AKORDA 1976.

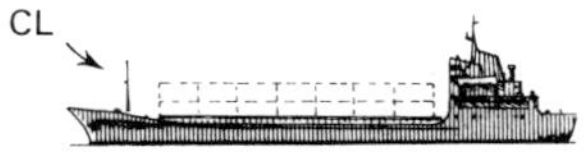

KMF H13
76100 ESTHER DEL MAR. Sp/Sp 1971; Con; 2000; 79.94 × 5.65 (262.27 × 18.54); M; 13; ex MANCHESTER RAPIDO 1977; launched as ESTHER DEL MAR: Sisters:(Sp flag): **76101 MERCEDES DEL MAR; 76102 BEATRIZ DEL MAR; 76103 FOLITA** ex MANCHESTER MERCURIO 1980.

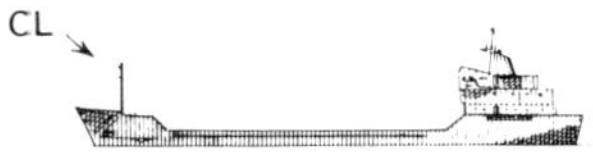

KMF H13
76110 CAREBEKA VIII. Ne/Ne 1976; C; 1600; 81.01 × 5.38 (265.78 × 17.65); M; 12.5; Sister: **76111 CAREBEKA IX** (Ne).

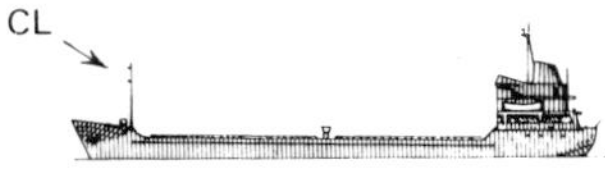

KMF H13
● **76120 FER BALTICO.** Sp/Sp 1976; C; 1600; 82.1 × 5.44 (269.36 × 17.85); M; 11.5; Sister: **76121 FER BALEAR** (Sp).

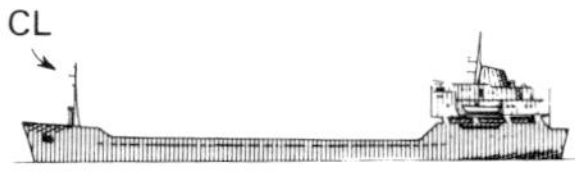

KMF H13
76130 BEEDING. Br/Sw 1971; C; 1600; 87.03 × 4.96 (285.53 × 16.27); M; 12; Sister: **76131 FALKENBERG** (FRG) ex PONTOS 1976; ex FALKENBERG 1973; launched as ISOTAT.

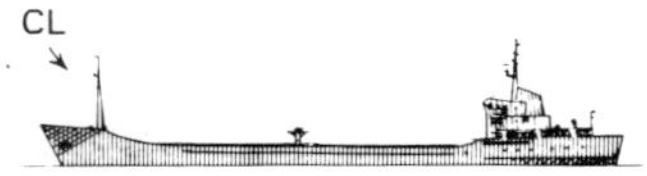

KMF H13
76140 LUMINENCE. Br/Br 1977; C; 1600; 91.24 × 5.15 (299.34 × 16.9); M; 13; Sister: **76141 KINDRENCE** (Br).

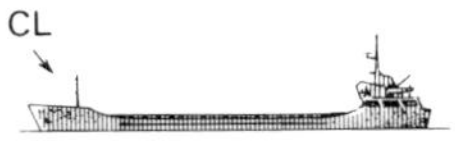

KMF H13
76150 DAUNT ROCK. Ih/Br 1976; C; 800; 64.01 × 3.8 (210.01 × 12.47); M; 11; Probable Sisters (Ih flag): **76151 SKELLIG ROCK; 76152 FASTNET ROCK;** Possible similar: **76153 TUSKAR ROCK.**

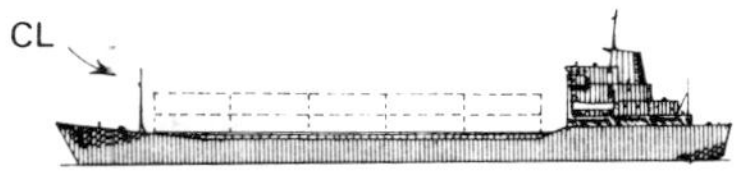

KMF H13
● **76160 BRATHAY FISHER.** Br/Ne 1971; Con; 2100/3600; 105.92 × 5.49/6.36 (347.51 × 18.01/20.87); M; 14.5; ex CALDERON 1979; ex BRATHAY FISHER 1976.

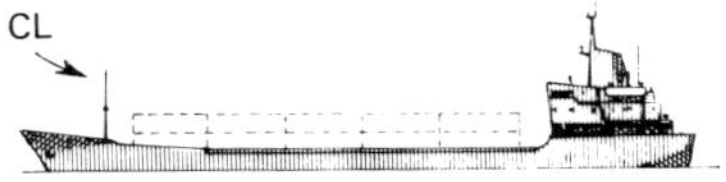

KMF H13
76170 AMERICAN ISLANDER. Li/Sp 1973; Con; 3100; 104.53 × 4.73 (342.95 × 15.52); M; 1675; ex AMERICAN MING 1977; Sisters: **76171 MARINE CONTAINER** (Pa) ex AMERICAN COMANCHE 1980; ex AMERICAN MIST 1978; **76172 STRAITS CONTAINER** (Li) ex AMERICAN MAIN 1978.

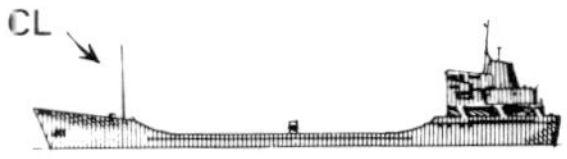

KMF H13
● **76180 ALSTERTAL.** Cy/Ne 1975; C; 1600; 81.67 × 5.38 (267.95 × 17.65); ex TELL 1977; Similar (Ne flag): **76181 BARENDSZ; 76182 VEERHAVEN.**

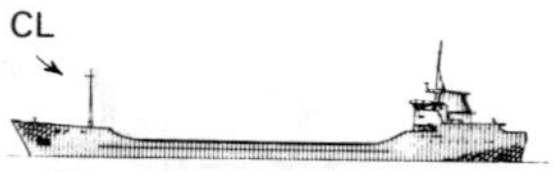

KMF H13
76190 FENJA. Ne/Ne 1977; C; 1600; 81.01 × 5.38 (265.78 × 17.65); M; 12.5; ex TINA HOWERDA 1977.

● 76195

KMF H13
76200 ALICIA. FRG/FRG 1970; C; 1000; 73.84 × 5.04 (242.26 × 16.54); M; 12.5; ex ALICIA D 1975; ex ALICIA 1972.

KMF H13
76210 TAKARI I. Ia/FRG 1966; C; 2300; 94.9 × 5.26 (311.35 × 17.26); M; 12.5; Sisters (Ia flag): **76211 TAKARI II; 76212 TAKARI III; 76213 TAKARI IV; 76214 TAKARI V; 76215 TAKARI VI; 76216 TAKARI VII; 76217 TAKARI VIII.**

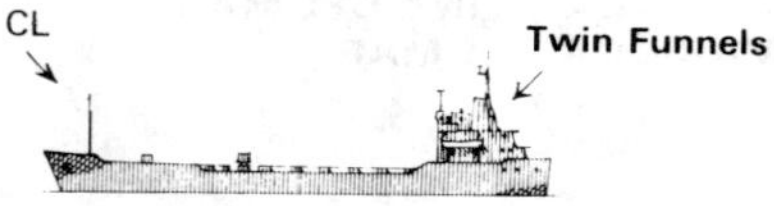

KMF H13
⋆76220 STAROGARD GDANSKI. Pd/Sp 1971; RoC; 1000; 79.33 × 4.7 (260.27 × 15.42); M; 14; ex COMETA 1973; Stern door **'Porter' type**. Sister: **76221 CHERCHELL** (Ag) ex ARDAN 1974.

KMF H13
76230 ODET. Fr/FRG 1975; WT/Ch; 1600; 90.1 × 5.72 (295.6 × 18.77); M; 13.5; Sister: **76231 RHONE** (Sd).

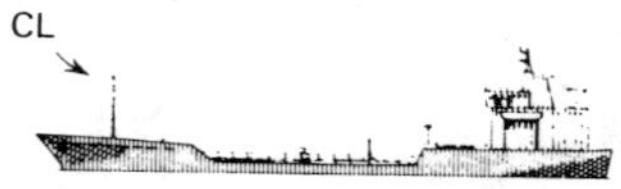

KMF H13
76240 ISMARA. Ag/FRG 1978; Tk/WT; 2000; 87.76 × 5.72 (287.93 × 18.77); Sisters (Ag flag): **76241 DAHRA; 76242 ZACCAR.**

KMF H13
● **⋆76250 DA QING No 216.** RC/Ma 1978; Tk; 3900; 106.28 × 6.88 (348.69 × 22.57); M; 13; Sister: **⋆76251 DA QING No 217.**

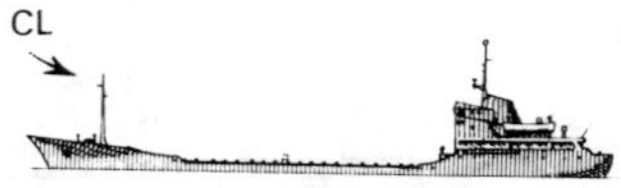

KMF H13
76260 CLERVILLE. Fr/Fr 1975; Tk/WT; 1600; 91.01 × 5.39 (298.6 × 17.68); M; 14.5.

KMF H13
76270 LEMAN. Sd/FRG 1965; Tk/WT; 1600; 79.51 × 5.99 (260.86 × 19.65); M; 13.5; ex STAINLESS ANNE; ex DANELAKE ex NORDENHAMERSAND 1972; Converted from cargo 1974.

KMF H13
76280 RIVER SHANNON. Br/Br 1970; Tk; 1600; 83.52 × 5.13 (274.02 × 16.83); M; 12; ex STEERSMAN 1976.

KMF H13
76290 POINTSMAN. Br/Br 1970; Tk; 2900; 99.29 × 6.17 (325.75 × 20.24); M; 12.

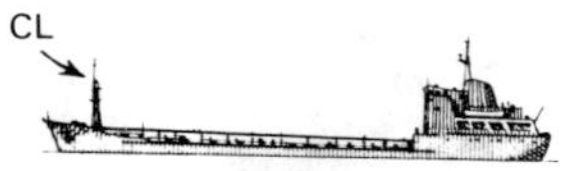

KMF H13
76300 PHILIP BROERE. Ne/Ne 1971; Tk/Ch; 1300; 81.11 × 4.97 (266.11 × 16.31); M; 13.

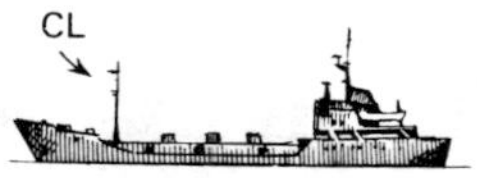

KMF H13
⋆76310 ALTAIR. Ru/It 1970; Tk/WT; 1200; 68.92 × 4.6 (226.12 × 15.09); M; 12; Sister: **⋆76311 ARKTUR**(Ru).

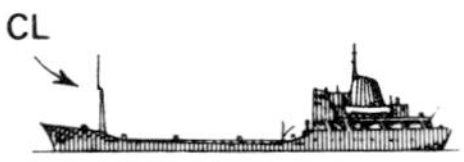

KMF H13
76320 LADY MARIANNA. It/FRG 1964; Tk; 1000; 64.57 × 5.19 (211.84 × 17.03); M; 12.25; ex HEINRICH ESSBERGER 1975.

KMF H13
76340 MARE LIBERUM. Ne/Ne 1964; Tk/Ch; 800; 76.08 × 4.19 (249.61 × 13.75); M; 11; Lengthened and deepened 1971; Sisters (Ne flag): **76341 MARE IRATUM; 76342 MARE SILENTUM.**

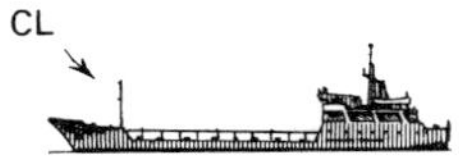

KMF H13
76350 NERVA. Sp/Sp 1976; Ch; 700; 62.21 × ×.23 (204.1 × 13.88); M; 11.5; Sister: **76351 NIEBLA** (Sp).

KMF H13
76370 KINGSABBEY. Br/Br 1966; LGC; 700; 56.7 × 3.43 (186.02 × 11.25); M; 11.5; ex RUDI M 1980; ex TEVIOT.

KMF H13
76390 PASS OF DRUMOCHTER. Br/Ne 1974; Ch; 1600; 80.75 × 5.56 (264.93 × 18.24); M; 13.5; Sister: **76391 PASS OF DIRRIEMORE** (Br).

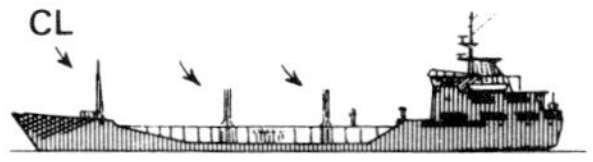

KMF H13
76410 MARE NOVUM. Ne/No 1977; Ch; 1600; 83.01 × 5.91 (272.34 × 19.4); M; 13; Sisters (Ne flag): **76411 MARE BONUM; 76412 MARE MAGNUM.**

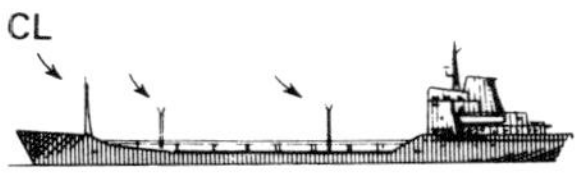

KMF H13
76430 ALCHIMIST LUBECK. Cy/FRG 1970; Ch; 1600; 87.03 × 5.1 (285.53 × 16.73); M; 12.5; Possible Sister: **76431 ALCHIMIST FLENSBURG** (Cy); ex CHEMATHENE 1980; ex ALCHIMIST FLENSBURG 1979.

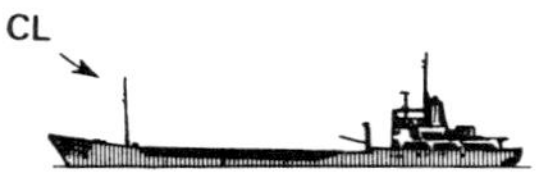

KMF H13
76330 BREDENBEK. FRG/FRG 1969; Tk; 1000; 74.05 × 4.63 (242.95 × 15.19); M; 11; Sisters (FRG flag): **76331 AMMERSBEK; 76332 SUSEBEK; 76333 OSTERBEK; 76334 GEFO BALTIC** ex TARPENBEK 1980; **76335 CORNELIS BROERE** (Ne) ex ISEBEK 1974.

KMF H13
76360 AUDACITY. Br/Br 1968; Tk; 700; 72.6 × 4.4 (238.19 × 14.44); M; —.

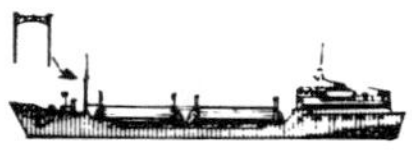

KMF H13
76380 CELIA. Sg/Fg 1963; LGC; 1200; 62.03 × 4.27 (203.51 × 14.01); M; 12; ex CELSIUS 1976.

KMF H13
76400 THUNTANK 7. Sw/Sw 1967; LGC; 1200; 72.95 × 5.17 (239.34 × 16.96); M; 12.5; ex THUNGAS 1975; ex THUNGAS 1 1974; ex PORSGRUNN 1974.

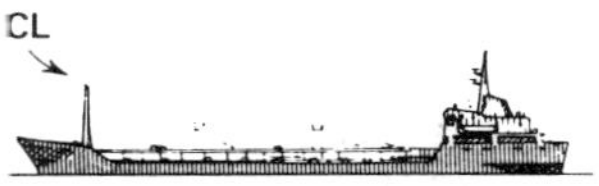

KMF H13
76420 ALCHIMIST ROTTERDAM. Cy/Sw 1973; Ch; 1600; 85.86 × 5.4 (281.69 × 17.72); M; 13.5; ex CHEMAPHRODITE 1980; ex ALCHIMIST MARATHON 1979; ex ALCHIMIST ROTTERDAM 1978; ex CHIMISTE NANTES 1977; Sisters: **76421 MULTITANK FRISIA** (Sg); ex OFRISIA 1974; ex FRISIA 1973; ex MONSUN 1972; **76422 MULTITANK HOLSATIA** (Sg); ex HOLSATIA 1974; Possibly similar: **76423 POINTE DU ROC** (Fr); **76424 POINTE DU VAN** (Fr); ex POINTE DE PENHARN.

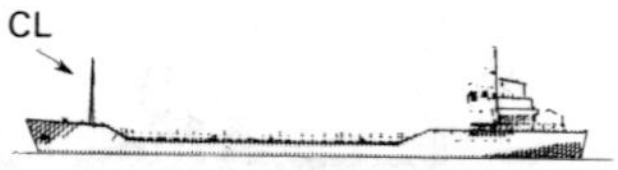

KMF H13
76440 PIC ST LOUP. Fr/FRG 1974; WT; 1600; 89.24 × 5.26 (192.78 × 17.26); M; —.

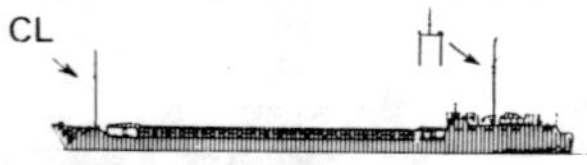

KMF H13
● **76460 ERIKA BOJEN.** FRG/FRG 1978; C(sea/river) 500; 81.62 × 3.28 (267.78 × 10.76); M; 11; Hinged masts; Sister (FRG flag): **76461 KONIGSEE 1;** Similar (higher bridge): **76462 LARISSASEE;** Similar (poop extends to stern): **76463 ALEXANDER;** Probably similar: **76464 HUBERNA.**

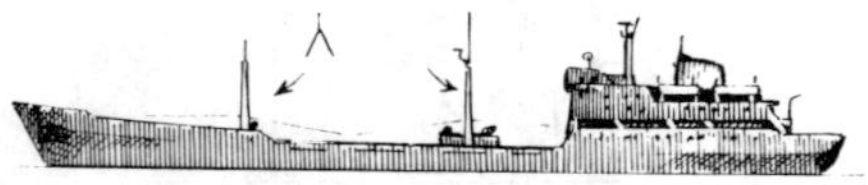

KMF H13
⋆**76490 IVAN AIVAZOVISKIY.** Ru/Ru 1963; FC; 6100; 130 × 7.17 (426.51 × 23.52); D-E; 16.5; Sisters (Ru flag): ⋆**76491 ALEKSEY VENETSIANOV;** ⋆**76492 VIKTOR VASTNETSOV;** ⋆**76493 ALEKSANDR IVANOV;** ⋆**76494 VASILIY PEROV;** ⋆**76495 ILYA REPIN;** ⋆**76496 VASILIY POLENOV;** ⋆**76497 MOLODAYA GVARDIYA;** ⋆**76498 IMENI 61 KOMMUNARA;** ⋆**76499 PIONER MURMANA;** ⋆**76500 HANS POGELMANN;** ⋆**76501 SEVERNYY VETER;** ⋆**76503 DEMYAN KOROTCHENKO;** ⋆**76504 MARSHAL ROKOSSOVSKIY;** ⋆**76505 GORETS;** ⋆**76506 ALMAZNYY;** ⋆**76507 SIBIR;** ⋆**76508 KONSTANTIN OLSHANSKIY;** ⋆**76509 ARKHIP KUINDZHI;** ⋆**76510 VIKTOR LYAGIN;** ⋆**76511 IVAN SHISHKIN;** ⋆**76512 VASILIY SURIKOV;** ⋆**76513 ZOLOTOY ROG;** ⋆**76514 KHUDOZHNIK S. GERASIMOV;** ⋆**76515 PIONER VOLKOV;** ⋆**76516 KAZIS PREYKSHAS;** ⋆**76517 ULAN-UDE;** ⋆**76518 POLYARNYE ZORI;** ⋆**76519 KHUDOZHNIK DEYNEKA;** ⋆**76520 KHUDOZHNIK VRUBEL;** ⋆**76521 GRANITNYY;** ⋆**76522 VASILY VERESCHCHAGIN;** ⋆**76523 IVAN KRAMSKOY;** ⋆**76524 VALENTIN SEROV;** ⋆**76525 KOSMONAUT GAGARIN;** ⋆**76526 OBUKHOVSKAYA OBORONA;** ⋆**76527 MARSHAL MALINOVSKIY;** ⋆**76528 POLYARNYY KRUG;** (Bu flag): ⋆**76529 SLANCHEV BRIAG;** ⋆**76530 ZLANTNI PIASATZI;** ⋆**76531 LAZUREN BRIAG;** ⋆**76532 ALBENA;** ⋆**76533 KITEN;** (DDR flag): ⋆**76534 EVERSHAGEN;** ⋆**76535 LUTTEN-KLEIN;** (Rm flag): ⋆**76536 POLAR I;** ⋆**76537 POLAR II.**

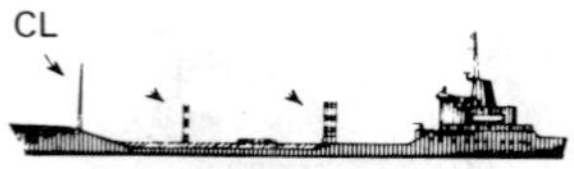

KMF H13
76450 ASTRAMAN. Br/Br 1973; Ch; 1600; 87.41 × 5.5 (286.74 × 18.04); M; 14; Sister: **76451 POLARISMAN** (Br).

KMF H13
76470 CONDOR. FRG/FRG 1978 C (sea/river); 900; 73.11 × 3.4 (239.86 × 11.15); M; 11; Hinged masts.

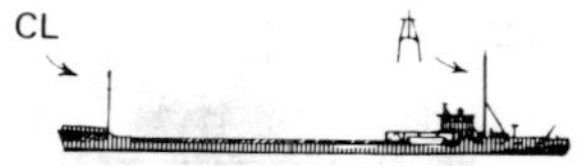

KMF H13
76480 CARGO-LINER I. FRG/Ne 1973; C (sea/river); 900; 80.02 × 3.18 (262.53 × 10.43); M; 10; Sister (FRG flag): **76481 CARGO-LINER II;** Possible sisters: **76482 CARGO-LINER III; 76483 CARGO-LINER IV; 76484 CARGO-LINER V; 76485 CARGO-LINER VI.**

KMF H13
76550 REEFER STAR. Si/FRG 1954; R; 3500; 114.99 × 6.57 (377.26 × 21.56); M; 15; ex NIKOLOAS 1980; ex KETTY 1979; ex ARAGON 1973.

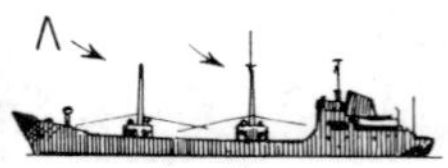

KMF H13
76560 GIANNIS DIMAKIS III. Gr/FRG 1956; C; 1000; 67.09 × 5.15 (220.11 × 16.9); M; 11; ex POLLENDAM 1977; ex VICTOR 1971; ex VORMANN RASS 1966.

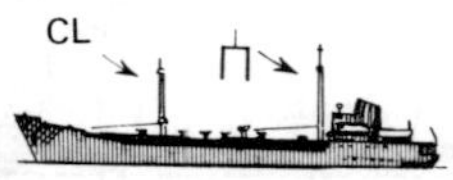

KMF H13
⋆**76570 COMBATE DE PALMAMOCHA.** Cu/Sw 1957; C; 487; 65.94 × 3.77 (216.34 × 12.37); M; 12; ex CORA 1964.

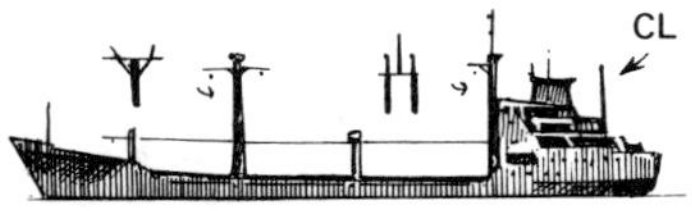

KMF H13
★76580 ABRAM ARKHIPOV. Ru/Fi 1973; C/TC; 3200; 97.31 × 6.7 (319.26 × 21.98); M; 14; Sisters (Ru flag): **★76581 VLADIMIR FAVORSKIY; ★76582 MITROFAN GREKOV; ★76583 VASILIY POLENOV; ★76584 NIKOLAY YAROSHENKO; ★76585 NIKOLAY KASATKIN; ★76586 KONSTANTIN YUON; ★76587 IGOR GRABAR; ★76588 IVAN SHADR; ★76589 MIKHAIL CHEREMNYKH; ★76590 VERA MUKINA; ★76591 YEKATERINA BELASHOVA.**

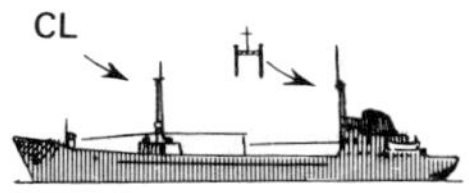

KMF H13
76600 GEVISA. It/FRG 1966; C; 500; 69.96 × 5.46 (229.53 × 17.91); M; 12; ex KOTIBE 1977; ex EDDA BUUR 1974; ex ELBA 1971; Sisters: **76601 CEDROS** (Po); ex IBIZA 1972; **76602 GORGULHO** (Po); ex MALLORCA 1972; **76603 LIMA** (Po); ex KORSIKA 1972; **76604 DINA R. E.** (Fr); ex MALTA 1971; **76605 RENEE R. E.** (Fr); ex KRETA 1971.

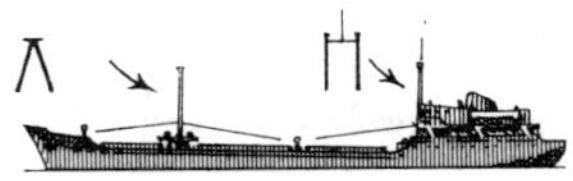

KMF H13
76610 BULK MERCHANT. Cy/Hu 1964; C; 1600; 84.44 × 4.93 (277.03 × 16.17); M; 11.5; ex FLEUR 1980; ex MARIAM 1974; ex FOFO; ex GEORGE X 1972; ex SAGALAND 1971; Lengthened 1976; Sisters (Cy flag): **76611 BULK PIONEER;** ex IXIA 1980; ex GARORM 1974; ex IRENE 1973; ex NICHOLAS X 1972; ex SAGAHORN 1971; **76612 BULK TRADER;** ex PRIMROSE 1980; ex GYRAM 1974; ex PAULINE 1973; ex PATRICIA X 1972; ex SAGAFJELL 1971.

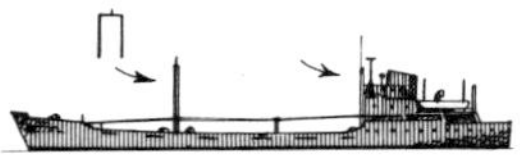

KMF H13
76620 MANDI. Pa/Br 1956; C; 1700; 78.92 × 4.8 (258.92 × 15.75); M; 12; ex KLIO 1980; ex SPARTA 1977; ex IRISH WILLOW 1969.

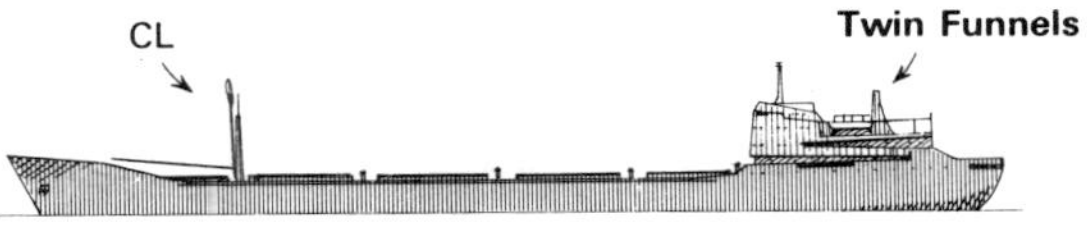

KMF H13
★76630 CHEMIK. Pd/Pd 1965; C/B; 7500/10600; 156.67 × 8.11/8.86 (514.01 × 26.61/29.07); M; 14.25; **'B512'** type; Probable sister: **★76631 ENERGETYK** (Pd).

KMF H13
● **★76640 HAJNOWKA.** Pd/Pd 1971; C; 800; 59.82 × 4.2 (196.26 × 13.78); M; 11.5; **'B 457'** type; Sisters (Pd flag): **★76641 BARLINEK; ★76642 RUCIANE.**

KMF H13
76650 PIAVE. It/It 1973; A/Wa; 5000 Dspl.

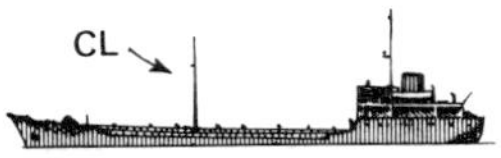

KMF H13
76660 PASS OF GLENCLUNIE. Br/Br 1963; Tk; 1400; 74.73 × 4.67 (245.18 × 15.32); M; 11.5.

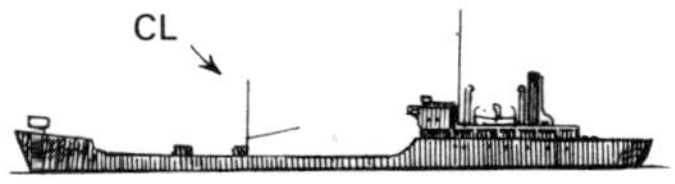

KMF H13
76670 THULA. Th/Ja 1942; FA/Tk; 4700 Dspl; 100 × 6.1 (338 × 20); T; —; Sister: **76671 MATRA** (Th).

KMF H13
76680 DUTCH SAILOR. Ne/Ne 1966; Tk/Ch; 600; 65.38 × 3.74 (214.5 × 12.27); M; —; Lengthened 1971; Sister: **76681 DUTCH MATE** (Ne).

KMF H13
76690 DELOS I. Pa/Fr 1957; WT; 1100; 70.21 × 4.33 (230.35 × 14.21); M; 12; ex CHERGUI 1975.

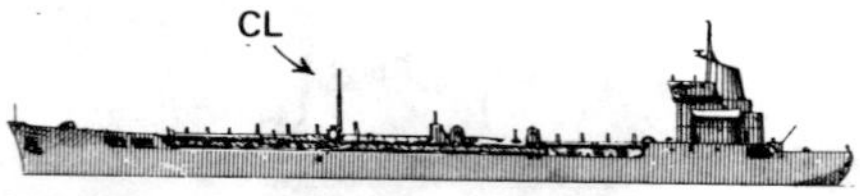

KMF H13
76700 PACIFIQUE. Fr/Br 1970; D; 7300; 131.68 × 7.49 (432.02 × 24.57); TSM; 13.

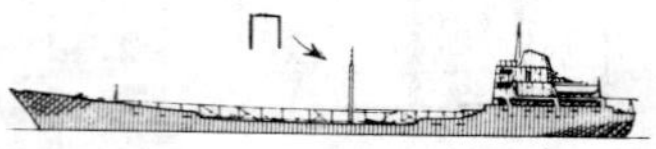

KMF H13
76710 SAINT MITRE. Fr/It 1965; Tk; 2700; 99.57 × 6.07 (326.67 × 19.91); M; —; Launched as SISINA PELLEGRINO.

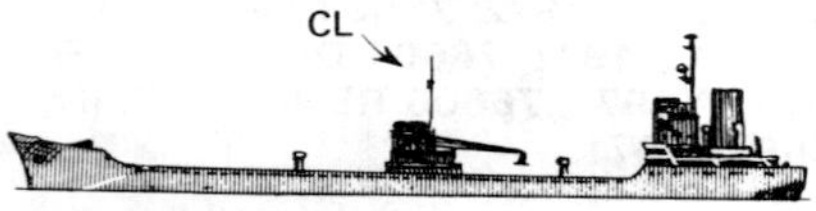

KMF H13
76720 UNYO MARU. Ja/Ja 1959; Cem; 5700; 127.06 × 7.42 (416.86 × 24.34); M; 11.5; Possibly similar: **76721 ZUIYO MARU** (Ja); **76722 GULFCEM** (Pa); ex KYUYO MARU 1975.

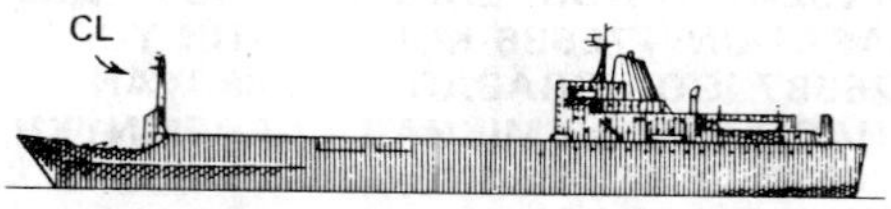

KMF H2
76730 FRECCIA BLU. It/It 1970; RoC; 4400; 163.96 × 5.98 (537.93 × 19.62); TSM; 21; Stern doors; lengthened 1977; (Note—drawing shows vessel before lengthening); Sister: **76731 FRECCIA ROSSA** (It).

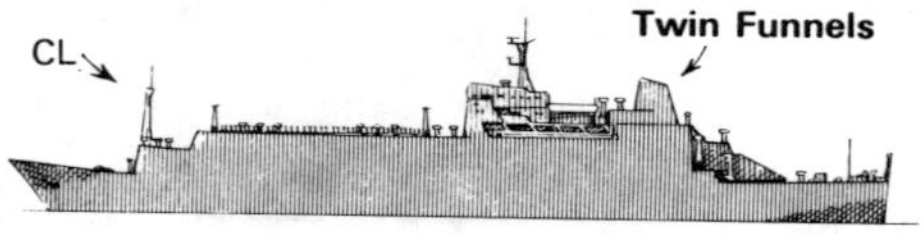

KMF H2
76740 GRIEG. Fr/Ne 1972; RoC; 4000; 138.26 × 7.01 (453.61 × 23); M; 18.5; Stern door; Sister: **76741 SIBELIUS** (Fr).

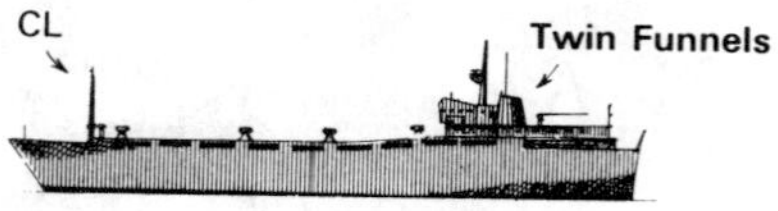

KMF H2
76750 NAVARCO. Fr/Fr 1972; RoC; 500; 100.51 × 3.99 (329.76 × 13.09); TSM; 17.5; ex MONTLHERY; Stern door; Sisters (Fr flag): **76751 MONACO; 76752 MONZA.**

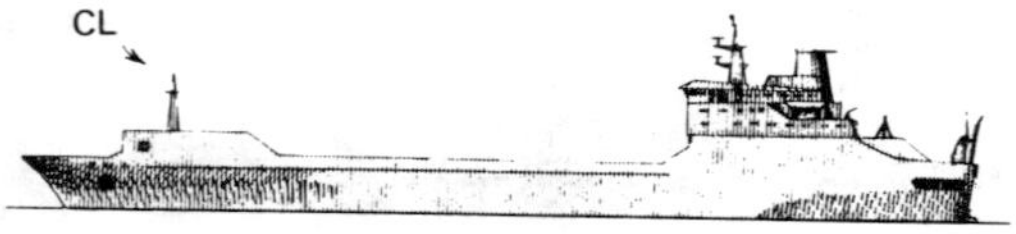

KMF H23
● **76760 ELK.** Br/Ko 1977; RoC; 5500; 151.01 × 7.32 (495.44 × 24.02); M; 18.5; Bow door/ramp; Stern door/ramp; Sisters: **76761 MERZARIO IONIA** (Br); ex STENA SHIPPER 1980; ex NORSKY 1980; **76762 HELLAS** (Gr); ex ALPHA PROGRESS 1979; ex STENA RUNNER 1977; **76763 SYRIA** (Gr); ex ALPHA ENTERPRISE 1980; **76764 ATLANTIC PROJECT** (Br); **76765 ATLANTIC PROSPER** (Br); **76766 TOR FELICIA** (Br); ex MERZARIO GRECIA; ex TOR FELICIA 1978; **76767 STENA FREIGHTER** (Sw); ex MERZARIO AUSONIA 1980; **76768 IMPARCA MIAMI** (Br); ex STENA CARRIER 1980; ex IMPARCA EXPRESS I 1980.

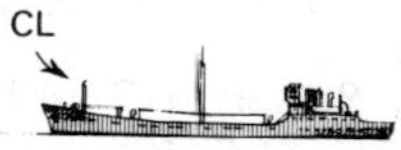

KMF H3
76780 CARSO. Br/It 1946; C; 859; 61.17 × 4.73 (200.69 × 15.52); M; 10; ex ALDER 1970; ex CARSO 1954; Similar: **76781 AMEL** (Pa); ex MARINELLO 1974; ex TAMARIS 1964; ex ISTAR 1960; ex ALBA 1955; ex GUNILIA; Possibly similar (lengthened): **76782 SPES** (Ar).

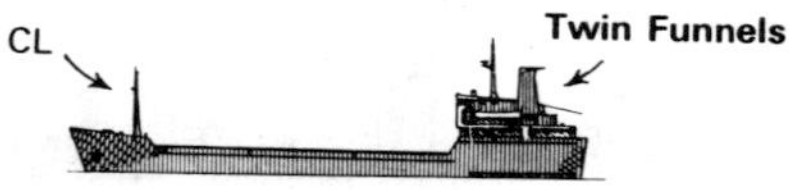

KMF H3
76790 ROF BEAVER. Br/FRG 1971; RoC; 1000; 80.7 × 4.14 (264.76 × 13.58); M; 14; ex HELGA I 1975; ex BIBIANA 1973; ex MONARCH FAME 1972; ex IRISH FAME 1971; ex BIBIANA 1971; Stern ramp.

KMF H3
76800 RIVAMAHON. Sp/Sp 1974; RoC; 684; 75.01 × 4.27 (246.1 × 14.01); M; 14; Sister: **76801 RIVANERVION** (Sp).

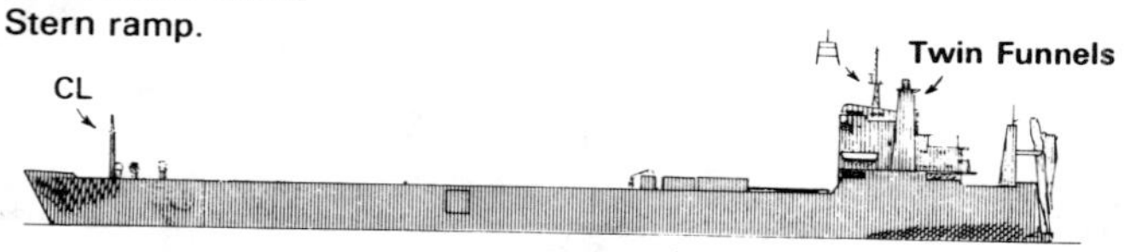

KMF H3
● **76810 LYRA.** US/FRG 1977; RoC; 14200; 193.33 × 8.61 (634.28 × 28.25); M; 19; ex REICHENFELS 1981; Slewing stern ramp; Stern door; Sister: **76811 NOREFJORD** (US); ex RHEINFELS 1981; Similar (Ja built): **76812 CYGNUS** (US); ex RABENFELS 1981; **76813 ESSEN** (FRG); ex RAUENFELS 1980.

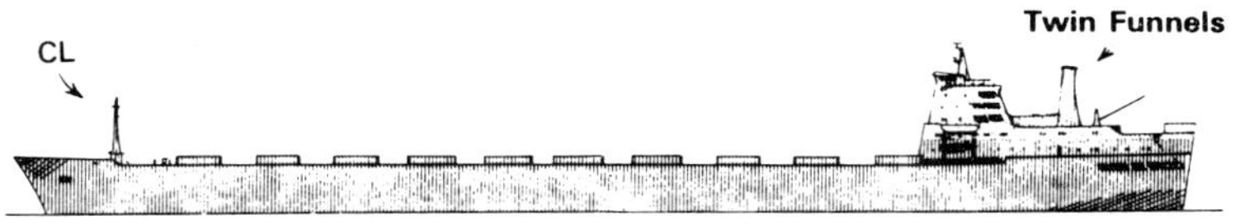

KMF H3
76820 ATLANTIC SONG. Sw/Fr 1967; RoC/Con; 14900; 223.02 × 9.15 (731.69 × 30.02); M; 21.5; Lengthened 1976; stern door; Sister: **76821 ATLANTIC STAR** (Ne).

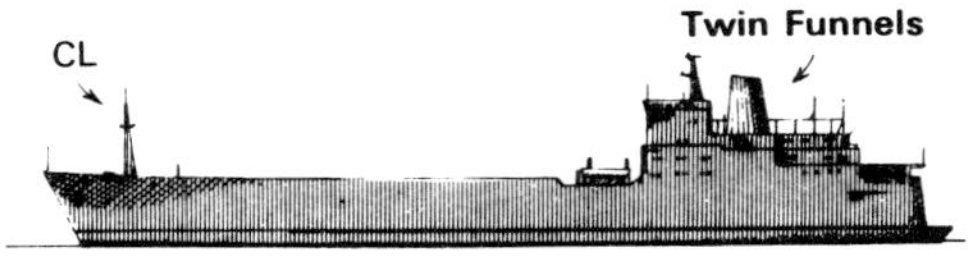

KMF H3
76830 LYSAGHT ENTERPRISE. Au/Au 1973; RoC; 7600; 168.05 × 7.7 (551.34 × 25.26); M; 18; Lengthened 1977; (Note—drawing shows vessel before lengthening); Stern door; Sister: **76831 LYSAGHT ENDEAVOUR** (Au).

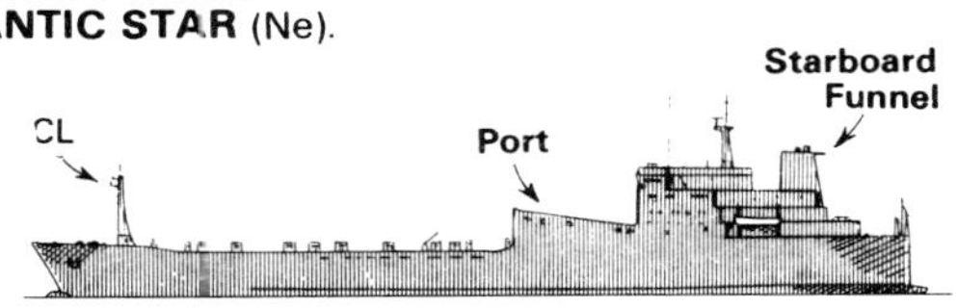

KMF H3
● **76840 MERZARIO GALLIA.** Sw/FRG 1977; RoC; 5100; 144.48 × 6.7 (474.02 × 21.98); TSM; 18.5; Stern door.

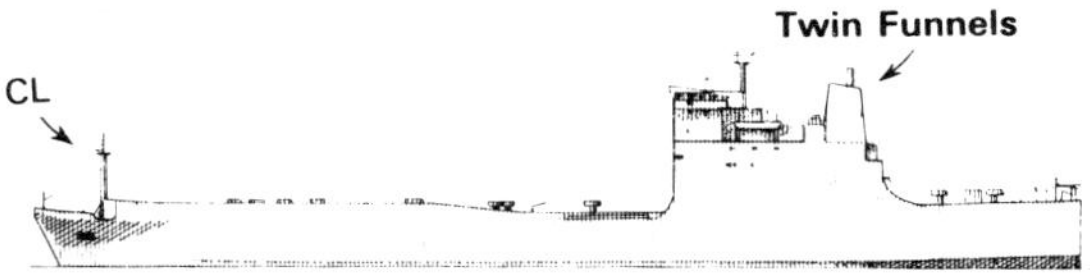

KMF H3
76850 FOSS DUNKERQUE. Fr/Fr 1978; RoC; 8700; 169.25 × 7.74 (555.2 × 25.3); M; 18.5; ex VILLE DE DUNKERQUE 1979; Stern door/ramp; Side doors; Sister: **76851 FOSS HAVRE** (Fr); ex VILLE DU HAVRE 1979; Similar: **76852 RO-RO MANHATTAN** (Fr); **76853 RO-RO GENOVA** (Fr); ex QATAR EXPRESS; ex RO-RO GENOVA.

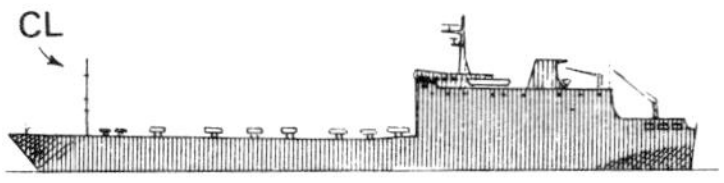

KMF H3
● **76860 CAP BENAT.** Fr/Fr 1977; RoC; 1600; 109.71 × 5.21 (359.94 × 17.09); TSM; 16; Stern door/ramp; Sisters (Fr flag): **76861 CAP CAMARAT; 76862 CAP LARDIER; 76863 CAP TAILLAT.**

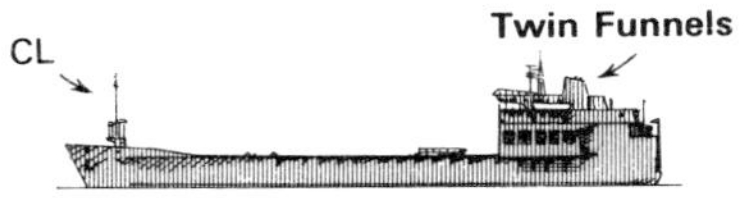

KMF H3
76870 BALDER MARACAI. NA/Ne 1979; RoC; 1200; 93.9 × 3.53 (308.07 × 11.58); TSM; 15; ex BALDER HAREN 1979; Stern door/ramp; Sister: **76871 BALDER EMS** (NA).

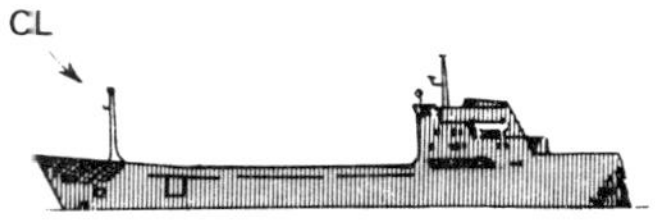

KMF H3
76880 RAAD. Si/Fr 1969; RoC/WT; 2100; 99.68 × 4.5 (327.03 × 14.76); TSM; 15.5; ex MONTE CINTO 1980; Stern door.

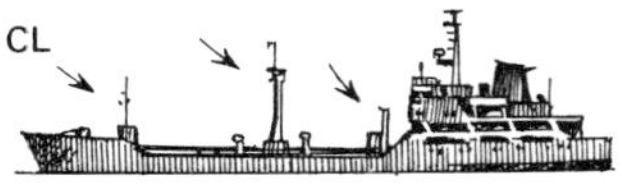

KMF H3
★**76890 ALIOT.** Ru/Fi 1970; WT/Ch; 3100; 93.88 × 6.5 (308.01 × 21.33); M; 14; Sisters (Ru flag): ★**76891 POLLUKS;** ★**76892 PROTSION.**

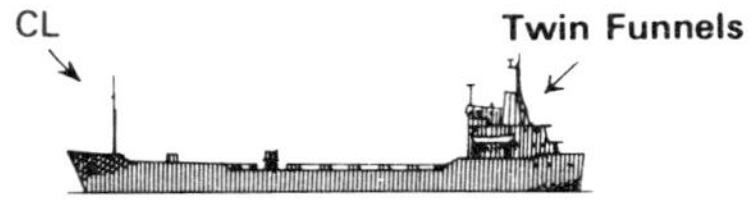

KMF H3
★**76900 STAROGARD GDANSKI.** Pd/Sp 1971; RoC; 1000; 79.33 × 4.7 (260.27 × 15.42); M; 14; ex COMETA; Stern door; **'Porter'** type; Sister: **76901 CHERCHELL** (Ag); ex ARDAN 1974.

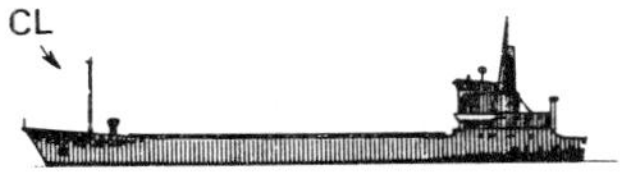

KMF H3
76910 BALTIC OSPREY. Br/FRG 1972; Con; 1000; 88.3 × 4.35 (289.7 × 14.27); M; 14; ex ATLANTIC VISCOUNT 1977; ex NAD PRINCE 1975; ex KALKGRUND 1974; Similar (probably with shorter funnel): **76911 STOLLER GRUND** (FRG).

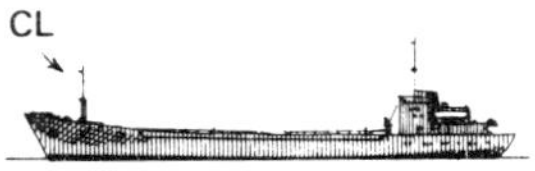

KMF H3
● **76920 RAMO.** Pa/Sw 1960; C; 1500; 86.95 × 4.53 (285.27 × 14.86); M; 13; ex RAUKEN 1975; ex CERES 1966; Lengthened 1968; May be some alterations to drawing.

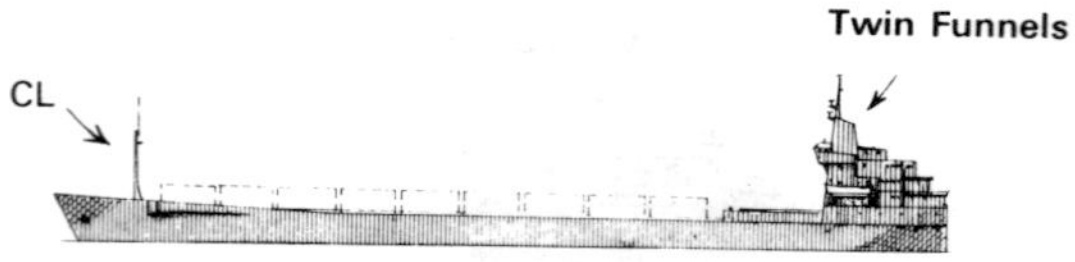

KMF H3
76930 BACAT 2. —/De; Bg; 6000 Dwt; 140 × — (459.32 × —); M; —; Under construction.

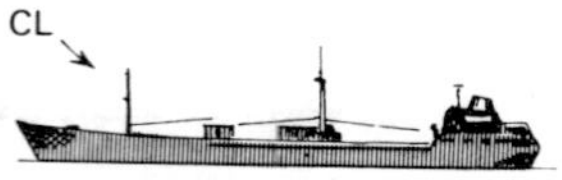

KMF H3
76940 BASTO. Fi/No; 1968; C; 1200; 81.44 × 3.8/5.02 (267.19 × 12.47/16.47); M; 16; ex FRIO TRADER 1973; Sister: **76941 BORGO** (Fi); ex FRIO CARRIER 1973.

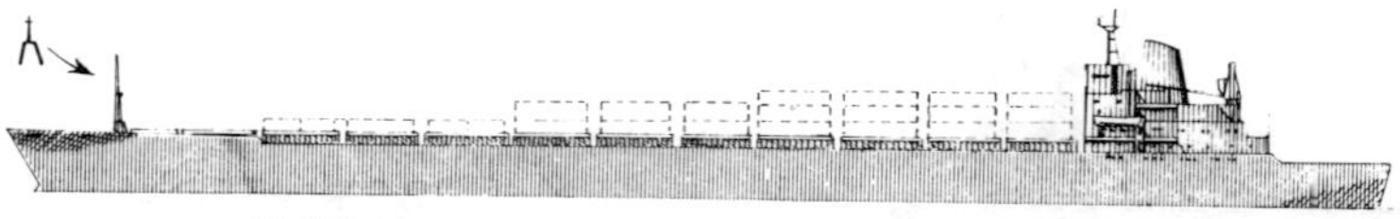

KMFC H
● **76950 DART EUROPE.** Be/Be 1970; Con; 31000; 231.55 × 10.08 (759.68 × 33.07); M; 21; Sisters (Br flag): **76951 DART ATLANTIC; 76952 DART AMERICA.**

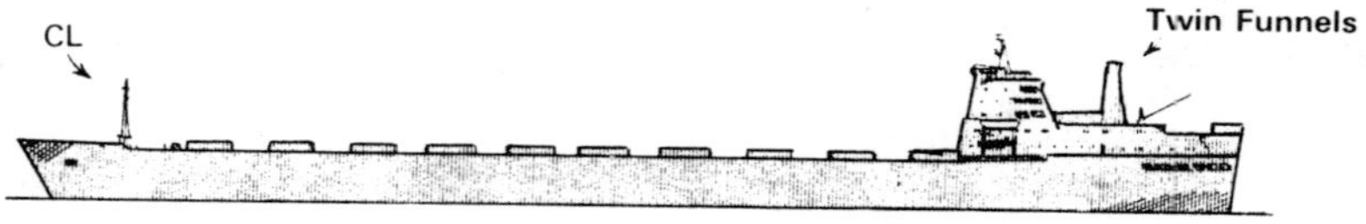

KMFC H
76960 ATLANTIC SONG. Sw/Fr 1967; RoC/Con; 14900; 223.02 × 9.15 (731.69 × 30.02); M; 21.5; Lengthened 1976; Stern door; Sister: **76961 ATLANTIC STAR** (Ne).

KMFC H
● **76970 MADOURI.** Cy/FRG 1966; RoC; 2260; 99.22 × 5.83 (325.52 × 19.13); M; 13; ex MOUNDRA 1977; ex SALOME 1973; Lengthened 1969; Side doors; Stern door/ramp; Sisters: **76971 ALPHA CONVEYOR** (Le); ex BELLMAN 1975; ex AIDA 1972; **76972 UNDINE** (FRG); **★76973 INSELSBERG** (DDR); ex BERWALD 1974; ex OTELLO 1972; (deck house forward of bridge).

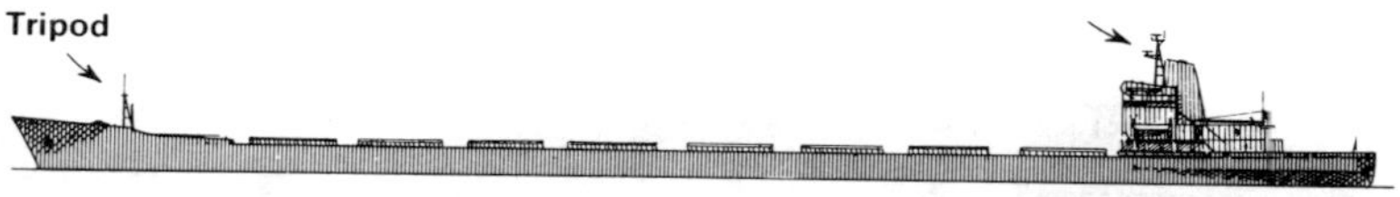

KMFC H1
76980 MINERAL MARCHIENNE. Be/Be 1973; B; 35900; 234.8 × 13.27 (770.34 × 43.54); M; 16; Sister: **76981 MINERAL ALEGRIA** (Be); Possible sister: **76982 BELGIUM** (Be); ex MINERAL BELGIUM.

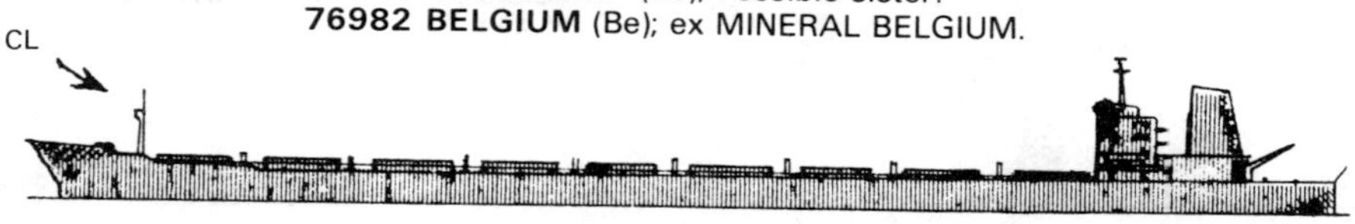

KMFC H1
● **76990 YOU ARE MY SUNSHINE.** Li/FRG 1976; B; 64100; 272.32 × 16.08 (893.44 × 52.76); M; 16; ex FERNSEA 1981; Sisters: **76991 FARLAND** (Br); ex NAWALA 1980; ex NAWADA; ex FERNBAY; **76992 ESTELLE J** (Pa); ex FERNHILL 1981; **76993 ENDEAVOR** (Li); ex SEALANE; ex FERNLANE 1978; **76994 PAN YOUNG** (Pa); ex SEALEAF 1980; ex FERNLEAF 1978.

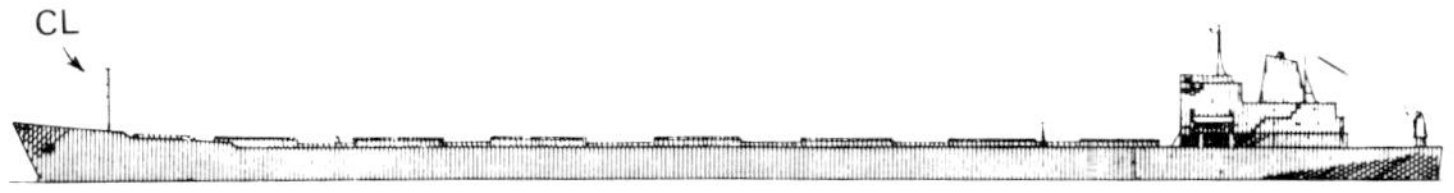

KMFC H1
77000 SEARADIANCE. Br/Br 1977; B; 39200; 228.12 × 14.05 (748.43 × 46.1); M; 15; ex ORIENT CITY 1978; Sister: **77001 WELSH CITY** (Br).

KMFC H1
77010 BASALT. FRG/Hu 1970; C; 1500; 76.41 × 5.31 (250.69 × 17.42); M; 11.5; Lengthened 1975; Sisters: **77011 DIORIT** (FRG); **77012 DIABAS** (FRG); **77013 GABBRO** (FRG); **77014 GRANIT** (Sg); Similar (fitted with satellite communication dome): **77015 DOLOMIT** (FRG).

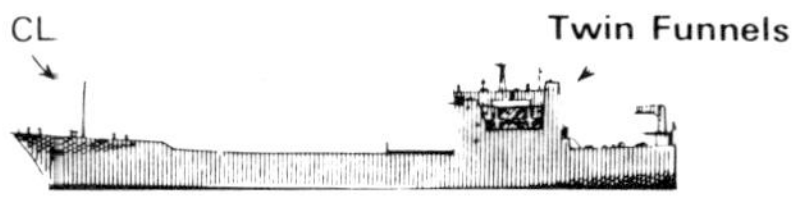

KMFC H1
● **77020 ARISTEOS.** Gr/Br 1971; RoC; 3700; 117.48 × 6.32 (385.43 × 20.73); TSM; 17.5; ex CARIBBEAN PROGRESS; ex IRANIAN PROGRESS 1976; ex CARIBBEAN PROGRESS 1975; May be spelt **ARISTAIOS;** Stern door; Sisters (FRG built): **77021 ARISTEFS** (Gr); ex CARIBBEAN ENDEAVOUR.

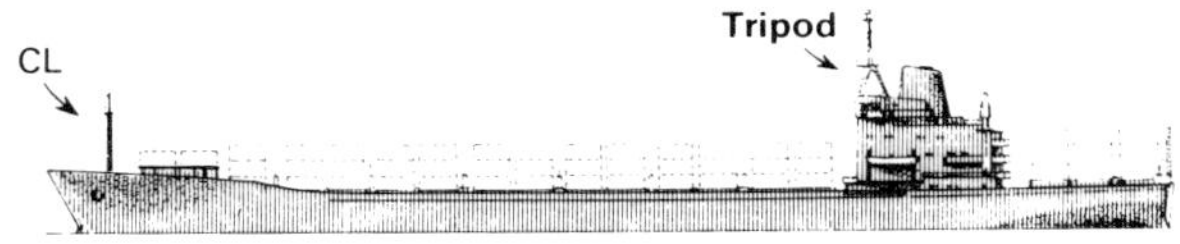

KMFC H1
● **77030 LEVERKUSEN EXPRESS.** FRG/FRG-FRG 1970/78; Con; 16700; 176.49 × 10.59 (579 × 34.74); M; —; ex LEVERKUSEN 1978; Converted from general cargo, lengthened and widened 1978; Sisters (FRG flag): **77031 ERLANGEN EXPRESS;** ex ERLANGEN 1979; **77032 HOECHST EXPRESS;** ex HOECHST 1978; **77033 LUDWIGSHAFEN EXPRESS;** ex LUDWIGSHAFEN 1979.

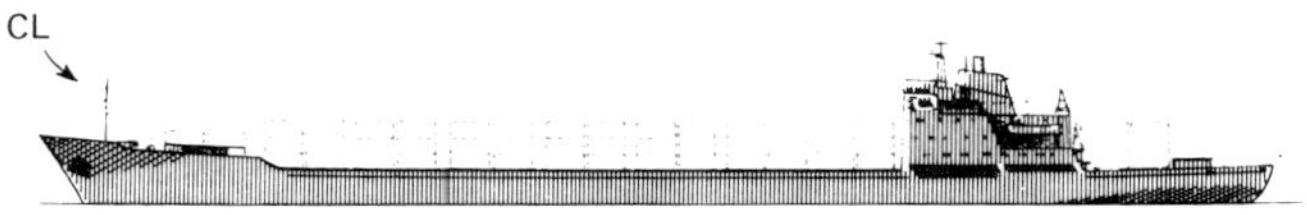

KMFC H1
77040 AL AHMADIAH. Ku/Ru-Sp 1969/80; Con; 14400; 194.33 × 9.5 (637.57 × 31.17); M; 18.5; Converted from cargo ship of 'FEODOSIYA' type; Sisters (Ku flag): **77041 AL RUMAITHIAH; 77042 AL SHAMIAH.**

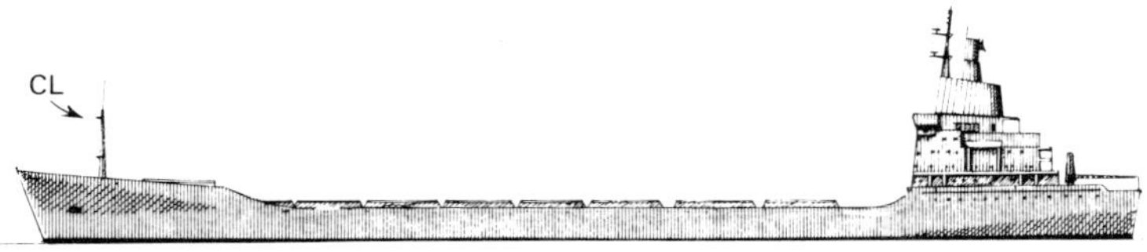

KMFC H13
77050 ENCOUNTER BAY. Br/FRG 1969; Con; 16800; 227.31 × 10.69 (745.77 × 35.07); T; 21.5; Sisters (Br flag): **77051 BOTANY BAY; 77052 DISCOVERY BAY; 77053 FLINDERS BAY; 77054 JERVIS BAY; 77055 MORETON BAY.**

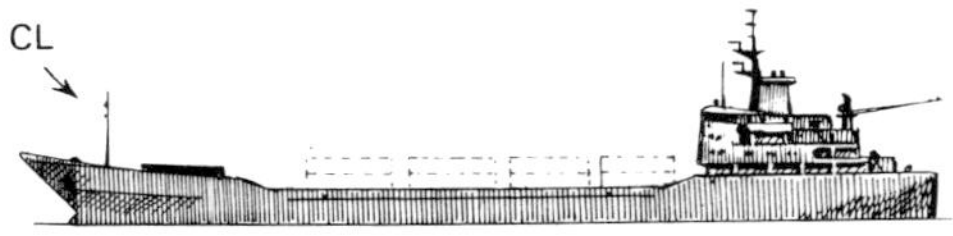

KMFC H13
⋆77060 ALEKSANDR FADEYEV. Ru/Ru 1973; Con; 6500; 130.21 × 7.5 (427 × 24.61); M; 17; Sisters (Ru flag): **⋆77061 ALEKSANDR PROKOFYEV; ⋆77062 ALEKSANDR TVARDOVSKIY; ⋆77063 MIKHAIL PRISHVIN; 77064 MIKHAIL SVETLOV.**

●
77067

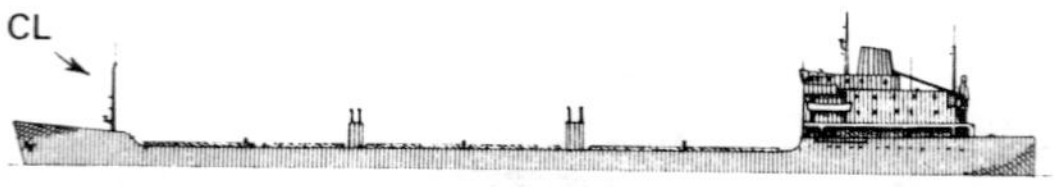

KMFC H13
★77070 DMITRIY DONSKOY. Ru/DDR 1977; B; 13500; 162.08 × 9.02 (531.76 × 29.59); M; 14.5; Sisters (Ru flag): **★77071 DMITRIY POZHARSKIY; ★77072 ALEKSANDR NEVSKIY; ★77073 ALEKSANDR SUVOROV; ★77074 MIKHAIL KUTUZOV; ★77075 ADMIRAL USHAKOV; ★77076 KUZMA MININ; ★77077 PETR VELIKIY; ★77078 STEPAN RAZIN; ★77079 YEMELYAN PUGACHEV.**

● ★77080

KMFC H13
77090 GERRINGONG. Au/Au 1965; O; 14500; 177.43 × 9.99 (582.02 × 32.78); M; 15; ex IRON GERRINGONG 1979; ex GERRINGONG 1977.

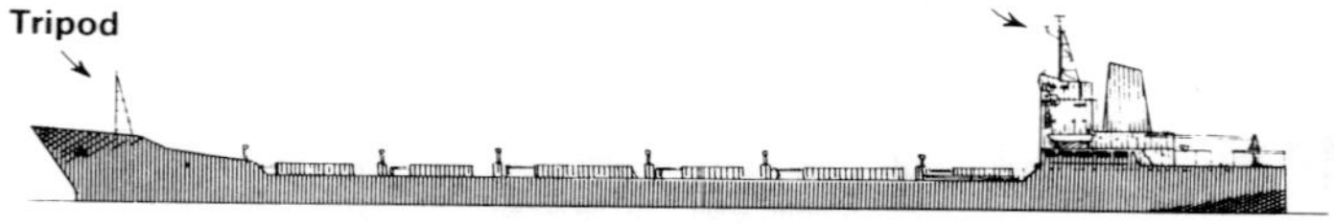

KMFC H13
77100 RIO VERDE. Bz/Bz 1977; B; 21700; 193.86 × 10.9 (636.02 × 35.76); M; 16; Possible Sisters: **77101 RIO NEGRO** (Bz); **77102 RIO BRANCO** (Bz); **77103 RIO GRANDE** (Bz); Possibly similar (may have cargo gear): **77104 MULHEIM** (FRG); **77105 GOLDEN RIO** (Li); ex WEINHEIM 1979.

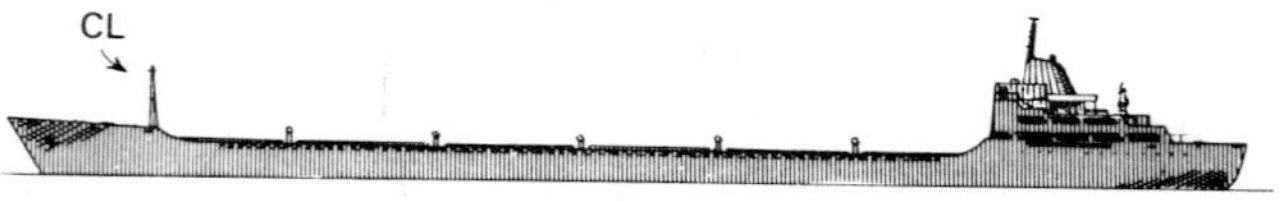

KMFC H13
77110 FIDES. It/It 1964; B; 16100; 193.63 × 10.35 (635.27 × 33.96); M; 16.

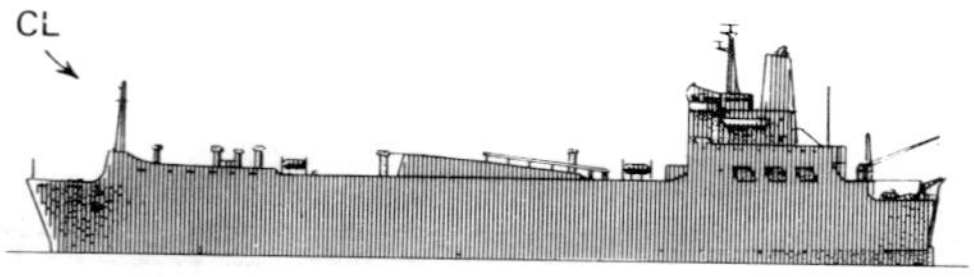

KMFC H2
77120 BELLMAN. Sg/Ja 1977; RoC/Tk/B; 9500; 143.85 × 7.8 (471.95 × 25.59); M; 14.75; **'BORO'** type; Sister: **77121 TAUBE** (Sg).

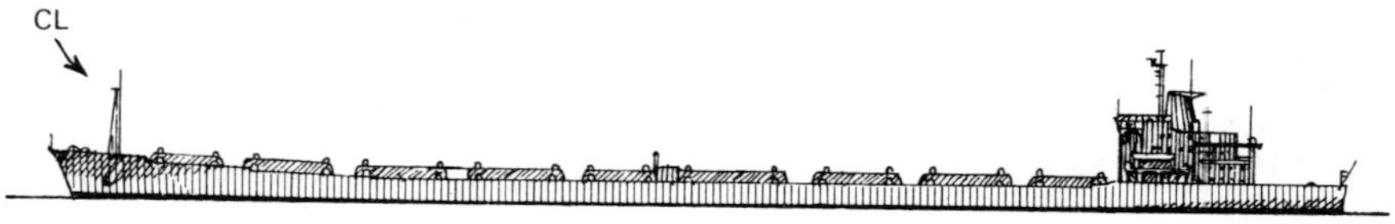

KMFK H
77130 GOLDEN FLAG. FRG/FRG 1972; B; 43500; 255.91 × 14.2 (839.6 × 46.59); M; 16; ex PROSERPINA 1981; Sister: **77131 PROPONTIS** (FRG); Similar (heavier Kingposts aft): **77132 WIKING BULKER** (FRG); ex JOHANN SCHULTE 1978.

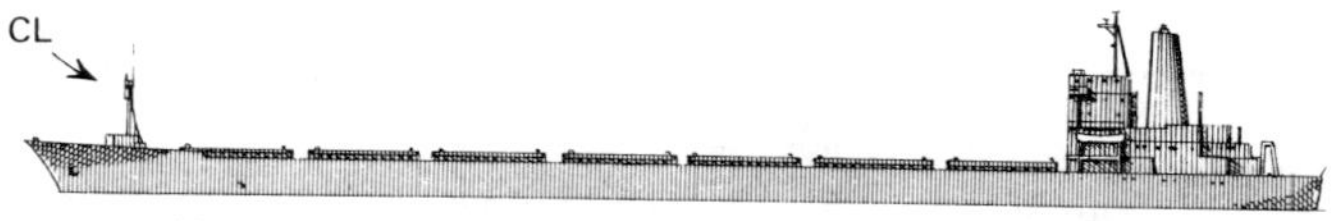

KMFK H
77140 LUTZ JACOB. FRG/Ih 1973; B; 28100; 205.49 × 12.33 (674.18 × 40.52); M; 15.5; Sisters (FRG flag): **77141 BABETTE JACOB; 77142 MARGOT JACOB; 77143 ROLF JACOB.**

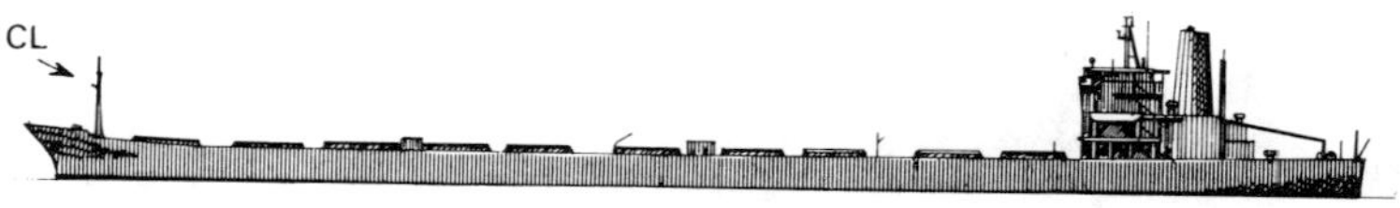

KMFK H
77150 ZEEBRUGGE. Be/Be 1974; B; 37700; 224.01 × 13.09 (734.94 × 42.95); M; 15.5; Sisters (Be flag): **77151 MARTHA; 77152 KYOTO; 77153 YAFFA; 77154 RUTH;** Possible sisters (In flag): **77155 MARATHA MARINER; 77156 MARATHA MELODY;** Possibly similar (larger): **77157 ARGOSY PACIFIC** (Br); **77158 LEON & PIERRE C** (Be).

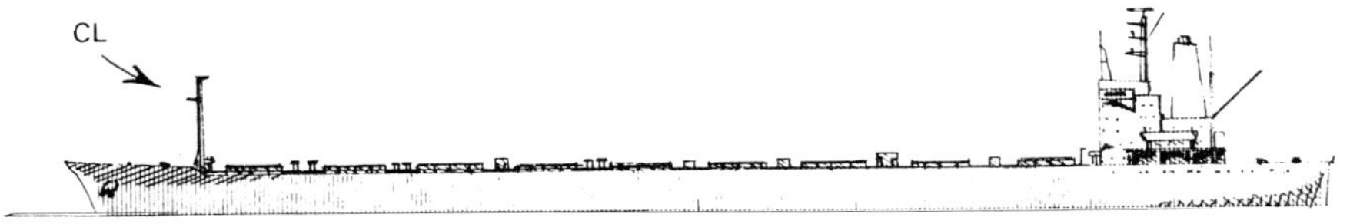

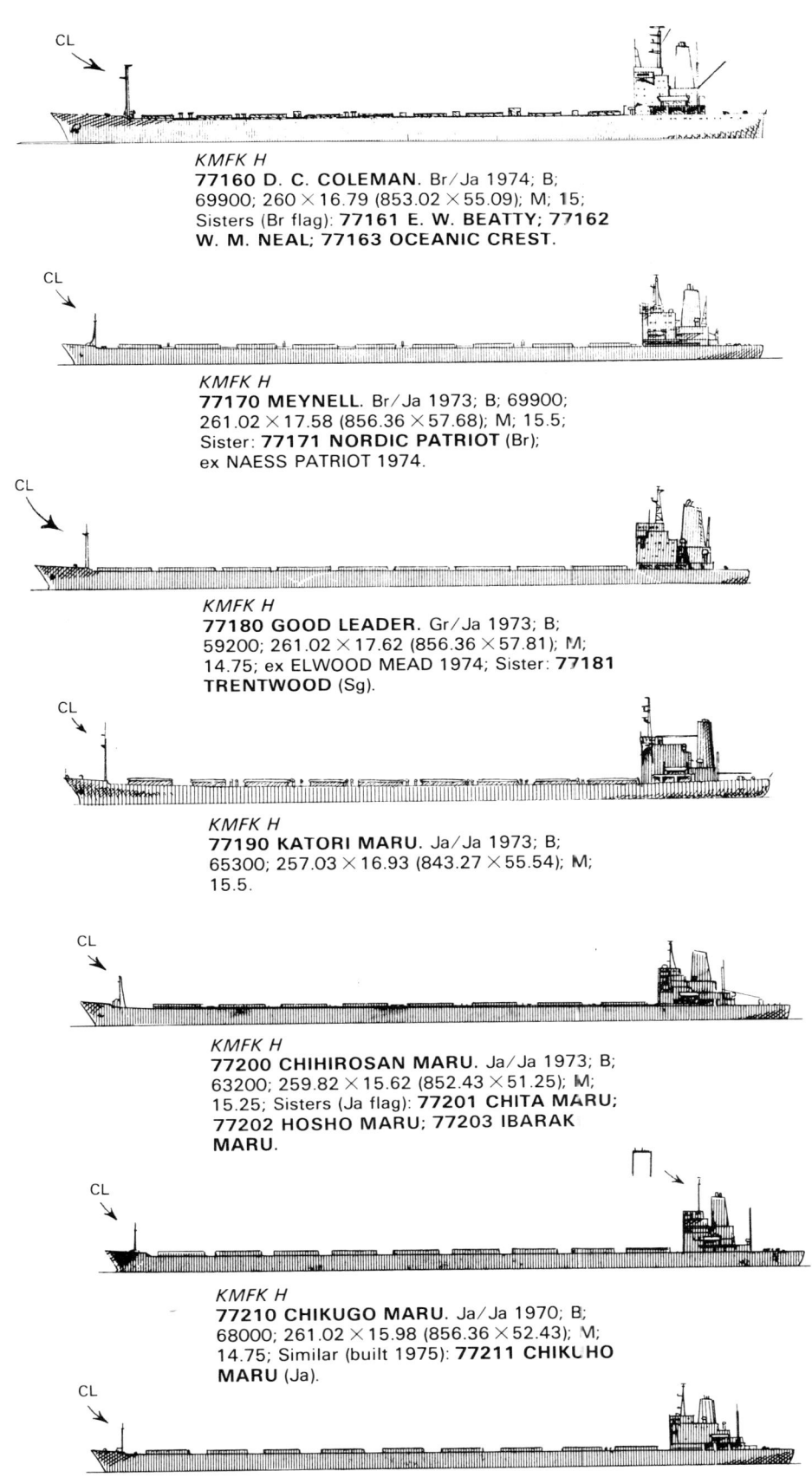

KMFK H
77160 D. C. COLEMAN. Br/Ja 1974; B; 69900; 260 × 16.79 (853.02 × 55.09); M; 15; Sisters (Br flag): **77161 E. W. BEATTY; 77162 W. M. NEAL; 77163 OCEANIC CREST**.

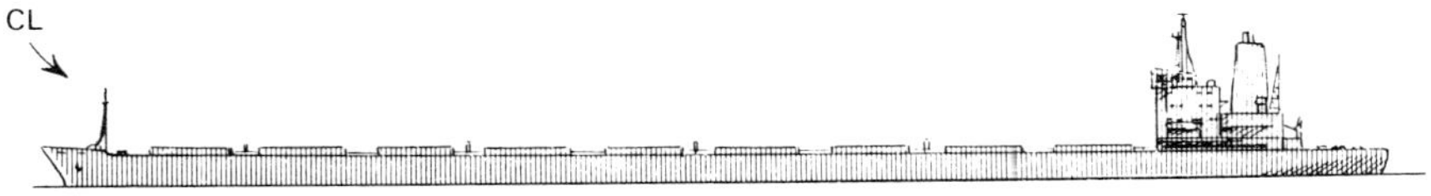

KMFK H
77170 MEYNELL. Br/Ja 1973; B; 69900; 261.02 × 17.58 (856.36 × 57.68); M; 15.5; Sister: **77171 NORDIC PATRIOT** (Br); ex NAESS PATRIOT 1974.

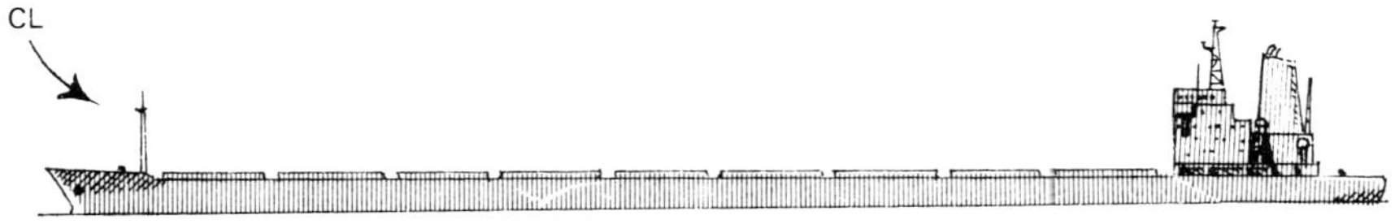

KMFK H
77180 GOOD LEADER. Gr/Ja 1973; B; 59200; 261.02 × 17.62 (856.36 × 57.81); M; 14.75; ex ELWOOD MEAD 1974; Sister: **77181 TRENTWOOD** (Sg).

KMFK H
77190 KATORI MARU. Ja/Ja 1973; B; 65300; 257.03 × 16.93 (843.27 × 55.54); M; 15.5.

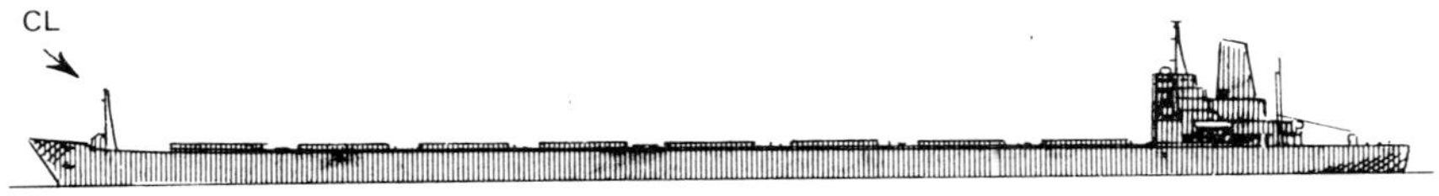

KMFK H
77200 CHIHIROSAN MARU. Ja/Ja 1973; B; 63200; 259.82 × 15.62 (852.43 × 51.25); M; 15.25; Sisters (Ja flag): **77201 CHITA MARU; 77202 HOSHO MARU; 77203 IBARAKI MARU**.

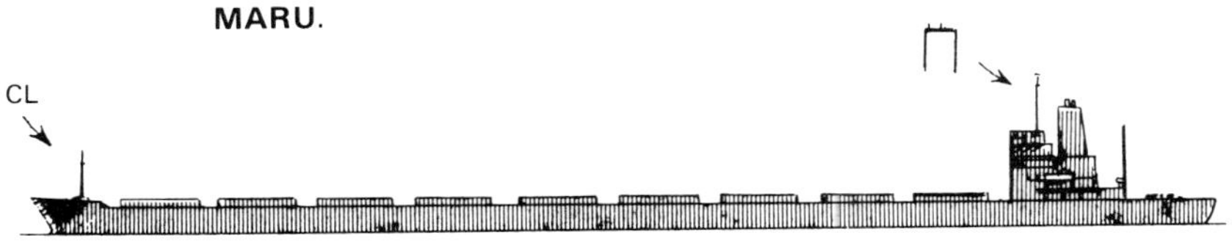

KMFK H
77210 CHIKUGO MARU. Ja/Ja 1970; B; 68000; 261.02 × 15.98 (856.36 × 52.43); M; 14.75; Similar (built 1975): **77211 CHIKUHO MARU** (Ja).

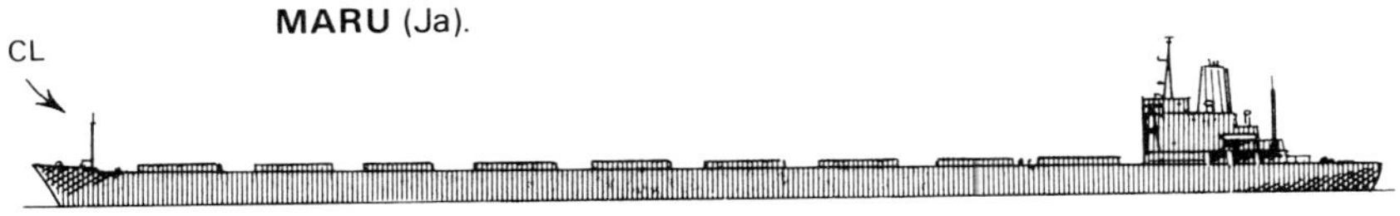

KMFK H
77220 SHINREI MARU. Ja/Ja 1973; B; 68200; 260.99 × 16.38 (856.27 × 53.74); M; 15.25; Sister: **77221 SHINZUI MARU** (Ja); Similar: **77222 JAPAN POPLAR** (Ja); **77223 GIBRALTAR PANSY** (Li); ex RIKO MARU 1974; **77224 THEODORE A.** (Li); ex TWEEDFIELD 1978; ex TWEED BRIDGE 1978; Possibly similar: **77225 CHOKAI MARU** (Ja); **77226 KASAGISAN MARU** (Ja).

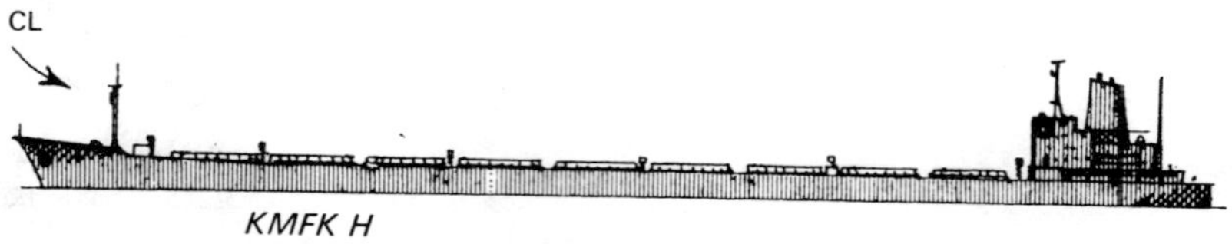

KMFK H
77230 SAMRAT ASHOK. In/Ja 1974; B; 72600; 261.02 × 17.58 (856.36 × 57.68); M; 15.5; ex GAUTAMA BUDDHA 1974.

KMFK H
● **77240 POLYVIKING.** No/Ja 1973; B; 64000; 260.03 × 16.45 (853.12 × 53.97); M; 16.5; Sisters (No flag): **77241 POLYCLIPPER; 77242 POLYCREST.**

KMFK H
77250 MARLIN. Li/Ja 1977; BO; 9400; 155,15 × 6.86 (509.02 × 22.51); TSM; 13; Sister: **77251 TARPON** (Li).

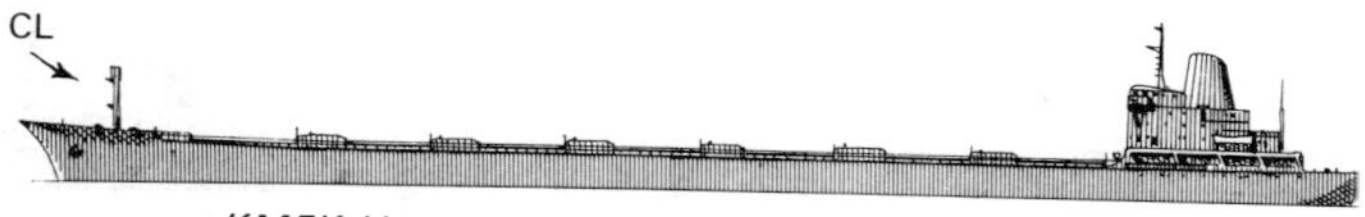

KMFK H
77260 NACIONAL SINES. Po/Sp 1971; B; 30400; 210.75 × 12.15 (691.44 × 39.86); M; 15; ex MANUEL YLLERA 1981.

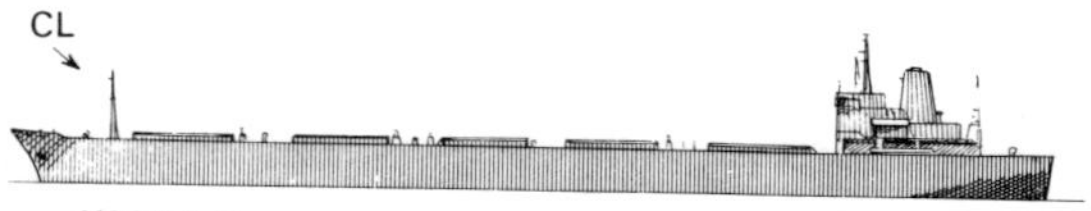

KMFK H
77270 NELSON MARU. Ja/Ja 1971; B; 17400; 165.11 × 9.72 (541.7 × 31.89); M; 14.75.

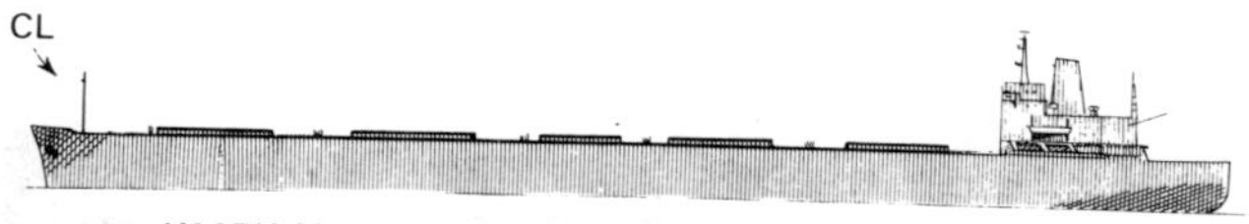

KMFK H
77280 BUNGA TEMBUSU. My/Ja 1972; BWC; 32300; 196.02 × 9.7 (643.11 × 31.82); M; 14.75; Sister: **77281 BUNGA MELAWIS**(My).

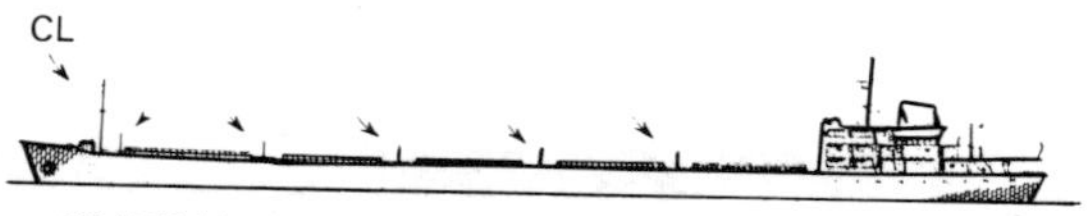

KMFK H
77290 WANDERER. Li/Sw-Ja 1953/64; B; 10200; 160.38 × 8.15 (526.18 × 26.74); M; —; Aft section built Sweden 1953. Forward & cargo section built Japan 1964; Sister: **77291 WAYFARER(Li).**

KMFK H
77300 SHINRYU MARU. Ja/Ja 1971; O; 88800; 292.44 × 17.91 (959.45 × 58.76); M; 15.75; Possibly similar (may be H1): **77301 SHINYU MARU**(Ja).

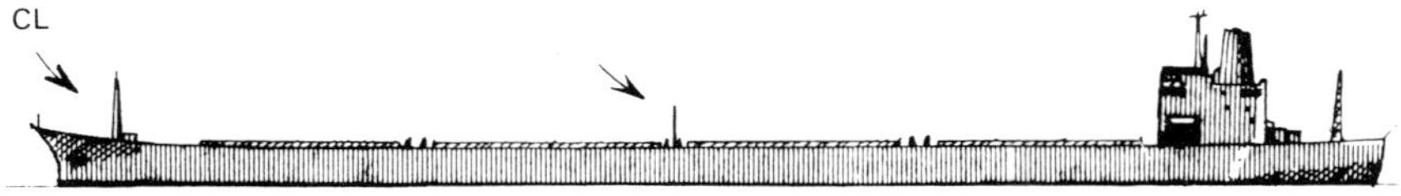

KMFK H
77310 SHINYO MARU. Ja/Ja 1973; O; 63100; 259.37 × 16.16 (850.95 × 53.02); M; 15.

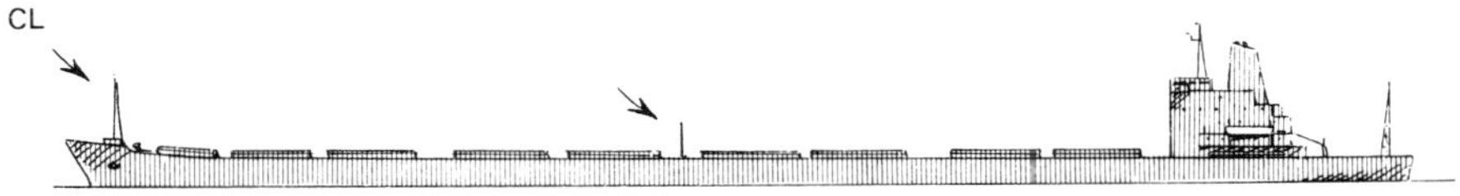

KMFK H
77320 BROCKMAN. Li/Ja 1974; O; 33900; 259.39 × 16.13 (851.02 × 52.92); M; 15; Sisters (Li flag): **77321 MARRA MAMBA; 77322 SEVEN TEAM;** ex SEVENSEAS CONQUEROR 1979.

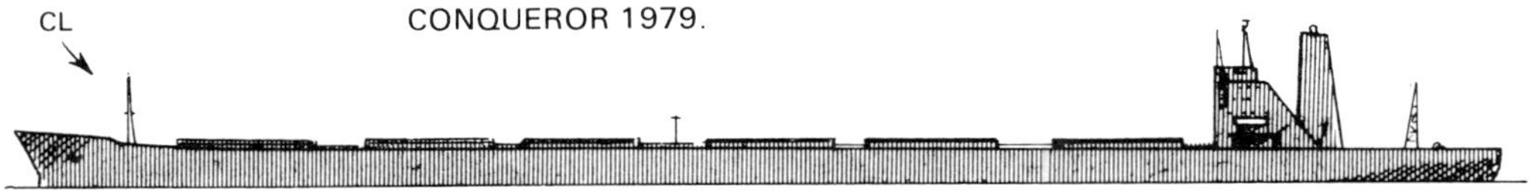

KMFK H
77330 NIIZURU MARU. Ja/Ja 1971; O; 92100; 313.62 × 16.99 (1028.94 × 55.74); M; 15.75.

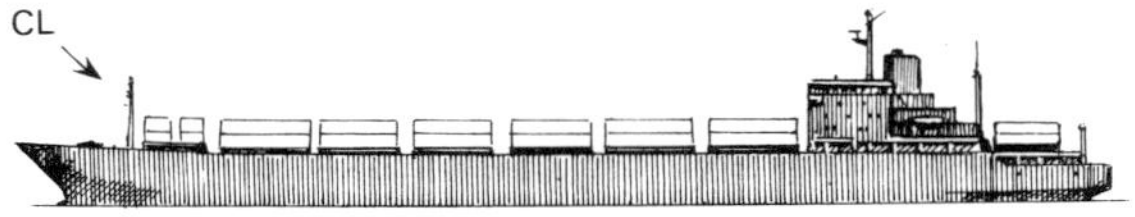

KMFK H
⋆77340 KHUDOZHNIK SARYAN. Ru/DDR 1975; Con; 17800; 169.63 × 9.2 (556.52 × 30.18); M; 20; **'Mercur' type;** Sisters (Ru flag): **⋆77341 KHUDOZHNIK IOGANSON; ⋆77342 KHUDOZHNIK PAKHOMOV; ⋆77343 KHUDOZHNIK PROROKOV; ⋆77344 KHUDOZHNIK REPIN; ⋆77345 KHUDOZHNIK ROMAS; ⋆77346 KHUDOZHNIK ZHUKOV; ⋆77347 NADEZHDA OBUKHOVA; ⋆77348 NIKOLAY GOLOVANOV; ⋆77349 MAKSIM MIKHAYLOV.**

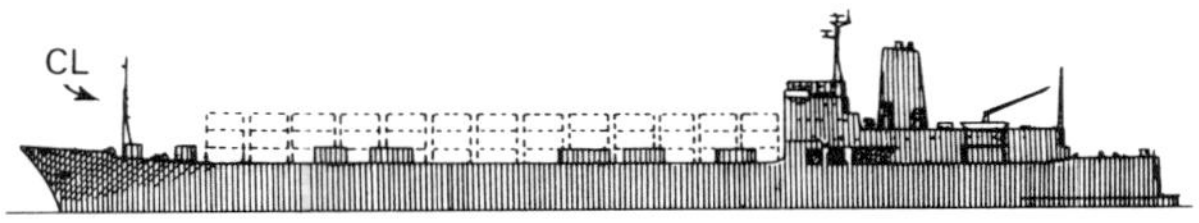

KMFK H
77360 HYOGO MARU. Ja/Ja 1973; RoC/Con. 9100; 181.74 × 8.98 (596.26 × 29.46); M; 21; Stern door; Similar (Au flag): **77361 AUSTRALIAN SEAROADER;** Similar (lengthened 1978); **77362 AUSTRALIAN ENTERPRISE; 77363 AUSTRALIAN EXPLORER;** ex MATTHEW FLINDERS 1975.

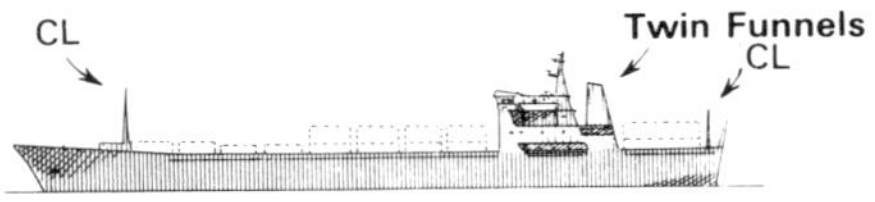

KMFK H
77370 SAND SHORE. No/Sw 1970; RoC; 2800; 112.71 × 6.82 (369.78 × 22.38); M; 16; ex NOPAL SHORE 1977; ex MIGNON 1974; Stern door.

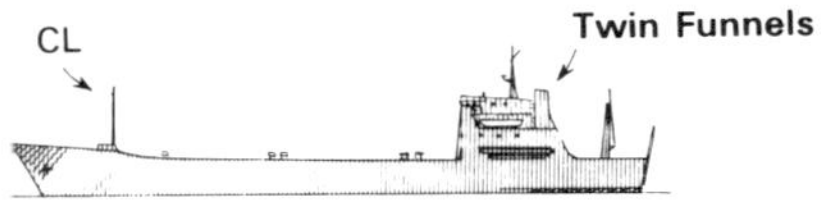

KMFK H
77380 JOLLY ROSSO. It/Sw 1968; RoC; 2300; 100.72 × 6.59 (330.45 × 21.62); M; 15.25; ex CLAUDE DEBUSSY 1973; ex NEVA 1971; ex ARABELLA 1969.

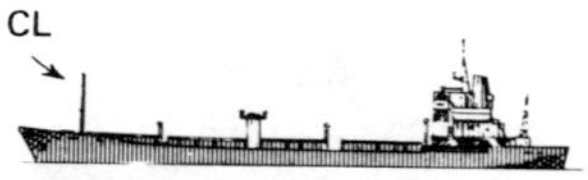

KMFK H

● **77390 GENEVE.** Li/Ja 1971; C/B; 3000; 85.83 × 7.45 (281.59 × 24.44); **'Camit' type;** Sisters (Li flag): **77391 AMSTERDAM; 77392 HAMBURG; 77393 GHENT; 77394 SAINT NAZAIRE; 77395 TARRAGONA;** (NA flag): **77396 EARLY BIRD;** ex SETE 1973.

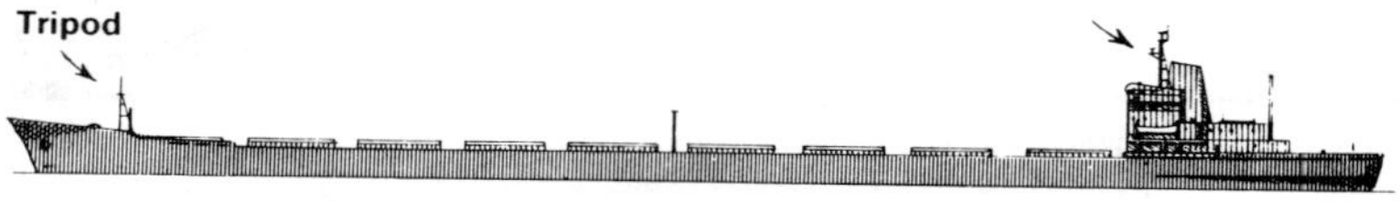

KMFK H1

77400 E R BRABANTIA. Be/Be 1971; B; 36800; 234.75 × 13.2 (770.18 × 43.31); M; 15; Sisters: **77401 E R ANTVERPIA** (Be); **77402 JAGAT SAMRAT** (In); Possibly similar: **77403 MARATHA MELODY** (In); **77404 MARATHA MARINER** (In).

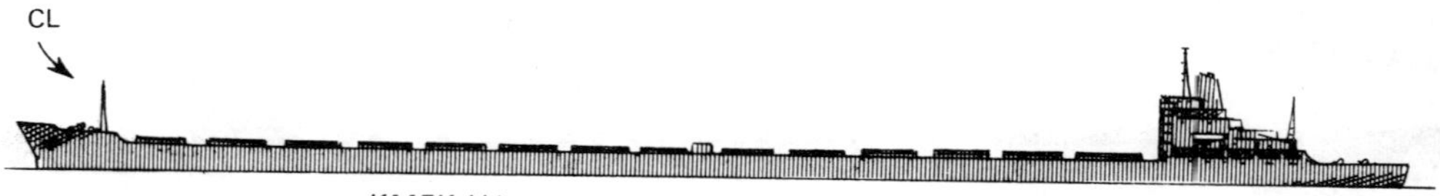

KMFK H1

77410 MARCONA EXPORTER. Li/Ja 1967; O; 44000; 303.74 × 17.44 (996.52 × 57.22); M; 14.75; Lengthened & deepened 1972.

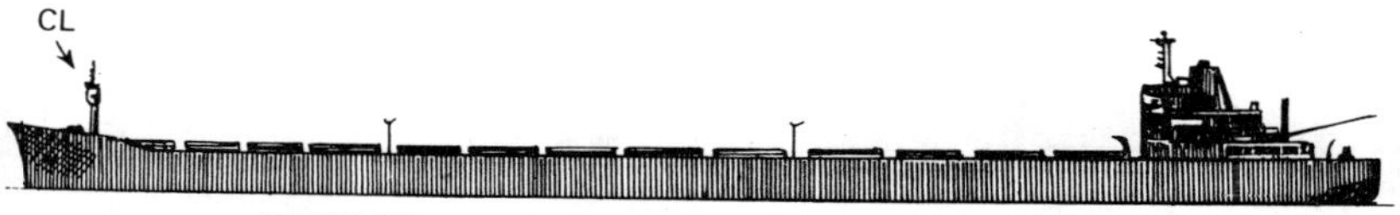

KMFK H1

77420 AEOLOS C. Pa/Br 1966; B; 40800; 249.94 × — (820.01 × —); M; 15; ex YALTA; ex BERGE SIGLION 1973; ex SIGLION 1971.

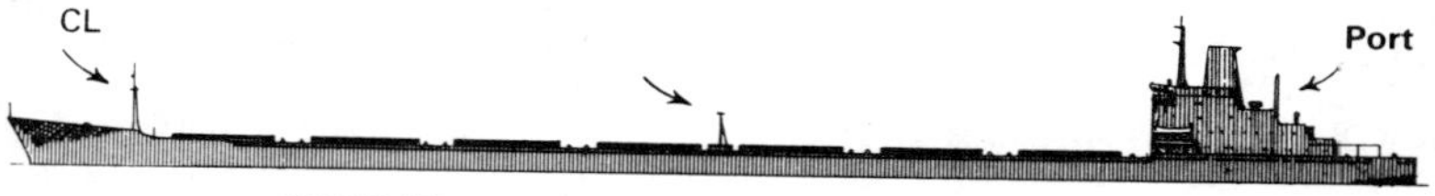

KMFK H1

77430 CATHAY SEATRADE. Li/Sw 1973; B; 35500; 224.06 × 13.1 (735.1 × 42.98); M; 16; ex LILI BILLNER 1978.

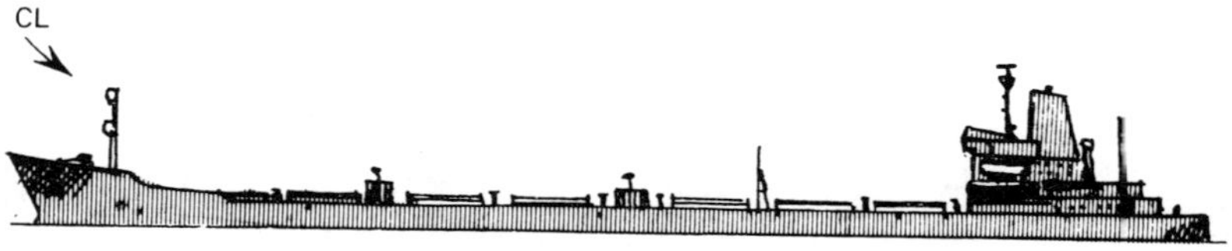

KMFK H1

● **77440 NEW WAYS.** Pa/Ys 1972; B; 40600; 243.75 × 12.91 (799.7 × 42.36); M; 15.5; ex MARIS HUNTSMAN 1981; ex RAGNA GORTHON 1978; Sisters: **77441 ROUNTON GRANGE** (Br) ex PACIFIC WASA 1980; **77442 CASSIOPEIA** (Sw); Similar: **77443 BIRTE OLDENDORFF** (Sg); **77444 DORA OLDENDORFF** (Sg); **77445 HELGA OLDENDORFF** (Sg); **77446 LUDOLF OLDENDORFF** (Sg); ⋆**77447 SHI TANG HAI** (RC) ex DIMITRIS A LEMOS 1980; Possibly similar: **77448 CETRA NORMA** (Fr).

KMFK H1
77460 JESSIE STOVE. No/No 1972; B; 60400; 265.62 × 15.78 (871.46 × 51.77); M; 15; Sisters (No flag): **77461 ARIEL; 77462 NEGO VICTORIA;** ex OLAV RINGDAL 1978; Possibly similar: **77463 BELCARGO; 77464 VIVA** ex COLUMBIA 1979.

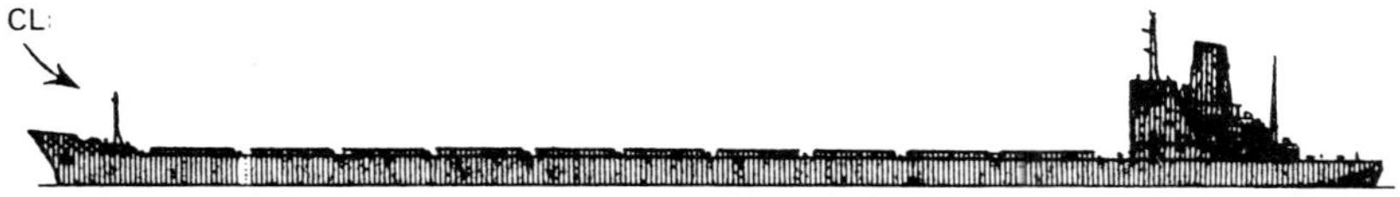

KMFK H1
77470 PORT LATTA MARU. Ja/Ja 1968; O; 50800; 249 × 14.15 (816.93 × 46.42); M; 15.25.

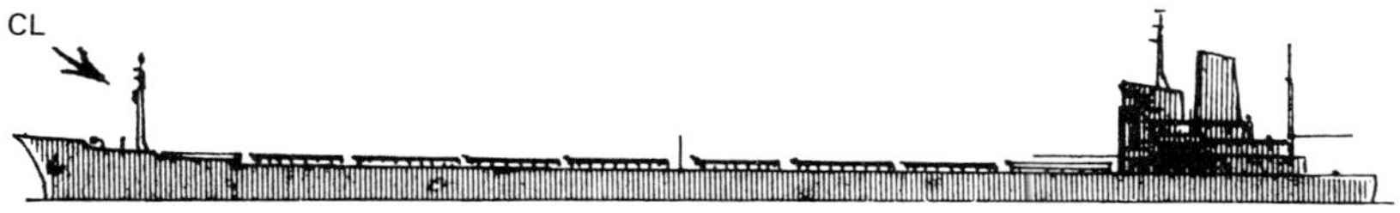

KMFK H1
⋆**77480 WEN DENG HAI.** RC/Br 1968; B. 41100; 251.47 × 14.26 (825.03 × 46.78); M; 16.5; ex ESSI KRISTINE 1978; Sisters (RC flag): ⋆**77481 DEN LONG HAI** ex FJORDAAS 1979; ⋆**77482 LUO SHAN HAI** ex THARA 1978.

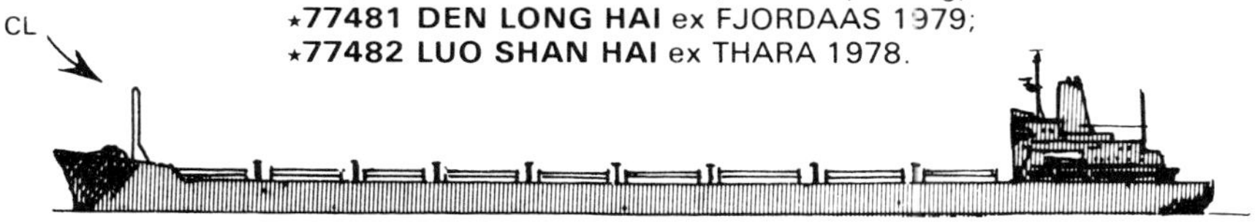

KMFK H1
77490 DORSETSHIRE. Br/Ja 1968; B; 44800; 246.9 × 14.53 (810.04 × 47.67); M; 16; ex ATLANTIC BRIDGE 1977; Sister: **77491 PETINGO** (Gr) ex PACIFIC BRIDGE 1974.

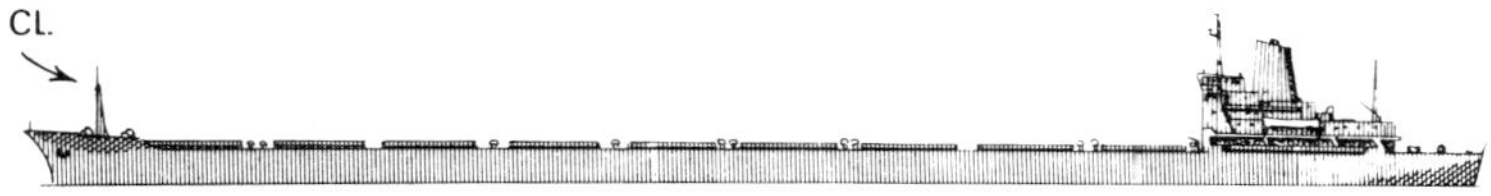

KMFK H1
77500 MIKUNISAN MARU. Ja/Ja 1967; B; 36900; 230 × 12.87 (754.59 × 42.22); M; 15.5; Similar (Ja flag): **77501 ROKKOHSAN MARU;** Similar (smaller): **77502 MITSUI MARU; 77503 TETSUZUI MARU; 77504 MITSUI MARU No 2.**

KMFK H1
77510 GUNGNIR X. Pa/Ja 1968; B; 28400; 226.42 × 12.9 (742.85 × 42.32); M; 16.25; ex GRISCHUNA 1980; Sister: **77511 EASTERN GRACE** (Li) ex PAMPERO 1978.

KMFK H1
⋆**77520 BAO QING HAI.** RC/Ja 1971; O; 45800; 239.07 × 14.36 (784.35 × 47.11); M; 15.5; ex MOSLANE 1978; Sister: **77521 MOSBROOK.**

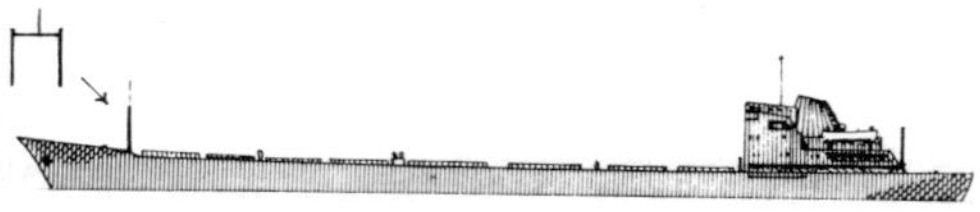

KMFK H1
77530 SANTO DOMINGO. Do/FRG 1959; B; 9400; 150.96 × 9.2 (495.28 × 30.18); M; —; ex PACSEA 1978; ex STAD GENT 1971; launched as HANS BERCKMEYER.

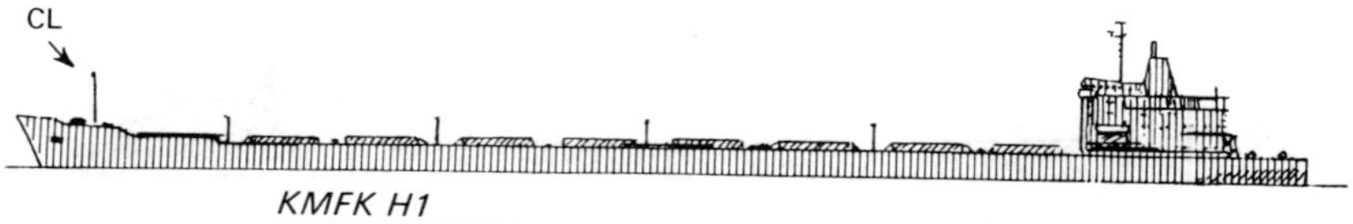

KMFK H1
77540 AUSTRALIAN PROSPECTOR. Au/FRG 1976; B; 74500; 282.07 × 16.43 (925.43 × 53.9); M; 15; Sister: **77541 AUSTRALIAN PROGRESS** (Au).

KMFK H1
77550 MARQUES DE BOLARQUE. Sp/Sp 1972; B; 44700; 256.22 × 14.44 (840.62 × 47.38); M; 15; May have deck cranes.

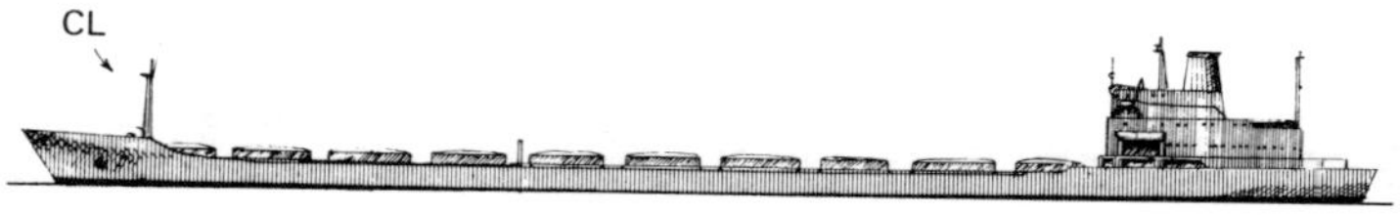

KMFK H1
● **77560 VIKING.** Li/Pd 1972; B; 33000; 220 × 12.43 (721.78 × 40.78); M; 15.75; ex PEARL SEA 1976; ex HAMPTON BRIDGE 1974; **'B-521'** type. Sister: **77561 GLOBAL E SUN** (Ko) ex POLITECHNIKA SZCZECINSKA; ex POLITECHNIKA GLIWICKA 1974; Possible sisters (May differ in appearance or coding): **77562 SERRAI** (Gr) ex INDUSTRY TRADER: EX JOTUNFJELL 1977; **77563 GENERAL GUISAN** (Sd) launched as LONDRINA: **77564 MOLISTA** (Gr) ex ANASTASIA; launched as POLITECHINIKA GDANSKA; **77565 KONITSA** (Gr) ex ENGIADINA; ex GUNNAR CARLSSON 1978; **77566 MASOVIA** (Li); **77567 JANA PRIYA** (In).

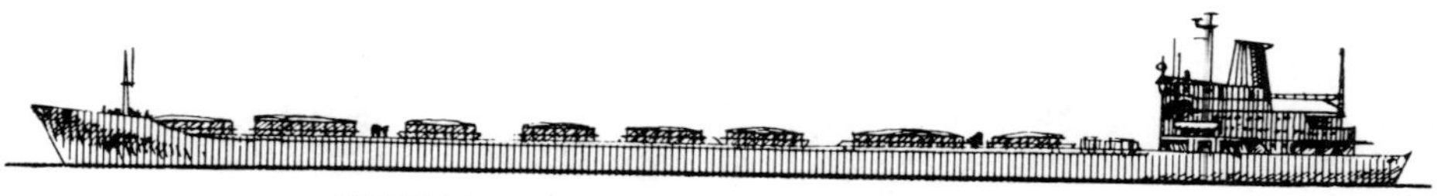

KMFK H1
● **77580 KNUT MARK.** Sw/Pd 1977; B; 39600; 251.16 × 12.35 (824.02 × 40.52); M; 15.25; **'B 526'** Type.

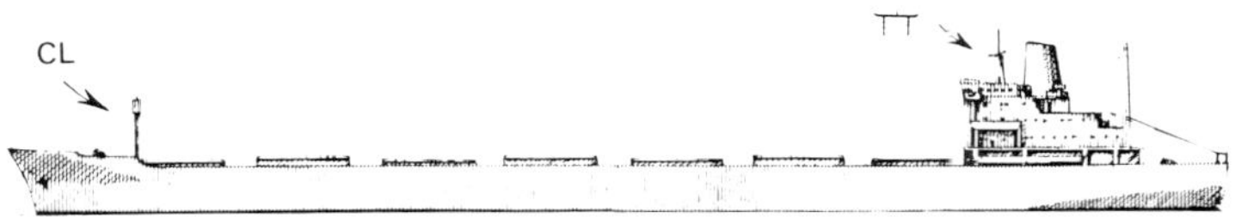

KMFK H1

● **77590 TAKARA.** No/Ja 1968; B; 36000; 244.01 × 12.24 (734.94 × 40.16); M; 15; Sister: **77591 TOLGA** (Sg) ex TONGA 1969; Similar: **77592 TACHIBANA** (No); **77593 TAKAMINE** (No); **77594 TAMBO RIVER** (Br) ex TAKASAGO 1975; **77595 MOUNT PARNASSOS** (Gr) ex TAKACHIHO 1978; **77596 CALORIC** (No).

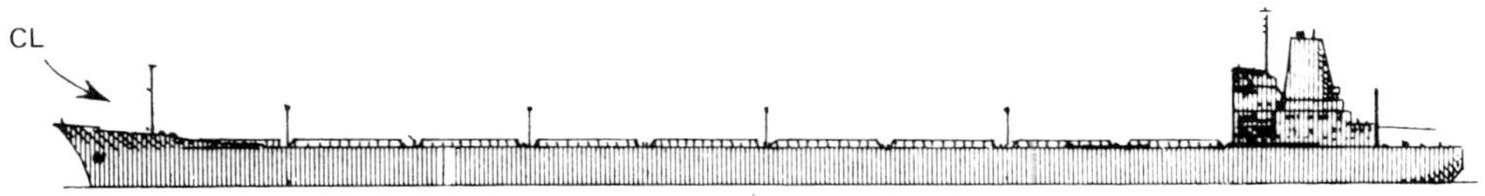

KMFK H1

77600 FUERTE VENTURA. FRG/FRG 1970; B; 74600; 282.23 × 16.42 (925.95 × 53.87); M; 15; ex STADT BREMEN 1979.

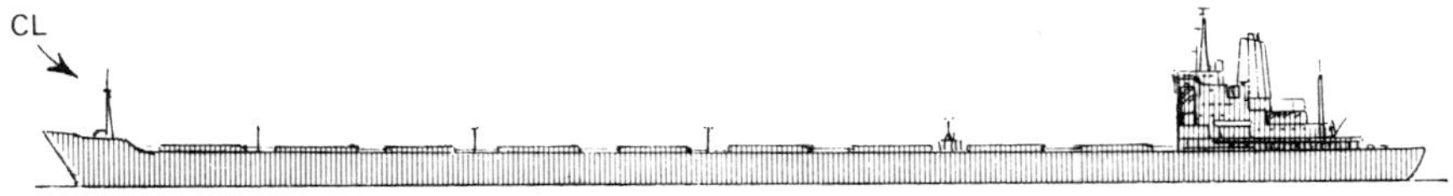

KMFK H1

77610 ERSKINE BRIDGE. Br/Ja 1973; E; 65900; 261.02 × 16.5 (856.36 × 54.13); M; 15; Sister: **77611 LAKE ALMANOR** (Li) ex SEVERN BRIDGE 1976; Similar: **77612 TAGELUS** (Ne) ex STIRLING BRIDGE 1979

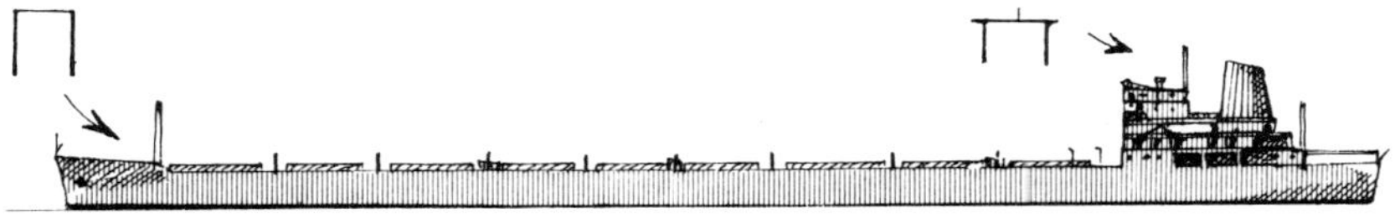

KMFK H1

77620 PANAMAX URANUS. Li/Br 1966; B; 40800; 249.94 × 13.36 (820.01 × 43.83); M; 15.5; ex NORDIC TRADER 1978; ex IRON PARKGATE 1975; ex NAESS PARKGATE 1974.

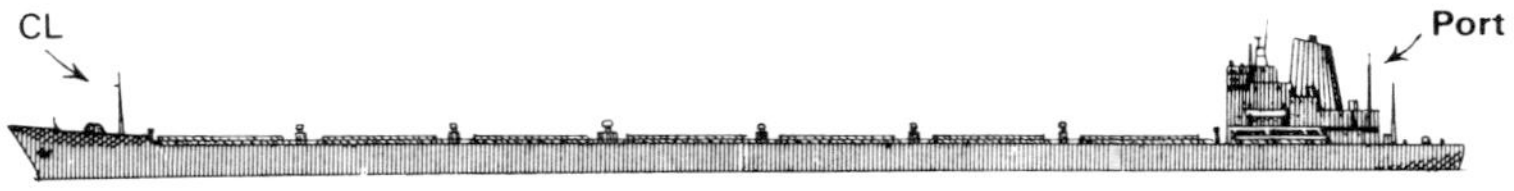

KMFK H1

77630 MAJESTY. Li/Ja 1972; B; 31900; 228.61 × 12.93 (750.03 × 42.42); M; 15.

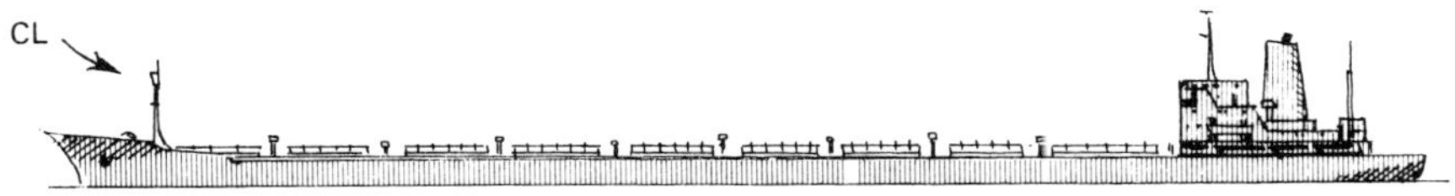

KMFK H1

77640 KONKAR INDOMITABLE. Gr/Ja 1972; B; 39200; 259.52 × 13.61 (851.44 × 44.65); M; 16; Sister: **77641 KONKAR VICTORY** (Gr).

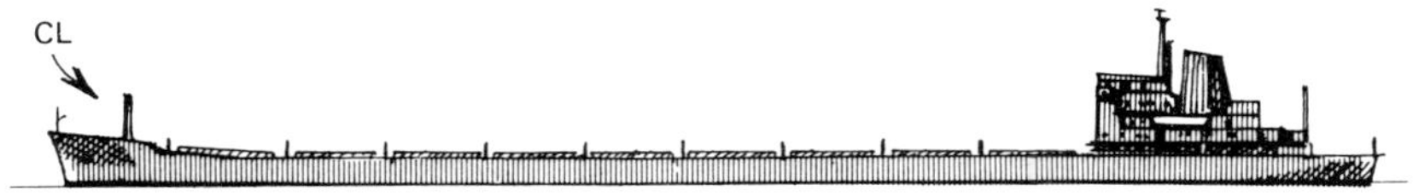

KMFK H1

77650 JHANSI KI RANI. In/Br 1975; B; 42100; 245.37 × 13.83 (805.02 × 45.37); M; 15.25; Sisters (In flag): **77651 JALAVIHAR; 77652 KASTURBA.**

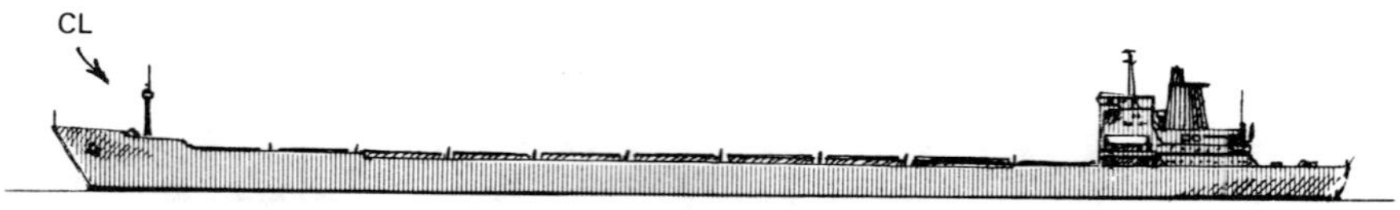

KMFK H1
77660 AEGIR. FRG/FRG 1968; B; 45800; 254.9 × 13.75 (836.29 × 45.11); M; 16; Sister: **77661 BRAGE** (FRG).

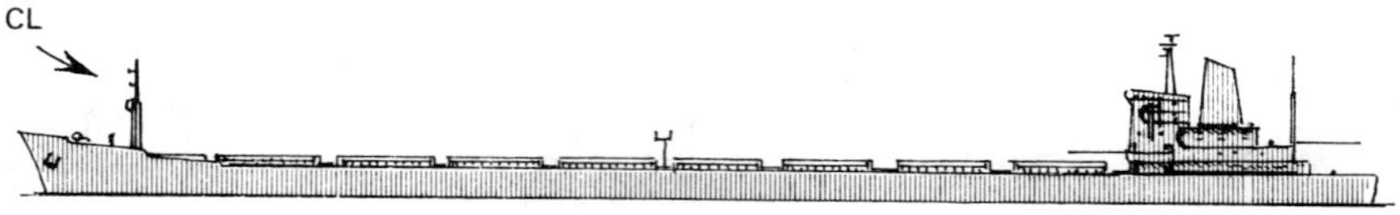

KMFK H1
● **77670 MOUNT PELION.** Gr/Br 1968; B; 57200; 260.61 × 14.8 (855.02 × 48.56); M; 15.25; ex SKAUFAST 1978; Similar: **77671 AINO** (No); **77672 WEST JUNORI** (Pa) ex BARBRO 1980; **77673 BELINDA** (No); **77674 BENWYVIS** (Br) ex ALNWICK CASTLE 1981; **77675 DUNSTANBURGH CASTLE** (Br); **77676 MOUNT NEWMAN** (Br); **77677 TECTUS** (Br) ex CANADIAN BRIDGE 1978.

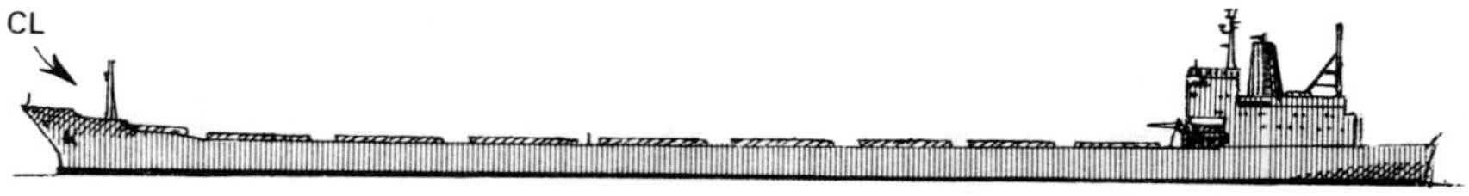

KMFK H1
77680 ESSI CAMILLA. No/Br 1975; B; 63500; 261.53 × 16.2 (858.04 × 53.15; M; 15.5; Similar: **77681 LACKENBY** (Br) ex OTTERPOOL 1977; Possibly similar: **77682 APPLEBY** (Br).

KMFK H1
● **77690 NAVIOS PATRIOT.** Li/De 1967; B; 38600; 255.63 × 14.03 (838.68 × 46.03); M; 16.75; ex LEISE MAERSK 1976; Sister: **77691 NAVIOS PIONEER** (Li) ex LOUIS MAERSK 1976.

KMFK H1
77700 AKRON. Li/Sw 1972; B; 63100; 263.66 × 15.89 (865.03 × 52.13); M; 15.5; ex NORSE LION 1978; Sisters: **77701 DELWIND** (Pa) ex CONSTANCE 1980; **77702 LOUSSIOS** (Gr) ex RONASTAR; Similar: **77703 ENTERPRISE** (Li) ex VARANGFJELL.

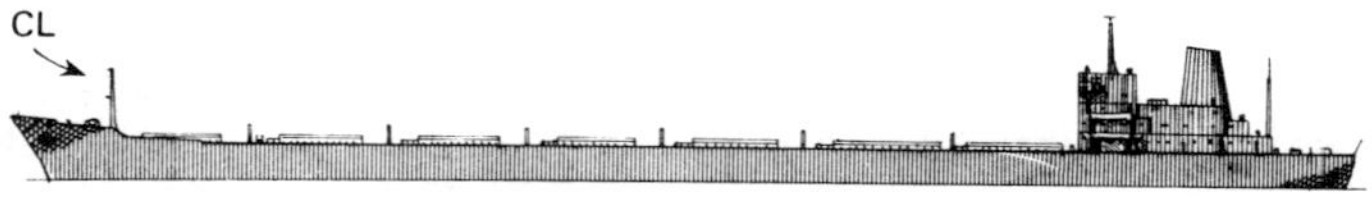

KMFK H1
77710 ARGONAUT. Gr/Br 1968; B; 24900; 211.44 × 12.22 (693.7 × 40.09); M; 15.75; Sister: **77711 NEPHELE** (Gr) ex G.M.LIVANOS 1978.

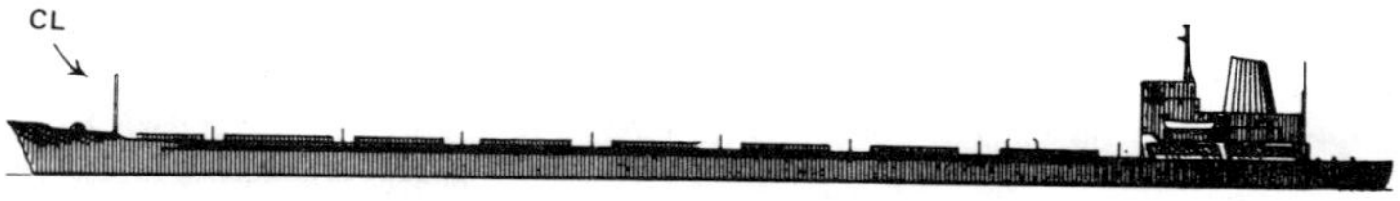

KMFK H1
● **77720 AMBER PACIFIC.** Br/Br 1969; B; 31400; 220.99 × 12.62 (725.03 × 41.4); M; 15; Sister: **77721 GOLDEN ENTERPRISE** (Li) ex AUGUST PACIFIC.

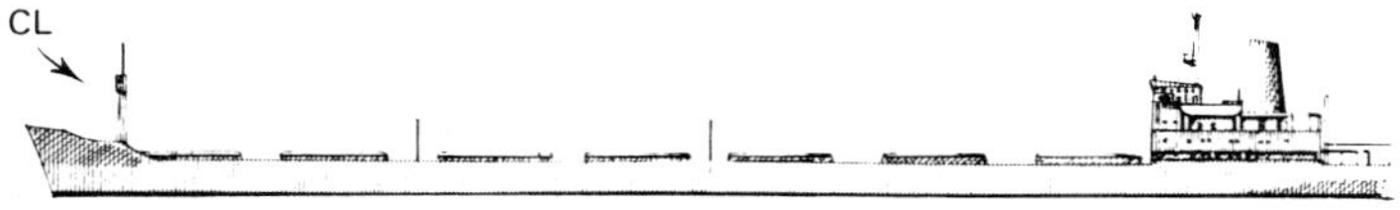

KMFK H1
77730 KING ALFRED. Br/Sw 1968; B; 29400; 217.58 × 12.82 (713.85 × 42.06); M; 14.75; Similar: **77731 LUCIANA DELLA GATTA** (It) ex EASTERN CHARM 1980; ex POLYHYMNIA 1979; Probably similar: **77732 MARITSA** (Gr) ex ORUNDA; **77733 FORT NORMAN** (Br) ex NORMAN TRADER; ex PILOT TRADER; ex RONA 1978.

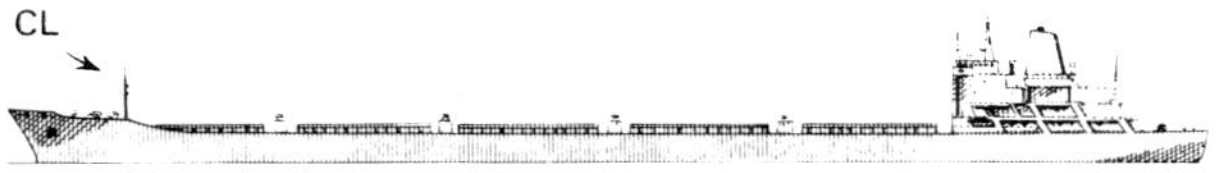

KMFK H1
77740 SUNDA CAREER. Pa/Ja 1964; B; 24600; 191.01 × 10.9 (626.67 × 35.76); M; 14.5; ex FUGO MARU 1978.

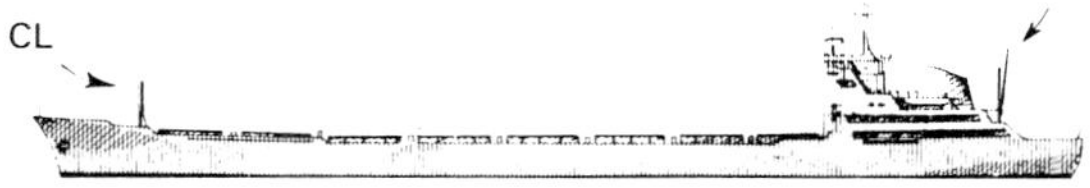

KMFK H1
77750 UNIMAR. Gr/Fr 1961; O; 10700; 165.92 × 9.58 (544.36 × 31.43); M; 14.5; ex LAODICE 1972; ex PENTELLINA 1972.

KMFK H1
77760 ANNIE. Li/Ja 1962; B; 25100; 217.13 × 11.63 (712.37 × 38.16); M; 15; ex NORDIC RANGER 1978; ex NAESS RANGER 1974; ex ROSS CAPE 1971.

KMFK H1
77770 YAMATO. Li/Br 1968; B; 35400; 246.59 × 14.47 (809.02 × 47.47); M; 16; ex HAR ADDIR 1975; Sisters (Li flag): **77771 CHIHAYA** ex HAR SAGGI 1970; **77772 MISAKA** ex MOUNT KATHERINA 1974; **77773 MOUNT EDEN**.

KMFK H1
77780 ALEXANDER STAR. Pa/FRG 1967; B; 23700; 202.11 × 10.82 (663.09 × 35.5); M; 16; ex STEENDORP 1978; ex SOGNEFJELL 1975; Sister: **77781 OCEAN JADE** (Pa) ex OMEGA 1978; ex IRONGATE 1978; ex HOLTEFJELL 1975; Similar (converted to container ship): **77782 ALTAIR** (Gr) ex CAST OTTER 1980; ex DOVREFJELL 1977.

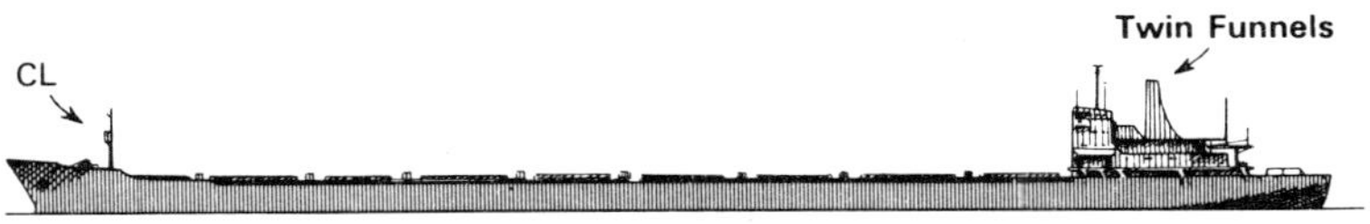

KMFK H1
77790 DAMODAR GENERAL T J PARK. In/FRG 1974; B; 31300; 229.12 × 12.57 (751.71 × 41.24); M; 15.25; Sister: **77791 JALVALLABH** (In).

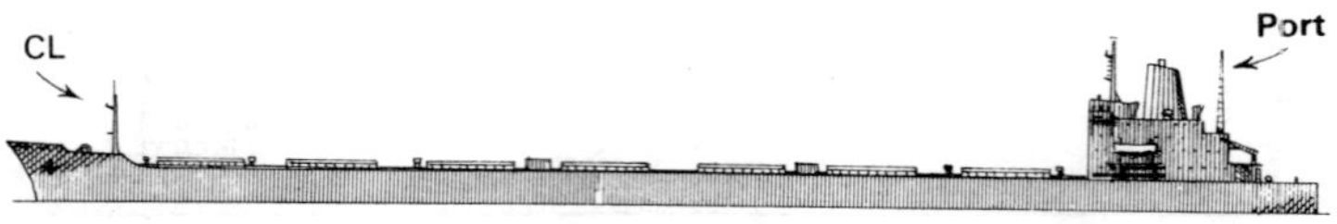

KMFK H1

● **77800 AMELIA TOPIC.** Li/Ja 1972; B; 30100; 223.02 × 12.82 (731.69 × 42.06); M; 14.75; Probable sisters: **77801 GALAXIA** (Pa) ex POLESTAR 1980; ex KYRIAKI 1979; **77802 OLGA TOPIC** (Li); Possible sisters: **77803 ANDROS MELTEMI** (Gr); **77804 GARDEN MOON** (Li); **77805 OCEAN HARMONY** (Li).

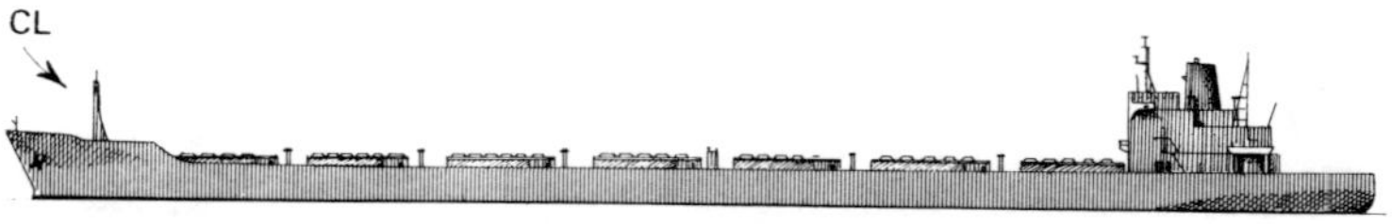

KMFK H1

77810 CHIEKAWA MARU. Ja/Ja 1968; B; 35000; 228.58 × (749.93 × 40.75); M; 15.25; Sister: **77811 YAKUMOKAWA MARU** (Ja).

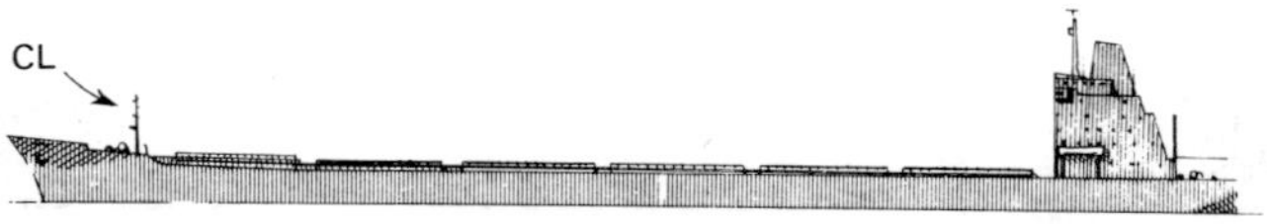

KMFK H1

77820 SUGAR ISLANDER. US/US 1972; B; 15500; 195.38 × 10.21 (641.01 × 33.5); M; 15.

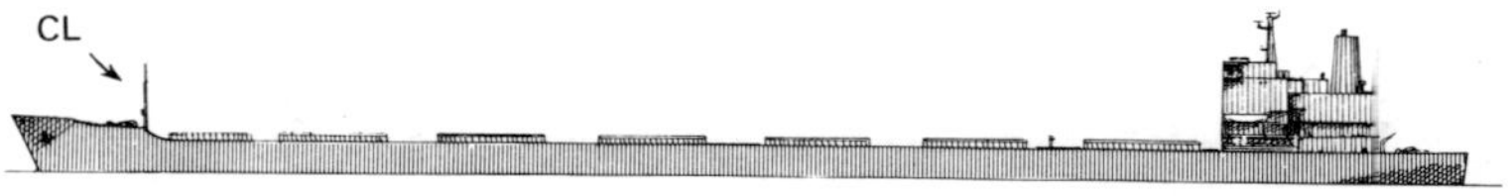

KMFK H1

77830 AEGEAN LION. Gr/Ja 1977; B; 38500; 232.75 × 13.85 (736.62 × 45.44); M; 15.5; Probable sister: **77831 ANTHONY III** (Li).

KMFK H1

77840 AMSTELMEER. Ne/Pd 1975; B; 34000; 221.47 × 12.4 (726.61 × 40.68); M; 16.5; launched as POLITECHNIKA GDANSKA; **'B-521'** type; Sister: **77841 BALTIC SEA** (Pa) ex POLITECHNIKA SLASKA 1980; ex POLITECHNIKA GLIWICKA 1974.

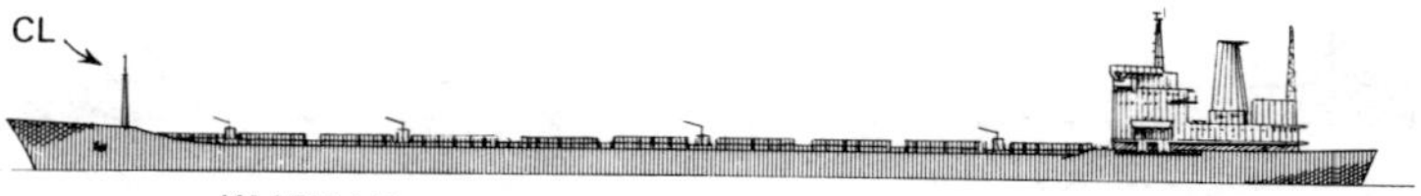

KMFK H1

77850 AMSTELMOLEN. Ne/Pd 1976; B; 34000; 221.47 × 12.4 (726.61 × 40.68); M; 15.75; **'B-521'** type.

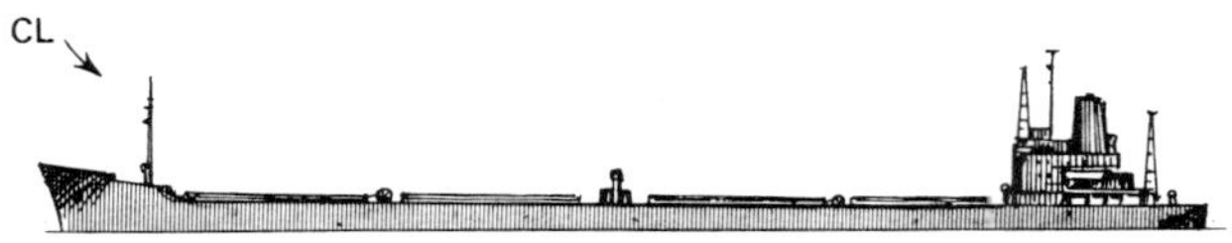

KMFK H1
77860 SHORYU MARU. Ja/Ja 1971; O; 20400; 188.02 × 9.15 (616.86 × 30.12); M; 14.5.

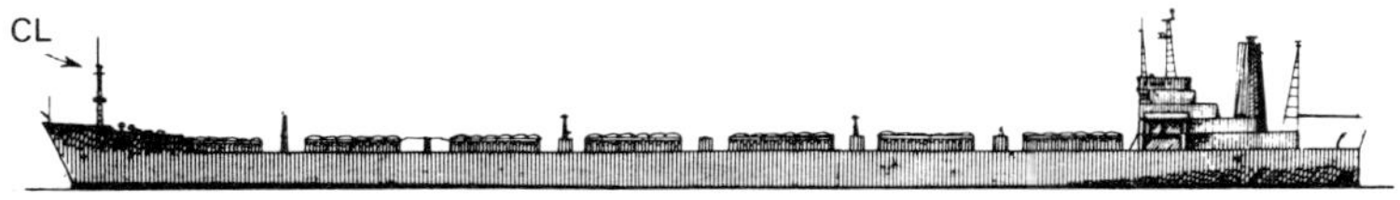

KMFK H1
77870 GOLDEN LAUREL. Li/Ja 1977; B; 29700; 225.03 × 12.4 (738.29 × 40.68); M; 14.75; Similar (May vary in details—particularly after Kingposts): **77871 OGDEN THAMES** (Li); **77872 OGDEN DANUBE** (Li); **77873 OSLO VENTURE** (Li); **77874 ARCHANGELOS** (Li); **77875 WORLD MEDAL** (Li); **77876 SAPPHIRE** (Li); **77877 PRIAMOS** (Li) ex SHOWA VENTURE 1975; **77879 CONTINENTAL FRIENDSHIP** (Li); **77879 CONTINENTAL TRADER** (Li); **77880 EVNIKI** (Li); **77881 CARYANDA** (Gr); **77882 MOUNT PINDOS** (Gr); **77883 HOAN MARU** (Ja); Possibly similar (May have kingposts); **77884 KYUKO MARU** (Ja); **77885 MARITIME KING** (Pa); **77886 PANAMAX MARS** (Li); **77887 ZANNIS MICHALOS** (Gr).

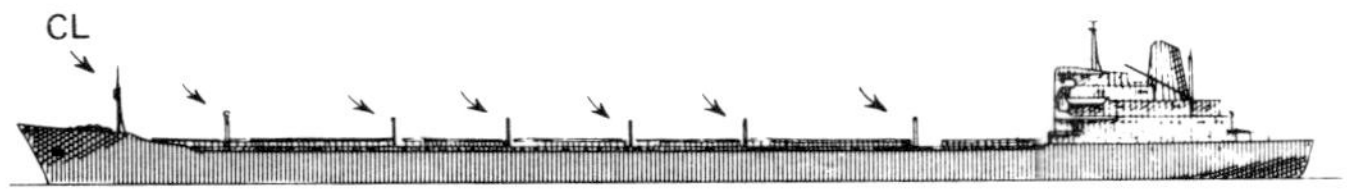

KMFK H1
77900 OTTO LEONHARDT. FRG/FRG 1967; B; 23400; 202.34 × 11.27 (663.85 × 36.98); M; 16.

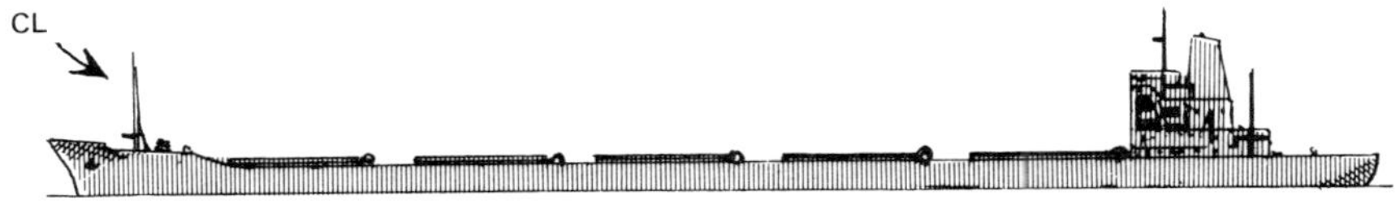

KMFK H1
77910 OWARI MARU. Ja/Ja 1969; O; 58800; 259.01 × 14.17 (849.77 × 47.24); M; 15.

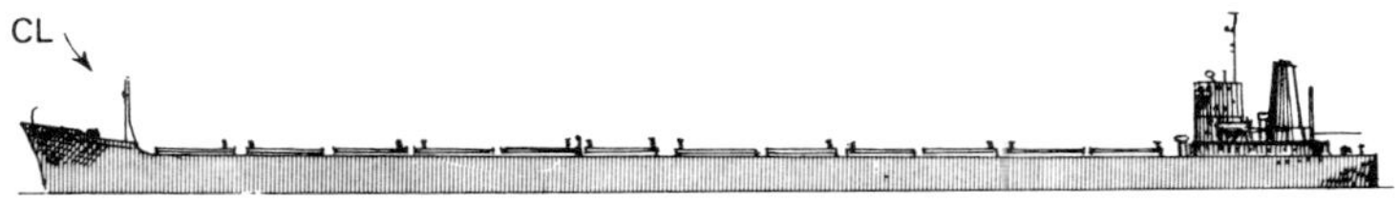

KMFK H1
77920 NEPTUNIA. Li/Ja 1965; B; 28000; 226.4 × 12.27 (742.78 × 40.26); M; —; ex THEODORE 1975; Sister: **77921 OCEANICA** (Li) ex DIMITRI 1968.

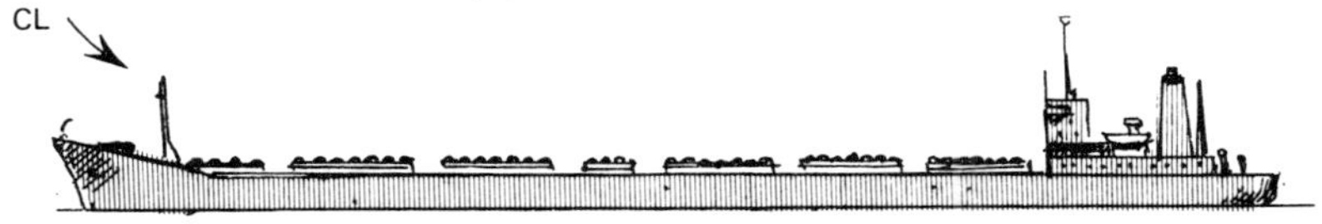

KMFK H1
77930 IMA. Li/Ja 1968; B; 28000; 226.42 × 12.4 (742.85 × 40.68); M; 16; Similar: **77931 VIRGINIA** (Li).

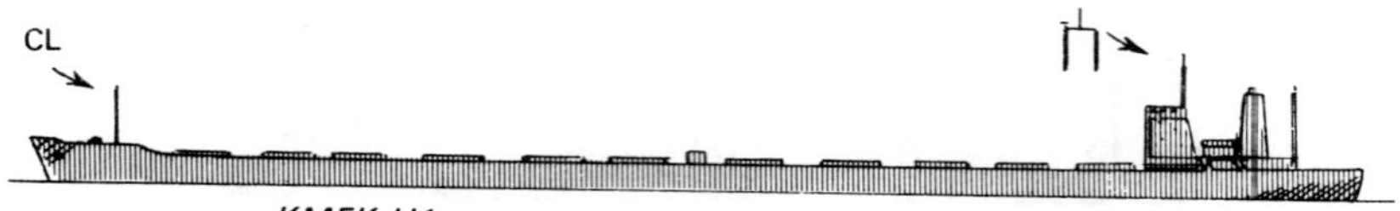

KMFK H1
77940 CHI SONG. Li/Ja 1966; B; 36600; 248.47 × 11,89 (815.19 × 39.01); M; 15.25; ex SHOBU MARU 1977.

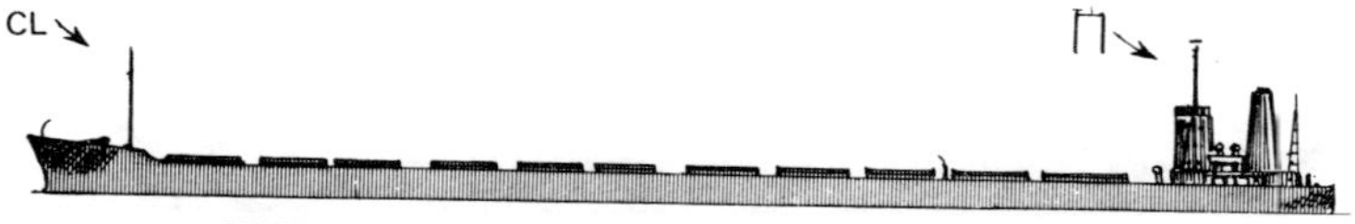

KMFK H1
77950 CHI CHING. Pa/Ja 1965; B; 33800; 226.4 × 11.61 (741.7 × 38.16); M; 15; ex SHOZAN MARU 1976.

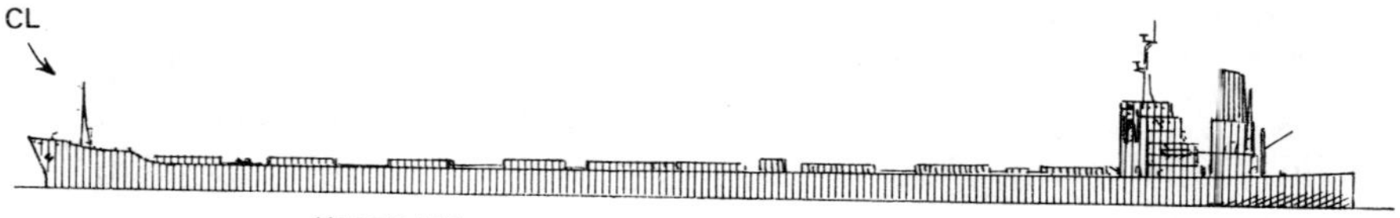

KMFK H1
77960 AFRICA MARU. Ja/Ja 1977; O; 74900; 267.01 × 16.6 (876.02 × 54.46); M; 14.75; Possible sister: **77961 OCEANIA MARU** (Ja).

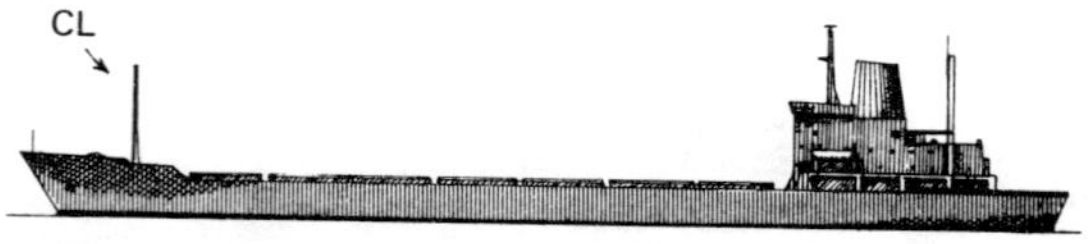

KMFK H1
77970 CP VOYAGEUR. Br/Br 1970; Con; 15700; 167.09 × 9.17 (548.2 × 30.9); M; 19; Sisters (Br flag): **77971 CP DISCOVERER; 77972 CP TRADER.**

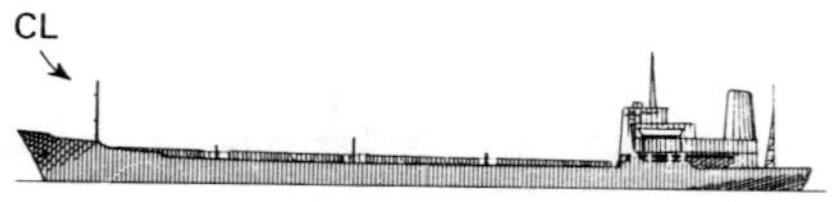

KMFK H1
⋆77980 LYULIN. Bu/Ja 1965; B; 6100; 126.02 × 7.6 (413.45 × 24.93); M; 13; Sisters (Bu flag): **⋆77981 PLANA; ⋆77982 BELASITZA; ⋆77983 HEMUS; ⋆77984 OGRAJDAN; ⋆77985 OSOGOVO.**

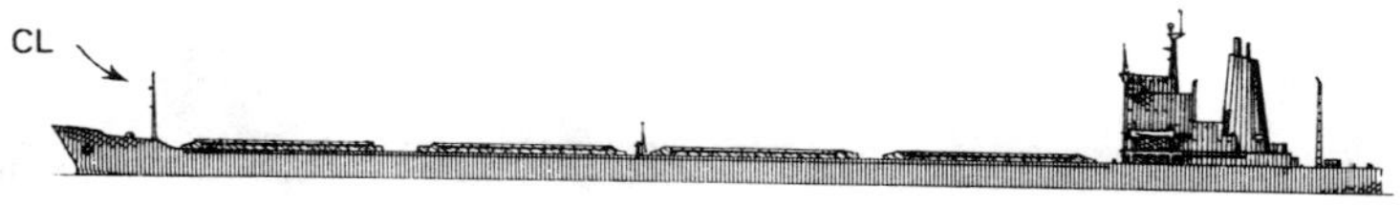

KMFK H1
77990 AZAR . Pa/Ja 1967; O; 32000; 219.36 × 11.61 (719.69 × 38.09); M; 15; ex SHINZAN MARU.

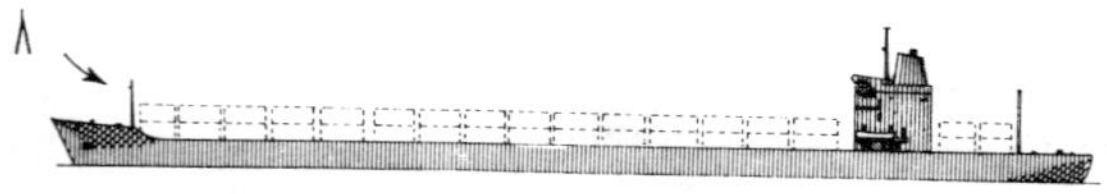

KMFK H1
78000 HELLENIC ADVENTURER. Gr/Fr 1973; Con; 13100; 163.91 × 7.8 (537.76 × 25.59); M; 19; ex SEATRAIN LE HAVRE 1980; ex MEDORFEA 1969; Sisters: **78001 HELLENIC FRIENDSHIP** (Gr); ex SEATRAIN BUNKER HILL 1980; ex ATLANTIC IBERIA 1977; ex MEDARIANA 1975; **78002 HELLENIC CONCORD** (Gr); ex SEATRAIN CONCORD 1980; ex MEDELENA 1977; Similar (lengthened): **78003 CHEVALIER DE BLOIS** (Fr); ex SEATRAIN TICONDEROGA 1980; ex AMERICAN ARROW 1979; ex ATLANTICA MARSEILLE.

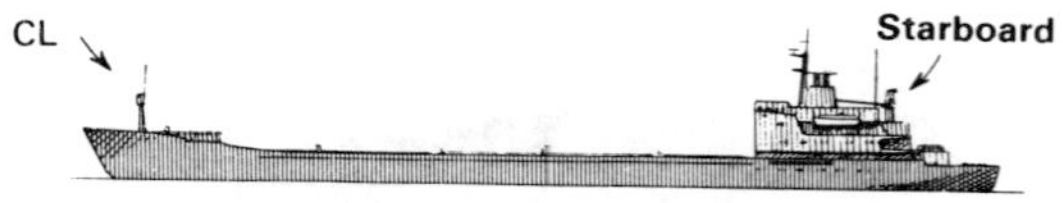

KMFK H1
⋆78010 KAPITAN PANFILOV. Ru/Ru 1975; B; 10100; 146.21 × 9.43 (479.69 × 30.94); M; 14; Sisters (Ru flag): **⋆78011 KAPITAN KHROMTSOV; ⋆78012 KAPITAN DUBININ; ⋆78013 KAPITAN IZHMYAKOV; ⋆78014 KAPITAN MESHCHRYAKOV; ⋆78015 KAPITAN REUTOV; ⋆78016 KAPITAN GUDIN; ⋆78017 KAPITAN STULOV; ⋆78018 KAPITAN VAVILOV; ⋆78019 IVAN NESTEROV.**

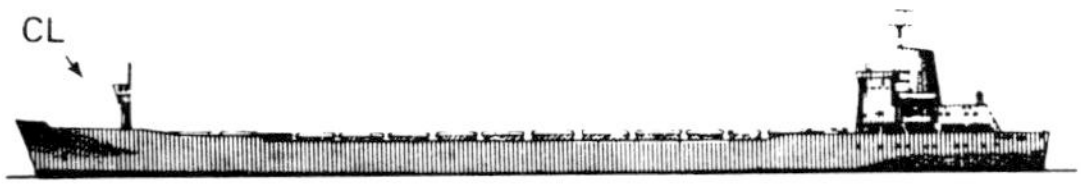

KMFK H1
78030 OCEAN CONTAINER. Pa/Br 1968; Con; 12000; 161.47 × 8.26 (529.76 × 27.1); M; 19.5; ex MANCHESTER CHALLENGE 1979; Sisters (Br flag): **78031 PACIFIC CONTAINER;** ex MANCHESTER COURAGE 1979; **78032 MANCHESTER CONCORDE; 78033 MANCHESTER CRUSADE; 78034 MANCHESTER RENOWN;** ex ASIAN RENOWN 1979; ex MANCHESTER RENOWN 1974; **78035 MANCHESTER REWARD;** ex ASIAN REWARD 1979; ex MANCHESTER REWARD.

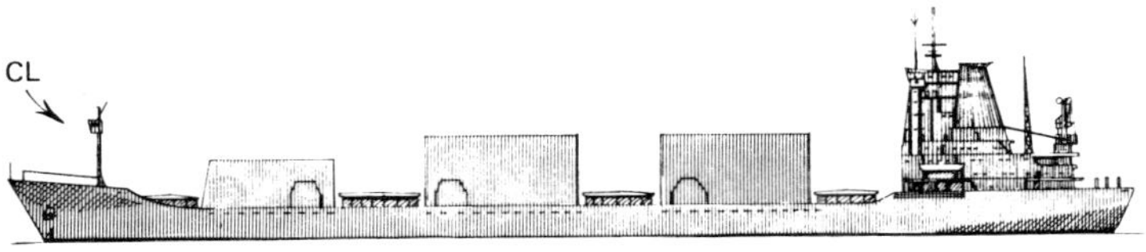

KMFK H1
78040 JUTHLANDIA. Li/Pd 1976; BC; 33000; 224.42 × 12.37 (736.29 × 40.58); M; 15.75; **'B-521'** type; Side doors.

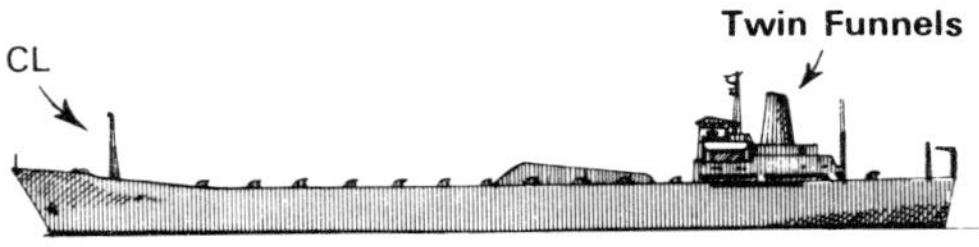

KMFK H1
78050 LEENA DAN. Br/Fi 1972; RoC; 1100; 162.36 × 7.72 (532.68 × 23.69); TSM; 17.5; ex UNION SYDNEY 1977; ex LEENA DAN 1974; ex MONT LAURIER 1973; Lengthened 1978; Stern door/ramp.

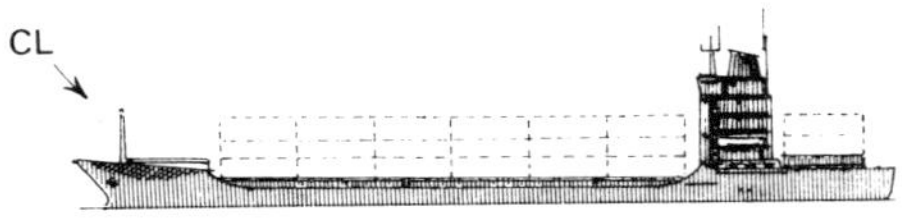

KMFK H13
78070 SIGAL. Is/Is 1977; Con; 6100; 129.85 × 8.07 (426.02 × 26.48); M; 17; Sisters (Is flag): **78071 PALMAH II; 78072 VERED;** ex ZIM MELBOURNE 1980; ex VERED 1978.

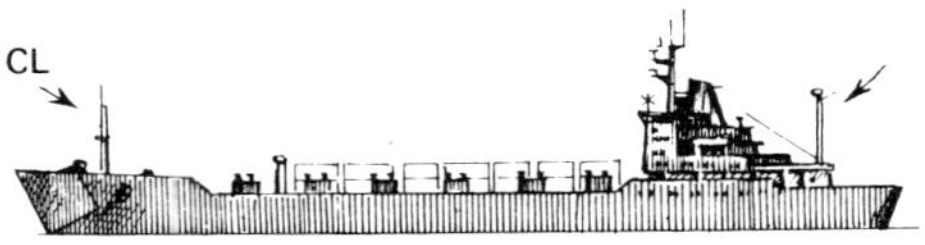

KMFK H1
● **⋆78060 IVAN SKURIDIN.** Ru/Ru 1975; RoC/Con; 4000; 139.6 × 6.62 (458 × 21.72); M; 17; Bow door; **'Neva'** type; Sisters (some have bow & stern doors—Ru flag): **⋆78061 GAVRILL KIRDISHCHEV; ⋆78062 YURIY SMIRNOV; ⋆78063 NIKOLAY VILKOV; ⋆78064 IVAN DERBENEV; ⋆78065 ZNAMYA OKTYABRYA; ⋆78066 EKATLERINA ZELENKO** (may be spelt **EKATERINA ZELENKO**); **⋆78067 ALEKSANDR OSIPOV; ⋆78068 TIMUR FRUNZE; ⋆78069 BORIS BUVIN.**

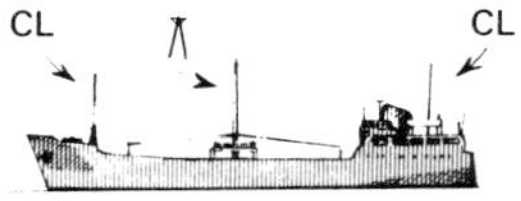

KMFK H13
78080 EKATERINI P. Gr/Br 1958; C; 1000; 70.74 × 4.03 (232.09 × 13.22); M; 12.5; ex PETROS P 1978; ex ABADAN 1977; ex GULF SKY 1977; ex DARLINGTON 1971; May be altered in appearance.

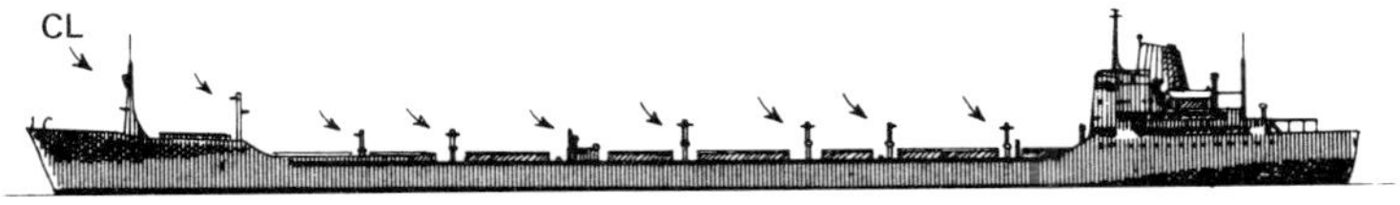

KMFK H13
78090 ARCHANGELOS III. Gr/FRG 1963; B; 22800; 217.99 × 11.59 (715.19 × 38.02); M; 15; ex NAESS LIBERTY 1974; Sister: **78091 PYTHEUS** (Gr); ex RUBYCORN 1980; ex FRIGGA 1973; Similar: **78092 TRADE LIGHT** (Gr); ex BALDUR 1978.

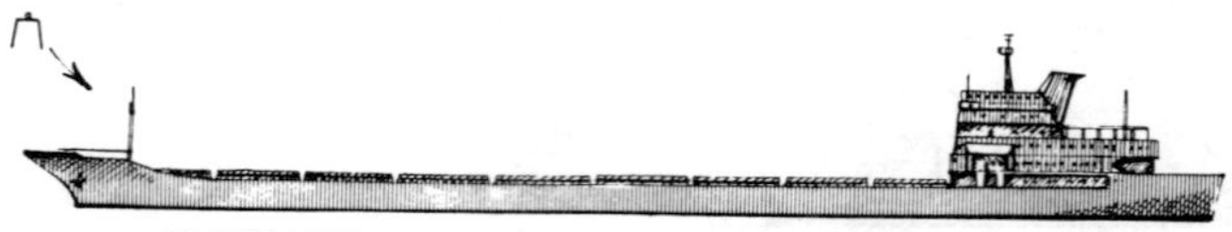

KMFK H13
78100 SAINT PIERRE. Li/Pd 1971; B; 19300; 202.34 × 10.71 (663.85 × 35.14); M; 15; **'B-447'** type; Sister: **78101 RIO CUANZA** (Po); Similar (centre-line KP forward with crows nest—Po flag): **78102 CASSINGA; 78103 RIO ZAMBEZE.**

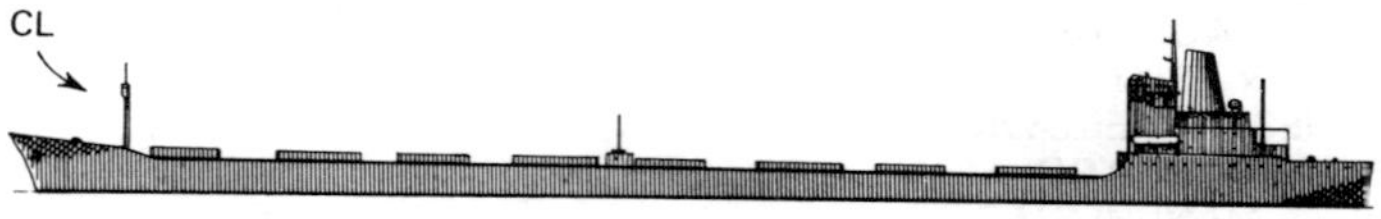

KMFK H13
78110 EVANGELIA C. Gr/Br 1967; B; 29400; 213.37 × 12.75 (700.32 × 41.83); M; 15; ex POLYFREEDOM 1978; Sister: **78111 PAN WESTERN** (Gr); ex NORSEMAN 1975.

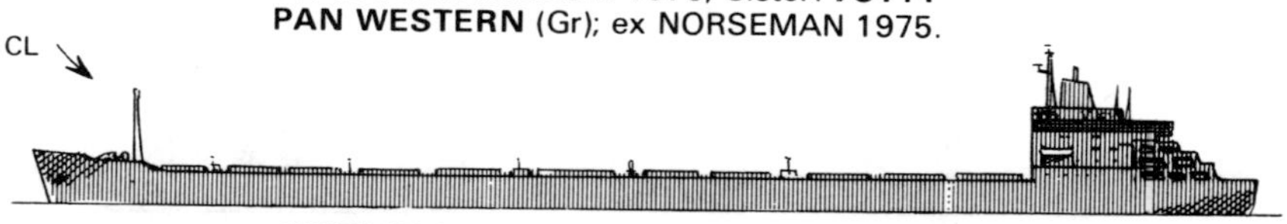

KMFK H13
78120 CURTIS CAPRICORN. Au/Au 1972; B; 48900; 255.43 × 15.14 (938.02 × 49.67); T; —; ex CLUTHA CAPRICORN 1977.

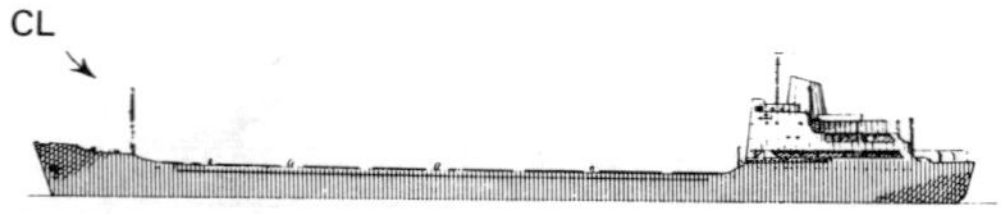

KMFK H13
★78130 YASINOVATYA. Ru/Sw 1962; B; 10600; 149.36 × 9.6 (490.03 × 31.5); M; 14; ex ANARIS &: Sisters: **★78131 YAVOROV** (Ru); ex AURIVAARA 1976; Possible sister (may be M_2FK): **★78132 YARTSEVO** (Ru); ex ADAK 1976.

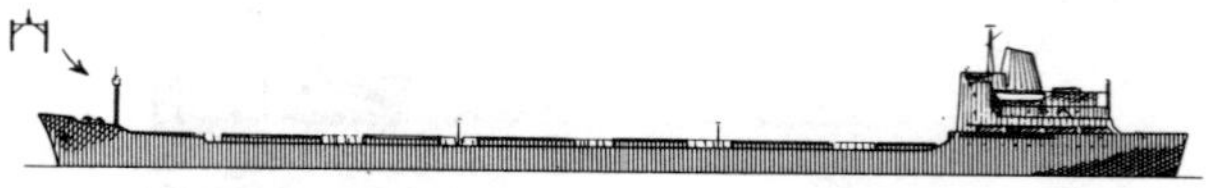

KMFK H13
★78140 ZIEMIA BYDGOSKA. Pd/Br 1967; B; 15700; 179.51 × 9.91 (588.94 × 32.51); M; 15; Sister: **★78141 ZIEMIA MAZOWIECKA** (Pd).

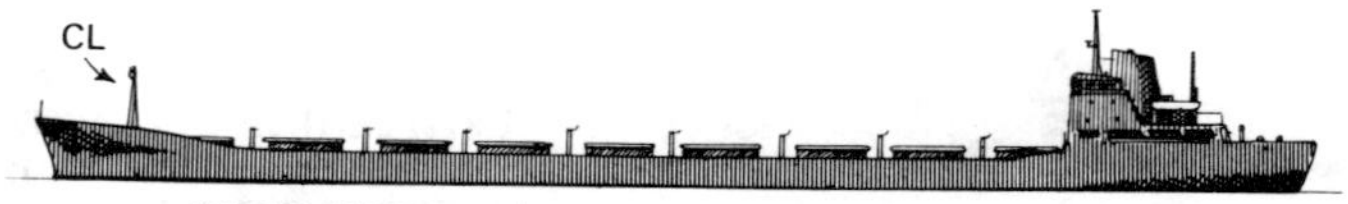

KMFK H13
78150 CHRISTOFFER OLDENDORFF. Li/FRG 1962; B; 17700; 200.01 × 9.81 (656.2 × 32.19); M; 16; Sister: **78151 HENNING OLDENDORFF** (Li); Similar: **78152 LABRADOR CURRENT** (Li); ex VULKAN 1972.

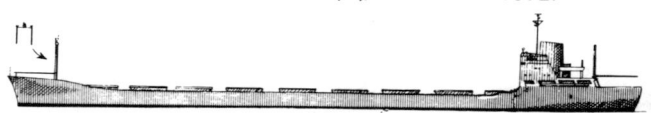

KMFK H13
78160 JORGE S. Ar/FRG 1962; B; 19800; 199.98 × 9.81 (656.1 × 32.19); M; 14.5; ex STAD GHENT 1976; ex STADT EMDEN 1974.

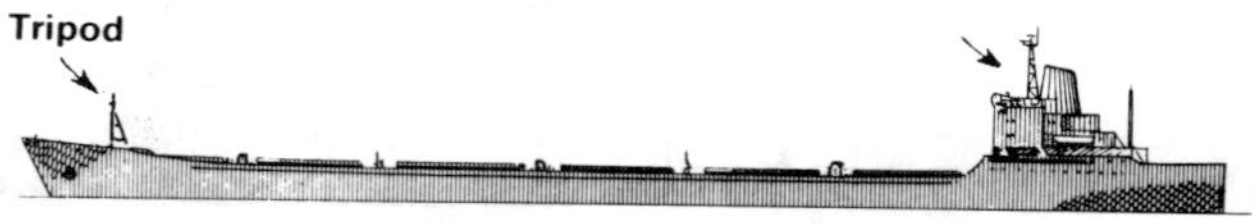

KMFK H13
78170 HASSELT. Be/Be 1974; B; 17600; 190 × 10.69 (623.36 × 35.07); M; —.

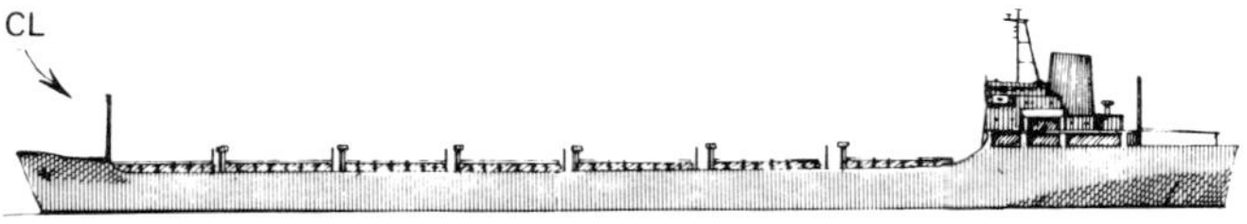

KMFK H13
78180 CHENNAI MUYARCHI. In/Sp 1973; B; 29300; 206.86 × 13.27 (678.67 × 43.54); M; 16.5; ex SENECA 1974; Sisters: **78181 CASTILLO MANZANARES** (Sp); **78182 NICHOLAS G. PAPALIOS** (Gr); Similar (pole masts): **78183 ERMUA** (Sp).

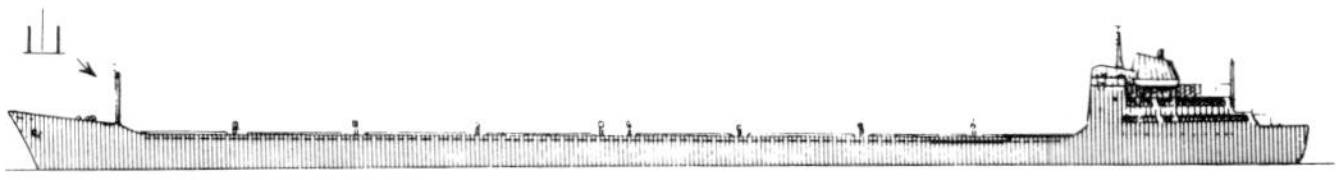

KMFK H13
78190 TIMNA. Is/FRG 1961; B; 19200; 206.08 × 10.87 (676.12 × 35.66); M; 15.

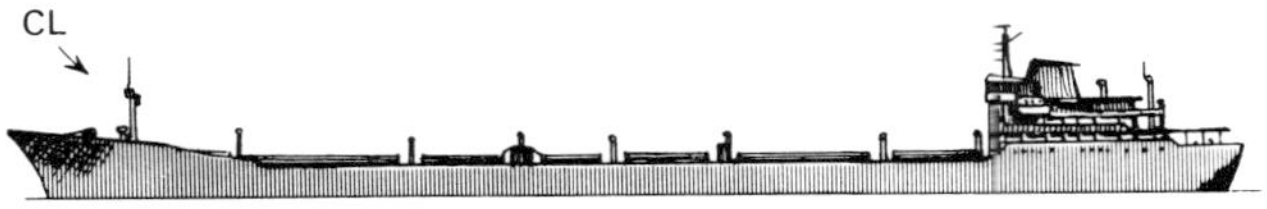

KMFK H13
78200 GOTHIC CHIEF. Pa/Sw 1964; B; 20800; 196.27 × 10.95 (643.93 × 35.93); M; 15; ex LOTUS 1974; ex MIMOSA 1970.

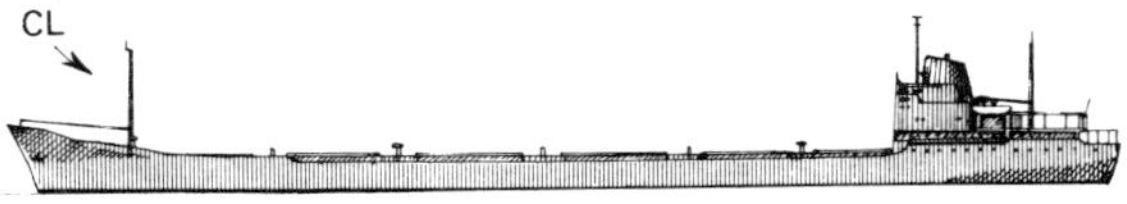

KMFK H13
78210 ARKADIA. Fi/FRG 1959; B; 13400; 176.79 × 9.89 (580.02 × 32.45); M; 13.5; ex SLESVIG 1974.

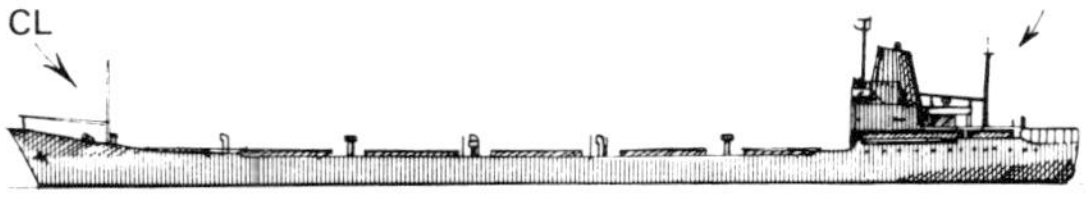

KMFK H13
78220 VITACARRIER. Gr/FRG 1959; B; 13400; 169.48 × 9.58 (556.04 × 31.43); M; 15; ex DORIC CHARIOT 1976; ex MULHEIM-RUHR 1967; Lengthened 1965.

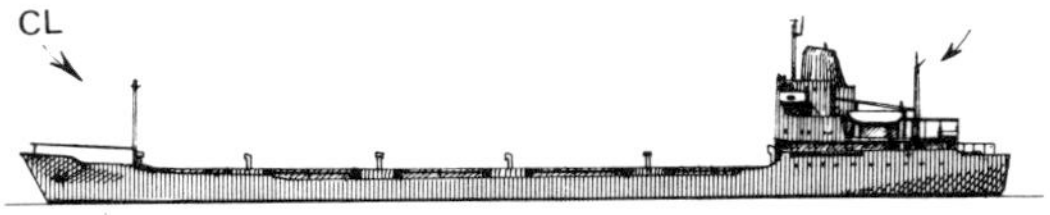

KMFK H13
78230 RUHRLAND. Pa/FRG 1960; B; 11500; 154.41 × 9.64 (506.59 × 31.63); M; 13.5; ex LINZERTOR 1977; ex CARSTEN RUSS 1970.

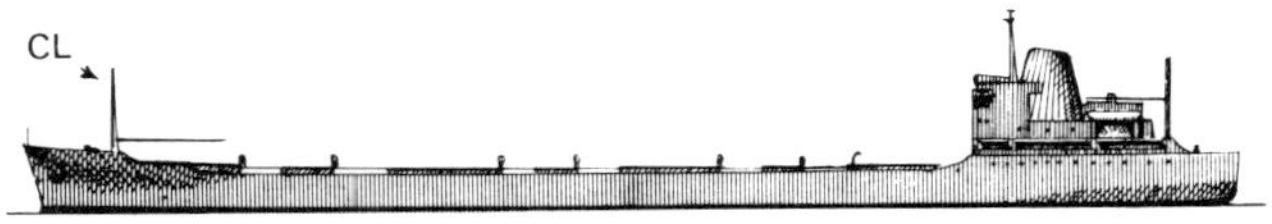

KMFK H13
78240 DELFI. Gr/Br 1965; B; 19000; 192.03 × 11.11 (630.02 × 36.45); M; 15.2; ex DREPANON 1977; ex ROMANDIE 1974.

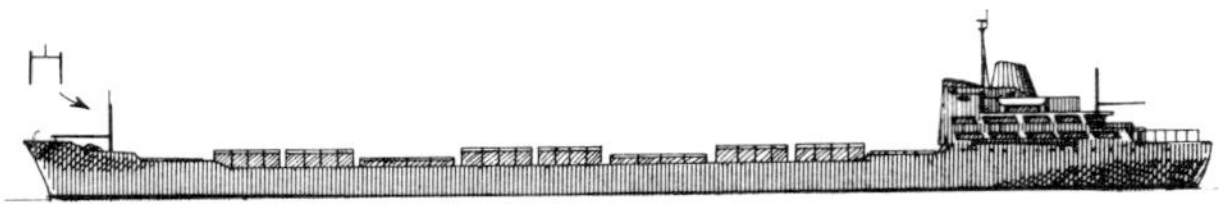

KMFK H13
78250 FRANCOIS L. D. Fr/Fr 1962; O; 16500; 188.02 × 10.02 (616.86 × 32.87); M; 16.25.

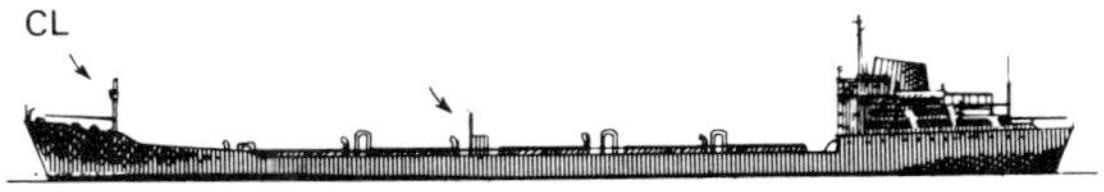

KMFK H13
● **78260 PROVIDENCE.** Pa/De 1959; B; 12000; 174.73 × 9.53 (573.26 × 31.27); M; 15.

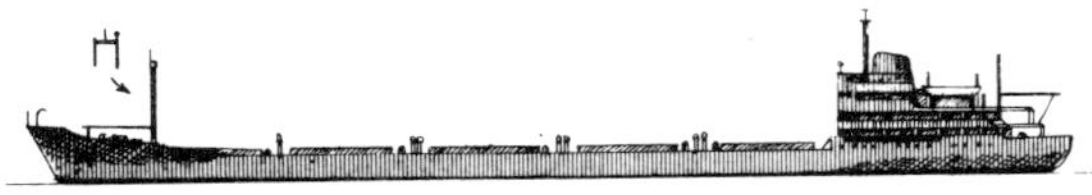

KMFK H13
78270 EPIMITHEFS. Gr/Ne 1959; B; 11800; 164.78 × 9.86 (540.62 × 32.35); M; 14.25; ex MEERDRECHT 1977; Sisters: **78271 VENI** (Gr); ex OSSENDRECHT 1978; **78272 SUCCESSOR** (Gr); ex HUANDOY 1976; ex ZWIJNDRECHT 1970; **78273 TOURMALIN BAY** (Pa); ex HOLENDRECHT 1978; **78274 AL TAQEE** (Sg); ex THUREDRECHT 1978.

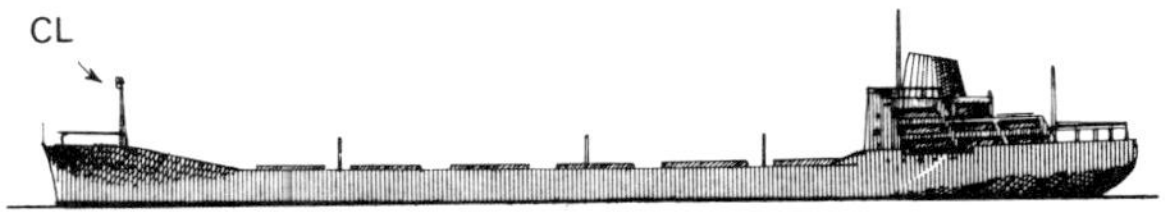

KMFK H13
★78280 HONG QI 302. RC/Br 1961; B; ex BEAUFORT SEA 1980; ex SUNPRINCE 1974; ex SUNMALKA 1970; ex MYLLA 1965.

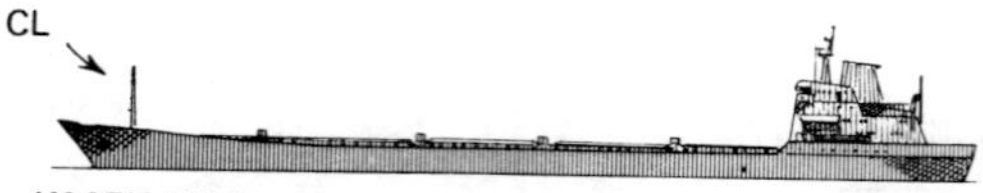

KMFK H13
★**78290 HUTA ZGODA.** Pd/FRG 1974; B; 9300; 145.65 × 8.35 (477.85 × 27.4); M; 15; Sisters (Pd flag): ★**78291 HUTA ZYGMUNT;** ★**78292 BUDOWLANY;** ★**78293 ROLNIK;** ★**78294 KOPALNIA SOSNOWIEC;** ★**78295 KOPALNIA WALBRZYCH;** ★**78296 KOPALNIA ZOFIOWKA.**

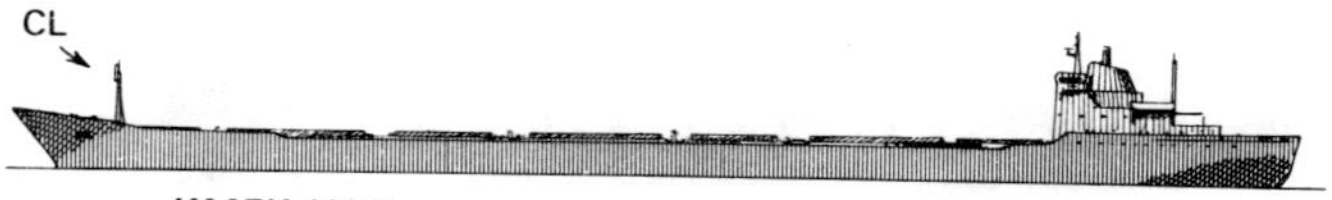

KMFK H13
78310 AMSTELWAL. Ne/Ne 1966; B; 23200; 205.32 × 10.83 (673.62 × 35.53); M; 18; ex WALCHEREN 1978.

KMFK H13
● **78320 ASEAN NATIONS.** Pi/Ne 1967; B; 232000; 205.19 × 11.32 (673.2 × 37.14); M; 17; ex FORELAND 1979.

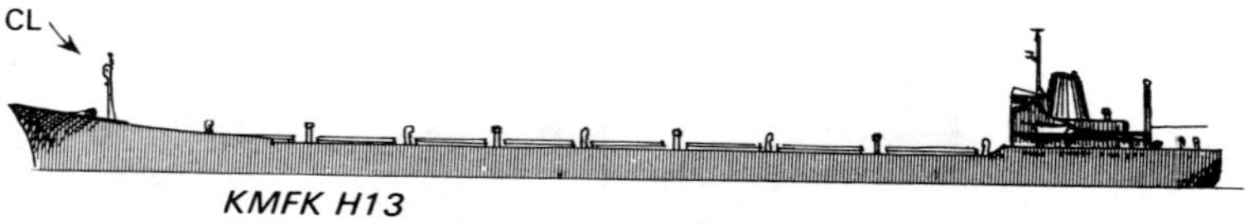

KMFK H13
78330 VASSILIOS BACOLITSAS. Gr/FRG 1964; B; 30600; 231.25 × 11.2 (758.69 × 36.75); M; 15; ex HEINRICH SCHULTE 1978.

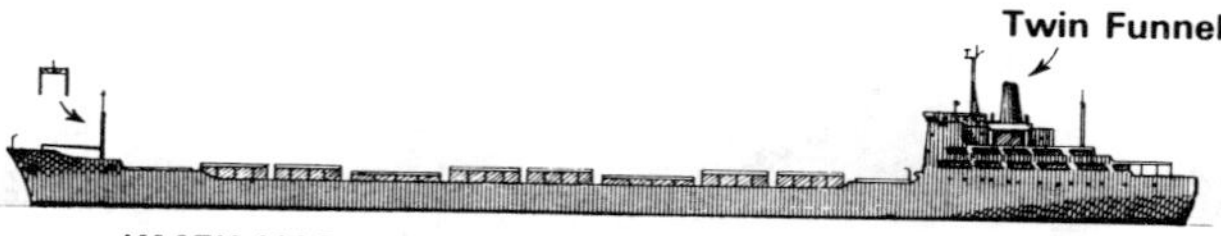

KMFK H13
78340 LAKE BIWA. Br/Fr 1963; B; 16600; 188.14 × 10.03 (617.26 × 32.91); M; 15.25; ex LA CHACRA 1981.

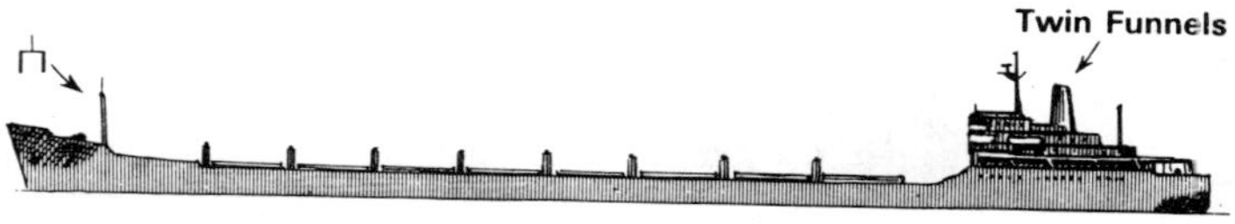

KMFK H13
78350 BRAVERY. Br/Br 1966; B; 28000; 219.46 × 12.34 (720 × 40.49); M; 15; ex LA SIERRA 1980; Sister: **78351 EMMANUEL COMNINOS** (Gr); ex LA ESTANCIA 1978.

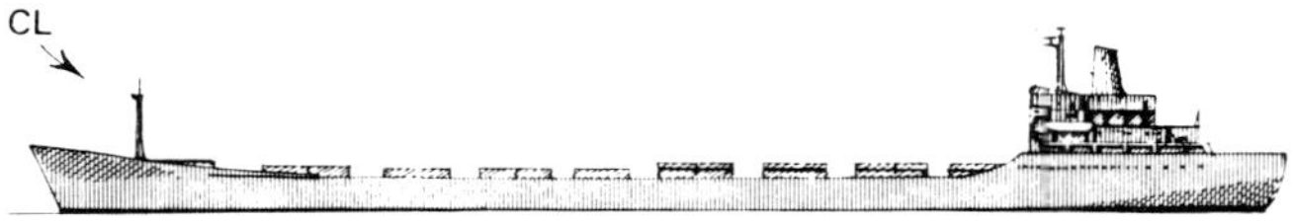

KMFK H13
78360 RIXTA OLDENDORFF. Sg/FRG 1967; B; 22100; 201.66 × 11.53 (661.61 × 37.83); M;

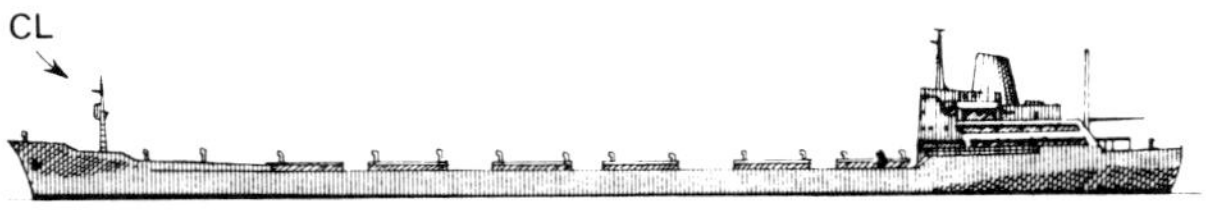

KMFK H13
78370 ANTARTICO. Pa/No 1963; B; 16300; 186.29 × 11.2 (611.19 × 36.75); M; 14.5; ex WILMARA 1977; Sister: **78371 SUNWAVE** (Br); ex MAR TERSO 1978; ex WILYAMA 1978.

KMFK H13
● **78380 ARCADIAN SEA.** Gr/FRG 1965; B; 21000; 191.27 × 11.32 (627.53 × 37.14); M; 15.25; ex ASTRAMARINA 1980; ex TORM HELVIG 1975; ex HELVIG 1974; Sisters: **78381 ASTRADIEGO** (Ar); ex TORM HERDIS 1975; ex HERDIS 1974; **78382 TRADE MASTER** (Gr); ex OCEAN MASTER 1977; **78383 ODYSSEUS** (Ar); ex TYROL 1978; ex FERNGLEN 1975.

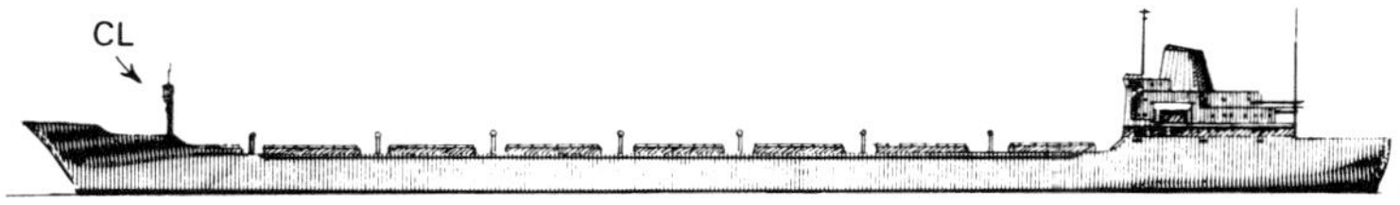

KMFK H13
78390 NAROTTAM MORARJEE. In/FRG 1967; B; 3000; 222.51 × 12.92 (730.02 × 42.39); M; 15; ex ORM JARL 1969; Sisters: **78391 STEPHANITOR** (FRG); ex GOLDEN MASTER 1969; **78392 RALLI** (Li); ex UNAS 1978; ex MOSBORG 1977; ex LEIV ERIKSSON 1970.

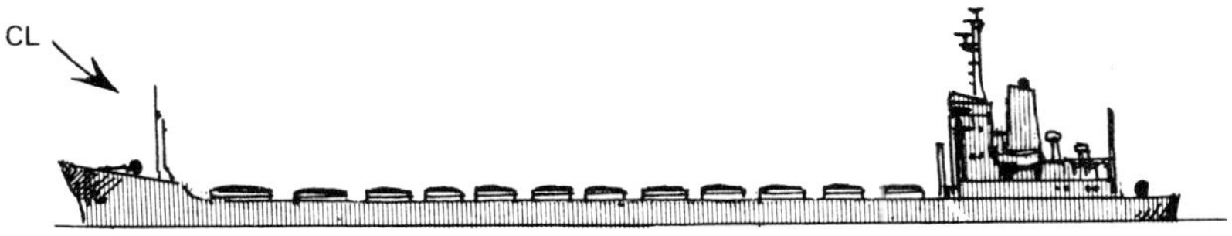

KMFK H13
78400 MARION. Gr/Ja 1967; B; 33600; 226.5 × 12.41 (743.11 × 40.72); M; 16.5; ex JARACONDA 1977; Sister: **78401 ORIENT ROSE** (Li); ex FORT ERIE 1981; ex NEMESIS 1980; ex JASAKA 1978; Similar: **78402 ASSIMINA** (Li); ex TEXADA 1971.

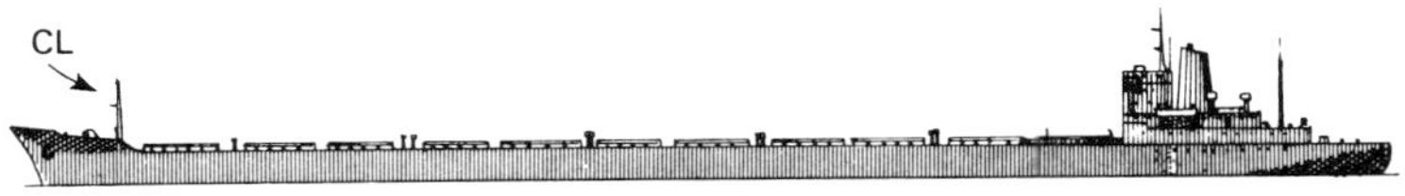

KMFK H13
78410 GUNGNIR X. Pa/Ja 1968; B; 28400; 226.42 × 12.9 (742.85 × 42.32); M; 16.25; ex GRISCHUNA 1980; Sister: **78411 EASTERN GRACE** (Li); ex EL PAMPERO 1978.

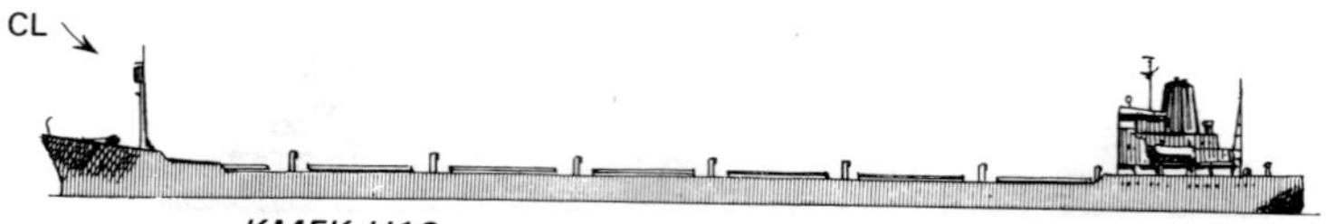

KMFK H13
78420 PAN UNION. Ko/Ja 1973; B; 36100; 219.01 × 13.62 (718.54 × 44.69); M; 15; ex SKEPPSBRON 1980; ex VOYWI 1975; Possible Sisters: **78421 NORSE DUKE** (No); **78422 ESPERANZA** (Li); ex CATHERINE; ex INGWI 1977; **78423 SOUTH BEAUTY** (Li); ex GARD 1978; **78424 MARO** (Gr); Similar: **78425 FAVORITA** (No); ex MOLDANGER 1977; **78426 JARILLA** (No); ex BERGANGER 1977.

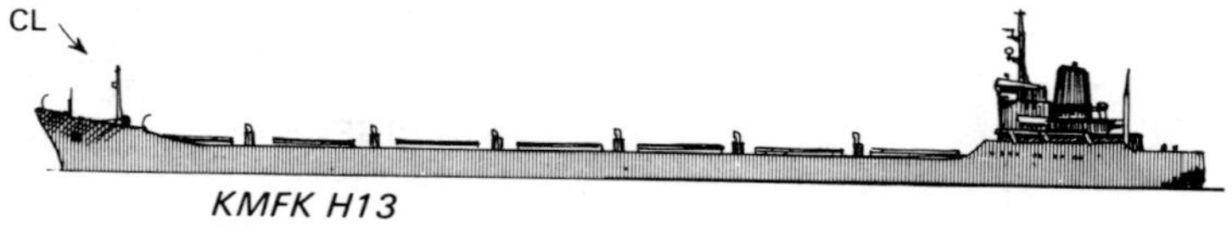

KMFK H13
78430 ST. PAUL. Li/Ja 1967; B; 30700; 219.01 × 12.5 (718.54 × 41.01); M; 16.5; Probable sister: **78431 LUIGI GRIMALDI** (It); ex OCEANIC FIRST 1973; Similar: **78432 RIRUCCIA** (Li).

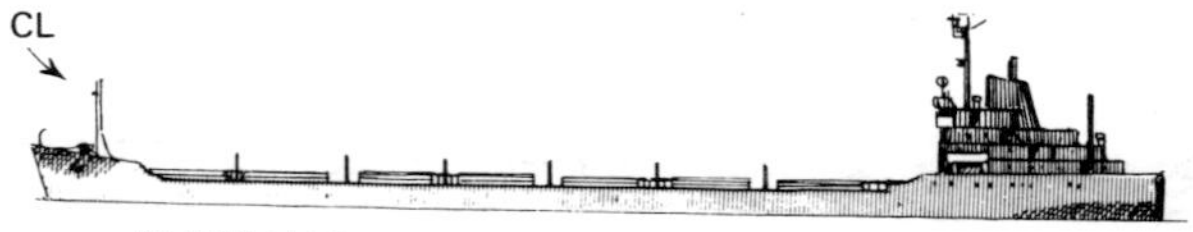

KMFK H13
78440 CABO SAN LUCAS. Li/Ne 1971; B; 19400; 181.72 × 11.21 (596.19 × 36.78); M; 16; ex BOCKENHEIM.

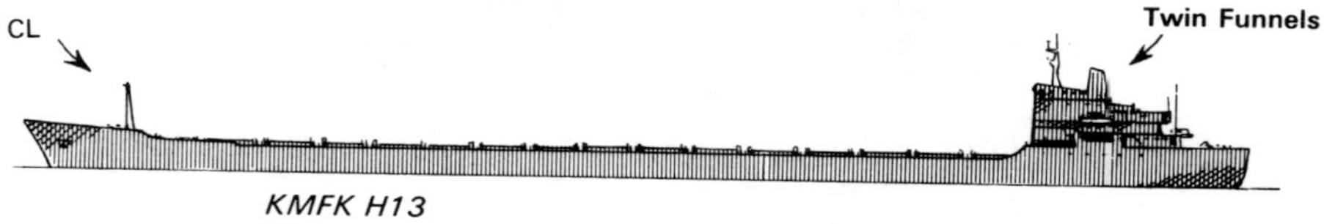

KMFK H13
78450 ANASTASIA L. Gr/Fr 1967; B; 53400; 264.24 × 13.72 (866.93 × 45.01); M; 14.5; ex CETRA COLUMBA 1978.

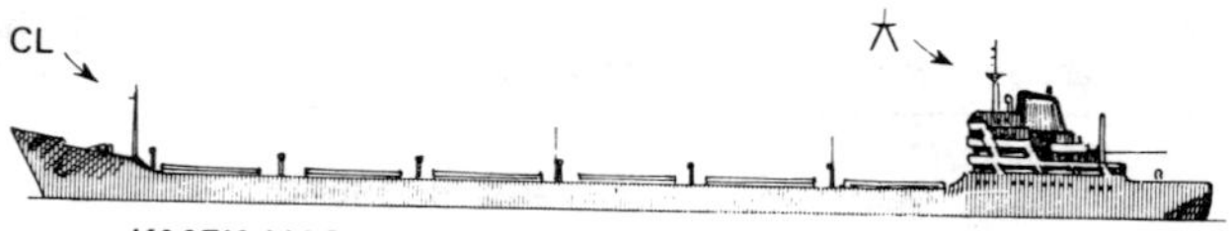

KMFK H13
78460 LUIGI ORLANDO. It/It 1964; B; 15600; 196.63 × 10.35 (645.11 × 33.96); M; —.

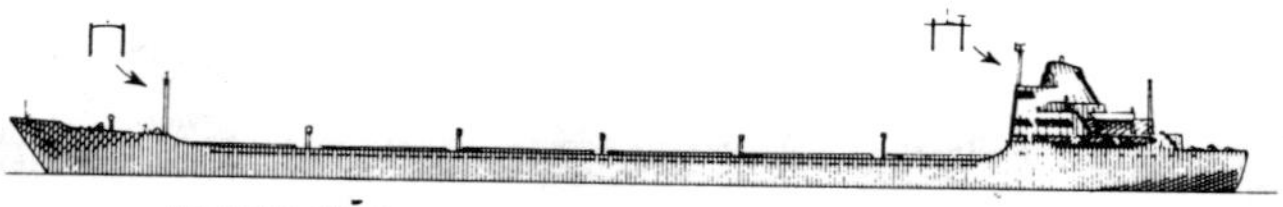

KMFK H13
78470 FIESTA 1. Pa/It 1962; B; 16000; 193.66 × 10.39 (635.37 × 34.09); M; —; ex FENICE 1977.

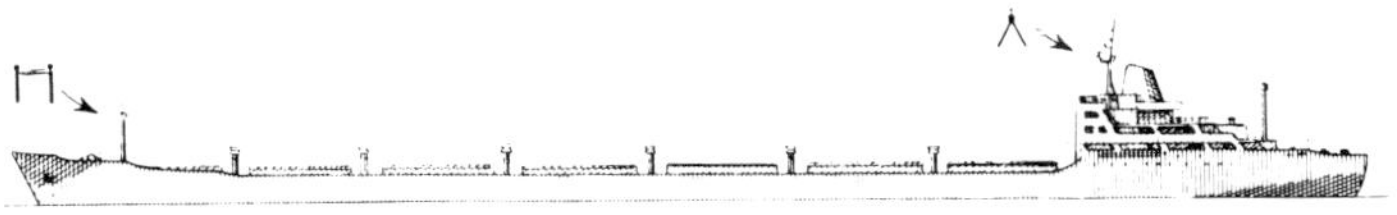

KMFK H13
78480 ELISA F. It/It 1967; B; 28200; 215.5 × 11.65 (707.02 × 38.22); M; —; Probable Sister: **78481 DESIDERIA F** (It).

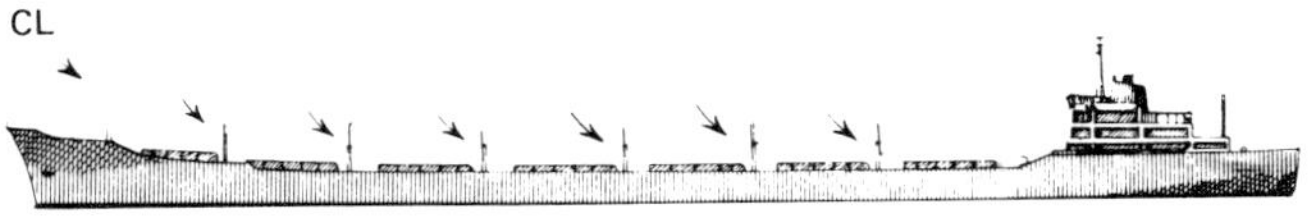

KMFK H13
● **78490 SUZANNE.** Gr/Br 1965; B; 21500; 201.78 × 11.18 (662.01 × 36.68); M; 15; ex GARTHNEWYDD 1972; ex CLUDEN 1972.

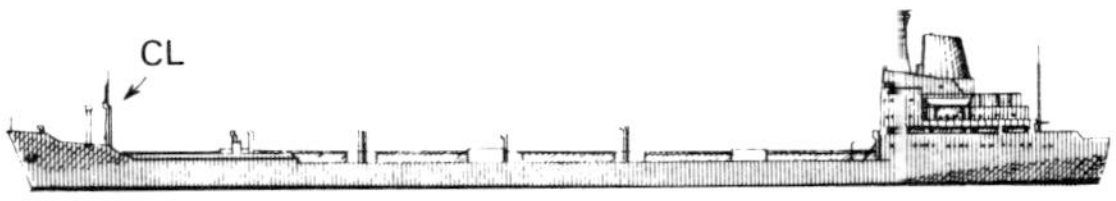

KMFK H13
78500 ORION. Gr/Sw 1963; B; 14600; 175.88 × 10.83 (577.03 × 35.53); M; 17.5.

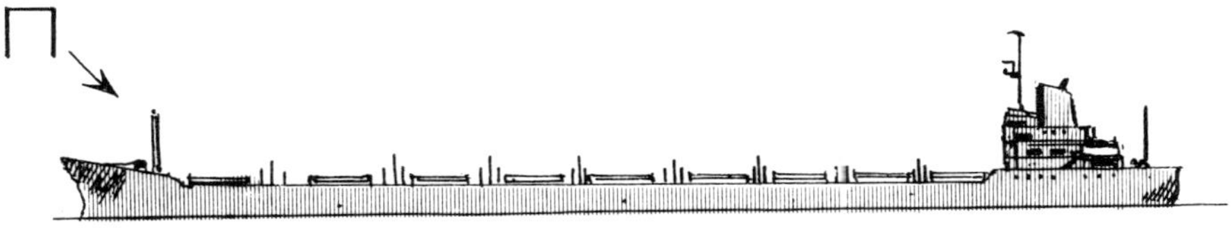

KMFK H13
78510 OREMAR. Li/Ja 1968; B; 35700; 261.58 × 13.58 (858.2 × 44.55); M; 16.25; ex MARKA L 1974.

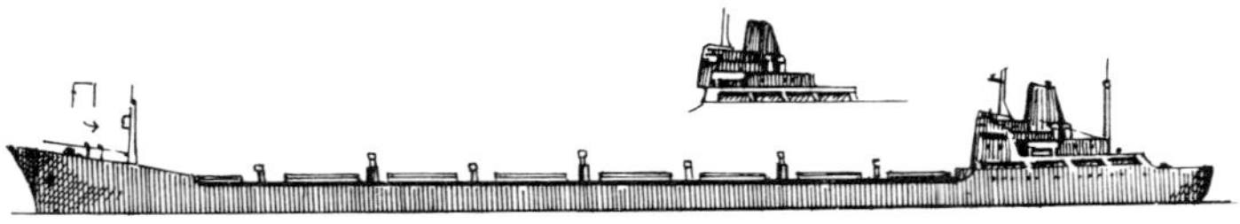

KMFK H13
⋆**78520 SOVFRACHT.** Ru/Ys 1967; B; 26000; 211.41 × 11.79 (693.6 × 38.68); M; 16; ex MAGDI 1973; ex SAARA AARNIO 1973; Sister: **78521 SUSAN TRIDENT** (Fr); ex KRITI; ex JOH. GORTHON 1977; Similar (inset): ⋆**78522 SOVINFLOT** (Ru); ex OLGA 1973; ex ANNUKKA ARNIO 1973.

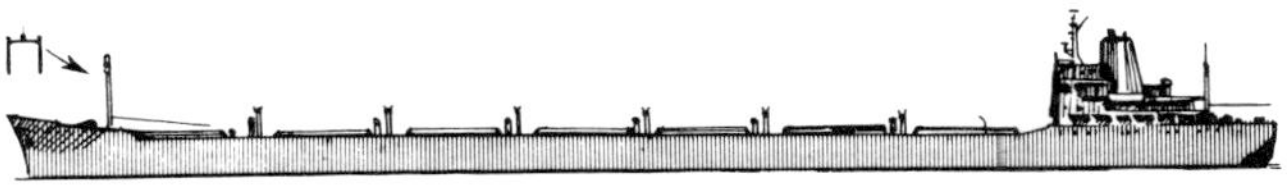

KMFK H13
⋆**78530 KOTOR.** Ys/Ys 1965; B; 23100; 199.52 × 11.48 (654.59 × 37.66); M; 15; Sisters (Ys flag): ⋆**78531 ZOZARA;** ⋆**78532 KRUSEVAC;** ⋆**78533 KUMANOVO.**

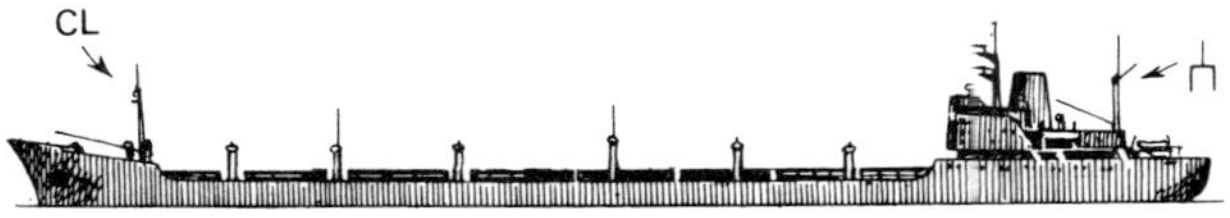

KMFK H13
⋆**78540 ZARECHENSK.** Ru/Ru 1967; B; 16000; 187.12 × 9.54 (614.17 × 31.3); M; 15.5; **'B-470'** type; Sisters (Ru flag): ⋆**78541 ZVENIGOROD;** ⋆**78542 ZAPOROZHYE;** ⋆**78543 ZAKARPATYE;** ⋆**78544 ZADONSK;** ⋆**78545 ZLATOUST;** ⋆**78546 ZORINSK;** Similar (Pd flag): ⋆**78547 ZIEMIA KRAKOWSKA;** ⋆**78548 ZIEMIA LUBELSKA;** ⋆**78549 ZAGLEBIE MIEDZIOWE.**

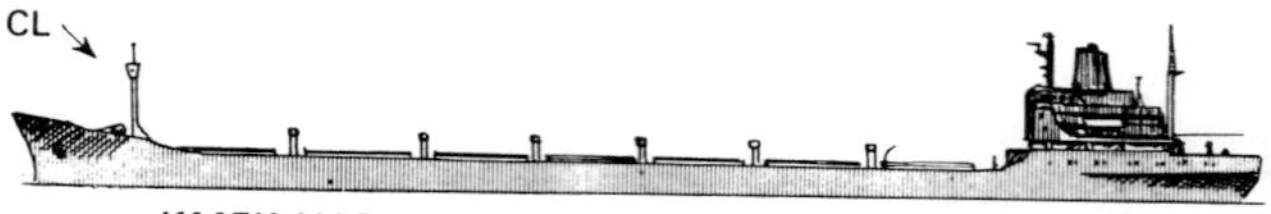

KMFK H13
78560 KONKAR RESOLUTE. Gr/Ja 1970; B; 25100; 203 × 12.49 (666 × 40.98); M; 16.

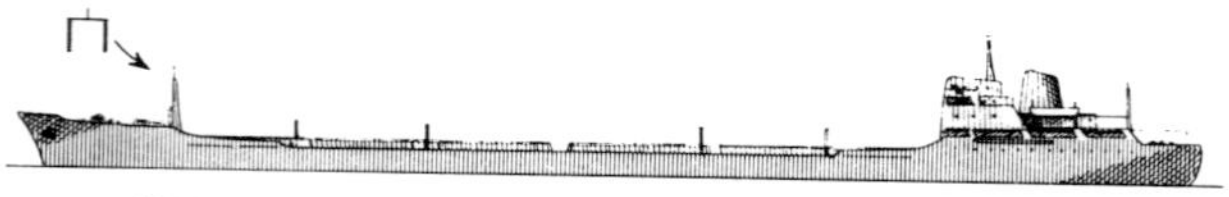

KMFK H13
78570 HALKIS EXPRESS. Gr/Br 1963; B; 19500; 187.46 × — (615.03 × —); M; 13; ex VICTORE 1979.

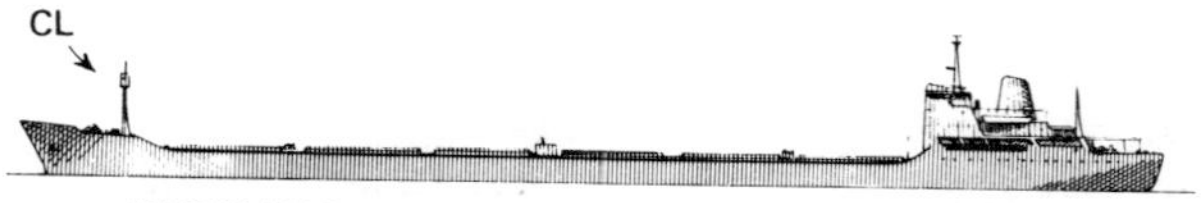

KMFK H13
⋆78580 BUCEGI. Rm/Ja 1966; B; 16600; 181.13 × 9.5 (594.26 × 31.17); M; 16; Sisters (Rm flag): **⋆78581 RESITA; ⋆78582 HUNEDOARA; ⋆78583 LUPENI; ⋆78584 CARPATI; ⋆78585 DUNAREA; ⋆78586 MARAMURES; ⋆78587 OLTUL.**

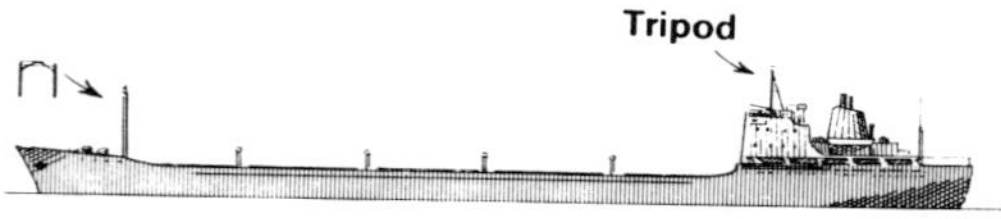

KMFK H13
78600 CHRISTOPHER S. Gr/Be 1958; B; 10200; 152.03 × 9.02 (498.79 × 29.6); M; 14; ex REGINA 1971.

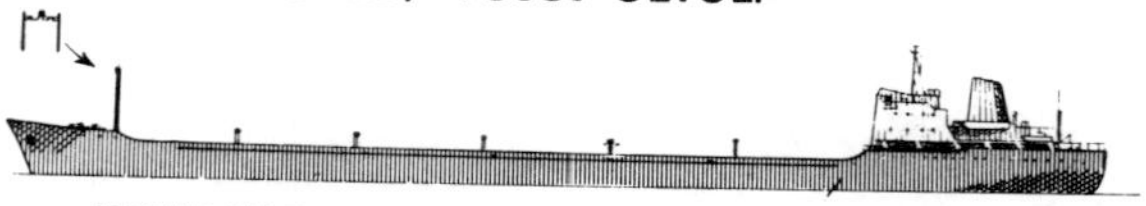

KMFK H13
● **78610 NICOLE 1.** Pa/Be 1959; B; 10700; 172.22 × 9.7 (565.03 × 31.82); M; 14.5; ex PHANTOM 1980; ex HUMBER 1977; ex ANTONAKI 1974; ex MARLY II 1973; Lengthened 1968; Sisters: **78611 MARGARITA** (Gr); ex GEORGIOS C 1980; ex TIELRODE 1974; ex TAMISE 1966; **⋆78612 CALBE** (DDR); ex MARLY I 1965.

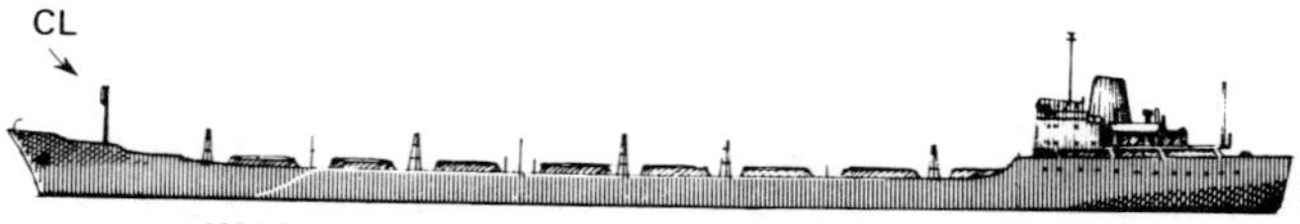

KMFK H13
78620 SUNRISE. Li/FRG 1963; B; 2300; 214.18 × 11.66 (702.69 × 38.26); M; 15; ex SKYLINE 1980; ex LEROS 1978; ex SPLENDID HONOUR 1977; ex DELPHINA 1974; Sister: **⋆78621 TIAN SHUI HAI** (RC).

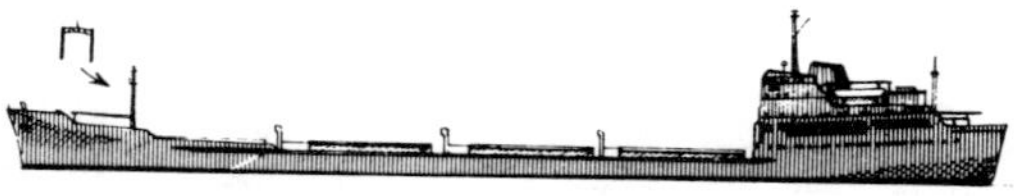

KMFK H13
78630 MARTHA ELLE. Pa/Sw 1959; O; 8600; 157.13 × 8.88 (515.52 × 29.13); M; 12.5; ex AMAX MINER 1980; ex FALCONDALE 1976; ex FAVORITA 1973; Similar: **78631 GALINI** (Gr); ex CARMENDALE 1980; ex CARMENCITA 1975; **78632 DAPO ANTIKLIA** (Gr); ex EVINDALE 1978; ex EVITA; **78633 MAREDALE** (Li); ex MARGARITA 1973.

KMFK H13
⋆78640 SKRADIN. Ys/Sw 1963; B; 12200; 157.92 × 9.7 (518.11 × 31.82); M; 14.5; ex BALTIC WASA 1975; ex ARGO 1971.

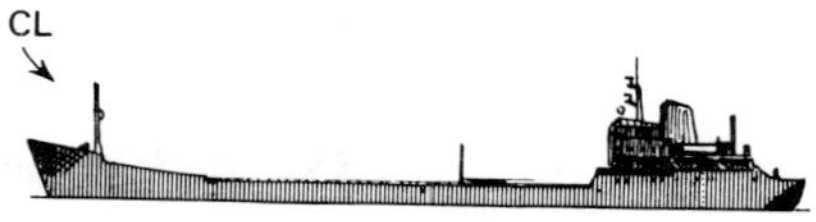

KMFK H13
78650 UNGAVA TRANSPORT. Ca/No 1959/71; Tk; 4700; 122.97 × 7.11 (403.44 × 23.33); M; 13; ex TOMMY WIBORG 1974; ex VARANGNES 1970; Converted from ore/oil 1971.

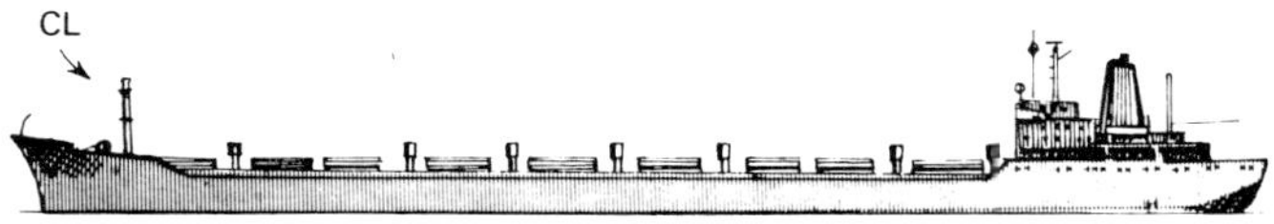

KMFK H13
78660 BRITSUM. Ne/Ja 1967; B; 25500; 207.37 × 11.72 (680.35 × 38.45); M; 14.5; Sister: **78661 FARMSUM** (Ne).

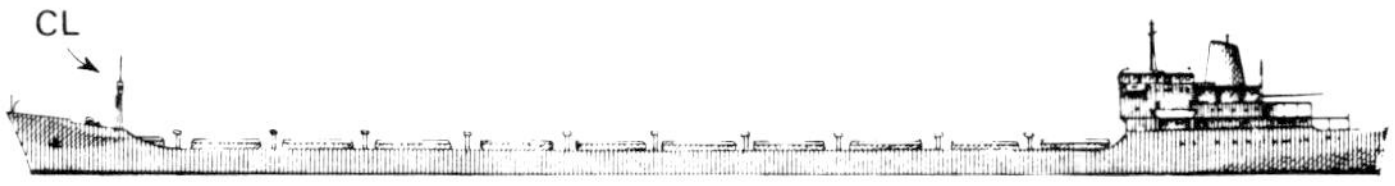

KMFK H13
78670 KYRAKATINGO. Gr/FRG 1967; B; 26500; 218.52 × 12.02 (716.93 × 39.44); M; 15.5; ex BRITTA 1973; Sister: **78671 HOWARD STAR** (Pa); ex BETTINA 1978.

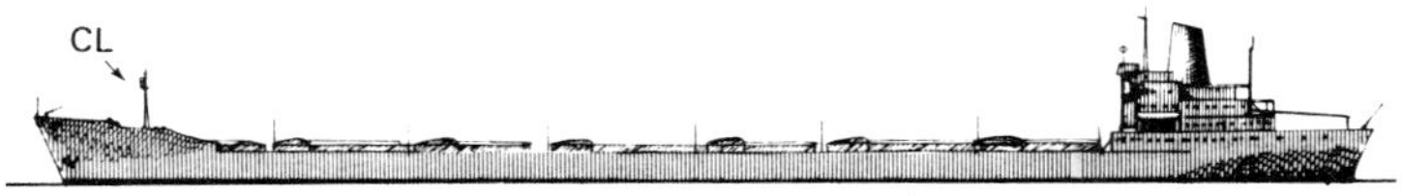

KMFK H13
● **78680 OLGA MAERSK**. De/De 1970; B; 3000; 218.85 × 12.1 (718 × 39.7); M; 16; Sisters: **78681 GLOBAL SUNSHINE** (Ko); ex OLIVIA MAERSK 1980; **78682 DANIELLE** (Li); ex DANITA 1978; **78683 MIRANDA** (Li); ex LISITA 1978; **78684 CAST BEAVER** (Gr); ex HOLTHAV 1977; **78685 CAST DOLPHIN** (Br); ex BERIT 1978; ***78686 UNIWERSYTET JAGIELLONSKI** (Pd); ***78687 UNIWERSYTET TORUNSKI** (Pd).

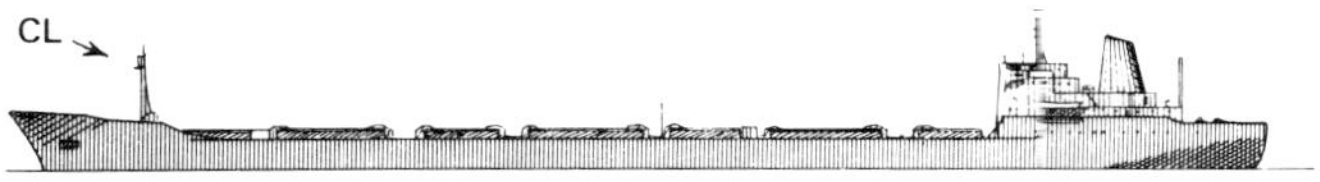

KMFK H13
● **78690 DELTADRECHT**. Ne/Fr 1966; B; 24700; 200.51 × 11.87 (657.84 × 38.94); M; 14.5; Sisters: **78691 DUIVENDRECHT** (Ne); **78692 IRENE S. LEMOS** (Gr); ex HEERING MILLE 1977; ex VILLE DE METZ 1972; **78693 DORDRECHT** (Ne).

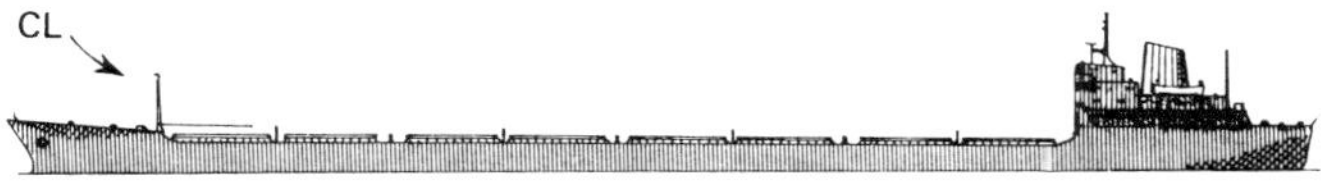

KMFK H13
78700 ATLANTICO. Li/Br 1965; B; 24300; 205.75 × 12.11 (675.03 × 39.73); M; 15.5; ex ARGO CASTOR 1977; ex BUCCLEUCH 1973; Sister: **78701 PACIFICO** (Li); ex ARGO POLLUX 9777; ex COTSWOLD 1973.

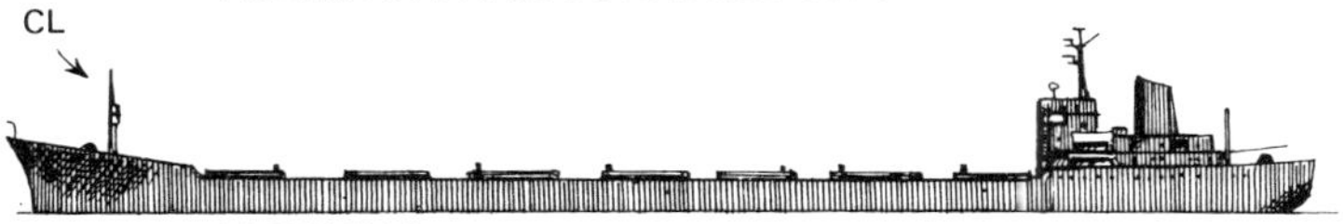

KMFK H13
78710 LUCY. Li/Br 1967; B; 27500; 218.45 × 12.56 (716.7 × 41.21); M; 16; ex ROSLAGEN 1973.

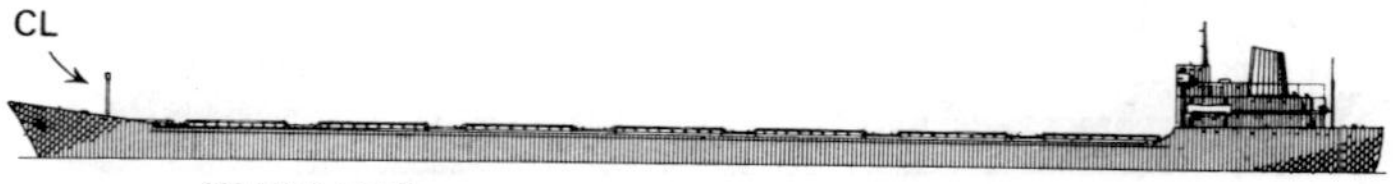

KMFK H13
78720 OCEANUS. Gr/Br 1967; B; 28000; 218.29 × 12.55 (716.17 × 41.17); M; 15.75; ex MYLLA 1968.

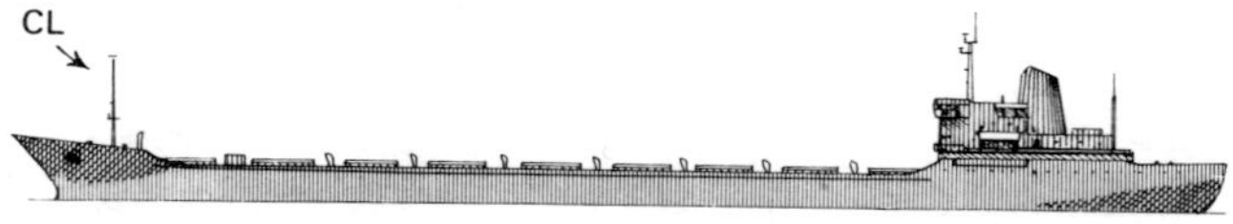

KMFK H13
★78730 GORLITZ. DDR/Ru 1974; B; 22800; 201.38 × 11.21 (660.7 × 36.78); M; 15.75; **'Baltika'** type; Sister: **★78731 GRODITZ** (DDR); Similar: **★78732 NIKOLAY VOZNESENSKIY** (Ru); Similar (with crane aft): **★78733 COLDITZ** (DDR).

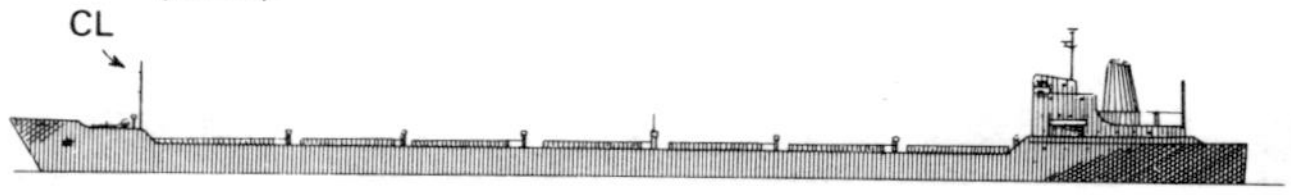

KMFK H13
78740 RIVERA. Li/Sp 1974; B; 19900; 196.02 × 11.15 (643.11 × 36.58); M; 15.25; ex FADURA; Similar (Sp flag): **78741 MARCOAZUL; 78742 MARCOVERDE.**

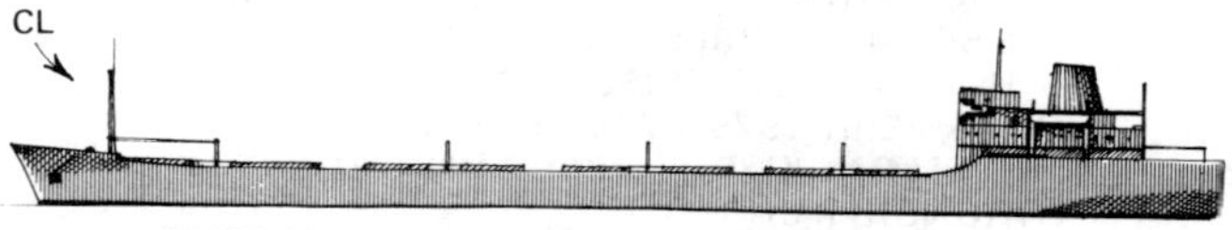

KMFK H13
78750 JANA VIJAY. In/Br 1966; B; 25400; 205.75 × 12.14 (675.03 × 39.83); M; 15.5; ex DUHALLOW 1974.

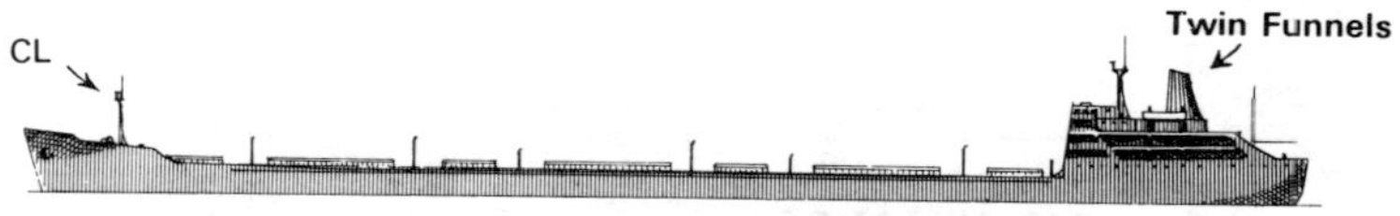

KMFK H13
78760 STONEPOOL. Br/Br 1966; B; 27000; 218.85 × 11.87 (718 × 38.94); M; 16.

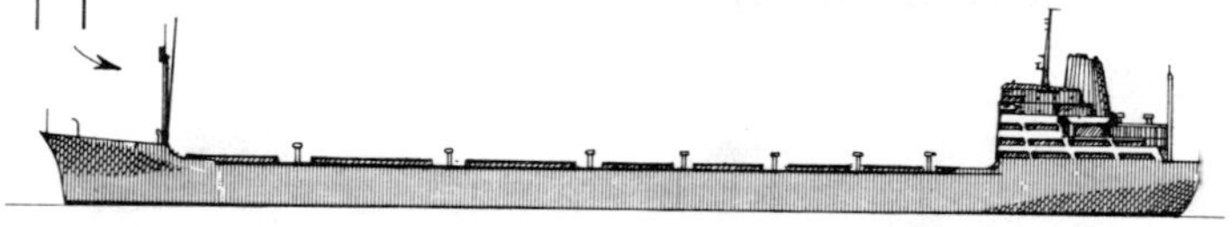

KMFK H13
78770 MATILDE. Li/Ja 1966; B; 26600; 209.4 × 12.56 (687.01 × 41.21); M; 15; Sister (lighter pole mast forward) (Li flag): **78771 ESMERALDA**: ex PAULINE 1980; **78772 PORTOFINO;** ex HAR MERON 1974; **78773 RIMINI;** ex HAR CASTEL 1975.

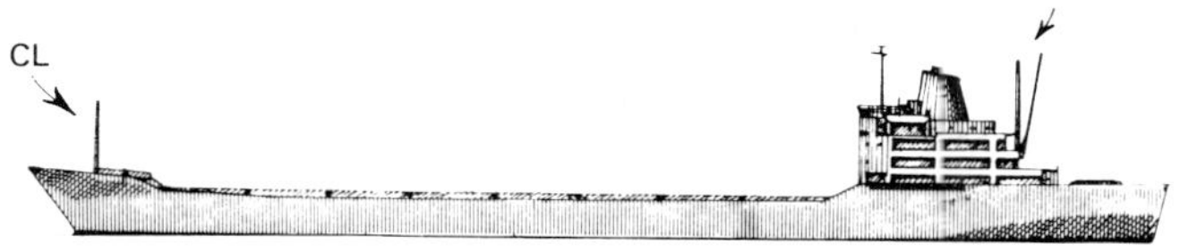

KMFK H13
78780 FALSTRIA. De/De 1971; Con; 20200; 201.86 × 9.48 (662.27 × 31.1); M; 21.5; Sister: **78781 MEONIA** (De).

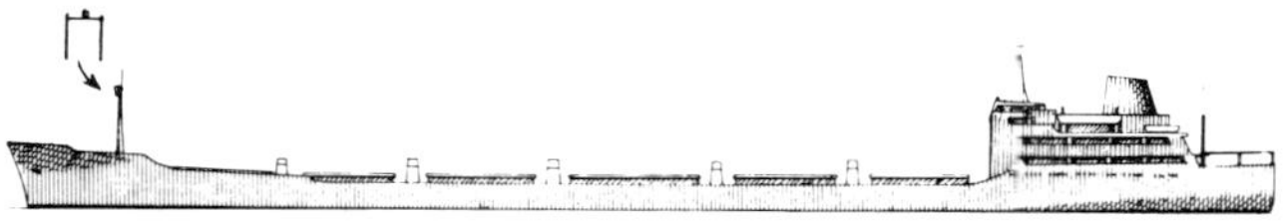

KMFK H13
78790 TRADE GREECE. Gr/No 1959; B; 16800; 200.97 × 10.03 (659.35 × 32.91); M; 15; ex MILBANK 1972; Lengthened 1966.

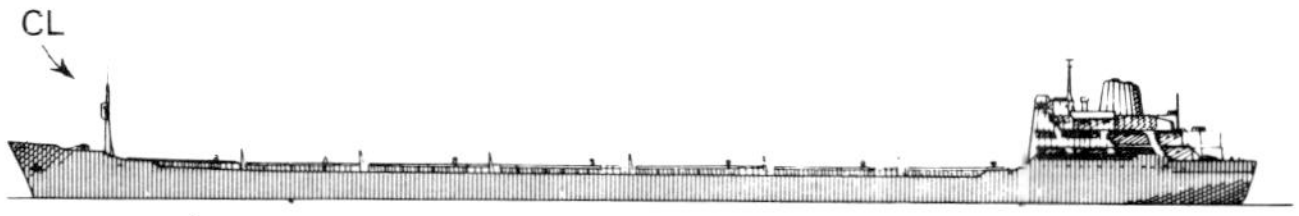

KMFK H13
78800 ACHILLEUS. Gr/Ja 1961; B; 16500; 198.08 × 10.53 (649.87 × 34.55); M; —; ex GAUCHO PAMPA 1978; ex SKAUBORG 1973; Lengthened 1965; Sisters: **78801 GRIGOROUSA** (Li); ex GAUCHO LAGUNA 1980; ex GOLAR COAL 1970; ex SKAUHOLT 1966; **78802 ST. LAWRENCE** (Ca); ex GAUCHO TAURA 1976; ex SKAUSTRAND 1973.

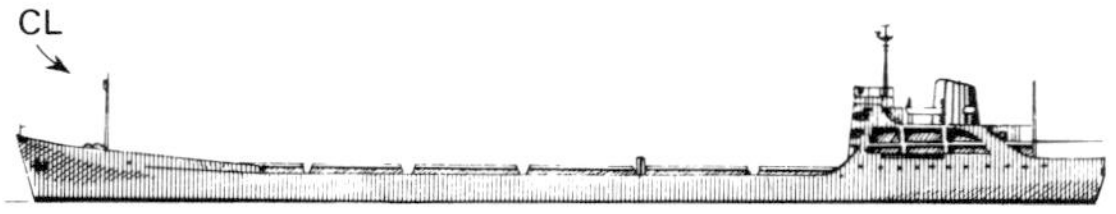

KMFK H13
● **78810 ELEANOR DUNBAR.** Br/Br 1961; B; 14400; 172.55 × 10.35 (566.11 × 33.96); M; 14.5; ex AURORA 1979; ex GATTOPARDO 1978; ex ATOMENA 1970.

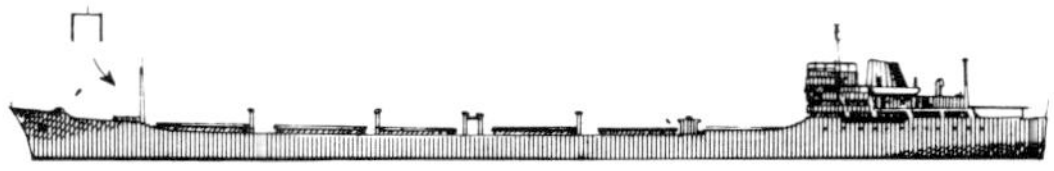

KMFK H13
● **78820 DON MANUEL.** Gr/Br 1961; O; 9900; 162.95 × 9.06 (534.61 × 29.72); M; 12; ex FINNAMORE MEADOW 1977.

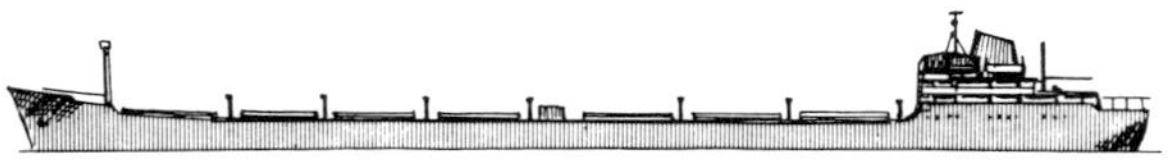

KMFK H13
78830 LUIS PEREDA. Sp/Sp 1965; B; 15300; 180.02 × 10.62 (590.62 × 34.84); M; 14.

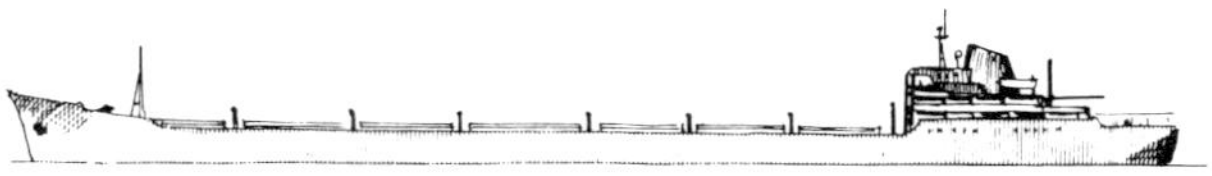

KMFK H13
78840 SPILIOS. Gr/Sp 1967; B; 15800; 185.2 × 10.27 (607.61 × 33.69); M; —; ex KONKORDIA; ex LEYRE 1975.

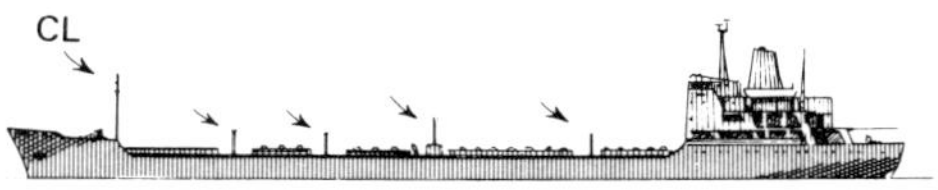

KMFK H13
★78850 MUSALA. Bu/Ja 1967; B; 9100; 139.83 × 9.26 (458.76 × 30.38); M; 14; Sisters (Bu flag): **★78851 RUEN; ★78852 VEJEN.**

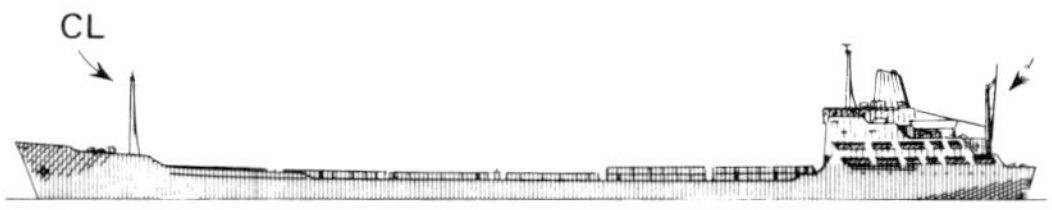

KMFK H13
78860 KATHERINE. Gr/Fr 1963; B; 8900; 165.41 × 8.27 (542.68 × 27.13); M; 15.5; ex CATHERINE 1977; Lengthened 1971; Sister: **78861 VITABULK** (Gr) ex MELTEMI II 1980; ex CHRISTINE 1974.

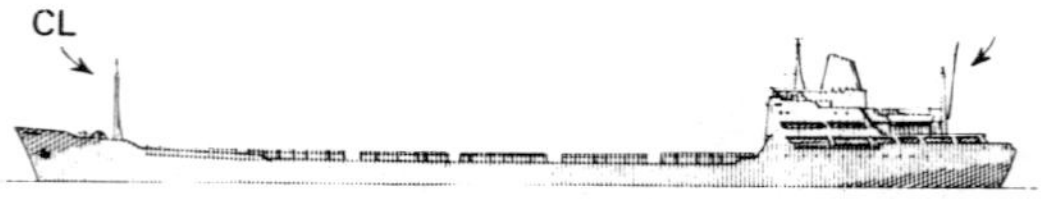

KMFK H13
78870 LENA. Gr/Fr 1961; O; 9200; 158.12 × 8.27 (518.77 × 27.13); M; 14; ex MELUSINE 1978; Lengthened 1969.

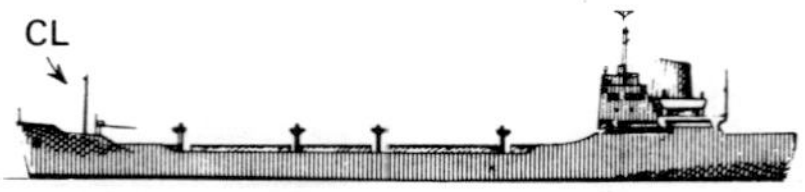

KMFK H13
78880 TONY. Gr/FRG 1962; B; 6200 121.34 × 8.51 (398.1 × 27.92); M; 13; ex ATLAS 1979; ex ECKENHEIM 1974; Sister: **78881 ATLANTIS** (Gr) ex LANGELSHEIM 1974.

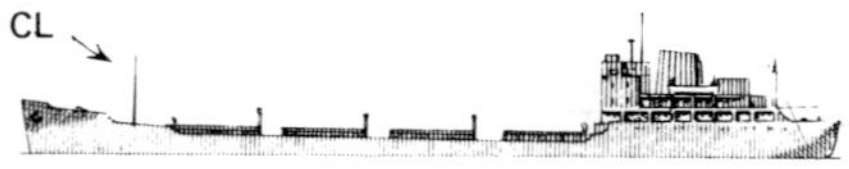

KMFK H13
⋆**78890 PODGORICA.** Ys/Br 1954; O; 6900; 130.16 × 8.1 (427.03 × 26.57); M; 11.5; ex MARILUCK 1974; ex OREOSA STAR 1973; ex OREOSA 1971.

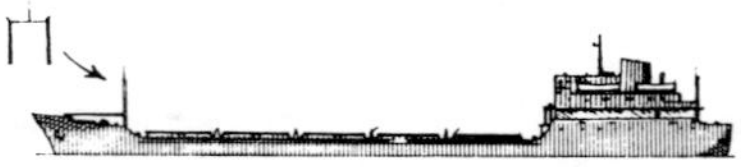

KMFK H13
78900 SALEM. Si/FRG 1962; OO/Ch; 4800; 109.81 × 7.43 (360.27 × 24.38); M; 13; ex SINGO 1978.

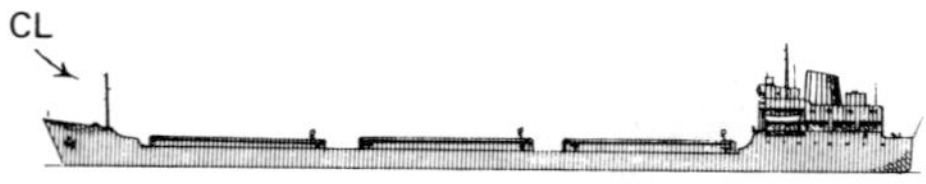

KMFK H13
● **78910 DALLINGTON.** Br/Ne 1975; B; 7700; 137.6 × 7.93 (451.44 × 26.02); M; 14; Sister: **78911 DONNINGTON** (Br).

KMFK H13
⋆**78920 HUAI HAI.** RC/FRG 1962; B; 14800; 179.38 × 10.92 (588.52 × 35.83); M; 14; ex GEORGIOS A GEORGILIS 1974; ex BENEDICTE 1969; Similar: ⋆**78921 HUANG HAI** (RC) ex AMUNDSEN SEA 1975; ex ANTONIS P LEMOS 1974; ex BEATRICE 1969.

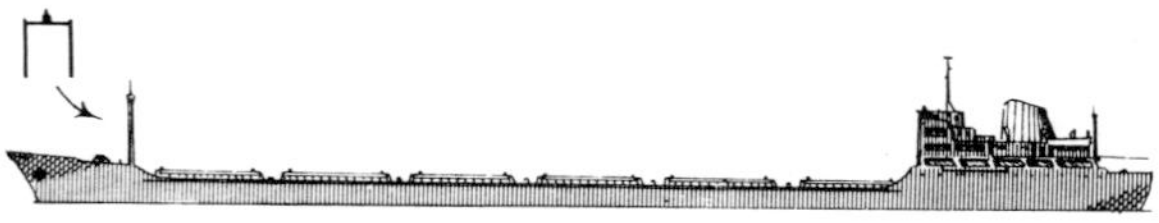

KMFK H13
● **78930 CARIBBEAN CARRIER.** Gr/Ys 1962; B; 16000; 180.68 × 6.82 (592.78 × 22.38); M; 14.5; ex CADIMARE 1973; ex SPLIT 1970; Similar: **78931 MEDITERRANEAN CARRIER** (Br) ex ARCOLA 1973; ex E H BIRD 1970.

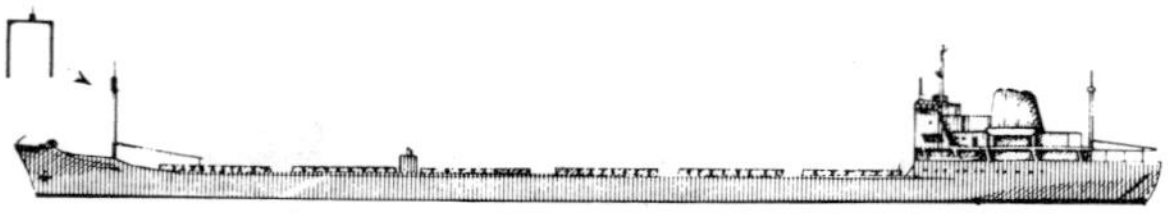

KMFK H13
⋆**78940 KOSICE.** Cz/Ja 1963; O; 16800; 181.21 × 9.91 (594.52 × 32.51); M; 16.

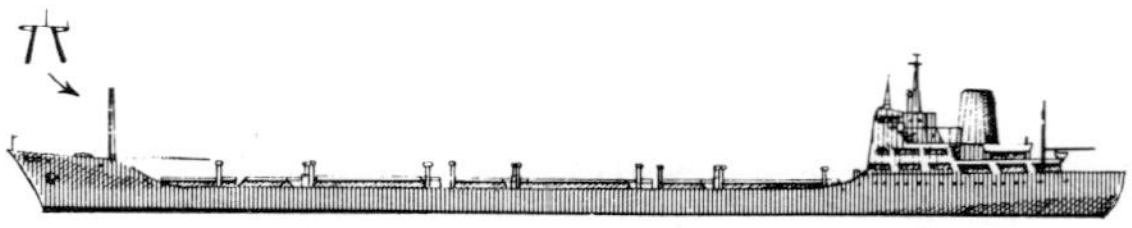

KMFK H13
78950 THOMAS K. Li/Ja 1961; C; 14000; 177.02 × 9.59 (580.77 × 31.46); M; 16; ex VELOS 1968; Launched as MONTEGO.

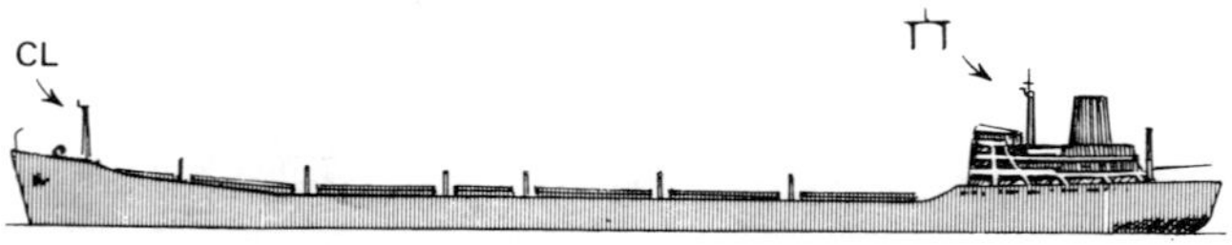

KMFK H13
78960 ANNA CH. Gr/Br 1966; B; 21900; 200.34 × 11.22 (657.28 × 36.81); M; 14.5; ex OINOUSSIAN MOTHER 1981; ex JERSEY BRIDGE 1972.

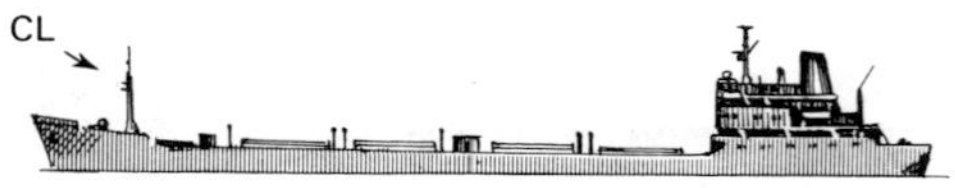

KMFK H13
⋆**78970 DESSAU.** DDR/Ru 1958/68; O; 7600; 145.5 × 8.42 (477.36 × 27.62); M; 12; ex LEUNA II 1968; Converted from tanker 1968.

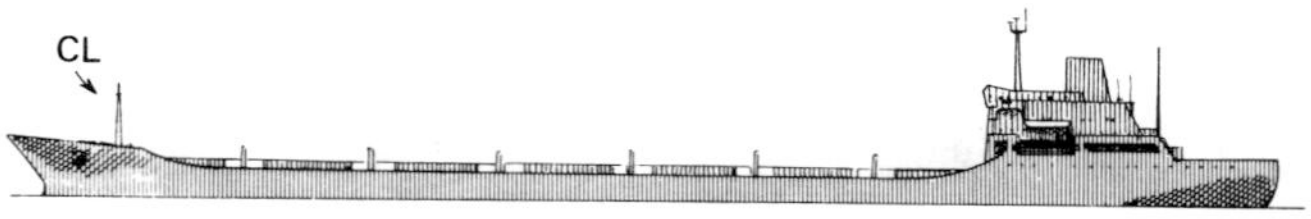

KMFK H13
⋆**78980 GENERAL SWIERCZEWSKI.** Pd/Bu 1973; B; 23300; 201.17 × 11.2 (660.01 × 36.75); M; 17; Sisters (Pd flag): ⋆**78981 GENERAL BEM;** ⋆**78982 GENERAL JASINSKI;** ⋆**78983 GENERAL MADALINSKI;** ⋆**78984 GENERAL PRADZYNSKI;** (Bu flag) ⋆**78985 JORDANKA NIKOLOVA;** ⋆**78986 PETIMATA OT RMS;** ⋆**78987 ADALBERT ANTONOV MALCHIKA** (may now be called **ADALBERT ANTONOV**).

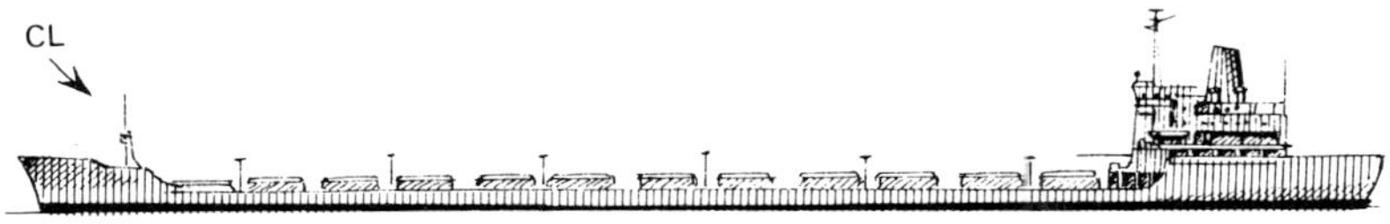

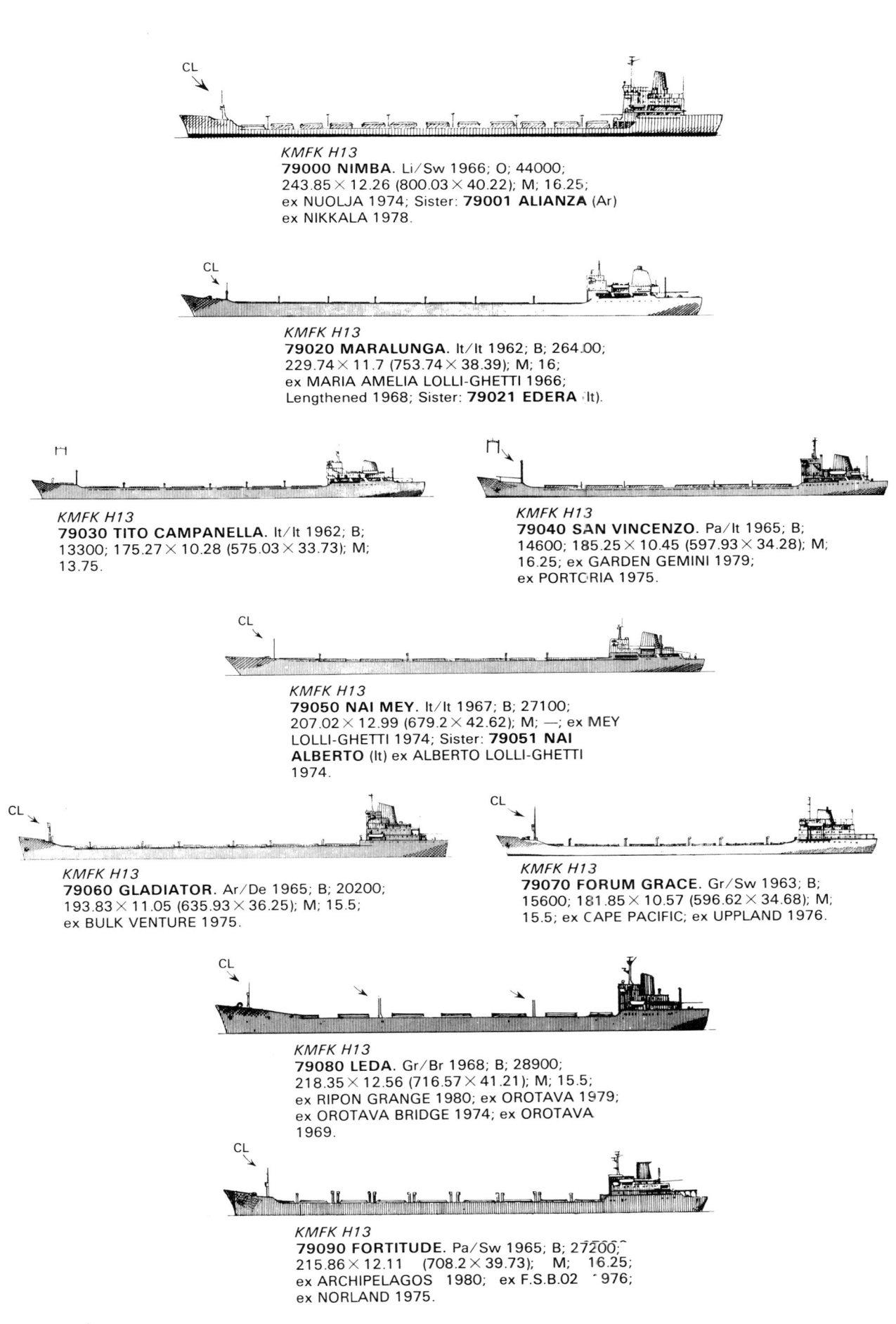

KMFK H13
79000 NIMBA. Li/Sw 1966; O; 44000; 243.85 × 12.26 (800.03 × 40.22); M; 16.25; ex NUOLJA 1974; Sister: **79001 ALIANZA** (Ar) ex NIKKALA 1978.

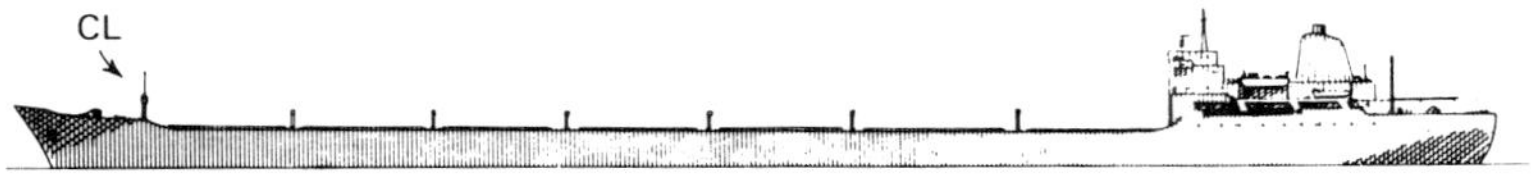

KMFK H13
79020 MARALUNGA. It/It 1962; B; 264.00; 229.74 × 11.7 (753.74 × 38.39); M; 16; ex MARIA AMELIA LOLLI-GHETTI 1966; Lengthened 1968; Sister: **79021 EDERA** (It).

KMFK H13
79030 TITO CAMPANELLA. It/It 1962; B; 13300; 175.27 × 10.28 (575.03 × 33.73); M; 13.75.

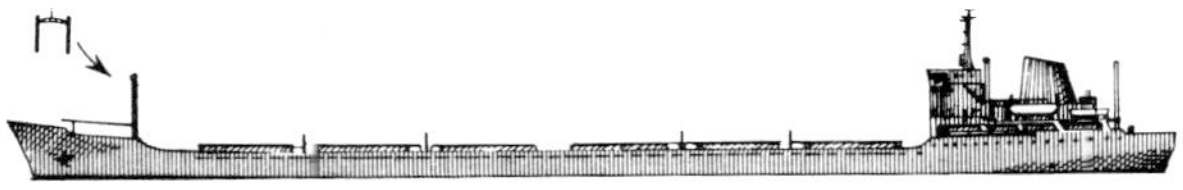

KMFK H13
79040 SAN VINCENZO. Pa/It 1965; B; 14600; 185.25 × 10.45 (597.93 × 34.28); M; 16.25; ex GARDEN GEMINI 1979; ex PORTORIA 1975.

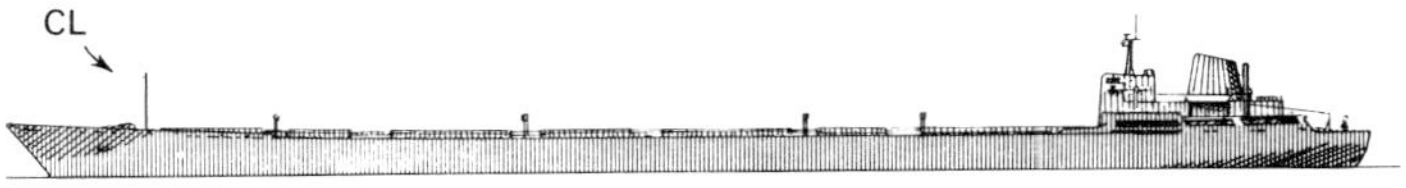

KMFK H13
79050 NAI MEY. It/It 1967; B; 27100; 207.02 × 12.99 (679.2 × 42.62); M; —; ex MEY LOLLI-GHETTI 1974; Sister: **79051 NAI ALBERTO** (It) ex ALBERTO LOLLI-GHETTI 1974.

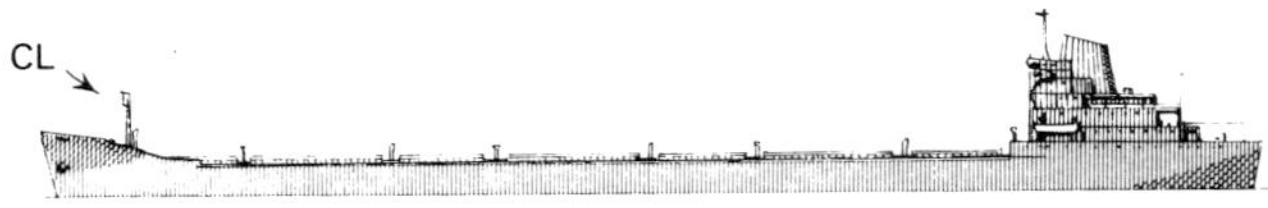

KMFK H13
79060 GLADIATOR. Ar/De 1965; B; 20200; 193.83 × 11.05 (635.93 × 36.25); M; 15.5; ex BULK VENTURE 1975.

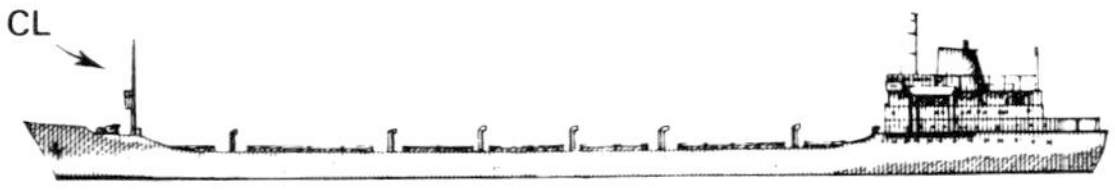

KMFK H13
79070 FORUM GRACE. Gr/Sw 1963; B; 15600; 181.85 × 10.57 (596.62 × 34.68); M; 15.5; ex CAPE PACIFIC; ex UPPLAND 1976.

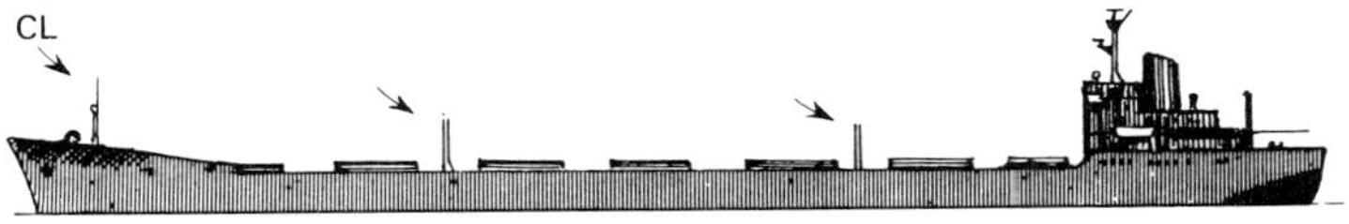

KMFK H13
79080 LEDA. Gr/Br 1968; B; 28900; 218.35 × 12.56 (716.57 × 41.21); M; 15.5; ex RIPON GRANGE 1980; ex OROTAVA 1979; ex OROTAVA BRIDGE 1974; ex OROTAVA 1969.

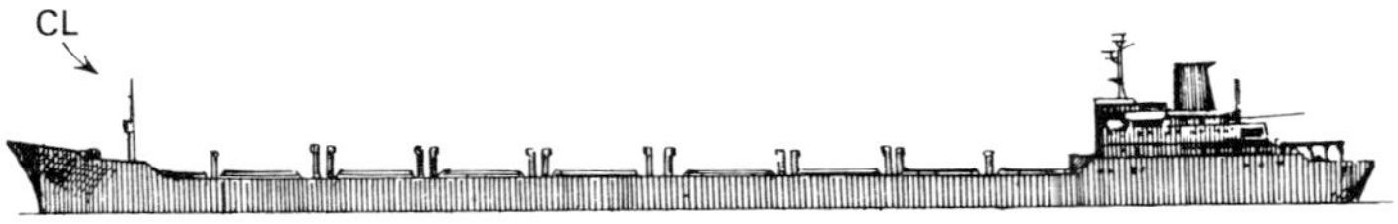

KMFK H13
79090 FORTITUDE. Pa/Sw 1965; B; 27200; 215.86 × 12.11 (708.2 × 39.73); M; 16.25; ex ARCHIPELAGOS 1980; ex F.S.B.02 1976; ex NORLAND 1975.

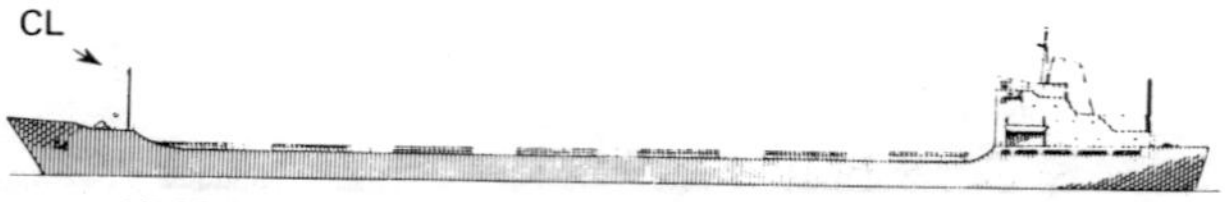

KMFK H13
79100 SAC MALAGA. Sp/Sp 1976; B; 17400; 190.66 × 10.69 (625.52 × 35.07); M; 15; Sister: **79101 CASTELLBLANCH** (Sp); launched as PONTE SAMPAYO; Probable sisters: **79102 DRY SACK** (Sp); launched as PONTE PASAJE; **BANDA AZUL** (Sp); launched as PONTE PEDRIDO.

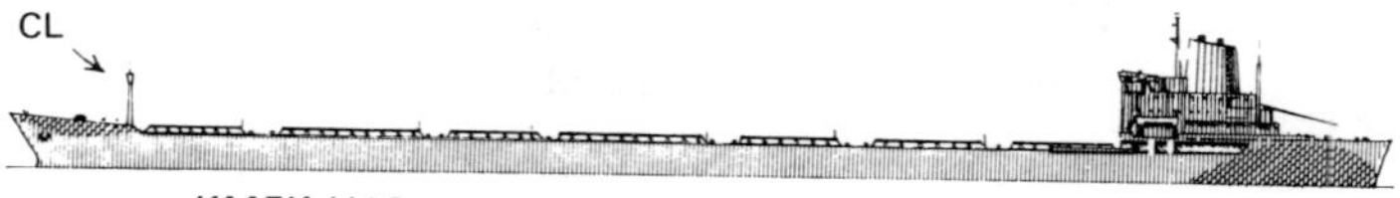

KMFK H13
79110 THORUNN. No/De 1973; B; 29700; 218.85 × 12.09 (718.01 × 39.66); M; 15.5; Similar: **79111 CARLOVA** (Gr); **79112 CAST ORCA** (Br) ex HECTOR 1979; ⋆**79113 UNIWERSYTET WARSZAWSKI** (Pd); ⋆**79115 UNIWERSYTET WROCLAWSKI** (Pd); **79116 SAMJOHN MARINER** (Li); **79117 JACARA** (No) ex HEERING CHRISTEL 1977.

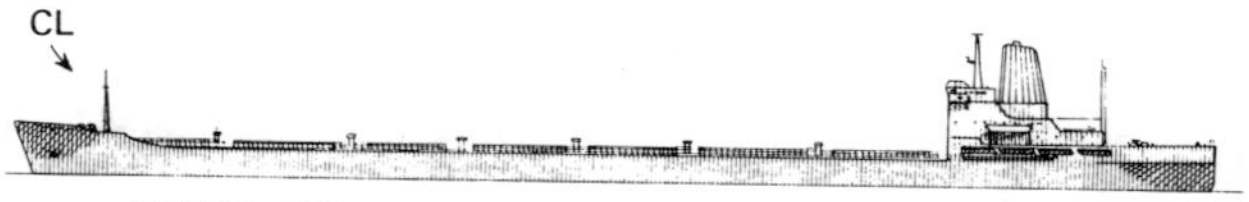

KMFK H13
79130 WORLD NEIGHBOUR. Li/Ja 1968; B; 23300; 194.52 × 12.1 (638.19 × 39.7); M; 14.5; Sisters (Li flag): **79131 WORLD NAUTILUS;** launched as WORLD HAPPINESS; **79132 WORLD NATURE;** Similar: **79133 NORTHERN NAIAD.**

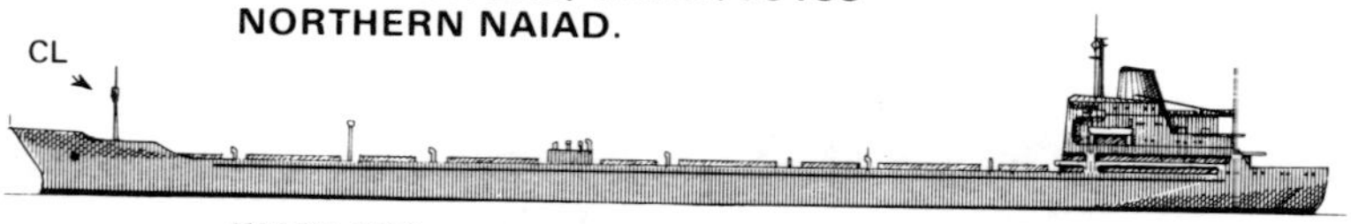

KMFK H13
79140 FRITZ THYSSEN. FRG/FRG 1965; B; 35000; 236.53 × 11.91 (776.02 × 39.07); M; 15.75; Sister: **79141 ODIN** (FRG).

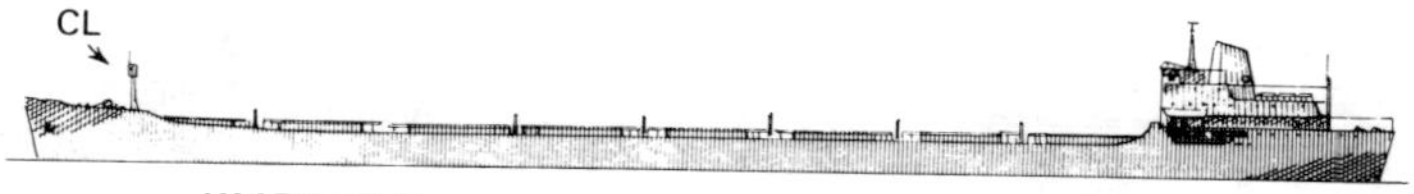

KMFK H13
79150 ACUMEN. Pa/Br 1967; B; 27400; 217.23 × 12.37 (712.7 × 40.58); M; 15.5; ex NORMAN MERCHANT 1980; ex PILOT MERCHANT; ex HAPPY DRAGON 1978.

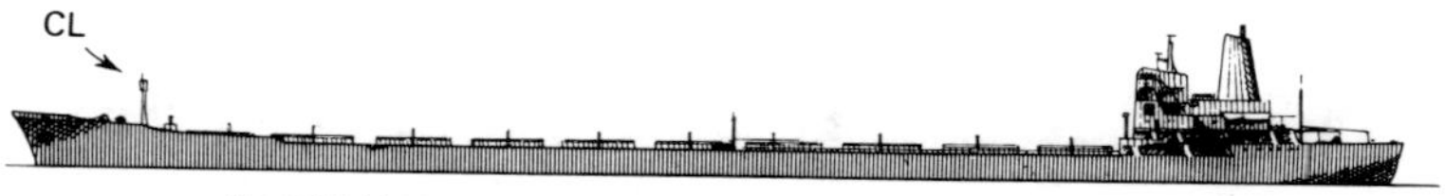

KMFK H13
79160 ANEMOS. Gr/Ja 1963; OO; 23300 (ore) 33000 (oil); 230.66 × 12.16 (756.76 × 39.9); T; —; Sisters (Gr flag): **79161 ASTRAPI; 79162 VRONTI.**

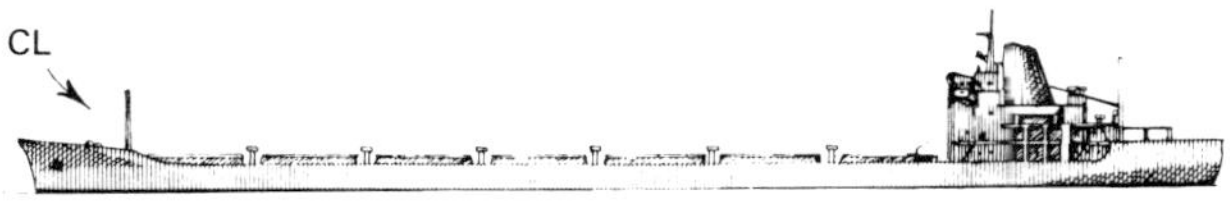

KMFK H13
79170 ANDROS CASTLE. Li/Ja 1968; B; 21400; 190 × 11.36 (623.36 × 37.27); M; 16; Sisters (Li flag): **79171 ANDROS CITY; 79172 ANDROS HILLS; 79173 ANDROS ISLAND; 79174 ANDROS MARINER**.

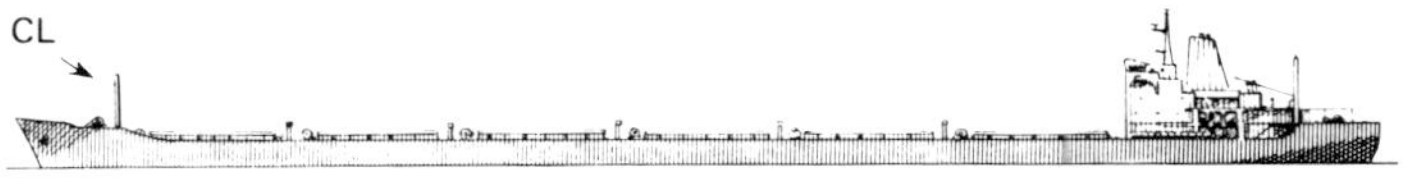

KMFK H13
79180 LEONIDAS D. Li/Ja 1967; B; 28600; 216.06 × 12.08 (708.86 × 39.63); M; —; Sister: **79181 EKATERINI M GOULANDRIS** (Gr).

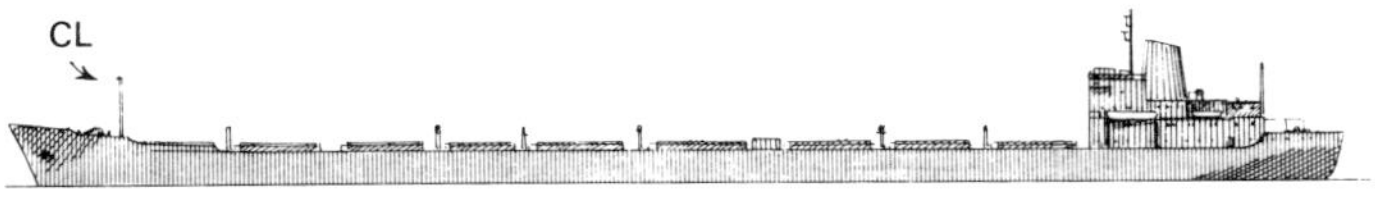

KMFK H13
79190 HAHNENTOR. FRG/FRG 1965; B; 23200; 212 × 10.18 (695.54 × 33.4); M; 15.

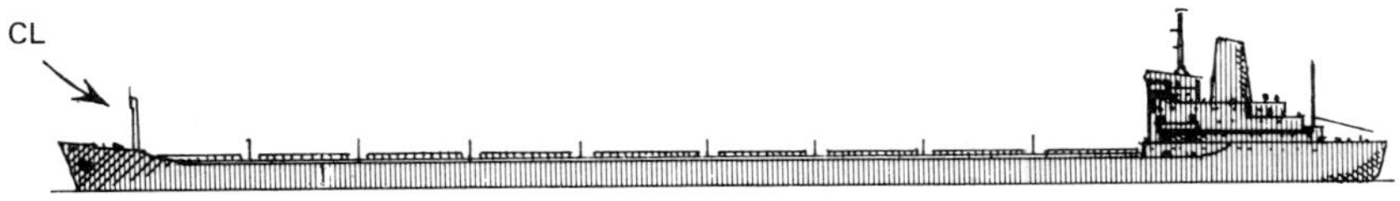

KMFK H13
79200 KING RICHARD. Br/De 1967; B; 42700; 249.21 × 14.33 (817.62 × 47.01); M; 15.75; ex ELBE ORE 1974; Similar (shorter funnel): **79201 MAIN ORE** (Li).

KMFK H13
79210 ORIENT HARMONY. Li/Br 1967; B; 29500; 215.96 × 12.43 (708.53 × 40.78); M; 16.75; ex GAUCHO GUEMES 1981 ex MARDULCE II ex FERNSPRING: Probable sister: **79211 WELFARE** (Gr) ex PILIO 1980 ex FERNRIVER 1978.

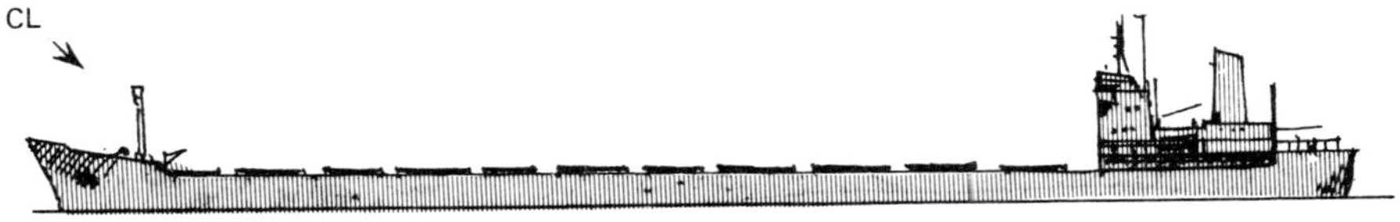

KMFK H13
79220 GOOD MOTHER. Gr/Be 1966; B; 36400; 266.73 × 13.11 (875.1 × 43.01); M; 16.25; ex ANASTASIA SUPER 1980; ex SAN MORITZ; ex TEMSE 1973.

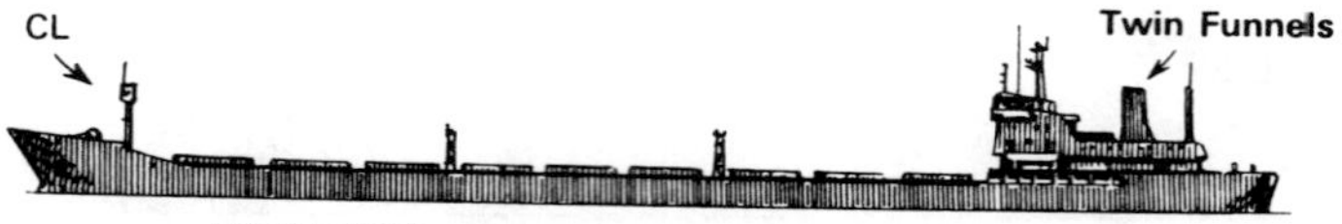

KMFK H13
★**79230 GEORGIY LEONIDZE.** Ru/Pd 1974; B; 20300; 202.34 × 10.64 (663.85 × 34.91); M; 15; **'B-447'** type; Sister (Ru flag): ★**79231 GENERAL LESELIDZE;** Similar (Cz flag): ★**79232 BRATISLAVA;** ★**79233 PRAHA;** ★**79234 TRINEC.**

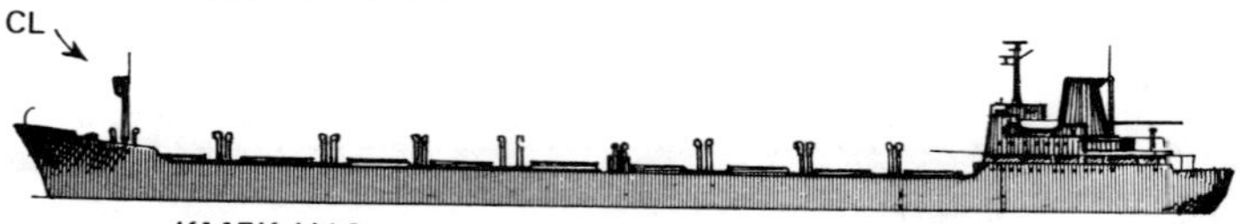

KMFK H13
★**79240 JU HAI.** RC/Sw 1966; B; 26500; 215.7 × 12.09 (707.68 × 39.67); M; 16; ex DRAKE SEA 1976; ex VARDAAS 1974.

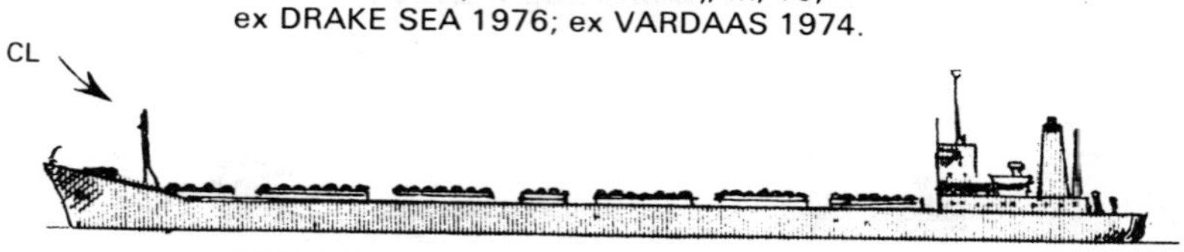

KMFK H13
79250 IMA. Li/Ja 1968; B; 28000; 226.42 × 12.4 (742.85 × 40.68); M; 16; Similar: **79251 VIRGINIA** (Li).

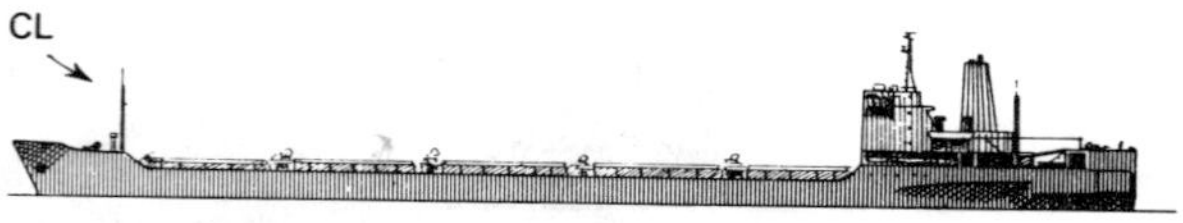

KMFK H13
79260 GOLD BOND CONVEYOR. Li/Ja 1974; O; 14900; 177.98 × 10.02 (583.92 × 32.87); M; 15.25; ex COLON BROWN 1975; Side doors. New mid body 1976; Sister: **79261 GOLD BOND TRAILBLAZER** (Li); Rebuilt from part of GOLD BOND CONVEYOR.

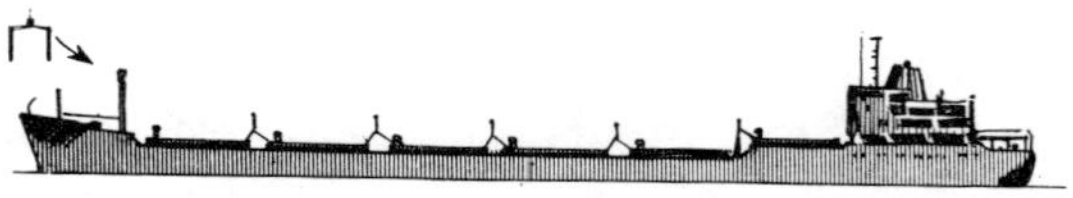

KMFK H13
79270 LAN HAI. RC/Sw 1960; B; 12100; 161.19 × 9.9 (528.84 × 32.48); M; 13; ex MARY XILAS 1974; ex SEA MASTER 1970.

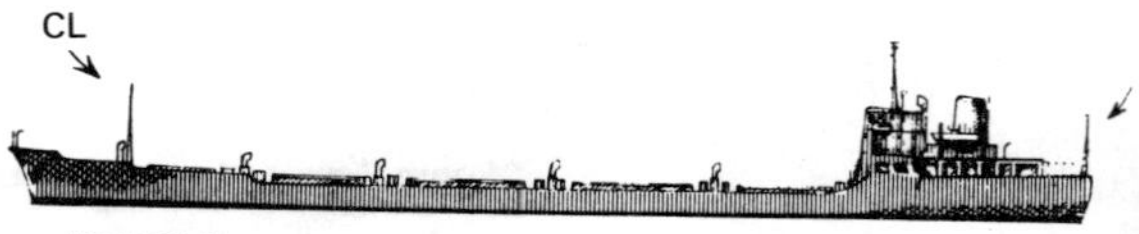

KMFK H13
79280 AGIA ANASTASIA. Gr/Ja 1959; C; 12300; 169.17 × 9.53 (555.02 × 31.27); M; 15.5; Similar: **79281 MENITES** (Gr) ex SAAS FEE 1977; ex BUTTERFLY 1972.

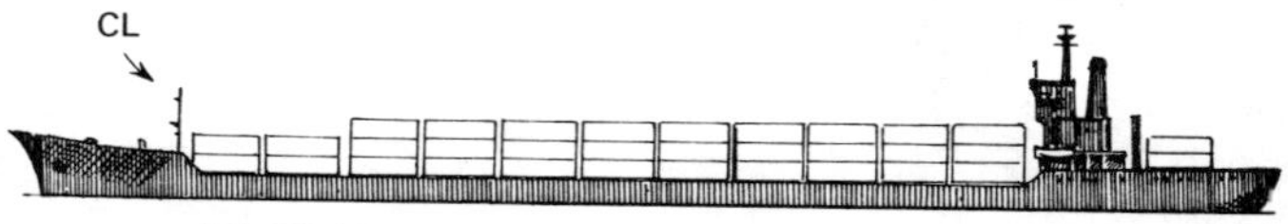

KMFK H13
79290 PANAMA. US/US 1945/66; Con; 17200; 208.77 × 9.18 (684.94 × 30.12); T; 16; ex MARINE JUMPER 1966; Converted from **'C-4'**type cargo ship 1966.

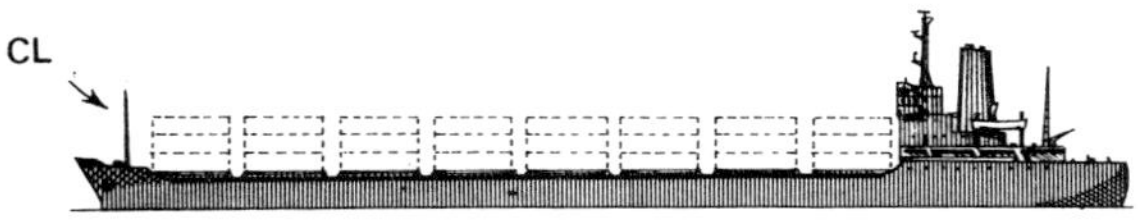

KMFK H13
79300 WERRA EXPRESS. Sg/Ja-Sg 1974/78; Con; 14200; 169.46 × — (555.97 × —); M; 18; ex FREUDENFELS 1980; ex DRACHENFELS 1976; ex ARISTOTELIS 1975; Converted from 'Mitsui-Concord' type cargo ship 1978; Sisters (Sg flag): **79301 NECKAR EXPRESS** ex FREIENFELS 1980; ex ARISTARCHOS 1975; **79302 FULDA EXPRESS** ex FRANKENFELS 1980; ex ARISTANDROS 1974; **79303 IBN AL SUWAIDI** ex FRAUENFELS 1980; ex ARISTIPOS 1974.

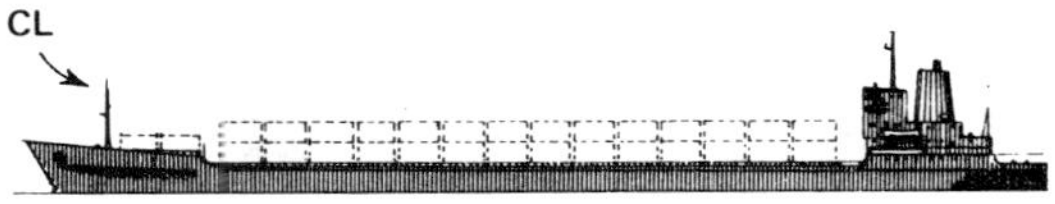

KMFK H13
● **79310 SEATRAIN ITALY.** Pa/FRG 1976; Con; 9100; 159.01 × 8.26 (521.69 × 27.1); M; 17.25; ex SOVEREIGN EXPRESS 1977; Sister: **79311 SOVEREIGN ACCORD** (Ja).

KMFK H13
79320 BREEZAND. Ne/FRG 1975; C; 1600; 79.51 × 5.55 (260.86 × 18.21); M; 12.5; Sisters (Br flag): **79321 CAIRNCARRIER; 79322 CAIRNFREIGHTER; 79323 CAIRNLEADER.**

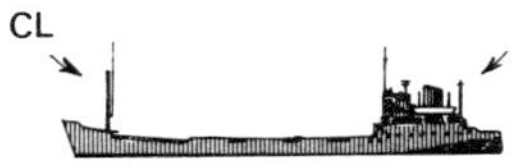

KMFK H13
● **79330 CONISTER.** Br/Br 1955; C/Con; 900; 68.2 × 4.59 (223.75 × 15.06); M; 11.5; ex SPANIEL 1973; ex BRENTFIELD 1959; Sister: **79331 TAURUS III** (Cy) ex POINTER 1975; ex BIRCHFIELD 1959.

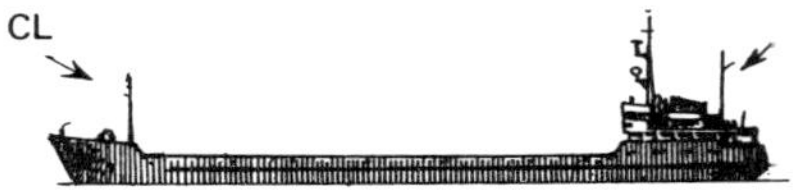

KMFK H13
★**79340 'SORMOVSKIY'** type. Ru/Ru 1967-79; C(Sea/river); 2500; 114.2 × 3.42 (374.67 × 11.22); TSM; 10.5; Sisters (Ru flag): ★**79341 SORMOVSKIY 2;** ★**79342 SORMOVSKIY 4;** ★**79343 SORMOVSKIY 5;** ★**79344 SORMOVSKIY 6;** ★**79345 SORMOVSKIY 7;** ★**79346 SORMOVSKIY 9;** ★**79347 SORMOVSKIY 11;** ★**79348 SORMOVSKIY 12;** ★**79349 SORMOVSKIY 13;** ★**79350 SORMOVSKIY 14;** ★**79351 SORMOVSKIY 17;** ★**79352 SORMOVSKIY 18;** ★**79353 SORMOVSKIY 19;** ★**79354 SORMOVSKIY 22;** ★**79355 SORMOVSKIY 27;** ★**79356 SORMOVSKIY 28;** ★**79357 SORMOVSKIY 29;** ★**79358 SORMOVSKIY 30;** ★**79359 SORMOVSKIY 31;** ★**79360 SORMOVSKIY 33;** ★**79361 SORMOVSKIY 34;** ★**79362 SORMOVSKIY 40;** ★**79363 SORMOVSKIY 42;** ★**79364 SORMOVSKIY 109;** ★**79365 SORMOVSKIY 110;** ★**79366 SORMOVSKIY 112;** ★**79367 SORMOVSKIY 117;** ★**79368 50 LET SOVIETSKOY VLASTI;** ★**79369 BUREVESTNIK REVOLYUTSKIY;** ★**79370 ALEKSANDR VERMISHEV;** ★**79371 LENINSKAYA SMENA;** ★**79372 VELIKIY POCHIN;** ★**79373 VOZNESENSK;** ★**79374 ALEKSANDR TSYURUPA;** ★**79375 DMITRY MANUILSKIY;** ★**79376 SHUSHENSKOYE;** ★**79377 STANISLAV KOSIOR;** ★**79378 ALEKSANDR PROKOFYEV;** ★**79379 GEROY MEKHTI;** ★**79380 PARIZHSKAYA KOMMUNA;** ★**79381 VISHNEVETS;** ★**79382 ANATOLIY VANEYEV;** ★**79383 GEROY MEKHTI;** ★**79384 PETR BOGDANOV;** ★**79385 STRANA SOVIETOV;** ★**79386 50 LET S.S.S.R;** ★**79387 NIKOLAY BAUMAN;** ★**79388 PETR ZAPOROZHETS;** ★**79389 IVAN KOLYSHKIN;** ★**79390 POET SABIR;** ★**79400 ALEKSANDR PASHKOV;** ★**79401 DESYATAYA PYATILETKA;** ★**79402 POET VIDADI;** ★**79403 DZHAMBUL DZHABAYEV;** ★**79404 GRIGORIY PETROVSKIY;** ★**79405 50 LET VLKSM;** ★**79406 VISHNEVOGORSK;** ★**79407 GORKY LENINSKOYE;** ★**79408 PETR ZALOMOV;** ★**79409 XVI SYEZD VLKSM;** ★**79410 DEVYATAYA PYATILETKA;** ★**79411 NIZHEGORODSKIY KOMSOMOLETS;** ★**79412 750—LETIYE GORODA GORKOGO;** ★**79413 XXIV SYEZD KPSS;** ★**79414 50 LET PIONERII;** ★**79415 KEMINE;** ★**79416 SOVIETSKIY SEVER;** ★**79417 VLADIMIR ZATONSKIY;** ★**79418 NASIMI;** ★**79419 PETR LIDOV;** ★**79420 XVII SYEZD VLKSM;** ★**79421 9 MAYA 1945 GODA;** ★**79422 SEMYON MOROZOV;** ★**79432 VITALIY PRIMAKOV;** ★**79424 ALEKSEY VIKHORYEV;** ★**79425 FEDOR PODTELKOV;** ★**79426 PROFESSOR I. I. KRAKOVSKIY;** ★**79427 ALIYA MOLDAGULOV;** ★**79428 XVIII SYEZD VLKSM;** ★**79429 GAZLI;** ★**79430 IVAN LESOVIKOV;** ★**79431 IVAN KUDRIYA;** ★**79432 LENINGRADSKIY KOMSOMOLETS;** ★**79433 MARSHAL VOROBYEV;** ★**79434 MIKHAIL KRIVOSHLIKOV;** ★**79435 MUKHTAR ASHRAFI;** ★**79436 PAVEL GRABOVSKIY;** ★**79437 PAVEL MOCHALOV;** ★**79438 PROFESSOR KERICHYEV;** ★**79439 60 LET VELIKOGO OKTYABR;** ★**79440 60 LET VLKSM;** ★**79441 TAVRIYA;** ★**79442 UZEIR GADZHIBEKOV;** ★**79443 YURIY KOTSYUBINSKY.**

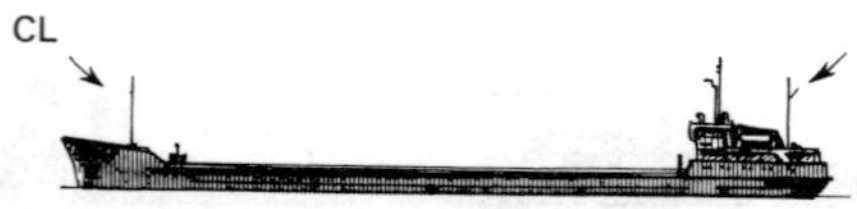

KMFK H13
★79450 'NEVTERUDOVOZ' type. Ru/Ru 1972-77; OO(Sea/river); 2700; 118.93 × 3.42 (390.19 × 11.22); TSM; 11; Sisters (Ru flag): from **★NEVTERUDOVOZ 8M** to **★NEVTERUDOVOZ 33M** inclusive.

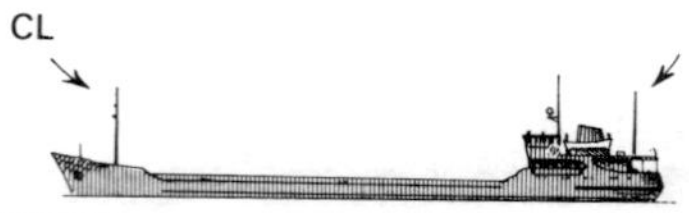

KMFK H13
★79500 'BALTIYSKIY' type. Ru/Ru 1962/68; C (sea/river); 1900; 96.02 × 3.26 (315.03 × 10.7); TSM; 10; Vessel illustrated is BALTIYSKIY 32; Some have lower funnels; Aftermast omitted on some vessels; Sisters (Ru flag): from **BALTIYSKIY 1** to **BALTIYSKIY 73** inclusive.

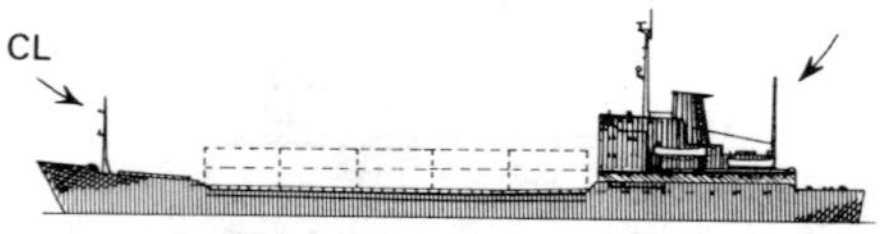

KMFK H13
★79550 PIONER NAKHODKI. Ru/Ru 1972; Con; 4800; 130.31 × 6.93 (427.53 × 22.74); M; 15; Sisters (Ru flag): **★79551 SESTRORETSK; ★79552 PIONER ODESSY; ★79553 PIONER VLADIVOSTOKA; ★79554 PIONER PRIMORYA; ★79555 PIONER VYBORGA.**

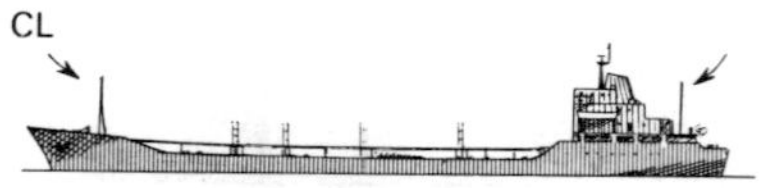

KMFK H13
79560 TUDELA. Sp/Sp 1977; Tk/Ch; 3900; 111.92 × 6.73 (367.19 × 22.08); M; 15.

KMFK H13
79570 PERTUSOLA. It/It 1975; Tk; 4000; 117.66 × 7.32 (386.02 × 24.02); M; 15.5; Sister: **79571 PUGLIOLA** (It).

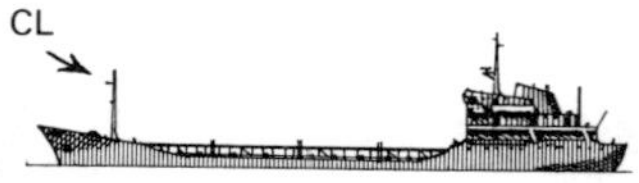

KMFK H13
79580 COMMANDANT HENRY. Fr/Fr 1975; WT/Ch; 1600; 90.99 × 5.52 (298.52 × 18.11); M; 14.5; Probably similar: **79581 POINTE DE LESVEN** (Fr).

KMFK H13
79590 BP JOUSTER. Br/Br 1972; Tk; 1600; 78.95 × 4.74 (259.02 × 15.55); M; 12; ex SWANSEA 1976; Sister (Br flag): **79591 SHELL EXPLORER;** ex DUNDEE 1979; Similar: **79592 SHELL DIRECTOR;** ex CAERNARVON 1979; **79593 SHELL SUPPLIER;** ex PLYMOUTH 1979.

KMFK H13
79600 SENKO MARU. Ja/Ja 1971; Ch; 1000; 68.03 × 4.01 (223.2 × 13.16); M; 12; Probable Sister: **79601 OGISHIMA MARU** (Ja); Possibly Similar (LGC): **79602 KOSHIN MARU No 3** (Ja).

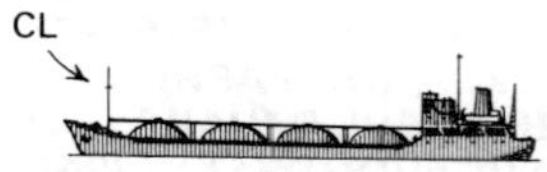

KMFK H13
79610 GREEN SEA. Li/Ja 1974; LGC; 1500; 73.18 × 4.62 (240.09 × 15.16); M; 12.

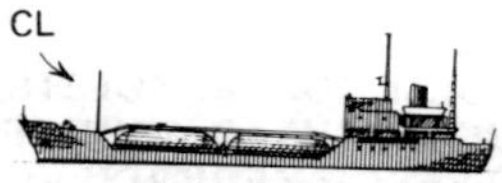

KMFK H13
79620 KOKUSHU MARU No 2. Ja/Ja 1976; LGC; 1600; 75.16 × 5.17 (246.6 × 16.96); M; 12.

KMFK H13
79630 BUTAUNO. Sp/Sp 1965; LGC; 1500; 79.56 × 4.93 (261.02 × 16.17); M; —; Sister: **79631 BUTADOS** (Sp).

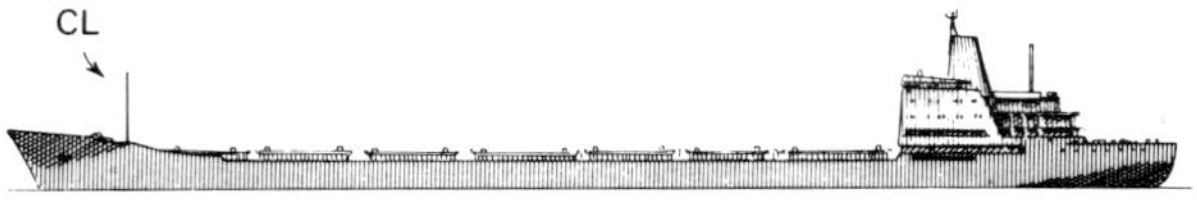

KMFK H13
79640 SOPHIA C. Gr/Bu 1971; B; 15700; 185.2 × 9.86 (607.61 × 32.35); M; 15.25; ex VIKHREN; Sisters (Bu flag): ⋆**79641 BELMEKEN;** ⋆**79642 GENERAL VLADIMIR ZAIMOV;** ⋆**79643 BALKAN;** (Pd flag): ⋆**79644 ZIEMIA BIALOSTOCKA;** ⋆**79645 ZIEMIA OLSZTYNSKA;** ⋆**79646 ZIEMIA OPOLSKI.**

KMFK H13
79650 KAITY. Gr/Ja 1965; B; 23000; 191.17 × 11.72 (627.2 × 38.45); M; —; Similar: **79651 ERO** (Gr).

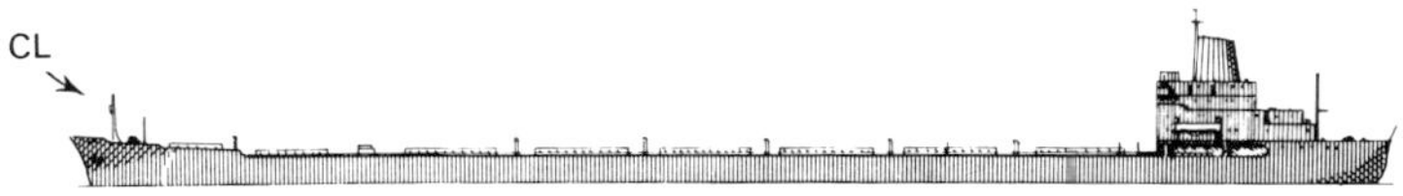

KMFK H13
79660 KUNIANG. Pa/Br 1967; B; 29000; 215.96 × 12.63 (708.53 × 41.44); M; 15.5 ex ELOUNDA; ex SHEAF TYNE 1978.

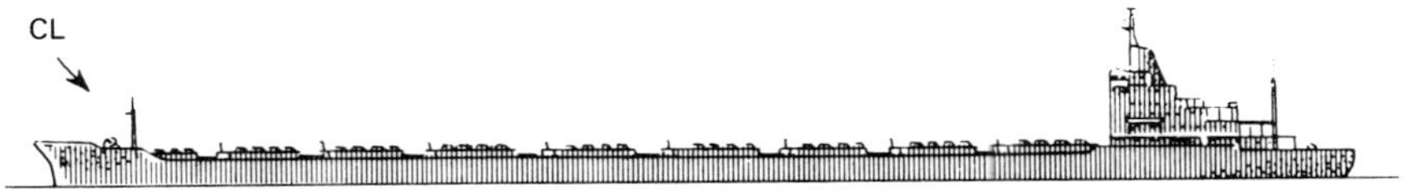

KMFK H13
79670 KEN VICTORY. Pa/Ja 1966; B; 35700; 254.16 × 12.92 (833.86 × 42.39); M; 16; ex MINORIES HOPE 1980; ex CRETAN BAY; ex WORLD SOYA 1975.

KMFK H13
79680 GYPSUM KING. Br/Ca 1975; B; 12800; 150.81 × 9.25 (494.78 × 30.35); T; 15; Sister: **79681 GYPSUM BARON** (Br).

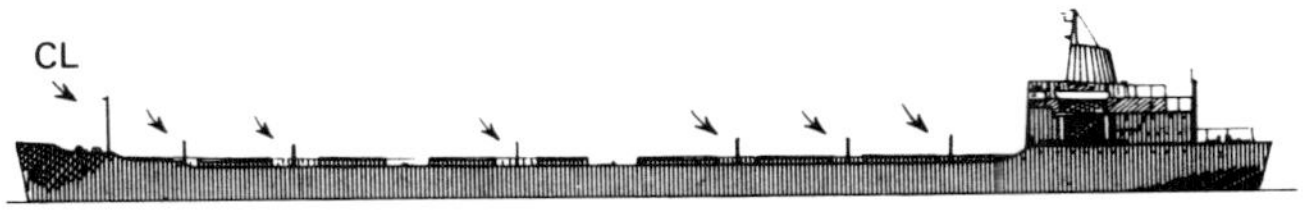

KMFK H13
79690 GENERAL M. MAKLEFF. Is/Br 1965; B; 22200; 196.76 × 11.65 (645.54 × 38.22); M; 16.5; ex OCEAN VALOUR 1980; ex ST PROVIDENCE 1976; ex SNEHOLT 1973; ex TOWER BRIDGE 1970; launched as SILVERHOW.

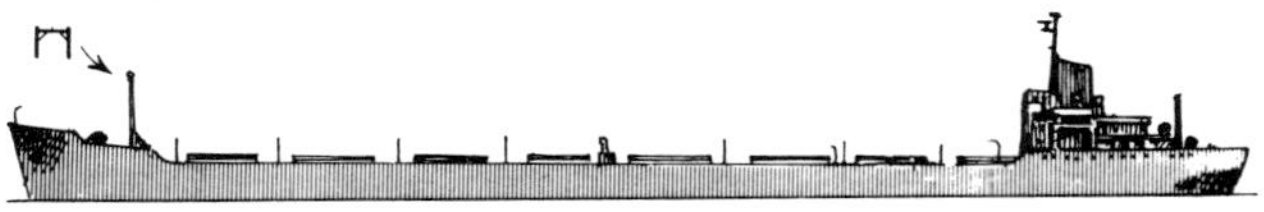

KMFK H13
79700 AL TAHIR. Sg/Br 1965; B; 22200; 196.76 × 11.71 (645.54 × 38.42); M; —; ex KIRRIEMOOR 1978.

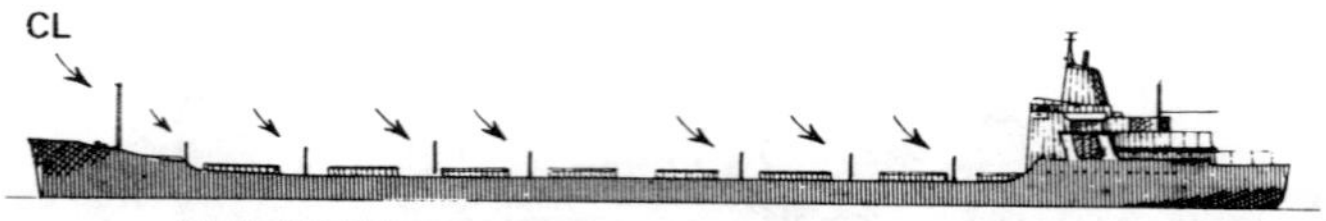

KMFK H13
79710 DRYS. Gr/Br 1965; B; 20200; 196.7 × 11.65 (645.34 × 38.22); M; 15; ex OAKWOOD 1971.

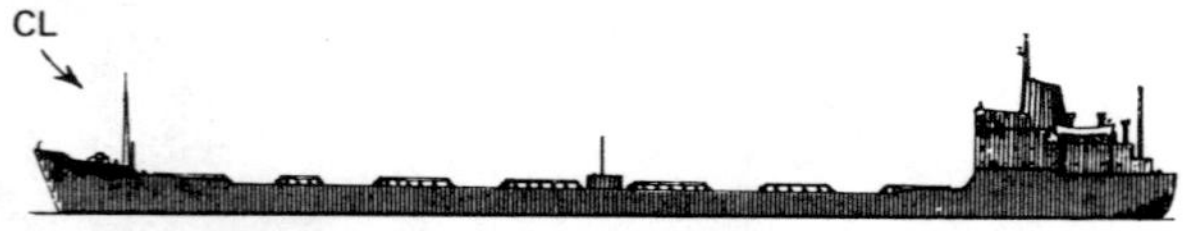

KMFK H13
79720 NEW FUTURE. Pa/Br 1968; B; 14000; 177.71 × 9.85 (583.04 × 32.32); M; 14.5; ex VANCOUVER TRADER; ex ESSEX TRADER 1971.

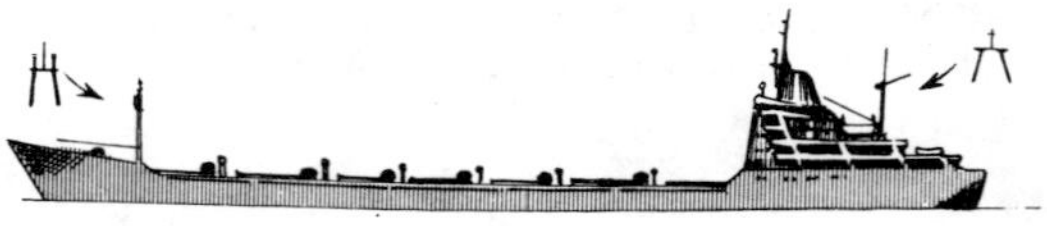

KMFK H13
⋆79730 LUBBENAU. DDR/DDR 1961; O; 8200; 151.59 × 8.31 (497.34 × 27.26); M; 15; Sisters (DDR flag): **⋆79731 MANSFELD; ⋆79732 ESPENHAIN; ⋆79733 SENFTENBERG; ⋆79734 TRATTENDORF; ⋆79735 VOCKERODE.**

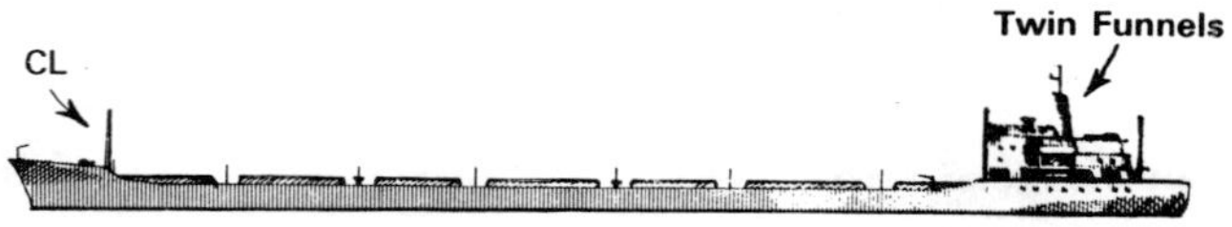

KMFK H13
79740 EGLANTINE. Fr/Fr 1968; B; 18700; 196.58 × — (644.95 × —); M; 17; Sister: **79741 HERMINE** (Fr).

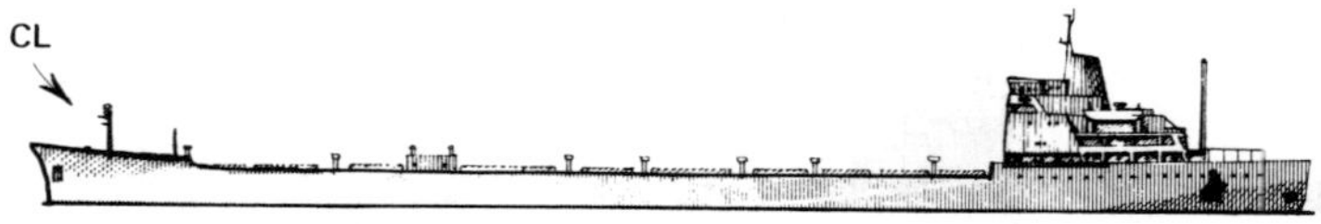

KMFK H13
79750 DISCOVERY BAY. Pa/Be 1963; B; 23300; 218.75 × 11.67 (717.68 × 38.29); M; 16; ex GOOD CARRIER 1979; ex EEKLO 1973.

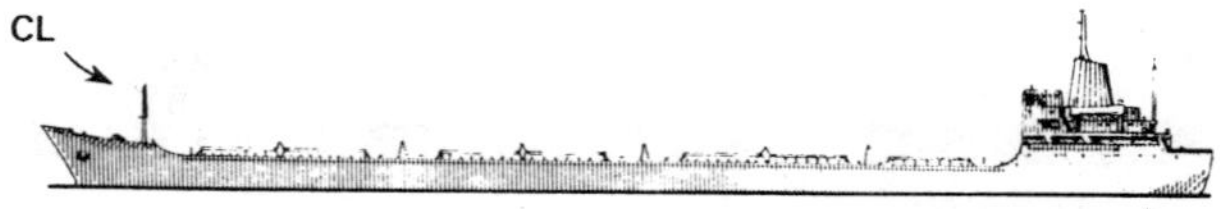

KMFK H13
79760 RIO LINDO. Gr/Ih 1964; B; 20000; 183.91 × 11.17 (603.35 × 36.65); M; 14; ex AMSTELHOF 1979; May now be fitted with cranes; Probable sister: **79761 CANADIAN BULKER** (Pa); ex SYNETOS 1981; ex RIJN 1975.

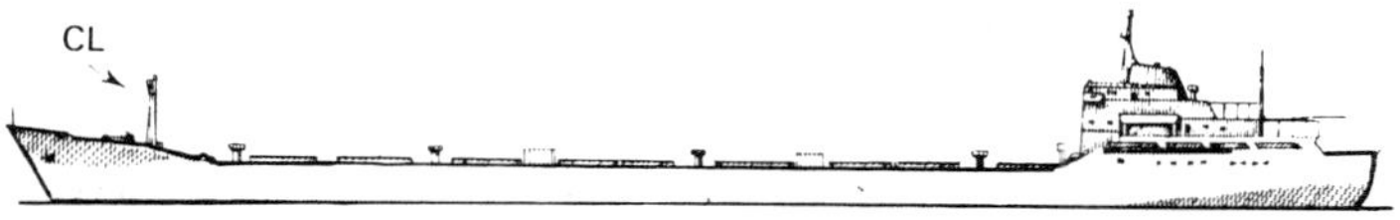

KMFK H13
79770 QUEBEC. Li/Ja 1965; B; 29200; 210.01 × 11.31 (718.85 × 37.11); M; 15.25 ex BARON HOLBERG 1967.

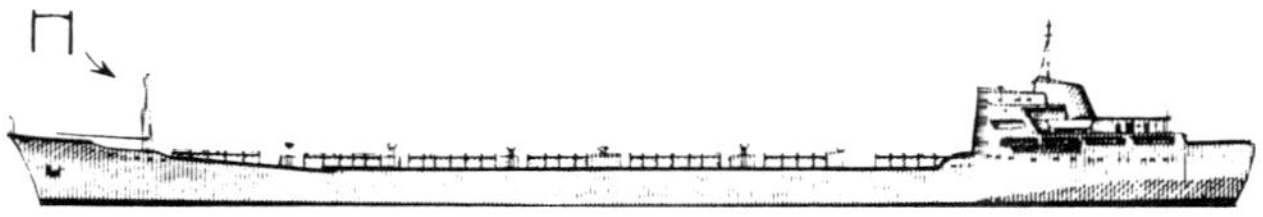

KMFK H13
79780 GEORGIOS T. KOROPOULIS. Gr/Ys 1964; B; 17500; 195.99 × 11.02 (643.01 × 36.15); M; 17; ex MYRON; Sisters (Li flag): **79781 DROMON; 79782 SKIRON.**

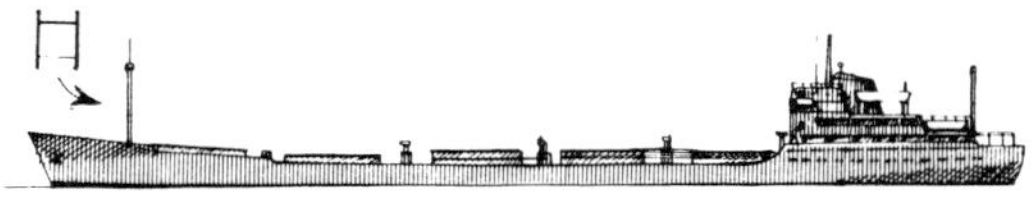

KMFK H13
● **79790 STAVFJORD.** Fi/FRG 1958; B; 10300; 157.82 × 9.45 (517.78 × 31); M; 14; ex MAGDALENA OLDENDORFF 1971.

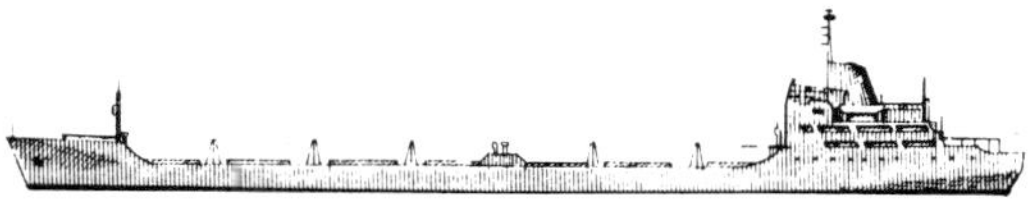

KMFK H13
⋆79800 FU HAI. RC/Ne 1963; B; 11300; 161.25 × 9.98 (529.04 × 32.74); M; 14; ex AEGNOUSSIOTIS 1974; ex POLYCROWN 1973; ex SUNPOLYCROWN 1970.

KMFK H13
79810 KORO SEA. Pa/Ys 1962; B; 13800; 170.44 × 9.56 (559.19 × 31.36); M; 14.5; ex BREGAGLIA 1972; Sister: **79811 PATVIN** (Pa); ex GALVIN 1980; ex ST. CERGUE 1978; ex BARILOCHE 1966.

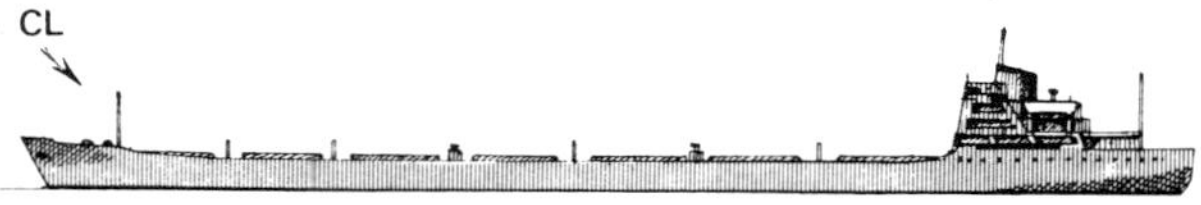

KMFK H13
79820 KAPETAN GEORGIS. Li/Br 1963; C; 16900; 186.09 × 10.85 (610.53 × 35.6); M; 14.

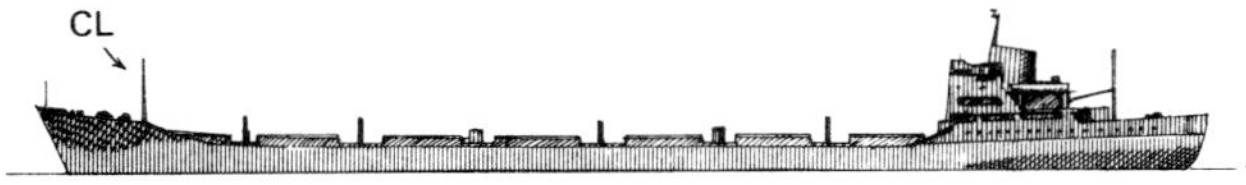

KMFK H13
79830 KARAISKAKI. Gr/Br 1965; B; 16900; 186.09 × 10.78 (610.53 × 35.37); M; 15.5; ex BRITISH MONARCH 1973; Sister: **⋆79831 LU HAI** (RC); ex OCEAN MARINER 1976; ex VENNACHAR 1973.

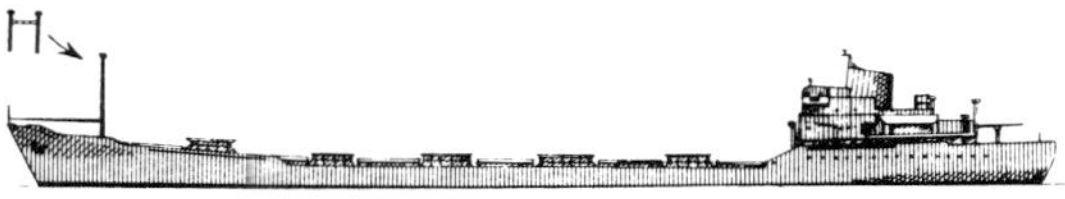

KMFK H13
⋆79840 HONG QI 301. RC/FRG 1958; B; 10400; 165 × 9.59 (541.34 × 31.46); M; 16; ex SALTON SEA 1980; ex ASMIDISKE 1973.

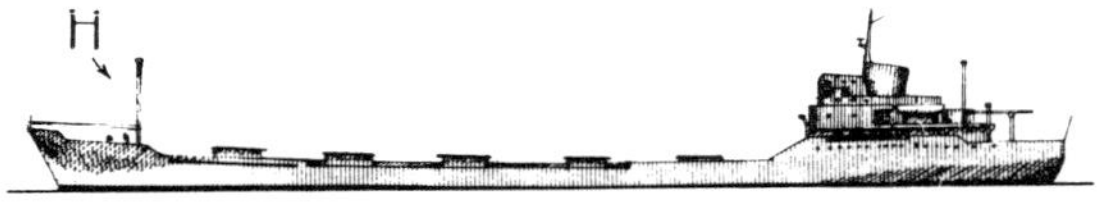

KMFK H13
● **79850 MATUMBA.** Gr/FRG 1958; B; 10500; 165.03 × 9.59 (541.44 × 31.46); M; 15; ex LUCIE SCHULTE 1976; ex NOORDWIJK 1969; Similar: **⋆79851 WU ZHI SHAN** (RC); ex CHUKCHI SEA 1978; ex ASTEROPE 1973.

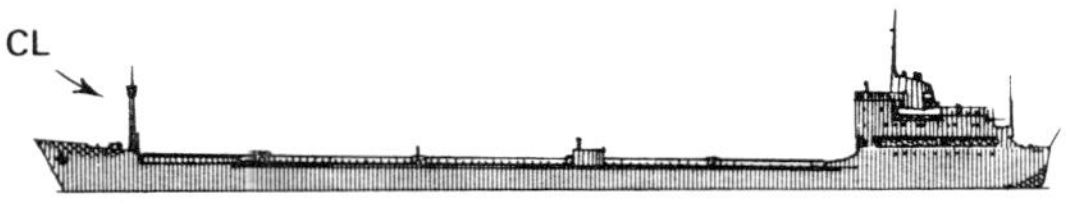

KMFK H13
79860 ASANO. Pa/Sw 1960; C; 9900; 157.26 × 9.13 (515.94 × 29.95); M; —; ex CAPE PALMAS 1978; ex ANNA BRODIN 1969.

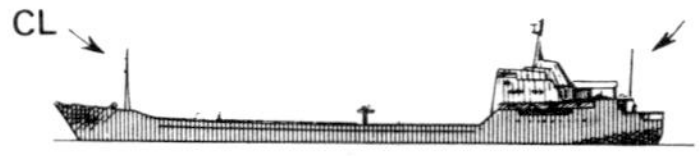

KMFK H13
⋆79870 SUWALKI. Pd/Bu 1969; C; 2400; 95.89 × 5.66 (314.6 × 18.57); M; 13; Sisters (Pd flag): **⋆79871 KUTNO II; ⋆79872 PIOTRKOW TRYBUNALSKI; ⋆79873 WADOWICE; ⋆79874 CIECHANOW; ⋆79875 STARACHOWICE; ⋆79876 PRZEMYSL.**

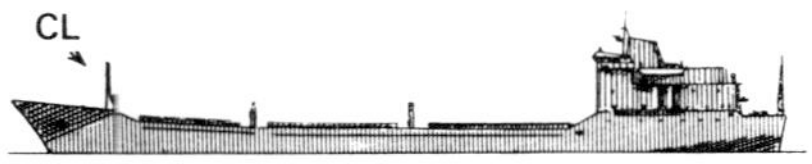

KMFK H13
79880 ZABAT DOS. Sp/Sp 1977; C; 5900; 119.64 × 7.99 (392.52 × 26.21); M; 14; Sister: **79881 ZABAT UNO** (Sp).

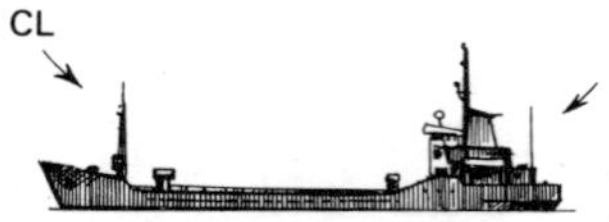

KMFK H13
79890 ALLUL. Sp/Sp 1974; C; 1600; 81.82 × 5.6 (268.44 × 18.37); M; 13.5; Sister: **79891 ALFER** (Sp).

KMFK H13
● **79900 FER BALTICO.** Sp/Sp 1976; C; 1600; 82.1 × 5.44 (269.36 × 17.85); M; 11.5; Sister: **79901 FER BALEAR** (Sp).

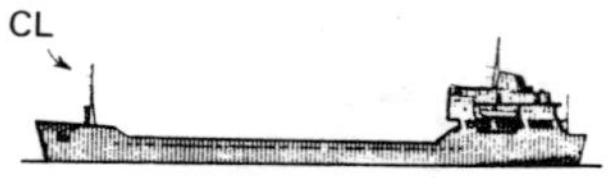

KMFK H13
79910 BEEDING. Br/Sw 1971; C; 1600; 87.03 × 4.96 (285.53 × 16.27); M; 12; Sister: **79911 FALKENBERG** (FRG); ex PONTOS 1976; ex FALKENBERG 1973; launched as ISOTAT.

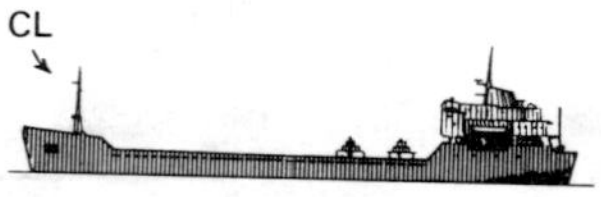

KMFK H13
79920 ANDERS. Sw/Sw 1971; C; 1600; 87.03 × 4.96 (285.53 × 16.27); M; 12.

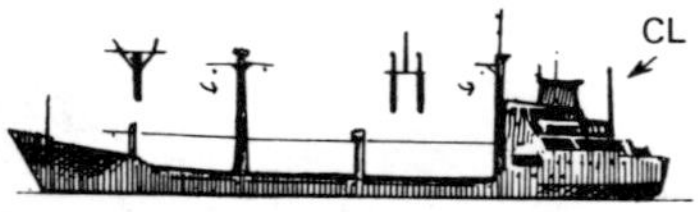

KMFK H13
⋆**79930 ABRAM ARKHIPOV.** Ru/Fi 1973; C/TC; 3200; 97.31 × 6.7 (319.26 × 21.98); M; 14; Sisters (Ru flag): ⋆**79931 VLADIMIR FAVORSKIY;** ⋆**79932 MITROFAN GREKOV;** ⋆**79933 VASILIY POLENOV;** ⋆**79934 NIKOLAY YAROSHENKO;** ⋆**79935 NIKOLAY KASATKIN;** ⋆**79936 KONSTANTIN YUON;** ⋆**79937 IGOR GRABAR;** ⋆**79938 IVAN SHADR;** ⋆**79939 MIKHAIL CHEREMNYKH;** ⋆**79940 VERA MUKINA;** ⋆**79941 YEKATERINA BELASHOVA.**

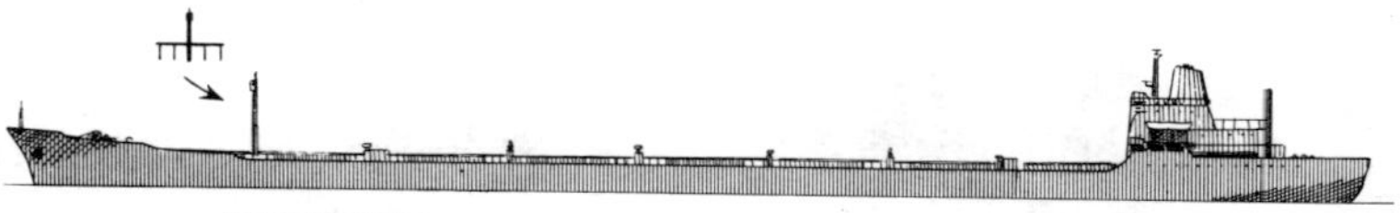

KMFK H13
79950 AEGEAN MONARCH. Gr/Ja 1967; B; 32500; 235.52 × 13.74 (772.7 × 45.08); M; 17; Sister: **79951 AEGEAN NEPTUNE** (Gr).

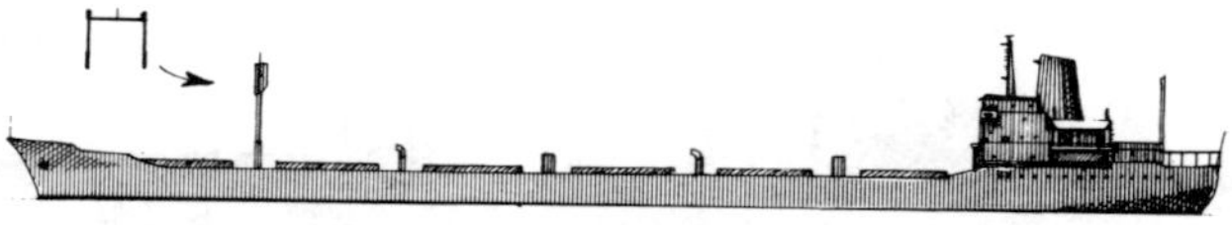

KMFK H13
79960 NYMPH C. Gr/Ja 1966; B; 22300; 193.55 × 11.84 (635.01 × 38.85); M; —; ex AEGEAN NYMPH 1980; Sister: **79961 AEGEAN SKY** (Gr).

KMFKC H1
79970 SEARADIANCE. Br/Br 1977; B; 39200; 228.12 × 14.05 (748.43 × 46.1); M; 15; ex ORIENT CITY 1978; Sister: **79971 WELSH CITY** (Br).

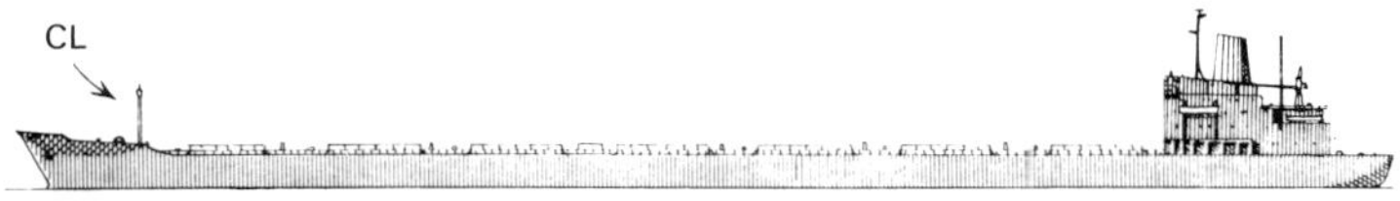

KMFKC H1
79980 PAN JUSTICE. Pa/Ja 1975; B; 35800; 224.01 × 13.32 (734.94 × 43.7); M; 14.5; ex HALLA GRIEG 1981.

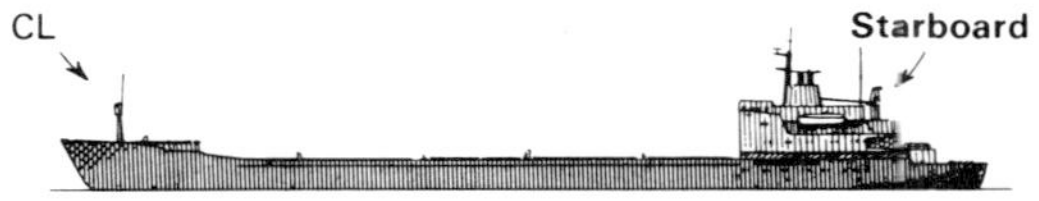

KMFKC H1
★79990 KAPITAN PANFILOV. Ru/Ru 1975; B; 10100; 146.21 × 9.43 (479.69 × 30.94); M; 14; Sisters (Ru flag): **★79991 KAPITAN KHROMTSOV; ★79992 KAPITAN DUBININ; ★79993 KAPITAN IZHMYAKOV; ★79994 KAPITAN MESHCHRYAKOV; ★79995 KAPITAN REUTOV; ★79996 KAPITAN GUDIN; ★79997 KAPITAN STULOV; ★79998 KAPITAN VANILOV; ★79999 IVAN NESTEROV.**

● ★80000

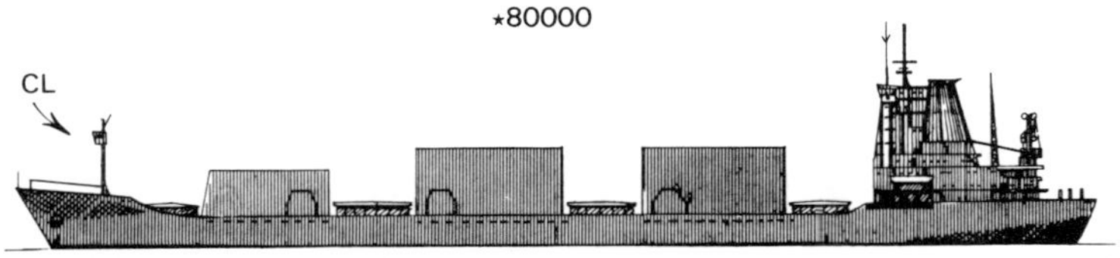

KMFKC H1
80010 JUTHLANDIA. Li/Pd 1976; BC; 33000; 224.42 × 12.37 (736.29 × 40.58); M; 15.75; **'B-521'** type; Side doors.

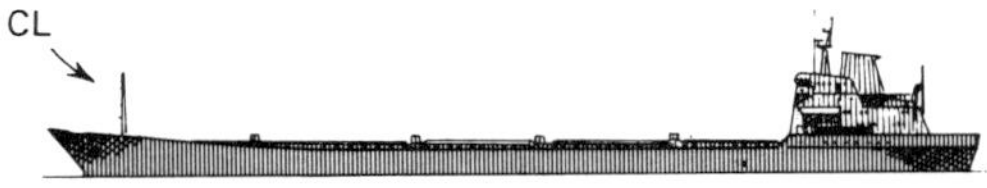

KMFKC H13
★80020 HUTA ZGODA. Pd/FRG 1974; B; 9300; 145.65 × 8.35 (477.85 × 27.4); M; 15; Sisters (Pd flag): **★80021 HUTA ZYGMUNT; ★80022 BUDOWLANY; ★80023 ROLNIK; ★80024 KOPALNIA SOSNOWIEC; ★80025 KOPALNIA WALBRZYCH; ★80026 KOPALNIA ZOFIOWKA.**

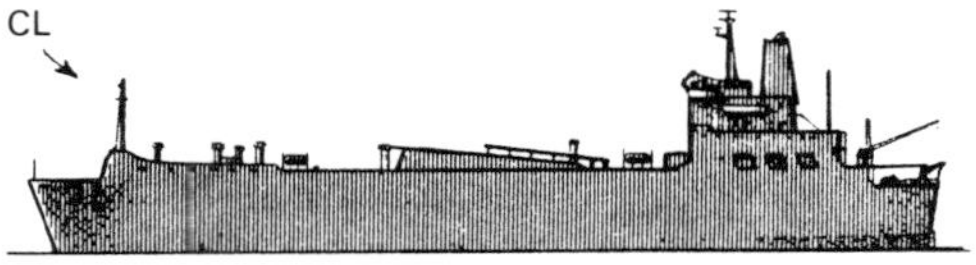

KMFKC H2
80030 BELLMAN. Sg/Ja 1977; RoC/Tk/B; 9500; 143.85 × 7.8 (471.95 × 25.59); M; 14.75; **'Boro'** type; Sister: **80031 TAUBE** (Sg).

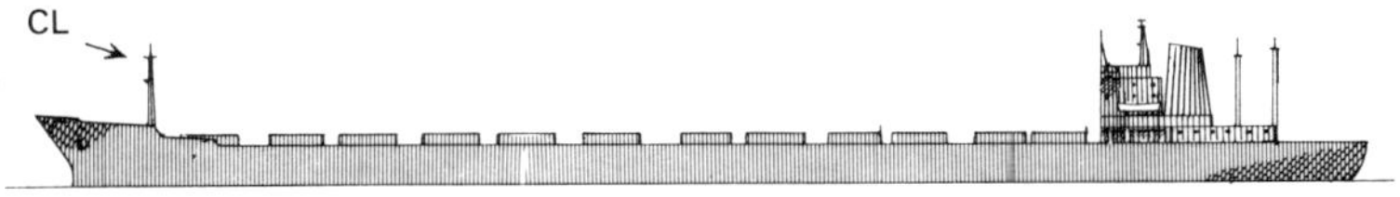

$KMFK_2$ H1
80040 T. AKASAKA. Br/Ja 1969; B; 33300; 226.88 × 12.3 (744.36 × 40.35); M; 15.5; Sister: **80041 W. C. VAN HORNE** (Br).

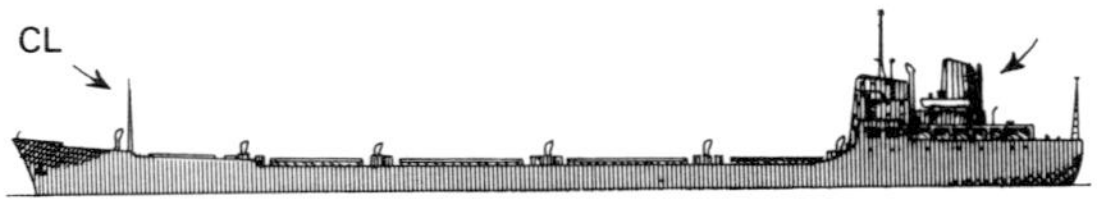

$KMFK_2$ H13
80050 AGIA ANASTASIA. Gr/Ja 1959; C; 12300; 169.17 × 9.51 (555.02 × 31.2); M; 15.5; ex SAAS GRUND 1976; ex DENEB 1972.

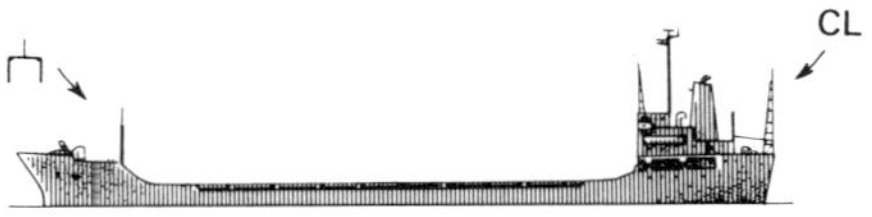

$KMFK_2$ H13
★80060 KAPITAN TOMSON. Ru/Ja 1977; RoC/Con; 4600; 113.49 × 6.87 (372.34 × 22.54); M; —; ex R. S. IXION 1978; launched as R. S. ONE; Sister: **★80061 KAPITAN YAKOVLEV** (Ru); ex R. S. JASON 1978.

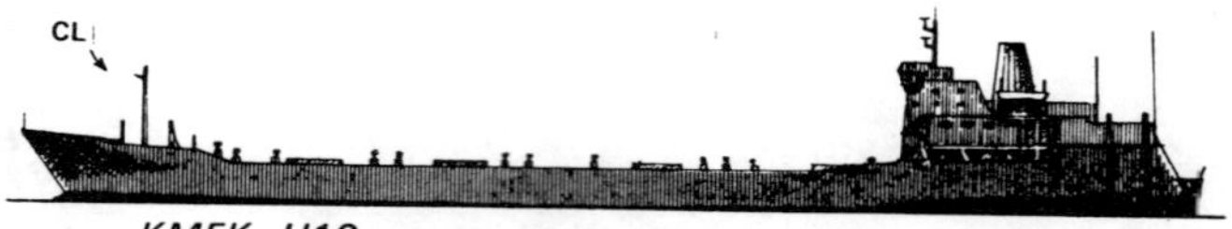

$KMFK_2$ H13
80070 GRAND ENCOUNTER. Pa/Ca 1972; RoC; 16400; 208.19 × 9.3 (683.04 × 30.51); TSM; 19; ex LAURENTIAN FOREST. Sister: **80071 AVON FOREST** (Br).

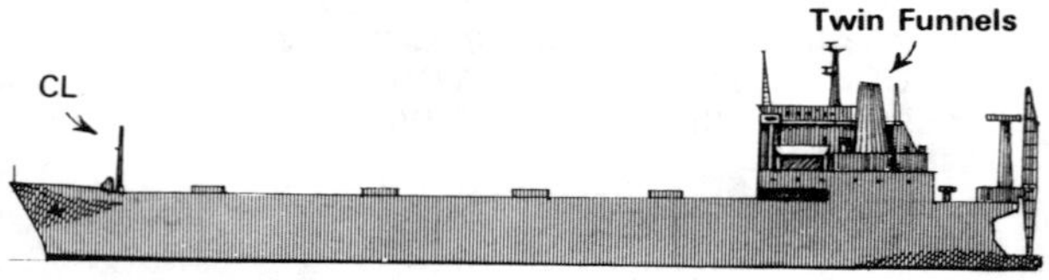

KMFKR H
80080 HELLENIC VALOR. Gr/Ja 1978; RoC; 17200; 190.53 × 11.9 (625.1 × 39.04); TSM; 17; Stern door/ramp; Sisters (Gr flag): **80081 HELLENIC EXPLORER; 80082 HELLENIC INNOVATOR.**

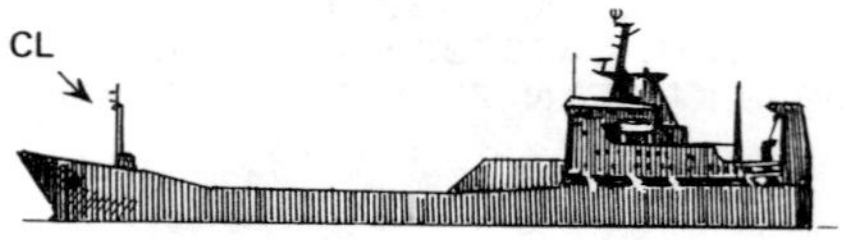

KMFKR H1
★80090 INZHENER MACHULSKIY. Ru/Fi 1975; RoC/Con; 4000; 124.21 × 6.6 (407.51 × 21.65); M; 16.75; Stern quarter ramp; Sisters (Ru flag): **★80091 INZHENER BASHKIROV;- ★80092 INZHENER SUKHORUKOV; ★80093 INZHENER KREYLIS; ★80094 MEKHANIK KONOVALOV;** Similar (stern ramp and no extension before bridgefront) (Ru flag): **★80095 INZHENER NECHIPORENKO; ★80096 MEKHANIK TARASOV; ★80097 MEKHANIK FEDOROV; ★80098 MEKHANIK YEVGRAFOV; ★80099 MEKHANIK GERASIMOV.**

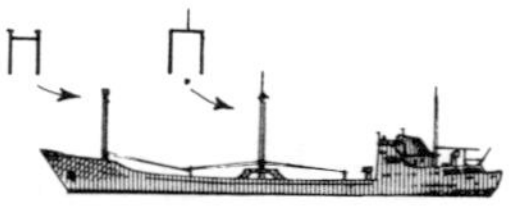

KMFM H1
80110 SVENDBORG GRACE. De/Ne 1963; C; 500; 72.67 × 3.82 (238.42 × 12.53); M; 13; ex KITTIWAKE 1974; launched as BREEWIJD; Sister: **8011 AQABA** (Jo); ex IMBER 1976.

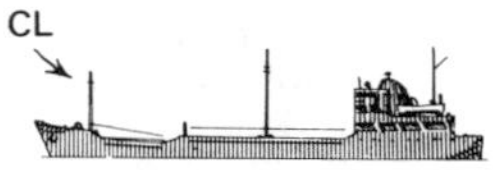

KMFM H12/123
80120 ESTLAND. Pa/Br 1961; B; 1100; 69.5 × 4.59 (228.02 × 15.06); M; 11; ex TURQUOISE; ex KYLEBANK 1975.

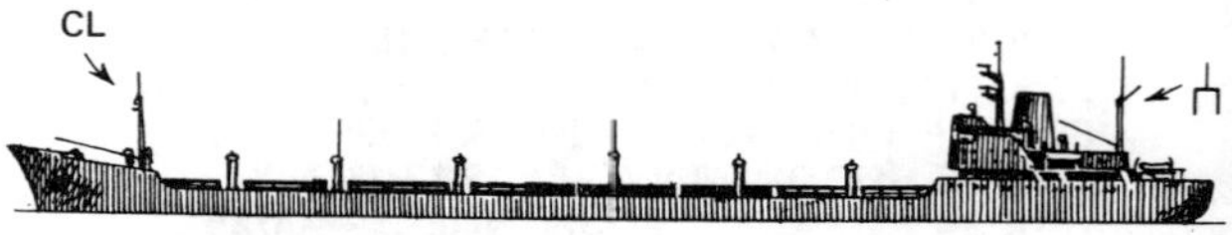

KMFM H13
★80130 ZARECHENSK. Ru/Ru 1967; B; 16000; 187.12 × 9.54 (614.17 × 31.3); M; 15.5; **'B-470'** type; Sisters (Ru flag): **★80131 ZVENIGOROD; ★80132 ZAPOROZHYE; ★80133 ZAKARPATYE; ★80134 ZADONSK; ★80135 ZLATOUST; ★80136 ZORINSK;** Similar (Pd flag): **★80137 ZIEMIA KRAKOWSKA; ★80138 ZIEMIA LUBELSKA; ★80139 ZAGLEBIE MIEDZIOWE.**

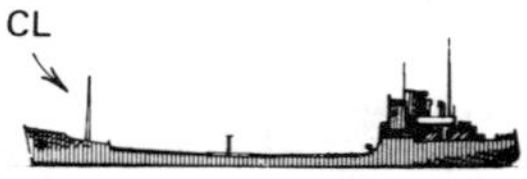

KMFM H13
80150 STEPHEN BROWN; Au/Br 1954; C; 1500; 77.27 × 4.43 (253.51 × 14.53); M; —.

KMFM H13
● **★80160 EUROBRIDGE PIONIR.** Ys/FRG 1973; Con; 4000; 118.88 × 6.4 (390.03 × 21); M; 15.5; ex PIONIR 1978; ex MARITIME CHAMP 1974; Sister: **80161 SUN FLOWER** (Ko); ex MARITIME ACE 1973.

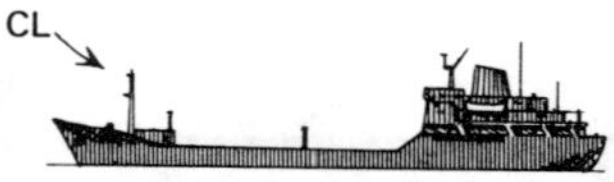

KMFM H13
80170 TYYSTERNIEMI. Fi/Fr 1967; Ch; 2000; 87 × 5.97 (285.43 × 19.59); M; 13.75.

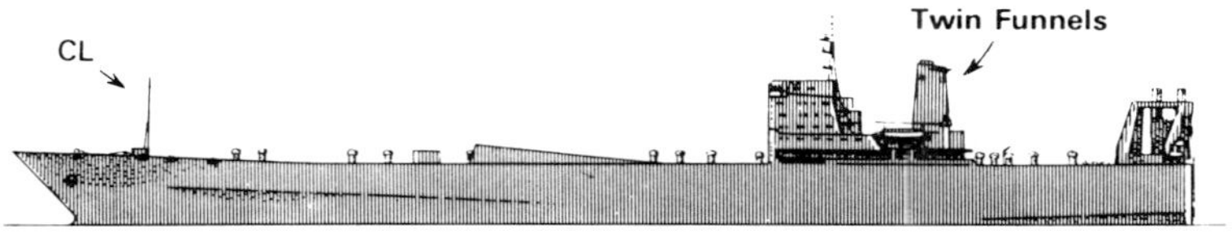

KMFR H
★**80180 KAPITAN SMIRNOV.** Ru/Ru 1979; RoC/Con; 14300; 227.3 × 9.87 (745.74 × 32.38); Ts GT/M; 25; Stern quarter ramp; Sisters (Ru flag): ★**80181 KAPITAN MEZENTSEV** (different design of ramp); ★**80182 INZHENER YERMOSHKIN.**

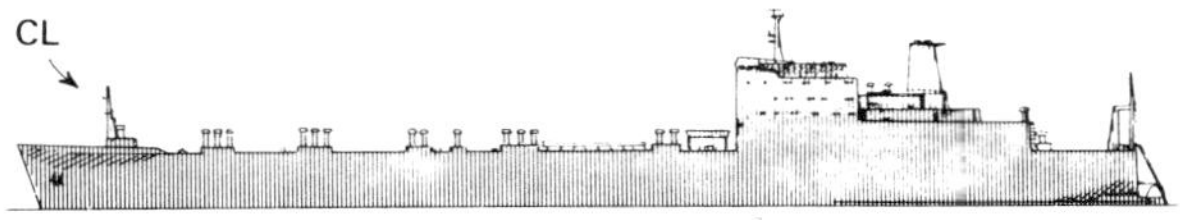

KMFR H
● **80190 EMIRATES EXPRESS.** Sw/Sw 1978; RoC; 9100; 183.5 × 8.44 (602.03 × 27.69); M; 18; Stern doors/ramp.

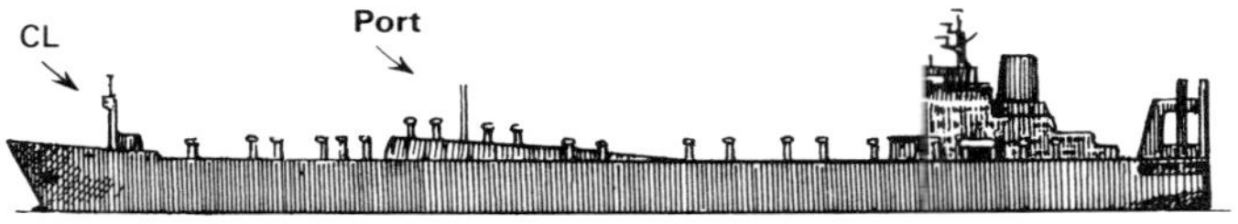

KMFR H
● ★**80200 MAGNITOGORSK.** Ru/Fi 1975; RoC; 15700; 205.8 × 9.7 (675.2 × 31.82); M; 22; Stern door/quarter ramp; Sisters (Ru flag): **80201 KOMSOMOLSK; 80202 ANATOLIY VASILYEV.**

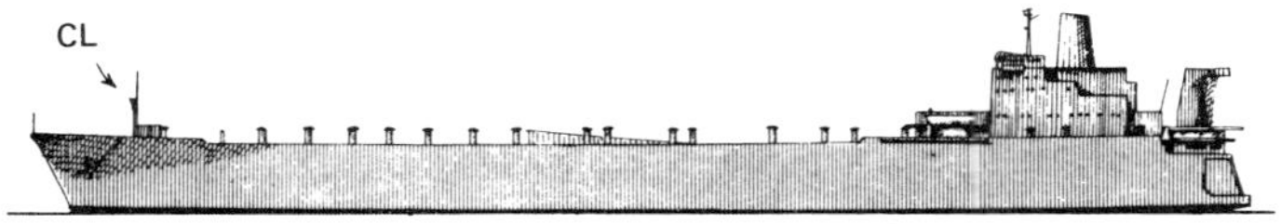

KMFR H
80210 LALANDIA. De/Sw 1974; RoC; 13900/24000; 207.4 × 9.58 (680.45 × 31.43); M; 22.75; Stern door; Similar (superstructure varies): **80211 BARRANDUNA** (Sw); **80212 TARAGO** (No); **80213 TOMBARRA** (No); **80214 TRICOLOR** (No); Similar (Fr built and flag): **80215 RODIN; 80216 ROSTAND; 80217 ROUSSEAU.**

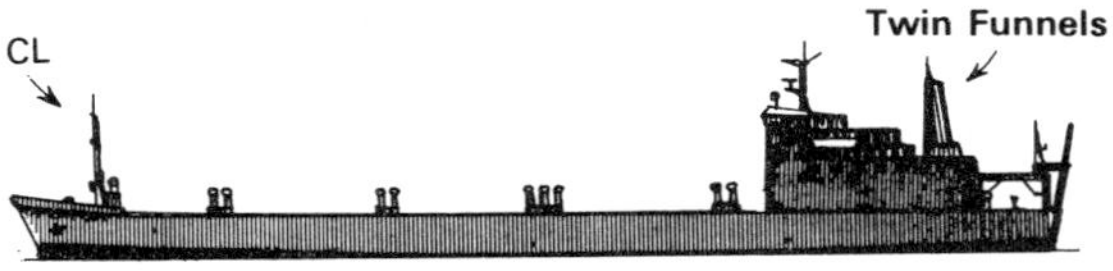

KMFR H
80220 KAPRIFOL. Sw/Sw 1977; RoC/Con; 5500; 162.11 × 6.6 (531.86 × 21.65); M; 17.25; Stern door/ramp; Sisters (Sw flag): **80221 VALLMO; 80222 LINNE** (funnel variation).

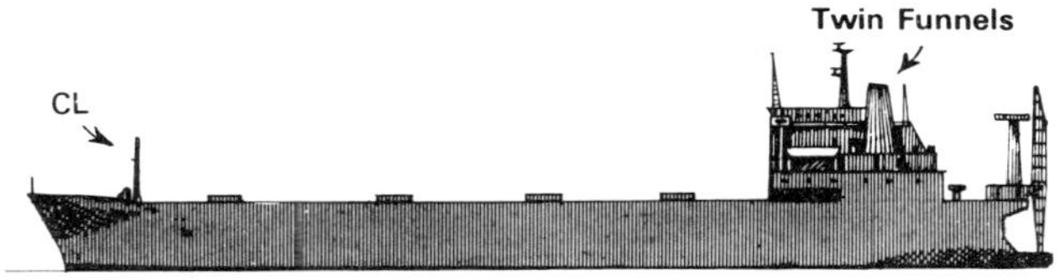

KMFR H
80230 HELLENIC VALOR. Gr/Ja 1978; RoC; 17200; 190.53 × 11.9 (625.1 × 39.04); TSM; 17; Stern door/ramp; Sisters (Gr flag): **80231 HELLENIC EXPLORER; 80232 HELLENIC INNOVATOR.**

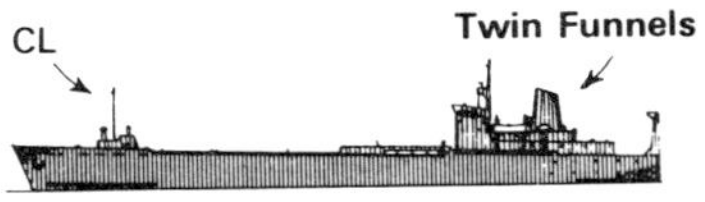

KMFR H
80240 MARY HOLYMAN. Br/Ne —; 2600; 101.2 × 5.18 (332.02 × 16.99); M; 15; Stern door.

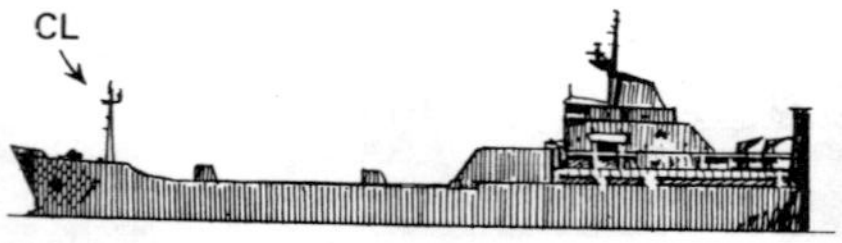

KMFR H1
⋆80250 **AKADEMIK ARTSIMOVICH.** Ru/Fr 1975; RoC; 3200; 119.03 × 5.77 (390.52 × 18.93); M; 17; Stern door; Sisters (Ru flag): **⋆80251 AKADEMIK GUBER; ⋆80252 AKADEMIK KUPREVICH; ⋆80253 AKADEMIK MILLIONSCHIKOV; ⋆80254 AKADEMIK STECHKIN; ⋆80255 AKADEMIK TUPOLEV.**

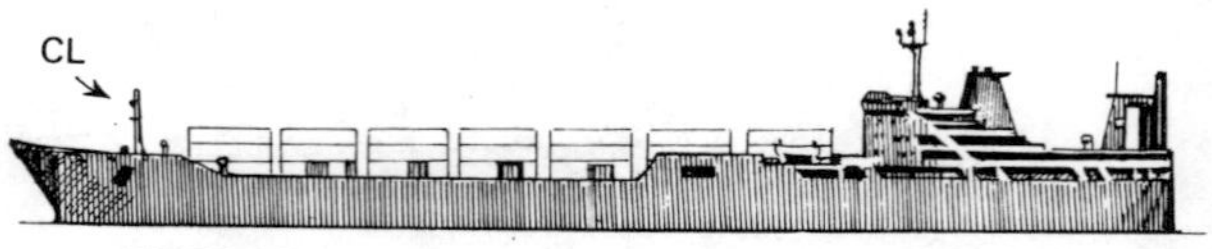

KMFR H1
● **80260 SKULPTOR KONENKOV.** Ru/Pd 1975; RoC/Con; 18500; 181.41 × 9.64 (595.18 × 31.63); M; 20.5; Stern door/quarter ramp **'B-481'** type; Sisters (Ru flag): **⋆80261 SKULPTOR VUCHETICH; ⋆80262 SKULPTOR GOLUBKINA; ⋆80263 SKULPTOR ZALKALNS; ⋆80264 NIKOLAY CHERKASOV; ⋆80265 AGOSTINHO NETO** ex BORIS LIMANOV.

KMFR H23
● **80270 ELK.** Br/Ko 1977; RoC; 5500; 151.01 × 7.32 (495.44 × 24.02); M; 18.5; Bow door/ramp. Stern door/ramp; Sisters: **80271 MERZARIO IONIA** (Br) ex STENA SHIPPER 1980; ex NORSKY 1980; **80272 HELLAS** (Gr) ex ALPHA PROGRESS 1979; ex STENA RUNNER 1977; **80273 SYRIA** (Gr) ex ALPHA ENTERPRISE 1980; **80274 ATLANTIC PROJECT** (Br); **80275 ATLANTIC PROSPER** (Br); **80276 TOR FELICIA** (Br) ex MERZARIO GRECIA; ex TOR FELICIA 1978; **80277 STENA FREIGHTER** (Sw) ex MERZARIO AUSONIA 1980; **80278 IMPARCA MIAMI** (Br) ex STENA CARRIER 1980; ex IMPARCA EXPRESS I 1980.

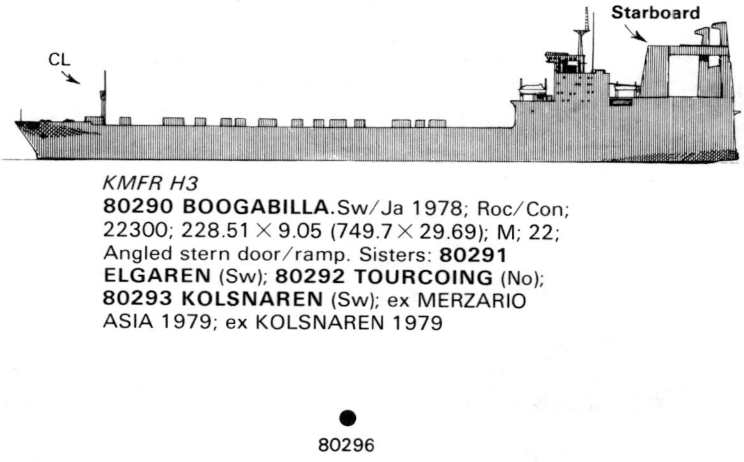

KMFR H3
80290 BOOGABILLA. Sw/Ja 1978; Roc/Con; 22300; 228.51 × 9.05 (749.7 × 29.69); M; 22; Angled stern door/ramp. Sisters: **80291 ELGAREN** (Sw); **80292 TOURCOING** (No); **80293 KOLSNAREN** (Sw); ex MERZARIO ASIA 1979; ex KOLSNAREN 1979

●
80296

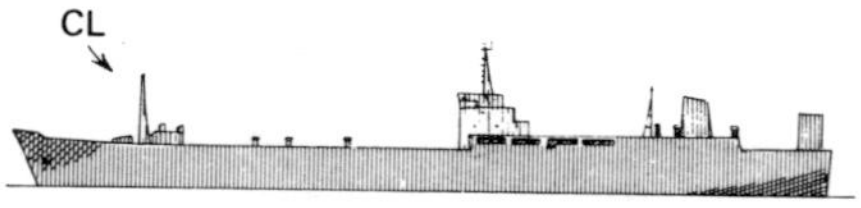

KMKF H
80300 KUSHIRO MARU. Ja/Ja 1974; RoC; 4700; 130 × 6.02 (426.51 × 19.75); M; 17.

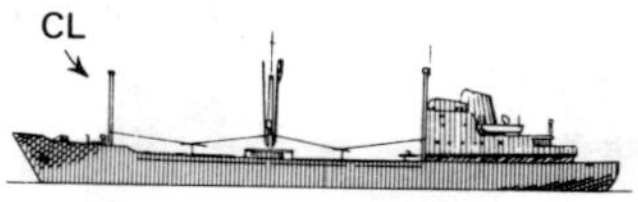

KMKF H1
80310 CARIBBEAN ARICHUNA. Br/FRG 1955; C; 3200; 96.06 × 6.71 (315.03 × 22.01); M; 12.5; ex COPPERLAND 1971; ex GYPTIS 1969; ex GERTRUD 1960.

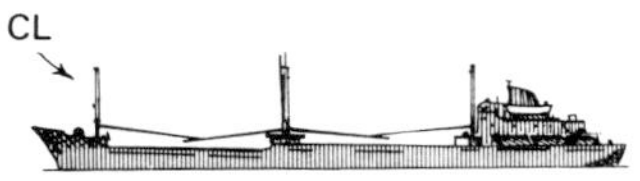

KMKF H1
80320 GOLD CLOUD. Pa/Sp 1964; C; 1800/2800; 92.39× —/7.13 (303.12× —/23.39); M; 12.5; ex JANCA 1975; ex CARMEN 1970.

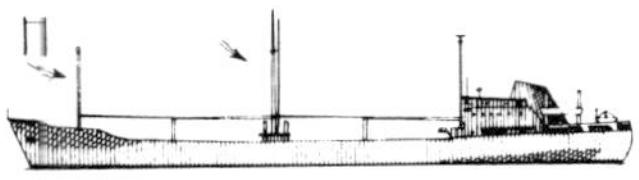

KMKF H1
80330 SOFIA. Le/Ne 1958; C; 3400; 99.65×5.74/7.15 (326.94×18.83/23.46); M; 12; ex SAALE 1980; ex OLIVIA WINTHER 1963.

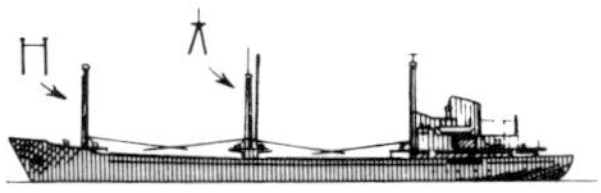

KMKF H1
80340 AYAN I. Tu/FRG 1967; C; 1800; 88.45×5.22 (290.19×17.13; M; 14; ex HIMNO I 1980; ex CAP HERO 1977; ex SCOMBER 1977; ex HIPPO SAILOR 1976; ex MARIE REITH 1975; Sisters: **80341 NANO K** (Gr) ex HIPPO LADY 1977; ex PERCA 1977; ex HIPPO LADY 1976; ex SUSANNE REITH 1974; **80342 EME** (Sg) ex EMIL P 1978; ex EMIL REITH 1978; Possible sister: **80343 CRESTENA** (Gr) ex RAJA 1977; ex HIPPO CARRIER 1976; ex ELISABETH REITH 1975.

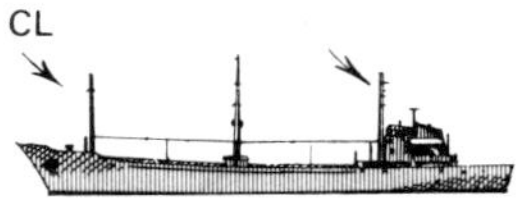

KMKF H1
80350 PREVEZE. Tu/Tu 1973; C; 1300; 80.02×5.51 (262.53×18.08); M; —; Sister (Tu flag): **80351 NIGBOLU;** Probable sisters: **80352 AGRI; 80353 ANTAKYA; 80354 ARTVIN; 80355 ANTALYA; 80356 CALDIRAN; 80357 MOHAC.**

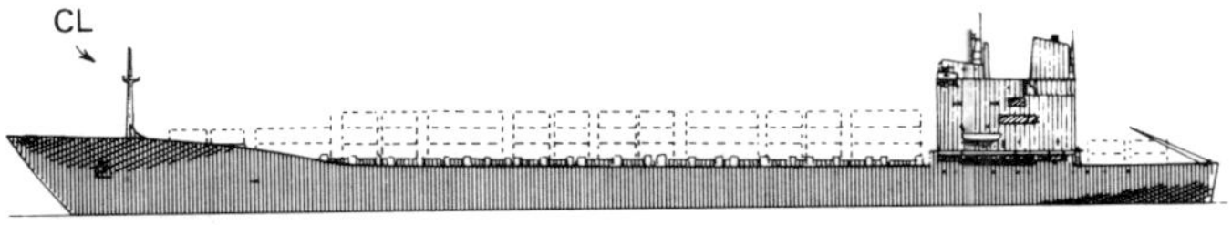

KMKF H1
● **80370 KOREAN JUPITER.** Ko/Fr 1975; Con; 21300; 208.19×9.27 (683.04×30.4); T; 23.5; ex ORIENTAL FINANCIER 1978; Sisters: **80371 ORIENTAL EXECUTIVE** (Li); **80372 ORIENTAL RESEARCHER** (Li); **80373 ORIENTAL STATESMAN** (Li); **80374 CHEVALIER VALBELLE** (Fr); Similar (lengthened): **80375 CHEVALIER ROZE** (Fr); **80376 CHEVALIER PAUL** (Fr); **80377 MERCATOR** (Be).

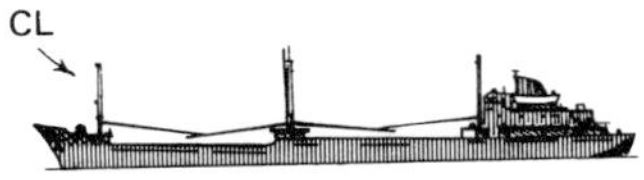

KMKF H12
80390 GOLD CLOUD. Pa/Sp 1964; C; 1800/2800; 92.39× —/7.13 (303.12× —/23.39); M; 12.5; ex JANCA 1975; ex CARMEN 1970.

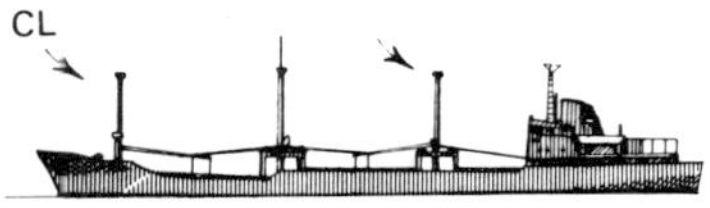

KMKF H12 & H123
80400 MONTONE. It/FRG 1963; C; 3000; 105.92×6 (347.51×19.69); M; 14.5; ex JOBST OLDENDORFF 1980; Sisters: **KATERINE** (Pa) ex CHRISTINE OLDENDORFF; **RIMA G** (Le) ex ERNA OLDENDORFF 1980; **LAMONE** (It) ex HANS OLDENDORFF 1980.

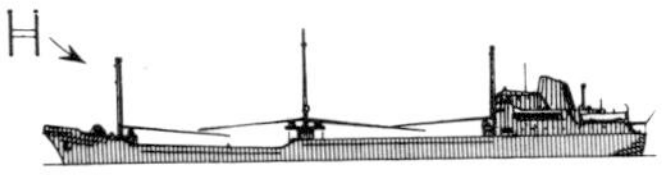

KMKF H123
80410 CIRO TERZO. It/FRG 1958; C; 2700; 96.7×6.1 (317.26×20.21); M; 13.75; ex ANGELIKI H 1980; ex PERSIA LYDIA 1973; ex COUDEBEC U.N. 2 1968; ex CAUDEBEC 1960.

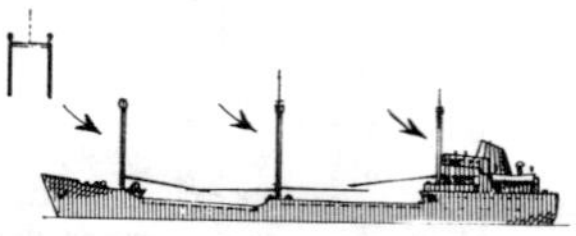

KMKF H123
80420 MERKET. Pa/FRG 1958; C; 1000/1800; 80.7 × 4.32/5.96 (264.76 × 14.17/19.55); M; 12.5; ex MOURA 1978; ex MARITA 1975; ex AKKO 1969; Sister: **80421 DUSK** (Pa) ex DUSAN 1978; ex RUNO 1975; ex ASHDOD 1969; Possibly similar: **80422 DADO** (Is) ex KESARYA 1978; ex JASPER 1975; ex KESARYA 1970.

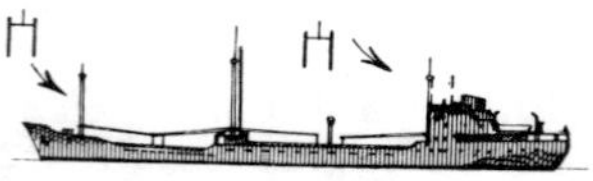

KMKF H123
80430 MARE AMICO. It/FRG 1953; C; 1600; 87.74 × 4.85 (287.86 × 15.91); M; 12.5; ex FRANCESCA SECONDA 1977; ex GRETKE OLDENDORFF 1971; ex MARY ROBERT MULLER 1961.

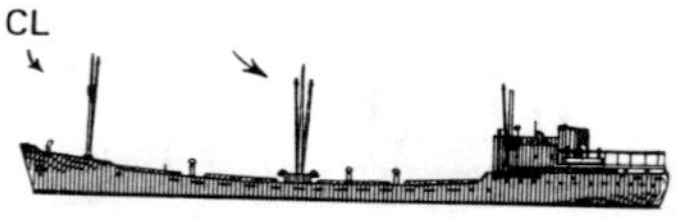

KMKF H13
● **80440 MALEA.** Pa/Br 1953; C; 3800; 108.69 × 8.66 (356.59 × 28.41); M; 11; ex MISTRAL 1977; ex BUSHWOOD 1971; ex LONGFELLOW 1961.

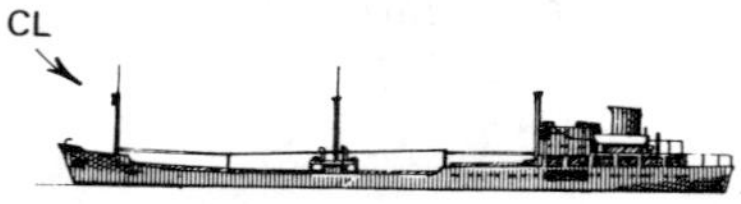

KMKF H13
80450 ARIES CARRIER. Br/Br 1956; C; 3900; 107.83 × 6.77 (353.77 × 22.21); M; —; ex FORESTAL 1 1975; ex PORTRIEUX 1972; ex SUGAR EXPORTER 1964.

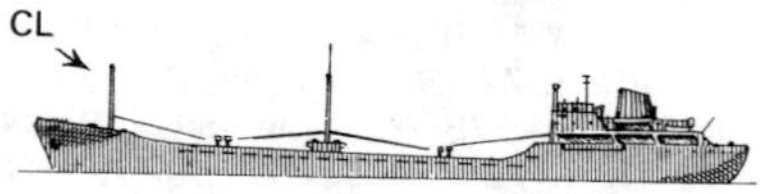

KMKF H13
80460 CONDE DEL CADAGUA. Sp/Sp 1959; C; 3900; 113.11 × 6.36 (371.1 × 20.87); M; 13.5.

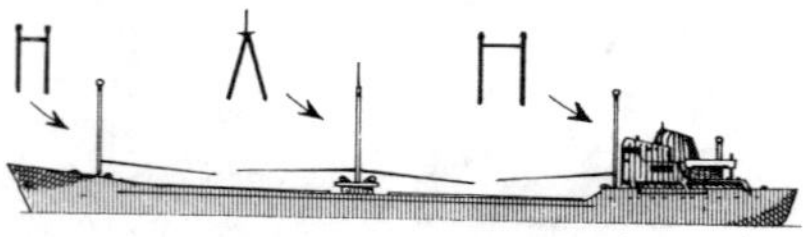

KMKF H13
80470 LINGAYEN. Li/FRG 1955; C; 2900; 134.55 × 6.08 (441.44 × 19.95); M; 18; ex BREMERHAVEN 1973.

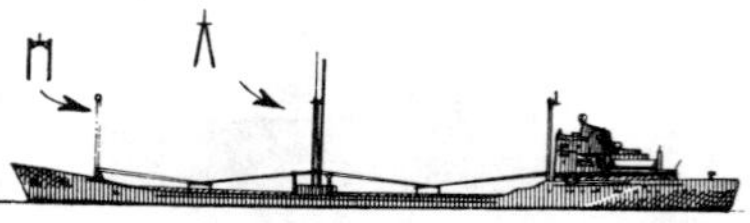

KMKF H13
80480 KARRABIO. Pa/Sp 1960; C; 3300; 116.62 × 6.8 (382.61 × 22.31); M; 12.75; ex JUPITER II 1978; ex ARRABIO 1976.

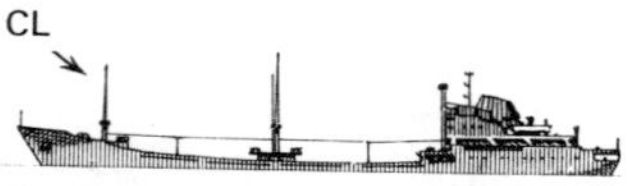

KMKF H13
80490 MASTROGIORGIS. Gr/FRG 1958; C; 3000; 95 × 6.9 (311.68 × 22.64); M; 14; ex PALMAH 1978; ex ATID 1960.

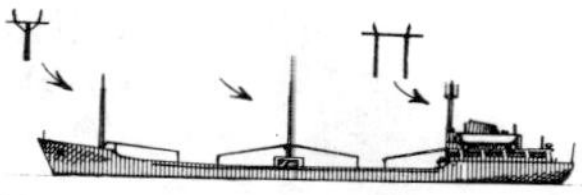

KMKF H13
80500 QUICKTHORN. Br/Br 1967; C; 1600; 85.35 × 4.93 (280.02 × 16.17); M; 13; ex TANMERACK 1973.

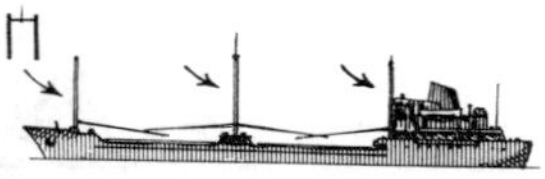

KMKF H13
80510 SONIA SOPHIA S. Cy/Sp 1966; C; 900/1700; 80.22 × —/5.79 (263.19 × —/19); M; —; ex NUESTRA SENORA DEL CARMEN SEGUNDO 1977.

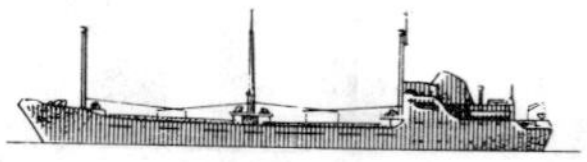

KMKF H13
80520 MAR DEL NORD. It/FRG 1956; C; 1200/1900; 83.98 × 4.97/6.1 (275.52 × 16.31/20.01); M; 12; ex REX 1973; ex FINNWOOD 1970; ex ORIZABA 1959; launched as EBBELLA; Sisters: **80521 MARIANNA DORMIO** (It) ex ANNA NIELSEN 1970; ex SIWEKA 1961: ⋆**80522 KORNAT** (Ys) ex FIDAS 1967; ex SUNNY BOY 1965; ex MONTEREY 1964; ex NORDFARER 1957.

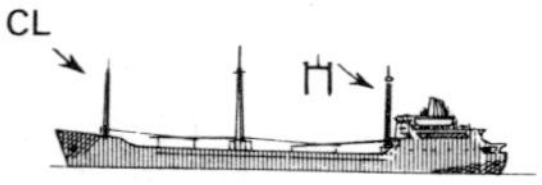

KMKF H13
80530 ANTHOULA I. Cy/No 1965; C; 500/1200; 71.73 × 3.77/5.31 (235.33 × 12.37/17.42); M; 12.5; ex CALANDPLEIN; ex MARMARA 1974; ex MARMORFJELL 1970; Probable sister: **80531 SEA CROWN** (No) ex MARMORHAV 1973; ex MARMORIAN 1968; ex MARMORHAV 1967.

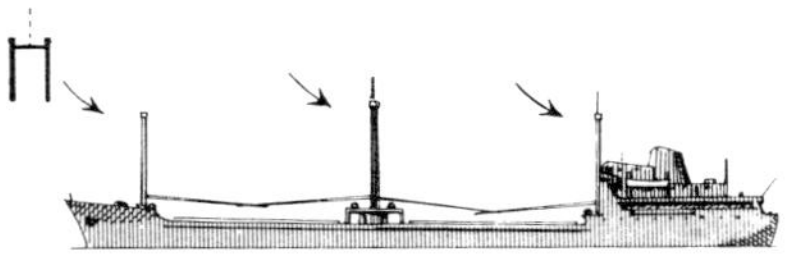

KMKF H13
80540 EVANGELIA. Gr/Sp 1964; C; 2800; 93.68 × 6.13 (307.35 × 20.11); M; —; ex ARGO 1974; ex MANGO 1969; launched as MALKENES.

KMKF H13
80560 GOLDEN SUMMER. Sg/Ne 1957; C; 850; 73.31 × 4.45 (240.52 × 14.6); M; 13; ex HOLMBURN 1975.

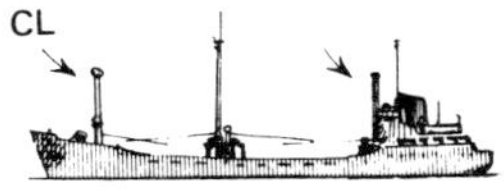

KMKF H13
80580 TZIMANIS. Pa/FRG 1952; C; 1200; 71.84 × 4.69 (235.7 × 15.39); M; 10; ex KATELINA 1977; ex MERIDIAN STAR 1976; ex TANGFOSS 1973; ex SKOTTFOSS 1972; ex WAKENITZ 1965; ex EDUARD BECKER 1960.

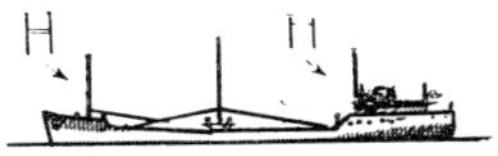

KMKF H13
80610 MYRTIDIOTISSA II. Gr/Br 1957; C; 1000; 65.41 × 4.07 (214.6 × 13.35); M; 12; ex KIRTONDYKE 1975.

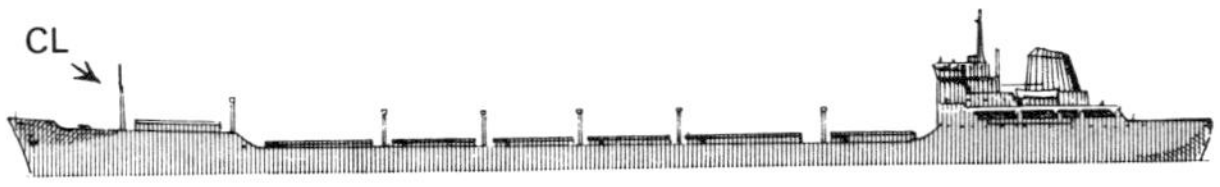

KMKF H13
80630 IDA TERESA. It/It 1965; B; 15900; 190.48 × 9.93 (624.93 × 32.98); M; —; Sisters (It flag): **80631 ELEONORA F; 80632 ALESSANDRA F;** (Pd flag—some have taller funnels): **⋆80633 ZIEMIA GDANSKA; ⋆80634 ZIEMIA LUBUSKA; ⋆80635 ZIEMIA SZCZECINSKA; ⋆80636 ZIEMIA WIELKOPOLSKA.**

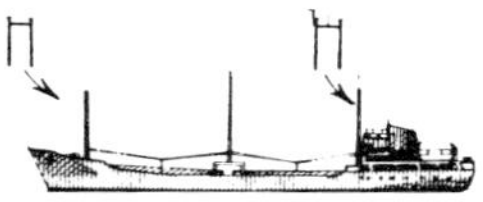

KMKF H13
80550 RAMSLI. No/FRG 1957; C; 1000; 71.38 × 4.7 (234.19 × 15.42); M; 12; ex AUSTVIK 1980; ex MARIA ALTHOFF 1967.

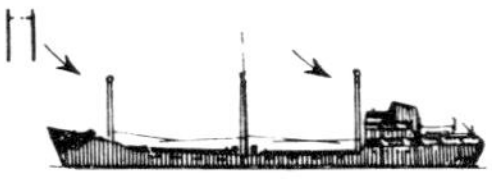

KMKF H13
80570 CHARTA. Pa/FRG 1958; C; 1000; 71.4 × 4.68 (234.25 × 15.35); M; 12; ex NEUWARDERSAND 1971; ex HAMME 1965. Sister: **80571 SEELAND** (Cy) ex GRETHE REITH 1969; ex BEROLINA 1964.

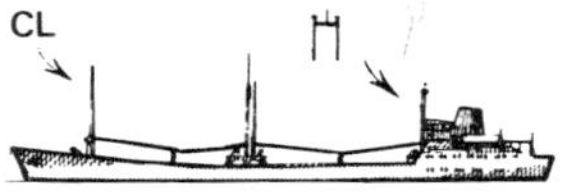

KMKF H13
80590 LAGO ATITLAN. Gu/FRG 1959; C; 2000; 86.06 × 5.64 (282.35 × 18.5); M; 14; ex ROTERSAND 1973.

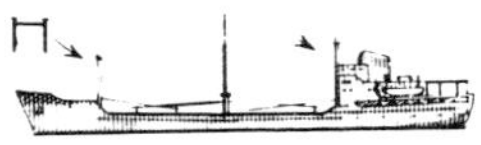

KMKF H13
● **80600 LE SCANDINAVE.** No/No 1957; C; 1400; 72.55 × 4.74 (238.02 × 15.55); M; 12.

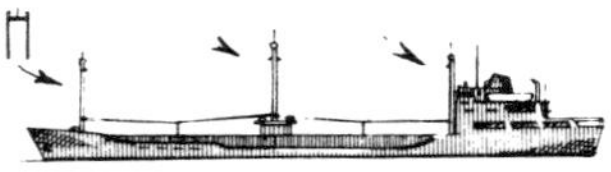

KMKF H13
80620 HTAN TAW YWA. Bm/FRG 1961; C; 2700; 91.5 × 6.03 (300.2 × 19.78); M; —; ex LINDO 1968; Similar (lengthened): **80621 DONGA** (Pa) ex GEORGIOS P P 1980; ex OLYMPIOS ATHINA 1980; ex EIRIN MARU 1979; ex HABERNIS 1974; ex BONGO 1969.

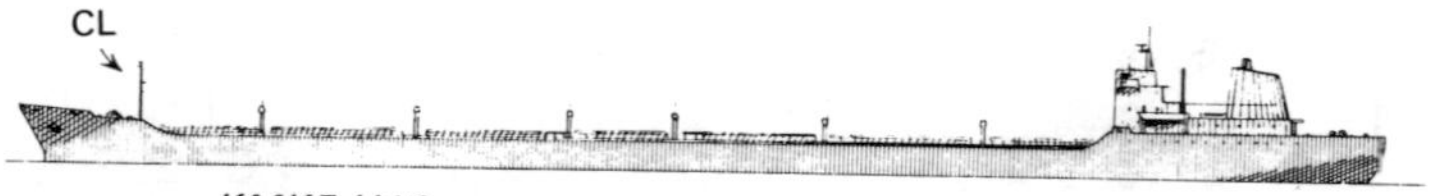

KMKF H13
80640 ANNA BIBOLINI. It/It 1967; B; 276.00; 213.32 × 12.51 (699.87 × 41.04); M; 17.25.

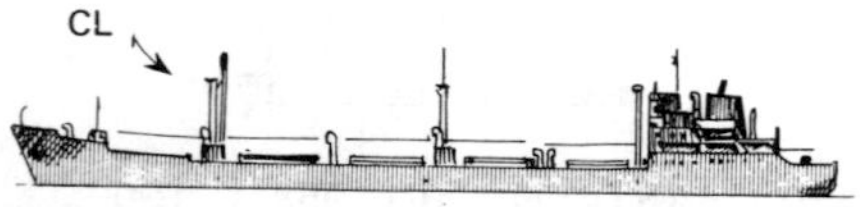

KMKF H13
80650 BANGLAR JOY. Bh/Br 1961; C; 4900/7200; 137.17 × 7.65/8.57 (450.03 × 25.1/28.12); M; 15; ex MARDULCE 1976; ex GILSLAND 1968.

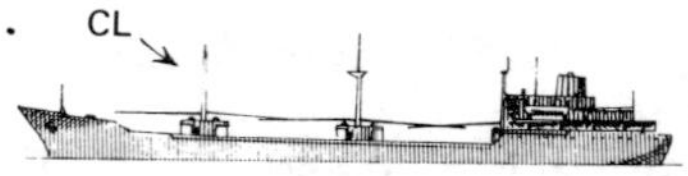

KMKF H13
80660 MINFU. Pa/FRG 1965; C; 2700/4300; 116.74 × 6.36/7.54 (383.01 × 20.87/24.74); M; 15; ex MARTIN SCHRODER; Sister: **80661 SHOU SHAN** (Pa) ex MONIQUE SCHRODER.

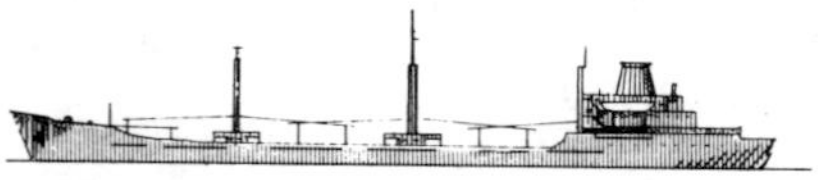

KMKF H13
● **80670 LOS CARIBES.** Pa/Br 1969; C; 3200/5100; 121.62 × 6.63/7.91 (399 × 21.75/25.95); M; 16; ex CARIBE VI 1977; ex CHRISTIANE BOLTEN 1977.

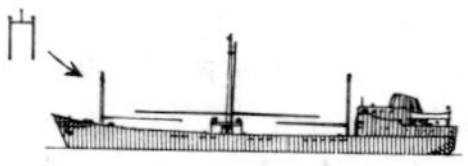

KMKF H3
80680 GOOD YEAR. Th/FRG 1953; C; 600; 63.71 × 5.06 (209.02 × 16.6); M; 12; ex HOLMNI; ex HOLMPARK 1974; ex COMMAND 1966; ex COMMANDANT MILLIASSEAU 1965.

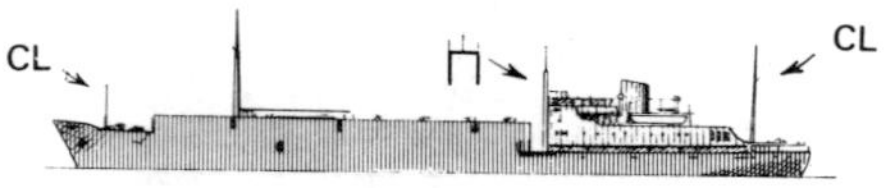

KMKFK H1
80690 GALLOWAY EXPRESS. Li/FRG 1960/77; LS; —; 119.49 × 5.68/6.41 (392.03 × 18.64/21.03; M; 16; Converted from general cargo 1977.

KMKFK H1
● **80700 ASUNCION.** Py/Ne 1961; C; 800; 77.17 × 4.02 (253.18 × 13.19); M; 11.25; ex ADARA 1973; Sisters **80701 VILLARRICA** (Py) ex SITULA 1973; **80702 FEDROS** (Br) ex TALITA 1977; **80703 FILON** (Gr) ex NASHABA 1977; **80704 RITSA M** (Gr) ex SOLON; ex NASHIRA 1977.

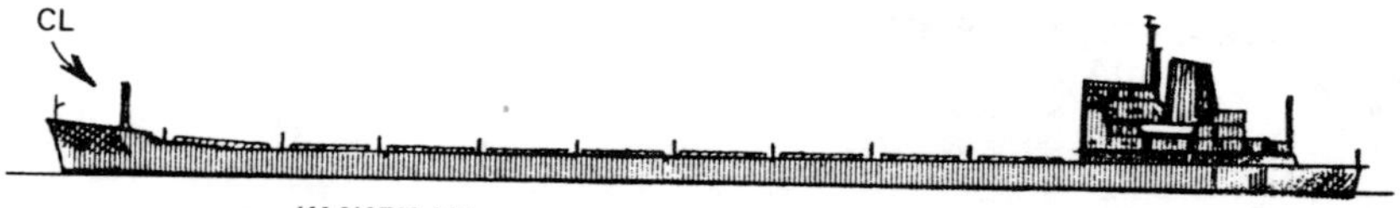

KMKFK H1
80710 JHANSI KI RANI. In/Br 1975; B; 42100; 245.37 × 13.83 (805.02 × 45.37); M; 15.25; Sisters: **80711 JALAVIHAR; 80712 KASTURBA.**

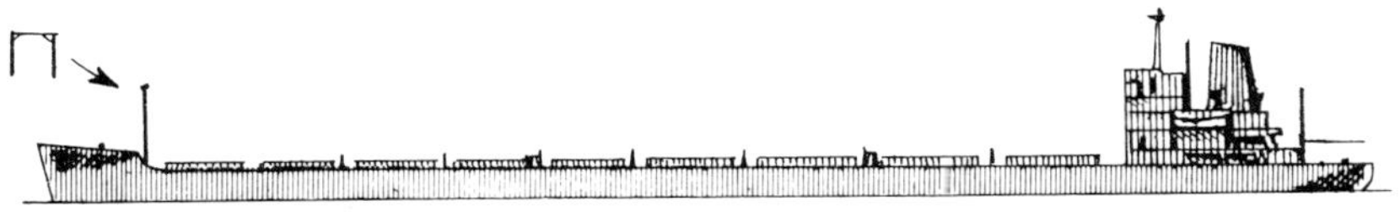

KMKFK H1
80720 BALTIC NEPTUNE. Li/Br 1966; B; 40800; 249.94 × 13.36 (820 × 43.83); M; 15; ex PANAMAX JUPITER 1980; ex NORDIC TALISMAN 1977; ex NAESS TALISMAN 1974.

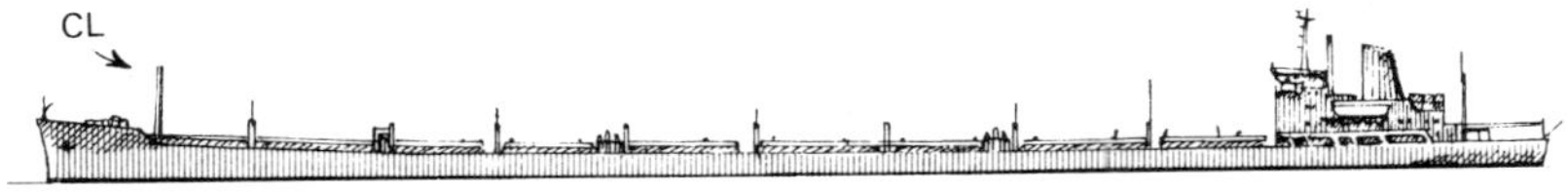

KMKFK H1
80730 SATYA KAILASH. In/Br 1967; B; 42200; 245.37 × 13.84 (805.02 × 45.41); ex GALLIC BRIDGE 1974; Sister: **80731 PROTEUS** (Gr) ex WESTMINSTER BRIDGE 1973.

KMKFK H1
80740 KEN SUCCESS. Pa/FRG 1963; B; 21300; 201.96 × 11.77 (662.6 × 38.62); M; 15.5; ex MYSTRAS 1980; ex NORDIC ROVER 1977; ex NAESS COMET 1974.

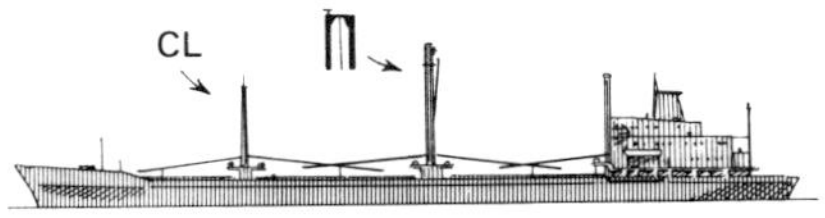

KMKFK H1
★**80750 LEONID TELIGA.** Pd/FRG 1969; C; 2800/5700; 125.18 × 6.45/7.64 (410.7 × 21.16/25.07); M; 12; ex SCOL EMINENT 1976; ex CAPE CANAVERAL 1974; ex CAPE RACE 1972; ex KATHE WIARDS 1970; Sisters: **80751 TRIMAR SKY** (Pa) ex INALOTTE BLUMENTHAL 1980; ex INRE 1979; ex INALOTTE BLUMENTHAL 1978; ex ADELHEID WIARDS 1972; **80752 EBN MAGID** (Ly) ex CAPE SEAR 1975; ex ADEL WEERT WIARDS 1973.

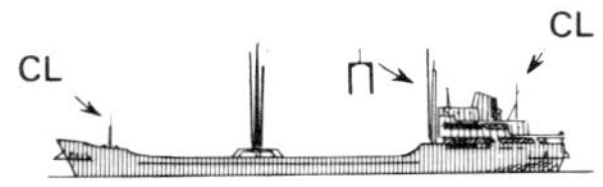

KMKFK H13
● **80760 BRIARTHORN.** Br/Ne 1962; RS; 1500; 80.6 × 4.77 (264.44 × 15.65); M; —; ex ANNE 1973; ex ANNE BOGELUND 1969; Converted from cargo.

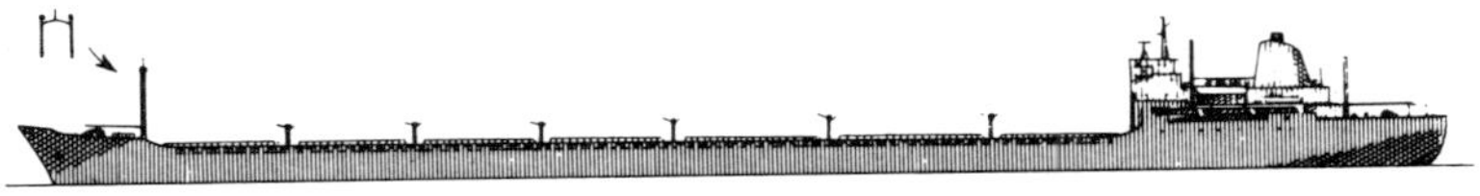

KMKFK H13
80770 CENTAURO. It/It 1962; B; 26400; 229.75 × 11.73 (753.77 × 38.48); M; 15; Lengthened 1967; Sisters (It flag): **80771 POSEIDON; 80772 VOLONTA** ex MAFIO Z 1978; launched as URSA MAJOR; Possibly similar: **80773 GALASSIA.**

KMKFK H13
80780 SAN VINCENZO. Pa/It 1965; B; 14600; 185.25 × 10.45 (597.93 × 34.28); M; 16.25; ex GARDEN GEMINI 1979; ex PORTORIA 1975.

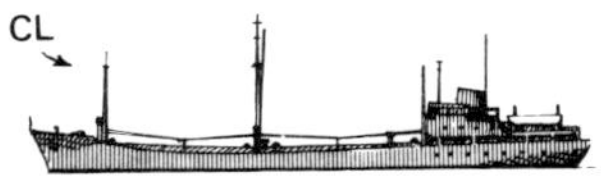

KMKFM H1
80790 VIJAYA AVTAR. In/FRG 1958; C; 1500/2400; 88.8 × 5.08/6.27 (291.34 × 16.67/20.57); M; 13.25; ex VISHVA MARG; ex CYRENE 1968; Sister: **80791 VISHVA VINAY** (In) ex SABRATHA 1968.

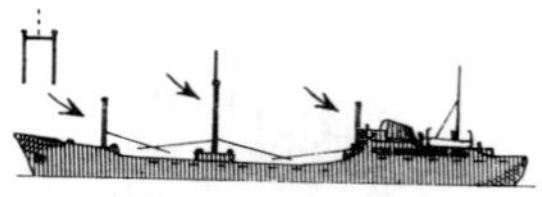

KMKFM H13
80800 PUERTO DE HUELVA. Sp/Sp 1959; C; 1500; 81.21 × 4.8 (266.44 × 15.75); M; 13.5.

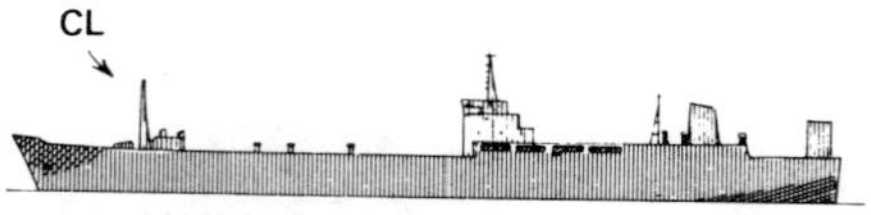

KMKFR H2
80810 KUSHIRO MARU. Ja/Ja 1974; RoC; 4700; 130 × 6.02 (426.51 × 19.75); M; 17.

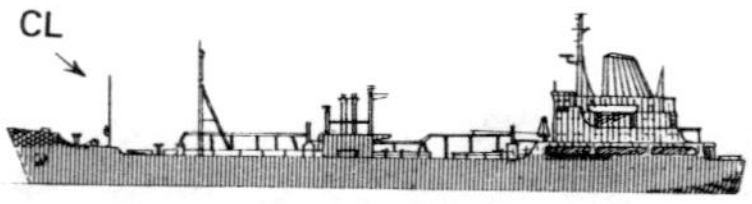

KMK$_2$CMF H1
80820 EIRIK RAUDE. No/FRG 1967; LGC; 6100; 116.31 × 7.77 (381.59 × 25.49); M; 15; ex MUNDOGAS BERMUDA 1976.

KMK$_4$MF H13
80830 TALETE. It/FRG 1967; LGC: 1600; 80.98 × 4.62 (265.68 × 15.16); M; 13; ex THALES 1972.

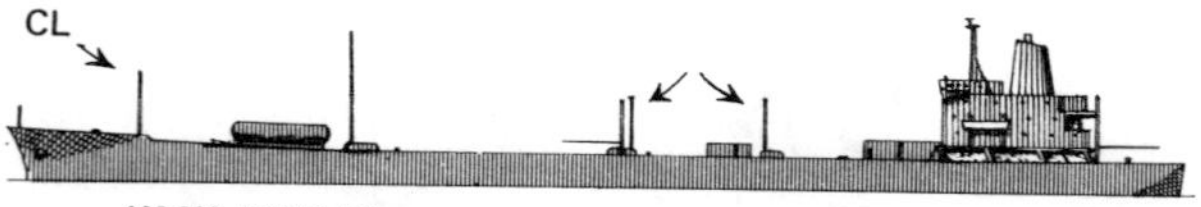

KMK$_3$MFK H
80840 FARADAY. Br/Br 1971; LGC; 19800; 186.85 × 9.75 (613.02 × 31.99); M; 15.75; Sister: **80841 LINCOLNSHIRE** (Br).

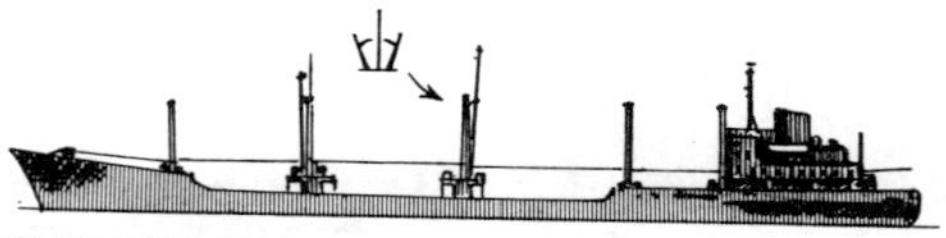

KMK$_3$MFK H13
80850 INDIAN VALOUR. In/FRG 1971; C; 7000/9600; 144.91 × 9.42 (475.43 × 30.91); M; 16; **'36-L'** type; Sister: **80851 INDIAN VENTURE** (In).

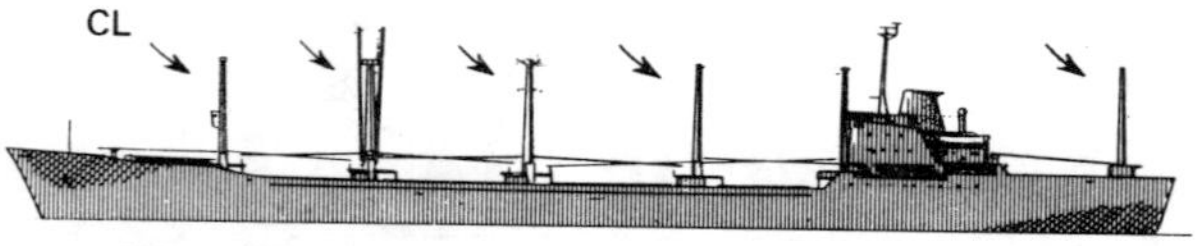

KMK$_3$MFK H13
80860 HOEGH OPAL. No/Fi 1967/75; C; 8200/12100; 182.61 × 8.05/9.4 (599.11 × 26.41/30.84); M; 17; lengthened 1975; Sisters: **80861 HOEGH ORCHID** (No); **80862 HOEGH ORRIS** (No); Similar (taller funnel etc.): **80863 HOEGH PILOT** (No); **80864 HOEGH PRIDE** (No).

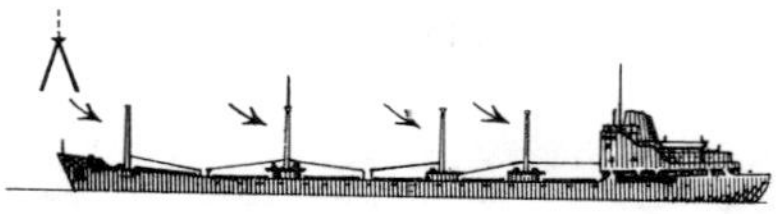

KMK$_2$MF H
80870 MILOS V. Gr/Sw 1954; C; 3700; 112.27 × 6.34 (368.34 × 20.8); M; 12; ex ARABERT; Sister: **80871 HIND G** (Le); ex ARABRITT 1979.

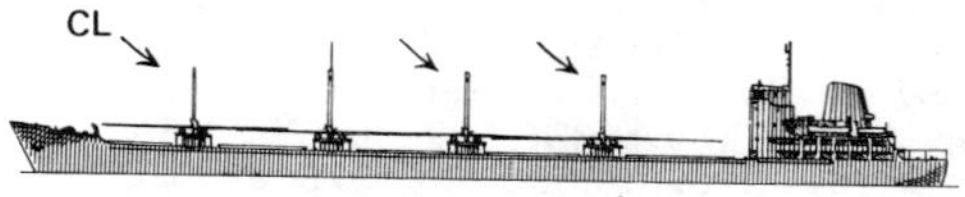

KMK$_2$MF H1
80880 LADY ERSI. Pa/Ja 1957; C; 8500; 147.48 × 8.8 (483.86 × 28.87); M; 14; ex IVI P 1980; ex SAINT LOUIS 1978; ex THAIS HOPE 1968.

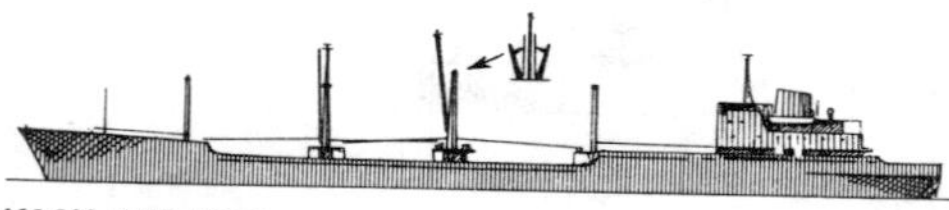

KMK$_2$MF H13
⋆**80890 ADAM ASNYK.** Pd/FRG 1974; C; 7000/9600; 145.04 × 8.23/9.43 (475.85 × 27/30.94); M; 16; **'36-L'** type; Sisters (RC flag): ⋆**80891 CHANGXING;** ⋆**80892 DEXING.**

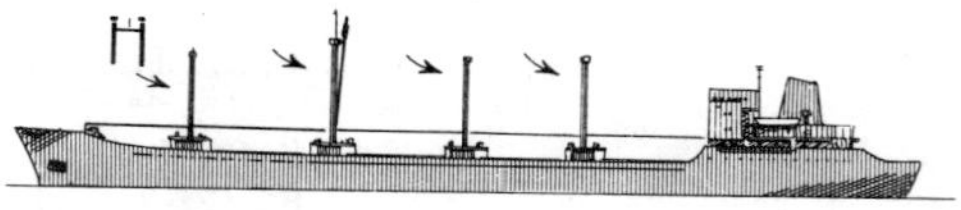

KMK$_2$MF H13
⋆**80900 PETKO R. SLAVEJNOV.** Bu/Ys 1968; C; 9100; 143.64 × 8.87 (471.26 × 29.1); M; 15; launched as ATRIA; Sister: ⋆**80901 IVAN VAZOV** (Bu); launched as ALMAK; Similar (heavier radar mast): **80902 OMDURMAN** (Su).

KMK$_2$MF H13
80910 TEXACO WARRIOR. Ca/Br 1970; Tk; 3300; 98.3 × 6.55 (322.51 × 21.49); M; 12.75; ex ANTERIORITY 1975; ex THUNTANK 6 1972; Sister: **80911 EKFJORD** (Sw); ex AMITY 1977; ex POINTE DE TOULINQUET 1976; ex AMITY 1975; ex THUNTANK 5 1972.

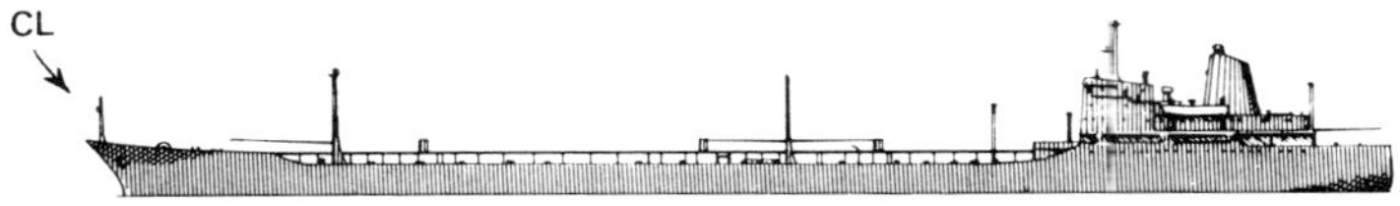

KMK$_2$MFK H13
⋆80920 LISICHANSK. Ru/Ru 1962; Tk; 23100; 207.04 × 11.11 (679.27 × 36.45); M; 16.5; Sisters (Ru flag): **⋆80921 LENKORAN; ⋆80922 LYUBOTIN.**

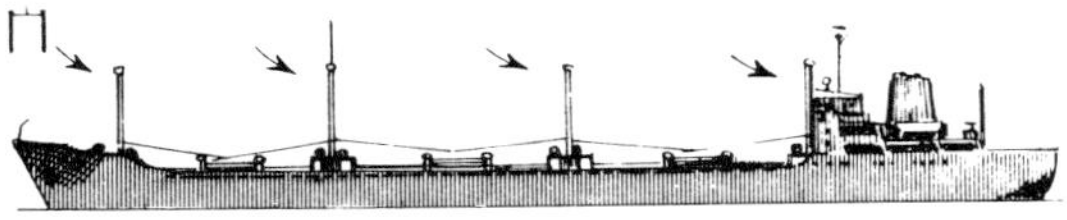

KMK$_2$MFK H13
80930 DOBROTA. Ma/Ja 1960; B; 11100; 161.96 × 9.21 (531.4 × 30.21); M; 14.75; ex ROSINA TOPIC; Sister: **80931 LJUTA** (Ma); ex SERAFIN TOPIC 1979.

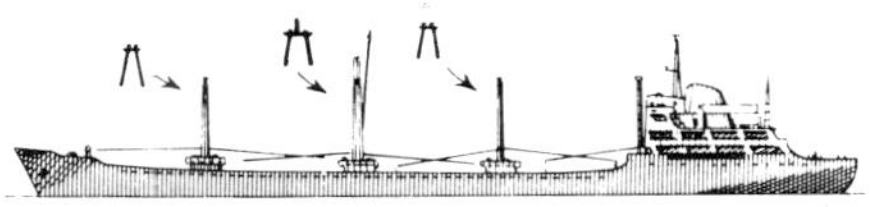

KMK$_2$MFK H13
80940 IRENE. Pi/Ja 1966; C; 7100; 131.93 × 7.6 (432.8 × 24.9); M; 15.

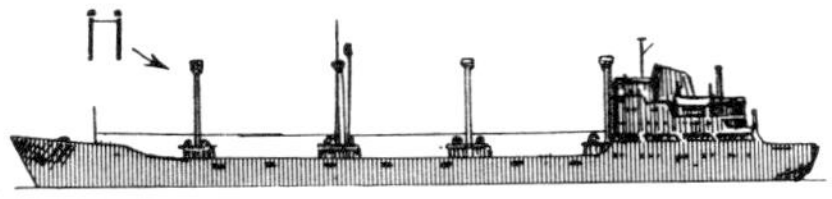

KMK$_2$MFK H13
80950 SHIQMA. Is/FRG 1961; Con; 6300; 127.36 × 7.27 (417.85 × 23.85); M; 15.5; ex PINE 1975; ex SHIQMA 1975; Converted from general cargo 1975; Drawing shows vessel before conversion; Cargo gear may now be removed; Sisters: **80951 ALON** (Is); ex PECAN 1976; ex ALON 1976; ex PECAN 1975; ex ALON 1974; **80952 ESHEL** (Is); ex PALM 1975; ex ESHEL 1974.

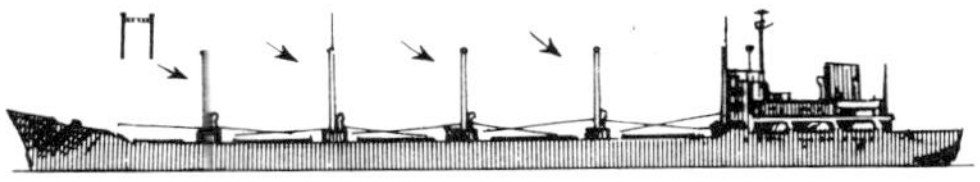

KMK$_2$M$_2$FK H13
80960 NOBLE FIVE. Pa/Ja 1959; B; 9000; 148.52 × 9.04 (487.27 × 29.66); M; 13.5; ex ARCHANGELOS MICHAIL 1980; ex KIKUSAI MARU 1970.

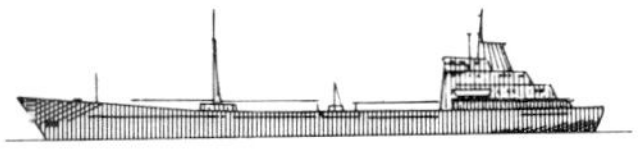

KMKMF H
80970 NYANAW. Gh/FRG 1969; R; 2000; 93.71 × 5.51 (307.45 × 18.08); M; 17.5; ex COOLER SCAN 1974.

KMKMF H
80980 FREEZER FINN. Fi/FRG 1968; R; 500/1200; 75.6 × 81/5 (248.03 × 12.5/16.4); M; 14.75; ex FREEZER SCAN 1973; Sisters: **80981 REEFER TRADER** (Cy); ex ICE FLOWER 1977; ex FRIGO SCAN 1973; **80982 JOKULFJELL** (Ic); ex BYMOS 1975; Probable sister: **80983 DANA FRIO** (Br); ex ZALAGH 1976; ex AHMOS 1972.

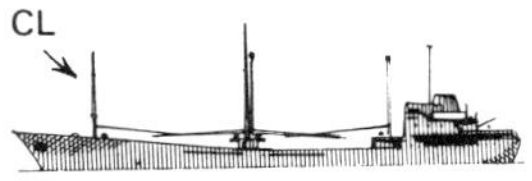

KMKMF H
80990 MINDANAO TRANSPORT. Pi/FRG 1961; C; 900/1500; 81.82 × —/5.27 (268.44 × —/17.29); M; 14.5; ex PISO 1974; ex VINLAND SAGA 1969.

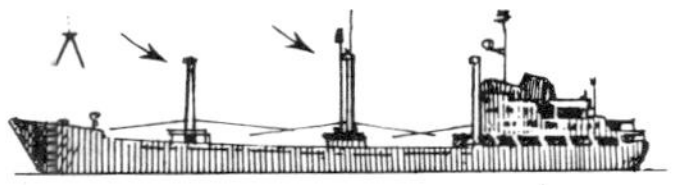

KMKMF H
⋆81000 NOVY BUG. Ru/Rm 1963; C; 3300; 100.59 × 6.55 (330.02 × 21.49); M; 12.5; Sisters (Ru flag): **⋆81001 NOVY DONBASS; ⋆81002 NOVAYA KAKHOVKA; ⋆81003 NOVORZHEV; 81004 NOVOSHAKHTINSK.**

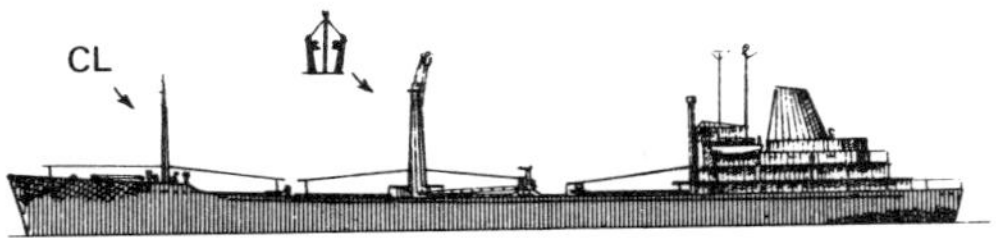

KMKMF H1
● **⋆81010 DA LONG TIAN.** RC/Ja 1966; C/HL; 7010/9450; 152.25 × 8.31/9.48 (499.5 × 27.2/31.1); M; 19; ex CROSTAFELS 1978; Sisters: **⋆81011 DA HONG QIAO** (RC); ex KYBFELS 1979; **⋆81012 WU YI SHAN** (RC); ex BIRKENFELS 1978; **⋆81013 DA QING SHAN** (RC); ex SCHONFELS; **81014 FALKENFELS** (Gr); **81015 HOHENFELS** (Gr).

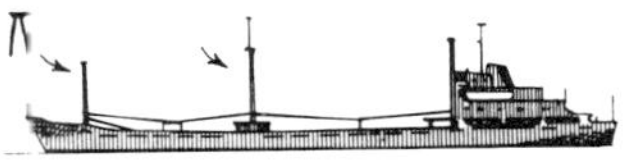

KMKMF H1
81020 MATINA. Gr/FRG 1963; C; 2900; 94.16/6.77 (308.92 × 22.21); M; —; ex BULWARK; ex NAHOON 1971; ex TRONSTAD 1967.

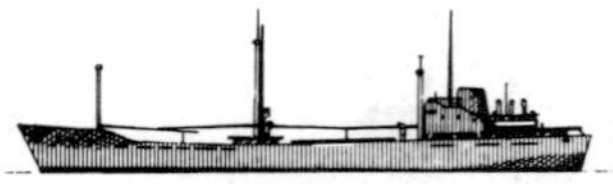

KMKMF H1
81030 ASTRON. Gr/FRG 1952; C; 1200/1900; 78.67 × —/6.24 (258.1 × —/20.47); M; 12; ex LEBANESE WIND 1970; ex SULAPHAT 1967; ex LEAMITRA 1963; ex LEADA.

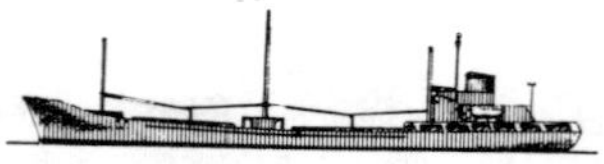

KMKMF H1
81040 MARIA K. Le/FRG 1962; C; 1800; 88.52 × 5.26 (290.42 × 17.26); M; 15.5; ex LA MOLINERA 1980; ex STEPHAN REITH 1972.

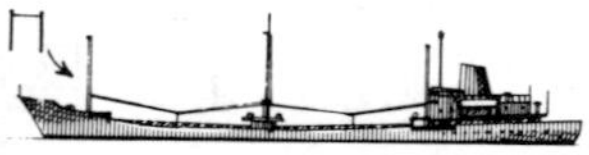

KMKMF H1
● **81050 HAJ ABDUL RAHMAN.** Cy/FRG 1966; C; 2100; 90.05 × 5.67 (295.44 × 18.6); M; 13.75; ex ISABELLE 1978; ex BOTANY BAY 1973; Sisters: **81051 RONA** (Pa); ex CAP FALCON 1980; ex STERN SIRIUS 1973; ex SIRIUS 1972; **81052 ABDUL LATIF** (Cy); ex STERN SATURN; ex SATURN 1974.

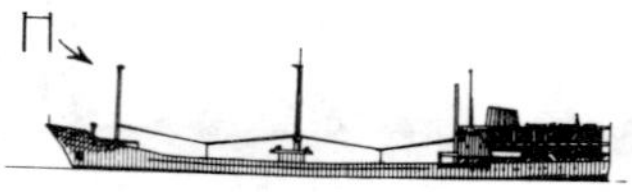

KMKMF H1
81060 ZAMBOANGA CITY. Pi/FRG 1966; CP; 2100; 90.05 × 5.67 (295.44 × 18.6); M; 13.5; ex LUZON TRANSPORT 1975; ex LEINSTER BAY 1973.

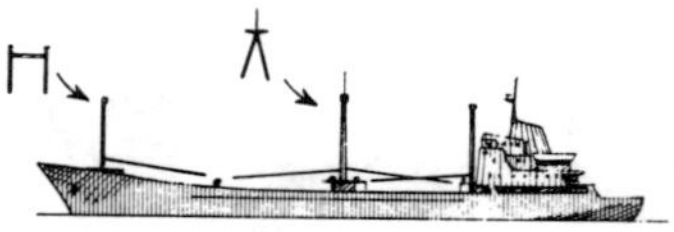

KMKMF H1
⋆**81070 KRUSEVO.** Ys/Sp 1967; C; 1700/2700; 95.54 × —/6.7 (313.45 × —/21.98); M; 14; ex IDRISSI 1969; Sister: **81071 MAGHREB** (In); ex MILJET 1974; ex TARIQ 1969.

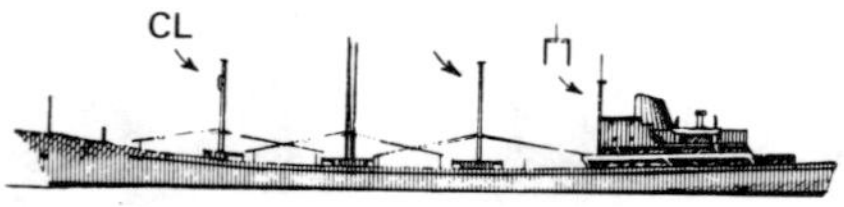

KMKMF H1
81080 MUSING. So/FRG 1957; C; 3900/5400; 130.41 × 6.89/7.77 (427.85 × 22.6/25.49); M; 15.5; ex RENDSBURG 1972; ex TOVE LILIAN 1965.

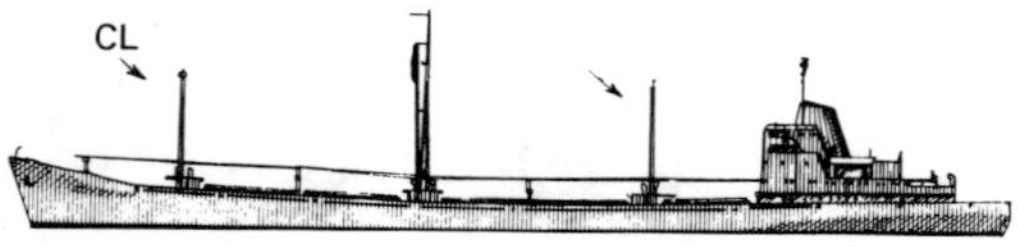

KMKMF H1
81090 OLYMPIAN. Gr/FRG 1962; C; 8200/11000; 158.5 × 8/9.2 (520 × 26.25/30.18); M; 15; ex MARATHA ENDEAVOUR 1971.

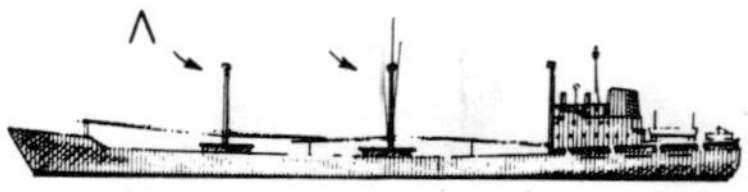

KMKMF H1
81100 BODRUM. Tu/FRG 1961; C; 3100/4400; 115.73 × —/7.16 (379.69 × —/23.49); M; —; Sisters (Tu flag): **81101 MARMARIS 1; 81102 MUGLA;** Similar: **81103 FETHIYE.**

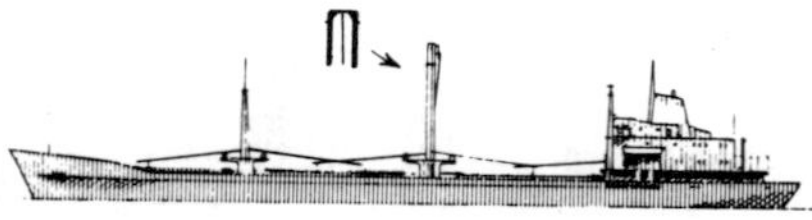

KMKMF H1
81110 JUNO. FRG/FRG 1969; C; 2800/5000; 124.97 × 6.53/7.67 (410 × 21.42/25.16); M; 16.5; Sister: **81111 JUPITER II** (Pa); ex JUPITER 1980.

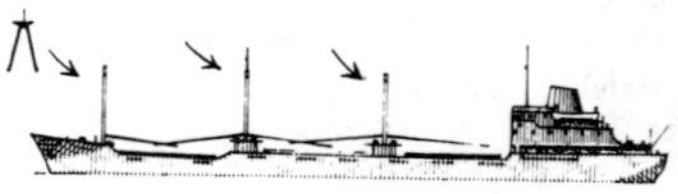

KMKMF H12
81120 PETROLA 30. Gr/FRG 1956; C; 2800; 101 × 6.25 (331.36 × 20.5); M; 12.5; ex PETROLA XXX 1976; ex YELLOW STAR 1 1975; ex ARRAS 1974; ex JULIUS HUGO STINNES 1971; ex MYLADY 1966; Sister: **81121 ISSA 1** (Le); ex VALERIANA 1980; ex SCALMIKE 1976; ex HOLNIS 1974; ex HUGO OLDENDORFF 1969; ex NORA HUGO STINNES 1964.

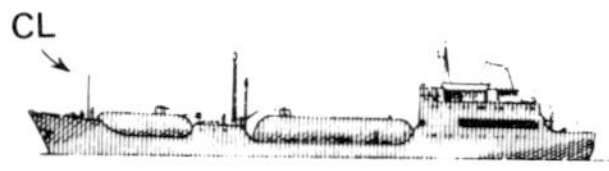

KMKMF H123

● **81130 SILVERSKY.** Br/FRG 1967; LGC; 2900; 90.56 × 6.1 (297.11 × 20.01); M; 12.5; ex MARCO POLO; ex GAZANIA 1970; Sisters: **81131 SILVERSEA** (Br); ex COLUMBUS; ex JANEGAZ 1970; **81132 BYZANTINE ENERGY** (Gr); ex FRIDTJOF NANSEN 1978; Similar: **81133 GAZ PROGRESS** (Pa); ex CORAL OBELIA 1979; ex ARCTIC PROPANE 1971.

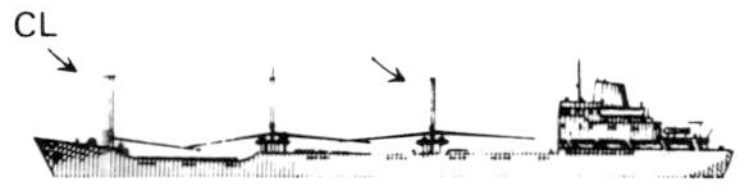

KMKMF H123

● **81140 AVLIS EXPRESS.** —/FRG 1960/70; C; 3500; 110.75 × 6.14 (360.93 × 19.72); M; 12.5; ex MARIA 1981; ex VAMOS 1979; ex BELLATRIX 1 1977; ex KOHOLYT 1971; ex KOHOLYT HUGO STINNES 1971; ex KOHOLYT 1962; Lengthened 1981; Sisters: **81141 ELOUNDA** (Gr); ex AQUILA 1 1977; ex ACHGELIS 1971; ex ACHGELIS HUGO STINNES; **81142 MARISA** (Li); ex MARISA KAR 1981; ex THERISSOS 1980; ex VELEROFONTIS 1975; ex COLUMBA 1975; ex MAK 1971; ex MAK HUGO STINNES 1971.

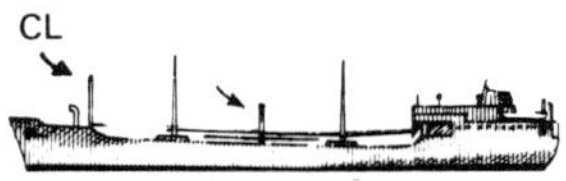

KMKMF H13

81150 NEAPOLIS. Gr/Sw 1952; C; 1500; 87.03 × 4.62 (285.53 × 15.16); M; 11.25; ex SUNNANHAV 1975; ex GAPERN 1967; ex STORFORS 1961.

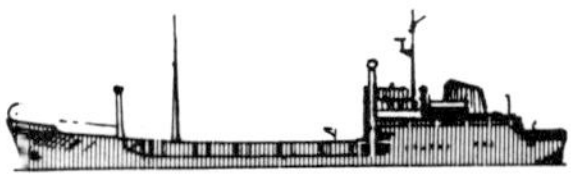

KMKMF H13

81160 PERMINA VIII. Ia/Ne 1954; Tk; 2400; 88.25 × 5.44 (289.53 × 17.85); M; 11.5; ex ELIZABETH BROERE 1966; ex ELIZABETH B. 1960.

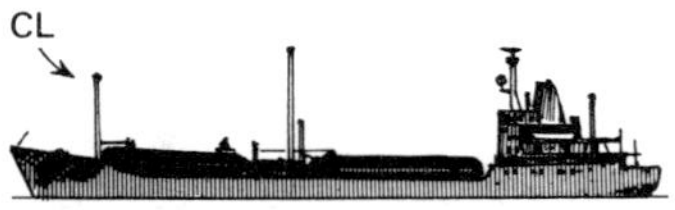

KMKMF H13

81170 THOR. Ma/No 1969; LGC; 3000; 101.94 × 5.72 (334.45 × 18.77); M; 13; ex THOR HEYERDAHL 1979.

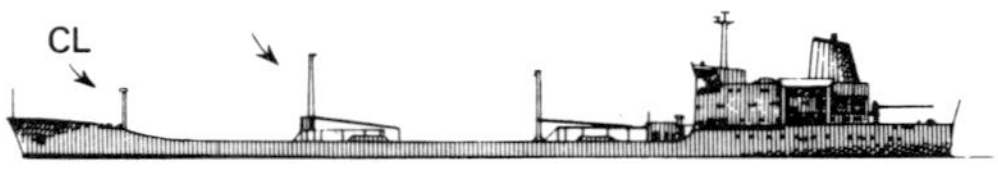

KMKMF H13

81180 MATADI PALM. Br/Br 1970; Tk; 8900; 147.83 × 8.55 (485 × 28.05); M; 15.

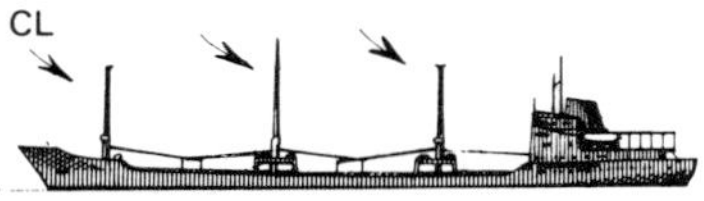

KMKMF H13

81190 LUANA. Pa/FRG 1965; C; 3200; 106.63 × 6.99 (349.84 × 22.93); M; 13.5; ex MAXI PORR 1980.

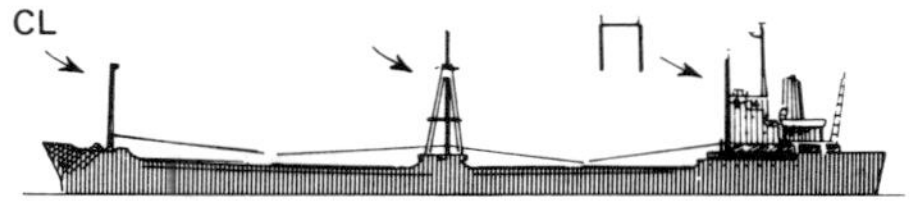

KMKMF H13

81200 SEIYO MARU. Ja/Ja 1971; C/HL; 7000; 131.81 × 8.23 (262.5 × 27); M; 14; Sister: **81201 SAKURA MARU** (Ja); Probable sister: **81202 FORUM STAR** (Gr); ex TACHIBANA MARU.

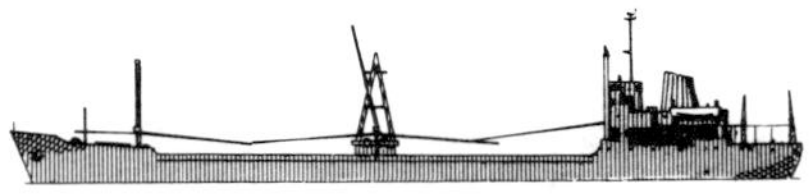

KMKMF H13

● **81210 SANIX ACE.** Pa/Ja 1960; C; 5400; 124.8 × 7.47 (409.45 × 24.51); M; 13.5; ex FUJI MARU 1978.

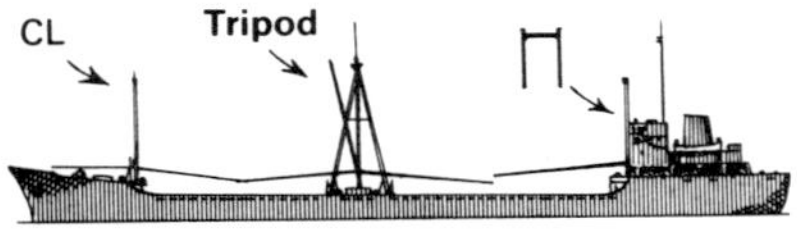

KMKMF H13

81220 CARIBBEAN STAR No 1. Pa/Ja 1959; C/HL; 5000; 122.81 × 7.39 (409.92 × 24.25); M; 13.5; ex KUMANO MARU 1975.

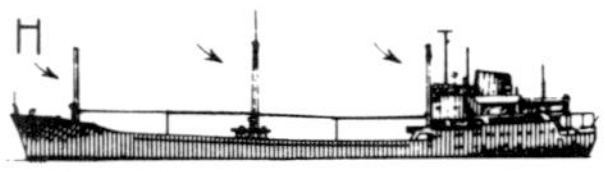

KMKMF H13

● **81230 REEM 1.** Gr/Ne 1971; C; 3000; 91.45 × 7.18 (300.03 × 23.56); M; 13.5; ex RAHA 1980; ex NELLY MAERSK 1976; Sister: **81231 ATLAS RIVER** (Gr); ex NIELS MAERSK 1976.

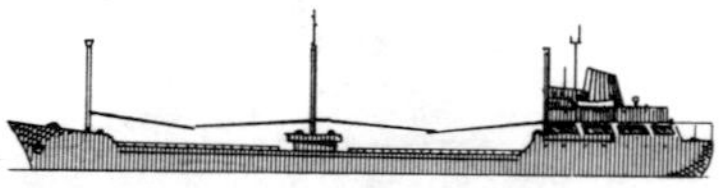

KMKMF H13
81240 LAGADA BAY. Gr/FRG 1968; C; 4400; 110.75 × 7.29 (363.35 × 23.92); M; —; ex INGE 1978; ex URSULA C. 1977; ex ALEXANDRA BOTELHO 1974; Sister: **81241 LAGADA BEACH** (Gr); ex EVA-MARIA C. 1978; ex LUISITA BOTELHO 1974.

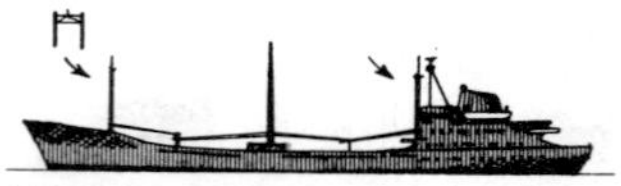

KMKMF H13
81250 NAVISTAR. Le/FRG 1959; C; 1500; 91.01 × 4.85 (298.59 × 15.91); M; 14; ex BALTIC JET.

KMKMF H13
81260 DIMACHK. Sy/No 1963; C; 2700; 91.52 × 6.03 (300.26 × 19.78); M; 12.25; ex ANNELIESE PORR 1975.

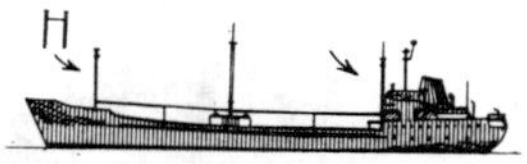

KMKMF H13
81270 MARANAR. Cy/FRG 1961; C; 800/1200; 76.1 × —/5.03 (249.67 × —/16.5); M; 12; ex LAUTER 1973; ex SIEGFRIED 1965; ex KARL-HEINZ PARCHMANN 1962.

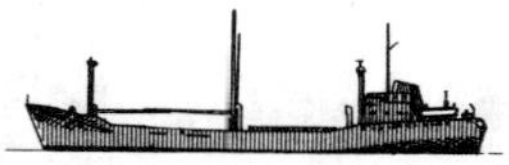

KMKMF H13
81280 MINOA. Cy/FRG 1953; C; 2000; 73.43 × 6.48 (240.91 × 21.26); M; 12; ex EL MINA 1972; ex JOHANNA 1965.

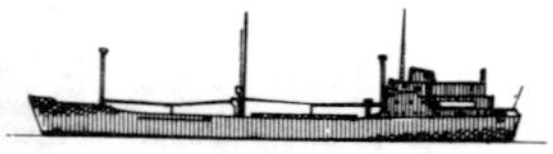

KMKMF H13
81290 NICOS A. Pa/FRG 1956; C; 1200/2200; 78.67 × 4.98/6.57 (258.1 × 16.34/21.56); M; —; ex RAMPART I 1977; ex RAMPART 1976; ex LEABETH 1966.

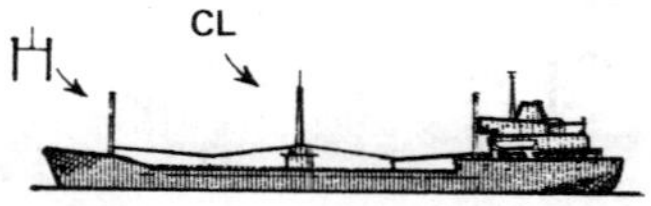

KMKMF H13
81300 LESLIE. Gr/FRG 1965; C; 2400; 92.06 × 5.6 (302.03 × 18.37); M; 13; ex ANNA REHDER 1973; Sister: ⋆**81301 KRKA** (Ys); ex MATTHIAS REHDER 1974.

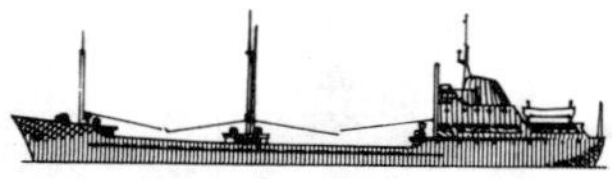

KMKMF H13
⋆**81310 CAMAGUEY.** Cu/Ja 1959; C; 2300; 93.22 × 5.77 (305.84 × 18.93); M; —.

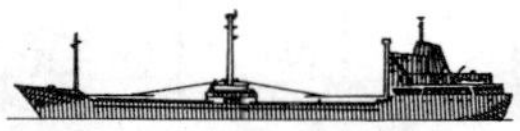

KMKMF H13
81320 SAUMATY. Fr/FRG 1967; C; 800/1400; 79.23 × 4.22/5.51 (259.9 × 13.85/18.08); M; 13.75; ex ASSER RIG 1973; ex VELA 1969; ex ASSER RIG 1968.

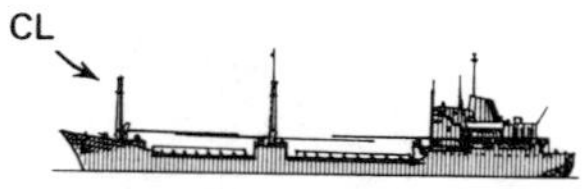

KMKMF H13
81330 MARINER. Pa/Ne 1962; C; 1500; 81.84 × 5.45 (268.5 × 17.88); M; 12.5; ex MARIANA III 1974; ex MARIANA 1973; ex MARION 1970; ex KAISA DAN 1969; Sister: **81331 ETAI** (Br); ex YTAI 1977; ex CARMELA 1976; ex BAROK 1974; ex RAILA DAN 1969.

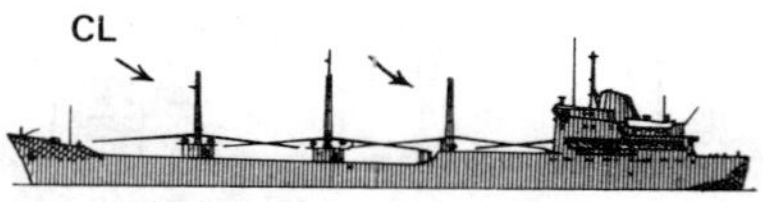

KMKMF H13
81340 TACAMAR VII. Pa/Fi 1965; C; 3200/4800; 118.01 × —/7.13 (387.17 × —/23.39); M; —; ex TAMANACO 1980; ex CITTA DI VIAREGGIO 1974; ex CONCORDIA FINN 1971; ex FINNMILL 1970; ex CONCORDIA FINN 1969; ex FINNMILL 1968; ex FINNBROD 1967.

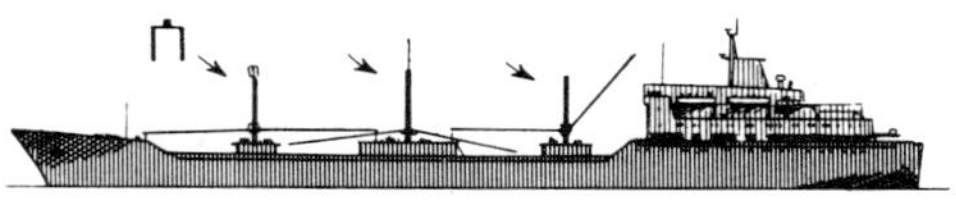

KMKMF H13
★81350 ZULAWY. Pd/Pd 1974; FC; 8100; 151.31 × 7.4 (496.42 × 24.28); M; 19; **'B 68'** type; Sisters (Pd flag): **★81351 KASZUBY II; ★81352 WINETA.**

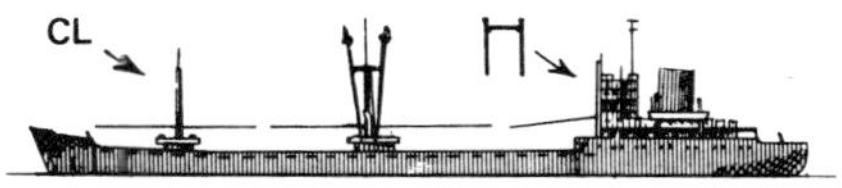

KMKMF H13
81360 AI FANOURIS. Gr/Ja 1956; C/HL; 4900; 122.81 × 7.37 (402.92 × 24.18); M; 14; ex ROYAL 1978; ex ATAGO MARU 1973.

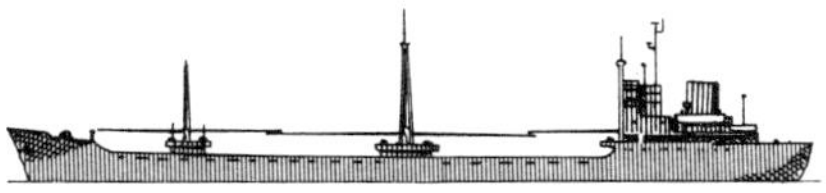

KMKMF H13
81370 UNION BALTIMORE. Pa/Ja 1958; C; 8700; 147.33 × 8.6 (483.37 × 28.22); M; 14; ex KIBI MARU 1978.

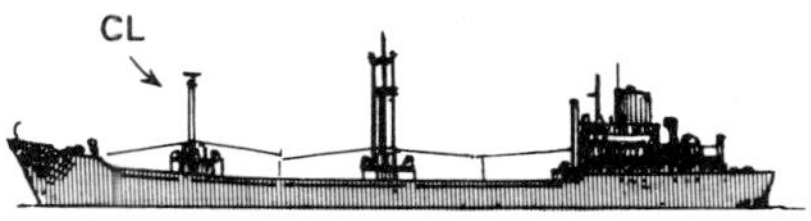

KMKMF H13
★81380 YONG CHENG. RC/Br 1968; C; 3200/5000; 121.62 × 6.61/7.89 (399 × 21.69/25.89); M; 16.5; ex PAUL SCHRODER 1981; Sister: **★81381 FANG CHENG** (RC); ex PETER SCHRODER 1981.

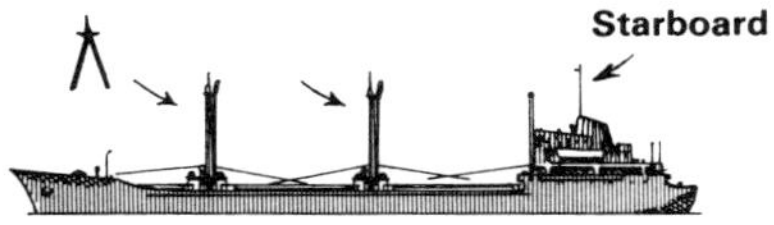

KMKMF H13
81390 ASTRID SCHULTE. Cy/FRG 1967; C; 2200/3600; 107.85 × 6.31/7.42 (353.84 × 20.7/24.34); M; 15.5; ex CAP MALEAS 1978; ex ASTRID SCHULTE 1976; Sister: **81391 MORITZ SCHULTE** (Cy).

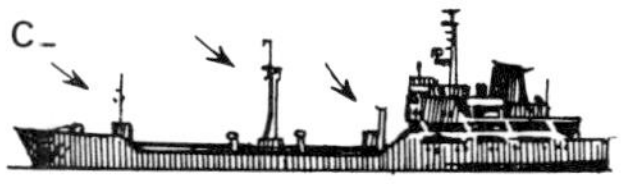

KMKMF H13
★81400 ALIOT. Ru/Fi 1970; WT/Ch; 3100; 93.88 × 6.5 (308.01 × 21.33); M; 14; Sisters (Ru flag): **★81401 POLLUKS; ★81402 PROTSION.**

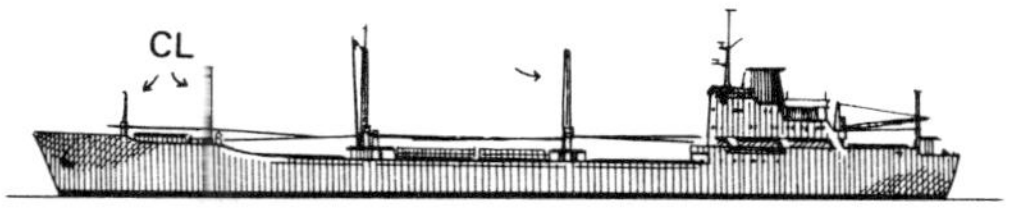

KMKMFCK H13
● **81410 FERNANDOEVERETT.** Li/Fi 1964/69; C/Con; 8700; 152 × 8.6 (500 × 28.7); M; 16; ex FINNHAWK; ex MALTESHOLM 1976; Converted from cargo and lengthened 1969; Sisters: **81411 CORDILLERA** (Pa); ex FINNARROW; ex VASAHOLM 1976; **81412 CORRAL** (Pa); ex MAH 1980; ex FINN-ENSO **81413 CONDOR** (Ch); ex PALLADIA; ex FINNMAID 1979; **81414 POYANG** (Br); ex ASIAN EXPORTER 1975; ex FINNBOSTON 1973; ex FINNENSO 1964.

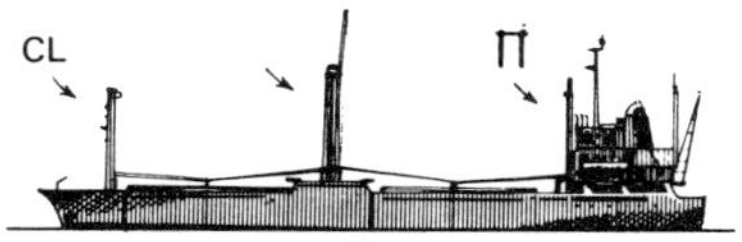

KMKMFK H
81420 EBN JUBAIR. Ly/Ja 1976; C; 3500/6200; 105.7 × 7.5/7.62 (346.78 × 24.61/25); M; 13; Sister: **81421 EBN BATUTA** (Ly).

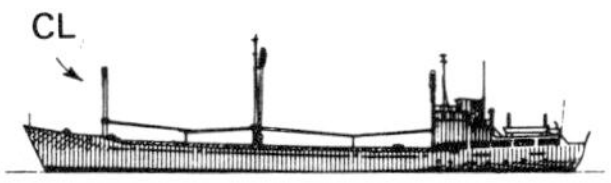

KMKMFK H1
81430 CIRCLE PIONEER. Pa/FRG 1959; C; 1600/2300; 88.85 × 5.08/6.27 (291.5 × 16.67/20.57); M; 13; ex STA MARIA 1975; ex MIEKE LEGENHAUSEN 1969.

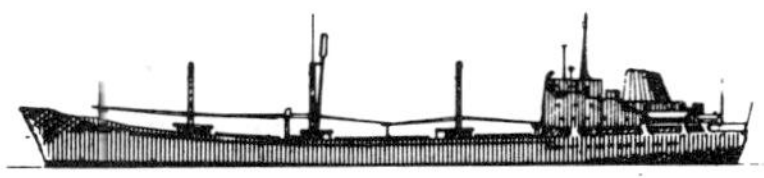

KMKMFK H1
★81440 RHON. DDR/Sw 1960; C; 2700/4300; 114.33 × —/7.19 (375 × —/23.59); M; 14.5; ex BINDAL 1964.

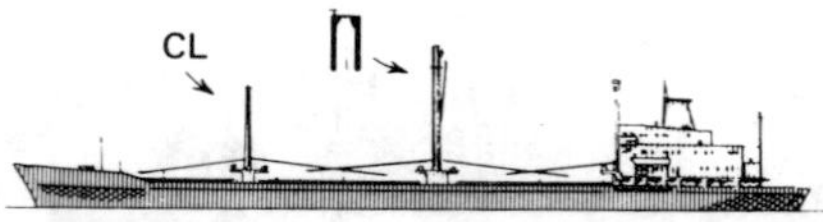

KMKMFK H1

● ⋆**81450 LEONID TELIGA.** Pd/FRG 1969; C; 2800/5700; 125.18 × 6.45/7.64 (410.7 × 21.16/25.07); M; 12; ex SCOL EMINENT 1976; ex CAPE CANAVERAL 1974; ex CAPE RACE 1972; ex KATHE WIARDS 1970; Sisters: **81451 TRIMAR SKY** (Pa); ex INALOTTE BLUMENTHAL 1980; ex INRE 1979; ex INALOTTE BLUMENTHAL 1978; ex ADELHEID WIARDS 1972; **81452 EBN MAGID** (Ly); ex CAPE SEAR 1975; ex ADEL WEERT WIARDS 1973.

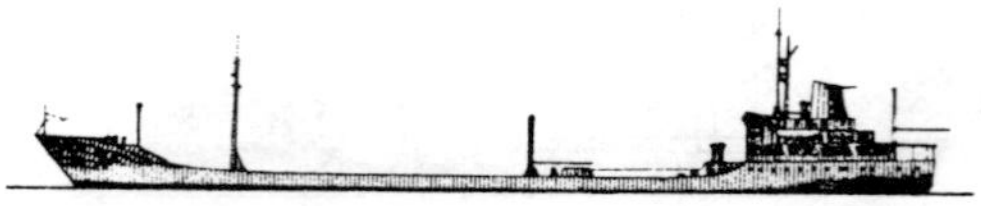

KMKMFK H13

81460 PERMINA 109. Ia/It 1973; Tk; 7700; 140.21 × 7.9 (460.01 × 25.92); M; 15; ex DONNA GABRIELLA 1974; Sister: **81461 ELISA d'ALESIO** (It); ex DONNA MARIELLA.

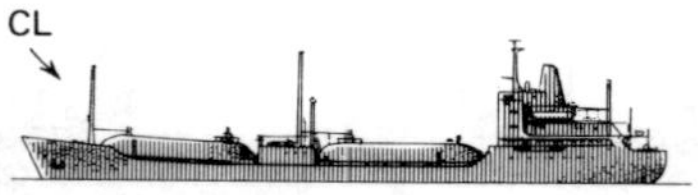

KMKMFK H13

81470 ELISABETTA MONTANARI. It/No 1969; LGC; 3300; 101.94 × 6.06 (334.45 × 19.88); M; 13.75; ex CATY MULTINA 1978; ex CABO TRES MONTES 1971; Sisters: **81471 CRISTINA MONTANARI** (It); ex HOEGH SCOUT 1974; launched as RITA; **81472 TROIKA** (No); Similar: **81473 THOR** (Ma); ex THOR HEYERDAHL 1979.

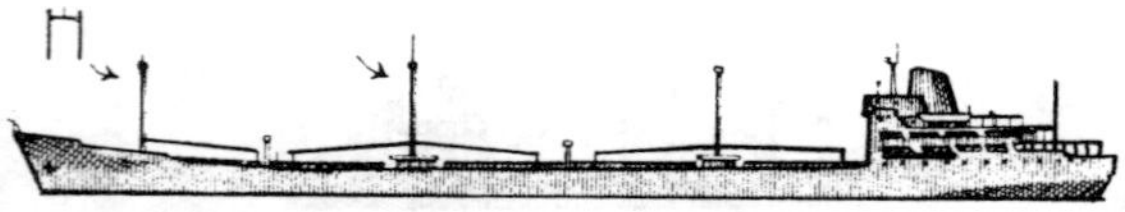

KMKMFK H13

81480 EOLIA. It/It 1964; B; 10600; 160.1 × 9.6 (525.26 × 31.5); M; 16; Probably similar (It flag): **81481 ILICE; 81482 ORFEO.**

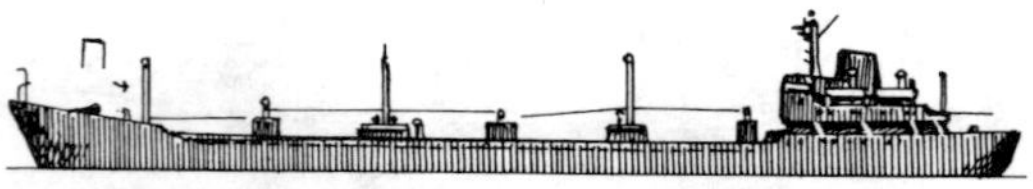

KMKMFK H13

⋆**81490 PRIBOY.** Ru/Sw 1964; FC; 10900; 156.93 × 7.4 (514.86 × 24.28); M; 18.25; Sisters (Ru flag): ⋆**81491 KARL LINNE;** ⋆**81492 KHIBINSKIE GORY;** ⋆**81493 KRYMSKIE GORY;** ⋆**81494 LENINSKIYE GORY;** ⋆**81495 URALJSKIE GORY.**

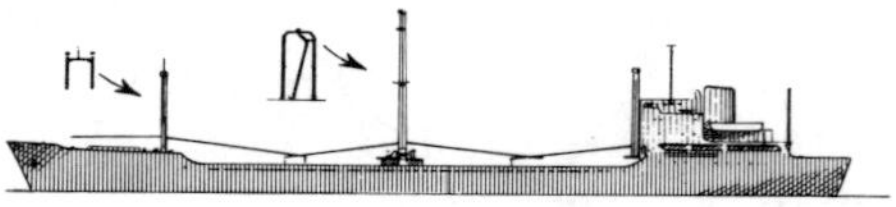

KMKMFK H13

81500 YACU WASI. Pe/Ja 1962; C/HL; 7400; 133.66 × 8 (438.52 × 26.25); M; 14; ex GOLIATH 1980; ex KOREAN DIAMOND 1980; ex WAKASA MARU 1978.

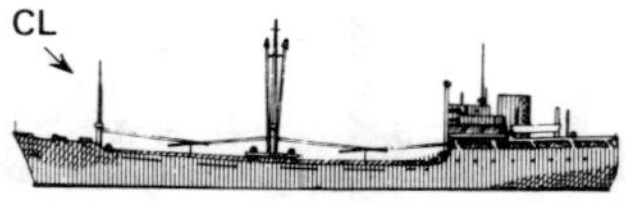

KMKMFK H13

● **81510 JOHNNY K.** Cy/FRG 1957; C; 3200; 95.89 × 7.39 (314.6 × 24.25); M; 13.25; ex KEKENIS 1973; ex PHONIZIEN 1971.

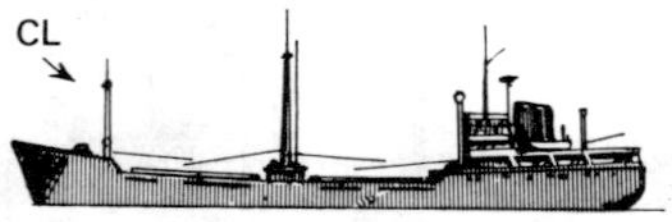

KMKMFK H13

81520 SKIPPER. Pa/FRG 1957; C; 2000/3100; 95.94 × 6.08/7.39 (314.76 × 19.95/24.25); M; 13; ex CONTI MED 1974; ex CLIPPER ARGONAUT 1974; ex SOVEREIGN CRYSTAL 1974; ex ERIKA 1970.

KMKMFK H13

81530 AEGEAN SEA. Pa/Fr 1962; C; 7500/11100; 160.2 × 8.1/10; (525.9 × 26.57/32.8); M; —; ex SILVERBEACH 1972; ex TOTEM STAR 1964; ex NORSE CORAL 1963; Launched as TOTEM STAR; Sister: **81531 NEW CORAL SEA** (Pa); ex CORAL SEA 1977; ex SILVERSEA 1972; ex TOTEM QUEEN 1964; launched as NORSE REEF.

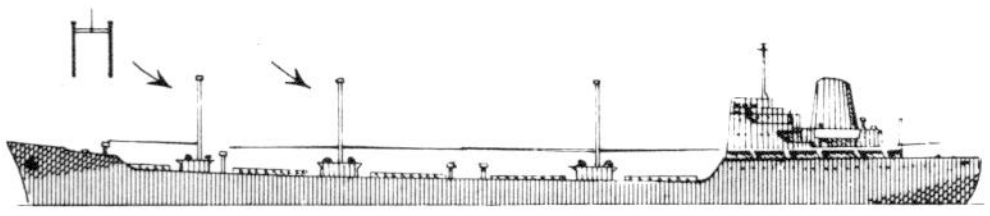

KMKMFK H13
81540 ALHAJA MAMA BAKARE. Pa/Ja 1957; C; 10300; 154.84 × 9.36 (508.01 × 30.71); T; —; ex THARROS 1977; Similar: **81541 DUPE BAKARE** (Pa); ex RYTHME 1977.

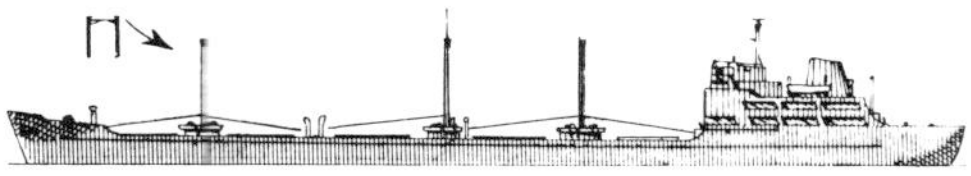

KMKMFK H13
81550 PANT AVRA. Gr/Ih 1962; C; 7700/10200; 152.25 × 8.61/9.38 (499.51 × 28.25/30.77); M; 14.5; ex AVRA 1978; ex IRISH ROWAN 1973; Sister: **81551 MALDIVE NOBLE** (Mv); ex ELIANE 1980; ex MARIA 1978; ex IRISH SYCAMORE 1973.

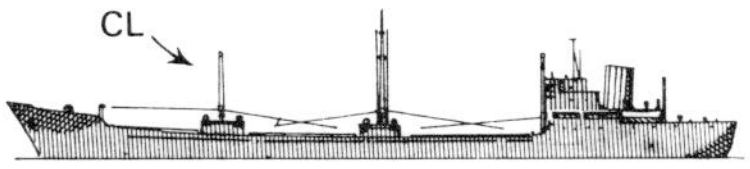

KMKMFK H13
● **81560 ZACAPA.** Li/FRG 1959; C; 2700/4200; 115.98 × 6.5/7.27 (380.51 × 21.33/23.85); M; 14; ex EMERALD SEA 1980; ex RAZA 1975; ex BOCKHOLM 1974; ex BYBLOS 1969.

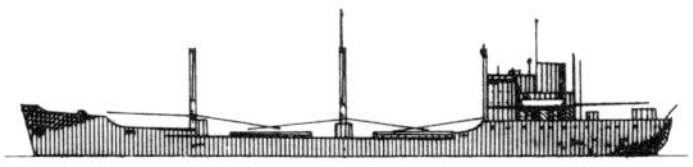

KMKMFK H13
81570 EUN HA. Ko/US 1945; C; 3700; 103.03 × 7.14 (338.02 × 23.43); M; 10; ex SAIGON MARU 1966; ex NORINDEI S 1957; ex SHEET BEND 1947; **'C1-M-AV1'**; type.

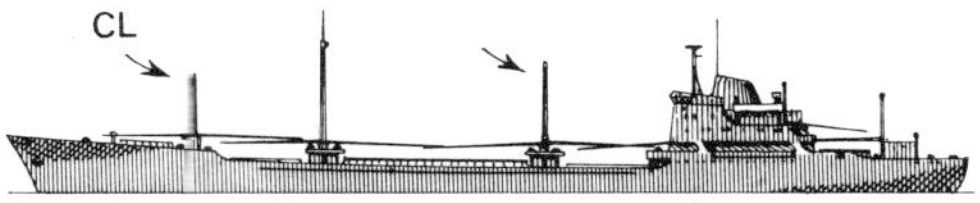

KMKMFKK H13
81580 BRADEVERETT. Li/FRG 1963/68; C; 6600/9000; 152.33 × 7.11/8.58 (499.77 × 23.33/28.15); M; 16; ex FINNFOREST 1979; Converted from general cargo and lengthened 1968; Sisters (Li flag): **81581 ROSSEVERETT;** ex FINNEAGLE 1979; ex TROLLEHOLM 1976; ex FINNEAGLE 1971; **81582 LEONOREVERETT:** ex FINNCLIPPER 1979.

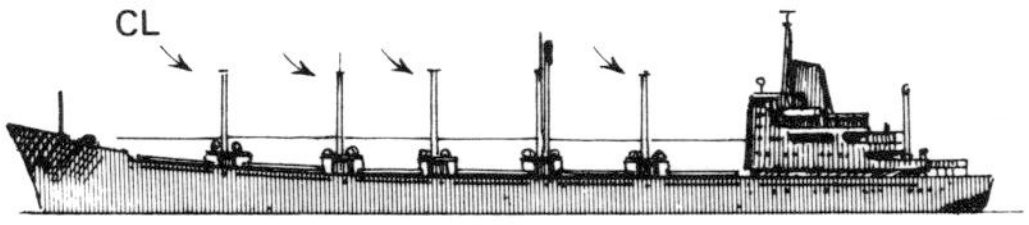

KMKMKMFK H1
81590 SELAS. Gr/Ne 1963; C; 8300/10900; 154.13 × 8.59/9.91 (505.68 × 18/32.51); M; 15; ex JAG ASHA 1976; ex DAGEID 1967.

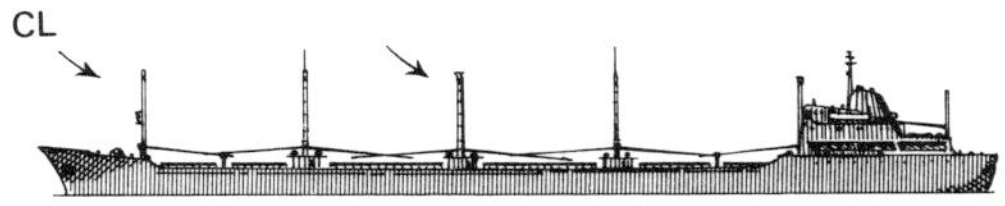

KMKMKMFK H13
● **81600 COPIHUE.** Ch/Fr 1963; C; 4700/7300; 151.62 × —/7.87 (497.44 × —/25.82); M; 16; ex HOEGH BEAVER 1978; ex MOOSE JAW 1968; ex N.O. ROGENAES 1964; Lengthened 1969.

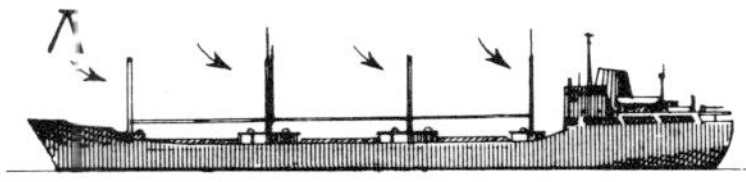

KMKM$_2$F H13
81610 GULF TRADER. Pa/No 1959; C; 4000; 111.77 × 7.83 (366.7 × 25.69); M; —; ex BRAVOTRADER 1980; ex LAURIE U 1976; ex ELGY 1973; ex ARLESIANA 1972; ex ELG 1970; ex ELG VIKING 1968; ex SUNBEAR 1965.

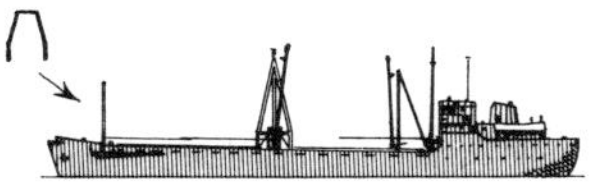

KMKM$_2$F H3
81620 BAHARI. Ia/Ne 1952; C/HL; 1100/1300; 84.51 × 4.15/4.74 (277.26 × 13.62/15.55); M; 12; ex MARIJKE IRENE 1974; ex ERASMUS 1965; ex RAMPART 1960; Lengthened 1965.

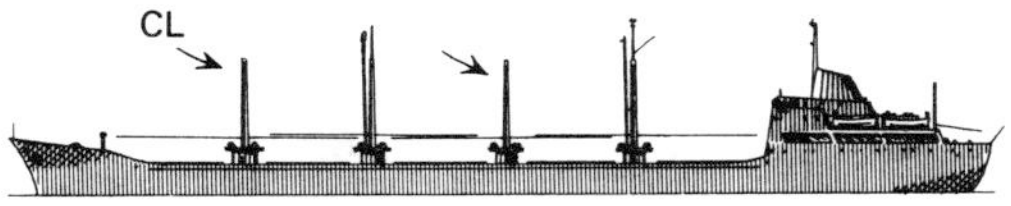

KMKM$_2$FK H13
81630 ARIADNI. Gr/Fr 1964; C; 6700/10100; 154.82 × 8.04/9.42 (507.94 × 26.38/30.91); M; 17.5; ex VILLE D'ANVERS 1976.

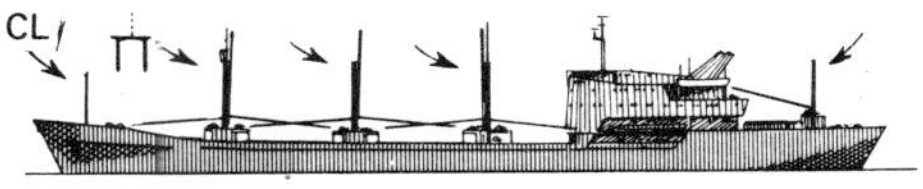

KMKM$_2$FK H13
⋆81640 ZAKOPANE. Pd/Pd 1968; C; 4200/6600; 135.41 × 6.78/7.67 (444.26 × 22.24/25.16); M; 17; **'B446'** type; Sisters: **⋆81641 ZAMOSC** (Pd); **⋆81642 ZAMBRZE** (Pd); **⋆81643 ZAMBROW** (Pd); **81644 ZAWICHOST** (Pd); **⋆81645 ZAWIERCIE** (Pd); **⋆81646 FENG CHENG** (RC); **⋆81647 YAN CHENG** (RC).

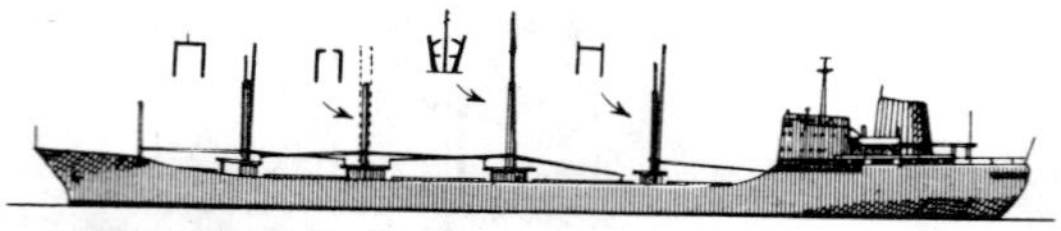

$KMKM_3F$ H13
81660 BAILUNDO. Po/Pd 1969; C; 7700/11600; 158.4 × 8.41/10.03 (519.69 × 27.59/32.91); M; 14; Launched as ARTEMONAS; **'B441'** type; Sister: **81661 CUNENE** (Po).

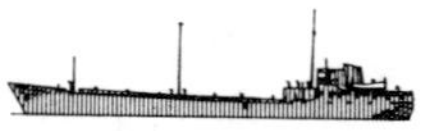

KM_2F H
● **81680 CRYOMAR.** It/Ne 1955/64; LGC; 1000; 63.23 × 3.77 (207.45 × 12.37); M; 12.25; ex CAPO CERVO 1972; ex ABBAS 1968; ex BROUGHTY 1963; Converted from general cargo 1964.

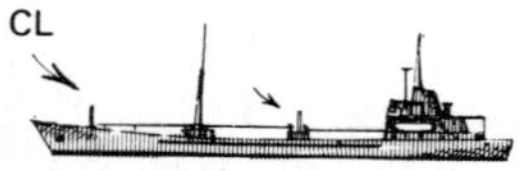

KM_2F H
81700 FREEZER FINN. Fi/FRG 1968; R; 500/1200; 75.6 × 3.81/5 (248.03 × 12.5/16.4); M; 14.75; ex FREEZER SCAN 1973; Sisters: **81701 REEFER TRADER** (Cy); ex ICE FLOWER 1977; ex FRIGO SCAN 1973; **81702 JOKULFELL** (Ic); ex BYMOS 1975; Probable sister: **81703 DANA FRIO** (Br); ex ZALAGH 1976; ex AHMOS 1972.

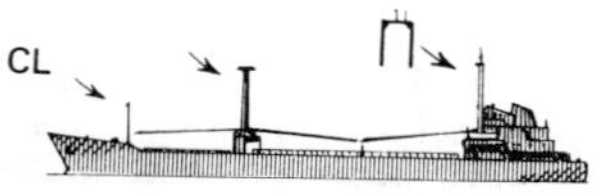

KM_2F H1
81720 DWEJRA II. Ma/Ne 1969; C; 1000; 84.26 × 5.11 (276.44 × 16.77); M; —; ex ASD IRIS 1976; ex IRIS 1973.

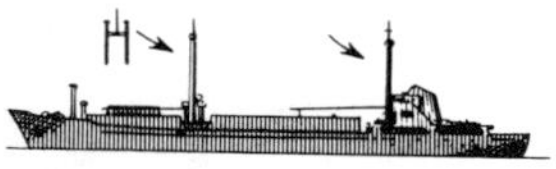

KM_2F H1
81740 NORMAND EXPRESS. Ne/Be 1959; LS; 1000; 82.3 × 4.83 (270.01 × 15.85); M; 13.5; ex LIVEOX 1975; ex SINJOOR 1973; ex MARIA 1967; Converted from general cargo.

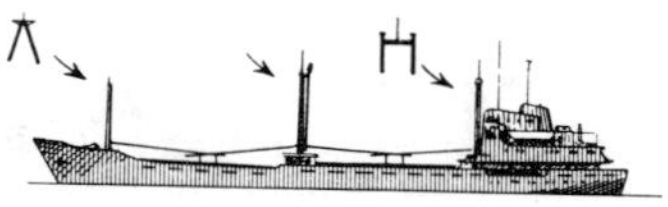

KM_2F H1
81760 FRANCISKA SCHULTE. Cy/FRG 1964; C; 2900; 94.29 × 8.61 (309.35 × 28.25); M; 14.5; ex FRIEDERIKE TEN DOORNKAT 1973.

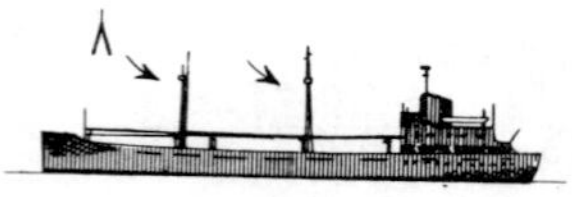

KM_2F H
81670 SELATAN MAJU. Sg/FRG 1956; C; 1600; 78.64 × 5.62 (258 × 18.44); M; 12.5; ex WOODCHUCK 1974; ex BAT GOLAN 1974; ex SHELDRAKE 1968; ex MANCHESTER VANGUARD 1963.

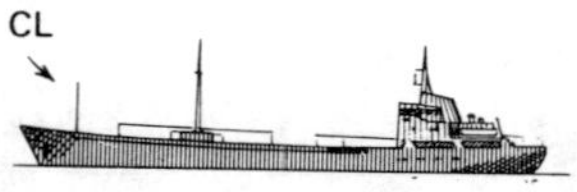

KM_2F H
● **81690 ALBAFRIGO.** Gr/Ne 1962; R; 1500; 83.57 × 4.82 (274.18 × 15.81); M; 14; ex CALANCA 1977; Possible Sisters: **81691 RISA PAULA** (Br); ex AZTEC 1979; ex RISA PAULA 1977; **81692 WINDFROST** (Cy); ex INCA 1977.

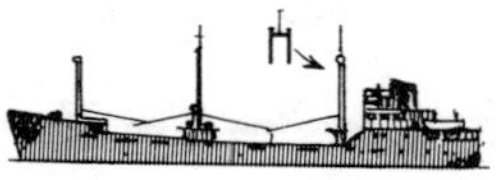

KM_2F H1
● **81710 CHINTA.** Cy/FRG 1950; C; 1500; 75.44 × 4.85 (247.51 × 15.91); M; 10.5; ex RALPH VON BARGEN 1975; ex IRMGARD JACOB 1967; ex ANNEMARIE 1963; Sister: **81711 STELLA A** (Cy); ex STELLA 1974; ex CALYPSO 1971; ex ELFRIEDE 1962.

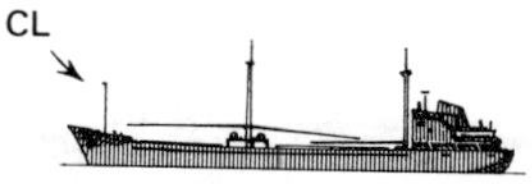

KM_2F H1
81730 SARAH ELIZABETH. NA/Ne 1965; C; 500; 69.35 × 3.72 (227.53 × 12.2); M; 11.5.

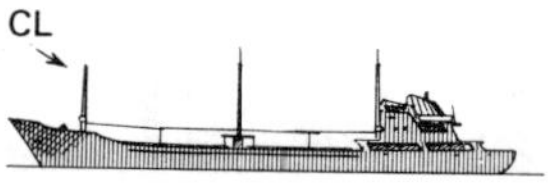

KM_2F H1
81750 GHADA. Pa/Ne 1966; C; 500/1500; 80.29 × 3.52/4.5 (263.42 × 11.55/14.76); M; 13; ex SELA 1980; ex GRECIAN 1974; ex ANDROMEDA 1969. Similar: **81751 LOTUS** (Eg); ex BRANDARIS 1980.

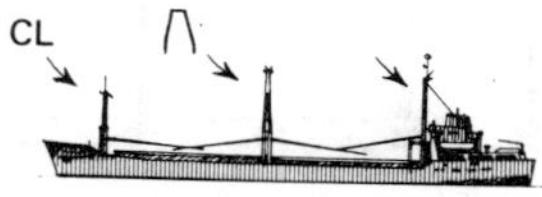

KM_2F H1
81770 ANNELIESE OLTMANN. FRG/No 1972; C; 1000; 77.09 × 5.1 (252.92 × 16.73); M; 14; Sisters (Pa flag): **81771 ESTEFLUT; 81772 ESTETAL.**

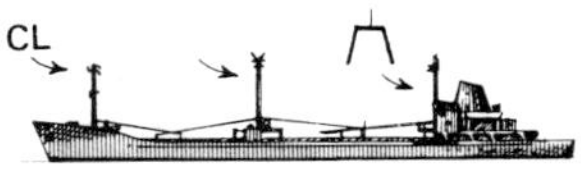

KM_2F H1
● **81780 RASHIDAH.** Qt/Br 1970; C; 1500; 86.87 × 5.07 (285 × 16.63); M; 13.5; ex QATAR 1 1979; ex CHEVIOT PRINCE 1978; ex MENDIP PRINCE 1974; Sisters (Br flag): **81781 CHILTERN PRINCE; 81782 MALVERN PRINCE; 81783 FIJIAN;** ex COTSWOLD PRINCE 1979.

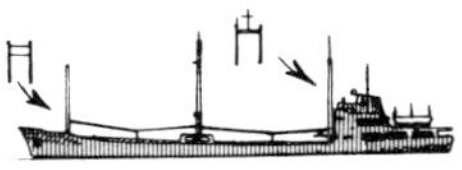

KM_2F H1
81810 CHRYSOULLA H. Cy/FRG 1954; C; 780/1000; 68.99 × 4.27/— (226.35 × 14.01/—); M; 10; ex DIAMONDSEA 1975; ex BEYROUTH 1973; ex NAIADE 1969; ex NAJADE 1958.

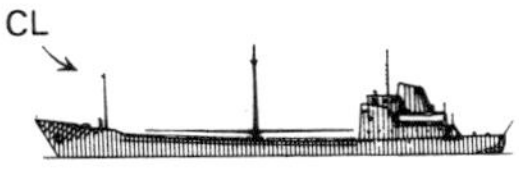

KM_2F H1
81830 ALNAIR. Pa/Ne 1968; C; 500/1100; 72.95 × —/5.21 (239.34 × —/17.09); M; —; ex PULPCA 1973.

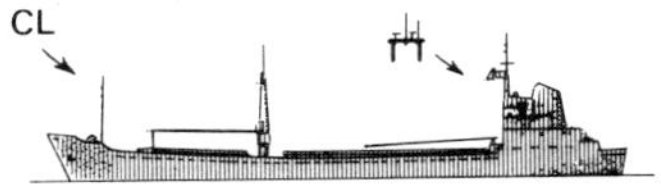

KM_2F H1
● **81840 MECHI VENTURE.** Li/In 1978; C; 1600; 91.19 × 5.58 (299.18 × 18.31); M; 14.5; ex GOMBA VENTURE 1979; Sisters: **81841 OUED SEBOU** (In); **81842 GOMBA NILE** (In) ex BALAKRAM; launched as GOMBA ENDEAVOUR; **81843 GOMBA ENDURANCE** (Li) ex SANTO VASTIRAM; ex VASTIRAM 1978; **81844 GOMBA VICTORIA** (Li) ex SANTO ALAKHRAM 1978; ex ALAKHRAM 1978; Probable sister: **81845 GOMBA ENDEAVOUR** (Li).

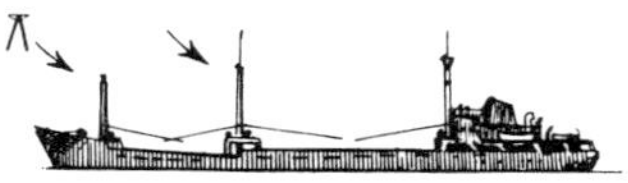

KM_2F H12
81880 GABRIELE. It/FRG 1956; C; 2200; 90 × 5.7 (295.28 × 18.7); M; 13; ex HILLE OLDENDORFF 1971.

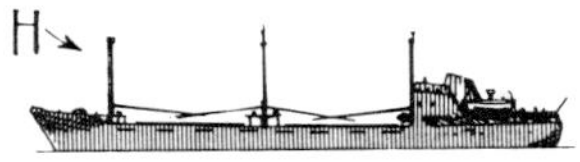

KM_2F H1
81790 LAVINIA COPPOLA. It/FRG 1957; C; 1800; 83.47 × 6.04 (273.95 × 19.85); M; 12; ex MEDOV GRECIA 1973; ex SIGURD RINDE 1967.

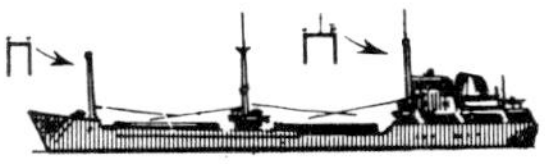

KM_2F H1
★**81800 LISKI.** Ys/No 1959; C; 1100/1800; 78.06 × 4.44/5.65 (256.1 × 14.57/18.54); M; 13; ex BESTUM 1974; ex SJOFNA 1962.

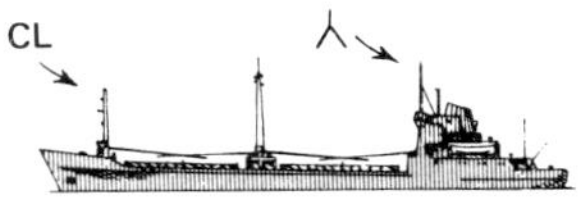

KM_2F H1
● **81820 ANNA VON BARGEN.** FRG/FRG 1970; C; 1000/2000; 83.8 × 5.05/6.33 (274.93 × 16.57/20.77); M; 13.5; Sister (FRG flag): **81821 FRIEDA GRAEBE** ex GITTA VON BARGEN 1974; **81822 SUSANN VON BARGEN; 81823 MOWENSTEERT; 81824 DUKEGAT;** Similar (lengthened—Pa flag): **81825 GROENLAND** ex VELA 1980.

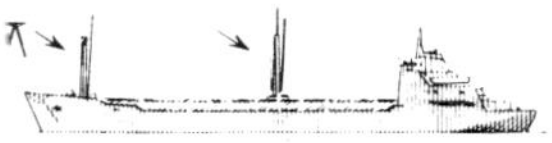

KM_2F H1
★**81850 DIKA.** Ys/Sw 1965; RoC; 800/2200; 80.85 × 3.77/6.53 (256.26 × 12.37/21.42); M; 12; ex DON JUAN 1972; Bow door; Sister: **81851 CARLA** (Ni) ex NOPAL SAND 1977; ex DON CARLOS 1973.

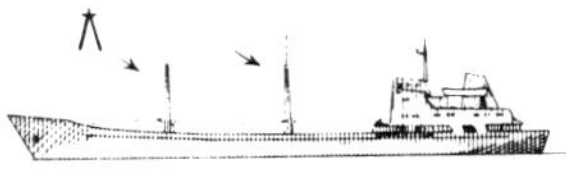

KM_2F H1
★**81860 IWONICZ ZDROJ.** Pd/Rm 1970; C; 1200/2000; 85.91 × 4.5/5.1 (281.86 × 14.76/16.73); M; 13; Sisters (Superstructure varies—Pd flag): ★**81861 BUSKO ZDROJ;** ★**81862 CIECHOCINEK;** ★**81863 DUSZNIKI ZDROJ;** ★**81864 POLCZYN ZDROJ;** ★**81865 CIEPLICE ZDROJ;** ★**81866 KARPACZ;** ★**81867 KUDOWA ZDROJ;** ★**81868 RABKA ZDROJ.**

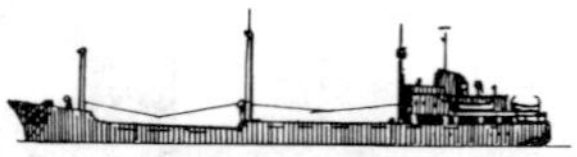

KM_2F H12
81890 GIOVANNI COPPOLA. It/FRG 1953; C; 1600; 84.26 × 5.52 (276.44 × 18.11); M; 12.5; ex IMME OLDENDORFF 1971.

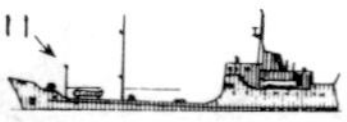

KM_2F H13
81910 CELTIC LEE. Br/Br 1960; Tk; 500; 52.02 × 3.54 (170.67 × 11.61); M; 9.5; ex ESSO TYNEMOUTH 1978.

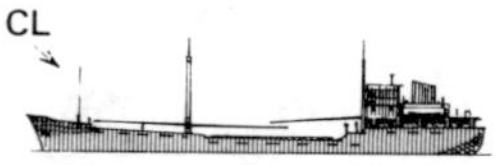

KM_2F H13
81930 GEORGIOS D. Gr/Ne 1958; C; 1000; 71.51 × 4.27 (234.6 × 14.01); M; 11; ex NUSAKAN 1979.

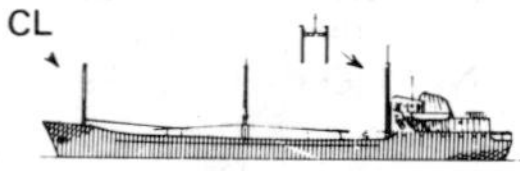

KM_2F H13
● ⋆**81950 DRIANOVO** Bu/Sp 1962; C; 500/1100; 74.91 × 3.56/4.93 (245.77 × 11.68/16.17); ex AMETHYST 1970; ex SLITAN 1966; Similar: **81951 PUERTO DE AMBERES** (Sp); **81952 MONTE BALERDI** (Sp) launched as MONTE CUARTO; **81953 CEDAR PRIDE** (Le) ex SAN BRUNO 1978; ex PUERTO DE PASAJES 1969 launched as MONTE DOS; **81954 HELLINORA** (Cy) ex PATRICIO 1977; ex MONTE CINCO 1977; **81955 TRIOS** (Pa) ex KAI KAVOOS 1975; ex ECO SOL 1975 launched as SKAGATIND; **81956 VIOLA** (Pa) ex KAI GHOBAD 1980; ex ECO GABRIELA 1975; **81957 KAI KHOSROW** (Ir) ex ECO LUISA 1975 launched as MONTE UNO.

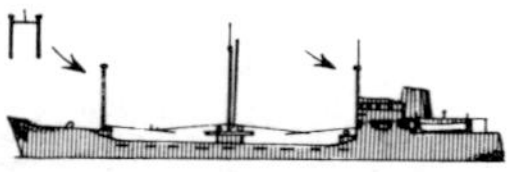

KM_2F H13
81990 SKIATHOS. Gr/Sw 1953; C; 1900; 77.7 × 5.97 (254.92 × 19.59); M; 12; ex GUNTHER SCHULTE 1970; ex KURT ARLT 1963.

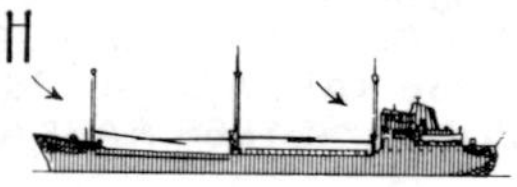

KM_2F H13
82010 MARA. Pa/FRG 1955; C; 900; 72.7 × 5.39 (238.52 × 17.68); M; 13; ex CARIBBEAN MARA 1976; ex VIGILANTE 1968; ex MONTROSE 1958.

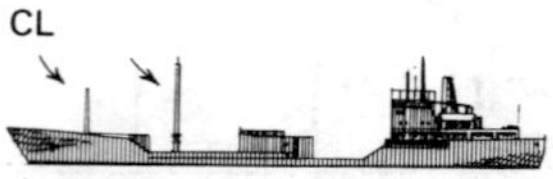

KM_2F H13
81900 CEMBULK. No/FRG 1973; Cem; 2200; 84.89 × 5.8 (278.51 × 19.03); 4.

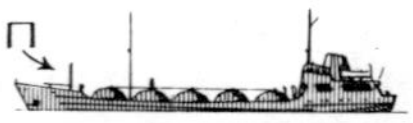

KM_2F H13
● **81920 SIGNE THOLSTRUP.** De/De 1957; LGC; 400; 59.62 × 3 (195.6 × 9.84); M; 11.5; Sister: **81921 SUSANNE THOLSTRUP** (De).

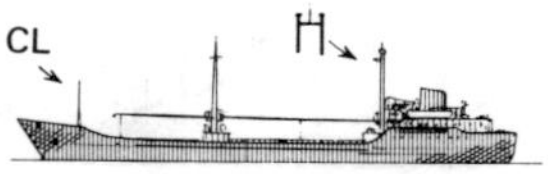

KM_2F H13
● **81940 ARANUI.** Pa/FRG 1967; C; 1000/1500; 76.66 × 4.59/5.81 (261.35 × 15.06/19.06); M; 13.5; ex CADIZ 1981; Sisters: **81941 HUELVA** (Pa); **81942 NIAGA XXIX** (Ia) ex SEVILLA 1980.

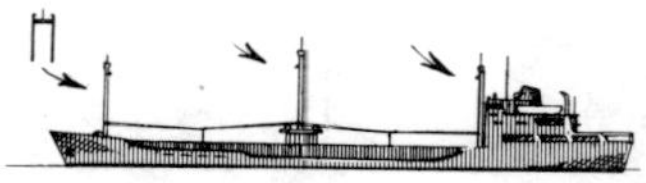

KM_2F H13
81970 HTAN TAW YWA. Bm/FRG 1961; C; 2700; 91.5 × 6.03 (300.2 × 19.78); M; —; ex LINDO 1968; Similar (lengthened): **81971 DONGA** (Pa) ex GEORGIOS P P 1980; ex OLYMPIOS ATHINA 1980; ex EIRIN MARU 1979; ex HABERNIS 1974; ex BONGO 1969.

KM_2F H13
81980 EUTERPE. Gr/FRG 1956; C; 1600; 77.5 × 5.72 (254.27 × 18.77); M; 12; ex MARGARETHA BISCHOFF 1962.

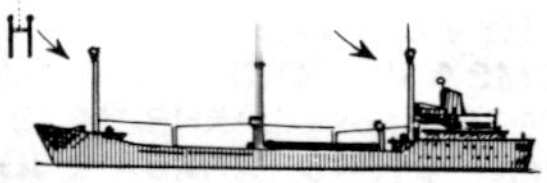

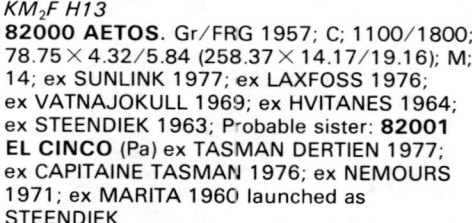

KM_2F H13
82000 AETOS. Gr/FRG 1957; C; 1100/1800; 78.75 × 4.32/5.84 (258.37 × 14.17/19.16); M; 14; ex SUNLINK 1977; ex LAXFOSS 1976; ex VATNAJOKULL 1969; ex HVITANES 1964; ex STEENDIEK 1963; Probable sister: **82001 EL CINCO** (Pa) ex TASMAN DERTIEN 1977; ex CAPITAINE TASMAN 1976; ex NEMOURS 1971; ex MARITA 1960 launched as STEENDIEK.

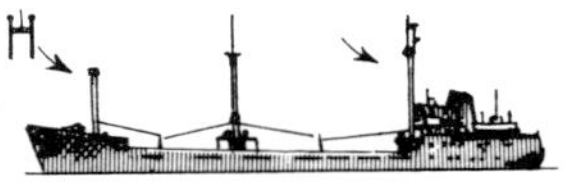

KM_2F H13
82020 CAPAL. Cy/FRG 1955; C; 1600; 81.78 × 5.7 (268.31 × 18.7); M; 12; ex GEORGIOS 1977; ex PATRICIA 1973; ex KORBACH 1970.

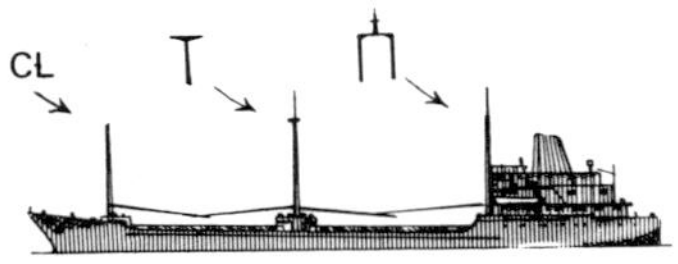

KM_2F H13
82040 WESER BROKER. FRG/FRG 1970; C; 1600/3300; 100.56 × 5.24/6.77 (329.92 × 17.19/22.21); M; 15.5.

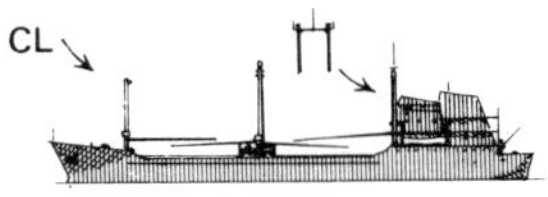

KM_2F H13
82060 SABA. Ne/Ne 1970; C; 800/1600; 79.69 × 4.56/5.89 (261.45 × 14.96/19.32); M; 13.5; ex SHIPMAIR V 1978; ex GAELIC 1974; ex HENDRIK BOS 1972; Sister: **82061 ALIANORA** (It) ex SHIPMAIR VI 1980; ex GERD 1974; ex GERD BOS 1973; Probable sister: **82062 TIBESTI** (Gr) ex SAFI; ex IRMGARD BOS 1976.

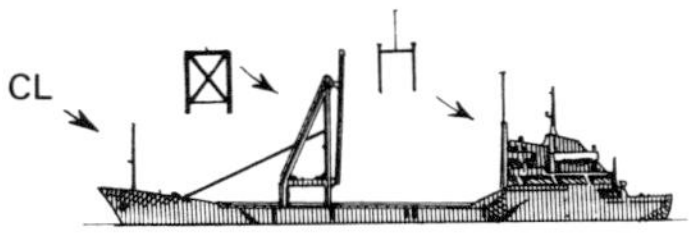

KM_2F H13
82080 GIANT. Li/Fr 1969; C/HL; 500/1400; 90.23 × — (296.03 × —); M; 15.5; ex LA GAVOTTE 1975; Converted from general cargo.

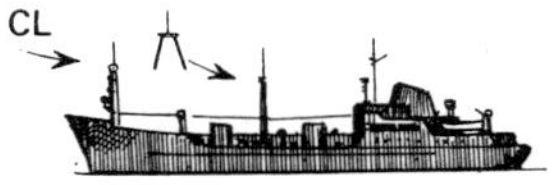

KM_2F H13
82090 HEREFORD EXPRESS. Ne/FRG 1958; LS; 600; 71.96 × 3.57 (236.09 × 11.71); M; 13.5; ex NORANIM I 1973; ex ALONDRA 1973; Similar (lengthened): **82091 LIMOUSIN EXPRESS** (Ne) ex NORANIM II 1973; ex ATHENE 1973.

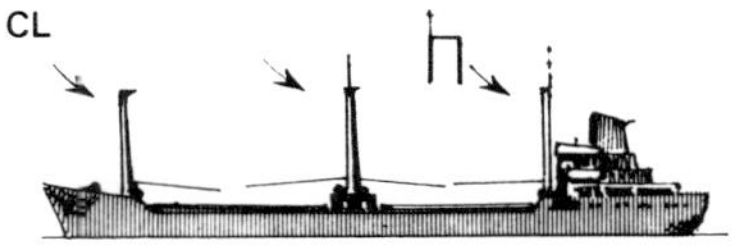

KM_2F H13
82030 FAITH. Sg/Ne 1971; C; 1600/3000; 103.51 × 5.14/6.52 (339.51 × 16.86/21.39); M; 15; ex CHESHIRE FAITH 1979; ex OSTERFEHN 1978; Sister: **82031 GANVIE** (Bi) ex FAROS 1978 launched as WESTERFEHN.

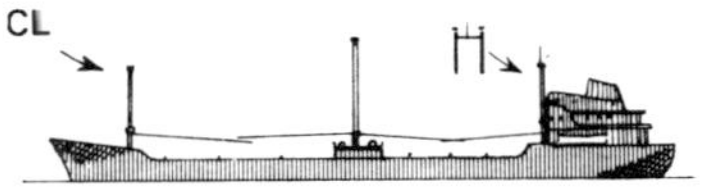

KM_2F H13
82050 VICTORIA. Gr/FRG 1970; C/Con; 1200/2800; 99.04 × 4.24/6.3 (324.93 × 13.91/20.67); M; 14; ex RABAT 1980; ex INO A 1974; ex BOSTON EXPRESS 1971 launched as INO; Similar: **82051 CURRENT TRADER** (Br) ex MERCHANT CLIPPER 1980; ex DWEJRA 1976; ex INO F 1975; **82052 CURRENT EXPRESS** (Br) ex MERCANDIAN EXPRESS 1980; ex CARIBIC 1975; ex KATHE BOS 1973; **82053 TINHINAN** (Ag) ex HOLMIA 1975; ex JOHANNES BOS 1973; **82054 HODNA** (Ag) ex ANNETTE BOS 1972.

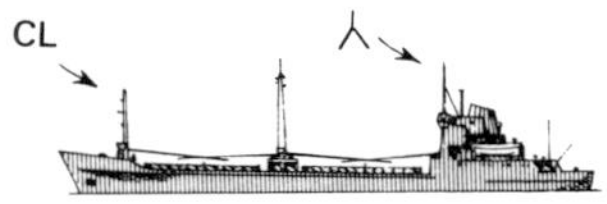

KM_2F H13
● **82070 ANNA VON BARGEN.** FRG/FRG 1970; C; 1000/2000; 83.8 × 5.05/6.33 (274.93 × 16.57/20.77); M; 13.5; Similar (FRG flag): **82071 FRIEDA GRAEBE** ex GITTA VON BARGEN 1974; **82072 SUSANN VON BARGEN; 82073 MOWENSTEERT; 82074 DUKEGAT;** Similar (lengthened—Pa flag): **82075 GROENLAND** ex VELA 1980.

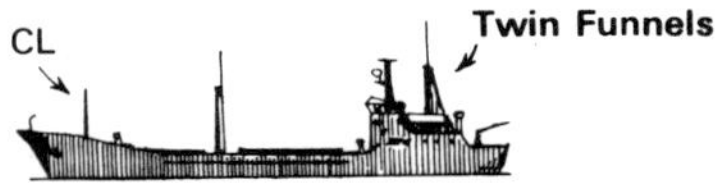

KM_2F H13
82100 OSTANHAV. Sw/Sw 1966; C; 1300; 73.77 × 5.6 (242.03 × 18.37); M; 12; ex TENTO 1974.

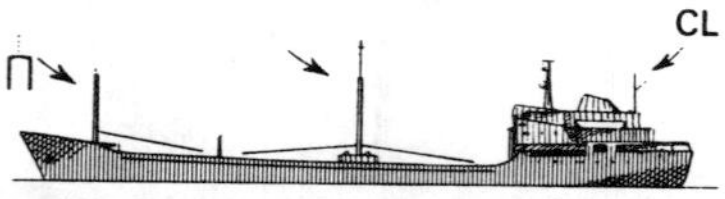

KM_2F H13
⋆82110 BRAD. Rm/Rm 1971; C; 2500/3500; 106.2 × —/7.06 (348.43 × —/23.16); M; 14; Sisters (Rm flag): **⋆82111 AZUGA; ⋆82112 TIRGU JIU; ⋆82113 CODLEA; ⋆82114 SULINA; ⋆82115 TIRNAVENI; ⋆82116 RIMNICU VILCEA; ⋆82117 PLOPENI; ⋆82118 SLATINA; ⋆82119 SLOBOZIA; ⋆82120 FALTICENI; ⋆82121 SACELE; ⋆82122 DUMBRAVENI; ⋆82123 CALARASI; ⋆82124 GHEORGHIENI; ⋆82125 SADU; ⋆82126 SADOVA; ⋆82127 SNAGOV; ⋆82128 TOPOLOVENI; ⋆82129 SOVEJA; ⋆82130 SOIATA; ⋆82131 SEGARCEA; ⋆82132 SAVINESTI; ⋆82133 SAVENI; ⋆82134 SUCEVITA; ⋆82135 SOUSA; ⋆82136 SALISTE; ⋆82137 SEBES;** (Bu flag): **⋆82138 LOVECH; ⋆82139 BAO AN** (RC)—may be **BEI AN; 82140 IRAN SHAHEED** (Ir) ex ARYA MARMAR 1980; **82141 IRAN TOWHEED** (Ir) ex ARYA NOOSH 1980.

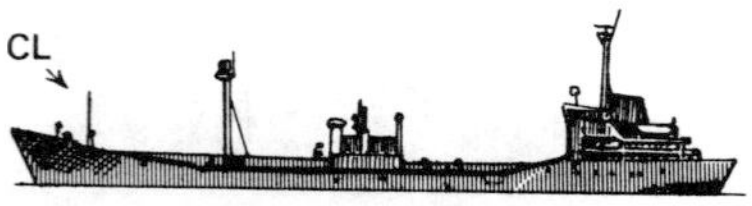

KM_2F H13
82180 CORAL MAEANDRA. NA/Ne 1969; LGC; 3400; 103.21 × 6.35 (338.61 × 20.83); M; 15.75.

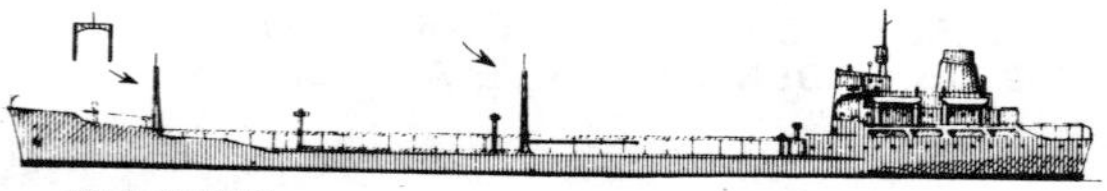

KM_2F H13
82200 GOGO RANGER. Li/Sw 1958; Tk; 12500; 170.57 × 9.58 (559.61 × 31.43); M; 15; ex POST RANGER 1977; ex ANCO STRIPE 1971; ex ANCO BERGLJOT 1969; ex BERGLJOT 1964.

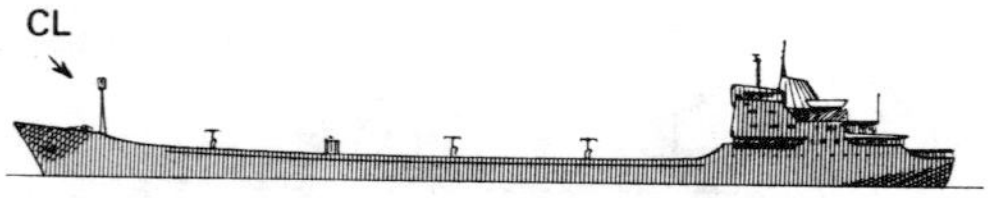

KM_2F H13
⋆82220 URICANI. Rm/Rm 1971; B; 9600; 148.72 × 7.93 (487.93 × 26.02); M; 12.5; Sisters (some have cranes and some have goalpost forward)(Rm flag): **⋆82221 PETROSANI; ⋆82222 ANINA; ⋆82223 CUGIR; ⋆82224 ROVINARI; ⋆82225 VULCAN; ⋆82226 MUSCEL; ⋆82227 CIMPULUNG; ⋆82228 AGNITA; ⋆82229 CALAN.**

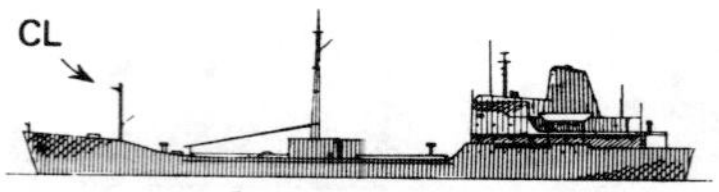

KM_2F H13
82150 CEMENTIA. Pa/FRG 1967; Cem; 3400; 106.61 × 6.74 (349.77 × 22.11); M; 14.75; Sister: **82151 DALIA** (Pa).

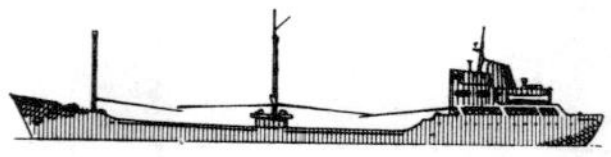

KM_2F H13
82160 MENELAOS TH. Gr/Sp 1968; C; 1300/2200; 93.02 × —/5.37 (305.18 × —/17.62); M; 15; ex ANAMILENA 1975; Sister: **82161 COSTIA PEFANIS** (Gr) ex ADRIANA 1965.

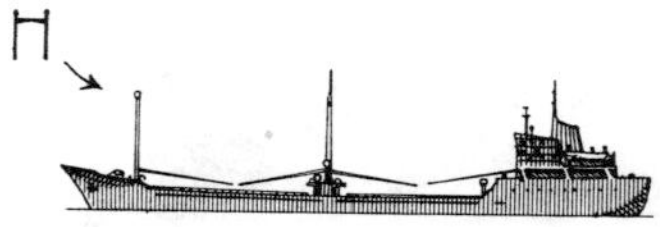

KM_2F H13
82170 FRISIAN TRADER. Ne/Ne 1976; C; 1600; 79.81 × 5.44 (261.84 × 17.85); M; 13.

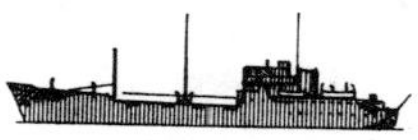

KM_2F H13
82190 CLEO. Gr/It 1947; Sal; 900; 61.68 × 4.1 (202.36 × 13.45); M; 11; ex GUTTORM JARL: Converted from general cargo 1970.

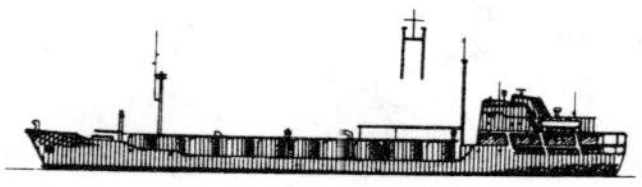

KM_2F H13
82210 FRED H BILLUPS. Li/Ne 1960; LGC; 2900; 99.32 × 5.12 (325.85 × 16.8); M; 13.

KM_2F H13
82240 FISKO. Fi/Fi 1974; R; 500/1300; 74.12 × 3.62/4.8 (243.18 × 11.88/15.75); M; 14; Sister: **82241 LINDO** (Fi).

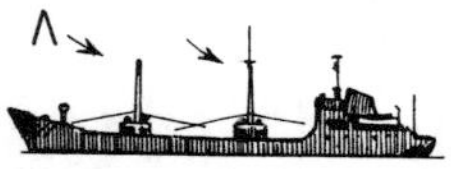

KM_2F H13
82250 GIANNIS DIMAKIS III. Gr/FRG 1956; C; 1000; 67.09 × 5.15 (220.11 × 16.9); M; 11; ex POLLENDAM 1977; ex VICTOR 1971; ex VORMANN RASS 1966.

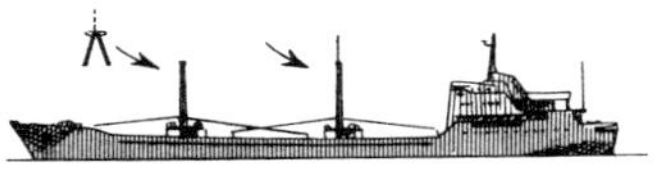

KM_2F H13
★**82260 WARNA.** Pd/Rm 1968; C; 2500; 95.89 × 5.64 (314.6 × 18.5); M; 13; Sisters (some have heavier radar mast and some have cowl round funnel top):(Pd flag): ★**82261 JELENIA GORA;** ★**82262 PLOCK;** ★**82263 KOLOBRZEG II;** ★**82264 ZYWIEC;** ★**82265 OSWIECIM;** ★**82266 CHRZANOW;** ★**82267 RYBNIK;** ★**82268 JELCZ II.**

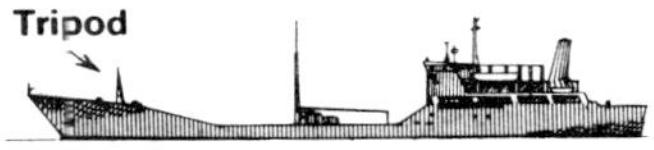

KM_2F H13
82280 CEMENT KING. NZ/No 1973; Cem; 2900; 98.66 × 5.51 (323.69 × 18.08); M; 14.

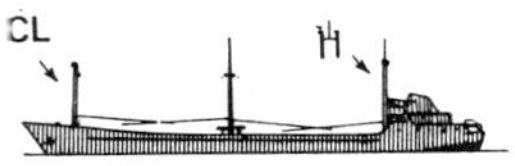

KM_2F H3
● **82290 EDELGARD.** FRG/FRG 1965; C; 500; 73.18 × 3.63 (240.09 × 11.91); M; 12.

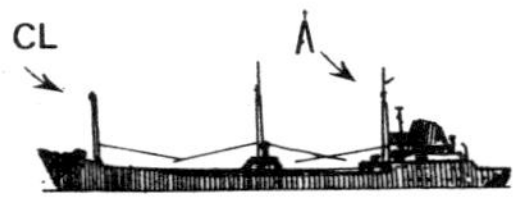

KM_2F H3
82300 ACQUAVIVA It/FRG 1957; C; 1300; 74.17 × 4.55 (243.34 × 14.93); M; 12.5; ex KOMTUR 1974; ex VOGELSAND 1968.

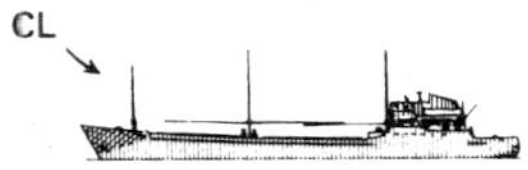

KM_2F H3
82310 DEEPA JUWITA. Ia/Ne 1967; C; 1200; 69.19 × 3.73 (227 × 12.24); M; 11; ex WESTMEEP 1977; ex MILDSTEDT 1975; ex WESTMEEP 1970.

KM_2FK H1
82320 NYMIT. Li/Ja 1970; RoC; 4500; 87.31 × — (286.45 × —); TSM; 11.5; ex COSMOS BELLATRIX 1977; ex COSMOS No2 1975.

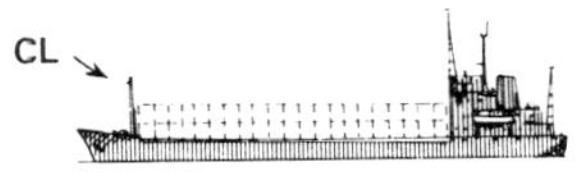

KM_2FK H1
82330 NIKKO MARU No35. Ja/Ja 1976; C/Con; 1900; 76.76 × 5.18 (251.84 × 17); TSM; 9.5; ex TUNGHO No1 1980; Probable sisters: **82331 TUNGHO No2** (Pa); **82332 WILCON V** (Pi) ex TUNGHO No3.

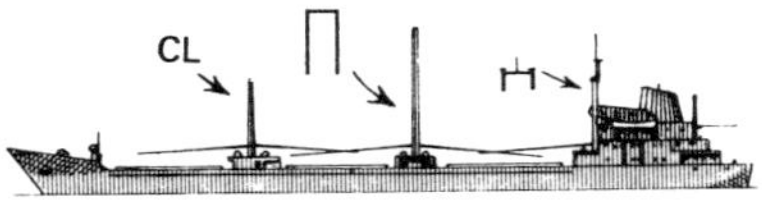

KM_2FK H1
82340 GEBE OLDENDORFF. Sg/FRG 1971; C; 1800/4800; 116.72 × 6.53/7.53 (382.94 × 21.42/24.7); M; 15; ex TERESOPOLIS 1973; ex GEBE OLDENDORFF 1971.

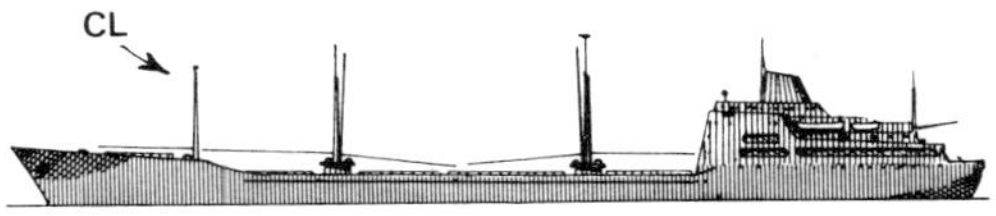

KM_2FK H13
● ★**82350 TU MEN JIANG.** RC/Fr 1964; C; 9100; 155.2 × 9.15 (509.19 × 30.02); M; 19.5; ex VILLE DE BORDEAUX 1977; Sisters: ★**82351 HEI LONG JIANG** (RC) ex VILLE DE LYON 1977; **82352 ALIAKMON LEADER** (Gr) ex VILLE DU HAVRE 1977; **82353 ALIAKMON LIGHT** (Gr) ex VILLE DE BREST 1977.

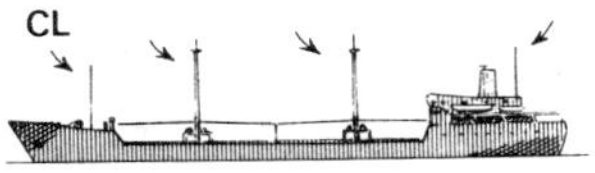

KM_2FK H13
● **82360 TROUP HEAD.** Br/Ne 1971; C; 1600; 87.61 × 5.37 (287.43 × 17.62); M; 12; Sister: **82361 TOD HEAD** (Br).

KM_2FK H13
● **82370 INTERNAVIS I.** Fr/FRG 1975; C/HL; 4000; 105.42 × 6.3 (345.87 × 20.67); M; 14; launched as MAMMOTH SCAN.

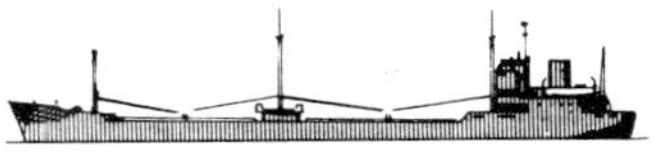

KM_2FK H13
82380 SHOHU MARU. Ja/Ja 1966; C; 3000; 98.35 × 6.25 (322.67 × 20.51); M; 13.

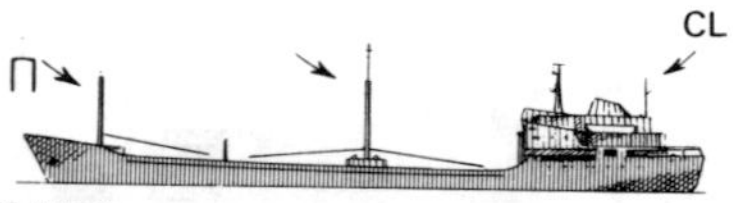

KM_2FK H13
⋆82390 BRAD. Rm/Rm 1971; C; 2500/3500; 106.2 × —/7.06 (348.43 × —/23.16); M; 14; Sisters (Rm flag): **⋆82391 AZUGA; ⋆82392 TIRGU JIU; ⋆82393 CODLEA; ⋆82394 SULINA; ⋆82395 TIRNAVENI; ⋆82396 RIMNICU VILCEA; ⋆82397 PLOPENI; 82398 SLATINA; ⋆82399 SLOBOZIA; ⋆82400 FALTICENI; ⋆82401 SACELE; ⋆82402 DUMBRAVENI; ⋆82403 CALARASI; ⋆82404 GHEORGHIENI; ⋆82405 SADU; ⋆82406 SADOVA; ⋆82407 SNAGOV; ⋆82408 TOPOLOVENI; ⋆82409 SOVEJA; ⋆82410 SOIATA; ⋆82411 SEGARCEA; ⋆82412 SAVINESTI; ⋆82413 SAVENI; ⋆82414 SUCEVITA; ⋆82415 SOUSA; ⋆82416 SALISTE; ⋆82417 SEBES;** (Bu flag): **⋆82418 LOVECH;** Possible sisters: **⋆82419 BAO AN** (RC) — may be **BEI AN; 82420 IRAN SHAHEED** (Ir) ex ARYA MARMAR 1980; **82421 IRAN TOWHEED** (Ir) ex ARYA NOOSH 1980

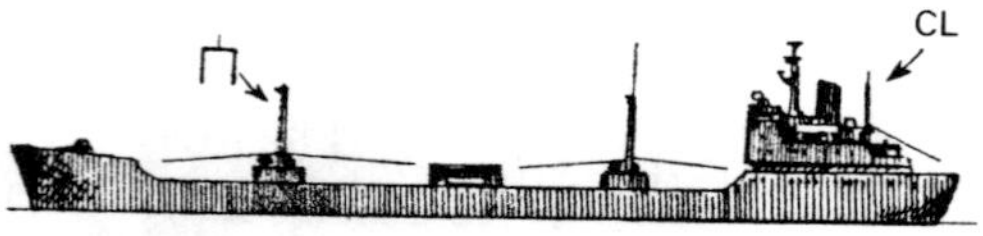

K_2MFK H13
⋆82460 OSTROV RUSSKIY. Ru/Sw 1969; FC; 9800; 150.55 × 7.47 (494 × 24.51); M; 18.25; Sisters (Ru flag): **⋆82461 OSTROV ATLASOVA; ⋆82462 OSTROV BERINGA; ⋆82462 OSTROV KARAKINSKIY; ⋆82463 OSTROV KOTLIN; ⋆82464 OSTROV LISYANSKOGO; ⋆82465 OSTROV LITKE; ⋆82466 OSTROV MEDNYY; ⋆82467 OSTROV SHMIDTA; ⋆82468 OSTROV SHOKALSKOGO; ⋆82469 OSTROV SIBIRYAKOVA; ⋆82470 OSTROV USHAKOVA.**

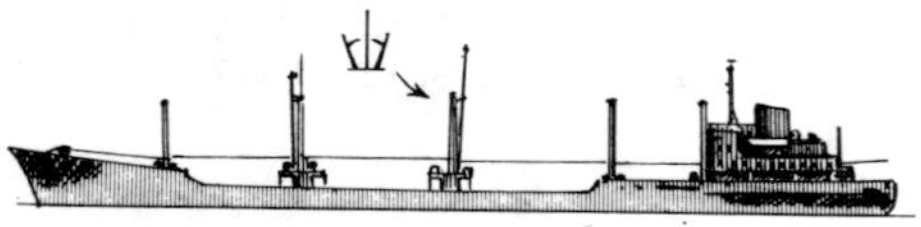

KM_2K_2MFK H13
82490 INDIAN VALOUR. In/FRG 1971; C; 7000/9600; 144.91 × 9.42 (475.43 × 30.91); M; 16; **'36L'** type; Sister: **82491 INDIAN VENTURE** (In).

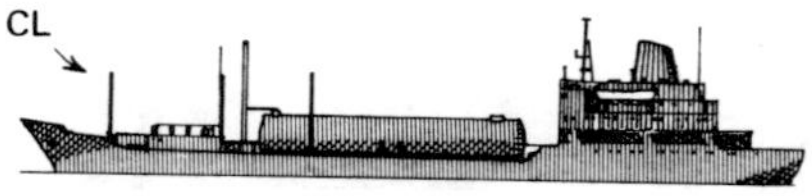

KM_2KMF H13
82510 MUNDOGAS ATLANTIC. Li/No 1969; LGC; 6800; 112.89 × 8.79 (403.18 × 28.84); M; 16.

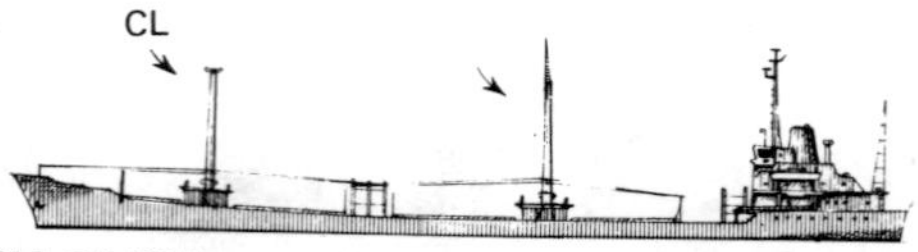

KM_2FK H13
82430 KYOTEN MARU. Ja/Ja 1970; C/TC; 8500; 141.28 × 8.84 (463.52 × 29); M; 14.5; Sister: **82431 KYOSEI MARU** (Ja).

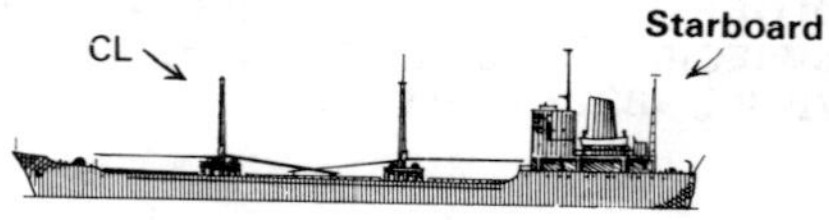

KM_2FK H13
82440 DAYAKA SATU. Ia/Ja 1966; C; 3700; 106.69 × 6.57 (350.03 × 21.56); M; 12.5; ex IZU MARU 1971.

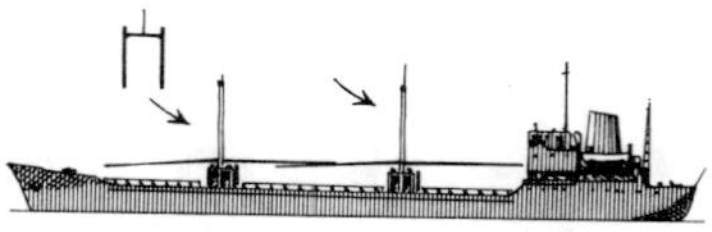

KM_2FK H13
82450 MIGHTINESS. Pa/Ja 1962; C; 3900; 108.92 × 6.83 (357.35 × 22.41); M; 12; ex PENDER 1980; ex MINGREN ENTERPRISE 1980; ex BUNG JOOP 1974; ex TOYO MARU No2 1971; Possible sisters: **82451 C K DOLAJI** (Ko) ex PRIME OCEAN 1973; ex ANYO MARU 1970; **82452 NITYA NANAK** (In) ex NODA WOOD MARU 1967; **82453 TONG** (Pa) ex MOUNT ZAO 1974; ex FUKUZAKI MARU 1971; **82454 NEW SPIRIT** (Pa) ex ZENOVIA D 1980; ex SHINYUBARI MARU 1976.

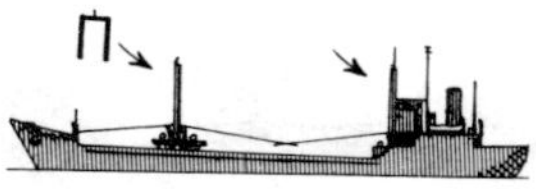

KM_2FK H13
82480 NAM SAN. Ko/Ko 1972; C; 1500; 82.66 × 5.26 (271.19 × 17.26); M; 11.

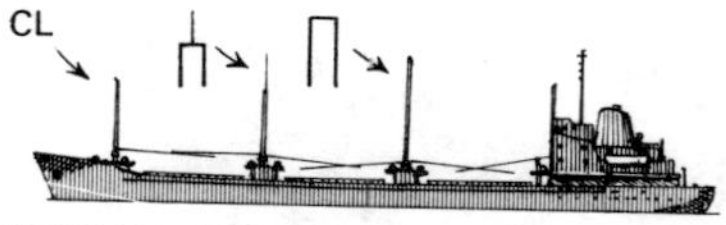

KM_2KMF H1
82500 GRYTTA. Pa/FRG 1961; C; 3000/4200; 115.42 × 6.4/7.16 (378.67 × 21/23.49); M; 15; ex AMBRI 1979; ex BOOKER VOYAGER 1978; ex EUGENIO 1973; ex HELGA WITT 1971.

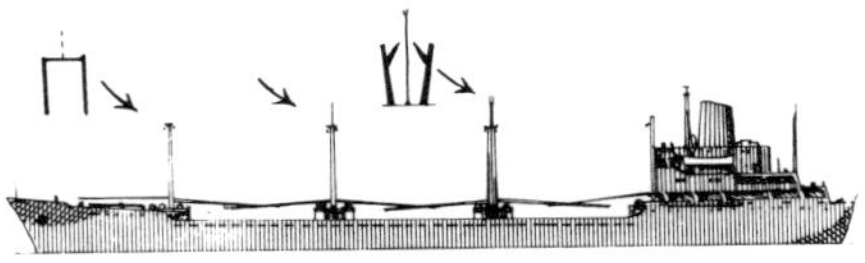

KM_2KMFK *H13*
82520 FANTI. Gh/Fr 1962; C; 5500/7600; 134.25 × 7.08/8.51 (440.45 × 23.23/27.92); M; 15; ex MOOSOU 1978; ex SAINT-MATTHIEU 1973.

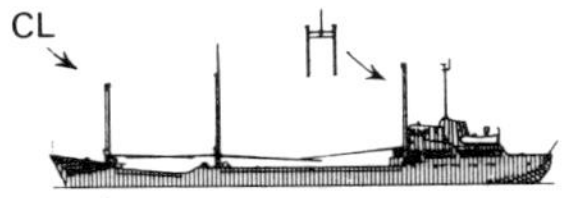

KM_3F *H123*
82540 CRUSADER. Gr/FRG 1958; C; 1600; 79.2 × 5.24 (259.84 × 17.19); M; 12; ex MARIE LOUISE 1978; ex INGA BASTIAN 1974; Lengthened 1959.

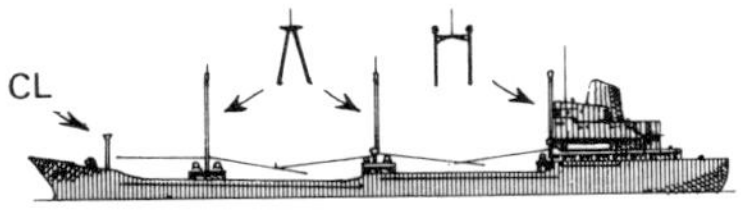

KM_3F *H123*
★82550 PAN SHAN. RC/FRG 1967; C; 2500/4200; 110.5 × —/7.57 (362.53 × —/24.84); M; 16.25; ex INGE KRUGER 1977; ex CAP DOUKATO 1977; ex INGE KRUGER 1975; ex THESSALIA 1970; ex INGE KRUGER 1967.

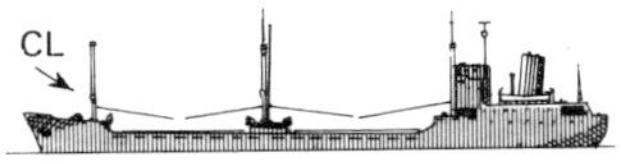

KM_3F *H13*
82570 SRI PHEN SINN. Th/Ja 1959; C; 2700; 92 × 5.77 (301.84 × 18.93); M; 11; ex IKUTA 1974; ex SEIKAI MARU 1971.

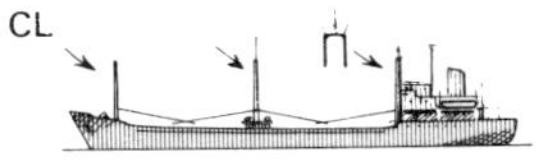

KM_3F *H13*
82580 TAI LAI. Tw/Ja 1962; C; 1000; 69.73 × 4.59 (228.77 × 15.06); M; 11; ex YAMATSUNE MARU 1969.

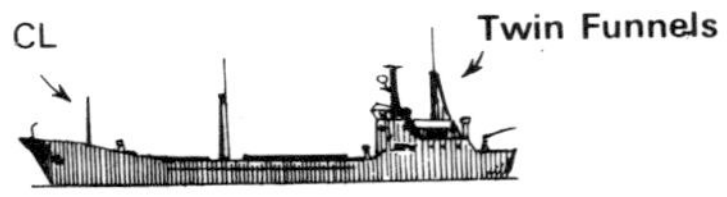

KM_3F *H13*
82600 OSTANHAV. Sw/Sw 1966; C; 1300; 73.77 × 5.6 (242.03 × 18.37); M; 12; ex TENTO 1974.

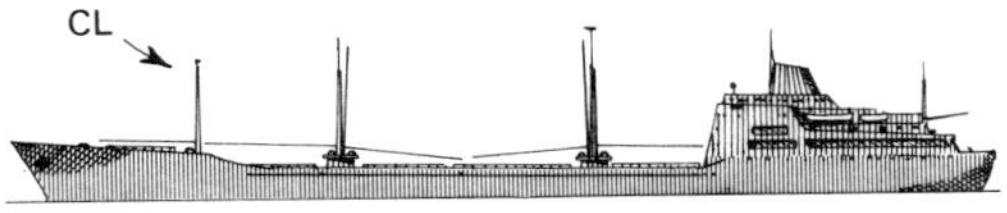

KM_3FK *H13*
● **★82620 TU MEN JIANG.** RC/Fr 1964; C; 9100; 155.2 × 9.15 (509.19 × 30.02); M; 19.5; ex VILLE DE BORDEAUX 1977; Sisters: **★82621 HEI LONG JIANG** (RC); ex VILLE DE LYON 1977; **82622 ALIAKMON LEADER** (Gr); ex VILLE DU HAVRE 1977; **82623 ALIAKMON LIGHT** (Gr); ex VILLE DE BREST 1977.

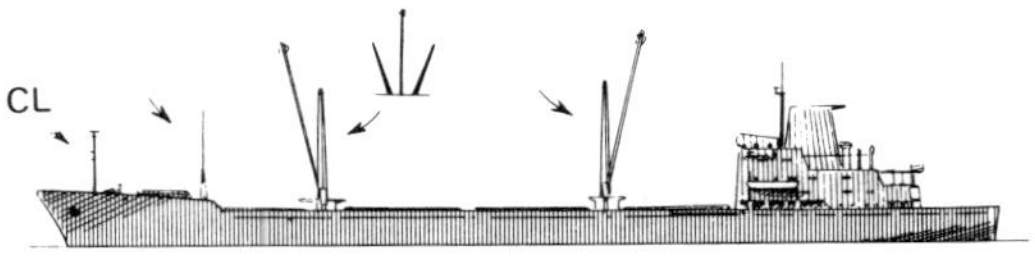

KM_3F *H1*
● **82530 TORM AMERICA.** Sg/FRG 1970; C/HL; 7500/10500; 153.27 × 9.01/10.01 (502.85 × 29.56/32.84); M; 20; ex GOLDEN FELS 1980; ex ATLANTICA MONTREAL 1976; ex GOLDENFELS 1972; Converted container ship; Sisters: **82531 TORM AMERICA** (Sg); ex DENEB 1981; ex GUTENFELS; ex ATLANTICA NEW YORK 1973; ex GUTENFELS 1972; The following may have deck cranes: **82532 LONE STAR** (Sg); ex STEINFELS 1980; **82533 EMILIA S** (Pa); ex STERNENFELS 1980; **82534 FRANCESCA** (Pa); ex STOCKENFELS 1980; **82535 MANILA** (Pi); ex STOLZENFELS 1980; **82536 ZAMBOANGA** (Pi); ex STRAHLENFELS 1980.

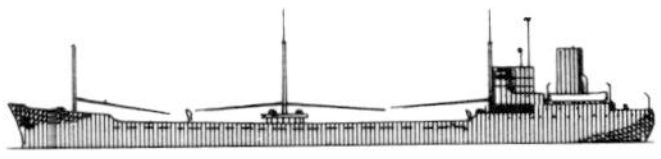

KM_3F *H13*
82560 NAM IL. Ko/Ja 1958; C; 3400; 102.39 × 6.46 (335.93 × 21.19); M; 12; ex SANSEI MARU 1966; Sister: **82561 CHUN SUNG** (Ko); ex MIZUKI MARU 1968; ex SUISEI MARU 1966; Possibly similar: **82562 DON HERNAN II** (Pi); ex NANYO MARU 1968.

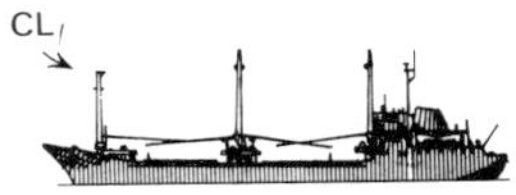

KM_3F *H13*
82590 PAMIR I. Pa/FRG 1965; C; 500; 73.44 × 3.65 (240.94 × 11.98); M; 11.5; ex HASLACH BEWA 1975; ex HASLACH 1971.

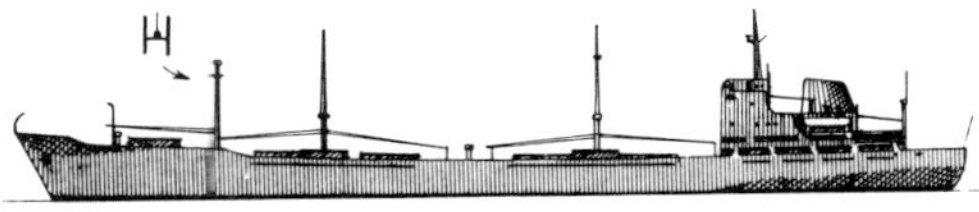

KM_3FK *H13*
82610 BARENTS SEA. Pa/FRG 1960; C; 6200/8800; 151.42 × 8.21/9.27 (496.78 × 26.94/30.41); M; 13.5; ex SAAB 1972; ex JARITA 1968.

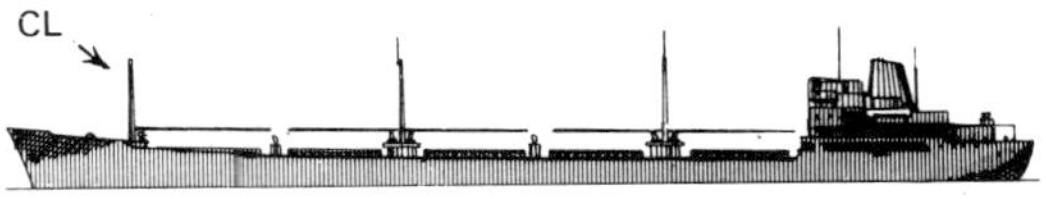

KM_3FK *H13*
82630 AMSTELVEEN. Ne/Ne 1963; C; 12300; 163.07 × 9.86 (535 × 32.35); M; 13.5.

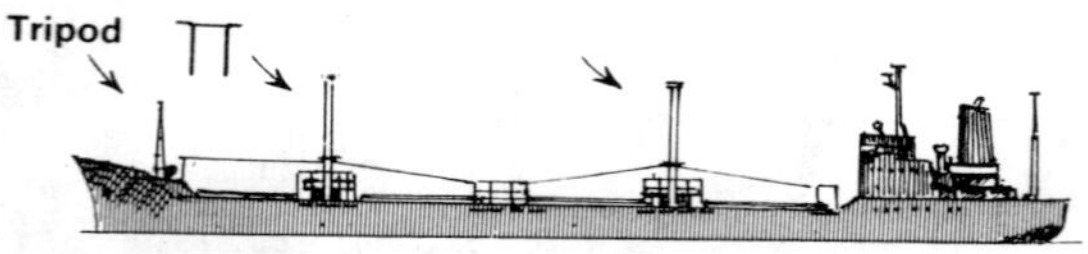

KM_3FK H13
82640 IRENES ECSTACY. Gr/Ja 1969; B; 10300; 154.05 × 9.19 (505.41 × 30.15); M; 14.75; ex MIDAS ARROW; ex NAGATO MARU 1971; Sisters: **82641 NIKOS N.** (Gr); ex DONA JUANA 1979; ex RETLADAWN 1979; ex OVERSEAS NAVIGATOR 1975; ex HAIKO MARU 1973; Possible sisters: **82642 NIKOLAOS A** (Gr); ex MIDAS PRINCE; ex ORIENTAL PRINCE 1971; ex YAMATO MARU 1970; **82643 MIDAS RHEIN** (Li); ex RHEIN MARU 1972; **82644 MONTROSE** (Li).

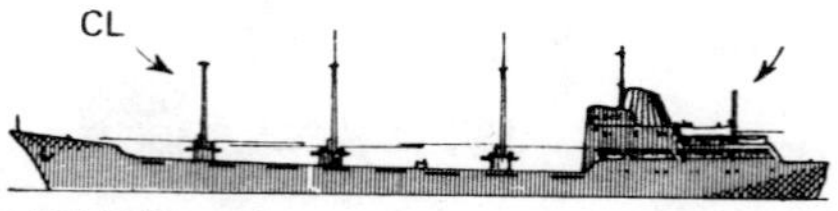

KM_3FK H13
82650 VILLE DE MAHEBOURG. Ms/Fr 1962; C; 6400; 130 × 7.49 (426.51 × 24.57); M; 15; ex KAMON 1973; ex VILLE DE DJIBOUTI 1972; ex SAINT FRANCOIS 1970.

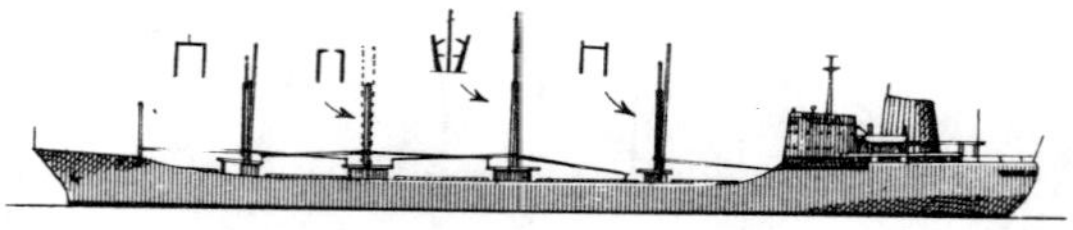

KM_5F H13
82660 BAILUNDO. Po/Pd 1969; C; 7700/11600; 158.4 × 8.41/10.03 (519.69 × 27.59/32.91); M; 14; launched as ARTEMONAS **'B441'** type; Sister: **82661 CUNENE** (Po).

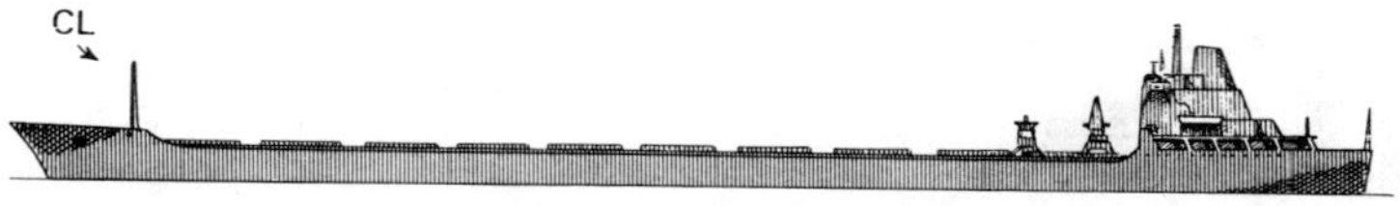

KNCMFK H13
82670 THEOGENNITOR. Gr/Ja 1968; B; 35500; 223.91 × 12.19 (734.61 × 39.99); M; 15.5; ex AGAMEMNON.

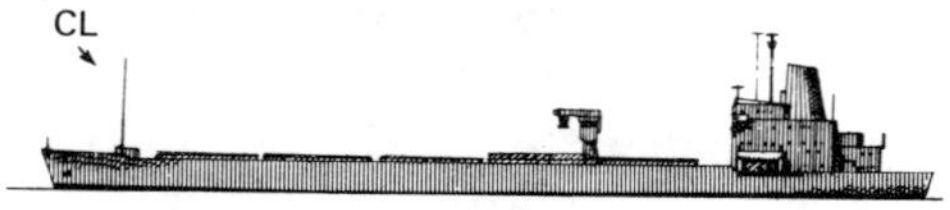

KNMF H
82680 WEYROC. Pa/FRG 1972; B/V; 8900; 141.61 × 7.27 (464.6 × 23.85); M; 16; Side doors and ramps.

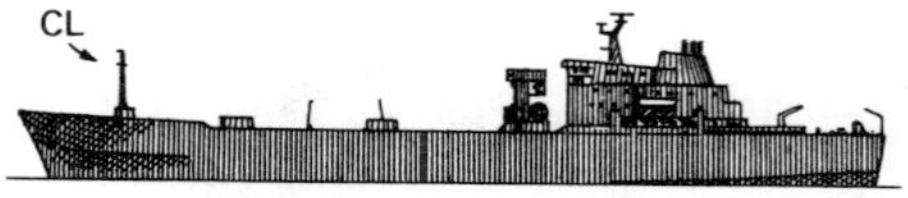

KNMF H
82690 NEDLLOYD ROCKANJE. Ne/Fi 1972; RoC; 4300; 137.52 × 6 64 (451.18 × 21.78); TSM; 18; ex RHEINFELS 1977; ex ANTARES 1975; Stern doors; Sisters: **82691 ORION** (Fi); **82692 SIRIUS** (Fi); **82693 BALTIC ENTERPRISE** (Br); **82694 BALTIC PROGRESS** (Br).

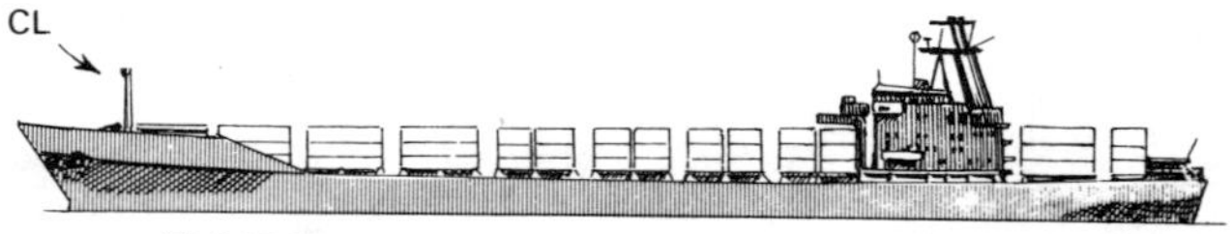

KNMF H1
82700 COLUMBUS AUSTRALIA. FRG/FRG 1971; Con; 19100; 193.94 × 10.85 (636.29 × 35.6); T; 22; Sisters (FRG flag): **82701 COLUMBUS AMERICA; 82702 COLUMBUS NEW ZEALAND.**

●
82706

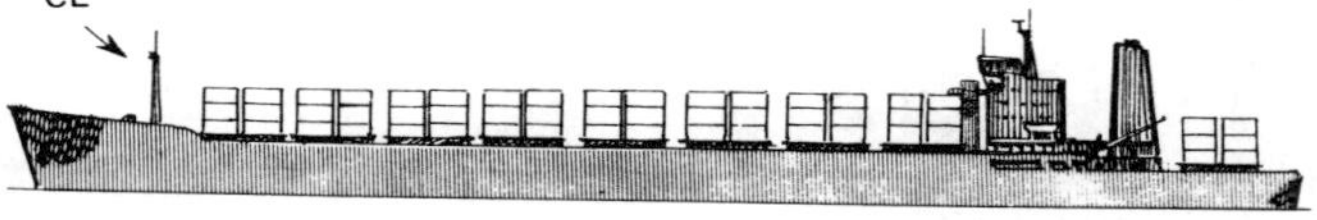

KNMF H1
● **82710 CARIBIA EXPRESS.** FRG/Pd 1976; Con; 27900; 203.99 × 10 (669.26 × 32.81); M; 22; **'B-463'** type; Sisters: **82711 CORDILLERA EXPRESS** (FRG); **82712 ALLEMANIA EXPRESS** (FRG); **82713 AMERICA EXPRESS** (FRG); **82714 ADVISER** (Br); **82715 ASTRONOMER** (Br); **82716 CARAIBE** (Fr); **82717 HOLLANDIA** (Ne); **82718 AUTHOR** (Br).

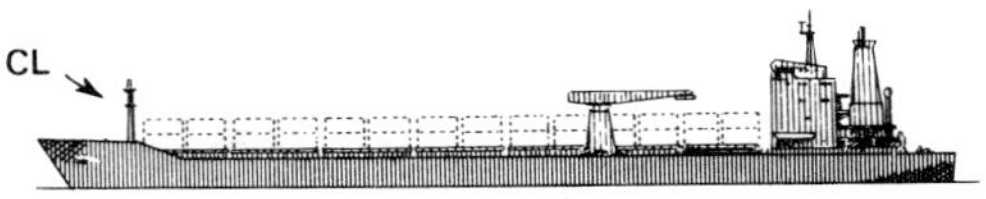

KNMF H1
82720 URUNDI. FRG/FRG 1977; Con; 10900; 145.01 × 9.02 (475.75 × 29.59); M; 19; ex GULF RANGER 1978; ex URUNDI 1977; Launched as BRABANT; Sisters (FRG flag): **82721 ULANGA:** ex GULF CLIPPER 1978; Launched as ULANGA; **82722 USAMBARA:** ex GULF LANCER 1978; ex USAMBARA 1977; Launched as ESCHENBACH.

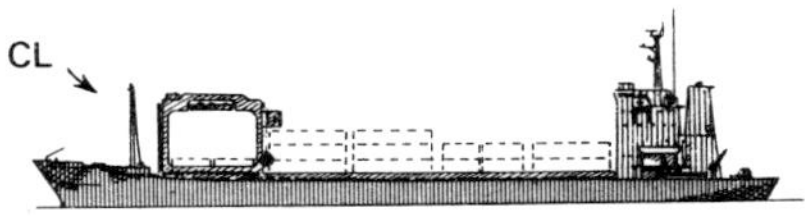

KNMF H1
● **82750 HODEIDAH CROWN.** Sg/Ja 1977; Con; 6200; 118.12 × 7.42 (387.53 × 24.34); M; —; ex RANGER 1979; ex STRATHKEITH 1979; Sister: **82751 CHENGTU** (Sg); ex JEDDAH CROWN 1981; ex TIMBER BAY 1979; ex STRATHKIRN 1979.

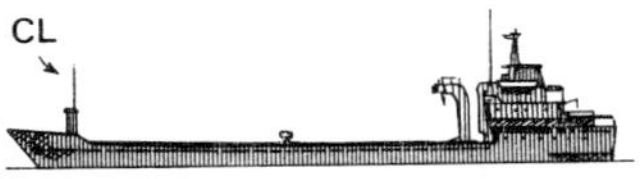

KNMF H13
● **82800 SATURNUS.** Sw/DDR 1971; C; 3200; 104.04 × 5.77; M; ex HANSA BAY 1978; Sisters: **82801 KLAREDON** (Br); ex LAREDO 1980; ex HANSA NORD 1979; **82802 RIO BRAVO** (Br); ex HANSA TRADE 1980; **82803 NAZIE BEAUTY** (Sh); ex HANSEAT 1980; **82804 ANATOLIA** (Pa); ex LARCH 1980; ex JOWOOD; **82805 HVALVIK** (Ic); ex MAMBO 1975; ex SAMBA 1972; **82806 JANJE** (Pa); ex JANJA 1979; ex RUMBA 1975; **82807 METEOR** (Sw); ex BENGATE 1977; ex JENKA 1974; **82808 ELISABETH** (Cy); ex ESKDALEGATE 1977; ex FREDERICKSGATE 1974; ex BRUNI 1974; **82809 WINDROVER** (Sw); ex SCOL ROVER 1980; ex SIMONSGATE 1976; ex HANSEL 1974.

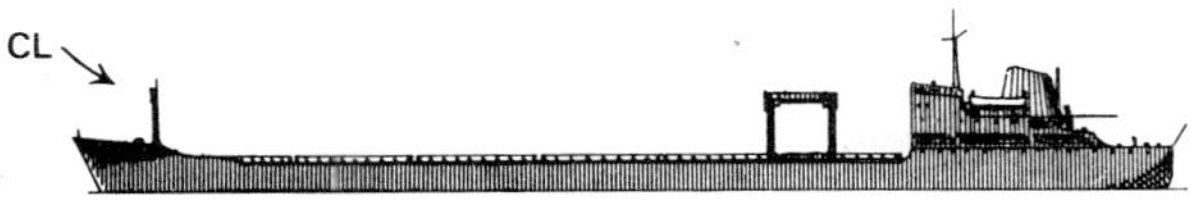

KNMF H13
● **82730 STAR SUPREME.** Pa/FRG 1959; B; 13200; 171.81 × 10.24 (563.68 × 33.6); M; 13.5; ex STAR BALLARAT 1976.

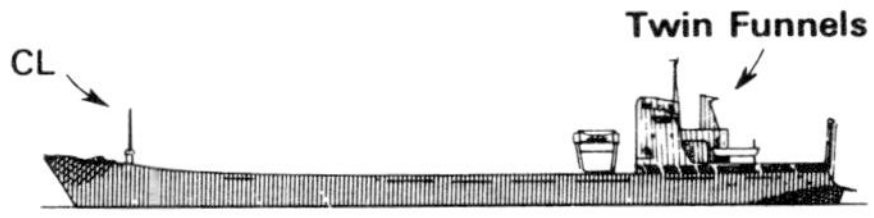

KNMF H1
82740 JOLLY ARANCIONE. It/FRG 1957/74; RoC; 2700; 126.4 × 5.43 (414.7 × 17.81); M; 15.25; ex ELSE REITH 1974; ex AQUILA 1972; Converted from general cargo 1974.

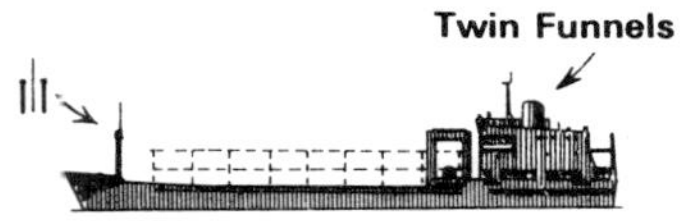

KNMF H13
● **82760 CAPTAIN PADDON.** Br/Ne 1971; RoC/Con; 1000/1600; 85.32 × 4.71 (279.92 × 15.45); M; 15; ex BRITIS 1974; ex ATLANTIC JAMAICAN 1973; Stern ramp; **'Tarros'** type; Sisters (Some Spanish built): **82761 MERZARIO ETRURIA** (Br); ex VENTO DI SCIROCCO 1976; **82762 DORLI** (Br); **82763 ASTRON** (Br); ex MERZARIO SARDINIA 1978; ex LONDIS 1976; ex ATLANTIC BERMUDIAN 1973; **82764 TARROS FIR** (Br); ex CHESHIRE ENDEAVOUR 1977; ex LAULA 1973; **82765 TARROS GAGE** (Br); ex LAHNECK 1978; ex BERGEN JUNO 1977; **82766 TARROS CEDAR** (Br); ex MERZARIO LIGURIA 1979; ex VENTO DI MAESTRALE 1976; **82767 TARROS PAXICON** (Br); ex TARROS HAZEL 1978; ex UNION SOUTH PACIFIC 1978; **82768 ZIM MANILA** (Br); ex TARROS ILEX; ex MARISUD PRIMA 1978; ex TARROS ILEX 1977; ex CHESHIRE VENTURE 1977; **82769 ZIM BANGKOK** (Br); ex TARROS JUNIPER 1979; ex MERZARIO SICILIA 1979; ex SWIFT ARROW 1976; **82790 PANAY** (Pi); ex TARROS ELM; ex ZIM MANILA; ex TARROS ELM; ex VOORLOPER 1978; launched as VENTO DI LIBECCIO.

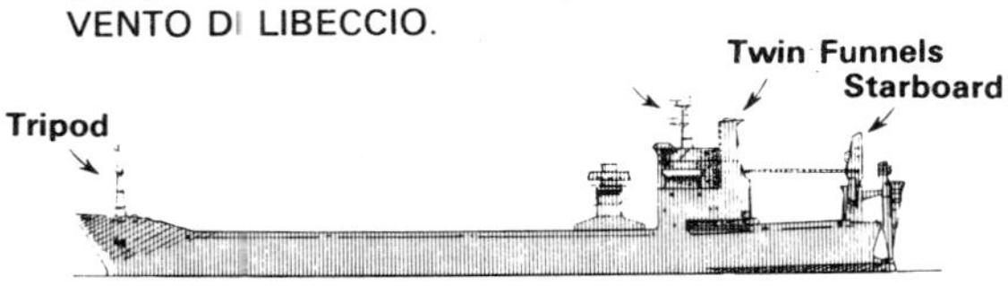

KNMFCR H1
⋆**82820 LEDENICE.** Ys/Ys 1979; Roc/Con/C; 5600; 144.4 × 6.5 (473.75 × 21.33); M; 17.9; Travelling gantry (with slewing deck crane); Stern slewing ramp; Probable Sister: ⋆**82821 BRIBIR.** (Ys).

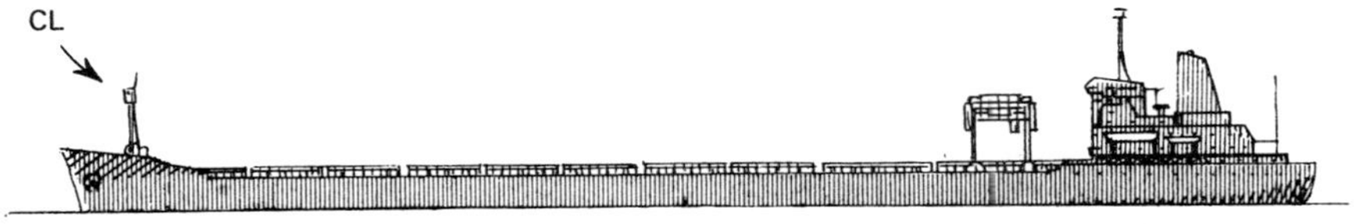

KNMFK H1
82830 THEOLIPTOS. Gr/FRG 1965; B; 41900; 250.02 × 13.8 (820.28 × 45.28); M; 15.5; ex MATHILDE SCHULTE 1976; ex SIGHANSA 1969.

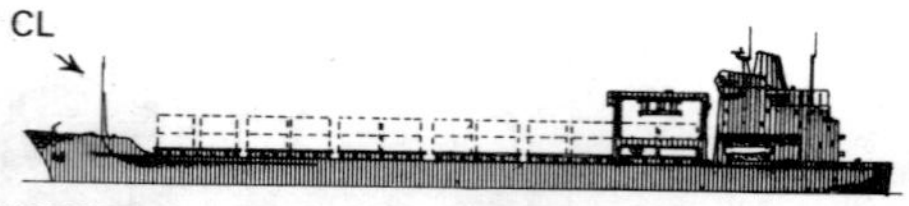

KNMFK H1
82840 BERG. SA/SA 1977; Con; 8200; 137.78 × 7.5 (452.03 × 24.61); M; 17; Sister: **82841 BREEDE** (SA).

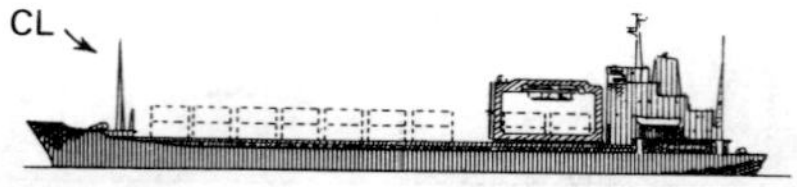

KNMFK H1
● **82850 PAPUAN CHIEF.** Br/Ja 1977; C/Con; 6400; 118.12 × 7.02 (387.53 × 23.03); M; 15; Sisters (Br flag): **82851 CORAL CHIEF; 82852 NIMOS.**

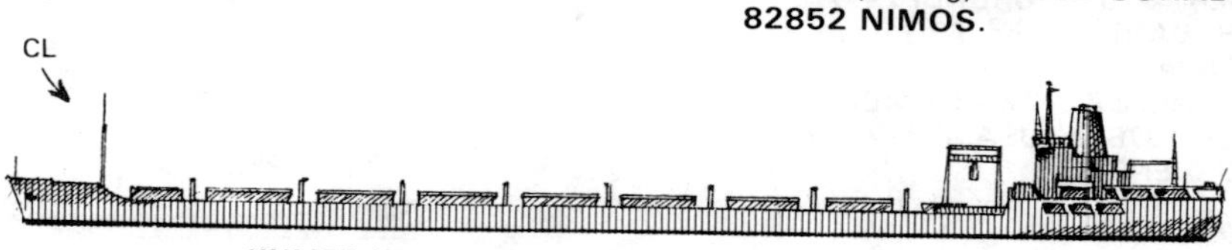

KNMFK H13
82860 PHOSPHORE CONVEYOR. Li/Ja 1969; B; 36500; 259.52 × 13.23 (851.44 × 43.41); M; 15.5.

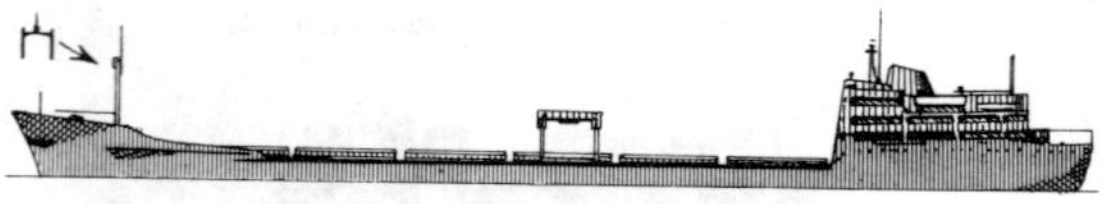

KNMFK H13
82870 STAR LIGHT. Gr/No 1961; B; 13200; 170.85 × 10.46 (560.53 × 34.32); M; 15; ex STAR BAY 1977; ex SONGA 1965.

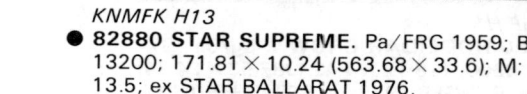

KNMFK H13
● **82880 STAR SUPREME.** Pa/FRG 1959; B; 13200; 171.81 × 10.24 (563.68 × 33.6); M; 13.5; ex STAR BALLARAT 1976.

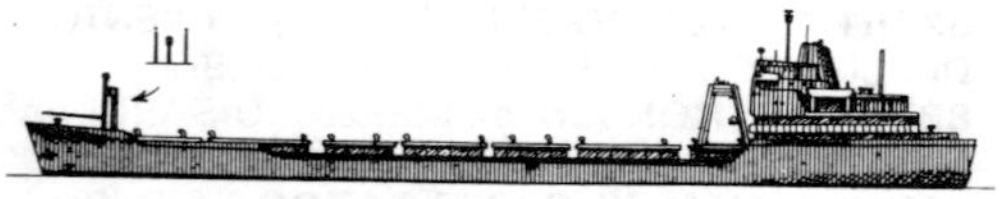

KNMFK H13
82890 ALPPILA. Fi/FRG 1963; B; 11500; 149.94 × 9.49 (491.93 × 31.14); M; 14.5; ex BINSHIP 1975; ex FINSHIP 1972; The twin kingposts on the forecastle may be removed (sister ANNA C has this appearance); Sisters: **82891 ANNA C** (Gr); ex BANAK 1978; **82892 LAS VEGAS** (Br); ex ARROWCANE 1980; ex BETH 1975; **82893 ANASTASIOS C** (Gr); ex HARIWA 1978; ex BARDU 1975; **82894 AEOLIAN SUN** (Gr); ex BAVANG 1974; Similar: **82895 TA LUANG** (Pa); ex COSTAS K 1979; ex HAVGA 1974.

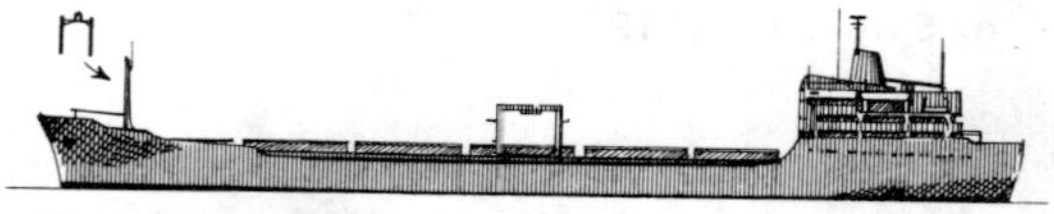

KNMFK H13
82900 STAR PRIDE. Gr/No 1962; B; 15600; 170.85 × 10.45 (560.53 × 34.28); M; 15.5; ex STAR FJELLANGER 1977; ex FJELLANGER 1972; ex SILJA 1965.

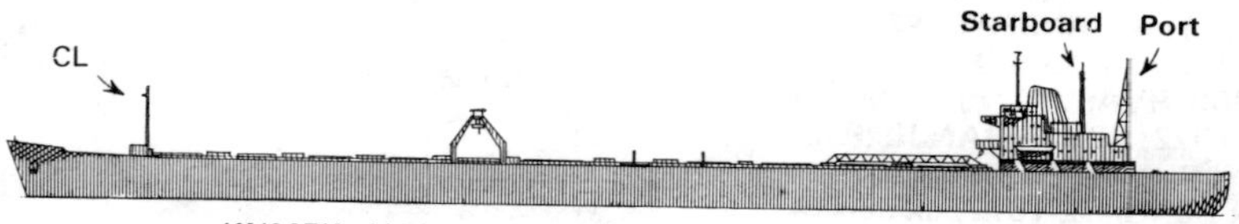

KNMFK$_2$ H13
82910 CONVEYOR. Li/Ja 1968; B; 39500; 143.59 × 14.55 (799.18 × 47.74); T; 15.5; ex UNIVERSE CONVEYOR 1980.

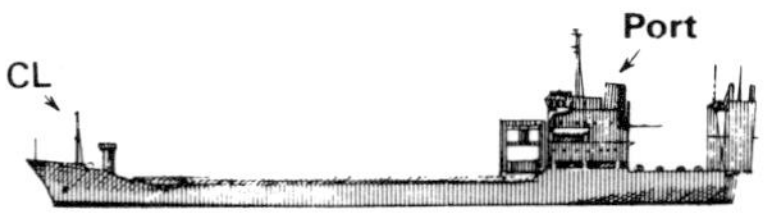

KNMFKR H13
● **82920 STRIDER AUSTRALIA.** Li/Ja 1975; RoC/Con; 3400; 119.61 × 7.47 (392.42 × 24.51); M; 16.75; ex MERZARIO IONIA 1978; ex MAERSK TEMPO 1976; Quarter ramp; **'Strider'** type; Sisters: **82921 STRIDER CRYSTAL** (Li); ex AQABA CROWN: **82922 STRIDER BROADSWORD** (Li); ex JEDDAH CROWN; ex STRIDER BROADSWORD 1976; **82923 STRIDER DIAMOND** (Br); ex SAUDI CROWN 1980; Similar (some have larger funnels): **82924 JADE BOUNTY** (Br); ex STRIDER GALLANT 1978; **82925 OPAL BOUNTY** (Br); **82926 SAPPHIRE BOUNTY** (Br); launched as STRIDER HERO 1978; **82927 TURQUOISE BOUNTY** (Br); Possibly similar (larger): **82928 FORUM NEW ZEALAND** (NZ); ex STRIDER ISIS 1982; **82828 STRIDER JUNO** (Br).

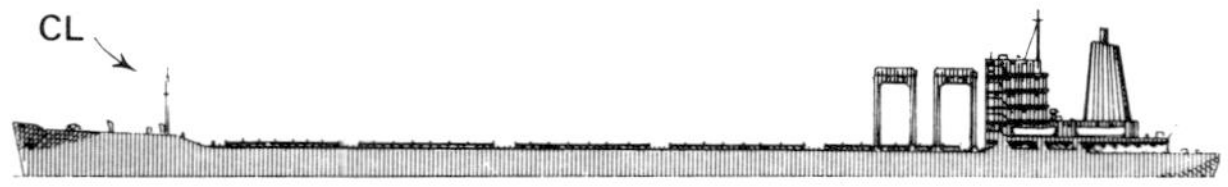

KN_2MF H1
82940 INGER. US/US-FRG 1945/62; B; 14200; 190.81 × 9.26 (626.02 × 30.38); T-E; 14; ex TRANSNORTHERN 1962; ex WANG HUNTER 1960; ex ATLANTIC EXPORTER; ex FORT CASPAR 1946; Converted from 'T-2' type tanker 1962.

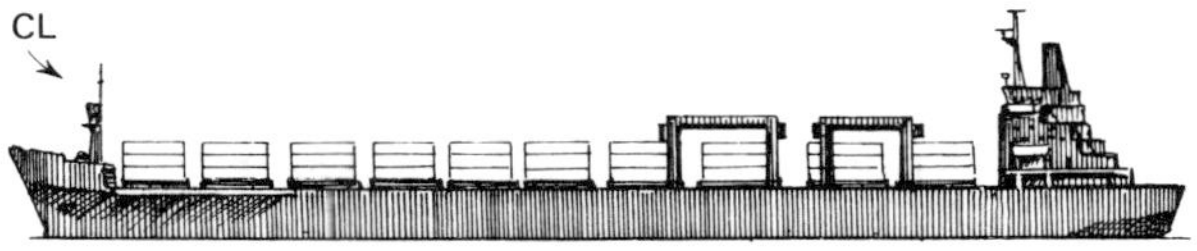

KN_2MF H1
● **82950 PACIFIC LUMBERMAN.** Br/Fi 1971; B/TC/V; 23600; 184.21 × 10.78 (604.36 × 35.37); M; 16.5; ex PACIFIC; Sister: **82951 PACIFIC FORESTER** (Li); ex SUECIA.

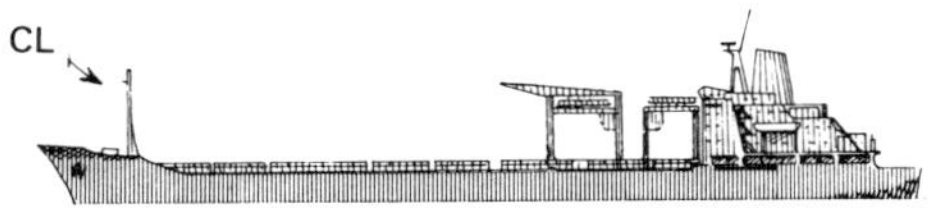

KN_2MF H1
82960 DARWIN TRADER. Au/Au 1970; B/Con; 10800; 139.6 × 9.15 (458 × 30.02); M; 15.

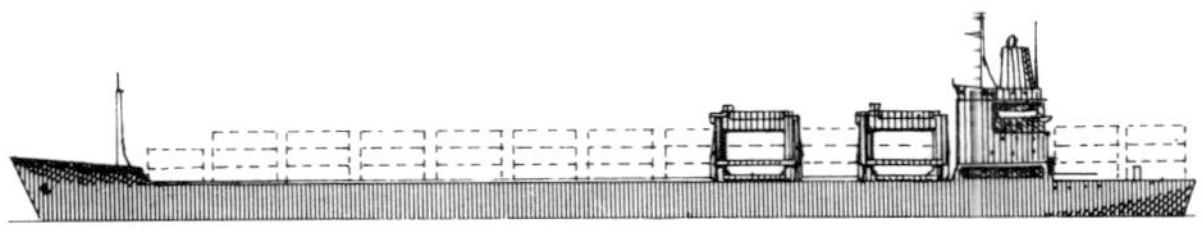

KN_2MF H1
82970 SEA-LAND LEADER. US/FRG-Ja 1962/78; Con; 17400; 201.84 × 8.28 (662.2 × 27.17); M; 18.5; ex ELIZABETHPORT 1978; Sisters (US flag): **82971 SEA-LAND ADVENTURER** ex SAN FRANCISCO 1978; **82972 SEA-LAND PACER** ex SAN JUAN 1978; **82873 SEA-LAND PIONEER** ex LOS ANGELES 1978.

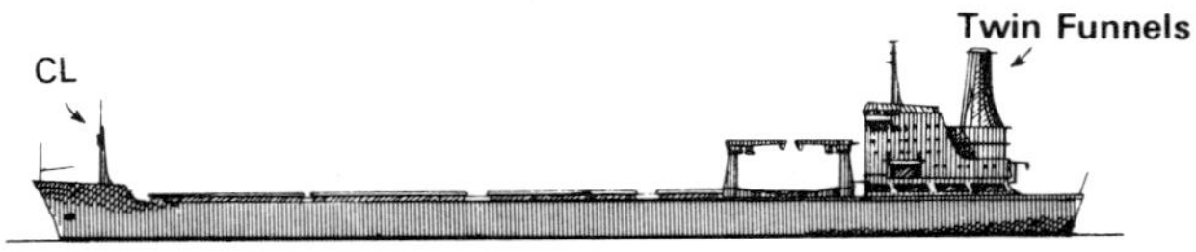

KN_2MF H1
82980 BORG. No/Be 1972; B/Ch; 19600; 172.52 × 10.52 (566 × 34.51); M; 15.25.

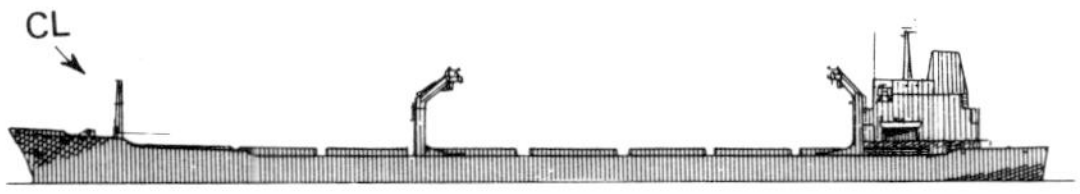

KN_2MF H1
82990 FALCON. Gr/Ja 1977; B; 13900; 164.34 × 9.4 (539.11 × 30.84); M; 15; **'Friendship'** type; Sisters: **82991 ANANGEL MIGHT** (Gr); **82992 ANANGEL SPIRIT** (Gr); **82993 PRESTIGIOUS** (Br); launched as EFDIM JUNIOR; **82994 ACE AUSTRALIA; 82995 GEORGE** (Gr); **82996 ANANGEL ENDEAVOUR** (Gr); Possible sisters: **82997 ANANGEL FIDELITY** (Gr); **82998 THEREAN MARINER** (Gr); **82999 AMETHYST** (Gr).

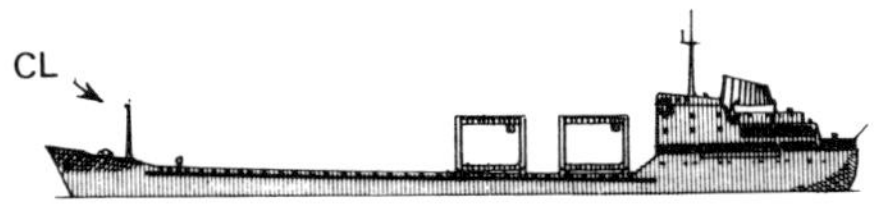

KN_2MF H13
83010 ISLAND CONTAINER. Pa/Au 1964; Con; 5700; 126.17 × 7.62 (413.94 × 25); M; 16; ex KOORINGA.

KN_2MF H13
83020 ANGELIC GLORY. Gr/Ja 1967; B; 24800; 206.03 × 10.9 (675.95 × 35.76); M; 15.25; ex NELSON C. WHITE 1970.

KN_2MF H13
● **83030 STAR CLIPPER.** Li/Sw 1969; B/Con; 16500; 171.91 × 10.41 (564 × 34.15); M; —; Similar (some have different gantries): **83031 STAR PERSEUS** (Gr); ex STAR EAST 1980; ex STAR HERANGER 1978; ex HERANGER 1972; **83032 STAR ORPHEUS** (Gr); ex STAR NAJD 1980; ex STAR TARANGER 1978; ex TARANGER 1972; **83033 STAR THESEUS** (Li); ex STAR OASIS 1980; ex STAR MALMANGER 1978; ex MALMANGER 1972; **83034 STAR DELTA** (Gr); ex STAR OLYMPIAN 1979; ex STAR COLUMBA 1977; **83035 STAR INDONESIA** (Pi); ex STAR IONIAN 1980; ex STAR ATLANTIC 1979; ex STAR ABADAN 1979; ex STAR ATLANTIC 1977; **83036 STAR LACONIAN** (Gr); ex ASTORIA 1979; ex STAR ASTORIA 1978; ex STAR ASSYRIA 1975; **83037 STAR MALAYSIA** (Pi); ex STAR RHODIAN 1980; ex STAR SHAHPOUR 1979; ex STAR ASAHI 1977; ex STAR ACADIA 1975; **83038 STAR DORIAN** (Gr); ex STAR AMALFI 1978; ex IRISH STARDUST 1976; **83039 STAR GAZER** (Gr); ex STAR ATHENIAN 1979; ex STAR CARIBOO 1978; **83040 STAR BULFORD** (Br); ex STAR PINEWOOD 1974; **83041 STAR BLACKFORD** (Br); ex BLACKFORD; ex STAR BLACKFORD 1978; ex STARWORTH; **83042 STAR SINGAPORE** (Pi); ex STAR DELPHIAN 1980; ex IRISH STAR 1978; **83043 AEOLIAN CARRIER** (Gr); ex STAR PROTEUS 1980; exSTAR SEA 1980; ex STAR DAVANGER 1978; ex DAVANGER 1972.

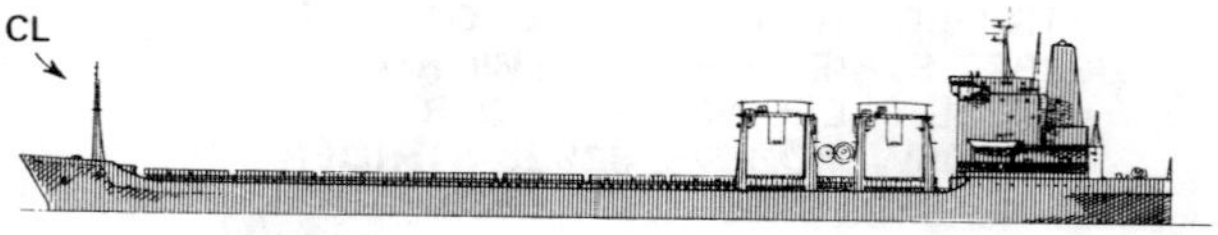

KN_2MF H13
83050 STAR MAGNATE. Br/Ja 1978; B/Con; 26900; 182.91 × 12.03 (600.1 × 39.47); M; 15; Sisters (Br flag): **83051 STAR HONG KONG; 83052 STAR WORLD**; Similar (No flag): **83053 STAR DIEPPE;** ex STAR SHIRAZ 1979; ex STAR DIEPPE 1977; **83054 STAR DOVER;** ex STAR ESFAHAN 1979; ex STAR DOVER 1977.

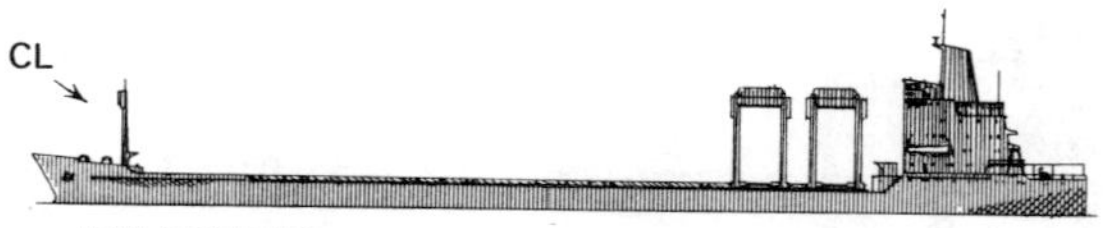

KN_2MF H13
83060 EAGLE ARROW. Br/Br 1970; B; 17200; 167.57 × 10.37 (549.77 × 34.02); M; 15; ex BULK EAGLE 1974; Sisters: **83061 POLYDEFKIS** (Gr); ex LA PAMPA; Similar: **83062 ANTAR** (Gr); ex HEINA; **83063 ALTAIR** (Gr); ex LISTA; Similar (built in Norway): **83064 OGNA** (No).

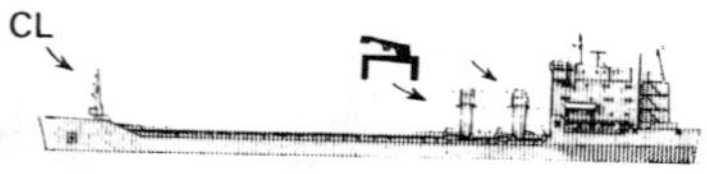

KN_2MF H13
83070 BOXY. Sw/Sw 1978; B/TC; 6200; 121 × 7.62 (396.98 × 25); M; 14.6; Travelling cranes; Jibs are normally stowed athwartships as shown in drawing; Sister: **83071 DANIA** (Sw).

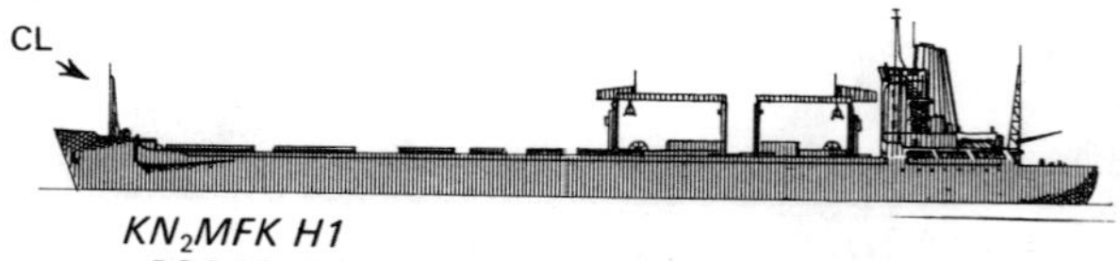

KN_2MFK H1
⋆**83080 DAI HAI.** RC/Ja 1967; B; 19900; 176 × 10.7 (577.43 × 35.1); M; 14.25; ex CHUETSUSAN MARU 1978.

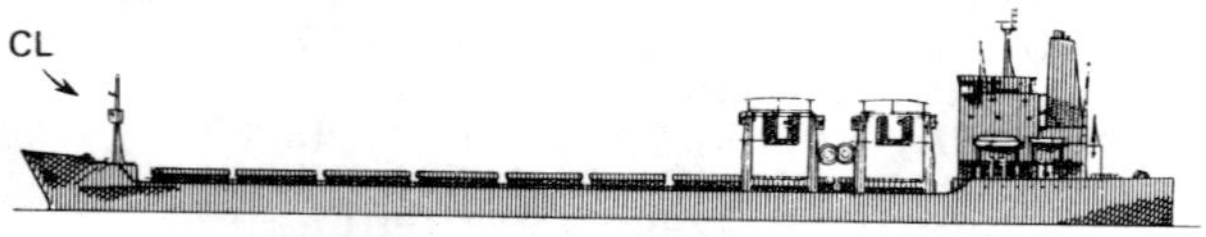

KN_2MFK H13
83090 STAR ENTERPRISE. Li/Ja 1978; B/Con; 25100; 183 × 12.05 (600.39 × 39.53); M; 14.6; Sister: **83091 STAR CARRIER** (Li).

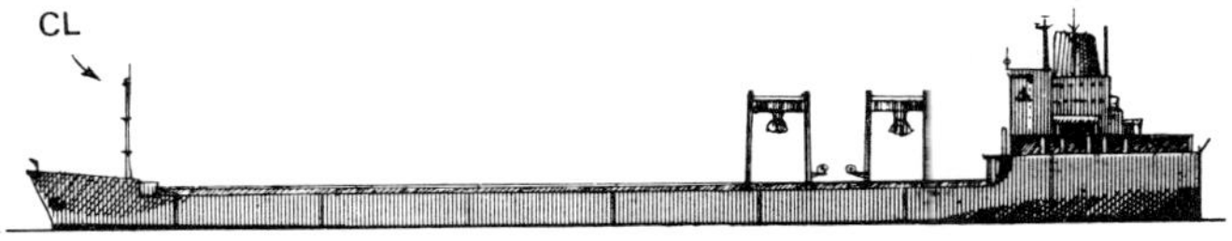

KN$_2$MFK H13
83100 HOEGH MALLARD. No/Ja 1977; B; 29200; 200.51 × 11.51 (657.84 × 37.62); M; 15.25; Sisters (No flag): **83101 HOEGH MASCOT; 83102 HOEGH MARLIN;** Possibly similar: **83103 HOEGH MERCHANT; 83104 HOEGH MERIT; 83105 HOEGH MINERVA; 83106 HOEGH MUSKETEER; 83107 HOEGH MIRANDA.**

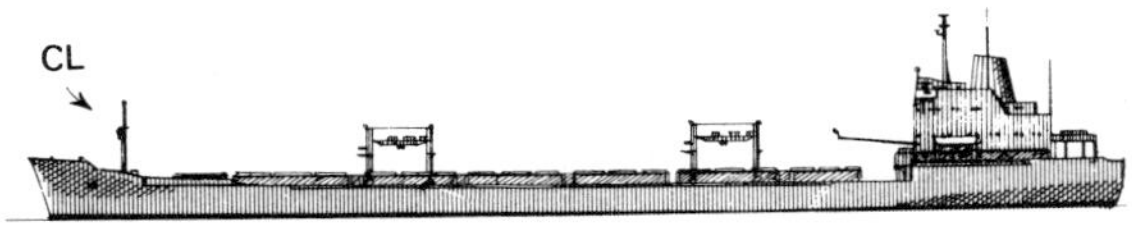

KN$_2$MFK H13
● **83110 STAR CLIPPER.** Li/Sw 1969; B/Con; 16500; 171.91 × 10.41 (564 × 34.15); M; —; Similar (some have different gantries): **83111 STAR PERSEUS** (Gr); ex STAR EAST 1980; ex STAR HERANGER 1978; ex HERANGER 1972; **83112 STAR ORPHEUS** (Gr); ex STAR NAJD 1980; ex STAR TARANGER 1978; ex TARANGER 1972; **83113 STAR THESEUS** (Li); ex STAR OASIS 1980; ex STAR MALMANGER 1978; ex MALMANGER 1972; **83114 STAR DELTA** (Gr); ex STAR OLYMPIAN 1979; ex STAR COLUMBA 1977; **83115 STAR INDONESIA** (Pi); ex STAR IONIAN 1980; ex STAR ATLANTIC 1979; ex STAR ABADAN 1979; ex STAR ATLANTIC 1977; **83116 STAR LACONIAN** (Gr); ex ASTORIA 1979; ex STAR ASTORIA 1978; ex STAR ASSYRIA 1975; **83117 STAR MALAYSIA** (Pi); ex STAR RHODIAN 1980; ex STAR SHAHPOUR 1979; ex STAR ASAHI 1977; ex STAR ACADIA 1975; **83118 STAR DORIAN** (Gr); ex STAR AMALFI 1978; ex IRISH STARDUST 1976; **83119 STAR GAZER** (Gr); ex STAR ATHENIAN 1979; ex STAR CARIBOO 1978; **83120 STAR BULFORD** (Br); ex STAR PINEWOOD 1974; **83121 STAR BLACKFORD** (Br); ex BLACKFORD; ex STAR BLACKFORD 1978; ex STARWORTH; **83122 STAR SINGAPORE** (Pi); ex STAR DELPHIAN ex IRISH STAR 1978; **83123 AEOLIAN CARRIER** (Gr); ex STAR PROTEUS 1980; ex STAR SEA 1980; ex STAR DAVANGER 1978; ex DAVANGER 1972.

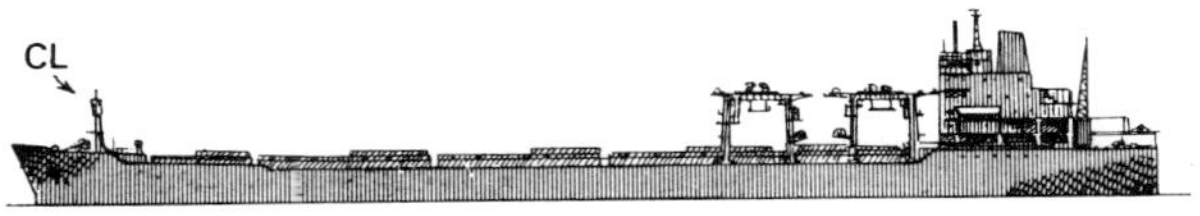

KN$_2$MFK H13
83130 FALCON ARROW. Br/Ja 1977; B; 15300; 182 × 11.55 (597.11 × 37.89); M; 14.5; Sister: **83131 SWAN ARROW** (No); Similar (Br flag): **83132 LA CORDILLERA; 83133 LA COSTA; 83134 LA PRIMAVERA; 83135 LA ENSENADA; 83136 TSURU ARROW; 83137 NANDU ARROW;** (No flag): **83138 GRENA; 83139 EGDA; 83140 MOLDA; 83141 STRINDA; 83142 KIWI ARROW; 83143 TOKI ARROW;** (Fr flag): **83144 ALAIN L-D; 83145 GERARD L-D; 83146 JEAN L-D; 83147 LOUIS L-D.**

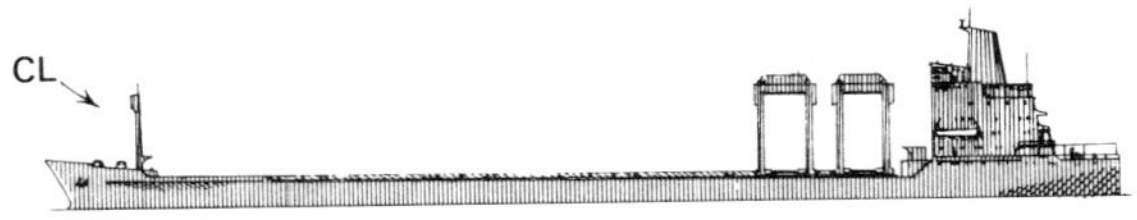

KN$_2$MFK H13
83160 EAGLE ARROW. Br/Br 1970; B; 17200; 167.57 × 10.37 (549.77 × 34.02); M; 15; ex BULK EAGLE 1974; Sisters: **83161 POLYDEFKIS** (Gr); ex LA PAMPA; Similar: **83162 ANTAR** (Gr); ex HEINA; **83163 ALTAIR** (Gr); ex LISTA; Similar (built in Norway): **83164 OGNA** (No).

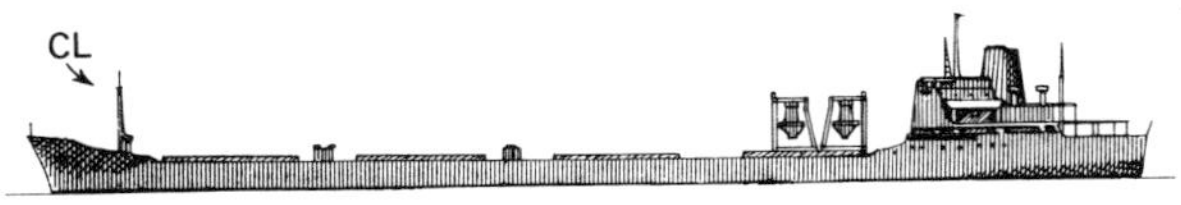

KN$_2$MFK H13
83170 SUGELA. Br/Ja 1965; B; 16400; 178.01 × 9.49 (584 × 31.14); M; 15; ex S.A. SUGELA 1977; launched as SUGELA; Gantries may have been removed.

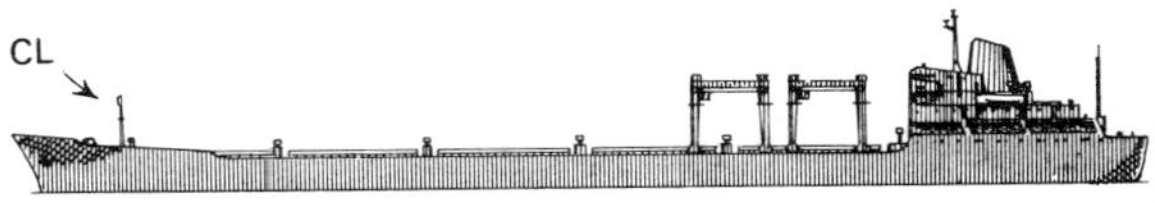

KN$_2$MFK H13
83180 PACIFIC RELIANCE. Li/Ja 1965; B; 16200; 178.64 × 10.19 (586.09 × 33.43); M; 15.5; ex TROPWOOD.

KN$_2$MFK H13
83190 MUNKSUND. Sw/Sw 1968; B; 9400; 153.4 × 8.4 (503.28 × 27.56); M; 16.5; Sisters (Sw flag): **83191 HOLMSUND; 83192 TUNADAL.**

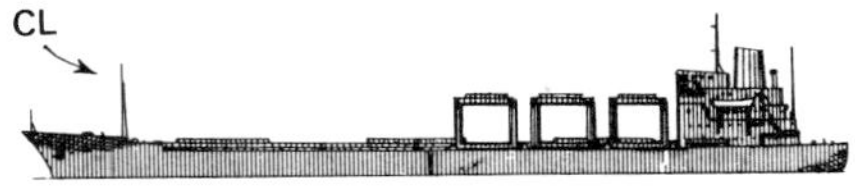

KN$_3$MFK H1
83200 AIFANOURIOS. Gr/Ja 1965; B; 8600; 128.71 × 9.64 (422.28 × 31.63); M; 14.25; ex SITKA MARU 1975.

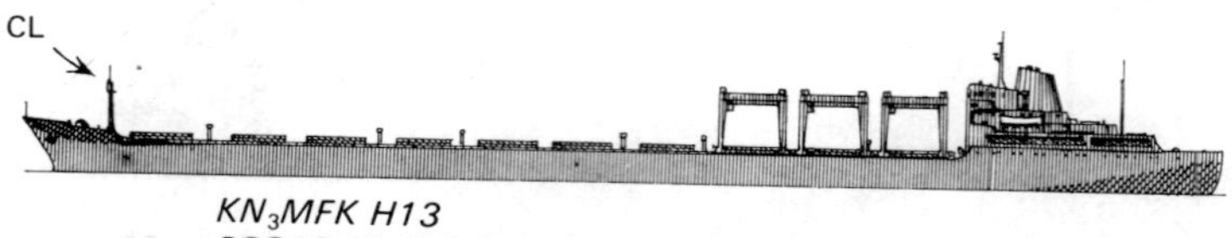

KN_3MFK H13
83210 TLALOC. Me/Ja 1967; B; 29100; 223.02 × 12.05 (731.69 × 39.53); M; 15.75; ex STRATHEARN.

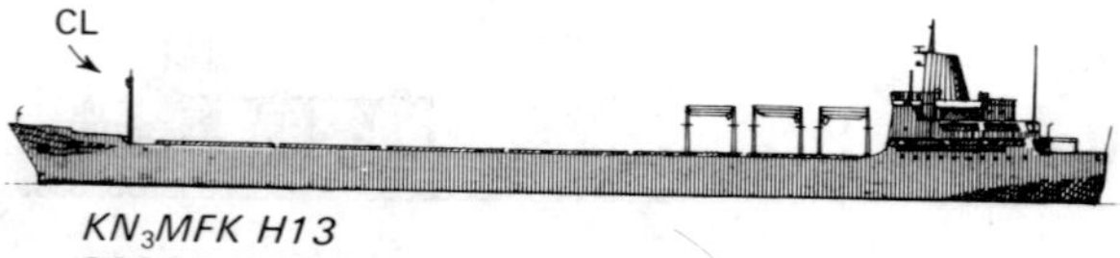

KN_3MFK H13
83220 WEST SUNORI. Pa/Ja 1968; B; 21400; 181.01 × 10.47 (593.86 × 34.35); M; 14.75; ex J.V. CLYNE; Sisters: **8322 GRAND RELIANCE** (Pa); ex H.R. MACMILLAN 1978; **83222 TEXISTEPEC** (Me); ex WEST JINORI; ex N.R. CRUMP 1979.

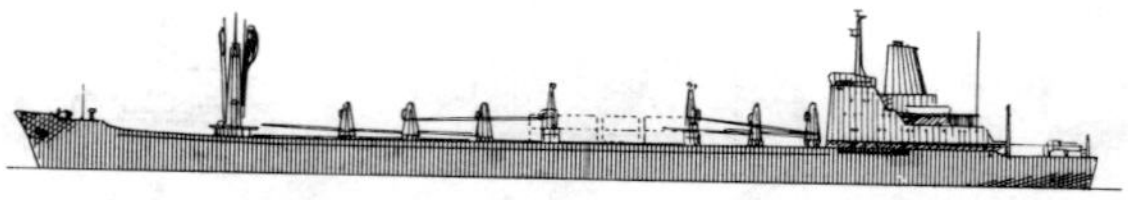

MC_7MFK H1
83230 SAINT BERNARD. Fr/Sw 1967/71; C/Con; 9000/12000; 172.19 × 8.41/9.38 (564.93 × 27.59/30.77); M; 19.5; ex TELENDOS 1980; ex TAMERLANE 1978; Converted from general cargo & lengthened 1971; Sister: **83231 SAINT BERTRAND** (Fr); ex TILOS 1980; ex TIRRANNA 1978.

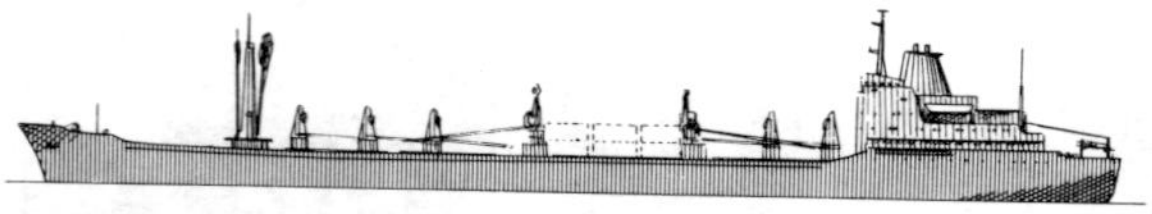

MC_7MFK H13
83240 TORRENS. Sg/Sw 1967/71; C/Con; 8900/12400; 174.71 × 8.47/9.39 (573.2 × 27.79/30.81); M; 19.5; Converted from general cargo & lengthened 1971; Sister: **83241 TARONGA** (Sg).

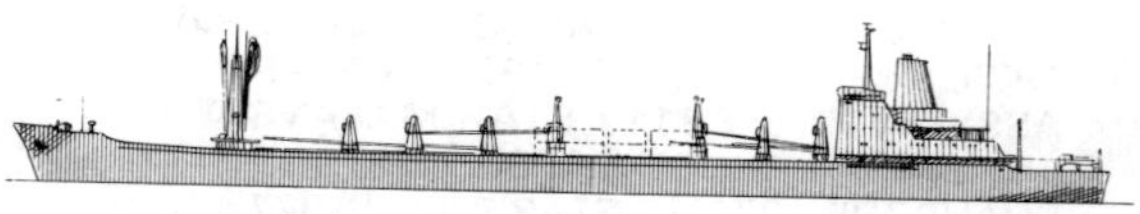

MC_7MFMK H1
83250 SAINT BERNARD. Fr/Sw 1967/71; C/Con; 9000/12000; 172.19 × 8.41/9.38 (564.93 × 27.59/30.77); M; 19.5; ex TELENDOS 1980; ex TAMERLANE 1978; Converted from general cargo & lengthened 1971; Sister: **83251 SAINT BERTRAND** (Fr); ex TILOS 1980; ex TIRRANNA 1978.

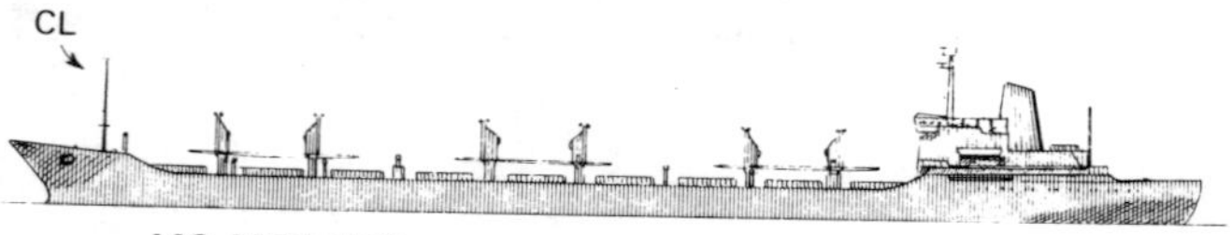

MC_6MFK H13
83260 ON YEUNG. Pa/Ru 1972; B; 23200; 199.9 × 11.23 (655.84 × 36.84); M; 16; **'Baltika'** type; Sister: **83261 SAINT ETIENNE** (Li); ex RAVENNA; ex NOPAL RAVENNA 1976; ex STAR RAVENNA 1975; Similar: **83262 ON LEE** (Pa); ex MADAME BUTTERFLY 1978; **83263 AKBAR** (Br); ex TRAVIATA 1977; **83264 WILLIAM** (Sg); ex AUGUST BOLTEN 1977; launched as RENATE; Possibly similar: **83265 LUIS BANCHERO** (Pe); **83266 COCKROW** (Pa); ex OSTRIA II 1980; ex GERLIN 1975; **83267 TRAMOUNTANA** (Li); ex GERLENA 1975.

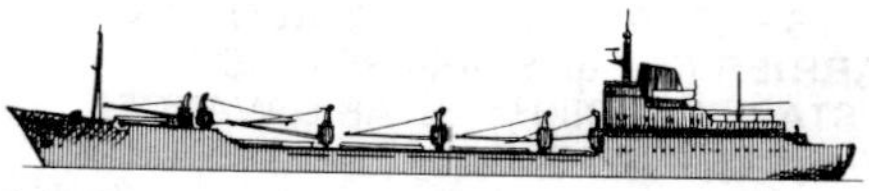

MC_6MFK H13
⋆83280 SONG HUONG. Vn/Sw 1965; C; 4600/6700; 134.17 × 7.99/8.99 (440.19 × 26.21/29.49); M; 17.5; ex ANDROS 1974; Sister: **⋆83281 DONG NAI** (Vn); ex LEMNOS 1975; Similar: **⋆83282 HAI PHONG** (Vn); ex MILOS 1975.

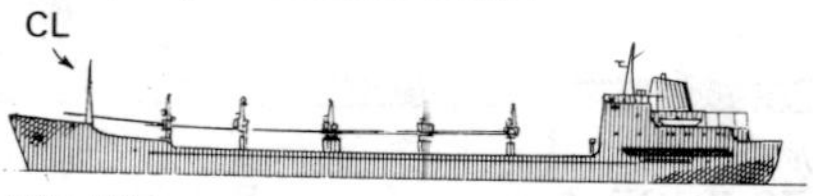

MC_5MF H1
38290 TESABA. Cy/Sp 1964; C; 2700/4300; 121.37 × 6.09/6.95 (398.19 × 19.98/228); M; 15; ex VALENCIA 1977; ex HISPANIA 1968; Sisters: **83291 TELINDA** (Cy); ex HANGVING 1977; ex GALLIA 1974; **83292 TEMURA** (Cy); ex INDUSTRIA 1977; **83293 BONNE BAY** (Li) 1978; ex SCANIA 1973; **83294 GADA** (Eg); ex IKARIA I 1974; ex ITALIA 1974; **83295 SCOL PRESIDENT** (Sw); ex SAGOLAND 1978; **⋆83296 XINDU** (RC); ex DALMATIA 1976.

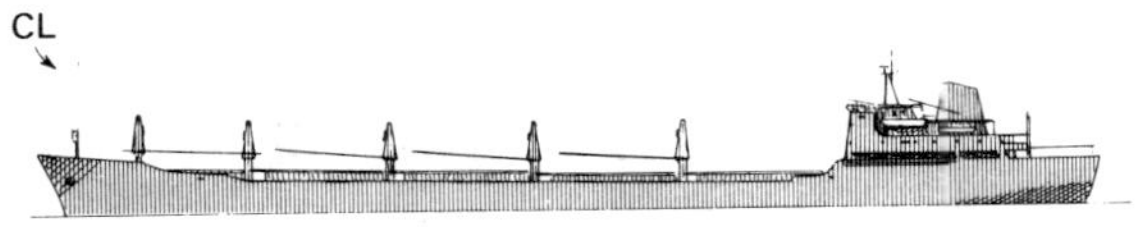

MC_5MFK H13

● **83300 SUNNINGDALE** Sg/No 1969; B; 11300; 165.67 × 9.31 (543.53 × 30.54); M; 15.5; ex STOVE TRADITION; Similar: **83301 EL JIANNI** (Gr) ex MELSOMVIK 1973; **83302 AGIOI VICTORES** (Gr) ex EXPECTATION 1976; **83303 MARIA X** (Gr) ex STOVE OCEAN 1977; ex BELOCEAN 1975; **83304 UNION AUCKLAND** (Br) ex COLUMBIA; **83305 DIMITRIS E** (Gr) ex BELBLUE 1975; **83306 GEORGIOS F** (Gr) ex FRIXOS D 1980; ex JAMES STOVE 1973; **83307 CAROLINE** (Pa) ex EASTWIND 1980; ex STOVE SCOTIA 1973; **83308 SANTA POLA** (Gr) ex RINGVARD 1973; ⋆**83309 AN JI HAI** (RC) ex STOVE FRIEND 1977.

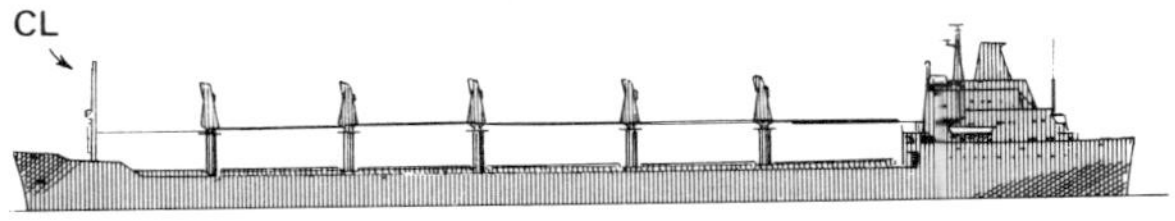

MC_5MFK H13

● **83320 ATHOLL FOREST.** Gr/Sw 1967; B; 17400; 175.22 × 9.88 (1574.86 × 32.41); M; 15.5; ex COLUMBIALAND 1976; Sister: **83321 KARAMU FOREST** (Sg) ex VICTORIA 1977; Similar: **83322 KANUKA FOREST** (Sg) ex GIMLELAND 1977; **83323 ASIAN FOREST** (Br) ex CALEDONIAN FOREST 1978; ex VIRGINIA 1976; ex GIMLESKOG 1972.

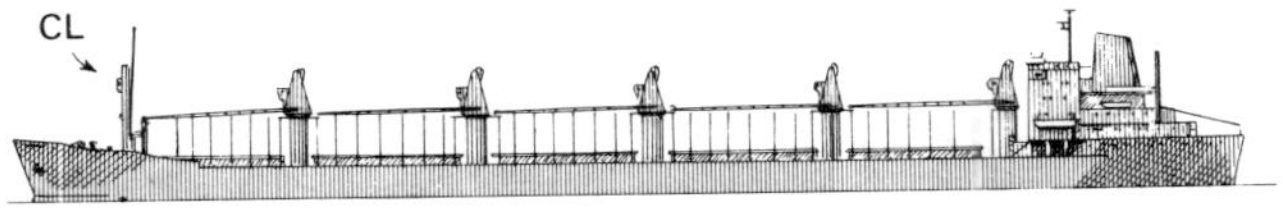

MC_5MFK H13

83330 JAVARA. No/De 1970; B; 25200; 192.06 × 10.12 (630.12 × 33.2); M; 15.5; ex SKOGSTAD 1976; Sisters: **83331 MANNHEIM** (FRG) ex ROLAND BREMEN 1974; **83332 KELKHEIM** (FRG) ex ROLAND KELKHEIM 1971; launched as KELKHEIM; Similar: **83333 JANEGA** (No).

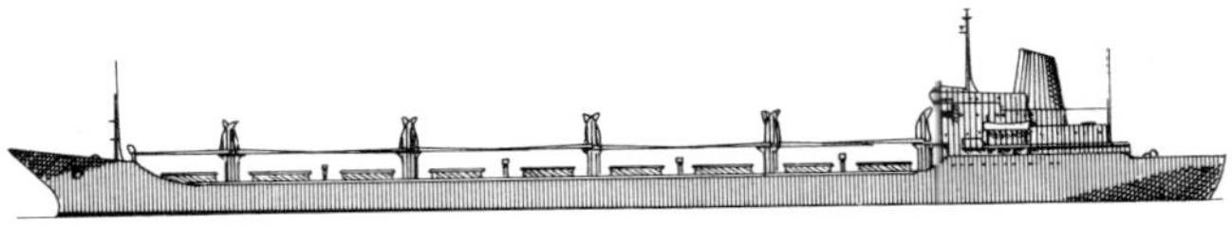

MC_5MFK H13

83340 CEBU. Sg/Ru 1972; B; 22700; 199.83 × 11.24 (655.61 × 36.88); M; 15.75; ex CARE 1980; ex CAROLA P 1978; **'Baltika'** type. Cranes are paired; Probable sister: **83341 LABO** (Sg) ex MARE 1980; ex MAGDALENA 1979; ex MAGDALENA REITH 1978; Possibly similar: **83342 CRESCO** (No).

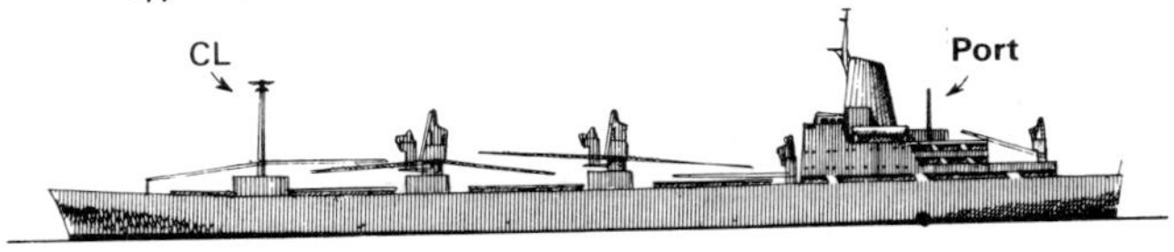

MC_5MFKC H

● **83350 GLOBE EXPRESS.** Sg/Br 1970; C; 12800; 182.73 × 9.32 (599.5 × 30.58); M; 21.5; ex BENLAWERS 1978.

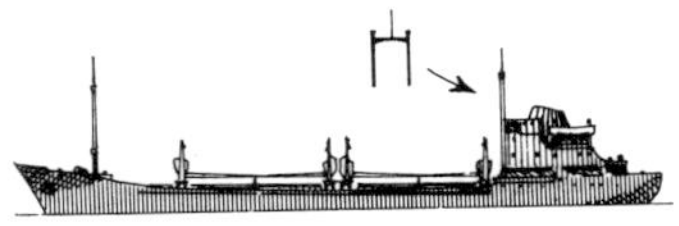

MC_4MF H1

● **83360 SUNRISE.** Li/Fi 1960; C; 1500/2700; 101.12 × 5.17/6.13 (331.76 × 16.96/20.11); M; 13; ex ARCTURUS 1981; Lengthened 1968; Sisters (Fi flag): **83361 BALTIC; 83362 CASTOR; 83363 CORONA; 83364 HEKTOS; 83365 LAPPONIA; 83366 OIHONNA;** (Gr flag): **83367 GOOD GUARDIAN** ex HEBE.

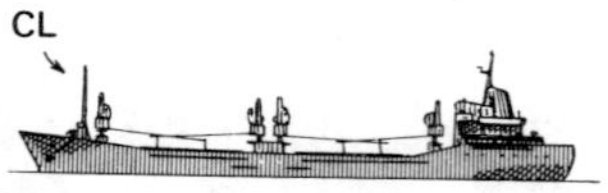

MC_4MF H13

● **83380 ALHALEMI.** Eg/Sp 1971; C; 1200; 87 × 4.87 (285.43 × 15.97); M; 13.5; ex BENIMUSA 1980; Sisters: **83381 BENIMAMET** (Sp); **83382 BENISALEM** (Sp); **83383 ALHAKEM** (Eg) ex BENIAJAN; **83384 NIAGA XXXV** (Ia) ex BENIFARAIG 1981; Similar (shorter): **83385 MARIA ZAKELINA S** (Gr) ex BENIMAR 1977; **83386 ALHAMBRA** (Eg) ex BENISA 1978; **83387 BENIALI** (Sp).

MC_4MFC H13

83400 NEDLLOYD WISSEKERK. Ne/Ne 1967; C; 7400/10700; 166.6 × 7.8/9.6 (546 × 25.6/31.6); M; 20; ex WISSEKERK 1977; Sisters (Ne flag): **83401 NEDLLOYD WAALEKERK** ex WAALEKERK 1977; **83402 NEDLLOYD WESTERKERK** ex WESTERKERK 1977; **83403 NEDLLOYD WILLEMSKERK** ex WILLEMSKERK 1977.

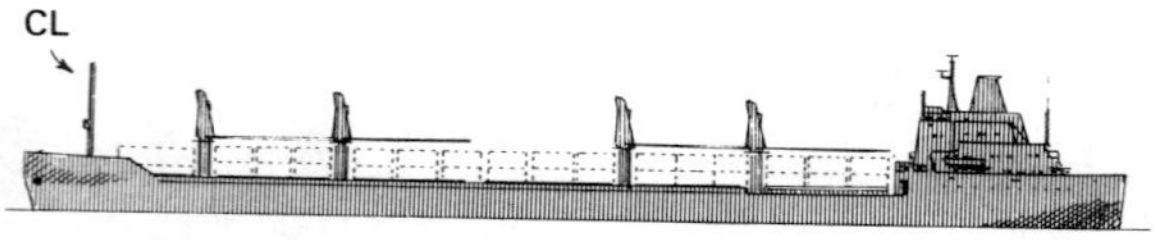

MC_4MFK H13

83410 ANDROS. Br/Sw 1968; C/Con; 17400; 172.22 × 9.9 (565.03 × 32.48); M; 16; ex FERMLAND 1975; Converted from bulk carrier 1975.

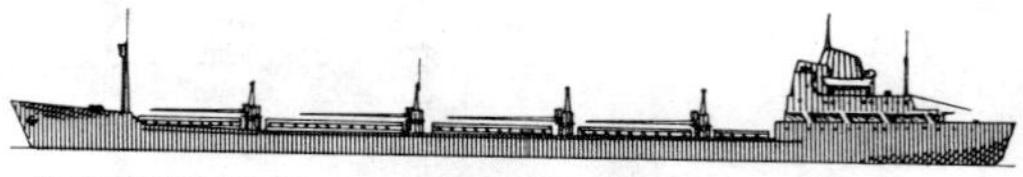

MC_4MFK H13

83420 PANDORA. Gr/Sw 1961; B; 10900; 157.97 × 9.4 (518.27 × 30.84); M; 15; ex FLORIDALAND 1970; ex ARALIZZ 1966.

MC_4MFM H13

★83430 DEBALTSEVO. Ru/DDR 1960; O; 6800; 139.5 × 8 (457.68 × 26.25); M; 14.25; Sisters (some may have 3 cranes) (Ru flag): **★83431 DOBRUSH; ★83432 DUBNO; ★83433 DUBOSSARY; ★83434 DZHANKOY; ★83435 DIMITROVO; ★83436 DOBROPOLJE; ★83438 DUDINKA; ★83439 DAGESTAN; ★83440 DASHAVA; ★83441 DNEPRODZERZHINSK; ★83442 DONSKOY; ★83443 DEDOVSK.**

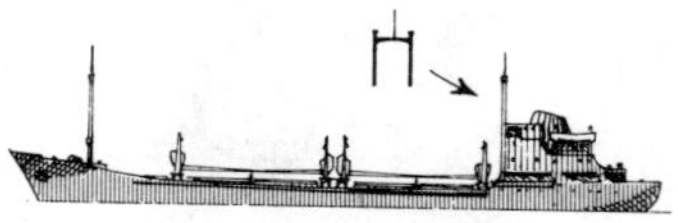

MC_3MF H1

● **83450 SUNRISE.** Li/Fi 1960; C; 1500/2700; 101.12 × 5.17/6.13 (331.76 × 16.96/20.11); M; 13; ex ARCTURUS 1981; Lengthened 1968; Sisters (Fi flag): **83451 BALTIC; 83452 CASTOR; 83453 CORONA; 83454 HEKTOS;83455 LAPPONIA; 83456 OIHONNA;** (Gr flag): **83457 GOOD GUARDIAN** ex HEBE.

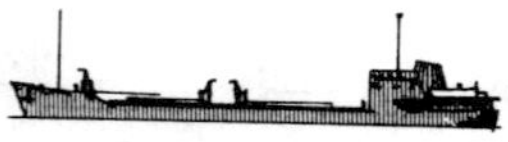

MC_3MF H1

83470 PHA SHWE GYAW YWA. Bm/De 1964; C; 800; 77.35 × 4.01 (253.77 × 13.16); M; 13.5; ex BERGENHUS 1968.

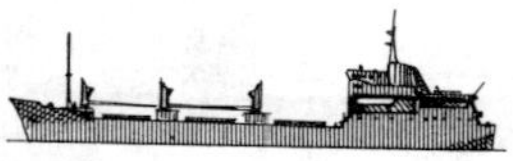

MC_3MF H13

83480 CARIBIC. Nc/No 1967; R; 500/1400; 75.77 × 3.7/6.02 (248.59 × 12.14/19.75); M; 15; ex CARIBIA 1979.

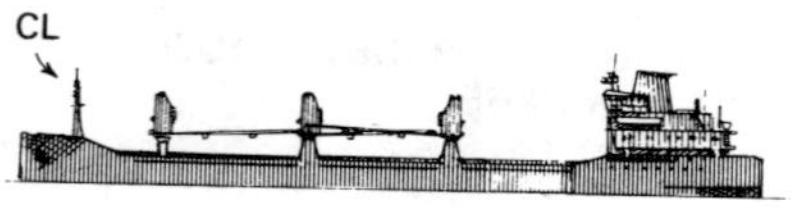

MC_3MF H13

● **83490 MARIA GORTHON.** Sw/Fi 1970; C; 3000/5600; 114.31 × 5.79/8.08 (375 × 18.99/28.47); M; 15; Lengthened 1975; Sisters (Sw flag): **83491 ADA GORTHON; 83492 CARL GORTHON.**

MC_3MF H13

83500 HAI HONG. Pa/Br 1948; C; 1600; 74.99 × 4.32 (246.03 × 14.17); M; 9; ex GOLDEN HILL 1978; ex APOLLO 1976; ex OUOLOF 1968.

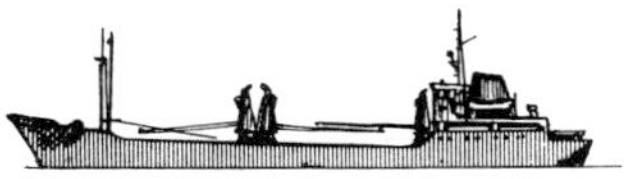

MC$_3$MF H13
83510 DETTIFOSS. Ic/De 1970; C; 2000/3000; 95.56 × 6.09/7.17 (313.52 × 19.98/23.52); M; 14; Sisters (Ic flag): **83511 GODAFOSS; 83512 MANAFOSS.**

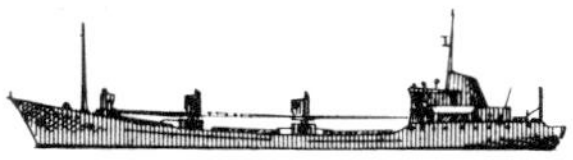

MC$_3$MF H3
83520 PINGUINO. Li/Sp 1970; R; 1000/1700; 88.8 × 15.25 (291.34 × —/17.22); M; 14.

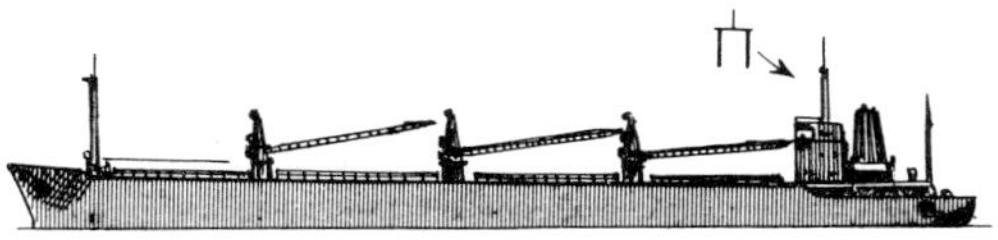

MC$_3$MFK H
83530 DIANA. Li/Ja 1969; B; 15900; 154.31 × 9.17 (506.27 × 30.09); M; 14.25; ex DAIAN MARU 1979.

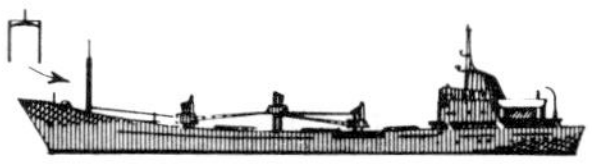

MC$_3$MFK H1
83540 PLAYA DEL MEDANO. Sp/Sp 1967; C; 1600; 91.01 × 5.56 (298.59 × 18.24); M; 16.

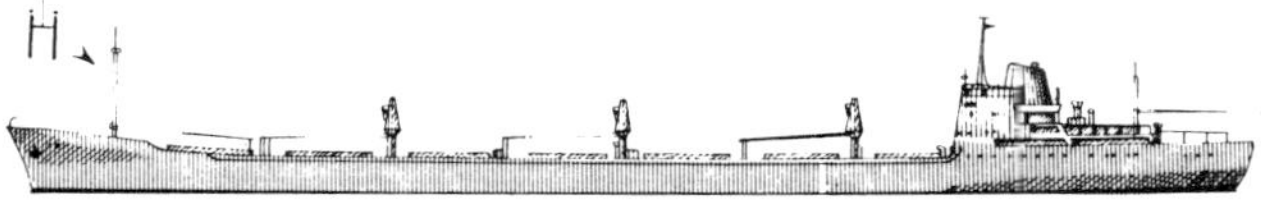

MC$_3$MFK H13
83550 HADJANNA. Gr/FRG 1965; B; 18000; 196.63 × 11.04 (645.11 × 36.22); M; —; ex AMICA 1974; Similar (RC flag): ★**83551 GUANG HAI** ex ANGELIC PROTECTOR 1975; ex AINO 1968; ★**83552 QIONG HAI** ex ARICA 1974.

MC$_3$MFK H3
83560 PINGUINO. Li/Sp 1970; R; 1000/1700; 88.8 × —/5.25 (291.34 × —/17.22); M; 14.

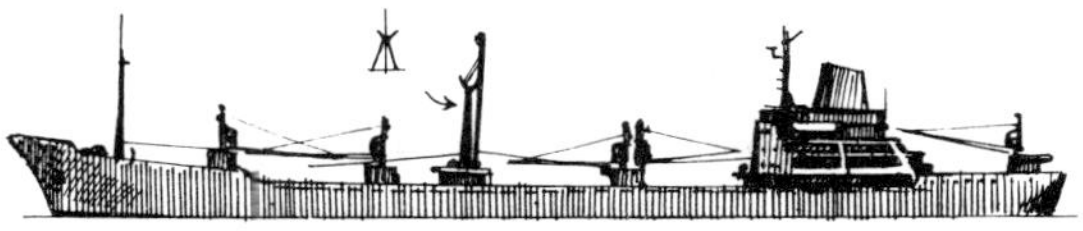

MC$_2$KC$_2$MFC H13
83570 RISHI ATRI. In/De 1966; C; 7700/11000; 164.65 × 8.64 (540.19 × 28.35); M; 20.75; ex ARANYA; Sisters: **83571 RISHI AGASTI** (In) ex AROSIA; **83572 AZUMA** (Gr).

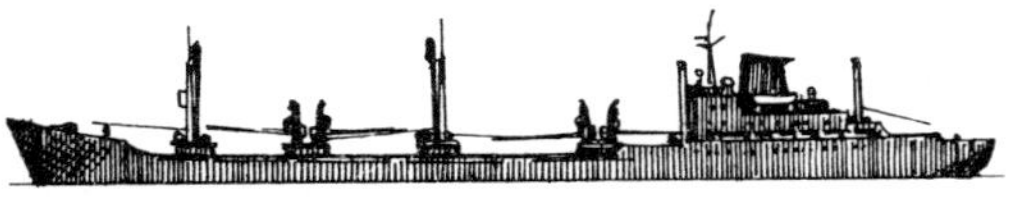

MC$_2$MC$_2$KMFK H13
83580 UNIQUE WINNER. Pa/Sw 1961; C; 9700; 155.48 × 8.45 (510 × 27.72); M; 17.5; ex TRIANON 1979; Similar (funnel design varies): **83581 KOTA MAKMUR** (Sg) ex BELALCAZAR 1980; ex TROJA 1979; ex TRICOLOR 1971; **83582 OCEAN DEFIANT** (Li) ex TEREPAIMA 1980; ex TONSBERG 1977; **83583 NEW DOLPHIN** (Sg) ex TOLEDO; **83584 HALLA PARTNER** (Ko) ex TARN 1978.

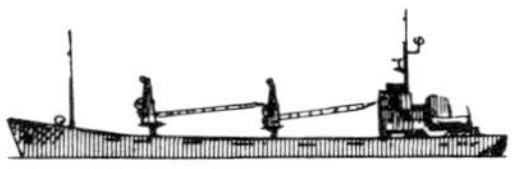

MC$_2$MF H
83590 ATHANASIOS - S. Cy/Ne 1962; C; 800; 79.18 × 4.1 (259 × 13.45); M; 12.5; ex TEXELSTROOM 1976.

MC_2MF H
● **83600 AVON.** Pa/DDR 1960; C; 550; 59.29 × 3.6 (194.52 × 11.81); M; 10; ex ATAIR 1980; Sisters (Some may be MCMF—DDR flag): **⋆83601 DENEBOLA; ⋆83602 GEMMA; ⋆83603 INSEL REIMS; ⋆83604 MALCHIN; ⋆83605 NORDSTERN; ⋆83606 POEL; ⋆83607 RERIK; ⋆83608 UCKERMUNDE; ⋆83609 ZINNOWITZ;** (Cy flag): **83610 ATHLOS I** ex EURABIA LAKE 1978; ex MARKAB 1977; **83611 ATHLOS II** ex EURABIA BAY 1978; ex ALDEBARAN 1977; **83612 VENUS DESTINY** ex WEGA 1977; **83613 VENUS GLORY** ex ARCTURUS 1977 (Vn flag); **83614 ALGENIB; 83615 SCHEDIR;** (These may have been re-named **DOAN KET & THONG NHAT**) (Pa flag): **83616 MERSEY** ex DENEB; **83617 FREDERIQUE LEONIE** ex VILM 1980; **83618 SEA CARRIER 1** ex WARREN 1980; (Ho flag): **83619 PETER** ex STAVENHAGEN; **83620 PALMA** ex PUTBUS 1980.

MC_2MF H13
83660 DON NICKY. Pa/FRG 1958; C; 2000; 82 × 5.52 (269.03 × 18.11); M; 12; ex STAVFOSS 1974; ex BANTRY 1971; ex STAVMOY 1968; ex MOSJOEN 1965.

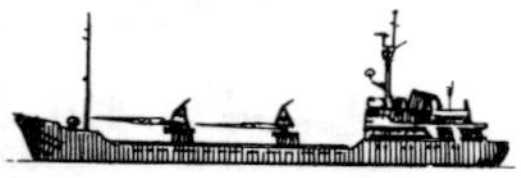

MC_2MF H13
⋆83680 CHEREPOVETS. Ru/Rm 1970; C; 1500; 80.27 × 4.9 (263.35 × 16.08); M; 12; Sisters (Ru flag): **⋆83681 SOSNOVETS; ⋆83682 SARATA; ⋆83683 SOSNOVKA; ⋆83684 SUVOROVO; ⋆83685 SERNOVODSK; ⋆83686 SNEZHNOGORSK; ⋆83687 SUDAK; ⋆83688 SLAUTNOYE; ⋆83689 SOFIYSK; ⋆83690 SURGUT;** (Rm flag): **⋆83691 NAZARCEA; ⋆83692 PALAS; ⋆83693 POIANA; ⋆83694 NOVACI.**

MC_2MF H13
⋆83720 BATAK. Bu/Bu 1966; C; 1300/1800; 80.65 × 4.35/5.29 (264.6 × 14.27/17.36); M; 12; Sisters (some are reported to have a 3rd crane on foc's'le. Some may be converted to container ships similar to ELENA—which see) (Bu flag): **⋆83721 SOPOT; ⋆83722 KALOFER; ⋆83723 BRACIGOVO; ⋆83724 PERUSTICA; ⋆83725 KOTEL; ⋆83726 TROJAN; ⋆83727 KOPRIVSTICA; ⋆83728 ZERAVNA;** (Bu flag): **⋆83729 KLISURA; ⋆83730 SAMOKOV; ⋆83731 ZLATOGRAD;** (RC flag): **⋆83732 MELNIK; ⋆83733 RAZLOG.**

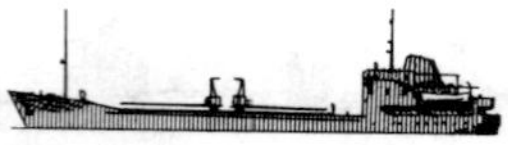

MC_2MF H1
83630 MADELEINE. Co/De 1959; C; 730; 77.35 × 4 (253.77 × 13.12); M; 13.5; ex C.T.M.A. 1975; ex KOLDINGHUS 1969.

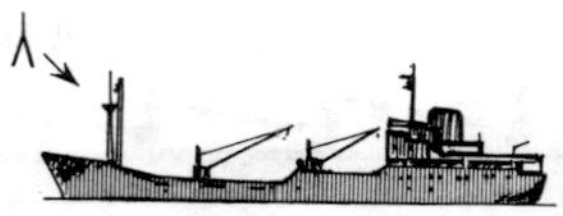

MC_2MF H12
83640 SIGURD JARL. No/FRG 1962; C; 1600; 83.83 × 5.91 (275.03 × 19.39); M; 13; Lengthened 1973; Sister: **83641 SOTE JARL** (No).

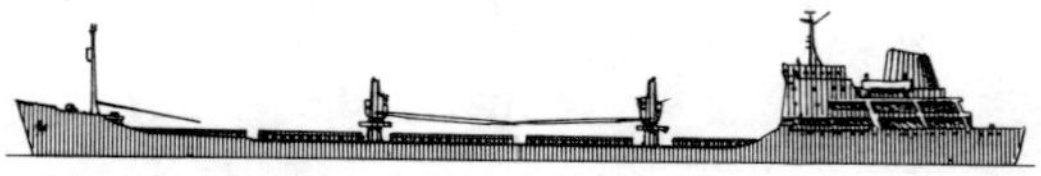

MC_2MF H13
83650 OCEAN ENDEAVOUR. Pk/Br 1965; B; 12000; 160.66 × 9.13 (527.1 × 29.95); M; 15.25; ex CAPE RODNEY 1971.

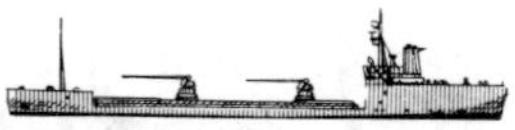

MC_2MF H13
● **83670 ESTHER SILVANA.** De/De 1975; C; 1400; 78.77 × 06 (258.43 × 16.6); M; 12.5; ex ESTHER BECH 1978; Travelling cranes; Sisters: **83671 LOUISE BRAVO** (De); **83672 SOFIE BRAVO** (Sg) ex LEILA BECH; **83673 OLGA BRAVO** (Sg) ex ANNA MARIE BECH 1978; Probable sister: **83674 SUSAN MAC** (De) ex SUSAN SILVANA 1980.

MC_2MF H13
⋆83700 ANKLAM. DDR/DDR 1955; C; 430; 50.07 × 3.2 (164.27 × 10.5); M; —; Sisters (DDR flag): **⋆83701 OSTSEEBAD; ⋆83702 WUSTROW; ⋆83703 SASSNITZ; ⋆83704 TIMMENDORF; ⋆83705 WOLGAST;** (Ru flag): **⋆83706 KERI; ⋆83707 MUKHU; ⋆83708 PRANGLI; ⋆83709 VAYNDLO** ex WARNEMUNDE; (Cy flag): **83710 LUCKY LADY** ex ELENA DEMET 1978; ex SANDRA DEMET 1976; ex BIBIA DEMET 1975; ex EVANGELIA; ex ZING 1975; ex ZINGST 1973; (Gr flag): **83711 AGIOS DIONISSIOS** ex POROS 1976; ex SEA CALM 1975; ex BAR 1974; ex BARHOFT 1973; **83712 MARIA DEMET** ex SEA WAVE 1974; ex ERO 1973; ex PREROW 1973; **83713 MYROVLITIS** ex GIANNIS 1974; ex GREI 1973; ex GREIFSWALD 1973; (No flag): **83714 ARGOVIND** ex AVALD 1973; ex DEANG 1972; ex KOSEROW 1971; **83715 FEANG** ex HERINGSDORF 1972.

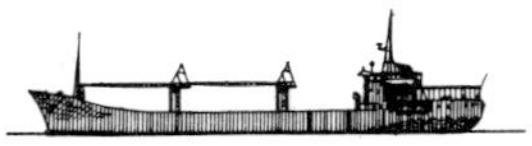

MC_2MF H13
83740 LA BONITA. Bs/FRG 1965; C; 1400; 72.8 × 5.31 (238.85 × 17.42); M; 13.

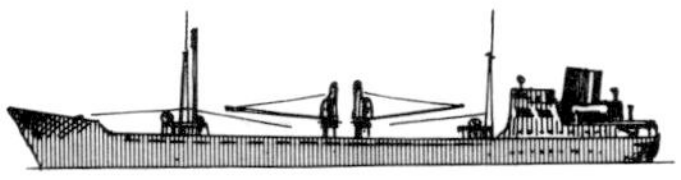

MC_2MF H13
83760 TANAMBI. Co/FRG 1959; VC; 1600; 100.84 × 4.64 (330.84 × 15.22); M; 12.5; ex VELOZ 1973; ex VALIENTE 1969; ex SPENSER 1961; Lengthened 1966; Similar (bi-pod masts): **83761 ACAIMA** (Co) ex VENIMOS 1973; **83762 PIGOANZA** (Co) ex VIAJERO 1973; **83763 HOLCOR I** (Le) ex VEEWAVE 1978; ex FALCON I 1978; ex ATAHUALPA 1976; ex VELOS 1967.

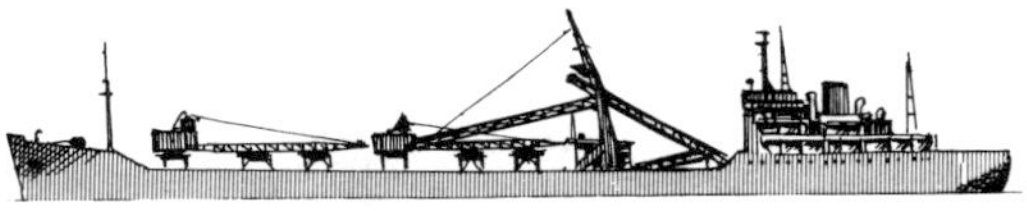

MC_2M_2FK H13
83800 SANJEEVANI. In/US-Ja 1945/69; B; 10300; 159.57 × 9.2 (523.52 × 30.18); T-E; —; ex NISSEI MARU 1964; ex KINGS CANYON 1951; Converted from 'T2' type tanker.

MCFM H13
83810 ALIDA. Cy/Fr 1957; C/WT; 2600; 101.33 × 5.89 (332.45 × 19.32); M; 15; ex PENTHIEVRE 1967; ex PENTHIEVRE II 1973.

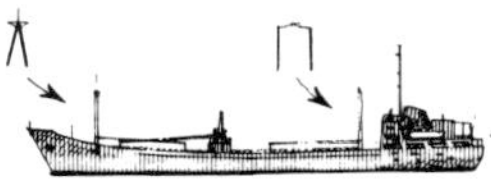

MCKMF H1
83830 KALLSO. Fi/Fi 1960; R; 500; 71.81 × 3.62 (235.6 × 11.88); M; 14.

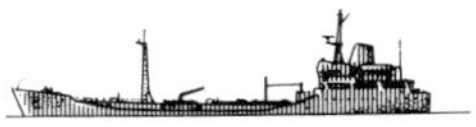

MCKMF H13
83850 BP SPRINGER. Br/Br 1969; Tk; 1100; 65.46 × 4.45 (214.76 × 14.6); M; 11.5; ex DUBLIN 1976; Sisters (Br flag): **83851 BP BATTLER** ex INVERNESS 1976; **83852 BP WARRIOR** ex GRANGEMOUTH 1976.

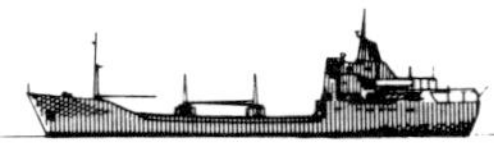

MC_2MF H13
83750 CABO FRIO. Cy/No 1960; R; 1600; 74.71 × 5.8 (245.11 × 19.03); M; 14.75.

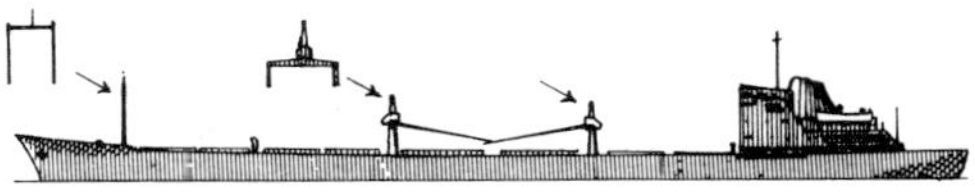

MC_2MFK H1
83770 RIO HAINA. Li/FRG 1960; B; 9400; 150.96 × 9.2 (495.28 × 30.18); M; —; ex PACSUN 1978; ex STAD ANTWERPEN 1971.

MC_2MFM H13
★83780 UGLEURALSK. Ru/DDR 1958; O; 5200; 133.69 × 7.42 (438.62 × 24.34); M; 15.5; Sisters (some may have 4 cranes—see No 83430): (Ru flag): **★83781 URITSK; ★83782 URGENTCH; ★83783 URYUPINSK; ★83784 URZHUM; ★83785 USOLJE; ★83786 USTYUZHNA; ★83787 USTILUG.**

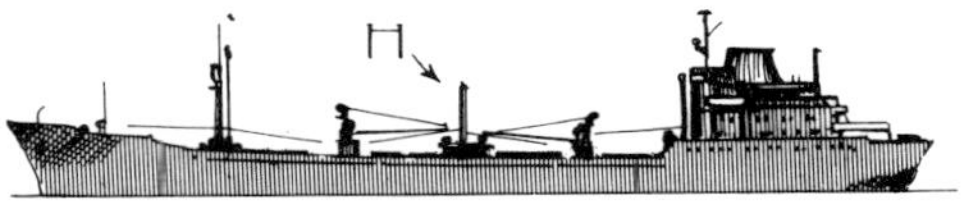

MCKCKMFK H13
83820 SANTOS. Gr/Sw 1961; C; 5700/8200; 144.23 × 7.74/8.97 (473.2 × 25.39/29.43); -m; 15; ex CANADIA 1973; ex SILVERLAND 1969; Sister: **83821 NESTOR SPIRIT** (Gr) ex IRENE M 1980; ex FINLAND 1973; ex MARIEHOLM 1967.

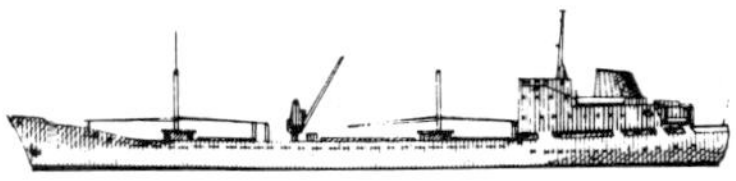

MCKMF H1
83840 AMIRA K. Le/Sw 1962; C; 2700/4500; 114.33 × 6.22/7.19 (375.09 × 20.4/23.59); M; 14.5; ex BOOKER VALIANCE 1973; ex JOHAN WESSEL 1963.

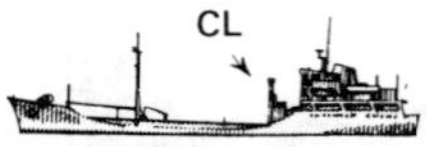

MCKMF H13

● **83860 SHELL MARINER.** Br/Br 1965; Tk; 1000; 61.45 × 4.22 (201.61 × 13.85); M; 11; ex FALMOUTH 1979; Sisters (Br flag): **83861 SHELL REFINER** ex HAMBLE 1979; **83862 BP SCORCHER** ex KILLINGHOLME 1976; Probable sister: **83863 SHELL SCIENTIST** ex PARTINGTON 1979; **83864 SHELL TRADER** ex TEESPORT 1979; Similar (lower superstructure, taller funnel): **83865 SHELL ENGINEER** ex DINGLE BANK 1979.

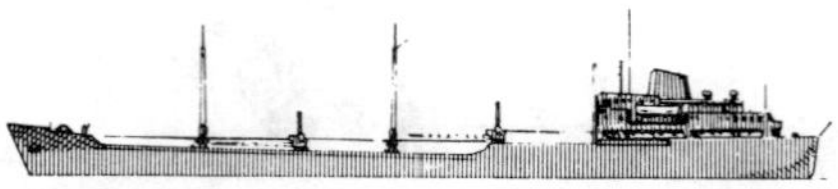

MCMCKMF H13

83870 SAN JUAN. Gr/De 1961; C; 4100/5900; 127.29 × 6.97/7.88 (417.62 × 22.87/25.85); M; 16.5; ex SALVADOR 1977; ex NORHOLT 1966.

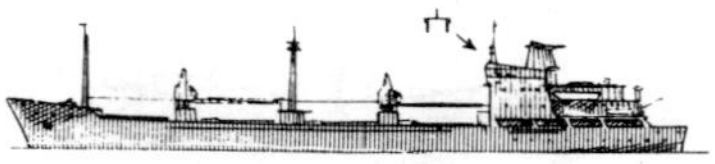

MCMCMF H1

83880 JOSE MARIA RAMON. Sp/Sp 1973; C/R; 1700; 108.39 × 4.16 (355.61 × 13.65); M; 18; Sister: **83881 PEDRO RAMIREZ** (Sp).

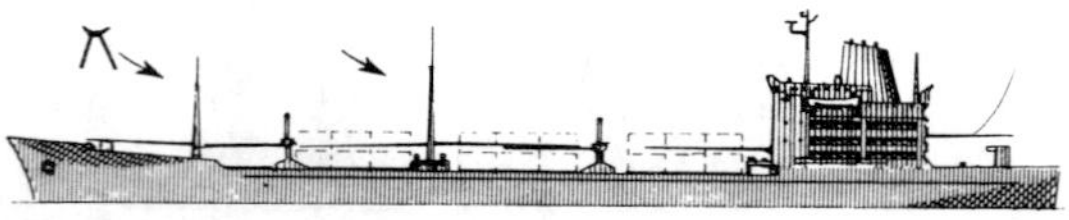

MCMCMFK H13

83890 ATREVIDA. Gr/De 1968; C/Con; 8900; 167.06 × 8.55 (548.1 × 28.05); M; 21.5; Cranes are on travelling gantries.

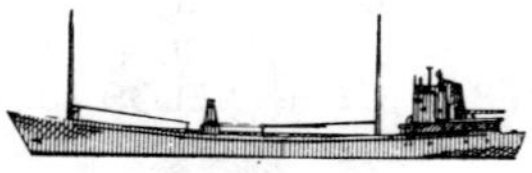

MCMF H

● **83900 FRIENDSHIP.** Cy/Sw 1962; C; 500; 61.3 × 3.77 (201.12 × 12.37); M; 11.5; ex MANOS 1977; ex RADIANT VICTOR 1976; ex VESTHOLM 1974; ex KALMARSUND I 1970.

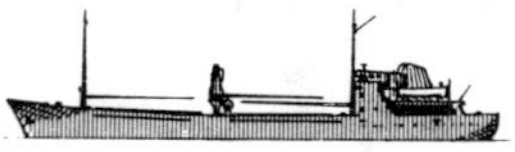

MCMF H

83910 NTAMA. Cy/De 1957; C; 1100; 77.65 × 4.19 (254.76 × 13.75); M; 12.5; ex TONNA 1975; Lengthened 1975.

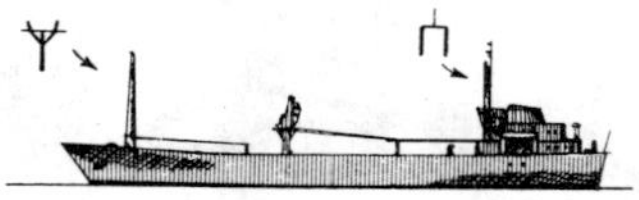

MCMF H

83920 SELA. Ic/No 1970; RoC/C; 1500; 87 × 6.13 (285.43 × 20.11); M; 15; ex BOMMA 1980; Stern door/ramp. Side doors: Sisters: **83921 BAROK** (No); **83922 BERBY** (No); **83923 SKAFTA** (Ic) ex BORRE 1981; ⋆**83924 PLATAK** (Ys) ex BARD 1975; ⋆**83925 SNJEZNIK** (Ys) ex BOLT 1975.

MCMF H

⋆**83930 BELLATRIX.** DDR/DDR 1961; C; 500; 59.47 × 3.66 (195.11 × 12.01); M; 10; (See 'AVON' MC_2MF for others of this class with this sequence).

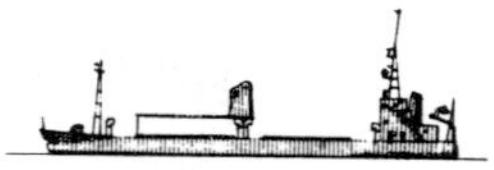

MCMF H

● **83940 MINI LADY.** Gr/Ja 1969; C/B; 1600; 65.51 × 4.95 (214.93 × 16.24); TSM; 10.25; Similar (some vessels have tandem cranes and some later ones have taller superstructure and funnel) (Gr flag): **83941 MINI LABOR; 83942 MINI LACE; 83943 MINI LAD; 83944 MINI LAGOON; 83945 MINI LAMP; 83946 MINI LANCE; 83947 MINI LANE; 83948 MINI LANTERN; 83949 MINI LAP; 83950 MINI LARK; 83951 MINI LASS; 83952 MINI LATRIA; 83953 MINI LAUD; 83954 MINI LAW; 83955 MINI LEAD; 83956 MINI LEAF; 83957 MINI LEAGUE; 83958 MINI LEE; 83959 MINI LEGEND; 83960 MINI LENS; 83961 MINI LIBRA; 83962 MINI LID; 83963 MINI LIDO; 83964 MINI LIFT; 83965 MINI LIGHT; 83966 MINI LINER; 83967 MINI LINK; 83968 MINI LION; 83969 MINI LIONESS; 83970 MINI LIZARD; 83971 MINI LOAF; 83972 MINI LOOM; 83973 MINI LORY; 83974 MINI LOT; 83975 MINI LOTUS; 83976 MINI LUCK; 83977 MINI LUX; 83978 MINI LYMPH; 83979 MINI LAMA;** ex AMERICAN MINX 1971; launched as MINI LAMA; **83980 MINI LOGIC;** ex AMERICAN MINI 1971; **83981 MINI LUNAR;** ex AMERICAN MING 1973; launched as MINI LUNAR; **83982 MINI LILAC; 83983 MINI LADY;** (Ko flag): **83984 AMERICAN MARK;** ex AMERICAN MACE 1974; launched as MINI LYRA; **83985 MORNING SUN;** ex MINI LIMIT 1975; **83986 KOREAN SHIPPER;** ex MINI LIFE 1972; **83987 GLOBAL CHALLENGER;** ex MINI LOOK 1974; ex AMERICAN MAIN 1973; launched as MINI LOOK; (Si flag): **83988 DALIA I;** ex MINI LAKE 1980; ex AMERICAN MUSE 1971; ex MINI LAKE 1970; **83989 DALIA II;** ex MINI LEO 1980; ex AMERICAN MARK 1971; ex MINI LEO 1970; (Pa flag): **83990 KIAEN;** ex GLOBAL TRADER 1979; (larger cranes-Ko flag): **83991 KOREAN FLOWER; 83992 KOREAN LIFTER.**

MCMF H1
84000 GOGO REEFER; Br/Ne 1962; R; 1800; 91.55 × 4.5 (300.36 × 14.76); M; 16; ex GOGOFRIO 1980; ex POOLSTER 1974.

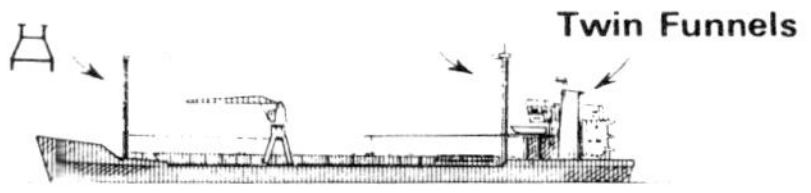

MCMF H1
84010 AMULET. De/De 1975; C; 1600; 94.39 × 5 77 (309.67 × 18.93); M; 13; Travelling crane; Sisters (De flag): **84011 TALISMAN; 84012 CHARM.**

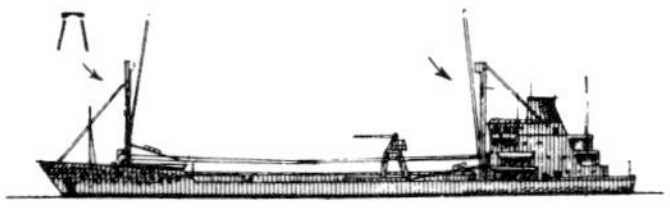

MCMF H1
84020 SAMSON SCAN. De/FRG 1976; C/HL; 3900; 94.49 × 7.9 (310 × 25.92); M; —; Travelling cranes; Sister: **84021 HERMES SCAN;** (De).

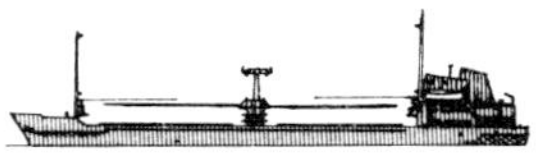

MCMF H1
84030 CELTIC CRUSADER; Br/Ne 1970; C; 700; 80.73 × 4.14 (264.86 × 13.58); M; 13.5; ex SUPREMITY.

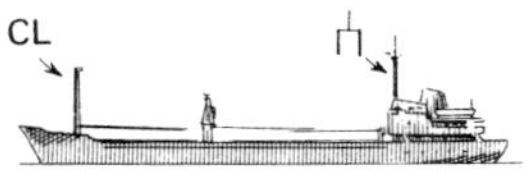

MCMF H1
84040 MANGEN. Ne/Ne 1969; C; 600/1500; 77.65 × 4.14/5.83 (254.75 × 13.58/19.12); M; 12; Sister: **84041 WADDENZEE** (Ne); ex UNDEN.

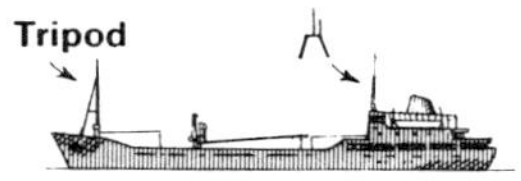

MCMF H1
84050 MARINE PACKER. Ca/No 1965; C; 1100; 70.8 × 3.62 (232.28 × 11.88); M; 12.5; ex BLIKUR 1974; Lengthened 1971.

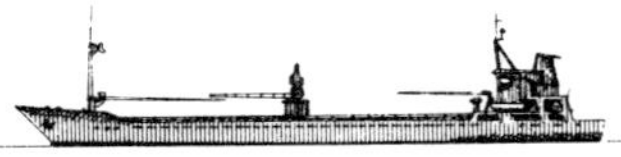

MCMF H1
● **84060 MERCANDIAN PRINCE.** De/De 1977; C; 1600; 96.53 × 5.64 (316.69 × 18.51); M; 12.25; **'Commander'** class; Sisters: **84061 POLYDORUS** (Ne); ex MERCANDIAN ADMIRAL; **84062 CASABLANCA** (FRG); ex MERCANDIAN AMBASSADOR 1980; **84063 SEVILLA** (FRG); ex MERCANDIAN COMMANDER 1980; **84064 MERCANDIAN QUEEN** (De).

MCMF H1
84070 ARNAFELL. Ic/De 1974; C; 700/1600; 78.52 × 4.⁄5.67 (257.61 × 13.12/18.6); M; 13; ex MERCANDIAN EXPORTER 1979; Sisters (Ic flag): **84071 LAGARFOSS;** ex MERCANDIAN IMPORTER 1977; **84072 HAIFOSS;** ex MERCANDIAN SUPPLIER 1977; **84073 LAXFOSS;** ex MERCANDIAN CARRIER 1977; **84074 HELGAFELL;** ex MERCANDIAN SHIPPER 1979; **84075 FJALLFOSS;** ex MERCANDIAN TRANSPORTER 1977; (Tu flag): **84076 SELIN;** ex SHIPMAIR VII 1977; ex MERCANDIAN SUPPLIER 1974; (Ag flag): **84077 CHELIA;** ex MERCANDIAN AGENT 1975.

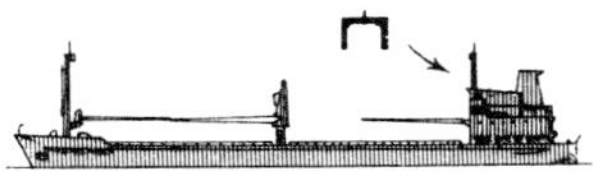

MCMF H1
84090 SINGULARITY. Br/Br 1977; C; 1600; 89.72 × 6.04 (294.36 × 19.82); M; 12.5.

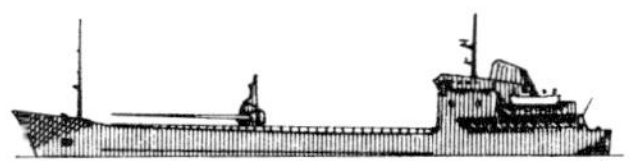

MCMF H1
84100 NAWAF. Si/It 1966; RoC; 1200; 94.19 × 3.73 (390.02 × 12.24); M; 14; ex SUFFOLK; ex NOPAL SPRAY 1976; ex SUFFOLK 1974; launched as FORENEDE; Stern door; Lengthened 1969; Sister: **84101 SATTAM** (Si); ex SUSSEX; ex NOPAL SURF 1975; ex SUSSEX 1974; launched as UNITED.

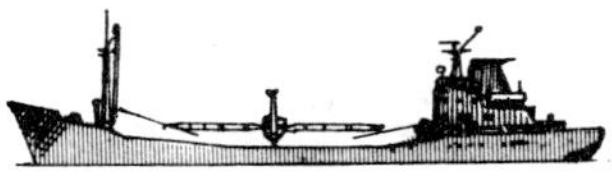

MCMF H1
84110 LUN SHAN; Pa/Fi 1964; C; 1600/2600; 91.57 × 5.42/6.67 (300.43 × 17.78/21.88); M; 14.5; ex FINNFIGHTER 1975; Sisters (Pa flag): **84111 DU SHAN;** ex FINNSTRIP 1975; ex REKOLA 1974; **84112 KUN SHAN;** ex FINNSEAL 1975; **84113 PING SHAN;** ex FINNTUBE 1975; ex LOTILA 1974.

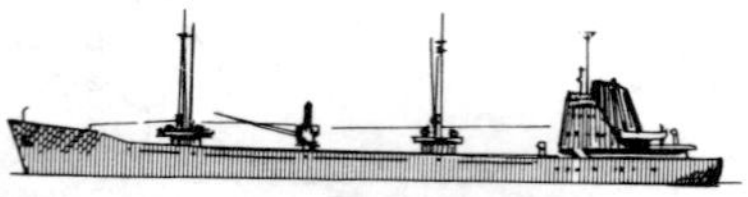

MCMF H1
84120 HOLSTENKAMP. FRG/FRG 1959; C; 2600/4000; 105.75 × 6.72/7.6 (346.95 × 22.05/24.93); M; 14; ex MIKES KASMAS 1974; ex BRUSNIS 1974; ex CAP DELGADO 1971; ex FUSAN 1960.

MCMF H13
84140 DON NICKY. Pa/FRG 1958; C; 2000; 82 × 5.52 (269.03 × 18.11); M; 12; ex STAVFOSS 1974; ex BANTRY 1971; ex STAVMOY 1968; ex MOSJOEN 1965.

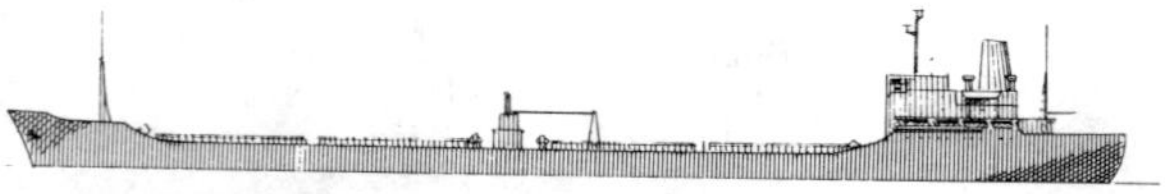

MCMF H13
84160 NIKKEI MARU No. 3. Ja/Ja 1969; O; 17900; 175.04 × 11 (574.28 × 36.09); M; 14.25.

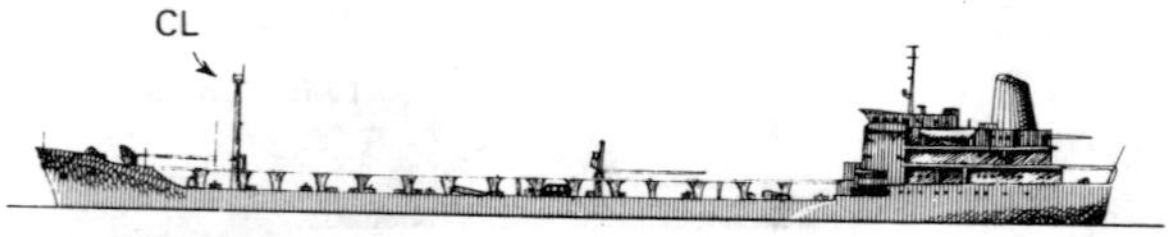

MCMF H13
● **84180 BRITISH LIBERTY.** Br/Sw 1968; Tk; 15100; 169.63 × 9.55 (556.52 × 31.33); M; 16; Similar (Br flag): **84181 BRITISH LOYALTY; 84182 BRITISH SECURITY; 84183 BRITISH TENACITY; 84184 BRITISH UNITY; 84185 BRITISH FIDELITY.**

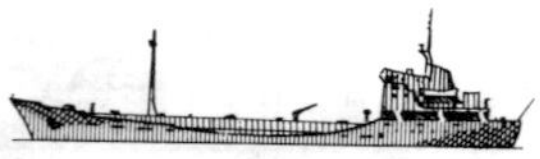

MCMF H13
● **84200 CASIMIR LE QUELLEC.** Fr/Fr 1969; Ch; 1400; 79.53 × 5.11 (260.93 × 16.77); M; 13.75.

MCMF H13
● ***84210 KAMTCHIA.** Bu/Bu 1960; C; 300; 49.31 × 3.09 (161.78 × 10.14); M; 9; Sisters (Bu flag): ***84211 KITEN; *84212 KOM; *84213 PAPIA.**

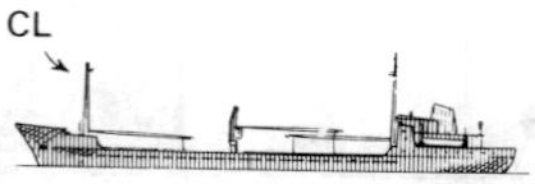

MCMF H13
84130 NIAGA XXVIII. Ia/Ne 1970; C; 1500; 78.75 × 5.84 (258.37 × 19.16); M; 12; ex HOLLAND; ex HEERENGRACHT 1979; ex HILVARENBEEK 1973; Sister: **84131 NIAGA XXXII** (Ia); ex NOORDWAL 1980; ex NOORBEEK 1979; ex TIMCA 1973.

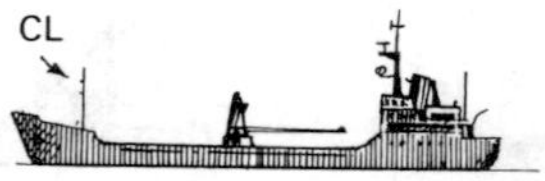

MCMF H13
***84150 BALKHASH.** Ru/Ru 1969; C; 1100; 72.12 × 4.63 (236.61 × 15.19); M; 11; Sisters (Ru flag): ***84151 BAKHCHISARAY; *84152 BELOMORYE.**

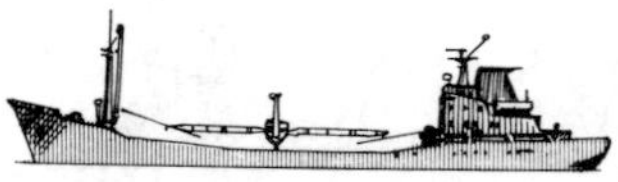

MCMF H13
84170 LUN SHAN. Pa/Fi 1964; C; 1600/2600; 91.57 × 5.42/6.67 (300.43 × 17.78/21.88); M; 14.5); ex FINNFIGHTER 1975; Sisters (Pa flag): **84171 DU SHAN;** ex FINNSTRIP 1975; ex REKOLA 1974; **84172 KUN SHAN;** ex FINNSEAL 1975; **84173 PING SHAN;** ex FINNTUBE 1975; ex LOTILA 1974.

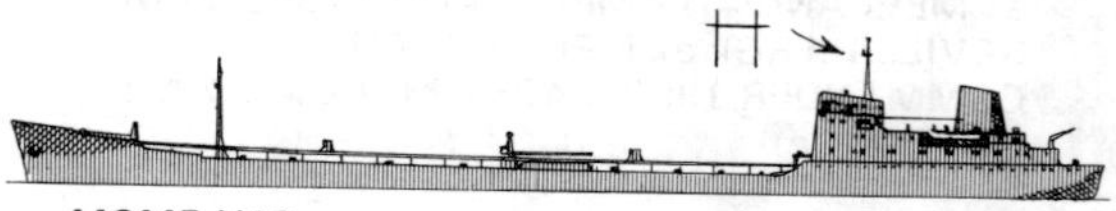

MCMF H13
● **84190 BORDER SHEPHERD.** Br/Br 1961; Tk; 13300; 174.35 × 9.91 (572 × 32.5); M; 14; Sisters (Br flag): **84191 BORDER CASTLE; 84192 BORDER FALCON; 84193 BORDER PELE;** (Gr flag): **84194 ACHILLET;** ex BORDER CHIEFTAIN.

MCM_2F H3
84220 OVERBECK. FRG/FRG 1969; V; 1000; 77.12 × 5.08 (253.02 × 16.63); M; 13.25.

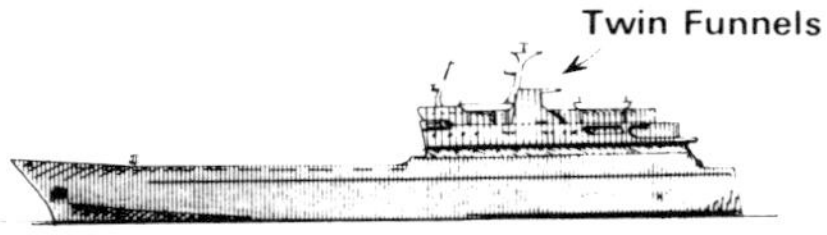

MF H
84230 MERENGUE EXPRESS. Br/It 1973; RoC/P; 3300; 115.12 × 5.97 (377.69 × 19.59); TSM; 20.5; ex SEASPEED CHALLENGER 1980; ex GISELLA 1974; ex MONICA RUSSOTTI 1974; Stern door/ramp; Sister: **84231 TAMBU EXPRESS** (Br); ex SEASPEED MASTER 1980; ex LAURA RUSSOTTI 1976.

MF H1
84240 BAT SHEVA. Is/Ne 1967; Transport; 900; 95 × 8 (311 × 26.9); M; 10.

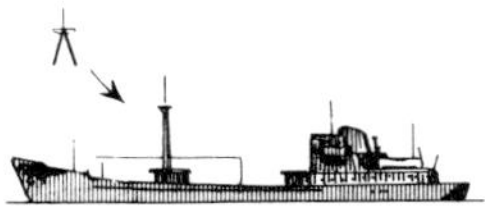

MF H1
84250 FRIGO KING. Gr/Ne 1960; R; 700/1200; 72.32 × —/4.48 (237.27 × —/14.7); M; 14; ex MEGREZ 1976; ex GERDA 1973; ex SILVER STAR 1969; ex SILVER COMET 1968.

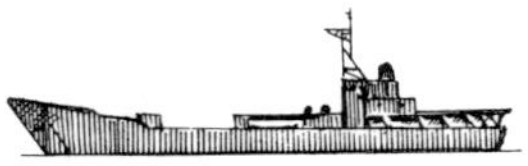

MF H1
84260 CHAMPLAIN. Fr/Fr 1974; Transport; 1400 Dspl; 80 × 2.4 (260 × 7.9); TSM; 16; **'BATRAL'** type; Helicopter platform; Sisters: **84261 FRANCIS GARNIER** (Fr); **84262 ABOU ABDALLAH EL AYACHI** (Mo); **84263 AHMED ES SAKAH** (Mo); **84264 DAOUD BEN AICHA** (Mo).

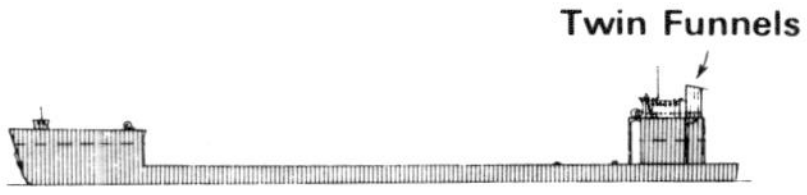

MF H1
84270 OCEAN SERVANT I. Ne/Ja 1976; RoC/HL; 7700; 108 × — (354 × —); M; —; Submersible—broken line shows line of maximum immersion; Sister: **84271 OCEAN SERVANT II** (Ne).

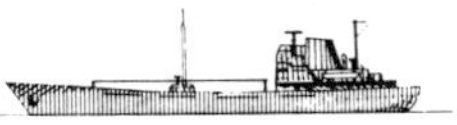

MFM H
84280 ARETOUSA. Gr/FRG 1958; R; 1100; 66.12 × 3.53 (216.93 × 11.58); M; 12; ex NORTHCAPE 1970; ex CLAUS HORN 1967; Sister: **84281 ATLANTIC FREEZE** (Pa); ex SEA SORCERESS 1977; ex WALDTRAUT HORN 1969.

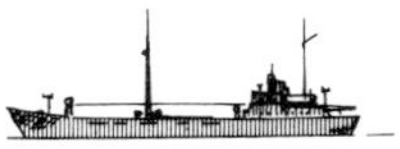

MFM H
84290 ATLANTIQUE. Ly/FRG 1952; C; 500; 57 × 3.51 (187.01 × 11.52); M; 10; ex BRUNNECK 1967; ex ACASTE 1955; Sister: **84291 TAT LEE No 2** (My); ex GETAH KINABALU 1980; ex BALTIQUE 1974; ex BAGHEERA; ex VILLE DE BASTIA 1970; ex MARIE THERESE LE BORGNE 1960.

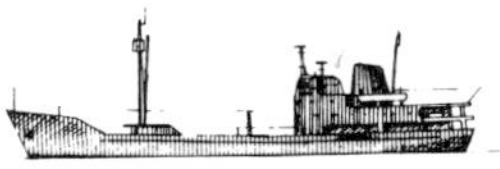

MFM H1
84300 THALA DAN. De/De 1957; PC; 2200; 75.14 × 6.29 (246.52 × 20.64); M; 12.

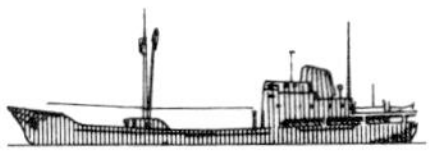

MFM H1
84310 BENJAMIN BOWRING. Br/De 1952; C/Sealer; 1200; 64.9 × 6 (212.93 × 19.69); M; 11.5; ex MARTIN KARLSEN; ex KISTA DAN 1967; Converted from general cargo 1968; Similar (Passenger cargo—extra superstructure deck): **84311 CALULO** (Pa); ex SAO NICOLAU; ex MAGGA DAN 1970.

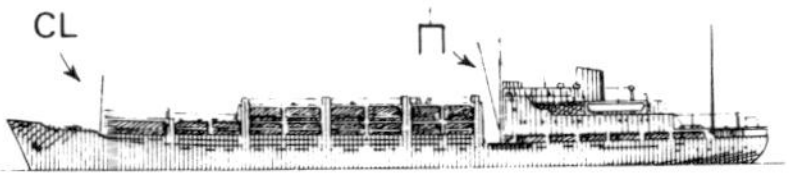

MFM H1
84320 MERINO EXPRESS. Li/Ne 1960; LS; 2400/3400; 119.49 × 5.68/6.41 (392.03 × 18.64/21.03); M; 16; ex CAP FARINA 1976; ex CARIBBEAN EXPRESS 1974; ex KREON 1973; Converted from cargo 1976.

MFM H12
★84330 ZVAYGZNE. Ru/De 1953; FC; 1600; 70.01 × 4.31 (229.69 × 14.14); M; 10.75; ex REFRIGERATOR No 7; Similar (Ru flag): **★84331 REFRIGERATOR No 4; ★84332 REFRIGERATOR No 5; ★84333 REFRIGERATOR No 6; ★84334 REFRIGERATOR No 8; ★84335 REFRIGERATOR No 12; ★84336 REFRIGERATOR No 13; ★84337 GELENDZHIK; ★84338 GORNOZAVODSK; ★84339 KRASNOGORSK; ★84340 SAMARKAND; ★84341 UGLEGORSK; ★84342 PROVORNY;** ex REFRIGERATOR No:11; **★84343 TRUDOLYUBIVYY;** ex REFRIGERATOR No 9.

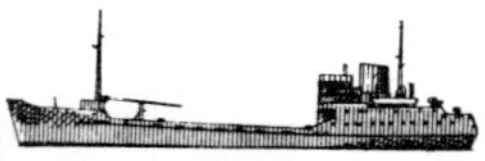

MFM H13
84380 RYUJIN MARU. Ja/Br 1954; Cem; 1600; 74.81 × 4.28 (245.44 × 14.04); TSM; 10.5; ex GOLDEN BAY 1976.

MFM H13
84400 SEA MEDWAY. Sg/Ja 1977; C; 700; 69.02 × 3.62 (226.44 × 11.88); M; 10.5; Sisters (Sg flag): **84401 SEA HUMBER; 84402 SEA AVON; 84403 SEA RHINE.**

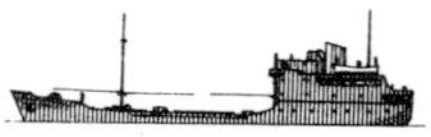

MFM H13
84420 ALKYON. Gr/Fi 1950; Tk; 900; 63.56 × 4.4 (208.53 × 14.44); M; 11; ex ISLA FINLANDIA 1972; ex ESSO FINLANDIA 1971.

MFM H3
84440 ATLANTIQUE. Ly/FRG 1952; C; 500; 57 × 3.51 (187.01 × 11.52); M; 10; ex BRUNNECK 1967; ex ACASTE 1955; Sister: **84441 TAT LEE No 2** (My); ex GETAH KINABALU 1980; ex BALTIQUE 1974; ex BAGHEERA 1972; ex VILLE DE BASTIA 1970; ex MARIE THERESE LE BORGNE 1960.

MKF H13
★84460 IRTISH. Ru/Sw 1951; Tk; 1100; 68.48 × 3.72 (224.67 × 12.2); M; 9; Similar (Ru flag): **★84461 KARADAG; ★84462 SUNGARI; ★84463 UKHTA; ★84464 KARTALY.**

MFM H12
★84350 DONETS; Ru/Sw 1951; C; 900; 61.52 × 4.29 (201.84 × 14.07); M; 13; Similar (Ru flag): **★84351 YENISEY; ★84352 MEDVEDITSA.**

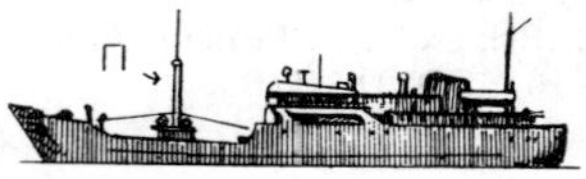

MFM H12
★84360 BOLON; Ru/DDR 1961; FC; 2300; 82.4 × 5.15 (270.34 × 16.9); M; 11; Similar (Ru flag): **★84361 EVORON; ★84362 KHANKA; ★84363 KIZI; ★84364 OREL; ★84365 BASKUNCHAK; ★84366 ELTON; ★84367 KHASAN; ★84368 MIKHAYLO LOMONOSOV.**

MFM H13
84390 PANORMITIS. Gr/Ne 1956; C; 1100; 70.11 × 4.74 (230.02 × 15.55); M; 12; ex MELISSA M. 1977.

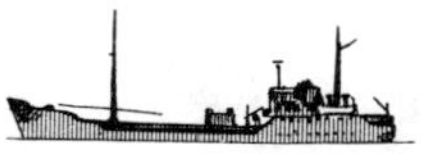

MFM H13
84410 PALMAIOLA. It/FRG 1954; Tk; 1000; 60.3 × 4.89 (197.83 × 16.04); M; 10; ex LUCY 1977; ex MICHAEL M. 1970.

MFM H13
84430 NORRIS CASTLE. Br/Br 1968; RoC/F; 900; 67.42 × — (221.19 × —); TSM; 14; Lengthened 1976.

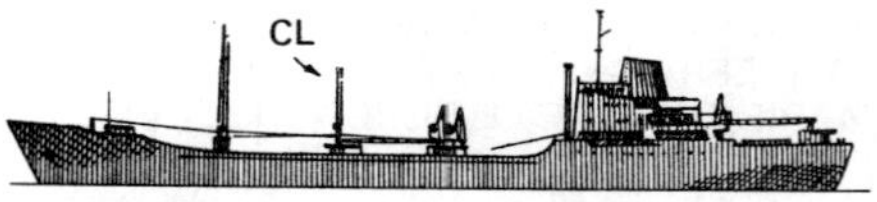

MKC_2KMFC H13
84450 SCHLOSS TARASP. Sd/Fi 1961; C; 6300; 134.65 × 8.61 (441.77 × 28.25); M; 16; ex TATRINA 1980; ex THEBELAND 1976; Sisters: **★84451 RUI CHANG** (RC); ex TYRUSLAND 1977; **84452 BRIGHTNESS** (Pa); ex TROJALAND 1978.

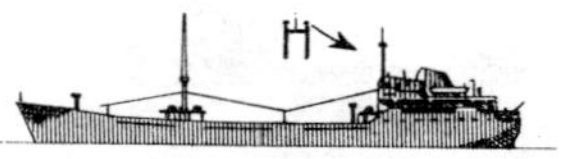

MKF H13
84470 DIMITRIS K. Gr/FRG 1956; C; 1800; 78.82 × 5.76 (258.6 × 18.9); M; 12; ex GIORGIOS K. 1977; ex HADAS 1974; ex ATZMAUT 1969; ex PALMAH 1960.

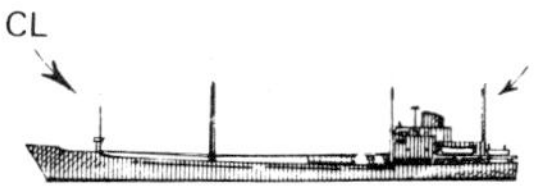

MKFK H1
● **84480 ASUNCION.** Py/Ne 1961; C; 800; 77.17 × 4.02 (253.18 × 13.19); M; 11.25; ex ADARA 1973; Sisters: **84481 VILLARRICA** (Py); ex SITULA 1973; **84482 FEDROS** (Br); ex TALITA 1977; **84483 FILON** (Gr); ex NASHABA 1977; **84484 RITSA M** (Gr); ex SOLON; ex NASHIRA 1977.

MKFM H1
84500 KUM YONG No 501. Ko/Ja 1954; C; 1900; 79.89 × 5 (262.11 × 16.4); M; 13; ex KUROSHIO MARU No 21 1976.

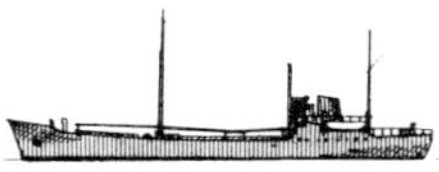

MKFM H3
● **84520 RABUNION VI.** Le/Ne 1958; C; 900; 64.85 × 4.56 (212.76 × 14.96); M; 10.75; ex PHOEBUS 1975; ex LEONIDAS 1974; Similar (Le flag): **84521 RABUNION V;** ex CROESUS 1975; ex BERTA 1973; ex LIBERTAS 1972; **84522 RABUNION XIII;** ex ARCAS 1978; **84523 RABUNION XIV;** ex CALCHAS 1978; **84524 RABUNION XV;** ex TARAS; **84525 RABUNION XVI;** ex BOREAS 1978; **84526 MAGA;** ex MAGAS 1973; **84527 AL SALAM II;** ex LA PERLA 1 1978; ex PALLAS 1978; ex SPALLA 1973; ex PALLAS 1972; (Gr flag): **84528 GIANNIS DIMAKIS II;** ex SMITHRA 1973; ex MITHRAS 1972; **84529 DIMITRIS;** ex PRODROMOS II 1980; **84530 ALEXIS K;** ex MARIA S; ex AMYNTAS 1972; **84531 STAVROULA XIII;** ex PHIDAS 1971; **84532 AMIN** (Sy); ex APOLLON 1980; ex PHILETAS 1972; **84533 GEENA** (Db); ex ABOTA 1973; ex LABOTAS 1972; **84534 ILIAS** (Ne); **84535 DIMITRIOS** (Cy); ex MYNIAS 1974; **84536 MARE 1** (Pa); ex ETAS 1976; ex ALCETAS 1972.

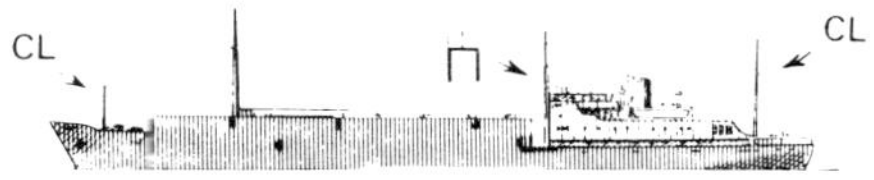

MKFK H1
84490 GALLOWAY EXPRESS. Li/FRG 1960/77; LS; 3400; 119.49 × 5.68/6.41 (392.03 × 18.64/21.03); M; 16; ex EUROPEAN EXPRESS 1977; ex CAP IVI 1976; ex EUROFEAN EXPRESS 1976; ex LADON 1974; Converted from general cargo & lengthened 1967.

MKFM H12
★**84510 PALEKH.** Ru/DDR 1959; FC; 2300; 82.4 × 5.15 (270.34 × 16.9); M; 11; ex BRATSK; This vessel is reported to have been converted to a research vessel.

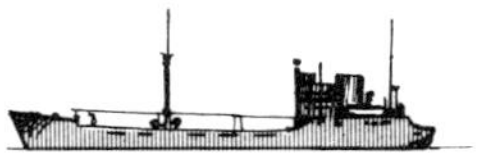

MKFM H3
★**84540 LOVRAN.** Ys/Br 1954; C; 900; 66.78 × 4.54 (219.09 × 14.9); M; 10; ex WOODWREN 1969; ex EDDYSTONE 1956.

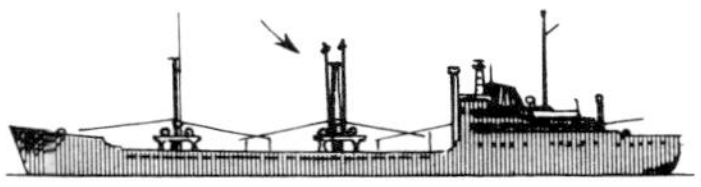

MK_2FMK H13
84550 ABIDIN DAVER. Tu/Tu 1955/60; C; 4400; 106.89 × 7.46 (350.69 × 24.48); M; —.

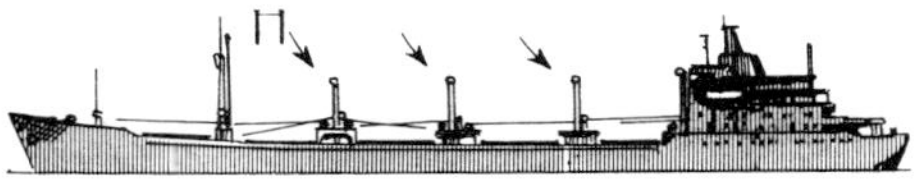

MK_4FK H13
★**84560 AN HUA.** RC/Sw 1960; C; 6300/8500; 143.9 × 7.74/8.97 (472.11 × 25.39/29.43); M; 15; ex BUKU 1974; ex SYDLAND 1972.

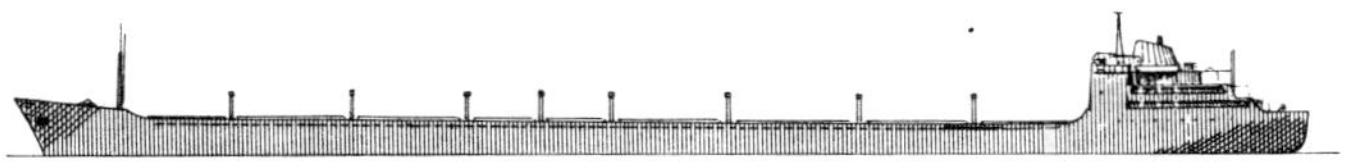

MK_8MFK H13
84570 HAR SINAI. Is/FRG 1961; B; 19000; 206.1 × 10.86 (676.18 × 35.63); M; —; Lengthened 1964.

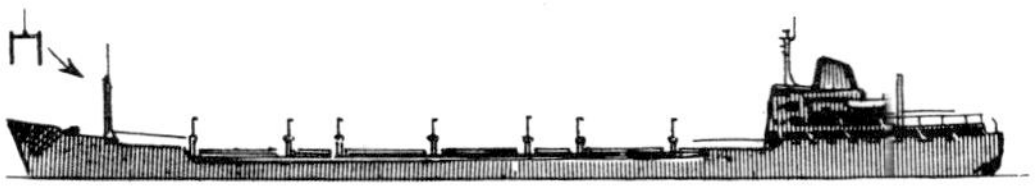

MK_7MFK H13
● **84580 RIO BRAVO.** Gr/Br 1960; B; 1200; 169.88 × 9.68 (557.35 × 31.76); M; 14.5; ex CUYO 1978; ex DRYMOS 1975; ex ST. MARY 1974; ex TRESFONN 1973; Sisters: **34581 SARANDI** (Ar); ex SAN FRANCESCO 1974; ex KROSSFONN 1972.

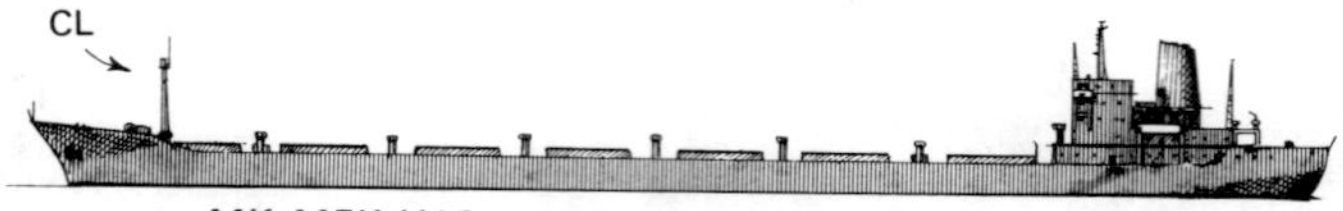

MK_6MFK H13
84590 NORTH EMPEROR. Li/Ja 1967; B; 25800; 206.03 × 12.2 (675.95 × 40.03); M; 16.5; Sister: **84591 NORTH KING** (Li).

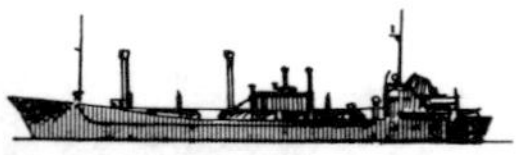

MK_4MF H
84600 LANRICK. Br/Sw 1957/69; LGC; 1200; 76.76 × 3.66 (251.84 × 12.01); M; 12.5; Converted from general cargo 1969.

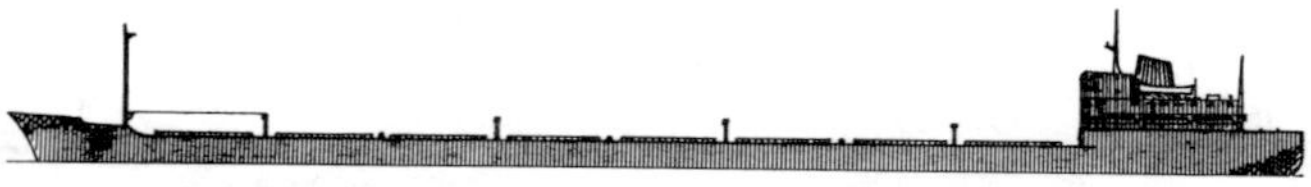

MK_4MF H13
84610 GOLDEAN ALLIANCE. Li/Ja 1965; B; 25100; 206.03 × 12.32 (675.95 × 40.42); M; 15; ex ATHERSTONE 1978.

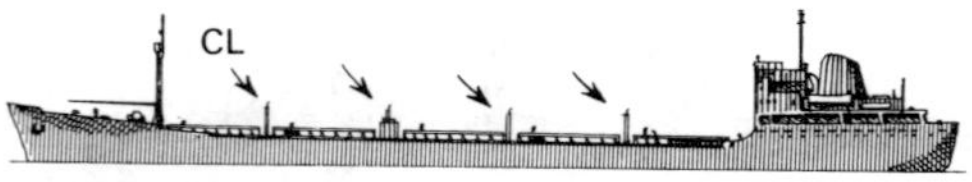

MK_4MF H13
84620 CRYSTAL. Pa/Br 1958; C; 10000; 148.72 × 9.37 (487.93 × 30.74); M; 13; ex SEALORD II 1980; ex STAMOLEON 1974; ex NAVISHIPPER 1973; ex NORTHERN VENTURE 1971; ex SUNHEIM 1970.

MK_4MF H13
84630 KIMOLIAKI AIGLI. Gr/Sw 1962; B; 10800; 152.56 × 9.16 (500.52 × 30.05); M; 14.25; ex OINOUSSIAN CAPTAIN 1981; ex FALSTER 1972; Sister: ⋆**84631 DING HAI** (RC); ex SUCCESSOR 1974; ex MATUMBA 1969.

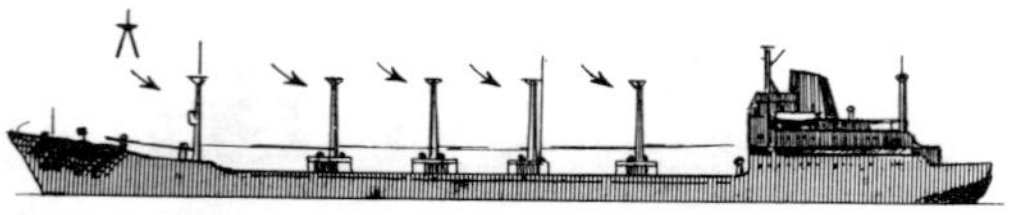

MK_4MFK H13
84640 MAHA JAG ANJLI. In/Sw 1963; C; 8600/11100; 154.84 × 8.59/9.91 (508 × 28.18/32.51); M; —; ex JAG ANJLI 1979; ex CYPRESS 1968.

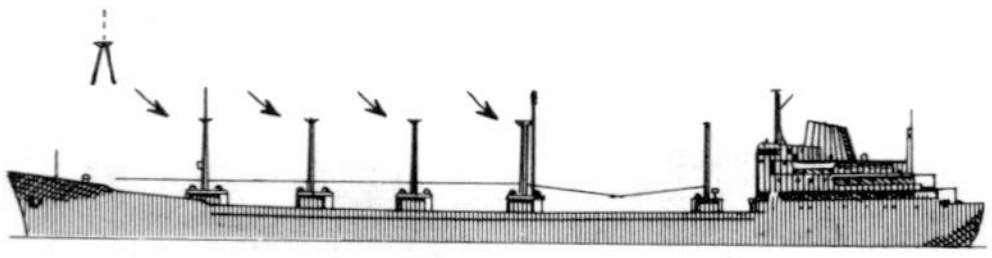

MK_4MFK H13
84650 IRAN HOJJAT. Ir/Sw 1964; C; 8200/11000; 154.84 × 8.59/9.48 (508.01 × 28.18/31.1); M; 14.5; ex ARYA FAR 1980; ex ARYA PEY 1973; ex VINSTRA 1969.

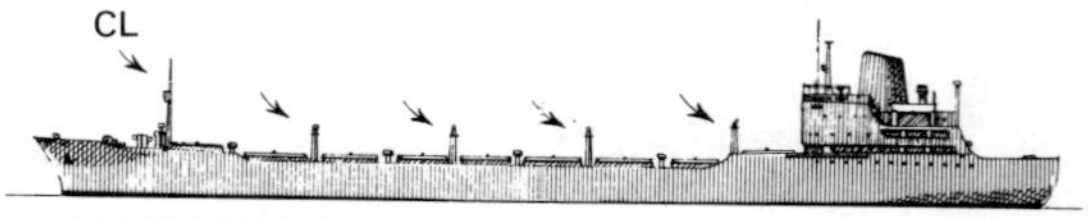

MK_4MFK H13
84660 JAGAT MOHINI. In/FRG 1958; B; 12200; 160.97 × 9.39 (528.12 × 30.8); M; 14; ex RHEINSTAHL 1969; Sister: **84661 JAGAT SWAMINI** (In); ex OTTO SPRINGORUM 1971.

MK_4MFK H13
● **84670 ATLAS CARRIER.** Ko/FRG 1962; B; 11700; 159.37 × 9.82 (522.87 × 32.22); M; 14.5; ex MILORA 1972; Sister: **84671 MARIGOULA** (Gr); ex ELMONA 1976; ex BELMONA 1972.

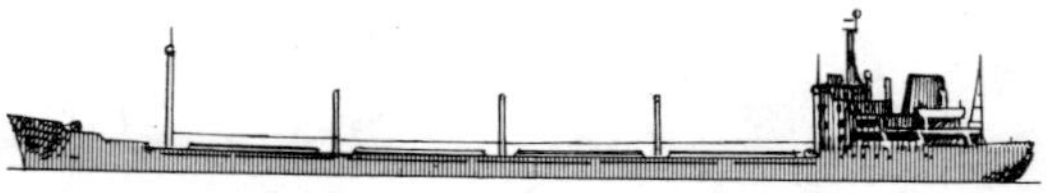

MK_4MFK H13
84680 LAWTONA. Pa/Ja 1960; O; 12300; 161.5 × 8.94 (529.86 × 29.33); M; 13; ex YOSHU MARU 1978; ex YAMAHIRO MARU 1961.

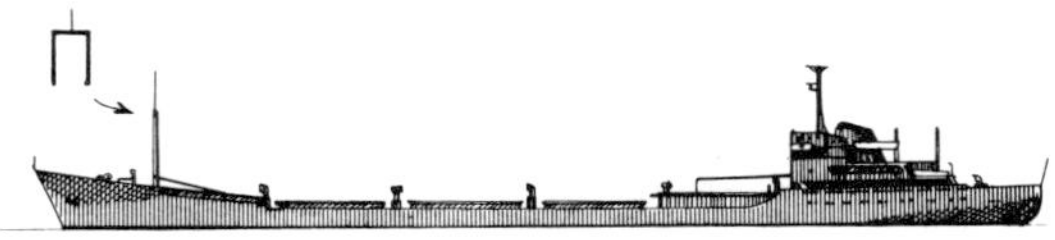

MK_4MFK H13
★84690 HONG QI 113. RC/FRG 1958; O; 10600; 159.34 × 9.42 (522.97 × 30.91); M; 13.5; ex CASPIAN SEA 1976; ex AUGUST LEONHARDT 1972; Sister (may have after KP removed): **84691 MARIE LEONHARDT** (Li).

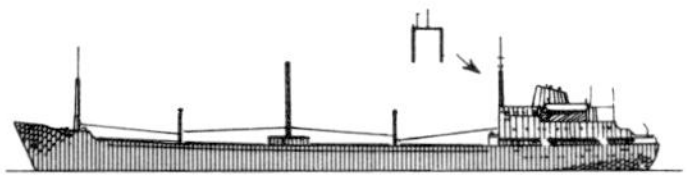

MK_3MF H1
★84710 BOTEVGRAD. Bu/No 1962; C; 2300; 102.77 × 6.01 (337.17 × 19.72); M; 14; ex GERMA 1969.

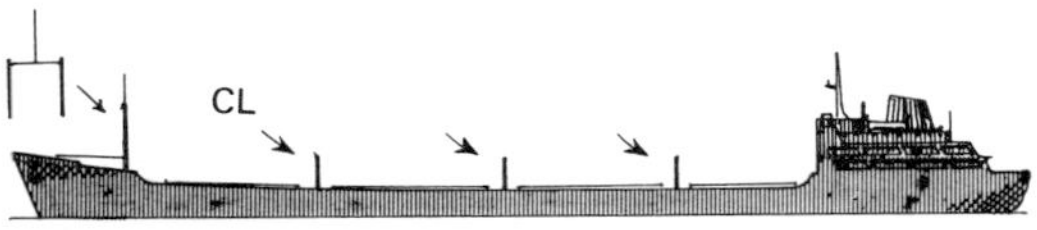

MK_3MF H13
84730 EVPO WAVE. Gr/Br 1961; B; 12200; 159.87 × 8.38 (524.5 × 27.49); M; 11.5; ex DAPO WAVE 1978; ex CAPE NELSON 1976.

MK_3MF H13
84750 TALETE. It/Fr 1967; LGC; 1600; 80.98 × 4.62 (265.68 × 15.16); M; 13; ex THALES 1972.

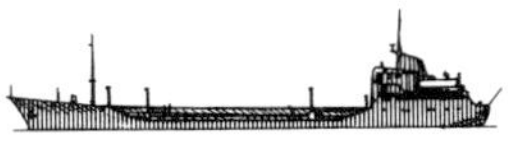

MK_3MF H13
84760 TAMAMES. Sp/Sp 1965; LGC; 1500; 75.72 × 5.25 (248.43 × 17.22); M; 12.5; Similar: **84761 ISLA DE MARNAY** (Sp).

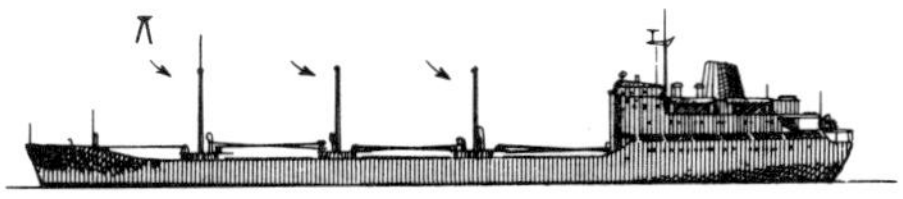

MK_3MF H13
84780 HALLDIS. No/Hong Kong 1960; C; 4000/6000; 130.89 × 6.97/7.89 (429.43 × 22.87/25.89); M; 15; ex BRAGERNES 1973; ex HALLDIS 1969.

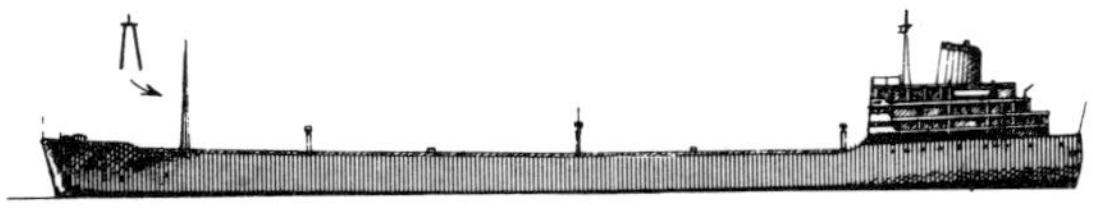

MK_3MF H13
84800 VORRAS. Gr/Ca 1958; B; 11500; 165.18 × 9.47 (541.93 × 31.07); T; 15; ex SUNRHEA 1971.

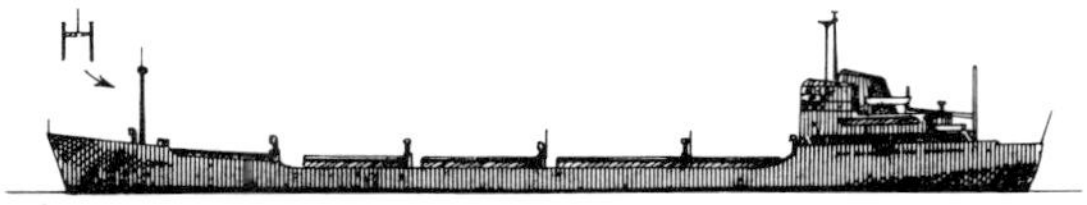

MK_4MFK H13
84700 STAVFJORD. Fi/FRG 1958; B; 10300; 157.82 × 9.45 (517.78 × 31); M; 14; ex MAGDALENA OLDENDORFF 1971.

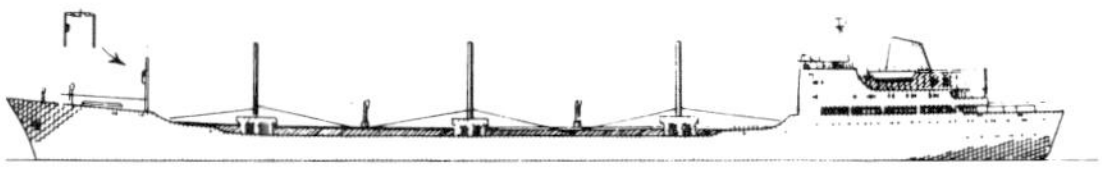

MK_3MF H13
84720 MIHALIOS XILAS. Gr/No 1961; B; 12700; 166.48 × 10.21 (546.19 × 33.5); M; 15; ex GREY MASTER 1970; Sister: **84721 NEW SULU SEA** (Pa); ex SULU SEA 1976; ex GJENDEFJELL 1972; ex ANGELINE 1968.

MK_3MF H13
84740 HERIOT. Br/FRG 1972; LGC; 1600; 78.11 × 6.22 (256.27 × 20.41); M; 14.5; Sisters: **84741 ANNA SCHULTE** (FRG); **84742 PENTLAND GLEN** (Br); ex ABBOTSFORD 1976; Probable sisters: **84743 LEIBNIZ** (Cy); ex ALEXANDER SCHULTE 1980; **84744 SOPHIE SCHULTE** (FRG).

MK_3MF H13
84770 TINE THOLSTRUP. De/FRG 1967; LGC; 1400; 71.2 × 4.52 (233.6 × 14.83); M; 12.

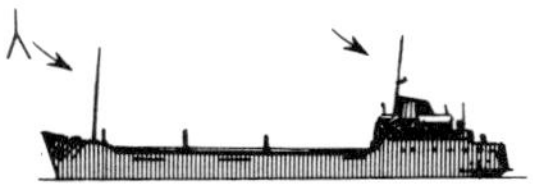

MK_3MF H13
84790 SPICE ISLAND GIRL. Pa/Br 1958; C; 1500; 73 72 × 4.33 (241.86 × 14.21); M; —; ex SPICE ISLAND 1979; ex ISLE OF ELY 1978.

MK_3MFK H13
★84810 LIVNY. Ru/Ja 1963; Tk; 22500; 207.04 × 11.11 (679.27 × 36.45); M; 17.25; Sisters (Ru flag): **★84811 LOZOVAYA; ★84812 LENINAKAN; ★84813 LYUDINOVO;** Probable sister: **★84814 NOVOROSSISKIY PARTIZAN;** ex LISKI 1976; Similar: **★84815 LENKORAN; ★84816 LISICHANSK; ★84817 LYUBOTIN.**

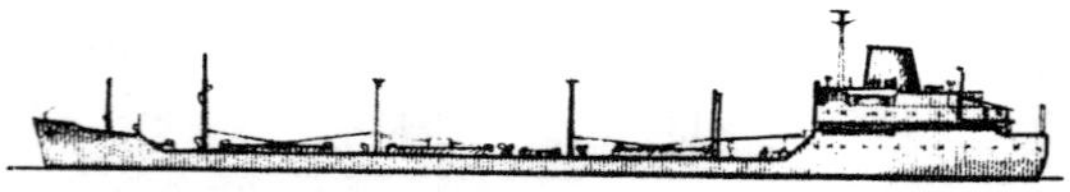

MK_3MFK H13
● **84820 OCEAN TRITON.** Gr/Sw 1963; B; 11900; 163.23 × 9.38 (535.53 × 30.77); M; 15.5; ex TROJA 1970.

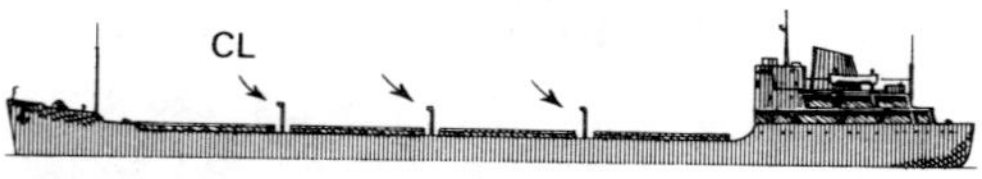

MK_3MFK H13
84840 RUBINI. Gr/Br 1960; O; 11600; 154.24 × 8.83 (506.04 × 28.97); M; 12.5; ex NIKOLAOS MALEFAKIS 1980; ex MABEL WARWICK 1976; Sister: **84841 HADIOTIS** (Gr); ex ST. MARGARET 1978; ex JOYA McCANCE 1966.

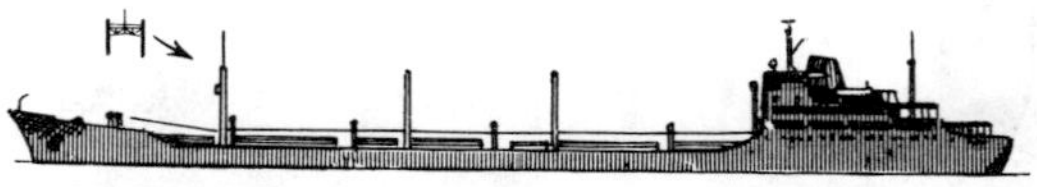

MK_3MFK H13
84830 MAUREEN B. Pa/No 1962; B; 12000; 159.65 × 9.95 (523.79 × 32.64); M; 15; ex GLYFADA SPIRIT 1980; ex GUDVANG 1974; ex NORBEGA 1969.

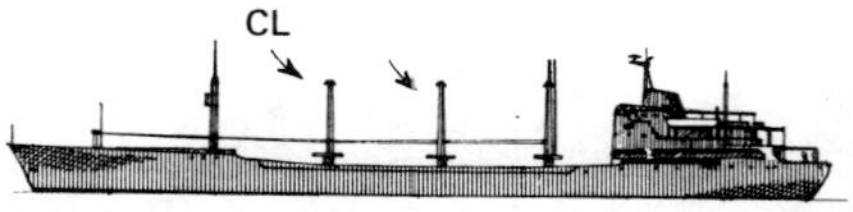

MK_3MFK H13
84850 DAVID SALMAN. Fi/Sw 1962; C; 7100; 129.29 × 7.94 (424.18 × 26.05); M; 16; ex GRIM 1976; ex DAVID SALMAN 1975.

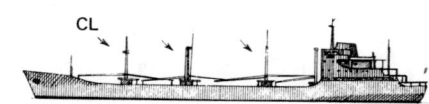

MK_3MFK H13
● **84860 AL KAHERA.** Eg/Sw 1961; C; 4100/5900; 126.93 × 6.81/8.14 (416.44 × 22.34/26.71); M; 16.25; ex SEAHORSE 1975; ex CONCORDIA SEAHORSE 1975; ex SEAHORSE 1972; ex SUNSEAHORSE 1972; ex SEAHORSE 1963.

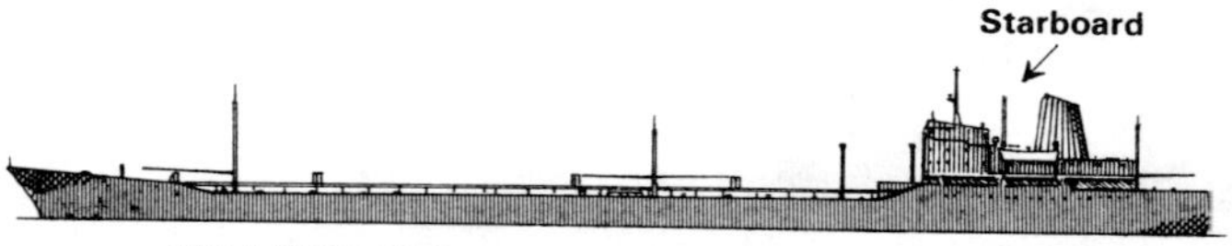

MK_3MKFK H13
★84870 LENINABAD. Ru/Ja 1964; Tk; 23100; 207.04 × 11.11 (679.27 × 36.45); M; 16.5; Sister: **★84871 LUTSK** (Ru).

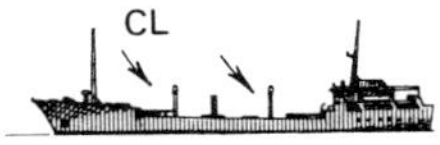

MK_2MF H
⋆84880 CAPITAN OLO PANTOJA. Cu/No 1965; Ch; 500; 63.71 × 3.89 (209.02 × 12.76); M; 11; ex RIER 1975; ex STAINLESS CARRIER 1974; Sister: **⋆84881 MARTINEZ TAMAYO** (Cu); ex STAIN 1975; ex STAINLESS TANKER 1974.

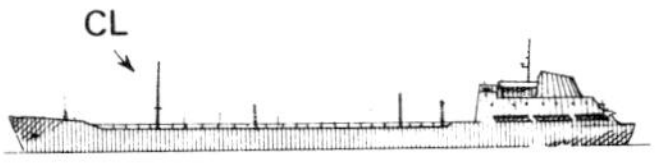

MK_2MF H1
84910 OTELIA. Sw/Sw 1969; Tk; 2700; 98.94 × 6.43 (324.61 × 21.1); M; 12; Sisters: **84911 OTTAWA** (Sw); **84912 KHALIJIAH** (Ku); ex OTELLO 1978; Similar: **84913 OTARU** (Sw); **84914 WOTONI** (Ma); ex OTONI 1977.

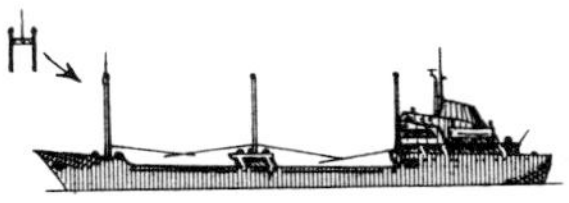

MK_2MF H13
84930 ZINGARA. It/DDR 1963; C; 900/1600; 82.4 × 4.26/5.75 (270.34 × 13.98/18.86); M; 12; ex ADAMASTOS 1980; ex KORMORAN 1976; Sisters (DDR flag): **⋆84931 BUSSARD; ⋆84932 CONDOR; ⋆84933 FALKE; ⋆84934 FLAMINGO; ⋆84935 PINGUIN.**

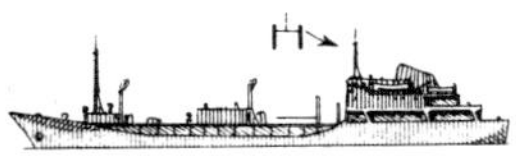

MK_2MF H13
84950 HERIOT. Br/FRG 1972; LGC; 1600; 78.11 × 6.22 (256.27 × 20.41); M; 14.5; Sisters: **84951 ANNA SCHULTE** (FRG); **84952 PENTLAND GLEN** (Br); ex ABBOTSFORD 1976; Probable sisters: **84953 LEIBNIZ** (Cy); ex ALEXANDER SCHULTE 1980; **84954 SOPHIE SCHULTE** (FRG).

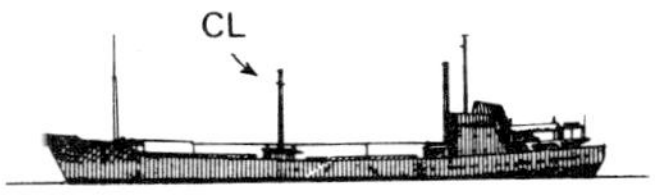

MK_2MF H1
84890 VIOCA. It/FRG 1957; C; 2700; 89.34 × 6.73 (293.1 × 22.08); M; 13; ex BAMBI 1969.

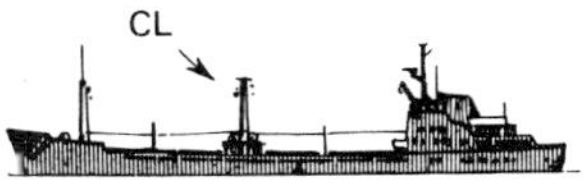

MK_2MF H1
84900 STUDLAFOSS. Ic/Br 1964; R; 2400; 89.46 × 5.35 (293.5 × 17.55); M; —; ex HOFSJOKULL 1977.

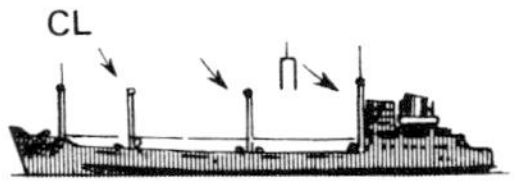

MK_2MF H13
84920 TACAMAR III. Pa/Br 1955; C; 1400; 76.82 × 3.98 (252 × 13.06); M; 12; ex ALFTAN 1976; ex VASILIA 1972; ex KELVIN 1968; ex ULSTER PREMIER 1963; Similar: **84921 HONG SHEN** (My); ex WOODBINE 1975; ex BAT SNAPIR 1973; ex TALISKER 1968; ex ULSTER PIONEER 1963.

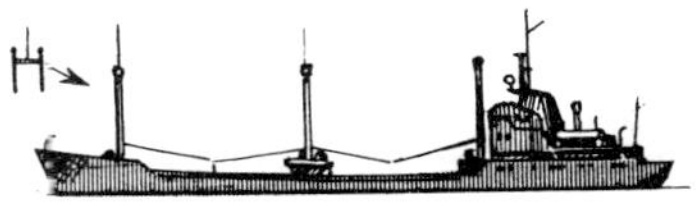

MK_2MF H13
⋆84940 OELSA. DDR/DDR 1967; C; 2500; 92.82 × 5.92 (304.53 × 19.42); M; 12.75; Sisters (DDR flag): **⋆84941 EISENBERG; ⋆84942 HELLERAU; ⋆84943 THEMAR; ⋆84944 ZEULENRODA.**

MK_2MF H13
84960 SULFURICO. Sp/Sp 1969; Ch; 1200; 77.32 × 4.76 (253.67 × 15.62); M; 12; Sisters: **84961 FOSFORICO** (Sp); **⋆84962 CAPITAN ALBERTO FERNANDEZ** (Cu); **84963 LITRIX** (It); ex NITRICO.

MK_2MF H13
84970 SILVERMERLIN. Br/Sw 1968; Tk/Ch; 1300; 77.32 × 4.8 (253.67 × 15.75); M; 12; Similar: **84971 SILVERFALCON** (Br).

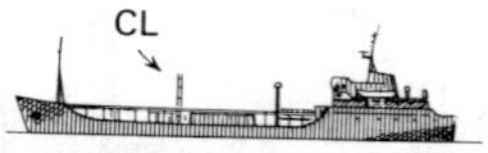

MK_2MF H13
84980 PASS OF CAIRNWELL. Br/Br 1970; Tk/Ch; 900; 70.16 × 4.19 (230.18 × 13.75); M; 11; ex CORDALE 1975; Lengthened 1972; Sister: **84981 PASS OF CHISHOLM** (Br); ex CORDENE 1975.

MK_2MF H13
85000 KIRSTEN THOLSTRUP. De/FRG 1961; LGC; 1000; 67.39 × 3.65 (221 × 11.98); M; 12.5; Sisters: **85111 BIRTHE THOLSTRUP** (De); **85002 ULLA THOLSTRUP** (De); Similar (lengthened): **85003 LISBET THOLSTRUP** (De); **85004 MAGALLANES** (Pi); ex HANNE THOLSTRUP 1974.

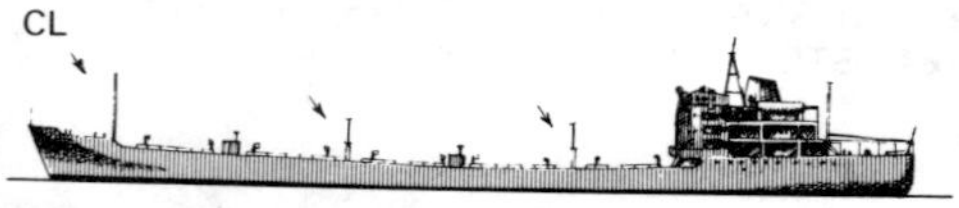

MK_2MFK H13
● **85020 GUNGNIR V.** Pa/Au 1957; B; 7300; 142.7 × 8.3 (468.18 × 27.23); M; 11.75; ex LAKE; ex LAKE BOGA 1978; Sisters: **85021 AL TOOS** (Li); ex LAKE SORELL 1980; **85022 AL TASLIM** (Sg); ex LAKE MACQUAIRE 1978.

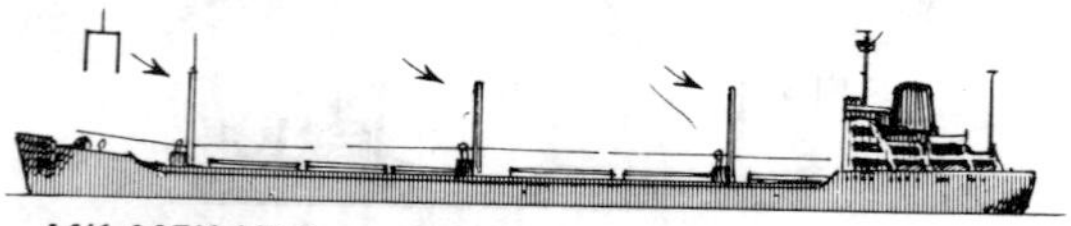

MK_2MFK H13
85040 OCEAN PROSPECT. Pa/Ja 1961; B; 12000; 160 × 9.17 (524.93 × 30.09); M; 14.25; ex LUNA 1976; ex TETSUKUNI MARU 1974.

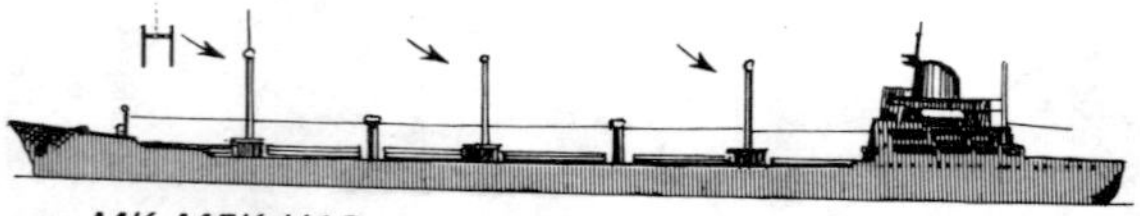

MK_2MFK H13
85060 KING LEONIDAS. Gr/Fr 1963; B; 15700; 177.27 × 10.56 (581.59 × 34.65); M; —.

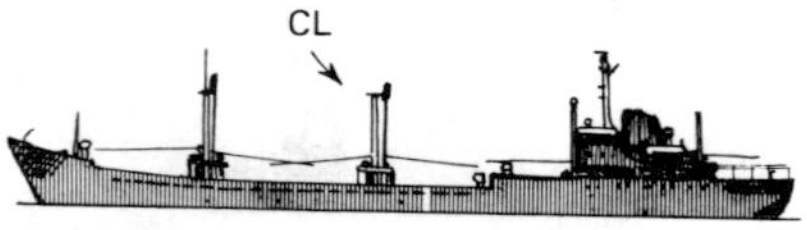

MK_2MFK H13
85080 14 JULY. Iq/Ja 1962; C; 3800/5700; 126.45 × 6.67/7.88 (414.86 × 21.88/25.85); M; 15.5; Sister: **85081 14 RAMADAN** (Iq) ex KASSIM 1963.

MK_2MF H13
84990 GAZ VICTORY. Gr/Fr 1964; LGC; 1700; 79.86 × 4.87 (262 × 15.98); M; 12; ex MED MULTINA 1980; ex CAP SOUNION 1974; ex CAP SICIE 1968; Similar: **84991 CAP PHAISTOS** (Gr); ex CAP FREHEL 1969; **84992 CAPO FALCONE** (It); ex YUKI MULTINA 1972; ex CAP GRIS-NEZ 1971.

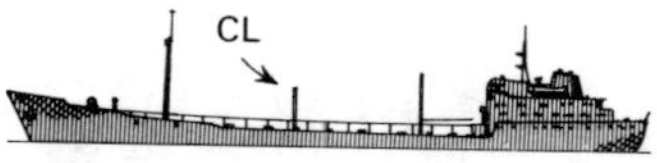

MK_2MF H13
● **85010 CHIQUITA.** Pa/No 1963; Tk/Ch; 2700; 101.45 × 5.81 (332.84 × 19.06); M; 12.25; ex MICHELLE F 1978; ex ST. PANTELEIMON 1975; ex EK 1974; Sister: **85011 TRADE WIND** (Pa); ex OAK 1974.

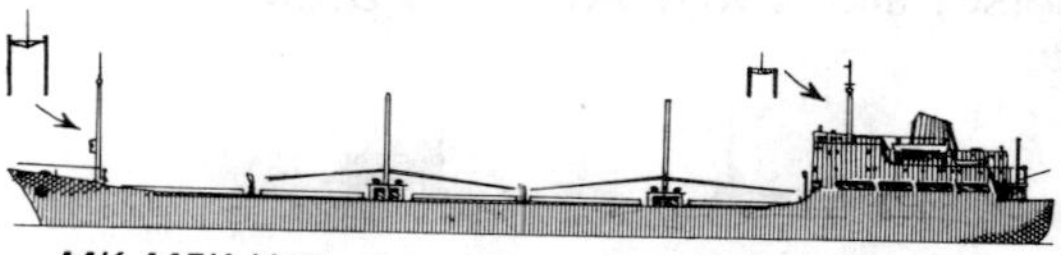

MK_2MFK H13
85030 ALMEA. Gr/No 1960; B; 10800; 166.48 × 10.22 (546.19 × 33.53); M; 14; ex FIONA 1 1978; ex ST. FOTINI 1977; ex BJORGHEIM 1969.

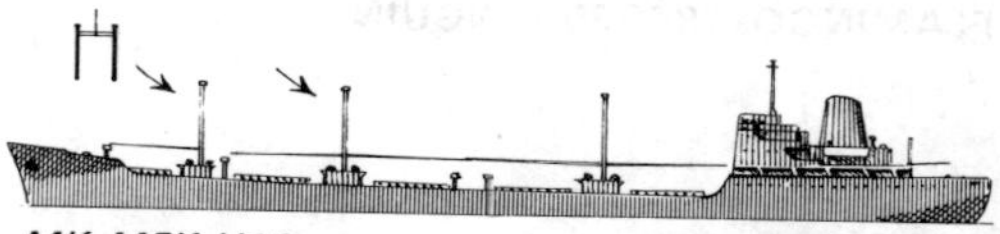

MK_2MFK H13
85050 ALHAJA MAMA BAKARE. Pa/Ja 1957; C; 10300; 154.84 × 9.36 (508.01 × 30.71); T; —; ex THARROS 1977; Similar: **85051 DUPE BAKARE** (Pa) ex RYTHME 1977.

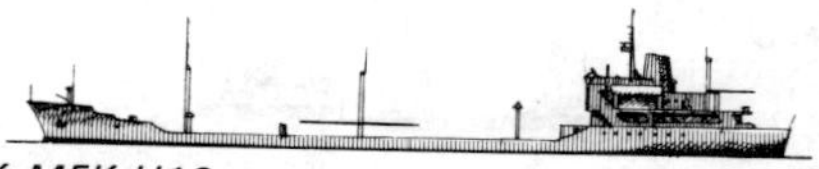

MK_2MFK H13
85070 UM EL FAROUD. Ly/Br 1969; Ch; 3100; 109.56 × 6.41 (359.45 × 21.03); M; 14; ex SEAFALCON 1973; Sister: **85071 STORNA** (Li) ex SEATERN 1975.

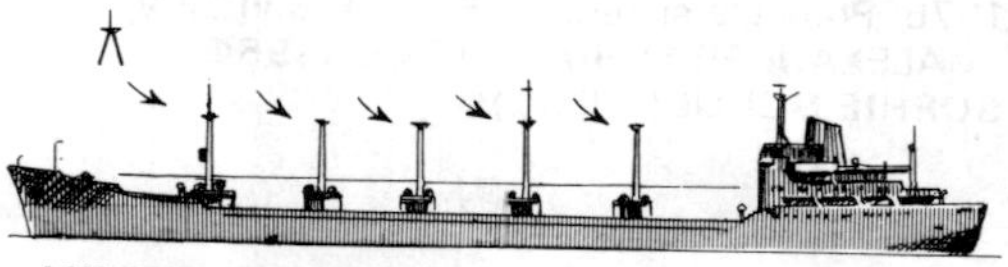

MK_2MKMFK H13
85090 OSWEGO PLANTER. Li/No 1963; C; 8100/10600; 155.25 × 8.83/9.47 (509.35 × 28.97/31.07); M; —; ex OLD DOMINION STATE 1972; ex NORBETH 1968.

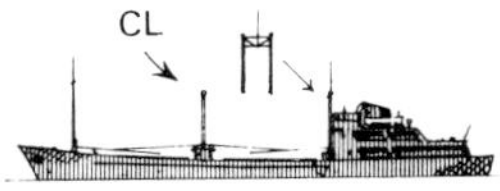

MKMF H
85100 SETE CIDADES. Po/Sw 1961; C; 1100; 74.5 × 3.67 (244.42 × 12.04); M; —; ex BRUSE 1972; ex NORDPOL 1964; Sister: **85101 LAGOA** (Po) ex BURE 1972; ex VAASA 1964.

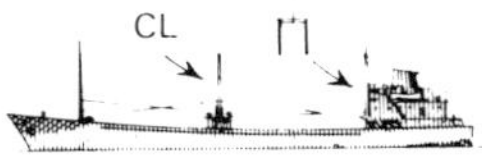

MKMF H
85110 VILI. To/Sw 1967; C; 500/1300; 73.41 × 3.62/5.72 (240.85 × 11.88/18.77); M; 13; ex NOGI 1979; ex MARIN 1974.

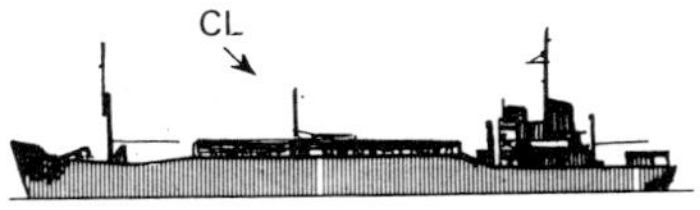

MKMF H
85120 ARISTOTLE. Pa/US 1945/58; LGC; 4700; 103.26 × 7.18 (338.78 × 23.56); M; 11.5; ex METHANE PIONEER 1967; ex NORMATI 1958; ex DON AURELIO 1951; ex MARLINE HITCH 1946; Converted from 'C1-M-AV1' type general cargo. Now used for storage.

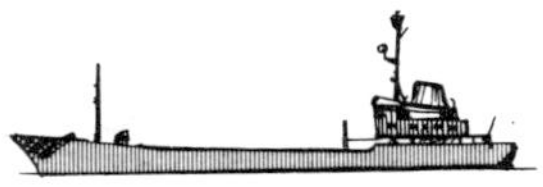

MKMF H
85130 LONE TERKOL. De/FRG 1972; Tk; 1300; 81.01 × 5.27 (265.78 × 17.29); M; 12; Possibly similar (lengthened 1976): **85131 OTTO** (FRG).

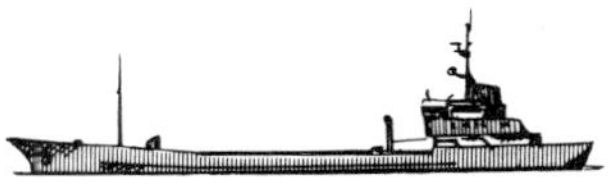

MKMF H
85140 BORKUM. FRG/FRG 1970; Tk; 1200; 92.97 × 5.21 (305 × 17.09); M; 12; lengthened 1975.

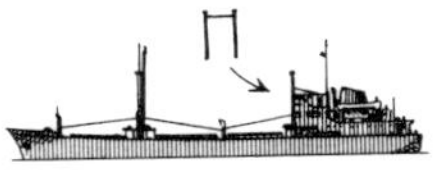

MKMF H
85150 SELAT MAKASSAR. Ia/Ja 1962; C; 1100; 64.98 × 4 (213.19 × 13.12); M; 12; Sister: **85151 SELAT KARIMATA** (Ia).

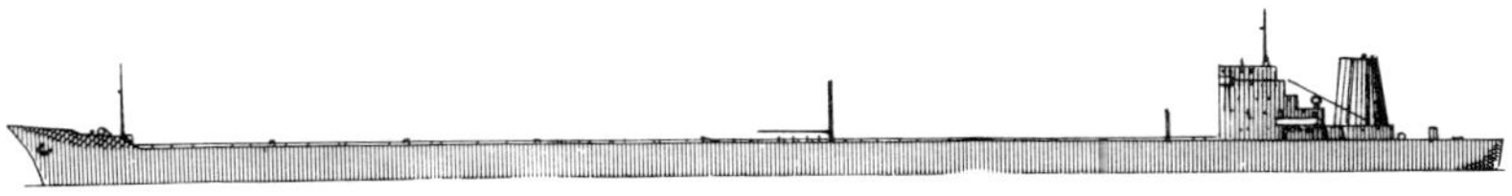

MKMF H1
● **85160 THAMES MARU.** Ja/Ja 1965; Tk; 42700; 245.57 × 12.35 (805.68 × 40.52); M; 16.25.

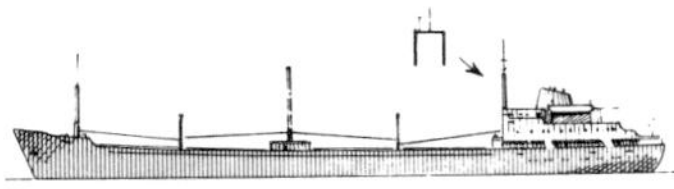

MKMF H1
⋆**85170 BOTEVGRAD.** Bu/No 1962; C; 2300; 102.77 × 6.01 (337.17 × 19.72); M; 14; ex GERMA 1969; Similar (without large vents in well): **85171 KARYATIS** (Gr) ex TARVA 1972; ex GERMONT 1962.

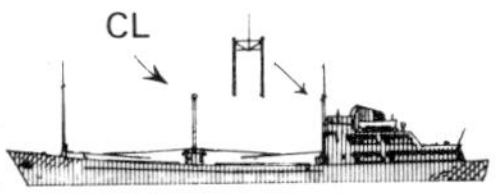

MKMF H1
85180 SETE CIDADES. Po/Sw 1961; C; 1100; 74.5 × 3.67 (244.42 × 12.04); M; —; ex BRUSE 1972; ex NORDPOL 1964; Sister: **85181 LAGOA** (Po) ex BURE 1972; ex VAASA 1964.

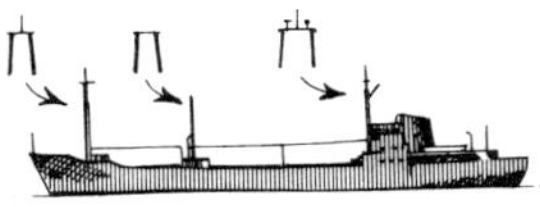

MKMF H1
85190 FIVE FLOWERS. Pa/De 1958; C; 1000/1500; 78.52 × 4.42/5.65 (257.61 × 14.5/18.54); M; —; ex BAKKAFOSS 1974; ex MILLE HEERING 1963; Similar: **85191 INGRID JUDITH** (Co) ex CATAIMA 1973; ex CHRISTEL HEERING 1962.

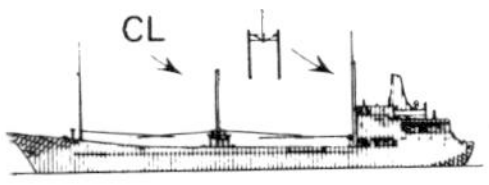

MKMF H1
85200 DIVONA. Pa/Sw 1966; C; 500; 73.41 × 3.62 (240.85 × 11.88); M; —; launched as SUNNANHAV.

MKMF H1
● **85210 SINGAPORE JATI.** Sg/Ne 1955; C/HL; 800/1200; 80.5 × 5.11/— (264.11 × 16.77/—); M; 10.5; ex BERNARD JOHN 1974; Gear amidships consists of quadpod and sheerlegs.

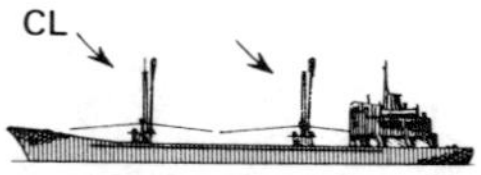

MKMF H1
85230 IBN JUBAIR. Eg/Sp 1970; C; 660/1180; 72.7 × 5.19 (238.5 × 16.96); M; —; ex ATLAN ESMERALDA 1974; Sister: **85231 IBN KORRA** (Eg) ex ATLAN RUBI 1975; Possibly similar: **85232 LUR TXORI** (Sp) ex JADE 1975; ex LIAN 1974; **85233 UR-TXORI** (Eg) ex TOPACIO 1976; ex LIAN DOS 1973.

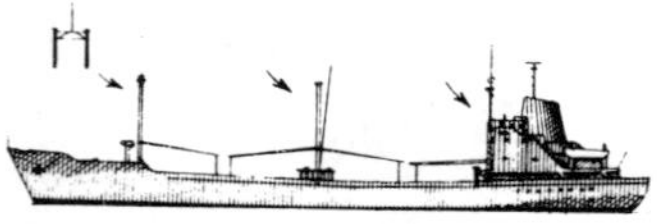

MKMF H1
85250 IOANNIS. Gr/Sw 1958; C; 2000/3100; 102.14 × 5.79/6.57 (335.1 × 21.56); M; 13.5; ex ODER 1980; ex CECILIA FALKLAND 1962.

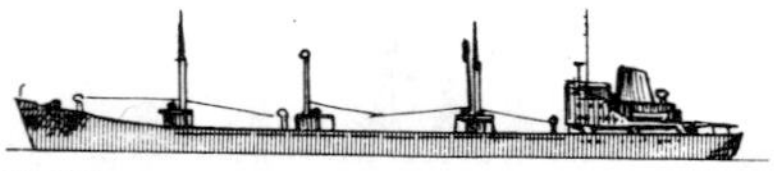

MKMF H1
85270 ZANET. Gr/Sw 1958; C; 4500; 114.33 × 7.21 (375 × 23.65); M; 14; ex BEAVERASH 1969; ex MIMER 1963.

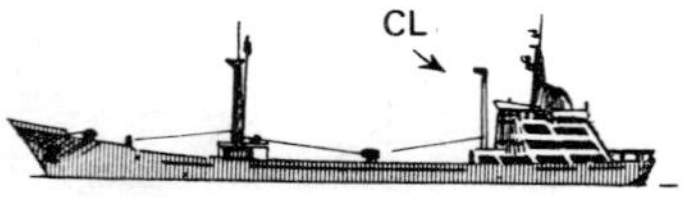

MKMF H1
85290 CORANTIJN. Sn/Ne 1968; C; 2700; 101.99 × 6.17 (334.61 × 20.24); M; 15.

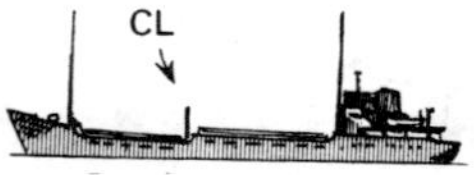

MKMF H12
85310 ESPERANZA No 2. Pa/Ne 1956/70; C; 1100; 70.85 × 4.4 (232.45 × 14.47); M; 11.25; ex ATLANTICO 1 1978; ex FIBROOK 1973; ex WARWICKBROOK 1972; lengthened 1970.

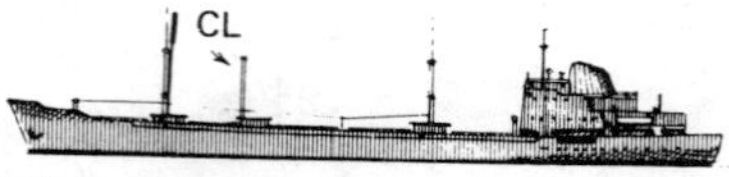

MKMF H1
● **85220 MINERVA.** Gr/No 1957; C; 2700/4400; 114.28 × 6.22/7.19 (374.93 × 20.41/23.59); M; 15; ex HELIOS 1978; ex KONGSHOLM 1963; Sister: **85221 MARTINA** (Gr) ex WANJA 1973; ex JEANETTE 1966; Similar: **85222 ATLANTICOS** (Gr) ex ATLANTIKOS 1980; ex LYDIA 1978; ex HERAKLES 1970; ex KONGSBORG 1959.

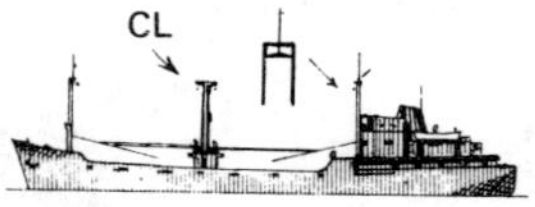

MKMF H1
85240 ANNA. Gr/Ne 1958; C; 1600; 78.64 × 4.47 (258 × 14.67); M; 12; ex CHARENTE 1970; Sister: **85241 MAYA** (Cy) ex MYRTO 1976; ex BISCAYA 1970.

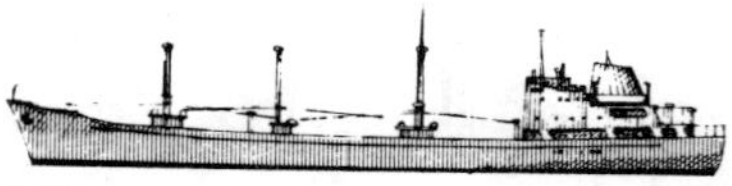

MKMF H1
*85260 ORLA.** DDR/Sw 1959; C; 2700/4300; 114.33 × 6.2/7.19 (375.1 × 20.34/23.59); M; 14.5; ex ARTENSIS 1968.

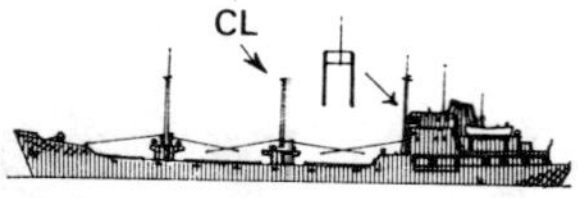

MKMF H1
85280 MUDISTAR .Pa/Ne 1959; C; 1400; 88.09 × 5.26 (289 × 17.26); M; 13; ex STALHEIM 1972; Sister: **85281 BONAWIND 1** (Sg) ex DALIASTAR 1980; ex STANFORD 1972.

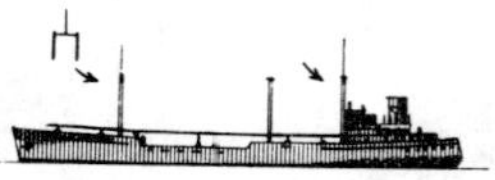

MKMF H12
85300 GEORGIOS. Gr/Br 1937; C; 1300; 72.24 × 5.12 (237 × 16.8); M; 11; ex VASILIOS 1978; ex MANTHOS 1971; ex PERTH 1963; ex LOCHEE 1948.

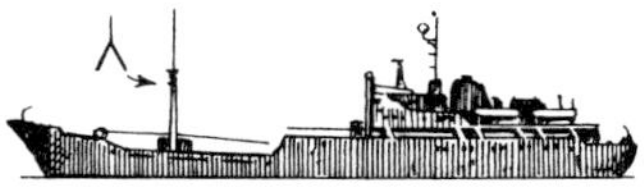

MKMF H12

● ⋆**85320 TAVRIYA.** Ru/Ru 1960; FC; 3000; 99.35 × 5.65 (325.95 × 18.54); D-E; 13; Sisters (some vary—taller funnels etc)— (Ru flag): ⋆**85321 DALNEVOSTOCHNY;** ⋆**85322 VOLZHSK;** ⋆**85323 ALBATROS;** ⋆**85324 ANDREY EVDANOV;** ⋆**85325 SOVIETSKAYA LATVIYA;** ⋆**85326 SOVIETSKAYA RODINA;** ⋆**85327 VITALIY BONIVUR;** ⋆**85328 BUREVESTNIK;** ⋆**85329 DMITRY CHASOVITIN;** ⋆**85330 KAZIS GERDIS;** ⋆**85331 RUDNYY;** ⋆**85332 ALTAIR;** ⋆**85333 MIKHAIL YANKO;** ⋆**85334 NEVELSKIY;** ⋆**85335 OKTYABRSK;** ⋆**85336 SEREBRYANSK;** ⋆**85337 SVETLYY;** ⋆**85338 IRBIT;** ⋆**85339 ISHIM;** ⋆**85340 ISKONA;** ⋆**85341 PRANAS ZIBERTAS;** ⋆**85342 SALNA;** ⋆**85343 SARMA;** ⋆**85344 PARSLA;** ⋆**85345 SAYANI;** ⋆**85346 SUKHINICHI;** ⋆**85347 GUTSUL;** ⋆**85348 MONGOL;** ⋆**85349 NANAYETS;** ⋆**85350 PFUSUNG;** ⋆**85351 AUGUST KORK;** ⋆**85352 BOEVOY;** ⋆**85353 LEDUS;** ⋆**85354;** ⋆**85355 MOLODYOZNYY;** ⋆**85356 MOREKHOD;** ⋆**85357 VETERAN;** ⋆**85358 DON;** ⋆**85359 KREUTSWALD;** ⋆**85360 NAMANGAN;** ⋆**85361 VIKTORAS YATSENYAVICHUS;** (Bu flag): ⋆**85362 KHAN OMTURAG** ex BETELGEUSE; (DDR flag): ⋆**85363 BREITLING;** (Gh flag): **85364 AGYASI MANKO.**

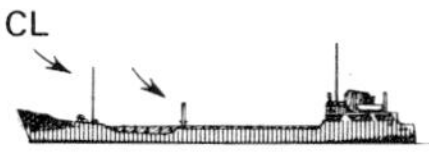

MKMF H123

85410 ALEX G. Gr/Br 1959; C; 850; 62.69 × 3.76 (205.67 × 12.33); M; 10.5; ex QUIESCENCE 1975.

MKMF H123

85430 ANN M. Br/Br 1961; C; 1200; 70.11 × 4.47 (230.02 × 14.67); M; 11.5.

MKMF H123

85370 GREEK SKY. Cy/Br 1955; C; 1300; 70.92 × 4.66 (232.68 × 15.29); M; 11; ex BRIGHT SKY 1976; ex SANDRINGHAM QUEEN 1972.

MKMF H123

85380 ANGELINA S. Br/Br 1965; C; 1100; 67.98 × 4.33 (223 × 14.21); M; 11; ex MARIYOS HOPE 1980; ex BALMERINO 1977; ex ARDGARVEL 1975.

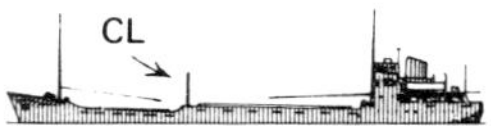

MKMF H123

85390 ORESTIS. Gr/Ne 1958; C; 1100; 73.94 × 4.4 (242.59 × 14.44); M; 11.25; ex HOUTMAN 1974; ex ERASMUS 1970; ex ARGONAUT 1968; lengthened 1971.

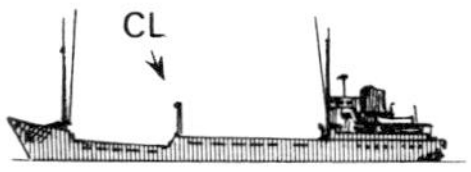

MKMF H123

85400 CRETE. Gr/Ne 1956; C; 1000; 66.45 × 4.42 (218 × 14.5); M; 11.25; ex MAHI 1978; ex WALLONA 1971; ex WINDSOR QUEEN 1969; ex MORTLAKE 1966; ex LOCKWOOD 1965; ex NORDGAS 1964; ex WINDSORBROOK 1963.

MKMF H123

85420 BREDAL. Br/FRG 1953; C; 1300; 80.52 × 4.43 (264.17 × 14.53); M; 10.5; ex BREDO 1972; ex JORUNA 1968; ex MARGARET C ERTEL 1963; lengthened 1957.

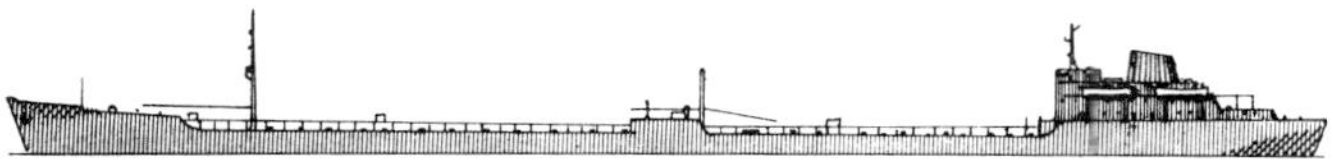

MKMF H123

85440 IOANNA V. Gr/Sw 1961; Tk; 22100; 208.03 × 11.56 (682.51 × 37.93); M; 16; ex ALBA 1977; ex HEMLAND 1972.

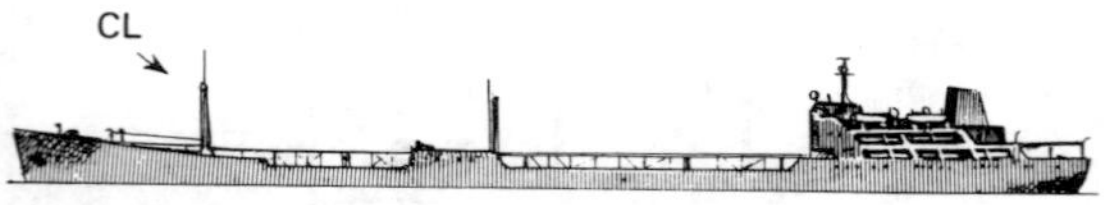

MKMF H123
⋆**85450 DUNAV.** Bu/Br 1961; Tk; 13600; 170.47 × 9.48 (559.28 × 31.1); M; 15; ex MONTANA 1963.

MKMF H13
85460 RESILIENCE. Br/Ne 1969; Starch carrier; 1000; 66.3 × 4.1 (217.52 × 13.45); M; 12.5.

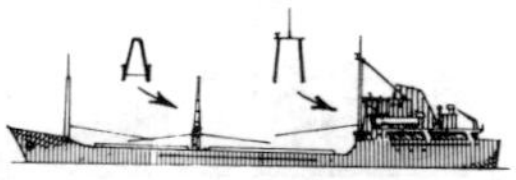

MKMF H13
● **85470 WESTFJORD.** FRG/No 1971; C; 1500; 77.07 × 4.73 (252.85 × 15.52); M; 12.5; Similar (tripod forward): **85471 CAREBEKA VII** (Ne) ex NORTRIO 1974; **85472 MAASPLEIN** (FRG) ex NORCATO 1974; **85473 MUNTE** (Ne) ex NORIMO 1974.

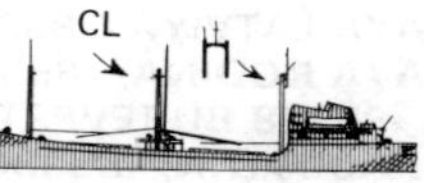

MKMF H13
85480 MAYA. Cy/FRG 1966; C; 800/1500; 74.81 × 4.02/5.75 (245.44 × 13.19/18.86); M; o3.5; ex ERIDAN 1980; ex AUSTRIAN SAILOR 1978; ex WIEN 1977; ex SEEADLER 1972.

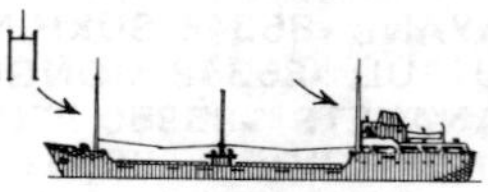

MKMF H13
85490 OTTO. Br/Ne 1955; C; 1300; 68.94 × 5.03 (226.18 × 16.5); M; 11.

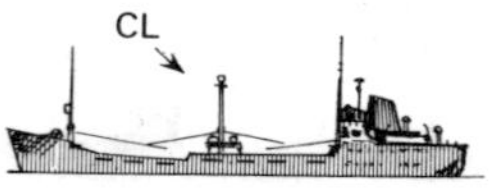

MKMF H13
⋆**85500 KOM.** Ys/FRG 1956; C; 1400; 74.48 × 5.22 (244.36 × 17.13); M; 12; ex HUM 1980; ex URANIA 1974; ex DOROTHEA G 1974; ex URANIA 1968.

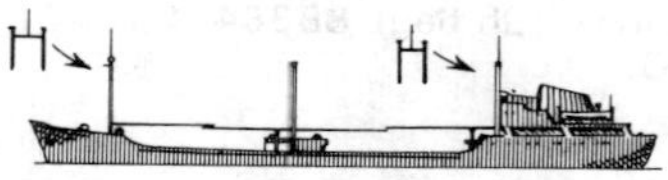

MKMF H13
⋆**85510 PUPNAT.** Ys/FRG 1959; C; 2200; 92.72 × 5.85 (304.2 × 19.19); M; 12.5; ex VICTOR 1973; ex I.G.NICHELSON 1972.

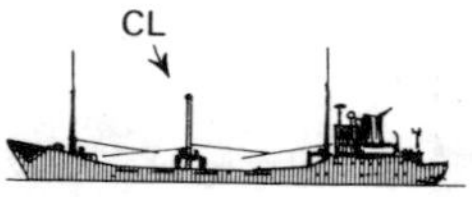

MKMF H13
● **85520 APOSTOLOS H.** Gr/FRG 1951; C; 1000; 72.32 × 4.61 (237.27 × 15.12); M; 11.5; ex ANNELIS CHRISTOPHERSEN 1975.

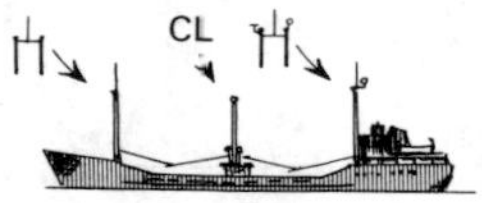

MKMF H13
● **85530 NICOLAOS M.** Gr/FRG 1951; C; 500; 63.15 × 3.9 (207.19 × 12.8); M; 10.5; ex DIETER KARL 1972; ex MARSUND 1968; ex KREUZBERG 1957; ex ANNELIESE GLEUE 1954.

MKMF H13
85540 MERCATOR. Pa/FRG 1952; C; 1100; 72.04 × 4.61 (236.35 × 15.12); M; 11; ex KATIE 1978; ex HAMMONIA 1965; ex ANNI AHRENS 1957.

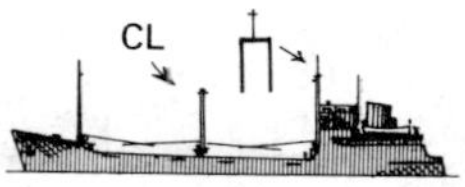

MKMF H13
85550 MANUEL. Pa/Br 1955; C; 900; 68.43 × 5.6 (224.51 × 18.37); ex PROODOS 1980; ex MICHALIS 1976; ex EVDELOS 1972; ex MOUNTSTEWART 1969; ex ESSEX COAST 1957.

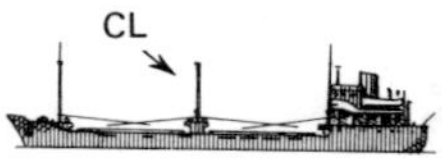

MKMF H13
85560 MARIO ATTANASIO. It/FRG 1952; C; 1000; 65.82 × 4.53 (215.98 × 14.86); M; 12; ex ELSE MULLER 1967.

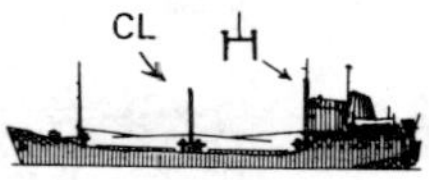

MKMF H13
85570 RAMSLAND. No/FRG 1956; C; 900; 64.95 × 4.31 (213.09 × 14.14); M; 11; ex SIMON 1975; ex ORTRUD MULLER 1965.

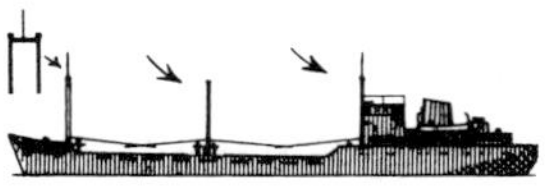

MKMF H13
85580 PETROLA 40. Gr/FRG 1958; C; 1800; 82 × 5.73 (269.03 × 18.8); M; 12.5; ex PETROLA XL 1976; ex VARODD 1975; ex ESTREMADURIAN 1970; ex VARODD 1968.

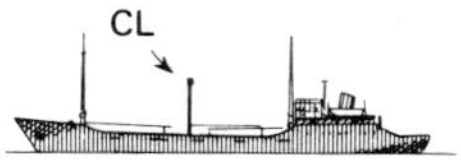

MKMF H13
● **85590 EVOIKOS.** Cy/FRG 1952; C; 1100; 66.42 × 4.62 (217.91 × 15.16); M; 11.75; ex SANTA MARINA 1975; ex MYRTO 1973; ex PYLADES 1971; ex EIFEL 1963.

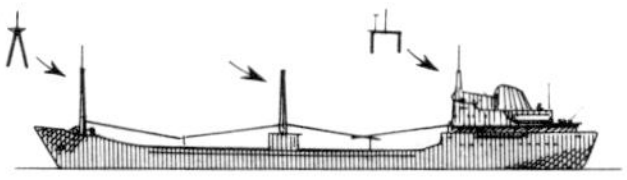

MKMF H13
85600 TABALO. Sy/Fi 1961; C; 1800; 85.81 × 5.39 (281.53 × 17.68); M; 13; ex GAIST 1977; ex ELSE REITH 1969; ex PULPTRADER 1966.

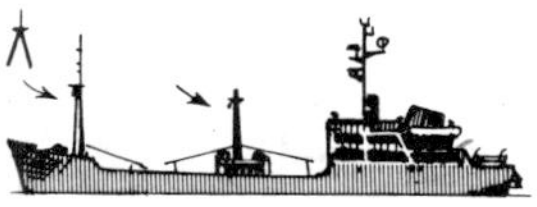

MKMF H13
● ⋆**85610 BIRA.** Ru/Ru; Sister: ⋆**85611 BUREYA** (Ru); No further details available. Probably used as naval transport or as landing craft.

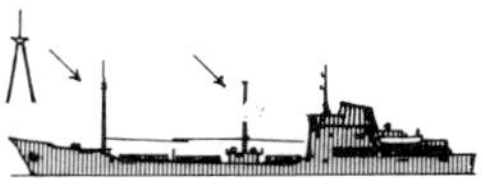

MKMF H13
85620 ARUBA BAY. NA/Sw 1964; R; 500/1300; 72.8 × 3.72 (238.85 × 12.2/16.47); M; 14.5; ex POLAR VIKING 1974; Similar: **85621 CARACAS BAY** (NA) ex HASTINGS 1973.

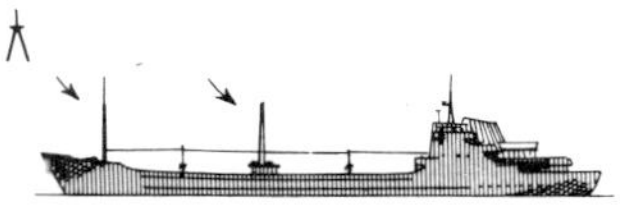

MKMF H13
⋆**85630 NAPALSAN.** RK/De 1961; R; 1900; 78.03 bp × 5.02 (256 bp × 5.02); M; 13; ex MAG 2 1968; ex DRANGAJOKULL 1968; Probably used as a fish carrier; Sister: ⋆**85631 PONGDESAN** (RK) ex MAG 1 1968; ex LANGJOKUL 1968.

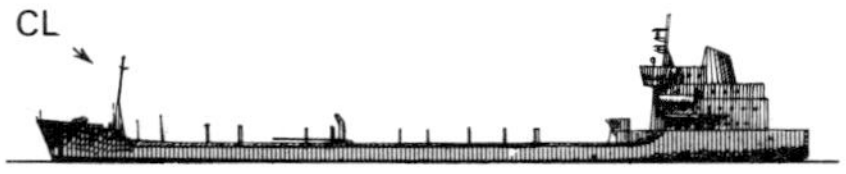

MKMF H13
85640 LAKESHELL. Ca/Ca 1969; Tk; 5700; 121.93 × 7.1 (400 × 23.29); M; 13.

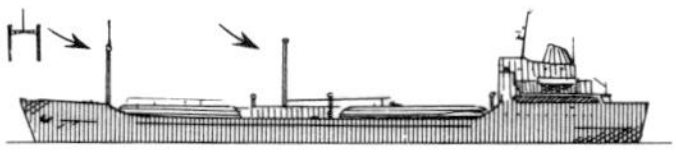

MKMF H13
85650 GAZ ATLANTIC. Gr/Fr 1965; LGC; 3000; 99.29 × 5.46 (325.75 × 17.91); M; 13.75; ex AMEDEO AVOGADRO 1980; ex URANUS 1971; Similar: **85651 GIOVANBATTISTA VENTURI** (It) ex JOULE 1970; (May be spelt **GIAMBATTISTA VENTURI**).

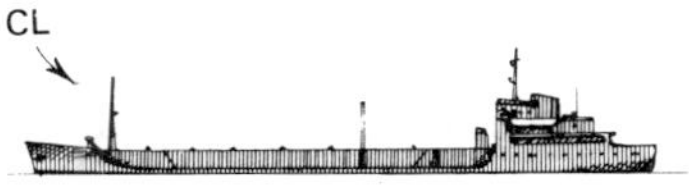

MKMF H13
85660 GIMONE. Fr/Fr 1969; Tk; 3400; 100.03 × 5.61 (328.18 × 18.41); TSM; 11.75.

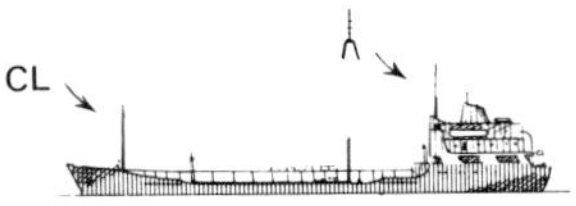

MKMF H13
85670 TARNFORS. Sw/No 1965; Tk; 1200; 76.03 × 4.6 (249.44 × 15.09); M; 11.5; ex WINJONA 1975; ex RUBISTREAM 1968.

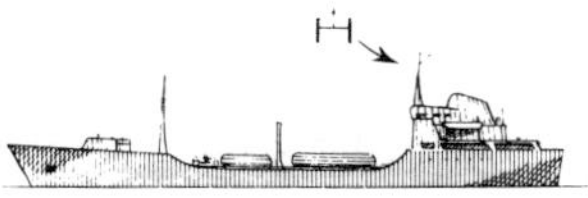

MKMF H13
85680 MELROSE. Br/FRG 1971; LGC; 2000; 86.95 × 6.12 (285.27 × 20.08); M; 14.

MKMF H13
● **85690 LA QUINTA.** Br/Ne 1969; Tk/Ch; 1500; 80.52 × 5.2 (264.17 × 17.06); M; 13.5; Sister: **85691 LA HACIENDA** (Br).

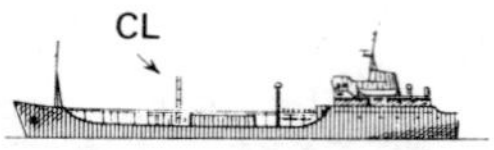

MKMF H13
85700 PASS OF CAIRNWELL. Br/Br 1970; Tk/Ch; 900; 70.16 × 4.19 (230.18 × 13.75); M; 11; ex CORDALE 1975; lengthened 1972; Sister: **85701 PASS OF CHISHOLM** (Br) ex CORDENE 1975.

MKMF H13
85710 PASS OF DRUMOCHTER. Br/Ne 1974; Ch; 1600; 80.75 × 5.56 (264.93 × 18.24); M; 13.5; Sister: **85711 PASS OF DIRRIEMORE** (Br).

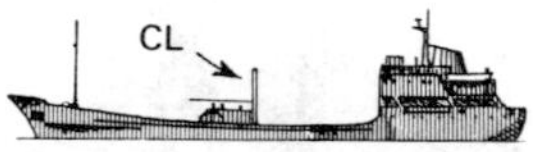

MKMF H13
85720 JOHN WILSON. NZ/Br 1961; Cem; 1600; 81.49 × 4.92 (267.36 × 16.14); D—E; 11.5.

MKMF H13
85730 PETROSTAR XIV. Si/FRG 1961; Tk; 1600; 87 × 5.26 (285.43 × 17.26); M; —; ex MARIA II 1980; ex GERTRUDE WIENER 1977.

MKMF H13
85740 DALAVIK. Sw/Sw 1966; Tk; 1000; 78.09 × 4.64 (256.2 × 15.22); M; —; Lengthened and deepened 1972.

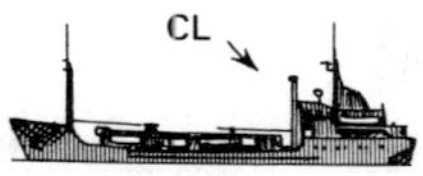

MKMF H13
85750 HALLIBURTON 602. Pa/No 1960; Cem; 900; 63.89 × 4.21 (209.61 × 13.81); M; 12; ex CEMENTINE 1978.

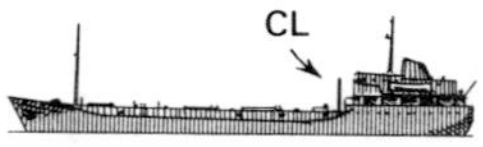

MKMF H13
85760 REDO. Sw/FRG 1963; TB; 1400; 72.95 × 4.64 (239.34 × 15.22); M; 11; ex NYNAS 1976.

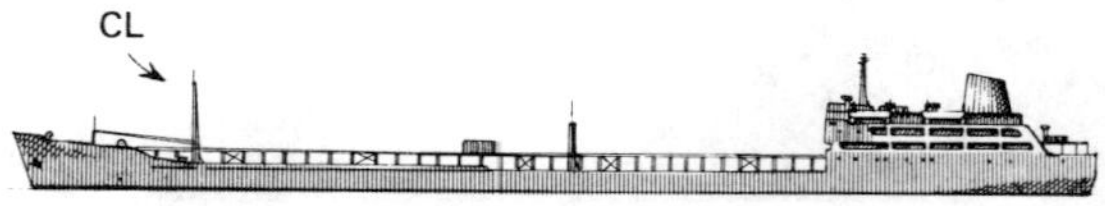

MKMF H13
85770 DOLPHIN OLIVIA. Cy/Sw 1960; Tk; 12800; 169.81 × 9.61 (557.12 × 31.53); M; 15; ex BRACONDA 1978.

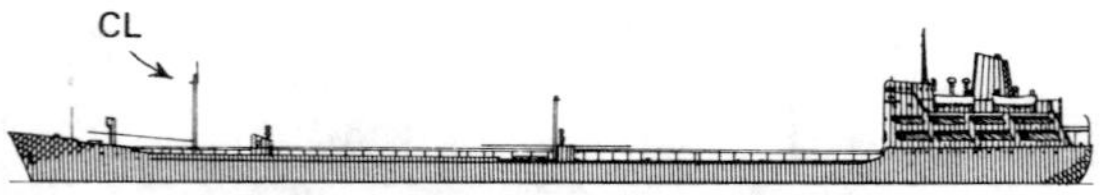

MKMF H13
85780 DOLPHIN II. Gr/Sw 1959; Tk; 12700; 169.81 × 9.57 (557.11 × 31.38); M; 15; ex VIBEKE 1978; Similar **⋆85781 DA QING No 41** (RC) ex ANELLA 1972; ex OSCAR GORTHON 1971; ex VINSTRA; Similar (asphalt tanker): **85782 VIBIT** (No).

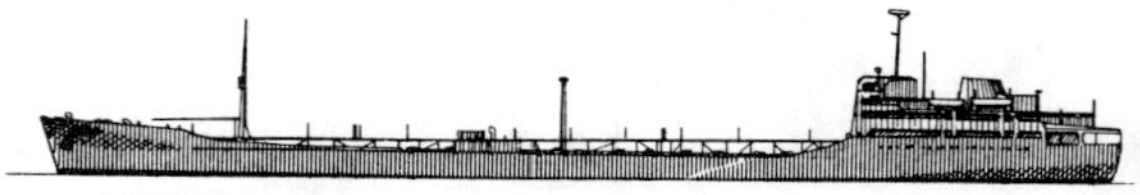

MKMF H13
85790 FIVE VALLEYS. Li/Ne 1960; Tk; 12300; 170.64 × 9.37 (559.84 × 30.74); M; 15.25; ex FOREST HILL 1973; Sisters: **85791 ANNA K** (Gr) ex STOLT ANNA 1977; ex FOREST LAKE 1973; **85792 NANCY HEATH** (Au) ex FOREST TOWN 1972; Similar: **85793 ORYX** (Gr) ex AEGEON 1980; ex HOPE SKY 1979; ex KEF EAGLE 1975; ex PEDRO 1973; ex BENWELL 1968; ex BELMAR 1962; **85794 ROAN** (Gr) ex MPENITSES 1980; ex TAMARA 1975.

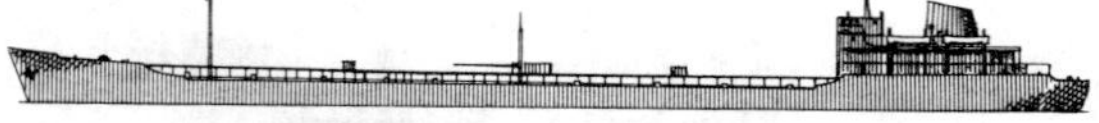

MKMF H13
● **85800 ORIENTAL WISDOM.** Li/Sw 1959; Tk; 12800; 170.64 × 9.37 (559.84 × 30.74); M; 14; ex TOPAZ 1978; ex LEADER COLOCOTRONIS 1977; ex KRISTINA 1968.

MKMF H13
● **85810 ARYADOOT.** In/Sw 1960; Tk; 12800; 170.67 × 9.64 (559.94 × 31.63); M; 14.5; ex KOLLBRIS 1973; Similar: **85811 ANIA** (Fi) ex NANNA 1980; ex FERMIA 1967; **85812 RIO GRANDE** (Gr) ex SUNARES 1979; ex BENARES 1974; ex ANGELUS 1966; ex LYSEFJELL 1959.

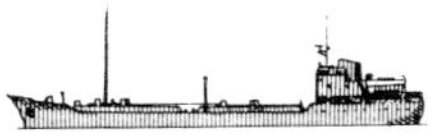

MKMF H13
85820 CARIBE No 1. Pa/De 1961; LGC; 800; 65.33 × 3.56 (214.34 × 11.68); M; 13; ex LILI THOLSTRUP 1971.

MKMF H13
85840 HARZ. FRG/FRG 1953; RT; 2600; 92.4 × 6.6 (303 × 21.7); M; 12; ex CLAERE JUNG 1963; In German naval service.

MKMF H13
85860 IRLA LUPE. De/De 1964; Tk/Ch; 1400; 79.66 × 5.21 (261.35 × 17.09); M; 12; ex IRLAND 1979.

MKMF H13
⋆**85880 KLYAZMA**. Ru/Fi 1952; Tk; 1100; 63.51 × 4.48 (208.37 × 14.7); M; 10; Sisters (Ru flag): ⋆**85881 NERCHA**; ⋆**85882 ORSK**; ⋆**85883 CHARDZHOV**; ⋆**85884 URZHUM**; ⋆**85885 AZNEFT**; ⋆**85886 NOVINSK**; ⋆**85887 GROSNEFT**; ⋆**85888 ELBAN**; ⋆**85889 KREKING**; ⋆**85890 BASHKIRNEFT**.

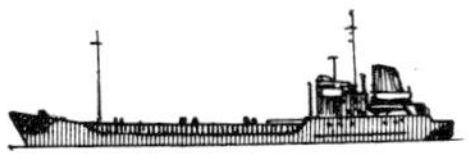

MKMF H13
85910 VASILIOS VII. Gr/FRG 1959; Tk; 1500; 85.55 × 4.67 (280.68 × 15.32); M; 11.5; ex SCHARHORN 1977; ex JOSEF JOHAM 1967; Lengthened 1968.

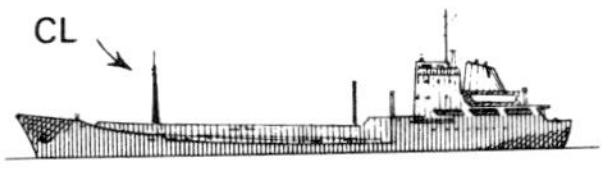

MKMF H13
85930 RATHOWEN. Ih/Sw 1965; Tk; 2250; 86.75 × 5.79 (284.6 × 19); M; 12; ex BELLONA 1974; ex LUNA 1974; Similar (one less deck on superstructure): **85931 WENA** (Ma) ex LENA 1977; Similar: **85934 LANA** (Sw); **85935 SIDON** (Gr) ex BELLONA 1978; ex LISA 1975; Possibly similar: **85936 BELLONA** (Sw) ex STELLA ATLANTIC 1978.

MKMF H13
85830 ENGELSBERG. Sw/Sw 1969; TB; 4500; 123.15 × 5.74 (404.03 × 18.83); M; 14.

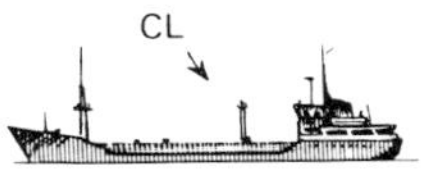

MKMF H13
85850 IVO DORMIO. It/FRG 1964; Ch; 800; 63.51 × 4.22 (208.37 × 13.85); M; 11.5; ex CHEMICOASTER 1972.

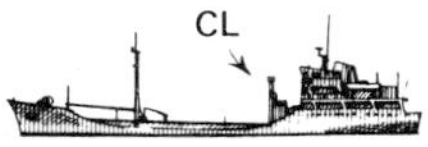

MKMF H13
● **85870 SHELL MARINER**. Br/Br 1965; Tk; 1000; 61.45 × 4.22 (201.61 × 13.85); M; 11; ex FALMOUTH 1979; Sisters (Br flag): **85871 SHELL REFINER** ex HAMBLE 1979; **85872 BP SCORCHER** ex SHELL SCIENTIST ex PARTINGTON 1979; **85874 SHELL TRADER** ex TEESPORT 1979; Similar (lower superstructure—taller funnel): **85875 SHELL ENGINEER** ex DINGLE BANK 1979.

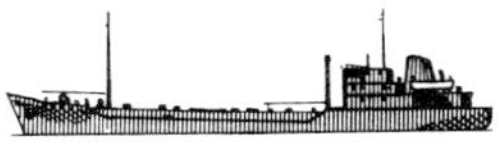

MKMF H13
85900 ROCAS. Po/Po 1965; Tk; 1400; 76.51 × 4.73 (251 × 15.52); TSM; 12; Possible sister: **85901 SACOR** (Po).

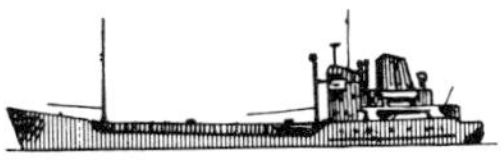

MKMF H13
85920 VASSILIOS I. Gr/FRG 1958; Tk; 1400; 76.51 × 4.65 (251 × 15.26); M; 11.5; ex EOLE 1974; ex ELLEN ESSBERGER 1958; Similar (lengthened): ⋆**85921 HERMANAS GIRALT** (Cu) ex BORKUM 1970.

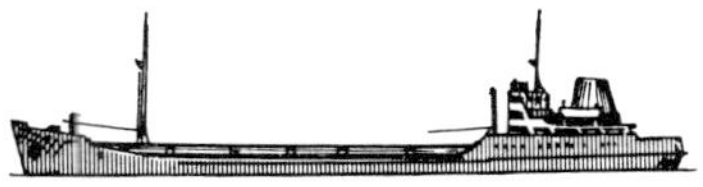

MKMF H13
85940 ESMERALDAS. Ec/Br 1960; Tk; 3600; 106.08 × 4.87 (348.03 × 15.98); TSM; 9.5; ex ANGLO 1976.

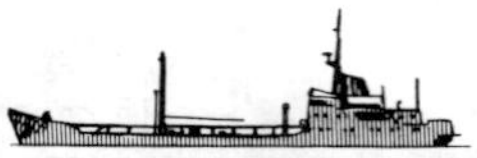

MKMF H13
85950 ESSO CAERNARVON. Br/Br 1962; Tk; 1100; 70.52 × 4.36 (231.36 × 14.3); M; 10; Similar: **85951 ESSO IPSWICH** (Br).

MKMF H13
⋆85970 KRIPTON. Ru/Ru 1964; Tk; 1800; 83.67 × 4.6 (274.51 × 15.09); M; 12.5; Sisters (some have taller funnels—Ru flag): **⋆85971 UKHTA; ⋆85972 GROZNYY; ⋆85973 ABAKAN; ⋆85974 AKADEMIK MAMEDALIEV; ⋆85975 EKIMCHAN; ⋆85976 LASPI; ⋆85977 EVENSK; ⋆85978 TEMRYUK; ⋆85979 KEKUR; ⋆85980 NARVA; ⋆85981 NIVA; ⋆85982 NEFTEGORSK; ⋆85983 NERCHINSK; ⋆85984 SOVIETSKIY POGRANICHNIK; ⋆85985 IMANT SUDMALIS; ⋆85986 NIKOPOL; ⋆85987 NOGINSK; ⋆85988 SEVAN; ⋆85989 FIORD; ⋆85990 KHANKA; ⋆85991 NOVIK; ⋆85992 KHRUSTALNYY; ⋆85993 SAMTREDIA; ⋆85994 SILVET; ⋆85995 BERDSK; ⋆85996 SOLNECHNYY; ⋆85997 STEPANOKERT; ⋆85998 BALADZHARY; ⋆85999 BELOYARSK; ⋆86000 BORISOGLEBSK; ⋆86001 KARAKUMNEFT; ⋆86002 KARELI; ⋆86003 NARYMNEFT; ⋆86004 BEREZOVNEFT; ⋆86005 ICHA; ⋆86006 ELTIGEN; ⋆86007 KUMBYSH; ⋆86008 NADEZHDA KURCHYENKO; ⋆86009 KERCHENSKIY KOMMUNIST;** (Bu flag): **⋆86010 CHAYA;** ex BENETNASH 1970; **⋆86012 VACHA;** ex BELLATRIX 1970.

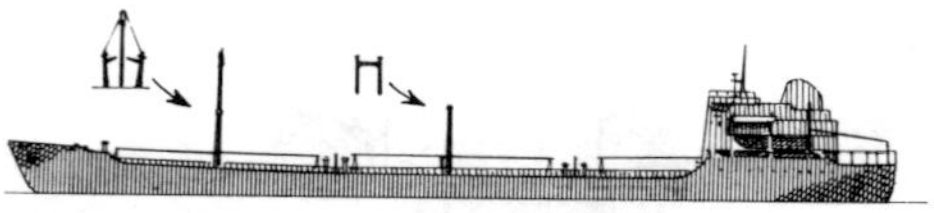

MKMF H13
⋆86050 UVERO. Cu/Fr 1960; C/HL; 9500; 141.13 × 9.3 (463 × 30.51); M; 13.5; ex BRIDGEDALE 1964; ex SOUTHWICK 1964; Similar (larger funnel): **86051 ARETI S.** (Gr); ex GRANTLEYHALL 1976; ex SKYCREST 1968.

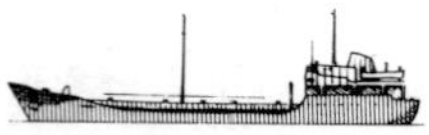

MKMF H13
85960 RATHGAR. Ih/FRG 1959; Tk; 1000; 65.99 × 4.35 (216.5 × 14.27); M; 11; ex PASS OF KILDRUMMY 1970.

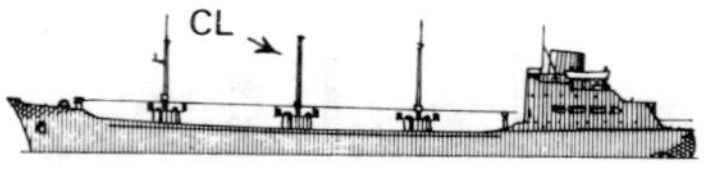

MKMF H13
86020 MALDIVE TRADER. Mv/Br 1959; C; 2200/3200; 108.29 × 5.4/— (355.28 × 17.72/—); M; 12.5; ex SANTONA 1974; Lengthened 1966; Sister: **86021 AKTIAN** (Gr); ex ANDREW C. CROSBIE 1977; ex COLINA 1967.

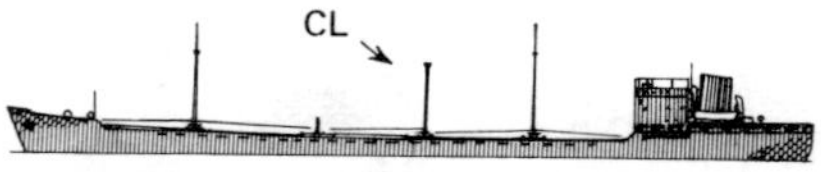

MKMF H13
86030 NISYROS ERA. Gr/Br 1958; C; 5300; 126.24 × 6.92 (414.17 × 22.7); M; —; ex SHERWOOD 1974; ex THACKERAY 1968; Lengthened 1966.

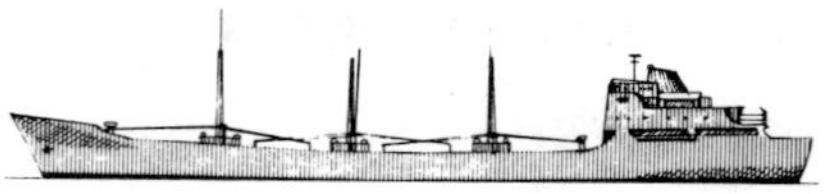

MKMF H13
86040 AZALEA. Gr/Sp 1964; C; 3800/5900; 127.67 × —/8.43 (418.86 × —/27.66); M; 15; ex CROSS RIVER 1977, ex STAMATIOS 1973; ex IRAN SEPAH 1973; ex STAMATIOS 1972; ex SUNDALE 1970; ex IMA SAM 1964.

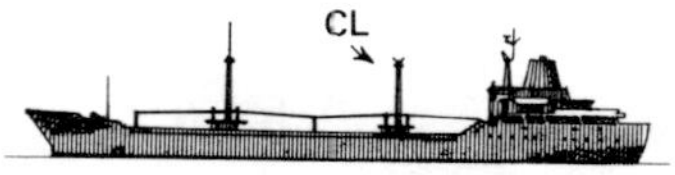

MKMF H13
86060 TIZI M'LIL. Mo/Sw 1970; R; 2000; 98.81 × 5.92 (324.18 × 19.42); M; 17.5; Sisters (Mo flag): **86061 TIZI N'TEST; 86062 TIZI N'TICHKA.**

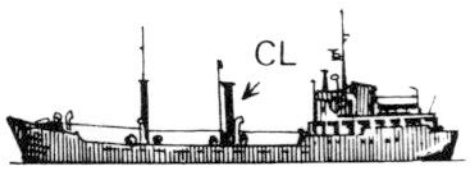

MKMF H13
★86070 'KORSAKOV' type. Ru/Hu 1949/61; C; 1300; 65.97 × 3.8 (216.44 × 12.47); TSM; 9.5; The existence of some of the following is doubtful and some have been reported as passenger/cargo; For similar vessels see BLAGOVESHCHENSK; Sisters (Ru flag): **★86071 KURILSK; ★86072 OKHA; ★86073 TYUMEN; ★86074 NALCHIK; ★86075 AKOP; ★86076 AKOPYAN; ★86077 TIKHORETSK; ★86078 TRUSKAVETS; ★86079 KALEV; ★86080 KEMERI; ★86081 SHEMAKHA; ★86082 VILSANDI; ★86083 EDUARD WILDE; ★86084 KAGUL; ★86085 KREMENETS; ★86086 NARYN; ★86087 SAAREMAA; ★86088 SULEV; ★86089 ZAYARSK; ★86090 AKHTUBA; ★86091 JAN KREUKS; ★86092 KANIN; ★86093 PESHT; ★86094 TAKELI; ★86095 BELBECK;** (RC flag): **★86096 FU CHOU No 651; ★86097 CHE HAI No 103; ★86098 LIEN YUN No 28;** (Le flag): **86099 GHADA;** ex RAMI 1977; ex RITA 1973; ex BALATON 1969.

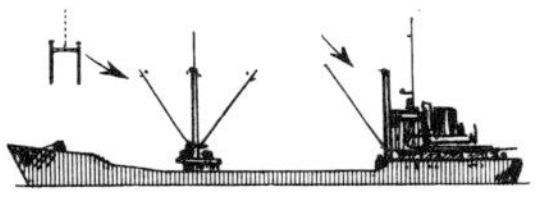

MKMF H13
86140 HONG HWA. Sg/Ja 1960; C; 1600; 80.75 × 5.2 (264.93 × 17.06); M; 11.5; ex SELAT BARU 1977; ex GOLDEN FISH 1976; ex GAY PHOENIX 1972; ex RED DRAGON 1970; ex MUI KIM 1967.

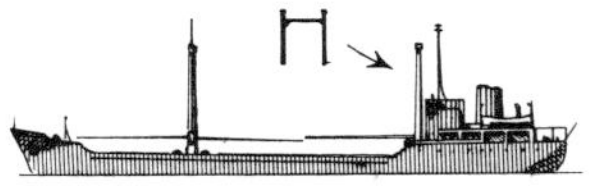

MKMF H13
● **86160 YAMAUME MARU No 2.** Ja/Ja 1962; C; 1900; 86.98 × 5.46 (285.37 × 17.91); M; 11; ex FUTUBA MARU No 3 1970.

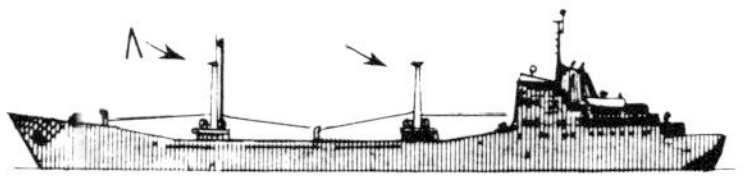

MKMF H13
86110 IRAN SEDAGHAT. Ir/Bu 1971; C; 4500; 114.26 × 6.55 (374.87 × 21.49); M; 13.75; ex ARYA RAD 1980; ex SLEVIK 1975; Sisters: **86111 IRAN SHAFAAT** (Ir); ex ARYA DAD 1980; ex WYVERN 1975; **86112 REMADA** (Tn); ex ONTARIO 1974; ex SARIBA 1973; **86113 KOHENG** (Pa); ex TAULOTO II; ex SAFIA 1973; **86114 WOOLGAR** (No); **★86115 TAI AN** (Rc); **★86118 TAI NING** (RC); **★86117 TAI SHUN** (RC); (Hu flag): **★86118 BUDAPEST; ★86119 HUNGARIA.**

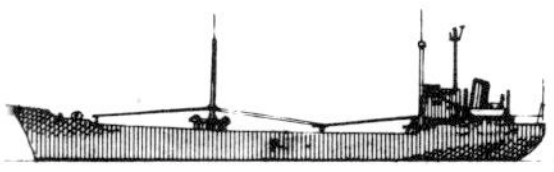

MKMF H13
86130 HIE. Pa/Ja 1964; C; 1900; 85.58 × 5.44 (280.77 × 17.85); M; 12; ex ICHIYO MARU 1972; Possible Sisters: **86131 NAM JUNG No 3** (Ko); ex EMPIRE 1980; ex HOUZAN 1974; ex HOUZAN MARU 1972; **86132 TA HANG** (Pa); ex SEIRYU; ex SEIRYU MARU 1972; ex KENSHO MARU 1969; **86133 ACE** (Ko); ex EASTERN ACE 1972; ex TSUSHIMA MARU 1971; ex KINYO MARU 1967.

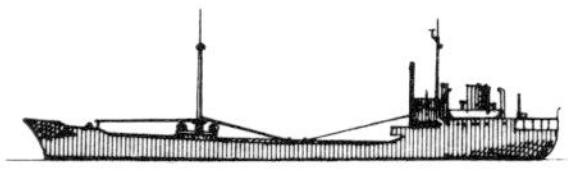

MKMF H13
86150 ZACHAROULA. Cy/Ja 1961; C; 1800; 84.89 × 5.66 (278.51 × 18.57); M; 11.5; ex SOUTH WING 1 1977; ex SOUTH WING 1976; ex ATSUTA 1976; ex SEIWA MARU 1971; ex FUKUHO MARU 1969; Similar: **86151 HWAPYUNG PUSAN** (Pa); ex SHOHO MARU 1973.

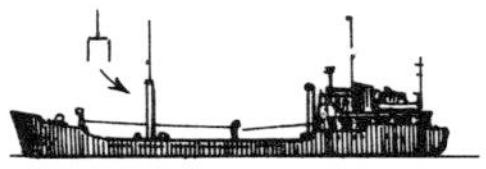

MKMF H13
86170 BLAGOVESHCHENSK. Ru/Hu 1953; C; 1200; 69.98 × 3.8 (229.6 × 12.47); TSM; 9.5; The existence of some of the following is doubtful and some are reported as cargo/passenger; See similar vessels 'KORSAKOV' type; Sisters (Ru flag): **★86171 IVAN ZEMNUKHOV; ★86172 SERGEY TYULENIN; ★86173 BORODIN; ★86174 LUGA; ★86175 OM; ★86176 TURA; ★86177 ARALSK; ★86178 GOMEL; ★86179 OLENSK; ★86180 TSELINOGRAD; ★86181 YUZHNO-SAKHALINSK; ★86182 BEZHETSK; ★86183 GDOV; ★86184 OSTROV; ★86185 PAVLIK MOROZOV;** ex PORKHOV: **★86186 ABAY KUNANBAYEV;** ex NERCHINSK; **★86187 DANILO NECHAY; ★86188 KOLA; ★86189 IVAN BOGUN; ★86190 YARENSK; ★86200 BELOGORSK; ★86201 SCHOLLAR; ★86202 SHONGAR; ★86203 TELMANSK; ★86204 TEMIR; ★86205 ALEKSANDR OBUKHOV;** ex MEGANOM; (Ia flag): **86206 TULUK WEDA;** ex BHIMA KARYA 1973; ex TELUK WEDA 1963; exBARNAUL; **86207 PAINAN;** ex TELUK BINTUNI 1962; ex BOLCHEREK 1958; (Sg flag): **86208 SILVILAI;** ex LAGOLIGO 1975; ex TELUK TOMINI 1975; ex TAIMYR 1958; Similar (Rm built-Rm flag): **★86209 BUZAU; ★86210 ARAD; ★86211 PITESTI; ★86212 ROMAN.**

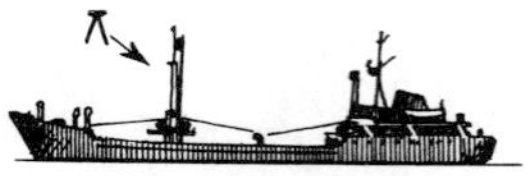

MKMF H13
● ★**86220 ANANYEV.** Ru/Hu 1960; C; 1200; 78.49×4.1 (257.51×13.45); M; 10.75; Some of the following have taller funnels and other smaller differences; For later ships in this class see KEKHRA—M²F; Sisters (Ru flag): ★**86221 HAAPSALU;** ★**86222 KOTOVSK;** ★**86223 PILTUN;** ★**86224 TARTU;** ★**86225 TERMEZ;** ★**86226 VILKOVO;** ★**86227 BELTSY;** ★**86228 KONOSHA;** ★**86229 NYANDOMA;** ★**86230 SERGEY KIROV;** ★**86231 SHKOTOVO;** ★**86232 TAMSALU;** ★**86233 PALDISKI;** ★**86234 PINEGA;** ★**86235 UST-BOLSHERETSK;** ★**86236 ZEYA;** ★**86237 GALICH;** ★**86238 GLUKHOV;** ★**86239 KIHELKONA;** ★**86240 UST-TIGIL;** ★**86241 VILYANDY;** ★**86242 ENGURE;** (Vn flag): ★**86243 SONG LO;** ex UST-KAMCHATSK; ★**86244 SONG KAU;** ex ELVA 1977; ★**86245 SONG THAO;** ex TYMLAT 1975; The following Ru. vessels are reported sold to Angola; ★**86246 HIYUMAA;** ★**86247 KEYLA.**

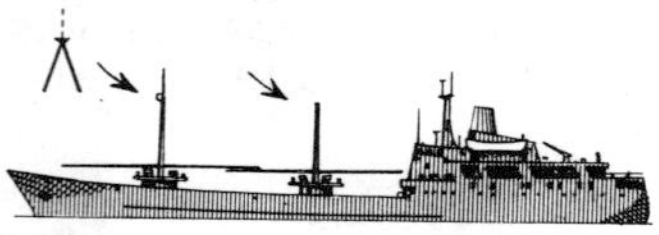

MKMF H3
86290 ST. HELENA. Br/Ca 1963; PC; 3200; 100.28×5.51 (329×18.08); M; —; ex NORTHLAND PRINCE 1977.

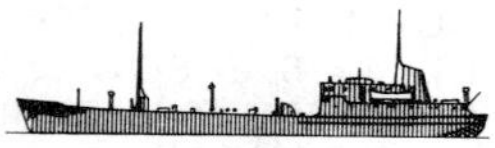

MKMF H3
86310 PIRAEUS 1. Gr/No 1966; Tk; 1000; 74.02×4.33 (242.85×14.21); M; 11; ex HEKTOR 1979; Lengthened 1970.

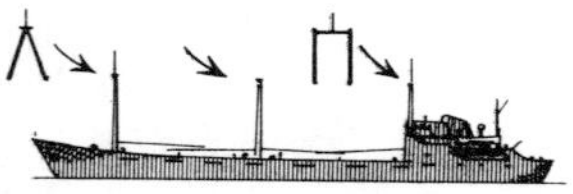

MKMFK H
86330 PANAGIA. Pa/Ne 1957; C; 1000; 82.12×4.64 (269.42×15.22); M; 14.5; ex OLYMPIOS HERMES 1977; ex OVAMBO 1976; ex MARC LAURENT V 1968.

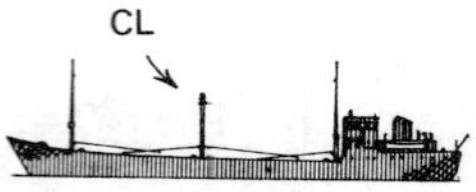

MKMF H3
86260 SPARTI. Gr/FRG 1952; C; 1300; 71.63×5 (235.01×16 4); M; 11; ex EYAL 1974; ex WULP 1961; ex BLOCKLAND 1956.

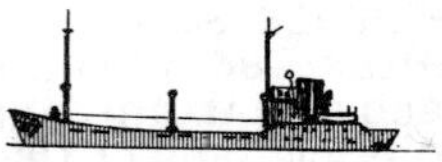

MKMF H3
86270 ALBORADA. Do/De 1953; C; 500; 63.51×3.63 (208.37×11.91); M; 11; ex DESPINA S; ex TELLO 1974.

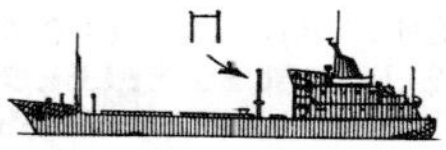

MKMF H3
86280 AN FIGHTER. Li/No 1966; Tk; 1100; 67.21×5.32 (220.51×17.45); M; 11; ex LINNEA 1973.

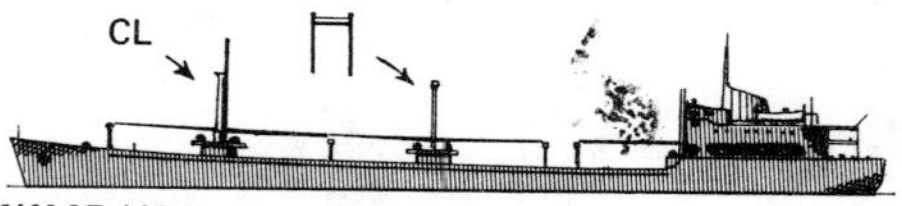

MKMF H3
● **86300 HWA CHU.** Sg/FRG 1957; C; 6600/9100; 152×—/9.01 (498.69×—/29.56); M; 14; ex STEENWIJK 1968.

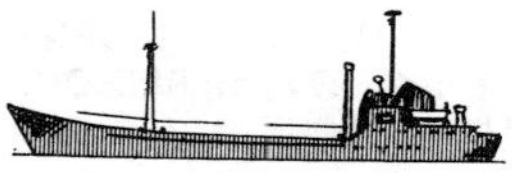

MKMF H3
● **86320 LAURA.** Si/Fr 1962; R; 1300; 79.48×4.8 (261.94×15.75); M; 14; ex LAURA CHRISTINA; Sisters: **86321 NORTH POLE** (NA); ex FRIO EXPRESS 1977; ex CORAL ACROPORA 1974; **86322 SOUTH POLE** (NA); ex IGLO EXPRESS 1977; ex CORAL ACTINIA 1974; **86323 MAYA** (Pa); ex MAYA V 1977; ex MAYA 1976.

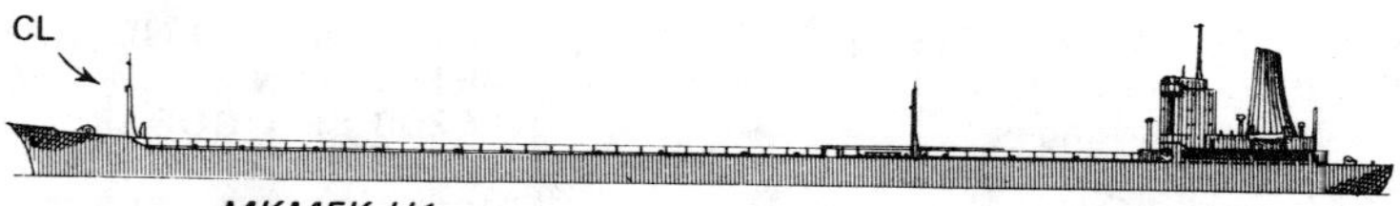

MKMFK H1
86340 BUENA ESPERANZA. Gr/Ja 1964; Tk; 32700; 225×12.38 (738.19×40.62); M; 16; ex JARELSA 1973.

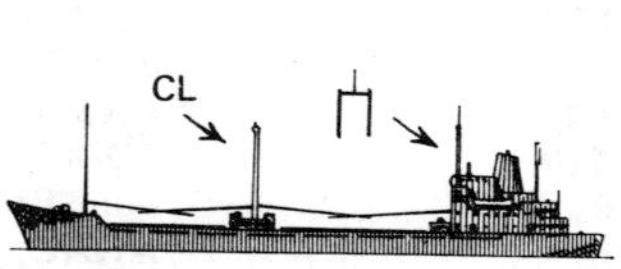

MKMFK H1
● **86350 KARLSBURG.** FRG/Ne 1971; C; 1500; 94.52×5.4 (310.1×17.72); M; 14.

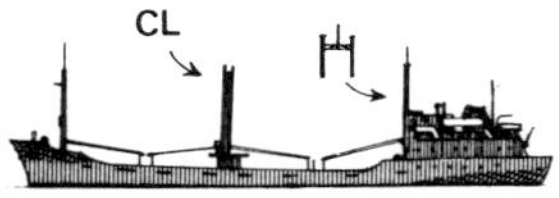

MKMFK H13
● **86360 EID.** Li/Ne 1960; C/Ch; 1900; 84.97 × 5.52 (278.77 × 18.11); M; 12.5; ex LAGA 1964.

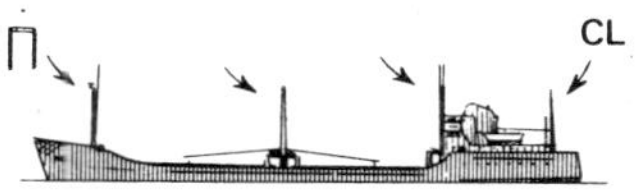

MKMFK H13
86370 ETHEL EVERARD. Br/Br 1966; C; 1600; 85.1 × 5.1 (279.2 × 16.73); M; 11.

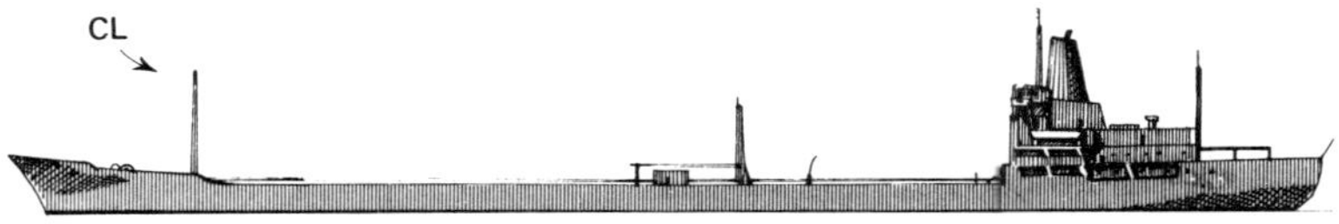

MKMFK H13
86380 GHIONA. Gr/Ja 1963; Tk; 30600; 225.03 × 12.24 (738.29 × 40.16); T; —; Sisters (Gr flag): **86381 GHERANIA; 86382 GHERESTOS.**

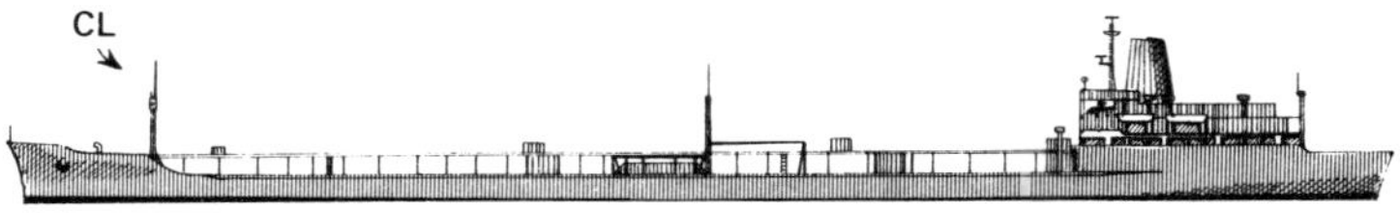

MKMFK H13
86390 SILVER LADY. Li/Sw 1966; Tk; 33700; 236.68 × 12.75 (776.51 × 41.83); M; 17; ex OKLAND 1977.

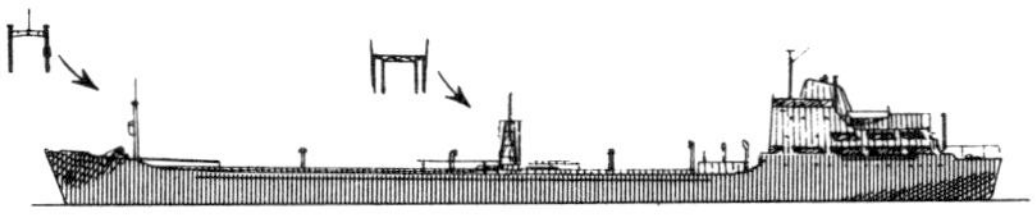

MKMFK H13
86400 ESSI KARI. No/Sw 1956/65; Ch; 10700; 149.36 × 9.38 (490.03 × 30.77); M; 13.5; ex ARJEPLOG 1965; Converted from ore carrier 1965.

MKMFK H13
86410 ESSI FLORA. No/FRG 1959/64; Ch; 12000; 157.69 × 9.34 (517.36 × 30.64); M; 13.75; ex ESSIFLORA 1963; Converted from bulk 1964.

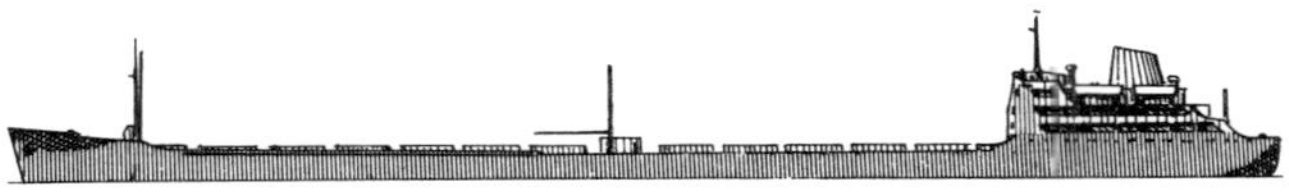

MKMFK H13
● ⋆**86420 EISENHUTTENSTADT.** DDR/Sw 1960; OO; 23400; 199.65 × 11.38 (655 × 37.34); M; 14.5; ex MERTAINEN 1970; Similar (both converted to tankers): **86421 FFM MATARENGI** (Sw); ex MATARENGI 1971; **86422 HOUSSAM B** (Pa); ex HELIOS 1976; ex COMMODORE CHARLES H. SMITH 1973; ex MALGOMAJ 1965.

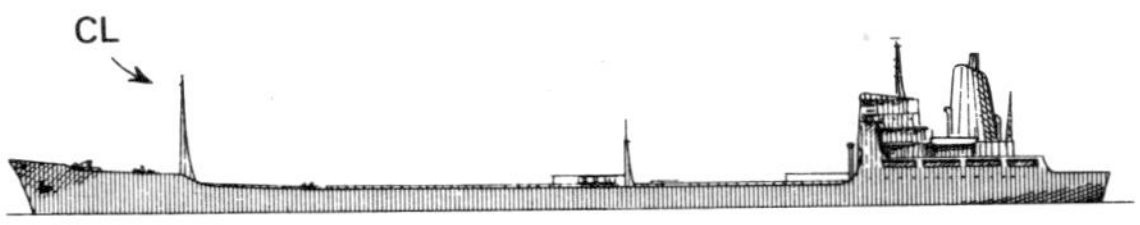

MKMFK H13
● **86430 TEXACO MELBOURNE.** Br/US-Ja 1945/67; Tk; 13900; 172.4 × 10 (565.62 × 32.81); T-E; 13.25; ex CALTEX MELBOURNE 1967; ex VICTORY LOAN 1951; Lengthened & converted from 'T-2' tanker 1967; Sisters: **86431 TEXACO WELLINGTON** (Br); ex CALTEX WELLINGTON 1968; ex PAULUS HOOK 1952; **86432 CHEVRON THE HAGUE** (Ne); ex CALTEX THE HAGUE 1967; ex BOONES BOROUGH 1950; **86433 TEXACO BOMBAY** (Br); ex CALTEX BOMBAY 1968; ex CASTLES WOODS 1951; **86434 TEXACO ROME** (Br); ex CALTEX ROME 1968; ex SIDELING HILL 1953; **86435 TEXACO KANSAS** (US); ex GREENPOINT 1960; ex CROWN POINT 1955; **86436 TEXACO NEW JERSEY** (US); ex NEW JERSEY 1961; ex LAKE ERIE 1947.

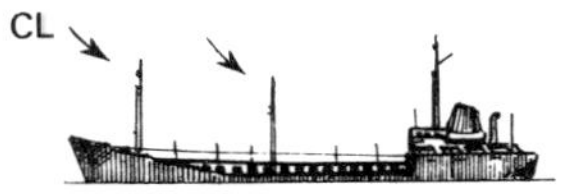

MKMFK H13
86450 ALLURITY. Br/Ne 1969; Tk; 700; 73.97 × 3.96 (242.68 × 12.99); M; 12; Sister: **86451 ACTIVITY** (Br).

MKMFK H13
86460 ALICIA 1. Pa/Ne 1970; LGC; 2100; 80.98 × 6.21 (265.68 × 20.37); M; 14; ex ALPHAGAS 1980; Sister: **86461 AMELIA** (Pa); ex BETAGAS 1980.

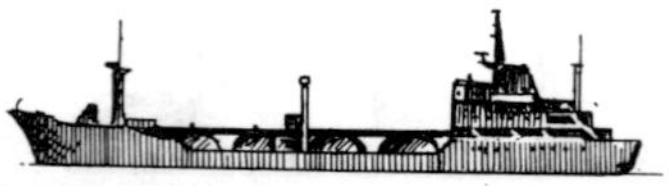

MKMFK H13
⋆**86470 KEGUMS.** Ru/Ja 1965; LGC; 3500; 96.53 × 5.02 (316.7 × 16.47); M; 13.75; Sister: ⋆**86471 KRASLAVA** (Ru).

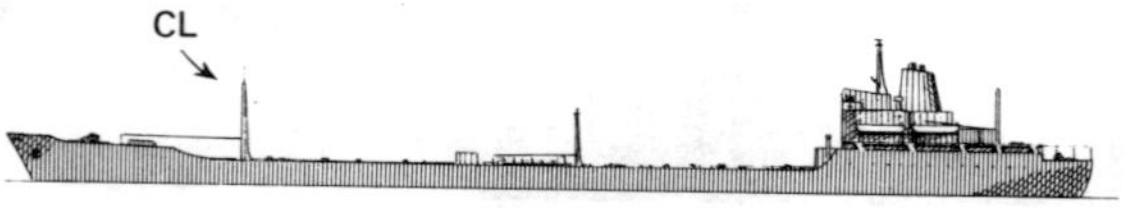

MKMFK H13
● **86480 BENITO JUAREZ.** Me/Ja 1968; Tk; 12800; 170.75 × 9.47 (560.2 × 31.07); M; 15.5; Sisters (Me flag): **86481 ALVARO OBREGON; 86482 FRANCISCO I MADERO; 86483 MECHOR OCAMPO; 86484 PLAN DE AYALA; 86485 PLAN DE AYUTLA; 86486 PLAN DE SAN LUIS**

MKMFK H13
● **86500 OVERSEAS ADVENTURER.** Br/FRG 1963; Tk; 13700; 170 49 × 9.37 (559.35 × 30.74); M; 14.5; ex CHERRYLEAF; ex OVERSEAS ADVENTURER 1973.

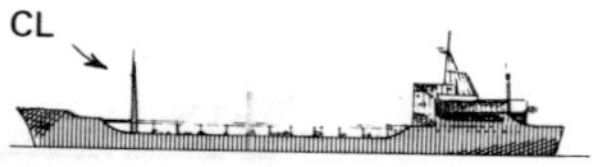

MKMFK H13
86510 PETROSTAR III. Si/Br 1968; Tk; 1900; 86.21 × 5.67 (282.84 × 18.6); M; 12; ex NETTE THERESA 1974; ex PRECIOSA 1972.

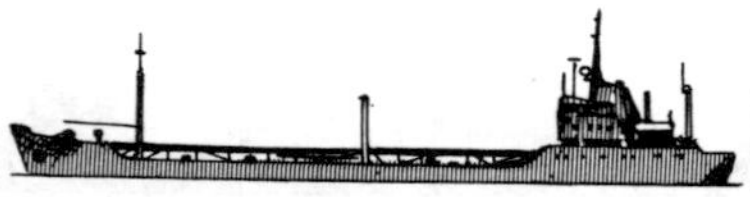

MKMFK H13
⋆**86520 POMORAVLJE.** Ys/Ys 1967; Tk; 2800; 98.53 × 6.23 (323.26 × 20.44); M; 14.25; Sister (Ys flag): ⋆**86521 PODUNAVLJE;** Similar (larger): ⋆**86522 PODRAVINA;** ⋆**86523 POSAVINA.**

MKMFK H13
86530 TSIMISARAKA. Mg/It 1966; Ch; 1600; 84.49 × 4.78 (277.2 × 15.68); TSM; 12.

MKMFK H13
⋆**86540 OZENOYE.** Ru/Pd 1962; Tk; 1300; 75.62 × 4.74 (248.1 × 15.55); M; 12.5; **'B-74'** type; Sisters: ⋆**86541 DIVNOGORSK** (Ru); ⋆**86542 PLAYA DUABA** (Cu); ex OGRE 1974; **86543 BULA** (Ia); ex OPALA; **86544 TARAKAN** (Ia); ex OZERSK

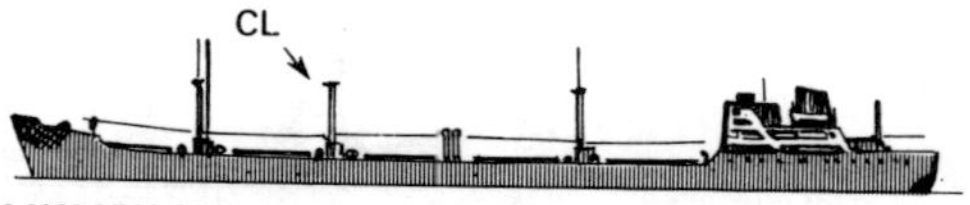

MKMFK H13
86550 EUGENIA M. Gr/Br 1961; C; 9000; 145.88 × 9.28 (478.6 × 30.45); M; 15; ex BLANCHLAND 1968.

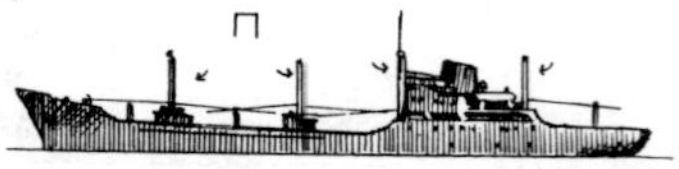

MKMFK H13
86560 ISORA. Sp/Sp 1967; C; 1600; 96.68 × 5.67 (317.19 × 18.6); M; —; ex LAGO SAN MAURICIO 1975.

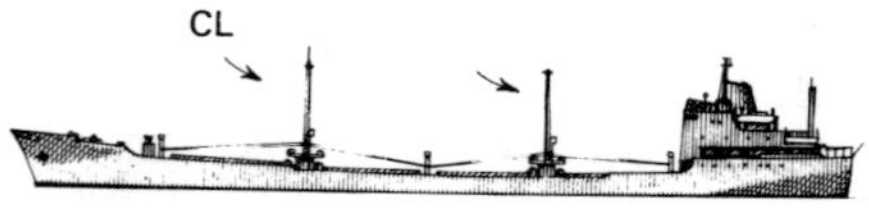

MKMFK H13
86570 OMEGA RHODOS. Gr/Fr 1960; O; 6000; 132.52 × 7.56 (434.78 × 24.8); M; 16.5; ex PENCHATEAU 1980; ex AEQUATOR 1980; ex QUEEN OF AMPELOS 1978; ex PENCHATEAU 1974.

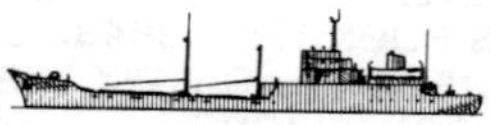

MKMFK H13
86580 KANO REEFER. Pa/Ja 1960/73; C/R; 1200; 74.25 × 4.75 (243.6 × 15.58); M; 12; ex KYOEI MARU 1978; ex AZUMA MARU No 21 1973; Converted from trawler 1973.

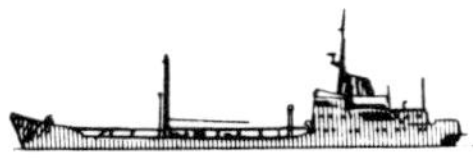

MKMFK H13
86590 ESSO CAERNARVON. Br/Br 1962; Tk; 1100; 70.52 × 4.36 (231.36 × 14.3); M; 10; Similar: **86591 ESSO IPSWICH** (Br).

MKMFK H13
86600 DOUGGA. Tn/Fr 1963; C/WT; 2100; 86.9 × 5.57 (285.1 × 18.27); M; 14; Sister: **86601 ZARZIS** (Tn).

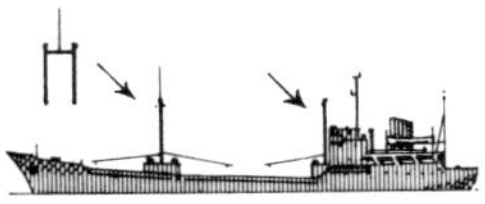

MKMFK H13
86610 OH DAI YANG No 106. Ko/Ja 1968; R; 2700; 104.5 × 5.84 (342.85 × 19.16); M; 15; ex BELA NICKERIE 1979; ex TONICHI MARU 1977; Sisters: **86611 MISHIMA MARU** (Ja); **86612 CHERRY ISLAND** (Pa); ex SAKURASHIMA MARU 1975; ex SUSUKASAN MARU 1971; ex NIPPONHAM MARU No 2 1969.

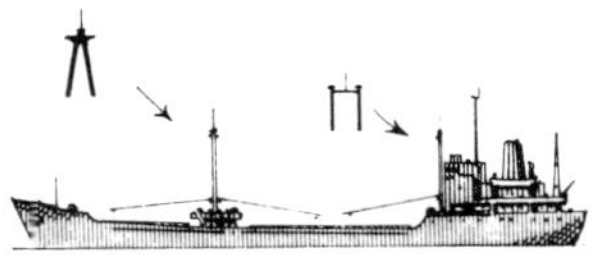

MKMFK H13
86620 HAI MING. Tw/Ja 1966; C; 2000; 90.48 × 5.59 (296.85 × 18.34); M; 12; ex EITOKU MARU 1972.

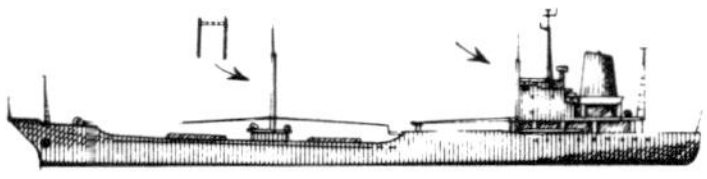

MKMFK H13
86630 NIPPONHAM MARU No 1. Ja/Ja 1972; R; 2900; 109.02 × 6.73 (357.68 × 22.08)); M; 16.5; Probably Similar: **86631 DAIRYO MARU** (Ja).

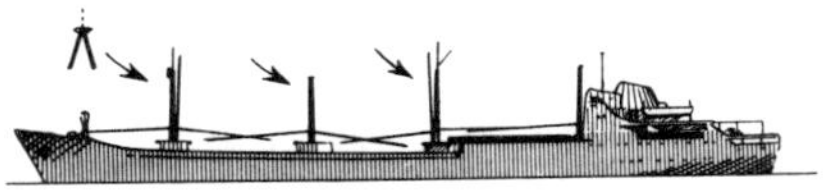

MKMKF H13
***86640 LU DING.** RC/Fi 1959; C; 2700/4800; 121.54 × 6.15/7.67 (398.75 × 20.18/25.16); M; 15; ex CHINGSING 1976; ex FLENSBURG 1971; ex AMAZONAS 1962.

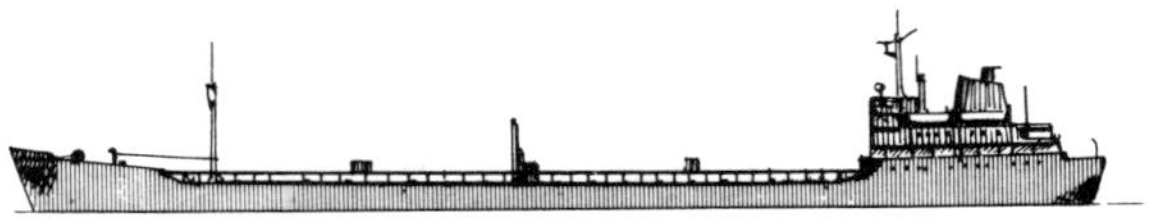

MKMKF H13
● **86650 ARYADOOT.** In/Sw 1960; Tk; 12800; 170.67 × 9.64 (559.94 × 31.63); M; 14.5; ex KOLLBRIS 1973; Similar: **86651 ANIA** (Fi); ex NANNA 1980; ex FERMIA 1967; **86652 RIO GRANDE** (Gr); ex SUNARES 1979; ex BENARES 1974; ex ANGELUS 1966; ex LYSEFJELL 1959.

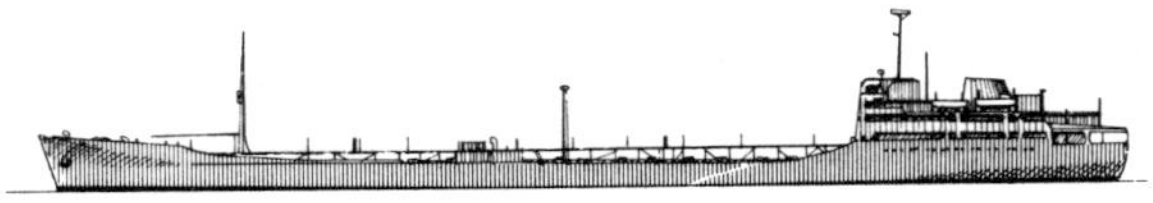

MKMKF H13
86660 FIVE VALLEYS. Li/Ne 1960; Tk; 12300; 170.64 × 9.37 (559.84 × 30.74); M; 15.25; ex FOREST HILL 1973; Sisters: **8661 ANNA K** (Gr); ex STOLT ANNA 1977; ex FOREST LAKE 1973; **86662 NANCY HEATH** (Au); ex FOREST TOWN 1972; Similar: **86663 ORYX** (Gr); ex AEGEON 1980; ex HOPE SKY 1979; ex KEF EAGLE 1975; ex PEDRO 1973; ex BENWELL 1968; ex BELMAR 1962; **86664 ROAN** (Gr); ex MPENITSES 1980; ex TAMARA 1975.

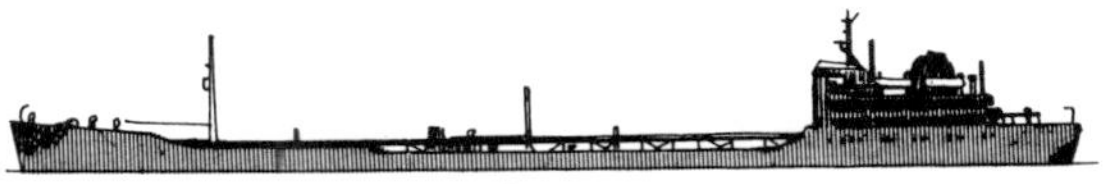

MKMKFK H13
● **86670 MONT-ALBEN.** Mn/Ne 1959; Tk; 12900; 170.64 × 9.37 (559.84 × 30.74); M; 14.5; ex PRESTO 1968; Sister: **86671 GOGO RIDER** (Pa); ex PRONTO 1978; Similar: **86672 GUADELUPE VICTORIA** (Me); ex PRESIDENTE GUADELUPE VICTORIA 1968; ex PÉMEX; ex SOLE 1965.

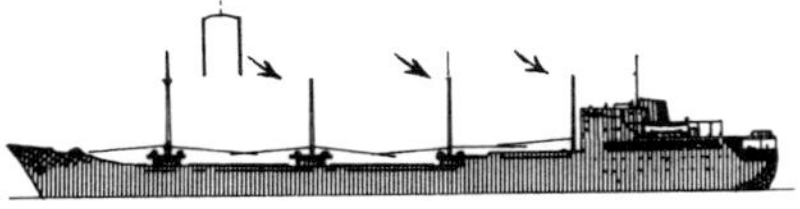

MKMKMF H13
● **86680 MARIVANA RENA.** Gr/No 1957; C; 3500/5200; 121.16 × 6.51/7.56 (397.51 × 21.36/24.8); M; —; ex ESPERANTO 1974; ex DOMSHEIDE 1970.

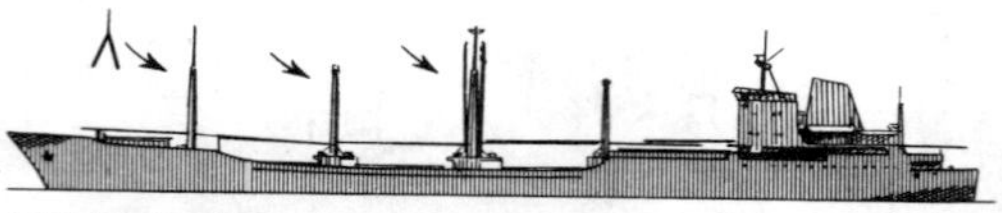

MKMKMFK H13
★**86690 BOLIVAR.** Cu/De 1976; C; 9700; 154.11 × 9.51 (505.61 × 31.2); M; 18; Sisters (Cu flag): ★**86691 JUAREZ;** ★**86692 O'HIGGINS;** ★**86693 SAN MARTIN;** ★**86694 SANDINO.**

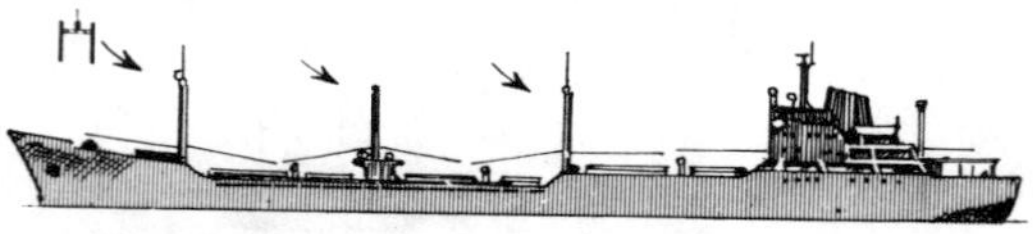

MKMKMFK H13
86720 TIARET. Ag/Fr 1963; B; 11400; 155.4 × 9.28 (509.84 × 30.45); M; 14.75; ex ARTHUR STOVE 1972; Similar: **86721 CAPE KAMARI** (Gr); ex KOSTOS M 1978; ex JOHS STOVE 1973; ex BRISSAC 1969; **86722 ALKOR** (Gr); ex TIMUR ENDURANCE 1980; ex LITA 1974; ex SNELAND 1972.

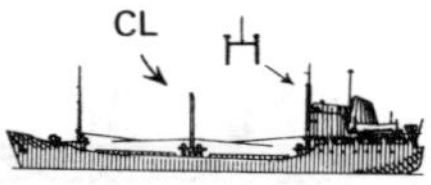

MKM$_2$F H13
86750 RAMSLAND. No/FRG 1956; C; 900; 64.95 × 4.31 (213.09 × 14.14); M; 11; ex SIMON 1975; ex ORTRUD MULLER 1965.

MKM$_2$FK H13
86770 HELLENIC LEADER. Gr/Ja 1962; C; 8900; 144.18 × 8.99 (473.03 × 29.49); M; 18; Sister: **86771 PACIFIC PIONEER** (Gr).

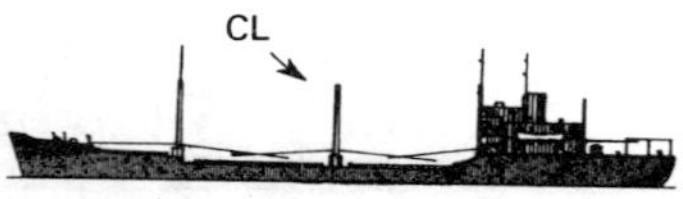

MKM$_2$FK H13
● **86790 CYPROS.** Gr/US 1945; C; 3800; 103.05 × 7.14 (338.09 × 23.43); M; 10.5; ex CIUDAD DE CARACAS 1961; ex DOUBLE LOOP 1947; **'C1-M-AV1'** type; Sister: **86791 ROTTERDAM** (Gr); ex I.C. ERTEL 1967; ex GERTRUD C. ERTEL 1966; ex ANDINO 1964; ex COASTAL CAPTAIN 1948.

MKMKMFK H13
86700 DITTE SKOU. De/De 1969; C; 6600/9600; 156.37 × 8.09/9.52 (513 × 26.54/31.23); M; 18; Sisters (De flag): **86701 DINNA SKOU; 86702 DORTE SKOU;** Similar: **86703 DAGMAR SKOU; 86704 DIANA SKOU; 86705 DOLLY SKOU; 86706 DORIT SKOU;** (Gr flag): **86707 PEARL BAY;** ex DAGNY SKOU.

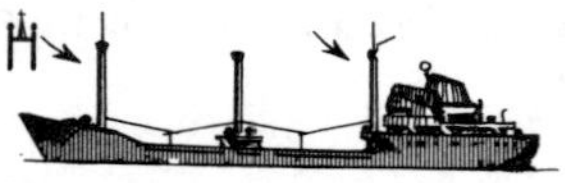

MKM$_2$F H13
★**86740 ALBATROS.** DDR/DDR 1961; C; 1000/1700; 82.45 × 4.26/5.75 (270.5 × 13.98/18.86); M; 11.5.

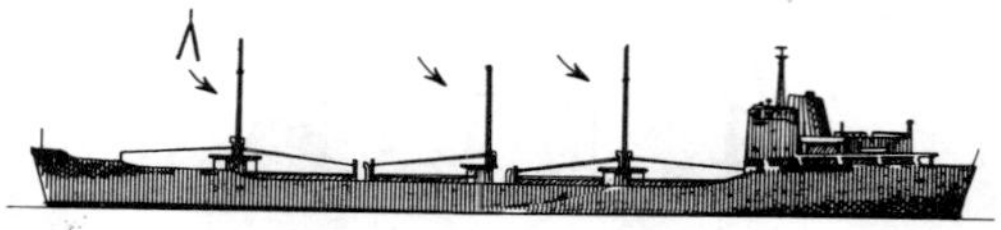

MKM$_2$F H13
86760 GALINI. Gr/Br 1960; C; 10200; 149.92 × 9.52 (491.86 × 31.23); M; —; ex REMBRANDT 1967.

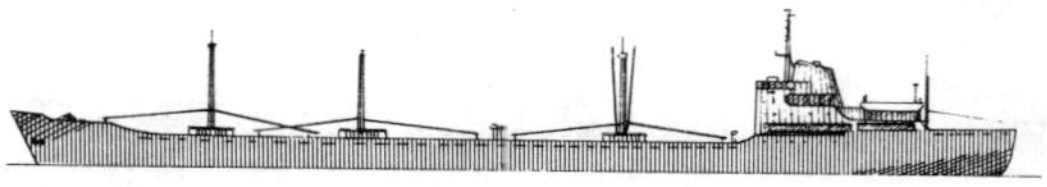

MKM$_2$FK H13
86780 DJATIPURA. Ia/Ja 1961; C; 9900; 157.03 × 9.02 (515.19 × 29.59); M; 15; ex SOUTH BREEZE 1976.

M$_2$ H3
86800 WESTERENCE. Br/Br 1977; C; 400; 45.55 × 3.25 (149.44 × 10.66); M; 9.5; ex GAINSBOROUGH MILLER 1980; Sister: **86801 XANTHENCE** (Br); ex HULL MILLER 1981.

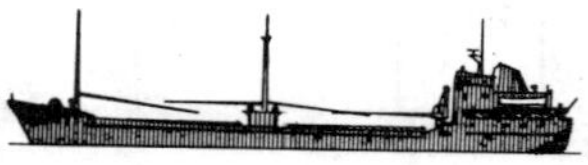

M$_2$CMF H13
86810 MAELIFELL. Ic/No 1964; C; 1900; 88.85 × 5.09 (291.5 × 16.7); M; 13.

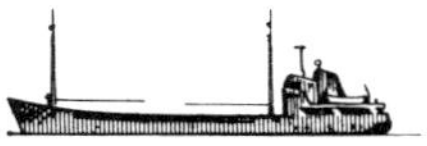

M_2F H
86820 THYELLA. Gr/FRG 1959; C; 700; 59.44 × 4.24 (195 × 13.91); M; 10; ex HERMES G 1977; ex VEGA 1977; ex LAXA 1974.

M_2F H
● **86830 UNION.** Gr/FRG 1952; C; 900; 61.93 × 4.41 (203.18 × 14.47); M; 11; ex GEORGIA P 1980; ex SKAANANG; ex JULIN 1965.

M_2F H
86840 GRACE CALABAR. Cy/FRG 1956; C; 1500; 84.49 × 5 (277.2 × 16.4); M; 12; ex STEPENITZ 1977; Lengthened & deepened 1971.

M_2F H
86850 CAYMAN. Br/Ne 1956; C; 900; 63.58 × 4.12 (208.6 × 13.52); M; 10.5; ex BRINDA. Lengthened & deepened 1969.

M_2F H
86860 REGINA VALERIA. Pa/FRG 1953; C; 800; 62.01 × 4.83 (203.44 × 15.85); M; 11; ex AZUERO UNO 1980; ex TAIFUN 1976; ex NEUWIED 1967.

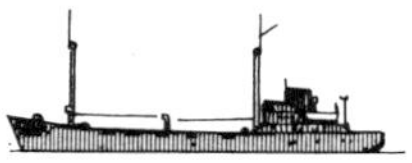

M_2F H
86870 APOLLO II. Pa/FRG 1952; C; 800; 57 × 4.66 (187 × 15.29); M; 10.5; ex DIAMANT 1971.

M_2F H
● **86880 FALLOW DEER.** Br/Br 1972; Con; 500; 76.66 × 3.7 (251.51 × 12.14); M; 13.75; ex FEDERAL BERMUDA 1977; ex FALLOW DEER 1976; Reported sold Norway 1981.

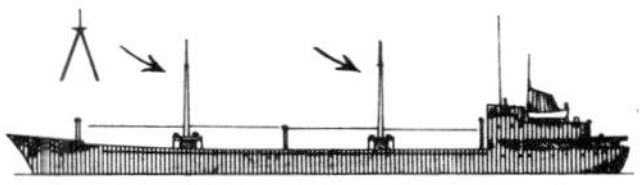

M_2F H
86890 CAPTAIN LEO. Gr/No 1962; C; 1900/3100; 99.22 × 6.52/— (325.52 × 21.39/—); M; 12.5; ex FROL 1972.

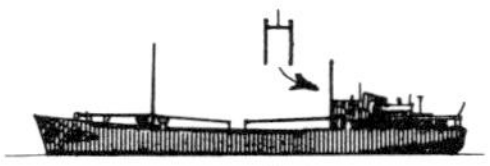

M_2F H
86900 ITALO. It/FRG 1953; C; 1300; 71.1 × 5.02 (233.27 × 16.47); M; 12; ex LELLO 1976; ex SONECK 1962.

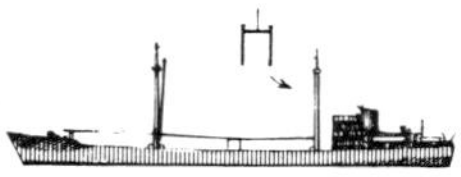

M_2F H
86910 CARIBBEAN TIUNA. Bs/FRG 1952; C; 700; 68.59 × 3.94 (225.03 × 12.93); M; 10.5; ex AUGUSTE SCHULTE 1968; ex VERIA 1961; ex AUGUSTE SCHULTE 1960; Sisters: **86911 MERCURIO** (Pe) ex MARIA SCHULTE 1964; **86912 KYPROS** (Gr) ex BERNI NUBEL 1968.

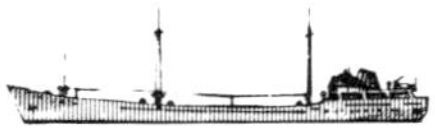

M_2F H
86920 AGIOS NIKOLAOS. Cy/FRG 1961; C; 500/1000; 66.81 × 3.66/— (219.19 × 12.01/—); M; 12; ex GAVINA 1974; ex HEENVLIET 1973.

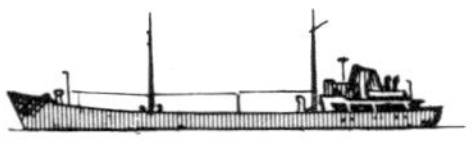

M_2F H
★**86930 PALE.** Ys/Ne 1960; C; 500; 68.81 × 4.02 (225.75 × 13.19); M; 10.5; ex NORDANHAV 1974; ex DAGNY 1965; ex INGER HOJSGAARD 1963; Lengthened 1969.

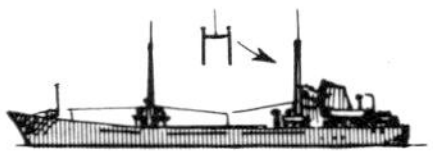

M_2F H
★**86940 KUPA.** Ys/FRG 1957; C; 900; 66.55 × 4.9 (218.34 × 16.08); M; 12; ex NORMANNVAAG 1974; ex BESTIK 1971.

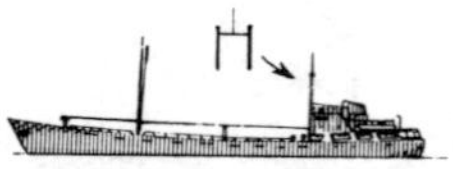

M_2F H

● **86950 SILVER RIVER.** My/FRG 1953; C; 800; 66.5 × 5.4 (218.18 × 17.72); M; 11.5; ex ISABEL MARINA 1978; ex MATHIOS 1973; ex VIKING 1970; ex NERISSA 1967; Similar: **86951 BISLIG TRANSPORT** (Pi) ex SAN MIGUEL MALSTER 1973; ex PICKHUBEN 1967; **86952 NONOC TRANSPORT** (Pi) ex SAN MIGUEL BREWER 1973; ex HUXTER 1966; **86953 LOUCY** (Gr) ex STAVROS K 1980; ex INDIZA 1979; ex DORNBUSCH 1963; **86954 CASTLE SPIRIT** (Br) ex INDOLA 1980; ex KAJEN 1963.

M_2F H

86980 KARIN. Ne/Ne 1968; C; 500/1500; 77.42 × 4.06/5.94 (254 × 13.32/19.49); M; 11.5; ex WESTERBEEK 1977.

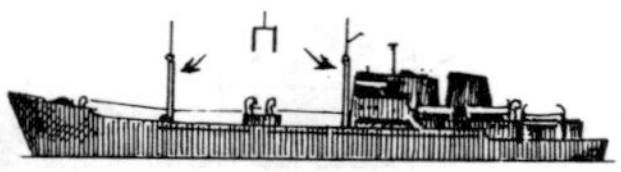

M_2F H

★87000 PERVOMAJSK. Ru/De 1959; FC; 3300; 94.8 × 4.37 (311.02 × 14.34); M; 13; Sisters(Ru flag): **★87001 NEVA; ★87002 PRIMORSK; ★87003 YULYUS YANONIS.**

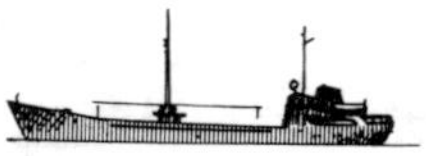

M_2F H

● **87020 ULTRA FREEZE.** Pa/FRG 1959; R; 500/900; 63.18 × 3.33/3.76 (207.28 × 10.93/12.34); M; 11.5; ex MARY B 1970; ex HERBERT HORN 1968; Sister: **87021 AFRICAN VIOLET** (Pa) ex ANTOINETTE CASTRO 1980; ex IRMGARD HORN 1969; Similar: **87022 LUPITA CASTRO** (Cy) ex DORA HORN 1968; **87023 MARIA CASTRO** (Li) ex STADT SCHLESWIG 1968; **87024 EVANGELISTRIA IV** (Gr) ex JUDITH R 1976; ex THERESE 1971; ex THERESE HORN 1965.

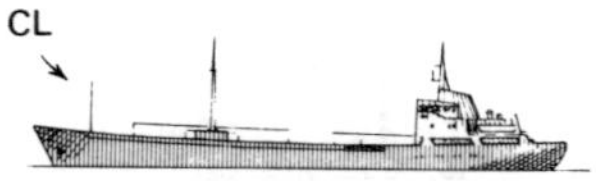

M_2F H

● **87050 ALBAFRIGO.** Gr/Ne 1962; R; 1500; 83.57 × 4.82 (274.18 × 15.82); M; 14; ex CALANCA 1977; Possible similar: **87051 AZTEC** (Li) ex RISA PAULA 1977; **87052 WINDFROST** (Cy) ex INCA 1977.

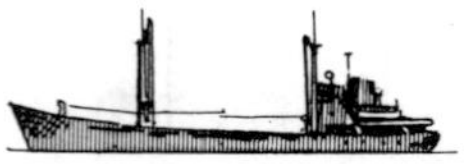

M_2F H

86960 DHOFAR. O/It 1958; C/TS; 550; 66.71 × 3.71 (218.86 × 12.17); M; 10.5; ex RESURGENCE 1971; ex SIGNORITA 1962; ex BERMUDIANA 1961; ex SIGNORITA 1958; Oman Navy.

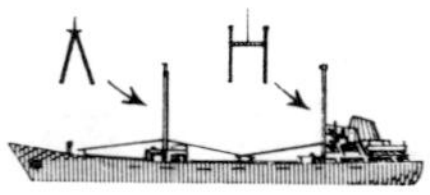

M_2F H

86970 PELKA. Gr/As 1957; C; 500/1000; 66.3 × 3.61/4.65 (217.52 × 11.84/15.26); M; 11.25; ex PERSEUS 1972; Sister: **86971 PROTEUS** (Pa).

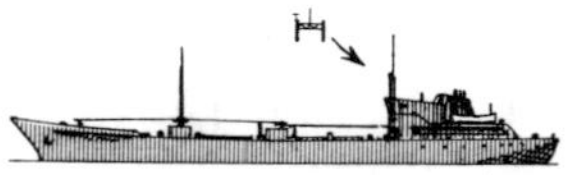

M_2F H

86990 BLAVET. Fr/Fr 1968; R; 1500; 86.67 × 6.21 (284.35 × 20.37); M; —; ex BARRAD WAVE 1977.

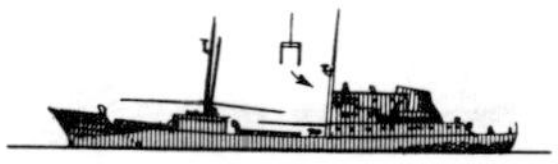

M_2F H

87010 WINSTON. Pa/Br 1955; LS; 900; 74.38 × 4.29 (244.03 × 14.07); M; 13; ex ROGNVALD 1978.

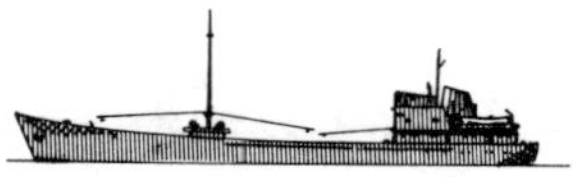

M_2F H

87030 MERIDIAN FRIO. Gr/FRG 1961; C/R; 1400; 81.21 × 4.86 (266.44 × 15.94); M; 14.5; ex BODIL SCAN 1977; ex ARCTIC SCAN 1975; ex GULDENSAND 1972; ex IBIRKA; ex GULDENSAND.

M_2F H

87040 NYANAW. Gh/FRG 1969; R; 2000; 93.71 × —/5.51 (307.45 × —/18.08); M; 17.5; ex COOLER SCAN 1974.

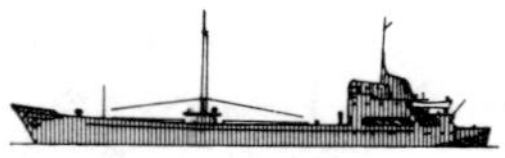

M_2F H

87060 AGIOS NEKTARIOS. Pa/FRG 1961; R; 900; 75.19 × 3.82 (246.69 × 12.53); M; 14; ex OLYMPOS 1979; ex CEDAR FREEZE 1975; ex DRAME OUMAR 1973; ex NEVE 1966; launched as OPTIMUM.

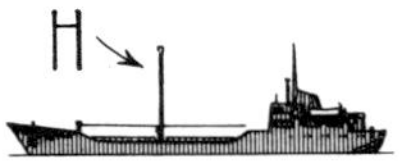

M_2F *H*
87070 BLUE MOON. Cy/Pd 1962; C/LS; 500; 59.85 × 3.42 (196.36 × 11.22); M; 11; ex EVON 1978; ex BORUTA 1973; **'B—475'** type; Sister: **87071 BLUE STAR** (Sg) ex ROBITA 1978; ex ROKITA 1973.

M_2F *H*
87080 CHEMIE CARRIER. Li/No 1970; No; 1400; 87.74 × 5.51 (287.86 × 18.08); M; 12.5; ex HOEGH VEDETTE 1972.

M_2F *H*
87090 MARIAN P BILLUPS. Li/Ne 1956; LGC; 1900; 87.1 × 4.61 (285.76 × 15.12); M; 13

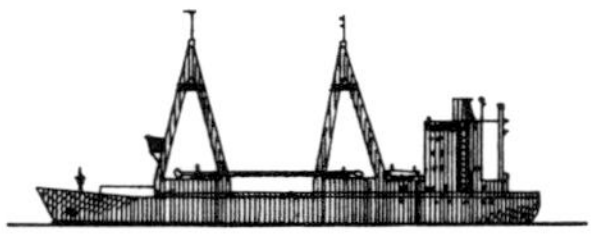

M_2F *H*
87100 GLORIA VIRENTIUM. Ne/FRG 1977; Roc/HL; 1600; 80.37 × 4.15 (263.68 × 13.62); TSM; 11.5; Stern ramp. Total lifting capacity 800 tons.

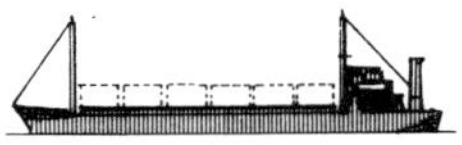

M_2F *H*
87110 SLETTER. No/No 1976; C; 300; 68.51 × 3.38 (224.77 × 11.09); M; 12.

M_2F *H*
87120 AUTO GULF. Gr/Fi 1972; RoC; 1300; 75.85 × 5.18 (248.85 × 16.99); TSM; 12; ex AEGEAN MARK 1978; ex RAH 1977; ex RA 1974; launched as NAVIRUS; Stern & side doors. Reported to be fitted with a 60 ton crane. crane.

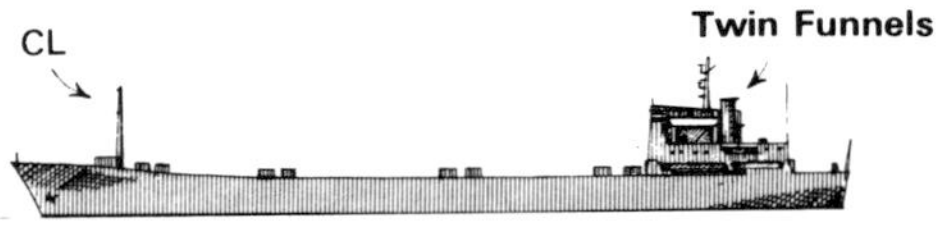

M_2F *H*
87130 VALERIE. Br/Sw 1972; RoC; 3400; 130.71 × 6.74 (428.84 × 22.11); M; 14.75; Stern & side doors; Sisters: **87131 TRANSCON** (Li) ex VALLANN; **87132 SAINT SERVAN** (Fr) ex ALPHA MARINER 1978; ex SAINT SERVAN 1977; ex VALLMO 1975.

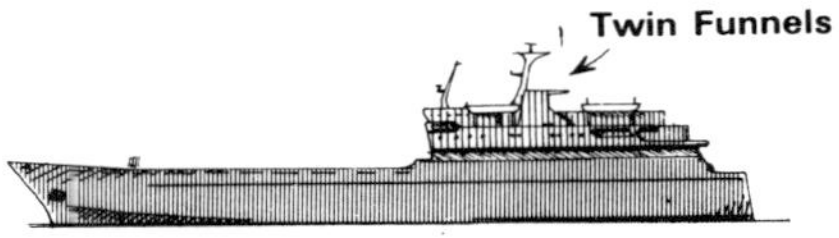

M_2F *H*
87140 MERENGUE EXPRESS. Br/It 1973; RoC/P; 3300; 115.12 × 5.97 (377.69 × 19.59); TSM; 20.5; ex SEASPEED CHALLENGER 1980; ex GISELLA 1974; Stern door/ramp; Sister: **87141 TAMBU EXPRESS** (Br) ex SEASPEED MASTER 1980; ex LAURA RUSSOTTI 1976.

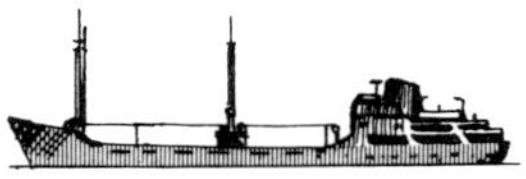

M_2F *H1*
● **87150 DESPO I.** Pa/De 1957; C; 1600; 78.52 × 4.37/5.36 (257.61 × 14.34/17.59); M; 13.5; ex A.E.S. 1975.

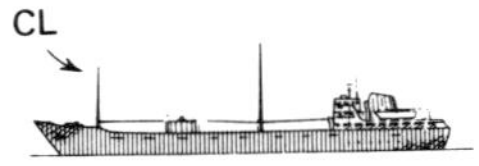

M_2F *H1*
87160 FRUCUBA. Cu/Fr 1956; R; 900; 64.62 × 4.51 (212.01 × 14.8); M; 12.5; ex ICE BIRD 1957; Sisters: **87161 AGIOS GEORGIOS** (Gr) ex SEA CHALLENGE 1973; ex ICE FLOWER 1968; ex ATLANTIC FLOWER 1966; ex ICE FLOWER 1965; **87162 SOL REEFER** (Br) ex ICE PEARL 1966; ex ATLANTIC PRINCESS 1966; ex ICE PEARL 1965.

M_2F *H1*
87170 MUSKETIER II. NA/Ne 1967; C; 500/1400; 79.61 × 3.98/5.77 (261.19 × 13.06/18.93); M; 12.5; ex BROUWERSGRACHT 1977; Sister: **87171 ALGENIB I** (Pa) ex SCHIPPERSGRACHT 1977.

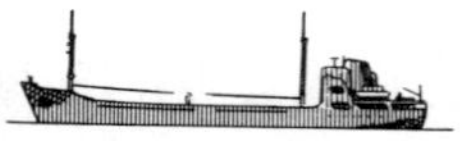

M_2F H1
87180 GHINA I. Pa/FRG 1957; C; 500/900; 66.02 × 3.66/4.8 (216.6 × 12.01/15.75); M; 11; ex THULE II 1975; ex KARIN K 1965.

M_2F H1
87190 PATRIA. It/FRG 1955; C; 900; 66.1 × 5.11 (216.86 × 16.77); M; 12; ex RACISCE 1970; ex STELLAPRIMA 1965.

M_2F H1
● **87200 KLASSEN.** Ca/FRG 1961; C; 600; 68 × 3.71 (223.1 × 12.17); M; 12; ex SIGRID 1972; ex SIGRID K 1969; Sister: **RUDAN** (Cy) ex INGRID K 1973.

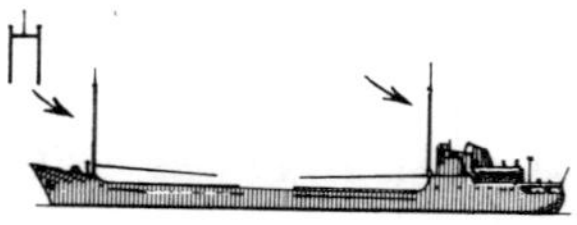

M_2F H1
● **87210 CAPTAIN PETROS.** Cy/Ne 1956; C; 800/1400; 73.84 × 4.4/— (242.26 × 14.44/—); M; —; ex BRUNEVAL 1974.

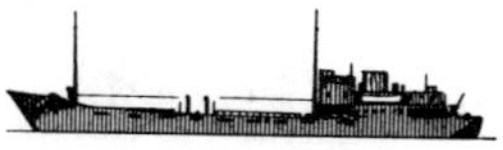

M_2F H1
87220 RAAFAT. Cy/Ne 1956; C; 700; 74.83 × 3.87 (245.5 × 12.7); M; 12; ex ANNE CHRISTINE.

M_2F H1
87230 RUSTRINGEN. FRG/FRG 1953; C; 600; 60.38 × 4.12 (198.1 × 13.52); M; 11; ex TIM II 1967; ex HUBERTGAT 1964; ex ELFRIEDE ROHDEN 1963; ex ANNELIESE PORR 1961.

M_2F H1
87240 VINDEMIA. Sw/No 1969; WT; 1400; 85.43 × 4.81 (280.28 × 15.78); M; 12.75.

M_2F H1
87250 UNA. Fi/Sw 1959; C/WT; 1100; 74.07 × 4.12 (243 × 13.52); M; 12; ex VINGARD 1980; ex VINIA 1979; Lengthened 1963.

M_2F H1
● **87260 CITY OF MILAN.** Br/Ne 1969; Con; 1600; 85.32 × 4.71 (279.92 × 15.45); M; 16; ex MINHO 1974; **'Hustler'** class. Sisters: **87261 CAPE HUSTLER** (Br) ex CITY OF LISBON 1980; ex TAGUS 1974; **87262 ECO GUADIANA** (Pa) ex CITY OF OPORTO 1980; ex TORMES 1974; **87263 CITY OF FLORENCE** (Br) ex TUA 1974; **87264 CITY OF GENOA** (Br) ex TAMEGA 1974; **87265 ATLANTIC CLIPPER** (Br) ex TIBER 1979; ex CITY OF NAPLES 1979; ex TIBER 1974; **87266 ATLANTIC RESOLUTE** (Br) ex CITY OF VENICE 1980; ex MONDEGO 1974; **87267 HUSTLER CHEYENNE** (Br) ex ISBRIT 1976; ex ENGLAND 1974; **87268 ATLANTIC INTREPID** (Br) ex TORONTO 1980; ex CITY OF LA SPEZIA; ex TRONTO 1974.

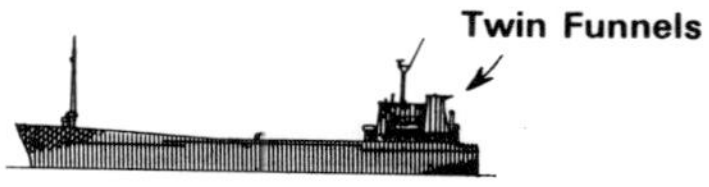

M_2F H1
● **87280 EL MALEK FAISAL.** Eg/FRG 1969; RoC; 500; 76.38 × 4.18 (250.59 × 13.71); M; 14.5; Stern & side doors; Sisters: **87281 EL MALEK KHALED** (Eg) ex COGOLIN 1977; **87282 RAS EL KHAIMA** (Eg) ex KING KHALED 1978; ex COTIGNAC 1977; ex CASSIS 1973; ex COTIGNAC 1971; **87283 AUSTRI** (No) ex CARNOULES 1974.

M_2F H1
87290 WIS. Br/Br 1977; C; 500; 45.93 × 3.88 (150.69 × 12.73); TSM; 9.75; Sister: **87291 WILKS** (Br).

M_2F H1
★**87300 LIWIEC.** Pd/Fr 1956; C; 900; 65.99 × 4.65 (216.5 × 15.26); M; 11.5; ex SEATERN 1958.

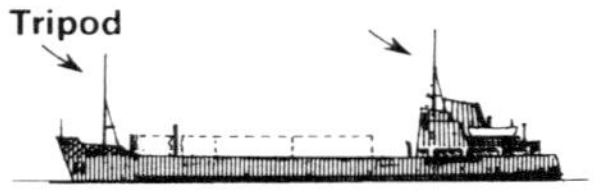

M_2F H1
87320 CONTAINER ENTERPRISE. Pa/Br 1958; C; 1000; 80.09 × 4.08 (262.76 × 13.39); M; 10; Sister: **87321 CONTAINER VENTURER** (Br).

M_2F H1
87330 LINDE. FRG/FRG 1967; C/Con; 500; 74.66 × 3.56 (244.95 × 11.7); M; 13; ex BELL VENTURE 1977; launched as ANKE; Sister: **87331 FALLWIND** (FRG) ex BELL VANGUARD 1977.

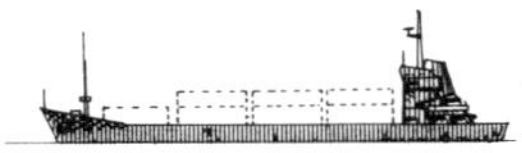

M_2F H1
● **87350 SENTA.** Cy/Ne 1968rcon; 500; 74.86 × 3.7 (244.62 × 12.14); M; 13.5; ex KYDOR PIONEER 1975; ex STADT ASCHENDORF 1973; Similar: **87351 ELINE** (Br) ex NIEUWLAND; **87352 KINI KERSTEN** (FRG) ex RELAY 1974; ex OSTERLAND 1973.

M_2F H1
● **87380 NASSIOUKA.** Gr/FRG 1959; C; 2200/3300; 99.7 × —/6.74 (327.1 × —/22.1); M; 13.5; ex NENI 1978; ex FINNRIVER 1973; ex TAINA 1971; ex MANJA DAN 1968.

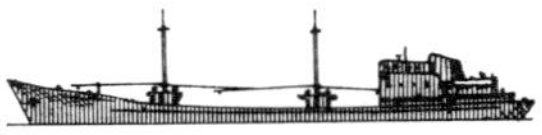

M_2F H1
87400 GELESIAE. It/It 1969; C; 1600; 82.81 × 4.81 (271.69 × 15.78); M; —.

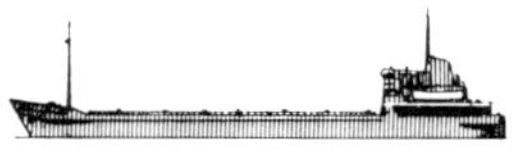

M_2F H1
● **87310 OWENGLAS.** Ih/Ne 1970; C/Con; 800; 78.47 × 4.03 (257.45 × 13.22); M; 12.5; ex IRISH COAST 1976; ex OWENGLAS 1971. Sister: **87311 COMMODORE CLIPPER** (Ih) ex MAYO 1974; ex HIBERNIAN ENTERPRISE 1971.

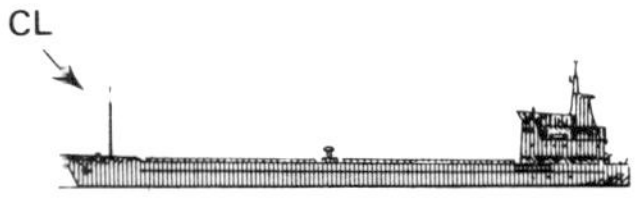

M_2F H1
87340 SPECIALITY. Br/Br 1977; C; 1600; 89.67 × 6.04 (294.19 × 19.82); M; 12.5; Possible sisters (may be geared like SINGULARITY—see MCMF) (Br flag): **87341 STABILITY; 87342 JACK WHARTON.**

M_2F H1
87360 SEA FREIGHTLINER I. Br/Br 1968; Con; 4000; 118.42 × 4.42 (388.52 × 14.5); TSM; 13.5; Sister: **87361 SEA FREIGHTLINER II** (Br).

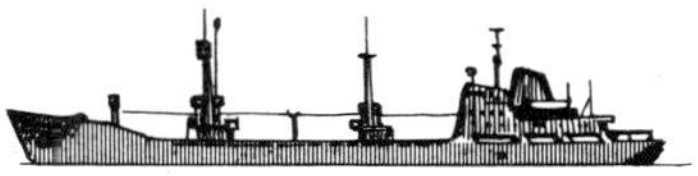

M_2F H1
87370 KUWAIT. Eg/Ne 1961; C; 3100; 96.96 × 6 64 (318.11 × 21.78); M; 13.5; ex KAKAWI 1975; ex RITVA DAN 1974; Sister: **87371 KOSTAS K** (Gr) ex SAIMA DAN 1975.

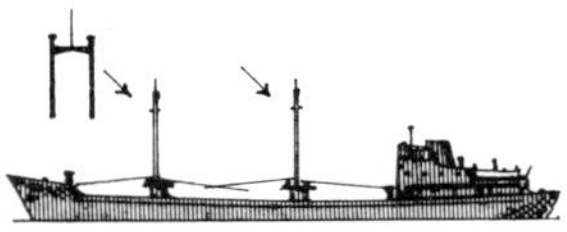

M_2F H1
87390 AVIOR. It/Sp 1964; C; 1300; 86.57 × 4.81 (284.02 × 15.78); M; 12; ex LA LAJA 1977; Sister: **87391 ARCO** (Cy) ex LA CINTA 1977; ex LA RABIDA 1967.

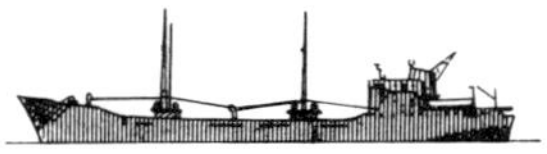

M_2F H1
● **87410 FALCON.** Gr/FRG 1953; C; 1500; 78.75 × —(258.37 × —); M; 12.5; ex ALEXIS G 1974; ex HERMANN SCHULTE 1970; ex ADOLPH GLEUE 1954; Sister: **87411 NIKOS M** (Gr) ex ROSA T 1977; ex MALABAR 1972; ex ERIKA SCHULTE 1970; ex ILSE E GLEUE 1954.

M_2F H1

● **87420 ATLANTIC SKY.** Br/Ne 1965; C; 500; 69.35 × 3.72 (227.53 × 12.2); M; 11.5; Sisters: **87421 ATLANTIC COMET** (NA); **87422 ATLANTIC SUN** (Br); **87423 AIDAN** (To) ex ATLANTIC TRADER 1973; ex FRANCINA 1965; **87424 DABEMA** (Pa) ex ALBAN 1975; ex ATLANTIC STAR 1973; **87425 MEREGHAN V** (Pa) ex ATLANTIC INTREPID 1977; Similar (lengthened): **87426 BILINGA** (Pa) ex ATLANTIC MERCHANT I 1975; ex ATLANTIC MERCHANT 1969.

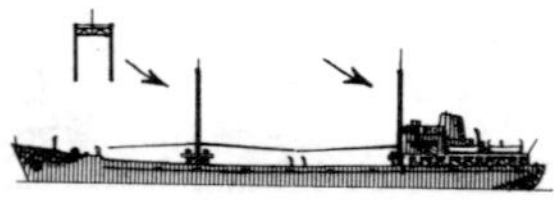

M_2F H1

87460 INDUS. Pa/It 1955/73; LS; 900; 82.48 × 4.57 (271.78 × 14.99); M; 13; Converted from general cargo 1973.

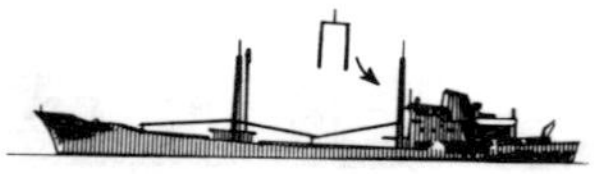

M_2F H1

● **87480 GLACIAR VERDE.** Sp/Sp 1966; R; 1600; 81.69 × 5 (267.88 × 16.4); M; 15; Sisters: **87481 GLACIAR GRIS** (Sp); **87482 GLACIAR ROJO** (Sp); **87483 GLACIAR NEGRO** (Sp); **87484 MAVUR** (Ic) ex GLACIAR AZUL 1976; **87485 EDDA** (Ic) ex GLACIAR BLANCO 1977; **87486 EL MANSOUR DHABI** (Mo).

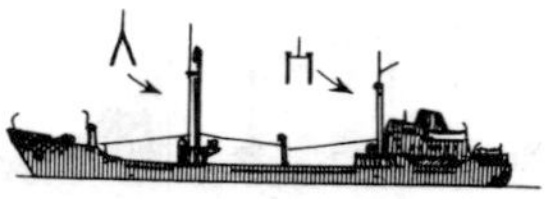

M_2F H1

● **87520 REPULSE BAY.** Li/No 1964; C; 1700; 80.04 × 4.41 (262.6 × 14.47); M; 13; ex SKANDERBORG 1973.

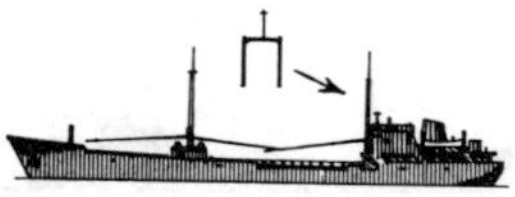

M_2F H1

87540 ZENITH. It/No 1956; C; 1600; 78.09 × 5.49 (256.2 × 18.01); M; 13; ex BLODD 1967; ex EIKA 1963.

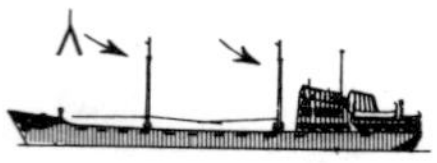

M_2F H1

● **87440 LUI.** Gr/Fr 1956; C; 900; 64.8 × 4.69 (212.6 × 15.39); M; 12; ex ELENI II 1975; ex EDDA 1968; ex JOMARA 1965; ex NICOTO 1963.

M_2F H1

87450 JETPUR CITY. Pa/It 1953; C; 1000; 82.5 × 4.57 (270.67 × 14.99); M; 13; ex MARINER 1980; ex RAINBOW 1980; ex SPEEDY 1976; ex LIONELLO C 1973; ex VEGA 1973.

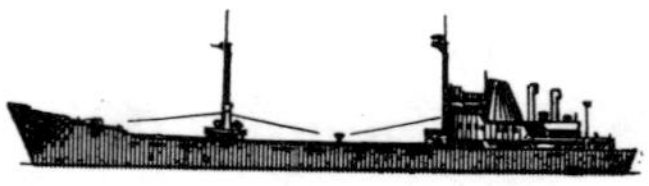

M_2F H1

***87470 HO PING.** RC/RC 1959; C; 2800; 99.36 × 5.49 (326 × 18); M; 12; Sisters(RC flag): ***87471 HO PING 60; *87472 HO PING 62; *87473 HO PING 63.**

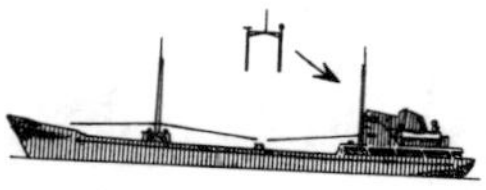

M_2F H1

87500 FRIGO ISABEL. Sp/Sp 1965; C; 1200; 75.14 × — (246.52 × —); M; 13.5; ex GUAYADEGUE 1975; ex COTOS 1970; 1970; ex SAN CYR 1966; May have been converted to passenger cargo.

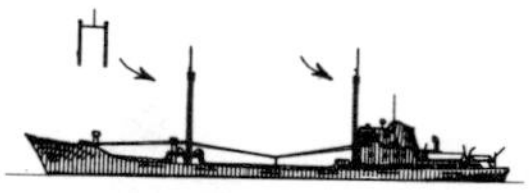

M_2F H1

87510 CAMARGO. Sp/Sp 1959; C; 1500; 76.66 × 5.91 (251.51 × 19.39); M; 11; ex ISABEL FLORES 1970.

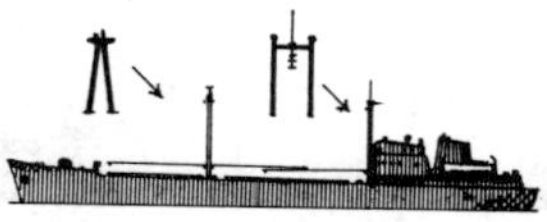

M_2F H1

87530 OCEAN FREEZE. Pa/FRG 1962; C; 1900; 83.29 × 4.37 (273.26 × 20.41); M; 13; ex HOLSTENAU 1977.

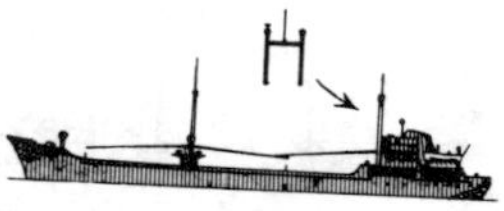

M_2F H1

87550 TROVADOR. Sp/Sp 1958; C; 1600; 76.36 × 5.72 (250.5 × 18.77); M; —; ex LAGO ENOL 1976; Sister (Sp flag): **87551 AZUERDO DOS** ex LABRADOR 1976; ex LAGO ISOBA 1976; Possibly similar: **87552 LAGO COMO; 87553 LAGO GARDA.**

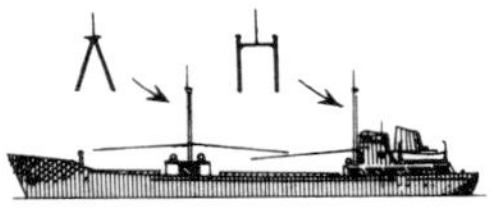

M_2F H1
87560 AGROTAI. Sp/Sp 1960; C; 700; 72.6 × 3.91 (238.19 × 12.83); M; 12.5.

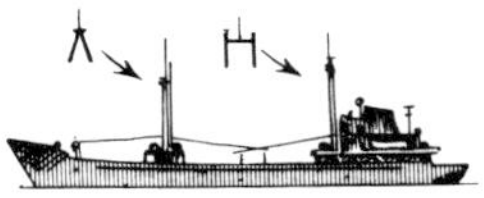

M_2F H1
87570 PUERTO DE ALICANTE. Sp/Sp 1960; C; 700; 72.6 × 3.91 (238.19 × 12.83); M; 12.25; Sisters: **87571 SIERRA URBION** (Sp) launched as LUKUS PRIMERO; **87572 TITI B** (Cy) ex VIRGEN DE LOS REYES 1978; ex ASTENE VEINTINUEVE 1960.

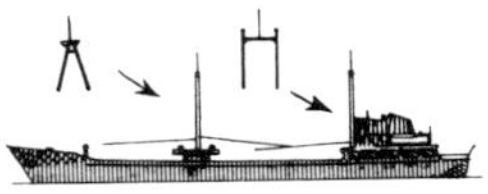

M_2F H1
87580 MARIMAR. Sp/Sp 1958; C; 700; 72.6 × 3.91 (238.19 × 12.83); M; 11.25.

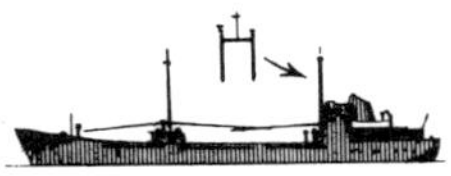

M_2F H1
87590 BATIK. Ia/FRG 1957; C; 900; 66.55 × 4.91 (218.34 × 16.11); M; 11.5; ex TROPIC VENTURE 1975; ex ARNE VIK 1974; ex NORMANNVIK 1973; ex SIRABUEN 1970; ex BLINK 1969.

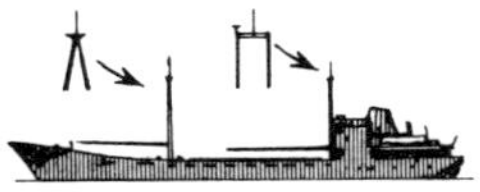

M_2F H1
87600 PELIKI. Gr/FRG 1957; C; 800/1300; 71.33 × 4.12/5.47 (234.02 × 13.5/17.95); M; 12; ex APOLLO 1972.

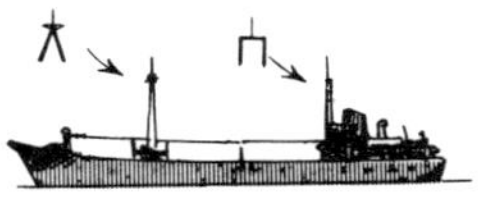

M_2F H1
87610 PELIAS. Gr/FRG 1955; C; 1200; 71.25 × 5.16 (233.76 × 16.93); M; 12; ex FRANZ DOERENKAMP 1968; Sister: **87611 PELOR** (Gr) ex KLOSTERFRAU 1968.

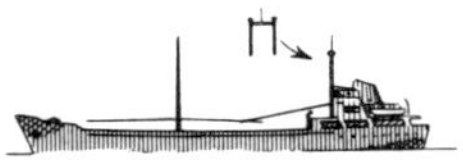

M_2F H1
⋆87620 FUNDADOR. Cu/FRG 1955; R; 700/1000; 66.27 × 3.67 (217.42 × 12.04); M; 11.5; ex FRIGUS 1957.

M_2F H1
87630 SELE. It/FRG 1959; C; 1000; 70.92 × 5.07 (232.68 × 16.63); M; 12; ex PARSIFAL 1971; ex HELMUT PARCHMANN 1962; Lengthened 1965.

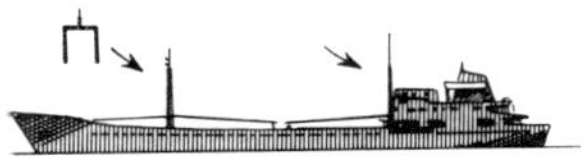

M_2F H1
⋆87640 BEGA. Rm/Rm 1972; C; 1900; 85.88 × 5.1 (281.76 × 16.73); M; 13.25; Sisters: **⋆87641 MEDIAS; ⋆87642 TIMIS; ⋆87643 DROBETA 1850.**

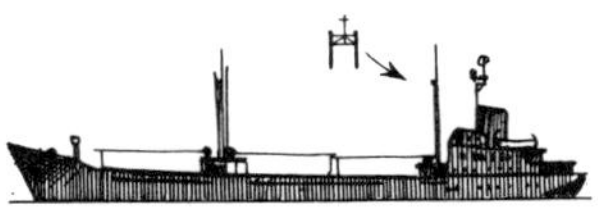

M_2F H1
87650 TRISTAR. Cy/FRG 1957; C; 1300/2000; 91.6 × —/5.72 (300.52 × —/18.77); M; 14; ex SUN 1977; ex GULF EXPRESS 1976; ex ZEPTRADER 1974; ex SEETEUFEL 1972; ex CARPATHIA 1968.

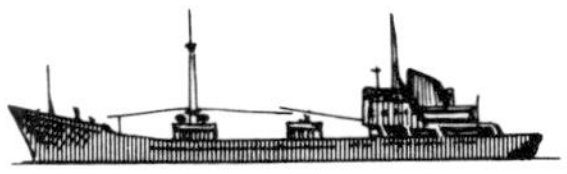

M_2F H1
87660 PLAYA DE MASPALOMAS. Sp/Sp 1965; R; 1600; 82.68 × 4.81 (271.26 × 15.78); M; 15.75; Sister: **87661 PLAYA DE LAS CANTERAS** (Sp).

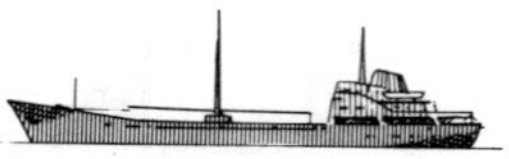

M_2F H1
87670 DONIBANE. Iv/FRG 1959; R; 800/1300; 75.09 × 3.86/4.5 (246.36 × 12.66/14.76); M; 13.5; ex ATLANTIC 1972; ex URSULA HORN 1969; ex URSULA H 1960; ex URSULA HORN 1960; Sisters: **87671 SEAFROST** (Cy) ex RADIANT BELLA 1976; ex VICTOR 1975; ex JAL EXPORTER 1973; ex AUCKLAND EXPORTER 1970; ex CAROLINE HORN 1968; **87672 TANGAROA** (NZ) ex WELLINGTON EXPORTER 1973; ex HARALD HORN 1968; **87673 NOVI T** (Le) ex ADIB 1980; ex JAL IMPORTER 1974; ex INGGA DAN 1973; ex JAL IMPORTER 1973; ex POLO SUR 1973; ex REEFER BASSE 1969; ex ORNEFJELL 1964; ex FJELL REEFER 1960; **87674 MUDI** (Le) ex JAMIL 1979; ex HEINZ HORN 1969.

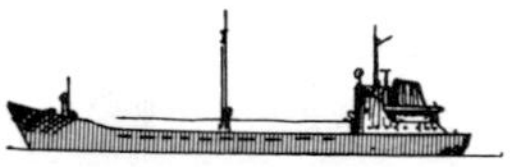

M_2F H1
87700 SCHILDMEER. Ne/Ne 1966; C; 500/1100; 73 × 3.82/5.02 (239.5 × 12.53/16.47); M; —; ex LOOIERSGRACHT 1975; Similar (some have mast from funnel): **87701 WENDY** (Ne); ex RAAMGRACHT 1973; ex AUKES 1969; **87702 ARMADA MARINER** (Ne); ex DICKY 1980; ex KRAFTCA 1975; **87703 ALNILAM** (Pa); ex ESBEEK 1973; ex BONTEKONING 1969; **87704 ANKO** (Cy); ex MOUNT ZERIA 1978; ex SILVER CLOUD 1977; ex SCHOONEBEEK 1974.

M_2F H1
87720 IDA HOYER. De/FRG 1967; LGC; 500; 62.31 × 3.5 (204.43 × 11.48); M; 12.

M_2F H1
⋆87740 KRASNAL. Pd/Pd 1959; C; 500/900; 66.2 × 3.68/— (217.19 × 12.07/—); M; 11.5; **'B-57'** type; Similar (some may be converted to cargo/container—see SKRZAT—Pd flag): **⋆87741 GOPLANA; ⋆87742 CHOCHLIK; ⋆87743 NIMFA; ⋆87744 RUSALKA; ⋆87745 SWIETLIK.**

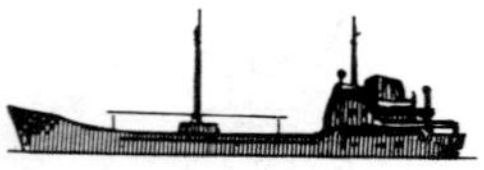

M_2F H1
● **87680 TINITO CASTRO.** Li/FRG 1959; R; 1100; 70.16 × 3.58/3.8 (230.18 × 11.75/12.47); M; 13; ex HILDE HORN 1969.

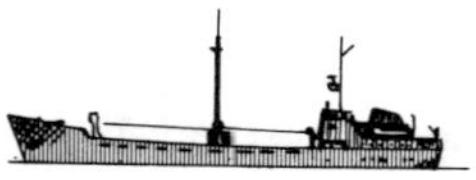

M_2F H1
87690 FIVE RIVERS. Pa/Ne 1957; C; 500/900; 68.89 × 3.96/5.01 (226.02 × 12.99/16.44); M; 10; ex SISTER AMALIA 1973; ex RIJSBERGEN 1968; Sisters: **87691 MATTERA MIMMO** (It) ex ZEVENBERGEN 1967; **87692 SAGEMAR SECONDA** (It) ex HEERENGRACHT 1970; **87693 KOSTAS** (Gr) ex COSTAS 1980; ex KATERINA EL; ex HELLA SCHAA 1976; ex UBBERGEN 1968; **87694 GALSTREAM** (Gr) ex SPITHEAD 1978; ex AERDENHOUT 1970.

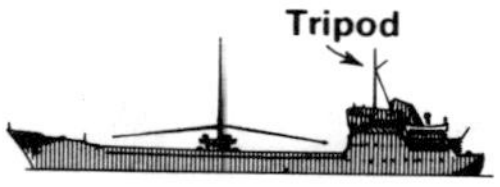

M_2F H1
87710 SOUTH SEA. Sg/FRG 1958; R; 1300; 75.19 × 4.13 (246.69 × 13.55); M; 13; ex SEA ENTERPRISE 1979; ex CARNELIAN 1973; ex LAKHISH 1970; Sister: **87711 CARIB FREEZE** (Pa); ex ARMIC 1974; ex TSEFAT 1970.

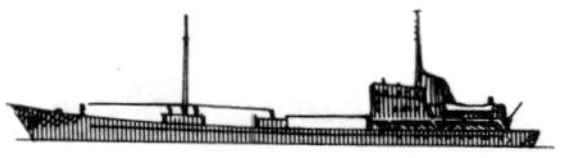

M_2F H1
87730 ISOLE. Fr/Ne 1967; R; 900/1500; 82.71 × 4.06/4.8 (271.36 × 13.32/15.75); M; 15; ex GORGOL 1969; Sisters: **87731 MEDITERRANEAN SPRINTER** (Cy); **87732 LAITA** (Fr).

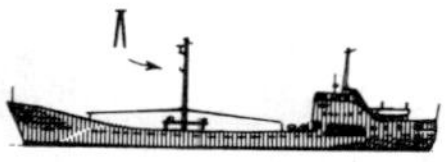

M_2F H1
⋆87750 KAPITAN KANSKI. Pd/Pd 1963; C; 1200; 69.02 × 4.45 (226.44 × 14.6); M; 12.5; **'B 458'** type; Sisters (Pd flag): **⋆87751 KAPITAN M. STANKIEWICZ; ⋆87752 KAPITAN ZIOLKOWSKI; ⋆87753 MARYNARZ MIGALA;** (some may be converted to cargo/container).

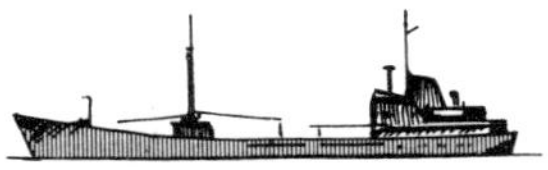

M_2F H1
87760 MERIDIAN ICE. Gr/FRG 1962; R; 1500; 81.82 × 4.75 (268.44 × 15.58); M; 14.5; ex THEOFILOS K. 1978; ex REEFER CARRIER 1975; ex SAMOSSAND 1974; ex RUNGHOLTSAND 1972; ex EL MANSOUR SAADI 1970; ex RUNGHOLTSAND 1968.

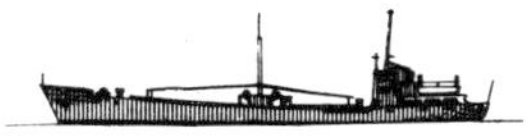

M_2F H1
87780 EMILIA DEL MAR. Sp/Sp 1960; C; 1400; 71.1 × 5.42 (233.27 × 17.78); M; 12; ex ECO MERCEDES 1973; ex LA PARED 1964; Converted to container ship; (Drawing shows vessel before conversion); Sister: **8771 BLANCA DEL MAR** (Sp); ex ECO MARIA 1973; ex HERADA 1964.

M_2F H1
87810 ATLANTIC SPRINTER. Cy/FRG 1971; C/HL; 500; 71.4 × 3.98 (234.25 × 13.06); M; 14; ex ATLAS SCAN 1979; Sister: **87811 BISCAYNE SUN** (Pa); ex UNIT SCAN.

M_2F H12
87830 BARRACUDA. Sg/Ne 1961; C; 1100; 66.12 × 4.48 (216.93 × 14.7); M 11; ex FAIR JENNIFER 1979; ex WESTMINSTERBROOK 1974.

M_2F H12
87850 BLACKTHORN. Br/Ne 1965; C; 1200; 72.27 × 4.53 (237.11 × 14.86); M; —; ex EDEN FISHER 1979.

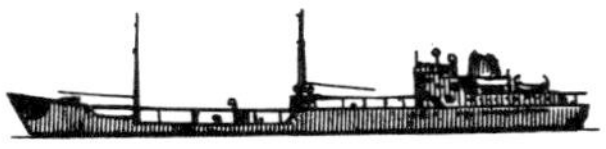

M_2F H12
● **87870 MAGID.** Si/FRG 1954; Tk; 2500; 96.12 × 5.69 (315.35 × 18.67); M; 12.5; ex BRITT 1976; ex FLEURTJE 1973; ex JOHANN HALTERMANN 1971; Lengthened 1960.

M_2F H1
⋆87770 BOGINKA. Pd/Pd 1964; C; 500; 60.66 × 3.45 (199 × 11.32); M; 11.5; **'B 476'** type; Sisters (Pd flag): **⋆87771 DZIWOZONA; ⋆87772 NEREIDA.**

M_2F H1
● **87790 ARQUITECTO GAUDI.** Sp/Sp 1965; Cem; 900; 64.78 × 4.85 (212.53 × 15.91); M; 11; ex CEMENTOS REZOLA TRES 1975; Sister: **87791 TERRA** (Sp); ex CEMENTOS REZOLA GALICIA 1977.

M_2F H1
87800 RIO GUAYAS. Ec/Br 1959; Tk; 1000; 66.91 × 4.27 (219.52 × 14.01); M; —; ex POINT FORTIN 1978; Sister: **87801 UNITED STAR** (Br); ex HALCYON STAR 1976; ex ORTOIRE 1974.

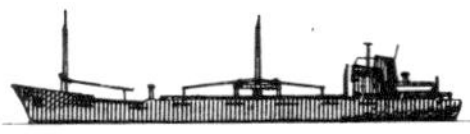

M_2F H12
87820 ADELINA TRICOLI. It/FRG 1956; C; 1600; 88.4 × 4.87 (290.03 × 15.98); M; 11; ex HUGO SELMER 1973; ex FALLSUND 1968; ex FLEETWING 1959; Lengthened 1968.

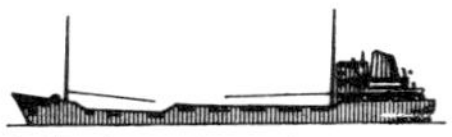

M_2F H12
87840 PARHAM. Br/Ne 1966; C; 1100; 66.12 × 4.52 (217.52 × 14.47); M; 11; ex DERWENT FISHER 1979; Similar: **87841 PELASGOS** (Gr); ex LUNE FISHER 1978.

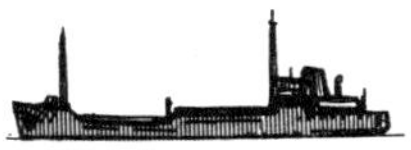

M_2F H12
87860 MARIYOS I. Br/Br 1963; C; 700; 60.05 × 3.65 (197.01 × 11.98); M; —; ex FOXTONGATE 1974.

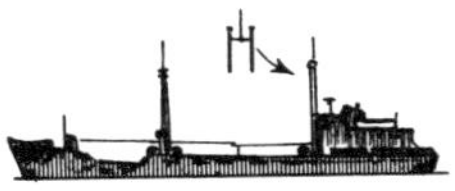

M_2F H12
87880 CAMILLA. It/Ne 1957; C; 1000; 67.06 × 4.47 (220 × 14.67); M; 12; ex TITA 1971; ex SALLING 1967.

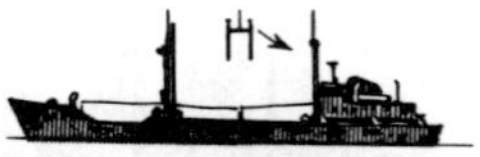

M_2F H12
87890 PARAVOLAS III. Cy/Ne 1958; C; 1100; 67.21 × 4.47 (220.5 × 14.67); M; 11.75; ex OCEAN TRADER 1974; ex HANGUDD 1973; ex STRIB 1968; Similar: **87891 QUIJOTE** (Ur); ex MURELL 1973; ex TERRIER 1972; ex STEGE 1963; ex EBBA ROBBERT 1959.

M_2F H12
87900 VELET. Br/Ne 1964; C; 1000; 66.12 × 4.52 (216.93 × 14.83); M; 11.5; ex HAVELET 1981; Sister: **87901 ABDULLAH** (Sy); ex PORTELET 1979.

M_2F H12
87910 NICOS S. Gr/FRG 1956; C; 1000; 68.48 × 4.88 (224.67 × 16.01); M; 11.5; ex VELOS 1978; ex KATINA 1973; ex FURSUND EFTYCHIA 1969; ex FURSUND 1966.

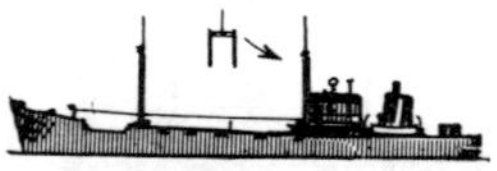

M_2F H12
87920 MAIA. Po/Fr 1954; C; 1000; 73.23 × 4.05 (240.26 × 13.29); GT; 12; ex CORVO 1974; ex MERIGNAC 1958; Lengthened 1955.

M_2F H12
87930 DE HOOP. Ne/Ne 1964; Hospital/Church Ship; 1100; 63.4 × 5.1 (208 × 16.73); M; 12.

M_2F H12
⋆87940 'KORSAKOV' class. Passenger/cargo conversions of class; See MKMF 'KORSAKOV' type & 'BLAGOVASHCHENSK'.

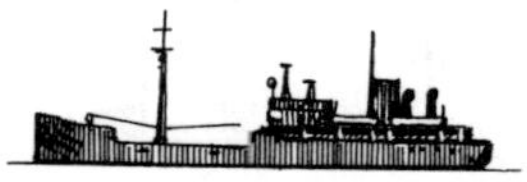

M_2F H12
⋆87950 ZVAYGZNE. Ru/De 1953; FC; 1700; 70.01 × 4.31 (229.69 × 14.14); M; 10.75; ex REFRIGERATOR No 7.

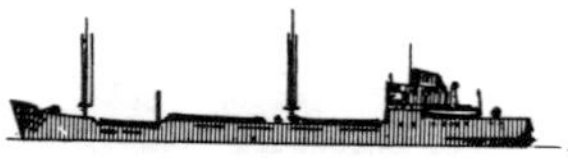

M_2F H123
87960 MANIA. Cy/Br 1952; C; 1600; 83.72 × 4.46 (274.67 × 14.63); M; 10.5; ex CAMEO 1976; ex GEM 1960.

M_2F H123
87970 GREEK SKY. Cy/Br 1955; C; 1300; 70.92 × 4.66 (232.68 × 15.29); M; 11; ex BRIGHT SKY 1976; ex SANDRINGHAM QUEEN 1972.

M_2F H123
87980 FYLRIX. Br/Ne 1962; C; 600; 61.91 × 3.54 (203.12 × 11.61); M; 10.5.

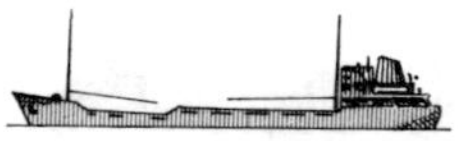

M_2F H123
87990 PARHAM. Br/Ne 1966; C; 1100; 66.12 × 4.52 (217.52 × 14.47); M; 11; ex DERWENT FISHER 1979; Similar: **87991 PELASGOS** (Gr); ex LUNE FISHER 1978.

M_2F H123
88000 BRENDONIA. Br/Br 1966; C; 600; 54.03 × 3.61 (177.26 × 11.84); M; —; Similar (Br flag): **88001 ECCTONIA; 88002 GLADONIA; 88003 TRENTONIA.**

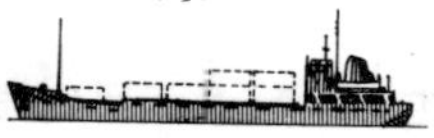

M_2F H123
88010 EL HUSSEIN. Eg/Br 1959; Con; 800/1200; 67.09 × 4.4/4.43 (220.11 × 14.43/14.53); M; 11.5; ex DORSET COAST 1979.

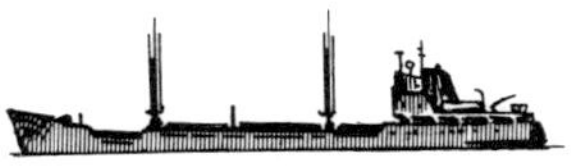

M_2F H123
88020 CHIOS AEINAFTIS. Gr/Br 1962; C; 2200; 86.87 × 5.57 (285.01 × 18.27); M; 14.5; ex GREENLAND.

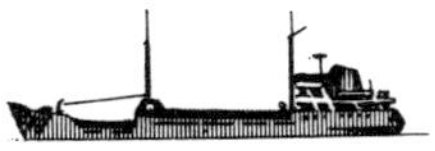

M_2F H123
88040 SAINT COLMAN. Br/Ne 1963; C; 900; 62.46 × — (204.92 × —); M; 12.

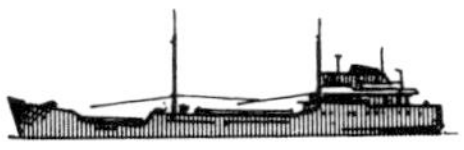

M_2F H123
88060 BRILLIANTE. Pa/Ne 1958; C; 1100; 68.36 × 4.3 (224.28 × 14.11); M; 11; ex SLEMISH 1980; ex BRILLIANT 1978.

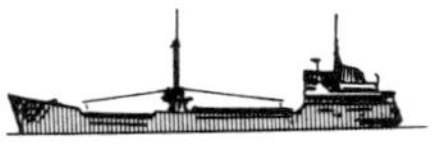

M_2F H123
88080 SAINT WILLIAM. Br/Br 1967; C; 800; 62.24 × 3.9 (204.2 × 12.8); M; 12.

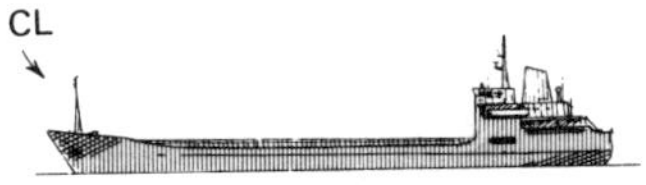

M_2F H13
● **88100 HFINO.** FRG/FRG 1971; C/Con; 1000; 88.5 × 5.28 (290.35 × 17.32); M; 14; ex SCOL VENTURE 1976; ex BALTIC UNIT 1973; ex HEINO 1971; Similar (some may have deck cranes) (FRG flag): **88101 IBESCA ALGERIA;** ex IBESCA ESPANA 1978; ex TWIEHAUSEN 1977; **88102 IBESCA BELGICA;** ex IBESCA BRITANNIA 1978; ex LUBBECKE 1977; **88103 NORRSUNDET;** ex URSA 1977; **88104 FRAUKE;** ex COMAR II 1974; ex FRAUKE 1972; **88105 MARGRET;** ex MARGRET KNUPPEL 1976; ex PINTO 1973; ex HANNES KNUPPEL 1973; **88106 BOMBERG;** ex ROXANE KERSTEN 1980; ex BOMBERG; **88107 NAUTIC.**

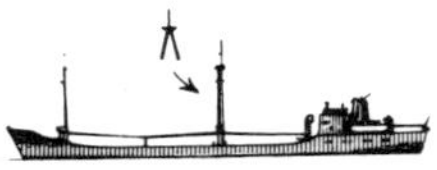

M_2F H13
88120 KARIN. It/FRG 1954; Ch; 1300; 66.12 × 5.54 (216.93 × 18.18); M; 11; ex KARIN CORDS 1968; Converted from general cargo 1969; (Drawing shows vessel before conversion).

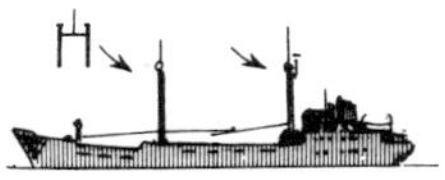

M_2F H123
88030 NIKE. It/FRG 1954; C; 1000; 66.71 × 6.2 (218.86 × 20.34); M; 11; ex ARMELIA 1970; ex SEECLIPPER 1967; Sister: **88031 SILVIA ONORATO** (It); ex SEETRAMPER 1965.

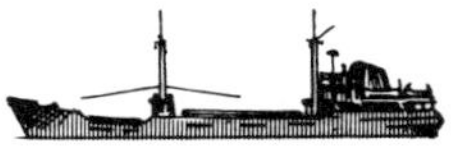

M_2F H123
88050 SAINT AIDAN. Br/Br 1962; C; 1000; 66.45 × 4.18 (218 × 13.71); M; 12.

M_2F H123
88070 THELMA. Pa/FRG 1953; C; 1400; 73.97 × 5.48 (242.68 × 17.98); M; 12; ex MARIANNE 1977; ex ROLANDIA 1971; ex CRUZ BAY 1967; ex CONCORDIA 1964.

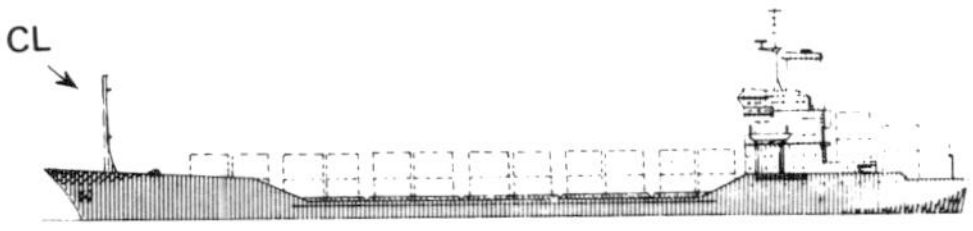

M_2F H13
● **88090 NEW ENGLAND HUNTER.** Li/Ne 1971; Con; 6700; 144.94 × 7.62 (475.52 × 25); M; 22; ex FIERY CROSS ISLE 1973; Sisters: **88091 GRAND HAVEN** (Li); ex NEW ENGLAND TRAPPER 1980; ex LORD OF THE ISLE 1973; **88092 WIBKE** (Gr); ex SPRINDRIFT; ex ATLANTICA MILANO 1977; ex NEW ENGLAND SCOUT 1976; ex SPINDRIFT ISLE 1973.

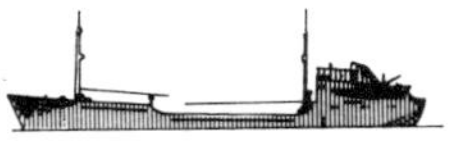

M_2F H13
88110 JENNY SMITS. Ne/Ne 1966; C; 600; 65.46 × 3.84 (214.76 × 12.6); M; 11; ex KALA PRIVA 1971; Lengthened 1973; Sisters: **88111 GERDA SMITS** (Ne); ex NORSTRAND PARTNER 1969; ex NORSTRAND PRIVA 1968; **88112 HEGA SMITS** (Ne); ex HEGA PRIVA 1971; **88113 WILLY SMITS** (Ne); ex GERDA PRIVA 1971; Similar (unlengthened): **88114 ANNA VERENA** (Ne); ex LADY ANNE 1980; ex PEDRO 1976; ex PAULINE LONBORG 1973; ex PEDRO SMITS 1971; **88115 ATLANTA** (Pa); ex LADY CARINA 1980; ex MICKY 1975; ex STACIA 1972; ex STACIA SMITS 1971.

M_2F H13
★**88130 YAKAN.** Ru/Fi 1952; C; 900; 59.47 × 4.57 (195.11 × 14.99); M; 10.

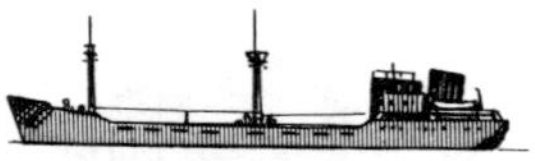

M_2F H13
88150 SEASWEEP. Ho/Ne 1955; C; 1500; 78.67 × 4.67 (258.1 × 15.32); M; 12; ex SELATAN JAYA 1980; ex CAPITAINE WALLIS 1974; ex AKELA 1970; Similar: **88151 KARTALA** (Mg); ex KELIBIA 1962.

M_2F H13
88170 HYBUR STAR. Br/Ne 1962; R; 500/1100; 74.12 × 3.76/4.73 (243.18 × 12.34/15.52); M; 13; ex ARCTIC 1977.

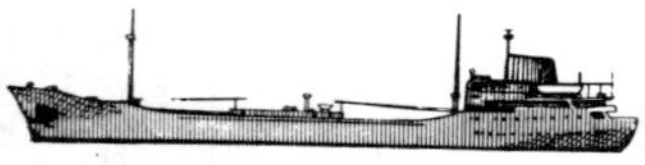

M_2F H13
88190 BANANA PLANTER. Pa/Ne 1963; R; 1900; 100.01 × 4.25 (328.12 × 13.94); M; 17; ex GEESTLAND 1971; Sister: **88191 BANANA REEFER** (Pa); ex GEESTSTAR 1971.

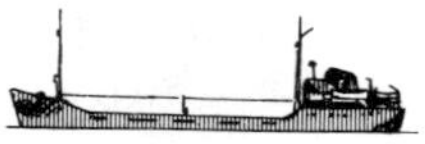

M_2F H13
88200 JANE-SEA. Br/Ne 1960; C; 700; 57.76 × 3.9 (189.5 × 12.8); M; 11; ex RUDYARD 1980; ex BLACKTHORN 1976.

M_2F H13
● **88220 CYPRESS POINT.** Br/FRG 1961; C; 1500; 82.4 × 4.71 (270.34 × 15.45); M; 15.5; ex HOYLAKE 1979; ex WARSTADE 1974; ex JENNY PORR 1969; ex BROSUND 1962; Lengthened 1969.

M_2F H13
88260 HANCOCK CLIPPER. Br/Br 1956; C; 500; 58.02 × 3.6 (190.35 × 11.81); M; 10; ex SOL ECLIPSE 1978; ex SANDY POINT No 1 1976; ex BLUE TRADER 1971; ex ESKWATER 1958.

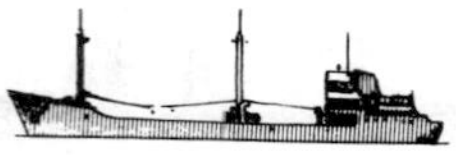

M_2F H13
88140 GRAN RIO. Sn/Ne 1957; C; 1000; 68.61 × 4.07 (225.1 × 12.35); M; —.

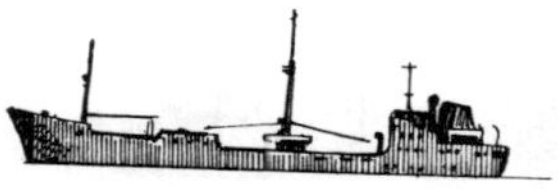

M_2F H13
★**88160 PEI CHING No 1.** RC/Fr 1957; R; 1200; 74.2 × 4.6 (243.44 × 15.09); M; —; ex ICE PRINCESS 1961; Sister: **88161 FRIGORA** (Br).

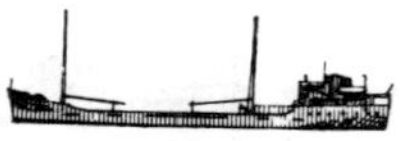

M_2F H13
88180 TRITON. Gr/FRG 1952/54; Tk; 600; 61.18 × 3.43 (200.72 × 11.25); M; 10; ex KONSTANTINOS 1971; ex DELTA 1969; ex BRODICK 1969; ex CHARLES ECKELMANN 1961; Aft section built 1952; Forward section built 1954.

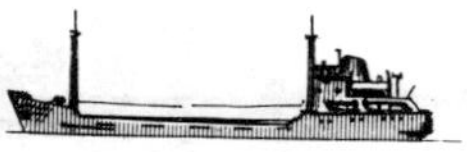

M_2F H13
88210 KOTA PAHLAWAN. Sg/Br 1958; C; 1300; 67.32 × 5.02 (220.87 × 16.47); M; —; ex CHANTALA FORTUNE 1977; ex MOANUI 1975; ex BAY FISHER 1970.

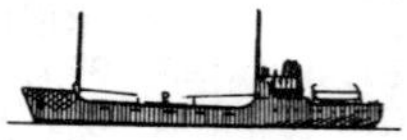

M_2F H13
★**88230 NAN HAI 136.** RC/Pd 1955; C; 600; 57.64 × 4.25 (189.11 × 13.94); M; 10.5; ex ORLOWO 1956; **'B-53'** type; **'Melitopol'** class; Sisters (Pd flag): ★**88231 REDA;** ★**88232 KARTUZY;** ★**88233 BRANIEWO;** ★**88234 RUMIA;** ★**88235 SOPOT;** (Ru flag): ★**88236 MINGECHAUR;** ★**88237 MONCHEGORSK;** ★**88238 NIKYEL;** ★**88239 OSIPENKO;** ★**88240 URALSK;** ★**88241 TIKHVIN;** ★**88242 UGLEGORSK;** ★**88243 GVARDEYSK;** ★**88244 KHOLMSK;** ★**88245 SIND;** (Gr flag): **88246 ANNOULA;** ex JASTARNIA 1976; **88247 DIMITRAKIS;** ex NOGAT 1976; Similar (Ru flag): ★**88248 MELITOPOL;** ★**88249 VORMSI.**

M_2F H13
88270 LISA HEEREN. FRG/FRG 1977; C; 1000; 72.8 × 4.5 (238.85 × 14.76); M; 12; Probable Sister: **88271 MARINA HEEREN** (FRG).

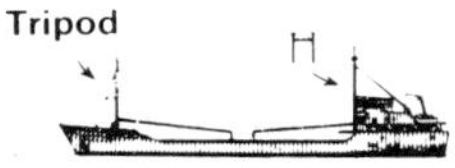

M_2F H13
88280 PECHUDO. Ne/Ne 1978; C; 1000; 65.84 × 4.3 (216.01 × 14.11); M; 12.

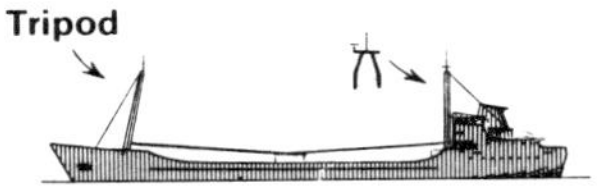

M_2F H13
● **88290 SUNDSVIKEN.** Ne/Ne 1978; C; 1600; 81.01 × 5.21 (265.78 × 17.09); M; 12.5; ex GERDA HOLWERDA 1978.

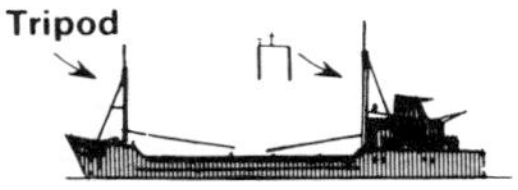

M_2F H13
● **88300 ELISABETH HOLWERDA.** Ne/Ne 1975; C; 900; 65.82 × 4.27 (215.94 × 14.01); M; 11; Sister: **88301 ROELOF HOLWERDA** (Ne); Similar (smaller funnel): **88302 FRISIAN** (Ne); Possibly similar: **88303 WILHELMINA V** (Ne).

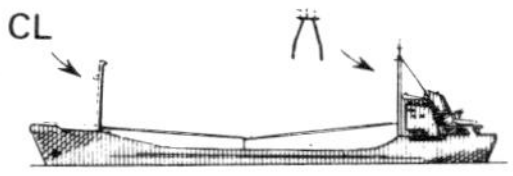

M_2F H13
88310 MARITTA JOHANNA. Ne/Ne 1978; C; 1600; 73(bp) × 5.45 (239.5 (bp) × 17.88); M; 12.5.

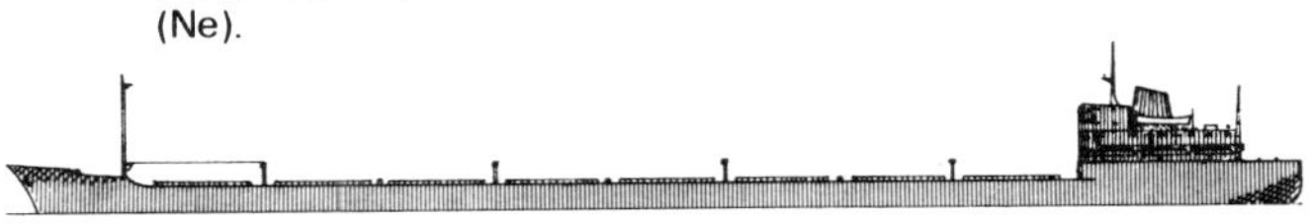

M_2F H13
88320 GOLDEAN ALLIANCE. Li/Ja 1965; B; 25100; 206.03 × 12.32 (675.95 × 40.42); M; 15; ex ATHERSTONE 1978.

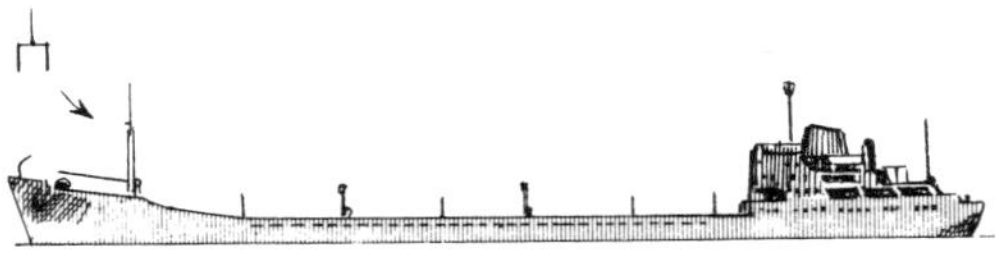

M_2F H13
88330 MALESSINA. Gr/No 1958; O; 10600; 153.93 × 9.19 (505.02 × 30.15); M; 11.75; ex GOOD TRADER 1975; ex MORDLAND 1972.

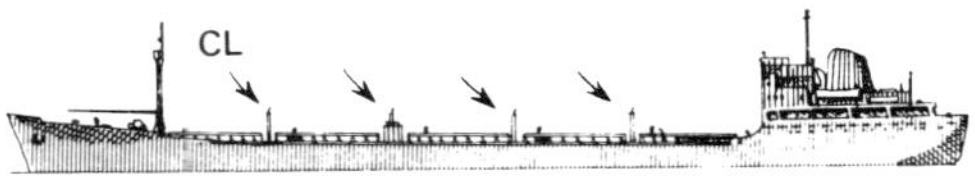

M_2F H13
88340 CRYSTAL. Pa/Br 1958; C; 10000; 148.72 × 9.37 (487.93 × 30.74); M; 13; ex SEALORD II 1980; ex STAMOLEON 1974; ex NAVISHIPPER 1973; ex NORTHERN VENTURE 1971; ex SUNHEIM 1970.

M_2F H13
88350 AUBADE. Pa/Ne 1961; B; 14900; 180.35 × 10.85 (591.7 × 35.6); M; —.

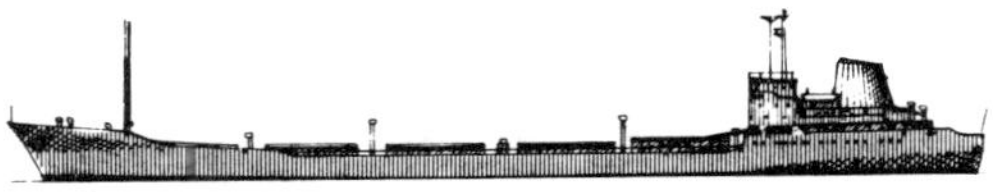

M_2F H13
88360 LIKE TWO. Li/FRG 1958; B; 8900; 155.38 × 9.49 (509.78 × 31.14); M; 14; ex OKAY 1975; ex KLAUS OLDENDORFF 1974; ex WALTER LEONHARDT 1961.

M_2F H13
88370 MINYEE. Pa/FRG 1958; B; 8800; 153.8 × 9.6 (504.59 × 31.5); M; —; ex UNIVERSAL KING 1977; ex TIEN CHEUNG 1972; ex INVERFIELD 1968.

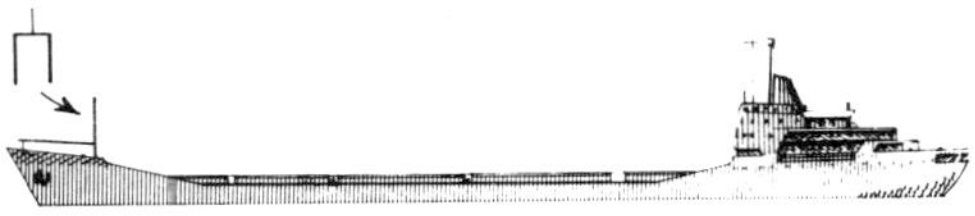

M_2F H13
⋆88380 ZAGLEBIE DABROWSKIE. Pd/Pd 1967; B; 11000; 156.37 × 9.51 (513.02 × 31.2); M; 15.5; **'B 520'** type; Sisters (Pd flag): **⋆88381 DOLNY SLASK; ⋆88382 GORNY SLASK; ⋆88383 PODHALE; ⋆88384 KUJAWY; ⋆88385 BIESZCZADY.**

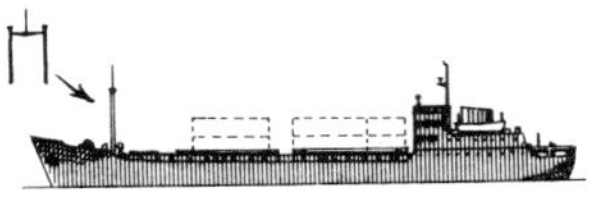

M_2F H13
88390 FORWARDER. Pa/Ne 1949; Con; 1000; 85.58 × 4.33 (280.77 × 14.21); M; 13.5; ex DOMBURGH 1975; Converted from general cargo.

M_2F H13
88400 CRAIGMORE. Br/Br 1966; C; 1400; 73.03 × 5.04 (239.6 × 16.54); M; 11.

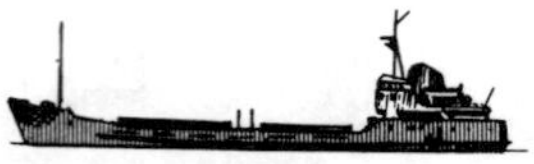

M_2F H13
88410 GORSETHORN. Br/Br 1963; C; 1600; 79.56 × 5.13 (261.02 × 16.83); M; 11; ex DIDO 1977.

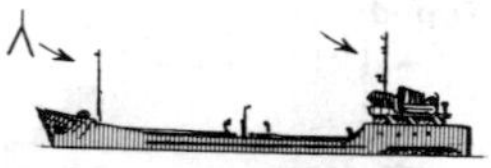

M_2F H13
88420 EMINENCE. Br/Br 1969; C; 1000; 67.67 × 4.22 (222.01 × 13.85); M; 10.5; Similar (lower poop, pole masts): **88421 SENTENCE** (Br).

M_2F H13
88430 CAMILLA WESTON. Br/Ne 1966; C; 500; 55.94 × 3.34 (183.53 × 10.96); M; 10.5; ex CROUCH 1971; Sister: **88431 BEN AIN** (Br); ex GRETCHEN WESTON 1976; ex DEBEN 1971.

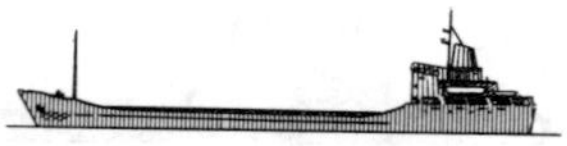

M_2F H13
88440 ATLANTIC COMET. Ne/Ne 1971; C; 1400; 82.1 × 4.53 (269.36 × 14.86); M; 13; ex CORNELIA BOSMA 1978; Lengthened 1977.

M_2F H13
88450 CIMBRIA. De/De 1971; Cem; 2800; 98.25 × 6.27 (322.34 × 20.57); M; 13.5.

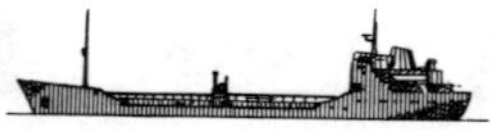

M_2F H13
***88460 TURQUINO.** Cu/Sw 1962; Cem; 1100; 72.37 × 3.86 (237.43 × 12.66); M; 13; ex RAPIDO 1972; ex RAPID 1972.

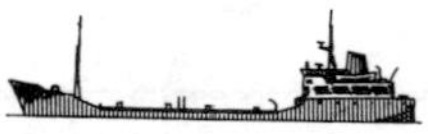

M_2F H13
88470 LEADSMAN. Br/Br 1968; Tk; 800; 62.49 × 4.19 (205 × 13.75); M; 11.

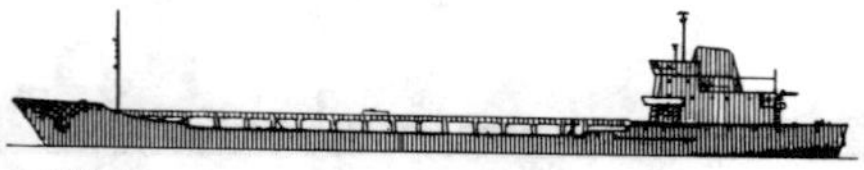

M_2F H13
88480 GULF GATINEAU. Ca/Ca 1976; Tk; 5900; 131.93 × 6.84 (432.84 × 22.44); M; 13.5; Sisters (Ca flag): **88421 GULF MACKENZIE; 88482 ARSENE SIMARD; 88483 ARTHUR SIMARD; 88484 LEON SIMARD;** Similar (Cu flag): ***88485 5 DE SEPTIEMBRE; *88486 PRIMERO DE MAYO.**

M_2F H13
88500 BASTIAAN BROERE. Ne/Ne 1968; Tk/Ch; 1300; 82.3 × 5 (270 × 16.4); M; 12.5; Sister: **88501 JACOBUS BROERE** (Ne).

M_2F H13
88510 DUTCH FAITH. Ne/Ne 1969; Tk/Ch; 1000; 69.5 × 4.98 (228.02 × 16.34); M; 11.5; Similar (lengthened): **88511 DUTCH SPIRIT** (Ne).

M_2F H13
88520 RATHDOWN. Ih/FRG 1965; Tk/Ch; 1400; 77.09 × 5.6 (252.92 × 18.37); M; —; ex THORHEIDE 1971; ex MIKHAL 1967; Similar: **88521 GEA PRIMA** (It) ex REFOLA 1975; ex THORALBE 1970.

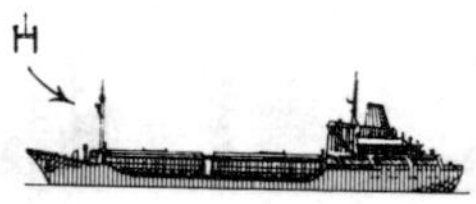

M_2F H13
88530 CLAUDE. Pa/FRG 1967; LGC; 1200; 67.67 × 5.03 (222.01 × 16.5); M; 12; Similar: **88531 BRIGITTA MONTANARI** (Pa) ex LIGUR 1973; **88532 SUNNY FELLOW** (Pa) ex LIBRA 1973.

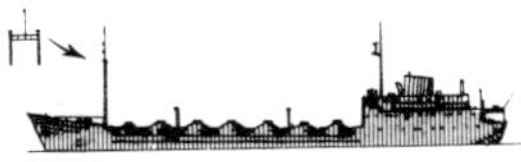

M_2F H13
88540 CAPO GALLO. It/Ne 1954; LGC; 1000; 64.11 × 4.03 (210.33 × 13.2.11; ex CAP CARBON 1966.

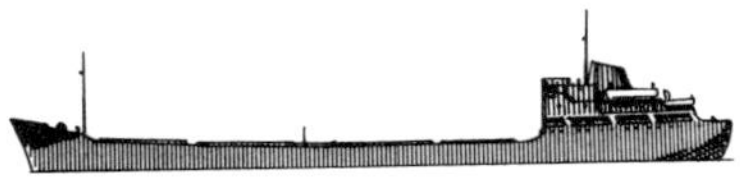

M_2F H13
88560 PULBOROUGH. Br/Br 1965; C; 5000; 112.76 × 7.39 (369.95 × 24.25); M; —; Sister: **88561 ROGATE** (Br).

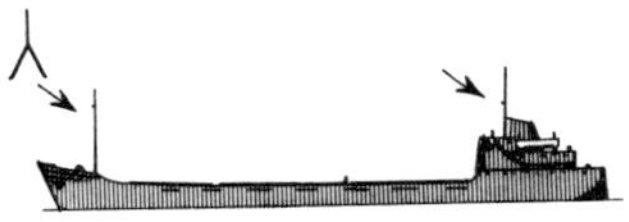

M_2F H13
88580 TAURUS II. Cy/Br 1959; Con; 1900; 90 × 18 × 4.43 (295.87 × 14.53); M; 13; ex COLCHESTER 1975; Converted from cargo and lengthened 1969.

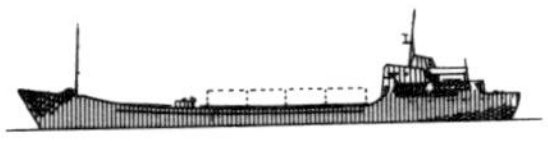

M_2F H13
***88600 ELENA.** Bu/Bu 1970; Con; 1300/1800; 80.73 × 4.35/5.31 (264.86 × 14.27/17.42); M; —; Converted from general cargo. Others of this class may be similarly converted.

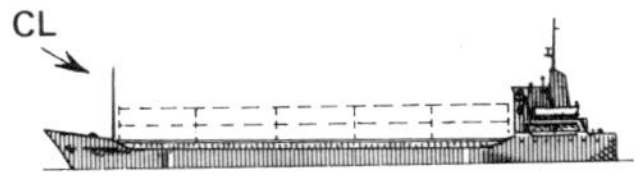

M_2F H13
88620 CARMEN DEL MAR. Sp/Sp 1970; Con; 2800; 88.22 × 5 (289.44 × 16.4); M; 12; ex ISLA DEL MEDITERRANEO 1974; Sisters: **88621 ISLA DEL ATLANTICO** (Sp); **88622 MING CHUN** (Tw) ex ECHUCA 1976; launched as ARDAN.

M_2F H13
88640 SOLWAY FISHER. Br/Ne 1968; Con; 1400; 90.12 × 4.64 (295.67 × 15.22); M; 14.5; Sister: **88641 ORWELL FISHER** (Br).

M_2F H13
88660 HAWTHORN. Br/FRG 1967; C; 1000; 75.24 × 4.42 (246.85 × 14.5); ex FRANCINAPLEIN 1977; ex HUNNAU 1973; ex ORTRUD MULLER 1969.

M_2F H13
88550 DUKE OF HOLLAND. Ne/Ne 1969; RoC; 800. 74.99 × 4.19 (246.03 × 13.75); M; 15; Stern door; Sister: **88551 DUKE OF NORFOLK** (Ne).

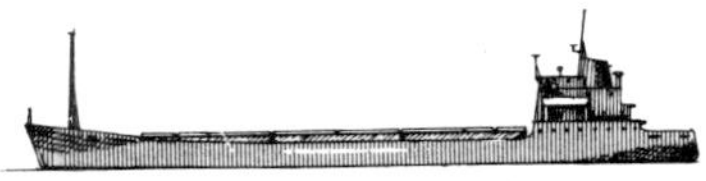

M_2F H13
88570 BRIAN BOROIME. Br/Ih 1970; Con; 4100; 107.14 × 4.44 (351.51 × 14.57); TSM; 14; Sister: **88571 RHODRI MAWR** (Br).

M_2F H13
88590 VENTURA. Ne/Ne 1972; C; 1300; 76.43 × 4.64 (250.75 × 15.22); M; 11.5.

M_2F H13
88610 ROCQUAINE. Br/Br 1977; C; 1000; 66.91 × 4.12 (219.52 × 13.52); M; 11; **88610 Modified 'COLNE' type;** Sisters (Br flag): **88611 BELGRAVE; 88612 PERELLE.**

M_2F H13
88630 WHITEGATE. Br/Ne 1972; C; 1600; 87.46 × 5.45 (286.94 × 17.88); M; 12; Sisters: **88631 MOIDART** (Br); **88632 MINGARY** (Br); **88633 REGENT'S PARK** (Br); Possible sisters: **88634 HIGHGATE** (Br); **88635 BONA FE** (Fi) ex NORRSTAL 1977.

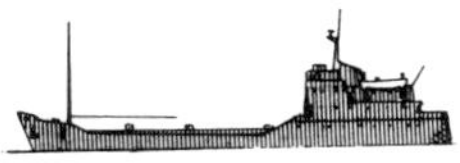

M_2F H13
88650 LIGAR BAY. NZ/Br 1964; Cem; 1300; 69.07 × 4.28 (226.61 × 14.04); TS D-E; 11.

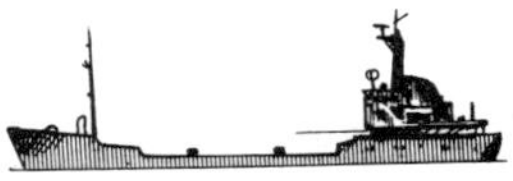

M_2F H13
88670 IONION. Gr/FRG 1964; AT; 1200; 73.72 × 4.8 (241.86 × 15.75); M; 11; ex SPIEKEROOG 1972; Sister: **88671 CHRISTINE FIRST** (Pa) ex DONNA LICIA 1974; ex ASPHALTJO 1973; ex WANGEROOG 1972.

M_2F $H13$
88680 SILVERMERLIN. Br/Sw 1968; Tk/Ch; 1300; 77.32 × 4.8 (253.67 × 15.75); M; 12; Similar: **88681 SILVERFALCON** (Br).

M_2F $H13$
88700 QUARTERMAN. Br/Br 1973; Tk; 1200; 72.85 × 4.92 (239 × 16.14); M; 11.5.

M_2F $H13$
88720 BREDENBEK. FRG/FRG 1969; Tk; 1000; 74.05 × 4.63 (243.95 × 15.19); M; 11; Sisters (FRG flag): **88721 AMMERSBEK; 88722 SUSEBEK; 88723 OSTERBEK; 88724 GEFO BALTIC** ex TARPENBEK 1980; **88725 CORNELIS BROERE** (Ne); ex ISEBEK 1974.

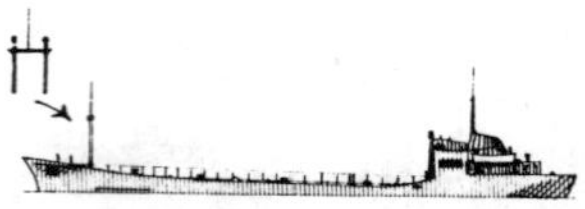

M_2F $H13$
88690 PETROSTAR XIV. Pa/FRG 1961; Tk; 1600; 87 × 5.26 (285.43 × 17.26); M; —; ex MARIA II 1980; ex GERTRUDE WIENER 1977.

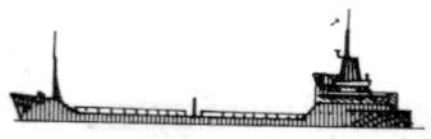

M_2F $H13$
88710 NELLIE M. Br/Br 1972; C; 1000; 72.73 × 3.76 (238.62 × 12.34); M; 12; Lengthened 1978. Drawing shows vessel before lengthening.

M_2F $H13$
88730 LADY RAFFAELLA. It/FRG 1964; Tk; 1000; 64.57 × 5.19 (211.84 × 17.03); M; 12.25; ex HEINRICH ESSBERGER 1975.

M_2F $H13$
88740 SAINT BRANDAN. Br/Br 1976; C/Roc; 900; 63.81 × 4.12 (209.35 × 13.52); M; 12; Bow ramp.

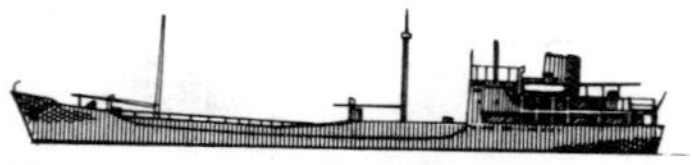

M_2F $H13$
88750 MONTE OLIVETO. It/No 1953; Tk; 3300; 105.11 × 6.21 (344.85 × 20.37); M; 13.5; ex RICHARD AMLIE 1966; Sister: **88751 COCCINELLA** (It) ex SUROIT 1972; ex VIBRAN 1965.

M_2F $H13$
***88770 PIONEER.** Bu/No 1954; Tk; 2500; 100.06 × 5.07 (328.28 × 16.63); M; 13.5; ex ROGN 1961; Probably similar: **88771 VALLAMBROSA** (It) ex HAFORNINN 1971; ex LONN 1966.

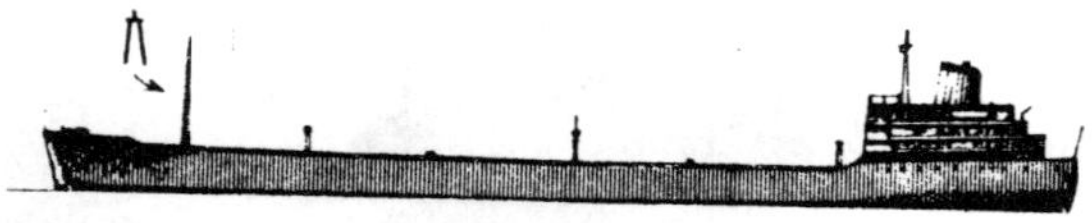

M_2F $H13$
88790 VORRAS. Gr/Ca 1958; B; 11500; 165.18 × 9.47 (541.93 × 31.07); T; 15; ex SUNRHEA 1971.

M_2F $H13$
88760 QUITO. Ec/Br 1953; Tk; 1400; 77.27 × 4.12 (253.51 × 13.52); TSM; 9.5; Kingposts abreast mainmast.

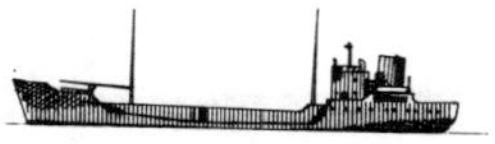

M_2F $H13$
88780 CAPUTERRA. It/Sw 1948; Tk; 1200; 71.2 × 4.57 (233.6 × 14.99); M; 11; ex LOUIS FREDERIC DEWULF 1963; ex JEAN GUITON 1953; ex RUNN 1953; ex BIE 1951; ex LOVO 1950; Sister: **88781 ZITMAR** (It) ex ZIT 1957; ex LIND 1949; Similar: **88782 AMAZONIA** (Bz) ex LIND 1959.

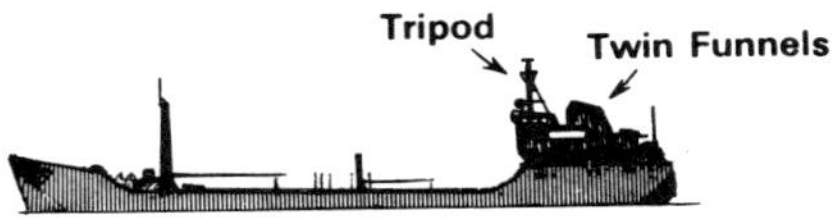

M_2F H13
88800 TEXACO COLON. Pa/No 1966; Tk/LGC; 3600; 103.66 × 5.93 (340.09 × 19.46); TSM; —; ex TEXACO PUERTO RICO 1971.

M_2F H13
88810 SAVE. Fr/Sw 1962; Tk; 4500; 118.78 × 6.86 (389.7 × 22.51); M; 14; ex ALOR STAR 1972; ex ROGN 1968.

M_2F H13
● ⋆**88820 OLIB.** Ys/Ys 1962; Tk; 1800; 84.89 × 5.23 (278.51 × 17.19); M; 12; Sister: ⋆**88821 VINJERAC** (Ys).

M_2F H13
88830 AMALIA. Gr/Br 1958; Tk; 1100; 70.72 × 4.2 (232.02 × 13.78); M; 11; ex KINGENNIE 1972.

M_2F H13
88840 FILICUDI. It/Br 1957; Tk; 2000; 87.58 × 4.94 (287.34 × 16.21); M; 11; ex REDROSE 1969; ex CHAILEY 1969.

M_2F H13
88850 BARBAROSSA. Gr/Br 1958; Tk; 1000; 71.25 × 4.19 (233.76 × 13.75); M; —; ex EFTYHIA 1980; ex PETWORTH 1978.

M_2F H13
88860 WHEELSMAN. Br/Br 1967; Tk; 2900; 98.3 × 6.08 (322.51 × 19.95); M; 12.75.

M_2F H13
88870 ANNUITY. Br/Br 1961; Tk; 1600; 81.16 × 4.83 (266.27 × 15.85); M; 10.

M_2F H13
88880 INGA THOLSTRUP. De/De 1965; LGC; 2000; 83.32 × 5.51 (273.36 × 18.08); M; 13.

M_2F H13
88890 THIRLMERE. Br/Ne 1955; Tk; 800; 60.3 × 4.03 (197.83 × 13.22); M; 10.5; ex KYNDILL 1974.

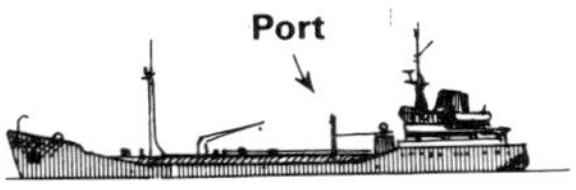

M_2F H13
88900 BP SPRINGER. Br/Br 1969; Tk; 1100; 65.46 × 4.45 (214.76 × 14.6); M; 11.5; ex DUBLIN 1976; Sisters (Br flag): **88901 BP BATTLER** ex INVERNESS 1976; **88902 BP WARRIOR** ex GRANGEMOUTH 1976.

M_2F H13
88910 CASTELLO. It/It 1964; Tk; 1200; 79.2 × 3.86 (259.84 × 12.66); M; 11.5; ex ANTONELLA MONTANARI 1967.

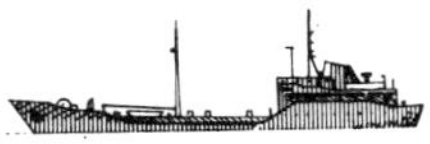

M_2F H13
88920 BURNLEY. Br/FRG 1957; Tk; 1000; 65.99 × 4.34 (216.5 × 14.24); M; 11; ex HERO 1972; ex ADRIAN M 1970.

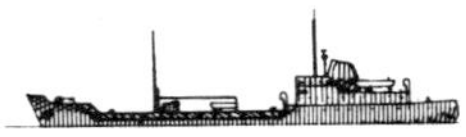

M_2F H13
88930 MARK VI. Gr/Br 1957; Tk; 1000; 68.08 × 4 (223.36 × 13.12); M; 10.5; ex RATHMINES 1976; ex STANSTED 1972.

M_2F H13
88940 ESMERALDA. It/FRG 1954; Tk; 1300; 77.09 × 4.48 (252.92 × 14.7); M; 12; ex MARIE BOETTGER 1967.

M_2F H13
88950 GHAZI—B. Si/Br 1959; Tk; 1000; 65.33 × 4.48 (214.34 × 14.7); M; 11; ex MALDIVE ENTERPRISE 1977; ex AGILITY 1976.

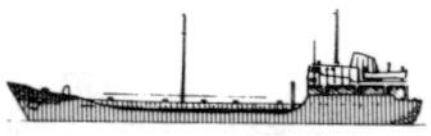

M_2F H13
88960 RATHGAR. Ih/FRG 1959; Tk; 1000; 65.99 × 4.35 (216.5 × 14.27); M; 11; ex PASS OF KILDRUMMY 1970.

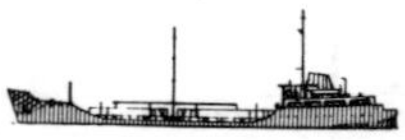

M_2F H13
88970 ANCHORMAN. Br/Br 1962; Tk; 800; 61.88 × 3.91 (203 × 12.83); M; 10.75.

M_2F H13
88980 KALI LIMENES. Gr/Br 1944; Tk; 900; 67.37 × 3.89 (221.03 × 12.76); R; 8; ex PASSAMARE 1965; ex PASS OF KINTAIL 1963; ex CHRISTINE 1956; ex MEDEA 1951; ex EMPIRE MULL 1946.

M_2F H13
88990 DELOS I. Pa/Fr 1957; WT; 1100; 70.21 × 4.33 (230.35 × 14.21); M; 12; ex CHERGUI 1975.

M_2F H13
89000 ATAR. Ma/Fr 1959; WT; 3000; 104.86 × 5.97 (344.03 × 19.59); M; 13.5; ex DAHRA 1978.

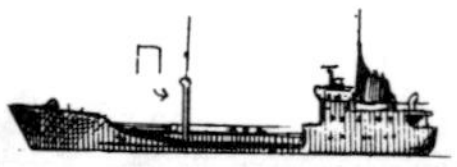

M_2F H13
⋆**89010 NAN HAI.** RC/No 1961; Tk; 900; 65.92 × 216.27 × 13.91); M; —; ex TIMUR STAR 1970; ex SLAMET TIMUR 1969; ex RUBISTAR 1968; ex RUSH 1965.

M_2F H13
● **89020 MAPLEHURST.** Br/Br 1961; Tk; 1500; 79.25 × 4.42 (260 × 14.5); M; 10.25; Lengthened 1971; Sisters (Br flag): **89021 FERNHURST; 89022 MIDHURST.**

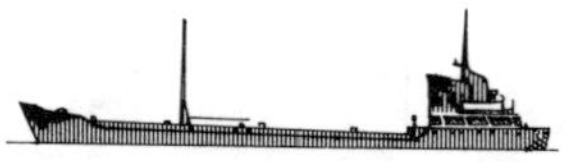

M_2F H13
89030 HUMBERGATE. Br/Br 1969; Tk; 1600; 84.66 × 4.9 (277.76 × 16.08); M; —; Similar: **89031 HULLGATE** (Br).

M_2F H13
● **89040 CASIMIR LE QUELLEC.** Fr/Fr 1969; Ch; 1400; 79.53 × 5.11 (260.93 × 16.77); M; 13.75.

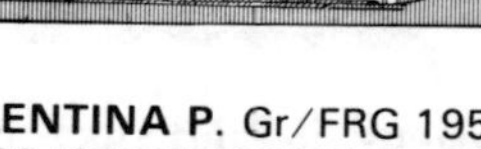

M_2F H13
89050 DUTCH SAILOR. Ne/Ne 1966; Tk/Ch; 600; 65.38 × 3.74 (214.5 × 12.27); M; —; Lengthened 1971; Sister: **89051 DUTCH MATE** (Ne).

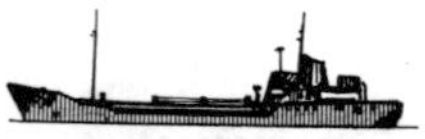

M_2F H13
89060 ANGLEZARKE. Br/FRG 1956; Tk; 600; 62.82 × 3.25 (206.1 × 10.66); M; 10.5; ex MABULI 1975; ex OTTO TERKOL 1971; ex OTTO 1968; ex NESSLAND 1967.

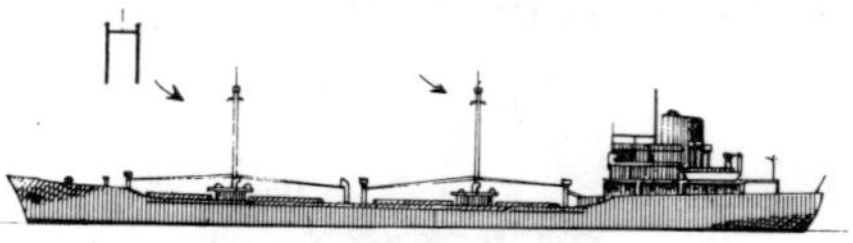

M_2F H13
89070 VALENTINA P. Gr/FRG 1954; C; 5500; 127.62 × 7.06 (418.7 × 23.16); T; 10.5; ex MARKUS 1973; ex AUNGTHITSA 1964.

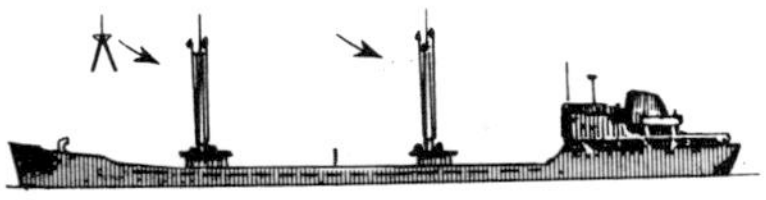

M_2F H13
89080 NIKE. Pa/Fr 1958; C; 4200; 116.69 × 6.4 (382.84 × 21); M; 12.5; ex PAROS TRADER 1978; ex KYRARINI 1976; ex RHEA 1972; ex JACQUELINE 1971.

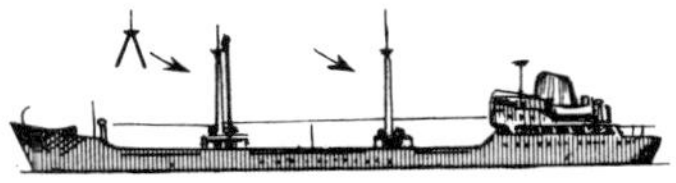

M_2F H13
89090 NAWEZA. Gr/FRG 1959; C; 3200; 100.16 × 6.87 (328.61 × 22.54); M; —; ex UNIPARAGON 1974; ex HOEGH BINNY; ex BINNY

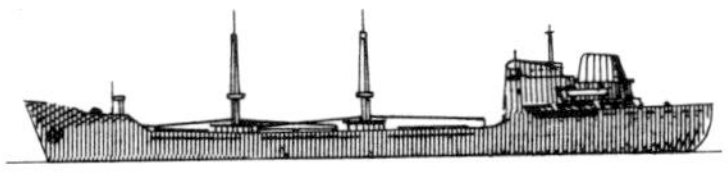

M_2F H13
89100 SERIFOS. Gr/Ne 1963; C/R; 3100/4000; 109.43 × 6.17/7.37 (359.02 × 20.24/24.18); M; —; Sister: **89101 SIFNOS** (Gr).

M_2F H13
89110 PAMBOLA. Gr/Br 1958; C; 2800; 102.42 × 5.5 (336.02 × 18.04); M; 12; ex GREATHOPE 1976; ex QUEENSLAND 1964.

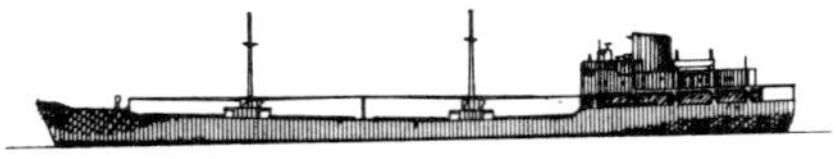

M_2F H13
● **89120 NICOLAS P.** Cy/Br 1957; C; 5000; 120.71 × 6.88 (396.03 × 22.57); M; 13; ex GALAXY FAITH 1976; ex INSCO PRODUCER 1971; ex SUGAR PRODUCER 1966; Sister: **89121 MOLLY** (Pa) ex SAILOR II 1979; ex NAVISAILOR 1978; ex ELARKADIA 1978; ex IRENES FAITH 1974; ex ARKADIA 1972; ex SUGAR REFINER 1967.

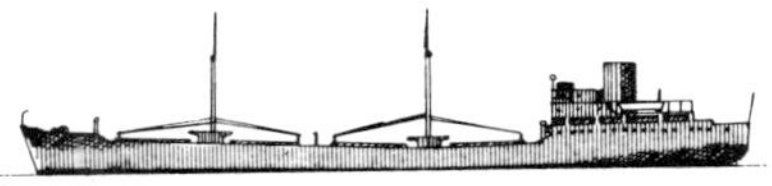

M_2F H13
⋆**89130 CUNSKI.** Ys/Br 1956; C; 4000; 116.31 × 6.62 (381.59 × 21.72); M; 11.5; ex SAMANTHA M 1975; ex LOTTINGE 1974.

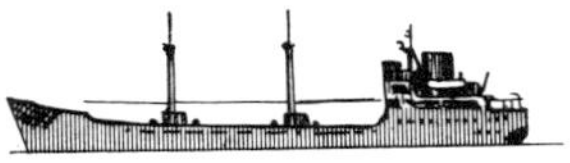

M_2F H13
89140 OCEAN GLORY No 6. Pa/Br 1958; C; 1400; 90.51 × 4.54 (296.95 × 14.9); M; —; ex OCEAN GLORY 1977; ex CATANIAN 1972.

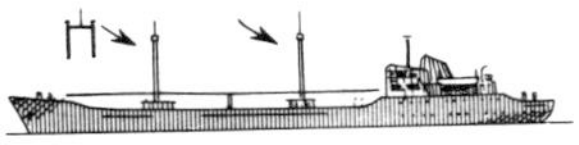

M_2F H13
⋆**89150 FRIMARO.** Cu/Sp 1966; R; 1700; 87 × 5.77 (285.43 × 18.93); M; —; ex FRIMAR 1972.

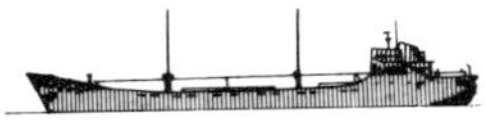

M_2F H13
89160 AIDA. Le/FRG 1956; C; 1400; 70.99 × 5.97 (232.91 × 19.59); M; 11; ex BLUE STONE 1975; ex HILDA WESCH 1972.

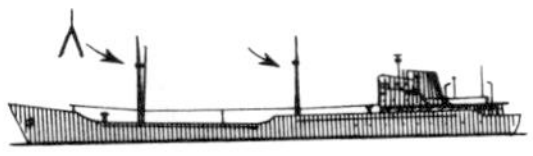

M_2F H13
89170 INCEM ARSEM. Pa/FRG 1958; C; 1800; 80.17 × 6.55 (263.02 × 21.49); M; —; ex OCEAN BLUE 1978; ex GEERTJE BUISMAN 1970.

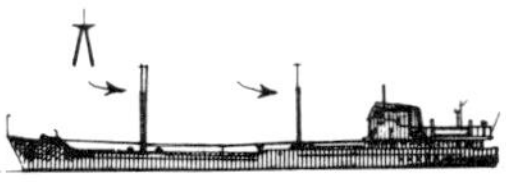

M_2F H13
● **89180 CORRADO.** Br/FRG 1956; C; 1200/1900; 78.97 × 4.75/6.07 (259.09 × 15.58/19.91); M; 12; ex NORDINA 1974; ex INGRID 1972; ex NORDHEIM 1969; ex ANNI NUBEL 1967; Sisters: **89181 BYZANTINE EAGLE** (Cy) ex TEHONGA 1977; ex MARIA ANNA SCHULTE 1970; **89182 UNISON II** (Sg) ex ORCHID FLOWER 1974; ex ELISE SCHULTE 1972.

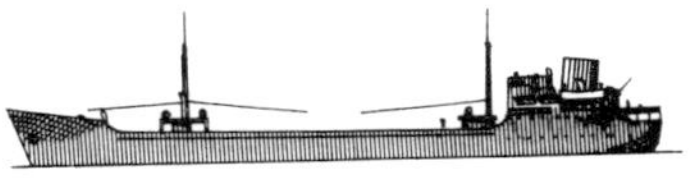

M_2F H13
89190 FAYROUZ. Gr/Br 1959; C; 1500; 100.49 × 4.64 (329.69 × 15.22); M; 12.5; ex KYDONIA 1976; ex VERAS 1973; ex SIDDONS 1962; Lengthened 1966.

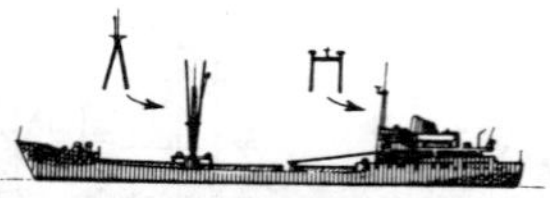

M_2F H13
★89200 KEKHRA. Ru/Hu 1966; C; 1200; 74.55 × 4.67 (244.59 × 15.32); M; 11.5; Sisters (Some of the Russian vessels have a large house ahead of bridge, and may be naval auxiliaries): **★89201 KUNDA; ★89202 OTEPYA; ★89203 ARTSIZ; ★89204 KUYVASTU; ★89206 MASSANDRA; ★89207 TIRASPOL; ★89208 VYANDRA; ★89209 KALMIUS; ★89210 SOLOMBALA; ★89211 VIRTSU; ★89212 BEREZINA; ★89213 OSMUSSAAR; ★89214 TAKHKUNA; ★89215 KARL KRUSHTEYN;** (Hu flag): **★89216 DEBRECEN; ★89217 HEVIZ; ★89218 HAJDUSZOBOSZLO; ★89219 HEREND; ★89220 SOMOGY; ★89221 TATA;** (Bh flag): **89222 CHATTAGRAM** ex RAPLA 1973; **89223 DACCA** ex AMBLA 1973;**89224 KHULNA** ex IMATRA 1972; (Cy flag): **89225 MYCENAE** ex NERINA 1973; ex PETRO STRANDA 1968; ex SAGASTRAND 1966; Probable sisters (Db flag): **89226 GULF EXPRESS** ex ARABIAN EXPRESS 1978; ex FREIGHTER 1977; ex VALZALL 1974; ex BO VIKING 1973; (Cy flag): **89227 OLYMPIA II** ex OLYMPIA 1975; ex HELENA 1973; ex PETRO HAUGE 1968; ex SAGATUN 1966;(Ia flag): **89228 KARIMATA; 89229 NARVA; 89230 SAWU; 89231 SELAYAR; 89232 ARU** ex LOVATJ 1964; **89233 MISOOL** ex PALANA 1964; The following vessels are now converted to wine/vegetable tankers; (Ru flag): **★89234 SEVERNYY DONETS; 89235 TARAKLIYA; ★89236 YARGORA.**

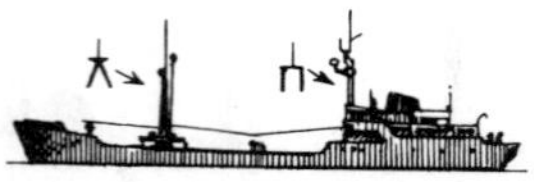

M_2F H13
★89250 SPARTAK. Ru/Hu 1967; C; 1500; 77.81 × 4.73 (255.28 × 15.52); M; 12.5; Sisters (Ru flag): **★89251 IVAN BOLOTNIKOV; ★89252 KONDRATIY BULAVIN; ★89253 NIKOLAY BAUMAN; ★89254 PETR KAKHOVSKIY; ★89255 SALAVAT YULAEV; ★89256 AEGNA; ★89257 ANGYAFOLD; ★89258 AUGUST KULBERG; ★89259 ANABAR; ★89260 MOKHNI; ★89261 ARAKS; ★89262 KABONA; ★89263 VITIM; ★89264 SEMYON ROSHAL; ★89265 TERIBERKA; ★89266 AMBLA; ★89267 RAPLA;** (Ye flag): **89268 ADEN;** ex MATE ZALKA 1974; (So flag): **89269 BOLIMOG;** ex ANABAR 1974.

M_2F H13
89280 JUAN NESPRAL. Sp/Sp 1964; C; 2800; 103.43 × 5.68 (339.34 × 18.64); M; 12.5; Lengthened 1970.

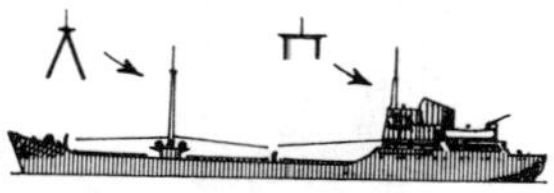

M_2F H13
89290 CALAMOS. Gr/Fr 1956; C; 2300; 84.87 × 5.95 (278.45 × 19.52); M; 11.5; ex TITSA 1976; ex ALEXIA 1976; ex PHEBE 1970; Similar (Cement carrier): **89291 NICOLAOS K HADJIKYRIAKOS** (Gr); ex ARISTEE 1963.

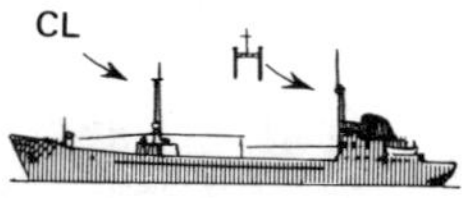

M_2F H13
89300 GEVISA. It/FRG 1966; C; 500; 69.96 × 5.46 (229.53 × 17.91); M; 12; ex KOTIBE 1977; ex EDDA BUUR 1974; ex ELBA 1971; Sisters: **89301 CEDROS** (Po); ex IBIZA 1972; **89302 GORGULHO** (Po); ex MALLORCA 1972; **89303 LIMA** (Po); ex KORSIKA 1972; **89304 DINA R. E.** (Fr); ex MALTA 1971; **89305 RENEE R. E.** (Fr); ex KRETA 1971.

M_2F H13
89310 SOUTH SEA. Sg/FRG 1958; C; 1300; 75.19 × 4.13 (246.69 × 13.55); M; 13; ex SEA ENTERPRISE 1979; ex CARNELIAN 1973; ex LAKHISH 1970; Sister: **89311 CARIB FREEZE** (Pa); ex ARMIC 1974; ex TSEFAT 1970.

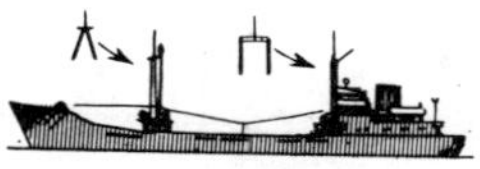

M_2F H13
89320 RASAJES. Cy/FRG 1956; C; 1400; 71.51 × 5.79 (234.61 × 19); M; 12.5; ex PASAJES 1973.

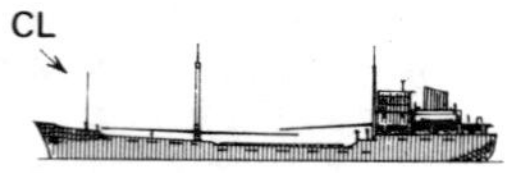

M_2F H13
89330 GEORGIOS D. Gr/Ne 1958; C; 1000; 71.51 × 4.27 (234.6 × 14.01); M; 11; ex NUSAKAN 1979.

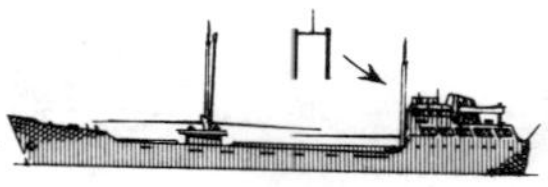

M_2F H13
89340 CHINDE. Mb/Po 1958; C; 1700; 81.67 × 4.01 (267.95 × 13.16); M; 11.5.

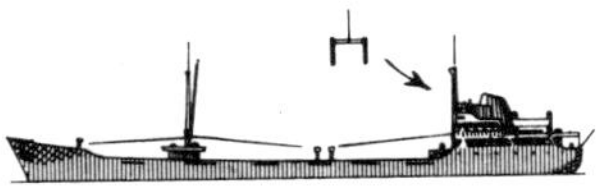

M_2F H13
89350 AXIOS. Pa/Fr 1957; C; 2300; 90.23 × 6.04 (296.03 × 19.82); M; 12; ex BORDER 1975; ex CASAMANCE 1965.

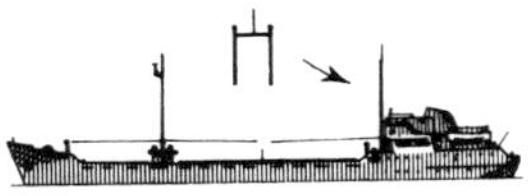

M_2F H13
89370 RAYES 1. Le/Ne 1960; C; 1200; 81.29 × 4.73 (266.7 × 15.52); M; 12; ex LEVENSAU; ex CITY OF CORK 1971.

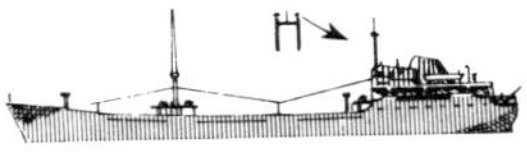

M_2F H13
89390 DIMITRIS K. Gr/FRG 1956; C; 1800; 78.82 × 5.76 (258.6 × 18.9); M; 12; ex GIORGIOS K 1977; ex HADAS 1974; ex ATZMAUT 1969; ex PALMAH 1960.

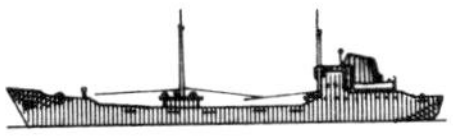

M_2F H13
● **89410 SOPHIA PAPPAS.** Gr/FRG 1954; C/WT; 700/1100; 69.04 × 3.7/4.35 (226.51 × 12.14/14.27); M; 12; ex STAVRAKIS 1979; ex GEIER 1970.

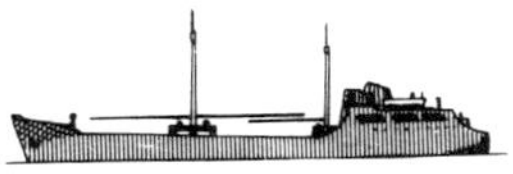

M_2F H13
89430 CHERRY BAGUS. Sg/Br 1959; C; 1700; 74.48 × 4.95 (244.36 × 16.24); M; 12; ex YORK 1969.

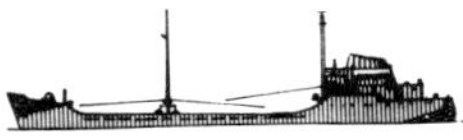

M_2F H13
● **89450 SAPPHIRE.** Br/Br 1966; C; 1300; 69.45 × 4.74 (227.85 × 15.55); M; 11.

M_2F H13
89490 LADY ROSLIN. Br/Br 1958; C; 700; 53.19 × 3.66 (174.51 × 12.01); M; —.

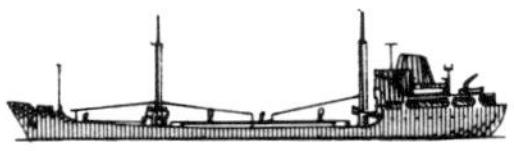

M_2F H13
● **89360 LEVEN FISHER.** Br/Br 1962; C; 1500; 79.25 × 5.11 (260 × 16.77); M; 12.25.

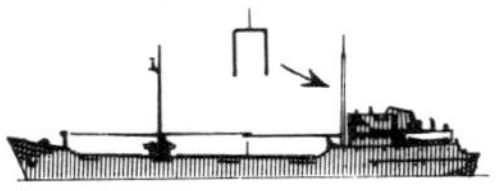

M_2F H13
89380 ILO. It/Ne 1954; C; 1300; 73.72 × 5.54 (241.86 × 18.18); M; 12; ex ILIAS 1970; ex BALLYGALLY HEAD 1968.

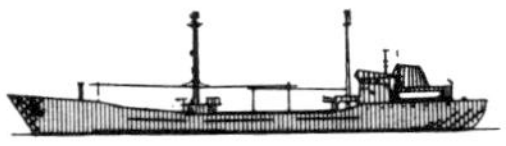

M_2F H13
89400 LANGA. Ic/FRG 1965; C; 800/1300; 74.73 × 4.2/5.4 (245.18 × 13.78/17.72); M; 11.5.

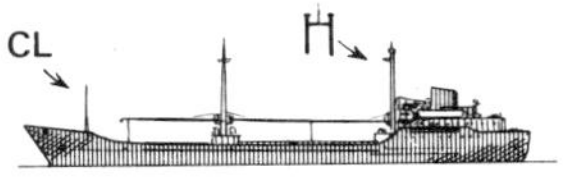

M_2F H13
● **89420 ARANUI.** Pa/FRG 1967; C; 1000/1500; 79.66 × 4.59/5.81 (261.35 × 15.06/19.06); M; 13.5; ex CADIZ 1981; Sisters: **89421 HUELVA** (Pa); **89422 NIAGA XXIX** (Ia); ex SEVILLA 1980.

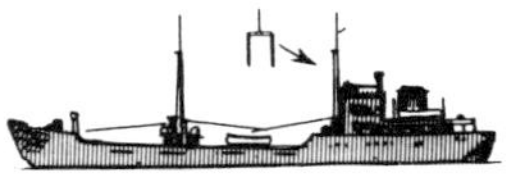

M_2F H13
89440 MAWAR. Sg/Ne 1952; C; 1300; 75.29 × 4.87 (247.01 × 15.98); M; 11; ex MINISTAR 1974; ex VESTA 1974.

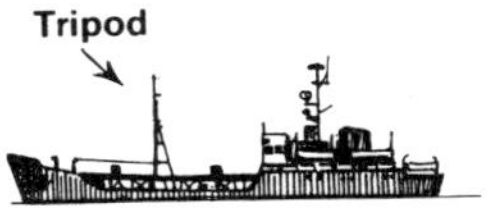

M_2F H13
⋆89460 LOKSA. Ru/Ru 1957; Tk; 800; 63.96 × 3.71 (209.84 × 12.17); TSM; 12.5; Sisters (Ru flag): **⋆89461 CHAIKA; ⋆89462 SUNGARY; ⋆89463 TITAN; ⋆89464 KOKCHETAV; ⋆89465 SAMBOR; ⋆89466 SULA; ⋆89467 BAYMAK; ⋆89468 BUGURUSLAN; ⋆89469 KANIN; ⋆89470 ALEKSANDR LEYNER; ⋆89471 ALITUS; ⋆89472 SIGULDA; ⋆89473 VYRU; ⋆89474 KANDAGACH; ⋆89475 YURYUZAN;** ex BARGUZIN 1966; **⋆89476 METAN.**

M_2F H13
⋆89500 YURILSK. Ru/Ru 1961; FC; 500; 51.9 × 2.94 (170.28 × 9.65); M; 9; Sisters (Ru flag): **⋆69501 AMGUN; ⋆89502 ARAKS; ⋆89503 ALDAN; ⋆89504 AYSBERG; ⋆89505 GRODEKOVO; ⋆89506 ANGARSK; ⋆89507 KAPITAN SCHUKIN; ⋆89508 KORIAKI; ⋆89509 ALPERIN; ⋆89510 KAPITAN KARTASHOV; ⋆89511 KIPARISOVO; ⋆89512 YELIZOVO**; Similar: **⋆89513 AMUR.**

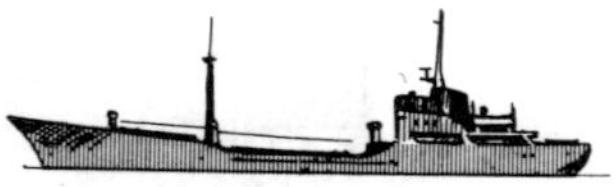

M_2F H13
89540 MARYN. Pa/Fr 1963; C/WT; 1600; 90.38 × 5.3 (296.52 × 17.39); M; 15; ex MAGUELONE 1977.

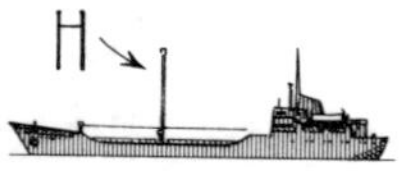

M_2F H13
89560 BLUE MOON. Cy/Pd 1962; C/Ls; 500; 59.85 × 3.42 (196.36 × 11.22); M; 11; ex EVON 1978; ex BORUTA 1973; **'B 475'** type; Sister: **89561 BLUE STAR** (Sg); ex ROBITA 1978; ex ROKITA 1973.

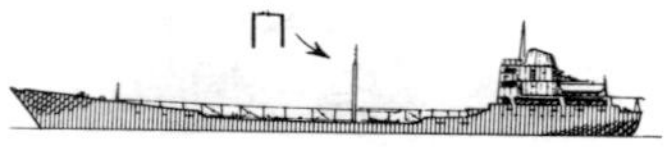

M_2F H13
89580 SAINT MITRE. Fr/It 1965; Tk; 2700; 99.57 × 6.07 (326.67 × 19.91); M; —; launched as SISINA PELLEGRINO.

M_2F H13
89600 GABRIELLA. NA/Ne 1974; C/HL 1300; 88.22 × 5.51 (289.44 × 18.08); M; 13.5; Sister: **89601 FAIRLOAD** (NA); Similar (built 1978): **89602 VALKENIER** (Ne).

M_2F H13
89620 FAIRLIFT. NA/Ne 1969; C/HL 900/1600; 78.72 × —/5.5 (258.27 × —/18.04); M; 12.5.

M_2F H13
89520 YUZBASI TOLUNAY. Tu/Tu 1951; FA/Tk; 3500 Dspl; 79 × 5.9 (260 × 19.5); TSM; 14.

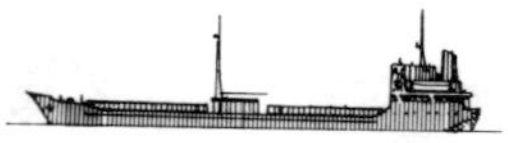

M_2F H13
89530 CARIBGAS DOS. Pa/It 1967; LGC; 1100; 71.51 × 4.37 (234.61 × 14.34); M; —; ex BIRGIT HOYER 1975; ex ALETTE STOVE 1972.

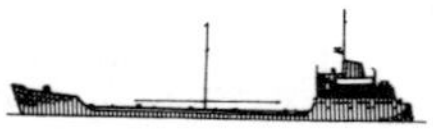

M_2F H13
89550 RIVER LEE. Br/Br 1967; Tk; 800; 61.88 × 3.91 (203.02 × 12.83); M; 10; ex CHARTSMAN 1976.

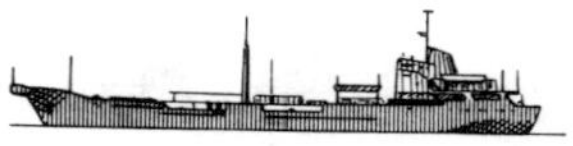

M_2F H13
89570 NORTHERN. De/Ne 1962/68; Cbl; 1700; 82 × 5.5 (269.03 × 18.04); M; 12; ex SIRPA DAN 1967; Converted from general cargo 1968.

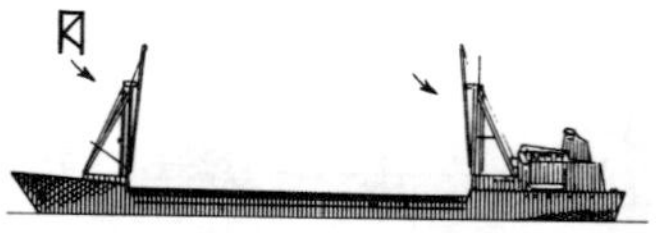

M_2F H13
89590 FAIRLANE. NA/Ne 1977; C/HL 1600/3800; 98.02 × 5.15/6 (321.59 × 16.9/19.69); TSM; 13; Sister: **89591 MIRABELLA** (NA).

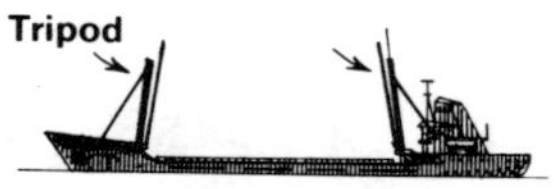

M_2F H13
89610 DANIELLA. NA/Ne 1969; C/HL; 1600; 77.65 × 5.5 (254.76 × 18.04); M; 12.5.

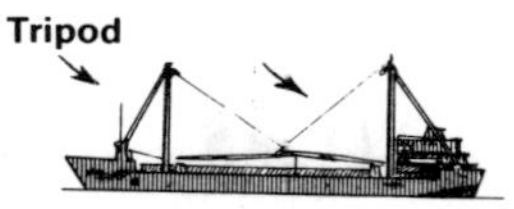

M_2F H13
89630 BISCAYNE STAR. Pa/De 1970; C/HL/RoC; 400; 66.1 × 3.44 (216.86 × 11.29); M; 11.5; ex TITAN SCAN; Bow door.

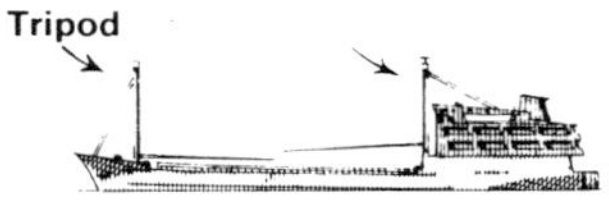

M_2F H13
89640 STOKKSUND. No/No 1974; C/HL; 1600; 79.66 × 5.32 (261.35 × 17.45); M; 15.

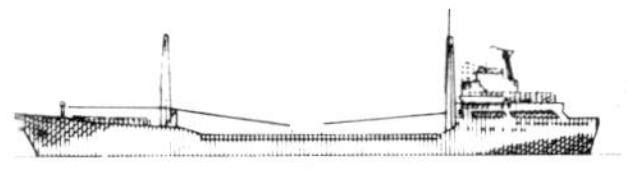

M_2F H13
89650 TROPIC STAR. Sg/Sw 1972; C; 1600; 93.22 × 5.13 (305.84 × 16.83); M; 15; ex JOTA.

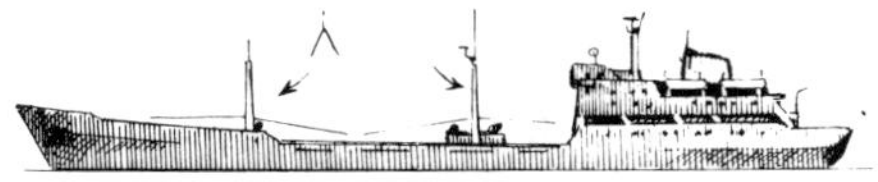

M_2F H13
★89660 IVAN AIVAZOVSKIY. Ru/Ru 1963; FC; 6100; 130 × 7.17 (426.51 × 23.52); D-E; 16.5; For list of sisters, see No 76490.

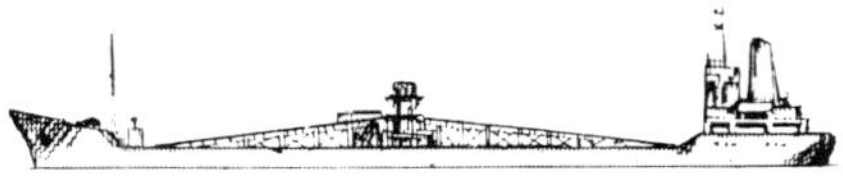

M_2F H13
89670 CHIKUMA MARU. Ja/Ja 1970; Cem; 6400; 131.5 × 7.82 (431.43 × 25.66); M; 12.75.

M_2F H13
★89680 SEVERODVINSKIY. Ru/Br 1966; D; 2000; 82.05 × 4.13 (269.19 × 13.55); TS D-E; 11.5; Sisters (Ru flag): **★89681 ARABATSKIY; ★89681 ONEGSKIY.**

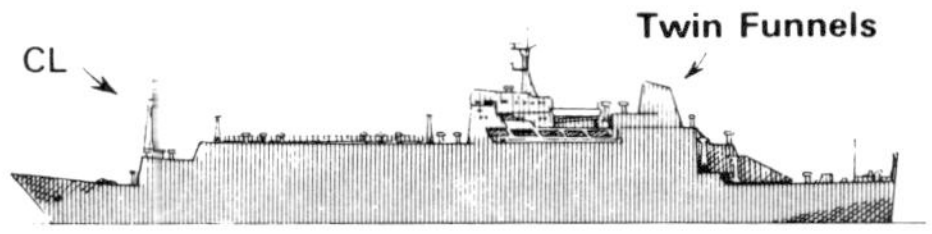

M_2F H2
89690 GRIEG. Fr/Ne 1972; RoC; 4000; 138.26 × 7.01 (453.61 × 23); M; 18.5; Stern door; Sister: **89691 SIBELIUS** (Fr).

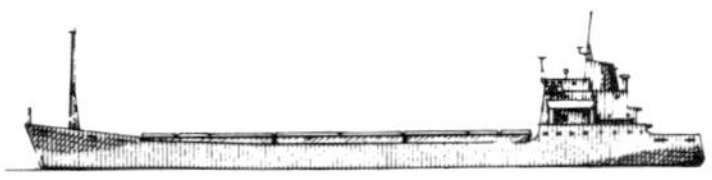

M_2F H3
89700 BRIAN BOROIME. Br/Ih 1970; Con; 4100; 107.14 × 4.44 (351.51 × 14.57); TSM; 14; Sister: **89701 RHODRI MAWR** (Br).

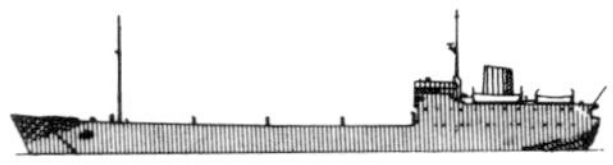

M_2F H3
89710 GHIBLI. Pa/FRG 1952/66; RoC; 1100; 90.91 × 4.06 (298.26 × 13.32); M; 11.5; ex ANNA CATHARINA 1965; Converted from tanker 1966.

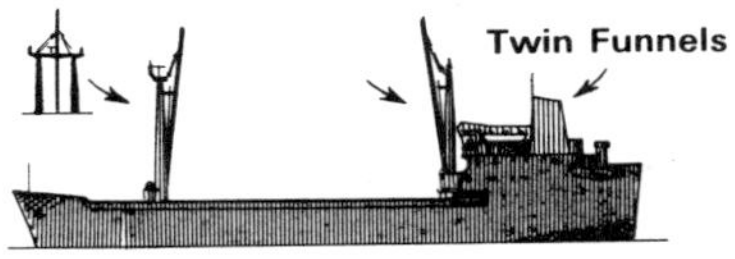

M_2F H3
89720 ATLAS. Fr/Fr 1972; C/HL/RoC; 2600; 100.06 × 6.35 (328.28 × 20.83); M; 14; Stern door; Sisters (Ag flag): **89721 GARA DJEBILET; 89722 TINDOUF.**

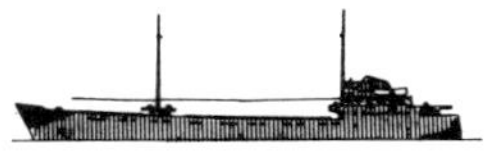

M_2F H3
89730 ISABELLA. Ch/FRG 1952; C; 1300; 70.41 × 5.28 (231 × 17.32); M; 10.5; ex HANS BROHAN 1960.

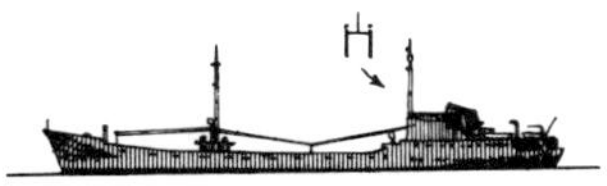

M_2F H3
● **89740 DOMINIC.** Pa/FRG 1952; C; 1800; 84.28 × 5.51 (276.51 × 18.08); M; —; ex WREN 1975; ex DUINO BAY 1973; ex MIRA 1970; ex TARRAGONA 1963; ex IRMGARD PLEUGER 1959.

M_2F H3
★89750 KENGARAGS. Ru/Ru 1973; FC; 600; 55 × 4.18 (180.45 × 13.71); M; 11.5; Probable Sisters (Ru flag): **★89751 BASTION; ★89752 PECHORSK; ★89753 KRISTALNYY; ★89754 MALAKHITOVYY; ★89755 RECHITSA; ★89756 REDUT; ★89757 KORALLOVYY; ★89758 AZURITOVYY; ★89759 RADUZHNYY; ★89760 KVARTSEVYY; ★89761 KORUNDOVYY; ★89762 VSEVOLOD TIMONOV; ★89764 MANGALI; ★89765 BAZALTOVYY.**

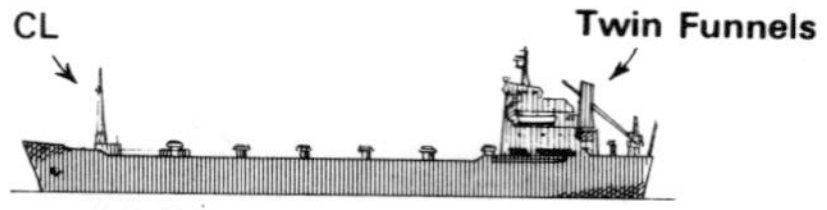

M_2FC H

● **89780 MADOURI.** Cy/FRG 1966; RoC; 2260; 99.22 × 5.83 (325.52 × 19.13); M; 13; ex MOUNDRA 1977; ex SALOME 1973; Lengthened 1969; Side doors; Stern door/ramp; Sisters: **89781 ALPHA CONVEYOR** (Le); ex BELLMAN 1975; ex AIDA 1972; **89782 UNDINE** (FRG); ★**89783 INSELSBERG** (DDR); ex BERWALD 1974; ex OTELLO 1972; (deck house forward of bridge).

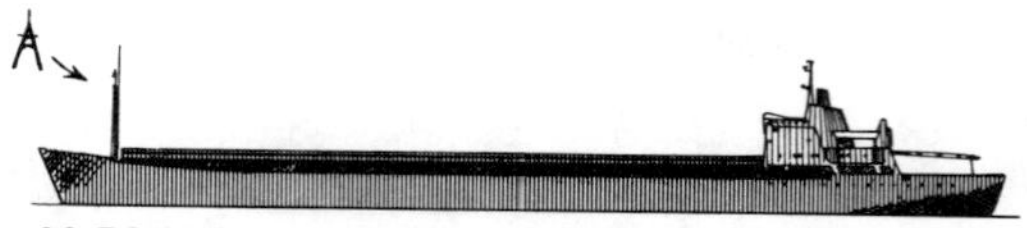

M_2FC H

89790 CHERRY BUNGA. Sg/Br 1967/71; Con; 11200; 153.02 × 8.73 (502.03 × 28.64); M; 17.5; ex MANCHESTER CONCEPT 1980; ex MANCHESTER PROGRESS 1972; Converted from general cargo 1971.

M_2FK H

89800 HALADI 1. Pa/FRG 1955; C; 1300; 70.69 × 5.03 (231.92 × 16.5); M; 12; ex MURTEN; ex LINORA 1966; ex KLAUS 1959.

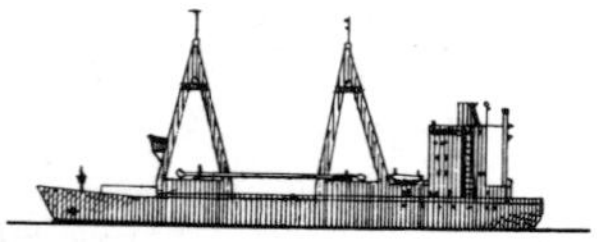

M_2FK H

89810 GLORIA VIRENTIUM. Ne/FRG 1977; RoC/HL; 1600; 80.37 × 4.15 (263.68 × 13.62); TSM; 11.5; Stern ramp; Total lifting capacity 800 tons.

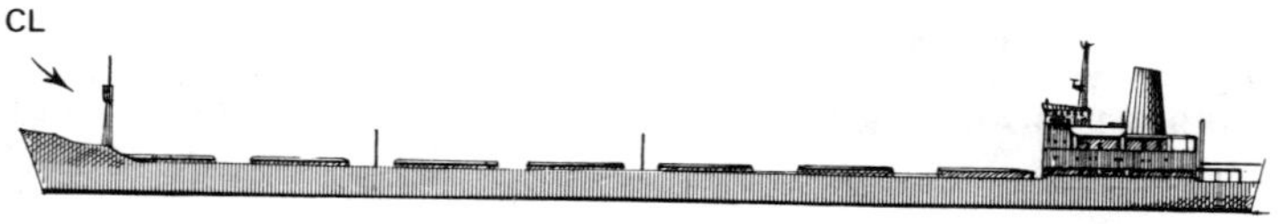

M_2FK H1

89820 KING ALFRED. Br/Sw 1968; B; 29400; 217.58 × 12.82 (713.85 × 42.06); M; 14.75; Similar: **89821 LUCIANA DELLA GATTA** (It); ex EASTERN CHARM 1980; ex POLYHYMNIA 1979; Probably similar: **89822 MARITSA** (Gr); ex ORUNDA; **89823 FORT NORMAN** (Br); ex NORMAN TRADER; ex PILOT TRADER; ex RONA 1978.

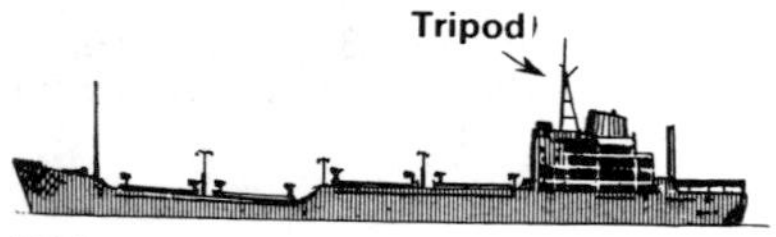

M_2FK H12

89830 IRANDA. Gr/Au 1957; C; 4700; 117.91 × 7.28 (386.84 × 23.88); M; —; Sister: **89831 UNITY** (Gr); ex THANASIS M 1980.

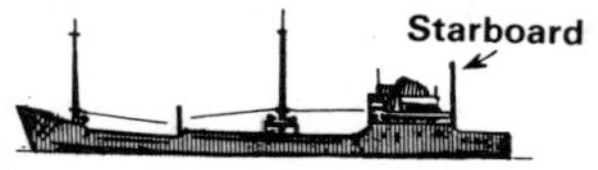

M_2FK H123

● **89840 GILLIAN EVERARD.** Br/Br 1963; C; 1600; 81.23 × 5.16 (266.5 × 16.93); M; —; Sisters (Br flag): **89841 PENELOPE EVERARD; 89842 ROSEMARY EVERARD; 89843 WILLIAM J. EVERARD;** Similar: **89844 STEYNING** (Br); ex GLANTON 1971; **89845 JUPITER** (Cy); ex CLAREBROOK 1976; **89846 ALMA** (Gr); ex KATJA 1980; ex CHESTERBROOK 1976; **89847 NEAPOLIS II** (Gr); ex CORKBROOK 1976.

M_2FK H123

89860 LOKMA 1. Cy/Br 1958; C; 1000; 67.59 × 4.36 (221.75 × 14.3); M; 10.5; ex MARY M 1977; ex YEWFOREST 1974; Sister: **89861 SILVERTHORN** (Br); ex YEWHILL 1974.

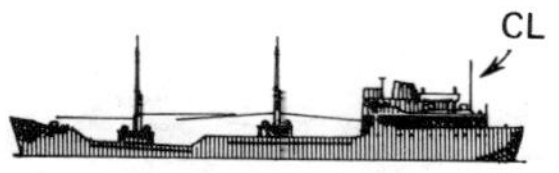

M_2FK H123

89870 NORTH SKY. To/Au 1957; C; 1600; 80.37 × 4.9 (263.68 × 16.08); M; 10; ex NORTH ESK.

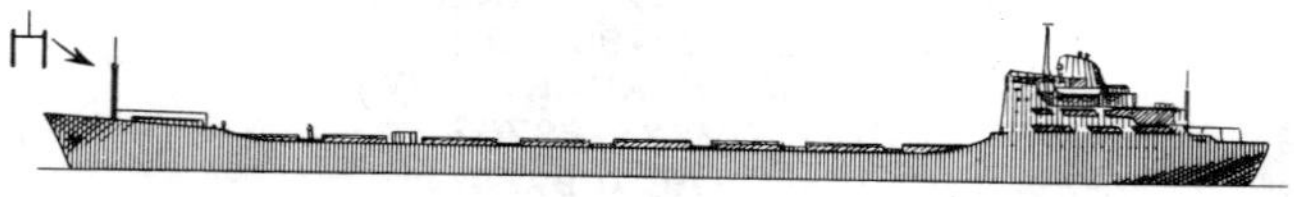

M_2FK H13

89880 THERESA. Li/No 1961; B; 18500; 194.67 × 11.21 (638.68 × 36.78); M; —; ex URANUS 1978; ex ELENI E.F. 1970; ex NORBULK 1970.

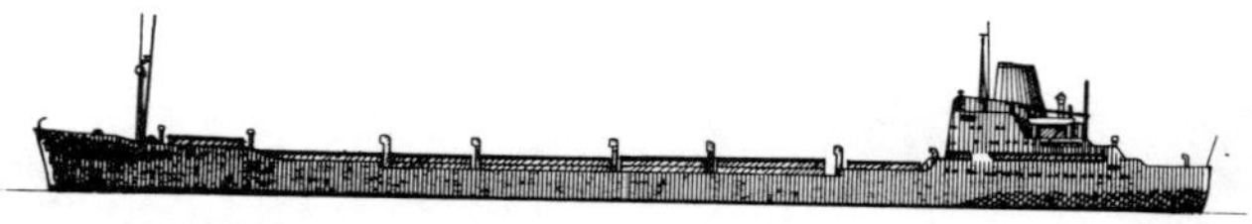

M_2FK H13

● **89890 PUERTO ACEVADO.** Li/FRG 1961; B; 16700; 189.01 × 10.31 (620.11 × 33.83); M; 14.75; ex PEARLSTONE 1975; ex TWINONE 1973; ex ANNELIESE 1972; Sisters: **89891 SHIN HUI** (Br); ex PUERTO ROCCA 1980; ex TWINTWO 1973; ex INGE 1972.

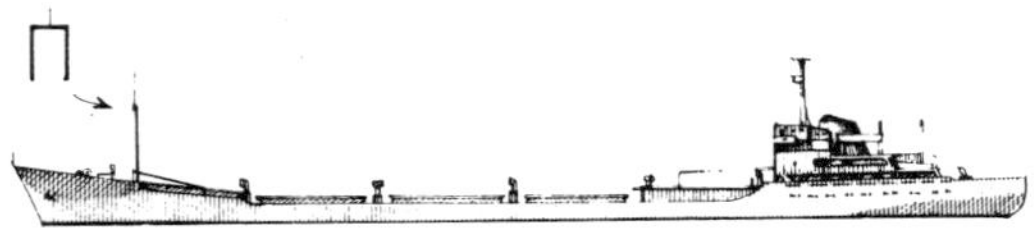

M_2FK H13
★89900 HONG QI 113. RC/FRG 1958; O; 10600; 159.34 × 9.42 (522.97 × 30.91); M; 13.5; ex CASPIAN SEA 1976; ex AUGUST LEONHARDT 1972; Sister (may have after KP removed): **89901 MARIE LEONHARDT** (Li).

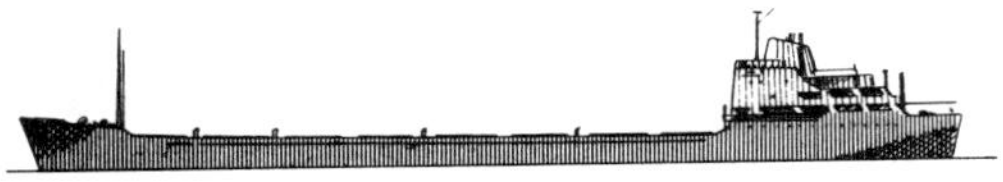

M_2FK H13
● **★89910 YAMPOL.** Ru/Sw 1959; B; 10600; 149.36 × 9.6 (490.03 × 31.5); M; 14.25; ex AVAFORS 1976; Sister: **★89911 YASNOGORSK** (Ru); ex ARVIDSJAUR 1976; Possible sister (may be KMFK): **★89912 YARTSYEVO** (Ru); ex ADAK 1976; Similar: **★89913 MIDJUR** (Bu); ex ALPHARD 1970; ex AVASAKSA 1966; **89914 TIGER BAY** (Br); ex VOLA 1980; ex ACHERNAR 1970; ex ALTA 1966; **89915 PRINCESS JADE** (Pa); ex ACANDI; ex PLUTON 1974; ex KOOKABURRA 1968.

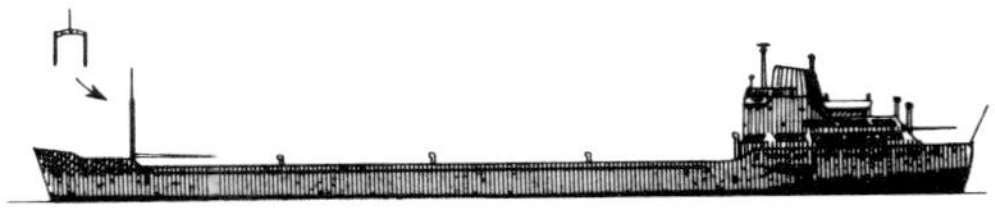

M_2FK H13
89905 FISONS REALF. No/Sw 1955; B; 10800; 149.36 × 9.6 (490.03 × 31.5); M; 14.5; ex ABISKO 1964.

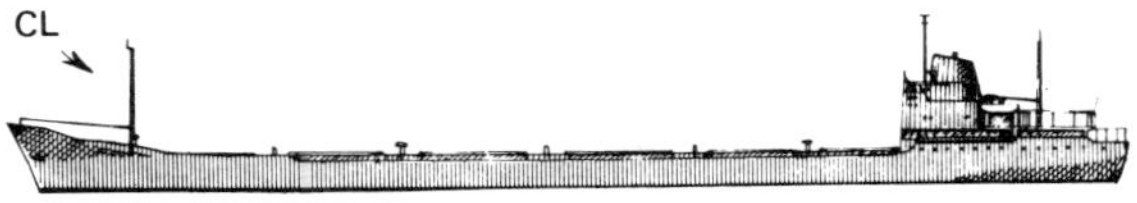

M_2FK H13
89920 ARKADIA. Fi/FRG 1959; B; 13400; 176.79 × 9.89 (580.02 × 32.45); M; 13.5; ex SLESVIG 1974.

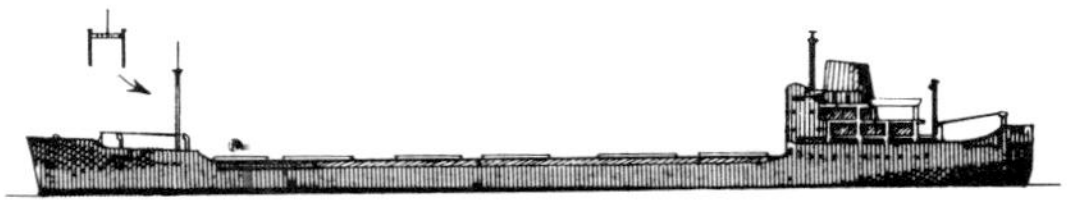

M_2FK H13
89930 MELVIN H. BAKER. Li/FRG 1956; O; 10200; 159.95 × 9.46 (524.77 × 31.04); M; 15.

M_2FK H13
89940 ARCHANGELOS III. Gr/FRG 1963; B; 22800; 217.99 × 11.59 (715.19 × 38.02); M; 15; ex NAESS LIBERTY 1974; Sister: **89941 PYTHEUS** (Gr); ex RUBYCORN 1980; ex FRIGGA 1973; Similar: **89942 TRADE LIGHT** (Gr); ex BALDUR 1978.

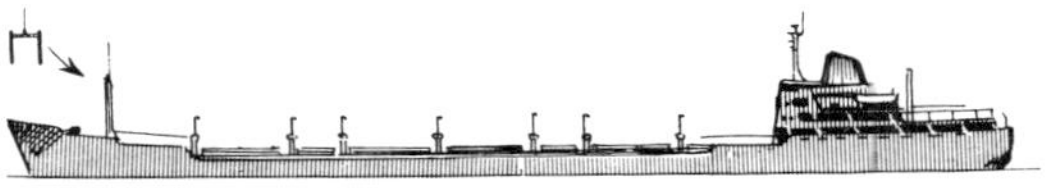

M_2FK H13
● **89950 RIO BRAVO.** Gr/Br 1960; B; 12000; 169.88 × 9.68 (557.35 × 31.76); M; 14.5; ex CUYO 1978; ex DRYMOS 1975; ex ST. MARY 1974; ex TRESFONN 1973; Sisters: **89951 SARANDI** (Ar); ex SAN FRANCESCO 1974; ex KROSSFONN 1972.

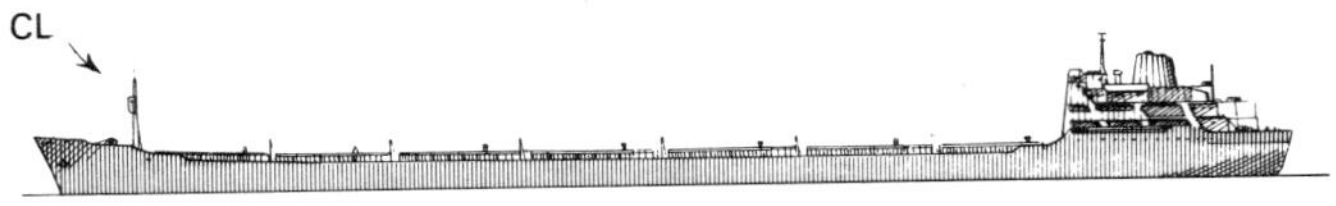

M_2FK H13
89960 ACHILLEUS. Gr/Ja 1961; B; 16500; 198.08 × 10.53 (649.87 × 34.55); M; —; ex GAUCHO PAMPA 1978; ex SKAUBORG 1973; Lengthened 1965; Sisters: **89961 GRIGOROUSA** (Li); ex GAUCHO LAGUNA 1980; ex GOLAR COAL 1970; ex SKAUHOLT 1966; **89962 ST. LAWRENCE** (Ca); ex GAUCHO TAURA 1976; ex SKAUSTRAND 1973.

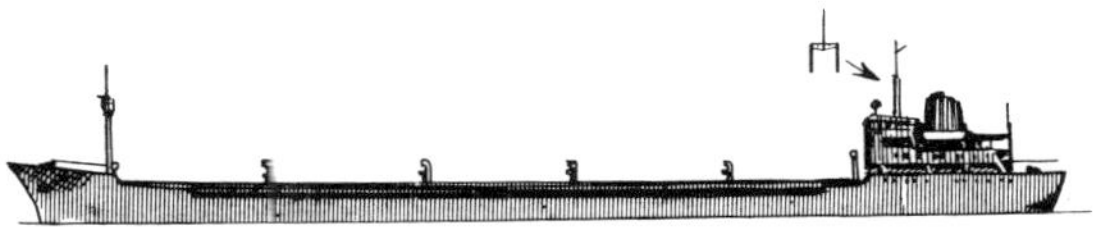

M_2FK H13
89970 KIMOLOS. Gr/No 1959; B; 12200; 166.48 × 10.24 (546.19 × 33.6); M; 15; ex ADONIS; ex HEMSEFJELL 1968.

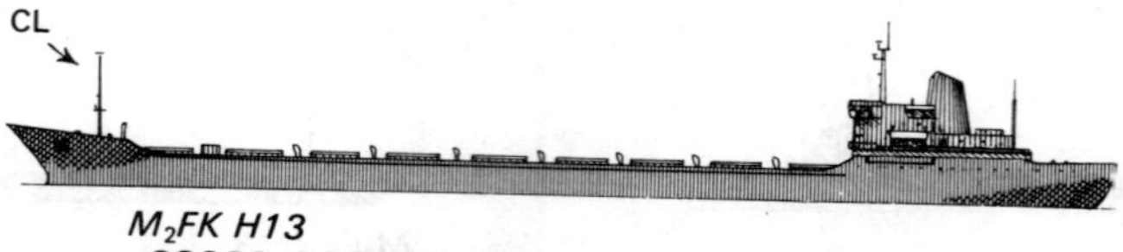

M_2FK H13
★89980 GORLITZ. DDR/Ru 1974; B; 22800; 201.38 × 11.21 (660.7 × 36.78); M; 15.5; **'Baltika'** type; Sister: **★89981 GRODITZ** (Ru); Similar: **★89982 NIKOLAY VOZNESENSKIY** (Ru); Similar (crane aft): **★89983 COLDITZ** (DDR).

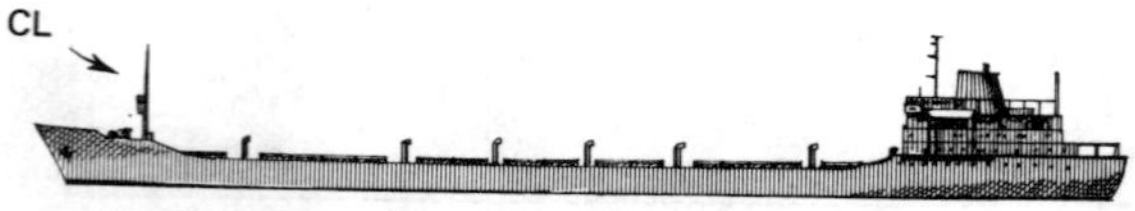

M_2FK H13
89990 FORUM GRACE. Gr/Sw 1963; B; 15600; 181.85 × 10.57 (596.62 × 34.68); M; 15.5; ex CAPE PACIFIC; ex UPPLAND 1976.

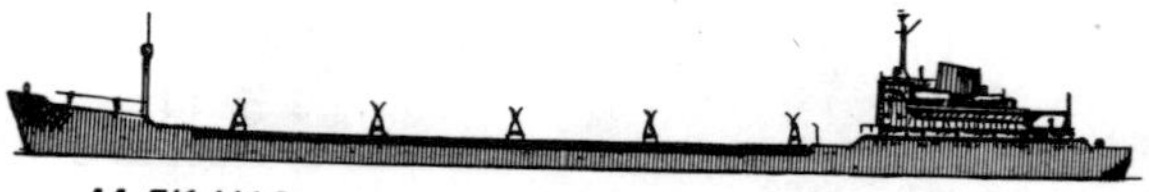

M_2FK H13
90000 ELISA. Gr/Sw 1958; B; 12000; 177.65 × 9.13 (582.84 × 29.95); M; 14; ex TROLLEGEN 1977; ex AKTION 1972; ex ALTAMIRA 1969; ex CERRO ALTAMIRA 1968.

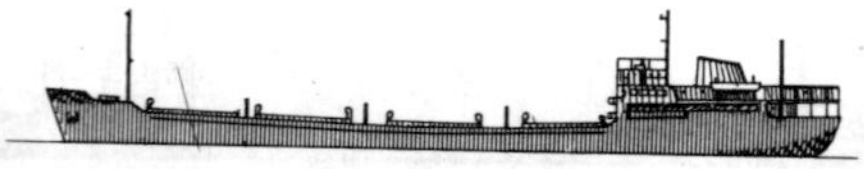

M_2FK H13
90010 MERINGA. Pa/Br 1958; C; 5500; 125.43 × 7.22 (411.52 × 23.69); M; 12.5.

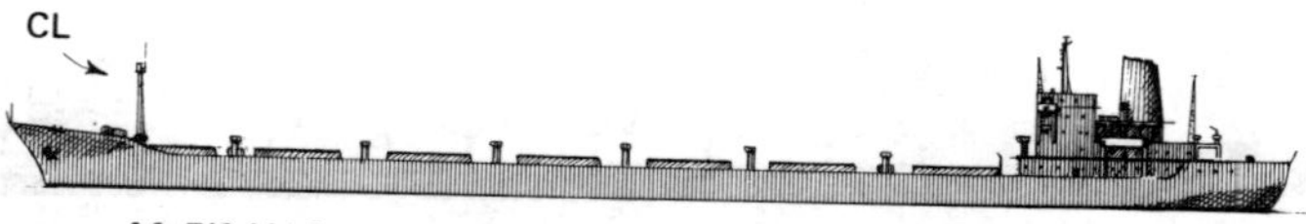

M_2FK H13
● **90020 NORTH EMPEROR.** Li/Ja 1967; B; 25800; 206.03 × 12.2 (675.95 × 40.03); M; 16.5; Sister: **90021 NORTH KING** (Li).

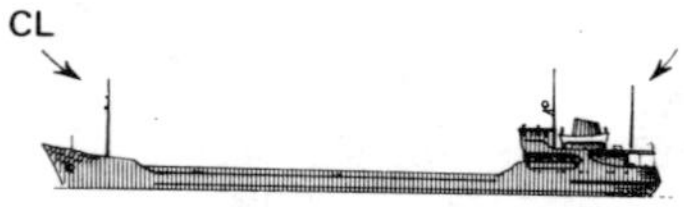

M_2FK H13
★90030 'BALTIYSKIY' type. Ru/Ru 1962/68; C (sea/river); 1900; 96.02 × 3.26 (315.03 × 10.7); TSM; 10; Vessel illustrated is BALTIYSKIY 32; Some have lower funnels; Aftermast omitted on some vessels; Sisters (Ru flag): from **BALTIYSKIY 1** to **BALTIYSKIY 73** inclusive.

M_2FK H13
90060 CECILE ERICKSON. Pa/Ja 1957; C; 3300; 113.54 × 6.24 (372.51 × 20.47); TrsM; 12.

M_2FK H13
90070 ROCQUAINE. Br/Br 1977; C; 1000; 66.91 × 4.12 (219.52 × 13.52); M; 11; Modified **'Colne'** type; Sisters (Br flag): **90071 BELGRAVE; 90072 PERELLE.**

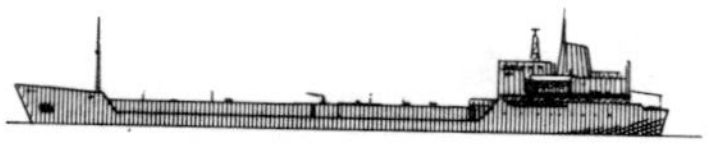

M_2FK H13
90080 BRIDGEMAN. Br/Br 1972; Tk; 3700; 103.64 × 6.99 (340.03 × 22.93); M; 13; Similar: **90081 HELMSMAN** (Br).

M_2FK H13
90090 ASSIDUITY. Br/Br 1964; Tk; 1200; 71.48 × 4.47 (234.51 × 14.67); M; —.

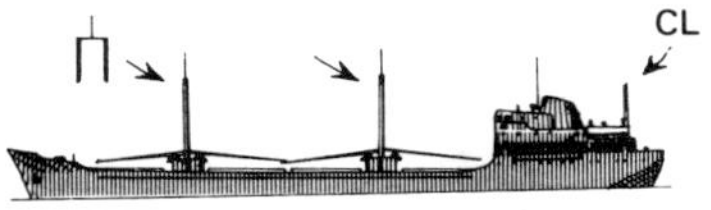

M_2FK H13
90100 PANAGIOTIS A. Gr/Be 1959; C; 2700; 103.66 × 6.41 (340.09 × 21.03); M; 14; ex GALAXY 1976; ex ANGARA 1970.

M_2FK H13
90120 JOHN M. Br/Br 1963; Tk; 1300; 70.11 × 4.83 (230 × 15.85); M; —.

M_2FK H13
90140 ALACRITY. Br/Br 1966; Tk/Ch; 900; 65.99 × 4.36 (216.5 × 14.3); M; —.

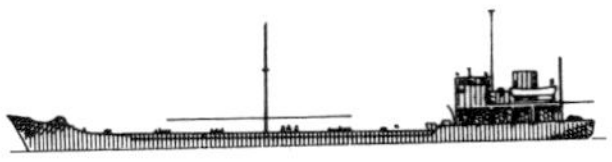

M_2FK H13
90160 DELBROS MT. APO II. Pi/Ja 1966; Tk; 2600; 92.79 × 6.3 (304.43 × 20.67); M; 11.75; ex NICHIYO MARU 1970; Possibly Similar: **90161 NISSHIN MARU** (Ja).

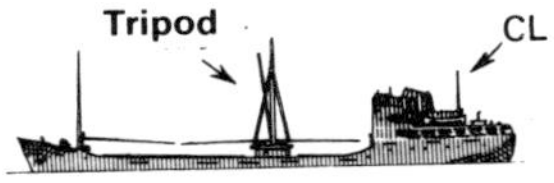

M_2FK H13
90180 GLORIA MARIS. Pa/Ne 1957; C/HL; 1500; 77.5 × 4.7 (254.27 × 15.42); M; 10.5.

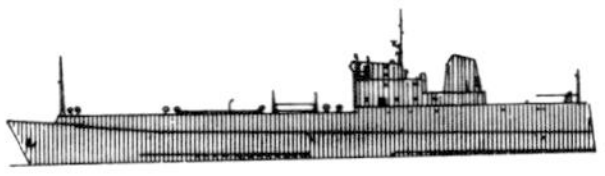

M_2FK H2
90200 AUTOSTRADA. Br/No 1971; RoVC; 600; 92.36 × 3.89 (303 × 12.76); M; 14.25; Stern door/ramp; Sister: **90201 AUTOLLOYD** (Bz); ex AUTOROUTE 1976.

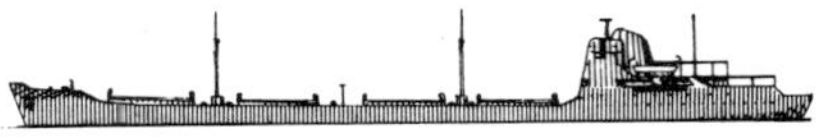

M_2FK H13
90110 AVANCE. Gr/Br 1960; B; 6600; 126.19 × 8.57 (414 × 28.12); M; 13; ex ARTHUR ALBRIGHT 1968.

M_2FK H13
90130 FRANK M. Br/Br 1965; Tk; 1300; 70.72 × 4.83 (232 × 15.85); M; —; Sister: **90131 NICHOLAS M** (Br).

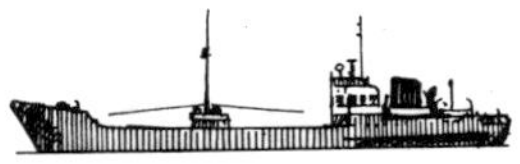

M_2FK H13
★**90150 KUSTANAY.** Ru/Sw 1955; FF; 1800; 79.25 × 6.12 (260 × 20.08); M; 11.5; Sisters (Ru flag): ★**90151 MAGADAN;** ★**90152 POLESSK;** ★**90153 SARANSK;** ★**90154 ZELENOGRAD.**

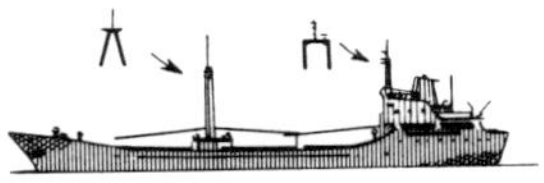

M_2FK H13
90170 KEMAL KOLOTOGLU. Tu/Tu 1978; C; 1600; 79.84 × — (261.94 × —); M; 12; Probable Sister: **90171 HACI ARIF KAPTAN** (Tu).

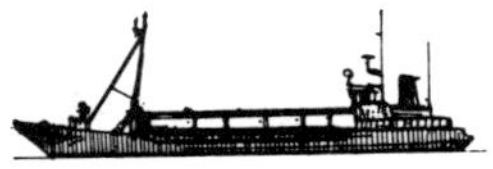

M_2FK H13
★**90190 YANA.** Ru/— 1974; D; —; 72 × — (236.22 × —); M; —; Sister: ★**90101 URENGOI** (Ru).

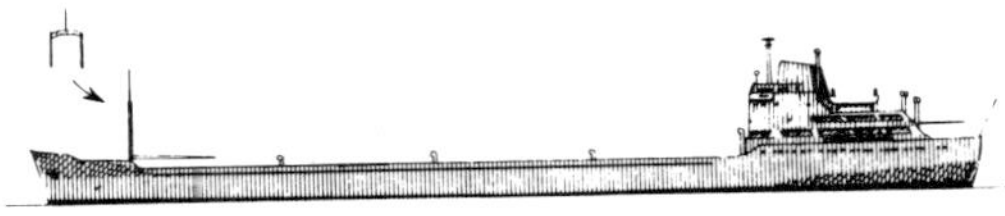

M_2FK_2 H13
90210 FISONS REALF. No/Sw 1955; B; 10800; 149.36 × 9.6 (490.03 × 31.5); M; 14.5; ex ABISKO 1964.

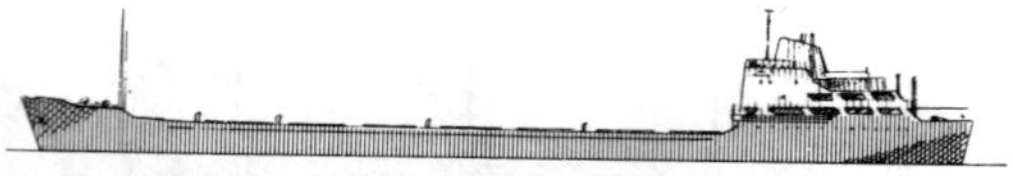

M_2FK_2 H13
⋆**90220 YAMPOL.** Ru/Sw 1959; B; 10600; 149.36 × 9.6 (490.03 × 31.5); M; 14.25; ex AVAFORS 1976; Sister: ⋆**90221 YASNOGORSK** (Ru); ex ARVIDSJAUR 1976; Possible sister (may be KMFK): ⋆**90222 YARTSYEVO** (Ru); ex ADAK 1976; Similar: ⋆**90223 MIDJUR** (Bu); ex ALPHARD 1970; ex AVASAKSA 1966; **90224 TIGER BAY** (Br); ex VOLA 1980; ex ACHERNAR 1970; ex ALTA 1966; **90225 PRINCESS JADE** (Pa); ex ACANDI; ex PLUTON 1974; ex KOOKABURRA 1968.

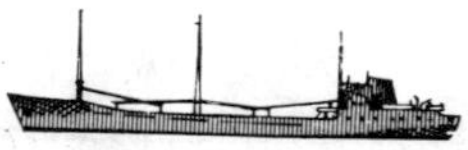

M_2KF H
⋆**90250 NERETVA.** Ys/FRG 1953; C; 800/1200; 71.66 × 4.52/5.59 (235.1 × 14.83/18.34); M; 11; ex KRKA 1973; ex HOLSTEIN 1964.

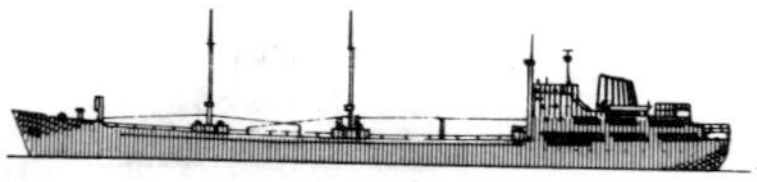

M_2KF H1
● **90270 ANDEN.** Br/No 1961; C; 2800/4500; 113.9 × 6.24/7.13 (373.69 × 20.47/23.39); M; 14.5; ex MANAURE II 1980; ex ARION 1975; ex BEAVERFIR 1972; Possible Sister: **90271 BOSNIA** (Pa); ex MAURITIUS 1978; ex CARINA 1975; ex POLLUX 1974; ex AILSA 1969.

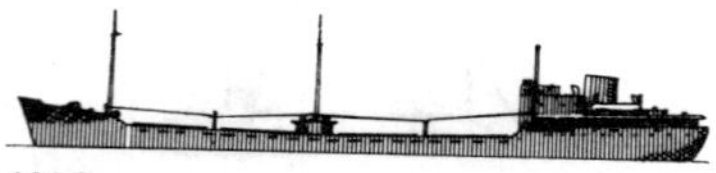

M_2KF H13
90290 GIANNA A. Gr/Br 1957; C; 3900; 108.69 × 6.65 (356.59 × 21.82); M; 11; ex ARLINGTON 1980; ex ASHINGTON 1978; ex TENNYSON 1968.

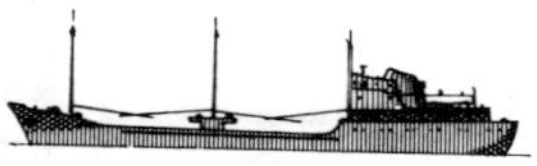

M_2KF H13
90310 REGINA EXPRESS. Pa/Ne 1962; C; 1500; 79.15 × 4.9 (259.68 × 16.08); M; 12; ex WINDLE SKY 1975; ex CAP FALCON 1973; ex LIS FRELLSEN 1967; Sister: **90311 DORTEA** (It); ex DORTHEA 1972; ex THEA DANIELSEN 1969.

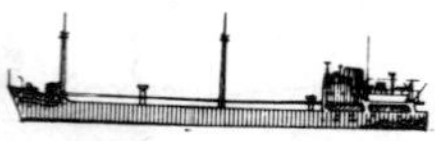

M_2FM H1
90230 FAROOQ. Bh/De 1956; C; 1000; 66.6 × 4.66 (218.5 × 15.29); M; 11.5; ex PELLA; ex SVANSUND 1971; ex IRIS 1968; ex HANNA DAN 1962; Sisters: **90231 KATERINA** (Gr); ex FREJ 1969; ex INGGA DAN 1962; **90232 LEDA** (Gr); ex KARNA DAN 1963.

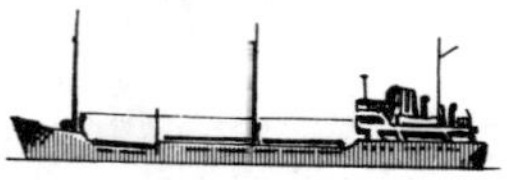

M_2FM H123
90240 LETA. Cy/Ne 1955; C; 1000; 71.94 × 4.85 (236 × 15.91); M; 11.5; ex EUROPEAN SKY 1978; ex CAROLINE H 1970; ex DURHAMBROOK 1969.

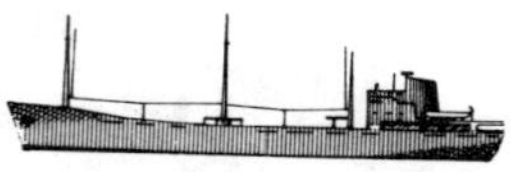

M_2KF H1
90260 NIKOPOLIS. Ho/FRG 1957; C; 1100/1800; 78.47 × —/4.9 (257.45 × —/16.08); M; 13; ex SEA HORSE 1 1979; ex SEA HORSE 1978; ex NORTHMAN 1978; ex INYULA 1977; ex ERNA WITT 1963.

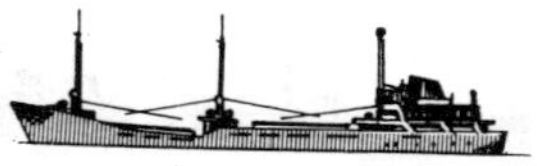

M_2KF H12
90280 FOTIS. Gr/FRG 1961; C; 1600; 77.81 × 5.4 (255.28 × 17.72); M; 12; ex NOLESE 1975; ex ELSE RETZLAFF 1971.

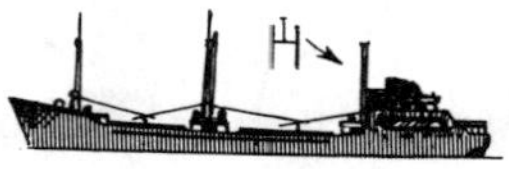

M_2KF H13
90300 ABDUL RAZZAK. Le/FRG 1956; C; 900/1400; 74.48 × 3.82/5.12 (244.36 × 12.53/16.8); M; 13; ex ATLANTA 1974; ex BONITA 1968.

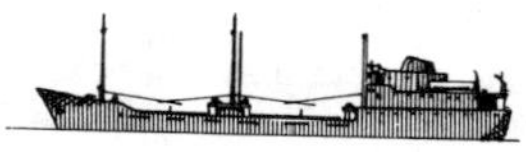

M_2KF H13
90320 OMAR EXPRESS. Pa/Ne 1962; C; 700/1400; 73.54 × 3.96/4.96 (241.27 × 12.99/16.27); M; 12.5; ex BIROONI 1971; ex NICO P.W. 1969.

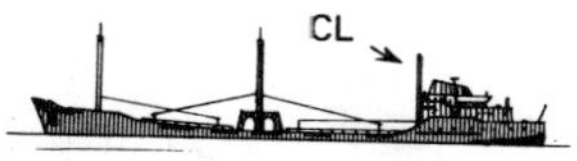

M_2KF H13
90330 TOPAZ. Br/Br 1962; C; 1600; 81.62 × 5.21 (267.78 × 17.09); M; 13.

M_2KF H13
90340 KYDONIA. Gr/Is 1965; C; 1300/2000; 84.31 × —/6.27 (276.61 × —/20.57); M; —; ex HANNA 1976; Sisters: **90341 MASSALIA** (Gr) ex LEA 1974; **90342 KOTA BANTENG** (Sg) ex EASTERN LUCK 1974; ex SARA 1974; **90343 KOTAH GAJAH** (Sg) ex EASTERN PROSPEROUS 1974; ex MIRYAM 1974; **90344 MAYA** (Gr) ex HAVIVA 1978; **90345 GREAT POINT** (Pa) ex RIVKA 1979.

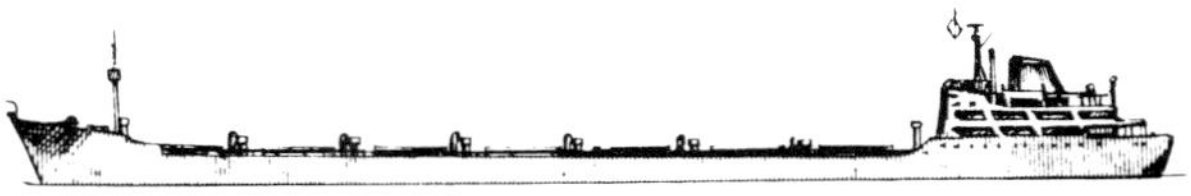

M_2KF H13
90350 AUBADE. Pa/Ne 1961; B; 14900; 180.35 × 10.85 (591.7 × 35.6); M; —.

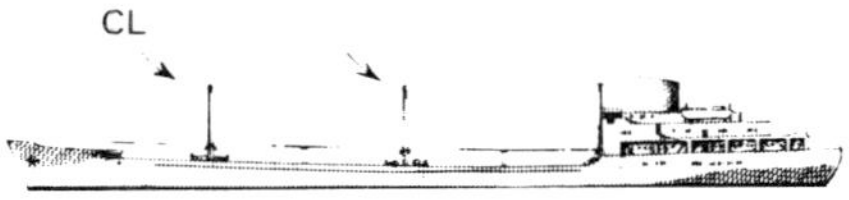

M_2KF H13
90360 OMEGA LEROS. Gr/Br 1960; C; 5800; 131.53 × 7.84 (431.53 × 25.71); M; 15.5; ex ELMINER 1980; ex VALLILA 1976; ex SUGAR CARRIER 1969.

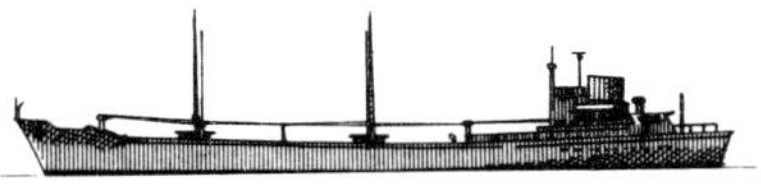

M_2KF H13
90370 BANG POO. Sg/De 1958; C; 5200; 125.56 × 7.82 (411.94 × 25.66); M; —; ex HANS MAERSK; Sisters: **90371 BANG LAMUNG** (Th) ex HARTVIG MAERSK; **90372 BANG NA** (Sg) ex ESTELLE MAERSK 1978.

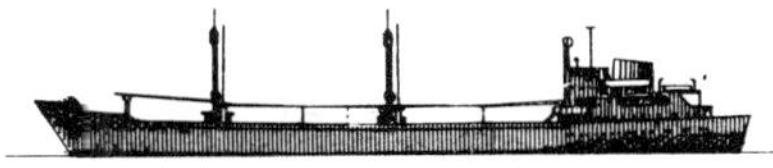

M_2KF H13
90380 MILOS VI. Cy/De 1959; C; 4700; 116.59 × 7.41 (382.51 × 24.31); M; 13; ex INTERSPIRIT 1980; ex HERTA MAERSK 1978; ex ROMO MAERSK 1972; Sisters: **90381 HIN ANN** (Pa) ex MARIJKE 1981; ex CHRISTINE SEAMONS 1979; ex MARIJKE 1979; ex HELENE MAERSK 1978; ex RAS MAERSK 1972; **90382 BANG PRA** (Th) ex HULDA MAERSK 1978; ex ROBERT MAERSK 1972.

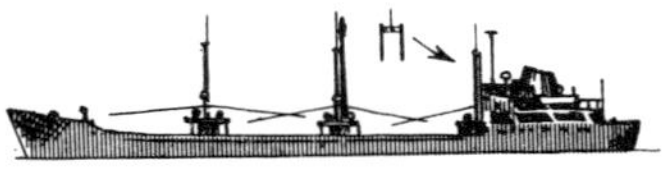

M_2KF H13
***90390 PINAR DEL RIO.** Cu/Br 1958; C; 3100; 101.94 × 6.29 (334.45 × 20.64); M; —; Sisters (Cu flag): ***90391 HABANA; *90392 LAS VILLAS; *90393 MATANZAS.**

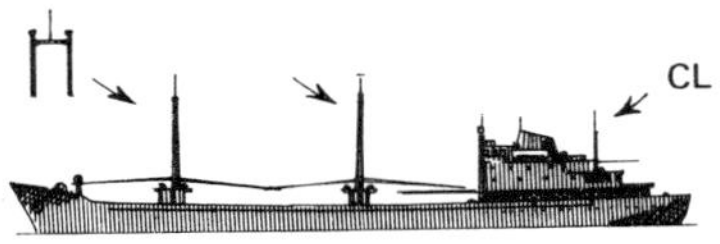

M_2KFK H1
90400 MILAS I. Tu/Sp 1964; C; 2600/4600; 107.12 × 6.45/7.53 (351.44 × 21.16/24.7); M; 14.5; ex VICTOR 1978; ex STUBBENHUK 1973; ex ALAR 1966.

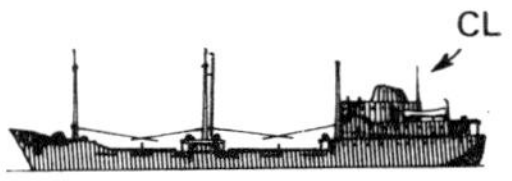

M_2KFK H13
90410 JOSE EXPRESS. Pa/Ne 1962; C; 1400; 73.54 × 4.96 (241.27 × 16.27); M; 12.5; ex ANY H 1971; ex ENY HOJSGAARD 1970.

M_2KFK H13
***90420 'VOLGONEFT'** type; Ru/Ru 1969-72; Tk; 3600; 135.01 × 3.5 (442.95 × 11.48); TSM; 10.5; This drawing represents the later vessels of this type. For earlier ships see 'VOLGONEFT' under M^4F. Names have the prefix 'VOLGONEFT' and a number. There are approx. 27 in the whole group.

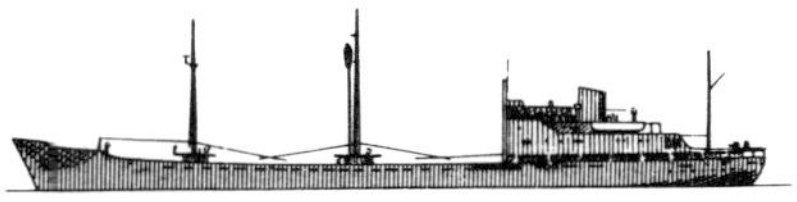

M_2KFM H1
● **90450 SOLOMON SEA.** Pa/Ne 1958; C; 2600/3800; 119.49 × 5.68/6.41 (392.03 × 18.64/21.03); M; 16; ex SEAMAID PROTO 1980; ex MEMNON 1973; Lengthened 1967; Sisters: **90451 MARATHON** (Gr) ex NIKI 1977; ex SAN SALAVADOR 1977; ex MARATHON 1973; **90452 PANORMUS** (Gr) ex EURABIA MOON; ex PARTHENON 1974; **90453 EFIE** (Gr) ex EURABIA SKY 1980; ex SINON 1974; **90454 ARTURO MICHELINA** (Ve) ex AMMON 1972; **90455 NELO ALTOMARE** (Ve) ex ARABIAN EXPRESS 1976; ex CHIRON 1974.

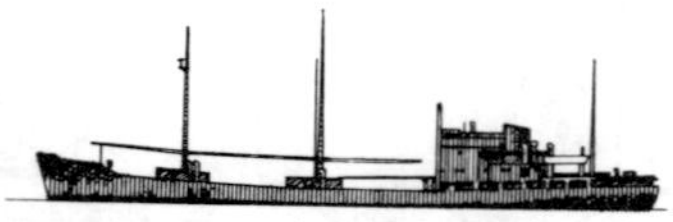

M_2KFM H1

● **90470 MALDIVE INDUSTRY.** Mv/Ne 1954; C; 2900; 98.3 × 6.27 (322.51 × 20.57); M; 13; ex CHARIS 1972; Sisters: **90471 KOTA BAHAGIA** (My) ex ADONIS 1972; **90472 KOTA HARAPAN** (My) ex ARTEMIS 1972; **90473 KOTA INDAH** (Sg) ex THEMIS 1972; **90474 MIMIS P** (Pa) ex ANNABA 1980; ex DAPHNIS 1971; **90475 SABAH A** (Si) ex THEODOROS 1979; ex GRACE 1976; ex ISA ANGELA 1974; ex ISIS 1970.

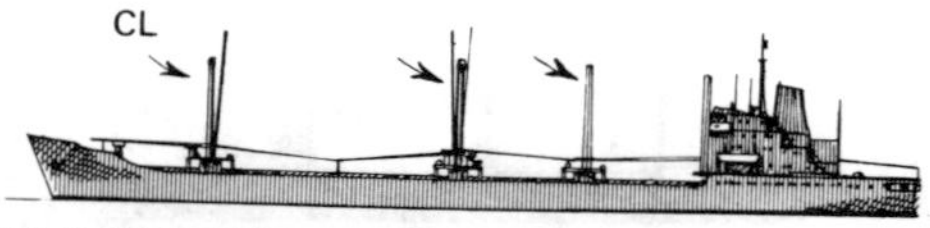

M_2K_2MFK H13

90500 ALPINA. Sd/FRG 1970; C; 6900/9600; 139.76 × 8.22/9.19 (458.53 × 26.97/30.15); M; 16; **90500 'German Liberty'** type; Possible sister: **90501 ASCONA** (Sd).

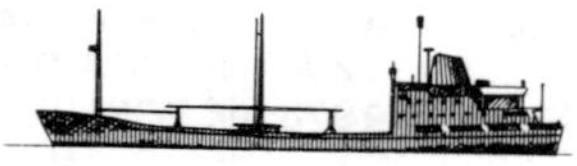

M_2KMF H1

● **90520 PERCY M CROSBIE.** Ca/No 1959; C; 2400; 83.83 × 6.05 (275.03 × 19.85); M; 12.5; ex PERLA DAN 1971.

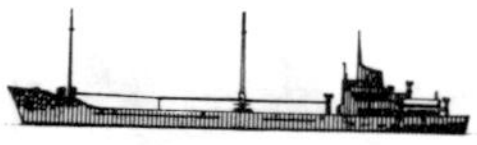

M_2KMF H1

● **90530 DORNACH.** Sd/Ne 1961; C; 1200; 73.51 × 4.57 (241.17 × 14.99); M; 12; ex ELFY NORTH 1969; Similar: **90531 ZEPHIR I** (Pa) ex MARIA MARE 1977; ex MALCHOW 1975; ex PERSEVERANCE BAY 1966; **90532 BEN MAJED** (Le) ex MAMAYA 1980; ex KRAKOW 1973; ex FORTUNA BAY 1965; **90533 SPYROS** (Gr) ex LIMPOPO 1977; ex BEREA 1975; ex KONGSHOLM 1968; **90535 AZIZA** (It) ex CORAL 1974; ex BIRTHE SCAN 1969; ex KNUDSHOLM 1968; **90535 EMEBORG** (Cy) ex SAEBORG 1977; ex PASSAT 1973; ex STAVHOLM 1969; ex KYHOLM 1965; **90536 HOURICO** (Li) ex JOVO 1979; ex VILSUND 1969; ex SKALS 1968; ex KLAUSHOLM 1968.

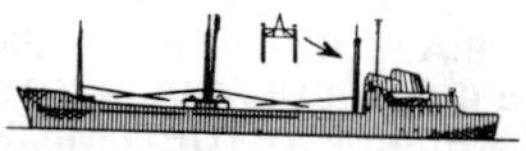

M_2KMF H13

● **90570 JEANNE D'ARC.** Le/FRG 1961; C/WT; 1100; 75.65 × 4.27 (248.2 × 14.01); M; —; ex NAZIH 1979; ex BARAKAT 1979; ex PALACIO 1977.

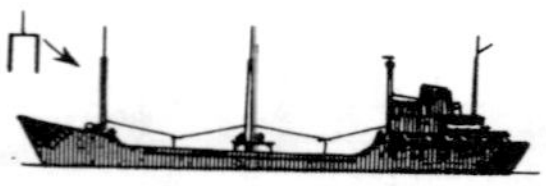

M_2KFM H13

90480 KETTY. It/Ne 1963; C; 1300; 80.68 × —(264.7 × —); M; 13; ex KETTY DANIELSEN 1970.

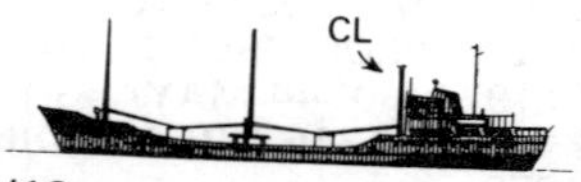

M_2KFM H13

● **90490 ARISTOTELIS.** Gr/Ne 1965; C; 1400; 80.68 × 5 (264.7 × 16.4); M; —; ex BREEVOORT 1977; ex FLYNDERBORG 1970; Sister: **90491 LEENA** (Ne) ex BREEVLIET 1975; ex FREDERIKSBORG 1970.

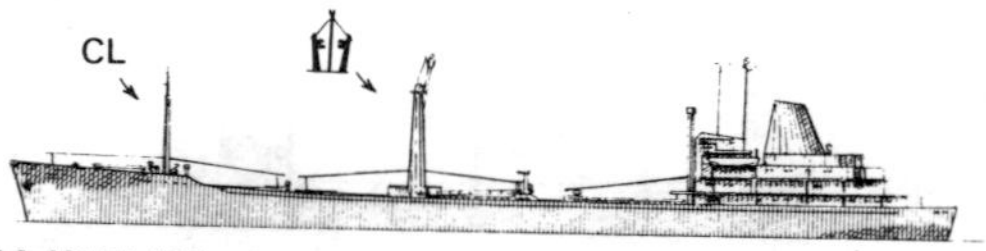

M_2KMF H1

● ***90510 DA LONG TIAN.** RC/Ja 1966; C/HL; 7010/9450; 152.25 × 8.31/9.48 (499.5 × 27.2/31.1); M; 19; ex CROSTAFELS 1978; Sisters: ***90511 DA HONG QIAO** (RC) ex KYBFELS 1979; ***90512 WU YI SHAN** (RC) ex BIRKENFELS 1978; ***90513 DA QING SHAN** (RC) ex SCHONFELS; **90514 FALKENFELS** (Gr); **90515 HOHENFELS** (Gr).

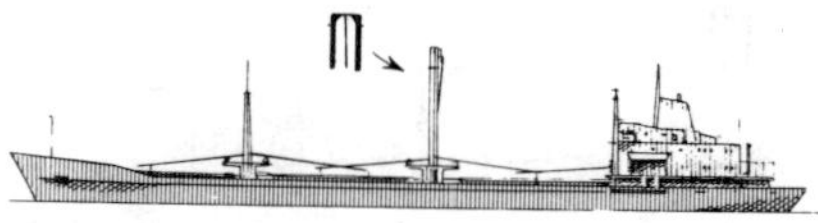

M_2KMF H1

90550 JUNO. FRG/FRG 1969; C; 2800/5000; 124.97 × 6.53/7.67 (410 × 21.42/25.16); M; 16.5; Sister: **90551 JUPITER II** (FRG) ex JUPITER 1980.

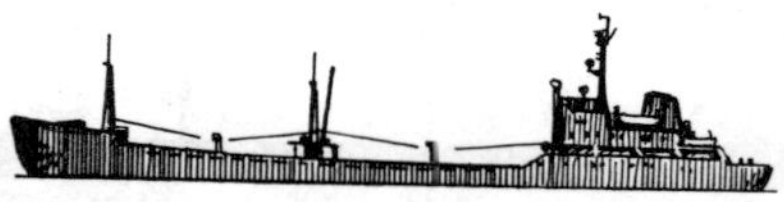

M_2KMF H13

***90560 MEZENLES.** Ru/Ru 1961; C; 4600; 121.77 × 7.16 (399.51 × 23.49); GT; 14.25; Sisters (Ru flag): ***90561 UMBALES; *90562 PECHORALES; *90563 TEODOR NETTE; *90564 JOHANN MAHMASTAL** (also spelt **IOHANN MAMASHAL**).

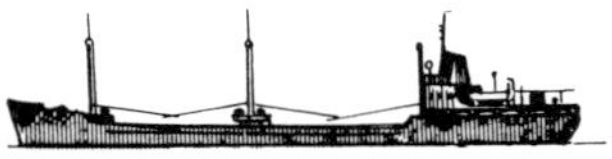

M_2KMF H13
⋆**90580 LIDIA DOCE.** Cu/No 1957; C; 2100; 91.27 × 5.82 (299.44 × 19.09); M; —; ex MARIA TERESA 1964.

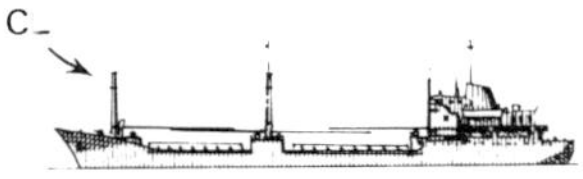

M_2KMF H13
90590 MARINER. Pa/Ne 1962; C; 1500; 81.84 × 5.45 (268.5 × 17.88); M; 12.5; ex MARIANA III 1974; ex MARIANA 1973; ex MARION 1970; ex KAISA DAN 1969; Sister: **90591 ETAI** (Br) ex YTAI 1977; ex CARMELA 1976; ex BAROK 1974; ex RAILA DAN 1969.

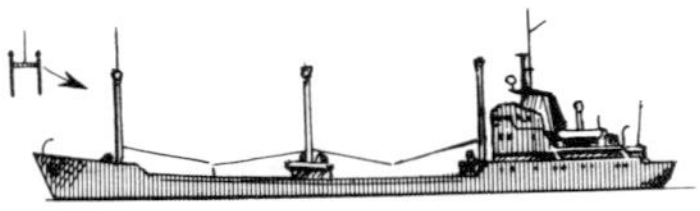

M_2KMF H13
● ⋆**90600 OELSA.** DDR/DDR 1967; C; 2500; 92.82 × 5.92 (304.53 × 19.42); M; 12.75; Sisters (DDR flag): ⋆**90601 EISENBERG;** ⋆**90602 HELLERAU;** ⋆**90603 THEMAR;** ⋆**90604 ZEULENRODA.**

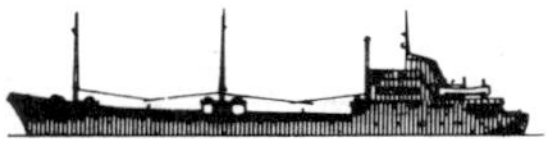

M_2KMF H13
90610 ATHINA. Gr/Sp 1966; C; 1000/1600; 82.5 × —/6 (270.67 × —/19.69); M; —; ex PROTON 1980; ex MARICHU 1976; Sisters: **90611 ANDROS** (Gr) ex ZEBRAS FORTUNE 1980; ex MARIA DOLORES TARTIERE 1977; **90612 DROMON** (Gr) ex BERNADOS 1978; ex IRUS 1977; **90613 MARIA DE ARANZAZU** (Sp); **90614 MARIA DE COVADONGA** (Sp).

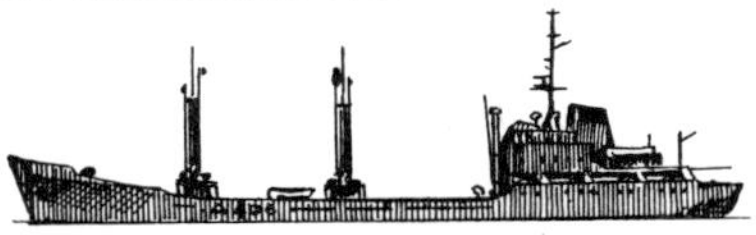

M_2KMF H13
90620 HEBE. Br/Br 1962; C/Sply; 4800; 115.6 × 6.73 (379.27 × 22.08); M; 15; Sister: **90621 BACCHUS** (Br).

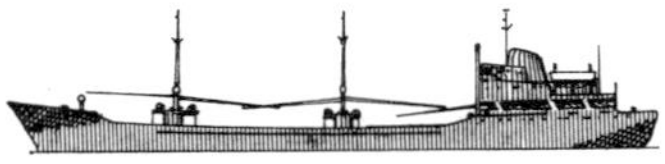

M_2KMF H13
90630 ULYSSES I. Pa/FRG 1959; C; 2300/3400; 103.33; ex YARDEN; ex GASOS 1978; ex YARDEN 1977; Sisters: **90631 KRANAOS** (Gr) ex ANTHOULA 1980; ex KINERET 1978; ex AGATE 1975; ex FABIO 1970; ex KINERET 1970.

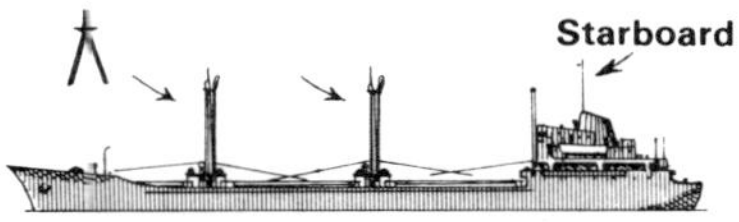

M_2KMF H13
90640 ASTRID SCHULTE. Cy/FRG 1967; C; 2200/3600; 107.85 × 6.31/7.42 (353.84 × 20.7/24.34); M; 15.5; ex CAP MALEAS 1978; ex ASTRID SCHULTE 1976; Sister: **90641 MORITZ SCHULTE** (Cy).

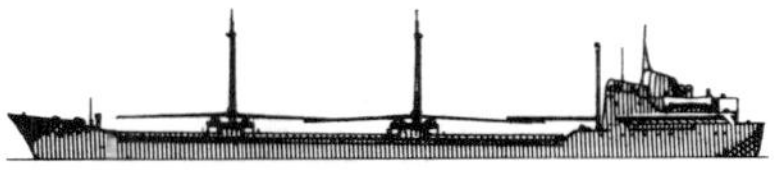

M_2KMF H13
90650 ACMI. Ag/Sp 1968; C; 4300; 117.96 × 6.71 (387.01 × 22.01); M; 14; ex SIERRA JARA; ex MIRENCHU 1972; Sister: **90651 ARIANNE LAURA** (Pa) ex KALLIDROMOS 1980; ex SPARTAN BAY 1976; ex ARCADIA WIEN 1973; ex MARTA 1971; Similar (taller funnel): **90652 LUCIE S** (Cy) ex JUPITER 1979.

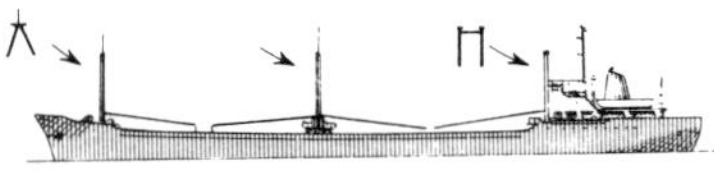

M_2KMFK H13
90660 TAIWAN MAHOGANY. Pa/Ja 1964; C; 3600; 105.29 × 6.25 (345.44 × 20.5); M; 12; ex SEIJUN MARU 1972; ex JUNSHO MARU 1969.

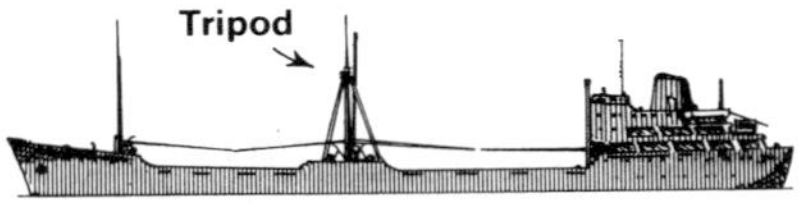

M_2KMFK H13
90670 ASAR. Pa/Ne 1957; C/HL; 3900/6000; 124.19 × —/8.19 (405.47 × —/26.86); M; 13; ex ELKINA; ex BELEVELYN 1972.

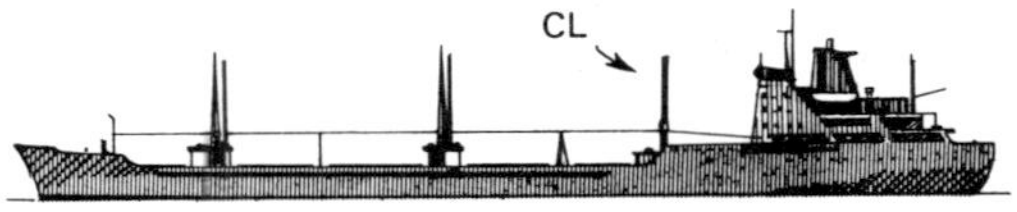

M_2KMFK H13
● **90680 AMPARO.** Pa/FRG 1967; C/HL; 8200/11400; 155.53 × —/9.44 (510.27 × —/30.97); M; 16.5; ex STAR ALCYONE 1974; ex HEERING LOTTE 1971; Sister: **90681 ELENA** (Pa) ex STAR PROCYON 1974; ex HEERING SUSAN 1969.

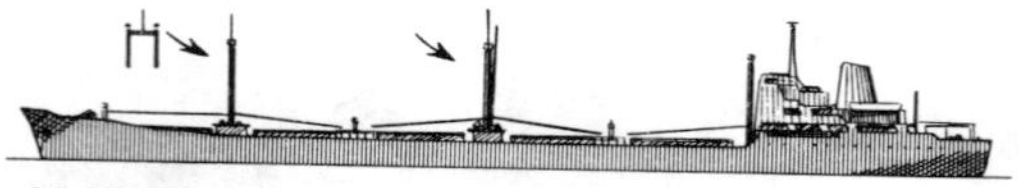

M_2KMFK H13
90690 ATROTOS. Gr/Ja 1961; C; 10900; 154.03 × 9.49 (505.35 × 31.14); M; —; ex APOLLONIA 1981; Similar: **90691 LINDOS** (Gr).

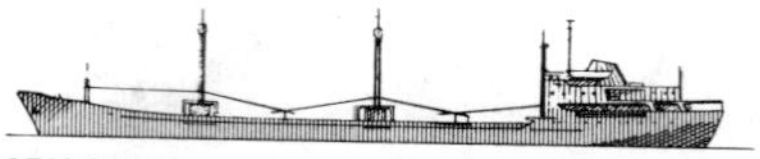

M_2KMFK H13
90700 MARKINA. Pa/Sp 1965; C; 3700; 111.69 × 6.09 (366.44 × 20); M; 12.75; ex MAURINE K 1980; ex HANNAH BLUMENTHAL 1975; ex PINTO 1969.

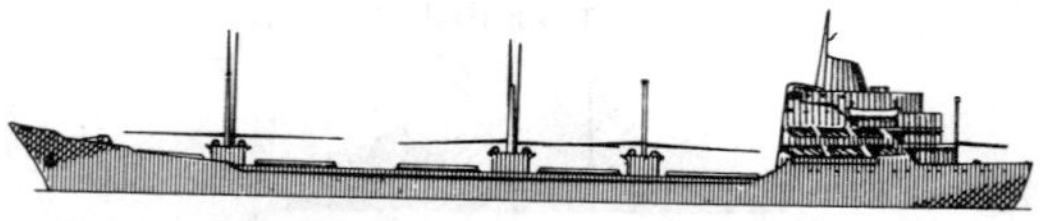

M_2KMFK H13
90710 PATRAIKOS. Gr/Fr 1962; C; 8800/11800; 162.64 × 8.69/10.05 (533.6 × 28.51/32.97); M; 16; ex DELPHIAN 1978; ex THORUNN 1971.

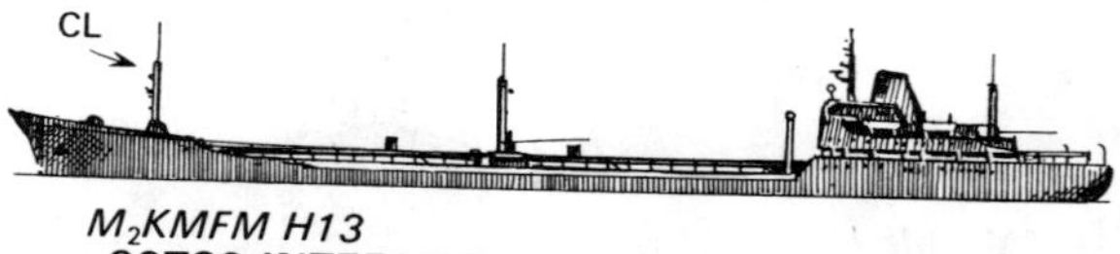

M_2KMFM H13
★90720 INTERNATSIONAL. Ru/Pd 1968; Tk; 14200; 177.27 × 9.37 (581.59 × 30.74); M; 16; **'B—72'** type; Sisters: **★90721 DRUZHBA NARADOV; ★90722 ISKRA; ★90723 LENINSKOE ZNAMYA; ★90724 NAKHODKA; ★90725 PROLETARSKAYA POBEDA; ★90726 PAMYAT LENINA; ★90727 PETR STUCHKA; ★90728 ZAVYETY ILYICHA.**

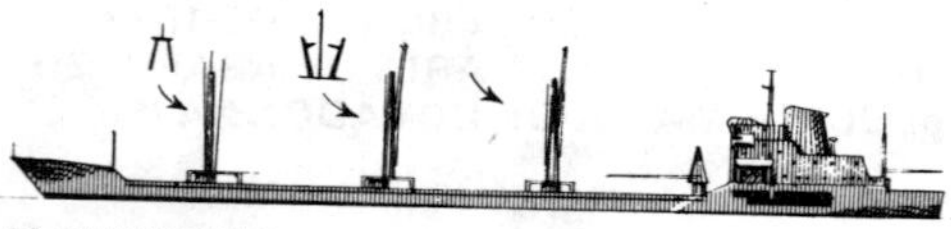

M_3CMFK H13
90740 NORTHWIND. Li/Sp 1970; B; 11300; 147.02 × 9.93 (482.35 × 32.58); M; 16; **'SANTA FE'** type; Sisters (Li flag): **90741 SOUTHWIND; 90742 WESTWIND.**

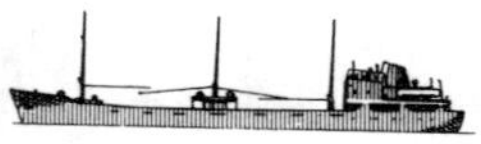

M_3F H
90750 DIES. It/FRG 1956; C; 900; 71.38 × 4.27 (234.19 × 14.01); M; 13 ex NORTHUMBRIAN QUEEN 1972; ex CHEVYCHASE 1972.

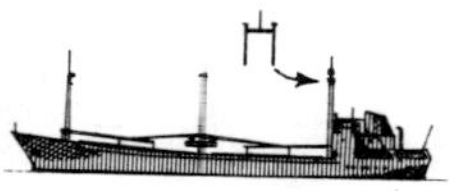

M_3F H
90760 RONNEBECK. FRG/FRG 1964; C; 500; 67.01 × 3.8 (219.85 × 12.47); M; 10; ex HEINRICH EHLER 1977; ex LEDINGERLAND 1969; Sisters: **90761 FRANZ HOLM** (FRG) ex ILSE WULFF 1971; **90762 MICHELE** (It) ex OSTERDEICH 1973.

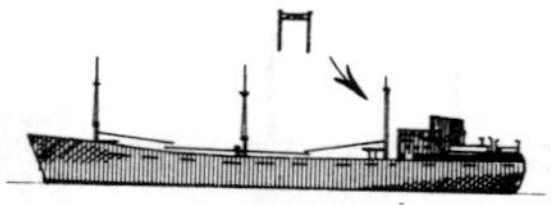

M_3F H
90770 KERKYRA. Cy/FRG 1965; C; 1600; 78.47 × 5.5 (257.45 × 18.04); M; 12.5; ex HAROULA 1976; ex SCHEERSBURG A 1970; ex SCHEERSBURG 1968.

M_3F H
90780 GRACE CALABAR. Cy/FRG 1956; C; 1500; 84.49 × 5 (277.2 × 16.4); M; 12; ex STEPENITZ 1977; Lengthened & deepened 1971.

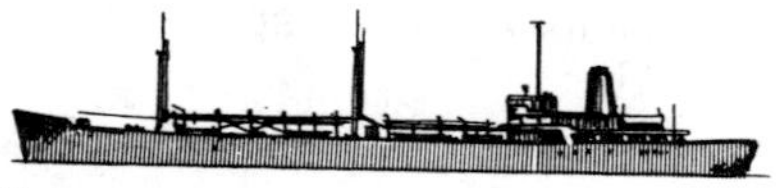

M_3F H
90790 MONOMER VENTURE. Pa/US-FRG 1945/62; LGC; 4600; 116.52 × 7.2 (382.28 × 23.62); M; 11; ex ESSO CENTRO AMERICA 1969; ex ESSO VENEZUELA 1962; ex MONTEBELLO 1947; ex TARAUCA 1945; Converted from 'T-1' type tanker and lengthened 1962.

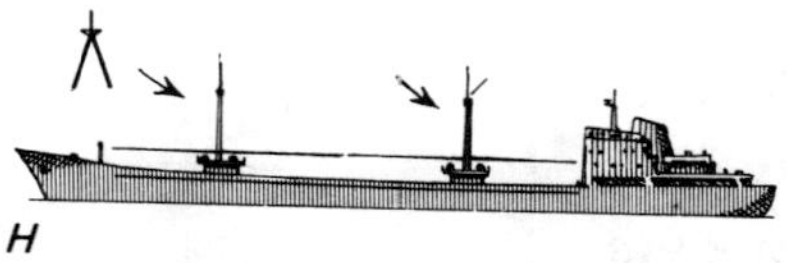

M_3F H
● **90800 MANAURE IV.** Ve/De 1962; C; 3100/4600; 119.54 × 6.07/7.01 (392.19 × 19.91/23); M; 15; ex LUCY BORCHARD 1978; ex HEERING ROSE 1969.

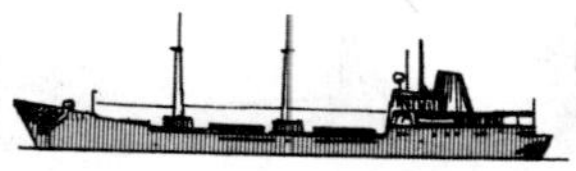

M_3F H
90810 REEFER MERCHANT. Cy/FRG 1967; R; 900/1700; 88.7 × 4.13/5.21 (291.01 × 13.55/17.09); M; —; ex FAHRMANNSAND 1974; Sisters: **90811 LUHESAND** (Cy); **★90812 HARMATTAN** (Pd) ex PAGENSAND 1972.

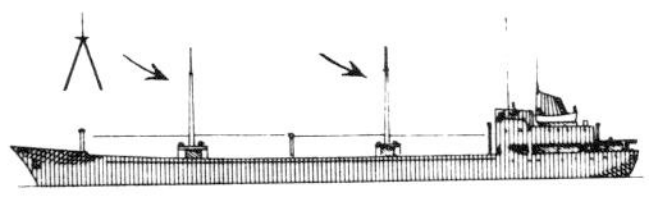

M_3F *H*
90820 CAPTAIN LEO. Gr/No 1962; C; 1900/3100; 99.22 × 6.52/— (325.52 × 21.39/—); M; 12.5; ex FROL 1972.

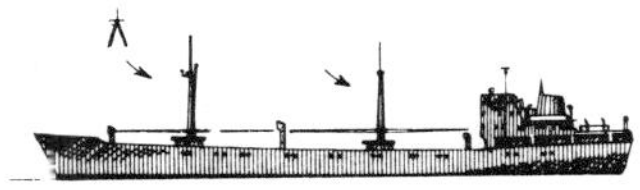

M_3F *H*
90830 IOS. Cy/No 1957; C; 2000; 96.12 × 5.75 (315.35 × 18.8); M; 12; ex LIA G 1979; ex DEKATRIA 1976; ex FORRA 1972; Similar: **90831 HELEN PAPPAS** (Gr) ex MARABOU 1980; ex SKAUMA 1971.

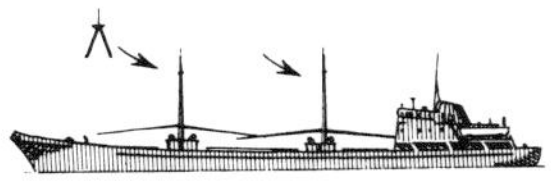

M_3F *H*
90840 RIO ASON. Sp/Sp 1965; R; 1500; 83.55 × 5.7 (274.11 × 18.7); M; 15; ex PUNTA UREKA 1967.

M_3F *H*
90850 RANNO. Fi/Fi 1966; R; 500/1100; 73.82 × 3 49/4.71 (242.19 × 11.45/15.45); M; 13.5; Sister: **90851 SAGGO** (Fi).

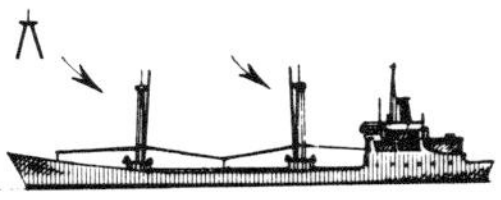

M_3F *H*
90860 ATLANTIC ISLE. Gr/Sp 1971; C; 800/1400; 77.4 × 4.07/5.32 (253.94 × 13.35/17.45); M; —; ex WICKENBURGH 1979; ex ATLAN TURQUESA 1975; Sister (Eg flag): **90861 AL BIRUNI** ex ATLAN ZAFIRO; **90862 AL IDRISI** ex ATLAN DIAMANTE 1975.

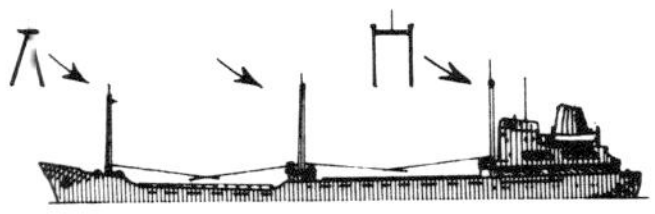

M_3F *H1*
● **90870 ESTHER CHARLOTTE SCHULTE.** Cy/FRG 1961; C; 2900; 94.01 × 6.77 (308.43 × 22.21); M; 13.5; Sisters (Cy flag): **90871 JOHANN CHRISTIAN SCHULTE; 90872 DONATA SCHULTE** ex JAN TEN DOORNKAAT 1973.

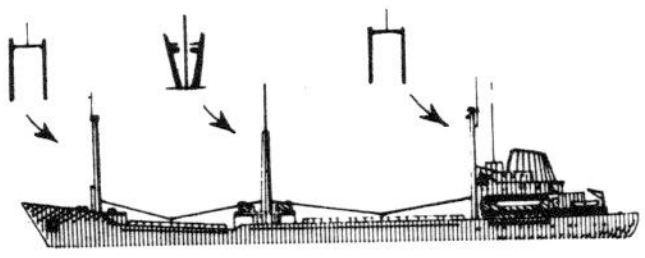

M_3F *H1*
⋆**90880 SECIL BRASIL.** Ys/FRG 1966; C/HL; 2000/3100; 98.84 × 5.72/.— (324.28 × 18.77/22.31); M; 15; ex PAPENBURG 1974.

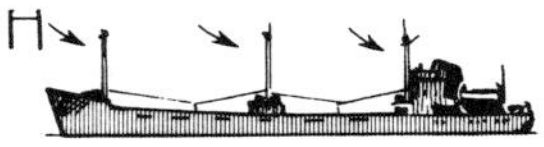

M_3F *H1*
● ⋆**90890 KURILA.** Ys/FRG 1958; C; 2000; 79.13 × 5.9 (259.61 × 19.36); M; 12; ex RAGNI 1974; Sisters: **90891 JAMEELA** (In) ex HIMING 1964; **90892 DOMINION TRADER** (Cy) ex FINNPINE 1967; ex NYX 1959; **90893 CRUZ DEL SUR** (Br) ex CARIBBEAN TAMANACO 1980; ex EVA 1969; ex TRONSTAD 1962; **90894 CRAZY HARRY** (Gr) ex SOFIA B 1980; ex NAVARINO 1975; ex MALKA 1968; ex NEGUS 1963; ex SUNNY GIRL 1962; **90895 TOUFIC** (Le) ex MAMMY YOKO 1978; ex CAPE COD 1975; ex HAMBURGER TOR 1972; ex ANGELICA SCHULTE 1969; **90896 HOE ONN** (Sg) ex NAIMBANA 1978; ex HAMBURGER MICHEL 1973; ex HEINRICH UDO SCHULTE 1970.

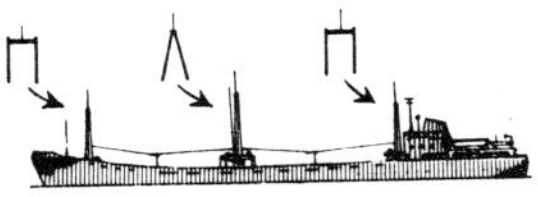

M_3F *H1*
90900 CHERRY CHANTEK. Sg/Ne 1959; C; 2000; 78.67 × 6.01 (258.1 × 19.72); M; 12; ex POLLUX 1974; ex FREUN 1959.

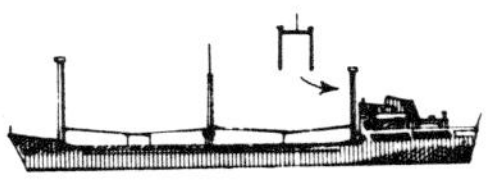

M_3F *H1*
90910 ARIES. Gr/Sp 1963; C; 1000; 74.78 × 4.89 (245.34 × 16.04); M; 13; ex ANAVISSOS 1976; ex SOUNION 1975; ex TEQUILA 1971; ex LINGLEE 1971; ex LINGLEA 1967.

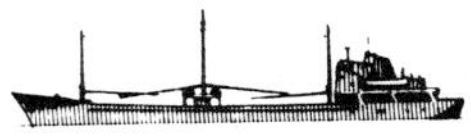

M_3F *H1*
● **90920 BIRKENHAIN.** Pa/FRG 1964; C; 500/1000; 69.8 × 3.72/4.96 (229 × 12.2/16.27); M; 12; ex ANNABELLA 1970.

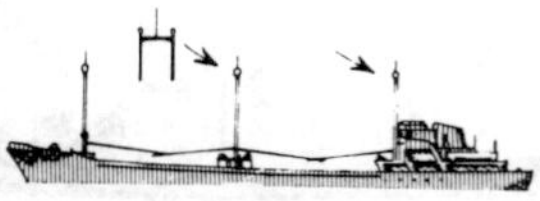

M_3F H1
90930 SALLY ANN. Pa/Sp 1963; C; 900/1600; 82.53 × 4.67/5.98 (270.77 × 15.32/19.62); M; 13; ex SIERRA ANDIA 1980; Sisters (Sp flag): **90931 SIERRA ARAMO; 90932 SIERRA ARANZAZU.**

M_3F H1
● **90950 SINGAPORE JATI.** Sg/Ne 1955; C/HL; 800/1200; 80.5 × 5.11/— (264.11 × 16.77/—); M; 10.5; ex BERNARD JOHN 1974; Gear amidships consists of quadpod & sheerlegs.

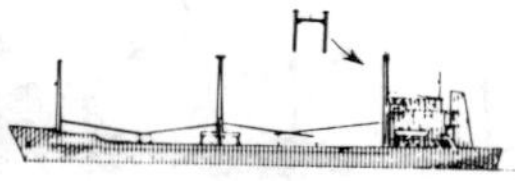

M_3F H1
● **90970 PIA DANIELSEN.** De/Ne 1976; C; 1000; 79.48 × 4.83 (260.76 × 15.85); M; 12.5; Similar: **90971 GUDRUN DANIELSEN** (De); **90972 HERMAN BODEWES** (Ne).

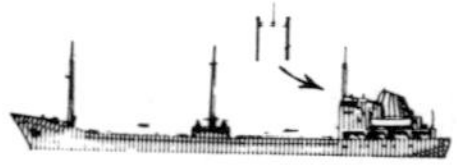

M_3F H1
90990 NORDWIK. FRG/FRG 1964; C; 500/1000; 68 × 3.82/5 (223.1 × 12.53/16.4); M; 11.25; ex PEP SEA 1974; ex SEEHAUSERSAND 1972.

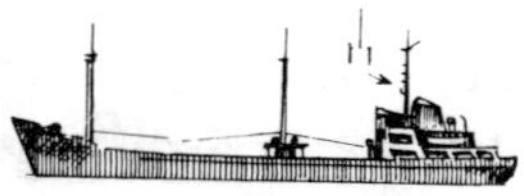

M_3F H1
91010 ANTARTIC. Ne/Ne 1967; R; 500/1400; 80.96 × 4.12/4.92 (265.62 × 13.52/16.14); M; 15; Similar: **91011 SANTA LUCIA** (Ne) ex COOLHAVEN 1975; ex FROST SCAN 1974; ex SPITSBERGEN 1972.

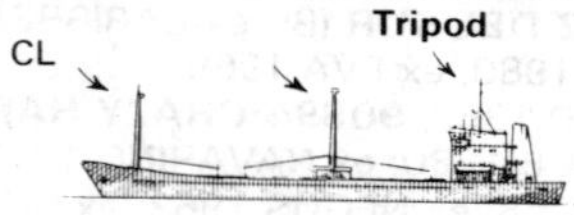

M_3F H1
● **91030 MIRA.** FRG/Ne 1974; C; 800; 76 × 4.45 (249.34 × 14.6); M; 11; ex AMIGO EXPRESS 1975; Similar (De flag): **91031 KASPAR SIF; 91032 JETTE SIF; 91033 ANN SANDVED; 91034 CHRIS ISA** ex BALTON 1975; **91035 RIKKE ISA; 91036 HERMAN SIF** ex GERDA LONBORG 1977; **91037 OTTO DANIELSEN** ex EGYPTIAN; launched as OTTO DANIELSEN; **91038 WINNI HELLESKOV; 91039 AMIGO FORTUNA;** (Ne flag): **91040 SWIFT; 91041 NIELSE DANIELSEN** ex AMIGO DEFENDER 1978; Possibly similar (De flag): **91042 INGE DANIELSEN** ex TROJAN PRINCE 1977; launched as INGE DANIELSEN; **91043 KETTY DANIELSEN; 91044 ERIK SIF; 91045 GRETE SIF; 91046 FRELLSEN HILLE** ex HILLE FRELLSEN 1980; (Fa flag): **91047 RUNATINDUR** ex LOTTE SCHEEL 1976.

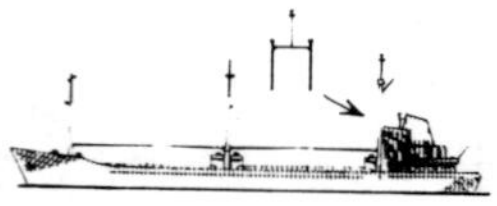

M_3F H1
90940 OCEANIA. De/De 1972; C; 500; 75.42 × 3.47 (247.44 × 11.38); M; 12; ex MOSS MAROC 1978; ex OCEANIA 1972; Sisters (De flag): **90941 ANNE METTE; 90942 ANNETTE S; 90943 ELIN S; 90944 SIGRID S.**

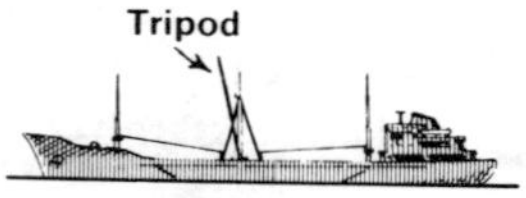

M_3F H1
90960 VALKENBURG. Ne/Ne 1966; C/HL; 500/1300; 75.42 × 3.99/5.01 (247.44 × 13.09/16.44); M; 10.

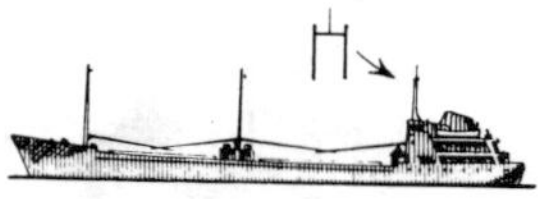

M_3F H1
● **90980 MINESOTA.** It/FRG 1968; C; 1000/1600; 80.09 × 5.11/6.05 (262.76 × 16.77/19.85); M; 13; ex ECKWARDERSAND 1981; Sisters: **90981 MINNEAPOLIS** (It) ex BOITWARDERSAND 1980; **90982 LEMWARDERSAND** (FRG).

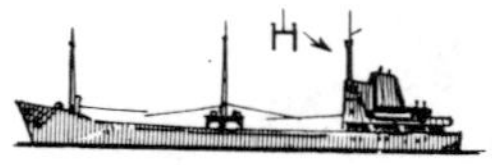

M_3F H1
91000 LADY SYLVIA. Cy/FRG 1965; C; 1000; 70.03 × 4.97 (229.76 × 16.31); M; 11.5; ex LIENERSAND 1972.

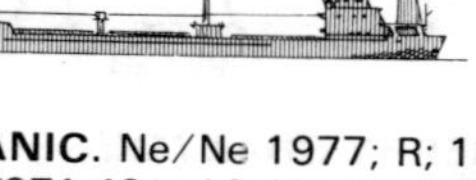

M_3F H1
91020 PACIFIC COUNTESS. Ne/De 1978; R; 1600; 74.5 × 5.01 (244.42 × 16.44); M; 13; ex GOMBA REEFER I 1980; **'613—B'** type; Sister: **91021 PACIFIC EMPRESS** (Ne) ex GOMBA REEFER II 1979.

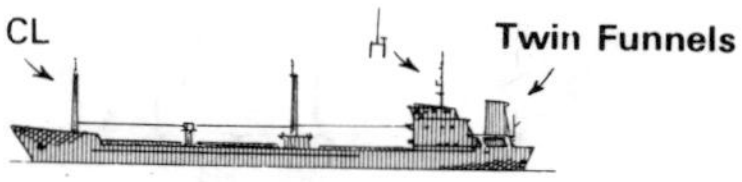

M_3F H1
91060 OCEANIC. Ne/Ne 1977; R; 1100; 82.73 × 5.01 (271.42 × 16.43); M; 13; Sister: **91061 ICELANDIC** (Ne).

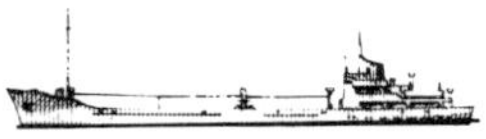

M_3F H1
● **91070 DORNACH.** Sd/Ne 1961; C; 1200; 73.51 × 4.57 (241.17 × 14.99); M; 12; ex ELFY NORTH 1969; Similar: **91071 ZEPHIR 1** (Pa); ex MARIA MARE 1977; ex MALCHOW 1975; ex PERSEVERANCE BAY 1966; **91072 BEN MAJED** (Le); ex MAMAYA 1980; ex KRAKOW 1973; ex FORTUNA BAY 1965; **91073 SPYROS** (Gr); ex LIMPOPO 1977; ex BEREA 1975; ex KONGSHOLM 1968; **91074 AZIZA** (It); ex CORAL 1974; ex BIRTHE SCAN 1969; ex KNUDSHOLM 1968; **91075 EMEBORG** (Cy); ex SAEBORG 1977; ex PASSAT 1973; ex STAVHOLM 1969; ex KYHOLM 1965; **91076 HOURICO** (Li); ex JOVO 1979; ex VILSUND 1969; exSKALS 1968; ex KLAUSHOLM 1968.

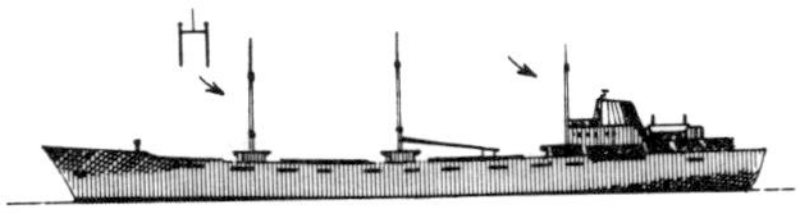

M_3F H1
● **91110 VIJAYA JYOTI.** In/FRG 1957; C; 3900; 114.05 × 6.12 (374.18 × 20.08); M; 15.5; ex VISHVA LALITA 1980; ex STERNENFELS 1968; ex NORPRADO 1957; This vessel capsized in harbour in 1980 and may be a total loss; Similar (In flag): **91111 VIJAYA JIWAN;** ex VISHVA ANAND 1980; ex STURMFELS 1968; ex NORTROPIC 1958; **91112 VISHVA PRATIBHA;** ex STOLZENFELS 1968; launched as NORCASTLE.

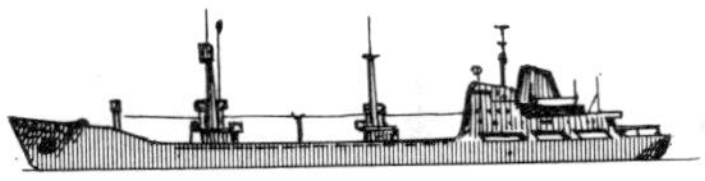

M_3F H1
91130 KUWAIT. Eg/Ne 1961; C; 3100; 96.96 × 6.64 (318.11 × 21.78); M; 13.5; ex KAKAWI 1975; ex RITVA DAN 1974; Sister: **91131 KOSTAS K** (Gr); ex SAIMA DAN 1975.

M_3F H1
91150 RIO ASON. Sp/Sp 1965; R; 1500; 83.55 × 5.7 (274.11 × 18.7); M; 15; ex PUNTA UREKA 1967.

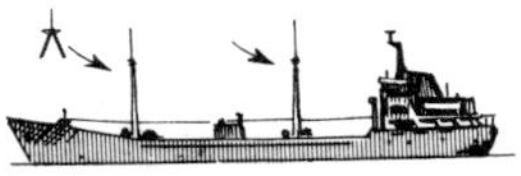

M_3F H1
91160 RANNO. Fi/Fi 1966; R; 500/1100; 73.82 × 3.49/4.71 (242.19 × 11.45/15.45); M; 13.5; Sister: **91161 SAGGO** (Fi).

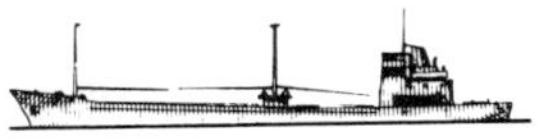

M_3F H1
91090 GERMA. Ly/Ne 1967; C; 500/1200; 76.87 × —/5.32 (252.2 × —/17.45); M; —; ex MARIETJE BOHMER 1972; Sister: **91091 LEONARD BOHMER** (Ne).

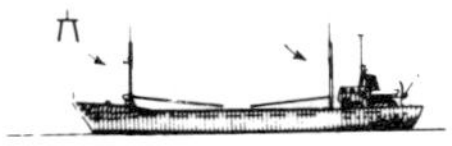

M_3F H1
⋆**91100 VELA LUKA.** Ys/FRG 1955; C; 300/600; 55.99 × 2.72/3.81 (183.69 × 8.92/12.5); M; 9.5; ex PIROL 1969; ex IPSWICH PIONEER 1968; ex MEISE 1960; Sisters: **91101 ALPHA** (FRG); ex STAR 1968; **91102 INGI** (Pa); ex PEWSUM 1973; ex UPPLAND 1971; ex SCHWALBE 1962; Some of these vessels may have the bipods removed, making the sequence KMF.

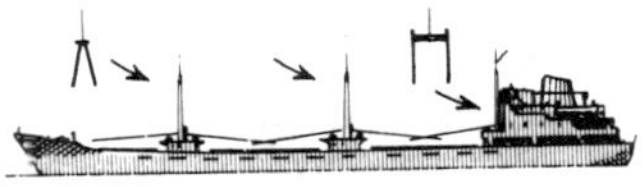

M_3F H1
91120 MARGO. Gr/FRG 1958; C; 1900/3000; 97.57 × —/6.69 (320.11 × —/21.95); M; 11.5; ex MALVINA 1980; ex RANGE 1972; ex SEADRAKE 1967.

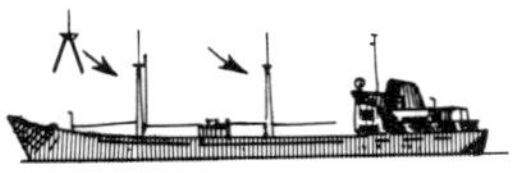

M_3F H1
● **91140 ASHRAF AL AWAL.** Si/Fi 1961; R; 500; 71.81 × 3.62 (235.6 × 11.88); M; 14; ex JARSO 1980; Similar: **91141 TINGO** (Fi); **91142 HERRO** (Fi); **91143 EVOCRYSTAL** (Fi); ex CRYSTAL GREEN 1975; ex CRYSTAL SCAN 1975; launched as ARCTIC SCAN; **91144 POLAR** (De); ex POLAR SCAN 1974; **91145 REEFER CARRIER** (Cy); ex EVOPEARL 1978; ex ICE PEARL 1975; ex REEFER SCAN 1973.

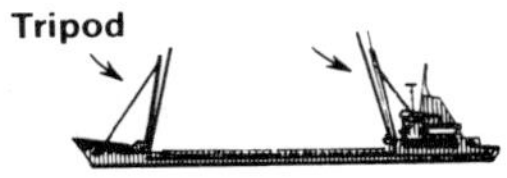

M_3F H1
91170 STELLANOVA. NA/Ne 1968; C/HL; 500/1500; 70.9 × 3.84/5.5 (232.61 × 12.6/18.04); M; 13.

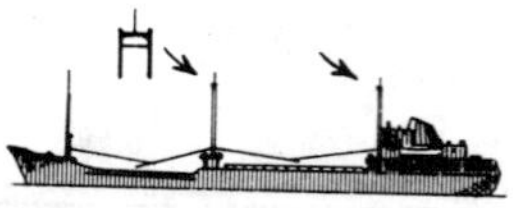

M_3F H12
91180 CLOUD. Cy/No 1963; C; 1200; 77.27 × 5.18 (253.51 × 16.99); M; 12; ex GULF AFRICA 1977; ex GRACIA 1974; Sister: **91181 PINGUIN** (It); ex DOMINIQUE 1978; ex SOKNA 1974; ex GLORIA 1971.

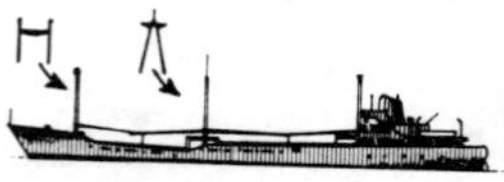

M_3F H12
91190 MABICA. It/FRG 1958; C; 1500; 76.59 × 5.32 (251.28 × 17.45); M; 12; ex EMMA RETZLAFF 1972; ex SEEFAHRER 1960.

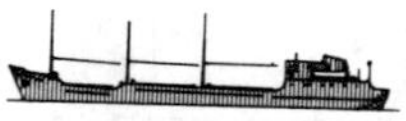

M_3F H123
91200 SATWAH. Db/Br 1962; C; 900; 59.44 × 4.28 (195 × 14.04); M; 11.25; ex YASIN 1980; ex SPRAY 1973.

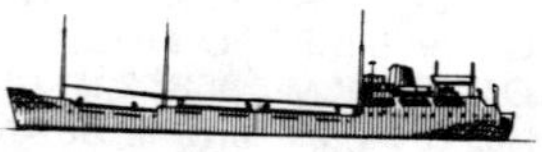

M_3F H123
91210 SAFRA PRIMA. It/Br 1957; C; 1900; 80.78 × 5.11 (265.03 × 16.77); M; 11; ex PALUMA 1978; ex MEDINA 1972; ex MARCHON TRADER 1969.

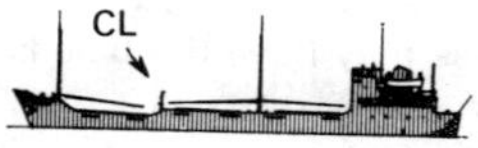

M_3F H123
● **91220 CARIGULF EXPRESS.** Pa/Br 1960; C; 1200; 70.03 × 4.59 (229.76 × 15.06); M; 11.5; ex MARY D 1978; ex TOWARD 1976; ex YEWGLEN 1974; ex TOLSTA 1971; Similar: **91221 RAYNESTONE** (Br); ex MAPLE 1974; ex MALTA FAITH 1973; ex SOUTRA 1970; **91222 RANA 1** (Le); ex ROSETHORN 1980; ex YEWKYLE 1974; ex LAKSA 1971; **91223 SABINA** (Sy); ex KATERINA PA; ex BELL CRUSADER 1976; ex AJAX 1971; ex FIDRA 1969; Possibly similar (converted to a cement carrier): **91224 ISLAND CEMENT** (Bs); ex LOGNA 1970.

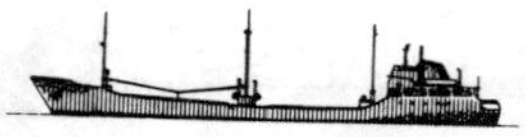

M_3F H13
91230 NEDA. Cy/FRG 1961; C; 1500; 74.68 × 5.65 (245.01 × 18.54); M; 12.5; ex MAX SIEGHOLD 1973.

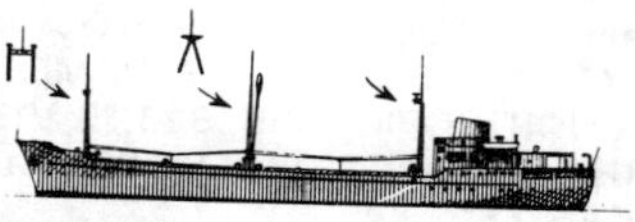

M_3F H13
91240 CASCIOTIS. Cy/De 1954; C; 1600; 93.1 × 5.35 (305.45 × 17.55); M; 13.5; ex FJALLFOSS 1977.

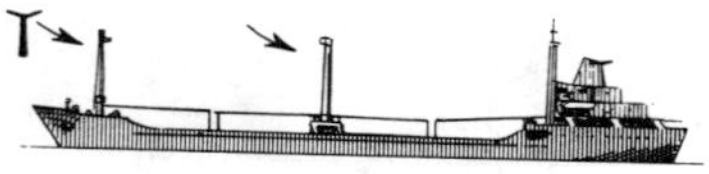

M_3F H13
91250 DOLLART. Sg/Sp 1971; C; 1500/3000; 104.25 × —/6.53 (342 × —/21.42); M; 15; ex AMBROSE 1976; ex DOLLART 1974.

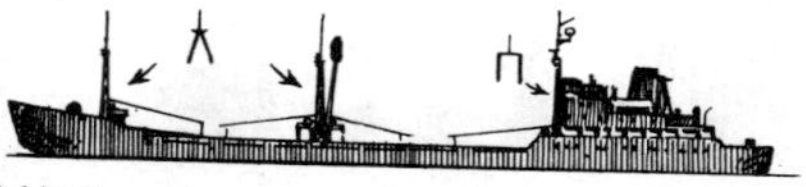

M_3F H13
⋆**91260 PAVLIN VINOGRADOV.** Ru/Ru 1960; C; 4600; 121.77 × 7.06 (399.51 × 23.16); GT; 14; See also MEZENLES—M^2KMF.

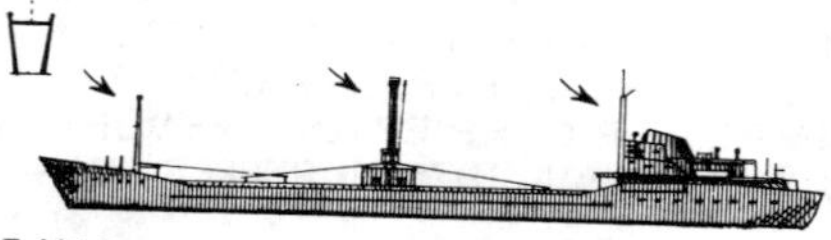

M_3F H13
91270 SOROLLA. Sp/Sp 1967; C; 5200; 124.21 × 6.66 (407.51 × 21.85); M; 13; Sister: **91271 RIBERA** (Sp); Similar: **91272 PINAZO** (Sp).

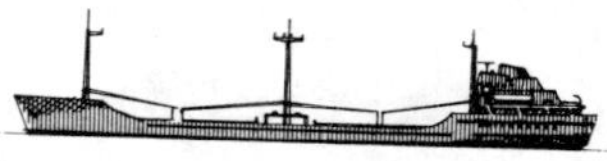

M_3F H13
91280 GEM. Br/Ne 1969; C; 1600; 92.72 × 5.19 (304.2 × 17.03); M; 12.

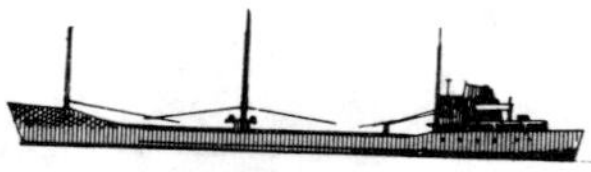

M_3F H13
91290 PEARL. Br/Br 1967; C; 1600; 92 × 5.2 (301.84 × 17.06); M; 11.5; ex SOMERSBYDYKE 1979.

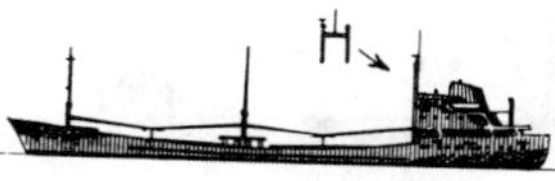

M_3F H13
91300 SUND. Pa/FRG 1967; C; 1600; 86.01 × 5.14 (282.19 × 16.86); M; 12.75; ex OSTESUND 1980; ex BREMERSAND 1973; Sisters: **91301 SIGRID** (Pa); ex WESERSAND; **91302 SARINE** (Li); ex NORDSEESAND 1977.

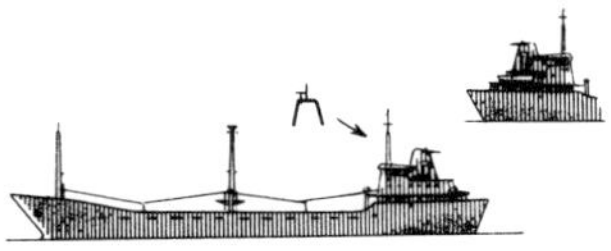

M_3F $H13$
● **91310 MERC CARIBIA.** De/De 1972; C; 500; 76.61 × 3.47 (251.35 × 11.38); M; 12; Starboard side superstructure differs—see inset; Sisters: **91311 ANGLIAN MERCHANT** (Br); ex MERC NORDIA 1977; **91312 LADY CONTINENTAL** (It); ex MERC CONTINENTAL 1981; **91313 NIAGA XXI** (Ia); ex MERC POLARIS 1979; **91314 NIAGA XXII** (Ia); ex MERC AEQUATOR 1979; **91315 PEP ORIENT** (De); ex MERC ORIENTALIS 1976; **91316 SLOT SCANDINAVIA** (No); ex MERC SCANDINAVIA 1980; **91317 TUNGUFOSS** (Ic); ex MERC ASIA 1974; **91318 UDAFOSS** (Ic); ex MERC AFRICA 1974; Similar: **91319 A.E.S.** (De); **91320 ADRIATIC** (Cy); ex PEDER MOST 1980; **91321 BRITANNIA** (De); **91322 CHARLOTTE S** (De); **91323 MOGENS S** (De); **91324 PATRICIA S** (De).

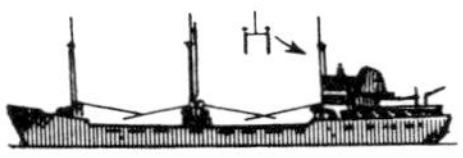

M_3F $H13$
91330 CHERRY MANIS. Sg/FRG 1957; C; 1000; 69.47 × 4.22 (227.92 × 13.85); M; 12; ex SINGAPORE MERANTI 1979; ex ARINA HOLWERDA 1974; ex HASELDORF 1970.

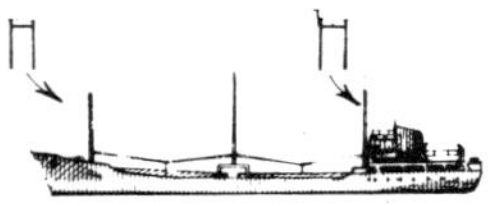

M_3F $H13$
91340 RAMSLI. No/FRG 1957; C; 1000; 71.38 × 4.7 (234.19 × 15.42); M; 12; ex AUSTV K 1980; ex MARIA ALTHOFF 1967.

M_3F $H13$
91350 PILION. Cy/FRG 1964; C; 1000; 71.63 × 4.93 (235 × 16.17); M; 11.25; ex CHRISTIAN MATTHIESEN 1978.

M_3F $H13$
91360 KANIELLE 1. Le/FRG 1953; C; 1600; 78.64 × 4.66 (258 × 15.29); M; 11.5; ex DANIELLE 1980; ex ARCHANGELOS 1980; ex BRAKERSAND 1972; ex FOSSUM 1961.

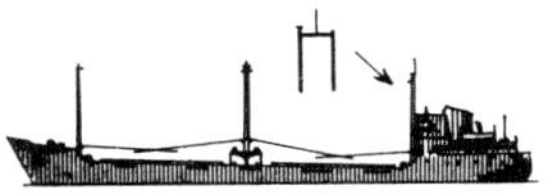

M_3F $H13$
91370 STONE AMBER. Br/Br 1958; C; 1600; 82.15 × 5.02 (269.52 × 16.47); M; 12; ex BURTON BARBER; ex KENTUCKY 1978; ex ALBI PIONEER 1977; ex C. BURTON BARBER 1976; ex MANTHOS M 1975; ex CANTICK HEAD 1971.

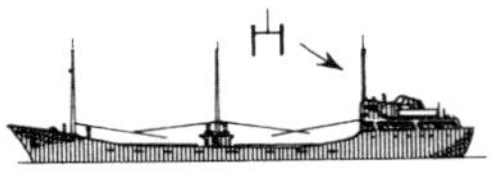

M_3F $H13$
91380 SIERRA. Pa/FRG 1959; C; 1000; 72.47 × 4.32 (237.76 × 14.17); M; 11; ex LIA 1979; ex ROTESAND 1975.

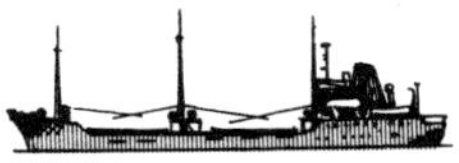

M_3F $H13$
91390 ANGELA. It/FRG 1957; C; 1000; 70.52 × 4.73 (231.36 × 15.52); M; 12; ex CONTENTIA 1970; Sisters: **91391 COSTAS G.** (Cy); ex KALI 1980; ex INANDA 1972; ex BERNHARD ALTHOFF 1959; ex PRUDENTIA 1957; **91392 THEOSKEPASTI** (Gr); ex REGNITZ 1971; ex FIDENTIA 1965.

M_3F $H13$
● **91400 ANNE OPEM.** No/DDR 1963; C; 500/1100; 75.24 × 3.6/5.19 (246.85 × 11.81/17.03); M; 11.5; ex SIRALYN 1975; ex HAVLYN 1973; ex BARI IV 1964; Sister: **91401 SIRAPIL** (No); ex HAVPIL 1973; ex BARI II 1964.

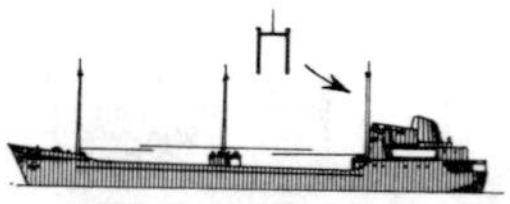

M_3F H13
91410 KEHDINGEN. FRG/FRG 1967; C; 500/1300; 75.34 × 3.71/5.55 (247.18 × 12.17/18.21); M; 13; Similar: **91411 HELGA WEHR** (FRG); **91412 WILKEN** (FRG); **91413 KREYVANG** (No) ex ANN-CARINA 1980; ex KUNSTEN 1979; ex CECILIA 1972.

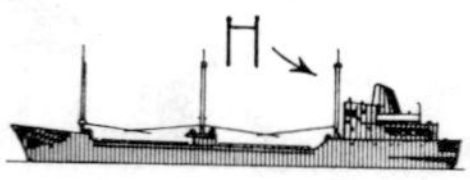

M_3F H13
91420 DISARFJELL. Ic/De 1967; C; 500/1200; 70.44 × 3.77/5.31 (231.1 × 12.37/17.42); M; 12.5; ex LENE NIELSEN 1973.

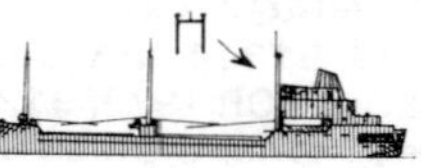

M_3F H13
91430 NIAGA XXV. Ia/De 1969; C; 500/1200; 70.44 × 5.3/5.54 (231.1 × 17.39/18.18); M; 12.5; ex DORTHE TY; ex BALCO 1975; ex LOTTE NIELSEN 1973.

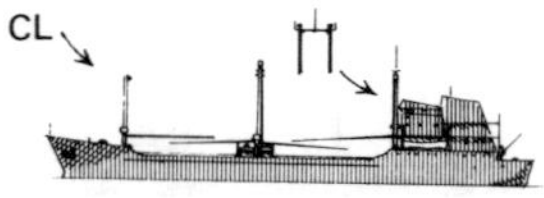

M_3F H13
91440 SABA. Ne/Ne 1970; C; 800/1600; 79.69 × 4.56/5.89 (261.45 × 14.96/19.32); M; 13.5; ex SHIPMAIR V 1978; ex GAELIC 1974; ex HENDRIK BOS 1972; Sister: **91441 ALIANORA** (It) ex SHIPMAIR VI 1980; ex GERD 1974; ex GERD BOS 1973; Probable sister: **91442 TIBESTI** (Gr) ex SAFI; ex IRMGARD BOS 1976.

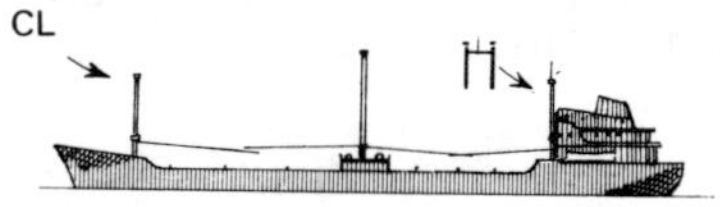

M_3F H13
91450 VICTORIA. Gr/FRG 1970; C/Con; 1200/2800; 99.04 × 4.24/6.3 (324.93 × 13.91/20.67); M; 14; ex RABAT 1980; ex INO A 1974; ex BOSTON EXPRESS 1971; launched as INO; Similar: **91451 CURRENT TRADER** (Br) ex MERCANDIAN CLIPPER 1980; ex DWEJRA 1976; ex INO F 1975; **91452 CURRENT EXPRESS** (Br) ex MERCANDIAN EXPRESS 1980; ex CARIBIC 1975; ex KATHE BOS 1973; **91453 TINHINAN** (Ag) ex HOLMIA 1975; ex JOHANNES BOS 1973; **91454 HODNA** (Ag) ex ANNETTA 1973; ex ANNETTE BOS 1972.

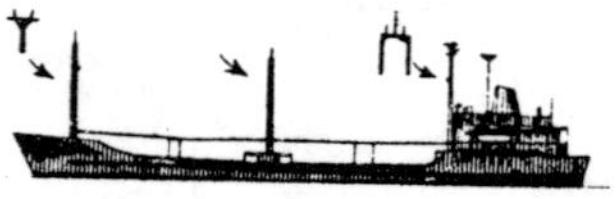

M_3F H13
91460 COLOMBO VENTURE. Pa/FRG 1970; C; 1700/3300; 100.56 × 5.47/6.76 (329.42 × 17.94/22.17); M; 15.25; ex ASHDOD Sister: **91461 APUS** (Is).

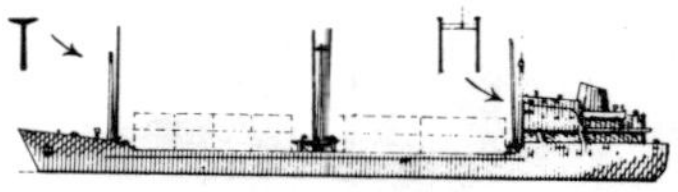

M_3F H13
● **91470 ILHA DE SAO MIGUEL.** Po/FRG 1970; Con; 2900; 102.42 × 6.24 (336.02 × 20.47); M; —; ex ANJA 1980; ex CHESHIRE CHALLENGE; ex ANJA 1974; launched as NORDERFEHN; Sister: **91471 PACIFIC** (FRG).

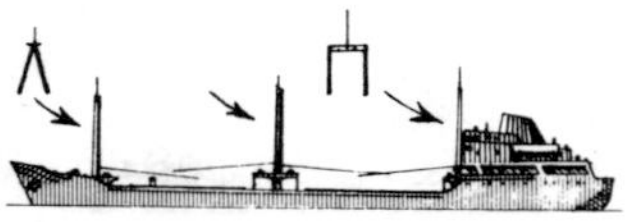

M_3F H13
91480 EDITH NIELSEN. De/De 1967; C; 1600/2700; 94.11 × 5.08/6.62 (308.76 × 16.67/21.72); M; 14.5.

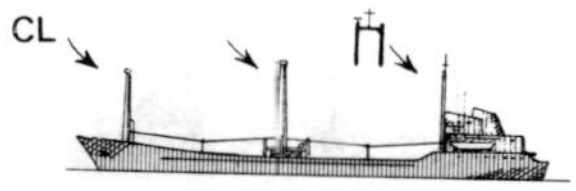

M_3F H13
91490 NIAGA XXIV. Ia/FRG 1969; C; 700/1500; 75.49 × 4.22/6 (247.6 × 13.84/19.68); M; 14; ex BILBAO; ex INGER 1973; ex TRURO 1971; launched as BELE; Sister: **91491 ELDVIK** (Ic) ex HEIDI 1975; ex TASSO 1971.

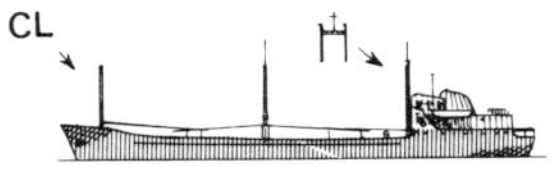

M_3F H13
● ★**91500 DRIANOVO.** Bu/Sp 1962; C; 500/1100; 74.91 × 3.56/4.93 (245.77 × 11.68/16.17); M; 12; ex AMETHYST 1970; ex SLITAN 1966; Similar: **91501 PUERTO DE AMBERES** (Sp); **91502 MONTE BALERDI** (Sp) launched as MONTE CUARTO; **91503 CEDAR PRIDE** (Le) ex SAN BRUNO 1978; ex PUERTO DE PASAJES 1969; launched as MONTE DOS; **91504 HELLINORA** (Cy) ex PATRICIO 1977; ex MONTE CINCO 1977; **91505 TRIOS** (Pa) ex KAI KAVOOS 1975; ex ECO SOL 1975; launched as SKAGATIND; **91506 VIOLA** (Pa) ex KAI GHOBAD 1980; ex ECO GABRIELA 1975; **91507 KAI KHOSROW** (Ir) ex ECO LUISA 1975; launched as MONTE UNO.

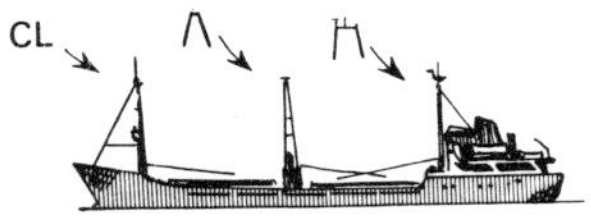

M_3F H13
● **91530 CAREBEKA VII.** Ne/No 1972; C; 1200; 77.17 × 4.76 (253.18 × 15.62); M; 13; ex NORTRIO 1974; Sister: **91531 MUNTE** (Ne) ex NORIMO 1974; Similar: **91532 MAASPLEIN** (Ne) ex NORCATO 1974.

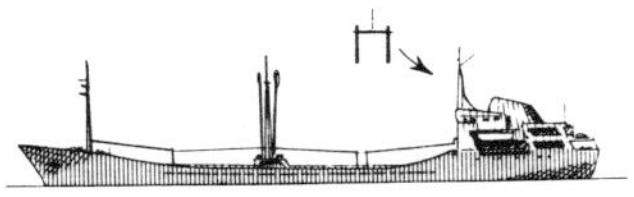

M_3F H13
● **91540 TEGELERSAND.** FRG/Ne 1969; C; 1000/2000; 92.33 × 4.65/6.1 (302.92 × 15.26/20.01); M; 15.

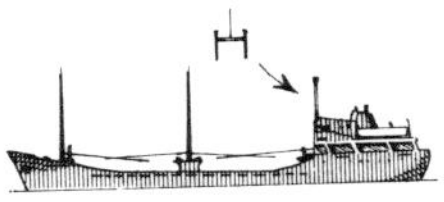

M_3F H13
91560 TITIKA D. Gr/FRG 1957; C; 1000; 65.31 × 4.29 (214.27 × 14.07); M; 12; ex STAR LION 1980; ex SKYLAB 1975; ex YEWARCH 1974; ex HINRICH SIEGHOLD 1960.

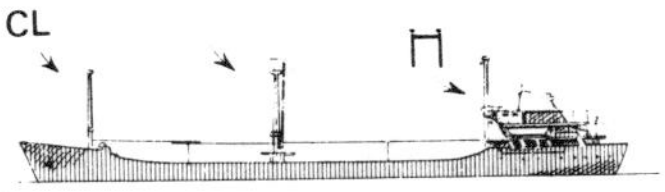

M_3F H13
● ★**91570 MIKULIC OREB.** Ys/FRG 1970; C; 2000; 95.28 × 5.53 (312.6 × 18.14); M; 14.5; ex BALTRUMERSAND. Sister: ★**91571 MARKO TASILO** (Ys) ex BORKUMERSAND 1980; Similar: **91572 MELLUMERSAND** (FRG).

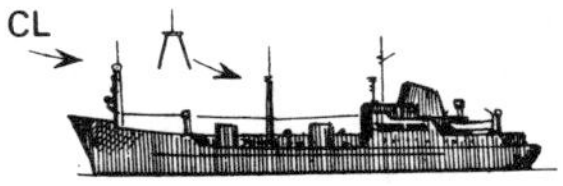

M_3F H13
91590 HEREFORD EXPRESS. Ne/FRG 1958; LS; 600; 71.96 × 3.57 (236.09 × 11.71); M; 13.5; ex NORANIM I 1973; ex ALONDRA 1973; Similar (lengthened): **91591 LIMOUSIN EXPRESS** (Ne) ex NORANIM II 1973; ex ATHENE 1973.

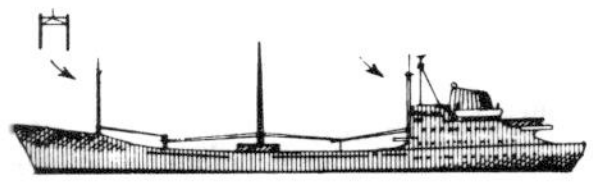

M_3F H13
91510 NAVISTAR. Le/FRG 1959; C; 1500; 91.01 × 4 85 (298.59 × 15.91); M; 14; ex BALTIC JET.

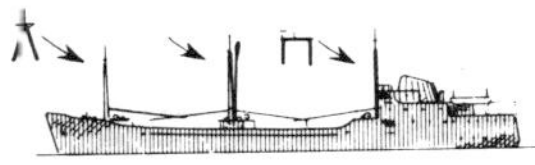

M_3F H13
★**91520 SUSAK.** Ys/Br 1963; C; 1100/1700; 74.73 × 4.31/5.77 (245.18 × 14.14/18.93); M; 13.5; ex PALOMARES 1973; Sister: **91521 PISANG PERAK** (Ia) ex BONAPART 1972; ex PELAYO 1971; Similar: ★**91522 SRAKANE** (Ys) ex PACHECO 1972.

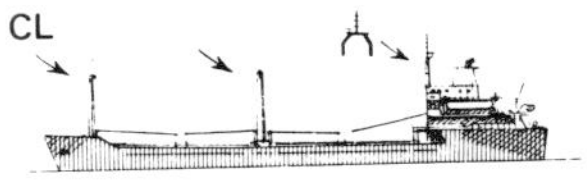

M_3F H13
91550 BREEKANT. Ne/No 1972; C; 1600; 79.91 × 5.28 (262.17 × 17.32); M; 14; ex KEIZERSGRACHT 1979; ex MINI SUN 1973; Sisters: **91551 BREEKADE** (Ne) ex MINI CLOUD 1978; **91552 CEBO MOON** (Sg) ex MINI MOON 1979; **91553 EERBEEK** (Ne) ex MINI SKY 1974; **91554 STROMBEEK** (Ne) ex MINI STAR 1973.

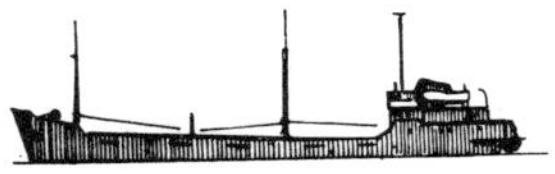

M_3F H13
91580 FAITH. Pa/Br 1958; C; 1600; 78.64 × 5.21 (258 × 17.09); M; 12; ex AMETHYST 1980.

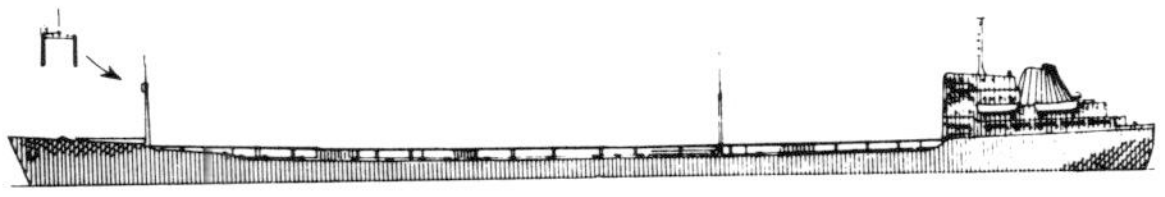

M_3F H13
91600 TEXACO BOGOTA. No/Sw 1960; Tk; 13600 181.67 × 9.57 (596.03 × 31.38); M; 14.5; lengthened and converted 1968.

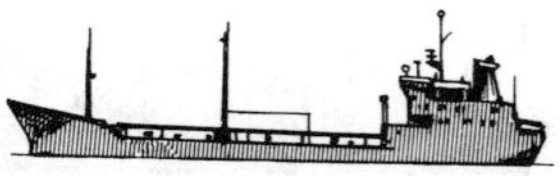

M_3F H13
91610 STELLA PROCYON. Ne/Ne 1978; TB; 2700; 83.62 × 6.61 (274.34 × 21.69); M; 11.75.

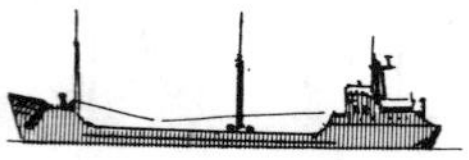

M_3F H13
91620 STAR ANN. Gr/Ne 1963; C; 900; 69.98 × 4.55 (229.59 × 14.93); M; 10.5; ex CAREBEKA II 1975.

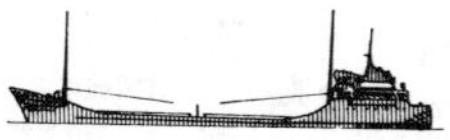

M_3F H13
91630 FIRETHORN. Br/Ne 1967; C; 1000; 67.21 × 4.59 (220.51 × 15.06); M; 12.

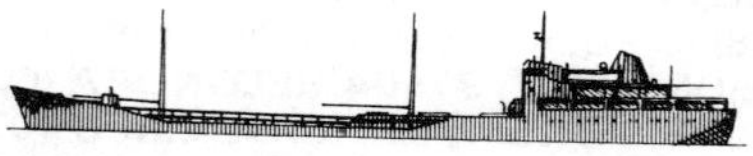

M_3F H13
91640 WADHURST. Br/No 1962; Tk; 3800; 114.28 × 6.54 (374.93 × 21.46); M; 13.25; ex SAPHIR 1970; Similar: **91641 BINTANG UTARA** (Pa) ex CALTEX SYDNEY 1975; ex WIDAN 1968.

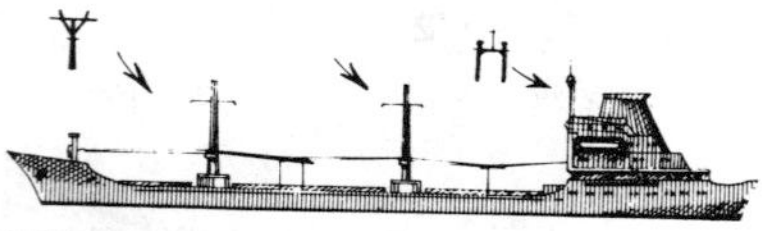

M_3F H13
★**91650 FU SHUN CHENG.** RC/FRG 1969; C; 3400/5400; 117.35 × 6.68/7.06 (385.01 × 21.92/23.16); M; 17; ex JORG KRUGER 1981; ex CAPARNAUTI 1975; ex JORG KRUGER 1974; Sister: ★**91651 PING XIANG CHENG** (RC) ex BRITTA KRUGER 1977.

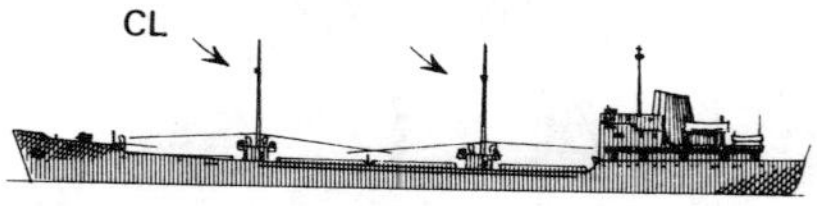

M_3F H13
91660 THOROLD. Ca/Br 1962; B; 5700; 125.05 × 7.58 (410.27 × 24.87); M; —; ex GOSFORTH 1972.

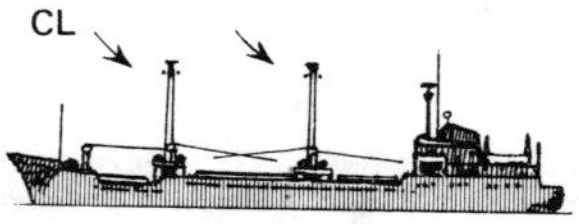

M_3F H13
91670 KRANTOR. Gr/Ne 1964; C; 1400/2300; 87.89 × —/6.31 (288.35 × —/20.7); M; 13; ex ASTRA 1980; ex RAHEL 1978; Sister: **91671 BRANT POINT** (Br) ex ORAN 1978; ex DEVORA 1978.

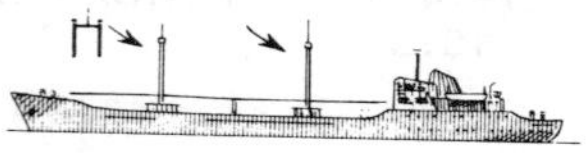

M_3F H13
★**91680 FRIMARO.** Cu/Sp 1966; R; 1700; 87 × 5.77 (285.43 × 18.93); M; —; ex FRIMAR 1978.

M_3F H13
91690 OCEAN GLORY No6. Pa/Br 1958; C; 1400; 90.51 × 4.54 (296.95 × 14.9); M; —; ex OCEAN GLORY 1977; ex CATANIAN 1972.

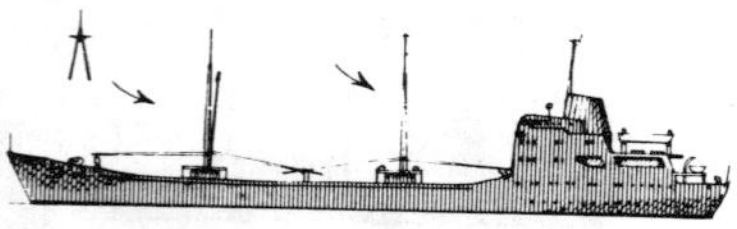

M_3F H13
★**91700 SOFIA.** Bu/Bu 1963; C; 2900/4400; 114.18 × 6.32/7.54 (374.61 × 20.73/24.74); M; 14; Sisters (Bu flag): ★**91701 PRESLAV;** ★**91702 VELIKO TIRNOVO.**

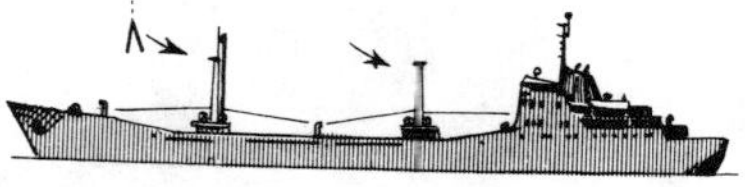

M_3F H13
91710 IRAN SEDAGHAT. Ir/Bu 1971; C; 4500; 114.26 × 6.55 (374.37 × 21.49); M; 13.75; ex ARYA RAD 1980; ex SLEVIK 1975; Sisters: **91711 IRAN SHAFAAT** (Ir) ex ARYA DAD 1980; ex WYVERN 1975; **91712 REMADA** (Tn) ex ONTATIO 1974; ex SARIBA 1973; **91713 KOHENG** (Pa) ex TAULOTO II; ex SAFIA 1973; **91714 WOOLGAR** (No); ★**91715 TAI AN** (RC); ★**91716 TAI NING** (RC); ★**91717 TAI SHUN** (RC); (Hu flag): ★**91718 BUDAPEST;** ★**91719 HUNGARIA.**

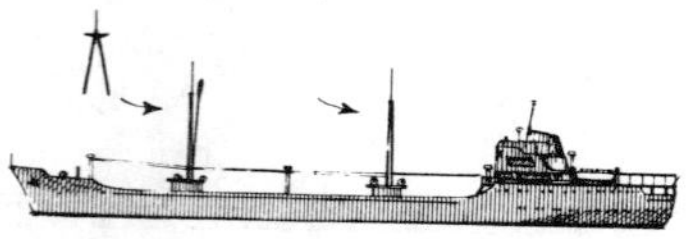

M_3F H13
● **91730 KEFALONIA.** Gr/No 1958; C; 2300/3700; 106.46 × 5.94/6.99 (349.28 × 19.49/22.93); M; 14.5; ex HAVEL; ex CEARA 1964.

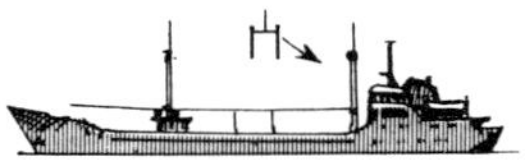

M_3F H13
91740 FALCON REEFER. Pa/Fr 1961; R; 900/1400; 7.04 × 3.87/4.92 (252.76 × 12.7/16.14); M; 13; ex DANIELA 1967.

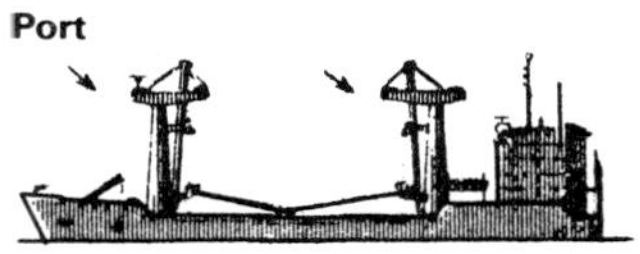

M_3F H13
91750 STAHLECK. FRG/FRG 1977; RoC/HL; 3500; 91.5 × 5.17 (300.2 × 16.96); TSM; 13.5; Similar (US flag): **91751 JOHN HENRY; 91752 PAUL BUNYAN.**

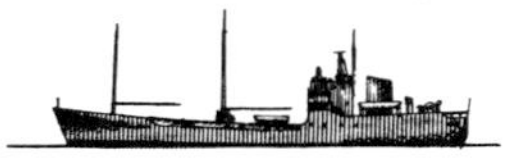

M_3F H3
91760 DEBORAH I. Pa/Br 1953; C/R; 1000; 65.11 × 3.98 (213.62 × 13.06); M; 11; ex ARGYRO; ex AVRA 1970; ex TERN 1964.

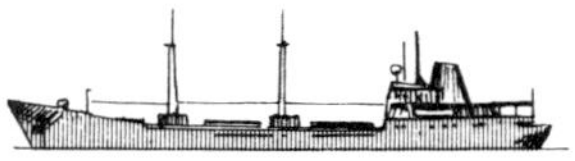

M_3F H3
91770 REEFER MERCHANT. Cy/FRG 1967; R; 900/1700; 88.7 × 4.13/5.21 (291.01 × 13.55/17.09); M; ex FAHRMANNSAND 1974; Sisters: **91771 LUHESAND** (Cy); ⋆**91772 HARMATTAN** (Pd) ex PAGENSAND 1972.

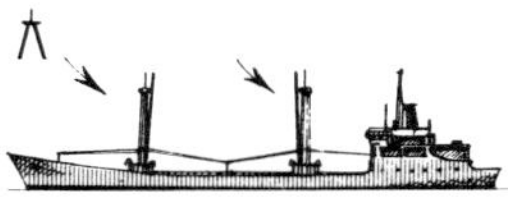

M_3F H3
91780 ATLANTIC ISLE. Gr/Sp 1971; C; 800/1400; 77.4 × 4.07/5.32 (253.94 × 13.35/17.45); M; —; ex WICKENBURGH 1979; ex ATLAN TURQUESA 1975; Sisters (Eg flag): **91781 AL BIRUNI** ex ATLAN ZAFIRO; **91782 AL IDRISI** ex ATLAN DIAMANTE 1975.

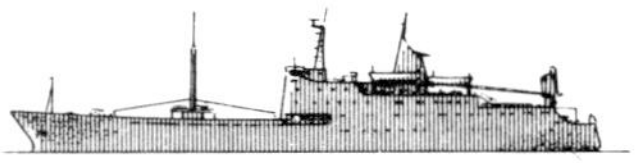

M_3FC H
⋆**91790 HAI OU.** RC/Ja 1973; PC; 3300; 100.51 × 5.68 (329.76 × 18.64); M; 14; Name also reported as **HAIO.**

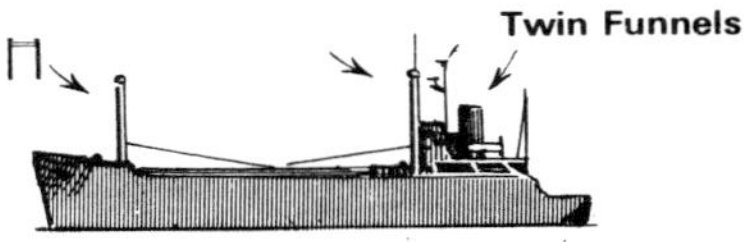

M_3FK H1
91800 NYMIT. Li/Ja 1970; RoC; 4500; 87.31 × — (286.45 × —); TSM; 11.5; ex COSMOS BELLATRIX 1977; ex COSMOS No2 1975.

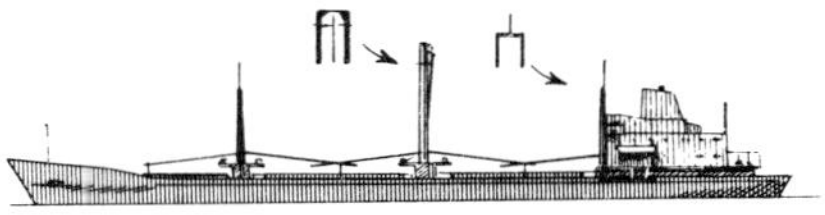

M_3FK H1
91810 PALLAS. FRG/FRG 1971; C; 2800/5000; 125.02 × 6.52/7.62 (410.17 × 21.39/25); M; 16.5; Possible sister: **91811 NEPTUN** (FRG).

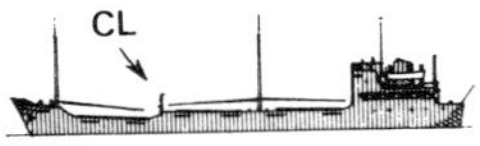

M_3FK H123
● **91820 CARIGULF EXPRESS.** Pa/Br 1960; C; 1200; 71.03 × 4.59 (229.76 × 15.06); M; 11.5; ex MARY D 1978; ex TOWARD 1976; ex YEWGLEN 1974; ex TOLSTA 1971; Similar: **91821 RAYNESTONE** (Br) ex MAPLE 1974; ex MALTA FAITH 1973; ex SOUTRA 1970; **91822 RANA I** (Le) ex ROSETHORN 1980; ex YEWKYLE 1974; ex LAKSA 1971; **91823 SABINA** (Sy) ex KATERINA PA 1979; ex BELL CRUSADER 1976; ex AJAX 1971; ex FIDRA 1969; Possibly similar (converted to a cement carrier): **91824 ISLAND CEMENT** (Bs) ex LOGNA 1970.

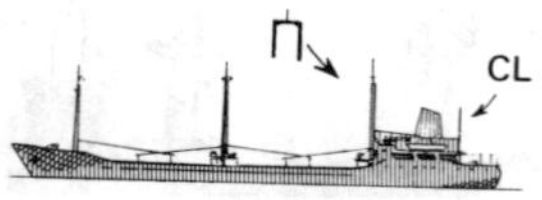

M_3FK H13

● **91830 ADINE.** Ne/Ne 1968; C; 700/1500; 77.55 × 4.31/5.74 (254.43 × 4.14/18.83); M; 12; ex NINA LONBORG 1976; ex TRONGATE 1973; ex HOLLAND PARK 1971; Sisters: **91831 GHADAMES** (Gr) ex ERIC; ex PASSAAT SANTOS 1977; ex SHIPMAIR III 1976; ex CAIRNVENTURE 1974; **91832 PELLINI** (Gr) ex HARCO 1980; ex CORATO 1978; **91833 PASSAAT CURACAO** (NA) ex SHIPMAIR II 1976; ex CILURNUM 1974; **91834 ARUBA** (NA) ex PASSAAT SANTOS 1980; ex PASSAAT BONAIRE 1978; ex SHIPMAIR IV 1976; ex VIDA 1974; ex VOREDA 1973; **91835 CELTIC ENDEAVOUR** (Br) ex EMBASSAGE 1978; **91836 OUADAN** (Gr) ex CALANDRIA; **91837 CAMARINA** (Br); **91838 VIRGILIA** (Br); **91839 PHOENICIA** (Pa) ex SUDRI 1977; ex ISBORG 1975; ex PHILIP LONBORG 1974; ex HYDE PARK 1973; **91840 LUSTAR** (Pa) ex SALTERSGATE 1977; Similar: **91841 BORMLA** (Ma) ex TUDOR PRINCE 1975; ex LISE NIELSEN 1974; **91842 NIAGA XXXIV** (Ia) ex MULTON 1980; ex BALTON 1978; ex GUDRUN DANIELSEN 1975; **91843 VAGERO** (It) ex WHITE CREST; ex BRITISH PRINCE 1973; ex WHITE CREST 1972; **91844 LADY SARAH** (Pa) ex BRETWALDA; ex NORDIC PRINCE 1978; ex BRETWALDA 1976; **91845 ADARA** (Ne) ex SAXON PRINCE 1976; ex CAIRNTRADER 1976; ex SAXON PRINCE 1975; launched as CAIRNTRADER; **91846 SITULA** (Ne) ex JYTTE DANIELSEN 1976; Similar (larger): **91847 CAIRNROVER** (Br); **91848 MOUNTPARK** (Br) ex CAIRNRANGER 1976; **91849 AIDEN** (Fi) ex JACKIE SILVANA 1980; ex THEA DANIELSEN 1978; Similar (Spanish built): **91850 LADY SERENA** (Pa) ex NARYA 1978.

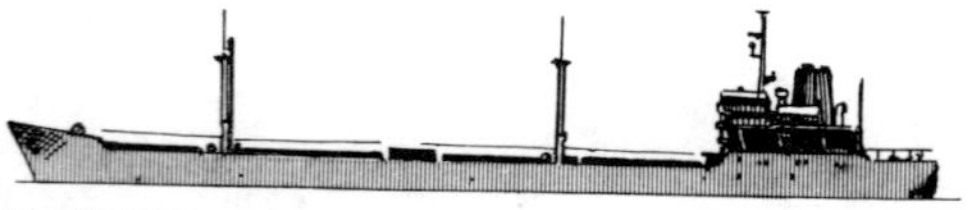

M_3FK H13

● **91890 APICO.** Gr/Ja 1964; C; 9700; 149.61 × 9.55 (490.85 × 31.33); M; 15; ex LOULWA AL KHALIFA; ex PAVLINA 1970; ex ARANETA MA—AO 1974; Sister: **91891 SARITA L** (Cy) ex AWATIF AL SABAH 1980; ex EFTHIMIS 1979; ex BACOLOD 1974; Possible sister (may have a heavy lift derrick): **91892 PUSHPA** (Cy) ex ANWAR AL SABAH 1980; ex TITIKA P 1979; ex TALISAY 1974.

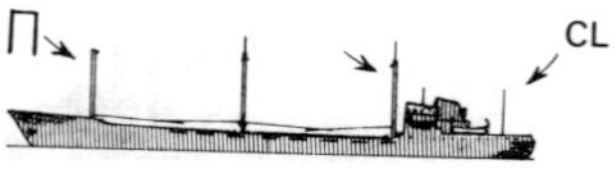

M_3FK H13

91860 ARMADA MEDLINER. Cy/Ne 1966; C; 600/1400; 83.5 × 3.65/4.3 (273.95 × 11.98/14.12); M; 14.25; ex SPYROS G II; ex OOSTEREEMS 1979; ex IONIAN 1977; ex OOSTEREEMS 1972; ex IONIAN 1971; ex OOSTEREEMS 1969.

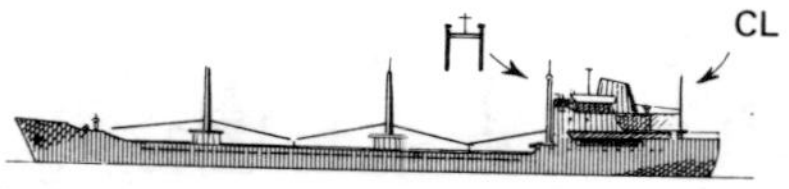

M_3FK H13

● **91870 JOYEID.** Li/No 1966; C; 2500; 111.33 × 6.33 (365.26 × 20.77); M; 13; EILERT RINDE 1974; Sisters: **91871 JUSTEID** (li) ex OLE RINDE 1974; **91872 DON ALEJO** (Pa) ex FOSSUM 1977.

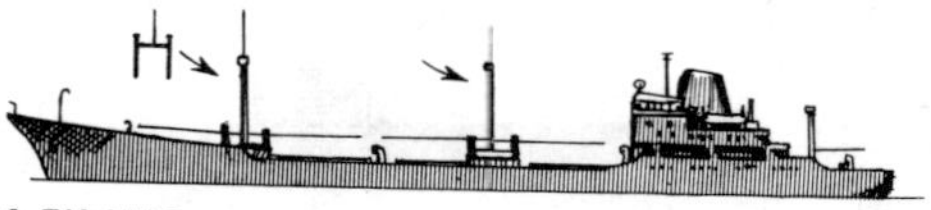

M_3FK H13

91880 GUIA. Pa/FRG 1960; C; 8400; 138.08 × 8.85 (453.02 × 29.04); M; 14.5; ex BAIE COMEAU 1978.

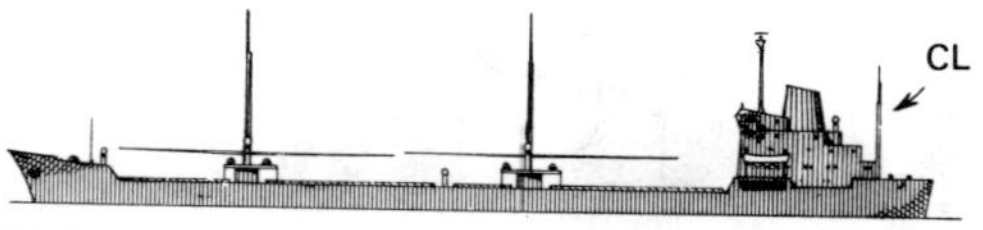

M_3FK H13

● **91900 PONTE PASAJE.** Sp/Sp 1978; C; 9600; 144.13 × 8.97 (472.87 × 29.43); M; 14; **'TD—15'** type: Sisters: **91901 PONTE PEDRIDO; 91902 PONTE SAMPAYO.**

M_3FK H13

⋆91910 KAMCHATSKIE GORY. Ru/Sw 1964; FC; 9700; 153.5 × 7.47 (503.61 × 24.51); M; 17; Sisters (Ru flag): **⋆91911 SAYANSKIE GORY; ⋆91912 SAKHALINSKIE GORY.**

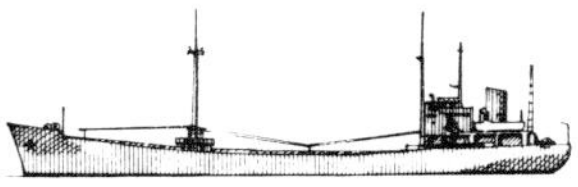

M_3FK H13
91920 ASIA LAKE. Pa/Ja 1967; C; 2000; 89.72 × 5.74 (294.36 × 18.83); M; 12; ex KYOSETSU MARU 1973; Sister: **91921 MEGHNA** (Pa) ex MEGNA 1978; ex NIKKAI MARU 1976; Possible sister: **91922 TUNG FAU** (Tw); Probable sisters: **91923 SEVEN LOG MASTER** (Pi) ex ASIA PACIFIC 1976; ex SHINKYO MARU 1973; **91924 WILRON** (Pa) ex GENERAL SANTOS CITY; ex KYOFUKU MARU 1978.

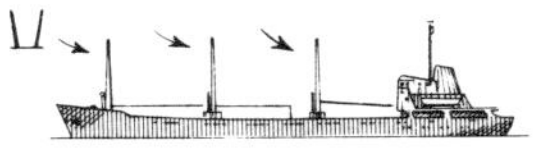

M_4F H1
● **91970 STOCKHORN.** Sd/FRG 1966; C; 1000; 71.61 × 4.98 (234.94 × 16.34); M; 11.5; ex UTHOERN 1976; ex UTHORN 1972.

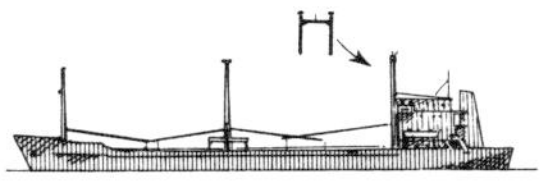

M_4F H1
91980 PIA DANIELSEN. De/Ne 1976; C; 1000; 79.48 × 4.83 (260.76 × 15.85); M; 12.25; Similar: **91981 HERMAN BODEWES** (Ne); **91982 GUDRUN DANIELSEN** (De).

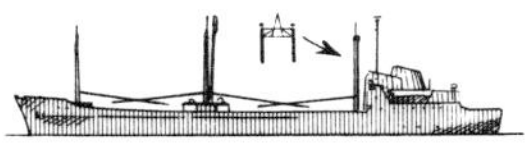

M_4F H13
● **91990 JEANNE D'ARC.** Le/FRG 1961; C/WT; 1100; 75.65 × 4.27 (248.2 × 14.01); M; —; ex NAZIH 1979; ex BARAKAT 1979; ex PALACIO 1977.

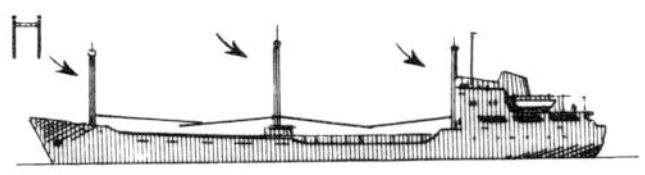

M_4F H13
92000 IRENE'S LUCK. Gr/FRG 1959; C; 2700; 91.52 × 6.03 (300.26 × 19.78); M; 12; ex PIRAEUS E 1971; ex IOANNINA 1970; ex THEODOROS KYRIAKOS 1968; ex PRESIDENT PIERRE ANGOT 1968; ex STELLA ORION 1962.

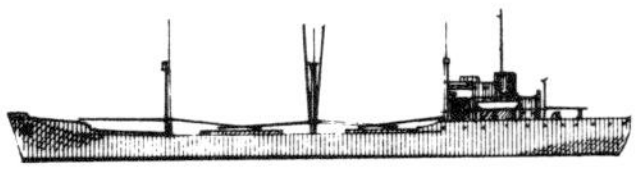

M_4F H13
⋆**92020 BAHIA DE NIPE.** Cu/US 1945; C; 3800; 98.73 × 7.14 (323.92 × 23.43); M; 10.5; ex COASTAL CHALLENGER 1948; **'C1—M—AV3'** type; Sister: ⋆**92021 BAHIA DE MARIEL** ex HALF HITCH 1948.

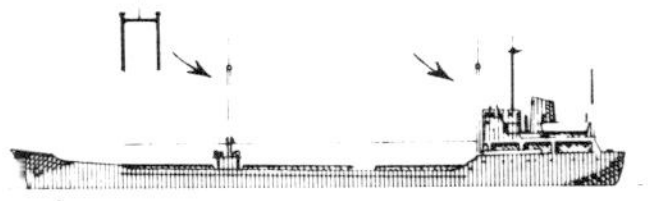

M_3FK H13
91930 ADHIGUNA MERANTI. Pa/Ja 1964; C; 3000; 96.7 × 6.3 (317.26 × 20.67); M; 12; ex YUZAN MARU 1972.

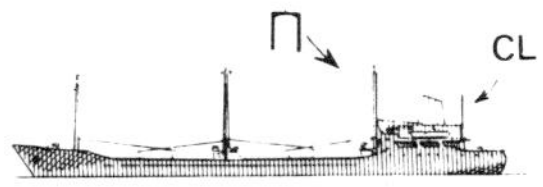

M_3FM H13
● **91940 ADINE.** Ne/Ne 1968; C; 700/1500; 77.55 × 4.31/5.74 (254.43 × 4.14/18.83); M; 12; ex NINA LONBORG 1976; ex TRONGATE 1973; ex HOLLAND PARK 1971; Sisters: **91941 GHADAMES** (Gr) ex ERIC; ex PASSAAT SANTOS 1977; ex SHIPMAIR III 1976; ex CAIRNVENTURE 1974; **91942 PELLINI** (Gr) ex HARCO 1980; ex CORATO 1978; **91943 PASSAAT CURACAO** (NA) ex PASSAAT SANTOS 1980; ex PASSAAT BONAIRE 1978; ex SHIPMAIR IV 1976; ex VIDA 1974; ex VOREDA 1973; **91945 CELTIC ENDEAVOUR** (Br) ex EMBASSAGE 1978; **91946 OUADAN** (Gr) ex CALANDRIA; **91947 CAMARINA** (Br); **91948 VIRGILIA** (Br);**91949 PHOENICIA** (Pa) ex SUDRI 1977; ex ISBORG 1975; ex PHILIP LONBORG 1974; ex HYDE PARK 1973; **91950 LUSTAR** (Pa) ex SALTERSGATE 1977; Similar: **91951 BORMLA** (Ma) ex TUDOR PRINCE 1975; ex LISE NIELSEN 1974; **91952 NIAGA XXXIV** (Ia) ex MULTON 1980; ex BALTON 1978; ex GUDRUN DANIELSEN 1975; **91953 VAGERO** (It) ex WHITE CREST; ex BRITISH PRINCE 1973; ex WHITE CREST 1972; **91954 LADY SARAH** (Pa) ex BRETWALDA; ex NORDIC PRINCE 1978; ex BRETWALDA 1976; **91955 ADARA** (Ne) ex SAXON PRINCE &: EX CAIRNTRADER 1976; ex SAXON PRINCE 1975; launched as CAIRNTRADER; **91956 SITULA** (Ne) ex JYTTE DANIELSEN 1976; Similar (larger): **91957 CAIRNROVER** (Br); **91958 MOUNTPARK** (Br) ex CAIRNRANGER 1976; **91959 AIDEN** (Fi) ex JACKIE SILVANA 1980; ex THEA DANIELSEN 1978; Similar (Spanish built): **91960 LADY SERENA** (Pa) ex NARVA 1978.

M_4F H13
92010 BUILDER III. Sg/FRG 1960; C; 2000; 84.69 × 5.6 (277.85 × 18.37); M; 12; ex JOHNSON HALE 1979; ex SIRAGARD 1974; ex AMRON 1973; ex FOSSHEIM 1966.

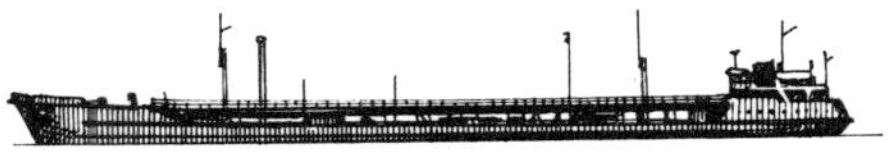

M_4F H13
⋆**92030 'VOLGONEFT' type.** Ru/Ru c1966-69; Tk; 3500; 132.59 × 3.58 (435 × 11.75); TSM; 10.5; This drawing represents the earlier vessels of this type. For later vessels see 'VOLGONEFT' under M^2KFK. Names have the prefix 'VOLGONEFT' and a number. Approx. 27 in the whole group.

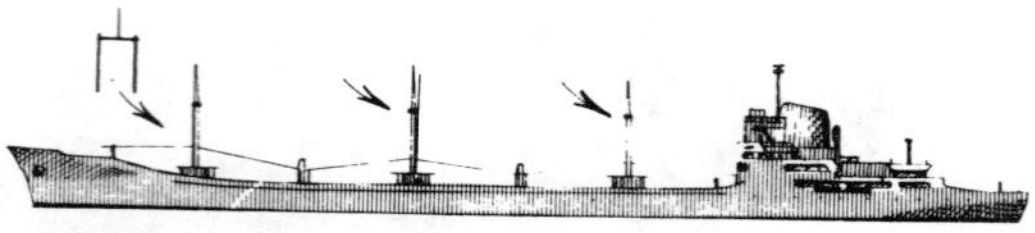

M_4FK H1
92060 ORIENTAL TRADER. Li/Ja 1956; C; 10200; 159.9 × 9.57 (524.61 × 31.4); M; —; ex PACIFIC PIONEER 1960.

M_5F H13
92080 GLORIA SIDERUM. Pa/Ne 1956-69; C/HL/Catamaran; 1000; 56.65 × 3.65 (185.86 × 11.98); TSM; —; Formed by joining two coasters 1969; Port Hull ex HADA II; Starboard Hull ex HERMES.

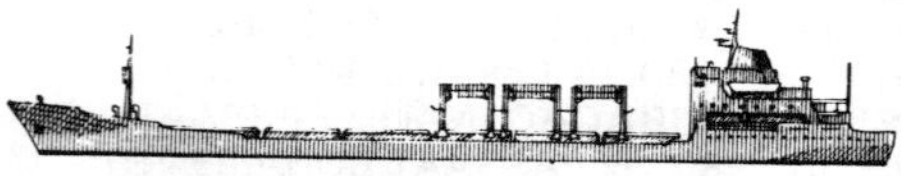

MN_3MFK H13
92110 BESSEGEN. Br/No 1963; B; 7400; 139.96 × 7.75 (459.19 × 25.43); M; 15; Sister: **92111 RONDEGGEN** (Br).

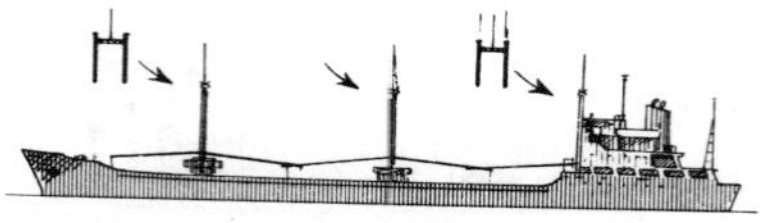

M_4FK H13
92070 RINA. Pa/Ja 1966; C; 4500; 113.59 × 6.85 (372.67 × 22.47); M; 15.5; ex KONG KIM 1980; ex FOH KIM 1978.

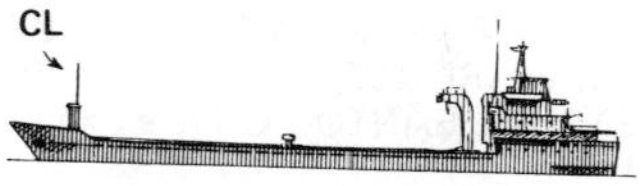

MNMF H13
92090 SATURNUS. Sw/DDR 1971; C; 3200; 104.04 × 5.77; M; ex HANSA BAY 1978; Sisters: **92091 KLAREDON** (Br); ex LAREDO 1980; ex HANSA NORD 1979; **92092 RIO BRAVO** (Br); ex HANSA TRADE 1980; **92093 NAZIE BEAUTY** (Sh); ex HANSEAT 1980; **92094 ANATOLIA** (Pa); ex LARCH 1980; ex JOWOOD; **92095 HVALVIK** (Ic); ex MAMBO 1975; ex SAMBA 1972; **92096 JANJE** (Pa); ex JANJA 1979; ex RUMBA 1975; **92097 METEOR** (Sw); ex BENGATE 1977; ex JENKA 1974; **92098 ELISABETH** (Cy); ex ESKDALEGATE 1977; ex FREDERICKSGATE 1974; ex BRUNI 1974; **92099 WINDROVER** (Sw); ex SCOL ROVER 1980; ex SIMONSGATE 1976; ex HANSEL 1974.

Profile 5

CMC_2KMF H1
⋆**92150 VOSTOCK.** Ru/Ru 1971; FF; 26400; 224.57 × 10.02 (736.78 × 32.87); TST; 19.

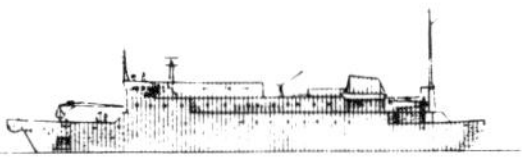

CMFM H2
● ⋆**92160 EMBA.** Ru/Fi 1980; Cbl; 1900; 75.9 × 3; (249 × 9.84); TSD-E; approx 11; 2 sisters ordered 1980.

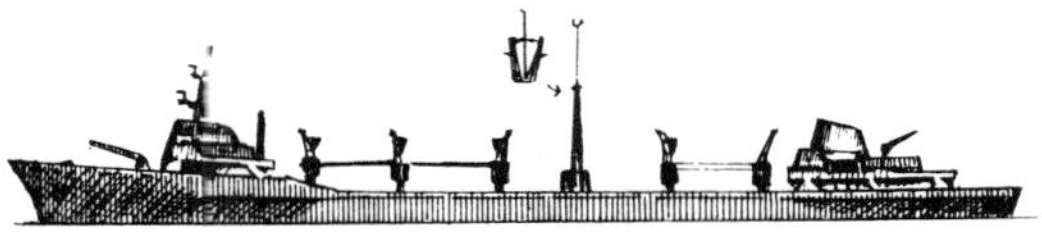

$CMKC_3MC_2FC$ H1
92170 DEL MUNDO. US/US 1968; C; 7100/10400; 159.11 × —/9.47 (522.01 × —31.07); T; 18.5; ex DELTA ARGENTINA 1980; Sisters (US flag): **92171 DEL CAMPO:** ex DELTA PARAGUAY 1980; **92172 DEL MONTE;** ex DELTA BRASIL 1980; **92173 DEL VIENTO**, ex DELTA MEXICO 1980; **92174 DEL VALLE;** ex DELTA URUGUAY 1980.

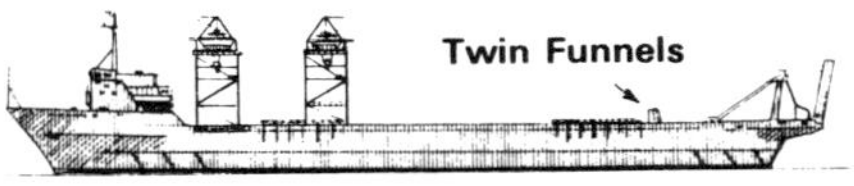

CMN_2FK_2 H1
92180 DOCKLIFT 2. NA/Ne 1967/74/78; Dk/Bg/HL; 3800; 129.78 × 5.95 (428.8 × 19.51); TrM; 12.5; ex LADY JANE 1974; Rebuilt from Ro/Ro ship 1974; Lengthened 1978; Stern ramp.

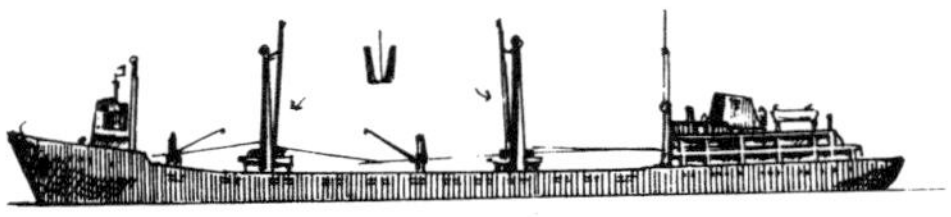

$KCMCM_2F$ H1
92190 TREUENBELS. Gr/FRG 1960; C/HL; 6800/9300; 139.48 × 8.57/9.19 (457.61 × 28.12/30.15); M; 14.5; ex TREUENFELS 1981.

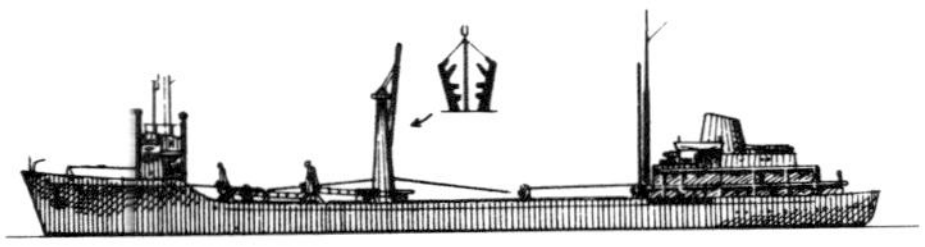

$K_2CKCMF/K_3C_2MF/K_3MF$ H1
⋆**92200 DADE.** RC/FRG 1962; C/HL: 6900/9600; 152.25 × 8.29/9.35 (499.51 × 27.2/30.68); M; 18.5; ex WERDENFELS 1973; Cranes move along main deck; Sisters (RC flag): ⋆**92201 DANING;** ex WACHTFELS 1972; ⋆**92202 DA SHI QIAO;** ex WALLENFELS 1978; ⋆**92203 DA JIN CHUAN;** ex WILDENFELS 1978; ⋆**92204 DA CHANG ZHEN;** ex WASSERFELS 1978.

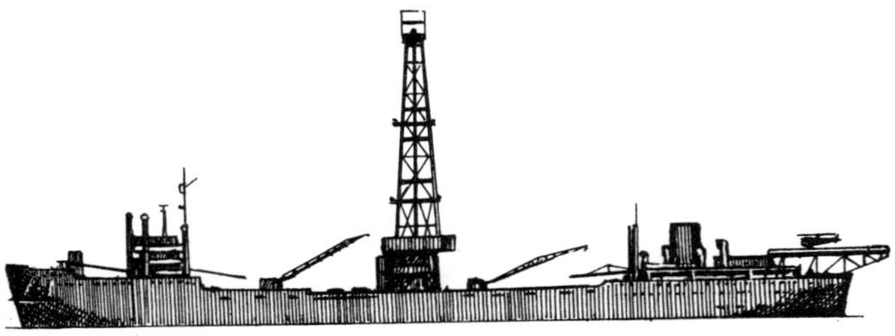

K_2MC_2KF H1
92210 J.W.BATES. Pa/De 1948/67; DS; 18400; 194.8 × 10.61 (639.1 × 34.8); TSM; —; ex SONDA 2 1972; ex DRILLSHIP 1970; ex STAR I 1970; ex DRILLSHIP 1969; ex THORSHOVDI 1967; Converted from whale factory 1967.

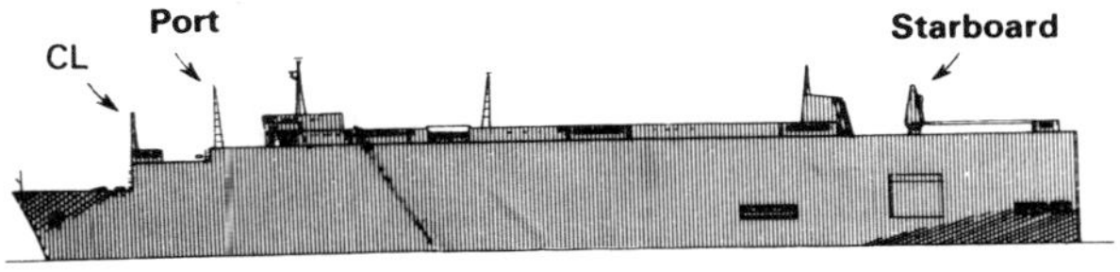

K_2MKMFC H2
92220 PRESIDENT. Pa/Ja 1977; V; 9200; 180.02 × 7.5 (590.62 × 24.61); M; 18; Side doors; Sister: **92221 NISSAN SILVIA** (Pa); Similar (goalpost radar mast): **92222 YOUNG SPLENDOR** (Li).

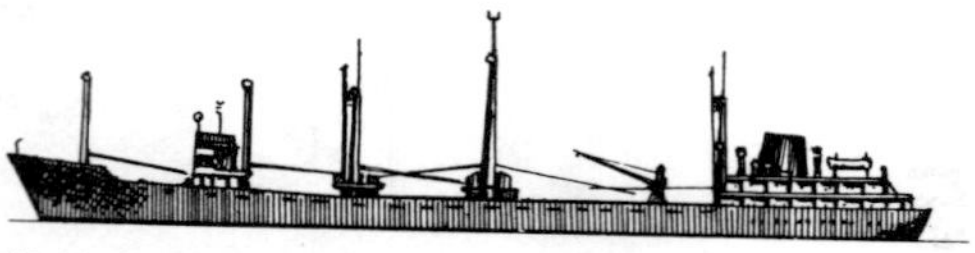

K_2M_2CMF H
⋆**92230 DATONG.** RC/FRG 1959; C/HL: 6800/9200; 145 × 8.57/9 (475.7 × 28.1/29.5); M; 14.5; ex TANNENFELS 1971; Sisters (RC flag): ⋆**92231 DAAN** ex SPITZFELS 1972; ⋆**92232 DAPU** ex NORTH SEA 1971; ex TRAUTENFELS 1971; ⋆**92233 DAMING** ex SCHWARZENFELS 1971.

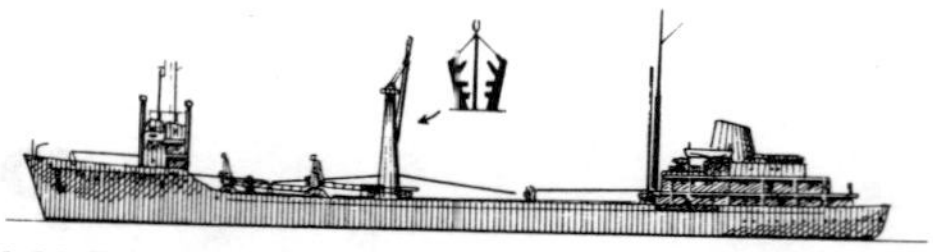

K_2M_2F H1
⋆**92240 DADE.** RC/FRG 1962; C/HL; 6900/9600; 152.25 × 8.29/9.35 (499.51 × 17.2/30.68); ex WERDENFELS 1973; Cranes move along main deck; Sisters (RC flag): ⋆**92241 DANING** ex WACHTFELS 1972; ⋆**92242 DA SHI QIAO** ex WALLENFELS 1978; ⋆**92243 DA JIN CHUAN** ex WILDENFELS 1978; ⋆**92244 DA CHANG ZHEN** ex WASSERFELS 1978.

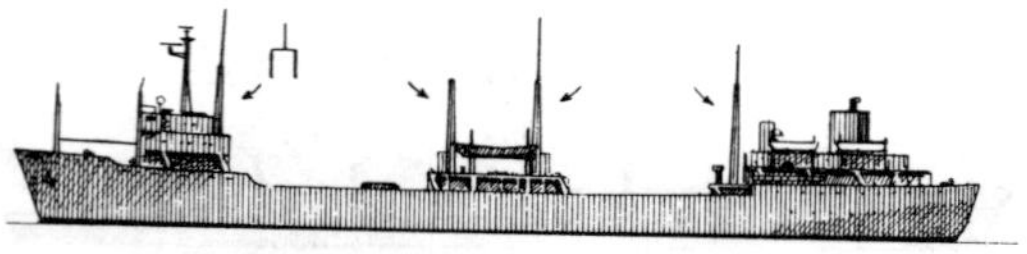

$K_2M_2KM_2F$ H13
92250 SHINANO MARU. Ja/Ja 1965/72/74; FF; 8900; 153.27 × 7.27 (502.8 × 23.85); M; 14; ex MEISEI MARU No 2 1972; Built as a Fish Factory converted to cargo 1972. Reconverted 1974.

KM H1
92260 KILDARE. Li/Hong Kong 1973; Sply/Con; 1200; 58.5 × 3.96 (191.9 × 12.9); TSM; —.

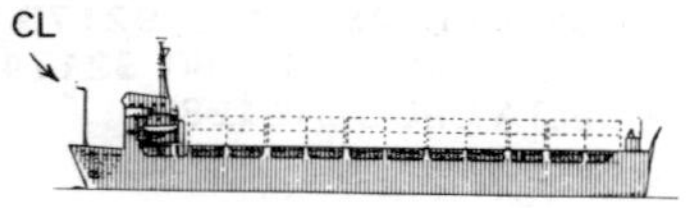

KM H3
92270 CONDOCK I. FRG/FRG 1979; Dk/Con/RoC; 1000; 92.4 × 4.58; (303.15 × 15.03); TSM; 12; Sister: **92271 CONDOCK II** (FRG).

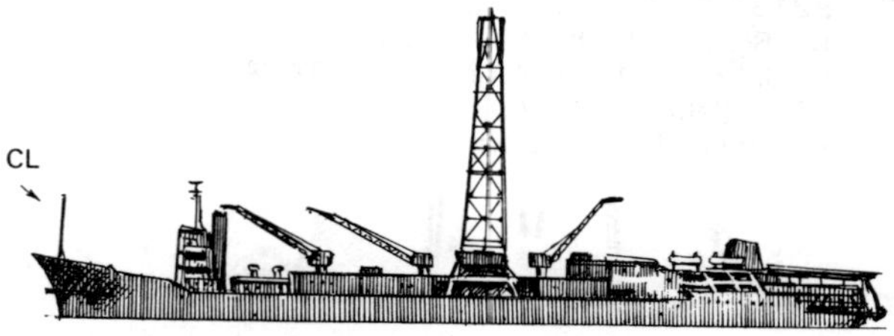

KMC_3F H13
92280 DANWOOD ICE. De/Fr 1959/74; DS; 13700; 172.5 × 10.05 (565.9 × 32.9); M; 16.25; ex JEAN SCHNEIDER; Converted ore carrier 1974.

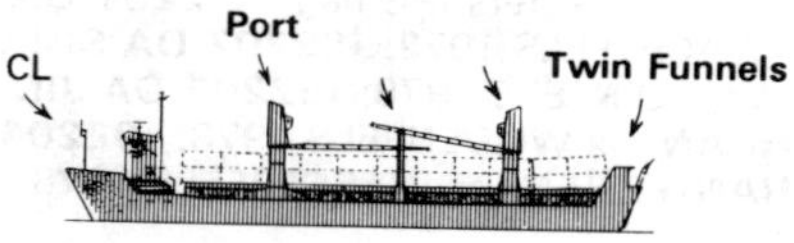

KMC_2F H1
92290 SLOMAN RANGER. FRG/FRG 1979; Roc/Con; 1000; 92.07 × 3.65; (302 × 11.98); TSM; 12.5; Stern ramp; Sisters (FRG flag): **92291 SLOMAN RECORD; 92292 SLOMAN RIDER; 92293 SLOMAN ROVER; 92294 SLOMAN ROYAL** launched as TILIA; **92295 SLOMAN RUNNER;** Similar: **92296 ADELE J** (FRG); **92297 BANGUI** (Cy); **92298 HEINRICH S** (FRG); ex PAOUA 1979; **92299 HEINRICH HUSMANN** (FRG); **922300 PETRA SCHEU** *(FRG).*

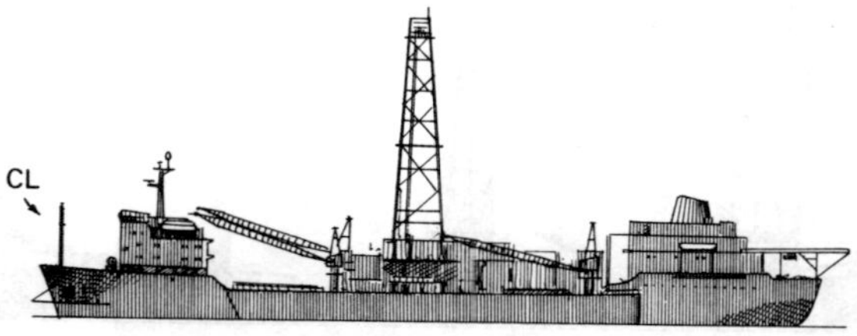

KMC_2F H13
92310 NEDDRILL I. Ne/Ne 1963/76; DS; 12400; 160.1 × 9.2 (525.2 × 30.18); M; 14.5; ex GOEREE 1976; Converted Ore Carrier 1976; Sister: **92311 NEDDRILL 2** (Ne) ex SCHOUWEN 1977.

KMC₂MF H13
92320 HUGHES GLOMAR EXPLORER. US/US 1973; DS/Sal/M; 27500; 188.58 × 11.63 (618.7 × 38.15); TS D—E; 12.

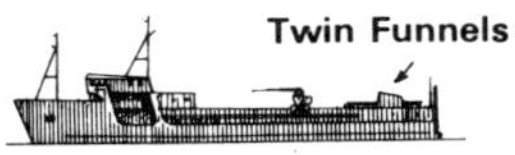

KMCF H1
92350 SASSARI I. It/No 1970; RoC/Con; 400; 67.95 × 3.01 (222.9 × 9.87); M; 10; ex FLORIANA 1974; ex CHANNELBRIDGE I 1974; ex MALTA CROSS 1972; Stern door/ramp. Bow door.

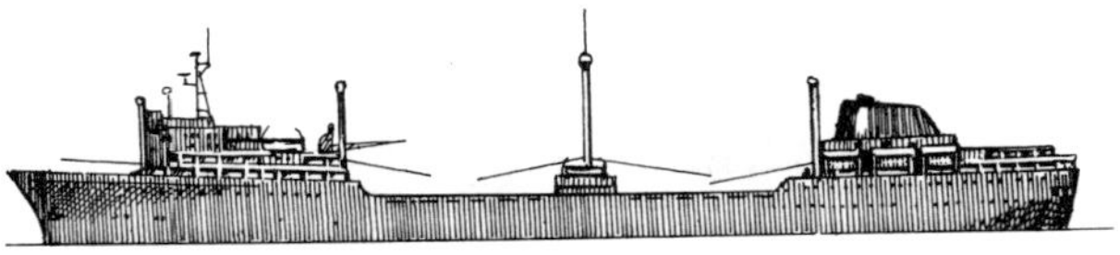

KMCKMKF H13
⋆**92380 VLADIVOSTOK.** Ru/FRG 1962; FF/WF; 17100; 181.9 × 8.89 (596.7 × 29.16); M; 14; Sister: ⋆**92381 DALNIY VOSTOK** (Ru).

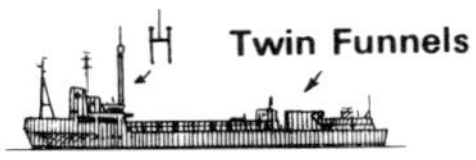

KMF H
92390 KAREN BRAVO. De/Ne 1969; C/RS; 500; 57.92 × 4.07 (190 × 13.35); M; 12.5.

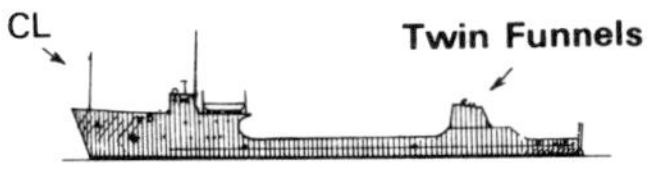

KMF H1
92410 INAGUA LIGHT. Pa/US 1970; RoC/LC; 800; 81.51 × 3.49 (267.4 × 11.45); Tr SM; 12; Bow doors; Sisters (Pa flag): **92411 INAGUA BEACH; 92412 INAGUA SOUND;** Possible sisters: **92413 INAGUA BAY; 92414 INAGUA SURF.**

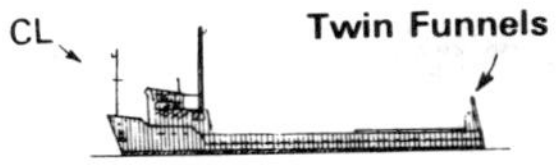

KMF H1
92430 KILDARE. Li/Hong Kong 1973; Sply/Con; 1200; 58.5 × 3.96 (191.9 × 12.9); TSM; —.

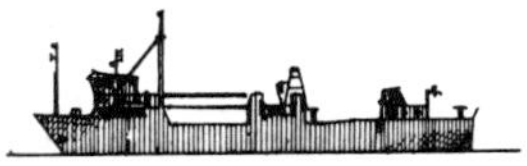

KMCF H
● **92330 PORSOY.** No/No 1977; Pal/Con; 500; 69.6 × 4.5 (228.3 × 14.7); M; 14; Side doors; Similar (No flag): **92331 FJELL; 92332 FJORD; 92333 LYNX; 92334 VELA;** Probably similar: **92336 NORDVAER.**

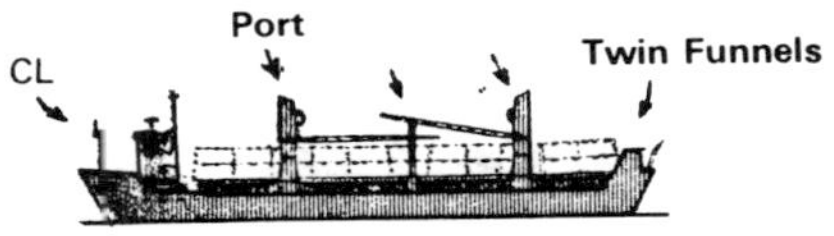

KMCKCF H1
92360 SLOMAN RANGER. FRG/FRG 1979; RoC/Con; 1000; 92.07 × 3.65; (302 × 11.98); TSM; 12.5; Stern ramp; Sisters (FRG flag): **92361 SLOMAN RECORD; 92362 SLOMAN RIDER; 92363 SLOMAN ROVER; 92364 SLOMAN ROYAL** launched as TILIA; **92365 SLOMAN RUNNER.**

KMF H
92400 IRIS. Is/Rm 1973; RoC; 8200; 128.33 × 6.58 (421 × 21.5); TSM; —; Stern door; Sister: **92401 NARCIS** (Is).

KMF H1
92420 SASSARI I. It/No 1970; RoC/Con; 400; 67.95 × 3.01 (222.9 × 9.87); M; 10; ex FLORIANA 1974; ex CHANNELBRIDGE I 1974; ex MALTA CROSS 1972; Stern door/ramp. Bow door.

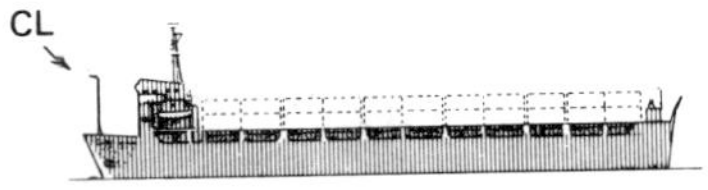

KMF H3
92440 CONDOCK I. FRG/FRG 1979; Dk/Con/RoC; 1000; 92.4 × 4.58 (303.15 × 15.03); TSM; 12; Sister; **92441 CONDOCK II** (FRG).

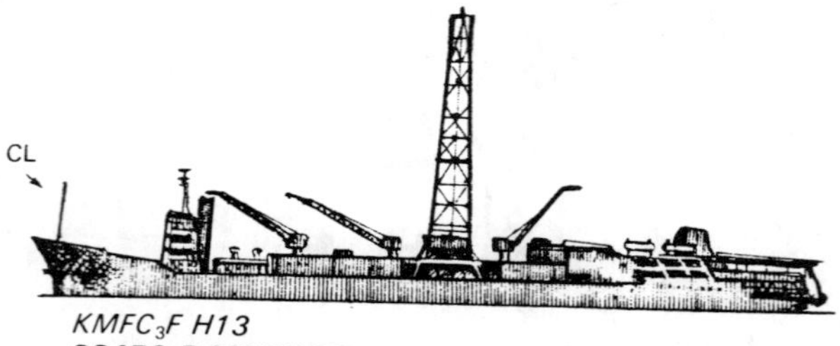

$KMFC_3F$ H13
92450 DANWOOD ICE. De/Fr 1959/74; DS; 13700; 172.5 × 10.05 (565.9 × 32.9); M; 16.25; ex JEAN SCHNEIDER; Converted Ore Carrier 1974.

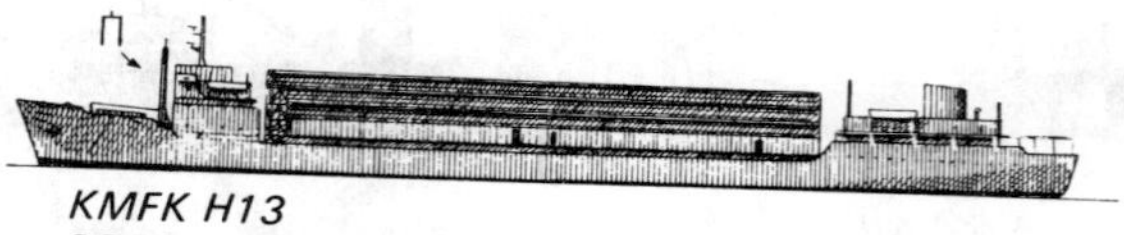

KMFK H13
92460 DANSBORG. Sg/No 1962/76; LS; 8600; 169.73 × 6.97 (556.8 × 31.7); M; 15.5; ex TEAM DANSBORG 1975; ex TEAM VEGA 1973; ex VEGA 1970; Converted tanker 1976.

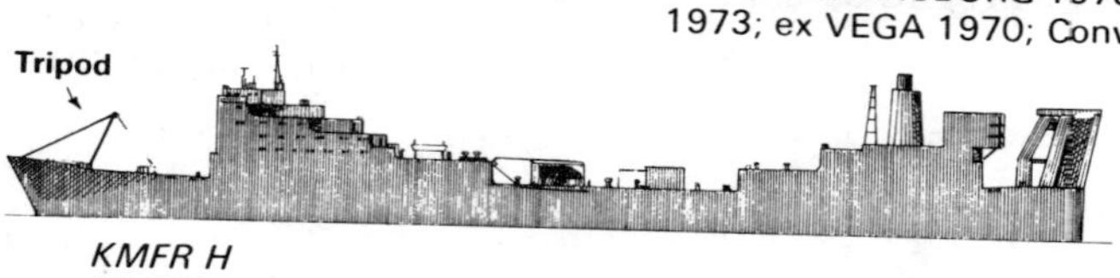

KMFR H
92470 UNION ROTORUA. NZ/Au 1976; RoC; 13000/24000; 203.21 × 8.04/9.53 (666.6 × 26.3/31.2); TSGT; 19; Bow ramp/Stern door. Sister: **92471 UNION ROTOITI** (NZ).

KMKF H1
92480 WESTERN EUROPE. Br/No 1974; Pal; 500/650; 59.14 × 4.5/— (194 × 14.7/—); TSM; —; ex BORN STAR.

KMKF H13
92490 VESTA. FRG/FRG 1979; Incinerator ship; 1000; 71.8 × 4.3 (235.56 × 14.11); M; 11.

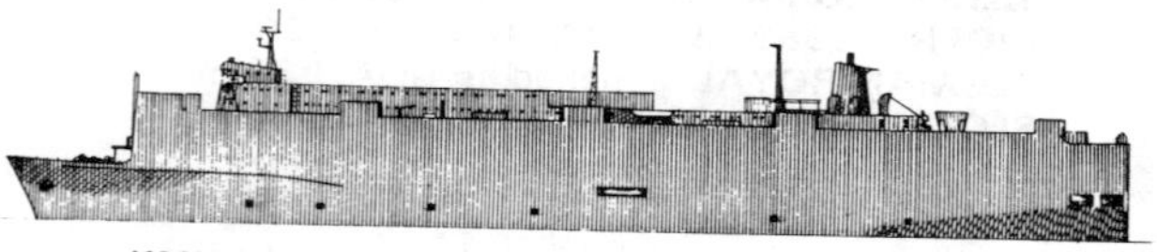

KMKF H2
92500 RIGOLETTO. Sw/Ja 1977; RoVC; 17500; 190.02 × 8.5 (623.4 × 27.8); M; 18.25; Sister: **92501 TRAVIATA** (Sw).

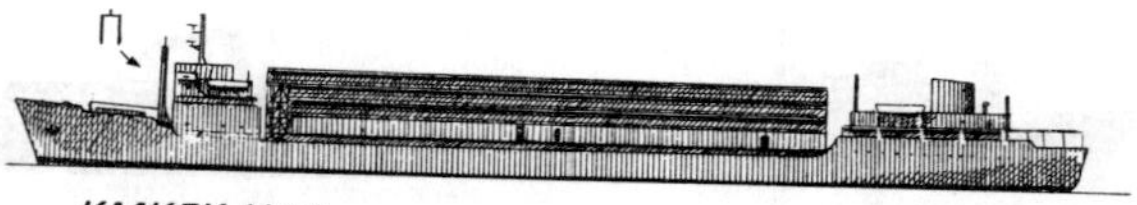

KMKFK H13
92510 DANSBORG. Sg/No 1962/76; LS: 8600; 169.73 × 6.97 (556.8 × 31.7); M; 15.5; ex TEAM DANSBORG 1975; ex TEAM VEGA 1973; ex VEGA 1970; Converted tanker 1976.

KMKFM H
92520 AKEBONO MARU No51. Ja/Ja 1961; ST; 1500; 79.46 × 5.61 (260.6 × 18.4); M; 12.5; Sister (Ja flag): **92521 AKEBONO MARU No 52;** Similar: **92522 AKEBONO MARU No 50; 92523 AKEBONO MARU No 53.**

KMKFR H
92530 UNION ROTORUA. NZ/Au 1976; RoC; 13000/24000; 203.21 × 8.04/9.53 (666.6 × 26.3/31.2); TSGT; 19; Bow ramp/Stern door; Sister: **92531 UNION ROTOITI** (NZ).

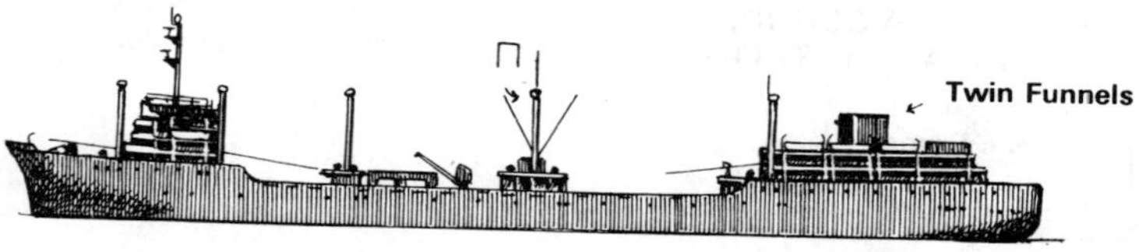

KMK_2CMKF H13
92540 GAE CHEOG. Ko/Ne 1955/67; FF; 23800; 206.51 × 10.73 (677.5 × 35.2); TSM; 14.5; ex GAE CHEOG HO No 2; ex YU SHIN 1979; ex WILLEM BARENDSZ 1973; Converted Whale-oil Factory ship 1967.

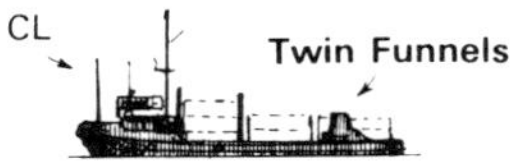

KMK$_2$F H1
92550 RIO HAINA. US/US 1968; Con; 400; 50.3 × 3.07 (165 × 10.07); M; 11.5.

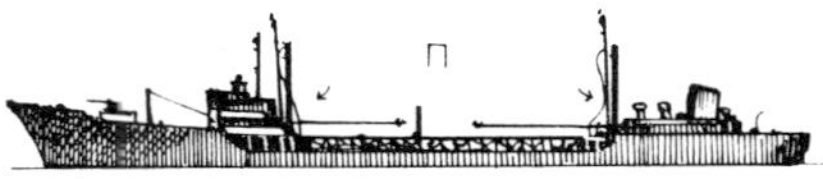

KMK$_2$F H13
92560 HAMANA. Ja/Ja 1962; RT/FA; 7600 Dspl; 128.1 × 6.3 (420 × 20.5); M; 16.

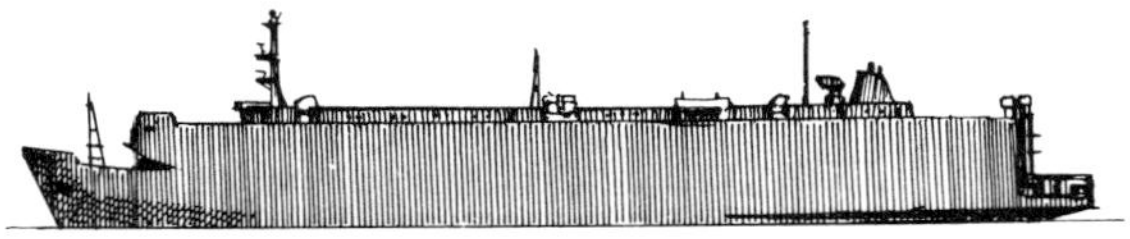

KMK$_2$F H2
92570 PRINCE MARU No 7. Ja/Ja 1973; V; 8500; 169.12 × 7.21 (554.8 × 23.6); M; 17.

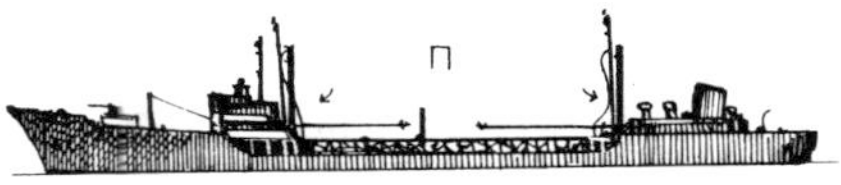

KMK$_3$F H13
92580 HAMANA. Ja/Ja 1962; RT/FA; 7600 Dspl; 128.1 × 6.3 (420 × 20.5); M; 16.

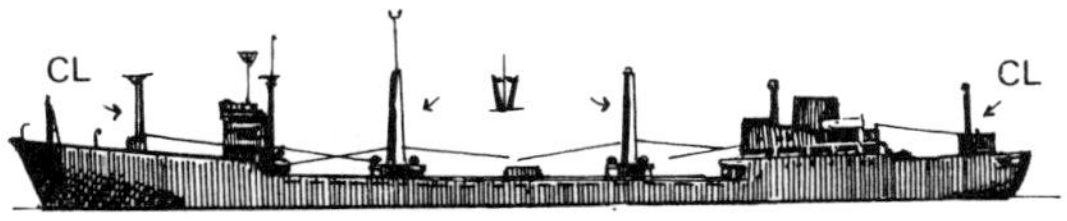

KMK$_3$FK'H13
92590 PETER RICKMERS. Sg/FRG 1962; C/HL; 9600; 159.7 × 9.37 (523.9 × 30.74); M; 17.

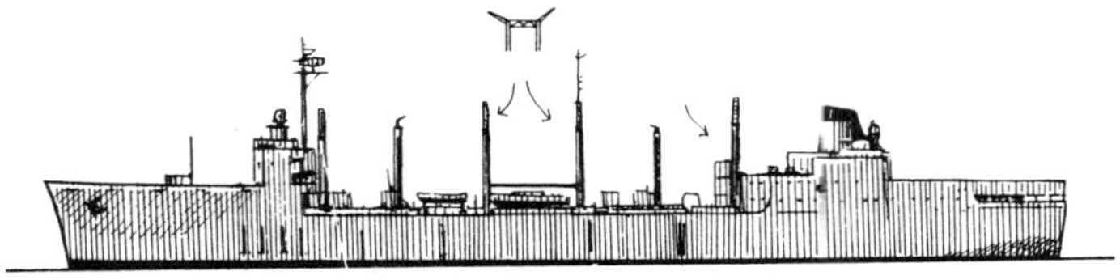

KMK$_2$MK$_2$F H13
92600 WICHITA. US/US 1969; RT/FA; 37400 Dspl; 206.9 × 10.2 (659 × 33.3); TST; 20; Helicopter deck & two helicopters; Sisters (US flag): **92601 KALAMAZOO; 92602 KANSAS CITY; 92603 MILWAUKEE; 92604 ROANOKE; 92605 SAVANNAH; 92606 WABASH.**

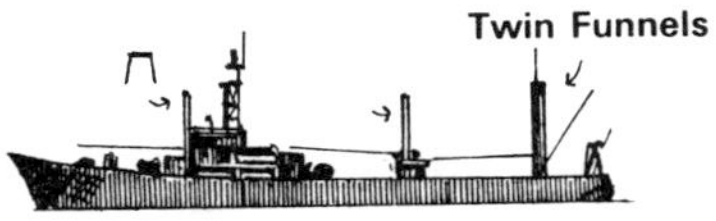

KMKMF H
92620 KOYO MARU No 2. Ja/Ja 1967; ST; 2900; 95.51 × 6 (313.3 × 19.6); M; 13.5; Sister (Ja flag): **92621 TAKACHIHO MARU;** Similar: **92622 ASO MARU; 92623 KIRISHIMA MARU.**

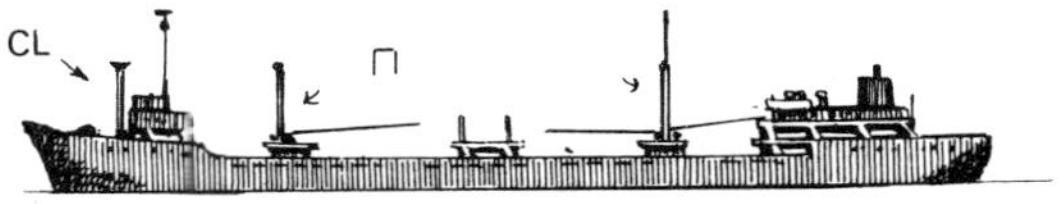

KMKMF H13
92630 CHALLWA V. Pe/Ja 1961; FF; 8000; 153.02 × 8.29 (502.03 × 27.19); M; 14; ex MEISEI MARU 1980.

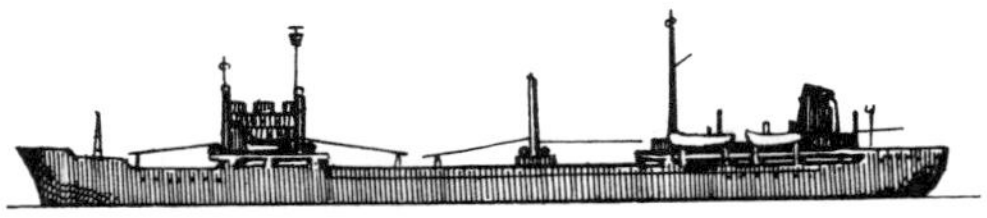

KMKMF H13
★92640 HAI YING 8001. RC/Ja 1960; C; 8000; 147.53 × 7.93 (484.02 × 26.01); M; 14.25; ex OHTSU MARU 1978.

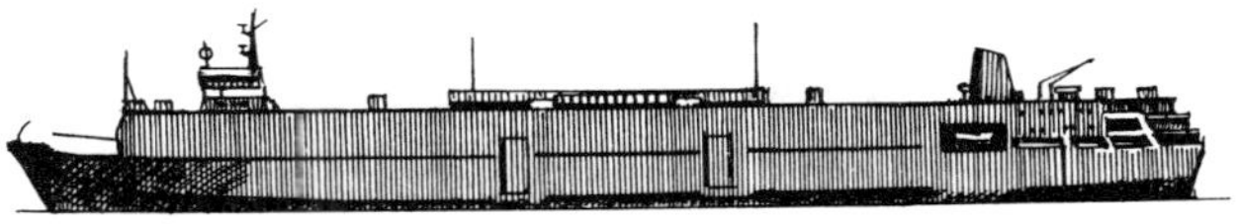

KMKMFC H
92650 HUAL SKAGERAK. No/Ne 1973; V; 7300; 187.51 × 8.01 (615.19 × 26.27); M; 18; ex DYVI SKAGERAK; Side doors; Sisters (No flag): **92651 DYVI KATTEGAT; 92652 HOEGH TARGET;** ex DYVI ADRIATIC 1975; **92653 HOEGH TRIGGER;** Similar (tall pipes from funnel): **92654 NOPAL SEL.**

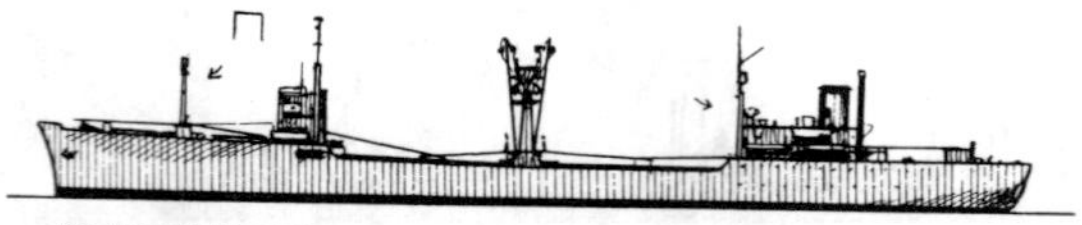

KMKMFK H13
92660 PVT. LEONARD C. BROSTROM. US/US 1943; C/FA; 13900 dwt; 158.5 × 10.1 (520 × 33); T; 15.8; ex MARINE EAGLE; **Modified 'C-4'** type.

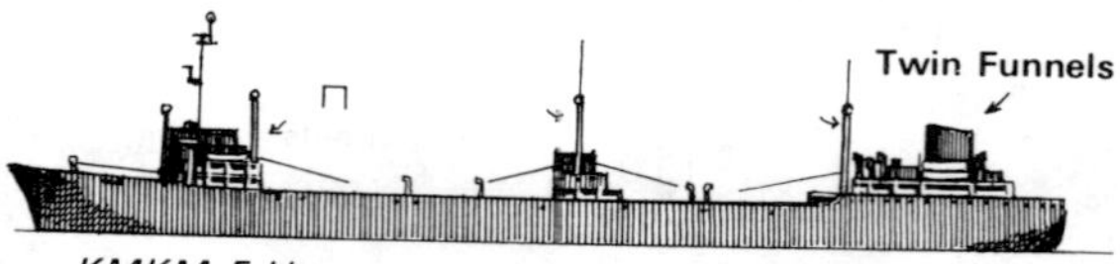

KMKM$_2$F H
92670 TONAN MARU No 2. Ja/Ja 1951/56; WF; 13100; 177.3 × 10.01 (581.6 × 32.9); M; 14; ex MATSUSHIMA MARU 1957; Converted tanker 1956.

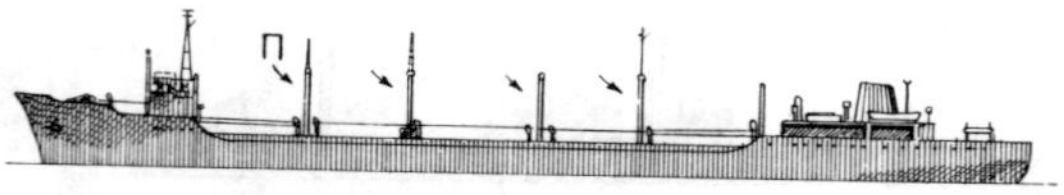

KMKM$_2$KMKF H13
● **92680 EVER GLORY.** Pa/Ja 1954; C; 9900; 162.21 × 8.26 (532.18 × 27.09); M; 13; ex NICHIRYU MARU 1969.

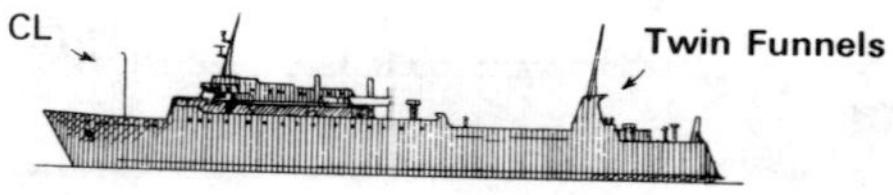

KM$_2$F H
92690 ANDERIDA. Br/No 1971; RoC; 1600; 106 × 4.94 (347.76 × 16.2); TSM; 17; Bow, stern and side doors.

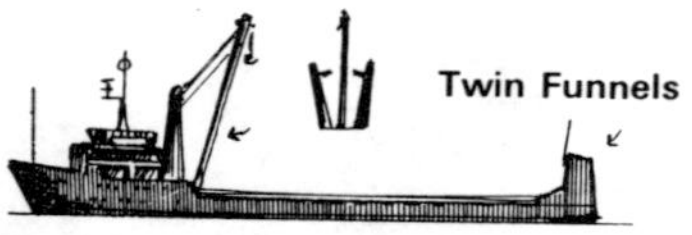

KM$_2$F H1
92700 STARMAN AFRICA. FRG/FRG 1977; RoC/HL; 2800; 93.53 × 64.65 (306.85 × 15.25); TSM; 12; Stern and side ramp; Sister: **92701 STARMAN ANGLIA** (Br).

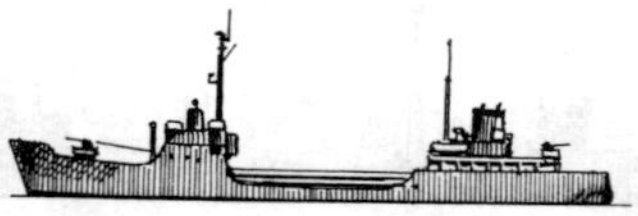

KM$_2$F H13
92710 BEAGLE. Ch/US 1944; Tk/FA; 4200 Dspl; 94.8 × 4.9 (310 × 16); TSD-E; 14; ex USS GENESEE; **'Patapsco'** class; Sisters: **92711 TUMACO** (Co); ex USS CHEWAUCAN; **92712 ARETHOUSA** (Gr); ex USS NATCHAUG; **92713 ARIADNI** (Gr); ex USS TOMBIGBEE; **92714 CHANG PEI** (Tw); ex USS PECATONICA; **92715 LUNG CHUAN** (Tw); ex HMNZS ENDEAVOUR; ex USS NAMAKAGON; **92716 HSIN LUNG** (Tw); ex USS ELKHORN.

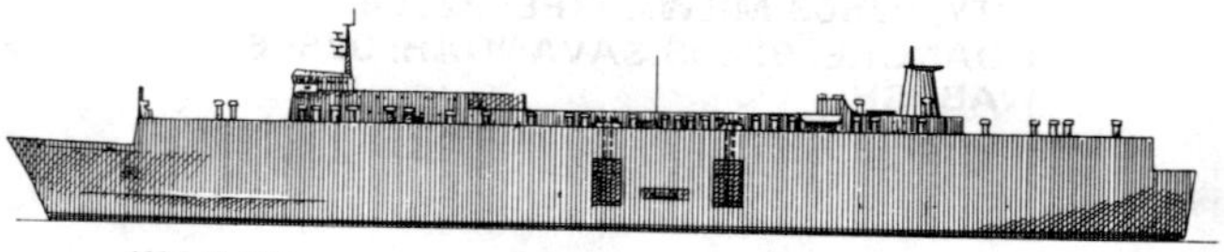

KM$_2$F H2
92730 DON CARLOS. Sw/Fi 1976; V; 14500; 202.62 × 8.48 (664.76 × 27.82); M; 19; Side doors; Sisters: **92731 DON JUAN** (Sw).

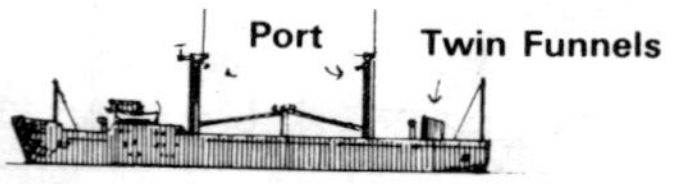

KM$_2$FM H2
● **92740 MARIAECK.** FRG/Ne 1969/75; RoC/HL; 700; 92 × 2.86 (301.83 × 9.38); TSM; 13; Bow & stern doors; Lengthened 1975.

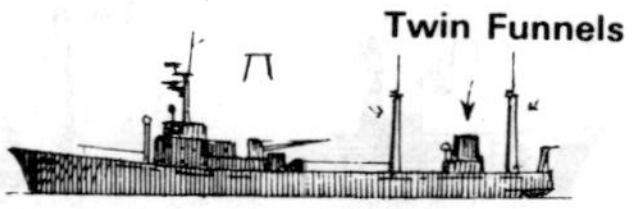

KM$_2$FM H1
92750 DONG BANG No 71. Ko/Ja 1972; ST; 1500; 80.75 × 5.2 (264.92 × 17.06); M; 14.

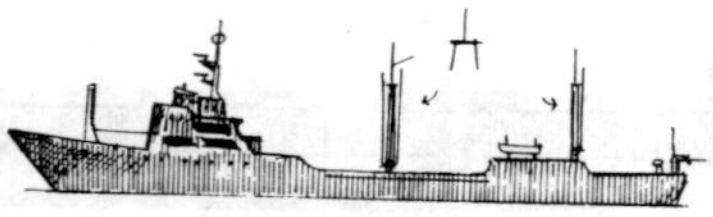

KM$_3$ H13
92760 MAR DE VIGO. Sp/Sp 1966; ST; 2900; 105.01 × 5.51 (344.52 × 18.07); TSM; 14.5; ex MAR DE ESPANA; **'ACSA 95'** type; Sister: ★**92761 MAR OCEANO** (Cu); ex PESCAFRIA CUARTO 1970.

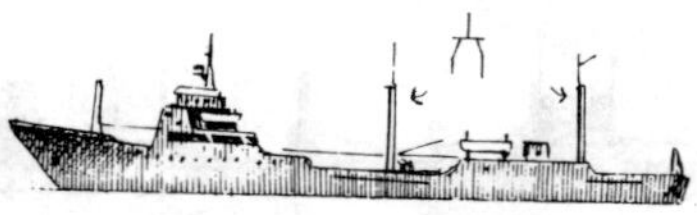

KM$_3$ H13
92770 BALTIM. Eg/Sp 1971; ST; 2400; 106 × 5.13 (347.76 × 16.83); TSM 15; Sister: **92771 RAS EL BAR** (Eg).

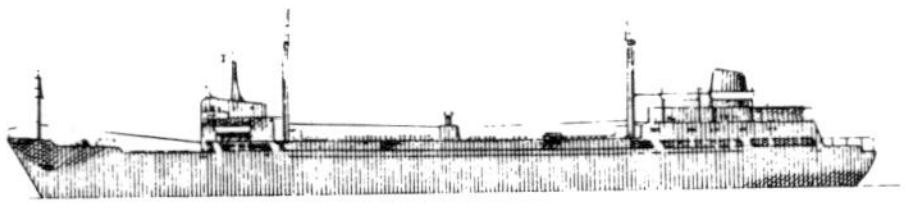

KM_3F H
★92780 CHIL BO SAN. RK/Ne 1969; FF; 10200; 138 × 6.81 (452.7 × 22.34); M; 15; Sister: **★92781 KEUM GANG SAN** (RK).

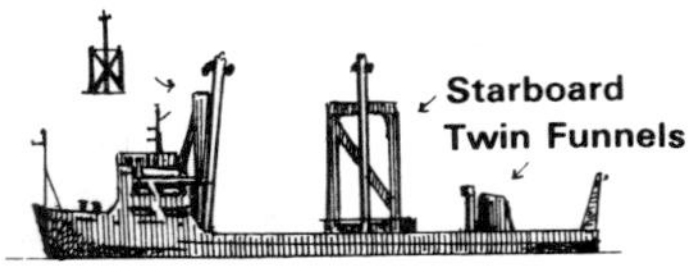

KM_2NF H1
92790 HAPPY PIONEER. Pa/Br 1964/70/73; RoC/HL; 1600; 89.74 × 4.5 (294.42 × 14.76); TSM; —; ex HARBO 1973; ex SIR JOSEPH RAWLINSON 1970; Converted sludge—carrier 1970; Converted cargo 1973.

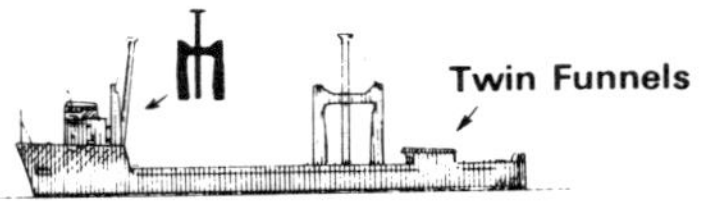

KMNF H1
92800 HAPPY RIDER. Ne/Ne 1976; RoC/HL; 1600; 81.82 × 5.55 (268.43 × 18.2); TSM; 12; Stern door; Sister: **92801 HAPPY RUNNER** (Ne).

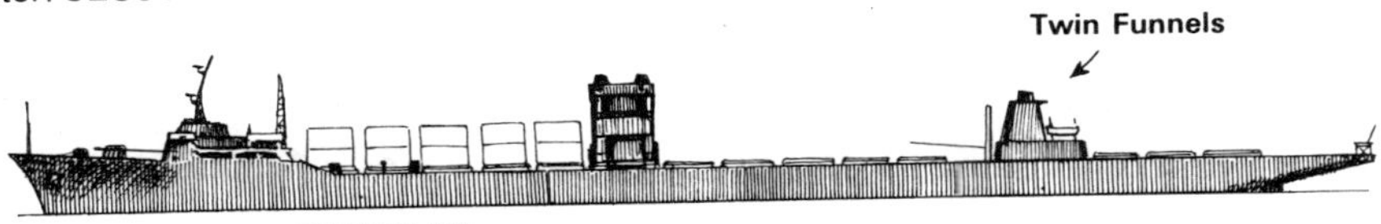

KMNKF H1
92810 ACADIA FOREST. Li/Ja 1969; Bg/Con; 37000; 261.42 × 12.12 (857.67 × 39.76); M; 19; **'Lash'** type; Sister: **92811 ATLANTIC FOREST** (Li).

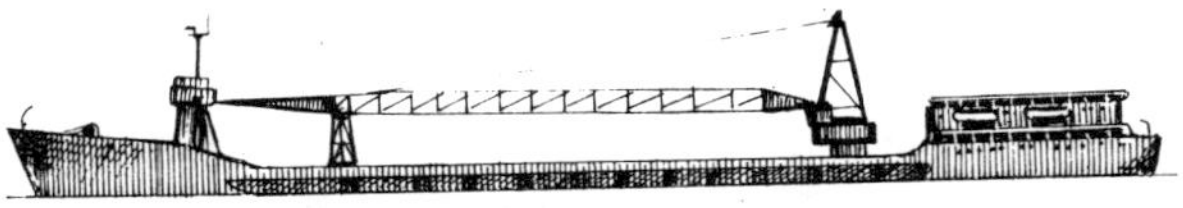

MC H13
92820 OCEAN BUILDER I. Li/Br-Ne; 1957/75; PLC/CS; 11900; 194.95 × 10.95; (639.59 × 35.92); M; —; ex SANTOS 1975; ex CUYAHOGA 1972; Converted from Ore/Oil & widened 1975.

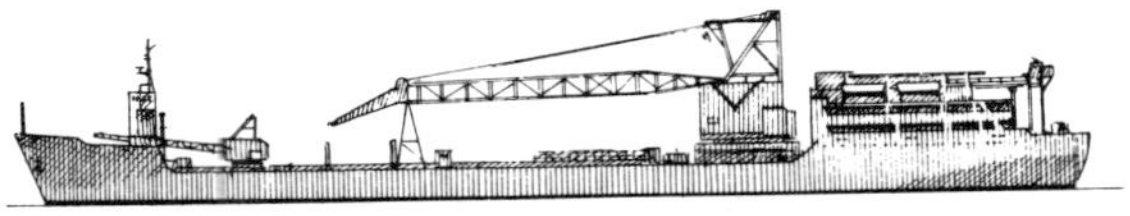

MC_2 H13
92830 ORCA. Pa/Sw-Ne 1954/72; PLC/CS; 9500; 181.62 × 10.03 (595.86 × 32.9); M; 15; ex SOYA-ATLANTIC 1972; Converted from Ore/Oil and widened 1972.

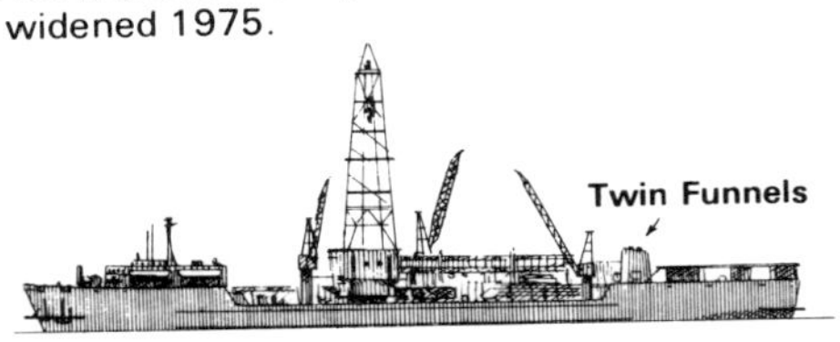

MC_3F H13
92840 SEDCO 445. Li/Ja 1971; DS; 6700; 136.05 × 7.61 (446.35 × 24.96); TSD-E; 14; Similar (Li flag): **92841 SEDCO 471; 92842 SEDCO 472**.

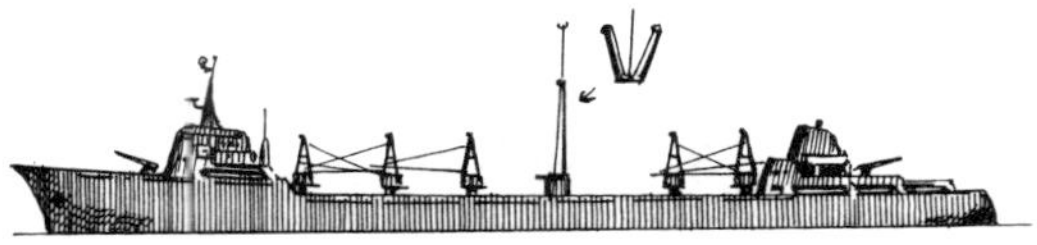

MC_3MC_2F H1
92850 DEL MUNDO. US/US 1968; C; 7100/10400; 159.11 × —/9.47 (522.01 × —31.07); T; 18.5; ex DELTA ARGENTINA 1980; Sisters (US flag): **92851 DEL CAMPO;** ex DELTA PARAGUAY 1980; **92852 DEL MONTE;** ex DELTA BRASIL 1980; **92853 DEL VIENTO;** ex DELTA MEXICO 1980; **92854 DEL VALLE;** ex DELTA URUGUAY 1980.

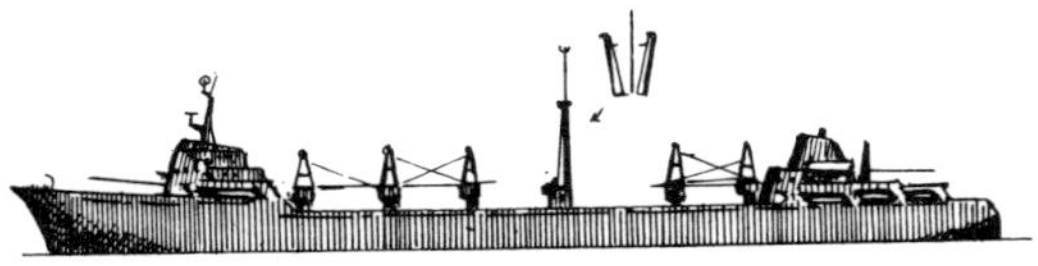

MC_3MC_2FK H1
92860 DEL ORO. US/US 1961; C; 7100/9800; 154.31 × —/9.48 (506.26 × —/31.1); T; 18; Sisters (US flag): **92861 DEL RIO; 92862 DEL SOL**.

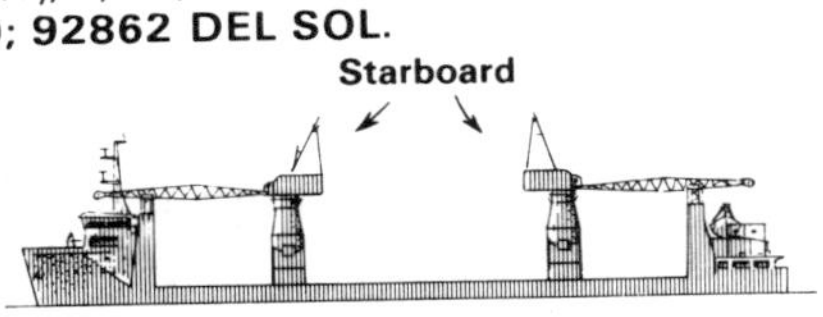

MC_2F H1
● **92870 HAIDA BRAVE**. Ca/Ca 1979; Log carrier; 10000 dwt; 121.5 × 5.82 (398.5 × 19.1); TS; 12.

MC_2F H13
92880 BEN OCEAN LANCER. Br/Br 1977; DS; 10800; 153.68 × 8 (504.19 × 26.2); TSD-E; 13; Similar: **92881 CANMAR EXPLORER III** (Ca); ex HAVDRILL 1976; **92882 PELERIN** (No); **92883 PETREL** (Be); **92884 PELICAN** (Fr).

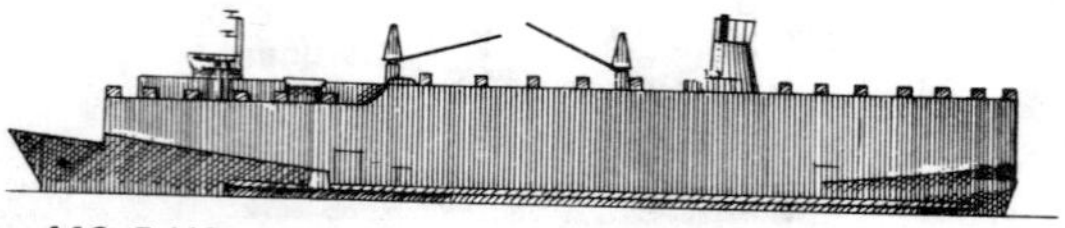

MC_2F H2
92890 NOPAL VERDE. No/Pd 1972/75; V; 14200; 190.58 × 9.93 (625.26 × 32.57); M; 19.5; ex JOANA 1973; Lengthened 1975; Converted general cargo 1975; Side doors/ramps; Sister: **92891 NOPAL BRANCO** (No); ex AMALIA 1973.

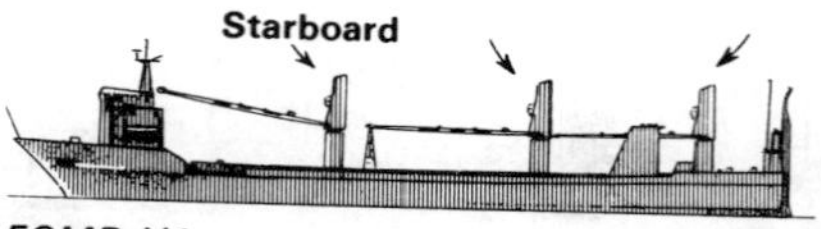

MC_2FCMR H1
92900 NEUGRABEN. FRG/FRG 1978; C/Con/RoC; 7100; 124 × 8.2 (406.8 × 26.9); TSM; 16.35; ex MERZARIO EMILIO; ex NEUGRABEN; Stern ramp; Funnel on port side only; Sister: **92901 UTA-SABINE** (FRG); ex MERZARIO LOMBARDIA; ex UTA-SABINE.

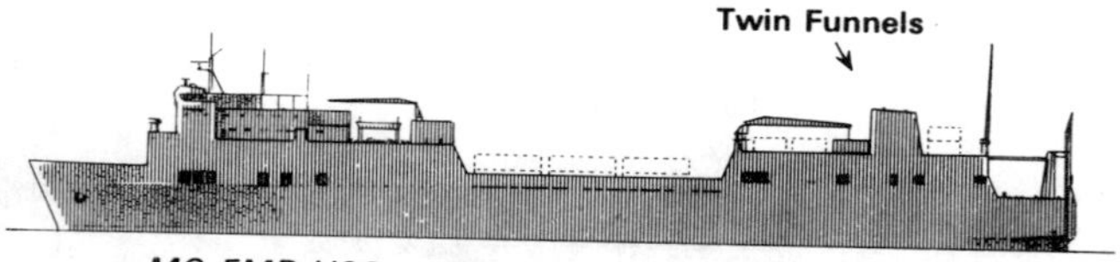

MC_2FMR H23
92910 FINNROSE. Sw/Sw; 1980; RoC/Con; 13400; 194.11 × 8.4 (636.84 × 27.56); TSM; 19; 2 stern ramps; Sister: **92911 FINNHAWK** (Sw).

MC_2MF H1
92920 ASPEN. Sw/Ne 1975; C; 3000; 88.02 × 6.67 (288.77 × 21.88); M; 12; Wood pulp carrier.

MC_2MF H13
92930 EMERALD. Sh/Br 1956; C; 2200; 79 × 5.04 (269.18 × 16.53); TSM; 8.5; ex LACHINEDOC 1975.

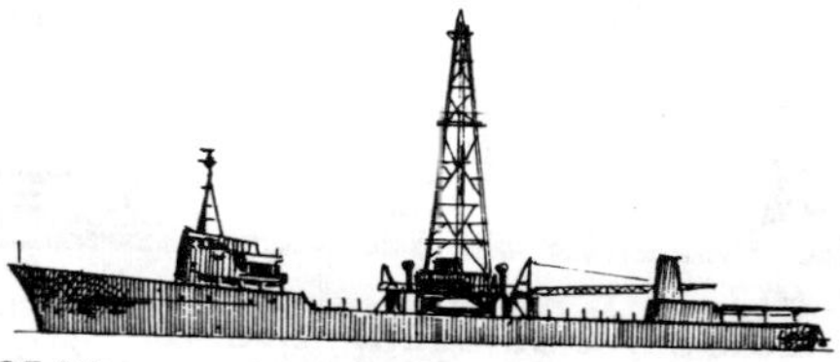

MCF H1
92940 SAIPEM DUE. It/It 1972; DS; 8500; 131.58 × 6.99 (431.69 × 22.93); TSD-E; 13.25.

MCF H1
● **92950 STEFI.** Li/Hong Kong 1975; C/Con; 1600; 76.23 × 3.83 (250.09 × 12.56); TSM; 11; ex DECKSHIP ARABELLA 1978; Stern ramp; **'Deckship'** type; Sisters: **92951 UNICON** (Sg); ex GHAZI 1980; ex CARINIA; **92952 LISSETTE** (Li); ex TAREK 1978; ex KHORRAMSHAHR 1976; ex DECKSHIP BRIGIDA 1976; **92953 DELICIA** (Li); **92954 PEGASUS PEACE** (Ko); Similar (stern ramp & new design of crane): **92955 FRANCESCA** (Li); **92956 FINNORIENT** (Li); ex ELEANORA.

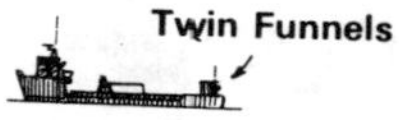

MCF H1
92970 LILLIAN XXII. Bn/No 1971; C; 150; 33 × 3.20 (108.26 × 10.5); TSM; 10; ex NANNA BUUR 1974; Sisters: **92971 LILLIAN XXIII** (Bn); ex TINA BUUR 1974, **92972 LILLIAN XXIV** (Bn); ex FENJA BUUR 1974; **92973 LILLIAN XXI** (Bn); ex FRIGGA BUUR 1974; **92974 CHIARA** (It); ex MERC CONTRACTOR 1977; ex TORA BUUR 1975.

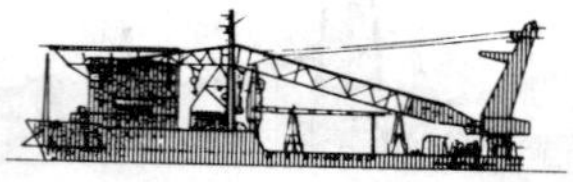

MCFC H1
92980 NORTHERN INSTALLER. Sg/Sg 1977; OSS; 2900; 77.91 × 4.61 (255.61 × 15.12); TSM; 11; Sister: **92981 PACIFIC INSTALLER** (Sg).

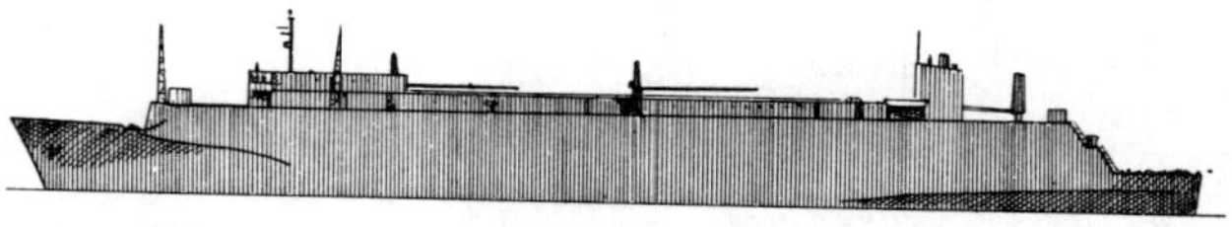

MCFC H2
92990 PACIFIC HIGHWAY. Ja/Ja 1977; V; 13500; 192.08 × 8.03 (630.18 × 26.34); M; 20.5; Sister: **92991 ATLANTIC HIGHWAY** (Li).

MCMF H
93000 KARMSUND. No/No 1979; Pal/Con; 500; 70.8 × 4.57 (232.28 × 14.99); M; 14; Side door (port); Sister: **93001 ROYKSUND** (No); Probable sister: **93002 ROGALAND** (No).

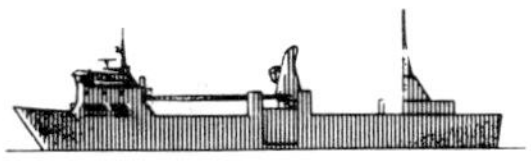

MCMF H
93010 NORDKYN. No/No 1979; Pal/Con; 700; 77.5 × 4.52 (254.27 × 14.83); M; 14; Side door (port); Possible sisters (No flag): **93011 BLIKUR; 93012 LOMUR.**

MCMF H1
93020 POINT SUSAN. US/US 1945/58; B; 16300; 193.71 × 10.21 (635.53 × 33.49); T-E; 15; ex AMERICAN BEAR 1978; ex AMERICAN WHEAT 1975; ex LUMBER QUEEN 1972; ex CONSOLIDATION COAL 1969; ex REDSTONE 1958; Converted from 'T-2' tanker 1958.

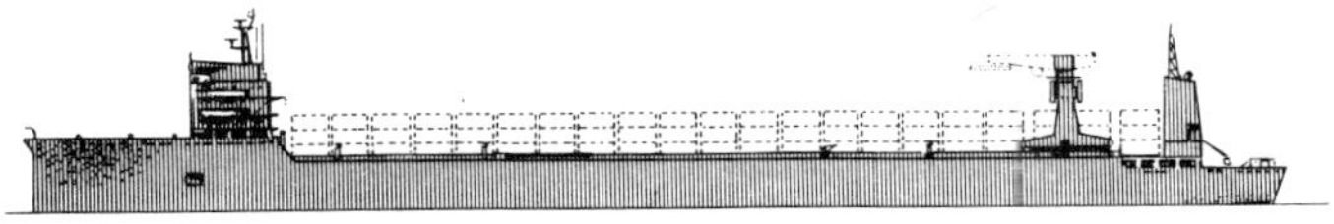

MCMF H1
93030 BACO-LINER 1. FRG/FRG 1979; Bg/Con; 23300; 204.1 × 6.67 (669.62 × 21.88); M; 15; Bow doors; Barges float on and off; Crane is shown in stowed position—dotted lines represent it swung fore—and—aft; Sister: **95031 BACO-LINER 2** (FRG).

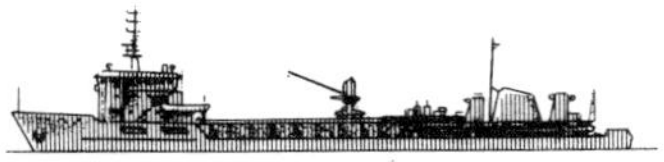

MCMF H1
93040 SCHELDE II. Be/Be 1979; D; 5700 dwt; 98.5 × 7 (323.16 × 22.97); M; 11; Trailing suction type.

MCMF H1
93050 CIUDAD DE BARRANQUILLA. Co/US 1949; D; 3700; 68.89 × — (226.01 × —); TSR; —.

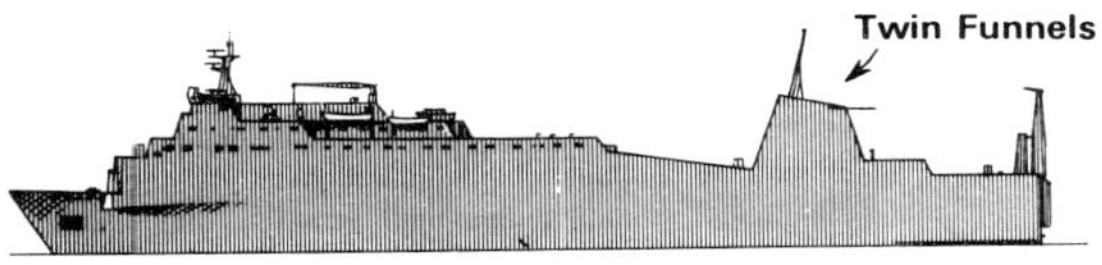

MCMFK H2
● **93060 ARIADNE.** Sw/Sw 1979; RoC; 8500; 166 × 7.9 (544.62 × 25.92); TSM; 18; Twin stern ramps (slewing); Sister: **93061 SCANDINAVIA** (Sw).

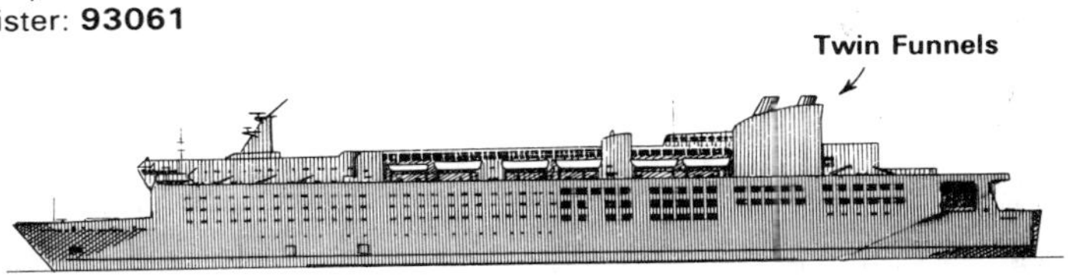

MF H
● **93070 FINNJET.** Fi/Fi 1977; RoPCf; 24600; 212.81 × 7.2 (698.2 × 23.62); TSGT/M; 30.5.

MF H
93080 IRIS. Is/Rm 1973; RoC; 8200; 128.33 × 6.58 (421 × 21.5); TSM; —; Stern door; Sister: **93081 NARCIS** (Is).

MF H
93090 MASHAL. Br/FRG 1977; RoC; 1600; 116.01 × 5.38 (380.61 × 17.65); TSM; 16; Sisters: **93091 SALAHALA** (Br); **94092 THOMAS WEHR** (FRG); ex WACRO EXPRESS; ex THOMAS WEHR; **93093 GABRIELE WEHR** (FRG); **93094 EMADALA** (Br).

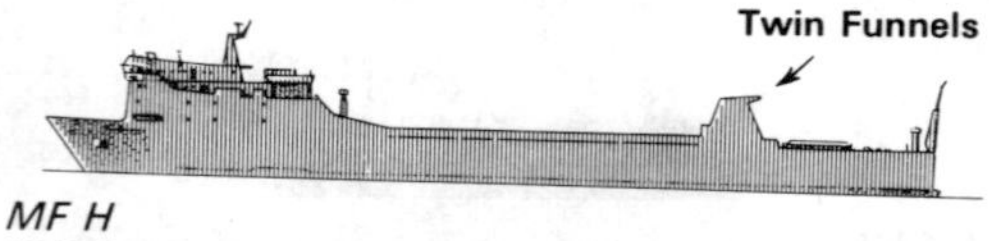

MF H
93100 FARHA. Cy/Ne 1973/75; RoC; 3900; 142.22 × approx. 5.94; TSM; 18; ex STENA SAILER 1976; Lengthened 1975; Bow and stern doors; Sister: **93101 BAHJAH** (Cy); ex SEATRADER 1976; launched as STENA SEATRADER.

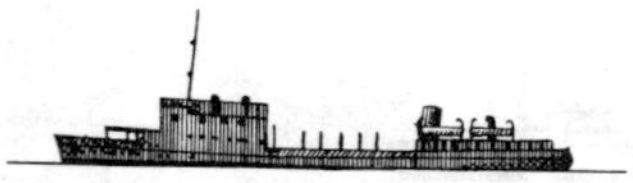

MF H
93120 CAMPECHE. Me/Br 1949; D; 1800; 82.63 × — (271.09 × —); TSR; —.

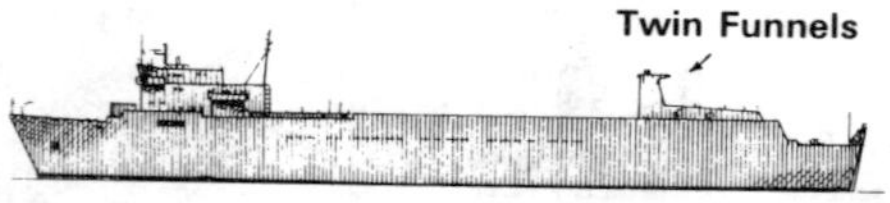

MF H2
93140 BAYARD. No/No 1975; RoC; 4000; 136.91 × 6.21 (449.17 × 20.37); TSM; 18.5; Stern door and ramp; Sisters (No flag): **93141 BOHEMUND; 93142 BALDUIN.**

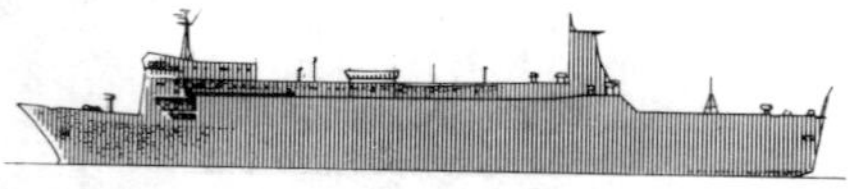

MF H2
● **93150 BRABANT.** FRG/FRG 1976; RoC; 3900; 127.03 × 5.41/6.55 (416 × 17.74/21.48); TSM; —; ex ARGO 1977; Stern door/ramp.

MF H2
93170 TAREK B. Pa/No 1975; RoC/F; 2400; 109.71 × 5.2 (359.94 × 17.06); TSM; 19; ex FALSTER 1980; ex PRINCE DE BRETAGNE 1975; ex FALSTER 1975; Bow door/ramp; Side door/ramp; Two stern doors/ramps.

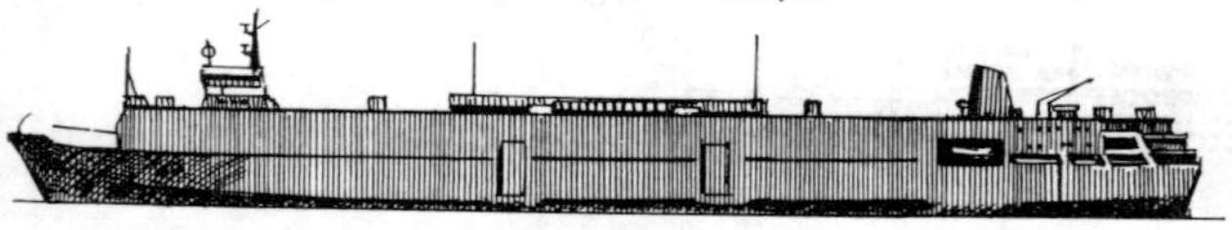

MFC H
93190 HUAL SKAGERAK. No/Ne 1973; V; 7300; 187.51 × 8.01 (615.19 × 26.27); M; 18; ex DYVI SKAGERAK; Side doors; Sisters (No flag): **93191 DYVI KATTEGAT; 93192 HOEGH TARGET**; ex DYVI ADRIATIC 1975; **93193 HOEGH TRIGGER**; Similar (tall pipes from funnel): **93194 NOPAL SEL.**

MF H
93110 CARRIER PRINCESS. Ca/US 1973; RoC/F; 4400; 115.83 × 4.88 (380.01 × 16.01); TSM; 18.

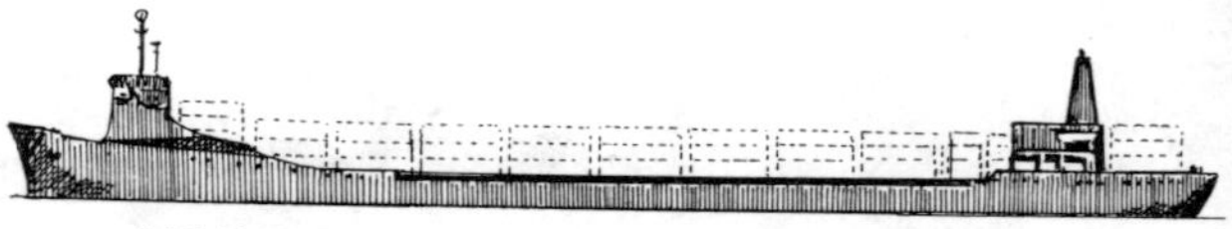

MF H13
93130 TRANSINDIANA. US/US 1944/69; Con; 13500; 192.92 × 8.93 (632.93 × 29.29); T; 16; ex GENERAL W. C. LANGFITT 1969; Converted 'C-4' type passenger/troopship 1969; Sisters (US flag): **93131 CAROLINA:** ex TRANSIDAHO 1975; ex GENERAL W. F. HASE 1969; **93132 AGUADILLA;** ex TRANSHAWAII 1975; ex GENERAL J. H. MCRAE 1969; **93133 MAYAGUEZ;** ex TRANSOREGON 1975; ex GENERAL W. G. HAAN 1969.

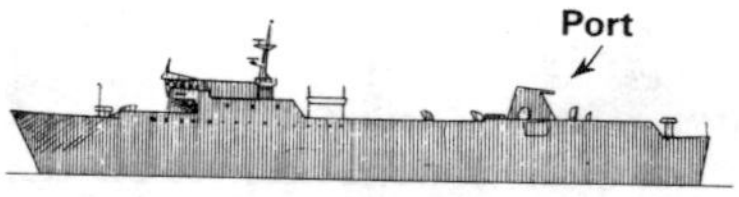

MF H2
93160 COUTANCES. Fr/Fr 1978; RoC; 2600; 110 × 4.5 (360.89 × 14.7); M; 17.5; Stern door; Bow door; Sister: **93161 PURBECK** (Fr).

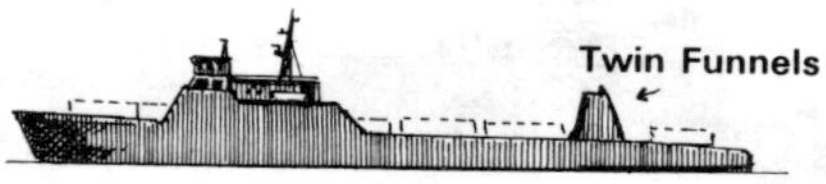

MF H2
93180 INCAN SUPERIOR. Ca/US 1974; RoC/F; 3800; 116.44 × 4.88 (382.02 × 16.01); TSM; 14; Possible sister: **93181 INCAN ST. LAURENT** (Ca).

MFK H1
● **93200 MANATI.** US/US 1970; RoC/Con; 500; 63.4 × 3.65 (208 × 11.97); TSM; —; Stern door.

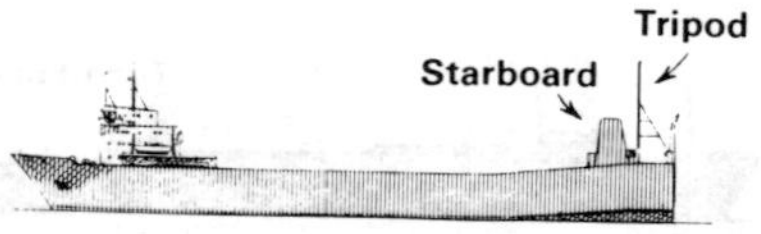

MFM H
93210 NOPAL OPTIMA. De/De 1978; RoC; 1600; 105.62 × 4.97 (346.52 × 16.31); M; 15.25; ex DANA OPTIMA; Stern door/ramp; Side doors; Sister: **93211 NOPAL MINERVA** (De); ex DANA MINERVA 1979.

MFM H
● **93220 FASGADAIR.** FRG/Ne 1969; RoC; 500; 76.99 × 2.85 (252.59 × 9.35); TSM; 13; ex BRUNNECK 1980; Bow door; Heavy cargoes; Now converted to pollution control vessel.

MFM H13
93230 EAGLESCLIFFE. Br/Br 1957; C; 2300; 78.95 × 5.51 (259.02 × 18.07); TSM; —; ex EAGLESCLIFFE HALL 1974.

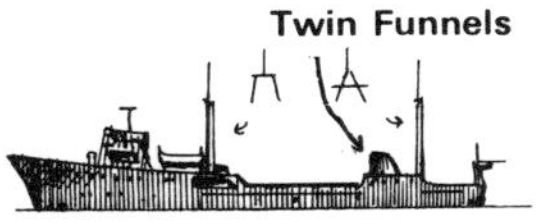

MFM H13
93240 USURBIL. Sp/Sp 1968; ST; 1300; 74.71 × 4.7 (245.11 × 15.41); M; 12.5; Sister: **93241 URQUIL** (Sp).

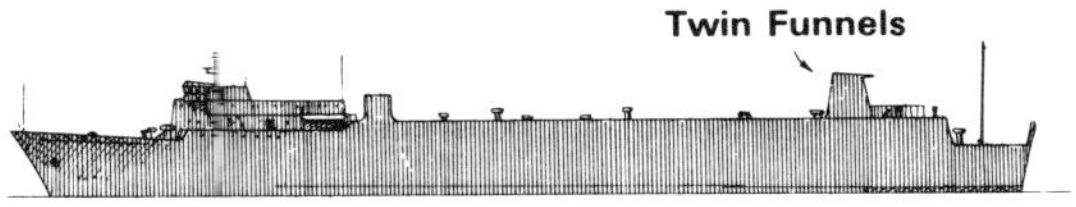

MFM H2
93250 TOR CALEDONIA. Br/No 1977; RoC; 5100; 162.77 × 6.2 (534.02 × 20.34); TSM; 18.5; Stern door; Similar (both lengthened) (Sw flag): **93251 TOR FINLANDIA; 93252 TOR DANIA:** ex BANDAR ABBAS EXPRESS 1979.

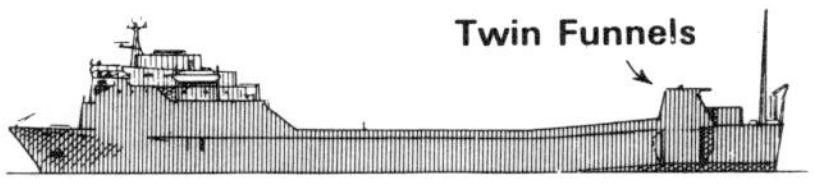

MFM H2
93260 ADMIRAL CARIBE. No/Ja 1977; RoC; 2600; 122.94 × 4.77 (403.35 × 15.65); TSM; 16.5; ex ADMIRAL NIGERIA; ex ADMIRAL CARIBE 1977; Stern door/ramp; Sisters (No flag): **93261 ADMIRAL ATLANTIC; 93262 ADMIRAL PACIFIC.**

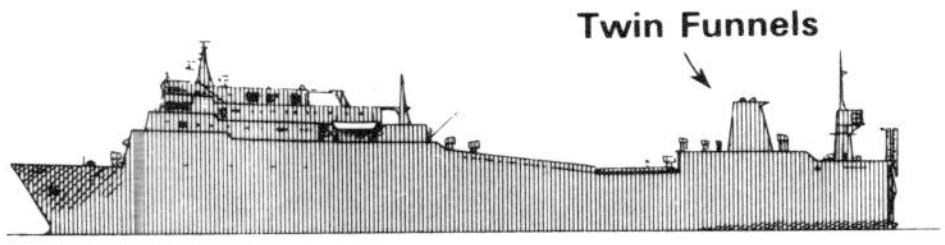

MFM H23
93270 TFL PROGRESS. Gr/Ja 1978; RoC; 5800; 140.85 × 7.65 (462.1 × 25); TSM; 14; Foreward ramp (starboard) and stern slewing ramp; Sister: **93271 TFL PROSPERITY** (Gr).

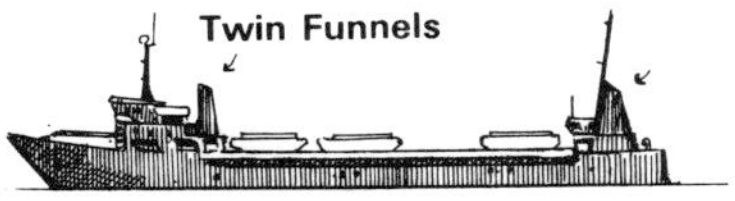

MFMF H
93280 BACAT I. In/De 1974; Bg; 1400; 103.51 × 5.42 (337.92 × 17.78); TSM; 11; Catamaran hull.

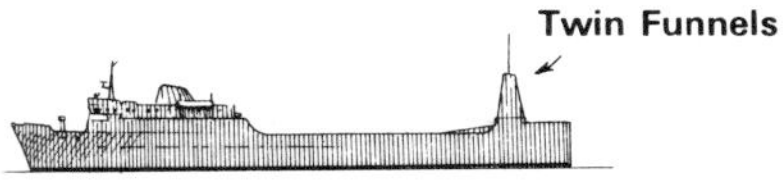

MFMF H2
93290 CALA MARSAL. Sp/Sp 1971; RoC; 900; 88.91 × 4.18 (291.69 × 13.71); M; 17; Sister: **93291 CALA LLONGA** (Sp).

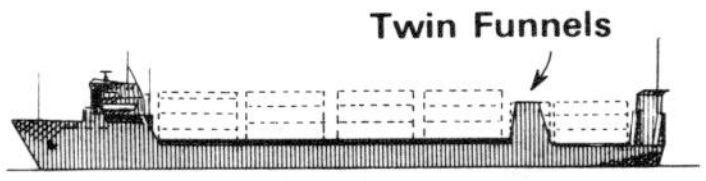

MFMR H1
● **93300 SEATRAIN LEONOR.** Do/No 1979; RoC/Con; 1500; 103.8 × 5.15 (340.55 × 16.9); M; 16; Stern quarter ramp; Sister: **93301 SEATRAIN LIBERTAD** (Do).

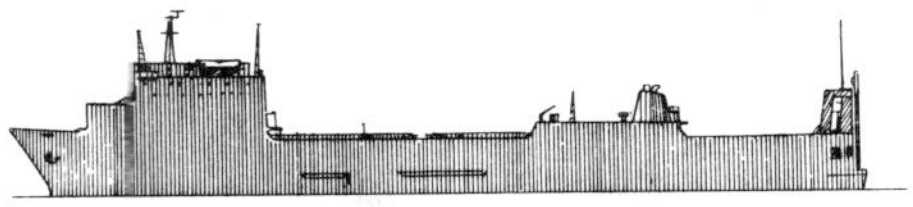

MFMR H2
⋆93310 NAN KOU. RC/Ja 1978; RoC; 3700; 136.19 × 6.81 (446.81 × 22.34); M; 17.7; ex OCEAN TRANSPORTER 1978; Sisters (RC flag): **⋆93311 BAI HEI KOU; ⋆93312 HUA YUAN KOU; ⋆93313 ZHI JIANG KOU; ⋆93314 TAI PING KOU; ⋆93315 XIAO SHI KOU.**

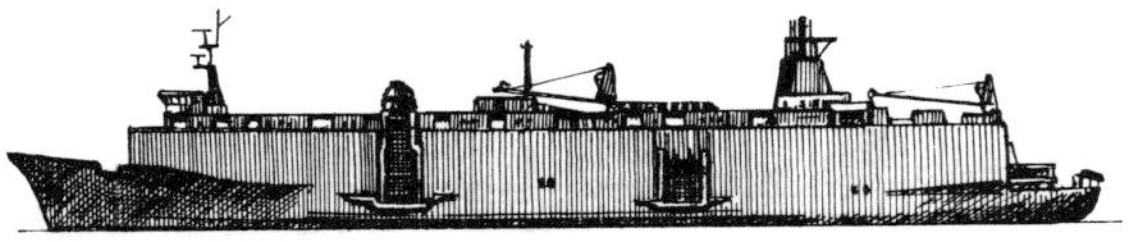

MKCFC H
93330 NOPAL ARGUS. Li/Ru-It 1970/73; RoVC; 7500; 169.63 × 8.31 (556.52 × 27.26); M; 18; Converted from general cargo 1973; Side doors.

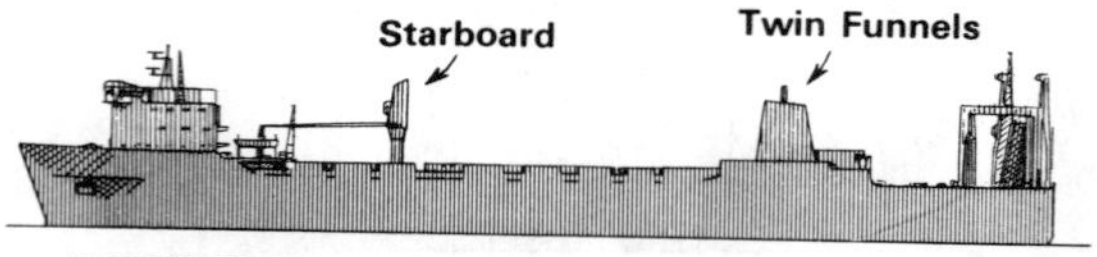

MKCFMR H13
93340 THEBELAND. Sw/Ja 1978; RoC/Con; 9400; 165 × 8 (541.34 × 26.25); TSM; 19.5; Stern quarter ramp/door; Sisters (Sw flag): **93341 TIMMERLAND; 93342 TYRUSLAND; 93345 VEGALAND;** Sisters (larger crane further aft): **93346 VIKINGLAND; 93347 VASALAND.**

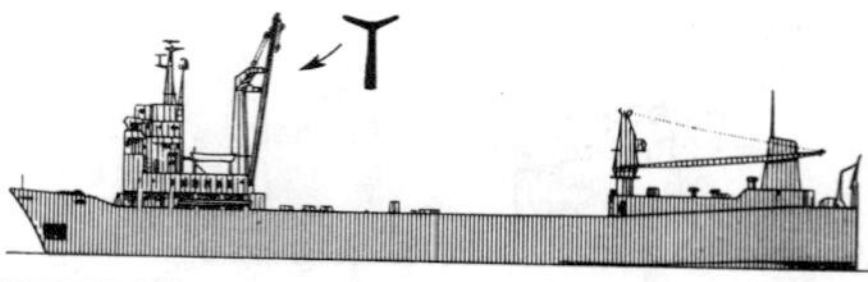

MKCMF H
93360 DANA AMERICA. Li/Ja 1979; RoC/Con/HL: 145.3 × 71.92 (442.91 × 21.92); M; 15.3; Stern ramp; 120 ton derrick; Sisters (Li flag): **93361 DANA AFRICA; 93362 DANA ARABIA; 93363 DANA CARIBIA.**

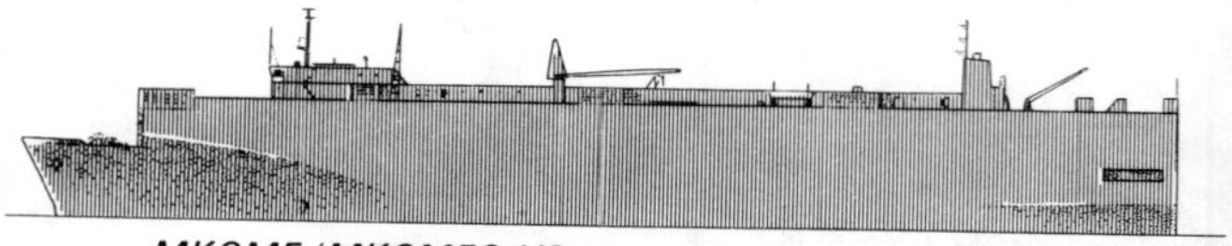

MKCMF/MKCMFC H2
93370 SCANDINAVIAN HIGHWAY. Ja/Ja 1978; RoVC; 20400; 197 × 9.52 (646.33 × 31.23); M; approx 18.8; Stern ramp; 2 side doors (P & S).

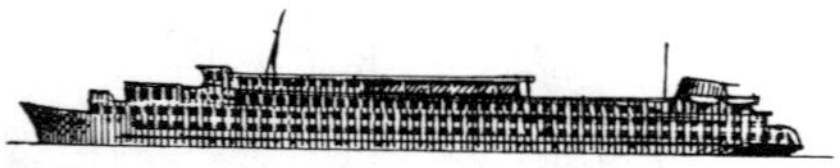

MKF H
⋆**93380 VLADIMIR ILYCH.** Ru/DDR 1976; Riv/P; 4900; 128.02 × —; (420 × —); —; —; Possible Sisters (Ru flag): ⋆**93381 MARIYA ULYANOVA;** ⋆**93382 SOVETSKAYA ROSSIYA;** ⋆**93383 60 LET OKTYABRYA.**

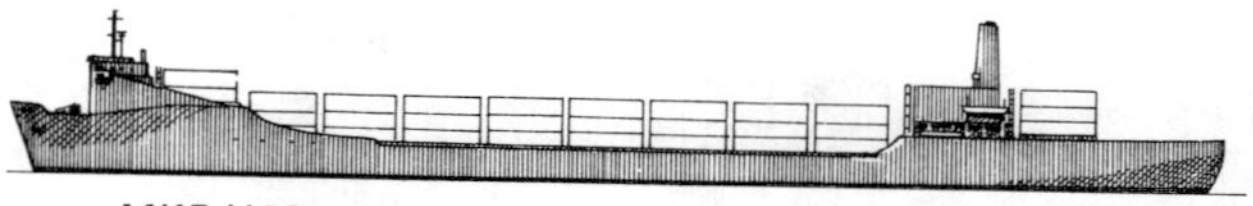

MKF H13
93390 TRANSINDIANA. US/US 1944/69; Con; 13500; 192.92 × 9.93 (632.93 × 29.29); T; 16; ex GENERAL W. C. LANGFITT 1969; Converted 'C-4' type passenger/troopship 1969; Sisters (US flag): **93391 CAROLINA:** ex TRANSIDAHO 1975; ex GENERAL W. F. HASE 1969; **93392 AGUADILLA:** ex TRANSHAWAII 1975; ex GENERAL J. H. MCRAE 1969; **93393 MAYAGUEZ:** ex TRANSOREGON 1975; ex GENERAL W. G. HAAN 1969.

MKFM H
93400 TAIYO MARU No 71. Ja/Ja 1962; ST; 1500; 75.52 × 5.51 (247.76 × 18.07); M; 12.25; Sister: **93401 CHALLWA No 2** (Pe); ex TAIYO MARU No 73 1976.

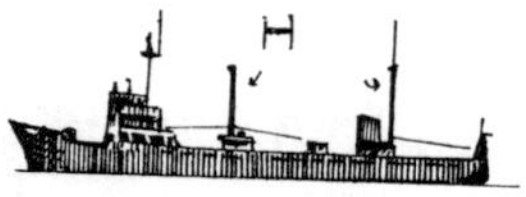

MKFM H
93410 TAIYO MARU No 65. Ja/Ja 1960; ST; 1300; 75.6 × 5.57 (248.03 × 18.27); M; 14.5; Sister (Ja flag): **93411 TAIYO MARU No 66;** Similar: **93412 BANSHU MARU No 5;** ex TAIYO MARU No 75; **93413 BANSHU MARU No 6;** ex TAIYO MARU No 76.

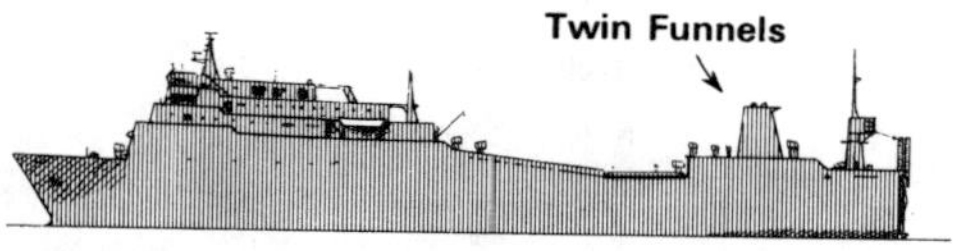

MKFM H23
93420 TFL PROGRESS. Gr/Ja 1978; RoC; 5800; 140.85 × 7.65 (462.1 × 25); TSM; 14; Foreward quarter ramp (starboard) and stern slewing ramp; Sister: **93421 TFL PROSPERITY** (Gr).

MKFMK H
93430 SWELLMASTER. Ca/Ca 1950; D; 1900; 76.21 × 4.57 (250.03 × 14.99); TSD-E; ex SANDPIPER.

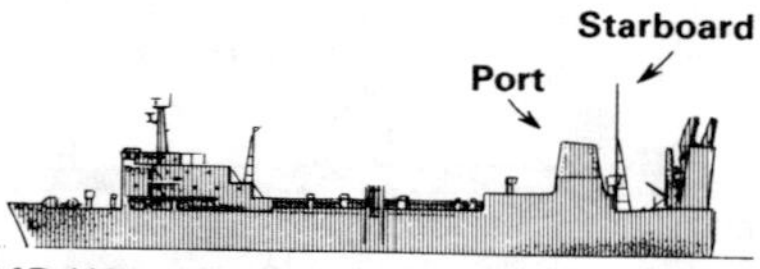

MKFMR H3
93440 SHINSEI MARU. Ja/Ja 1978; RoC; 3100; 112.53 × 6.01 (369.2 × 19.72); M; 17; Stern ramp.

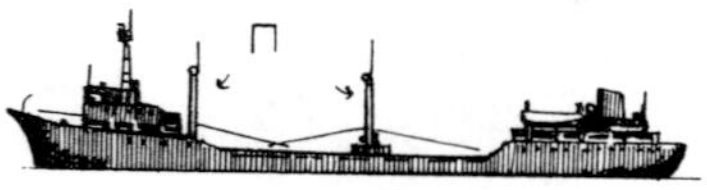

MK_2F H13
93450 KAZUSHIMA MARU. Ja/Ja 1962; C; 3700; 105.01 × 6.22 (344.52 × 20.4); M; 12.75.

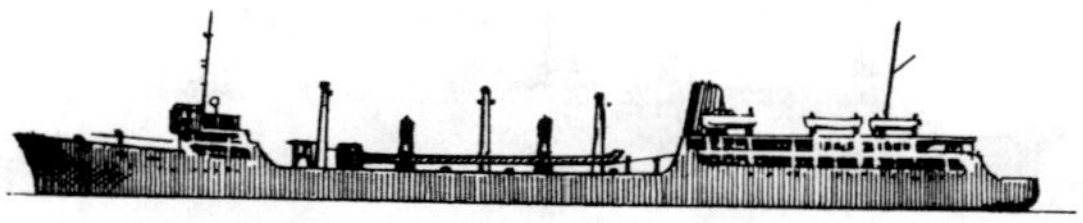

MK_5FM H
93460 ESSAYONS. US/US 1950; D; —; 160.05 × 8.22 (525.1 × 27); TSM; 15.5.

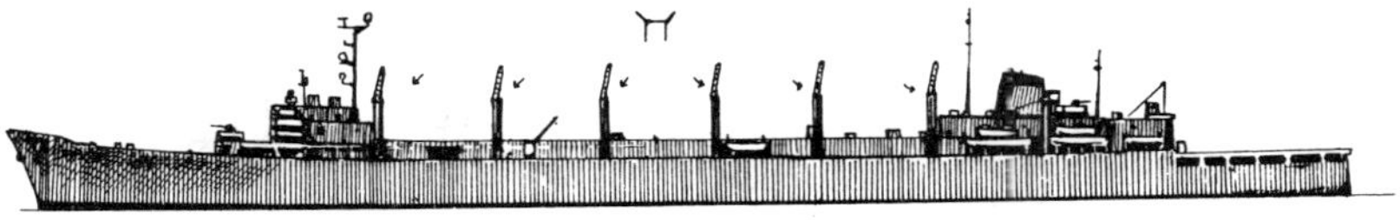

MK$_6$MFK H
93470 SACRAMENTO. US/US 1964; Spt/FA; 53600 dspl; 241.7 × 12 (793 × 29.3); TST; 26; Helicopter deck and two helicopters; Sisters (US Flag): **93471 CAMDEN; 93472 DETROIT; 93473 SEATTLE.**

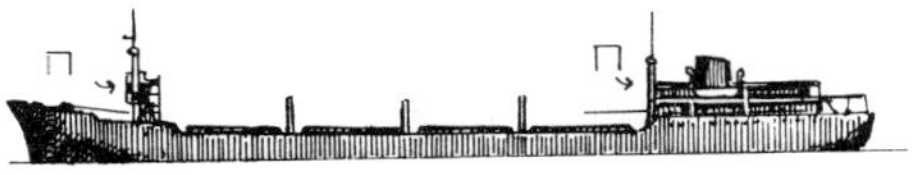

MK$_3$MF H13
93480 TOPIRA. Br/Br 1954; OO; 6900; 134.75 × 6.1 (442.09 × 20.01); R; 10; ex SUNBRAYTON 1979.

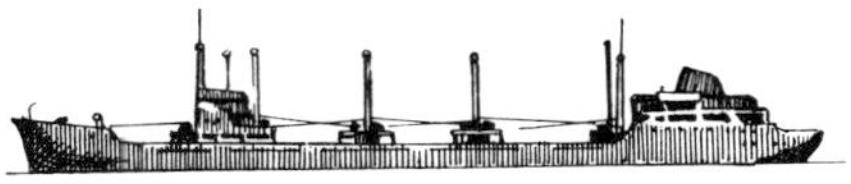

MK$_3$MF H13
93490 TODOS OS SANTOS. Bz/Fi 1960; C; 4000/6400; 126.8 × 6.78/— (416.01 × 22.24/—); M; —; Sisters (Bz flag): **93491 ALBERTO MONTEIRO;** ex GUANABARA 1980; **93492 TURIACU.**

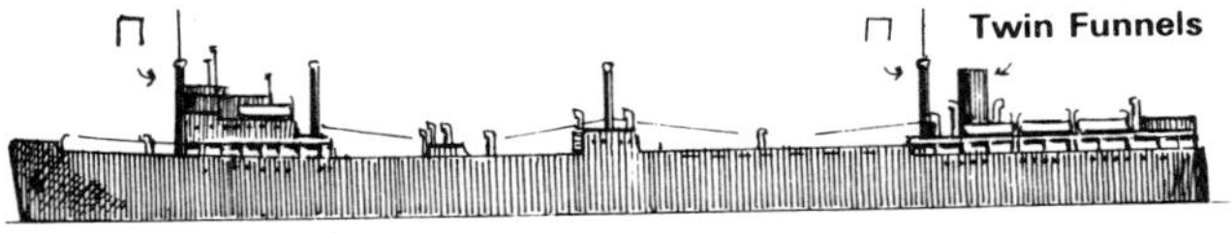

MK$_2$MF H
93500 NISSHIN MARU No 2. Ja/FRG 1937; FF; 27100; 193.45 × 12.19 (634.67 × 39.99); TSM; 14.75; ex ABRAHAM LARSEN 1957; ex EMPIRE VICTORY 1950; ex UNITAS 1945.

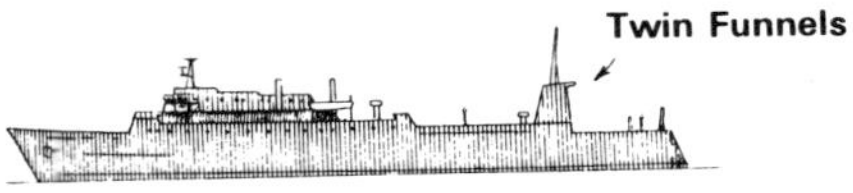

MK$_2$MF H
● **93510 ULIDIA.** Br/No 1970; RoC; 1600; 105.9 × 4.95 (347.44 × 16.24); TSM; 17; ex STENA CARRIER 1974; Bow, stern and side doors; Sister: **93511 VIKING TRADER** (Br); ex STENA TRADER 1980; ex DALRIADA 1980; ex STENA TRAILER 1971; Similar: **93512 ANDERIDA** (Br).

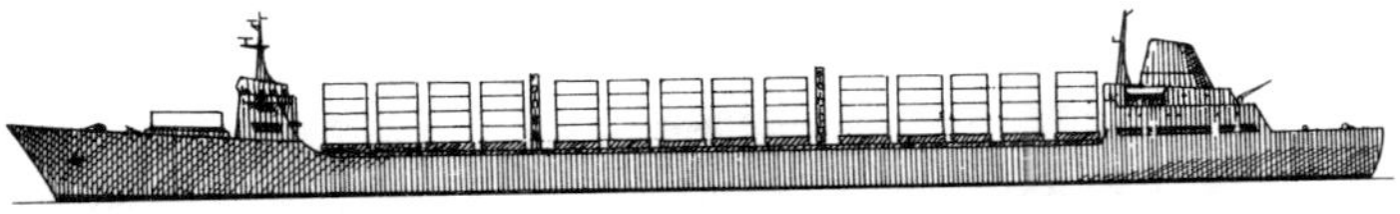

MK$_2$MF H1
93520 MANUKAI. US/US 1970; Con; 23800; 219.62 × 10.4 (720.53 × 34.12); T; 23; ex HAWAIIAN ENTERPRISE; Sister (US flag): **93521 MANULANI:** ex HAWAIIAN PROGRESS; Similar (bridge superstructure one deck lower): **93522 SEA-LAND ECONOMY;** ex SL 818 1973; ex H. P. BALDWIN; **93523 SEA-LAND VENTURE;** ex SL 180 1973; ex S. T. ALEXANDER; **93524 SEA-LAND CONSUMER;** ex AUSTRALIA BEAR 1973; **93525 SEA-LAND PRODUCER;** ex NEW ZEALAND BEAR; Similar (bridge further foreward and one deck higher): **93526 MAUI; 93527 KAUAI.**

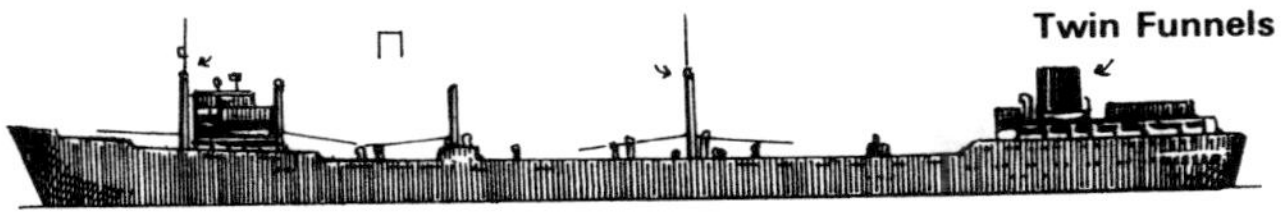

MK$_2$MF H13
93540 NISSHIN MARU No 3. Ja/Sw 1947; FF; 22800; 194.62 × 10.71 (638.51 × 35.13); M; 12.5.

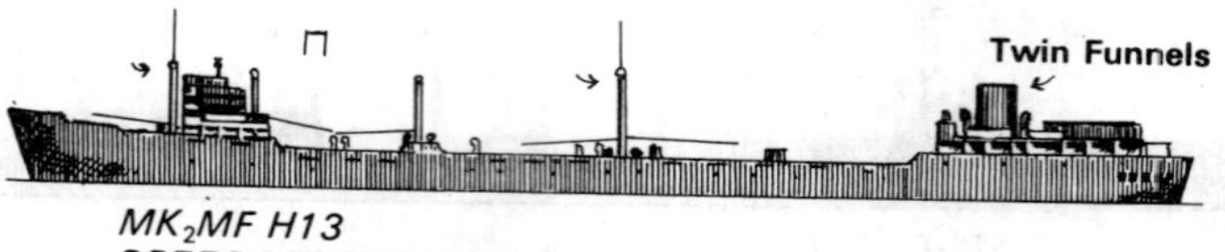

MK_2MF H13
93550 L'INTERPECHE. Br/Br 1948/66; FF; 18900; 204.6 × — (671.25 × —); TSM; 10.5; ex SUIDERKRUIS 1971; ex KOSMOS V 1967; Converted from whale factory 1966.

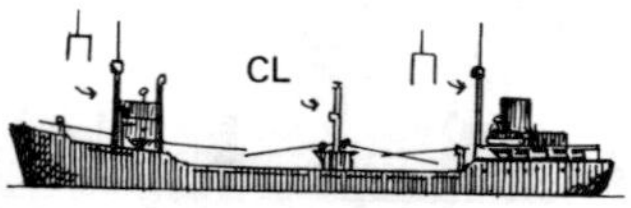

MK_2MF H13
93560 ELEISTRIA III. Cy/No 1952; C; 2600; 94.6 × 6.02 (310.36 × 19.75); M; 12.5; ex HINRICH PETERS 1972; ex GUDVIN 1964; ex GERMA 1961; Sister: **93561 TACAMAR II** (Pa); ex GELTING 1974; ex AUN 1968; ex GERSTAD 1964; ex FERM 1964.

MK_2MF H13
93570 HILLAH. Iq/Ne 1969; D; 6300; 120 × 6.72 (393.7 × 22.04); TSR; 14.

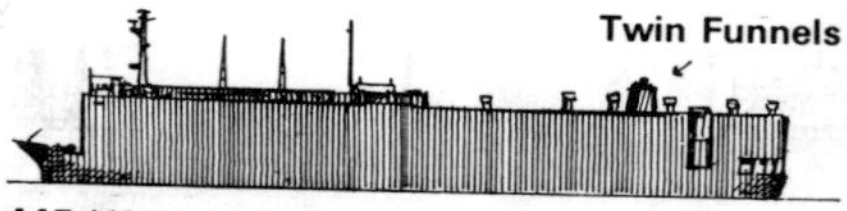

MK_2MF H2
93580 EMILY MOON. Pa/Ja 1976; V; 4700; 120.1 × 8.93 (394.02 × 29.29); M; 17; ex BLUE ANDROMEDA 1977; Side doors. Sister: **93581 EMILY STAR** (Pa) ex BLUE CASSIOPEIA 1977.

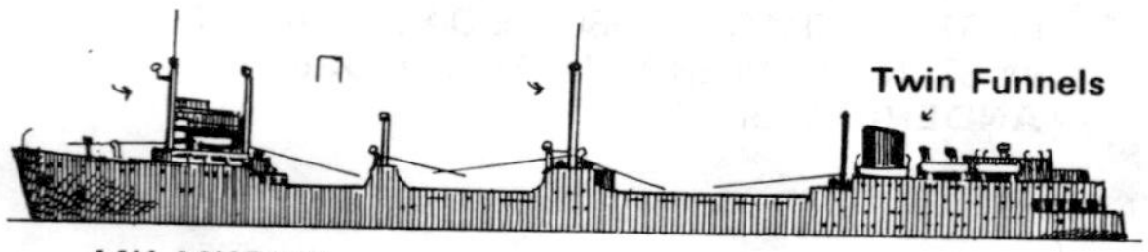

MK_2MKF H1
93590 KYOKUSEI MARU. Ja/FRG 1937/51; WF; 13900; 183.06 × 8.89 (600.59 × 29.16); TSM; 12; ex KOSMOS IV 1971; ex WALTER RAU 1946; lengthened 1951.

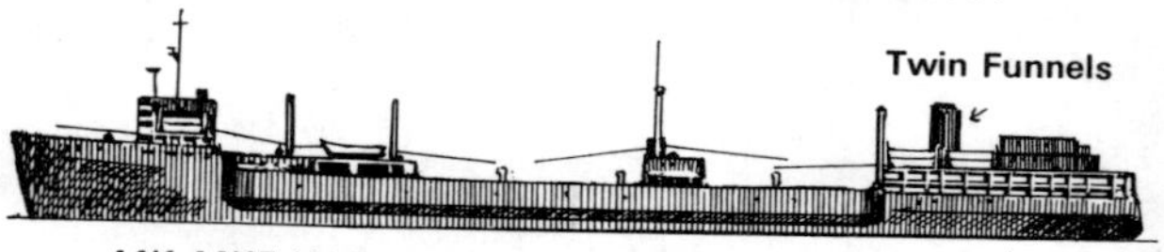

MK_2MKF H13
93600 KYOKUYO MARU No3. Ja/Br 1946; WF; 23100; 169.17 × 10.59 (555.01 × 34.74); TSM; 13; ex BALAENA 1960.

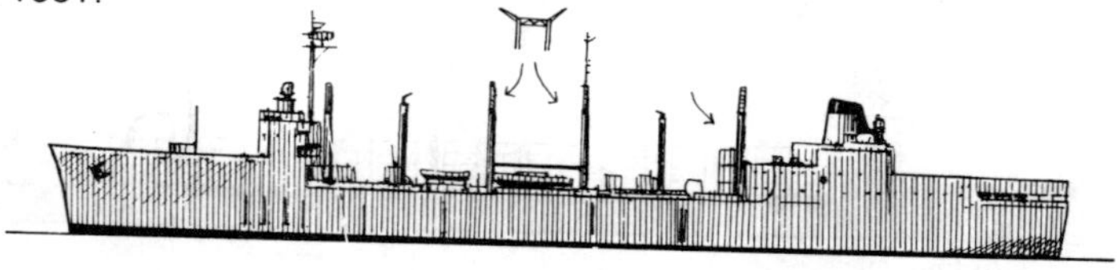

MK_2MK_2F H13
93610 WICHITA. US/US 1969; RT/FA; 37400 Dspl; 206.9 × 10.2 (659 × 33.3); TST; 20; Helicopter deck & two helicopters. Sisters (US flag): **93611 KALAMAZOO; 93612 KANSAS CITY; 93613 MILWAUKEE; 93614 ROANOKE; 93615 SAVANNAH; 93616 WABASH.**

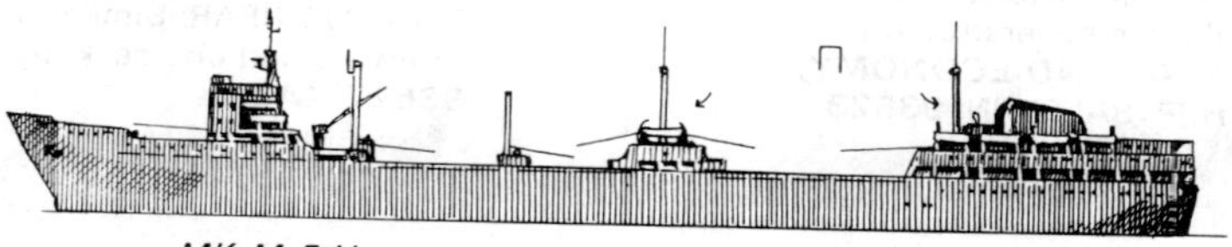

MK_2M_2F H
⋆93630 SOVIETSKAYA ROSSIA. Ru/Ru 1961; WF; 33200; 217.51 × 10.85 (713.61 × 35.59); TSM; 16.

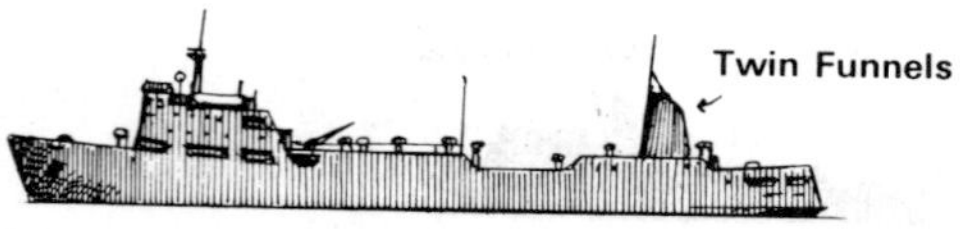

MKMF H
93640 AFRICAN TRADER. Pa/Br 1969 RoC; 3000; 130.99 × 6.62 (429.75 × 21.71); TSM; —; ex JOLLY GIALLO 1980; ex MAHENO 1977; Stern door. Sister: **93641 MARAMA** (NZ).

MKMF H
93650 AKORA. Gh/Ja 1965; ST; 2000; 79.5 × 4.97 (260.82 × 16.3); M; 14.5. Sisters (Gh flag): **93651 ASEBU; 93652 BANKO; 93653 SUBIN.**

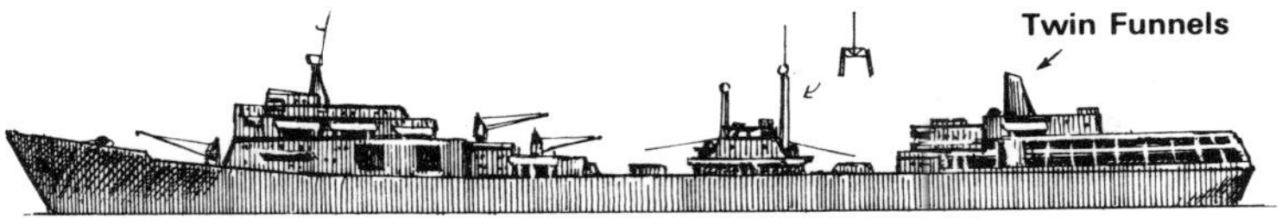

MKMF H1
***93660 VOSTOCK.** Ru/Ru 1971; FF; 26400; 224.57 × 10.02 (736.78 × 32.87); TST; 19.

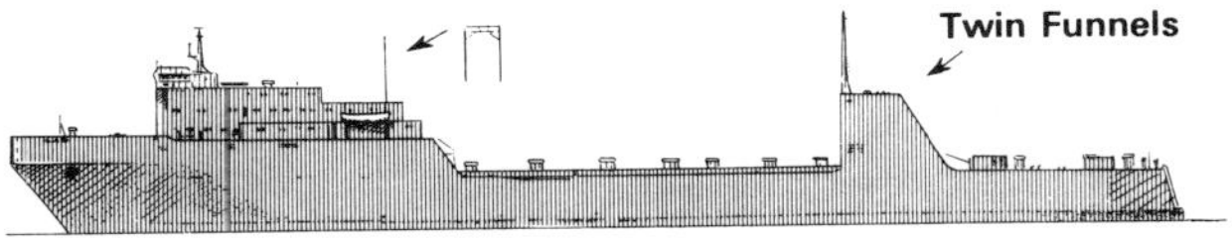

MKMF H1
***93670 GEROITE NA SEVASTOPOL.** Bu/No 1978; RoC/TF; 9600; 185.45 × 7.42 (608.43 × 24.34); TSM; 19; Stern door. Sister: ***93671 GEROITE NA ODESSA** (Bu); Similar (Ys built): ***93672 GEROI PLEVNY** (Ru); ***93673 GEROI SHIPKI** (Ru).

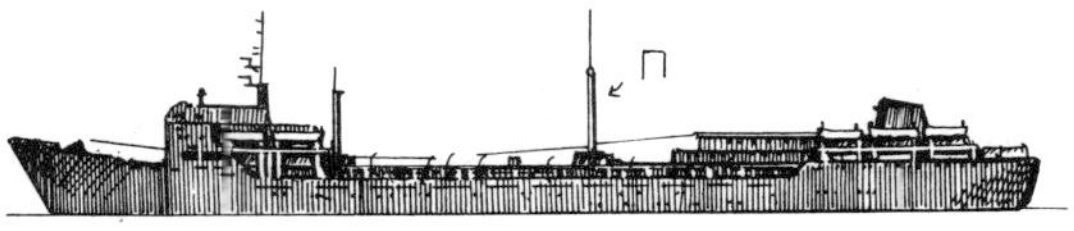

MKMF H13
***93680 ANDREY ZAKHAROV.** Ru/Ru 1960; FF; 12700; 162.16 × 7.02 (532.02 × 23.03); TSM; 12.5. Sisters (Ru flag): ***93681 PAVEL CHEBOTNYAGIN; *93682 ALEKSANDR OBUKHOV; *93683 EVGENIY NIKISHIN; *93684 KONSTANTIN SUKHANOV; *93685 VASILIY BLUKHER; *93686 MIKHAIL TUKACHEVSKIY; *93687 PAVEL POSTYSHEV; *93688 SERGEY LAZO; *93689 VASILIY PUTINTSEV; *93690 ALEKSANDR KOSAREV; *03691 KRONID KORENOV; *93692 IERONIM UBOREVICH; *93693 KORABLESTROITYEL KLOPOTOV.**

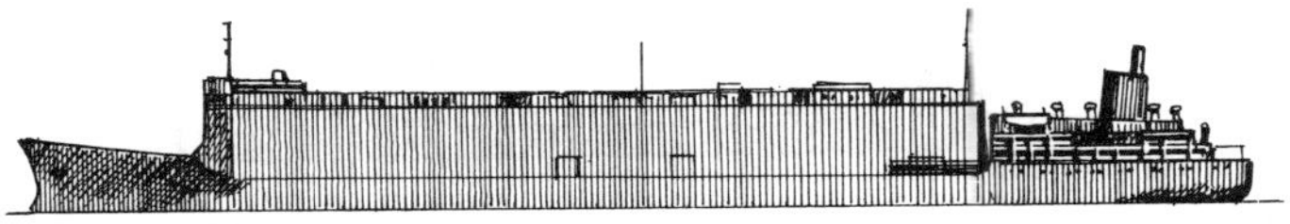

MKMF H13
93710 HUAL TRADER. Li/It 1958/70; V; 21400; 211.26 × 11.12 (693.11 × 36.48); T; 16.5; ex HOEGH TRADER 1978; ex ESSO GENOVA 1969; ex ESSO WINDSOR 1963. Side doors. Converted tanker 1970.

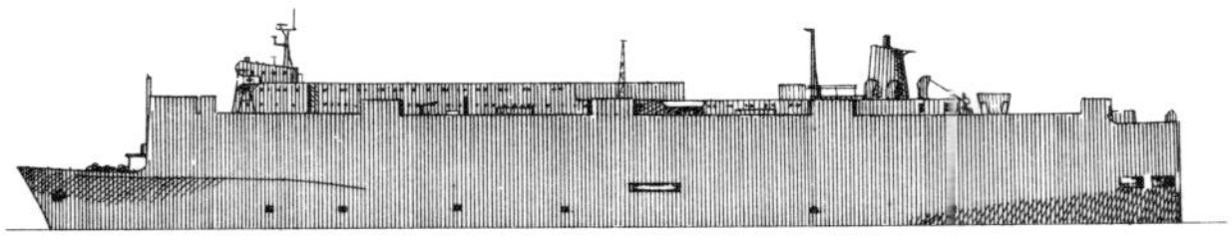

MKMF H2
93720 RIGOLETTO. Sw/Ja 1977; RoVC. 17500; 190.02 × 8.5 (623.4 × 27.8); M; 18.25. Sister: **93721 TRAVIATA** (Sw).

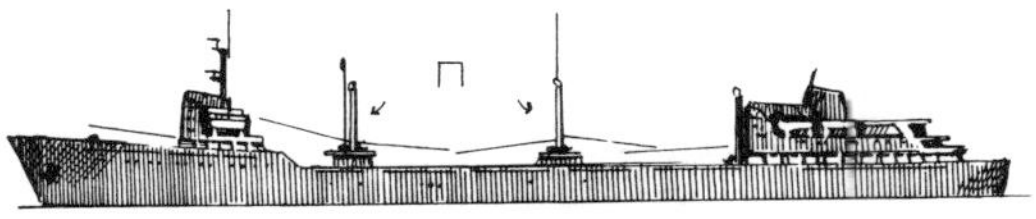

MKMKF H1
***93730 PROFESSOR BARANOV.** Ru/Pd 1967; FF; 13600; 164.02 × 8.08 (538.09 × 26.5); M; 15.25. **'B—69** type. Similar (Ru flag): ***93731 FELIKS KON; *93732 NAKHICHEVAN; *93733 ROBERT EYKHE; *93734 YULIAN MARKHLEVSKIY; *93735 KALININGRADSKIY KOMSOMOLETS; *93736 SEVERNYY POLYUS; *93737 SOVIETSKIY ZAPOLYARYE; *93738 TOMSK; *93739 LENINSKAYA ISKRA; *93740 MARSHAL MERETSKOV; *93741 NOVAYA KAKHOVKA; *93742 NOVAYA LADOGA; *93743 ARKTIKA; *93744 OROCHON; *93745 PALANGA; *93746 SOVIETSKOYE PRIMORYE; *93747 AVACHA; *93748 RYBAK BALTIKA; *93749 ANTARKTIKA; *93750 LENINSKIY PUT; *93751 SOVIETSKAYA SIBIR; *93752 YUZHINO—SAKJALINSK; *93753 PRIBALTIKA; *93754 RIZHSKOYE VZMORYE; *93755 50 LET OKTYABRYA** (or **PYATIDYESYATILYETIYE OKTYABRYA**) ***93756 VINTSAS MITSKYAVICHUS—KAPSUKAS** ex VINTSAS MITSKYAVICHUS 1973; ex ZAPRYBA 1971; ***93757 SOVIETSKAYA BURYATYA; *93758 ALEKSANDROVSK SAKHALINSKIY; *93759 KOMSOMOLETS MAGADANA; *93760 KOMSOMOLSK NA AMURE; *93761 MARSHAL SOKOLOVSKIY; *93762 RYBAK LATVII; *93763 ZEMLYA KOLSKAYA; *93764 POGRANICHNIK LEONOV.**

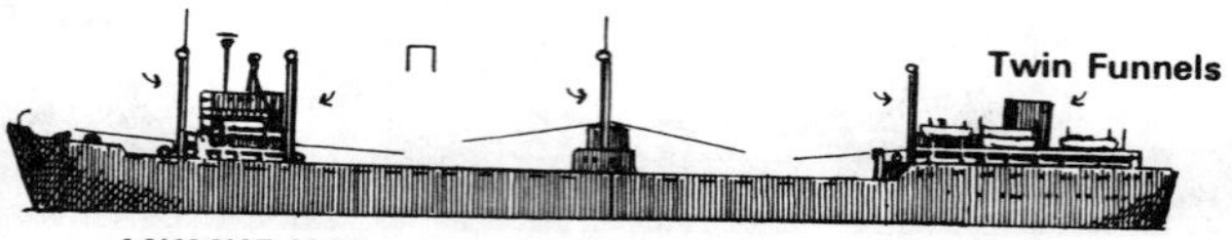

MKMKF H13
93770 NISSHIN MARU. Ja/Ja 1951; WF; 20800; 189.54 × 10.8 (621.85 × 35.43); M; 13.

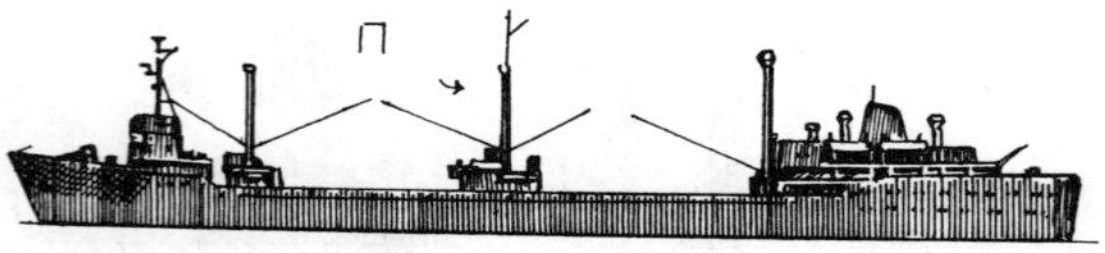

MKMKF H13
⋆93780 VILIS LACIS. Ru/FRG 1966; FF; 16500; 167.24 × 7.49 (548.68 × 24.57); M; 14; ex MORSKAYA SLAVA 1966; Sisters (Ru flag): **⋆93781 BOEVAYA SLAVA; ⋆93782 RYBATSKAYA SLAVA; ⋆93783 TRUDOVAYA SLAVA; ⋆93784 BALTIYSKAYA SLAVA; ⋆93785 CHERNOMORSKAYA SLAVA; ⋆93786 KRONSHTADTSKAYA SLAVA; ⋆93787 LENINGRADSKAYA SLAVA.**

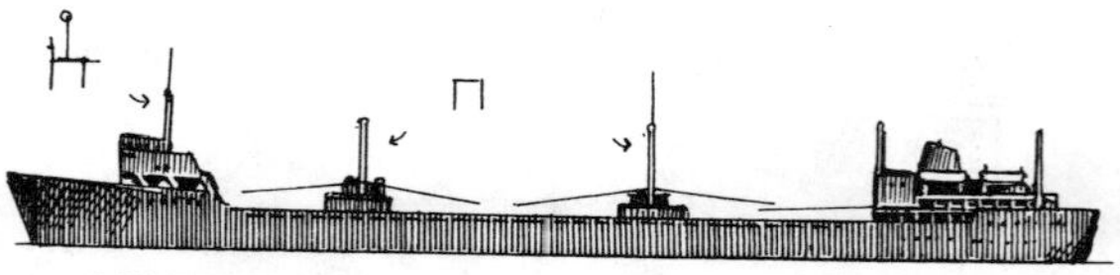

MKMKFK H13
● **⋆93800 SEVERODONETSK.** Ru/Ja 1966; FF; 18000; 174.33 × 7.32 (571.94 × 24.01); M; 14.5; Sisters (Ru flag): **⋆93801 SEVEROURALSK; ⋆93802 SHALVA NADIBAIDZE; ⋆93803 SLAVYANSK; ⋆93804 SPASSK; ⋆93805 SUKHONA; ⋆93806 SULAK; ⋆93807 SUZDAL.**

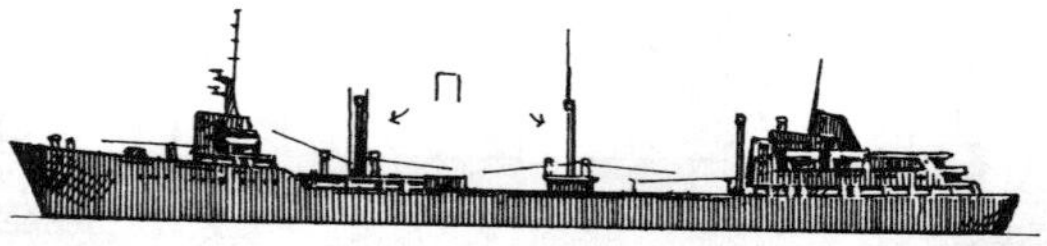

MKMKMF H1
⋆93820 POGRANICHNIK LEONOV. Ru/Pd 1972; FF; 13100; 164.01 × 8.08 (538.09 × 26.5); M; 15.25; **'B-69'** type; Similar (Ru flag);**⋆93821 FELIKS KON; ⋆93822 NAKHICHEVAN; ⋆93823 ROBERT EYKHE; ⋆93824 YULIAN MARKHLEVSKIY; ⋆93825 KALININGRADSKIY KOMSOMOLETS; ⋆93826 SEVERNYY POLYUS; ⋆93827 SOVIETSKIY ZAPOLYARYE; ⋆93828 TOMSK; ⋆93829 LENINSKAYA ISKRA; ⋆93830 MARSHAL MERETSKOV; ⋆93831 NOVAYA KAKHOVKA; ⋆93832 NOVAYA LADOGA; ⋆93833 ARKTIKA; ⋆93834 OROCHON; ⋆93835 PALANGA; ⋆93836 SOVIETSKOYE PRIMORYE; ⋆93837 AVACHA; ⋆93838 RYBAK BALTIKA; ⋆93839 ANTARKTIKA; ⋆93840 LENINSKIY PUT; ⋆93841 SOVIETSKAYA SIBIR; ⋆93842 YUZHINO-SAKHALINSK; ⋆93843 PRIBALTIKA; ⋆93844 RIZHSKOYE VZMORYE; ⋆93845 50 LET OKTYABRYA** (or **PYATIDYESYATILYETIYE OKTYABRYA); ⋆93846 VINTSAS MITSKYAVICHUS-KAPSUKAS;** ex VINTSAS MITSKYAVICHUS 1973; ex ZAPRYBA 1971; **⋆93847 SOVIETSKAYA BURYATYA; ⋆93848 ALEKSANDROVSK SAKHALINSKIY; ⋆93849 KOMSOMOLETS MAGADANA; ⋆93850 KOMSOMOLSK NA AMURE; ⋆93851 MARSHAL SOKOLOVSKIY; ⋆93852 RYBAK LATVII; ⋆93854 PROFESSOR BARANOV.**

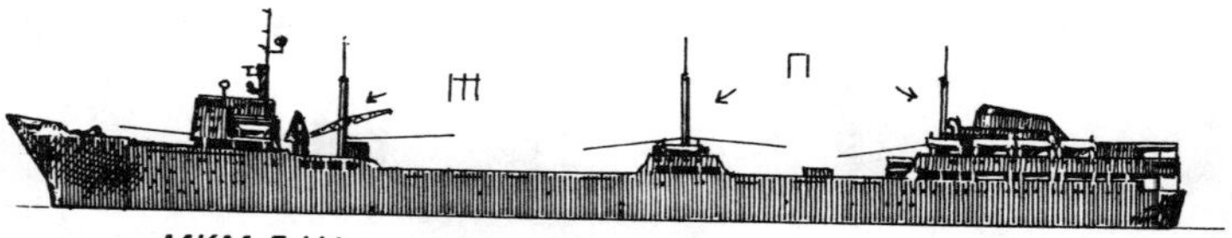

MKM$_2$F H1
⋆93860 SOVIETSKAYA UKRAINA. Ru/Ru 1959; WF; 32000; 217.51 × 10.85 (713.61 × 35.59); TSM; 16.

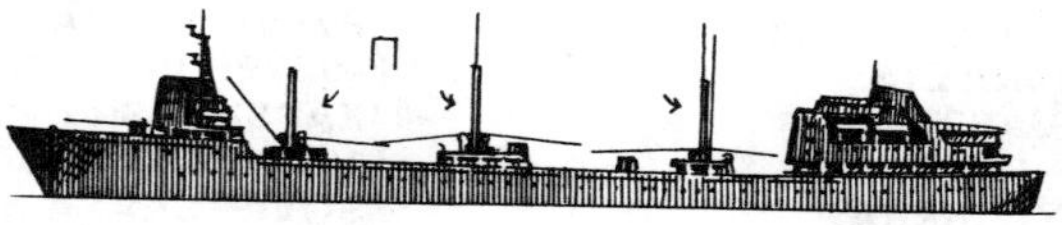

MKM$_2$F H1
93870 PIONERSK. Ru/Pd 1963; FF; 13600; 165.46 × 8.1 (542.84 × 26.57); M; 14.25; **'B-64'** type; Sisters (Ru flag): **⋆93871 DAURIYA; ⋆93872 MATOCHKIN SHAR; ⋆93873 RYBNYY MURMAN; ⋆93874 FRYDERYK CHOPIN; ⋆93875 POLYARNAYA ZVEZDA; ⋆93876 SEVRYBA; ⋆93877 ALEKSEY KHLOBYSTOV; ⋆93878 ALEKSEY POZDNYAKOV; ⋆93879 GRIGORIY LYSENKO; ⋆93880 NIKOLAY DANILOV; ⋆93881 SERGEY VASILISIN;** Similar: **'B-67'** type (Pd flag): **⋆93882 POMORZE; ⋆93883 GRYF POMORSKY.**

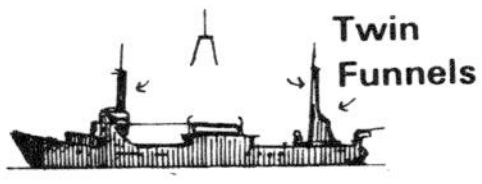

M_2 H2
93885 UCHI. Ar/Sp 1968; ST; 700; 53.8 × 4.7 (176.51 × 15.42); M; —; ex BUENO GONZALEZ 1975.

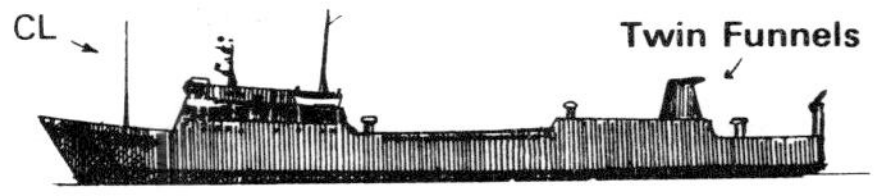

M_2F H
93890 GREY MASTER. No/No 1973; RoC; 1900; 124.19 × 4.98 (407.45 × 16.34); TSM; 16; Bow, side and stern doors; Similar: **93891 LEON** (Gr); ex LEO 1976; **93892 NORMANDIA** (Fr); ex JUNO.

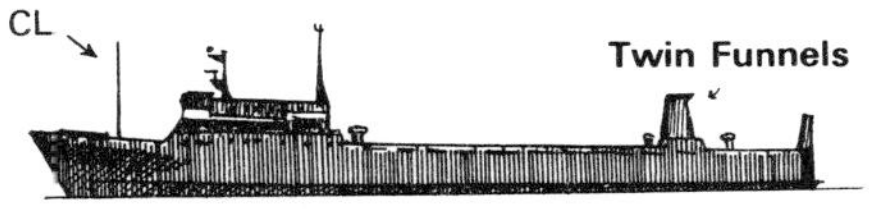

M_2F H
93900 BEGONIA. NA/No 1974; RoC; 1900; 124.59 × 4.98 (408.76 × 16.34); TSM; 17; ex FERNHILL.

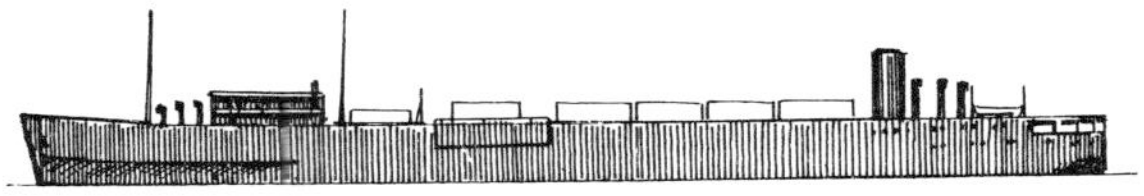

M_2F H
93910 GEORGIA. US/US 1951/62; RoC; 9700; 169.88 × 8.25 (557.35 × 27.07); T; 16; ex SEATRAIN GEORGIA; Lengthened 1962; May have 2 cranes; Sister: **93911 LOUISIANA** (US); ex SEATRAIN LOUISIANA.

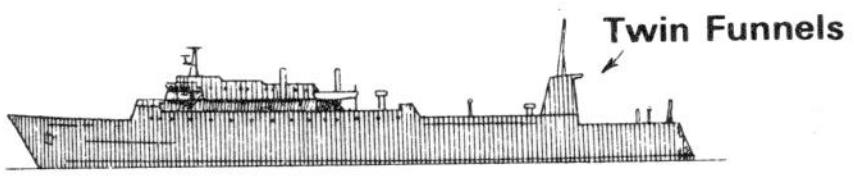

M_2F H
● **93920 ULIDIA.** Br/No 1970; RoC; 1600; 105.9 × 4.95 (347.44 × 16.24); TSM; 17; ex STENA CARRIER 1974; Bow, stern and side doors; Sister: **93921 VIKING TRADER** (Br); ex STENA TRADER 1980; ex DALRIADA 1980; ex STENA TRAILER 1971; Similar: **93922 ANDERIDA** (Br).

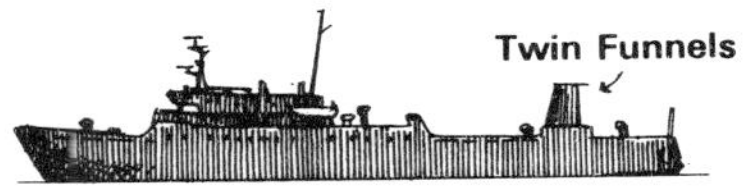

M_2F H
93930 JAGUAR. Br/No 1971; RoC; 2000; 106.28 × 4.97 (348.69 × 16.31); TSM; 19; ex PENDA 1980; ex ASD METEOR 1975; ex HOLMIA 1973; Also known as **'n. f. JAGUAR'**; Bow door, stern ramp; Similar (larger): **93931 GUNILLA** (Fi); **93932 ARONA** (Fi); **93933 GRANO** (Fi); **93934 COASTAL TRADER** (NZ); ex SILVIA 1973; **93935 DERNA** (Ly); **93936 GHAT** (Ly).

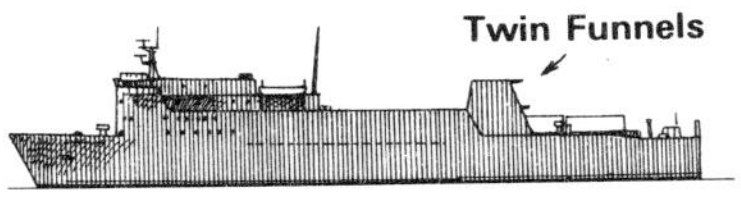

M_2F H
93950 MARINE EVANGELINE. Br/No 1974; RoC; 2800; 110.14 × 5.75 (361.35 × 18.86); TSM; 18.5; ex DUKE OF YORKSHIRE 1978; Bow, side and stern doors.

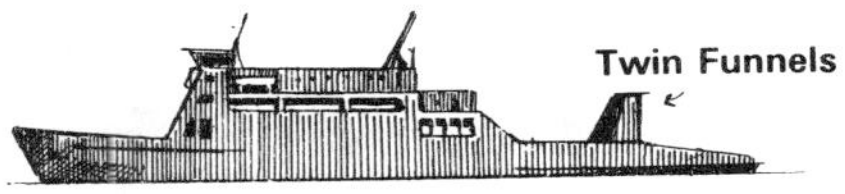

M_2F H
93960 CARRIER PRINCESS. Ca/US 1973; RoC/F; 4400; 115.83 × 4.88 (380.01 × 16.01); TSM; 18.

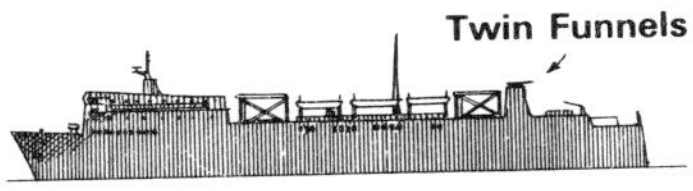

M_2F H
93970 MONTE CONTES. Sp/Sp 1975; RoPCF; 2800; 101.66 × 5.67 (333.53 × 18.6); TSM; 18; Stern door/ramp; Sisters: **93971 MONTE CORONO** (Sp); **93972 MANX VIKING** (Br); ex MONTE CASTILLO 1978; bow & stern doors.

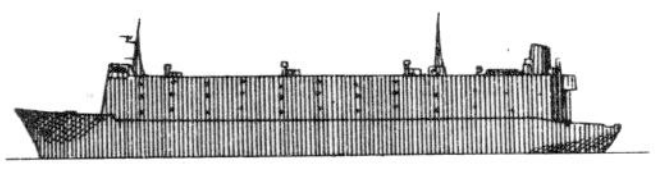

M_2F H
93980 AICHI MARU. Ja/Ja 1967; RoC; 2600; 96.7 × 4.8 (317.26 × 15.75); M; 13.5.

M_2F H
93990 KIRSTEN BRAVO. De/FRG 1974; RS/C; 500; 57.92 × 3.99 (190.03 × 13.09); M; 8.5; Possible sister: **93991 ANNE BRAVO** (De).

M_2F H
● **94000 SOBY FAERGEN.** De/Sw 1966; RoC; 300; 49.2 × 3.2 (161.42 × 10.5); M; 12; ex SOBY-FAABORG 1980; ex OSTBORNHOLM 1980; Side doors; Possible Sister: **94001 CAMILLA HENRIKSEN** (De); ex NORDBORNHOLM 1968.

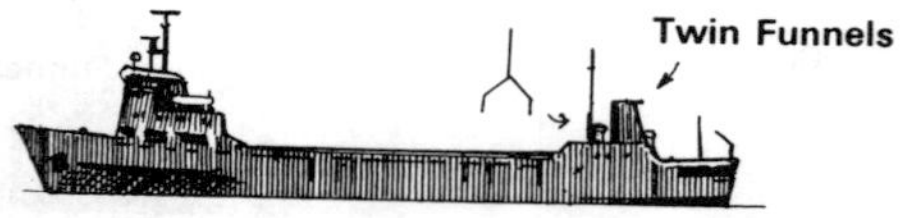

M_2F H
94010 AETOS. Gr/Fi 1972; RoC; 3100; 113.52 × 6.25 (372.44 × 20.51); M; 16; ex BORE VII; Stern door; Similar: ★**94011 ASCHBERG** (DDR); ex BORE IX 1977; ★**94012 BEERBERG** (DDR); ex BORE X; **94013 BORE XI** (Sw).

M_2F H
94020 BUENAVISTA. Ne/No 1971/74; RoC/TF; 3300; 106.43 × 6.25 (349.18 × 20.51); TSM; 19; Stern and side doors; Lengthened 1974; Sister: **94021 BENCHIJGUA** (Sp); ex BONANZA 1980; (may not be lengthened).

M_2F H
● **94030 CAPITAINE LE GOFF.** Fr/No 1972; RoC; 500; 91.04 × 4.42 (298.69 × 14.5); TSM; 16; ex ADMIRAL CARRIER I; Stern door; Sister: **94031 LA GOULETTE** (Tn); ex OLAU VIG 1974; ex ADMIRAL CARRIER 1974.

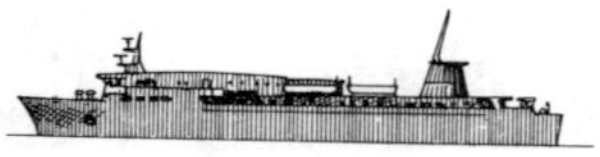

M_2F H
94040 HANSTHOLM. No/No 1973; RoPF; 1600; 86.54 × 4.92 (283.92 × 16.14); TSM; —; ex BASTO V 1980; Bow, stern and side doors; Sister: **94041 SUILVEN** (Br).

M_2F H
94050 RHONE. Fr/FRG 1970; RoC; 2500; 104.02 × 5.03 (341.27 × 16.5); TSM; 17.5; ex RHONETAL; ex NORCAPE 1974; ex RHONETAL; Similar: **94051 MAR CARIBE** (Li).

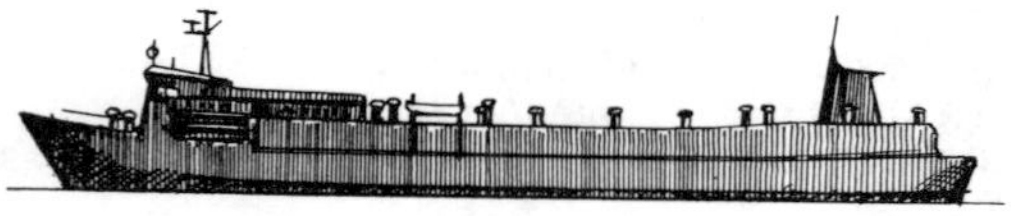

M_2F H
94060 AQUILA. FRG/FRG 1973/76; RoC; 4100; 149.23 × 6.41 (489.6 × 21.03); M; 18; ex NAHOST PIONEER; ex EHRENFELS 1977; ex IPSWICH PIONEER II 1976; ex AQUILA; Lengthened 1976.

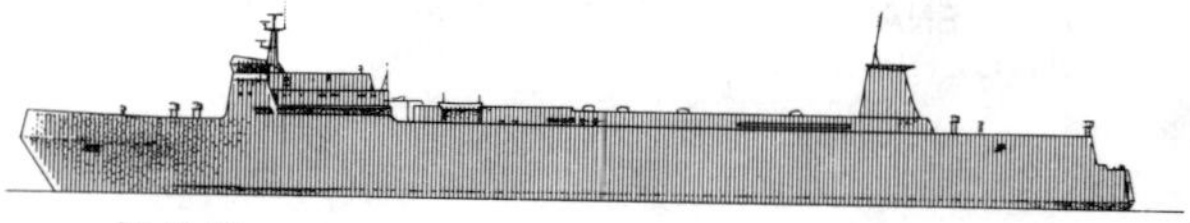

M_2F H
94070 RAILSHIP 1. FRG/FRG-FRG 1975/80; RoC/TF; —; 177.22 × — (581.43 × —); TSM; approx. 20; Stern door/ramp; Lengthened 1980.

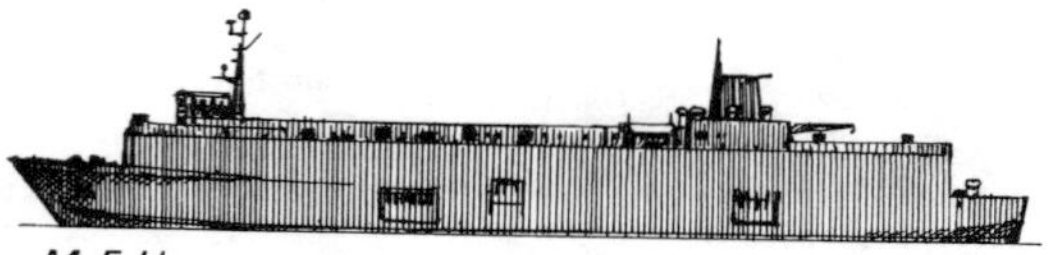

M_2F H
94080 LAURITA. No/FRG 1969; V; 6500; 180.02 × 6.8 (590.62 × 22.31); M; 21; Side doors; Sisters (No flag): **94081 SAVONITA; 94082 TORINITA.**

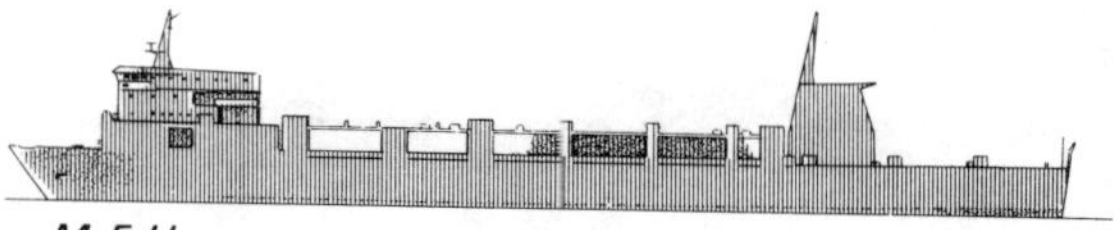

M_2F H
● **94090 AMBASSADOR.** US/FRG 1980; RoC; 13400; 168.8 × 6.45 (553.8 × 21.16); M; 17; Stern ramp; Sister; **94091 DIPLOMAT** (US).

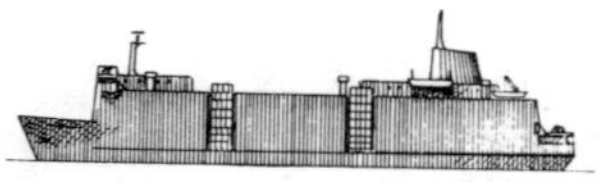

M_2F H
93100 JOLLY VERDE. It/Br 1967; RoC; 1600; 88.55 × 4.34 (290.52 × 14.24); M; 14; ex CARWAY 1973.

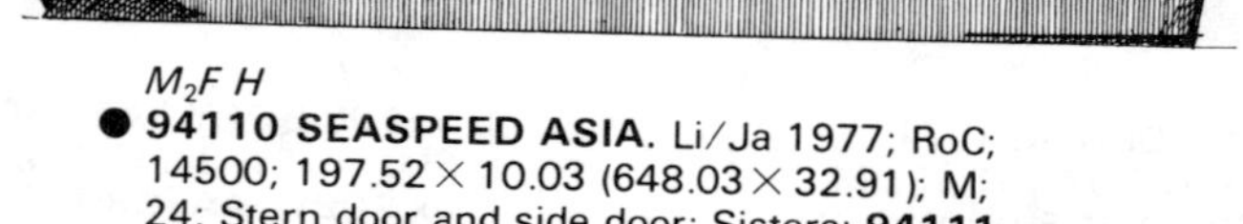

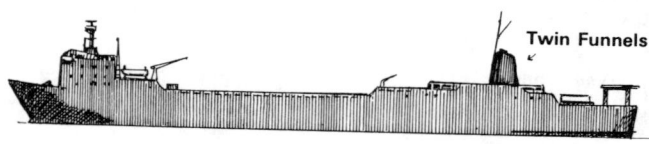

M_2F H
● **94110 SEASPEED ASIA.** Li/Ja 1977; RoC; 14500; 197.52 × 10.03 (648.03 × 32.91); M; 24; Stern door and side door; Sisters: **94111 SEASPEED AMERICA** (Gr); **94112 SEASPEED ARABIA** (Li).

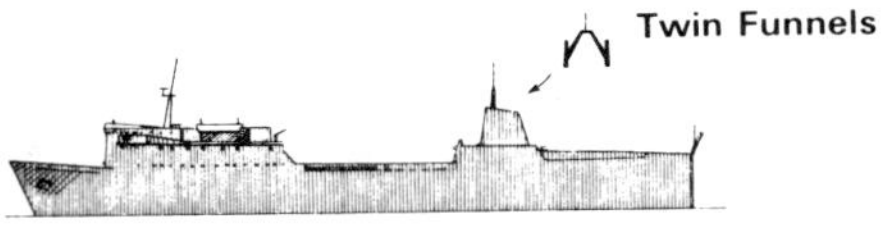

M_2F *H*
94120 CHARLES SCHIAFFINO. Fr/Sp 1977; RoC; 2000; 110.6 × 5.61 (362.86 × 18.41); M; 15.5; ex CALA D'OR 1977; Lengthened 1977.

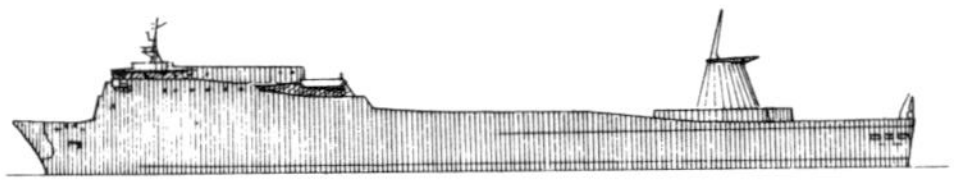

M_2F *H*
● **94140 FEDERAL NOVA.** Ca/As-FRG 1977; RoC; 3800; 144.07 × 5.7 (472.67 × 18.7); TSM; 18; ex GOYA; ex STENA TENDER 1977; Bow door and stern ramp; Completed in Romania and lengthened in West Germany 1977.

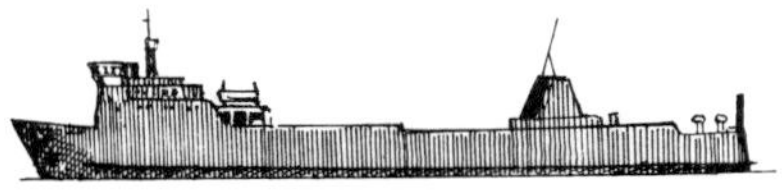

M_2F *H*
94160 MASHALA. Br/FRG 1977; RoC; 1600; 116.01 × 5.38 (380.61 × 17.65); TSM; 16; Sisters: **94161 SALAHALA** (Br); **94162 THOMAS WEHR** (FRG); ex WACRO EXPRESS; ex THOMAS WEHR; **94163 GABRIELE WEHR** (FRG); **94164 EMADALA** (Br).

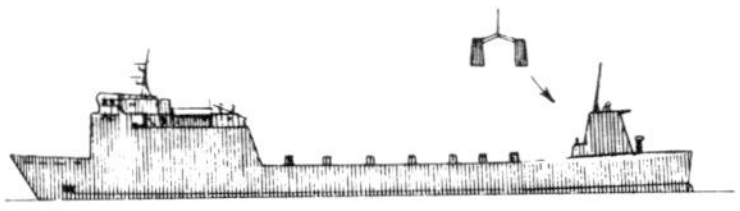

M_2F *H*
● **94190 MIRIAM.** Li/FRG 1977; RoC; 1500; 109 × — (357 × —); TSM; 15.

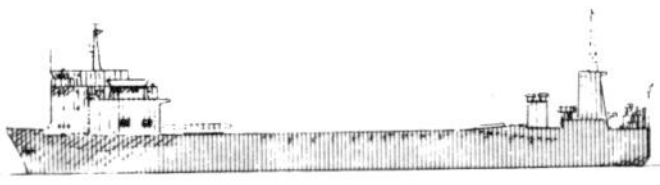

M_2F *H*
94210 IVA. Pa/Ja 1978; RoC; 900; 93.81 (bp) × 3.52 (307.78 (bp) × 11.55); TSM; 13; Stern door/ramp; Sister: **94211 ANI** (Pa).

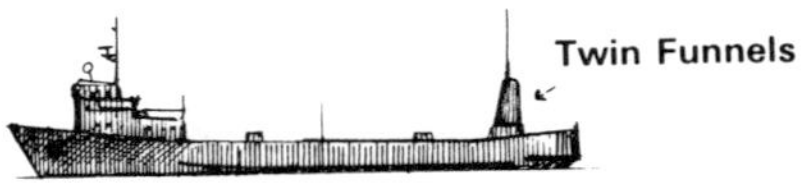

M_2F *H*
● **94230 MICHEL.** FRG/No 1972; RoC; 600; 91.9 × 3.16 (301.51 × 10.37); TSM; 15; ex VECHTSTROOM; ex OSTEND EXPRESS 1973; Side door.

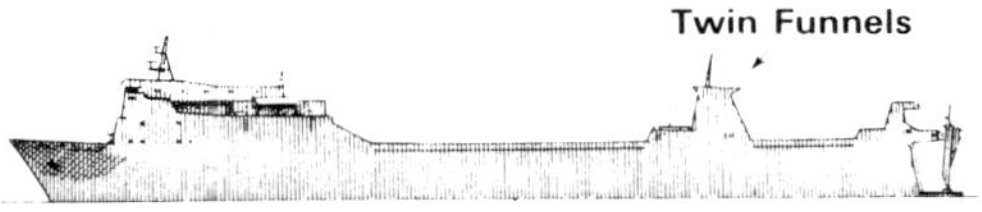

M_2F *H*
94130 ANZERE. Sd/Ne 1978; RoC; 5000; 151 × 6.2 (495.41 × 20.34); M; 18.

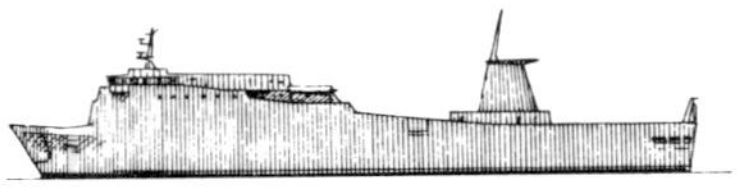

M_2F *H*
94150 STENA TIMER. Sw/As 1977; RoC; 2500; 114.38 × 5.7 (375.26 × 18.7); TSM; 18; ex JAGUAR 1979; ex STENA TIMER 1977; Sister: **94151 DARNIA** (Br); ex STENA TRADER 1978.

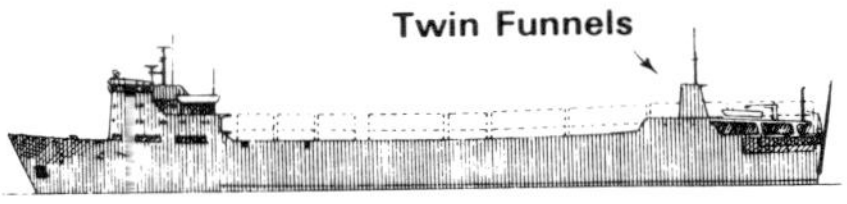

M_2F *H*
● **94170 ABHA.** NA/Fi 1977; RoC; 3800; 128.91 × 6.3 (422.93 × 20.67); M; 17.25; Sister: **94171 BURAIDAH.**

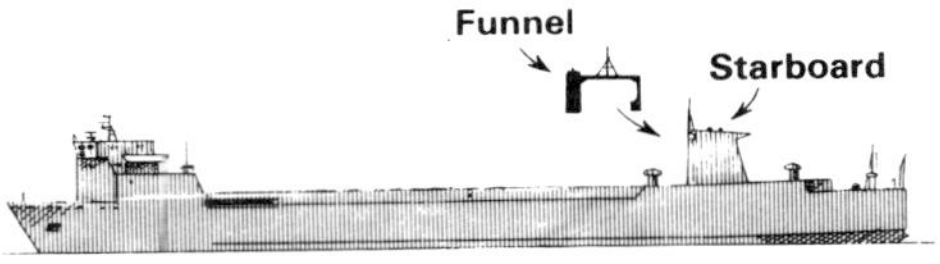

M_2F *H*
94180 BRITTA ODEN. Sw/Sw 1978; RoC; 4500; 143.26 × 5.2 (470 × 17.06); TSM; 15.25; Stern door/ramp; Sisters (Sw flag): **94181 ANNA ODEN; 94182 EVA ODEN.**

M_2F *H*
94200 BACAT I. In/De 1974; Bg; 1400; 103.51 × 5.42 (337.92 × 17.78); TSM; 11; Catamaran Hull.

M_2F *H*
94220 ALICE LANGLI. De/De 1977; RoC/Ccn; 400; 57.08 × 3.47 (187.27 × 11.38); M; 10; Sister: **94221 SEADRAKE** (No); ex NOPAL SEA 1980.

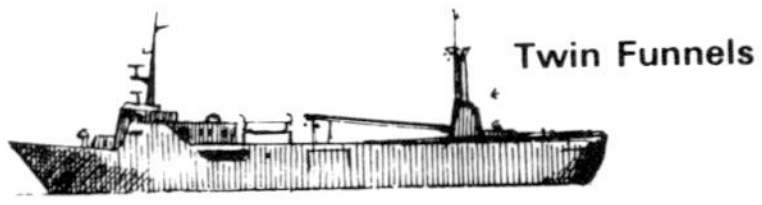

M_2F *H*
● **94240 VOLCAN DE YAIZA.** Sp/It 1967; RoC; 300; 51.08 × 3.3 (167.59 × 10.83); M; 11.5; ex FIRLINGEN 1973; Sisters: **94241 LINDINGER SATELITE** (De); ex VOLCAN DE TAHICHE 1975; ex ROLLINGEN 1973; ex RAVENNA 1967; **94242 LINDINGER SURVEYOR (De); ex TUMLINGEN 1974; ex RAPALLO 1967; 94243 FLORNES** (No); ex TRILLINGEN 1971.

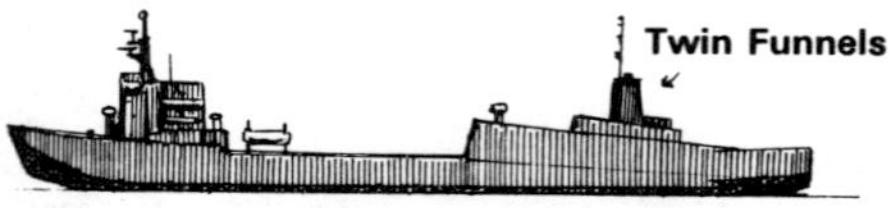

M_2F H
94250 BIA. Gr/Fi 1975; RoC; 2500/7200; 129.85 × 5.33/6.4 (458.83 × 17.49/21); TSM; 15; ex MERZARIO NUBIA 1979; ex BIA 1976; Stern door/ramp; **'Katatran'** type; Semi-catamaran hull.

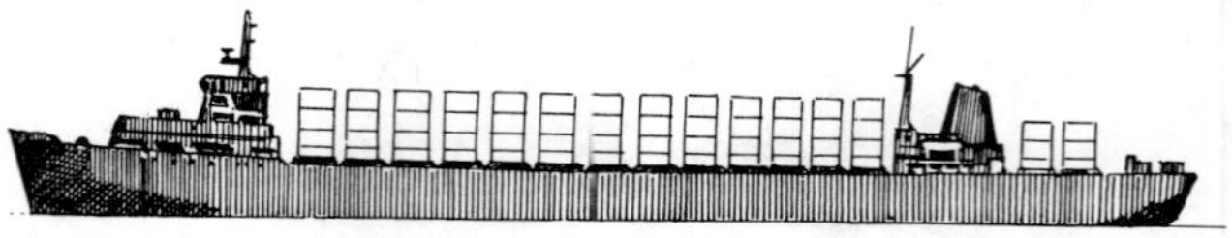

M_2F H
94260 HAWAIIAN QUEEN. US/US 1944/65; Con/V; 17500; 184.78 × 10.03 (606.23 × 32.91); T; 17; ex MARINE DEVIL 1965; Lengthened and deepened 1965; Converted from 'C-4' type cargo ship 1965; Sister: **94261 HAWAIIAN MONARCH** (US); ex MARINE DRAGON 1965.

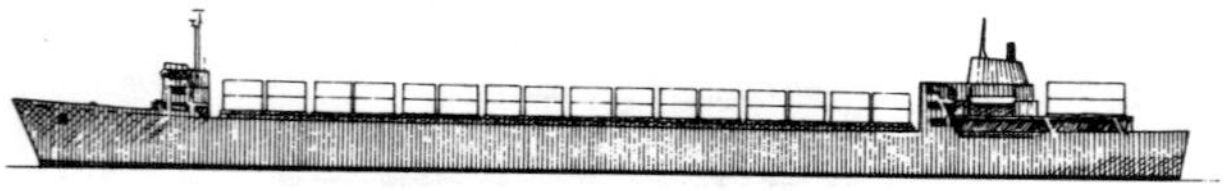

M_2F H
94270 C. V. LIGHTNING. US/US 1969; Con; 17900; 185.93 × 9.63 (610.01 × 31.59); T; 21; Sisters (US flag): **94271 C. V. STAGHOUND; 94272 CHEMICAL DISCOVERER;** ex C. V. SEA WITCH 1977—may be converted to chemical tanker; **94273 EXPORT FREEDOM; 94274 EXPORT LEADER; 94275 EXPORT PATRIOT; 94276 ARGONAUT; 94277 RESOLUTE.**

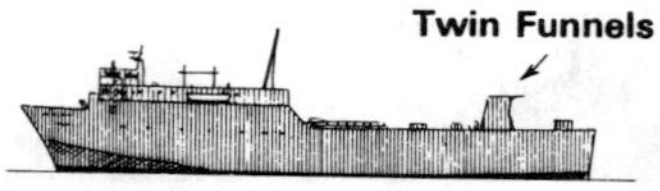

M_2F H1
94290 MATHILDA. Fr/Fr 1977; RoC; 1100; 90.71 × — (297.57 × —); M; 14; Sisters (Fr flag): **94291 L'AUDE; 94292 L'ARDECHE; 94293 AURELIA; 94294 ANTHENOR; 94295 LUBERON.**

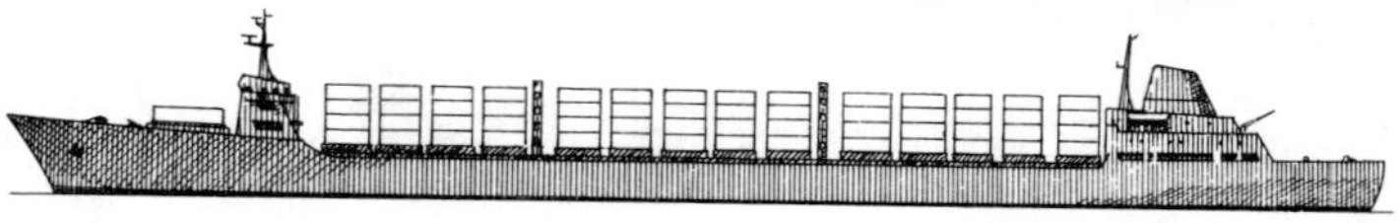

M_2F H1
94310 MANUKAI. US/US 1970; Con; 23800; 219.62 × 10.4 (720.53 × 34.12); T; 23; ex HAWAIIAN ENTERPRISE; Sister (US flag): **94311 MANULANI;** ex HAWAIIAN PROGRESS; Similar (bridge superstructure one deck lower): **94312 SEA-LAND ECONOMY;** ex SL 181 1973; ex H. P. BALDWIN; **94313 SEA-LAND VENTURE;** ex SL 180 1973; ex S. T. ALEXANDER; **94314 SEA-LAND CONSUMER;** ex AUSTRALIA BEAR 1973; **94315 SEA-LAND PRODUCER;** ex NEW ZEALAND BEAR; Similar (bridge further foreward and one deck higher): **94316 MAUI; 94317 KAUAI.**

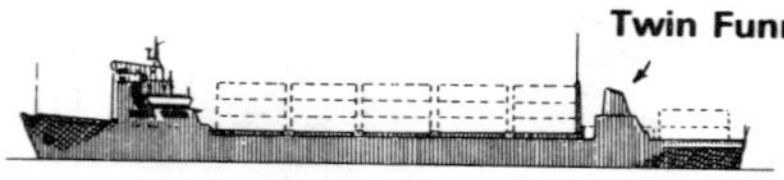

M_2F H1
94330 FLYING SCOT. Sg/Ne 1970; Con; 1600; 114.51 × 4.15 (375.69 × 13.62); TSM; 14.5; ex GREYHOUND 1972.

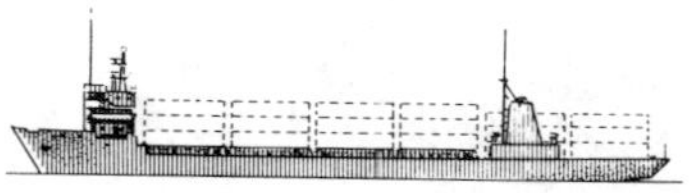

M_2F H1
94340 DESAFIO. Sp/Sp 1979; Con; 2000; 103.45 × 6.43 (339.4 × 21.1); M; 15.

M_2F H1
94350 KAIRYU MARU. Ja/Ja 1961; D; 2900; 88.97 × 5.61 (291.9 × 18.41); TSD-E; —.

M_2F H1
94360 BALI. Ia/FRG 1957; D; 1400; 73.03 × 4.18 (239.6 × 13.71); TSR; 10.

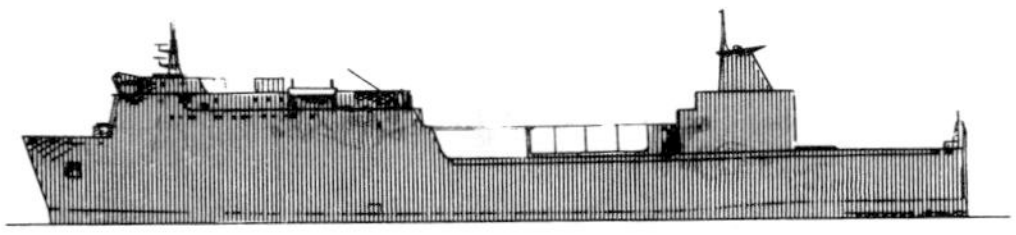

M_2F H1
94370 NORSEA. Br/Ja 1979; RoC; 6300; 150 × 5.12 (492 × 16.8); TSM; 19; ex IBEX 1981; Stern door/ramp; Sister: **94371 TIPPERARY** (Br); ex PUMA 1979.

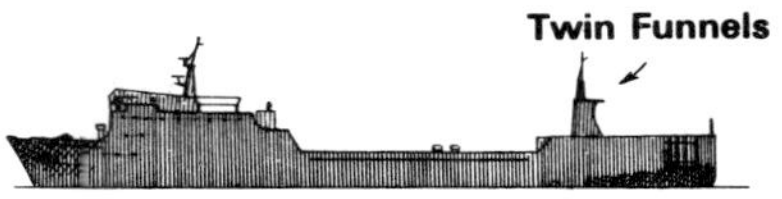

M_2F H13
94380 ROLON NORTE. Sp/Sp 1977; RoC; 1800; 111.03 × 4.6 (364.27 × 15.09); M; 14; Sister: **94381 ROLON SUR** (Sp).

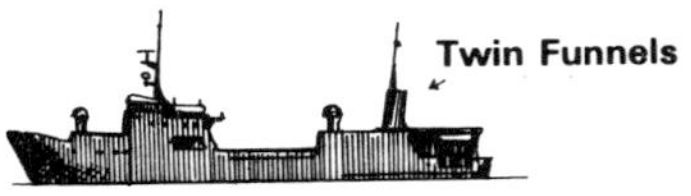

M_2F H13
94390 ROLON PLATA. Sp/Sp 1970; RoC; 800; 76.51 × 3.76 (251.02 × 12.34); M; 15; Sister: **94391 ROLON ORO** (Sp).

M_2F H13
94400 DUNGENESS. Ch/Ne 1970; RoC; 500; 84 × 3.62 (275.59 × 11.88); M; 15; ex ASD ASTOR 1980; ex ASTOR 1973; ex LIBYAVILLE 1971; Similar: **94401 LAMARA** (Sg); ex ORIENTVILLE 1976.

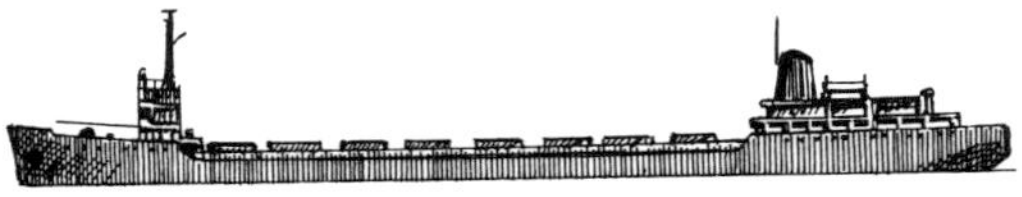

M_2F H13
94410 PYRAMID VENUS. Br/Br 1952; O; 10800; 157.89 × 8.48 (518.01 × 27.82); T; 15; ex CARL SCHMEDEMAN 1973; ex PYRAMID VEGA; ex CARL SCHMEDEMAN.

M_2F H13
94420 GYPSUM EMPRESS. Br/FRG 1956; B; 8200; 134.45 × 7.72 (440.78 × 25.33); T; 13; May have unloading gear; Sister: **94421 GYPSUM DUCHESS** (Br).

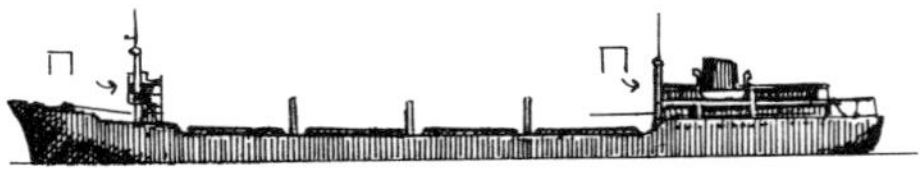

M_2F H13
94430 TOPIRA. Br/Br 1954; OO; 6900; 134.75 × 6.1 (442.09 × 20.01); R; 10; ex SUNBRAYTON 1979.

M_2F H13
94440 BULK QUEEN. Pa/US 1947; B; 8000; 132.9 × 7.57 (436.02 × 24.84); T; 12.25; ex GYPSUM QUEEN 1978.

M_2F H13
● ★**94450 LENA.** Ru/Ru 1961; Spt/Tk; 7200 Dspl; 121.1 × 6.2 (400.3 × 20.3); TSM; 17; 'Uda' class; Similar (Ru flag): ★**94451 DUNAY;** ★**94452 KOIDA;** ★**94453 SHEKSNA;** ★**94454 TEREK;** ★**94455 VISHERA;** Ships vary in appearance; Some have guns; KOIDA has a short kingpost on the starboard side abaft the bridge; **94456 BALIKPAPAN** (Ia—navy).

M_2F H13
94470 MIZAN. Ia/FRG 1963; BT; 1700; 77.98 × — (255.84 × —); R; 14; Sister: **94471 MAJANG** (Ia).

M_2F H13
94480 AGW VII. FRG/Br 1917; SDT; 1000; 67.01 × 4.56 (219.85 × 14.96); R; 8; ex ELMOL 1962; Converted from tanker.

M_2F H2
94490 MELBOURNE TRADER. Au/No 1975; RoC; 4500; 139.91 × 7.16 (459.02 × 23.49); M; 18; Stern door/ramp; Similar: ★**94491 FICHTELBERG** (DDR); ex TOR CALEDONIA.

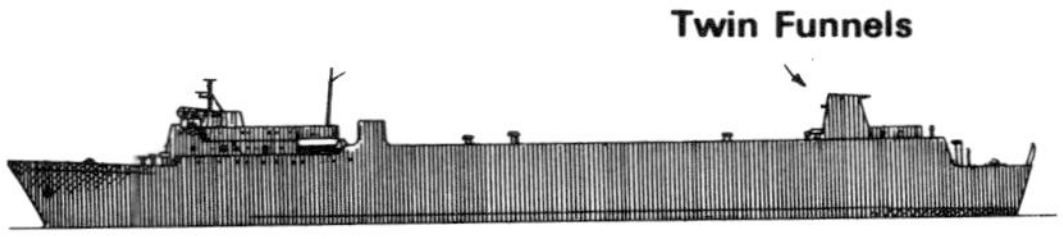

M_2F H2
● **94500 TOR GOTHIA.** Br/No 1971/77; RoC; 5200; 152.8 × 7.17 (501.31 × 23.52); TSM; 18.5; Stern door; Lengthened 1977; Sisters (Pa flag): **94501 NERLANDIA;** ex TOR NERLANDIA 1979; **94502 BELGIA;** ex TOR BELGIA 1979.

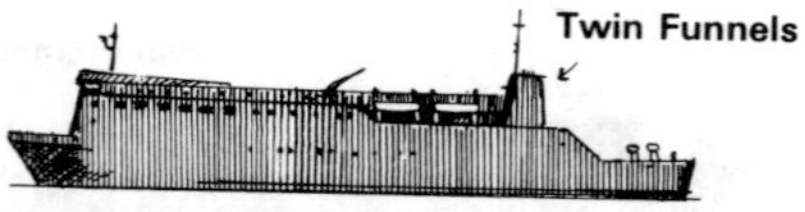

M_2F H2
94510 TAREK B. Pa/No 1975; RoC/F; 2400; 109.71 × 5.2 (359.94 × 17.06); TSM; 19; ex FALSTER 1980; ex PRINCE DE BRETAGNE 1975; ex FALSTER 1975; Bow door/ramp; Side door/ramp; Two stern doors/ramps.

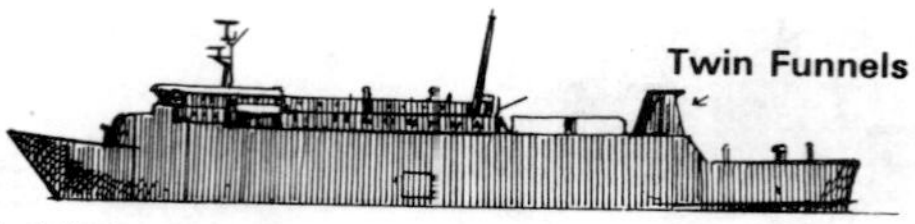

M_2F H2
● **94520 SEASPEED DANA.** Li/No 1976; RoC; 3500; 132.52 × 6.58 (434.78 × 21.59); M; 18.5; Sisters: **94521 DIMA** (Ma); ex SEASPEED DIMA 1980; **94522 INGER EXPRESS** (Sw); ex SEASPEED DORA 1978.

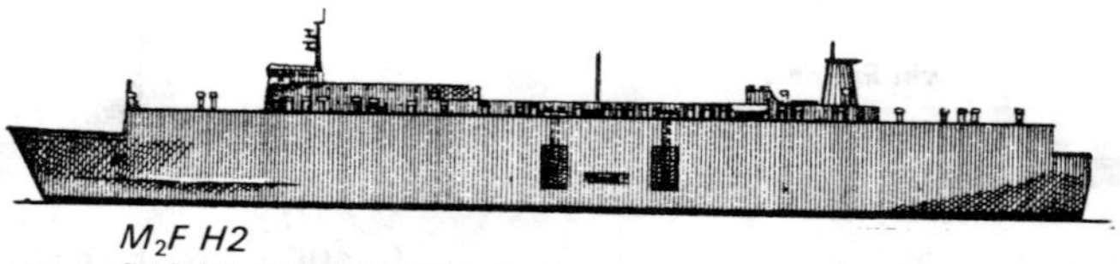

M_2F H2
94530 DON CARLOS. Sw/Fi 1976; V; 14500; 202.62 × 8.48 (664.76 × 27.82); M; 19; Side doors; Sister: **94531 DON JUAN** (Sw).

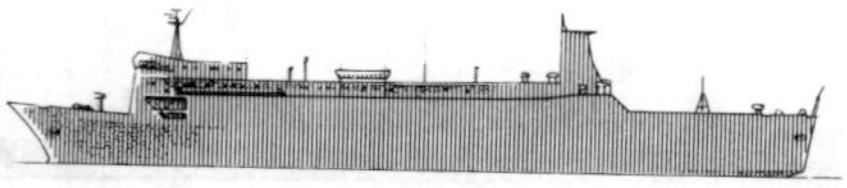

M_2F H2
● **94540 BRABANT.** FRG/FRG 1976; RoC; 3900; 127.03 × 5.41/6.55 (416 × 17.74/21.48); TSM; —; ex ARGO 1977; Stern door/ramp.

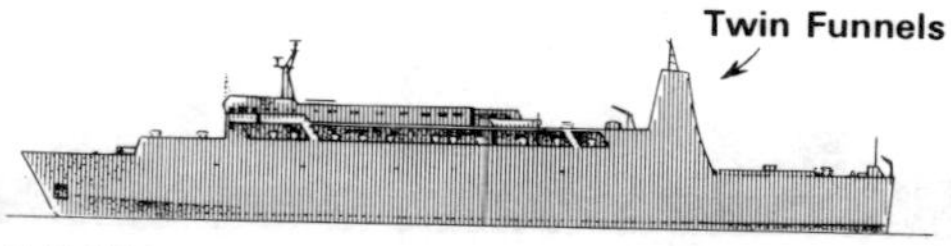

M_2F H2
94550 BALTIC EAGLE. Br/Fi 1979; RoC; 6400; 137.12 × 8.21 (449.87 × 26.94); TSM; 18; Two stern doors/ramps; Sister: **★94551 INOWROCLAW** (Pd).

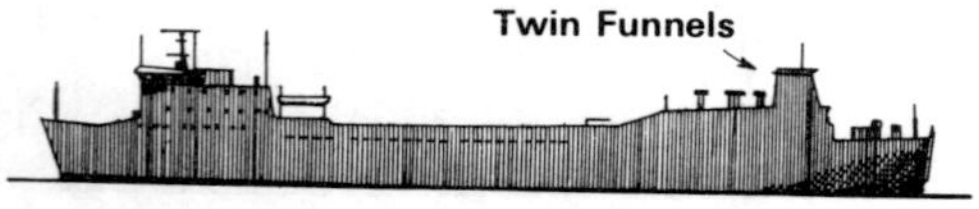

M_2F H2
94560 BORE SKY. Fi/No 1977; RoC; 4700; 142.22 × 7 (466.6 × 22.97); TSM; 18; Sisters (Fi flag): **94561 BORE SUN; 94562 FINNFOREST;** ex ROLITA 1979.

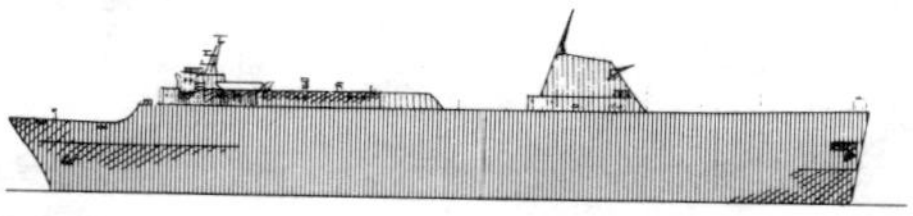

M_2F H2
94570 DORA BALTEA. It/It 1975; RoC; 3500; 135.52 × 6 (444.62 × 19.67); TSM; 18.5; Stern door/ramp; Side doors/ramps; Sister: **94571 PO** (It); Similar (larger): **94572 DORA RIPARIA** (It).

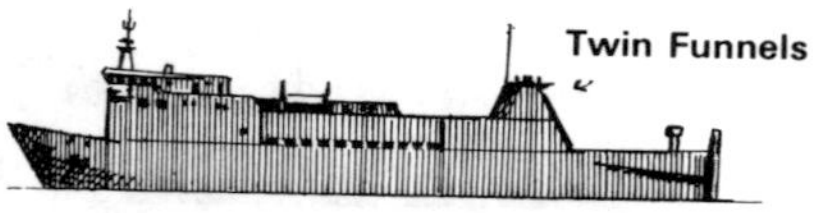

M_2F H2
94580 RAED B. Pa/No 1974; RoPVF; 2200; 109.61 × 4.92 (359.61 × 16.14); TSM; 19; ex SCANDINAVIA 1980; Bow, side & stern doors.

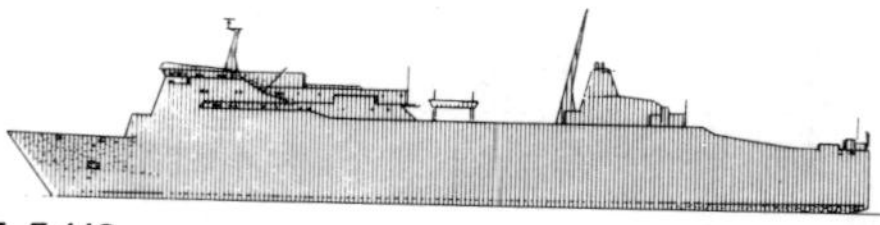

M_2F H2
94590 TRANSGERMANIA. FRG/FRG 1976; RoC; 5600; 135.45 × 6.05 (444.39 × 19.85); TSM; 19; Stern ramp.

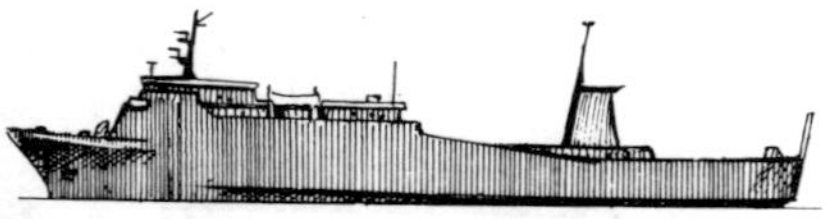

MMF H2
94600 BUFFALO. Br/FRG 1975; RoC; 3500; 125 × 3.79 (410.1 × 12.43); TSM; 18; Stern door.

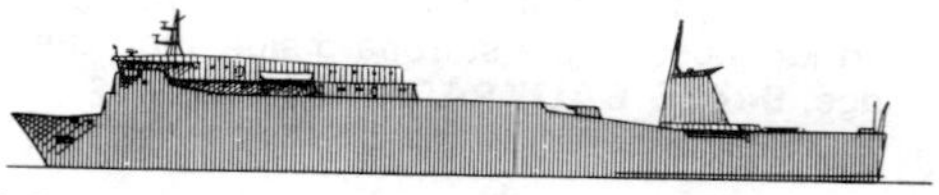

M_2F H2
94610 PUMA. Br/FRG 1975; RoC; 4000; 141.81 × 5.81 (465.26 × 19.06); TSM; 18; ex UNION MELBOURNE 1980; Lengthened 1975; Stern door/ramp; Similar: **94611 BISON** (Br).

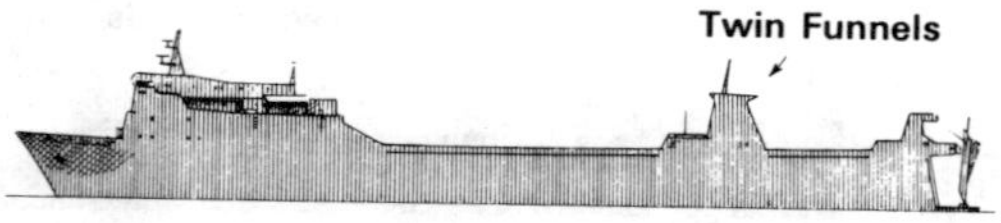

M_2F H2
94620 ANZERE. Sd/Ne 1978; RoC; 5000; 151 × 6.2 (495.41 × 20.34); M; 18.

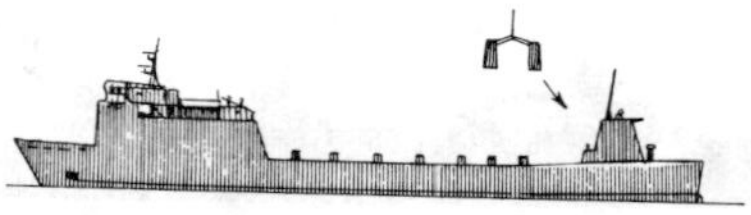

M_2F H2
● **94630 MIRIAM.** Li/FRG 1977; RoC; 1500; 109 × — (357 × × —); TSM; 15.

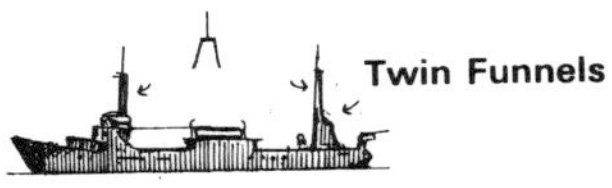

M_2F *H2*
94640 UCHI. Ar/Sp 1968; ST; 700; 53.8 × 4.7 (176.51 × 15.42); M; —; ex BUENO GONZALEZ 1975.

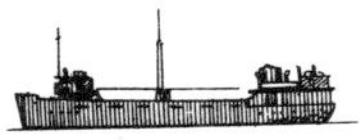

M_2F *H3*
94660 HONG LEE. My/Hong Kong 1958; C; 400; 51.08 × 3.11 (187.27 × 10.2); M; 10; ex GIANG LEE 1976; Sister: **94661 HONG SOON** (My); ex GIANG ANN 1976.

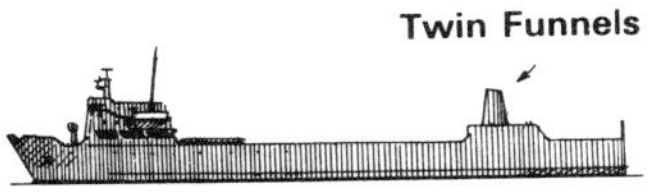

M_2F *H3*
94670 LA DURANCE. Fr/Sp 1972; RoC; 2200; 99.17 × 5.81 (325.36 × 19.06); TSM; 16; ex KERISNEL 1974; ex LILAC 1972; Stern door; Sister: **94671 GUAYCURA** (Me); ex JASMINE.

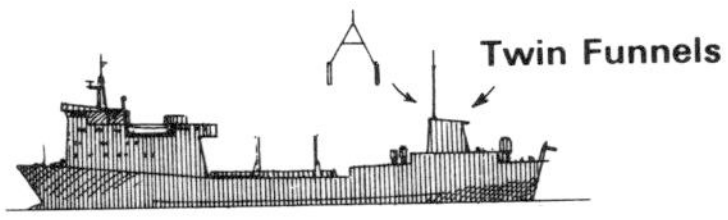

M_2F *H3*
● **94690 ADOR.** Sg/Ne 1972; RoC; 1500; 98 × 3.85 (321.52 × 12.63); TSM; 15; ex SAINT CHRISTOPHE 1975; ex ADOR; Bow and stern doors; Sister: **94691 EVANGELISTO** (Ch); ex CONDOR 1980.

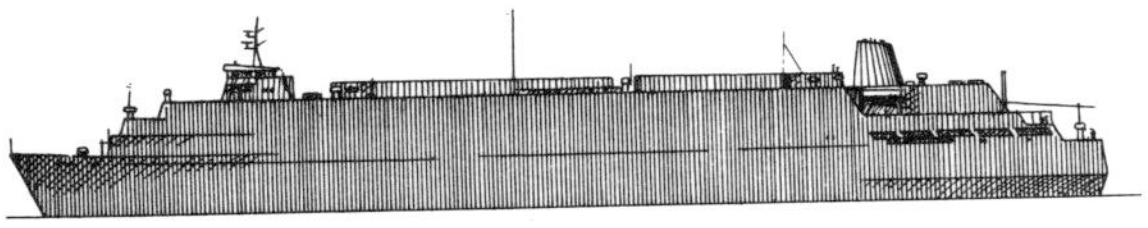

M_2FK *H*
94710 DYVI OCEANIC. No/No 1968; V; 5400; 175.8 × 6.86 (576.77 × 22.51); M; 18.5; Side doors; Sister: **94711 DYVI PACIFIC** (No).

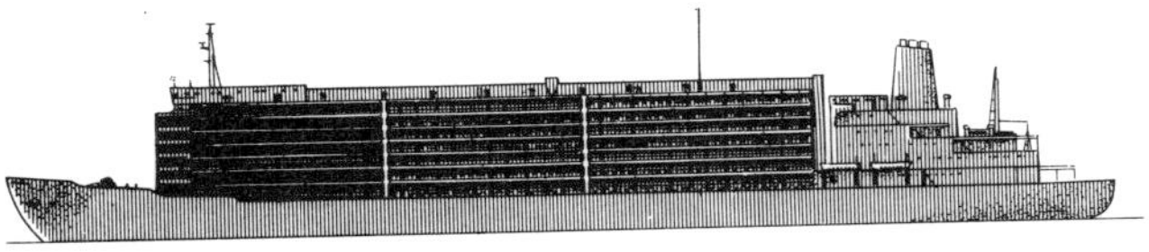

M_2FK *H1*
94730 AL-SHUWAIKH. Ku/Ja-FRG 1967/80; LS; 34400; 195 × — (639.8 × —); M; approx. 16; ex ERVIKEN 1980; Converted from tanker and shortened 1980.

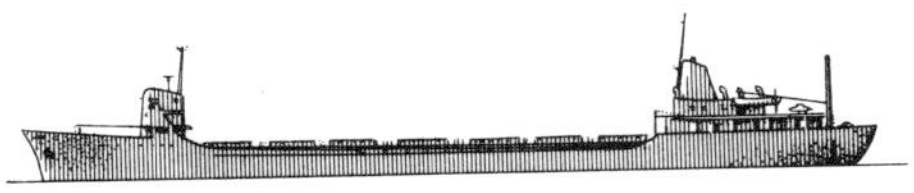

M_2FK *H13*
94750 GYPSUM COUNTESS. Br/Fr 1960; B; 8200; 135.9 × 7.72 (445.87 × 25.33); T; 12.

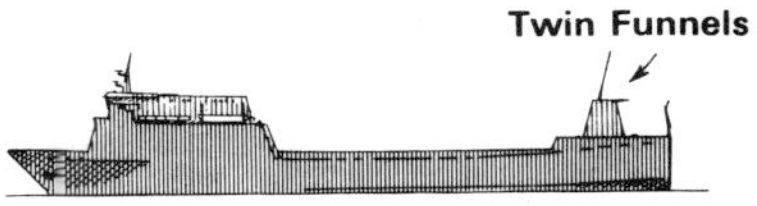

M_2F *H23*
● **94650 MERCANDIAN TRANSPORTER II.** De/De 1978; RoC; 1600; 105.62 × 4.97 (346.52 × 16.31); M; 15; Stern door/ramp; **'Merc. Multiflex'** type; Sisters (Ic flag): **94651 ALAFOSS;** ex DANA ATLAS 1980; **94652 EYRARFOSS;** ex MERCANDIAN IMPORTER II 1980; **94653 MERCANDIAN CARRIER II; 94654 MERCANDIAN EXPORTER II; 94655 MERCANDIAN TRADER II.**

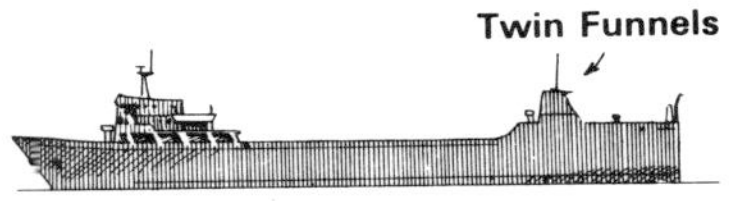

M_2F *H3*
94680 ANTONIO SUARDIAZ. Sp/Sp 1976; RoC; 2000; 106.36 × 6.2 (348.95 × 20.34); M; 16.

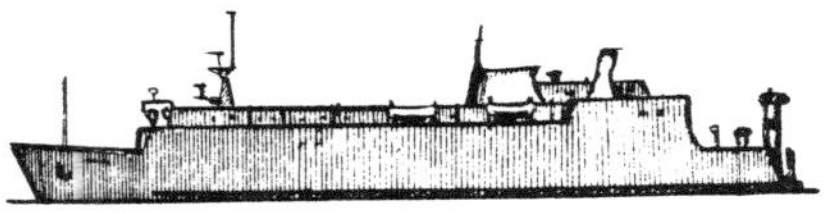

M_2F_2 *H2*
⋆**94700 MIKOLAJ KOPERNIK.** Pd/No 1974; RoPVF/TF; 2900; 125.61 × 4.5 (412.11 × 14.76); TSM; 16.5; Similar: ⋆**94701 JAN HEWELIUSZ** (Pd).

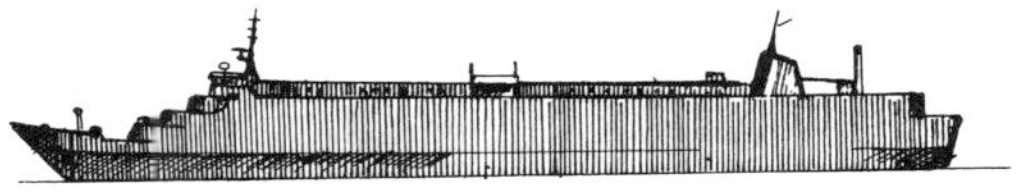

M_2FK *H*
94720 DYVI ATLANTIC. No/No 1965; V; 1900; 148.6 × 5.27 (487.53 × 17.29); M; 17; Side doors.

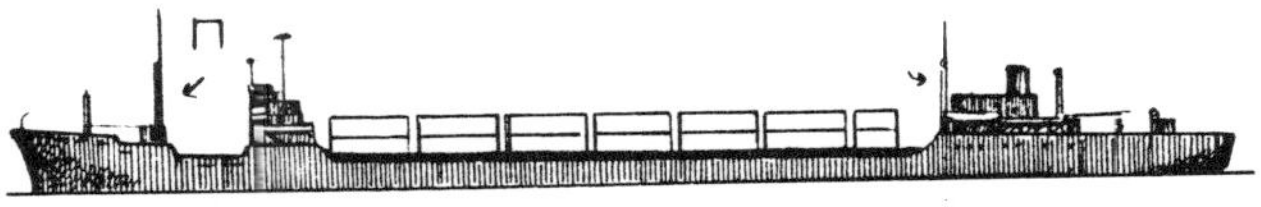

M_2FK *H123*
● **94740 CALIFORNIAN.** US/US 1946/54/60; C/Con; 13600; 193 × 10.5 (633.2 × 32.97); T; 16.75; ex MOUNT GREYLOCK 1951; Converted from 'C-4' type cargo ship & lengthened 1954; Converted from Ore/Oil 1960.

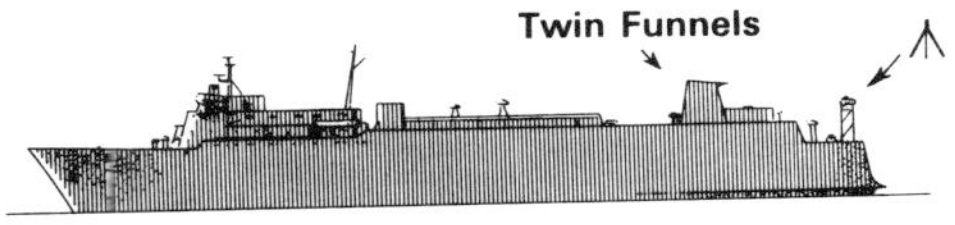

M_2FK *H2*
94760 UNION HOBART. Br/No 1976; RoC; 4400; 135.79 × 7.17 (445.5 × 23.52); TSM; 18.5; Stern door; Sister: **94761 UNION LYTTELTON** (Br).

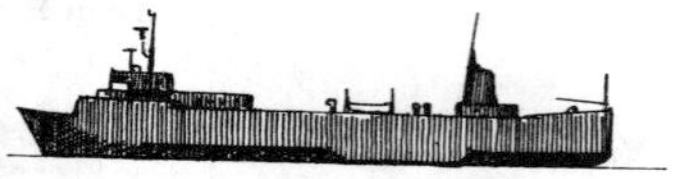

M_2FK H2
94770 AUTOBAHN. No/No 1972; RoVC; 500; 92.46 × 3.88 (303.35 × 12.73); TSM; 14; Stern door.

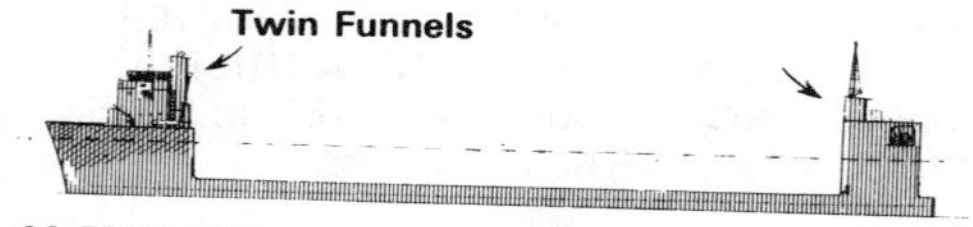

M_2FMF H13
94790 SUPER SERVANT 1. Ne/Ja 1979; RoC/HL; 10200; 139 × 6.18 (456 × 20.28); TSM; 13; Submersible; Broken line shows maximum extent of immersion.

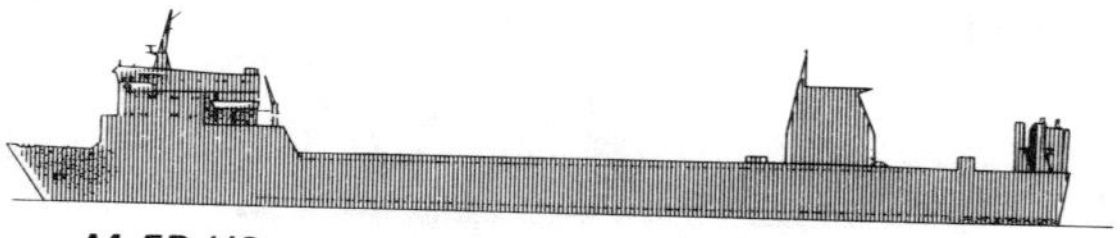

M_2FR H2
94810 NESTOR. FRG/FRG 1980; RoC/Con; 5100; 168.8 × 6.45 (553.8 × 21.16); M; 19; Stern quarter ramp.

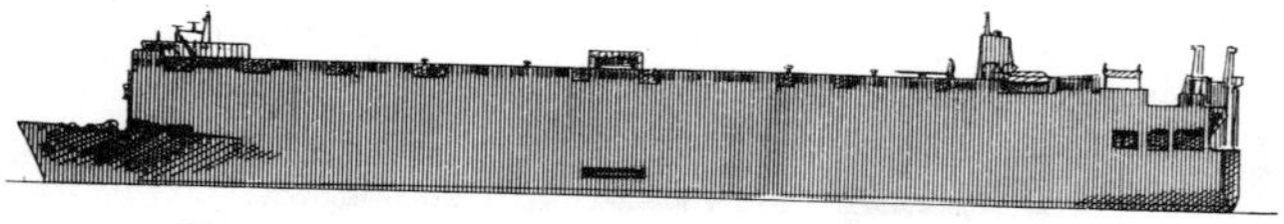

M_2FR H2
94820 NOPAL MASCOT. No/Ja 1978; RoVC; 17600; 194.52 × 8.2 (638.19 × 26.9); M; 19.5; Side door/ramp; Stern door/ramp.

M_2KF H13
94840 DON AMANDO. Pi/Ja 1958/68; C; 2500; 79.76 × 5.31 (261.68 × 17.42); M; —; ex ESTANCIA 1963; Converted from a factory ship 1968; Appearance may be altered.

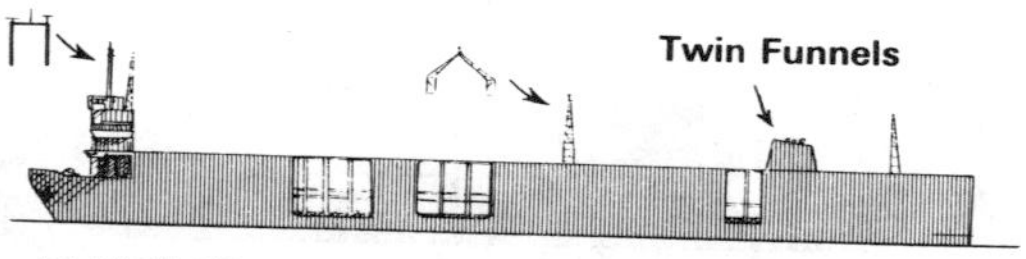

M_2KFK H2
94850 OAK. Li/Ja 1978; Bg/Dk; 1900; 134.5 × 4.8 (441.27 × 15.75); TSM; 10.25; ex MAMMOTH OAK 1978; **'L-19'** type; Barges float on and off through stern; The openings in the hull will not be apparent when barges are stowed; Sister: **94851 WILLOW** (Li); ex MAMMOTH WILLOW 1978.

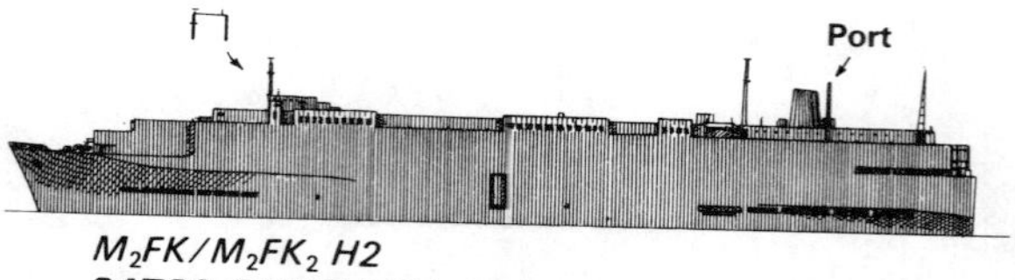

M_2FK/M_2FK_2 H2
94780 OLIVE ACE. Pa/Ja 1977; V; 12300; 176.26 × 9.03 (578.28 × 29.63); M; 19; Sister: **94781 SUZUKASAN MARU** (Ja); Probable sister: **94782 ORANGE ACE** (Pa).

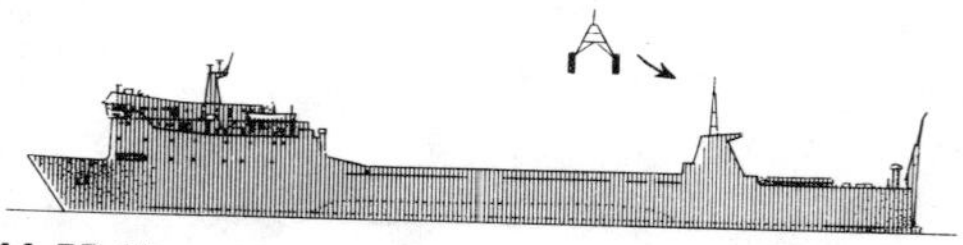

M_2FR H
94800 SPEEDLINK VANGUARD. Br/Ne 1973/77; RoC/TF; 3200; 142.27 × 5.92 (466.77 × 19.42); TSM; 18; ex STENA SHIPPER; ex ALPHA EXPRESS; ex UNION WELLINGTON 1977; launched as STENA SHIPPER; Stern door; Lengthened 1977.

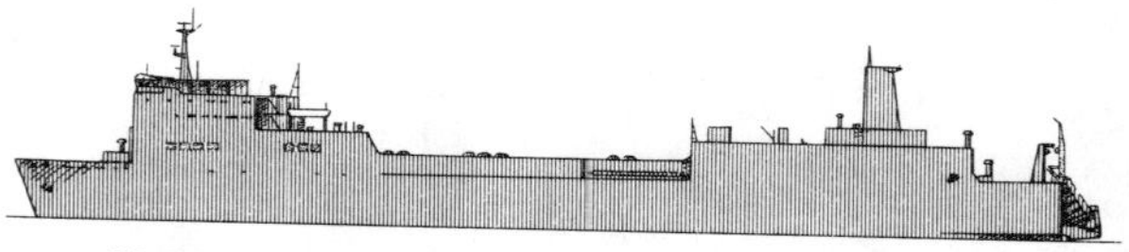

M_2FR H23
● **94830 QATAR EXPRESS.** Sw/Sw 1979; RoC/Con; 8800; 183.14 × 8.47 (600.85 × 27.79); M; 18.5; ex FINNEAGLE 1981; Two stern ramps (slewing); Sister (Sw flag): **94831 FINNCLIPPER;** ex GULF EXPRESS 1979; Similar: **94832 SAUDI EXPRESS;** ex BANDAR ABBAS EXPRESS 1980.

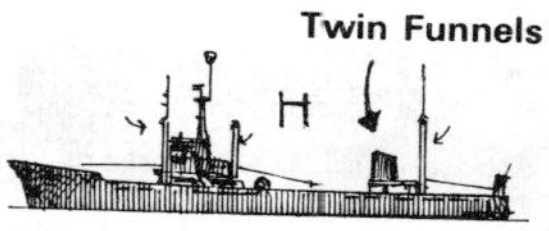

M_2KFM H
94860 DAISHIN MARU No 11. Ja/Ja 1962; ST; 1500; 75 × 5.53 (246.06 × 18.14); M; 13.

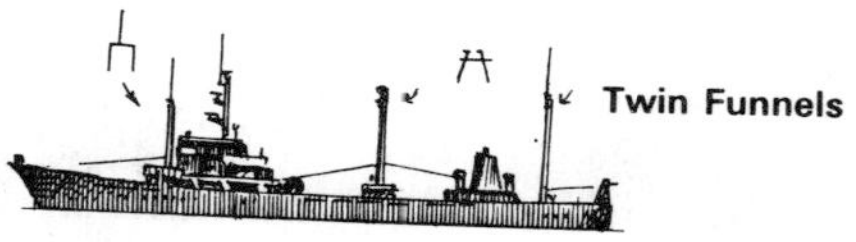

M_2KFM H
94870 KAI YANG. Ko/Ja 1970; ST; 3000; 95.61 × 6.71 (313.68 × 22.01); M; 14.5; May be **'GAE YANG HO';** Sisters (Ko flag): **94871 CHEOG YANG** (may be **CHEOG YANG HO**); **94872 SEO YANG; 94873 POONG YANG.**

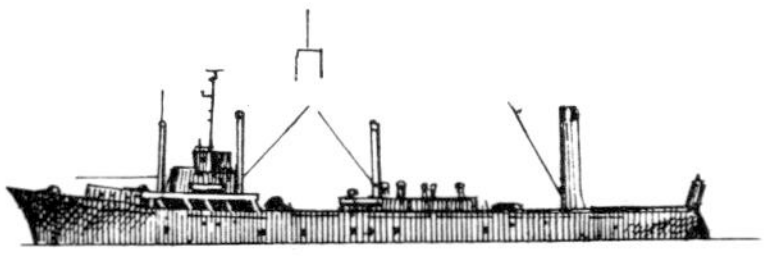

M_2K_2F *H*
94880 CHIKUBU MARU. Ja/Ja 1971; FT; 5500; 110.72 × 6.7 (363.25 × 21.98); M; 14.

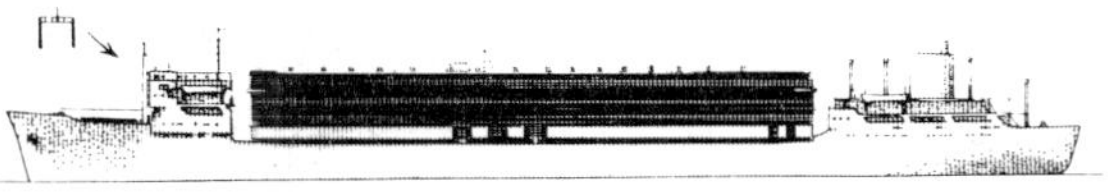

$M_2K_2FK_2$ *H13*
94890 ROSBORG. Sg/De-Sg 1958/76; LS; 13100; 170.69 × 9.76 (560 × 32.02); M; 15; ex HAUKANGER 1976; Converted from tanker 1976.

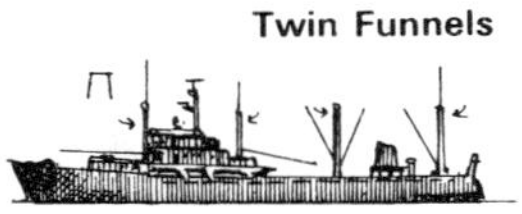

M_2K_2FM *H*
94900 TAIYO MARU No 83. Ja/Ja 1965; ST; 1500; 73.79 × 5 (242.09 × 16.4); M; 12.5. Similar (larger—Ja flag): **94901 SHOYO MARU; 94902 ZUIYO MARU No 2**.

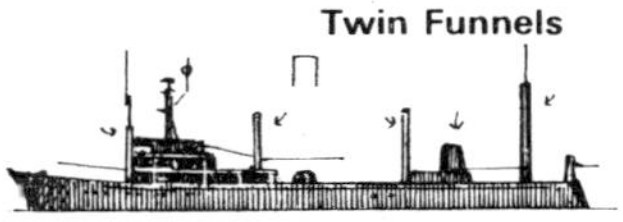

M_2K_2FM *H*
94910 DAISHIN MARU No 12. Ja/Ja 1963; ST; 2800; 94.52 × 6.01 (310.1 × 19.72); M; 13.25. Similar: **94911 DAISHIN MARU No 22** (Ja) ex SHIKA MARU 1969.

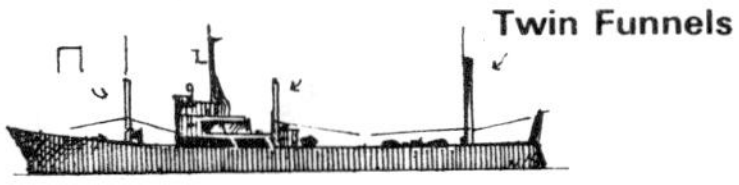

M_2KMF *H*
94920 SHIRANE MARU. Ja/Ja 1966; ST; 2500; 83.93 × 5.16 (275.36 × 19.63); M; 13.5. Sister: **94921 ZAO MARU** (Ja).

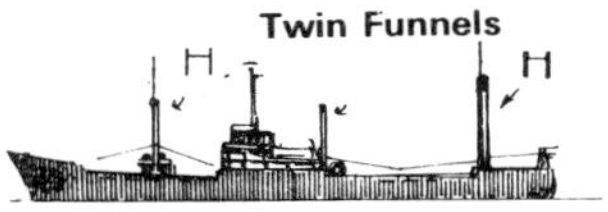

M_2KMF *H*
94930 KISO MARU. Ja/Ja 1963; ST; 2500; 84.97 × 5.31 (278.77 × 17.42); M; 12.5.

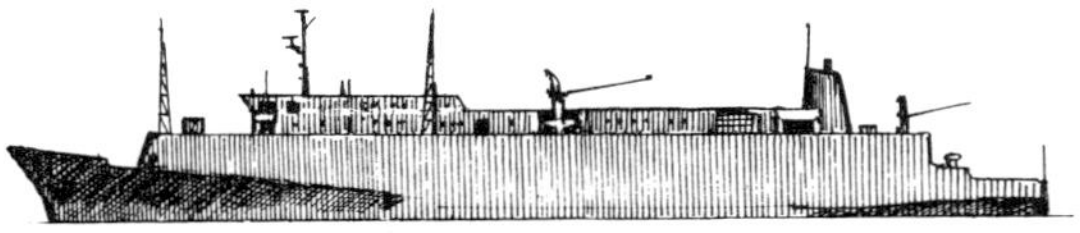

M_3CMFM *H2*
94940 TOYOTA MARU No 10. Ja/Ja 1970; V; 12500; 160 × 7.52 (524.93 × 24.67); M; 18. Sisters (Ja flag): **94941 TOYOTA MARU No 11; 94942 TOYOTA MARU No 12**.

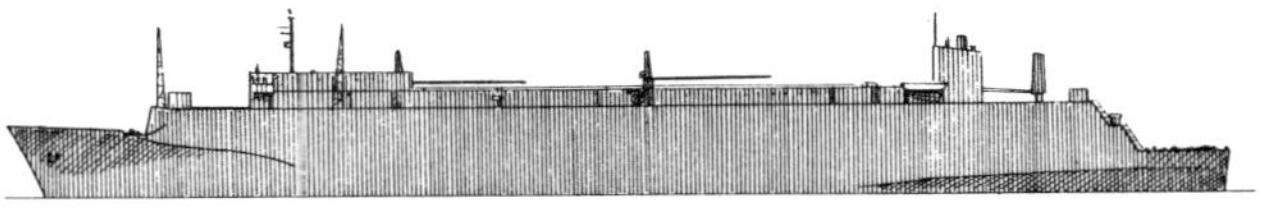

M_3C_2MFC *H2*
94950 PACIFIC HIGHWAY. Ja/Ja 1977; V; 13500; 192.08 × 8.03 (630.18 × 26.34); M; 20.5. Sister: **94951 ATLANTIC HIGHWAY** (Li).

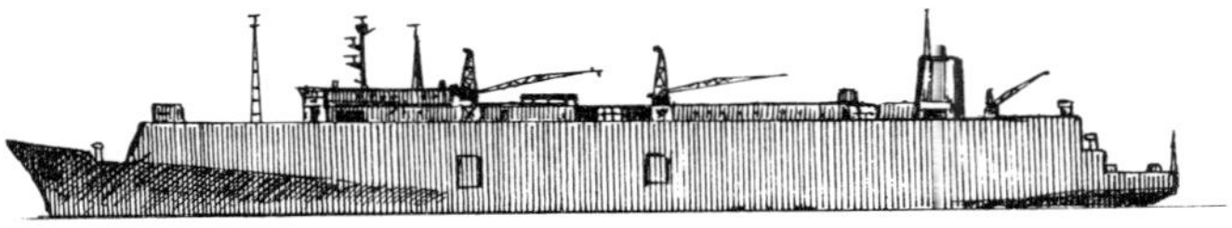

M_3C_2MFC *H2*
94960 EUROPEAN HIGHWAY. Ja/Ja 1973; RoVC; 13500; 197.14 × 8.99 (646.78 × 29.49); M; 20. Similar: **94961 TOYOTA MARU No 15** (Ja); **94962 TOYOTA MARU No 18** (Ja); **94963 UNIVENTURE No 1** (Li); **94964 SOUTHERN CROSS** (Li) ex NOPAL LANE 1980.

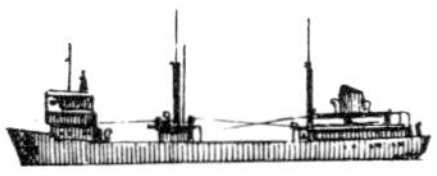

M_3F *H*
94970 PERLIS. Sg/Br 1954; C; 1400; 64.34 × 3.37 (211.09 × 11.06); M; 14. Sister: **94971 PERAK** (Sg); Similar: **94972 PETALING** (Sg).

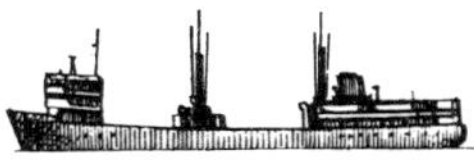

M_3F *H*
94980 AUBY. My/Br 1954; C; 1700; 69.73 × 3.59 (228.77 × 11.78); TSM; 10.5.

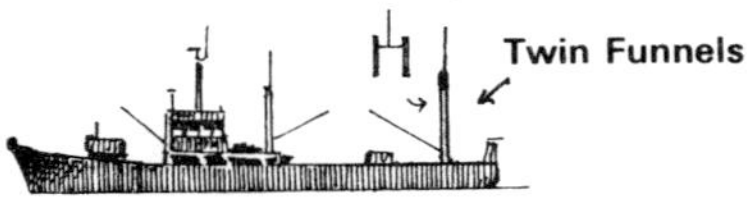

M_3F *H*
94990 AKORA. Gh/Ja 1965; ST; 2000; 79.5 × 4.97 (260.82 × 16.3); M; 14.5. Sisters (Gh flag): **94991 ASEBU; 94992 BANKO; 94993 SUBIN**.

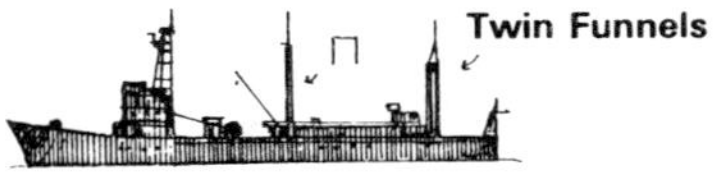

M_3F *H*
95000 GOLDEN DRAGON No 1. Tw/Ja 1967; ST; 1900; 78.49 × 5.79 (257.51 × 19); M; 14.

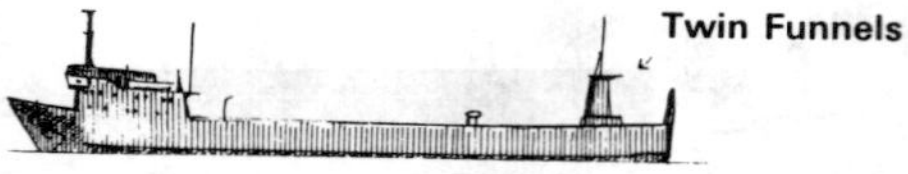

M_3F H
● **95010 LEON R.E.** Fr/No 1973; RoC; 1300; 105.39 × 3.52 (345.77 × 11.55); TSM; 15; ex STENA TRANSPORTER 1975; ex JARL TRANSPORTER 1975; Bow & stern doors. Sister: **95011 KIRK TRAILER** (Br) ex STENA TRAILER; ex NOPAL SKY 1977; ex STENA TRAILER 1974.

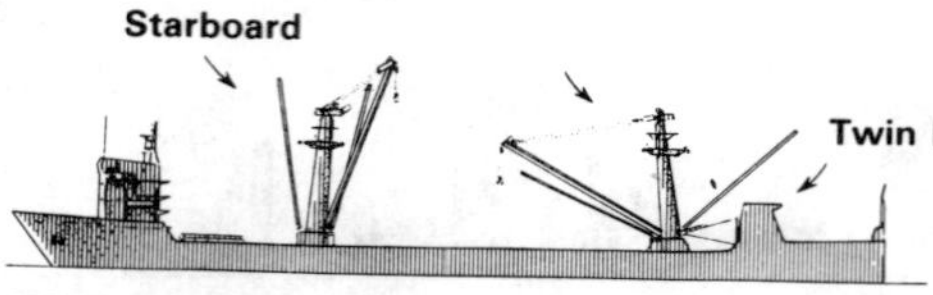

M_3F H13
● **95020 PROJECT AMERICAS.** FRG/FRG 1979; RoC/HL; 9800; 138.95 × 8.5 (455.87 × 27.89); M; 16; Can carry containers. Stern ramp.

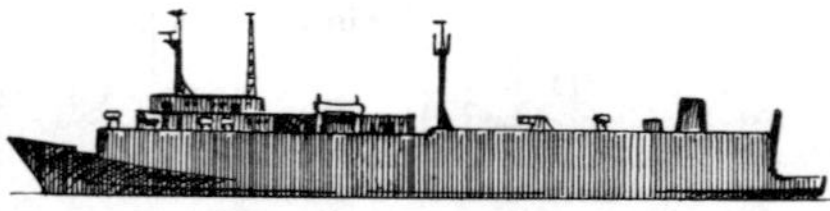

M_3F H2
95030 DAISHIN MARU. Ja/Ja 1972; RoVC; 3300; 130.59 × 6.32 (428.44 × 20.73); M; 17.

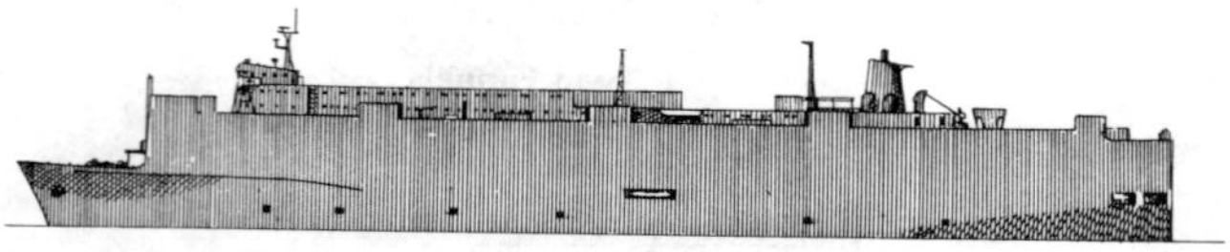

M_3F H2
95040 RIGOLETTO. Sw/Ja 1977; RoVC; 17500; 190.02 × 8.5 (623.4 × 27.8); M; 18.25. Sister: **95041 TRAVIATA** (Sw).

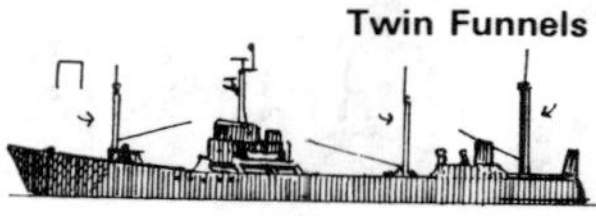

M_3FM H
95050 DAISHIN MARU No 23. Ja/Ja 1966; ST; 2400; 91.29 × 5.51 (299.51 × 18.08); M; 15.25; ex YUTAKA MARU 1971.

M_3FM H
95060 DAISHIN MARU No 15. Ja/Ja 1964; ST; 1500; 77.81 × 5.53 (255.28 × 18.16); M; 12.5. Sister: **95061 DAISHIN MARU No 16** (Ja).

M_3KFM H
95070 TAIYO MARU No 83. Ja/Ja 1965; ST; 1500; 73.79 × 5 (242.09 × 16.4); M; 12.5. Similar (Ja flag): **95071 SHOYO MARU; 95072 ZUIYO MARU No 2.**

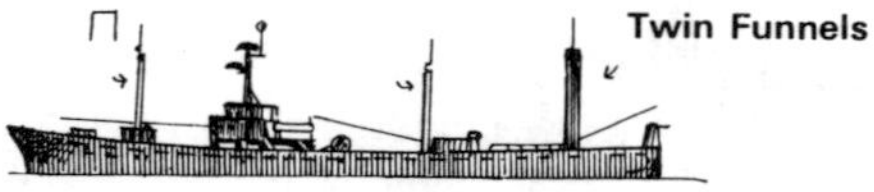

M_4F H
95080 FUJI MARU. Ja/Ja 1968; FT; 3900; 102.27 × 5.97 (335.53 × 19.59); M; 13.75. Sisters (Ja flag): **95081 HARUNA MARU; 95082 KASUGA MARU; 95083 KONGO MARU; 95084 NIITAKA MARU; 95085 ROKKO MARU.**

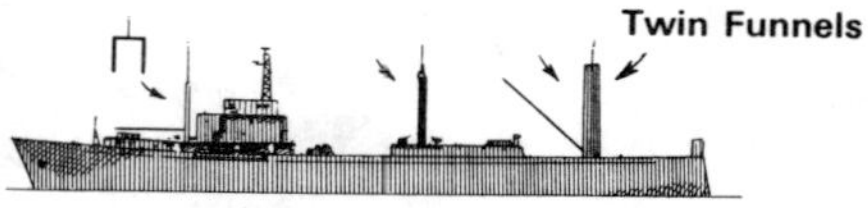

M_4F H1
95100 TSUDA MARU. Ja/Ja 1972; FT; 5500; 110.7 × 6.78 (363.19 × 22.24); M; 14.

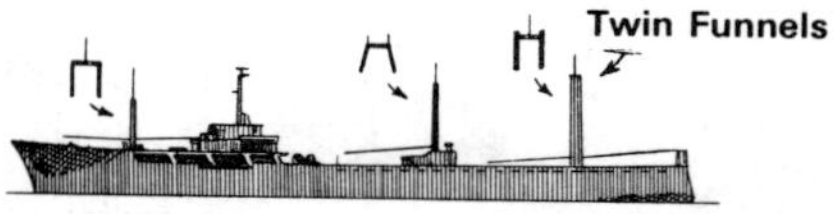

M_4F H1
95110 YAMATO MARU. Ja/Ja 1970; FT; 4000; 108.95 × 6.2 (357.45 × 20.34); M; 14.25. Sister: **95111 RIKUZEN MARU** (Ja).

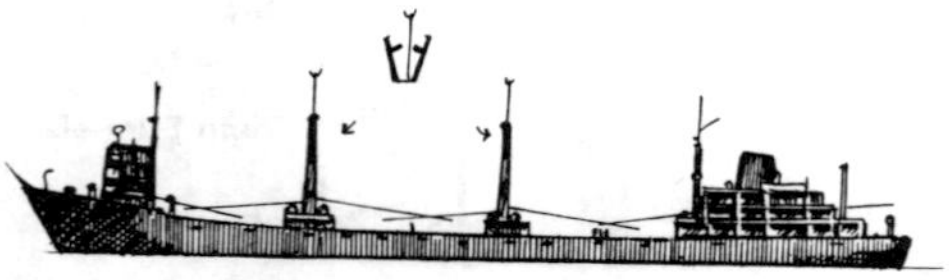

M_4FK H1
● **95120 PENELOPE V.** Gr/FRG 1956; 6600; 140.47 × 8.03 (460.86 × 26.35); M; 15.75; ex SILVER LIGHT 1980; ex RABENFELS 1977; New engines 1967. Sisters (Gr flag): **95121 SILVER GLORY**ex OCKENFELS 1978; **95122 SILVER PORT** ex NEUENFELS 1978.

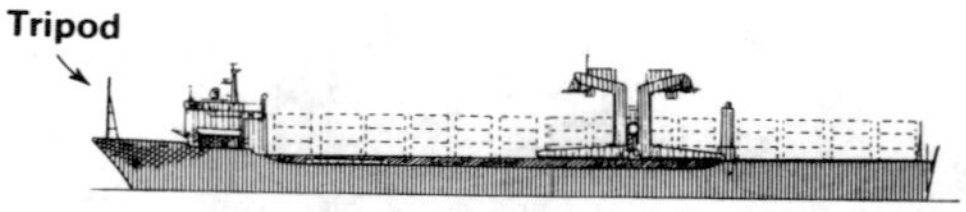

M_2N_2F H1
● **95130 LEVANTE EXPRESS.** Cy/Ja 1978; RoC/Con; 5700; 133.94 × 6.51 (439.44 × 21.36); M; 17.75; **'BOXER'** type. Stern ramp. Sisters (Cy flag): **95131 FENICIA EXPRESS; 95132 BOXER CAPTAIN COOK** (no stern ramp).

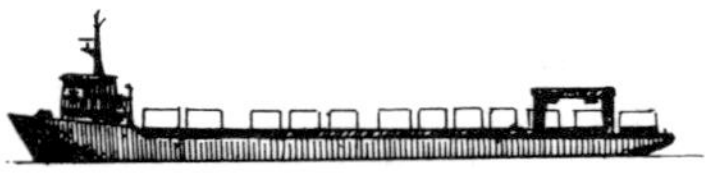

MN H1
95140 HAWAIIAN PRINCESS. US/US 1967; Con; 3900; 103.1 × 5.57 (338.25 × 18.27); TSM; 10.

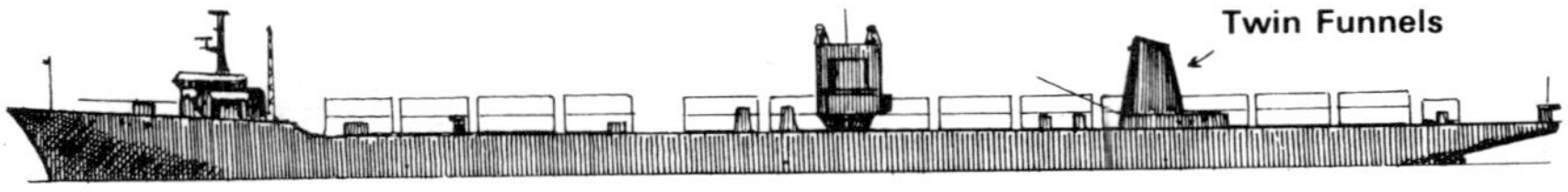

MNF H1
95150 BILDERDYK. Ne/Be 1972; Bg/Con; 37000; 261.42 × 11.27 (857.68 × 36.98); M; 18; **'LASH'** type. Similar (Li flag): **95151 ACADIA FOREST; 95152 ATLANTIC FOREST.**

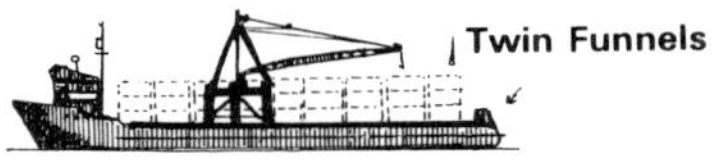

MNF H1
● **95160 STEFI.** Li/Hong kong 1975; C/Con; 1600; 76.23 × 3.83 (250.09 × 12.56); TSM; 11; ex DECKSHIP ARABELLA 1978. Stern ramp **'DECKSHIP'** type. Sisters: **95161 UNICON** (Sg) ex GHAZI 1980; ex CARINIA; **95162 LISSETTE** (Li) ex TAREK 1978; ex KHORRAMSHAHR 1976; ex DECKSHIP BRIGIDA 1976; **95163 DELICIA** (Li); **95164 PEGASUS PEACE** (Ko); Similar (stern ramps & new design of crane): **95165 FRANCESCA** (Li); **95166 FINNORIENT** (Li) ex ELEANORA.

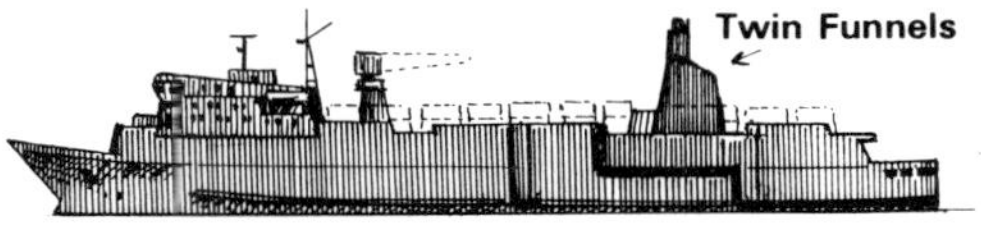

MNF H2
95180 DANA FUTURA. De/De 1975; RoVC; 6000; 144 × 7.08 (472.44 × 23.23); TSM; 22.5; ex DROSSELFELS 1977; ex DAMMAM EXPRESS 1976; ex DANA FUTURA 1976; Bow & stern coors. Sister: **95181 DANA HAFNIA** (De) ex DRACHENFELS 1977; ex DANA GLORIA 1976.

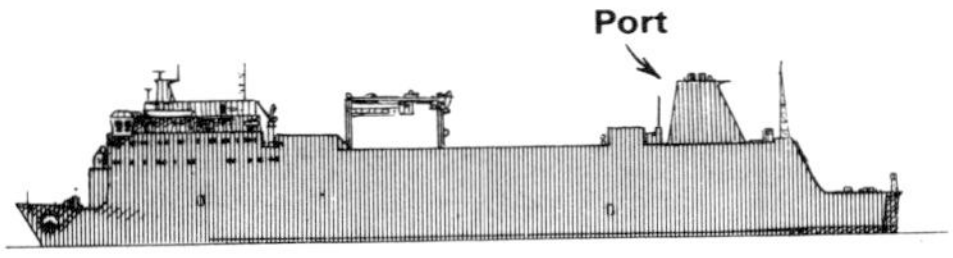

MNFM H2
95190 DANA MAXIMA. De/Ja 1978; RoC/Con; 4900; 141.51 × 6.56 (464.27 × 21.52); TSM; 18.2; Stern doors/ramps.

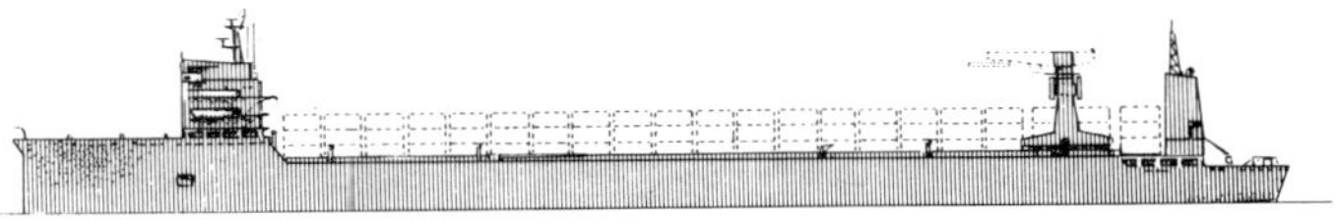

MNMF H1
95200 BACO—LINER 1. FRG/FRG 1979; Bg/Con; 23300; 204.1 × 6.67 (669.6 × 21.88); M; 15; Bow doors. Barges float on and off. Crane is shown in stowed position—dotted lines represent it swung Fore-and-aft. Sister: **95201 BACO—LINER 2** (FRG).

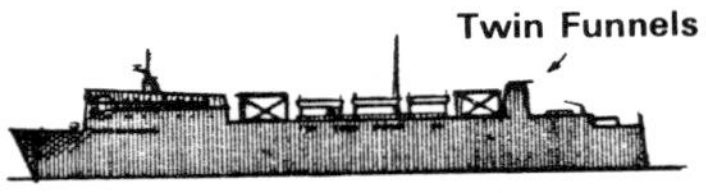

MNMNF H
95210 MONTE CONTES. Sp/Sp 1975; RoPCF; 2800; 101.66 × 5.67 (333.53 × 18.6); TSM; 18; Stern door/ramp. Sisters: **95211 MONTE CORONA** (Sp); **95212 MANX VIKING** (Br) ex MONTE CASTILLO 1978; bow and stern doors.

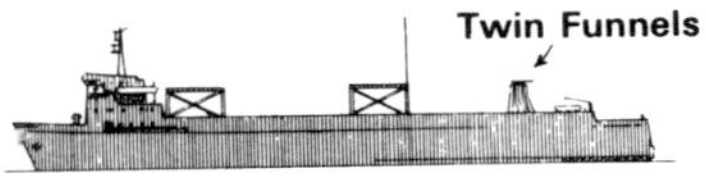

MNMNF/MN_2F *H*
95220 MONTE BANDERAS. Sp/Sp 1976; RoC; 2000; 101.66 × 5.66 (333.53 × 18.57); TSM; 13; Stern door. Probable sisters (Sp flag): **95221 MONTE BUITRE; 95222 MONTE BUSTELO.**

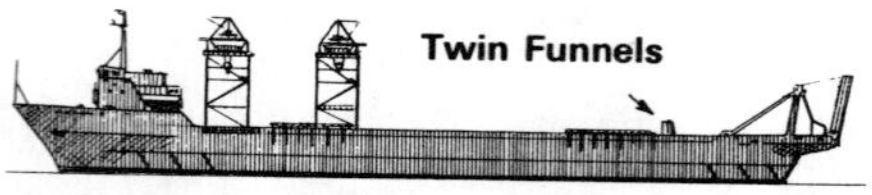

MN_2F/MN_2FK_2 H1
95230 DOCKLIFT 2. NA/Ne 1967/74/78; Dk/Bg/HL; 3800; 129.78 × 5.95 (428.8 × 19.51); TrM; 12.5; ex LADY JANE 1974; Rebuilt from Ro/Ro ship 1974. Lengthened 1978. Stern ramp.

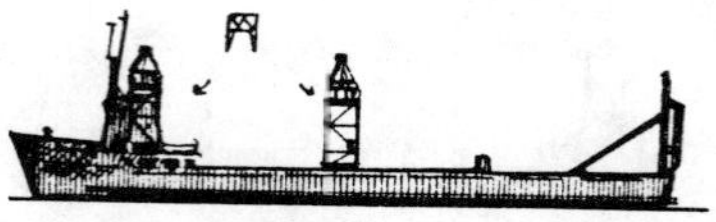

MN_2FM H1
95240 DOCKLIFT 1. Pa/Ne 1972; Dk/HL/Bg; 2400; 105.7 × 4.97 (346.78 × 16.31); TSM; 12.75; Stern ramp.

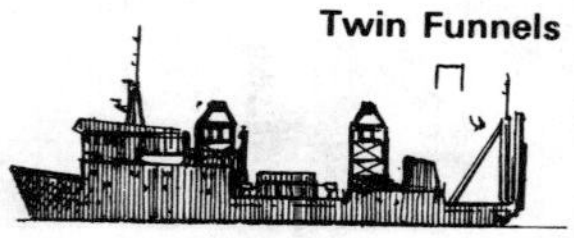

MN_2FM H1
★95250 BROCKEN. DDR/Ne 1976; RoC/HL; 1200; 81.01 × 3.95 (265.78 × 12.96); TSM; 11.75; Bow door.

INDEX

USING THE INDEX

For names which consist of two or more words, look for the first word alone. If there are a number of names beginning with that word it is then necessary to look at the second word, and so on. For example, GOLDEN BAY will appear before GOLDENALPA as it is entered as GOLDEN initially. Initials are treated in the same way; for example, the name D. C. COLEMAN is regarded as three words, the first being D. Therefore, it is initially placed under D and will come at the beginning of the D section. It is often very difficult to establish whether a name consists of initials. Prefixes such as CP and BP, although known to be initials, appear as words because that is how they appear on ships. The answer, when in doubt, is to check both places. Abbreviations of titles, such as ST for SAINT or DR for DOCTOR, are inserted under their abbreviated form.

With names such as D'ARTAGNAN, disregard the apostrophe and consider it as DARTAGNAN.

When a name is suffixed with a numeral it comes before names suffixed with a letter, e.g. MARIA 1 will come before MARIA A. If the numeral is spelt, however, it is considered to be a word and is inserted alphabetically. Names which begin with a numeral are inserted within the index but for ease of identification they are listed separately at the end of the main index on page 1021.

If a vessel has two or more entries its name appears several times rather than several numbers following one entry. If there are six entries for MARIA, for example, they may be six different vessels or some may be alternative entries for the same vessel.

For further names see the separate index for the Appendix.

A

AFGHANISTAN	35378
AFOVOS	36390
AFOVOS	52141
AFOVOS	52532
AFRAM RIVER	13311
AFRAM RIVER	34830
AFRAN ENERGY	64206
AFRAN ENERGY	68656
AFRAN EQUATOR	58342
AFRAN EQUATOR	63992
AFRAN JUPITER	70054
AFRAN LEEWARD	68670
AFRAN MERIDIAN	58770
AFRAN MERIDIAN	62510
AFRAN NEPTUNE	70055
AFRAN STREAM	67947
AFRAN TIDE	66010
AFRAN WAVE	64150
AFRIC STAR	02560
AFRIC STAR	02660
AFRICA	08808
AFRICA	09140
AFRICA.	10710
AFRICA CUBA	10100
AFRICA MARU	73340
AFRICA MARU	77960
AFRICA PALM	05450
AFRICAN AMBER	06067
AFRICAN BERYL	05400
AFRICAN CORRAL	06068
AFRICAN DIAMOND	07773
AFRICAN EXPRESS	05074
AFRICAN EXPRESS	05326
AFRICAN LION	13640
AFRICAN PIONEER	08050
AFRICAN TRADER	93640
AFRICAN VIOLET	87021
AFRIKA type	34960
AFROS	48771
AGADIR	19260
AGAPI	26400
AGAPI	60074
AGAPI II	27650
AGAT	12383
AGATE	06626
AGATE ISLANDS	29930
AGATHON	60075
AGATOVYY	11916
AGDAM	50772
AGELIKI III	45440
AGELIKI III	52761
AGELOS MICHAEL	57750
AGENOR	45500
AGENOR	49790
AGENOR	60076
AGENT	15703
AGHIA MARINA	00300
AGHIA MARINA	40421
AGHIA MARINA	42331
AGHIA MARINA	42591
AGHIA THALASSINI	06911
AGHIOS ERMOLAOS	40190
AGHIOS GEORGIOS III	07261
AGHIOS NICOLAOS	00383
AGIA ANASTASIA	74730
AGIA ANASTASIA	79280
AGIA ANASTASIA	80050
AGIA ANNA	42701
AGIA EFIMIA	26750
AGIA ERINI II	56980
AGIA IRINI I	41840
AGIA MARINA	10622
AGIA MARINA	15372
AGIA MARINA	28850
AGIA SKEPI	06537
AGIA VARVARA	26881
AGIAPARASKEVI	28730
AGILITY	00931
AGILITY	10150
AGINOR	30322
AGIOI VICTORES	46522
AGIOI VICTORES	83302
AGIOS CONSTANTINOS	61970
AGIOS DIMITROS	41520
AGIOS DIONISSIOS	83711
AGIOS FANOURIS III	31500
AGIOS FANOURIOS V	41140
AGIOS FANOURIOS V	42580
AGIOS FANOURIOS VI	28931
AGIOS GEORGIOS	19610
AGIOS GEORGIOS	43030
AGIOS GEORGIOS	72961
AGIOS GEORGIOS	87161
AGIOS GERASSIMOS	26100
AGIOS GERASSIMOS	29370
AGIOS GERASSIMOS	42510
AGIOS GIANNIS	02941
AGIOS IOANNIS	51634
AGIOS KONSTANTINOS	06414
AGIOS NECTARIOS	23200
AGIOS NECTARIOS	67300
AGIOS NEKTARIOS	87060
AGIOS NICOLAOS	01321
AGIOS NICOLAOS	12130
AGIOS NICOLAOS IV	41730
AGIOS NIKOLAOS	86920
AGIOS NIKOLAOS III	57001
AGIOS NIKOLAS	52410
AGIOS PANDELEIMON	06110
AGIOS SPYRIDON	75878
AGIOS VLASIOS V	36760
AGIP ABRUZZO	62854
AGIP ABRUZZO	67534
AGIP ANCONA	65310
AGIP CAMPANIA	62855
AGIP CAMPANIA	67535
AGIP GELA	66197
AGIP GENOVA	65311
AGIP LAZIO	62856
AGIP LAZIO	67536
AGIP MARCHE	62857
AGIP MARCHE	67537
AGIP RAVENNA	66198
AGIP SARDEGNA	62851
AGIP SARDEGNA	67531
AGIP SICILIA	62850
AGIP SICILIA	67530
AGIP TRIESTE	65040
AGIP TRIESTE	74180
AGNIC II	61130
AGNITA	82228
AGOI ANARGYROI III	42210
AGOSTINHO NETO	80265
AGOSTINO LAURO	18890
AGRI	80352
AGROTAI	87560
AGUA GRANDE	65860
AGUADILLA	93132
AGUADILLA	93392
AGUILA II	42551
AGW VII	94480
AGYASI MANKO	85364
AGYIMFRA	27211
AHMAD AL-FATEH	49403
AHMAD AL-FATEH	50963
AHMED ES SAKAH	84263
AHMOS	01416
AHMOS	01676
AI FANOURIS	81360
AICHI MARU	93980
AIDA	89160
AIDAN	87423
AIDE	15702
AIDEN	91849
AIDEN	91959
AIFANOURIOS	83200
AIGEORGIS	55090
AIHUA	13240
AIKATERINA	65061
AIKATERINA	65951
AIKATERINE K.	61600
AIKO MARU	54490
AIKO MARU	54920
AIKO MARU	55720
AILSA PRINCESS	32791
AIMEE LYKES	00081
AIMEE LYKES	00231
AIMIN	13241
AIN ZALAH	69571
AINIKOLAS	21140
AINO	77671
AINOS	19410
AIS GIORGIS	26113
AIS GIORGIS	26841
AIU-DAG	11801
AJAN	31849
AJANTA	56781
AJAX	46581
AJDABYA	63282
AKAD	49060
AKADEMIK ARTSIMOVICH	80250
AKADEMIK BERG	12573
AKADEMIK CHOCHLOV	10752
AKADEMIK EVGENIY PATON	02671
AKADEMIK FILATOV	02526
AKADEMIK GUBER	80251
AKADEMIK IOSIF ORBELI	02527
AKADEMIK KHOKHLOV	10753
AKADEMIK KNIPOVICH	12570
AKADEMIK KOROLYOV	12000
AKADEMIK KRYLOV	02460
AKADEMIK KRYLOV	63571
AKADEMIK KUPREVICH	80252
AKADEMIK KURCHATOV.	07620
AKADEMIK MAMEDALIEV	85974
AKADEMIK MILLIONSCHIKOV	80253
AKADEMIK PAVLOV	63572
AKADEMIK RYKACHEV	02528
AKADEMIK SECHENOV	63573
AKADEMIK SHIMANSKIY	01561
AKADEMIK SHIRSHOV	12001
AKADEMIK SHUKHOV	02529
AKADEMIK STECHKIN	80254
AKADEMIK TUPOLEV	80255
AKADEMIK VERNADSKIY	07621
AKADEMIK YANGEL	03968
AKADEMIK YURYEV	02530
AKADEMOS	58171
AKANE MARU	18800
AKARNANIA	06534
AKASHI MARU	18801
AKBAR	46093
AKBAR	60960
AKBAR	83263
AKDENIZ	01580
AKEBONO MARU	18802
AKEBONO MARU No 50	92522
AKEBONO MARU No 51	92520
AKEBONO MARU No 52	92521
AKEBONO MARU No 53	92523
AKEBONO REEFER	05193
AKEN	61710
AKEN	71080
AKHALTSIKHE	70767
AKHILLEON	13652
AKHILLES	11802
AKHTARSKIY LIMAN	33621
AKHTUBA	11803
AKHTUBA	35315
AKHTUBA	36861
AKHTUBA	86090
AKHUN	11804
AKIHIRO MARU	61642
AKIS S	28150
AKIS S	31910
AKLAN	33770
AKMOLINSK	11805
AKOP	86075
AKOPYAN	86076
AKORA	93650
AKORA	94990
AKRA AKTION	41510
AKRA DREPANON	06930
AKRA RION	25881
AKRA RION	53170
AKRA SIGRI	49621
AKRA SOUNION	25880
AKRA TENARON	53171
AKRATA	60140
AKRITAS	58142
AKRON	77700
AKROPOLIS	26130
AKSAY	36894
AKSAY	43794
AKSTAFA	50773
AKTASH	36893
AKTASH	43793
AKTAU	70761
AKTEA	47371
AKTIAN	86021
AKTINJA	23441
AKTION	61035
AKTION	71195
AKTYUBINSK	70762
AKTYUBINSK	45210
AKUSTIK	11806
AKVAMARIN	23549
AL-ABEDIN	45399
AL AHAD	58561
AL AHMADIAH	09010
AL AHMADIAH	77040
AL AHOOD	67741
AL AHWAR	23470
AL AIN	64360
AL AKBER	42220
AL AKBER	42740
AL AMIRAH	51171
AL ANDALAS	58311
AL ANDALUS	62500
AL ANDALUS	63960
AL ANOUD	19630
AL ARIDHIAH	45371
AL BADIAH	52390
AL-BAKRY	40840
AL BARAT	05270
AL BATTANI	66884
AL BIRUNI	90861
AL BIRUNI	91781
AL DAHRAN	25910
AL DAMMAM 1	71502
AL DHAID STAR	74322
AL ESRAA	03630
AL FARWANIAH	45380
AL FUJAIRAH	49400
AL FUJAIRAH	50960
AL GHASSANI	66580
AL GILANI	26071
AL GURAINIAH	45372
AL HAMRAA	03631
AL HARAMAIN	63031
AL HASAN	26830
AL HODEIDAH	66880
AL HOFUF	71500
AL HUSSEIN B.	37740
AL IDRISI	90862
AL IDRISI	91782
AL JABIRIAH	45374
AL KADISIAH	45377
AL KAHERA	84860
AL KAHERAH	57580
AL KAHLA	23471
AL KHAFJI	71501
AL KHAIRAT	01310
AL-KHALEEJ	33040
AL-KHALEEJ	33340
AL KHALIDIAH	45373
AL KHLOOD	60820
AL KHLOOD	70840
AL KULSUM	10340
AL-KUWAIT	60511
AL LOULOUAH	32030
AL MADANI	23260
AL MALAZ	65541
AL MANSOURIAH	45375
AL MESSILAH	10630
AL MORGAN	38141
AL MUBARAKIAH	49398
AL MUBARAKIAH	50958
AL MUHARRAQ	49401
AL MUHARRAQ	50961
AL ODALIAH	45376
AL OMARIAH	45378
AL OSMAN	51710
AL OSMAN	52370
AL PASHA	23790
AL PETRI	44108
AL QASEEM	26200
AL QASIM	57920
AL QASIM	62920
AL RAFIDAIN	63280
AL RAHIM	60175
AL RAHMAN	60176
AL RAKEEB	60150
AL RASHED	60151
AL RAWDATAIN	58000
AL RAYYAN	49402
AL RAYYAN	50962
AL RAZAK	60152
AL RAZAZA	23472
AL RAZIQ	60177
AL REDHA	60178
AL REKKAH	54492
AL REKKAH	54922
AL REKKAH	55722
AL RIYAD	16740
AL RIYADH	06370
AL RIYADH	16740
AL RUMAITHIAH	09011
AL RUMAITHIAH	77041
AL SABAHIAH	45379
AL-SABBIYAH	51370
AL SADIQ	58172
AL SALAAM	58173
AL SALAM I	49993
AL SALAM II	84527
AL SALEHIAH	45383
AL SALIMI V	37060
AL SALIMIAH	49397
AL SALIMIAH	50957
AL SAMAD	58174
AL SAMIE	58175
AL SAUDIA	68691
AL SHAMIAH.	09012
AL SHAMIAH	77042
AL SHAN	47240
AL SHEHABIA	13350
AL SHIDADIAH	45381
AL SHUWAIKH	13382
AL-SHUWAIKH	94730
AL SOLAIBIAH	45382
AL SUDAN	18391
AL SULTANA	52050
AL-TAHA	57350
AL TAHIR	79700
AL TAIF	22390
AL TAJDAR	46060
AL TAMMAR	47480
AL TAMMAR	47980
AL TAQEE	78274
AL TASLIM	60932
AL TASLIM	85022
AL TAWWAB	74690
AL TOOS	60931
AL TOOS	85021
AL WASEL	64210
AL YAMAMAH	49399
AL YAMAMAH	50959
AL YARMOUK	03633
AL ZAHER	19840
ALA	22061
ALA WAI	61614
ALABAMA GETTY	64160
ALABAMA GETTY	68480
ALACRITY	90140
ALAFOSS	94651
ALAGIR	36905
ALAGIR	43805
ALAIN L-D	83144
ALAMAK	59680
ALAMAR	35991
ALAMO	69030
ALAMOS	13450
ALAND	51622
ALAND	72685
ALANFUSHI	50701
ALAPAEVSK	01021
ALAPAYEVSK	00341
ALAPAYEVSKLES	24033
ALARIC	47800
ALASKA	33500
ALASKA I	34201
ALASKA MARU	09850
ALASKAN	65900
ALASKAN TRADER	36450
ALASKAN TRADER	43430
ALASSIR	31410
ALATYR	40013
ALATYRLES	24034
ALAUNIA	34216
ALBA	11939
ALBA IULIA	06142
ALBAFORTH	61311
ALBAFORTH	62611
ALBAFRIGO	81690
ALBAFRIGO	87050
ALBAKORA	22331
ALBATROS	12311
ALBATROS	85323
ALBAY HAKKI BURAK	75050
ALBENA	76532
ALBERT J. MEYER	22741
ALBERT MAERSK	08672
ALBERT MAERSK	09002
ALBERTO MONTEIRO	39531
ALBERTO MONTEIRO	93491
ALBERTOEMME	00921
ALBIN KOBIS	06384
ALBIN KOBIS	15413
ALBION	59350
ALBIREO	32581
ALBIS	26871
ALBORADA	86270
ALBRIGHT EXPLORER	74921
ALBRIGHT PIONEER	74920
ALCA	47520
ALCAZAR	71551
ALCHATBY	50702
ALCHEMIST	53630
ALCHEMIST	53670
ALCHEVSK	25552
ALCHIMIST FLENSBURG	59051
ALCHIMIST FLENSBURG	76431
ALCHIMIST LAUSANNE	56250
ALCHIMIST LAUSANNE	75230
ALCHIMIST LUBECK	59050
ALCHIMIST LUBECK	76430
ALCHIMIST ROTTERDAM	59070
ALCHIMIST ROTTERDAM	76420
ALCOUTIM	07970
ALCYONE	35680
ALDABI	04350
ALDABI	52820
ALDAN	31855
ALDAN	89503
ALDANLES	24035
ALDEA	04461
ALDEBARAN	50551
ALDENBURG	33922
ALDERAMIN	12232
ALDERAMINE	35810
ALDERAMINE	41580
ALDO CECCONI	43410
ALDONZA MANRIQUE	19190
ALDRICH	61681
ALE	23670
ALEA	60153
ALECOS M	65461
ALEDREESI	63680
ALEGRIA DE PIO	48214
ALEKSANDER ZAWADSKI	10572
ALEKSANDER ZAWADSKI	15342
ALEKSANDR BARANOV	17922
ALEKSANDR BLOK	14371
ALEKSANDR BOGOLYUBOV	23518
ALEKSANDR DOVZHENKO	09970
ALEKSANDR DOVZHENKO	11510
ALEKSANDR FADEYEV	77060
ALEKSANDR GERTSEN	14372
ALEKSANDR GRIN	14373
ALEKSANDR IVANOV	76493
ALEKSANDR IVANOVICH VOEYKOV	23770
ALEKSANDR KOSAREV	93690
ALEKSANDR LEYNER	89470
ALEKSANDR MAKSUTOV	12385
ALEKSANDR MATROSOV	73291
ALEKSANDR MIROSHNIKOV	50295
ALEKSANDR NEVSKII	17501
ALEKSANDR NEVSKIY	77072
ALEKSANDR OBUKHOV	86205
ALEKSANDR OBUKHOV	93682
ALEKSANDR OSIPOV	78067
ALEKSANDR PANKRATOV	50282
ALEKSANDR PASHKOV	79400
ALEKSANDR POKALCHUK	49241
ALEKSANDR POPOV	17923
ALEKSANDR PROKOFYEV	79378
ALEKSANDR PROKOVYEV	77061
ALEKSANDR PUSHKIN.	01750
ALEKSANDR RYLKE	14481
ALEKSANDR SERAFIMOVIC	14374
ALEKSANDR SUVOROV	15400
ALEKSANDR SUVOROV	77073
ALEKSANDR TEREKHIN	17924
ALEKSANDR TORTSYEV	00142
ALEKSANDR TSYURUPA	03962
ALEKSANDR TSYURUPA	79374
ALEKSANDR TVARDOVSKIY	77062

ALEKSANDR ULYANOV 03065
ALEKSANDR ULYANOV 03657
ALEKSANDR VERMISHEV 14375
ALEKSANDR VERMISHEV 79370
ALEKSANDR VINOKUROV 03771
ALEKSANDR VINOKUROV 04011
ALEKSANDRA ARTYUKHINA 03772
ALEKSANDRA ARTYUKHINA 04012
ALEKSANDRA KOLLONTAY 10721
ALEKSANDRIT 23528
ALEKSANDROVSK 00330
ALEKSANDROVSK 11808
ALEKSANDROVSK SAKHALINSKIY 93758
ALEKSANDROVSK SAKHALINSKIY 93848
ALEKSEY BORDUNOV 11809
ALEKSEY CHIRIKOV 10432
ALEKSEY CHIRIKOV 22181
ALEKSEY GMYREV 12386
ALEKSEY KHLOBYSTOV 93877
ALEKSEY KRYLOV 41151
ALEKSEY KRYLOV 44951
ALEKSEY MAKHALIN 12387
ALEKSEY POZDNYAKOV 93878
ALEKSEY TOLSTOY 07919
ALEKSEY VENETSIANOV 76491
ALEKSEY VIKHORYEV 79424
ALEKSEYEVKA 36902
ALEKSEYEVKA 43802
ALEKSEYEVSK 36903
ALEKSEYEVSK 43803
ALEKSIN 36907
ALEKSIN 43807
ALENDALE 65973
ALEPPO 46001
ALESSANDRA F 80632
ALEUTIAN DEVELOPER 32071
ALEX G 65080
ALEX G 85410
ALEXA 11370
ALEXANDER 72122
ALEXANDER 76463
ALEXANDER STAR 73110
ALEXANDER STAR 77780
ALEXANDER THE GREAT 54391
ALEXANDERS FAITH 07181
ALEXANDERS TRUST 07180
ALEXANDRA 28513
ALEXANDRA 61626
ALEXANDRA CONWAY 37460
ALEXANDRA DYO 64082
ALEXANDRA DYO 72082
ALEXANDRA K. II 72500
ALEXANDRA N 46610
ALEXANDRA N. 52780
ALEXANDRA T 56051
ALEXANDRIA. 03972
ALEXANDROS 09391
ALEXANDROS 31141
ALEXANDROS 35713
ALEXANDROS 41423
ALEXANDROS A 25580
ALEXANDROS A 31660
ALEXANDROS G. TSAVLIRIS 49110
ALEXANDROS K 17791
ALEXANDROS K 24961
ALEXANDROS P 25691
ALEXANDROUPOLIS 28410
ALEXI H 29871
ALEXIA 21850
ALEXIA 44626
ALEXION HOPE 06508
ALEXIS G 43491
ALEXIS G 43551
ALEXIS K 84530
ALEYSK 36906
ALEYSK 43806
ALFA 74040
ALFA CEMENTA 43950
ALFER 79891
ALFEUS 23442
ALFITO 35901
ALFITO 41591
ALFONSAS CHEPONIS 12384
ALFONSO CUARTO 74190
ALFRED REHDER 56111
ALFRED REHDER 59801
ALGAZAYER 33760
ALGENIB 50371
ALGENIB 83614
ALGENIB I 87171
ALGERIA 74022
ALGONQUIN II type 61770
ALGOSEA 52560
ALHAJA MAMA BAKARE 61730
ALHAJA MAMA BAKARE 81540
ALHAJA MAMA BAKARE 85050
ALHAKEM 47323
ALHAKEM 83383
ALHALEMI 47320
ALHALEMI 83380
ALHAMBRA 07321
ALHAMBRA 47326
ALHAMBRA 83386
ALHENA 04351
ALHENA 52821
ALIAKMON 57185
ALIAKMON BREEZE 25710
ALIAKMON LEADER 82352
ALIAKMON LEADER 82622
ALIAKMON LIGHT 82353
ALIAKMON LIGHT 82623
ALIAKMON PROSPERITY 05901
ALIANORA 82061
ALIANORA 91441
ALIANZA 74771
ALIANZA 79001
ALIARTOS 26873
ALIBRAHIMIYA 50703
ALICAMPOS 55080
ALICAMPOS 57340
ALICE LANGLI 94220
ALICIA 76200
ALICIA 1 86460
ALIDA 83810
ALIDA SMITS 50500
ALIDADE 20910
ALIKI 74880
ALIKI I. P. 71852
ALIMAR 49650
ALINDA 37013
ALINDA 37510
ALINDA 44212
ALIOSHA POPOVICH 17502
ALIOT 12233
ALIOT 76890
ALIOT 81400
ALISHER NAVOI 14376
ALITA 73794
ALITHIA 71510
ALITUS 89471
ALIYA MOLDAGULOV 79427
ALKA 11807
ALKA 11956
ALKAIOS 05238
ALKAIOS 61036
ALKAIOS 71196
ALKEOS C 72261
ALKHANSAA 63682
ALKMAAR 15712
ALKMAN 47954
ALKMINI 42390
ALKMINI 58571
ALKMINI A 18480
ALKOR 61292
ALKOR 86722
ALKYON 34898
ALKYON 47860
ALKYON 84420
ALKYONIA 61153
ALKYONIS 58143
ALLA TARASOVA 02341
ALLEGIANCE 36640
ALLEGIANCE 43680
ALLEGRO 68980
ALLEMAGNA EXPRESS 18002
ALLEMANIA EXPRESS 73402
ALLEMANIA EXPRESS 82712
ALLIANCE 75501
ALLIANCE SUCCESS 34952
ALLIGATOR III 45720
ALLISON LYKES 00082
ALLISON LYKES 00232
ALLISON STAR 35750
ALLISON STAR 37093
ALLUL 79890
ALLUNGA 52631
ALLURITY 66470
ALLURITY 86450
ALLY 62025
ALMA 11810
ALMA 89846
ALMA-ATA 44103
ALMAK 12234
ALMANDARAH 49681
ALMAR 61041
ALMAR II 28855
ALMARIS 47053
ALMATEVSK 01022
ALMAZ 12388
ALMAZ 48310
ALMAZNYY 76506
ALMEA 85030
ALMEDA STAR 02561
ALMEDA STAR 02661
ALMERIA LYKES 08860
ALMERIA STAR 02564
ALMERIA STAR 02664
ALMETYEVSK 00342
ALMIRANTE 63731
ALMIRANTE 72901
ALMIRANTE GRACA ARANHA 55011
ALMIRANTE GRACA ARANHA 55881
ALMIRANTE GRACA ARANHA 56551
ALMIRANTE IRIZAR. 22210
ALMIRANTE IRIZAR 23650
ALMIRANTE JORGE MONTT 44450
ALMIRANTE LOBO 10200
ALMIRANTE LUIS BIRON 19184
ALMIRANTE STORNI 06676
ALMIZAR 65260
ALMONA 24260
ALMOUNTAZAH 1 49682
ALMUSTANSIRIYAH 63391
ALMUT BORNHOFEN 71847
ALMY 42251
ALNAIR 81830
ALNAIR II 60727
ALNAJDI 70480
ALNASL 33301
ALNASL 34991
ALNATI 04352
ALNATI 52822
ALNILAM 87703
ALON 80951
ALPAC AFRICA 09941
ALPAC ASIA 09940
ALPAMAYO 59757
ALPERIN 89509
ALPHA 91101
ALPHA BAY 03980
ALPHA BAY 35520
ALPHA CEMENTA 44380
ALPHA CONVEYOR 76971
ALPHA CONVEYOR 89781
ALPHACCA 04353
ALPHACCA 52823
ALPILLES 49960
ALPILLES 51821
ALPINA 57480
ALPINA 90500
ALPPILA 82890
ALPRO 65030
ALQADISIAH 63392
ALRAI 64620
ALRANA 25280
ALRUBAYIA 35760
ALRUBAYIA 35790
ALSACE 18630
ALSACE 57830
ALSAD ALAALY 36970
ALSAD ALAALY 37480
ALSALMA 13030
ALSATIA 34222
ALSTER EXPRESS 73512
ALSTERBERG 51623
ALSTERBERG 72686
ALSTERTAL 76180
ALSU 11811
ALSYTA SMITS 50505
ALTAI 17503
ALTAI MARU 51210
ALTAIF 22390
ALTAIR 50370
ALTAIR 73112
ALTAIR 76310
ALTAIR 77782
ALTAIR 83063
ALTAIR 83163
ALTAIR 85332
ALTAJ 58123
ALTANIN 64621
ALTANO 48085
ALTAPPEN 75560
ALTAVIA 58594
ALTAVIA 60474
ALTAY 70760
ALTAY 11301
ALTAYLES 24048
ALTCAR 03522
ALTE LIEBE 02030
ALTENBURG. 03870
ALTHEA 47370
ALTIS 58567
ALTMARK 56140
ALTMARK 71720
ALTNES 50120
ALUKSNE 36891
ALUKSNE 43791
ALUPKA 01962
ALUPKA 12235
ALUSHTA 01963
ALUSHTA 12236
ALVA BAY 68680
ALVA MAERSK 08677
ALVA MAERSK 09007
ALVA SEA 68681
ALVARO OBREGON 69991
ALVARO OBREGON 86481
ALVARO PEREZ 48215
ALWAHA 29290
ALZAHRAA 20140
ALZAWRAA 63681
AMADO 45921
AMAGI MARU 61637
AMAK 72433
AMAL EXPRESS 24250
AMALI 66940
AMALIA 04801
AMALIA 24381
AMALIA 39690
AMALIA 88830
AMALIA II 63470
AMALIE ESSBERGER 72560
AMALINDA 12861
AMALTHEA 12211
AMAMI MARU 22630
AMANDA 1 66883
AMANDA MILLER 64590
AMANDA MILLER 67630
AMANDA MILLER 69040
AMANDA SMITS 50503
AMANDAEVERETT 34340
AMAR 26673
AMAR 31735
AMARALINA 05360
AMARALINA 15660
AMARANTE 07971
AMAREL 23449
AMARYLLIS 11270
AMASTRA 37512
AMASTRA 44210
AMAZON 58572
AMAZON MARU 63100
AMAZON MARU 68140
AMAZONIA 49601
AMAZONIA 51051
AMAZONIA 51542
AMAZONIA 88782
AMBARCHIK 11302
AMBASADOR 32090
AMBASSADOR 15700
AMBASSADOR 94090
AMBER 35010
AMBER ISLANDS 30622
AMBER PACIFIC 73170
AMBER PACIFIC 77720
AMBERES 22490
AMBERMA 11812
AMBLA 89266
AMBRONIA 69540
AMBRONIA 71620
AMBROSE SHEA 19540
AMBURAN 43520
AMCO 1 53930
AMCO 1 71660
AMDERMA 25551
AMEL 76781
AMELIA 86461
AMELIA TOPIC 77800
AMER B 38410
AMERICA 49600
AMERICA EXPRESS 73403
AMERICA EXPRESS 82713
AMERICA MARU 09760
AMERICA STAR 12700
AMERICA SUN 63410
AMERICAN ACCORD 09724
AMERICAN ACE 09720
AMERICAN ALLIANCE 09721
AMERICAN APOLLO 09716
AMERICAN AQUARIUS. 09717
AMERICAN ARCHER 09723
AMERICAN ARGOSY 09722
AMERICAN ASTRONAUT 09715
AMERICAN CHALLENGER 05670
AMERICAN CHAMPION 05671
AMERICAN CHARGER 05672
AMERICAN CHEROKEE 73947
AMERICAN CHIEFTAIN 05673
AMERICAN CORSAIR 05674
AMERICAN COURIER 05675
AMERICAN EXPLORER 36800
AMERICAN ISLANDER 76170
AMERICAN LANCER 09710
AMERICAN LARK 09713
AMERICAN LEADER 09725
AMERICAN LEGACY 09726
AMERICAN LEGEND 09727
AMERICAN LEGION 09711
AMERICAN LIBERTY 09712
AMERICAN LYNX 09714
AMERICAN MARK 83984
AMERICAN RACER 05930
AMERICAN RANGER 05931
AMERICAN RELIANCE 05932
AMERICANA 06170
AMERICANA 64720
AMERICANO 40720
AMERIGO VESPUCCI 24332
AMERIKANIS 08270
AMERSFOORT 15713
AMETHYST 82999
AMETHYSTOS 57360
AMETIST 12389
AMGA 11813
AMGA 45730
AMGUEMA 21610
AMGUEMA 34100
AMGUN 70763
AMGUN 69501
AMICA 63281
AMIGO FORTUNA 64859
AMIGO FORTUNA 91039
AMILLA 58144
AMIN 84532
AMINA 31720
AMINAH A 26982
AMINUL BAHR 36150
AMIRA K 83840
AMIRAL S ALTINCAN 30811
AMIRAL S OKAN 30810
AMMERSBEK 76331
AMMERSBEK 88721
AMOCO BALTIMORE 69821
AMOCO BRISBANE 69820
AMOCO CAIRO 60300
AMOCO CAIRO 68520
AMOCO CHICAGO 63174
AMOCO CHICAGO 71543
AMOCO CREMONA 69822
AMOCO EUROPA 63171
AMOCO EUROPA 71541
AMOCO MILFORD HAVEN 63172
AMOCO MILFORD HAVEN 71542
AMOCO SEAFARER 59910
AMOCO SINGAPORE 63173
AMOCO SINGAPORE 71540
AMOCO TRINIDAD 60302
AMOCO TRINIDAD 68522
AMOCO VOYAGER 68790
AMOCO WHITING 60301
AMOCO WHITING 68521
AMOCO YORKTOWN 69823
AMOKURA 66143
AMOKURA 70583
AMORGOS 27781
AMOUN 01414
AMOUN 01674
AMPARO 90680
AMPERE 18640
AMPHION 05239
AMPHIOPE 37390
AMPHIOPEA 36370
AMPOL SAREL 53060
AMSTELBRINK 59353
AMSTELBURCHT 46140
AMSTELDIEP 46860
AMSTELDREEF 46861
AMSTELLAAN 47752
AMSTELLAND 34820
AMSTELMEER 77840
AMSTELMOLEN 77850
AMSTELPARK 47751
AMSTELVAART 48153
AMSTELVEEN 82630
AMSTELVLIET 48152
AMSTELVOORN 48154
AMSTELWAL 78310
AMSTERDAM 03140
AMSTERDAM 21690
AMSTERDAM 25970
AMSTERDAM 72631
AMSTERDAM 77391
AMU-DARYA 35316
AMULET 51350
AMULET 52700
AMULET 84010
AMUNDSEN SEA 73388
AMUR 50570
AMUR 89513
AMUR MARU 54544
AMUR MARU 63904
AMURIYAH 63390
AMURSK 12390
AMURSK 36896
AMURSK 43796
AMURSKIY ZALIV 61101
AMURSKLES 24050
AMYNTAS 60077
AN DA HAI 46446
AN FIGHTER 86280
AN HAI 46006
AN HENG 31112
AN HUA 84560
AN JI HAI 46529
AN JI HAI 83309
AN LEE 62090
ANABAR 89259
ANABELA 74260
ANADRIA 61261
ANADYR 10430
ANADYR 35335
ANADYRLES 24036
ANAHITA 72521
ANAHUAC II 51950
ANAHUAC II 75700
ANAKENA 06654
ANAKLIYA 70765
ANAMARIA 34130
ANANGEL DILIGENCE 61442
ANANGEL ENDEAVOUR 82996
ANANGEL FIDELITY 82997
ANANGEL FORTUNE 58165
ANANGEL FRIENDSHIP 58870
ANANGEL GLORY 58145
ANANGEL HAPPINESS 58166
ANANGEL HARMONY 54100
ANANGEL HARMONY 54600
ANANGEL HONOUR 58146
ANANGEL HOPE 58147
ANANGEL LIBERTY 58148
ANANGEL MIGHT 82991
ANANGEL PEACE 58167
ANANGEL PROSPERITY 58149
ANANGEL PRUDENCE 58871
ANANGEL SPIRIT 82992

ANANGEL TRIUMPH	58150
ANANGEL WISDOM	58151
ANANYEV	86220
ANAPA	36908
ANAPA	43808
ANAPKA	36899
ANAPKA	43799
ANASSA	12960
ANASSA	14560
ANASTASIA	18192
ANASTASIA	49112
ANASTASIA L	74590
ANASTASIA L	78450
ANASTASIOS	12373
ANASTASIOS	46448
ANASTASIOS C	82893
ANASTASIS	04131
ANASTASSIA	56792
ANATOLI	69390
ANATOLIA	82804
ANATOLIA	92094
ANATOLIY BREDOV	11625
ANATOLIY KHALIN	04521
ANATOLIY LUNACHARSKIY	03063
ANATOLIY LUNACHARSKIY	03654
ANATOLIY VANEYEV	79382
ANATOLIY VASILYEV	71532
ANATOLIY VASILYEV	80202
ANAVISSOS	06502
ANCAP SEXTO	40850
ANCAP SEXTO	41060
ANCHAN	02760
ANCHANA	67491
ANCHISES	46582
ANCHORMAN	88970
ANCO CHALLENGER	65720
ANCO CHALLENGER	75660
ANCO CHAMPION	65721
ANCO CHAMPION	75661
ANCO CHARGER	65722
ANCO CHARGER	75662
ANCO CHASER	65723
ANCO CHASER	75663
ANCO EMPRESS	70090
ANCO ENDEAVOUR	65724
ANCO ENDEAVOUR	75664
ANCO ENERGIE	65727
ANCO ENERGIE	75667
ANCO ENTENTE	65726
ANCO ENTENTE	75666
ANCO ENTERPRISE	65725
ANCO ENTERPRISE	75665
ANCO GLORY	65560
ANCO PRINCESS	70091
ANCO SCEPTRE	70092
ANCO SOVEREIGN	70093
ANCO STANE	70094
ANCO TEMPLAR	70095
ANCORA	64580
ANCORA	69210
ANDALUCIA STAR	02562
ANDALUCIA STAR	02662
ANDALUSIA	71850
ANDAMAN SEA	45810
ANDANIA	34209
ANDEN	90270
ANDERIDA	92690
ANDERIDA	93512
ANDERIDA	93922
ANDERS	50860
ANDERS	79920
ANDERS MAERSK	08670
ANDERS MAERSK	09000
ANDERSO	50554
ANDES	04720
ANDES	04940
ANDES MARU	51561
ANDES MARU	67870
ANDHIKA ADIRAJA	61563
ANDINE	66680
ANDINO	24380
ANDIZHAN	22840
ANDIZHAN	34470
ANDOMALES	24037
ANDRA	51541
ANDRE DELMAS	48260
ANDREA MANTEGNA	02391
ANDREA SMITS	50501
ANDREAS A	42230
ANDREAS A	42750
ANDRES BONIFACIO	64317
ANDREY ANDREYEV	03773
ANDREY ANDREYEV	04013
ANDREY ANDREYEV	11318
ANDREY EVDANOV	85324
ANDREY IVANOV	50286
ANDREY KIZHEVATOV	50746
ANDREY LAVROV	03963
ANDREY MARKIN	11780
ANDREY VILKITSKIY	22182
ANDREY ZAKHAROV	93680
ANDRIA	34223
ANDRIAN GONCHAROV	69322
ANDRIOTIS	44490
ANDROMACHI	61154
ANDROMEDA	11640
ANDROMEDA	12237
ANDROMEDA	35811
ANDROMEDA	41581
ANDROMEDA	46471
ANDROS	28470
ANDROS	48030
ANDROS	62140
ANDROS	83410
ANDROS	90611
ANDROS ANTARES	68230
ANDROS ARIES	68231
ANDROS ATLAS	68232
ANDROS CASTLE	79170
ANDROS CHRYSSI	56404
ANDROS CHRYSSI	59924
ANDROS CHRYSSI	67784
ANDROS CITY	79171
ANDROS HILLS	79172
ANDROS ISLAND	79173
ANDROS MARINER	79174
ANDROS MASTER	68233
ANDROS MELTEMI	77803
ANDROS MENTOR	58152
ANDROS OCEANIA	47207
ANDROS TITAN	68234
ANDROS TRANSPORT	58176
ANDRUS YOKHANI	12575
ANDRZEJ STRUG	15300
ANDRZWJ BOROWY	73840
ANDY'S PRIDE	67004
ANEL D'AZUR	00600
ANEMOS	39673
ANEMOS	50180
ANEMOS	70400
ANEMOS	75260
ANEMOS	79160
ANG PANGARAP	60880
ANG PANGARAP	70940
ANG PANGULO	09290
ANGARA	17811
ANGARLES	24051
ANGARSK	28070
ANGARSK	34540
ANGARSK	89506
ANGARSKLES	24038
ANGE SCHIAFFINO	28870
ANGEARCTIC	61026
ANGEARCTIC	71186
ANGEATLANTIC	61019
ANGEATLANTIC	71179
ANGEBALTIC	45571
ANGEL	30880
ANGEL PARK	37940
ANGEL PARK	43600
ANGEL PARK	44530
ANGELA	91390
ANGELA F	44200
ANGELA SMITS	50502
ANGELBURG	33921
ANGELIC GLORY	83020
ANGELIC POWER	28741
ANGELICA SCHULTE	73992
ANGELIKE DYNAMIS	35210
ANGELIKI	01112
ANGELIKI	28612
ANGELIKI G	63200
ANGELINA	31400
ANGELINA S	85380
ANGELITA	61478
ANGELO SCINICARIELLO	40841
ANGLEZARKE	89060
ANGLIA EXPRESS	18001
ANGLIAN MERCHANT	91311
ANGLO	66802
ANGOL	06653
ANGY	27990
ANGYAFOLD	89257
ANI	94211
ANIA	67941
ANIA	85811
ANIA	86651
ANIELLO	59433
ANINA	82222
ANINGA	36290
ANINGA	37870
ANINGA	43080
ANINGA	44460
ANIS III	41850
ANISIMOVKA	12391
ANITA	24190
ANITA	57600
ANITA	62026
ANITA	62240
ANITA SMITS	50504
ANIVA	36904
ANIVA	43804
ANK WINSEMIUS	73821
ANKARA	18770
ANKLAM	83700
ANKO	87704
ANN M	85430
ANN SANDVED	64853
ANN SANDVED	91033
ANNA	59311
ANNA	85240
ANNA BAKKE	29390
ANNA BECKER	73951
ANNA BIBOLINI	80640
ANNA BROERE	66590
ANNA BROERE	75160
ANNA C	13591
ANNA C	82891
ANNA CH	78960
ANNA DRACOPOULOS	06484
ANNA DRENT	75876
ANNA I. ANGELICOUSSI	64061
ANNA K	85791
ANNA K	86611
ANNA MADRE	37160
ANNA MAERSK	08673
ANNA MAERSK	09003
ANNA MARIA LAURO	22530
ANNA MARTINI	22910
ANNA ODEN	94181
ANNA PRESTHUS	57554
ANNA SCHULTE	84741
ANNA SCHULTE	84951
ANNA ULYANOVA	03064
ANNA ULYANOVA	03656
ANNA VERENA	88114
ANNA VON BARGEN	81820
ANNA VON BARGEN	82070
ANNA XYLA	69180
ANNAFLORA	21403
ANNAJM	00280
ANNAJM	00570
ANNARITA SECONDA	18460
ANNE BRAVO	93991
ANNE CATHARINA	72759
ANNE METTE	90941
ANNE OPEM	91400
ANNELIESE OLTMANN	81770
ANNELIESE OLTMANN	64740
ANNEMARIE KRUGER	57560
ANNETTE	52120
ANNETTE S	90942
ANNIE	77760
ANNIE JOHNSON	04270
ANNIE JOHNSON	16301
ANNIKA	50811
ANNIKA	74030
ANNIKA N	46831
ANNITA	71710
ANNITSA L.	49280
ANNOOR	06920
ANNOULA	60078
ANNOULA	88246
ANNOULA II	14082
ANNOULA K	17800
ANNOULA TSIRIS	34751
ANNUITY	88870
ANONA	06317
ANSON	35951
ANTAGORAS	00301
ANTAIOS	57191
ANTAKYA	80353
ANTALYA	80355
ANTANAS SNECHKUS	62687
ANTAR	83062
ANTAR	83162
ANTARCTIC	34202
ANTARES	10541
ANTARES	10543
ANTARES	12238
ANTARES	70772
ANTARES	39460
ANTARES	50550
ANTARES	66790
ANTARES	72580
ANTARKTIKA	33750
ANTARKTIKA	93749
ANTARKTIKA	93839
ANTARTIC	91010
ANTARTICO	78370
ANTCHAR	12392
ANTCLIZO	43651
ANTHEMIOS	60079
ANTHENOR	94294
ANTHI L	22440
ANTHIA	31440
ANTHIA	31610
ANTHONY III	77831
ANTHOS	58568
ANTHOULA I	80530
ANTIGONI	48130
ANTIGONI TSIRIS	27500
ANTIGUA	62141
ANTILLA BAY	56442
ANTILLA BAY	68352
ANTILLA CAPE	56450
ANTILLA CAPE	60010
ANTILLIA	49602
ANTILOPE	03521
ANTINEA	72520
ANTING.	05370
ANTIOCHA	61157
ANTIOPI	58565
ANTIPOLO	07651
ANTJE SCHULTE	53410
ANTJE SCHULTE	64940
ANTLIA	11647
ANTOFAGASTA	69332
ANTON-BUYUKLY	31868
ANTON CHEKOV	14377
ANTON DOHRN	24170
ANTON GUBARYEV	67010
ANTON IVANOV	40580
ANTON LOPATIN	11629
ANTON MAKARENKO	07925
ANTON ROTH	28370
ANTON SAEFKOW.	06380
ANTON SAEFKOW	15410
ANTON STJEPOV	55910
ANTON TAMMSAARE	12393
ANTONELLO	43160
ANTONELLO DA MESSINA	01340
ANTONELLOESSE	43280
ANTONI GARNUSZEWSKI.	07860
ANTONIA	25080
ANTONIA JOHNSON	04101
ANTONIA NEDZHDANOVA	02342
ANTONIO D'ALESSIO	70262
ANTONIO GRAMSCI	70591
ANTONIO M	66807
ANTONIO SUARDIAZ	94680
ANTONIOS C	10364
ANTONIOS G	55470
ANTONIOS G	56340
ANTONIOTTO USODIMARE	24331
ANTONIS P LEMOS	46911
ANTONY	28920
ANTRIM PRINCESS	32790
ANTS LAYKMAA	12394
ANTXON MARI	73850
ANUI	06120
ANVERSA	28122
ANVERSA	28562
ANWAR	36190
ANYI	05420
ANYUY	70775
ANZERE	94130
ANZERE	94620
AOI MARU	08570
AOTEA	09870
APAPA PALM	55872
APAPA PALM	56602
APE	36892
APE	43792
APETIT	09384
APHRODITE	01830
APHRODITE	46110
APHRODITE B	69730
APHRODITE TRANSOCEANIC	37190
APICO	91890
APILIOTIS	59251
APILIOTIS	62521
APJ AKASH	41260
APJ AKASH	44980
APJ AMBIKA	15231
APJ ANJLI	41261
APJ ANJLI	44981
APJ PRIYA	15232
APJ SUSHMA	44070
APJ SUSHMA	44500
APLI CHAU	24270
APOGEY	13654
APOIKIA	37960
APOLLO	26190
APOLLO	52760
APOLLO II	86870
APOLLO III	16580
APOLLON	20520
APOLLON	56863
APOLLON II	17640
APOLLONIA	18070
APOLLONIAN LIGHT	21370
APOLLONIUS	61771
APOSTOLOS A	30680
APOSTOLOS H	85520
APOSTOLOS K	14870
APOSTOLOS M	30050
APOSTOLOS M	31801
APOSTOLOS M IV	39060
APPIA	20600
APPLE BLOSSOM	33890
APPLEBY	77682
APRICITY	74350
APSHERON	11461
APSHERON	66172
APSHERONSK	36897
APSHERONSK	43797
APTMARINER	46650
APUS	66871
APUS	91461
AQABA	80111
AQUA STAR	21000
AQUACHARM	48170
AQUAFAITH	48171
AQUAGEM	48177
AQUAGLORY	48172
AQUAGRACE	48173
AQUAJOY	48174
AQUAMARINE	09491
AQUAMARINE	60080
AQUARAMA	02505
AQUARIUS	32650
AQUARIUS	35460
AQUARIUS	66140
AQUARIUS	70580
AQUILA	32380
AQUILA	94060
AQUILEIA	24710
AQUILON	03490
AQUILON	03580
AQUITANE	57831
ARA	72751
ARAB ALHIJAZ	01690
ARAB ALRIYAD	49851
ARAB ALRIYAD	50091
ARAB DABBOR	02611
ARAB DABBOR	04331
ARAB NAJAD	49852
ARAB NAJAD	50092
ARABAT	13655
ARABATSKIY	89681
ARABI	20850
ARABIAN ENDEAVOUR	46251
ARABIAN LULUAH	50030
ARABIAN STRENGTH	46250
ARABIAN VICTORY	27930
ARACAJU	06580
ARACTOS BRIDGE	26380
ARACTOS GLORY	28710
ARAD	57421
ARAD	86210
ARAFAT	18580
ARAFAT	49404
ARAFAT	50964
ARAFURA	09880
ARAFURA MARU	63270
ARAGON	13903
ARAGON	63160
ARAGONIT	11917
ARAGRACE	71991
ARAGRACE	72111
ARAGUA	04372
ARAGVI	21220
ARAHANGA	19970
ARAHANGA	23340
ARAKS	36898
ARAKS	43798
ARAKS	89261
ARAKS	89502
ARALAR	52500
ARALDA	39870
ARALSK	12395
ARALSK	86177
ARAMIL	23170
ARAMIS	60081
ARAMIS	64330
ARAN	58573
ARANUI	19960
ARANUI	81940
ARANUI	89420
ARARAT	70768
ARAS	07881
ARAS	15644
ARATIKA	19950
ARATU	65861
ARAUCANO	37980
ARAUCO	47052
ARAXOS	26761
ARBERIA	71995
ARBERIA	72115
ARC MINOS	61704
ARC MINOS	71074
ARCADIA	28180
ARCADIA	54413
ARCADIA	57873
ARCADIAN FAITH	62171
ARCADIAN SEA	74670
ARCADIAN SEA	78380
ARCADIAN SKY	62170
ARCADIAN STAR	29071
ARCAMARE	34131
ARCAMARE	34730
ARCHANGELOS	35900
ARCHANGELOS	41590
ARCHANGELOS	77874
ARCHANGELOS G	32010
ARCHANGELOS III	53700
ARCHANGELOS III	78090
ARCHANGELOS III	89940
ARCHANGELSK	00850
ARCHIMEDES	61040
ARCHIMEDES	61770
ARCHONTAS	64337
ARCHONTISSA KATINGO	63540
ARCO	87391
ARCO ANCHORAGE	64241
ARCO FAIRBANKS	64242
ARCO JUNEAU	64240
ARCO PRUDHOE BAY	64250
ARCO SAG RIVER	64251
ARCTIC	47231
ARCTIC	47511
ARCTIC	48020
ARCTIC FREEBOOTER	17700
ARCTIC MARINER	33972
ARCTIC OCEAN	06330
ARCTIC STAR	38411
ARCTIC TOKYO	53871

ARCTIC TROLL	48970
ARCTIC WASA	47811
ARCTURUS	10544
ARCTURUS	07891
ARDATOV	11815
ARDATOV	36911
ARDATOV	43811
ARDENHALL	06461
ARDMAY	58860
ARDMAY	65740
ARDMORE	58861
ARDMORE	65741
AREF	35641
AREF	41301
ARENAL	74321
ARENDSEE	46379
ARENDSEE	47079
ARETHOUSA	48321
ARETHOUSA	92712
ARETI	58153
ARETI S.	86051
ARETOUSA	84280
ARETUSA	51638
ARGIRO	07230
ARGIRO	07430
ARGIRO	48490
ARGO	12239
ARGO	02590
ARGO	33300
ARGO	34990
ARGO	46420
ARGO CHALLENGE	59591
ARGO FAITH	59592
ARGO GLORY	59593
ARGO HOPE	59594
ARGO PIONEER	59590
ARGO SPIRIT	59595
ARGO VALOUR	59596
ARGOLICOS GULF	48240
ARGOLICOS GULF	48540
ARGOLIKOS	60480
ARGOLIS	70641
ARGON	36890
ARGON	43790
ARGONAUT	23443
ARGONAUT	07020
ARGONAUT	16610
ARGONAUT	77710
ARGONAUT	94276
ARGONAUT II	03523
ARGONAVI	61262
ARGOS	42550
ARGOS	60082
ARGOSY PACIFIC	72357
ARGOSY PACIFIC	77157
ARGOVIND	83714
ARGUN	11816
ARGUN	24049
ARGUS	12576
ARGUS	18670
ARGYRO M	41761
ARHON	70370
ARIA	47819
ARIADNE	06486
ARIADNE	19130
ARIADNE	47820
ARIADNE	93060
ARIADNE E	44830
ARIADNI	81630
ARIADNI	92713
ARIAKE	08770
ARIAKE	73364
ARIAKE REEFER	05192
ARIANA	23161
ARIANE	06731
ARIANE	20970
ARIANE	31190
ARIANE I	06322
ARIANE II	34080
ARIANNE LAURA	90651
ARIEL	45910
ARIEL	56751
ARIEL	77461
ARIEL I	03524
ARIES	11648
ARIES	28640
ARIES	90910
ARIES CARRIER	80450
ARIETTA	55550
ARIETTA	56522
ARIETTA	63380
ARIETTA GREGOS	48150
ARILD MAERSK	08676
ARILD MAERSK	09006
ARION	00360
ARION	17570
ARION	48603
ARION	58168
ARIS	12970
ARIS	25320
ARIS	40250
ARIS	44627
ARIS	60083
ARIS V	39744
ARIS VI	37340
ARIS VI	45200
ARISTAGELOS	60481
ARISTAIOS	74050
ARISTAIOS	77020
ARISTANAX	60482
ARISTARCHOS	60084
ARISTARKH BELOPOLSKIY	10741
ARISTEFS	74051
ARISTEFS	77021
ARISTEOS	74050
ARISTEOS	77020
ARISTEUS	60085
ARISTIDES	56752
ARISTOFILOS	12103
ARISTOFILOS	13892
ARISTOTELES	34893
ARISTOTELIS	25090
ARISTOTELIS	90490
ARISTOTLE	85120
ARISTOTLE S ONASSIS	54418
ARISTOTLE S ONASSIS	57878
ARKADIA	04290
ARKADIA	78210
ARKADIA	89920
ARKADIY KAMANIN	15511
ARKADY GAYDAR	14378
ARKANDROS	60154
ARKAS	32580
ARKHANGELSK	17935
ARKHANGELSKLES	24039
ARKHIMED	34881
ARKHIP KUINDZHI	76509
ARKOVO	12396
ARKTIKA	12660
ARKTIKA	93743
ARKTIKA	93833
ARKTUR	76311
ARLBERG	47222
ARMADA MARINER	87702
ARMADA MEDLINER	91860
ARMADALE	04840
ARMAN	25841
ARMAND HAMMER	53790
ARMAND HAMMER	68550
ARMANDO REVERON	45651
ARMAVIR	25553
ARMENIYA	02163
ARMENIYA	11817
ARMONIKOS	58750
ARMONIKOS	60530
ARMORIQUE	32210
ARNAFELL	84070
ARNEB	72581
ARNIS	72752
ARNOLD MAERSK.	08678
ARNOLD MAERSK.	09008
ARNON	60022
ARONA	06741
ARONA	31201
ARONA	93932
AROS ATHENE	49880
AROS OLYMPIC	73952
ARPA	30310
ARPA SUN	13041
ARPAD	46900
ARPOADOR	05365
ARPOADOR	15665
ARQUITECTO GAUDI	87790
ARRAN	20860
ARSENE SIMARD	88482
ARSENEYEV	12397
ARSENIY MOSKVIN	50283
ARSENYEV	45113
ARTADI	45981
ARTEAGA	54520
ARTEAGA	55440
ARTEAGA	55730
ARTEK	11818
ARTEMIDA	11941
ARTEMIDI IV	10360
ARTEMIS	70461
ARTEMIS	73993
ARTEMIS GAROFALIDIS	58341
ARTEMIS GAROFALIDIS	63991
ARTERN	71915
ARTHUR BECKER	23412
ARTHUR MAERSK	08674
ARTHUR MAERSK	09004
ARTHUR PHILLIP	53540
ARTHUR SIMARD	88483
ARTICO	15670
ARTISIZ	89203
ARTLENBURG	33923
ARTURO MICHELINA	90454
ARTVIN	80354
ARTYOM	36251
ARTYOM	42801
ARU	89232
ARUBA	91834
ARUBA BAY	85620
ARUNACHAL PRADESH	47046
ARUNAKAMAL	12912
ARUNTO	66800
ARVEPRINS KNUD	18930
ARWAD	63713
ARYADOOT	85810
ARYADOOT	86650
ARZAMAS	11819
ARZAMAS	31830
ARZEW	60646
ARZEW	62606
'AS—300' type	75580
ASA-THOR	21960
ASAHAN	38940
ASAHAN	39090
ASAKAZE MARU	03560
ASANO	79860
ASAR	90670
ASCARYA	30100
ASCHBERG	94011
ASCONA	57481
ASCONA	90501
ASD HEKTOR	51850
ASEAN GREATNESS	68391
ASEAN KNOWLEDGE	65820
ASEAN KNOWLEDGE	69950
ASEAN LIBERTY	65822
ASEAN LIBERTY	69952
ASEAN MISSION	65820
ASEAN MISSION	65821
ASEAN MISSION	69951
ASEAN NATIONS	78320
ASEAN OBJECTIVE	45820
ASEAN PIONEER	51860
ASEAN PIONEER	64910
ASEAN PROSPERITY	51861
ASEAN PROSPERITY	64911
ASEAN VENTURE	51862
ASEAN VENTURE	64912
ASEBU	93651
ASEBU	94991
ASHANTI	39730
ASHKHABAD	12341
ASHKHABAD	39973
ASHLEY LYKES	00060
ASHRAF AL AWAL	91140
ASHTABULA	35960
ASHUG ALEKSER	50760
ASHURST	70960
ASIA-AFRIKA	30740
ASIA CARRIER	25276
ASIA CARRIER III	25277
ASIA FIDELITY	56700
ASIA FIDELITY	57730
ASIA FLAMINGO	48041
ASIA GOLD	48042
ASIA GRACE	71141
ASIA HAWK	47921
ASIA HERON	48995
ASIA HUNTER	46480
ASIA INDUSTRY	48996
ASIA LAKE	91920
ASIA LOYALTY	48043
ASIA MARU	04701
ASIA MARU	05011
ASIA MARU	10020
ASIA MORALITY	48040
ASIA PALMO	25706
ASIA SPICA	61647
ASIA SWALLOW	47922
ASIAFREIGHTER.	08583
ASIALINER	08582
ASIAN ADVENTURESS	46114
ASIAN FOREST	46643
ASIAN FOREST	83323
ASIAN GLORY	63140
ASIAN PALM	61620
ASIAN REEFER	05112
ASIATIC	62960
ASIR	28851
ASK	71901
ASKANIYA	11303
ASKOLD.	07460
ASKOLD	12398
ASMAA	03632
ASMAA	50201
ASMAA	75971
ASO MARU	92622
ASPA QUARTO	23851
ASPAKI	17780
ASPASSIA M	27410
ASPASSIA M.	38930
ASPEN	92920
ASPERITY	75070
ASPHALT MERCHANT	44320
ASPHERON	11814
ASPIA	59471
ASPIDOFOROS	74941
ASPINDZA	70776
ASPIS	29091
ASPRA	69541
ASPRA	71620
ASPRELLA	37513
ASPRELLA	44213
ASPROPYRGOS	43020
ASPYR	28280
ASSALAMAH	03350
ASSIDUITY	90090
ASSIMINA	78402
ASSOCIATED GRAIN	04475
ASSOMATOS	60086
ASTA	51141
ASTAKOS	51651
ASTAKOS	64421
ASTARA	50777
ASTARTE	48604
ASTERI	16220
ASTERION	58154
ASTEROID	11940
ASTEROID	34895
ASTILLERO	00640
ASTIR	58155
ASTONDO	76089
ASTORIA	67760
ASTRA	12399
ASTRA PEAK	46050
ASTRACHUBUT	40530
ASTRADIEGO	74671
ASTRADIEGO	78381
ASTRAEA	70463
ASTRAMAN	59060
ASTRAMAN	76450
ASTRAPI	70401
ASTRAPI	79161
ASTREA	50553
ASTREA	52600
ASTRID	11390
ASTRID SCHULTE	81390
ASTRID SCHULTE	90640
ASTRO	40540
ASTRON	81030
ASTRON	82763
ASTRONAFTIS	27430
ASTRONOM	11820
ASTRONOMER	73405
ASTRONOMER	82715
ASUBONE	27213
ASUNCION	80700
ASUNCION	84480
ATA	38680
ATACAMA	47051
ATAKOY	32162
ATALANTA II	59731
ATALANTA II	67221
ATALANTE	33180
ATALANTI	05476
ATALANTI	16221
ATALAYA	50552
ATAR	89000
ATHANASIA COMNINOS	36470
ATHANASIOS I	42130
ATHANASIOS - S	83590
ATHANASSIA	06487
ATHEN SKY	13830
ATHENA	06485
ATHENA	10921
ATHENA	70360
ATHENAIS	29090
ATHENE	64316
ATHENIAN	38131
ATHENIAN HORIZON	44191
ATHENIC	53150
ATHENIC	66300
ATHENS DAY	13200
ATHENS EXPRESS	20530
ATHENS SEA	25901
ATHENS WAY	13042
ATHINA	37700
ATHINA	44250
ATHINA	59230
ATHINA	90610
ATHINA ZAFIRAKIS	57188
ATHINAI	25010
ATHINOULA	13220
ATHLON	58569
ATHLOS I	83610
ATHLOS II	83611
ATHOL	58193
ATHOLL FOREST	46640
ATHOLL FOREST	83320
ATHOS	60087
ATHOS	63032
ATIGUN PASS	58030
ATILOLA	42090
ATILOLA	42300
ATKARSK	00331
ATLAND	70172
ATLANT	12574
ATLANTA	22800
ATLANTA	45760
ATLANTA	88115
ATLANTIC	52170
ATLANTIC	52580
ATLANTIC BARON	73733
ATLANTIC BOUNTY	64490
ATLANTIC BOUNTY	68580
ATLANTIC CAUSEWAY	08350
ATLANTIC CHAMPAGNE	08354
ATLANTIC CHARITY	45570
ATLANTIC CINDERELLA	08352
ATLANTIC CLIPPER	73885
ATLANTIC CLIPPER	87265
ATLANTIC COGNAC	08353
ATLANTIC COMET	87421
ATLANTIC COMET	88440
ATLANTIC CONVEYOR	08351
ATLANTIC COUNT	73732
ATLANTIC CROWN	08355
ATLANTIC CURRENT	58600
ATLANTIC EAGLE	35904
ATLANTIC EAGLE	41594
ATLANTIC EARL	73731
ATLANTIC EMPEROR	63800
ATLANTIC EMPEROR	55750
ATLANTIC ENDEAVOUR	64491
ATLANTIC ENDEAVOUR	68581
ATLANTIC EXPRESS	46180
ATLANTIC EXPRESS	49300
ATLANTIC FOREST	35101
ATLANTIC FOREST	92811
ATLANTIC FOREST	95152
ATLANTIC FREEZE	84281
ATLANTIC FREEZER	21350
ATLANTIC FREEZER	26310
ATLANTIC HAWK	57181
ATLANTIC HELMSMAN	57182
ATLANTIC HERITAGE	57183
ATLANTIC HERO	57180
ATLANTIC HIGHWAY	92991
ATLANTIC HIGHWAY	94951
ATLANTIC HOPE	57240
ATLANTIC HORIZON	57184
ATLANTIC INTREPID	73888
ATLANTIC INTREPID	87268
ATLANTIC ISLE	90860
ATLANTIC ISLE	91780
ATLANTIC MARQUESS	68871
ATLANTIC NEPTUNE	05770
ATLANTIC OCEAN	14171
ATLANTIC PRELUDE	74061
ATLANTIC PREMIER	74060
ATLANTIC PRINCESS	68872
ATLANTIC PROGRESS	63583
ATLANTIC PROJECT	76764
ATLANTIC PROJECT	80274
ATLANTIC PROSPER	76765
ATLANTIC PROSPER	80275
ATLANTIC RESOLUTE	73886
ATLANTIC RESOLUTE	87266
ATLANTIC SAGA	72780
ATLANTIC SEA	49840
ATLANTIC SKOU	56771
ATLANTIC SKY	62350
ATLANTIC SKY	87420
ATLANTIC SONG	72800
ATLANTIC SONG	76820
ATLANTIC SONG	76960
ATLANTIC SPAN	72790
ATLANTIC SPLENDOUR	64470
ATLANTIC SPRINTER	87810
ATLANTIC STAR	35905
ATLANTIC STAR	41695
ATLANTIC STAR	72801
ATLANTIC STAR	76821
ATLANTIC STAR	76961
ATLANTIC SUN	64318
ATLANTIC SUN	75484
ATLANTIC SUN	87422
ATLANTIC SWAN	73870
ATLANTIC TRADER	69220
ATLANTICA	46550
ATLANTICO	14350
ATLANTICO	78700
ATLANTICOS	85222
ATLANTIDE	21391
ATLANTIK	18721
'ATLANTIK' type	11800
'ATLANTIK' type	07470
ATLANTIKA	26960
ATLANTIQUE	84290
ATLANTIQUE	84440
ATLANTIS	20460
ATLANTIS	33140
ATLANTIS	33830
ATLANTIS	55421
ATLANTIS	72340
ATLANTIS	73913
ATLANTIS	78881
ATLANTISCH	67492
ATLAS	01860
ATLAS	10367
ATLAS	46470
ATLAS	47311
ATLAS	48761
ATLAS	89720
ATLAS 1	53360
ATLAS CARRIER	84670
ATLAS CHALLENGER	56750
ATLAS COUNSELLOR	57210
ATLAS MARU	51560
ATLAS PREMIER	29570
ATLAS RIVER	59541
ATLAS RIVER	81231
ATLE	33000
ATOLL	11821
ATOMIC	53153
ATOMIC	66303
ATRA	15170
ATREO	24890
ATREUS	58169
ATREVIDA	83890
ATROMITOS	14511
ATROTOS	90690

ATSUMI	72940
ATTICA	58156
ATTIKA HOPE	58606
ATTIKI	45170
ATTIKON	35682
ATTIKOS	14120
ATTILIO IEVOLI	29170
AUBADE	88350
AUBADE	90350
AUBRAC	05452
AUBY	94980
AUCTORITAS	35594
AUCTORITAS	36494
AUDACIA	18380
AUDACIA	33931
AUDACITY	76360
AUE	70230
AUGUST ALLE	12400
AUGUST FORK	85351
AUGUST JAKOBSON	45122
AUGUST KULBERG	89258
AUGUST MOON	71153
AUGUSTO MONTENEGRO	08331
AUKSHAYTIKA	13653
AULICA	37514
AULICA	44214
AUNIS	05381
AURELIA	26872
AURELIA	33474
AURELIA	58892
AURELIA	94293
AURELIA DI MAIO	13150
AURELIAN	60551
AURELIAN	65203
AURELIAN	67413
AURELIAN	69481
AURELLA	20630
AURES	64964
AURIGA	11643
AURIGA	35462
AURIGA	48800
AUROBINDO	71631
AURORA	26112
AURORA	26840
AURORA	35813
AURORA	41583
AURORA	45761
AURORE	31192
AUSEKLIS	70773
AUSONIA	10050
AUSTRAL	56971
AUSTRAL ENDURANCE	11351
AUSTRAL ENSIGN	11350
AUSTRAL ENTENTE	11341
AUSTRAL ENVOY	11340
AUSTRAL LIGHTNING	00013
AUSTRAL LIGHTNING	02483
AUSTRAL LIGHTNING	35133
AUSTRAL MOON	02484
AUSTRAL PIONEER	11342
AUSTRAL PURITAN	11343
AUSTRALIA MARU	04700
AUSTRALIA MARU	05010
AUSTRALIA STAR	02870
AUSTRALIAN EMBLEM	09800
AUSTRALIAN EMBLEM	10040
AUSTRALIAN ENDEAVOUR	74502
AUSTRALIAN ENTERPRISE	09551
AUSTRALIAN ENTERPRISE	33310
AUSTRALIAN ENTERPRISE	77362
AUSTRALIAN ESCORT	09801
AUSTRALIAN ESCORT	10041
AUSTRALIAN EXPLORER	33311
AUSTRALIAN EXPLORER	77363
AUSTRALIAN EXPLORER	09552
AUSTRALIAN EXPORTER	51943
AUSTRALIAN EXPORTER	52433
AUSTRALIAN PIONEER	72410
AUSTRALIAN PROGRESS	77541
AUSTRALIAN PROSPECTOR	77540
AUSTRALIAN PURPOSE	72411
AUSTRALIAN SEAROADER	09552
AUSTRALIAN SEAROADER	33312
AUSTRALIAN SEAROADER	77361
AUSTRALIAN VENTURE	08440
AUSTRALIC	03520
AUSTRI	87283
AUSTRIAN EXPLORER	04460
AUSTRIAN IMPORTER	27691
AUSTRIAN MERCHANT	26752
AUSTRIAN TRADER	27240
AUTHENTIC	62963
AUTHOR	73408
AUTHOR	82718
AUTHORITY	75071
AUTO GULF	87120
AUTOBAHN	94770
AUTOLLOYD	90201
AUTOROUTE	12810
AUTOROUTE	15690
AUTOSTRADA	90200
AUTOWEG	36160
AUTSE	70769
AVA	13270
AVACHA	93747
AVACHA	93837
AVALO	41990
AVANCE	90110
AVANT	66801
AVANTI	21245
AVARE	22420
AVAX	28614
AVE	75272
AVEDAT	53830
AVEDAT	69460
AVELONA STAR	02563
AVELONA STAR	02663
AVETIK ISAAKYAN	50742
AVIATOR	11822
AVIN OIL GERANI	55692
AVIN OIL GERANI	58302
AVIN OIL LEADER	57840
AVIN OIL TRADER	63840
AVIN OIL TRADER	67610
AVIOR	87390
AVLIS	58570
AVLIS EXPRESS	81140
AVON	61812
AVON	83600
AVON FOREST	74951
AVON FOREST	80071
AVONBANK	26026
AVRA	15910
AVRA	18450
AVRA	28680
AVRA	32020
AVRA	70460
AXEL JOHNSON	04271
AXEL JOHNSON	16300
AXEL MAERSK	08675
AXEL MAERSK	09005
AXIOS	89350
AY-PETRI	01964
AY-PETRI	11823
AYAN 1	53390
AYAN I	80340
AYENI	45300
AYESHA	14794
AYESHA	48320
AYKHAL	70766
AYNAZHI	70770
AYON	70771
AYSBERG	89504
AYSEN	58113
AYTODOR	01965
AYUTHIA	38931
AYVALIK	15810
AYVAZOVSKIY	20650
AZALEA	86040
AZALEA BREEZE	14680
AZAR	77990
AZARPAD	63360
AZELIA	59480
AZERBAIJAN	43244
AZERBAYDZHAN	20372
AZGAD III	27217
AZIM	10998
AZIM	34156
AZIZ BHATTI	39231
AZIZA	90535
AZIZA	91074
AZNEFT	85885
AZORES STAR	52161
AZOV	13656
AZOV SEA	10362
AZTEC	87051
AZTECA	49120
AZUERDO DOS	87551
AZUGA	82111
AZUGA	82391
AZUMA	15872
AZUMA	83572
AZUR	16940
AZURE SEAS	36360
AZURIT	11824
AZURITOVYY	89758

B

'B-15' type	11640
'B-15' type	11660
'B-15' type	12610
'B-22' type	11700
'B-23' type	22330
'B-25' type	57350
'B-26' type	11580
'B-26' type	11610
'B-26' type	45950
'B-26' type	47690
'B-26' type	56500
'B-29' type	18740
'B-30' type	42960
'B-31' type	10430
'B-31' type	17920
'B-31' type	23760
'B-31' type	33730
'B-31' type	33740
'B-32' type	10640
'B-32' type	12140
'B-40/401' type	05620
'B-40/401' type	14450
'B-41' type	10570
'B-41' type	15160
'B-41' type	15340
'B-41' type	15370
'B-42' type	10290
'B-43' type	10610
'B-44' type	07900
'B-46' type	03770
'B-46' type	04010
'B-49' type	31180
'B-50' type	26990
'B-51' type	72510
'B-53' type	88230
'B-54' type	07290
'B-54' type	13010
'B-54' type	13370
'B-54' type	14580
'B-54' type	14700
'B-54' type	15180
'B-54' type	15280
'B-54' type	15300
'B-55' type	14290
'B-55' type	14300
'B-55' type	14310
'B-57' type	73650
'B-57' type	87740
'B-59' type	15450
'B-62' type	25840
'B-64' type	93870
'B-67' type	93882
'B-68' type	59690
'B-68' type	81350
'B-69' type	93730
'B-69' type	93820
'B-70' type	38610
'B-72' type	60680
'B-76' type	54130
'B-76' type	54250
'B-80' type	07860
'B-80' type	09080
'B-80' type	15000
'B-88' type	02270
'B-89' type	22350
'B400' type	34880
'B413' type	04170
'B414' type	10540
'B417' type	11790
'B418' type	23440
'B419' type	23440
'B422' type	17950
'B424' type	11690
'B430' type	55870
'B430' type	56590
'B430' type	56600
'B431' type	58730
'B431' type	59610
'B431' type	66980
'B431' type	71900
'B431' type	71920
'B432' type	03230
'B432' type	03620
'B433' type	10260
'B433' type	10760
'B434' type	05810
'B434' type	08080
'B436' type	54710
'B436' type	55280
'B437' type	10740
'B441' type	81660
'B441' type	82660
'B442' type	06040
'B442' type	06090
'B442' type	14450
'B442' type	14770
'B442' type	14800
'B443' type	10720
'B444' type	05360
'B445' type	14910
'B445' type	15720
'B446' type	81640
'B447' type	59220
'B447' type	60900
'B447' type	70540
'B447' type	74540
'B447' type	78100
'B447' type	79230
'B448' type	51470
'B449' type	49120
'B450' type	16250
'B454' type	10560
'B454' type	15380
'B455' type	15080
'B455' type	15090
'B457' type	67050
'B457' type	76640
'B458' type	73840
'B458' type	87750
'B459' type	59600
'B459' type	71930
'B459' type	76010
'B463' type	73400
'B463' type	82710
'B464' type	53370
'B464' type	62760
'B466' type	52920
'B467' type	54970
'B467' type	71810
'B469' type	62760
'B470' type	62460
'B470' type	78540
'B470' type	80130
'B471' type	42070
'B472' type	51260
'B474' type	06140
'B475' type	87070
'B475' type	89560
'B476' type	87770
'B478' type	06142
'B481' type	80260
'B490' type	08170
'B512 type	47600
'B512' type	47610
'B512' type	72170
'B512' type	76630
'B513' type	34370
'B514' type	24030
'B515' type	50020
'B516' type	10280
'B516' type	15190
'B517' type	65850
'B517' type	67690
'B520' type	75730
'B520' type	88380
'B521' type	73280
'B521' type	77560
'B521' type	77840
'B521' type	77850
'B521' type	78040
'B521' type	80010
'B523' type	50680
'B524' type	68250
'B524' type	68800
'B525' type	58390
'B526' type	77580
'B540' type	54714
'B540' type	55284
'B550' type	55580
'B550' type	56460
'B670' type	45270
B. P. 1	43180
BA SHAN	10590
BA SHAN	13393
BAABDA	17781
BAARN	71992
BAARN	72112
BABA GURGUR	69570
BABOR	48906
BABUSHKIN	45356
BABYLON	45385
BACAB	54681
BACAB	66161
BACAT I	93280
BACAT I	94200
BACAT 2	76930
BACAU	41318
BACCARAT	39381
BACCHIS	13080
BACCHUS	90621
BACO-LINER 1	93030
BACO-LINER 1	95200
BACO-LINER 2	95031
BACO-LINER 2	95201
BADEN	64093
BADGER	19561
BADR	24701
BADR	58020
BAEK DU SAN	71330
BAFFIN	22130
BAFFIN TRANSPORT	41710
BAGAS	42200
BAGH-E-DACCA	15251
BAGH-E-KARACHI	15250
BAGHDAD	45384
BAGRATION	17504
BAGRATIONOVSK	13659
BAGRU	50410
BAGRU	50820
BAHAGIA VI	25340
BAHAMA MARU	07763
BAHAMA MARU	07810
BAHARI	81620
BAHIA AGUIRRE	23250
BAHIA AGUIRRE	34700
BAHIA BLANCA	03910
BAHIA BUEN SUCESO	23251
BAHIA BUEN SUCESO	34701
BAHIA DE COCHINOS	31012
BAHIA DE MARIEL	92021
BAHIA DE NIPE	92020
BAHIA SANTIAGO DE CUBA	33711
BAHJAH	93101
BAHLUI	13731
BAHMA	50411
BAHMA	50821
BAI HEI KOU	93311
BAI YUN HAI	46336
BAI YUN HAI	55930
BAI YUN SHAN	15021
BAIA DE SAO BRAS	50211
BAIA MARE	39660
BAILADILA	53222
BAILADILA	64431
BAILU	70891
BAILUNDO	81660
BAILUNDO	82660
BAIMA	30844
BAIPAO	30845
BAIRE	12790
BAJAR	05650
BAJKA	50683
BAKAR	50684
BAKAYEVO	12401
BAKHCHISARAY	11942
BAKHCHISARAY	52021
BAKHCHISARAY	84151
BAKLAN	12556
BAKU	50770
BAKURIANI	45357
BALABAC	45080
BALADZHARY	85998
BALAKHNALES	24052
BALAKLAVA	12240
BALAKLAVA	38611
BALAO	50685
BALASHIKHA	45363
BALASHOV	28063
BALBINA	60350
BALBINA	68490
BALDBUTTE	37262
BALDER B	52090
BALDER EMS	76871
BALDER LONDON	67440
BALDER MARACAI	76870
BALDONE	38612
BALDUIN	93142
BALI	94360
BALIKPAPAN	94456
BALINTAWAK	07650
BALKAN	79643
BALKAN REEFER	05113
BALKHASH	20791
BALKHASH	33991
BALKHASH	52020
BALKHASH	84150
BALLENITA	18440
BALLYCASTLE	42720
BALLYKERN	75482
BALLYLESSON	42460
BALLYLORAN	42461
BALLYRORY	42470
BALLYRUSH	42471
BALMORAL	18900
BALMORAL UNIVERSAL	06351
BALTA	11825
BALTA	36252
BALTA	42802
BALTIC	52171
BALTIC	52581
BALTIC	83361
BALTIC	83451
BALTIC EAGLE	33280
BALTIC EAGLE	94550
BALTIC ENTERPRISE	15783
BALTIC ENTERPRISE	82693
BALTIC FREEZER	18330
BALTIC FREEZER	33651
BALTIC NEPTUNE	80720
BALTIC OSPREY	72730
BALTIC OSPREY	76910
BALTIC PROGRESS	15784
BALTIC PROGRESS	82694
BALTIC SEA	77841
BALTIC STAR	02440
BALTIC STAR	18030
BALTIC VALIANT	48870
BALTIC VENTURE	48690
BALTIC VIKING	51510
BALTICA	49903
BALTICA	50343
BALTICLAND	57558
BALTIKA	18010
'BALTIKA' type	46090
'BALTIKA' type	46900
'BALTIKA' type	78730
'BALTIKA' type	83260
'BALTIKA' type	83340
'BALTIKA' type	89980
BALTIM	92770
BALTIMORE	73420
BALTIMORE TRADER	35650
BALTIYSK	00851
BALTIYSK	21601
BALTIYSKAYA SLAVA	93784
'BALTIYSKIY'	75350
'BALTIYSKIY'	79500
'BALTIYSKIY'	90030
BALTIYSKIY	90031
BALTIYSKIY	90073
BALTIYSKIY 1-73	79500
BALTIYSKIY 1-73	90030
BALTIYSKIY 101	75380
BALTIYSKIY 102	75381
BALTIYSKIY 103	75382
BALTIYSKIY 104	75383

Name	Number
BALTIYSKIY 105	75384
BALTIYSKIY 106	75385
BALTIYSKIY 107	75386
BALTIYSKIY 108	75387
BALTIYSKIY 109	75388
BALTIYSKIY 110	75389
BALTIYSKIY 111	75390
BALVY	38613
BAM	70028
BAMMEN	51610
BAMSA DAN	58620
BAMSA DAN	64990
BANANA EXPRESS	31642
BANANA PLANTER	88190
BANANA REEFER	88191
BANANG	42110
BANAT	15320
BANAT	55780
BANAT	56480
BANDA AZUL	79103
BANDA CAREER	29790
BANDAK	56040
BANDERAS	48070
BANDIM	56240
BANDUNDU	62711
BANDUNDU	62751
BANG LAMUNG	90371
BANG NA	90372
BANG POO	90370
BANG PRA	90382
BANGKOK 2	00311
BANGLAR ALO	35740
BANGLAR ASHA	09072
BANGLAR BAANI	06642
BANGLAR DOOT	25785
BANGLAR JOY	80650
BANGLAR KHEYA	35940
BANGLAR MAAN	49711
BANGLAR MAITRI	29921
BANGLAR MITA	49710
BANGLAR NOOR	64100
BANGLAR NOOR	71580
BANGLAR POLYXENI	24863
BANGLAR PREETI	30101
BANGLAR PROGOTI	15131
BANGLAR SWAPNA	15130
BANGLAR TARANI	30270
BANGLAR UPOHAR	09071
BANGOR	50412
BANGOR	50822
BANGPLEE	49731
BANGPRA-IN	49730
BANGRAK	29830
BANGUI	92297
BANI	50413
BANI	50823
BANIJA	61780
BANJA LUKA	74510
BANKO	93652
BANKO	94992
BANNER	36641
BANNER	43681
BANSHU MARU No 5	93412
BANSHU MARU No 6	93413
BANSIN	75333
BANTA	50686
BAO AN	82139
BAO AN	82419
BAO FENG.	01770
BAO HU	60723
BAO QING HAI	53800
BAO QING HAI	77520
BAO SHAN	07823
BAO SHAN	10590
BAO SHAN	13391
BAO XING	44514
BAOTING.	04860
BAR	13960
BAR HAVEN	22090
BARABASH	12403
BARABINSK	12404
BARABINSK	22841
BARABINSK	34471
BARADA	03634
BARAHONA	60088
BARAKUDA	22332
BARANJA	74511
BARAO DE JACEGUAY	26770
BARAO DO RIO BRANCO	26771
BARAUNI	53221
BARAUNI.	64432
BARBA	22810
BARBARA	25330
BARBARA LEONHARDT	46282
BARBARA WESTON	75872
BARBARA B	28840
BARBARA-BRITT	73795
BARBARA-CHRIS	73796
BARBAROSSA	88850
BARBATA	22333
BARBER MEMNON	54191
BARBER MEMNON	54341
BARBER MENELAUS	54190
BARBER MENELAUS	54340
BARBER MENESTHEUS	54192
BARBER MENESTHEUS	54342
BARBER NARA	52642
BARBER PERSEUS	52644
BARBER PRIAM	52643
BARBER TAIF	52641
BARBER TOBA	52645
BARBER TONSBERG	52640
BARBETTE JACOB	77141
BARCELONA	08420
BARCELONA	08980
BARCELONA	63170
BARCELONA	71544
BARCELONA MARU	04551
BARCOLA	65390
BARDALAND	57559
BARDU	50021
BARENBELS	52980
BARENDSZ	76181
BARENTS SEA	82610
BARENTSEE	18722
BARFONN	70910
BARGUZIN	15461
BARIS	60320
BARIT	11918
BARKENKOPPEL	72680
BARLINEK	67051
BARLINEK	76641
BARNAUL	24056
BARO	50687
BAROGRAF	07471
BAROJA	51890
BAROK	83921
BARON BELHAVEN	74931
BARON MACLAY	47460
BARON NAPIER	47872
BARON PENTLAND	47873
BARON WEMYSS	47391
BARON WEMYSS	47961
BAROUK	24382
BARRACUDA	87830
BARRANCA	35121
BARRANDUNA	80211
BARRIAN	44083
BARRIAN	44393
BARRIER	41810
BARRY	50022
BARRY	61813
BARS	22161
BARU	42890
BARU HOPE	00880
BARWA	50688
BARWENA	22334
BASALT	73830
BASALT	77010
BASARGIN	12405
BASCA	61660
BASHKIR	45121
BASHKIRIYA	02140
BASHKIRNEFT	85890
BASIL III	61870
BASILEA	59514
BASILEA	59824
BASKA	15240
BASKUNCHAK	11460
BASKUNCHAK	84365
BASRAH	45386
BASSEIN	13271
BASTIAAN BROERE	88500
BASTION	89751
BASTION ALPHA	57042
BASTO	72890
BASTO	76940
BASTO III	19030
BAT SHEVA	84240
BATAK	83720
BATALLA DE STA. CLARA	71340
BATALLA DE STA. CLARA	67340
BATALLA DE YAGUAJAY	71341
BATALLA DE YAGUAJAY	67341
BATANGHARI	21570
BATAYSK	23760
BATE BRIDGE	05481
BATE BRIDGE	06812
BATIK	87590
BATILLUS	52950
BATILLUS	55480
BATILMAN	13657
'BATRAL' type	84260
BATROUN	28200
BATUMI;	11826
BATUMI	44140
BAUCHI	50023
BAUCIS	51811
BAUPRE ISLAND	30480
BAUSKA	38610
BAVANG	50024
BAVARIA	04641
BAY	14553
BAY	35600
BAYAMON	08341
BAYANO	35120
BAYARD	93140
BAYBRIDGE	48841
BAYERN	64094
BAYKAL	02120
BAYKAL	12402
BAYKAL	17812
BAYKAL	20792
BAYKAL	33990
BAYKALLES	04181
BAYKONUR	24059
BAYMAK	45364
BAYMAK	89467
BAYNUNAH	15142
BAYU	57606
BAYU	62249
BAYVILLE	11114
BAZALT	11827
BAZALTOVYY	89765
BEACON POINT	66751
BEACON POINT	75801
BEAGLE	92710
BEATRICE	55382
BEATRICE	66956
BEATRICE	70996
BEATRIZ DEL MAR	76102
BEAUFORT MARINER	70420
BEAUGENCY	57991
BEAUMARIS	65202
BEAUMARIS	67412
BEAUMONT	56413
BEAUMONT	67833
BEAUMONT	68433
BEAURIVAGE	56414
BEAURIVAGE	67834
BEAURIVAGE	68434
BEAUTY ROSE	21900
BEAVERBANK	05231
BEBEDOURO	71031
BECENA	13461
BECKNES	46313
BECKNES	46563
BECKUMERSAND	67000
BEDOUIN BIRKNES	46315
BEDOUIN BIRKNES	46565
BEEDING	76130
BEEDING	79910
BEERBERG	94012
BEGA	87640
BEGONA DEL MAR	76081
BEGONIA	93900
BEI AN	82139
BEI AN	82419
BEI HAI	56880
BEI SHAN	02770
BEIRA	13570
BEISHU MARU	04702
BEISHU MARU	05012
BEITEDDINE	28350
BEJAIA	55316
BEJAIA	70060
BEKAS	11957
BELA KHUN	05634
BELA KHUN	14463
BELA KOSMO	61561
BELA ROZO	61562
BELASITZA	77982
BELBECK	86095
BELCARGO	77463
BELEN	03221
BELEN	03891
BELGIA	94502
BELGICA	51750
BELGIUM	73002
BELGIUM	76982
BELGOROD DNESTFOVSKIY	45365
BELGRAD	36862
BELGRAVE	88611
BELGRAVE	90071
BELGULF MERCURY	70050
BELI	28540
BELINDA	77673
BELINSKIY	12361
BELINSKIY	20790
BELITSK	01071
BELL RACER	73771
BELL RAIDER	73772
BELL RANGER	73773
BELL REBEL	73774
BELL RELIANT	73777
BELL RENOWN	73776
BELL RESOLVE	73778
BELL RIVAL	73779
BELL ROVER	73770
BELL RULER	73775
BELLA MAERSK	55960
BELLA MAERSK	56720
BELLAMYA	52951
BELLAMYA	55481
BELLARY	53220
BELLARY	64430
BELLATRIX	07892
BELLATRIX	83930
BELLE ISLE	04786
BELLE ROSE	04787
BELLEA	61700
BELLEA	71070
BELLMAN	77120
BELLMAN	80030
BELLNES	46314
BELLNES	46564
BELLOC	05322
BELLONA	66494
BELLONA	85936
BELMEKEN	79641
BELOBO	63510
BELOBO	68280
BELOGORSK	12299
BELOGORSK	86200
BELOMORSKLES	24047
BELOMORYE	11304
BELOMORYE	52022
BELOMORYE	84152
BELONA	22330
BELORETSK	01070
BELORUSSIYA	10433
BELOVODSK	01072
BELOYARSK	85999
BELOZERSKLES	24057
BELSTAR	46000
BELTSY	86227
BELVAUX	12690
BEN AIN	88431
BEN FRANKLIN	53650
BEN FRANKLIN	53740
BEN MAJED	90532
BEN MAJED	91072
BEN OCEAN LANCER	92880
BENADIR	21240
BENALDER	08410
BENARTY	14730
BENAVON	08411
BENCHIJGUA	94021
BENCLEUCH	66611
BENCLEUCH	75131
BENDEARG	05000
BENEFACTOR	05470
BENGAWAN	21571
BENGHAZI	58480
BENGUELA CURRENT	26751
BENHA	12162
BENHOPE	67640
BENHOPE	71430
BENIALI	47327
BENIALI	83387
BENIGNITY	58185
BENIMAMET	47321
BENIMAMET	83381
BENISALEM	47322
BENISALEM	83382
BENITO JUAREZ	19371
BENITO JUAREZ	69990
BENITO JUAREZ	86480
BENJAMAS	02761
BENJAMIN BOWRING	84310
BENJAMIN HARRISON	01056
BENLEDI	72334
BENMACDHUI	66612
BENMACDHUI	75132
BEN-MY-CHREE	20501
BENNEVIS	49140
BENSTAC	05920
BENVANNOCH	13291
BENVENUE	66610
BENVENUE	75130
BENWYVIS	77674
BENYA RIVER	15270
BENYA RIVER	35041
BERANE	43400
BERANE	43540
BERBY	83922
BERDIKARI	61475
BERDJANSK	00332
BERDSK	85995
BERDY KERBAEAYEV	50743
BERESFORD	39380
BEREZEN	11828
BEREZINA	89212
BEREZINALES	24058
BEREZNIK.	06770
'BEREZNIK' class.	07550
'BEREZNIK' class	07600
BEREZNIKI	01074
BEREZNIKI	11314
BEREZOVKA	45366
BEREZOVNEFT	86004
BEREZOVO	70022
BERG	82840
BERGA	59161
BERGA	66511
BERGE ADRIA	65191
BERGE BRIONI	65190
BERGE COMMANDER	60791
BERGE DUKE	58010
BERGE DUKE	59810
BERGE EMPEROR	56380
BERGE EMPRESS	56381
BERGE KING	67820
BERGE LORD	58012
BERGE LORD	59812
BERGE ODEL	64551
BERGE PRINCE	67822
BERGE PRINCESS	67823
BERGE QUEEN	67821
BERGE SAGA	55643
BERGE SAGA	55843
BERGE SEPTIMUS	58011
BERGE SEPTIMUS	59811
BERGE SISAR	55642
BERGE SISAR	55842
BERGE SISU	55641
BERGE SISU	55841
BERGEBONDE	64550
BERGEN MARU	04552
BERGENSFJORD	61411
BERGLJOT	50689
BERGO	50025
BERILL	12406
BERING SEA	29246
BERING SEA	47831
BERINGOV PROLIV	71821
BERINGOV PROLIV	58511
BERISLAV	45358
BERJAYA	25371
BERJAYA	34772
BERJAYA	70952
BERKSHIRE	56870
BERKUT	13658
BERLIN	58362
BERNADETTE No 1	29740
BERNARDINO CORREA	05364
BERNARDINO CORREA	15664
BERNARDO HOUSSAY	60870
BERNBURG	03871
BERNHARD BASTLEIN	06385
BERNHARD BASTLEIN	15414
BERNHARD KELLERMANN	10251
BERNHARD KELLERMANN	12631
BERNHARD OLDENDORFF	72250
BERNHARD S.	50260
BERRY	37330
BERTHA FISSER	62104
BERTOLT BRECHT	12620
BERTRAM RICKMERS	52810
BERYTE	17782
BESSEGEN	92110
BETACRUX	59142
BETELGEUSE	07890
BETH	50020
BETHIOUA	55317
BETHIOUA	70061
BETIS	57234
BETTY	67283
BETULA	19080
BEXLEY	40320
BEYKOZ	16730
BEZHETSK	86182
BHADRAVATI	29190
BHAGAT SINGH	59906
BHAGAT SINGH	67666
BHAGIRATHI	39400
BHAIRAB	16280
BHANGURANSI	34970
BHARATA	56840
BHASKARA	55220
BHASKARA	57250
BHOJA MARINER	27960
BIA	94250
BIA RIVER	07990
BIA RIVER	15275
BIAFRA	31650
BIAKH	50414
BIAKH	50824
BIAN	18151
BIANCO	18191
BIANKA LEONHARDT	57500
BIBAN	48907
BIBI	12800
BIELSKO	12160
BIESZCZADY	75735
BIESZCZADY	88385
BIFROST	56280
BIHOR	47550
BIJELA	59400
BIJELA	62160
BIKIN	12407
BIKIN	22842
BIKIN	34472
BILBAO	37731
BILBAO	37841
BILBARAKAH	45650
BILDERDYK	35102
BILDERDYK	95150
BILINGA	87426
BILKIS	27261
BILLESBORG	75060
BIMA	43198
BIMBO	66651
BIN HAI	46750
BINTANG BOLONG	52100
BINTANG SAMUDRA III	37320
BINTANG SAMUDRA IV	45070
BINTANG UTARA	91641
BIOSFERA	13660
BIRA	85610
BIRCHBANK	05232
BIRD OF PARADISE	22080
BIRIM RIVER	13312
BIRIM RIVER	34831
BIRKENHAIN	90920
BIRKHALL	35560
BIRLING	75920
BIRSHTONAS	12409

BIRTE OLDENDORFF	77443
BIRTHE THOLSTRUP	85111
BIRYUSINSK	11742
BIRYUSINSK	34632
BIRYUZA	12410
BIRYUZA	15462
BIRYUZA	70781
BISCAYA GOLF	31560
BISCAYNE SEA	72740
BISCAYNE SEA	73700
BISCAYNE SKY	72741
BISCAYNE SKY	73701
BISCAYNE STAR	89630
BISCAYNE SUN	87811
BISCHOFSTOR	47205
BISLIG TRANSPORT	86951
BISMILLAH	63721
BISON	11598
BISON	94611
BISTRITA	13732
BIYO MARU	63310
BIYSK	01075
BIZERTE	51290
BJORGHOLM	63455
BLACK PRINCE	16351
BLACK SEA	29610
BLACK WATCH	16350
BLACKPOOL	36170
BLACKPOOL	41900
BLACKTHORN	87850
BLACKWELL POINT	36070
BLACKWELL POINT	41790
BLAGOVESHCHENSK	07552
BLAGOVESHCHENSK	86170
BLANCA DEL MAR	87781
BLANIK	15093
BLANKENBURG	03872
BLANKENSEE	46380
BLANKENSEE	47080
BLAVET	86990
BLENHEIM	16360
BLESSING FIVE	00390
BLIKUR	93011
BLITAR	00740
BLIX	50690
BLOIS	57990
BLOUDAN	40101
BLUE BAY	09591
BLUE MASTER	48631
BLUE MOON	87070
BLUE MOON	89560
BLUE NILE	49351
BLUE OCEAN	21130
BLUE OCEAN	55580
BLUE OCEAN	56460
BLUE PEARL	27010
BLUE SEA	40090
BLUE SKY	08040
BLUE SKY	40091
BLUE SKY	44480
BLUE SPIRIT	58720
BLUE SPIRIT	59660
BLUE STAR	52361
BLUE STAR	87071
BLUE STAR	89561
BLUE WAVE	26029
BLUE WAVE	30198
BLUEBIRD	48311
BLUENOSE	20240
BLUMENTHAL	06281
BO CHURN	61640
BOA ESPERANCA	51050
BOA VISTA 1	52280
BOBERG	51624
BOBERG	72687
BOBRUYSKLES	24060
BOCA TABLA	51812
BOCCACCIO	32540
BOCHNIA	03231
BOCHNIA	03621
BODAYBO	24062
BODE THOMAS	18650
BODO UHSE	17980
BODRUM	81100
BOEVAYA SLAVA	93781
BOEVOY	85352
BOGDAN	39130
BOGDAN KHMELNITSKY	28750
BOGINKA	87770
BOGOWONTO	21572
BOHEME	08250
BOHEMUND	93141
BOHENE	17050
BOIN	51090
BOIN	51480
BOIZENBURG	03873
'BOIZENBURG' type	50440
'BOIZENBURG' type	52000
BOJNICE	35480
BOKA.	04470
BOKA	10990
BOKA	34150
BOKELNBURG	73671
BOKSIT	11919
BOLA No 1	30990
BOLD KNIGHT	36340
BOLDURI	63641
BOLESLAW CHOBRY	14920
BOLESLAW CHOBRY	15730
BOLESLAW KRZYWOUSTY	14922
BOLESLAW KRZYWOUSTY	15732
BOLESLAW PRUS	71857
BOLESLAW SMIALY	14921
BOLESLAW SMIALY	15731
BOLESLAWIEC	50460
BOLGRAD	57541
BOLIMOG	89269
BOLIVAR	34210
BOLIVAR	86690
BOLIVIA	04640
BOLNES	46310
BOLNES	46560
BOLON	84360
BOLSHEVIK	16623
BOLSHEVIK KARAYEV	44100
BOLSHEVIK SUKHANOV	13011
BOLSHEVO	12241
BOLTENHAGEN	75320
BOMBERG	75296
BOMBERG	88106
BOMIN II	44920
BONA FE	75935
BONA FE	88635
BONA TIDE	39741
BONAHOPE	42940
BONAIRE CROSS	69550
BONANZA	27660
BONAVISTA	22010
BONAWIND I	85281
BONG SAN	69452
BONITA	34200
BONITA 1	26570
BONITO	23450
BONN	58360
BONNIEWAY	72332
BONNY	68660
BONTRADER	72320
BOOKER CHALLENGE	57552
BOOKER COURAGE	57557
BOOKER CRUSADE	57553
BOOKER VULCAN	51470
BORA	18271
BORDABARRI	00384
BORDABEKOA	07232
BORDABEKOA	07432
BORDAGAIN	06991
BORDATXOA	04900
BORDER CASTLE	84191
BORDER FALCON	84192
BORDER PELE	84193
BORDER SHEPHERD	84190
BORE MOON	74070
BORE SKY	94560
BORE SUN	94561
BORE XI	94013
BOREA	01800
BOREA	67150
BORELLA	50080
BORG	82980
BORGA	58450
BORGA	64650
BORGEN	20620
BORGESTAD	46260
BORGNES	46311
BORGNES	46561
BORGO	72891
BORGO	76941
BORINQUEN	74470
BORIS BUTOMA	63570
BORIS BUVIN	78069
BORIS CHILIKIN	59880
BORIS DAVIDOV	22183
BORIS GORBATOV	07920
BORIS GORINSKIY	12408
BORIS LAVRENEV	07926
BORIS NIKOLAICHUK	31874
BORIS TSINDELIS	13661
BORIS ZHEMCHUZIN.	03072
BORIS ZHEMCHUZIN	03652
BORISLAV	57542
BORISOGLEBSK	86000
BORISPOL	11734
BORISPOL	34624
BORIYA TSARIKOV	15512
BORKUM	85140
BORLA	67761
BORMLA	91841
BORMLA	91951
BORNHEIM	74561
'BORO' type	77120
'BORO' type	80030
BORODIN	86173
BORODINO	36881
BOROVICHI	11380
BOROVNICA	13173
BOROVNICA	34800
BORUSSIA	04642
BORZHOMI	60629
BORZHOMI	62589
BOSANKA	61781
BOSFOR	12413
BOSHNYAKOVO	17925
BOSNIA	90271
BOSTON MARU	30510
BOSTONSAND	67001
BOSUT	66951
BOSUT	70991
BOSWELL	05323
BOSWICK	61680
BOTAFOGA	15663
BOTAFOGO	05363
BOTANY BAY	77051
BOTEVGRAD	84710
BOTEVGRAD	85170
BOTNIA EXPRESS	19294
BOTNIA EXPRESS	23705
BOTNICHESKIY ZALIV	61102
BOTSMAN MOSHKOV	54730
BOTSMAN MOSHKOV	55300
BOTSMAN ZOTOV	22843
BOTSMAN ZOTOV	34473
BOTTENVIKKEN	75531
BOUAR	21540
BOUGAINVILLE	03133
BOUGAINVILLE	03343
BOURGOGNE	73949
BOW ELM	60863
BOW ELM	70903
BOW FAGUS	54552
BOW FLOWER	54553
BOW FORTUNE	54130
BOW FORTUNE	54250
BOW SEA	54131
BOW SEA	54251
BOW SKY	54132
BOW SKY	54252
BOW SPRING	54133
BOW SPRING	54253
BOW STAR	54134
BOW STAR	54254
BOW SUN	54135
BOW SUN	54255
BOX TRADER	75891
'BOXER' type	95130
BOXER CAPTAIN COOK	95132
BOXY	50480
BOXY	83070
BP. BATTLER	83851
BP. BATTLER	88901
BP. JOUSTER	70880
BP. JOUSTER	79590
BP. SCORCHER	83862
BP. SCORCHER	85872
BP. SPRINGER	83850
BP. SPRINGER	88900
BP. WARRIOR	83852
BP. WARRIOR	88902
BRABANT	17310
BRABANT	33290
BRABANT	93150
BRABANT	94540
BRACIGOVO	83723
BRAD	82110
BRAD	82390
BRADEVERETT	14720
BRADEVERETT	81580
BRADFORD	36171
BRADFORD	41901
BRADING	20930
BRAENNAREN	66670
BRAGA	63720
BRAGANCA	63932
BRAGD	67462
BRAGE	73161
BRAGE	73742
BRAGE	77661
BRAILA	39672
BRAINPOWER	69333
BRALANTA	63398
BRALI	68690
BRANDAL	22370
BRANIEWO	88233
BRANIK	13174
BRANIK	34801
BRANSFIELD	16240
BRANT POINT	67251
BRANT POINT	91671
BRANTAS	21573
BRAS	67460
BRASILIA	02720
BRASILIA	51637
BRASLAV	12411
BRASLAVLES	24061
BRASOV	41313
BRATHAY FISHER	76160
BRATISLAVA	36863
BRATISLAVA	79232
BRATSK	00852
BRATSKLES	24054
BRATSTVO	01562
BRATSTVO	21721
BRATTINGSBORG	75061
BRAVENES	64312
BRAVENES	46562
BRAVERY	78350
BRAVIK	72841
BRAVO ARES	34890
BRAVO CERES	34894
BRAVO DENIS	13420
BRAVO KATERINA	34900
BRAVO MARIA	13400
BRAVO MARIA	13400
BRAVOALTONA	24251
BRAVUR	67461
BRAZILIAN EXPRESS	05078
BRAZILIAN EXPRESS	06130
BRAZILIAN EXPRESS	07840
BRAZILIAN FRIENDSHIP	69050
BRAZILIAN HOPE	58363
BRAZILIAN TRADER	71451
BRAZILIAN VITORIA	71450
BRAZILIAN WEALTH	64520
BRAZILIAN WEALTH	68470
BREAKSEA	24991
BREDA	71993
BREDA	72113
BREDAL	85420
BREDENBEK	76330
BREDENBEK	88720
BREEDE	82841
BREEHELLE	59621
BREEHOEK	59624
BREEHORN	59620
BREEKADE	66971
BREEKADE	91551
BREEKANT	66970
BREEKANT	91550
BREEZAND	75600
BREEZAND	79320
BREEZE	40390
BREEZE	74990
BREITLING	85363
BREIZH-IZEL	33220
BREMEN	26082
BREMEN	58361
BREMEN EXPRESS	08370
BREMEN MARU	04550
'BREMEN PROGRESS' type	48510
'BREMEN PROGRESS' type	56130
BREMER HORST BISCHOFF	47330
BREMERHAVEN	06280
BREMERHAVEN	33570
BRENDONIA	88000
BREST	71030
BRESTSKAYA KREPOST	33901
BREUGHEL	15331
BREZICE	13175
BREZICE	34802
BREZZA	35812
BREZZA	41582
BRIAN BOROIME	88570
BRIAN BOROIME	89700
BRIARTHORN	80760
BRIBIR	15791
BRIBIR	52321
BRIBIR	82821
BRICK DECIMO	42444
BRICK DODICESIMO	42950
BRICK NONO	42441
BRICK OTTAVO	42442
BRICK UNDICESIMO	42443
BRIDGEMAN	90080
BRIDGESTONE MARU V	54460
BRIDGESTONE MARU V	54910
BRIGHT FRUIT	21150
BRIGHT MOON	62311
BRIGHT SKY	61632
BRIGHTNESS	24242
BRIGHTNESS	84452
BRIGIT MAERSK	55961
BRIGIT MAERSK	56721
BRIGITTA	75681
BRIGITTA MONTANARI	88531
BRIGITTE GRAEBE	73791
BRILLIANT	12412
BRILLIANT STAR	61211
BRILLIANTE	88060
BRIMANGER	54136
BRIMANGER	54256
BRINTON LYKES	00061
BRIONI.	01680
BRIS	21261
BRISBANE TRADER	33061
BRISE II	72990
BRISKNES	46317
BRISKNES	46567
BRISSAC	57980
BRISTOL	07014
BRITANIA	47270
BRITANIS	09150
BRITANNIA	91321
BRITANNIA TEAM	63452
BRITISH AVON	53341
BRITISH BEECH	53121
BRITISH CENTAUR	51662
BRITISH CENTAUR	73212
BRITISH COMMERCE	51660
BRITISH COMMERCE	73210
BRITISH COMMODORE	51661
BRITISH COMMODORE	73211
BRITISH DART	53340
BRITISH DRAGOON	51380
BRITISH DRAGOON	65510
BRITISH ESK	53342
BRITISH EXPLORER	62490
BRITISH EXPLORER	71560
BRITISH FIDELITY	51975
BRITISH FIDELITY	84185
BRITISH FORTH	53343
BRITISH GULL	38340
BRITISH GULL	44700
BRITISH HAWTHORN	53122
BRITISH HAZEL	53123
BRITISH HOLLY	53120
BRITISH HUMBER	53344
BRITISH IVY	53124
BRITISH KENNET	53345
BRITISH LAUREL	53125
BRITISH LIBERTY	51970
BRITISH LIBERTY	84180
BRITISH LOYALTY	51971
BRITISH LOYALTY	84181
BRITISH MAPLE	53126
BRITISH NORNESS	57941
BRITISH PATIENCE	57861
BRITISH PIONEER	60270
BRITISH PIONEER	63830
BRITISH POPLAR	53127
BRITISH PRIDE	57850
BRITISH PROGRESS	58330
BRITISH PROMISE	57860
BRITISH PURPOSE	58331
BRITISH RANGER	57942
BRITISH RELIANCE	57943
BRITISH RENOWN	57940
BRITISH RESOLUTION	57944
BRITISH RESOURCE	57945
BRITISH RESPECT	58320
BRITISH SCIENTIST	60271
BRITISH SCIENTIST	63832
BRITISH SECURITY	51972
BRITISH SECURITY	84182
BRITISH SPEY	53346
BRITISH TAMAR	53347
BRITISH TAY	53348
BRITISH TENACITY	51973
BRITISH TENACITY	84183
BRITISH TEST	53349
BRITISH TRENT	53350
BRITISH TRIDENT	57946
BRITISH TWEED	53351
BRITISH UNITY	51974
BRITISH UNITY	84184
BRITISH VINE	53128
BRITISH VISCOUNT	24010
BRITISH VOYAGER	11990
BRITISH WILLOW	53129
BRITISH WYE	53352
BRITSUM	78660
BRITTA I	73948
BRITTA LEONHARDT	57501
BRITTA ODEN	94180
BRNO	72171
BROCKEN	95250
BROCKMAN	68290
BROCKMAN	77320
BRODNICA	14300
BROLAND	70171
BRONISLAW LACHOWICZ	14482
BRONTE	05324
BROOKNES	46316
BROOKNES	46566
BROOKS RANGE	58031
BROTHER STAR	62431
BROWNING	05325
BRUARFOSS	15990
BRUAS	40391
BRUCE BALI	66350
BRUCE BAWGAN	66351
BRUCE BINTAN	66352
BRUCE BUATAN	66353
BRUCE SURABAYA	66354
BRUCE TORRES	70571
BRUMAIRE	57832
BRUNELLA	24530
BRUNELLA	31293
BRUNHORN	61702
BRUNHORN	71072
BRUNLA	61701
BRUNLA	71071
BRUNO TESCH	23413
BRUNSBUTTEL	21242
BRUNSHAUSEN	21241
BRUNSKAMP	33850
BRUNSLAND	14172
BRUNSRODE	33940
BRUNSWICK	33941
BRYANSKIY MASHINOSTROITEL	01386
BRYANSKIY MASHINOSTROITEL	01646
BRYANSKIY RABOCHIY	45362
BRYANSKLES	24040
BUARQUE	55014
BUARQUE	55884
BUARQUE	56554
BUCCANEER	02250
BUCEGI	78580

BUCHAREST	36841
BUCHENSTEIN	13980
BUCKINGHAM	43181
BUCURESTI	15420
BUDAPEST	36842
BUDAPEST	45850
BUDAPEST	86118
BUDAPEST	91718
BUDOWLANY	78292
BUDOWLANY	80022
BUDVA	62024
BUENA ESPERANZA	69080
BUENA ESPERANZA	86340
BUENA FORTUNA	41080
BUENA SUERTE	68693
BUENAVISTA	94020
BUENO	40451
BUENOS AIRES	02724
BUFFALO	32370
BUFFALO	61195
BUFFALO	66192
BUFFALO	94600
BUGA	38360
BUGURUSLAN	39990
BUGURUSLAN	89468
BUILDER	35601
BUILDER	35643
BUILDER	41303
BUILDER II	42077
BUILDER III	92010
BUKAVU	62712
BUKAVU	62752
BUKHARA	24055
BUKHTARMA	15463
BUKOVINA	02351
BUKOVINA	35371
BULA	86543
BULGARIA	73296
BULK MERCHANT	76610
BULK PIONEER	76611
BULK QUEEN	94440
BULK TRADER	74360
BULK TRADER	76612
BULKNES	62432
BULSOOK	27361
BULUNKHAN	50744
BUNA	52070
BUNA	75170
BUNGA ANGSANA	09750
BUNGA BINDANG	48932
BUNGA BUTANG	24661
BUNGA BUTANG	26271
BUNGA CHEMPAKA	54653
BUNGA CHEMPAKA	55074
BUNGA DAHLIA	50351
BUNGA GELANG	48933
BUNGA KESUMBA	60610
BUNGA KESUMBA	70070
BUNGA MAS	48931
BUNGA MAWAR	68102
BUNGA MELATI	03202
BUNGA MELATI	03602
BUNGA MELAWIS	77281
BUNGA MELOR	03211
BUNGA ORKID	03200
BUNGA ORKID	03600
BUNGA PENAGA	50350
BUNGA PERMAI	08470
BUNGA PERMAI	09560
BUNGA RAYA	03210
BUNGA SELASIH	60611
BUNGA SELASIH	70071
BUNGA SEPANG	60612
BUNGA SEPANG	70072
BUNGA SEROJA	03203
BUNGA SEROJA	03603
BUNGA SETAWAR	48930
BUNGA SURIA	08471
BUNGA SURIA	09561
BUNGA TANJONG	03201
BUNGA TANJONG	03601
BUNGA TERATAI	09751
BUNKO MARU	51020
BUNKO MARU	52880
BURAIDAH	94171
BURAN	10260
BURAN	22222
BURAN	23512
BURAN	10760
BURDIGALA	66882
BUREVESTNIK	11829
BUREVESTNIK	12312
BUREVESTNIK	85328
BUREVESTNIK REVOLYUTSKIY	79369
BUREYA	85611
BUREYALES	24053
BURG	61709
BURG	71079
BURGAS	28991
BURGAS	36874
BURGENSTEIN	13981
BURHAVERSAND	67002
BURJA	21262
BURMAH ENDEAVOUR	56401
BURMAH ENDEAVOUR	59921
BURMAH ENDEAVOUR	67781
BURMAH ENTERPRISE	56402
BURMAH ENTERPRISE	59922
BURMAH ENTERPRISE	67782
BURMAH LEGACY	64147
BURMAH SPAR	60728
BURNLEY	88920
BURNSIDE	36522
BURNSIDE	43502
BUSKO ZDROJ	81861
BUSSARD	84931
BUSSOL	09375
BUSTENI	47547
BUTACUATRO	70831
BUTADOS	79631
BUTATRES	70830
BUTAUNO	79630
BUTRON	54521
BUTRON	55441
BUTRON	55731
BUTTON GWINNETT	01052
BUYER	35602
BUZAU	86209
BUZLUDJA	49160
BUZOVNY	44115
BUZURGAN	69572
BYDGOSZCZ	14301
BYELKINO	12414
BYELOKAMENKA	17953
BYELOMORSK	11722
BYELOMORSK	34612
BYELORUSSIYA	20370
BYELOVO	11830
BYEREZINA	17954
BYKOVO	11721
BYKOVO	34611
BYTOM	50466
BYZANTINE EAGLE	89181
BYZANTINE ENERGY	81132
BYZANTINE ENTERPRISE	18220
BYZANTINE MONARCH	26600
BYZANTION	64271
BYZANTION	68591

C

'C-1' type	26140
'C-1' type	26150
'C-1' type	28580
'C-1' type	30210
'C1-M-AV1' type	86790
'C1-M-AV1' type	81570
'C1-M-AV1' type	92020
'C-2' type	07690
'C-2' type	13330
'C-2' type	13840
'C-3' type	29640
'C 3' type	07720
'C 3' type	07730
'C-4' type	79290
'C-4' type	92660
'C5-5-AX1' type	39560
'C5-214' type	18183
'C 37' type	39301
C.K. APOLLO	57270
C K DOLAJI	82451
C.S. IRIS	02411
C.S. IRIS	32941
C.S. MONARCH	02410
C.S. MONARCH	32940
C.V. LIGHTNING	94270
C.V. STAGHOUND	94271
C.W. KITTO	55708
C.W. KITTO	58278
CABLE ENTERPRISE	23400
CABLE RESTORER	08920
CABO BOJADOR	14531
CABO BOJEADOR	21170
CABO BOLINAO	21401
CABO CORRIENTES I	38192
CABO DE SANTA MARTA	14311
CABO DE SAO ROQUE	14310
CABO FRIO	14312
CABO FRIO	83750
CABO SAN AGUSTIN	21171
CABO SAN LUCAS	78440
CABO SANTA ANA	14150
CABO VERDE	14532
CABOT	50150
CABRITE	64314
CACICA ISABEL	32321
CACICA ISABEL	17171
CACIULATA	47561
CADMUS	28451
CAESAREA	20510
CAGAYAN DE ORO	21030
CAICARA	04802
CAIRNCARRIER	75601
CAIRNCARRIER	79321
CAIRNFREIGHTER	75602
CAIRNFREIGHTER	79322
CAIRNLEADER	75603
CAIRNLEADER	79323
CAIRNROVER	91847
CAIRNROVER	91957
CAIRU	55540
CAIRU	63340
CALA LLONGA	23741
CALA LLONGA	93291
CALA MARSAL	23740
CALA MARSAL	93290
CALABRIA	01720
CALAFIA	64871
CALAGARIBALDI	06291
CALAMOS	89290
CALAN	82229
CALANDA	50421
CALANDRINI	14492
CALARASI	82123
CALARASI	82403
CALATRAVA	65270
CALBE	54302
CALBE	78612
CALDERETA	48086
CALDIRAN	80356
CALEDONIA	32280
CALEDONIA	46252
CALEDONIA	70470
CALEDONIAN PRINCESS	19850
CALIFORNIA	08005
CALIFORNIA STAR	08880
CALIFORNIAN	43440
CALIFORNIAN	94740
CALIMANESTI	47544
CALIXTO CARCIA	06614
CALLAO	02571
CALOOSAHATCHEE	35961
CALORIC	77596
CALULO	84311
CALVADOS	51074
CALYPSO	75502
CALYPSO N	61020
CALYPSO N	71180
CAM AYOUS	07172
CAM AZOBE	07173
CAM BUBINGA	59701
CAM BUBINGA	61401
CAM DOUSSIE	59702
CAM DOUSSIE	61402
CAMAGUEY	81310
CAMARA	46447
CAMARGO	87510
CAMARGUE	64370
CAMARINA	91837
CAMARINA	91947
CAMBRIDGE FERRY	33090
CAMDEN	93471
CAMELIA	26101
CAMELLIA B	35731
CAMELLIA B	41431
CAMELLIA B	41560
CAMERONA	62022
CAMILLA	87880
CAMILLA HENRIKSEN	94001
CAMILLA WESTON	88430
CAMILLE B	69311
CAMINITO	10400
'CAMIT' type	60020
'CAMIT' type	72630
'CAMIT' type	77390
CAMPANAR	38521
CAMPANIA FELIX	01280
CAMPANIA PRIMA	16724
CAMPANIA SECONDA	16725
CAMPAZAS	38522
CAMPEADOR	65700
CAMPEADOR	69800
CAMPECHE	24990
CAMPECHE	93120
CAMPEON	66131
CAMPHOR	61420
CAMPO DURAN	66193
CAMPOALEGRE	37050
CAMPOAZUR	38673
CAMPOAZUR	44843
CAMPOBLANCO	38901
CAMPOBLANCO	44762
CAMPOCERRADO	38672
CAMPOCERRADO	44842
CAMPOCERRADO	44882
CAMPODARRO	40921
CAMPOGENIL	40922
CAMPOGRIS	44760
CAMPOGULES	38671
CAMPOGULES	44841
CAMPOLLANO	37051
CAMPOLONGO	67142
CAMPOMAYOR	65701
CAMPOMAYOR	69801
CAMPOMINO	65791
CAMPONALON	40920
CAMPONAVIA	65790
CAMPONEGRO	44761
CAMPONUBLA	66130
CAMPOO	42990
CAMPORRASO	44880
CAMPORROJO	38670
CAMPORROJO	44840
CAMPORRUBIO	38674
CAMPORRUBIO	44844
CAMPORRUBIO	44881
CAMPOSALINAS	67141
CAMPOSECO	37052
CAMPOTEJAR	67140
CAMPOVERDE	38900
CAMPROVIN	42991
CAMSELL	09920
CANABAL	39420
CANADA MARU	39180
CANADA MARU	45230
CANADIAN BULKER	79761
CANADIAN HIGHLANDER	70660
CANADIAN OWL	63941
CANADIAN OWL	71591
CANADIAN PROGRESS	52150
CANADIAN REEFER	05110
CANADON SECO	66194
CANALGRANDE	39743
CANBERRA	36130
CANBERRA MARU	08620
CANBERRA MARU	09820
CANDEIAS	65862
CANDIA	32910
CANG SHAN	25104
CANGURO BIANCO	20271
CANGURO BRUNO	20272
CANGURO CABO SAN JORGE	16531
CANGURO CABO SAN JORGE	17591
CANGURO CABO SAN SEBASTIAN	16530
CANGURO CABO SAN SEBASTIAN	17590
CANGURO FULVO	22383
CANGURO VERDE	20273
CANIS MAJOR	61490
CANISTEO	35962
CANMAR CARRIER	49371
CANMAR EXPLORER III	92881
CANMAR KIGORIAK	09060
CANMAR KIGORIAK	17330
CANOPUS	22280
CANOPUS	73942
CANOPY	47160
CANOVA	71913
CANSO TRANSPORT	55330
CANSO TRANSPORT	70300
CANTAL	51073
CANTUARIA	14491
CAP BAITAR	61690
CAP BENAT	76860
CAP BIZERTA	61691
CAP BRETON	53408
CAP BRETON	64938
CAP CAMARAT	76861
CAP FALCONERA	33050
CAP LARDIER	76862
CAP PALMAS	40300
CAP PHAISTOS	84991
CAP PINEDE	48500
CAP SAN AUGUSTIN	02291
CAP SAN DIEGO	02292
CAP SAN LORENZO	02293
CAP SAN MARCO	02294
CAP SAN NICOLAS	02290
CAP SERRAT	51540
CAP TAILLAT	76863
CAPAL	82020
CAPE ANTIBES	47396
CAPE ANTIBES	47966
CAPE AVANTI DUE	59291
CAPE AVANTI DUE	61331
CAPE DON	02090
CAPE FREELS	50160
CAPE FREELS	50710
CAPE GRENVILLE	47394
CAPE GRENVILLE	47964
CAPE HAWK	47392
CAPE HAWK	47962
CAPE HENLOPEN	02500
CAPE HORN	47395
CAPE HORN	47965
CAPE HUSTLER	73881
CAPE HUSTLER	87261
CAPE ITEA	45452
CAPE ITEA	48712
CAPE KAMARI	61291
CAPE KAMARI	86721
CAPE KENNEDY	60090
CAPE MONTEREY	60091
CAPE MORETON	02091
CAPE MUSTANG	71222
CAPE ORTEGAL	47870
CAPE PILLAR	02092
CAPE RACE	74930
CAPE RACE	74930
CAPE RION	06536
CAPE RODNEY	47871
CAPE STROVILI	46710
CAPE YORK	22640
CAPECREST	76091
CAPETAN ALECOS MILONAS	40950
CAPETAN COSTAS	24862
CAPETAN COSTIS 1	56986
CAPETAN GEORGIS	30630
CAPETAN GIORGIS	29480
CAPETAN GIORGIS Z	61441
CAPETAN LUKIS	05300
CAPETAN MANOLIS HAZIMANOLIS	55210
CAPETAN MARKOS	06529
CAPETAN NICOLAS	00170
CAPETAN PSARROS	61772
CAPETAN RAHIOTIS	61773
CAPETAN TASSOS	56791
CAPIRA	62280
CAPIRONA	72470
CAPITAINE COOK	08132
CAPITAINE LA PEROUSE	08134
CAPITAINE LA PEROUSE	31160
CAPITAINE LE GOFF	94030
CAPITAINE WALLIS	28871
CAPITAN ALBERTO	55431
CAPITAN ALBERTO FERNANDEZ	84962
CAPITAN CARLO	36400
CAPITAN OLO PANTOJA	84880
CAPITANO FRANCO V	69431
CAPO BIANCO	32350
CAPO CORSO	39480
CAPO EMMA	64600
CAPO FALCONE	84992
CAPO GALLO	88540
CAPO MADRE	40260
CAPO MADRE	41490
CAPO MANNU	36320
CAPO MELE	50400
CAPO MELE	50830
CAPO OVEST	55850
CAPO SAN MARCO	10170
CAPRAIA	39160
CAPRICORN	39311
CAPRICORN	65501
CAPRICORNUS	73384
CAPRIOLO	03991
CAPT. F. GAIGNEROT	59080
CAPTAIN CONSTANTINOS	17150
CAPTAIN DEMOSTHENES	57290
CAPTAIN GEORGE L.	49281
CAPTAIN GLYPTIS	31480
CAPTAIN GREGOS	39880
CAPTAIN JOHN	30847
CAPTAIN JOHN L	35501
CAPTAIN LEMOS	62221
CAPTAIN LEMOS	71131
CAPTAIN LEO	86890
CAPTAIN LEO	90820
CAPTAIN LYGNOS	06990
CAPTAIN NICOLAS	48140
CAPTAIN PADDON	82760
CAPTAIN PAPPIS	59260
CAPTAIN PAPPIS	61301
CAPTAIN PAPPIS	62530
CAPTAIN PAPPIS	62621
CAPTAIN PETROS	87210
CAPTAIN VENIAMIS	56820
CAPUTERRA	88780
CAR EXPRESS	41980
CARA	56972
CARACAS	03142
CARACAS BAY	85621
CARAIBE	73406
CARAIBE	82716
CARAIBI	38520
CARAIMAN	11706
CARAVAGGIO	19181
CARAVELLE	73811
CARBAY	68323
CARBET	58552
CARBET	71872
CARCAPE	68324
CARCHESTER	68300
CARDIFF	22491
'CARDIFF' class	46430
'CARDIFF' class	46460
'CARDIFF' class	46470
'CARDIFF' class	47870
CARDIFF CITY	46870
CARDIGAN BAY	08401
CARDUCCI	32541
CAREBEKA I	66803
CAREBEKA VI	59604
CAREBEKA VI	71934
CAREBEKA VII	85471
CAREBEKA VII	91530
CAREBEKA VIII	76110
CAREBEKA IX	76111
CARENERO	31303
CARGO - LINER I	72140
CARGO - LINER I	76480
CARGO - LINER II	72141
CARGO - LINER II	76481
CARGO - LINER III	72142
CARGO - LINER III	76482
CARGO - LINER IV	72143
CARGO - LINER IV	76483
CARGO - LINER V	72144
CARGO - LINER V	76484
CARGO - LINER VI	72145
CARGO - LINER VI	76485
CARIB	75879
CARIB FREEZE	87711
CARIB FREEZE	89311
CARIBBEAN ARICHUNA	80310

CARIBBEAN ARROW	21470
CARIBBEAN CARRIER	78930
CARIBBEAN NOSTALGIA	45871
CARIBBEAN STAR No 1	81220
CARIBBEAN TIUNA	86910
CARIBBEAN UNIVERSAL	06222
CARIBBEAN UNIVERSAL	07453
CARIBE	16970
CARIBE No 1	85820
CARIBGAS DOS	89530
CARIBIA EXPRESS	73400
CARIBIA EXPRESS	82710
CARIBIC	83480
CARIBSTAR	18420
CARIDDI	17430
CARIGULF EXPRESS	91220
CARIGULF EXPRESS	91820
CARIMARE	58553
CARIMARE	71873
CARINA	11715
CARINA	75011
CARINTHIA	14173
CARISLE	68325
CARL GORTHON	83492
CARL KAMPE	33550
CARL WIEDERKEHR	33560
CARLA	81851
CARLA C	01230
CARLANTIC	68322
CARLEVERETT	21420
CARLO CANEPA	35583
CARLO CANEPA	36434
CARLO M	47206
CARLO SCHONHAAR	23414
CARLOS BORGES	57523
CARLOS MANUEL DE CESPEDES	06612
CARLOVA	79111
CARMANIA	14174
CARMEN	01470
CARMEN A	02772
CARMEN DEL MAR	76030
CARMEN DEL MAR	88620
CARNIVALE	06240
CAROL MERCUR	48730
CAROLA	19361
CAROLINA	50381
CAROLINA	93131
CAROLINA	93391
CAROLINE	46527
CAROLINE	83307
CAROLINE OLDENDORFF	71841
CAROLINE P	58177
CAROLINE WESTON	75871
'CAROLINER' type	48920
'CAROLINER' type	56320
CAROLYN	37430
CAROLYN	39190
CARPATI	78584
CARRAS	48175
CARRIE	72050
CARRIER PRINCESS	93110
CARRIER PRINCESS	93960
CARSO	76780
CARSTEN RUSS	54940
CARTAGENA DE INDIAS	07370
CARTAGENA DE INDIAS	15176
'CARTAGO' class	48210
CARTHAGO-NOVA	63130
CARUAO	51683
CARVALHO ARAUJO	03097
CARYANDA	77881
CASABLANCA	51742
CASABLANCA	64872
CASABLANCA	84062
CASCIOTIS	91240
CASIMIR LE QUELLEC	84200
CASIMIR LE QUELLEC	89040
CASON	59755
CASPIAN SEA	47832
CASPIAN TRADER	53682
CASPIAN TRADER	53812
CASPIAN TRADER	68532
'CASPIAN-VOLGO-BALT' type	50770
CASPIANA	59310
CASSANDRA	59270
CASSINGA	78102
CASSIO	18711
CASSIOPEIA	77442
CAST BEAVER	78684
CAST CORMORANT	64481
CAST DOLPHIN	46731
CAST DOLPHIN	78685
CAST FULMAR	53090
CAST FULMAR	63480
CAST GANNET	58402
CAST GANNET	64562
CAST GULL	63552
CAST GULL	68262
CAST HERON	53091
CAST HERON	63481
CAST KITTIWAKE	63493
CAST NARWHAL	58290
CAST ORCA	79112
CAST OSPREY	58400
CAST OSPREY	64560
CAST PETREL	63551
CAST PETREL	68261
CAST PORPOISE	45780
CAST PUFFIN	63553
CAST PUFFIN	68263
CAST RORQUAL	63191
CAST RORQUAL	67561
CAST SEAL	46730
CAST SKUA	58401
CAST SKUA	64561
CAST TERN	68841
CAST WALRUS	47031
CASTALIA	32640
CASTELLBLANCH	79101
CASTELLO	88910
CASTILLO DE LA MOTA	73130
CASTILLO MANZANARES	78181
CASTLE GLORY	18430
CASTLE GLORY	21830
CASTLE POINT	74830
CASTLE SPIRIT	86954
CASTLETON	68880
CASTOR	07340
CASTOR	83362
CASTOR	83452
CATALINA DEL MAR	76074
CATALUNYA	66062
CATAMARCA	69861
CATAMARCA II	53101
CATAMARCA II	53331
CATHARINA OLDENDORFF	06581
CATHAY SEATRADE	68740
CATHAY SEATRADE	77430
CATHERINE	27301
CATHERINE	38650
CATHERINE ANN	61033
CATHERINE ANN	71193
CATHERINE L	46691
CATHRIN	46280
CATTLEYA	55564
CATTLEYA	62944
CAUCASUS MARU	53686
CAUCASUS MARU	53816
CAUCASUS MARU	68536
CAUSEWAY	72333
CAVACO	39220
CAVALIER BULKER	60391
CAVALLO	33261
CAVENDISH	54901
CAVO AZURO	19230
CAVO DORO	29080
CAVO SIDERO	23240
CAYENNE	03496
CAYENNE	03586
CAYMAN	86850
CAYMAN TRADER	39520
CAYUGA	51671
CEAHLAU	11707
CEBO MOON	66972
CEBO MOON	91552
CEBU	46901
CEBU	83340
CEBU CITY	33460
CECILE ERICKSON	90060
CECILIE MAERSK	01440
CEDAR PRIDE	81953
CEDAR PRIDE	91503
CEDARBANK	05233
CEDROS	60360
CEDROS	76601
CEDROS	89301
CEDYNIA	70541
CEFALLONIAN AMBITION	29450
CEFALLONIAN AMBITION	30600
CEFALLONIAN DESTINY	31662
CEFALLONIAN GLORY	26280
CEFALLONIAN GRACE	31661
CEFALLONIAN SEA	10922
CEFALLONIAN SKY	10923
CEFALLONIAN SPIRIT	11530
CEFALLONIAN STAR	28820
CEGLED	35482
CELEBES	55661
CELEBES	55861
CELEBES CAREER	29770
CELEBES CAREER	30910
CELEBES SEA	29860
CELEBES SEA	29245
CELESTINO	04891
CELESTINO	35080
CELESTINO	57521
CELIA	54170
CELIA	71760
CELIA	76380
CELINA TORREALBA	04804
CELJE	57443
CELLANA	51980
CELTIC	52172
CELTIC	52582
CELTIC CRUSADER	84030
CELTIC ENDEAVOUR	91835
CELTIC ENDEAVOUR	91945
CELTIC LEE	81910
CELTIC SKY	46950
CELTIC VENTURE	66932
CELTIC VENTURE	70982
CEMBULK	65110
CEMBULK	81900
CEMENT CARRIER	56710
CEMENT KING	82280
CEMENTIA	82150
CEMENTO PUERTO RICO	39650
CEMENTO PUERTO RICO	40070
CENTAUR	03180
CENTAURMAN	59000
CENTAURMAN	75180
CENTAURO	54010
CENTAURO	80770
CENTAUROS	31670
CENTAURUS	11663
CENTRAL CRUISER	61530
CENTRAL CRUISER	72030
CENTURION BULKER	60392
CENTURY	55820
CENTURY	56621
CEPHALONIA	38220
CEPHEUS	66221
CERAM SEA	14210
CERDIC FERRY	23330
CERESIO	06600
CERINTHUS	48751
CERINTHUS	75571
CERNA	13734
CERRO PELADO	12791
CERVANA	65972
CERVINIA II	29510
CERVO	03992
CESARE D'AMICO	26231
CETRA CENTAURUS	65840
CETRA NORMA	77448
CETRA VELA	68101
CETUS	11664
CEUTA	65974
CEZANNE	48401
CHAC	54680
CHAC	66160
CHACO	48371
CHAI TRADER	08120
CHAIKA	89461
CHAITEN	06311
CHALLENGER I	45740
CHALLWA No 2	22771
CHALLWA No 2	93401
CHALLWA V	92630
CHALMEVERETT	21440
CHAMBORD	57947
CHAMNARN SAMUT	61655
CHAMPAGNE	68100
CHAMPEX	15292
CHAMPLAIN	84260
CHAMWINO	06063
CHANAKYA	55221
CHANAKYA	57251
CHANDA	48141
CHANG AN	41321
CHANG CHUN	61550
CHANG CHUN	72040
CHANG HAI	55950
CHANG HAI	57080
CHANG HU	65540
CHANG HUA	29280
CHANG HUA	29522
CHANG PEI	92714
CHANGDE	30930
CHANGDU	30423
CHANGMING	10366
CHANGNING	10579
CHANGNING	15349
CHANGSHU	01170
CHANGTING	05371
CHANGXING	80891
CHANTALA FORTUNE	48590
CHANTENAY	75877
CHANTILLY	20020
CHAPAEV	33914
CHAPARRAL	44730
CHAPAYEVSK	12141
CHAR CHUN	07490
CHAR HANG	24293
CHAR HO	05071
CHAR HOONG	45833
CHAR HUI	03400
CHAR HWA	14791
CHAR KANG	24292
CHAR KUO	03401
CHAR LOONG	45832
CHAR LY	24294
CHAR MOU	03402
CHAR TAH	03403
CHAR YIH	14620
CHAR YUENG	24291
CHARALAMBOS	70380
CHARALAMBOS F	56988
CHARALAMBOS M. PATERAS	31930
CHARDZHOV	85883
CHARISMA N	46611
CHARISMA N.	52781
CHARITY	26791
CHARLES LYKES	52521
CHARLES PIGOTT	55703
CHARLES PIGOTT	58273
CHARLES SCHIAFFINO	94120
CHARLESTON	74478
CHARLIE	38150
CHARLOTTE BASTIAN	61705
CHARLOTTE BASTIAN	71075
CHARLOTTE KOGEL	71849
CHARLOTTE LYKES	00083
CHARLOTTE LYKES	00233
CHARLOTTE S	91322
CHARLOTTENBORG	04420
CHARM	51352
CHARM	52702
CHARM	84012
CHARRUA	23600
CHARTA	80570
CHARTRES	19910
CHASTINE MAERSK	01442
CHATTAGRAM	89222
CHATYR-DAG	11943
CHAUMONT	57948
CHAVEZ	46711
CHAYA	86010
CHAZHMA	07551
CHAZHMA	39110
CHE HAI No 1	33680
CHE HAI No 2	33681
CHE HAI No 103	86097
CHEBOKSARY	39987
CHECHEKU	27214
CHEER KING	29750
CHEER MAY	56660
CHEER SONG	07410
CHEER SPIRIT	28000
CHEKHOV	12342
CHELIA	84077
CHELM	03233
CHELM	03622
CHELSEA PIONEER	70250
CHELYABINSK	22844
CHELYABINSK	34474
CHEMICAL CHALLENGER	41770
CHEMICAL DISCOVERER	94272
CHEMIE CARRIER	87080
CHEMIK	47612
CHEMIK	76630
CHEMIST LUTETIA	56251
CHEMIST LUTETIA	75231
CHEMTRANS WEGA	63650
CHENAB	15252
CHENGTU	82751
CHENNAI JAYAM	45960
CHENNAI MUYARCHI	78180
CHENNAI OOKKAM	45961
CHENNAI PERUMAI	45962
CHENNAI SADHANAI	45963
CHENNAI SELVAM	45964
CHENONCEAUX	57949
CHEOG YANG	94871
CHEOG YANG HO	94870
CHEONGWIND	17371
CHERCHELL	76221
CHERCHELL	76901
CHEREMKHOVO	10434
CHEREPOVETS	83680
CHERNIGOV	31875
CHERNISHEVSKIY	20793
CHERNOGORSK	12142
CHERNOMORSKAYA SLAVA	93785
CHERNOVTSY	39979
CHERNYAKHOVSK	00343
CHERNYAKHOVSK	01023
CHERNYAKHOVSK	21602
CHERNYSHEVSKIY	12362
CHERRY	14175
CHERRY	58170
CHERRY BAGUS	89430
CHERRY BARON	44030
CHERRY BUNGA	89790
CHERRY CHANTEK	90900
CHERRY CHEPAT	40120
CHERRY CRYSTAL	15260
CHERRY EARL	44820
CHERRY FLOWER	58157
CHERRY ISLAND	86612
CHERRY JET	44910
CHERRY LAJU	29831
CHERRY LORD	69860
CHERRY MANIS	91330
CHERRY MOLEK	27450
CHERRY NES	67380
CHERRY PARK	44170
CHERRY SINDIA	29832
CHERRY SINGA	01201
CHERRY VESTA	38250
CHERRYFIELD	61074
CHERRYFIELD	71264
CHERVONOGRAD	12143
CHESHIRE	56871
CHESLEY A. CROSBIE	67200
CHEUNG CHAU	26930
CHEUNG CHAU	13994
CHEVALIER DARBY	14600
CHEVALIER DE BLOIS	78003
CHEVALIER PAUL	73446
CHEVALIER PAUL	80376
CHEVALIER ROZE	73445
CHEVALIER ROZE	80375
CHEVALIER VALBELLE	73444
CHEVALIER VALBELLE	80374
CHEVRON ARIZONA	53274
CHEVRON ARIZONA	58434
CHEVRON BRUSSELS	58240
CHEVRON CALIFORNIA	64253
CHEVRON COLORADO	53271
CHEVRON COLORADO	58431
CHEVRON COPENHAGEN	55704
CHEVRON COPENHAGEN	58274
CHEVRON EDINBURGH	55705
CHEVRON EDINBURGH	58275
CHEVRON EINDHOVEN	38050
CHEVRON FELUY	55702
CHEVRON FELUY	58272
CHEVRON HAWAII	64254
CHEVRON LONDON	58241
CHEVRON LOUISIANA	53272
CHEVRON LOUISIANA	58432
CHEVRON MADRID	43990
CHEVRON MISSISSIPPI	64255
CHEVRON NAGASAKI	55700
CHEVRON NAGASAKI	58270
CHEVRON NEDERLAND	43991
CHEVRON NORTH AMERICA	54494
CHEVRON NORTH AMERICA	54924
CHEVRON NORTH AMERICA	55724
CHEVRON OREGON	53273
CHEVRON OREGON	58433
CHEVRON PERTH	55701
CHEVRON PERTH	58271
CHEVRON SOUTH AMERICA	54493
CHEVRON SOUTH AMERICA	54923
CHEVRON SOUTH AMERICA	55723
CHEVRON THE HAGUE	69592
CHEVRON THE HAGUE	86432
CHEVRON WASHINGTON	53270
CHEVRON WASHINGTON	58430
CHEYENNE	51670
CHI CHING	77950
CHI GRAND	10152
CHI HO	26024
CHI KONG	31240
CHI LEE	07150
CHI SONG	77940
CHI STAR	46334
CHI TAI	41680
CHI YUEN	12201
CHIARA	92974
CHIBA	46515
CHIDAMBARAM	06800
CHIEFTAIN	48053
CHIEFTAIN BULKER	60390
CHIEH HSING	29760
CHIEH JEN	05750
CHIEH JEN	30700
CHIEH LAI	29780
CHIEH SHENG	28090
CHIEH TEH	13921
CHIEH TEH	14831
CHIEKAWA MARU	77810
CHIEN SHE No 9	43070
CHIEN SHE No 12	43071
CHIGIRIN	12145
CHIHAYA	73271
CHIHAYA	77771
CHIHIROSAN MARU	77200
CHIKUBU MARU	94880
CHIKUGO MARU	77210
CHIKUHO MARU	77211
CHIKUMA MARU	75710
CHIKUMA MARU	89670
CHIL BO SAN	92780
CHILBAR	37260
CHILLAN	06321
CHILTERN PRINCE	81781
CHIMISTE SAYID	56254
CHIMISTE SAYID	75234
CHIMO	50151
CHINA CONTAINER	09830
CHINDE	89340
CHINON	57950
CHINTA	12760
CHINTA	81710
CHIOS AEINAFTIS	88020
CHIOS CAPTAIN	62436
CHIOS CLIPPER	34225
CHIOS MERCHANT	53471
CHIOS PRIDE	34208
CHIPKA	21800
CHIQUITA	85010
CHITA	71361
CHITA	67351
CHITA MARU	77201
CHITOS ARK	14621
CHIYODA	61901
CHKALOV	17505
CHKALOV DZERZHINSK	39983
CHLOE	46585
CHOAPA	21360
CHOCANO	07941
CHOCHLIK	87742
CHOKAI MARU	77225
CHOKO MARU	54570
CHOKO MARU	54950

CHOLGUAN	06324
CHONGMING	24980
CHOPIN	45030
CHORZOW	50461
CHRIS ISA	64854
CHRIS ISA	91034
CHRISOULA K	27690
CHRISTA THIELEMANN	51760
CHRISTIAN IV	19150
CHRISTIAN MAERSK	01443
CHRISTIAN VIELJEUX	05121
CHRISTIAN VIELJEUX	59871
CHRISTIANA TRANSOCEANIC	41190
CHRISTIANE SCHULTE	73990
CHRISTIANSBORG	04421
CHRISTINA	02851
CHRISTINA	24120
CHRISTINA	38241
CHRISTINA	38711
CHRISTINA	62027
CHRISTINA B	34870
CHRISTINA C.	61300
CHRISTINA C	62620
CHRISTINA CLAUSEN	74340
CHRISTINA TH	42340
CHRISTINE I	41760
CHRISTINE FIRST	88671
CHRISTL HERMANN	07510
CHRISTO BOTEV	49471
CHRISTO BOTEV	49741
CHRISTO BOTEV	48431
CHRISTO SMIRNENSKI	28950
CHRISTOFFER OLDENDORFF	53711
CHRISTOFFER OLDENDORFF	78150
CHRISTOFOROS	36072
CHRISTOFOROS	41792
CHRISTOPHER LYKES	00084
CHRISTOPHER LYKES	00234
CHRISTOPHER S	78600
CHRISTOS K	30230
CHRISTOS K	61465
CHRISTOS M	27961
CHRISTOS S.T. ARAPAKIS	05760
CHRISTOS S T ARAPAKIS	30670
CHRYANTHI	29730
CHRYS	28856
CHRYSANTHEMUM	19200
CHRYSANTHI G L	57186
CHRYSANTHY H	39340
CHRYSANTHY M LEMOS	62791
CHRYSANTHY M LEMOS	67551
CHRYSOULLA H	81810
CHRYSOVALANDOU TRIA	09600
CHRYSSI	68983
CHRYSSOPIGI II	00840
CHRYSSOULA II	25131
CHRZANOW	82266
CHUGUYEV	12144
CHUKOTKA	22721
CHUKOTKA	25842
CHULMLES	11431
CHUMIKAN	39111
CHUN HU	36742
CHUN JIN	61551
CHUN JIN	72041
CHUN SUNG	82561
CHUN UNG	61479
CHUN WOO	54523
CHUN WOO	55443
CHUN WOO	55733
CHUNLIN	06031
CHURKIN	45115
CICERO	33260
CIDADE DE ALCANTARA	22837
CIDADE DE AVEIRO	24200
CIDLA	56241
CIECHANOW	79874
CIECHOCINEK	81862
CIELO BIANCO	52205
CIELO BIANCO	65155
CIELO DI GENOVA	48973
CIELO DI NAPOLI	55790
CIELO DI NAPOLI	64651
CIELO DI ROMA	66199
CIELO DI SALERNO	66200
CIELO ROSSO	44850
CIEPLICE ZDROJ	81865
CIKOLO	66952
CIKOLO	70992
'CIMARRON' class	45040
CIMBRIA	88450
CIMPULUNG	82227
CINDERELLA	47530
CINDREWL	13735
CINULIA	40201
CIRCLE PIONEER	81430
CIRO SECONDO	39250
CIRO SECONDO	39272
CIRO TERZO	80410
CIROLANA	22300
CIRON	58940
CIS BROVIG	58911
CIS BROVIG	65301
CISSUS	61198
CITIALI	69862
CITTA DI GENOVA	28591
CITTA DI META	22710
CITTA DI NAPOLI	01270
CITTA DI NUORO	01271
CITTA DI SAVONA	38720
CITY OF CANTERBURY	48512
CITY OF DUNDEE	23141
CITY OF DUNDEE	28341
CITY OF DUNDEE	32003
CITY OF DURBAN	08421
CITY OF DURBAN	08981
CITY OF EDINBURGH	08412
CITY OF FLORENCE	73883
CITY OF FLORENCE	87263
CITY OF GENOA	73884
CITY OF GENOA	87264
CITY OF HARTLEPOOL	75582
CITY OF HYDRA	11240
CITY OF IPSWICH	75583
CITY OF LEEDS	23143
CITY OF LEEDS	28343
CITY OF LEEDS	32004
CITY OF MIDLAND 41	19560
CITY OF MILAN	73880
CITY OF MILAN	87260
CITY OF OXFORD	75584
CITY OF PERTH	75581
CITY OF PIRAEUS	22060
CITY OF PLYMOUTH	75580
CITY OF RHODOS	16431
CITY OF TEMA	51150
CITY OF WINCHESTER	48510
CITY OF YORK	48513
CIUDAD DE ARMENIA	53373
CIUDAD DE ARMENIA	62763
CIUDAD DE BADAJOZ	16532
CIUDAD DE BADAJOZ	17592
CIUDAD DE BARCELONA	33400
CIUDAD DE BARRANCABERMEJA	69010
CIUDAD DE BARRANQUILLA	07371
CIUDAD DE BARRANQUILLA	15174
CIUDAD DE BARRANQUILLA	93050
CIUDAD DE BOGOTA	04850
CIUDAD DE BUCARAMANGA	04851
CIUDAD DE BUENAVENTURA	04852
CIUDAD DE BURGOS	33401
CIUDAD DE CACERES	16534
CIUDAD DE CACERES.	17594
CIUDAD DE CADIZ	18050
CIUDAD DE CALI	08081
CIUDAD DE COLONIA	17630
CIUDAD DE COMPOSTELA	01291
CIUDAD DE CUCUTA	04853
CIUDAD DE FORMOSA	17450
CIUDAD DE GRANADA	33402
CIUDAD DE HUESCA	33410
CIUDAD DE IBAGUE.	08082
CIUDAD DE IBIZA	20980
CIUDAD DE LA LAGUNA	19280
CIUDAD DE LA PLATA	17451
CIUDAD DE MANIZALES	04440
CIUDAD DE MANTA	08080
CIUDAD DE MARCAIBO	12992
CIUDAD DE MEDELLIN	04441
CIUDAD DE NEIVA	53371
CIUDAD DE NENA	62761
CIUDAD DE PAMPLONA	24440
CIUDAD DE PASTO	15171
CIUDAD DE PASTO	53374
CIUDAD DE PASTO	62764
CIUDAD DE PEREIRA	15172
CIUDAD DE POPAYAN	53370
CIUDAD DE POPAYAN	62760
CIUDAD DE QUITO	53375
CIUDAD DE QUITO	62765
CIUDAD DE SANTA MARTA	53372
CIUDAD DE SANTA MARTA	62762
CIUDAD DE SEVILLA	08180
CIUDAD DE SEVILLA	09440
CIUDAD DE SEVILLA	16533
CIUDAD DE SEVILLA	17593
CIUDAD DE TARIFA	17210
CIUDAD DE TOLEDO	10110
CIUDAD DE TUNJA	15175
CIUDAD DE TUNYA	07372
'CL 10' type	45530
'CL 10' type	53560
'CL 10' type	59720
'CL 10' type	67240
CLABUCET	11679
CLAIRE A. TSAVLIRIS	49111
CLAN GRAHAM	07660
CLAN MACGILLIVRAY	07770
CLAN MACGREGOR	07771
CLANSMAN	18160
CLARA CLAUSEN	50880
CLARA MAERSK	01444
CLARE	07264
CLARITA	28440
CLASSIC	62962
CLAUDE	75680
CLAUDE	88530
CLAUDIA KOGEL	06622
CLAYMORE	22360
CLEMENTINE	06317
CLEO	45250
CLEO	82190
CLEON	43650
CLEOPATRA	13760
CLEOPATRA	18251
CLEOPATRA II	39010
CLERK-MAXWELL	54740
CLERK-MAXWELL	66110
CLERVAUX	12691
CLERVILLE	76260
CLIFF QUAY	42440
CLIFFORD MAERSK	01445
CLIMAX EMERALD	28600
CLIMAX JADE	34920
CLIMAX PEARL	11540
CLIMAX RUBY	08100
CLIMAX SAPPHIRE	28601
CLIMAX TOPAZ	34921
CLODIA	33471
CLOUD	91180
CLOVERBANK	05236
CLUJ	39661
CLYDE	43340
'CLYDE' class	51270
'CLYDE' class	52410
CLYDEBANK	03671
CLYDEBANK	03731
CLYMENE	61703
CLYMENE	71073
CLYMENIA	48110
CLYTONEUS	65781
CLYTONEUS	70201
CO-OP GRAIN	73365
CO-OP GRAIN II	73368
COALINGA	59941
COALINGA	67931
COASTAL CALIFORNIA	38810
COASTAL SPIRIT	70520
COASTAL TEXAS	37200
COASTAL TEXAS	38380
COASTAL TRADER	93934
COASTAL TRANSPORT	55331
COASTAL TRANSPORT	70301
COBALT MARU	32470
COBAN	41361
COBAN	41531
COBARGO	27870
COBARGO	34420
COBETAS	48058
COBRES	39421
COCKROW	83266
COCLERDUE	35584
COCLERDUE	36433
COCLERTRE	35593
COCLERTRE	36493
CODLEA	82113
CODLEA	82393
COFFEE TRADER	02940
COHO	17230
COLDITZ	78733
COLDITZ	89983
COLLO	75651
'COLNE'	88610
'COLNE' type (Modified)	90076
COLOMBIA MARU	07764
COLOMBIA MARU	07817
COLOMBO VENTURE	66870
COLOMBO VENTURE	91460
COLONEL PLEVIN II	02330
COLORADO	05091
COLOSSUS	06621
COLUMBA	11660
COLUMBA	16701
COLUMBIA	16370
COLUMBIA	66340
COLUMBIA STAR	08881
'COLUMBUS 44' type	47220
COLUMBUS AMERICA	73531
COLUMBUS AMERICA	82701
COLUMBUS AUSTRALIA	73530
COLUMBUS AUSTRALIA	82700
COLUMBUS CALIFORNIA	56121
COLUMBUS CALIFORNIA	59771
COLUMBUS COROMANDEL	49642
COLUMBUS NEW ZEALAND	73532
COLUMBUS NEW ZEALAND	82702
COLUMBUS VENTURE	10390
COLUMBUS VERONICA	06430
COLUMBUS VICTORIA	73520
COLUMBUS VIRGINIA	73521
COLUMBUS WELLINGTON	73522
COMANDANTE VILC ACUNA	75950
COMARA	22520
COMBATE DE PALMAMOCHA	76570
COMBI TRADER	52720
COMELUCK GLORY	10999
COMELUCK GLORY	34157
COMET	05960
COMET	60089
COMMANDANT HENRY	79580
COMMANDANTE CAMILO CIENFUEGOS	10276
COMMANDANTE CAMILO CIENFUEGOS	15186
'COMMANDER' class	51740
'COMMANDER' class	84060
COMMENCEMENT	25072
COMMODORE CLIPPER	87311
COMMODORE ENTERPRISE	73610
COMMONWEALTH	37770
COMMONWEALTH	38800
COMPIEGNE	19670
COMTE DE NICE	32431
CONALCO	36520
CONALCO	43500
CONASTOGA	66210
CONCEPCION MARINO	17170
CONCEPCION MARINO	32320
'CONCORD' type	52850
'CONCORD' type	53040
CONCORDE	65940
CONCORDIA	67940
CONCORDIA DANAOS	30902
CONCORDIA ION	30900
CONCORDIA LAGO	07060
CONCORDIA SKY	13320
CONCORDIA STAR	48424
CONCORDIA STAR	49464
CONCORDIA STAR	49514
CONCORDIA TADJ	13540
CONCORDIA TALEB	13541
CONCORDIA TAREK	13542
CONCORDIA VIKING	14000
CONDATA	06315
CONDE DEL CADAGUA	80460
CONDOCK I	92270
CONDOCK I	92440
CONDOCK II	92271
CONDOCK II	92441
CONDOR	14284
CONDOR	71743
CONDOR	72130
CONDOR	76470
CONDOR	81413
CONDOR	84932
CONDORA	06314
CONFEDERATION	19020
CONFIDENCE	25101
CONG HUA	61950
CONGO	10672
CONGO	13511
CONISTER	74200
CONISTER	79330
CONNACHT	16490
CONNIE	39320
CONNY	26061
CONQUEROR BULKER	60393
CONRADO BENITEZ	27070
CONSORTIUM I	22691
CONSTANCE	60155
CONSTANCIA	53480
CONSTANCIA	61280
CONSTANTA	17661
CONSTANTINE	58931
CONSTANTINOS T	13750
CONSTANTINOS T	14780
CONSTELLATION	09160
CONSTELLATION	09431
CONTAINER ENTERPRISE	87320
CONTAINER VENTURER	87321
CONTI ALMANIA	58714
CONTI ALMANIA	59644
CONTI ALMANIA	61724
CONTI LIBAN	45340
CONTI MISR	58660
CONTINENTAL CARRIER	46886
CONTINENTAL FRIENDSHIP	77879
CONTINENTAL PIONEER	52801
CONTINENTAL SHIPPER	52800
CONTINENTAL TRADER	77879
CONTMAR	75831
CONTOVELLO	35630
CONTOVELLO	69400
CONTRACT CARRIER	51871
CONTRACT MARINER	51870
CONTRACT TRADER	51872
CONVEYOR	82910
COPACABANA	03091
COPIAPO II	34951
COPIHUE	81600
CORABANK	03670
CORABANK	03730
CORAGGIO	54512
CORAIN 1	04667
CORAIN 2	04668
CORAJE	59371
CORAL	27201
CORAL	38750
CORAL	46160
CORAL CHIEF	82851
CORAL ISIS	60372
CORAL ISIS	64683
CORAL MAEANDRA	82180
CORAL PRINCESS	09490
CORAL VOLANS	57611
CORAL VOLANS	62252
CORANTIJN	85290
CORDI	28791
CORDIALITY	48100
CORDILLERA	14281
CORDILLERA	71741
CORDILLERA	81411
CORDILLERA EXPRESS	73401
CORDILLERA EXPRESS	82711
CORIANDER	03513
CORINA	55001
CORINA	71691
CORINTHIAKOS	40291
CORINTHIAN	69930
CORINTHIAN REEFER	33930
CORINTO MARU	04410
CORIOLANUS	18710
CORK	24361
CORMORAN	16021
CORNELIA MAERSK	01441
CORNELIS BROERE	76334
CORNELIS BROERE	88724
CORNER BROOK	51701
CORNER BROOK	52291
CORNUAILLES	33210
COROMUEL	19295
COROMUEL	23703
CORONA	20642
CORONA	83363
CORONA	83453
CORONA AUSTRALE	35461
CORONA BOREALE	35591
CORONA BOREALE	36491
CORONIA	61152
CORRADO	89180
CORRAGIO	63892
CORRAL	14282
CORRAL	71742
CORRAL	81412
CORREGIDOR	05431
CORREZE	51072
CORRIE BROERE	66602
CORRIE BROERE	75152
CORRIENTES II	48370
CORRIERE DEL SUD	08511
CORSE	32430
CORSICA MARINA	19191
CORSICA NOVA	19141
CORSICA SERENA	19381
CORSICA STAR	19580
CORSICA VIVA	32721
CORSICANA	66211
CORTEMAGGIORE	35820
CORTINA	03280
COSMAS	57650
COSMOPOLITAN	40590
COSMOPOLITAN II	43920
COSMOS	34896
COSMOTOR ACE	47020
COSTA RICA	56595
COSTAMAR	39620
COSTAS	50070
COSTAS G.	91391
COSTIA PEFANIS	82161
COSTIS	47214
COSWIG	71916
COTENTIN	32951
COTES DU NORD	51071
COTINGA	75483
COURAGE	13803
COURSON	14926
COURSON	15737
COUTANCES	17300
COUTANCES	93160
COVADONGA	08051
COVADONGA	12990
COVADONGA	52300
COVE	14554
COVE COMMUNICATOR	38550
COVE EXPLORER	65502
COVE LEADER	38820
COVE SAILOR	38031
COVE SPIRIT	44560
COVE TRADE	36655
COVODORO	36330
COWAL	20862
COYOLES	11170
CP DISCOVERER	77971
CP TRADER	77972
CP VOYAGEUR	77970
CRAFTSMAN	51240
CRAIGABOY	73620
CRAIGANTLET	73760
CRAIGANTLET	75860
CRAIGMORE	88400
CRAIGWOOD	73761
CRAIGWOOD	75861
CRAIOVA	41311
CRANIA	40202
CRATER	11661
CRAZY HARRY	90894
CREDO	64148
CRESCENCE	74210
CRESCO	46904
CRESCO	83342
CRESTBANK	04770
CRESTENA	53393
CRESTENA	80343
CRETE	85400
CREUSE	51070
CRISANA	55781
CRISANA	56481
CRISPI	14404

CRISTINA MONTANARI 81471
CRISTOBAL 07380
CRISTOFORD COLOMBO 09110
CRNA GORA 00770
CROWN PRINCE 75585
CRUSADER 82540
CRUZ DEL SUR 90893
CRUZEIRO DO SOL 46940
CRUZEIRO DO SOL 47100
CRYOMAR 63740
CRYOMAR 81680
CRYSTAL 27490
CRYSTAL 84620
CRYSTAL 88340
CRYSTAL ISLAND 40425
CRYSTAL ISLAND 42335
CRYSTAL ISLAND 42595
CSOKONAI 06140
CUBA 36921
CUBA 43821
CUBAHAMA 42530
CUGIR 82223
CUMULUS 29301
CUMULUS 34070
CUNARD CONQUEST 16861
CUNARD COUNTESS 16860
CUNENE 81661
CUNENE 82661
CUNEWALDE 46371
CUNEWALDE 47071
CUNSKI 89130
CUPID 59612
CUPID 71922
CURACAO MARU 04411
CURITIBA 06700
CURRENT EXPRESS 82052
CURRENT EXPRESS 91452
CURRENT TRADER 82051
CURRENT TRADER 91451
CURRO 64149
CURTEA DE ARGES 06143
CURTIS CAPRICORN 74630
CURTIS CAPRICORN 78120
CUU LONG I 35920
CUU LONG II 35921
CUZCO 31900
CYCLOPS 65780
CYCLOPS 70200
CYCLOPUS 59830
CYCNUS 76812
CYGNUS 11662
CYGNUS 66222
CYMBELINE 75250
CYNTHIA G 04927
CYNTHLEMA 26820
CYPRESS KING 63000
CYPRESS POINT 88220
CYPRIAN 56415
CYPRIAN 67835
CYPRIAN 68435
CYPROS 86790
CYRNOS 20670
CYRUS 49831
CYS INTEGRITY 69253
CYS INTEGRITY 70553
CZANTORIA 68921
CZESTOCHOWA 15081
CZWARTACY AL 59223
CZWARTACY AL 74543

D

'D-9' class 08680
D. C. COLEMAN 72290
D. C. COLEMAN 77160
DA CHANG ZHEN 92204
DA CHANG ZHEN 92244
DA HONG QIAO 58611
DA HONG QIAO 81011
DA HONG QIAO 90511
DA JIN CHUAN 92203
DA JIN CHUAN 92243
DA LONG TIAN 58610
DA LONG TIAN 81010
DA LONG TIAN 90510
DA MOSTO 03461
DA QING No 10 40662
DA QING No 11 40663
DA QING No 13 41050
DA QING No 14 40810
DA QING No 15 40060
DA QING No 15 42980
DA QING No 16 40560
DA QING No 17 38614
DA QING No 34 36950
DA QING No 35 40670
DA QING No 36 35720
DA QING No 37 36700
DA QING No 38 70290
DA QING No 39 40820
DA QING No 41 65551
DA QING No 41 85781
DA QING 136 38331
DA QING 136 44691
DA QING No 216 76250
DA QING No 217 76251
DA QING 235 44690
DA QING 235 38330
DA QING 250 65290
DA QING No 251 38700
DA QING No 252 60724
DA QING No 253 38690
DA QING No 410 39930
DA QING No 410 40570
DA QING SHAN 58613
DA QING SHAN 81013
DA QING SHAN 90513
DA SHA PING 71853
DA SHI QIAO 92202
DA SHI QIAO 92242
DA SHI ZHAI 71854
DA VERRAZANO 04050
DAAN 92231
DABEMA 25271
DABEMA 87424
DACCA 40760
DACCA 89223
DACEBANK 04670
DACHENG 62190
DACHENG 62450
DACIA 55782
DACIA 56482
DADABHAI NAOROJI 71632
DADE 92200
DADE 92240
DADO 80422
DAE YANG 61636
DAFFODIL B 36830
DAFFODIL B 37990
DAFNOS 30172
DAGESTAN 83439
DAGMAR SKOU 86703
DAGNY 38191
DAGNY 38741
DAGONYS 57200
DAGUS 33670
DAHRA 66621
DAHRA 76241
DAI HAI 83080
DAIRYO MARU 71381
DAIRYO MARU 86631
DAISETSU 32571
DAISHIN MARU 95030
DAISHIN MARU No 11 94860
DAISHIN MARU No 12 94910
DAISHIN MARU No 15 95060
DAISHIN MARU No 16 95061
DAISHIN MARU No 22 94911
DAISHIN MARU No 23 95050
DAITOKU MARU No 31 69340
DAIWA MARU 31580
DALAVIK 85740
D'ALBERTIS 03460
DALIA 82151
DALIA I 83988
DALIA II 83989
DALIA A 28860
DALLIA 53146
DALLIA 66076
DALLINGTON 78910
DALMA 58310
DALMA 63962
DALMACIJA 02450
DALMAR 71200
DALMOR 11641
DALNEGORSK 15464
DALNERECHENSK 22845
DALNERECHENSK 34475
DALNEVOSTOCHNY 85321
DALNIY 22846
DALNIY 34476
DALNIY VOSTOK 92381
DALSLAND 51620
DAMAN 22400
DAMIAN 31301
DAMING 92233
DAMMAM 23090
DAMODAR GANGA 54116
DAMODAR GANGA 54586
DAMODAR GENERAL T.J. PARK 73080
DAMODAR GENERAL T J PARK 77790
DAMODAR TANABE 47700
DAMODAR TASAKA 47701
DAN HU 69870
DANA 02260
DANA AFRICA 93361
DANA AMERICA 93360
DANA ANGLIA 17080
DANA ARABIA 93362
DANA CARIBIA 93363
DANA CORONA 01901
DANA FRIO 80983
DANA FRIO 81703
DANA FUTURA 35110
DANA FUTURA 95180
DANA GLORIA 19180
DANA HAFNIA 95181
DANA MAXIMA 95190
DANA REGINA 32200
DANA SCARLETT 19360
DANA SIRENA 01900
DANAE 01711
DANAE 16391
DANAH 49405
DANAH 50965
DANAOS 25911
DANBJORN 23940
DANE 42033
DANGULF MAERSK 67100
DANIA 24000
DANIA 50481
DANIA 73741
DANIA 83071
DANIA HAFNIA 35111
DANIAN GAS 55350
DANIELA 13386
DANIELLA 89610
DANIELLE 78682
DANILA 55964
DANILA 56724
DANILO NECHAY 86187
DANING 92201
DANING 92241
DANISH ARROW 67470
DANISH DART 67471
DANJIANG 26520
DANKO 12415
DANMARK 20090
DANNEBROG 18620
DANSBORG 92460
DANSBORG 92510
DANUBE 69430
DANWOOD ICE 92280
DANWOOD ICE 92450
DAOUD BEN AICHA 84264
DAPHNA 55190
DAPHNE 01710
DAPHNE 16390
DAPHNE 42000
DAPHNE 46107
DAPHNE 53147
DAPHNE 66077
DAPHNE 70361
DAPHNEMAR 12914
DAPO ALECOS 39140
DAPO ALECOS 45190
DAPO ANTIKLIA 57432
DAPO ANTIKLIA 78632
DAPO SAILOR 36211
DAPO SAILOR 36411
DAPO STAR 36212
DAPO STAR 36412
DAPO TRADER 69451
DAPU 92232
DARASUN 24063
DARIEN 12994
DARIEN 33811
DARINA 66080
DARNIA 94151
DARNITZA 36912
DARNITZA 43812
DARPO DUA 40371
DARPO SATU 39640
DART AMERICA 76952
DART ATLANTIC 76951
DART CANADA 74520
DART EUROPE 76950
D'ARTAGNAN 63033
DARVISH VANANCA 42320
DARWIN TRADER 82960
DARYAL 11831
DARYAL 15401
DASHAKI 48641
DASHAKI 49011
DASHAVA 83440
DASHWOOD 64471
DATIAN 62191
DATIAN 62451
DAUGAVA 22847
DAUGAVA 34477
DAUGAVPILS 60620
DAUGAVPILS 62580
DAUNT ROCK 76150
DAUPHIN DE CHERBOURG 08501
DAURIYA 11462
DAURIYA 93871
DAVAO 33810
DAVAO 33880
DAVAO CITY 26170
DAVID P. REYNOLDS 52550
DAVID SALMAN 84850
DAVID SIQUEIROS 70593
DAVOS 29880
DAVYDOV 09381
DAWN 05961
DAYAKA DUA 67270
DAYAKA SATU 82440
DAYAKA TIGA 61651
DAYNAVA 23547
DAYSPRING 57141
D'AZEGLIO 14405
DE DU. 04610
DE HOOP 87930
DE HUA 29553
DE KASTRI 18350
DE RODE TULP 74371
DE WITTE TULP 74372
DE YIN 14051
DE YIN 14231
DEA BROVIG 37550
DEA MARIS 65471
DEBALTSEVO 83430
DEBLIN 34370
DEBORAH I 91760
DEBRAEVERETT 33831
DEBRECEN 70791
DEBRECEN 89216
'DECKSHIP' type 92950
'DECKSHIP' type 95160
DECORATOR 35644
DECORATOR 41304
DEDOVSK 83443
DEEPA RAYA 22930
DEEPA SAKTI 42075
DEEPSEA MINER II 36530
DEFIANCE 01490
DEFIANCE 17710
DEGAS 48400
DEKA NAVIGATOR 45830
DEKABRIST 03704
DEKABRIST 03823
DEKKA CONCORD 72081
DEL CAMPO 92171
DEL CAMPO 92851
DEL MONTE 92172
DEL MONTE 92852
DEL MUNDO 92170
DEL MUNDO 92850
DEL ORO 92860
DEL RIO 92861
DEL SOL 92862
DEL VALLE 92174
DEL VALLE 92854
DEL VIENTO 92173
DEL VIENTO 92853
DELAWARE 65801
DELAWARE 74781
DELAWARE 74781
DELAWARE GETTY 36852
DELAWARE SUN 38540
DELAWARE SUN 44810
DELBROS MT. APO II 90160
DELDONA 44050
DELEDDA 32550
DELEDDA 33370
DELESEA 44680
DELFBORG 50240
DELFI 78240
DELFIN 23451
DELFIN ADRIATICO 27711
DELFIN DE SALAZAR 27710
DELFIN DEL CANTABRICO 27712
DELFINI V 24541
DELICIA 92953
DELICIA 95163
DELIMA 30150
DELLYS 75650
DELORIS 73011
DELOS 16551
DELOS 60092
DELOS I 76690
DELOS I 88990
DELPHIC MIRACLE 46712
DELPHIC REEFER 15071
DELPHIC SKY 61890
DELPHINUS 73386
DELTA 59625
DELTA 74010
DELTA BAY 04280
DELTA CARIBE 00018
DELTA CARIBE 02488
DELTA CARIBE 35137
DELTA DUNARII 11705
DELTA MAR 00015
DELTA MAR 02485
DELTA MAR 35134
DELTA NORTE 00017
DELTA NORTE 02487
DELTA NORTE 35136
DELTA SIGMA PI 26290
DELTA SUD 00016
DELTA SUD 02486
DELTA SUD 35135
DELTADRECHT 78690
DELTAGAS 60370
DELTAGAS 64681
DELWIND 77701
DEMARG 09912
DEMETRIOS 46190
DEMETRIS. 12210
DEMOSTHENES V 44360
DEMYAN BEDNYY 14379
DEMYAN KOROTCHENKO 76503
DEN LONG HAI 77481
DENA 39612
DENEB 12242
DENEBOLA 11672
DENEBOLA. 07893
DENEBOLA 83601
DENIS 42040
DENIS M 34891
DENIZATI 63670
DENIZHANLAR 28570
DENIZHANLAR 28310
DENIZLI 34590
DEPUTAT LUTSKIY 13012
DERNA 93935
DERWENT 05321
DESAFIO 33150
DESAFIO 94340
DESANMAR 10490
DESANMAR 15261
DESANMAR 22830
DESCARTES 53860
DESDEMONA 18250
DESEADO 00200
DESERT PRINCE 47933
DESERT QUEEN 47934
DESERT WIND 46501
DESIDERIA F 78481
DESNA 38950
DESNA 39112
DESNA 41940
DESPINA 06491
DESPINA 31750
DESPINA 67321
DESPINA AII 25450
DESPINA A.L. 65990
DESPINA A.L. 70530
DESPINA GIAVRIDIS 45860
DESPINA GIAVRIDIS 46020
DESPO I 87150
DESSAU 78970
DESTRO 32971
DESYATAYA PYATILETKA 11768
DESYATAYA PYATILETKA 34659
DESYATAYA PYATILETKA 79401
DETLEF SCHMIDT 75621
DETROIT 93472
DETTIFOSS 83510
DEUSTO 48059
DEUTSCHLAND 32510
DEUTSCHLAND EXPRESS 05900
DEVA 41313
DEVALI 1 60541
DEVARAYA 56841
DEVON CITY 46871
DEVON CURLEW 59030
DEVON CURLEW 75110
DEVON EXPRESS 14860
DEVONIA 06160
DEVONSHIRE 55601
DEVOTION 47223
DEVYATAYA PYATILETKA 79410
DEWI 31820
DEXENA 18400
DEXENA 22952
DEXING 80892
DEXTER 14530
DHALIT 47753
DHARINI 11410
DHOFAR 86960
DIABAS 73832
DIABAS 77012
DIADEMA 53142
DIADEMA 66072
DIAKAN MASCOT 40340
DIAKAN MASCOT 41132
DIAKAN MASCOT 44942
DIAKLIS 29554
DIALA 64190
DIAMANDO 10401
DIAMANT CAPTAIN 12915
DIAMANTENIA 29541
DIAMANTENIA 30770
DIAMANTIS 29410
DIAMOND 30070
DIAMOND 61120
DIAMOND SUN 53402
DIAMOND SUN 64932
DIANA 23931
DIANA 25400
DIANA 28831
DIANA 55000
DIANA 71690
DIANA 73725
DIANA 83530
DIANA II 20360
DIANA SKOU 86704
DIANE 60740
DIAS 57192
DIAVOLEZZA 46941
DIAVOLEZZA 47101
d IBERVILLE 10850
DICLE 07882
DICLE 15645
DICTO 48341
DIDYMI 61191
DIEGO 13481
DIEGO DE BLASIO 66841
DIEGO SUAREZ 39791
DIERHAGEN 75321
DIES 90750
DIETRICH OLDENDORFF 74720
DIGNITY 26792
DIKA 81850

E

EBALINA	52313
EBN BATUTA	62371
EBN BATUTA	81421
EBN JUBAIR	62370
EBN JUBAIR	81420
EBN MAGID	80752
EBN MAGID	81452
EBO	06644
EBURNA	52310
ECCTONIA	88001
ECKERT OLDENDORFF	72451
ECLAIR	56031
ECO DOURO	72670
ECO GUADIANA	73882
ECO GUADIANA	87262
ECO SADO	50202
ECO SADO	75972
ECO TEJO	50203
ECO TEJO	75973
ECOL SPEZIA	36930
ECUADORIAN REEFER	05111
EDDA	87485
EDDY	30140
EDDYFIRTH	43780
EDELGARD	82290
EDERA	53971
EDERA	79021
EDESSA	56311
EDGAR ANDRE	04231
EDGAR JOURDAIN	66820
EDINBURGH UNIVERSAL	06223
EDINBURGH UNIVERSAL	07452
EDITA	56120
EDITA	59770
EDITH ESSBERGER	72561
EDITH NIELSEN	91480
EDOUARD L.D.	53643
EDOUARD SIMARD	65880
EDOUGH	64967
EDRA	11260
EDUARD CLAUDIUS	13663
EDUARD SYRMUS	12420
EDUARD TOLL	35423
EDUARD VEYDENBAUM	12421
EDUARD WILDE	86083
EDWARD DEMBOWSKI	27180
EDWARD RUTLEDGE	01057
EDWARD STEVINSON	37220
EDY 1	59670
EEKLO	63790
EEKLO	73190
EEMHAVEN	15560
EERBEEK	66973
EERBEEK	91553
EFCHARIS	30220
EFCHARIS	30360
EFDIM HOPE	58574
EFDIM JUNIOR	58575
EFFIGYNY	22480
EFFY	31970
EFI	12165
EFORIE	00530
EFPLOIA	56989
EFSTATHIA	00881
EFSTATHIOS	07200
EFTHITIS	60094
EFTYHIA	45392
EFYRA	69510
EGDA	83139
EGE	01590
EGE MELTEMI	63689
EGEON	37560
EGERSHELD	45114
EGIDIA	09640
EGLANTINE	79740
EGMOND	63422
EGNATIA	20260
EGNAZIA	35700
EGNAZIA	41424
EGORYEVSK	44621
EGTON	06940
EGVEKINOT	31843
EHIME MARU	48950
EIBE OLDENDORFF	06583
EICHSFELD	71682
EICHWALDE	46377
EICHWALDE	47077
EID	86360
EIDANGER	05612
EIDER	64830
EIDER	75622
EIFEL	37290
EIFFEL	49550
EIFFEL	49570
EIGAMOIYA	16260
EIKO MARU	67991
EILDON	75456
EILENBURG	03874
EIR	71902
EIRA	75793
EIRAMA	69231
EIRIK RAUDE	80820
EIRINI L	41780
EIRINI L	45260
EISENBERG	84941
EISENBERG	90601
EISENHUTTENSTADT	86420
EISHO MARU	63362
EISK	11834
EITOKU MARU	60040
EKA DAYA SAMUDERA	01080
EKATERINI	65460
EKATERINI M GOULANDRIS	79181
EKATERINI P	78080
EKATLERINA ZELENKO	78066
EKENES	73600
EKFJORD	56191
EKFJORD	80911
EKHOLOT	09376
EKIMCHAN	85975
EKMAN	72060
EKTON	61380
EKTOR	61990
EKVATOR	12577
EL ARISH	32620
EL CHAMPION	48054
EL CINCO	82001
EL DJAZAIR	34090
EL FLAMINGO	39570
EL GAUCHO	18200
EL GRECO	08210
EL HAG ABDALLA	12164
EL HASSAN	21060
EL HUSSEIN	88010
EL JEM	47061
EL JIANNI	83301
EL JIGUE	12792
EL MALEK FAISAL	87280
EL MALEK KHALED	87281
EL MANSOUR DHABI	87486
EL MEXICANO	55012
EL MEXICANO	55882
EL MEXICANO	56552
EL NIL	21700
EL PASO CONSOLIDATED	53641
EL PASO PAUL KAYSER	63640
EL PASO SONATRACH	53642
EL PODRERO	18201
EL PODRERO	21100
EL QUETZAL	24580
EL SALVADOR	25120
EL SALVADOR	27590
EL TAMBO	39761
EL TOR	32621
EL ZANJON	31520
ELA MANA MOU	74601
ELA MANA MOU	74601
ELAFI	56521
ELAFINA	60410
ELAFINA	69360
ELAMIR FAHD	15881
ELAT	53721
ELAZIG	06730
ELAZIG	31191
ELAZIG	71110
ELBA	39161
ELBAN	85888
ELBE	73902
ELBE EXPRESS	73513
ELBE MARU	08390
ELBIA	59470
ELBJORN	23830
ELBREEZE	00130
ELBRUS	11305
ELBRUS	39993
ELCANO	22650
ELDE	28330
ELDIR	65092
ELDRID	59613
ELDRID	71923
ELDVIK	66831
ELDVIK	91491
ELEANOR DUNBAR	78810
ELEFSIS	59560
ELEFTHERIA	00120
ELEFTHERIOS	61150
ELEFTHERIOS T	06421
ELEISTRIA	47602
ELEISTRIA 1	72173
ELEISTRIA II	36064
ELEISTRIA II	41804
ELEISTRIA III	93560
ELEISTRIA IV	39630
ELEISTRIA V	27570
ELEISTRIA VIII	41280
ELEISTRIA VIII	44990
ELEKRENAY	12422
ELEKTROSTAL	24066
ELENA	43570
ELENA	88600
ELENA	90681
ELENA P	16630
ELENA PEREZ	48211
ELENI A	26410
ELENI K	27571
ELENI V	70860
ELEO MAERSK	48920
ELEO MAERSK	56320
ELEONORA F	80631
ELETS	17931
ELEUROPA	48283
ELFWAIHAT	63396
ELGAVA	44370
ELGER	65091
ELGURDABIA	63397
ELIAS	27821
ELIAS ANGELAKOS	62551
ELIAS K	47754
ELIKON	00410
ELIN S	90943
ELINA	33971
ELINE	87351
ELIOS	51636
ELIPIDA	04510
ELISA	90000
ELISA d'ALESIO	60841
ELISA d'ALESIO	81461
ELISA F	78480
ELISABETH	64511
ELISABETH	82808
ELISABETH	92098
ELISABETH BERG	07501
ELISABETH HOLWERDA	88300
ELISABETH J	37120
ELISABETH MAERSK	48923
ELISABETH MAERSK	56323
ELISABETH OLDENDORFF	71844
ELISABETH ROTH	62103
ELISABETTA MONTANARI	81470
ELISSAR	49853
ELISSAR	50093
ELIZA	56050
ELIZABETH A	18780
ELIZABETH II	52201
ELIZABETH II	65151
ELIZABETH LYKES	05580
ELIZABETH LYKES	14420
ELIZABETH LYKES	14890
ELJIANNI	46521
ELK	76760
ELK	80270
ELLEROS	28810
ELLI	26630
ELLI	42780
ELLINIS	09180
ELLITSA	21550
ELLOBA	26180
ELMINA	69123
ELOCEAN	45800
ELOISEID	59040
ELOISEID	75120
ELOUNDA	81141
ELPEDIO BERVIDES	75961
ELPIDA	28270
ELPIDA	31940
ELPIDA	59252
ELPIDA	62522
ELPIDA	62871
ELPINIKI K	39691
ELPIREA	43520
ELPIS	29461
ELPIS	41210
ELPIS	60095
ELPIS C	25260
ELPIS N	40880
ELQUI	37130
ELS TEEKMAN	75504
ELSA	42570
ELSA K	12893
ELSFLETH	33820
ELTIGEN	86006
ELTON	84366
ELVIRA	66812
ELVIRA EISENSCHNEIDER	23415
ELVIUBA	24899
EMADALA	93094
EMADALA	94164
EMANUEL	11160
EMBA	44122
EMBA	92160
EME	53392
EME	80342
EMEBORG	90535
EMEBORG	91075
EMEKSIZ	32169
EMERALD	60156
EMERALD	75921
EMERALD	92930
EMERALD SEAS	17390
EMERAUDE	63251
EMETSK	22848
EMETSK	34478
EMILIA	33473
EMILIA DEL MAR	87780
EMILIA PLATER	14580
EMILIA S	51031
EMILIA S	82533
EMILIA UNO	71761
EMILIE MAERSK	48922
EMILIE MAERSK	56322
EMILY MOON	93580
EMILY STAR	93581
EMINENCE	75440
EMINENCE	88420
EMIRATES EXPRESS	80190
EMMA BAKKE	24302
EMMA JOHANNA	45841
EMMA MAERSK	48921
EMMA MAERSK	56321
EMMA OLDENDORFF	72450
EMMANUEL COMNINOS	78351
EMMANUEL MARCOU	07240
EMMAPLEIN	75505
EMOULI	43870
EMPRESS OF AUSTRALIA	16410
EMPROS	05328
EMSLAND	19480
EMSLAND	42790
EN GEDI	53831
EN GEDI	69461
ENAK	65090
ENAMEL	24571
ENARXIS	25810
ENARXIS	30960
ENATON	55101
ENATON	57591
ENAYATALLAH	36331
ENCOUNTER BAY	77050
ENDEAVOR	73203
ENDEAVOR	76993
ENDEAVOUR	29110
ENDURANCE	29210
ENDURANCE	68511
ENDURANCE EXPRESS	60157
ENDURANCE FRIENDSHIP	60158
ENERGETYK	47613
ENERGETYK	76631
ENERGY ENDURANCE	60790
ENERGY EVOLUTION	69610
ENERGY GENERATION	69612
ENERGY GREATION	69611
ENERGY GROWTH	54371
ENERGY GROWTH	54820
ENERGY GROWTH	62981
ENERGY MOBILITY	69613
ENERGY PRODUCTION	69614
ENERGY PROSPERITY	68701
ENERGY RESOURCE	69615
ENERGY TRANSPORT	37750
ENERGY VITALITY	69616
ENGELSBERG	85830
ENGLAND	01920
ENGLAND MARU	03680
ENGURE	86242
ENIM	41962
ENNA G	26090
ENRICO C	12740
ENRIQUETA	07667
ENSKERI	36120
ENSKERI	37900
ENTERPRISE	77703
ENTRE RIOS II	48372
EOLIA	61140
EOLIA	81480
EOS	50810
EPAPHUS	12820
EPAPHUS	14440
EPHESTOS	66261
EPIFAN KOVTYUKH	62593
EPIFAN KOVTYUKH	60633
EPIMELIA	60096
EPIMENIDIS	06501
EPIMITHEFS	78270
EPIROS	66370
EPOMEO PRIMO	16650
EPOS	60097
EPSILONGAS	60371
EPSILONGAS	64682
EPTA DAFNES	55200
EPTA VELI	57330
EPTANISSOS	65350
ERAWAN	66051
ERCOLE LAURO	09020
ERDEMIR	57237
EREBUS	36913
EREBUS	43813
ERECHTHION	25270
EREDINE	72339
ERGINA I	61860
ERICH STEINFURTH	23416
ERICSON	13330
ERIDAN	12244
ERIK SIF	64864
ERIK SIF	91044
ERIK WEINERT	12621
ERIKA BOJEN	72120
ERIKA BOJEN	76460
ERIKA BOLTEN	49950
ERIKA BOLTEN	58500
ERIKA JACOB	71412
ERIKA NABER	58551
ERIKA NABER	71871
ERINI PATERA	00381
ERITHIANI	56520
ERLANGEN EXPRESS	08831
ERLANGEN EXPRESS	09031
ERLANGEN EXPRESS	77031
ERLING JARL	17770
ERMA	44127
ERMINIA PRIMA	73030
ERMIS	61991
ERMUA	78183
ERNE	58880
ERNST HAECKEL	17670
ERNST KRENKEL	02271
ERNST MORITZ ARNDT	34215
ERNST SCHNELLER	04232
ERNST TELMAN	17509
ERNST THALMANN	05623
ERNST THALMANN	14453
ERNST THALMANN	62681
ERO	79651
EROFFREY KHABAROV	22223
EROS	08281
ERRADALE	54654
ERRADALE	55075
ERSKINE BRIDGE	54930
ERSKINE BRIDGE	77610
ERVILIA	52311
ERZURUM	57236
ESHEL	80952
ESHKOL	05490
ESHKOL	07950
ESHKOL	61750
ESKISEHIR	26050
ESLA	75270
ESMERALDA	78771
ESMERALDA	88940
ESMERALDAS	85940
ESPANA	74023
ESPENHAIN	79732
ESPERANZA	61350
ESPERANZA	78422
ESPERANZA No 2	85310
ESPEROS	27020
ESPRESSO AZZURRO	20270
ESPRESSO CORINTO	02170
ESPRESSO LIGURIA	32980
ESPRESSO LIVORNO	17271
ESPRESSO LOMBARDIA.	32984
ESPRESSO OLBIA	19120
ESPRESSO RAVENNA	17273
ESPRESSO ROSSO	20274
ESPRESSO SARDEGNA	32981
ESPRESSO SICILIA	32982
ESPRESSO TOSCANA	32983
ESPRESSO VENEZIA	17272
ESQUILINO	24341
ESSAYONS	93460
ESSEN	76813
ESSEX FERRY	21950
ESSI BALTIC	67170
ESSI CAMILLA	77680
ESSI CORAL	67171
ESSI FLORA	86410
ESSI KARI	70220
ESSI KARI	86400
ESSO ABERDEEN	54620
ESSO AFRICA	62842
ESSO ALBANY	65635
ESSO ALBANY	70005
ESSO ANTWERP	66100
ESSO BAHAMAS	70136
ESSO BANGKOK	58840
ESSO BANGKOK	65650
ESSO BATAAN	58850
ESSO BATAAN	65660
ESSO BILBAO	54531
ESSO BILBAO	54791
ESSO BOMBAY	58841
ESSO BOMBAY	65651
ESSO BONAIRE	57808
ESSO BONAIRE	59858
ESSO BONN	57810
ESSO BONN	59860
ESSO BREGA	55630
ESSO BRETAGNE	62805
ESSO BRISBANE	65633
ESSO BRISBANE	70003
ESSO CAERNARVON	85950
ESSO CAERNARVON	86590
ESSO CALEDONIA	57801
ESSO CALEDONIA	59851
ESSO CALLUNDA	65636
ESSO CALLUNDA	70006
ESSO CAMBRIA	57802
ESSO CAMBRIA	59852
ESSO CARDIFF	51360
ESSO CARDIFF	65520
ESSO CARIBBEAN	56400
ESSO CARIBBEAN	59920
ESSO CARIBBEAN	67780
ESSO CASTELLON	66101
ESSO CHILE	38480
ESSO CHITTAGONG	58851
ESSO CHITTAGONG	65661
ESSO CLYDE	58821
ESSO CLYDE	65621
ESSO COPENHAGEN	55453
ESSO COPENHAGEN	57803
ESSO COPENHAGEN	59853
ESSO COPENHAGEN	62804
ESSO DALRIADA	64320
ESSO DEMETIA	64321
ESSO DEUTSCHLAND	54510
ESSO DEUTSCHLAND	63890
ESSO EUROPA	57804
ESSO EUROPA	59854

ESSO EUROPOORT	57807
ESSO EUROPOORT	59857
ESSO EVERETT	65690
ESSO EVERETT	70120
ESSO FAWLEY	65611
ESSO FAWLEY	71891
ESSO FLAME	75690
ESSO FLANDRE	57812
ESSO FLANDRE	59862
ESSO FUJI	59900
ESSO GUAM	65634
ESSO GUAM	70004
ESSO HAFNIA	65637
ESSO HAFNIA	70007
ESSO HALIFAX	65680
ESSO HALIFAX	70110
ESSO HIBERNIA	55451
ESSO HIBERNIA	62801
ESSO HONOLULU	54530
ESSO HONOLULU	54790
ESSO HUMBER	58852
ESSO HUMBER	65662
ESSO INTERAMERICA	58845
ESSO INTERAMERICA	65655
ESSO INVERNESS	75090
ESSO IPSWICH	85951
ESSO IPSWICH	86591
ESSO KARACHI	58846
ESSO KARACHI	65656
ESSO KOBE	58844
ESSO KOBE	65654
ESSO KURE	58849
ESSO KURE	65659
ESSO LIGURIA	55631
ESSO MALACCA	58847
ESSO MALACCA	65657
ESSO MEDITERRANEAN	56403
ESSO MEDITERRANEAN	59923
ESSO MEDITERRANEAN	67783
ESSO MERSEY	58820
ESSO MERSEY	65620
ESSO MILFORD HAVEN	65610
ESSO MILFORD HAVEN	71890
ESSO MONTREAL	65681
ESSO MONTREAL	70111
ESSO NAGASAKI	58848
ESSO NAGASAKI	65658
ESSO NAGOYA	65632
ESSO NAGOYA	70002
ESSO NASSAU	70137
ESSO NEDERLAND	57805
ESSO NEDERLAND	59855
ESSO NORMANDIE	62840
ESSO NORTHUMBRIA	55450
ESSO NORTHUMBRIA	62800
ESSO ORIENT	64411
ESSO OSAKA	54532
ESSO OSAKA	54792
ESSO PENZANCE	75091
ESSO PHILIPPINES	66091
ESSO PICARDIE	62841
ESSO PORT DICKSON	58842
ESSO PORT DICKSON	65652
ESSO PORT JEROME	58830
ESSO PORT JEROME	60570
ESSO PORT JEROME	65638
ESSO PORT JEROME	70008
ESSO PORTOVENERE	55632
ESSO PROVENCE	62806
ESSO PROVIDENCE	65691
ESSO PROVIDENCE	70121
ESSO PURFLEET	70820
ESSO SABA	57809
ESSO SABA	59859
ESSO SAINT JOHN	65682
ESSO SAINT JOHN	70112
ESSO SAINT PETERSBURG	65692
ESSO SAINT PETERSBURG	70122
ESSO SCOTIA	57800
ESSO SCOTIA	59850
ESSO SEVERN.	58822
ESSO SEVERN	65622
ESSO SKANDIA	55454
ESSO SKANDIA	57806
ESSO SKANDIA	59856
ESSO SKANDIA	62803
ESSO SLAGEN	70210
ESSO TENBY	66440
ESSO TORONTO	65693
ESSO TORONTO	70123
ESSO ULIDIA	55452
ESSO ULIDIA	62802
ESSO WARWICKSHIRE	38071
ESSO WESTERNPORT	54210
ESSO WILHELMSHAVEN	57811
ESSO WILHELMSHAVEN	59861
ESSO YOKOHAMA	58843
ESSO YOKOHAMA	65653
ESSO YORK	36850
ESSO ZURICH	66090
ESTADO DA GUANABARA	37890
ESTAFETA OKTYABRYA	12423
ESTEBAN S	21501
ESTEBLICK	59730
ESTEBLICK	67220
ESTEBOGEN	49900
ESTEBOGEN	50340
ESTEFLUT	64741
ESTEFLUT	81771
ESTELLE J	73202
ESTELLE J	76992
ESTELLE MAERSK	48924
ESTELLE MAERSK	56324
ESTETAL	64742
ESTETAL	81772
ESTHER CHARLOTTE SCHULTE	90870
ESTHER DEL MAR	76100
ESTHER SILVANA	50330
ESTHER SILVANA	83670
ESTLAND	80120
ESTONIA	02160
ESTRELLA	11171
ESTRELLA	40040
ESTRELLA	44961
ESTRELLA ANTARTICA	70280
ESTRELLA ARGENTINA	37230
ESTRELLA DEL MAR	15840
ESTRELLA PATAGONICA	65440
ETAI	81331
ETAI	90591
ETERNITY	40690
ETHA RICKMERS	07750

ETHEL EVERARD	70970
ETHEL EVERARD	86370
ETHNIC	59925
ETHNIC	67785
ETROG	05491
ETROG	07951
ETROG	61751
ETTORE	35675
ETTORE	52460
ETTRICK	75457
EUCADIA	00611
EUCLIDE	54760
EUDOCIA	27820
EUGEN SCHONHAAR	23417
EUGENIA II	38731
EUGENIA II	44872
EUGENIA M	86550
EUGENIA V	26340
EUGENIE COTTON	75773
EUGENIE LIVANOS	55551
EUGENIE LIVANOS	63381
EUGENIO C	01240
EUGENIO C	35230
EUGENIUSZ KWIATKOWSKI	14483
EUN HA	81570
EUPLECTA	52312
EURABIA FRIENDSHIP	39080
EURABIA OCEAN	26020
EURABIA PROGRESS	58715
EURABIA PROGRESS	59645
EURABIA PROGRESS	61725
EURABIA WIND	25960
EURO PRINCESS	48640
EURO PRINCESS	49010
EUROBRIDGE PIONIR	75280
EUROBRIDGE PIONIR	80160
EUROCARRIER	71481
EUROFREIGHTER	08581
EUROLINER	08580
EUROLOGGER	62320
EUROPA	08809
EUROPA	09240
'EUROPA' type	58360
EUROPAFARJAN III	17030
EUROPAFARJAN IV	23821
EUROPE	14081
EUROPE II	14080
EUROPEAN EXPRESS	05327
EUROPEAN EXPRESS	12900
EUROPEAN HIGHWAY	94960
EUROPEAN LIBERTY	12890
EUROPEAN MARCHIONESS	26531
EUROPEAN MASTER	49191
EUROPEAN MASTER	52791
EUROPIC FERRY	23310
EUROSAILOR	29870
EUROSEA	46914
EUROTRANSPORT	48312
EUROUNITY	46915
EURYDICE	23140
EURYDICE	28340
'EUSKALDUNA 27' type	48050
EURYLOCHUS	07700
EUSTATHIA	39810
EUTERPE	39020
EUTERPE	44930
EUTERPE	81980
EUTHYMENES	66701
EVA	69450
EVA	71903
EVA ODEN	94182
EVALD TAMMLAAN	12424
EVALI	25273
EVANDROS	34170
EVANGELIA	80540
EVANGELIA C	70680
EVANGELIA C	78110
EVANGELIA S	07210
EVANGELISTO	94691
EVANGELISTRIA	20820
EVANGELISTRIA	22110
EVANGELISTRIA	57130
EVANGELISTRIA IV	23840
EVANGELISTRIA IV	87024
EVANGELOS B	27860
EVANGELOS D	61077
EVANGELOS D	71267
EVANGELOS LEMOS	62550
EVANGELOS M 1	29411
EVANTHIA	68950
EVDOKIA TSIRIS	13203
EVDORI	69511
EVDOXIA K	43330
EVELYN	54560
EVELYN	54960
EVELYN MAERSK	48925
EVELYN MAERSK	56325
EVENSK	36909
EVENSK	43809
EVENSK	85977
EVER	39700
EVER FAITH	62222
EVER FAITH	71132
EVER GLORY	92680
EVER HARMONY	07640
EVER HONOR	46883
EVER RELIANCE	62028
EVER SHINE	10000
EVER SPLENDOR	71221
EVER SPRING	10001
EVER SUMMIT	10002
EVER SUPERB.	10003
EVER VALIANT	08890
EVER VALIANT	74390
EVER VALOR	08895
EVER VALOR	74395
EVER VALUE	08896
EVER VALUE	74396
EVER VICTORY	08891
EVER VICTORY	74391
EVER VIGOR	08893
EVER VIGOR	74393
EVER VITAL	08894
EVER VITAL	74394
EVER VOYAGER	08892
EVER VOYAGER	74392
EVERETT F. WELLS	58233
EVERGREEN	71152
EVERGREEN STATE	18980
EVERSHAGEN	76534
EVGENA	45391
EVGENIA 1	40730

EVGENIY CHAPLANOV	31876
EVGENIY NIKISHIN	93683
EVGENIY NIKONOV	50284
EVGENIY ONUFRIEV	50287
EVIA	26491
EVIMERIA	58158
EVITA	64363
EVITA TH	21500
EVLALIA	06962
EVNIA	60098
EVNIKI	77880
EVOCRYSTAL	91143
EVOICOS GULF	07270
EVOIKOS	85590
EVORON	84361
EVPO ARAMIS	43390
EVPO WAVE	84730
EVRIKA	11944
EVROS	35907
EVROS	41597
EVY L	46694
EWALDEVERETT	21411
EXCELSIOR REEFER	06300
EXPORT BANNER	35603
EXPORT DEFENDER	07850
EXPORT DIPLOMAT	07851
EXPORT FREEDOM	94273
EXPORT LEADER	94274
EXPORT PATRIOT	94275
EXPRESSO CAGLIARI	17270
EXTRAMAR ESTE	76071
EXTRAMAR NORTE	76070
EXTRAMAR OESTE	76072
EXTRAMAR SUR	76073
EXXON BALTIMORE	38011
EXXON BALTIMORE	38881
EXXON BANGOR	37794
EXXON BATON ROUGE	53551
EXXON BATON ROUGE	55571
EXXON BOSTON	38010
EXXON BOSTON	38880
EXXON CHESTER	37791
EXXON FLORENCE	37790
EXXON GETTYSBURG	38570
EXXON HOUSTON	66092
EXXON HUNTINGTON	37792
EXXON JAMESTOWN	38571
EXXON LEXINGTON	38572
EXXON NEW ORLEANS	66093
EXXON NEWARK	37793
EXXON PHILADELPHIA	53552
EXXON PHILADELPHIA	55572
EXXON SAN FRANCISCO	53550
EXXON SAN FRANCISCO	55570
EXXON SEATTLE	37263
EXXON WASHINGTON	38573
EYRARFOSS	94652
EYSK	22849
EYSK	34479
EYSKIY LIMAN	33620
EYZHEN BERG	67655
EYZHENS BERGS	59895

F

F.C. WEISKOPF	12622
FABIAN	56410
FABIAN	67830
FABIAN	68430
FABIO SAVERIO	36075
FABIC SAVERIO	41795
FABIOLAVILLE	16190
FADEL	64760
FADI B	65340
FAETHON	05471
FAGARAS	47546
FAGET	47541
FAHAD	40160
FAILAKA	70164
FAIR ISLAND	53470
FAIR ISLAND	62050
FAIR LADY	19300
FAIR REEFER	21341
FAIR STAR	01210
FAIR WIND	47670
FAIRFIELD ARCHER	65490
FAIRFIELD ARCHER	70430
FAIRLANE	89590
FAIRLIFT	89620
FAIRLOAD	89601
FAIRNESS	47209
FAIRSEA	01221
FAIRSEA	16791
FAIRSHIP	25460
FAIRWIND	01220
FAIRWIND	16790
FAITH	37251
FAITH	66890
FAITH	82030
FAITH	91580
FAITH FIVE	35880
FAIZI	30130
FAJAR	58126
FALCON.	04373
FALCON	82990
FALCON	87410
FALCON AROW	83130
FALCON BAY	65810
FALCON BAY	74790
FALCON REEFER	91740
FALCONERA	54670
FALESHTY	21560
FALISEA	23100
FALKE	84933
FALKENBERG	76131
FALKENBERG	79911
FALKENFELS	58614
FALKENFELS	81014
FALKENFELS	90514
FALKENSTEIN	73955
FALLOW DEER	86880
FALLWIND	87331
FALSTAFF	50662
FALSTRIA	78780
FALTICENI	82120
FALTICENI	82400
FAMILY ANGEL	06950
FAMILY DELTA	05700
FAMILY UNITY	07010
FANARI	66020

FANEROMENI	09610
FANG CHENG	81381
FANIS	42453
FANNY	67421
FANOMA	27215
FANTI	82520
FAR EAST VANGUARD	61631
FARAB	21561
FARADAY	80840
FARES REEFER	05710
FARHA	93100
FARIDPUR	27330
FARLAND	73201
FARLAND	76991
FARMER	65380
FARMSUM	78661
FARNES	50510
FAROOQ	90230
FAROS	25360
FARSA 1	39580
FASGADAIR	93220
FAST BREEZE	24680
FASTNET ROCK	76152
FASTOV	17830
FATEZH	17831
FATHER PANOS	60260
FATHULKHAIR	49406
FATHULKHAIR	50966
FAULAD SARDAR	13560
FAULAD SARDAR	25611
FAUNA	48601
FAUREI	47545
FAUST	63420
FAVORITA	03495
FAVORITA	03585
FAVORITA	78425
FAY C	10151
FAY III	13372
FAYROUZ	89190
FAYZABAD	21562
FEANG	83715
FEATHER	41020
FEAX	05477
FEAX	07960
FEDERAL CALUMET	53901
FEDERAL CLYDE	53900
FEDERAL FRASER	61180
FEDERAL MAPLE	23620
FEDERAL NOVA	94140
FEDERAL PIONEER	48822
FEDERAL RHINE	53902
FEDERAL SCHELDE	53903
FEDERAL ST. CLAIR	47399
FEDERAL ST. CLAIR	47969
FEDERAL SUMIDA	61181
FEDERAL TYNE	42001
FEDERICO C	08160
FEDERICO C	09100
FEDON	01530
FEDOR BREDIKHIN	10742
FEDOR GLADKOV	07927
FEDOR GLADKOV	11835
FEDOR KRAYNOV	12425
FEDOR LITKE	22184
FEDOR LITKE	22224
FEDOR MATISEN	39173
FEDOR PETROV	03774
FEDOR PETROV	04014
FEDOR PODTELKOV	79425
FEDOR POLETAEV	38581
FEDOR SHALYAPIN	06201
FEDOR VARAKSIN	54731
FEDOR VARAKSIN	55301
FEDROS	80702
FEDROS	84482
FEDYA GUBANOV	44101
FEI CHU HAI	46680
FEI CHU HAI	47110
FELANIA	51691
FELICIA V	48861
FELICIE	00630
FELICITY	10120
FELICITY	14020
FELIKS DZERZHINSKY	02121
FELIKS DZIERZYNSKI	65850
FELIKS DZIERZYNSKI	67690
FELIKS KON	93731
FELIKS KON	93821
FELIPES	51692
FELIX	47559
FELLOWSHIP	71032
FENBANK	04771
FENCHURCH	64800
FENERBAHCE	32150
FENG BAO	02320
FENG CHENG	81646
FENG GUANG	02322
FENG HUANG SHAN	58593
FENG HUANG SHAN	60473
FENG LANG	02321
FENG QING	14630
FENICIA EXPRESS	95131
FENIKS	11642
FENIX	12313
FENJA	76190
FENNIA	19250
FENNIA	48671
FENNIA	48811
FEODOR OKK	23534
FEODOSIYA	12245
'FEODOSIYA' type	02790
'FEODOSIYA' type	09010
FEOSO AMBASSADOR	38270
FEOSO STAR	37420
FER BALEAR	76121
FER BALEAR	79901
FER BALTICO	76120
FER BALTICO	79900
FERAX	27580
FERDINAND FREILIGRATH	33870
FERE	24770
FERIAL	13171
FERIAL	34804
FERNANDAEMME	13460
FERNANDO ESCANO	33020
FERNANDOEVERETT	14283
FERNANDOEVERETT	71740
FERNANDOEVERETT	81410
FERNHURST	89021
FERNWAVE	60861
FERNWAVE	70901
FERO CADIZ	48831

G

GAMID SULTANOV	20324
GAMMAGAS	64680
GAN JIANG	51551
GAN QUAN	72900
GAN QUAN	63730
GANDA	11180
GANGUT	11773
GANGUT	34664
GANN	18100
GANN	18610
GANVIE	66891
GANVIE	82031
GAO HU	60722
GAO SHAN	15950
GAOPENG	04980
GARA DJEBILET	89721
GARBIS	65831
GARBIS	69491
GARCIA MUNTE	06750
GARCILASO	07940
GARDEN GREEN	68103
GARDEN MOON	77804
GAREFOWL	61992
GARGI	58800
GARGI	65410
GARI	53582
GARI	53732
GARIFALIA C	02730
GARNATA	16951
GARNELA	23452
GARNES	50121
GARNET	01090
GARPUNNER PROKOPYENKO	13670
GARRISON POINT	73560
GARTHNEWYDD	60911
GARWOLIN	03233
GARWOLIN	03623
GARYVILLE	63320
GARYVILLE	68240
GARZA	73810
GARZA OCEAN	61473
GARZUF	44351
GAS AL-AHMADI	54042
GAS AL-BURGAN	54043
GAS AL-KUWAIT	54044
GAS AL-MINAGISH	54045
GAS ENTERPRISE	54041
GAS PILOT	57680
GAS RISING SUN	55640
GAS RISING SUN	55840
GASTOR	53890
GASTRANA	53583
GASTRANA	53733
GATOOMA	65960
GAUCHO MOREIRA	73090
GAUGUIN	48404
GAVANA	18270
GAVILAN	66850
GAVRIIL DERZHAVIN	14382
GAVRIL SARITCHEV	22189
GAVRILL KIRDISHCHEV	78061
GAY LUSSAC	54900
GAYTA	07300
GAZ ATLANTIC	85650
GAZ MED	56172
GAZ PIONEER	56170
GAZ PROGRESS	60890
GAZ PROGRESS	71770
GAZ PROGRESS	81133
GAZ UNITY	56171
GAZ VICTORY	84990
GAZANA	58071
GAZANA	62391
GAZELLA	03990
GAZELLE	72753
GAZIANTEP	67800
GAZLI	79429
GDANSK	36868
GDOV	23520
GDOV	86183
GDYNIA	36864
GDYNIA II	15082
GDYNSKI KOSYNIER	10757
GEA PRIMA	88521
GEBE OLDENDORFF	82340
GEDIZ	07884
GEDIZ	15647
GEDSER	17280
GEENA	84533
GEEST-TIDE	03260
GEESTCREST	03261
GEESTLAND	03262
GEESTSTAR	03263
GEFEST	13669
GEFO BALTIC	76335
GEFO BALTIC	88725
GEIZER	09361
GEKKO MARU	63361
GELA	00090
GELENDZHIK	40009
GELENDZHIK	84337
GELESIAE	87400
GELINDA	48580
GELIOGRAF	11836
GELTING	19140
GEM	91280
GEMA	21490
GEMILANG	13600
GEMINI	11674
GEMLIK	15811
GEMMA	83602
GEMPITA	13341
GEMURUH	13340
GENERAL A. F. CEBESOY	05641
GENERAL A. F. CEBESOY	14470
GENERAL ASLANOV	53161
GENERAL BABAYAN	53162
GENERAL BAGRATION	59897
GENERAL BAGRATION	67657
GENERAL BELGRANO.	06678
GENERAL BEM	78981
GENERAL BOCHAROV	60641
GENERAL BOCHAROV	62601
GENERAL CHERNIAKOVSKI	17512
GENERAL FR. KLEEBERG	54972
GENERAL GUISAN	77563
GENERAL JASINSKI	78982
GENERAL JOSE ARTIGAS	17140
GENERAL K. ORBAY	05642
GENERAL K. ORBAY	14471
GENERAL KARBYSHEV	60630
GENERAL KARBYSHEV	62590
GENERAL KLEEBERG	71812
GENERAL KRAVTSOV	60642
GENERAL KRAVTSOV	62602
GENERAL LESELIDZE	60901
GENERAL LESELIDZE	79231
GENERAL LIM	59461
GENERAL M. MAKLEFF	53850
GENERAL M. MAKLEFF	79690
GENERAL MADALINSKI	78983
GENERAL MERKVILADZE	67681
GENERAL OSTRYAKOV	13671
GENERAL PRADZYNSKI	78984
GENERAL R. GUMUSBALA	05643
GENERAL R. GUMUSBALA	14472
GENERAL RACHIMOW	11649
GENERAL SHKODUNOVICH	60643
GENERAL SHKODUNOVICH	62603
GENERAL STANISLAW POPLAWSKI	14487
GENERAL SWIERCZEWSKI	78980
GENERAL VLADIMIR ZAIMOV	03958
GENERAL VLADIMIR ZAIMOV	79642
GENERAL Z. DOGAN	05644
GENERAL Z. DOGAN	14473
GENERAL ZHDANOV	60625
GENERAL ZHDANOV	62585
GENEVE	72630
GENEVE	77390
GENEVIEVE LYKES	05582
GENEVIEVE LYKES	14423
GENEVIEVE LYKES	14893
GENIE	07050
GENNARGENTU	16570
GENOTA	53585
GENOTA	53735
GENRIK GASANOV	59882
GENTILE DA FABRIANO	02390
GEOKCHAY	50774
GEOMITRA	53584
GEOMITRA	53734
GEOPOTES VII	43590
GEOPOTES 12	44060
GEORG BUCHNER	25220
GEORG BUCHNER	29710
GEORG HANDKE	15674
GEORG KURZ	53412
GEORG KURZ	64942
GEORG SCHUMANN	06388
GEORG SCHUMANN	15417
GEORG WEERTH	33871
GEORGE	82995
GEORGE GEORGIU-DEZH	36872
GEORGE M KELLER	63910
GEORGE S. EMBIRICOS	57002
GEORGE WYTHE	01054
GEORGES	64180
GEORGES VIELJEUX	05123
GEORGES VIELJEUX	59872
GEORGI BENKOVSKI	67311
GEORGI DIMITROV.	01980
GEORGI SAVA RAKOVSKY	06260
GEORGIA	64143
GEORGIA	93910
GEORGIAN GLORY	49190
GEORGIAN GLORY	52790
GEORGIOS	07000
GEORGIOS	44071
GEORGIOS	44501
GEORGIOS	44720
GEORGIOS	58530
GEORGIOS	85300
GEORGIOS D	81930
GEORGIOS D	89330
GEORGIOS F	46526
GEORGIOS F	83306
GEORGIOS G	42521
GEORGIOS M II	43860
GEORGIOS MATSAS	60102
GEORGIOS PARAVALOS	60103
GEORGIOS T. KOROPOULIS	79780
GEORGIOS TSAKIROGLOU	56872
GEORGIOS VENTOURIS	42180
GEORGIOS XYLAS	46670
GEORGIS A GEORGILIS	46910
GEORGIS GERONTAS	46601
GEORGIS PROIS	56984
GEORGIY CHICHERIN	14451
GEORGIY DIMITROV	05622
GEORGIY DMITROV	14452
GEORGIY LEONIDZE	60900
GEORGIY LEONIDZE	79230
GEORGIY MAKSIMOV	39174
GEORGIY SEDOV	22225
GEORGIY USHAKOV	02272
GEORGIY VASILIEV	09971
GEORGIY VASILIEV	11511
GEORGY	06910
GEORTINA	61024
GEORTINA	71184
GERAKL	11946
GERARD L-D	83145
GERD MAERSK	51681
GERDA GRAEBE	72757
GERDA SMITS	88111
GERDT OLDENDORFF	71843
GERINA	65151
GERINGSWALDE	46374
GERINGSWALDE	47074
GERMA	91090
GERMA FONDAL	51781
GERMA FOREST	51782
GERMA FRAM	51783
GERMA KARMA	74000
GERMA LINA	51784
GERMA LIONEL	51785
GERMA PRIDE	51786
GERMA TARA	51780
GERMA TEAM	51787
GERMAINE R E	47310
GERMAINE R.E.	48760
'GERMAN LIBERTY' type	56570
'GERMAN LIBERTY' type	57480
'GERMAN LIBERTY' type	58590
'GERMAN LIBERTY' type	58600
'GERMAN LIBERTY' type	59740
'GERMAN LIBERTY' type	59750
'GERMAN LIBERTY' type	60470
'GERMAN LIBERTY' type	62100
'GERMAN LIBERTY' type	62630
'GERMAN LIBERTY' type	62710
'GERMAN LIBERTY' type	62750
'GERMAN LIBERTY' type	90500
GERMANIC	59732
GERMANIC	67222
GERMUNDO	47500
GEROI ADZHIMUSHKAYA	07473
GEROI ADZHIMUSHKAYA	11837
GEROI BRESTA	36875
GEROI PANFILOVTSKY	49751
GEROI PANFILOVTSY	48441
GEROI PANFILOVTSY	49481
GEROI PLEVNY	31152
GEROI PLEVNY	93672
GEROI SHIPKI	31153
GEROI SHIPKI	93673
GEROI ZAPOLYARYA	11741
GEROI ZAPOLYARYA	34631
GEROITE NA ODESSA	31151
GEROITE NA ODESSA	93671
GEROITE NA SEVASTOPOL	31150
GEROITE NA SEVASTOPOL	93670
GEROY MEKHTI	79379
GEROY MEKHTI	79383
GERRINGONG	77090
GERT STAERKE	63691
GERTRUD JACOB	71411
GETALDIC	58128
GEVISA	76600
GEVISA	89300
GEYA	13665
GHADA	81750
GHADA	86099
GHADAMES	60950
GHADAMES	91831
GHADAMES	91941
GHAT	93936
GHAZI—B	88950
GHENT	72633
GHENT	77393
GHEORGHIENI	82124
GHEORGHIENI	82404
GHERANIA	70511
GHERANIA	86381
GHERENUK	59431
GHERESTOS	70512
GHERESTOS	86382
GHIBLI	89710
GHIKAS	58576
GHINA I	87180
GHIONA	70510
GHIONA	86380
GIAMAICA	51520
GIAMBATTISTA VENTURI	85651
GIANNA A	90290
GIANNIS DIMAKIS I	84528
GIANNIS DIMAKIS II	76560
GIANNIS DIMAKIS II	82250
GIANNIS M	06509
GIANNIS N	69910
GIANNIS XILAS	06490
GIANT	82080
GIANT PILOT	61753
GIANT PIONEER	15601
GIBRALTAR	63161
GIBRALTAR PANSY	77223
GIEWONT II	64091
GILLIAN EVERARD	89840
GIMI	53882
GIMONE	66480
GIMONE	85660
GINO JULIANO	46030
GIOACCHINO LAURO	59432
GIORGIS	06533
GIORGOS	14307
GIORGOS K	72051
GIOVANBATTISTA VENTURI	85651
GIOVANNA C	13592
GIOVANNELLA D'AMICO	43760
GIOVANNI CEFALU	43530
GIOVANNI COPPOLA	81890
GISMATALLAH	18520
GIULIANA 1	65420
GIUSEPPE DI VITTORIO	05624
GIUSEPPE DI VITTORIO	14454
GIUSEPPE GARIBALDI	36940
GIUSEPPE VERDI	60500
GIZHIGA	12578
GIZHIGA	21612
GJERTRUD MAERSK	66181
GJERTRUD MAERSK	67731
GLACIAR GRIS	87481
GLACIAR NEGRO	87483
GLACIAR ROJO	87482
GLACIAR VERDE	87480
GLACIER BAY	63411
GLADIATOR	79060
GLADONIA	88002
GLADSTONE STAR	12930
GLAFKI	70700
GLAFKOS	57187
GLAROS	63600
GLARUS	11959
GLASGOW	06649
GLEB KRZHIZHANOVSKIY	03775
GLEB KRZHIZHANOVSKIY	04015
GLEB SEDIN	75331
GLEB USPENSKIY	12363
GLEB USPENSKY	28970
GLENCOE	42660
GLENPARK	46721
GLETCHER	09362
GLIWICE II	61096
GLOBAL CHALLENGER	83987
GLOBAL E SUN	77561
GLOBAL STAR	46353
GLOBAL STAR	46923
GLOBAL SUN	55201
GLOBAL SUNSHINE	78681
GLOBAL TRADER	00380
GLOBE	67710
GLOBE COMET	65760
GLOBE CONSTELLATION	70052
GLOBE EXPRESS	47090
GLOBE EXPRESS	83350
GLOBE GALAXY	70053
GLOBE MARITIMA	44860
GLOBE NOVA	60560
GLOBE NOVA	70240
GLOBE TRADER	05318
GLOBE VENUS	70051
GLOBTIK LONDON	57971
GLOBTIK LONDON	63331
GLOBTIK TOKYO	57970
GLOBTIK TOKYO	63330
GLOGOW	31181
GLORIA L	01471
GLORIA MARIS	90180
GLORIA PEAK	46051
GLORIA SIDERUM	92080
GLORIA VIRENTIUM	87100
GLORIA VIRENTIUM	89810
GLORIASTAR	00451
GLORIC	53151
GLORIC	66301
GLORIOUS TRADER	60250
GLORY	40661
GLORY	64205
GLORY	67500
GLORY	68655
GLORY II	01600
GLUKHOV	86238
GLYFADA	55966
GLYFADA	56726
GLYFADA BREEZE	57150
GLYFADA FAITH	46333
GLYFADA MIMI	61820
GLYFADA SUN	48120
GNIEZNO II	50464
GODAFOSS	83511
GOGO RANGER	62640
GOGO RANGER	82200
GOGO REEFER	84000
GOGO RIDER	86671
GOGO RIVER	43652
GOGOL	12331
GOGOL	17513
GOLAR FREEZE	54081
GOLAR FREEZE	72211
GOLAR FROST	55644
GOLAR FROST	55844
GOLAR KANSAI	63853
GOLAR KANTO	63852
GOLAR ROBIN	63851
GOLCONDA	06000
GOLD ALISA	51270
GOLD BEETLE	07282
GOLD BOND CONVEYOR	79260
GOLD BOND TRAILBLAZER	79261
GOLD BRIDGE	07280
GOLD CLOUD	80320
GOLD CLOUD	80390
GOLD CORAL	61302
GOLD CORAL	62622
GOLD HILLA	51271
GOLD LEAF	07281
GOLD MARINE	61625
GOLD MOUNTAIN	13301
GOLD ORLI	51272
GOLD PILOT	05492
GOLD PILOT	07952
GOLD STAR	05211
GOLD STATE	61612
GOLD STREAM	13300
GOLD VARDA	51273
GOLDBEACH	07190
GOLDEAN ALLIANCE	84610
GOLDEAN ALLIANCE	88320
GOLDEAN ENTERPRISE	73171
GOLDEAN ENTERPRISE	77721
GOLDEN ANNE	46441
GOLDEN ARROW	09700
GOLDEN CAMEO	55670
GOLDEN CAMEO	72370
GOLDEN CAMEROON	58605
GOLDEN CAMEROON	60495
GOLDEN CANARY	70056
GOLDEN CAPE	70057
GOLDEN CHALLENGER	47952
GOLDEN CHARIOT	61166
GOLDEN CHASE	61161
GOLDEN CITY	07671
GOLDEN CLOVER	63110
GOLDEN CROWN	61167
GOLDEN DAISY	54650
GOLDEN DAISY	55071
GOLDEN DOLPHIN	54651
GOLDEN DOLPHIN	55072
GOLDEN DRAGON	61078
GOLDEN DRAGON	71268
GOLDEN DRAGON No 1	95000
GOLDEN EAGLE	14792
GOLDEN EASTERN	44040
GOLDEN EXPLORER	61028
GOLDEN EXPLORER	71188
GOLDEN FLAG	72440
GOLDEN FLAG	77130
GOLDEN GATE BRIDGE	08730
GOLDEN GHANA	58602
GOLDEN HARVEST	61644
GOLDEN HERO	14622
GOLDEN HORIZON	61162
GOLDEN LAUREL	77870
GOLDEN LION	06440
GOLDEN LOTUS	47152
GOLDEN MARINER	62880
GOLDEN MIRANDA	55967
GOLDEN MIRANDA	56727
GOLDEN NICHOLAS	46211
GOLDEN NIGERIA	07341
GOLDEN ODYSSEY	16520
GOLDEN ODYSSEY	17610
GOLDEN ORCHID	47153
GOLDEN ORIOLE	46440
GOLDEN PANAGIA	61163
GOLDEN PIONEER	61029
GOLDEN PIONEER	71189
GOLDEN POLYDINAMOS	47953
GOLDEN PRINCESS	16560
GOLDEN RIO	74965
GOLDEN RIO	74965
GOLDEN RIO	77105
GOLDEN SEAGULL	71700
GOLDEN SHIMIZU	61164
GOLDEN SKY	13911
GOLDEN SKY	14821
GOLDEN SOURCE	44041
GOLDEN SPEAR	61168
GOLDEN STAR	20511
GOLDEN STATE	52360
GOLDEN SUMMER	80560
GOLDEN SUN	01281
GOLDEN SUNRAY	63940
GOLDEN SUNRAY	71590
GOLDEN SWORD	61169
GOLDEN TENNYO	61160
GOLDEN TOGO	51550

GOLDEN TRADER	47951
GOLDEN TULIP	63111
GOLDEN VENTURE	67280
GOLDENROD	71151
GOLFO DE BATABANO	06303
GOLFO DE GUACANAYBO	06304
GOLFO DE GUANAHACABIBES	06305
GOLFO DI PALERMO	54090
GOLFO PARADISO	15060
GOLFSTRIM	11306
GOLIATH	52060
GOMASA	61060
GOMBA ENDEAVOUR	81845
GOMBA ENDURANCE	81843
GOMBA NILE	81842
GOMBA VICTORIA	81844
GOMEL	86178
GONCALO	57524
GONCHAROV	12592
GONZALEZ LINES	10275
GONZALEZ LINES	15185
GOOD BREEZE	07016
GOOD CHAMPION	71490
GOOD DOLPHIN	06504
GOOD FAITH	05319
GOOD FRIEND	58120
GOOD GUARDIAN	83367
GOOD GUARDIAN	83457
GOOD HERALD	08020
GOOD HERALD	72100
GOOD ISLANDER	72910
GOOD LEADER	72280
GOOD LEADER	77180
GOOD LION	07015
GOOD LORD	06506
GOOD MOTHER	79220
GOOD OCEAN	47350
GOOD PATRIOT	06507
GOOD SKIPPER	13440
GOOD SPIRIT	07032
GOOD SUN	06505
GOOD WIND	57510
GOOD WIND	62000
GOOD YEAR	80680
GOOILAND	05540
GOPLANA	87741
GORAN KOVACIC.	05655
GORANKA	10311
GORECHJE	12246
GORETS	76505
GORGULHO	76602
GORGULHO	89302
GORI	60623
GORI	62583
GORIZONT	34711
GORJ	47556
GORKOVSKAYA KOMSOMOLIYA	49242
GORKY	35318
GORKY LENINSKOYE	79407
GORLICE	31182
GORLITZ	78730
GORLITZ	89980
GORLOVKA	42962
GORNIK	47601
GORNO-ALTAYSK	15465
GORNOPRAVDINSK	70023
GORNOZAVODSK	84338
GORNY SLASK	75732
GORNY SLASK	88382
GORNYAK	49246
GORODETSKIY	17927
GOROKHOVETS	75353
GORSETHORN	88410
GOSPIC	47215
GOTALAND	16981
GOTALAND	19980
GOTALAND	51621
GOTH	42030
GOTHIA	66860
GOTHIA TEAM	63453
GOTHIC CHIEF	78200
GOTLANDIA	19370
GOTZE DELCHEV	48432
GOTZE DELCHEV	49472
GOTZE DELCHEV	49742
GOULDIA	53586
GOULDIA	53736
GOULIAS	46331
GOURI SHANKAR	00612
GOVORA	47566
GRACE BONNY II	74370
GRACE CALABAR	86840
GRACE CALABAR	90780
GRACE L	46692
GRACECHURCH	48491
GRAD	23550
GRADIENT ENERGY	60321
GRAN RIO	88140
GRANAT	12429
GRAND ALLIANCE	56471
GRAND BRILLIANCE	56470
GRAND CONCORDANCE	56472
GRAND ENCOUNTER	74950
GRAND ENCOUNTER	80070
GRAND FELICITY	61444
GRAND HAVEN	74421
GRAND HAVEN	88091
GRAND RELIANCE	83221
GRAND REXTAR	56420
GRANIK	22336
GRANIT	13668
GRANIT	73834
GRANIT	77014
GRANITNYY	76521
GRANITNYY BEREG	62693
GRANITZ	12317
GRANO	93933
GRANUAILE	42420
GRANVIK	65100
GRATIAN	58351
GREAT CONCORD	14850
GREAT COSMOS	70951
GREAT LAND	08710
GREAT POINT	90345
GREAT REPUBLIC	01491
GRECIAN FLAME	61880
GRECIAN LEGEND	55040
GRECIAN SPIRIT	55041
GRECIAN TEMPLE	56790
GREEK SKY	85370
GREEK SKY	87970
GREEN SEA	79610
GREENPORT	19800
GREENVILLE	11112
GREGERSO	47232
GREGERSO	47512
GREGOS	59390
GREMIKHA	17962
GRENA	83138
GRESHAM	55530
GRESHAM	63350
GRETCHEN WESTON	75873
GRETE MAERSK	66182
GRETE MAERSK	67732
GRETE SIF	64865
GRETE SIF	91045
GRETE WALTER	23418
GRETKE OLDENDORFF	71845
GREY MASTER	93890
GREY WARRIOR	60310
GREZ	58124
GRIBOYEDOV	12364
GRIEG	76740
GRIEG	89690
GRIGORIOS C IV	04785
GRIGORIOS D	13500
GRIGORIS	41870
GRIGORIY ACHKANOV	60621
GRIGORIY ACHKANOV	52581
GRIGORIY ALEKSEEV	50670
GRIGORIY KOVALCHUK	69314
GRIGORIY LYSENKO	93879
GRIGORIY ORDZHONIKIDZE	02122
GRIGORIY OVODOVSKIY	13672
GRIGORIY PETRENKO	49476
GRIGORIY PETRENKO	49746
GRIGORIY PETRENKO	48436
GRIGORIY PETROVSKIY	79404
GRIGORIY POLUYANOV	11581
GRIGORIY SHELIKOV	12430
GRIGORIY TEREMTYEV	13667
GRIGORIY VAKULENCHUK	39981
GRIGOROUSA	78801
GRIGOROUSA	89961
GRIMMEN	69720
GRINWAL	23453
GRIPEN	48570
GRIPO	65012
GRISHA AKOPIAN	15466
GRISHA PODOBEDOV	67012
GROBNIK	15242
GRODEKOVO	24065
GRODEKOVO	89505
GRODITZ	78731
GRODITZ	89981
GRODNO	39984
GROENLAND	81825
GROENLAND	82075
GRONLAND	64901
GROOTSAND	59510
GROOTSAND	59820
GROSNEFT	85887
GROSSER BELT	18723
GROZNY	39974
GROZNYY	66171
GROZNYY	85972
GRUDZIADZ	31180
GRUMANT	09360
GRUMANT	15467
GRUNDARFOSS	75974
GRUNDARFOSS	50204
GRUNWALD	10351
GRUZIYA	20371
GRYF	32310
GRYF POMORSKY	93883
GRYNGE	45470
GRYTTA	82500
GUADALUPE 1	52301
GUADELUPE VICTORIA	86672
GUALOMA	42880
GUANG HAI	49151
GUANG HAI	83551
GUANG PING	26800
GUANGHE	53300
GUANGHUA	00980
GUANGSHUI;	01532
GUATARI	13940
GUATEMALA	56593
GUAYAMA	74477
GUAYANA	72020
GUAYAQUIL	11172
GUAYCURA	94671
GUBERTAS BORISA	12431
GUDERMES	43240
GUDERMES	66174
GUDRID	59614
GUDRID	71924
GUDRUN	12180
GUDRUN DANIELSEN	90971
GUDRUN DANIELSEN	91982
GUDRUN MAERSK	66180
GUDRUN MAERSK	67730
GUERVEUR	09500
GUGLIELMO MARCONI	01761
GUI HAI	47911
GUIA	91880
GUIRIA	13810
GUIYIN	28231
GULANG YU	16430
GULBENE	15468
'GULF ANDES' class	05250
GULF BANKER	05250
GULF BEAR	08343
GULF COAST	52771
GULF EAGLE	07262
GULF EXPRESS	89226
GULF FALCON	13290
GULF FARMER	05251
GULF GATINEAU	88480
GULF HERON	07670
GULF MACKENZIE	88421
GULF MERCHANT	05252
'GULF PRIDE' class	00060
GULF SHIPPER	05253
GULF TRADER	05254
GULF TRADER	81610
GULFCEM	76722
GULFDEER	44570
GULFLION	44571
GULFTIGER	44572
GULUNGAN	13995
GUN	66650
GUNDA BROVIG	70261
GUNDULIC	58129
GUNGNIR 1	52200
GUNGNIR 1	65150
GUNGNIR V	52910
GUNGNIR V	60930
GUNGNIR V	85020
GUNGNIR X	77510
GUNGNIR X	78410
GUNILLA	93931
GUNUNG DJATI	17410
GURAMI	04591
GURIEV	01966
GURIYA	12247
GURJEVSK	12248
GURZUF	12249
GUS-KHRUSTALNYY	06771
GUS-KHRUSTALNYY	07581
GUSTAV AV KLINT	16750
GUSTAV VASA	16512
GUTSUL	85347
GVARDEYSK	21603
GVARDEYSK	88243
GWARDIA LUDOWA	10573
GWARDIA LUDOWA	15343
GYPSUM BARON	75781
GYPSUM BARON	79681
GYPSUM COUNTESS	94750
GYPSUM DUCHESS	94421
GYPSUM EMPRESS	94420
GYPSUM KING	75780
GYPSUM KING	79680
GYURGYAN	44104

H

HA LONG	20550
HAAPSALU	86221
HABANA	90391
HABIB	16930
HABICHT II	20810
HACI ARIF KAPTAN	90171
HADA	55791
HADA	64652
HADI	15930
HADIOTIS	84841
HADJANNA	49150
HADJANNA	83550
HADJI AGUS SALIM	15380
HADOKASAN MARU	31101
HADRIAN	60552
HADRIAN	69482
HAE YUNG EASTERN	47390
HAE YUNG EASTERN	47960
HAE YUNG GOLD	47393
HAE YUNG GOLD	47963
HAGEN	04661
HAGENOW	50441
HAGENOW	52001
HAHNENTOR	79190
HAI CHENG	64815
HAI FENG	42370
HAI HONG	83500
HAI LEE	31250
HAI MING	86620
HAI MOON	61571
HAI OU	35000
HAI OU	91790
HAI PHONG	83282
HAI QUAN	02570
HAI RYONG	33720
HAI YING 8001	92640
HAIDA BRAVE	92870
HAIFENG	05391
HAIFENG.	05830
HAIFOSS	84072
HAIMEN.	05440
HAINING	10580
HAINING	15350
HAIO	35000
HAIO	91790
HAITI MARU	07766
HAITI MARU	07814
HAJ ABDUL RAHMAN	81050
HAJDUK	23454
HAJDUSZOBOSZLO	89218
HAJNOWKA	76640
HAJNOWKA	67050
HAKKODA MARU	19682
HAKON JARL	16100
HAKOZAKI MARU	09890
HAKUHO MARU	34720
HAKUREI MARU	01850
HAKUREI MARU	02220
HAKUSAN MARU	09851
HALADI 1	89800
HALCYON ISLE	41660
HALCYON MED	51663
HALCYON MED	73213
HALIA	40750
HALIA	41480
HALIFAX STAR	01500
HALKI	69630
HALKIS EXPRESS	78570
HALLA PARTNER	83584
HALLA PILOT	48470
HALLA PILOT	49520
HALLA PILOT	49775
HALLA PRIDE	48471
HALLA PRIDE	49521
HALLA PRIDE	49776
HALLAREN	01550
HALLBORG	49712
HALLDIS	84780
HALLDOR	72160
HALLE;	04918
HALLEY	33230
HALLIBURTON 602	85750
HALLVARD	72161
HALNIAK	10761
HALNIAK	10261
HALSINBORG	19010
HALSSKOV	18942
HALUL	69111
HALUL	71461
HAMANA	92560
HAMANA	92580
HAMAYU	32634
HAMBURG	04662
HAMBURG	72632
HAMBURG	77392
HAMBURG EXPRESS	08371
HAMBURG EXPRESS	14570
HAMEN	43930
HAMID	35570
HAMILTON LOPES	64130
HAMLET	19400
HAMLET	54417
HAMLET	57877
HAMLET ARABIA	57761
HAMLET ARABIA	62481
'HAMLET MULTIFLEX' type	49350
'HAMLET MULTIFLEX' type	57760
'HAMLET MULTIFLEX' type	62480
HAMLET SAUDIA	57762
HAMLET SAUDIA	62482
HAMMERSHUS	32220
HAMMONIA	04643
HAMNO	47522
HAMPSHIRE	55600
HAMPTON MARU	30511
HAMPTON MARU	63010
HAN BORI	30520
HAN CHEONG	05730
HAN CHUAN	05101
HAN GARAM	05971
HAN GARAM	31000
HAN GEONG	30440
HAN NURI	31001
HAN YIN	58591
HAN YIN	60471
HANAN	27810
HANBORI	29320
HANCOCK CLIPPER	88260
HAND FORTUNE	61073
HAND FORTUNE	71263
HAND LOONG	61072
HAND LOONG	71262
HANDARA	01611
HANDYMARINER	46651
HANGETE	47230
HANGETE	47510
HANGZOU	35271
HANIA T	50220
HANJIANG	38335
HANJIANG	44695
HANKA SAWICKA	15280
HANKYU No. 16	32230
HANKYU No. 17	32231
HANNATU	63712
HANNO GUNTHER	23419
HANNOVER	04663
HANNOVERLAND	15630
HANOI	10270
HANOI	15180
HANS GUTZEIT.	08522
HANS LIEBERECHT	12432
HANS POGELMANN	76500
HANS SACHS	73022
HANSA	25170
'HANSA' type	28940
'HANSA' type	29000
HANSE	23960
HANSTHOLM	94040
HANYANG	55991
HAOUD L'HAMRA	60583
HAPPY	23010
HAPPY PIONEER	92790
HAPPY RIDER	92800
HAPPY RUNNER	92801
HAPPY WILLING	27480
HAR CARMEL	55050
HAR SINAI	84570
HARALD JARL	01350
HARBIYE	32160
HARDANGER	60862
HARDANGER	70902
HARENGUS	34030
HARGHITA	11676
HARGHITA	11680
HARIS	53510
HARLANDSVILLE	11113
HARLANDSVILLE	34141
HARLEKIN	19231
HARMATTAN	90812
HARMATTAN	91772
HARMEN OLDENDORFF	72251
HARMONIC	53155
HARMONIC	66304
HARMONY SEA	62037
HARMONY VENTURE	56351
HARMONY VENTURE	68051
HARNGJIN	67285
HAROLD H. JAQUET	56020
HARRIET	41650
HARRIET	43890
HARRIET	62029
HARRY C. WEBB	53770
HARRY C. WEBB	53920
HARRY POLLITT	03060
HARRY POLLITT.	03650
HARSHA VARDHANA	08940
HARTFORD EXPRESS	64780
HARUKAZE MARU	03561
HARUNA MARU	09781
HARUNA MARU	35091
HARUNA MARU	95081
HARVEST	05040
HARVEST TRADER	55370
HARZ	85840
HASSAN B	60770
HASSAN B	69670
HASSAYAMPA	45052
HASSELT	78170
HASSI R'MEL	54020
HATEG	47564
HATI BAIK	29200
HATI SENANG	34771
HATI SENANG	25370
HATTAN	37530
HATTINGEN	04665
HAU GIANG	57760
HAU GIANG	62480
HAUDA BEAUTY	61080
HAUDA BEAUTY	71270
HAUNDOY	56524
HAUSSMANN	49551
HAUSSMANN	49571
HAVANA	18270
HAVANA	36865
HAVBJORN	50680
HAVDROTT	63430
HAVFALK	50011
HAVFROST	62421

HAVFRU 50415
HAVFRU 50825
HAVIS 56150
HAVJO 50012
HAVKATT 50681
HAVMANN 50416
HAVMANN 50826
HAVORN 50010
HAVPRINS 63456
HAVSO 52092
HAVTROLL 50682
HAWAII 02990
HAWAII 03030
HAWAIIAN CITIZEN 09580
HAWAIIAN MONARCH 94261
HAWAIIAN PRINCESS 95140
HAWAIIAN QUEEN 94260
HAWAIIAN SEA 65971
HAWTHORN 88660
HAYASHIKANE MARU NO.1 03440
HAYASHIKANE MARU NO.1 03570
HAYASHIKANE MARU NO.2 03441
HAYASHIKANE MARU NO.2 03571
HAYASHIO MARU 34380
HAYATOMO MARU 19520
'HD16F' type 50550
HE LAN SHAN 64818
HEAVY SCAN 63714
HEBE 21480
HEBE 34310
HEBE 90620
HEBRIDES 16700
HECHT V 67160
HEGA SMITS 88112
HEHALUZ II 73571
HEI LONG JIANG 82351
HEI LONG JIANG 82621
HEIDE LEONHARDT 59753
HEIDELBERG 04664
HEIDENHEIM 72004
HEINERSDORF 68870
HEINLAID 75643
HEINO 75290
HEINO 88100
HEINRICH HUSMANN 92299
HEINRICH S 92298
HEINRICH WESCH 66886
HEINZ KAPELLE 15411
HEINZ KAPELLE 06381
HEINZ KAPELLE 23420
HEINZ PRIESS 23421
HEJAZ 28852
HEJO 73670
HEKTOR 53406
HEKTOR 64936
HEKTOS 83364
HEKTOS 83454
HEL. 04340
HEL. 04400
HELEN 02553
HELEN 45971
HELEN 73010
HELEN PAPPAS 90831
HELEN SCHULTE 57608
HELEN SCHULTE 62242
HELENA C 13281
HELENA C 14661
HELENA OLDENDORFF 74650
HELENE DELMAS 48880
HELENE GRAEBE 72760
HELENE PRESTHUS 57550
HELENE ROTH 58550
HELENE ROTH 71870
HELGA OLDENDORFF 77445
HELGA WEHR 91411
HELGAFELL 84074
HELGE FOLMER 75914
HELIOS MARU 61646
HELLA 45420
HELLAN 29951
HELLAS 16320
HELLAS 76762
HELLAS 80272
HELLAS IN ETERNITY 56862
HELLENIC ADVENTURER 78000
HELLENIC CARRIER 04781
HELLENIC CHALLENGER 04782
HELLENIC CHAMPION 04780
HELLENIC CONCORD 78002
HELLENIC DESTINY 29380
HELLENIC EXPLORER 80081
HELLENIC EXPLORER 80231
HELLENIC FAITH 04711
HELLENIC FAITH 04881
HELLENIC FRIENDSHIP 78001
HELLENIC GLORY 24490
HELLENIC GRACE 08022
HELLENIC GRACE 72102
HELLENIC HERO 14030
HELLENIC IDEAL 04783
HELLENIC INNOVATOR 80082
HELLENIC INNOVATOR 80232
HELLENIC LAUREL 29381
HELLENIC LEADER 86770
HELLENIC NAVIGATOR 04784
HELLENIC PATRIOT 03290
HELLENIC PRIDE 04710
HELLENIC PRIDE 04880
HELLENIC SEA 04712
HELLENIC SEA 04882
HELLENIC SEAMAN 45771
HELLENIC SEAMAN 48411
HELLENIC SKY 08021
HELLENIC SKY 72101
HELLENIC SPIRIT 14031
HELLENIC SPLENDOUR 29382
HELLENIC STAR 04713
HELLENIC STAR 04883
HELLENIC SUN 04714
HELLENIC SUN 04884
HELLENIC TORCH 24491
HELLENIC VALOR 80080
HELLENIC VALOR 80230
HELLENIC WAVE 04715
HELLENIC WAVE 04885
HELLERAU 84942
HELLERAU 90602
HELLINORA 81954
HELLINORA 91504
HELME 49247
HELMSMAN 90081
HELSINGOR 19011
HELTERMAA 15469
HELWAN. 40102
HEMINA 65070
HEMUS 77983
HENG CHUN HAI 57193
HENG SHAN 35050
HENGIST 19900
HENGSHUI 15962
HENNIGSDORF 46341
HENNING MAERSK 37701
HENNING MAERSK 44251
HENNING OLDENDORFF 53712
HENNING OLDENDORFF 78151
HENON 27980
HENRI BARBUSSE 10722
HENRIETTE SCHULTE 60953
HENRY STAHL 72770
HENRY STAHL 73710
HENRYK JENDZHA 10281
HENRYK LEMBERG 03234
HENRYK LEMBERG 03624
HEPING 25030
HERA 13260
HERA 55383
HERA 59180
HERALD OF FREE ENTERPRISE 20211
HERBERT BAUM 23422
HERBERT TSCHAPE 23423
HERCEGOVINA 46074
HERCULES 67960
HERCULUS 15173
HEREFORD EXPRESS 82090
HEREFORD EXPRESS 91590
HEREND 89219
HERIOT 84740
HERIOT 84950
HERKULES 12250
HERMAEA 20451
HERMAN BODEWES 90972
HERMAN BODEWES 91981
HERMAN SIF 64856
HERMAN SIF 91036
HERMANAS GIRALT 85921
HERMES 33080
HERMES 1 75262
HERMES SCAN 84021
HERMIA 73601
HERMINE 79741
HERMINIOS 43750
HERMION 25990
HERMIONE 63210
HERMOD 73261
HEROIC 66281
HEROIC SAILOR 35674
HEROJ KOSTA STAMENKOVIC 48450
HEROJ KOSTA STAMENKOVIC 49490
HEROJ KOSTA STAMENKOVIC 49760
HEROJ PAIC 49489
HEROJ PAIC 48449
HEROJ PAIC 49759
HEROJ SENJANOVIC 48451
HEROJ SENJANOVIC 49491
HEROJ SENJANOVIC 49761
HEROS 59181
HERRO 91142
HERTA LINDER 23424
HERVANG 64142
HESPERIA 57540
HESPERUS 60866
HESPERUS 70906
HESSEN 18700
HESTIA 65071
HETTSTEDT 61708
HETTSTEDT 71078
HEUNG AH No 7 17910
HEVER 64831
HEVIZ 89217
HEWELIUSZ 15191
'Hi Bulk 50' type 51020
'Hi Bulk 50' type 52880
HIBISCUS 34050
HICKORY 70950
HIDLEFJORD 02565
HIDLEFJORD 02665
HIE 86130
HIGASHIKAWA MARU 61463
HIGHGATE 75934
HIGHGATE 88634
HIGHSEA PRIDE 60200
HIGHSEA PROMISE 45560
HIJAZ 49407
HIJAZ 50967
HILARY B 61082
HILARY B 71272
HILARY WESTON 75870
HILCO GIRL 34211
HILCO SCAMPER 02651
HILCO SPEEDSTER 02652
HILCO SPRINTER 02650
HILDA KNUDSEN 54511
HILDA KNUDSEN 63891
HILDA WESCH 59735
HILDA WESCH 67225
HILDE 47342
HILDEGARD 59611
HILDEGARD 71921
HILDEGARD WULFF 49891
HILDESHEIM 72000
HILLAH 93570
HILLE OLDENDORFF 06584
HILLI 53881
HILTONA 47600
HIMALAYA MARU 51211
HIMKI 50781
HIN ANN 90381
HIND G 80871
HIND-D 39770
HINRICH OLDENDORFF 06585
HINTHA 01610
HIOS 26510
HIPPO 37540
HIRA MARU 08740
HIRA MARU 09790
HIRATSUKA MARU 47002
HIRMA 66910
HIRO MARU 52363
HISPANIA 52981
HISTORIAN 02810
'HITACHI STANDARD 18' type 55080
'HITACHI STANDARD 18' type 57340
'HITACHI STANDARD 19' type 61150
'HITACHI UT-20' type 48360
'HITACHI UT-20' type 50870
HITAKA MARU 23730
HIYAMA MARU 19700
HIYAMA MARU 23731
HIYUMAA 86246
HIZB-UL-BAHR 20960
HO CHI MIN 14456
HO CHIN MIN 05627
HO PING 87470
HO PING 60 87471
HO PING 62 87472
HO PING 63 87473
HOAN MARU 77883
HODEIDAH CROWN 82750
HODNA 82054
HODNA 91454
HODO 71300
HOE AIK 21710
HOE HING 27260
HOE ONN 90896
HOECHST EXPRESS 08832
HOECHST EXPRESS 09032
HOECHST EXPRESS 77032
HOEGH APAPA 56594
HOEGH ELAN 04590
HOEGH GANDRIA 54080
HOEGH GANDRIA 72210
HOEGH HILL 63871
HOEGH HILL 67601
HOEGH HOOD 63870
HOEGH HOOD 67600
HOEGH LAUREL 64019
HOEGH LAUREL 68409
HOEGH MALLARD 83100
HOEGH MARLIN 83102
HOEGH MASCOT 83101
HOEGH MERCHANT 83103
HOEGH MERIT 83104
HOEGH MINERVA 83105
HOEGH MIRANDA 83107
HOEGH MUSKETEER 83106
HOEGH OPAL 14140
HOEGH OPAL 80860
HOEGH ORCHID 14141
HOEGH ORCHID 80861
HOEGH ORRIS 14142
HOEGH ORRIS 80862
HOEGH PILOT 14143
HOEGH PILOT 80863
HOEGH PRIDE 14144
HOEGH PRIDE 80864
HOEGH RAINBOW 63500
HOEGH RAINBOW 68220
HOEGH RANGER 64270
HOEGH RANGER 68590
HOEGH RIDER 63503
HOEGH RIDER 68223
HOEGH ROVER 63501
HOEGH ROVER 68221
HOEGH SKEAN 55620
HOEGH SWIFT 55581
HOEGH SWIFT 56461
HOEGH SWORD 55582
HOEGH SWORD 56462
HOEGH TARGET 92652
HOEGH TARGET 93192
HOEGH TRIGGER 92653
HOEGH TRIGGER 93193
HOELIEN 48670
HOELIEN 48810
HOGGAR 32632
HOHENFELS 58615
HOHENFELS 81015
HOHENFELS 90515
HOHKOKUSAN MARU 49000
HOJI YA HENDA 06643
HOKO MARU 57791
HOKO MARU 62771
HOKUO MARU 52420
HOKUSEI MARU 52490
HOKUTO MARU 10820
HOKUTO MARU 11220
HOLCOR I 83763
HOLGER DANSKE 20170
HOLLAND 31070
HOLLAND MARU 04971
HOLLANDIA 25011
HOLLANDIA 73407
HOLLANDIA 82717
HOLMON 66805
HOLMSUND 83191
HOLSATIA 04644
HOLSTENCLIPPER 57491
HOLSTENKAMP 84120
HOLSTENLAND 45640
HOLSTENLAND 51580
HOLSTENSAILOR 57490
HOLSTENSAND 45641
HOLSTENSAND 51581
HOLSTENSTEIN 01421
HOLSTENTAL 05382
HOLSTENTRADER 57492
HOLSTENWALL 27390
HOLY 56650
HOLY 62210
HOLYHEAD 20490
HOMAR 10814
HOMER 10640
HOMERUS 19730
HONAM JADE 68041
HONAM PEARL 68040
HONAM RUBY 63850
HONAM TOPAZ 63855
HONDURAS 27300
HONDURAS MARU 07761
HONDURAS MARU 07811
HONEST SPRING 33846
HONESTAS 38660
HONESTY 58186
HONG CHUN 24730
HONG ENG 26760
HONG GU CHENG 51431
HONG HA 22882
HONG HOI 12842
HONG HU 38620
HONG HU 71610
HONG HWA 86140
HONG KONG CONTAINER 04952
HONG KONG EXPRESS 74860
HONG KONG SUCCESS 34810
HONG LEE 94660
HONG MING 28220
HONG MING 31920
HONG QI 31040
HONG QI 105 41410
HONG QI 106 29070
HONG QI No 107 25981
HONG QI No 108 25980
HONG QI 112 35980
HONG QI 112 35990
HONG QI 113 84690
HONG QI 113 89900
HONG QI 115 28191
HONG QI 116 28190
HONG QI 118 24895
HONG QI 119 12961
HONG QI 119 14561
HONG Q1 120 30040
HONG QI 126 38991
HONG Q1 134 30091
HONG QI 137 12962
HONG QI 137 14562
HONG QI 138 26810
HONG QI 150 41322
HONG QI 151 41323
HONG QI 152 41324
HONG QI 153 41325
HONG QI 159 12159
HONG Q1 165 30332
HONG QI 301 79840
HONG QI 302 78280
HONG QI 303 57110
HONG SHAN 25102
HONG SHEN 84921
HONG SHOU SHAN 03130
HONG SHOU SHAN. 03340
HONG SOON 94661
HONG YIN 14050
HONG YIN 14230
HONGKONG CONTAINER 08611
HONGKONG EXPRESS 08372
HONGKONG ISLAND 10332
HONOLULU 02850
HONOR SEA 00859
HOOP 67080
HOOSIER MARINER 07853
HOP 71905
HOPE 26371
HOPECLIPPER 66250
HOPECLIPPER 69920
HOPEDALE 02100
HOPING 25030
HOPING CHI SHI CHI 25520
HOPING CHI SHI CHIU 00150
HOPING CHI SHI LIU 00151
HOPING CHI SHI WU 00152
HOPING CHI SHI WU 00780
HOPING ER SHI CHI 00153
HOPING ER SHI CHIU 00460
HOPING ER SHI ER 25567
HOPING ER SHI I 25568
HOPING ER SHI SAN 10460
HOPING ER SHI SSU 10461
HOPING SAN SHI 00154
HOPING SAN SHI 00154
HOPING SAN SHI CHI 10462
HOPING SAN SHI CHIU 10463
HOPING SAN SHI ER 10464
HOPING SAN SHI I 25570
HOPING SAN SHI PA 10465
HOPING SAN SHI SAN 25569
HOPING SAN SHI WU 12154
HOPING SHI CHIU 25572
HOPING SHI PA 25571
HOPING SHI SAN 00155
HOPING SSU SHI 12156
HOPING SSU SHI 1 12155
HOPING SSU SHI CHI 01040
HOPING SSU SHI ER 12157
HOPING SSU SHI PA 00830
HOPING WU SHI 00156
HOPING WU SHI I 00157
HOPING WU SHI WU 00700
HORIZON 31193
HORIZONA 24550
HORNED OWL 69421
HORNGOLF 14191
HORNWIND 14192
HOROL 22850
HOROL 34480
HOROL 50783
HORSA 19901
HORSA 71940
HORTA BARBOSA 64131
HORUS 67380
HORYU MARU 36600
HOSHA MARU 77202
HOUDA STAR 25920
HOUNSLOW 40321
HOURICO 90536
HOURICO 91076
HOUSSAM B 86422
HOUSTON 72480
HOUSTON GETTY 64362
HOVE 49881
HOWA MARU 05952
HOWA MARU 30470
HOWARD STAR 78671
HOWARD W BELL 63911
HOWELL LYKES 05583
HOWELL LYKES 14424
HOWELL LYKES 14894
HOYU MARU 61480
HRELJIN 74440
HSIEH YUNG 62270
HSIEN YUAN 64201
HSIEN YUAN 68651
HSIN LUNG 92716
HSING MAY 67282
HTAN TAW YWA 80620
HTAN TAW YWA 81970
HU PO HAI 46007
HUA HAI 56850
HUA LIEN 32635
HUA TAI 35903
HUA TAI 41593
HUA YIN 62100
HUA YUAN KOU 93312
HUAI AN 41326
HUAI HAI 74870
HUAI HAI 78920
HUAI YIN 13120
HUAL AKARITA 29260
HUAL JASMINE 50663

HUAL ROSAL	50664
HUAL SKAGERAK	93190
HUAL SKAGERAK	92650
HUAL TRADER	93710
HUAL TRAVELLER	17180
HUAL TROTTER	17181
HUAN JIANG	63687
HUANG HAI	74871
HUANG HAI	78921
HUANG PU JIANG	15022
HUANGSHI.	07080
HUATING;	05372
HUBERNA	72124
HUBERNA	76464
HUDSON	02190
HUDSON	66341
HUDSON DEEP	61011
HUDSON DEEP	71171
HUDSON VENTURE	51140
HUELVA	81941
HUELVA	89421
HUGHES GLOMAR EXPLORER	92320
HUGHEVERETT	04752
HUGO	69871
HUGO BRINKMAN	75506
HUGO OLDENDORFF	71842
HUI JIU 101	34401
HULIN	06030
HULLGATE	89031
HUMACAO	74476
HUMANIST	47771
HUMANITY	26790
HUMBAK	23455
HUMBER	06961
HUMBER ARM	51700
HUMBER ARM	52290
HUMBER RIVER	04281
HUMBERGATE	89030
HUMBOLDT	59160
HUMBOLDT	66510
HUMBOLT	52461
HUNEDOARA	78582
HUNG HSING	30790
HUNG MING	61552
HUNG MING	72042
HUNG YU	22680
HUNGARIA	86119
HUNGARIA	91719
HUPEH	05200
HUSTLER CHEYENNE	73887
HUSTLER CHEYENNE	87267
'HUSTLER' class	73880
'HUSTLER' class	87260
HUSUM	73672
HUTA ZGODA	78290
HUTA ZGODA	80020
HUTA ZYGMUNT	78291
HUTA ZYGMUNT	80021
HUTNIK	47611
HVALVIK	82805
HVALVIK	92095
HVASSAFELL	50800
HVASSAFELL	52610
HWA CHU	67520
HWA CHU	86300
HWA GEK	07120
HWAPYUNG PUSAN	86151
HYANG SAN	25705
HYBUR STAR	88170
HYDE PARK	75480
HYDRA	49540
HYDRA GLAMOUR	13900
HYDRA GLORY	13901
HYDROMOS	61192
HYOGO MARU	09550
HYOGO MARU	33313
HYOGO MARU	77360
HYOK SIN.	07100

I

I. D. SINCLAIR	68942
IALOMITA	11973
IANEVERETT	18290
IAPETOS	55170
IASI	41315
IASON	05473
IBARAKI MARU	77203
IBERIA	51040
IBERIA	52890
IBERVILLE	07713
IBESCA ALGERIA	75291
IBESCA ALGERIA	88101
IBESCA BELGICA	75292
IBESCA BELGICA	88102
IBESCA PORTUGAL	73959
IBN ABDOUN	46770
IBN AL-ATHEER	49381
IBN AL-ATHEER	50941
IBN AL-HAITHAM	46771
IBN AL-MOATAZ	49383
IBN AL-MOATHAZ	50943
IBN AL-NAFEES	49382
IBN AL-NAFEES	50942
IBN AL SUWAIDI	79303
IBN ALBANNA	58971
IBN ALBANNA	65171
IBN ALBEITAR	49384
IBN ALBEITAR	50944
IBN ASAKIR	49385
IBN ASAKIR	50945
IBN BADIS	64961
IBN BAJJAH	46772
IBN BASSAM	49386
IBN BASSAM	50946
IBN BATOUTA	64962
IBN BATTOTAH	49387
IBN BATTOTAH	50947
IBN DURAID	49388
IBN DURAID	50948
IBN HAYYAN	49389
IBN HAYYAN	50949
IBN HAZM	46773
IBN JUBAIR	65000
IBN JUBAIR	85230
IBN JUBAYR	46776
IBN KHALDOON	33591
IBN KHALDOON	49390
IBN KHALDOON	50950
IBN KHALDOUN II	64969
IBN KHALLIKAN	49391
IBN KHALLIKAN	50951
IBN KORRA	65001
IBN KORRA	85231
IBN MALIK	49392
IBN MALIK	50952
IBN OTMAN	58972
IBN OTMAN	65172
IBN QUTAIBAH	49393
IBN QUTAIBAH	50953
IBN ROCHD	58970
IBN ROCHD	64960
IBN ROCHD	65170
IBN RUSHD	49394
IBN RUSHD	50954
IBN SHUHAID	49380
IBN SHUHAID	50940
IBN SINA	28854
IBN SINA	46774
IBN SINA	58973
IBN SINA	65173
IBN SINA II	64970
IBN SIRAJ	64963
IBN TUFAIL	49395
IBN TUFAIL	50955
IBN YOUNUS	49396
IBN YOUNUS	50956
IBN ZUHR	46775
ICE MERCHANT	33641
ICE PILOT	33640
ICE STAR	49980
ICELAND	34207
ICELANDIC	64881
ICELANDIC	91061
ICHA	21402
ICHA	86005
ICHA	18310
IDA HOYER	87720
IDA TERESA	80630
IDAHO	05090
IDEFIX	63591
IDEFIX	68331
IDEFJORD	29160
IERONIM UBOREVICH	93692
IEZER	11677
IFEWARA	38941
IFEWARA	39091
IFNI	34217
IGARKA	12661
IGARKALES	45682
IGGESUND	72840
IGNACIO AGRAMONTE	06613
IGNATIY SERGEYEV	14450
IGNATIY SERGEYEV	05620
IGOR GRABAR	76587
IGOR GRABAR	79937
IGRIM	70033
IHABI	15880
IHSAN	32163
IJZER	23360
IKAGURI	58682
IKAM	12761
IKAN BILIS	73360
IKEJA PALM	12913
IKERIAN REEFER	18301
IKHNATON	01417
IKHNATON	01677
IKHTIANDR	23570
IKTINOS	05474
IKUTA MARU	61652
IKUYO MARU	56390
IKUYO MARU	67920
ILE DE FRANCE	73734
ILE DE LA CITE	68692
ILE DE LA MARTINIQUE	28881
ILE DE SAINT PIERRE	18230
ILENA	46912
ILEOLUJI	29248
ILHA DE COMO	67496
ILHA DE SAO MIGUEL	66900
ILHA DE SAO MIGUEL	91470
ILIA	41327
ILIAS	84534
ILICE	61141
ILICE	81481
ILICHOVO	07554
ILIM	70788
ILIOS	10600
ILIRIJA	32290
ILITCH	17514
ILKON TAK	37920
ILLERBERG	53405
ILLERBERG	64935
ILLINOIS	52622
ILLIRIA	09680
ILMATAR	20300
ILMEN	11838
ILMEN	21910
ILMENLES	45687
ILO	52660
ILO	89380
ILOSANGI	58684
ILSE	13790
ILYA KATUNIN	11582
ILYA KULIK	02672
ILYA METCHNIKOV	10751
ILYA METCHNIKOV	34240
ILYA MUROMETS	17515
ILYA MUROMETS	22226
ILYA REPIN	76495
ILYA SELVINSKIY	50754
ILYA ULYANOV	03067
ILYA ULYANOV	03659
ILYA VOLYNKIN	11781
ILYCH	16160
ILYICHYOVSK	11839
ILYINSK	07553
IMA	77930
IMA	79250
IMAD S	39790
IMAN	36916
IMAN	43816
IMANDRA	25557
IMANT SUDMALIS	12433
IMANT SUDMALIS	85985
IMENI 61 KOMMUNARA	76498
IMERITI	11840
IMILCHIL	34218
IMME OLDENDORFF	06586
IMOUZZER	34219
IMPALA	59733
IMPALA	67223
IMPARCA MIAMI	76768
IMPARCA MIAMI	80278
IMPERIAL SARNIA	43220
IMPERIAL SKEENA	45580
IMPERIAL STAR	34923
IN-AMENAS	64335
IN-NAHALA	69110
IN-NAHALA	74160
IN-SAFRA	64334
INA	72510
INABUKWA	58681
INACHUS STAR	48290
INAGO	43751
INAGUA BAY	92413
INAGUA BEACH	92411
INAGUA LIGHT	92410
INAGUA SOUND	92412
INAGUA SURF	92414
INARAN	58680
INAU	11681
INAYAMA	65220
INAYAMA	69880
INCA	64874
INCAN ST. LAURENT	39391
INCAN ST. LAURENT	93181
INCAN SUPERIOR	39390
INCAN SUPERIOR	93180
INCEM ARSEM	89170
INCONFIDENTE	00510
INCOTRANS SPEED	04111
INCOTRANS SPIRIT	04110
INDEPENDENCIA	70041
INDEPENDENCIA I	66214
INDEPENDENCIA II	66215
INDIA	62330
INDIA ROSEWOOD	34350
INDIAN FAITH	60230
INDIAN FAME	60231
INDIAN FORTUNE	60232
INDIAN FRATERNITY	60234
INDIAN FREEDOM	60235
INDIAN GLORY	54117
INDIAN GLORY	54587
INDIAN GRACE	54118
INDIAN GRACE	54588
INDIAN INDUSTRY	10510
INDIAN OCEAN	06331
INDIAN PRESTIGE	57460
INDIAN PROGRESS	57461
INDIAN PROSPERITY	57462
INDIAN RELIANCE	13620
INDIAN RENOWN	13621
INDIAN SECURITY	13563
INDIAN TRIBUNE	07772
INDIAN TRIUMPH	13561
INDIAN TRUST	13562
INDIAN VALOUR	80850
INDIAN VALOUR	82490
INDIAN VENTURE	80851
INDIAN VENTURE	82491
INDIGA	11490
INDIGIRKA	17810
INDIGIRKA	21581
INDIGIRKA	35319
INDUS	10545
INDUS	87460
INESSA ARMAND	05628
INESSA ARMAND	14457
INEY	21190
INFANTE DOM HENRIQUE	09450
INGA	48560
INGA THOLSTRUP	88880
INGE BECH	67481
INGE DANIELSEN	64862
INGE DANIELSEN	91042
INGE MAERSK	60860
INGE MAERSK	70900
INGELHEIM	72002
INGENIERO VILLA	52651
INGENIERO VILLA	71601
INGER	73641
INGER	82940
INGER EXPRESS	94522
INGERSEKS	59530
INGI	91102
INGRID JUDITH	85191
INGUL.	02110
INGUL	12146
INGUL	22163
INGUL	23060
INGUL	35170
'INGUL' class	22161
INGUR	21221
INGURI.	04210
INGURI	35190
INICIATIVA	57041
INIKIOS EXPRESS No 2	33320
INKERMAN	36914
INKERMAN	43814
INKILAP	32165
INKURLES	45683
INLAND	70170
INNAREN	29923
INNISFALLEN	32720
INOWROCLAW	33281
INOWROCLAW	94551
INSEL REIMS	83603
INSELSBERG	76973
INSELSBERG	89783
INSTALLER I	51440
INTAN	43060
INTER II	09962
INTERAMICITY	27150
INTERDOS	09960
INTERFELICITY	35906
INTERFELICITY	41596
INTERHARMONY	26890
INTERNACIONAL	15184
INTERNACIONAL	10274
INTERNATSIONAL	60680
INTERNATSIONAL	90720
INTERNAVIS I	82370
INTISAR	64336
INVENTOR	00020
INVENTOR	35470
INZHEHIER AGEYEV	70743
INZHENER KREYLIS	80093
INZHENER MACHULSKIY	80090
INZHENER NECHIPORENKO	80095
INZHENER SUKHORUKOV	80092
INZHENER YERMOSHKIN	80182
INZHENIER BELOV	50771
INZHENIER YAMBURENKO	69323
IO	06503
IOANIS XILAS	26401
IOANNA V	85440
IOANNIS	06760
IOANNIS	10230
IOANNIS	40424
IOANNIS	42334
IOANNIS	42594
IOANNIS	49223
IOANNIS	85250
IOANNIS III	22836
IOANNIS K	42270
IOANNIS MARTINOS	46913
IOANNIS ZAFIRAKIS	57190
IOHANNES LAURISTIN	03779
IOHANNES LAURISTIN	04019
IOHANN MAMASHAL	90564
IOKHAN KYOLER	12434
IOKHANNES SEMPER	23535
ION	05475
ION SOLTYS	73292
IONA	22070
IONA YAKIR	05629
IONA YAKIR	14458
IONAS BILYUNAS	12435
IONIAN CAREER	07762
IONIAN CAREER	07812
IONIAN CARRIER	48055
IONIAN COMMANDER	38441
IONIAN MARINER	36021
IONIAN SEA	39050
IONIAN STAR	19331
IONIAN STAR	23710
IONIC	00201
IONIC	53156
IONIC	66305
IONIO	44190
IONIO	57230
IONION	88670
IOS	03430
IOS	90830
IOSIF DUBROVINSKIY	03776
IOSIF DUBROVINSKIY	04016
IOSIF LAPUSHKIN	13673
IOZAS VITAS	12436
IPANEMA	70561
IQBALBAKSH	13190
IQBALBAKSH	14640
IRAN ABAD	51162
IRAN ABAD	51531
IRAN BAYAN	49037
IRAN BESAT	05143
IRAN BORHAN	49033
IRAN CREMONA	16020
IRAN EHSAN	49034
IRAN EKRAM	14923
IRAN EKRAM	15734
IRAN ELHAM	14924
IRAN ELHAM	15733
IRAN EMAMAT	56301
IRAN ERSHAD	51163
IRAN ERSHAD	51533
IRAN GHEYAM	14925
IRAN GHEYAM	15735
IRAN HEJRAT	05140
IRAN HEMMET	07661
IRAN HOJJAT	55033
IRAN HOJJAT	84650
IRAN JAHAD	51164
IRAN JAHAD	51534
IRAN JENAN	49036
IRAN KALAM	07444
IRAN KALAM	15311
IRAN KEYHAN	56302
IRAN MEEAD	51160
IRAN MEEAD	51530
IRAN MEELAD	51161
IRAN MEELAD	51532
IRAN MEEZAN	49031
IRAN NAHAD	15312
IRAN NAHAD	51230
IRAN NEHZAT	05141
IRAN OKHUVAT	07662
IRAN REZVAN	49030
IRAN SALAM	07443
IRAN SEDAGHAT	86110
IRAN SEDAGHAT	91710
IRAN SEEYAM	07440
IRAN SEEYAM	15310
IRAN SEPEHR	56303
IRAN SHAD	05142
IRAN SHAFAAT	86111
IRAN SHAFAAT	91711
IRAN SHAHAB	56304
IRAN SHAHEED	82140
IRAN SHAHEED	82420
IRAN SHAMS	56300
IRAN SOKAN	49032
IRAN TOWHEED	82141
IRAN TOWHEED	82421
IRAN VOJDAN	49035
IRANDA	89830
IRATI	70560
IRBENSKIY PROLIV	58512
IRBENSKIY PROLIV	71822
IRBIT	85338
IRBITLES	45684
IRENA DAN	72380
IRENE	57570
IRENE	62023
IRENE	80940
IRENE D	11131
IRENE LEMOS	62792
IRENE LEMOS	67552
IRENE PATERAS	73120
IRENE S. LEMOS	78692
IRENES BANNER	10160
IRENES CHARITY	28761
IRENES CHARITY	30371
IRENES ECSTACY	61050
IRENES ECSTACY	82640
IRENES EMERALD	57470
IRENES FANTASY	56970
IRENES FRIENDSHIP	49220
IRENES GRACE	12892
IRENES LOGIC	05421
IRENES LOGIC	06121
IRENES LUCK	92000
IRENES MAGIC	05550
IRENES RHAPSODY	70670
IRENES SAPPHIRE	57471

IRENES SEA	58713
IRENES SEA	59643
IRENES SEA	61723
IRENES SINCERITY	50360
IRENES SINCERITY	74700
IRENES SINCERITY	74700
IRENES SUCCESS	46337
IRENES SUN	58712
IRENES SUN	59642
IRENES SUN	61722
IRENES ZEAL	55968
IRENES ZEAL	56728
IRENES ZEST	55965
IRENES ZEST	56725
IRFON	64081
IRINA	73642
IRINI G.F	07030
IRINI M	44150
IRINI S.K.	28430
IRINIO	58411
IRINIO	64571
IRIS	15110
IRIS	26950
IRIS	74173
IRIS	92400
IRIS	93080
IRISH CEDAR	46810
IRISH LARCH	46442
IRISH MAPLE	46443
IRISH OAK	46444
IRISH PINE	46445
IRISH ROWAN	46811
IRISH SEA	57194
IRISH WASA	56920
IRKUT	56271
IRKUT	62731
IRKUTSK	02520
IRKUTSK.	45116
IRKUTSKLES	45681
IRLA LUPE	85860
IRMA DELMAS	48881
IRON ARNHEM	47581
IRON BARON	59703
IRON BARON	61403
IRON CAPRICORN	46318
IRON CAPRICORN	46568
IRON CARPENTARIA	51250
IRON CARPENTARIA	53620
IRON CUMBERLAND	46115
IRON CURTIS	51251
IRON CURTIS	53621
IRON DUKE	72191
IRON KERRY	47884
IRON KESTREL	47885
IRON MONARCH	72190
IRON SIRIUS	73040
IRON TRANSPORTER	51633
IRON YORK	47580
IRPINIA	09400
IRSHALES	45685
IRTISH	84460
IRTYSHLES	45688
IRVING ARCTIC	65694
IRVING ARCTIC	70124
IRVING ESKIMO	65695
IRVING ESKIMO	70125
IRVINGWOOD	35620
ISABEL	73640
ISABELA	58683
ISABELITA	29650
ISABELLA	89730
ISABELLE	58391
ISADORE HECHT	18381
ISAKOGORKA	11432
ISAR	53409
ISAR	64939
ISBJORN	23941
ISCHIA	32130
ISE MARU	05075
ISE MARU	67787
ISERE	38080
ISEULT	63241
ISFONN	55360
ISHER	31420
ISHIKARI	32570
ISHIKARI MARU	19690
ISHIKARI MARU	23732
ISHIM	85339
ISIDOR BARAKHOV	50753
ISIS	01413
ISIS	01673
ISKENDERUN	18060
ISKONA	85340
ISKRA	60683
ISKRA	90722
ISLA BALTRA	14489
ISLA DE COCHE	19321
ISLA DE CUBAGUA	19320
ISLA DE LA JUVENTUD	18691
ISLA DE MARNAY	84761
ISLA DE MENORA	16690
ISLA DEL ATLANTICO	76031
ISLA DEL ATLANTICO	88621
ISLA GENOVESA	05482
ISLA GENOVESA	06813
ISLA LEONES	43010
ISLA PINTA	05480
ISLA PINTA	06810
ISLA SANTAY	14488
ISLA VERDE	33950
ISLAND ARCHON	56690
ISLAND CEMENT	91224
ISLAND CEMENT	91824
ISLAND CONTAINER	74840
ISLAND CONTAINER	74840
ISLAND CONTAINER	83010
ISLAND JESTER	59020
ISLAND KING	75962
ISLAND MARINER	46892
ISLAND OF MARMARA	23144
ISLAND OF MARMARA	28344
ISLAND OF MARMARA	32000
ISLAND PRINCESS	16831
ISLAND PRINCESS	16831
ISLAND SKY	61025
ISLAND SKY	71185
ISLAND SUPPLIER	41880
ISLAND TRADER	12870
ISLAS GALAPAGOS	04140
ISLAS GEORGIAS	41160
ISLAS MALVINAS	41161
ISMAILIYA	03969

ISMARA	66620
ISMARA	76240
ISMENE	53570
ISNES	66958
ISNES	70998
ISOBEL	26122
ISOLDA	22750
ISOLE	87730
ISONZO	24351
ISORA	06740
ISORA	31200
ISORA	71120
ISORA	86560
ISPARTA	46890
ISSA 1	81121
ISTIKBAL	00620
ISTRA	02451
ISTRA	45690
ISVANIA	74150
ISYK KOL	20794
ITABERA	05361
ITABERA	15661
ITAGIBA	03085
ITAIMBE	03080
ITAITE	03081
ITALIA	01450
ITALIA	35260
ITALIAN EXPRESS	64750
ITALICA	06171
ITALICA	64721
ITALMARE	52660
ITALMARE	73380
ITALO	86900
ITANAGE	03082
ITAPAGE	03086
ITAPARICA	65863
ITAPE	03087
ITAPUCA	03087
ITAPUI	03083
ITAPURA	03089
ITAQUATIA	03088
ITAQUICE	03084
ITASSUCE	03090
ITATINGA	05362
ITATINGA	15662
ITEL TAURUS	49284
ITELMAN	12437
ITHACA	10770
ITHAKI	06494
ITHAKI SAILOR	39900
ITHAKI SAILOR	40220
ITORORO	70562
IVA	94210
IVAN AIVAZOVSKIY	76490
IVAN AIVAZOVSKIY	89660
IVAN BABUSHKIN	28980
IVAN BOGUN	86189
IVAN BOLOTNIKOV	89251
IVAN BUBNOV	59883
IVAN BYELOSTOTSKIY	03777
IVAN BYELOSTOTSKIY	04017
IVAN CHERNOPYATKO	12439
IVAN CHERNYKH	11433
IVAN DERBENEV	78064
IVAN DVORSKIY	12438
IVAN FEDEROV	25843
IVAN FRANKO	01751
IVAN GOLUBETS	12251
IVAN GONCHAROV	07922
IVAN GREN	23513
IVAN KIREYEV	39175
IVAN KOLYSHKIN	79389
IVAN KOROBTSOV	03957
IVAN KOROTEYEV	69318
IVAN KRAMSKOY	76523
IVAN KRUZENSHTERN	22228
IVAN KUDRIYA	79431
IVAN KULIBIN	10749
IVAN LESOVIKOV	79430
IVAN MAZURANIC	34262
IVAN MOSKALENKO	48440
IVAN MOSKALENKO	49750
IVAN MOSKVIN	28491
IVAN MOSKVITIN	22227
IVAN MUSKALENKO	49480
IVAN NESTEROV	78019
IVAN NESTEROV	79999
IVAN PANOV	12440
IVAN PAVLOV	34241
IVAN POKROVSKIY	03778
IVAN POKROVSKIY	04018
IVAN POLZUNOV	10748
IVAN RYABOV	17926
IVAN SECHENOV	34242
IVAN SHADR	76588
IVAN SHADR	79938
IVAN SHEPETKOV	48439
IVAN SHEPETKOV	49479
IVAN SHEPETKOV	49749
IVAN SHISHKIN	76511
IVAN SIVKO	00143
IVAN SKURIDIN	78060
IVAN STEPANOV	45214
IVAN STROD	50734
IVAN SYRYKH	54711
IVAN SYRYKH	55281
IVAN VAZOV	80901
IVAN ZAGUBANSKI	49470
IVAN ZAGUBANSKI	49740
IVAN ZAGUBANSKI	48430
IVAN ZEMNUKHOV	41152
IVAN ZEMNUKHOV	44952
IVAN ZEMNUKHOV	86171
IVANOVO	39985
IVER HERON	53000
IVER HERON	53290
IVER SWAN	57664
IVI	39674
IVO DORMIO	85850
IVO VOJNOVIC	58130
IVORY	54961
IVORY	54561
IVORY ISLANDS	41540
IVORY ISLANDS	44090
IVORY MARU	32471
IVORY TELLUS	59704
IVORY TELLUS	61404
IVYBANK	03673
IVYBANK	03733
IWASHIRO MARU	05073
IWONICZ ZDROJ	81860
IXIA	56010

IYO MARU	05076
IYO MARU	32480
IYUN KORAN	11782
IZ	38640
IZGUTTY AYTYKOV	73293
IZHEVSK	00853
IZHEVSK	12344
IZHEVSKLES	45686
IZHMA	22851
IZHMA	34481
IZHMALES	45680
IZHORA	02521
IZHORA	70811
IZHORALES	45689
IZMAIL	02522
IZMAIL	11841
IZMIR	01591
IZU MARU No 3	23720
IZU MARU No. 3	32240
IZU MARU No 11	23721
IZU MARU No 11	32241
IZUMI MARU	05072
IZUMISAN MARU	54220
IZUMO MARU	05070
IZUMRUD	12441
IZUMRUD	35390
IZUMRUDNYY	11922
IZUMRUDNYY BEREG	62692
IZVESTIYA	57764
IZVESTIYA	62484
IZYASLAV	39996

J

J.J. SISTER	16421
J.R. GREY	57901
J.R. GREY	62991
J.R. ONE	25440
J W BATES	92210
JAAN KOORT	12442
JACARA	79117
JACK WHARTON	73682
JACK WHARTON	87342
JACKSONVILLE	72481
JACOB RUSS	54941
JACOBUS BROERE	88501
JACOPO TINTORETTO	32690
JACQUES DUCLOS	70595
JACY RAMOS	26772
JADE	14240
JADE	59603
JADE	64040
JADE	71933
JADE BAY	06495
JADE BOUNTY	82924
JADE STAR	57280
JADRAN	68760
JAG DARSHAN	54110
JAG DARSHAN	54580
JAG DEESH	54111
JAG DEESH	54581
JAG DHARMA	54112
JAG DHARMA	54582
JAG DHIR	54113
JAG DHIR	54583
JAG DOOT	54114
JAG DOOT	54584
JAG JYOTI	70102
JAG LAADKI	68831
JAG LAXMI	63457
JAG LEELA	63458
JAG REKHA	51083
JAG SHAKTI	48050
JAG SHANTI	48051
JAGAT MOHINI	55400
JAGAT MOHINI	84660
JAGAT NETA	53820
JAGAT PRIYA	54115
JAGAT PRIYA	54585
JAGAT SAMRAT	68392
JAGAT SAMRAT	77402
JAGAT SWAMINI	55401
JAGAT SWAMINI	84661
JAGAT VIJETA	53821
JAGRANDA	64332
JAGUAR	93930
JAINARAYAN VYAS	71633
JAKHONT	12443
JAKOB MAERSK	53190
JAKOV ALKSNIS	10730
JAKOV KUNDER	50288
JAKOV SMUSHKEVICH	12444
JALABALA	47042
JALADHRUV	25610
JALADUHITA	04490
JALADURGA	25770
JALADUTA	25771
JALAGIRIJA	25730
JALAGOMATI	27030
JALAGOURI	28290
JALAJAYA	04250
JALAJYOTI	15230
JALAKALA	30751
JALAKANTA	30754
JALAKENDRA	30752
JALAKIRTI	30750
JALAKRISHNA	30753
JALAMANGALA	05825
JALAMANGALA	06012
JALAMANI	05822
JALAMANI	06013
JALAMATSYA	05826
JALAMATSYA	06014
JALAMAYUR	06017
JALAMAYUR	05824
JALAMOHAN	05823
JALAMOHAN	06015
JALAMOKAMBI	05820
JALAMOKAMBI	06010
JALAMORARI	05821
JALAMORARI	06011
JALAMOTI.	05827
JALAMOTI	06016
JALAMUDRA	04911
JALAMURUGAN	04912
JALANIDHI	09660
JALAPANKHI	07663
JALAPUTRA	06641
JALARAJAN	05170
JALARAJAN	14321
JALARASHMI	05172

JALARASHMI	14320
JALARATNA	05171
JALARATNA	14322
JALATARANG	67290
JALAVIHAR	77651
JALAVIHAR	80711
JALAYAMINI	15681
JALAYAMUNA	15680
JALENGI	39350
JALINGA	60280
JALINGA	68420
JALTIPAN	74701
JALVALLABH	73081
JALVALLABH	77791
JAMAICA FAREWELL	48360
JAMAICA FAREWELL	50870
JAMAICA PRODUCER	04150
JAMBUR	69573
JAMEELA	90891
JAMES E. O'BRIEN	63150
JAMES LYKES	00062
JAMES ROWAN	42451
JAMHURI	20990
JAMILK	27770
JAMUNDA	60281
JAMUNDA	68421
JAN	66840
JAN	73721
JAN ANVELT	10435
JAN BERZIN	12445
JAN FABRITSIUS	12446
JAN HEWELIUSZ	09251
JAN HEWELIUSZ	33381
JAN HEWELIUSZ	94701
JAN KARS	73954
JAN KREUKS	86091
JAN MATEJKO	14582
JAN MAYEN	18724
JAN RAINBERG	13674
JAN RUDZUTAK	12447
JAN TAVENIER	50230
JAN WILHELM	50841
JAN WILLEM	64870
JAN ZIZKA	14302
JANA	02111
JANA	21580
JANA	35171
JANA PRIYA	77567
JANA VIJAY	78750
JANAKI	27950
JANALES	11491
JANE MAERSK	53191
JANE-SEA	88200
JANE STOVE	69112
JANE STOVE	71462
JANEGA	46993
JANEGA	83333
JANEK KRASICKI	14583
JANI	13230
JANJE	82806
JANJE	92096
JANUSHA	27640
JAPAN ACE	08720
JAPAN ADONIS	54545
JAPAN ADONIS	63905
JAPAN AMBROSE	08640
JAPAN CANELA	03741
JAPAN CANELA	51121
JAPAN CAOBO	03740
JAPAN CAOBO	51120
JAPAN CARNATION	55461
JAPAN CARNATION	62781
JAPAN COSMOS	54801
JAPAN COSMOS	68031
JAPAN LUPINUS	55460
JAPAN ORCHID	56350
JAPAN ORCHID	68050
JAPAN POPLAR	77222
JAPAN TUNA No 2	50890
JAPAN VIOLET	54370
JAPAN VIOLET	62980
JAPAN WISTERIA	69120
JAPANA	72343
JAPIN LUPINUS	62780
JAPURA	68203
JARABELLA	60282
JARABELLA	68422
JARI	68204
JARICHA	64331
JARILLA	78426
JARITA	64333
JARLI	64310
JAROSLAW	66980
JASLO	16270
JASNOMORSK	22853
JASNOMORSK	34483
JASON	20461
JASTARNIA-BOR	04341
JASTARNIA-BOR	04401
JASTARNIA-BOR	04401
JASTELLA	60283
JASTELLA	68423
JATULI	58350
JAVARA	46990
JAVARA	83330
JAVRON	03750
JAWAHARLAL NEHRU	67770
JAWAHARLAL NEHRU	69190
JAY DURGA	56991
JAYA PUTRA II	42310
JEAN CHARCOT	02510
JEAN L-D	83146
JEAN LYKES	00063
JEANNE D'ARC	90570
JEANNE D'ARC	91990
JEANNE LABOURBE	05630
JEANNE LABOURBE	14459
JEANNIE	62030
JEANNIE	74942
JEBEL ALI 2	30350
'JEEP' type	25520
JEFF DAVIS	02300
JELA TOPIC	61930
JELA TOPIC	72090
JELAU	61076
JELAU	71266
JELCZ II	82268
JELENIA GORA	82261
JENA	47818
JENNIFER	43670
JENNY GRAEBE	72755
JENNY SMITS	88110

K

KAPITAN SOROKIN	02230
KAPITAN STULOV	78017
KAPITAN STULOV	79997
KAPITAN TELOV	00144
KAPITAN TOMSON	80060
KAPITAN VANILOV	78018
KAPITAN VANILOV	79998
KAPITAN VASILYEVSKIY	54727
KAPITAN VASILYEVSKIY	55297
KAPITAN VISLOBOKOV	45360
KAPITAN VOOLENS	22854
KAPITAN VOOLENS	34484
KAPITAN VORONIN	23972
KAPITAN YAKOVLEV	80061
KAPITAN ZAMYATIN	54728
KAPITAN ZAMYATIN	55298
KAPITAN ZARUBIN	22203
KAPITAN ZIOLKOWSKI	87752
KAPPA VICTORY	69440
KAPRELA	23445
KAPRIFOL	72820
KAPRIFOL	80220
KAPRIJE	66950
KAPRIJE	70990
KAPSUKAS	06772
KAPSUKAS	07592
KAPTAI	52681
KAPTAMICHALIS	06535
KAPTAN NECDET OR	32991
KAPTAN SAIT OZEGE	32990
KAPUAS	61476
KARA	06774
KARA	07580
KARA	48080
KARA CAREER	05950
KARA SEA	29247
KARACHAJEVO-CHERKESSIJA	03043
KARACHAJEVO-CHERKESSIJA	50913
KARA-DAG	11948
KARADAG	84461
KARADENIZ	01581
KARAGA	31877
KARAGACH	11925
KARAGANDA	02523
KARAGAT	23536
KARAISKAKI	79830
KARAKUM KANAL	44119
KARAKUMNEFT	86001
KARAKUMY	11316
KARAMA MAERSK	54451
KARAMA MAERSK	63371
KARAMAN	50142
KARAMU FOREST	46641
KARAMU FOREST	83321
KARANA AMPAT	30450
KARANA ENAN	31810
KARE	49861
KARELI	86002
KARELIYA	20373
KARELYALES	04184
KAREN	57610
KAREN	62241
KAREN BRAVO	92390
KAREN MAERSK	54452
KAREN MAERSK	63372
KAREN WINTHER	64890
KAREPO	03530
KARGOPAL	23531
KARHU	23981
KARIMATA	89228
KARIN	75508
KARIN	86980
KARIN	88120
KARIN BORNHOFEN	71848
KARIN VATIS	48151
KARINA	39680
KARINA	40080
KARINA RIO GRANDE	74231
KARKONOSZE	70065
KARKONOSZE	55314
KARL KRUSHTEYN	89215
KARL LIEBKNECHT	05631
KARL LIEBKNECHT	14460
KARL LIEBKNECHT	17516
KARL LIEBKNECHT	62680
KARL LINNE	61271
KARL LINNE	81491
KARL MARX	03150
KARL MARX	17517
KARL MARX STADT;	04920
KARL WOLF	23425
KARLIS ZIEDINS	10724
KARLSBURG	86350
KARLSVIK	75532
KARMSUND	93000
KAROLINE MAERSK	54453
KAROLINE MAERSK	63373
KAROLIS POZHELA	12454
KAROLOS	22920
KAROSSA	18153
KAROTUA	00800
KARPACZ	81866
KARPATY	11313
KARPOGORY	11326
KARRABIO	80480
KARSKOYE MORE	55130
KARTALA	88151
KARTALY	84464
KARTHAGO	50130
KARTLI	12255
KARTUZY	88232
KARUKERA	33960
KARYATIS	85171
KASAGISAN MARU	77226
KASAYSAYAN	22962
KASEM SAMUT	31960
KASHIMA MARU	72400
KASHIMASAN MARU	68010
KASHINO	06773
KASHINO	07583
KASHU MARU	08750
KASIMOV	03040
KASIMOV	50910
KASIMPASA	19041
KASKAD	12455
KASPAR SIF	64851
KASPAR SIF	91031
KASPIJSK	03045
KASPIJSK	50914
KASPIY	35310
KASPIY	50780
KASPROWY WIERCH	64090
KASSANDRA	48340
KASSANTINA	60952
KASSIOPEYA	12256
KASSOS	18371
KASSOS	21200
KASSOS	27291
KASSOS	45951
KASTAV	05653
KASTELLORIZON	00420
KASTOR	12611
KASTOR	29300
KASTRIANI III	25130
KASTURBA	77652
KASTURBA	80712
KASUGA MARU	51280
KASUGA MARU	52690
KASUGA MARU	95082
KASUGAI MARU	48942
KASZALOT	10812
KASZUBY II	59691
KASZUBY II	81351
KATAL	13791
KATANGLI	31862
'KATATRAN' type	94250
KATAWA	51788
KATE MAERSK	54454
KATE MAERSK	63374
KATENDRECHT	47421
KATERINA	35661
KATERINA	56990
KATERINA	90231
KATERINA DRACOPOULOS	06540
KATERINA E	47398
KATERINA E	47968
KATERINA K	41340
KATERINA V	43480
KATERINA V	43510
KATERINE	80401
KATHE JOHANNA	73970
KATHERINE	78860
KATHERINE ALEXANDRA	60721
KATHLEEN	75890
KATIA	17820
KATIE	10365
KATINA	31700
KATINA C	45171
KATINA MATHEO	30791
KATIPUNAN	18805
KATJANA	47250
KATORI MARU	51281
KATORI MARU	52691
KATORI MARU	72300
KATORI MARU	77190
KATRINA	72660
KATRINE MAERSK	54455
KATRINE MAERSK	63375
KATRISA	69410
KATSINA PALM	12871
KATSURA MARU	62301
KATTEGAT	18725
KATUN	35180
KATUNJ	02280
KATUNJ	35180
KATY	51170
KATYN	02280
KAUAI	93527
KAUAI	94317
KAUNAS	40004
KAVALEROVO	31878
KAVKAZ	17518
KAVKAZ	63982
KAVO ALKYON	28610
KAVO DELFINI	28611
KAVO GROSSOS	07021
KAVO MALEAS	63950
KAVO MATAPAS	48200
KAVO PEIRATIS	48201
KAVO SPATHI	65530
KAVO XIFIAS	36381
KAVO XIFIAS	37401
KAVO YOSSONAS	07022
KAVO YOSSONAS	37710
KAVRAY	11926
KAWISHIWI	45053
KAYESON	37221
KAZAKHSTAN	12456
KAZAKHSTAN	20374
KAZALINSK	23539
KAZAN	12322
KAZATIN	23542
KAZATIN	31869
KAZBEK	39975
'KAZBEK' class	39970
'KAZBEK' class	44890
KAZIS GERDIS	85330
KAZIS PREYKSHAS	76516
KAZUKAWA MARU	08721
KAZUSHIMA MARU	93450
KAZUTAMA MARU	58060
KDD MARU	02430
KDD MARU	35450
KEA	54671
KEBAN	07880
KEBAN	15648
KEBON AGUNG	18152
KEDAYNYAY	06777
KEDAYNYAY	07591
KEDZIERZYN	75771
KEFALONIA	91730
KEFALONIA LIGHT	57380
KEFALONIA SPIRIT	09070
KEFALONIA STAR	59293
KEFALONIA STAR	61333
KEFALONIA SUN	47750
KEFALONIA WIND	59292
KEFALONIA WIND	61332
KEGOSTROV	11381
KEGUMS	86470
KEHARITOMENI	40290
KEHDINGEN	91410
KEHREA	57100
KEKHRA	89200
KEKUR	85979
KELEKAR	41963
KELKHEIM	46992
KELKHEIM	83332
KELLYEVERETT	21421
KELO	48081
KEM	31857
KEMAL KOLOTOGLU	90170
KEMERI	86080
KEMEROVO	10435
KEMINE	79415
KEN SHENG	12190
KEN SUCCESS	80740
KEN VICTORY	79670
KENAN MARU	71158
KENFIG	35291
KENGARAGS	89750
KENINGAU	18140
KENNEMERLAND	13410
KENTAVROS	16620
KENTUCKY HOME	46587
KENWA MARU	28001
KEPLERO	66540
KERASOUS	10900
KERASOUS	34120
KERCH	12230
KERCH	39976
KERCH	59894
KERCH	67654
KERCHENSKIY	12302
KERCHENSKIY KOMMUNIST	86009
KERI	83706
KERKYRA	90770
KERO	00110
KERO	36040
KESNAR	13530
KESSULAID	75640
KETA LAGOON	04834
KETTY	90480
KETTY DANIELSEN	64863
KETTY DANIELSEN	91043
KEUM GANG SAN	92781
'KEY 12' type	57490
'KEY 26' type	47430
'KEY 26' type	47900
'KEY 40' type	64640
KEYLA	86247
KEYSTONE CANYON	58032
KEYSTONER	38170
KHABAROVSK	02123
KHABAROVSK	12345
KHADIJAAN	29920
KHALIJ COOLER	05467
KHALIJ EXPRESS	06190
KHALIJ FREEZER	05465
KHALIJ FROST	05466
KHALIJ REEFER	05463
KHALIJ SKY	26210
KHALIJIAH	58492
KHALIJIAH	84912
KHAN ASPARUKH	52440
KHAN OMTURAG	85362
KHANAQUIN	69574
KHANKA	84362
KHANKA	85990
KHANNUR	53880
KHARITON LAPTEV	22190
KHARK	55464
KHARK	62784
KHARLOV	07565
KHARLOVKA.	17975
KHAROVSK	11757
KHAROVSK	34648
KHASAN	25550
KHASAN	67352
KHASAN	71362
KHASAN	84367
KHATANGA	24071
KHATANGALES	11492
KHAYRYUZOVO	23554
KHENDRIK KUYVAS	67013
KHERMAN ARBON	12457
KHERSON	67682
KHERSONES	70778
KHIAN CAPTAIN	58091
KHIAN ENGINEER	58092
KHIAN HILL	58093
KHIAN ISLAND	58094
KHIAN SAILOR	58095
KHIAN SEA	58096
KHIAN STAR	58097
KHIAN SUN	58098
KHIAN WAVE	58099
KHIAN ZEPHYR	58100
KHIBINSKIE GORY	61272
KHIBINSKIE GORY	81492
KHIBINY	11320
KHIRURG VISHNEVSKIY	01564
KHOLMOGORY	11307
KHOLMOGORY	22852
KHOLMOGORY	34482
KHOLMSK	24072
KHOLMSK	26160
KHOLMSK	88244
KHOOBCHAND	06982
KHRONOMETR	11949
KHRUSTAL	12459
KHRUSTALNYY	11927
KHRUSTALNYY	85992
KHUDOZHNIK DEYNEKA	76519
KHUDOZHNIK IOGANSON	77341
KHUDOZHNIK KUINDZHA	50737
KHUDOZHNIK PAKHOMOV	77342
KHUDOZHNIK PLASTOV	50748
KHUDOZHNIK PROROKOV	77343
KHUDOZHNIK REPIN	77344
KHUDOZHNIK ROMAS	77345
KHUDOZHNIK S. GERASIMOV	76514
KHUDOZHNIK SARYAN	77340
KHUDOZHNIK V. KRAYNEV	10438
KHUDOZHNIK VRUBEL	76520
KHUDOZHNIK ZHUKOV	77346
KHULIO ANTONIO MELYA	36876
KHULNA	89224
KIAEN	83990
KIAN AN	59250
KIAN AN	62520
KIDRIC B	55993
KIELDRECT	47420
KIETA	40910
KIETA	45150
KIEV	02071
KIFANGONGO	05312
KIGILYAKH	50745
KIHELKONA	86239
KII MARU	20390
KIISLA	75220
KIKA	56987
KIKCHETAV	89464
KIKCHIK	06792
KIKHCHIK	07584
KIKI	12840
KIKI YEMELOS	46040
KIKUKO MARU	48282
KILDARE	64480
KILDARE	92260
KILDARE	92430
KILDIN	11434
KILDIN	11583
KILIYA	31860
KILIYA	75351
KILKENNY	72710
KIM ANN	17760
KIM GUAN	37360
KIM GUAN	44130
KIMANIS	00950
KIMBERLEY	57765
KIMBERLEY	62485
KIMBERLY	57842
KIMITETSU MARU	69291
KIMITSU MARU	69290
KIMKO STORK	25261
KIMOLIAKI AIGLI	54690
KIMOLIAKI AIGLI	84630
KIMOLOS	19830
KIMOLOS	33951
KIMOLOS	40970
KIMOLOS	60771
KIMOLOS	69671
KIMOLOS	89970
KIMOVSK	03046
KIMOVSK	50915
KIMRY	07590
KINDRENCE	76141
KING ALFRED	77730
KING ALFRED	89820
KING BIRD	41956
KING CADMUS	69530
KING CHARLES	60910
KING EAST	28841
KING EGBERT	34214
KING GEORGE	73230
KING HORSE	27910
KING HORSE	34440
KING LEONIDAS	85060
KING LION	41955
KING NESTOR	61881
KING ON	40426
KING ON	42336
KING ON	42596
KING RICHARD	79200
KING STAR	27920
KING STAR	63592
KING STAR	68332
KING WILLIAM	73231
KINGAN	12458
KINGFORD	25173
KINGISEPP	06778
KINGISEPP	07572
KINGSABBEY	66720
KINGSABBEY	76370
KINGSNORTH	54270
KINGSNORTH FISHER	23991
KINI KERSTEN	87352
KINKO MARU	48280
KINKO MARU	56330
KINKO MARU	68020
KINPURNIE UNIVERSAL	06352
KIPARISOVO	89511
KIRENSK	31863
KIRGHIZSTAN	02352
KIRGHIZSTAN	35372
KIRIR	23555
KIRISHIMA MARU	92623
KIRK EXPRESS	17260
KIRK TRAILER	95011
KIRKELLA	31130
KIRKUK	69575
KIROVABAD	44121
KIROVOGRAD	11844
KIROVSK	00854
KIROVSK	11602
KIROVSKLES.	04180
KIRRIBILLI	15980
KIRSTEN BRAVO	93990
KIRSTEN MAERSK	54450
KIRSTEN MAERSK	63370
KIRSTEN SKOU	31302
KIRSTEN SMITS	52110
KIRSTEN SMITS	67060
KIRSTEN THOLSTRUP	85000
KIRSTEN WESCH	57607
KIRSTEN WESCH	62251
KISANGANI	62713
KISANGANI	62753
KISHINEV	49240
KISLOVODSK	00333
KISO MARU	09810
KISO MARU	10180
KISO MARU	94930
KITANO MARU	33601
KITANO MARU	62312
KITEN	76533
KITEN	84211
KITHNOS	52930
KITMEER	24574
KITTY PORR	60951
KIVACH	11308
KIWI ARROW	83142
KIZI	84363
KIZKULESI	19040
KLAHOWYA	18981
KLAMONO/PERMINA 1016	65181
KLARA ZETKIN	10420
KLARA ZETKIN	10725
KLAREDON	82801
KLAREDON	92091
'KLASMA' class	02110
'KLASMA' class	02280
'KLASMA' class	35170
'KLASMA' class	35180
'KLASMA' class	35190
KLASSEN	87200
KLAUS LEONHARDT	59754
KLAVDIA	45393
KLAYPEDA	39960
KLEK	07981
KLEMENT GOTTWALD	70599
KLIM VOROSHILOV	03965
KLIMOVO	11929
KLIN	03930
KLIO	29911
KLISURA	83729
KLORTE LAGOON	07993

KLORTE LAGOON	15278
KLOSTERFELDE	59650
KLYAZMA	12257
KLYAZMA	85880
KLYUCHEYSKOY	23556
KNIAZIK	18744
KNIEPSAND	59513
KNIEPSAND	59823
KNOSSOS	20151
KNUD JESPERSEN	57766
KNUD JESPERSEN	62486
KNUDSHOVED	18940
KNUT MARK	77580
KOBULETI	11845
KOCAELI 1	58192
KOCEVJE	71157
KOCHANOWSKI	06890
KODINO	11494
KOERIER	52091
KOH EUN	71159
KOHENG	86113
KOHENG	91713
KOHSHO MARU	72310
KOIDA	94452
KOITELI	47492
KOKAN SEWAK	33440
KOKAN SEWAK	33610
KOKAND	36258
KOKAND	42808
KOKHTLA	15471
KOKKO MARU	54541
KOKKO MARU	63901
KOKUSHU MARU No 2	79620
KOLA	70777
KOLA	86188
KOLANDIA	71630
KOLASIN	58131
KOLEN	18745
KOLGUYEV	11498
KOLIAS	23461
KOLIMA	43170
KOLKHIDA	02350
KOLKHIDA	12258
KOLKHIDA	35370
KOLLBRIS	64364
KOLN EXPRESS	08781
KOLOBRZEG II	82263
KOLOMNA	28060
KOLPINSEE	46384
KOLPINSEE	47084
KOLSKIY	11585
KOLTSOV	12365
KOLYA MYGATIN	15514
KOLYMA	35323
KOLYMALES	04185
KOM	84212
KOM	85500
KOMANDARM FEDKO	67680
KOMANDARM GAY	50752
KOMANDARM MATVEYEV	03966
KOMERING	18155
KOMETA	11580
KOMILES	24043
KOMISSAR POLUKHIN	45126
KOMMUNAR	13678
KOMMUNARSK	03937
KOMMUNIST	05632
KOMMUNIST	12460
KOMMUNIST	14461
'KOMMUNIST' class	05620
'KOMMUNIST' class	14450
KOMMUNIST UKRAINY	12461
KOMMUNISTICHESKOYE ZNAMYA	05633
KOMMUNISTICHESKOYE-ZNAMYA	14462
KOMPAS	09385
KOMSOMOL	23543
KOMSOMOL	40007
KOMSOMOL UKRAINI	12462
KOMSOMOLETS	01385
KOMSOMOLETS	01645
KOMSOMOLETS	07569
KOMSOMOLETS	12303
KOMSOMOLETS ADZHARII	01399
KOMSOMOLETS ADZHARII	01659
KOMSOMOLETS ARMENII	01389
KOMSOMOLETS ARMENII	01649
KOMSOMOLETS AZERBAYDZHANA	01390
KOMSOMOLETS AZERBAYDZHANA	01650
KOMSOMOLETS BYELORUSSII	01400
KOMSOMOLETS BYELORUSSII	01660
KOMSOMOLETS ESTONII	03931
KOMSOMOLETS GRUZII	01391
KOMSOMOLETS GRUZII	01651
KOMSOMOLETS KAZAKHSTANA	01398
KOMSOMOLETS KAZAKHSTANA	01658
KOMSOMOLETS KIRGIZII	03932
KOMSOMOLETS KUBANI	36873
KOMSOMOLETS LATVII	03933
KOMSOMOLETS LENINGRADA	36879
KOMSOMOLETS LITVY	03934
KOMSOMOLETS MAGADANA	93759
KOMSOMOLETS MAGADANA	93849
KOMSOMOLETS MOLDAVII	01392
KOMSOMOLETS MOLDAVII	01652
KOMSOMOLETS NAKHODKI	01393
KOMSOMOLETS NAKHODKI	01653
KOMSOMOLETS PRAVDA	01402
KOMSOMOLETS PRAVDA	01662
KOMSOMOLETS ROSSII	01397
KOMSOMOLETS ROSSII	10657
KOMSOMOLETS SPASSKA	01394
KOMSOMOLETS SPASSKA	01654
KOMSOMOLETS TADZHIKISTANA	03935
KOMSOMOLETS TURKMENII	01401
KOMSOMOLETS TURKMENII	01661
KOMSOMOLETS UKRAINY	39994
KOMSOMOLETS USSURIYSKA	01395
KOMSOMOLETS USSURIYSKA	01655
KOMSOMOLETS UZBEKISTANA	03936
KOMSOMOLETS VLADIVOSTOKA	01396
KOMSOMOLETS VLADIVOSTOKA	01656
KOMSOMOLSK	71531
KOMSOMOLSK	80201
KOMSOMOLSK NA AMURE	93760
KOMSOMOLSK NA AMURE	93850
KOMSOMOLSKAYA SLAVA	02681
KONDA	21582
KONDOPOGO	31858
KONDOR	09386
KONDOR	11960
KONDRATIY BULAVIN	89252
KONG FREDERIK IX	19590
KONG HAAKON VII	60550
KONG HAAKON VII	69480
KONG OLAV	01940
KONG OLAV V	01910
KONG SVERRE	33430
KONGER	22337
KONGO MARU	35092
KONGO MARU	95083
KONIGSEE	72121
KONIGSEE 1	76461
KONIN	14474
KONIN	05645
KONINGIN FABIOLA	20060
KONINGIN JULIANA	20470
KONISTRA	07141
KONISTRA	29021
KONITSA	77565
KONKAN SHAKTI	33441
KONKAN SHAKTI	33611
KONKAR DINOS	63441
KONKAR INDOMITABLE	77640
KONKAR RESOLUTE	78560
KONKAR VICTORY	77641
KONOSHA	86228
KONPIRA	56080
KONSTANTIN KORSHUNOV	50289
KONSTANTIN OLSHANSKIY	76508
KONSTANTIN PETROVSKIY	54717
KONSTANTIN PETROVSKIY	55287
KONSTANTIN SAVELYEV	50285
KONSTANTIN SHESTAKOV	50281
KONSTANTIN SUKHANOV	93684
KONSTANTIN TSIOLKOVSKIY	59896
KONSTANTIN TSIOLKOVSKIY	67656
KONSTANTIN YUON	76586
KONSTANTIN YUON	79936
KONSTANTIN ZANKOV	69315
KONSTANTIN ZASLONOV	50735
KONSTANTINOVKA	12147
KONSTANTIS YEMELOS	06498
KONSTITUTSIYA SSSR	45270
KONTEA	09651
KONTULA	47190
KOOPERATSIYA	22451
KOPALNIA GRZYBOW	48660
KOPALNIA JEZIORKO	49211
KOPALNIA KLEOFAS	61091
KOPALNIA MACHOW	48661
KOPALNIA MARCEL	61092
KOPALNIA MOSZCZENICA	61090
KOPALNIA PIASECZNO	49210
KOPALNIA SOSNICA	61093
KOPALNIA SOSNOWIEC	78294
KOPALNIA SOSNOWIEC	80024
KOPALNIA SZCZYGLOWICE	61094
KOPALNIA WALBRZYCH	78295
KOPALNIA WALBRZYCH	80025
KOPALNIA WIREK	61096
KOPALNIA ZOFIOWKA	78296
KOPALNIA ZOFIOWKA	80026
KOPER	62180
KOPET-DAG	11300
KOPORYE	06779
KOPORYE	07582
KOPRIVSTICA	83727
KORABLESTROITYEL KLOPOTOV	93693
KORALL	12463
KORALLE	28530
KORALLOVYY	89757
KORCULA	71010
KORDUN	68761
KOREA BANNER	55563
KOREA BANNER	62943
KOREA DONGHAE	63854
KOREA EDINBURGH	38160
KOREA STAR	55562
KOREA STAR	62942
KOREA SUN	55561
KOREA SUN	62941
KOREA SUNNYHILL	69254
KOREA SUNNYHILL	70554
KOREAN COMMANDER	08800
KOREAN DONGHAE II	63304
KOREAN FIR	61032
KOREAN FIR	71192
KOREAN FLOWER	83991
KOREAN JUPITER	73440
KOREAN JUPITER	80370
KOREAN LEADER	73483
KOREAN LIFTER	83992
KOREAN LOADER	73491
KOREAN PEARL	48270
KOREAN PRIDE	61031
KOREAN PRIDE	71191
KOREAN RUNNER	14690
KOREAN SHIPPER	83986
KOREIZ	12260
KOREIZ	31864
KORENGA	23558
KORIAKI	89508
KORINTHOS	12980
KORLE LAGOON	15272
KORLE LAGOON	35043
KORMORAN I	73590
KORNAT	80522
KORO SEA	79810
KOROLENKO	12366
KOROLENKO	20795
KOROTAN	10310
KORRIGAN	09690
KORSAKOV	31844
'KORSAKOV' type	86070
'KORSAKOV' type	87940
KORSNES	50122
KORSOR	19100
KORTENAER	76010
KORUND	11846
KORUNDOVYY	89761
KORWIN	18746
KOS	18372
KOS	21201
KOSCIERZYNA	50468
KOSHIN MARU No 3	70922
KOSHIN MARU No 3	79602
KOSICE	78940
KOSMAJ	68762
KOSMAS K	24670
KOSMONAUT	01073
KOSMONAUT GAGARIN	76525
KOSMONAUT KOMAROV	45127
KOSMONAUT PAVEL BELYAYEV	11430
KOSMONAUT VLADISLAV VOLKOV	11435
KOSMOS	11584
KOSMOS	40930
KOSOVO	62060
KOSSOU	25274
KOSTA KHETAGUROV	50762
KOSTAKIS	43121
KOSTAR	62225
KOSTAR	71135
KOSTAS	87693
KOSTAS K	87371
KOSTAS K	91131
KOSTAS MELAS	56890
KOSTER	33540
KOSTINO	06781
KOSTINO	07579
KOSTRENA	15291
KOSTROMA	40003
KOSTROMALES	11493
KOSZALIN	34371
KOTA ABADI	10363
KOTA AGUNG	12090
KOTA ALAM	00893
KOTA BAHAGIA	90471
KOTA BAKTI	13385
KOTA BALI	01510
KOTA BANTENG	90342
KOTA BENAR	13384
KOTA BERANI	13482
KOTA BINTANG	07532
KOTA BUANA	10520
KOTA CAHAYA	05801
KOTA CANTIK	05800
KOTA CEMPAKA	08131
KOTA DJAJA	42160
KOTA FAJAR	26460
KOTA HARAPAN	90472
KOTA INDAH	90473
KOTA JADE	48493
KOTA JASA	13990
KOTA JATI	15622
KOTA JAYA	13092
KOTA MAHA	34560
KOTA MAJU	15612
KOTA MAKMUR	83581
KOTA MANIS	31550
KOTA MAS	00900
KOTA MAWAR	10652
KOTA MEGAH	11363
KOTA MELATI	10651
KOTA MELUR	29430
KOTA MEWAH	07231
KOTA MEWAH	07431
KOTA MOLEK	00892
KOTA MUNI	30110
KOTA PAHLAWAN	88210
KOTA PANJANG	00580
KOTA PANJANG	27790
KOTA RAJA	08122
KOTA RAKYAT	26021
KOTA RAKYAT	30191
KOTA RATNA	17870
KOTA RATU	08121
KOTA RIA	17871
KOTA RUKUN	17872
KOTA SABAS	00711
KOTA SEJARAH	13590
KOTA SEJATI	13531
KOTA SELAMAT	15602
KOTA SENTOSA	13992
KOTA SETIA	31060
KOTA SILAT XII	43149
KOTA SUBUR	07360
KOTA SUBUR	31260
KOTA TANJONG	30090
KOTA TIMUR	30490
KOTAH GAJAH	90343
KOTAYKA	23557
KOTEL	83725
KOTELNICH	11324
KOTHEN	61712
KOTHEN	71082
KOTKANIEMI	47790
KOTLAS	28064
KOTLASLES	04186
KOTOR	78530
KOTOVSK	86222
KOTOVSKIY	20796
KOTOVSKIY	33910
KOTUKU	53111
KOTUKU	53181
KOUTOURIARIS S.V.	32080
KOVDA	24073
KOVDALES	04189
KOVDOR	15472
KOVEL	34485
KOVEL	22855
'KOVEL' type	22790
'KOVEL' type	22840
'KOVEL' type	34470
KOVROV	03047
KOVROV	50916
KOWLOON BAY	08402
KOWLOON VOYAGER	27380
KOYALI	67401
KOYO MARU	34390
KOYO MARU	38980
KOYO MARU	52590
KOYO MARU No 2	92620
KOZELSK	50736
KOZEROG	12304
KOZYREVSK	07559
KR. AVINASH	25172
KRAGUJEVAC	40241
KRAIGHER B	55994
KRAKOW	15080
KRALJEVICA	05651
KRAMATORSK	45218
KRANAOS	90631
KRANJ	57442
KRANJCEVIC	05654
KRANSK	24070
KRANSNOBORSK	07573
KRANTOR	21920
KRANTOR	67250
KRANTOR	91670
KRAPANJ	71020
KRAS	55270
KRASICA	04922
KRASIN	20872
KRASKINO	24067
KRASLAVA	86471
KRASNAL	87740
KRASNAYA GORKA	11436
KRASNAYA PRESNYA	01565
KRASNOARMEYSK	31865
KRASNOBORSK	06780
KRASNODAR	12259
KRASNODON	03940
KRASNOE SELO	03944
KRASNOE ZNAMYA	01566
KRASNOGORSK	84339
KRASNOGORSKLES	04187
KRASNOGRAD	03049
KRASNOGRAD	50918
KRASNOGVARDEYETS	23559
KRASNOGVARDEYSK	03938
KRASNOKAMSK	03939
KRASNOPOLYE	31866
KRASNOPUTILOVETS	11614
KRASNOTURINSK	31867
KRASNOUFIMSK	03048
KRASNOUFIMSK	03941
KRASNOUFIMSK	50917
KRASNOURALSK	03942
KRASNOYARSK	07566
KRASNOYARSKI KOMSOMOLETS	01388
KRASNOYARSKI KOMSOMOLETS	01648
KRASNOZAVODSK	03943
KRASNYY LUCH	71671
KRASNYY-OKTYABAR	01567
KRASZEWSKI	15580
KRATILAOS	31491
KRAYEV	12464
KRECHET	23521
KREKING	85889
KREMEN	11928
KREMENCHUG	39997
KREMENETS	86085
KREML	01568
KRETAN GLORY	28512
KRETAN GLORY	30323
KRETAN SPIRIT	28511
KRETAN SPIRIT	30321
KRETINGA	07558
KREUTSWALD	85359
KREYVANG	91413
KRIOS	16070
KRIOS	31490
KRIOS	36510
KRIPTON	85970
KRIS MADURA	49611
KRIS MELELA	49610
KRISGAIL	72514
KRISHYANS VOLDEMARS	12367
KRISTALL	12465
KRISTALNYY	89753
KRISTIN BAKKE	12730
KRISTINA	52480
KRISTINA BRAHE	20830
KRISTINE MAERSK	54456
KRISTINE MAERSK	63376
KRISTIONAS DONELAYTIS	12466
KRISTO MARINOVIC	35511
KRISTYAN RAUD	12467
KRITI	08200
KRITI	42900
KRITI LAND	69141
KRITI STAR	69140
KRITI WAVE	69142
KRIVAN	15090
KRIVBASS	63984
KRK	04923
KRKA	59571
KRKA	81301
KRONID KORENOV	03691
KRONOS	05341
KRONOS	23080
KRONOS	61790
KRONOS 1	00820
KRONPRINS FREDERIK	16032
KRONPRINS FREDERIK	19992
KRONPRINS HARALD	16920
KRONPRINSESSAN VICTORIA	16910
KRONSHTADT	11736
KRONSHTADT	34626
KRONSHTADTSKAYA SLAVA	93786
KROPELIN	75335
KRPAN	62181
KRUNG SIAM	23040
KRUPSKAYA	17519
KRUSAU	64981
KRUSEVAC	78532
KRUSEVO	81070
KRUSZWICA	14303
KRUTYNIA	72511
KRYLOV	17520
KRYM	63980
KRYMSK	31861
KRYMSKIE GORY	61273
KRYSTINA F	14290
KSAR CHELLALA	49451
KSAR EL BOUKHARI	49452
KSAR ETTIR	49450
KUAKA	53110
KUAKA	53180
KUAN CHENG	64812
KUANG HAI	45890
KUBA	12468
KUBA	18280
KUBAN	02141
KUBAN	63981
KUBATLY	50784
KUBBAR	49410
KUBBAR	50970
KUDOWA ZDROJ	81867
KUDU	59430
KUJAWY	75734
KUJAWY	88384
KULBAK	18747
KULBIN	18748
KULOY	21583
KULPAWN RIVER	13313
KULPAWN RIVER	34832
KULUNDA	31879
KUM YONG No 501	84500
KUMANOVO	78533
KUMBYSH	86007
KUN SHAN	84112
KUN SHAN	84172
KUNATKA	18749
KUNDA	89201

KUNGUR	24068
KUNGURLES	04188
KUNIANG	79660
KUNMING	13101
KUNTSEVO	06784
KUNTSEVO	07589
KUNUNGUAK	12110
KUPA	86940
KUPISHKIS	06783
KUPISHKIS	07576
KUPRIN	12593
KURA	21222
KURA	35322
KURAMA MARU	33602
KURE	50040
KURENAI MARU	20710
KURGAN	45211
KURILA	90890
KURILSK	86071
KUROSHIO MARU	02420
KUROSHIO MARU	08990
KUROSHIO MARU	15030
KUROSHIO MARU	35410
KURS	09364
KURSHAYA DUGA	13676
KURSK	40008
KURSOGRAF	07474
KURUSHIMA MARU	64120
KURUSHIMA MARU	68600
KUSHIRO MARU	80300
KUSHIRO MARU	80810
KUSHKA	23560
KUSKOV	17933
KUSTANAY	31870
KUSTANAY	90150
KUSU ISLAND	26672
KUSU ISLAND	31732
KUTAISI	70610
KUTINA	63715
KUTNO II	79871
KUULUNDA	23519
KUURTANES	74901
KUURTANES	74901
KUWAIT	87370
KUWAIT	91130
'KUWAIT' class	46770
'KUWAIT' class	49380
'KUWAIT' class	50940
KUYBYSHEVGES	45221
KUYVASTU	89204
KUZBASS	10439
KUZBASS	63983
KUZGUNCUK.	32170
KUZMA MININ	77076
KUZMINKI	06782
KUZMINKI	07578
KUZNETSK	31871
KUZNICA	04344
KUZNICA	04403
KUZNICA	04403
KVADRANT	11847
KVARNER	28620
KVARTS	23514
KVARTSEVYY	89760
KVIKSHOLM	74171
KWAI	60729
KWANGCHOW	14270
KWANTUNG	07252
KWEI YING	22961
KWIDZYN	51260
KYARDLA	22856
KYARDLA	34486
KYDON	42020
KYDONIA	90340
KYLIX	40753
KYLIX	41483
KYLLINI	43210
KYMA	06850
KYMO	37180
KYMO	44011
KYNOSSOURA	70620
KYOHO MARU	69422
KYOKKO MARU	54542
KYOKKO MARU	63902
KYOKUSEI MARU	93590
KYOKUYO MARU No3	93600
KYOMEI MARU	06450
KYOSEI MARU	71231
KYOSEI MARU	82431
KYOSEKI MARU No 3	66520
KYOTEN MARU	71230
KYOTEN MARU	82430
KYOTO	72352
KYOTO	77152
KYPROS	62870
KYPROS	86912
KYPU	15473
KYRA	06131
KYRA	07841
KYRAKATINGO	78670
KYRGO	66410
KYRIA	09650
KYRIAKI	22700
KYRIAKOULA D. LEMOS	47470
KYRNICOS E	63580
KYUKO MARU	77884

L

'L 19' type	94850
L. JALABERT BONTANG	48909
L.L. CHILE	06551
L.L. COLOMBIA	06553
L.L. EQUADOR	06552
L.L. PERU	06550
L.W. FUNKHAUSER	55707
L. W. FUNKHAUSER	58277
LA BAHIA	59010
LA BAHIA	67090
LA BONITA	83740
LA CHARENTE	40640
LA COLINA	75210
LA CORDILLERA	83132
LA COSTA	83133
LA DURANCE	94670
LA ENSENADA	83135
LA FALDA	59011
LA FALDA	67091
LA FLECHE	69650
LA GOULETTE	94031
LA GUAIRA	15710
LA HACIENDA	85691
LA LIBERTAD	71491
LA LIMA	21230
LA MINERA	56100
LA MINERA	57530
LA NINA	58773
LA NINA	62513
LA PAIX	49990
LA PALLICE	48900
LA PALMA	08280
LA PAZ	20120
LA PRADERA	75211
LA PRIMAVERA	83134
LA QUINTA	85690
LA RIOJA	53102
LA RIOJA	53332
LA ROCHELLE	48901
LA SAONE	40210
LA VALLETTA	32740
LABINSK	13013
LABIOSA	53325
LABIOSA	63225
LABO	46905
LABO	83341
LABORE	49860
LABRADOR	09520
LABRADOR	14402
LABRADOR	23561
LABRADOR CURRENT	53710
LABRADOR CURRENT	78152
LACERTA	11711
LACKENBY	77681
LACON	60104
LACONIAN	69241
LACONIC	66310
LACONICA	57930
LADOGA	20797
'LADOGA' type	75360
LADOGA 1	75361
LADOGA 2	75362
LADOGA 3	75363
LADOGA 4	75364
LADOGA 5	75365
LADOGA 6	75366
LADOGA 7	75367
LADOGA 9	75368
LADOGA 11	75401
LADOGA 12	75402
LADOGA 13	75403
LADOGA 14	75404
LADOGA 15	75405
LADOGA 16	75406
LADOGA 17	75407
LADOGA 18	75408
LADOGA 19	75409
LADOGA 20	75410
LADY AUGUSTA	54150
LADY CATHERINE	17192
LADY CATHERINE	32962
LADY CONTINENTAL	91312
LADY DOROTHY	39911
LADY DOROTHY	40831
LADY EMA	66231
LADY ERA	27040
LADY ERSI	80880
LADY ISABEL	06620
LADY JOSEPHINE	15390
LADY M.A. CROSBIE	73750
LADY M A CROSBIE	75840
LADY MADONNA	06350
LADY MARIANNA	76320
LADY NINA	17190
LADY NINA	32960
LADY OF MANN	20181
LADY PARKES	17720
LADY RAFFAELLA	88730
LADY ROSLIN	89490
LADY SARAH	91844
LADY SARAH	91954
LADY SERENA	91850
LADY SERENA	91960
LADY SYLVIA	91000
LADY TONE	17191
LADY TONE	32961
LADY VICTORIA	57220
LAERTES	48458
LAERTES	49498
LAERTES	49768
LAERTIS	12105
LAERTIS	13894
LAFUMINA	64460
LAGADA BAY	81240
LAGADA BEACH	81241
LAGADA STAR	21630
LAGARFOSS	84071
LAGENA	51310
LAGO ALUMINE	24450
LAGO ARGENTINO	24451
LAGO ATITLAN	80590
LAGO COMO	87552
LAGO GARDA	87553
LAGO HUALAIHUE	58114
LAGO IZABAL	39251
LAGO IZABAL	39271
LAGO LACAR	24284
LAGO LANALHUE	58115
LAGO LLANQUIHUE	58116
LAGO MAIHUE	58117
LAGO NAHUEL HUAPI	24283
LAGO PUYEHUE	58118
LAGO TRAFUL	24285
LAGOA	85101
LAGOA	85181
LAGOS EXPRESS	00890
LAGOS PALM	12910
LAGOVEN CARACAS	38561
LAGOVEN MARACAIBO	38560
LAGOVEN QUIRIQUIRE	66175
LAGOVEN SANTA RITA	66176
LAGUNA	12469
LAIETA	55633
LAIRAN	43191
LAITA	87732
LAJPAT RAI	69810
LAKE	14555
LAKE ALMANOR	54931
LAKE ALMANOR	77611
LAKE ANETTE	70101
LAKE ANIARA	70270
LAKE ANJA	70260
LAKE ARROWHEAD	63490
LAKE BERRYESSA	68830
LAKE BIWA	78340
LAKE BOSOMTWE	13314
LAKE BOSOMTWE	34837
LAKE CHARLES	72208
LAKE KATYA	65580
LAKE LOTHING	35290
LAKE MENDOCINO	63550
LAKE MENDOCINO	68260
LAKE PALOURDE	35800
LAKE SHASTA	68850
LAKE TAHOE	64450
LAKESHELL	85640
LAKHTA	22791
LAKHTA	31856
LAKOR	43192
LAKOTA	43193
LAKY	05870
LALANDIA	80210
LALANG	43190
LALAZAR	15140
LALLI	32963
LAMARA	94401
LAMBROS TSAGLIO¯IS	05762
LAMDA	40410
LAMIA STAR	43124
LAMINATORE	35592
LAMINATORE	36492
LAMMA ISLAND	10331
LAMONE	80403
LAMTONG CHAU	25940
LAMUT	43300
LAMYRA	70391
LAN CAN JIANG	60241
LAN HAI	79270
LAN SHAN	25103
LANA	66492
LANA	85934
LANAI	02852
LANCASTERBROOK	75911
LANDING	42700
LANDU	43194
LANGA	89400
LANGEAIS	69690
LANGELAND	51629
LANGELAND	72684
LANGELAND II	32860
LANGELAND TO	32860
LANGKOES	00741
LANGUST	12261
LANGUSTA	10817
LANISTES	57931
LANKA DEVI	13160
LANKA KALYANI	28170
LANKA KANTHI	02960
LANKA KEERTI	26023
LANKA KEERTI	30193
LANKA RANI	10370
LANKA RATNA	10361
LANKA SHANTHI	11130
LANRICK	84600
LANTAO ISLAND	10330
LANZHOU	35272
LAODIKI	72170
LAODONG	13840
LAPLANDIYA	17951
LAPONDA	43195
LAPPONIA	83365
LAPPONIA	83455
LAPU LAPU	40200
LARA	13251
LARA	14671
LARA MIKHEYENKO	15515
LARA S	60105
L'ARDECHE	94292
LARGS BAY	08430
LARINA	63105
LARINA	68145
LARISA REYSNER	10723
LARISSASEE	72123
LARISSASEE	76462
LARRY L	46690
LARYMNA	72991
LAS ARENAS	09980
LAS ARENAS	09980
LAS COLORADAS	48212
LAS MINAS	39651
LAS MINAS	49971
LAS MOROCHAS	13812
LAS PALMAS	21880
LAS PALMAS DE GRAN CANARIA	01292
LAS VEGAS	82892
LAS VILLAS	90392
'LASH' type	00010
'LASH' type	01050
'LASH' type	02480
'LASH' type	35100
'LASH' type	35130
'LASH' type	92810
'LASH' type	95150
LASH ATLANTICO	00010
LASH ATLANTICO	02480
LASH ATLANTICO	35130
LASH ITALIA	00011
LASH ITALIA	02481
LASH ITALIA	35131
LASH PACIFICO	00012
LASH PACIFICO	02482
LASH PACIFICO	35132
LASKARA	18740
LASPI	85976
LASS	25350
LATAKIA	33730
LATERNA	18750
LATIA	53324
LATIA	63224
LATIRUS	53323
LATIRUS	63223
LATONA	53320
LATONA	63220
LATVII	23544
LATVIYA	02161
L'AUDE	94291
LAUDERDALE	58291
LAURA	59630
LAURA	86320
LAURA CHRISTINA	64873
LAURA PRIMA	51632
LAUREL	39280
LAUREL	54410
LAUREL	57870
LAUREL WREATH	63090
LAUREL WREATH	67890
LAURENTINE	48060
LAURIE U	56610
LAURIERGRACHT	49814
LAURITA	94080
LAURO EXPRESS	22020
LAURO SODRE	08332
LAUTAN ENAM	45671
LAUTAN RANI	47180
LAVENDER	28790
LAVINIA COPPOLA	81790
LAVINIA V	48860
LAVOISIER	59162
LAVOISIER	66512
LAWAK	43196
LAWANDRA	43197
LAWANTI	13380
LAWTONA	55240
LAWTONA	84680
LAXA	51320
LAXFOSS	84073
LAXMI	56843
LAZAREV	22857
LAZAREV	34487
LAZARO CARDENAS	37280
LAZULI	13893
LAZUREN BRIAG	76531
LAZURIT	12470
LAZURNYY	11615
LAZURNYY BEREG	62689
LE CONTE	19810
LE DU	50430
LE GOELO	66806
LE HAVRE ABETO	25250
LE MANS	33360
LE ROVE	58711
LE ROVE	59641
LE ROVE	61721
LE SCANDINAVE	80600
LEADSMAN	88470
LEAGE	05980
LEBED	12558
LEBEDIN	62571
LEBEDIN	60661
LEBLON	22833
LEBORK	51261
LEDA	53321
LEDA	55032
LEDA	60920
LEDA	62380
LEDA	63221
LEDA	79080
LEDA	90232
LEDA MAERSK	14110
LEDEA	39260
LEDENICE	82820
LEDENICE.	04120
LEDENICE	15790
LEDENICE	52320
LEDNICE	35481
LEDUS	85353
LEE SHARON	49830
LEELAVATI	55222
LEELAVATI	57252
LEENA	90491
LEENA DAN	78050
LEFKAS	44270
LEFKAS	66851
LEFTERIS II	44521
LEFTHERO	57101
LEGAZPI	22651
LEI SHAN	12751
LEIBNIZ	84743
LEIBNIZ	84953
LEIDENSCHAFT	62110
LEIDSEGRACHT	49811
LEIF STAERKE	64817
LEILA	48840
LEILA ONE	42600
LEINSTER	16491
LEIV EIRIKSSON	59200
LEIXOES	31470
LEKEITIO	48071
LELA	25071
LELEWEL	07292
LELIEGRACHT	49810
LELLO DI MAIO	14760
LELLO DI MAIO	13610
LEMAN	76270
LEMATANG	18156
LEMBIT PERN	13680
LEMBULUS	62831
LEMBULUS	68081
LEMPA	39470
LEMWARDERSAND	90982
LENA	11120
LENA	78870
LENA	94450
LENA	25060
LENA	35314
LENALES.	07600
LENDOUDIS EVANGELOS	26500
LENDOUDIS KIKI	07024
LENINABAD	57770
LENINABAD	84870
LENINAKAN	84812
LENINAKAN	57632
LENINGRAD	02072
LENINGRAD	10574
LENINGRAD	11634
LENINGRAD	15344
LENINGRAD	39970
LENINGRADETS	35324
LENINGRADSKAYA SLAVA	93787
LENINGRADSKIY KOMSOMOLETS	79432
LENINGRADSKIY OPOLCHENETS	50292
LENINGRADSKIY PARTIZAN	50293
LENINO	10571
LENINO	15341
LENINO	60664
LENINO	62574
LENINOGORSK	11848
LENINOGORSK	13010
LENINSK	40005
LENINSK-KUZNETSKIY	70030
LENINSKAYA GVARDIYA	03770
LENINSKAYA GVARDIYA	04010
LENINSKAYA ISKRA	93739
LENINSKAYA ISKRA	93829
LENINSKAYA SMENA	79371
LENINSKIY	20798
LENINSKIY KOMSOMOL	31050

LENINSKIY LUCH	71670
LENINSKIY PIONER	01569
LENINSKIY PUT	93750
LENINSKIY PUT	93840
LENINSKIYE GORY	81494
LENINSKIYE GORY	61274
LENINSKIYE ISKRY	01387
LENINSKIYE ISKRY	01647
LENINSKOE ZNAMYA	90723
LENINSKOE ZNAMYA	60684
LENKORAN	57634
LENKORAN	80921
LENKORAN	84815
LENKORAN	60671
LENTINI	40270
LEO	72920
LEO SCHRODER	56112
LEO SCHRODER	59802
LEO SOLING	25890
LEO STAR	25891
LEON	56503
LEON	93891
LEON & PIERRE C	77158
LEON & PIERRE C	72358
LEON OF CHAERONEA	28069
LEON PAEGLE	12471
LEON POPOV	03780
LEON POPOV	04020
LEON PROM	29270
LEON R.E	95010
LEON SIMARD	88484
LEONARD BOHMER	91091
LEONARDO DA VINCI	38582
LEONCE VIELJEUX	05120
LEONCE VIELJEUX	59870
LEONID KRASIN	25590
LEONID LEONIDOV	28492
LEONID SEVRYUKOV	12262
LEONID SMIRNYKH	31872
LEONID SOBINOV	06200
LEONID TELIGA	80750
LEONID TELIGA	81450
LEONIDAS	65480
LEONIDAS D	79180
LEONIDAS Z. CAMBANIS	56800
LEONIS HALCOUSSIS	60141
LEONOREVERETT	81582
LEOPARD	32501
LEOPARDI	32541
LEOPARDIS	60741
LEOPOLD STAFF	71858
LEOPOLDO PERES	08330
LEPTON	62830
LEPTON	68080
LEPUS	11710
LERMONTOV	12368
LEROS	35610
LESKOV	12590
LESKOV	12594
LESLIE	59570
LESLIE	81300
LESLIE GAULT	48750
LESLIE GAULT	75570
LESNOY	12305
LESOGORSK	12472
LESOZAVODSK	13014
30-LET POBEDY	34637
50 LET VLKSM	79405
50 LET OKTYABRYA	93845
50 LET OKTYABRYA	93755
50 LET PIONERII	79414
50 LET S.S.S.R	79386
50 LET SOVIET SOVIETSKOY	05625
50 LET SOVIETSKOY UKRAINY	14455
50 LET SOVIETSKOY VLASTI	79368
50 LET SSSR	71820
50 LET VLKSM	12426
50 LET VLKSM	35334
60 LET VELIKOGO OKTYABR	79439
60 LET VLKSM	79440
60 LET OKTYABRYA	93383
LETA	90240
LETING	05130
LETITIA LYKES	05584
LETITIA LYKES	14425
LETITIA LYKES	14895
750—LETIYE GORODA GORKOGO	79412
30-LETIYE POBEDY	11747
30-LETIYE POBEDY	01665
LETO	18850
LETO	70462
30—LETYE POBEDY	01405
LEV TOLSTOY	12369
LEV TOLSTOY	28971
LEVANT	69780
'LEVANT' type	22790
'LEVANT' type	22840
'LEVANT' type	34470
LEVANT CLIPPER	39751
LEVANTE EXPRESS	95130
LEVANTES	30860
LEVANTINO	74940
LEVEN FISHER	89360
LEVERKUSEN EXPRESS	08830
LEVERKUSEN EXPRESS	09030
LEVERKUSEN EXPRESS	77030
LEWANT II	31770
LEWANTER.	10262
LEWANTER.	10762
LEYTE GULF	18190
LI CHENG	64816
LI SHAN	26351
LI SHAN	31691
LI SHUI;	01531
LIA PERO	12901
LIAN HUA CHENG	51430
LIAN JIANG	63686
LIAN YUN SHAN	03031
LIAN YUN SHAN	03341
LIAO YUAN	25051
LIAZI.	04500
LIBERIAN STATESMAN	46130
LIBERTADOR GENERAL JOSE DE SAN MARTIN	06673
LIBERTADOR SAN MARTIN	52650
LIBERTADOR SAN MARTIN	71600
LIBERTADOR SIMON BOLIVAR	12991
LIBERTE	20671
'LIBERTY' type	07460
'LIBERTY' type	15400
LIBRA	00691
LIBRA.	11716
LIBURNIJA	32710
LICHIANG	07666
LICHTENHAGEN	62700
LICORNE OCEANE	68450
LICUNGO	29060
LIDA DEMESH	67014
LIDIA DOCE	90580
LIDO	00690
LIDROTT	72921
LIEBENWALDE	47070
LIEBENWALDE	46370
LIECHTENSTEIN	62111
LIELUPE	63644
LIEN CHANG	13210
LIEN YUN No 28	86098
LIEPAYA	44622
LIESELOTTE HERRMANN	06382
LIESELOTTE HERRMANN	15412
LIFT-ON	74300
LIGAR BAY	88650
LIGOVO	07567
LIGURIA	01501
LIH FONG	25190
LIHO	00692
LIJNBAANSGRACHT	49812
LIKA	10991
LIKA	34151
LIKA PETKA	04471
LIKA PETKA	04471
LIKE ONE	69300
LIKE TWO	88360
LIKHOSLAVL	60662
LIKHOSLAVL	62572
LIKODYN	18751
LIKOMUR	18752
LIKOSAR	18753
LIKOWAL	18754
LILAC ACE	61658
LILIANE	24700
LILLA	21890
LILLGAARD	67480
LILLIAN XXI	92973
LILLIAN XXII	92970
LILLIAN XXIII	92971
LILLIAN XXIV	92972
LILY H	66030
LILY H	67720
LILY VENTURE	62231
LILY VENTURE	71251
LIM GLORY	69423
LIMA	29400
LIMA	30552
LIMA	76603
LIMA	89303
LIMAN	11849
LIMATULA	53071
LIMBAZHI	38531
LIMENDA	17956
LIMING	10625
LIMING	15375
LIMNEA	53073
LIMON	33900
LIMOPSIS	53074
LIMOUSIN	63400
LIMOUSIN EXPRESS	82091
LIMOUSIN EXPRESS	91591
LIMOZA	11961
LIN HAI	46210
LINA FISSER	59750
LINAKHAMARI	11755
LINAKHAMARI	34645
LINARD LAYTSEN	12473
LINCOLN	15760
LINCOLNBROOK	75912
LINCOLNSHIRE	80841
LINDA DAN	64900
LINDAUNIS	73797
LINDBLAD EXPLORER	32840
LINDE	87330
LINDENGRACHT	49813
LINDENHALL	06462
LINDINGER SATELITE	94241
LINDINGER SURVEYOR	94242
LINDO	59790
LINDO	62360
LINDO	82241
LINDOS	90691
LINERA	36074
LINERA	41794
LING HU	69640
LING LONG HAI	48010
LING YUNG	05610
LINGA	53070
LINGAYEN	80470
LINGUIST	03331
LINK FAITH	29363
LINK FAITH	30581
LINK HARMONY	10932
LINK LOVE	10931
LINK TRUST	06761
LINNE	72822
LINNE	80222
LINO MANCINO	12170
L'INTERPECHE	93550
LINTONG	13371
LINYIN	29611
LION	19470
LION OF ETHIOPIA	04580
LION OF ETHIOPIA	34910
LIONELLO L	71880
LIOTINA	51311
LIPARI	09270
LIPARUS	53072
LIPETSK.	12140
LIPS	60106
LIPSK N/BIEBRZA	58731
LIRA	12306
LIRIJA	12152
LIRYC	66280
LISA HEEREN	88270
LISANA	55100
LISANA	57590
LISBET THOLSTRUP	85003
L'ISERE	32103
LISICHANSK	80920
LISICHANSK	84816
LISICHANSK	57635
LISICHANSK	60670
LISKI	81800
LISSA	42770
LISSETTE	92952
LISSETTE	95162
LITA	48090
LITA 1	28760
LITA I	30370
LITIOPA	57932
LITO	30162
LITORAL SANTAFECINO	74230
LITRIX	84963
LITTLE NIKOS	45020
LITVA	02124
LIU KIANG	26521
LIU PAN SHAN	00721
LIULINHAI	46009
LIVADIYA	12263
LIVERPOOL BAY	08400
LIVNY	57630
LIVNY	84810
LIWIEC	87300
LIZA CHAYKINA	41154
LIZA CHAYKINA	44956
LJGOV	00340
LJGOV	01020
LJUBLJANA	04871
LJUBLJANA	07801
LJUTA	56931
LJUTA	80931
LJUTOMER.	04870
LJUTOMER.	07800
LLAIMA	70340
LLARANES	72240
LLOYD ALEGRETE	04807
LLOYD ALTAMIRA	49663
LLOYD ALTAMIRA	50933
LLOYD ANTUERPIA	06554
LLOYD BAGE	03470
LLOYD BAGE	03540
LLOYD BALTIMORE	50540
LLOYD BRAS	06558
LLOYD CUIABA	49661
LLOYD CUIABA	50931
LLOYD GENOVA	06559
LLOYD HAMBURGO	06555
LLOYD HUMAITA	49660
LLOYD HUMAITA	50930
LLOYD LIVERPOOL	06556
LLOYD MANDU	04800
LLOYD MARABA	49662
LLOYD MARABA	50932
LLOYD MARSELHA	06560
LLOYD NEW YORK	50051
LLOYD ROTTERDAM	06557
LLOYD SANTAREM	49664
LLOYD SANTAREM	50934
LLOYD SANTOS	03471
LLOYD SANTOS	03541
LLOYD SYDNEY	15631
LLOYD TUPIARA	04806
LLOYD VIRGINIA	60954
LLOYDIANA	74412
LNG AQUARIUS	72200
LNG ARIES	72201
LNG CAPRICORN	72202
LNG GEMINI	72203
LNG LEO	72204
LNG LIBRA	72205
LNG TAURUS	72206
LNG VIRGO	72207
LO SHAN	32661
LOBITO	24720
LOBO D'ALMADA.	08333
LOCARNO	35550
LOCARNO	35581
LOCARNO	36431
LOCH LOMOND	02861
LOCH LOMOND	03001
LOCH MAREE	02860
LOCH MAREE	03000
LODOWIK	18755
LODS	15083
LOFOTEN	02370
LOFOTEN	35360
LOFOTEN	18726
LOGOS	21120
LOIDA	64641
LOK SEVAK	71093
LOK SEVAK	71643
LOK VAIBHAV	30870
LOKATOR	09377
LOKBATAN	40664
LOKKY	48781
LOKMA 1	89860
LOKSA	89460
LOKSA	22858
LOKSA	34488
LOLA DEL MAR	76084
LOMBARD	55531
LOMBARD	63351
LOMONOSOVO	07560
LOMUR	93012
LOMZA	50469
LONDINON	25180
LONDOGE	05313
LONDON BARON	47690
LONDON CONFIDENCE	38370
LONDON EARL	47691
LONDON ENTERPRISE	55770
LONDON GLORY	55771
LONDON PRIDE	54480
LONDON PRIDE	64322
LONDON TEAM	58403
LONDON TEAM	64563
LONDON TRADER	64296
LONDON VISCOUNT	47692
LONDONBROOK	75910
LONDRINA	62352
LONE EAGLE	07265
LONE STAR	51030
LONE STAR	82532
LONE STAR MARINER	07852
LONE TERKOL	85130
LONG BEACH	60185
LONG BEACH	74471
LONG CHARITY	57140
LONG CHUAN JIANG	57450
LONG CHUAN JIANG	71780
LONG HAI	57370
LONG HAI	61960
LONG LINES	02400
LONG PHOENIX	38000
LONG PHOENIX	44580
LONGHUA	26730
LONGLIN.	06037
LONGMEN	05392
LONGTIME	26753
LONGVA	34010
LONGVA	34460
LONTUE	58596
LONTUE	60476
LOO CHONG	21520
LOOIESGRACHT	49815
LOON MAU	39631
LORANA	35861
LORD BYRON	62070
LORD CREVECOEUR	18341
LORD CREVECOEUR	33842
LORD DE FRANCE	18342
LORD DE FRANCE	33841
LORD D'ORLEANS	33844
LORD FLEUR D'EPEE	18343
LORD FLEUR D'EPEE	33843
LORD MOUNT STEPHEN	60710
LORD NELSON	22760
LORD NIAGARA	18344
LORD NIAGARA	33845
LORD SELKIRK	16770
LORD STRATHCONA	60711
LORD TRINITE	15391
LORENZO d'AMICO	12950
LORENZO HALCOUSSI	66272
LORENZO HALCOUSSI	69902
LORETO	25703
LORETTA	57543
LORNA	11962
LOS CARIBES	80670
LOS TEQUES	51190
LOT	38339
LOT	44699
LOTILA	47290
LOTTIA	51312
LOTUS	81751
LOUCAS N	58159
LOUCY	86953
LOUIS L-D	83147
LOUIS S. ST. LAURENT	01840
LOUISE	74680
LOUISE	74680
LOUISE BRAVO	50331
LOUISE BRAVO	83671
LOUISE LYKES	05585
LOUISE LYKES	14426
LOUISE LYKES	14896
LOUISE WESTON	75874
LOUISIANA	72209
LOUISIANA	93911
LOULLIA	28801
LOUSSIOS	77702
LOVCEN	26321
LOVECH	82138
LOVECH	82418
LOVOZYERO	11723
LOVOZYERO	34613
LOVRAN	84540
LOYALTY	06483
LOZOVAYA	57631
LOZOVAYA	84811
LSCO AMIHAN	42820
LSCO CAMRANH	42822
LSCO CANTHO	42821
LSCO PIONEER	41620
LSCO TAWI-TAWI	36440
LSCO TAWI-TAWI	43420
LSCO TRANSASIA	42830
LSCO TRIDENT	37110
LSCO TRIDENT	43910
LU CHENG	14500
LU CHIANG	30240
LU CHUN	07664
LU DING	86640
LU HAI	79831
LU LIANG SHAN	00722
LUANA	59500
LUANA	81190
LUBBENAU	79730
LUBECA	73792
LUBEN KARAVELOV	48433
LUBEN KARAVELOV	49473
LUBEN KARAVELOV	49743
LUBERON	94295
LUBLIN	15084
LUBNA	40870
LUBNY	60663
LUBNY	62573
LUC NGAN	06270
LUCENDRO	48178
LUCENT STAR	61210
LUCERNA	69011
LUCERO DEL MAR	02515
LUCHANA	09900
LUCHEGORSK	23480
LUCHEGORSK	23490
LUCIANA DELLA GATTA	77731
LUCIANA DELLA GATTA	89821
LUCIDITY	12101
LUCIDITY	13890
LUCIE DELMAS	48882
LUCIE S	90652
LUCIEN DELMAS	48261
LUCILLE	13361
LUCINA	53322
LUCINA	62034
LUCINA	63222
LUCJAN SZENWALD.	06091
LUCJAN SZENWALD	14801
LUCK WAVE	60159
LUCKENWALDE	46372
LUCKENWALDE	47072
LUCKY	16080
LUCKY LADY	83710
LUCKY PENNY	25671
LUCKY TRADER	42610
LUCKY TWO	24461
LUCNAM	05315
LUCTOR I	42870
LUCY	21661
LUCY	23150
LUCY	25121
LUCY	27591
LUCY	46893
LUCY	78710
LUCY MAUD MONTGOMERY	19350
LUDOGORETZ	49162
LUDOLF OLDENDORFF	77446
LUDWIG	59120
LUDWIG TUREK	13740
LUDWIGSHAFEN EXPRESS	08833

LUDWIGSHAFEN EXPRESS 09033
LUDWIGSHAFEN EXPRESS 77033
LUDWIK SOLSKI 14584
LUDZA 22859
LUDZA 34489
LUFENG 05393
LUFENG 05831
LUGA 86174
LUGANO 61360
LUGANSK 62570
LUGANSK 60660
LUHESAND 90811
LUHESAND 91771
LUI 87440
LUIGI CASALE 54780
LUIGI CASALE 67450
LUIGI D'AMICO 30410
LUIGI D'AMICO 34930
LUIGI GARDELLA 75760
LUIGI GRIMALDI 78431
LUIGI MARTINI 22940
LUIGI ORLANDO 78460
LUIS BANCHERO 46095
LUIS BANCHERO 83265
LUIS PEREDA 78830
LUISA 37380
LUISE BORNHOFEN 71840
LUISE BORNHOFEN 71980
LUJAN DE CUYO 37721
LUJUA 46120
LUK CHAU 00891
LUKA BOTIC 06412
LUKHOVITSY 60667
LUKHOVITSY 62577
LUMIERE 71503
LUMINENCE 76140
LUMINETTA 71504
LUMUMBA 62710
LUMUMBA 62750
LUN 35670
LUN SHAN 84110
LUN SHAN 84170
LUNAMAR 69661
LUNG CHUAN 92715
LUNG YUNG 62271
LUNJ 11599
LUNNI 51990
LUNNI 65160
LUNNIK 12595
LUNOKHOD I 23486
LUO DING 28160
LUO SHAN HAI 77482
LUPENI 78583
LUPITA CASTRO 87022
LUPUS 73389
LUR TXORI 85232
LURLINE 08950
LUR-TXORI 65002
LUSITANIA 74024
LUSTAR 91840
LUSTAR 91950
LUTETIAN 56821
LUTJAN 18756
LUTSK 57771
LUTSK 84871
LUTTEN-KLEIN 76535
LUTZ JACOB 77140
LUTZ SCHRODER 56113
LUTZ SCHRODER 59803
LUTZKENDORF 60800
LUTZKENDORF 69830
LUZON 31980
LUZYTANKA 18757
LVOV 11850
LYCAON 48457
LYCAON 49497
LYCAON 49767
LYDIA 60107
LYDIA P 39891
LYNDA 68791
LYNGENFJORD 52851
LYNGENFJORD 53041
LYNTON GRANGE 56501
LYNX 92333
LYONYA GOLIKOV 07610
LYONYA GOLYKOV 15516
LYRA 68970
LYRA 75010
LYRA 75010
LYRA 76810
LYRA 11713
LYRIA 53075
LYSAGHT ENDEAVOUR 72811
LYSAGHT ENDEAVOUR 76831
LYSAGHT ENTERPRISE 72810
LYSAGHT ENTERPRISE 76830
LYSPOL 71906
LYUBAN 06785
LYUBAN 07571
LYUBERTSY 36900
LYUBERTSY 43800
LYUBERTSY 60666
LYUBERTSY 62576
LYUBLINO 60665
LYUBLINO 62575
LYUBOTIN 80922
LYUBOTIN 84817
LYUBOTIN 57636
LYUBOTIN 60672
LYUBOV ORLOVA 02343
LYUBOV SHEVTSOVA 41153
LYUBOV SHEVTSOVA 44953
LYUDAS GIRA 12474
LYUDINOVO 84813
LYUDINOVO 57633
LYUDMILA PAVLICHENKO 13679
LYUDMILA STAL 03781
LYUDMILA STAL 04021
LYULIN 77980

M

M. ALEXAND 10920
M. BORISOV 11851
M. EFES 65823
M. EFES 69953
M. EREGLI 39210
M.G. TSANGARIS 48176
M H THAMRON 30921
M. ISTANBUL K 72260
M.O.P 225-C 41930
M. P. GRACE 58080
M. URITSKIY 02126
MAASBREE 55490
MAASBREE 62950
MAASKADE 70130
MAASKANT 70131
MAASKERK 70132
MAASKROON 70133
MAASPLEIN 85472
MAASPLEIN 91532
MABICA 91190
MABUHAY 27782
MACAPA 52281
MACARENA 57235
MACASSAR MARU 05500
MACASSAR MARU 14410
MACEDON 25361
MACHITIS 10901
MACHITIS 34121
MACOMA 63303
MADELEINE 83630
MADIMAR 50081
MADINIA 40480
MADOURI 76970
MADOURI 89780
MAELIFELL 86810
MAERSK ANGUS 65932
MAERSK BUCHAN 65931
MAERSK CADET 55963
MAERSK CADET 56723
MAERSK COMMANDER 55962
MAERSK COMMANDER 56722
MAERSK MONDO 64770
MAERSK NEPTUN 72330
MAERSK PINTO 55110
MAERSK RANDO 64771
MAERSK TRITON 72331
MAFFO 12793
MAGA 84526
MAGADAN 90151
MAGALI 74261
MAGALLANES 85004
MAGAR 72950
MAGDA 37580
MAGDALENA 03761
MAGDALENA 64876
MAGDALENA DEL MAR 47711
MAGDEBURG 03876
MAGDUS 43940
MAGED 35640
MAGED 41300
MAGHREB 81071
MAGIC SUN 46702
MAGICIAN 02811
MAGID 55891
MAGID 58691
MAGID 87870
MAGNA SPES 13070
MAGNISI 42850
MAGNIT 09374
MAGNITOGORSK 71530
MAGNITOGORSK 80200
MAGNUS JENSEN 49970
MAGNUS POSER 23426
MAGO 67367
MAGO 71363
MAH 2 25861
MAHA JAG ANJLI 84640
MAHABIR 30721
MAHAJAK FOUNDER 26063
MAHAKIRAN 51082
MAHAPRIYA 07171
MAHARASHMI 25862
MAHARISHI DAYANAND 63459
MAHARISHI KARVE 63460
MAHAVIJAY 30720
MAHDIA 42380
MAHINDA 74943
MAHMOUD 12940
MAHSURI 05712
MAHTRA 22860
MAHTRA 34490
MAI RICKMERS 28711
MAIA 87920
MAID OF KENT 20010
MAIJIN 24781
MAIK 66811
MAIK PRIMO 59628
MAIN EXPRESS 73514
MAIN ORE 79201
MAINE 50383
MAIRANGI BAY 08443
MAIRI EVERARD 75459
MAIROULA 49270
MAISTROS 57003
MAJA—M 75623
MAJANG 94471
MAJESTIC 57310
MAJESTIC 66311
MAJESTY 77630
MAJOR SUCHARSKI 07441
MAKEDONIA STAR 70471
MAKEDONIJA 28300
MAKELIS BUKA 07475
MAKELIS BUKA 11930
MAKEVERETT 13352
MAKHACHKALA 40001
MAKHACHKALA 66173
MAKHTUM-KULI 14383
MAKIRI SMITS 50192
MAKRA 06532
MAKRAN 45935
MAKRAN 47445
MAKSIM AMMOSOV 50755
MAKSIM MIKHAYLOV 77349
MALACCA 72341
MALACCA MARU 51420
MALAGA 71550
MALAKHIT 12475
MALAKHITOVYY 89754
MALAKHOV KURGAN 10880
MALANGE 14750
MALANGEN 18727
MALARVIK 73860
MALASPINA 20130
MALAYA VISHERA 35060
MALAYA ZEMLYA 13683
MALAYA ZEMLYA 42963
MALAYAN REEFER 21390
MALCHIN 83604
MALDIS SKREYA 67015
MALDIVE AMBASSADOR 34924
MALDIVE AMITY 42930
MALDIVE CARRIER 22890
MALDIVE CORAL 38350
MALDIVE COURAGE 06710
MALDIVE CREST 27610
MALDIVE ENVOY 29130
MALDIVE EXPLORER 31261
MALDIVE EXPRESS 27880
MALDIVE IMAGE 07070
MALDIVE INDUSTRY 90470
MALDIVE LOYALTY 11541
MALDIVE LOYALTY 28201
MALDIVE NAVIGATOR 26851
MALDIVE NEIGHBOUR 24921
MALDIVE NOBLE 81551
MALDIVE NOVEL 29073
MALDIVE PEACE 24920
MALDIVE PIONEER 39042
MALDIVE PLEDGE 59410
MALDIVE PRIZE 28630
MALDIVE PROGRESS 24930
MALDIVE PROMOTER 09951
MALDIVE REPUBLIC 25390
MALDIVE REPUBLIC 34760
MALDIVE SEAFARER 24860
MALDIVE STAR 27230
MALDIVE SWIFT 48330
MALDIVE TRADER 86020
MALDIVE TRUST 34180
MALDIVE UNITY 13930
MALEA 53460
MALEA 80440
MALENE OSTERVOLL 17650
MALESSINA 74850
MALESSINA 88330
MALIAKOS 31450
MALIGAYA 17860
MALKI 23562
MALLECO 72150
MALLING 50170
MALLORY LYKES 05586
MALLORY LYKES 14427
MALLORY LYKES 14897
MALMROS MONSOON 02581
MALMROS MONSOON 02951
MALOYAROSLAVYETS 35061
MALTA EXPRESS 32530
MALUKA 40913
MALUKA 45153
MALVERN PRINCE 81782
MAMAIA 13850
MAMANI 27890
MAMANI 34430
MAMAYEV KURGAN 13681
MAMIN SIBIRYAK 12597
MAMIN SIBIRYAK 20799
MAMIN-SIBIRYAK 12476
MAMMOTH FIR 61196
MAMMOTH PINE 61197
MAN AN 28700
MAN CHENG 64810
MAN CHEONG 26360
MAN SING 30941
MAN WAH 28240
MANAFOSS 83512
MANAGUA 25122
MANAGUA 27592
MANATI 93200
MANAURE 39760
MANAURE IV 90800
MANAURE V 74091
MANAURE VI 74090
MANCHESTER CONCORDE 73502
MANCHESTER CONCORDE 78032
MANCHESTER CRUSADE 73503
MANCHESTER CRUSADE 78033
MANCHESTER FAITH 73904
MANCHESTER RENOWN 73504
MANCHESTER RENOWN 78034
MANCHESTER REWARD 73505
MANCHESTER REWARD 78035
MANCHESTER ZEAL 75900
MANDAMA 05713
MANDI 76620
MANDO V 70134
MANDOULA 28080
MANGALI 89764
MANGANESE 18260
MANGEN 51730
MANGEN 84040
MANGYSHLAK 44120
MANGYSHLAK 53160
MANHATTAN 36590
MANHATTAN KING 54035
MANIA 59370
MANIA 87960
MANICA 10670
MANICA 13512
MANIFEST LIPCOWY 73280
MANILA 30950
MANILA 51033
MANILA 82535
MANILA BAY 31690
MANILAID 75641
MANISTEE 03760
MANITOU 67110
MANKOADZE 12559
MANNHEIM 46991
MANNHEIM 83331
MANOKA 15821
MANOLOEVERETT 04750
MANSART 49552
MANSART 49572
MANSFELD 79731
MANSOOR 28770
MANSOUR 41920
MANTA 23462
MANTINIA 40650
MANUEL 85550
MANUEL ASCUNCE 27071
MANUEL AVILA COMACHO 70040
MANUEL MEJIA 07373
MANUEL SOTO 16420
MANUKAI 93520
MANUKAI 94310
MANULANI 93521
MANULANI 94311
MANX MAID 20500
MANX VIKING 93972
MANX VIKING 95212
MANXMAN 18820
MANYCH 15474
MANYCH 45590
MANZANARES 03762
MANZONI 32543
MAOLIN 06422
MAPLE LEAF 28380
MAPLEHURST 89020
MAR CADIZ 48832
MAR CANTABRICO 04620
MAR CANTABRICO 05080
MAR CANTABRICO 30400
MAR CARIBE 32390
MAR CARIBE 94051
MAR CORRUSCO 43881
MAR DE VIGO 92760
MAR DEL NORD 80520
MAR GRANDE 00490
MAR OCEANO 92761
MARA 82010
MARABOU 60108
MARACAIBO 15711
MARACANA I 29364
MARAJO 65870
MARAKAZ 18840
MARALUNGA 53970
MARALUNGA 79020
MARAMA 93641
MARAMURES 78586
MARANAR 81270
MARAO 64390
MARAO 68610
MARAT KOZEY 15517
MARAT KOZLOV 67016
MARATHA ENVOY 61940
MARATHA MARINER 68394
MARATHA MARINER 72355
MARATHA MARINER 77155
MARATHA MARINER 77404
MARATHA MELODY 68393
MARATHA MELODY 72356
MARATHA MELODY 77156
MARATHA MELODY 77403
MARATHA PROGRESS 55150
MARATHON 90451
MARATHON LAKE 62010
MARAZUL 1 56754
MARBONITA 58111
MARCALAN 62150
MARCHEN MAERSK 47380
MARCHEN MAERSK 47650
MARCIA 04928
MARCO POLO 24330
MARCOAZUL 78741
MARCONA CONVEYOR 52540
MARCONA EXPORTER 77410
MARCONA TRADER 69260
MARCONA TRANSPORTER 51650
MARCONA TRANSPORTER 64420
MARCOPLATA 48101
MARCOS M F 61230
MARCOS SOUZA DANTAS 51060
MARCOVERDE 78742
MARDAKYANY 44117
MARDI GRAS 06830
MARE 1 84536
MARE AMICO 80430
MARE ANTARTICO 33860
MARE ARABICO 31640
MARE ARTICO 33861
MARE AUSTRALE 33862
MARE BONUM 59101
MARE BONUM 76411
MARE BOREALE 33863
MARE CARIBICO 31641
MARE FELICE 54660
MARE IRATUM 76341
MARE ITALICO 47850
MARE LIBERUM 76340
MARE LIGURE 53661
MARE LIGURE 73381
MARE MAGNUM 59102
MARE MAGNUM 76412
MARE NOVUM 59100
MARE NOVUM 76410
MARE PLACIDO 54661
MARE SERENO 54662
MARE SILENTUM 76342
MARE TIRRENO 53662
MARE TIRRENO 73382
MARE TRANQUILLO 54663
MAREA NEAGRA 11701
MAREDALE 57433
MAREDALE 78633
MARELLA 32770
MARESOL 49224
MARFRIO 01620
MARGARET 27682
MARGARET JOHNSON 04272
MARGARET JOHNSON 16302
MARGARETHA SMITS 50190
MARGARITA 47680
MARGARITA 54301
MARGARITA 78611
MARGARITA L 01480
MARGARITE 56985
MARGELAN 07902
MARGIO 56530
MARGO 91120
MARGOT JACOB 77142
MARGRET 75295
MARGRET 88105
MARGRETHE MAERSK 47381
MARGRETHE MAERSK 47651
MARHABA 14403
MARI 06488
MARI 25290
MARI BOEING 48361
MARI BOEING 50871
MARI CHANDRIS 47681
MARIA 06500
MARIA 18401
MARIA 22951
MARIA 25070
MARIA 28660
MARIA 51901
MARIA 66050
MARIA 72551
MARIA A 40462
MARIA A 44902
MARIA BERLINGIERI 42522
MARIA C 43561
MARIA CASTRO 87023

MARIA COSTA	39541
MARIA DA PENHA	05367
MARIA DA PENHA	15667
MARIA DE ARANZAZU	90613
MARIA DE COVADONGA	90614
MARIA DEMET	83712
MARIA DORMIO	66954
MARIA DORMIO	70994
MARIA E	40740
MARIA G.L	46880
MARIA GORTHON	48820
MARIA GORTHON	83490
MARIA GRAEBE	72758
MARIA ISABELLA	58930
MARIA K	06499
MARIA K	81040
MARIA L	47208
MARIA LEMOS	61312
MARIA LEMOS	62612
MARIA MONICA	66933
MARIA MONICA	70983
MARIA N	58160
MARIA OLDENDORFF	71846
MARIA PAOLINA G	34040
MARIA POLIVANOVA	04522
MARIA SIGMA	22590
MARIA SMITS	50193
MARIA SOFIA	24470
MARIA TOPIC	47210
MARIA U	56611
MARIA X	46523
MARIA X	83303
MARIA XILAS	55102
MARIA XILAS	57592
MARIA YERMOLOVA	02340
MARIA ZAKELINA S	47325
MARIA ZAKELINA S	83385
MARIAECK	92740
MARIAELENA T	10500
MARIAM	09930
MARIAM	42260
MARIAM	58410
MARIAM	64570
MARIAN BUCZEK	07442
MARIAN BUCZEK	15314
MARIAN P BILLUPS	87090
MARIANN	51902
MARIANN	66990
MARIANN	72552
MARIANNA	70135
MARIANNA VI	09420
MARIANNA VII	64365
MARIANNA DORMIO	80521
MARIANNE	50990
MARIANNE	51460
MARIANNE BOLTEN	55662
MARIANNE BOLTEN	55862
MARIANNE ROTH	53414
MARIANNE ROTH	64944
MARIANNINA	59840
MARIANNINA	67510
MARIANO ESCOBEDO	54741
MARIANO ESCOBEDO	66111
MARIANO MOCTEZUMA	70044
MARIANTHE	02642
MARIAS	45040
MARIB	23290
MARIBELLA	60700
MARIBELLA	69840
MARIBOR	57441
MARIE	28460
MARIE BAKKE	47131
MARIE DELMAS	48883
MARIE LEONHARDT	84691
MARIE LEONHARDT	89901
MARIE MAERSK	37830
MARIE MAERSK	44420
MARIE SKOU	31304
MARIETTA	01110
MARIETTA	42560
MARIGO	60109
MARIGOLD	61474
MARIGOULA	84671
MARIGOULA G	40151
MARIINSK	07903
MARIJKE SMITS	50191
MARIKA	49930
MARIKA	50630
MARIKA J. LEMOS	13172
MARIKA J. LEMOS	34805
MARIKA T	34892
MARILENA	08550
MARILENA	51631
MARILENA	53010
MARILIA	62353
MARILIA	68733
MARILYN L	46695
MARIMAR	87580
MARIMO	32582
MARIMO	34980
MARINA	18880
MARINA	27700
MARINA	35070
MARINA	51900
MARINA	61900
MARINA	72550
MARINA DEL CANTONE	69330
MARINA DI ALIMURI	46320
MARINA DI CASSANO	55990
MARINA DI EQUA	46321
MARINA GRANDE	46500
MARINA HEEREN	88271
MARINA P	13280
MARINA P	14660
MARINA RASKOVA	10726
'MARINDUS' type	48900
'MARINDUS' type	51070
MARINE ATLANTICA	16990
MARINE CHEMIST	58960
MARINE CONTAINER	76171
MARINE CRUISER	19600
MARINE EAGLE	64660
MARINE EVANGELINE	93950
MARINE NAUTICA	16991
MARINE PACKER	84050
MARINE TRANSPORT	42500
MARINELLA D'AMICO	43761
MARINER	81330
MARINER	90590
'MARINER' class	07710
'MARINER' class	07850
MARINGA	03095.
MARINIQUAIS	24531
MARINULA	63290
MARINUS SMITS	50194
MARINUS SMITS	52111
MARINUS SMITS	67061
MARIO ATTANASIO	85560
MARION	78400
MARION DUFRESNE	06180
MARION DUFRESNE	07520
MARIONA DEL MAR	76075
MARIPOSA	06841
MARIPRIMA	37630
MARIPRIMA	44160
MARISA	81142
MARITA LEONHARDT	59756
MARITIME ACE	54630
MARITIME ACE	55060
MARITIME ALLIANCE	49671
MARITIME BRILLIANCE	47150
MARITIME CHALLENGE	54631
MARITIME CHALLENGE	55061
MARITIME DOMINION	47151
MARITIME EAGLE	68861
MARITIME EXPLORER	06860
MARITIME EXPLORER	32050
MARITIME FORTUNE	54632
MARITIME FORTUNE	55062
MARITIME HARMONY	54636
MARITIME HARMONY	55066
MARITIME HAWK	68860
MARITIME JUSTICE	54633
MARITIME JUSTICE	55063
MARITIME KING	77885
MARITIME OPTIMUM	07291
MARITIME PIONEER	55081
MARITIME PIONEER	57341
MARITIME RESOURCE	52730
MARITIME STAR	56060
MARITIME STAR	71730
MARITIME TRADER	54634
MARITIME TRADER	55064
MARITIME UNITY	54635
MARITIME UNITY	55065
MARITIME VICTOR	61017
MARITIME VICTOR	71177
MARITSA	77732
MARITSA	89822
MARITSA III	15550
MARITSA P. LEMOS	46070
MARITTA JOHANNA	74290
MARITTA JOHANNA	88310
MARITZA	59901
MARITZA	67661
MARIVANA RENA	86680
MARIVIC	36380
MARIVIE	37400
MARIYA	00760
MARIYA SAVINA	02344
MARIYA ULYANOVA	02125
MARIYA ULYANOVA	93381
MARIYOS I	87860
MARIZINA	69500
MARJAN	75509
MARJORIE LYKES	00068
MARK RESHETNIKOV	12477
MARK VI	88930
MARK VII	66460
MARKHOR	07211
MARKINA	62340
MARKINA	90700
MARKINCH	48753
MARKINCH	75573
MARKO MARULIC.	06410
MARKO MILAT	35512
MARKO POLO	21211
MARKO TASILO	53441
MARKO TASILO	91571
MARKOS N	71140
MARLEN	27630
MARLEN	28480
MARLENE S	58650
MARLI	44330
MARLIN	23463
MARLIN	77250
MARLINDA	58112
MARLOW	50440
MARLOW	52000
MARLY	56570
MARMARAS	05890
MARMARIS 1	81101
MARMORICA	17132
MARNEULI	07904
MARO	78424
MAROFA	64391
MAROFA	68611
MARON	54194
MARON	54344
MAROUKO	26880
MARQUES DE BOLARQUE	77550
MARQUISE	72421
MARRA MAMBA	68291
MARRA MAMBA	77321
MARS - 2	23565
MARSA	04300
MARSA EL HARIGA	69181
MARSDIEP	18971
MARSHA	06601
MARSHAL BIRYUZOV	60626
MARSHAL BIRYUZOV	62586
MARSHAL BUDENYY	68250
MARSHAL BUDENYY	68800
MARSHAL GOVOROV	24740
MARSHAL GOVOROV	31380
MARSHAL KONYEV	68801
MARSHAL MALINOVSKIY	76527
MARSHAL MERETSKOV	93740
MARSHAL MERETSKOV	93830
MARSHAL ROKOSSOVSKIY	68252
MARSHAL ROKOSSOVSKIY	68802
MARSHAL ROKOSSOVSKIY	76504
MARSHAL SOKOLOVSKIY	93761
MARSHAL SOKOLOVSKIY	93851
MARSHAL VOROBYEV	79433
MARSHAL YAKUBOVSKIY	00145
MARSHAL ZHUKHOV	68253
MARSHAL ZHUKHOV	68803
MARSHALL CLARK	65222
MARSHALL CLARK	69882
MARSHALL KONYEV	68251
MARSMAN	58991
MARSMAN	75191
MARSO	22570
MART SAAR	12478
MARTERESA	22100
MARTHA	72351
MARTHA	77151
MARTHA BAKKE	24300
MARTHA ELLE	57430
MARTHA ELLE	78630
MARTIN ANDERSEN NEXO	17990
MARTINA	37930
MARTINA	85221
MARTINDYKE	75458
MARTINEZ TAMAYO	84881
MARTINIQUAIS	31294
MARTINIQUE	48680
MARTIS	62540
MARUN	53353
MARVALIENTE	14330
MARY	35872
MARY	43951
MARY	44381
MARY HOLYMAN	72870
MARY HOLYMAN	80240
MARY K	23000
MARY K	61464
MARY R. KOCH	64522
MARY R. KOCH	68472
MARYBETH	03492
MARYBETH	03582
MARYLAND	50384
MARYLISA	59351
MARYN	89540
MARYNARZ MIGALA	87753
MARYS KETCH	40420
MARYS KETCH	42330
MARYS KETCH	42590
MARYSTAR	00452
MARYUT	49683
MASBON	60050
MASHAL	93090
MASHALA	94160
MASHITAGI	44118
MASHU MARU	19683
MASHUK	22162
MASLUCK	60053
MASON LYKES	05587
MASON LYKES	14428
MASON LYKES	14898
MASOVIA	77566
MASSA	70850
MASSACHUSETTS GETTY	69161
MASSALIA	16942
MASSALIA	90341
MASSANDRA	89206
MASSIMO PRIMO	54701
MASSIMO PRIMO	74761
MASTER JOHN	58780
MASTER PETROS	35873
MASTER STEFANOS	46671
MASTER TONY K	24540
MASTRO MANOLIS	12880
MASTROGIORGIS	80490
MATA PRIMA	38510
MATADI PALM	58950
MATADI PALM	81180
MATANGI	06881
MATANUSKA	32190
MATANZAS	90393
MATCO AVON	37950
MATE ZALKA	70590
MATEMATIK	23481
MATHIAS THESEN	06389
MATHIAS THESEN	15418
MATHIAS THESEN	62686
MATHILDA	45831
MATHILDA	64877
MATHILDA	94290
MATHILDE	35908
MATHILDE	41599
MATHILDE	75550
MATHILDE MAERSK	47383
MATHILDE MAERSK	47653
MATHIOS	18471
MATHIOS	26900
MATHIOS	62011
MATILDE	78770
MATINA	05260
MATINA	81020
MATIS PLUGDON	12479
MATKO LAGINJA	34261
MATOCHKIN SHAR	93872
MATRA	76671
MATROS KOSHKA	10881
MATROSOV	17521
MATSESTA	07901
MATSONIA	08951
MATSUMAE MARU	19684
MATTERA MIMMO	87691
MATUMBA	79850
MATVEY MURANOV	03782
MATVEY MURANOV	04022
MAUI	93526
MAUI	94316
MAULE	72153
MAUMEE	38420
MAUREEN B	84830
MAURICE THOREZ	36869
MAURICIO DE OLIVEIRA	73581
MAURITIUS	24140
MAVRO VETRANIC	58132
MAVUR	87484
MAWAR	89440
MAW-LA-MYAING	71302
MAX REICHPIETSCH	06386
MAX REICHPIETSCH	15415
MAXHUTTE	43100
MAXHUTTE	36270
MAXIM LITVINOV	03783
MAXIM LITVINOV	04023
MAXIMO GOMEZ	05311
MAXIMUS	00930
MAXSIM GORKIY	16810
MAYA	64875
MAYA	85241
MAYA	85480
MAYA	86323
MAYA	90344
MAYA FARBER	70330
9 MAYA 1945 GODA	79421
MAYA I	41360
MAYA I	41530
MAYAGUEZ	93133
MAYAGUEZ	93393
MAYAKOVSKIY	12370
'MAYAKOVSKIY' class	12360
'MAYAKOVSKIY' class	12380
'MAYAKOVSKIY' class	12570
27 MAYIS	34582
MAYKOP	39971
MAYKOP	66170
MAYON	03840
MAYORI	63645
MAYSTAR	30190
MAZATEC	03763
MAZATLAN	20440
MAZDA	27120
MAZOWIA	08172
MAZOWSZE	02010
MAZZINI	14400
MB 18	22150
MB 15	22151
MB 105	22152
MB 119	22153
MBANDAKA	62714
MBANDAKA	62754
MBUJI-MAYI	62715
MBUJI-MAYI	62755
McKINNEY MAERSK	47382
MCKINNEY MAERSK	47652
MEADOWBANK	03674
MEADOWBANK	03734
MECHI VENTURE	81840
MECIS FLAG	10700
MECIS LEADER	10702
MECIS PIONEER	10701
MED FREEZER	18331
MED FREEZER	33650
MED SUN	20861
MED TRADER	27140
MED VICTORY	49340
MEDANITO	66195
MEDCAPE	24480
MEDCEMENT CARRIER	74750
MEDIAS	87641
MEDIK	23563
MEDI-SUN	13050
MEDITERRANEA	08806
MEDITERRANEAN CARRIER	78931
MEDITERRANEAN EXPRESS	41981
MEDITERRANEAN ISLAND	10060
MEDITERRANEAN SEA	16800
MEDITERRANEAN SKY	16801
MEDITERRANEAN SPRINTER	87731
MEDITERRANEAN SUN	17581
MEDMARE	28400
MEDNOGORSK	14701
MEDORA	63300
MEDROCK	31360
MEDVEDITSA	84352
MEDWAY	49862
MEDYN	07906
MEERDRECHT	47220
MEGAMA	41950
MEGANOM	11852
MEGAS	68731
MEGHNA	91921
MEI ABETO	25240
MEI GUI HAI	46010
MEI JIANG	06652
MEI PYA	22730
MEIHOU MARU	49330
MEIKI	13471
MEIKO MARU	54543
MEIKO MARU	63903
MEIRU	13470
MEISTERSINGER	73020
MEITAI MARU	59960
MEITAI MARU	62400
MEJEAN III	53400
MEJEAN III	64930
MEKHANIK AFANASYEV	36880
MEKHANIK BONDIK	10440
MEKHANIK FEDOROV	80097
MEKHANIK GERASIMOV	80099
MEKHANIK GORDYENKO	54718
MEKHANIK GORDYENKO	55288
MEKHANIK KALUSHNIKOV	20800
MEKHANIK KONOVALOV	80094
MEKHANIK KULUBIN	20801
MEKHANIK RYBASHUK	24075
MEKHANIK TARASOV	80096
MEKHANIK YEVGRAFOV	80098
MELAMPUS	54193
MELAMPUS	54343
MELANITA	11963
MELANTHO C	24542
MELANTHO C	31305
MELBOURNE EXPRESS	74490
MELBOURNE TRADER	94490
MELCHOR OCAMPO	69993
MELCHOR OCAMPO	86484
MELETE	53781
MELETE	68771
MELILLA	21870
MELINA	16550
MELINA	59631
MELINA TSIRIS	39440
MELITA	41953
MELITI	35753
MELITI	37090
MELITON	60110
MELITOPOL	11853
MELITOPOL	88248
'MELITOPOL' class	88230
MELLUMERSAND	53442
MELLUMERSAND	91572
MELNIK	83732
MELPO	00190
MELPO LEMOS	62790
MELPO LEMOS	67550
MELROSE	66500
MELROSE	85680
MELSOMVIK	45990
MELTEM UNIVERSAL	06365
MELTEMI	64640
MELTEMI II	08221
MELTON CHALLENGER	73961
MELVIN H. BAKER	89930
MEMBERSHIP	71033
MEMLING	15332
MEMPHIS	01418
MEMPHIS	01678
MENA	66061
MENANTIC	54416
MENANTIC	57876

MOGES AGATHIS 61615
MOGILEV 25559
MOHAC 80357
MOHAMMED ABBAS 00810
MOHAWK 63454
MOIDART 75931
MOIDART 88631
MOIRA 33030
MOJAIL 5 12841
MOKARIA 31370
MOKHA 58710
MOKHA 59640
MOKHA 61720
MOKHNI 89260
MOKRAN 53355
MOKSTEIN 48790
MOLARA 39890
MOLAT 47212
MOLDA 83140
MOLDAVIA 02353
MOLDAVIA 35373
MOLDOVEANU 11702
MOLIRO 25704
MOLISTA 77564
MOLLENDO 36743
MOLLY 89121
MOLOCHANSK 07912
MOLODAYA GVARDIYA 76497
MOLODECHNO 40006
MOLODOGVARDEYSK 07915
MOLODYOZNYY 85355
MOMBAKA 50417
MOMBAKA 50827
MONACO 76751
MONARCH 02792
MONARCH 59623
MONA'S QUEEN 20180
MONCADA 06611
MONCALVO 25211
MONCHEGORSK 88237
MONEMVASIA 36740
MONEMVASIA 67946
MONET 48403
MONGE 54040
MONGIBELLO 19001
MONGOL 85348
MONGOLIYA 12483
MONIA 45060
MONIMBO 51112
MONIMBO 51492
MONIUSZKO 44511
MONOMER VENTURE 90790
MONOWAI 04060
MONS CALPE 17240
MONSONE UNIVERSAL 06364
MONSOON 02793
MONSUN 55874
MONSUN 56604
MONT-ALBEN 86670
MONT BLANC MARU 09770
MONTAIGLE 06050
MONTAN 38890
MONTANA 05093
MONTANA 46944
MONTANA 47104
MONTCALM 08850
MONTCALM 72412
MONTE ALTO 06567
MONTE BALERDI 81952
MONTE BALERDI 91502
MONTE BANDERAS 95220
MONTE BRASIL 17840
MONTE BUITRE 95221
MONTE BUSTELO 95222
MONTE CARLO 10930
MONTE CASSINO 22820
MONTE CHRISTO 29440
MONTE CONTES 93970
MONTE CONTES 95210
MONTE CORONO 93971
MONTE CORONO 95211
MONTE CRISTO 06568
MONTE CRISTO 30610
MONTE D'ORO 72590
MONTE OLIVETO 88750
MONTE PASCOAL 06569
MONTE ZALAMA 46081
MONTE ZAMBURU 46122
MONTE ZAPOLA 46121
MONTE ZARAYA 46123
MONTEBELLO 38830
MONTELEON 70310
MONTEMURO 64392
MONTEMURO 68612
MONTENAKEN 06051
MONTEREY 06840
MONTERREY 01430
MONTERREY 56444
MONTERREY 68354
MONTESA 58771
MONTESA 62511
MONTEVIDEO 02723
MONTFORT 06052
MONTICELLO VICTORY 36650
MONTONE 80400
MONTPELIAR VICTORY 36651
MONTROSE 61054
MONTROSE 82644
MONTSALVA. 06053
MONZA 76752
MOORDRECHT 47226
MOR 67494
MORANT 05261
MORAYBANK 03675
MORAYBANK 03735
MOREKHOD 17932
MOREKHOD 85356
MORELIA 72342
MORESBY CHIEF 67490
MORETON BAY 77055
MORILLO 14170
MORITZ SCHULTE 81391
MORITZ SCHULTE 90641
MORMACALTAIR 04560
MORMACALTAIR 07792
MORMACARGO 04930
MORMACARGO 07790
MORMACCAPE 14551
MORMACDAWN 05933
MORMACDRACO 04561
MORMACDRACO 07795
MORMACGLEN 14550
MORMACLYNX 04931
MORMACLYNX 07791
MORMACMOON 05934
MORMACRIGEL 04932
MORMACRIGEL 07793
MORMACSAGA 08000
MORMACSEA 08002
MORMACTIDE 08003
MORMACTRADE 14552
MORMACVEGA 04933
MORMACVEGA 07794
MORMACWAVE 08004
MORNING GLORY 61216
MORNING SUN 83985
MORS 23457
MORSHANSK 07913
MORUKA 42140
MORVEN 35970
MORVIKEN 05310
MORZHOVETS 11382
MOS SHOVGENOV 60635
MOS SHOVGENOV 62595
MOSBROOK 53801
MOSBROOK 77521
MOSCENICE 04924
MOSCHA D 24892
MOSCHANTHY 10970
MOSCLIFF 55501
MOSCLIFF 63021
MOSCLIFF 67911
MOSEL EXPRESS 73511
MOSEL ORE 52380
MOSEL ORE 64440
MOSELLE 54415
MOSELLE 57875
MOSELSTEIN 13630
MOSKALVO 40000
MOSKOVSKIY KOMSOMOLETS 01403
MOSKOVSKIY KOMSOMOLETS 01663
MOSKVA. 02070
MOSLAKE 47631
MOSLAVINA 15211
MOSQUEIRO 22831
MOSRIVER 47630
MOSTEFA BEN BOULAID 53651
MOSTEFA BEN BOULAID 53741
MOSTOLES 65975
MOSTUN SANKO 53683
MOSTUN SANKO 53813
MOSTUN SANKO 68533
MOTAGUA 05262
MOTILAL NEHRU 63560
MOTOBU 72941
MOTOVUN 04925
MOUNT ATHOS 47950
MOUNT CARIBBEAN 31220
MOUNT EDEN 73273
MOUNT EDEN 77773
MOUNT NEWMAN 77676
MOUNT OTHRYS 56860
MOUNT PALMA 61659
MOUNT PARNASSOS 77595
MOUNT PELION 77670
MOUNT PINDOS 77882
MOUNT VERNON VICTORY 36653
MOUNT WASHINGTON 36652
MOUNTCREST 76090
MOUNT NAVIGATOR 44801
MOUNTPARK 91848
MOUNTPARK 91958
MOUTSAINA 61707
MOUTSAINA 71077
MOWENSTEERT 81823
MOWENSTEERT 82073
MOZART 60340
MOZART 68500
MOZHAISK 07911
MOZYR 07916
MOZYR 36253
MOZYR 42803
'MP 20' type 54190
'MP 20' type 54340
MPOLO 25707
MRAMOR 12484
MRAMORNY 11931
MTSENSK 07905
MTSKHETSA 12264
MU DAN JIANG 71856
MU DAN JIANG 71981
MUDI 87674
MUDISTAR 85280
MUGGELSEE 46382
MUGGELSEE 47082
MUGLA 81102
MUHLHAUSEN 03706
MUHLHAUSEN 03826
MUHUTI 51085
MUI KIM 62272
MUKACHEVO 07914
MUKALLA 59671
MUKHTAR ASHRAFI 79435
MUKHU 83707
MULDE 26064
MULHEIM 74964
MULHEIM 77104
MULTI FROST 21210
MULTITANK BADENIA 54750
MULTITANK BADENIA 56210
MULTITANK FRISIA 59071
MULTITANK FRISIA 76421
MULTITANK HAMMONIA 54751
MULTITANK HAMMONIA 56211
MULTITANK HOLSATIA 59072
MULTITANK HOLSATIA 76422
MULTITANK WESTFALIA 54752
MULTITANK WESTFALIA 56212
MUNAKATA MARU 31391
MUNATONES 58772
MUNATONES 62512
MUNDOGAS AMERICA 55610
MUNDOGAS ATLANTIC 82510
MUNDOGAS BRASILIA 62560
MUNDOGAS EUROPE 54470
MUNDOGAS PACIFIC 54472
MUNDOGAS RIO 55830
MUNDSBURG 24360
MUNETAMA MARU 57960
MUNETAMA MARU 59930
MUNKSUND 83190
MUNSTER 32730
MUNSTERLAND 41690
MUNSTERLANDES 10671
MUNSTERLANDES 13514
MUNTE 85473
MUNTE 9153'
MUNTENIA 55783
MUNTENIA 56483
MUOSTAKH 49248
MURASAKI MARU 20711
MURASAKI MARU 43290
MURES 11976
MURGAB 50775
MURGASH 49161
MURMAN 15475
MURMANSELD 11767
MURMANSELD 34658
MURMANSK 02073
MURMANSK 12346
MURMANSK 11200
MURMASH 22862
MURMASHI 34492
MUROM 07917
MUROMSK 11600
MURRAYEVERETT 04753
MURTAJA 23980
MUSA 05263
MUSA DZHALIL 14384
MUSALA 55410
MUSALA 78850
MUSCEL 82226
MUSI 18157
MUSING 81080
MUSKETIER II 87170
MUSSON 02270
MUSSON 18272
MUSTYARV 13682
MUTAN CAREER 58125
MUTIARA 01460
MUTIARA 08560
MUTSU 35400
MUTSU 35540
MUXIMA 10673
MUXIMA 13513
MYASSAR 43490
MYASSAR 43550
MYCENAE 89225
MYKONOS 03190
MYKONOS 03590
MYKONOS 55793
MYKONOS 64654
MYOMA YWA 52671
MYRIAM DEL TORO 76080
MYRINA 64260
MYRMIDON 54196
MYRMIDON 54346
MYROVLITIS 83713
MYRTEA 53080
MYRTEA 55794
MYRTEA 63230
MYRTEA 64655
MYRTIA 39252
MYRTIA 39270
MYRTIA V 53520
MYRTIDIOTISSA 28670
MYRTIDIOTISSA II 80610
MYRTOS 28291
MYS ARKTICHESKIY 11737
MYS ARKTICHESKIY 34627
MYS BABUSHKIN 11786
MYS BABUSKIN 34671
MYS BARANOVA 23496
MYS BELKINA 23489
MYS BOBROVA 23491
MYS BUDYONNOGO 11748
MYS BUDYONNOGO 34638
MYS CHAKO 13684
MYS CHASOVOY 11763
MYS CHASOVOY 34654
MYS CHAYKOVSKOGO 11764
MYS CHAYKOVSKOGO 34655
MYS CHELYUSKIN 11749
MYS CHELYUSKIN 34639
MYS DALNIY 11778
MYS DALNIY 34669
MYS FRUNZE 11750
MYS FRUNZE 34640
MYS GAMOVA 23492
MYS GRINA 23497
MYS GROTOVYY 11724
MYS GROTOVYY 34614
MYS GROZNYY 11765
MYS GROZNYY 34656
MYS ILMOVYY 11760
MYS ILMOVYY 34651
MYS KRONOTSKIY 11751
MYS KRONOTSKIY 34641
MYS KRYLOVA 23493
MYS KURILSKIY 11725
MYS KURILSKIY 34615
MYS KUZNETSOVA 11761
MYS KUZNETSOVA 34652
MYS LAZARYEVA 23494
MYS LOPATKA 11724
MYS LOPATKA 34616
MYS MALTSYEVA 23498
MYS NADEZHDY 23499
MYS OBRUCHYEVA 23495
MYS OREKHOVA 23500
MYS OSIPOVA 23501
MYS OSTROVSKOGO 11787
MYS OSTROVSKOGO 34672
MYS OTRADNYY 11752
MYS OTRADNYY 34642
MYS PROKOFYEVA 11727
MYS PROKOFYEVA 34617
MYS RATMONOVA 11728
MYS RATMONOVA 34618
MYS SHELIKHOVA 23538
MYS SILINA 11762
MYS SILINA 34653
MYS SINYAVINA 23482
MYS SKALISTYY 11766
MYS SKALISTYY 34657
MYS SVOBODNYY 11770
MYS SVOBODNYY 34661
MYS TAYMYR 11729
MYS TAYMYR 34619
MYS TIKHIY 11777
MYS TIKHIY 34668
MYS VAYGACH 11730
MYS VAYGACH 34620
MYS VODOPADNYY 11753
MYS VODOPADNYY 34643
MYS VORONINA 11731
MYS VORONINA 34621
MYS YEGOROVA 23483
MYS YELAGINA 23484
MYS YERMAK 23502
MYS YUDINA 23503
MYS YUNONY. 11788
MYS YUNONY. 34673
MYSTRAS 21840
MYTHIC 66271
MYTHIC 69901
MYTILENE 66040
MYTILUS 63302
MYTISHCHI 07918
MYUNG JIN 62226
MYUNG JIN 71136

N

N. B. McLEAN 17550
n. f. JAGUAR 93930
n. f. PANTHER 32781
n. f. TIGER 32780
N. FILCHENKOV 12268
N. GASTELLO 17523
NABIL 16050
NACALA 06020
NACALA 08010
NACELLA 64221
NACIONAL MONCHIQUE 73070
NACIONAL SINES 77260
NADE RIBAKOVAYTE 67017
NADER 14840
NADEZHDA 11857
NADEZHDA KRUPSKAYA 03705
NADEZHDA KRUPSKAYA 03824
NADEZHDA KURCHYENKO 86008
NADEZHDA OBUKHOVA 77347
NADEZHDINSK 12485
NADIA 1 74310
NADINA 49920
NADINA 50620
NADIR 12267
NADIR 24970
NADYM 70024
NAESBORG 70890
NAFSIKA L 41040
NAFTILOS 05342
NAGAEVO 22863
NAGAEVO 34493
NAGARA 02582
NAGARA. 02952
NAGARAT 23031
NAGLAN 31300
NAGOS 62012
NAHED 21740
NAI ALBERTO 79051
NAI ASSIA 74580
NAI ASSIA 74580
NAI CAROLINA 47910
NAI DI STEFANO 62859
NAI DI STEFANO 67539
NAI LUISA 51590
NAI LUISA 52340
NAI MARIA AMELIA 51635
NAI MARIO PERRONE 62858
NAI MARIO PERRONE 67538
NAI MATTEINI 62860
NAI MATTEINI 67540
NAI MEY 79050
NAI MONREALE 24410
NAI ROCCO PIAGGIO 62861
NAI ROCCO PIAGGIO 67541
NAIAD 53782
NAIAD 68772
NAIEFF 20720
NAIRA 42680
NAIRNBANK 07023
NAJADE 25900
NAJD 20080
NAJD 21300
NAJD II 20082
NAKHICHEVAN 44123
NAKHICHEVAN 93732
NAKHICHEVAN 93822
NAKHODA VANANCA 28110
NAKHODKA 12486
NAKHODKA 60685
NAKHODKA 90724
NAKORNTHON 14160
NAKWA 14250
NAKWA RIVER 15271
NAKWA RIVER 35042
NALANDA 56782
NALCHIK 86074
NALECZOW 74140
NAM IL 82560
NAM JUNG No 3 86131
NAM SAN 82480
NAM SHAN 32662
NAMANGAN 22864
NAMANGAN 34494
NAMANGAN 85360
NAMYANG BAY 61572
NAMYANG DRAGON 26102
NAN A. 61540
NAN FUNG 48091
NAN GUAN LING 61471
NAN HAI 89010
NAN HAI 136 88230
NAN HAI 145 00160
NAN HAI 155 28067
NAN HAI 156 28068
NAN HAI 157 10470
NAN HAI 158 12158
NAN HAI 169 39461
NAN HAI 175 33710
NAN HAI 502 04220
NAN HAI 502 04260
NAN KOU 93310
NAN SHANG 02771
NANAYETS 85349
NANCHENG 13493
NANCOWRY 25310
NANCY HEATH 85792
NANCY HEATH 86662
NANCY LYKES 00066
NAND KAVITA 67432
NAND KAVITA 71402
NANDU ARROW 83137
NANGKA 42071

NANHUA	13490
NANHUEI	13130
NANJIANG	43731
NANKUO	13492
NANNY	64050
NANO K	53391
NANO K	80341
NANOULA	47740
NANOULA	49310
NANPING	31460
NANSHIN MARU	61621
NANTAO	13491
NANWU	13631
NANXIANG	29360
NANXING	30991
NAOUSSA	57050
NAPALSAN	85630
NAPOLEON	20660
NARA	48422
NARA	49462
NARA	49512
NARCIS	92401
NARCIS	93081
NARICA	64220
NAROCH	11732
NAROCH	34622
NARODNYY OPOLCHENETS	13692
NARODOV	60682
NAROTTAM MORARJEE	78390
NARVA	85980
NARVA	89229
NARVAL	03494
NARVAL	03584
NARVSKAYA ZASTAVA	11632
NARVSKAYA ZASTAVA	50290
NARVSKIY ZALIV	61106
NARWAL	10813
NARWIK II	70543
NARYAN—MAR	24077
NARYMNEFT	86003
NARYN	86086
NASAUD	01410
NASAUD	01670
NASIA RIVER	13315
NASIA RIVER	34833
NASIM II	23321
NASIMI	79418
NASOS	29680
NASSAU I	73621
NASSIOUKA	87380
NATA	60111
NATALIA KOVCHOVA.	04520
NATALIE BOLTEN	49951
NATALIE BOLTEN	58501
NATHALIE D	21751
NATICINA	52970
NATIONAL STEEL FOUR	61083
NATIONAL STEEL FOUR	71273
NATIONAL STEEL TWO	30651
NATKO NODILO	06411
NAUKA	12307
NAULI	42683
NAUMBURG	03878
NAUSHON	16710
NAUSICAA	48423
NAUSICAA	49463
NAUSICAA	49513
NAUTIC	75297
NAUTIC	88107
NAUTILUS	67497
NAVARCO	76750
NAVARIN	21618
NAVARIN	34107
NAVARINO	09230
NAVASHINO	50785
NAVASOTA	38921
NAVIGATOR	09365
NAVIGIA	73945
NAVIKAPOL	26300
NAVIKAPOL	29490
NAVIOS CHALLENGER	71471
NAVIOS COURIER	68811
NAVIOS CRUSADER	64500
NAVIOS PATRIOT	73220
NAVIOS PATRIOT	77690
NAVIOS PIONEER	73221
NAVIOS PIONEER	77691
NAVISTAR	81250
NAVISTAR	91510
NAWAF	84100
NAWEZA	89090
NAXOS	13202
NAXOS	60112
NAZAR GUBIN	11437
NAZARCEA	83691
NAZIE BEAUTY	82803
NAZIE BEAUTY	92093
NAZIM KHIKMET	14384
NEAJLOV	11977
NEAPOLIS	81150
NEAPOLIS II	89847
NEBIT DAG	44109
NECHES	66342
NECKAR EXPRESS	79301
NECTARINE	06319
NEDA	91230
NEDDRILL I	92310
NEDDRILL 2	92311
NEDI	66060
NEDLLOYD ADELAIDE	03161
NEDLLOYD ALBANY	03165
NEDLLOYD AMSTERDAM	03160
NEDLLOYD AUCKLAND	03162
NEDLLOYD BAHRAIN	49420
NEDLLOYD BALTIMORE	49421
NEDLLOYD BANGKOK	49422
NEDLLOYD BARCELONA	49423
NEDLLOYD DEJIMA	08374
NEDLLOYD DELFT	08375
NEDLLOYD EBRO	15610
NEDLLOYD EEMS	15611
NEDLLOYD FORCADOS	08075
NEDLLOYD FRANKLIN	12711
NEDLLOYD FRAZER	12713
NEDLLOYD FREETOWN	12712
NEDLLOYD FREMANTLE	12710
NEDLLOYD FRESCO	08074
NEDLLOYD FUKUOKA	08076
NEDLLOYD HOBART	02751
NEDLLOYD HOLLAND	02750
NEDLLOYD HONG KONG	02753
NEDLLOYD HONSHU	02752
NEDLLOYD HOORN	08431
NEDLLOYD KARAKORUM	15620
NEDLLOYD KATWIJK.	04394
NEDLLOYD KATWIJK.	52904
NEDLLOYD KEMBLA	04390
NEDLLOYD KEMBLA	52900
NEDLLOYD KIMBERLEY	04391
NEDLLOYD KIMBERLEY	52901
NEDLLOYD KINGSTON	04392
NEDLLOYD KINGSTON	52902
NEDLLOYD KOBE	10681
NEDLLOYD KOREA	10680
NEDLLOYD KYOTO	04393
NEDLLOYD KYOTO	52903
NEDLLOYD LEUVE	03300
NEDLLOYD LINGE	03302
NEDLLOYD LOIRE	03301
NEDLLOYD MADISON	07684
NEDLLOYD MADISON	07834
NEDLLOYD MAIN	07683
NEDLLOYD MAIN	07833
NEDLLOYD NAGASAKI	02710
NEDLLOYD NAGASAKI	47640
NEDLLOYD NAGOYA	02711
NEDLLOYD NAGOYA	47641
NEDLLOYD NAPIER	02712
NEDLLOYD NAPIER	47642
NEDLLOYD NASSAU	02713
NEDLLOYD NASSAU	47643
NEDLLOYD NIGER	62630
NEDLLOYD RHONE	13520
NEDLLOYD RIJN	13521
NEDLLOYD ROCKANJE	15780
NEDLLOYD ROCKANJE	82690
NEDLLOYD SCHELDE	07681
NEDLLOYD SCHELDE	07831
NEDLLOYD SCHIE	07682
NEDLLOYD SCHIE	07832
NEDLLOYD SEINE	07680
NEDLLOYD SEINE	07830
NEDLLOYD SEROOSKERK	13430
NEDLLOYD SIMONSKERK	13431
NEDLLOYD SINOUTSKERK	08071
NEDLLOYD SPAARNEKERK	08070
NEDLLOYD STEENKERK	08072
NEDLLOYD STREEFKERK	08073
NEDLLOYD TALBOT	51080
NEDLLOYD TASMAN	74411
NEDLLOYD TAURANGA	51081
NEDLLOYD WAALEKERK	15831
NEDLLOYD WAALEKERK	72181
NEDLLOYD WAALEKERK	83401
NEDLLOYD WESER	15621
NEDLLOYD WESTERKERK	15833
NEDLLOYD WESTERKERK	72182
NEDLLOYD WESTERKERK	83402
NEDLLOYD WILLEMSKERK	15832
NEDLLOYD WILLEMSKERK	72183
NEDLLOYD WILLEMSKERK	83403
NEDLLOYD WISSEKERK	15830
NEDLLOYD WISSEKERK	72180
NEDLLOYD WISSEKERK	83400
NEDON	21471
NEDROMA	46930
NEERLANDIA	49871
NEFELI	37181
NEFELI	44010
NEFERTITI	01412
NEFERTITI	01672
NEFTECHALA	44104
NEFTEGORSK	70789
NEFTEGORSK	85982
NEFTEKAMSK	70792
NEGAM	73995
NEGO MAY	60163
NEGO TRIABUNNA	50600
NEGO TRIABUNNA	52350
NEGO VICTORIA	77462
NEGOIU	11703
NEIL ARMSTRONG	38260
NEKRASOV	12323
NEKTARIOS	17780
NELE MAERSK	53021
NELE MAERSK	53051
NELLA DAN	22620
NELLIE M	88710
NELLY MAERSK	53022
NELLY MAERSK	53052
NELO ALTOMARE	90455
NELSON MARU	77270
NELY P	44960
NEMA	43391
NEMAN	21584
NEMEA	58578
NEMEA	68621
NEMEMCHA	46931
NEMIROVICH-DANCHENKO	28493
NEMURO	72942
NEN JIANG	57763
NEN JIANG	62483
NEOCHO	45050
NEOTIS	06512
NEPHELE	77711
NEPTUN	07862
NEPTUN	12579
NEPTUN	12612
NEPTUN	91811
'NEPTUN' type	57550
'NEPTUN' type	59700
'NEPTUN' type	61400
NEPTUN HERCULES	52710
NEPTUNE	05964
NEPTUNE	20700
NEPTUNE	22740
NEPTUNE AGATE	03020
NEPTUNE ARIES	70190
NEPTUNE CYPRINE	60201
NEPTUNE EMERALD	03010
NEPTUNE IOLITE	60202
NEPTUNE IRIS	60203
NEPTUNE KIKU	60204
NEPTUNE ORION	70191
NEPTUNE PERIDOT	60205
NEPTUNE RUBY	60206
NEPTUNE SAPPHIRE	03011
NEPTUNE SARDONYX	60207
NEPTUNE SPINEL	60208
NEPTUNE STAR	57281
NEPTUNE TOURMALINE	60209
NEPTUNE TURQUOISE	60210
NEPTUNE VOLANS	57613
NEPTUNE VOLANS	62254
NEPTUNE WORLD	54500
NEPTUNIA	20110
NEPTUNIA	77920
NEPTUNO	08220
NER	72512
NERCHA	85881
NERCHINSK	85983
NEREIDA	87772
NERETVA	90250
NERLANDIA	94501
NERVA	60553
NERVA	69483
NERVA	76350
NESTEFOX	66560
NESTEGAS	66550
NESTOR	52180
NESTOR	53891
NESTOR	56510
NESTOR	94810
NESTOR SPIRIT	83821
NESTOS	35909
NESTOS	41598
NETUNO	03103
NEUBOKOW	50444
NEUBOKOW	52004
NEUBRANDENBURG	03883
NEUGRABEN	92900
NEUHAUSEN	59651
NEUQUEN II	06675
NEVA	22501
NEVA' type	78060
NEVA	87001
NEVALES	11495
NEVEL.	11383
NEVELSKIY	85334
NEVER	15476
NEVERITA	64222
NEVEZHIS	35311
NEVKA	35312
NEVSEHIR	26052
'NEVTERUDOVOZ' type	79450
NEVTERUDOVOZ 8M-33M	79450
NEVYANSK	11733
NEVYANSK	34623
NEW APOLLO	47661
NEW BEAR	08110
NEW CASTLE	14793
NEW CORAL SEA	81531
NEW DOLPHIN	83583
NEW DOVE	14092
NEW EAGLE	07665
NEW ENGLAND HUNTER	74420
NEW ENGLAND HUNTER	88090
NEW FUTURE	70720
NEW FUTURE	79720
NEW GLOBE	29242
NEW GOLDEN PHOENIX	03681
NEW HERO	21651
NEW HERO	27561
NEW HYDE	21650
NEW HYDE	27560
NEW HYSAN	30161
NEW INDEPENDENCE	48944
NEW JERSEY MARU	08650
NEW JERSEY SUN	38543
NEW JERSEY SUN.	44813
NEW LARK	24870
NEW PANDA	06629
NEW PENGUIN	67190
NEW SEA PIONEER	25660
NEW SPIRIT	82454
NEW STAR	10130
NEW STAR	10320
NEW STAR	23162
NEW SULU SEA	55921
NEW SULU SEA	84721
NEW SWAN	14091
NEW WAN FU	26111
NEW WAYS	77440
NEW WESTMINSTER CITY	46436
NEW WHALE	06590
NEW YELLOW SEA	10131
NEW YELLOW SEA	10321
NEW YORK GETTY	36851
NEW YORK MARU	09860
NEW ZEALAND CARIBBEAN	02820
NEW ZEALAND PACIFIC	08444
NEW ZEALAND STAR	02871
NEWARK	26027
NEWBEACH	26028
NEWBEACH	30197
NEWCREST	26025
NEWCREST	30194
NEWFOUNDLAND COAST	43130
NEWFOUNDLAND CONTAINER	73930
NEWHAM	40322
NEWHAVEN	57331
NEWTIDE	24865
NEWTON	24861
NEWTON	63770
NEXUS	50205
NEXUS	75975
NEZLA	60582
NGAHERE	45881
NGAKUTA	45882
NGAPARA	45880
N'GOLA	10674
N'GOLA	13510
NGOMEI CHAU	13993
NIAGA XX	52093
NIAGA XXI	91313
NIAGA XXII	91314
NIAGA XXIV	66830
NIAGA XXIV	91490
NIAGA XXV	91430
NIAGA XXVI	71941
NIAGA XXVIII	52190
NIAGA XXVIII	84130
NIAGA XXIX	81942
NIAGA XXIX	89422
NIAGA XXXII	52191
NIAGA XXXII	84131
NIAGA XXXIV	91842
NIAGA XXXIV	91952
NIAGA XXXV	47324
NIAGA XXXV	83384
NIC TRADER	73944
NICE KATHRINE	72970
NICHIO MARU	67990
NICHOLAS	68990
NICHOLAS G. PAPALIOS	78182
NICHOLAS M	90131
NICIA	04805
NICOLA VAPTZAROV	07863
NICOLAI MAERSK	53023
NICOLAI MAERSK	53053
NICOLAOS CH	67310
NICOLAOS G	25530
NICOLAOS K HADJIKYRIAKOS	89291
NICOLAOS M	85530
NICOLAOS RIGAS	23890
NICOLAS MIHANOVICH	19770
NICOLAS P	89120
NICOLE 1	78610
NICOLE I	54300
NICOLINE MAERSK	53024
NICOLINE MAERSK	53054
NICOLO MARIA	22900
NICOS A	81290
NICOS I. VARDINOYANNIS	63590
NICOS I. VARDINOYANNIS	68330
NICOS S	87910
NICOS V	39840
NIDA	23566
NIEBLA	76351
NIEDERSACHSEN	63425
NIELS HENRIK ABEL	59210
NIELS HENRIK ABEL	66740
NIELS MAERSK	53025
NIELS MAERSK	53055
NIELSE DANIELSEN	64861
NIELSE DANIELSEN	91041
NIENBURG	03879
NIENBURG	33822
NIENHAGEN	75322
NIEWIADOW	58730
NIGBOLU	80351
NIGER BASIN	06645
NIGER VALLEY	06646
NIHON	08480
NIHON	09570
NIHON ALPHA	57040
NIHON MARU	10800
NIIHATA MARU	72390
NIITAKA MARU	35093
NIITAKA MARU	95084
NIIZURU MARU	77330
NIKA	74330
NIKE	88030
NIKE	89080
NIKEA	46943
NIKEA	47103
NIKI	06513
NIKI R	34899
NIKIFOR ROGOV	53164
NIKITA MITCHENKO	48437
NIKITA MITCHENKO	49477
NIKITA MITCHENKO	49747
NIKITAS	37170
NIKITAS	43960
NIKITAS F	07013
NIKKEI MARU No 3	52220
NIKKEI MARU No 3	84160
NIKKO MARU No35	82330
NIKO NIKOLADZE	59221
NIKO NIKOLADZE	74541
NIKOFOR PAVLOV	13689
NIKOLA TESLA	11100
NIKOLAI ZUBOV	22180
NIKOLAKIS	35673
NIKOLAOS A	26110
NIKOLAOS A	61052
NIKOLAOS A	82642
NIKOLAOS G	25500
NIKOLAOS K	40130
NIKOLAY ANANYEV	48443
NIKOLAY ANANYEV	49483
NIKOLAY ANANYEV	49753
NIKOLAY BAUMAN	79387
NIKOLAY BAUMAN	89253
NIKOLAY BERAZIN	13688
NIKOLAY BOSHNYAK	17929
NIKOLAY BROVTSYEV	11858
NIKOLAY BURDYENKO	34243
NIKOLAY CHERKASOV	80264
NIKOLAY CHERNYSHEVSKIY	28981
NIKOLAY DANILOV	93880
NIKOLAY DUBROLYUBOV	14386
NIKOLAY EMELYANOV	50296
NIKOLAY FILCHENKOV	12268
NIKOLAY GOGOL	14387
NIKOLAY GOLOVANOV	77348
NIKOLAY GRIBANOV	13691
NIKOLAY ISAYENKO	43301
NIKOLAY KARAMZIM	14388
NIKOLAY KASATKIN	76585
NIKOLAY KASATKIN	79935
NIKOLAY KOLOMEYTSYEV	35425
NIKOLAY KONONOV	11607
NIKOLAY KOPERNIK	10740
NIKOLAY KREMLYANSKIY	05636
NIKOLAY KREMLYANSKIY	14465
NIKOLAY KRYLENKO	03068
NIKOLAY KRYLENKO	03660
NIKOLAY MAKSIMOV	48444
NIKOLAY MAKSIMOV	49484
NIKOLAY MAKSIMOV	49754
NIKOLAY MIRONOV	24078
NIKOLAY MOROZOV	69313
NIKOLAY NEKRASOV	07923
NIKOLAY NOVIKOV	54710
NIKOLAY NOVIKOV	55280
NIKOLAY OGARYEV	14389
NIKOLAY OSTROVSKIY	12347
NIKOLAY OSTROVSKIY	12487
NIKOLAY OSTROVSKIY	28982
NIKOLAY PAPIVIN	23567
NIKOLAY PIROGOV	34244
NIKOLAY PODVOYSKIY	60644
NIKOLAY PODVOYSKIY	62604
NIKOLAY POGODIN	03069
NIKOLAY POGODIN	03661
NIKOLAY PRZHEVALSKIY	10442
NIKOLAY SEMASHKA	03786
NIKOLAY SEMASHKO	04026
NIKOLAY SHCHETININ	49243
NIKOLAY SHCHORS	33911
NIKOLAY SHCHUKIN	69320
NIKOLAY SHVERNIK.	03787
NIKOLAY SHVERNIK	04027
NIKOLAY SIPYAGIN	59893
NIKOLAY SIPYAGIN	67653
NIKOLAY TSYGANOV	13690
NIKOLAY VILKOV	78063

NIKOLAY VOZNESENSKIY	78732
NIKOLAY VOZNESENSKIY	89982
NIKOLAY YAROSHENKO	76584
NIKOLAY YAROSHENKO	79934
NIKOLAY YEVGENOV	35424
NIKOLAY ZAZOLOTSKIY	50756
NIKOLAY ZHUKHOV	69312
NIKOLAY ZHUKOVSKIY	63574
NIKOLAY ZYSTSTAR	45123
NIKOLAYEV	11859
NIKOLAYEV	45353
NIKOLAYEVSK	02127
NIKOLAYEVSKIY KOMSOMOLETS	23532
NIKOLAYEVSKIY KORABEL	11779
NIKOLAYEVSKIY KORABEL	34670
NIKOLOZ BARATASHVILI	60632
NIKOLOZ BARATASHVILI	62592
NIKOLSK	12269
NIKOPOL	85986
NIKOPOLIS	90260
NIKOS	12966
NIKOS	14566
NIKOS	15671
NIKOS A	27670
NIKOS M	87411
NIKOS N	61051
NIKOS N	82641
NIKYEL	11626
NIKYEL	88238
NILE MARU	71790
NILE U	05512
NILS DACKE	16513
NILS DACKE	17040
NIMBA	74770
NIMBA	79000
NIMERTIS	39910
NIMERTIS	40830
NIMFA	87743
NIMOS	21781
NIMOS	82852
NIN	58196
NINA KUKOVEROVA	15518
NINA SAGAYDAK	15519
9 DE ABRIL	59904
9 DE ABRIL	67664
NINFEA	65570
NING HUA	25950
NINGDU	30132
NIOBE	57381
NIPPON MARU	09161
NIPPON MARU	09430
NIPPON MARU No 3	67810
NIPPONHAM MARU No 1	71380
NIPPONHAM MARU No 1	86630
NIPPONICA	08807
NIPPOU MARU	49331
NIRITOS	58900
NIRITOS	65362
NIRVANA	62853
NIRVANA	67533
NISHNIJ TAGIL	11438
NISSAN MARU	47000
NISSAN SILVIA	92221
NISSEI MARU	57972
NISSEI MARU	63332
NISSEKI MARU	57973
NISSEKI MARU	63333
NISSHIN MARU	90161
NISSHIN MARU	93770
NISSHIN MARU No 2	93500
NISSHIN MARU No 3	93540
NISSOS ANDROS	31210
NISSOS CHIOS	32750
NISSOS ITHAKI	00790
NISSOS KEFALLINIA	40620
NISSOS MYKONOS	14061
NISSOS RHODOS	21180
NISYROS ERA	86030
NITSA	66220
NITTOKU MARU	60041
NITYA NANAK	82452
NIUGINI EXPRESS	46231
NIUVAKAI	40092
NIVA	85981
NIVES	37342
NIVES	45202
NIZAMI	50757
NIZHEGORODSKIY KOMSOMOLETS	79411
NIZHNEUDINSK	15477
NIZHNEVARTOVSK	70025
NJEGOS	16723
NJORD	23663
NOAH VI	38338
NOAH VI	44698
NOBLE FIVE	55260
NOBLE FIVE	80960
NODAWAY	42825
NOGA	09460
NOGA	15050
NOGA	64361
NOGAR LOIRA	28890
NOGINSK	85987
NOKUYEV	11315
NOMENTANA	33472
NONA	22011
NONNA RAFFAELLA	58127
NONOC TRANSPORT	86952
NOOR JEHAN	10101
NOORD NEDERLAND	19070
NOORDLAND	52030
NOPAL ARGUS	93330
NOPAL BRANCO	92891
NOPAL MASCOT	94820
NOPAL MINERVA	93211
NOPAL OPTIMA	93210
NOPAL SEL	92654
NOPAL SEL	93194
NOPAL VEGA	13581
NOPAL VERDE	92890
NORA MAERSK	53020
NORA MAERSK	53050
NORBAY	65201
NORBAY	67411
NORBEGA	64020
NORBEGA	67620
NORBIRD	65200
NORBIRD	67410
NORBORN	56417
NORBORN	67837
NORBORN	68437
NORBRIGHT	56418
NORBRIGHT	67838
NORBRIGHT	68438
NORCAN	50110
NORDANGER	54137
NORDANGER	54257
NORDBAY	51543
NORDFELS	57602
NORDFELS	62245
NORDGARD	50221
NORDHAUSEN	03707
NORDHAUSEN	03827
NORDHEIM	57601
NORDHEIM	62244
NORDHOLM	57603
NORDHOLM	62246
NORDHVAL	49174
NORDIC CLANSMAN	63190
NORDIC CLANSMAN	67560
NORDIC FAITH	58040
NORDIC LOUISIANA	52450
NORDIC LOUISIANA	53210
NORDIC PATRIOT	72271
NORDIC PATRIOT	77171
NORDIC PRINCE	16871
NORDIC SPIRIT	58041
NORDIC TEXAS	52451
NORDIC TEXAS	53211
NORDKAP	49170
NORDKAP	53401
NORDKAP	64931
NORDKYN	49173
NORDKYN	93010
NORDLAND V	34206
NORDLYS	01300
NORDMARK	57604
NORDMARK	62247
NORDMEER	18728
NORDNORGE	01950
NORDON	66804
NORDPOL	49171
NORDSCHAU	19650
NORDSEE	36080
NORDSEE	73912
NORDSEE	18720
NORDSEE I	20780
NORDSTERN	83605
NORDSTJERNEN	01301
NORDSTRAND	64933
NORDSTRAND	53403
NORDTRAMP	49172
NORDVAER	92336
NORDVIK	24076
NORDWIK	90990
NORDWIND	26081
NORDWIND	73790
NOREFJORD	76811
NORFOLK FERRY	21951
NORGE	22000
NORILSK	23880
NORITA	47360
NORITA	47890
NORLAND	17060
NORLAND	32600
NORLAND	51840
NORMAN ATLANTIC	63542
NORMAN LADY	63630
NORMAN LADY	72220
NORMAN PACIFIC	59970
NORMAN PACIFIC	68310
NORMAN VENTURE	54566
NORMAN VENTURE	54966
NORMAND EXPRESS	81740
NORMANDIA	93892
NORMANDIE	57833
NORNED THOR	75880
NORPPA	75369
NORRBOTTEN	75530
NORRIS CASTLE	84430
NORRSUNDET	75293
NORRSUNDET	88103
NORSE	42031
NORSE DUKE	78421
NORSE HERALD	46439
NORSE KING	64011
NORSE KING	68401
NORSE MARSHAL	46438
NORSE PILOT	46437
NORSE QUEEN	64012
NORSE QUEEN	68402
NORSE RIVER	46172
NORSE TRANSPORTER	55120
NORSE VIKING	46170
NORSEA	94370
NORSEMAN	64016
NORSEMAN	68406
NORSK BARDE	51985
NORSTAR	17061
NORSTAR	32601
NORTEMAR	26140
NORTH COUNTESS	26440
NORTH EMPEROR	84590
NORTH EMPEROR	90020
NORTH EMPRESS	26441
NORTH KING	84591
NORTH KING	90021
NORTH POLE	86321
NORTH SEA	05720
NORTH SKY	89870
NORTH WAVE	26981
NORTHERN	89570
NORTHERN CRUISER	20480
NORTHERN HORIZON	31133
NORTHERN ICE	23910
NORTHERN INSTALLER	92980
NORTHERN LION	59945
NORTHERN LION	67935
NORTHERN NAIAD	79133
NORTHERN STAR	67942
NORTHIA	64381
NORTHRIDGE	66920
NORTHUMBRIA ROSE	76088
NORTHWIND	53380
NORTHWIND	90740
NORTRANS VISION	46902
NORTREFF	33010
NORWAVE	17120
NORWAVE	32440
NORWAY	09165
NORWEGIAN SEA	47830
NORWID	30430
NORWIND	17121
NORWIND	32441
NOSTOS	43740
NOTIS	10300
NOTRE DAME D'AFRIQUE	58670
NOTUS	65130
NOVA GORICA	61194
NOVACI	83694
NOVAYA ERA	12488
NOVAYA KAKHOVKA	81002
NOVAYA KAKHOVKA	93741
NOVAYA KAKHOVKA	93831
NOVAYA LADOGA	93742
NOVAYA LADOGA	93832
NOVAYA LADOGA	11439
NOVAYA ZEMLYA	10443
NOVAYA ZEMLYA	11440
NOVEMBER SEVENTH	26260
NOVGOROD	00550
NOVGOROD	02690
NOVGOROD	03110
NOVI T	87673
NOVI VINODOLSKI	15243
NOVIA	58595
NOVIA	60475
NOVIGRAD	58197
NOVIK	85991
NOVIKOV-PRIBOY	12324
NOVINSK	85886
NOVO REDONDO	62660
NOVOALTAISK	02697
NOVOALTAISK	03117
NOVOCHERKASSK	67353
NOVOCHERKASSK	71364
NOVODRUZHESK	02700
NOVODRUZHESK	03120
NOVOGRUDOK	02703
NOVOGRUDOK	03123
NOVOKUIBYSHEVSK	02693
NOVOKUIBYSHEVSK	03113
NOVOKUIBYSHEVSK	11616
NOVOKUZNETSK	02692
NOVOKUZNETSK	03112
NOVOLVOVSK	02701
NOVOLVOVSK	03121
NOVOMIRGOROD	02698
NOVOMIRGOROD	03118
NOVOMOSKOVSK	02694
NOVOMOSKOVSK	03114
NOVOPOLOTSK	02699
NOVOPOLOTSK	03119
NOVOROSSISKIY PARTIZAN	84814
NOVORZHEV	81003
NOVOSHAKHTINSK	81004
NOVOSIBIRSK	02691
NOVOSIBIRSK	03111
NOVOSOKOLNIKI	13693
NOVOTROITSK	02695
NOVOTROITSK	03115
NOVOVOLYNSK	02704
NOVOVOLYNSK.	03124
NOVOVORONEZH	15501
NOVOVYATSK	02696
NOVOVYATSK	03116
NOVOZYBKOV	03122
NOVY BUG	81000
NOVY DONBASS	81001
NOVYY MIR	11744
NOVYY MIR	34634
NOVZYBKOV	02702
NOWOWIEJSKI	44513
NOWY SACZ	75772
NTAMA	83910
N'TCHENGUE	55773
NUEVA ESPARTA	31194
NUITS ST. GEORGE	32680
NURAGE	42681
NUREK	44110
NURNBERG EXPRESS	08782
NWAKUSO	21941
NYANAW	80970
NYANAW	87040
NYANDA	15101
NYANDOMA	86229
NYHOLT	54550
NYHORN	54551
NYMIT	82320
NYMIT	91800
NYMPH C	79960
NYOMBE	33953
NYON	73366
NYURA KIZHEVATOVA	67018

O

OAK	94850
OAKLAND	60186
OAKLAND	74472
OAKWOOD	01190
OB	25062
OB	35325
OBERNAI	53361
OBESTAIN	24370
OBO QUEEN	68851
OBORISHTE	49163
OBRONCY POCZTY	74544
OBRONCY POCZTY	59224
OBSERVER	44540
OBUKHOVSKAYA OBORONA	76526
OCEAN	28613
OCEAN ACE	15570
OCEAN ACE	46777
OCEAN ACE	62232
OCEAN ACE	71252
OCEAN BEAUTY	46778
OCEAN BUILDER I	92820
OCEAN CHALLENGE	50531
OCEAN CHALLENGER	51866
OCEAN CHALLENGER	64916
OCEAN CONTAINER	73500
OCEAN CONTAINER	78030
OCEAN CROWN	46779
OCEAN DEFIANT	83582
OCEAN DIAMOND	14090
OCEAN DUKE	46780
OCEAN DYNAMIC	60420
OCEAN DYNAMIC	69350
OCEAN ENDEAVOUR	83650
OCEAN ENDURANCE	03550
OCEAN ENVOY	06650
OCEAN FREEZE	87530
OCEAN FRESH	60421
OCEAN FRESH	69351
OCEAN GIRL	67180
OCEAN GLORY	15571
OCEAN GLORY	89140
OCEAN GLORY No 6	91690
OCEAN GREEN	05790
OCEAN HARMONY	77805
OCEAN JADE	73111
OCEAN JADE	77781
OCEAN KING	06230
OCEAN LADY	74810
OCEAN LEADER	51863
OCEAN LEADER	64913
OCEAN LINK	74080
OCEAN LION	71552
OCEAN PARK	54522
OCEAN PARK	55442
OCEAN PARK	55732
OCEAN PEGASUS	47760
OCEAN PROGRESS	51864
OCEAN PROGRESS	64914
OCEAN PROMOTER	51865
OCEAN PROMOTER	64915
OCEAN PROSPECT	61850
OCEAN PROSPECT	85040
OCEAN QUEEN	33390
OCEAN ROYAL	14623
OCEAN SERVANT I	84270
OCEAN SERVANT II	84271
OCEAN SKY	60030
OCEAN SKY	68360
OCEAN SKY	71970
OCEAN SOVEREIGN	59240
OCEAN TRADER	55211
OCEAN TRADERS	24600
OCEAN TRITON	57260
OCEAN TRITON	84820
OCEAN VENTURE	69122
OCEAN VICTORY	65976
OCEANIA	90940
OCEANIA MARU	73341
OCEANIA MARU	77961
OCEANIC	01250
OCEANIC	22140
OCEANIC	35220
OCEANIC	64880
OCEANIC	91060
OCEANIC CONSTITUTION	09190
OCEANIC CREST	72293
OCEANIC CREST	77163
OCEANIC ENERGY	69090
OCEANIC INDEPENDENCE	09191
OCEANIC VICTORY	69201
OCEANIC WINNER	65062
OCEANIC WINNER	65952
OCEANICA	77921
OCEANIS	60113
OCEANO ANTARTICO	21280
OCEANO ARTICO	06307
OCEANO ATLANTICO	06306
OCEANO PACIFICO	04142
OCEANOS	08282
OCEANUS	68710
OCEANUS	78720
OCHAKOV SAMARKAND	39982
OCTAVIAN	60554
OCTAVIAN	69484
ODEN	23950
ODESSA	16960
ODET	56200
ODET	59090
ODET	76230
ODIGITRIA B	28930
ODIN	45600
ODIN	73943
ODIN	79141
ODLI	34373
ODORHEI	47554
ODYSEFS	05150
ODYSSEUS	33924
ODYSSEUS	74673
ODYSSEUS	78383
ODYSSEY 10	46881
OELAND	51628
OELAND	72683
OELSA	84940
OELSA	90600
OFELIA	19401
OFELIA	23446
OFFIN RIVER	13316
OFFIN RIVER	34834
OGAN	18158
OGDEN AMAZON	72434
OGDEN CHALLENGER	38030
OGDEN CHAMPION	58425
OGDEN CHARGER	58420
OGDEN DANUBE	77872
OGDEN EXPORTER	59360
OGDEN IMPORTER	59361
OGDEN LEADER	58421
OGDEN NELSON	59940
OGDEN NELSON	67930
OGDEN OTTAWA	69012
OGDEN SAGUENAY	69013
OGDEN SUNGARI	55500
OGDEN SUNGARI	63020
OGDEN SUNGARI	67910
OGDEN THAMES	77871
OGDEN WABASH	58426
OGDEN WILLAMETTE	58427
OGISHIMA MARU	70921
OGISHIMA MARU	79601
OGLASA	17133
OGNA	83064
OGNA	83164
OGNYAN NAYDOV	50759
OGRAJDAN	77984
OH DAI YANG No 106	86610
O'HIGGINS	86692
OHIO	30171
OHIO	50385
OHRMAZD	14880
OHSHIMA MARU	57910
OHTORI	58181
OHTSUKAWA MARU	69150
OIHONNA	83366
OIHONNA	83456
OIL ENDEAVOUR.	09040
OINOUSSAI ALPHA	57142
OINOUSSIAN DESTINY	61220
OINOUSSIAN FRIENDSHIP	61221
OINOUSSIAN LEADERSHIP	61222

OINOUSSIAN PRESTIGE 61223
OINOUSSIAN VIRTUE 61224
OJCOW 15451
OJI MARU No 1 48948
OKA 11441
OKA 35313
OKAH 10780
OKEAN 02273
OKEANIS 59580
OKHA 86072
OKHANEFT 66381
OKHOTSK 03271
OKHOTSK 49721
OKHOTSKOYE MORE 55131
OKINAWA MARU 34450
OKINOSHIMA MARU 54440
OKLAHOMA 38390
OKLAHOMA GETTY 69160
OKPO PEARL 62200
OKTANT 11860
OKTAVIUS 65711
OKTAVIUS 67701
OKTURUS 65710
OKTURUS 67700
OKTYABRSK 85335
OKTYABRSKAYA 45367
OKTYABRSKOYE 11861
OLA 01541
OLA 45630
OLANCHO 06313
OLANESTI 47551
OLAU FINN 20160
OLAU KENT 19290
OLAU KENT 23700
OLDENBURG 01990
OLEG KOSHEVOY 44950
OLEG KOSHEVOY 41150
OLEKMA 39120
OLEKO DUNDICH 60627
OLEKO DUNDICH 62587
OLENEGORSK 11587
OLENEGORSK 15478
OLENSK 86179
OLENTUY 11603
OLESNICA 14291
OLGA 21760
OLGA ANDROVSKAYA 02345
OLGA BRAVO 50333
OLGA BRAVO 83673
OLGA MAERSK 78680
OLGA SADOVSKAYA 02346
OLGA TOPIC 77802
OLGA ULYANOVA 03070
OLGA ULYANOVA 03662
OLGA VARENTSOVA 03788
OLGA VARENTSOVA 04028
OLIB 88820
OLINDA 03096
OLIVA 65320
OLIVE ACE 94780
OLIVEBANK 26010
OLIVER 63660
OLIVER DRESCHER 50050
OLIVER DRESCHER 47280
OLIVIA 47050
OLIVINE 04970
OLIWA 15452
OLKAS 73091
OLKUSZ 15450
OLMEDA 45330
OLNA 45331
OLOHAVA 33170
OLOIBIRI 67402
OLTUL 78587
OLUSHA 11964
OLWEN 45332
OLYMPIA 12020
OLYMPIA II 89227
OLYMPIAN 81090
OLYMPIAN REEFER 15070
OLYMPIAS 12860
OLYMPIC ACCORD 67971
OLYMPIC ACTION 62910
OLYMPIC ALLIANCE 67970
OLYMPIC ANTHEM 62911
OLYMPIC ARCHER 69170
OLYMPIC ARROW 69171
OLYMPIC ASPIRATION 62912
OLYMPIC AVENGER 62913
OLYMPIC BOND 57820
OLYMPIC BOND 59950
OLYMPIC CHARIOT 65231
OLYMPIC CHIVALRY 65230
OLYMPIC DREAM 70163
OLYMPIC GAMES 65242
OLYMPIC GARLAND 69710
OLYMPIC GATE 65241
OLYMPIC GLORY 69611
OLYMPIC GOAL 69712
OLYMPIC GRACE 65240
OLYMPIC HARMONY 48057
OLYMPIC HISTORY 48056
OLYMPIC HOPE 57238
OLYMPIC PALM 59340
OLYMPIC PEACE 59345
OLYMPIC PEARL 59341
OLYMPIC PEGASUS 59342
OLYMPIC PHAETHON 59343
OLYMPIC PIONEER 59344
OLYMPIC POWER 59346
OLYMPIC PRESTIGE 59347
OLYMPIC PRIDE 59348
OLYMPIC PROGRESS 59349
OLYMPIC SPLENDOUR 58340
OLYMPIC SPLENDOUR 63990
OLYMPIC STAR 52441
OLYMPIOS ZEUS 29180
OLYNTHIA 61158
OLYUTORKA 11496
OLYUTORKA 21625
OM 86175
OMALOŠ 39072
OMALOS 41292
OMALOS 45001
OMANIAH 53760
OMANIAH 25200
OMAR 22660
OMAR 23111
OMAR B 38140
OMAR EXPRESS 90320
OMBRINA 52203
OMBRINA 65153
OMDURMAN 80902
OMEGA KASSOS 25860
OMEGA LEROS 53450
OMEGA LEROS 90360
OMEGA PATMOS 65120
OMEGA RHODOS 71350
OMEGA RHODOS 86570
OMID 29150
OMIS 34263
OMNIUM PRIDE 74714
OMOA 06312
OMOLON 31851
OMSK 03270
OMSK 49720
OMSK 70782
ON DING 49080
ON LEE 46092
ON LEE 83262
ON PING 04653
ON SHUN 04650
ON SUNG 65401
ON SUNG 69791
ON TAT 04651
ON TUNG 46903
ON WO 04652
ON YEUNG 46090
ON YEUNG 83260
ONBAK FADJAR 17890
ONCU 66430
ONDINA 37270
1 CONGRESO DEL PARTIDO 06610
ONE SKY 59141
ONE STAR 59140
ONE WEST No 8 56312
ONEGA 20802
ONEGSKIY 89681
ONEKOTAN 11604
ONESSILUS 74570
ONEZHSKIY ZALIV 61107
ONGE 18600
ONGE 22541
ONOBA 53230
ONOE MARU 74970
ONOE MARU 74970
ONORATO 74944
ONWARD ELITE 05970
ONYX ISLANDS 29810
OPAL 26560
OPAL BOUNTY 82925
OPAL CITY 46872
OPAL ISLANDS 30621
OPALA 12489
OPALIA 65330
OPALINE BAY 00351
OPALINE BAY 26211
OPOLE 12161
OPULENCE 05483
OPUSO 40450
ORADEA 41310
ORAN 75430
ORANGE ACE 94782
ORANIENBURG 03880
ORANJESTAD 37381
ORAVITA 47565
ORBITA 12598
ORCA 92830
ORCADIA 18170
ORCHID VENTURE 40392
ORCYN 23464
ORDUNA 65977
ORDZHONIKIDZENNEFT 44112
ORE JUPITER 37150
ORE MERIDIAN 37151
ORE METEOR 37152
ORE NEPTUNE 37153
ORE PRINCE 37140
ORE SATURN 37154
ORE VENUS 37155
OREANDRA 12270
OREKHOV 01542
OREKHOV 45632
OREKHOVO-ZUYEVO 24079
OREL 84364
OREL 11862
OREMAR 78510
ORENBURG 03272
ORENBURG 49722
ORESTIA 61155
ORESTIS 85390
ORESUND 20760
ORFEO 61142
ORFEO 81482
ORGEO 74250
ORIANA 01260
ORICA 06310
ORIENT 18510
ORIENT 21841
ORIENT CLIPPER 17850
ORIENT CORAL 57161
ORIENT ENTERPRISE 52140
ORIENT ENTERPRISE 52530
ORIENT FISHER 61070
ORIENT FISHER 71260
ORIENT HARMONY 74980
ORIENT HARMONY 79210
ORIENT HORIZON 57090
ORIENT HORIZON 57780
ORIENT LONDON 13910
ORIENT LONDON 14820
ORIENT PINE 49222
ORIENT ROSE 78401
ORIENT SUCCESS 31430
ORIENT TRADER 59380
ORIENT TRUST 49221
ORIENT UNION 46888
ORIENT VENTURE 57321
ORIENT VENTURE 74560
ORIENT VICTORY 29660
ORIENTAL ANTELOPE 61650
ORIENTAL BANKER 38333
ORIENTAL BANKER 44693
ORIENTAL CHAMPION 03326
ORIENTAL CHAMPION 04386
ORIENTAL COMMANDER 73482
ORIENTAL CONFIDENCE 60750
ORIENTAL CONFIDENCE 69750
ORIENTAL DRAGON 37760
ORIENTAL EDUCATOR 73481
ORIENTAL ENVOY 56030
ORIENTAL EXECUTIVE 73441
ORIENTAL EXECUTIVE 80371
ORIENTAL EXPLORER 65060
ORIENTAL EXPLORER 65950
ORIENTAL HERO 12830
ORIENTAL LADY 12831
ORIENTAL LEADER 73480
ORIENTAL MERCHANT 03327
ORIENTAL MERCHANT 04387
ORIENTAL NAVIGATOR 44300
ORIENTAL PEACE 38334
ORIENTAL PEACE 44694
ORIENTAL PHOENIX 63321
ORIENTAL PHOENIX 28241
ORIENTAL QUEEN 05520
ORIENTAL RESEARCHER 73442
ORIENTAL RESEARCHER 80372
ORIENTAL RULER 12832
ORIENTAL STAR 71420
ORIENTAL STATESMAN 73443
ORIENTAL STATESMAN 80373
ORIENTAL SURVEYOR 27962
ORIENTAL TAIO 48961
ORIENTAL TRADER 58540
ORIENTAL TRADER 92060
ORIENTAL UNITY 38332
ORIENTAL UNITY 44692
ORIENTAL VANGUARD 08601
ORIENTAL VENTURE 08600
ORIENTAL VENUS 57300
ORIENTAL WISDOM 85800
ORION 09300
ORION 15781
ORION 69470
ORION 73958
ORION 78500
ORION 82691
ORION 12271
ORJEN 68763
ORJULA 18570
ORKA 10815
ORKNEY 47813
ORKNEY 18729
ORLA 85260
ORLEN 23465
ORLETS 11863
ORLINOYE 11864
ORLOWO 15453
ORNEN 20750
ORNETA 15454
OROCHON 93744
OROCHON 93834
ORONMONTE 58190
OROPESA 56581
OROSEI 23070
OROSI 74320
OROYA 56580
ORPHEUS 20580
ORPHEUS 23780
ORPHEUS 28230
ORPHEUS 33920
ORQUE 03493
ORQUE 03583
ORSA MINORE 35585
ORSA MINORE 36435
ORSHA 01543
ORSHA 45633
ORSINO 18713
ORSK 85882
ORSOLA 41030
ORTEGA 04721
ORTEGA 04941
ORTELIUS 08460
ORUDA 18532
ORWELL FISHER 88641
ORYX 85793
ORYX 86663
OSADO MARU 19530
OSAKA BAY 08403
OSAKA REEFER 60033
OSAKA REEFER 68363
OSAKA REEFER 71973
OSAM 54871
OSAM 68561
OSBORNE CASTLE 22711
OSCAR 27940
OSCO LINEA 53310
OSCO SAGONA 66150
OSCO SIERRA 53312
OSCO SPIRIT 53311
OSCO STRIPE 53313
OSCO TAMPIMEX EAGLE 66230
OSETIYA 02354
OSETIYA. 35379
OSHEA EXPRESS 43320
OSHIMA MARU 23733
OSIA IRINI CHRYSOVALANDOU 25740
OSIA IRINI CHRYSOVALANDOU III 09630
OSIJEK 08530
OSIP PYATNITSKIY 03789
OSIP PYATNITSKIY 04029
OSIPENKO 88239
OSKAR LUTS 12490
'OSKOL' class 45540
'OSKOL III' class 45700
OSLO 63451
OSLO VENTURE 77873
OSLOFJORD 61410
OSMUSSAAR 89213
OSOGOVO. 77985
OSTANHAV 82100
OSTANHAV 82600
OSTECLIPPER 73941
OSTERBEK 76333
OSTERBEK 88723
OSTEREMS 50842
OSTERHEIDE 73953
OSTETURM 75940
OSTROGOZHSK 45634
OSTROGOZHSK 01544
OSTROLEKA 03235
OSTROLEKA 03625
OSTROV 86184
OSTROV ATLASOVA 82461
OSTROV ATLASOVA 71311
OSTROV BERINGA 82462
OSTROV BERINGA 71312
OSTROV KARAKINSKIY 82462
OSTROV KARAKINSKIY 71313
OSTROV KOTLIN 82463
OSTROV KOTLIN 71314
OSTROV LISYANSKOGO 82464
OSTROV LISYANSKOGO 71315
OSTROV LITKE 82465
OSTROV LITKE 71316
OSTROV MEDNYY 82466
OSTROV MEDNYY 71317
OSTROV RUSSKIY 82460
OSTROV RUSSKIY 71310
OSTROV SHMIDTA 82467
OSTROV SHMIDTA 71318
OSTROV SHOKALSKOGO 82468
OSTROV SHOKALSKOGO 71319
OSTROV SIBIRYAKOVA 82469
OSTROV SIBIRYAKOVA 71320
OSTROV USHAKOVA 82470
OSTROV USHAKOVA 71321
OSTSEEBAD 83701
OSWEGO CONCORD 37440
OSWEGO PEACE 37441
OSWEGO PLANTER 85090
OSWEGO STAR 64700
OSWESTRY GRANGE 75251
OSWIECIM 82265
OTARU 55810
OTARU 58493
OTARU 84913
OTCHI RIVER 13317
OTCHI RIVER 34835
OTELIA 58490
OTELIA 84910
OTEPYA 89202
OTHELLO 18712
OTHON 28671
OTI RIVER 07991
OTI RIVER 15276
OTOK 18531
OTOL 23466
OTOMAR OSHKALIN 10727
OTOME MARU 17470
OTRADNOE. 01540
OTRADNOE 45631
OTROG 12491
OTTAWA 58491
OTTAWA 84911
OTTO 85131
OTTO 85490
OTTO DANIELSEN 64857
OTTO DANIELSEN 91037
OTTO GROTEVOHL 36870
OTTO GROTEVOHL 62682
OTTO LEONHARDT 53960
OTTO LEONHARDT 77900
OTTO N. MILLER 55706
OTTO N. MILLER 58276
OTTO RYASTAS 23515
OTTO SCHMIDT 00540
OUADAN 91836
OUADAN 91946
OUARSENIS 64968
OUARZAZATE 73921
OUED SEBOU 81841
OUEZZANE 73920
OUIRGANE 73922
OURANIA 13040
OURANOUPOLIS 23270
OUTOKUMPU 71960
OVANES TUMANYAN 14390
OVERBECK 84220
OVERSEA FRUIT 05570
OVERSEAS ADVENTURER 86500
OVERSEAS ALASKA 64256
OVERSEAS ALICE 58422
OVERSEAS ARCTIC 64257
OVERSEAS ARGONAUT 55772
OVERSEAS JOYCE 36654
OVERSEAS JUNEAU 64243
OVERSEAS NATALIE 36610
OVERSEAS VALDEZ 58423
OVERSEAS VIVIAN 58424
OWARI MARU 77910
OWENGLAS 87310
'OZEAN' type 05380
'OZEAN' type 05390
'OZEAN' type 05400
'OZEAN' type 05420
'OZEAN' type 05450
'OZEAN' type 05820
'OZEAN' type 05830
'OZEAN' type 06010
'OZEAN' type 06120
'OZEAN' type 06720
OZENOYE 86540
OZERSK 12272
OZYORNYE KLYUCHI 12492

P

P.S. PALIOS 46740
PABLO NERUDA 70592
PABLO V 52990
PABLO V 53030
PABLOEVERETT 01141
PACBARON 46885
PACBARONESS 46894
PACDUCHESS 46887
PACDUKE 46895
'PACER' class 00060
PACGLORY 58179
PACIFIC 51111
PACIFIC 51491
PACIFIC 66312
PACIFIC 66901
PACIFIC 91471
PACIFIC ACE 05761
PACIFIC ACE 30671
PACIFIC ARROW 08660
PACIFIC CONTAINER 73501
PACIFIC CONTAINER 78031
PACIFIC CONVOY 75311
PACIFIC COUNTESS 91020
PACIFIC COURIER 75310
PACIFIC CURRENT 29580
PACIFIC DEFENDER 46540
PACIFIC DESPATCHER 76060
PACIFIC EMPRESS 91021
PACIFIC ERA 56680
PACIFIC EXPRESS 09780
PACIFIC FISHER 72700
PACIFIC FORESTER 82951
PACIFIC HIGHWAY 92990
PACIFIC HIGHWAY 94950
PACIFIC INSTALLER 92981
PACIFIC JASMIN 73310
PACIFIC LADY 45410

PACIFIC LUMBERMAN	82950
PACIFIC MARCHIONESS	45411
PACIFIC MARU	63011
PACIFIC MASTER	47660
PACIFIC MULIA	27621
PACIFIC OCEAN	03531
PACIFIC OCEAN	21361
PACIFIC PIONEER	86771
PACIFIC PRINCESS	16830
PACIFIC PRINCESS	49940
PACIFIC QUEEN	45412
PACIFIC QUEEN	71150
PACIFIC REEFER	06301
PACIFIC RELIANCE	83180
PACIFIC RIDE	30730
PACIFIC SAGA	56681
PACIFIC SKOU	56770
PACIFIC VENTURE	48945
PACIFICO	26993
PACIFICO	78701
PACIFIQUE	76700
PACLOG SEALINK	29243
PACPRINCE	60164
PACPRINCESS	60165
PACTOLOS	25275
PADANG	35490
PADEREWSKI	44510
PADJONGE	43140
PADMA	27110
PAGNET	47430
PAGNET	47900
PAHEPA	43146
PAINAN	86207
PAJANGAN	43141
PAKALONG SERAYA	61657
PAKHACHA	12493
PAKPANNANG	42670
PALACE TOKYO	63620
PALANA	18351
PALANA	07563
PALANGA	93745
PALANGA	93835
PALANGA	02901
PALAS	83692
PALASAUR	28661
PALATINO	24340
PALAU	40790
PALAU	41450
PALAWAN	05430
PALDISKI	86233
PALE	86930
PALEKH	84510
PALEKH	03691
PALEKH	03811
PALEMBANG	48910
PALIAT	43145
PALIZZI	29231
PALLADA	12273
PALLADE	74740
PALLAS	45912
PALLAS	91810
PALLIUM	37850
PALLIUM	44431
PALM B	40770
PALM B	41240
PALM TRADER	56560
PALMA	07942
PALMA	83620
PALMA MOCHA	48213
PALMA SORIANO	16760
PALMAH II	78071
PALMAIOLA	84410
PALMIRA ZETA	43880
PALMIRO TOGLIATTI	36871
PALMIS	00382
PALMYRA	69232
PALOMA DEL MAR	64510
PALUDINA	66120
PALUDINA	70081
PALVA	36091
PALVA	36221
PAMBOLA	89110
PAMELA	48082
PAMELA	61460
PAMINA	48089
PAMIR	02902
PAMIR	11309
PAMIR	22163
PAMIR I	82590
PAMPA ARGENTINA	11111
PAMPA ARGENTINA	34142
PAMPANA	14341
PAMPERO	48092
PAMPERO	53418
PAMPERO	64948
PAMPERO UNIVERSAL	06361
PAMYAT 26 KOMISSAROV	44102
PAMYAT LENINA	90726
PAMYAT LENINA	60687
PAMYATI KIROVA	23590
PAN ANTILLES	32070
PAN DYNASTY	46002
PAN JUSTICE	79980
PAN KOREA	61030
PAN KOREA	71190
PAN PACIFIC	61811
PAN SHAN	82550
PAN UNION	78420
PAN VIGOR	39200
PAN WESTERN	70681
PAN WESTERN	78111
PAN YOUNG	73204
PAN YOUNG	76994
PANAGHIA LOURION	12104
PANAGHIA LOURION	13895
PANAGHIA P	05551
PANAGHIS VERGOTTIS	06514
PANAGIA	43580
PANAGIA	86330
PANAGIA CHRYSSOPIGI	21820
PANAGIA ELEOUSSA	06981
PANAGIA MYRTIDIOTISSA	57511
PANAGIA MYRTIDIOTISSA	62001
PANAGIOTIS A	90100
PANAGIOTIS A.L	08060
PANAGIOTIS S	46080
PANAGIOTIS XILAS	25801
PANAGIS C	39043
PANAGIS K	37921
PANAGURISHTE	21790
PANAMA	70181
PANAMA	74473
PANAMA	79290
PANAMAX MARS	77886
PANAMAX URANUS	77620
PANAMIN II	34690
PANARMA	56910
PANAY	18410
PANAY	82790
PANCALDO	03462
PANDELIS	01810
PANDORA	83420
PANEHAN	43142
PANETOLIKON	00560
PANGANI	45389
PANKY	11520
PANOCEANIC FAME	58740
PANORMITIS	84390
PANORMOS	29000
PANORMUS	90452
PANSEPTOS	07170
PANT AVRA	81550
PANTAI	42682
PANTANASSA	17881
PANTAZIS CAIAS	13770
PANTAZIS CAIAS	34860
PANTELEYMON LEPESHINSKIY	03790
PANTELEYMON LEPESHINSKIY	04030
PANTERA	13480
PANTHER	32781
PANTJARAN SINAR	29530
PAOLA	65753
PAOLA C	06690
PAOLINO	72650
PAOLO D'AMICO	26230
PAPACAROLOS	55160
PAPACAROLOS	62670
PAPACOSTAS	31711
PAPADO	43143
PAPAGAYO UNIVERSAL	06363
PAPIA	84213
PAPILIONA	61613
PAPUAN CHIEF	82850
PARACLETE	04000
PARAGGI	62852
PARAGGI	67532
PARAGON	15120
PARALLA	52630
PARALLAKS	11601
PARALOS	61341
PARAMOUNT	07290
PARAMUSHIR	02903
PARANA	43311
PARANA STAR	06647
PARANAGUA	70182
PARAVOLAS III	87890
PARFENTIY GRECHANYY	73294
PARGA	32041
PARGOLOVO	02905
PARHAM	87840
PARHAM	87990
PARIATA	51684
PARIS	30382
PARIZHSKAYA KOMMUNA	79380
PARIZHSKAYA KOMMUNA	01572
PARKHOMENKO	33912
PARMA	23458
PARNASS	73960
PARNASSOS	69453
PAROMAY	02904
PAROS	16000
PAROS	43730
PAROS	54672
PARSLA	85344
PARTHENON	74110
PARTIZAN BONNIVUR	13015
PARTIZANI	12153
PARTIZANSKAYA ISKRA	45359
PARTIZANSKAYA SLAVA	45361
PARTNERSHIP	71034
PARTULA	37851
PARTULA	44430
PARVATI	56844
PASABAHCE	32152
PASADENA	06320
PASADENA	70180
PASCOLI	32544
PASIGI	43144
PASIONARIYA	12494
PASOSO	43147
PASS OF BALMAHA	57700
PASS OF BALMAHA	60811
PASS OF BRANDER	57701
PASS OF BRANDER	60810
PASS OF CAIRNWELL	84980
PASS OF CAIRNWELL	85700
PASS OF CHISHOLM	84981
PASS OF CHISHOLM	85701
PASS OF DIRRIEMORE	76391
PASS OF DIRRIEMORE	85711
PASS OF DRUMOCHTER	76390
PASS OF DRUMOCHTER	85710
PASS OF GLENCLUNIE	76660
PASSAAT CURACAO	91833
PASSAAT CURACAO	91943
PASSAT	18273
PASSAT	58210
PASSAT	63750
PASSAT	73956
PASSAT	02274
PASSAT - 2	23568
PASSAT UNIVERSAL	06360
PASSUMPSIC	38924
PASUDU	43148
PASVALIS	34884
PATAGONIA	70183
PATAGONIA ARGENTINA	11110
PATAGONIA ARGENTINA	34143
'PATAPSCO' class	92710
PATEVERETT	14670
PATMOS	60114
PATRAI	27720
PATRAI	34190
PATRAIKOS	90710
PATRAS	27310
PATRIA	46391
PATRIA	73946
PATRIA	87190
PATRICIA	21040
PATRICIA	46171
PATRICIA	48093
PATRICIA L	46693
PATRICIA S	24532
PATRICIA S	31295
PATRICIA S	91324
PATRICIA U	13020
PATRICIA V	48862
PATRICK VIELJEUX	05125
PATRICK VIELJEUX	59875
PATRIS	34191
PATRIZIA	08531
PATROCLOS	30380
PATROCLUS	03320
PATROCLUS	04381
PATROKL	13694
PATVIN	79811
PAUDZHA	23533
PAUL BUNYAN	67212
PAUL BUNYAN	91752
PAUL HEROULT	35300
PAUL L FAHRNEY	57900
PAUL L. FAHRNEY	62990
PAUL RICKMERS	24780
PAUL ROBESON	70598
PAULINA BRINKMAN	75500
PAVEL CHEBOTNYAGIN	93681
PAVEL DAUGE	03799
PAVEL DAUGE	04039
PAVEL DYBENKO	60638
PAVEL DYBENKO	62598
PAVEL GRABOVSKIY	79436
PAVEL MOCHALOV	79437
PAVEL PARENAGO	10744
PAVEL PONOMARYEV	21619
PAVEL PONOMARYEV	34111
PAVEL POSTYSHEV	93687
PAVEL RYBIN	50671
PAVEL SHTERNBERG	10745
PAVLIK LARISHKIN	15520
PAVLIK MOROZOV	86185
PAVLIN VINOGRADOV	91260
PAVLO	29773
PAVLODAR	03692
PAVLODAR	03812
PAVLOGRAD	03693
PAVLOS V	38210
PAVLOS V	38760
PAVLOVO	02906
PAVLOVO	09368
PAVLOVSK	45354
PAVOLGRAD	03813
PAVONIS	75510
PAWCATUCK	38922
PAYAS	43741
PAYDE	15499
PAYIME	45402
PAZ	25690
PAZIN	05652
PEACE	42650
PEACE ROSE	31390
PEACE VENTURE	54962
PEACE VENTURE	54562
PEARL	91290
PEARL BAY	86707
PEARL CITY	26572
PEARL DELTA	26590
PEARL FRUIT	18345
PEARL ISLAND	31441
PEARL ISLAND	31611
PEARL VALLEY	29980
PEARLEAF	38490
PEBANE	45394
PECAN	06318
PECHENGA	02907
PECHENGA	12495
PECHENGA	25845
PECHENGA	56272
PECHENGA	62732
PECHEUR BRETON	59490
PECHORA	67019
PECHORALES	90562
PECHORSK	89752
PECHUDO	88280
PECONIC	54414
PECONIC	57874
'PECONIC' class	42820
PEDOULAS	38300
PEDRIN	40741
PEDRO RAMIREZ	83881
PEDRO TEIXEIRA	51052
PEER GYNT	17090
PEGAS	12308
PEGAS	23862
PEGASOS	61910
PEGASUS	09590
PEGASUS	14190
PEGASUS PEACE	92954
PEGASUS PEACE	95164
PEGASUS TIMBER	47810
PEGAZ	12613
PEGNY	68661
PEI CHING No 1	74220
PEI CHING No 1	88160
PEIKIANG	25650
PEISANDER	03325
PEISANDER	04385
PEKIN	10271
PEKIN	15181
PEKIN	36840
PELAGOS	46150
PELAGOS	50181
PELAGOS	75261
PELASGOS	87841
PELASGOS	87991
PELENGATOR	09369
PELERIN	92882
PELEUS	26780
PELIAS	87610
PELICAN	92884
PELIKAN	12314
PELIKI	87600
PELINA	49850
PELINA	50090
PELINDABA	45400
PELITA DELI	42070
PELKA	86970
PELLA	58579
PELLEAS	60115
PELLINI	91832
PELLINI	91942
PELOPIDAS	69940
PELOR	87611
PELTI	66842
PEMA	07541
PEMBA	01140
PENCHATEAU	72413
PENDIK	32167
PENELOPE	15150
PENELOPE II	12981
PENELOPE V	95120
PENELOPE A	09620
PENELOPE EVERARD	89841
PENERF	46700
PENHORS	38341
PENHORS	44701
PENMARCH	46663
PENMEN	48061
PENN AR BED	32250
PENN HILLS	54990
PENNSYLVANIA GETTY	69162
PENNSYLVANIA SUN	38040
PENNY	51200
PENNY S	07821
PENTA	02740
PENTA	48380
PENTA-Y	09950
PENTELI	68620
PENTLAND GLEN	84742
PENTLAND GLEN	84952
PENZHINA	21611
PENZHINA	34108
PEP ATLANTIC	63688
PEP COMET	51131
PEP COMET	51501
PEP CORAL	51130
PEP CORAL	51500
PEP ICE	51132
PEP ICE	51502
PEP ORIENT	91315
PEP SIRIUS	50313
PEP SPICA	50312
PEP STAR	50310
PEP SUN	50311
PEPITO TEY.	05880
PERA	64400
PERAK	94971
PERAST	26874
PERAST.	08320
PERCH	62872
PERCY M CROSBIE	90520
PEREDOVIK	11865
PEREDOVIK	43040
PEREIRA d'ECA	03100
PEREKAT	12496
PEREKOP	45351
PERELIK	36391
PERELLE	88612
PERELLE	90072
PEREMYSHLJ	09370
PERENNIAL ACE	36550
PERESLAVL-ZALESSIK	15480
PERESVET	22230
PERICLES	34901
PERIGEY	13696
PERKUN	20880
PERLA	04462
PERLAMUTR	11590
PERLIS	94970
PERM	02900
PERMATARIS	00730
PERMINA VIII	81160
PERMINA IX	43270
PERMINA XXVII	66355
PERMINA XXIX	70570
PERMINA XXX	66356
PERMINA XXXI	66357
PERMINA 101	40780
PERMINA 102	40781
PERMINA 107	37030
PERMINA 108	40700
PERMINA 109	60840
PERMINA 109	81460
PERMINA SAMUDRA V	37020
PERMINA SAMUDRA V	43850
PERMINA SAMUDRA VII	38290
PERMINA SAMUDRA XIV	37670
PERMINA SAMUDRA XIV	38591
PERMLES	45691
PERNA	59601
PERNA	71931
PERNAMBUCO	43312
PERNAT	43162
PERSEUS	04383
PERSEUS	63393
PERSEUS	73387
PERSEUS	11673
PERSEY	12274
PERSEY	23863
PERSEY III	12571
PERSIA	08930
PERSIAN REEFER	06332
PERTOMINSK	02908
PERTUSOLA	53990
PERTUSOLA	79570
PERUSTICA	83724
PERUVIAN TRADER	12911
PERVOMAJSK	87000
PERVOMAYSK	03701
PERVOMAYSK	03825
PERVOURALSK	11499
PESHT	86093
PESQUERA	25171
PESTOVO	03694
PESTOVO	03814
PETALING	94972
PETALUMA	42826
PETEN II	31780
PETER	48083
PETER	83619
PETER BERON	24630
PETER GORING	23427
PETER KAST	10252
PETER KAST	12633
PETER L	35500
PETER NELL	10253
PETER NELL	12634
PETER PAN	17070
PETER RICH	30290
PETER RICKMERS	92590
PETER WESSEL	16452
PETERSBERG	62224
PETERSBERG	71134
PETIMATA OT RMS	78986
PETINGO	77491
PETKA	10992
PETKA	34152
PETKO R. SLAVEJNOV	80900
PETOFI	45370

PETR ALEKSEYEV	60628
PETR ALEKSEYEV	62588
PETR BOGDANOV	79384
PETR DUTOV	48438
PETR DUTOV	49478
PETR DUTOV	49748
PETR GUTCHENKO	49244
PETR KAKHOVSKIY	89254
PETR KRASIKOV	03791
PETR KRASIKOV	04031
PETR LEBEDEV	17560
PETR LIDOV	79419
PETR LIZYUKOV	11866
PETR SGIBNEV	00140
PETR SHIRSHOV	39991
PETR SMIDOVICH	54723
PETR SMIDOVICH	55293
PETR STAROSTIN	69321
PETR STRELKOV	54734
PETR STRELKOV	55304
PETR STUCHKA	90727
PETR STUCHKA	12497
PETR STUCHKA	60688
PETR VELIKIY	77077
PETR YEMTSOV	48445
PETR YEMTSOV	49485
PETR YEMTSOV	49755
PETR ZALOMOV	79408
PETR ZAPOROZHETS	79388
PETRA	42630
PETRA CROWN	50420
PETRA SCHEU	92300
PETRADI	58604
PETRADI	59758
PETRAIA	48111
PETRARCA	32545
PETREL	92883
PETRELO	61061
PETRO BOUSCAT	42631
PETRO SOULAC	59150
PETROCLIS	43481
PETROCLIS	43511
PETRODVORETS	18130
PETRODVORETS	03695
PETRODVORETS	03815
PETRODVORETS	12498
PETROGAS I	65910
PETROGRADSKAYA STORONA	13699
PETROKREPOST	02909
PETROKREPOST	23540
PETROLA 1	43000
PETROLA 11	40751
PETROLA 11	41481
PETROLA 13	36230
PETROLA 17	40752
PETROLA 17	41482
PETROLA 20	42860
PETROLA 23	37411
PETROLA 26	65280
PETROLA 27	38070
PETROLA 30	81120
PETROLA 31	70500
PETROLA 32	43660
PETROLA 33	35690
PETROLA 33	37100
PETROLA 34	35691
PETROLA 34	37101
PETROLA 36	37810
PETROLA 40	85580
PETROLINA I	40610
PETROMAR BAHIA BLANCA	37412
PETROMAR BAHIA BLANCA	44230
PETROMAR BAHIA BLANCA II	65630
PETROMAR BAHIA BLANCA II	70000
PETROMAR CAMPANA	37797
PETROMAR CAMPANA II	65631
PETROMAR CAMPANA II	70001
PETROMAR CORDOBA	37450
PETROMAR CORDOBA	44221
PETROMAR MENDOZA	43720
PETROMAR ROSARIO	37451
PETROMAR ROSARIO	44220
PETRON GASUL	54880
PETRON GASUL	60000
PETROPAVLOVSK	02128
PETROPAVLOVSK— KAMCHATSKIY	10444
PETROPOLIS	57522
PETROS	22980
PETROS	28100
PETROS	68982
PETROS V	61883
PETROSANI	82221
PETROSHIP A	68570
PETROSHIP B	68571
PETROSTAR III	70870
PETROSTAR III	86510
PETROSTAR IV	44180
PETROSTAR V	66660
PETROSTAR VI	66661
PETROSTAR XIV	85730
PETROSTAR XIV	88690
PETROSTAR XV	68930
PETROVSK	17940
PETROVSKIY	02910
PETROZAVODSK	02911
PETROZAVODSK	23530
PETYA KOVALYENKO	67020
PETYA SHITIKOV	67021
PEVEK	11310
PEVEK	36250
PEVEK	42800
PEYPSI	13697
PEZZATA ROSA	51930
PEZZATA ROSA	74172
PFUSUNG	85350
PHA SHWE GYAW YWA	83470
PHAEDON II	07540
PHAEDRA	47340
PHAEDRA	62142
PHAEDRA E	43980
PHAISTOS	42400
PHEMIUS	03321
PHEMIUS	04382
PHENIAN	10272
PHENIAN	15182
PHENIAN	36843
PHILADELPHIA	74475
PHILEMON	73991
PHILIP BROERE	76300
PHILIP OF MACEDON	68890
PHILIPP MULLER	23428
PHILIPPE NOIR	69230
PHILIPPI	45900
PHILIPPINE ANTONIA LUNA	14816
PHILIPPINE ANTONIO LUNA	30801
PHILIPPINE BATAAN	14817
PHILIPPINE BATAAN	30800
PHILIPPINE ORCHID	50661
PHILIPPINE PRESIDENT ROXAS	14815
PHILIPPINE RIZAL	14818
PHILIPPINES FRUIT	05571
PHILLIPS ENTERPRISE	64013
PHILLIPS ENTERPRISE	68403
PHILLIPS OREGON	38391
PHILLIPS TEXAS	38060
PHOENICIA	91839
PHOENICIA	91949
PHOENIX	27730
PHOENIX STAR	38280
PHOENIX TRADER	71942
PHOEVOS	06531
PHOINIKAS	63881
PHOINIKAS	68461
PHOLEGANDROS	54673
PHOSPHORE CONVEYOR	82860
PHRONTIS	03322
PHRONTIS	04380
PIA COSTA	39540
PIA DANIELSEN	90970
PIA DANIELSEN	91980
PIAMAR	04511
PIAVE	24711
PIAVE	76650
PIBIDUE	35821
PIBIMARE PRIMA	36960
PIBIMARE PRIMA	43901
PIBIMARE PRIMA	44601
PIC D'AGOU	71301
PIC ST LOUP	76440
PICHINCHA	12993
PICHIT SAMUT	25870
PICOBLANCO	09960
PICOVERDE	09961
PICT	42034
PIENINY II	55315
PIENINY II	70066
PIERRA DELLA FRANCESCA	17131
PIERRE GUILLAUMAT	52952
PIERRE GUILLAUMAT	55482
PIERRE VIDAL	33490
PIERRE VIELJEUX	05124
PIERRE VIELJEUX	59873
PIETER WINSEMIUS	73820
PIETRO	66955
PIETRO	70995
PIETRO NOVELLI	17130
PIGOANZA	83762
PIKEBANK	04671
PILAR DEL MAR	76085
PILAR MARIA	52501
PILION	91350
PILOTO PARDO	01740
PILTUN	86223
PINA DEL AGUA	48210
PINAGORIY	11617
PINAR DEL RIO	90390
PINAZO	91272
PINDAROS	10620
PINDAROS	15370
PINDOS	37820
PINEGA	86234
PINEGA	67022
PINELOPI	24761
PINELOPI	29542
PINELOPI	30772
PING CHAU	29241
PING DING SHAN	62105
PING HAI	57371
PING HAI	61961
PING SHAN	84113
PING SHAN	84173
PING XIANG CHENG	67231
PING XIANG CHENG	91651
PING YIN	30000
PING YIN	30981
PINGUIN	12100
PINGUIN	84935
PINGUIN	91181
PINGUINO	83520
PINGUINO	83560
PINGVIN	11965
PINSK	25560
PINYA	07420
PIONEER	20950
PIONEER	88770
'PIONEER' type	45560
'PIONEER' type	54100
'PIONEER' type	54110
'PIONEER' type	54580
'PIONEER' type	54600
PIONEER COMMANDER	05676
PIONEER CONTENDER	05677
PIONEER CONTRACTOR	05678
PIONEER CRUSADER	05679
PIONEER LOUISE	53950
PIONEER LOUISE	54000
PIONEER MOON	05680
PIONEER No 1	47730
PIONEER No 2	47731
PIONEER No 3	47732
PIONER	15510
PIONER	15521
PIONER ARKHANGELSKA	71041
PIONER AYKUTII	71054
PIONER BELORUSSII	71055
PIONER BURYATII	71050
PIONER CHUKOTKI	71044
PIONER ESTONII	71047
PIONER KAMCHATKI	71048
PIONER KARELII	71056
PIONER KAZAKHSTANA	71057
PIONER KHOLMSKA	71045
PIONER KIRGIZII	71058
PIONER LITVY	71051
PIONER MOLDAVII	71059
PIONER MOSKVY	71040
PIONER MURMANA	76499
PIONER NAKHODKI	79550
PIONER ODESSY	79552
PIONER ONEGI	71046
PIONER PRIMORYA	79554
PIONER ROSSII	71049
PIONER SAKHALINA	71042
PIONER SEVERODVINSKA	71052
PIONER SLAVYANKI	71053
PIONER UKRAINY	12499
PIONER UZBEKISTANA	71060
PIONER VLADIVOSTOKA	79553
PIONER VOLKOV	76515
PIONER VYBORGA	79555
PIONER YUZHNO SAKHALINSKA	71043
PIONER ZAPOLYARYA	12500
PIONERSK	93870
PIONERSKAYA PRAVDA	15522
PIONERSKAYA ZOFKA	15523
PIOTR DUNIN	10576
PIOTR DUNIN	15346
PIOTRKOW TRYBUNALSKI	79872
PIRAEUS 1	86310
PIRAN	62061
PIREAS	49931
PIREAS	50631
PIRIN	49040
PIRIT	11932
PIRKKOLA	61706
PIRKKOLA	71076
PIROT	21511
PIRYATIN	36254
PIRYATIN	42804
PISANG PERAK	91521
PISANG RAJA	41000
PISATEL	11867
PISCES	65503
PISOLO	43392
PISTIS	29460
PISTIS	40800
PISTIS	41470
PISTIS	58161
PITESTI	86211
PITSUNDA	01968
PITSUNDA	11868
PIVIERE	35580
PIVIERE	36430
PKHEN HOA	28992
PLAN DE AYALA	69994
PLAN DE AYALA	86485
PLAN DE AYUTLA	69995
PLAN DE AYUTLA	86486
PLAN DE GUADELUPE	69997
PLAN DE SAN LUIS	69998
PLAN DE SAN LUIS	86487
PLANA	77981
PLANERIST	11869
PLANETA	11588
PLANTA DE BETANIA	49800
PLANTA DE MAMONAL	49801
PLATAK	83924
PLATON OYUNSKIY	50758
PLATONIC	53152
PLATONIC	66302
PLAYA BLANCA	03411
PLAYA BLANCA	15971
PLAYA COLORADO	11968
PLAYA DE EZARO	49991
PLAYA DE EZARO	50640
PLAYA DE LAS CANTERAS	87661
PLAYA DE LAS NIEVES	03410
PLAYA DE LAS NIEVES	15970
PLAYA DE MASPALOMAS	87660
PLAYA DEL MEDANO	83540
PLAYA DUABA	86542
PLAYA DUABA	11969
PLAYA GIRON	11970
PLAYA HIRON	18274
PLAYA LARGA	31011
PLAYA VARADERO	11972
PLAYAS	21244
PLAYITAS	11971
PLEIAS	25720
PLESETSK	02912
PLETWAL	10818
PLISKA	37310
PLITVICE	40240
PLOCK	82262
PLOD	21310
PLOPENI	82117
PLOPENI	82397
PLOTINOS	10621
PLOTINOS	15371
PLOVDIV	37300
PLUG	22231
PLUMA RICO	07041
PLUMLEAF	38500
PLUNGE	34882
PLUTON	23860
PLUTON	11870
PLUTONIY	11589
PLYAVINYAS	38530
PO	94571
PO SEA	47241
POBJEDA	21720
POBYEDA OKTYABRYA	67651
POBYEDA OKTYABRYA	59891
POBYEDINO	24084
POCAHONTAS	02841
POCANTICO	02840
PODGORA	29102
PODGORICA	78890
PODHALE	75733
PODHALE	88383
PODMOSKOVYE	11311
PODRAVINA	86522
PODUNAVLJE	86521
POEL	83606
POEL	39300
POET	11881
POET SABIR	79390
POET VIDADI	79402
POETIC	66290
POETIC	69890
POGRANICHNIK LEONOV	93764
POGRANICHNIK LEONOV	93820
POHENG	31113
POIANA	83693
POINT CLEAR	68810
POINT JULIE	44573
POINT SUSAN	93020
POINTE DE LESVEN	79581
POINTE DU ROC	59073
POINTE DU ROC	76423
POINTE DU VAN	59074
POINTE DU VAN	76424
POINTE LA ROSE	02621
POINTE MADAME	02622
POINTE SANS SOUCI	02620
POINTER	32953
POINTSMAN	76290
POITIERS	48902
POITOU	64372
POJUCA	65864
POKKINEN	47296
POLA	60166
POLANA	45388
POLANICA	14292
POLAR	91144
'POLAR' type	62680
POLAR ALASKA	53870
POLAR ARGENTINA	09260
POLAR BRASIL	09261
POLAR COLOMBIA	09262
POLAR ECUADOR	09263
POLAR EXPRESS	32300
POLAR I	76536
POLAR II	76537
POLAR III	62696
POLAR IV	62697
POLAR V	62698
POLAR VI	62699
POLAR PARAGUAY	09264
POLAR SEA	01781
POLAR STAR	01780
POLAR URUGUAY	09265
POLARIS	08520
POLARISMAN	59061
POLARISMAN	76451
POLARLYS	01302
POLCZYN ZDROJ	81864
POLESSK	90152
POLESSK	03696
POLESSK	03816
POLESYE	11312
POLEVOD	11871
POLHEM	19390
POLIKOS	16640
POLINA OSIPENKO	10728
POLINNIA	54700
POLINNIA	74760
POLLENGER	54070
POLLENGER	72221
POLLUCE	37590
POLLUKS	76891
POLLUKS	81401
POLLUX	46390
POLLUX	10546
POLLY	62020
POLNORD	05453
POLOTSK	11611
POLOTSK	45352
POLTAVA	11872
POLTAVA	45350
POLYARNAYA ZVEZDA	93875
POLYARNOYE SIYANIE	11608
POLYARNYE ZORI	76518
POLYARNYY	11591
POLYARNYY	22865
POLYARNYY	34495
POLYARNYY KRUG	76528
POLYCLIPPER	77241
POLYCREST	77242
POLYCRUSADER	73330
POLYDEFKIS	83061
POLYDEFKIS	83161
POLYDORA	30901
POLYDORUS	51741
POLYDORUS	84061
POLYKARP	37680
POLYKARP	44261
POLYMICHANOS	11191
POLYS	66240
POLYSAGA	68120
POLYSTAR	34630
POLYSTAR	44780
POLYTIMI ANDREADIS	35890
POLYTIMI ANDREADIS	41670
POLYTRADER	64140
POLYTRAVELLER	64141
POLYTROPOS	61165
POLYUS	33980
POLYVICTORIA	64017
POLYVICTORIA	68407
POLYVIKING	77240
POLYVOS	35730
POLYVOS	41430
POLYXENE G	24620
POLYXENI	74610
POMALAA	38932
POMELLA	66121
POMELLA	70080
POMONA	34301
POMORAVLJE	86520
POMORYE	02913
POMORZE	93882
POMPOSA	60167
PONCE	08340
PONCE	15770
PONCHATOULA	45055
PONGDESAN	85631
PONGOLA	45401
PONOY	02914
PONTA DELGADA	08230
PONTA GARCIA	33530
PONTE PASAJE	91900
PONTE PEDRIDO	91901
PONTE SAMPAYO	91902
PONTENEGRO	47181
PONTEVEDRA	15360
PONTOS	34300
POOLSTER	35250
POOLTA	03450
POONG YANG	94873
POPI	01522
POPI	45611
POPLAT	59602
POPLAT	71932
PORECHIE	12275
PORKHOV	11442
PORONIN	24080
POROZINA	08321
PORSANGER	54138
PORSANGER	54258
PORSOY	92330
PORT ALBERNI CITY	46431
PORT ALFRED	06880
PORT CAROLINE	01120
PORT CHALMERS	01130
PORT HAWKESBURY	68941
PORT ILYICH	44124

PORT LATTA MARU	77470
PORT LAUNAY	03901
PORT PYLOS	23101
PORT QUEBEC	72337
PORT RENARD	44280
PORT SAID	03970
PORT SAID	27841
PORT TUDY	66450
PORT VANCOUVER	72338
'PORTER' type	76220
'PORTER' type	76900
PORTFIELD	36341
PORTO	14751
PORTOFINO	78772
POSAVINA	86523
POSEIDON	19220
POSEIDON	32700
POSEIDON	54011
POSEIDON	80771
'POSEIDON' class	67350
'POSEIDON' class	71360
POSEIDON C	24610
POSEIDON C	26370
POSEIDONIA	11470
POSEYDON.	12580
POSIDON	10190
POSSIDONIA	36010
POSTIRA	08322
POSYET	12501
POSYET	22866
POSYET	34496
POTENZA	60168
POTI	12276
POTI	39977
POTIRNA	59600
POTIRNA	71930
POTOMAC.	02842
POUNENTES	60116
POVL ANKER	20350
POVOLZHYE	11325
POVONETS	15502
'POVONETS' type	15500
'POVONETS' type	15460
POWSTANIEC SLASKI	74545
POWSTANIEC SLASKI	59225
POWSTANIEC WIELKOPOLSKI	70544
POYANG	14280
POYANG	71744
POYANG	81414
POZEGA	60169
PRA RIVER	13310
PRA RIVER	34836
PRABHU PARVATI	25613
PRABHU SAKHI	25612
PRABHU SATRAM	61260
PRACTICIAN	47770
PRAG	45851
PRAGA	36844
PRAHA	79233
PRAHOVA	41630
PRAIRIAL	52953
PRAIRIAL	55483
PRANAS EYDUKYAVICHUS	12504
PRANAS ZIBERTAS	85341
PRANGLI	83708
PRAVDA	07561
PRAVDINSK	03697
PRAVDINSK	03817
PRAVOVYED	11873
PRECIOUS STAR	28960
PREDEAL	48481
PREMUDA BIANCA	66191
PREMUDA ROSA	66190
PRESERVER	40170
PRESIDENT	92220
PRESIDENT ADAMS	31120
PRESIDENT CLEVELAND	31121
PRESIDENT DELCOURT	56180
PRESIDENT DELCOURT	58980
PRESIDENT DELCOURT	60850
PRESIDENT EISENHOWER	11360
PRESIDENT FILLMORE	10532
PRESIDENT FILLMORE	11552
PRESIDENT GARCIA	05951
PRESIDENT HARRISON	15200
PRESIDENT J KASAVUBU	05050
PRESIDENT JACKSON	31122
PRESIDENT JEFFERSON	11352
PRESIDENT JOHNSON	11355
PRESIDENT KENNEDY	11361
PRESIDENT MADISON	11353
PRESIDENT MAGSAYSAY	30840
PRESIDENT McKINLEY	10533
PRESIDENT MCKINLEY	11553
PRESIDENT MONROE	15201
PRESIDENT PIERCE	11354
PRESIDENT PIK	13695
PRESIDENT POLK	15202
PRESIDENT QUIRINO	30842
PRESIDENT ROOSEVELT	11362
PRESIDENT ROXAS	30843
PRESIDENT TAFT	10530
PRESIDENT TAFT.	11550
PRESIDENT TAYLOR	31124
PRESIDENT TRUMAN	11363
PRESIDENT VAN BUREN	10531
PRESIDENT VAN BUREN	11551
PRESIDENT WILSON	31123
PRESIDENTE ALLENDE	46589
PRESIDENTE CASTILLO	00520
PRESIDENTE DEODORO	37910
PRESIDENTE DEODORO	38860
PRESIDENTE DIAZ ORDAZ	32260
PRESIDENTE FLORIANO	37911
PRESIDENTE FLORIANO	38861
PRESIDENTE KENNEDY	55010
PRESIDENTE KENNEDY	55880
PRESIDENTE KENNEDY	56550
PRESLAV	91701
PRESTIGIOUS	82993
PREVEZE	80350
PREYLI	38532
PREZHEVALSK	02916
PRIAMOS	26970
PRIAMOS	77877
PRIAMURYE	02129
PRIAMURYE	09210
PRIAMURYE	12502
PRIBALTIKA	93753
PRIBALTIKA	93843
PRIBOY	61270
PRIBOY	81490
PRIBOY	02275
PRIDE	14556
PRIDE OF FREE ENTERPRISE	20212
PRIDE OF TEXAS	47216
PRIDNEPROVSK	45355
PRIDYATLES	24082
PRIGNITZ	71680
PRIKARPATYE	11322
PRIKUMSK	25561
PRILIV	02276
PRILIV	11874
PRILUKI	09371
PRIMA	70058
PRIMA KING	38460
PRIMAROSA	62862
PRIMAROSA	67542
PRIMAVERA	47204
PRIMERA PEAK	46052
PRIMERO	36630
PRIMERO DE JUNIO	26940
PRIMERO DE MAYO	88486
PRIMO ARABIA	28140
PRIMO ARABIA	30340
PRIMORJE	12040
PRIMORLES	24044
PRIMORSK	87002
PRIMORSK	03698
PRIMORSK	03818
PRIMORSK	10445
PRIMROSE	54381
PRIMROSE	63071
PRIMULA	47203
'PRINASA 26/15' type	47050
'PRINASA 26/15' type	49110
'PRINASA 121' type	04800
PRINCE GEORGE	20430
PRINCE IVANHOE	20932
PRINCE LAURENT	19931
PRINCE MARU No 2	72600
PRINCE MARU No 7	92570
PRINCE NOVA	17220
PRINCE OF BRITTANY	16450
PRINCE OF TOKYO	48951
PRINCE RUPERT CITY	46432
PRINCESS ANNE	24210
PRINCESS ANNE-MARIE	70390
PRINCESS AURORA	49670
PRINCESS EMERALD	30911
PRINCESS JADE	73430
PRINCESS JADE	89915
PRINCESS JADE	90225
PRINCESS MARGUERITE	17420
PRINCESS OF ACADIA	18810
PRINCESS OF NEGROS	22040
PRINCESS OF VANCOUVER	19720
PRINCESS PATRICIA	17421
PRINCESSAN CHRISTINA	32810
PRINCESSE ASTRID	20030
PRINCESSE MARGARETHE	01911
PRINCESSE MARIE CHRISTINE	19940
PRINKIPOS	69070
PRINS ALBERT	19942
PRINS JOACHIM	16030
PRINS JOACHIM	19990
PRINS PHILIPPE	19930
PRINSEN	01930
PRINSES BEATRIX	18961
PRINSES BEATRIX	32760
PRINSES CHRISTINA	18950
PRINSES IRENE	18962
PRINSES MARGRIET	18960
PRINSES MARGRIET	22050
PRINSES MARIA ESMERALDA	19941
PRINSES PAOLA	20040
PRINSESSAN BIRGITTA	20330
PRINSESSAN DESIREE	20290
PRINSESSE ANNE-MARIE	19570
PRINSESSE BENEDIKTE	19591
PRINSESSE ELISABETH	20610
PRINSESSE RAGNHILD	20560
PRINZ HAMLET	16511
PRINZ OBERON	16510
PRIONEZHYE	11327
PRIOZERSK	10446
PRIOZERSK	12503
PRIVATE RAMON CASTILLO	06674
PRIVOLZHSK	10447
PRIVOLZHSK	45219
PRIZVANIE	13730
PROCYON	16010
PROCYON	16850
PROCYON	76050
PROFESOR K BOHDANOWICZ	73551
PROFESOR SIEDLECKI	11690
PROFESSOR	15000
PROFESSOR	11951
PROFESSOR ANICHKOV	09082
PROFESSOR BARANOV	93730
PROFESSOR BARANOV	93854
PROFESSOR BOGOROV	39170
PROFESSOR BOGUCKI	23467
PROFESSOR BUZNIK	03967
PROFESSOR DERYUGIN	12572
PROFESSOR I. I. KRAKOVSKIY	79426
PROFESSOR KERICHYEV	79438
PROFESSOR KLYUSTIN	09085
PROFESSOR KUDREVICH	09081
PROFESSOR KURENTSOV	39171
PROFESSOR MESYATSYEV	11952
PROFESSOR MINYAYEV.	09088
PROFESSOR NESTOR SMYERNOV	17969
PROFESSOR PAVLENKO	09083
PROFESSOR POPOV	10750
PROFESSOR RYBALTOVSKIY	09084
PROFESSOR SERGEY DOROFEYEV	17968
PROFESSOR SHCHYOGOLEV	09080
PROFESSOR UKHOV	09087
PROFESSOR VISE	12002
PROFESSOR VODYANITSKIY	39172
PROFESSOR YUSHENKO	09086
PROFESSOR ZUBOV	12003
PROFITIS ELIAS	26522
PROGRESS	75892
PROGRESS	11606
PROGRESS	23571
PROGRESS 1	10301
PROGRESSIST	47772
PROJECT AMERICAS	95020
PROKOPIY GALUSHIN	31853
PROKOPYEVSK	02915
PROKOPYEVSK	09372
PROLETARSK	12148
PROLETARSKAYA POBEDA	90725
PROLETARSKAYA POBEDA	60686
PROLIV	11875
PROLIV LAPERUZA	58513
PROLIV LAPERUZA	71823
PROLIV SANNIKOVO	58514
PROLIV SANNIKOVO	71824
PROLIV VILKITSKOGO	58515
PROLIV VILKITSKOGO	71825
PROMETHEUS	26674
PROMETHEUS	31733
PROMOTEY	13698
PROMYSLOVIK	11876
PRONAOS	61635
PROODOS	28120
PROODOS	28560
PROOF SPIRIT	56260
PROOF SPIRIT	75240
PROOF TRADER	56261
PROOF TRADER	75241
PROPAGANDIST	11877
PROPONTIS	72441
PROPONTIS	77131
PROSO	47840
PROSPATHIA	60117
PROSPERITY	55560
PROSPERITY	62940
PROSVETITEL	11878
PROTEA	04130
PROTECTEUR	40171
PROTECTOR ALPHA	55660
PROTECTOR ALPHA	55860
PROTEKTOR	74640
PROTESILAUS	03324
PROTESILAUS	04384
PROTEUS	80731
PROTEUS	86971
PROTOKLITOS	62080
PROTOKLITOS	62440
PROTOPOROS	46583
PROTSION	76892
PROTSION	81402
PROVENCE	16440
PROVENCE	32520
PROVIDENCE	61002
PROVIDENCE	70710
PROVIDENCE	78260
PROVIDENCE GETTY	42823
PROVIDER	38960
PROVORNYY	84342
PRUT	70810
PRUZANIY	34883
PRZEMYSL	79876
PSARA	29511
PSILI	55940
PSKOV	03699
PSKOV	03819
PSKOV	23527
PSKOVITYANKA	35326
PUBLIKIST	11879
PUEBLA	55013
PUEBLA	55883
PUEBLA	56553
PUERTO ACEVADO	89890
PUERTO CADIZ	48830
PUERTO DE ALICANTE	87570
PUERTO DE AMBERES	81951
PUERTO DE AMBERES	91501
PUERTO DE HUELVA	80800
PUERTO DE VITA	25200
PUERTO MONTT	19110
PUERTO RICO	08344
PUERTO RICO	50380
PUERTO ROSALES	66196
PUERTO VALLARTA	19296
PUERTO VALLARTA	23704
PUFFIN PRIDE	56982
PUGLIOLA	53991
PUGLIOLA	79571
PUHOS	48084
PULA	10924
PULA	14370
PULAO BATAM	06066
PULAU BALI	13580
PULAU NIAS	30180
PULAWY	48410
PULAWY	45770
PULBOROUGH	88560
PULKOVO	02917
PULKOVO	12505
PULKOVSKIY MERIDIAN	10870
PULKOWNIK DABEK	15361
PUMA	94610
PUNAT.	08323
PUNTA ANGELES	36741
PUNTA ATALAYA	13250
PUNTA ATALAYA	14672
PUNTA BIANCA	02833
PUNTA BIANCA	03420
PUNTA BRAVA	51076
PUNTA DELGADA	45140
PUNTA DELGADA	45240
PUNTA MALVINA	51075
PUNTA MEDANOS	45100
PUNTA SOLE	02832
PUNTA STELLA	02830
PUNTA VERDE	02831
PUPNAT	85510
PURBECK	17301
PURBECK	93161
'PUSHKIN' class	12320
'PUSHKIN' class	12330
PUSHKIN	12332
PUSHKIN	12340
PUSHLAKHTA	02918
PUSHPA	91892
PUSSUR	06400
PUSTOZERSK	02919
PUTIVL	03700
PUTIVL	03820
PUTIVL	12506
PUTNA	13738
PUTYATIN	24083
PVT. LEONARD C. BROSTROM	92660
PYARNU	15500
PYATIDYESYATILETIYE KOMSOMOLA	01100
PYATIDYESYATILETIYE KOMSOMOLA	01180
PYATIDYESYATILYETIYE OKTYABRYA	93730
PYATIDYESYATILYETIYE OKTYABRYA	93820
PYATIDYESYATILYETIYE OKTYABRYA	36878
PYATIDYESYATILYETIYE SOVETSKOY GRUZII	60637
PYATIDYESYATILYETIYE SOVETSKOY GRUZII	62597
PYATIDYESYATILYETIYE SSSR	45290
PYATIDYESYATILYETIYE SSSR	58510
PYATIDYESYATILYETIYE SSSR	71820
PYATIGORSK	11880
PYATIGORSK	25562
PYOTR OVCHINNIKOV	12507
PYOTR SGIBNEV	00146
PYRAMID VENUS	94410
PYRAMIDS U	14810
PYRGOS STAR	48492
PYRROS V	36781
PYTHAGORE	54781
PYTHAGORE	67451
PYTHEAS 0053701 PYTHEUS	66700
PYTHEUS	78091
PYTHEUS	89941

Q

QAROUH	49409
QAROUH	50969
QATAR EXPRESS	94830
QI LI HAI	36350
QI LIN HU	36720
QIAN TANG JIANG	51461
QIAN TANG JIANG	50991
QIANJIN	10560
QIMEN.	05390
QINGHAI	45980
QINGSHUI	15960
QINLING	61071
QINLING	71261
QIONG HAI	83552
QIONG HAI	49152
QORMI	08500
QUARTERMAN	88700
QUARTZ	06627
QUE LIN	38990
QUEBEC	79770
QUEDLINBURG	03881
QUEEN ELIZABETH 2	01700
QUEEN MARY	18830
QUEEN OF ALBERNI	18990
QUEEN OF BURNABY	17164
QUEEN OF COQUITLAM	18920
QUEEN OF COWICHAN	18921
QUEEN OF ESQUIMALT	17163
QUEEN OF NANAIMO	17165
QUEEN OF NEW WESTMINISTER	17166
QUEEN OF PRINCE RUPERT	19440
QUEEN OF SAANICH	17162
QUEEN OF SHEEBA	04581
QUEEN OF SHEEBA	34911
QUEEN OF SIDNEY	16680
QUEEN OF SURREY	16500
QUEEN OF THE ISLANDS	19060
QUEEN OF TSAWWASSEN	19780
QUEEN OF VANCOUVER	17161
QUEEN OF VANCOUVER	32271
QUEEN OF VICTORIA	17160
QUEEN OF VICTORIA	32270
QUEEN SEA	26910
QUELIMANE	29560
QUELLIN	48891
QUELLIN	49321
QUESTNORTH	07350
QUI JIANG	60242
QUICKTHORN	80500
QUIJOTE	87891
QUIMICO LEIXOES	56253
QUIMICO LEIXOES	75233
QUIMICO LISBOA	56252
QUIMICO LISBOA	75232
QUINCY	05510
QUINGSHAN.	04600
QUINTANA ROO	33130
QUIRINALE	24342
QUITAUNA	52250
QUITO	88760
QUIXADA	52251

R

R A EMERSON	70151
R.S.A.	31950
RAAD	72880
RAAD	76880
RAAFAT	87220
RAAMGRACHT	49816
RABA	27460
RABAC	18571
RABIGH BAY I	55312
RABIGH BAY I	70063
RABIGH BAY 3	64371
RABKA ZDROJ	81868
RABOCHAYA SMENA	01406
RABOCHAYA SMENA	01666
RABUNION IV	40370
RABUNION V	84521
RABUNION VI	84520
RABUNION XIII	84522
RABUNION XIV	84523
RABUNION XV	84524
RABUNION XVI	84525
RAD	35671
RADAUTI	47540
RADE KONCAR	69020
RADEBERG	59652
RADHOST	15091
RADIANT	12120
RADIANT MED	61648
RADIANT STAR	61212
RADIANT VENTURE	47200
RADIOSA	20730
RADISHEV	12371
RADISHEV	20803
RADIY	36917
RADIY	43817
RADNOTI	06141
RADOM	15085

Name	No.
RADOMYSHI	67363
RADOMYSHI	71374
RADUGA	12309
RADUZHNYY	89759
RADVILISKIS	35328
RADZIONKOW	03230
RADZIONKOW	03620
RAED B	94580
RAFAEL	60502
RAFFAELE CAFIERO	66320
RAFFAELLA	41070
RAFFAELLO	09201
RAFFLES BAY	64612
RAFI AHMED KIDWAI	71634
RAFIG II	27760
RAGNA BAKKE	24301
RAGNI BERG	07500
RAGNVALD JARL	02381
RAGNVALD JARL	35351
RAIKO MARU	65782
RAIKO MARU	70202
RAILSHIP 1	94070
RAIMOL	47431
RAIMOL	47901
RAINBOW	61654
RAINBOW STAR	61580
RAINBOW VOLANS	57612
RAINBOW VOLANS	62253
RAINFROST	27190
RAJAAN	29952
RAJAH BROOKE	41350
RAJAH MAS	00040
RAJAH SARAWAK	42690
RAJENDRA PRASAD	68090
RAKHOV	67360
RAKHOV	71371
RAKOW	50445
RAKOW	52006
RAKVERE	22867
RAKVERE	34497
RALIDA	11966
RALLYTIME 1	44660
RALLYTIME II	65370
RALPH O. RHOADES	65451
RALU	78392
RAMADA	22338
RAMBUTAN	42076
RAMIN	55180
RAMIRO PEREZ	25140
RAMO	76920
RAMONA	40423
RAMONA	42333
RAMONA	42593
RAMONEVERETT	30170
RAMSES II	01411
RAMSES II	01671
RAMSGATE	72570
RAMSLAND	85570
RAMSLAND	86750
RAMSLI	80550
RAMSLI	91340
RANA 1	91222
RANA 1	91822
RAND-1	35336
RAND-2	35337
RAND-3	35338
RAND-4.	35339
RANE	73740
RANENFJORD	52850
RANENFJORD	53040
RANGAMATI	15641
RANGATIRA	20000
RANIA B	43161
RANNO	90850
RANNO	91160
RANTIH GUMALA	59782
RAPANA	63821
RAPEL	01424
RAPHAEL	60502
RAPLA	89267
RAPOCA	15061
RAPOLAS CHARNAS	12508
RAS AL HADD	13801
RAS DEDGEN	10221
RAS EL BAR	92771
RAS EL KHAIMA	87282
RAS MAERSK	54430
RAS MAERSK	54810
RAS TANURA	69520
RASA	28541
RASAJES	89320
RASAMALA	59391
RASELTIN	50700
RASHIDAH	81780
RATHDOWN	88520
RATHGAR	85960
RATHGAR	88960
RATHOWEN	66490
RATHOWEN	85930
RATNA KIRTI	49701
RATNA KIRTI	52861
RATNA MANORAMA	49700
RATNA MANORAMA	52860
RATNA USHA	10313
RATNA VANDANA	47883
RATNO	67362
RATNO	71373
RAUMA	70779
RAUTARUUKKI	74900
RAVA RUSSKAYA	44890
RAVENS	34850
RAVENSTVO	01573
RAVENSWOOD	59441
RAVENSWOOD	60941
RAVI	00614
RAVNANGER	31350
RAVNI KOTARI.	58198
RAVU	60215
RAWAS	41960
RAY	48501
RAYCHIKHINSK	24093
RAYES 1	89370
RAYMOND J. BUSHEY	43260
RAYNESTONE	91221
RAYNESTONE	91821
RAZDOLNOYE	22868
RAZDOLNOYE	34498
RAZELM	11708
RAZLIV	22870
RAZLIV	34500
RAZLIV	35327
RAZLOG	83733
REA	06515
REA	16060
REA	21290
REA B	03380
READY	18671
REALENGRACHT	49817
REBECCA	73050
REBECCA ELYSE	61034
REBECCA ELYSE	71194
RECHITSA	89755
RECHLIN	75336
RECIFE	58370
RECIFE	64350
RECORDER	11570
RED ARROW	61217
RED JACKET	01492
RED RIVER	44574
REDA	88231
REDO	85760
REDSEA EXPRESS	51830
REDUT	89756
REEFER CARRIER	91145
REEFER CITY	33510
REEFER GIULIA	65011
REEFER MERCHANT	90810
REEFER MERCHANT	91770
REEFER PRINCESS	05711
REEFER QUEEN	24510
REEFER STAR	74100
REEFER STAR	76550
REEFER TRADER	80981
REEFER TRADER	81701
REEM 1	59540
REEM 1	81230
REEM B	66400
REFORMA	70042
REFRIGERATOR No 4	84331
REFRIGERATOR No 5	84332
REFRIGERATOR No 6	84333
REFRIGERATOR No 8	84334
REFRIGERATOR No 12	84335
REFRIGERATOR No 13	84336
REGAL SCOUT	61801
REGAL SKY	55390
REGAL STAR	36310
REGAL STAR	43090
REGENSTEIN	14040
REGENT	41740
REGENT PIMPERNEL	53684
REGENT PIMPERNEL	53814
REGENT PIMPERNEL	68534
REGENT'S PARK	75933
REGENT'S PARK	88633
REGGIO	19750
REGINA	60956
REGINA	64018
REGINA	68408
REGINA CELI	06561
REGINA EXPRESS	90310
REGINA MAERSK	54433
REGINA MAERSK	54813
REGINA MARIS	23630
REGINA OLDENDORFF	74651
REGINA S	24273
REGINA S	60187
REGINA VALERIA	86860
REGINE	73720
REGULA	19081
REGULIERSGRACHT	49818
REGULUS	10540
REGULUS	50143
REIHO MARU	71155
REINA DEL FRIO	21070
REINE ASTRID	20081
REIYO MARU	09990
REKIN	23459
RELIANT	60118
RELUME	51920
REMADA	86112
REMADA	91712
REMCO	34803
REMJAY	33450
REMUERA BAY	08360
RENA K	26022
RENA K	30192
RENACIMIENTO	62223
RENACIMIENTO	71133
RENAICO	01423
RENATA B	13811
RENATE SCHULTE	60955
RENATO GUITART	28733
RENEE	21530
RENEE R. E.	76605
RENEE R. E.	89305
RENEE RICKMERS	52811
RENI	22871
RENI	34501
RENO MARU	34600
RENOIR	48402
REPINO	12277
REPINO	22872
REPINO	34502
REPUBLICA DE COLOMBIA	04854
REPUBLICA DEL ECUADOR	04856
REPULSE BAY	87520
RERIK	83607
RESILIENCE	85460
RESITA	78581
RESOLUTE	54390
RESOLUTE	94277
RESOLUTION BAY	08442
RESOURCE	41741
RESURGENCE	74373
RESURGENCE EXPRESS	25701
RETAVAS	13700
RETEZATUL	11700
RETHIMNON	32911
RETRIEVER	23401
REUNION	07390
REUTOV	67361
REUTOV	71372
REVDA	22869
REVDA	34499
REVERE	36521
REVERE	43501
REVOLUCION	70043
REVOLYUTSIYA	11592
REVOLYUTSIYA	45368
REWI	48605
REYNOLDS	61993
REYNOSA	56443
REYNOSA	68353
REZEKI	51151
REZEKNE	60639
REZEKNE	62599
REZVAYA	59902
REZVAYA	67662
RHEA	45911
RHEIN EXPRESS	73515
RHEIN MARU	61184
RHETORIC	68780
RHIN	59081
RHINE MARU	33603
RHINE ORE	64521
RHINE ORE	68471
RHINO	44790
RHODRI MAWR	88571
RHODRI MAWR	89701
RHON	71750
RHON	81440
RHONE	32391
RHONE	56201
RHONE	59091
RHONE	76231
RHONE	94050
RIA LUNA	58191
RIBEIRA GRANDE	17841
RIBERA	91271
RIBICONE	66808
RICE TRADER	56561
RICHARD SORGE	36877
RICHARDAS BUKAUSKAS	67023
RICKY	25191
RIDGE	53415
RIDGE	64945
RIEDERSTEIN	14041
RIENZI	49641
RIGA	25846
RIGA	38533
RIGEL	35681
RIGEL	69850
RIGHTEOUS	56504
RIGI	66885
RIGOLETTO	27370
RIGOLETTO	92500
RIGOLETTO	93720
RIGOLETTO	95040
RIHENG	28910
RIJEKA	60640
RIJEKA	62600
RIJNBORG	45430
RIJNHAVEN	52721
RIJPGRACHT	49819
RIKHARD MIRRING	23569
RIKKE ISA	64855
RIKKE ISA	91035
RIKUZEN MARU	95111
RIMA G	80402
RIMAC	52661
RIMBA DUA	61653
RIMBA DUA	72052
RIMBA MERANTI	46960
RIMBA RAMIN	46961
RIMINI	78773
RIMNICU VILCEA	82396
RIMNICU VILCEA	82116
RIMON	61121
RIMULA	63820
RINA	62260
RINA	92070
RINCON	42824
RINGGRACHT	49820
RINGNES	75611
RINI	14571
RINOULA	06516
RIO ABAUCAN	05530
RIO AMAZONAS	04141
RIO AMAZONAS	29670
RIO ASON	90840
RIO ASON	91150
RIO ATRATO	10210
RIO BABAHOYA	07504
RIO BALSAS	30841
RIO BELEN	29721
RIO BELGRANO	29722
RIO BERMEJO	29720
RIO BESAYA	50210
RIO BRANCO	06870
RIO BRANCO	74962
RIO BRANCO	77102
RIO BRAVO	82802
RIO BRAVO	84580
RIO BRAVO	89950
RIO BRAVO	92092
RIO CALCHAQUI	05290
RIO CALCHAQUI	14360
RIO CALINGASTA	05533
RIO CARCARANA	24281
RIO CHONE	07502
RIO CINCEL	05281
RIO COLORADO	24282
RIO CORRIENTES	24280
RIO CUANZA	78101
RIO CUARTO	24430
RIO CUYAMEL	10755
RIO DE JANERIO	16170
RIO DE LA PLATA	05291
RIO DE LA PLATA	14361
RIO DESEADO	05282
RIO DIAMANTO	23145
RIO DIAMANTO	28345
RIO DIAMANTO	32002
RIO DULCE	30530
RIO ESMERALDAS	07503
RIO ESQUEL	05280
RIO EXPLORER	62250
RIO FRIO	02853
RIO GRANDE	74963
RIO GRANDE	77103
RIO GRANDE	85812
RIO GRANDE	86652
RIO GRANDE DO NORTE	43313
RIO GRANDE DO SUL	43314
RIO GUALEGUAY	05294
RIO GUALEGUAY	14364
RIO GUAYAS	87800
RIO HAINA	83770
RIO HAINA	92550
RIO IGUAZU	05292
RIO IGUAZU	14362
RIO JIBACOA	00270
RIO LIMAY	05283
RIO LINDO	79760
RIO LOS SAUCES	05531
RIO MAGDALENA	04855
RIO MARAPA	05534
RIO NEGRO	74961
RIO NEGRO	77101
RIO NEGRO II	48374
RIO NEUQUEN	05535
RIO NUNEZ	73121
RIO OLIVIA	05284
RIO PARANA	05293
RIO PARANA	14363
RIO PILCOMAYO	05532
RIO PLATA	47920
RIO QUEQUEN	28130
RIO QUINTO	24431
RIO SALADO	30531
RIO SAMO	23300
RIO SAN JUAN	26430
RIO SEGUNDO	00320
RIO SIXAOLA	10754
RIO SULACO	10756
RIO SUN	65830
RIO SUN	69490
RIO VERDE	74960
RIO VERDE	77100
RIO ZAIRE	49200
RIO ZAMBEZE	78103
RION	37681
RION	44260
RION	22500
RIRUCCIA	78432
RISA PAULA	81691
RISANGER	54139
RISANGER	54259
RISHI AGASTI	15871
RISHI AGASTI	83571
RISHI ATRI	15870
RISHI ATRI	83570
RISNJAK	48770
RISTNA	15494
RITA MAERSK	14100
RITA MARIA	27740
RITINA	62863
RITINA	67543
RITSA M	80704
RITSA M	84484
RIVA	10623
RIVA	15373
RIVA 1	69660
RIVAMAHON	76800
RIVANERVION	76801
RIVER ABOINE	04821
RIVER ADADA	04730
RIVER ANDONI	04826
RIVER ASAB	04822
RIVER BENUE	15221
RIVER ETHIOPE	15222
RIVER GUMA	04827
RIVER GURARA	04734
RIVER HADEJIA	55875
RIVER HADEJIA	56605
RIVER IKPAN	04830
RIVER JIMINI	04820
RIVER KERAWA	04828
RIVER LEE	89550
RIVER MADA	04825
RIVER MAIDUH	04732
RIVER MAJE	04737
RIVER NGADA	04829
RIVER NIGER	15220
RIVER OGBESE	04736
RIVER OGUN	15223
RIVER OJI	04731
RIVER OLI	04733
RIVER OSHUN	04735
RIVER OSSE	04823
RIVER RIMA	04824
RIVER SHANNON	76280
RIVER SIDE	29140
RIVERA	78740
RIVERBANK	05234
RIVERINA	59442
RIVERINA	60942
RIVIERA	47991
RIXTA OLDENDORFF	74621
RIXTA OLDENDORFF	78360
RIZCUN HONG KONG	58607
RIZCUN HONG KONG	59759
RIZHSKIY ZALIV	61100
RIZHSKOYE VZMORYE	93754
RIZHSKOYE VZMORYE	93844
ROACHBANK	04672
ROALD ADMUNDSEN	59191
ROALD AMUNDSEN	56161
ROAN	85794
ROAN	86664
ROANA	18860
ROANOKE	92604
ROANOKE	93614
ROBERT EYDEMAN	12509
ROBERT EYKHE	93733
ROBERT EYKHE	93823
ROBERT KOCH	40422
ROBERT KOCH	42332
ROBERT KOCH	42592
ROBERT KOCH	22550
ROBERT M	41090
ROBERT MAERSK	54431
ROBERT MAERSK	54811
ROBERT MILLER	53200
ROBERTO	60494
ROBERTS BANK	72435
ROBIN	61624
ROBINSON	54513
ROBINSON	63893
ROCADAS	02790
ROCAS	85900
ROCHEFORT	48903
ROCHE'S POINT	75080
ROCHFORD	00500
ROCK FERRY	13000
ROCKHAMPTON STAR	12920
ROCKNES	75612
ROCKY GIANT	72620
ROCQUAINE	88610
ROCQUAINE	90070
RODANTHI A	00990
RODIN	80215
RODINA	17524
RODINA	24310
RODINA	39450
RODINA	73297
RODONAS	13800

RODONIT	07476
RODONIT	11933
RODOPI	40500
RODOS	08190
RODOS	27681
RODOSTO	35950
RODOSTO	38751
RODRIGUES CABRILHO	73580
ROEBUCK	59440
ROEBUCK	60940
ROELOF HOLWERDA	88301
ROF BEAVER	75630
ROF BEAVER	76790
ROGALAND	93002
ROGALIN	17580
ROGATE	88561
ROGERS TRADER	07250
ROGET	05493
ROGET	07953
ROGET	61752
ROGOZNICA	66953
ROGOZNICA	70993
ROI BAUDOUIN	20050
ROKISHKIS	35329
ROKKO MARU	95085
ROKKOHSAN MARU	77501
ROKOS V	38430
ROLAND PACIFIC	57556
ROLAND VON BREMEN	08290
ROLF JACOB	77143
ROLLNES	75613
ROLNIK	78293
ROLNIK	80023
ROLON NORTE	94380
ROLON ORO	94391
ROLON PLATA	94390
ROLON SUR	94381
ROMAN	42032
ROMAN	86212
ROMAN PAZINSKI	14485
ROMAN REEFER	06333
ROMAN ROLLAN.	07928
ROMANDIE	46942
ROMANDIE	47102
ROMANTIC	68781
ROMANTICA	18080
ROMANZA	01730
ROMEO BRAGA	55015
ROMEO BRAGA	55885
ROMEO BRAGA	56555
ROMER	10280
ROMMY	59610
ROMMY	71920
ROMNY	67357
ROMNY	71368
ROMO MAERSK	54432
ROMO MAERSK	54812
RONA	81051
RONCESVALLES	03220
RONCESVALLES	03890
RONDEGGEN	92111
RONG CHENG	47041
RONHILL	10241
RONIREL	21243
RONNEBECK	90760
RONNEBURG	03884
RONSON	10240
RORO ANGLIA	32101
RORO CIMBRIA	32102
RORO DANIA	32100
RO-RO GENOVA	08963
RO-RO GENOVA	76853
RO-RO MANHATTAN	08962
RO-RO MANHATTAN	76852
ROSA	40350
ROSA DANIA	63684
ROSA LUXEMBURG	05638
ROSA LUXEMBURG	14467
ROSA LUXEMBURG	62684
ROSA ROTH	50161
ROSA ROTH	50711
ROSANA	61000
ROSANDRA	24350
ROSARIO	02721
ROSARIO	06517
ROSARIO DOS	25700
ROSARITA	45461
ROSARITA	48721
ROSARITO	43250
ROSBORG	94890
ROSE BAY	61581
ROSE MALLOW	60031
ROSE MALLOW	68361
ROSE MALLOW	71971
ROSELEN	27530
ROSELINE	46664
ROSELLA	20341
ROSEMARY	06316
ROSEMARY EVERARD	89842
ROSENORT	31760
ROSINA TOPIC	47201
ROSLAVL	12278
ROSLAVL	67365
ROSLAVL	71376
ROSS ILLUSTRIOUS	17731
ROSS KELETCHEKIS	43125
ROSS SEA	29230
ROSS VANGUARD	17730
ROSSANA	62021
ROSSELLAEMME	00920
ROSSEVERETT	30481
ROSSEVERETT	81581
ROSSIYA	16040
ROSTAND	80216
ROSTOCK	03882
ROSTOK	67350
ROSTOK	71360
ROSY	21380
ROSYTH	74890
ROTALIA	23447
ROTNA	19380
ROTTERDAM	03141
ROTTERDAM	12030
ROTTERDAM	86791
ROUMANIA	29120
ROUNTON GRANGE	77441
ROUSSEAU	80217
ROUSSILLON	17091
ROVENSCA	42100
ROVINARI	82224
ROVNO	39998
ROYAL FORTUNE	05940
ROYAL LYNX	68510
ROYAL PRINCE	75586
ROYAL RUBY	05077
ROYAL RUBY	07842
ROYAL SEA	03480
ROYAL SEA	24151
ROYAL SKY	03481
ROYAL STAR	21247
ROYAL VIKING SEA	16821
ROYAL VIKING SKY	16811
ROYAL VIKING STAR	16820
ROYAN	48904
ROYKSUND	93001
ROZEL BAY	59280
ROZENGRACHT	49821
ROZMARY	42120
RU YUNG	06100
RUBENS	04722
RUBENS	04942
RUBENS	07220
RUBENS	46630
RUBEZHNOYE	67358
RUBEZHNOYE	71369
RUBIN	12510
RUBINI	84840
RUBINOVYY	11934
RUBIS	63250
RUBTSOVSK	24086
RUCIANE	76642
RUCIANE	67052
RUDAN	87201
RUDDBANK	04673
RUDDERMAN	75020
RUDESHEIM	72001
RUDI ARNT	23429
RUDNYY	85331
RUDNYY	67356
RUDNYY	71367
RUDO	47213
RUDOLF BLAUMANIS	12511
RUDOLF BREITSCHEID	15413
RUDOLF BREITSCHIED	06383
RUDOLF DIESEL	46378
RUDOLF DIESEL	47078
RUDOLF LEONHARD.	10254
RUDOLF LEONHARD	12635
RUDOLF SCHWARZ	23430
RUDOLF SIRGE	23504
RUDOLF VAKMAN	23505
RUEN	55411
RUEN	78851
RUEY HSING	14790
RUGARD	51770
RUGEN	32890
RUHR EXPRESS	73431
RUHR ORE	63822
RUHRLAND	78230
RUI CHANG	84451
RUI CHANG	24241
RUKHULLA AKHUNDOV	53165
RUMAILA	69576
RUMBALA	70793
RUMIA	88234
RUMIJA	06651
RUNATINDUR	64867
RUNATINDUR	91047
RUPEA	47563
RUPIT	41961
RUSALKA	87744
RUSHANY	67355
RUSHANY	71366
RUSLAN	12279
RUSNE	23485
RUSSE	37211
RUSSELSHEIM	72003
RUSTAVI	12280
RUSTRINGEN	87230
RUTH	67943
RUTH	72354
RUTH	77154
RUTH LYKES	05588
RUTH LYKES	14429
RUTH LYKES	14899
RUZA	12281
RUZA	24085
RYAZAN	67364
RYAZAN	71375
RYAZHSK	25563
RYBACHIY	11593
RYBACHKA	23411
RYBAK	23410
RYBAK BALTIKA	93748
RYBAK BALTIKA	93838
RYBAK CHUKOTKI	45273
RYBAK KAMCHATSKIY	45271
RYBAK LATVII	93762
RYBAK LATVII	93852
RYBAK MORSKI	22350
RYBAK PRIMORIYA	45272
RYBATSKAYA SLAVA	93782
RYBINSK	67366
RYBINSK	71377
RYBNIK	82267
RYBNYY MURMAN	93873
RYLYEV	17525
RYSHKANY	67354
RYSHKANY	71365
RYSY	41910
RYSY II	64092
RYTTERHOLM	26141
RYUJIN MARU	84380
RZESZOW	15086
RZHEV	11319
RZHEV	67359
RZHEV	71370

S

S. A. AGULHAS	04070
S.A. ALPHEN	04691
S.A. CONSTANTIA	04680
S.A. HELDERBERG	08381
S.A. HUGUENOT	04690
S.A. LANGEBERG	08810
S.A. MORGENSTER	04681
S.A. SEDERBERG	08380
S.A. SKUKUZA	46590
S.A. VERGELEGEN	04682
S.A. WATERBERG	08382
S.A. WINTERBERG.	08383
S.G. THOLSTRUP	53931
S. G. THOLSTRUP	71661
SAADEDDIN	28590
SAADYARV	13705
SAAR ORE	52381
SAAR ORE	64441
SAAREMAA	86087
SAATLY	50786
SABA	82060
SABA	91440
SABAH A	90475
SABIE	46588
SABIK	39041
SABINA	91223
SABINA	91823
SABINE	37795
SABINE 1	40470
SABIRABAD	50782
SABLE	43770
SABOGAL	07943
SABRINA	30222
SABRINA	30362
SABUNCHI	44113
SAC BARCELONA	21670
SAC MALAGA	79100
SACELE	82121
SACELE	82401
SACHA	06602
SACHEM	66212
SACKR AL JAZIRAH	10840
SACOR	85901
SACRAMENTO	93470
SACRAMENTO MARU	02550
SACRAMENTO MARU	45970
SADKO	11882
SADKO	22232
SADOVA	82126
SADOVA	82406
SADU	82125
SADU	82405
SAFINA SALAMAH	70521
SAFINA SAUDIA	65970
SAFINA—E—ARAB	14070
SAFINA-E-HAIDER	07330
SAFINA-E-ISMAIL	00601
SAFINA-E-REHMAT	24898
SAFOCEAN NEDERBURG	14181
SAFOCEAN WELTEVREDEN	14180
SAFRA PRIMA	91210
SAGACITY	75451
SAGAFJORD	08140
SAGAMI MARU	39031
SAGAMI MARU	43372
SAGAR	18680
SAGARDEEP	02470
SAGEMAR SECONDA	87692
SAGGO	90851
SAGGO	91161
SAGITA	23448
SAGITTA	10542
SAGITTA	63180
SAGITTA	73900
SAHEL	42640
SAI JONG	25951
SAIBURI	23190
SAIKYO MARU	14740
SAINI	26690
SAINT AIDAN	88050
SAINT BERNARD	83230
SAINT BERNARD	83250
SAINT BERTRAND	83231
SAINT BERTRAND	83251
SAINT BRANDAN	88740
SAINT COLMAN	88040
SAINT ELOI	32560
SAINT ETIENNE	38790
SAINT ETIENNE	46091
SAINT ETIENNE	83261
SAINT FRANCOIS	45550
SAINT GERMAIN	19660
SAINT JACQUES	45790
SAINT KILLIAN	16464
SAINT LUC	45791
SAINT LUCIA	64315
SAINT MARCEL	35910
SAINT MARCEL	38792
SAINT MARCET	54380
SAINT MARCET	63070
SAINT MARCET	67912
SAINT MARY	39920
SAINT MARY	40680
SAINT MITRE	76710
SAINT MITRE	89580
SAINT NAZAIRE	72634
SAINT NAZAIRE	77394
SAINT NECTARIOS	00370
SAINT NICHOLAS	65250
SAINT NICOLAS	71280
SAINT PATRICK	16451
SAINT PAULIA	32630
SAINT PIERRE	78100
SAINT RAPHAEL	35911
SAINT RAPHAEL	38791
SAINT SERVAN	72832
SAINT SERVAN	87132
SAINT SPYRIDON	65360
SAINT WILLIAM	88080
SAIPEM DUE	92940
SAIRYU MARU	58050
SAKARTVELO	11883
SAKHALIN	12512
SAKHALIN	22722
SAKHALIN - 1	20310
SAKHALIN -2	20311
SAKHALIN -3	20312
SAKHALIN - 4	20313
SAKHALIN - 5.	20314
SAKHALINLES	24087
SAKHALINNEFT	70794
SAKHALINSKIE GORY	91912
SAKUMO LAGOON	15272
SAKUMO LAGOON	35040
SAKURA	14260
SAKURA	39000
SAKURA MARU	18804
SAKURA MARU	50521
SAKURA REEFER	05191
SAKURU MARU	81201
SALAH ALDEEN	49411
SALAH ALDEEN	50971
SALAHALA	93091
SALAHALA	94161
SALAJ	01409
SALAJ	01669
SALAJAR	15457
SALAMBO	35830
SALAMIS	47815
SALAMIS	61340
SALANTI	13701
SALAT	40600
SALAVAT	10611
SALAVAT YULAEV	89255
SALCANTAY	62038
SALDUS	11500
SALEEMA	39780
SALEKHARD	23572
SALEKHARD	24091
SALEM	78900
SALERNUM	10010
SALGIR	12282
SALI	17790
SALI	24960
SALINA DE MANAURE	49802
SALINAS	34221
SALISTE	82136
SALISTE	82416
SALKHINO	11884
SALLA	47293
SALLY ANN	90930
SALLY I	65761
SALLY I	67711
SALLY II	65762
SALLY II	67712
SALMIAH COAST	40030
SALMO	04170
SALNA	85342
SALOMEYA NERIS	10448
SALONAE	09911
SALONAE	12770
SALSK	22873
SALSK	34503
SALTA	06670
SALTERSGATE	50492
SALTERSGATE	75614
SALTIKOV SHCHEDRIN	12325
SALTNES	61321
SALTYKOV-SHCHEDRIN	28972
SALVADOR ALLENDE	03702
SALVADOR ALLENDE	03821
SALVATORE d'AMICO	73362
SALVISCOUNT	33070
SALYANY	50778
SALYUT	11631
SAM HOUSTON	01052
SAM RATULANGIE	15382
SAM SOO	57383
SAM WON No 27	22772
SAMAINA	23810
SAMARA	23541
SAMARGA	12513
SAMARIA	04631
SAMARIA	04761
SAMARKAND	40011
SAMARKAND	84340
SAMBOR	89465
SAMBURG	70026
SAMENA	23020
SAMI	00191
SAMJOHN GOVERNOR	52411
SAMJOHN MARINER	79116
SAMJOHN PIONEER	52412
SAMOA	45930
SAMOA	47440
SAMOAN REEFER	05180
SAMOAN REEFER	06334
SAMOKOV	83730
SAMOS	54280
SAMOS PROGRESS	06519
SAMOS SEA	21460
SAMOS SKY	13231
SAMOS STORM	21461
SAMOS SUN	15890
SAMOTLOR	70020
SAMPO	23982
SAMRAT ASHOK	77230
SAMSHIT	23506
SAMSON SCAN	84020
SAMSUN	18061
SAMTREDIA	85993
SAMUDRA	18681
SAMUDRA VIJAY	30071
SAMUDRAGUPTA	56845
SAMUIL MARSHAK	07924
SAMULUN	39742
SAN BENITO	03512
SAN BERNARDINO	21330
SAN BLAS	03510
SAN BRUNO	03511
SAN DENIS	41500
SAN FELICE	04480
SAN FELICE	12650
SAN FRANCESCO DI PAOLA	19760
SAN FRANCISCO	04100
SAN FRANCISCO MARU	02551
SAN FRANCISCO MARU	45972
SAN GEORGE	06518
SAN GEORGE	21930
SAN GEORGE	48550
SAN JOAQUIN VALLEY	02541
SAN JOHN	51300
SAN JOHN	61250
SAN JORGE	43460
SAN JOSE	27200
SAN JUAN	53103
SAN JUAN	53333
SAN JUAN	74474
SAN JUAN	83870
SAN LUIS	53104
SAN LUIS	53334
SAN MARCOS	37796
SAN MARTIN	86693
SAN MING	28222
SAN MING	31921
SAN NICOLAOS	26680
SAN NICOLAS	40140
SAN NIKITAS	44272
SAN PEDRO	61016
SAN PEDRO	71176
SAN REMO	48610
SAN SALVADOR	44610
SAN SALVADOR	44750
SAN SPYRIDON IV	28360
SAN VINCENZO	79040
SAN VINCENZO	80780

SEIYO MARU	59520
SEIYO MARU	81200
SEIZAN MARU	61622
SEJWAL	10810
SEKI ROKAKO	48390
SEKI ROKEL	48391
SEKONDI	56591
SELA	83920
SELAMAT	22510
SELANDIA	08490
SELAS	62650
SELAS	81590
SELAT KARIMATA	85151
SELAT MAKASSAR	85150
SELATAN MAJU	81670
SELAYAR	89231
SELE	87630
SELEMDZHA	15482
SELENA	13709
SELENE G	32040
SELENGA	31850
SELENGALES	24094
SELFOSS	15991
SELIGER	11612
SELIN	84076
SELINTI	40601
SELMA	55318
SELMA	59130
SELMA	70067
SELNES	75610
SEMELI	57030
SEMEN CHELYUSKIN	22234
SEMENIC	11678
SEMI	56973
SEMIPALATINSK	10612
SEMIRA	61800
SEMIRAMIS	06562
SEMLOW	50447
SEMLOW	52008
SEMYON CHELYUSKIN	22185
SEMYON DEZHNEV	12515
SEMYON DEZHNEV	22186
SEMYON DEZHNEV	22233
SEMYON EMELYANOV	12284
SEMYON KOSINOV	11444
SEMYON MOROZOV	79422
SEMYON ROSHAL	89264
SENANG ISLAND	00131
SENDAI	48943
SENECA	68320
SENEGAL	71520
SENEZH	23864
SENFTENBERG	79733
SENG KONG No 1	69420
SENIOR K	31510
SENKAKU MARU	66710
SENKO MARU	70920
SENKO MARU	79600
SENLAC	19902
SENORITA MARIA	36540
SENTA	87350
SENTENCE	75441
SENTENCE	88421
SENTOSA	70953
SENTOSA BAY	64611
SEO YANG	94872
SEQUOIA	36291
SEQUOIA	37871
SEQUOIA	43081
SEQUOIA	44461
SEQUOIA	68321
SERAFIMOVICH	12326
SERANTES	46124
SERDOLIK.	07477
SERDOLIK	11938
SEREBRYANKA	17952
SEREBRYANSK	02673
SEREBRYANSK	85336
SERENELL	75981
SERENISSIMA EXPRESS	18000
SERENITY	75452
SERGEI LAZO	33913
SERGEI TSENSKAY	20804
SERGEI VAVILOV	17561
SERGEY BOTKIN	34245
SERGEY BURYACHEK	49249
SERGEY EYZENSHTEYN	09972
SERGEY EYZENSHTEYN	11512
SERGEY GRITSEVETS	50749
SERGEY GUSEV	03792
SERGEY GUSEV	04032
SERGEY KANDACHIK	11886
SERGEY KIROV	86230
SERGEY KRAVKOV	35440
SERGEY LAZO	93688
SERGEY LYULIN	13702
SERGEY TYULENIN	41155
SERGEY TYULENIN	44954
SERGEY TYULENIN	86172
SERGEY VASILIEV	11513
SERGEY VASILISIN	93881
SERGEY VASILYEV	09973
SERGEY YESENIN	12516
SERGEY YESENIN	14391
SERIFOS	03191
SERIFOS	03591
SERIFOS	89100
SERIR	69182
SERNOVODSK	83685
SEROGLAZKA	12517
SEROV	02677
SERPA PINTO	02791
SERPUKOV	25174
SERRA AZUL	06563
SERRA BRANCA	06564
SERRA DOURADA	06565
SERRA VERDE	06566
SERRAI	77562
SERTAN	73980
SERVIA	04633
SERVIA	04763
SESTRORETSK	79551
SETE CIDADES	85100
SETE CIDADES	85180
SETIABUDHI	30920
SETIF	61980
SEVAN	02674
SEVAN	11465
SEVAN	20805
SEVAN	85988
SEVASTOPOL	45111
SEVEN DAFFODIL	61075
SEVEN DAFFODIL	71265
7 DE NOVIEMBRE	59905
7 DE NOVIEMBRE	67665
SEVEN LOG MASTER	91923
SEVEN SEAS BRIDGE	04951
SEVEN SEAS BRIDGE	08612
SEVEN TEAM	68292
SEVEN TEAM	77322
SEVERLES	24045
SEVERNAYA PALMIRA	12518
SEVERNAYA ZEMLYA	10450
SEVERNOYE SIYANIE	12348
SEVERNYY DONETS	89234
SEVERNYY POLYUS	93736
SEVERNYY POLYUS	93826
SEVERNYY VETER	76501
SEVERODONETSK	02678
SEVERODONETSK	93800
SEVERODVINSK	25840
SEVERODVINSKIY	89680
SEVEROMORSK	10451
SEVEROMORSKIY KOMSOMOLETS	12519
SEVEROURALSK	93801
SEVERSK	11771
SEVERSK	34662
SEVERYANIN	11624
SEVILLA	51743
SEVILLA	84063
SEVILLAN REEFER	18300
SEVONIA TEAM	58405
SEVONIA TEAM	64565
SEVORODVINSK	15483
SEVRYBA	93876
SEYHAN	21770
SHABELLE	60510
SHABNAM	14662
SHABONEE	67431
SHABONEE	71401
SHADRINSK	24088
SHAHJEHAN	56846
SHAIKAH AL QURAICHI	73730
SHAKHTERSK	12149
SHAKHTY	10452
SHALAMAR	15141
SHALVA NADIBAIDZE	93802
SHAMA	27216
SHAMKHOR	50776
SHAMS	31630
SHAN YIN	30001
SHAN YIN	30980
SHANGHAI	25230
SHANI Z	26121
SHANTA ROHAN	48520
SHANTA SHIBANI	57233
SHANTAR	11953
SHAO YAO	16330
SHARON H	37350
SHARPNES	61324
SHAT-AL ARAB	58364
SHATURA	24092
SHEARWATER BAY	45620
SHEARWATER BAY	45660
SHEDAR	12310
SHEKSNA	94453
SHEKSNALES	11501
SHELDON LYKES	00085
SHELDON LYKES	00235
SHELL CRAFTSMAN	67390
SHELL DIRECTOR	70882
SHELL DIRECTOR	79592
SHELL ENGINEER	83865
SHELL ENGINEER	85875
SHELL EXPLORER	70881
SHELL EXPLORER	79591
SHELL MARINER	83860
SHELL MARINER	85870
SHELL REFINER	83861
SHELL REFINER	85871
SHELL SCIENTIST	83863
SHELL SUPPLIER	70883
SHELL SUPPLIER	79593
SHELL TRADER	83864
SHELL TRADER	85874
SHEMAKHA	86081
SHEN NON	64202
SHEN NON	68652
SHENANDOAH	46586
SHENKURSK	22875
SHENKURSK	34505
SHERBRO	55871
SHERBRO	56601
SHEREMTYEVO	11740
SHEREMTYEVO	34630
SHEVCHENKO	12520
SHI JING SHAN	58603
SHI TANG HAI	77447
SHI ZUI SHAN	64819
SHIEH FU	34550
SHIELDHALL	39490
SHIGEO NAGANO	65221
SHIGEO NAGANO	69881
SHIKISHIMA MARU	36000
SHILKA	15484
SHIN-EN MARU	68000
SHIN HUI	89891
SHIN SAKURA MARU	02970
SHINANO MARU	92250
SHINIAS	07012
SHINING STAR	61213
SHINJU MARU	63760
SHINKAWA MARU	51113
SHINKAWA MARU	51493
SHINKO MARU	54540
SHINKO MARU	61619
SHINKO MARU	63900
SHINPO MARU	61491
SHINREI MARU	77220
SHINRYO ETHYLENE MARU	57710
SHINRYU MARU	77300
SHINSEI MARU	93440
SHINTOKU MARU	11230
SHINWA	52206
SHINWA	65156
SHINYO MARU	77310
SHINYU MARU	77301
SHINZUI MARU	77221
SHIQMA	80950
SHIRANE MARU	94920
SHIRDEL VANANCA	42321
SHIRLEY	67944
SHIRRABANK	07011
SHIRVANNEFT	44114
SHKIPER GIEK	17920
SHKOTOVO	86231
SHKVAL	21450
SHKVAL	34290
SHOHU MARU	82380
SHOJU MARU	38470
SHOKAKU MARU	66711
SHOMAR SHAIMA	42840
SHONGA	55870
SHONGA	56600
SHONGAR	86202
SHORTHORN EXPRESS	40360
SHORYU MARU	77860
SHOSHONE	38421
SHOTA RUSTAVELI	01752
SHOTA RUSTAVELI	12285
SHOU SHAN	80661
SHOUSH	60272
SHOUSH	63831
SHOYO MARU	94901
SHOYO MARU	95071
SHOZEN MARU	73180
SHTURMAN YELAGIN	12521
SHU YU QUAN	10491
SHUANG FENG HAI	68150
SHUI HSIEN	17620
SHUN OH	58182
SHUNKO MARU	57790
SHUNKO MARU	62770
SHUNYO MARU	52872
SHURA BURLACHENKO	49245
SHURA KOBER	15510
SHUSENSKOYE.	07593
SHUSHENSKOYE	79376
SHUWA MARU	61079
SHUWA MARU	71269
SHVENTOY	11887
SHYAULYAY	12522
SIAM	53145
SIAM	66075
SIAM RAINBOW	24703
SIAM VENTURE	48350
SIARKOPOL	73552
SIBELIUS	76741
SIBELIUS	89691
SIBIR	22723
SIBIR	76507
SIBIRKIJ	04083
SIBIRLES	31841
SIBIRNEFT	70795
SIBIRTSYEVO	31845
SIBIRYAK	12523
SIBIU	41317
SIBOEN	64540
SIBOEN	73250
SIBONEY	51191
SIBOSIX	63512
SIBOSIX	68282
SIBOTEM	63541
SIBOTO	64541
SIBOTO	73251
SIBOTRE	64542
SIBOTRE	73252
SICILIA	01722
SICILMOTOR	38630
SIDERIS	46584
SIDON	66493
SIDON	85935
SIDOR KOVPAK	03951
SIEKIERKI	59226
SIEKIERKI	74546
SIEMIATYCZE	03238
SIEMIATYCZE	03628
SIENA	45933
SIENA	47443
SIENKIEWICZ	24560
SIERADZ	50465
SIERRA	91380
SIERRA ARAMO	90931
SIERRA ARANZAZU	90932
SIERRA GRANA	50611
SIERRA GRANERA	50612
SIERRA GREDOS	50610
SIERRA GUADELUPE	50613
SIERRA GUARDARRAMA	50614
SIERRA LUCENA	49910
SIERRA LUNA	49911
SIERRA MAESTRA	35273
SIERRA NEVADA	34212
SIERRA URBION	87571
'SIETAS type 81'	73910
SIFNOS	49102
SIFNOS	49713
SIFNOS	54674
SIFNOS	89101
SIG	71900
SIGAL	78070
SIGGEN	72681
SIGI SIGI	51084
SIGMA	72061
SIGNAL	64921
SIGNE THOLSTRUP	81920
SIGRID	59615
SIGRID	71925
SIGRID	91301
SIGRID S	90944
SIGULDA	22877
SIGULDA	34507
SIGULDA	89472
SIGURD JARL	83640
SIGURD JORSALFAR	59211
SIGURD JORSALFAR	66741
SIJILMASSA	34224
SILAGA	06628
SILBA	36751
SILESIA	08171
SILJA STAR	20640
SILJESTAD	63262
SILK	31800
SILVAPLANA	56983
SILVER ATHENS	60125
SILVER CITY	12102
SILVER CITY	13891
SILVER CLIPPER	62035
SILVER CLOUD	06523
SILVER DRAGON	31590
SILVER EAGLE	31320
SILVER FERN	71210
SILVER FIR	36200
SILVER GATE	12850
SILVER GLORY	95121
SILVER ISLAND	44470
SILVER LADY	69680
SILVER LADY	86390
SILVER PACE	36782
SILVER PHOENIX	03682
SILVER PIT	18730
SILVER PORT	95122
SILVER RAYS	07630
SILVER RIVER	86950
SILVER SHELTON	57311
SILVER ZEPHYR	46884
SILVERCORN	59261
SILVERCORN	61303
SILVERCORN	62531
SILVERCORN	62623
SILVEREAGLE	66640
SILVERFALCON	84971
SILVERFALCON	88681
SILVERFJORD	48630
SILVERLAND	64492
SILVERLAND	68582
SILVERMAIN	46262
SILVERMERLIN	84970
SILVERMERLIN	88680
SILVEROSPREY	66641
SILVERSEA	81131
SILVERSKY	81130
SILVERTHORN	89861
SILVET	85994
SILVIA	75561
SILVIA ONORATO	88031
SILVICULTURE	50601
SILVICULTURE	52351
SILVILAI	86208
SILWON	54151
SIMALI 1	23930
SIMALI 1	28830
SIMBA	45932
SIMBA	47442
SIMEIZ	12286
SIMERIA	47555
SIMFEROPOL	10610
SIMFEROPOL	45112
SIMONBURN	66142
SIMONBURN	70582
SIMONETTA	46300
SIMYAVINO	23487
SINAIA	48480
SINALITHIA	30261
SINALOA	45934
SINALOA	47444
SINAR SURYA	27900
SINCERE No 3	67284
SINCERE ORIENT	40900
SINCERE TRADER	60251
SINCERITY	75471
SINCLAIR TEXAS	65920
SIND	88245
SINDBAD	45387
SINE MAERSK	60865
SINE MAERSK	70905
SINEGORSK	22879
SINEGORSK	34509
SINEGORSK	36901
SINEGORSK	43801
SINEGORSK	15460
SING TAO	11532
SINGAPORE 2	24830
SINGAPORE CAR	56810
SINGAPORE FORTUNE	10624
SINGAPORE FORTUNE	15374
SINGAPORE JATI	85210
SINGAPORE JATI	90950
SINGAPORE MERCHANT	62233
SINGAPORE MERCHANT	71253
SINGAPORE RAMIN	42760
SINGAPORE VOYAGER	67331
SINGAPURA	57605
SINGAPURA	62248
SINGELGRACHT	49823
SINGULARITY	84090
SINGWIND	17370
SINKAI	14220
SINNI	71914
SINNO M.E.	72491
SINNO M.E.	72981
SINNO M. E. II	21532
SINOE	11704
SINOIA	65400
SINOIA	69790
SIPCA DAMMAM	55742
SIPCA DAMMAM	63812
SIR ALEXANDER GLEN	63492
SIR BEDIVERE	50390
SIR CHARLES HAMBRO	56416
SIR CHARLES HAMBRO	67836
SIR CHARLES HAMBRO	68436
SIR FRED PARKES	17721
SIR GALAHAD	50392
SIR GERAINT	50393
SIR HUMPHREY GILBERT	08852
SIR JOSEPH BAZALGETTE	40323
SIR LANCELOT	50391
SIR PERCIVAL	50394
SIR ROBERT BOND	11560
SIR TRISTRAM	50395
SIR WILLIAM WALKER	42452
SIRAPIL	91401
SIREN	18661
SIRENA	55380
SIRENIA	55760
SIRENIA	64063
SIRET	11978
SIRIUS	11675
SIRIUS	12287
SIRIUS	00030
SIRIUS	15782
SIRIUS	16340
SIRIUS	22281
SIRIUS	52770
SIRIUS	82692
SIRLAD	40490
SIRLAD	42350
SIROCCA	39820
SIROCO	74945
SISAK	49020
SISAL TRADER	62740
SISES	25680
SISSILI RIVER	04833
SISU	33003
SIT-TWAY	71303
SITHONIA	60126

SITNO 15092
SITULA 91846
SITULA 91956
SIULI 27360
SIVAND 62492
SIVAND 71562
SIVASH 11888
SIVASH 25490
'613-B' type 91020
'16 BC5' type 56650
'16 BC5' type 62210
SIYANIE 11605
SKAFTA 83923
SKAFTAFELL 50801
SKAFTAFELL 52611
SKAGERN 51611
SKAGERRAK 18733
SKALISTYY 11889
SKALISTYY BEREG 62694
SKANDIA 17490
SKANDYNAWIA 19143
SKANE 19240
SKAUBORD 35530
SKAUGRAN 36110
SKAUGRAN 36560
SKAZOCHNIK ANDERSEN 09366
SKELLIG ROCK 76151
SKENDERBEG 28990
SKIATHOS 81990
SKIKDA 60645
SKIKDA 62605
SKIPPER 81520
SKIRON 79782
SKLERION 06524
SKOCZOW 03237
SKOCZOW 03627
SKODSBORG 03860
SKOPELOS 40050
SKOPELOS SEA 35672
SKOPJE 33581
SKORPIOS 42271
SKRADIN 78640
SKRYPLEV 09380
SKRZAT 73650
SKULE 18540
SKULPTOR GOLUBKINA 80262
SKULPTOR KONENKOV 80260
SKULPTOR VUCHETICH 80261
SKULPTOR ZALKALNS 80263
SKYMNOS 06340
SKYPTRON 46003
SKYRIAN ROVER 58700
SKYRIAN ROVER 62410
SKYRON II 69770
SKYROS 64101
SKYROS 71581
SKYWARD 01871
SLAGEN 70752
SLANCHEV BRIAG 76529
SLATINA 82118
SLATINA 82398
SLAURNOYE 83688
SLAVA SEVASTOPOLYA 10882
SLAVGOROD 11620
SLAVGOROD 39986
SLAVIJA 19170
SLAVISA VAJNER 69023
SLAVONIJA 04472
SLAVONIJA 10993
SLAVONIJA 34153
SLAVONIJA 04472
SLAVSK 10613
SLAVSK 12288
SLAVYANKA 25564
SLAVYANSK 02679
SLAVYANSK 93803
SLENSVIK 70755
SLETTA 70753
SLETTER 87110
SLIDRE 40440
SLIEDRECHT 72431
SLITAN 70754
SLIVEN 29011
SLOBODA 21722
SLOBOZIA 82119
SLOBOZIA 82399
SLOMAN MERCUR 56090
SLOMAN MIRA 48731
SLOMAN MIRA 56091
SLOMAN NAJADE 45531
SLOMAN NAJADE 67241
SLOMAN NEREUS 45530
SLOMAN NEREUS 67240
SLOMAN RANGER 92290
SLOMAN RANGER 92360
SLOMAN RECORD 92291
SLOMAN RECORD 92361
SLOMAN RIDER 92292
SLOMAN RIDER 92362
SLOMAN ROVER 92293
SLOMAN ROVER 92363
SLOMAN ROYAL 92294
SLOMAN ROYAL 92364
SLOMAN RUNNER 92295
SLOMAN RUNNER 92365
SLORA 70751
SLOT SCANDINAVIA 91316
SLUPSK 34363
SLURRY EXPRESS 68160
SLUSKEN 22610
SLUTSK 10614
SMARA 34203
SMELA 28062
SMENA 01407
SMENA 01667
SMINARCHOS FRANGISTAS 05981
SMINARCHOS FRANGISTAS 07401
SMOLNY 10577
SMOLNYY 11610
SMOLNYY 22450
SMYRIL 19182
SNABZHENETS PERVYY 12524
SNAGOV 82127
SNAGOV 82407
SNELAND 47397
SNELAND 47967
SNEZHNOGORSK 83686
SNIADECKI 15192
SNJEZNIK 83925
SNOLNY 15347
SNOW BALL 02601
SNOW BALL 02631
SNOW CRYSTAL 02602
SNOW CRYSTAL 02632
SNOW DRIFT 02603
SNOW DRIFT 02633
SNOW FLAKE 02600
SNOW FLAKE 02630
SNOW FLOWER 02604
SNOW FLOWER 02634
SNOW LAND 02605
SNOW LAND 02635
SNOW STORM 02606
SNOW STORM 02636
SOBOLEVO 22876
SOBOLEVO 34506
SOBY FAERGEN 94000
SOCHI 02682
SOCONY-VACUUM 44562
SOCRATES 54610
SOCRATES 74160
SOCRATIS 39310
SOFALA 05811
SOFIA 80330
SOFIA 91700
SOFIA A 43581
SOFIA PEROVSKAYA 06789
SOFIA PEROVSKAYA 07586
SOFIE 55310
SOFIE BRAVO 50332
SOFIE BRAVO 83672
SOFIE MAERSK 60864
SOFIE MAERSK 70904
SOFIYA 36860
SOFIYSK 83689
SOGNEFJORD 09510
SOHANLAL 61830
SOHIO INTREPID 63412
SOHIO RESOLUTE 63413
SOIATA 82130
SOIATA 82410
SOKNATUN 71907
SOKOL 03952
SOKOLICA 68922
SOKOLINOYE 11890
SOKORRI 48102
SOKOTO 56590
SOL LAILA 59706
SOL LAILA 61406
SOL PHRYNE 32900
SOL REEFER 72962
SOL REEFER 87162
SOL TULLA 59707
SOL TULLA 61407
SOLA 72513
SOLDEK 42960
SOLEDAD MARIA 50000
SOLEDAD MARIA 50650
SOLENTBROOK 64791
SOLENTBROOK 66771
SOLIDOR 32820
SOLNECHNOGORSK. 13016
SOLNECHNYY 85996
SOLNECHNYY BEREG 62690
SOLNECHNYY LUCH 71672
SOLNTSEDAR 11891
SOLOGNE 64373
SOLOMBALA 89210
SOLOMON SEA 90450
SOLON 57921
SOLON 62921
SOLON TURMAN 00067
SOLOVIETSKIY 11739
SOLOVIETSKIY 34629
SOLOVKI; 01970
SOLSTAD 63263
SOLVENT EXPLORER 55680
SOLVENT EXPLORER 72530
SOLVENT VENTURER 55681
SOLVENT VENTURER 72531
SOLVIKEN 55792
SOLVIKEN 64653
SOLWAY FISHER 88640
SOMERI 45870
SOMERSET 34781
SOMERSETBROOK 64792
SOMERSETBROOK 66772
SOMES 11979
SOMIO 76086
SOMMERSTAD 63260
SOMOGY 89220
SONDERHAUSEN. 03709
SONDERHAUSEN 03829
SONG DUONG 05317
SONG GIANH 10522
SONG HUA JIANG 60243
SONG HUONG 83280
SONG JIANG 26920
SONG KAU 86244
SONG KHAN 22884
SONG KHAN 34514
SONG LIM 40660
SONG LO 86243
SONG NHUE 31330
SONG OF NORWAY 16870
SONG THAO 86245
SONG TRA LY 22960
SONGDA 22883
SONGDA 34513
SONGKHLA 47450
SONGKHLA 48230
SONGLIN 06032
SONIA 57362
SONIA SOPHIA S 80510
SONID 46830
SONJA 55311
SONJA 70062
SONORA 25640
SOON HENG 40150
SOPHIA 40310
SOPHIA II 29922
SOPHIA C 79640
SOPHIA PAPPAS 89410
SOPHIE C 47932
SOPHIE RICKMERS 07751
SOPHIE SCHULTE 84744
SOPHIE SCHULTE 84954
SOPHOCLES 05511
SOPKA GEROYEV 11892
SOPOT 34360
SOPOT 83721
SOPOT 88235
SORACH MARU 23734
SORACHI MARU 19701
'SORMOVSKIY' type 79340
SORMOVSKIY 2 79341
SORMOVSKIY 4 79342
SORMOVSKIY 5 79343
SORMOVSKIY 6 79344
SORMOVSKIY 7 79345
SORMOVSKIY 9 79346
SORMOVSKIY 11 79347
SORMOVSKIY 12 79348
SORMOVSKIY 13 79349
SORMOVSKIY 14 79350
SORMOVSKIY 17 79351
SORMOVSKIY 18 79352
SORMOVSKIY 19 79353
SORMOVSKIY 22 79354
SORMOVSKIY 27 79355
SORMOVSKIY 28 79356
SORMOVSKIY 29 79357
SORMOVSKIY 30 79358
SORMOVSKIY 31 79359
SORMOVSKIY 33 79360
SORMOVSKIY 34 79361
SORMOVSKIY 40 79362
SORMOVSKIY 42 79363
SORMOVSKIY 109 79364
SORMOVSKIY 110 79365
SORMOVSKIY 112 79366
SORMOVSKIY 117 79367
SOROKOS 60170
SOROLLA 91270
SORONG 44440
SORRENTO 72461
SOSNOGORSK. 03950
SOSNOVETS 83681
SOSNOVKA 83683
SOTE JARL 83641
SOTIR 22290
SOTIR 36311
SOTIR 43091
SOTKA 51991
SOTKA 65161
SOUFFLOT 49553
SOUFFLOT 49573
SOUGERKA 25160
SOULA K 12060
SOUND OF ISLAY 17250
SOUNION 59290
SOUNION 61330
SOUSA 82135
SOUSA 82415
SOUTH ANGELA 63930
SOUTH BEAUTY 78423
SOUTH FOUNDATION 62491
SOUTH FOUNDATION 71561
SOUTH PACIFIC 34925
SOUTH POLE 86322
SOUTH RAINBOW 73367
SOUTH SEA 87710
SOUTH SEA 89310
SOUTH SKY 73363
SOUTH STAR 01425
SOUTH VIVIEN 63931
SOUTH WIND 49370
SOUTHERN CONQUEROR 37651
SOUTHERN CONQUEST 37650
SOUTHERN CROSS 94964
SOUTHERN DIAMOND 72152
SOUTHERN ENTERPRISE 29800
SOUTHERN FIGHTER 31134
SOUTHERN FRIENDSHIP 60171
SOUTHERN GLORY 33190
SOUTHERN LION 59944
SOUTHERN LION 67934
SOUTHERN RANGER 17680
SOUTHGATE 50491
SOUTHLAND STAR 03610
SOUTHSEA 20931
SOUTHWARD 17000
SOUTHWEST CAPE 37602
SOUTHWEST CAPE 44312
SOUTHWIND 53381
SOUTHWIND 90741
SOVEJA 82129
SOVEJA 82409
SOVEREIGN ACCORD 74461
SOVEREIGN ACCORD 79311
SOVEREIGN RUBY 23041
SOVEREIGN VENTURE 47202
SOVETSKAYA NEFT 63985
SOVETSKAYA ROSSIYA 93382
SOVETSKIY POGRANICHNIK 50294
SOVETSKIY VOIN 50280
SOVFRACHT 78520
SOVGANSKIY KOMSOMOLETS 11772
SOVGANSKIY KOMSOMOLETS 34663
SOVGAVAN 12525
SOVIETSK 09382
SOVIETSK. 10615
SOVIETSKAYA ARKTIKA 26220
SOVIETSKAYA ARKTIKA 31680
SOVIETSKAYA BURYATYA 93757
SOVIETSKAYA BURYATYA 93847
SOVIETSKAYA KAMCHATKA 25847
SOVIETSKAYA LATVIYA 85325
SOVIETSKAYA LITVA 25849
SOVIETSKAYA RODINA 85326
SOVIETSKAYA ROSSIA 93630
SOVIETSKAYA SAKHALIN 25848
SOVIETSKAYA SIBIR 93751
SOVIETSKAYA SIBIR 93841
SOVIETSKAYA UKRAINA 93860
SOVIETSKAYA YAKUTIYA 50730
SOVIETSKIE PROFSOYUZY 12526
SOVIETSKIY AZERBAIDZHAN 20320
SOVIETSKIY KAZAKHSTAN 20322
SOVIETSKIY MORYAK 50297
SOVIETSKIY POGRANICHNIK 85984
SOVIETSKIY SEVER 79416
SOVIETSKIY SOYUZ 12010
SOVIETSKIY TURKMENISTAN 20321
SOVIETSKIY UZBEKISTAN 20323
SOVIETSKIY ZAPOLYARYE 93737
SOVIETSKIY ZAPOLYARYE 93827
SOVIETSKIYE PROFSOYUZY 49487
SOVIETSKIYE PROFSOYUZY 49757
SOVIETSKIYE PROFSOYUZY 48447
SOVIETSKOYE PRIMORYE 93746
SOVIETSKOYE PRIMORYE 93836
SOVINFLOT 78522
SOYA 34000
SOYUZ 3 11893
SOZER BIRADESLER 11400
SPACIOUS 60189
SPAN QUARTA 35660
SPAROS 73793
SPARTA 05740
SPARTAK 89250
SPARTAN 19562
SPARTAN REEFER 03900
SPARTI 86260
SPASSK 93804
SPASSK-DALNIY 15485
SPECIALIST 72335
SPECIALITY 73680
SPECIALITY 87340
SPEEDLINK VANGUARD 94800
SPERO 48342
SPERUS 22670
SPES 66760
SPES 67482
SPES 69000
SPES 76782
SPETSAI 35752
SPETSAI 37091
SPETSES ISLAND 57551
SPEY BRIDGE 69200
SPEYER 04666
SPHINX U 14814
SPICE ISLAND GIRL 84790
SPIEGELGRACHT 49824
SPIJKENISSE 01203
SPILIOS 78840
SPINANGER 54140
SPINANGER 54260
SPIRIT OF FREE ENTERPRISE 20210
SPIRIT OF LIBERTY 58428
SPIROS 65472
SPLENDID HOPE 56960
SPLENDID HOPE 62120
SPLIT 60622
SPLIT 62582
SPOKANE 18910
SPRAVEDLIVYY 04081
SPRAY DERRICK 54572
SPRAY DERRICK 54952
SPRAYNES 61323
SPRING ODESSA 53685
SPRING ODESSA 53815
SPRING ODESSA 68535
SPRINGDALE 22091
SPRINGTIME 36420
SPROGO 18941
SPRUT 34880
SPUTNIK 12599
SPYROS 18521
SPYROS 90533
SPYROS 91073
SPYROS A LEMOS 63880
SPYROS A LEMOS 68460
SPYROS V 47720
SRAKANE 91522
SRBIJA 00660
SREDNA GORA 49041
SRETENSK 00334
SRI CHOL 22970
SRI PHEN SINN 82570
SRI KAILASH 62742
SRI KANDI 61510
SRI THAMARACH 25470
SRYMSKIE GORY 81493
ST. ANSELM 19460
ST. ANTONIUS 75624
ST. CHRISTOPHER 19461
ST. CLAIR 23820
ST. CLEMENS 64642
ST. COLUMBA 19890
ST. DAVID 19462
ST. DEMETRIUS 29521
ST. EDMUND 19880
ST. FRANCOIS 01360
ST. GEORGE 16380
ST. HELENA 86290
ST. JASON 17740
ST. JASPER 17741
ST. JEROME 17742
ST. JOHN 02640
ST. LAWRENCE 78802
ST. LAWRENCE 89962
ST. MAGNUS 32952
ST MARCOS 62821
ST MARCOS 67571
ST. MARGARETS 09280
ST NICOLAS 38240
ST. NICOLAS 38710
ST. OLA 32870
ST. PAUL 01361
ST. PAUL 45551
ST. PAUL 78430
ST VINCENT 62820
ST VINCENT 67570
STABENKO 60591
STABENKO 69961
STABILITY 73681
STABILITY 87341
STADION 61199
STADIONGRACHT 49825
STAFFETTA ADRIATICA 22380
STAFFETTA JONICA 22381
STAFFETTA TIRRENICA 22382
STAFFORD 34780
STAFFORDSHIRE 54060
STAFFORDSHIRE 55590
STAHLECK 67210
STAHLECK 91750
STAKARA 60590
STAKARA 69960
STAKHANOVETS 04082
STAKHANOVETS KOTOV 35150
STAKHANOVETS PETRASH 35151
STAKHANOVETS YERMOLENKO 35152
STALAND 57813
STALAND 59863
STALO 2 46335
STAMATA II 41100
STAMATIOS G. EMBIRICOS 24800
STAMENIS 60592
STAMENIS 69962
STAMY 54565
STAMY 54965
STANISLAV KOSIOR 79377
STANISLAVSKIY 28490
STANISLAW DUBOIS 10578
STANISLAW DUBOIS 15348
STANYUKOVICH 12527

SWEDE SURPRISE	41010
SWEDE TONIA	28650
SWEE LEAN	71274
SWEE LEAN	61084
SWEET FAITH	02050
SWEET GRACE	21020
SWEET HOME	06210
SWEET ROSE	21090
SWELLMASTER	93430
SWIDNICA	14304
SWIERADOW ZDROJ	74142
SWIETLIK	87745
SWIFT	64860
SWIFT	91040
SWIFT SEAGULL	27320
SWIFTNES	61320
SWINOUJSIE	74141
SYBILLE	51626
SYBILLE	72689
SYDNEY EXPRESS	74410
SYDNEY TRADER	33060
SYKTYVKAR	15488
SYLVANIA	64014
SYLVANIA	68404
SYLVIA ALPHA	75540
SYLVIA BETA	75541
SYLVIA DELTA	75542
SYLVIA EPSILON	75543
SYLVIA GAMMA	75544
SYLVIA OMEGA	75545
SYLVO	47817
SYMMETRIA	39801
SYMON	21780
SYMPHONIC	62961
SYN PULKU	70540
SYNARISTIA	29451
SYNARISTIA	30260
SYNEBORIA	10650
SYNTOMIA	39800
SYRENKA	73651
SYRIA	33761
SYRIA	76763
SYRIA	80273
SYROS	12862
SYROS	33642
SYRVE	22878
SYRVE	34508
SYZRAN	02675
SZCZAWNICA	14305
SZEKESFEHERVAR	35483
SZYMANOWSKI	44512

T

'T - 1' type	42820
'T - 1' type	45140
'T - 2' type	41460
'T - 3' type	45040
T. AKASAKA	80040
T. BELLINGSGAUSEN	22187
T. G. SHAUGNESSY	68940
T.W. NELSON	14950
TA HANG	86132
TA LUANG	82895
TABALO	85600
TABARKA	42381
TABORA	50980
TABOU	41720
TABUK	49413
TABUK	50973
TACAMAR II	93561
TACAMAR III	84920
TACAMAR VI	26720
TACAMAR VII	81340
TACHIBANA	77592
TACHIRA	04370
TACHIRA	04430
'TACKLER' type	15750
TACKLER ARABIA	15750
TACKLER DOSINIA	15751
TACLOBAN CITY	33800
TACNA	29441
TACNA	30611
TACOMA CITY	46435
TACOMA MARU	29322
TACOMA MARU	30521
TACOMA MARU	31270
TACTIC	54034
TACUARI	29590
TADEUSZ OCIOSZYNSKI	14486
TADZHAKISTAN	02355
TADZHAKISTAN	35374
TADZHIKISTAN	12529
TAFELBERG	45010
TAGAMA	50981
TAGANROG	11896
TAGANROG	26991
TAGANROGSKIY ZALIV	61108
TAGELUS	54932
TAGELUS	77612
TAGIL	45591
TAI AN	86115
TAI AN	91715
TAI CHEUNG	63511
TAI CHEUNG	68281
TAI HU	60720
TAI JOHN	61370
TAI LAI	59550
TAI LAI	82580
TAI LIENG	57400
TAI NING	04990
TAI NING	86118
TAI NING	91716
TAI PING KOU	93314
TAI SHAN	32660
TAI SHING	62032
TAI SHOU	41270
TAI SHUN	86117
TAI SHUN	91717
TAI SUN	04991
TAI TUNG	55230
TAI WU SHAN	35662
TAI YANG No 11	00001
TAI YANG SHAN	35663
TAI YUAN	21160
TAI YUNG	28040
TAIBAH	00470
TAICHEE	40132
TAICHUNG 2	00312
TAIFUN	53419
TAIFUN	64949
TAIHO	49672
TAIHO	61520
TAIKAI MARU	48941
TAIKO	72151
TAILIAT	17792
TAILIAT	24962
TAINARON	35280
TAIPING	07391
TAIPOOSEK	30300
TAISEI MARU	11420
TAISEI MARU No 98	60970
TAISETU MARU	19681
TAISHAN	26710
TAITUNG	23160
TAIWAN MAHOGANY	61500
TAIWAN MAHOGANY	90660
TAIXING	13110
TAIYO MARU No 62	22770
TAIYO MARU No 63	22773
TAIYO MARU No 65	93410
TAIYO MARU No 66	93411
TAIYO MARU No 67	22774
TAIYO MARU No 67	34021
TAIYO MARU No 68	22775
TAIYO MARU No 68	34020
TAIYO MARU No 71	34022
TAIYO MARU No 71	22776
TAIYO MARU No 71	93400
TAIYO MARU No 72	22777
TAIYO MARU No 72	34023
TAIYO MARU No 73	34024
TAIYO MARU No 83	95070
TAIYO MARU No 83	94900
TAJ	05126
TAJ	59876
TAJAMI	73962
TAJIN	15752
TAJO	75271
TAKA	36282
TAKA	36482
TAKACHIHO MARU	32611
TAKACHIHO MARU	92621
TAKAMINE	77593
TAKAMIYA MARU	54441
TAKARA	77590
TAKARI I	52240
TAKARI I	76210
TAKARI II	52241
TAKARI II	76211
TAKARI III	52242
TAKARI III	76212
TAKARI III	52243
TAKARI IV	76213
TAKARI IV	52244
TAKARI V	76214
TAKARI V	52245
TAKARI VI	76215
TAKARI VI	52246
TAKARI VII	76216
TAKARI VII	52247
TAKARI VIII	76217
TAKARI VIII	61610
TAKASAGO MARU No 12	55520
TAKASAKA MARU	54850
TAKASE MARU	56370
TAKASE MARU	86094
TAKELI	89214
TAKHKUNA	27100
TAKIS ALEXAKOS	53143
TAKIS E	66073
TAKIS E	24702
TAKIS H	54852
TAKOAKA MARU	56372
TAKOAKA MARU	14710
TALAVERA	80830
TALETE	84750
TALETE	51351
TALISMAN	52701
TALISMAN	84011
TALISMAN	39978
TALLIN	02356
TALLINN	35375
TALLINN	41460
TALLULAH	03247
TALNIKI	03644
TALNIKI	38535
TALSY	45041
TALUGA	39030
TAMA MARU	43370
TAMA MARU	84760
TAMAMES	11466
TAMAN	12531
TAMAN	35332
TAMAN	02580
TAMARA	02950
TAMARA	07130
TAMARA	05380
TAMATAVE	28880
TAMBA	77594
TAMBO RIVER	84231
TAMBU EXPRESS	87141
TAMBU EXPRESS	28020
TAMIL ANNA	27060
TAMIL PERIYAR E.V.R.	38211
TAMMANNA	38761
TAMMANNA	53240
TAMMO	53430
TAMMO	72482
TAMPA	07592
TAMPERE	18040
TAMPOMAS	86232
TAMSALU	13717
TAMULA	13353
TAMURAEVERETT	31221
TAMY	61412
TANAFJORD	25272
TANAGREA	83760
TANAMBI	31620
TANG YIN	15673
TANGA	87672
TANGAROA	08510
TANGO EXPRESS	25952
TANGSHAN	18402
TANIA	22950
TANIA	29362
TANIA	30580
TANIA P	27620
TANIT	52462
TANJA HOLWERDA	41750
TANNHAUSER	73023
TANO RIVER	04831
TANTA	12163
TANTAL	11783
TANTALUS	62900
TANTALUS	68170
TANYA KARPINSKAYA	67024
TAOLIN	06036
TAQUIPE	65865
TARA	13860
TARA	36621
TARAGO	80212
TARAGONA	72635
TARAKAN	86544
TARAKAN MARU	61553
TARAKAN MARU	72043
TARAKLIYA	89235
TARAS SHEVCHENKO	01753
TARAS SHEVCHENKO	17526
TARASOVSK	03248
TARASOVSK	03645
TARBATNESS	00032
TARBELA	52680
TARCOOLA	72414
TAREK	16090
TAREK B	93170
TAREK B	94510
TARKHANKUT	70790
TARKHANSK	03239
TARKHANSK	03635
TARMO	23661
TARN	70100
TARNFORS	66420
TARNFORS	85670
TARNOBRZEG	73550
TARNOW	75770
TARONGA	83241
TARPOL	22339
TARPON	77251
TARPON SANTIAGO	60990
TARPON SEALANE	46111
TARPON SENTINEL	57382
TARRAGONA	77395
TARRING	36060
TARRING	41800
'TARROS' class	82760
TARROS CEDAR	82766
TARROS FIR	82764
TARROS GAGE	82765
TARROS PAXICON	82767
TARTU	86224
TARUSA	11720
TARUSA	34610
TASERGAL	22340
TASIA	57320
TASMAN REX	04740
TASMAN SEA	49090
TASMANIA	47814
TASSIA	68720
TASSILI	19500
TASSO	38132
TASSOS K	28514
TASSOS K	30324
TAT LEE No 2	84291
TAT LEE No 2	84441
TATA	89221
TATAI	51720
TATAI QUEEN	47300
TATAI SEA	47301
TATARIYA	02357
TATARIYA	35376
TATIANA	64080
TATIANGELA	42290
TATRY	70064
TATRY	55313
TATSUNO MARU	54230
TAUBE	77121
TAUBE	80031
TAURAGE	13714
TAUROS	62036
TAURUS	11714
TAURUS	22310
TAURUS	48632
TAURUS	51680
TAURUS II	88580
TAURUS III	74201
TAURUS III	79331
TAUYSK	00350
TAVDA	02284
TAVERNER	02101
TAVRIDA	11897
TAVRIYA	79441
TAVRIYA	85320
TAXIARCHIS	06527
TAXIARCHIS	42360
TAXILA	05240
TAXILA	15643
TAYABAS BAY	27000
TAYBOLA	17961
TAYFUN	21263
TAYGA	23866
TAYGA	24100
TAYGONOS	24097
TAYLAN KALKAVAN	42970
TAYMYR	11445
TAYSHEN	24101
TAYSHET	12530
TAZAR	23468
TBILISI	12290
TBILISI	39995
TCHAIKA	12315
'TD—15' type	91900
TEAKBANK	57561
TEAKWOOD	01191
TEBOSTAR	75031
TECALLI	66330
TECONA	53413
TECONA	64943
TECTUS	77677
TEDDE	71571
TEDDE	72541
TEES BAY	43380
TEGAL	29420
TEGAL	30640
TEGELERSAND	91540
TEIDE	39950
TEISTEN	19183
TEL - AVIV	57420
TELAMON	26980
TELANCA	15931
TELEGONOS	39830
TELEMAQUE	41120
TELEORMAN	47548
TELFAIR CHALLENGER	60127
TELFAIR LEADER	60172
TELFAIR PIONEER	60179
TELINDA	46241
TELINDA	83291
TELLHOLM	36281
TELLHOLM	36481
TELLO	07944
TELMANSK	86203
TEMA	61627
TEMA	69331
TEMANTA	46243
TEMI	25291
TEMIR	86204
TEMPESTA	40890
TEMRYUCHANIN	13713
TEMRYUK	85978
TEMURA	46242
TEMURA	83292
TENCHBANK	04674
TENES	75652
TENIERS	15333
TENNESSEE MARU	05763
TENO	45572
TEODOR NETTE	12532
TEODOR NETTE	90563
TER	10941
TERAAKA	09350
TERAAKA	33420
TEREK	94454
TEREKHOVSK	03241
TEREKHOVSK	03637
TERENGA	53417
TERENGA	64947
TERIBERKA	89265
TERMANCIA	75273
TERMEZ	86225
TERNEY	12533
TERNEY	31846
TERNOVSK	03242
TERNOVSK	03638
TERPANDROS	27270
TERRA	87791
TERRA NOVA	67201
TERVI	36090
TERVI	36220
TERZIA	46281
TESABA	46240
TESABA	38290
TESEY	11936
TESSIN	75334
TESTBANK	53561
TESTBANK	59721
TETA M	37690
TETE OLDENDORFF	74620
TETI N	60128
TETIEN	61861
TETSUZUI MARU	77503
TEUTA	74240
TEVEGA	31170
TEVEGA	33520
TEXACO ALASKA	44000
TEXACO AMSTERDAM	58250
TEXACO AMSTERDAM	63921
TEXACO ANACORTES	36770
TEXACO BALTIC	65731
TEXACO BERGEN	65730
TEXACO BOGOTA	65890
TEXACO BOGOTA	91600
TEXACO BOMBAY	69593
TEXACO BOMBAY	86433
TEXACO BRASIL	54437
TEXACO BRASIL	54817
TEXACO BRIGHTON	36771
TEXACO BRUSSELS	65670
TEXACO CARIBBEAN	54419
TEXACO CARIBBEAN	57879
TEXACO COLON	88800
TEXACO DENMARK	55740
TEXACO DENMARK	63810
TEXACO GEORGIA	36670
TEXACO GHENT	65671
TEXACO GLOUCESTER	36683
TEXACO GREENWICH	44740
TEXACO IDAHO	43700
TEXACO IRELAND	54435
TEXACO IRELAND	54815
TEXACO ITALIA	55709
TEXACO ITALIA	58279
TEXACO JAPAN	55710
TEXACO JAPAN	58280
TEXACO KANSAS	69595
TEXACO KANSAS	86435
TEXACO KENTUCKY	41180
TEXACO LIVERPOOL	43710
TEXACO LONDON	63131
TEXACO MAINE	36772
TEXACO MARYLAND	36671
TEXACO MASSACHUSETTS	36672
TEXACO MELBOURNE	69590
TEXACO MELBOURNE	86430
TEXACO MONTANA	36673
TEXACO NEDERLAND	54436
TEXACO NEDERLAND	54816
TEXACO NEW JERSEY	69596
TEXACO NEW JERSEY	86436
TEXACO NORGE	36681
TEXACO NORTH DAKOTA	41170
TEXACO NORWAY	55741
TEXACO NORWAY	63811
TEXACO OHIO	41181
TEXACO OSLO	36682
TEXACO OSLO	36991
TEXACO PANAMA	58251
TEXACO PANAMA	63920
TEXACO PENNSYLVANIA	41182
TEXACO PLYMOUTH	38400
TEXACO PLYMOUTH	43992
TEXACO PLYMOUTH	44742
TEXACO RHODE ISLAND	36674
TEXACO ROCHESTER	36660
TEXACO ROCHESTER	43690
TEXACO ROME	69594
TEXACO ROME	86434
TEXACO ROTTERDAM	65672
TEXACO SKANDINAVIA	36680
TEXACO SOUTH AMERICA	63132
TEXACO SOUTHAMPTON	44741
TEXACO STOCKHOLM	65732
TEXACO TEXAS	41183
TEXACO VENEZUELA	37240
TEXACO VERAGUAS	54420
TEXACO VERAGUAS	57880

U

V

VANESSA	75992
VANGUARD 8	61467
VANGUARD ALPHA	46511
VANINO	22881
VANINO	34511
VANJA	64299
VANKAREM	21620
VANKAREM	34109
VANTAGE	73940
VANYA KOVALYEV	67027
VARAZDIN	21510
VARDE	47341
VARENNA	68840
VARI	43470
VARJAKKA	47295
VARKIZA	37080
VARMA	23662
VARNA	10070
VARNA	36866
VARSHAVA	36845
VARSHUGA	17966
VARUNA ADHAR	26812
VARUNA KACHHAPI	06640
VARUNA YAMINI	40460
VARUNA YAMINI	44900
VARUNA YAN	40461
VARUNA YAN	44901
VARVARA	64501
VASALAND	93347
VASHA GORDIYENKO	67028
VASIL KOLAROV	01971
VASIL KOLAROV	01981
VASIL LEVSKY	48435
VASIL LEVSKY	49475
VASIL LEVSKY	49745
VASILIOS VII	85910
VASILIS	06980
VASILIY BLUKHER	93685
VASILIY BYELOKONYENKO	69316
VASILIY CHERNYSHYEV	45291
VASILIY DOKUCHAEV	28983
VASILIY FEDOSEYEV	21621
VASILIY FEDOSEYEV	34110
VASILIY FESENKOV	10746
VASILIY FOMIN	13721
VASILIY GOLOVNIN	10455
VASILIY GOLOVNIN	22188
VASILIY KACHALOV	28494
VASILIY KIKVIDZE	59900
VASILIY KIKVIDZE	67660
VASILIY KOSENKHOV	11618
VASILIY MUSINSKIY	54724
VASILIY MUSINSKIY	55294
VASILIY PEROV	76494
VASILIY POLENOV	76496
VASILIY POLENOV	76583
VASILIY POLENOV	79933
VASILIY PORIK	60624
VASILIY PORIK	62584
VASILIY POYARKHOV	22235
VASILIY PRONCHISHCHEV	22236
VASILIY PUTINTSEV	93689
VASILIY REVYAKIN	13723
VASILIY STRUVE	10747
VASILIY SURIKOV	76512
VASILIY YAN	50741
VASILY GOLOVKIN	11903
VASILY KLOCHKOV	48442
VASILY KLOCHKOV	49482
VASILY KLOCHKOV	49752
VASILY SHELGUNOV	03796
VASILY SHELGUNOV	04036
VASILY VERESCHCHAGIN	76522
VASILY VINEVITIN	12542
VASLUI	41316
VASSILAKIS	00180
VASSILIKI	26994
VASSILIOS I	85920
VASSILIOS BACOLITSAS	78330
VASSILIS	35850
VASSILIS	41640
VASSILIS IV	36062
VASSILIS IV	41802
VASSILIS KATSIKIS	28731
VASTANVIK	73861
VASYA ALEKSEEV	11446
VASYA KOROBKO	15533
VASYA KURKA	67030
VASYA SHISHKOVSKIY	15534
VASYA STABROVSKIY	67029
VATUTINO	08032
VAUCLUSE	24290
VAVY K	21640
VAYGACH	11619
VAYNDLO	83709
VEEJUMBO	07260
VEENDAM	19741
VEER VARUNA	54119
VEER VARUNA	54589
VEERHAVEN	76182
VEESTAR	24871
VEGA	11670
VEGA	12293
VEGA	27280
VEGA	51682
VEGA SEAL	63502
VEGA SEAL	68222
VEGALAND	93345
VEGAMAN	59001
VEGAMAN	75181
VEGESACK	03500
VEGESACK	04090
VEJEN	55412
VEJEN	78852
VELA	19490
VELA	54564
VELA	54964
VELA	64300
VELA	92334
VELA LUKA	91100
VELEBIT	26322
VELEKA	59903
VELEKA	67663
VELENJE	57440
VELET	87900
VELIKIY OKTYABR	59890
VELIKIY OKTYABR	67650
VELIKIY POCHIN	79372
VELIKIY USTYUG	07574
VELIKIYE LUKI	06060
VELIKIYE USTYUG	06791
VELIKO TIRNOVO	91702
VELIZH	06062
VELMA LYKES	05590
VELMA LYKES	14431
VELMA LYKES	14901
VELOX	76021
VELSK	17930
VENATOR	55821
VENATOR	56620
VENDEE	52470
VENERA IV	11904
VENEZIA	39601
VENEZUELA	03143
VENEZUELA MARU	07813
VENI	78271
VENICE	12080
VENTOUX	24533
VENTOUX	31291
VENTSPILS	36255
VENTSPILS	42805
VENTURA	66152
VENTURA	88590
VENTURE AMERICA	57890
VENTURE AMERICA	63060
VENTURE BRITAIN	59980
VENTURE CANADA	54383
VENTURE CANADA	63073
VENTURE ESPANA	67740
VENTURE EUROPE	54382
VENTURE EUROPE	63072
VENTURE INDEPENDENCE	57891
VENTURE INDEPENDENCE	63061
VENTURE ITALIA	65800
VENTURE ITALIA	74780
VENTURE ITALIA	74780
VENTURE LOUISIANA	38310
VENTURE LOUISIANA	44650
VENTURE OKLAHOMA	60701
VENTURE OKLAHOMA	69841
VENTURE SEA	40280
VENTURE TEXAS	38870
VENTUS	73994
VENUS	16351
VENUS	32920
VENUS	57841
VENUS DEL MAR	01521
VENUS DEL MAR	45612
VENUS DESTINY	83612
VENUS GLORY	83613
VENUS II	22580
VENUS II	23210
VENUTA	22792
VERA LEBEDYEVA	03794
VERA LEBEDYEVA	04034
VERA MUKINA	76590
VERA MUKINA	79940
VERACRUZ 1	09340
VERED	78072
VEREYA	06061
VERGA	32551
VERGA	33371
VERGE	53416
VERGE	64946
VERGINA	23800
VERGO	68812
VERGRAY	06469
VERGSTAR	06468
VERILA	75790
VERKHOVINA	11769
VERKHOVINA	34660
VERKHOYANSKLES	31840
VERKHOYANY	11328
VERNA	30335
VERRAZANO BRIDGE	04950
VERRAZANO BRIDGE	08610
VESLETS	75791
VESPASIAN	56412
VESPASIAN	67832
VESPASIAN	68432
VESTA	19491
VESTA	92490
VESTAL	18672
VESTANHAV	50812
VESTERALEN	17772
VESTLAND	59705
VESTLAND	61405
VESTRI	59170
VESTRI	72010
VESUVIO	51401
VESYEGONSK	66388
VETER	21264
VETERAN	85357
VETUGALES	24104
VIANA	37231
VIBIT	65552
VIBIT	85782
VICMAR STAR	29910
VICTOR BUGAEV	02277
VICTORIA	39662
VICTORIA	08310
VICTORIA	63426
VICTORIA	82050
VICTORIA	91450
VICTORIA 1	03163
VICTORIA CITY	46433
VICTORIA DE GIRON	31010
VICTORIA K	21531
VICTORIA U	25811
VICTORIA U	30961
VICTORIA VENTURE	65413
VICTORY	13060
VICTORY	17750
VICTORY	29630
VICTORY	52773
VICTORY	65600
VICTORY	75991
'VICTORY' type	13760
VICTORY FIVE	30221
VICTORY FIVE	30361
VICTORY KING	31110
VICTORY QUEEN	13912
VICTORY QUEEN	14822
VIDA	55381
VIDAL DE NEGREIROS	55541
VIDAL DE NEGREIROS	63341
VIDEN	75792
VIDNOYE	66389
VIET BAO	21680
VIETNAM HEROICO	16111
VIETNAM THUONG TIN I	24910
VIGNEMALE	60730
VIGNES	50123
VIIRELAID	75644
VIJAYA AVTAR	80790
VIJAYA JIWAN	91111
VIJAYA JYOTI	91110
VIJAYA VISANT	27951
VIKI-LAM	47620
VIKING	77560
VIKING 1	19291
VIKING I	23701
VIKING III	19431
VIKING IV	32400
VIKING IV	42010
VIKING VI	32881
VIKING SAGA	17010
VIKING SALLY	16880
VIKING SALLY	20680
VIKING SONG	17011
VIKING TRADER	44400
VIKING TRADER	93511
VIKING TRADER	93921
VIKING VALIANT	20221
VIKING VENTURER	20220
VIKING VICTORY	19430
VIKING VISCOUNT	20222
VIKING VOYAGER	20223
VIKINGLAND	93346
VIKTOR KHUDYAKOV	23488
VIKTOR KURNATOVSKIY	03795
VIKTOR KURNATOVSKIY	04035
VIKTOR LYAGIN	76510
VIKTOR VASTNETSOV	76492
VIKTORAS YATSENYAVICHUS	85361
VIKTORIO CODOVILLA	70594
VILI	85110
VILIS LACIS	93780
VILKOVO	86226
VILLA DE AGAETE	19270
VILLA DE BILBAO	24441
VILLABLANCA	49590
VILLABLANCA	49630
VILLAFRANCA	49591
VILLAFRANCA	49631
VILLAFRIA	49592
VILLAFRIA	49632
VILLANDRY	20280
VILLANGER	05613
VILLARRICA	80701
VILLARRICA	84481
VILLAVERDE	49593
VILLAVERDE	49633
VILLE D'ANVERS	48420
VILLE D'ANVERS	49460
VILLE D'ANVERS	49510
VILLE DE BORDEAUX	48421
VILLE DE BORDEAUX	46461
VILLE DE BORDEAUX	49511
VILLE DE BREST	49530
VILLE DE GENES	49441
VILLE DE MAHEBOURG	82650
VILLE DE MARSEILLE	51000
VILLE DE MARSEILLE	51180
VILLE DE NANTES	51001
VILLE DE NANTES	51181
VILLE DE REIMS	49531
VILLE DE ROTTERDAM	03841
VILLE DE ROUEN	49532
VILLE DE STRASBOURG	51002
VILLE DE STRASBOURG	51182
VILLE DE VALENCE	49440
VILLE D'ORIENT	75901
VILLIERS	51810
VILSANDI	86082
VILYANDY	86241
VILYANY	15491
VILYUY	22793
VILYUYLES	34106
VILYUYSK	36256
VILYUYSK	42806
VILYUYSK	70029
VIMINALE	24343
VINCITA	66151
VINDEMIA	87240
VINGAREN	01551
VINGASJO	66690
VINGAVAG	75030
VINJERAC	88821
VINNITSA	39988
VINTSAS MITSKYAVICHUS— KAPSUKAS	93756
VINTSAS MITSKYAVICHUS- KAPSUKAS	93846
VIOCA	84890
VIOLA	81956
VIOLA	91506
VIOLANDO	60284
VIOLANDO	68424
VIOLET	39281
VIRA	26860
VIRGEN DE AFRICA	08311
VIRGEN DEL CAMINO	18690
VIRGILIA	91838
VIRGILIA	91948
VIRGINIA	77931
VIRGINIA	79251
VIRGINIA LILY	64121
VIRGINIA LILY	68601
VIRGINIA M.	39510
VIRGINIA M	40400
VIRGINIA M	40520
VIRGINIA RHEA	61560
VIRGINIA STAR	64122
VIRGINIA STAR	68602
VIRGO	11645
VIRGO	02591
VIRGO	46421
VIRGO	65500
VIRPAZAR	27350
VIRTSU	89211
VIRTUOUS	62033
VIRTUS	06603
VISAYAS	21590
VISBY	16900
VISCAYA	64502
VISCOUNT	76020
VISEVICA	07982
VISHERA	94455
VISHNEVETS	79381
VISHNEVOGORSK	79406
VISHVA ABHA	45398
VISHVA ASHA	45397
VISHVA BANDHAN	15593
VISHVA BINDU	14911
VISHVA BINDU	15720
VISHVA CHETANA	14910
VISHVA CHETANA	15721
VISHVA JYOTI	25780
VISHVA KALYAN	10292
VISHVA KARUNA	15590
VISHVA KAUMUDI	04916
VISHVA KAUSHAL	71090
VISHVA KAUSHAL	71640
VISHVA KIRTI	25781
VISHVA MADHURI	15591
VISHVA MAHIMA	10291
VISHVA MAMTA	15592
VISHVA MANGAL	25782
VISHVA MAYA	25783
VISHVA MOHINI	04913
VISHVA NANDINI	04914
VISHVA NIDHI	25620
VISHVA PRABHA	10314
VISHVA PRATAP	10950
VISHVA PRATAP	15440
VISHVA PRATIBHA	91112
VISHVA PRAYAS	04915
VISHVA PREM	71091
VISHVA PREM	71641
VISHVA RAKSHA.	10293
VISHVA SANDESH	14912
VISHVA SANDESH	15722
VISHVA SEVA	30755
VISHVA SUDHA	40252
VISHVA TARANG	45396
VISHVA TIRTH	30756
VISHVA UMANG	45395
VISHVA VIBHUTI	10290
VISHVA VIJAY	71092
VISHVA VIJAY	71642
VISHVA VIKAS	14913
VISHVA VIKAS	15723
VISHVA VINAY	80791
VISHVA VIVEK	12070
VISKO REEFER	58220
VISKO REEFER	72930
VISPY	66957
VISPY	70997
VISSION BELINSKIY	14393
VISTAFJORD	08150
VISTAFJORD	09330
VISTEN	50250
VISURGIS	74430
VISVESVARAYA	59908
VISVESVARAYA	67668
VIT	37102
VITABULK	78861
VITACALM	10980
VITACARRIER	78220
VITALITY	48094
VITALIY BONIVUR	12543
VITALIY BONIVUR	85327
VITALIY KRUCHINA	69317
VITALIY PRIMAKOV	79432
VITASEA	26731
VITAUTAS MONTVILA	12544
VITAUTAS PUTNA	12545
VITIM	89263
VITINA	45950
VITKOVICE	75720
VITREA	65430
VITTORE CARPACCIO	01330
VITTORIO GARDELLA	39360
VITTORIO GARDELLA	42430
VITUS BERING	09383
VITUS BERING	10456
VITYA CHALENKO	15535
VITYA KHONENKO	15536
VITYA NOVITSKIY	67031
VITYA SITNITSA	15537
VIVA	77464
VIVARAIS	24534
VIVARAIS	31290
VIVITA	58912
VIVITA	65050
VIVITA	65302
VIYTNA	13719
VKP (b)	43243
VLADAS REKASHYUS	12546
VLADIMIR	40010
VLADIMIR ATLASOV	12547
VLADIMIR FAVORSKIY	76581
VLADIMIR FAVORSKIY	79931
VLADIMIR ILYCH	03071
VLADIMIR ILYCH	03663
VLADIMIR ILYCH	93380
VLADIMIR KAVRAYSKIY	23640
VLADIMIR KOLECHITSKY	59884
VLADIMIR KOROLENKO	14394
VLADIMIR MAYAKOVSKIY	14395
VLADIMIR MORDVINOV	54712
VLADIMIR MORDVINOV	55282
VLADIMIR NAZOR	16720
VLADIMIR RUSANOV	22237
VLADIMIR SUKHOTSKIY	35428
VLADIMIR TIMOFEYEV	54713
VLADIMIR TIMOFEYEV	55283
VLADIMIR ZATONSKIY	79417
VLADIVOSTOK	02074
VLADIVOSTOK	45216
VLADIVOSTOK	92380
VLAS CHUBAR	75352
VLAS NICHKOV	54719
VLAS NICHKOV	55289
VLORA	24880
VNUKOVO	11743
VNUKOVO	34633
VOCE	21430
VOCKERODE	79735
VOIKOV.	10690
VOIMA	02240
VOIMA	22260
VOLCAN DE YAIZA	94240
VOLCHANSK.	05410
VOLCHANSK	45124
VOLDEMAR AZIN	23511
VOLENDAM	19740
VOLERE	62864
VOLERE	67544
VOLFRAM	36915
VOLFRAM	43815
VOLGA	24109
VOLGA MARU	53681
VOLGA MARU	53811
VOLGA MARU	68531
VOLGOBALT	11317
VOLGODON	39972

VOLGOGRAD 15402
VOLGOLES 24030
'VOLGONEFT' type 90420
'VOLGONEFT' type 92030
VOLGONEFTGAROZ 44125
VOLINE 73660
VOLISSOS 01322
VOLKERFREUNDSCHAFT 10090
VOLKHOV 40014
VOLKHOVSTROY 11905
VOLNA. 02278
VOLNOMER 11906
VOLNOVAKHA 42961
VOLO 25573
VOLOCHAYEVSK 45217
VOLODARSKIY 10480
VOLODYA SCHERBATSEVICH 15538
VOLOGDA 45125
VOLOGDALES. 04190
VOLONTA 54012
VOLONTA 80772
VOLOPAS 12294
VOLTA RIVER 04832
VOLUNTAS 35710
VOLUNTAS 41420
VOLVULA 44771
VOLZHANIN 23573
VOLZHSK 08033
VOLZHSK 85322
VOMAR 57189
VOO SHEE 64200
VOO SHEE 68650
VOORSPELER 16200
VORKUTA 10457
VORKUTA 24110
VORMSI 88249
VORONEZH 06788
VORONEZH 07588
VOROSHILOVGRAD 13722
VOROSMARTY 48460
VOROSMARTY 49500
VOROSMARTY 49770
VORRAS 36882
VORRAS 84800
VORRAS 88790
VORTIGERN 19920
VOSGES 52471
VOSKHOD 11447
VOSKHOD 11595
VOSKHOD 12548
VOSRESENSK 24107
VOSTOCK 92150
VOSTOCK 93660
VOSTOK 2 11448
VOSTOK 5 11449
VOSTOK 6 11450
VOULLA 31990
VOUNITSO 14010
VOZNESENSK 79373
VRANCEA 25786
VRONTI 70402
VRONTI 79162
VROUWE ALIDA 74280
VSEVELOD KOCHETOV 67683
VSEVOLOD BERYEZKIN 39410
VSEVOLOD PUDOVKIN. 09974
VSEVOLOD PUDOVKIN. 11514
VSEVOLOD TIMONOV 89762
VSPOLOKH 11596
VUK KARADZIC 16721
VULCAN 82225
VULCANUS 65020
VULCANUS 67750
VULKAN 23517
VYACHESLAV DENISOV 50298
VYACHESLAV SHISHKOV 10458
VYANDRA 89208
VYATKALES 31847
VYAZMA 08032
VYBORG. 08030
VYBORGSKAYA STORONA 11621
VYBORGSKAYA STORONA 50291
VYCHEGDA 35333
VYCHEGDALES 24105
VYMPEL 11622
VYOVSK 34666
VYRU 15492
VYRU 89473
VYSHINSKII 17529
VYSHOGOROD 11776
VYSHOGOROD 34667
VYSOVSK 11775
VYTEGRA 11451
VYUGA 22239
VZMORYE 11907
VZMORYE 31852

W

W A MATHER 70152
W. C. VAN HORNE 80041
W. M. NEAL 72292
W. M. NEAL 77162
WABASH 92606
WABASH 93616
WACCAMAW 38923
WADDENZEE 51731
WADDENZEE 84041
WADEEVERETT 21412
WADHURST 91640
WADOWICE 79873
WAH FAI 23232
WAH FAT 49283
WAH HING 49282
WAH SHAN 18790
WAH SHUN 48000
WAHENO 23230
WAHRAN 58365
WAHYUNI 61643
WAIAL 55890
WAIAL 58690
WAIGANI EXPRESS 46230
WAITAKI 60020
WAJABULA 18210
WAKAGIKU MARU 51012
WAKAKUSA MARU 56632
WAKAKUSA MARU 57622
WAKAMATSU MARU 56630
WAKAMATSU MARU 57620
WAKAMIZU MARU 51011
WAKANAMI MARU 51010
WAKASHIO MARU 07870
WAKASHIO MARU 15040
WAKATAKE MARU 51013
WAKAUME MARU 51220
WAKAURA MARU 56631
WAKAURA MARU 57621
WAKAZURA MARU 63102
WAKAZURA MARU 68142
WAKENITZ 71943
WAKO MARU 54200
WAKO MARU 67840
WAKOLO 24131
WALCHAND 58406
WALCHAND 64566
WALEN 23460
WALKA MLODYCH 65851
WALKA MLODYCH 67691
WALKURE 56122
WALKURE 59772
WALLA-WALLA 18911
WALTER BARTH 23431
WALTER DEHMEL 10250
WALTER DEHMEL 12630
WALTER ULBRICHT 03703
WALTER ULBRICHT 03822
WAN FU 00670
WAN FU 30390
WANDA 55980
WANDEBORI 24132
WANDERER 46661
WANDERER 54240
WANDERER 77290
WANGKOLL 64146
WANGLI 64144
WANGSKOG 64145
WANGTING; 05374
WAPPEN VON HAMBURG 02020
WARBAH 51371
WARIN 75332
WARISANO 24133
WARNA 82260
WARNEMUNDE. 03690
WARNEMUNDE. 03810
WARNEMUNDE 17480
WARRIOR 46662
WARSAK 52682
WARSCHAU 45840
WARSZAWA 15087
WASA EXPRESS 19293
WASA EXPRESS 23702
WASHINGTON TRADER 37600
WASHINGTON TRADER 44310
WASSIMA 44770
WATAMPONE 24130
WATERLAND 05350
WATUDAMBO 24134
WAVE 41200
WAVERLEY 17440
WAWEL 19330
WAWEL 23711
WAYFARER 46660
WAYFARER 54241
WAYFARER 77291
WEI HAI 48001
WEIDA 01631
WEIKO 29700
WEIKUO 30831
WEILEE 36580
WEILEE 37370
WEILI 29701
WEILI 30821
WEIRBANK 24872
WEISSERITTZ 16071
WEJHEROWO 51262
WELFARE 74981
WELFARE 79211
WELL KEEPER 28091
WELL SPEEDER 44081
WELL SPEEDER 44391
WELL VOY No 1 25210
WELLAMO 20643
WELLINGTON STAR 03611
WELLPARK 48300
WELSH CITY 77001
WELSH CITY 79971
WELSH TROUBADOUR 06470
WEN DENG HAI 77480
WENA 66491
WENA 85931
WENDY 87701
WENDY WESTON 75875
WENJIANG 38337
WENJIANG 44697
WENSHUI; 01534
WERA JACOB 73025
WERBELLINSEE 46383
WERBELLINSEE 47083
WERNER KUBE 23432
WERNER SEELENBINDER. 04233
WERRA EXPRESS 79300
WESER 73903
WESER BROKER 82040
WESER EXPRESS 73510
WESERMUNDE 03501
WESERMUNDE 04091
WESERTAL 33202
WEST BAY 71909
WEST CLIFF 71910
WEST END 71912
WEST JINORIWON 58520
WEST JINORIWON 60450
WEST JUNORI 77672
WEST REEF 71911
WEST RIVER 56900
WEST SUNORI 83220
WEST WONORI 51639
WESTBON 62433
WESTERENCE 86800
WESTERMOOR 49870
WESTERN ARCTIC 23850
WESTERN EUROPE 92480
WESTERN LION 59943
WESTERN LION 67933
WESTERN NAV 26671
WESTERN NAV 31731
WESTERN SUN 38542
WESTERN SUN 44812
WESTERPLATTE 10352
WESTFALEN 63427
WESTFALIA 04656
WESTFJORD 85470
WESTGATE 22990
WESTGATE 45390
WESTLAND 04788
WESTRIDGE 41830
WESTWARD HO 20920
WESTWARD VENTURE 08345
WESTWIND 53382
WESTWIND 90742
WEYROC 82680
WHEELSMAN 88860
WHITE BEACH 37500
WHITE BEACH 44340
WHITE JASMIN 60032
WHITE JASMIN 68362
WHITE JASMINE 71972
WHITE NILE 49350
WHITE RIVER 35596
WHITE RIVER 36496
WHITE SEA 26877
WHITE SHARK 24950
WHITEGATE 75930
WHITEGATE 88630
WHITEHALL 29220
WHITEHEAD 51340
WIBKE 74422
WIBKE 88092
WICHITA 92600
WICHITA 93610
WICKLOW 72711
WIDAR 73260
WIELAND 73723
WIELICZKA 03236
WIELICZKA 03629
WIELUN 50470
WIEN 73024
WIIDSWAL 52162
WIKING 73901
WIKING BULKER 77132
WILA 73652
WILCON 1 50560
WILCON V 82332
WILD CORMORANT 06220
WILD CORMORANT 07450
WILD CURLEW 06221
WILD CURLEW 07451
WILD FULMAR 34213
WILD GANNET 11150
WILD GREBE 11151
WILD MALLARD 04361
WILD MARLIN 04360
WILDRAKE 17340
WILHELM FLORIN. 04230
WILHELM PIECK 62683
WILHELMINA 01630
WILHELMINA V 88303
WILHELMINE ESSBERGER 63428
WILHELMSHAVEN 19210
WILKEN 91412
WILKS 87291
WILLI BREDEL 17981
WILLIAM 46094
WILLIAM 83264
WILLIAM DAMPIER 70465
WILLIAM FOSTER 03062
WILLIAM FOSTER 03653
WILLIAM HOOPER 01055
WILLIAM J. EVERARD 89843
WILLIAM LARIMER MELLON 65450
WILLIAM R ADAMS 46820
WILLIAM R. GRACE 70650
WILLIAM SHAKESPEARE 59741
WILLINE TOYO 49181
WILLOW 94851
WILLOWBANK 02880
WILLY SMITS 88113
WILMINGTON 75810
WILNORA 63402
WILRON 91924
WILTSHIRE 55340
WILTSHIRE 57670
WIND EAGLE 64301
WIND ENTERPRISE 64302
WIND ESCORT 64303
WINDFROST 81692
WINDFROST 87052
WINDRATI 36240
WINDROVER 82809
WINDROVER 92099
WINDSOR LION 58231
WINETA 59692
WINETA 81352
WINHO 21860
WINNETOU 67111
WINNI HELLESKOV 64858
WINNI HELLESKOV 91038
WINSTON 59352
WINSTON 87010
WINSTON CHURCHILL 18663
WINSTON CHURCHILL 20570
WINSUM 57143
WINTER MOON 02931
WINTER SEA 02932
WINTER STAR 02933
WINTER SUN 02934
WINTER WATER 02930
WINTER WAVE 02935
WIS 87290
WISHFORD 30281
WISLICA 14306
WISMAR 34960
WISTARIA CORAL 60211
WISTARIA PEARL 60212
WISTERIA 73031
WITSHUTTLE 41622
WITTENBERG 34963
WITTSAND 59511
WITTSAND 59821
WLADYSLAW BRONIEWSKI 15301
WLADYSLAW JAGIELLO 14914
WLADYSLAW JAGIELLO 15724
WLADYSLAW LOKIETEK 14915
WLADYSLAW LOKIETEK 15725
WLADYSLAW ORKAN 06090
WLADYSLAW ORKAN 14800
WLADYSLAWOWO. 04343
WLADYSLAWOWO. 04404
WLADYSLAWOWO 04404
WLOCZNIK 11790
WOLFE 08851
WOLFEN 38732
WOLFEN 44871
WOLGAST 83705
WOLIN 34372
WOLRAAD WOLTEMADE 22171
WOO YANG 71240
WOOLGAR 86114
WOOLGAR 91714
WOOSTER KING 61670
WORLD ACHILLES II 46116
WORLD ADMIRAL 55462
WORLD ADMIRAL 62782
WORLD AEGEUS 46117
WORLD AGAMEMNON 46104
WORLD AJAX 46103
WORLD AMBASSADOR 55463
WORLD AMBASSADOR 62783
WORLD AMPHION 46113
WORLD APOLLO 46101
WORLD ARES 46102
WORLD ARETUS 46105
WORLD ARGUS 46100
WORLD AZALEA 54031
WORLD BARONESS 67980
WORLD BERMUDA 54400
WORLD BERMUDA 63080
WORLD BRIGADIER 54030
WORLD CANADA 54384
WORLD CANADA 63074
WORLD CANDOUR 61214
WORLD CHALLENGER 68131
WORLD CHALLENGER 71441
WORLD CHIEF 68900
WORLD CITY 54502
WORLD COMET 54032
WORLD CONCORD 53941
WORLD CREATION 53942
WORLD CROWN 59942
WORLD CROWN 67932
WORLD DIPLOMAT 63363
WORLD DISCOVERER 32850
WORLD DUCHESS 69618
WORLD DUKE 54360
WORLD DUKE 62970
WORLD EMPIRE 54033
WORLD EMPIRE 54860
WORLD EMPIRE 68070
WORLD ENDEAVOUR 56353
WORLD ENDEAVOUR 68053
WORLD ERA 62902
WORLD ERA 68172
WORLD EULOGY 58932
WORLD FIELD 69270
WORLD FINANCE 48990
WORLD GALA 64530
WORLD GENERAL 69619
WORLD GUARD 68130
WORLD GUARD 71440
WORLD HAPPINESS 68110
WORLD HERCULES 61022
WORLD HERCULES 71182
WORLD HORIZON 68111
WORLD KINDNESS 68910
WORLD KNOWLEDGE 68911
WORLD LADY 62903
WORLD LADY 68173
WORLD MARINE 46106
WORLD MEDAL 77875
WORLD MITSUBISHI 54851
WORLD MITSUBISHI 56371
WORLD NATURE 79132
WORLD NAUTILUS 79131
WORLD NAVIGATOR 54980
WORLD NAVIGATOR 55140
WORLD NEGOTIATOR 54981
WORLD NEGOTIATOR 55141
WORLD NEIGHBOUR 79130
WORLD NEWS 54982
WORLD NEWS 55142
WORLD NOBILITY 54983
WORLD NOBILITY 55143
WORLD NOMAD 54984
WORLD NOMAD 55144
WORLD PHILIPPINES 54036
WORLD PRESTIGE 67992
WORLD PROBITY 61215
WORLD PROGRESS 54501
WORLD PROMISE 70160
WORLD PROTECTOR 70161
WORLD PROVIDER 70162
WORLD RECOVERY 63440
WORLD RENAISSANCE 23380
WORLD RUBY 54652
WORLD RUBY 55073
WORLD SAGA 56354
WORLD SAGA 68054
WORLD SCHOLAR 63193
WORLD SCHOLAR 67563
WORLD SCORE 63192
WORLD SCORE 67562
WORLD SOVEREIGN 54037
WORLD SPLENDOUR 63112
WORLD SUN 64319
WORLD SYMPHONY 64295
WORLD TRUTH 63872
WORLD TRUTH 67602
WORLD UNICORN 58234
WORLD VANGUARD 54963
WORLD VANGUARD 54563
WORLD VICTORIA 69617
WORLD VIGOUR 53943
WORLD WOOD 48960
WORTHY 36063
WORTHY 41803
WOTAN 45601
WOTAN 73911
WOTONI 58494
WOTONI 84914
WU CHANG 03173
WU JIANG 60245
WU SHENG HAI 46071
WU TAI SHAN 03132
WU TAI SHAN 03342
WU XING 41610
WU YI SHAN 58612
WU YI SHAN 81012
WU YI SHAN 90512
WU ZHI SHAN 79851
WUDU 30131
WUPPERTAL 23580
WUPPERTAL 33203
WUSTROW 83702
WUXI 33660
WYOMING 05094
WYSPIANSKI 06891

WYSZKOW 50462
WYUNA 20890

X

XANADU 20740
XANTHENCE 86801
'XD' type 03870
XI JIANG 63710
XIANG CHENG 47040
XIANG SHAN 12750
XIANG YIN 29950
XIAO SHI KOU 93315
XIN AN 41328
XIN AN JIANG 58592
XIN AN JIANG 60472
XIN HUA 18020
XINCHANG 30420
XINDU 46246
XINDU 83296
XINFENG 05395
XINFENG 05832
XING CHENG. 04910
XING HU 19340
XING HUA 29551
XING HUO 00400
XING KONG 13550
XING MING 28250
XINGNING 10582
XINGNING 15352
XIONG ER SHAN 64811
XIONG YUE CHENG 06811
xiushan 10591
XIUSHAN 13392
XUAN CHENG 60244
XUAN HUA 30060
XUAN HUA 31020
XUCHANG 00856
XI FESTIVAL 48456
XI FESTIVAL 49496
XI FESTIVAL 49766
XIII CONGRESO 58194
XV SYEZD PROFSOYUZOV 23522
XVI SYEZD VLKSM 79409
XVI SZEZD PROFSOYUZOV 11784
XVII SEYEZD VLKSM 11785
XVII SYEZD VLKSM 79420
XVIII SYEZD VLKSM 79428
XX ANIVERSARIO 16110
XXIV SYEZD KPSS 79413
XXV SYEZD KPSS 58516
XXV SYEZD KPSS 71826

Y

YA CHENG 64814
YAAN ANVELT 03797
YAAN ANVELT 04037
YACU CASPI 34897
YACU RUNA 27402
YACU TAITO 25871
YACU WASI 81500
YAETT 1 61649
YAFFA 72353
YAFFA 77153
YAGOTIN 49101
YAGUAR 22160
YAKAN 88130
YAKHROMA 61840
YAKOV BONDARENKO 48446
YAKOV BONDARENKO 49486
YAKOV BONDARENKO 49756
YAKOV GAKKEL 39412
YAKOV REZNICHENKO 50299
YAKOV SVERDLOV 28984
YAKUB KOLAS 50733
YAKUMOKAWA MARU 77811
YAKUTSKLES 31848
YALTA 12295
YAMAHIDE MARU 54890
YAMAHIRO MARU 73369
YAMAL 11452
YAMASHIN MARU 08591
YAMASHIN MARU 09731
YAMATO 73270
YAMATO 77770
YAMATO MARU 61616
YAMATO MARU 95110
YAMAUME MARU No 2 86160
YAMAZURA MARU 63103
YAMAZURA MARU 68143
YAMPOL 89910
YAMPOL 90220
YAN CHENG 81647
YAN HE 46360
YAN SHAN 52830
YAN SHAN 52940
YANA 31854
YANA 02110
YANA 90190
YANA 35170
YANBU 64110
YANG CHUN 56310
YANG QUAN 02572
YANG ZONG HAI 61814
YANGI-YUL 50779
YANGLIN 06034
YANGOS 41220
YANGTING 05375
YANIS LENTSMANIS 10729
YANIS RAYNIS. 10720
YANKA KUPALA 50738
YANKEE CLIPPER 73950
YANMAR 40342
YANMAR 41130
YANMAR 44940
YANNIS 31230
YANNIS 51091
YANNIS 51481
YANNIS HALCOUSSIS 60132
YANNIS K 36980
YANTAR 12549
YANTARNIY BEREG 62691
YANTARNYY 07557
YANTARNYY 45120
YANXILAS 69760
YAOHUA 09480
YARA 14130
YARACUY 13813
YARENSK 86190
YARGORA 89236
YARKIY LUCH 71673
YARONIMAS UBORYAVICHUS 12550
YAROSLAVL 12327
YAROSLAVL 45220
YARTSEVO 78132
YARTSYEVO 89912
YARTSYEVO 90222
YASENYEVO 49100
YASHIMA MARU 08631
YASHIMA MARU 09741
YASHMA 12551
YASINOVATYA 78130
YASNOGORSK 89911
YASNOGORSK 90221
YASNOYE 46620
YAT HING 00221
YAT LEE 24640
YAT SHING 24641
YAVOROV 78131
YEGORLIK 70783
YEH YUNG 05611
YEKATERINA BELASHOVA 76591
YEKATERINA BELASHOVA 79941
YELENE STASOVA 04038
YELIZOVO 89512
YELNYA 44623
YELNYA 70780
YELSK 44620
YEMANJA 58371
YEMANJA 64351
YEMELYAN PUGACHEV 77079
YEMELYAN YAROSLAVSKIY. 03801
YEMELYAN YAROSLAVSKIY 04041
YEMEN 33731
YENISEY 25061
YENISEY 84351
YENISEYSK 25565
YENISEYSK 70032
YEOTA E. 58790
YEREWA 18601
YEREWA 22540
YERMAK 20870
YERUPAJA 57351
YESILADA 19160
YESSENTUKI 44624
YEVGENIY LEBEDYEV 45292
YEVPATORIYE 12296
YI 06970
YI CHI 28857
YI NING HAI 56691
YI SHANG 25161
YI XING 10273
YI XING 15183
YIANNIS 74600
YIANNIS DIMAKIS 41890
YICHANG 03172
YICHUN 12721
YIDU 30421
YIN CHUAN 05102
YIN HU 37640
YIN SHAN HAI 46722
YING GE HAI 49130
YING SHAN 13383
YOKO MARU 54800
YOKO MARU 68030
YONA B 69310
YONAVA 13726
YONG CHENG 81380
YONG CHUN 12720
YONG DING 29552
YONG FENG HAI 56992
YONG KANG 26060
YONG KANG 31740
YONG MING 28221
YONG MING 31922
YONGCHANG 03174
YONGMEN 05394
YONGNING. 10583
YONGNING 15353
YORKSAND 59512
YORKSAND 59822
YORKSHIRE 58343
YORKSHIRE 63993
YORKTOWN 58583
YOTEI MARU 19680
YOU ARE MY SUNSHINE 73200
YOU ARE MY SUNSHINE 76990
YOU YI 25830
YOUHAO 38840
YOUNG AMERICA 01493
YOUNG SPLENDOR 92222
YOUNG SPORTSMAN 51100
YOUNG STATESMAN 61001
YOUSSEF B 37210
YOUTH GIANT 27090
YPAPANTI 66021
YU HU 58891
YU HUA 16150
YU JIANG 45941
YU KONG 60520
YU M SHOKALSKIY 23771
YU QUAN SHAN 00720
YU TSAO 64203
YU TSAO 68653
YUBILEY OKTYABRYA 12551
YUEN CHAU 29240
YUG 23392
YUG 23867
YUGANSK 70784
YUGLA 36920
YUGLA 43820
YUHAI 26062
YUHENG 27693
YUKHAN SMUUL 11908
YUKON 38422
YULIAN MARKHLEVSKIY 93734
YULIAN MARKHLEVSKIY 93824
YULIMISTE 11909
YULIN 06035
YULIUS FUCHIK 00240
YULIUS FUCHIK 14975
YULIYA ZHEMAYTE 10436
YULSAN POSEIDON 58184
YULYUS YANONIS 87003
YUMA 67112
YUMEN 06065
YUN CHENG 47044
YUN HAI 57010
YUN TAI SHAN 51087
YUNAM No 9 72063
YUNG LEE 61570
YUNGLUTATION 00290
YUNOST 12552
YUNYY LENINETS 01577
YUNYY PARTIZAN 67032
YUOZAS GARYALIS 12553
YUOZAS VAREYKIS 12554
YUQUAN 30333
YURBARKAS 13725
YURIY DOLGORUKIY 24390
YURIY GAGARIN 01578
YURIY KOSTIKOV 11636
YURIY KOTSYUBINSKY 79443
YURIY LISYANSKIY 22238
YURIY MALAKHOV 11910
YURIY SAVINOV 54729
YURIY SAVINOV 55299
YURIY SMIRNOV 78062
YURMALA 13724
YURMALA 63640
YURNIEKS 11911
YURYUZAN 89475
YUSHAN 10592
YUSHO 63610
YUSHO 67580
YUTA BONDAROVSKAYA 15539
YUTING 05376
YUVALI 26350
YUYO MARU No 2 70490
YUZBASI TOLUNAY 89520
YUZHINO-SAKHALINSK 93842
YUZHINO—SAKHALINSK 93752
YUZHNO-SAKHALINSK 86181
YUZHNOMORSK 11912
YUZHNYY KREST 12297
YZONA 26740

Z

ZABAT DOS 79880
ZABAT UNO 79881
ZABAYKALSK 24111
ZABAYKALYE. 09211
ZABAYKALYE 45128
ZACAPA 81560
ZACCAR 66622
ZACCAR 76242
ZACHARIA T 60540
ZACHARIAS Z 17880
ZACHAROULA 86150
ZADAR 10925
ZADONSK 62463
ZADONSK 78544
ZADONSK 80134
ZADORIE 17971
ZAGLEBIE DABROWSKIE 75730
ZAGLEBIE DABROWSKIE 88380
ZAGLEBIE MIEDZIOWE 62469
ZAGLEBIE MIEDZIOWE 78549
ZAGLEBIE MIEDZIOWE 80139
ZAGLEBIE SIARKOWE 73553
ZAGORIANA 17957
ZAGORSKIY 17972
ZAGREB 33583
'ZAGREB' type 07890
ZAHARI STOIANOV 47569
ZAISAN 34512
ZAK 26490
ZAKARPATYE 62462
ZAKARPATYE 78543
ZAKARPATYE 80133
ZAKAVKAZYE 11323
ZAKHARIY PALIASHVILI 59898
ZAKHARIY PALIASHVILI 67558
ZAKHAROVO 17963
ZAKIR HUSSAIN 68091
ZAKOPANE 81640
ZAKYNTHOS 38770
ZALAU 49492
ZALAU 49762
ZALAU 48452
ZALESOVO 17955
ZAMBESI 61015
ZAMBESI 71175
ZAMBEZE 01060
ZAMBOANGA 30940
ZAMBOANGA 51034
ZAMBOANGA 82536
ZAMBOANGA CITY 81060
ZAMBROW 81643
ZAMBRZE 81642
ZAMENHOF 45031
ZAMENHOF 41611
ZAMIRA 21472
ZAMOSC 81641
ZAMZAM 22410
ZANET 14401
ZANET 85270
ZANGELAN 50787
ZANNIS MICHALOS 77887
ZANOOBIA 63683
ZAO MARU 94921
ZAPADNAYA DVINA 25566
ZAPATA COURIER 58441
ZAPATA COURIER 63971
ZAPATA PATRIOT 58440
ZAPATA PATRIOT 63970
ZAPATA RANGER 58442
ZAPATA RANGER 63972
ZAPATA ROVER 58443
ZAPATA ROVER 63973
ZAPOLYARNYY. 09387
ZAPOLYARNYY 15493
ZAPOLYARYA 34647
ZAPOROZHYE 62461
ZAPOROZHYE 78542
ZAPOROZHYE 80132
ZARAYSK 12298
ZARECHENSK 62464
ZARECHENSK 78540
ZARECHENSK 80130
ZARKA 67493
ZARNITSA 11597
ZARNITSA 23391
ZARNITZA 17320
ZARZIS 86601
ZASHCHITNIK ZAPOLYARYA 34646
ZASHCHITNIK ZAPOLYARYA 11756
ZASLONOVO 17958
ZAVOLZHSK 12351
ZAVOLZHYE 11329
ZAVYETY ILYICHA 60689
ZAVYETY ILYICHA 90728
ZAWICHOST 81644
ZAWIERCIE 81645
ZAWRAT 68920
ZAYARSK 86089
ZEA BEACH 13390
ZEA SILVER 30020
ZEA SKY 28121
ZEA SKY 28561
ZEA STAR 07760
ZEA STAR 07816
ZEEBRUGGE 01061
ZEEBRUGGE 72350
ZEEBRUGGE 77150
ZEENA 26811
ZEFIR 13729
ZEIDA 66930
ZEIDA 70980
ZEITZ 38200
ZEJTUN 49960
ZEJTUN 51820
ZELANDE 01062
ZELENETS 11635
ZELENOBORSK 09373
ZELENOGORSK 21600
ZELENOGRAD 90154
ZELEZNOGORSK 11745
ZELEZNOGORSK 34635
ZEMLYA KOLSKAYA 93763
ZEMUN 21512
ZENA 27771
ZENAIDE A 39931
ZENAIDE A 40571
ZENIT 34710
ZENITH 87540
ZENTA OZOLA 10731
ZEPHIR 1 91071
ZEPHIR I 90531
ZERALDA 32631
ZERAVNA 83728
ZERHOUN 66931
ZERHOUN 70981
ZEROMSKI 24561
ZETA 10997
ZEULENRODA 84944
ZEULENRODA 90604
ZEUNG SAN 72172
ZEUS 03102
ZEUS 40131
ZEYA 02283
ZEYA 86236
ZEYALES. 11502
ZGORZELEC 50467
ZHALGIRIS 70785
ZHAN DOU 13 00961
ZHAN DOU 14 33700
ZHAN DOU 16 33690
ZHAN DOU 27 01030
ZHAN DOU No 28 25020
ZHAN DOU 30 01031
ZHAN DOU 44 28065
ZHAN DOU 45 28066
ZHAN DOU 47 01040
ZHAN DOU 48 00830
ZHAN DOU No 49 25540
ZHAN DOU 50 01032
ZHAN DOU 51 00960
ZHAN DOU 52 01033
ZHAN DOU 53 00940
ZHAN DOU 55 00700
ZHAN DOU No 65 25541
ZHAN DOU No 66 25542
ZHAN DOU No 71 25040
ZHAN DOU No 72 25050
ZHAN DOU 75 00780
ZHAN DOU 76 00962
ZHAN DOU 77 25520
ZHAN DOU 79 00963
ZHAO YANG HAI 46073
ZHDANOV 39961
ZHDANOVSKIY KOMSOMOLETS 01404
ZHDANOVSKIY KOMSOMOLETS 01664
ZHELEZNOVODSK 11913
ZHEMAYTIYA 11914
ZHEMCHUYNYY BEREG 62695
ZHEN HAI 61884
ZHEN RONG HAI 46340
ZHEN ZHU QUAN 01200
ZHENJIANG 35030
ZHI JIANG KOU 93313
ZHIGANSK 44126
ZHIGULEVSK. 12353
ZHIHAI 57000
ZHITOMIR 39989
ZHONG TIAO SHAN 58590
ZHONG TIAO SHAN 60470
ZHU HAI 61885
ZHUKOVSKIY 12372
ZIAD 42540
ZIEMIA BIALOSTOCKA 79644
ZIEMIA BYDGOSKA 74660
ZIEMIA BYDGOSKA 78140
ZIEMIA GDANSKA 80633
ZIEMIA KIELECKA 73140
ZIEMIA KOSZALINSKA 73141
ZIEMIA KRAKOWSKA 62467
ZIEMIA KRAKOWSKA 78547
ZIEMIA KRAKOWSKA 80137
ZIEMIA LUBELSKA 62468
ZIEMIA LUBELSKA 78548
ZIEMIA LUBELSKA 80138
ZIEMIA LUBUSKA 80634
ZIEMIA MAZOWIECKA 74661
ZIEMIA MAZOWIECKA 78141
ZIEMIA OLSZTYNSKA 79645
ZIEMIA OPOLSKI 79646
ZIEMIA SZCZECINSKA 80635
ZIEMIA WIELKOPOLSKA 80636
ZIGMAS ANGARETIS 12555
ZIKONIYA 11967
ZIM BANGKOK 82769
ZIM CALIFORNIA 08801
ZIM GENOVA 08802
ZIM HAIFA 08803
ZIM HONG KONG 74451
ZIM MANILA 82768
ZIM MONTREAL 74450
ZIM NEW YORK 08804
ZIM NORTHLAND 73722

ZIM TOKYO	08805
ZINA PORTNOVA	15540
ZINGARA	84930
ZINI	61023
ZINI	71183
ZINNIA	56760
ZINNOWITZ	83609
ZIRIA	61062
ZITMAR	88781
ZIWAY HAIQ	41621
ZIYA KALKAVAN II	26051
ZLANTNI PIASATZI	76530
ZLARIN	01472
ZLATOGRAD	83731
ZLATOUST	12352
ZLATOUST	62465
ZLATOUST	78545
ZLATOUST	80135
ZNA	02282
ZNA	35182
ZNAMYA KERCHIL	13728
ZNAMYA OKTYABRYA	78065
ZNAMYA POBEDY	11746
ZNAMYA POBEDY	34636
ZODCHIY	11633
ZODIAC	23868
ZOE	68732
ZOE II	23900
ZOELLA LYKES	00070
ZOLOTITZA.	11453
ZOLOTOY KOLOS	11915
ZOLOTOY ROG	36257
ZOLOTOY ROG	42807
ZOLOTOY ROG	76513
ZORINSK	62466
ZORINSK	78546
ZORINSK	80136
ZOYA KOSMODEMYANSKAYA	73290
ZOZARA	78531
ZSCHOPAU	52071
ZSCHOPAU	75170
ZUBARYEVO	17973
ZUBOVO	17965
ZUGDIDI	70786
ZUHAIR	42730
ZUIDER SEA	29244
ZUIDERKRUIS	35240
ZUIDWAL	59626
ZUIHO MARU	63104
ZUIHO MARU	68144
ZUIYO MARU	76721
ZUIYO MARU No 2	94902
ZUIYO MARU No 2	95072
ZULAIHA	29840
ZULAWY	59690
ZULAWY	81350
ZUND	11954
ZUNHUA	29550
ZUROW	50449
ZUROW	52010
ZUSSOW	50450
ZUSSOW	52011
ZVAYGZNE	84330
ZVAYGZNE	87950
ZVENIGOROD	62460
ZVENIGOROD	78541
ZVENIGOROD	80131
ZVEZDA	13727
ZVEZDA	23390
ZVEZDA KRIMA	11955
ZVIR.	07983
ZVYAGIMO	17960
ZVYEROBOY	17950
ZVYERYEVO	17964
ZWICKAU	43110
ZWICKAU	36302
ZWICKAU	36462
ZWIJNDRECHT	72432
ZYEMCHUSNYY	11937
ZYGMUNT AUGUST	14916
ZYGMUNT AUGUST	15726
ZYGMUNT III WAZA	14918
ZYGMUNT III WAZA	15728
ZYGMUNT STARY	14917
ZYGMUNT STARY	15727
ZYGOS	26640
ZYGOS	61193
ZYKOVO	17959
ZYRARDOW.	10759
ZYWIEC	82264

NUMERICAL SECTION

1 CONGRESO DEL PARTIDO	06610
5 DE SEPTIEMBRE	88485
7 DE NOVIEMBRE	59905
7 DE NOVIEMBRE	67665
9 DE ABRIL	59904
9 DE ABRIL	67664
9 MAYA 1945 GODA	79421
13 DE DICIEMBRE	43450
13 DE MARZO	12794
14 JULY	85080
14 RAMADAN	85081
15 SYEZD VLKSM	12427
16 BC5 type	56650
16 BC5 type	62210
22 type	58830
22 type	60570
26 BC-5 type	46350
26 BC-5 type	46920
27 MAYIS	34582
30 DE NOVIEMBRE	48455
30 DE NOVIEMBRE	49495
30 DE NOVIEMBRE	49765
30 LET POBEDY	34637
30 LETIYE POBEDY	11747
30 LETIYE POBEDY	01665
30 LETYE POBEDY	01405
36 L type	49030
36 L type	53100
36 L type	53330
36 L type	71840
36 L type	71980
36 L type	71990
36 L type	72000
36 L type	72110
36 L type	80850
36 L type	80890
36 L type	82890
50 LET OKTYABRYA	93845
50 LET OKTYABRYA	93755
50 LET PIONERII	79414
50 LET S.S.S.R.	79386
50 LET SOVIET SCVIETSKOY	05625
50 LET SOVIETSKOY UKRAINY	14455
50 LET SOVIETSKOY VLASTI	79368
50 LET SSSR	71820
50 LET SSSR	45290
50 LET VLKSM	12426
50 LET VLKSM	35334
50 LET VLKSM	79405
50 LETIYE KOMSOMOLA	01100
50 LETIYE KOMSOMOLA	01180
50 LETIYE OKTYABRYA	36878
50 LETIYE SOVETSKOY GRUZII	60620
50 LETIYE SOVETSKOY GRUZII	62580
60 LET OKTYABRYA	93383
60 LET VELIKOGO OKTYABR	79439
60 LET VLKSM	79440
613 B type	91020
750 LETIYE GORODA GORKOGO	79412

APPENDIX

ADDITIONAL DRAWINGS SECTION

The numbers represent the exact position that the drawing will take between the entries in the main drawing sections.

Profile 2

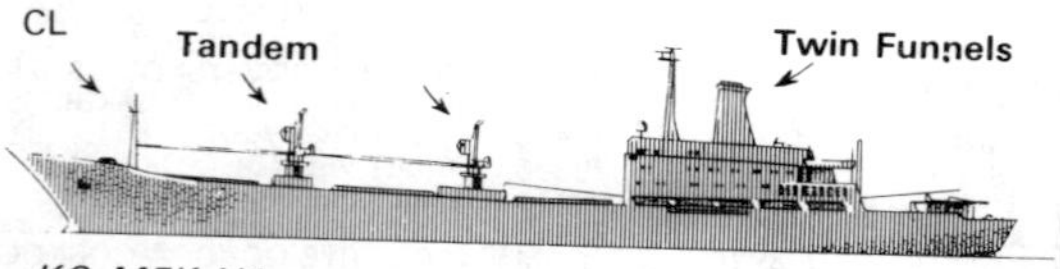

KC_2MFK H1
03545 GEESTBAY. Br/Br 1981; R/CP; 7700; 159.07 × 8.82 (521.8 × 28.94); M; 20; Sister **03546 GEESTPORT** (Br).

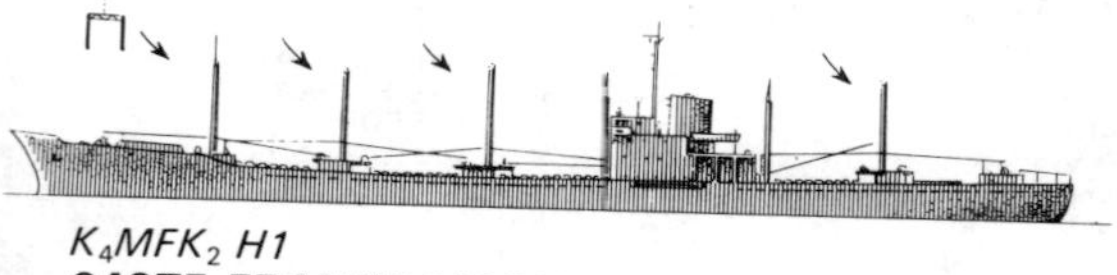

K_4MFK_2 H1
04975 FRANCE MARU. Ja/Ja 1967; C; 10800; 167.01 × 9.58 (547.93 × 31.43); M; 20; Sisters (Ja flag) **04976 ITALY MARU. 04977 PORTUGAL MARU. 04978 SPAIN MARU.**

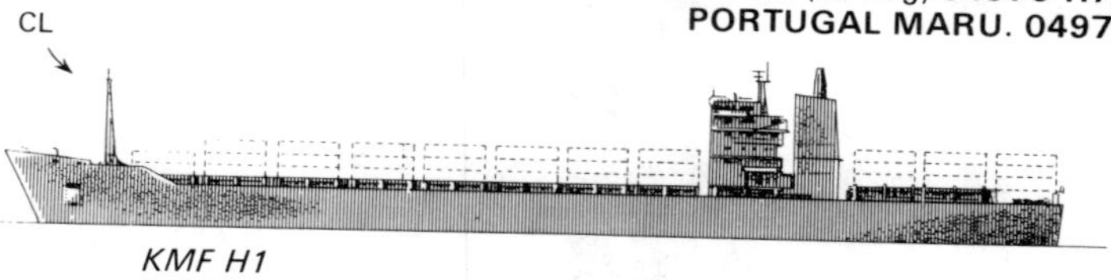

KMF H1
08775 ZIM KEELUNG. Is/Ne 1981; Con; 29400; 210.22 × 11.5 (689.7 × 37.73); M; 22.5; Sisters (Is flag): **08776 ZIM SAVANNAH 08777 ZIM BARCELONA.**

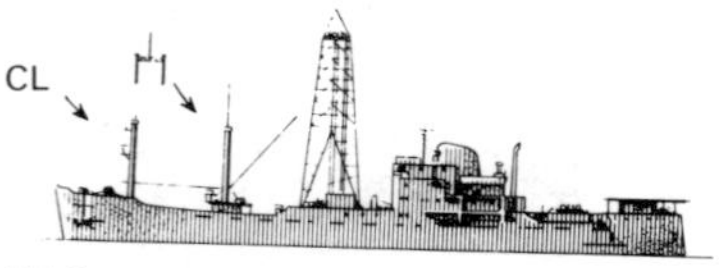

KMFK H13
10005 PHOLAS. Br/Br 1958/74; DS; 3800; 99.12 × 7 (325.2 × 22.97); M; 10; ex WIMPEY SEALAB 1980; ex ELIZABETH BOWATER 1972; Converted from general cargo 1974 Helicopter platform aft.

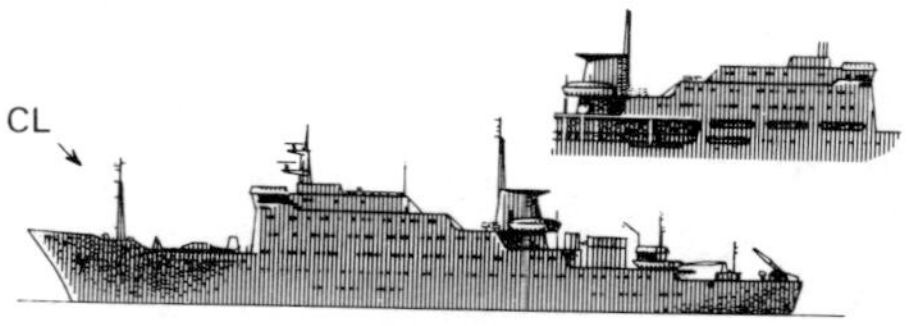

KM_2F H1
⋆14955 AKADEMIK MSTISLAV KELDYSH. Ru/Fi 1981; RS; 5500; 122.21 × 5.9 (400.95 × 19.36); TSM; 16; Inset drawing shows detail of starboard side superstructure.

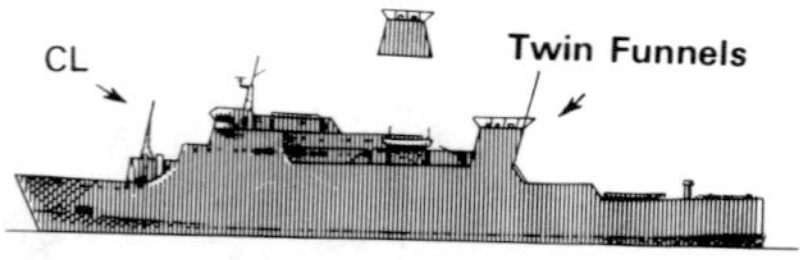

KM_2F H2
14976 EUROPEAN CLEARWAY. Br/FRG 1976; RoC; 3300; 118.32 × 5.82 (388.2 × 19.09); TSM; 18.5; Bow door/ramp and stern door/ramp; Sister **14977 EUROPEAN TRADER** (Br); Similar (funnel shape differs-see inset); **14978 EUROPEAN ENTERPRISE** (Br); Similar (lengthened by 8 metres); **14979 EUROPEAN GATEWAY** (Br); launched as European Express.

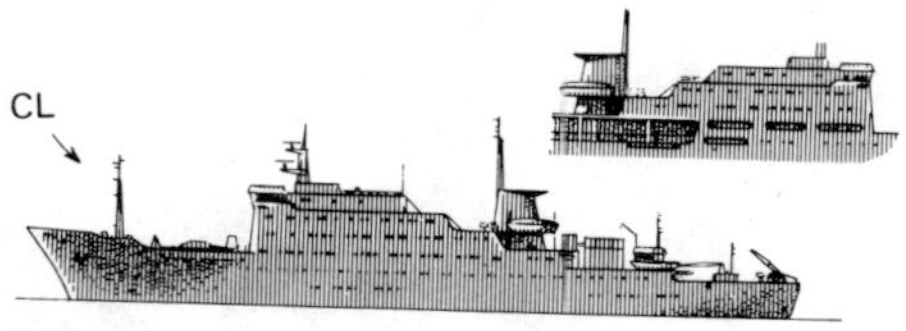

KM_2FK H1
⋆15095 AKADEMIK MSTISLAV KELDYSH. Ru/Fi 1981; RS; 5500; 122.21 × 5.9 (400.95 × 19.36); TSM; 16; Inset drawing shows detail of starboard side superstructure.

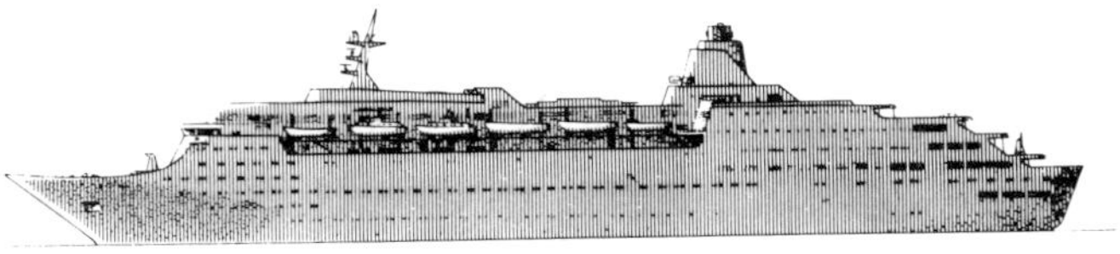

MF H
16875 EUROPA. FRG/FRG 1981; P; 35000; 196 × 8.35 (643 × 27.4); TSM; 22;

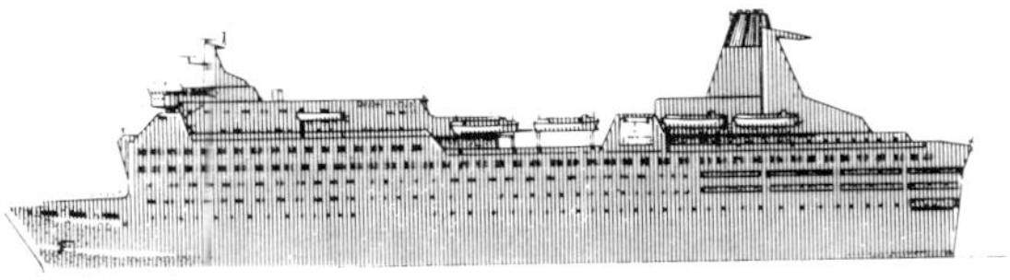

MF H
16895 FINLANDIA. Fi/Fi 1981; RoPF; 25700; 166.02 × 6.72 (544.69 × 22.05); TSM; —; Bow door/ramp and 2 stern door/ramps. Sister (Sw flag); **16896 SILVIA REGINA.**

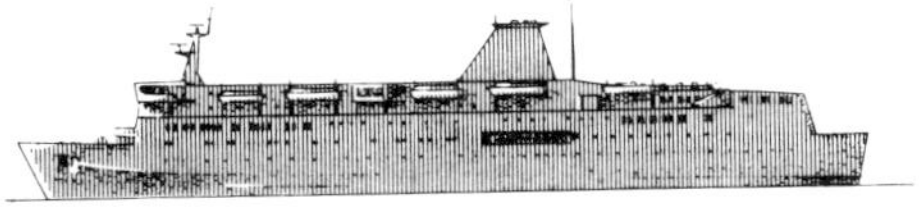

MFM H
⋆20353 GEORG OTS. Ru/Pd 1980; RoPF; 11496; 134 × 5.46 (439.6 × 17.91); TSM; 19; "B493" type; Sisters (some are "B492" type) (Ru flag); **⋆20354 DMITRIY SHOSTAKOVICH ⋆20355 LEV TOLSTOY ⋆20356 KONSTANTIN SIMONOV ⋆20357 VASILIY SOLOVYEV SEDOY.**

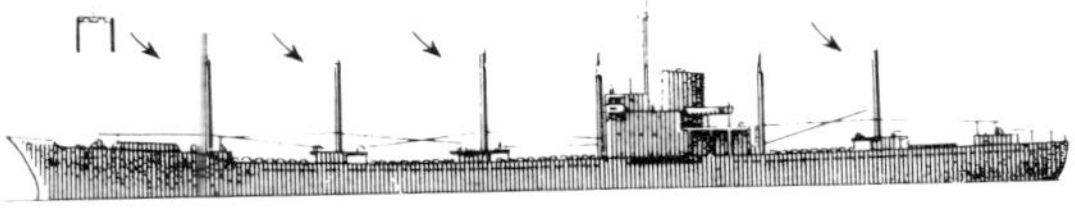

MK_3MFK_2 H1
30425 FRANCE MARU. Ja/Ja 1967; C; 10800; 167.01 × 9.58 (547.93 × 31.43); M; 20; Sisters (Ja flag); **30426 ITALY MARU 30427 PORTUGAL MARU 30428 SPAIN MARU.**

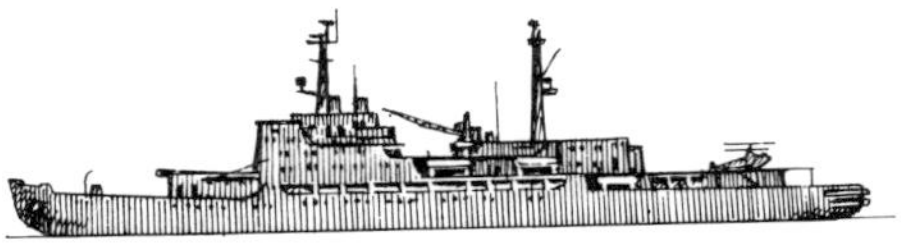

M_2 H
⋆32065 LENIN. Ru/Ru 1959; IB; 14100; 134 × 10.5 (440 × 34.6); TrS N T-E; 18; New reactors fitted c.1971.

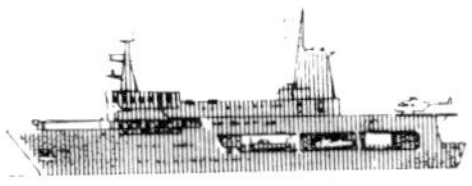

M_2F H1
33095 JOHAN NORDENANKAR. Sw/Sw 1980; RS; 1800; 73 × 3.8 (239.5 × 12.47); M; 13; Helicopter deck aft.

Profile 3

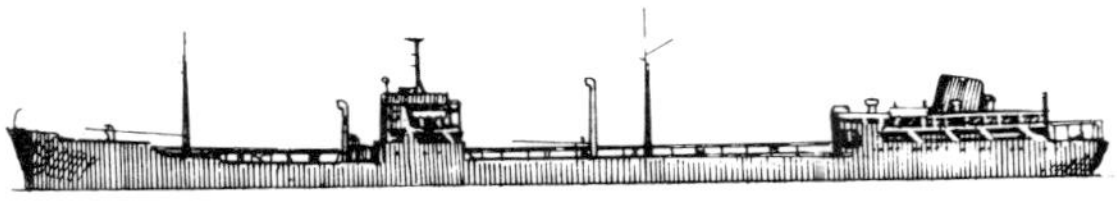

MK_2MF H123
39875 DANIMAR. Pa/No 1959; Tk; 12600; 170.69 × 9.61 (560 × 31.53); M; 14.5; ex TREFALCON LOGIC 1980; ex HARALD STANGE 1974.

Profile 4

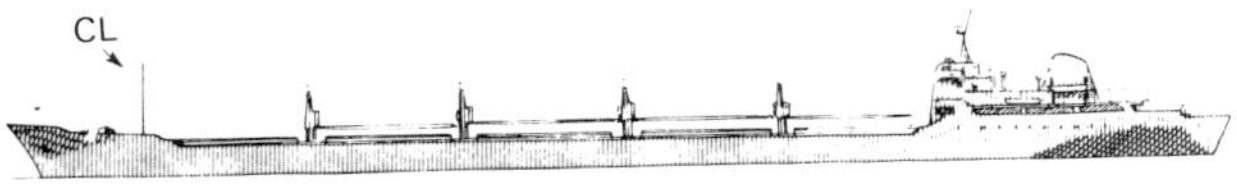

KC_4MF H13
47375 MANUELA PRIMA. It/It 1965; B; 17300; 192 × 10.59 (629.92 × 34.74); M; —.

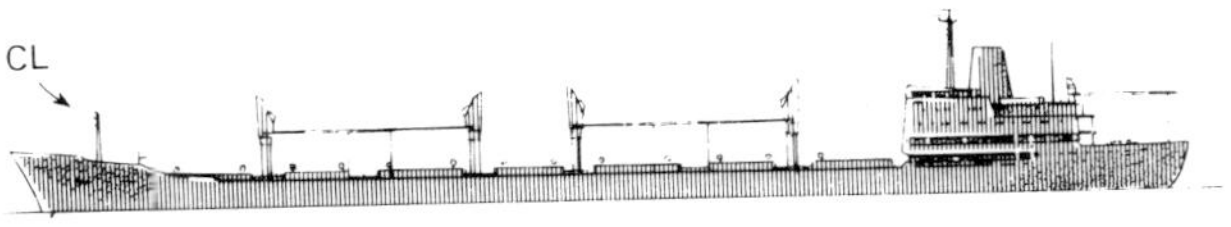

KC_6MFKC H13
48383 ANWAR. Mo/Bu 1975; B; 16200; 185.43 × 10.25 (608.37 × 33.63); M; 15; Sister **48384 BOUJNIBA** (Mo); Similar: **⋆48385 ROJEN** (Bu); probably similar: (Cu flag); **⋆48386 26 DE JULIO; ⋆48387 ANTONIO MACEO.**

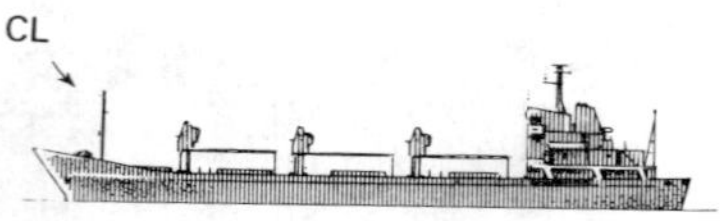

KC_3MFK H1
49021 FRIGO AMERICA. Sp/Sp 1980; R; 3600; 103.74 × 6.3 (340.35 × 20.67); M; —; Sisters (Sp flag) **49022 FRIGO AFRICA 49023 FRIGO ASIA 49024 FRIGO ESPANA 49025 FRIGO EUROPA 49026 FRIGO OCEANIA 49027 FRIGO LAS PALMAS** launched as POLO SUR; **49028 FRIGO TENERIFE.**

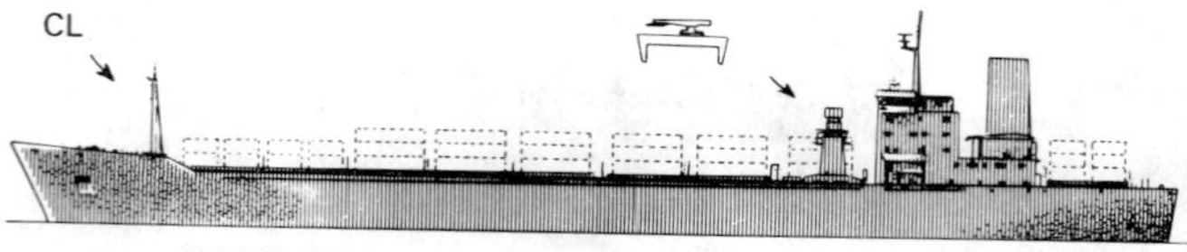

KCMF H1
51895 BENATTOW. Ne/Ne 1980; Con; 28400; 204.02 × 10.21 (669.36 × 33.5); M; —; ex ZEELANDIA 1980.

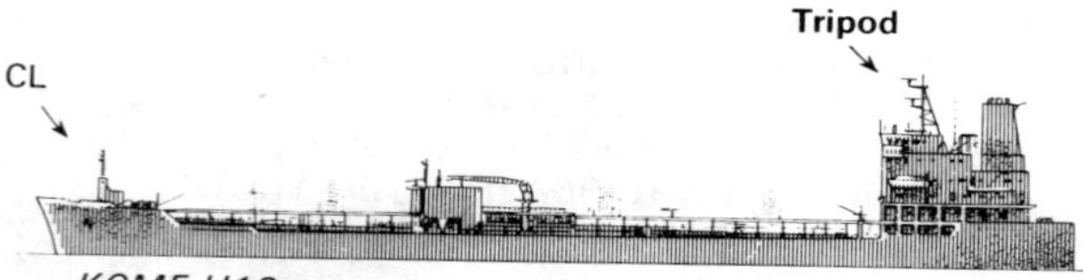

KCMF H13
52265 JOHNSON CHEMSTAR. Sw/Sw 1980; Ch; 22200; 175.01 × 10.7 (574.18 × 35.1); TSM; 16.3 (Trials); Sister **52266 JOHNSON CHEMSUN** (Sw).

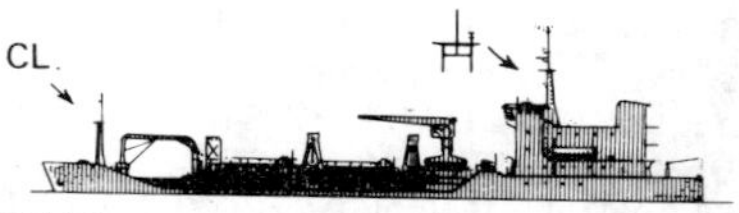

KCMF H13
52285 JAMES ENSOR. Be/Be 1980; D; 4200; 105.21 × 6 (345.18 × 19.69); TSM; 12.5; Trailing suction hopper dredger.

K_4MF H13
56185 SILVERHAWK Br/Br 1969; Tk/Ch; 6800; 130.21 × 7.53 (427.2 × 24.7); M; 14.5.

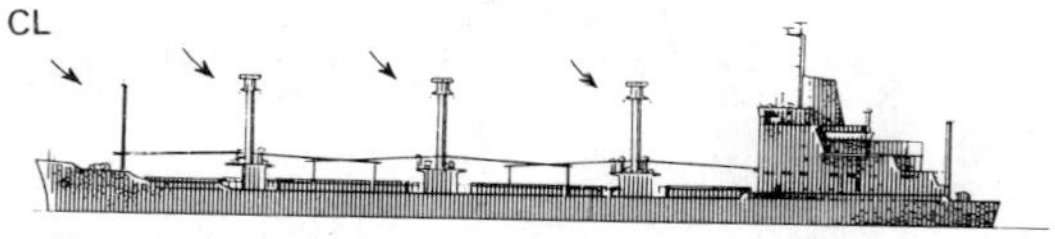

K_4MFK H1
56575 MURREE. Pk/Br 1981; C; 7900/11900; 152.03 × 9.49/— (498.79 × 31.14/—); M; —; **"SD 18"** type; (Pk flag); Sisters (Pk flag) **56576 AYUBIA 56577 KAGHAN.**

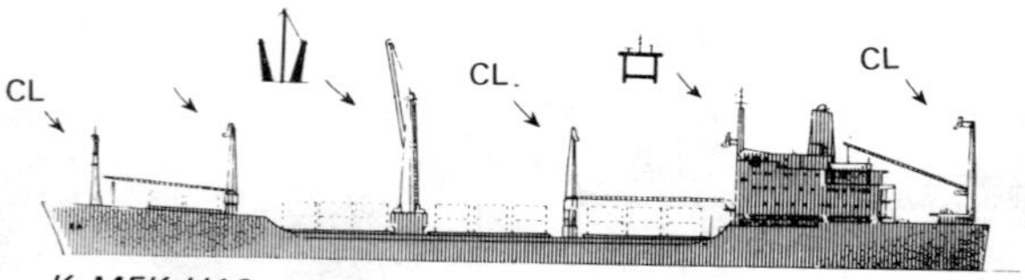

K_4MFK H13
56636 STRATHFIFE. Br/Ja 1978; C/Con/HL; 7900/13400; 169 × —/9.75 (554.46 × —/31.99); M; 18.75; Sister **56637 STRATHFYNE** (Br).

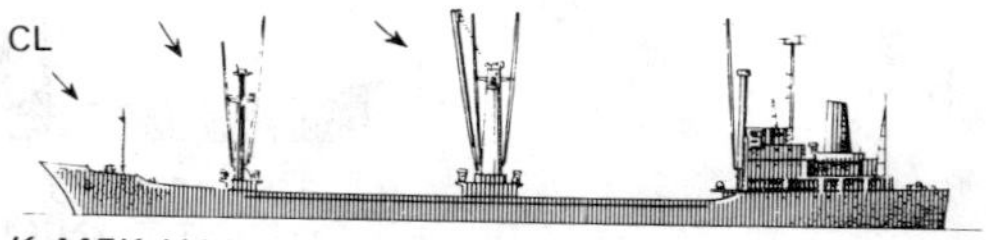

K_4MFK H13
56695 AMAZON MARU. Ja/Ja 1974; C/HL; 8300; 143.52 × 8.36 (470.87 × 27.43); M; 15.

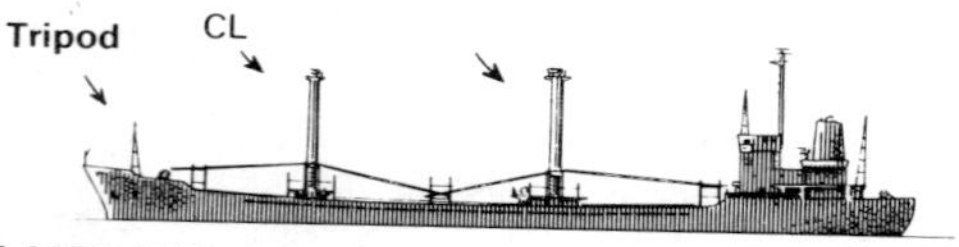

K_4MFK H13
57614 YUE RIVER. Ja/Ja 1975; C/TC; 6200; 129.98 × 7.75 (426.4 × 25.43); M; 13.25; ex KONG HOI 1976; Sisters **57615 YUE MAN** (Pa); **57616 BRIGHT MELBOURNE** (Pa); possible sisters: **57617 AGATHA** (Gr) ex PEARL LOTUS 1979; **57618 EXTRACO 1** (Pi) ex PEARL RIVER 1979; **57619 EXTRACO II** (Pi) ex OCEAN EXPLOTAR 1978; **57619A GREAT HONOR** (Pa) ex GREAT SUCCESS 1976; **57619B CARIBBEAN HOPE** (Pa) ex RUBY LOTUS 1979; **57619C HO CHUNG** (Pa); **57619D MARIA MARIOS H** (Gr) ex SUNNY SYDNEY 1979; **57619F SUN ALKES** (Ja) ex MATSUFUKUJIN MARU; **57619G TIMBER LEADER** (Pa); **57619H TYCHE** (Pa); **57619J VIRGO** (Pa) ex SUN ANTARES 1979; **57619K WONJIN** (Ko) ex NAMYANG CROWN 1980; ex NANPO MARU 1976.

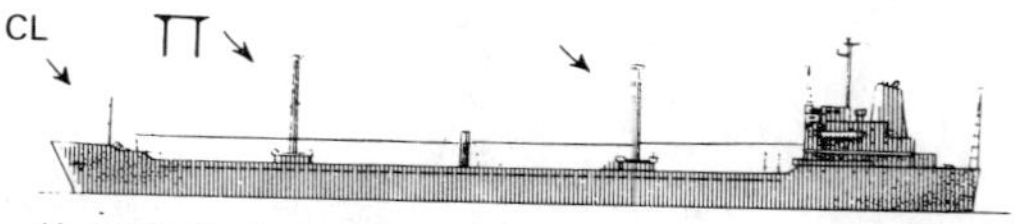

K_4MFK H13
57625 GLORY OCEAN. Ja/Ja 1977; C/TC; 10700; 146.08 × 9.31 (479.27 × 30.54); M; 14; Similar **57626 PACIFIC CHARGER** (Li)

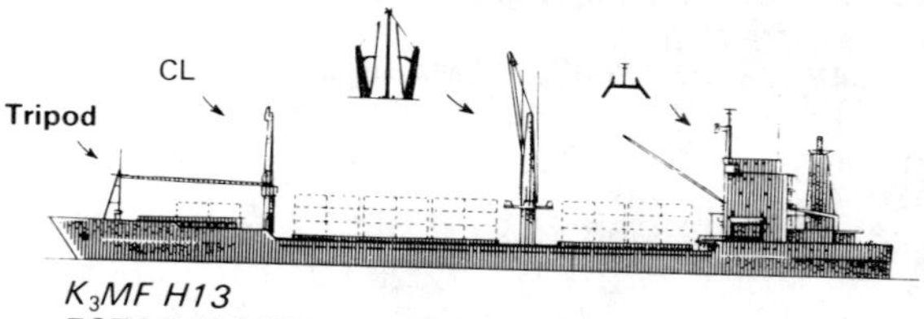

K_3MF H13
59710 MOSEL. FRG/FRG 1978; C/Con/HL; 7800/13100; 163.02 × 26.6/31.56); M; 16.5; Sister **59711 ELBE** (FRG).

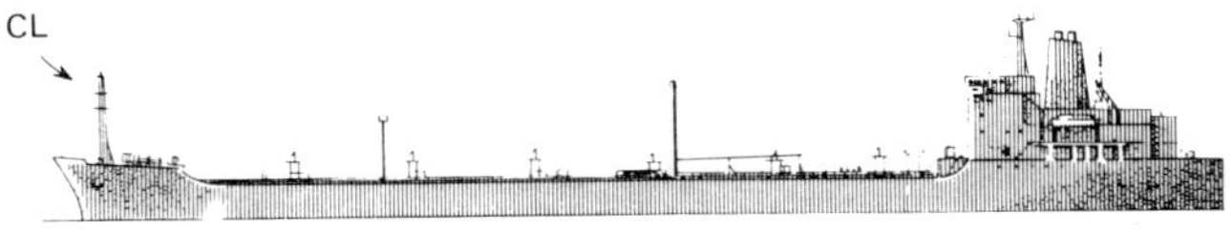

K_3MFK H13
60565 ESSO PALM BEACH. Pa/Ja 1978; Tk; 27400; 196.53 × 11.28 (644.78 × 37.01); M; 16.25; Sisters (Li flag); **60566 ESSO BAYWAY; 60567 ESSO PORTLAND.**

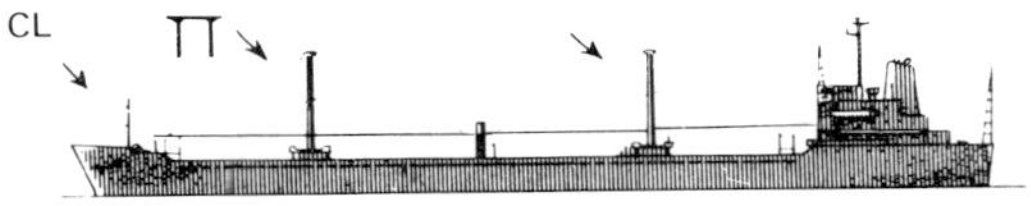

K_3MFK H13
61045 GLORY OCEAN. Ja/Ja 1977; C/TC; 10700; 146.08 × 9.31 (479.27 × 30.54); M; 14; Similar **61046 PACIFIC CHARGER** (Li)

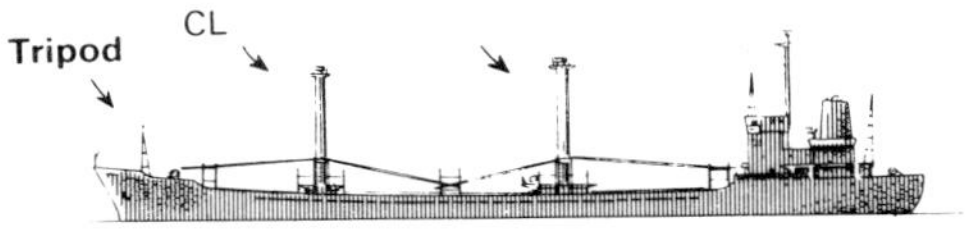

K_3MFK H13
61055 YUE RIVER. Ja/Ja 1975; C/TC; 129.98 × 7.75 (426.4 × 25.43); M; 13.25; ex KONG HOI 1976; Sisters **61056 YUE MAN** (Pa); **61057 BRIGHT MELBOURNE** (Pa); Possible sisters: **61058 AGATHA** (Gr) ex PEARL LOTUS 1979; **61059 EXTRACO 1** (Pi) ex PEARL RIVER 1979; **61059A EXTRACO II** (Pi) ex OCEAN EXPLOTAR 1978; **61059B GREAT HONOR** (Pa) ex GREAT SUCCESS 1976; **61059C CARIBBEAN HOPE** (Pa) ex RUBY LOTUS 1979; **61059D HO CHUNG** (Pa); **61059E MARIA MARIOS H** (Gr) ex SUNNY SYDNEY 1979; **61059F SUN ALKES** (Ja); ex MATSUFUKUJIN MARU; **61059G TIMBER LEADER** (Pa); **61059H TYCHE** (Pa); **61059J VIRGO** (Pa); ex SUN ANTARES 1979; **61059K WONJIN** (Ko); ex NAMYANG CROWN 1980; ex NANPO MARU 1976.

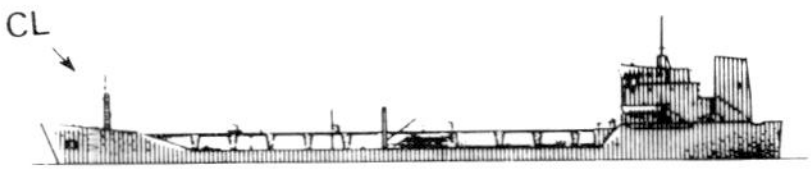

K_2MF H13
66577 CABLEMAN. Br/Br 1980; Tk; 4900; 116.52 × 7.2 (382.28 × 23.62); M; 13.

K_2MF H13
66635 SILVERHAWK. Br/Br 1969; Tk/Ch; 6800; 130.21 × 7.53 (427.2 × 24.7); M; 14.5.

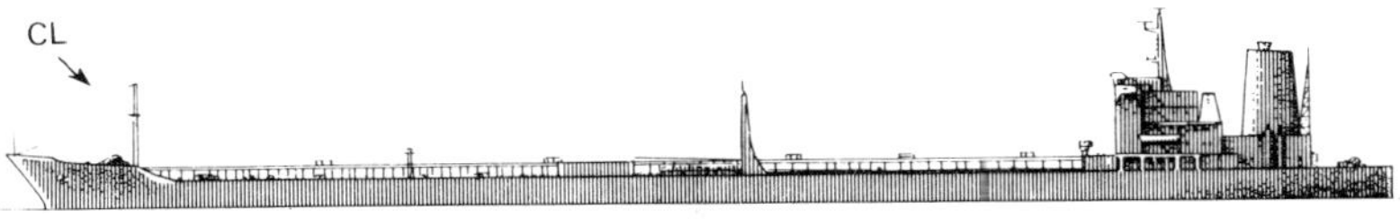

K_2MFK H1
68551 NIGMA Pa/Ja 1976; Tk; 47300; 242.98 × 14.5 (797.18 × 47.57); M; 16; ex CUMBERLANDIA 1980; Similar; (some Sg built) **68552 MOORFIELDS MONARCH** (Sg); **68553 MAMMOTH MONARCH** (Li) ex EUROASIA MONARCH 1978; **68554 NEPTUNE LEO** (Sg); **68555 NORTHERN VICTORY** (Sg); **68556 OLYMPIC RAINBOW** (Gr); ex OCEANIC ERIN 1980; **68557 SANKO HONOUR** (Sg); **68558 TATINA** (Gr); ex NOGA 1980; **68559 PAGEANTRY** (li); **68559A PALMSTAR CHERRY** (Sg); **68559B PALMSTAR ORCHID** (Sg); **68559C BRILLIANCY** (Sg); **68559D GYOKO MARU** (Ja); ex BRUCE RUTHI II 1978; **68559E CONTINENTAL MONARCH** (Li) **68559F ASIA MARU No2** (Ja); ex OCEANIC KRISTIN 1979.

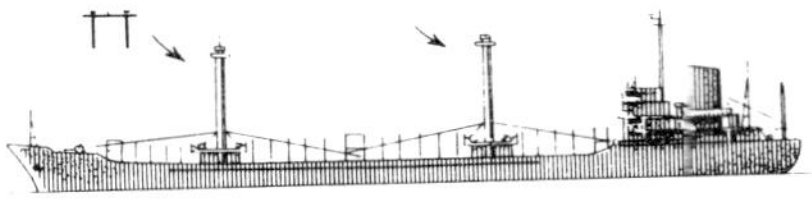

K_2MFK_2 H13
71505 IRENES MELODY. Cy/Ja 1969; C/TC; 6100; 127.41 × 7.25 (418 × 23.79); M; 12.75; ex EASTERN BEAUTY 1978; Similar (Superstructure varies); **71506 ALLIED ENTERPRISE** (Li); possibly similar: **71507 ELONA** (Gr) ex SALUTE 1975; ex MOKUSEI MARU 1974; **71508 SILVERDOLPHIN** (Li) ex KOSEI MARU 197U; **71509 SUMMER DAY** (Gr) ex IRENES TRUST 1980; ex DIADEM 1975; ex RINSEI MARU 1973; **71509A SUMMER SKY** (Gr) ex CRYSTAL CAMELLIA 1979.

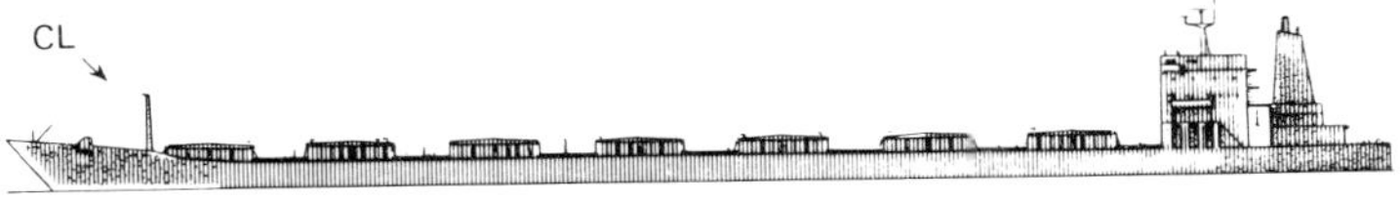

KMF H
72383 DANELOCK. Li/De 1981; B; 33500; 225 × 13.1 (738.19 × 42.98); M; 15; Sisters (Li flag); **72384 HYDROLOCK; 72385 BAUMARE; 72386 SUSAN B; 72387 KAREN Y.**

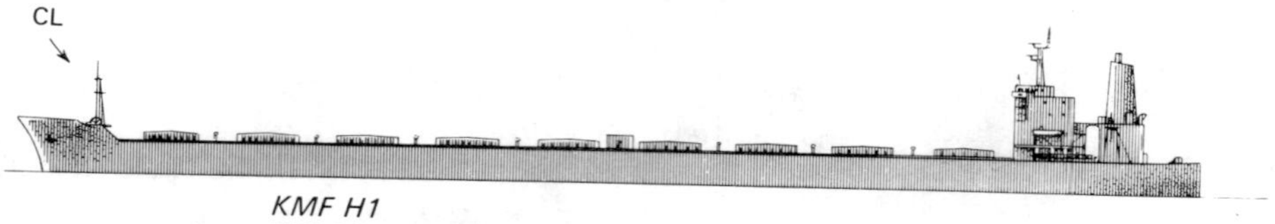

KMF H1
73335 WORLD DULCE. Pa/Ja 1981; B; 63100; 270.9 × 16.35 (888.78 × 53.64); M; —;

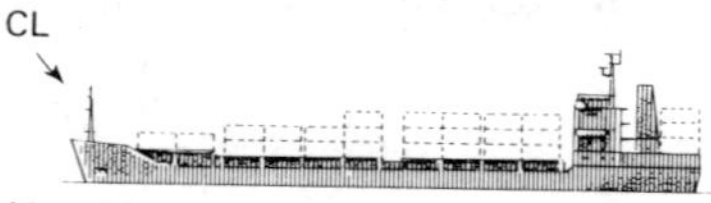

KMF H1
74015 YMIR. FRG/FRG 1980; C/Con; 1600; 99.95 × 5.09 (327.92 × 16.7); M; 12.25.

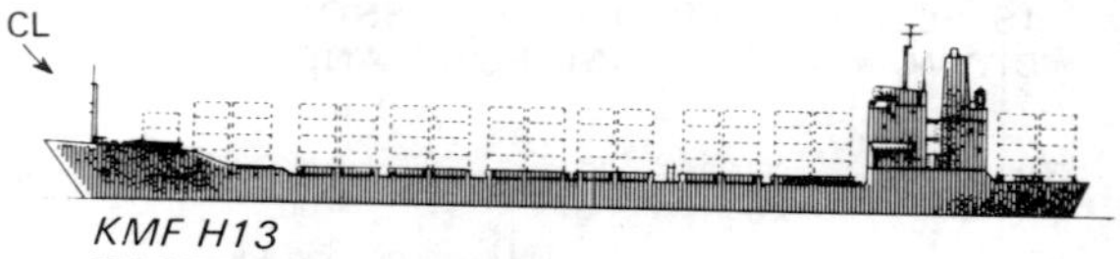

KMF H13
74435 TFL WASHINGTON. FRG/FRG 1980; Con; 15000; 170.21 × 9.65 (558.43 × 31.66); M; 19; launched as AMBROSIA; Sister (FRG flag) **74436 TFL ADAMS.**

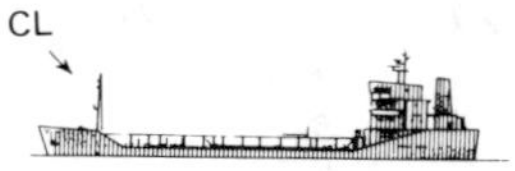

KMF H13
75085 ESSO PLYMOUTH. Br/Br 1980; Tk; 1400; 70.82 ×4.71 (232.35 × 15.45); M; 11.75.

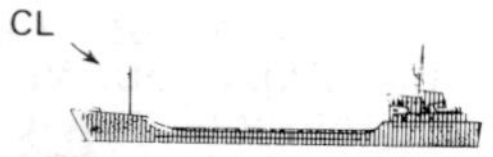

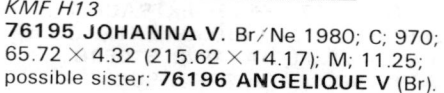

KMF H13
76195 JOHANNA V. Br/Ne 1980; C; 970; 65.72 × 4.32 (215.62 × 14.17); M; 11.25; possible sister: **76196 ANGELIQUE V** (Br).

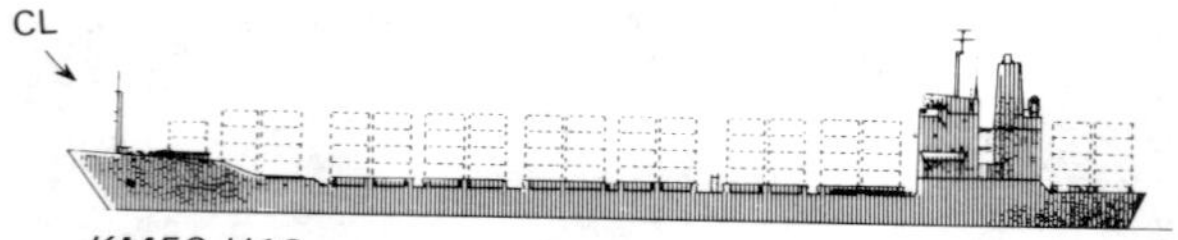

KMFC H13
77067 TFL WASHINGTON. FRG/FRG 1980; Con; 15000; 170.21 × 9.65 (558.43 × 31.66); M; 19; launched as AMBROSIA; Sister (FRG flag); **77068 TFL ADAMS.**

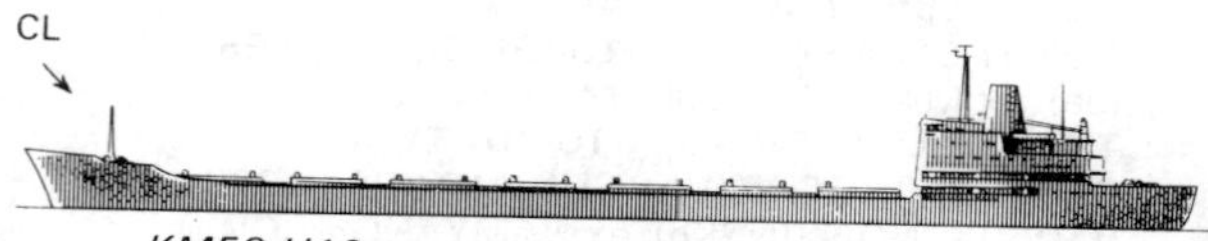

KMFC H13
★77080 KHUDOZHNIK FEDOROVSKIY. Ru/Bu 1978; B; 15600; 185.22 × 10.1 (607.68 × 33.14); M; 15.25; This vessel may be fitted with 4 deck cranes. This could also apply to the sisterships; Sisters (Ru flag); **★77081 KHUDOZHNIK A GERASIMOV; ★77082 KHUDOZHNIK GABASHVILI; ★77083 KHUDOZHNIK KASIYAN; ★77084 KHUDOZHNIK KUSTODIYEV; ★77085 KHUDOZHNIK TOIDZE; ★77086 KHUDOZHNIK VLADIMIR SEROV; ★77087 SOVIETSKIY KHUDOZHNIK;** (Bu flag); **★77088 CHIPKA** (or **SHIPKA**); **★77089 RILA; ★77089A RODOPI; ★77089B VITOCHA; ★77089C MILIN KAMAK; ★77089D SLAVIANKA.**

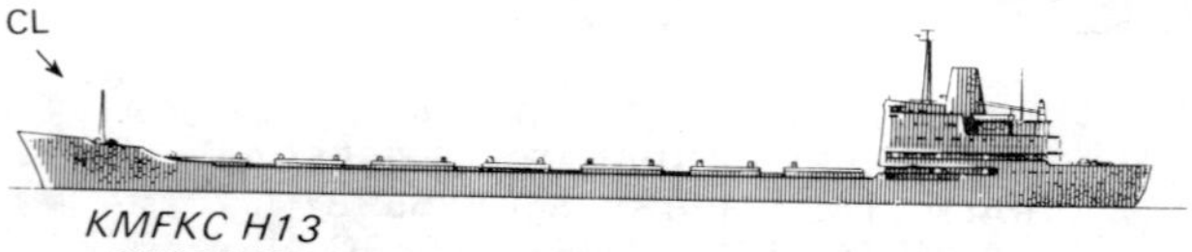

KMFKC H13
★80000 KHUDOZHNIK FEDOROVSKIY. Ru/Bu 1978; B; 15600; 185.22 × 10.1 (607.68 × 33.14); M; 15.25; This vessel may be fitted with 4 deck cranes. This could also apply to the sisterships; Sisters (RuFlag); **★80001 KHUDOZHNIK A GERASIMOV; ★80002 KHUDOZHNIK GABASHVILI; ★80003 KHUDOZHNIK KASIYAN; ★80004 KHUDOZHNIK KUSTODIYEV; ★80005 KHUDOZHNIK TOIDZE; ★80006 KHUDOZHNIK VLADIMIR SEROV; ★80007 SOVIETSKIY KHUDOZHNIK;** (Bu flag); **★80008 CHIPKA** (or **SHIPKA**); **★80009 RILA; ★80009A RODOPI; ★80009B VITOCHA; ★80009C MILIN KAMAK; ★80009D SLAVIANKA.**

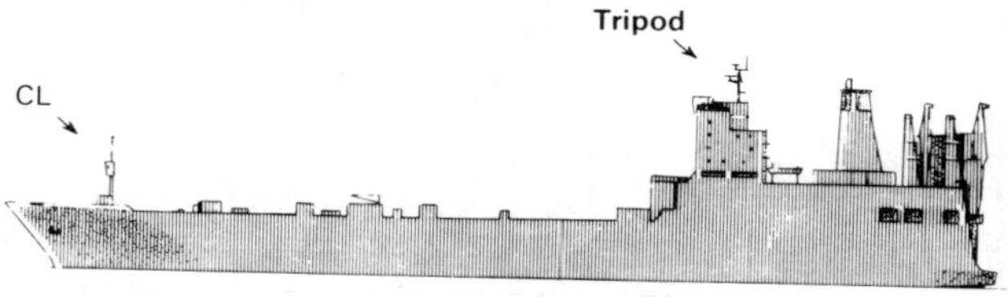

80296 ANDREA MERZARIO. It/It 1980; RoC/Con; 21300; 194.37 × 10.8 (637.7 × 35.43); M; 19.15; quarter ramp on starboard side; Sister **80297 COMANDANTE REVELLO (It).**

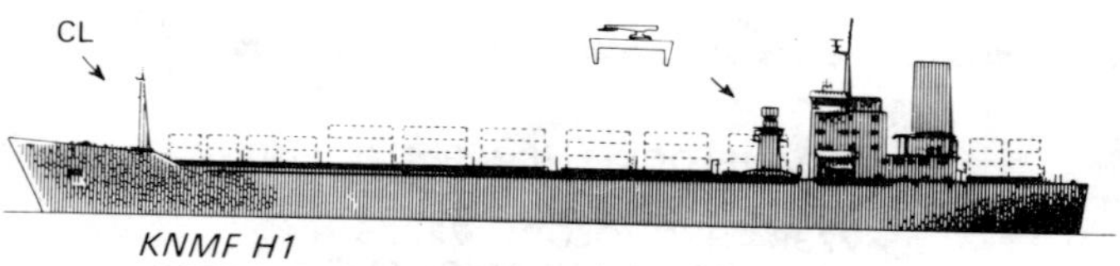

KNMF H1
82706 BENATTOW. Ne/Ne 1980; Con; 28400; M; —; ex ZEELANDIA 1980.

NUMERICAL SECTION

The amendments are given in numerical order corresponding to the entries in the main drawings section. The individual amendments are grouped to correspond with the numbers under one entry and a line separates the entries.
Where a ship has changed name, the date of the change appears after the new name.

00010 add further sister
00019 **AUSTRAL MOON** (US); ex AUSTRALIA BEAR 1975; ex PHILIPPINE BEAR 1975.

00020 **INVENTOR → PENTA WORLD** (Sg) 1981.

00140 add further sister.
*00147 **ALEKSEY GENERALOV** (Ru).

00190 **MELPO → DESPOULA K** (Gr) 1980.

00200 **DESEADO → SAN GEORGE** (Gr) 1981.

00220 **EASTERN JADE**—broken up.

00250 **SEA-LAND COMMERCE**
00252 **SEA-LAND EXCHANGE**
00253 **SEA-LAND FINANCE**
00256 **SEA-LAND MARKET**
00257 **SEA-LAND RESOURCE**
00258 **SEA-LAND TRADE**
All transferred to U.S. Navy.

00300 **AGHIA MARINA → BRAZEN EAGLE** (Pa) 1979.
Later broken up.

00351 add sister.
00352 **KHALIJ SKY** (Gr); ex TARPON 1978.

00390 **BLESSING FIVE**—broken up.

00452 **MARYSTAR**—broken up.

00560 **PANETOLIKON → SHABAAN** (Pa) 1981.

00580 **KOTA PANJANG**—broken up.

00611 **EUCADIA → SIGIRIYA** (Sr) 1981.

00620 **ISTIKBAL**—broken up.

00691 **LIBRA**—amend to **LIRA**. Now broken up.
00692 **LIHO**—broken up.

00721 **LIU PAN SHAN**—broken up.

01200 add further sister.
01204 **DINA** (Pa); ex MAHABHAKTI 1980; ex TRIKORA DJAYA 1973; ex SUMATRA BREEZE 1971; ex BAMORA 1971.

01281 **GOLDEN SUN**—broken up.

01393 **KOMSOMOLETS NAKHODKI**—total loss.

01440 **CECILIE MAERSK**
01441 **CORNELIA MAERSK**
01442 **CHASTINE MAERSK**
01443 **CHRISTIAN MAERSK**
01444 **CLARA MAERSK**
01445 **CLIFFORD MAERSK**
Delete entire entry. All being rebuilt as container ships.

01520 **MIRRABOOKA.** At least one of this class (maybe all) has had the mast and kingpost in the well replaced by sets of tandem cranes.
01522 **POPI → ATHINAI** (Gr) 1980.

*01560 add further sisters.
*01579 **FIZIK KURCHATOV** (Ru)
*01579A **KHIMIK ZELINSKI** (Ru)

01620 **MARFRIO**—delete from entry. Sequence is now CK$_2$MFMC.
01621 **SEA FROST**—May be similarly modified.

01631 **WEIDA → ARAMEDIA** (Gr) 1981.

*01653 **KOMSOMOLETS NAKHODKI**—total loss.

01830 **APHRODITE**—Amend flag to Cy.

01930 **PRINSEN → WID** (Si) 1978
01931 **MIN FUNG**—amend to **MINFUNG.** renamed***JI MEI** (RC) 1981.

02290 **CAP SAN NICOLAS → NICOLA** (Pa) 1981
02293 **CAP SAN LORENZO → LORENZ** (Pa) 1981.

02340 Note: some of the later units of this class have a small mast aft instead of on funnel.

*02354 **OSETIYA**—rebuilt with extended superstructure and taller funnel.

02480 **AUSTAL LIGHTNING**—amend to **AUSTRAL LIGHTNING.**

02540 **ACONCAGUA VALLEY → PISANG** (Sg) 1981
02541 **SAN JOAQUIN VALLEY → DURIAN** (Sg) 1981.

02550 **SACRAMENTO MARU → MULTI CARRIER** (Pa)
02551 **SAN FRANCISCO MARU → CHAOHU CAREER** (Pa)
02553 **HELEN → ELENA** (Ma) 1981.

02581 **MALMROS MONSOON**—amend flag to Br.

02590 **ARGO → LEENOR** (Is) 1981
02591 **VIRGO → LEEOR** (Is) 1981

02601 **SNOW BALL → MALAYAN QUEEN** (Pi) 1981
02606 **SNOW STORM**—amend flag to Br.

02631 **SNOW BALL → MALAYAN QUEEN** (Pi) 1981
02636 **SNOW STORM**—amend flag to Br.

02651 **HILCO SCAMPER → SCAMPER UNIVERSAL** (Pa)
02652 **HILCO SPEEDSTER → STIRLING UNIVERSAL** (Br)

*02676 to *02682 Amend 'Similar' ships in class to Simila- (Smaller cranes, arranged in pairs).

02721 **ROSARIO → ZACAPA** (Gu) 1980.
02723 **MONTEVIDEO → ROCK** (Pa) 1981.

02810 **HISTORIAN → CHERRY ORIENT** (Sg) 1981
02811 **MAGICIAN → CHERRY CRYSTAL** (Sg) 1981.

02860 **LOCH MAREE → AL SALAMA** (Sh) 1981
02861 **LOCH LOMOND → AL ZAHRA** (Sh) 1981.

02951 **MALMROS MONSOON**—amend flag to Br.

02981 **TOYU MARU → EASTERN REEFER** (Pa) 1980.

03000 **LOCH MAREE → AL ZAHRA** (Sh) 1981
03001 **LOCH LOMOND → AL SALAMA** (Sh) 1981.

03080 Delete following sisters, converted to container ships.
03081 **ITAITE**
03082 **ITANAGE**
03086 **ITAPAGE**
03087 **ITAPE**
03088 **ITACUATIA**
One more Sister will probably be converted.

*03239 to 03248 Delete all Russian flag sisters from entry.

03260 **GEEST-TIDE →*KULDIGA** (Ru) 1981
03261 **GEESTCREST →*KANDARA** (Ru) 1981.

03350 **ASSALAMAH** (Gr) **→ APOLLON** (Gr) 1980.

03412 **USHAIA**—amend to **USHUAIA.**

03430 **IOS**—amend to **IOS 1.**

03482 **FRIGO TIETE → ADRIATIC FREEZER** (Gr) 1981.

03490 **AQUILON → HORNCAP** (Li) 1981
03491 **FORT SAINTE MARIE → HORNBAY** (Li) 1981.

03513 **CORIANDER → MALAYAN PRINCESS** (Pi) 1981.

03580 **AQUILON → HORNCAP** (Li) 1981
03581 **FORT SAINTE MARIE → HORNBAY** (Li) 1981.

*03635 to *03645 Delete all Russian flag sisters from entry.

03750 **JAVRON → BOUNTY III** (Fr) 1981.

03841 **VILLE DE ROTTERDAM → PUERTO PRINCESA** (Pi).

03901 **PORT LAUNAY → KHALIJ CRYSTAL** (Li) 1981.

04050 **DA VERRAZANO → REA B** (Pa) 1980.

04150 **JAMAICA PRODUCER → MIRANDA** (Pa) 1981. Now used as livestock carrier—may be altered in appearance.

04170 **SALMO**—delete entry — now rebuilt.

*04100 Amend sequence to KCMFMC
*04182 **KAMALES.** Delete -has different appearance.

04361 **WILD MALLARD → MACEDONIAN REEFER** (Gr) 1981.

04460 **AUSTRIAN EXPLORER → NIGERIAN EXPLORER** (Pa) 1980 Further renamed **BELLERIVE** 1980. Further renamed **CEFALLONIAN WAVES** (Gr) 1981.

04590 **HOEGH ELAN → GABUS** 1979. Further renamed **UNION NORFOLK** (Pa) 1982
04591 **GURAMI → UNION AUCKLAND** (Pa) 1981.

04665 **HATTINGEN →*MIAO FENG SHAN** (RC) 1979
Has stulcken as third KP. Others may be similar.

04710 to 04715 Four ships of this class are to be converted to cellular containerships in 1982.

04781 **HELLENIC CARRIER**—total loss.

04800 Delete following sisters—appearance differs
04801 **AMALIA**
04802 **CAICARA**
04803 **JOANA**
04804 **CELINA TORREALBA**
04805 **NICIA**
04807 **LLOYD ALEGRETE**
The following is confirmed as a sister
04806 **LLOYD TUPIARA.**

04840 **ARMADALE → DIDO** (Gr) 1981.

04880 to 04885 Four ships of this class are to be converted to cellular containerships in 1982.

04916 **VISHVA KAUMUNDI** amend to **VISHVA KAUMUDI.**

05000 **BENDEARG → NEW PANTHER** (Sg) 1981.

05040 **HARVEST →★YANG CHENG** (RC) 1979.

05072 **IZUMI MARU → FAMILY ARROW** (Gr) 1981.

05078 **BRAZILIAN EXPRESS**—amend flag to Pi.

05090 **IDAHO → AMERICAN SPITFIRE** (US) 1981
05091 **COLORADO → AMERICAN TITAN** (US) 1981
05092 **MICHIGAN → AMERICAN SPARTAN** (US) 1981
05093 **MONTANA → AMERICAN TROJAN** (US) 1981
05094 **WYOMING → AMERICAN MONARCH** (US) 1981.

05121 **CHRISTIAN VIELJEUX → SANTA RITA** (Pe) 1981
05125 **PATRICK VIELJEUX → CUZCO II** (Pe) 1981
05126 **TAJ → STEPHANE VIELJEUX** 1979
Further renamed **LIMA II** (Pe) 1981.

05200 **HUPEH → SUN OPAL** (Pa) 1981.

05211 **GOLD STAR → GOLEMI** (Li) 1981.

05230 **FLEETBANK → FLORIDA** (Li) 1981.
05231 **BEAVERBANK → SANJOHN BAY** (Gr) 1981.
05232 **BIRCHBANK → CALIFORNIA** (Li) 1981.
05236 **CLOVERBANK → COLORADO** (Li) 1981.

05291 **RIO DE LA PLATA**—delete—sequence is different.

05310 **'SD 14'** type.
05312 **KIFANGONGO**—amend to **KIFANGONDO**
05318 **GLOBE TRADER**—delete and transfer to **06606**
Add further sisters
★05329 **YUANJIANG** (RC)
★05330 **HUNJIANG** (RC)

05382 **HOLSTENTAL → KARIN** (Pi) 1981
Delete ship from entry—appearance differs.

05468 **FREEZER ACE**—amend flag to Pa.

05471 **FAETHON**—delete as a sister and add as similar ship.

05481 **BATE BRIDGE → ISLA FERNANDINA** (Pa) 1981.

05491 **ETROG → ROGA** (Pa) 1981.

05710 **FARES REEFER → BEACON HILL** (Br) 1981.

05760 **CHRISTOS S. T. ARAPAKIS**—probable total loss.

05891 **DONGA → DIAMANT MERCHANT** (Gr) 1981.

05910 **FINN-AMER → IMPERIAL** (Li) 1981.

05911 **FINNBUILDER → NORTHERN SAPPIRE** (Li) 1981. Further renamed **COPIAPO** (Li) 1981.

05912 **FINNSAILOR → ACONCAGUA** (Ch) 1981.

05940 **ROYAL FORTUNE → YENBO** 1978. **→ UNION BANGKOK** 1979 **→ UNION YENBO** (Si) 1979.

05960 **COMET → CAPE ALAVA** (US-govt.) 1980.

06068 **AFRICAN CORRAL**—amend to **AFRICAN CORAL.**

06080 **MIGHTY → ETERNAL PEACE** (Gr) 1981.

06110 **AGIOS PANDELEIMON → PROTOKLITOS** (Gr) 1981.

06130 **BRAZILIAN EXPRESS**—amend flag to Pi.

06190 **KHALIJ EXPRESS**—amend flag to Si.

06220 **WILD CORMORANT → ATTICA REEFER** (Gr) 1981
06221 **WILD CURLEW → ATHENIAN REEFER** (Gr) 1981.

06280 **BREMERHAVEN → BRAZILIAN REEFER** (Bs) 1981
06281 **BLUMENTHAL → BELGIAN REEFER** (Bs) 1981.

06291 **CALAGARIBALDI → GAFREDO** (Pa) 1981.

06320 **PASADENA → PASADENA I** (Li) 1981
06322 **ARIANE I**—amend flag to Li.

06340 **SKYMNOS**—probable total loss.

06353 **DOVER UNIVERSAL → GOLDEN SEA** (Gr) 1981.

06361 **PAMPERO UNIVERSAL → AEGEAN WAVE** (Gr) 1981.

06414 **AGIOS KONSTANTINOS**—amend to **AGIOS CONSTANTINOS.**

06460 **'SD 14'** type
06461 **ARDENHALL → MOOLCHAND** (Pa) 1981
06494 **ITHAKI → DANIELLA** (Pa) 1981
06516 **RINOULA → UNITY** (Gr) 1981
06519 **SAMOS PROGRESS → FORTUNE KING** (Pa) 1981
06529 **CAPETAN MARKOS → CALY** (Pa) 1981
06536 **CAPE RION → TORTUGAS** (Br) 1981
06603 **VIRTUS → POMONA** (Pa) 1981
06605 **DURBAN CARRIER → IRINI II** (Gr) 1981
06646 **NIGER VALLEY → HONESTY II** (Pa) 1981.
Add further sisters
06538 **FEDORA** (Gr); ex RODRIGO TORREALBA 1981
06606 **GLOBE TRADER** (Li).

06674 **PRIVATE RAMON CASTILLO**—amend to **PRESIDENTE RAMON CASTILLO**

06678 **GENERAL BELGRANO**— amend to **GENERAL MANUEL BELGRANO.**

★06811 **XIONG YUE CHENG → OPULENCE** (Pa) 1981
06812 **BATE BRIDGE → ISLA FERNANDINA** (Pa) 1981.

06930 **AKRA DREPANON**—broken up.

06962 **EVLALIA**—amend flag to Gr.

07000 **GEORGIOS → MASTRO GIORGIS** (Gr) 1978.

07011 **SHIRRABANK → AL BASEER** (Li) 1981

07040 **UNION LISBON → YUH DONG** (Ko) 1981.

07130 **TAMARA → AMAR** (Gr) 1980.

07170 **PANSEPTOS → CHERRY RUBY** (Sg) 1980
07172 **CAM AYOUS → COPPER TRADER** (Gr) 1981
07173 **CAM AZOBE → COTTON TRADER** (Gr) 1981.

07190 **GOLDBEACH → NICOLAS K** (Gr)
Later broken up.

07232 **BORDABEKOA → SEA RELIANCE** (Pa) 1981.

07250 Delete similar ships
07251 **STRAITS STAR**
07252 **KWANGTUNG.**

07264 **CLARE → RESOLVE** (Pa) 1981
07265 **LONE EAGLE → ANJO ONE** (Pa) 1980.

07280 **GOLD BRIDGE → TRANS VASSILIKI** (Gr) 1981.

07371 **CIUDAD DE BARRANQUILLA → CEFALLONIAN CHARIS** (Gr) 1981.

07391 **TAIPING → SEA HORSE** 1979. Further renamed **EVER LUCK** 1980 and broken up.

07432 **BORDABEKOA → SEA RELIANCE** (Pa) 1981.

07450 **WILD CORMORANT → ATTICA REEFER** (gr) 1981
07451 **WILD CURLEW → ATHENIAN REEFER** (Gr) 1981.

07490 **CHAR CHUN → CHAR CHENG** (Pa) 1979
Broken up 1981.

07501 **ELISABETH BERG → ZAIN AL-QAWS** (Iq) 1981.

07510 **CHRISTL HERMANN**—amend flag to Cy.

07530 **SEA GLORY → BIRBA** (Pa) 1981
07531 **EASTERN FORTUNE → JOO HENG** (Ho) 1980.

07540 **PHAEDON II**—total loss.

07660 **CLAN GRAHAM → MARI ANNE** (Pa) 1981.

07700 **EURYLOCHUS → AL MAHROUSA** (Ku) 1981
Now broken up.

07750 **ETHA RICKMERS**—amend flag to Pa.

07761 **HONDURAS MARU → HALMAHERA CAREER** 1978
Further renamed **BALDER CHUANCHOW** (Pa) 1981
07762 **IONIAN CAREER → BALDER ZEA DAWN** (Gr) 1980.

07770 **CLAN MACGILLIVRAY → CLAN MACBOYD** (Br) 1981
07771 **CLAN MACGREGOR → ANGELIKA P** (Gr) 1981.

07780 **TOBIAS MAERSK → SIBUYAN CAREER** (Pa) 1981
07781 **THOMAS MAERSK → SARIKA B** (Pa) 1981
07782 **TREIN MAERSK → NEW STALLION** (Pa) 1981.

07795 **MARMACDRACO**—amend to **MORMACDRACO.**

07811 **HONDURAS MARU → HALMAHERA CAREER** 1978
Further renamed **BALDER CHUANCHOW** (Pa) 1981
07812 **IONIAN CAREER → BALDER ZEA DAWN** (Gr) 1980.

07822 **FILOMENA LEMBO → CER ALSIRAT** (Pa) 1981.

07840 **BRAZILIAN EXPRESS**—amend flag to Pi.

07951 **ETROG → ROGA** (Pa) 1981.

07960 **FEAX**—add note: See BENEFACTOR etc under K_3MFK— **05470**
07961 **FAETHON** (Gr)—added as sister.

★07980 **TUHOBIC → ABU RASHID** (Eg) 1981.

08004 **MARMACWAVE**—amend to **MORMACWAVE.**

08040 **BLUE SKY → BLUE LION** (1980) Now broken up.

08051 **COVADONGA → COVADONGA 1** (Li) 1980. Further renamed **AFRICAN MARINER** (Li) 1980.

08400 **LIVERPOOL BAY**—amend engines to TSM.

08580 **EUROLINER → SEAPAC TRENTON** (FRG) 1981
Further renamed **ORIENTAL GOVERNOR** (Pa) 1981.
08581 **EUROFREIGHTER → SEAPAC VALLEY FORGE** (FRG) 1981
Further renamed **ORIENTAL KNIGHT** (Pa) 1981.

08601 **ORIENTAL VANGUARD → MANCHESTER VANGUARD** (Br) 1981.

08804 **ZIM NEW YORK**—amend flag to Is.
08805 **ZIM TOKYO**—amend flag to Is.

08831 **ERLANGEN EXPRESS → INCOTRANS PROGRESS** (FRG) 1981.
08832 **HOECHST EXPRESS → INCOTRANS PROMISE** (FRG) 1981.

08870 **SEATRAIN ORISKANY**—amend length to 583.96ft.
Renamed **SEAPAC ORISKANY** (Li) 1981. Further renamed **DART BRITAIN** (Br) 1981.
08871 **SEATRAIN BENNINGTON → TFL FRANKLIN** (FRG) 1981
08872 **SEATRAIN CHESAPEAKE → SEAPAC CHESAPEAKE** (Li) 1981.
Further renamed **DART ATLANTIC** (Br) 1981.
08873 **SEATRAIN YORKTOWN → SEAPAC YORKTOWN** (Li) 1981
Further renamed **DART CONTINENT** (Br) 1981.

08874 **SEATRAIN INDEPENDENCE** → **SEAPAC INDEPENDENCE** (Li) 1981
Further renamed **DART AMERICANA** (Br) 1981.

09031 **ERLANGEN EXPRESS** → **INCOTRANS PROGRESS** (FRG) 1981.
09032 **HOECHST EXPRESS** → **INCOTRANS PROMISE** (FRG) 1981.

09110 **CRISTOFORO COLOMBO**—broken up.

09240 **EUROPA** → **COLUMBUS** (It).

09552 **AUSTRALIAN EXPORTER**—amend to **AUSTRALIAN EXPLORER.**

09600 **CHRYSOVALANDOU TRIA** → **KOMARINE No 9** (Ko) 1981.

09610 **FANEROMENI** → **FILOTHEI** (Gr) 1979.

09620 **PENELOPE A** → **STAVROULA K** (Gr) 1981.

09640 **EGIDIA** → **SEA VICTORY** (Pa) 1981.

09890 Add similar.
09891 **HIEI MARU** (Ja)
Add similar (pole radar mast).
09892 **BEISHU MARU** (Ja).

10110 **CUIDAD DE TOLEDO**—broken up.

10130 **NEW STAR**—broken up.

10140 **MINSHAN** →***LONG SHAN** (RC) 1978.

*10274 **INTERNACIONAL**—add ex GUO JI 1963.

10313 **RATNA USHA** → **SAMUDRA JYOTI** (In) 1980.
10314 **VISHVA PRABHA**—broken up.

10320 **NEW STAR**—broken up.

10364 **ANTONIOS C** → **HONOUR FIVE** (Pa) 1981.

10380 **STATE OF KUTCH**—broken up.
10381 **STATE OF ORISSA**—broken up.

10400 **CAMINITO** → **BRAZIL** (Pa) 1981.
10401 **DIAMANDO** → **POLANA** (Gr) 1980.

*10440 **MEKHANIK BONDIK**—broken up.
*10442 **NIKOLAY PRZHEVALSKIY**—broken up.
*10446 **PRIOZERSK**—broken up.
*10447 **PRIVOLZHSK**—broken up.
*10456 **VITUS BERING**—broken up.

*10578 **STANISLAW DUBIOS**—amend to **STANISLAW DUBOIS**. Sunk 1981.

10622 **AGIA MARINA** → **OLYMPIAKOS** (Gr) 1981.

10630 **AL MESSILAH** → **MUKAIRISH ALTHALETH** (Si) 1981.

10740 Some of the sisters have a light pole on the forecastle, making sequence K_2MFM.
10754 **RIO SIXAOLA**—amend flag to Pa.
Add further sister.
*10759A **AKADEMIK ARTOBOLEVSKY** (Ru)

10840 **SACKR AL JAZIRAH**—sank 1980.

10890 **MILETO** → **MAKIS K** (Gr) 1981.

10922 **CEFALLONIAN SEA** → **GIANNOULA K** (Gr) 1981.
10923 **CEFALLONIAN SKY** → **NATALIA K** (Gr) 1981.

10940 **DUERO**—converted to Ro/Ro Ship and renamed **CABORJA** -delete from entry.

10999 **COMELUCK GLORY** → **ASSOCIATED GRAIN** (Tw) 1980.

11111 **PAMPA ARGENTINA** → **SANTIAGO** (Pa) 1981.

11120 **LENA**—amend flag to Ma.

11191 **POLYMICHANOS** → **INTRA TRADER** (Pa) 1981.
11192 **THARALEOS** → **INTRA TRAVELLER** (Pa) 1981.

11220 Add similar (CL Kingpost foreward).
11221 **TAISEI MARU** (Ja).

11254 **SANTA MARIA DEL PINO**—broken up.

11350 **AUSTRAL ENSIGN** → **AMERICAN MARKETER** (Us) 1981.
11351 **AUSTRAL ENDURANCE** → **AMERICAN MERCHANT** US) 1981.

11370 **ALEXA**—broken up.

*11430 Delete the following from entry.
*11430 **KOSMONAUT PAVEL BELYAYEV.**
*11435 **KOSMONAUT VLADISLAV VOLKOV.**
*11437 **NAZAR GUBIN.**
*11444 **SEMYON KOSINOV.**

11480 **AFAMIA STAR**—amend to **AFAMI STAR.**
Now renamed **FARID M** (Le) 1980.

*11490 Add further sister.
*11503 **KAMALES** (Ru)

*12080 **VENICE**—amend flag to RC.

12130 **AGIOS NICOLAOS**—broken up.

12220 **STATE OF MAINE**—amend name to **EMPIRE STATE.**

*12230 Delete following vessels—appearance differs.
*12317 **GRANITZ.**
*12318 **STUBNITZ**
*12323 **NEKRASOV**—broken up.

*12331 **GOGOL**—broken up.
*12332 **PUSHKIN**—broken up.

*12368 **LERMONTOV**—broken up.

*12680 Add further sister.
*12682 **INZHENER YERMOSHKIN** (Ru).

12730 **KRISTIN BAKKE** → **CER ACTIVITY** (Li) 1981.

12761 **IKAM**—amend name to **IKAN.**

12880 Add sister.
12881 **MAGDALINI K** (Gr); ex IONIAN SKY 1981; ex ELENMA 1977; ex AKASSA PALM 1972.

12892 **IRENES GRACE**—broken up.
12893 **ELSA K**—amend to **ELSA SK.** Now renamed **ETERNAL SEA** (Gr) 1981.

12900 **EUROPEAN EXPRESS** →***HUANG JIN SHAN** (RC)

12910 **LAGOS PALM** → **LAGOS PALM II** (Br) 1981.
12911 **PERUVIAN TRADER** → **RICHMOND** (Br) 1981.

12960 **ANASSA**—broken up.
12966 **NIKOS**—broken up.

13042 **ATHENS WAY**—broken up.

13050 **MEDI-SUN** → **CITY OF CREMORNE** (Cy) 1981.

13090 **TOM** (Gr)—probable total loss.

13190 **IQBALBAKSH**—broken up.

13200 **ATHENS DAY**—broken up.
13202 **NAXOS** → **GULF PRIDE** (Pa) 1981.

13310 **PRA RIVER** → **NOTOS** (Gr) 1981.
13313 **KULPAWN RIVER** → **CATHY** (Cy) 1981.
13314 **LAKE BOSOMTWE** → **CHARMYL** (Cy) 1981.
13316 **OFFIN RIVER** → **NICOL MYLO** (Cy) 1981.

13363 **KOTA MEGAH**—broken up.

13370 **FLORIAN CEYNOWA** → **PRESIDENT OSMENA** (Pi).

13382 **AL SHUWAIKH**—delete from entry. Converted to livestock carrier and renamed.

13390 **ZEA BEACH** → **MAN PO** (Pa) 1980.

13410 **KENNERMERLAND** → **SAUDI VENTURE** (Si) 1981.

13420 **BRAVO DENIS**—broken up.

13430 **NEDLLOYD SEROOSKERK** → **SAUDI EAGLE** (Si) 1981.
13431 **NEDLLOYD SIMONSKERK** → **SAUDI FALCON**(Si) 1981.

13460 **FERNANDAEMME**—broken up.

13521 **NEDLLOYD RIJN** → **SAUDI AMBASSADOR** (Si) 1981.

13560 **FAULAD SARDAR** → **SUCCESS** (Pa) 1981.

13591 **ANNA C** → **DAMENHAN** (Pa) 1981.

13600 **GEMILANG**—broken up.

*13650 Delete.
*13685 **PERIGEY**
Add further sister.
*13741 **ORFEY** (Ru)

13801 **RAS EL HADD** amend to **RAS AL HADD** Now broken up.

13820 **STERNAL TRADER** → **SOCRATES** (Gr) 1981.

13913 **UNION NEW YORK** → broken up.

13920 **SWAN RIVER** → **MUKAIRISH** (Si) 1981.

13980 **BUCHENSTEIN** → **SAUDI ROSE** (Si) 1981.
13981 **BURGENSTEIN** → **SAUDI PALM** (Si) 1981.

13992 **KOTA SENTOSA**—sank 1981.

14000 **CONCORDIA VIKING** → **CONCORDIA VENUS** (Bz) 1980.

14110 **LEDA MAERSK** → **SAUDI CLOUD** (Si) 1981.

14192 **HORNWIND** → **HATTINGEN** Further renamed **ANDROMEDA** (Gr) 1981.

14250 **NAKWA**—burnt out 1981.

14280 **POYANG** →***HUE LU** (RC) 1981.
14281 **CORDILLERA**—amend flag to Ch.

14290 **KRYSTINA F** → **BIG ORANGE** (Sg) 1981.
*14291 **OLESNICA** → **MICHALIS** (Gr) 1981.

*14304 **SWIDNICA** → **KOSTIS** (Gr) 1981.

14330 **MARVALIENTE**—total loss 1981.

14340 **TILLY TUSS** → **TILLY** (Pa) 1980.

14361 **RIO DE LA PLATA**—delete—sequence is different.

*14370 Delete the following sisters and re-enter as Sisters (may be converted to gearless container ships).
*14374 **ALEKSANDR SERAFIMOVICH**
*14377 **ANTON CHEKHOV**
*14382 **GAVRILL DERZHAVIN**
*14386 **NIKOLAY DOBROLYUBOV**
*14387 **NILOLAY GOGOL**
*14394 **VLADIMIR KOROLENKO.**

14402 **LABRADOR** → **VIBORG** (Li) 1980. May be converted to livestock carrier.

14484 **MIECZYSLAW KAUNOWSKI**—amend to **MIECZYSLAW KALINOWSKI.**

14520 **FINNCLIPPER**—amend tonnages to 6500/8800. Renamed **LEONOREVERETT** (Li) 1978.

14540 Add Similar
14542 **OLYMPUS** (Gr); ex ARTEAGA 1981; ex ELYSIA 1969; ex HIGHLAND 1968.

14552 **MORMACTRADE** → **SOUTHERN CROSS**(US) 1980
14554 **COVE** → **MORNING LIGHT** (US) 1980
Both vessels Military Sealift Command.

14560 **ANASSA**—broken up
14566 **NIKOS**—broken up.

14570 **HAMBURG EXPRESS** → **EXPRESS** (Pa) 1980.

14640 **IQBALBAKSH**—broken up.

14730 **BENARTY** → **KOTA PETANI** (Sg) 1981

14780 **CONSTANTINOS T** → **CAPETAN COSTIS** 1978
Further renamed **STYLIANI** 1981. Further renamed **MALDIVE PRIVILEGE** (Mv) 1981.

14810 Add probably similar
14819 **PONTALVA** (Pa); ex GALLEON RUBY 1980; ex PHILIPPINES 1978
14812 **GALLEON PEARL** → **PEARL K** (Pa) 1981.

14830 **SWAN RIVER** → **MUKAIRISH** (Si) 1981.

14840 **NADER** → **SAMAD 1** (Pa) 1980. Later broken up.

15173 **HERCULUS**—amend name to **CEFALLONIAN AMBITION** (Gr). Amend ex name to: ex CIUDAD DE GUAYAQUIL 1980
15174 **CIUDAD DE BARRANQUILLA** → **CEFALLONIAN CHARIS** (Gr) 1981.

*15210 **SUMADIJA**
*15211 **MOSLAVINA**
Delete entry. Sequence now altered—see 15320.

15312 **IRAN NAHAD**—amend name to **IRAN SALAM**.

*15320 Add further sisters:
*15322 **SUMADIJA** (Ys)
*15323 **MOSLAVINA** (Ys).

15330 **JORDAENS** → **CHAR NING** (Pa) 1981.

15360 **PONTEVEDRA** → **GAY FORTUNE** (Gr) 1981.

15372 **AGIA MARINA** → **OLYMPIAKOS** (Gr) 1981.

*15452 **OLIWA** → **ZAHI** (Le) 1980.

15600 **JUTHA DHIPYA**—broken up.

15610 **NEDLLOYD EBRO** → **KOTA MURNI** (Sg) 1981.

15672 **STELLENBOSCH** → **TSAVO** (Li)
15673 **TANGA** → **LLOYD BRISBANE** (As) 1981
Further renamed **BALDER JIANGCHOW** (Pa) 1981.

15712 **ALKMAAR** → **LLOYD AUCKLAND** (Ne) 1980
Further renamed **ALKMAAR** (Ne) 1981.

15720 Amend sequence *KM_4FK_2*.'

15910 **AVRA**—broken up.

15931 **TELANCA** → **TAIPAN PRIDE** (Pa) 1980.

16000 **PAROS**—delete entry—sequence now altered.

16021 **CORMORAN** → **ETAIWI 1** (Si) 1980.

16180 **TINOS** → **POPI** (Gr) 1980.

16360 **BLENHEIM** → **SCANDINAVIAN SEA** (Bs) 1981.

16450 **PRINCE OF BRITTANY**—amend flag to Fr.

16471 **DJURSLAND II** → **DJURSLAND** (De) 1980.

16480 **TRAVEMUNDE** →***NJEGOS** (Ys) 1980.

16500 **QUEEN OF SURREY** → **QUEEN OF THE NORTH** (Ca) 1980.

16513 **NILS DACKE**—delete from entry.

16530 **CANGURO CABO SAN SEBASTIAN** → **CIUDAD DE PALMA** (Sp) 1981.

16551 **DELOS** → **BELLA MARIA** (Gr) 1980.

16560 **GOLDEN PRINCESS**—sank 1980.

16590 **FIESTA**—broken up.

16700 **HEBRIDES**
16701 **COLUMBA**
Delete entire entry—sequence now KMF.

16724 **CAMPANIA PRIMA** → **CASAICCIOLA EXPRESS** (It) 1980.

16941 **SCANDINAVICA** → **TREGOR** 1981.

16970 **CARIBE** → **SCANDINAVIAN SUN** (Bs) 1981.

16992 **STENA NORDICA** → **HELLAS** (Sw) 1980.

17040 **NILS DACKE** → **QUIBERON** 1981.

17091 **ROUSSILON** → **KAMIROS** (Gr) 1980.

17100 **FINNSTAR** → **PEARL OF SCANDINAVIA** (1981)—to be rebuilt and converted.

17180 **HUAL TRAVELLER** → **TRAVELLER** (Li) 1980
Later broken up
17181 **HUAL TROTTER** → **TROTTER** (Li) 1980
Later broken up.

17190 Add further sister
17193 **LALLI** (FRG).

17310 **BRABANT** → **ARGO-HELLAS** (FRG) 1978.

17381 **SUBSEA 1** → **PACIFIC HORIZON** 1981
Delete from entry—now rebuilt.

17451 **CIUDAD DE LA PLATA** → **CIUDAD DE MAR DEL PLATA** (Ar) 1980.

*17580 **ROGALIN**—amend flag to Pd.

17590 **CANGURO CABO SAN SEBASTIAN** → **CIUDAD DE PALMA** (Sp) 1981.

17792 **TAILIAT** → **NEW FORMULA II** (Pa) 1980.

17850 **ORIENT CLIPPER**—broken up.

*17940 **PETROVSK**—broken up.

18050 **CIUDAD DE CADIZ**—broken up.

18200 Delete sister
18201 **EL PODRERO.**

18230 **ILE DE SAINT PIERRE** → **ALINDA** (Gr) 1981.

18370 **DIMITRIOS K**—broken up.

18400 **DEXENA** → **SANG THAI STEEL** (Th) 1981
18401 **MARIA**—total loss 1981
18402 **TANIA** → **ELHAWI STAR** (Si) 1981.

18430 **CASTLE GLORY**—abandoned—aground 1981.

18510 **ORIENT**—broken up.

18850 **LETO**—delete entry—altered in appearance.

19090 **SVEA SCARLETT**—amend flag to De.

19100 **KORSOR**—broken up.

*19143 **SKANDYNAWIA** → **TIEN HU** (Pa) 1981.

19180 **DANA GLORIA** →***BALKANIJA** (Ys) 1981.

19290 **OLAU KENT** → **GELTING NORD** (De) 1980.

19381 **CORSICA SERENA**—add ex TANGER 1975; ex JULIE:
Now renamed **GIOTTO** (It) 1980.

19390 **POLHEM** → **NEREUS** (Gr) 1981.

19510 **KAMOME** → **DONG YANG EXPRESS FERRY No 2** (Ko) 1979.

19860 **EARL SIWARD** → **SOL EXPRESS** (Cy) 1981.

19870 **EARL LEOFRIC**—broken up.

20180 The following is a definite sister
20181 **LADY OF MANN.**

*20310 Add further sisters
*20315 **SAKHALIN—6** (Ru)
*20316 **SAKHALIN—7** (Ru).

20510 **CAESAREA** → **AESAREA** (Pa) 1981.

20540 **DRONNING MARGRETHE II**—delete entry—now lengthened.

20560 **PRINSESSE RAGNHILD** → **JANINA** (No) 1980
Further renamed **AMATISTA** (Li) 1981.

20620 **BORGEN**—delete entry—now rebuilt.

20643 **WELLAMO** → **DANA GLORIA** 1981.

20671 **LIBERTE**—delete from entry.

20750 **ORNEN** → **SARONIC SUN** (Gr) 1981.

20840 **JUAN**—sank after fire 1981.

20861 **MED SUN**—amend name to **MEDITERRANEAN SUN.**

20932 **PRINCE IVANHOE**—holed, beached—total loss 1981.

20950 **PIONEER**—delete entry—now rebuilt.

20960 **HIZBUL BAHR** → **SHAHEED SALAMUDDIN** (Bh) 1981.

21100 **EL PODRERO**—delete entry—now converted to livestock carrier.

21130 **BLUE OCEAN**—broken up.

21243 **RONIREL** → **PACIFIC FRUIT** (Sg) 1978. Further renamed **COMFORT** (Tw) 1981
21245 **AVANTI**—broken up.

21320 **SANSTEFANO**—broken up.

21350 **ATLANTIC FREEZER**—broken up.

21380 **ROSY** → **SAFINA REEFER** (Si) 1980.

21403 **ANNAFLORA** → **NISSOS SAMOS** 1978—broken up 1981.

21471 **NEDON** → **ALMA M** (Pa) 1980
21473 **FORTUNE CARRIER** → **SIDERI**—broken up.

21540 **BOUAR** → **NOURAN** (Le) 1979—broken up.

21550 **ELLITSA** → **TIMBU** (SL) 1981.

21670 **SAC BARCELONA**—broken up.

21690 **AMSTERDAM** → **JETPUR DELIGHT** (Pa) 1981.

21760 **OLGA**—broken up.

21780 **SYMON** → **ANEMOS** (1976)—now broken up.

21830 **CASTLE GLORY**—abandoned—aground 1981.

21841 **ORIENT**—broken up.

21880 **LAS PALMAS → KATLA.** Delete entry—now converted to ferry.

21890 **LILLA**—broken up.

21980 **SANTA MARIA DEL PINO**—broken up.

22070 **IONA**—delete entry—now rebuilt.

*22185 **SEJMEN CHELYUSKIN**—amend to **SEMYON CHELYUSKIN**
*22186 **SEJMEN DEZHNEV**—amend to **SEMYON DEZHNEV.**

22520 Delete entire entry.

22711 **OSBORNE CASTLE → LE GOBELET D'ARGENT** (Ca) 1980.

22800 **ATLANTA**—delete entry—altered in appearance.

*22820 **MONTE CASSINO → DARLING** (Pa) 1981.

22830 **DESANMAR → THEODOROS II** (Cy) 1980.

22854 **KAPITAN VOOLENS → LENIN** (An) 1978.

22890 **MALDIVE CARRIER**—delete entry—changed in appearance, cargo gear removed.

22950 **TANIA → ELHAWI STAR** (Si) 1981
22951 **MARIA**—damaged by fire—total loss 1981
22952 **DEXENA → SANG THAI STEEL** (Th) 1981.

23101 **PORTO PYLOS → GULF FRIO** (Gr) 1981.

23143 **CITY OF LEEDS**—total loss.

23180 **SEA BEAUTY**—broken up.

23330 **CERDIC FERRY → ATLAS I** (Gr) 1981
23331 **DORIC FERRY → ATLAS II** (Gr) 1981.

23700 **OLAU KENT → GELTING NORD** (De) 1980.

23931 **DIANA → APOSTOLOS M II** (Gr) 1978. Further renamed **DIMITRIS** (Gr) 1980.

24140 **SEEFREEZE ATLANTIC**—amend to **SEAFREEZE ATLANTIC.**

24210 **PRINCESSE ANNE → POLAR PRINCE** (Ca)—to be converted to seismographic survey.

24252 **TUNDRALAND → ARCTIC TIDE** (Br) 1981.

24284 **LAGO LACAR**—delete from entry—cranes before bridge have been removed. Some, or all, of the others in the class may be similarly altered.

24290 **VAUCLUSE → CHAR KWEI** (Pa) 1981.

24300 Add further similar ships
24303 **LLOYD BAKKE** (No)
24304 **SANTOS** (Pa); ex GUDRUN BAKKE 1981
24302 **EMMA BAKKE → HAI MENG** (Pa) 1981.

*24310 Add **'B-406'** type and add sisters (Ru flag)
*24311 **TIORA**
*24312 **TROCHUS**
*24313 **UVAROVSK**
*24314 **IVAN BORZOV**
*24315 **UZGORSK**
*24316 **ZEMLYANSK**
*24317 **GORYACHEGORSK**
*24318 **YEVGENIY PREOBRAZENSKIY**
*24319 **TRYDAKNA.**

24370 **OBESTAIN**—broken up.

24380 **ANDINO**—amend flag to Pe.

24440 **CIUDAD DE PAMPLONA → KOTA SINGAPURA** (Sg) 1981.
24441 **VILLA DE BILBAO → NEW PHOENIX** (Sg) 1981.

24470 **MARIA SOFIA**—probable total loss

24573 **FILIA → CALIOPE** (Gr) 1981
24574 **KITMEER**—amend flag to Pa

24580 **EL QUETZAL → STAR 1** (Gr) 1980

24620 **POLYXENE G → PATRICIA T** (Gr) 1981

24661 **BUNGA BUTANG**—broken up

24700 **LILIANE → RUBINI F** (Pa) 1980.

24710 **AQUILEIA → INTRA SPRAY** (Pa) 1981
24711 **PIAVE → INTRA SUN** (Pa) 1981

24790 **TONG HONG → COSMOS MERCHANT**—now broken up.

24860 **MALDIVE SEAFARER**—broken up
24862 **CAPETAN COSTAS**—amend flag to Gr.

24872 **WEIRBANK → SARONIC SKY** (Gr)—now a total loss.

24894 **THEANO → EFMAR**—now broken up.

24962 **TAILIAT → NEW FORMULA II** (Pa) 1981.

25011 **HOLLANDIA**—broken up.

25070 **MARIA → JETPUR VICTORY** (Sg) 1981
25071 **LELA → JETPUR VICEROY** (Sg) 1980
25072 **COMMENCEMENT → CARIBBEAN** (Gr) 1981. Further renamed **MELPOL** (Br) 1981.

25080 **ANTONIA → VIVI** (Gr) 1980.

25131 **CHRYSSOULA II**—broken up.

25180 **LONDINON**—amend flag to Cy.

25271 **DABEMA → ASIA CARRIER I**—now broken up
25276 **ASIA CARRIER**—amend to **ASIA CARRIER II**—now broken up
25277 **ASIA CARRIER III**—broken up.

25400 **DIANA**—delete entire entry.

25530 **NICOLAOS G → SYRIA STAR** (Sy) 1981.

25573 **VOLO**—broken up.

25710 **ALIAKMON BREEZE → KOUKOUNARIES K** (Gr) 1981.

25720 **PLEIAS → SPYROS G** (Gr) 1981.

25750 Add similar ships
25751 **CALIFORNIA** (Pa); ex KWANGTUNG 1978; ex NORMAN 1966; ex KWANGTUNG 1965
25752 **STRAITS STAR** (Br); ex BANGKOK STAR; ex NEW GUINEA CHIEF 1977; ex KWANGSI 1971.

25861 **MAH 2**—amend to **MAH II.**

25880 **AKRA SOUNION → SOUNION 1979.** Further renamed **LEFKADIAN SKY** (Gr) 1980
25881 **AKRA RION → RION 1979.** Further renamed **DATSUN** (1981). Further renamed **CEYOCEAN** (Ce) 1981.

25900 **NAJADE → DALIA D** (Pa) 1981.

25920 **HOUDA STAR**—broken up.

25960 **EURABIA WIND → RAW LINES** (Le) 1980.

25970 **AMSTERDAM → JETPUR DELIGHT** (Pa) 1981.

26061 **CONNY**—broken up.

26111 **NEW WAN FU → CHAR CHENG** (Pa)—now broken up.

26122 **ISOBEL → INTRA TRADITION** (Pa) 1981.

26240 **DINA** → DINA NED 1978 → **MERCURY 1 1980 → ZEA PORT (Gr) 1980 → STAMATIA (Gr) 1981.**

26271 **BUNGA BUTANG**—broken up.

26320 **TRIGLAV →*CIKAT** (Ys) 1980
26322 **VELEBIT →*DOLFIN** (Ys) 1980.

26340 **EUGENIA V**—explosion—Total loss 1981.

26401 **IOANIS XILAS**—broken up.

26420 **SANIX BELLE**—broken up.

26441 **NORTH EMPRESS → SKYRIAN EMPRESS** (Gr) 1981.

26570 **BONITA → MAYSUN II** (Gr) 1981.

26590 **PEARL DELTA**—broken up.

26670 **EASTAR → EASTERN NAV** (Pa) 1979.

26690 **SAINI → TARA** (Pa) 1981.

26752 **AUSTRIAN MERCHANT**—broken up.

26791 **CHARITY**—sank 1981.

26801 **SANTIAGO → AGRILIA** (Pa) 1981.

26872 **AURELIA**—probably total loss.

*26990 **STAVROPOL**—broken up.

27060 **TAMIL PERIYAR E.V.R.**—broken up.

27080 **DONA KATERINA**—broken up.

27090 **YOUTH GIANT**—broken up.

27250 **MICHAEL K → JETPUR MUSAFIR** 1980. Since broken up.

27320 **SWIFT SEAGULL**—broken up.

27361 **BULSOOK → AL BADR** (Pa) 1980.

27410 **ASPASIA M → SEA RENOWN** (Pa) 1980.

27500 **ANTIGONI TSIRIS**—broken up.

27571 **ELENIK** amend to **ELENI K.** Now renamed **CATHY P** (Pa) 1981.

27600 **DIONI → ANTONIS** (Gr) 1980. Further renamed **MIMIE** (Pa). Now broken up.

27620 **TANIA P**—broken up.

27690 **CHRISOULA K**—total loss
27691 **AUSTRIAN IMPORTER → NIGERIAN IMPORTER** (Pa) 1980. Further renamed **COLIBRI 1** 1980. Further renamed **CEFALLONIAN SUN** (Gr) 1981.

27781 **AMORGOS → YASHOO** 1979. Further renamed **GULF STAR** 1980. Now broken up.

27790 **KOTA PANJANG**—broken up.

27850 **SCALRAY → ROBIN HOOD** (Cy) 1980.

27860 **EVANGELOS B**—broken up.

27950 **JANAKI → SAI NANAK** (In) 1980.

28030 **SEA KING → A-TRADER** (1981).

28080 **MANDOULA**—broken up.

28121 **ZEA SKY → KETTY** (Gr) 1980. Further renamed **NIMAS II** (Gr) 1981.

28260 **KALLIXENOS → ARION** (Gr) 1981.

28290 **JALAGOURI → JALDOOT ASHOK** (In) 1981.

28310 **DENIZHANLAR**—broken up.

28343 **CITY OF LEEDS**—broken up.

28360 **SAN SPYRIDON IV**—broken up.

★28494 **VASILIY KACHALOV**—broken up.

28561 **ZEA SKY** → **KETTY** (Gr) 1980. Further renamed **NIMAS II** (Gr) 1981

28570 **DENIZHANLAR**—broken up.

28660 **MARIA** → **MORIAS** 1978 → **THRACIAN NANA** (Gr) 1979 → **PARNASSUS** (Gr) 1981.

28831 **DIANA** → **APOSTOLOS M II** (Gr) 1978. Further renamed **DIMITRIS** (Gr) 1980.

28840 **BARBARA B**—total loss.

28856 **CHRYS**—broken up.

28871 **CAPITAINE WALLIS**—broken up.

28990 **MIR** → ★**PYONG HWA** (RK).

29010 **JISKRA** → **PIERROS** (Gr) 1980.

29080 **CAVO DORO** → **LUZON** (Ho) 1980. Later broken up.

29160 **IDEFJORD** → **NEW PEACOCK** (Sg) 1981.

29170 **ATTILIO IEVOLI** → **MIZAR** (It) 1980.

29180 **OLYMPIOS ZEUS** → **GEORGIOS G** (Cy) 1980.

29220 **WHITEHALL**—broken up.

29245 **CELEBES SEA** → ★**HONG QI 102** (RC).

29260 **HUAL AKARITA** → **AKARITA** (Li) 1980.

29301 **CUMULUS**—broken up.

29322 **TACOMA MARU** → **EASTERN PEARL** (Pa) 1981.

29330 **MERCURY GULF** → **SAUDI SUNRISE** (Pa) 1981.

29363 **LINK FAITH** → **EUROPEAN FAITH** (Gr) 1981
29364 **MARACANA I** → **PARACALLAK** (Si) 1981.

29400 **LIMA** → **MAYFLOWER** (Pa) 1981.

29450 **CEFALLONIAN AMBITION** → **HERCULUS** (Gr) 1980
29451 **SYNARISTIA** → **EVEREST** (Gr) 1981.

29470 **SEAHORSE**—broken up.

29670 **RIO AMAZONAS** → **MAZON** (Pa) 1980.

29700 **WEIKO**—amend to **WEIKUO.**

29810 **ONYX ISLANDS**—delete entry—sequence altered.

29832 **CHERRY SINDIA**—broken up.

29952 **RAJAAN** → **PARDESI** (Pa) 1981—also reported as **PARADESI.**

29980 **PEARL VALLEY** → **VIVACIOUS** 1981—now broken up.

30020 **ZEA SILVER** → **PANOS** (Gr) 1980 → **KOTINOS** 1980 → **INTRA SKY** (Pa) 1981.

30080 **EASTERN ACADEMY**—amend flag to Si.

30162 **LITO**—sank 1981.

30240 **LU CHIANG**—broken up.

30260 **SYNARISTIA** → **EVEREST** (Gr) 1981.

30300 **TAIPOOSEK** → **STAR SHIP** (Gr) 1981.

30382 **PARIS** → **TITHIS**—now broken up.

30450 **KARANA AMPAT**—probable total loss.

30521 **TACOMA MARU** → **EASTERN PEARL** (Pa) 1981.

30552 **LIMA** → **MAYFLOWER** (Pa) 1981.

30581 **LINK FAITH** → **EUROPEAN FAITH** (Gr) 1981.

30600 **CEFALLONIAN AMBITION** → **HERCULUS** (Gr) 1980.

30670 **CHRISTOS S. T. ARAPAKIS**—probable total loss.

30680 **AEOLIAN WIND**—broken up.

30940 **ZAMBOANGA** → **ZAMBOANGA I** 1980. Further renamed **ZAMBO** (Pa) 1981.

30950 **MANILA** → **MANILA 1** (Pi) 1980.

30990 **BOLA No1**—total loss.

31160 **CAPITAINE LA PEROUSE** → **BOUNTY** (Fr) 1981.

31170 **TEVEGA** → **DIMMER** (Pa) 1981.

31193 **HORIZON** → **HELMAR** (Gr) 1980.

31270 **TACOMA MARU** → **EASTERN PEARL** (Pa) 1981.

31303 **CARENERO** → **ANTZELA** (Gr) 1981.

★31380 **MARSHAL GOVOROV**—probably broken up.

31400 **ANGELINA**—sunk 1981.

31560 **BISCAYA GOLF** → **NEW DAWN** (Sg) 1981.

31600 **TRADER** → **BENGAL PRIDE** (Bh) 1981.

31640 **MARE ARABICO** → **BANANERA** (Pa) 1981.

31650 **BIAFRA** → **BIANCA** (Bs) 1981.

★31680 **SOVIETSKAYA ARTIKA**—amend to **SOVIETSKAYA ARKTIKA.**

31720 **AMINA** → **AMINA-1** (Pa) 1980.

31800 **SILK** → **GALAXY II** (Gr) 1981

31800 add further sister
31803 **DRAGON EXPRESS** (Tw); ex TA PENG No 3 1979; ex CELEBES MARU 1970.

31922 **YONG FING**—amend to **YONG MING.**

31930 **CHARALAMBOS M. PATERAS**—amend to **CHARALAMBOS N. PATERAS**—now renamed **CAPTAIN ANDREADIS** (Gr) 1980.

31960 **KASEM SAMUT** → **ELDE** (Gr).

31980 **LUZON**—broken up.

31990 **VOULLA** → **BEGONIA D** (Pa) 1980.

32004 **CITY OF LEEDS**—total loss.

32020 **AVRA** → **MIGHT WIND** (Pa) 1981.

32310 **GRYF** → **EOLOS** (Gr) 1981.

32330 **DONA MONTSERRAT**—amend to ★**XING HU** (RC).

32460 **FUJI** → **ILIGAN CITY.** Further renamed **OZAMIS CITY** (Pi) 1980.

32540 Delete entire entry. All vessels transferred to 32550.

32550 Add further sisters
32552 **BOCCACCIO**
32553 **CARDUCCI**
32554 **LEOPARDI**
32555 **MANZONI**
32556 **PASCOLI**
32557 **PETRARCA.**

32770 **MARELLA** → **ALCAEUS** (Gr) 1981.

32801 **DJURSLAND II** → **DJURSLAND** (De) 1980
32802 **TRAVEMUNDE** → ★**NJEGOS** (Ys) 1980.

32972 **STARMARK** → **RIO TRADER** (Gr) 1981.

32982 **ESPRESSO SICILIA** → **EASTERN ISLE** (Li) 1981.

33290 **BRABANT** → **ARGO-HELLAS** (FRG) 1978.

33350 **GLEN SANNOX**—delete entry—now rebuilt.

33410 **CIUDAD DE HUESCA**—broken up.

33450 **REMJAY** → **POLAR B.V.** (Pa) 1981.

33520 **TEVEGA** → **DIMMER** (Pa) 1981.

33540 **KOSTER** → **SPORT ROVER** (Pa) 1980.

33780 **DONA ANA** → **DONA MARILYN** (Pi) 1980.

33810 **DAVAO** → **CHION TRADER** (Gr) 1981
33811 **DARIEN** → **CHION CARRIER** (Gr) 1981.

33930 Amend sister to similar
33391 **AUDACIA**
Add further similar
33932 **ISADORE HECHT** (Pa); ex CLYDEFIRTH 1980; ex VIKFRIO 1974; ex THORSOY 1972.

33953 **NYOMBE** → **TURTLE** (Bs) 1981.

34080 **ARIANE II**—amend name to **FIORITA** (Pa) —amend ex names to ex AMSTERDAM 1970.

34142 **PAMPA ARGENTINA** → **SANTIAGO** (Pa) 1981.

34209 **ANDANIA** → **EUROPA FREEZER** (Gr) 1981
34216 **ALAUNIA** → **OCEANIA FREEZER** (Gr) 1981
34222 **ALSATIA** → **AMERICA FREEZER** (Gr) 1981
34223 **ANDRIA** → **AUSTRALIA FREEZER** (Gr) 1981.

★34260 **FRANO SUPILO** → **CER ALACRITY** (Li) 1981
★34261 **MATKO LAGINJA** → **CER AMITY** (Pa) 1981
★34262 **IVAN MAZURANIC** → **CER AGILITY** (Pa) 1981.

34280 **MINDANAO**—broken up.

34350 **INDIA ROSEWOOD** → **ROSEWOOD** (Pa) 1980—broken up 1981.

★34372 **WOLIN** → **MAHMOUDY** (Eg) 1981.

34484 **KAPITAN VOOLENS** → **LENIN** (An) 1978.

34530 **TWIGHT**—amend to **TWILIGHT**—amend ex names to read: ex EVER GRACE 1980; ex TWILIGHT 1979; ex GREENLAKE 1977; ex NASIPIT MARU 1972.

★34646 **ZASHCHITNIK**—amend to **ZASHCHITNIK ZAPOLYARYA.**

34781 **SOMERSET** → **PURCELL LIVESTOCK**—delete from entry -converted to livestock carrier.

34832 **KULPAWN RIVER** → **CATHY** (Cy) 1981
34834 **OFFIN RIVER** → **NICOL MYLO** (Cy) 1981
34836 **PRA RIVER** → **NOTOS** (Gr) 1981
34837 **LAKE BOSOMTWE** → **CHARMYL** (Cy) 1981.

34950 **ACONCAGUA II**—broken up
34951 **COPIAPO II**—broken up
34952 **ALLIANCE SUCCESS**—broken up.

35020 **SANSHIN PIONEER** → **EURO NAUTILUS** (Gr) 1981.

35130 add further sister
35138 **AUSTRAL MOON** (US); ex AUSTRALIA BEAR 1975; ex PHILIPPINE BEAR 1975.

35274 **SAUDI INDEPENDENCE**—amend name to **SAUDI TRADER**
35275 **SAUDI TRADER**—amend name to **SAUDI INDEPENDENCE.**

35291 **KENFIG** → **HEDON SAND** (Br) 1981.

35470 **INVENTOR** → **PENTA WORLD** (Sg) 1981.

35584 **COCLERDUE**—broken up.

35660 **SPAN QUARTA** → **ARISTON** (It) 1980.

35660 **KATERINA**—amend to **KATERINA A.**

35675 **ETTORE** → **NATHALIE** 1978. Further renamed **NATHALI** (Cy) 1981.

35750 **ALLISON STAR** → **SANIKA** (Pa) 1981—since broken up.
35751 **ABELARDO L. RODRIGUEZ**—broken up.

35813 **AURORA**—broken up.

35902 **THEOFANO LIVANOS** → **CALLIROY** (Gr) 1980.

35951 **ANSON** → **CORAL GEORGE.** Further renamed **CELESTE** (Pa) 1980.

36063 **WORTHY** → **ANTIGONI P** (Pa) 1980
36064 **ELEISTRIA II**—broken up.

36071 **GRAINVILLE**—now has a funnel. Possible total loss.

36210 **MICHALIS** → **TAXIARCHIS** (Gr) 1980.

36240 **WINDRATI**—amend flag to Pa.

36280 Add similar ship
36283 **FORUM PLESSOT** (Gr); ex JIHAD 1981; ex TOMMY II 1981; ex ARGO LEADER 1976; ex WORLD SEAFARER 1972.

36390 **AFOVOS** → **MIKI** (Pa) 1981.

36400 **CAPITAN CARLO** → **POLYKLIS** (Gr) 1980.

36410 **MICHALIS** → **TAXIARCHIS** (Gr) 1980.

36433 **COCLERDUE**—broken up.

36480 Add further similar ship
36483 **FORUM PLESSOT** (Gr); ex JIHAD 1981; ex TOMMY II 1981; ex ARGO LEADER 1976; ex WORLD SEAFARER 1972.

36620 **MIZAR** → **UNITED COURAGE** (Pa) 1980—since broken up.

36683 **TEXACO GLOUCESTER** → **FIVE LAKES** (Pa) 1981.

*36710 **JIN HU** → **WAH FU** (Pa) 1981.

36850 **ESSO YORK**—broken up.

36980 **YANNIS K**—broken up.

37060 **AL SALIMI V**—add ex MARIA PIA ESSE before other ex names.

37092 **ABELARDO L. RODRIGUEZ**—broken up
37093 **ALLISON STAR** → **SANIKA**—later broken up.

37152 **ORE METEOR**—broken up
37153 **ORE NEPTUNE**—broken up.

37221 **KAYESON—AOUNALLAH** (Pa) 1981.

37231 **VIANA**—broken up.

37240 **TEXACO VENZUELA**—broken up.

37260 **CHILBAR**—delete from entry—rebuilt.

37342 **NIVES** → **IVE** (It) 1980.

37350 **SHARON H**—broken up.

37450 **PETROMAR CORDOBA**—broken up.

37460 **ALEXANDRA CONWAY**—broken up.

37550 **DEA BROVIG**—amend flag to Li.

37560 **EGEON**—broken up.

37660 **TYCHOS**—broken up.

37760 **ORIENTAL DRAGON**—broken up.

37770 **COMMONWEALTH** → **GAMMA** (Pa)—then broken up.

37850 **PALLIUM**—broken up
37851 **PARTULA** → **LUSSIN** (It) 1981.

37940 **ANGEL PARK**—broken up.

37960 **APOIKIA** → **KALYMNOS**—then broken up.

38000 **LONG PHOENIX**—delete entry—now rebuilt.

38060 **PHILLIPS TEXAS**—broken up.

38070 **PETROLA 27** → **POLASIA 27**—then broken up.

38110 **MOBIL COMET** → **MONTANA** (Li) 1981.

38132 **TASSO**—broken up.

38280 **PHOENIX STAR**—broken up.

38335 **HANJIANG** → **NEWHAVEN** (Pa) 1981.

38350 **MALDIVE CORAL**—broken up.

38370 **LONDON CONFIDENCE**—broken up.

38480 **ESSO CHILE**—broken up.

*38611 **BALAKLAVA**—has a shorter funnel and the forepart of the after accommodation is more open.

38750 **CORAL**—amend name to **CORAL GEORGE**— renamed **CELESTE** (Pa) 1980.

38790 **SAINT ETIENNE** → **GUNGNIR III** 1979. Further renamed **SAN MARCO** (Pa) 1980.

38800 **COMMONWEALTH** → **GAMMA** (Pa)—then broken up.

38870 **VENTURE TEXAS**—broken up.

38890 **MONTAN**—broken up.

38901 **CAMPOBLANCO**—is confirmed as a sister.

38941 **IFEWARA** → **NORB** (Br) 1981.

38970 **FRANCES**—amend flag to Pa.

38990 Add similar
38992 **ATHENS STAR** (Gr); ex SILVER COAST 1980; ex KANDELFELS 1977.

39091 **IFEWARA** → **NORB** (Br) 1981.

39161 **ELBA**—broken up.

39180 **CANADA MARU** → **CANADIAN ACE** (Pa) 1980.

*39410 Add further sisters—(Ru flag)
*39413 **DALNIYE ZELYENTSK**
*39414 **ISKATEL**
*39415 **ISSLEDOVATEL**
*39416 **LEV TITO**
*39417 **MORSKOY GEOFIZIK**
*39418 **RUDOLF SAMOYLOVICH**
*39419 **VULKANLOG.**

39440 **MELINA TSIRIS**—broken up.

*39450 Add **'B 406'** type. Add sisters (Ru flag);
*39451 **TIORA**
*39452 **UVAROVSK**
*39453 **UZGORSK**
*39454 **GORYACHEGORSK**
*39455 **TROCHUS**
*39456 **IVAN BORZOV**
*39457 **ZEMLYANSK**
*39458 **YEVENIY PREOBRAZENSKIY**
*39459 **TRYDAKNA.**

39470 **LEMPA**—broken up.

39500 **UHENFELS** → **UHENBELS** (Gr) 1980.

39520 **CAYMEN TRADER**—amend to **CAYMAN TRADER.**

39541 **EL FLAMINGO**—broken up.

39570 **KARINA**—total loss.

39780 **SALEEMA** → **VIJAYA DARSHANA** (In) 1980.

39801 **SYMMETRIA** → **NIMAS 1** (Gr) 1981.

39931 **ZENAIDE A**—broken up.

*39970 **LENINGRAD** → **SVETLOMOR** (Ru) 1979. Now converted to oil pollution control vessel. May be altered in appearance
*39984 **GRODNO**—now a storage hulk
*40005 **LENINSK** → **SLAV MARU**—now broken up
*40012 **DZERZHINSK**—broken up.

40270 **LENTINI** → **ERSILIA L** (It) 1980. Further renamed **IRENE** (It) 1981.

40280 **VENTURE SEA** → **ELNICO** (Gr) 1980. Further renamed **DINIE S** (Gr) 1980.

40291 **CORINTHIAKOS** → **EASTERN GUARDIAN** (Pa) 1980.

40300 **CAP PALMAS** → **PALMAS** (FRG) 1979.

40341 **EASTERN GRAND** → **TIMUR GRAND** (Pa) 1980—broken up
40342 **YANMAR**—broken up.

40410 **LAMDA** → **BLUE DANUBE** (Li) 1980.

40480 **MADINIA** → **SUNLIGHT** (Pa) 1980.

40571 **ZENAIDE A**—broken up.

40590 **COSMOPOLITAN** → **KANG SUN**—later broken up.

40650 **MANTINIA**—broken up.

40700 **PERMINA 108**—broken up.

40740 **MARIA E** → **GULF STAR**—later broken up.

40780 **PERMINA 101**—broken up.

40800 **PISTIS**—broken up.

40880 **ELPIS N** → **ATLANTIS 1** (Cy) 1980.

40930 **KOSMOS** → **APUS** (Pa) 1980.

40950 **CAPETAN ALECOS MILONAS** → **ALECOS** (Pa) 1980.

41130 **YANMAR**—broken up
41131 **EASTERN GRAND** → **TIMUR GRAND** (Pa) 1980—broken up.

41160 **ISLAS GEORGIAS**—broken up.

41170 **TEXACO NORTH DAKOTA** → **BLANCO** (US) 1981.

41261 **APJ ANJLI**—broken up.

41350 **RAJAH BROOKE**—broken up.

41440 **VALNY**—broken up.

41470 **PISTIS**—broken up.

41510 **AKRA AKTION**—grounded—total loss.

41570 **STAR**—amend flag to Gr.

41583 **AURORA**—broken up.

41592 **THEOFANO LIVANOS** → **CALLIROY** (Gr) 1980.

41730 **AGIOS NICOLAOS IV**—amend to **AGIOS NIKOLAOS IV** Amend flag to Gr.

41750 **TANJA HOLWERDA** → **JENSON II** 1981.

41780 **EIRINI L**—broken up.

41791 **GRAINVILLE**—delete from entry—now has a funnel. May be a total loss.

41803 **WORTHY** → **ANTIGONI P** (Pa) 1980
41804 **ELEISTRIA II**—broken up.

41840 **AGIA IRINI 1** → **EKATERINI STR.** (Cy) 1980
41870 **GRIGORIS** → **MELINA** (Gr) 1980.

41980 **CAR EXPRESS** → **BRAHMAN EXPRESS** (Va) 1981.

42001 **FEDERAL TYNE** → **KERRY EXPRESS**—delete from entry—rebuilt as Livestock Carrier.

42461 **BALLYLORAN** → **ALLA EL DEEN** (Si) 1981.

42490 **THALASSITRA**—broken up.

42720 **BALLYCASTLE** → **AREF** (Le) 1981.

42760 **SINGAPORE RAMIN**—amend flag to Pa.

42770 **LISSA** → **ELVINA** (Gr) 1979. Further renamed **JOYCE CLARE** (Cy) 1980. May be spelt **JOYCE CLAIR.**

42823 **PROVIDENCE GETTY** → **CRISTINA E** (Pa) 1980.

43148 **PASUDU** → **SABANG** (Ia) 1980.

43230 **DOMENICO IEVOLI** → **PUNTA GAUDIO** (Pa) 1980. Further renamed **GUNGA DIN II** 1980.

43380 **TEES BAY** → **SWANSEA BAY** (Br) 1979.

43391 **NEMA**—broken up.

43440 **CALIFORNIAN** → **CALIFORNIA** (US) 1980.

43491 and 43551 **ALEXIS G** → **ATHENS LUCK** (Gr) 1981.

43570 **ELENA** → **ADVENTURE 1** (Gr) 1980.

43600 **ANGEL PARK**—broken up.

43651 **ANTCLIZO**—broken up.

43670 **JENNIFER**—broken up.

43700 **TEXACO IDAHO**—broken up
43701 **TEXACO VIRGINIA**—broken up.

43760 **GIOVANNELLA D'AMICO**—broken up.

43900 **MIRAMAR**—broken up.

43950 **ALFA CEMENTA**—delete from entry.

43990 **CHEVRON MADRID**—broken up.

44080 **AEGEAN SEA** → **WEALTHY STAR** (Pa) 1981.
44082 **SEALORD 1** → **MALDIVE NATION** (Mv) 1980
44083 **BARRIAN** → **ARION** (Gr) 1981.
Add further sister
44084 **NIKY** (Gr); ex VESTLAND 1970.

44200 **ANGELA F** → **SHOMAR HANAN** (Si)—in use as a bunkering vessel at Jeddah.

44221 **PETROMAR CORDOBA**—broken up.

44290 **TOXOTIS** → **JAGUAR** (Cy) 1980. Further renamed **TOXOTIS** (Cy) 1981.

44320 **ALPHA CEMENTA**—delete from entry.

44390 **AEGEAN SEA** → **WEALTHY STAR** (Pa) 1981
44392 **SEALORD 1** → **MALDIVE NATION** (Mv) 1980
44393 **BARRIAN** → **ARION** (Gr) 1981.
Add further sister
44394 **NIKY** (Gr); ex VESTLAND 1970.

44430 **PARTULA** → **LUSSIN** (It) 1981
44431 **PALLIUM**—broken up.

44470 **SILVER ISLAND** → **AMALIA** (Gr) 1981.

44530 **ANGEL PARK**—broken up.

44572 **GULFTIGER** → **SUZANNE** (US) 1981.

44600 **MIRAMAR**—broken up.

44640 **URANUS**—broken up.

44695 **HANJIANG** → **NEWHAVEN** (Pa) 1981.

44730 **CHAPARRAL**—broken up.

44762 **CAMPOBLANCO**—delete as possible sister.

44770 **WASSIMA**—broken up.

44920 **BOMIN II** → **BOMIN WILHELMSHAVEN** (Sg) 1981.

44940 **YANMAR**—broken up
44941 **EASTERN GRAND** → **TIMUR GRAND** (Pa) 1980—broken up.

44981 **APJ ANJLI**—broken up.

45202 **NIVES** → **IVE** (It) 1980.

45230 **CANADA MARU** → **CANADIAN ACE** (Pa) 1980.

45260 **EIRINI L**—broken up.

*45270 Add further sisters—(Ru flag)
*45274 **PISHCHEVAYA PROMYSHIENNOST**
*45275 **RYBAK VLADIVOSTOKA**
Delete '2 more on order'

45376 **AL ODAILIAH** → **ROSA S** (Pa) 1981
45377 **AL KADISIAH** → **ALEXA II** (Pa) 1981
45388 **POLANA**—amend flag to Li
45389 **PANGANI** → **ALBANY** (Sg) 1980.

45451 **TIMI** → **HAPPY MED** (Li) 1981.

45460 **TONY'S LUCK** → **MIRAMAR PRIMA** (It) 1980.

45470 **GRYNGE**—delete from entry. Now converted to chemical tanker.

45572 **TENO** → **BUDI** (Li) 1981.

45610 **MIRRABOOKA**—At least one of this class (maybe all) has had the mast & kingpost in the well replaced by sets of tandem cranes
45611 **POPI** → **ATHINAI** (Gr) 1980.

45790 **SAINT JACQUES** → **WOOLLAHRA** (Sw) 1981.

45820 **ASEAN OBJECTIVE** → **MISTI** (Pe) 1981. Note: now converted to bulk/container, may have some alterations in appearance.

45862 **SUNWARD** → **ATLANTIC MARINER** (Li) 1980.

45883 **KAPETAN ANTONIS** → **ANTONY O** 1981. Further renamed **FADEL G** (Le) 1981.

45970 **SACRAMENTO MARU** → **MULTI CARRIER** (Pa)
45971 **HELEN** → **ELENA** (Ma) 1981
45972 **SAN FRANCISCO MARU** → **CHAOHU CAREER** (Pa).

46022 **SUNWARD** → **ATLANTIC MARINER** (Li) 1980.

46114 **ASIAN ADVENTURESS** → **ANITA DAN** (Bs) 1981.

46130 **LIBERIAN STATESMAN** → **MINORIES PRIDE** (Pa) 1981.

46170 **NORSE VIKING** → **NORSE CAPTAIN** (Bs) 1980.

46211 **GOLDEN NICHOLAS** → **ADELFA** (Pa) 1981.

46310 **BOLNES** → **EASTERN ALLIANCE** (Li) 1981.

46360 **YAN HE**—amend sequence to KC_5MF.

46370 add further sisters (DDR Flag);
*46385 **INSELSEE.**
*46386 **RHINSEE.**
*46387 **SCHWIELOSEE.**
*46388 **TRENNTSEE** (may be spelt **TRENTSEE).**

46420 **ARGO** → **LEENOR** (Is) 1981.
46421 **VIRGO** → **LEEOR** (Is) 1981.

46439 **NORSE HERALD** → **NORSE CARRIER** (Bs) 1981.
46447 **CAMARA** → **ELPIDOFOROS** (Gr) 1981.

46471 **ANDROMEDA** → **ARION** (Li) 1981.

46512 **TOYOTA MARU No 7** → **ELENI M** (Ma) 1981.

46522 **AGIOI VICTORES** → **NEGEV ORON** (Is) 1981.
46528 **SANTA POLA** → **TELFAIR TRADER** (Li) 1981.

46560 **BOLNES** → **EASTERN ALLIANCE** (Li) 1981.

46641 **KARAMU FOREST** → **OCEAN VENUS** (Pa) 1981.

46650 add further sisters (Br Flag):
46652 **NOSIRA LIN.**
46653 **NOSIRA SHARON.**

46700 **PENERF** → **ANBOTO** (Li) 1981.

46720 **SCOTSPARK** → **NAN TA** (Sg) 1981.

46873 **STAR EMERALD** → **PROTOMACHOS** (Gr) 1981.

47001 **KANAGAWA MARU** → **SILVER EXPRESS** (Pa) 1980.
47002 **HIRATSUKA MARU**—amend flag to Ja.

47030 **E. R. BRUGGE**—amend tonnage to 13400.
47031 **CAST WALRUS**—amend ex names as follows: ex E. R. BRUSSEL 1981; ex C. P. HUNTER 1980; ex E. R. BRUSSEL 1980.

47070 add further sisters (DDR flag):
*47085 **INSELSEE.**
*47086 **RHINSEE.**
*47087 **SCHWIELOSEE.**
*47088 **TRENNTSEE** (may be spelt **TRENTSEE)**

47090 **GLOBE EXPRESS** → **UNICEB** (It) 1981.

47203 **PRIMULA** → **PAN EXPRESS** (Ko) 1981.
47204 **PRIMAVERA** → **PRIMAVERA I** 1980 further renamed **PAN QUEEN** (Ko) 1981
add further sister (US built):
47217 **STAR OF TEXAS** (US).

47250 **KATJANA**—amend flag to Pa.
47251 **STEINDAMM** → **TROPIC DAWN** (Sg) 1981.

47322 **BENISALEM** → **NIAGA XXXVI** (Ia) 1981.

47341 **VARDE** → **ADA** (Pa) 1981.
47342 **HILDE** → **IDA I** (Pa) 1981.

47395 **CAPE HORN** → **TANJONG TOKONG** (Sg) 1981.
47399 **FEDERAL ST. CLAIR** → **TRANSOCEAN PEARL** (Pi) 1981.

47410 add probable sisters (Tw flag):
47414 **TAI HSIUNG.**
47415 **TAI LUNG.**

47530 **CINDERELLA**—delete entire entry—now converted to Livestock carrier (renamed AL MESILAH).

47540 add further sisters (Rm flag):
*47570 GIURGU
*47571 HIRSOVA.
*47572 HUSI.
47568 SEFAN KARADJA amend to STEFAN KARADJA.

47780 ADVARA—amend flag to Sg.

47930 add similar:
47935 CHRISTINA C (Gr).

47965 CAPE HORN → TANJONG TOKONG (Sg) 1981.
47969 FEDERAL ST. CLAIR → TRANSOCEAN PEARL (Pi) 1981.

48053 CHIEFTAIN → GREAT CITY (Pa) 1981.

48102 SOKORRI → ROG (Li) 1981.

48150 ARIETTA GREGOS—amend builder to Bu.

48183 AEGIS BALTIC—probable total loss.

48220 add probable sisters (Tw flag):
48224 TAI HSIUNG.
48225 TAI LUNG.

48301 STAR BAY → CLARKSPEY 1981 further renamed LAMMA FOREST (Br) 1981.

48321 ARETHOUSA—delete from entry—sequence is *KC_2MFK*.

48370 add further sisters (Ar flag):
48378 SANTA FE II
48379 CHUBUT.

48420 VILLE D'ANVERS → HAPAG LLOYD TRIER (Fr) 1981
48421 VILLE DE BORDEAUX → HAPAG LLOYD KIEL (Fr) 1981.

48430 add further sisters (Gr flag):
48460 ATHINA K
48461 FAMILY FOTINI
48462 FAMILY ANTHONY.

48500 CAP PINEDE → CLAUDIA (Pa) 1981.

48510 CITY OF WINCHESTER → ARC ODYSSEUS (Gr) 1981
48512 CITY OF CANTERBURY → ARC AEOLOS (Gr) 1981.

48550 SAN GEORGE → MAHA NUWARA (Sr) 1980.

48632 TAURUS → ARICA (Pa) 1981.

48690 BALTIC VENTURE—amend to GULF VENTURE (Cy).

48711 TIMI → HAPPY MED (Li) 1981.

48720 TONY'S LUCK → MIRAMAR PRIMA (It) 1980.

48730 CAROL MERCUR → SLOMAN MERCUR (FRG) 1980.

48820 add further sister:
48823 AGIOS MATTHEOS (Gr) ex IVAN GORTHON 1981.

48980 TROLL FOREST → WILLINE TARO (Sg) 1980.

49112 ANASTASIA—delete from entry.

49180 VANCOUVER FOREST—amend flag to Sg
49181 WILLINE TOYO—amend flag to Sg.

49284 ITEL TAURUS → WAH LEE 1980. Further renamed WAH LOK (Pa) 1981.

49371 CANMAR CARRIER—broken up.

49460 VILLE D'ANVERS → HAPAG LLOYD TRIER (Fr) 1981.
49461 VILLE DE BORDEAUX → HAPAG LLOYD KIEL (Fr) 1981.

49470 add further sisters (Gr flag):
49500 ATHINA K.
49501 FAMILY FOTINI.
49502 FAMILY ANTHONY.

49510 VILLE D'ANVERS → HAPAG LLOYD TRIER (Fr) 1981.
49511 VILLE DE BORDEAUX → HAPAG LLOYD KIEL (Fr) 1981.

49540 HYDRA—amend name to YDRA.

49642 COLUMBUS COROMANDEL → SENTA 1980 Further renamed MONTE PASCOAL 1981 Further renamed MUSCAT BAY (FRG) 1981.

49650 ALIMAR → ELISABETH (Gr) 1981.

49670 PRINCESS AURORA → TAIWO (Li) 1981.

49700 add similar:
49702 AEGIS BLAZE (Gr) add probably similar (Gr flag):
49703 AEGIS HARVEST
49704 AEGIS STOIC
49705 AEGIS WISDOM.

49740 add further sisters (Gr flag):
49769A ATHINA K
49769B FAMILY FOTINI
49769C FAMILY ANTHONY.

49810 add further sisters (Ne flag):
49826 BAKENGRACHT
49827 BARENTZGRACHT
49828 BEURSGRACHT
49829 BONTEGRACHT
49829A BICKERSGRACHT.

49850 PELINA → MELINA I (Pa) 1980.

49900 add further sister:
49905 NORRSUNDET (FRG) ex URSA 1977.
49903 BALTICA—amend flag to Pa.

50051 LLOYD NEW YORK → MACAELA DRESCHER (FRG) 1980.

50070 COSTAS → COSTAS II (Pa) 1980.

50081 MADIMAR—total loss.

50090 PELINA → MELINA I (Pa) 1980.

50130 add sister:
50131 KALKARA (FRG).

50202 ECO SADO → MERIAN (Mo) 1981.

50230 JAN TAVENIER → FRISIAN LINER (Ne) 1981.

50260 add sister:
50261 KARIN (FRG).

50330 ESTHER SILVANA → CARIB DAWN (Br) 1981.

50340 add further sister:
50345 NORRSUNDET (FRG) ex URSA 1977.
50343 BALTICA—amend flag to Pa.

50540 LLOYD BALTIMORE → CORINNA DRESCHER (FRG) 1980.

50590 DORRIT CLAUSEN → OM ALQORA (Si) 1981.

50600 NEGO TRIABUNNA → TRIABUNNA (Li) 1980.

50660 FIDELIO → NEMESIS (Gr) 1981.
50662 FALSTAFF → POSIDON (Gr) 1981.
50663 HUAL JASMINE → PHILIPPINE JASMINE (Pi) 1980.
50664 HUAL ROSAL → PHILIPPINE ROSAL (Pi) 1980.

50687 BARO → LA GUAJIRA (Co) 1981.

50811 ANNIKA—delete from entry.

51030 LONE STAR → VALERIA (Li) 1981.

51102 VAN HAWK—delete from entry.

51170 KATY → FRANKY (Gr) 1981.

51280 KASUGA MARU—amend length to 145.0 (478.7).

51370 AL-SABBIYAH—broken up.

51543 NORDBAY → MAHONIA (Sg) 1980.

51600 SCANDINAVIAN EXPRESS → SINNO M.E. IV (Le) 1981.

51625 MESSBERG—delete from entry.

51634 AGIOS IOANNIS—broken up.

51740 MERCANDIAN PRINCE → PEP REGULUS (De) 1981
51744 MERCANDIAN QUEEN → PEP RIGEL (De) 1981.

51784 GERMA LINA—delete from entry
51787 GERMA TEAM → GERMA DOLPHIN (Sg) 1981.

51861 ASEAN PROSPERITY → OCEAN PROSPERITY (Pa) 1981.

51880 UNIVERSE KURE → KURE (Li) 1980.

51890 add further sister:
51892 GURIDI (Sp).

51901 MARIA → CARIA (Br) 1981.

51970 BRITISH LIBERTY → FOLGOET (Fr) 1981
51971 BRITISH LOYALTY → HALA (Si) 1981
51974 BRITISH UNITY → SEBASTIANO (Pa) 1981.

51990 LUNNI—amend type to Tk/IB.

52160 SCHOONEBEEK → WESTWAL (Ne) 1981
52161 AZORES STAR → LOIRA (It) 1981.

52201 ELIZABETH II → ROBERTA 1 (Pa) 1981
52202 SARISSOLA → DRASTIRIOS (Gr) 1981
52203 OMBRINA → FILIKOS (Gr) 1981
52294 SCRIVIA → IRINIKOS (Gr) 1981.

52210 SANTA CRISTINA PRIMA → ELEFTHEROS (Gr) 1981.

52230 SVEALAND → TEQUILA SUNRISE (FRG) 1981.

52350 NEGO TRIABUNNA → TRIABUNNA (Li) 1980.

52362 SUNWAY → ORIENT PEGASUS (Pa) 1980.

52390 AL BADIAH—broken up.

52622 ILLINOIS → MERCURY (US) 1980 (now operated by U.S. Navy).

52710 NEPTUN HERCULES → TATAI (Gr)

52730 MARITIME RESOURCE → NAVESA NORMA (Cy) 1980.

52772 DIMITRIS—total loss.
52773 VICTORY—broken up.

52840 TRIFELS → TRIBELS (Gr) 1980.

52850 RANENFJORD → HAE WOO 3 (Ko) 1981.
52851 LYNGENFJORD—now confirmed as sister.

52860 add similar:
52862 AEGIS BLAZE (Gr)
add probably similar (Gr flag):
52863 AEGIS HARVEST.
52864 AEGIS STOIC.
52865 AEGIS WISDOM.

52981 HISPANIA → ATLAS (Gr) 1981.

53040 RANENFJORD → HAE WOO 3 (Ko) 1981.
52851 LYNGENFJORD—now confirmed as a sister.

53070 LINGA → ARABIAN SEA (Br) 1981.
53071 LIMATULA → ARABIAN SKY (Br) 1981.

53125 **BRITISH LAUREL → MARIBRUNA IV** (Pa) 1981.
53126 **BRITISH MAPLE → MANAMARIA** (Gr) 1981.

53140 **DIONE → STROFADES II** (Gr) 1981.
53141 **DOSINA → YEROTSAKOS** (Gr) 1981.

53300 **GUANGHE.**
53301 **ABEL SANTAMARIA.**
53302 **FRANK PAIS**
delete entire entry.

53325 **LABIOSA → AUTAN** (Fr) 1981.

53370 delete similar ships (appearance differs):
53373 **CIUDAD DE ARMENIA.**
53375 **CIUDAD DE QUITO.**
note:
53374 **CIUDAD DE PASTO** may also differ in appearance although not confirmed.

53401 **NORDKAP → DIAMOND MOON** (Gr) 1981.
53416 **VERGE → RANGE** (SA) 1981.

53442 **MELLUMERSAND → KALOS I** (Pa) 1981.

53460 **MALEA**—broken up.

53490 **TROUP HEAD → MOHANNAD** (Le) 1981.
53491 **TOD HEAD → NAZIR** (Pa) 1981.

53500 **JOYEID → JOY** (Li) 1981.

53510 **HARIS → PEARL** (Li) 1981.

53610 **SUNNY BABY → HAPPY FALCON** (Pa) 1981.
53611 **SUNNY BOY → HAPPY FELLOW** (Pa) 1981.

53643 **EDOUARD L.D.**—delete from entry.

53660 add further sisters (It Flag):
53663 **URSA MAJOR.**
53664 **CAPRICORNUS.**
53665 **DRACO.**
53666 **DELPHINUS.**
53667 **PERSEUS**
(Pa Flag):.
53668 **AMUNDSEN SEA** ex SEXTUM 1979
add probable sister:
53669 **LUPUS** (It)

53681 **VOLGA MARU → BRIOLETTE** (Li) 1981 note: This vessel has been converted to a tanker and may be altered in appearance.
53663 **MOSTUN SANKO → MOSTUN** (No) 1980.
53685 **SPRING ODESSA** is also converted to a tanker. The following may also be converted:
53680 **DONAU MARU.**
53686 **CAUCASUS MARU.**

53750 **ULTRAGAS**—amend flag to Pa.

53790 **ARMAND HAMMER**—delete entry-rebuilt.

53811 **VOLGA MARU → BRIOLETTE** (Li) 1981 note: This vessel has been converted to a tanker and may be altered in appearance.
53813 **MOSTUN SANKO → MOSTUN** (No) 1980.
53815 **SPRING ODESSA** is also converted to a tanker the following may also be converted:
53810 **DONAU MARU.**
53816 **CAUCASUS MARU.**

53900 add similar (Be built-Be flag):
53904 **FEDERAL DANUBE.**
53905 **FEDERAL MAAS.**
53906 **FEDERAL OTTAWA.**
53907 **FEDERAL THAMES.**

53980 **SUZANNE → SUZANNE H** (Pa) 1980.

54036 **WORLD PHILIPPINES → EASTERN LAUREL** (Pa) 1980.

54151 **SILWON → INGER WONSILD** (De) 1981.

54194 **MARON → STUDLAND BAY** (Br) 1981.
54195 **MENTOR → CITY OF LONDON** (Br) 1981.

54270 **KINGSNORTH → DORITAL** (Pa) 1981.

54302 **CALBE → TONJE** (Pa) 1981.

54320 **DON MANUEL → PALAMIDI** (Gr) 1981.

54344 **MARON → STUDLAND BAY** (Br) 1981.
54345 **MENTOR → CITY OF LONDON** (Br) 1981.

54413 **ACADIA**—amend to **ARCADIA.**

54434 **ADELE → TENARON** (Li) 1981.

54460 add similar ships (Pa Flag):
54461 **OGDEN BRIDGESTONE.**
54462 **WORLD BRIDGESTONE.**

54562 **PEACE VENTURE → GLOBAL PEACE** (Ko) 1981.

54638 **EASTERN JADE → SAMICK ATLANTIC** (Ko) 1981.
54651 **GOLDEN DOLPHIN → ABU SALAMA** (Si) 1981.

54662 **MARE SERENO → MARBELLA** (Li) 1981.

54674 **SIFNOS**—broken up.

54700 **POLINNIA → ARCTIC OCEAN** (Cy) 1981.
54702 **UMBERTO D'AMATO → TRADE WIND** (Gr) 1980.

54814 **ADELE → TENARON** (Li) 1981.

54900 **GAY LUSSAC → GAS FOUNTAIN** (Pa) 1981.

54962 **PEACE VENTURE → GLOBAL PEACE** (Ko) 1981.

55015 **ROMEO BRAGA → BRAVO GEORGE** (Gr) 1981.

55041 **GRECIAN SPIRIT**—amend flag to Gr.

55068 **EASTERN JADE → SAMICK ATLANTIC** (Ko) 1981.
55072 **GOLDEN DOLPHIN → ABU SALAMA** (Si) 1981.

55110 **MAERSK PINTO → LUISE LEONHARDT** (FRG) 1981.

55210 **CAPETAN MANOLIS HAZIMANOLIS** amend ex names as follows: ex SEATRAIN BALTIMORE 1980; ex CAPETAN MANOLIS HAZIMANOLIS; ex HAMBURGER WAPPEN 1977.

55320 **STOLT LION → MERCATOR G** (Br) 1981.

55460 **JAPAN LUPINUS**—broken up.

55640 add further sister:
55645 **BERGE SUND** (No).

55690 **UNIVERSE IRELAND → AVIN OIL EPISKOPI** 1981 Further renamed **HAQL EPISKOPI** (Si) 1981.

55750 **ATLANTIC EMPOROR**—amend to **ATLANTIC EMPEROR.**

55761 **FLYING CLOUD**—broken up.

55840 add further sister:
55845 **BERGE SUND** (No).

55885 **ROMEO BRAGA → BRAVO GEORGE** (Gr) 1981.

55962 **MAERSK COMMANDER → SUNWARD II** (Br) 1981.
55964 **DANILA → JAY GOURI** (In) 1981.

56030 **ORIENTAL ENVOYS**—amend to **ORIENTAL ENVOY.**

56111 **ALFRED REHDER → ALFRED** (Pa) 1980.

56140 **ALTMARK → KASSIAN GLORY** (Gr) 1981.

56250 **ALCHIMIST LAUSANNE → CHEMICAL LAUSANNE** (Li) 1980.

56280 **BIFROST → GEM TRANSPORTER** (Sh) 1981.

56310 **YANG CHUN**—probable total loss.

56420 **GRAND REXTAR → ISAVENA** (Pa) 1981.

56555 **ROMEO BRAGA → BRAVO GEORGE** (Gr) 1981.

56595 **COSTA RICA**—amend flag to Li.

56670 **UNITED FAITH**—broken up.

56722 **MAERSK COMMANDER → SUNWARD II** (Br) 1981.
56724 **DANILA → JAY GOURI** (In) 1981.

56920 **IRISH WASA → FLORES** (Li) 1981.

56973 **SEMI → DESPINA Z** (Gr) 1981.

57020 **MITERA ITENA**—amend to **MITERA IRENE.**

57220 **LADY VICTORIA → MOIRA V** (Gr) 1980.

57260 **OCEAN TRITON → EVELINE** (Gr) 1981.

57500 **BIANKA LEONHARDT →*KARIPANDE** (An) 1981.
57501 **BRITTA LEONHARDT →*KASSAMBA** (An) 1981.

57550 add further similar:
57562 **WILHELM WESCH** (Sg) ex LLOYD MARYLAND 1981; ex WILHELM WESCH 1980; ex ILRI 1979; ex NEWFOUNDLAND 1975; ex ANA LUISA 1974; ex ILRI 1972.
57555 **FREEDEBURG → ROLAND ATLANTIC** (Pa) 1979.

57761 **HAMLET ARABIA → PILBARA** (Au) 1981.
57762 **HAMLET SAUDIA → KOOLINDA** (Au) 1981.

57800 **ESSO SCOTIA**—broken up.
57802 **ESSO CAMBRIA**—broken up.

57820 **OLYMPIC BOND**—delete entire entry.

57873 **ACADIA**—amend to **ARCADIA.**

57990 **BLOIS → ZAFER** (Tu) 1981.

58020 **BADR → LANIA** (Gr) 1981.

58041 **NORDIC SPIRIT → EASTERN ENTERPRISE** (Br) 1981.

58113 **AYSEN → POYANG CAREER** (Pa) 1981.
58118 **LAGO PUYEHUE → MARIA GLYPTIS** (Gr) 1981.
58121 **THEOHARIS → ADONIS T** (Gr) 1980

58140 add further sisters:
58176A **AUSTRALIAN GRAIN** (Li)
58186A **JASPER** (Pa)
58199 **CHIMO** (No)
58192 **KOCAELI I → KOCAELI** (Tu) 1980

58290 **CAST NARWHAL**—amend flag to Li.

58300 **UNIVERSE IRELAND → AVIN OIL EPISKOPI** 1981 further renamed **HAQL EPISKOPI** (Si) 1981.

58353 **SEA SWIFT → SAFINA SWIFT** (Si) 1980.

58400 **CAST OSPREY → CAST SHEARWATER** (Pa) 1981.
58405 **SEVONIA TEAM → NAVIOS CONQUEROR** (Li) 1981.

58440 **ZAPATA PATRIOT → PATRIOT** (US) 1981.
58441 **ZAPATA COURIER → COURIER** (US) 1981.
58442 **ZAPATA RANGER → RANGER** (US) 1981.
58443 **ZAPATA ROVER → ROVER** (US) 1981.

58560 add further sisters (Gr Flag):
58584 **AMARANTOS.**

58586 NAXOS ISLAND.
58587 POROS ISLAND
58561 AL AHAD → ANANGEL ARES (Gr)

58601 JOSEF STEWING → THEOCHARIOS (Pa) 1981 amend ex names as follows: ex JOSEF STEWING 1981; ex FJORD LINER; ex JOSEF STEWING; ex VIGRAFJORD 1977; ex JOSEF STEWING 1976; ex RHEINFELS 1970; launched as JOSEF STEWING.

58614 FALKENFELS → AIAS (Gr) 1989.
58615 HOHENFELS → HOHENBELS (Gr)

58630 STOCKHORN → BULK NAVIGATOR (Cy) 1981.

58700 add sister:
58701 NORTHERN NAV (Pa) ex SEA EAGLE 1980; ex CALLIROY 1975; ex SUNCORONA 1970.

58710 MOKHA—amend Flag to Si.
58712 IRENES SUN → TRITON (Gr) 1980.
58713 IRENES SEA → ORION (Gr) 1981.
58715 EURABIA PROGRESS → SANAA (Si).

58770 AFRAN MERIDIAN—broken up.

58911 CIS BROVIG—amend Flag to Li.

59140 ONE STAR → ONESTAR (Sg) 1980.

59260 CAPTAIN PAPPIS → GRANIKOS (Gr) 1980.

59420 FISKARDO → AEGEAN SUN (Gr) 1981.

59451 FJORDNES → GENERAL LUNA (Pi) 1981.

59460 FOSSNES → AKRANES (Ic) 1981.

59480 AZELIA—broken up.

59541 ATLAS RIVER → MARIANNA (Gr) 1980.

59603 JADE → EVANGELINA (Cy) 1981.

59640 MOKHA—amend flag to Si.
59642 IRENES SUN → TRITON (Gr) 1980.
59643 IRENES SEA → ORION (Gr) 1981.
59645 EURABIA PROGRESS → SANAA (Si).

59706 SOL LAILA → LLOYD MANHATTAN (No) 1979.

59732 GERMANIC → KAIROS (Pa) 1980.
59734 ADRIA I → PHAROS (Pa) 1980.

59801 ALFRED REHDER → ALFRED (Pa) 1980.

59850 ESSO SCOTIA—broken up.
59852 ESSO CAMBRIA—broken up.

59871 CHRISTIAN VIELJEUX → SANTA RITA (Pe) 1981.
59875 PATRICK VIELJEUX → CUZCO II (Pe) 1981.
59876 TAJ → STEPHANE VIELJEUX 1979 further renamed LIMA II (Pe) 1981.

60075 AGATHON—probable total loss.
60081 ARAMIS → RAJAAN (Li) 1981.
60088 BARAHONA → JOHN A. (Pa) 1981.
60119 SANTO FORTUNE → GALLANTRY (Pa)
60123 SEA FALCON →★GUI JIANG (RC) 1980.
60127 TELFAIR CHALLENGER → CAPE SUPERIOR (Gr) 1981.

60270 BRITISH PIONEER → TISH PION 1981 further renamed M. CEYHAN (Tu) 1981.
60271 BRITISH SCIENTIST—broken up.

60310 GREY WARRIOR → CELTIC LINK (Br) 1981.

60541 DEVALI I → PARALOS (Gr) 1981.

60590 STAKARA → MESSINIAKI AVRA (Gr) 1981.
60591 STABENKO → MESSINIAKI ANATOLI (Gr) 1981.
60592 STAMENIS → MESSINIAKI AVGI (Gr) 1981.
60593 STAWANDA → MESSINIAKI AKTI (Gr) 1981.

60760 TRADE ENDEAVOR—broken up.

60790 ENERGY ENDURANCE—broken up.
60791 BERGE COMMANDER → STELIOS (Gr) 1981.

60880 ANG PANGARAP → SARRAT (Pi) 1980.

60911 GARTHNEWYDD → NACIONAL BRAGANCA (Po) 1981.

60931 AL TOOS—broken up.

60955 RENATE SCHULTE—add ex names as follows: ex VILLE DE SAINT PIERRE 1981; ex RENATE SCHULTE 1981.

61014 SWAKOP—amend flag to Pa.
61017 MARITIME VICTOR → BO AH (Ko) 1980.

61084 SWEELEAN—amend to SWEE LEAN.

61197 MOMMOTH PINE—amend to MAMMOTH PINE.

61220 OINOUSSIAN DESTINY → IRAN ENGHELAB (Ir) 1981.

61230 MARCOS M.F. → CARIBBEAN DREAMS (Gr) 1980.

61301 CAPTAIN PAPPIS → GRANIKOS (Gr) 1980.

61321 SALTNES → BEAGLE (Sg) 1980.
61325 SURENES → MED TRANSPORTER (Tu) 1981.

61406 SOL LAILA → LLOYD MANHATTAN (No) 1979.

61410 OSLOFJORD → AMBIKA (Li) 1981.
61411 BERGENSFJORD → ARIMBI (Li) 1981.
61412 TANAFJORD → AMBALIKA (Ia) 1981.

61441 CAPETAN GIORGIS Z—delete from entry.

61460 PAMELA → ARCADIAN SUN (Gr) 1981.

61472 TRES MAR → ASIA REGULUS (Pa) 1981.

61540 NAN A → RYUSEI MARU (Pa) 1981.

61572 NAMYANG BAY → HAE YUNG (Ko) 1979. Amend ex names as follows: ex NAMYANG BAY 1979; ex WALSONG 1976; ex SHINJITSU MARU 1970.

61613 PAPILIONA → OASIS EMPEROR (Pa) 1980.
61622 SEIZAN MARU → MOUNT ORO (Pa) 1980.
61626 ALEXANDRA → EKOWATI (Pa) 1981.
61627 TEMA—amend flag to Ko.

61652 IKUTA MARU → OASIS VISCOUNT (Pa) 1980.

61700 BELLEA → BELLE ISLE (Sg) 1981.

61720 MOKHA—amend flag to Si.
61722 IRENES SUN → TRITON (Gr) 1980.
61723 IRENES SEA → ORION (Gr) 1981.
61725 EURABIA PROGRESS → SANAA (Si).

61751 ETROG → ROGA (Pa) 1981.

61890 DELPHIC SKY → KYRIAKOULA 1980. Further renamed ANTONIA (Gr) 1980.

62023 IRENE → FRANCES (Li) 1981.
62030 JEANNIE → FLORENCE (Li) 1981.

62140 ANDROS—probable total loss.

62233 SINGAPORE MERCHANT—confirmed as sister.
62231 LILY VENTURE → CHARLOTTE (Li) 1981.

62254 NEPTUNE VOLIANS—amend to NEPTUNE VOLANS.

62300 JESAMINE → BONA (Pa) 1981.

62320 EUROLOGGER → SEALOGGER (Ma) 1981.

62330 INDIA → ENTELI (Pa) 1981.

62410 add sister:
62411 NORTHERN NAV (Pa) ex SEA EAGLE 1980; ex CALLIROY 1975; ex SUNCORONA 1970.

62421 HAVFROST → OCEAN FROST (Li) 1981.

62430 MINORIES LUCK → DIMITRIOS (Gr) 1981.

62481 HAMLET ARABIA → PILBARA (Au) 1981.
62482 HAMLET SAUDIA → KOOLINDA (Au) 1981.

62490 BRITISH EXPLORER—broken up.

62510 AFRAN MERIDIAN—broken up.

62530 CAPTAIN PAPPIS → GRANIKOS (Gr) 1980.

62621 CAPTAIN PAPPIS → GRANIKOS (Gr) 1980.

62760 delete similar ships (appearance differs):
62763 CIUDAD DE ARMENIA.
62765 CIUDAD DE QUITO.
note:
62764 CIUDAD DE PASTO may also differ in appearance although not confirmed.

62831 LEMBULUS → ANNIE (Fi) 1981.

62911 OLYMPIC ANTHEM—broken up.

63000 CYPRESS KING → ELENI P. (Pa) 1981.

63130 add further similar (Sp flag):
63133 MONICA MARIA.
63134 MUNDACA.
63135 MUNGUIA.

63180 SAGITTA → PILIO (Li) 1981.

63225 LABIOSA → AUTAN (Fr) 1981.

63250 RUBIS—broken up.
63251 EMERAUDE—broken up.

63300 MEDORA—delete from entry. Now a self-propelled floating storage unit.
63302 MYTILUS → GREGORIO DEL PILAR (Pi) 1981.

63310 BIYO MARU → NOTOS (Gr) 1981.

63399 JOHNAKI → SIR JOHN (Gr) 1981.
63400 LIMOUSIN → MARGAUX (Gr) 1981.

63452 BRITANNIA TEAM → OBO PRINCESS (No) 1981.
63455 BJORGHOLM → FJORDAAS (No) 1981.

63685 MERCANDIAN SUN → PEP ALTAIR (De) 1981.
63690 MERCANDIAN SKY → PEP ANTARES (De) 1981.

63740 CRYOMAR → MINOGAZ I (Gr) 1980.

63830 BRITISH PIONEER → TISH PION 1981. Further renamed M. CEYHAN (Tu) 1981.
63832 BRITISH SCIENTIST—broken up.
63861 MOBIL PRIDE → YANBU PRIDE (Li) 1981.
63862 MOBIL PROGRESS → YANBU PROGRESS (Li) 1981.
63863 MOBIL PETROLEUM → AL BILAD (Li) 1980.

63970 ZAPATA PATRIOT → PATRIOT (US) 1981.
63971 ZAPATA COURIER → COURIER (US) 1981.
63972 ZAPATA RANGER → RANGER (US) 1981.
63973 ZAPATA ROVER → ROVER (US) 1981.

64040 JADE → YIANNIS II (Gr) 1981.

64062 **FLYING CLOUD**—broken up.
64082 **ALEXANDRA DYO**—amend to **ALEXANDRA DIO.**
64170 **TIHAMA**—broken up.
64210 **AL WASEL**—delete entire entry.
64260 **MYRINA**—broken up. (Note: entry is wrongly numbered).
64290 **SEA SAINT → SAFINA SAHARA** (Si) 1981.
64312 **SEA SWIFT → SAFINA SWIFT** (Si) 1980.
64381 **NORTHIA**—now converted for use as a North Sea shuttle tanker.
64471 **DASHWOOD → TIFFANY** (Li) 1981.
64513 **VICTORIA VENTURE → OBO KING** (No) 1981.
64560 **CAST OSPREY → CAST SHEARWATER** (Pa) 1981.
64565 **SEVONIA TEAM → NAVIOS CONQUEROR** (Li) 1981.
64680 **GAMMAGAS**—amend flag to Pa.
64740 **ANNELISE OLTMANN**—amend to **ANNELIESE OLTMANN.**
64760 **FADEL**—amend flag to Le.
64770 **MAERSK MONDO → MONDO** 1980. Further renamed **FONDO** (Li) 1981.
64771 **MAERSK RANDO → RANDO** 1980. Further renamed **PANCHABHA** (In) 1981.
64858 **WINNI HELLESKOV → ILHA DO PORTO SANTO** (Po) 1981.
64863 **KETTY DANIELSEN**—delete ex name.
64866 **FRELLSEN HILLE**—delete from entry.
64911 **ASEAN PROSPERITY → OCEAN PROSPERITY** (Pa) 1981.
64931 **NORDKAP → DIAMOND MOON** (Gr) 1981.
64946 **VERGE → RANGE** (SA) 1981.
64960 the following sisters have a stulcken derrick:
64969 **IBN KHALDOUN II.**
64970 **IBN SINA II.**
65140 **SANTA CRISTINA PRIMA → ELEFTHEROS** (Gr) 1981.
65151 **ELIZABETH II → ROBERTA I** (Pa) 1981.
65152 **SARISSOLA → DRASTIRIOS** (Gr) 1981.
65153 **OMBRINA → FILIKOS** (Gr) 1981.
65154 **SCRIVIA → IRINIKOS** (Gr) 1981.
65250 **SAINT NICHOLAS → MANOLIS M.** (Gr) 1981.
65280 **PETROLA 26**—broken up.
65301 **CIS BROVIG**—amend flag to Li.
65451 **RALPH O. RHOADES → TAXIARHIS** (Li) 1981.
65471 **DEA MARIS**—broken up.
65490 **FAIRFIELD ARCHER → CORALI** (Li) 1981.
65631 **PETROMAR CAMPANA II**—amend ex name as follows: ex ESSO BAYWAY 1978.
65633 **ESSO BRISBANE → ESSO GENOVA** (It) 1981.
65690 add further possible sister:
65696 **IRVING OCEAN** (Ca).
65693 **ESSO TORONTO → PETROMAR SANTA CRUZ** (Ar) 1981.
65750 **MOBIL MARKETER**—add note: kingpost abreast funnel on port side.
65760 **GLOBE COMET → THOR ASGARD** (FRG) 1981.
65820 The following vessels have been converted to bulk/container and may have alterations to appearance:
65820 **ASEAN KNOWLEDGE** (not ASEAN MISSION as text).
65821 **ASEAN MISSION.**
65822 **ASEAN LIBERTY.**
65920 **SINCLAIR TEXAS → PETERSBURG** (Li) 1981.
65960 **GATOOMA**—broken up.
66010 **AFRAN TIDE → HARALABOS** (Li) 1981.
66070 **DIONE → STROFADES II** (Gr) 1981.
66071 **DOSINA → YEROTSAKOS** (Gr) 1981.
66182 **GRETE MAERSK → CASTOR** (Bs) 1981.
66220 add further sister:
66223 **LIBRA** (Gr).
66330 **TECALLI → ANNETA** (Pa) 1980. later broken up.
66350 **BRUCE BALI → PERMINA XXII** (Ia) 1981.
66353 **BRUCE BUATAN → PERMINA XXIII** (Ia) 1981.
66384 **MYSSAYEH**—amend to **MYS SARYCH.**
66385 **MYS SARYCH**—delete from entry
add further sisters (Ru flag):
*66390 **LINKUVA.**
*66391 **DELEGAT.**
*66392 **KROPOTKIN.**
*66393 **MYS KHRUSTALNYY.**
*66394 **UST-ILIMSK.**
*66395 **UST-KAN.**
*66397 **MYS KODOSH.**
*66398 **LUKOMORYE.**
66410 **KYRGO → BATU** (Tu) 1981.
66640 **SILVEREAGLE → YAU FOOK** (Br) 1981.
66641 **SILVEROSPREY → KYRGO** (Br) 1981.

66730 **SUNNY BABY → HAPPY FALCON** (Pa) 1981.
66731 **SUNNY BOY → HAPPY FELLOW** (Pa) 1981.
66860 **GOTHIA → STRAITS VENTURE** (Sg) 1981.
66901 **PACIFIC → AL MANSOURA** (Qt) 1980.
67001 **BOSTONSAND → AMIR** (My) 1981.
67002 **BURHAVERSAND → AUDAX** (Pa) 1981.
67003 **STOLLHAMMERSAND → PAROUTH** (Gr) 1981.
67040 **SVEALAND → TEQUILA SUNRISE** (FRG) 1981.
67050 **HAJNOWKA**—delete from entry. Amidships kingpost removed. The sisters may also be modified:
67051 **BARLINEK.**
67052 **RUCIANE.**
67222 **GERMANIC → KAIROS** (Pa) 1980.
67224 **ADRIA 1 → PHAROS** (Pa)1980.
67380 **HORUS → TROPICANA** (Gr)1981.
67481 **INGE BECH → ENI** (It) 1981.
67497 **NAUTILUS → PRACETIA** Ia) 1981.
67520 **HWA CHU → GRAND SUCCESS** (Pa) 1981.
67680 add further sisters (Ru flag):
*67684 **ALEKSANDR KORNEYCHUK**
*67685 **ALEKSANDR TSULUKIDZE**
*67686 **DMITRIY MEDVEDEV**
*67687 **GRIGORIY NIKOLAYEV**
*67688 **JAN SUDRABKALN**
*67689 **NATA VACHNADZE**
*67689A **VLADIMIR GAVRILOV**
add possible sisters (Cy flag):
67689B **ATHENIAN OLYMPICS** ex MOSCOW OLYMPICS 1981:
67689C **ATHENIAN VICTORY**
67689D **ATHENIAN XENOPHON.**
67732 **GRETE MAERSK → CASTOR** (Bs) 1981.
67741 **AL AHOOD**—amend flag to Si.
67942 **NORTHERN STAR**—delete from entry. Converted to bulk carrier.
67970 **OLYMPIC ALLIANCE**—broken up
67971 **OLYMPIC ACCORD**—broken up.
67992 **WORLD PRESTIGE**—broken up.
68081 **LEMBULUS → ANNIE** (Fi) 1981.
68150 **SHUANG FENG HAI**—delete from entry—rebuilt
68151 **FUKUYAMA MARU → GOONZARAN** (Ko) 1981 (may be spelt **GOONJARAN**).
68204 **JARI**—total loss.
68233 **ANDROS MASTER**—broken up.
68325 **CARISLE → CAPE CLEAR** (Ih) 1981.
68531 **VOLGA MARU → BRIOLETTE** (Li) 1981
note: This vessel has been converted to a tanker and may be altered in appearance
68533 **MOSTUN SANKO → MOSTUN** (No) 1980
68535 **SPRING ODESSA** is also converted to a tanker
The following may also be converted:
68530 **DONAU MARU**
68536 **CAUCASUS MARU.**
68550 **ARMAND HAMMER**—delete entry—now rebuilt.
68692 **ILE DE LA CITE → ATIA C** (Gr) 1981.
68841 **CAST TERN → CAST RAZORBILL** (Li) 1981.
68990 **NICHOLAS**—broken up.
69100 **TULA → SHINYON** (Pa) 1981.
69120 **JAPAN WISTERIA → CATHARINA** (Pa) 1981
69126 **TSURUSAKI MARU → ACACIA** (Ko) 1981.
69170 **OLYMPIC ARCHER**—broken up
69171 **OLYMPIC ARROW**—broken up.
69370 **TINA LENTOUDIS → LEVANTE C** (Gr) 1980.
69390 **ANATOLI → NYALA** (Gr) 1981.
69421 **HORNED OWL → PHILIPPINE PINE** (Pi) 1980.
69440 **KAPPA VICTORY → ANNABELLE E** (Gr) 1980.
69594 **TEXACO ROME**—broken up.
69619 **WORLD GENERAL**—broken up.
69710 **OLYMPIC GARLAND → AFTHOROS** (Gr) 1981.
69740 **MISTRAL → THANASSIS M** (Gr) 1981.
69862 **CITIALI**—amend to **CITLALI.**
69950 The following vessels have been converted to bulk/container and may have alterations to appearance:
69950 **ASEAN KNOWLEDGE**
69951 **ASEAN MISSION**
69952 **ASEAN LIBERTY.**
69960 **STAKARA → MESSINIAKI AVRA** (Gr) 1981
69961 **STABENKO → MESSINIAKI ANATOLI** (Gr) 1981
69962 **STAMENIS → MESSINIAKI AVGI** (Gr) 1981
69963 **STAWANDA → MESSINIAKI AKTI** (Gr) 1981.
70003 **ESSO BRISBANE → ESSO GENOVA** (It) 1981.

70051 **GLOBE VENUS** → **MYRICA** (Li) 1981.
70052 **GLOBE CONSTELLATION** → **GOGO RAMBLER** (Li) 1981.

70091 **ANCO PRINCESS** → **MOLAVENTURE** (Li) 1981.

70120 add further possible sister:
70126 **IRVING OCEAN** (Ca).
70123 **ESSO TORONTO** → **PETROMAR SANTA CRUZ** (Ar) 1981.

70160 **WORLD PROMISE** → **VALIANT PORPOISE** (Li) 1981.
70162 **WORLD PROVIDER** → **RIO PANUCO** (Me) 1981.

70261 **GUNDA BROVIG** → **PRETTY** (Li) 1981.

70430 **FAIRFIELD ARCHER** → **CORALI** (Li) 1981.

70471 **MAKEDONIA STAR** → **OBO MAKEDONIA STAR** (Li) 1981.

70490 **YUYO MARU No 2** → **KATINA** (Ja) 1981.

70590 **MATE ZALKA**—add note: some sisters have a taller funnel.

70710 **PROVIDENCE**—broken up.

70910 **BARFONN** → **BERNARDO HOUSSAY** (Ar) 1980.

70940 **ANG PANGARAP** → **SARRAT** (Pi) 1980.

71032 **FELLOWSHIP** → **FOMALHAUT** (Li) 1981.

71040 add possible sister:
71061 **JUGO NAVIGATOR** (Li).

71070 **BELLEA** → **BELLE ISLE** (Sg) 1981.

71100 **JOYEID** → **JOY** (Li) 1981.

71141 **ASIA GRACE** → **PACIFIC MARINER** (Li) add ex names as follows: ex UNITED GRACE 1981; ex ASIA GRACE 1981; ex UNITED GRACE 1980; ex ASIA GRACE 1980.

71174 **SWAKOP**—amend flag to Pa.
71177 **MARITIME VICTOR** → **BO AH** (Ko) 1980.

71220 add similar:
71221 **DONA ROSSANA** (Li).

71240 **WOO YANG**—amend to **WOO YONG** now renamed **AMGIS KATASYRTI** (Gr).

71253 **SINGAPORE MERCHANT**—confirmed as a sister.
71251 **LILY VENTURE** → **CHARLOTTE** (Li) 1981.

71491 **LA LIBERTAD** → **GOOD HARVEST** (Gr) 1981.

71520 **SENEGAL** → **CRISANTHI I** (Pa)1980 later broken up.

71530 add further similar (Ru flag):
*71533 **SMOLENSK.**

71560 **BRITISH EXPLORER**—broken up.

71720 **ALTMARK** → **KASSIAN GLORY** (Gr) 1981.

71741 **CORDILLERA**—amend flag to Ch.
71744 **POYANG** →***HUE LU** (RC) 1981.

71760 add similar (De built):
71762 **VILLIA** (Pa) ex TORBEN MAERSK 1981.

71850 **ANDALUSIA** →***NEI JIANG** (RC) 1981.

71933 **JADE** → **EVANGELINA** (Cy) 1981.

71940 **HORSA** → **FRIGARD** (Fi) 1989.
71942 **PHOENIX TRADER** → **FARIDA** (Eg) 1981.

71991 **ARAGRACE**—amend flag to Sg.

72111 **ARAGRACE**—amend flag to Sg.

72122 **ALEXANDER** has the same appearance as 72123 **LARISSASEE.**

72171 **BRNO** → **ULYSSUS** (Gr) 1981.

72240 **LLARANES** → **NACIONAL AVEIRO** (Po) 1981.

72339 **EREDINE** → **BENALBANACH** (Br) 1981.
72343 **JAPANA** → **PIONEER JAPAN** (Li) 1981.

72431 **SLIEDRECHT** → **ASTYANAX** (Gr) 1981.
72432 **ZWIJNDRECHT** → **ROLLON** (Gr) 1981.

72490 **AEGEAN STAR** → **CUERNAVACA** (Br) 1981.
72492 **SUNSETTER**—amend name to **ANIARA.**

72500 **ALEXANDRA K.II** → **LARA DIANA** (Ho) 1981.

72510 **INA**—delete from entry. sequence is M_2F. Others in class may be similarly altered.

72551 **MARIA** → **CARIA** (Br) 1981.

72581 **ARNEB** → **ANGELIKI IV** (Cy) 1981.

72631 **AMSTERDAM** → **SULU** (Fi) 1981.
72634 **SAINT NAZAIRE** → **BOHOL** (Pi) 1981.

72689 **MESSBERG**—confirmed as a sister.

72750 add further similar (FRG flag):
72762 **KIEFERNBERG.**
72763 **JAN GRAEBE** ex MUNKBRON 1973; launched as JAN GRAEBE.
72754 **FUCHSBERG** → **CAROLINE GRAEBE** (FRG) 1980.

72840 **IGGESUND** → **TUULIA** (Fi) 1981.

72980 **AEGEAN STAR** → **CUERNAVACA** (Br) 1981.
72982 **SUNSETTER**—amend name to **ANIARA.**

73091 **OLKAS** → **ANTARTICO** (Ar) 1980.

73171 **GOLDEN ENTERPRISE**—amend to **GOLDEAN ENTERPRISE.**

73200 **YOU ARE MY SUNSHINE**—amend to **YOU'RE MY SUNSHINE.**

73220 **NAVIOS PATRIOT** → **GOOD HORIZON** (Gr) 1981.
73221 **NAVIOS PIONEER** → **GOOD TARGET** (Gr) 1981.

73408 **AUTHOR** → **BENARMIN** (Br) 1981.

73440 **KOREAN JUPITER** → **KOREAN WONIS-SUN** (Ko) 1980.

73481 **ORIENTAL EDUCATOR** → **ORIENTAL SCHOLAR** 1981 further renamed **OMEX PIONEER** (Sg) 1981.
73483 **KOREAN LEADER** → **KOREAN WONIS-ONE** (Ko) 1980.

73490 **SEATRAIN PRINCETON** → **PLUVIUS** (FRG) 1981.

73514 **MAIN EXPRESS** → **NGAN CHAU** (Pa) 1981.
73515 **RHEIN EXPRESS** → **GREEN ISLAND** (Pa) 1981.

73620 **CRAIGABOY** → **RUBIN** 1979 further renamed **BISCAYNE SURF** (Pa) 1980.

73650 add further similar (lengthened):
*73653 **WROZKA** (Pd).

73690 **TRIMAR GUY**—amend name and flag to **LYNDARET** (FRG)

73730 **SHAIKAH AL QURAICHI** → **ATLANTIC KING** 1979 further renamed **BONA VENTURE II** (Ca) 1981.

73740 **RANE** → **VERNIA** (Sw) 1980.

73797 **LINDAUNIS** → **ISLE OF MAN** (FRG) 1980.

73880 **CITY OF MILAN** → **ECO MONDEGO** (Pa) 1980.

73900 add further sister:
73905 **ROXANE KERSTEN** (FRG) ex JANNE WEHR 1980.

74000 add sisters:
74001 **GERMA FONDAL** (No)
74002 **GERMA GARANT** (Pa) ex GERMA LINA 1980; ex LINA 1980.

74030 **ANNIKA**—add note: may now be fitted with 2 deck cranes.

74051 **ARISTEFS** → **SUCRE** (Ve) 1981.

74130 **TITOV VELES** → **HAIDER A** (Br) 1981.

74140 add further sister:
*74143 **SWIERADOW ZDROJ** (Pd)

74171 **KVIKSHOLM**—delete from entry Kingpost amidships replaced by crane. Others in the class may be similarly modified.

74200 **CONISTER**—broken up.

74210 **CRESCENCE** → **CRESSET** (Br) 1981.

74380 **SEATRAIN ORISKANY** amend length to 583.96ft renamed **SEAPAC ORISKANY** 1981 further renamed **DART BRITAIN** (Br) 1981
74381 **SEATRAIN BENNINGTON** → **TFL FRANKLIN** (FRG) 1981
74382 **SEATRAIN CHESAPEAKE** → **SEAPAC CHESAPEAKE** (Li) 1981 Further renamed **DART ATLANTIC** (Br) 1981
74383 **SEATRAIN YORKTOWN** → **SEAPAC YORKTOWN** (Li) 1981 further renamed **DART CONTINENT** (Br) 1981
74384 **SEATRAIN INDEPENDENCE** → **SEAPAC INDEPENDENCE** (Li) 1981 further renamed **DART AMERICANA** (Br) 1981.

74420 **NEW ENGLAND HUNTER** → **CATHY** (Gr) 1981.

74460 **SEATRAIN ITALY** → **HERMES ACE** (Ja) 1981.

74476 **HUMACAO** → **EASTERN LIGHT** (Pa) 1981
74477 **GUAYAMA** → **EASTERN KIN** (Pa) 1981.

74520 **DART CANADA** → **CANADIAN EXPLORER** (Br) 1981.

74671 **ASTRADIEGO** → **VERA** (Gr) 1981.

74760 **POLINNIA** → **ARCTIC OCEAN** (Cy) 1981
74762 **UMBERTO D'AMATO** → **TRADE WIND** (Gr) 1980.

74944 **ONORATO** → **HERAKLIA** (Pa) 1981
74945 **SIROCO** → **SKYROS** (Pa) 1981.

75230 **ALCHIMIST LAUSANNE** → **CHEMICAL LAUSANNE** (Li) 1980.

75280 **EUROBRIDGE PIONIR**—amend to***PIONIR** (Ys).

75291 **IBESCA ALGERIA** → **TWIEHAUSEN** (Pa) 1980
75292 **IBESCA BELGICA** → **LUBBECKE** (FRG) 1980
75293 **NORRSUNDET**—delete from entry. Now Fitted with deck cranes.

75369 **NORPPA** →***LADOGA 8** (Ru) 1981.

75505 **EMMAPLEIN** → **POLARIS** (Ne) 1981
75507 **FLEVO** → **PLATO** (Ne) 1981.

75520 **MERAK** → **GEZIENA** (Ne) 1980.

75583 **CITY OF IPSWICH** → **MANCHESTER FULMAR** (Br) 1981.

75610 add similar (centre-line kingpost Foreward):
75615 **RAFNES** (No)
75616 **RADNES** (No)
75617 **RAMNES** (No)
75618 **REFSNES** (No)
75619 **REKSNES** (No)
75619A **RIKNES** (No)
75619B **ROGNES** **(No)**
75619C **RONNES** (No)
75619D **ROSSNES** (No).

75770 **TARNOW**—amend B447 type to B522 type.

75793 **EIRA** → **FLAG TRADER** (Gr) 1981.

75892 **PROGRESS** → **ST. ANN'S BAY** (Jm) 1981.

75900 **MANCHESTER ZEAL** → **SEA HAWK** (Sg) 1981.

75912 **LINCOLNBROOK**—delete from entry. Now Fitted with deck cranes.

75920 add further sister:
75922 **HARTING** (Br).

75972 **ECO SADO** → **MERIAN** (Mo) 1981.

76021 **VELOX**—confirmed as sister.

76120 **FER BALTICO** → **FLORIDA STAR** (Pa) 1981.

76180 **ALSTERTAL** → **ANTIKLEA**(Cy) 1981.

76250 add further sister:
★76252 **DA QING 218** (RC).

76463 **ALEXANDER** has the same appearance as 76462 **LARISSASEE.**

76640 **HAJNOWKA**—delete from entry. Amidships kingpost removed. the sister ships may also be modified:
76641 **BARLINEK**
76642 **RUCIANE.**

76761 **MERZARIO IONIA** → **CONSTELLATION ENTERPRISE** (Gr) 1981
76763 **SYRIA**—delete from text. Now rebuilt
76764 **ATLANTIC PROJECT** → **MERZARIO HISPANIA** (Ma) 1981
76765 **ATLANTIC PROSPER** → **STENA IONIA** 1981 further renamed **MERZARIO IONIA** (Ma) 1981.

76813 **ESSEN** → **KONGSFJORD** (FRG) 1981.

76840 **MERZARIO GALLIA** → **PROJECT WASA** 1981.

76861 **CAP CAMARAT** → **AL HOCEIMA** (Mo) 1981
76863 **CAP TAILLAT** → **ANWAL** (Mo) 1981.

76920 **RAMO**—total loss.

76951 **DART ATLANTIC** → **CP AMBASSADOR** (Br) 1981
76952 **DART AMERICA** → **MANCHESTER CHALLENGE** (Br) 1981.

76970 **MADOURI** → **TRANS LINK** (Cy) 1980.

76990 **YOU ARE MY SUNSHINE**—amend to **YOU'RE MY SUNSHINE.**

77021 **ARISTEFS** → **SUCRE** (Ve) 1981.

77031 **ERLANGEN EXPRESS** → **INCOTRANS PROGRESS** (FRG) 1981
77032 **HOECHST EXPRESS** → **INCOTRANS PROMISE** (FRG) 1981.

77240 **POLYVIKING** → **WEST DAORI** (Pa) 1981.

77391 **AMSTERDAM** → **SULU** (Fi) 1981
77394 **SAINT NAZAIRE** → **BOHOL** (Pi) 1981.

77440 **NEW WAYS**—amend to **NEWAYS.**

77560 **VIKING** → **MARE NORDICO** (It) 1981.

77580 **KNUT MARK** → **TENOCH** (Me) 1981.

77596 **CALORIC** → **DERBY** (Gr) 1981.

77675 **DUNSTANBURGH CASTLE** → **GLOBAL AMBITION** (Ko) 1981.

77690 **NAVIOS PATRIOT** → **GOOD HORIZON** (Gr) 1981
77691 **NAVIOS PIONEER** → **GOOD TARGET** (Gr) 1981.

77721 **GOLDEN ENTERPRISE**—amend to **GOLDEAN ENTERPRISE.**

77801 **GALAXIA** → **JADE GLORIOUS** (Pa) 1980.

★78060 add further sister:
★78070 **VERA KHORUZHKAYA** (Ru)
★78066 **EKATLERINA ZELENKO**—amend to **KATYA ZELENKO.**

78260 **PROVIDENCE**—broken up.

78320 **ASEAN NATIONS**—now converted to bulk/container —may have alterations to appearance.

78381 **ASTRADIEGO** → **VERA** (Gr) 1981.

78490 **SUZANNE** → **SUZANNE H** (Pa) 1980.

78612 **CALBE** → **TONJE** (Pa) 1981.

78680 **OLGA MAERSK** → **ASYA** (Tu) 1981.

78690 **DELTADRECHT** → **BANDAR DEMAK** (Ia) 1981
78691 **DUIVENDRECHT** → **BANDAR DEMTA** (Ia) 1981
78693 **DORDRECHT** → **BANDAR DENPASAR** (Ia) 1981.

78810 **ELEANOR DUNBAR**—amend name to **DIVONNE** (Pa).

78820 **DON MANUEL** → **PALAMIDI** (Gr) 1981.

78910 add further sister:
78912 **DURRINGTON** (Br).

78931 **MEDITERRANEAN CARRIER**—amend flag to Gr.

79310 **SEATRAIN ITALY** → **HERMES ACE** (Ja) 1981.

79330 **CONISTER**—broken up.

79790 **STAVFJORD** → **FOUR FLAGS II** (Gr).

79850 **MATUMBA**—broken up.

79900 **FER BALTICO** → **FLORIDA STAR** (Pa) 1981.

80160 **EUROBRIDGE PIONIR**—amend name to ★**PIONIR** (Ys).

80190 **EMIRATES EXPRESS** → **ABUJA EXPRESS** (Sw) 1981.

80200 add further similar:
★80203 **SMOLENSK** (Ru).

80260 add further sister:
★80266 **PETR MASHEROV** (Ru).

80271 **MERZARIO IONIA** → **CONSTELLATION ENTERPRISE** (Gr) 1981
80273 **SYRIA**—delete from text. Now rebuilt
80274 **ATLANTIC PROJECT** → **MERZARIO HISPANIA** (Ma) 1981
80275 **ATLANTIC PROSPER** → **STENA IONIA** 1981 further renamed **MERZARIO IONIA** (Ma) 1981.

80370 **KOREAN JUPITER** → **KOREAN WONIS-SUN** (Ko) 1981.

80440 **MALEA**—broken up.

80600 **LE SCANDINAVE** → **VATSY** (Mg) 1979.

80670 add sister:
80671 **LINHAVEN** (Cy) ex NAUSICA 1981; ex LYDIA; ex HELEN MILLER; ex ANA RENATA 1973; ex HELEN MILLER 1972.

80700 **ASUNCION** → **NERA** (Br) 1981
80701 **VILLARRICA** → **YOKAMU** (Br) 1981.

80760 **BRIARTHORN** → **GEODRILL** (Br) 1981.

81014 **FALKENFELS** → **AIAS** (Gr) 1980
81015 **HOHENFELS** → **HOHENBELS** (Gr).

81051 **RONA** → **ANNA** 1981.

81132 **BYZANTINE ENERGY** → **CAP AKRITAS** (Gr) 1981.

81141 **ELOUNDA** → **AGGELA** (Gr) 1981.

81210 **SANIX ACE**—broken up.

81231 **ATLAS RIVER** → **MARIANNA** (Gr) 1980.

81411 **CORDILLERA**—amend flag to Ch
81414 **POYANG** → ★ **HUE LU** (RC) 1981

81450 add similar:
81453 **FAIRSKY F** (Pa) ex FAIRSKY 1980; ex STEPHAN REITH 1979.

81510 **JOHNNY K** → **MICHALIS K** (Cy) 1980.

81560 **ZACAPA** → **EMERALD SEA** (Li) 1980.

81600 **COPIHUE** → **SHENG LI** (Li) 1981.

81680 **CRYOMAR** → **MINOGAZ 1** (Gr) 1980.

81690 add sister:
81693 **CASTANEDA** (Br) ex ALBACORE 1980; ex CASTANEDA 1977.

81710 **CHINTA** → **AGIOS ELEFTHERIOS** (Cy) 1980.

81781 **CHILTERN PRINCE** → **FRIENDSHIP** (Pa) 1981
81782 **MALVERN PRINCE** → **VICTORY 1** (Pa) 1981
81783 **FIJIAN** → **ONEHUNGA** (NZ) 1981.

81820 **ANNA VON BARGEN** → **LAUTOKA** 1981. Further renamed **ADI VITI** (Fiji) 1981.

81840 **MECHI VENTURE** → **PACIFIC VIOLET** (Pa) 1981
81842 **GOMBA NILE** → **PACIFIC LILY** (Pa) 1980
81843 **GOMBA ENDURANCE** → **PACIFIC TULIP** (Pa) 1981
81844 **GOMBA VICTORIA** → **PACIFIC FREESIA** (Pa) 1981
81845 **GOMBA ENDEAVOUR** → **PACIFIC ROSE** (Li) 1981.

81920 **SIGNE THOLSTRUP** → **POLAR GAS** (Pa) 1981.

81941 **HUELVA** → **DIANA CLAUSEN** (De) 1981.

81957 **KAI KHOSROW** → **AGAETE** (Pa) 1980.

82070 **ANNA VON BARGEN** → **LAUTOKA** 1981 further renamed **ADI VITI** (Fiji) 1981.

82290 **EDELGARD** → **VICTORIOUS** (Cy) 1981.

82353 **ALIAKMON LIGHT** → **MARIKA** (Gr) 1981.

82360 **TROUP HEAD** → **MOHANNAD** (Le) 1981
82361 **TOD HEAD** → **NAZIR** (Pa) 1981.

82370 **INTERNAVIS 1** → **STELLA PRIMA** (NA) 1981.

82532 **LONE STAR** → **VALERIA** (Li) 1981.

82623 **ALIAKMON LIGHT** → **MARIKA** (Gr) 1981.

82718 **AUTHOR** → **BENARMIN** (Br) 1981.

82730 **STAR SUPREME** → **STAR YORK** (Br) 1981.

82750 **HODEIDAH CROWN** → **RANGER** 1981 further renamed **KOTA SAHABAT** (Sg) 1981.

82769 **ZIM BANGKOK** → **TARROS JUNIPER** 1980 further renamed **DADIANGAS** (Pi) 1980.

82808 **ELISABETH** → **LISSY SCHULTE** (FRG) 1980.

82850 **PAPUAN CHIEF**—now lengthened
Sisters may also be lengthened in the future.

82880 **STAR SUPREME** → **STAR YORK** (Br) 1981.

82921 **STRIDER CRYSTAL** → **NEDLLOYD CRYSTAL** (Br) 1980
82923 **STRIDER DIAMOND** → **INDIAN COURIER** (In) 1981
82926 **SAPPHIRE BOUNTY** → **NEDLLOYD BOUNTY** (Br) 1980.

82951 **PACIFIC FORESTER** → **KEMANO** (Br) 1981.

83030 **STAR CLIPPER** → **STAR LANAO** (Pi) 1981
83031 **STAR PERSEUS** → **STAR VISAYAS** (Pi) 1981
83032 **STAR ORPHEUS** → **STAR LUZON** (Pi) 1981
83033 **STAR THESEUS** → **STAR MINDANAO** (Pi) 1981
83036 **STAR LACONIAN** → **STAR THAILAND** (Pi) 1981
83038 **STAR DORIAN** → **STAR PHILIPPINES** (Pi) 1980.

83110 **STAR CLIPPER** → **STAR LANAO** (Pi) 1981
83111 **STAR PERSEUS** → **STAR VISAYAS** (Pi) 1981
83112 **STAR ORPHEUS** → **STAR LUZON** (Pi) 1981
83113 **STAR THESEUS** → **STAR MINDANAO** (Pi) 1981

83116 **STAR LACONIAN** → **STAR THAILAND** (Pi) 1981
83118 **STAR DORIAN** → **STAR PHILIPPINES** (Pi) 1980.

83302 **AGIOI VICTORES** → **NEGEV ORON** (Is) 1981
83308 **SANTA POLA** → **TELFAIR TRADER** (Li) 1981.

83321 **KARAMU FOREST** → **OCEAN VENUS** (Pa) 1981.

83350 **GLOBE EXPRESS** → **UNICEB** (It) 1981.

83361 **BALTIC** → **BALTICO** (Br) 1981 (now converted to cable ship)
83363 **CORONA** → **SUNSHINE** (Le) 1981
83364 **HEKTOS** → **PACIFIC CARRIER** (Sg) 1981.

83382 **BENISALEM** → **NIAGA XXXVI** (Ia) 1981.

83451 **BALTIC** → **BALTICO** (Br) 1981 (now converted to cable ship)
83453 **CORONA** → **SUNSHINE** (Le) 1981
83454 **HEKTOS** → **PACIFIC CARRIER** (Sg) 1981.

83490 add further sister:
83493 **AGIOS MATTHEOS** (Gr) ex IVAN GORTHON 1981.

83600 **AVON** → **MY DESTINY** (Cy) 1981
83601 **DENEBOLA** → **SEVERN** 1979 further renamed **MY CHARM** (Cy) 1981
83612 **VENUS DESTINY** → **MONA S** (Le) 1981
83613 **VENUS GLORY** → **MANAL S** (Le) 1981
83614 **ALGENIB** → ⋆**DOC LAP** (Vn) (delete reference to **DOAN KET** in text)
83615 **SCHEDIR** → ⋆**THON NHUIT** (Vn) (delete reference to **TONG NHAT** in text)
83618 **SEA CARRIER 1** → **BETTY S** (Pa) 1981
83620 **PALMA** → **ALEXANDROS G** (Gr) 1981 amend ex names as follows: ex PALMA 1981; ex HUMBER 1979; ex SIRRAH 1979
add further sister:
83621 **ARCHON** (Gr) ex AURORA 1980; ex PUTBUS 1979.

83670 **ESTHER SILVANA** → **CARIB DAWN** (Br) 1981.

83861 **SHELL REFINER** → **METRO STAR** (Ca) 1981
83863 **SHELL SCIENTIST** → **METRO SUN** (Ca) 1981.

83900 **FRIENDSHIP** → **AGIOI ANARGYROI** (Pa) 1981.

83945 **MINI LAMP** → **DEL CHAP** (Me) 1981.

84060 **MERCANDIAN PRINCE** → **PEP REGULUS** (De) 1981
84064 **MERCANDIAN QUEEN** → **PEP RIGEL** (De) 1981.

84180 **BRITISH LIBERTY** → **FOLGOET** (Fr) 1981
84181 **BRITISH LOYALTY** → **HALA** (Si) 1981
84184 **BRITISH UNITY** → **SEBASTIANO** (Pa) 1981.

84190 **BORDER SHEPHERD** → **MARIVERDA IV** (Pa) 1981
84191 **BORDER CASTLE** → **FIVE BROOKS** (Pa) 1981
84193 **BORDER PELE** → **FIVE STREAMS** (Pa) 1981.

84200 **CASIMIR LE QUELLEC** → **IVORY** (Pa) 1981.

84210 **KAMTCHIA** → ⋆**GALATA** (Bu) 1981.

84480 **ASUNCION** → **NERA** (Br) 1981
84481 **VILLARRICA** → **YOKAMU** (Br) 1981.

84531 **STAVROULA XIII** → **HUSSEIN** (Le) 1981.

84581 **SARANDI** → **LEROS ISLAND** (Gr) 1981.

84671 **MARIGOULA** → **AQUATIC** (Pa) 1981.

79790 **STAVFJORD** → **FOUR FLAGS II** (Gr).

84820 **OCEAN TRITON** → **EVELINE** (Gr) 1981.

84860 **AL KAHERA**—amend to **AL KAHERAH.**

85010 **CHIQUITA**—amend flag to Ec.

85021 **AL TOOS**—broken up.

85160 **THAMES MARU** → **RIVER THAMES** 1979 later broken up.

85210 **SINGAPORE JATI**—amend flag to Pa.

85221 **MARTINA** → **SKOPELOS STAR** (Gr) 1981.

85323 **ALBATROS**—broken up.

85472 **MAASPLEIN** → **NIAGA XXXIII** (Ia) 1981.

85520 **APOSTOLOS H**—broken up.

85530 delete entire text and replace with the following: **NICOLAOS M** Cy/FRG; 1954; C; 836; 65.69 x 3.8 (215.5 x 12.47); M; 11.5; ex HOMER 1973; ex KATERINA K 1972; ex KURT BASTIAN 1970.

85590 **EVOIKOS** → **OGUY** (Le) 1980 later a total loss.

85610 **BIRA**—add further details as Follows: tonnage: 2100 dspl; dimensions: 75 ×— (246 ×—); Engines: M; speed 12; Type: transports (converted From landing craft).

85690 **LA QUINTA** → **CAPO NOLI** (It) 1981.

85800 **ORIENTAL WISDOM**—broken up.

85810 **ARYADOOT**—broken up.

85871 **SHELL REFINER** → **METRO STAR** (Ca) 1981
add further sister:
85876 **METRO SUN** (Ca) ex SHELL SCIENTIST 1981; ex PARTINGTON 1979.

85160 **YAMAUME MARU No2** → **YAMAUME No2** (Ko) 1981.

86237 **GALICH**—broken up.

86300 **HWA CHU** → **GRAND SUCCESS** (Pa) 1981.

86322 **SOUTH POLE** → **JANICE ANN** (Br) 1981.

86350 **KARLSBURG** → **NIAGA XXXVII** (Ia) 1981.

86360 **EID**—total loss.

86422 **HOUSSAM B.**—broken up.

86434 **TEXACO ROME**—broken up.

86486 **PLAN DE SAN LUIS**—amend from sister and amend to possible similar
add further sisters (Me flag):
86488 **JOSE MARIA MORELOS**
86489 **PLAN DE GUADELUPE.**

86500 **OVERSEAS ADVENTURER** → **PETROSTAR XVI** (Si) 1981.

86650 **ARYADOOT**—broken up.

86672 **GUADELUPE VICTORIA**—amend ex names to: ex PRESIDENTE GUADELUPE VICTORIA 1968; ex PEMEX 65-1; ex SOLE 1965.

86680 **MARIVANA RENA**—broken up
amend ex names as Follows: ex DAFRA PAUL 1974; ex PACIFIC PAUL 1973; ex FERNWOOD 1970.

86790 **CYPROS**—broken up
86791 **ROTTERDAM**—broken up.

86830 **UNION**—amend flag to Ne.

86880 **FALLOW DEER** → **GRUNNVAAG** (No) 1981.

86952 **NONOC TRANSPORT**—total loss
86953 **LOUCY**—total loss
86954 **CASTLE SPIRIT**—amend flag to Gr.

87022 **LUPITA CASTRO** → **CASUARINA** (Cy) 1980.

87050 add sister:
87053 **CASTANEDA** (Br) ex ALBACORE 1980; ex CASTANEDA 1977.

87150 **DESPO 1**—total loss.

87201 **RUDAN** → **RACHAD** (Le) 1981.

87210 **CAPTAIN PETROS**—total loss.

87280 **EL MALEK FAISAL** → **SAHIWAL EXPRESS** (Ne) 1981.

87310 **OWENGLAS**—amend flag to Pa.

87352 **KINI KERSTEN** → **EUROTRADER** (FRG) 1980.

87380 **NASSIOUKA** → **PACIFIC SKY** (Fiji) 1980.

87410 **FALCON**—broken up
87411 **NIKOS M.** → **ANGSA MAS** (Pa) 1981 amend ex names as Follows: ex ADELAIDE 1981; ex PEARL NILE 1981; ex NIKOS M. 1980; ex ROSA T. 1977; ex MALABAR 1972; ex ERIKA SCHULTE 1970; ex ILSE E. GLEUE 1954.

87421 **ATLANTIC COMET** → **HAIFFA AL KULAID** (Ku) 1981.

87440 **LUI**—broken up.

87482 **GLACIAR ROJO** → **M.A. ULUSOY** (Tu) 1981.

87520 **REPULSE BAY** → **ALEJANDRA G.** (Pa) 1981.

87680 **TINITO CASTRO** → **JACARANDA** (Cy) 1980.

87791 **TERRA** → **CARIBBEAN CEMENT** (Pa) 1981.

87870 **MAGID** → **NADIA** (Si) 1981.

88090 **NEW ENGLAND HUNTER** → **CATHY** (Gr) 1981.

88101 **IBESCA ALGERIA** → **TWIEHAUSEN** (Pa) 1980
88102 **IBESCA BELGICA** → **LUBBECKE** (FRG) 1980
88103 **NORRSUNDET**—delete from entry. Now fitted with deck cranes.

88220 **CYPRESS POINT** → **MANA** (Pa) 1981.

88290 **SUNDSVIKEN** → **SAMSUN EXPRESS** (Ne) 1980.

88300 add further sister:
88304 **EENDRACHT** (Ne).

88820 **OLIB** → **JET V** (Gr) 1981.

89020 **MAPLEHURST** → **VASILIKI II** (Gr) 1981.

89040 **CASIMIR LE QUELLEC** → **IVORY** (Pa) 1981.

89120 **NICOLAS P.** → **TARA** (Pa) 1981.

89182 **UNISON II** → **VONNY** (Sg) 1980.

89360 **LEVEN FISHER**—now converted to nuclear-Fuel carrier. May be altered in appearance.

89410 **SOPHIA PAPPAS**—amend to **SOFIA PAPPAS** now renamed **ELEFTHERIA** (Gr).

89421 **HUELVA** → **DIANA CLAUSEN** (De) 1981.

89450 **SAPPHIRE** → **APOLLONIA VII** (Cy) 1981.

89740 **DOMINIC** → **ZULA** (Pa) 1980.

89780 **MADOURI** → **TRANS LINK** (Cy) 1980.

89840 amend all similar ships to sisters (nos. 89844-89847)
89844 **STEYNING** → **JULIA** (Pa) 1981
add further sister:
89848 **STAR** (Gr) ex MERIDIAN SKY 1980; ex CAERNARVONBROOK 1976.

89890 **PUERTO ACEVADO** → **ABUELO GIORGIO** (Li) 1981
89891 **SHIN HUI** (Br)—amend name & flag to **FLAG WILLIAMS** (Gr).

89913 **MIDJUR** → **BUANA** (Pa) 1980
89914 **TIGER BAY** → **VOLARE** (Gr) 1980 now a total loss.

89951 **SARANDI** → **LEROS ISLAND** (Gr) 1981.

90223 **MIDJUR → BUANA** (Pa) 1980
90224 **TIGER BAY → VOLARE** (Gr) 1980 now a total loss.

90270 **ANDEN**—amend Flag to Pe.

90451 **MARATHON**—amend Flag to Ec.

90470 **MALDIVE INDUSTRY**—broken up.

90491 **LEENA → SIBYLLA** (Gr) 1981.

90514 **FALKENFELS → AIAS** (Gr) 1980
90515 **HOHENFELS → HOHENBELS** (Gr).

90520 **PERCY M. CROSBIE → BAIE JAMES** (Ca) 1981.

90531 **ZEPHIR 1 → ZUNA** (Le) 1981.

90570 **JEANNE D'ARC**—amend to **JEAN D'ARC** renamed **JEAN DARK** further renamed **AL JAMAL** (Le) 1981.

90621 **BACCHUS → CHERRY LANKA** (Sg) 1981.

90681 **ELENA → SAMIA** further renamed **JALAPA** (Me) 1981.

90800 **MANAURE IV → NORSUN** (Li) 1980.

90870 **ESTHER CHARLOTTE SCHULTE → TUKWILA CHIEF** (Pa) 1980
90872 **DONATA SCHULTE → NADA G** (Le) 1980.

90894 **CRAZY HARRY → HONG HING** (My) 1981.

90920 **BIRKENHAIN**—total loss.

90950 **SINGAPORE JATI**—amend flag to Pa.

90970 add similar (sloping uprights to goalpost):
90973 **FRELLSEN HILLE** (De) ex HILLE FRELLSEN 1980.

90982 **LEMWARDERSAND → BELL COMET** (Gr) 1981.

91038 **WINNI HELLESKOV → ILMA DO PORTO SANTO** (Po) 1981
91046 **FRELLSEN HILLE**—delete from entry.

91071 **ZEPHIR 1 → ZUNA** (Le) 1981.

91112 **VISHVA PRATIBHA → VIJAYA VAIBHAV** (In) 1981.

91143 **EVOCRYSTAL → NORRO** (Fi) 1981.

91223 **SABINA → ADHAM 1** (Sy) 1980.

91310 **MERC CARIBIA → ILEIGH** (Mo) 1981
91311 **ANGLIAN MERCHANT → DAKHLA** (Mo) 1981.

91401 **SIRAPIL → MERIAM** (Eg) 1981.

91471 **PACIFIC → AL MANSOURA** (Qt) 1980.

91507 **KAI KHOSROW → AGAETE** (Pa) 1980.

91532 **MAASPLEIN → NIAGA XXXIII** (Ia) 1981.

91540 **TEGELERSAND → ASTOR** (Pa) 1981.

91572 **MELLUMERSAND → KALOS 1** (Pa) 1981.

91730 **KEFALONIA**—amend to **KEFALLONIA** now renamed **GEORGIOS A** (Gr) 1981.

91823 **SABINA → ADHAM 1** (Sy) 1980.

91830 **ADINE → MUHIEDDINE** (Le) 1981
91849 **AIDEN → DOMENICO SCOTTO** (It) 1981.

91870 **JOYEID → JOY** (Li) 1981.

91892 **PUSHPA → HYDO** (Cy) 1981.

91900 **PONTE PASAJE → LADY GABRIELA** (Li)
91902 **PONTE SAMPAYO → LADY VERONICA** (Li) 1981.

91940 **ADINE → MUHIEDDINE** (Le) 1981
91955 **ADARA**—amend ex names as Follows: ex SAXON PRINCE 1976; ex CAIRNTRADER 1976; ex SAXON PRINCE 1975; launched as CAIRNTRADER.
91959 **AIDEN → DOMENICO SCOTTO** (It) 1981.

91970 **STOCKHORN → BULK NAVIGATOR** (Cy) 1981.

91990 **JEANNE D'ARC**—amend to **JEAN D'ARC** renamed **JEAN DARK** Further renamed **AL JAMAL** (Le) 1981.

*92160 add further sisters (Ru Flag):
*92161 **NEPRYADVA**
*92162 **SETUN.**

92330 delete all similar ships:
92331 **FJELL**
92332 **FJORD**
92333 **LYNX**
92334 **VELA**
92336 **NORDVAER.**

92680 **EVER GLORY**—broken up.

92690 **ANDERIDA → TRUCKTRADER** (Gr) 1981.

92740 **MARIAECK → MARI-LIFT** (Pa) 1981.

92870 **HAIDA BRAVE**—amend engines to TSM.

92952 **LISSETTE → BEULAH** (Li) 1980
add further similar:
92957 **MAERSK ASTRO** (Li) ex GISELA 1980.

93060 **ARIADNE → *SOCA** (Bu) 1980
93061 **SCANDINAVIA**—amend Flag to Bu.

93070 **FINNJET**—amend engines to TSGT/M.

93150 **BRABANT → ARGO-HELLAS** (FRG) 1978.

93200 **MANATI → ARCTIC SALVOR** (US) 1980.

93220 **FASGADAIR**—delete entire entry, Now rebuilt.

93300 **SEATRAIN LEONOR → LARIMAR** (Do) 1981
93301 **SEATRAIN LIBERTAD → AMBAR** (Do) 1981.

93510 **ULIDIA → AUTO TRADER** (Gr) 1981.

93511 **VIKING TRADER**—amend Flag to Sw
93512 **ANDERIDA → TRUCKTRADER** (Gr) 1981.

93800 **SEVERODONETSK**—delete from entry. Now has a goalpost before funnel, making sequence MKM_2FK. This could apply to others, or all, in the class.

93920 **ULIDIA → AUTO TRADER** (Gr) 1981
93921 **VIKING TRADER**—amend Flag to Sw
93922 **ANDERIDA → TRUCKTRADER** (Gr) 1981.

94001 **CAMILLA HENRIKSEN → HERTHA** (De) 1980.

94030 **CAPITAINE LE GOFF → AL ZAHER II** (Si) 1981.

94091 **DIPLOMAT** can be distinguished from AMBASSADOR by extra housing above the bridge, adjoining the foremast.

94110 **SEASPEED ASIA → SAUDI MAKKAH** (Si) 1981
94112 **SEASPEED ARABIA → SAUDI RIYADH** (Si) 1981.

94140 **FEDERAL NOVA → CARIBBEAN SKY** (Br) 1981.

94150 **STENA TIMER → LORETO** (Me) 1981.

94171 **BURAIDAH → BORE SEA** (Fi) 1979.

94190 **MIRIAM → CORAL GABLES** (Br) 1981.

94230 **MICHEL → TRANSIT** 1979 further renamed **SOL GEORGIOS** (Cy) 1980.

94240 delete the following from entry:
94241 **LINDINGER SATELITE**
94242 **LINDINGER SURVEYOR.**

94450 **LENA**—delete from entry—modified in appearance
94454 **TEREK**—delete from entry—modified in appearance.

94501 **NERLANDIA → JOLLY ORO** (Pa) 1980
94502 **BELGIA → JOLLY ARGENTO** (Pa) 1980.

94520 **SEASPEED DANA → DANA** (Ma) 1981
94522 **INGER EXPRESS → MARCEL C.** (Be) 1981.

94540 **BRABANT → ARGO-HELLAS** (FRG) 1978.

94630 **MIRIAM → CORAL GABLES** (Br) 1981.

94650 the following sisters have a ramp on the starboard quarter:
94654 **MERCANDIAN EXPORTER II**
94655 **MERCANDIAN TRADER II**
add further sisters (Do flag):
94656 **MERCANDIAN MERCHANT II**
94657 **MERCANDIAN SUPPLIER II.**

94690 **ADOR → ROSE SCHIAFFINO** (Fr) 1980
94691 **EVANGELISTO**—amend to **EVANGELISTAS.**

94740 **CALIFORNIAN → CALIFORNIA** (US) 1980.

94831 **FINNCLIPPER → GULF EXPRESS** (Sw) 1981.

95011 **KIRK TRAILER → CARIBBEAN TRAILER** (Br) 1980.

95020 add sister:
95021 **PROJECT ORIENT** (NA).

95120 add further sister:
95123 **DIONYSIS V** (Gr) ex SILVER BIRD 1981; ex LIEBENFELS 1978.

95130 **LEVANTE EXPRESS**—amend Flag to It
95131 **FENICIA EXPRESS**—amend Flag to It.

95162 **LISSETTE → BEULAH** (Li) 1980
add further similar:
95167 **MAERSK ASTRO** (Li) ex GISELA 1980.

APPENDIX INDEX

This index contains only names which do not appear in the main index of this book, i.e. new names of vessels which have changed name, additional sisters and similar ships, and amendments of names. Names which appear in the Additional Drawings section are indicated thus +.

ELEFTHERIA 89410
ELEFTHEROS 52210
ELEFTHEROS 65140
ELENA 02553
ELENA 45971
ELENI K. 27571
ELENI M. 46512
ELENI P. 63000
ELHAWI STAR 18402
ELHAWI STAR 22950
ELISABETH 49650
ELONA +71507
ELPIDOFOROS 46447
ELSA SK 12893
EMERALD SEA 81560
EMPIRE STATE 12220
ENI 67481
ENTELI 62330
EOLOS 32310
ESSO BAYWAY +60566
ESSO GENOVA 65633
ESSO GENOVA 70003
ESSO PALM BEACH +60565
ESSO PLYMOUTH +75085
ESSO PORTLAND +60567
ETAIWI I 16021
ETERNAL PEACE 06080
ETERNAL SEA 12893
EURO NAUTILUS 35020
EUROPA +16875
EUROPA FREEZER 34209
EUROPEAN CLEARWAY +14976
EUROPEAN ENTERPRISE +14978
EUROPEAN FAITH 29363
EUROPEAN FAITH 30581
EUROPEAN GATEWAY +14979
EUROPEAN TRADER +14977
EUROTRADER 87352
EVANGELINA 59603
EVANGELINA 71933
EVANGELISTAS 94691
EVELINE 57260
EVELINE 84820
EVEREST 29451
EVEREST 30260
EXPRESS 14570
EXTRACO I +57618
EXTRACO I +61059
EXTRACO II +57619
EXTRACO II +61059

F

FADEL G 45883
FAETHON 07961
FAIRSKY F 81453
FAMILY ANTHONY 48462
FAMILY ANTHONY 49502
FAMILY ANTHONY 49769 C
FAMILY ARROW 05072
FAMILY FOTINI 48461
FAMILY FOTINI 49501
FAMILY FOTINI 49769 B
FARID M 11480
FARIDA 71942
FEDERAL DANUBE 53904
FEDERAL MAAS 53905
FEDERAL OTTAWA 53906
FEDERAL THAMES 53907
FEDORA 06538
FILIKOS 52203
FILIKOS 65153
FILOTHEI 09610
FIORITA 34080
FINLANDIA +16895
FIVE BROOKS 84191
FIVE LAKES 36683
FIVE STREAMS 84193
FIZIK KURCHATOV 01579
FJORDAAS 63455
FLAG TRADER 75793
FLAG WILLIAMS 89891
FLORENCE 62030
FLORES 56920
FLORIDA 05230
FLORIDA STAR 76120
FLORIDA STAR 79900
FOLGOET 51970
FOLGOET 84180
FOMALHAUT 71032
FONDO 64770
FORTUNE KING 06519
FORUM PLESSOT 36283
FORUM PLESSOT 36483
FOUR FLAGS II 79790
FOUR FLAGS II 84700
FRANCE MARU +04975
FRANCE MARU +30425
FRANCES 62023
FRANKY 51170
FRELLSEN HILLE 64866
FRELLSEN HILLE 90973
FRIENDSHIP 81781
FRIGARD 71940
FRIGO AFRICA +49022
FRIGO AMERICA +49021
FRIGO ASIA +49023
FRIGO ESPANA +49024
FRIGO EUROPA +49025
FRIGO LAS PALMAS +49027
FRIGO OCEANIA +49026
FRIGO TENERIFE +49028
FRISIAN LINER 50230

G

GAFREDO 06291
GALATA 84210
GALAXY II 31800
GALLANTRY 60119
GAY FORTUNE 15360
GAZ FOUNTAIN 54900
GEESTBAY +03545
GEESTPORT +03546
GELTING NORD 19290
GELTING NORD 23700
GEM TRANSPORTER 56280
GENERAL LUNA 59451
GENERAL MANUEL BELGRANO 06678
GEODRILL 80760
GEORG OTS +20353
GEORGIOS A. 91730
GEORGIOS G. 29180
GERMA DOLPHIN 51787
GERMA FONDAL 74001
GERMA GARANT 74002
GEZIENA 75520
GIANNOULA K. 10922
GIOTTO 19381
GIURGU 47450
GLOBAL AMBITION 77675
GLOBAL PEACE 54962
GLOBAL PEACE 54562
GLOBE TRADER 06606
GLORY OCEAN +57625
GLORY OCEAN +61045
GOGO RAMBLER 70052
GOLDEAN ENTERPRISE 73171
GOLDEAN ENTERPRISE 77721
GOLDEN SEA 06353
GOLEMI 05211
GOOD HARVEST 71491
GOOD HORIZON 73220
GOOD HORIZON 77690
GOOD TARGET 73221
GOOD TARGET 77691
GOONJARAN 68151
GOONZARAN 68151
GORYACHEGORSK 14317
GORYACHEGORSK 39454
GRAND SUCCESS 67520
GRAND SUCCESS 86300
GRANIKOS 59260
GRANIKOS 61301
GRANIKOS 62530
GRANIKOS 62621
GREAT CITY 48053
GREAT HONOR +57619
GREAT HONOR +61059
GREEN ISLAND 73515
GREGORIO DEL PILAR 63302
GRIGORIY NIKOLAYEV 67687
GRUNNVAAG 86880
GUI JIANG 60123
GULF EXPRESS 94831
GULF FRIO 23101
GULF PRIDE 13202
GULF VENTURE 48690
GUNGA DIN II 43230
GURIDI 51892
GYOKO MARU +68559 D

H

HAE WOO 3 52850
HAE WOO 3 53040
HAE YUNG 61572
HAI MENG 24302
HAIDER 74130
HAIFFA AL KULAIB 87421
HAJE NAIME 76160
HALA 51971
HALA 84181
HAPAG LLOYD KIEL 48421
HAPAG LLOYD KIEL 49461
HAPAG LLOYD KIEL 49511
HAPAG LLOYD TRIER 48420
HAPAG LLOYD TRIER 49460
HAPAG LLOYD TRIER 49510
HAPPY FALCON 53610
HAPPY FALCON 66730
HAPPY FELLOW 53611
HAPPY FELLOW 66731
HAPPY MED 45451
HAPPY MED 48711
HAQL EPISKOPI 55690
HAQL EPISKOPI 58300
HARALABOS 66010
HARTING 75922
HEDON SAND 35291
HELLAS 16992
HELMAR 31193
HERAKLIA 74944
HERCULUS 29450
HERCULUS 30600
HERMES ACE 74460
HERMES ACE 79310
HERTHA 94001
HIEI MARU 09891
HIRSOVA 47571
HO CHUNG +57619C
HO CHUNG +61059D
HOHENBELS 58615
HOHENBELS 81015
HOHENBELS 90515
HONESTY II 06646
HONG HING 90894
HONG QI 102 29245
HONOUR FIVE 10364
HORNBAY 03491
HORNBAY 03581
HORNCAP 03490
HORNCAP 03580
HUANG JIN SHAN 12900
HUE LU 71744
HUE LU 81414
HUNJIANG 05330
HUSI 47572
HUSSEIN 84531
HYDO 91892
HYDROLOCK +72384

I

IDA I 47342
IKAN 12761
ILEIGH 91310
ILHA DO PORTO SANTO 64858
ILHA DO PORTO SANTO 91038
IMPERIAL 05910
INCOTRANS PROGRESS 08831
INCOTRANS PROGRESS 09031
INCOTRANS PROGRESS 77031
INCOTRANS PROMISE 08832
INCOTRANS PROMISE 09032
INCOTRANS PROMISE 77032
INDIAN COURIER 82923
INGER WONSILD 54151
INSELSEE 46385
INSELSEE 47085
INTRA SKY 30020
INTRA SPRAY 24710
INTRA SUN 24711
INTRA TRADER 11191
INTRA TRADITION 26122
INTRA TRAVELLER 11192
INZHENER YERMOSHKIN 12682
IOS I 03430
IRAN ENGHELAB 61220
IRAN SALAM 15312
IRENE 40270
IRENES MELODY +71505
IRGIZ 85612
IRINI II 06605
IRINIKOS 52204
IRINIKOS 65154
IRVING OCEAN 65696
IRVING OCEAN 70126
ISADORE HECHT 33932
ISAVENA 56420
ISKATEL 39414
ISLA FERNANDINA 05481
ISLA FERNANDINA 06812
ISLE OF MAN 73797
ISSLEDOVATEL 39415
ITALY MARU +04976
ITALY MARU +30426
IVAN BORZOV 24314
IVAN BORZOV 39456
IVE 37342
IVE 45202
IVORY 84200
IVORY 89040

J

JACARANDA 87680
JADE GLORIOUS 77801
JALAPA 90681
JALDOOT ASHOK 28290
JAMES ENSOR +52285
JAN GRAEBE 72763
JAN SUDRABKALN 67688
JANICE ANN 86322
JASPER 58186
JAY GOURI 55964
JAY GOURI 56724
JEBEL ALI 2 30350
JENSON II 41750
JET V 88820
JETPUR DELIGHT 21690
JETPUR DELIGHT 25970
JETPUR VICEROY 25071
JETPUR VICTORY 25070
JI MEI 01931
JOHAN NORDENANKAR +33095
JOHANNA V +76195
JOHN A. 60088
JOHNSON CHEMSTAR +52265
JOHNSON CHEMSUN +52266
JOLLY ARGENTO 94502
JOLLY ORO 94501
JOO HENG 07531
JOSE MARIA MORELOS 86488
JOY 53500
JOY 71100
JOY 91870
JOYCE CLAIR 42770
JOYCE CLARE 42770
JUGO NAVIGATOR 71061
JULIA 89844

K

KAGHAN +56577
KAIROS 59732
KAIROS 67222
KALKARA 50131
KALOS I 53442
KALOS I 91572
KAMALES 04182
KAMALES 11503
KAMIROS 17091
KANDARA 03261
KAREN Y +72387
KARIN 50261
KARIN 05382
KARIPANDE 57500
KASSAMBA 57501
KASSIAN GLORY 56140
KASSIAN GLORY 71720
KATERINA A. 35661
KATINA 70490
KATYA ZELENKO 78066
KEFALONIA 91730
KEMANO 82951
KHALIJ CRYSTAL 03901
KHALIJ SKY 00352
KHIMIK ZELINSKIY 01579 A
KHOPER 85613
KHUDOZHNIK A. GERASIMOV +77081
KHUDOZHNIK A. GERASIMOV +80001
KHUDOZHNIK FEDOROVSKIY +77080
KHUDOZHNIK FEDOROVSKIY +80000
KHUDOZHNIK GABASHVILI +77082
KHUDOZHNIK GABASHVILI +80002
KHUDOZHNIK KASIYAN +77083
KHUDOZHNIK KASIYAN +80003
KHUDOZHNIK KUSTODIYEV +77084
KHUDOZHNIK KUSTODIYEV +80004
KHUDOZHNIK TOIDZE +77085
KHUDOZHNIK TOIDZE +80005
KHUDOZHNIK VLADIMIR SEROV +77086
KHUDOZHNIK VLADIMIR SEROV +80006
KIEFERNBERG 72762
KIFANGONDO 05312
KOCAELI 58192
KOMARINE No. 9 09600
KONGSFJORD 76813
KONSTANTIN SIMONOV +20356
KOOLINDA 57762
KOOLINDA 62482
KOREAN WONIS-ONE 73483
KOREAN WONIS-SUN 73440
KOREAN WONIS-SUN 80370
KOSTIS 14304
KOTA MURNI 15610
KOTA PETANI 14730
KOTA SAHABAT 82750
KOTA SINGAPURA 24440
KOUKOUMARIES 25710
KROPOTKIN 66392
KULDIGA 03260
KURE 51880
KYRGO 66641

L

LA GUAJIRA 50687
LADOGA 8 75369
LADY GABRIELA 91900
LADY VERONICA 91902
LAGOS PALM II 12910
LALLI 17193
LAMMA FOREST 48301
LANIA 58020
LARA DIANA 72500
LARIMAR 93300
LE GOBELET D'ARGENT 22711
LEENOR 02590
LEENOR 46420
LEEOR 02591
LEEOR 46421
LEFKADIAN SKY 25880
LENIN 22854
LENIN +32065
LENIN 34484
LEONOREVERETT 14520
LEOPARDI 32554
LEROS ISLAND 34581
LEROS ISLAND 89951
LEV TITO 39416
LEV TOLSTOY +20355
LEVANTE C 69370
LIBRA 66223
LIMA II 05126
LIMA II 59376
LINHAVEN 80671
LINKUVA 66390
LIRA 00691
LISSY SCHULTE 82808
LLOYD BAKKE 24303
LLOYD MANHATTAN 59706
LLOYD MANHATTAN 61406
LOIRA 52161
LONG SHAN 10140
LORENZ 02293
LORETTO 94150
LUBBECKE 75292
LUBBECKE 88102
LUISE LEONHARDT 55110
LUKOMORYE 66398
LUPUS 53669
LUSSIN 37851
LYNDARET 73680

M

M. A. ULUSOY 87482
M. CEYHAN 60270
M. CEYHAN 63830
MACAELA DRESCHER 50051
MACEDONIAN REEFER 04361
MAERSK ASTRO 92957
MAERSK ASTRO 95167
MAGDALINI K 12881
MAH II 25861
MAHA NUWARA 48550
MAHMOUDY 34372
MAHONIA 51543
MAKIS K 10890
MALAYAN PRINCESS 03513
MALAYAN QUEEN 02601
MALDIVE NATION 44082
MALDIVE NATION 44392
MALDIVE PRIVILEGE 14780
MAMMOTH MONARCH +68553
MAMMOTH PINE 61197
MAN PO 13390
MANA 88220
MANAL S. 83613
MANAMARIA 53126
MANCHESTER CHALLENGE 76952
MANCHESTER FULMAR 75583
MANCHESTER VANGAURD 08601
MANILA 30950
MANOLIS M 65250
MANUELA PRIMA 47375
MANZONI 32555
MARBELLA 54662
MARCEL C 94522
MARE NORDICO 77560
MARGAUX 63400
MARI ANNE 07660
MARIA GLYPTIS 58118
MARIA MARIOS H +57619
MARIA MARIOS H +61059
MARIANNA 59541
MARIANNA 81231
MARIBRUNA IV 53125
MARIKA 82353
MARIKA 82623
MARI-LIFT 92740
MARIVERDA IV 84190
MARYSTAR 00452
MASTRO GIORGIS 07000
MAYFLOWER 29400
MAYSUN II 26570
MAZON 29670
MED TRANSPORTER 61325
MEDITERRANEAN SUN 20861
MELINA 41870
MELINA I 49850
MELINA I 50090
MELPOL 25072
MERCANDIAN MERCHANT II 94656
MERCANDIAN SUPPLIER II 94657
MERCATOR G 55320
MERCURY 52622
MERIAM 91401
MERIAN 50202
MERIAN 75972
MERZARIO HISPANIA 76764
MERZARIO HISPANIA 80274
MERZARIO IONIA 76765
MERZARIO IONIA 80275
MESSINIAKI AKTI 60593
MESSINIAKI AKTI 69963

U

V

W

X

Y

Z

NUMERICAL